O9-AID-564
9G
VOL 28

BUSINESS INFORMATION RESOURCES

REFERENCE

MAR 23 2021

2021

Twenty-Eighth Edition

BUSINESS INFORMATION RESOURCES

GREY HOUSE PUBLISHING

PRESIDENT: Richard Gottlieb
PUBLISHER: Leslie Mackenzie
EDITORIAL DIRECTOR: Laura Mars

PRODUCTION MANAGER & COMPOSITION: Kristen Hayes
MARKETING DIRECTOR: Jessica Moody

Grey House Publishing, Inc.
4919 Route 22
Amenia, NY 12501
518.789.8700
Fax: 518.789.0545
www.greyhouse.com
books@greyhouse.com

While every effort has been made to ensure the reliability of the information presented in this publication, Grey House Publishing neither guarantees the accuracy of the data contained herein nor assumes any responsibility for errors, omissions or discrepancies. Grey House accepts no payment for listing; inclusion in the publication of any organization, agency, institution, publication, service or individual does not imply endorsement of the editors or publisher.

Errors brought to the attention of the publisher and verified to the satisfaction of the publisher will be corrected in future editions.

Except by express prior written permission of the Copyright Proprietor no part of this work may be copied by any means of publication or communication now known or developed hereafter including, but not limited to, use in any directory or compilation or other print publication, in any information storage and retrieval system, in any other electronic device, or in any visual or audio-visual device or product.

This publication is an original and creative work, copyrighted by Grey House Publishing, Inc. and is fully protected by all applicable copyright laws, as well as by laws covering misappropriation, trade secrets and unfair competition.

Grey House has added value to the underlying factual material through one or more of the following efforts: unique and original selection; expression; arrangement; coordination; and classification.

Grey House Publishing, Inc. will defend its rights in this publication.

Copyright © 2021 Grey House Publishing, Inc.
All rights reserved

First edition published 1992
Twenty-eighth edition published 2021

Printed in Canada
The directory of business information resources. – 1992-2021

v. ; 27.5 cm.
Annual
Other title: Business information resources

1. Business information services – United States – Directories. 2. Reference books – Business – Bibliography – Periodicals. 3. Association, institutions, etc. – United States – Directories. 4. Business – Databases – Directories. 5. Trade shows – Directories. I. Title: Business information resources.

HF54.52.U5 D56
016.65
ISBN: 978-1-64265-809-5 softcover
ISSN: 1549-7224

Table of Contents

Indexes

Introduction

This twenty-eighth edition of *Business Information Resource,* the premier reference book for business researchers since 1992, includes comprehensive coverage of 104 of the most significant industries in today's economy. Users will find: new customers and ways to improve the bottom line; ways to maintain customers during these uncertain economic times; and paths to new business opportunities that have presented themselves due to the current climate. As the pandemic and political divide continue to wreak havoc on American business as we know it, current business information is more valuable than ever.

This reference work offers an unequaled collection of valuable, industry-specific resources. Reach out to new customers through industry **Associations, Directories, Databases,** and **Trade Shows**. Find new ways to cut costs and improve efficiency through **Magazines, Journals** and **Newsletters**. Learn what your competitors are up to by visiting the latest, most important **Web Sites**.

The industry coverage in this new edition of *Business Information Resources* is far-reaching, and reflects current trends. Recently added chapters include Gaming, Robotics & AI, Advertising in the 21st Century and Computers & Software Services. Other important coverage includes Cyber Security, Law Enforcement & Public Safety, and National Security & International Affairs. Users will find Marketing, E-Commerce and Social Media, as well as Alternative Energy, Brewing & Distilling, Environment & Conservation, International Trade, Pharmaceutical Drugs & Devices, Real Estate, Social Media, Transportation and Water Supply.

We have added hundreds of new records and made thousands of updates across all chapters. With 24,764 listings, this edition is the most comprehensive guide to business information on the market today. All listings include name, address, phone, fax, web site, email, key contacts and a brief description, making your research focused and productive. When available, we have indicated an association's social media presence.

The value of the focused, comprehensive data in *Business Information Resources*, compiled with the business researcher in mind, cannot be overstated. Online-only information is often confusing, unreliable, and outdated. This edition provides immediate assistance with your business: attend industry Trade Shows to promote your product and find new customers; subscribe to Publications to stay competitive and ahead of the curve; join Associations for business support and educational opportunities.

The content in this 2021 edition breaks down as follows: 6,665 Associations; 2,999 Newsletters; 5,173 Magazines and Journals; 4,115 Trade Shows; 2,479 Directories and Databases; 3,081 Industry Web Sites; and 252 International Resources. Plus you'll find 57,476 contact names, 18,294 fax numbers, 18,946 web sites, and 12,870 e-mail addresses.

Front Matter for 2021

This section includes six reports from the U.S. Small Business Administration:

- **2020 Small Business Profile** offers data on employment, income & finance, self-employment, turnover; and small business by industry;
- **December 2020 Economic Bulletin** glimpses at proprietors' income, job creation, loans, and delinquency rates;
- **What's New With Small Business** looks at demographic breakdown from gender to minority to veteran firms;
- **The Pulse of Small Business: An Industry Breakdown** shows the continued impact of COVID-19 by industry, and how various industries have changed the way they operate;
- **Small Business Facts (1)** show that black owners experienced the biggest decline in business activity;
- **Small Business Facts (2)** show the staggering plummet of employment in leisure and hospitality, and how restaurants and bars continue to struggle.

- **Content Summary of Chapter Listings:** Lists more than 1,600 specific businesses under each chapter name. For example, *Accounting* lists auditors, bookkeepers, payroll and taxes; *Engineering* includes cost engineers, geologists, and robotics; *Restaurants* covers bakers, cookware and caterers.
- **NAICS and SIC Reference Tables**: Enable users to approach their topic based on the North American Industry Classification System (NAICS), or the Department of Labor's Standard Industrial Classification System (SIC).

User Guide and Key: Defines fields for entry type. In addition to name, address, phone, fax, web site, e-mail, and description, *Associations* include number of members, dues and founding year. *Publications* include cost and frequency. *Trade shows* include location, number of exhibitors and attendees.

Two Indexes

- *Entry Index*—Alphabetical list of all entries
- *Publisher Index*—Alphabetical list of publishers of industry literature, or sponsors of trade shows, etc. The entry number listed identifies the title of the published material/trade show listed in this directory. Note that publishers often offer additional material not included here.

Business Information Resources answers the need for well-organized, accessible business information for market researchers, advertising agencies, job placement and career planning offices, public relations personnel, and business schools and colleges—a need well-documented by one of the identified high-growth sectors: Information.

Praise for previous editions:

> *"...convenient, efficient vehicle for locating sources of information on U.S. businesses... recommended for academic libraries... ideal for collection development."*
>
> **American Reference Books Annual**

> *"...continues to be an essential reference source..."*
>
> **Choice**

> *"...a worthy addition to academic and large public libraries serving business researchers..."*
>
> **Booklist**

> *"...substantial reference, recommended for marketing and industry research collections..."*
>
> **Library Journal**

Business Information Resources is available for subscription online at http://gold.greyhouse.com for even faster, easier access to this vast array of information. With a subscription, users can search by keyword, geographic area, organization type, key contact name and so much more. Visit the site or call 800-562-2139 to set up a free trial of the Online Database.

User Guide

Descriptive listings in *The Directory of Business Information Resources* are organized into 98 industry chapters. You will find the following types of listings throughout the book: Associations; Newsletters; Magazines & Journals; Trade Shows; Directories & Databases; and Web Sites.

Below is a sample listing illustrating the kind of information that is or might be included in an Association entry, with additional fields that apply to publication and trade show listings. Each numbered item of information is described in the paragraphs on the following page.

---

(1) **12345**

(2) **National Association of Big Band Musicians**

(3) 2061 Ryders Avenue
Westerville, OH 43081

(4) 002-208-0843

(5) 800-208-0845

(6) 002-208-0844

(7) info@bigb.com

(8) www.bigb.com

(9) Linda Whare, Executive Director
Keith Fallon, Secretary
Bill Jenkins, Editor

(10) A national organization that supports those musicians and instructors whose main interest is big band music. Committed to furthering the art of big bands through teaching, performance, compositions and scholarly research. Also promotes the growth and establishment of big band literature and libraries, and offers musicians and teachers guidance in instrument maintenance and performing venues.

(11) 1M *Members*

(12) *Founded*: 1984

(13) Bi Monthly

(14) $59.00

(15) 110,000

(16) **Special Issues:**
Top 100 Music Dealers
January

(17) 3,000 Attendees

(18) April

Resources User Key

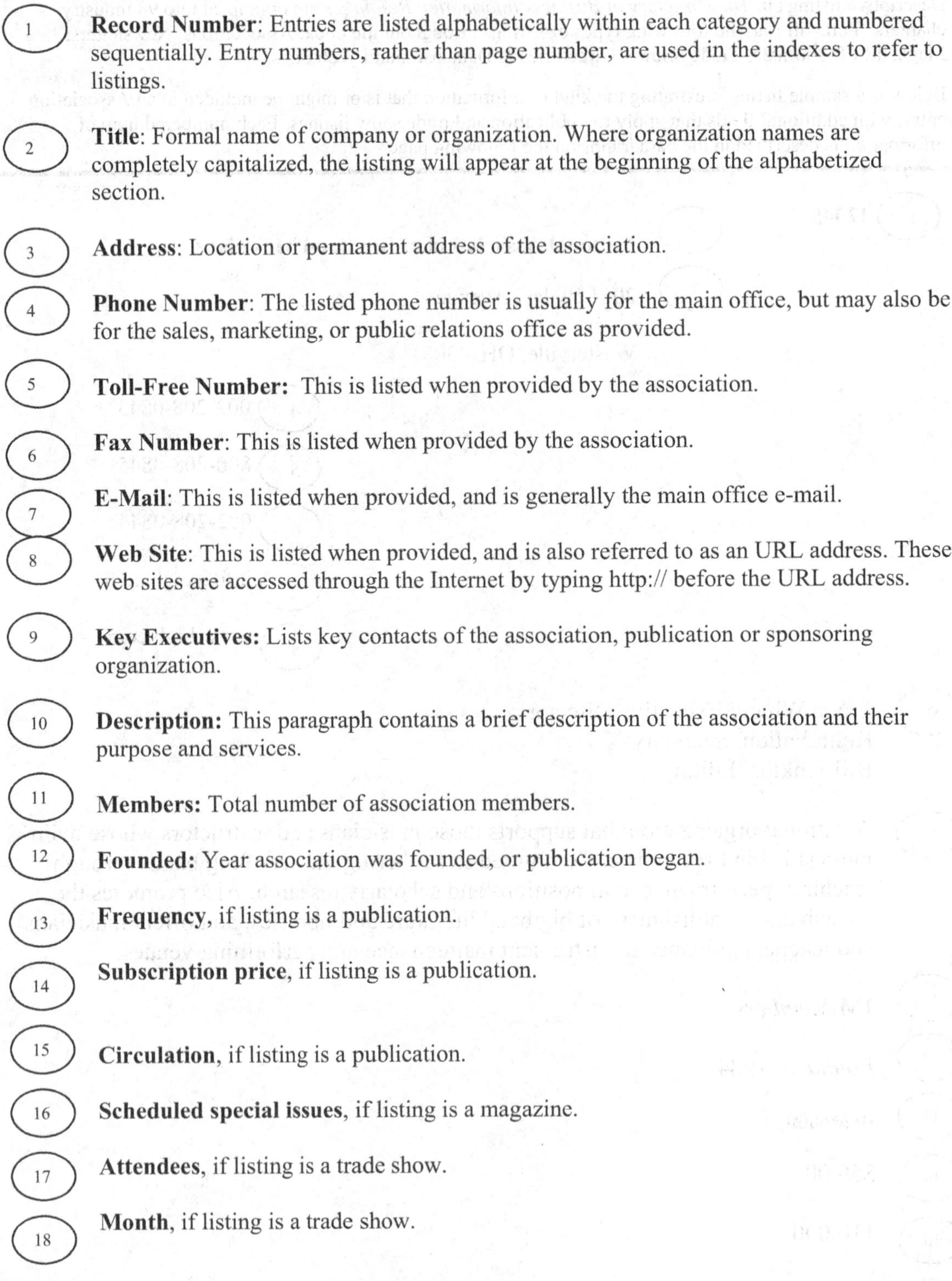

1 **Record Number**: Entries are listed alphabetically within each category and numbered sequentially. Entry numbers, rather than page number, are used in the indexes to refer to listings.

2 **Title**: Formal name of company or organization. Where organization names are completely capitalized, the listing will appear at the beginning of the alphabetized section.

3 **Address**: Location or permanent address of the association.

4 **Phone Number**: The listed phone number is usually for the main office, but may also be for the sales, marketing, or public relations office as provided.

5 **Toll-Free Number:** This is listed when provided by the association.

6 **Fax Number**: This is listed when provided by the association.

7 **E-Mail**: This is listed when provided, and is generally the main office e-mail.

8 **Web Site**: This is listed when provided, and is also referred to as an URL address. These web sites are accessed through the Internet by typing http:// before the URL address.

9 **Key Executives:** Lists key contacts of the association, publication or sponsoring organization.

10 **Description:** This paragraph contains a brief description of the association and their purpose and services.

11 **Members:** Total number of association members.

12 **Founded:** Year association was founded, or publication began.

13 **Frequency**, if listing is a publication.

14 **Subscription price**, if listing is a publication.

15 **Circulation**, if listing is a publication.

16 **Scheduled special issues**, if listing is a magazine.

17 **Attendees**, if listing is a trade show.

18 **Month**, if listing is a trade show.

Content Summary of Chapter Listings

Chapters in this directory often include a wide range of topics. The following list of keywords from the Association listings shows the subjects covered in each chapter.

Accounting
Accounting Historians
Accounting Standards
Accreditation
Auditors
Black Accountants
Bookkeepers
Broadcast Cable Financial Management
Budget & Program Analysis
Computerized Accounting
Construction Financial Management
Cost Estimating
Government Accountability
Government Financial Officers
Healthcare Financial Management
Hospitality Financial Management
Insolvency
Insurance
Latino Accountants
Military Comptrollers
Newspapers Financial Management
Payroll
Public Accountants
Taxes
Trucking Financial Management
Valuation
Women Accountants

Advertising
Advertising Agencies
Advertising Research
Cable TV Advertising
Children's Advertising
Commercials
Communications
E Marketing
Educational Advertising
Exhibition Management
Newspaper Advertising
Outdoor Advertising
Photographers
Point of Purchase
Public Opinion
Railroad Advertising
Signs
Transportation Advertising
Women in Advertising

Agriculture
4-H
Agricultural Aviation
Agricultural Communications
Agricultural Consultants
Agricultural County Agents
Agricultural Economics
Agricultural Education
Agricultural Engineers
Agricultural Fairs
Agricultural History
Agricultural Law
Agricultural Management
Agricultural Manufacturers
Agricultural Marketing
Agricultural Research
Agricultural Retail
Agricultural Teachers
Agronomy
Alfalfa
Angus
Animal Health
Animal Hides
Animal Science
Aquatics
Arid Lands
Bedding Plants
Bee Keeping
Beef
Bio-Dynamic Farming
Biomolecular Study
Blacksmiths
Blueberries
Brahman Beef
Canola
Cereal
Christmas Trees
Conservation
Corn
Cotton
Cottonseed
Cranberries
Crops
Dairy
Ecological Farming
Eggs
Enology
Entomology
Family Farming
Feed
Fertilizer
Fisheries
Florals
Foresters
Gardening
Grain
Grapes
Grasslands
Guernsey
Hay
Herbs
Hereford
Holstein
Horticulture
Irrigation
Jersey Cattle
Livestock
Maple Syrup
Millers
Oil Seed
Onions
Organic
Pesticides
Phytopathology
Pork
Potato
Poultry
Produce
Santa Gertrudis
Seeds
Sheep
Soil
Soybean
Sugar
Sunflowers
Veal
Walnuts
Weeds
Wheat

Alternative Energy
Biodiesel
Biogas
Biomass
Clean Energy
Energy Recovery
Ethanol
Geothermal Energy
Hydrogen
Lignite Energy
Low Impact Hydropower
Ocean Renewable Energy
Renewable Energy
Solar Energy
Sustainable Energy
Thermal Energy
Wind Energy

Amusement & Entertainment
Amusement Equipment Manufacturers
Amusement Equipment Rentals
Amusement Industry Marketing
Amusement Parks
Amusement Safety
Aquariums
Caves
Circus
Coin Operated
Concessions
Gambling
Game Developers
Go-Karts
Haunted Attractions
Jugglers
Kiddie Rides
Laser Attractions
Motor Sports
Roller Coasters
Spectator Sports
Theaters
Themed Amusements
Ticketing
Water Parks
Zoos

Apparel & Accessories
Cashmere & Camel Hair Manufacturers
Clothing Contractors
Clothing Manufacturers
Costume Designers
Cotton
Cotton Shippers
Fashion Designers
Footwear
Fur Manufacturers
Fur Merchants
Headwear
Home Sewing/Crafts
Hosiery
Infant & Children Wear
Intimate Apparel
Knitting
Leather
Millners, Dressmakers & Tailors
Neckwear
Needlework
Sportswear
Sunglasses
Uniform Manufacturers
Union Manufacturers & Distributors
Western & English Tack Apparel

Appliances
Manufacturers
Parts Suppliers
Repair
Retail Dealers
Service

Architecture
Accessibility for the Disabled
Architectural Historians
Building Officials
Cast Stone
Code Administrators
Concrete
Conservation
Design Drafting
Education
Environmental Design
Impact Assessment
Insulated Cable Engineers
Intelligent Buildings
Landscape Architects
Livable Communities
Marine Engineers
Naval Architects
Precasts
Preservation
Schools of Architecture
Sustainable Buildings
Urban Design

Art & Antiques
Aesthetics
American History
Animal Artists
Antique Dealers
Appraisal
Art Dealers
Art Education
Art Libraries
Art Materials
Art Museums
Art Placement
Art Research
Art Therapy
Auctioneers
Blacksmiths
College Art
Collectors
Conservation
Fine Arts
Fine Print Dealers
Illustrators
Library Art
Limited Edition Dealers
Photography
Picture Framers
Preservation Technology
School Programs
State Art Agencies

Automotive
Aftermarkets
Air Conditioning
Antique Trucks
Auto Auctions

Content Summary of Chapter Listings

Retail Lumber
Roof Coatings
Roof Tile
Rubber Pavements
Safety Glazing
Scaffolds
Screen Manufacturers
Senior Housing
Slag
Slurry Surfacing
Steel Joists
Steel Windows
Stone, Sand & Gravel
Structural Insulated Panel
Stucco Manufacturers
Subcontractors
Tech Home
Terrazzo & Mosaic
Tile Contractors
Tilt-Up Concrete
Timber Framers
Tools & Fasteners
Truck Mixer
Underground Construction
Unions
Utility Contractors
Wall & Ceiling Industries
Western Building Material
Women In Construction
Woodwork

Chemicals
Acrylonitrile
Adhesion
Aerosol
Agricultural Chemicals
Alkyl Amines
Analytical & Life Science Systems
Analytical Chemists
Analytical Communities
Bioanalysts
Biochemistry & Molecular Biology
Brewing Chemists
Cadmium
Catalysis
Chemical Engineers
Chemical Heritage
Chemical Manufacturers
Chemical Marketing Research
Chemical Recyclers
Chemical Strategies
Chlorine
Chlorine Chemistry
Chlorine Free
Chlorobenzene Producers
Clinical Chemistry
Coatings Technology
Coke & Coal Chemicals
Colorists
Consumer Specialty Chemicals
Cosmetic Chemists
Crystal Growth
Drug, Chemical & Allied Trades
Electrochemical
Embalming Chemical Manufacturers
Fiber Manufacturers
Hydrogen
Leather Chemists
Liquid Terminals
Lubricant Manufacturers
Mass Spectrometry
Materials Technology
Methanol
Oil Chemists
Oxygenated Fuels
Ozone
Pest Management
Pesticide Applicators
Phosphate Chemicals
Pine Chemicals
Polyisocyanurate Insulation
Polyurethane Foam
Powder Coating
Process Equipment Manufacturers
Spectroscopy
Synthetic Organic Chemicals
Textile Chemists
Toxicology

Cleaners & Laundries
Building Service Contractors
Diaper Services
Drycleaners
Environmental Management
Fabricare
Halogenated Solvents
Kitchen Exhaust
Linens
Power Washers
Uniform & Textile Service

Communications & Media
Abstracting & Information Services
Freedom Information Center
Information & Image Management
Information Systems
Information Technology
Medical Illustrators
Newspapers
Personal Achievement
Postal Commerce
Regional Magazines
Speakers
Technology in Education
Telecommunications Industry
Toastmasters
Translators
Writers

Computers & Data Processing
Alpha Micro Users
Artificial Intelligence
Audiovisual Catalogers
Automated Reasoning
Data Interchange Standards
Digital Dealers
Educational Communications & Technology
Electronic Engineers
Event Marketing
Identification Manufacturers
Imaging Science
Image Management
Information Display
Information Networking
Information Processing
Information Science
Information Systems Management
Intelligence
Interactive Multimedia
Knowledge Engineers
Language Instruction
Managing Human Resource Information
Medical Imaging
Medical Information
Open Applications
Optical Engineering
Precision Engineering
Recognition Technologies
Regional Sciences
Reprographic
Science Association
Security
Serial Storage Architecture
Software Users
Systems Management Technology
Technology in Education

Cosmetics, Perfumes & Personal Care
Aesthetics Manufacturers & Distributors
Aloe Science
Aromatics
Color
Consumer Healthcare Manufacturers
Cosmetology
Drug, Chemical & Allied Trades
Fragrance Research
Fragrances
Nail & Beauty
Nail Manufacturers
Tanning Manufacturers

Credit & Lending Services
Bankruptcy
Business Producers Credit
Commercial Collectors
Commercial Finance
Consumer Data
Consumer Debt Counseling
Credit Union Research & Consulting
Electronic Transactions
Financial Services
Fraud & Theft
Mortgage Brokers
Recovery Association
Risk Management

Cyber Security
Cyber Crime
Cyber Forensics
Automated Teller Machines
Intelligence Communities
Homeland Security
Defense Security
Microcomputers
Professional Certifications
Information Technology
Security Research
Firewalls
Intrusion Prevention
Advanced Technology Crimes
Information Security
Assurance
Risk Management
Governance
Federal Bureau of Investigation
National Security
Corporate Security
Cyber Crime Threats
Forensics
Cyber Watch

Direct Marketing
Art Directors
Digital Concepts
E-Marketing
Hispanic Marketing
Mail Marketing
Mobile Telecommunications
Publication Designers
Teleservices
Third Party Mailing
Writers

Drugs & Pharmaceuticals
Clinical
Clinical Laboratory
Distribution
Education
Efficient Operation
Ethical Pharmacies
Excipients
Generic
Health System
History of Pharmacy
Hospitals
Managed Care
Oil Chemists
Outsourcing Research
Parenteral & Enteral Nutrition
Pharmacy Law
Pharmaceutical Alliance
Pharmacy Cooperative
Senior Care
Standardization
Wholesale Druggists

E-Commerce & Internet
Advertising
Computing in Education
eMarketing
Hispanic Chamber
Public Technology
Security
Software Alliance
Uniform Council
Women in ECommerce

Electrical
Apparatus Service
Bioelectrmagnetics
Contractors
Electrical Instruments
Electrochemical
Electronic Assembly
Electronic Measuring Instruments
Engineers
Generating Systems
Insulated Cable
Intercommunications Applications
Laser and Electro-Optic
Magnetic
Microelectronics
Microwave
Overstress/Electrostatic
Public Owned Utilities
Relay Electronics
Research
Rural Electric Cooperative
Safety
Sound Systems
Technical Certifications
Testing
Variable Resistive Products

Electronics
Agricultural
Aircraft
Armed Forces
Assembly
Certified Technicians
Commercialization Research
Consumer Electronics
Environmental
Instrumentation & Measurement
Interactive Services
Marine Electronics
Metals
Microchip Industry
Microelectronics
Minerals

Content Summary of Chapter Listings

Society of Arboriculture

Gifts
Christmas
Handmade
Holiday
International
Museums
Salespeople Association
Souvenirs
Toy and Hobby

Glass & Ceramics
China Clay Producers
Flint Glass Workers Union
Glazing Industry Code Committee
Industrial Sand Association
Insulating Glass
Porcelain Enamel Institute
Refractory Ceramic Fiber

Government
Access Professionals
Board of National Labor Relations
Border Patrol Council
Center for Neighborhood
Chiefs of Police
Citizens Against Government Waste
Community Development
Conference of Mayors
Council of State Housing
Council on the Homeless
Council on Water Policy
County and City Health Officials
Emergency Management
Fire Chiefs
Governmental Purchasing
Housing Law Project
Interstate Oil and Gas
League of Cities
Local Air Pollution
Milk Control Agencies
Procurement Round Table
Rural Housing Coalition
Search and Rescue
State Community Service Programs
Study of the Presidency
Trust for Public Land
Urban and Regional Information
Urban Economic Development
Weatherization Assistance
World Federalist Association

Graphic Design
Graphic Arts
Graphic Communications
Illustrators
Imaging
Printing
Publication Designers
Urban Art

Hardware
Doors
Equipment Lessors
Hand Tools
Locksmiths
Lumbermen
Metal Detectors

Healthcare
Applied Psychophysiology
Association for Worksite Health
Promotion
Athletic Trainers
Blood Banks
Bone and Mineral Research
Breast Cancer
Cataract & Refractive Medicine
Cell Biology
Chiropractics
Cleft Palate Craniofacial
Clinical Nutrition
Compliance Packaging
Continuity of Care
Council on the Aging
County Health Facility Administration
Crematin
Dental
Gerantological Society
Headaches
Health Plans
Healthcare Recruitment
Home Care
Human Genetics
Human Services
Laser Medicine
Medical Imaging
Medical Instrumentation
Medical Libraries
Mental Retardation
Nonprescription Medicines
Nuclear Medicine
Pain
Pharmacology
Postgraduate Medicine
Psychiatry
Psychologyl
Radiology
Sleep Products
Speech-Language-Hearing
State Medicaid Directors
Suicidology
Textile Rental Services
Tissue Banks
Worksite Health

Heating & Air Conditioning
Air Balance Consultants
Flexible Air Duct
Gas Appliance Manufacturers
Masonry Heater
Microwave Power Institute
Mobile Air Conditioning
Power Engineers
Refrigeration
Solar Energy
Wholesalers

Hobbies & Games
American Craft Council
American Quilts
Archery
Camping
Home Sewing
Hooking Artists
Miniatures
Model Railroad
Philatelic Society
Society of Craft Designers

Hotels & Motels
Asian/American Hotel Owners
Executive Housekeepers
Facility Management
Hospitality Financial & Technology
Hotel and Motel Brokers
Hotel and Restaurant Employees
Resort Development
Small Luxury Hotels

Industrial Equipment
Abrasive Manufacturers
Asphalt Recycling and Reclaiming
Casting Industry Suppliers
Coatings
Composite Can and Tube Institute
Composite Fabricators
Corrugated Steel Pipe
Electroplaters Surface Finishers
Fluid Controls
Hack and Band Saw Manufacturers
Heat Processing Equipment
Hoist Manufacturers
Industrial Diamonds
Industrial Engineers
Industrial Security
Spray Equipment
Tribologists & Lubrication

Insurance
American Prepaid Legal Services
Arbitration Forums
Association of Retired Persons
Cargo War Risk Reinsurance
Certified Insurance Counselors
Committee for Arson Control
Crop Insurers
Defense & Corporate Counsel
Fire Investigators
Highway Loss Data Institute
Insurance Law
National Viatical Association
Property Insurance Loss Register
Registered Mail Insurance
Self Insurance Institute
Shipowners Claim
Transportation Consumer Protection
Underwriters Laboratories
Workers Compensation Reinsurance

Interior Design, Decorating & Lighting
Can Manufacturers
Carpets and Rugs
Decorative Fabric Distributors
Floor Covering
Florists
Home Furnishings
Illuminating Engineering
Kitchen and Bath
Lighting Association
Paint and Decorating
Picture Framers
Upholstery
Window Coverings

International Trade
Academy of International Business
American League for Exports
Security Assistance
Hong Kong Trade Development
International Chambers of Commerce
Latin American Studies
Oil and Gas of Russian Far East
US China Business Council

Jewelry & Watches
Appraisers Association
Cultured Pearl Information
Diamond Council
Estate Jewelry
Gemological Institute
Gold Prospectors
Goldsmiths
Indian Arts & Crafts
Jewelers Vigilance Committee
Silversmiths
Traveling Jewelers
World Gold Council

Journalism
Collegiate Press
Environmental Journalists
Gay and Lesbian Press
Hollywood Foreign Press
Investigative Reporters and Editors
Overseas Press Club of America
Society for News Design
Society of American Travel Writers

Law Enforcement & Public Safety
Academy of Criminal Justice Science
American Jail Association
American Polygraph Association
Arson Investigators
Bloodhounds
Bombs
Drug Enforcement Officers
Footprint Association
Forensic Dentists
Livestock Theft
National Constables Association
Society of Criminology

Leather Products
Pedorthic Footwear Association
Restorers
Saddle Markers
Sponge and Chamois Institute

Legal
American Bar Foundation
American Institute of Parliamentarians
American Society of Family & Conciliation
American Society for Legal History
American Society for Trial Consultants
Arbitration Association
Center on Children and the Law
Commission on Mental Retardation & Physical Disability Law
Council on Legal Education Opportunity
Council on State Government
Equal Justice Works
Family Mediators
First Amendment Lawyers Association
Japanese American Society for Legal Studies
Legal Investigators
Mineral Law
Native American Rights Fund
People Against Racist Terror
Psychiatry and the Law

Libraries
American Archivists
American Indian Library
Art Libraries Society
Asian/Pacific American Librarians
Center for Children's Books
Library Blinding Institute
Library Needs of Nurses
Population/Family Planning
Recorded Sound

Content Summary of Chapter Listings

2020 Small Business Profile

U.S. SMALL BUSINESS ADMINISTRATION
OFFICE OF ADVOCACY
REGULATION • RESEARCH • OUTREACH

United States

31.7 million Small Businesses
99.9% of United States Businesses

60.6 million Small Business Employees
47.1% of United States Employees

EMPLOYMENT
1.6 million
net new jobs

DIVERSITY
5.2 million
self-employed minorities

TRADE
285,334
small business exporters

A note on COVID-19: This report uses the most up-to-date government data to present a unique snapshot of small businesses. The BLS employment estimates capture the early stages of the pandemic. All other sources reflect data collected prior to the pandemic.

Overall Economy

- In the fourth quarter of 2019, the United States grew at an annual rate of 2.1%. The United States' 2019 overall growth rate of 2.3% was down from the 2018 rate of 2.9%. (Source: BEA)
- In April 2020, the unemployment rate was 14.7%, up from 3.6% in April 2019. (Source: CPS)

Employment

Figure 1: United States Employment by Business Size (Employees)

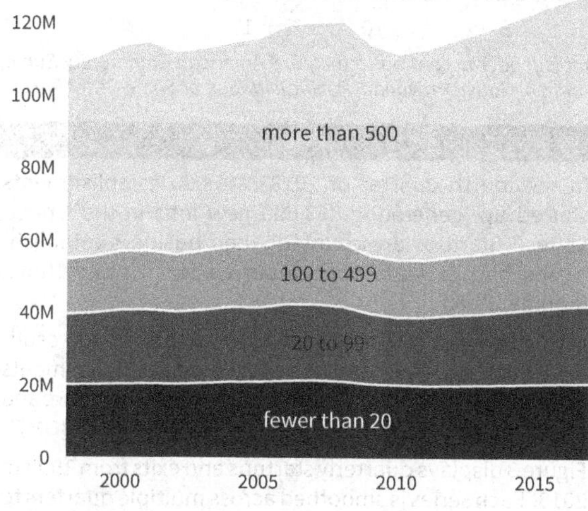

- United States small businesses employed 60.6 million people, or 47.1% of the private workforce, in 2017. (Source: SUSB)
- Firms with 20 to 99 employees have the largest share of small business employment. Figure 1 provides further details on firms with employees. (Source: SUSB)
- Private-sector employment decreased 14.6% during the 12-month period ending in April 2020. This was below the increase of 1.6% during the prior 12-month period. (Source: CES)
- The number of proprietors increased in 2018 by 3.1% relative to the previous year. (Source: BEA)
- Small businesses created 1.6 million net jobs in 2019. Firms employing fewer than 20 employees experienced the largest gains, adding 1.1 million net jobs. The smallest gains were in firms employing 100 to 499 employees, which added 249,900 net jobs. (Source: BDM)

The Small Business Profiles are produced by the US Small Business Administration's Office of Advocacy (http://advocacy.sba.gov). These profiles define small businesses as firms with fewer than 500 employees. Net small business job change, self-employed minorities, and exporter share statistics are based on 2019 Business Employment Dynamics (BDM), 2018 American Community Survey (ACS), and 2018 International Trade Administration (ITA) data, respectively.

Income and Finance

- The median income for self-employed individuals at their own incorporated businesses was $51,816 in 2018. For self-employed individuals at their own unincorporated firms, median income was $26,084. (Source: ACS)
- The total number of banks decreased by 239 between June 2018 and June 2019 to 5,303 banks. During the same period, the number of banks with assets under $1 billion decreased by 261 to 4,511 banks. (Source: FDIC)
- In 2018, United States lending institutions reporting under the Community Reinvestment Act issued 6.6 million loans under $100,000, a total value of $98.2 billion. (Source: FFIEC)

Median income represents earnings from all sources. Unincorporated self-employment income includes unpaid family workers, a very small percent of the unincorporated self-employed. The decline in the number of banks with assets under $1 billion may exceed the change in the total number of banks due to mergers and asset balance changes.

Self-Employment Demographics

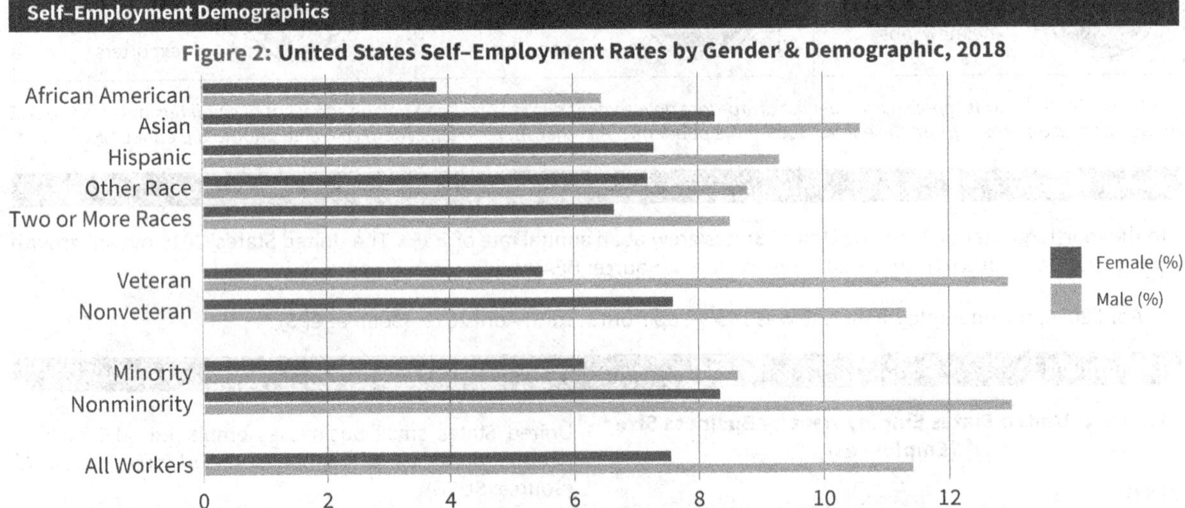

Figure 2 shows the self-employment rate for each demographic group by gender according to the 2018 American Community Survey (ACS). Other Race includes those who selected Alaska Native, American Indian, Native Hawaiian, Pacific Islander, or Some Other Race.

Turnover among Establishments with Employees

Figure 3: United States Quarterly Startups and Exits

200K
100K
0
-100K
-200K
Startups
Net New Establishments
Exits
1995 2000 2005 2010 2015

- In the fourth quarter of 2018, 249,000 establishments started up, generating 863,000 new jobs in the United States. Startups are counted when business establishments hire at least one employee for the first time. (Source: BDM)
- In the same period, 222,000 establishments exited, resulting in 762,000 jobs lost. Exits occur when establishments go from having at least one employee to having none, and then remain closed for at least one year. (Source: BDM)
- Figure 3 displays quarterly startups and exits from 1993 to 2018. Each series is smoothed across multiple quarters to highlight long-run trends. (Source: BDM)

The BDM data covers only business establishments with employees. BDM refers to startups as births and exits as deaths. These terms are distinct from the BDM openings and closings categories. Openings include seasonal re-openings and closings include seasonal shutterings. Quarterly startup and exit values may not align with Figure 3 due to smoothing.

International Trade

- A total of 292,793 firms exported goods from the United States in 2018. Of these, 285,334, or 97.5%, were small firms, which generated 32.0% of the United States' $1.5 trillion in total exports. (Source: ITA)

Small Business Employment by Industry and Self-Employment by County

Table 1: United States Employment by Industry, 2017

Industry	Small Business Employment	Total Private Employment	Small Business Employment Share
Health Care and Social Assistance	8,984,159	20,241,438	44.4
Accommodation and Food Services	8,542,661	14,088,211	60.6
Retail Trade	5,526,296	15,705,808	35.2
Construction	5,373,702	6,533,061	82.3
Professional, Scientific, and Technical Services	5,190,980	8,905,549	58.3
Manufacturing	5,039,772	11,721,785	43.0
Other Services (except Public Administration)	4,697,878	5,534,978	84.9
Administrative, Support, and Waste Management	3,754,463	11,897,056	31.6
Wholesale Trade	3,413,157	6,115,476	55.8
Finance and Insurance	1,909,993	6,408,168	29.8
Transportation and Warehousing	1,685,388	4,866,282	34.6
Educational Services	1,645,962	3,688,541	44.6
Real Estate and Rental and Leasing	1,451,546	2,148,006	67.6
Arts, Entertainment, and Recreation	1,428,531	2,368,928	60.3
Information	984,379	3,507,966	28.1
Management of Companies and Enterprises	423,295	3,462,498	12.2
Mining, Quarrying, and Oil and Gas Extraction	244,367	578,098	42.3
Agriculture, Forestry, and Fishing and Hunting	136,591	164,046	83.3
Utilities	111,747	644,703	17.3
Industries Not Classified	11,214	11,214	100.0
Total	**60,556,081**	**128,591,812**	**47.1**

Figure 4: United States Self-Employment Rates by County, 2018

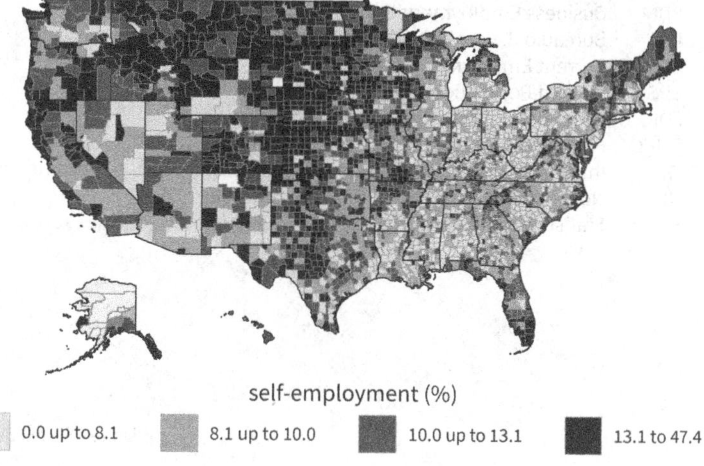

Small Businesses by Industry

Table 2: United States Small Businesses by Industry and Firm Size, 2017

Industry	1–19 Employees	1–499 Employees	Nonemployer Firms	Total Small Firms
Other Services (except Public Administration)	649,612	695,268	3,740,305	4,435,573
Professional, Scientific, and Technical Services	757,638	807,932	3,535,071	4,343,003
Construction	643,304	700,393	2,494,089	3,194,482
Real Estate and Rental and Leasing	295,084	308,106	2,784,753	3,092,859
Retail Trade	589,200	645,685	2,093,459	2,739,144
Health Care and Social Assistance	561,991	650,689	1,941,097	2,591,786
Administrative, Support, and Waste Management	305,247	343,791	2,143,437	2,487,228
Transportation and Warehousing	163,167	182,688	2,205,648	2,388,336
Arts, Entertainment, and Recreation	112,643	129,287	1,436,152	1,565,439
Finance and Insurance	220,285	236,657	732,196	968,853
Accommodation and Food Services	413,464	537,443	402,772	940,215
Educational Services	73,163	92,148	741,870	834,018
Wholesale Trade	253,458	294,909	399,261	694,170
Manufacturing	185,612	244,098	348,476	592,574
Information	67,876	78,430	349,905	428,335
Agriculture, Forestry, and Fishing and Hunting	21,184	22,535	250,537	273,072
Mining, Quarrying, and Oil and Gas Extraction	15,808	18,720	88,882	107,602
Utilities	4,535	5,752	13,761	19,513
Total	**5,339,918**	**5,976,761**	**25,701,671**	**31,678,432**

Tables 1 and 2 display data from the 2017 Statistics of U.S. Businesses (SUSB). Table 2 includes additional data from the 2017 Nonemployer Statistics (NES). Figure 4 provides estimates of the rate of self-employment among employed civilians, 16 years and over, including both incorporated and unincorporated businesses, from the 2018 American Community Survey (ACS). Data for areas shown in white in Figure 4 were withheld by the Census Bureau because they do not meet publication standards or could disclose information regarding individual businesses.

References

The Small Business Profiles, source data, and methodology are available at https://go.usa.gov/xvSPA.

ACS	American Community Survey, US Census Bureau
BEA	Bureau of Economic Analysis, US Department of Commerce
BDM	Business Employment Dynamics, BLS
BLS	Bureau of Labor Statistics, US Department of Labor
CES	Current Employment Statistics, BLS
CPS	Current Population Survey, BLS
FDIC	Federal Deposit Insurance Corporation
FFIEC	Federal Financial Institutions Examination Council
ITA	International Trade Administration, US Department of Commerce
NES	Nonemployer Statistics, US Census Bureau
SUSB	Statistics of US Businesses, US Census Bureau

Economic Bulletin

U.S. SMALL BUSINESS ADMINISTRATION
OFFICE OF ADVOCACY
REGULATION • RESEARCH • OUTREACH

December 2020

Small Business at a Glance

Prior to the COVID-19 pandemic, small firms were still slowly recovering from the Great Recession. Now, in the midst of the pandemic, self-employment levels have held, but proprietors' income changes have been choppy and a lack of contemporaneous data on business closures makes their true status unknown.

General

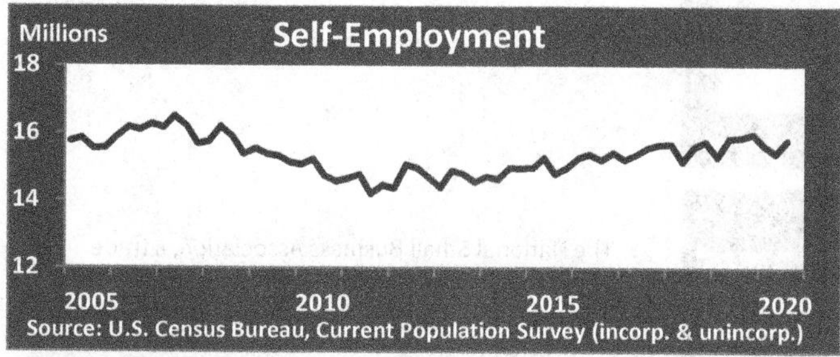

Self-employment (primary occupation, not seasonal adjusted) was slowly increasing for the last decade but remains below the pre-Great Recession peak. On a quarterly basis, the small drop in self-employment experienced in the first half of the year was mostly erased in the 3rd quarter. Note that the COVID-19 pandemic may have put the business of many of the self-employed on a pause or hiatus. However, they remain self-employed.

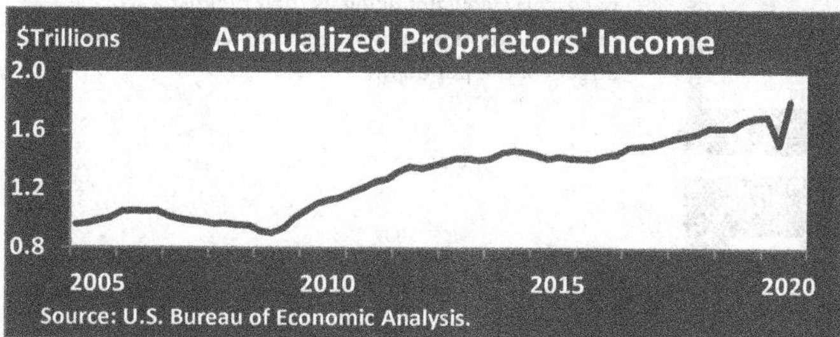

While self-employment figures indicate the number of proprietors has been mostly consistent over time, their income declined 13% annualized in the second quarter of 2020. This is the largest quarterly decline in history (quarterly data began in 1947). However in the most recent quarter, proprietors' income recovered. It is not clear if this is a temporary recovery related to short term federal COVID-19 financial assistance.

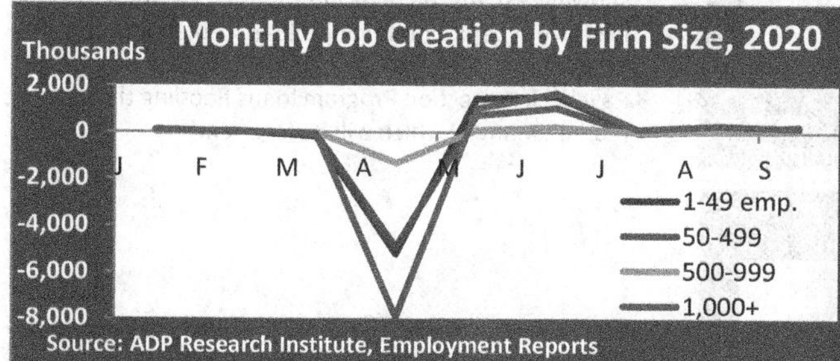

The Bureau of Labor Statistics' firm size job creation figures show small firms (<500 employees) accounting for 63 percent of the private net job creation from 2010 to 2019, but 2020 had a labor market shock. For 2020, payroll services firm ADP estimates that firms with 1,000 or more employees had the biggest monthly job decline in the spring in terms of number of employees. The size classes quickly recovered some of the losses, and gains since have been muted. Small firms lost more jobs in the spring but gained more since, and overall, in 2020 they lost 4.8 million net jobs vs 5.3 million for large firms.

Census' High-Propensity Business Applications, which indicate business openings, have been relatively stable for fifteen years. However, the number of applications have recently spiked. It is not clear if the spike is from recently closed businesses reforming or from brand new businesses. The next few months will indicate if the spike is a trend or a data anomaly.

advocacy.sba.gov

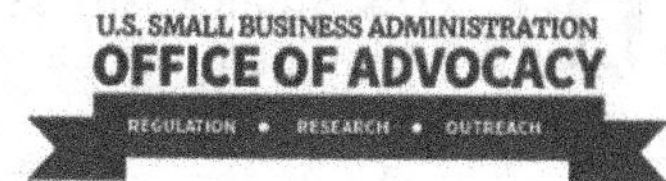

Finance

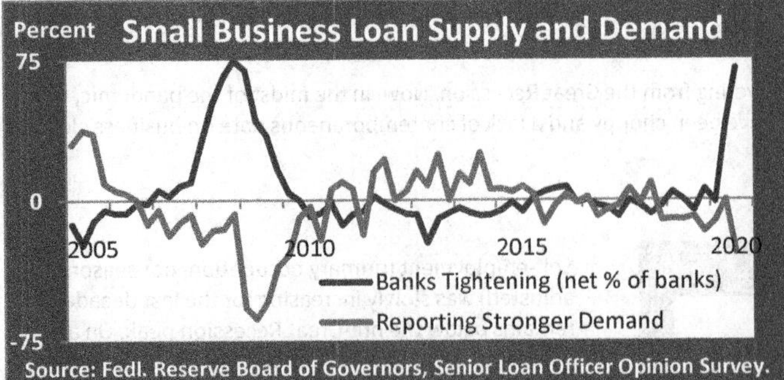

Due to the COVID-19 pandemic and weakening economic outlook, small business lenders were quick to tighten lending standards while loan demand also dropped. The demand in loans had been trending down prior to the pandemic as well.

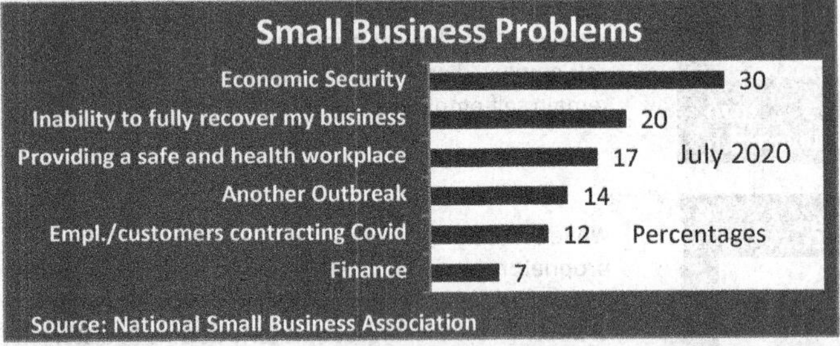

The National Small Business Association, a trade association for small businesses, points out that the largest concern of small businesses is essentially sales and economic worries. Small businesses do not necessarily view financing as their biggest problem/solution, and are instead worried about the effects of the pandemic.

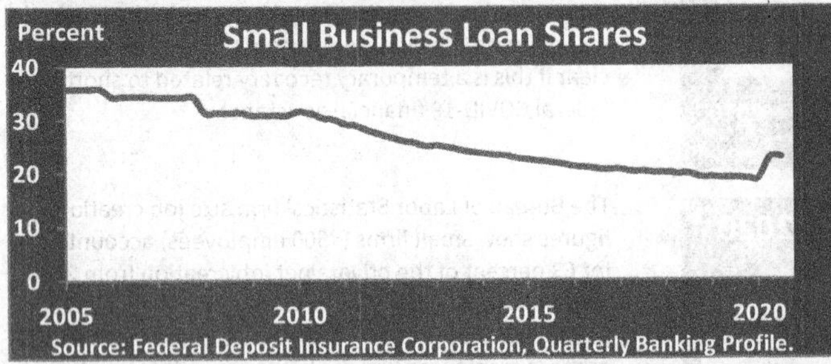

The small business loan share (loans $1 million or less) of total loans declined for nearly a decade before showing a slight rise in recent months. The increase is likely from banks limiting new loans, outstanding amounts on existing loans being slowly paid down, and Paycheck Protection Program loans flooding the market, many of which will be forgiven.

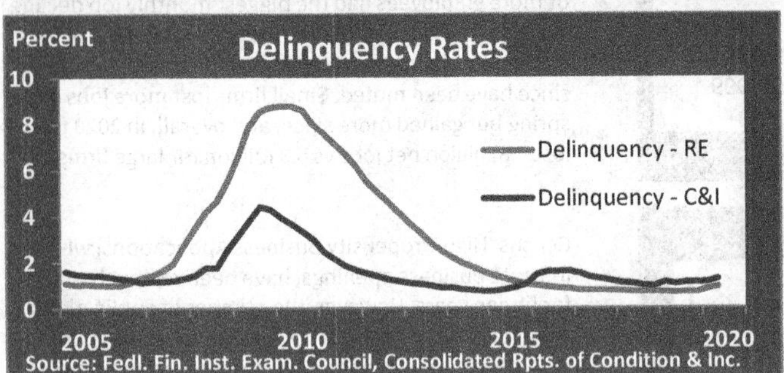

Delinquency rates for commercial and industrial loans (C&I) and commercial real estate loans (CRE) have been slightly increasing in 2020. While the increase is minimal, it could be an indicator of a trend as sales suffer for many businesses impacted by the pandemic.

By Brian Headd and Victoria Williams

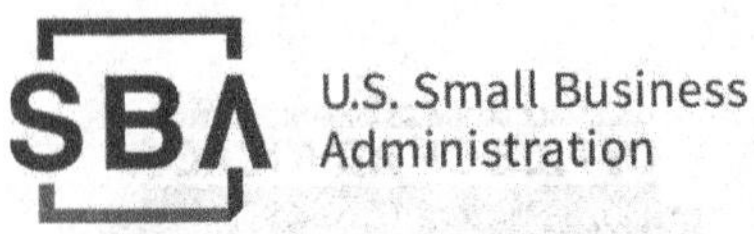

advocacy.sba.gov

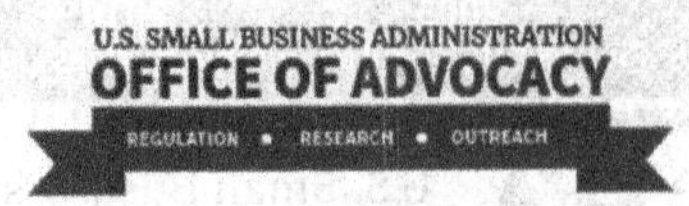

WHAT'S NEW WITH SMALLBUSINESS?

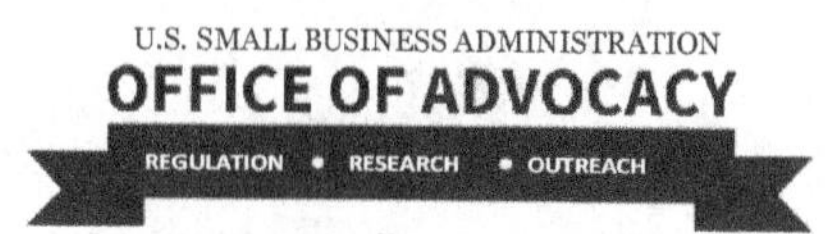

October 2020

WHAT IS A SMALL BUSINESS?

A small business is an independent business with fewer than 500 employees.

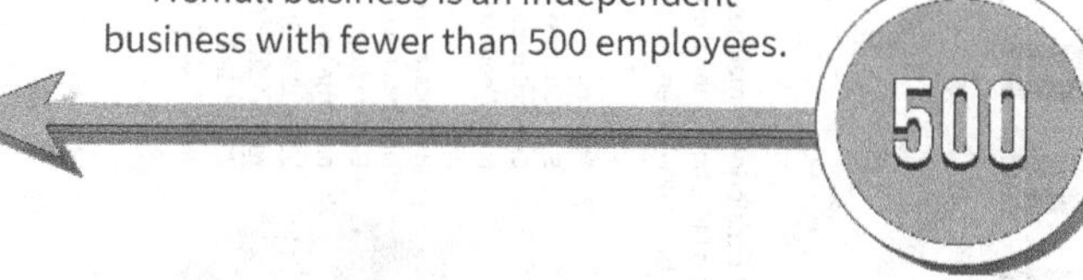

NET NEW JOBS

65%

NET NEW JOBS

Small businesses accounted for 65% of net new jobs. BED [2000-2019]

Small Businesses Comprise:

SUSB, NES, ITA

ALL FIRMS	ALL FIRMS with paid Employees	EXPORTING FIRMS	KNOWN EXPORT VALUE	PRIVATE SECTOR EMPLOYEES	PRIVATE SECTOR PAYROLL
99.9%	99.7%	97.5%	32.0%	47.1%	40.3%

31.7M SMALL BUSINESSES IN THE U.S.

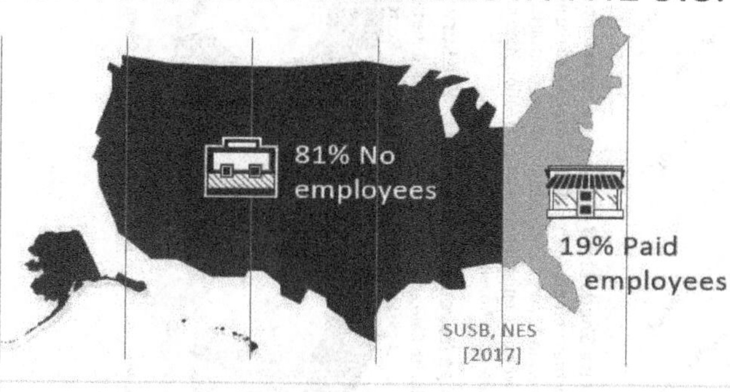

Change in Establishments

898K Closings

1M Openings

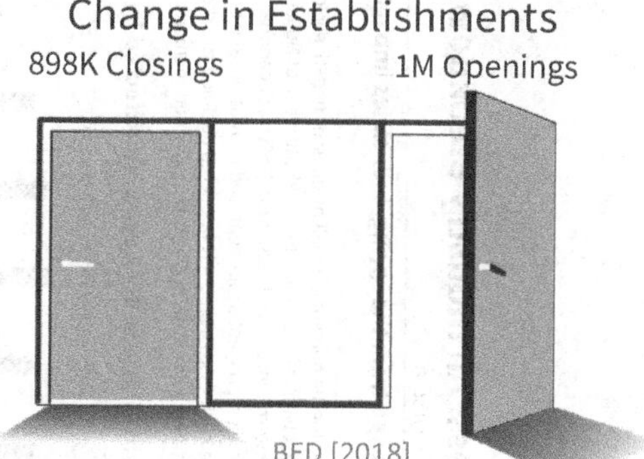

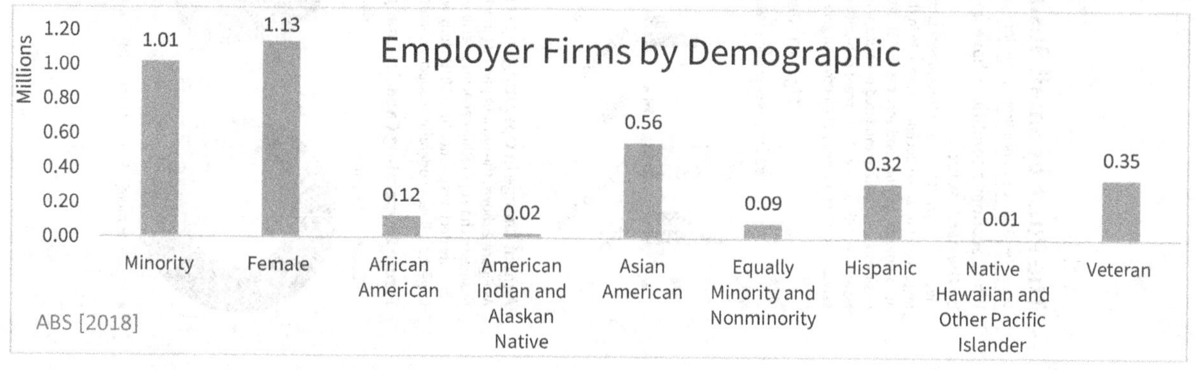

SOURCES

ABS Annual Business Survey
BED Business Employment Dynamics
ITA International Trade Administration
NES Nonemployer Statistics
SUSB Statistics of US Businesses

SBA For even more information visit advocacy.sba.gov

Small Business Facts

The Pulse of Small Business: An Industry Breakdown

December 2020 By Daniel Brown, Regulatory Economist

While economic conditions have improved from the spring, industries impacted the most at the beginning of the pandemic continue to be the hardest hit.

Figure 1 analyzes March and November estimates for the percent of small businesses negatively impacted by the COVID-19 epidemic. The total share of small businesses negatively impacted declined from 51% in the first week of the survey to 29.7% the week of November 16th. In the April 26th survey, the four most impacted industries were accommodation and food services (84%); arts, entertainment, and recreation (75%); educational services (74%); and health care (70%). While the amount of small businesses negatively impacted in education services; arts, entertainment, and recreation; and accommodation and food services remained relatively high in the November 16th survey, the percent of health care businesses negatively impacted declined to 33%. This was due in large part to the necessary nature of many health care services and the recovery of elective surgery numbers after many states had suspended them from March until May.

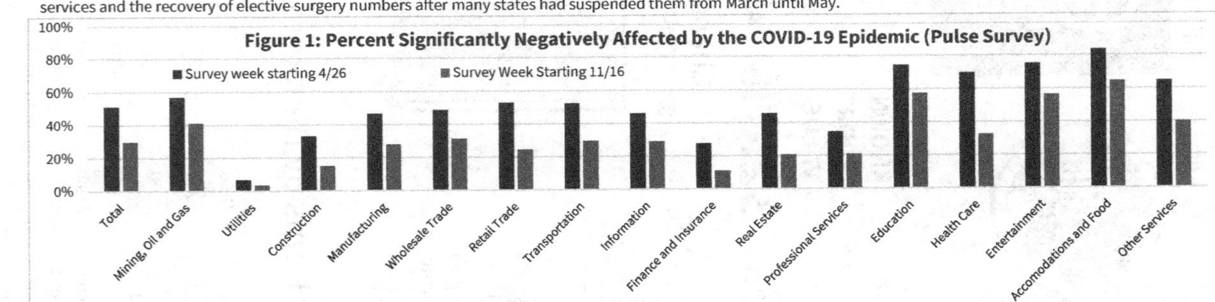

Figure 1: Percent Significantly Negatively Affected by the COVID-19 Epidemic (Pulse Survey)

Annual Change in Operating Capacity Sheds Light on Most Impacted Industries

As Figure 2 shows, the most impacted industries from November 2019-2020 also had the highest reduction in operation capacity. While the majority of small health care businesses had operating capacities decline, most saw capacity declines of less than 50%. Like Figure 1, accommodation and food services (46% have annual operating capacity declines greater than 50%) along with arts, entertainment and recreation (45% have annual operating capacity declines greater than 50%) experienced the largest declines in operating capacity compared to November 2019.

Figure 2: Operating Capacity Change November 2019-2020 (Pulse Survey)

Educational Services | Health Care and Social Assistance | Arts, Entertainment and Recreation | Accomodation and Food Services

■ Up 50% or more ■ Up less than 50% ■ No Change ■ Down less than 50% ■ Down 50% or more

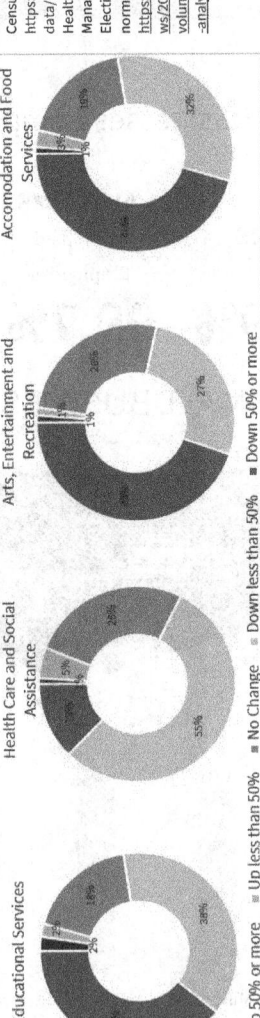

Sources:
Small Business Pulse Survey, US Census Bureau, https://portal.census.gov/pulse/data/
Healthcare Financial Management Association, Elective surgery volume near normal in late July, https://www.hfma.org/topics/news/2020/07/elective-surgery-volume-near-normal-in-late-july--analysis-finds.html

Small Business Facts

BLACK BUSINESS OWNERS HIT HARD BY PANDEMIC

August 2020 · By Daniel Wilmoth, PhD

U.S. SMALL BUSINESS ADMINISTRATION OFFICE OF ADVOCACY REGULATION • RESEARCH • OUTREACH

Black owners show biggest decline in business activity

Effects of the COVID-19 pandemic on business owners have varied across demographic groups. Data on demographic characteristics and self-employment are collected through the Current Population Survey and available through IPUMS. In July 2020, the total number of people who were self-employed and working was 7.3 percent lower than in July 2019. That decline was a partial recovery from April 2020, when the decline was 20.2 percent relative to April 2019. Declines have been largest for Black self-employed workers, with a decline of 37.6 percent in April and a partial recovery to a decline of 18.4 percent in July. The effects of the pandemic have varied by industry, and demographic differences in the effects of the pandemic reflect demographic differences in distributions across industries.

The decline in business activity among Black owners has been nearly three times the decline among other owners

Black women show bigger decline than Black men

In April 2020, the total number of Black women who were working and self-employed was 40.8 percent lower than in April 2019, while the decline for Black men was 35.7 percent. After a partial recovery, the decline for Black women in July was 19.8 percent, while the decline for Black men was 17.6 percent. Relatively few business owners are Black women, and the large declines among Black women have reduced their representation in recent months. In January 2010, Black women accounted for 5.9 percent of all workers but only 1.8 percent of self-employed workers. The share of self-employed workers who were Black women had risen to 3.1 percent by March 2020 before falling to 2.0 percent in April and then recovering to 2.7 percent in July.

Change in total working self-employed

Everyone	-7.3%
Asian	-4.7%
Black	-18.4%
White	-6.2%
All other groups	-13.5%
Hispanic	-2.7%
Men	-8.0%
Women	-6.0%

Change from July 2019 to July 2020.
Source: Current Population Survey; BLS, Census, and IPUMS

Change in Black self-employment by gender

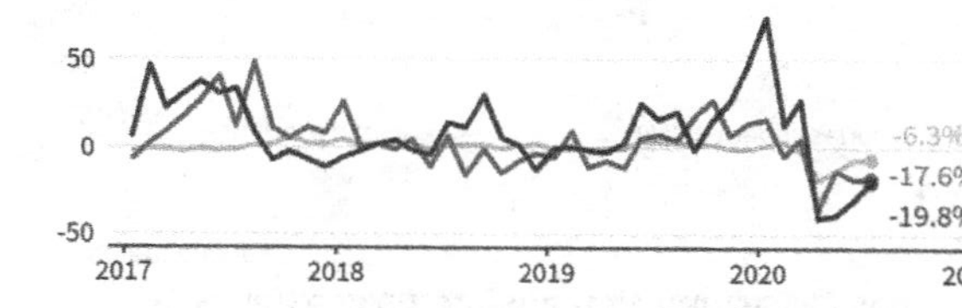

Change relative to 12 months prior.
Source: Current Population Survey; BLS, Census, and IPUMS

Small Business Facts

RESTAURANTS AND BARS STAGGERED BY PANDEMIC

June 2020 · By Daniel Wilmoth, PhD

Leisure and hospitality employment plunges

The COVID-19 pandemic caused a decline in employment in leisure and hospitality that was more than twice the decline for any other industry group. The Bureau of Labor Statistics (BLS) measures employment by industry group through the Current Employment Statistics (CES) program. In May 2020, employment in leisure and hospitality was down 41 percent relative to May 2019. Declines for other groups monitored through the CES program ranged from 2 percent for financial activities to 18 percent for miscellaneous services. Before the pandemic, leisure and hospitality accounted for 13 percent of total private employment, and small businesses accounted for 61 percent of employment in leisure and hospitality. As of June 20, 2020, the Small Business Administration had approved over $49 billion in emergency funding for small businesses in leisure and hospitality.

Restaurants and bars, a category dominated by small businesses, have suffered disproportionate declines in employment

Restaurants and bars struggle despite partial recovery

The two largest categories of businesses within the leisure and hospitality group before the pandemic were accommodation, which accounted for 13 percent of group employment, and food services and drinking places, which accounted for 73 percent. Small businesses accounted for 42 percent of employment in accommodation and 64 percent of employment in food services and drinking places. In May 2020, employment in accommodation was 50 percent lower than in May 2019, and employment in food services and drinking places was 37 percent lower. The decline for food services and drinking places was a substantial improvement from April, when employment was down by 48 percent relative to April 2019.

Change in employment by industry group

Percent change

Financial activities

Miscellaneous services

Leisure and hospitality

Share of employment in small businesses

Change relative to prior year. Symbol size reflects share of total employment.
Source: CES (BLS), SUSB 2017 (Census)

Employment changes within leisure and hospitality

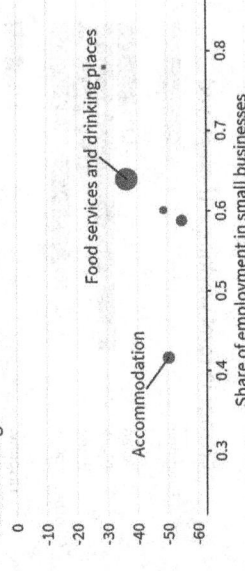

Percent change

Food services and drinking places

Accommodation

Share of employment in small businesses

Change relative to prior year. Symbol size reflects share of group employment.
Source: CES (BLS), SUSB 2017 (Census)

The North American Industry Classification System (NAICS, pronounced Nakes) was developed as the standard for use by Federal statistical agencies in classifying business establishments for the collection, analysis, and publication of statistical data related to the business economy of the U.S. NAICS was developed under the auspices of the Office of Management and Budget (OMB), and adopted in 1997 to replace the old Standard Industrial Classification (SIC) system (see page xxiii). Below are all relevant NAICS codes and descriptions. For a more detailed explanation of the NAICS, visit www.naics.com.

11 **Agriculture, Forestry, Fishing and Hunting**
11141 Food Crops Grown Under Cover
11191 Tobacco Farming
114 Fishing, Hunting and Trapping
115 Support Activities for Agriculture and Forestry

21 **Mining**
211111 Crude Petroleum and Natural Gas Extraction
212 Mining (except Oil and Gas)

22 **Utilities**
22131 Water Supply and Irrigation Systems

23 **Construction**
236 Construction of Buildings
237 Heavy and Civil Engineering Construction
23815 Glass and Glazing Contractors
23821 Electrical Contractors
23822 Plumbing, Heating, and Air-Conditioning Contractors
2383 Building Finishing Contractors

31-33 **Manufacturing**
311 Food Manufacturing
3111 Animal Food Manufacturing
31121 Flour Milling and Malt Manufacturing
3113 Sugar and Confectionery Product Manufacturing
3114 Fruit and Vegetable Preserving and Specialty Food Manufacturing
3115 Dairy Product Manufacturing
3117 Seafood Product Preparation and Packaging
3118 Bakeries and Tortilla Manufacturing
31191 Snack Food Manufacturing
31192 Coffee and Tea Manufacturing
31193 Flavoring Syrup and Concentrate Manufacturing
31194 Seasoning and Dressing Manufacturing
312 Beverage and Tobacco Product Manufacturing
3141 Textile Furnishings Mills
315 Apparel Manufacturing
315211 Men's and Boys' Cut and Sew Apparel Contractors
315212 Women's, Girls', and Infants' Cut and Sew Apparel Contractors
315292 Fur and Leather Apparel Manufacturing
3159 Apparel Accessories and Other Apparel Manufacturing
316 Leather and Allied Product Manufacturing
3162 Footwear Manufacturing
321 Wood Product Manufacturing
322 Paper Manufacturing
323 Printing and Related Support Activities
324 Petroleum and Coal Products Manufacturing
325 Chemical Manufacturing
3252 Resin, Synthetic Rubber, and Artificial Synthetic Fibers and Filaments Manufacturing
3253 Pesticide, Fertilizer, and Other Agricultural Chemical Manufacturing
3254 Pharmaceutical and Medicine Manufacturing
3255 Paint, Coating, and Adhesive Manufacturing
3256 Soap, Cleaning Compound, and Toilet Preparation Manufacturing
32591 Printing Ink Manufacturing
32592 Explosives Manufacturing
325992 Photographic Film, Paper, Plate, and Chemical Manufacturing
326 Plastics and Rubber Products Manufacturing
3262 Rubber Product Manufacturing
32621 Tire Manufacturing
32622 Rubber and Plastics Hoses and Belting Manufacturing
32629 Other Rubber Product Manufacturing
327 Nonmetallic Mineral Product Manufacturing
32711 Pottery, Ceramics, and Plumbing Fixture Manufacturing
32712 Clay Building Material and Refractories Manufacturing
3272 Glass and Glass Product Manufacturing
3273 Cement and Concrete Product Manufacturing
3274 Lime and Gypsum Product Manufacturing
32791 Abrasive Product Manufacturing
331 Primary Metal Manufacturing
332 Fabricated Metal Product Manufacturing
3325 Hardware Manufacturing
333 Machinery Manufacturing
3331 Agriculture, Construction, and Mining Machinery Manufacturing
3333 Commercial and Service Industry Machinery Manufacturing
3334 Ventilation, Heating, Air-Conditioning, and Commercial Refrigeration Equipment Manufacturing
3335 Metalworking Machinery Manufacturing
3336 Engine, Turbine, and Power Transmission Equipment Manufacturing
334 Computer and Electronic Product Manufacturing
3342 Communications Equipment Manufacturing
33422 Radio and Television Broadcasting and Wireless Communications Equipment Manufacturing
3343 Audio and Video Equipment Manufacturing
3344 Semiconductor and Other Electronic Component Manufacturing
3345 Navigational, Measuring, Electromedical, and Control Instruments Manufacturing
334518 Watch, Clock, and Part Manufacturing
3346 Manufacturing and Reproducing Magnetic and Optical Media
335 Electrical Equipment, Appliance, and Component Manufacturing
3353 Electrical Equipment Manufacturing
336 Transportation Equipment Manufacturing
3361 Motor Vehicle Manufacturing
3363 Motor Vehicle Parts Manufacturing
3364 Aerospace Product and Parts Manufacturing
3365 Railroad Rolling Stock Manufacturing
3366 Ship and Boat Building
336991 Motorcycle, Bicycle, and Parts Manufacturing
336992 Military Armored Vehicle, Tank, and Tank Component Manufacturing
337 Furniture and Related Product Manufacturing
3372 Office Furniture (including Fixtures) Manufacturing
3391 Medical Equipment and Supplies Manufacturing
33991 Jewelry and Silverware Manufacturing
33992 Sporting and Athletic Goods Manufacturing
33993 Doll, Toy, and Game Manufacturing
33994 Office Supplies (except Paper) Manufacturing
33995 Sign Manufacturing

42 **Wholesale Trade**
423 Merchant Wholesalers, Durable Goods
424 Merchant Wholesalers, Nondurable Goods
425 Wholesale Electronic Markets and Agents and Brokers

44-45 **Retail Trade**
441 Motor Vehicle and Parts Dealers
442 Furniture and Home Furnishings Stores
443 Electronics and Appliance Stores
444 Building Material and Garden Equipment and Supplies Dealers
445 Food and Beverage Stores
446 Health and Personal Care Stores
451 Sporting Goods, Hobby, Book, and Music Stores
453 Miscellaneous Store Retailers
454 Nonstore Retailers

48-49 **Transportation and Warehousing**
481 Air Transportation
482 Rail Transportation
483 Water Transportation
484 Truck Transportation

485 Transit and Ground Passenger Transportation
486 Pipeline Transportation
487 Scenic and Sightseeing Transportation
4885 Freight Transportation Arrangement
493 Warehousing and Storage

51 Information
511 Publishing Industries (except Internet)
5111 Newspaper, Periodical, Book, and Directory Publishers
5121 Motion Picture and Video Industries
51223 Music Publishers
515 Broadcasting (except Internet)
516 Internet Publishing and Broadcasting
517 Telecommunications
518 Data Processing, Hosting and Related Services
51912 Libraries and Archives
51913 Internet Publishing and Broadcasting and Web Search Portals

52 Finance and Insurance
522 Credit Intermediation and Related Activities
52211 Commercial Banking
522292 Real Estate Credit
522293 International Trade Financing
52311 Investment Banking and Securities Dealing
52392 Portfolio Management
52399 All Other Financial Investment Activities
524 Insurance Carriers and Related Activities
525 Funds, Trusts, and Other Financial Vehicles
5251 Insurance and Employee Benefit Funds
52593 Real Estate Investment Trusts

53 Real Estate and Rental and Leasing
531 Real Estate
5321 Automotive Equipment Rental and Leasing
53212 Truck, Utility Trailer, and RV (Recreational Vehicle) Rental and Leasing
53221 Consumer Electronics and Appliances Rental
53223 Video Tape and Disc Rental
5324 Commercial and Industrial Machinery and Equipment Rental and Leasing
533 Lessors of Nonfinancial Intangible Assets (except Copyrighted Works)

54 Professional, Scientific, and Technical Services
5411 Legal Services
5412 Accounting, Tax Preparation, Bookkeeping, and Payroll Services
5413 Architectural, Engineering, and Related Services
54135 Building Inspection Services
54141 Interior Design Services
54143 Graphic Design Services
541613 Marketing Consulting Services
54162 Environmental Consulting Services
5418 Advertising and Related Services
54182 Public Relations Agencies
54183 Media Buying Agencies
541921 Photography Studios, Portrait

56 Administrative and Support and Waste Management and Remediation Services
561422 Telemarketing Bureaus
56145 Credit Bureaus
5615 Travel Arrangement and Reservation Services
5616 Investigation and Security Services
5617 Services to Buildings and Dwellings
56191 Packaging and Labeling Services
562 Waste Management and Remediation Services

61 Educational Services
6114 Business Schools and Computer and Management Training

71 Arts, Entertainment, and Recreation
711 Performing Arts, Spectator Sports, and Related Industries
713 Amusement, Gambling, and Recreation Industries
71321 Casinos (except Casino Hotels)
71394 Fitness and Recreational Sports Centers

72 Accommodation and Food Services
7211 Traveler Accommodation
72111 Hotels (except Casino Hotels) and Motels
72112 Casino Hotels
7212 RV (Recreational Vehicle) Parks and Recreational Camps
722 Food Services and Drinking Places
7221 Full-Service Restaurants

81 Other Services (except Public Administration)
8111 Automotive Repair and Maintenance
811211 Consumer Electronics Repair and Maintenance
8113 Commercial and Industrial Machinery and Equipment (except Automotive and Electronic) Repair and Maintenance
81141 Home and Garden Equipment and Appliance Repair and Maintenance
8121 Personal Care Services
81231 Coin-Operated Laundries and Drycleaners
813211 Grantmaking Foundations
813312 Environment, Conservation and Wildlife Organizations

92 Public Administration
921 Executive, Legislative, and Other General Government Support
922 Justice, Public Order, and Safety Activities
924 Administration of Environmental Quality Programs
92612 Regulation and Administration of Transportation Programs
92613 Regulation and Administration of Communications, Electric, Gas, and Other Utilities
92614 Regulation of Agricultural Marketing and Commodities
928 National Security and International Affairs

The Standard Industrial Classification (SIC) is a United States government system for classifying industries by a four-digit code. Established in 1937, it has been supplanted by the six-digit North American Industry Classification System (NAICS) (see page ixx), which was released in 1997; however certain government departments and agencies, such as the U.S. Securities and Exchange Commission (SEC), still use SIC codes. Below are all major SIC codes and descriptions. For a more detailed explanation of the SIC system, visit http://www.census.gov/epcd/www/sic.html.

01 Agricultural Production - Crops

07 Agricultural Services

09 Fishing, Hunting and Trapping

10 Metal Mining

12 Coal Mining

13 Oil and Gas Extraction

14 Mining and Quarrying of Nonmetallic Minerals, Except Fuels

15 Building Construction - General Contractors & Operative Builders

16 Heavy Construction, Except Building Construction - Contractors

17 Construction - Special Trade Contractors

20 Food and Kindred Products

21 Tobacco Products

22 Textile Mill Products

23 Apparel and Other Finished Products Made From Fabrics and Similar Materials

24 Lumber and Wood Products, Except Furniture

25 Furniture and Fixtures

26 Paper and Allied Products

27 Printing, Publishing, and Allied Industries

28 Chemicals and Allied Products

29 Petroleum Refining and Related Industries

30 Rubber and Miscellaneous Plastics Products

31 Leather and Leather Products

32 Stone, Clay, Glass, and Concrete Products

33 Primary Metal Industries

34 Fabricated Metal Products, Except Machinery and Transportation Equipment

35 Industrial and Commercial Machinery and Computer Equipment

36 Electronic and Other Electrical Equipment and Components, Except Computer Equipment

37 Transportation Equipment

38 Measuring, Analyzing, and Controlling Instruments; Photographic, Medical and Optical Goods; Watches

39 Miscellaneous Manufacturing Industries

41 Local and Suburban Transit and Interurban Highway Passenger Transportation

42 Motor Freight Transportation and Warehousing

44 Water Transportation

45 Transportation By Air

47 Pipelines, Except Natural Gas

47 Transportation Services

48 Communications

49 Electric, Gas and Sanitary Services

50 Wholesale Trade-Durable Goods

51 Wholesale Trade-Non-Durable Goods

60 Depository Institutions

61 Non-Depository Credit Institutions

63 Insurance Carriers

65 Real Estate

73 Business Services

75 Automotive Repair, Services, and Parking

76 Miscellaneous Repair Services

78 Motion Pictures

79 Amusement and Recreation Services

80 Health Services

81 Legal Services

82 Educational Services

84 Museums, Art Galleries, and Botanical and Zoological Gardens

87 Engineering, Accounting, Research, Management, and Related Services

92 Justice, Public Order, and Safety

94 Administration of Human Resource Programs

95 Administration of Environmental Quality and Housing Programs

96 Administration of Economic Programs

97 National Security and International Affairs

Associations

1 **AGN International - North America**
13918 E. Mississippi Avenue
Suite 63308
Aurora, CO 80012

303-743-7880
info@agn.org
www.agn.org
Twitter, LinkedIn

Lisa Hastings, Chair
Robert Watts, Vice Chair
Jim Rollins, Treasurer
Kevin Doyle, Secretary
Cindy Frey, Regional Director

Worldwide association of separate and independent accounting and consulting firms. Composed of CPA consulting firms who share information and resources via the association programs. AGN-NA operates under the premise that by sharing information and resources, members' growth and quality goals can be achieved more quickly.
53 Members
Founded in 1978

2 **ARMA International**
11880 College Boulevard
Suite 450
Overland Park, KS 66210

913-444-9174
844-565-2120; Fax: 913-257-3855
headquarters@armaintl.org
www.arma.org
Facebook, Twitter, LinkedIn

Nate Hughes, Exec. Dir, Operations
Jennifer Millett, National Account Manager
Heather Lehman, Sr. Manager, Membership

ARMA International is a not-for-profit association and a source for authoritative education, the latest legislative updates, standards & best practices. The association was established in 1955. Its approximately 27,000 members include records managers, archivists, corporate librarians, imaging specialists, legal professionals, IT managers, consultants, and educators, all of whom work in a wide variety of industries.
27000 Members
Founded in 1955

3 **Academy of Accounting Historians**
9009 Town Center Parkway
Lakewood Ranch, FL 34202

941-921-7747; Fax: 941-923-4093
AAHWebmaster@aaahq.org
aaahq.org/AAH

Gary Spraakman, President
Stephan A. Fafatas, Vice President, Communications
Martin E. Persson, Vice President, Partnerships
Yvette J. Lazdowski, Treasurer
Stephanie D. Moussalli, Secretary

Section of the American Accounting Association that aims to ecourage research, publication, teaching and personal interchanges in all phases of accounting history and its interrelation with business and economic history including the environment within which they developed.
Founded in 1973

4 **Accounting & Financial Women's Alliance**
2365 Harrodsburg Road
Suite A325
Lexington, KY 40504

859-219-3532
800-326-2163
afwa@afwa.org
www.afwa.org
Facebook, Twitter, LinkedIn, Instagram, Pinterest

Cindy Stanley, Executive Director
Catherine Schaefer, Member Engagement & Ops. Specialist
Kara Hamilton, Member Services
Rachel Gates, Member Services

Their mission is to enable women in all accounting and related fields to achieve their full personal, professional and economic potential and to contribute to the future development of their profession.
Founded in 1938

5 **Accreditation Council for Accountancy and Taxation**
1330 Braddock Place
Suite 540
Alexandria, VA 22314

888-289-7763
info@acatcredentials.org
www.acatcredentials.org

Cynthia Hunt, President
Janet Downs, Secretary/Treasurer
John Rice, Executive Director

A non-profit independent testing, accrediting and monitoring organization that seeks to identify professionals in independent practice who specialize in providing financial, accounting and taxation services to individuals and small to mid-size businesses.
Founded in 1973

6 **Affordable Housing Association of Certified Public Accountants**
459 N. 300 W.
Suite 11
Kaysville, UT 84037

801-547-0809; Fax: 801-547-5070
info@ahacpa.org
www.ahacpa.org

Les Sparks, President
Kathy Christensen, Manager
Kennen Sparks, Technology & Tool Development

AHACPA is a national association of CPAs and financial professionals providing financial services, support and education for the affordable housing and HUD-approved lender communities, informing members of financial requirements and providing specific guidance on how to efficiently implement those requirements.
500 Members
Founded in 1998
Mailing list available for rent

7 **American Accounting Association**
9009 Town Center Parkway
Lakewood Ranch, FL 34202

941-921-7747; Fax: 941-923-4093
info@aaahq.org
aaahq.org
Facebook, Twitter

Yvonne Hinson, CEO
Julie Smith David, Chief Innovation Officer
Barbara Brady, Sr. Director, Operations
Erlinda L. Jones, Sr. Director, Meetings & Programs

The American Accounting Association promotes worldwide excellence in accounting education, research and practice. The Association is a voluntary organization of persons interested in accounting education and research.
9000 Members
Founded in 1916

8 **American Association for Budget and Program Analysis**
P.O. Box 1157
Falls Church, VA 22041

aabpa@aabpa.org
www.aabpa.org
Facebook, Twitter, LinkedIn, GovLoop

Justin Theal, President
John Buhl, Vice President, Communications
Courtney Timberlake, Vice President, Partnerships
Karen Kunz, Vice President, Events
Beth Blue, Treasurer

Helps federal, state, and local government managers and analysts, corporate executives and academic specialists meet the unique challenges of their careers. By helping members keep up with the latest developments in their fields, establish and maintain contacts with colleagues, represent their interests and share opportunities, AABPA serves the key difference between simply having a job and being part of a highly respected and well trained profession.
400 Members
Founded in 1976
Mailing list available for rent

9 **American Association of Attorney-Certified Public Accountants**
P.O. Box 706
Warrendale, PA 15095

703-352-8064
888-288-9272; Fax: 703-352-8073
info@attorney-cpa.com
www.attorney-cpa.com
Facebook, Twitter, LinkedIn

Howard O. Bernstein, President
Michele B. Friend, Vice President
Deron R. Harrington, Treasurer
Marc L. Schwartz, Secretary
Kimmy Headland, Director, Membership & Chapters

The AAA-CPA is the only association in the nation whose members are comprised of professionals dually qualified as both attorneys and certified public accountants. Their mission is to provide members with quality education, opportunities to interface with other Attorney-CPAs, and resources to support and develop their professional practices.
Founded in 1964

10 **American Association of Finance & Accounting**

Home Page: www.aafa.com
Facebook, Twitter, LinkedIn

An alliance of executive search firms specializing in the recruiting of finance and accounting professionals.
Founded in 1978

11 **American College of Trust and Estate Counsel**
901 15th Street, NW
Suite 525
Washington, DC 20005

202-684-8460; Fax: 202-684-8459
www.actec.org
Facebook, Twitter, LinkedIn

Stephen R. Akers, President
Ann B. Burns, President-Elect
Robert W. Goldman, Vice President
Kurt A. Sommer, Treasurer
Susan D. Snyder, Secretary

Nonprofit association of lawyers that advises clients on planning for tax efficient transfer of wealth during life and after death, preparing real estate planning documents, administering

trusts, guardianships, planning for employee benefits, etc.
2500+ Members
Founded in 1949

12 **American Council of Life Insurers**
101 Constitution Avenue NW.
Suite 700
Washington, DC 20001-2133

202-624-2000
webadmin@acli.com
www.acli.com
Facebook, Twitter, LinkedIn

Daniel Houston, Chair
Susan K. Neely, President & CEO
David C. Turner, EVP & Corporate Secretary
Joyce Y. Meyer, EVP, Government Relations
Jill Kozeny, SVP, Comm. & Public Affairs

Trade association advocating federal, state, and international forums for public policy that supports the industry marketplace. ACLI members offer life insurance, annuities, retirement plans, long-term care, disability income insurance, and reinsurance.
290 Members
Founded in 1976

13 **American Institute of Certified Public Accountants**
220 Leigh Farm Road
Durham, NC 27707-8110

919-402-4500; Fax: 919-402-4505
www.aicpa.org
Facebook, Twitter, LinkedIn, YouTube

Barry C. Melancon, CPA, CGMA, President & CEO

Professional organization of CPAs in the United States. The AICPA serves as an advocate before legislative bodies, public interest groups and other professional organizations and develops standards for audits of private companies and other services by CPAs.
429K Members
Founded in 1887

14 **American Institute of Professional Bookkeepers**
6001 Montrose Road
Suite 500
Rockville, MD 20852

800-622-0121; Fax: 800-541-0066
info@aipb.org
www.aipb.org

Stanley Hartman, Co-Pres. & Executive Director
Stephen Sahlein, Co-Pres. & Director, Publishing
Barbara Regotti, General Manager, Education

An association established to achieve recognition of bookkeepers as accounting professionals, keep bookkeepers up to date on changes in bookkeeping, accounting and tax, answer questions on bookkeeping and accounting, and certify bookkeepers.
30000 Members
Founded in 1987

15 **American Payroll Association**
660 N. Main Avenue
Suite 100
San Antonio, TX 78205

210-224-6406; Fax: 210-224-6038
www.americanpayroll.org
Facebook, Twitter, LinkedIn, YouTube, Instagram

Daniel Maddux, Executive Director

The American Payroll Association is the leading advocate for the advancement of payroll professionals and a catalyst for connecting the payroll industry with employers and government. Their vision is to create opportunities and forge a community by providing the education, skills, and resources necessary for payroll professionals to become successful leaders and strategic partners within their organizations.
20000 Members
Founded in 1982

16 **American Property Tax Counsel**
77 W. Washington
Suite 900
Chicago, IL 60602

Home Page: www.aptcnet.com
Facebook, Twitter, LinkedIn

Linda Terrill, President

An organization of law firms providing major portfolio owners with a single source for all their property tax reporting and tax reduction needs.
100 Members
Founded in 1994

17 **American Society of Military Comptrollers**
415 N. Alfred Street
Alexandria, VA 22314

703-549-0360
800-462-5637; Fax: 703-549-3181
www.asmconline.org
Facebook, Twitter, LinkedIn

Al Runnels, Executive Director
Libby Long, Deputy Director, Memberships
Phara G. Rodrigue, Associate Director, Certification
Catherine Kenol, Associate Director, Communications
Judson Lineberger, Financial Operations Manager

ASMC is the non-profit educational and professional organization for persons, military and civilian, involved in the overall field of military comptrollership. ASMC promotes the education and training of its members, and supports the development and advancement of the profession of military comptrollership. The society sponsors research, provides professional programs to keep members abreast of current issues and encourages the exchange of techniques and approaches.
20000 Members
Founded in 1948

18 **Appraisers Association of America**
212 W. 35th Street
11th Floor South
New York, NY 10001

212-889-5404; Fax: 212-889-5503
referrals@appraisersassociation.org
www.appraisersassociation.org
Facebook, Twitter, LinkedIn

Linda Selvin, Executive Director
Teresa Caputo, Program Manager
Patrick McIntyre, Membership Manager
Yasemin Yeldener, Communications Coordinator
Jennifer Buonocore, CASP Coordinator

A national association of personal property appraisers who focus on fine and decorative arts. Appraiser Association appraisers work with private and corporate art collections as well as partner with collectors, attorneys, accountants, museums, educational institutions, trusts, brokers and insurance carriers to reflect the highest industry standards.
900+ Members
Founded in 1949

19 **Association for Accounting Marketing**
201 E. Main Street
Suite 1405
Lexington, KY 40507

859-402-9769
info@accountingmarketing.org
www.accountingmarketing.org
Facebook, Twitter, LinkedIn, Instagram

Becca Davis, President
Rhonda Clark, Association Manager
Heather Scott, Project Coordinator

The Association for Accounting Marketing (AAM) is a national organization and is the only trade association of its kind that provides resources, education, seminars, workshops, support and a global network to the accounting marketing industry. Membership includes accounting firm marketers from Big Four and other national, regional, local and sole proprietor firms. Others include sales and business development professionals, accounting partners, firm administrators, and students.
843 Members
Founded in 1989

20 **Association of Certified Fraud Examiners**
716 W. Avenue
Austin, TX 78701-2727

512-478-9000
800-245-3321; Fax: 512-478-9297
memberservices@acfe.com
www.acfe.com
Facebook, Twitter, LinkedIn, Instagram

Joseph T. Wells, Chair
Bruce Dorris, President & CEO
John D. Gill, VP, Education
John Warren, VP & General Counsel
Jeanette LeVie, VP & COO

The ACFE is reducing business fraud world-wide and inspiring public confidence in the integrity and objectivity within the profession.
85000 Members
Founded in 1988

21 **Association of Chartered Accountants in the United States**
admin@acaus.org
www.acaus.org
Facebook, LinkedIn

Conall McGonagle, President
Chris Easton, Vice President
Mark Billings, Treasurer
Veronica Beilby, Secretary
David Powell, Acting Chief Executive

ACAUS is a nonprofit professional and educational organization representing interests of U.S. based chartered accountants from the institutes of Chartered Accountants across the globe.
8000+ Members
Founded in 1980

22 **Association of College & University Auditors**
4400 College Boulevard
Suite 220
Overland Park, KS 66211

913-222-8663; Fax: 913-222-8606
ACUA-info@kellencompany.com
www.acua.org
Facebook, Twitter, LinkedIn, YouTube

Julia Hann, President
Emily Burch, Executive Director
Kristin Miodonski, Association Manager
Hannah Janvrin, Education Program Administrator

The Association of College & University Auditors (ACUA) is a professional organization comprised of audit professionals from all over the globe. They strive to continually improve the internal operations and processes of the individual institutions they serve, through continued professional development and the dissemination of individual internal audit experiences in an open forum with friends and colleagues.
Founded in 1958

23 **Association of Credit Union Internal Auditors**
332 Commerce Street
Suite 100
Alexandria, VA 22314

703-688-2284; Fax: 703-348-7602
acuia@acuia.org
www.acuia.org
Facebook, Twitter, LinkedIn

Bobby Nichols, Chair
Jill Meznarich, Vice Chair
Dean Swenson, Secretary
Barry Lucas, Treasurer

ACUIA is an international professional organization dedicated to the practice of internal auditing in credit unions. ACUIA's objectives are: to unify and encourage cooperative relationships among credit union internal auditors; to facilitate the exchange of information and ideas; to provide educational opportunities for developing and enhancing audit and leadership skills; and to promote the internal auditing profession.
600 Members
Founded in 1990

24 **Association of Government Accountants**
2208 Mount Vernon Avenue
Alexandria, VA 22301-1314

703-684-6931
800-242-7211; Fax: 703-519-0039
communications@agacgfm.org
www.agacgfm.org
Facebook, Twitter, LinkedIn, Flickr

Ann M. Ebberts, Chief Executive Officer
Susan Fritzlen, Chief Operating Officer
Cristina Barbudo, Dir., Finance & Administration
Katya Silver, Dir., Professional Certification

AGA supports the careers and professional development of government finance professionals working in federal, state and local governments as well as the private sector and academia. Through education, research, publications, certification and conferences, AGA reaches thousands of professionals and offers more than 100,000 continuing professional education (CPE) hours annually.
14K+ Members
Founded in 1950

25 **Association of Healthcare Internal Auditors**
One Parkview Plaza
Suite 800
Oakbrook Terrace, IL 60181

303-327-7546
888-275-2442; Fax: 720-881-6101
info@ahia.org
www.ahia.org
LinkedIn, YouTube

Mary Jane Schroeder, Chair
Cavell Alexander, Vice Chair
Todd Havens, Secretary/Treasurer
Michelle Cunningham, Executive Director

The Association of Internal Auditors (AHIA) is a network of experienced healthcare internal auditing professionals who come together to share tools, knowledge and insight on how to assess and evaluate risk within a complex and dynamic healthcare environment. AHIA is an advocate for the profession, continuing to elevate and champion the strategic importance of healthcare internal auditors with executive management and the Board.
Founded in 1981

26 **Association of Independent Accounting Professionals**
staff@aiaponline.com
www.aiaponline.com

An online resource designed for today's independent accountant; provides practice expansion opportunities, information, and resources.

27 **Association of Insolvency Advisors and Restructuring Advisors**
221 W. Stewart Avenue
Suite 207
Medford, OR 97501

541-858-1665; Fax: 541-858-9187
aira@aira.org
www.aira.org

Jim Lukenda, Executive Director
Terry Jones, Director, CIRA & CDBV Programs
Michael Stull, Director, Information Technology
Michele Michael, Director, Member Services

AIRA is a nonprofit professional association serving the bankruptcy, restructuring and turnaround practice area. AIRA's membership consists of accountants, financial advisors, investment bankers, attorneys, workout consultants, trustees, and others in the field of business turnaround, restructuring and bankruptcy. AIRA members are among the most trusted and sought-after professionals in matters dealing with limited capital resources and deteriorating operating performance.
2000+ Members
Founded in 1982

28 **Association of Latino Professionals in Finance and Accounting**
1717 W. 6th Street
Suite 410
Austin, TX 78703

855-692-5732
carlos.perez@national.alpfa.org
www.alpfa.org
Facebook, Twitter, LinkedIn, YouTube, Instagram

Damian Rivera, Chief Executive Officer
Selene Benavides, Chief Financial Officer
Justin Lopez, Chief Operating Officer
Ann Marquez, Chief of Staff

ALPFA is the leading professsional association dedicated to enhancing opportunities for Latinos in the accounting, finance and related professions. ALPFA is a nonprofit entity registered with the IRS.
72000 Members
Founded in 1972

29 **Association of Local Government Auditors**
859-276-0686
kyoung@nasact.org
algaonline.org
Twitter, LinkedIn, RSS

Larry Stafford, President
Lisa Monteiro, Secretary
Justin Anderson, Treasurer

A professional organization committed to supporting and improving local government auditing through advocacy, collaboration, education, and training.
2500+ Members
Founded in 1989

30 **Association of Public Pension Fund Auditors**
P.O. Box 16064
Columbus, OH 43216-6064

webmaster@appfa.org
www.appfa.org

Sandra Vice, President
Leslie Nagel, Vice President
Yikchau Sze, Secretary
Cheryl Cervantes Dietz, Treasurer

A professional association consisting of internal auditors dedicated to providing comprehensive professional development and networking opportunities for its members.
Founded in 1991

31 **Beta Alpha Psi**
220 Leigh Farm Road
Durham, NC 27707

919-402-4044
bap@bap.org
www.bap.org
Facebook, Twitter, LinkedIn, Instagram

Rita Grant, President
Margaret Fiorentino, Executive Director
Lisa Wicker, Manager, Chapter Services
Lauren Peck, Manager, Marketing

Beta Alpha Psi is an honor organization for financial information students and professionals. The primary objective of Beta Alpha Psi is to encourage and give recognition to scholastic and professional excellence in the business information field. This includes promoting the study and practice of accounting, finance and information systems; providing opportunities for self-development, service and association among members and practicing professionals.
300K Members
Founded in 1919

32 **Broadcast Cable Credit Association**
550 W. Frontage Road
Suite 3600
Northfield, IL 60093

847-881-8757; Fax: 847-784-8059
info@bccacredit.com
www.bccacredit.com
Twitter, LinkedIn

Mary Collins, President & CEO
Jamie Grande, Director, Operations
Arcelia Pimentel, Sales/Membership
Dawn Stenstrom, Credit Investigator
Colette Pinter, Credit Investigator

BCCA, a subsidiary of Media Financial Management Association, represents credit and collection professionals from TV, radio, cable, system operators, newspaper, and magazine organizations in the U.S. and Canada. BCCA functions as a central clearinghouse for credit information on advertisers, agencies and buying services, both locally and nationally.
Founded in 1972

33 **CPA Associates International**
65 Harristown Road
Suite 210
Glen Rock, NJ 07452

201-857-8656
info@cpaai.com
www.cpaai.com
Twitter, LinkedIn, YouTube

Roger Isaacs, International Co-Chair
Jim Holmes, International Co-Chair
Joe Tarasco, North America Regional Manager

CPA Associates International was established as a global group of high-quality independent CPA and chartered accounting firms; it is market exclusive, with members in major cities throughout the world. The organized association provides members with the capabilities of

the largest firm, yet allows each to maintain its local practice while avoiding costly overhead and unnecessary controls.
113 Members
Founded in 1957

34 **CPA Firm Management Association**
136 S. Keowee Street
Dayton, OH 45402

937-222-0030
info@cpafma.org
www.cpafma.org
Facebook, Twitter, LinkedIn

Kim Fantaci, President
Jeanie Price, Chair
Alan Alexander, Vice Chair
Larry Sheftel, Secretary/Treasurer

The CPA Firm Management Association enables accounting firm administrators to communicate with one another and provide each other with the benefits of everyone's experiences in what was a new and emerging profession.
900 Members
Founded in 1984

35 **CPAsNET**
P.O. Box 4827
Boulder, CO 80306

609-890-0800
cpasnet@cpasnet.com
www.cpasnet.com

Sarah Johnson Dobek, President

An association of accounting and business consulting firms who havepooled their resources to provide their clients with the local, national, and international perspective needed to prosper.
Founded in 1994

36 **Construction Financial Management Association**
100 Village Boulevard
Suite 200
Princeton, NJ 08540-5783

609-452-8000
888-421-9996; Fax: 609-452-0474
info@cfma.org
www.cfma.org
Facebook, Twitter, LinkedIn, YouTube

Stuart Binstock, President & CEO
Brian Summers, VP, Operations
Catherine Wasner, VP, Member Services
Samantha Lake, VP, Marketing
Stacey Scholl, Director, Finance

CFMA is the only organization dedicated to bringing together construction financial professionals and those partners serving their unique needs. CFMA has 98 chapters located throughout the US and Canada.
8600 Members
Founded in 1981

37 **Construction Industry CPA/Consultants Association**
4531 Bohemia Drive
Pensacola, FL 32504

850-723-0372
info@cicpac.com
www.cicpac.com
Facebook, LinkedIn

Mike Karlins, President
Wes Winborne, Vice President
Bryan Eto, Secretary/Treasurer
Kathleen Baldwin, Executive Director

The Construction Industry CPAs/Consultants Association (CICPAC) is a national association of CPA firms recognized in their respective markets for providing high quality financial and consulting services. Each firm is the exclusive member in its area and must demonstrate proficiency in construction industry services and a reputation for high-quality work and integrity.
Founded in 1989

38 **Federal Accounting Standards Advisory Board**
441 G Street NW.
Suite 1155
Washington, DC 20548

202-512-7350; Fax: 202-512-7366
fasab@fasab.gov
www.fasab.gov
Twitter, LinkedIn

Monica Valentine, Executive Director
Melissa Batchelor, Assistant Director
Robin Gilliam, Assistant Director
Ross Simms, Assistant Director
Domenic N. Savini, Assistant Director

Establishes accounting standards for financial reporting entities of the United States Government.
Founded in 1990

39 **Federation of Schools of Accountancy**
220 Leigh Farm Road
Durham, NC 27707-8110

919-402-4825
mtarasi@aicpa.org
www.thefsa.org

Richard Dull, President
Anne Magro, Secretary
Norma Ramirez Montague, Treasurer

Promotes and supports high-quality graduate accounting programs andachieves public trust in the accounting profession through leadership in supporting and shaping high quality accounting education.
Founded in 1978

40 **Federation of Tax Administrators**
444 N. Capitol Street NW.
Suite 348
Washington, DC 20001

202-624-5890
support@taxadmin.org
www.taxadmin.org

Gale Garriott, Executive Director
Verenda Smith, Deputy Director
Ronald Alt, Sr. Manager, Economic & Tax
Cindy Anders-Robb, Sr. Manager, Motor Fuel & Tobacco
Ryan Minnick, Manager, Special Projects

A nonprofit corporation designed to improve the quality of state tax administration by providing services to state tax authorities and administrators. These services include research and information exchange, training, and intergovernmental and interstate coordination.
53 Members
Founded in 1937

41 **Financial Accounting Standards Board**
401 Merritt 7
P.O. Box 5116
Norwalk, CT 06856-5116

203-847-0700; Fax: 203-849-9714
www.fasb.org
Facebook, LinkedIn, RSS, YouTube

Hillary H. Salo, Chair
Peter C. Proestakes, Assistant Director
Alicia A. Posta, Assistant Director
Alex Casas, Assistant Director
Jeffrey D. Mechanick, Assistant Director

The mission of the FASB is to establish and improve standards of financial accounting and reporting that foster financial reporting by nongovernmental entities that provides decision-useful information to investors and other users of financial reports. That mission is accomplished through a comprehensive and independent process that encourages broad participation, objectively considers all stakeholder views, and is subject to oversight by the Financial Accounting Foundation's Board of Trustees.
Founded in 1973

42 **Financial Executives International**
1250 Headquarters Plaza
West Tower, 7th Floor
Morristown, NJ 07960

973-765-1000; Fax: 973-765-1018
membership@financialexecutives.org
www.financialexecutives.org
Facebook, Twitter, LinkedIn, Instagram

Andreas Rothe, National Chair
Andrej Suskavcevic, President/CEO
Kevin McBride, National Vice Chair
Alice Jolla, National Secretary
Bret Lawson, National Treasurer

FEI strives to be recognized globally as the leading organization for senior-level financial executives. Connects members through: interaction: providing local and international forums for connecting with peers, information: providing insight to assist with informed business decisions, influence: providing authoritative representation for members' interests, and integrity: providing the tools to advance the profession through ethical leadership.
10000 Members
Founded in 1931

43 **Financial Management Association International**
University of South Florida
4202 E. Fowler Avenue
BSN 3403
Tampa, FL 33620-5500

813-974-2084; Fax: 813-974-3318
fma@coba.usf.edu
www.fma.org
Facebook, Twitter, LinkedIn, YouTube

Michelle Lui, Executive Director
Dawn Appleby, Program Assistant
Matt Staton, Managing Editor
Kieara Nunez, Manager, Marketing & Communications
Shannon Tompkins, Director, Student Programs

Serving the global finance community by: Promoting the development of high-quality research that extends the frontier of financial knowledge; Promoting the understanding of basic and applied research and of sound financial practices; Enhancing the quality and relevance of education in finance; Providing opportunities for professional interaction between and among academics, practitioners, and students.
Founded in 1970

44 **Financial Managers Society**
1 North LaSalle Street
Suite 3100
Chicago, IL 60602-4003

312-578-1300
800-275-4367; Fax: 312-578-1308
info@fmsinc.org
www.fmsinc.org
Facebook, Twitter, LinkedIn

John A. Carrozza, Chair
Alana Vartanian, Chief Operating Officer
Taylor Weathers, Director, Membership
Jennifer Lindberg, Director, Marketing & Communication
Mark Loehrke, Editor/Writer

Provides service to financial personnel such as savings and loan financial officers, and to community commercial banks and credit unions.
Founded in 1948

45 **Government Finance Officers Association**
203 N. LaSalle Street
Suite 2700
Chicago, IL 60601-1210
312-977-9700; Fax: 312-977-4806
www.gfoa.org
Facebook, Twitter, LinkedIn, YouTube

Marion M. Gee, President
Chris Morrill, Executive Director
Mike Mucha, Deputy Executive Director
John Jurkash, Chief Financial Officer
Randall Towns, Director, Education

Represents public finance officials throughout the United States and Canada and promotes the professional management of governmental financial resources by indentifying, developing, and advancing fiscal strategies, policies, and practices for the public benefit.
Founded in 1906

46 **Healthcare Financial Management Association**
3 Westbrook Corporate Center
Suite 7600
Westchester, IL 60154-5723
708-531-9600
800-252-4362; Fax: 708-531-0032
jfifer@hfma.org
www.hfma.org
Facebook, Twitter, LinkedIn, YouTube

Joseph J. Fifer, FHFMA, CPA, President & Chief Executive Officer
Joyce Zimowski, FHFMA, CPA, Executive Vice President & CFO
Susan Brenkus, VP, HR & Chapter Relations
Richard L. Gundling, VP, Healthcare Financial Practices

HFMA is the nation's leading membership organization for healthcare financial management executives and leaders. HFMA's vision is to be the indispensable resource for healthcare finance.
40000 Members
Founded in 1950

47 **Hospitality Financial and Technology Professionals**
11709 Boulder Lane
Suite 110
Austin, TX 78726
512-249-5333
800-646-4387; Fax: 512-249-1533
Membership@hftp.org
www.hftp.org
Facebook, Twitter, LinkedIn

Daniel N. Conti, Jr., CHAE, CAM, President
Arlene Ramirez, Vice President
Frank I Wolfe, Ex Officio
Lyle Worthington, CHTP, Treasurer
Jerry M. Trieber, Immediate Past President

HFTP is an international, professional association providing a global network, continuing education and resources to the hospitality, finance and technology communities.
4600 Members
Founded in 1952

48 **INPACT Americas**
PO Box 495
Frederick, MD 21705-0495
301-694-8580; Fax: 301-694-5804
gloria@inpactam.org
www.inpactglobal.org

Bruce C. Levine, President
Gloria Parsley, Executive Director
James Valk, Treasurer
Loraine Koepenick, Dir. Communicaiotns & Program Devt.

A nonprofit association focused on contributing to the profitability and success of North America's accounting and consulting firms through management and marketing programs and resources.

49 **Information Resources Management Association**
701 E Chocolate Avenue
Suite 200
Hershey, PA 17033-1240
717-533-8845; Fax: 717-533-8661
member@irma-international.org
www.irma-international.org

Mehdi Khosrowpour, Executive Director
Sherif Kamel, VP, Information Management

An international professional organization dedicated to advancing the concepts and practices of information resources management in modern organizations. The primary objective of IRMA is to assist organizations and professionals in enhancing the overall knowledge and understanding of effective information resource management in the early 21st century and beyond.

50 **Information Systems Audit & Control Association (ISACA)**
Rolling Meadows, IL
847-660-5505
844-472-2246
www.isaca.org
Facebook, Twitter, LinkedIn

David Samuelson, CEO
Robb Micek, Chief Financial Officer
Mader Qaimari, Chief Learning Officer
Simona Rollinson, Chief Technology Officer

With members in more than 180 countries, ISACA is a recognized worldwide leader in IT governance, control, security and assurance. Sponsors international conferences, publishes the thw ISACA Journal and develops international information systems auditing and control standards.
9000+ Members
Founded in 1967

51 **Institute for Professionals in Taxation**
600 Northpark Town Center
1200 Abernathy Rd., Suite L-2
Atlanta, GA 30328-1040
404-240-2300; Fax: 404-240-2315
website@ipt.org
www.ipt.org

David H. LeVan, CMI, President
Chris G. Muntifering, CMI, Executive Director
Agnieszka Aburto, Finance Manager
Emily Archer, Certification Officer

A nonprofit educational association that provides educational programs, certifies, and establishes strict codes of conduct for state and local income, property, and sales.
4100+ Members
Founded in 1976

52 **Institute of Internal Auditors**
247 Maitland Ave
Altamonte Springs, FL 32701-4201
407-937-1111; Fax: 407-937-1101
CustomerRelations@theiia.org
na.theiia.org
Facebook, Twitter, LinkedIn, Auditchannel.tv

Jenitha John, Chair
Nancy Haig, North American Chair
Richard F. Chambers, President & CEO

Independent, objective assurance and consulting activity designed to add value to an organization's operations. It helps an organization accomplish its objectives by bringing a systematic, disciplined approach to evaluate and improve the effectiveness of risk management, control and governance processes. Representation from more than 100 countries.
18000 Members
Founded in 1941

53 **Institute of Management & Administration**
3 Bethesda Metro Center
Suite 250
Bethesda, MD 20814-5377
800-372-1033
703-341-3500; Fax: 800-253-0332
blawhelp@bna.com
www.bna.com
Facebook, Twitter, LinkedIn, YouTube

Josh Eastright, CEO
Mike McCarty, Chief Financial Officer
Christina Correira, Chief Human Resources Officer
Cesca Antonelli, Editor-In-Chief

An independent source of exclusive business management information for experienced senior and middle management proessionals.

54 **Institute of Management Accountants**
10 Paragon Dr
Suite 1
Montvale, NJ 07645-1760
201-573-9000
800-638-4427; Fax: 201-474-1600
ima@imanet.org
www.imanet.org
Facebook, Twitter, LinkedIn, YouTube

Paul E. Juras, Chair
Jeffrey C. Thomson, President and CEO

Professional organization devoted exclusively to management accounting and financial management. Goals are to help members develop both personally and professionally, by means of education, certification and association with other business professionals.
90K Members
Founded in 1919

55 **Insurance Accounting & Systems Association, Inc.**
3511 Shannon Road
Suite 160
Durham, NC 27707
919-489-0991; Fax: 919-489-1994
info@iasa.org
www.iasa.org
Facebook, Twitter, LinkedIn, YouTube

Laurie Macklosky, President
Kerry Crockett, CEO
Chuck Gunkel, VP, Business Development
Parshy Phillips, Director, Marketing & Communication
Kelli Bohannon, Director, Membership

A nonprofit, education association that strives to enhance the knowledge of insurance professionals and participants from similar organizations closely allied with the insurance industry by facilitating the exchange of ideas and information.

56 **International Cost Estimating and Analysis Association**
8221 Old Courthouse Rd
Suite 106
Vienna, VA 22182
703-938-5090; Fax: 703-938-5091
iceaa@iceaaonline.org
www.iceaaonline.org
Facebook, Twitter

Rick Collins, President
Bob Hunt, Executive Vice President
Christian Smart, VP, Professional Development

3 1326 00553 9905

Christina Snyder, Secretary
Jeffrey Moore, Treasurer

A non-profit organization dedicated to improving cost estimating and analysis in government and industry by enhancing the competence and achievements of its professional members
2015 Members
Founded in 2012

57 **International Federation of Accountants**
529 5th Avenue
6th Floor
New York, NY 10017

212-286-9344; Fax: 212-286-9570
communications@ifac.org
www.ifac.org
Facebook, Twitter, LinkedIn, YouTube

Alan Johnson, President
Kevin Dancey, Chief Executive Officer
Russell Guthrie, Chief Financial Officer
Jennifer DiClerico, Head, Communications
Damarys Albino, Head, Human Capital

IFAC is the global organization for the accountancy profession. It works with members and associates in 123 countries and jurisdictions to protect the public interest by encouraging high quality practices by the world's accountants.
175 Members
Founded in 1977

58 **National Academy of Public Administration**
1600 K Street NW
Suite 400
Washington, DC 20006

202-347-3190; Fax: 202-223-0823
feedback@napawash.org
www.napawash.org
Facebook, Twitter, LinkedIn, Vimeo

David Wennergren, Chair
Norton N. Bonaparte, Jr., Vice Chair
Teresa Gerton, President & CEO
Jane Fountain, Secretary
David Mader, Treasurer

An independent, nonprofit, and non-partisan organization that helpsthe Federal government address its critical management challenges through in-depth studies and analyses, advisory services and technical assistance, Congressional testimony, forums and conferences, and online stakeholder engagement.
800 Members
Founded in 1967

59 **National Association of Black Accountants**
7474 Greenway Center Drive
Suite 1120
Greenbelt, MD 20770

301-474-6222
888-571-2939; Fax: 301-474-3114
customerservice@nabainc.org
www.nabainc.org
Facebook, Twitter, LinkedIn, YouTube

Walter J. Smith, President/CEO
Kim R. Wilson, Chief Programs Officer
Herschel Frierson, Chair
Shon McGhee, Controller
Loleta Holmes, Director, Programs

Nationwide professional association with the primary purpose of developing, encouraging and serving as a resource for greater participation by African-Americans and other minorities in the accounting and finance professions.
Founded in 1969

60 **National Association of Certified Valuators and Analysts (NACVA)**
5217 South State Street
Suite 400
Salt Lake City, UT 84107

801-486-0600
800-677-2009; Fax: 801-486-7500
nacva1@nacva.com
www.nacva.com
Facebook, Twitter, YouTube

Alina Rivera, Chairman
Brien K. Jones, COO/EVP
Melissa Cardwell, Director of Project Management
Parnell Black, CEO
Jonathan Jackson, Executive Director

Global, professional association that supports the business valuation and litigation consulting disciplines within the CPA and professional communities. Along with its training and certification programs, NACVA offers a range of support services, reference materials, software, & customized databases to enahnce the professional capabilities and capacities of its members.
6500 Members
Founded in 1990

61 **National Association of Computerized Tax Processors**
H&R Block
4400 Main Street
Kansas City, MO 64111

816-328-8485; Fax: 800-996-3526
www.nactp.org
Facebook

Rebecca McCaulley, President
Jared Ballew, Vice President
Christina Taylor, Treasurer
Julie Sforza-Smith, Secretary
Carl Paduch, Webmaster

Nonprofit association that represents tax processing software and hardware developers, electronic filing processors, tax form publishers and tax processing service bureaus. The association promotes standards in tax processing and works closely with the Internal Revenue Service and state governments to promote efficient and effective tax filing.
14100 Members
Founded in 1969

62 **National Association of Construction Auditors**
7305 Hancock Village Drive
Suite 519
Chesterfield, VA 23832

804-608-8703; Fax: 888-702-1059
info@thenaca.org
www.thenaca.org
Facebook, Twitter, LinkedIn

Brian D. Felix, Chairman/Founder
Carl E. Hansen, Vice Chairman
Randall K. Hart, Secretary/Treasurer

Provides resources, information, and leadership for NACA members, their clients, and the public to ensure the highest standard of construction control environments possible.

63 **National Association of Enrolled Agents**
1730 Rhode Island Avenue, NW
Suite 400
Washington, DC 20036-3953

202-822-6232
855-880-6232; Fax: 202-822-6270
info@naea.org
www.naea.org
Facebook, Twitter, LinkedIn, YouTube

Donald Rosenberg, President
Michael Nelson, Interim Executive Vice President
Michael Hamilton, Director of Membership

Members are individuals who are enrolled to represent taxpayers before the Internal Revenue Service. We advise, represent and prepare tax returns for individuals, partnerships, corporations, estates, trusts and any entities with tax reporting requirements.
11000 Members
Founded in 1972

64 **National Association of Insurance and Financial Advisors**
2901 Telestar Court
Falls Church, VA 22042-1205

877-866-2432
www.naifa.org
Facebook, Twitter, LinkedIn, YouTube

Cammie Scott, President
Tom Michel, President Elect
Lawrence Holzberg, Secretary
Brock Jolly, Treasurer
Kevin M. Mayeux, CAE, Chief Executive Officer

Serves and represents insurance and financial advisors, advocates for a positive legislative and regulatory environment, enhances business and professional skills, and promotes the ethical conduct of its members.
Founded in 1890

65 **National Association of Mutual Insurance Companies**
3601 Vincennes Road
Indianapolis, IN 46268

317-875-5250; Fax: 317-879-8408
www.namic.org
Facebook, Twitter, LinkedIn, YouTube, RSS

Randall K. Druvenga, Chair
Robert M. Zak, Chair Elect
Steven C. Sliver, Vice Chair
Charles Chamness, President/CEO
Steven D. Linkous, Secretary/Treasurer

The largest property/casualty insurance trade association that has educational and advocacy programs to promote public policy solutions that benefit policyholoders and the NAMIC member companies that exist to serve them.
Founded in 1920

66 **National Association of Personal Financial Advisors**
8700 W. Bryn Mawr Avenue
Suite 700N
Chicago, IL 60631

847-483-5400
888-333-6659; Fax: 847-483-5415
info@napfa.org
www.napfa.org
Facebook, Twitter, LinkedIn, YouTube

Lydia Sheckels, Chair
Geoffrey Brown, CEO
Jeff Jones, Treasurer
Susan Weiner, Managing Editor

Professional association of Fee-Only financial advisors who advocate for client-focused financial planning with a Fee-Only compensation.
Founded in 1983

67 **National Association of State Auditors, Comptrollers and Treasurers**
449 Lewis Hargett Circle
Suite 290
Lexington, KY 40503-3590

859-276-1147; Fax: 859-278-0507
www.nasact.org

Elaine Howle, President
Richard Eckstrom, First Vice President
Manju Ganeriwala, Second Vice President

R. Kinney Poynter, CPA, Executive Director
Dianne Ray, Secretary

Serves as the premier organization working to bring together state auditors, state comptrollers and state treasurers to cooperatively address government financial management issues.

68 **National Association of State Boards of Accountancy**
150 Fourth Ave North
Suite 700
Nashville, TN 37219-2417

615-880-4200; Fax: 615-880-4290
nasba.org
Facebook, Twitter, LinkedIn, YouTube, Instagram

Ken L. Bishop, President & CEO
Colleen K. Conrad, EVP & COO
Michael R. Bryant, SVP & CFO
Jeff Oliver, Chief Information Officer

Enhances the effectiveness and advances the common interests of theBoards of Accountancy by creating a forum for accounting regulators and practitioners to address issues relevant to the viability of the accounting profession.
Founded in 1908

69 **National Association of State Budget Officers**
444 North Capitol Street NW
Suite 642
Washington, DC 20001

202-624-5382; Fax: 202-624-7745
nasbo-direct@nasbo.org
www.nasbo.org
Facebook, Twitter, LinkedIn, Google+

Kate Nass, President
Margaret Kelly, President Elect
Shelby Kerns, Executive Director
Keely Martin Bosler, Director, Finance

Provides a range of publications, services, and knowledge-sharing opportunities for its members and others interested in state finance issues.

70 **National Association of Tax Professionals**
PO Box 8002
Appleton, WI 54912-8002

800-558-3402; Fax: 800-747-0001
natp@natptax.com
www.natptax.com
Facebook, Twitter, LinkedIn, MySpace, YouTube

Brett Rosser, President
Jaimee Hammer, Vice President
Melissa Bowman, Treasurer
Sherri Hoskisson, Secretary

NATP members have access to a wide range of the most reliable industry resources, which ultimately save time and money. Members enjoy the support and knowledge that comes from joining the only professional organization that is 100% devoted to tax expertise.
Founded in 1979

71 **National CPA Health Care Advisors Association**
1801 West End Avenue
Suite 800
Nashville, TN 37203

615-373-9880
800-231-2524; Fax: 615-377-7092
info@hcaa.com
www.hcaa.com
Twitter

Helen Connolly, President
Boyle Henderson, Vice President
Christina Saunders, Secretary
Peter Matwijiw, Treasurer

HCAA is an association of CPA firms that provide services to health care providers beyond traditional compliance work. Members are admitted on a territorial exclusive basis, one member in each territory.

72 **National Conference of CPA Practitioners**
22 Jericho Turnpike
Suite 110
Mineola, NY 11501

516-333-8282
888-488-5400; Fax: 516-333-4099
go.nccpap.org
Facebook, Twitter, LinkedIn, Flickr, YouTube

Mark Stewart, President
Frank Sands, Executive Vice President

NCCAP is a group of CPA professionals that allows small CPA firms and the sole practitioner to have a greater community impact and presence. This organization also gives back through its local chapters and at the national level.

73 **National Society of Accountants**
1330 Braddock Place
Suite 540
Alexandria, VA 22314-1574

703-549-6400
800-966-6679; Fax: 703-549-2984
members@nsacct.org
www.nsacct.org
Facebook, Twitter, LinkedIn

Curtis Lee, Jr., President
Marchelle Foshee, First Vice President
Debra Cope, Second Vice President

Professional society of practicing accountants and tax practitioners that sponsors the Accreditation Council for Accountancy and Taxation and supports the National Society of Public Accountants Political Action Committee and NSPA Scholarship Foundation.
30000 Members
Founded in 1945

74 **National Society of Accountants for Cooperatives**
136 South Keowee Street
Dayton, OH 45402

937-222-6707; Fax: 937-222-5794
info@nsacoop.org
www.nsacoop.org
Facebook

Kim Fantaci, Executive Director
Nick Mueting, President
Dave Antoni, Vice President
Jeff Roberts, Association Executive
Krista Saul, Client Accounting Manager

A professional society involved with the financial management and planning of cooperative business. It also provides educational programming, networking opportunities, and a directory of other professionals.
2000 Members
Founded in 1936

75 **National Tax Association**
725 15th St. NW
Ste. 600
Washington, DC 20005-2109

202-737-3325; Fax: 202-737-7308
natltax@aol.com
www.ntanet.org

William Gale, President
James Alm, First Vice President
James Mackie, Second Vice President
Adam Cole, Secretary
Eric Toder, Treasurer

A nonpartisan, nonpolitical educational association of tax professionals dedicatd to advancing understanding of the theory and practice of public finance.
Founded in 1907

76 **PKF North America**
1745 N. Brown Road
Suite 350
Lawrenceville, GA 30043

770-279-4560; Fax: 770-279-4566
www.pkfna.com
Facebook, Twitter, LinkedIn, YouTube

Carolyn Morgan, Director, North America Region
Donna Raper, Corrdinator, North America Region

An association of legally independently-owned accounting and consulting firms with offices in North America and throughout the world through its affiliation with PKF International.
402 Members

77 **PrimeGlobal**
3235 Satellite Bvld Bldg. 400
Suite 300
Duluth, GA 30096

678-417-7730; Fax: 678-999-3959
kmead@primeglobal.net
www.primeglobal.net
Facebook, Twitter, LinkedIn, YouTube

Michelle Arnold, Executive Director, North America
Stephen Heathcote, CEO
Gary Owen, Executive Director, Finance & Ops
Stacey Sanchez, Director, Global Events
Gorana Stojanovic, Executive Director, Communications

PrimeGlobal is an international affiliation of independent accounting and consulting firms.
200 Members
Founded in 1978

78 **Society of Actuaries**
475 N Martingale Rd
Suite 600
Schaumburg, IL 60173-2252

847-706-3500
888-697-3900; Fax: 847-706-3599
customerservice@soa.org
www.soa.org
Twitter, LinkedIn, YouTube

Greg Heidrich, Executive Director
Stacy Lin, Deputy Executive Director/CFO
Ken Guthrie, Managing Director Of Education
Richard Veys, General Counsel
Michael Boot, Managing Director of Sections

An educational, research and professional organization dedicated to serving the public and society members. The vision is for actuaries to be recognized as the leading professional in the modeling and management of risk.
17000 Members
Founded in 1889
Mailing list available for rent: 17000 names at $300 per M

79 **Society of Financial Examiners**
12100 Sunset Hills Rd
Suite 130
Reston, VA 20190-3221

703-234-4140
800-787-7633; Fax: 888-436-8686
sofe@sofe.org
www.sofe.org
Facebook, LinkedIn

Joanne Campanelli, President
Cindy Dodson, Executive Director
Rhenda Davis, Membership & Customer Care
Katie McRee, Assistant Executive Director

The Society of Financial Examiners is a professional society for examiners of insurance com-

panies, banks, savings and loans, and credit unions.
1700+ Members
Founded in 1973

80 **Society of Financial Service Professionals**
3803 West Chester Pike
Suite 225
Newtown Square, PA 19073-3239

610-526-2500
800-392-6900; Fax: 610-359-8115
info@societyoffsp.org
national.societyoffsp.org
Facebook, Twitter, LinkedIn, YouTube, Flickr, RSS

David M. Maola, Chief Executive Officer
Michael J. McGlothlin, President
Brian D. Horn, Chief Operating/Information Officer
Donna M. Conrad, Chief Financial Officer

Provides financial products and planning services in order to help individuals, families, and businesses achieve financial security.
9000 Members
Founded in 1928
Mailing list available for rent

81 **The American Society of Tax Problem Solvers**
2250 Wehrie Drive
Suite 3
Williamsville, NY 14221

716-630-1650; Fax: 716-630-1651
info@astps.org
www.astps.org

Lawrence M. Lawler, National Director
John J. Witkowski, Secretary/Treasurer
Mitchell Piper, National Marketing Director
Carolyn Ryer, National Membership Director
Hannah Sojka, Membership Coordinator

A select group of licensed tax professionals located in communities across the United States to help taxpayers end individual and business IRS problems.

82 **The Professional Accounting Society of America**
Home Page: www.thepasa.org

A professional organization designed specifically for entry-level and mid-level associates working at accounting firms across America.
Founded in 2005

83 **Wholesale & Specialty Insurance Association (WSIA)**
4131 N. Mulberry Drive
Suite 200
Kansas City, MO 64116

816-741-3910
info@wsia.org
www.wsia.org
Twitter, LinkedIn

Brady Kelley, Executive Director
Julie Fritz, Director of Operations
Susan Henderson, Director of Marketing
Bryan Sanders, President
Davis Moore, Vice President

Formed in 2017 through the merger of the American Association of Managing General Agents (AAMGA) and the National Association of Professional Surplus Lines Offices (NAPSLO), the WSIA is a world-class member service organization representing the entirety of the wholesale, specialty and surplus lines industry.
Founded in 2017

Newsletters

84 **AAA Report**
CPA Firm Management Association
136 S. Keowee Street
Dayton, OH 45402

937-222-0030
info@cpafma.org
www.cpafma.org

Kim Fantaci, President
Jeanie Price, Chair
Alan Alexander, Vice Chair
Larry Sheftel, Secretary/Treasurer

Qarterly newsletter for the professional manager.
Frequency: Quarterly
Founded in 1984

85 **AAACPA Newsletter**
American Association of Attorney-CPAs
P.O. Box 706
Warrendale, PA 15095

703-352-8064
888-288-9272; Fax: 703-352-8073
info@attorney-cpa.com
www.attorney-cpa.com

Robert Driegert, President
Domenick Lioce, President Elect
Joseph Cordell, Treasurer
John Pramberg, Secretary

To promote the study and understanding of law and accounting and those related professions.
Frequency: Quarterly
Founded in 1964

86 **AAM Minute**
Association for Accounting Marketing
201 E. Main Street
Suite 1405
Lexington, KY 40507

859-402-9769
info@accountingmarketing.org
www.accountingmarketing.org

Rhonda Clark, Association Manager

A monthly e-newsletter that provides timely information about topics that impact accounting marketing and practice growth. It is available to anyone interested in what is happening in accounting marketing.
Frequency: Monthly
Founded in 1989

87 **AHACPA Newsletter**
AHACPA
459 N. 300 W.
Suite 11
Kaysville, UT 84037

801-547-0809; Fax: 801-547-5070
info@ahacpa.org
www.ahacpa.org

Les Sparks, President
Kathy Christensen, Manager

A newsletter for AHACPA members.
Founded in 1998

88 **AICPA Tax Insider**
American Institute of Certified Public Accountants
220 Leigh Farm Road
Durham, NC 27707-8110

919-402-4500; Fax: 919-402-4505
www.aicpa.org

Barry C. Melancon, CPA, CGMA, President & CEO

Delivers need-to-know news of the profession, hard-hitting commentary, recommended products and professional development resources to its subscribers.
Frequency: Monthly
Founded in 1887

89 **ALGA Newsletter**
Association of Local Government Auditors
859-276-0686
kyoung@nasact.org
algaonline.org

Kathleen Young, Publications Contact

e-Newsletter with news about current activities and member audit shops.
Frequency: Monthly
Founded in 1989

90 **ARCH**
Society of Actuaries
475 N Martingale Rd
Suite 600
Schaumburg, IL 60173-2252

847-706-3500; Fax: 847-706-3599
webmaster@soa.org
www.soa.org

Greg Heidrich, Executive Director
Stacy Lin, Deputy Executive Director/CFO
Ken Guthriw, Managing Director, Education
Richard Veys, General Counsel

ARCH is an informal communication providing current actuarial research to friends and members of the actuarial community. Its primary goal is the speedy dissemination of current thinking and aids to research.

91 **ASMC Connection**
American Society of Military Comptrollers
415 N. Alfred Street
Alexandria, VA 22314

703-549-0360
800-462-5637; Fax: 703-549-3181
www.asmconline.org
Facebook, Twitter, LinkedIn

Al Runnings, Executive Director
Catherine Kenol, Associate Director, Communications

Provides insight into defense financial news, chapter spot lights, and other society news.
Founded in 1948

92 **ASMC National Newsletter**
American Society of Military Comptrollers
415 N. Alfred Street
Alexandria, VA 22314

703-549-0360
800-462-5637; Fax: 703-549-3181
www.asmconline.org
Facebook, Twitter, LinkedIn

Al Runnings, Executive Director
Catherine Kenol, Associate Director, Communications

Focuses on society information such as training, events, and other issues related to supporting the membership of ASMC.
Frequency: Monthly
Founded in 1948

93 **ATEC Newsletter**
American College of Trust and Estate Counsel
901 15th Street, NW
Suite 525
Washington, DC 20005

202-684-8460; Fax: 202-684-8459
www.actec.org

Charles D. Fox IV, President
Stephen R. Akers, Vice President
John A. Terrill II, President-Elect

A newsletter for ATEC members.
Founded in 1949

94 **AWSCPA News**
American Woman's Society of CPAs
136 South Keowee Street
Dayton, OH 45402

937-222-1872
800-297-2721; Fax: 937-222-5794
info@awscpa.org
www.awscpa.org

Amy Knowles-Jones, President
Kelly Welter, President Elect
Alexandra Miller, Secretary/Treasurer
Cynthia Cox, VP - Member Services

Available electronically.
Frequency: Quarterly
Circulation: 1500
Founded in 1933
Printed in 4 colors

95 **Accounting Alerts**
Grant Thornton
175 W Jackson Blvd
20th Floor
Chicago, IL 60604-2687

312-856-0001; Fax: 312-602-8099
www.grantthornton.com
Twitter

Stephen Chipman, CEO
Lou Grabowsky, COO
Russ Wieman, Chief Financial Officer

Periodic newsletter that highlights important accounting developments.
Founded in 1924

96 **Accounting Education News**
American Accounting Association
9009 Town Center Parkway
Lakewood Ranch, FL 34202

941-921-7747; Fax: 941-923-4093
info@aaahq.org
aaahq.org

Yvonne Hinson, CEO
Nate Smith, Co-Director, Publishing
Stephanie Austin, Co-Director, Publishing

Information on industry development and associations, the newsletter is only available to members.
Frequency: Quarterly
Founded in 1916

97 **Accounting Historians Notebook**
Academy of Accounting Historians
9009 Town Center Parkway
Lakewood Ranch, FL 34202

941-921-7747; Fax: 941-923-4093
acchistory@case.edu
aaahq.org/AAH

Gary Spraakman, President
Tiffany Schwendeman, Academy Administrator

Published by the Academy of Accounting Historians, the Notebook provides information about the Academy, its members, conference, and publications. As of 2018 the Notebook is an online-only publication.
Frequency: Monthly
Founded in 1978

98 **Accounting Office Management & Administration Report**
Institute of Management and Administration
3 Bethesda Metro Center
Suite 250
Bethesda, MD 20814-5377

800-372-1033
703-341-3500; Fax: 800-253-0332
customercare@bna.com
www.ioma.com

Designed for use by anyone responsible for the day-to-day management of a CPA firm. Provides actionable information that readers can use to manage their firms efficiently and profitably.
Cost: $469.00
Frequency: Monthly
Founded in 1984

99 **Accounting and Auditing Update Service**
Thomson Reuters
2395 Midway Rd
Carrollton, TX 75006

817-332-3709
800-431-9025; Fax: 888-216-1929
trta.lei-support@thomsonreuters.com
www.ria.thomsonreuters.com

Elaine Yadlon, Plant Manager
Thomas H Glocer, CEO & Director
Robert D Daleo, Chief Financial Officer
Kelli Crane, Senior Vice President & CIO

Analyzes FASB and AICPA pronouncements.
Cost: $465.00
Frequency: Bi-Weekly
Founded in 1935

100 **BAP Quarterly Newsletter**
Beta Alpha Psi
220 Leigh Farm Road
Durham, NC 27707

919-402-4044
bap@bap.org
www.bap.org

Rita Grant, President
Margaret Fiorentino, Executive Director

A newsletter sent to BAP members in order to stay up-to-date on BAP news and updates.
Frequency: Quarterly
Founded in 1919

101 **Business Valuation Monitor**
Grant Thornton
175 W Jackson Blvd
20th Floor
Chicago, IL 60604-2687

312-856-0001; Fax: 312-602-8099
www.grantthornton.com
Twitter, LinkedIn

Stephen Chipman, CEO
Lou Grabowsky, COO
Russ Wieman, CFO

Newsletter covering value creation perspectives for corporate executives and the investment community in the areas of financial reporting, transaction support, damage calculations in disputes, intellectual property, bankruptcy proceedings and corporate tax planning.
Founded in 1924

102 **CAE Bulletin**
Institute of Internal Auditors
247 Maitland Ave
Altamonte Spgs, FL 32701-4201

407-830-7600; Fax: 407-937-1101
custserv@theiia.org
www.theiia.org

J. Michael Pepper, Chairman
Carolyn Saint, Senior Vice President
John Wxzelaki, Vice Chairman - Finance/Security

Newsletter that alerts members to news, guidance and information that helps professionals become as effective as possible in their jobs.
Frequency: Twice Monthly

103 **CPA Insider**
American Institute of Certified Public Accountants
220 Leigh Farm Road
Durham, NC 27707-8110

919-402-4500; Fax: 919-402-4505
www.aicpa.org

Barry C. Melancon, CPA, CGMA, President & CEO

Delivers need-to-know news of the profession, hard-hitting commentary, recommended products and professional development resources.
Frequency: Weekly
Founded in 1887

104 **Chapter Weekly**
National Association of Tax Professionals
PO Box 8002
Appleton, WI 54912-8002

800-558-3402; Fax: 800-747-0001
natp@natptax.com
www.natptax.com
Facebook, Twitter, MySpace

Brett Rosser, President
Jaimee Hammer, Vice President

E-Newsletter features Chapter events and updates.
Frequency: Weekly

105 **Client Information Bulletin**
WPI Communications
55 Morris Ave
Springfield, NJ 07081-1422

973-467-8700
800-323-4995; Fax: 973-467-0368
info@wpicommunications.com
www.wpicomm.com

Steve Klinghoffer, Owner
Lori Klinghoffer, Executive Vice President
Marilyn Lang, Circulation Manager
Sandy McMurray, Sales Manager
Anna Cooley, Managing Editor

This monthly newsletter covers important new tax developments, general business principles, financial planning, estate planning and other related topics.
4 Pages
Frequency: Monthly
Founded in 1952
Printed in 2 colors

106 **Contractor Chronicles**
CPAsNET
P.O. Box 4827
Boulder, CO 80306

609-890-0800
cpasnet@cpasnet.com
www.cpasnet.com

Sarah Johnson Dobek, President

A newsletter for CPAsNET members.
Founded in 1994

107 **Controller's Report**
Institute of Management and Administration
3 Bethesda Metro Center
Suite 250
Bethesda, MD 20814-5377

800-372-1033
7033413500; Fax: 800-253-0332
customercare@bna.com
www.ioma.com

Aimed at corporate controllers in companies of all sizes.
Cost: $437.00
20 Pages
Frequency: Monthly
Founded in 1984
Printed in 2 colors

108 **Controller's Tax Letter**
Institute of Management and Administration

3 Bethesda Metro Center
Suite 250
Bethesda, MD 20814-5377

800-372-1033
7033413500; Fax: 800-253-0332
customercare@bna.com
www.ioma.com

Focuses on the tax implications of business decisions and provides readers in corporate finance/accounting details on recently settled cases from US Tax Court, with full citations for those who want to know more. CTL also shows controllers, accounting managers and tax managers the effects of business decisions as they relate to a company's strategic planning for new sales efforts, expanding their overseas or foreign presence, and exemptions and deductions available where laws have changed.
Cost: $259.00
Frequency: Monthly
Founded in 1984

109 **Controllers Update**
Institute of Certified Management Accountants
10 Paragon Drive
Suite 1
Montvale, NJ 07645-1718

800-638-4427; Fax: 201-474-1600
ima@imanet.org
www.imanet.org
Facebook, Twitter, LinkedIn

Jeffrey C. Thomson, President and CEO
Paul E. Juras, Chair

Monthly newsletter with useful information for chief financial officers, plant controllers and financial management personnel.
Frequency: Monthly
Circulation: 2,200

110 **Currency**
Grant Thornton
175 W Jackson Blvd
20th Floor
Chicago, IL 60604-2687

312-856-0001; Fax: 312-602-8099
www.grantthornton.com
Twitter, LinkedIn

Stephen Chipman, CEO
Lou Grabowsky, COO
Russ Wieman, Chief Financial Officer

Electronic newsletter for bank executives that covers issues and trends in the financial institutions industry.
Founded in 1924

111 **E@lert**
National Association of Enrolled Agents
1120 Connecticut Avenue NW
Suite 460
Washington, DC 20036-3922

202-822-6232; Fax: 202-822-6270
info@naea.org
www.naea.org
Facebook, Twitter, LinkedIn

Donald Rosenberg, President
Michael Nelson, Interim Executive Vice President
Kathy Brown, Secretary

Newsletter that provides brief updates on the latest tax news affecting clients and practices.
11000 Members

112 **FASAB Bimonthly Newsletter**
Federal Accounting Standards Advisory Board
441 G Street NW.
Suite 1155
Washington, DC 20548

202-512-7350; Fax: 202-512-7366
fasab@fasab.gov
www.fasab.gov

Monica Valentine, Executive Director

Provides highlights of recent Board actions and issues.
Founded in 1990

113 **FSA Newsletter**
Federation of Schools of Accountacy
220 Leigh Farm Road
Durham, NC 27707-8110

919-402-4825
mtarasi@aicpa.org
www.thefsa.org

Richard Dull, President
Megan Tarasi, Contact

Provides information, news, and updates about the Federation of Schools of Accountacy.
Frequency: Bi-Annually
Founded in 1978

114 **FSA Times**
Institute of Internal Auditors
247 Maitland Ave
Altamonte Spgs, FL 32701-4201

407-937-1100; Fax: 407-937-1101
custserv@theiia.org
www.theiia.org

J. Michael Pepper, Chairman
Carolyn Saint, Senior Vice President
John Wxzelaki, Vice Chairman - Finance/Security

Quarterly publication provided to members of the Institute of Internal Auditors' Financial Services Auditor Group to support knowledge development for financial services auditors.
Frequency: Quarterly

115 **Financial Bulletin**
Grant Thornton
175 W Jackson Blvd
20th Floor
Chicago, IL 60604-2687

312-856-0001; Fax: 312-602-8099
www.grantthornton.com
Twitter, LinkedIn

Stephen Chipman, CEO
Lou Grabowsky, COO
Russ Wieman, Chief Financial Officer

Electronic publication that covers regulations and developments affecting financial services industry.
Founded in 1924

116 **Focus on Forensics**
Grant Thornton
175 W Jackson Blvd
20th Floor
Chicago, IL 60604-2687

312-856-0001; Fax: 312-602-8099
www.grantthornton.com
Twitter, LinkedIn

Stephen Chipman, CEO
Lou Grabowsky, COO
Russ Wieman, Chief Financial Officer

Periodic newsletter providing valuable forensic accounting insights into some of the most complex and critical challenges that businesses and legal counsel face today.
Founded in 1924

117 **General Ledger**
American Institute of Professional Bookkeepers
6001 Montrose Road
Suite 500
Rockville, MD 20852

800-622-0121; Fax: 800-541-0066
info@aipb.org
www.aipb.org

Stanley Hartman, Co-Pres. & Executive Director
Stephen Sahlein, Co-Pres. & Director, Publishing

The latest bookkeeping, accounting and tax news. Keep current on bookkeeping and reporting techniques, time and money-saving charts, practical tips, sharpen skills with a Bookkeeper's Quiz in every issue, and monthly and annual rates and numbers are included.
Frequency: Monthly
Founded in 1987

118 **Government Accounting and Auditing Update**
Thomson Reuters
2395 Midway Rd
Carrollton, TX 75006

817-332-3709
800-431-9025; Fax: 888-216-1929
trta.lei-support@thomsonreuters.com
www.ria.thomsonreuters.com

Elaine Yadlon, Plant Manager
Thomas H Glocer, CEO & Director
Robert D Daleo, Chief Financial Officer
Kelli Crane, Senior Vice President & CIO

Includes changes taking place in government accounting and financial reporting, analysis of the latest developments, explanations of how they affect work and practical guidance on adapting to these changes.
Cost: $370.00
8 Pages
Frequency: Monthly
Founded in 1935
Mailing list available for rent: 5000 names
Printed in 2 colors on glossy stock

119 **Governmental Accounting Standards Board Action Report**
Governmental Accounting Standards Board
401 Merritt 7
PO Box 5116
Norwalk, CT 06856-5116

203-847-0700; Fax: 203-849-9714
webmaster@gasb.org
www.gasb.org
Twitter, LinkedIn

David A. Vaudt, Chairman
David Bean, Director Research/Technical Active

Action Report newsletter that includes developments in the standards-setting process and the status of technical projects.
Cost: $155.00
Frequency: Monthly

120 **IIA Insight**
Institute of Internal Auditors
247 Maitland Ave
Altamonte Spgs, FL 32701-4201

407-937-1100; Fax: 407-937-1101
custserv@theiia.org
www.theiia.org
Facebook, Twitter, LinkedIn

J. Michael Pepper, Chairman
Carolyn Saint, Senior Vice President
John Wxzelaki, Vice Chairman - Finance/Security

Member newsletter designed to instruct members on using IIA services, products, and training opportunities.
Frequency: Monthly

121 **IIA Today**
Institute of Internal Auditors

247 Maitland Ave
Altamonte Spgs, FL 32701-4201

407-830-7600; Fax: 407-937-1101
custserv@theiia.org
www.theiia.org

J. Michael Pepper, Chairman
Carolyn Saint, Senior Vice President
John Wxzelaki, Vice Chairman - Finance/Security

Provides relevent and timely information on internal audit news. In print and electronic formats available.
Frequency: Twice Monthly

122 **IMA Educational Case Journal**
Institute of Management Accountants
10 Paragon Dr
Suite 1
Montvale, NJ 07645-1760

800-638-4427; Fax: 201-474-1600
ima@imanet.org
www.imanet.org
Facebook, Twitter, LinkedIn

Jeffrey C. Thomson, President and CEO
Paul E. Juras, Chair

The journal publishes teaching cases and research related to case writing or teaching with cases in management accounting and related fields.
Cost: $250.00
60000 Members
Frequency: Quarterly

123 **IOMA's Report on Salary Surveys**
Institute of Management and Administration
3 Bethesda Metro Center
Suite 250
Bethesda, MD 20814-5377

800-372-1033
7033413500; Fax: 800-253-0332
customercare@bna.com
www.ioma.com

Analyzes data from major salary surveys released during the year by the biggest compensation survey companies, WorldatWork, SHRM, state HR societies, and the Big Four accounting firms, to give readers an overview of those expensive, hard-to-manage services.
Cost: $445.00
Founded in 1984

124 **Infoline**
Hospitality Financial & Technology Professionals
11709 Boulder Lane
Suite 110
Austin, TX 78726-1832

512-249-5333
800-646-4387; Fax: 512-249-1533
membership@hftp.org
www.hftp.org

Frank I Wolfe, Executive VP/CEO
Lucinda Hart, COO
Thomas Atzenhofer, CFO
Eliza Selig, Director of Communications

Provides information regarding chapter and officer activities.
Frequency: Monthly
Founded in 1952

125 **Information Management Newsletter**
Information Resources Management Association
701 E Chocolate Avenue
Suite 200
Hershey, PA 17033-1240

717-533-8845; Fax: 717-533-8861
member@irma-international.org
www.irma-international.org

Mehdi Kwosrowpour, Executive Director
Sherif Kamel, VP, Information Management

This practical, informative newsletter is a leading publication of information technology resources management. Short, concise articles give objective, professional views of newly emerging technologies and trends.
Cost: $60.00
Frequency: Semi-Annually
ISSN: 1080-286X

126 **Inside IMA**
Institute of Management Accountants
10 Paragon Dr
Suite 1
Montvale, NJ 07645-1760

201-573-9000
800-638-4427; Fax: 201-474-1600
ima@imanet.org
www.imanet.org
Facebook, Twitter, LinkedIn, YouTube

Latest news, events and developments for IMA's general membership.

127 **Internal Auditing Report**
Thomson Reuters
2395 Midway Rd
Carrollton, TX 75006

817-332-3709
800-431-9025; Fax: 888-216-1929
trta.lei-support@thomsonreuters.com
www.ria.thomsonreuters.com

Elaine Yadlon, Plant Manager
Thomas H Glocer, CEO & Director
Robert D Daleo, Chief Financial Officer
Kelli Crane, Senior Vice President & CIO

Perfect for keeping up to date on new auditing standards and developments. Offers guidance on managing internal auditing departments, covers new audit technology, offers new audit techniques used by successful audit management practices, and provides practitioner level feedback on current Institute of Internal Auditors standards.
Cost: $320.00
12 Pages
Frequency: Six Times/Year
Circulation: 5000
Founded in 1935
Mailing list available for rent: 5000 names
Printed in 2 colors on glossy stock

128 **Jacobs Report**
Offshore Press
PO Box 8137
Prairie Village, KS 66208-2824

913-362-9667
888-516-3177; Fax: 913-432-7174

Vernon K Jacobs, President

Contains International tax news.
Frequency: Daily
Founded in 1981

129 **Letter Ruling Review**
Tax Analysts
400 S Maple Ave
Suite 400
Falls Church, VA 22046-4245

703-533-4400
800-955-2444; Fax: 703-533-4444
cservice@tax.org
www.taxanalysts.com

Chris Bergin, CEO
Martin Lobel, Chairman of the Board

Publication analyzes significant private letter rulings issued by the Internal Revenue Service during the month.
4 Pages
Frequency: Monthly
Founded in 1970
Printed in one color on matte stock

130 **Management & Administration Report (ADMAR)**
Institute of Management and Administration
3 Bethesda Metro Center
Suite 250
Bethesda, MD 20814-5377

800-372-1033
7033413500; Fax: 800-253-0332
customercare@bna.com
www.ioma.com

How to manage corporate accounting departments more effectively, boost staff productivity, reduce operation costs and adopt new systems and technology, and take charge of your dealings with auditors and lenders.
Founded in 1984

131 **Managing Accounts Payable**
Institute of Management and Administration
3 Bethesda Metro Center
Suite 250
Bethesda, MD 20814-5377

800-372-1033
7033413500; Fax: 800-253-0332
customercare@bna.com
www.ioma.com

The source of information for accounts payable and those responsible for the function. Each issue contains 5-7 articles, 6-10 short news clips, a manager's forum on the back page and calendar of upcoming seminars and conferences.
Cost: $419.00
Frequency: Monthly
Founded in 1984

132 **Managing the General Ledger**
Institute of Management and Administration
3 Bethesda Metro Center
Suite 250
Bethesda, MD 20814-5377

800-372-1033
7033413500; Fax: 800-253-0332
customercare@bna.com
www.ioma.com

Aimed at controllers and corporate accounting managers and shows the most current techniques for efficient monthly closings and AICPA approved methods for general ledger entries.
Cost: $308.14
Frequency: Monthly
Founded in 1984

133 **NSPA Washington Reporter**
National Society of Public Accountants
1010 N Fairfax St
Alexandria, VA 22314-1574

703-549-6400
800-966-6679; Fax: 703-549-2984
members@nsacct.org
www.nsacct.org
Facebook, Twitter, LinkedIn

Curtis Lee, Jr., President
Marchelle Foshee, First Vice President
Debra Cope, Second Vice President

Coverage of NSPA activity with the government, and news on members in various states.
Frequency: Monthly
Founded in 1955

134 **National Estimator**
Society of Cost Estimating and Analysis
8221 Old Courthouse Rd
Suite 106
Vienna, VA 22182

703-938-5090; Fax: 703-938-5091
scea@sceaonline.org
www.sceaonline.org

Erin Whittaker, Executive Director
Sharon Burger, Certification Program Admin
Brittany Walker, Membership Coordinator
Debra Lehman, Treasurer

Information on cost estimating and analysis, earned value management, budget and financial analysis, and program control.
Cost: $55.00
2015 Members
Frequency: Biannual
Founded in 1990

135 **New Developments Summary**
Grant Thornton
175 W Jackson Blvd
20th Floor
Chicago, IL 60604-2687

312-856-0001; Fax: 312-602-8099
www.grantthornton.com
Twitter, LinkedIn

Stephen Chipman, CEO
Lou Grabowsky, COO
Russ Wieman, Chief Financial Officer

Periodic bulletin providing a detailed summary of a recent technical development or accounting pronouncement.
Founded in 1924

136 **News Plus**
National Association of Black Accountants
7474 Greenway Center Dr
Suite 1120
Greenbelt, MD 20770-3504

301-474-6222
888-571-2939; Fax: 301-474-3114
newsplus@nabainc.org
www.nabainc.org
Facebook, Twitter, LinkedIn, YouTube

Walter J. Smith, President/CEO

Updates on accounting proposals and regulations.
Cost: $20.00
Frequency: Quarterly
Founded in 1969

137 **Nonprofit Examiner**
CPAsNET
P.O. Box 4827
Boulder, CO 80306

609-890-0800
cpasnet@cpasnet.com
www.cpasnet.com

Sarah Johnson Dobek, Director

A newsletter for CPAsNET members.
Founded in 1994

138 **Nonprofit Report: Accounting, Taxation Management**
Thomson Reuters
2395 Midway Rd
Carrollton, TX 75006

817-332-3709
800-431-9025; Fax: 888-216-1929
trta.lei-support@thomsonreuters.com
www.ria.thomsonreuters.com

Elaine Yadlon, Plant Manager
Thomas H Glocer, CEO & Director
Robert D Daleo, Chief Financial Officer
Kelli Crane, Senior Vice President & CIO

Offers CPAs with nonprofit clients, and professionals working in the nonprofit sector. A practical, timely look at today's key nonprofit issues, including IRS rulings and pronouncements, AICPA changes and legislation governing the financial management of most nonprofit organizations.
Cost: $250.00
Frequency: Monthly
Founded in 1935
Mailing list available for rent
Printed in 2 colors on glossy stock

139 **On the Horizon**
Grant Thornton
175 W Jackson Blvd
20th Floor
Chicago, IL 60604-2687

312-856-0001; Fax: 312-602-8099
www.grantthornton.com
Twitter, LinkedIn

Stephen Chipman, CEO
Lou Grabowsky, COO
Russ Wieman, Chief Financial Officer

Updates on announcements, meetings and proposals from the accounting standards-setting bodies and industry regulators.
Frequency: Weekly
Founded in 1924

140 **Partner's Report for Law Firm Owners**
Institute of Management and Administration
3 Bethesda Metro Center
Suite 250
Bethesda, MD 20814-5377

800-372-1033
703-341-3500; Fax: 800-253-0332
customercare@bna.com
www.ioma.com

Keeps partners up-to-date on salary guidelines and benefits, as well as provides the reader with tips on increasing profit margins and exercising leadership skills.
Cost: $464.00
Frequency: Monthly
Founded in 1984

141 **PayState Update**
American Payroll Association
660 N. Main Avenue
Suite 100
San Antonio, TX 78205

210-224-6406; Fax: 210-224-6038
www.americanpayroll.org

Daniel Maddux, Executive Director

Association e-newsletter offering members news on updates in state and local payroll compliance. Sold in one-year increments.
Cost: $397.00
Founded in 1982

142 **Payroll Currently**
American Payroll Association
660 N. Main Avenue
Suite 100
San Antonio, TX 78205

210-224-6406; Fax: 210-224-6038
www.americanpayroll.org

Daniel Maddux, Executive Director

Member newsletter containing information on new legislation affecting payroll, benefits, and human resources.
Frequency: Monthly
Founded in 1982

143 **Payroll Manager's Report**
Institute of Management and Administration
3 Bethesda Metro Center
Suite 250
Bethesda, MD 20814-5377

800-372-1033
703-341-3500; Fax: 800-253-0332
www.ioma.com

Written for payroll practitioners working with small and large employers. Provides how-to information on managing a payroll department cost effectively and service-efficiently.
Cost: $399.00
Frequency: Monthly
Founded in 1984

144 **Payroll Practitioner's Monthly**
Institute of Management and Administration
3 Bethesda Metro Center
Suite 250
Bethesda, MD 20814-5377

800-372-1033
703-341-3500; Fax: 800-253-0332
customercare@bna.com
www.ioma.com

Shows payroll professionals what they need to do and how to do it when it comes to the many rules, regulations and laws they must follow to prepare and distribute a corporate payroll.
Cost: $399.00
16 Pages
Frequency: Monthly
Founded in 1984

145 **Payroll Tax Alert**
Institute of Management and Administration
3 Bethesda Metro Center
Suite 250
Bethesda, MD 20814-5377

800-372-1033
703-341-3500; Fax: 800-253-0332
customercare@bna.com
www.ioma.com

Used by payroll managers and professionals in accounting or human resources. Provides quick, hard hitting updates on changes to federal and state payroll policy (wage-hour rules, industrial orders, new posting requirements and tax issues) from every agency that has a hand in corporate payroll & benefits administration.
Cost: $240.00
Frequency: Monthly
Circulation: 2000
Founded in 1984

146 **Pocket MBA**
Practising Law Institute
810 Seventh Avenue
21st Floor
New York, NY 10019-5818

212-824-5700
800-260-4754; Fax: 212-581-4670
info@pli.edu
www.pli.edu
Facebook, Twitter

Victor J Rubino, President
Nickola Francis, Subscription Manager

Provides information every lawyer needs to know about business and finance.
Cost: $1295.00
Frequency: Weekly
Founded in 1933

147 **Polaris International Newsletter**
Polaris International

9200 South Dadeland Boulevard
Suite 510
Miami, FL 33156

305-670-0580; Fax: 305-670-3818
www.accountants.org
Facebook, Twitter, LinkedIn, Youtube

Kevin Mead, President
Lydie Jubin, Chief Regional Officer
Anne Hampson, CFO
Pedro Figueroa, Administrative Manager

Newsletter containing information regarding events, activities and recent news for accounting and consulting firms.
Frequency: Quarterly
Founded in 1978

148 **Practicing CPA**
American Institute of Certified Public Accountants
220 Leigh Farm Road
Durham, NC 27707-8110

919-402-4500; Fax: 919-402-4505
www.aicpa.org

Barry C. Melancon, CPA, CGMA, President & CEO

Provides information on practice management issues and new technical developments and delivers related practitioner perspective from all firm sizes on potential opportunities and creative strategies and solutions for practice management success.
Frequency: Monthly
Founded in 1887

149 **Public Accounting Desk Book**
Strafford Publications
590 Dutch Valley Road
PO Box 13729
Atlanta, GA 30324-0729

404-881-1141
800-926-7926; Fax: 404-881-0074
customerservice@straffordpub.com
www.straffordpub.com
Twitter

Richard Ossoff, President
Jon McKenna, Executive Editor

Provides public accounting firms with authoritative news and analysis of developments in the accounting profession today and emerging trends for the future. Also reports SEC auditor changes, mergers, acquisitions, personnel changes and related events.
Cost: $39.00
Frequency: Annual
ISSN: 0161-309X
Founded in 1984

150 **Public Accounting Report**
CCH
2700 Lake Cook Rd
Riverwoods, IL 60015-3867

847-940-4600
800-835-5224; Fax: 773-866-3095
www.cch.com

Mike Sabbatis, President
Douglas M Winterrose, Vice President & CFO
Jim Bryant, EVP Software Products

Written for public accounting firm partners and professionals, it is renowned for its straight reporting and analysis of the news, developments, and trends that have influenced the profession for more than 20 years.
Cost: $449.00
8 Pages
Frequency: Bi-Weekly

151 **SEC Accounting Report**
Thomson Reuters
2395 Midway Rd
Carrollton, TX 75006

817-332-3709
800-431-9025; Fax: 888-216-1929
trta.lei-support@thomsonreuters.com
www.ria.thomsonreuters.com

Elaine Yadlon, Plant Manager
Thomas H Glocer, CEO & Director
Robert D Daleo, Chief Financial Officer
Kelli Crane, Senior Vice President & CIO

For senior executives needing monthly news and insights on emerging SEC issues. The SEC Accounting Report can help you to understand SEC changes and their subsequent compliance requirements.
Cost: $365.00
8 Pages
Frequency: Monthly
Circulation: 5000
Founded in 1935
Mailing list available for rent: 5000 names
Printed in 2 colors on glossy stock

152 **Strategic TechNotes**
Institute of Management Accountants
10 Paragon Dr
Suite 1
Montvale, NJ 07645-1774

201-573-9000
800-638-4427; Fax: 201-474-1600
ima@imanet.org
www.imanet.org
Facebook, Twitter, LinkedIn

Jeffrey C. Thomson, President and CEO
Paul E. Juras, Chair

Award-winning technology e-newsletter designed for IMA members and others who want a look into the world of today's and tomorrow's technological trends and tools.
60000 Members
Frequency: 2 Times/Month

153 **TAXPRO Monthly**
National Association of Tax Professionals
PO Box 8002
Appleton, WI 54912-8002

800-558-3402; Fax: 800-747-0001
natp@natptax.com
www.natptax.com
Facebook, Twitter, MySpace

Brett Rosser, President
Jaimee Hammer, Vice President

Covers the latest news in detail and explores critical new developments in federal tax laws while providing practical applications of tax laws and procedures.
Frequency: Monthly

154 **TAXPRO Weekly**
National Association of Tax Professionals
PO Box 8002
Appleton, WI 54912-8002

800-558-3402; Fax: 800-747-0001
natp@natptax.com
www.natptax.com
Facebook, Twitter, MySpace

Brett Rosser, President
Jaimee Hammer, Vice President

Members receive e-Newsletter featuring tax alerts and news briefs hot off the press.
Frequency: Weekly

155 **Tax Hot Topics**
Grant Thornton
175 W Jackson Blvd
20th Floor
Chicago, IL 60604-2687

312-856-0001; Fax: 312-602-8099
www.grantthornton.com
Twitter, LinkedIn

Stephen Chipman, CEO
Lou Grabowsky, COO
Russ Wieman, Chief Financial Officer

Electronic newsletter addressing a wide range of tax issues, including Internal Revenue Service rulings, tax-related litigation, and state, local and international tax developments
Frequency: Biweekly
Founded in 1924

156 **Tax Incentives Alert**
Strafford Publications
590 Dutch Valley Road NE
PO Box 13729
Atlanta, GA 30324-0729

404-881-1141
800-926-7926; Fax: 404-881-0074
customerservice@straffordpub.com
www.straffordpub.com

Richard Ossoff, President
Jon McKenna, Executive Editor

Reports on the new and ever-evolving array of federal and state tax credits, exemptions, deductions, abatements and other incentives.
Cost: $467.00
Frequency: Monthly
ISSN: 0161-309X
Founded in 1984

157 **Tax Letter and Social Security Report**
Scott Peyron & Associates
209 Main Street
Suite 200
Boise, ID 83702-7356

208-388-3800; Fax: 208-388-8898
www.peyron.com

Scott Peyron, Owner

Covers taxes, social security tax, benefit tips and information for middle income individuals and professionals.
Cost: $56.00
4 Pages
Frequency: Monthly
Circulation: 2000
Printed in one color on matte stock

158 **The CPA Letter Daily**
American Institute of Certified Public Accountants
220 Leigh Farm Road
Durham, NC 27707-8110

919-402-4500; Fax: 919-402-4505
www.aicpa.org

Barry C. Melancon, CPA, CGMA, President & CEO

A free e-newsletter published each weekday and covers the 10-12 most important stories in business, finance and accounting, as well as AICPA information.
Frequency: Daily
Founded in 1887

159 **The Gaming Auditorium**
Institute of Internal Auditors
247 Maitland Ave
Altamonte Spgs, FL 32701-4201

707-937-1100; Fax: 407-937-1101
custserv@theiia.org
www.theiia.org

J. Michael Pepper, Chairman
Carolyn Saint, Senior Vice President
John Wxzelaki, Vice Chairman - Finance/security

Quarterly publication provided to members of the Institute of Internal Auditors' Gaming Audit Group to support knowledge development for gaming audit professionals.
Frequency: Quarterly

160 **The Profit Counselor**
CPAsNET
P.O. Box 4827
Boulder, CO 80306
609-890-0800
cpasnet@cpasnet.com
www.cpasnet.com
Sarah Johnson Dobek, President
A newsletter for CPAsNET members.
Founded in 1994

161 **Tone at the Top**
Institute of Internal Auditors
247 Maitland Ave
Altamonte Spgs, FL 32701-4201
407-937-1100; Fax: 407-937-1101
custserv@theiia.org
www.theiia.org
J. Michael Pepper, Chairman
Carolyn Saint, Senior Vice President
John Wxzelaki, Vice Chairman - Finance/security
Newsletter that provides executive management, boards of directors, and audit committees with concise, leading-edge information in issues such as risk, internal control, governance, ethics, and the changing role of internal auditing.
Frequency: Quarterly

162 **Topics Newsletter**
Association of Government Accountants
2208 Mount Vernon Avenue
Alexandria, VA 22301-1314
703-684-6931
800-242-7211; Fax: 703-519-0039
communications@agacgfm.org
www.agacgfm.org
Ann M. Ebberts, Chief Executive Officer
Mary Margaret Yodzis, Editor/Copywriter
Designed to give national exposure to chapter events, community service projects and member accomplishments while offering the most up-to-date Association news, released every other Monday morning by e-mail to members.
Frequency: Weekly
Founded in 1950

Magazines & Journals

163 **AABPA Symposium**
AABPA
P.O. Box 1157
Falls Church, VA 22041
aabpa@aabpa.org
www.aabpa.org
Facebook, Twitter, LinkedIn, GovLoop
Karen Kunz, Vice President, Symposia
A symposium of the American Association for Budget and Program Analysis that allows budget and program analysis professionals the chance to learn from leaders in the public sector about major changes in budgeting at the federal, state and local levels. Attendees are also able to join dicussions with other professionals, policy researchers, and experts from state and local governments, federal agencies and academia.
Frequency: Annually
Founded in 1916

164 **AIRA Journal**
Association of Insolvency & Restructuring Advisors
221 W. Stewart Avenue
Suite 207
Medford, OR 97501
541-858-1665; Fax: 541-858-9187
aira@aira.org
www.aira.org
Jim Lukenda, Executive Director
Valda Newton, Managing Editor
A quarterly publication of the Association of Insolvency & Restructuring Advisors that publishes professional papers, articles and commentary by members as well as other professionals in the turnaround, bankruptcy, restructuring and related fields, such as banking, tax, law and government.
Frequency: Quarterly
Founded in 1982

165 **ALGA Newsletter**
Association of Local Government Auditors
859-276-0686
kyoung@nasact.org
algaonline.org
Kathleen Young, Publications Contact
e-Newsletter with news about current activities and member audit shops.
Frequency: Monthly
Founded in 1989

166 **ATA Journal of Legal Tax Research**
American Accounting Association
9009 Town Center Parkway
Lakewood Ranch, FL 34202
941-921-7747; Fax: 941-923-4093
info@aaahq.org
aaahq.org
Yvonne Hinson, CEO
Blaise M. Sonnier, Editor
Publishes creative and innovative studies employing legal research methodologies that logically and clearly identify, decribe and illuminate important current tax issues, propose improvements in tax systems and unique solutions to problems, and critically analyze proposed or recent tax rule changes from both technical and policy perspectives. JLTR is online-only and publishes semi-annually, and is indexed in ESCI.
Frequency: Semi-Annually
Founded in 1916

167 **Accountants SEC Practice Manual**
CCH
2700 Lake Cook Rd
Riverwoods, IL 60015-3867
847-940-4600
800-835-5224; Fax: 773-866-3095
www.cch.com
Mike Sabbatis, President
Douglas M Winterrose, Vice President & CFO
Jim Bryant, EVP Software Products
Offers guidance for preparing and filing financial statements with the SEC, including regulations, forms and helpful summaries and checklists.
Cost: $819.00
Frequency: Annual
Founded in 1913

168 **Accounting Historians Journal**
Academy of Accounting Historians
9009 Town Center Parkway
Lakewood Ranch, FL 34202
941-921-7747; Fax: 941-923-4093
AHJ@aaahq.org
aaahq.org/AAH
Gary Spraakman, President
Bill Black, Senior Editor
Chelsea Matthews, Publications Assistant
Published by the Academy of Accounting Historians, the Journal provides research on the evolution of accounting thought and accounting practice. Subscription to the semi-annual publication is included in membership to the Academy.
Frequency: Semi-Annual
Founded in 1973

169 **Accounting Horizons**
American Accounting Association
9009 Town Center Parkway
Lakewood Ranch, FL 34202
941-921-7747; Fax: 941-923-4093
info@aaahq.org
aaahq.org
Yvonne Hinson, CEO
Nate Smith, Managing Editor
Papers focusing on the scholarship of integration and application. It prints quarterly in March, June, September, and December and is an A journal indexed in both Scopus and SSCI.
Frequency: Quarterly
Founded in 1916

170 **Accounting Today**
Accountants Media Group & SourceMedia, Inc.
1 State Street Plaza
25th Floor
New York, NY 10004
212-258-8445
800-221-1809; Fax: 212-292-5216
www.accountingtoday.com
Facebook, Twitter, LinkedIn
Michael Cohn, Editor-in-Chief
Tamika Cody, Managing Editor
Daniel Hood, Editor in Chief
Seth Fineberg, Technology Editor
Covers accounting and auditing standards, taxation and practice management.
Cost: $99.00
48 Pages
Circulation: 34991
ISSN: 1044-5714
Founded in 1987
Printed in 4 colors on glossy stock

171 **Accounting and Tax Highlights**
Thomson Reuters
2395 Midway Rd
Carrollton, TX 75006
817-332-3709
800-431-9025; Fax: 888-216-1929
trta.lei-support@thomsonreuters.com
www.ria.thomsonreuters.com
Elaine Yadlon, Plant Manager
Thomas H Glocer, CEO & Director
Robert D Daleo, Chief Financial Officer
Kelli Crane, Senior Vice President & CIO
Covers current news and developments in the field. Audiocassette program for CPAs for continuing professional education. Accepts advertising.
Cost: $112.00
28 Pages
Frequency: Monthly
Founded in 1935

172 **Accounting and the Public Interest**
American Accounting Association
9009 Town Center Parkway
Lakewood Ranch, FL 34202
941-921-7747; Fax: 941-923-4093
info@aaahq.org
aaahq.org
Yvonne Hinson, CEO
Amy M. Hageman, Editor
An academic journal taking the view that accounting has broad societal responsibilities, and thus accounting-related activities have consequences for a wide spectrum of constituencies. Studies submitted to the journal should be linked to the public interest by situating them within a

historical, social, or political context, and findings should ultimately provide guidance for responsible action. API is an online-only journal that publishes annually and is indexed in Scopus.
Frequency: Periodically
Founded in 1916

173 **Achieve**
National Association of Black Accountants
7474 Greenway Center Dr
Suite 1120
Greenbelt, MD 20770-3504

301-474-6222
888-571-2939; Fax: 301-474-3114
customerservice@nabainc.org
www.nabainc.org
Facebook, Twitter, LinkedIn, YouTube

Walter J. Smith, President/CEO

Magazine for NABA student members. Discussed are issues relevant to student academic, career, and personal aspirations.
Frequency: 2 Times/Year
Founded in 1969

174 **Actuary Magazine**
Society of Actuaries
475 N Martingale Rd
Suite 600
Schaumburg, IL 60173-2252

847-706-3500; Fax: 847-706-3599
webmaster@soa.org
www.soa.org

Greg Heidrich, Executive Director
Stacy Lin, Deputy Executive Director/CFO

Provides informative feature articles that focus on a variety of actuarial topics, plus career information, SOA education initiatives and trends in international business.
Frequency: Bimonthly
Printed in 4 colors on glossy stock

175 **Armed Forces Comptroller**
American Society of Military Comptrollers
415 N. Alfred Street
Alexandria, VA 22314

703-549-0360
800-462-5637; Fax: 703-549-3181
www.asmconline.org
Facebook, Twitter, LinkedIn

Al Runnels, Executive Director
Catherine Kenol, Associate Director, Communications

Leading industry journal from the American Society of Military Comptrollers, being one of the Society's means of sharing professional information. Articles are received from a variety of sources, such as academia, the government, and our members.
Founded in 1948

176 **Audit Report**
Association of Credit Union Internal Auditors
332 Commerce Street
Suite 100
Alexandria, VA 22314

703-688-2284; Fax: 703-348-7602
acuia@acuia.org
www.acuia.org
Facebook, Twitter, LinkedIn

Bobby Nichols, Chair
Jill Maznarich, Vice Chair
Dean Swenson, Secretary
Barry Lucas, Treasurer

Articles of interest to those in the auditing profession.
Frequency: Quarterly
Founded in 1990

177 **Auditing: A Journal of Practice & Theory**
American Accounting Association
9009 Town Center Parkway
Lakewood Ranch, FL 34202

941-921-7747; Fax: 941-923-4093
info@aaahq.org
aaahq.org

Yvonne Hinson, CEO
Christopher P. Agoglia, Senior Editor

The journal is distributed to members of the Auditing section of the Association, as well as libraries. Papers report results of original research that embody improvements in auditing theory or auditing methodology, discussion and analysis of current issues that bear on prospects for developments in auditing practice and in auditing research, and practices and developments in auditing in different countries.
Frequency: Quarterly
Founded in 1916

178 **Behavioral Research in Accounting**
American Accounting Association
9009 Town Center Parkway
Lakewood Ranch, FL 34202

941-921-7747; Fax: 941-923-4093
info@aaahq.org
aaahq.org

Yvonne Hinson, CEO
Nate Smith, Managing Editor

Original research relating to accounting and how it affects and is affected by individuals and organizations.
Frequency: Semi-Annually
Founded in 1916

179 **CFMA Building Profits**
Construction Financial Management Association
100 Village Boulevard
Suite 200
Princeton, NJ 08540-5783

609-452-8000
888-421-9996; Fax: 609-452-0474
info@cfma.org
www.cfma.org
Facebook, Twitter, LinkedIn, YouTube

Stuart Binstock, President & CEO
Brian Summers, VP, Operations

Information for financial managers and CPAs concerned with financial management.
Frequency: Bi-Monthly
Circulation: 8,600
Founded in 1981

180 **CPA Practice Management Forum**
CCH
2700 Lake Cook Rd
Riverwoods, IL 60015-3867

847-940-4600
800-835-5224; Fax: 773-866-3095
www.cch.com

Mike Sabbatis, President
Douglas M Winterrose, Vice President & CFO
Jim Bryant, EVP Software Products

Mini-journal that includes articles featuring best practices, tips and advice from the nation's leading practice management experts.
Cost: $529.00
24 Pages
Frequency: Monthly

181 **CPA Technology Advisor**
Cygnus Publishing
1233 Janesville Avenue
Fort Atkinson, WI 53538-0803

800-547-7377
shari.dodgen@cygnuspub.com

John French, CEO
Paul Bonaiuto, CFO
Ed Wood, VP
Kris Flitcroft, EVP

The magazine is a resource for accountants and managers that features a Buyer's Guide that lists hundreds of businesses, manufacturers and professionals that can assist public accounting firms in delivering a variety of services to their clients in various industries.
Cost: $48.00
Circulation: 50,000+
Founded in 1991
Printed in 4 colors on glossy stock

182 **CPA Wealth Provider**
Accountants Media Group & SourceMedia, Inc.
One State Street Plaza
25th Floor
New York, NY 10004

212-258-8445
800-221-1809; Fax: 212-292-5216
www.accountingtoday.com
Facebook

Michael Cohn, President and CEO
Joseph Wells, Chairman
John Gill, VP of Education
John Warren, VP and General Counsel

Offers financial planning strategies, product information and practivve-building advice in an environment that recognizes the special needs of accountants.
Frequency: Quarterly
Circulation: 37000
Founded in 1968
Printed in 4 colors on glossy stock

183 **College and University Auditor Journal**
Association of College & University Auditors
4400 College Boulevard
Suite 220
Overland Park, KS 66211

913-222-8663; Fax: 913-222-8606
ACUA-info@kellencompany.com
www.acua.org

Emily Burch, Executive Director
Marilyn Carnevale, Editor

The College and University Auditor is written and edited specifically for college and university internal auditors. Articles published cover a wide variety of topics related to internal auditing in higher education including: accounting, auditing, risk assessment and management, computer security and information systems, fraud, legislation and regulatory issues, and international higher education issues.
Frequency: 3x Year
Founded in 1958

184 **Computers in Accounting**
Thomson Reuters
2395 Midway Rd
Carrollton, TX 75006

817-332-3709
800-431-9025; Fax: 888-216-1929
trta.lei-support@thomsonreuters.com
www.ria.thomsonreuters.com

Elaine Yadlon, Plant Manager
Thomas H Glocer, CEO & Director
Robert D Daleo, Chief Financial Officer
Kelli Crane, Senior Vice President & CIO

Contains the latest information on accounting, tax and business software, electronic spread-

sheets, and available hardware.
Cost: $58.00
40 Pages
Founded in 1935

185 **Controller's Cost & Profit Report**
Thomson Reuters
2395 Midway Rd
Carrollton, TX 75006

817-332-3709
800-431-9025; Fax: 888-216-1929
trta.lei-support@thomsonreuters.com
www.ria.thomsonreuters.com

Elaine Yadlon, Plant Manager
Thomas H Glocer, CEO & Director
Robert D Daleo, Chief Financial Officer
Kelli Crane, Senior Vice President & CIO

Targets cash flow issues, risk/reward decisions, personnel trends, ways to increase productivity while reducing overhead costs, and technology updates for the new millennium.
Cost: $195.50
Frequency: SemiMonthly
Founded in 1935

186 **Current Issues in Auditing**
American Accounting Association
9009 Town Center Parkway
Lakewood Ranch, FL 34202

941-921-7747; Fax: 941-923-4093
info@aaahq.org
www.aaahq.org

Tracey Sutherland, Executive Director
Lisa Milici Gaynor, Co-Editor
Dan Sutherland, Co-Editor

Devoted to advancing the dialogue between academics and practitioners on current issues facing the auditing practice community (e.g., new opportunities and challenges, emerging areas, global developments, effects of new regulations or pronouncements, and effects of technological or market developments on audit processes). CIIA is an online only publication that publishes twice a year and is indexed in Scopus and ESCI.
Frequency: 2x Year
Founded in 1916

187 **EA Journal**
National Association of Enrolled Agents
1120 Connecticut Avenue NW
Suite 460
Washington, DC 20036-3922

202-822-6232; Fax: 202-822-6270
info@naea.org
www.naea.org
Facebook, Twitter, LinkedIn

Donald Rosenberg, President
Michael Nelson, Interim Executive Vice President
Nancy Lyman, Treasurer
Kathy Brown, Secretary

EA Journal brings information that helps set professionals apart from other tax practitioners.
12000 Members
Frequency: Every Other Month
Founded in 1972

188 **Financial Executive**
200 Campus Drive
PO Box 674
Florham Park, NJ 07932

973-360-0177; Fax: 973-898-4649
www.financialexecutives.org

Andrej Suskavcevic, President & CEO

Award-winning flagship publication of FEI, providing senior-level financial executives with financial, business and management news, trends and strategies to help them work better, faster and smarter. Covers professional, strategic and technological practices and developments that affect financial executives' day-to-day and longer-term issues, reflecting the financial executive's increasing involvement in the general management of their companies.
15M Members
Frequency: 10x/ Year
Founded in 1931

189 **Financial Executive Magazine**
Financial Executives International
1250 Headquarters Plaza
West Tower, 7th Floor
Morristown, NJ 07960

973-765-1000; Fax: 973-765-1018
membership@financialexecutives.org
www.financialexecutives.org

Andrej Suskavcevic, President & CEO

Addresses accounting and treasury subjects, as well as overall strategies in corporate financial management.
72 Pages
Frequency: 10x/yr
Circulation: 17000
ISSN: 0895-4186
Founded in 1931
Printed in 4 colors on glossy stock

190 **Financial Management**
Financial Management Association International
University of South Florida
4202 E. Fowler Avenue, BSN 3403
Tampa, FL 33620-5500

813-974-2084; Fax: 813-974-3318
fma@coba.usf.edu
www.fma.org

Utpal Bhattacharya, Executive Editor

Financial Management serves the profession by publishing significant new scholarly research in finance that is of the highest quality. The principal criteria for publishability are originality, rigor, timeliness, practical relevance and clarity.
Frequency: Quarterly

191 **Financial Manager**
Broadcast Cable Credit Association
550 W. Frontage Road
Suite 3600
Northfield, IL 60093-1243

847-881-8757; Fax: 847-784-8059
info@bccacredit.com
www.bccacredit.com

Mary Collins, President & CEO
Jamie Smith, Director, Operations
Arcelia Pimentel, Sales/Membership

A bi-monthly magazine published by the Broadcast Cable Credit Association.
Frequency: Bi-Monthly

192 **Fraud Magazine**
Association of Certified Fraud Examiners
716 W. Avenue
Austin, TX 78701-2727

512-478-9000
800-245-3321; Fax: 512-478-9297
memberservices@acfe.com
www.fraud-magazine.com

Bruce Dorris, President & CEO
Kevin Taparauskas, Director, Communications

Articles on white-collar crime and fraud examination techniques. Free for ACFE members.
Cost: $65.00
Frequency: Bi-Monthly
Founded in 1988

193 **ISACA Journal**
Information Systems Audit & Control Association
Rolling Meadows, IL

847-660-5505
844-472-2246
www.isaca.org
Facebook, Twitter, LinkedIn

David Samuelson, CEO

Provides professional development information to those spearheading IT governance and those involved with information systems audit, control and security.
9000+ Members
Frequency: Bimonthly
Circulation: 35000
Founded in 1967

194 **Information Management**
ARMA International
11880 College Boulevard
Suite 450
Overland Park, KS 66215

913-444-9174
844-565-2120; Fax: 913-257-3855
headquarters@armaintl.org
magazine.arma.org
Facebook, Twitter, LinkedIn

Nick Inglis, Exec. Dir., Content & Programming
Jeff Whited, Sr. Content Writer
Ann Snyder, Manager, Content Development

Also known as ARMA Magazine, it is a major source of information on topics and issues central to the management of records and information worldwide. Each issue features articles written by experts in the management of records and information.
61 Pages
Frequency: 6/Year
Founded in 1955

195 **Insight**
Illinois CPA Society
550 W Jackson Blvd
Suite 900
Chicago, IL 60661-5742

312-993-0407
800-993-0407; Fax: 312-993-9954
www.icpas.org
Facebook, Twitter, LinkedIn, YouTube

Elaine Weiss, President & CEO
Todd Shapiro, CFO & VP Finance & Administration
Judy Giannetto, INSIGHT Director

Editorial content focuses on practical issues affecting professional development.
Frequency: Monthly
Circulation: 23000
Founded in 1980

196 **Internal Auditing**
Thomson Reuters
2395 Midway Rd
Carrollton, TX 75006

817-332-3709
800-431-9025; Fax: 888-216-1929
trta.lei-support@thomsonreuters.com
www.ria.thomsonreuters.com

Elaine Yadlon, Plant Manager
Thomas H Glocer, CEO & Director
Robert D Daleo, Chief Financial Officer
Kelli Crane, Senior Vice President & CIO

Provides solutions to internal auditing problems. Only professional resource written exclusively by leading practitioners.
Cost: $275.00
Frequency: Annual+
Founded in 1935

197 **Internal Auditor Magazine**
Institute of Internal Auditors
247 Maitland Ave
Altamonte Spgs, FL 32701-4201

407-937-1100; Fax: 407-937-1101
iia@theiia.org

www.theiia.org
Facebook, Twitter, LinkedIn

J. Michael Pepper, Chairman
Carolyn Saint, Senior Vice President
John Wxzelaki, Vice Chairman - Finance/security

World's leading publication covering the internal audit profession. Shares timely, helpful- indispensable -information for professionals who want to keep pace with the diverse, dynamic field of internal auditing.
160M Members
Founded in 1941

198 **International Journal of Business Data Communications and Networking**
Information Resources Management Association
701 E Chocolate Avenue
Suite 200
Hershey, PA 17033-1240

717-533-8845; Fax: 717-533-8661
member@irma-international.org
www.irma-international.org

Mehdi Khosrowpour, Executive Director
Sherif Kamel, VP, Information Management

This journal examines the impact of data communications and networking technologies, policies, and management on business organizatios, capturing their effect on IT-enabled management practices.
Cost: $545.00
Frequency: Quarterly
ISSN: 1548-0631

199 **Interpreter Magazine**
Insurance Accounting Systems Association
PO Box 51340
Durham, NC 27717-1340

919-489-0991; Fax: 919-489-1994
info@iasa.org
www.iasa.org
Facebook, Twitter

Laurie Macklosky, President
Kerry Crockett, CEO
Parshy Phillips, Director, Marketing & Communication
Kelli Bohannon, Director, Membership

This magazine includes reports on actions by the NAIC, interviews with business leaders, reports on industry trends and news about IASA activities.
Cost: $45.00
12 Pages
Frequency: Quarterly
Founded in 1940

200 **Issues in Accounting Education**
American Accounting Association
9009 Town Center Parkway
Lakewood Ranch, FL 34202

941-921-7747; Fax: 941-923-4093
info@aaahq.org
aaahq.org

Yvonne Hinson, CEO
Nate Smith, Managing Editor

Publishes research, commentaries, and instructional resources that assist accounting faculty in teaching and that address important issues in accounting education. It prints quarterly in February, May, August, and November and is a top journal indexed in both Scopus and ESCI.
Frequency: Quarterly
Founded in 1983

201 **Journal of Accountancy**
American Institute of Certified Public Accountants
220 Leigh Farm Road
Durham, NC 27707-8110

919-402-4500; Fax: 919-402-4505
www.aicpa.org
Facebook, Twitter, LinkedIn

Kim Nilsen, Publisher
Rocky S. Rosen, Managing Editor

AICPA publication that focuses on the latest news and developments in accounting.
Frequency: Monthly
Founded in 1887

202 **Journal of Accounting Research**
University of Chicago Booth School of Business
5807 S Woodlawn Ave
Chicago, IL 60637-1656

773-702-7743; Fax: 773-702-2225
jar@chicagobooth.edu
www.chicagobooth.edu
Facebook, Twitter, LinkedIn, YouTube

Ted Snyder, Manager
Nicholas Dopuch, Consulting Editor

Publishes original research using analytical, empirical, experimental, and field study methods in accounting research.
Cost: $49.00
Frequency: 5 Times/Year
Circulation: 2800
Founded in 1963

203 **Journal of Accounting and Public Policy**
Elsevier
3251 Riverport Lane
Maryland Heights, MO 63043

314-447-8878
877-839-7126; Fax: 314-447-8077
journalcustomerservice-usa@elsevier.com
www.elsevier.com

Ron Mobed, CEO
David Lomas, CFO
Gavin Howe, EVP, Human Resources

Publishes research papers that focus on the intersection between accounting and public policy. It offers articles on accounting including public administration, political science and the law.
Cost: $126.00
Frequency: 6x Yearly
ISSN: 0278-4254
Founded in 1997

204 **Journal of Applied Corporate Finance**
Financial Management Association International
University of South Florida
4202 E. Fowler Avenue BSN 3403
Tampa, FL 33620-5500

813-974-2084; Fax: 813-974-3318
fma@coba.usf.edu
www.fma.org

Matt Staton, Managing Editor

The Journal of Applied Corporate Finance's goal is to be the leading bridging journal between practitioners and academics. The mission is to publish well-crafted papers of interest to practitioners and of use to academics in stimulating research and in their teaching function.
Frequency: 2 Times/Year

205 **Journal of Construction Accounting & Taxation**
Thomson Reuters
2395 Midway Rd
Carrollton, TX 75006

817-332-3709
800-431-9025; Fax: 888-216-1929
trta.lei-support@thomsonreuters.com
www.ria.thomsonreuters.com

Elaine Yadlon, Plant Manager
Thomas H Glocer, CEO & Director
Robert D Daleo, Chief Financial Officer
Kelli Crane, Senior Vice President & CIO

Authoritative, targeted articles and experience-based columns cover several areas, including job-costing, risk assessment, dispute resolution, financial reporting, and benchmarking contractor performance.
Cost: $270.00
Frequency: 6 Times/Year
Circulation: 3400
Founded in 1935

206 **Journal of Cost Analysis and Parametrics**
Society of Cost Estimating and Analysis
8221 Old Courthouse Rd
Suite 106
Vienna, VA 22182

703-938-5090; Fax: 703-938-5091
scea@sceaonline.org
www.sceaonline.org

Erin Whittaker, Executive Director
Sharon Burger, Certification Program Admin
Brittany Walker, Membership Coordinator

The Journal of Cost Analysis and Parametrics is a joint publication with the International Society of Parametric Analysts. It is dedicated to promoting excellence in cost estimating, cost analysis, and cost management.
Cost: $ 55.00
2015 Members
Frequency: Twice/Year
Founded in 1990

207 **Journal of Cost Management**
Thomson Reuters
2395 Midway Rd
Carrollton, TX 75006

817-332-3709
800-431-9025; Fax: 888-216-1929
trta.lei-support@thomsonreuters.com
www.ria.thomsonreuters.com

Elaine Yadlon, Plant Manager
Thomas H Glocer, CEO & Director
Robert D Daleo, Chief Financial Officer
Kelli Crane, Senior Vice President & CIO

Journal of modern cost management (including cost and managerial accounting topics), especially activity-based costing, activity-based management, performance measurement, target costing and investment justification. Accepts advertising.
Cost: $275.00
64 Pages
Founded in 1935

208 **Journal of Emerging Technologies in Accounting**
American Accounting Association
9009 Town Center Parkway
Lakewood Ranch, FL 34202

941-921-7747; Fax: 941-923-4093
info@aaahq.org
aaahq.org

Yvonne Hinson, CEO
Miklos A. Vasarhelyi, Editor

This journal is distributed to members of the AI/Emerging Technologies section of the Association, as well as libraries. Designed to encourage, support, and disseminate the production of a stream of high-quality research focused on emerging technologies and artificial intelligence applied or applicable to a wide set of accounting related problems. It prints

semi-annually in Spring and Fall, and is indexed in Scopus and ESCI.
Frequency: Semi-Annually
Founded in 1916

209 **Journal of Government Financial Management**
Association of Government Accountants
2208 Mount Vernon Avenue
Alexandria, VA 22301-1314

703-684-6931
800-242-7211; Fax: 703-519-0039
communications@agacgfm.org
www.agacgfm.org

Ann M. Ebberts, Chief Executive Officer
Mary Margaret Yodzis, Editor/Copywriter

Provides valuable information for governmental decision makers. Examines budgeting, accounting, auditing and data process developments.
Cost: $33.00
Frequency: Quarterly
Circulation: 14,250
Founded in 1950

210 **Journal of Information Systems**
American Accounting Association
9009 Town Center Parkway
Lakewood Ranch, FL 34202

941-921-7747; Fax: 941-923-4093
info@aaahq.org
aaahq.org

Yvonne Hinson, CEO
Alexander Kogan, Co-Editor
Patrick R. Wheeler, Co-Editor

Publishes academic and educational research, and the reports of practice advances related to information systems and information technology to support, promote, and improve information systems and information technology research, education, and practice. JIS prints 3 issues a year in Spring, Summer, and Fall, and is indexed in Scopus and ESCI.
Frequency: 3x Year
Founded in 1916

211 **Journal of International Accounting Research**
American Accounting Association
9009 Town Center Parkway
Lakewood Ranch, FL 34202

941-921-7747; Fax: 941-923-4093
info@aaahq.org
aaahq.org

Yvonne Hinson, CEO
Joanna Ho, Editor

Publishes articles that increase understanding of the development and use of international accounting and reporting practices or attempt to improve extant practices. It prints three times a year in Spring, Summer, and Fall, and is indexed in Scopus and ESCI.
Frequency: 3x Year
Founded in 1916

212 **Journal of Management Accounting Research**
American Accounting Association
9009 Town Center Parkway
Lakewood Ranch, FL 34202

941-921-7747; Fax: 941-923-4093
info@aaahq.org
aaahq.org

Yvonne Hinson, CEO
Eva Labro, Senior Editor

Devoted exclusively to management accounting research. Contributes to improving the theory and practice of management accounting by promoting high-quality applied and theoretical research. Papers relate to internal reporting and decision making, the interface between internal and external reporting, profit and not-for-profit organizations, service and manufacturing organizations and domestic, foreign and multinational organizations.
Frequency: 3x Year
Founded in 1916

213 **Journal of Organizational and End User Computing**
Information Resources Management Association
701 E Chocolate Avenue
Suite 200
Hershey, PA 17033-1240

717-533-8845; Fax: 717-533-8661
member@irma-international.org
www.irma-international.org

Mehdi Khosrowpour, Executive Director
Sherif Kamel, VP, Information Management

The Journal of Organizational and End User Computing (JOEUC) provides a forum to information technology educators, researchers, and practitioners to advance the practice and understanding of organizational and end user computing. The journal features a major emphasis on how to increase organizational and end user productivity and performance, and how to achieve organizational, strategic and competitive advantage.
Cost: $125.00
Frequency: Quarterly
ISSN: 1546-2234

214 **Journal of the American Taxation Association**
American Accounting Association
9009 Town Center Parkway
Lakewood Ranch, FL 34202

941-921-7747; Fax: 941-923-4093
info@aaahq.org
aahq.org

Yvonne Hinson, CEO
Connie D. Weaver, Senior Editor

Promotes the study of, and the acquisition of knowledge about, taxation. Dedicated to disseminating a wide variety of tax knowledge and publishes research that employs quantitative, analytical, experimental, and descriptive methods to address tax topics of interest to its readership. It prints semi-annually in Spring and Fall, and is indexed in Scopus and ESCI.
Frequency: Semi-Annually
Founded in 1916

215 **Local Government Auditing Quarterly**
Association of Local Government Auditors

859-276-0686
kyoung@nasact.org
algaonline.org

Kathleen Young, Publications Contact
Alicia Cline, Editor

Professional journal of the Association of Local Government Auditors.
Frequency: Quarterly
Founded in 1989

216 **Main Street Practitioner**
National Society of Accountants
1330 Braddock Place
Suite 540
Alexandria, VA 22314

800-966-6679
members@nsacct.org
www.nsacct.org
Facebook, Twitter, LinkedIn

Digital magazine for tax and accounting professionals.
Frequency: 5 issues/yr

217 **National Public Accountant**
National Society of Accountants
1010 N Fairfax St
Alexandria, VA 22314-1574

703-549-6400
800-966-6679; Fax: 703-549-2984
members@nsacct.org
www.nsacct.org
Facebook, Twitter, LinkedIn

Curtis Lee, Jr., President
Marchelle Foshee, First Vice President
Debra Cope, Second Vice President

News for practicing accountants and tax practitioners.
48 Pages
Circulation: 20000
ISSN: 0027-9978
Founded in 1945

218 **New Accountant**
REN Publishing
3550 W Peterson Avenue
Suite 403
Chicago, IL 60659

773-866-9900; Fax: 773-866-9881
inquiries@RenPublishing.com
www.renpublishing.com/

Steven N Polydoris, President/Publisher/Editor

A professional publication for accounting students and the accounting profession. Each issue includes articles to introduce students to the many and diverse career opportunities available to accounting majors and to prepare college accounting students and recent graduates to sit for the CPA exam. Also available in an online format.
Cost: $85.00
17 Pages
Frequency: Monthly
Circulation: 68000
Founded in 1883

219 **North American Actuarial Journal**
Society of Actuaries
475 N Martingale Rd
Suite 600
Schaumburg, IL 60173-2252

847-706-3500; Fax: 847-706-3599
webmaster@soa.org
www.soa.org

Greg Heidrich, Executive Director
Stacy Lin, Deputy Executive Director/CFO
Harry H Panjer, Editor

Scientically addresses domestic and international problems, interests and concerns of actuaries, their customers, and public policy decision makers.
Frequency: Quarterly
Circulation: 22800
ISSN: 1092-0277
Founded in 1997
Mailing list available for rent: 17000 names at $105 per M

220 **Payroll Administration Guide**
Bureau of National Affairs
3 Bethesda Metro Center
Suite 250
Bethesda, MD 20814

800-372-1033; Fax: 800-253-0332
customercare@bna.com
www.bna.com

Josh Eastright, CEO

A notification and reference service for payroll professionals. Covers federal and state employment tax, wage-hour and wage-payment laws.
Cost: $896.00
Frequency: Bi-Weekly
Founded in 1929

221 **Paytech**
American Payroll Association
660 N. Main Avenue
Suite 100
San Antonio, TX 78205

210-224-6406; Fax: 210-224-6038
www.payroll.org

Daniel Maddux, Executive Director

A monthly magazine that covers payroll management, technology, new and pending legislation, professional development, and trends shaping the payroll industry and profession.
Frequency: Monthly
Founded in 1982

222 **Practical Tax Strategies**
Thomson Reuters
2395 Midway Rd
Carrollton, TX 75006

817-332-3709
800-431-9025; Fax: 888-216-1929
trta.lei-support@thomsonreuters.com
www.ria.thomsonreuters.com

Elaine Yadlon, Plant Manager
Thomas H Glocer, CEO & Director
Robert D Daleo, Chief Financial Officer
Kelli Crane, Senior Vice President & CIO

Features offer in-depth articles and technical notes on taxation.
Cost: $185.00
64 Pages
Frequency: Monthly
Circulation: 12000
Founded in 1935

223 **Public Budgeting and Finance**
AABPA
PO Box 1157
Falls Church, VA 22041

703-941-4300; Fax: 703-941-1535
aabpa@aabpa.org
www.aabpa.org
Facebook, Twitter, LinkedIn, GovLoop

Judy Thomas, President
Melissa Neuman, President Elect
Anthony Rainey, VP
Patrick Vallely, Treasurer

Presents research and experiences on government finance, from universities, private/nonprofit research centers, those involved in public financial markets, government agencies, and those who practice government budgeting and finance. Free online access is given to members of the American Association for Budget and Program Analysis.
400 Members
Frequency: Monthly
Founded in 1976

224 **Real Estate Taxation**
Thomson Reuters
2395 Midway Rd
Carrollton, TX 75006

817-332-3709
800-431-9025; Fax: 888-216-1929
trta.lei-support@thomsonreuters.com
www.ria.thomsonreuters.com

Elaine Yadlon, Plant Manager
Thomas H Glocer, CEO & Director
Robert D Daleo, Chief Financial Officer
Kelli Crane, Senior Vice President & CIO

Timely source of new ideas, trends and legal developments in real estate taxation. This journal gives you complete, ongoing coverage of all aspects of real estate tax planning.
Cost: $350.00
Frequency: Quarterly
Founded in 1935

225 **Review of Taxation of Individuals**
Thomson Reuters
2395 Midway Rd
Carrollton, TX 75006

817-332-3709
800-431-9025; Fax: 888-216-1929
trta.lei-support@thomsonreuters.com
www.ria.thomsonreuters.com

Elaine Yadlon, Plant Manager
Thomas H Glocer, CEO & Director
Robert D Daleo, Chief Financial Officer
Kelli Crane, Senior Vice President & CIO

Offers information on the taxation of individuals, legislation, etc.
Cost: $58.00
Frequency: Monthly
Founded in 1935

226 **Sales & Use Tax Monitor**
Strafford Publications
590 Dutch Valley Road NE
PO Box 13729
Atlanta, GA 30324-0729

404-881-1141
800-926-7926; Fax: 404-881-0074
customerservice@straffordpub.com
www.straffordpub.com
Twitter

Richard Ossoff, President
Jon McKenna, Executive Editor

Provides updates on compliance requirements and tax avoidance opportunities in every state.
Cost: $487.00
Frequency: 2 Times/Month
ISSN: 0161-309X
Founded in 1984

227 **Spectrum Magazine**
National Association of Black Accountants
7474 Greenway Center Dr
Suite 1120
Greenbelt, MD 20770-3504

301-474-6222
888-571-2939; Fax: 301-474-3114
www.nabainc.org
Facebook, Twitter, LinkedIn, YouTube

Walter J. Smith, President/CEO

Provides a communication mechanism whereby readers are kept abreast of key topics of interest within the accounting, finance, and business professions.
Frequency: Annual

228 **State Income Tax Monitor**
Strafford Publications
590 Dutch Valley Road NE
PO Box 13729
Atlanta, GA 30324-0729

404-881-1141
800-926-7926; Fax: 404-881-0074
customerservice@straffordpub.com
www.straffordpub.com

Richard Ossoff, President
Jon McKenna, Executive Editor

This journal is a comprehensive briefing on the latest revenue rulings, tax codes, regulations, court decisions and more in every state.
Cost: $467.00
Frequency: 2 Times/Month
ISSN: 0161-309X
Founded in 1984

229 **Strategic Finance**
Institute of Management Accountants
10 Paragon Dr
Suite 1
Montvale, NJ 07645-1774

201-573-9000
800-638-4427; Fax: 201-474-1600
ima@imanet.org
www.imanet.org
Facebook, Twitter, LinkedIn

Jeffrey C. Thomson, President and CEO
Paul E. Juras, Chair

IMA's award winning magazine that provides the latest information about practices and trends in finance, accounting, and information management that will impact members and their jobs.
Cost: $195.00
Frequency: Monthly
Printed in 4 colors on glossy stock

230 **TAXPRO Journal**
National Association of Tax Professionals
PO Box 8002
Appleton, WI 54912-8002

800-558-3402; Fax: 800-747-0001
natp@natptax.com
www.natptax.com
Facebook, Twitter, MySpace

Brett Rosser, President
Jaimee Hammer, Vice President

In-depth tax information and timely feature articles on such issues as new tax acts, practical tax applications, and solutions to the day-to-day challenges of running a tax practice.
Frequency: Quarterly

231 **Tax Management Estates, Gifts and Trusts Journal**
Bureau of National Affairs
3 Bethesda Metro Center
Suite 250
Bethesda, MD 20814

800-372-1033; Fax: 301-294-6760
www.bna.com

Josh Eastright, CEO

Provides articles by leading tax practitioners and proven techniques for estate planning and planning opportunities. It also features reviews of legislative, administrative and judicial developments.
Frequency: Bimonthly

232 **Tax and Business Advisor**
Grant Thornton
175 W Jackson Blvd
Suite 20
Chicago, IL 60604-2687

312-856-0001; Fax: 312-602-8099
www.grantthornton.com
Twitter, LinkedIn

Stephen Chipman, CEO
Lou Grabowsky, COO
Russ Wieman, Chief Financial Officer

Current tax and general business issues.
Founded in 1924

233 **The Accounting Review**
American Accounting Association
9009 Town Center Parkway
Lakewood Ranch, FL 34202

941-921-7747; Fax: 941-923-4093
info@aaahq.org
aaahq.org

Yvonne Hinson, CEO
Mary E. Barth, Senior Editor
Stephanie Austin, Managing Editor

The premier journal for publishing articles reporting the results of accounting research and explaining and illustrating related research methodology. It publishes six issues per year in January, March, May, July, September, and November and is indexed in Scopus and SSCI.
Frequency: 6x Year
Founded in 1916

234 **The Bottomline**
Hospitality Financial & Technology Professionals
11709 Boulder Lane
Suite 110
Austin, TX 78726-1832

512-249-5333
800-646-4387; Fax: 512-249-1533
membership@hftp.org
www.hftp.org

Frank I Wolfe, Executive VP/CEO
Lucinda Hart, COO
Thomas Atzenhofer, CFO
Eliza Selig, Director of Communications

The Bottomline chronicles the most important industry news with focuses on both finance, technology and general management in hospitality.
4800 Members
Frequency: 10x/Year
Founded in 1952

235 **The Compass**
American Society of Women Accountants
1760 Old Meadow Road
Suite 500
McLean, VA 22102

703-506-3265
800-326-2163; Fax: 703-506-3266
aswa@aswa.org
www.aswa.org
Facebook, Twitter, LinkedIn

Cheryl E Heitz, President
Catherine Mulder, President-elect
Berranthia Brown, VP

Each e-magazine includes content in the areas of accounting & auditing, controllership, leadership, and tax and quick and easy links to the popular sections of the American Society of Women Accountants web site.
Frequency: Monthly
Founded in 1938

236 **The Tax Adviser**
American Institute of Certified Public Accountants
220 Leigh Farm Road
Durham, NC 27707-8110

919-402-4500; Fax: 919-402-4505
www.aicpa.org
Twitter, LinkedIn

Kim Nilsen, Publisher
Alistair M. Nevius, Editor-in-Chief
Rocky S. Rosen, Managing Editor

A monthly publication of the American Institute of CPAs, providing tax practitioners with timely, in-depth, practical, and comprehensive information on federal and state tax developments.
Frequency: Monthly
Founded in 1887

237 **Today's CPA**
Texas Society of CPAs
14651 Dallas Pkwy
Suite 700
Dallas, TX 75254-7408

972-687-8500
800-428-0272; Fax: 972-687-8646
www.tscpa.org
Facebook, Twitter, LinkedIn

Fred Timmons, Chairman
William Hornberger, Chairman/Elect
Stephen W Parker, Treasurer
Roxie Samaniego, Secretary

Includes articles, news and professional tips.
Cost: $28.00
27000 Members
Frequency: Bimonthly

Trade Shows

238 **AAM Summit**
Association for Accounting Marketing
201 E. Main Street
Suite 1405
Lexington, KY 40507

859-402-9769
info@accountingmarketing.org
www.accountingmarketing.org

Rhonda Clark, Association Manager

Annual educational and networking conference designed to provide educational events through keynote speakers and breakout sessions featuring sole presenters, co-presenters and panel presentations.
Founded in 1989

239 **ACFE Global Fraud Conference**
Association of Certified Fraud Examiners
716 W. Avenue
Austin, TX 78701-2727

512-478-9000
800-245-3321; Fax: 512-478-9297
memberservices@acfe.com
www.fraudconference.com

Bruce Dorris, President & CEO
Leslie Simpson, Director, Events

A conference for professionals in the fraud industry to network with colleagues and learn new ways fraud is being committed and tactics to prevent, detect and deter it.
Cost: $1800.00
3000 Attendees
Frequency: Annual
Founded in 1988

240 **ACUA Annual Conference**
Association of College & University Auditors
4400 College Boulevard
Suite 220
Overland Park, KS 66211

913-222-8663; Fax: 913-222-8606
ACUA-info@kellencompany.com
www.acua.org

Emily Burch, Executive Director
Caitlin Arnold, Meetings Manager

Annual conference for professionals in the auditing profession.
Frequency: Annual
Founded in 1958

241 **ACUIA Annual Conference & One-Day Seminar**
Association of Credit Union Internal Auditors
332 Commerce Street
Suite 100
Alexandria, VA 22314

703-688-2284; Fax: 703-348-7602
acuia@acuia.org
www.acuia.org

Bobby Nichols, Chair
Jill Meznarich, Vice Chair
Dean Swenson, Secretary
Barry Lucas, Treasurer

This four-day event covers the latest developments and features some of the industry's most popular speakers.
600 Members
Founded in 1990

242 **AGA National Leadership Training**
Association of Government Accountants
2208 Mount Vernon Avenue
Alexandria, VA 22301-1314

703-684-6931
800-242-7211; Fax: 703-519-0039
communications@agacgfm.org
www.agacgfm.org

Ann M. Ebberts, Chief Executive Officer
Susan Fritzlen, Chief Operating Officer
Jerome Bruce, Director, Meetings & Expositions

Presents new tools, innovations and insights from financial management and accountability leaders, as well as their strategies, mistakes, and new management techniques; and the most current standards and regulations updates. The event is worth up to 14 CPE hours.
Cost: $800.00
Frequency: Annual/February
Founded in 1950

243 **AGA Professional Development Training**
Association of Government Accountants
2208 Mount Vernon Avenue
Alexandria, VA 22301-1314

703-684-6931
800-242-7211; Fax: 703-519-0039
communications@agacgfm.org
www.agacgfm.org

Ann M. Ebberts, Chief Executive Officer
Susan Fritzler, Chief Operating Officer
Jerome Bruce, Director, Meetings & Expositions

Worth 25 CPE hours, the conference covers the latest research and information about the American Recovery Act, the constantly changing rules and standards, new management techniques, technological advances and practical tips for bringing greater efficiency to government operations.
Cost: $1075.00
Frequency: Annual
Founded in 1950

244 **AGN North American Regional Meeting**
AGN International - North America
13918 E. Mississippi Avenue
Suite 63308
Aurora, CO 80012

303-743-7880
info@agn.org
www.agn.org
Twitter, LinkedIn

Lisa Hastings, Chair
Robert Watts, Vice Chair
Jim Rollins, Treasurer
Kevin Doyle, Secretary
Cindy Frey, Regional Director

Annual meeting of the North American Region of AGN, a worldwide association of separate and independent accounting and consulting firms.
53 Members
Founded in 1978

245 **AHIA Annual Conference**
Association of Healthcare Internal Auditors
One Parkview Plaza
Suite 800
Oakbrook Terrace, IL 60181

303-327-7546
888-275-2442; Fax: 720-881-6101
info@ahia.org
www.ahia.org

Mary Jane Schroeder, Chair
Cavell Alexander, Vice Chair
Todd Havens, Secretary/Treasurer
Michelle Cunningham, Executive Director

Exhibits concerning cost containment and increased productivity in health care institutions through internal auditing.
Founded in 1981

246 **AIRA Bankruptcy & Restructuring Conference**
Association of Insolvency & Restructuring Advisors
221 W. Stewart Avenue
Suite 207
Medford, OR 97501

541-858-1665; Fax: 541-858-9187
aira@aira.org
www.aira.org

Jim Lukenda, Executive Director
Cheryl Campbell, Conference Director

A conference for AIRA members to connect and network with colleages, as well as learn from experts in the field.
Frequency: Annual
Founded in 1982

247 **ALGA Annual Conference**
Association of Local Government Auditors

859-276-0686
dmaloy@nasact.org
algaonline.org

Kathleen Young, General Contact
Donna Maloy, Conference Contact

A conference for ALGA members to connect and network with colleagues.
Frequency: Annual
Founded in 1989

248 **ALPFA Convention**
ALPFA
1717 W. 6th Street
Suite 410
Austin, TX 78703

855-692-5732
carlos.perez@national.alpfa.org
www.alpfa.org
Facebook, Twitter, LinkedIn, YouTube, Instagram

Damian Rivera, Chief Executive Officer
Selene Benavides, Chief Financial Officer
Justin Lopez, Chief Operating Officer
Ann Marquez, Chief of Staff

Conference of the Association of Latino Professionals in Finance and Accounting, dedicated to enhancing opportunities for Latinos in the accounting, finance and related professions.
Frequency: Annual
Founded in 1972

249 **AM&AA Summer Conference**
Alliance of Merger and Acquisition Advisors
200 E. Randolph Street
24th Floor
Chicago, IL 60601

312-856-9590
877-844-2535; Fax: 312-729-9800
info@amaaonline.org
www.amaaonline.com

Matthew C Hawkins, Conference Chairman

Hosts many of the world's leading mid-market M&A executives, top tier speakers, as well as an invaluable networking opportunity.
Frequency: Semi-Annual

250 **AM&AA Winter Conference**
Alliance of Merger and Acquisition Advisors
200 E. Randolph Street
24th Floor
Chicago, IL 60601

312-856-9590
877-844-2535; Fax: 312-729-9800
info@amaaonline.com
www.amaaonline.com

Matthew C Hawkins, Conference Chairman

The conference covers a wide range of current topics of interest to members, such as new accounting and tax regulations, value-added intermediary services, financing, licensure, marketing and business development services and networking opportunities.
Frequency: Semi-Annual

251 **APLG/FSA Joint Annual Seminar**
Federation of Schools of Accountacy
220 Leigh Farm Road
Durham, NC 27707-8110

919-402-4825
mtarasi@aicpa.org
www.thefsa.org

Richard Dull, President
Megan Tarasi, Contact

Provides a forum for the interchange of ideas among participants from schools desiring to develop or improve professional five-year accounting programs, as well as a forum for major officials from the accounting profession, industry, and government to present and discuss their views and concerns for professional accounting education.
Frequency: Annual/February
Founded in 1978

252 **APPFA Annual Conference**
Association of Public Pension Fund Auditors
P.O. Box 16064
Columbus, OH 43216-6064

Home Page: www.appfa.org

Sandra Vice, President
Leslie Nagel, Vice President

A conference for APPFA members to conect and network with colleagues, and to learn from experts in the industry.
Frequency: Annual
Founded in 1991

253 **ARMA InfoCon**
ARMA International
11880 College Boulevard
Suite 450
Overland Park, KS 66210

913-444-9174
844-565-2120; Fax: 913-257-3855
headquarters@armaintl.org
www.arma.org
Facebook, Twitter, LinkedIn

Nate Hughes, Exec. Dir., Operations
Jennifer Millett, National Account Manager
Karen Skaggs, Sales & Events Specialist

Conference, seminar, workshop, banquet, award ceremony and 175 exhibits of micrographics, optical disk, automated document storage and retrieval systems and more technology of interest to information professionals.
3500 Attendees
Frequency: Annual
Founded in 1956

254 **ASWA/AWSCPA Joint Annual Conference**
American Woman's Society of CPAs
136 S Keowee Street
Dayton, OH 45402

937-222-1872
800-297-2721; Fax: 937-222-5794
info@awscpa.org
www.awscpa.org
Facebook, Twitter, LinkedIn

Amy Knowles-Jones, President
Kelly Welter, President Elect
Alexandra Miller, Secretary/Treasurer
Cynthia Cox, VP - Member Services

The conference presents an opportunity to learn from leading experts on ways to develop a variety of your skills, leadership development, networking, education and fun.
Frequency: Annual/September
Founded in 2001

255 **ASWA/AWSCPA Joint National Conference**
American Society of Women Accountants
1760 Old Meadow Road
Suite 500
McLean, VA 22102

703-506-3265
800-326-2163; Fax: 703-506-3266
aswa@aswa.org
www.aswa.org
Facebook, Twitter, LinkedIn

Julia Merrill, Annual Conference Contact

Banquet, luncheon, tours and exhibits of accounting, business and employment opportunities. In conjunction with American Women's Society of CPAs
400 Attendees
Frequency: Annual

256 **ATEC Annual Meeting**
American College of Trust and Estate Counsel
901 15th Street, NW
Suite 525
Washington, DC 20005

202-684-8460; Fax: 202-684-8459
www.actec.org

Stephen R. Akers, President
Ann B. Burns, President-Elect
Robert W. Goldman, Vice President

A conference for ATEC members to meet and network with colleagues.
Frequency: Annual
Founded in 1949

257 **Accounting Technology New York Show & Conference**
Flagg Management
353 Lexington Avenue
New York, NY 10016

212-286-0333; Fax: 212-286-0086
flaggmgmnt@msn.com
www.flaggmgmt.com

Russell Flagg, President

The free Show focuses on new computer-savvy systems for accounting practices and client operations. See new products offered for the first time. The Conference offers CPE sessions with more than 100 exhibitors and nationally recognized speakers.
Frequency: Annual

258 **All Star Conference**
Institute of Internal Auditors
247 Maitland Avenue
Altamonte Springs, FL 32701-4201

407-371-1100; Fax: 407-937-1101
iia@theiia.org
www.theiia.org

J. Michael Pepper, Chairman
Carolyn Saint, Senior Vice President
John Wxzelaki, Vice Chairman - Finance/security

Event features concurrent sessions in tracks focusing on strategies for excellence, risk management, emerging issues, organization best practices, and preventing fraud.
400 Members
Frequency: October/Annual

259 **Alliance of Merger & Acquisition Advisors Semi-Annual Conference**
200 E Randolph St
24th Floor
Chicago, IL 60601-6435

312-856-9590
877-844-2535; Fax: 312-729-9800
info@amaaonline.org
www.amaaonline.com

Michael Nall, Owner

AM&AA is the premier International Organization serving the educational and resource needs of the middle market M&A profession. Conferences cover a wide range of current topics of interest to our members, such as new accounting and tax regulations, value-added intermediary services, financing, licensure, marketing and business development services and networking.
Frequency: Semi-Annual
Founded in 1998

260 **American Accounting Association Annual Meeting**
American Accounting Association
9009 Town Center Parkway
Lakewood Ranch, FL 34202

941-921-7747; Fax: 941-923-4093
info@aaahq.org
aaahq.org

Yvonne Hinson, CEO
Julie Smith David, Chief Innovation Officer
Barbara Brady, Director of Operations
Erlinda L. Jones, Sr. Director, Meetings & Programs

The Association's annual meeting and conference on teaching and learning in accounting.
9000 Members
Founded in 1916

261 **American Association of Attorney-Certified Public Accountants Annual Meeting**
American Association of Attorney-CPAs
P.O. Box 706
Warrendale, PA 15095

703-352-8064
888-288-9272; Fax: 703-352-8073
info@attorney-cpa.com
www.attorney-cpa.com

Howard O. Bernstein, President
Kimmy Headland, Director, Membership & Chapters
Jennifer Welding, Meetings Manager

Exhibits for persons licensed both as attorneys and CPAs for learning and networking purposes.
Frequency: Annual/July
Founded in 1964
Mailing list available for rent

262 **American Payroll Association Annual Congress**
American Payroll Association
660 N. Main Avenue
Suite 100
San Antonio, TX 78205

210-224-6406; Fax: 210-224-6038
www.americanpayroll.org

Daniel Maddux, Executive Editor

The Annual Congress is the premier payroll event of the year. With over 190 workshops and special programs and entertainment, Congress is an excellent opportunity for payroll and other financial professionals to learn and network.
1500 Attendees
Frequency: Annual
Founded in 1982

263 **American Payroll Association Capital Summit**
American Payroll Association
660 N. Main Avenue
Suite 100
San Antonio, TX 78205

210-224-6406; Fax: 210-224-6038
www.americanpayroll.org

Daniel Maddux, Executive Director

APA hosts the Capital Summit in Washington, D.C. This conference offers attendees the opportunity to meet with government officials and learn about the latest compliance initiatives.
Cost: $950.00
Frequency: Annual
Founded in 1982

264 **American Payroll Association Educational Institutions Payroll Conference**
American Payroll Association
660 N. Main Avenue
Suite 100
San Antonio, TX 78205

210-224-6406; Fax: 210-224-6038
www.americanpayroll.org

Daniel Maddux, Executive Director

This conference focuses on compliance issues impacting payroll professionals working in the higher education community.
Cost: $1510.00
Frequency: Annual
Founded in 1982

265 **American Payroll Association Payroll Leaders Conference**
American Payroll Association
660 N. Main Avenue
Suite 100
San Antonio, TX 78205

210-224-6406; Fax: 210-224-6038
www.americanpayroll.org

Daniel Maddux, Executive Director

APA's Payroll Leaders Conference offers training through four certificate programs, aimed at managers and professionals looking to become leaders.
Frequency: Annual
Founded in 1982

266 **Annual ACFE Fraud Conference and Exhibition**
716 West Ave
Austin, TX 78701-2727

512-478-9070
800-245-3321; Fax: 512-478-9297
accounting@acfe.com
www.acfe.com
Facebook, Twitter, LinkedIn

James D Ratley, President and CEO
Scott Grossfeld, Chief Executive Officer

The ACFE is the world's largest anti-fraud organization and premier provider of anti-fraud training and education.
50000 Members

267 **Annual Conference for Women in Accounting**
1760 Old Meadow Road
Suite 500
McLean, VA 22102

703-506-3265
800-326-2163; Fax: 703-506-3266
www.aswa.org
Facebook, Twitter, LinkedIn, ASWA Presidents Blog

Barbara W Cornington, President
Monika P Miles CPA, VP of Membership
Tracy L Johnson CPA, VP of Chapter Partnering
Vivian L Moller CPA, VP of Communications

Provides a program that offers a myriad of opportunities to help you meet your continuing education goals, whether technical or soft-skills focused, as well as an opportunity to network with other women of similar backgrounds.
4000 Members
Founded in 1938

268 **Appraisers Association of America National Conference**
Appraisers Association of America
212 W. 35th Street
11th Floor South
New York, NY 10001

212-889-5404; Fax: 212-889-5503
referrals@appraisersassociation.org
www.appraisersassociation.org

Linda Selvin, Executive Director
Yasemin Yeldener, Communications Coordinator

Exhibits of interest to appraisers, workshops, and presentations.
Founded in 1949

269 **BCCA Distance Learning Seminars**
Broadcast Cable Credit Association
550 W. Frontage Road
Suite 3600
Northfield, IL 60093

847-881-8757; Fax: 847-784-8059
info@bccacredit.com
www.bccacredit.com

Mary Collins, President & CEO
Jamie Grande, Director, Operations
Arcelia Pimentel, Sales/Membership

Teleconference and online seminars educating members on important areas of the broadcast and cable industry.
Founded in 1972

270 **BCCA Media Credit Seminar**
Broadcast Cable Credit Association
550 W. Frontage Road
Suite 3600
Northfield, IL 60093

847-881-8757; Fax: 847-784-8059
info@bccacredit.com
www.bccacredit.com

Mary Collins, President & CEO
Jamie Grande, Director, Operations
Arcelia Pimentel, Sales/Membership

A subsidiary of the Media Financial Management Association, BCCA provides credit information, education, and networking opportunities which enables members to efficiently manage credit risk and increase profitability.
Frequency: Annual
Founded in 1972

271 **CFMA Annual Conference & Exhibition**
Construction Financial Management Association
100 Village Boulevard
Suite 200
Princeton, NJ 08540

609-452-8000; Fax: 609-452-0474
info@cfma.org
www.cfma.org

Stuart Binstock, President & CEO
Brian Summers, VP, Operations

A resource for construction financial professionals.
Frequency: Annual/May

272 **CICPAC Annual Conference**
Construction Industry CPA/Consultants Association

4531 Bohemia Drive
Pensacola, FL 32504

850-723-0372
info@cicpac.com
www.cicpac.com

Mike Karlins, President
Wes Winborne, Vice President
Bryan Eto, Secretary/Treasurer
Kathleen Baldwin, Executive Director

This conference brings together CICPAC members for networking and educational opportunities.
Founded in 1989

273 **CPAAI International Conference**
65 Harristown Road
Suite 210
Glen Rock, NJ 07452

201-857-8656
info@cpaai.com
www.cpaai.com

Roger Isaacs, International Co-Chair
Jim Holmes, International Co-Chair
Felicia Solimini, North American Regional Manager

CPA Associates International was established as a global group of high-quality independent CPA and chartered accounting firms; it is market exclusive, with members in major cities throughout the world. The organized association provides members with the capabilities of the largest firm, yet allows each to maintain its local practice while avoiding costly overhead and unnecessary controls.
Frequency: Annual
Founded in 1957

274 **Club and Hotel Controllers Conference**
11709 Boulder Lane
Suite 110
Austin, TX 78726

512-249-5333
800-646-4387; Fax: 512-249-1533
www.hftp.org
Facebook, Twitter, LinkedIn

Frank I Wolfe, Executive VP/CEO
Lucinda Hart, COO
Thomas Atzenhofer, CFO
Eliza Selig, Director of Communications

The program offers a range of sessions that reflect diverse responsibilities, from technology to taxes, human resource management to personal inspiration.
4600 Members
Founded in 1952

275 **Conf-IRM**
Association for Information Systems
Member Service Center
PO Box 2712
Atlanta, GA 30301-2712

404-413-7445
membership@aisnet.org
aisnet.org

Lise Fitzpatrick, Chief Operating Officer
Robina Wahid, Conference Director

Provides forums for researchers and practitioners to share leading-edge knowledge in the global information resource management area.

276 **Current Financial Reporting Issues Conference**
Financial Executives International
1250 Headquarters Plaza
West Tower, 7th Floor
Morristown, NJ 07960

973-765-1000; Fax: 973-765-1018
membership@financialexecutives.org
www.financialexecutives.org

Andrej Suskavcevic, President & CEO

The conference focuses on FASB/IASB technical accounting, revenue recognition, accounting for leases by lessors and lessees, financial instruments-recognition, measurement, hedging and expected loss model, Washington tax update, and the latest SEC happenings.
Founded in 1931

277 **Detecting & Deterring Financial Reporting Fraud**
200 Campus Drive
PO Box 674
Florham Park, NJ 07932

973-360-0177; Fax: 973-898-4649
www.financialexecutives.org

Andrej Suskavcevic, President & CEO

Executive workshop for exploring strategies for building an ethical philosophy that deters fraud, employs skepticism-an enemy of fraud- in management's attitude and developing a culture of collaboration and knowledge sharing to deter and detect fraud.
15M Members
Frequency: 10x/Year
Founded in 1931

278 **FMA Annual Meeting**
Financial Management Association International
University of South Florida
4202 E. Fowler Avenue BSN 3403
Tampa, FL 33620-9951

813-974-2084; Fax: 813-974-3318
fma@coba.usf.edu
www.fma.org

Michelle Lui, Executive Director
Dawn Appleby, Program Assistant
Karen Wright, Special Events Coordinator

The Financial Management Association International (FMA) is the global leader in developing and disseminating knowledge about financial decision making. FMA's members include adademicians and practitioners worldwide.
Founded in 1970

279 **Financial Leadership Summit**
Financial Executives International
1250 Headquarters Plaza
West Tower, 7th Floor
Morristown, NJ 07960

973-765-1000; Fax: 973-765-1018
membership@financialexecutives.org
www.financialexecutives.org

Andrej Suskavcevic, President & CEO

Forum to help advance the success of senior-level financial executives.
Founded in 1931

280 **Gaming Conference**
Institute of Internal Auditors
247 Maitland Avenue
Altamonte Springs, FL 32701-4201

407-371-1100; Fax: 407-937-1101
iia@theiia.org
www.theiia.org

J. Michael Pepper, Chairman
Carolyn Saint, Senior Vice President
John Wxzelaki, Vice Chairman - Finance/security

A must attend event for knowledge-seeking auditors, compliance officers, regulators, and professionals from gaming sectors.
300 Members
Frequency: April/Annual

281 **General Audit Management Conference**
Institute of Internal Auditors
247 Maitland Avenue
Altamonte Springs, FL 32701-4201

407-371-1100; Fax: 407-937-1101
iia@theiia.org
www.theiia.org

J. Michael Pepper, Chairman
Carolyn Saint, Senior Vice President
John Wxzelaki, Vice Chairman - Finance/security

The premiere opportunity for chief audit executives (CAEs), audit directors, and audit leaders to network with peers, benchmark against best practices, and tap into the knowledge of the profession's highest-level practitioners.
800 Members
Frequency: March/Annual

282 **Governance, Risk and Control Conference**
Institute of Internal Auditors
247 Maitland Avenue
Altamonte Springs, FL 32701-4201

407-371-1100; Fax: 407-937-1101
iia@theiia.org
www.theiia.org

J. Michael Pepper, Chairman
Carolyn Saint, Senior Vice President
John Wxzelaki, Vice Chairman - Finance/security

Develop and enhance your auditing skills.
400 Members
Frequency: August/Annual

283 **HITEC**
11709 Boulder Lane
Suite 110
Austin, TX 78726

512-249-5333
800-646-4387; Fax: 512-249-1533
www.hftp.org
Facebook, Twitter, LinkedIn

Frank I Wolfe, Executive VP/CEO
Lucinda Hart, COO
Thomas Atzenhofer, CFO
Eliza Selig, Director of Communications

Attend HITEC and network with the industry's innovators, gain knowledge from an expert-led education program and find technology products and services to take your organization to the next level.
4600 Members
Founded in 1952

284 **Hall of Fame Gala**
Financial Executives International
1250 Headquarters Plaza
West Tower, 7th Floor
Morristown, NJ 07960

973-765-1000; Fax: 973-765-1018
membership@financialexecutives.org
www.financialexecutives.org

Andrej Suskavcevic, President & CEO

Providing recognition to senior-level financial executives who have epitomized the performance, leadership and integrity of the most exemplary financial professionals throughout their careers and in doing so, have made significant contributions to the betterment of their respective organizations and to the profession as a whole.
Founded in 1931

285 **IASA Annual Conference**
Insurance, Accounting & Systems Association
PO Box 51340
Durham, NC 27717-1340

919-489-0991; Fax: 919-489-1994
info@iasa.org
www.iasa.org
Facebook, Twitter

Laurie Macklosky, President
Kerry Crockett, CEO

Provides comprehensive education programs targeted for financial and technology professionals in the industry.
1800 Attendees
Frequency: Annual

286 **IFRS Boot Camp**
200 Campus Drive
PO Box 674
Florham Park, NJ 07932

973-360-0177; Fax: 973-898-4649
www.financialexecutives.org

Andrej Suskavcevic, President & CEO

Provides an update on various recent convergence and regulatory/ statutory matters impacting U.S. GAAP and IFRS reporting companies. Provides financial executives with practical information for addressing global accounting convergence in their organizations, including potential operational considerations rellated to topics such as leases and revenue recognition.
15M Members
Frequency: 10x/Year
Founded in 1931

287 **IMA's Annual Conference & Exposition**
10 Paragon Dr
Suite 1
Montvale, NJ 07645-1774

201-573-9000
800-638-4427; Fax: 201-474-1600
ima@imanet.org
www.imanet.org
Facebook, Twitter, LinkedIn

Jeffrey C. Thomson, President and CEO
Paul E. Juras, Chair

Offers three days of knowledge building, education, networking, optional pre-conference workshops, and opportunities to earn NASBA-approved credits.
67000 Members
Founded in 1919

288 **IMA's Student Leadership Conference**
10 Paragon Dr
Suite 1
Montvale, NJ 07645-1774

201-573-9000
800-638-4427; Fax: 201-474-1600
ima@imanet.org
www.imanet.org
Facebook, Twitter, LinkedIn

Jeffrey C. Thomson, President and CEO
Paul E. Juras, Chair

Offers three days of learning and career networking opportunities for college students and educators. Accounting, finance, and business students will learn from veteran practitioners about the critical role of accountants and financial professionals within business.
67000 Members
Founded in 1919

289 **Joint ISPA/SCEA Conference & Workshop**
Society of Cost Estimating & Analysis
8221 Old Courthouse Rd
Suite 106
Vienna, VA 22182

703-938-5090; Fax: 703-938-5091
scea@sceaonline.org
www.sceaonline.net

Erin Whittaker, Executive Director
Sharon Burger, Certification Program Admin
Brittany Walker, Membership Coordinator
Debra Lehman, Treasurer

Speakers and panel sessions, integrated training tracks, informative workshops and vendor exhibits. Three of every four years, the annual conference is a joint conference with the International Society of Parametric Analysts (ISPA). Certification exams are offered at the conference for a separate fee.
2015 Members
400 Attendees
Frequency: Annual/June
Founded in 1990

290 **MFMA/BCCA Annual Conference: Media Finance Focus**
Broadcast Cable Credit Association
550 W. Frontage Road
Suite 3600
Northfield, IL 60093

847-881-8757; Fax: 847-784-8059
info@bccacredit.com
www.mediafinancefocus.org

Mary Collins, President & CEO
Jamie Grande, Director, Operations
Arcelia Pimenetal, Sales/Membership

Offers professional education targeting media financial and business executives; CPE opportunities; exhibitors; roundtables; and networking opportunities.
Frequency: Annual
Founded in 1972

291 **NASBA Annual Meeting**
Ntl. Assn. of State Boards of Accountancy
150 Fourth Ave North
Suite 700
Nashville, TN 37219-2417

615-880-4200; Fax: 615-880-4290
nasba.org

Ken L Bishop, President & CEO

292 **NATP National Conference and Expo**
National Association of Tax Professionals
PO Box 8002
Appleton, WI 54912-8002

800-558-3402; Fax: 800-747-0001
natp@natptax.com
www.natptax.com
Facebook, Twitter, MySpace

Brett Rosser, President
Jaimee Hammer, Vice President

Four days filled with top-notch tax education, fun social events, networking, and much more.
Frequency: Annual

293 **National Practice Management Conference**
136 S. Keowee Street
Dayton, OH 45402

937-222-0030
info@cpafma.org
www.cpafma.org

Kim Fantaci, President
Jeanie Price, Chair
Alen Alexander, Vice Chair
Larry Sheftel, Secretary/Treasurer

Conference of the CPA Firm Management Association, devoted to helping participants manage accounting firms of varying sizes.
Founded in 1984

294 **SCEA/ISPA Joint Annual Conference & Training Workshop**
Society of Cost Estimating and Analysis
8221 Old Courthouse Rd
Suite 106
Vienna, VA 22182

703-938-5090; Fax: 703-938-5091
scea@sceaonline.org
www.sceaonline.org

Erin Whittaker, Executive Director
Sharon Burger, Certification Program Admin
Brittany Walker, Membership Coordinator

Features training sessions to help attendees enhance their skill set or prepare for the CCEA or CPP exams, study sessions, Professional Papers give attendees the chance to hear about best practices, lessons learned and the latest developments in the field.
2015 Members
500+ Attendees
Frequency: Annual
Founded in 1990

295 **Society of Actuaries Annual Meeting & Exhibit**
Society of Actuaries
475 N Martingale Road
Suite 600
Schaumburg, IL 60173

847-697-3900
customerservice@soa.org
www.soa.org

Greg Heidrich, Executive Director
Stacy Lin, Deputy Executive Director/CFO

Sessions and keynote presentations about cutting edge research, and discussions, networking opportunities, the latest and greatest technologies, sponsorship opportunities; sometimes held in conjunction with the Academy Luncheon. Registration fees begin at $55 for the luncheon and go to $995 for full meeting attendance.
1,700 Attendees
Frequency: Annual/November

296 **SourceMedia Conferences & Events**
SourceMedia
One State Street Plaza
27th floor
New York, NY 10004

212-803-6093
800-803-3424; Fax: 212-803-8515
www.sourcemedia.com/

James M Malkin, Chairman & CEO
William Johnson, CFO
Steve Andreazza, VP, Sales & Customer Service
Celie Baussan, SVP, Operations
Anne O'Brien, EVP Marketing & Strategic Planning

SourceMedia Conferences & Events attract over 20,000 attendees worldwide. The content embraces a variety of formats, including: conferences, executive roundtables, expositions, Web seminars, custom events and pod casts. With over 70 events annually, participants are provided with premier content as well as access to the industry's top solution providers. Markets served include: accounting; banking; capital markets; financial services; information technology; insurance; and real estate.

297 **Technology and Office Productivity (TOP) Conference**
National Association of Tax Professionals
PO Box 8002
Appleton, WI 54912-8002

800-558-3402; Fax: 800-747-0001
natp@natptax.com

www.natptax.com
Facebook, Twitter, MySpace

Brett Rosser, President
Jaimee Hammer, Vice President

Two days filled with valuable education on what it takes to run a small business, fun social events, networking, and more.
Frequency: Annual

298 **The IIA's International Conference**
The Institute of Internal Auditors
247 Maitland Avenue
Altamonte Springs, FL 32701-4201

407-937-1100; Fax: 407-937-1101
iia@theiia.org
www.theiia.org

William J Mulcahy, Conference Chairman
Richard Chambers, President & CEO

Annual conference that features and unprecedented number of concurrent sessions on today's top issues, industry best practices, and unique challenges to help you add value to your organization.
84000 Attendees
Frequency: Annual
Founded in 1941

299 **The World Congress Annual Leadership Summit on Mergers & Acquisitions**
200 E Randolph St
24th Floor
Chicago, IL 60601-6435

312-856-9590
877-844-2535; Fax: 312-729-9800
info@amaaonline.org
www.amaaonline.com

Michael Nall, Owner

AM&AA is the premier International Organization serving the educational and resource needs of the middle market M&A profession.
Founded in 1998

300 **VALCON**
ABI/AIRA
221 W. Stewart Avenue
Suite 207
Medford, OR 97501

541-858-1665; Fax: 541-858-9187
aira@aira.org
www.aira.org

Jim Lukenda, Executive Director
Cheryl Campbell, Conference Director

A joint conference by the American Bankruptcy Association and the Association of Insolvency & Restructuring Advisors where professionals can connect with leadinge experts and dealmakers in the distressed-debt, restructuring and valuation industry.
Frequency: Annual
Founded in 1982

301 **Valcon**
Association of Insolvency & Restructuring Advisors
221 Stewart Avenue
Suite 207
Medford, OR 97501

541-858-1665; Fax: 541-858-9187
aira@aira.org
www.airacira.org

Anthony Sasso, President
Thomas Morrow, Vice President
Mathew Schwartz, Treasurer
Joel Waite, VP
Matthew Schwartz, Treasurer

Join leading restructuring and valuation experts - attorneys, private equity investors, bankers, financial advisors and workout specialists - to discuss cutting-edge valuation issues and market developments.
Frequency: Annual/February
Founded in 1984

302 **WSIA Annual Marketplace**
Wholesale & Specialty Insurance Association
4131 N. Mulberry Drive
Suite 200
Kansas City, MO 64116

816-741-3910
info@wsia.org
www.wsia.org

Brady Kelley, Executive Director
Julie Fritz, Director of Operations
Jaqueline Schaendorf, President

A conference that includes three days of business meetings and networking opportunities.
4500 Attendees
Frequency: Annual/September
Founded in 2017

303 **WSIA Underwriting Summit**
Wholesale & Specialty Insurance Association
4131 N. Mulberry Drive
Suite 200
Kansas City, MO 64116

816-741-3910
info@wsia.org
www.wsia.org

Brady Kelley, Executive Director
Julie Fritz, Director of Operations
Jaqueline Schaendorf, President

This conference will include networking for the underwriting and delegated authority segment of the WSIA membership and an opportunity for the leadership of all member firms to collaborate on strategic issues facing the marketplace.
1500 Attendees
Frequency: Annual/February
Founded in 2017

304 **Women Who Count Conference**
Accounting & Financial Women's Alliance
2365 Harrodsburg Road
Suite A325
Lexington, KY 40504

859-219-3532
800-326-2163
afwa@afwa.org
www.afwa.org/women-who-count

Cindy Stanley, Executive Director
Catherine Schaefer, Member Engagement & Ops. Specialist
Kara Hamilton, Member Services
Rachel Gates, Member Services

Education and professional development event presented by The Accouting and Financial Women's Alliance.
Founded in 1938

Directories & Databases

305 **ARMA International's Buyers Guide**
ARMA International
11880 College Boulevard
Suite 450
Overland Park, KS 66215

913-444-9174
844-565-2120; Fax: 913-257-3855
headquarters@armaintl.org
armabuyersguide.org
Facebook, Twitter, LinkedIn

Nick Inglis, Exec. Dir., Content & Programming
Jeff Whited, Sr. Content Writer
Ann Snyder, Manager, Content Development

75-100 companies listed. Free.
Frequency: Annual

306 **Accountancy: A Professional Reference Guide**
Georgia State University
35 Broad Street
5th Floor
Atlanta, GA 30302-3991

404-413-7200; Fax: 404-413-7203
admissions@gsu.edu

Carla Hines, Administrative Coordinator
Allison Jacobs, Director of Student Services

Listings of accounting firms, associations, regulatory agencies and schools offering accredited accounting programs.
Cost: $99.95
450 Pages
Frequency: Hardcover

307 **Accounting Research Directory**
Markus Wiener Publishing
231 Nassau St
Princeton, NJ 08542-4601

609-921-1141; Fax: 609-921-1140
www.markuswiener.com
Facebook

Markus Wiener, Owner
Lawrence D Brown, Editor
Markus Wiener, President

Quick guide arranged by author's names for key articles. It can enable those interested in quantitative literature analysis to test and verify much of the work in this area by the authors in this book.
Cost: $79.95
Frequency: Hardcover
ISBN: 1-558760-68-7

308 **Accounting, Tax & Banking Collection**
ProQuest Information and Learning
789 E Eisenhower Parkway
PO Box 1346
Ann Arbor, MI 48106-1346

734-761-4700
800-889-3358; Fax: 800-864-0019
www.proquest.com
Facebook, Twitter, LinkedIn

Offers comprehensive global scholarly journals and key resources on a range of topics relating to accoutning and finance

309 **American Association of Attorney-Certified Public Accountants Directory**
American Association of Attorney-CPAs
P.O. Box 706
Warrendale, PA 15095

703-352-8064
888-288-9272; Fax: 703-352-8073
info@attorney-cpa.com
www.attorney-cpa.com

Howard O. Bernstein, President
Kimmy Headland, Director, Membership & Chapters

Offers names, addresses and biographical data on members licensed as both attorneys and CPAs for a one-time rental.
Founded in 1964

310 **Directory of Actuarial Memberships**
Society of Actuaries
475 N Martingale Rd
Suite 600
Schaumburg, IL 60173-2252

847-706-3500; Fax: 847-706-3599
webmaster@soa.org

www.soa.org
Twitter, LinkedIn

Greg Heidrich, Executive Director
Stacy Lin, Deputy Executive Director/CFO
Ken Guthrie, Managing Director, Education
Richard Veys, General Counsel
Roy Goldman, Preident

Lists member names, affiliations and contact information for major US and international actuarial professional associations.
Cost: $150.00
Mailing list available for rent: 17000 names at $300 per M

311 **Federal Tax Coordinator 2D**
Thomson Reuters
2395 Midway Rd
Carrollton, TX 75006

817-332-3709
800-431-9025; Fax: 888-216-1929
trta.lei-support@thomsonreuters.com
www.ria.thomsonreuters.com

Elaine Yadlon, Plant Manager
Thomas H Glocer, CEO & Director
Robert D Daleo, Chief Financial Officer
Kelli Crane, Senior Vice President & CIO

Provides verbatim text of the Internal Revenue Code and IRS Regulations. Information is arranged by subject rather than in Code order. Professional tax preparers are heavy users of this service because of the thorough authoritative analysis it provides.
Cost: $2460.00
Founded in 1935

312 **Future Actuary**
Society of Actuaries
475 N Martingale Rd
Suite 600
Schaumburg, IL 60173-2252

847-706-3500; Fax: 847-706-3599
webmaster@soa.org
www.soa.org

Greg Heidrich, Executive Director
Stacy Lin, Deputy Executive Director/CFO

Full coverage on topics like career development, non-traditional careers, grading systems, study tips, professional conduct and ethics and the structure of actuarial organizations.
Mailing list available for rent: 17000 names at $300 per M

313 **International Guide to Accounting Journals**
Markus Weiner Publishers
231 Nassau St
Princeton, NJ 08542-4601

609-921-1141; Fax: 609-921-1140
www.markuswiener.com

Markus Wiener, Owner
Surendra Agrawal, Editor

Approximately 300 journals in accounting and related areas, including about 150 published in the US and 150 from 33 other countries that are published in English.
Cost: $49.95
ISBN: 1-558760-67-9

314 **National Society of Public Accountants Yearbook**
National Society of Public Accountants
1010 N Fairfax St
Alexandria, VA 22314-1574

703-549-6400
800-966-6679; Fax: 703-549-2984
members@nsacct.org
www.nsacct.org
Facebook, Twitter, LinkedIn

Curtis Lee, Jr., President
Marchelle Foshee, First Vice President
Debra Cope, Second Vice President

Association members and committees, lists of affiliated state organizations and members of governing board.
Frequency: Annual

315 **Salem Press Online Platform**
Grey House Publishing
4919 Route 22
PO Box 56
Amenia, NY 12501

800-221-1592; Fax: 201-968-0511
csr@salempress.com
online.salempress.com

The new Salem Press platform houses more than 500 titles including all of Salem's Health, Literature, History and Science titles in addition to select titles from the Grey House Publishing and H.W. Wilson product lines. Online access is free with each print purchase and includes an unlimited number of simultaneous users and remote access.

Industry Web Sites

316 **www.aabpa.org**
American Assoc for Budget and Program Analysis
LinkedIn
The American Association for Budget and Program Analysis helps federal, state and local government managers and analysts, corporate executives and academic specialists meet the unique challenges of their careers related to the fields of public budgeting and program analysis.

317 **www.acatcredentials.org**
Accreditation Council for Accountancy and Taxation
Identifies and accredits specialists in accountancy and federal taxation who serve the financial needs of individuals and small to mid-sized business entities. Offers 4 credentials: Accreditation in Accountancy/Accredited Business Accountant, Accredited Tax Preparer and Accredited Tax Advisor, and Accredited Retirement Advisor.

318 **www.acaus.org**
Association of Chartered Accountants in the U.S.
ACAUS is a nonprofit professional and educational organization representing interests of over 7,000 U.S. based chartered accountants from the institutes of Chartered Accountants across the globe.

319 **www.acfe.com**
Association of Certified Fraud Examiners
The ACFE is the world's largest anti-fraud organization and premier provider of anti-fraud training and education.

320 **www.agacgfm.org**
Association of Government Accountants
AGA is an educational association dedicated to enhancing public financial management by serving the professional interests of governmental managers and public accounting firms.

321 **www.agn.org**
Accountants Global Network International
Composed of CPA consulting firms who share information and resources via the associated programs.

322 **www.ahia.org**
Association of Healthcare Internal Auditors
Promotes cost containment and increased productivity in health care institutions through internal auditing. Serves as a forum for the exchange of experience, ideas, and information among members; provides continuing professional education courses and informs members of developments in health care internal auditing. Offers employment clearinghouse services.

323 **www.aiaponline.com**
Assn. of Independent Accounting Professional
An online resource designed for today's independent accountant; provides practice expansion opportunities, information, and resources.

324 **www.aicpa.org**
American Institute of Certified Public Accountants
The American Institute of Certified Public Accountants is the national, professional organization for all Certified Public Accountants. Its mission is to provide members with the resources, information, and leadership that enables them to provide valuable services in the highest professional manner to benefit the public as well as employers and clients.

325 **www.aipb.org**
American Institute of Professional Bookkeepers
Established to help achieve recognition of bookkeepers as accounting professionals, to keep bookkeepers up-to-date on changes in bookkeeping, accounting and tax, to answer bookkeepers everyday bookkeeping and accounting questions, and to certify bookkeepers who meet high national standards.

326 **www.amaaonline.com**
Alliance of Merger & Acquisition Advisors
AM&AA is the premier International Organization serving the educational and resource needs of the middle market M&A profession.

327 **www.americanpayroll.org**
American Payroll Association
American Payroll Association provides numerous opportunities for payroll education and information.

328 **www.aswa.org**
American Society of Women Accountants
Organization for networking and information exchange in pursuit of professional development.

329 **www.attorney-cpa.com**
American Association of Attorney-CPAs
Seeks to safeguard the professional and legal rights of CPA attorneys.

330 **www.awscpa.org**
American Woman's Society of CPAs
Provides supportive environment that promotes equity and provides opportunities for the achievement of career goals in a competitive and rapidly changing profession.

331 **www.bap.org**
Beta Alpha Psi
Beta Alpha Psi is an honor organization for financial information students and professionals. The primary objective is to encourage and give recognition to scholastic and professional excellence in the business information field.

332 **www.bccacredit.com**
Broadcast Cable Credit Association
Information on Credit Inquiry Service, credit and collection seminars yearly, credit personnel directories, surveys and on-line services.

333 **www.computercpa.com**
Accountant's Home Page
Provides information on general accounting for manufacturing, contstruction, service, not-for-profit, e-commerce and more.

334 **www.cpa.net**
Mark Dietrich, CPA, PC
Includes information on social security and alternatives, bill presentation and payment.

335 **www.cpaadmin.org**
CPA Firm Management Association
Enables accounting firm administrators to communicate with one another and share experiences in the profession.

336 **www.cpaai.com**
CPA Associates International
CPA Associates International was established as a global group of high-quality independent CPA and chartered accounting firms; it is market exclusive, with members in major cities throughout the world. The organized association provides members with the capabilities of the largest firm, yet allows each to maintain its local practice while avoiding costly overhead and unnecessary controls.

337 **www.cpatechadvisor.com**
The CPA Technology Advisor
Online resource for accountants and managers. The Web site features a Buyer's Guide that lists hundreds of businesses, manufacturers, and professionals that can assist public accounting firms in delivering a variety of services to their clients in various industries.

338 **www.expresscarriers.com**
Express Carriers Association
A member organization of chief financial officers within the American Trucking Association.

339 **www.fma.org**
Financial Management Association International
Strives to facilitate exchanges of ideas among persons in financial management.

340 **www.gasb.org**
Governmental Accounting Standards Board
Establishes and improves standards of state and local governmental accounting and financial reporting that will result in useful information for users of financial reports and guide and educate the public, including issuers, auditors and users of those financial institutions.

341 **www.grantthornton.com**
Grant Thornton LLP
Grant Thornton LLP is the U.S. member firm of Grant Thornton International Ltd., one of the six global audit, tax and advisory organizations.

342 **www.greyhouse.com**
Grey House Publishing
Authoritative reference directories for business information and general reference, including accounting, banking and financial markets. Users can search the online databases with varied search criteria allowing for custom searches by product category, geographic area, sales volume, keyword, subject and more. Full Grey House catalog and online ordering also available.

343 **www.hftp.org**
Hospitality Financial & Technology Professionals
HFTP is the global professional association for financial and technology personnel working in hotels, clubs, and other hospitality-related businesses.

344 **www.iasa.org**
Insurance, Accounting & Systems Association
The Insurance Accounting & Systems Association Web site offers information about membership in the organization, accounting seminars, events, publications and textbooks.

345 **www.ifac.org**
International Federation of Accountants
IFAC is the global organization for the accountancy profession. It works with its 157 members and associates in 123 countries and jurisdictions to protect the public interest by encouraging high quality practices by the world's accountants.

346 **www.igafworldwide.org**
International Group of Accounting Firms
IGAF Worldwide is one of the oldest, largest, and most well-respected accounting associations in the world. It was founded for the purpose of providing member firms with the tools and resources they need to furnish a broad spectrum of efficient, cost-effective accounting, auditing and management services to clients around the globe.

347 **www.imanet.org**
Institute of Management Accountants
Professional organization devoted exclusively to management accounting and financial management. Goals are to help members develop both personally and professionally, by means of education, certification, and association with other business professionals.

348 **www.nabainc.org**
National Association of Black Accountants
Nationwide professional association with the primary purpose of developing, encouraging and serving as a resource for greater participation by African-Americans and other minorities in the accounting and finance professions.

349 **www.nactp.org**
Nat'l Association of Computerized Tax Processors
A nonprofit association that represents tax processing software and hardware developers, electronic filing processors, tax form publishers and tax processing service bureaus. The association promotes standards in tax processing and works closely with the Internal Revenue Service and state governments to promote efficient and effective tax filing.

350 **www.nacva.com**
National Assoc of Certified Valuation Analysts
Global, professional association that supports the business valuation and litigation consulting disciplines within the CPA and professional communities. Along with its training and certification programs, NACVA offers a range of support services, marketing tools, software programs, reference materials and customized databases to enhance the professional capabilities of its members.

351 **www.naea.org**
National Association of Enrolled Agents
Members are enrolled to represent taxpayers before the Internal Revenue Service. We advise, represent and prepare tax returns for individuals, partnerships, corporations, estates, trusts and any entities with tax reporting requirements.

352 **www.nsacct.org**
National Society of Accountants
Professional society of practicing accountants and tax practitioners that sponsors the Acceditation Council for Accountancy and Taxation and supports the National Society of Public Accountants Political Action Committee and NSPA Scholarship Foundation.

353 **www.sceaonline.org**
Society of Cost Estimating and Analysis
Dedicated to improving cost estimating and analysis in government and industry. Offers a unique collection of educational and training materials on cost estimating, cost analysis, earned value management and related disciplines through its professional development program.

354 **www.taxsites.com**
Tax and Accounting Sites Directory
A comprehensive index of internet resources, designed to be a starting point for people who are searching for tax and accounting information and services.

355 **www.theiia.org**
Institute of Internal Auditors
International organization of internal auditors, corporate executives and board members. Contact and current development information.

Associations

356 **Advertising Council Inc**
815 Second Avenue
9th Floor
New York, NY 10017-4503

212-922-1500
info@adcouncil.org
www.adcouncil.org
Facebook, Twitter, LinkedIn, YouTube, Instagram

Lisa Sherman, President & CEO
Kathy Kayse, Chief Media Strategy Officer
Heidi Arthur, EVP, Campaign Development
Kate Emanuel, EVP, Business Operations & Strategy
Paula Veale, EVP, Marketing & Communications

The Ad Council marshals volunteer talent from the advertising and communications industries, the facilities of the media, and the resources of the business and non-profit communities to create awareness, foster understanding and motivate action. The council utilizes new technological developments such as programmatic, mobile, VR and AI to achieve their goals.
100 Members
Founded in 1942

357 **Advertising Educational Foundation**
10 Grand Central, 155 E. 44th Street
3rd Floor
New York, NY 10017

212-986-8060; Fax: 212-986-8061
gm@aef.com
www.aef.com
Facebook, Twitter, LinkedIn, YouTube, Instagram

Gord McLean, President & CEO
Elliot Lum, SVP, Talent Strategy & Program Dev.
Marcia Soling, VP & Content Manager
Sharon Hudson, VP & Program Manager
Sara Parrish, VP & Program Manager

The AEF is supported by ad agencies, advertisers and media companies. The foundation acts as a bridge between the advertising, marketing and academic communities, fostering a better understanding of of marketing and advertising in society. As of 2015, the AEF is the educational foundation of the Association of National Advertisers.
48 Members
Founded in 1983

358 **Advertising Media Credit Executives Association**
PO Box 740031
Louisville, KY 40201-7431

502-582-4327; Fax: 502-582-4330
myounger@gannett.com
www.amcea.org

Norman Taylor, President
Kimberly Archibald Russell, Vice President
Newt Collins, Secretary/Treasurer
Vickie Bolinger, Immediate Past President
Sandra Lawson, Director

The objectives of the AMCEA: To improve the professionalism, principles, understanding and techniques of media credit management by encouraging the exchange of ideas, methods and procedures within the membership; To provide additional education and training in the business fundamentals of media credit and credit policies; and in the related areas of finance, accounting, law and economics for the purpose of enhancing the career development of the members.
Founded in 1953

359 **Advertising Research Foundation**
432 Park Avenue S.
6th Floor
New York, NY 10016

212-751-5656; Fax: 212-689-1859
www.thearf.org
Facebook, Twitter, LinkedIn, YouTube

Scott McDonald, President & CEO
Paul Donato, Chief Research Officer
Tom Higgins, COO & CFO
Rachael Feigenbaum, SVP & Events Program Producer
Michael Heitner, EVP, Member Needs & Value

The Advertising Research Foundation (ARF) conducts research, experiments, and market tests to better guide marketers in the use of evolving technology. Research areas include ad effectiveness & ROI, analytics & data science, audience & media measurement, and creative & branded content.
400 Members
Founded in 1936

360 **Advertising Self-Regulatory Council**
112 Madison Avenue
3rd Floor
New York, NY 10016

212-705-0104
acalixte@bbbnp.org
www.asrcreviews.org
Facebook, Twitter, YouTube

Eric D. Reicin, President & CEO
Vickie McCormick, CFO & COO
Harley Bledsoe, Chief Information Officer
Jim Boyle, Chief Marketing & Comms. Officer
Amy J. Clark, Chief Human Resources Officer

Establishes the policies and procedures for advertising industry self-regulation. The self-regulatory system is administered by the Council of Better Business Bureaus.

361 **Advertising Specialty Institute**
4800 Street Road
Trevose, PA 19053

800-546-1350
ideas@asicentral.com
www.asicentral.com
Facebook, Twitter, LinkedIn, YouTube, Instagram, Pinterest

Norman Unger Cohn, Chair
Timothy Andrews, President & CEO
Steve Bright, EVP & General Counsel
Nancy Carmona, SVP, Business Strategy & Analysis
Andy Cohen, SVP, Editorial

The Advertising Specialty Institute (ASI) is a membership organization for the promotional product industry, offering media, technology, marketing, and educational services to members.
26000 Members
Founded in 1950

362 **Alliance for Audited Media**
48 W. Seegers Road
Arlington Heights, IL 60005-3913

224-366-6939
800-285-2220
auditedmedia.com
Facebook, Twitter, LinkedIn, YouTube, Instagram

Tom Drouillard, President, CEO & Managing Director
Brian Condon, EVP, Commercial Development
Scott Hanson, EVP, Audit Service
Mark Wachowicz, EVP, Business Innovation

A nonprofit, member-based organization that works with media companies, advertising technology providers, ad agencies, and advertisers to provide them with independently verified data and information critical to evaluating and purchasing media.
Founded in 1914

363 **American Academy of Advertising**
support@aaasite.org
www.aaasite.org
Facebook, Twitter

Eric Haley, President
Debbie Treise, Executive Director

The American Academy of Advertising (AAA) is an organization of advertising scholars and professionals with an interest in advertising and advertising education.
600 Members
Founded in 1958

364 **American Advertising Federation**
1101 K Street NW
Suite 420
Washington, DC 20005

202-898-0089
www.aaf.org
Facebook, Twitter, LinkedIn

Steve Pacheco, President & CEO
Lisa Rubin, EVP, Events & Corporate Services
Clark Rector, EVP, Government Affairs
Adrianne Lipscomb, VP, Creative Services
Kesha Robinson, VP, Information Technology

The AAF is the oldest national advertising trade association, and protects and promotes the well-being of advertising. The AAF accomplishes this through a unique, nationally coordinated grassroots network of advertisers, agencies, media companies, local advertising clubs and college chapters.
40000 Members
Founded in 1905

365 **American Association for Public Opinion Research**
One Parkview Plaza
Suite 800
Oakbrook Terrace, IL 60181

847-686-2230; Fax: 847-686-2251
info@aapor.org
www.aapor.org
Facebook, Twitter, LinkedIn

Delia Murphy, Executive Director
Meagan Comerford, Director, Communications
Linda Arcangeli-Story, Meetings Director
Sam Nysetvold, Program Manager, Membership
Daniel Choppa, Program Admin, Ops. & Education

The AAPOR community includes producers and users of survey data from a variety of disciplines. Members span a range of interests including election polling, market research, statistics, research methodology, health related data collection and education.
1700 Members
Founded in 1947
Mailing list available for rent: 1000 names at $400 per M

366 **American Association of Advertising Agencies**
1065 Avenue of the Americas
16th Floor
New York, NY 10018

212-682-2500
www.aaaa.org
Facebook, Twitter, LinkedIn, YouTube, Instagram

Marla Kaplowitz, President & CEO
Adam Cotumaccio, COO
Alison Pepper, EVP, Government Relations
Mollie Rosen, EVP, Member Engagement & Dev.
Donna Tobin, EVP, Marketing & Communications

Dedicated to helping brands create, distribute, and measure effective and insightful advertising and marketing through the use of new technology and techniques.
600+ Members
Founded in 1917

367 **American Marketing Association**
130 E. Randolph Street
22nd Floor
Chicago, IL 60601

800-262-1150
customersupport@ama.org
www.ama.org
Facebook, Twitter, LinkedIn

Russ Klein, Chief Executive Officer
Julie Schnidman, VP, Alliances
Adara Bowen, VP, Growth
Molly Soat, VP, Professional Development
Jeremy Van Ek, Chief Operations Officer

The AMA is a professional association for individuals and organizations leading the practice, teaching and development of marketing knowledge worldwide. Their principle role is to serve as a forum to connect like-minded individuals and foster knowledge sharing, provide resources, tools and training and support marketing practice and thought leadership around the globe.
40000 Members
Founded in 1953

368 **American Photographic Artists**
5042 Wilshire Boulevard
Suite 321
Los Angeles, CA 90036

executivedirector@apanational.com
apanational.org
Facebook, Twitter, LinkedIn, Vimeo, Instagram

Tony Gale, President
R.J. Muna, Executive Vice President
Juliette Wolf-Robin, National Executive Director
Dana Hursey, Senior Vice President
Inti S. Clair, Vice President

Formerly known as Advertising Photographers of America, APA's membership includes professional photographers, photo assistants, educators, and students, as well as individuals from associated fields. APA seeks to help members navigate the world of commercial photography and run a more profitable business. Chapters are located in Atlanta, Los Angeles, Chicago, New York, San Diego, San Francisco, Charlotte, the Northwest, and Washington, DC.
Founded in 1981

369 **Asian American Advertising Federation**
6230 Wilshire Boulevard
Suite 1216
Los Angeles, CA 90048

ghomfranzen@3af.org
www.3af.org
Facebook, Twitter, YouTube, Instagram

Jay Kim, President
Iris Yim, Vice President
Sandra Lee, Treasurer
Genny Hom-Franzen, Executive Director

3AF consists of Asian American advertising agency principals, media, advertisers and strategic partners that seek to grow the Asian American advertising and marketing industry, raise public awareness of the Asian community, and increase professionalism within the industry.

370 **Association for Education in Journalism and Mass Communication**
234 Outlet Pointe Boulevard
Suite A
Columbia, SC 29210-5667

803-798-0271; Fax: 803-772-3509
www.aejmc.org
Facebook, Twitter, LinkedIn, YouTube, Pinterest, Instagram

Tim P. Vos, President
Jennifer McGill, Executive Director
Belinda Pearson, Association Business Manager
Felicia G. Brown, Assistant Executive Director
Lillian Coleman, Newsletter Editor/Project Manager

AEJMC promotes the highest possible standards for education in journalism and mass communication, encouraging the widest possible range of communication research and the implementation of a multi-cultural society in the classroom and curriculum, defending and maintaining the freedom of expression in day-to-day living.
Founded in 1912

371 **Association of Canadian Advertisers**
21 St. Clair Avenue E.
Suite 1201
Toronto, ON M4T 1L9

416-964-3805
800-565-0109; Fax: 416-964-0771
communications@acaweb.ca
www.acaweb.ca
Twitter, LinkedIn

Ron Lund, President & CEO
Judy Davey, VP, Media Policy & Marketing
Davina Wong, Director, Membership
Jessica Yared, Manager, Digital Marketing

The Association of Canadian Advertisers (ACA) is a national, not-for-profit association exclusively dedicated to serving the interests of companies that market and advertise their products and services in Canada. Membership in the ACA is restricted to client marketers only, making it the premier Canadian marketing association. It cuts across all products and service sectors, and speaks on behalf of over 200 companies.
Founded in 1914

372 **Association of Marketing Service Providers**
1800 Diagonal Road
Suite 320
Alexandria, VA 22314-2806

703-836-9200; Fax: 703-548-8204
kgarner@mfsanet.org
www.amsp.org

Joseph P. Truncale, President & CEO
Ken Garner, Chief Operating Officer
Dean D'Ambrosi, Chief Financial Officer
Andrew D. Paparozzi, SVP & Chief Economist
Leo Raymond, VP, Postal & Member Relations

Formerly known as the Mailing & Fulfillment Service Association, the Association of Marketing Service Providers provides educational content, networking opportunities, and legislative advocacy.

373 **Association of National Advertisers**
Association of National Advertisers
10 Grand Central, 155 E. 44th Street
New York, NY 10017

212-697-5950; Fax: 212-687-7310
info@ana.net
www.ana.net
Facebook, Twitter, LinkedIn, Instagram

Bob Liodice, Chief Executive Officer
Christine Manna, President & COO
Brian Davidson, EVP, Membership
Mark Liebert, SVP, Marketing Training & Dev.
Kathleen Hunter, EVP, Marketing Knowledge Center

The Association of National Advertisers (ANA) is the advertising industry's oldest trade association. Currently, the ANA leads the marketing community by providing its members insights, collaboration, and advocacy. ANA's membership includes 20,000 brands that collectively spend over $400 billion in marketing communications and advertising. ANA acquired the Brand Activation Association and the Business Marketing Association in 2014, and the Data and Marketing Association in 2018.
1000 Members
Founded in 1910

374 **Culture Marketing Council**
8280 Willow Oaks Corporate Drive
Suite 600
Fairfax, VA 22031

703-745-5531; Fax: 703-610-0227
info@culturemarketingcouncil.org
culturemarketingcouncil.org
Facebook, Twitter, LinkedIn, YouTube

Gonzalo Del Fa, Chair
Isabella Sanchez, Treasurer
Horacio Gavilan, Executive Director

Formerly known as the Association of Hispanic Advertising Agencies and AHAA: The Voice of Hispanic Marketing, the Culture Marketing Council represents the Hispanic marketing, communications and media industry.
45000 Members
Founded in 1996

375 **EMarketing Association**
251 W. 30th Street
6th Floor
New York, NY 10001

212-678-2520
admin@emarketingassociation.com
www.emarketingassociation.com
Twitter, LinkedIn, YouTube

International association of eMarketing professionals committed to enriching the marketing community and its members through recognition, research, advocacy, education, and service.
Founded in 1997

376 **Financial Communications Society**
368 Ninth Avenue
9th Floor
New York, NY 10001

908-858-0427
admin@thefcs.org
thefcs.org

Tim Hart, Chair
Tom Jago, Vice Chair
Katherine Divney, Secretary
Kevin Windorf, CEO

The FCS is devoted to improving professional standards in financial marketing communications, with a membership comprised of managers in advertising, marketing, PR, IR, corporate communications, and social and digital media.
Founded in 1967

377 **Geopath**
561 7th Avenue
12th Floor
New York, NY 10018

212-972-8075
geekout@geopath.org
geopath.org
Facebook, Twitter, LinkedIn, YouTube, Instagram

Kym Frank, President

Formerly known as the Traffic Audit Bureau for Media Measurement, Geopath is a non-profit

organization whose historical mission has been to audit the circulation of out-of-home media in the United States. The group's role has expanded to encompass audience location measurement, consumer insight, and market research utilizing state-of-the-art data, technology, and methodologies.
220+ Members
Founded in 1933

378 **Insights Association**
1156 15th Street NW
Suite 700
Washington, DC 20005

202-800-2545
www.insightsassociation.org

Melanie Courtright, CEO
Nicole Symelidis, VP, Membership
Jonathan Saxe, VP, Revenue
Art Flanagan, VP, Communications
Howard Fienberg, VP, Advocacy

Insights Association is a community of marketing research and data analytics. They strive to represent, advance and grow the research profession and indutry through legislative, regulatory and judicial means.
Founded in 2017

379 **Insurance Marketing & Communications Association**
4248 Park Glen Road
Minneapolis, MN 55416

952-928-4644; Fax: 952-929-1318
info@imcanet.com
www.imcanet.com
Facebook, Twitter, LinkedIn, Youtube

Valerie Foster, Chair
Christopher Nance, Executive Vice-Chair
Hank Pinkowski, Treasurer
Megan Flanagan, Executive Director

An international organization of insurance communications professionals who specialize in marketing, marketing communications, advertising, sales promotion, and public relations.
Cost: $350.00
120+ Members
Frequency: Annual Membership Fee
Founded in 1923
Mailing list available for rent

380 **Insurance and Financial Communications Association**
515 East Grant Rd Ste 141
Box 250
Tucson, AZ 85705

602-350-0717; Fax: 866-402-7336
info@ifcaonline.com
www.ifcaonline.com
Facebook, Twitter, LinkedIn, YouTube

Jaimee Niles, President
Ralph Chaump, Vice President
Laurie Swinton, Past President
Katherine Gebhardt, Director, Communications
Tara Haselden, Director, Social Media

IFCA's primary objective is to encourage and promote the exchange of experience and ideas among its members through an extensive program of formal schools, workshops, seminars, Newsletters, research studies, networking, international awards competition and IFCA's showcase event: the three-day annual meeting. The IFCA name reflects the diversity of its members and helps recruit new members from more companies.
700 Members
Founded in 1933

381 **Interactive Advertising Bureau**
116 E. 27th Street
6th Floor
New York, NY 10016

212-380-4700
learning@iab.com
www.iab.com
Facebook, Twitter, LinkedIn, YouTube, Instagram

David Cohen, Board President & CEO
Dennis Buchheim, President
Randall Rothenberg, Executive Chair
Dave Grimaldi, EVP, Public Policy
Sheryl Goldstein, SVP, Member Engagement & Dev.

The Interactive Advertising Bureau (IAB) is comprised of leading media and technology companies that are responsible for selling the majority of online advertising in the United States. On behalf of its members, the IAB is dedicated to the growth of the interactive advertising marketplace, of interactive's share of total marketing spend, and of its members' share of total marketing spend. The IAB educates marketers, agencies, and media companies about the value of interactive advertising.
650+ Members
Founded in 1996

382 **Intermarket Advertising Network**
401 Mendocino Avenue
Santa Rosa, CA 95401

info@theengineisred.com
www.intermarketnetwork.com

Alicia Wadas, President
Tom Flynn, Vice President
Dan Borgmeyer, Membership Chair

The Intermarket Agency Network (IAN) is a forum for leaders of noncompetitive marketing agencies to openly exchange knowledge in a collaborative setting. A nationwide association of carefully selected agencies, its members meet twice annually to freely discuss important issues like new business, financials, HR, creativity, growth and much more. No topic is off limits.
13 Members
Founded in 1967

383 **International Advertising Association**
114 E. 25th Street
Suite 915
New York, NY 10009

646-722-2612; Fax: 646-722-2501
iaa@iaaglobal.org
www.iaaglobal.org
Facebook, Twitter, LinkedIn

Joel Nettey, Chair & World President
Sasan Saeidi, Senior Vice President
Suresh Mathai, VP, Area Director, USA
Fredrik Borestrom, VP, Corporate Members
Dagmara Szulce, Managing Director, IAA Global

International network comprising thousands of members working in all areas of marketing communications.
Founded in 1938

384 **International Association of Better Business Bureaus**
3033 Wilson Boulevard
Suite 600
Arllington, VA 22201

703-276-0100; Fax: 703-525-8277
www.bbb.org
Facebook, Twitter, LinkedIn, YouTube, Pinterest, Instagram

Colleen Rudio, Interim Executive Director
Sam McMakin, Chief Operating Officer
Steve Salter, Chief Development Officer
Katherine Hutt, Chief Communications Officer
Richard Woods, VP & General Counsel

The BBB is a leader in public services related to ethical business practices and dispute resolution. They promote honesty and integrity in the marketplace and are guided by trust, respect and fairness.
Founded in 1912

385 **International Communications Agency Network**
P.O. Box 3417
Nederland, CO 80466

720-215-6674
info@icomagencies.com
www.icomagencies.com
Facebook, Twitter, LinkedIn, Instagram

Emma Keenan, Executive Director
Nancy Giges, Media Relations Manager
Diane Venturino, International Meeting Planner
Alice Freeman, Finance Manager
Jennifer Henderson, Online Manager

ICOM is one of the world's largest networks of independent advertising and marketing communications agencies. Their mission is: To provide effective integrated communications resources to clients internationally; To provide a free exchange of ideas, information & support for members.
80+ Members
Founded in 1950

386 **International Sign Association**
1001 N. Fairfax Street
Suite 301
Alexandria, VA 22314

703-836-4012; Fax: 703-836-8353
info@signs.org
www.signs.org
Facebook, Twitter, LinkedIn, YouTube, Instagram

Lori Anderson, President & CEO
Alicia Auerswald, VP, Marketing, Membership & Comms.
David Hickey, VP, Advocacy
Lisa Queeney, VP, Finance
Alison Kent, Director, Workforce Development

The International Sign Association (ISA) supports, promotes and improves the sign industry through government advocacy, education and training programs, as well as technical resources, stakeholder outreach and networking events. Members are manufacturers, users and suppliers of on-premise signs and other similar systems.
2600 Members
Founded in 1944

387 **Internet Marketing Association**
200 Spectrum Center Drive
Irvine, CA 92618

949-443-9300
info@imanetwork.org
imanetwork.org
Facebook, Twitter, LinkedIn, YouTube

Sinan Kanatsiz, Chair & Founder
Sean Conrad, CEO
Lei Lani Fera, Head Of Creative
Hall Roosevelt, General Manager
Marcus Volpe, Executive Director

Seeks to provide members with the chance to learn, network, and establish Internet Marketing best practices. Members are in fields such as sales, marketing, business ownership, programming, and creative development.
Founded in 2001

388 **Junior Billboard Association**
P.O. Box 582096
Elk Grove, CA 95758

800-874-3387
www.juniorbillboard.org
Facebook

Carla Osmus, Chair
Peter Maloney, President
Mike Cossota, Vice President
Stuart Rayburn, Secretary/Treasurer

Formerly known as the Eight-Sheet Outdoor Advertising Association, the organization has helped establish and enforce industry standards for eight-sheet billboard advertising.
140 Members
Founded in 1953

389 **MAGNET: Marketing & Advertising Global Network**
226 Rostrevor Place
Pittsburgh, PA 15202

412-415-1282
melissa@magnetglobal.org
www.magnetglobal.org
Facebook, Twitter

Scott Morgan, Chair
Melissa Lentz, CEO
Melissa King, Operations Manager

MAGNET is a group of non-competing, independently owned advertising agencies in major markets throughout the world. The network is comprised of leading agencies sharing a desire to pursue and achieve excellence in the marketing profession. Three executive-level meetings are held each year.
40+ Members
Founded in 1999

390 **News Media Alliance**
4401 N. Fairfax Drive
Suite 300
Arlington, VA 22203

571-366-1000
info@newsmediaalliance.org
www.newsmediaalliance.org
Facebook, Twitter, LinkedIn, YouTube

David Chavern, President & CEO
Robert Walden, Chief Financial Officer
Rebecca Frank, VP, Research & Insights
Danielle Coffey, SVP & General Counsel
Paul Boyle, SVP, Public Policy

Formerly known as the Newspaper Association of America, the News Media Alliance represents large daily papers, non-daily/small-market publications, as well as digital and multiplatform products across North America.
2000 Members
Founded in 1992

391 **Outdoor Advertising Association of America**
1850 M Street NW
Suite 1040
Washington, DC 20036

202-833-5566; Fax: 202-833-1522
oaaa.org
Facebook, Twitter, LinkedIn, Pinterest, YouTube, Instagram

Anna Bager, President & CEO
Ken Klein, EVP, Government Affairs
Stephen Freitas, Chief Marketing Officer
Marci Welinich, SVP, Membership & Administration

Out-of-Home and Digital Out-of-Home advertising industry association, focused on emerging new technologies that are advancing the industry. Members are media companies, advertisers, agencies, ad-tech providers, and suppliers.
800+ Members
Founded in 1891

392 **Promotional Products Association International**
3125 Skyway Circle N.
Irving, TX 75038

888-426-7724
webmaster@ppai.org
www.ppai.org
Facebook, Twitter, LinkedIn

Ira Neaman, Chair
Paul Bellantone, President & CEO
Cory Halliburton, General Counsel

Seeks to provide knowledge, resources, and community to members within the promotional products industry.
15000 Members
Founded in 1903

393 **She Runs It**
1460 Broadway
New York, NY 10036

212-221-7969
info@sherunsit.org
sherunsit.org
Facebook, Twitter, LinkedIn, Instagram

Lynn Branigan, President & CEO
Rebekah Walter, Director, Business Development
Megan Heady, Director, Programming
Cheri Carpenter, Communications Lead

Formerly known as the League of Advertising Women and Advertising Women of New York, the organization was founded as the first women's association in the communications industry. Members now include women in marketing, media, and tech.
1700 Members
Founded in 1912

394 **Shop! Environments Association**
4651 Sheridan Street
Suite 470
Hollywood, FL 33021

954-893-7300; Fax: 954-893-7500
welcome@shopassociation.org
www.shopassociation.org
Facebook, Twitter, LinkedIn, Instagram, Pinterest

Todd Dittman, Executive Director
Susan Kimelman, Director, Member Marketing Partners
Scott Savodnik, Director, Membership
Madeline Baumgartner, Director, Education & Research
Karen Benning, Director, Communications

Formed in the merger of the Association for Retail Environments and Point of Purchase Advertising International, Shop! is a global trade association devoted to enhancing retail environments and experiences for members through research, education, and networking.
2000 Members
Founded in 2015

395 **Transworld Advertising Agency Network: TAAN**
814 Watertown Street
Newton, MA 02465

617-795-1706; Fax: 419-730-1706
info@taan.org
www.taan.org
Facebook, Twitter, LinkedIn

Andrew Eklund, Chair
Peter Gerritsen, President
Rodrigo Rodrigues, Governor - International
David Maricich, Governor - North America

TAAN exists to enhance the intelligence, expertise, reach and personal effectiveness of the owners of its member agencies: Intelligence, through the sharing of best practices, management information, processes and technologies; Expertise, through cooperative utilization of the talents, skills and experience of each member; Reach, through hands-on affiliations with local independent agencies around the world; Personal Effectiveness, through education and close, confidential, trusted relations.
47+ Members
Founded in 1936

396 **Video Advertising Bureau**
830 3rd Avenue
2nd Floor
New York, NY 10022

212-508-1200
info@thevab.com
thevab.com
Twitter, LinkedIn

Sean Cunningham, President & CEO
Danielle Delauro, EVP
Jason Wiese, SVP & Director, Strategic Insights
Marianne Vita, SVP & Director, Integrated Strategy
Lauren Liff, VP, Public Relations & Comms.

VAB is a research and marketing organization for the video industry, providing insights and custom analysis, while embracing emerging technologies.

Newsletters

397 **ACT Newsletter**
Advertising Communications Times
29 Bala Ave
Suite 114
Bala Cynwyd, PA 19004

484-562-0063; Fax: 484-562-0068
adcomtimes@aol.com
www.phillybizmedia.com

Joseph H. Ball, Publisher/Executive Editor
Elena Cruz, Executive Assistant

Business to business newsletter for company owners and executives in Philadelphia, Eastern Pennsylvania, Southern New Jersey & Delaware.
Frequency: Monthly
Circulation: 40000

398 **AEJMC News**
AEJMC
234 Outlet Pointe Boulevard
Suite A
Columbia, SC 29210-5667

803-798-0271; Fax: 803-772-3509
www.aejmc.org

Jennifer McGill, Executive Director
Lillian Coleman, Newsletter Editor/Project Manager

Newsletter of the Association for Education in Journalism and Mass Communication.
Frequency: Monthly
Circulation: 3425
Founded in 1912

399 **AdvertisEd**
American Advertising Federation
1101 K Street NW
Suite 420
Washington, DC 20005

202-898-0089
www.aaf.org

Steve Pacheco, President & CEO
Adrianne Lipscomb, VP, Creative Services

Monthly newsletter for student and faculty members of the AAF.

400 **Associated Spring Newsletter**
Associated Spring

18 Main St
Bristol, CT 06010-6581
860-582-9581
800-528-3795; Fax: 860-589-3122
www.asbg.com

Paulo Coit, Manager

Offers news, conferences and seminars.
Frequency: Quarterly

401 **Business Owner**
Mailing & Fulfillment Service Association
1421 Prince Street
Suite 410
Alexandria, VA 22314-2806

703-836-9200; Fax: 703-548-8204
www.mfsanet.org
Facebook, Twitter, LinkedIn

Ken Garner, President/CEO
Leo Raymond, Vice President
Karen Loveridge, Executive Assistant

Distributed to the owner or CEO of all member companies as a dues-supported benefit of membership. Developed specifically to communicate with owners and CEOs on issues unique to them.
Frequency: Bi-Monthly

402 **DMA Daily Digest**
Direct Marketing Association
1120 Avenue of the Americas
New York, NY 10036-6700

212-768-7277; Fax: 212-302-6714
customerservice@the-dma.org
www.the-dma.org
Facebook, Twitter, LinkedIn

Lawrence M Kimmel, CEO

A summary of today's industry news from trade publications and national media. Also available as an e-mail newsletter.

403 **Direct Hit**
Midwest Direct Marketing Association
PO Box 75
Andover, MN 55304

763-607-2943; Fax: 763-753-2240
www.mdma.org

Beth Gervais, President
Vicki Erickson, Secretary/Treasurer

Brings members news of meetings, activities, local and regional events, pertinent articles and changes in legislation and postal requirements that affect the direct marketing industry.
Frequency: Bi-Monthly
Circulation: 600

404 **Dos and Dont's in Advertising**
Council of Better Business Bureaus
4200 Wilson Blvd
Suite 800
Arlington, VA 22203-1838

703-276-0100; Fax: 703-525-8277
webmaster@bbb.org
www.bbb.org

Stephen A Cox, CEO

Provides in-depth coverage of the laws and regulations governing the advertising industry. Helps you to write, place and manage ads that foster consumer trust and confidence, follow federal and state ad rules, regulations and laws. It has helped legal and advertising professionals produce advertising that is ethical and correct for 50 years.
4000 Pages
Frequency: Monthly
Founded in 1970

405 **Employment Points**
Mailing & Fulfillment Service Association
1421 Prince Street
Suite 410
Alexandria, VA 22314-2806

703-836-9200; Fax: 703-548-8204
www.mfsanet.org

The content is written for business owners and operators who want to stay informed about current employment issues. The editorial is targeted on human resource issues and employment practices in the mailing and fulfillment services industry.
Frequency: 4x/Year
Circulation: 2000

406 **Globe Newsletter**
International Communications Agency Network
1649 Lump Gulch Road
PO Box 490
Rollinsville, CO 80474-0490

303-258-9511; Fax: 303-484-4087
info@icomagencies.com
www.icomagencies.com
Facebook, Twitter

Bob Morrison, Director
Joe Phelps, North American Member at Large

A review of industry trends, member agency news and network happenings.
Frequency: Monthly
Circulation: 150

407 **IMCA Newsletter**
Insurance Marketing & Communications Association
4248 Park Glen Road
Minneapolis, MN 55416

952-928-4644; Fax: 952-929-1318
info@imcanet.com
www.imcanet.com

Megan Flanagan, Executive Director

Available to members of the Insurance Marketing & Communications Association.
Mailing list available for rent

408 **ISA Report**
International Sign Association
1001 N. Fairfax Street
Suite 301
Alexandria, VA 22314

703-836-4012; Fax: 703-836-8353
info@signs.org
www.signs.org

Lori Anderson, President & CEO
Alicia Auerswald, VP, Marketing & Communications

Industry Trends report contributed to Signs of the Times magazine.
Frequency: Monthly

409 **Industry Tracker**
International Sign Association
1001 N. Fairfax Street
Suite 301
Alexandria, VA 22314

703-836-4012; Fax: 703-836-8353
info@signs.org
www.signs.org

Lori Anderson, President & CEO
Alicia Auerswald, VP, Marketing & Communications

Weekly e-newsletter, providing industry developments, new technology, and special offers from ISA.
Frequency: Weekly/Online

410 **InsideAPA Newsletter**
Advertising Photographers of America
27 W 20th Street
Suite 601
New York, NY 10011

212-807-0399; Fax: 212-727-8120
jocelyn@apany.com
www.apanational.com

Theresa Raffetto, National President
Michael Grecco, VP
George Simian, Treasurer

InsideAPA is a blog style newsletter focused on photographers and the membership of the Advertising Photographers of America, APA.

411 **MAGNET Minute**
MAGNET: Marketing & Advertising Global Network
226 Rostrevor Place
Pittsburgh, PA 15202

412-415-1282
melissa@magnetglobal.org
www.magnetglobal.org

Melissa Lentz, CEO

MAGNET network updates for members.
Frequency: Bi-Monthly

412 **Outdoor Advertising**
Junior Billboard Association
P.O. Box 582096
Elk Grove, CA 95758

800-847-3387
www.juniorbillboard.org

Available to members of the Junior Billboard Association.

413 **PPB Newslink**
Promotional Products Association International
3125 Skyway Circle N.
Irving, TX 75038

888-426-7724
webmaster@ppai.org
www.ppai.org

Paul Bellantone, President & CEO

Electronic newsletter providing news and information about PPAI and the industry with links to articles in the online version of PPB Magazine.
Frequency: Weekly

414 **Platform News You Can Use**
Newspaper Association of America
4401 N. Fairfax Drive
Suite 300
Arlington, VA 22203

571-366-1000
info@newsmediaalliance.org
www.newsmediaalliance.org

David Chavern, President & CEO
Michael Maloon, VP, Innovation & Communications
Rebecca Frank, VP, Research & Insights
Lindsey Loving, Manager, Communications
Jennifer Peters, Reporter, Trends & Insights

Members-only e-newsletter with developments on large tech platforms and their relationships with the news industry and journalism.
Frequency: Monthly

415 **PostScripts**
Association of Marketing Service Providers
1800 Diagonal Road
Suite 320
Alexandria, VA 22314-2806

703-836-9200; Fax: 703-548-8204
kgarner@mfsanet.org
www.amsp.org

Joseph P. Truncale, President & CEO

Each issue of PostScripts highlights a theme relevant to mailing or fulfillment operations, such as

production management or information technology.
Frequency: Monthly

416 **Postal Points**
Mailing & Fulfillment Service Association
1421 Prince Street
Suite 410
Alexandria, VA 22314-2806
703-836-9200; Fax: 703-548-8204
www.mfsanet.org
Facebook, Twitter, LinkedIn
Leo Raymond, Editor
Deals exclusively with current and pending postal and delivery issues. Here you will find the facts and analysis of developing postal issues.
Frequency: 18x/Year

417 **STORES First Edition**
Retail Advertising & Marketing International
325 7th St Nw
Suite 1100
Washington, DC 20004-2818
202-661-3052; Fax: 202-737-2849
www.rama-nrf.org
Facebook, Twitter
Kevin Brown, RAMA Chairman
Rob Gruen, Vice Chairman
Gwen Morrison, CEO
Julie Gardner, CMO
E-newsletter alerting readers to new stories including web only content as well as STORES and NRF events taking place in the upcoming month.
Frequency: Monthly

418 **STORES Retail Deals**
Retail Advertising & Marketing International
325 7th St Nw
Suite 1100
Washington, DC 20004-2818
202-661-3052; Fax: 202-737-2849
www.rama-nrf.org
Kevin Brown, RAMA Chairman
Rob Gruen, Vice Chairman
Gwen Morrison, CEO
Julie Gardner, CMO
Provides coverage of retail industry product and service provider news.
Frequency: Semi-Monthly

419 **Shopping Center Ad Trends**
National Research Bureau
320 Valley St
Burlington, IA 52601-5513
319-752-5415; Fax: 319-752-3421
www.national-research-bureau.com
Diane M Darnall, President
Nancy Heinzel, Editor
Advertising and marketing information for the clothing and furniture industry.
Frequency: Monthly
Founded in 1993

420 **Signline**
International Sign Association
1001 N Fairfax Street
Suite 301
Alexandria, VA 22314
703-836-4012
866-WHY-SIGN; Fax: 703-836-8353
info@signs.org
www.signs.org
ISA's newsletter developed especially for sign users, sign companies, planners, building and zoning officials, and other government groups connected with the sign industry. Find important legal and planning information on signage, as well as information on traffic safety, amortization, the economic value of on-premise signs, and other related topics.
2600 Members
Frequency: Weekly/Online

421 **SmartBrief**
Culture Marketing Council
8280 Willow Oaks Corporate Drive
Suite 600
Fairfax, VA 22031
703-745-5531; Fax: 703-610-0227
info@culturemarketingcouncil.org
culturemarketingcouncil.org
Horacio Gavilan, Executive Director
E-mail newsletter of the Culture Marketing Council (formerly the Association of Hispanic Advertising Agencies).

422 **dailyXchange**
Newspaper Association of America
4401 N. Fairfax Drive
Suite 300
Arlington, VA 22203
571-366-1000
info@newsmediaalliance.org
www.newsmediaalliance.org
David Chavern, President & CEO
Michael Maloon, VP, Innovation & Communications
Rebecca Frank, VP, Research & Insights
Lindsey Loving, Manager, Communications
Jennifer Peters, Reporter, Trends & Insights
Members-only e-newsletter with relevant Alliance and industry news from the past day.
Frequency: Daily

423 **newsXchange**
Newspaper Association of America
4401 N. Fairfax Drive
Suite 300
Arlington, VA 22203
571-366-1000
info@newsmediaalliance.org
www.newsmediaalliance.org
David Chavern, President & CEO
Michael Maloon, VP, Innovation & Communications
Rebecca Frank, VP, Research & Insights
Lindsey Loving, Manager, Communications
Jennifer Peters, Reporter, Trends & Insights
News brief from the News Media Alliance with news media industry news, as well as information on digital, advertising, trends, and Alliance products and services.
Frequency: Weekly (Wed.)

Magazines & Journals

424 **AAPOR News**
American Association for Public Opinion Research
One Parkview Plaza
Suite 800
Oakbrook Terrace, IL 60181
847-686-2230; Fax: 847-686-2251
info@aapor.org
www.aapor.org
Delia Murphy, Executive Director
Meagan Comerford, Director, Communications
Quarterly newsletter of the American Association for Public Opinion Research.
Frequency: Quarterly
Founded in 1948

425 **ANA Magazine**
Association of National Advertisers
10 Grand Central, 155 E. 44th Street
New York, NY 10017
212-697-5950; Fax: 212-687-7310
info@ana.net
www.ana.net
Bob Liodice, Chief Executive Officer
Duke Fanelli, EVP & CMO
The latest news and insights from the Association of National Advertisers.

426 **Ad Age**
Crain Communications
684 Third Ave
New York, NY 10017
212-210-0100
adage.com
Facebook, Twitter, LinkedIn
Josh Golden, Publisher
Heidi Waldusky, Assoc. Publisher & General Manager
Editorial insights, exclusive analysis and proprietary data take readers beyond the day's news, helping our audience understand ongoing and emerging trends.
Frequency: Weekly
Circulation: 56650
Founded in 1930

427 **Advantages**
Advertising Specialty Institute
4800 Street Road
Trevose, PA 19053
800-546-1350
ideas@asicentral.com
www.asicentral.com
Timothy Andrews, President & CEO
Dave Vagnoni, Editor
Written especially for the promotional products sales professional, with tips and sales tactics.
Frequency: 15x/Year

428 **Advertiser**
The Pohly Company
253 Summer Street
Floor 3
Boston, MA 02210
617-451-1700
800-383-0888; Fax: 617-338-7767
info@pohlyco.com
www.pohlyco.com
Facebook, Twitter, LinkedIn
Diana Pohly, President & CEO
Bill Pryor, Media Sales General Manager
Kevin Miller, Chief Creative Officer
Bill Dugan, VP/General Manager, FuelNet
Matt Thorsen, Director of Operations & Production
Reports on today's most critical marketing issues such as measuring brand equity, using emerging technologies and global marketing. It also contains articles on key benchmarks and industry trends.
Frequency: 6x/Year

429 **Advertising & Society Quarterly**
Advertising Educational Foundation
10 Grand Central, 155 E. 44th Street
3rd Floor
New York, NY 10017-5813
212-986-8060; Fax: 212-986-8061
gm@aef.com
www.aef.com
William O'Barr, Editor
Ed Timke, Associate Editor
Online peer-reviewed scholarly journal of the Advertising Educational Foundation, directed to professors and students in liberal arts colleges, universities and professional schools. It is an academic publication that publishes articles, essays and other scholarships about adver-

tising in society, culture, history and the economy.

430 **Advertising and Marketing Law in Canada**
Association of Canadian Advertisers
21 St. Clair Avenue E.
Suite 1201
Toronto, ON M4T 1L9

416-964-3805
800-565-0109; Fax: 416-964-0771
communications@acaweb.ca
www.acaweb.ca

Ron Lund, President & CEO
Judy Davey, VP, Media Policy & Marketing
Davina Wong, Director, Membership
Jessica Yared, Manager, Digital Marketing
Current information on advertising and marketing law in Canada, including the latest on social media advertising practices and changes to online behavioural advertising.
Founded in 1914

431 **Adweek**
Prometheus Global Media
770 Broadway
7th Floor
New York, NY 10003-9595

212-493-4100; Fax: 646-654-5368
www.prometheusgm.com
Facebook, Twitter

Richard D. Beckan, CEO
James A. Finkelstein, Chairman
Madeline Krakowsky, Vice President Circulation
Tracy Brater, Executive Director Creative Service
Adweek is the source for advertising and agency news, information and opinion. Covering the industry from an agency perspective, Adweek focuses on the image makers and those who create the strategy and the ads as well as those who buy the media and handle client relations.
Cost: $149.00
Frequency: Weekly
Circulation: 36000
Founded in 1978

432 **B-to-B Marketer**
Association of National Advertisers
10 Grand Central, 155 E. 44th Street
New York, NY 10017

212-697-5950; Fax: 212-687-7310
info@ana.net
www.ana.net

Bob Liodice, Chief Executive Officer
Duke Fanelli, EVP & CMO
Best practices, case studies and expert advice from the Association of National Advertisers.

433 **Billboard Magazine**
Prometheus Global Media
770 Broadway
7th Floor
New York, NY 10003-9595

212-493-4100; Fax: 646-654-5368
www.prometheusgm.com
Facebook, Twitter, RSS

Richard D. Beckman, CEO
James Finkelstein, Chairman
Madeline Krakowsky, Vice President Circulation
Tracy Brater, Executive Director Creative Service
Packed with in-depth music and entertainment features including the latest in new media and digital music, global coverage, music and money, touring, new artists, radio news and retail reports.
Cost: $149.00
Frequency: Weekly
Founded in 1894

434 **Brandweek**
Prometheus Global Media
770 Broadway
7th Floor
New York, NY 10003-9595

212-493-4100; Fax: 646-654-5368
www.prometheusgm.com

Richard D. Beckman, CEO
James A. Finkelstein, Chairman
Madeline Krakowsky, Vice President Circulation
Tracy Brater, Executive Director Creative Service
Focuses on marketing strategy and services, brand identity, sponsorships, licensing, media usage and distribution and promotions.
Frequency: Weekly
Circulation: 26000
Founded in 1991

435 **BtoB Magazine**
Crain Communications, Inc.
1155 Gratiot Ave
Detroit, MI 48207-2732

313-446-6000
info@crain.com
www.crain.com

Keith Crain, Chairman
Rance Crain, President
Mary Kay Crain, Treasurer/Assistant Secretary
Merrilee P. Crain, Secretary/Assistant Treasurer
Robert Felsenthal, Vice President/Publisher
Dedicated to integrated business to business marketing. Every page is packed with substance news, reports, technologies, benchmarks, and best practices served up by the most knowledgeable journalists.
Frequency: Monthly
Circulation: 45000

436 **Corporate Logo Magazine**
Virgo Publishing LLC
3300 N Central Ave
Suite 300
Phoenix, AZ 85012-2532

480-675-9925; Fax: 480-990-0819
kkennedy@vpico.com
www.vpico.com

Jenny Bolton, President
Provides promotional products distributors with tools to grow their businesses in a competitive marketplace.
Circulation: 20000
Founded in 1986
Printed in on glossy stock

437 **Counselor**
Advertising Specialty Institute
4800 Street Road
Trevose, PA 19053

800-546-1350
ideas@asicentral.com
www.asicentral.com

Timothy Andrews, President & CEO
Andy Cohen, VP, Editorial & Marketing Services
Counselor covers marketing trends and new products, and is aimed at distributor principals.
Frequency: Monthly

438 **Creativity**
Ad Age Group/Division of Crain Communications
1155 Gratiot Ave
Detroit, MI 48207-2732

313-446-6000
info@crain.com
www.crain.com

Norm Feldman, Manager
Information, insight and inspiration in the brand creativity world. Each month we showcase the best work and take readers inside the making of ground breaking brand communications and experiences, while exploring the issues facing those in the idea business.
Frequency: Monthly
Circulation: 33000

439 **Forward**
Association of National Advertisers
10 Grand Central, 155 E. 44th Street
New York, NY 10017

212-697-5950; Fax: 212-687-7310
info@ana.net
www.ana.net

Bob Liodice, Chief Executive Officer
Duke Fanelli, EVP & CMO
Thought leadership newsletter from the Association of National Advertisers.

440 **Hispanic Business Magazine**
Hispanic Business Inc
425 Pine Ave
Santa Barbara, CA 93117-3709

805-964-4554; Fax: 805-964-5539
www.hnmagazine.com

Jesus Chavarria, President
Our feature stories highlight significant trends in the US Hispanic market and include profiles of successful entrepreneurs, analysis of economic trends and news and data on such topics as government procurement, workplace diversity, politics, advertising, entertainment and events.
Frequency: Monthly
Circulation: 225000
Founded in 1979

441 **Hospitality Style**
ST Media Group International
11262 Cornell Park Dr
Cincinnati, OH 45242-1812

513-421-2050
800-421-1321; Fax: 513-421-5144
customer@stmediagroup.com
www.stmediagroup.com

Tedd Swormstedt, CEO
Brian Foos, CFO
Publication for design and architecture of hotels, restaurants, spas, resorts, casinos, complexes or convention centers. Covers hospitality design with the eye of a fashion magazine, identifying trends and showcasing them seasonally in a photo-rich format.
Frequency: Monthly
Circulation: 17000
Founded in 1906

442 **IQ News Adweek**
Prometheus Global Media
770 Broadway
7th Floor
New York, NY 10003-9595

212-493-4100; Fax: 646-654-5368
www.prometheusgm.com
Facebook, Twitter, RSS

Richard D. Beckman, CEO
James A. Finkelstein, Chairman
Madeline Krakowsky, Vice President Circulation
Tracy Brater, Executive Director Creative Service
Adweek IQ Daily goes out every weekday morning with a briefing of the most important news on interactive advertising, the latest moves by major brands and agencies in terms of content creation, media partnerships and distribution strategies in the digital realm.
Frequency: Daily

443 **In-Store Marketer**
In-Store Marketing Institute
7400 Skokie Blvd
Skokie, IL 60077-3339

847-675-7400; Fax: 847-675-7494
pdproducts_editor@instoremarketer.org
www.instoremarketer.org
Facebook, Twitter, LinkedIn

Peter Hoyt, President

Members-only e-newsletter highlights new content added to the Institute's website, including research, audio-enabled presentations, image galleries and trends articles.
Frequency: Bi-Monthly
Circulation: 15000
Printed in 4 colors on glossy stock

444 **Industrial + Specialty Printing**
ST Media Group International
11262 Cornell Park Dr
Cincinnati, OH 45242-1812

513-421-2050
800-421-1321; Fax: 513-421-5144
customer@stmediagroup.com
www.stmediagroup.com

Tedd Swormstedt, CEO
Brian Foos, CFO

Covers functional and decorative printing done as part of the manufacturing process, examining the challenges printers face when setting up and maintaining efficient workflows and provides the solutions to keep production on track in industrial printing operations.
Frequency: Monthly
Circulation: 17000
Founded in 1906

445 **International Archive Magazine**
Luerzer's Archive Inc
106 West 29th St
New York, NY 10001

212-643-4297; Fax: 646-619-4264
www.luerzersarchive.net

Sandra Lehnst, CEO
Michael Weinzettl, Publisher
Christina Hrdlicka, Managing Editor
Michael Weinzettl, Editor in Chief

Presents new and innovative TV, magazine, poster and newspaper ads from 20 countries. Devoted to presentation of ads. Translations are provided.
Frequency: Bi-Monthly

446 **Journal of Advertising**
American Academy of Advertising

Home Page:
www.aaasite.org/journal-of-advertising

Shintaro Okazaki, Editor-in-Chief

Quarterly academic journal covering the latest developments in advertising theory and practice.
Frequency: Quarterly

447 **Journal of Advertising (JA)**
American Academy of Advertising
24710 Shaker Blvd.
Beachwood, OH 44122

512-471-8149; Fax: 512-471-7018
jaeditor@austin.utexas.edu
www.journalofadvertising.org
Facebook, Twitter

Herbert J Rotfeld, President
Debbie Treise, President Elect
Steve Edwards, Vice President
Margie Morrison, Treasurer
Wei-Na Lee, Ph.D, Editor

The premier academic publication covering significant intellectual development pertaining to advertising theories and their relationship with practice. The goal is to provide a public forum that reflects the current understanding of advertising as a process of communication, its role in the changing environment, and the relationships between these and other components of the advertising business and practice.
600 Members
Frequency: Quarterly
Founded in 1957

448 **Journal of Advertising Education**
AEJMC
234 Outlet Pointe Boulevard
Suite A
Columbia, SC 29210-5667

803-798-0271; Fax: 803-772-3509
www.aejmc.org

Jay Newell, Editor

Peer-reviewed academic journal devoted to research and commentary on instruction, curriculum, and leadership in advertising education. Official journal of the Advertising Division of the Association for Education in Journalism and Mass Communication, and available to members of the American Academy of Advertising.

449 **Journal of Advertising Research**
Advertising Research Foundation
432 Park Avenue S.
6th Floor
New York, NY 10016

212-751-5656; Fax: 212-689-1859
www.thearf.org

Scott McDonald, President & CEO
Paul Donato, Chief Research Officer

The mission of the Journal of Advertising Research is to act as the research and development vehicle for professionals in all areas of marketing including media, research, advertising and communications
Frequency: Quarterly

450 **Journal of Current Issues and Research in Advertising**
American Academy of Advertising

Home Page: www.aaasite.org/journals

Barbara J. Phillips, Editor-in-Chief

Current issues, the latest research, literature reviews and conceptual papers.
Frequency: Biannual

451 **Journal of Euromarketing**
Taylor & Francis Inc
325 Chestnut St
Suite 800
Philadelphia, PA 19106-2614

215-625-8900
800-354-1420; Fax: 215-625-2940
www.taylorandfrancis.com

Kevin Bradley, President

Aims to meet the needs of academicians, practitioners, and public policymakers in the discussion of marketing issues pertaining to Europe. It helps to increase our understanding of the strategic planning aspects of marketing in Europe and the marketing aspects of the trading relationship between European and foreign firms.
Frequency: Quarterly
ISSN: 1049-6483

452 **Journal of Interactive Advertising**
American Academy of Advertising

Home Page:
www.aaasite.org/journal-of-interactive-advertising

Jooyoung Kim, Editor

A refereed online publication designed to promote the understanding of interactive advertising, marketing and communication in a networked world.
Frequency: Biannual
Circulation: 7000

453 **Journal of International Marketing**
American Marketing Association
130 E. Randolph Street
22nd Floor
Chicago, IL 60601

800-262-1150
customersupport@ama.org
www.ama.org/ama-academic-journals

Kelly Hewett, Editor-in-Chief

Presents scholarly and managerially relevant articles on international marketing.
Frequency: Quarterly
ISSN: 1069-031X

454 **Journal of Marketing**
American Marketing Association
130 E. Randolph Street
22nd Floor
Chicago, IL 60601

800-262-1150
customersupport@ama.org
www.ama.org/ama-academic-journals

Christine Moorman, Editor-in-Chief

Scholarly journal of the marketing discipline.
Frequency: Bimonthly
ISSN: 0022-2429
Founded in 1936

455 **Journal of Marketing Research**
American Marketing Association
130 E. Randolph Street
22nd Floor
Chicago, IL 60601

800-262-1150
customersupport@ama.org
www.ama.org/ama-academic-journals

Rajdeep Grewal, Editor-in-Chief

Covers a wide range of marketing research concepts, methods and applications.
Frequency: Bimonthly
ISSN: 0022-2437
Mailing list available for rent

456 **Journal of Public Policy & Marketing**
American Marketing Association
130 E. Randolph Street
22nd Floor
Chicago, IL 60601

800-262-1150
customersupport@ama.org
www.ama.org/ama-academic-journals

Scot Burton, Co-Editor
Pam Ellen, Co-Editor
Josh Weiner, Co-Editor

Each issue features a wide ranging forum for the research, findings and discussion of marketing subjects related to business and government.
Frequency: Semiannual
ISSN: 0743-9156

457 **Journal of Shopper Research**
Shop! Environments Association
4651 Sheridan Street
Suite 470
Hollywood, FL 33021

954-893-7300; Fax: 954-893-7500
editor@journalofshopperresearch.com
www.journalofshopperresearch.com

Todd Dittman, Executive Director
Raymond Burke, Editor-in-Chief
Madeline Baumgartner

Academic journal focused on the shopper's journey and behavior, with academic and commercial research.
Frequency: Quarterly

458 **Journal of Survey Statistics and Methodology**
American Association for Public Opinion Research
One Parkview Plaza
Suite 800
Oakbrook Terrace, IL 60181
847-686-2230; Fax: 847-686-2251
info@aapor.org
www.aapor.org
Delia Murphy, Executive Director
Meagan Comerford, Director, Communications
Journal sponsored by AAPOR and the American Statistical Association, with scholarly articles on statistical and methodological issues.
Founded in 1948

459 **Journalism & Mass Communication Quarterly (JMCQ)**
AEJMC
234 Outlet Pointe Boulevard
Suite A
Columbia, SC 29210-5667
803-798-0271; Fax: 803-772-3509
www.aejmc.org
Jennifer McGill, Executive Director
Louisa Ha, Editor
Published by the Association for Education in Journalism and Mass Communication, the JMC Quarterly focuses on research in journalism and mass communication. Each issue features reports of original investigation, presenting the latest developments in theory and methodology of communication, international communication, journalism history, and social and legal problems. Also contains book reviews. Refereed. Four times per year. (est. 1924)
Circulation: 4800
Mailing list available for rent

460 **MAGNET Matters**
MAGNET: Marketing & Advertising Global Network
226 Rostrevor Place
Pittsburgh, PA 15202
412-415-1282
melissa@magnetglobal.org
www.magnetglobal.org
Melissa Lentz, CEO
MAGNET network magazine for members.
Frequency: 3x Year

461 **Media**
Media Index Publishing
PO Box 24365
Seattle, WA 98124-0365
206-382-9220
800-332-1736; Fax: 206-382-9437
media@media-inc.com
www.media-inc.com
Katie Sauro, Editor
James Baker, President
Contains the most up-to-date information and issues that are important to you as a member of the marketing, advertising, broadcast, film and video production, multimedia and creative services industries, along with special focus segments and lists each issue, helpful advice from industry leaders and insightful reporting.
Frequency: Bi-Monthly
Circulation: 10,000
Mailing list available for rent: 35M names

462 **Mediaweek**
Prometheus Global Media
770 Broadway
7th Floor
New York, NY 10003-9595
212-493-4100; Fax: 646-654-5368
www.prometheusgm.com
Facebook, Twitter, RSS
Richard D. Beckman, CEO
James A. Finkelstein, Chairman
Madeline Krakowsky, Vice President Circulation
Tracy Brater, Executive Director Creative Service
Highly targeted circulation covers media decision makers at the top 350 ad agencies in America, all top buying services and client media departments.
Frequency: Weekly
Circulation: 21000
Founded in 1991

463 **News & Views**
Advertising Media Credit Executives Association
8840 Columbia 100 Parkway
Columbia, MD 21045-2158
410-992-7609; Fax: 410-740-5574
amcea@amcea.org
www.amcea.org
Sheila Wroten, President
Mary Younger, Vice President
Josie Salazar, Secretary/ Treasurer
Vickie Bolinger, Director
Grace Carter, Director
Our magazine reports on current trends and legal issues while offering tips on customer service, time management and collections.
Frequency: Quarterly

464 **Outdoor Advertising Magazine**
Outdoor Advertising Magazine
Rapid City, SD 57702
877-926-5406
www.oam.net
Facebook, Twitter, LinkedIn
Randall Williamson, Publisher
A major source for the outdoor and out-of-home advertising industry. Contains the latest information on products, services, supplies, technology, creative ideas, financial and industry news.
Cost: $24.95
Founded in 1920

465 **PC Today**
Promotional Products Association International
3125 Skyway Circle N.
Irving, TX 75038
888-426-7724
webmaster@ppai.org
www.ppai.org
Paul Bellantone, President & CEO
Quick-read, daily, electronic newsletter serves the unique educational needs of distributor salespeople.
Frequency: Weekly

466 **POP Design**
In-Store Marketing Institute
7400 Skokie Blvd
Skokie, IL 60077-3339
847-675-7400; Fax: 847-675-7494
pdproducts_editor@instoremarketer.org
www.instoremarketer.org
Facebook, Twitter, LinkedIn
Peter Hoyt, President
Serves the news and product information needs of producers and designers of in-store displays, signs and fixtures. Each issue features the latest trends and technologies vital to building and designing successful in-store merchandising.
Frequency: Bi-Monthly
Circulation: 15000
Printed in 4 colors on glossy stock

467 **PPB Magazine**
Promotional Products Association International
3125 Skyway Circle N.
Irving, TX 75038
888-426-7724
webmaster@ppai.org
www.ppai.org
Paul Bellantone, President & CEO
Coverage concentrates on news activities and events of the promotional products industry.
Cost: $72.00
Frequency: Monthly

468 **Package Design Magazine**
ST Media Group International
11262 Cornell Park Dr
Cincinnati, OH 45242-1812
513-421-2050
800-421-1321; Fax: 513-421-5144
customer@stmediagroup.com
www.stmediagroup.com
Tedd Swormstedt, CEO
Brian Foos, CFO
Full of the news and information professional package designers need to stay abreast of the latest innovations, materials, and technology driving the packaging industry. Presents readers with the useful insights they need to succeed in competitive retail markets.
Frequency: Monthly
Circulation: 17000
Founded in 1906

469 **Politically Direct**
Direct Marketing Association
1120 Avenue of the Americas
New York, NY 10036-6713
212-768-7277; Fax: 212-302-6714
customerservice@the-dma.org
www.the-dma.org
Facebook, Twitter, LinkedIn
Matt Blumberg, Chairman
Glenn Eisen, Vice Chairman
Rick Erwin, Treasurer
Published in both print and digital versions, this newsletter on DMA advocacy efforts keeps DMA members informed and involved in the politics and policies that impact them today and ahead of the curve on developments that will affect them tomorrow.
Frequency: Quarterly

470 **Promotional Consultant Magazine**
Promotional Products Association International
3125 Skyway Cir N
Irving, TX 75038-3539
972-252-0404; Fax: 972-258-3004
ppb@ppai.org
www.ppai.org
Facebook, Twitter, YouTube
Paul Bellantone, President
Steven Meyer, Chairman of the Board
Marc Simon, Chair-Elect
Featuring short, sales-specific articles, relevant trends, targeted strategies, expert voices and compelling case studies.
Frequency: Bi-Monthly
Circulation: 20000

471 **Public Opinion Quarterly**
American Association for Public Opinion Research

One Parkview Plaza
Suite 800
Oakbrook Terrace, IL 60181

847-686-2230; Fax: 847-686-2251
info@aapor.org
www.aapor.org

Delia Murphy, Executive Director
Meagan Comerford, Director, Communications

Offers articles about the science and practice of survey and opinion research to give people a voice in the decisions that affect their daily lives.
Frequency: Quarterly
Founded in 1948
Mailing list available for rent: 1000 names at $400 per M

472 **Response**
201 Sandpointe Ave
Suite 500
Santa Ana, CA 92707-8700

714-338-6700
800-854-3112; Fax: 714-513-8482
thaire@questex.com
www.responsemagazine.com
Facebook, Twitter, LinkedIn, YouTube

Thomas Haire, Editor
Don Rosenberg, VP
Kristina Kronenberg, Marketing Director

Magazine of direct response television reporting. Educates marketers and advertising executives on how to sell products, generate leads and drive store sales through infomercials, short-form commercials, televised shopping and multi-media retailing.
Frequency: Monthly
Circulation: 12000
Founded in 1987

473 **STORES Magazine**
Retail Advertising & Marketing International
325 7th St NW
Suite 1100
Washington, DC 20004-2818

202-661-3052; Fax: 202-737-2849
www.rama-nrf.org

Kevin Brown, RAMA Chairman
Rob Gruen, Vice Chairman
Gwen Morrison, CEO
Julie Gardner, CMO

A publication devoted to retail news and trends as well as notification of conferences and meetings.
Frequency: Monthly

474 **Screen Printing Magazine**
ST Media Group International
11262 Cornell Park Dr
Cincinnati, OH 45242-1812

513-421-2050
800-421-1321; Fax: 513-421-5144
customer@stmediagroup.com
www.stmediagroup.com

Tedd Swormstedt, CEO
Brian Foos, CFO

Leading publication and trusted source of information for the screen-printing industry. Landmark coverage of the latest techniques and technologies that save time, energy and money.
Frequency: Monthly
Circulation: 17000
Founded in 1906

475 **Shop! Retail Environments Magazine**
Shop! Environments Association
4651 Sheridan Street
Suite 470
Hollywood, FL 33021

954-893-7300; Fax: 954-893-7500
editor@journalofshopperresearch.com
www.journalofshopperresearch.com

Todd Dittman, Executive Director
Jo Rossman, Publisher/Editor

Official magazine of Shop! Association, devoted to the business of the retail landscape.
Circulation: 25000

476 **Shopper Marketing**
In-Store Marketing Institute
7400 Skokie Blvd
Skokie, IL 60077-3339

847-675-7400; Fax: 847-675-7494
pdproducts_editor@instoremarketer.org
www.instoremarketer.org
Facebook, Twitter, LinkedIn

Peter Hoyt, President

The leading information source for news and information surrounding the shopper marketing industry. Each month, more than 18000 marketers, manufacturers, agencies and retailers of consumer products or services who buy and specify in-store marketing solutions turn to Shopper Marketing to learn about the latest insights, data and trends surrounding the industry.
Frequency: Bi-Monthly
Circulation: 15000
Printed in 4 colors on glossy stock

477 **Shopper Marketing Newswire**
In-Store Marketing Institute
7400 Skokie Blvd
Skokie, IL 60077-3339

847-675-7400; Fax: 847-675-7494
pdproducts_editor@instoremarketer.org
www.instoremarketer.org
Facebook, Twitter, LinkedIn

Peter Hoyt, President

Delivered to a powerful audience of brands, retailers, agencies and solution providers. Offering personnel updates, company news, research/ data reports, path-to-purchase innovations, co-marketing initiatives across FDM and specialty chains and more.
Frequency: Bi-Monthly
Circulation: 15000
Printed in 4 colors on glossy stock

478 **Sign & Digital Graphics**
National Business Media Inc
2800 W Midway Boulevard
PO Box 1416
Broomfield, CO 80020

303-469-0424
800-669-0424; Fax: 303-469-5730
mdixon@nbm.com
www.nbm.com/sb
Facebook, Twitter

James Kochevar, Publisher
Ken Mergentime, Executive Editor
Matt Dixon, Managing Editor

A comprehensive monthly trade publication covering the business of visual communications offering a broad range of in-depth reporting for professionals. Topics covered include commercial signage, wide-format commercial printing, electric signs and letters, architectural signage, electronic displays, vehicle wraps and graphics and much more.
Cost: $38.00
120 Pages
Frequency: Monthly
Circulation: 18300
Founded in 1986
Mailing list available for rent: 1000 names at $225 per M
Printed in 4 colors

479 **Sign Builder Illustrated**
Simmons-Boardman Publishing Corporation
345 Hudson St
12th Floor
New York, NY 10014-7123

212-620-7200; Fax: 212-633-1165
www.simmonsboardman.com

Arthur J McGinnis Jr, President

How-to magazine featuring the latest products, technology and techniques to enhance the sign maker's craft.
Frequency: Monthly
Circulation: 19055

480 **Sign Business**
National Business Media Inc
2800 W Midway Boulevard
PO Box 1416
Broomfield, CO 80020

303-469-0424
800-669-0424; Fax: 303-469-5730
mdixon@nbm.com
www.nbm.com/sb

James Kochevar, Publisher
Ken Mergentime, Executive Editor
Matt Dixon, Managing Editor

Contains information on electrical illuminated signage, outdoor advertising and commercial sign shops.
Cost: $38.00
120 Pages
Frequency: Monthly
Circulation: 18348
Founded in 1986
Mailing list available for rent: 1000 names at $225 per M
Printed in 4 colors

481 **SignCraft Magazine**
SignCraft Publishing Company
PO Box 60031
Fort Myers, FL 33906

239-939-4644
800-204-0204; Fax: 239-939-0607
signcraft@signcraft.com
www.signcraft.com

Tom McIltrot, Editor

Each issue includes an inside look at several sign shops, plus articles on techniques, materials, pricing, sales and computer aided sign making and puts hundreds of layout ideas at your fingertips.
Frequency: Monthly
Circulation: 14000
Mailing list available for rent: 25M names

482 **Signs of the Times Magazine**
ST Media Group International
11262 Cornell Park Dr
Cincinnati, OH 45242-1812

513-421-2050
800-421-1321; Fax: 513-421-5144
customer@stmediagroup.com
www.stmediagroup.com

Tedd Swormstedt, CEO
Brian Foos, CFO

It is our mission to educate and inspire signage and graphics professionals worldwide through award winning editorial perspectives, technology updates, CAS reports, new product reviews, one of a kind Electric, CAS and Commercial State of the Industry reports, graphics techniques and much more.
Frequency: Monthly
Circulation: 17000
Founded in 1906

483 **Supplier Global Resource**
Advertising Specialty Institute

4800 Street Road
Trevose, PA 19053

800-546-1350
ideas@asicentral.com
www.asicentral.com

Timothy Andrews, President & CEO
Michele Bell, Editorial Director

News on international commerce and forecasts for the promotional products industry.
Frequency: 6x/Year

484 **Survey Practice**
American Association for Public Opinion Research
One Parkview Plaza
Suite 800
Oakbrook Terrace, IL 60181

847-686-2230; Fax: 847-686-2251
info@aapor.org
www.aapor.org

Delia Murphy, Executive Director
Meagan Comerford, Director, Communications

E-journal of AAPOR, offering public opinion and survey research articles and commentary.
Frequency: Quarterly
Founded in 1948
Mailing list available for rent: 1000 names at $400 per M

485 **TelevisionWeek**
Crain Communications
1155 Gratiot Ave
Detroit, MI 48207-2732

313-446-6000
info@crain.com
www.crain.com

Norm Feldman, Manager
Chuck Ross, Managing Director

Covers all aspects of the business programming and production, distribution and talent, broadcast, cable and satellite, advertising and media, government and regulation, finance and emerging technologies.
Founded in 1982

486 **The Big Picture**
ST Media Group International
11262 Cornell Park Dr
Cincinnati, OH 45242-1812

513-421-2050
800-421-1321; Fax: 513-421-5144
customer@stmediagroup.com
www.stmediagroup.com

Tedd Swormstedt, CEO
Brian Foos, CFO

Provides real-world solutions to today's design and production challenges. This publication reports on digital printing of visual communications with coverage of digital printing from image capture and processing to finishing and display.
Frequency: Monthly
Circulation: 17000
Founded in 1906

487 **VMSD**
ST Media Group International
11262 Cornell Park Dr
Cincinnati, OH 45242-1812

513-421-2050
800-421-1321; Fax: 513-421-5144
customer@stmediagroup.com
www.stmediagroup.com

Tedd Swormstedt, CEO
Brian Foos, CFO

Leading magazine for retail designers and store display professionals, showcasing the latest store designs and visual presentations, presents merchandising strategies and new products, and reports on industry news and events.
Frequency: Monthly
Circulation: 17000
Founded in 1906

488 **Wearables**
Advertising Specialty Institute
4800 Street Road
Trevose, PA 19053

800-546-1350
ideas@asicentral.com
www.asicentral.com

Timothy Andrews, President & CEO
C.J. Mittica, Editor

Serves the apparel and accessories segment of the advertising specialty industry.
Frequency: 10x/Year

489 **Winning at Retail**
In-Store Marketing Institute
7400 Skokie Blvd
Skokie, IL 60077-3339

847-675-7400; Fax: 847-675-7494
pdproducts_editor@instoremarketer.org
www.instoremarketer.org
Facebook, Twitter, LinkedIn

Peter Hoyt, President

Shares insights, case studies and lessons learned from thousands of studies conducted by Perception Research Services, the leading company in packaging and shopper marketing research.
Frequency: Bi-Monthly
Circulation: 15000
Printed in 4 colors on glossy stock

Trade Shows

490 **3AF Asian Marketing Summit**
Asian American Advertising Federation
6230 Wilshire Boulevard
Suite 1216
Los Angeles, CA 90048

ghomfranzen@3af.org
www.3af.org
Facebook, Twitter, YouTube, Instagram

Genny Hom-Franzen, Executive Director

Two-day event aimed at Asian members of the marketing profession.
Frequency: Annual

491 **4A's Data Summit**
American Association of Advertising Agencies
1065 Avenue of the Americas
16th Floor
New York, NY 10018

212-682-2500
www.aaaa.org

Marla Kaplowitz, President & CEO
Mollie Rosen, EVP, Member Engagement & Dev.

One-day event exploring how data will impact the advertising industry.

492 **4A's Talent@2030**
American Association of Advertising Agencies
1065 Avenue of the Americas
16th Floor
New York, NY 10018

212-682-2500; Fax: 212-682-8391
www.aaaa.org
Twitter, Instagram, YouTube

Marla Kaplowitz, President & CEO
Mollie Rosen, EVP, Member Engagement & Dev.

Event explores how technology, social media and data are impacting people and culture.

493 **AAPOR Annual Conference**
American Association for Public Opinion Research
One Parkview Plaza
Suite 800
Oakbrook Terrace, IL 60181

847-686-2230; Fax: 847-686-2251
info@aapor.org
www.aapor.org

Delia Murphy, Executive Director
Amy Metzgar, Meetings Coordinator
Linda Arcangeli-Story, Meetings Director

Features cutting edge research and informal access to leaders in the fields.
Founded in 1948

494 **ADMERICA**
American Advertising Federation
1101 K Street NW
Suite 420
Washington, DC 20005

202-898-0089
www.aaf.org

Steve Pacheco, President & CEO
Lisa Rubin, EVP, Events & Corporate Services
Karen Cohn, SVP, Conference & Meetings
Beatrice Santacroce, Sr. Manager, Special Events

Connects all aspects of the advertising industry. Influential agencies, clients, media companies, suppliers, and colleges from across the country will address how to thrive in a recovering economy and how the changing culture of business and consumers is impacting our industry.

495 **AEJMC Annual Conference**
AEJMC
234 Outlet Pointe Boulevard
Suite A
Columbia, SC 29210-5667

803-798-0271; Fax: 803-772-3509
www.aejmc.org

Jennifer McGill, Executive Director
Amanda Caldwell, Confernece/Meetings Manager

Annual conference of the Association for Education in Journalism and Mass Communication.
2000 Attendees
Frequency: August
Founded in 1912

496 **AMA Annual Conference**
American Marketing Association
130 E. Randolph Street
22nd Floor
Chicago, IL 60601

800-262-1150
customersupport@ama.org
www.ama.org
Facebook, Twitter, LinkedIn

Russ Klein, Chief Executive Officer
Jeremy Van Ek, Chief Operating Officer

Premier educational and networking event of the American Marketing Association.

497 **AMCEA Conference**
Advertising Media Credit Executives Association
8840 Columbia 100 Parkway
Columbia, MD 21045-2158

410-992-7609; Fax: 410-740-5574
amcea@amcea.org
www.amcea.org

J Dee Stevenson, President
Kimberly Riley, VP
Vickie Bolinger, Director

The conference encompasses four days and is a networking extravaganza. Top attorneys discuss

bankruptcy and legal issues. We invite advertising agencies to discuss network buying and liability problems.
Frequency: Annual

498 **AMSP Annual Conference**
Association of Marketing Service Providers
1800 Diagonal Road
Suite 320
Alexandria, VA 22314-2806

703-836-9200; Fax: 703-548-8204
kgarner@mfsanet.org
www.amsp.org

Joseph P. Truncale, President & CEO
Leo Raymond, VP, Postal & Member Relations

Opportunity for marketing professionals to network, collaborate, and learn.
Frequency: Annual

499 **ANA Advertising Financial Management Conference**
Association of National Advertisers
10 Grand Central, 155 E. 44th Street
New York, NY 10017

212-697-5950; Fax: 212-687-7310
info@ana.net
www.ana.net

Bob Liodice, Chief Executive Officer
Kristen McDonough, SVP, Conferences

Brings together top marketing finance and procurement professionals from the client side with agency CFOs and other key industry stakeholders interested in efficiencies, cost savings, return on investment, and delivering greater value to organizations.

500 **ANA Advertising Law & Public Policy Conference**
Association of National Advertisers
10 Grand Central, 155 E. 44th Street
New York, NY 10017

212-697-5950; Fax: 212-687-7310
info@ana.net
www.ana.net

Bob Liodice, Chief Executive Officer
Kristen McDonough, SVP, Conferences

Keeping up with the digital revolution is becoming a nearly impossible task. This conference enters the battlefield by putting together a stellar faculty, including leading regulators, top practitioners, and serious critics, capped off by a session that puts it all together led by a leading law professor.

501 **ANA Brand Activation Marketing Conference**
Association of National Advertisers
10 Grand Central, 155 E. 44th Street
New York, NY 10017

212-697-5950; Fax: 212-687-7310
info@ana.net
www.ana.net

Bob Liodice, Chief Executive Officer
Kristen McDonough, SVP, Conferences

Coordinated brand activation strategies from top marketers.

502 **ANA Brand Masters Conference**
Association of National Advertisers
10 Grand Central, 155 E. 44th Street
New York, NY 10017

212-697-5950; Fax: 212-687-7310
info@ana.net
www.ana.net

Bob Liodice, Chief Executive Officer
Kristen McDonough, SVP, Conferences

Effective brand marketing approaches from CMOs and marketing leaders. Conference presented by Twitter.

503 **ANA Chicago Nonprofit Conference**
Association of National Advertisers
10 Grand Central, 155 E. 44th Street
New York, NY 10017

212-697-5950; Fax: 212-687-7310
info@ana.net
www.ana.net

Bob Liodice, Chief Executive Officer
Kristen McDonough, SVP, Conferences

Marketing, fundraising, and collaborative ideas to help nonprofits expand their donor base.

504 **ANA DC Nonprofit Conference**
Association of National Advertisers
10 Grand Central, 155 E. 44th Street
New York, NY 10017

212-697-5950; Fax: 212-687-7310
info@ana.net
www.ana.net

Bob Liodice, Chief Executive Officer
Kristen McDonough, SVP, Conferences

Marketing, fundraising, and collaborative ideas to help nonprofits expand their donor base.

505 **ANA Data & Measurement Conference**
Association of National Advertisers
10 Grand Central, 155 E. 44th Street
New York, NY 10017

212-697-5950; Fax: 212-687-7310
info@ana.net
www.ana.net

Bob Liodice, Chief Executive Officer
Kristen McDonough, SVP, Conferences

506 **ANA Digital & Social Media Conference**
Association of National Advertisers
10 Grand Central, 155 E. 44th Street
New York, NY 10017

212-697-5950; Fax: 212-687-7310
info@ana.net
www.ana.net

Bob Liodice, Chief Executive Officer
Kristen McDonough, SVP, Conferences

Discussing how to use social media and digital technology to impact consumer decisions and how to effectively partner with other companies to maximize social media reach and more.

507 **ANA Email Evolution Conference**
Association of National Advertisers
10 Grand Central, 155 E. 44th Street
New York, NY 10017

212-697-5950; Fax: 212-687-7310
info@ana.net
www.ana.net

Bob Liodice, Chief Executive Officer
Kristen McDonough, SVP, Conferences

A look at regulatory changes, privacy concerns, and technical advances in email marketing.

508 **ANA In-House Agency Conference**
Association of National Advertisers
10 Grand Central, 155 E. 44th Street
New York, NY 10017

212-697-5950; Fax: 212-687-7310
info@ana.net
www.ana.net

Bob Liodice, Chief Executive Officer
Kristen McDonough, SVP, Conferences

Conference devoted to all aspects of in-house agencies, including digital asset management, culture and talent, the evolution of in-house agencies, starting a new agency, and more.

509 **ANA Influencer Marketing Conference**
Association of National Advertisers
10 Grand Central, 155 E. 44th Street
New York, NY 10017

212-697-5950; Fax: 212-687-7310
info@ana.net
www.ana.net

Bob Liodice, Chief Executive Officer
Kristen McDonough, SVP, Conferences

510 **ANA Masters of B2B Marketing**
Association of National Advertisers
10 Grand Central, 155 E. 44th Street
New York, NY 10017

212-697-5950; Fax: 212-687-7310
info@ana.net
www.ana.net

Bo Liodice, Chief Executive Officer
Kristen McDonough, SVP, Conferences

Insights into successful B2B approaches.

511 **ANA Masters of Data & Technology**
Association of National Advertisers
10 Grand Central, 155 E. 44th Street
New York, NY 10017

212-697-5950; Fax: 212-687-7310
info@ana.net
www.ana.net

Bob Liodice, Chief Executive Officer
Kristen McDonough, SVP, Conferences

Discussions on the ever-changing marketing technology ecosystem.

512 **ANA Masters of Marketing Conference**
Association of National Advertisers
10 Grand Central, 155 E. 44th Street
New York, NY 10017

212-697-5950; Fax: 212-687-7310
info@ana.net
www.ana.net

Bob Liodice, Chief Executive Officer
Kristen McDonough, SVP, Conferences

The conference offers an opportunity to learn from and engage with the leaders of the industry as they build brands, leverage the expanding array of media, make marketing more accountable and improve the quality of their marketing organizations.
2500 Attendees

513 **ANA Media Conference**
Association of National Advertisers
10 Grand Central, 155 E. 44th Street
New York, NY 10017

212-697-5950; Fax: 212-687-7310
info@ana.net
www.ana.net

Bob Liodice, Chief Executive Officer
Kristen McDonough, SVP, Conferences

Actionable insights into today's important issues.

514 **ANA Multicultural Marketing & Diversity Conference**
Association of National Advertisers
10 Grand Central, 155 E. 44th Street
New York, NY 10017

212-697-5950; Fax: 212-687-7310
info@ana.net
www.ana.net

Bob Liodice, Chief Executive Officer
Kristen McDonough, SVP, Conferences

515 **ANA Nonprofit Federation Leadership Summit**
Association of National Advertisers

10 Grand Central, 155 E. 44th Street
New York, NY 10017

212-697-5950; Fax: 212-687-7310
info@ana.net
www.ana.net

Bob Liodice, Chief Executive Officer
Kristen McDonough, SVP, Conferences

516 **ANA/BAA Marketing Law Conference**
Association of National Advertisers
10 Grand Central, 155 E. 44th Street
New York, NY 10017

212-697-5950; Fax: 212-687-7310
info@ana.net
www.ana.net

Bob Liodice, Chief Executive Officer
Kristen McDonough, SVP, Conferences

517 **Ad Age A-List & Creativity Awards**
Ad Age
684 Third Ave
New York, NY 10017

212-210-0100
aaevents@adage.com
adage.com
Facebook

Editorial insights, exclusive analysis and proprietary data take readers beyond the day's news, helping our audience understand ongoing and emerging trends.
Founded in 2016

518 **Ad:tech Adweek**
Prometheus Global Media
770 Broadway
7th Floor
New York, NY 10003-9595

212-493-4100; Fax: 646-654-5368
www.prometheusgm.com
Facebook, Twitter, RSS

Richard D. Beckman, CEO
James A. Finkelstein, Chairman
Madeline Krakowsky, Vice President Circulation
Tracy Brater, Executive Director Creative Service

An interactive advertising and technology conference and exhibition. Worldwide shows blend keynote speakers, topic driven panels and workshops to provide attendees with the tools and techniques they need to compete in a changing world.

519 **Advertising Media Credit Executives Association Annual Conference**
Advertising Media Credit Executives Association
PO Box 433
Louisville, KY 40201

502-582-4327; Fax: 502-582-4330
amcea@amcea.org
www.amcea.org

Cheryl E Szluzer, President
Sheila Wroten, Vice President

Media credit managers, editors, business mangers and other professionals gather for exhibits of advertising media such as newspapers, magazines, radio and television.
400 Attendees
Frequency: Annual
Founded in 1896

520 **Annual Action Taker Series**
Retail Advertising & Marketing International
325 7th Street NW
Suite 1100
Washington, DC 20004

202-661-3052; Fax: 202-737-2849
www.rama-nrf.org

Kevin Brown, RAMA Chairman
Rob Gruen, Vice Chairman
Gwen Morrison, CEO
Julie Gardner, CMO

Come hear real case studies and inspiring concepts from today's retail creative leaders.
400 Attendees
Frequency: Annual

521 **Annual Advertising Conference**
Advertising Women of New York
25 W 45th Street
Suite 403
New York, NY 10036

212-221-7969; Fax: 212-221-8296
www.awny.org
Facebook, Twitter, LinkedIn, You tube

Carol Watson, President
Melissa Goidel, VP

To meet some of the top people in the field of advertising; to discover techniques of career planning that can help you get the job of your choice with greater ease; to network with some of the most influential advertising executives of the time from a variety of disciplines.
600 Attendees

522 **Annual Global Marketing Summit**
International Advertising Association - NY Chapter
World Serivce Center
275 Madison Avenue Suite 2102
New York, NY 10016

212-338-0222; Fax: 212-983-0455
coordinator@iaany.org
www.iaany.org
Facebook, Twitter, LinkedIn

Tom Brookbanks, President
Larry Levy, Treasurer
Sean Lough, Secretary

Designed to provide participants with the knowledge, tools and inspiration needed to market global brands. Various registration options. Visit website for details.
1000 Attendees
Frequency: Annual

523 **Annual Proceedings Conference**
American Academy of Advertising
24710 Shaker Blvd.
Beachwood, OH 44122

786-393-3333
patrose@aaasite.org
www.aaasite.org
Facebook, Twitter

Eric Haley, President

Every year the American Academy of Advertising holds a conference at which advertising research findings and theories are presented, as well as papers concerning methods of teaching advertising.
600 Members
Founded in 1957

524 **Asian-Pacific Conference**
American Academy of Advertising
24710 Shaker Blvd.
Beachwood, OH 44122

786-393-3333
www.aaasite.org
Facebook, Twitter

Eric Haley, President
Debbie Treise, Executive Director

Focusing on issues in the Asian-Pacific region, this conference welcomes research on any aspect of advertising as broadly defined in one or more Asian-Pacific countries or in multiple countries involving at least one Asian-Pacific country. This conference is co-sponsored by China Advertising Association of Commerce and Communication University of China.
600 Members
Founded in 1957

525 **AudiencexScience**
Advertising Research Foundation
432 Park Avenue S.
6th Floor
New York, NY 10016

212-751-5656; Fax: 212-689-1859
www.thearf.org

Scott McDonald, President & CEO
Rachael Feigenbaum, SVP & Events Program Producer

Conference devoted to audience measurement and growth.
400 Members
Founded in 1936

526 **CMC Annual Summit**
Association of Hispanic Advertising Agencies
8280 Willow Oaks Corporate Drive
Suite 600
Fairfax, VA 22031

703-745-5531; Fax: 703-610-0227
info@culturemarketingcouncil.org
culturemarketingcouncil.org

Horacio Gavilan, Executive Director

Examines the myriad of changes facing Hispanic agencies in and beyond including shifts in approaches to communications planning, demographics and client needs.

527 **Cable Advertising Conference**
Cabletelevision Advertising Bureau
830 3rd Avenue
2nd Floor
New York, NY 10022

212-508-1200; Fax: 212-832-3268
www.thecab.tv

Sean Cunningham, President

Annual conference and exhibits of advertising-supported cable television networks and services to support local advertising sales.
2000 Attendees
Frequency: Annual/April

528 **Channel Partners Conference & Expo**
Virgo Publishing LLC
3300 N Central Ave
Suite 300
Phoenix, AZ 85012-2532

480-675-9925; Fax: 480-990-0819
kkennedy@vpico.com
www.vpico.com

John Siefert, CEO
Kelly Ridley, CFO
Jon Benninger, VP
John LyBarger, Director of IT

The communications industry's only event designed exclusively for indirect sales organizations - agents, VARs, systems integrators, interconnects and consultants - focused on transforming their businesses to become converged solutions providers.
Circulation: 20000
Founded in 1986
Printed in on glossy stock

529 **Comprehensive CRM & Database Marketing**
Direct Marketing Association

1120 Avenue of the Americas
New York, NY 10036-6700

212-768-7277; Fax: 212-302-6714
customerservice@the-dma.org
www.the-dma.org
Facebook, Twitter, LinkedIn

Lawrence M Kimmel, CEO

In an increasingly digital marketing landscape, metrics and ROI are being scrutinized and recalibrated like never before. Whether interested in classic database statistics or emerging trends in web analytics, the insights gained in our classes will add up to success.

530 **DMA Annual Conference & Exhibition**
Direct Marketing Association
1120 Avenue of Americas
New York, NY 10036-6700

212-768-7277; Fax: 212-302-6714
dmaconferences@the-dma.org
www.the-dma.org
Facebook, Twitter, LinkedIn

Lawrence M Kimmel, CEO
Julie A Hogan, SVP Conferences/Education Services

Offers a progressive marketers to help better engage customers and improve bottom line results in all channels, including social, search, monile, video and more.
12000 Attendees
Frequency: Annual/October

531 **Direct Marketing Institute**
Direct Marketing Association
1120 Avenue of the Americas
New York, NY 10036-6700

212-768-7277; Fax: 212-302-6714
customerservice@the-dma.org
www.the-dma.org
Facebook, Twitter, LinkedIn

Lawrence M Kimmel, CEO

A three-day intensive direct marketing seminar, the DMI iwll give step-by-step tactics to maximize the ROI of your campaigns.

532 **Effective Email Marketing**
Direct Marketing Association
1120 Avenue of the Americas
New York, NY 10036-6700

212-768-7277; Fax: 212-302-6714
customerservice@the-dma.org
www.the-dma.org
Facebook, Twitter, LinkedIn

Lawrence M Kimmel, CEO

The online world presents a myriad of options for establishing and developing customer and community relationships. If you want to segment and target your email database or launch a mobile campaign, we can teach you the best practices and strategies you need to meet and exceed your goals.

533 **Email Evolution Conference**
Direct Marketing Association
1120 Avenue of Americas
New York, NY 10036-6700

212-768-7277; Fax: 212-302-6714
www.the-dma.org
Facebook, Twitter, LinkedIn

Lawrence M Kimmel, CEO
Julie A Hogan, SVP Conferences/Education Services

Focuses on the ever-changing and evolving world of email marketing, providing attendees with the best ways to capitalize on the high ROI this low-cost communication tool can provide both on its own, and integrated with social, search, mobile, video and other email enhancers.
10M Attendees
Frequency: Annual/February

534 **FCS Race for Kids**
Financial Communications Society
368 Ninth Avenue
9th Floor
New York, NY 10001

908-858-0427
admin@thefcs.org
thefcs.org

Tim Hart, Chair
Tom Jago, Vice Chair
Katherine Divney, Secretary
Kevin Windorf, CEO

Charity event and marketing summit held by the Financial Communications Society.
Founded in 1967

535 **Global Shop Conference**
Nielsen Business Media
1145 Sanctuary Parkway
Suite 355
Alpharetta, GA 30074

770-569-1540; Fax: 770-569-5105
www.globalshop.org
Facebook, Twitter, LinkedIn

David Loechner, President
Michael Alicea, SVP/Human Resources
Denise Bashem, VP/Finance

Retail designers and brand marketers find the most innovative concepts, newest products and services to create unique store design and in-store marketing solutions.
50000 Attendees
Frequency: Annual/March

536 **Hospitality Match**
ST Media Group International
11262 Cornell Park Dr
Cincinnati, OH 45242-1812

513-421-2050
800-421-1321; Fax: 513-421-5144
customer@stmediagroup.com
www.stmediagroup.com

Tedd Swormstedt, CEO
Brian Foos, CFO

A series of targeted and exclusive invitation-only events that bring key decision makers from top design firms, purchasing companies and hotel groups together with relevan suppliers, face-to-face for a weekend of serious business and exceptional networking events. Suppliers will meet with pre-qualified hospitality buyers through pre-arranged one-on-one meetings.
Frequency: Monthly
Circulation: 17000
Founded in 1906

537 **IAA World Congress**
International Advertising Association
114 E. 25th Street
Suite 915
New York, NY 10009

646-722-2612; Fax: 646-722-2501
iaa@iaaglobal.org
www.iaaglobal.org

Dagmara Szulce, Managing Director, IASA Global

Bi-annual event attracts more than a thousand marketing communications professionals from all over the world.
1200 Attendees
Frequency: Bi-annual

538 **IAB ALM**
Interactive Advertising Bureau
116 E. 27th Street
6th Floor
New York, NY 10016

212-380-4700
learning@iab.com
www.iab.com
Facebook, Twitter, LinkedIn, YouTube, Instagram

David Cohen, Board President & CEO
Dennis Buchheim, President
Randall Rothenberg, Executive Chair
Dave Grimaldi, EVP, Public Policy
Sheryl Goldstein, SVP, Member Engagement & Dev.

AdTech conference hosted by the Interactive Advertising Bureau, dedicated to exploring the devices, systems, networks, regulations, and applications shaping marketing and media.
Cost: $2695.00
Frequency: Registration Fee
Founded in 1996

539 **IAB Annual Leadership Meeting**
Interactive Advertising Bureau
116 East 27th Street
6th Floor
New York, NY 10016

212-380-4700
www.iab.net
Facebook, Twitter, LinkedIn

Randall Rothenberg, President & CEO

Addresses head-on issues taking place right now in the digital industry.

540 **ICOM World Meeting**
International Communications Agency Network
P.O. Box 3417
Nederland, CO 80466

720-215-6674
info@icomagencies.com
www.icomagencies.com

Emma Keenan, Executive Director
Diane Venturino, International Meeting Planner

Networking opportunity with new business opportunities and information on industry developments.
Frequency: Annual

541 **IFCA Annual Conference**
Insurance and Financial Communications Association
1037 N 3rd Ave
Tucson, AZ 85705

602-350-0717
info@ifcaonline.com
www.ifcaonline.com
Facebook, Twitter, LinkedIn, YouTube

Susan o'Neill, President
Ralph Chaump, VP
Kim Schultz, Secretary

Offers networking among peers, education through platform speeches and practical workshops, display of the best industry communications work being done and volunteer opportunities.

542 **IMCA Annual Conference**
Insurance Marketing & Communications Association
4248 Park Glen Road
Minneapolis, MN 55416

952-928-4644; Fax: 952-929-1318
info@imcanet.com
www.imcanet.com

Megan Flanagan, Executive Director

To promote education and development of its members.
Mailing list available for rent

543 **ISA Converge**
International Sign Association
1001 N. Fairfax Street
Suite 301
Alexandria, VA 22314

703-836-4012; Fax: 703-836-8353
info@signs.org
www.signs.org

Lori Anderson, President & CEO
Iain Mackenzie, VP, Meetings & Events

The conference featured a slate of experts speaking on a wide range of topics specifically of interest to companies that sell to sign manufacturers.
Frequency: Annual

544 **ISA International Sign Expo**
International Sign Association
1001 N. Fairfax Street
Suite 301
Alexandria, VA 22314

703-836-4012; Fax: 703-836-8353
info@signs.org
www.signs.org

Lori Anderson, President & CEO
Iain Mackenzie, VP, Meetings & Events

ISA's annual internation sign Expo is a premier platform for the sign industry to conduct business. 600 exhibitors.
20600 Attendees

545 **International Career Developmemt Conference**
DECA Inc
1908 Association Drive
Reston, VA 20191

703-860-5000; Fax: 703-860-4013
www.deca.org

Jacklyn Schiller, President
Jim Brock, President-elect
Lynore Levenhagen

Gathering of members, advisors, businesspersons and alumni who attend. Most of the participants are competitors in one of DECA's competency based competitive events.
15000 Attendees

546 **MFSA Midwinter Executive Conference**
Mailing & Fulfillment Service Association
1421 Prince Street
Suite 410
Alexandria, VA 22314-2806

703-836-9200; Fax: 703-548-8204
www.mfsanet.org

Ken Garner, President
Jennifer Root, Director
Bill Stevenson, Director Marketing

Addresses financial operations and business valuation, marketing your own company, the changing world of postal regulations, technology in fulfillment, building a sales team, being strong in digital printing and the landscape of employment law.

547 **MIXX Conference & Expo**
Interactive Advertising Bureau
116 E 27th Street
7th Floor
New York, NY 10016

212-380-4700
www.iab.net

Lisa Milgram, Events Director
Margaret Southwell, Events Coordinator

The preeminet event for marketing and agency professionals-and the publishers and technology firms who help drive their efforts. Brings together the industry's most prominent and influential figures to share insights on the most pressing topics in advertising.
Frequency: Annual

548 **Mailer Strategies Conference**
Mailing & Fulfillment Service Association
1421 Prince Street
Suite 410
Alexandria, VA 22314-2806

703-836-9200; Fax: 703-548-8204
www.mfsanet.org

Ken Garner, President
Jennifer Root, Director
Bill Stevenson, Director Marketing

This conference will focus solely on postal issues that are important to your operations.

549 **Multicultural Council Meeting**
Interactive Advertising Bureau
116 E 27th Street
7th Floor
New York, NY 10016

212-380-4700
www.iab.net
Facebook, Twitter, LinkedIn

Randall Rothenberg, President/CEO

IAB members contributing information on the interactive advertising marketplace.
Frequency: Monthly

550 **NCDM Conference**
Direct Marketing Association
1120 Avenue of Americas
New York, NY 10036-6700

212-768-7277; Fax: 212-302-6714
dmaconferences@the-dma.org
www.the-dma.org
Facebook, Twitter, LinkedIn

Julie A Hogan, SVP Conferences/Events

Presents industry experts and hard-hitting case studies from a variety of verticles, such as financial services, retail, automotive, publishing, non-profit and many more, who will share the latest strategies and methodologies in gathering, analyzing, leveraging and protecting the most valuable business asset, customer data.
10M Attendees
Frequency: Annual/December

551 **NRF Annual Convention & EXPO**
Retail Advertising & Marketing International
325 7th Street NW
Suite 1100
Washington, DC 20004

202-661-3052; Fax: 202-737-2849
www.rama-nrf.org

Kevin Brown, RAMA Chairman
Rob Gruen, Vice Chairman
Gwen Morrison, CEO
Julie Gardner, CMO

RAMA is undertaking in important transformation to become an organization that's representative of the changes that are affecting the retail marketing community with a strategic view that includes the integration of mobile, digital and traditional media.
400 Attendees
Frequency: Annual

552 **National Conference on Operations & Fulfillment (NCOF)**
Direct Marketing Association
1120 Avenue of Americas
New York, NY 10036-6700

212-768-7277; Fax: 211-302-6714
dmaconferences@the-dma.org
www.the-dma.org
Facebook, Twitter, LinkedIn

Julie A Hogan, SVP Conference/Events
Lawrence M Kimmel, CEO

Focuses on innovative solutions for the warehouse, distribution, operations, and ecommerce needs in the ever-changing world of operations and fulfillment.
10M Attendees

553 **New York Nonprofit Conference**
Direct Marketing Association
1120 Avenue of Americas
New York, NY 10036-6700

212-768-7277; Fax: 212-302-6714
dmaconferences@the-dma.org
www.the-dma.org
Facebook, Twitter, LinkedIn

Lawrence M Kimmel, CEO
Julie A Hogan, SVP Conferences/Education Services

Discover which acknowledgement problems work best and why, increase revenue with membership options-as well as traditional fundraising appeals, learn how the internet and e-mail campaigns can improve fundraising, lowering costs and increase advocacy.
10M Attendees

554 **OAAA Media Conference and Expo**
Outdoor Advertising Association of America
1850 M Street NW
Suite 1040
Washington, DC 20036

202-833-5566; Fax: 202-833-1522
nfletcheter@oaaa.org
www.oaaa.org

Anna Bager, President & CEO
Marci Welinich, SVP, Membership & Administration

Out-of-Home advertising conference geared towards media, advertising agencies, advertisers, and all types of suppliers.
Frequency: Annual

555 **OAAA\TAB National Convention + Expo**
Outdoor Advertising Association of America
1850 M St. NW
Suite 140
Washington, DC 20036

202-833-5566; Fax: 202-833-1522
www.oaaa.org

Responsibility for the program alternates between the Outdoor Advertising Association of America (OAAA) and Traffic Audit Bureau (TAB).
Frequency: Annual

556 **PPAI Brand**
Promotional Products Association International
3125 Skyway Circle N.
Irving, TX 75038

888-426-7724
webmaster@ppai.org
www.ppai.org

Paul Bellantone, President & CEO

The industry's most highly regarded incentive products showcase, gives an all-access pass to the $46 billion incentives market.

557 **PPAI Decorate**
Promotional Products Association International

3125 Skyway Circle N.
Irving, TX 75038

888-426-7724
webmaster@ppai.org
www.ppai.org

Paul Bellantone, President & CEO

The best in screen printing, embroidery and digital technology. Experience demonstrations of the newest products and equipment.

558 **PPAI Expo**
Promotional Products Association International
3125 Skyway Circle N.
Irving, TX 75038

888-426-7724
webmaster@ppai.org
www.ppai.org

Paul Bellantone, President & CEO

Large and long-running promotional products event.

559 **PPAI MASCAS**
Promotional Products Association International
3125 Skyway Cir N
Irving, TX 75038-3539

972-252-0404; Fax: 972-258-3004
ppb@ppai.org
www.ppai.org
Facebook, Twitter, LinkedIn, YouTube

Paul Bellantone, President
Steven Meyer, Chairman of the Board
Marc Simon, Chair-Elect

Master Advertising Specialist (MAS) and Certified Advertising Specialist (CAS) are the promotional products industry's professional designations.

560 **RAMA CMO Summit**
Retail Advertising & Marketing International
325 7th Street NW
Suite 1100
Washington, DC 20004

202-661-3052; Fax: 202-737-2849
www.rama-nrf.org

Kevin Brown, RAMA Chairman
Rob Gruen, Vice Chairman
Gwen Morrison, CEO
Julie Gardner, CMO

To provide a networking and discussion forum for senior retail marketing executives.
50 Attendees

561 **RAMACON: Thoughtful Topics, Fearless Ideas Remarkable People**
Retail Advertising & Marketing International
325 7th Street NW
Suite 1100
Washington, DC 20004

202-661-3052; Fax: 202-737-2849
www.rama-nrf.org

Kevin Brown, RAMA Chairman
Rob Gruen, Vice Chairman
Gwen Morrison, CEO
Julie Gardner, CMO

RAMA is undertaking in important transformation to become an organization that's representative of the changes that are affecting the retail marketing community with a strategic view that includes the integration of mobile, digital and traditional media.
400 Attendees
Frequency: Annual

562 **Re:Think The ARF Annual Convention & Expo**
Advertising Research Foundation
432 Park Avenue S.
6th Floor
New York, NY 10016

212-751-5656; Fax: 212-689-1859
www.thearf.org

Scott McDonald, President & CEO
Rachael Feigenbaum, SVP & Events Program Producer

Re:Think is a research forum where the ad industry gathers to dispense, explore and challenge the latest knowledge driving the advertising and marketing industry. Showcases innovative market research services and products, high-level networking, free education, and leading-edge industry resources.
400 Members
Founded in 1936

563 **Response Expo**
201 Sandpointe Ave
Suite 500
Santa Ana, CA 92707-8700

714-338-6700
800-854-3112; Fax: 714-513-8482
thaire@questex.com
www.responsemagazine.com
Facebook, Twitter, LinkedIn, YouTube

Thomas Haire, Editor
Don Rosenberg, VP
Kristina Kronenberg, Marketing Director

Focuses on the evolution of consumers from passive watchers to active and empowered brand evangelists. Technology and social media have enabled and encouraged consumers to engage and interact with content. Learn how to take DR marketing from traditional campaign management to the future of customer engagement.
Frequency: Monthly
Circulation: 12000
Founded in 1987

564 **Shopper Marketing Expo**
In-Store Marketing Institute
7400 Skokie Blvd
Skokie, IL 60077-3339

847-675-7400; Fax: 847-675-7494
pdproducts_editor@instoremarketer.org
www.instoremarketer.org
Facebook, Twitter, LinkedIn

Peter Hoyt, President

The premier annual event in the in-store industry filled with symposia, seminars, exhibits and awards dedicated to integrating the wide variety of solutions, tools and expertise needed to influence decision-making along the path to purchase.
Circulation: 15000
Printed in 4 colors on glossy stock

565 **Shopper Marketing Summit**
In-Store Marketing Institute
7400 Skokie Blvd
Skokie, IL 60077-3339

847-675-7400; Fax: 847-675-7494
www.instoremarketer.org
Facebook, Twitter, LinkedIn

Peter Hoyt, President

A world-class senior level conference offering ideas and solutions to retailers, manufacturers and marketers of consumer products and services, agencies and other solution providers who are looking to achieve new heights at retail.
Printed in 4 colors on glossy stock

566 **Signage and Graphics Summit**
ST Media Group International
11262 Cornell Park Dr
Cincinnati, OH 45242-1812

513-421-2050
800-421-1321; Fax: 513-421-5144
customer@stmediagroup.com
www.stmediagroup.com

Tedd Swormstedt, CEO
Brian Foos, CFO

Three days of education and networking for high-volume sign companies, screen printers and digital print shops.
Founded in 1906

567 **Stratconn**
In-Store Marketing Institute
7400 Skokie Blvd
Skokie, IL 60077-3339

847-675-7400; Fax: 847-675-7494
www.instoremarketer.org
Facebook, Twitter, LinkedIn

Peter Hoyt, President

Gathering the leading designers/producers of displays, signs and fixtures together with teams of merchandising experts from leading CPG manufacturers and retailers.
Printed in 4 colors on glossy stock

568 **SupplySide International Tradeshow and Conference**
Virgo Publishing LLC
3300 N Central Ave
Suite 300
Phoenix, AZ 85012-2532

480-675-9925; Fax: 480-990-0819
kkennedy@vpico.com
www.vpico.com

John Siefert, CEO
Kelly Ridley, CFO
Jon Benninger, VP
John LyBarger, Director of IT

The world's largest event for healthy and innovative ingredients. Food, beverage, dietary supplement and cosmeceutical manufacturers, marketers and formulators attend to source cutting edge ingredients and learn from outstanding educational presentations at the largest event of its kind.
Founded in 1986

569 **SurveyFest**
American Association for Public Opinion Research
One Parkview Plaza
Suite 800
Oakbrook Terrace, IL 60181

847-686-2230; Fax: 847-686-2251
info@aapor.org
www.aapor.org

Delia Murphy, Executive Director
Amy Metzgar, Meetings Coordinator
Linda Arcangeli-Story, Meetings Director

Half-day conference and networking event for undergraduate and graduate students, encouraging them to consider careers studies in public opinion and survey research.
Founded in 1948

570 **VMSD International Retail Design Conference**
ST Media Group International
11262 Cornell Park Dr
Cincinnati, OH 45242-1812

513-421-2050
800-421-1321; Fax: 513-421-5144
customer@stmediagroup.com
www.stmediagroup.com

Tedd Swormstedt, CEO
Brian Foos, CFO

The premier educational event created especially for members of the retail design community.
Circulation: 17000
Founded in 1906

571 **adXchange**
News Media Alliance
4401 N. Fairfax Drive
Suite 300
Vienna, VA 22203
571-366-1000
info@newsmediaalliance.org
www.newsmediaalliance.org
David Chavern, President & CEO
Rachel Fox, Event Planner & Executive Assistant
Hosted by the News Media Alliance to bring members of the news industry together with advertisers.
Frequency: Annual

572 **impactSHOW**
Internet Marketing Association
200 Spectrum Center Drive
Irvine, CA 92618
949-443-9300
info@imanetwork.org
imanetwork.org
Facebook, Twitter, LinkedIn, YouTube
Sinan Kanatsiz, Chair & Founder
Sean Conrad, CEO
Lei Lani Fera, Head Of Creative
Hall Roosevelt, General Manager
Marcus Volpe, Executive Director
Conference of the Internet Marketing Association.
Founded in 2001

Directories & Databases

573 **AMCEA Member Handbook & Roster**
Advertising Media Credit Executives Association
8840 Columbia 100 Parkway
Columbia, MD 21045-2158
410-992-7609; Fax: 410-740-5574
amcea@amcea.org
www.amcea.org
J Dee Stevenson, President
Kimberly Riley, VP
Vickie Bolinger, Director
Inside you will find direct telephone numbers to every credit manager in our association along with numbers for credit references and fax inquiries. We also include their e-mail addresses and computer hardware and software information.

574 **Advertisers and Agency Red Book Plus**
Canon Communications Pharmaceutical Medial Group
300 American metro Bvld
Newtown, PA 18940
215-944-9800; Fax: 215-867-0053
sandra.baker@cancom.com
www.pharmalive.com
Karl Engel, President
Styli Engel, Executive VP/Editor-in-Chief
James Hannan, CEO/Group Publisher
Lisa Aberman, CFO/COO
Advertising information.
Cost: $1788.00
Frequency: Quarterly
Founded in 1982

575 **Advertising Growth Trends**
Schonfeld & Associates Inc
1931 Lynn Circle
Libertyville, IL 60048-1323
847-816-4870
800-205-0030; Fax: 847-816-4872
saiinfo@saibooks.com
www.saibooks.com
Carol Greenhut, Publisher
Information on publicly owned corporations that spend on advertising. Measures of profitability and effectiveness of the company's advertising expenditures are shown.
Cost: $395.00
217 Pages
Frequency: Annual
ISBN: 1-932024-84-0

576 **Advertising Ratios & Budgets**
Schonfeld & Associates Inc
1931 Lynn Circle
Libertyville, IL 60048-1323
847-816-4870
800-205-0030; Fax: 847-816-4872
saiinfo@saibooks.com
www.saibooks.com
Carol Greenhut, Publisher
The detailed annual report covers over 5,000 companies and 300 industries with information on current advertising budgets, ad-to-sales ratios and ad-to-gross margin ratios, as well as budgets and growth rate forecasts. Use it to track competition, win new ad agency clients, set and justify ad budgets, sell space and time or plan new media ventures and new products. Includes industry and advertiser ad spending rankings.
Cost: $395.00
186 Pages
Frequency: Annual
ISBN: 1-932024-80-8

577 **Advertising Red Books**
PO Box 1514
Summit, NJ 07902
800-908-5395
info@redbooks.com
www.redbooks.com
Advertising Red Books has been providing competitive intelligence and prospecting data to media companies, advertising agencies, manufacturers, libraries, advertising service and suppliers.
Founded in 1922

578 **Advertising and Marketing Intelligence**
New York Times
1719 State Route 10
#A
Parsippany, NJ 07054-4507
hartman-center@duke.edu
www.library.duke.edu
Contains abstracts of articles from over 75 publications on advertising, marketing and the media.

579 **Adweek Directory**
Prometheus Global Media
770 Broadway
7th Floor
New York, NY 10003-9595
212-493-4100; Fax: 646-654-5368
www.prometheusgm.com
Facebook, Twitter
Richard D. Beckman, CEO
James A. Finkelstein, Chairman
Madeline Krakowsky, Vice President Circulation
Tracy Brater, Executive Director Creative Service
Adweek Directories Online is where you will find searchable databases with comprehensive information on ad agencies, brand marketers and multicultural media.
Frequency: Annual
Circulation: 800
Founded in 1981

580 **Brands and Their Companies**
Gale/Cengage Learning
PO Box 09187
Detroit, MI 48209-0187
248-699-4253
800-877-4253; Fax: 248-699-8049
www.gale.com
Facebook, Twitter, LinkedIn, YouTube
Patrick C Sommers, President
This source lists manufacturers and distributors from small businesses to large corporations, from both the public and private sectors offering complete coverage of more than 426,000 US consumer brands.
Frequency: Annual
ISBN: 1-414434-26-X

581 **Buyers Guide to Outdoor Advertising**
DoMedia LLC
247 Marconi Boulevard
Suite 400
Columbus, OH 43215
866-939-3663
www.domedia.com
FC Miller, Publisher
Robert Gainey, Circulation Manager
Offers valuable information on outdoor advertising companies and their markets.

582 **CMC Hispanic Market Guide**
Association of Hispanic Advertising Agencies
8400 Westpark Drive
2nd Floor
McLean, VA 22102
703-610-9014; Fax: 703-610-0227
info@culturemarketingcouncil.org
culturemarketingcouncil.org
Horacio Gavilan, President
Digital guide with advertising, media and marketing companies that specialize in the Hispanic market.

583 **Circulation**
Standard Rate & Data Services
1700 E Higgins Rd
Des Plaines, IL 60018-5610
847-375-5000
800-851-7737; Fax: 847-375-5001
contact@srds.com
www.srds.com
George Carens, Executive Vice President
Trish Delaurier, Publisher
This print service provides complete circulation, penetration and consumer demographic information on your newspaper options so you can make objective comparisons in multi newspaper markets and across markets. You'll be able to analyze circulation, number of households, retail sales, average household income and market rankings to determine what papers deliver your target audience.
Frequency: Annual
Circulation: 1000+

584 **Co-op Advertising Programs Sourcebook**
National Register Publishing

430 Mountain Ave.
Suite 400
New Providence, NJ 07974

800-473-7020; Fax: 908-673-1189
nrpeditorial@marquiswhoswho.com
www.co-opsourcebook.com

The best source for media companies, wholesalers, retailers and others for finding available advertising dollars to fund co-op programs. Includes 52 product classifications.
Frequency: Semi-Annual

585 **Consumer Magazine Advertising Source**
Standard Rate & Data Services
1700 E Higgins Rd
Des Plaines, IL 60018-5610

847-375-5000
800-851-7737; Fax: 847-375-5001
contact@srds.com
www.srds.com

George Carens, Executive Vice President
Joseph Hayes, Publisher

This service provides complete planning information on US consumer magazines, including standardized ad rates, dates, contact information and links to online media kits, Web sites and audit statements that provide additional facts on readership information and positioning.
Frequency: Semi-Annual
Circulation: 2000+

586 **Creative Industry Director**
Black Book Inc
740 Broadway
Suite 202
New York, NY 10003-9518

212-979-6700
800-841-1246; Fax: 212-673-4321
www.blackbook.com

Joe Resudek, Janet

Designed to meet the needs of professionals who seek creative services in every aspect of media, advertising, production and the fashion industry.
Frequency: Annual

587 **Fashion and Print Directory: Madison Avenue Handbook**
Peter Glenn Publications
777 E Atlantic Ave
Suite C2337
Delray Beach, FL 33438

561-404-4209
888-332-6700; Fax: 561-892-5786
gjames@pgdirect.com
www.pgdirect.com

Gregory James, Publisher
Todd Heustess, Editor

The most reliable and comprehensive entertainment resource includes over 400 pages of national information including everyone you need to know within the advertising, fashion and print industries.
Frequency: Annual
Founded in 1956

588 **IQ Directory Adweek**
Prometheus Global Media
770 Broadway
7th Floor
New York, NY 10003-9595

212-493-4100; Fax: 646-654-5368
www.prometheusgm.com

Richard D. Beckman, CEO
James A. Finkelstein, Chairman
Madeline Krakowsky, Vice President Circulation
Tracy Brater, Executive Director Creative Service

Profile of companies at the leading edge of digital marketing, has the specifics you'll need to investigate, launch and/or expand your digital presence. Profiles over 2,200 interactive agencies, web developers, brand marketers, online media, CD-ROM developers, POP/Kiosk designers and multimedia creative companies
Founded in 1981

589 **IRS Corporate Financial Ratios**
Schonfeld & Associates Inc
1931 Lynn Circle
Libertyville, IL 60048-1323

847-816-4870
800-205-0030; Fax: 847-816-4872
saiinfo@saibooks.com
www.saibooks.com

Carol Greenhut, Publisher

An ideal reference for CPAs, controllers, bankers, CFOs, tax lawyers, financial analysts, investment advisors and corporate planners, this reference book features 70-plus key financial ratios calculated from the latest income statement and balance sheet data available from the IRS.
Cost: $225.00
293 Pages
Frequency: Annual
ISBN: 1-932024-79-4

590 **ISA Membership & Buyer's Guide**
International Sign Association
1001 N Fairfax Street
Suite 301
Alexandria, VA 22314

703-836-4012
866-WHY-SIGN; Fax: 703-836-8353
info@signs.org
www.signs.org

Alicia Auerswald, VP, Marketing, Membership & Comms.

Discover a new supplier or distributor. Use our database to search members by company, location, products, services or equipment.
2600 Members

591 **Illustrated Guide to P.O.P. Exhibits and Promotion**
Creative Magazine
31 Merrick Avenue
Merrick, NY 11566

516-378-0800; Fax: 516-378-0884
info@creativemag.com
www.creativemag.com

Larry Flasterstein, Publisher

The Illustrated Guide serves over 15,000 P.O.P buyers, sales promotion and event managers in the leading corporations in North America with quick, up to the minute information about the resources in this industry.
Frequency: Annual

592 **Infomercial Marketing Sourcebook**
Prometheus Global Media
770 Broadway
7th Floor
New York, NY 10003-9595

212-493-4100; Fax: 646-654-5368
www.prometheusgm.com

Richard D. Beckman, CEO
James A. Finkelstein, Chairman
Madeline Krakowsky, Vice President Circulation
Tracy Brater, Executive Director Creative Service

A complete resource guide for everyone involved in the infomercial industry.

593 **Journalism and Mass Communication Directory**
AEJMC
234 Outlet Pointe Boulevard
Suite A
Columbia, SC 29210-5667

803-798-0271; Fax: 803-772-3509
www.aejmc.org

Jennifer McGill, Executive Director

Published by the Association for Education in Journalism and Mass Communication. Features over 3,000 professionals, academics and graduate students; more than 400 journalism and mass communications schools and departments in four-year colleges and universities.
Frequency: Annual
Circulation: 5000
Founded in 1983
Mailing list available for rent

594 **Mediaweek Multimedia Directory**
Prometheus Global Media
770 Broadway
7th Floor
New York, NY 10003-9595

212-493-4100; Fax: 646-654-5368
www.prometheusgm.com

Richard D. Beckman, CEO
James A. Finkelstein, Chairman
Madeline Krakowsky, Vice President Circulation
Tracy Brater, Executive Director Creative Service

Focuses on the most powerful segments covering 9,000 media companies from the top 100 media markets for radio, broadcast TV, cable TV and daily newspapers. Also includes the top 300 consumer magazines, the top 150 trade magazines, networks, syndicators, sales representatives, multi-media holding companies, trade associations and rating organizations.
Frequency: Annual
Circulation: 800

595 **Medical Marketing and Media**
Haymarket Media Inc
114 W 26th St
4th Floor
New York, NY 10001-6812

212-206-0606; Fax: 212-638-6117
custserv@haymarketmedia.com
www.haymarket.com

William Bekover, Chief Executive Officer

Offers a comprehensive editorial resource to leaders, thinkers and executives dedicated to the promotion and commercialization of prescription drugs and other medical products and services in the US.
Frequency: Monthly
Circulation: 15000
Founded in 1996

596 **Navigator**
Promotional Products Association International
3125 Skyway Circle N
Irving, TX 75038-3539

972-252-0404; Fax: 972-258-3004
ppb@ppai.org
www.ppai.org

Paul Bellantone, President
Steven Meyer, Chairman of the Board
Marc Simon, Chair-Elect

An invaluable resource designed to educate distributors about PPAI supplier and business services members and the products they offer.
Frequency: Annual

597 **Online Advertising Playbook**
John Wiley & Sons

111 River St
Hoboken, NJ 07030-5790

201-748-6000; Fax: 201-748-6088
info@wiley.com
www.wiley.com

Stephen Smith, President & Chief Executive Officer
Vincent Marzano, Vice President

The book focuses on the enduring strategies necessary for marketers to have the knowledge base necessary to execute winning campaigns.

598 **Planning for Out of Home Media**
Traffic Audit Bureau for Media Measurement
271 Madison Ave
Suite 1504
New York, NY 10016-1012

212-972-8075; Fax: 212-972-8928
inquiry@tabonline.com
www.tabonline.com

Joseph Philport, President
Larry Hennessy, Vice President

Reference book contains up-to-date descriptions of O-O-H media and their production specifications, O-O-H local and national case history success stories and creative guidelines, travel trend data, new technologies and a glossary of O-O-H terminology.

599 **Print Media Production Source**
Standard Rate & Data Services
1700 E Higgins Rd
Des Plaines, IL 60018-5610

847-375-5000
800-851-7737; Fax: 847-375-5001
contact@srds.com
www.srds.com

Trish Delaurier, Publisher
George Carens, Executive Vice President

This service provides complete data on all critical ad production specifications for business and consumer magazines and newspapers. Production, traffic and graphic design personnel use this current, accurate resource to confirm essential production information so they can control production deadlines and budgets.
Frequency: Quarterly
Circulation: 800+

600 **R&D Ratios & Budgets**
Schonfeld & Associates Inc
1931 Lynn Circle
Libertyville, IL 60048-1323

847-816-4870
800-205-0030; Fax: 847-816-4872
saiinfo@saibooks.com
www.saibooks.com

Carol Greenhut, Publisher

The comprehensive annual report covers over 4,700 companies and 280 industries with information on current R&D budgets, R&D-to-sales ratios and R&D-to-gross margin ratios. Use it to track competition, set and justify R&D budgets, screen potential acquisitions, sell the laboratory and technology markets or plan new ventures and develop new products. Includes industry and R&D spender rankings.
Cost: $395.00
163 Pages
Frequency: Annual
ISBN: 1-932024-81-6

601 **Radio Creative Resources Directory**
Radio Advertising Bureau
1320 Greenway Dr
Suite 500
Irving, TX 75038-2547

972-753-6700
800-232-3131; Fax: 972-753-6727
jhaley@rab.com
www.rab.com

Erica Farber, President
Van Allen, EVP and CFO

A list of radio production companies and studios in response to advertisers and agencies who want to find companies that specialize in writing, casting and producing great radio spots. Our current edition contains over 60 companies including many Radio-Mercury Award winners.
Frequency: Annual

602 **Research & Development Growth Trends**
Schonfeld & Associates Inc
1931 Lynn Circle
Libertyville, IL 60048-1323

847-816-4870
800-205-0030; Fax: 847-816-4872
saiinfo@saibooks.com
www.saibooks.com

Carol Greenhut, Publisher

Information on publicly owned corporations that spend on R&D.
Cost: $395.00
273 Pages
Frequency: Annual
ISBN: 1-932024-85-9

603 **Salem Press Online Platform**
Grey House Publishing
4919 Route 22
PO Box 56
Amenia, NY 12501

800-221-1592; Fax: 201-968-0511
csr@salempress.com
online.salempress.com

The new Salem Press platform houses more than 500 titles including all of Salem's Health, Literature, History and Science titles in addition to select titles from the Grey House Publishing and H.W. Wilson product lines. Online access is free with each print purchase and includes an unlimited number of simultaneous users and remote access.

604 **Shop! Buyer's Guide**
Shop! Environments Association
4651 Sheridan Street
Suite 470
Hollywood, FL 33021

954-893-7300; Fax: 954-893-7500
service@shopassociation.org
www.shopassociation.org

Todd Dittman, Executive Director
Jo Rossman, Publisher/Editor
Karin Pryor, Director, Marketing
Karen Benning, Director, Communications

Guide to Shop! Association members: providers of store fixtures, POP displays, retail design services, visual presentation products, signage, materials, installation, and more.
Cost: $175.00
Frequency: Annual

605 **Suppliers Directory**
Eight-Sheet Outdoor Advertising Association
1244 Lake Park Ave
Galt, CA 95632

209-251-7622
800-847-3387; Fax: 209-251-7658
ddjesoaa@comcast.net
www.esoaa.com

Rebecca Lambert, Editor

Lists suppliers to the Eight-Sheet outdoor billboard industry; arranged by specialty. Includes definitions of basic industry terms.
Frequency: Annual
Circulation: 800

606 **The Art & Science of Managing a Content Marketing Strategy**
Direct Marketing Association
1120 Avenue of the Americas
New York, NY 10036-6700

212-768-7277; Fax: 212-302-6714
customerservice@the-dma.org
www.the-dma.org
Facebook, Twitter, LinkedIn

Lawrence M Kimmel, CEO

Effective Search Engine Optimization and Search Engine Marketing can have a dramatic effect on a website's performance and ROI. From optimization techniques to keyword bidding, our Search course offerings will give the insights and strategies to improve search results and efficiency.

607 **U.S. Sourcebook of R&D Spenders**
Schonfeld & Associates Inc
1931 Lynn Circle
Libertyville, IL 60048-1323

847-816-4870
800-205-0030; Fax: 847-816-4872
saiinfo@saibooks.com
www.saibooks.com

Carol Greenhut, Publisher

A directory of publicly owned corporations that spend on R&D, published annually. Corporate name, address, telephone number, and website are provided along with the names and titles of three senior executives, R&D budgets, sales, fiscal year closing, and more. Organized by state and ZIP code. The ideal reference for sales people who call on R&D centers and for economic development agencies.
Cost: $395.00
157 Pages
Frequency: Annual
ISBN: 1-932024-83-2

608 **US Source Book of Advertisers**
Schonfeld & Associates Inc
1931 Lynn Circle
Libertyville, IL 60048-1323
847-816-4870
800-205-0030; Fax: 847-816-4872
saiinfo@saibooks.com
www.saibooks.com

Carol Greenhut, Publisher

A directory of publicly owned corporations that advertise. Corporate name, address, telephone number and website are provided along with the names and titles of three senior executives, ad budgets, sales, fiscal year closing and more. The ideal reference for media sales, ad agency new business development and selling corporate services.
Cost: $395.00
224 Pages
Frequency: Annual
ISBN: 1-932024-55-7

609 **Who's Who: MASA Buyer's Guide to Blue Ribbon Mailing Services**
Mailing & Fulfillment Service Association
1421 Prince Street
Suite 410
Alexandria, VA 22314-2806

703-836-9200; Fax: 703-548-8204
www.mfsanet.org

Ken Garner, President
Bill Stevenson, Director Marketing

Offers a detailed listing of suppliers of equipment, products and services to the direct mail industry, most containing a description of the specific products they provide.
Frequency: Annual

610 **Workbook**
Scott & Daughters Publishing
6762 Lexington Avenue
Los Angeles, CA 90038-2482

323-856-0008
800-547-2688; Fax: 323-856-4368
www.workbook.com
Facebook, Twitter

Alexis Scott, Owner
Susan Haller, Managing Editor
Bill Daniels, Publisher

This directory, offered in four volumes, lists over 25,000 advertising agencies, art directors and freelance illustrators in the United States.
Frequency: Annual
Circulation: 35,000

611 **Workforce Growth Trends**
Schonfeld & Associates Inc
1931 Lynn Circle
Libertyville, IL 60048-1323

847-816-4870
800-205-0030; Fax: 847-816-4872
saiinfo@saibooks.com
www.saibooks.com

Carol Greenhut, Publisher

Information on all publicly owned corporations. Study is ordered by U.S. Department of Commerce SIC(Standard Industrial Classification) and alphabetically by company name within each SIC. Each companys historical information, average annual percent change, sales and shares are displayed.
Cost: $495.00
565 Pages
Frequency: Annual
ISBN: 1-932024-87-5

612 **Workforce Ratios & Forecasts**
Schonfeld & Associates Inc
1931 Lynn Circle
Libertyville, IL 60048-1323

847-816-4870
800-205-0030; Fax: 847-816-4872
saiinfo@saibooks.com
www.saibooks.com

Carol Greenhut, Publisher

This comprehensive annual study by Schonfeld & Associates covers over 6,600 companies and 420 industries. The information reported includes current number of employees, a forecast of projected employee headcount and growth rates, as well as sales per employee and gross margin per employee. Use it to track competition, set and justify manpower budgets, screen potential acquisitions, plan new ventures and develop new businesses. Includes rankings by size and growth rate.
Cost: $495.00
243 Pages
Frequency: Annual
ISBN: 1-932024-86-7

Industry Web Sites

613 **www.3af.org**
Asian American Advertising Federation
3AF consists of Asian American advertising agency principals, media, advertisers and strategic partners that seek to grow the Asian American advertising and marketing industry, raise public awareness of the Asian community, and increase professionalism within the industry.

614 **www.aaaa.org**
American Association of Advertising Agencies
To improve and strengthen the advertising agency business in the United States by counseling members on operations and management.

615 **www.aaasite.org**
American Academy of Advertising
An organization of advertising scholars and professionals with an interest in advertising and advertising education.

616 **www.aaf.org**
American Advertising Federation
The American Advertising Federation protects and promotes the wellbeing of advertising.

617 **www.aapor.org**
American Association for Public Opinion Research
The American Advertising Federation protects and promotes the wellbeing of advertising.

618 **www.acaweb.ca**
Association of Canadian Advertisers
The Association of Canadian Advertisers (ACA) is a national, not-for-profit association exclusively dedicated to serving the interests of companies that market and advertise their products and services in Canada. Resources for marketers are available on their website, including Confidential Consultations reports on areas such as agency remuneration, agency searches, agency contracts, performance reviews, production, legal issues, and programmatic advertising/marketing.

619 **www.adcouncil.org**
Advertising Council
The Ad Council is a private, non-profit organization that marshals volunteer talent from the advertising and communications industries, the facilities of the media, and the resources of the business and non-profit communities to deliver critical messages to the American public.

620 **www.aef.com**
Advertising Educational Foundation
The advertising industry's provider and distributor of educational content to enrich the understanding of advertising and it's role in culture, society and the economy.

621 **www.ahaa.org**
Association of Hispanic Advertising Agencies
Mission to grow, strengthen and protect the Hispanic marketing and advertising industry by providing leadership in raising awareness of the value of the Hispanic market opportunities and enhancing the professionalism of the industry.

622 **www.amsp.org**
Association of Marketing Service Providers
Formerly known as the Mailing & Fulfillment Service Association, the Association of Marketing Service Providers provides educational content, networking opportunities, and legislative advocacy.

623 **www.ana.net**
Association of National Advertisers
Provides indispensable leadership that drives marketing excellence and champions, promotes and defends the interests of the marketing community.

624 **www.apanational.com**
Advertising Photographers of America
Our goal is to establish, endorse and promote professional practices, standards and ethics in the photographic and advertising community.

625 **www.bbb.org**
Better Business Bureau
To be the leader in advancing marketplace trust.

626 **www.greyhouse.com**
Grey House Publishing
Authoritative reference directories for business information and general reference including advertising, communications, marketing and media markets. Users can search the online databases with varied search criteria allowing for custom searches by product category, geographic area, sales volume, keyword, subject and more. Full Grey House catalog and online ordering also available.

627 **www.iaany.org**
International Advertising Association
Promoting the value of advertising globally, advocacy of freedom of commercial speech and consumer choice and encouraging industry self regulation.

628 **www.iab.net**
Interactive Advertising Bureau
Dedicated to the growth of the interactive advertising marketplace, of interactive's share of total marketing spend, and of its members' share of total marketing spend

629 **www.icomagencies.com**
International Communications Agency Network
The international organization of museums and museum professionals which is committed to the conservation, continuation and communication to society of the world's natural and cultural heritage, present and future, tangible and intangible.

630 **www.ifcaonline.com**
Insurance and Financial Communicators Association
An international association for insurance and financial communicators offering professional development and networking.

631 **www.imanetwork.org**
Internet Marketing Association
Seeks to provide members with the chance to learn, network, and establish Internet Marketing best practices. Members are in fields such as sales, marketing, business ownership, programming, and creative development.

632 **www.juniorbillboard.org**
Junior Billboard Association
Formerly known as the Eight-Sheet Outdoor Advertising Association, the organization has helped establish and enforce industry standards for eight-sheet billboard advertising.

633 **www.magnetglobal.org**
MAGNET: Marketing & Advertising Global Network
Provides a way for member agencies to share their experience, knowledge and ideas with other agencies in other parts of the world.

634 **www.marketingpower.com**
American Marketing Association
It is a professional association for individuals and organizations involved in the practice, teaching and study of marketing and advertising worldwide.

635 **www.mfsanet.org**
Mailing & Fulfillment Service Association
The national trade association for the mailing and fulfillment services industry.

636 **www.newsmediaalliance.org**
News Media Alliance
Formerly known as the Newspaper Association of America, the News Media Alliance repre-

sents large daily papers, non-daily/small-market publications, as well as digital and multiplatform products across North America.

637 **www.oaaa.org**
Outdoor Advertising Association of America
To provide leadership, services and standards to promote, protect and advance the outdoor advertising industry.

638 **www.ppa.org**
Promotional Products Association International
To lead the industry by expanding the market, providing indispensable products and services, and enhancing our members' professionalism and success.

639 **www.sherunsit.org**
She Runs It
Formerly known as the League of Advertising Women and Advertising Women of New York, the organization was founded as the first women's association in the communications industry. Members now include women in marketing, media, and tech.

640 **www.shopassociation.org**
Shop! Environments Association
Formed in the merger of the Association for Retail Environments and Point of Purchase Advertising International, Shop! is a global trade association devoted to enhancing retail environments and experiences for members through research, education, and networking.

641 **www.signs.org**
International Sign Association
Supports, promotes and improves the sign industry, which sustains the nation's retail industry.

642 **www.tabonline.com**
Traffic Audit Bureau for Media Measurement
An independent third party provider of standardized and valid circulation measures for out of home media.

643 **www.thearf.org**
Advertising Research Foundation
The Advertising Research Foundation (ARF) conducts research, experiments, and market tests to better guide marketers in the use of evolving technology. Research areas include ad effectiveness & ROI, analytics & data science, audience & media measurement, and creative & branded content.

644 **www.thefcs.org**
Financial Communications Society
The FCS is devoted to improving professional standards in financial marketing communications, with a membership comprised of managers in advertising, marketing, PR, IR, corporate communications, and social and digital media.

645 **www.thevab.Com**
Video Advertising Bureau
VAB is a research and marketing organization for the video industry, providing insights and custom analysis, while embracing emerging technologies.

646 **www.tradepromo.org**
Trade Promotion Management Association
Provides members with information, education and research on the dynamic world of trade promotion, including co op advertising, market development funds, slotting fees, off invoice deductions, channel promotions and more.

Associations

647 **AACC International**
3340 Pilot Knob Road
St. Paul, MN 55121-2055

651-454-7250
800-328-7560; Fax: 651-454-0766
aacc@scisoc.org
www.aaccnet.org
Facebook, Twitter, LinkedIn, Pinterest

Lydia Tooker Midness, Chair of the Board
Robert L. Cracknell, President
Dave L. Braun, Treasurer
Samuel Millar, Director
Anne M. Birkett, Director

Formerly the American Association of Cereal Chemists, a non-profit organization of members who are specialists in the use of cereal grains in foods.
2000 Members
Founded in 1915

648 **Agribusiness Council(ABC)**
P.O. Box 5565
Washington, DC 20016

202-296-4563; Fax: 202-244-4694
info@agribusinesscouncil.org
www.agribusinesscouncil.org

Nicholas E. Hollis, President/CEO

The Agribusiness Council (ABC) is a private, nonprofit/tax-exempt, membership organization dedicated to strengthening U.S. agro-industrial competitiveness through programs which highlight international trade and development potentials as well as broad issues which encompass several individual agribusiness sectors and require a food systems approach. Examples of such issues are commercialization of new tech/crops, environmental impacts, human resource development, trade and investment policy.
Founded in 1967

649 **Agricultural & Applied Economics Association**
555 E Wells Street
Suite 1100
Milwaukee, WI 53202-6600

414-918-3190; Fax: 414-276-3349
info@aaea.org
www.aaea.org
Facebook, Twitter, LinkedIn, Blogger, Google+

Dawn Thilmany McFadden, President
Madhu Khanna, President-Elect

The Agricultural & Applied Economics Association (AAEA) is a not-for-profit association serving the professional interests of members working in agricultural and broadly related fields of applied economics. Members of the AAEA are employed by academic or government institutions, as well as in industry and not-for-profit organizations, and engage in a variety of teaching, research, and extension/outreach activities.
3000 Members
Founded in 1910

650 **Agricultural Retailers Association**
1156 15th St NW
Suite 500
Washington, DC 20005-1745

202-457-0825; Fax: 202-457-0864
info@aradc.org
www.aradc.org
Facebook, Twitter

Rod Wells, Chair
Daren Coppock, President & CEO
Richard Gupton, SVP, Public Policy & Counsel
Donnie Taylor, VP, Membership & Corp Relations
Melisa Augusto, Dir., Comm. & Marketing

The Agricultural Retailers Association (ARA) is a nonprofit trade association that serves as the political voice of agricultural retailers and distributors. We're advocates, educators, and champions for the American ag retailer. The Agricultural Retailers Association (ARA) is a nonprofit trade association that serves as the political voice of agricultural retailers and distributors. We're advocates, educators, and champions for the American ag retailer.
Frequency: Annual
Founded in 1993

651 **Agriculture Council of America**
11020 King St
Suite 205
Overland Park, KS 66210-1201

913-491-1895; Fax: 913-491-6502
www.agday.org
Facebook, Twitter, Flickr, YouTube

Greg Horstmeier, Chair
Jonathon Ebert, Vice Chair
Amy Bradford, Secretary/Treasurer

The Agriculture Council of America (ACA) is an organization uniquely composed of leaders in the agriculture, food and fiber communities dedicated to increasing the public awareness of agriculture's vital role in our society.
75 Members
Founded in 1973

652 **Agriculture Federal Credit Union**
1400 Independence Ave SW
Room SM2
Washington, DC 20250

202-479-2270
800-368-3552; Fax: 202-479-3877
members@agriculturefcu.org
www.agfed.org
Facebook, Twitter

Margie Click, President/CEO
Theodora Ezekwerre, Senior Vice President
Tom Bowles, Senior Vice President
Clifton Jeter, Chair
Stephen J Hawkins, Vice Chair

Agriculture Federal Credit Union meets the highest standards for long term financial soundness. AgFed's workplace environment motivates and empowers employees to provide quality service to our members. AgFed offers a wide range of financial services and products to satisfy the diverse needs of our members throughout their lifetimes. AgFed has state-of-the-art technology designed to meet our members' needs.
23000 Members
Founded in 1934

653 **American Agricultural Law Association**
P.O. Box 5861
Columbia, SC 29250

803-728-3200; Fax: 360-423-2287
ellenberg@aglaw-assn.org
www.aglaw-assn.org

Mike Traxinger, President
Scott Heidner, Executive Director

The AALA is a membership organization that focuses on the legal needs of the agricultural community.
600 Members
Founded in 1980

654 **American Agriculture Movement**
AAM National Secretary/Treasurer
11232 Road K
Liberal, KS 67901

620-482-6306
aaminc.org

David Senter, President
Crystal Carson, Executive Vice President
Arthur Chaney, Vice President
Jacqueline Reed, Recording Secretary
John Willis, Treasurer

The creation of the AAM has provided a farmer-created, farmer-built organization within which farmers themselves have been the leaders, speakers and organizers; empowering farmers as they had not been in the past, to speak for and advocate for themselves.
Founded in 1977

655 **American Angus Association**
3201 Frederick Ave
St Joseph, MO 64506-2997

816-383-5100; Fax: 816-233-9703
angus@angus.org
www.angus.org
Facebook, Twitter, Pinterest, Youtube, Vimeo

Mark McCully, CEO
David A. Dal Porto, President
Jerry Connealy, Vice President
Chuck Grove, Treasurer

The American Angus Association is the nation's largest beef registry association. Our goal is to serve the beef cattle industry, and increase the production of consistent, high quality beef that will better satisfy consumers throughout the world.
36000 Members
Founded in 1873

656 **American Association of Crop Insurers**
1 Massachusetts Ave NW
Suite 800
Washington, DC 20001-1401

202-789-4100; Fax: 202-408-7763
aaci@mwmlaw.com
www.cropinsurers.com

Michael Davenport, President

The American Association of Crop Insurers is a nonprofit industry service organization representing the interests of insurance companies, agents, and adjusters involved in the Federal crop insurance program. AACI's reinsured company members write more than 80 percent of the crop insurance sold by private companies nationwide. AACI's primary purpose is governmental relations with Congress, the U.S. Department of Agriculture, and other executive agencies whose decisions influence the program.
25 Members
Founded in 1980

657 **American Beekeeping Federation**
3525 Piedmont Road
Bldg 5 Suite 300
Atlanta, GA 30305-1509

404-760-2875; Fax: 404-240-0998
info@abfnet.org
www.abfnet.org

Molly Sausaman, Executive Director

The ABF is a national organization that continually works in the interest of all beekeepers, large or small, and those associated with the industry to ensure the future of the honey bee. Our members share a common interest to work toward better education and information for all segments of the industry in the hope of increasing our chances for survival in today's competitive world.
4700 Members
Founded in 1943

658 **American Brahman Breeders Association**

3003 South Loop West
Suite 520
Houston, TX 77054

713-349-0854; Fax: 713-349-9795
abba@brahman.org
www.brahman.org
Facebook, Twitter, YouTube, Instagram

Craig Fontenot, President
Mike England, Vice President
Pasquale Swaner, Secretary/Treasurer

American Brahman Breeders is a beef crossbreeding organization that plays a big role in the United States and beyond.
Founded in 1924

659 **American Dairy Science Association**

1800 South Oak Street
Suite 100
Champaign, IL 61820-6974

217-356-5146; Fax: 217-398-4119
adsa@assochq.org
www.adsa.org
RSS

Rich Erdman, President
Paul Kindstedt, Vice President
Catharine Kuber Perry, Executive Director
Paul Kononoff, Editor-in-Chief

The American Dairy Science Association (ADSA) is an international organization of educators, scientists, and industry representatives who are committed to advancing the dairy industry and keenly aware of the vital role the dairy sciences play in fulfilling the economic, nutritive, and health requirements of the world's population. Together, ADSA members have discovered new methods and technologies that have revolutionized the dairy industry.
3000 Members
Founded in 1998
Mailing list available for rent

660 **American Farm Bureau Federation**

600 Maryland Ave SW
Suite 1000 W
Washington, DC 20024

202-406-3600
www.fb.org
Facebook, Twitter, Instagram, YouTube

Zippy Duvall, President
Dale Moore, Executive VP
Sarah Brown Dirkes, Executive Dir., Industry Relations
Lynne Finerty, Exec. Dir., Presidential Initiative

Federation of state Farm Bureaus with 6 million member families.
Founded in 1919

661 **American Feed Industry Association**

American Feed Industry Association
2101 Wilson Blvd
Suite 916
Arlington, VA 22201-3047

703-524-0810; Fax: 703-524-1921
afia@afia.org
www.afia.org
Facebook, Twitter, LinkedIn, YouTube

Constance Cullman, President & CEO
Rob Cooper, Executive Director Of IFEEDER
Victoria Broehm, Communications Director
Louise Calderwood, Regulatory Affairs Director
Paul Davis, Dir., Quality, Education & Safety

AFIA is the world's largest organization devoted exclusively to representing the business, legislative and regulatory interests of the U.S. animal feed industry and its suppliers. AFIA also is the recognized leader on international industry developments. Members include more than 500 domestic and international companies and state, regional and national associations.
690 Members
Founded in 1909

662 **American Forage and Grassland Council**

PO Box 867
Berea, KY 40403

800-944-2342
tina.bowling@afgc.org
www.afgc.org
Facebook, Twitter, YouTube

The American Forage and Grassland Council (AFGC) is an international organization made up of 20 affiliate councils in the United States and Canada. Our primary objective is to promote the profitable production and sustainable utilization of quality forage and grasslands. Mission is to be recognized as the leader and voice of economically and environmentally sound forage agriculture.
2700 Members

663 **American Guernsey Association**

1224 Alton Darby Creeek Road
Suite G
Columbus, OH 43228

614-864-2409; Fax: 614-864-5614
info@usguernsey.com
www.usguernsey.com

David Coon, President
Chris Lang, 1st Vice President
Brian Dinderman, 2nd Vice President
Robin Alden, Executive Secretary
Victoria L. Baker, Purebred Publishing President

The AGA's mission is to provide and promote programs and services to enhance the value and profitability of the Guernsey breed for the members, owners and dairy industry worldwide.
900 Members
Founded in 1877

664 **American Hemp Association**

Home Page:
www.americanhempassociation.com
Facebook

Jason Lauve, Contact

Dedicated to promoting hemp farmers and companies in the Americas through education, advocacy, and expansion.
Founded in 2012

665 **American Hereford Association**

PO Box 014059
Kansas City, MO 64101

816-842-3757; Fax: 816-842-6931
aha@hereford.org
www.hereford.org
Facebook

Jack Ward, Executive Vice President
Shane Bedwell, Chief Operating Officer
Leslie Matthews, Chief Financial Officer
Amy Cowen, Youth Activities Director
Diane Meyer, Communications Director

Association for people in the Hereford cattle industry.
Founded in 1910

666 **American Jersey Cattle Association**

6486 E Main Street
Reynoldsburg, OH 43068-2362

614-861-3636; Fax: 614-861-8040
www.usjersey.com
Facebook, Twitter

Neal Smith, CEO/Executive Secretary
Vickie J. White, Treasurer
Kimberly Billman, Director Of Communications
Cari Wolfe, Director Of Research
Kristin Paul, Director of Field Service

They improve and promote the Jersey cattle breed.
2178 Members
Founded in 1868

667 **American Livestock Breeds Conservancy (ALBC)**

PO Box 477
33 Hillsboro St
Pittsboro, NC 27312

919-542-5704; Fax: 919-545-0022
www.livestockconservancy.org
Facebook, Twitter, LinkedIn, Blogger, YouTube

Alison Martin, Executive Director
Angelique Thompson, Operations Director
Michele Brane, Information Manager
Charlene Couch, Program Manager
Brittany Sweeney, Communications Manager

The American Livestock Breeds Conservancy is a nonprofit membership organization working to protect over 180 breeds of livestock and poultry from extinction. Included are asses, cattle, goats, horses, sheep, pigs, rabbits, chickens, ducks, geese, and turkeys.
Founded in 1977

668 **American Meat Science Association**

201 W Springfield Ave
Ste 1202
Champaign, IL 61822-7676

217-356-5370
800-517-AMSA; Fax: 888-205-5834; Fax: 217-356-5370
information@meatscience.org
www.meatscience.org
Facebook, Twitter, LinkedIn, Vimeo

Dean Pringle, President
Collette Kaster, Chief Executive Officer
Deidrea Mabry, Chief Operating Officer
Morgan Pfeiffer, Membership & Marketing Manager
Rachel Adams, Youth Programs Coordinator

The American Meat Science Association is a broad-reaching organization of individuals that discovers, develops, and disseminates its collective meat science knowledge to provide leadership, education, and professional development. Our passion is to help meat science professionals achieve previously unimaginable levels of performance and reach even higher goals.
Founded in 1964

669 **American Phytopathological Society**

3340 Pilot Knob Road
Saint Paul, MN 55121-2097

651-454-7250
800-328-7560; Fax: 651-454-0766
aps@scisoc.org
www.apsnet.org
Facebook, Twitter, LinkedIn, YouTube, Pinterest

Amy Hope, Executive VP
Carol Ericson, Director, Operations
Kim Davis, Director, Finance
Greg Grahek, Director, Publications
Linda Schmitt, Dir., Foundation, Award Program

APS is a diverse global community of scientists that: provides credible and beneficial information related to plant health; advocates and participates in the exchange of knowledge with the public, policy makers, and the larger scientific community; and promotes and provides opportunities for scientific communication, career preparation, and professional development for its members.
4500 Members
Founded in 1908

670 **American Poultry Association**
PO Box 306
Burgettstown, PA 15021

724-729-3459
www.amerpoultryassn.com

Mark Podgwaite, President
Bart Pals, Vice President

The mission of the association is to promote and protect the standard bred poultry industry in all its phases. To encourage and protect poultry shows as being the show window of the industry, an education for both breeders and the public and a means of interesting young future breeders.

671 **American Seed Trade Association**
1701 Duke Street
Suite 275
Alexandria, VA 22314-3415

703-837-8140; Fax: 703-837-9365
info@amseed.com
www.betterseed.org
Facebook, Twitter, YouTube, Google+

John Latham, Chair
Andrew LaVigne, President/CEO
Bethany Shively, VP, Strategic Communications
Fan-Li Chou, VP, Scientific Affairs & Policy
Ann Jorss, Chief Operating Officer

ASTA's mission is to be an effective voice of action in all matters concerning the development, marketing and movement of seed, associated products and services throughout the world. ASTA promotes the development of better seed to produce better crops for a better quality of life.
700+ Members
Founded in 1883

672 **American Sheep Industry Association**
9785 Maroon Circle
Suite 360
Englewood, CO 80112

303-771-3500; Fax: 303-771-8200
eatlamb@wildblue.net
www.sheepusa.org
Facebook, Twitter

Benny Cox, President
Susan Shultz, Vice President
Peter Orwick, Executive Director
Larry Kincaid, Chief Financial Officer
Rita Kourlis Samuelson, Deputy Dir. & Dir., Wool Marketing

ASI is the national organization representing the interests of sheep producers located throughout the United States. From East to West, farm flocks to range operations, ASI works to represent the interests of all producers. ASI is a federation of 45 state sheep associations as well as individual members.
82000 Members
Founded in 1865

673 **American Society for Enology and Viticulture**
PO Box 1855
Davis, CA 95617-1855

530-753-3142; Fax: 530-753-3318
society@asev.org
www.asev.org
Twitter, LinkedIn, Picasa

Patty Skinkis, President
Dan Howard, Executive Director
Daniel Friedlander, Publications & Tech Coordinator
Dean Spencer, Office Coordinator
Michelle Taillon, Event Coordinator

The American Society for Enology and Viticulture (the sciences of winemaking and grape growing) is a 501 (c)(6), tax exempt professional society dedicated to the interests of enologists, viticulturists, and others in the fields of wine and grape research and production throughout the world. Our membership includes professionals from wineries, vineyards, academic institutions and organizations.
2400+ Members
Founded in 1950

674 **American Society for Horticultural Science**
1018 Duke Street
Alexandria, VA 22314

703-836-4606; Fax: 703-836-2024
webmaster@ashs.org
www.ashs.org
Facebook, Twitter, LinkedIn, Pinterest

Louise Ferguson, President
Michael W. Neff, Executive Director
Heather Hilko, Member Services & Subscriptions
Negar Mahdavian, Conferences
Sylvia DeMar, Publication Submissions

A cornerstone of research and education in horticulture and an agent for active promotion of horticultural science.
1200 Members
Founded in 1903

675 **American Society of Agricultural Consultants**
605 Columbus Ave South
New Prague, MN 56071

952-758-5811; Fax: 952-758-5813
asac@gandgcomm.com
www.agconsultants.org
Facebook, Twitter, LinkedIn, YouTube

Amy Keith McDonald, Executive Vice President

An association representing the full range of agricultural consultants which serves as an information, resource, and networking base for its members. The specific purpose of ASAC is to foster the science of agricultural consulting in all its varied fields; to promote the profession and maintain high standards under which the members conduct their service to the public; hold meetings for the exchange of ideas and the study of the profession of agricultural consulting;
181 Members
Founded in 1963

676 **American Society of Agricultural and Biological Engineers**
2950 Niles Rd
St Joseph, MI 49085-8607

269-429-0300
800-371-2723; Fax: 269-429-3852
hq@asabe.org
www.asabe.org
Facebook, Twitter, LinkedIn, YouTube

Darrin Drollinger, Executive Director
Joe Walker, Publication Director
Dolores Landeck, Director/Public Affairs
Scott Cedarquist, Dir., Standards & Tech Activities
Mark Crossley, Director/Membership

The American Society of Agricultural and Biological Engineers is an educational and scientific organization dedicated to the advancement of engineering applicable to agricultural, food, and biological systems. With members in more than 100 countries. The Society's Agricultural, Food and Biological Engineers develop efficient and environmentally sensitive methods of producing food, fiber, timber, and renewable energy sources.
8000 Members
Founded in 1907
Mailing list available for rent: 10000 names at $120 per M

677 **American Society of Agronomy**
5585 Guilford Road
Madison, WI 53711-5801

608-273-8080; Fax: 608-273-2021
membership@agronomy.org
www.agronomy.org
Facebook, Twitter, LinkedIn, RSS

Nick Goeser, Chief Executive Officer
Wes Meixelsperger, CFO & Director, Meetings
Sara Uttech, Director, Governance
Susan Chapman, Director, Member Services
Ian Popkewitz, Director, IT & Operations

Promote human welfare through advancing the acquisition and dissemination of scientific knowledge concerning the nature, use improvement and interrelationships of plants, soils, water and environment. The society shall promote effective research, disseminate scientific information, facilitate technology transfer, foster high standards of education, strive to maintain high standards of ethics, promote advancements in this profession and cooperate with other organizations of similar objectives.
11000 Members
Founded in 1907

678 **American Society of Animal Science**
PO Box 7410
Champaign, IL 61826-7410

217-356-9050; Fax: 217-568-6070
asas@asas.org
www.asas.org
Facebook, Twitter, LinkedIn, YouTube

Glenn C. Duff, President
Meghan C. Wulster-Radcliffe, Chief Executive Officer
Justin E. Bartlett, Director, Programming & Operations

The American Society of Animal Science is a membership society that supports the careers of scientists and animal producers in the United States and internationally. The American Society of Animal Science fosters the discovery, sharing and application of scientific knowledge concerning the responsible use of animals to enhance human life and well-being.
ISSN: 0021-8812
Founded in 1908

679 **American Society of Consulting Arborists**
9707 Key West Avenue
Suite 100
Rockville, MD 20850-3992

301-947-0483; Fax: 301-990-9771
asca@mgmtsol.com
www.asca-consultants.org
Twitter, LinkedIn, Pinterest

Richard Adkins, President
Th,rŠse Oetegen Clemens, Executive Director
Grace Jan, Senior VP, Meetings Management
Julianne Clark, Coordinator, Member Services
Julie Hill, Marketing Director

The industry's premier professional association focusing solely on arboricultural consulting. Consulting Arborists are authoritative experts on trees, consulting property owners, municipalities, attorneys, insurance professionals and others on tree disease, placement, preservation and dispute resolution in addition to providing consulting and expert testimony in the legal, insurance and environmental arenas.
Founded in 1967

680 **American Society of Farm Managers and Rural Appraisers (ASFMRA)**
720 S. Colorado Boulevard
Suite 360-S
Glendale, CO 80246

303-758-3513; Fax: 303-758-0190
info@asfmra.org

www.asfmra.org
Facebook, Twitter, LinkedIn, Plaxo

Brian Stockman, Executive VP/CEO
Alex Clark, Dir., Membership/Marketing/Comm.
Mya Sadler, Dir., Education/Accreditation
Brian Sheppelman, Dir., Finance/Administration

The ASFMRA provides members with the resources, information, and leadership that enable them to provide valuable services to the agricultural community. The focus of the ASFMRA is providing education and networking opportunities for a professional group of members providing farm and ranch management, rural and real property appraising, review appraisal, and agricultural consulting services to the private and public sectors and to the governmental and lending communities.
2100+ Members
Founded in 1929

681 **American Soybean Association**
12125 Woodcrest Executive
Suite 100
Creve Coeur, MO 63141-5009

314-576-1770
800-688-7692; Fax: 314-576-2786
info@soy.org
www.soygrowers.com
Facebook, Twitter, YouTube, RSS

Steve Censky, CEO
Vickie Wilks, COO
Brian Vaught, CFO
Christy Seyfert, Exec. Director, Government Affairs
Bill Schuermann, Exec. Director, Industry Relations

The American Soybean Association (ASA) is recognized by the majority of U.S. soybean growers and industry for its vital role as their domestic and international policy advocate. ASA is clearly leading an expanding soybean value-chain, with farmers capturing a growing percentage. ASA's development of influential and effective grower leaders is recognized throughout the agriculture industry.
22000 Members
Founded in 1920

682 **American Trade Association for Cannabis & Hemp**
712 H St. NE
Suite 712
Washington, DC 20002

atach.email@gmail.com
www.atach.org

Michael Bronstein, Co-Founder & Lead Consultant

Promotes the expansion, protection, and preservation of businesses in the legal trade of industrial, medical, and recreational cannabis and hemp products.

683 **Animal Agriculture Alliance**
2101 Wilson Blvd
Suite 916-13
Arlington, VA 22201

703-562-5160; Fax: 703-524-1921
info@animalagalliance.org
www.animalagalliance.org
Facebook, Twitter

Sarah Novak, Chair
Kay Johnson Smith, President and CEO
Hannah Thompson, VP, Communications
Casey Kinler, Director, Membership & Marketing
Emily Solis, Communications Specialist

The Animal Agriculture Alliance, is a broad based coalition of individual farmers, ranchers, producer organizations, suppliers, packer-processors, scientists, veterinarians and retailers. The Alliance with its members are interested in helping consumers better understand the role animal agriculture plays in providing a safe, abundant food supply to a hungry world.
3000 Members
Founded in 1987

684 **Aquatic Plant Management Society**
7922 NW 71st Street
Gainesville, FL 32653

FAX 601-634-5502
webmaster@apms.org
www.apms.org
Facebook, Twitter, LinkedIn, Bloggr

The Aquatic Plant Management Society, Inc. is an international organization of scientists, educators, students, commercial pesticide applicators, administrators, and concerned individuals interested in the management and study of aquatic plants. The Aquatic Plant Management Society (APMS) strives to promote environmental stewardship through scientific innovation and development of technology related to integrated plant management in aquatic and riparian systems.
Founded in 1961

685 **Association for Arid Lands Studies**
601 Indiana Avenue
PO Box 45004
Lubbock, TX 79409-5004

806-742-3667; Fax: 806-742-1286
gay.riggan@ttu.edu
www.iaff.ttu.edu
Facebook

Jorge Salazar-Bravo, International Director

To promote the university's special mission of the interdisciplinary study of arid and semi-arid environments and the human relationship to these environments from an international perspective.
200 Members
Founded in 1977

686 **Association of American Feed Control Officials**
1800 South Oak Street
Suite 100
Champaign, IL 61820-6974

217-356-4221; Fax: 217-398-4119
aafco@aafco.org
www.aafco.org
Facebook

The Association of American Feed Control Officials (AAFCO) is a voluntary membership association of local, state and federal agencies charged by law to regulate the sale and distribution of animal feeds and animal drug remedies.Although AAFCO has no regulatory authority, the Association provides a forum for the membership and industry representation to achieve two main goals: Ensure consumer protection and safeguarding the health of animals and humans.
Founded in 1909

687 **Association of American Seed Control Officials**
Utah Department of Agriculture
350 N Redwood Road
PO Box 146500
Salt Lake City, UT 84114-6500

801-848-8543; Fax: 801-538-7189
walshm@purdue.edu
www.seedcontrol.org

Jason Goltz, President
Jeff Claxton, First Vice President
Jan Morawski, Second Vice President
Greg Helmbrecht, Treasurer
Don Robison, Secretary

The Association of American Seed Control Officials is an organization of seed regulatory officials from the United States and Canada. The members meet to discuss mutual concerns of seed law enforcement, to be updated on new developments in the seed industry, and to update the Recommended Uniform State Seed Law which the organization developed and maintains as model law.
Founded in 1949

688 **Association of Equipment Manufacturers**
6737 West Washington Street
Suite 2400
Milwaukee, WI 53214-5647

414-272-0943; Fax: 414-272-1170
aem@aem.org
www.aem.org
Facebook, Twitter, LinkedIn, YouTube

Jeffrey R. Reed, Chair

A trade association that provides global services to companies that manufacture equipment and products in the following industries: Agriculture, Construction, Forestry, Mining and Utility.
900+ Members

689 **Biodynamic Farming and Gardening Association**
1661 N Water Street
Suite 307
Milwaukee, WI 53202

262-649-9212; Fax: 262-649-9213
info@biodynamics.com
www.biodynamics.com
Facebook

Thea Maria Carlson, Executive Director
Kaitlin Downs, Community Outreach Coordinator
Anna McAvoy-Emerick, Director, Operations & Finance
Rebecca Briggs, Communications Coordinator
Raphael Guzman, Special Events Organizer

The Biodynamic Farming and Gardening Association (BDA) is an association of individuals and organizations in North America who are committed to the transformation of the whole food system, from farm to table, and who draw inspiration from the spiritual-scientific insights of Rudolf Steiner. Biodynamics is a worldwide movement for the renewal of agriculture based on an understanding of the spiritual forces at work in nature and in human social life.
Founded in 1938

690 **Canadian Hemp Trade Alliance**
6815 8 St. NE
Suite 200
Calgary, AB T2E 7H7

403-219-6262
ted@hemptrade.ca
www.hemptrade.ca
Twitter, YouTube

Ted Haney, President
Danielle Burges, Office Manager

Promotes Canadian hemp and hemp products globally. Members include farmers, processors, manufacturers, researchers, entrepreneurs, and marketers.
Founded in 2003

691 **Cape Cod Cranberry Growers' Association**
1 Carver Square Boulevard
PO Box 97
Carver, MA 02330

508-866-7878; Fax: 508-866-4220
info@cranberries.org
www.cranberries.org
Facebook

Steve Ward, President
Brian Wick, Executive Director

Bonnie Soule, Special Projects Coordinator
Patti Silvia, Membership & Office Coordinator
Dawn Gates, Dir., Member & Financial Services

Promotes the success of US and Canadian cranberry growers through health, agricultural and environmental stewardship research and education.
Founded in 1888

692 **Communicating for AMERICA**
112 E Lincoln Avenue
PO Box 677
Fergus Falls, MN 56537

218-739-3241
800-432-3276; Fax: 218-739-3832
memberbenefits@cainc.org
www.communicatingforamerica.org
Facebook

Stephen Rufer, Chair & General Council
Patty Strickland, President/ Chief Operations Officer
Angela Nelson, Chief Financial Officer
Milt Smedsrud, Founder & Chair Emeritus

Strives to promote health, well-being and advancement of people in agriculture and agribusiness.
40M Members
Founded in 1972

693 **Community Alliance with Family Farmers**
36355 Russell Boulevard
PO Box 363
Davis, CA 95616

530-756-8518
800-892-3832; Fax: 530-756-7857
info@caff.org
www.caff.org
Facebook, Twitter, YouTube, Flickr

Paul Towers, Executive Director
David Runsten, Policy Director
Holly Markham, Development & Admin. Director
Ben Thomas, Program Director, Farm To Market
Evan Wiig, Dir., Membership & Communications

Mission is to build a movement of rural and urban people to foster family-scale agriculture that cares for the land, sustains local economies and promotes social justice.
Cost: $47.95
Founded in 1978

694 **Corn Refiners Association**
1701 Pennsylvania Ave NW
Suite 950
Washington, DC 20006-5806

202-331-1634; Fax: 202-331-2054
comments@corn.org
www.corn.org
Facebook, Twitter, LinkedIn, StumbleUpon, Google+

John Bode, President & CEO
Rob Ritchie, Chair
Steve Gardner, Chief Operating Officer
Keniece Barbee, Director, Member Services
Johnelle Brown, Director, Operations

Supports carbohydrate research programs through grants to colleges, government laboratories and private research centers.
8 Members
Founded in 1913

695 **Council for Agricultural Science and Technology**
4420 West Lincoln Way
Ames, IA 50014-3447

515-292-2125
cast@cast-science.org
www.cast-science.org
Facebook, Twitter, LinkedIn, YouTube, Blogspot, Schooltube

Kent G. Schescke, Executive Vice President
Melissa Sly, Director, Council Operations
Dan Gogerty, Managing Communications Editor
Megan Wickham, Scientific Editor
Gale Osborne, Office Manager/Events Coordinator

CAST, through its network of experts, assembles, interprets, and communicates science-based information to policymakers, the media, the private sector, and the public. Its primary work is the publication of task force reports, commentaries, special publications, and issue papers written by volunteer experts-economists, legal experts and scientists from many disciplines. These documents cover issues related to food sciences, agricultural technology, animal sciences, and plant and soil sciences.
700+ Members
Founded in 1972

696 **Crop Insurance and Reinsurance Bureau Inc.**
440 First St NW
Suite 500
Washington, DC 20001

202-544-0067; Fax: 202-330-5255
mtorrey@cropinsurance.org
www.cropinsurance.org

Zane Vaughn, Chair
Mike Torrey, Executive Vice President
Tara Smith, Federal Affairs Vice President
Barbara Patterson, Director of Government Relations
Perry Harlow, Manager Of Membership & Events

The Crop Insurance Research Bureau is a national trade association made up of insurance providers and related organizations that provide a variety of insurance products to farmers. CIRB companies are big and small and offer private hail/fire coverage on growing crops, as well as participate in the federal crop insurance program which offers a greater variety of subsidized insurance products from yield based coverages to revenue products.
Founded in 1964

697 **Crop Science Society of America**
5585 Guilford Road
Madison, WI 53711-1086

608-273-8086; Fax: 608-273-2021
membership@agronomy.org
www.agronomy.org
Facebook, Twitter, LinkedIn

Nick Geoser, Chief Executive Officer
Wes Meixelsperger, Chief Financial Officer
Sara Uttech, Director, Governance
Susan Chapman, Director, Member Services
Ian Popkewitz, Director, IT & Operations

Seeks to advance research, extension, and teaching of all basic and applied phases of the crop sciences.
4700 Members
Founded in 1955

698 **CropLife America**
1156 15th St NW
Suite 400
Washington, DC 20005-1752

202-296-1585; Fax: 202-463-0474
Info@croplifeamerica.org
www.croplifeamerica.org
Facebook, Twitter, LinkedIn, YouTube, RSS Feeds

Christopher Novak, President & CEO
Kellie Bray, Chief Of Staff
Beau Greenwood, EVP, Gov. Relations & Pub. Affairs
Rachel G. Lattimore, EVP, Legal & General Counsel
Genevieve O'Sullivan, VP, Communications & Marketing

A trade association of the manufacturers, formulators, and distributors of agricultural crop protection, pest control, and biotechnology products. Membership is composed of companies that produce, sell and distribute virtually all the active ingredients used in crop protection chemicals.
86 Members
Founded in 1933

699 **Ecological Farming Association**
2901 Park Ave.
Suite D-2
Soquel, CA 95073

831-763-2111
info@eco-farm.org
eco-farm.org
Facebook, Twitter, Instagram

Andy Fisher, Executive Director
Abbie Erskine, Administrative Coordinator
Deborah Yashar, Marketing & Communications Director
Emily Becker, Conference Manager
Gabi Salazar, Program Director

EcoFarm is a nonprofit educational organization that promotes sustainable agriculture.
Founded in 1981

700 **Equipment Marketing & Distribution Association (EMDA)**
PO Box 1347
Iowa City, IA 52244

319-354-5156
pat@emda.net
www.emda.net
Facebook, Twitter, LinkedIn

Patricia A. Collins, Executive Vice President

EMDA is the result of the 2008 merger of FEWA and AIMRA. EMDA members are devtoed to the marketing of specialized equipment: agricultural, outdoor power, light industrial, forestry, irrigation, turf and grounds maintenance, lawn and garden and parts/components for thosesegments of industry.
250 Members
Founded in 1945

701 **Farm Equipment Manufacturers Association**
1000 Executive Parkway Drive
Suite 100
St. Louis, MO 63141-6369

314-878-2304
info@farmequip.org
www.farmequip.org
Facebook, Twitter, LinkedIn

Matt Westendorf, President
Vernon Schmidt, Executive Vice President
Tricia Kidd, Accounting & Meeting Services
Kristi Ruggles, Communications Director
Sarah Stevener, Meetings & Membership

An information gathering and distributing organization for farm equipment manufacturers and suppliers. The association offers a forum for marketing equipment through networking, communications, and technology.
730+ Members
Founded in 1950

702 **Farm Foundation**
1301 W 22nd St
Suite 615
Oak Brook, IL 60523-2197

630-571-9393; Fax: 630-571-9580
mary@farmfoundation.org
www.farmfoundation.org

Facebook, Twitter, YouTube, RSS Feeds, Blogger

Shari Rogge-Fidler, President & CEO
Time Brennan, VP, External Relations
Martha King, VP, Programs & Projects
Jessie Atchison, VP, Marketing & Communications
Amy Keane, Senior Director, Finance

A publicly supported nonprofit organization working to improve the economic health and social well-being of US agriculture, the food system and rural people by helping private and public sector decision makers identify and understand forces that will shape the future.
Founded in 1993

703 **Fertilizer Institute**
425 Third Street, SW
Suite 950
Washington, DC 20024

202-962-0490; Fax: 202-962-0577
information@tfi.org
www.tfi.org
Facebook, Twitter, LinkedIn, YouTube

Corey Rosenbusch, President & CEO
Bradley Cheng, Director, Accounting
Mariana Gallo, Senior Director, Conferences
Christopher Glen, Director, Communications
Roberta Rosenberg, Senior Director, Marketing

TFI is the leading voice in the fertilizer industry, representing the public policy, communication and statistical needs of producers, manufacturers, retailers and transporters of fertilizer. Issues of interest to TFI members include security, international trade, energy, transportation, the environment, worker health and safety, farm bill and conservation programs to promote the use of enhanced efficiency fertilizer.
325 Members
Founded in 1883

704 **Foundation for Agronomic Research**
107 S State St
Suite 300
Monticello, IL 61856-1968

605-692-6280
www.farmresearch.com

John Jones, Director

The Foundation for Agronomic Research (FAR) is a non-profit (501(c)(3) research and education foundation, created in 1980 by the Board of Directors of the Potash & Phosphate Institute (PPI), now the International Plant Nutrition Institute (IPNI), to expand its research efforts beyond that possible with PPI's resources and mandate. The mission of FAR is to improve the economic vigor and sustainability of agriculture in N.A. and around the world, while protecting and enhancing the environment.
Founded in 1980

705 **Fresh Produce Association of the Americas**
590 East Frontage Road
PO Box 848
Nogales, AZ 85628

520-287-2707; Fax: 520-287-2948
info@freshfrommexico.com
www.freshfrommexico.com

Lance Jungmeyer, President
Allison Moore, Vice President
Emmis Yubeta, Director, Membership Programs
Georgina Felix Berrueto, Director, Operations
Conchita Singh, Dir., Accounting & Human Resources

The Fresh Produce Association of the Americas and its members help to ensure North America's uninterrupted access to fresh, high-quality, healthy and delicious Mexican-grown fruits and vegetables. The FPAA is the leading agent of produce trade at the U.S.-Mexico border and across the country.
125+ Members
Founded in 1944

706 **Fresh Produce and Floral Council**
2400 E. Katella Ave.
Ste. 330
Anaheim, CA 92806

714-739-0177; Fax: 714-739-0226
info@fpfc.org
www.fpfc.org

Don Gann, Interim Executive Director
Emma McBride-Taylor, Event & Communication Specialist

Promotes through communication and education, fresh fruit, vegetable and floral products. Acts as a trade organization providing an environment for better communication within the industry.
600+ Members
Founded in 1965

707 **Hemp Industries Association**
707-874-3648
www.thehia.org
Instagram

Jody McGinness, Executive Director
Sarah Gardner, Membership Director
Ryann Hinch, Operations Director

Advances the hemp economy and educates the market for the benefit of our members, the public, and the planet.
Founded in 1994

708 **Herb Growing and Marketing Network**
PO Box 245
Silver Springs, PA 17575-0245

717-393-3295; Fax: 717-393-9261
herbworld@aol.com
www.herbworld.com

Maureen Rogers, Director

The Herb Growing & Marketing Network is the largest trade association for the herb industry. We are an information service. We have a library of over 3000 books, subscribe to over 200 periodicals, monitor blogs of all types and search the Web looking for resources and research on the herb industry that we can pass on to our members.
Cost: $48.00
1000 Members
Founded in 1990

709 **Holstein Association USA**
1 Holstein Place
PO Box 808
Brattleboro, VT 05302-0808

802-254-4551
800-952-5200; Fax: 802-254-8251
info@holstein.com
www.holsteinusa.com
Facebook, Twitter, You Tube

Corey Geiger, President
Jonathan Lamb, Vice President
John M. Meyer, Executive Secretary
Barbara Casna, Treasurer

Holstein Association USA maintains records on over 22 million Registered Holsteinsr, collecting and analyzing production, type and genetic data to provide useable information that enables dairy producers to improve their businesses by breeding better cows. The Holstein Association works to help dairy producers recognize the full potential of their herds.
30000 Members
Founded in 1885

710 **Institute of Food and Agricultural Sciences**
University of Florida
PO Box 110180
Gainesville, FL 32611-0180

352-392-1971
ifas.ufl.edu
Facebook, Twitter

Ruth Borger, Asst. Vice President

Research and development for Florida's agriculture, natural resources and food-related industries.

Founded in 1964

711 **International Association of Fairs and Expositions**
3043 E Cairo Street
PO Box 985
Springfield, MO 65802

417-862-5771
800-516-0313; Fax: 417-862-0156
iafe@fairsandexpos.com
www.fairsandexpos.com
Facebook, Twitter, You Tube

Marla Calico, President/CEO

The International Association of Fairs and Expositions (IAFE) is a voluntary, non-profit corporation whose members provide services and products that promote the overall development and improvement of fairs, shows, expositions, and allied fields. Mission is to lead in representing and facilitating the evolving interests of agricultural fairs, exhibitions and show associations.

1300 Members
Founded in 1885

712 **International Association of Operative Millers**
12351 w. 96th Terrace
Suite 100
Lenexa, KS 66215

913-338-3377; Fax: 913-338-3553
info@iaom.info
www.iaom.info
Facebook, Twitter, LinkedIn

Melinda Farris, CEO
Annette Peterson, Office Coordinator
Cynthia Malone, Director, Meetings & Exhibitions

The International Association of Operative Millers (IAOM) is comprised of grain millers and allied trades representatives devoted to the advancement of education and training opportunities in the grain milling industries. Among its members, IAOM promotes a spirit of fellowship and cooperation, enhances their proficiency, and advances their interests in industry activities.

1500 Members
Founded in 1896

713 **International Fruit Tree Association**
16020 Swingley Ridge Rd.
Suite 300
Chesterfield, MO 63017

636-449-5083; Fax: 636-449-5051
dungey@ifruittree.org
www.ifruittree.org
Facebook, Twitter

Lisa Jenereaux, President
Jeff Cleveringa, Vice President
Chris Hedges, Treasurer

The association promotes research on, and understanding of, Intensive Orchard Systems.

Founded in 1958

714 **International Maple Syrup Institute**
5072 Rock St.
RR#4
Spencerville, ON KOE 1XO

860-974-1235; Fax: 802-868-5445
agrofor@ripnet.com
www.internationalmaplesyrupinstitute.com

Pam Greene, President
Tom Zaffis, Vice President
Daivd Campbell, Treasurer
Jean Lamontagne, Executive Director

The International Maple Syrup Institute (IMSI) was founded to promote and protect pure maple syrup and other pure maple products. The organization provides an important international framework for communication, information exchange and cooperation on a variety of issues related to the production, sale and marketing of pure maple syrup. In addition, the Institute has been a strong monitor for adulteration around the world, protecting the integrity of maple products.
15M Members
Founded in 1975

715 **International Weed Science Society**
University of Arkansas
1366 W. Altheimer Drive
Fayetteville, AR 72704

479-575-3984; Fax: 479-575-3975
secretary@iwss.info
www.iwss.info

Samunder Singh, President
Do-Soon Kim, Vice President
Te-Ming Paul Tseng, Treasurer
Luis Avila, Secretary

The International Weed Science Society (IWSS) was formed in 1975, by individuals from Europe, North America, South America, and the Asian-Pacific area, to deal with global weed science issues. The IWSS is a worldwide scientific organization, open to all who are interested in weeds and their control. The formation of IWSS was promoted actively by the six existing regional weed science societies. The purpose of IWSS is to supplement and complement their vital role.
Founded in 1975

716 **Irrigation Association**
8280 Willow Oaks Corp. Dr.
Suite 400
Fairfax, VA 22031-4507

703-536-7080; Fax: 703-536-7019
info@irrigation.org
www.irrigation.org

Deborah M. Hamlin, Chief Executive Officer
Rebecca J. Bayless, Finance Director
Brad Binzer, Operations Coordinator
Anne Blankenbiller, Senior Communications Manager
Janie C. Hakim, Membership Manager

Membership organization for irrigation equipment and system manufacturers, dealers, distributors, designers, consultants, contractors and end users.
1600 Members
Founded in 1949

717 **Livestock Marketing Association**
10510 NW Ambassador Drive
Kansas City, MO 64153-1278

816-891-0502
800-821-2048; Fax: 816-891-0552
lmainfo@lmaweb.com
www.lmaweb.com
Facebook, Twitter, YouTube, Instagram

Mark Mackey, Chief Executive Officer
Sheri Crist, Chief Financial Officer
Jennifer Aiman, Vice President, Operations
Chelsea Good, VP, Government & Industry Affairs
Kristen Parman, Vice President, Membership Services

We are committed to the support and protection of the local livestock auction markets. Auctions are a vital part of the livestock industry, serving producers and assuring a fair, competitive price through the auction method of selling.
800 Members
Founded in 1947

718 **Marijuana Business Association**

info@mjba.net
www.mjba.net
Facebook, Twitter, YouTube

A leading national business-to-business organization in legal cannabis. Provides members with business intelligence, networking, and business opportunities.
Founded in 2013

719 **Maryland and Virginia Milk Producers Cooperative**
1985 Isaac Newton Square West
Reston, VA 20190-5094

703-742-6800; Fax: 703-742-7459
www.mdvamilk.com

Lindsay P. Reames, Director, External Relations

Known for being a leader in the dairy industry, the Eastern Milk Producers Cooperative has a reputation for integrity, service and high quality products.
Founded in 1920

720 **Mid-America Christmas Tree Association**

740-815-6107
midamericachristmastreeassoc@gmail.com
www.midamericachristmastree.com

Donna Cackler, Executive Administrator

Represents members in the Christmas tree industry and provides them with up-to-date information.

721 **Midwest-SouthEastern Equipement Dealers Association**
5330 Wall St
Suite 100
Madison, WI 53718-7929

608-240-4700; Fax: 608-240-2069
gmanke@medaassn.com
mseda.com

Gary W. Manke, President & CEO
Lance Formwalt, Legal Counsel
Jay Dee Shattuck, Legislative Director
Denise Collins, Accounting Department

Our mission is to promote the farm, industrial, outdoor power equipment, dairy and farmstead mechanization industry and to provide services that will assist Association members in becoming more profitable and better equipped to operate in today's business environment.
Founded in 1991

722 **NCBA CLUSA**
1401 New York Ave NW
Suite 1100
Washington, DC 20005-2160

202-638-6222; Fax: 202-638-1374
ncba@ncba.coop
www.ncba.coop
Facebook, Twitter, YouTube, Google+

Doug O'Brien, President & CEO
Valeria Roach, EVP & CFO
Larry Thomas, Chief HR & Admin. Officer
Tamela Blalock, VP, Cooperative Relations
Matthew Buzby, VP, International Operations

Leading US organization strengthening the cooperative form of business to empower people and improve quality of life worldwide. To make cooperatives a strong, distinct and unified sector, recognized by the American public. Our member co-ops operate in the areas including, agricultural supply and marketing, children, energy, food distribution, healthcare and housing.
1800 Members
Founded in 1916

723 **National 4-H Council**
7100 Connecticut Ave
Chevy Chase, MD 20815-4934

301-961-2800; Fax: 301-961-2894
info@fourhcouncil.edu
www.4-h.org
Facebook, Twitter, LinkedIn, Google+, Pinterest, YouTube

Jennifer Sirangelo, President/CEO
Gary Tang, Chief Financial Officer
Andy Ferrin, SVP & Chief Strategy Officer
Artis Stevens, SVP & Chief Marketing Officer
Jill Bramble, SVP & Chief Development Officer

Works to advance the 4-H youth development movement, building a world in which youth and adults learn, grow, and work together as catalysts for positive change. National 4-H Council partners with the Cooperative Extension System and other organizations to provide technical support and training, develop curricula, create model programs and promote positive youth development to fulfill its mission. National 4-H Council also manages the National 4-H Conference.
7M Members
Founded in 1902

724 **National Agri-Marketing Association**
11020 King St
Suite 205
Overland Park, KS 66210-1201

913-491-6500; Fax: 913-491-6502
agrimktg@nama.org
www.nama.org
Facebook, Twitter, LinkedIn, Flicker, You Tube

Jennifer Pickett, Executive VP & CEO
Sherry Pfaff, Chief Operating Officer
Janae Prewitt, Manager, Information Services
Debbie Brummel, Student Coordinator

Marketing and communication suppliers, including trade publications, radio and television broadcast sales organizations, premium/incentive manufacturers, printers, marketing research firms, photographers and related professionals.
3500 Members
Founded in 1957

725 **National Agricultural Aviation Association**
1440 Duke Street
Alexandria, VA 22314

202-546-5722; Fax: 202-546-5726
information@agaviation.org
www.agaviation.org
Facebook

Andrew Moore, Chief Executive Officer
Lindsay Barber, Director, Meetings & Marketing
Marisa Beam, Registration, Membership & Programs
Deanna Burke, Director, Finance & Operations
Jay Calleja, Manager, Communications

NAAA supports the interests of small business owners and pilots licensed as professional commercial aerial applicators who use aircraft to enhance food, fiber and bio-fuel production, protect forestry and control health-threatening pests. NAAA provides networking, educational, government relations, public relations,

recruiting and informational services to its members.
1900 Members
Founded in 1966

726 **National Alliance of Independent Crop Consultants**
349 E Nolley Dr
Collierville, TN 38017-3538

901-861-0511; Fax: 901-861-0512
AllisonJones@NAICC.org
www.naicc.org

Matt Winslow, President
Grant McMillan, President Elect
Laurie Bennett, Secretary
Angela Dawson, Treasurer

The national society of agricultural professionals who provide research and advisory services. Memebers comprise 40 states and several foreign countries, and have expertise in the production of most crops grown around the world.
500+ Members
Founded in 1978

727 **National Association of Agricultural Educators (NAAE)**
300 Garrigus Building
University of Kentucky
Lexington, KY 40546-0215

859-257-2224
800-509-0204; Fax: 859-323-3919
jay_jackman@ffa.org
www.naae.org
Facebook, Twitter, YouTube, Pinterest, Flickr

Alissa Smith, Chief Executive Officer
Wm. Jay Jackman, Executive Director
Olivia Thomas, Specialist, Marketing & Comm.
Ashley Hood, Membership Coordinator
Sarah Warren, Meeting Planner & Program Assistant

Professionals providing agricultural education for the global community through visionary leadership, advocacy and service. NAAE seeks to advance agricultural education and promote the professional interests and growth of agriculture teachers as well as recruit and prepare students who have a desire to teach agriculture.
7800+ Members
Founded in 1948

728 **National Association of Agricultural Fairs**
Tennessee Department of Agriculture
440 Hogan Road
PO Box 40627
Nashville, TN 37220

615-837-5160
800-342-8206; Fax: 615-837-5194
pick.tn@tn.gov
www.picktnproducts.org
Facebook, Twitter, Pinterest

US and Canadian representatives of state/provincial agencies that are responsible for the support of educational and agricultural fairs.
35 Members
Founded in 1966

729 **National Association of Animal Breeders**
PO Box 1033
Columbia, MO 65205-1033

573-445-4406; Fax: 573-446-2279
naab-css@naab-css.org
www.naab-css.org

Paul Hunt, Chair
Christopher England, Director
Bobby Fair, Director
Earl Souva, Director
Roy Wilson, Director

The purpose of the National Association of Animal Breeders (NAAB) as defined by its By-Laws is to unite those individuals and organizations engaged in the artificial insemination of cattle and other livestock into an affiliated federation operating under self-imposed standards of performance and to conduct and promote the mutual interest and ideals of its members.
20 Members
Founded in 1975

730 **National Association of Cannabis Businesse s**
1918 E. Lafayette Place
Milwaukee, WI 53202

720-926-6881
info@nacb.com
www.nacb.com
Facebook, Twitter, LinkedIn

Gina Kranwinkel, Chief Executive Officer
Mark Gorman, Executive VP & COO
Tom Nolasco, Dir., Legal & Strategic Initiatives
Meggan Hau, Operations Manager
Mary Clifton, Cannabis Research Advisor

A self-regulatory organization devoted to transparency, accountability, and legal compliance in the cannabis industry. The organization and its members are committed to building a successful, profitable industry that promotes public health and safety, ethical conduct, corporate responsibility, and social justice.

731 **National Association of County Agricultural Agents**
6584 W Duroc Road
Maroa, IL 61756

217-794-3700; Fax: 217-794-5901
exec-dir@nacaa.com
www.nacaa.com
Facebook, Twitter

J. Craig Williams, President
Bill Burdine, President-Elect
Phillip Durst, Vice President
Connie Strunk, Secretary
Lenny Rogers, Treasurer

The NACAA strives to: Advance the professional status of Extension agents and specialists with agriculture-related Extension appointments. Encourage, promote, and provide professional improvement for all members. Provide for the exchange of ideas, methods, and techniques. Represent professional interests of members in matters of public policy and affairs. Promote public confidence, esteem, and respect for Cooperative Extension. Recognize excellence in Cooperative Extension nationwide.
3850 Members
Founded in 1917
Mailing list available for rent: 3500 names at $500 per M

732 **National Association of Extension 4-H Youth Development Professionals**
701 Exposition Place
Suite 206
Raleigh, NC 27615

919-232-0112
contact@nae4hydp.org
www.nae4hydp.org
Facebook, Twitter

Suzanne Boarts, President
Robby Kelly, VP, Finance & Operations
Steve McKinley, VP, Professional Development
Bernie Wiesen, VP, Marketing & Outreach
Alyssa Walden, VP, Programs

Designed to meet the needs of youth development professionals by maximizing the use of technology, provide progressive levels of professional development, elevate the quality of youth development work through scholarship, research and practice, advocate for the 4-H youth development profession.
3600 Members
Founded in 1946

733 **National Association of State Departments of Agriculture**
4350 North Fairfax Drive
#910
Arlington, VA 22203

202-296-9680; Fax: 703-880-0509
nasda@nasda.org
www.nasda.org
Facebook, Twitter

Barb Glenn, Chief Executive Officer
Martha Dale, Chief Financial & Strategy Officer
Amanda Culp, Communications & Events Director
Elizabeth Rowland, Human Resources Director
Lisa Benson, NASDA Foundation Executive Director

Represents the state departments of agriculture in the development, implementation and communication of sound public policy and programs which support and promote the American agricultural industry, while protecting consumers and the environment.
Founded in 1916

734 **National Association of Wheat Growers**
415 Second St NE
Suite 200
Washington, DC 20002

202-547-7800; Fax: 202-546-2638
wheatworld@wheatworld.org
www.wheatworld.org
Facebook, Twitter

Chandler Goule, CEO
Josh Tonsager, VP, Policy & Communications
Caitlin Eannello, Director, Communications

Represents wheat producers in Washington, D.C.
Founded in 1950

735 **National Bison Association**
8690 Wolff Court
Suite 200
Westminster, CO 80031

303-292-2833; Fax: 303-845-9081
david@bisoncentral.com
www.bisoncentral.com
Facebook

Dave Carter, Executive Director
Jim Matheson, Assistant Director
Barb Dowdy, Bookkeeper
Karen Conley, Communications Director
Anita Shaver, Design & Production Manager

Formed to promote the production, marketing and preservation of bison. The mission of the National Bison Association is to bring together stakeholders to celebrate the heritage of American bison/buffalo, to educate, and to create a sustainable future for our industry.
1100+ Members
Founded in 1995

736 **National Christmas Tree Association**
16020 Swingley Ridge Rd
Suite 300
Chesterfield, MO 63017-6030

636-449-5070; Fax: 636-449-5051
info@realchristmastrees.org
www.realchristmastrees.org
Facebook, Twitter, YouTube, Blogger

Tim O'Connor, Executive Director
Ann O'Connor, Director, Programs & Membership
Dugald Kell, Jr., President
Steve Meier, President-Elect

The National Christmas Tree Association (NCTA) is the national trade association representing the Christmas tree industry. NCTA represents more than 700 active member farms, 29 state and regional associations, and more than 4,000 affiliated businesses that grow and sell Christmas trees or provide related supplies and services.
700 Members
Founded in 1955
Mailing list available for rent: 5100 names

737 **National Cotton Council of America**
National Cotton Council of America
7193 Goodlett Farms Pkwy
Cordova, TN 38016

901-274-9030; Fax: 901-725-0510
www.cotton.org

Kent Fountain, Chair
Gary Adams, President & Chief Executive Officer
Ken Burton, Exec. Dir. US Cotton Trust Protocol
Bruce Atherley, Exec. Dir. Cotton Council Intl.
John Gibson, Vice President, Member Services

The National Cotton Council is a unifying force of the U.S. cotton industry, bringing together representatives from the seven industry segments in the 17 cotton-producing states of the Cotton Belt to work out common problems and develop programs of mutual benefit.
35 Members

738 **National Cottonseed Products Association**
866 Willow Tree Circle
Cordova, TN 38018-6376

901-682-0800; Fax: 901-682-2856
info@cottonseed.com
www.cottonseed.com

National association of cottonseed products. NCPA is an organization of firms and individuals engaged in the processing of cottonseed and the marketing of cottonseed products, as well as cottonseed. These include oil mills, refiners, product dealers and product brokers.
200 Members
Founded in 1929

739 **National Council of Agricultural Employers**
525 9th Street, NW
Suite 800
Washington, DC 20004

202-629-9320; Fax: 202-728-0303
www.ncaeonline.org
Facebook

Michael Marsh, President & CEO
Jon Devaney, Chair
Michael Lalich, Vice-Chair
Maureen Torrey, Treasurer
Diane Kurrle, Secretary

NCAE represents Agricultural Employer interests before Congress and Regulatory/Administrative bodies such as the Departments of Labor, Homeland Security, Agriculture, the Occupational Safety and Health Administration, and the Environmental Protection Agency.
250 Members
Founded in 1964

740 **National Crop Insurance Services**
8900 Indian Creek Pkwy
Suite 600
Overland Park, KS 66210-1567

913-685-2767
800-951-6247; Fax: 913-685-3080
webmaster@ag-risk.org
www.ag-risk.org
Facebook, Twitter

Dr. Thomas P. Zacharias, President & CEO
Linda Kovelan, Director Executive Services
Laurie Langstraat, VP, Public Relations
Sherri Scharff, VP, Membership Services
Dana Ford, Director, Human Resources

NCIS is an association of insurance companies writing insurance for damage by hail, fire and other weather perils to growing crops.
60+ Members
Founded in 1915

741 **National Dairy Herd Information Association**
PO Box 930399
Verona, WI 53593-0399

608-848-6455; Fax: 608-260-7772
jmattison@requestltd.com
www.dhia.org

Allen Chester, President
Kevin Haase, Vice President
Jay Mattison, CEO/Administrator
Leslie Thoman, Accounting/Bookkeeping
Steven Sievert, Quality Certification Services

The objective is to promote accuracy, credibility and uniformity of DHI records. To represent the DHI system on issues involving other National and International organizations
65M Members

742 **National Farmers Organization**
528 Billy Sunday Road
Suite 100, PO Box 2508
Ames, IA 50010-2508

515-292-2000
800-247-2110; Fax: 866-629-3976
nfo@nfo.org
www.nfo.org
Facebook, Twitter, YouTube

Paul Olson, President, Chair of the Board
Bruce Shultz, Vice President

National Farmers defines itself by its sophisticated commodity marketing and ag risk management programs and services. Through National Farmers MaximumMarketing, producers market their commodities in pooled groups, and their bank accounts benefit.
30M Members
Founded in 1955

743 **National Farmers Union**
20 F Street NW
Suite 300
Washington, DC 20001

202-554-1600
800-347-1961; Fax: 202-554-1654
nfu.org
Facebook, Twitter, YouTube, Instagram

Rob Larew, President
Patty Edelburg, Vice President
Dave Velde, General Counsel
Ethan Whitmore, Vice President, Operations
Martha Van Dale, Director, Finance

Farmers Union helped shape national policy, organized cooperative businesses that thrive today, delivered educational programs designed to build rural leaders, and provided farmers and ranchers with opportunities to be at the table.
Founded in 1902

744 **National Fisheries Institute**
7918 Jones Branch Dr
Suite 700
Mc Lean, VA 22102-3319

703-752-8880; Fax: 703-752-7583
bsb@nfi.org
www.aboutseafood.com
Facebook, Twitter, LinkedIn, Pinterest, google+

John Connelly, President

The National Fisheries Institute is a non-profit organization dedicated to education about seafood safety, sustainability, and nutrition. From vessels at sea to your favorite seafood restaurant, our diverse member companies bring delicious fish and shellfish to American families. NFI promotes the US Dietary Guidelines that suggest Americans include fish and shellfish in their diets twice per week for longer, healthier lives.
241 Members
Founded in 1945

745 **National Future Farmers of America Organization**
PO Box 68960
6060 FFA Drive
Indianapolis, IN 46268-0960

317-802-6060
www.ffa.org
Facebook, Twitter, LinkedIn, Instagram, YouTube

Mark Poeschl, Chief Executive Officer
David Schapker, Chief Financial Officer
Christine White, Chief Program Officer

Organization prepares future generations for careers in agriculture.
650K Members
Founded in 1928

746 **National Grain and Feed Association**
1250 I St NW
Suite 1003
Washington, DC 20005-3939

202-289-0873; Fax: 202-289-5388
ngfa@ngfa.org
www.ngfa.org
Facebook, Twitter, LinkedIn, Flickr

Randall Gordon, President & CEO
Todd E. Kemp, Vice President of Marketing
Charles M. Delacruz, SVP, General Counsel & Secretary
David A. Fairfield, SVP, Feed Services
Sarah Gonzalez, Dir. Comm & Digital Media

NGFA is the national trade association of grain elevators, feed and feed ingredient manufacturers, grain and oilseed processors, exporters, livestock and poultry integrators, and firms providing products and services to the industry.
Founded in 1896

747 **National Hay Association**
Ellington Agricultural Center
432 Hogan Rd.
Nashville, TN 37220

615-837-5560
800-707-0014; Fax: 615-523-1385
NHAExecOffice@gmail.com
www.nationalhay.org
Facebook

Dan Wray, President
John Russell, First Vice President
Clayton Geralds, Second Vice President
Sue Arnold, Executive Director

The National Hay Association is made up of people that are involved in the production, sale and transportation of forage products across the United States and the world. As an organization we work for the good of the hay industry through knowledge among members, to following government legislation. We operate as an independent organization with no commitments or ties to any government groups.
750 Members
Founded in 1895

748 **National Hemp Association**
80 M St. SE
Suite 130
Washington, DC 20003

202-706-3911
www.nationalhempassociation.org
Facebook, Twitter, Google+

Erica Stark, Executive Director
Anna Chanthavongseng, Assistant Executive Director

Supports the growth and development of all aspects of the industrial hemp industry through education, creating community, and working with government, scientific, and industry professionals.

749 **National Institute for Animal Agriculture**
13570 Meadowgrass Dr
Suite 201
Colorado Springs, CO 80921-3058

719-538-8843; Fax: 719-538-8847
niaa@animalagriculture.org
www.animalagriculture.org
Facebook, Twitter, LinkedIn, YouTube

J.J. Jones, Executive Director
Morgan Young, Director, Communications & Outreach
Emily Grund, Communications Coordinator

NIAA is an organization that satisfies your needs, concerns and interests about the animal agriculture industry. NIAA's purpose is quite simple - to provide a source for individuals, organizations, and the entire animal agriculture industry to obtain information, education and solutions for challenges facing animal agriculture.
250 Members

750 **National Oilseed Processors Association**
1300 L St NW
Suite 1020
Washington, DC 20005-4168

202-842-0463; Fax: 202-842-9126
thammer@nopa.org
www.nopa.org

Thomas A. Hammer, President
David J. Hovermale, EVP, Gov. Relations
Katie Vassalli, Director, Regulatory Affairs
Jeanne L. Seibert, Office Administrator
Steve O'Nan, Chair

NOPA now represents oilseed crushers of soybeans, canola, flaxseed, safflower seed and sunflower seed. NOPA represents twelve (12) regular member firms engaged in the actual processing of oilseeds, and eight (8) associate member firms who are consumers of vegetable oil or oilseed meal, including some refiners.
Founded in 1989

751 **National Onion Association**
822 7th St
Suite 510
Greeley, CO 80631-3941

970-353-5895; Fax: 970-353-5897
kreddin@onions-usa.org
www.onions-usa.org
Twitter, LinkedIn, Pinterest, RSS

Greg Yielding, Executive Vice President
Doug Bulgrin, President
Rene Hardwick, Dir., Public & Industry Relations
Courtney Herbst, Admin. Assistant & Accounting

The National Onion Association (NOA) is the official organization representing growers, shippers, brokers, and commercial representatives of the U.S. onion industry.
500 Members
Founded in 1913
Mailing list available for rent: 600 names

752 **National Pork Producers Council**
122 C Street NW
Suite 875
Washington, DC 20001

202-347-3600
800-937-7675; Fax: 202-347-5265
news@nppc.org
www.nppc.org
Facebook, Twitter, LinkedIn, Pinterest, Flickr, Swinecast

Neil Dierks, Chief Executive Officer
Jeff Smouse, Chief Financial Officer
Liz Wagstrom, Chief Veterinarian
Nick Giordano, VP & Counsel, Global Gov. Affairs
Dallas Hockman, VP, Industry Relations

The National Pork Producers Council conducts public-policy outreach on behalf of its affiliated state associations, enhancing opportunities for the success of U.S. pork producers and other industry stakeholders by establishing the U.S. pork industry as a consistent and responsible supplier of high-quality pork to the domestic and world markets.
44 Members

753 **National Potato Council**
1300 L St NW
Suite 910
Washington, DC 20005-4107

202-682-9456; Fax: 202-682-0333
spudinfo@nationalpotatocouncil.org
www.nationalpotatocouncil.org
Facebook, Twitter, YouTube

Kam Quarles, Chief Executive Officer
Mike Wenkel, Chief Operating Officer
Hollee Alexander, VP, Industry Relations & Events
Hillary Hutchins, Dir., Member Outreach & Programs
Mark Szymanski, Director, Public Relations

The National Potato Council is the advocate for the economic well-being of U.S. potato growers on federal legislative, regulatory, environmental, and trade issues.
45000 Members
Founded in 1948

754 **National Potato Promotion Board**
4949 S. Syracuse St.
#400
Denver, CO 80237

303-369-7783; Fax: 303-369-7718
potatoesusa.com
Facebook, Twitter, YouTube, Pinterest, Instagram

Blair Richardson, President & CEO
Carrie Connelly, Exec. Admin. & Human Resources Dir.
Monica Heath, VP, Finance & Policy
John Toaspern, Chief Marketing Officer
Chelsea Gray, Meetings & Events Manager

Also known as the US Potato Board. Organized to operate a national marketing program to position potatoes as low calorie, nutritious vegetables and to facilitate market expansion into domestic and export sales.
2500+ Members
Founded in 1971

755 **National Sunflower Association**
2401 46th Avenue SE
Suite 206
Mandan, ND 58554-4829

701-328-5100
888-718-7033; Fax: 701-328-5101
larryk@sunflowernsa.com
www.sunflowernsa.com
Facebook, YouTube

John Sandbakken, Executive Director
Tina Mittelsteadt, Business & Office Manager

Trade association for the sunflower industry.
20000 Members
Founded in 1981
Printed in 4 colors on glossy stock

756 **National Turkey Federation**
1225 New York Avenue NW
Suite 400
Washington, DC 20005

202-898-0100; Fax: 202-898-0203
info@turkeyfed.org
www.eatturkey.com
Facebook, Twitter, YouTube, Pinterest

Joel Brandenberger, President
Beth Breeding, VP, Communications & Marketing
Hayden Demos, Coordinator, Member Services
Shelby Shaw, Manager, Communications

(NTF) is the national Advocate for all segments of the $8 billion turkey industry, providing services and conducting activities that increase demand for its members' products. The federation also protects and enhances its members' ability to effectively and profitably provide wholesome, high quality, nutritious turkey products.
264 Members
Founded in 1947

757 **National Young Farmer Educational Association**
PO Box 20326
Montgomery, AL 36120

334-546-9951
888-332-2668; Fax: 334-213-0421
nyfea-main@nyfea.org
www.nyfea.org
Facebook, Twitter, Google+

Gordon Store, Executive Vice President
Donnie Carter, President-Elect
Clovia Ketchum, Secretary

To promote the personal and professional growth of all people involved in agriculture.

758 **Nebraska Alfalfa Dehydrators Association**
8810 Craig Dr
Overland Park, KS 66212-2916

913-341-0562
800-678-9192; Fax: 913-341-0564
wcobbkc@sbcglobal.net
www.nebada.org

Carlton Bert, President
David Rhea, Vice President
Chris Healey, Director

Information for the processors and suppliers in the alfalfa industry.
Founded in 1941

759 **North American Farm Show Council**
590 Woody Hayes Drive
Columbus, OH 43210

614-292-4278; Fax: 614-292-9448
gamble.19@osu.edu
www.farmshowcouncil.org

Matt Jungmann, President
Jerry Sinift, First Vice President
Marti Smith, Executive Coordinator

Members are agriculture trade show sponsors and suppliers of services to these shows. Provides members with education, communication and evaluation. Provides the best possible marketing showcase for exhibitors and related products to the farmer/rancher/producer customer.
37 Members
Founded in 1972

760 North American Millers' Association
600 Maryland Ave SW
Suite 825 W
Washington, DC 20024

202-484-2200; Fax: 202-488-7416
generalinfo@namamillers.org
www.namamillers.org
Facebook, Twitter, LinkedIn, Flickr

Jane DeMarchi, President
Dale Nellor, VP, Government & Technical Affairs
Christopher Clark, VP, Communications & Administration
Kim Cooper, Manager, Government Affairs
Holly Wiedemann, Administrative Coordinator

Trade association representing the wheat, corn, oat and rye milling industry. NAMA members operate one hundred and seventy mills in thirity-eight states and Canada. Their aggregate production of more than one hundred and sixty million pounds per day is approximately ninety-five percent of the industry capacity in the U.S.
45 Members
Founded in 1902

761 Northeastern Weed Science Society
P.O. Box 25
Woodstown, NJ 08098

315-209-7580
northeasternweedscience@hotmail.com
www.newss.org

Serves the Northeastern US by bringing together those who are concerned with the knowledge of weeds and their control, cooperates with other scientific societies to promote research, education and outreach activities and publishes scientific and practical information of value concerning weed sciences and other fields.
Founded in 1946

762 Oregon Tilth
2525 SE 3rd Street
Corvallis, OR 97333

503-378-0690
877-378-0690; Fax: 541-753-4924
organic@tilth.org
www.tilth.org
Facebook, Twitter, Instagram

Chris Schreiner, Executive Director
Chris Roddy, Director, Communcations & Marketing
Sarah Brown, Director, Education & Advocacy
Renee Kempka, Director, Finance & Administration
Kim Nelson, Director, Human Resources

Oregon Tilth is a nonprofit research and education membership organization dedicated to biologicaly sound and socially equitable agriculture. Oregon Tilth offers educational events throughout the state of Oregon, and provides organic certification services to organic growers, processors and handlers internationally.
Founded in 1974

763 Organic Crop Improvement Association
1340 North Cotner Boulevard
Lincoln, NE 68505-1838

402-477-2323; Fax: 402-477-4325
info@ocia.org
www.ocia.org
Facebook, Twitter

Amanda Brewster, Executive Director
Deana McKinstry, Director, Finance
Angie Tunink, Director, Marketing
Cindy Elder, Director, Accredation
Shelby Workman, Office Clerk

OCIA International is a farmer owned international program of certification, which adheres to strict organic standards. It currently certifies thousands of farmers and processors in North, Central and South America and Asia. OCIA International is IFOAM accredited and adheres to the USDA ISO Guide 65, Japan Agriculture Standards and the Quebec Accreditation Council. OCIA has also been accredited from the USDA National Organic Program and Costa Rica Ministry of Agriculture.
3500 Members
Founded in 1985
Mailing list available for rent: 3500 names at $50 per M

764 Organic Seed Alliance
PO Box 772
Port Townsend, WA 98368

360-385-7192; Fax: 360-385-7455
info@seedalliance.org
www.seedalliance.org
Facebook, Twitter

Cara Loriz, Executive Director
Micaela Colley, Program Director
Kiki Hubbard, Advocacy & Communications Director
Cathleen McCluskey, Outreach Director
Jennifer Turney, Financial Manager

Supports the ethical development and stewardship of the genetic resources of agricultural seed.
Founded in 2003

765 Produce Marketing Association
Po Box 6036
Newark, DE 19714-6036

302-738-7100; Fax: 302-731-2409
solutionctr@pma.com
www.pma.com
Facebook, Twitter, YouTube, Flickr, Pinterest

Cathy Burns, CEO
Doug Bohr, Executive Director
Yvonne Bull, Chief Financial Officer
Lauren Scott, Chief Marketing Officer
Max Teplitski, Chief Science Officer

The Produce Marketing Association is a not-for-profit trade association serving members who market fresh fruits, vegetables, and floral products worldwide. Its members are involved in the production, distribution, retail, and foodservice sectors of the industry.
2500 Members
Founded in 1949

766 Professional Farmers of America
1818 Market Street 31st Floor
Philadelphia, PA 19103

319-277-1278
800-772-0023
editors@profarmer.com
www.profarmer.com
Facebook, Twitter, LinkedIn

Provides farmers with marketing strategies and market-trend data, as well as seminars and home study courses.
25M Members
Founded in 1973

767 Santa Gertrudis Breeders International
PO Box 1257
Kingsville, TX 78364-1257

361-592-9357; Fax: 361-592-8572
jford@santagertrudis.com
santagertrudis.com
Facebook

Webb Fields, Executive Director
Diana L. Ruiz, Association Services
Emma Remirez, Member Services
Melissa Braden, DNA Coordinator
Darren Richmond, Member Services Representative

America's First Beef Breed developed in 1918 at the famous King Ranch in Texas. Recognized in 1940 by the USDA. Famous for raid and efficient growth, solid red color, hardiness and good disposition. They are adaptable to many environments and are present throughout the US and in other countries.

768 Society of American Foresters
5400 Grosvenor Ln
Bethesda, MD 20814-2198

301-897-8720
866-897-8720; Fax: 301-897-3690
membership@safnet.org
www.safnet.org
Facebook, Twitter, LinkedIn

Terry Baker, Chief Executive Officer
Susi Metz, Director, Finance & Administration
Danielle Watson, Director, Policy & Public Affairs
Angela Colonna, Manager, Marketing & Communications
Steven Glover, Director, Membership

Provides access to information and networking opportunities to prepare members for the challenges and the changes that face natural resource professionals.
Founded in 1900

769 Society of Commercial Seed Technologists
653 Constitution Avenue NE
Washington, DC 20002

202-870-2412; Fax: 607-273-1638
scst@seedtechnology.net
www.analyzeseeds.com
Facebook, Twitter

Jess Peterson, Executive Director
Kelly Polzin, Director, Membership Services
Kelly Fogarty, Annual Meeting Coordinator
Kristen Albers, Finance
Lia Biondo, Communications

Professionals involved in the testing and analysis of seeds, including research, production and handling based on botanical and agricultural sciences.
250 Members
Founded in 1922

770 Soil and Plant Analysis Council
347 North Shores Circle
Windsor, CO 80550

970-686-5702; Fax: 402-476-0302
www.spcouncil.org

Promotes uniform soil test and plant analysis methods, use, interpretation and terminology.
250 Members
Founded in 1969

771 Southern Cotton Ginners Association
874 Cotton Gin Pl
Memphis, TN 38106-2588

901-947-3104; Fax: 901-947-3103
www.southerncottonginners.org
Facebook

Timothy L. Price, Executive Vice President
William Lindamood, Director, Safety
Andrea Steadman, Specialist, Marketing Communication
Carol Carlson, Bookkeeper

Operates in a five state area as an information center covering safety and governmental regu-

lations. Serves its members by providing safety, training and regulatory representation. Sponsors certification programs and hosts the industry's leading trade show, The Mid-South Farm & Gin Show.
700 Members
Founded in 1967

772 **Texas Agribusiness Market Research Center**
600 John Kimbrough Blvd.
Suite 371 - 2124 TAMU
College Station, TX 77843

979-845-5911; Fax: 979-845-6378
afcerc.tamu.edu
Facebook, LinkedIn

Gary Williams, Co-Director & COO
Oral Capps, Jr., Co-Dir./Chief Resources Dev. Offr.
Victoria Salin, Co-Director & CFO
Loren Burns, Program Manager

Provide a single point to all agricultural resources on the internet. Objective is to promote agribusiness and to enhance agricultural product marketing and research.

773 **The National Grange**
1616 H Street NW
Suite 10
Washington, DC 20006

202-628-3507
888-447-2643; Fax: 202-347-1091
www.nationalgrange.org
Facebook, Twitter, YouTube, RSS Feeds

Betsy Huber, National President
Samantha Wilkins, Operations Coordinator
Joseph Stefenoni, Leadership & Membership Director
Amanda Leigh Brozana-Rios, Communications Director
Loretta Washington, Sales, Benefits & Programs Director

Non-partisan fraternal organization with its roots in rural agriculture.
160K Members
Founded in 1867

774 **The William H. Miner Agricultural Research Institute**
1034 Miner Farm Road
PO Box 90
Chazy, NY 12921

518-846-7121; Fax: 518-846-8445
www.whminer.com
Facebook, Google+

Richard Grant, President
Kirk Beattie, VP, Administration & Finance
Catherine Ballard, Director, Research
Rachel Dutil, Public Relations & Marketing Coord.
Wanda Emerich, Dairy Outreach Coordinator

Miner Institute conducts integrated, cutting-edge education, research, and demonstration programs that optimize the biological and economic relationships among forage-crop production, dairy and equine management, and environmental stewardship.We envision a vital agricultural community in northern New York and surrounding regions built on effective use of forage crops and management technologies that optimize animal production and well-being while sustaining the natural environment.
Founded in 1903

775 **USA Dry Pea & Lentil Council**
2780 W. Pullman Road
Moscow, ID 83843

208-882-3023; Fax: 208-882-6406
pulse@pea-lentil.com
www.pea-lentil.com

Tim D. McGreevy, CEO
Jeff Rumney, VP, Marketing
Todd Scholz, VP, Research & Member Services
Becky Garrison, Director, Domestic Marketing
Drex Rhoades, Director, Communications

The USA Dry Pea & Lentil Council(USADPLC) is a non-profit organization to promote and protect the interests of growers, processors, warehousemen and sellers of dry peas, lentils and chickpeas in the United States.
Founded in 1965

776 **USA Rice Federation**
USA Rice Federation
2101 Wilson Bvld
Suite 610
Arlington, VA 22201

703-226-2300; Fax: 703-236-2301
riceinfo@usarice.com
www.usarice.com
Facebook, Twitter, LinkedIn, Pinterest, YouTube, Google+

Betsy Ward, President & CEO
Rebecca Greenway, Chief Financial Officer
Michael Klein, VP, Communications & Domestic Promo
Ben Mosely, VP, Government Affairs
Jeanette Davis, Sr. Dir., Meetings & Member Service

The global advocate for all segments of the U.S. rice industry with a mission to promote and protect the interests of producers, millers, merchants and allied businesses. USA Rice is made up of the USA Rice Grower's Assoc, USA Rice Millers' Assoc, USA Rice Council, and the USA Rice Merchants' Association.

777 **United Fresh Produce Association**
1901 Pennsylvania Ave NW
Suite 1100
Washington, DC 20006-3412

202-303-3400; Fax: 202-303-3433
united@unitedfresh.org
www.unitedfresh.org
Facebook, Twitter, LinkedIn, YouTube

Thomas Stenzel, President/CEO
Robert Guenther, SVP, Public Policy
Mary Coppola, VP, Marketing & Communication
Julian Gamez, VP, Finance & Operations
Miriam Wolk, VP, Member Services

Equipment, supplies, cartons, packaging machinery, computers, sorting and sizing equipment, harvesting equipment, film wrap manufacturing and commodity organizations.
1000+ Members
Founded in 1904

778 **United Producers**
8351 N High St
Sute 250
Columbus, OH 43235-1440

614-890-6666
800-456-3276; Fax: 614-890-4776
webmaster@uproducers.com
www.uproducers.com
Facebook, LinkedIn

A cooperative marketing organization owned by farmers and ranchers in the United States' corn belt, midwest and southeast.
36000 Members
Frequency: Annual Meetings
Founded in 1962

779 **United States Animal Health Association**
4221 Mitchell Ave.
St Joseph, MO 64507

816-671-1144; Fax: 816-671-1201
usaha@usaha.org
www.usaha.org
Facebook, Twitter

Marty Zaluski, President
Ben Richey, Executive Director
Kelly Janicek, Executive Assistant

Seeks to prevent, control and eliminate livestock diseases.
1400 Members
Founded in 1897

780 **United States Canola Association**
600 Pennsylvania Ave SE
Suite 320
Washington, DC 20003-6300

202-969-8113; Fax: 202-969-7036
info@uscanola.com
www.uscanola.com
Facebook, Twitter, YouTube

John Gordley, Executive Director
Dale Thorenson, Assistant Director
Angela Dansby, Communications Director
Blair Elias, Advertising Sales Representative

USCA members are producers and processors of canola and grapeseed.
Founded in 1989

781 **United States Egg Marketers**
4500 Hugh Howell Road
Suite 270
Tucker, GA 30084

770-360-9220; Fax: 770-360-7058
www.unitedegg.org
Facebook, Twitter, RSS Feed

Chad Gregory, President & CEO
Oscar Garrison, SVP, Food Safety
Larry Sadler, VP, Animal Welfare
Sherry Shedd, VP, Finance
Kathy Bryan, Director, Communications

A producer cooperative established specifically for the purpose of exporting large quantities of U.S. Shell Eggs.

782 **United States Grains Council**
20 F Street NW
Suite 600
Washington, DC 20001

202-789-0789; Fax: 202-898-0522
grains@grains.org
www.grains.org
Facebook, Twitter, LinkedIn, YouTube, Flickr, Pinterest

Jim Raben, Chair
Ryan LeGrand, President and CEO
Josh Miller, Secretary/Treasurer
Chad Willis, Vice Chair
Greg Hibner, Agribusiness Sector Director

Motivated by the grain sorghum, barley and corn producer associations and representatives of the agricultural community. Provides commodity export market development.
175 Members
Founded in 1960

783 **United States Hide, Skin & Leather Association**
1150 Connecticut Ave, NW
12th Floor
Washington, DC 20036

202-587-4250
ssothmann@meatinstitute.org
www.ushsla.org

Jay Jensen, Chair
Stephen Sothmann, President
Sarah Little, VP, Communications

Exclusive representative of the hides and skin industry in the United States. Members range in size from small family-owned businesses to large corporations. Participates in two annual trade shows in Asia as a cooperator through the US Department of Agriculture's Foreign Agriculture Service.
35 Members

784 **Veal Quality Assurance Program & Veal Issues Management Program**
7501 NW Tiffany Springs Parkway
Suite 200
Kansas City, MO 64153

717-823-6995
info@vealfarm.com
www.vealfarm.com

Members include veal producers and processors.
1300 Members
Founded in 1984

785 **Walnut Council**
Wright Forestry Center
1007 N 725 W
West Lafayette, IN 47906-9431

765-583-3501; Fax: 765-583-3512
walnutcouncil@walnutcouncil.org
www.walnutcouncil.org

Bill Hammitt, President
John Katzke, Quartermaster
Liz Jackson, Executive Director
Bill Hoover, Treasurer

A science based organization that encourages research, discussion, and application of knowledge about growing hardwood trees.
1000 Members
Founded in 1970

786 **Weed Science Society of America**
810 East 10th St.
Lawrence, KS 66044-7065

785-865-9250
800-627-0326; Fax: 785-843-1274
jlancaster@allenpress.com
www.wssa.net
Facebook, Twitter, LinkedIn, RSS, YouTube

Joyce Lancaster, Executive Secretary
Beverly Lindeen, Managing Editor
John Madsen, Secretary
Ian Burkel, Treasurer

Promotes research, education and extension outreach activities related to weeds, provides science-based information to the public and policy makers; and fosters awareness of weeds and their impacts on managed and natural ecosystems.
2000 Members
Founded in 1956

787 **Western Equipment Dealers Association**
638 West 39th St.
P.O. Box 419264
Kansas City, MO 64141-6264

816-561-5323
800-762-5616; Fax: 816-561-1249
www.westerneda.com
Facebook, Twitter, LinkedIn

John Schmeiser, CEO
Jennifer Luce, COO
Eric Wareham, VP, Government Affairs (US)
Larry Hertz, VP, Canada
Katie Clark, Member Services Coordinator

An advocacy association that advances the interests of agriculture, industrial, forestry, and outdoor equipment dealers.
Founded in 1899

788 **Western Fairs Association**
1776 Tribute Rd
Suite 210
Sacramento, CA 95815-4495

916-927-3100; Fax: 916-927-6397
info@fairsnet.org
www.fairsnet.org
Facebook, Twitter, YouTube, Instagram

Sarah Cummings, President & CEO
Taylor Corder, Communications Manager
Cliff Munson, Chair

A non-profit association with members throughout the Western United States and Canada that strives to promote industry standards. Membership includes access to conventions and trade shows, educational training programs as well as legislative advocacy support.
2000 Members
Founded in 1922

789 **Western United States Agricultural Trade Association**
4601 NE 77th Avenue
Suite 240
Vancouver, WA 98662-2697

360-693-3373; Fax: 360-693-3464
export@wusata.org
www.wusata.org
Facebook, Twitter, LinkedIn

Andy Anderson, Executive Director
Rebecca Roberts, Executive Administrator
Tricia Stein, Chief Of Staff
Terri Curtis, Office Coordinator
Monica Quenette, Outreach & Communications Coord.

The Western United States Agricultural Trade Association (WUSATAr) is a non-profit trade association whose members are the thirteen western state departments of agriculture. WUSATA is administered by the USDA 's Foreign Agricultural Service (FAS) and funded through the Market Access Program (MAP) with a mission to support and assist members and agribusinesses in the thirteen Western States in developing and enhancing international markets for U.S. food and agricultural products.
Founded in 1980

790 **Women Grow**
contact@womengrow.com
www.womengrow.com
Facebook, Twitter, LinkedIn, Instagram, Vimeo

Chanda Macias, Chief Executive Officer
Gia Moron, Executive Vice President
Arielle Paredes, Communications Assistant
Lauren Rudick, Counsel
Parisa Rad, Director, Market Leader Program

Connects, educates, and empowers diverse leaders in all segments of the cannabis industry across the U.S. and Canada.
Founded in 2014

Newsletters

791 **AAM Newsletter**
American Agriculture Movement
24800 Sage Creek Road
Scenic, SD 57780

605-993-6201; Fax: 605-993-6185
jjobgen@hotmail.com

Larry Matlack, President
Arthur Chaney, Executive Vice President
John Willis, Vice President
Jim Rice, Secretary/Treasurer
John Willis, Vice President

The creation of the AAM has provided a farmer-created, farmer-built organization within which farmers themselves have been the leaders, speakers and organizers; empowering farmers as they had not been in the past, to speak for and advocate for themselves. Updates about events, news, articles and letters to the editor.
Founded in 1977
Mailing list available for rent

792 **ALBC News**
American Livestock Breeds Conservancy
PO Box 477
Pittsboro, NC 27312

919-542-5704; Fax: 919-545-0022
www.albc-usa.org
Facebook, Blogger

Charles Bassett, Executive Director

Provides in-depth information about current ALBC activities, breed information, member updates, and more.
Frequency: Bi-Monthly

793 **ARA Retailer Facts**
Agricultural Retailers Association
1156 15th St Nw
Suite 500
Washington, DC 20005-1745

202-457-0825; Fax: 202-457-0864
ara@aradc.org
www.aradc.org
Facebook, Twitter, RSS Feed

Daren Coppock, President and CEO
Richard Gupton, SVP
Donnie Taylor, VP of Membership
Gary Baise, General Counsel

The Agricultural Retailers Association advocates before Congress and the Executive Branch to ensure a profitable business environment for members.
Frequency: Daily

794 **ARClight**
National Agri-Marketing Association
11020 King St
Suite 205
Overland Park, KS 66210-1201

913-491-6500; Fax: 913-491-6502
agrimktg@nama.org
www.nama.org
Facebook, Twitter, LinkedIn, Flicker, You Tube

Jennifer Pickett, CEO

Agricultural Relations Council - a national association with members involved in agricultural public relations. Electronic newsletter of interest to association members.

795 **ASA Today**
American Soybean Association
12125 Woodcrest Executive
Suite 100
Saint Louis, MO 63141-5009

314-576-1770
800-688-7692; Fax: 314-576-2786
www.soygrowers.com
Facebook, Twitter, RSS Feed

Steve Censky, CEO

For members only
Frequency: Weekly

796 **ASAC News**
American Society of Agricultural Consultants
N78W14573 Appleton Ave
#287
Menomonee Falls, WI 53051

262-253-6902; Fax: 262-253-6903
cmerry@countryside-marketing.com
www.agconsultants.org
Facebook, LinkedIn

~the American Society of Agricultural Consultants (ASAC) is a non-profit organization oriented around raising the standards and image of professional agricultural consultants. ASAC is the only association representing the full range of agricultural consultants.
Frequency: Quarterly
Founded in 1963

797 **Ag Equipment Intelligence**
Lessiter Media
P.O. Box 624
Brookfield, WI 53008-0624

262-782-4480
800-645-8455; Fax: 262-782-1252
dkanicki@lessitermedia.com
www.agequipmentintelligence.com
Facebook, Twitter

Frank Lessiter, Chair & Editorial Director
Dave Kanicki, Editor & Publisher
Alex Zank, Data Editor
Kim Schmidt, Managing Editor
Jack Zemlicka, Technology Editor

Farm equipment industry news, information, and analysis. Each issue contains inside stories from top ag equipment analysts, consulting groups, dealers, and manufacturers worldwide.
Cost: $499.00
Frequency: Monthly

798 **AgNews**
ASFMRA
720 S. Colorado Boulevard
Suite 360-S
Glendale, CO 80246

303-758-3513; Fax: 303-758-0190
info@asfmra.org
www.asfmra.org

Brian Stockman, Executive VP/CEO
Andrew Eames, Content Coordinator

Provides professionals involved in rural property issues such as management and appraisal, with information on the industry as well as educational opportunities. Includes membership and information from the American Society of Farm Manager and Rural Appraisers.
Frequency: Weekly
Founded in 1929

799 **Agri Times Northwest**
PO Box 1626
Pendleton, OR 97801

541-276-6202; Fax: 541-278-4778
editor@agritimesnw.com
www.agritimesnw.com

Sterling Allen, Publisher
Jim Eardley, Editor
Brianna Walker, Graphics

Contains news stories and columns pertaining to rural life and agri-business, designed to keep farmers and ranchers up to date with agriculture in their backyard.
Cost: $20.00
Frequency: Bi-Monthly
Founded in 1981

800 **AgriMarketing Weekly**
Henderson Communications LLC
1422 Elbridge Payne Rd
Suite 250
Chesterfield, MO 63017-8544

636-728-1428; Fax: 636-777-4178
info@agrimarketing.com
www.agrimarketing.com

Lynn Henderson, Publisher/Editorial Director
Stephanie Wobbe, Editorial Assistant
Audrey Evans, Customer Service Manager

It includes a recap of the most important news within the industry during the prior week.
Frequency: Weekly
Circulation: 4500

801 **Agricultural Law Update**
American Agricultural Law Association
127 Young Rd
Kelso, WA 98626

360-200-5699; Fax: 360-432-2287
www.aglaw-assn.org

Mike Traxinger, President
Scott Heidner, Executive Director

Articles written about environmental and agricultural issues.

802 **Agweek**
Grand Forks Herald
375 2nd Avenue N
Grand Forks, ND 58206-6008

701-780-1100; Fax: 701-780-1211
www.gfherald.com
RSS Feed

Matthew C Cory, Managing Editor
Tom Dennis, Editorial/Opinion Page Editor
Mary Jo Hotler, Editor

Features classifieds, weather information, farming, ranch news and opinion for the Upper Midwest
Cost: $32.00
Frequency: Weekly

803 **Alliance Link Newsletter**
Animal Agriculture Alliance
2101 Wilson Blvd
Suite 916-B
Arlington, VA 22201

703-562-5160; Fax: 703-524-1921
info@animalagalliance.org
www.animalagalliance.org
Facebook, Twitter

Kay Johnson, Executive VP
Emily Solis, Communications Specialist

Helps members and industry stakeholders stay informed about the key issues impacting animal agriculture
Frequency: Monthly

804 **American Beekeeping Federation Newsletter**
American Beekeeping Federation
3525 Piedmont Rd NE
Bldg 5 Suite 300
Atlanta, GA 30305-1509

404-760-2875; Fax: 404-240-0998
info@abfnet.org
www.abfnet.org

Molly Sausaman, Executive Director

Newsletter for members of the American Beekeeping Federation.
Cost: $35.00
24 Pages
Frequency: Bi-Monthly
Circulation: 1750
Founded in 1943

805 **American Feed Industry Newlsetter**
American Feed Industry Association
2101 Wilson Boulevard
Suite 916
Arlington, VA 22201

703-524-0810; Fax: 703-524-1921
afia@afia.org
www.afia.org
Facebook, Twitter, LinkedIn

Constance Cullman, President & CEO
Victoria Broehm, Communications Director

Newsletter published every two weeks by the American Feed Industry for members only.
Frequency: Bi-Monthly
Circulation: 700
Founded in 1909

806 **Aquatic Plant News**
Aquatic Plant Management Society
PO Box 821265
Vicksburg, MS 39182-1265

FAX 601-634-5502
dpetty@ndrsite.com
www.apms.org
Facebook, LinkedIn

Terry Goldsby, President
Mike Netherland, President-elect
Sherry Whitaker, Treasurer

Aquatic Plant News is produced 3 times each year, and is distributed primarily by email.
Frequency: 3x Yearly
Founded in 1961

807 **Association of American Seed Control Officials Bulletin**
Utah Department of Agriculture
350 N Redwood Road
PO Box 146500
Salt Lake City, UT 84114-6500

801-538-7100; Fax: 801-538-7126
agriculture@utah.gov
www.ag.utah.gov
Facebook, Twitter, YouTube

Stephen T Burningham, Control Officer
Leonard Blachham, Commissioner
Jed Christenson, Marketing

Seed laws in the United States and Canada.
Frequency: Annual+
Circulation: 5000

808 **CSA News**
5585 Guilford Road
Madison, WI 53711-1086

608-273-8080; Fax: 608-273-2021
headquarters@agronomy.org
www.agronomy.org
Facebook, Twitter, LinkedIn

Matt Nilsson, Managing Editor

The official magazine for members of the American Society of Agronomy, Crop Science Society of America, and Soil Science Society of America.
11000 Members
Founded in 1907

809 **Chaff Newsletter**
American Association of Grain Inspection
PO Box 26426
Kansas City, MO 64196

816-569-4020; Fax: 816-221-8189
www.aagiwa.org

Larry Kitchen, President
Mark Fulmer, VP

Welcomes member information about new products, business changes, personnel changes and other items that may be of interest to AAGIWA members.
Frequency: Monthly

810 **Council for Agricultural Science and Technology Newsletter**
Council For Agricultural Science and Technology
4420 Lincoln Way
Ames, IA 50014-3447

515-292-2125; Fax: 515-292-4512
info@cast-science.org
www.cast-science.org
Facebook, Twitter, LinkedIn, YouTube

Kent G. Schedcke, Executive Vice President
Melissa Sly, Director, Council Operations
Dan Gogerty, Managing Communications Editor
Megan Wickham, Scientific Editor
Gale Osborne, Officer Manager/Events Coordinator

Identifies food, fiber, environmental and other agricultural issues for all stake holders, including legislators, policy makers and the public.
Founded in 1972

811 **Country Folks**
Lee Publications
6113 State Highway 5
PO Box 121
Palatine Bridge, NY 13428-0121

518-673-3237
888-596-5329; Fax: 518-673-2699
subscriptions@leepub.com
www.countryfolks.com
Facebook, Twitter

Frederick Lee, Publisher
Joan Kark-Wren, Editor
Bruce Button, President
Larry Price, Marketing Manager
Ian Hitchener, Sales Manager

Agricultural news from national, state and local levels. Some features on farm and agricultural industry, rural interest, etc.
75 Pages
Frequency: Weekly
Circulation: 27000
Founded in 1973

812 **Country Folks Grower**
Lee Publications
6113 State Hwy. 5
P.O. Box 121
Palatine Bridge, NY 13428

518-673-3237
800-836-2888; Fax: 518-673-3245
info@leepub.com
www.leepub.com

Frederick Lee, Publisher
Joan Kark-Wren, Editor
Bruce Button, President
Larry Price, Marketing Manager
Ian Hitchener, Sales Manager

A business-to-business publication coverings all aspects of growing and marketing fresh market and ornamental crops. Available in three regional editions: Eastern, Midwest, Western
Frequency: Monthly

813 **Country World Newspaper**
Echo Publishing Company
401 Church St
Sulphur Springs, TX 75482-2681

903-885-0861
800-245-2149; Fax: 903-885-8768
scott@ssecho.com

Scott Key, President
Kari Arnold, Editor

A newspaper offering agricultural information to farmers, ranchers, dairyfarmers, and agribusinesses.
Frequency: Weekly
Founded in 1981

814 **Dair-e-news**
American Dairy Science Association
1800 S. Oak Street
Suite 100
Champaign, IL 61820-6974

217-356-5146; Fax: 217-398-4119
adsa@assochq.org
www.adsa.org
Facebook

Catharine Kuber Perry, Executive Director

Timely topics and important announcements, industry calendar of events, and news of the Association.

815 **DairyProfit Weekly**
6437 Collamer Road
East Syracuse, NY 13057-1031

315-703-7979
800-334-1904; Fax: 315-703-7988
dgarno@dairybusiness.com
www.dairybusiness.com
Facebook, Twitter, YouTube

Keeps readers up to date with a quick, timely summary of news, markets and trends that impact your business.
Frequency: Weekly
Founded in 1904

816 **Decision Support Systems for Agrotechnology Transfer**
ICASA
2440 Campus Road
PO Box 527
Honolulu, HI 96822

808-956-2713; Fax: 808-956-2711
www.dssat.net

Jeffrey White, Co-Chair
Martin Ittersum, Co-Chair
Gordon Tsuji, Secretariat

Systems analysis and crop simulation models for agrotechnology transfers and risk assessment. Reference guides and models for maize, wheat, rice, sorghum, millet, barley, soybean, peanut and potato are included. Linked to GIS software.

817 **Doane's Agricultural Report**
Doane Agricultural Services
77 Westport Plz
Suite 250
St Louis, MO 63146-3121

314-569-2700
866-647-0918; Fax: 314-569-1083
www.doane.com

Rich Pottorff, Chief Economist
Marty Foreman, Senior Economist
Sam Funk, Senior Economist

Provides information to US farmers and agricultural professionals. Doane keeps you up to date on factors affecting your farm program benefits and production costs too.
Frequency: Weekly

818 **Farm Equipment E-Watch Daily**
Lessiter Media
P.O. Box 624
Brookfield, WI 53008-0624

262-782-4480
800-645-8455; Fax: 262-782-1252
info@farm-equipment.com
www.farm-equipment.com

Mike Lessiter, Editor & Publisher
Dave Kanicki, Executive Editor
Michael Ellis, Director of Sales

An e-newsletter delivered Monday-Saturday and produced by the editors of Farm Equipment Magazine. Contains information of interest to farm equipment dealers including industry news, best practices, videos, and more.
Frequency: Daily

819 **Farm Equipment Weekly Digest**
Lessiter Media
P.O. Box 624
Brookfield, WI 53008-0624

262-782-4480
800-645-8455; Fax: 262-782-1252
info@farm-equipment.com
www.farm-equipment.com
Facebook, Twitter, LinkedIn, YouTube

Mike Lessiter, Editor & Publisher
Dave Kanicki, Executive Editor
Michael Ellis, Director of Sales

An e-newsletter delivered each Sunday and produced by the editors of Farm Equipment Magazine. Contains a summary of the week's biggest developments in farm equipment dealing.
Frequency: Weekly

820 **Farm and Ranch Guide**
2401 46th Avenue SE
Mandan, ND 58554

701-255-4905; Fax: 701-255-2312
office@farmandranchguide.com
www.farmandranchguide.com
Facebook, Twitter, RSS Feed

Brian Kroshus, Group Publisher
Mark Conlon, Editor
Patrick Sitter, General Manager
Andrea Johnson, Assistant Editor

Inform and entertain while serving as a conduit between our valued advertising customers and our loyal readers
Cost: $32.95
Frequency: Bi-Monthly
Circulation: 38,000

821 **Farmer's Friend**
116 Main Street
Towanda, PA 18846

570-265-2151
800-253-3662; Fax: 570-265-6130
kandrus@thedailyreview.com
www.farmers-friend.com

Ronald W Hosie, Editor
Kelly Andrus, Managing Editor
Debbie Bump, Circulation

Farming news.
Frequency: Weekly
Founded in 1977

822 **Feedstuffs**
The Miller Publishing Company
5810 W. 78th St
Suite 200
Bloomington, MN 55339

952-931-0211; Fax: 952-938-1832
smuirhead@feedstuffs.com
www.feedstuffs.com

Sarah Muirhead, Publisher/Editor
Rod Smith, Staff Editor/Livestock & Poultry
Tim Lundeen, Staff Editor/Nutrition & Health
Jacqui Fatka, Staff Editor/Policy
Kristin Bakker, Editorial Production Manager

A newspaper for agribusiness, each week of the month focuses on a different animal species. Topics include nutrition, health, marketing issues and the popular Bottom Line of Nutrition section.
Cost: $144.00
24 Pages
Frequency: Weekly
Circulation: 16600
Founded in 1895

823 **Fencepost**
The Fencepost

423 Main Street
Windsor, CO 80550-5129

970-686-5691; Fax: 970-686-5694
www.thefencepost.com

Gary Loftus, Publisher
Amiella Diaz, Editor
Robyn Scherer, Staff Reporter

Farming news and reports.
Cost: $39.00
Frequency: Weekly
Founded in 1980

824 **Forestry Source**
Society of American Foresters
5400 Grosvenor Ln
Bethesda, MD 20814-2198

301-897-8720
866-897-8720; Fax: 301-897-3690
www.safnet.org
Facebook, Twitter, LinkedIn

Morgan Fincham, Director, Publications
Steve Wilent, Editor

Offers the latest information on national forestry trends, the latest developments in forestry policy at the federal, state, and local levels, the newest advances in forestry-related research and technology, and up-to-date information about SAF programs and activities
Cost: $35.00
Frequency: Monthly
Founded in 1990

825 **Friday Notes**
Council For Agricultural Science and Technology
4420 West Lincoln Way
Ames, IA 50014-3447

515-292-2125
cast@cast-science.org
www.cast-science.org

Kent G. Schescke, Executive Vice President
Dan Gogerty, Managing Communications Editor

E-Newsletter featuring lead articles on current topics being discussed in agriculture, congressional updates, announcements of upcoming CAST publications and activities, and information about CAST's scientific society, company, and nonprofit members.
Frequency: Weekly
Circulation: 4000
Founded in 1972

826 **Global Dairy Update**
DairyBusiness Communications
6437 Collamer Road
East Syracuse, NY 13057-1031

315-703-7979
800-334-1904; Fax: 315-703-7988
dgarno@dairybusiness.com
www.dairybusiness.com
Facebook, Twitter, YouTube

Dave Natzke, Editor
Scott Smith, Chairman/Co-CEO
John Montandon, President/Co-CEO
Joel Hastings, President, Dairy Business

Focuses on dairy developments throughout the world.
Founded in 1904

827 **Goats on the Move**
Meat & Livestock Australia
1401 K Street NW
Suite 602
Washington, DC 20005

202-521-2551; Fax: 202-521-2699
info@mla.com.au
www.mla.com.au
Facebook, Twitter, YouTube

Don Heatley, Chairman
David Palmer, Managing Director
Bernie Bindon, Director
Chris Hudson, Director

eNewsletter providing information on the latest developments in MLA's goat program and the broader Australian goatmeat industry.
Frequency: Quarterly
Founded in 1998

828 **Greenhouse Product News**
Scranton Gillette Communications
3030 W Salt Creek Lance
Suite 201
Arlington Heights, IL 60005-5025

847-391-1000; Fax: 847-390-0408
www.gpnmag.com

Bob Bellew, VP/Group Publisher
Tim Hodson, Editorial Director
Jasmina Radjevic, Managing Editor

Features the industry's leading Buyer's Guide directory, the PGR table and the bookstore are just a few reasons the industry's buyers keep coming back to GPN.
Frequency: Monthly
Mailing list available for rent: 19,000 names

829 **Hay Market News**
US Department of Agriculture
1400 Independence Ave., S.W.
Washington, DC 20250-0506

202-690-7650; Fax: 509-457-7132
www.usda.gov

Tom Vilsack, Secretary
Chris Smith, Chief Information Officer
Matt Paul, Director of Communications
Ramona Romero, General Counsel

Federal newsletter offering information and updates on crops and farming.
Cost: $40.00
8 Pages
Circulation: 180
Founded in 1862

830 **Holstein Association News**
Holstein Association
1 Holstein Place
PO Box 808
Brattleboro, VT 05302-0808

802-254-4551
800-952-5200; Fax: 802-254-8251
info@holstein.com
www.holsteinusa.com

Corey Geiger, President

Bimonthly newsletter provides active customers with information on the association programs and services and how to integrate them into their dairy operations.
Founded in 1885

831 **Holstein Pulse**
Holstein Association USA Inc
1 Holstein Place
PO Box 808
Brattleboro, VT 05302-0808

802-254-4551
800-052-5200; Fax: 802-254-8251
info@holstein.com
www.holsteinusa.com

Corey Geiger, President

Includes information relevant to our members, new developments in the industry, as well as updates from the CEO and President.
Cost: $2.00
Frequency: Quarterly
Founded in 1885

832 **Irrigation Association E-Newsletter**
Irrigation Association
8280 Willow Oaks Corp. Dr.
Suite 400
Fairfax, VA 22031-4507

703-536-7080; Fax: 703-536-7019
info@irrigation.org
www.irrigation.org

Deborah M. Hamlin, Chief Executive Officer
Sarah Bunyea, Digital Content Editor

Published on a quarterly basis, this e-newsletter provides updates on Foundation activities and accomplishments.
Frequency: Quarterly
Founded in 1949

833 **Irrigation Association IA Times**
Irrigation Association
8280 Willow Oaks Corp. Dr.
Suite 400
Fairfax, VA 22031

703-536-7080; Fax: 703-536-7019
membership@irrigation.org
www.irrigation.org

Deborah Hamlin, CEO
Kyle Brown, Editor-In-Chief

Reports on federal and state policies and legislation that affect the irrigation industry. Status updates on industry initiatives, and information on the latest association events, programs, services and awards.
1600 Members
Founded in 1949

834 **Kiplinger Agricultural Letter**
Kiplinger Washington Editors
1100 13th St. NW
Washington, DC 20005

202-887-6400
800-544-0155; Fax: 202-778-8976
sub.services@kiplinger.com
www.kiplinger.com
Facebook, Twitter, RSS

Knight A Kiplinger, President, Editor-in-Chief
Ed Maixner, Editor

Forecasts and judgments on wages, income, food packaging, processing and marketing techniques.
Cost: $137.00
Frequency: Biweekly
Founded in 1929

835 **MJ Business Week**
Marijuana Business Association

info@mjba.net
www.mjnewsnetwork.com
Facebook, Twitter, YouTube

A weekly e-newsletter bringing you the latest cannabis industry business news.
Frequency: Weekly
Founded in 2013

836 **MJ Headline News**
Marijuana Business Association

info@mjba.net
www.mjnewsnetwork.com
Facebook, Twitter, YouTube

A daily e-newsletter bringing you the latest cannabis industry news.
Frequency: Daily
Founded in 2013

837 **NAMA Newsletter**
North American Millers' Association

600 Maryland Ave SW
Suite 825 W
Washington, DC 20024

202-484-2200; Fax: 202-488-7416
generalinfo@namamillers.org
www.namamillers.org

Jane DeMarchi, President
Christopher Clark, VP, Communications & Administration

Trade association representing the wheat, corn, oat and rye milling industry. NAMA members operate one hundred and seventy mills in thrirty-eight states and Canada. Their aggregate production of more than one hundred and sixty million pounds per day is approximately ninety-five percent of the industry capacity in the U.S.
Frequency: Monthly
Circulation: 250

838 **NASDA News**
1156 15th St NW
Suite 1020
Washington, DC 20005-1711

202-296-9680; Fax: 202-296-9686
nasda@nasda.org
www.nasda.org
Facebook, Twitter

Barb Glenn, CEO

Represents the state departments of agriculture in the development, implementation and communication of sound public policy and programs which support and promote the American agricultural industry, while protecting consumers and the environment.
Founded in 1915

839 **NBA Weekly Update**
National Bison Association
8690 Wolff Ct
200
Westminster, CO 80031

303-292-2833; Fax: 303-845-9081
www.bisoncentral.com

Dave Carter, Executive Director

Mailed exclusively to all Life, Active and Allied Industry members. Contains the most up to date information available on the bison industry.
Frequency: Weekly

840 **NCPA Newsletter**
National Cottonseed Products Association
866 Willow Tree Cir
Cordova, TN 38018-6376

901-682-0800; Fax: 901-682-2856
info@cottonseed.com
www.cottonseed.com

Providing members with information on legislation, administrative rulings, federal regulations and court decisions affecting their business.
Founded in 1897

841 **National Honey Report**
Federal Market News Service
1400 Independence Avenue SW
STOP 0238
Washington, DC 20250

202-720-2175; Fax: 202-720-0547
www.ams.usda.gov/mnreports/fvmhoney.pdf

Billy Cox, Director
Becky Unkenholz, Deputy Director
Joan Shaffer, Senior Public Affairs Specialist

Current honey market information and colony conditions in the United States and other countries.
16 Pages
Frequency: Monthly
Founded in 1915

842 **National Onion Association Newsletter**
National Onion Association
822 7th St
Suite 510
Greeley, CO 80631-3941

970-353-5895; Fax: 970-353-5897
wmininger@onions-usa.org
www.onions-usa.org
Twitter

Greg Yielding, Executive Vice President
Doug Bulgrin, President

Newsletter published by and only for the National Onion Association.
Frequency: Monthly
Circulation: 600
Founded in 1913
Mailing list available for rent: 600 names

843 **Nebraska Alfalfa Dehydrators Bulletin**
Nebraska Alfalfa Dehydrators Association
8810 Craig Dr
Overland Park, KS 66212-2916

913-648-6800; Fax: 913-648-2648
wcobbkc@sbcglobal.net
www.nebada.org

Carlton Bert, President
David Rhea, Vice President
Chris Healey, Director

Information for the processors and suppliers in the alfalfa industry.
Frequency: Weekly
Founded in 1941

844 **New England Farm Bulletin and Garden**
Jacob's Meadow Inc.
PO Box 67
Townton, MA 02780

Home Page: www.jacobsmeadow.org

Articles explore relevant topics; extensive farm clasifieds, doings around New England, book reviews and discount prices.

845 **News of the Association of Official Seed Analysts**
Association of Official Seed Analysts (AOSA)
101 East State Street
#214
Ithaca, NY 14850

607-256-3313; Fax: 607-273-1638
www.aosaseed.com

Dan Curry, President
Michael Stahr, Vice President
Janine Maruschak, Secretary/Treasurer

News items, technical reports, rules changes for testing seeds, surveys, identification and tax news, legislative updates and updates on the Association's programs and publications in progress.

846 **No-Till Farmer**
Lessiter Media
P.O. Box 624
Brookfield, WI 53008-0624

262-782-4480
800-645-8455; Fax: 262-782-1252
info@no-tillfarmer.com
www.no-tillfarmer.com
Facebook, Twitter, LinkedIn, YouTube

Frank Lessiter, Owner
Darrell Bruggnik, Executive Editor/Publisher
Mark McNeely, Managing Editor
John Dobberstein, Senior Editor

Management information for farmers interested in conservation tillage.

847 **North American Millers' Association Newsletter**
600 Maryland Ave SW
Suite 825 W
Washington, DC 20024

202-484-2200; Fax: 202-488-7416
generalinfo@namamillers.org
www.namamillers.org

Jane DeMarchi, President

Trade association representing the wheat, corn, oat and rye milling industry. NAMA members operate one hundred and seventy mills in thrirty-eight states and Canada. Their aggregate production of more than one hundred and sixty million pounds per day is approximately ninety-five percent of the industry capacity in the U.S.
45 Members
Founded in 1902

848 **Northeastern Weed Science Society Newsletter**
PO Box 307
Fredericksburg, PA 17026

814-574-4067
northeasternweedscience@hotmail.com
www.newss.org

Serves the Northeastern US by bringing together those who are concerned with the knowledge of weeds and their control, cooperates with other scientific societies to promote research, education and outreach activities and publishes scientific and practical information of value concerning weed sciences and other fields.
Founded in 1946

849 **OCIA Communicator Newletter**
1340 North Cotner Boulevard
Lincoln, NE 68505-1838

402-477-2323; Fax: 402-477-4325
info@ocia.org
www.ocia.org

Amanda Brewster, Executive Director

A quarterly newsletter published by the Organic Crop Improvement Association International (OCIA).
Cost: $50.00
Frequency: Quarterly
Circulation: 300
Mailing list available for rent: 3500 names at $50 per M

850 **Organic Report**
Organic Trade Association
28 Vernon St
Suite 413
Brattleboro, VT 05301

202-403-8520
info@ota.com
www.ota.com
Facebook, Twitter, LinkedIn

Danielle Cote, Membership Manager

Targets an audience of manufacturers, growers, retailers, importers, distributors, and consultants in the organic food and fiber industry.
Frequency: Monthly
Circulation: 2500
Founded in 1985

851 **Peterson Patriot**
Peterson Patriot Printers-Publishers
202 Main Street
PO Box 126
Peterson, IA 51047-0126

712-295-7711

Roger Stoner, Publisher
Jane Stoner, Editor/Circulation Manager

Agricultural news.
Cost: $18.00
12 Pages
Frequency: Weekly
Circulation: 549

852 **Precision Farming Dealer Daily**
Lessiter Media
P.O. Box 624
Brookfield, WI 53008-0624

262-782-4480
800-645-8455; Fax: 262-782-1252
info@precisionfarmingdealer.com
www.precisionfarmingdealer.com
Facebook, Twitter, LinkedIn, YouTube

Mike Lessiter, Editor/Publisher
Dave Kanicki, Executive Editor
Michael Ellis, Director of Sales

An e-newsletter delivered Monday-Saturday and produced by the editors of Precision Farming Dealer magazine. Contains information of interest to precision dealers including industry news, best practices, and videos.
Frequency: Daily

853 **Precision Farming Dealer Weekly Digest**
Lessiter Media
P.O. Box 624
Brookfield, WI 53008-0624

262-782-4480
800-645-8455; Fax: 262-782-1252
info@precisionfarmingdealer.com
www.precisionfarmingdealer.com
Facebook, Twitter, LinkedIn, YouTube

Mike Lessiter, Editor/Publisher
Dave Kanicki, Executive Editor
Michael Ellis, Director of Sales

An e-newsletter delivered each Sunday and produced by the editors of Precision Farming Dealer magazine. Contains a summary of the week's biggest news in precision farming dealing
Frequency: Weekly

854 **Pro Farmer**
Farm Journal Media
1550 N Northwest HW
Suite 403
Park Ridge, IL 60068

215-578-8900
800-320-7992; Fax: 215-568-6782
www.farmjournalmedia.com

Andy Weber, Chief Executive Officer
Steve Custer, Executive Vice President/Publishing
Jeff Pence, Division President
Chuck Roth, Senior Vice President
Mitch Rouda, President, eMedia

Farm market news, analysis and management advice.
8 Pages
Frequency: Weekly
Founded in 1973

855 **Rural Lifestyle Dealer Weekly Digest**
Lessiter Media
P.O. Box 624
Brookfield, WI 53008-0624

262-782-4480
800-645-8455; Fax: 262-782-1252
info@rurallifestyledealer.com
www.rurallifestyledealer.com

Michael Ellis, Publisher
Dave Kanicki, Executive Editor

An e-newsletter delivered each Sunday and produced by the editors of Rural Lifestyle Dealer magazine. Contains the week's biggest stories in the industry.
Frequency: Weekly

856 **SHORTLINER**
Farm Equipment Manufacturers Association
1000 Executive Parkway Dr
Suite 100
St Louis, MO 63141-6369

314-878-2304; Fax: 314-732-1480
info@farmequip.org
www.farmequip.org
Twitter

Matt Westendorf, President
Vernon Schmidt, Executive Vice President
Tricia Kidd, Accounting & Meeting Services
Kristi Ruggles, Publications Editor

A review of news stories, press reports, and government actions affecting the farm equipment manufacturing industry.
8 Pages
Frequency: Bi-Weekly
Circulation: 1000
Founded in 1950

857 **Salt & Trace Mineral Newsletter**
Salt Institute
700 N Fairfax Street
Suite 600
Alexandria, VA 22314-2040

703-549-4648; Fax: 703-548-2194
info@saltinstitute.org
www.saltinstitute.org

Lori Roman, President
Morton Satin, VP/Science & Research

Information on animal nutrition.
Frequency: Quarterly
Founded in 1914

858 **Seed News**
PO Box 772
Port Townsend, WA 98368

360-385-7192; Fax: 360-385-7455
info@seedalliance.org
www.seedalliance.org
Facebook, Twitter

Cara Loriz, Executive Director

Information covering events, seminars and meetings.
Cost: $8.00
8 Pages

859 **Seed Technologist Newsletter**
Association of Official Seed Analysts (AOSA)
101 East State Street
#214
Ithaca, NY 14850

607-256-3313; Fax: 607-273-1638
www.aosaseed.com

Dan Curry, President
Michael Stahr, Vice President
Janine Maruschak, Secretary/Treasurer

News items, technical reports, rules changes for testing seeds, surveys, identification and tax news, legislative updates and updates on the Association and publications in progress.
Cost: $20.00
Frequency: TriAnnual
Circulation: 500

860 **Signals Newsletter**
Association for Communication Excellence
ACE Headquarters
59 College Road, Taylor Hall
Durham, NH 03824

603-862-1564; Fax: 603-862-1585
ace.info@unh.edu
www.aceweb.org

Faith Peppers, President
Joanne Littlefield, Vice President
Elaine Edwards, Treasurer
Emily Eubanks, Professional Development Director
Jason Ellis, Research Director

The newsletter includes articles with a professional development focus; updates from special interest groups, states and regions; announcements about upcoming workshops and conferences; and write-ups about members' awards and accomplishments, job changes and more.
Cost: $75.00
Frequency: Bimonthly

861 **Smart Choices Newsletter**
Communicating for America
112 E Lincoln Avenue
Fergus Falls, MN 56537

218-739-3241
80- 43- 327; Fax: 218-739-3832
info@cabenefits.org
www.cabenefits.org

Milt Smedsrud, CEO
Wayne Nelson, President

Filled with updates on legislative accomplishments and advocacy, articles about healthy living and first-hand accounts from those participating in CA Education Programs.
40M Members
Founded in 1972

862 **Society for Laboratory Automation and Screening**
100 Illinois Street
Suite 242
St. Charles, IL 60174

630-256-7527
877-990-7557; Fax: 630-741-7527
slas@slas.org
www.slas.org
Facebook, Twitter, LinkedIn, YouTube

Greg Dummer, CEO
Mary Geismann, Manager
Carol Brady, Coordinator

Provides forums for education and information exchange to encourage the study of and advance science and technology for the drug discovery, agrochemical, biotechnology, chemical, clinical diagnostic, consumer product, energy, forensic, pharmaceutical, security and other industries.
Frequency: Bi-Monthly

863 **Southern Cotton Ginners Association Newsletter**
874 Cotton Gin Pl
Memphis, TN 38106-2588

901-947-3104; Fax: 901-947-3103
carmen.griffin@southerncottonginners.org
www.southerncottonginners.org
Facebook

Timothy Price, Executive Vice President

Operates in a five state area as an information center covering safety and governmental regulations. Serves its members by providing safety, training and regulatory representation. Sponsors certification programs and hosts the industry's leading trade show, The Mid-South Farm & Gin Show.
Founded in 1950

864 **Strip-Till Farmer**
Lessiter Media
P.O. Box 624
Brookfield, WI 53008-0624

262-782-4480
800-645-8455; Fax: 262-782-1252
dbruggink@lessitermedia.com
www.striptillfarmer.com
Facebook, Twitter, YouTube

Frank Lessiter, Editor
Darrell Bruggink, Executive Editor/Publisher

Features content on strip-till farmers, strip-till management, and trending practices in strip-till.
Cost: $19.95
Frequency: Quarterly

865 **The Agrarian Advocate**
36355 Russell Boulevard
P.O. Box 363
Davis, CA 95617

530-756-8518
800-892-3832; Fax: 530-756-7857
judith@fullbellyfarm.com
www.caff.org
Facebook, Twitter, YouTube

Provides timely reporting on the food and farming issues
Cost: $47.95
Frequency: 3x/Year
Founded in 1978

866 **The Alliance Link**
Animal Agriculture Alliance
2101 Wilson Blvd
Suite 916-B
Arlington, VA 22201

703-562-5160
info@animalagalliance.org
www.animalagalliance.org
Facebook, Twitter

Kay Johnson, President and CEO
Emily Meredith, Communications Specialist

Provides information about specific animal rights organizations and their campaigns, referenced quotes by the activists themselves, as well as information to help with security at your facilities.
Frequency: Monthly

867 **The Exchange**
Agricultural & Applied Economics Association
555 E Wells Street
Suite 1100
Milwaukee, WI 53202-6600

414-918-3190; Fax: 414-276-3349
jsaunders@aaea.org
www.aaea.org

Dawn Thilmany McFadden, President

Electronic newsletter for members of the American Agricultural Economics Association featuring association announcements, membership news, and updates from the profession.
3000 Members
Frequency: Bi-Monthly
Founded in 1910

868 **The Patrons Chain**
1616 H Street NW
Suite 10
Washington, DC 20006

202-628-3507
888-447-2643; Fax: 202-347-1091
www.nationalgrange.org/news/weekley-e-news letter

Official e-newsletter of The National Grange.

869 **USA Rice Daily**
USA Rice Federation
2101 Wilson Blvd
Suite 610
Arlington, VA 22201

703-226-2300; Fax: 703-236-2301
riceinfo@usarice.com
www.usarice.com
Facebook, Twitter, RSS, You Tube

Betsy Ward, President/CEO

The latest news on issues and activities for the U.S. rice industry.

870 **WSSA Newsletter**
P.O.Box 7065
Lawrence, KS 66044-7065

785-429-9622
800-627-0629; Fax: 785-843-1274
wssa@allenpress.com
www.wssa.net

Rod Lym, President
Joe DiTomaso, Vice President
John Madsen, Secretary
Ian Burke, Treasurer
James Anderson, Director Publications

Promotes research, education and extension outreach activities related to weeds, provides science-based information to the public and policy makers; and fosters awarenes of weeds and their impacts on managed and natural ecosystems.
Founded in 1956

871 **Webster Agricultural Letter**
Webster Communications Corporation
3835 9th St N
Suite 401W
Arlington, VA 22203-5812

703-525-4512; Fax: 703-852-3534
www.agletter.com

James C Webster, President
Marilyn Webster, Vice President

Agricultural politics and policy issues.
Cost: $397.00
6 Pages
Frequency: 2x Monthly
ISSN: 1073-4813
Founded in 1980
Printed in one color on matte stock

872 **Weekly Livestock Reporter**
PO Box 7655
Fort Worth, TX 76111-0655

817-831-3147; Fax: 817-831-3117
service@weeklylivestock.com
www.weeklylivestock.com

Ted Gouldy, Publisher
Phil Stoll, CEO/President
Mickey Schwarz, Circulation Manager

Offers comprehensive weekly information for cattle farmers and livestock agricultural professionals.
Cost: $18.00
Frequency: Weekly
Circulation: 10000
Founded in 1897

873 **Weekly Weather and Crop Bulletin**
NOAA/USDA Joint Agricultural Weather Facility
1400 Independence Ave SW
Washington, DC 20250

202-720-2791
www.usda.gov

Douglas LeComte, Publisher
Annette Holmes, Secretary

Provides a vital source of information on weather, climate and agricultural developments worldwide, along with detailed charts and tables of agrometeorological information that are appropriate for the season.
Cost: $60.00
Frequency: Weekly
Circulation: 1,500
Founded in 1862

Magazines & Journals

874 **AFIA Journal**
American Feed Industry Association
2101 Wilson Boulevard
Suite 916
Arlington, VA 22201

703-524-0810; Fax: 703-524-1921
afia@afia.org
www.afia.org
Facebook, Twitter, LinkedIn

Constance Cullman, President & CEO
Victoria Broehm, Communications Director

Variety of topics about the animal feed industry and its suppliers.
Frequency: Quarterly
Founded in 1909

875 **Acreage Magazine**
Heartland Communications Group
1003 Central Avenue
Fort Dodge, IA 50501

515-955-1600
800-247-2000
www.acreagelife.com
Facebook

Francis McLean, Publisher

Cultural news and features edited for rural farm producers magazine.
Cost: $5.00
40 Pages
Frequency: Monthly
Founded in 1985

876 **Acres USA**
5321 Industrial Oaks Boulevard
Suite 128
Austin, TX 78735

51- 8-2 44
800-355-5315; Fax: 512-892-4448
info@acresusa.com
www.acresusa.com
Facebook, Twitter, LinkedIn

Fred C Walters, CEO/President

Commercial-scale organic/ sustainable farming news.
Cost: $27.00
Frequency: Monthly
Circulation: 19000
ISSN: 1076-4968
Founded in 1970

877 **Agri Marketing Magazine**
Henderson Communications LLC
1422 Elbridge Payne Rd
Suite 250
Chesterfield, MO 63017-8544

636-728-1428; Fax: 636-777-4178
info@agrimarketing.com
www.agrimarketing.com

Lynn Henderson, Editorial Director
Audrey Evans, Customer Service Manager
Stephanie Wobbe, Editorial Assistant
Judy Henderson, Artist

Covers the unique interests of corporate agribusiness executives, their marketing communications agencies, the agricultural media, ag trade associations and other ag-related professionals.
Circulation: 8000
Founded in 1962

878 **AgriSelling Principles and Practices**
Henderson Communications LLC
1422 Elbridge Payne Rd
Suite 250
Chesterfield, MO 63017-8544

636-728-1428; Fax: 636-777-4178
info@agrimarketing.com
www.agrimarketing.com

Lynn Henderson, Editorial Director
Audrey Evans, Customer Service Manager
Stephanie Wobbe, Editorial Assistant
Judy Henderson, Artist

This 448-page book is utilized by many major agribusiness corporations and academic institutions for training its sales and marketing staff and or students.
Founded in 1962

879 **Agribusiness Fieldman**
Western Agricultural Publishing Company
4969 E Clinton Way
Suite 104
Fresno, CA 93727-1549

559-252-7000
westag@psnw.com

For the professional agricultural consultant, featuring the latest information on chemical regulation, pest control techniques and feature stories on PCA and PCO community.

880 **Agrichemical Age**
Farm Progress Publishers
191 S Gary Ave
Carol Stream, IL 60188-2024

630-690-5600
800-441-1410; Fax: 630-462-2869
www.farmprogress.com

Jeffry M Lapin, President
John Vogel, Editor
Willie Vogt, Corporate Editorial Director
John Otte, Economics Editor
Dan Crummett, Executive Editor

Information for fertilizer/pesticide dealers, distributors, commercial applicators and crop consultants.

881 **Agricultural Aviation**
National Agricultural Aviation Association
1440 Duke Street
Alexandria, VA 22314

202-546-5722; Fax: 202-546-5726
information@agaviation.org
www.agaviation.org

Andrew Moore, Chief Executive Officer

Official publication for legislative updates, industry trends, new products and more.
Frequency: 6x Yearly
Founded in 1978

882 **Agricultural History**
The Sheridan Press
MSU History Department
PO Box H
Mississippi State, MS 39762

662-268-2247
aimarcus@history.msstate.edu
www.aghistorysociety.org

Claire Strom, Editor
James C Giesen, Executive Secretary
Alan I Marcus, Treasurer

Traces historical lineage of agriculture in the US.
Cost: $47.00
Frequency: Quarterly
Circulation: 900
Founded in 1924

883 **Agriculture Research Magazine**
Agricultural Research Service
George Washington Carver Center
5601 Sunnyside Avenue
Beltsville, MD 20705-5130

301-504-1651; Fax: 301-504-1641
info@ars.usda.gov
www.ars.usda.gov/ar

Robert Sowers, Editor/Circulation Manager
William Johnson, Art Director
Edward Knipling, CEO
Carol Durflinger, Secretary
Cost: $50.00
27 Pages
Frequency: Monthly
Circulation: 45000
Founded in 1954

884 **Agronomy Journal**
5585 Guilford Road
Madison, WI 53711-1086

608-273-8080; Fax: 608-273-2021
headquarters@agronomy.org
www.agronomy.org
Facebook, Twitter, LinkedIn

Emily Mueller, Managing Editor

Journal of agriculture and natural resource sciences. Articles convey original research in soil science, crop science, agroclimatology, agronomic modeling, production agriculture, instrumentation, and more.
Founded in 1907

885 **Agweek**
Grand Forks Herald
375 2nd Avenue N
Grand Forks, ND 58203

701-780-1100
800-477-6572; Fax: 701-780-1123
onlineteam@gfherald.com
www.agweek.com
RSS

Michael Jacobs, Publisher/Editor
Tom Dennis, Editorial/Opinion Page Editor
Dawn Zimney, Circulation Director
Cory Matt, Managing Editor

Agweek features classified, weather information, farming, ranch news and opinions for the Upper Midwest.
Cost: $32.00
80 Pages
Frequency: Weekly
Circulation: 25,000
Founded in 1879
Printed in 4 colors

886 **Alimentos Balanceados Para Animales**
WATT Publishing Company
303 N Main Street
Rockford, IL 61101

815-966-5400; Fax: 815-966-6416
www.wattnet.com

Jim Watt, Chairman/CEO
Clayton Gill, Editorial Director
Christina Karmer, Human Resources Consultant

For feed industry professionals in Latin America.
Founded in 1994

887 **American Agriculturist**
Farm Progress Companies
5227 B Baltimore Park
Littlestown, PA 17340

717-359-0150
800-441-1410; Fax: 717-359-0250
jvogel@farmprogress.com
www.farmprogress.com

John Vogel, Editor
Willie Vogt, Corporate Editorial Director
Dan Crummett, Executive Editor

Serves Northeast producers with information to help them maximize their productivity and profitability. Each issue is packed with information, ideas, news and analysis.
Cost: $26.95
Frequency: Monthly
Founded in 1842

888 **American Bee Journal**
Dadant and Sons
51 S 2nd St
Hamilton, IL 62341-1397

217-847-3324
888-922-1293; Fax: 217-847-3660
editor@americanbeejournal.com
www.americanbeejournal.com
Facebook, Twitter

Tim C Dadant, President
Marta Menn, Advertising
Dianne Behnke, Publisher
Eugene Makovec, Editor

Read by commercial and hobby beekeepers and entomologists.
Cost: $22.95
80 Pages
Frequency: Monthly
Circulation: 11000
ISSN: 0002-7626
Founded in 1861
Printed in 4 colors on glossy stock

889 **American Christmas Tree Journal**
National Christmas Tree Association
16020 Swingley Ridge Rd
Suite 300
Chesterfield, MO 63017-6030

636-449-5070; Fax: 636-449-5051
info@realchristmastrees.org
www.realchristmastrees.org

Tim O'Connor, Executive Director
Ann O'Connor, Director, Programs & Membership
Dugald Kell, Jr., President
Steve Meier, President-Elect

Covers production and research topics, marketing advice, feature stories, legislative updates, tax and business management info, NCTA news and more
Cost: $57.00
Frequency: Quarterly
Circulation: 1500
ISSN: 0569-3845

890 **American Feed Industry Association Journal**
2101 Wilson Blvd
Suite 916
Arlington, VA 22201-3047

703-524-0810; Fax: 703-524-1921
afia@afia.org
www.afia.org
Facebook, Twitter, LinkedIn

Constance Cullman, President & CEO
Victoria Broehm, Communications Director

Includes a variety of topics about the animal feed industry and its suppliers.
Founded in 1909

891 **American Fruit Grower**
Meister Media Worldwide
37733 Euclid Ave
Willoughby, OH 44094-5992

440-942-2000
800-572-7740; Fax: 440-975-3447
info@meistermedia.com
www.meistermedia.com

Gary Fitzgerald, Chairman and CEO
Michael Deluca, President
Donald Hohmeier, VP and CFO

Specialized production and marketing information and industry-wide support for fruit growers.
Cost: $19.95
66 Pages
Frequency: Monthly
Circulation: 14000
Founded in 1880

892 **American Journal of Enology and Viticulture**
1784 Picasso Avenue, Suite D
PO Box 1855
Davis, CA 95617-1855

530-753-3142; Fax: 530-753-3318
society@asev.org

www.asev.org
Twitter, LinkedIn

Dan Howard, Executive Director
Daniel Friedlander, Publications & Tech Coordinator
Rosemary O'Brien, Publications Coordinator
Raquel Abad, Managing Editor

The official journal of the American Society for Enology and Viticulture and is the premier journal dedicated to scientific research on winemaking and grapegrowing.
Frequency: Quarterly
Founded in 1950

893 **American Small Farm Magazine**
Back 40 Group
P.O. Box 8
Hartshorn, MO 65479

573-858-3244
866-284-9844; Fax: 573-858-3245
www.smallfarm.com

Paul Berg, Editor
Herman Beck-Chenoweth, Publisher

Published for the owner/operator of farms from 5 to 300 acres. Focuses on production agriculture including alternative and sustainable farming ideas and technology, case studies, small farm lifestyle and tradition.
Cost: $18.00
Frequency: Monthly
Circulation: 62,444
ISSN: 1064-7473
Founded in 1992

894 **American Vegetable Grower**
Meister Media Worldwide
37733 Euclid Ave
Willoughby, OH 44094-5992

440-942-2000
800-572-7740; Fax: 440-975-3447
www.growingproduce.com/americanvegetablegrower/

Gary Fitzgerald, President
Rosemary Gordon, Editor
Jo Monahan, Publisher
Brian Sparks, Group Editor
Paul Rusnak, Managing Editor

American Vegetable Grower magazine provides insight on field, greenhouse and organic production, marketing, and new varieties and products.
Cost: $19.95
Frequency: Monthly
Circulation: 26000
Founded in 1908

895 **Animal & Dairy News**
American Dairy Science Association
2441 Village Green Pl
Champaign, IL 61822-7676

217-356-5146; Fax: 217-398-4119
adsa@assochq.org
www.adsa.org

Rich Erdman, President
Paul Kononoff, Editor-In-Chief

A Publication of ADSA
Founded in 1898
Mailing list available for rent

896 **Applied Economic Perspectives and Policy**
Agricultural & Applied Economics Association
555 E Wells Street
Suite 1100
Milwaukee, WI 53202-6600

414-918-3190; Fax: 414-276-3349
cggunder@illinois.edu
www.aaea.org/publications/aepp

Dawn Thilmany McFadden, President

Publishes research articles for an audience of agricultural and applied economists as well as a general audience.
3000 Members
Founded in 1910

897 **Beef Today**
Farm Journal Media
1818 Market Street
31st Floor
Philadelphia, PA 19103-3654

215-578-8900
800-331-9310; Fax: 215-568-6782
jstruyk@farmjournal.com
www.agweb.com/livestock/beef
Facebook, Twitter, YouTube

Andy Weber, Chief Executive Officer
Steve Custer, Executive Vice President
Jeff Pence, President, Electronic Media
Chuck Roth, Senior Vice President
Boyce Thompson, Editorial Director

This is the only nationwide publication that currently serves beef producers of all sizes-large and small. It delivers the tools cattlemen need to make sustainable and profitable choices to transition their herd to the next generation. Topics include genetics, animal health, business planning, pasture management, wildlife management and market analysis.
Frequency: Weekly
Founded in 1973

898 **Belt Pulley**
Belt Pulley Pub Company
PO Box 58
Jefferson, WI 53549-1341

920-674-9732
www.beltpulley.com

Katie Elmore, Publisher
Jane Aumann, Managing Editor

Covers antique tractors and farm machinery of all makes and models.
Cost: $20.00
Frequency: Monthly
Circulation: 3500
Founded in 1987

899 **Better Crops International Magazine**
Potash and Phosphate Institute
3500 Parkway Lane
Suite 550
Norcross, GA 30092-2844

770-447-0335; Fax: 770-448-0439
http://www.ipni.net/wave

Terry Roberts, President
Steve Couch, VP Administration
Gavin Sulewski, Editor

Researchers report on nutrient-related topics for corn, wheat, groundnut, oil palm, sugarcane, rice, crop rotations, and fish ponds. The issue concludes with a back cover commentary explaining why support of agricultural development is the right thing to do.

900 **Biodynamics Journal**
PO Box 944
East Troy, WI 53120-0944

26- 6-9 92
888-516-7797; Fax: 26- 6-9 92
info@biodynamics.com
www.biodynamics.com
Facebook

Thea Maria Carlson, Executive Director

Provides a thoughtful collection of original articles centered on a theme of interest to the biodynamic community. Recent themes have included urban agriculture, biodynamic community, earth healing, raw milk, and the biodynamic preparations.

901 **Capital Press**
Press Publishing Company
1400 Broadway NE
PO Box 2048
Salem, OR 97308-2048

503-364-4431
800-882-6789; Fax: 503-370-4383
www.capitalpress.com
Facebook, Twitter, LinkedIn, MySpace, Stumble Upon

Mike Forrester, President
John Perry, COO
Michael O'Brien, Publisher
Joe Beach, Editor

For the agricultural and forest community of the Pacific Northwest.
Cost: $44.00
60 Pages
Frequency: Weekly
Circulation: 37000
Founded in 1928
Printed in 4 colors

902 **Carrot Country**
Columbia Publishing
8405 Ahtanum Rd
Yakima, WA 98903-9432

509-248-2452
800-900-2452; Fax: 509-248-4056
dbrent@columbiapublications.com
www.carrotcountry.com

Brent Clement, Editor/Publisher
Mike Stoker, Publisher

Includes information on carrot production, grower and shipper feature stories, carrot research, new varieties, market reports, spot reports on overseas production and marketing and other key issues and trends of interest to US and Canadian carrot growers.
Cost: $10.00
Frequency: Quarterly
Circulation: 2500
ISSN: 1071-6653
Founded in 1993
Printed in 4 colors on glossy stock

903 **Cattle Guard**
Colorado Cattlemen's Agricultrual Land Trust
8833 Ralston Road
Arvada, CO 80002-2239

303-431-6422; Fax: 303-431-6446
www.coloradocattle.org

T Wright Dickinson, President
Frank Daley, First VP
Tim Canterbury, Treasurer
Terry Frankhauser, Executive VP
Heidi Brown, Membership and Operations Manager

A full overview of information is given through this magazine for cattle farmers and breeders.
Founded in 1867

904 **Cattleman**
Texas & Southwestern Cattle Raisers Association
1301 W 7th St
Suite 201
Fort Worth, TX 76102-2665

817-332-7064
800-242-7820; Fax: 817-332-8523
tscra@tscra.org
www.texascattleraisers.org
Facebook, Twitter

Joe Parker, President
Eldon White, Executive VP and CEO
Clay Birdwell, First VP
Pete Bonds, Second VP
Matt Brockman, Manager

Full overview of information for the cattle producer in Texas and Oklahoma.
Cost: $25.00
130 Pages
Frequency: Monthly
Circulation: 16000
Founded in 1877
Printed in 4 colors on glossy stock

905 **Cereal Foods World**
AACC International
3340 Pilot Knob Rd
St. Paul, MN 55121-2055

651-454-7250; Fax: 651-454-0766
akohn@scisoc.org
www.aaccnet.org

Robert L. Cracknell, President
Lydia Tooker Midness, Chair of Board
Dave L. Braun, Treasurer

Articles on scientific studies that focus on advances in grain based food science.
Founded in 1915

906 **Choices**
Agricultural & Applied Economics Association
555 E Wells Street
Suite 1100
Milwaukee, WI 53202-6600

414-918-3190; Fax: 414-276-3349
Alison.Davis@uky.edu
www.choicesmagazine.org
Twitter

Jill McCluskey, President
Janet Perry, Editor
Kynda Curtis, Editor
Alison Davis, Co-Editor
Amy Bekkerman, Technical Editor

Provides current coverage on economic implications of food, farm, resource or rural community issues. Subjects covered include agriculture and trade, resources and the environment, consumers and markets, agribusiness and finance.
3000 Members
Frequency: Quarterly
Founded in 1910

907 **Christmas Tree Lookout**
Pacific Northwest Christmas Tree Association
4093 12th Street SE
PO Box 3366
Salem, OR 97302

503-364-2942; Fax: 503-581-6819
info@christmas-tree.com
www.nwtrees.com

Bruce Wiseman, President
John Tillman, VP- Washington
Jan Hupp, Secretary/Treasurer
Mike Ramsby, V.P. Oregon
Bryan Ostlund, Executive Director

Marketing research and industry information for Christmas tree growers. Mailing list available.
Cost: $25.00
80 Pages
Frequency: Quarterly
Circulation: 1500
Founded in 1955
Printed in 4 colors on glossy stock

908 **Christmas Trees**
Tree Publishers
PO Box 304
Nevada, MO 64772

785-249-6769
ctreesmag@gmail.com
www.christmastreesmagazine.com
Facebook, Twitter

Catherine Meacham, Publisher & Editor
Becky Evatt, Director of Advertising

The world's leading magazine for Christmas tree growers. All aspects of Christmas tree production are covered from soil basics and planting to marketing and sales. Christmas Trees Magazine accepts advertising for Christmas tree seedlings, nurseries, tools, equipment, supplies, services, and other products sold to the real Christmas tree industry.
Cost: $16.00
44 Pages
Frequency: Quarterly
Circulation: 3200
ISSN: 0149-0217
Founded in 1973
Printed in 4 colors on glossy stock

909 **Citrus & Vegetable Magazine**
Vance Publishing
400 Knightsbridge Pkwy
Lincolnshire, IL 60069

847-634-2600; Fax: 847-634-4379
info@vancepublishing.com
www.vancepublishing.com

Shawn Etheridge, VP and Publishing Director
Matthew Morgan, Director
Greg Johnson, Editorial Director
Vicky Boyd, Editor

Devlivers profitable production and management strategies to commercial citrus and vegetable growers in Florida.
Cost: $45.00
Frequency: Monthly
Circulation: 12000
Founded in 1937
Printed in 4 colors on glossy stock

910 **Citrus Industry**
Southeast AgNet Publications
5053 NW Hwy 225-A
Ocala, FL 34482

352-671-1909; Fax: 888-943-2224
www.citrusindustry.net

William Cooper, President
Robin Loftin, Vice President
Ernie Neff, Editor

News, facts and data of interest to citrus growers, processors and shippers.
Cost: $24.00
64 Pages
Frequency: 6 issues per year
Circulation: 9900
Founded in 1920
Printed in 4 colors on glossy stock

911 **Cotton Farming**
One Grower Publishing, LLC
Collierville, TN 38117-5710

901-853-5067; Fax: 901-853-2197
lguthrie@onegrower.com
www.cottonfarming.com
Twitter, RSS, Flickr

Mike Rolfs, President
Lia Guthrie, Publisher
Tommy Horton, Editor
Carroll Smith, Senior Writer
Debbie Gibbs, Sales Manager

For commercial cotton growers across the United States Cotton Belt.
52 Pages
Frequency: Monthly
Circulation: 36300
Founded in 1993
Printed in 4 colors on glossy stock

912 **Country Living**
Arens Publications
395 S High Street
Covington, OH 45318-0069

937-473-2028; Fax: 937-473-2500
www.arenspub.com

Gary Godfrey, Owner
Connie Didier, Manager
Don Selanders, Sales Manager

Current news and features devoted to the agricultural industry.
Cost: $13.95
Frequency: Monthly
Circulation: 17000
Founded in 1954

913 **Country Woman**
Reiman Publications
5400 S 60th St
Greendale, WI 53129-1404

414-423-0100
888-861-1264; Fax: 414-423-1143
www.reimanpub.com
Facebook, Twitter

Barbara Newton, President
Marylin Kruse, Editor
Lisa Karpinski, Director/Marketing
Reese Ludewig, Marketing Manager

Offers recipes, stories, profiles and articles pertaining to the country woman.
Cost: $14.98
68 Pages
Frequency: 6 issues in a year
Circulation: 50,000 +
Founded in 1970

914 **Countryside and Small Stock Journal**
Countryside Publications
145 Industrial Dr
Medford, WI 54451-1711

715-785-7979
800-551-5691; Fax: 715-785-7414
customerservice@countrysidemag.com
www.countrysidemag.com

Mike Campbell, Publisher
Anne-Marie Belanger, Managing Editor
Elen Grunseth, Circulation & Fulfillment

Offers information for homesteaders seeking a self-reliant lifestyle.
Cost: $18.00
132 Pages
Circulation: 115000
ISSN: 8750-7595
Founded in 1917
Printed in on newsprint stock

915 **County Agents**
National Association of County Agricultural Agents
6584 W Duroc Road
Maroa, IL 61756

217-794-3700; Fax: 217-794-5901
exec-dir@nacaa.com
www.nacaa.com
Facebook, Twitter

J. Craig Williams, President

Members receive professional improvement, news of association activities, shared education efforts from other states and reports from NACAA leadership and member states.
Cost: $10.00
Frequency: Quarterly
Circulation: 5000
Founded in 1916
Mailing list available for rent: 3850 names at $125 per M
Printed in 4 colors on matte stock

916 **Cranberries Magazine**
Cranberries Magazine

PO Box 190
Rochester, MA 02770

508-763-8080; Fax: 508-763-4141

Carolyn Gilmore, Editor/Publisher

Containing up-to-date news, technical articles, new product information, grower profiles, economic data and other related features regarding the cranberry industry. Accepts advertising.
Cost: $25.00
28 Pages
Frequency: Monthly
Circulation: 850
Founded in 1936

917 **Crop Insurance Today**
National Crop Insurance Services
8900 Indian Creek Pkwy
Suite 600
Overland Park, KS 66210-1567

913-685-2767; Fax: 913-685-3080
webmaster@ag-risk.org
www.ag-risk.org

Thomas Zacharias, President & CEO

A quarterly magazine published by the National Crop Insurance Services. Includes current rate information, tips and advice, industry news, forecasts, and resources.
Cost: $13.00
Frequency: Quarterly
Circulation: 18000
Founded in 1915
Printed in 4 colors on glossy stock

918 **Crop Science**
Crop Science Society of America
5585 Guilford Road
Madison, WI 53711-5801

608-273-8080; Fax: 608-273-2021
headquarters@crops.org
www.crops.org
Facebook, Twitter, LinkedIn

Ellen Bergfeld, CEO
Wes Meixelsperger, CFO

Publishes original research in crop breeding and genetics, crop physiology and metabolism, crop ecology, production and management, and much more.
Founded in 1955

919 **DVM Magazine**
Advanstar Communications
8033 Flint St
Lenexa, KS 66214-3335

913-492-4300
800-225-6864; Fax: 913-871-3808
dverdon@advanstar.com
www.dvm360.com
Facebook, Twitter

Margaret Rampey, Editor
Marnette Falley, Principal
Sabrina Wilcox, COO
Dot Theisen, Sales Manager
Mindy Valcarcel, Senior Editor

The leading news in veterinary medicine covering news, features, practice management and new products and services.
Cost: $48.00
Frequency: Monthly
Circulation: 20000+
ISSN: 0012-7337
Founded in 1992

920 **Dairy Herd Management**
Vance Publishing
400 Knightsbridge Parkway
Lincolnshire, IL 60069

847-634-2600; Fax: 847-634-4379
info@vancepublishing.com
www.vancepublishing.com

Tom Quaife, Editor/Associate Publisher
Matthew Morgan, Director

Helps top dairy producers prepare for and adapt to the different management skills needed in this increasingly evolving industry
Cost: $60.00
Frequency: Monthly
Circulation: 61638

921 **Dairy Today**
Farm Journal
30 S 15th Street
Suite 900
Philadelphia, PA 19102-4803

215-578-8900
800-320-7992
www.farmjournal.com
Facebook, Twitter, RSS, You Tube

Charlene Finck, Editor
Katie Humphreys, Managing Editor
Beth Snyder, Art Director
Sara Schafer, Business & Crops Online Editor

Award-winning editorial covers the broad spectrum of production, nutrition and marketing information. It serves dairy producers who milk 40+ cows or are members of the Dairy Herd Improvement Association.
Frequency: Monthly
Circulation: 125000
Founded in 1989

922 **Dealer & Applicator**
Vance Publishing
400 Knightsbridge Pkwy
Lincolnshire, IL 60069-3628

847-634-2600; Fax: 847-634-4379
www.vancepublishing.com

Peggy Walker, President
Dean Horowitz, VP eMedia & Marketing
Steve Reiss, VP Salon & Woodworking
William C. Vance, CEO
Shawn Etheridge, VP Produce & Raw Crop

Serves as the reader's business partner to provide full-service dealers and custom applicators with management and business strategies to increase profitability.
Founded in 1937

923 **Drovers**
Vance Publishing
400 Knightsbridge Parkway
Lincolnshire, IL 60069

847-634-2600; Fax: 847-634-4379
info@vancepublishing.com
www.vancepublishing.com

William C Vance, Chairman
Peggy Walker, President

Recognized as the beef industry leader for more than 130 years, valued for its management, production and marketing information.
Cost: $60.00
Frequency: Monthly
Circulation: 92000
Founded in 1873

924 **Eastern DairyBusiness**
DairyBusiness Communications
6437 Collamer Road
East Syracuse, NY 13057-1031

315-703-7979
800-334-1904; Fax: 315-703-7988
kjentz@dairybusiness.com
www.dairybusiness.com
Facebook, Twitter, YouTube

Joel P Hastings, President
John Montandon, President & Co-CEO
Scott A Smith, Chairman / Co-CEO

Reports on milk production and prices, quotes on hay and feed markets, animal health and nutrition, and the newest innovations in dairying technology, specifically tailored to the Eastern parts of the United States
Cost: $49.95
67 Pages
Frequency: Monthly
Circulation: 14000
ISSN: 1528-4360
Founded in 1904
Printed in 4 colors on glossy stock

925 **Egg Industry**
WATT Publishing Company
303 N Main Street
Suite 500
Rockford, IL 61101

815-966-5400; Fax: 815-966-6416
tokeefe@wattnet.net
www.wattnet.com

James Watt, Chairman
Greg Watt, President/CEO
Terrance O'Keefe, Content Director

Regarded as the standard for information on current issues, trends, production practices, processing, personalities and emerging technology. A pivotal source of news, data and information for decision-makers in the buying centers of companies producing eggs and further-processed products.
Cost: $36.00
Frequency: Monthly
Circulation: 2500

926 **Executive Guide to World Poultry Trends**
WATT Publishing Company
303 N Main Street
Suite 500
Rockford, IL 61101

815-966-5400; Fax: 815-966-6416
www.wattnet.com

James Watt, Chairman/CEO
Greg Watt, President/COO
Jeff Swanson, Publishing Director

Offers detailed analysis on a country-by-country and market-by-market basis.

927 **FFA New Horizons**
National FFA Organization
6060 FFA Drive
P.O. Box 68960
Indianapolis, IN 46268

317-802-6060
800-772-0939; Fax: 317-802-6051
newhorizons@ffa.org
www.ffanewhorizons.org
Facebook, Twitter

Jessy Yancey, Association Editor
Christina Carden, Associate Production Director
Julie Woodard, FFA Publications Manager

The official member magazine of the FFA contains information about agricultural education, career possibilities, chapter and individual accomplishments and news on FFA. Now available online.
100 Pages
Frequency: Bi-Monthly
Circulation: 525000
ISSN: 1069-806x
Founded in 1928
Printed in 4 colors

928 **FRONTIER**
Meat & Livestock Australia
1401 K Street NW
Suite 602
Washington, DC 20005

202-521-2551; Fax: 202-521-2699
info@mla.com.au
www.mla.com.au
Facebook, Twitter, YouTube

Don Heatley, Chairman
David Palmer, Managing Director
Bernie Bindon, Director
Chris Hudson, Director

Offers northern beef producers practical information on how to best manage their cattle enterprise and improve on-property profits and sustainability.
30000 Members
Frequency: Quarterly
Founded in 1998

929 **Farm Chemicals International**
Meister Media Worldwide
65 Germantown Ct.
Suite 202
Cordova, TN 38018

901-756-8822
800-572-7740
www.farmchemicalsinternational.com
Facebook, Twitter, RSS

William Miller II, President
Rosemary Gordon, Editor
Robert White, COO
Roger Hercl, CFO
Richard Meister, Director

Information on production, marketing and application of crop protection chemicals and fertilizers.
Circulation: 8000
Founded in 1986

930 **Farm Equipment**
Lessiter Media
P.O. Box 624
Brookfield, WI 53008-0624

262-782-4480
800-645-8455; Fax: 262-782-1252
dkanicki@lessitermedia.com
www.farm-equipment.com
Facebook, Twitter, LinkedIn, YouTube

Mike Lessiter, Editor & Publisher
Dave Kanicki, Executive Editor
Michael Ellis, Director of Sales

Delivers coverage of the farm equipment dealership market. Topics include: streamling your operation, business trends and outlooks, industry news and trends.
Frequency: 8/Year

931 **Farm Equipment Guide**
Heartland Communications
1003 Central Avenue
PO Box 1115
Fort Dodge, IA 50501-1115

515-955-1600
800-247-2000; Fax: 515-574-2182
dustin@agdeal.com
www.farmershotline.com
Facebook, Twitter

Sandra J Simonson, Group Publisher
Tracy Roper, Production Manager
Tammy Sweeney, Operational Manager
Dustin Hector, Sales Manager
Chet Frahm, Advertising Sales Associate

A subscription that includes an annual blue book of specifications, serial numbers and average pricing on farm machinery with monthly updates that list thousands of pieces for sale and thousands of actual auction values.
120 Pages
Frequency: Monthly
Circulation: 20,000
ISSN: 1047-725X
Founded in 1981
Printed in 4 colors on glossy stock

932 **Farm Impact**
314 E Church Street
Mascoutah, IL 62258-2100

618-566-8282; Fax: 618-566-8283

Greg Hoskins, Publisher
Michael King, Advertising Manager

Offers information to farmers.
Frequency: Monthly

933 **Farm Journal**
30 S 15th Street
Suite 900
Philadelphia, PA 19102-4803

215-557-8900
800-523-1538; Fax: 215-568-4436
scuster@farmjournal.com
www.farmjournalmedia.com

Andrew J Weber Jr, CEO/President
Crain Freiberg, Editor
Steve Custer, President/Publishing
Chuck Roth, Senior Vice President/Project Dev

Published for operators and owners of commercial farms and ranches. Provides timely, useful marketing and management information to help them produce more efficiently, buy more wisely, sell their products at the highest possible prices, and retain as much of their income as possible.
Cost: $24.75
182 Pages
Frequency: Monthly
Circulation: 440,000
Founded in 1878

934 **Farm Reporter**
Meridian Star
814 22nd Avenue
PO Box 1591
Meridian, MS 39302

601-693-1551; Fax: 601-485-1210
www.meridianstar.com
Facebook, Twitter

Michael Stewart, Executive Editor
Steve Gillespie, Assistant Editor
Ida Brown, Staff Writer
Briand Livingston, Staff Writer
Otha Barham, Outdoors Page

Reports on every phase of farming including timber, cattle, poultry and all growing crops.
Cost: $2.00
Frequency: Monthly

935 **Farm Review**
Lewis Publishing Company
PO Box 153
Lynden, WA 98264-0153

360-354-4444; Fax: 360-354-4445
www.lyndentribune.com

Michael D Lewis, Publisher
Calvin Bratt, Editor
Diane Partlow, Circulation Manager

Offers a review of farming techniques and trends nationwide.
Cost: $30.00
Frequency: Quarterly
Circulation: 7000
Founded in 1888

936 **Farm Show Magazine**
Farm Show Publishing
Johnson Building
PO Box 1029
Lakeville, MN 55044-1029

952-469-5572
800-834-9665; Fax: 952-469-5579
www.farmshow.com/
Facebook

Mark Newhall, Editor/Publisher
Bill Gergen, Associate Editor

Focuses on latest agricultural products, and product evaluation. Contains no advertising.
Cost: $17.95
Founded in 1977

937 **Farm Talk**
Farm Talk
1801 S Highway 59
PO Box 601
Parsons, KS 67357-4900

620-421-9450
800-356-8255; Fax: 620-421-9473
farmtalk@terraworld.net
www.farmtalknewspaper.com

Mark Parker, Publisher
Ted Gum, Manager

Agriculture for Eastern Kansas, Western Missouri, Northeast Oklahoma and Northwest Arkansas.
Cost: $30.00
60 Pages
Frequency: Weekly
Circulation: 10000
Founded in 1974

938 **Farm World (Farm Week)**
Mayhill Publications
27 N Jefferson Street
PO Box 90
Knightstown, IN 46148-1242

317-326-2235
800-876-5133; Fax: 765-345-3398

Dave Blower Jr, Editor
Richard Lewis, Publisher
Diana Scott, Marketing Manager

Agriculture, farming, and related areas in Indiana, Ohio and Kentucky. Accepts advertising.
Cost: $28.50
84 Pages
Frequency: Monthly

939 **Farm and Dairy**
Lyle Printing and Publishing Company
185 E State Street
PO Box 38
Salem, OH 44460

330-337-3419
800-837-3419; Fax: 330-337-9550
farmanddairy@aol.com
www.farmanddairy.com

Scot Darling, Chief Executive Officer, Publisher
Susan Crowell, Editor
Billy Sekely, Advertising Manager
Howard Marsh, Circulation Manager

Briefs of research reports from experiment stations in agriculture, success stories concerning farmers of Ohio, Pennsylvania and West Virginia, sale and livestock market reports, auctions and more. Accepts advertising.
Cost: $ 28.00
132 Pages
Circulation: 33500
ISSN: 0014-7826
Founded in 1914
Printed in 4 colors on n stock

940 **Farm and Ranch Living**
Reiman Publications

5400 S 60th St
Greendale, WI 53129-1404

414-423-0100
888-858-5417; Fax: 414-423-1143
editors@farmandranchliving.com
www.reimanpub.com

Barbara Newton, President
Catherine Cassidy, SVP/Editor-in-Chief
Ann Kaiser, Editor
Lisa Karpinski, Marketing & Circulation Manager
Gretchen Trautman, Membership Director

Includes stories written by working farm families, antique tractor events and rural photo contests.
Cost: $3.99
68 Pages
Frequency: Bimonthly
Founded in 1978

941 **FarmWorld**
DMG World Media
27 N Jefferson Street
PO Box 90
Knightstown, IN 46148-1242

765-345-5133
800-876-5133; Fax: 765-345-5133
webmaster@farmworldonline.com
www.farmworldonline.com

Tony Gregory, Publisher
David Blower Jr, Editor
Meggie Foster, Assistant Editor
Toni Hodson, Advertising Manager

Agriculture, farming, and related areas in Indiana, Ohio and Kentucky. Accepts advertising.
Cost: $38.95
84 Pages
Frequency: Weekly
Founded in 1955
Printed in 4 colors on newsprint stock

942 **Farmers Digest**
Heartland Communications
1003 Central Avenue
PO Box 1115
Fort Dodge, IA 50501-1115

515-955-1600
800-247-2000; Fax: 515-574-2182
www.agdeal.com

Sandra J Simonsoa, Group Publisher
Melanie Filloon, Subscription Coordinator

Straightforwarded, commonsense articles on every aspect of farming and ranching edited with one goal in mind - to make you a better farmer or rancher.
Founded in 1941

943 **Farmers Hot Line**
Heartland Communications
1003 Central Avenue
Fort Dodge, IA 50501-1052

515-955-1600
800-247-2000; Fax: 515-955-1668
www.agdeal.com
Facebook, Twitter

Gale W McKinney II, President/CFO
Mary Gonnerman, Vice President
Sandy Simonson, Publisher
Dustin Hector, Sales Manager
Chet Frahm, Advertising Sales Associate

Distributed to manufacturers, farmers, auctioneers and service companies nationwide. Designed to help buyers and sellers of new and used farm machinery, auctions, farm real estate, services and supplies.
Cost: $9.95
Circulation: 50000
Founded in 1988

944 **Farmers' Advance**
Camden Publications
331 E Bell Street
PO Box 130
Camden, MI 49232

517-368-0365
800-222-6336; Fax: 517-368-5131
www.farmersadvance.com/
Facebook

Don Lee, Circulation Manager
Richard Aginian, President
Ken Ungar, Senior Vice President
Kyle Hupfer, Director

Farming technology magazine.
Cost: $25.00
Frequency: Weekly
Circulation: 20000
Founded in 1898

945 **Farmers' Exchange**
Exchange
PO Box 490
Fayetteville, TN 37334

931-433-9737; Fax: 931-433-0053

William Thomas, Publisher/Editor/CEO
Jim Bowers, Sales/Marketing Manager

Magazine offers a forum for the exchange of farming ideas and information country-wide.
56 Pages
Frequency: Monthly
Circulation: 30000
Founded in 1987

946 **Farmshine**
Dieter Krieg
State and Main Streets
PO Box 219
Brownstown, PA 17508

717-656-8050
866-724-6455; Fax: 717-656-8188
www.farmshine.com

Dieter Krieg, Publisher/Editor
Tammy Krieg, Ad Sales

Information pertaining to the farming community.
Cost: $12.00
Frequency: Weekly
ISSN: 0745-7553
Founded in 1979
Printed in on newsprint stock

947 **Fastline Catalog**
Fastline Publications
4900 Fox Run Road
P.O. Box 248
Buckner, KY 40010

502-222-0146
800-626-6409; Fax: 502-222-0615
www.fastline.com
Facebook, Twitter, YouTube, Flickr

William G Howard, President/Editor
Susan Arterburn, Marketing Director
Pat Higgins, Vice President, Sales

Nationwide and regional picture buying guides for the farming industry.
Frequency: Monthly
Founded in 1978

948 **Feed & Grain**
Cygnus Business Media
1233 Janesville Ave
Fort Atkinson, WI 53538

631-845-2700
800-547-7377
info@cygnus.com

John French, CEO
Paul Bonaiuto, CFO
Edward Wood, Vice President, HR & Communications

Provides techniques and solutions on ways yo increase productivity and profitability for the commercial feed, grain and allied processing industry.
Frequency: Bi-Monthly
Circulation: 16,500

949 **Feed Additive Compendium**
The Miller Publishing Company
5810 W 78th St
Suite 200
Bloomington, MN 55439

952-931-0211; Fax: 952-938-1832
smuirhead@feedstuffs.com
www.feedstuffs.com

Sarah Muirhead, Publisher
Rod Smith, Staff Editor/Livestock & Poultry
Sally Schuff, Staff Editor/Washington Bureau
Jacqui Fatka, Staff Editor/Grains & Ingredients
Kristin Baker, Editorial Production Manager

This magazine takes a closer look at the food additives and agriculture industries.
Cost: $260.00
Frequency: Weekly
Founded in 1935

950 **Feed International**
WATT Publishing Company
303 N Main Street
Suite 500
Rockford, IL 61101

815-966-5400; Fax: 815-966-6416
www.wattnet.com

James Watt, Chairman/CEO
Greg Watt, President/COO
Ken Jennison, Editor

Provides feed formulators and manufacturers outside North America with the latest feed and grain market developments, management strategies, and information on nutrition and regulations to efficiently and safely formulate, process and market animal feeds and become more competitive in the world market.
Cost: $48.00
Frequency: Monthly
Circulation: 19191
ISSN: 9274-5771
Founded in 1980
Mailing list available for rent: 19,191 names at $225 per M
Printed in 4 colors

951 **Feed Management**
WATT Publishing Company
303 N Main Street
Suite 500
Rockford, IL 61101

815-966-5400; Fax: 815-966-6416
www.wattnet.com

Jim Watt, Chairman/CEO
Greg Watt, President/COO
Ken Jennison, Editor

Covers the latest news in feed production, nutritional developments and trends, food safety and regulatory developments, grain markets, management strategies and new products.
Cost: $48.00
Circulation: 20,250
ISSN: 0014-956X
Founded in 1950
Mailing list available for rent: 20,249 names at $155 per M
Printed in 4 colors on glossy stock

952 **Flue Cured Tobacco Farmer**
Tabacco Farmer.Com

3101 Poplarwood Court
Suite 115
Raleigh, NC 27604

91- 8-2 47; Fax: 919-876-6531
www.tobaccofarmer.com

Dayton Matlick, Chairman
Taco Tuinstra, Editor in Chief
Noel Morris, Publisher

Business of farming publication for commercial tobacco producers. Feature articles deal with the research-backed production, harvesting and marketing aspects of the flue cured tobacco.
Cost: $25.00
Circulation: 14000
ISSN: 0015-4512
Founded in 1964
Printed in 4 colors on glossy stock

953 **Food Aid Needs Assessment**
US Department of Agriculture
1400 Independence Avenue SW
Washington, DC 20250

202-690-7650
800-999-6779; Fax: 202-720-2030
www.usda.gov
Facebook, Twitter, LinkedIn, YouTube, Flickr

Gene Mathia, Branch Chief

This annual report assesses the food situation in 60 developing countries. Most of the data are presented by region; crisis countries are covered individually.
Cost: $30.00
Founded in 1862

954 **Forest Science**
5400 Grosvenor Ln
Bethesda, MD 20814-2198

301-897-8720
866-897-8720; Fax: 301-897-3690
www.safnet.org
Facebook, Twitter, LinkedIn

Morgan Fincham, Director, Publications

Provides access to information and networking opportunities to prepare members for the challenges and the changes that face natural resource professionals.
Founded in 1900

955 **Fresh Cut Magazine**
Great American Publishing
75 Applewood Drive, Suite A
PO Box 128
Sparta, MI 49345

616-887-9008; Fax: 616-887-2666
fcedit@freshcut.com
www.freshcut.com

Matt McCallum, Publisher
Kimberly Baker, Director of Media Services
Beecky Bosserd, Circulation Manager
Lee Dean, Editorial Director

Covers all sectors of the international value-added produce industry. Features industry profiles, research reports, governmental legislation coverage, industry columnists, news reports, new equipment showcases and much more.
Cost: $15.00
40 Pages
Frequency: Monthly
ISSN: 1072-2831
Founded in 1993
Printed in 4 colors on glossy stock

956 **Fresh Digest**
Fresh Produce & Floral Council
16700 Valley View Ave
Suite 130
La Mirada, CA 90638-5844

714-739-0177; Fax: 714-739-0226
info@fpfc.org
www.fpfc.org

Addresses issues concerning the Western US, with heavy emphasis on the important California market, read by thousands of professionals in the produce and floral industries.
600+ Members
Founded in 1965

957 **Fruit Country**
Clintron Publishing
PO Box 547
Yakima, WA 98907-0547

509-248-2452
800-869-7923; Fax: 509-248-4056

Clintke Withers, Publisher
John M Dahlin, Editor

Written for and about growers, their operations and their needs. Stories on growers and shippers, developments and trends in the fruit industry, human interest stories and politics, new products, chemicals and supplies, avant garde management techniques, cultural practices and tips on profitability. Advertising equipment and services to the fruit industry and distribution system.
Cost: $12.00
Frequency: Monthly
Circulation: 11,500

958 **Futures Magazine**
Futures Magazine
111 W Jackson Blvd
7th Floor
Chicago, IL 60604-4139

312-977-0999; Fax: 312-846-4638
www.aip.com

Steve Lown, Manager
James T Holter, Editor

Agriculture commodities charted by various technical studies, plus analysis.
Cost: $39.00
24 Pages
Frequency: Monthly
Founded in 1972

959 **Game Bird Breeders, Agiculturists, Zoologists and Conservationists**
Game Bird Breeders
1155 W 4700 S
Salt Lake City, UT 84123
George Allen, Editor

Articles on how to keep and breed all types of game birds.
Cost: $18.00
45 Pages
Frequency: Monthly
Founded in 1974

960 **Good Day! Magazine**
1616 H Street NW
Suite 10
Washington, DC 20006

202-628-3507
888-447-2643; Fax: 202-347-1091
www.nationalgrange.org/news/weekley-e-news letter

General interest publication from The National Grange.
Cost: $7.00
Frequency: Quarterly

961 **Grape Grower**
Western Agricultural Publishing Company
4969 E Clinton Way
Suite 104
Fresno, CA 93727

559-252-7000; Fax: 559-252-7387
westag@psnw.com

Paul Baltimore, Co Publisher
Jim Baltimore, Co Publisher
Randy Bailey, Editor
Robert Fujimoto, Assistant Editor

The West's most widely read authority on the cultivation of table grapes, raising grapes and wine grapes. All aspects of production are covered with the most current university, government and private research.

962 **Greenhouse Grower**
Meister Media Worldwide
37733 Euclid Ave
Willoughby, OH 44094-5992

440-942-2000
800-572-7740; Fax: 440-975-3447
www.meistermedia.com

Gary Fitzgerald, President
Rick T Melnick, Corporate Editorial Director

Industry-leading voice for the commercial floriculture industry in the United States. Compiles buyers' directories and annual reports on the largest growers in the nation, produces vibrant emedia products and manages industry-leading events and awards programs.
Frequency: Monthly
Circulation: 20000
Founded in 1932

963 **Grower**
Vance Publishing
400 Knightsbridge Parkway
Lincolnshire, IL 60069

847-634-2600; Fax: 847-634-4379
info@vancepublishing.com
www.vancepublishing.com

William C Vance, Chairman
Peggy Walker, President

Positioned as the key source of profitable production and management strategies to commercial producers who control 90% of the U.S. fruit and vegetable market.
Cost: $45.00
Frequency: Monthly
Circulation: 22,000
Founded in 1937

964 **Growertalks Magazine**
Ball Publishing
622 Town Road
PO Box 1660
West Chicago, IL 60186

630-231-3675
888-888-0013; Fax: 630-231-5254
info@ballpublishing.com
www.growertalks.com

Chris Beytes, Editor/Publisher
Jennifer Zurko, Managing Editor

Specializes in the publishing of horticulture information, primarily related to floriculture production and marketing.
Frequency: Monthly
Circulation: 12000
Founded in 1937

965 **Guernsey Breeders' Journal**
Purebred Publishing Inc
1224 Alton Darby Creeek Road
Suite G
Columbus, OH 43228

614-864-2409; Fax: 614-864-5614
info@usguernsey.com
www.usguernsey.com

Seth Johnson, Executive Secretary-Treasurer
Brian Schnebly, Programs Coordinator

Katie Hensen, Editor
Ashley Shaffer, Assistant Editor

The journal discusses breeder stories, management trends and events in the Guernsey industry.
Frequency: 10x Yearly

966 **Gulf Coast Cattleman**
EC Larkin
11201 Morning Court
San Antonio, TX 78213-1300

210-334-8300; Fax: 210-344-4258
info@gulfcoastcattleman.com
www.gulfcoastcattleman.com
Facebook

EC Larkin, Jr., President/Editor
Joan Dover, Circulation/Office Manager
Chel Terrell, Managing Editor

Services commercial cattlemen along the Gulf Coast states with industry news, management and herd health related articles.
Cost: $15.00
64 Pages
Frequency: Monthly
Circulation: 16000
ISSN: 0017-5552
Founded in 1935
Printed in 4 colors on glossy stock

967 **Hereford World**
American Hereford Association
PO Box 014059
Kansas City, MO 64101

81- 8-2 37; Fax: 816-842-6931
aha@hereford.org
www.hereford.org

Craig Huffhines, Executive VP

Trade magazine for breeders of registered Polled Hereford cattle.
Frequency: Monthly
Circulation: 9500
Founded in 1742

968 **High Country News**
High Country Foundation
119 Grand Avenue
P.O. Box 1090
Paonia, CO 81428

970-527-4898
800-905-1155; Fax: 970-527-4897
circulation@hcn.org
www.hcn.org
Facebook, Twitter, LinkedIn, YouTube, Instagram, Google+

Paul Larmer, Executive Director/Publisher
Brian Calvert, Managing Editor
Gretchen King, Director, Engagement
Laurie Milford, Director, Development

High Country News is the nation's leading source of reporting on the American West. Its mission is to inform and inspire people - through in-depth jurnalism - to act on behalf of the West's diverse natural and human communities.
32000 Members
Founded in 1970
Mailing list available for rent: 53,000 names

969 **High Plains Journal/Midwest Ag Journal**
High Plains Publishing Company
1500 E Wyatt Earp Boulevard
PO Box 760
Dodge City, KS 67801

620-227-1834
800-452-7171; Fax: 620-227-7173
journal@hpj.com
www.hpj.com

Tom Tayor, Publisher/CEO
Holly Martin, Editor
John Seatvet, Sales Manager
Sarah Farlee, Marketing Director

Farming news for the central states.
Cost: $46.00
Frequency: Weekly
Circulation: 50000
Printed in 4 colors on glossy stock

970 **Hog Producer**
Farm Progress
6200 Aurora Avenue
Suite 609 E
Urbandale, IA 50322-2838

515-278-6693; Fax: 515-278-7797
jotte@farmprogress.com
www.farmprogress.com

Sara Wyant, Publisher
John Otte, Editor

Management publication to help pork producers in the production, housing, genetics, health care and marketing of hogs.

971 **Holstein Pulse**
Holstein Association USA
PO Box 808
Brattleboro, VT 05302-0808

802-254-4551
800-965-5200; Fax: 802-254-8251
info@holstein.com
www.holsteinusa.com

Corey Geiger, President
Frequency: Quarterly
Circulation: 19000

972 **Holstein World**
Dairy Business Communications
6437 Collamer Road
East Syracuse, NY 13057

315-703-7979
800-334-1904; Fax: 315-703-7988
www.holsteinworld.com

Joel P Hastings, Publisher/Editor
Janice Barrett, Associate Editor

Showcases breeders who own America's genetically superior cattle. Elite group of progressive dairymen who have income, herd size, and milk production considerably above the national average.
Cost: $38.95
123 Pages
Frequency: Monthly
Circulation: 12000
ISSN: 0199-4239
Founded in 1904
Printed in 4 colors on glossy stock

973 **HortScience**
American Society for Horticultural Science
1018 Duke Street
Alexandria, VA 22314-2851

703-836-4606; Fax: 703-836-2024
webmaster@ashs.org
www.ashs.org

Michael Neff, Executive Director

HortScience is a monthly journal concentrating on significant research, education, extension findings, and methods.
Cost: $85.00
160 Pages
Frequency: Monthly
Circulation: 2500
ISSN: 0018-5345
Founded in 1903
Mailing list available for rent: 2500 names at $100 per M

974 **Implement & Tractor**
Farm Journal Media
1818 Market Street
31st Floor
Philadelphia, PA 19103-3654

215-578-8900
800-331-9310; Fax: 215-568-6782
jstruyk@farmjournal.com
www.agweb.com/machinery/implement_tractor.aspx

Andy Weber, Chief Executive Officer
Steve Custer, Executive Vice President
Jeff Pence, President, Electronic Media
Chuck Roth, Senior Vice President

Implement & Tractor is a bimonthly publication providing news and insights for dealers, distributors, OEMs, engineers and the associations that make up the more than $40 billion dealer and wholesaler equipment industry.
Frequency: Bimonthly
Founded in 1885

975 **International Journal of Vegetable Science**
Taylor & Francis Group LLC
325 Chestnut St
Suite 800
Philadelphia, PA 19106-2614

215-625-8900
800-354-1420; Fax: 215-625-2940
haworthorders@taylorandfrancis.com
www.taylorandfrancis.com

Vincent M. Russo, Editor

Features innovative articles on all aspects of vegetable production, including growth regulation, pest management, sustainable production, harvesting, handling, storage, shipping and final consumption.
Frequency: Quarterly

976 **International Poultry Exposition Guide**
WATT Publishing Company
122 S Wesley Ave
Mt Morris, IL 61054-1451

815-734-7937; Fax: 815-734-4201
www.wattnet.com

Jim Watt, Chairman/CEO
Lisa Thornton, Managing Editor
Clay Schreiber, Publisher

977 **Invasive Plant Science and Management Journal**
P.O.Box 7065
Lawrence, KS 66044-7065

785-429-9622
800-627-0326; Fax: 785-843-1274
wssa@allenpress.com
www.wssa.net

Dale Shaner, President
Jeff Derr, VP
Tom Mueller, Secretary
Dave Gealy, Treasurer
Michael Foley, Director Publications

Promotes research, education and extension outreach activities related to weeds, provides science-based information to the public and policy makers; and fosters awarenes of weeds and their impacts on managed and natural ecosystems.
2000 Members
Founded in 1956

978 **Jojoba Happenings**
John S Turner Public Relations
805 N 4th Avenue
Unit 404
Phoenix, AZ 85003-1304

FAX 602-252-5722

John Turner, Publisher
Ken Lucas, Editor

Jojoba farming. Accepts advertising.
8 Pages
Frequency: Bi-Monthly

979 **Journal of Agricultural & Food Chemistry**
American Chemical Society
1155 16th St NW
Washington, DC 20036-4892

202-872-4600
800-227-9919; Fax: 202-872-4615
www.pubs.acs.org

Madeleine Jacobs, CEO
John W Finley, Associate Editor
Elizabeth Waters, Associate Editor

Research results in pesticides, fertilizers, agricultural and food processing chemistry.
Cost: $146.00
Frequency: Monthly
Circulation: 159000
Founded in 1856

980 **Journal of Animal Science (JAS)**
PO Box 7410
Champaign, IL 61826

217-356-9050; Fax: 217-398-4119
www.asas.org
Facebook, Twitter, RSS

Meghan Wulster-Radcliffe, CEO

Premier journal for animal science and serves as the leading source of new knowledge and perspective in this area. JAS consistently ranks as on of the top journals in the category of Agriculture, Dairy, and Animal Sciences.
Frequency: Monthly
ISSN: 0021-8812
Founded in 1908

981 **Journal of Applied Communications**
Association for Communications Excellence
University of Florida
407 Rolfs Hall
Gainesville, FL 32611-0540

352-273-2094; Fax: 352-392-8583
rwtelg@ufl.edu
www.aceweb.org

Katie Abrams, Executive Editor
Courtney Meyers, Managing Editor

A referred journal offering professional development for educational communicators who emphasize agriculture, natural resources, and life and human sciences.
Frequency: Quarterly
ISSN: 1051-0834

982 **Journal of Applied Communications (JAC)**
ACE
448 Agricultural Hall
Stillwater, OK 74078

40- 7-4 04
866-941-3048
www.journalofappliedcommunications.org

Dwayne Cartmell, Executive Editor
Ricky Telg, Editorial Board Chair

The Journal of Applied Communications is a refereed journal offering professional development for educational communicators who emphasize agriculture, natural resources, and life and human sciences.
Frequency: Quarterly
Founded in 1970

983 **Journal of Aquatic Plant Management**
PO Box 821265
Vicksburg, MS 39182-1265

FAX 601-634-5502
webmaster@apms.org
www.apms.org
Facebook, LinkedIn

Terry Goldsby, President
Cody Gray, VP
Sherry Whitaker, Treasurer
Jeff Schardt, Secretary
Robert J. Richardson, Editor

A publication of the Aquatic Plant Management Society, Inc.
Founded in 1961

984 **Journal of Biomolecular Screening**
36 Tamarack Ave
Suite 348
Danbury, CT 06811

203-778-8828; Fax: 203-748-7557
www.sbsonline.org

Jeff Paslay, President
Michelle Palmer, Executive Director
Christine Giordano, Executive Director

The leading peer-reviewed journal focusing on drug-discovery sciences. Delivers the latest advancements in quantitative biomolecular sciences.
Cost: $175.00
Frequency: 10x/Year

985 **Journal of Dairy Science**
American Dairy Science Association
2441 Village Green Pl
Champaign, IL 61822-7676

217-356-5146; Fax: 217-398-4119
adsa@assochq.org
www.adsa.org

Rich Erdman, President
Paul Kononoff, Editor-In-Chief

Official Journal of the American Dairy Science Association
3000 Members
Founded in 1898
Mailing list available for rent

986 **Journal of Environmental Quality**
5585 Guilford Road
Madison, WI 53711-1086

608-273-8080; Fax: 608-273-2021
headquarters@agronomy.org
www.agronomy.org
Facebook, Twitter, LinkedIn

Ann Edahl, Managing Editor

Published by ASA, CSSA, and SSSA. Papers are grouped by subject matter and cover water, soil, and atmospheric research as it relates to agriculture and the environment.
11000 Members
Founded in 1907

987 **Journal of Forestry**
Society of American Foresters
5400 Grosvenor Ln
Bethesda, MD 20814-2198

301-897-8720
866-897-8720; Fax: 301-897-3690
www.safnet.org
Facebook, Twitter, LinkedIn

Morgan Fincham, Director, Publications

To advance the profession of forestry by keeping professionals informed about significant developments and ideas in the many facets of forestry: economics, education and communication, entomology and pathology, fire, forest ecology, geospatial technologies, history, international forestry, measurements, policy, recreation, silviculture, social sciences, soils and hydrology, urband and community forestry, utilization and engineering, and wildlife management.
Cost: $85.00
Frequency: 8x Yearly
ISSN: 0022-1201
Founded in 1902

988 **Journal of Natural Resources & Life Sciences Education**
5585 Guilford Road
Madison, WI 53711-1086

608-273-8080; Fax: 608-273-2021
headquarters@agronomy.org
www.agronomy.org
Facebook, Twitter, LinkedIn

Susan Ernst, Managing Editor

Today's educators look here for the latest teaching ideas in the life sciences, natural resources, and agriculture.
11000 Members
Founded in 1907

989 **Journal of Plant Registrations**
Crop Science Society of America
5585 Guilford Road
Madison, WI 53711-5801

608-273-8080; Fax: 608-273-2021
headquarters@crops.org
www.crops.org
Facebook, Twitter, LinkedIn

Maria Gallo, President
Jeffrey Volenec, President-elect

Publishes cultivar, germplasm, parental line, genetic stock, and mapping population registration manuscripts.
4700 Members
Founded in 1955

990 **Journal of Soil and Water Conservation**
Soil and Water Conservation Society
945 SW Ankeny Rd.
Ankeny, IA 50023

515-289-2331; Fax: 515-289-1227
pubs@swcs.org
www.swcs.org

Annie Binder, Director of Publications/Editor
Jorge A. Delgado, Research Editor
Jody Thompson, Editorial Assistant

A multidisciplinary journal of natural resource conservation research, practice, policy, and perspectives. The journal has two sections: the A Section containing various departments and features and the Research Section containing peer-reviewed research papers.
Cost: $99.00
Frequency: 6x Yearly
Circulation: 2000
ISSN: 0022-4561
Founded in 1945

991 **Journal of Sustainable Agriculture**
Taylor & Francis Group LLC
325 Chestnut St
Suite 800
Philadelphia, PA 19106-2614

215-625-8900
800-354-1420; Fax: 215-625-2940
www.taylorandfrancis.com

Stephen R. Gliessman, Editor

Focuses on new and unique systems in which resource usage and environmental protection are kept in balance with the needs of productivity, profits, and incentives that are necessary for the agricultural marketplace. It increases professional and public awareness and gains support for these necessary changes in our agricultural industry.
Frequency: 8x Yearly

992 **Journal of Vegetable Science**
Taylor & Francis Group LLC

825 Chestnut Street
Suite 800
Philadelphia, PA 19106

215-625-8900
800-354-1420; Fax: 215-625-2940
www.haworthpress.com

Vincent M Russo PhD, Editor

Features innovative articles on all aspects of vegetable production, including growth regulation, pest management, sustainable production, harvesting, handling, storage, shipping and final consumption.
Frequency: Quarterly
ISSN: 1931-5260

993 **Journal of the American Society of Farm Managers and Rural Appraisers**
ASFMRA
720 S. Colorado Boulevard
Suite 360-S
Glendale, CO 80246

303-758-3513; Fax: 303-758-0190
info@asfmra.org
www.asfmra.org

Brian Stockman, Executive VP/CEO

Provides the most up-to-date studies, research, practices, and methodologies proposed by the leading academic, management, appraisal and consulting members of our professions.
Frequency: Annual
Founded in 1929

994 **Land**
Free Press Company
418 S 2nd Street
PO Box 3169
Mankato, MN 56001

507-344-6395
800-657-4665

Kevin Schulz, Editor
Lynnae Schrader, Assistant Editor
Kim Henrickson, Advertising Manager
Ken Lingen, Manager

Agricultural news
Cost: $20.00
48 Pages
Frequency: Weekly
Circulation: 40000
ISSN: 0279-1633
Founded in 1976
Printed in 4 colors on newsprint stock

995 **Landscape Management**
Advanstar Communications
7500 Old Oak Blvd
Cleveland, OH 44130-3343

440-243-8100
800-225-4569; Fax: 440-891-2740
www.ubmamericas.com

Ron Hall, Editor-in-Chief
Jason Stahl, Managing Editor

Covers news, market trends, business and operations management, technical information on horticulture and agronomy for professional landscape contractors, lawncare operators and in-house grounds managers.
Cost: $3.83
Circulation: 60014
Founded in 1962
Printed in 4 colors on glossy stock

996 **Meat Science Journal**
American Meat Science Association
2441 Village Green Pl
Champaign, IL 61822-7676

217-356-5368
800-517-AMSA; Fax: 888-205-5834; Fax: 217-356-5370
information@meatscience.org
www.meatscience.org

Dean Pringle, President
Collette Kaster, Chief Executive Officer

The official journal of AMSA. Peer-reviewed resource is the best way to stay current on the latest research in meat science across all meat products and in all aspects of meat production and processing.

997 **MidAmerican Farmer Grower**
MidAmerica Farm Publications
19 N Main Street
PO Box 323
Perryville, MO 63775

573-547-2244
877-486-6997; Fax: 573-547-5663
publisher@mafg.net
www.mafg.net

John M LaRose, CEO/Publisher
Barbara Galeski, Editor
Jack Thompson II, Marketing

Offers farming news for the middle states.
Cost: $19.00
Frequency: Weekly

998 **Midwest DairyBusiness**
DairyBusiness Communications
6437 Collamer Road
East Syracuse, NY 13057-1031

315-703-7979; Fax: 315-703-7988
www.dairybusiness.com/midwest

Dave Natzke, Editorial Director
Joel P Hastings, Publisher
JoDee Sattler, Associate Editor
Tom Vilsack, Secretary

Business resource for successful milk producers. Only business-oriented dairy publication exclusively for the large herd, Midwest milk producer.
Cost: $45.00
43 Pages
Frequency: Monthly
Circulation: 27500
ISSN: 1087-7096
Founded in 1904
Printed in 4 colors on glossy stock

999 **Milling Journal**
3065 Pershing Court
Decatur, IL 62526

217-877-9660
800-728-7511; Fax: 217-877-6647
webmaster@grainnet.com
www.grainnet.com

Mark Avery, Publisher
Arvin Donley, Editor
Jody Sexton, Production Manager

Mailed to all active AOM members in the US, Canada, and internationally, including wheat flour/corn mills and corn/oilseed processors in US and Canada.
Frequency: Quarterly
Circulation: 1224

1000 **Mushroom News**
American Mushroom Institute
1284 Gap Newport Pike
Suite 2
Avondale, PA 19311-9503

610-268-7483; Fax: 610-268-8015
ami@mwmlaw.com
www.americanmushroom.org

For growers and scientists in the mushroom production.
Cost: $275.00
Frequency: Monthly
Founded in 1955

1001 **NWAC News: National Warmwater Aquaculture Center**
127 Experiment Station Road
PO Box 197
Stoneville, MS 38776

662-686-3302; Fax: 662-686-3568
www.msstate.edu/dept/tcnwac

Jammy Avery, Publisher
J Charles Lee, President
Frequency: Bi-annually
Circulation: 1000
Founded in 1993
Printed in 3 colors on matte stock

1002 **National Hog Farmer**
7900 International Dr
Suite 300
Minneapolis, MN 55425-2562

952-851-4710; Fax: 952-851-4601
www.nationalhogfarmer.com

Dale Miller, Manager
Steve May, Publisher
John Frinch, President
Robert Moraczewski, Senior Vice President
Susan Rowland, Marketing Manager

Offers production information for hog farming business managers.
Cost: $35.00
Frequency: Monthly
Circulation: 31000
Founded in 1956
Mailing list available for rent: 84M names
Printed in 4 colors on glossy stock

1003 **National Wheat Growers Journal**
National Association of Wheat Growers
415 2nd St NE
Suite 300
Washington, DC 20002-4993

202-547-7800; Fax: 202-546-2638
wheatworld@wheatworld.org
www.wheatworld.org
Facebook, Twitter

David Cleavinger, Publisher
Chandler Goule, CEO

Information for wheat growers.
Founded in 1950

1004 **North Africa and Middle East Int'l Agricultural and Trade Report**
US Department of Agriculture
200 Independence Ave SW
Washington, DC 20201-0007

202-690-7650
800-999-6779; Fax: 202-512-2250
www.usda.gov

Michael Kurrzig, Editor
Chris Smith, Chief Information Officer
Matt Paul, Director of Communications
Ramona Romero, General Counsel

Information on current and projected agriculture production and trade in North Africa and the Middle East. Reports include trade and production data, highlights United States and European trade with the region.
Frequency: Annual
Founded in 1862

1005 **North American Deer Farmers Magazine**
North American Deer Farmers Association

4501 Hills and Dales Rd NW
Suite C
Canton, OH 44708

330-454-3944; Fax: 330-454-3950
info@nadefa.org
www.nadefa.org

Shawn Schafer, Executive Director
Tim Condict, First VP
Bill Pittenger, Second VP

National association of deer farming and ranching. Membership dues include this quarterly magazine.
Cost: $15.00
32 Pages
Frequency: Quarterly
Circulation: 1000
ISSN: 1084-0583
Founded in 1983
Printed in 4 colors on glossy stock

1006 **Northeast Dairy Business**
DairyBusiness Communications
6437 Collamer Road
East Syracuse, NY 13057-1031

315-703-7979
800-334-1904; Fax: 315-703-7988
www.dairybusiness.com/northeast

Eleanor Jacobs, Editor
Susan Harlow, Managing Editor
Joel Hasting, CEO/Publisher
Tom Vilsack, Secretary
Sue Miller, Circulation Manager

Business resource for successful milk producers. Devoted exclusively to the business and dairy management needs of milk producers in the 12 northeastern states.
Cost: $3.00
51 Pages
Frequency: Monthly
Circulation: 17500
ISSN: 1523-7095
Founded in 1904
Printed in 4 colors on glossy stock

1007 **Nut Grower**
Western Agricultural Publishing Company
4969 E Clinton Way
Suite 119
Fresno, CA 93727-1549

559-252-7000; Fax: 559-252-7387
westag@psnw.com

Paul Baltimore, Co Publisher
Jim Baltimore, Co Publisher
Randy Bailey, Editor
Robert Fujimoto, Assistant Editor

Covers production topics, the latest in research developments, and crop news on almonds, walnuts, pistachios, pecans and chestnuts.

1008 **OEM Off-Highway**
1233 Janesville Avenue
Fort Atkinson, WI 53538-2738

920-563-6388
800-547-7377; Fax: 920-563-1701
Leslie.Shalabi@cygnuspub.com

Richard Reiff, President
Leslie Shalabi, Publisher
Chad Elmore, Associate Editor
James S. Rank, VP
Kathy Scott, Director of Public Relations

Offers information on off-road machinery and farm equipment.
Founded in 1966

1009 **Onion World**
Columbia Publishing
8405 Ahtanum Rd
Yakima, WA 98903-9432

509-248-2452
800-900-2452; Fax: 509-248-4056
www.onionworld.net

Brent Clement, Editor
Mike Stoker, Publisher
Includes information on onion production and marketing, grower and shipper feature stories, onion research, from herbicide and pesticide studies to promising new varieties, martket reports, feedback from major onion meetings and conventions, spot reports on overseas production and marketing, and other key issues and trends of interest to US and Canadian onion growers.
Cost: $16.00
32 Pages
Circulation: 6500
Founded in 1984
Printed in 4 colors on glossy stock

1010 **Organic World**
Loft Publishing
3939 Leary Way NW
Seattle, WA 98107-5043

206-632-2767; Fax: 206-632-7055

Covers the news of organic gardening.
Cost: $15.00
Frequency: Quarterly

1011 **Pacific Farmer-Stockman**
999 W Riverside
PO Box 2160
Spokane, WA 99201

509-595-5385
800-624-6618; Fax: 509-459-5102
www.farmerstockmaninsurance.com

Michael R Craigen, General Manager
Tracy Sikes, Manager
Kathy Bergloff, Manager
Michelle Musgrave, Administrative Assistant

Offers farming news and information for farmers and herdsmen located in the Pacific states.

1012 **Peanut Farmer**
Specialized Agricultural Publications
5808 Faringdon Place
Suite 200
Raleigh, NC 27609

919-872-5040; Fax: 919-876-6531
www.peanutfarmer.com

Dayton H Matlick, Chairman
Mary Evans, Publisher/Sales Director
Mary Ann Rood, Editor

Offers peanut farmers profitable methods of raising, marketing and promoting peanuts, plus key related issues.
Cost: $15.00
24 Pages
Frequency: Monthly January-July
Circulation: 18,500
Founded in 1965
Printed in 4 colors on glossy stock

1013 **Peanut Grower**
Vance Publishing
10901 W 84th Ter
Suite 200
Lenexa, KS 66214-1631

913-438-5721; Fax: 913-438-0697
mweeks@vancepublishing.com
www.vancepublishing.com

Cliff Becker, VP
William C Vance, CEO

Written for the US peanut farmers. Covers disease, weed and insect control, legislation, farm equipment, marketing and new research.

1014 **Pesticide Chemical News Guide**
FCN Publishing
2200 Clarendon Blvd
Suite 1401
Arlington, VA 22201

888-732-7070
www.agra-net.com

Jason Huffman, Editor-in-Chief

Reference tool on pesticides and chemicals.
Frequency: Monthly

1015 **Pig International**
WATT Publishing Company
303 N Main Street
Suite 500
Rockford, IL 61101

815-966-5400; Fax: 815-966-6416
www.wattnet.com

James Watt, Chairman/CEO
Greg Watt, President/COO
Roger Abbott, Editor

Covers nutrition, animal health issues, feed procurement, and how producers can be profitable in the world pork market.
Frequency: Monthly
Circulation: 17600
ISSN: 0191-8834
Founded in 1971
Mailing list available for rent
Printed in 4 colors on glossy stock

1016 **Plant Disease**
American Phytopathological Society
3340 Pilot Knob Road
St. Paul, MN 55121-2097

651-454-7250
800-328-7560; Fax: 651-454-0766
aps@scisoc.org
www.apsnet.org
Facebook, Twitter, LinkedIn, YouTube

R. Michael Davis, Editor-in-Chief
Brian Simdars, Publications - Submissions

Published to stimulate plant disease research and to enable those throughout the world to benefit from the advances made in this environmentally important science.
Frequency: Monthly
Circulation: 1200
ISSN: 0191-2917

1017 **Pork**
Vance Publishing
400 Knightsbridge Parkway
Lincolnshire, IL 60069

847-634-2600; Fax: 847-634-4379
info@vancepublishing.com
www.vancepublishing.com

William C Vance, Chairman
Peggy Walker, President

Delivers practical, how-to information on production management, business techniques, industry trends and market analysis to the pork industry.
Cost: $50.00
Frequency: Monthly
Circulation: 16,000
Mailing list available for rent

1018 **Pork Report**
PO Box 10383
Clive, IA 50325

515-223-6186; Fax: 515-223-2646

Charles Harness, Publisher

Hog farming news and information.

1019 **Potato Country**
Columbia Publishing

8405 Ahtanum Rd
Yakima, WA 98903-9432

509-248-2452
800-900-2452; Fax: 509-248-4056
www.potatocountry.com

Brent Clement, Editor/Publisher
Mike Stoker, Publisher

Edited for potato growers and allied industry people throughout the Western fall-production states. Editorial material covers production, seed, disease forecast, equipment, fertilizer, irrigation, pest/weed management, crop reports and annual buyers guide.
Cost: $18.00
32 Pages
Frequency: Daily
Circulation: 7500
ISSN: 0886-4780
Founded in 1993
Printed in 4 colors on glossy stock

1020 **Potato Grower**
Harris Publishing Company
360 B Street
Idaho Falls, ID 83402

208-524-4217; Fax: 208-522-5241
www.potatogrower.com

Jason Harris, Publisher
Gary Rawlings, Editor

Current news on growing potatoes, market trends, technology.
Cost: $20.95
48 Pages
Frequency: Monthly
Founded in 1971
Printed in on glossy stock

1021 **Poultry Digest**
WATT Publishing Company
122 S Wesley Ave
Mt Morris, IL 61054-1451

815-734-7937; Fax: 815-734-4201
www.wattnet.com

Jim W Watt, Chairman/CEO
Charles G Olentine Jr PhD, VP/Publisher
Clay Schreiber, Publisher
Jim Wessel, Circulation Director

A magazine serving the production side of the entire poultry industry.

1022 **Poultry International**
WATT Publishing Company
303 N Main Street
Suite 500
Rockford, IL 61101

815-966-5400; Fax: 815-966-6416
mclements@wattnet.net
www.wattnet.com

James Watt, Chairman/CEO
Greg Watt, President/COO
Mark Clements, Editor

Viewed by commercial poultry integrators as the leading international source of news, data and information for their businesses.
68 Pages
Frequency: Monthly
Circulation: 20,000
ISSN: 0032-5767
Founded in 1962
Printed in 4 colors

1023 **Poultry Times**
Poultry & Egg News
345 Green Street NW
PO Box 1338
Gainesville, GA 30503

770-536-2476; Fax: 770-532-4894
www.poultrytimes.net
Facebook

Christopher Hill, Publisher/Editor
David Strickland, Editor
Barbara Olejnik, Associate Editor
Dinah Winfree, National Sales Representative
Stacy Louis, National Sales Representative

The only newspaper in the poultry industry. We deliver the most up to date news in teh poultry industry.
Cost: $22.00
Frequency: Twice Monthly
Circulation: 13000
Founded in 1954

1024 **Poultry USA**
WATT Publishing Company
303 N Main Street
Suite 500
Rockford, IL 61101

815-966-5400; Fax: 815-966-6416
www.wattnet.com

James Watt, Chairman/CEO
Greg Watt, President/COO
Jeff Swanson, Publishing Director

The only resource focused on the entire integrated poultry market, delivering relevant and timely information to industry professionals across the entire poultry supply chain - from farm to table.
Frequency: Monthly

1025 **Practical Winery & Vineyard**
58 Paul Dr
Suite D
San Rafael, CA 94903-2054

415-479-5819; Fax: 415-492-9325
Office@practicalwinery.com
www.practicalwinery.com

A bi-monthly magazine of wine-growing and winemaking news and reviews.
Cost: $31.00
Circulation: 7500
Founded in 1985

1026 **Prairie Farmer**
Prairie Farm Dairy
300 E Washington St
PO Box 348
Pana, IL 62557-1239

217-562-3956; Fax: 217-877-9695
info@prairiefarms.com
www.prairiefarms.com

James R Smith, Manager
Mike Wilson, Editor

Agricultural news.

1027 **Precision Farming Dealer**
Lessiter Media
P.O. Box 624
Brookfield, WI 53008-0624

262-782-4480
800-645-8455; Fax: 262-782-1252
dkanicki@lessitermedia.com
www.precisionfarmingdealer.com

Mike Lessiter, Editor/Publisher
Dave Kanicki, Executive Editor
Michael Ellis, Director of Sales

Contains information on selling, servicing, and supporting precision farming technology. Topics include: streamlining your operation, business trends and outlooks, industry news and trends.
Frequency: 3/Year

1028 **Progressive Farmer**
2100 Lakeshore Drive
Birmingham, AL 35209-6721

205-445-6000; Fax: 205-445-6422
bruce_thomas@timeinc.com
www.progressivefarmer.com

Bruce Thomas, Publisher
Jack Odle, Editor
Allen Vaughan, Business Manager

Farming news with regional focus on the midwest, midsouth and southwest.
Cost: $18.00
106 Pages
Frequency: 6 issues/Year
Circulation: 610000
ISSN: 0033-0760
Founded in 1886

1029 **RF Design**
RFD News
131 E Main Street
Bellevue, OH 44811-1449

419-483-7410; Fax: 419-483-3737

Barry LeCerf, Publisher

Comprehensive source of rural agricultural news and information for farmers and the general public.
Frequency: Weekly

1030 **Rice Farming**
Vance Publishing
400 Knightsbridge Pkwy
Lincolnshire, IL 60069-3628

847-634-2600
800-888-9784; Fax: 847-634-4379
vlboyd@worldnet.att.net
www.vancepublishing.com

Peggy Walker, President
William Vance, Chairman
Judy Riggs, Director
Vicky Boyd, Editor

Profitable production strategies for commercial rice growers.
Founded in 1937

1031 **Rice Journal**
Specialized Agricultural Publications
3000 Highwoods Boulevard
Suite 300
Raleigh, NC 27604-1029

919-878-0540; Fax: 919-876-6531
www.ricejournal.com

Dayton H Matlick, President
Mary Evans, Publisher

Offers rice growers profitable methods of producing, marketing and promoting rice, plus key related issues.
Founded in 1897

1032 **RuraLife**
William Johnston
1172 Orangeburg Mall Circle
Orangeburg, SC 29115-3439

803-534-1980

Jaun Maults, Executive Director
Gary Grimmond, Editor

Farm and agricultural news.

1033 **Rural Heritage**
Allan Damerow
281 Dean Ridge Ln
Gainesboro, TN 38562-5039

931-268-0655
info@ruralheritage.com
www.ruralheritage.com

Gail Damerow, Owner

Publication for people who farm and log with horses and other draft animals.
Cost: $26.00
100 Pages
Frequency: Bi-Monthly
Circulation: 8500
ISSN: 0889-2970
Founded in 1976
Printed in 4 colors on matte stock

1034 **Rural Lifestyle Dealer**
Lessiter Media
P.O. Box 624
Brookfield, WI 53008-0624

262-782-4480
800-645-8455; Fax: 262-782-1252
info@rurallifestyledealer.com
www.rurallifestyledealer.com

Michael Ellis, Publisher
Dave Kanicki, Executive Editor

Contains information of interest to the rural equipment dealership market. Topics include: streamlining your operation, business trends and outlooks, industry news and trends.
Frequency: Quarterly

1035 **Rural Living**
Michigan Farm Bureau
7373 W Saginaw Highway
PO Box 30960
Lansing, MI 48909-8460

517-323-7000; Fax: 517-323-6793
mifarmnews@michfb.com
www.michiganfarmbureau.com

Dennis Rudat, Editor
Paul W Jackson, President
Brigette Leach, Director
Earl Butz, Secretary

Editorial emphasis on consumer food news, travel information and issue analysis.
24 Pages
Frequency: Quarterly
Circulation: 200000

1036 **Santa Gertrudis USA**
Caballo Rojo Publishing
PO Box 1257
Kingsville, TX 78364-1257

361-592-9357; Fax: 361-592-8572
www.santagertrudis.com

Ervin Kaatz, Executive Director

Official Journal of the Breed developed in 1918 at the famous King Ranch in Texas. Famous solid red color, hardiness and good disposition. They are adaptable to many environments and are present throughout the US and in other countries.

1037 **Seed Industry Journal**
Freiberg Publishing Company
2701 Minnetonka Dr
PO Box 7
Cedar Falls, IA 50613-1531

319-553-0642; Fax: 319-277-3783
www.care4elders.com

Bill Freiberg, Owner
Carol Cutler, Editor

International seed industry news.

1038 **Seed Technology Journal**
Society of Commerical Seed Technologists
101 E State Street
Suite 214
Ithaca, NY 14850

607-256-3313; Fax: 607-256-3313
www.analyzeseeds.com

Jess Peterson, Executive Director

Published jointly with the Association of Official Seed Analysts. an international journal containing scientific and technological papers in all areas of seed science and technology. The emphasis is on applied and basic research in seed physiology, pathology and biology that may relate to seed development, maturation, germination, dormancy and deterioration.
Cost: $125.00
Frequency: Members Cost: $75.00
Founded in 1922

1039 **Seed Today**
Grain Journal Publishing Company
3065 Pershing Ct
Decatur, IL 62526-1564

217-877-9660
800-728-7511; Fax: 217-877-6647
webmaster@grainnet.com
www.grainnet.com

Mark Avery, Publisher
Joe Funk, Editor
Kay Merryfield, Circulation Administrator
Ayanna Green, Manager

Information for individuals related to seeds.
Frequency: Quarterly
Circulation: 4000
Founded in 1978

1040 **Seed World**
Scranton Gillette Communications
380 E Northwest Highway
Suite 200
Des Plaines, IL 60016-2282

847-298-6622; Fax: 847-390-0408
www.seedworld.com

E S Gillette, Publisher
Angela Dansby, Editor

Seed marketers.
Cost: $30.00
48 Pages
Frequency: Monthly
Circulation: 5000
ISSN: 0037-0797
Founded in 1915

1041 **Seed and Crops Industry**
Freiberg Publishing Company
2701 Minnetonka Dr
Cedar Falls, IA 50613-1531

319-553-0642
800-959-3276; Fax: 319-277-3783
www.care4elders.com

Bill Freiberg, Owner

Offers information for farmers related to crop protection.
Frequency: Monthly

1042 **Self Employed Country**
Communicating for Agriculture & the Self Employed
112 E Lincoln Ave
Fergus Falls, MN 56537-2217

218-739-3241
800-432-3276; Fax: 218-739-3832
www.selfemployedcountry.org

Milt Smedsrud, Owner
Jerry Barney, Production Manager

For members of Communicating for Agriculture, including legislation relating to CA activities, exchange program activities, rural seniors news, health and insurance material, feature stories and columns.
Cost: $6.00
Frequency: Quarterly
Founded in 1985

1043 **Shorthorn Country**
Durham Management Company
5830 S 142nd St
Siote A
Omaha, NE 68137-2894

402-827-8003; Fax: 402-827-8006
www.durhamstaffingsolutions.com

Machael Durham, President
Tracy Duncan, Editor
Peggy Gilliland, Circulation Manager

Magazine published for cattle producers who breed and sell registered Shorthorn and Polled Shorthorn cattle.
Cost: $24.00
Circulation: 3000
ISSN: 0149-9319
Founded in 1956

1044 **Soil Science**
Lippincott Williams & Wilkins
351 W Camden St
Baltimore, MD 21201-2436

410-949-8000
800-638-6423; Fax: 410-528-4414
www.lww.com

J Arnold Anthony, Operations

Covers investigations in environmental soils.
Cost: $205.00
Frequency: Monthly
Circulation: 2800
ISSN: 0038-075X

1045 **Soil Science of America Journal**
Soil Science Society of America
677 S Segoe Rd
Madison, WI 53711-1086

608-273-8095; Fax: 608-273-2021
headquarters@soils.org
www.soils.org

Ellen Bergfeld, CEO

For those involved in research, teaching and extension activities in physics, chemistry, mineralogy, microbiology, soil fertility and plant nutrition
Cost: $600.00
Circulation: 4000
Founded in 1961

1046 **Southeast Farm Press**
14920 US Highway 61
Clarksdale, MS 38614

662-624-8503
866-505-7173; Fax: 662-627-1977
www.southeastfarmpress.com

Grey Frey, Publisher
Paul Hollis, Editor

Offers farming news for the southeastern states.
Founded in 1989

1047 **Southeastern Peanut Farmer**
Southern Peanut Farmer's Federation
110 E 4th Street
Po Box 706
Tifton, GA 31794

229-386-3470; Fax: 229-386-3501
info@gapeanuts.com
www.gapeanuts.com

Joy Carter, Editor

Offers information to peanut farmers.
Cost: $25.00
20 Pages
Frequency: Monthly
Circulation: 8400
ISSN: 0038-3694
Founded in 1961
Printed in 4 colors on glossy stock

1048 **Southwest Farm Press**
Farm Press Publications

2104 Harvell Circle
Bellevue, NE 68005

402-505-7173
866-505-7173; Fax: 402-293-0741
sscs@pbsub.com
southwestfarmpress.com

Greg Frey, Publisher
Ron Smith, Editor
Hembree Brandon, Editorial Director
Forrest Laws, Executive Editor
Darrah Parker, Marketing Manager

Farming news.
Cost: $40.00
Frequency: Fortnightly
Circulation: 33,100
Founded in 1974

1049 **Soybean South**
6263 Poplar Avenue
Suite 540
Memphis, TN 38119-4736

901-385-0595; Fax: 901-767-4026

John Sowell, Publisher
Jeff Kehl, Circulation Director

Profitable prediction strategies for soybean farmers.
Frequency: 5 per year
Printed in 4 colors on glossy stock

1050 **Speedy Bee**
American Beekeeping Federation
3525 Piedmont Road NE
Bldg 5 Suite 300
Atlanta, GA 30305-1509

404-760-2875; Fax: 404-240-0998
info@abfnet.org
www.abfnet.org

Troy Fore, Publisher/Editor

The latest news affecting the beekeeping and honey industry.
Cost: $17.95
16 Pages
Frequency: Monthly
Circulation: 1500
ISSN: 0190-6798
Founded in 1972
Printed in on newsprint stock

1051 **Spudman Magazine**
Great American Publishing
Po Box 128
Suite A
Sparta, MI 49345-0128

616-887-9008; Fax: 616-887-2666
www.spudman.com

Matt McCallum, Owner
Kimberly Warren, Managing Editor
Erica Bernard, Circulation Manager
Marnie Draper, Advertising Manager
Jill Peck, Creative Director

Information for potato farming and marketing.
Circulation: 15500
Printed in on glossy stock

1052 **Successful Farming**
Meredith Corporation
1716 Locust St
Des Moines, IA 50309-3023

515-284-3000
800-678-2659; Fax: 515-284-3563
shareholderhelp@meredith.com
www.meredith.com

Stephen M Lacy, CEO
Sandy Williams, Production Manager
William Kerr, CEO
Tom Davis, Publisher

U.S. commerical farmers, ranchers and those employed in those operations or a directly related occupation.
Cost: $15.95
Frequency: Monthly
Circulation: 442000
Founded in 1902
Mailing list available for rent: 500M names at $75 per M
Printed in 4 colors on glossy stock

1053 **Sugar: The Sugar Producer Magazine**
Harris Publishing Company
360 B Street
Idaho Falls, ID 83402

208-524-4217
800-638-0135; Fax: 208-522-5241
www.sugarproducer.com

Jason Harris, Publisher
David FairBourn, Editor
Rob Erickson, Marketing
Eula Endecott, Circulation Manager

Sugar beet industry information.
Cost: $15.95
Frequency: Monthly
Circulation: 16000
Founded in 1975

1054 **Sugarbeet Grower**
Sugar Publications
503 Broadway
Fargo, ND 58102-4416

701-476-2111; Fax: 701-476-2182
www.sugarpub.com

Provides news and feature articles pertaining to sugarbeet production practices, research, legislation and marketing, along with profiles of industry leaders and outstanding producers. Primary audience is United States and Canadian sugarbeet growers.
Cost: $12.00
Circulation: 11,300
Founded in 1963

1055 **Sunflower Magazine**
National Sunflower Association
Ste 206
2401 46th Ave SE
Mandan, ND 58554-4829

701-328-5100
888-718-7033; Fax: 701-328-5101
www.sunflowernsa.com

John Sandbakken, Executive Director
Tina Mittelsteadt, Business & Office Manager

Magazine geared to sunflower products.
Cost: $9.00
Circulation: 29300
Founded in 1981
Printed in 4 colors

1056 **Sunflower and Grain Marketing Magazine**
Sunflower World Publishers
3307 Northland Drive
Suite 130
Austin, TX 78731-4964

512-407-3434; Fax: 512-323-5118

Ed R Allen, Editor

Offers news and information on the sunflower and grain industries.
Circulation: 15,000

1057 **Super Hay Today Magazine**
Mt Adams Publishing and Design
14161 Fort Road
White Swan, DC 98552-9786

509-848-2706
800-554-0860; Fax: 509-848-3896

Vee Graves, Editor
Julie LaForge, Advertising Manager

1058 **Swine Practitioner**
10901 W 84th Terrace
Suite 200
Lenexa, KS 66214-1649

913-438-8700
800-255-5113; Fax: 913-438-0695
info@vancepublishing.com
www.vancepublishing.com

Kristal Arnold, Editor
Kevin Murphy, Sales/Marketing Manager
Bill Newham, Publishing Director
Cliff Becker, Group Publisher
Lori Eppel, Chief Financial Officer

Offers technical information, primarily on swine health and related production areas, to veterinarians and related industry professionals.
Frequency: Monthly
Circulation: 4800
Mailing list available for rent

1059 **The American Journal of Agricultural Economics (AJAE)**
Agricultural & Applied Economics Association
555 E Wells Street
Suite 1100
Milwaukee, WI 53202-6600

414-918-3190; Fax: 414-276-3349
junjie.wu@oregonstate.edu
www.aaea.org/publications/ajae

Dawn Thilmany McFadden, President

Journal presenting research and policy articles about agricultural economics. The journal contains scholarly materials on the economics of agriculture and food, natural resources and the environment, and rural and community development.
3000 Members
Frequency: 5x Yearly
Founded in 1910

1060 **The Forestry Source**
5400 Grosvenor Ln
Bethesda, MD 20814-2198

301-897-8720; Fax: 301-897-3690
safweb@safnet.org
www.safnet.org
Facebook, Twitter, LinkedIn

Morgan Fincham, Director, Publications
Steve Wilent, Editor

Provides access to information and networking opportunities to prepare members for the challenges and the changes that face natural resource professionals.
Founded in 1900

1061 **The Grower**
Vance Publishing
400 Knightsbridge Parkway
Lincolnshire, IL 60069

847-634-2600; Fax: 847-634-4379
info@vancepublishing.com
www.vancepublishing.com
Facebook, Twitter

William C Vance, Chairman
Peggy Walker, President

The key source of profitable production and management strategies to commercial producers who control 90% of the U.S. fruit and vegetable market.
Cost: $45.00
Frequency: Monthly
Circulation: 22,004
Founded in 1937
Printed in 4 colors on glossy stock

1062 **The Plant Genome**
Crop Science Society of America

5585 Guilford Road
Madison, WI 53711-5801

608-273-8080; Fax: 608-273-2021
headquarters@crops.org
www.crops.org
Facebook, Twitter, LinkedIn

Maria Gallo, President
Jeffrey Volenec, President-Elect

Electronic journal that provides readership with a short publication of the latest advances and breakthroughs in plant genomics research.
Founded in 1955

1063 **Today's Farmer**
MFA
201 Ray Young Dr
Columbia, MO 65201-3599

573-874-5111; Fax: 573-876-5521
www.mfa-inc.com

William Streeter, CEO
J Brian Griffith, Senior Vice President of Operations

Management and marketing news.
Cost: $12.00
Founded in 1914

1064 **Tomato Country**
Columbia Publishing
8405 Ahtanum Rd
Yakima, WA 98903-9432

509-248-2452
800-900-2452; Fax: 509-248-4056
www.tomatomagazine.com

Brent Clement, Editor/Publisher
Mike Stoker, Publisher

Includes information on tomato production and marketing, grower and shipper feature stories, tomato research, from herbicide and pesticide studies to new varieties, market reports, feedback from major tomato meetings and conventions, along with other key issues and points of interest for USA and Canada tomato growers.

1065 **Top Producer**
Farm Journal Media
1818 Market Street
31st Floor
Philadelphia, PA 19103-3654

215-578-8900
800-320-7992; Fax: 215-568-6782
topproducer@farmjournal.com
www.agweb.com/topproducer

Andy Weber, Chief Executive Officer
Steve Custer, Executive Vice President
Jeff Pence, President, Electronic Media
Chuck Roth, Senior Vice President

Top Producer is the premier magazine devoted to the business of farming. The focus on industry leaders, entrepreneurs and innovators in agriculture make this magazine the authoritative business resource for commercial farm operators.
Frequency: Weekly
Founded in 1973

1066 **Tree Farmer Magazine, the Guide to Sustaining America's Family Forests**
American Forest Foundation
1111 19th St NW
Suite 780
Washington, DC 20036

202-463-2700; Fax: 202-463-2785
info@forestfoundation.org
www.forestfoundation.org

Tom Martin, President & CEO
Brigitte Johnson APR, Director Communications, Editor

The official magazine of ATFS, this periodical provides practical, how-to and hands-on information and techniques, and services to help private fore landowners to become better stewards, save money and time, and add to the enjoyment of their land.

1067 **Tree Fruit**
Western Agricultural Publishing Company
4969 E Clinton Way
Suite 104
Fresno, CA 93727-1546

559-252-7000; Fax: 559-252-7387
westag@psnw.com

Paul Baltimore, Co Publisher
Jim Baltimore, Co Publisher
Randy Bailey, Editor
Robert Fujimoto, Assistant Editor

For tree fruit growers in California.

1068 **Valley Potato Grower**
420 Business Highway 2
PO Box 301
East Grand Forks, MN 56721

218-773-7783; Fax: 218-773-6227
vpgsales@nppga.org
www.nppga.org

Todd Phelph, CEO
Duane Maatz, Chairman

Information on potato farming.
Circulation: 10600
Founded in 1946

1069 **Vegetable Growers News**
Great American Publishing
75 Applewood Drive Suite A
PO Box 128
Sparta, MI 49345

616-887-9008; Fax: 616-887-2666
www.vegetablegrowersnews.com

Matt McCallum, Executive Publisher
Brenda Bradford, Advertising
Kimberly Warren, Managing Editor
Erica Bernard, Circulation Department
Jill Peck, Creative Director

Market and marketing news.
Cost: $12.00
Frequency: Monthly

1070 **Vegetables**
Western Agricultural Publishing Company
4969 E Clinton Way
#104
Fresno, CA 93727-1549

559-252-7000; Fax: 559-252-7387
westag@psnw.com

Paul Baltimore, Co Publisher
Jim Baltimore, Co Publisher
Randy Bailey, Editor
Robert Fujimoto, Assistant Editor

The definitive source for information on all aspects of western vegetable production.

1071 **Vegetarian Journal**
Vegetarian Resource Group
PO Box 1463
Baltimore, MD 21203

410-366-8343; Fax: 410-366-8804
vrg@vrg.org
www.vrg.org

Debra Wasserman, Director
Jeanne Yacoubou, Research Director

Journal covering health, ecology, and ethics topics as relates to vegetarianism and veganism. Included are informative articles, recipes, book reviews, notices about vegetarian events, product evaluations, and tips on where to find vegetarian products and services. All nutrition information is based on scientific studies.
10000 Members
Frequency: Quarterly
Founded in 1982

1072 **Vineyard and Winery Management**
PO Box 2358
Winsdor, CA 95492

707-366-6820
800-535-5670; Fax: 607-535-2998
www.vwm-online.com

Robert Merletti, Publisher
Tom Loid, General Manager
Dennis Black, General Manager
Suzanne Webb, Marketing Director

To be the bottom line resource for growers and vintners; to keep our readers tuned and primed for profit.
Cost: $37.00
100 Pages
Circulation: 6000
ISSN: 1047-4951
Founded in 1975
Printed in 4 colors on glossy stock

1073 **Wallaces Farmer**
Farm Progress Companies
255 38th Avenue
Suite P
St Charles, IL 60174-5410
630-462-2224
800-441-1410
rswoboda@farmprogress.com
www.farmprogress.com

Rod Swoboda, Editor
Willie Vogt, Corporate Editorial Director
Frank Holdmeyer, Executive Editor

Serves Iowa farmers and ranchers with information to help them maximize their productivity and profitability. Each issue is packed with information, ideas, news and analysis.
Cost: $26.95
ISSN: 0043-0129
Founded in 1855

1074 **Weed Science Journal**
P.O.Box 7065
Lawrence, KS 66044-7065

785-429-9622
800-627-0629; Fax: 785-843-1274
wssa@allenpress.com
www.wssa.net

Dale Shaner, President
Jeff Derr, VP
Tom Mueller, Secretary
Dave Gealy, Treasurer
Michael Foley, Director Publications

Promotes research, education and extension outreach activities related to weeds, provides science-based information to the public and policy makers; and fosters awarenes of weeds and their impacts on managed and natural ecosystems.
2000 Members
Founded in 1956

1075 **Weed Technology Journal**
P.O.Box 7065
Lawrence, KS 66044-7065

785-429-9622
800-627-0629; Fax: 785-843-1274
wssa@allenpress.com
www.wssa.net

Dale Shaner, President
Jeff Derr, VP
Tom Mueller, Secretary
Dave Gealy, Treasurer
Michael Foley, Director Publications

Promotes research, education and extension outreach activities related to weeds, provides science-based information to the public and policy makers; and fosters awarenes of weeds and their impacts on managed and natural ecosystems.
Founded in 1956

1076 **Western DairyBusiness**
DairyBusiness Communications

6437 Collamer Road
East Syracuse, NY 13057-1031

315-703-7979
800-334-1904; Fax: 315-703-7988
bbaker@dairyline.com
www.dairybusiness.com

Joel P Hastings, Editor
John Montandon, President & Co-CEO
Debbie Morneau, Marketing Coordinator

Business resource for successful milk producers. Covers 13 Western states. Provides information and news that is helpful in the daily operations of dairymen.
Cost: $49.95
67 Pages
Frequency: Monthly
Circulation: 14000
ISSN: 1528-4360
Founded in 1904
Printed in 4 colors on glossy stock

1077 **Western Farm Press**
Penton Media
249 W 17th Street
New York, NY 10011

212-204-4200
westernfarmpress.com

Greg Frey, VP
Hembree Brandon, Editorial Director
Harry Cline, Editor

Provides growers and agribusiness with in-depth coverage of the region's major crops plus the legislative, environmental and regulatory issues that affect their businesses.

1078 **Western Fruit Grower**
Meister Media Worldwide
37733 Euclid Ave
Willoughby, OH 44094-5992

440-942-2000
800-572-7740; Fax: 440-975-3447
rljones@meistermedia.com
www.meisternet.com

Gary Fitzgerald, President
John Monahan, Publisher
Richard Jones, Editor

Edited for commercial growers of deciduous crops, citrus fruit and nut grape crops in the Western US.
Cost: $19.95
66 Pages
Frequency: Monthly
Circulation: 36000
Founded in 1933

1079 **Western Livestock Journal**
Crow Publications
7355 E Orchard Road
Suite 300
Greenwood Village, CO 80111

303-722-7600
800-850-2769; Fax: 303-722-0155
editorial@wlj.net
www.wlj.net

Pete Crow, Publisher

Offers its readers the best coverage of timely, necessary news and information that affects the livestock industry, particularly cattle.
Cost: $45.00
Frequency: Weekly
Circulation: 30000+
Founded in 1922

Trade Shows

1080 **AACC International Annual Meeting**
3340 Pilot Knob Road
St. Paul, MN 55121-2055

651-454-7250
800-328-7560; Fax: 651-454-0766
aacc@scisoc.org
www.aaccnet.org
Facebook, Twitter, LinkedIn

Robert L. Cracknell, President
Lydia Tooker Midness, Chairman
Dave L. Braun, Treasurer

Formerly the American Association of Cereal Chemists, the AACC meeting offers a chance to come together, network with peers, discuss critical issues in the science and discover the methods of others.
Frequency: Annual/October
Founded in 1915

1081 **AAEA Annual Meeting**
Agricultural & Applied Economics Association
555 E Wells Street
Suite 1100
Milwaukee, WI 53202-6600

414-918-3190; Fax: 414-276-3349
jsaunders@aaea.org
www.aaea.org

Dawn Thilmany McFadden, President

Annual meeting and trade show for those interested in the fields of agricultural and applied economics.
3000 Members
Frequency: Annual/August
Founded in 1910

1082 **AAEA Symposia**
555 E Wells Street
Suite 1100
Milwaukee, WI 53202-6600

414-918-3190; Fax: 414-276-3349
info@aaea.org
www.aaea.org

Otto C Doering III, President
Yvonne C Bennett, Executive Director

Providing a platform for research on the economics related to the role of consumers' food environments on their choices and health outcomes. The conference is aimed at providing insights into the influence of the food environment on the quality, price, and availability of food, associatec health or environmental impacts, and to uncover the impact of policies aimed at influencing the food production and choice.
3000 Members
Frequency: Annual
Founded in 1910
Mailing list available for rent

1083 **AAFCO Meeting**
Association of American Feed Control Officers
PO Box 478
Oxford, IN 47971

765-385-1029; Fax: 765-385-1032
www.aafco.org

Frequency: Annual/July/August

1084 **AAW Annual Convention**
American Agri-Women
2103 Zeandale Road
Manhattan, KS 66502

785-537-6171; Fax: 785-537-9727
www.americanagriwomen.org
Facebook, Twitter

Karen Yost, President
Jody Elrod, Secretary
Peggy Clark, Treasurer

Tradeshow consisting of products of interest to women in agribusiness, farms and ranches.
350 Attendees
Frequency: Annual/November
Founded in 1974

1085 **AEM Annual Conference**
Association of Equipment Manufacturers
6737 West Washington Street
Suite 2400
Milwaukee, WI 53214-5647

414-272-0943; Fax: 414-272-1170
aem@aem.org
www.aem.org

Jeffrey R. Reed, Chair

Conference for executives of the off-road equipment industry.
Frequency: Annual/November

1086 **AFIA Pet Food Conference**
American Feed Industry Association
2101 Wilson Blvd
Suite 916
Arlington, VA 22201-3047

703-524-0810; Fax: 703-524-1921
afia@afia.org
www.afia.org
Facebook, Twitter, LinkedIn

Constance Cullman, President & CEO
Rob Cooper, Executive Director Of IFEEDER
Paul Davis, Director, Animal Food Safety

Organization devoted to representing companies in the animal feed industry and its suppliers.
690 Members
Founded in 1909

1087 **ALBC Conference**
American Livestock Breeds Conservancy
PO Box 477
Pittsboro, NC 27312

919-542-5704; Fax: 919-545-0022
www.albc-usa.org
Facebook

Charles Bassett, Executive Director

An educational opportunity where members can share their knowledge with other members by sharing posters at the annual conference, subtting articles to the newsletter and more.
Frequency: Annual

1088 **AMSA Reciprocal Meat Conference**
American Meat Science Association
2441 Village Green Place
Champaign, IL 61822

217-356-5370
800-517-AMSA; Fax: 888-205-5834; Fax: 217-356-5370
information@meatscience.org
www.meatscience.org\rmc

Dean Pringle, President
Collette Kaster, Chief Executive Officer

RMC is the annual meeting for AMSA, featuring an interactive program tailored to bring attendees the very best and inspiring educational experience. Attendees are professionals in academia, government and industry, as well as students in the meat, food and animal science fields.

1089 **AOSA/SCST Annual Meeting-Association of Official Seed Analysts**
PMB #411
101 East State Street
Suite 214
Ithaca, NY 14850

607-256-3313; Fax: 607-273-1638
www.aosaseed.com

Ellen Chirco, President
Wayne Guerke, VP
Dan Curry, Secretary/Treasurer
Aaron Palmer, Certificate/Analysis
Larry Nees, Membership

Seed testing and laboratory equipment, supplies and services; workshops and discussions.
Frequency: Annual/June

1090 **APA National Meet**
American Poultry Association
PO Box 306
Burgettstown, PA 15021

724-729-3459
www.amerpoultryassn.com

Mark Podgwaite, President
Bart Pals, Vice President

Poultry show and banquet.

1091 **ARA Conference & Expo**
1156 15th St NW
Suite 500
Washington, DC 20005-1745

202-457-0825; Fax: 202-457-0864
info@aradc.org
www.aradc.org

Daren Coppock, President & CEO
Melisa Augusto, Marketing Director

Advocates in the ag retail and distribution industry.
Frequency: Annual
Founded in 1993

1092 **ARBA National Convention**
American Rabbit Breeders Association
8 Westport Court
Bloomington, IL 61704

309-664-7500; Fax: 309-664-0941
www.arba.net

Mike Avesing, President
Erik Bengtson, Vice-President
Eric Stewart, Executive Director
David Freeman, Treasurer

Seminar, banquet, luncheon and 1500 rabbit breeders exhibits.
3000 Attendees
Frequency: Annual/April
Founded in 1910

1093 **ASA-CSSA-SSSA International Annual Meeting**
American Society of Agronomy
5585 Guilford Road
Madison, WI 53711-5801

608-273-8080; Fax: 608-273-2021
pscullion@agronomy.org
www.agronomy.org
Facebook, Twitter, LinkedIn

Wes Meixelsperger, Director, Meetings
Jeanne Pluemer, Senior Meetings Manager
Stacey Giesen, Meetings Manager

Society members are dedicated to the conservation and wise use of natural resources to produce food, feed and fiber crops while maintaining and improving the environment. Annual meeting and exhibits of agricultural equipment, supplies and services.
Frequency: Annual/Fall

1094 **ASABE Annual International Meeting**
American Society of Agricultural & Bio-Engineers
2950 Niles Road
St. Joseph, MI 49085-9659

269-429-0300
800-371-2723; Fax: 269-429-3852
www.asabe.org
Facebook, Twitter, YouTube

Melissa Moore, Exec VP/Meetings & Conference Dir
Donna Hull, Publication Director

A forum to expand awareness of industry trends, promote and acknowledge innovations in design and technology, and provide opportunities for professional development. Networking, trade show, technical workshops and presentations, specialty sessions, and career fair.
Frequency: Annual/June
Founded in 1907

1095 **ASAS-ADSA Annual Meeting**
American Society of Animal Science
1800 S. Oak Street
Suite 100
Champaign, IL 61820-6974

217-356-9050; Fax: 217-398-4119
www.asas.org
Facebook, Twitter

Glenn Duff, President
Mike D. Tokach, President-Elect
Meghan Wulster-Radcliffe, Chief Executive Officer

Professional organization for animal scientists designed to help members provide effective leadership through research, extension, teaching and service for the dynamic and rapidly changing livestock and meat industries. Containing 45 booths. Always a joint meeting with ADSA, and usually with one or more of these organizations: CSAS, AMPA, WSASAS, and PSA.
2000 Attendees
Frequency: Annual/July
Founded in 1908

1096 **ASCA Annual Conference**
American Society of Consulting Arborists
9707 Key West Avenue
Suite 100
Rockville, MD 20850-3992

301-947-0483; Fax: 301-990-9771
asca@mgmtsol.com
www.asca-consultants.org
Twitter, LinkedIn

Th,rŠse Oetegen Clemens, Executive Director

Recognized as a high quality, in depth conference with cutting edge speakers. Combining the best forum for discussion of current and relevant arboricultural issues, as well as consulting practice management issues and key consulting topics such as the role of the expert witness, risk assessment and tree appraisal
300 Attendees
Frequency: Annual
Founded in 1967

1097 **ASEV National Conference**
American Society for Enology and Vinticulture
PO Box 1855
Davis, CA 95617-1855

530-753-3142; Fax: 530-753-3318
society@asev.org
www.asev.org
LinkedIn

Patty Skinkis, President
Dan Howard, Executive Director

Provides a forum for the presentation of research in the fields of enology and viticulture or related sciences.
Frequency: Annual/June
Founded in 1950

1098 **ASFMRA Annual Conference**
ASFMRA
720 S. Colorado Boulevard
Suite 360-S
Glendale, CO 80246

303-758-3513; Fax: 303-758-0190
info@asfmra.org
www.asfmra.org

Brian Stockman, Executive VP/CEO

A conference for anyone involved with rural property and rural property assets - managing, consulting, valuing and brokering on behalf of clients and landowners throughout the United States.
Frequency: Annual
Founded in 1929

1099 **ASHS Annual Conference**
American Society for Horticultural Science
1018 Duke Street
Alexandria, VA 22314-2851

703-836-4606; Fax: 703-836-2024
webmaster@ashs.org
www.ashs.org
Facebook, Twitter, LinkedIn

Louise Ferguson, President
Michael W. Neff, Executive Director
Angie Lower, Conferences Manager
Negar Mahdavian, Conference Manager

Facilitating the mutual exchange of ideas and information concerning horticultural research, extension, education, and industry.
Cost: $560.00
Frequency: Annual

1100 **ATA Annual Conference**
Animal Transportation Association
12100 Sunset Hills Road
Suite 130
Reston, VA 20190

703-437-4377; Fax: 703-435-4390
info@animaltransportationassociation.org
www.animaltransportationassociation.org

Robin Turner, Association Director
Lisa Schoppa, AATA President
Erik Liebegott, President-Elect
Chris Santarelli, Secretary/Treasurer

The latest information and technology relating to the transportation of animals. Subtopics include welfare, stress, meat quality, environmental control, biosecurity guidelines, training programs, and new transport designed crates and trailers.
150 Attendees
Frequency: Annual

1101 **AVMA Annual Convention**
American Veterinary Medical Association
1931 N Meacham Road
Suite 100
Schaumburg, IL 60173

800-248-2862; Fax: 847-925-1329
www.avma.org
Facebook, Twitter, Flickr, YouTube

Rene Carlson, President
Douglas Aspros, President-Elect
Jan Strother, Vice President
Barbara Schmidt, Treasurer
W. Ron DeHaven, Executive Vice President

Seminar and more than 300 exhibits of products, materials, equipment, data, and services for veterinary medicine. Education and hands-on labs, exhibit hall, charitable events and networking.
10000 Attendees
Frequency: Annual/July

1102 **Acres USA Conference**
5321 Industrial Oaks Boulevard
Suite 128
Austin, TX 78735

512-892-4446
800-355-5315; Fax: 512-892-4448
info@acresusa.com
www.acresusa.com
Facebook, Twitter, LinkedIn

Fred C Walters, Publisher/Editor
1300 Attendees
Founded in 1970
Printed in on newsprint stock

1103 **Ag Progress Days**
College of Agricultural Sciences
Penn State University
420 Agricultural Admin Building
University Park, PA 16802

814-865-2081; Fax: 814-865-1677
www.apd.psu.edu

Bob Oberheim, Manager

Agricultural trade show focusing on the innovations and progress made in the agricultural industry. More than 400 commercial exhibitors, interactive educational exhibits, guided tours and workshops, machinery and field demonstrations, live animals and equine seminars and demonstrations.
50M Attendees
Frequency: Annual/August
Founded in 1976

1104 **Agri News Farm Show**
Agri News
18 1st Avenue SE
Rochester, MN 55904-6118

507-857-7707
800-533-1727; Fax: 507-281-7436
www.agrinew.com

John Losness, Publisher
Rosie Allen, Advertsising Manager
Mychal Wilmes, Managing Editor

Annual show of 123 exhibitors of farming equipment, supplies and services.
7,500 Attendees
Frequency: Annual/March

1105 **Agricultural Retailers Association Convention and Expo**
Agricultural Retailers Association
1156 15th Street
Suite 302
Washington, DC 20005

202-570-0825
800-535-6272; Fax: 314-567-6808
www.aradc.org
Facebook, Twitter

Daren Coppock, President/CEO
Richard Gupton, Sr, VP, Public Policy
Melisa Augusto, Dir., Comm. & Marketing

Annual show of 120 manufacturers, suppliers and distributors of agricultural chemicals and fertilizers. Seminar, conference and banquet.
1200 Attendees
Frequency: Annual/December
Founded in 1993

1106 **Allied Social Sciences Association Annual Meeting**
555 E Wells Street
Suite 1100
Milwaukee, WI 53202-6600

414-918-3190; Fax: 414-276-3349
info@aaea.org
www.aaea.org

Otto C Doering III, President
Yvonne C Bennett, Executive Director

The professional association for agricultural economists and related fields.
3000 Members
Frequency: Annual
Founded in 1910
Mailing list available for rent

1107 **America Trades Produce Conference**
590 East Frontage Road
PO Box 848
Nogales, AZ 85628

520-287-2707; Fax: 520-287-2948
info@freshfrommexico.com
www.fpaota.org

Lee Frank, President
Alicia Bon Martin, Vice Chair
Allison Moore, Communications Director
Jose Luis Obregon, Deputy Director
Martha Rascon, Public Affairs Director

Represents companies involved in growing, harvesting, marketing and importing of Mexican produce entering the US.
125+ Members
Founded in 1944

1108 **American Farriers Association Annual Convention Marketplace**
American Farriers Association
4059 Iron Works Parkway
Suite 1
Lexington, KY 40511

859-233-7411; Fax: 859-231-7862
info@americanfarriers.org
www.americanfarriers.org
Facebook

Buck McClendon, President
Thomas Trosin, President Elect
John Blombach, Vice President
Alan Larson, Treasurer
Jason Knight, Secretary

One-hundred and seventy exhibits of equipment and supplies for farriers, seminar, banquet, luncheon and tours.
1500 Attendees
Frequency: Annual/February
Founded in 1971

1109 **American Livestock Breeds Convervancy ALBC Conference**
PO Box 477
Pittsboro, NC 27312

919-542-5704; Fax: 919-545-0022
www.albc-usa.org
Facebook, Blogger

Charles Bassett, Executive Director

Ensuring the future of agriculture through genetic conservation and the promotion of endangered breeds of livestock and poultry. A nonprofit membership organization working to protect over 180 breeds of livestock and poultry from extinction.

1110 **American Seed Trade Association Annual Conference**
1701 Duke Street
Suite 275
Alexandria, VA 22314-2878

703-837-8140; Fax: 703-837-9365
www.amseed.com

Andy Lavigna, CEO

Producers of seeds for planting purposes. Consists of companies involved in seed production and distribution, plant breeding and related industries in North America.
850 Members
Founded in 1883

1111 **Americas Food & Beverage Show**
4601 NE 77th Avenue
Suite 200
Vancouver, WA 98662-2697

360-693-3373; Fax: 360-693-3464
www.wusata.org

Andy Anderson, Executive Director
Monica Quenette, Outreach Coordinator

A nonprofit organization that promotes the export of food and agricultural products from the Western region of the US Comprised of 13 state funded agricultural promotion agencies.

1112 **Annual Agricultural Law Symposium**
127 Young Rd.
Kelso, WA 98626

360-200-5699; Fax: 360-423-2287
roberta@aglaw-assn.org
www.aglaw-assn.org

Mike Traxinger, President
Scott Heidner, Executive Director

Bringing opportunities and ideas.
Frequency: Annual/October
Founded in 1980

1113 **Annual Board of Delegates Meeting**
1400 K St NW
Suite 1200
Washington, DC 20005-2449

202-789-0789; Fax: 202-898-0522
grains@grains.org
www.grains.org

Ryan LeGrand, President & CEO

Motivated by the grain sorghum, barley and corn producer associations and representatives of the agricultural community. Provides commodity export market development.
Founded in 1960

1114 **Annual Convention of the American Assoc. of Bovine Practitioners**
American Association of Bovine Practicioners
PO Box 3610
Auburn, AL 36831-3610

334-821-0442; Fax: 334-821-9532
aabphq@aabp.org
www.aabp.org

Brian J. Gerloff, President
Nigel B. Cook, President-Elect
Daniel L. Grooms, Vice President
Brian K. Reed, Treasurer
Charles W. Hatcher, Exhibits Chairman

130 exhibits of pharmaceutical and biological manufacturers, equipment and agricultural companies, computer programs and supplies.
1905 Attendees
Frequency: Annual/September
Founded in 1967

1115 **Annual Meeting and Professional Improvement Conferences (AM/PIC)**
6584 W Duroc Road
Maroa, IL 61756

217-794-3700; Fax: 217-794-5901
exec-dir@nacaa.com
www.nacaa.com
Facebook, Twitter

J. Craig Williams, President

Hundreds of NACAA members from all over the country, every one relates to the same challenges faced every day on the job. Networking with other professional organizations.
Founded in 1917
Mailing list available for rent: 3500 names at $500 per M

1116 **Aquatic Plant Management Society Annual Meeting**
Aquatic Plant Management Society
PO Box 821265
Vicksburg, MS 39182-1265

FAX 601-634-5502
dpetty@ndrsite.com
www.apms.org
Facebook, LinkedIn

Tyler Koschnick, President
Mike Netherland, VP
Sherry Whitaker, Treasurer
Jeff Schardt, Secretary
Craig Aguillard, Director

An international organization of educators, scientists, commercial pesticide applicators, administrators and individuals interested in aquatic plant species and plant management.
Founded in 1961

1117 **Argi-Marketing Conference**
11020 King St
Suite 205
Overland Park, KS 66210-1201

913-491-6500; Fax: 913-491-6502
agrimktg@nama.org
www.nama.org
Facebook, Twitter, LinkedIn, YouTube, Flickr

Jennifer Pickett, CEO

Marketing and communication suppliers, including trade publications, radio and television broadcast sales organizations, premium/incentive manufacturers, printers, marketing research firms, photographers and related professionals.
Founded in 1957

1118 **Asia Pacific Leather Fair**
1150 Connecticut Ave, NW
12th Floor
Washington, DC 20036

202-587-4250
www.ushsla.org

Stephen Sothmann, President

Exclusive representative of the hides and skin industry in the United States. Members range in size from small family-owned businesses to large corporations. Participates in two annual trade shows in Asia as a cooperator through the US Department of Agriculture's Foreign Agriculture Service.

1119 **Beltwide Cotton Conference**
National Cotton Council of America
7193 Goodlett Farms Parkway
Cordova, TN 38016

901-274-9030; Fax: 901-725-0510
www.cotton.org

Gary Adams, President & CEO

Offers a forum for agricultural professionals.
Frequency: Annual/January

1120 **Big Iron Farm Show and Exhibition**
Red River Valley Fair Association
1805 Main Ave. W
West Fargo, ND 58058-0797

701-282-2200
800-456-6408; Fax: 701-282-6909
info@redrivervalleyfair.com
www.bigironfarmshow.com
Facebook

Bryan Schulz, Manager

Annual show of 750 manufacturers of agricultural machinery and related products with over 1,000 exhibit spaces.
Frequency: Annual/September
Founded in 1980

1121 **Breeders of the Carolinas Field Day**
PO Box 1257
Kingsville, TX 78364-1257

361-592-9357; Fax: 361-592-8572
www.santagertrudis.com

Ervin Kaatz, Executive Director

Devoted to the interests and the needs of the breed developed in 1918 at the famous King Ranch in Texas. Recognized in 1940 by the USDA, and famou for efficient growth, solid red color, hardiness and good disposition. They areadaptable to many environments and are present throughout the US and in other countries.

1122 **COSA Annual Meeting**
Committee on Organic and Sustainable Agriculture
5585 Guilford Road
Madison, WI 53711-5801

608-273-8080; Fax: 608-273-2021
www.cosagroup.org

Ann-Marie Fortuna, Chair

COSA is a committee of the Tri-Societies for agronomy. The annual committee meeting is held in conjunction with the ASA-CSSA-SSSA Annual Meeting.
Frequency: Annual/Fall

1123 **CPMA Convention**
590 East Frontage Road
PO Box 848
Nogales, AZ 85628

520-287-2707; Fax: 520-287-2948
info@freshfrommexico.com
www.fpaota.org

Lee Frank, President
Alicia Bon Martin, Vice Chair
Allison Moore, Communications Director
Jose Luis Obregon, Deputy Director
Martha Rascon, Public Affairs Director

Represents more than 125 member companies involved in growing, harvesting, marketing and importing of mexican produce entering the US at Nogales, Arizona.
125+ Members
Founded in 1944

1124 **California Cannabis Business Conference**
National Cannabis Industry Association
1501 India St.
Suite 103-60
San Diego, CA 92101

888-409-4418
luke@gsmiweb.com
www.seedtosaleshow.com
Facebook, Twitter, Instagram, YouTube

F. Aaron Smith, Executive Director
Shannon Hayden, Chief Operating Officer
Michael Correia, Director, Government Relations
Morgan Fox, Director, Media Relations
Brooke Gilbert, Director, Events & Education

Brings together over 3,000 cannabis industry professionals, policymakers, entrepreneurs and newcomers to discuss best practices, policy issues, and share secrets for business success.
2000 Members
3000+ Attendees
Frequency: Annual, Fall
Founded in 2010

1125 **Cannabis Business Summit & Expo**
National Cannabis Industry Association
1501 India St.
Suite 103-60
San Diego, CA 92101

888-409-4418
luke@gsmiweb.com
www.seedtosaleshow.com
Facebook, Twitter, Instagram, YouTube

F. Aaron Smith, Executive Director
Shannon Hayden, Chief Operating Officer
Michael Correia, Director, Government Relations
Morgan Fox, Director, Media Relations
Brooke Gilbert, Director, Events & Education

Brings together cannabis industry professionals and exhibitors. Shop for your business-to-business needs, attend keynotes, panels and workshops.
2000 Members
7500+ Attendees
Frequency: Annual, Summer
Founded in 2010

1126 **Citrus Expo**
Southeast AgNet Publications/Citrus Industry Mag
5053 NW Hwy 225-A
Ocala, FL 34482

352-671-1909; Fax: 888-943-2224
www.citrusexpo.net

Maryann Holland, Show Manager

Citrus Trade Show with seminars, containing 150 exhibits. Complimentary attendance and lunch are provided to bona-fide grove owners & managers, citrus production managers, professional crop advisors, association execs & board members, government & legislative officials and the citrus research community.
1500 Attendees
Frequency: Annual/August
Founded in 1992

1127 **Commodity Classic**
Commodity Classic: ASA, NWGA, NCGA, NSP
632 Cepi Drive
Chesterfield, MO 63005-6397

636-733-9004; Fax: 636-733-9005
corninfo@ncga.com
www.commodityclassic.com

Dave Burmeister, Registration Information
Kristi Burmeister, Exhibitor Information
Susan Powers, Media/Press Information
Beth Musgrove, General Information
Peggy Findley, Sponsorship Information

550 booths of equipment, seed and chemicals. Lecture series, classes, entertainment, awards, annual meetings of several agri-organziations/associations, and the trade show.
4000 Attendees
Frequency: February

1128 **Contractor Summit**
6540 Arlington Blvd
Falls Church, VA 22042-6638

703-536-7080; Fax: 703-536-7019
info@irrigation.org
www.irrigation.org

Deborah Hamlin, Chief Executive Officer

Promotes education and use of irrigation in many areas of agriculture.
1600 Members
Founded in 1949

1129 **Country Elevator Conference & Trade Shows**
1250 I St NW
Suite 1003
Washington, DC 20005-3939

202-289-0873; Fax: 202-289-5388
ngfa@ngfa.org
www.ngfa.org

Randall Gordon, President & CEO
Todd E, Kemp, Vice President Of Marketing

NGFA is the national trade association of grain elevators, feed and feed ingredient manufacturers, grain and oilseed processors, exporters, livestock and poultry integrators, and firms providing products and services to the industry.
Founded in 1896

1130 **Dealership Minds Summit**
Lessiter Media
P.O. Box 624
Brookfield, WI 53008-0624

262-432-0388
866-839-8455; Fax: 262-786-5564
info@farm-equipment.com
www.farm-equipment.com
Facebook, Twitter, LinkedIn, YouTube

Bree Greenawalt, Event Manager
Michael Ellis, Sponsorship Opportunities
Dallas Ziebell, Group Attendance Discounts

A summit for farm equipment dealers to network and learn new marketing strategies.
Frequency: Annual

1131 **EMDA Industry Showcase**
Equipment Marketing & Distribution Association
PO Box 1347
Iowa City, IA 52244

319-354-5156
pat@emda.net
www.emda.net

Patricia A. Collins, Executive Vice President

Annual convention and 130 exhibits of equipment, supplies and services for wholesaler-distributors and independent manufacturer's representatives of shortline and specialty farm equipment, light industrial, lawn and garden, turf care equipment, estate and park maintenance equipment.
600 Attendees
Frequency: Annual/November

1132 **Eastern Milk Producers Cooperative Annual Meeting**
1985 Isaac Newton Square West
Reston, VA 20190-5094

703-742-6800; Fax: 703-742-7459
www.mdvamilk.com

Known for being a leader in the dairy industry, the Eastern Milk Producers Cooperative has an 85-plus year reputation for integrity, service and high quality products.
ISSN: west-

1133 **EcoFarm Conference**
Ecological Farming Association
2901 Park Ave.
Suite D-2
Soquel, CA 95073

831-763-2111
info@eco-farm.org
eco-farm.org

Emily Becker, Conference Manager

The largest sustainable agriculture conference in the western US, with a technical focus.
Frequency: Annual
Founded in 1980

1134 **El Foro**
WATT Publishing Company
122 S Wesley Avenue
Mount Morris, IL 61054

815-734-4171; Fax: 815-734-4201
www.wattnet.com

Jim Watt, Chairman/CEO

A trade show and technical symposium for the Latin American poultry, pig and feed industries. Containing 50 booths and 150 exhibits.
275 Attendees
Frequency: July

1135 **Empire State Expo**
Lee Publications
6113 State Hwy. 5
P.O. Box 121
Palatine Bridge, NY 13428-0121

518-673-3237
888-596-5329; Fax: 518-673-2699
kmaring@leepub.com
www.leetradeshows.com

Ken Maring, Show Manager

A comprehensive trade show and educational conference for fruit and vegetable growers and marketers in New York and surrounding states, as well as Eastern Canada.
Frequency: Annual

1136 **Equipment Manufacturers Conference**
American Feed Industry Association
2101 Wilson Blvd
Suite 916
Arlington, VA 22201-3047

703-524-0810; Fax: 703-524-1921
afia@afia.org
www.afia.org
Facebook, Twitter, LinkedIn

Constance Cullman, President & CEO

Organization devoted to representing companies in the animal feed industry and its suppliers.
690 Members
Founded in 1909

1137 **European Seafood Exposition**
4601 NE 77th Avenue
Suite 200
Vancouver, WA 98662-2697

360-693-3373; Fax: 360-693-3464
www.wusata.org

Andy Anderson, Executive Director
Monica Quenette, Outreach Coordinator

A nonprofit organization that promotes the export of food and agricultural products from the Western region of the US Comprised of 13 state funded agricultural promotion agencies.

1138 **FPAA Convention & Golf Tournament**
590 East Frontage Road
PO Box 848
Nogales, AZ 85628

520-287-2707; Fax: 520-287-2948
info@freshfrommexico.com
www.fpaota.org

Lee Frank, President
Alicia Bon Martin, Vice Chair
Allison Moore, Communications Director
Jose Luis Obregon, Deputy Director
Martha Rascon, Public Affairs Director

Represents companies involved in growing, harvesting, marketing and importing of Mexican produce entering the US.
125+ Members
Founded in 1944

1139 **Farm Equipment Manufacturers Association Spring Conference**
Farm Equipment Manufacturers Association
1000 Executive Parkway Drive
Suite 100
St. Louis, MO 63141-6369

314-878-2304
info@farmequip.org
www.farmequip.org

Matt Westendorf, President
Vernon Schmidt, Executive Vice President
Tricia Kidd, Accounting & Meeting Services
Kristi Ruggles, Communications Director

Event for those involved in the farm equipment manufacturing industry. The conference includes a supplier product showcase.
730+ Members
Founded in 1950

1140 **Farm Progress Show**
Farm Progress Companies
255 38th Avenue
Suite P
St Charles, IL 60174-5410

630-462-2224
800-441-1410
mjungmann@farmprogress.com
www.farmprogressshow.com

Matt Jungman, National Shows Manager

Annual farm show of 400 exhibitors representing various types of agricultural products and services for farmers and agribusiness, including small operations to top producers.
Frequency: August/September

1141 **Farm Science Review**
Ohio State University
590 Woody Hayes Drive
232 Ag Engineering Building
Columbus, OH 43210-1057

614-926-6691
800-644-6377; Fax: 614-292-9448
gamble.18@osu.edu
fsr.osu.edu

Chuck Gamble, Manager
Mattk Sullivan, Assistant Manager
Suzanne Steel, Media Coordinator

Annual show of 600 exhibitors of agricultural equipment, supplies and services.
140M Attendees
Frequency: Annual/September

1142 **Farm/Ranch Expo**
Bacon Hedland Management
475 S Frontage Road
Suite 101
Burr Ridge, IL 60527

630-323-6880; Fax: 630-898-3550

Gene Bacon, Show Manager

160 booths
7M Attendees
Frequency: January

1143 **Farmfest**
Farm Fairs
Highway 60 West
PO Box 731
Lake Crystal, MN 56055

507-726-6863; Fax: 507-726-6750

Annual show of 450 manufacturers, suppliers and distributors of farm equipment and machinery, computers and software products, chemicals, seeds and crops, and techniques of planting, tillage and harvesting.
50M Attendees

1144 **Fertilizer Outlook and Technology Conference**
425 Third Street SW
Suite 950
Washington, DC 20002-8037

202-962-0490; Fax: 202-962-0577
information@tfi.org
www.tfi.org

Mariana Gallo, Senior Director, Conferences

Gain perspective on the outlook for agriculture and major fertilizer materials and inputs from industry experts.
Founded in 1970

1145 **Fresh Summit International Convention & Expo**
1500 Casho Mill Road
PO Box 6036
Newark, DE 19714-6036

302-738-7100; Fax: 302-731-2409
pma@pma.com
www.pma.com
Facebook, Twitter, Flickr, YouTube, Xchange

Cathy Burns, CEO

PMA brings together leaders from around the world and from every segment of the supply chain. Participants throughout the global fresh produce and floral supply chains come together as a community to learn, network, build relationships, and do business.
Founded in 1949

1146 **GEAPS Operations, Management, & Technology Seminar**
Grain Elevator & Processing Society
4248 Park Glen Road
Minneapolis, MN 55416

952-928-4640; Fax: 952-929-1318
info@geaps.com
www.geaps.com

David Krejci, Executive VP/Secretary
Darren Grahsl, Manager/Member & Chapter Services
Chuck House, Manager/Comm & Professional Dev
Amy McGarrigle, Manager/Member Ser & Information
Jason Stones, Manager/Member Ser & Publications

Offered in collaboration with the National Grain and Feed Association, boasted a faculty of industry experts covering topics including contamination, purity and salvage; handling, storage and incident response; theft protection and inventory management beset practices; and natural disaster response and preparedness
2,000 Attendees
Frequency: March
Founded in 1937

1147 **GIE+EXPO - Green Industry & Equipment Expo**
Professional Lawncare Network, Inc
222 Pearl Street
Suite 300
New Albany, IN 47150

812-949-9200
800-558-8767; Fax: 812-949-9600
info@gie-expo.com
www.gie-expo.com
Facebook, Twitter

Annual show of 400 manufacturers, suppliers and distributors of lawn care equipment, supplies and services, including fertilizers, weed control materials, insurance information and power equipment, plus education sessions and presentations and demos.

1148 **Government Affairs Conference**
USA Rice Federation
4301 N Fairfax Drive
Suite 425
Arlington, VA 22203

703-226-2300; Fax: 703-236-2301
riceinfo@usarice.com
www.usarice.com

Ben Mosely, VP, Government Affairs
Jeanette Davis, Sr. Dir., Meetings & Member Service
Jamison Cruce, Director, Government Affairs

Discuss issues and activities for the U.S. rice industry, legislation, training, and seminars.
Frequency: Annual

1149 **Grain Feed Association Trade Show**
National Grain and Feed Association
1250 I Street NW
Suite 1003
Washington, DC 20005-3922

202-289-0873; Fax: 202-289-5388
ngfa@ngfa.org
www.ngfa.org

Randall Gordon, President & CEO

One hundred and thirty booths exhibiting agribusiness products, supplies and services.
1.3M Attendees
Frequency: March

1150 **Grape Grower Magazine Farm Show**
Western Agricultural Publishing Company
4974 E Clinton Way
Suite 123
Fresno, CA 93727-1520

559-261-0396; Fax: 559-252-7387

Phill Rhoads, Manager

Seminars, exhibits and prizes for grape growers. Contianing 80 booths and exhibits.

1151 **Green Industry Conference - GIC**
Professional Lawncare Network, Inc (PLANET)
950 Herndon Parkway
Suite 450
Herndon, VA 20170

703-736-9666
800-395-2522; Fax: 703-736-9668
www.landscapeprofessionals.org

Held in conjunction with the GIE+EXPO, the conference offers leadership series, workshops, educational opportunities, events, and new member orientation.
Frequency: Annual

1152 **GrowerExpo**
Ball Publishing
335 N River Street
PO Box 9
Batavia, IL 60510-0009

630-208-9080
800-456-5380; Fax: 630-208-9350
info@ballpublishing.com

Diane Blazek, President

A trade show devoted to horticulture and floriculture production and marketing. 200 booths.
2M Attendees
Frequency: January

1153 **Hawkeye Farm Show**
Midwest Shows
PO Box 737
Austin, MN 55912

507-437-7969; Fax: 507-437-7752
www.farmshowsusa.com

Penny Swank, Show Manager
18000 Attendees
Frequency: March

1154 **Hemp Industries Association**

707-874-3648
www.thehia.org
Instagram

Jody McGinness, Executive Director
Sarah Gardner, Membeship Director
Ryann Hinch, Operations Director

Advances the hemp economy and educates the market for the benefit of our members, the public, and the planet.
Founded in 1994

1155 **Hemp Industries Association Annual Confere nce**
Hemp Industries Association

707-874-3648
www.thehia.org
Instagram

Jody McGinness, Executive Director
Sarah Gardner, Membership Director
Ryann Hinch, Operations Director

A leading business-to-business hemp industries tade show. Features the annual general meeting, exhibits, discussions, focused educational tracks, and industry awards.
Founded in 1994

1156 **Holstein Association USA Regional Meeting**
1 Holstein Place
PO Box 808
Brattleboro, VT 05302-0808

802-254-4551
800-965-5200; Fax: 802-254-8251
info@holstein.com
www.holsteinusa.com

Corey Geiger, President

Dairy cattle breed association with a membership base of people with strong interests in breeding, raising and milking Holstein cattle.
Founded in 1885

1157 **Horticulture Industries Show**
P.O. Box 75495
Oklahoma City, OK 73147

405-696-3079
hortindustriesshow@gmail.com
www.hortindustriesshow.org
Facebook

A horticulture educational conference in the areas of Christmas trees, sustainable agriculture, fruit, vegetables, farmers markets and master gardeners.
Frequency: Annual

1158 **IAOM Conferences and Expos**
International Association of Operative Millers
10100 West 87th Street
Suite 306
Overland Park, KS 66212

913-338-3377; Fax: 913-338-3553
info@iaom.info
www.iaom.info
Facebook, LinkedIn

Melinda Farris, CEO
Cynthia Malone, Director, Meetings & Exhibitions

Premier educational events for grain milling and seed processing professionals. The annual events gather milling and allied trade professionals from around the world for several days of education, networking and fellowship.
Frequency: Annual/May
Founded in 1896

1159 **IFTA Annual Conference**
International Fruit Tree Association
16020 Swingley Ridge Rd.
Suite 300
Chesterfield, MO 63017

636-449-5083; Fax: 636-449-5051
dungey@ifruittree.org
www.ifruittree.org

Lisa Jenereaux, President
Jeff Cleveringa, Vice President
Chris Hedges, Treasurer

Distinguished speakers, workshops and a regional orchard tour are highlights of the association's annual conference.
Frequency: Annual
Founded in 1958

1160 **International Feed Expo**
American Feed Industry Association
2101 Wilson Blvd
Suite 916
Arlington, VA 22201-3047

703-524-0810; Fax: 703-524-1921
afia@afia.org
www.afia.org
Facebook, Twitter, LinkedIn

Constance Cullman, President & CEO
Paul Davis, Director, Animal Food Safety
Rob Cooper, Executive Director Of IFEEDER

Organization devoted to representing companies in the animal feed industry and its suppliers.
Founded in 1909

1161 **International Hoof-Care Summit**
American Farriers Journal
PO Box 624
Brookfield, WI 53008-0624

262-432-0388
866-839-8455; Fax: 262-786-5564
info@americanfarriers.com
www.americanfarriers.com
Facebook, Twitter, LinkedIn, YouTube

Frank Lessiter, Owner
Jeremy McGovern, Sponsorship Opportunities
Dallas Ziebell, Group Attendance Discounts

Attendees will receive unparalleled hoof-care education through engaging general sessions, practical hoof-care classrooms, hoof-care roundtables, and how-to clinics. The summit features farriers, veterinarians, and researchers.
800 Attendees
Frequency: Annual, January

1162 **International Marketing Conference & Annual Membership Meeting**
1400 K St NW
Suite 1200
Washington, DC 20005-2449

202-789-0789; Fax: 202-898-0522
grains@grains.org
www.grains.org

Ryan LeGrand, President & CEO

Motivated by the grain sorghum, barley and corn producer associations and representatives of the agricultural community. Provides commodity export market development.
Founded in 1960

1163 **International Off-Highway and Power Plant Meeting and Exposition**
Society of Automotive Engineers
400 Commonwealth Drive
Warrendale, PA 15096-0001

724-776-4841; Fax: 724-776-4026
www.sae.org

Diane Rogne, Show Manager
Sam Barill, Treasurer
Andrew Brown, Treasurer

Annual show of 270 suppliers of parts, components, materials and systems utilized in farm and industrial machinery and off-road and recreational vehicles.
5000 Attendees
Circulation: 84,000

1164 **International Sweets & Biscuits Fair (ISM)**
4601 NE 77th Avenue
Suite 200
Vancouver, WA 98662-2697

360-693-3373; Fax: 360-693-3464
www.wusata.org

Andy Anderson, Executive Director
Monica Quenette, Outreach Coordinator

A nonprofit organization that promotes the export of food and agricultural products from the Western region of the US Comprised of 13 state funded agricultural promotion agencies.

1165 **Irrigation Show**
Irrigation Association
8280 Willow Oaks Corp. Dr.
Suite 400
Fairfax, VA 22031-4507

703-536-7080; Fax: 703-536-7019
info@irrigation.org
www.irrigation.org

Deborah M. Hamlin, Chief Executive Officer
Rebecca J. Bayless, Finance Director
Tiffany Wilson, Senior Trade Show Manager
Anne Blankenbiller, Senior Communications Manager
Janie C. Hakim, Membership Manager

The Irrigation Show is the industry's one-stop event. Discover innovations on the show floor and in technical sessions, make connections with industry experts, business partners, and peers and build expertise with targeted education and certification.
3.5M Attendees
Frequency: Annual/November

1166 **KFYR Radio Agri International Stock & Trade Show**
KFYR Radio
3500 East Rosser Avenue
PO Box 1658
Bismarck, ND 58501

701-580-0550
800-472-2170; Fax: 701-255-8155
mwall@clearchannel.com
www.kfyr.com

Syd Stewart, General Manager
Neil Cary, Manager
Jim Lowe, Manager

Annual show of 400 exhibitors of agricultural equipment, livestock and services.
15M Attendees
Frequency: February

1167 **Kentucky Grazing Conference**
151 Treasure Island Cswy. #2
St. Petersburg, FL 33706-4734

727-367-9702
800-707-0014; Fax: 727-367-9608
darthay@yahoo.com
www.nationalhay.org

Dan Wray, President

NHA is the trade group that represents the interests of the hay industry throughout the United States and internationally.
Founded in 1895

1168 **Kosherfest**
4601 NE 77th Avenue
Suite 200
Vancouver, WA 98662-2697

360-693-3373; Fax: 360-693-3464
www.wusata.org

Andy Anderson, Executive Director
Monica Quenette, Outreach Coordinator

A nonprofit organization that promotes the export of food and agricultural products from the Western region of the US Comprised of 13 state funded agricultural promotion agencies.

1169 **Legislative Action Conference National Pork Producers Council**
122 C Street NW
Suite 875
Washington, DC 20001

202-347-3600
800-937-7675; Fax: 202-347-5265
warnerd@nppc.org
www.nppc.org
Facebook, Twitter

Neil Dierks, Chief Executive Officer
Doug Fricke, Director, Trade Show Marketing

National Pork Producers Council hosts a legislative action conference twice a year for pork producers from around the nation to learn about, discuss and lobby on agriculture legislation important to the U.S. pork industry.

1170 **Legislative Conference**
6540 Arlington Blvd
Falls Church, VA 22042-6638

703-536-7080; Fax: 703-536-7019
info@irrigation.org
www.irrigation.org

Deborah Hamlin, Chief Executive Officer

Promotes education and use of irrigation in many areas of agriculture.
Founded in 1949

1171 **Liquid Feed Symposium**
American Feed Industry Association
2101 Wilson Blvd
Suite 916
Arlington, VA 22201-3047

703-524-0810; Fax: 703-524-1921
afia@afia.org
www.afia.org
Facebook, Twitter, LinkedIn

Constance Cullman, President & CEO
Paul David, Director, Animal Food Safety
Rob Cooper, Executive Director IFEEDER

Organization devoted to representing companies in the animal feed industry and its suppliers.
Founded in 1909

1172 **Mid South Farm Gin Supply Exhibit**
Southern Cotton Ginners Association
874 Cotton Gin Place
Memphis, TN 38106

901-947-3104; Fax: 901-947-3103
www.southerncottonginners.org

Timothy Price, Executive Vice President

Exhibits new technology and practices for those in the cotton industry.
Frequency: Annual/February

1173 **Mid-America Christmas Tree Association Sum mer Show**
Mid-America Christmas Tree Association

740-815-6107
midamericachristmastreeassoc@gmail.com
www.midamericachristmastree.com

Donna Cackler, Executive Administrator

Industry leaders share information and insights. Vendors sell stockfor the upcoming season.
Frequency: Annual

1174 **Mid-America Farm Show**
Salina Area Chamber of Commerce

120 W Ash St.
PO Box 586
Salina, KS 67401

785-827-9301; Fax: 785-827-9758
www.salinakansas.org

Don Weiser, Show Manager

Annual show of 325 exhibitors of agricultural equipment, supplies and services, including irrigation equipment, fertilizer, farm implements, hybrid seed, agricultural chemicals, tractors, feed, farrowing crates and equipment, silos and bins, storage equipment and farm buildings.
13M Attendees
Frequency: Annual/March
Founded in 1911

1175 **Mid-America Horticulture Trade Show**
Mid Am Trade Show
401 N. Michigan Ave.
Suite 2200
Chicago, IL 60611

312-321-5130
800-300-6103; Fax: 312-673-6882
mail@midam.org
www.midam.org
Facebook, Twitter, LinkedIn, YouTube

Barbara Rosborough, President
Bill Vogel, Vice President
Jim Melka, Secretary
Dave Story, Treasurer

Mid-Am is a green-industry event featuring more than 650 leading suppliers offering countless products, equipment, and services for the horticulture industry. Mid-Am also offers a variety of educational seminars featuring the best and the brightest in the horticultural and business communities to help keep you informed of the latest trends.
Frequency: Annual/January

1176 **Midwest Ag Expo: OH**
590 Woody Hayes Drive
Room 232
Columbus, OH 43210

614-292-4278; Fax: 614-292-9448
gamble.19@osu.edu
www.worldagexpo.com

Doug Wagner, President
Dennis Alford, 1st Vice President
Chip Blalock, 2nd Vice President
Chuck Gamble, Secretary-Treasurer

Members are agriculture trade show sponsors and suppliers of services to these shows. Provides members with education, communication and evaluation. Provides the best possible marketing showcase for exhibitors and related products to the farmer/rancher/producer customer.
Founded in 1972

1177 **Midwest Expo: IL**
Illinois Fertilizer & Chemical Association
130 W Dixie Highway
PO Box 186
Saint Anne, IL 60964-0186

815-939-1566
800-892-7122; Fax: 815-427-6573

Jean Trobec, President

Annual show of 130 manufacturers, suppliers and distributors of agricultural chemical and fertilizer application equipment, supplies and services.
2500 Attendees
Frequency: August, Danville

1178 **Midwest Farm Show**
North Country Enterprises
5330 Wall St
Suite 100
Madison, WI 53718

608-240-4700; Fax: 608-240-2069
medaassn.com

Bill Henry, President
Massey Ferguson, Vice-President
Julie Roisum, Executive Assistant

250 booths. Top farm show exhibiting dairy and Wisconsin's tillage equipment, feed and seed.
175 Members
11M+ Attendees
Frequency: January

1179 **NACB Symposiums**
National Association of Cannabis Businesses
1918 E. Lafayette Place
Milwaukee, WI 53202

720-926-6881
info@nacb.com
www.nacb.com
Facebook, Twitter, LinkedIn

Gina Kranwinkel, Chief Executive Officer
Mark Gorman, Executive VP & COO
Tom Nolasco, Dir., Legal & Strategic Initiatives
Meggan Hau, Operations Manager
Mary Clifton, Cannabis Research Advisor

A series of day-long symposiums on the most pressing legal and business issues facing the cannabis industry. Features presentations by premier law, accounting, and advisory firms.

1180 **NCTA Convention & Trade Show**
National Christmas Tree Association
16020 Swingley Ridge Rd
Suite 300
Chesterfield, MO 63017-6030

636-449-5070; Fax: 636-449-5051
info@realchristmastrees.org
www.realchristmastrees.org

Tim O'Connor, Executive Director
Ann O'Connor, Director, Programs & Memberships
Dugald Kell, Jr., President
Steve Meier, President-Elect

Draws christmas tree growers, retailers and suppliers from around the world for education, contests, networking and the trade show.
500 Attendees
Frequency: Annual/August

1181 **NDHIA Annual Meeting**
National Dairy Herd Improvement Association
421 S Nine Mound Round
PO Box 930399
Verona, WI 53593-0399

608-848-6455; Fax: 608-848-7675
info@dhia.org
www.dhia.org

Jay Mattison, CEO
Allen Chester, President
250 Attendees

1182 **NFU Women's Conference**
20 F Street NW
Suite 300
Washington, DC 20001

202-554-1600
800-347-1961; Fax: 202-554-1654
www.nfu.org
Facebook, Twitter, YouTube, Instagram

Business planning, marketing and networking for women in agriculture.

1183 **NHA Annual Convention**
National Hay Association
151 Treasure Island Cswy
#2
St. Petersburg, FL 33706

727-367-9702
800-707-0014; Fax: 727-367-9608
darthay@yahoo.com
www.nationalhay.org

Information and technology affecting the Hay industry.
Frequency: Annual/September

1184 **National 4-H Conference**
4-H
National 4-H Conference Center
7100 Connecticut Ave.
Chevy Chase, MD 20815

Home Page: www.4-h.org/4-h-conference

Annual leadership and personal development event for 4-H members, 15 to 19 years old.
Frequency: Annual
Founded in 1927

1185 **National Agri-Marketing Association Conference**
National Agri-Marketing Association
11020 King Street
Suite 205
Overland Park, KS 66210

913-491-6500; Fax: 913-491-6502
agrimktg@nama.org
www.nama.org

Jennifer Pickett, Executive VP & CEO

Annual show of 60 exhibitors of marketing and communication suppliers, including trade publications, radio and television broadcast sales organizations, premium/incentive manufacturers, printers, marketing research firms and photographers.
1400 Attendees
Frequency: April

1186 **National Agricultural Plastics Congress**
American Society for Plasticulture
526 Brittany Drive
State College, PA 16803

814-238-7045; Fax: 814-238-7051
www.plasticulture.org

William Tietjen, President
Jodi Fleck-Arnold, VP
Edward Cary, Secretary/Treasurer
Patricia Heuser, Executive Director

Congress of research presentations, with exhibit area of equipment, supplies and services relating to greenhouse production and mulch film production of agricultural and horticultural crops.
225 Attendees
Frequency: March

1187 **National Alliance of Independent Crop Consultants Annual Meeting**
349 E Nolley Dr
Collierville, TN 38017-3538

901-861-0511; Fax: 901-861-0512
jonesnaicc@aol.com
www.naicc.org

Represents individual crop consultants and contract researchers.
500+ Members
Founded in 1978

1188 **National Association Extension 4-H Agents Convention**
University of Georgia
Hoke Smith Annex
Athens, GA 30602

706-542-8804

Bo Ryles, State 4-H Leader
Heather Schultz, Live Stock Coordinator

50 booths for young people, youth staff and volunteers involved in 4-H.
1.2M Attendees
Frequency: November

1189 **National Association of Agricultural Educators (NAAE) Convention**
300 Garrigus Building
University of Kentucky
Lexington, KY 40545

859-257-2224
800-509-0204; Fax: 859-323-3919
www.naae.org

Alissa Smith, Chief Executive Officer
Wm. Jay Jackman, Executive Director

A federation of 50 affiliated state vocational agricultural teacher associations.
7600 Members
Founded in 1948

1190 **National Association of County Agricultural Agents Conference**
National Association of County Agricultural Agents
6584 W Duroc Road
Maroa, IL 61756

217-794-3700; Fax: 217-794-5901
exec-dir@nacaa.com
www.nacaa.com
Facebook, Twitter

J. Craig Williams, President

Annual conference and exhibits for county agricultural agents and extension workers.
Frequency: Annual

1191 **National Association of Wheat Growers Convention**
National Association of Wheat Growers
415 2nd St NE
Suite 300
Washington, DC 20002-4993

202-547-7800; Fax: 202-546-2638
wheatworld@wheatworld.org
www.wheatworld.org
Facebook, Twitter

Chandler Goule, CEO

Convention and trade show for the wheat, corn, soybean and sorghum industries.
Frequency: Annual/February
Founded in 1950

1192 **National Cotton Council Annual Meeting**
7193 Goodlett Farms Parkway
Cordova, TN 38016

901-274-9030; Fax: 901-725-0510
www.cotton.org

Gary Adams, President/CEO

Membership consists of approximately 300 delegates named by cotton interests in the cotton-producing states.
35 Members

1193 **National Custom Applicator Exposition**
Agribusiness Association of Iowa
900 Des Moines Street
Suite 150
Des Moines, IA 50309-5549

515-262-8323; Fax: 515-262-8960
info@agribiz.org
www.agribiz.org

Ed Beaman, President/CEO

Annual show of 70 manufacturers, suppliers and distributors of agrichemicals, fertilizers, spray equipment, tanks, agriplanes and agricomputer and flotation equipment.
2500 Attendees
Frequency: August

1194 **National FFA Convention & Expo**
PO Box 68960
6060 FFA Drive
Indianapolis, IN 46268-0960

317-802-6060
www.ffa.org/events/conventionandexpo
Facebook, Twitter, Snapchat, Instagram

Mark Poeschl, Chief Executive Officer

Agricultural, food science and natural resource education show.
63K Attendees

1195 **National FFA Week**
PO Box 68960
6060 FFA Drive
Indianapolis, IN 46268-0960

317-802-6060
www.ffa.org/participate/events/ffa-week
Facebook, Twitter, Snapchat, Instagram

Annual week-long celebration of the FFA's contributions to local schools, communities and the agriculture industry.
Founded in 1947

1196 **National Farm Machinery Show & Tractor Pull**
590 Woody Hayes Drive
Room 232
Columbus, OH 43210

614-292-4278; Fax: 614-292-9448
gamble.19@osu.edu
www.worldagexpo.com

Doug Wagner, President
Dennis Alford, 1st Vice President
Chip Blalock, 2nd Vice President
Chuck Gamble, Secretary-Treasurer

Members are agriculture trade show sponsors and suppliers of services to these shows. Provides members with education, communication and evaluation. Provides the best possible marketing showcase for exhibitors and related products to the farmer/rancher/producer customer.
37 Members
Founded in 1972

1197 **National Farm Machinery Show and Championship Tractor Pull**
Kentucky Fair and Exposition Center
937 Phillips Lane
PO Box 37130
Louisville, KY 40233-7130

502-367-5000; Fax: 502-367-5299
www.farmmachineryshow.org

Harold Workman, President/CEO

Annual show of 800 plus exhibitors of agricultural products, equipment, supplies and services.
293M Attendees
Frequency: February

1198 **National Farmers Union Convention**
20 F Street NW
Suite 300
Washington, DC 20001

202-554-1600
800-347-1961; Fax: 202-554-1654
www.nfu.org
Facebook, Twitter, YouTube, Instagram

Promotes educational, cooperative and legislative activities of farm families in 26 states.

1199 **National Grain Feed Association Annual Convention**
National Grain Feed Association
1250 I Street NW
Suite 1003
Washington, DC 20005

202-289-0873; Fax: 202-289-5388
ngfa@ngfa.org
www.ngfa.org

Randall Gordon, NGFA President
Todd Kemp, Vice President Of Marketing

Committee meetings addressing issues essential to the business; Ag Village exhibitors and speakers.
1.3M Attendees
Frequency: March/April
Founded in 1896

1200 **National Grange Convention**
1616 H Street NW
Suite 10
Washington, DC 20006

202-628-3507
888-447-2643; Fax: 202-347-1091
www.nationalgrange.org/events/future-national-grange-conventions

Samantha Wilkins, Operations Coordinator

Annual policy- and agenda-setting meeting.

1201 **National Hemp Association Annual Meeting**
National Hemp Association
80 M St. SE
Suite 130
Washington, DC 20003

202-706-3911
www.nationalhempassociation.org
Facebook, Twitter, Google+

Erica Stark, Executive Director
Anna Chanthavongseng, Assistant Executive Director

A meeting to discuss all aspects of the industrial hemp industry including education, community, legislation, and scientific and industry news.
Frequency: Annual

1202 **National No-Tillage Conference**
Lessiter Media
P.O. Box 624
Brookfield, WI 53008-0624

262-432-0388
866-839-8455; Fax: 262-786-5564
info@no-tillfarmer.com
www.no-tillfarmer.com/nntc
Facebook, Twitter, LinkedIn

Frank Lessiter, Owner
Bree Greenawalt, Event Manager
Darrell Bruggink, Sponsorship Opportunities
Joanne Volkert, Group Attendance Discounts

Conference held for America's leading most innovative no-till farmers.
Frequency: January

1203 **National Orange Show Fair**
National Orange Show
689 South E Street
San Bernardino, CA 92408

909-888-6788; Fax: 909-889-7666
http://nationalorageshow.com
Facebook

Five days of entertainment, art, exhibits, music, food and rides celebrating and educating the community on the California orange.
80000 Attendees
Frequency: Annual/May
Founded in 1889

1204 **National Potato Council Annual Meeting**
1300 L St NW
Suite 910
Washington, DC 20005-4107

202-682-9456; Fax: 202-682-0333
spudinfo@nationalpotatocouncil.org
www.nationalpotatocouncil.org
Twitter

Kam Quarles, Chief Executive Officer

Connect with other grower leaders from across the country on shaping national public policy impacting potato production and distribution. Such issues as keeping potatoes in schools, finalizing free trade agreements, and gearing up for the next Farm Bill will be reviewed and strategies will be developed.
45000 Members
Founded in 1948

1205 **National Strip-Tillage Conference**
Lessiter Media
P.O. Box 624
Brookfield, WI 53008-0624

262-432-0388
800-645-8455; Fax: 262-786-5564
info@striptillfarmer.com
www.striptillfarmer.com
Facebook, Twitter, YouTube

Frank Lessiter, Owner
Michael Ellis, Sponsorship Opportunities
Dallas Ziebell, Group Attendance Discounts

Assembles the best strip-tillers, agronomists and researchers in one location to share cutting-edge ideas, techniques and strategies to raise your level of strip-till profitability, efficiency and efficacy. Features session speakers, classrooms, roundtables, and networking opportunities.
Frequency: Annual, August

1206 **North American Beekeeping Conference & Tradeshow**
American Beekeeping Federation
3525 Piedmont Road
Bldg 5 Suite 300
Atlanta, GA 30305-1509

404-760-2875; Fax: 404-240-0998
info@abfnet.org
www.abfnet.org

Molly Sausaman, Executive Director

Expert talks and discussions about beekeeping hot topics; exhibits and introduction of new products; and workshops.
Frequency: Annual/January
Founded in 1943

1207 **North American Deer Farmers Association Annual Conference & Exhibit**
North American Deer Farmers Association
104 S Lakeshore Drive
Lake City, MN 55041-1266

651-345-5600; Fax: 651-345-5603
info@nadefa.org
www.nadefa.org

Carolyn Laughlin, President
Dave McQuaig, First VP
Glenn Dice Jr, Second VP

Annual show of 30+ exhibitors of deer farming equipment, supplies and services.
300 Attendees
Frequency: February
Founded in 1983

1208 **North American Farm and Power Show**
Tradexpos
811 W Oakland Avenue
PO Box 1067
Austin, MN 55912

507-437-4697
800-949-3976; Fax: 507-437-8917
steve@tradexpos.com
www.tradexpos.com

Steve Guenthner, Show Director

Agri-business farm show for the 5-state region. Free admission and parking.
28M Attendees
Frequency: March

1209 **North American Fertilizer Transportation Conference**
425 Third Street SW
Suite 950
Washington, DC 20002-8037

202-962-0490; Fax: 202-962-0577
information@tfi.org
www.tfi.org

Mariana Gallo, Senior Director, Conferences

Co-hosted by The Fertilizer Institute and the Canadian Fertilizer Institute. Provides and opportunity for shippers and carriers to discuss issues of concern and work to reach mutually-beneficial solutions to logistical problems.
325 Members
Founded in 1970

1210 **North American International Livestock Exposition**
Kentucky Fair and Exposition Center
937 Phillips Lane
PO Box 37130
Louisville, KY 40209-7130

502-367-5000; Fax: 502-367-5139
www.livestockexpo.org

Debbie Burda, Booking/Events
Ellen Anderson, Event Contact

Purebred livestock show with more than 20,000 entries in eight major divisions: dairy cattle, dairy goats, llamas, quarter horses, draft horses, market swine, beef cattle, sheep. Held at Kentucky Fair and Exposition Center in Louisville, Kentucky.
Frequency: November

1211 **Northwest Agricultural Congress**
4991 Drift Creek Rd SE
Sublimity, OR 97385-9764

503-769-8940; Fax: 503-769-8946
www.nwagshow.com

Jim Heater, Show Manager

Second largest agricultural show on the west coast. Show is produced by the Northwest Horticultural Congress which is a partnership between Oregon Horticultural Society, the Oregon Association of Nurseries and Northwest Nut Growers Association. Show held in conjunction with annual meetings and seminars by all three of the horticultural groups.
21000 Members

1212 **Nut Grower Magazine Farm Show**
Western Agricultural Publishing Company
4974 E Clinton Way
Suite 123
Fresno, CA 93727-1520

559-252-7000; Fax: 559-252-7387

Phill Rhoads, Manager

Productions seminars, guest speakers, prizes and exhibits for nut growers. Containing 80 booths and exhibits.

1213 **Organic Seed Growers Conference**
PO Box 772
Port Townsend, WA 98368

360-385-7192; Fax: 360-385-7455
info@seedalliance.org
www.seedalliance.org
Facebook, Twitter

Cara Loriz, Executive Director

Supports the ethical development and stewardship of the genetic resources of agricultural seed.
Founded in 1975

1214 **Ozark Fall Farmfest**
Ozark Empire Fair
3001 North Grant Street
PO Box 630
Springfield, MO 65308

417-833-2660; Fax: 417-833-3769
www.ozarkempirefair.com

Pat Lloyd, Manager

Annual show of 700 exhibitors with about 600 booths of agricultural products and services, including livestock.
40M Attendees
Frequency: October

1215 **PMA Convention & Exposition**
Produce Marketing Association
1500 Casho Mill Road
Newark, DE 19711-3547

302-738-7100; Fax: 302-731-2409
pma@pma.com
www.pma.com
Twitter, Flickr, YouTube

Cathy Burns, CEO
Doug Bohr, Executive Director
Yvonne Bull, CFO

A trade association of companies engaged in the marketing of fresh and safe produce and floral products. Show will inlcude 600 exhibitors with 1,600 booths.
16000 Attendees
Frequency: Annual/October
Founded in 1949

1216 **PMA Fresh Summit**
590 East Frontage Road
PO Box 848
Nogales, AZ 85628

520-287-2707; Fax: 520-287-2948
info@freshfrommexico.com
www.fpaota.org

Lee Frank, President
Alicia Bon Martin, Vice Chair
Allison Moore, Communications Director
Jose Luis Obregon, Deputy Director
Martha Rascon, Public Affairs Director

Represents more than 125 member companies involved in growing, harvesting, marketing and importing of mexican produce entering the US at Nogales, Arizona.
125+ Members
Founded in 1944

1217 **Pest World**
National Pest Management Association
9300 Lee Highway
Suite 301
Fairfax, VA 22031

703-738-8330; Fax: 703-352-3031
www.pestworld.org

Robert Lederer, Executive VP
Dominique Broyles, Director Conventions/Meetings

240 booths.
4000 Attendees
Frequency: October

1218 **Potato Expo**
1300 L St NW
Suite 910
Washington, DC 20005-4107

202-682-9456; Fax: 202-682-0333
spudinfo@nationalpotatocouncil.org
www.nationalpotatocouncil.org
Twitter

Kam Quarles, Chief Executive Officer
Hollee Alexander, VP, Industry Relations & Events
Hillary Hutchins, Dir., Member Outreach & Programs

Largest conference and tradeshow for the potato industry held in North America. Offers educational programming covering the top issues facing the potato industry, provides networking opportunities with key decision makers and showcases the latest products and services for potato production and distribution.
45000 Members
Founded in 1948

1219 **Power Show**
590 Woody Hayes Drive
Room 232
Columbus, OH 43210

614-292-4278; Fax: 614-292-9448
gamble.19@osu.edu
www.worldagexpo.com

Doug Wagner, President
Dennis Alford, 1st Vice President
Chip Blalock, 2nd Vice President
Chuck Gamble, Secretary-Treasurer

Members are agriculture trade show sponsors and suppliers of services to these shows. Provides members with education, communication and evaluation. Provides the best possible marketing showcase for exhibitors and related products to the farmer/rancher/producer customer.
37 Members
Founded in 1972

1220 **Prairie Farmer Farm Progress Show**
Farm Progress Publishers
1301 E Mound Road
Decatur, IL 62526-9394

217-877-9070; Fax: 217-877-9695

Sherry Stout, Editor
Jeffrey Smith, Advertising

One of the largest farm shows in the country.

1221 **Precision Farming Dealer Summit**
Lessiter Media
P.O. Box 624
Brookfield, WI 53008-0624

262-432-0388
866-839-8455; Fax: 262-786-5564
info@precisionfarmingdealer.com
www.precisionfarmingdealer.com
Facebook, Twitter, LinkedIn, YouTube

Bree Greenawalt, Event Manager
Michael Ellis, Sponsorship Opportunities
Luke Weigel, Group Attendance Discounts

A dealer-only conference that equips companies to run a more profitable precision farming business through education and networking.
Frequency: Annual

1222 **Pro Farmer Midwest Crop Tour**
1818 Market Street 31st Floor
Philadelphia, PA 19103

800-772-0023
editors@profarmer.com
www.profarmer.com
Twitter

Sue King, Contact

Join the Pro Farmer editors at these seminars to discuss commodity markets, world economy, farm policy, land prices and more.
25M Members
Founded in 1973

1223 **Produce Executive Development Program**
1901 Pennsylvania Ave NW
Suite 1100
Washington, DC 20006-3412

202-303-3400; Fax: 202-303-3433
united@unitedfresh.org
www.uffva.org
Facebook, Twitter, YouTube

Thomas E Stenzel, CEO
Nicholas J Tompkins, Chair
Robert A Grimm, Executive Committee
Daniel G Vache, Secretary/Treasurer

Equipment, supplies, cartons, packaging machinery, computers, sorting and sizing equipment, harvesting equipment, film wrap manufacturing and commodity organizations.
1000+ Members
Founded in 1904

1224 **Produce Inspection Training Program**
1901 Pennsylvania Ave NW
Suite 1100
Washington, DC 20006-3412

202-303-3400; Fax: 202-303-3433
united@unitedfresh.org
www.uffva.org
Facebook, Twitter, YouTube

Thomas E Stenzel, CEO
Nicholas J Tompkins, Chair
Robert A Grimm, Executive Committee
Daniel G Vache, Secretary/Treasurer

Equipment, supplies, cartons, packaging machinery, computers, sorting and sizing equipment, harvesting equipment, film wrap manufacturing and commodity organizations.
1000+ Members
Founded in 1904

1225 **Produce for Better Health Annual Meeting**
590 East Frontage Road
PO Box 848
Nogales, AZ 85628

520-287-2707; Fax: 520-287-2948
info@freshfrommexico.com
www.fpaota.org

Lee Frank, President
Alicia Bon Martin, Vice Chair
Allison Moore, Communications Director
Jose Luis Obregon, Deputy Director
Martha Rascon, Public Affairs Director

Represents companies involved in growing, harvesting, marketing and importing of Mexican produce entering the US.
125+ Members
Founded in 1944

1226 **Profit Briefing Professional Farmers of America**
1818 Market Street 31st Floor
Philadelphia, PA 19103

800-772-0023
editors@profarmer.com
www.profarmer.com
Twitter

Sue King, Contact

Join the Pro Farmer editors at these seminars to discuss commodity markets, world economy, farm policy, land prices and more.
25M Members
Founded in 1973

1227 **Purchasing & Ingredient Suppliers Conference**
American Feed Industry Association
2101 Wilson Blvd
Suite 916
Arlington, VA 22201-3047

703-524-0810; Fax: 703-524-1921
afia@afia.org
www.afia.org
Facebook, Twitter, LinkedIn

Constance Cullman, President & CEO
Paul Davis, Director, Animal Food Safety
Rob Broehm, Executive Director Of IFEEDER

Organization devoted to representing companies in the animal feed industry and its suppliers.
690 Members
Founded in 1909

1228 **Quarterly Cannabis Caucus**
National Cannabis Industry Association
126 C Street NW
3rd Floor
Washington, DC 20001

888-683-5650
info@thecannabisindustry.org
www.thecannabisindustry.org
Facebook, Twitter, LinkedIn, Instagram

F. Aaron Smith, Executive Director
Shannon Hayden, Chief Operating Officer
Michael Correia, Director, Government Relations
Morgan Fox, Director, Media Relations
Brooke Gilbert, Director, Events & Education

This business-to-business networking event series provides an opportunity to meet with the cannabis industry's leading executives and policymakers and advance the cannabis industry nationally. Hosted in the industry's eight most active regions in the first month of each quarter.
2000 Members
Frequency: Quarterly
Founded in 2010

1229 **SAF National Convention**
5400 Grosvenor Ln
Bethesda, MD 20814-2198

301-897-8720; Fax: 301-897-3690
safweb@safnet.org
www.safnet.org

Terry Baker, Chief Executive Officer

Provides access to information and networking opportunities to prepare members for the challenges and the changes that face natural resource professionals.
Founded in 1900

1230 **SBS Conference & Exhibition**
Society for Biomolecular Sciences
100 Illinois Street
Suite 242
St. Charles, IL 60174

630-256-7527
877-990-7527; Fax: 630-741-7527
slas@slas.org
www.slas.org
Facebook, Twitter, LinkedIn

Michelle Palmer, Ph.D, President
David Dorsett, Vice President
Erick Rubin, Ph.D, Treasurer
Andy Zaayenga, Secretary

Scientists, innovators, researchers and industry analysts from around the world will converge to learn about the latest trends and basic and applied research that are transforming the way new pharmaceuticals are developed.
2000 Attendees
Frequency: Annual

1231 **Santa Gertrudis Breeders International Annual Meeting**
PO Box 1257
Kingsville, TX 78364-1257

361-592-9357; Fax: 361-592-8572
www.santagertrudis.com

Ervin Kaatz, Executive Director

Information and issues regarding America's First Beef Breed developed in 1918 at the famous King Ranch in Texas. Recognized in 1940 by the USDA. Famous for rapid and efficient growth, solid red color, hardiness and good disposition. They are adaptable to many environments and are present throughout the US and in other countries.

1232 **Seed to Sale Show**
National Cannabis Industry Association
1501 India St.
Suite 103-60
San Diego, CA 92101

888-409-4418
luke@gsmiweb.com
www.seedtosaleshow.com
Facebook, Twitter, Instagram, YouTube

F. Aaron Smith, Executive Director
Shannon Hayden, Chief Operating Officer
Michael Correia, Director, Government Relations
Morgan Fox, Director, Media Relations
Brooke Gilbert, Director, Events & Education

Brings together cannabis industry innovators for business-to-business networking, exchanging knowledge, and discussing policy. Focuses on technology and science in the seed to sale cycle and features keynote speakers, educational sessions, and exhibitors.
2000 Members
3000+ Attendees
Frequency: Annual, Spring
Founded in 2010

1233 **Society for Biomolecular Screening**
Society for Biomolecular Screening
36 Tamarack Avenue
Suite 348
Danbury, CT 06810

203-788-8828; Fax: 203-748-7557
www.sbsonline.org

Al Kolbh, President
Christine Giordano, Executive Director
Larry Walker, Editor-in-Chief
Marietta Manono, Manager Meetings/Exhibitions

Technical sessions, exhibits, exhibitor tutorials, short courses, discussion groups related to discovery in the pharmaceutical and agrochemical industry and 181 exhibits.

1234 **Soil and Water Conservation Society Annual International Conference**
Soil and Water Conservation Society
945 SW Ankeny Rd.
Ankeny, IA 50021

515-289-2331; Fax: 515-289-1227
www.swcs.org

Clare Lindahl, Chief Executive Officer
Courtney Allen, Event/Professional Development Dir.
Catherine DeLong, Special Project/Policy Director

Explores ways to improve the linkages among conservation science, policy and application at local, national, and international scales. The conference will provide participants an opportunity to teach skills, learn techniques, compare successes, and improve understanding.
1200 Attendees
Frequency: Annual/July

1235 **Southern Farm Show**
590 Woody Hayes Drive
Room 232
Columbus, OH 43210

614-292-4278; Fax: 614-292-9448
gamble.19@osu.edu
www.worldexpo.com

Doug Wagner, President
Dennis Alford, 1st Vice President
Chip Blalock, 2nd Vice President
Chuck Gamble, Secretary-Treasurer

Members are agriculture trade show sponsors and suppliers of services to these shows. Provides members with education, communication and evaluation. Provides the best possible marketing showcase for exhibitors and related products to the farmer/rancher/producer customer.
37 Members
Founded in 1972

1236 **St. Louis All Equipment Expo**
SouthWestern Association
P.O. Box 419264
Kansas City, MO 64141

816-762-5616
800-561-5323; Fax: 816-561-1249
www.swassn.com

Jeffrey Flora, CEO
Cory Hayes, Director of Education

Manufacturers, suppliers and distributors of farm equipment, outdoor power equipment, supplies and agriculture products. Containing 350 booths.
15M Attendees
Frequency: December

1237 **State Masters Conference**
1616 H St NW
Suite 10
Washington, DC 20006-4999

202-628-3507
888-447-2643; Fax: 202-347-1091
www.nationalgrange.org

Betsy Huber, National President
Amanda Leigh Brozana-Rios, Communications Director
Burton Eller, Legislative Director
Mandy Bostwick, Director Youth\Young Adult

Promotes general welfare and agriculture through local organizations. Presides over the advancement and promotion of the farming and agriculture industry.
300k Members
Founded in 1960

1238 **Sunbelt Agricultural Exposition**
Sunbelt Ag Expo
290-G Harper Boulevard
Moultrie, GA 31788-2157

229-985-1968; Fax: 229-890-8518
info@sunbeltexpo.com
www.sunbeltexpo.com
Facebook

Over 1,200 exhibitors showing the latest agricultural technology in products and equipment plus harvesting and tillage demonstrations in the field. Largest farm show in North America's premier farm show.
200M Attendees
Frequency: Annual/October

1239 **Sustainable Foods Summit**
1340 North Cotner Blvd
Lincoln, NE 68505

402-477-2323; Fax: 402-477-4325
info@ocia.org
www.ocia.org

Amanda Brewster, Executive Director

OCIA International is a farmer owned international program of certification, which adheres to strict organic standards. It currently certifies thousands of farmers and processors in North, Central and South America and Asia. OCIA International is IFOAM accredited and adheres to the USDA ISO Guide 65, Japan Agriculture Standards and the Quebec Accreditation Council. OCIA has also been accredited from the USDA National Organic Program and Costa Rica Ministry of Agriculture.
3500 Members
Founded in 1985
Mailing list available for rent: 3500 names at $50 per M

1240 **Sweetener Symposium**
2111 Wilson Blvd
Suite 600
Arlington, VA 22201-3051

703-351-5055; Fax: 703-351-6698
info@sugaralliance.org
www.sugaralliance.org

James Johnson, President
Jack Roney, Director Economics/Policy Analysis
Luther Markwart, Executive Vice President
Carolyn Cheney, Vice President

Covering a broad range of timely issues affecting the industry.
Founded in 1983

1241 **TFI Fertilizer Marketing & Business Meeting**
425 Third Street SW
Suite 950
Washington, DC 20002-8037

202-962-0490; Fax: 202-962-0577
information@tfi.org
www.tfi.org

Roberta Rosenberg, Senior Director, Marketing

Brings together members from each sector of the fertilizer industry for two days of networking and conducting business leading up to the spring planting season.
325 Members
Founded in 1970

1242 **TFI World Fertilizer Conference**
425 Third Street SW
Suite 950
Washington, DC 20002-8037

202-962-0490; Fax: 202-962-0577
information@tfi.org
www.tfi.org

Mariana Gallo, Senior Director, Conferences

Provides two days of networking and conducting business with industry leaders from as many as 60 different countries that represent all sectors of the fertilizer industry.
325 Members
Founded in 1970

1243 **Tree Fruit Expo**
Western Agricultural Publishing Company
4974 E Clinton Way
Suite 123
Fresno, CA 93727-1520

559-252-7000; Fax: 559-252-7387

Phill Rhoads, Manager

Productions seminars, dessert contest, guest speakers, prizes and exhibits for tree fruit growers. Containing 80 booths and exhibits.

1244 **U.S. Cannabis Conference & Expo**
Milestone Trade Shows
14300 N. Northsight Blvd.
Suite 101
Scottsdale, AZ 85260

954-309-5578
info@usccexpo.com

www.usccexpo.com
Facebook, Twitter, Instagram

Brandy Shapiro-Babin, Contact

A series event that takes place in different cities throughout the year. Brings together business leaders and professionals for thought-provoking presentations, discussions, workshops, and exhibits.

1245 **USA Rice Outlook Conference**
USA Rice Federation
4301 N Fairfax Drive
Suite 425
Arlington, VA 22203

703-226-2300; Fax: 703-236-2301
riceinfo@usarice.com
www.usarice.com

Betsy Ward, President & CEO
Jeanette Davis, Sr. Dir., Meetings & Member Service

Discuss issues and activities for the U.S. rice industry, legislation, training, and seminars.
Frequency: Annual

1246 **USHSLA Annual Convention**
United States Hide, Skin & Leather Association
1150 Connecticut Avenue, NW
12th Floor
Washington, DC 20036

202-587-4250
www.ushsla.org

Jay Jensen, Chair
Stephen Sothmann, President

Represents the hide, skin and leather industries. Members range from small family-owned businesses to large corporations.
Frequency: Annual

1247 **United Fresh Convention**
590 East Frontage Road
PO Box 848
Nogales, AZ 85628

520-287-2707; Fax: 520-287-2948
info@freshfrommexico.com
www.fpaota.org

Lee Frank, President
Alicia Bon Martin, Vice Chair
Allison Moore, Communications Director
Jose Luis Obregon, Deputy Director
Martha Rascon, Public Affairs Director

Represents companies involved in growing, harvesting, marketing and importing of Mexican produce entering the US.
125+ Members
Founded in 1944

1248 **United Fresh Fruit and Vegetable Association Annual Convention**
United Fresh Fruit & Vegetable Association
1901 Pennsylvania Avenue NW
Suite 1100
Washington, DC 20006

202-624-4989; Fax: 202-303-3433
united@uffva.org
www.uffva.org

Thomas Stenzel, CEO
Mark Overbay, Manager Communications
30000 Attendees

1249 **United States Animal Health Association Annual Meeting**
4221 Mitchell Ave.
St Joseph, MO 64508

816-671-1144; Fax: 816-671-1201
usaha@usaha.org
www.usaha.org

Benjamin Richey, Executive Director
Kelly Janicek, Executive Assistant

Seeks to prevent, control and eliminate livestock diseases.
1400 Members
Founded in 1897

1250 **United States Hide, Skin & Leather Assoc. - Asia Pacific Leather Fair**
1150 Connecticut Ave, NW
12th Floor
Washington, DC 20036

202-587-4250
www.ushsla.org

Stephen Sothmann, President

Buyers will see the complete spectrum of the leather sector featuring the latest technology and products for leather making and footwear, as well as the widest range of leathers from around the globe displayed under one roof.
35 Members

1251 **Virginia Farm Show**
Lee Publications
6113 State Highway 5
PO Box 121
Palatine Bridge, NY 13428-0121

518-673-3237
888-596-5329; Fax: 518-673-2699
kmaring@leepub.com
www.leetradeshows.com

Ken Maring, Trade Show Manager

This show caters to the full-time farmer, with exhibits of all the major lines of equipment and services, and seminars presented by industry experts in dairy, beef and crop production.
Frequency: Annual, January
Founded in 1982

1252 **WEDA International Dealer Conference**
Western Equipment Dealers Association
638 West 39th St.
P.O. Box 419264
Kansas City, MO 64141-6264

816-561-5323
800-762-5616; Fax: 816-561-1249
www.westerneda.com
Facebook, Twitter, LinkedIn

John Schmeiser, CEO
Jennifer Luce, COO
Eric Wareham, VP, Government Affairs (US)
Larry Hertz, VP, Canada
Katie Clark, Member Services Coordinator

Features insights from industry-leading experts, practical sales advice, updates on the business economy, and networking.
Founded in 1899

1253 **Walnut Council Annual Meeting**
1011 N 725 W
West Lafayette, IN 47906-9431

765-583-3501; Fax: 765-583-3512
walnutcouncil@walnutcouncil.org
www.walnutcouncil.org

Liz Jackson, Executive Director

Inviting scientists with the latest research on hardwood forestry, black walnut in particular, to present.
1000 Members
Founded in 1970

1254 **Washington Public Policy Conference**
United Fresh Produce Association
1901 Pennsylvania Ave NW
Suite 1100
Washington, DC 20006-3412

202-303-3400; Fax: 202-303-3433
united@unitedfresh.org
www.uffva.org
Facebook, Twitter, YouTube

Thomas E Stenzel, CEO
Nicholas J Tompkins, Chair
Robert A Grimm, Executive Committee
Daniel G Vache, Secretary/Treasurer

Equipment, supplies, cartons, packaging machinery, computers, sorting and sizing equipment, harvesting equipment, film wrap manufacturing and commodity organizations.
1000+ Members
Founded in 1904

1255 **Water Conference**
6540 Arlington Blvd
Falls Church, VA 22042-6638

703-536-7080; Fax: 703-536-7019
info@irrigation.org
www.irrigation.org

Deborah Hamlin, Chief Executive Officer

Promotes education and use of irrigation in many areas of agriculture.
1600 Members
Founded in 1949

1256 **Western Fairs Association Convention & Trade Show**
1776 Tribute Rd
Suite 210
Sacramento, CA 95815-4495

916-927-3100; Fax: 916-927-6397
stephenc@fairsnet.org
www.fairsnet.org

Sarah Cummings, President & CEO

A non-profit association with members throughout the Western United States and Canada that strives to promote industry standards. Membership includes access to conventions and trade shows, educational training programs as well as legislative advocacy support.
2000 Members
Founded in 1922

1257 **Western Farm Show**
Western Equipment Dealers Association
638 W 39th Street
P.O. Box 419264
Kansas City, MO 64141-6264

816-561-5323
800-762-5616; Fax: 816-561-1249
kdean@westerneda.com
www.westernfarmshow.com
Facebook, Twitter

Ken Dean, Show Manager
Lisa Stock, Farm Show Coordinator

Annual show of close to 500 exhibitors. Features products and servicing for all aspects of agribusiness, including farm implements, livestock equipment, seed and feed, chemicals, and computers. Full-time, part-time, and hobby farmers welcome.
35M Attendees
Frequency: Annual, February
Founded in 1962

1258 **Wheat Industry Conference**
415 2nd Street NE
Washington, DC 20002-4993

202-547-7800; Fax: 202-546-2638
wheatworld@wheatworld.org
www.wheatworld.org
Facebook, Twitter, YouTube

Chandler Goule, CEO

Nonprofit partnership of US wheat growers, by combining their strengths, voices and ideas are working to ensure a better future for themselves, their industry and the general public.
Founded in 1950

1259 **Winter Fancy Food Show**
4601 NE 77th Avenue
Suite 200
Vancouver, WA 98662-2697

360-693-3373; Fax: 360-693-3464
www.wusata.org

Andy Anderson, Executive Director
Monica Quenette, Outreach Coordinator

A nonprofit organization that promotes the export of food and agricultural products from the Western region of the US Comprised of 13 state funded agricultural promotion agencies.

1260 **Women Grow Annual Leadership Summit**
Women Grow

contact@womengrow.com
www.womengrow.com
Facebook, Twitter, LinkedIn, Instagram, Vimeo

Chanda Macias, Chief Executive Officer
Gia Moron, Executive Vice President
Arielle Paredes, Communications Assistant
Lauren Rudick, Counsel

Lighting talks, breakout sessions, and networking opportunities for diverse leaders in all segments of the cannabis industry.
Frequency: Annual
Founded in 2014

1261 **Women Grow Monthly Networking Events**
Women Grow

Home Page: www.womengrow.com
Facebook, Twitter, LinkedIn, Instagram, Vimeo

Chanda Macias, Chief Executive Officer
Gia Moron, Executive Vice President
Arielle Paredes, Communications Assistant
Lauren Rudick, Counsel

Connects newcomers and established cannabis professionals on the first Thursday of every month to network and listen to educational speakers. Events are held in cities across North America.
Frequency: Monthly
Founded in 2014

1262 **World Dairy Expo**
151 Treasure Island Cswy. #2
St. Petersburg, FL 33706-4734

727-367-9702
800-707-0014; Fax: 727-367-9608
darthay@yahoo.com
www.nationalhay.org

Dan Wray, President

NHA is the trade group that represents the interests of the hay industry throughout the United States and internationally.
750 Members
Founded in 1895

1263 **World Pork Expo**
122 C Street NW
Suite 875
Washington, DC 20001

202-347-3600
800-937-7675; Fax: 202-347-5265
warnerd@nppc.org
www.nppc.org
Facebook, Twitter

Neil Dierks, Chief Executive Officer
Doug Fricke, Director, Trade Show Marketing

The world's largest pork-specific trade show featuring business seminars, hundreds of exhibitors, breed shows and sales, and plenty of food and entertainment for everyone.
44 Members

Directories & Databases

1264 **AGRICOLA**
US National Agricultural Library
10301 Baltimore Ave
Beltsville, MD 20705-2351

301-504-5755; Fax: 301-504-5675
www.agricola.nal.usda.gov/

Simon Y Liu, Director
Chris Cole, Acting Deputy Director

A database containing more than 3.3 million citations to journal literature, government reports, proceedings, books, periodicals, theses, patents, audiovisuals, electronic information, and other materials related to agriculture and its allied sciences.
Founded in 1962

1265 **ARI Network**
Ari Network Services
10850 W Park Pl
Suite 1200
Milwaukee, WI 53224-3636

414-973-4300
800-558-9044; Fax: 414-973-4619
www.arinet.com
Facebook, Twitter, LinkedIn, YouTube

Roy W. Olivier, President & CEO
Darin R. Janecek, CFO
Brian E. Dearing, Chairman

Offers current information on agricultural business, financial and weather information as well as statistical information for farmers.

1266 **Ag Ed Network**
ARI Network Services
10850 W Park Pl
Suite 900
Milwaukee, WI 53224-3636

414-973-4300
800-558-9044; Fax: 414-973-4619
info@arinet.com
www.arinet.com

Roy W Olivier, Chief Executive Officer
John C Bray, New Market Development

Offers access to more than 1500 educational agriculture lessons covering farm business management and farm production.
Frequency: Full-text

1267 **AgriMarketing Services Guide**
Henderson Communications LLC
1422 Elbridge Payne Rd
Suite 250
Chesterfield, MO 63017-8544

636-728-1428; Fax: 636-777-4178
info@agrimarketing.com
www.agrimarketing.com

Richard A Herrett, Executive Director

AgriMarketing Services Guide is published each December and is commonly referred to as the Who's Who in the North American ag industry sector.
Frequency: Annual/December

1268 **Agricultural Research Institute: Membership Directory**
Agricultural Research Institute
9650 Rockville Pike
Bethesda, MD 20814-3998

301-530-7122; Fax: 301-571-1816

Richard A Herrett, Executive Director

125 member institutions; also lists study panels and committees interested in environmental issues, pest control, agricultural meteorology, biotechnology, food irradiation, agricultural policy, research and development, food safety, technology transfer and remote sensing.
Cost: $50.00
Frequency: Annual

1269 **American Feed Industry Association: Software Directory**
American Feed Industry Association
2101 Wilson Blvd
Suite 916
Arlington, VA 22201-3047

703-524-0810; Fax: 703-524-1921
afia@afia.org
www.afia.org

Constance Cullman, President/CEO
Erica Burson, Membership & Database Specialist

Companies that design software programs applicable to the feed industry.
Cost: $25.00

1270 **American Fruit Grower: Source Book Issue**
Meister Media Worldwide
37733 Euclid Ave
Willoughby, OH 44094-5992

440-942-2000
800-572-7740; Fax: 440-975-3447
joe_monahan@meistermedia.com
www.meistermedia.com

Richard T Meister, Chairman
Gary T Fitzgerald, President
Joe Monahan, Group Publisher

Offers a list of manufacturers and distributors of equipment and supplies for the commercial fruit growing industry.
Cost: $19.95
66 Pages
Circulation: 35,143

1271 **American Meat Science Association Directory of Members**
American Meat Science Association
2441 Village Green Place
Champaign, IL 61822

217-356-5370
800-517-AMSA; Fax: 888-205-5834; Fax: 217-356-5370
information@meatscience.org
www.meatscience.org

Dean Pringle, President
Collette Kaster, Chief Executive Officer
Morgan Pfeiffer, Membership & Marketing Manager

Directory for American Meat Science members only.
Cost: $20.00
230 Pages
Frequency: Biennial

1272 **American Society of Consulting Arborists: Membership Directory**
American Society of Consulting Arborists
9707 Key West Ave
Suite 100
Rockville, MD 20850-3992

301-947-0483; Fax: 301-990-9771
asca@mgmtsol.com
www.asca-consultants.org

Th,rŠse Oetegen Clemens, Executive Director
Julianne Clark, Coordinator, Member Services

About 270 persons specializing in the growth and care of urban shade and ornamental trees; includes expert witnesses and monetary appraisals.
Frequency: Annual

1273 **Biological & Agricultural Index**
HW Wilson Company

950 Dr Martin Luther King Jr Blvd
Bronx, NY 10452-4297

718-588-8405
800-367-6770; Fax: 718-590-1617
www.hwwilson.com

Harold Regan, President & CEO
Ann Case, Vice President, Editorial
Phillip Taylor, Customer Service Director
Amy Rosenbaum, Senior Manager
Kathleen McEvoy, Director of Public Relations

Provides fast access to core literature. In addition to citations to research and feature articles, users finding indexing of reports of symposia and conferences, and citations to current book reviews. Available on Web and disc.
359 Pages
Founded in 1898

1274 **Citrus & Vegetable Magazine: Farm Equipment Directory Issue**
Vance Publishing
10901 W 84th Ter
Suite 200
Lenexa, KS 66214-1631

913-438-5721; Fax: 913-438-0697
cvmscott@compuserve.com
www.vancepublishing.com

Michael H Ross, President, Chief Operating Officer
William C Vance, Chairman, Chief Executive Officer
Judy Riggs, Director/Research Marketing

Offers information on a list of manufacturers of produce and citrus growing, handling, picking and packaging equipment.
Cost: $25.00
48 Pages
Frequency: Annual
Circulation: 12,000
ISSN: 0009-7586
Founded in 1938

1275 **Complete Guide to Gardening and Landscaping by Mail**
Mailorder Gardening Association
5836 Rockburn Woods Way
Elkridge, MD 21075-7302

410-540-9830; Fax: 410-540-9827
www.mailordergardening.com

Bruce Frasier, President
Jim Bryant, First Vice President
Roberta Simpson, Second Vice President
Jean Vivlamore Norton, Treasurer
Camille Cimino, Executive Director

Member catalogers who sell gardening and nursery stock and supplies to consumers.
Cost: $2.00
Frequency: Annual
Founded in 1934

1276 **Contemporary World Issues: Agricultural Crisis in America**
ABC-CLIO
130 Cremona Drive
PO Box 1911
Santa Barbara, CA 93117-1911

805-681-1911
800-422-2546; Fax: 805-685-9685
CustomerService@abc-clio.com
www.abc-clio.com

Ron Boehm, President/CEO

List of agencies and organizations in the US concerned with agricultural issues.
Cost: $50.00
Founded in 1953

1277 **Crop Protection Reference**
Vance Communications Corporation
315 W 106th St
Suite 504
New York, NY 10025-3473

212-932-1727
800-839-2420; Fax: 646-733-6010
GreenbookCustomerService@Greenbook.net
www.greenbook.net

Hilda Vazquez, Director Marketing, Sales

A single comprehensive source of up-to-date label information of crop protection products marketed in the United States by basic manufacturers and formulators. Extensive product indexing helps to locate products by: brand name, manufacturer crop site, mode of action, disease, insect, week, product category, common name, tank mix.
Cost: $50.00
Frequency: Annual

1278 **Directory for Small-Scale Agriculture**
US Department of Agriculture
Secretary oF Agriculture
Whitten Building/Room 200A
Washington, DC 20250-0001

202-012-2000

Offers information on persons involved with projects and activities relating to small-scale agriculture.
Cost: $5.50
119 Pages

1279 **Directory of American Agriculture**
Agricultural Resources & Communications
P.O.Box 283
Wamego, KS 66547-0283

785-456-9705
800-404-7940; Fax: 785-456-1654
chris@agresources.com
www.agresources.com

Christina Wilson, President

This directory lists over 7,000 state and national associations involved in providing products and services related to food and fiber industries, in 27 categories. There are categorical indexes as well. Includes guide to Washington, D.C. offices, USDA listings, and guide to ag commodity commissions. Available on CD for $99.
Cost: $64.95
350 Pages
ISSN: 0897-1919
Founded in 1988
Printed in on matte stock

1280 **EMDA Membership Directory**
Equipment Marketing & Distribution Association
PO Box 1347
Iowa City, IA 52244

319-354-5156
pat@emda.net
www.emda.net

Patricia A. Collins, Executive Vice President

Annual directory of FEWA-AIMRA members, includes address, phone, fax, web, e-mail, territory covered (with map) product descriptions, key personnel, and a descriptive paragraph.
Cost: $50.00

1281 **Electronic Pesticide Reference: EPR II**
Vance Communications Corporation
315 W 106th St
Suite 504
New York, NY 10025-3473

212-932-1727; Fax: 646-733-6020
GreenbookCustomerService@Greenbook.net
www.greenbook.net

Hilda Vazquez, Director Marketing, Sales

Complete electronic reference to our 1,500 crop protection products; a full range of product information: full text labels and supplemental labels, full text MSDS's, product summaries, list of labeled tank mixes, worker protection information, DOT shipping information, SARA Title III reporting information. Search by brand name, manufacturer, common name crop, plant, site, weed, disease, insect plus much more. All versions of EPR II are provided on CD-ROM for windows.

1282 **Farm Equipment Membership Directory**
Farm Equipment Manufacturers Association
1000 Executive Parkway Drive
Suite 100
St. Louis, MO 63141-6369

314-878-2304
info@farmequip.org
www.farmequip.org

Matt Westendorf, President
Vernon Schmidt, Executive Vice President
Tricia Kidd, Accounting & Meeting Services
Kristi Ruggles, Communications Director
Sarah Stevener, Meetings & Membership

Index featuring services and products of members of the Farm Equipment Manufacturers Association.
Founded in 1950

1283 **Food & Beverage Marketplace**
Grey House Publishing
4919 Route 22
PO Box 56
Amenia, NY 12501

518-789-8700
800-562-2139; Fax: 845-373-6390
books@greyhouse.com
www.greyhouse.com
Facebook, Twitter

Richard Gottlieb, President
Leslie Mackenzie, Publisher

The most comprehensive resource in the food and beverage industry. Available in a three-volume printed directory, a subscription-based Online Database, as well as mailing list and database formats.
Cost: $595.00
2000 Pages
ISBN: 1-592373-61-5
Founded in 1981

1284 **Food & Beverage Marketplace: Online Database**
Grey House Publishing
4919 Route 22
PO Box 56
Amenia, NY 12501

518-789-8700
800-562-2139; Fax: 845-373-6390
gold@greyhouse.com
gold.greyhouse.com
Facebook, Twitter

Richard Gottlieb, President
Leslie Mackenzie, Publisher

This complete updated Food & Beverage Market Place: Online Database is the go-to source for the food and beverage industry. Anyone involved in the food and beverage industry needs this 'industry bible' and the important contacts to develop critical research data that can make for successful business growth.
Frequency: Annual
Founded in 1981

1285 **Food and Agricultural Export Directory**
National Technical Information Service

5285 Port Royal Rd
Springfield, VA 22161-0001
703-605-6000
800-553-6847; Fax: 703-605-6900
info@ntis.gov
www.ntis.gov

Linda Davis, Vice President
Patrik Ekstr"m, Business Development Manager
Reuel Avila, Managing Director

Includes up to date listings of federal and state agencies, trade associations and a host of other organizations that can help you penetrate foreign markets. Includes phone and fax numbers.
100 Pages
Frequency: Annual

1286 **Food, Hunger, Agribusiness: A Directory of Resources**
Center For Third World Organizing
1218 E 21st St
Oakland, CA 94606-3132

510-533-7583; Fax: 510-533-0923
www.ctwo.org

Lian Cheun, MAAP Director
Dan Ringer-Barwick, Operations Director

Offers information on organizations and publishers of books and other materials on food, hunger and agribusiness overseas.
Cost: $12.95
160 Pages

1287 **Grain & Milling Annual**
Sosland Publishing Company
4801 Main St
Suite 100
Kansas City, MO 64112-2513

816-756-1000; Fax: 816-756-0494
www.sosland.com

Offers a list of milling companies, mills, grain companies and cooperatives.
Cost: $100.00
Frequency: Annual
Circulation: 6,000
ISSN: 1098-4615

1288 **Guernsey Breeders' Journal: Convention Directory Issue**
Purebred Publishing Inc
7616 Slate Ridge Blvd
Reynoldsburg, OH 43068-3126

614-575-4620; Fax: 614-864-5614
sjohnson@usguernsey.com
www.usguernsey.com

Seth Johnson, Manager
Dale Jensen, President
Tom Ripley, VP

A convention directory offering a list of officers and national members of the American Guernsey Cattle Association.
Cost: $20.00
Frequency: 10x Yearly

1289 **Hort Expo Northwest**
Mt Adams Publishing and Design
14161 Fort Road
White Swan, WA 98952-9786

509-848-2706
800-554-0860; Fax: 509-848-3896

Vee Graves, Editor
Julie LaForge, Advertising Manager

The directory is mailed to subscribers and is also available complimentary at horticulture shows in the Northwest.
32 Pages
Frequency: Annually
Circulation: 8,700
Founded in 1989
Printed in 4 colors on glossy stock

1290 **Industrial Economic Information**
Global Insight
800 Baldwin Tower
Eddystone, PA 19022

610-490-4000
800-933-3374; Fax: 610-490-2557
www.globalinsight.com

Joseph E Kasputys, Chair/President/CEO
Pricella Trumbull, Chief Operations Officer
Vicki Van Mater, VP
Kenneth J McGill, Product Management

Global Insight's unique perspective provides the most comprehensive economic and financial coverage of countries, regions and industries from any source.

1291 **International Green Front Report**
Friends of the Trees Society
PO Bo 253
Twisp, WA 98856

509-997-9200; Fax: 509-997-4812
www.friendsofthetrees.net

Michael Pilarski, Director

Organizations and periodicals concerned with sustainable forestry and agriculture and related fields.
Cost: $7.00
192 Pages
Frequency: Irregular
Circulation: 8,000
Founded in 1978

1292 **International Soil Tillage Research Organization**
International Soil Tillage Research
1680 Madison Avenue
Wooster, OH 44691-4114

330-263-3700; Fax: 330-263-3658

A Franzluebbers, Editor-in-Chief

More than 750 individuals and institutions in 72 countries involved in the research or application of soil tilage and related subjects.
Cost: $100.00
Frequency: 10 per year

1293 **Journal of the American Society of Farm Managers and Rural Appraisers**
ASFMRA
720 S. Colorado Boulevard
Suite 360-S
Glendale, CO 80246

303-758-3513; Fax: 303-758-0190
info@asfmra.org
www.asfmra.org

Brian Stockman, Executive VP

Provides the most up-to-date studies, research, practices, and methodologies proposed by the leading academic, management, appraisal and consulting members of our professions.
Frequency: Annual
Founded in 1929

1294 **Landscape & Irrigation: Product Source Guide**
Adams Business Media
11 Hanover Square
Suite 501
New York, NY 10005

212-566-7600; Fax: 212-566-7877
lenadams@acgresources.com
www.acgresources.com

Len Adams, CEO

Offers information on suppliers, distributors and manufacturers serving the professional agriculture and landscaping community.
Circulation: 37,000

1295 **Material Safety Data Sheet Reference**
Vance Communications Corporation
315 W 106th St
Suite 504
New York, NY 10025-3473

212-932-1727; Fax: 646-733-6020
GreenbookCustomerService@Greenbook.net
www.greenbook.net

Susan J Vannucci, Manager

Regulatory and product safety requirements. Contains full text MSDS's for products listed in the 1999 15th Edition Crop Protection Reference plus additional safety information such as DOT shipping information, SARA Title III regulations, Hazardous Chemical inventory reporting information plus much more.

1296 **Meat and Poultry Inspection Directory**
US Department of Agriculture
Administration Building
Room 344
Washington, DC 20250-0001

202-690-7650; Fax: 202-512-2250
www.access.gpo.gov

Offers valuable information on all meat and poultry plants that ship meat interstate and therefore come under the US Department of Agriculture inspection.
Cost: $16.00
600 Pages
Frequency: SemiAnnual

1297 **NACB Signals**
National Association of Cannabis Businesses
1918 E. Lafayette Place
Milwaukee, WI 53202

720-926-6881
info@nacb.com
www.nacb.com
Facebook, Twitter, LinkedIn

Gina Kranwinkel, Chief Executive Officer
Mark Gorman, Executive VP & COO
Tom Nolasco, Dir., Legal & Strategic Initiatives
Maggan Hau, Operations Manager
Mary Clifton, Cannabis Research Advisor

A cannabis, marijuana, and hemp legislation tracking tool available only to members of the NACB.

1298 **NASDA Directory**
National Association of State Dept of Agriculture
1156 15th St NW
Suite 1020
Washington, DC 20005-1711

202-296-9680; Fax: 202-296-9686
nasda@nasda.org
www.nasda.org

Barb Glenn, Chief Executive Officer

Top agricultural officials in 50 states and four territories.
Cost: $100.00
Frequency: Annual

1299 **National Agri-Marketing Association Directory**
11020 King St
Suite 205
Overland Park, KS 66210-1201

913-491-6500; Fax: 913-491-6502
agrimktg@nama.org
www.nama.org
Facebook, Twitter, LinkedIn, Flickr, YouTube

Jennifer Pickett, Executive VP & CEO

Orginated as the Chicago Area Agricultural Advertising Association with 39 charter members. In 1963 the name was changed to the National

Agricultural Advertising and Marketing Association and the present name was assumed in 1973.
Cost: $150.00
2500 Pages
Frequency: Annual
Founded in 1956

1300 **National Organic Directory**
Community Alliance with Family Farmers
36355 Russell Boulevard
PO Box 363
Davis, CA 95617-0363
530-756-8518
800-892-3832; Fax: 530-756-7857
info@caff.org
www.caff.org

Wriiten for all sectors of the booming organic food and fiber industry. Offers international listing with full contact information and extensive, cross-referenced index. Also provides regulatory updates, essays by industry leaders and other ressources.
Cost: $47.95
400 Pages
Frequency: Annual
Circulation: 2,500
ISBN: 1-891894-04-8
Founded in 1983

1301 **Organic Pages Online North American Resource Directory**
Organic Trade Association
28 Vernon St.
Suite 413
Brattleboro, VT 05301
802-275-3800; Fax: 802-275-3801
info@ota.com
www.ota.com
Facebook, Twitter, LinkedIn
Matt McLean, President
Sarah Bird, Vice President
Todd Linsky, Secretary
Kristen Holt, Treasurer

Provides over 1,300 listings by company name, brand name, business type, supply chain, product and service.

1302 **Produce Marketing Association Membership Directory and Buyer's Guide**
Produce Marketing Association
PO Box 6036
Newark, DE 19714-6036
302-738-7100; Fax: 302-731-2409
pma@pma.com
www.pma.com
Cathy Burns, CEO
Dan Stark, Chief Content Officer

A list of over 2,000 members that are involved in retail grocery and foodservice marketing businesses, including international companies.
Cost: $70.00
280 Pages
Frequency: Annual

1303 **Professional Workers in State Agricultural Experiment Stations**
US Department of Agriculture
200 Independence Ave SW
Whitten Bldg/Room 200A
Washington, DC 20201-0007
202-690-7650; Fax: 202-512-2250
www.access.gpo.gov
Mike Johanns, Secretary of Agriculture

This directory offers information on academic and research personnel in all agricultural, forestry, aquaculture and home economics industries.
Cost: $15.00
289 Pages
Frequency: Annual
Founded in 1963

1304 **Turf & Ornamental Reference**
Vance Communications Corporation
315 W 106th St
Suite 504
New York, NY 10025-3473
212-932-1727; Fax: 646-733-6020
GreenbookCustomerService@Greenbook.net
www.greenbook.net
Susan J Vannucci, Manager

Professional guide to plant protection problems. Provides the turf and ornamental industry with a single comprehensive source of up to date label and MSDS information of plant protection products marketed in the United States by basic manufacturers and formulators. Extensive product indexing helps to locate products by: brand name; manufacturer; plant site; mode of action; disease, insect, weed; product category; common name; tank mix.
Cost: $159.00

1305 **USAHA Report of the Annual Meeting**
United States Animal Health Association
4221 Mitchelle Ave.
St Joseph, MO 64507
816-671-1144; Fax: 816-671-1201
usaha@usaha.org
www.usaha.org
Benjamin Richey, Executive Director
Kelly Janicek, Executive Assistant

Held in conjunction with the American Association of Veterinary Laboratory Diagnosticians. (AAVLD)
Founded in 1897

1306 **Warehouses Licensed Under US Warehouse Act**
Farm Service Agency-US Dept. of Agriculture
1400 Independence Avenue SW
Stop Code 0506
Washington, DC 20013-2415
202-720-7809; Fax: 202-690-0014
Eric Parsons, Chief Public Affairs

Agricultural warehouses voluntarily licensed under the US Warehouse Act governing public storage facilities.
Frequency: Annual

1307 **Who's Who International**
WATT Publishing Company
303 N Main Street
Suite 500
Rockford, IL 61101
815-966-5400; Fax: 815-966-6416
www.wattnet.com
James Watt, Chairman/CEO
Greg Watt, President/COO
Jeff Swanson, Publishing Director

Contains a detailed statistical section of key contacts in the industry. Includes industry phone book, genetic hatcheries and products, company directories, poultry marketers by city and state, refrigerated warehouses and federal agencies and associations.
310 Pages

1308 **Who's Who in the Egg & Poultry Industry in the US and Canada**
WATT Publishing Company
303 N Main Street
Suite 500
Rockford, IL 61101
815-966-5400; Fax: 815-966-6416
www.wattnet.com
James Watt, Chairman/CEO
Greg Watt, President/CEO
Jeff Swanson, Publishing Director

Contains a detailed statistical section of key contacts in the industry. Includes industry phone book, genetic hatcheries and products, company directories, poultry marketers by city and state, refrigerated warehouses and federal agencies and associations.
Cost: $105.00
Frequency: Annual
ISSN: 0510-4130

1309 **World Databases in Agriculture**
National Register Publishing
430 Mountain Ave.
Suite 400
New Providence, NJ 07974
800-473-7020; Fax: 908-673-1189
nrpeditorial@marquiswhoswho.com

Agricultural information on databases, including CD-ROM, magnetic tape, diskette, online, fax or databroadcast worldwide.

Industry Web Sites

1310 **http://gold.greyhouse.com**
G.O.L.D Grey House OnLine Databases

Grey House Publishing's online database platform, GOLD, includes Quick Search, Keyword Search and Expert Search for most business sectors including agriculture and food markets. The GOLD platform makes finding the information you need quick and easy. All of Grey House's directory products are available for subscription on the GOLD platform.

1311 **www.aaccnet.org**
AACC International

A non-profit organization of members who are specialists in the use of cereal grains in foods.

1312 **www.aaea.org**
Agricultural & Applied Economics Association
Facebook, Twitter, LinkedIn, Blogger, Google+

A nonprofit association serving the professional interests of those working in agricultural and broadly related fields of applied economics.

1313 **www.aafco.org**
Association of American Feed Control Officials

Provides a mechanism for develping and implementing uniform and equitab;e laws, regulations, standrads and enforcement policies for regulating the manufacture, distribution and sale of animal feeds; resulting in safe, effective, and useful feeds.

1314 **www.aagiwa.org**
American Assoc of Grain Inspection & Weighing

The national association representing grain inspection and weighing agencies. These agencies provide official inspection services to measure the quantity of grain being bough and sold in the United States.

1315 **www.aapausa.org**
AFIA Alfalfa Processors Council

Information for the processors and suppliers in the alfalfa industry.

1316 **www.abfnet.org**
American Beekeeping Federation
A national organiation with about 1,000 members that continually works in the interest of all beekeepers, large or small, and those associated with the industry to ensure the future of the honeybee.

1317 **www.aceweb.org**
Agricultural Communicators in Education
An international association of communicators and information technologists. Develops professional skills of its members to extend knowledge about agriculture, natural resources and life and human sciences to people worldwide.

1318 **www.adsa.org**
American Dairy Science Association
Provides leadership in scientific and technical support to sustain and grow the global dairy through generation, dissemination, and exchange of information and services.

1319 **www.aem.org**
Association of Equipment Manufacturers
A trade association that provides services for companies that offer equipment, products and services used in the following industries: Agriculture, Construction, Forestry, Mining and Utility.

1320 **www.afgc.org**
American Forage and Grassland Council
Dedicated to advancing the use of forage as a prime feed resource. Members present the academic community, producers, private industry, institutes and foundations.

1321 **www.afia.org**
American Feed Industry Association
Represents the total feed industry, as a key segment of the food chain, and member copmanies' interests, with one industry leadership voice on matters involving federal/state legislation and regulation

1322 **www.agconsultants.org**
American Society of Agricultural Consultants
A non-profit organization oriented around raising the standards and image of professional agricultural consultants.

1323 **www.agday.org**
Agriculture Council of America
A nonprofit organization composed of leaders in the agricultural, food and fiber community, dedicating its efforts to increasing the public's awareness of agriculture's role in modern society.

1324 **www.agnic.org**
Agriculture Network Information Center
A voluntary alliance of members based on the concept of centers of excellence. The member institutions are dedicated to enhancing collective information and services among the members and their partners for all those seeking agriculture information over the Internet.

1325 **www.agribusiness.com**
National Agri-Marketing Association
The nation's largest professional association for professionals in marketing and agribusiness

1326 **www.amseed.com**
American Seed Trade Association
Promotes the development of better seed to produce better crops for a better quality of life.

1327 **www.angus.org**
American Angus Association
The nation's largest beef registry association with over 30,000 adult and junior members. The goal is to serve the beef cattle industry, and increase the production of consistent, high quality beef that will better satisfy consumers throughout the world.

1328 **www.animalalliance.org**
Animal Agricultural Alliance
A non-profit organization that is dedicated to the protection of wildlife, the alleviation of animal suffering and the preservation of our environment.

1329 **www.aomillers.org**
International Association of Operative Millers
An international organization, comprised of flour millers, cereal grain and seed processors and allied trades representatives and companies devoted to the advancement of technology in the flour milling and cereal grain processing industries.

1330 **www.apms.org**
Aquatic Plant Management Society
An international organization of scientists, educators, students, commercial pedticide applicators, administrators, and concerned individuals interested in the management and study of aquatic plants.

1331 **www.asabe.org**
American Society of Agricultural & Biological Eng
An educational and scientific organization dedicated to the advancement of engineering applicable to agriculture, food, and biological systems.

1332 **www.asas.org**
American Society of Animal Science
Discover, disseminate and apply knowledge for sustainable use of animals for food and other human needs.

1333 **www.asca-consultants.org**
American Society of Consulting Arborists
The industry's premier professional association focusing solely on arboricultural consulting. Consulting Arborists are authoritative experts on trees, consulting property owners, municipalities, attorneys, insurance professionals and others on tree disease, placement, preservation and dispute resolution in addition to providing consulting and expert testimony in the legal, insurance and environmental arenas.

1334 **www.asev.org**
American Society for Enology and Viticulture
A tax exempt professional society dedicated to the interests of enologists, viticulturists, and others in the fields of wine and grape research and production throughout the world.

1335 **www.biodynamics.com**
Biodynamic Farming and Gardening Association
A non-profit, membership organization that fosters tknowledge of the practices and principles of the biodynamic method of agriculture, horticulture, and forestry in the North American continent

1336 **www.cast-science.org**
Council for Agricultural Science and Technology
A nonprofit organization composed of scientific societies an many individual, student, copmany, nonprofit, and associate society members.

1337 **www.christmastree.org**
National Christmas Tree Association
Strives to be one voice representing Christmas Tree Professionals and promoting the use of Real Christmas Trees

1338 **www.corn.org**
Corn Refiners Association
The national trade association representing the corn refining (wet milling) industry of the United States.

1339 **www.cottonseed.com**
National Cottonseed Products Association
An organization of firms and individuals engaged in the processing of cottonseed and the marketing of cottonseed products, as well as cottonseed. These include oil mills, refiners, product dealers and product brokers.

1340 **www.cropinsurance.org**
Crop Insurance Research Bureau
Working to improve crop insurance through unity and leadership

1341 **www.croplifeamerica.org**
CropLife America
Represents the developers manufacturers, formulators and distributors of plant science solutions for agriculture and pest management in the Unted States.

1342 **www.crops.org**
Crop Science Society of America
Seeks to advance research, extension, and teaching of all basic and applied phases of the crop sciences.

1343 **www.dhia.org**
National Dairy Herd Improvement Association
Promote accuracy, credibility, and uniformity of DHI records; represent the DHIA system on issues involving other National and International organizations; organize industry activities that benefit members of National DHIA

1344 **www.eap.mcgill.ca/cfbmc.htm**
Canadian Farm Business Management Council
To share and co-ordinate informatio non farm business management in order to help prevent duplication, encourage cost-sharing and build partnerships; to act as a forum for dialogue on farm business management issues of concern nationally or in more than on province of the country; to develop, adapt and distribute information products in farm business management to help increase the competitiveness of Canadian Agriculture.

1345 **www.farmequip.org**
Farm Equipment Manufacturers Association
Facebook, Twitter, LinkedIn
An association for farm equipment manufacturers and suppliers.

1346 **www.farmers-friend.com**
Farmers Friend
Farming news.

1347 **www.farmshowcouncil.org**
Farm Show Council
Strives to improve the value of its member shows through education, communication and evaluation. Provides the best possible marketing showcase for exhibitors of agricultural equipment and related products to the farmer/rancher/producer customer.

1348 **www.fb.org**
American Farm Bureau Federation
The unified national voice of agriculture, working through our grassroots organization to en-

hance and strengthen the lives of rural American and to build strong, prosperous agricultural communities

1349 **www.fewa-aimra.org**
FEWA-AIMRA Marketing & Distribution Association
Merged with AIMRA to form the leading association devoted to the marketing of specialized equipment.

1350 **www.fourhcouncil.edu**
National 4-H Council
Empowers youth to reach their full potential, working and learning in partnership with caring adults.

1351 **www.fpaota.org**
Fresh Produce Association of the Americas
A non-profit trade group of more than 100 members who are involved in the growth, harvest, import and distribution of the finest produce from Mexico.

1352 **www.fpfc.org**
Fresh Produce and Floral Council
Stimulates the promotion and sale of fresh fruit, vegetables and floral products; improves communications between all segments of the fresh produce and floral industries; and to exchange ideas on better and more economical handling of fresh fruit, vegetables and floral products from the farm to table.

1353 **www.freshcut.com**
Great American Publishing
Information on carrot production, growers and shippers.

1354 **www.grains.org**
US Grains Council
Develops export markets for U.S. barley corn, grain sorghum and related products. A private, non-profit corporation with nine international offices and programs in more than 50 countries.

1355 **www.greyhouse.com**
Grey House Publishing
Authoritative reference directories for business information and general reference, including agriculture and food markets. Users can search the online databases with varied search criteria allowing for custom searches by product category, geographic area, sales volume, keyword, subject and more. Full Grey House catalog and online ordering also available.

1356 **www.hereford.org**
American Hereford Association
For the raising and breeding of stock in the hereford cattle industry.

1357 **www.holsteinusa.com**
Holstein Association USA
The largest breed organization in the world, comprised of members who have a strong interest in breeding, raising and milking Holstein cattle.

1358 **www.iaff.ttu.edu/aals**
Association for Arid Land Studies

1359 **www.iaom.info**
International Association of Operative Millers
An international organization, comprised of flour millers, cereal grain and seed processors and allied trades representatives and companies devoted to the advancement of technology in the flour milling and cereal grain processing industries.

1360 **www.ifas.ufl.edu**
Institute of Food & Agriculture/Univ of Florida
For college students professionally interested in communications related to agriculture, food, natural resources and allied fields.

1361 **www.ipaa.net**
International Pesticide Applicators Association
Provides education and information for the professional horticultural applicator. Legislative work involves the states of Washington, Oregon, Idaho in the area of laws and regulations.

1362 **www.irrigation.org**
Irrigation Association
Membership organization for irrigation equipment and system manufacturers, dealers, distributors, designers, consultants, contractors and end users.

1363 **www.mailordergardening.com**
Mailorder Gardening Association
nonprofit organization serving the needs of companies involved in marketing gardening products to consumers

1364 **www.meatami.org**
American Meat Institute
Dedicated to increasing the efficiency, profitability and safety of meat and poultry worldwide.

1365 **www.naab-css.org**
National Association of Animal Breeders
To unite thos individuals and organizations engaged in the artificial insemination of cattle and other livestock into an affiliated federation operating under self-imposed standards of performance and to conduct and promote the mutual interest and ideals of its members.

1366 **www.nacaa.com**
National Association County Agricultural Agents
For agents focusing on educational programs for the youth of the community.

1367 **www.naicc.org**
National Alliance of Independent Crop Consultants
A professional society that represents the nation's crop porduction and research consultants.

1368 **www.nama.org**
National Agri-Marketing Association
Professional association for professionals in marketing and agribusiness.

1369 **www.nationalgrange.org**
Nat'l Grange of the Order of Patrons of Husbandry
Provides opportunities for individuals and families to develop to their highest potential in order to build stronger communities and states, as well as a stronger nation.

1370 **www.nationalhempassociation.org**
A source for news and information on all aspects of the industrial hemp industry, including scientific, legislative, and industry news.

1371 **www.nationalplantboard.org**
National Plant Board
A non-profit organization of the plant pest regulatory agencies opf each of the staes and Commonwealth of Puerto Rico.

1372 **www.nationalpotatocouncil.Org**
National Potato Council
The advocate for the economic well-being of U.S. potato growers on federal legislative, regulatory, environmental and trade issues.

1373 **www.nfu.org**
National Farmers Union
Protects and enhances the economic well-being and quality of life for family farmers and ranchers and their rural communities

1374 **www.nppc.org**
National Pork Producers Council
Conducts public-policy outreach on behalf of its 43 affiliated state associations, enhancing opportunities for the success of U.S. pork producers and other industry stakeholders by establishing the U.S. pork industry as a consistent and responsible supplier of high-quality pork to the domestic and world markets.

1375 **www.ocia.org**
Organic Crop Improvement Association International
Dedicated to providing the highest quality organic certification serices and access to global organic markets

1376 **www.onions-usa.org**
National Onion Association
The official organization representing growers, shippers, brokers, and commerical representatives of the U.S. onion industry.

1377 **www.ota.com**
Organic Trade Association
A membership-based business association that focuses on the organic business community in North America. Promotes and protects the growth of organic trade to benefit the environment, farmers, the public and the economy.

1378 **www.pma.com**
Produce Marketing Association
Global trade association serving the entire produce and floral supply chains by enhancing the marketing of produce, floral, and related products and services worldwide.

1379 **www.profarmer.com**
Professional Farmers of America
Gives customers a competitive edge in marketing and financial management through timely delivery and accurate analysis of market-sensitive news and views.

1380 **www.sbsonline.org**
Society for Biomolecular Sciences
Non-profit scientific society dedicated to drug discovery and its related disciplines. Provides a forum for global educationand information exchange among professionals in the chemical, pharmaceutical, biotech and agrochemical industries.

1381 **www.seedtechnology.net**
Society Commercial Seed Technologists
An organization comprised of commercial, independent and government seed technologists.

1382 **www.sheepusa.org**
American Sheep Industry Association
The national organization representing the interests of sheep producers located throughout the United States.

1383 **www.southerncottonginners.org**
Southern Cotton Ginners Association
Serves its members by providing safety, training, and regulatory representation.

1384 **www.southwesternassn.com**
SouthWestern Association

Established by a progressive group of independent hardware and farm implement/mercantile dealers to help increase their profitability and solve common problems.

1385 **www.soygrowers.com**
American Soybean Association

Represents U.S. soybean farmers through policy advocacy and international market development.

1386 **www.sugaralliance.org**
American Sugar Alliance

A natinoal coalition of sugarcane and sugarbeet farmers, processoris, refiners, suppliers, workers and others dedicated to preserving a strong domestic sugar industry.

1387 **www.sunflowernsa.com**
National Sunflower Association

A non-profit commodity organization working on problems and opportunities for the improvement of all members.

1388 **www.tfi.org**
Fertilizer Institute

The leading voice in the fertilizer industry, representing the public policy, communication and statistical needs of producers, manufacturers, retailers and transporters of fertilizer.

1389 **www.turfweeds.net**
Turfgrass Weed Science/Virginia Polytech Institute

Provides weed management information and research reports to turfgrass managers.

1390 **www.unitedfresh.org**
United Fresh Produce Association

Commited to driving the growth and success of produce companies and their partners. Represents the interests of member companies throughout the global, fresh produce supply chain, including family-owned, private and publicly traded businesses as well as regional, national and international companies.

1391 **www.usguernsey.com**
American Guernsey Association

Register and deliver guernsey cattle throughout the United States.

1392 **www.uspotatoes.com**
United States Potato Board

The central organizing force in implementing programs that will increase demand for potatoes.

1393 **www.vealfarm.com**
Veal Quality Association Program

For veal producers and processors.

1394 **www.wawgg.org**
Washington Association of Wine Grape Growers

Advocates for the Washington wine growing industry by educating, promotin, representing, and unifying the industry and fostering a positive business environment for continued growth and production of world-class, Washington-grown wines.

1395 **www.wildblueberries.com**
Wild Blueberry Association of North America

For processors and growers of wild blueberries in Eastern Canada and Maine.

Associations

1396 **Advanced BioFuels USA**
507 North Bentz Street
Frederick, MD 21701

301-644-1395
advancedbiofuelsusa.info

Joanne M. Ivancic, President/Executive Director
Robert E. Kozak, Treasurer
Dr. Craig Laufer, Secretary

A nonprofit organization that advocates for the adoption of advanced biofuels as an energy security, military flexibility, economic development andclimate change mitigation/pollution control solution though its promotion of public understanding, acceptance, and research.

1397 **Advanced Biofuels Association**
800 17th Street, NW
Suite 1100
Washington, DC 20006

Home Page:
www.advancedbiofuelsassociation.com
Facebook, Twitter, LinkedIn, YouTube

Wayne Simmons, Chairman
Chris Ryan, Vice Chairman
Michael McAdams, President
Andrew Rojeski, Secretary
Christopher Higby, Treasurer

Organization that seeks to help America transform to a low carbon economy by supporting and advocating for public policies that are technology neutral, use sustainable feedstocks, and offering financial support to its member companies to bring products to market that are competitive and compatible with petroleum-based fuels and byproducts.
40 Members

1398 **Alliance for Affordable Energy**
P.O. Box 751133
New Orleans, LA 70175

504-208-9761
all4energy.org
Facebook, Twitter, LinkedIn, YouTube, Instagram, Flickr

Casey DeMoss, Chief Executive Officer
Logan Atkinson Burke, Manager, Admin & Reg. Affairs
John Williams, Treasurer
Logan Atkinson, Office Development Manager
Logan Williams, Volunteer & Intern Manager

An environmental advocacy organization that promotes fair, affordable, environmentally responsible energy.
Founded in 1985

1399 **Alliance to Save Energy**
1850 M Street NW
Suite 610
Washington, DC 20036

202-857-0666
www.ase.org
Facebook, Twitter, LinkedIn, YouTube, Google+, Flickr

Jason Hartke, President
Kara O'Connell, Chief Operating Officer
Ross Robinson, Chief Financial Officer
Susanna Silvan, Manager, Events/Executive Affairs
Ben Somberg, Manager, Communications

Organization that leads worldwide energy efficiency initiatives in policy advocacy, research, education and technology deployment.
Founded in 1977

1400 **Alternative Energy Association**
1061 East Indiantown Road
Suite 400
Jupiter, FL 33477

561-776-8600
alternativeenergyassn@gmail.com

Organization that uses marketing campaigns, seminars, and eduactional activities to promote awareness of clean, renewable sources of power generation as alternatives to the use of fossil fuels for energy production.

1401 **Alternative Energy Resources Organization**
432 N. Last Chance Gulch
Helena, MT 59601

406-443-7272; Fax: 406-442-9120
aero@aeromt.org
www.aeromt.org
Facebook, Twitter, Myspace, Pinterest, Google+

Jennifer Hill-Hart, Executive Director
Corrie Williamson, Comm. & Membership Director
Rosie Goldich, Abundant Montana Intern

A grassroots nonprofit organization dedicated to solutions that promote resource conservation and local economic vitality. By bringing people together, AERO offers a vehicle for collective action and a sense of common purpose for citizens within their communities to shape a more sustainable future.
Founded in 1974

1402 **American Biogas Council**
1211 Connecticut Ave NW
Suite 600
Washington, DC 20036-2701

202-640-6595
info@americanbiogascouncil.org
www.americanbiogascouncil.org
Twitter, LinkedIn, YouTube, Flickr

Bernie Sheff, PE, Chairman
Paul Greene, Vice-Chair
Melissa VanOrnum, Treasurer
Mark Stoermann, Vice-Chair
Patrick Serfass, Executive Director (ex-officio)

Mission is to create jobs, environmental sustainability and energy independence by growing the American biogas industry.
Mailing list available for rent

1403 **American Coalition for Ethanol**
5000 South Broadband Lane
Suite 224
Sioux Falls, SD 57108

605-334-3381
cbeck@ethanol.org
ethanol.org
Facebook, Twitter

Ron Alverson, President
Duane Kristensen, Vice President
Brian Jennings, Executive Vice President
Ron Lamberty, Senior Vice President
Chuck Beck, Director of Communications

Environmental advocacy organization that promotes the use of ethanol as the most successful renewable energy platform in the world.
Founded in 1987

1404 **American Council On Renewable Energy**
1600 K Street NW
Suite 650
Washington, DC 20006

202-393-0001
info@acore.org
www.acore.org
Facebook, Twitter, LinkedIn

Greg Wetstone, President and CEO
Todd Foley, SVP, Policy & Govt. Affairs
Gil Jenkins, VP, Communications
Lesley Hunter, VP, Programs
Gerald Borenstein, SVP, Finance & Administration

Works to bring all forms of renewable energy into the mainstream of America's economy and lifestyle. Members include every aspect and sector of the renewable energy industries and their trade associations, including wind, solar, geothermal, biomass and biofuels, hydropower tidal/current energy and waste energy.
Founded in 2001

1405 **American Council for an Energy-Efficient Economy**
529 14th Street N.W
Suite 600
Washington, DC 20045-1000

202-507-4000; Fax: 202-429-2248
www.aceee.org
Facebook, Twitter, RSS

Alison Silverstein, President
Timothy M Stout, Treasurer
Peter A. Molinaro, Secretary
Roland J. Risser, Special Advisor
Jim Barrett, Chief Economist

A nonprofit organization that seeks to advance energy efficiency policies, programs, technologies, investments, and behaviors.

1406 **American Hydrogen Association**
P.O. Box 4205
Mesa, AZ 85201

480-234-5070
help@clean-air.org
www.americanhydrogenassociation.org
Facebook, YouTtube

Roy McAlister, President
Ben Ferguson, Vice President
Douglas Hawley, Secretary/Treasurer

Providing information on the use of hydrogen as a fuel.

1407 **American Solar Energy Society**
2525 Arapahoe Ave
Ste E4-253
Boulder, CO 80302

303-443-3130; Fax: 303-443-3212
info@ases.org
www.ases.org
Facebook, Twitter, LinkedIn, Instagram

Carly Rixham, Executive Director

The nation's leading association of solar professionals & advocates. Mission is to inspire an era of energy innovation and speed the transition to a sustainable energy economy. Advancing education, research and policy.
Founded in 1954

1408 **American Water Works Association**
6666 W Quincy Ave.
Denver, CO 80235

303-794-7711
800-926-7337; Fax: 303-347-0804
www.awwa.org
Facebook, Twitter, LinkedIn, YouTube

Melissa Elliott, President
Aurel Arndt, Treasurer
David B. LaFrance, Chief Executive Officer

The professional society of North American drinking water experts. Develop standards and support research programs in waterworks design, construction, operation, and management. Conducts in-service training schools and offers placement service.
Founded in 1881

1409 **American Wind Energy Association**
1501 M Street NW
Suite 900
Washington, DC 20005

202-383-2500
engage.awea.org
Facebook, Twitter, LinkedIn, YouTube, Instagram

Tom Kiernan, Chief Executive Officer
Heather Graving, Manager, Executive Services
Joshua DeShong, Public Affairs Coordinator
Mark Bakke, Manager, Member Relations/Exhibits
Angela Bell, Manager, Member Relations

Promotes wind energy as a clean source of electricity for consumers around the world. Representing wind power project developers, equipment suppliers, services providers, parts manufacturers, utilities, researchers, and others involved in the wind industry.

1410 **Association of Energy Engineers**
3168 Mercer University Drive
Atlanta, GA 30341

770-447-5083
www.aeecenter.org
Facebook, Twitter, LinkedIn, YouTube

Lary Good, Dir., International Member Devel.
Stephen A. Roosa, Dir., Sustainable & Local Programs
Timothy B. Janos, Dir., Special Project
Eric Oliver, Dir., Governmental Affairs
Albert Thumann, Executive Director

Promotes energy certification, management and education.
17500 Members
Founded in 1977

1411 **Association of Energy Engineers (AEE)**
3168 Mercer University Drive
Atlanta, GA 30341

770-447-5083
www.aeecenter.org
Facebook, Twitter, YouTube

Lary Good, Dir., International Member Devel.
Stephen A. Roosa, Dir., Sustainable & Local Programs
Timothy B. Janos, Dir., Special Projects
Eric Oliver, Dir., Governmental Affairs
Albert Thumann, Executive Director

Promotes energy certification, management and education.
17500 Members
Founded in 1977

1412 **Biomass Energy Research Association**
901 D Street, S.W
Suite 100
Washington, DC 20024

410-953-6202; Fax: 410-290-0377

Joan Pellegrino, President/Treasurer
Phillip C. Badger, Secretary/Director
Mark A. Paisley, Director
Janis L. Tabor, Director
Dr. Evan Hughes, Director

An association of bioenergy researchers, companies, and advocates that promotes education and research on renewable biomass energy and waste-to-energy systems.

1413 **Biomass Power Association**
100 Middle St.
PO Box 9729
Portland, ME 04104-9729

202-494-2493
carrie@usabiomass.org
www.usabiomass.org

Bob Cleaves, President & CEO
Carrie Annand, VP of External Affairs
Nicholas Mazuroski, Director of Operations and Research
Katherine A. Pe□a, Web Director

The nation's leading organization working to expand and advance the use of clean, renewable biomass power. Educates policymakers at the state and federal level about the benefits of biomass and provides regular briefings and research to keep members fully informed about public policy impacting the biomass industry. Members include local owners and operators of existing biomass facilities, suppliers, plant developers and others.
80 Members

1414 **Biomass Thermal Energy Council**
1211 Connecticut Avenue NW
Suite 600
Washington, DC 20036-2701

202-596-3974; Fax: 202-223-5537
info@biomassthermal.org
www.biomassthermal.org
Facebook, Twitter, LinkedIn, SlideShare, Vimeo

Dan Wilson, Chairman
Joel Stronberg, Executive Director
Dayanita Ramesh, Project Assistant
Emanuel Wagner, Programs Director
Ben Bell Walker, Technical Affairs

An association of biomass fuel producers, appliance manufacturers and distributors, supply chain companies and non-profit organizations that view biomass thermal energy as a renewable, responsible, clean and energy-efficient pathway to meeting America's energy needs. BTEC engages in research, education, and public advocacy for the fast growing biomass thermal energy industry.
Founded in 2009

1415 **Business Council for Sustainable Energy**
805 15th Street, NW
Suite 708
Washington, DC 20005

202-785-0507; Fax: 202-785-0514
bcse@bcse.org
www.bcse.org
Facebook, Twitter, LinkedIn

Mark Wagner, Chair
Rob Gramlich, Vice Chair
Scott Crider, Vice Chair
Lisa Jacobson, President
Ruth McCormick, Director, Federal and State Affairs

A coalition of companies and trade associations from the energy efficiency, natural gas and renewable energy sectors, and includes independent electric power producers, investor-owned utilities, public power, commercial end-users and project developers and service providers for environmental markets.

1416 **Canadian Renewable Fuels Association(CRFA)**
350 Sparks Street
Suite 605
Ottawa, ON K1R 7S8

613-594-5528; Fax: 613-594-3076
www.greenfuels.org
Facebook, Twitter, LinkedIn, Instagram

Andrea Kent, President
Deborah Elson, VP, Public Affairs & Membership
Tyler Bjornson, Executive Director
William Meyer, Manager, Communication
Jim Grey, Chair

Promotes and advances the use of renewable fuels for transporation- to protect our environment by reducing harmful emissions and to grow our economy by creating the good, green-energy jobs of the future.
Founded in 1984

1417 **Center for Energy Efficiency and Renewable Technologies**
1100 11th Street
Suite 311
Sacramento, CA

916-442-7785
info@ceert.org
ceert.org
Facebook, Twitter, LinkedIn

Jonathan M. Weisgall, Chairman
Ralph Cavanagh, Vice Chair
V. John White, Executive Director
John Shahabian, Director of Operations
Kevin Lynch, Secretary/Treasurer

A partnership of major environmental groups and private-sector clean energy companies that advocate for policies that promote global warming solutions and increased reliance on clean, renewable energy sources for California andthe West.
Founded in 1990

1418 **Clean Energy Group**
50 State St
Suite 1
Montpelier, VT 05602

802-223-2554; Fax: 802-223-4967
info@cleanegroup.org
www.cleanegroup.org
Facebook, Twitter, LinkedIn, Vimeo

Lewis Milford, President
Seth Mullendore, Vice President

A leading nonprofit advocacy organization working in the US and internationally on innovative clean energy technology, finance, and policy programs. Supported by major foundations, as well as state, federal and international energy agencies.
Founded in 1998

1419 **Distributed Wind Energy Association**
P.O. Box 721866
Norman, OK 73070

405-301-9329
info@distributedwind.org
distributedwind.org
Facebook, Twitter, LinkedIn

Russell Tencer, President
James Duffy, Secretary
Mike Bergey, Treasurer

A collaborative group comprised of manufacturers, distributors, project developers, dealers, installers, and advocates, whose primary mission is to promote and foster all aspects of the American distributed wind energy industry.

1420 **Ducks Unlimited**
One Waterfowl Way
Memphis, TN 38120

901-758-3825
800-45D-UCKS
www.ducks.org
Facebook, Twitter, YouTube, Instagram

George Dunklin, Jr., Chairman
Paul R. Bonderson, Jr., President
Dale Hall, Chief Executive Officer
Rogers Hoyt, Jr., First Vice President
Wendell Weakley, Treasurer

Conserves, restores, and manages wetlands and associated habitats for North America's waterfowl.
Founded in 1937

1421 **Efficient Windows Collaborative**
21629 Zodiac Street NE
Wyoming, MN 55092

efficientwindowscollaborative@gmail.com
www.efficientwindows.org
Facebook, Twitter, LinkedIn

A nonprofit organization that partners with window, door, skylight,and component manufacturers, research organizations, federal, state and local government agencies, and others interested in expanding the market for high-efficiency fenestration products.

1422 **Electric Auto Association**
PO Box 639
Los Altos, CA 94024-0639

831-688-8669; Fax: 831-688-8669
freund.ron@gmail.com
www.electricauto.org
Facebook, Twitter, LinkedIn

Ron Freund, Chairman
Guy Hall, Secretary
Gint Federas, Treasurer
Will Beckett, Membership
Carl Vogel, Board Member

Nonprofit educational organization promoting the advancement and adoption of electric vehicles by educating the public on the benefits of this alternative.
Founded in 1967

1423 **Energy Recovery Council**
2200 Wilson Boulevard
Suite 310
Arlington, VA 22201

202-467-6240
tmichaels@energyrecoverycouncil.org
www.energyrecoverycouncil.org

Ted Michaels, President

Represents the waste-to-energy industry and communities that own waste-to-energy facilities. Current ERC members own and operate modern waste-to-energy facilities that operate nationwide, safely disposing of municipal solid waste, while at the same time generating renewable electricity using modern combustion technology equipped with state-of-the-art emission control systems.

1424 **Environmental and Energy Study Institute**
1112 16th Street, NW
Suite 300
Washington, DC 20036-4819

202-628-1400; Fax: 202-204-5244
info@eesi.org
www.eesi.org
Facebook, Twitter, LinkedIn, Vimeo

Jared Blum, Chairman
Carol Werner, Executive Director
David Robison, Director of Finance & Admin
Susan Williams, Director of Development
Alison Alford, Programs & Administrative Assistant

A nonprofit organization that advances innovative policy solutions that set us on a cleaner, more secure and sustainable energy path.
Founded in 1984

1425 **Export Council for Energy Efficiency**

Home Page: www.ecee.org

Laura Gubisch, Executive Director

A nonprofit association that promotes the export of energy efficient products, services, and technologies worldwide.
Founded in 1994

1426 **Florida Solar Energy Center**
1679 Clearlake Rd.
Cocoa, FL 32922-5703

321-638-1000; Fax: 321-638-1010
www.fsec.ucf.edu
Facebook

James Fenton, Director

Created by the State of Florida in 1975, FSEC is the largest publicly-supported alternative energy research institute in the United States.
Founded in 1975

1427 **Fuel Cell and Hydrogen Energy Association**
1211 Connecticut Avenue Northwest
#600
Washington, DC 20036

202-261-1337
info@fchea.org
www.fchea.org
Facebook, Twitter, LinkedIn, Google+

Morry B. Markowitz, President
Bud DeFlaviis, Director of Government Affairs
Jennifer Gangi, Director of Comm. & Outreach
Sandra Curtin, Research & Comm. Manager
Connor Dolan, Director Of External Affairs

A trade association for the fuel cell and hydrogen energy industry,and is dedicated to the commercialization of fuel cells and hydrogen energy technologies.
Founded in 2010

1428 **Geothermal Energy Association**
209 Pennsylvania Avenue SE
Washington, DC 20003

202-454-5261; Fax: 202-454-5265
jgreco@terra-genpower.com
www.geo-energy.org
Facebook, Twitter, LinkedIn, YouTube, Wordpress

Karl Gawell, Executive Director
Leslie Blodgett, Geothermal News Specialist
Kathy Kent, Sr. Director of Marketing
Mihaela-Daniela Lobontiu, Business Manager
Yoram Bronicki, President

Advocates for public policies that will promote the development and utilization of geothermal resources, provides a forum for the industry to discuss issues and problems, encourages research and development to improve geothermal technologies, presents industry views to governmental organizations, and conducts education and outreach projects.

1429 **Geothermal Exchange Organization**
312 S. Fourth St
Suite 100
Springfield, IL 62701

888-255-4436
www.geoexchange.org
Facebook, Twitter, LinkedIn, Google+

Douglas Dougherty, President & CEO
Ted Clutter, Manager of Outreach

A nonprofit trade association that promotes the manufacture, designand installation of GeoExchange systems—an energy efficient and environmentallyfriendly heating and cooling technology.

1430 **Geothermal Resources Council**
630 Pe¤a Dr.
Ste. 400
Davis, CA 95618-5476

530-758-2360; Fax: 530-758-2839
grc@geothermal.org
www.geothermal.org
Facebook, Twitter, LinkedIn, YouTube, Flickr, Pinterest, Bl

Steve Ponder, Executive Director
Ian Crawford, Director of Communications, Editor
Estela M. Smith, GRC Office Manager
Anh Lay, Office Associate
Chi-Meng Moua, Graphic Designer

Nonprofit, educational association actively seeking to expand its role as a primary professional educational association for the international geothermal community.
1300+ Members
Founded in 1970

1431 **Intergovernmental Renewable Energy Organization**
884 2nd Avenue, UN Centre
No. 20050
New York, NY 10017

917-862-6444; Fax: 212-202-4100
www.ireoigo.org
Facebook, Twitter

Dr. Anthony James Watson, Chairman
Heidi Walters, Chief Protocol Officer
Diane Mello, Executive Director Operations
John Hill, Secretary-General
Michael Rubin, Under Secretary

Promotes the urgent transition to renewable energy sources and sustainable development through collaborative effort and the implementation of projects that improve the lives of people while preserving the environment and our resources for future generations of humans.
Founded in 2008

1432 **International Association for Energy Economics**
28790 Chagrin Blvd
Suite 350
Cleveland, OH 44122-4642

216-464-5365; Fax: 216-464-2737
www.iaee.org
Facebook, LinkedIn

David Newbery, President
Jacques Percebois, Vice President for Publications
Christophe Bonnery, Vice President for Business & Govt.
G□rkan Kumbaroglu, Vice President for Conferences
Ricardo B. Raineri, Vice President for Academic Affairs

Association for those involved in energy economics including publications, consultants, energy database software.
3400 Members
Founded in 1977
Mailing list available for rent

1433 **International Association for Hydrogen Energy**
5794 SW 40 St.
#303
Miami, FL 33155

info@iahe.org
www.iahe.org

Dr. T. Nejat Veziroglu, President
John W. Sheffield, Vice President
Juan Carlos Bolcich, Vice President for South America
Ibrahim Din‡er, Vice President for Strategy
Bruno Pollet, Vice President for South Africa

An association that stimulates the exchange of information in the Hydrogen Energy field through its publications and sponsorship of international workshops, short courses and conferences and endeavors to inform the general public of the important role of Hydrogen Energy in the planning of an inexhaustible and clean energy system.

1434 **International District Energy Association**
24 Lyman Street
Suite 230
Westborough, MA 1581

508-366-9339; Fax: 508-366-0019
idea@districtenergy.org
www.districtenergy.org
Facebook, Twitter, YouTube, Flickr, RSS

Bruce Ander, Chair
Tim Griffin, Vice Chair
Chris Lyons, Second Vice Chair
James Adams, Secretary/Treasurer
Ken Smith, Past Chair

An organization that actively works to foster the success of its members as leaders in providing reliable, economical, efficient and environmentally sound district heating, district cooling and cogeneration (combined heat and power) services.
Founded in 1909

1435 **International Ground Source Heat Pump Association**
1201 S. Innovation Way Dr.
Suite 400
Stillwater, OK 74074

405-744-5175
800-626-4747; Fax: 405-744-5283
igshpa@okstate.edu
www.igshpa.okstate.edu
Facebook, Twitter, Youtube, Google+

John Turley, President
Gail Ezepek, Conference and Membership Assistant
Janet Reeder, Technical Writer
Ben Champlin, Graphic Designer
Roshan Revankar, Manager

Member-driven organization established to advance ground source heat pump technology on local, state, national and international levels. IGSHPA utilizes state-of-the-art facilities for conducting GSHP system installation training and geothermal research. Mission is to promote the use of ground source heat pump technology worldwide through education and communication.
Founded in 1987

1436 **Interstate Renewable Energy Council**
PO Box 1156
Latham, NY 12110-1156

518-458-6059
info@irecusa.org
www.irecusa.org
Facebook, Twitter, LinkedIn, Pinterest, YouTube

Larry Shirley, Chair
Jane Weissman, President and CEO
Larry Sherwood, Vice President, COO
Maryteresa Colello, Administrative Coordinator
Louise Urgo, Administration

Works with industry, government, educators and other stakeholders to ensure that the broader use of renewable energies is possible, safe, affordable and practical, particularly for the individual consumer.
Founded in 1982

1437 **Lignite Energy Council**
1016 E. Owens Avenue
PO Box 2277
Bismarck, ND 58502-2277

701-258-7117
800-932-7117; Fax: 701-258-2755
lec@lignite.com
www.lignite.com
Facebook, Twitter, YouTube, RSS Feeds

Jason Bohrer, President/CEO
Marie Hoerner, Dir., Finance & Benefit Resources
Mike Jones, Ph. D., VP, Research and Development
Steve Van Dyke, Vice President of Communications
Kay LaCoe, Director of Membership Marketing

Regional Trade Association - promotes policies and activities that maintain a viable lignite industry and enhance development of our regions' lignite resources.
355 Members
Founded in 1974

1438 **Low Impact Hydropower Institute**
PO Box 194
Harrington Park, NJ 07640

201-906-2189; Fax: 206-984-3086
www.lowimpacthydro.org
Facebook, Twitter, Google+ Pinterest

Julie Keil, Chair
John Seebach, Vice-Chair
Michael J. Sale, PhD, Executive Director
Dana Hall, Deputy Director
Jacob Palmer, Treasurer

Dedicated to reducing the impacts of hydropower generation through the certification of hydropower projects that have avoided or reduced their environmental impacts pursuant to the Low Impact Hydropower Institute's criteria. Mission is to reduce the impacts of hydropower dams through market incentives.

1439 **NABCEP**
56 Clifton Country Rd.
Suite 202
Clifton Park, NY 12065

800-654-0021; Fax: 518-899-1092
info@nabcep.org
www.nabcep.org
Facebook

Don Warfield, Chair
Richard Lawrence, Executive Director
Kathryn Casey, Program Manager
Sue Pratt, Business Manager
Melissa Bell, Program Assistant

Mission is to support, and work with, the renewable energy and energy efficiency industries, professionals, and stakeholders. Goal is to develop voluntary national certification programs that will; promote renewable energy, provide value to practitioners, promote worker safety and skill, and promote consumer confidence.
Founded in 2002

1440 **National Association of Energy Service Companies**
1615 M Street, NW
Suite 800
Washington, DC 20036

202-822-0950; Fax: 202-822-0955
info@naesco.org
www.naesco.org
Facebook, LinkedIn

David Weiss, Chairman
Mike Kearney, Vice Chair
Terry E. Singe, Executive Director
Donald Gilligan, President
Scott Ririe, Secretary

An organization that promotes energy efficiency at state, federal, and international facilities; ensures the key role of ESCOs in delivering energyefficiency resources; and builds new market opportunities while growing existingmarkets.

1441 **National Association of State Energy Officials**
2107 Wilson Boulevard
Suite 850
Arlington, VA 22201

703-299-8800; Fax: 703-299-6208
energy@naseo.org
www.naseo.org
Facebook, Twitter, LinkedIn, YouTube, Flickr

Janet Streff, Chair
Robert Jackson, Vice Chair
David Terry, Executive Director
Jeffrey C. Genzer, General Counsel
Marion Gold, Treasurer

A national nonprofit association that facilitates peer learning among state energy officials, serves as a resource for and about state energy offices, and advocates the interests of the state energy offices to Congress and federal agencies.
Founded in 1986

1442 **National Biodiesel Board**
605 Clark Avenue
PO Box 104898
Jefferson City, MO 65110-4898

573-635-3893
800-841-5849; Fax: 573-635-7913
info@biodiesel.org
www.biodiesel.org
Facebook, Twitter, YouTube, RSS Feeds, Google+

Chad Stone, Chairman
Mike Rath, Vice Chairman
Rob Shaffer, 2nd Vice Chairman
Ryan Pederson, Treasurer
Troy Alberts, Secretary

Representing AmericaBs clean diesel replacement fuels, the National Biodiesel Board will advance the interests of its members by supporting sustainable biodiesel, renewable diesel, and renewable jet industry growth. NBB serves as the industryBs central coordinating entity for technical and quality assurance programs and will be the strongest voice for its advocacy, communications, and market development.

1443 **National Fenestration Rating Council**
6305 Ivy Lane
Suite 140
Greenbelt, MD 20770

301-589-1776; Fax: 301-589-3884
info@nfrc.org
www.nfrc.org
Facebook, Twitter, LinkedIn, YouTube

James C. Benney, Chief Executing Officer
Deborah Callahan, Chief Operating Officer
Jessica Finn, Membership Coordinator
Cheryl Gendron, Meeting Manager
Scott Hanlon, Program Director

A nonprofit organization that administers an independent rating andlabeling system for the energy performance of windows, doors, skylights, and attachment products.
Founded in 1989

1444 **National Hydropower Association**
601 New Jersey Ave NW
Suite 660
Washington, DC 20001
202-750-8402; Fax: 202-682-9478
help@hydro.org
www.hydro.org
Facebook, Twitter

Linda Church Ciocci, Executive Director
Steve Wenke, Vice President
John McCormick, President
Debbie Mursch, Treasurer
John Suloway, Secretary

Dedicated to promoting the growth of clean, affordable US hydropower. Seeks to secure hydropower's place as a climate-friendly, renewable and reliable energy source that serves national environmental, energy, and economic policy objectives. Members are involved in projects throughout the US hydropower industry, including both federal and non-federal hydroelectric facilities.

1445 **National Renewable Energy Association**
629 North Main Street
Hattiesburg, MS 39401
601-582-3330; Fax: 601-582-3354
nrea@megagate.com

A nonprofit organization dedicated to helping Americans use less energy and to use more renewable energy in the future.
Founded in 2007

1446 **National Renewable Energy Laboratory**
15013 Denver West Parkway
Golden, CO 80401
303-275-3000
www.nrel.gov
Facebook, Twitter, LinkedIn, YouTube

Dr. Dan Arvizu, President
Dr. Dana Christensen, Deputy Laboratory Director
Bobi Garrett, Deputy Laboratory Director
David Post, Acting Deputy Lab Director/COO
Howard Branz, Research Fellow

Develops renewable energy and energy efficiency technologies and practices, advances related science and engineering, and transfers knowledge and innovations to address the nation's energy and environmental goals.

1447 **National Wind Coordinating Collaborative**
1110 Vermont Ave NW
Suite 950
Washington, DC 20005
202-656-3303
info@awwi.org
nationalwind.org

Lauren Flinn, Facilitator
Abby Arnold, Senior Mediator

Provides a neutral forum for various stakeholders to pursue the shared objective of developing environmentally, economically, and politically sustainable commercial markets for wind power in the United States.
Founded in 1994

1448 **Natural Resources Defense Council**
40 West 20th Street
New York, NW 10011
212-727-2700; Fax: 212-727-1773
webmaster@nrdc.org
www.nrdc.org
Facebook, Twitter, YouTube, Tumblr, RSS

Daniel R. Tishman, Chairman
Frederick A.O. Schwarz, Chair Emeritus
Patricia Bauman, Vice Chair
Mary Moran, Treasurer
Alan F. Horn, Vice Chair

A nonprofit environmental action group that works to restore the natural elements, defend endangered species, and strives to safeguard the Earth: its people, its plants and animals and the natural systems on which all life depends.
14000 Members

1449 **North American Board of Certified Energy Practitioners**
56 Clifton Country Rd
Suite 202
Clifton Park, NY 12065
800-654-0021; Fax: 518-899-1092
info@nabcep.org
www.nabcep.org
Facebook

Don Warfield, Chair
Richard Lawrence, Executive Director
Kathryn Casey, Program Manager
Sue Pratt, Business Manager
Melissa Bell, Program Assistant

Offers entry level knowledge assessment, professional certification, and company accreditation programs to renewable energy professionals throughout North America.
Founded in 2002

1450 **Northeast Sustainable Energy Association**
50 Miles Street
Greenfield, MA 01301-3255
413-774-6051; Fax: 413-774-6053
nesea@nesea.org
www.nesea.org
Facebook, Twitter, LinkedIn, YouTube

Jennifer Marrapese, Executive Director
Miriam Aylward, Director of Program Development
Mary Biddle, Deputy Executive Director
Gina Sieber, Business manager
Jenny Goldberg, Outreach & Event Coordinator

The nation's leading regional membership organization focused on promoting the understanding, development and adoption of energy conservation and non-polluting, renewable energy technologies.
1802 Members
Founded in 1974

1451 **Ocean Renewable Energy Coalition**
12909 Scarlet Oak Drive
Darnestown, MD 20878
301-869-3790; Fax: 301-869-5637
info@oceanrenewable.com
www.oceanrenewable.typepad.com
Facebook, Twitter, RSS

Sean O'Neill, President
Carolyn Elefant, General and Regulatory Counsel

Exclusively dedicated to promoting marine and hydrokinetic energy technologies from clean, renewable ocean resources. Organization embraces a wide range of renewable technologies; including wave, tidal, current, offshore wind, ocean thermal, marine biomass and all other technologies that utilize renewable resources from oceans, tidal areas and other unimpounded water bodies to produce electricity, desalinized water, hydrogen, mariculture and other by products.
40+ Members
Founded in 2005

1452 **Office of Energy Efficiency & Renewable Energy**
Forrestal Building
1000 Independence Avenue, SW
Washington, DC 20585
202-586-8302
energy.gov/eere/office-energy-efficiency-renewable-energy
Facebook, Twitter, LinkedIn

David Danielson, Assistant Secretary
David Friedman, Principal Deputy Assis Secretary
Michael Budney, Director of Business Operations
John Lushetsky, Strategic Programs Director
Kathleen Hogan, Deputy Assistant Secretary

Leads the U.S. Department of Energy's efforts to develop and deliver market-driven solutions for energy-saving homes, buildings, and manufacturing;sustainable transportation; and renewable electricity generation.

1453 **One Sky**
One Sky
1635 Grandview Road
Gibsons, BC V0N 1V5
604-886-0508
www.onesky.ca

Michael S. Smithers, Executive Director
Lisa Gibson, Nigeria Integral Leadership Coord.
Gail Hochachka, Integral Program Coordinator

Explores and promotes practical solutions and appropriate technologies for our environmental. social and economic challenges in a global setting.
Founded in 2000

1454 **Pellet Fuels Institute**
1901 North Moore St
Suite 600
Arlington, VA 22209
703-522-6778; Fax: 703-522-0548
hedrick@pelletheat.org
www.pelletheat.org
Facebook, Twitter, LinkedIn

Stephen Faehner, Chairman
Jennifer Hedrick, Executive Director
Andrew Estep, Association Executive
John Crouch, Director of Public Affairs
Chris Amey, Vice Chairman

Promotes energy independence throught the effiecient use of clean, renewable, densified biomass fuel.
Founded in 1985

1455 **Portable Rechargeable Battery Association**
1776 K Street
4th Floor
Washington, DC 20006
202-719-4978
www.prba.org

Charlie Monahan, Chairman
Stephen P. Victor, President & COO
Chris Carlson, Vice President of Logistics
Andrew J. Sirjord, Vice President
Mark HickoK, Director

A nonprofit trade association that develops plans for workable battery recycling programs to be used industry wide and that serves as the voice of the Rechargeable Power Industry, representing its members on legislative, regulatory

and standards issues at the state, federal and international level.
Founded in 1991

1456 **Renewable Energy Markets Association (REMA)**
1211 Connecticut Ave NW
Suite 650
Washington, DC 20036-2701

202-640-6597; Fax: 202-223-5537
info@renewablemarketers.org
www.renewablemarketers.org
Facebook, Twitter

Richard Anderson, President
Ian McGowan, Vice President
Patrick Serfass, General Manager
Joel Stronberg, Director - Policy and Gov. Affairs
Kevin Maddaford, Treasurer

A nonprofit association dedicated to maintaining and growing strong markets for renewable energy in the United States. Representing organizations that sell, purchase, or promote renewable energy products.

1457 **Renewable Energy and Efficiency Business Association, Inc.**
1245 Farmington Avenue
Suite 354
West Hartford, CT 06107

860-338-3728
pmichaud@murthalaw.com
www.reeba.org

Jim Daylor, Chairman & Treasurer
Mitchell Wurmbrand, Secretary
Paul Michaud, Esq., Executive Director & Founder
Kathryn Dube, Operations & Membership Director

The mission of the business association is to support the renewable energy industry by promoting energy efficiency and offering legislative advocacy, collaboration, networking opportunities, and more. Members include renewable energy developers, energy services companies, and municipalities with an interest in energy technology.
100+ Members
Founded in 2010

1458 **Renewable Fuels Association (RFA)**
425 Third Street SW
Suite 1150
Washington, DC 20024

202-289-3835; Fax: 202-289-7519
www.ethanolrfa.org
Facebook, Twitter, LinkedIn, YouTube, Google+, Instagram

Randall Doyal, RFA Chairman
Bob Dinneen, President & CEO
Kelly Davis, Director of Regulatory Affairs
Samantha Slater, Vice President, Government Affairs
Tony Jackson, Communications Director

The national trade association for the US ethanol industry promoting policies, regulations and research and development initiatives that will lead to the increased production and use of fuel ethanol. Membership includes a broad cross-section of businesses, individuals and organizations dedicated to the expansion of the US fuel ethanol industry.
181 Members
Founded in 1981

1459 **Rocky Mountain Institute**
1820 Folsom Street
Boulder, CO 80302

303-245-1003
www.rmi.org
Facebook, Twitter, YouTube

Amory B. Lovins, Chief Scientist/Chair Emeritus
Marty Pickett, JD, Managing Director
Jules Kortenhorst, Chief Executive Officer
Robert Hutchinson, Senior Fellow
Kathy Wight, Executive Assistant

Emphasizes integrative design, advanced technologies working with the private sector as well as civil society and government to drive the transition from coal and oil to efficiency and renewables.
Founded in 1982

1460 **Solar Electric Light Fund**
1612 K Street NW
Suite 300
Washington, DC 20006

202-234-7265
info@self.org
self.org
Facebook, Twitter, YouTube

Robert A. Freling, Executive Director
Jeff Lahl, Project Director
John Alejandro, Communications Director
Darren Anderson, Project Manager
Lisa Esler, Finance Director

Designs and implements solar energy solutions to assist people living in energy poverty with their economic, educational, health care, and agricultural development.
Founded in 1990

1461 **Solar Electric Power Association**
1220 19th Street, NW,
Suite 800
Washington, DC 20036-2405

202-857-0898
www.solarelectricpower.org
Facebook, Twitter, LinkedIn, YouTube

Steve Malnight, Chair
Joseph Forline, Chair Elect
Julia Hamm, President & CEO
John Hewa, Secretary
Ervan Hancock, Treasurer

An educational nonprofit association dedicated to advancing utilityintegration of solar through collaborative solutions, objecive information and shared benefits to the utility, its customers, and the public good.
Founded in 1992

1462 **Solar Energy Industries Association**
600 14th Street NW
Suite 400
Washington, DC 20005

202-682-0556
info@seia.org
www.seia.org
Facebook, Twitter, LinkedIn, YouTube

Abigail Ross Hopper, President & CEO

Works with its member companies to make solar a mainstream and significant energy source by expanding markets, removing market barriers, strenghtening the industry and educating the public on the benefits of solar energy.
1000 Members

1463 **Solar Energy International**
39845 Mathews Lane
Paonia, CO 81428

970-527-7657
www.solarenergy.org
Facebook, Twitter, LinkedIn, YouTube

Ed Marston, Chairperson
Sarah Bishop, President

A nonprofit educational organization that provides industry-leadingtechnical training and expertise in renewable energy to empower people, communities, and businesses worldwide.
Founded in 1991

1464 **Solar Living Institute**
PO Box 836
13771 S. Hwy 101
Hopland, CA 95449

707-472-2450; Fax: 707-472-2498
sli@solarliving.org
solarliving.org
Facebook, Twitter, LinkedIn, YouTube

John Schaeffer, Founder/Board President
Brad Elliott, Staff
Shaylene Marino, Staff

A nonprofit solar training and sustainability organization. Mission is to promote sustainable living through inspirational environmental education.
Founded in 1998

1465 **The Solar Foundation**
1717 Pennsylvania Ave NW
Suite 750
Washington, DC 20006

202-469-3750
info@solarfound.org
www.thesolarfoundation.org
Facebook, Twitter, LinkedIn

Andrea Luecke, President & Executive Director
Ed Gilliland, Senior Director

Nonprofit committed to the advancement of solar technology.
Founded in 1977

1466 **The Solutions Project**

info@thesolutionsproject.org
thesolutionsproject.org
Facebook, Twitter, Instagram, YouTube

Sarah Shanley Hope, Executive Director
Stacey Heras, Operations Manager
Rudi Navarra, Program Officer

Organization committed to accelerating the transition to renewable energy use in the United States.
Founded in 2011

1467 **The Sustainable Biodiesel Alliance**
P.O. Box 1677
Kahului, HI 96732

512-410-7841; Fax: 512-410-7841
test.sustainablebiodieselalliance.com/SBA/
Facebook, Twitter

Kelly King, Chair
Annie Nelson, Vice-Chair
Mike Nasi, Treasurer
Ed Zwick, Secretary

An organization founded to support and encourage sustainable production and use of the renewable fuel biodiesel. Its primary mission is the completion of an independent sustainability certification system for U.S. Biodiesel Feedstock.
Founded in 2006

1468 **UNEP SEF Alliance**
Clean Energy Group

50 State St.
Suite 1
Montpelier, VT 05602

802-223-2554; Fax: 802-223-4967
RTyler@cleanegroup.org

The only convening body in the international system for public finance agencies in the clean energy sector. Members are visionary organizations from various countries pushing the forefront of how to do public finance for clean energy.

1469 **US Renewable Energy Association**
PO Box 0550
Lexington, MI 48450

810-359-2250
support@usrea.org
www.usrea.org
Facebook, Twitter, Google+, YouTube

Gerry Zack, President & CEO
Vivian Cywink, Vice President/Managing Director

A volunteer renewable energy advocacy group working to educate and promote advanced technologies in the R.E. industry.

1470 **United States Clean Heat & Power Association**
1875 Connecticut Ave. NW
10th Floor
Washington, DC 20009

202-888-0708
www.chpassociation.org
Facebook, Twitter, Rss Feeds

Chrissy Borskey, Chair
Dale Louda, Executive Director
Debbie Chance, Vice Chair
Jim Kerrigan, Secretary
Paul Lemar, Treasurer

Providing superior advocacy, networking, education and market information to companies in the business of clean, local energy generation. Documents the benefits of clean heat and power to the public and to decision-makers. Also participates in federal agency programs to promote clean distributed energy.
Founded in 1999

1471 **United States Energy Association**
1300 Pennsylvania Ave NW
Suite 550
Washington, DC 20004

202-312-1230; Fax: 202-682-1682
reply@usea.org
www.usea.org
Twitter

Barry K Worthington, Executive Director
Brian Kearns, Chief Financial Officer
Will Polen, Senior Director

U.S. member of World Energy Council represents broad interests of the U.S. energy sector.

1472 **Wind Energy Foundation**
1501 M Street NW
Suite 900
Washington, DC 20005

202-383-2500; Fax: 202-383-2505
windenergyfoundation.org
Facebook, Twitter, LinkedIn

John Kostyack, Executive Director
Kevin O'Rourke, Director, Public Affairs

Nonprofit raises public awareness of clean, domestic wind power.

1473 **Women of Renewable Industries and Sustainable Energy**
155 Water St
Brooklyn, NY 11201

718-260-9550
info@wrisenergy.org
wrisenergy.org
Facebook, Twitter, LinkedIn, Instagram

Kristen Graf, Executive Director
E'Lon Hall, Operations Manager

Nonprofit dedicated to building a diverse workforce in the renewable energy economy.
Founded in 2005

1474 **Women's Council on Energy and the Environment**
816 Connecticut Ave NW
Suite 200
Washington, DC 20006

202-997-4512; Fax: 202-478-2098
www.wcee.org
Facebook, Twitter, LinkedIn

Robin Cantor, President
Mary Brosnan-Sell, Vice President
Joyce Chandran, Executive Director
Barbara Tyran, Treasurer
Alice Grabowski, Secretary

Supports women involved in the environmental community with education, research, new trend information and several publications.

1475 **World Resources Institute(WRI)**
10 G Street NE
Suite 800
Washington, DC 20002

202-729-7600; Fax: 202-729-7686
cpotochny@gmail.com
www.wri.org
Facebook, Twitter, LinkedIn, YouTube, RSS

James A. Harmon, Chair
Andrew Steer, President & CEO
Steve Barker, CFO/Chief Administrative Officer
Manish Bapna, EVP/Managing Director
Lawrence MacDonald, VP, Communications

WRI takes research and puts ideas into action, working globally with governments, business and civil society to build transformative solutions that protect the earth and improve people's lives.
Founded in 1982

Newsletters

1476 **BTEC Newsletter**
Biomass Thermal Energy Council
1211 Connecticut Avenue NW
Suite 600
Washington, DC 20036-2701

202-596-3974; Fax: 202-223-5537
info@biomassthermal.org
www.biomassthermal.org
Facebook, Twitter

Joseph Seymour, Executive Director
Charlie Niebling, Chairman
T.J. Morice, Vice-Chairman
Jon Strimling, Secretary
Bob Sourek, Treasurer

Provides member news, industry updates, upcoming events, and breaking BTEC news.
Frequency: Monthly
Founded in 2009

1477 **Biogas News**
American Biogas Council
1211 Connecticut Ave NW
Suite 600
Washington, DC 20036-2701

202-596-3974; Fax: 202-223-5537
info@americanbiogascouncil.org
www.americanbiogascouncil.org

Paul Greene, Chairman
Norma McDonald, Vice-Chair
Melissa VanOrnum, Treasurer
Nora Goldstein, Secretary

Members only publication includes everything from legislative updates to industry news and funding opportunities.
Frequency: Bi-Weekly

1478 **Clean Energy Direct**
IHS, Inc.

855-417-4155
energy@omeda.com
www.theenergydaily.com
RSS

George Lobsenz, Executive Editor
Sabrina Ousmaal, Associate Publisher
Eric Lindeman, Contributing Editor

Get analysis of regulation, technology and industry news of renewables, top news in the clean energy industry as well as access to clean energy articles and archives.
Cost: $695.00
Frequency: Weekly

1479 **Climate Change News**
Environmental and Energy Study Institute
1112 16th Street, NW
Suite 300
Washington, DC 20036-4819

202-628-1400; Fax: 202-204-5244
cwerner@eesi.org
www.eesi.org
Facebook, Twitter, YouTube

Carol Werner, Executive Director
Jared Blum, Chair
Shelley Fidler, Treasurer
Richard L. Ottinger, Chair Emeritus

Recounts the top climate science, business, and politics stories of the week and includes a list of upcoming events and pending federal legislation.
Frequency: Weekly
Founded in 1984

1480 **Coal Outlook**
Pasha Publications
1600 Wilson Boulevard
Suite 600
Arlington, VA 22209-2509

703-528-1244
800-424-2908; Fax: 703-528-1253

Harry Baisden, Group Publisher
Michael Hopps, Editor
Kathy Thorne, Circulation Manager

Primary strategic information source that keeps coal marketing executives and utilities up-to-date on who's getting coal contracts and at what price.
Cost: $795.00
Frequency: Weekly

1481 **Coal Week International**
McGraw Hill
2 Penn Plz
Suite 25
New York, NY 10121-0101

212-904-2000
800-752-8878; Fax: 720-548-5701
support@platts.com
www.mcgraw-hill.com

Peter C Davis, President
David Stellfox, Editor

Harry Sachinis, CEO
Larry Barth, Marketing Manager

A market management intelligence service for executives concerned with world trade metallurgical and steam coal.
Cost: $987.00
8 Pages
Frequency: Weekly
Founded in 1888

1482 **Coal and Synfuels Technology**
Pasha Publications
1600 Wilson Boulevard
Suite 600
Arlington, VA 22209-2510

703-528-1244
800-424-2908; Fax: 703-528-1253

Harry Baisden, Group Publisher
Michael Hopps, Editor

Reports on the US and international advances in clean coal technologies, synthetic fuels and clean air issues.
Cost: $790.00
Frequency: Weekly
Founded in 1985

1483 **Connecting to the Grid**
Interstate Renewable Energy Council
PO Box 1156
Latham, NY 12110-1156

518-458-6059
info@irecusa.org
www.irecusa.org

Laurel Varnado, Editor
Ken Jurman, Chair
David Warner, Vice Chair
Jane Pulaski, Secretary
Jennifer Szaro, Treasurer

Focusing on the latest news on interconnection and net metering in the US.
Frequency: Monthly

1484 **Council on Women in Energy and Environmental Leadership Newsletter**
Association of Energy Engineers
3168 Mercer University Drive
Atlanta, GA 30341

770-447-5083
www.aeecenter.org
Facebook, Twitter, LinkedIn, YouTube

Albert Thumann, Executive Director

Addressing the high cost of energy, present and future sources of energy, and the impact of energy on the environment.
17500 Members
Founded in 1977

1485 **EESI Update**
Environmental and Energy Study Institute
1112 16th Street, NW
Suite 300
Washington, DC 20036-4819

202-628-1400; Fax: 202-204-5244
cwerner@eesi.org
www.eesi.org
Facebook, Twitter, YouTube

Carol Werner, Executive Director
Jared Blum, Chair
Shelley Fidler, Treasurer
Richard L. Ottinger, Chair Emeritus

Updating supporters about the current work of EESI.
Frequency: 3x Yearly
Founded in 1984

1486 **Electric Auto Association News**
Electric Auto Association
PO Box 639
Los Altos, CA 94024-0639

831-688-8669; Fax: 831-688-8669
freund.ron@gmail.com
www.electricauto.org
Facebook, Twitter, LinkedIn

Ron Freund, Chairman
Guy Hall, Secretary
Gint Federas, Treasurer
Will Beckett, Membership
Carl Vogel, Board Member

News about current events relevant to those interested in promoting the use of electric vehicles.
Founded in 1967

1487 **Energy Insight**
Association of Energy Engineers
3168 Mercer University Drive
Atlanta, GA 30341

770-447-5083
www.aeecenter.org
Facebook, Twitter, YouTube

Albert Thumann, Executive Director

Written by, about and for the AEE member. Electronic publication includes information on AEE news, officers, award programs, nominations, certification, chapter news, operations report, presidents' message, study missions, upcoming events, and more.
Frequency: Tri-Annually
Founded in 1977
Mailing list available for rent

1488 **GRC Bulletin**
Geothermal Resources Council
20001 Second Street
Suite 5
Davis, CA 95618-5476

530-758-2360; Fax: 530-758-2839
grc@geothermal.org
www.geothermal.org
Facebook, Twitter, LinkedIn, YouTube, Flickr

Curt Robinson, Ph.D, Executive Director

Features articles on technical topics and geothermal development issues, as well as commentaries and news briefs.
Frequency: 6x Yearly
Founded in 1970

1489 **Geothermal Energy Weekly**
Geothermal Energy Association
209 Pennsylvania Avenue SE
Washington, DC 20003

202-454-5241
jgreco@terra-genpower.com
www.geo-energy.org

Karl Gawell, Executive Director
Leslie Blodgett, Editor-in-Chief
Paul Thomsen, President
Jonathan M. Weisgall, Chairman

Electronic newsletter providing updates on the national, state, and international levels, and includes news from GEA member companies. Upcoming events, job opportunities, and Requests for Proposals are also found here.
Frequency: Weekly

1490 **NABCEP News**
56 Clifton Country Rd.
Suite 202
Clifton Park, NY 12065

800-654-0021; Fax: 518-899-1092
info@nabcep.org
www.nabcep.org

Ezra Auerbach, Executive Director
Don Warfield, Chair
Jane Weissman, Vice Chair
Les Nelson, Treasurer
Jeff Spies, Secretary

Newsletter from the North American Board of Certified Energy Practitioners featuring news, updates, technical issues and accomplishments of their certificants. Available electronically only.
Frequency: Bi-Monthly
Founded in 2000

1491 **NHA Today**
National Hydropower Association
25 Massachusetts Ave, NW
Suite 450
Washington, DC 20001

202-682-1700; Fax: 202-682-9478
help@hydro.org
www.hydro.org
Facebook, Twitter

Linda Church Ciocci, Executive Director
David Moller, President
James Crew, Treasurer
John Ragonese, Vice President
Tim Oakes, Secretary

Offers the latest information on regulatory and legislative policy, regional concerns, and issues on the horizon. Available electronically to members of NHA only.
Frequency: Bi-Weekly

1492 **OREC Newsletter**
Ocean Renewable Energy Coalition

301-869-3790
info@oceanrenewable.com

Sean O'Neill, President
Carolyn Elefant, General Counsel

Striving to keep members, legislators, regulators, the media and the public at large up to date with OREC's activities as well as ongoing developments in this emerging industry.
40+ Members
Frequency: Weekly
Founded in 2005

1493 **Pellet Fuels Institute**
Pellet Fuels Institute.
1901 North Moore Street
Suite 600
Arlington, VA 22209

703-522-6778; Fax: 703-522-0548
pfimail@pelletheat.org
www.pelletheat.org

Jennifer Hedrick, Executive Director
Jason Berthiaume, Membership/Gov't Affairs
John Crouch, Director of Public Affairs

Newsletter with industry news, updates published quarterly

1494 **REEBA Hot Topics newsletter**
Renewable Energy and Efficiency Business Assoc
1245 Farmington Avenue
Suite 354
West Hartford, CT 06107

860-338-3728
pmichaud@murthalaw.com
www.reeba.org

Jim Daylor, Chairman & Treasurer
Mitchell Wurmbrand, Secretary
Paul Michaud, Esq., Executive Director & Founder
Kathryn Dube, Operations & Membership Director

Newsletter exploring the subject of renewable energy trends, including industry updates affecting business for members of the Renewable Energy and Efficiency Business Association, Inc. (REEBA).
100+ Members
Founded in 2010

1495 **Resilient Power**
Clean Energy Group

50 State St
Suite 1
Montpelier, VT 05602

802-223-2554; Fax: 802-223-4967
info@cleanegroup.org
www.cleanegroup.org
Facebook, Twitter, LinkedIn

Seth Mullendore, Project Director

Monthly newsletter of the Resilient Power Project, an initiative to speed up the market development of clean energy solutions.

1496 **Small Wind Energy**
Interstate Renewable Energy Council
PO Box 1156
Latham, NY 12110-1156

518-458-6059
info@irecusa.org
www.irecusa.org

Larry Sherwood, Editor
Ken Jurman, Chair
David Warner, Vice Chair
Jane Pulaski, Secretary
Jennifer Szaro, Treasurer

Featuring updates and news about small wind energy issues.
Frequency: Quarterly

1497 **Sun Times**
Alternative Energy Resources Organization
432 N. Last Chance Gulch
Helena, MT 59601

406-443-7272; Fax: 406-442-9120
aero@aeromt.org
www.aeromt.org
Facebook, Twitter, Myspace

Bryan von Lossberg, Executive Director

Stay up to date on AERO news and events.
Frequency: Monthly
Founded in 1974

1498 **Sustainable Bioenergy, Farms, and Forests**
Environmental and Energy Study Institute
1112 16th Street, NW
Suite 300
Washington, DC 20036-4819

202-628-1400; Fax: 202-204-5244
cwerner@eesi.org
www.eesi.org
Facebook, Twitter, YouTube

Carol Werner, Executive Director
Jared Blum, Chair
Shelley Fidler, Treasurer
Richard L. Ottinger, Chair Emeritus

A look at sustainable bioenergy, farm, and forest policy issues.
Frequency: Weekly
Founded in 1984

1499 **The Biodiesel Bulletin**
National Biodiesel Board
605 Clark Avenue
PO Box 104898
Jefferson City, MO 65110-4898

573-635-3893
800-841-5849; Fax: 573-635-7913
info@biodiesel.org
www.biodiesel.org
Facebook, Twitter, YouTube

Chad Stone, Chairman
Mike Rath, Vice Chairman
Rob Shaffer, 2nd Vice Chairman
Ryan Pederson, Treasurer
Troy Alberts, Secretary

Electronic publication keeping members up to date on the biodiesel industry and technology.
Frequency: Monthly
Mailing list available for rent

1500 **The Energy Daily**
IHS, Inc.

855-417-4155
energy@omeda.com
www.theenergydaily.com

George Lobsenz, Executive Editor
Sabrinal Ousmaal, Associate Publisher
Erica Lengermann, Manager, Sales

Keeping readers at the forefront of all major developments in the energy industry. Through in-depth analysis of issues, cutting-edge reporting and unbiased journalism, The Energy Daily continues to deliver the news readers need for business success.
Cost: $2497.00
Frequency: Daily

1501 **The Energy Roundup**
IHS, Inc.

855-417-4155
energy@omeda.com
www.theenergydaily.com

George Lobsenz, Executive Editor
Sabrinal Ousmaal, Associate Publisher
Erica Lengermann, Manager, Sales

The most important developing stories delivered weekly.
Frequency: Weekly

1502 **The IREC Report**
Interstate Renewable Energy Council
PO Box 1156
Latham, NY 12110-1156

518-458-6059
info@irecusa.org
www.irecusa.org

Jane Pulaski, Editor
Ken Jurman, Chair
David Warner, Vice Chair
Jane Pulaski, Secretary
Jennifer Szaro, Treasurer

A monthly recap of the latest news about IREC's programs, policies and best practices in renewable energy.
Frequency: Monthly

1503 **The ISPQ Insider**
Interstate Renewable Energy Council
PO Box 1156
Latham, NY 12110-1156

518-458-6059
info@irecusa.org
www.irecusa.org

Jane Pulaski, Editor
Ken Jurman, Chair
David Warner, Vice Chair
Jane Pulaski, Secretary
Jennifer Szaro, Treasurer

A monthly recap of the latest news, policies and best practices from the ISPQ credentialing program for renewable energy, weatherization and the energy retrofit sector.
Frequency: Monthly

1504 **The SITN Quarterly**
Interstate Renewable Energy Council
PO Box 1156
Latham, NY 12110-1156

518-458-6059
info@irecusa.org
www.irecusa.org

Jane Pulaski, Editor
Ken Jurman, Chair
David Warner, Vice Chair
Jane Pulaski, Secretary
Jennifer Szaro, Treasurer

Summary of the latest news, policies and best practices from the Solar Instructor Training Network.
Frequency: Quarterly

1505 **Utility Reporter: Fuels, Energy and Power**
InfoTeam
PO Box 15640
Plantation, FL 33318-5640

954-473-9560; Fax: 954-473-0544

Randy M Allen CPA, Editor

Focuses on activities involving: power generation, combustion, delivery and transmission; alternative energy devices and systems; heat transfer, storage and utilization; and myriad of related topics.
Cost: $289.00
20 Pages
Frequency: Monthly
ISBN: 0-890298-4 -
Printed in one color on matte stock

Magazines & Journals

1506 **Biodiesel Magazine**
BBI International
308 2nd Avenue North
Suite 304
Grand Forks, ND 58203

866-746-8385; Fax: 701-746-5367
service@bbiinternational.com
www.biodieselmagazine.com
Twitter, YouTube

Trade journal dedicated to objective, independent coverage of biodiesel news, events and information relevant to the global industry. With editorial focus on US and international methyl ester manufacturing, trade, distribution and markets, Biodiesel Magazine also provides valuable insight into feedstock and market share competition from the non-ester renewable diesel sector.
Frequency: Monthly

1507 **Biomass Power & Thermal**
Biomass Thermal Energy Council
1211 Connecticut Avenue NW
Suite 600
Washington, DC 20036-2701

202-596-3974; Fax: 202-223-5537
info@biomassthermal.org
www.biomassthermal.org
Facebook, Twitter

Joseph Seymour, Executive Director
Charlie Niebling, Chairman
T.J. Morice, Vice-Chairman
Jon Strimling, Secretary
Bob Sourek, Treasurer

Tailored for industry professionals engaged in utilizing biomass for the generation of electricity, thermal energy, or both (CHP). Maintains a core editorial focus on biomass logistics; generating, cultivating, collecting, transporting, processing, marketing, procuring and utilizing sustainable biomass for power and heat.
Frequency: Monthly
Founded in 2009

1508 **Distributed Generation & Alternative Energy Journal**
Association of Energy Engineers
3168 Mercer University Drive
Atlanta, GA 30341

770-447-5083
www.aeecenter.org
Facebook, Twitter

Albert Thumann, Executive Director
Jorge B. Wong, Ph.D, Editor-in-Chief

An authoritative publication which provides readers with detailed information on the latest innovations and developments in the distrib-

uted generation and related alternative energy fields.
17500 Members
Frequency: Quarterly
Founded in 1977

1509 **Energy Law Journal**
Federal Energy Bar Association
1990 M St Nw
Suite 350
Washington, DC 20036-3429
202-223-5625; Fax: 202-833-5596
admin@eba-net.org
www.eba-net.org
Lorna Wilson, Administrator
Clinton A. Vince, Editor-in-Chief
Lawyers and consultants engaged in energy and public utility law.
Cost: $35.00
Frequency: Monthly
Circulation: 2600
ISSN: 0270-9163
Founded in 1946
Printed in 2 colors on matte stock

1510 **Geo Outlook**
International Ground Source Heat Pump Association
1201 S Innovation Way
Suite 400
Stillwater, OK 74074
405-744-5175
800-626-4747; Fax: 405-744-5283
igshpa@okstate.edu
www.igshpa.okstate.edu
Jim Bose, Ph.D, Executive Director
Shelly Fitzpatrick, Conference & Membership Coordinator
John Turley, Chairman
Jack Henrich, Vice Chairman
The official publication of the geoexchange industry.
Frequency: Quarterly
Circulation: 50000

1511 **Home Power Magazine**
312 N. Main Street
Phoenix, OR 97535
541-512-0201
800-707-6585
www.homepower.com
Facebook, Twitter
Claire Anderson, Associate Editor
For renewable energy and sustainable living enthusiasts- homeowners and industry professionals alike. Specializing in hands-on, practical information about RE technologies, and presenting technical material in an easy-to-use format.
Frequency: Bi-Monthly

1512 **IEEE Power and Energy Magazine**
IEEE Power Electronics Society
445 Hoes Lane
Piscataway, NJ 08854
732-981-0061; Fax: 732-981-9667
pels-staff@ieee.org
www.ieee-pels.org
Mel Olken, Editor
Susan Schneiderman, Business Development
Dedicated to disseminating information on all matters of interest to electric power engineers and other professionals involved in the electric power industry. Feature articles focus on advanced concepts, technologies, and practices associated with all aspects of electric power from a technical perspective in synergy with nontechnical areas such as business, environmental, and social concerns.
Cost: $260.00
82 Pages
Frequency: Monthly
Circulation: 23000
ISSN: 1540-7977
Founded in 2003
Mailing list available for rent
Printed in on glossy stock

1513 **International Journal of Energy Management**
Association of Energy Engineers
3168 Mercer University Drive
Atlanta, GA 30341
770-447-5083
www.aeecenter.org
Facebook, Twitter
Albert Thumann, Executive Director
Steven Marker, Editor
Exclusively written for engineers, energy managers, facility managers, utility professionals, VP's of operations, governmental energy managers and plant engineers involved in the design and application of energy management and facility improvement technologies.
15M Members
Frequency: Monthly
Founded in 1904

1514 **Renewables Global Status Report**
REN21
REN21 Secretariat c/o UNEP
15, Rue de Milan 75441
Paris, France CEDEX 09
+33 1 44 3714 5090
secretariat@ren21.net
www.ren21.net
Mohamed El-Ashry, Chair-UN Foundation
Michael Eckhart, VP- Citygroup
Kevin Nassiep, VP
Christine Lins, Executive Secretary
The Global Status Report(GSR) is the collaborative effort of over 400 authors, contributors and reviewers and is today the most frequently referenced report on renewable energy market, industry and policy trends. it provides testimony of the undeterred growth of electricity. heat and fuel production capacities from renewable energy sources including solar PV, wind power, solar hot water/heating, biofuels, hydropower and geothermal.

1515 **Solar Energy**
Elsevier Science
655 Avenue of the Americas
PO Box 945
New York, NY 10010-5107
212-633-3800; Fax: 212-633-3850
www.elsevier.com
Young Suk Chi, Manager
Devoted exclusively to the science and technology of solar energy applications. Presents information not previously published in journals on any aspect of solar energy research, development, application, measurement or policy.
Frequency: Monthly
Circulation: 6400

1516 **Solar Today**
American Solar Energy Society
2525 Arapahoe Ave
Suite E4-253
Boulder, CO 80302
303-443-3130; Fax: 303-443-3212
www.ases.org
Facebook, Twitter
With the renewable energy industry changing at an unprecedented pace, Solar Today helps readers understand the changes, where the industry is headed, and how it's affecting the country.
Frequency: 6 issues/yr

1517 **Solar@Work**
American Solar Energy Society
2525 Arapahoe Ave
Suite E4-253
Boulder, CO 80302
303-443-3130; Fax: 303-443-3212
www.ases.org
Facebook, Twitter
Bi-weekly collection of stories from the solar energy industry.
Frequency: Bi-weekly

1518 **Strategic Planning for Energy and the Environment**
Association of Energy Engineers
3168 Mercer University Drive
Atlanta, GA 30341
770-447-5083
www.aeecenter.org
Facebook, Twitter
Albert Thumann, Executive Director
Stephen Roosa, Editor
Concentrates on the background, new developments and policy issues which impact corporate planning for energy savings, operational efficiency, and environmental concerns.
17500 Members
Frequency: Quarterly
Founded in 1977

1519 **The Ally**
BlueGreen Alliance
1020 19th Street NW
Suite 600
Washington, DC 20036
202-706-6910
www.bluegreenalliance.org
Facebook, Twitter, flickr, YouTube
David Foster, Executive Director
A biweekly update providing reports, letters, press releases and other publications along with clean energy industry news.

1520 **The Energy Journal**
International Association for Energy Economics
28790 Chagrin Blvd
Suite 350
Cleveland, OH 44122-4642
216-464-5365; Fax: 216-464-2737
www.iaee.org
Facebook, LinkedIn
Mine Yucel, President
Lars Bergman, President-Elect
David L. Williams, Executive Director
Promotes the advancement and dissemination of new knowledge concerning energy and related topics. Publishing a blend of theoretical, empirical and policy related papers in energy economics.
3400 Members
Founded in 1977

Trade Shows

1521 **ACORE Finance West**
American Council On Renewable Energy
1600 K Street NW
Suite 650
Washington, DC 20006
202-393-0001
info@acore.org
acorefinancewest.com
Facebook, Twitter, LinkedIn, Flickr
Assesses developments and opportunities in renewable energy finance in the Western U.S.

1522 **ACORE National Renewable Energy Policy Forum**
American Council On Renewable Energy

1600 K Street NW
Suite 650
Washington, DC 20006

202-393-0001
info@acore.org
www.acorepolicyforum.org
Facebook, Twitter, LinkedIn, Flickr

Cindi Eck, Director, Leadership Programs
Tracy Aliaga, Corporate Relations Associate
Anna Hahnemann, Communications Manager

Industry leaders and elected officials discuss challenges and opportunities in renewable energy policy.

1523 **AERO Annual Meeting**
Alternative Energy Resources Organization
432 N. Last Chance Gulch
Helena, MT 59601

406-443-7272; Fax: 406-442-9120
aero@aeromt.org
www.aeromt.org
Facebook, Twitter, Myspace

Bryan von Lossberg, Executive Director

Sustainability Begins at Home.
Frequency: Annual/ October
Founded in 1974

1524 **ASES Solar Conference**
American Solar Energy Society
2525 Arapahoe Ave
Ste E4-253
Boulder, CO 80302

303-443-3130; Fax: 303-443-3212
info@ases.org
www.ases.org/conference
Facebook, Twitter, LinkedIn

America's premier educational event for solar energy professionals. The conference introduces you to the leaders, innovators and technologies moving the industry forward.

1525 **AWEA CLEANPOWER**
American Wind Energy Association
1501 M Street NW
Suite 900
Washington, DC 20005

202-383-2500
conference@awea.org
engage.awea.org/events
Facebook, Twitter, LinkedIn

Tom Kiernan, Chief Executive Officer
Mark Bakke, Manager, Member Relations/Exhibits

Bringing together attendees and exhibitors from every aspect of the industry. Exhibitors display the latest industry products and services from manufacturing leaders, component suppliers, and other wind energy organizations. This conference combines education, exhibition, and networking creating a perfect venue for business development.
7000 Attendees
Frequency: Annual/June

1526 **AWEA Offshore WINDPOWER**
American Wind Energy Association
1501 M Street NW
Suite 900
Washington, DC 20005

202-383-2500
engage.awea.org/events
Facebook, Twitter, LinkedIn, YouTube, Instagram

Tom Kiernan, Chief Executive Officer
Mark Bakke, Manager, Member Relations/Exhibits

Brings together exhibitors and attendees from all over the world who are interested in becoming players in this new and highly promising market.
Frequency: Annual/October

1527 **Annual Algae Biomass Summit**
Biomass Power Association
100 Middle St.
PO Box 9729
Portland, ME 04104-9729

703-889-8504
www.usabiomass.org

Bob Cleaves, President & CEO
Gary Melow, State Projects Coordinator

This dynamic event unites industry professionals from all sectors of the world's algae utilization industries including, but not limited to; financing, algal ecology, genetic systems, carbon partitioning, engineering & analysis, biofuels, animal feeds, fertilizers, bioplastics, supplements and foods.
80 Members
Frequency: Annual/October

1528 **Annual National Ethanol Conference**
Renewable Fuels Association
425 Third Street SW
Suite 1150
Washington, DC 20024

202-289-3835; Fax: 202-289-7519
necregistration@bbiinternational.com
www.ethanolrfa.org
Facebook, Twitter, YouTube, Flickr

Bob Dinneen, President & CEO
Christina Martin, Executive Vice President
Alex Obuchowski, CFO

Recongnized as the preeminent conference for delivering accurate, timely information on marketing, legislative and regulatory issues facing the ethanol industry. Meet and interact with key stakeholders and take part in shaping the future of the ethanol industry.
1250+ Attendees
Frequency: Annual/February
Founded in 1981

1529 **Annual North American Waste-to-Energy Conference**
Solid Waste Association of North America - SWANA

800-GOS-WANA; Fax: 301-589-7068
www.nawtec.org

Co-sponsored by ERC, ASME and SWANA, in partnership with WTERT, the conference and trade show focuses on municipal waste-to-energy operational issues and policy, technology and research initiatives.

1530 **Annual Renewable Energy Technology Conference & Exhibition (RETECH)**
American Council on Renewable Energy
1600 K Street NW
Suite 700
Washington, DC 20006

202-393-0001
Facebook, Twitter, LinkedIn, YouTube

Dennis V. McGinn, President

Conference sessions deliver unparalleled educational content including business development opportunities, topical professional development, current trends, the newest technologies and important up-to-date information on the changing legislative and regulatory landscapes. Exhibition offers the best opportunity to meet, network and connect with companies and organizations in the renewable energy industry.
3000+ Attendees
Frequency: Annual/October
Founded in 2001

1531 **Bioenergy Fuels & Products Conference & Expo**
Biomass Thermal Energy Council
1211 Connecticut Avenue NW
Suite 600
Washington, DC 20036-2701

202-596-3974; Fax: 202-223-5537
info@biomassthermal.org
www.biomassthermal.org
Facebook, Twitter

Joseph Seymour, Executive Director
Charlie Niebling, Chairman
T.J. Morice, Vice-Chairman
Jon Strimling, Secretary
Bob Sourek, Treasurer

Speakers and moderators who will address a range of topics including raw material, product and market developments and bio-process technologies.
Frequency: Annual/March
Founded in 2009

1532 **Biomass Thermal DC Summit**
Biomass Thermal Energy Council
1211 Connecticut Avenue NW
Suite 600
Washington, DC 20036-2701

202-596-3974; Fax: 202-223-5537
info@biomassthermal.org
www.biomassthermal.org
Facebook, Twitter

Joseph Seymour, Executive Director
Charlie Niebling, Chairman
T.J. Morice, Vice-Chairman
Jon Strimling, Secretary
Bob Sourek, Treasurer

Summit participants engage policy makers and renewable energy - related groups on the substantial benefits of biomass thermal energy use; increased rural economic activity, energy independence, healthier forests, and effective tax policy.
Frequency: Annual/November
Founded in 2009

1533 **Building Energy**
Northeast Sustainable Energy Association
50 Miles St
Greenfield, MA 01301-3255

413-774-6051; Fax: 413-774-6053
nesea@nesea.org
www.nesea.org
Facebook, Twitter, LinkedIn

David Barclay, Executive Director
Sonia Hamel, Vice Chair
Daniel Sagan, Secretary
Michael Skelly, Treasurer

Oldest and largest regional renewable energy event in the country, known for showcasing next-generation thinkers and game-changing ideas.
1802 Members
Founded in 1974
Mailing list available for rent

1534 **Geothermal Energy Expo**
Geothermal Energy Association
209 Pennsylvania Avenue SE
Washington, DC 20003

202-454-5261; Fax: 202-454-5265
jgreco@terra-genpower.com
www.geo-energy.org

Karl Gawell, Executive Director
Leslie Blodgett, Editor-in-Chief
Paul Thomsen, President
Jonathan M. Weisgall, Chairman
Kathy Kent, Director of Events

The world's largest gathering of vendors providing support for geothermal resource exploration, characterization, development, production and management. Provides a unique opportunity for exhibitors to showcase their projects,

equipment, services and state of the art technology to the geothermal community.
Frequency: Annual/October

1535 **GlobalCon Conference & Expo**
Biomass Thermal Energy Council
1211 Connecticut Avenue NW
Suite 600
Washington, DC 20036-2701
202-596-3974; Fax: 202-223-5537
info@biomassthermal.org
www.biomassthermal.org
Facebook, Twitter
Joseph Seymour, Executive Director
Charlie Niebling, Chairman
Dan Arnett, Vice-Chairman
John Ackerly, Secretary
Mike Jostrom, Treasurer
Designed specifically to facilitate those seeking to expand their knowledge of fast-moving developments in the energy field, explore promising new technologies, compare energy supply options, and learn about innovative and cost-conscious project implementation strategies.
Frequency: Annual/March
Founded in 2009

1536 **IGSHPA Conference & Expo**
International Ground Source Heat Pump Association
1201 S Innovation Way
Suite 400
Stillwater, OK 74074
405-744-5175
800-626-4747; Fax: 405-744-5283
igshpa@okstate.edu
www.igshpa.okstate.edu
Jim Bose, Ph.D, Executive Director
Shelly Fitzpatrick, Conference & Membership Coordinator
Jack Henrich, Chairman
Greg Wells, Vice Chairman
Jim Bose, Executive Director
The largest technical conference in the US dedicated solely to geothermal. Conference features technical classes, which attract many industry newcomers each year.
Frequency: Annual/October

1537 **International Bioenergy and Bioproducts Conference (IBBC)**
Technical Association of the Pulp & Paper Industry
15 Technology Parkway S
Norcross, GA 30092
770-446-1400
800-322-8686; Fax: 770-446-6947
webmaster@tappi.org
www.tappi.org
Norman F. Marsolan, Chair
Thomas J. Garland, Vice Chair
Larry N. Montague, President & CEO
Focusing on technical advancements and commercialization of bioconversion technologies that leverage the forest products manufacturing infrastructure and will include technical presentations, expert panels, case studies, and reports from projects that address feedstock and harvesting improvements to increase yield and quality of biomass, and much more.
500 Attendees
Frequency: Annual/October

1538 **International Biomass Conference & Expo**
Biomass Thermal Energy Council
1211 Connecticut Avenue NW
Suite 600
Washington, DC 20036-2701
202-596-3974; Fax: 202-223-5537
info@biomassthermal.org
www.biomassthermal.org
Facebook, Twitter
Joseph Seymour, Executive Director
Charlie Niebling, Chairman
Dan Arnett, Vice-Chairman
John Ackerly, Secretary
Mike Jostrom, Treasurer
This dynamic event unites industry professionals from all sectors of the world's interconnected biomass utilization industries - biobased power, thermal energy, fuels and chemicals. Where future and existing producers of biobased power, fuels and thermal energy products go to network with waste generators and other industry suppliers and technology providers.
Frequency: Annual/April
Founded in 2009

1539 **International Topical Meeting on Advances in Reactor Physics**
555 N Kensington Ave
La Grange Park, IL 60526-5592
708-352-6611
800-323-3044; Fax: 708-352-0499
advertising@ans.org
www.ans.org
Facebook, Twitter, LinkedIn
Jack Tuohy, Executive Director
James S Tulenko, VP
William F Naughton, Treasurer
Advances in reactor physics being the main topic of discussion. Promoting the awareness and understanding of the application of nuclear science and technology.
10500 Members
Founded in 1954

1540 **NABCEP Continuing Education Conference**
NABCEP
56 Clifton Country Rd.
Suite 202
Clifton Park, NY 12065
800-654-0021; Fax: 518-899-1092
www.nabcep.org
Ezra Auerbach, Executive Director
Don Warfield, Chair
Jane Weissman, Vice Chair
Les Nelson, Treasurer
Jeff Spies, Secretary
The objective of this conference is to offer NABCEP certified installers and technical sales professionals an opportunity that allows them to fulfill the majority of their CE requirements at a single event. In combination with manufacturer's training sessions, conference registrants will be able to attend workshops on the NEC, financial analysis, safety, and emerging fire codes.
Frequency: Annual/March
Founded in 2000

1541 **National Biodiesel Conference & Expo**
National Biodiesel Board
605 Clark Avenue
PO Box 104898
Jefferson City, MO 65110-4898
573-635-3893
800-841-5849; Fax: 573-635-7913
info@biodiesel.org
www.biodieselconference.org
Facebook, Twitter, YouTube
Chad Stone, Chairman
Mike Rath, Vice Chairman
Rob Shaffer, 2nd Vice Chairman
Ryan Pederson, Treasurer
Troy Alberts, Secretary
The only event that gathers biodiesel decision-makers from across the U.S. and the world. Opportunities abound for attendees and exhibitors to network connect and learn. Event explores the topics of governmental policy, technical issues and marketing trends in the biodiesel industry.
Frequency: Annual/January

1542 **National Hydropower Association Annual Conference**
National Hydropower Association
25 Massachusetts Ave, NW
Suite 450
Washington, DC 20001
202-682-1700; Fax: 202-682-9478
help@hydro.org
www.hydro.org
Facebook, Twitter
Linda Church Ciocci, Executive Director
David Moller, President
Eric Van Deuren, Treasurer
Cherise Oram, Vice President
Suzanne Grassell, Secretary
Program will provide a unique opportunity to hear first-hand from the Administration, Congress, federal regulators and resource agencies on the issues and policies that directly affect individual businesses and projects.
Frequency: Annual/April

1543 **Pellet Fuels Institute Annual Conference**
1901 North Moore Street
Suite 600
Arlington, VA 22209
703-522-6778; Fax: 703-522-0548
pfimail@pelletheat.org
www.pelletheat.org
Jennifer Hedrick, Executive Director
Jason Berthiaume, Membership/ Gov't Affairs Associate
John Crouch, Director of Public Affairs
Conference educates industry members on the latest information including new program development and what to expect in upcoming months. Speakers, roundtable panels, annual golf tournament and a beach bash.

1544 **REFF - Wall Street**
American Council On Renewable Energy
1600 K Street NW
Suite 650
Washington, DC 20006
202-393-0001
info@acore.org
www.reffwallstreet.com
Facebook, Twitter, LinkedIn
Renewable Energy Finance Forum - Wall Street assesses the current state of renewable energy finance.
500 Attendees

1545 **Renewable Energy Finance Forum (REFF) -Wall Street**
American Council on Renewable Energy
1600 K Street NW
Suite 700
Washington, DC 20006
202-393-0001
Facebook, Twitter, LinkedIn, YouTube
Dennis V. McGinn, President
Estelle Lloyd, Managing Editor & Co-Founder
Tom, Naylor, Ronan
Murphy Managing Editor
Bringing together the top leaders of the USA's renewable energy industry, drawing attendees from the entire value chain, including financiers, manufacturers and developers.
700 Attendees
Frequency: Annual/June
Founded in 2001

1546 **Renewable Energy Markets Conference**
Renewable Energy Markets Association
1211 Connecticut Ave NW
Suite 600
Washington, DC 20036-2701

202-640-6597; Fax: 202-223-5537
www.renewablemarketers.org
Facebook, Twitter

Richard Anderson, President
Ian McGowan, Vice President
Kevin Maddaford, Treasurer
Sarah Smith, Secretary
Josh Lieberman, General Manager

Bridging the interests of renewable energy generators, sellers, and utilities with those of purchasers, policymakers, and the communities that benefit from clean energy, this is the nation's premier forum for the energy community to gather, learn from each other, and recognize best practices for promoting renewable energy.
400 Attendees
Frequency: Annual/November

1547 **Solar Power International**
Solar Energy Industries Association
600 14th Street NW
Suite 400
Washington, DC 20005

202-682-0556
info@seia.org
www.seia.org
Facebook, Twitter

Largest solar show in North America.

1548 **Solar Thermal**
Interstate Renewable Energy Council
PO Box 1156
Latham, NY 12110-1156

518-458-6059
info@irecusa.org
www.irecusa.org

Jane Weissman, Executive Director
Lary Sherwood, Vice Chaie
David Warner, Chair
Jane Pulaski, Secretary
Jennifer Szaro, Treasurer

A two-day conference and networking event for industry professionals including; installers, manufacturers, distributors, engineers, designers, policy makers, code officials, and trainers. A national solar heating and cooling conference.
Frequency: Annual/December

1549 **U.S. Clean Heat & Power Association's Annual Spring CHP Forum**
U.S. Clean Heat & Power Association
105 North Virginia Avenue
Suite 204
Falls Church, VA 22046

703-436-2257
www.uschpa.org
Twitter

Jessica Bridges, Executive Director
Joe Allen, Chair
Warren Ferguson, Vice Chair
John Rathbun, Secretary
Paul Lemar, Treasurer

Showcasing a series of knowledgeable speakers sharing their expertise on policies and best practices that have facilitated CHP deployment in overseas markets and offering advice on how to break down barriers to CHP deployment and replicate those successes stateside. Listen to national and international trade and policy authorities, US government officials, and CHP business leaders discuss CHP challenges, success stories, and market expansion opportunities.
Frequency: Annual/May
Founded in 1999

1550 **UNEP SEF Alliance Annual Meeting**
Clean Energy Group/ UNEP SEF Alliance
50 State St.
Suite 1
Montpelier, VT 05602

802-223-2554; Fax: 802-223-4967

Members engage in candid discussion with peer agencies about current challenges faced, latest programme developments, and plans for future programme design. Experts speak about specialized topics, and proposals for new areas of collaboration are presented and discussed.
Frequency: Annual/September

1551 **USEA State of the Energy Industry Forum**
United States Energy Association
1300 Pennsylvania Ave NW
Suite 550
Washington, DC 20004

202-312-1230; Fax: 202-682-1682
reply@usea.org
www.usea.org
Twitter

U.S. member of World Energy Council represents broad interests of the U.S. energy sector.
200 Attendees
Founded in 2005

1552 **World Shale Gas Conference & Exhibition**
Institute of Gas Technology
1700 S Mount Prospect Rd
Des Plaines, IL 60018-1804

847-768-0664; Fax: 847-768-0669
www.gastechnology.org
Facebook, Twitter, LinkedIn, YouTube

David Carroll, President & CEO
Ronald Snedic, Vice President/ Corporate Devel.
Paul Chromek, General Counsel & Secretary

Unique platform to uncover the real impact of shale on the global gas market. Provides a valuable opportunity to develop business, explore future prospects and unlock the potential of shale gas globally. Share knowledge and experience among industry professionals, government operators and solution providers.

Directories & Databases

1553 **Association of Energy Service Companies Directory**
Association of Energy Service Companies
6060 N Central Expy
Dallas, TX 75206-5209

214-692-0771
800-692-0771; Fax: 214-692-0162
www.aesc.net

Patty Jordan, Publisher

About 750 energy service companies and industry suppliers.
Frequency: Bi-Monthly
Circulation: 10,000

1554 **Database of State Incentives for Renewables & Efficiency (DSIRE)**
North Carolina State University
Campus Box 7504
Raleigh, NC 27695-7504

919-515-3470; Fax: 919-515-2556
DSIREinfo@ncsu.edu
www.dsireusa.org
Facebook, Twitter

Amanda Vanega, Program Manager

Funded by the US Department of Energy's Office of Energy Efficiency and Renewable Energy. A comprehensive source of information on state, local, utility and federal incentives and policies that promote renewable energy and energy efficiency.
Founded in 1995

1555 **Energy**
WEFA Group
800 Baldwin Tower Boulevard
Eddystone, PA 19022-1368

610-490-4000; Fax: 610-490-2770
info@wefa.com
www.wefa.com

Peter McNabb

This database covers energy supply and demand, including weekly rig count and gasoline prices by states; reserves, stocks, production, consumption and trade of petroleum products.

1556 **Energy Science and Technology**
US Department of Energy
PO Box 62
Oak Ridge, TN 37831-0062

865-574-1000; Fax: 865-576-2865
www.osti.gov

This large database offers over 3 million citations, with abstracts, to literature pertaining to all fields of energy.

1557 **Handbook: Solar Energy System Design**
American Society of Plumbing Engineers
2980 S River Rd
Des Plaines, IL 60018-4203

847-296-0002; Fax: 847-296-2963
info@aspe.org
www.aspe.org

Tom Govedarica, Executive Publisher
Richard Albrecht, Publication Coordinator
Gretchen Pienta, Managing Editor

This manual provides the know-how on solar hot-water systems, collectors, thermal storage and much more.
Cost: $20.00

1558 **Membership Roster and Registry of Geothermal Services & Equipment**
Geothermal Resources Council
20001 Second Street
Suite 5
Davis, CA 95618-5476

530-758-2360; Fax: 530-758-2839
grc@geothermal.org
www.geothermal.org
Facebook, Twitter, LinkedIn, YouTube, Flickr

Curt Robinson, Ph.D, Executive Director
Steve Ponder, Interim Executive Director
Estela M. Smith, Office Manager
Ian Crawford, Managing Editor
Chi-Meng Moua, Library Associate

A unique publication that provides business, consulting and research contacts throughout the international geothermal community.
Frequency: Annual
Founded in 1970

1559 **REEBA Associate Members**
Renewable Energy and Efficiency Business Assoc

1245 Farmington Avenue
Suite 354
West Hartford, CT 06107

860-338-3728
pmichaud@murthalaw.com
www.reeba.org

Jim Daylor, Chairman & Treasurer
Mitchell Wurmbrand, Secretary
Paul Michaud, Esq., Executive Director & Founder
Kathryn Dube, Operations & Membership Director

Business directory listing member companies of the Renewable Energy and Efficiency Business Association, Inc. Members include renewable energy developers, energy services companies, and municipalities with an interest in energy technology.
100+ Members
Founded in 2010

1560 **REFIN Directory**
American Council on Renewable Energy
1600 K Street NW
Suite 700
Washington, DC 20006

202-393-0001
Facebook, Twitter, LinkedIn, YouTube

Dennis V. McGinn, President
Douglas Llyod, CEO and Co-Founder
Estelle Llyod, Managing Editor

Connects suppliers of capital and expertise with industry participants engaged in the scale-up of renewable energy.
Frequency: Annually
Founded in 2001

1561 **Salem Press Online Platform**
Grey House Publishing
4919 Route 22
PO Box 56
Amenia, NY 12501

800-221-1592; Fax: 201-968-0511
csr@salempress.com
online.salempress.com

The new Salem Press platform houses more than 500 titles including all of Salem's Health, Literature, History and Science titles in addition to select titles from the Grey House Publishing and H.W. Wilson product lines. Online access is free with each print purchase and includes an unlimited number of simultaneous users and remote access.

1562 **The Source for Renewable Energy**
Momentum Technologies, LLC
PO Box 460813
Glendale, CO 80246

303-229-4841; Fax: 408-705-2031
energy@mtt.com
energy.sourceguides.com

A comprehensive buyer's guide and business directory to more than 18,000 renewable energy businesses and organizations worldwide.

1563 **Wind Energy Conversion Systems**
South Dakota Renewable Energy Association
PO Box 491
Pierre, SD 57501-0491

605-224-8641

Offers valuable information for electrical-output wind machine manufacturers.
Cost: $2.00
45 Pages
Frequency: Annual

Industry Web Sites

1564 **energy.sourceguides.com**
Momentum Technologies, LLC

A comprehensive buyer's guide and business directory to more than 18,000 renewable energy businesses and organizations worldwide.

1565 **http://gold.greyhouse.com**
G.O.L.D Grey House OnLine Databases

Grey House Publishing's online database platform, GOLD, offers Quick Search, Keyword Search and Expert Search for most business sectors including mining, petroleum and alternative energy markets. The GOLD platform makes finding the information you need quick and easy. All of Grey House's directory products are available for subscription on the GOLD platform.

1566 **staging.unep.org**
UNEP

The only convening body in the international system for public finance agencies in the clean energy sector. Members are visionary organizations from various countries pushing the forefront of how to do public finance for clean energy.

1567 **www.acore.org**
American Council on Renewable Energy

Works to bring all forms of renewable energy into the mainstream of America's economy and lifestyle. Members include every aspect and sector of the renewable energy industries and their trade associations, including wind, solar, geothermal, biomass and biofuels, hydropower tidal/current energy and waste energy.

1568 **www.aeecenter.org**
Association of Energy Engineers

Promotes energy certification, management and education.

1569 **www.aeromt.org**
Alternative Energy Resources Organization

A grassroots nonprofit organization dedicated to solutions that promote resource conservation and local economic vitality. By bringing people together, AERO offers a vehicle for collective action and a sense of common purpose for citizens within their communities to shape a more sustainable future.

1570 **www.americanbiogascouncil.org**
American Biogas Council

Mission is to create jobs, environmental sustainability and energy independence by growing the American biogas industry.

1571 **www.americanhydrogenassociation.org**
American Hydrogen Association

Providing information on the use of hydrogen as a fuel.

1572 **www.ases.org**
American Solar Energy Society

The nation's leading association of solar professionals & advocates. Mission is to inspire an era of energy innovation and speed the transition to a sustainable energy economy. Advancing education, research and policy.

1573 **www.awea.org**
American Wind Energy Association

Promotes wind energy as a clean source of electricity for consumers around the world. Representing wind power project developers, equipment suppliers, services providers, parts manufacturers, utilities, researchers, and others involved in the wind industry.

1574 **www.biodiesel.org**
National Biodiesel Board

Representing AmericaBs clean diesel replacement fuels, the National Biodiesel Board will advance the interests of its members by supporting sustainable biodiesel, renewable diesel, and renewable jet industry growth. NBB serves as the industryBs central coordinating entity for technical and quality assurance programs and will be the strongest voice for its advocacy, communications, and market development.

1575 **www.biomassthermal.org**
Biomass Thermal Energy Council

An association of biomass fuel producers, appliance manufacturers and distributors, supply chain companies and non-profit organizations that view biomass thermal energy as a renewable, responsible, clean and energy-efficient pathway to meeting America's energy needs. BTEC engages in research, education, and public advocacy for the fast growing biomass thermal energy industry.

1576 **www.cleanegroup.org**
Clean Energy Group

A leading nonprofit advocacy organization working in the US and internationally on innovative clean energy technology, finance, and policy programs. Supported by major foundations, as well as state, federal and international energy agencies.

1577 **www.dsireusa.org**
DSIRE Database

Funded by the US Department of Energy's Office of Energy Efficiency and Renewable Energy. A comprehensive source of information on state, local, utility and federal incentives and policies that promote renewable energy and energy efficiency.

1578 **www.eesi.org**
Environmental and Energy Study Institute

A nonprofit organization that advances innovative policy solutions that set us on a cleaner, more secure and sustainable energy path.

1579 **www.energyrecoverycouncil.org**
Energy Recovery Council

Represents the waste-to-energy industry and communities that own waste-to-energy facilities. Current ERC members own and operate modern waste-to-energy facilities that operate nationwide, safely disposing of municipal solid waste, while at the same time generating renewable electricity using modern combustion technology equipped with state-of-the-art emission control systems.

1580 **www.ethanolrfa.org**
Renewable Fuels Association

The national trade association for the US ethanol industry promoting policies, regulations and research and development initiatives that will lead to the increased production and use of fuel ethanol. Membership includes a broad cross-section of businesses, individuals and organizations dedicated to the expansion of the US fuel ethanol industry.

1581 **www.geo-energy.org**
Geothermal Energy Association

Advocates for public policies that will promote the development and utilization of geothermal resources, provides a forum for the industry to discuss issues and problems, encourages research and development to improve geothermal technologies, presents industry views to governmental organizations, and conducts education and outreach projects.

1582 **www.geothermal.org**
Geothermal Resources Council

Nonprofit, educational association actively seeking to expand its role as a primary professional educational association for the international geothermal community.

1583 **www.greyhouse.com**
Grey House Publishing

Authoritative reference directories for business information and general reference, including alternative energy, mining and petroleum markets. Users can search the online databases with varied search criteria allowing for custom searches by product category, geographic area, sales volume, keyword, subject and more. Full Grey House catalog and online ordering also available.

1584 **www.hydro.org**
National Hydropower Association

Dedicated to promoting the growth of clean, affordable US hydropower. Seeks to secure hydropower's place as a climate-friendly, renewable and reliable energy source that serves national environmental, energy, and economic policy objectives. Members are involved in projects throughout the US hydropower industry, including both federal and non-federal hydroelectric facilities.

1585 **www.iaee.org**
International Association for Energy Economics

Association for those involved in energy economics including publications, consultants, energy database software.

1586 **www.igshpa.okstate.edu**
International Ground Source Heat Pump Association

Member-driven organization established to advance ground source heat pump technology on local, state, national and international levels. IGSHPA utilizes state-of-the-art facilities for conducting GSHP system installation training and geothermal research. Mission is to promote the use of ground source heat pump technology worldwide through education and communication.

1587 **www.irecusa.org**
Interstate Renewable Energy Council

Works with industry, government, educators and other stakeholders to ensure that the broader use of renewable energies is possible, safe, affordable and practical, particularly for the individual consumer.

1588 **www.ireoigo.org**
Intergovernmental Renewable Energy Organization

Promotes the urgent transition to renewable energy sources and sustainable development through collaborative effort and the implementation of projects that improve the lives of people while preserving the environment and our resources for future generations of humans.

1589 **www.lignite.com**
Lignite Energy Council

Regional Trade Association - promotes policies and activities that maintain a viable lignite industry and enhance development of our regions' lignite resources.

1590 **www.nabcep.org**
N. American Board of Cert. Energy Practitioners

Mission is to support, and work with, the renewable energy and energy efficiency industries, professionals, and stakeholders. Goal is to develop voluntary national certification programs that will; promote renewable energy, provide value to practitioners, promote worker safety and skill, and promote consumer confidence.

1591 **www.nesea.org**
Northeast Sustainable Energy Association

The nation's leading regional membership organization focused on promoting the understanding, development and adoption of energy conservation and non-polluting, renewable energy technologies.

1592 **www.reeba.org**
Renewable Energy and Efficiency Business Assoc

Business association dedicated to supporting the renewable energy industry.

1593 **www.seia.org**
Solar Energy Industries Association

Works with its member companies to make solar a mainstream and significant energy source by expanding markets, removing market barriers, strenghtening the industry and educating the public on the benefits of solar energy.

1594 **www.solarliving.org**
Solar Living Institute

A nonprofit solar training and sustainability organization. Mission is to promote sustainable living through inspirational environmental education.

1595 **www.usabiomass.org**
Biomass Power Association

The nation's leading organization working to expand and advance the use of clean, renewable biomass power. Educates policymakers at the state and federal level about the benefits of biomass and provides regular briefings and research to keep members fully informed about public policy impacting the biomass industry. Members include local owners and operators of existing biomass facilities, suppliers, plant developers and others.

1596 **www.usrea.org**
US Renewable Energy Association

A nonprofit organization dedicated to helping Americans use more renewable energy by promoting sustainable, alternative energy through education.

1597 **www.wcee.org**
Women's Council on Energy and the Environment

Supports women involved in the environmental community with education, research, new trend information and several publications.

Associations

1598 **Academy of Science Fiction Fantasy and Horror Films**
334 W 54th St
Los Angeles, CA 90037-3806

323-752-5811; Fax: 323-752-5811
saturn.awards@ca.rr.com
www.saturnawards.org
Facebook, Twitter

Robert Holguin, CEO & President
David Bilbrey, Executive Administrator
Michael Laster, Director of Operations
Jeff Rector, Official Spokesperson
Kurt Reichenbach, Art Designer

Honors, recognizes and promotes genre films. Annually presents the prestigious Saturn Awards. In recent years, have added television and home entertainment categories to the media mix. Widened the scope of our awards by celebrating achievement in additional genres including action, adventure, and thrillers as well as international cinema.
Founded in 1972

1599 **American Amusement Machine Association**
450 E Higgins Rd
Suite 201
Elk Grove Village, IL 60007

847-290-9088
866-372-5190; Fax: 847-290-9121
info@coin-op.org
coin-op.org
Facebook, Twitter, Instagram

Peter Gustafson, Exec. VP
Ashley Ritschdorff, Marketing Coordinator
Tina Schwartz, Business and Finance Manager

Non-profit trade association representing the manufacturers, distributors and part suppliers to the coin-operated and out-of-home amusement industry.
Founded in 1981

1600 **American Association of Cheerleading Coaches and Administration**
6745 Lenox Center Court
Suite 318
Memphis, TN 38115

800-533-6583; Fax: 901-251-5851
www.aacca.org
Facebook, Twitter

Lauri Harris, Executive Director
Jim Lord, Director, Education & Programs
Jessica Chatto, Exec. Asst. & Director, STUNT Ops.

AACCA,is a non-profit educational association for cheerleading coaches across the United States. Members of the association include: youth, junior high school, high school, all star, and college or university coaches/advisors, as well as leading national cheerleading instructional companies dedicated to the safe and responsible practice of student cheerleading.
70000 Members
Founded in 1987

1601 **American Coaster Enthusiasts**
P.O. Box 540261
Grand Prairie, TX 75054-0261

469-278-6223; Fax: 740-452-2552
info@aceonline.org
www.aceonline.org
Facebook, Twitter, RSS

Robert Ulrich, President
Jeremy Delong, Membership Director
Lee Ann Draud, Publications Director
Elizabeth Ringas, Communications Director
Scott Short, Operations Director

ACE is the world's largest ride enthusiast organization, and its members are the most educated, dedicated, and passionate amusement park guests. ACE's activities include publications, action-packed events, and preservation efforts. ACE is highly visible in the mainstream media. Local television stations and newspapers often consider ACE events in their area to be major news items.
6000 Members
Founded in 1978

1602 **American Disc Jockey Association**
20118 N 67th Avenue
Suite 300-605
Glendale, CA 85308

888-723-5776; Fax: 866-310-4676
office@adja.org
www.adja.org
Facebook, Twitter, YouTube
Rob Snyder, Director

An association of professional mobile entertainers. Encourages success for its members through continuous education, camaraderie, and networking. The primary goal is to educate Disc Jockeys so that each member acts ethically and responsibly.

1603 **Amusement & Music Operators Association**
380 Terra Cotta Rd
Suite F
Crystal Lake, IL 60012

815-893-6010
800-937-2662; Fax: 815-893-6248
amoa.memberclicks.net
Facebook, Twitter, LinkedIn, YouTube

Lori Schneider, Executive VP
Ann Choulnard, Exec. Office & Meetings Assistant
Laura McGowen, Communications Coordinator
Maggie Kapinos, Manager, Marketing & Membership

AMOA was created when 68 jukebox owners from around the country banded together to fight the repeal of the jukebox royalty exemption. The modest beginning, created by a common cause, revealed a fierce passion-shared by many-about their business. Harnessing the collective strength, energy, knowledge and entrepreneurial spirit of a growing number of volunteer members, AMOA quickly established itself as a major force.
Founded in 1948

1604 **Amusement Expo International**
American Amusement Machine Association
450 E Higgins Rd
Suite 201
Elk Grove Village, IL 60007

847-290-9088
866-372-5190; Fax: 847-290-9121
info@coin-op.org
coin-op.org
Facebook, Twitter

Peter Gustafson, Exec. VP
Ashley Ritschdorff, Marketing Coordinator
Tina Schwartz, Business and Finance Manager

Non-profit trade association representing the manufacturers, distributors and part suppliers to the coin-operated and out-of-home amusement industry.

1605 **Amusement Industry Manufacturers & Suppliers International**
P.O. Box 92366
Nashville, TN 37209

714-425-5747; Fax: 714-276-9666
info@aimsintl.org
www.aimsintl.org
Facebook

Mary Jane Brewer, Executive Director
Holly Coston, Seminar Manager
Darlene Reese, Curriculum & Certification Manager

The Amusement Industry Manufacturers and Suppliers (AIMS) Trade Association evolved from the American Recreational Equipment Association. The Associations purpose is to establish communications and foster working relations using the highest degree of professionalism with other Amusement Industry Trade Associations, Local, State, and Federal Government entities in order to promote and preserve the prosperity of the Amusement Industry.
Founded in 1994

1606 **Association of College Unions International**
120 W Seventh Street
One City Centre, Suite 200
Bloomington, IN 47404

812-245-2284; Fax: 812-245-6710
acui@acui.org
www.acui.org
Facebook, Twitter, YouTube

John Taylor, Chief Executive Officer
Dave Teske, Director, Finance & Administration
Devon Bray, Marketing Coordinator
Jake Dawes, Events & Operations Coordinator
Scarlett Winters, Online Engagement Specialist

The association is a non-profit organization and has member institutions in a number of countries. ACUI members work at and attend urban and rural campuses at both the two and four year levels and are dedicated to building community on campus through programs, services and publications with the common goal of unifying the union and activities fields.
1000 Members
Founded in 1914

1607 **Association of Zoos and Aquariums**
8403 Colesville Rd
Suite 710
Silver Spring, MD 20910-3314

301-562-0777; Fax: 301-562-0888
membership@aza.org
www.aza.org
Facebook, Twitter, Pinterest, Instagram, YouTube

Dan Ashe, President & CEO
Craig Hoover, Executive Vice President
Jack Keeney, Jr., General Counsel
Phil Wagner, Chief Financial Officer
Melissa Howerton, SVP, Member Services

A nonprofit organization dedicated to the advancement of accredited zoos and aquariums in the areas of animal care, wildlife conservation, education and science.
200 Members
Founded in 1924

1608 **Canadian Game Studies Assocation**

Home Page: gamestudies.ca
Twitter

The CGSA is devoted to the interdisciplinary study of digital games, and supports the work of researchers, graduate students, artists, game designers, programmers, theorists, and others working in the industry.
Mailing list available for rent

1609 **Circus Fans Association of America**
2704 Marshall Avenue
Lorain, OH 44052-4315

360-452-1919
circusvern@aol.com
www.circusfans.org

Jan Biggerstaff, President
Maxine House, Executive Secretary-Treasurer
Daniel Kleintop, President Elect
Vanessa Gagne, Webmaster & Social Media Director
Bruce Johnson, Public Relations & Media Director

Established to enjoy and preserve the circus as an institution. CFA offers you an opportunity interact with fellow circus enthusiasts in many ways. Local geographic groups (called TENTS) provide a chance for folks who live in the same geographic area to attend shows together and to meet to discuss the circus scene. State organizations (called TOPS) organize larger gatherings and special events.
Founded in 1926

1610 **Circus Historical Society**
3100 Parkside Lane
Williamsburg, VA 23185

757-259-0412
CircusHistoricalSociety@gmail.com
circushistoricalsociety.org
Facebook, Twitter

Don Covington, President
Kat Vechhio, Webmaster
Kristen Lee, Secretary/Treasurer & Membership
Greg Parkinson, Bandwagon Editor

The Circus Historical Society, Inc. (CHS) is a tax-exempt, not-for-profit educational organization dedicated to recording the history of the American circus from the first one in Philadelphia during 1793 to today. Membership includes historians, scholars, circus personnel, memorabilia collectors, Americana specialists who share both a love of the circus and a desire to preserve and disseminate its great heritage.
1000 Members
Founded in 1939

1611 **Clowns of America International**
PO Box 112
Eustis, FL 32727

352-357-1676
877-816-6941
coaioffice@aol.com
mycoai.com

Adam Schill, President
Carrie Ray, Director, Membership
Frank Bunton, Director, Conventions
Alene Kraus, Director, Education
Gloria Sterett, Director, Alley & Regional Support

The purpose of Clowns of America International Website is to share, educate, and act as a gathering place for serious minded amateurs, semiprofessionals, and professional clowns. COAI provides its membership with necessary resources that allow them to further define and improve their individual clown character. Visitors who are interested in the clown arts will find a variety of resources that will stimulate their interest, foster their curiosity and offer pathways to valuable information.

1612 **Corporate Esports Association**

administrator@cea.gg
cea.gg
Twitter, YouTube

Brad Tenenholtz, Chief Executive Officer
Michael Pleasant, Co-Founder & Chair
Terence Southard, Co-Founder & Board Member

Facilitates online esport tournaments for corporate professionals on Discord, to enocurage team-building and donate the proceeds to charity.

1613 **Council for Amusement & Recreational Equipment Safety**
PO Box 8236
Des Moines, IO 50301-8236

617-727-3200
217-558-7194
www.uscancares.org

Mark Mooney, President
Kathy Fackler, System Administrator

CARES is a voluntary organization of chief government officials who are responsible for the enforcement of amusement ride and recreational equipment regulations within their jurisdiction. Fosters cooperation among regulatory officials and amusement equipment industries to promote public safety. CARES membership has grown to more than two dozen regulatory agencies in the United States and Canada, and includes the informal participation of the U.S. Consumer Product Safety.

1614 **Digital Games Research Association**

coordinator@digra.org
www.digra.org

William Huber, President
Hanna Wirman, Vice President
Allan Fowler, Secretary
Jussi Holopainen, Treasurer
Cody Mejeur, Diversity Officer

DiGRA is an international association of academics and professionals interested in research into digital games and related products. It features a Digital Library, Gamesnetwork mailing list, and the ToDiGRA journal.
Founded in 2003
Mailing list available for rent

1615 **Entertainment Consumers Association**

Home Page: www.theeca.com

Hal Halpin, Founder & President
Heather Ellertson, VP, Marketing
Jennifer Mercurio, VP & General Counsel
Brett Schenker, Advocacy Director
Mike Conley, Digital Marketing Coordinator

Non-profit representing the interests of consumers of digital entertainment in the US and Canada.

1616 **Entertainment Software Association**
601 Massachusetts Avenue NW
Suite 300
Washington, DC 20001

esa@theesa.com
www.theesa.com
Facebook, Twitter, LinkedIn

Stanley Pierre-Louis, President & CEO
Gina Vetere, SVP & General Counsel
Andrew Bowins, SVP, Comm. & Public Affairs
Ana Molina, CFO
Michael O'Leary, SVP, Government Affairs

The trade association of the video game industry.
Founded in 2000

1617 **Entertainment Software Association of Canada**
#408, 130 Spadina Avenue
Toronto, ON M5V 2L4

416-620-7171
theesa.ca
Facebook, Twitter, Instagram, YouTube

Jayson Hilchie, President & CEO
Corinne Crichlow, Director, Communications & PR
Paul Fogolin, Director, Policy & Gov. Affairs
Dylan Boyd, Digital Content Manager

The ESAC is devoted to video game developers, publishers, and distributors in Canada

1618 **Entertainment Software Rating Board**
New York, NY

marketing@esrb.org
www.esrb.org
Facebook, Twitter

Patricia E. Vance, President
David Kassack, SVP, Finance & Operations
Bill Garrity, SVP, Ratings
John Falzone, VP, ESRB Privacy Certified
Randy Walker, SVP, Marketing & Communications

Non-profit, self-regulatory body devoted to informing consumers (especially parents) about the video games they play. The ESRB established and maintains a ratings system for all video games, from E for Everyone to AO for Adults Only.
Founded in 1994

1619 **Esports Trade Association**
541 N. Fairbanks Court
Suite 2200
Chicago, IL 60611

708-680-7133
info@esportsta.org
esportsta.org
Facebook, Twitter, LinkedIn, YouTube, Instagram

Megan Van Petten, Founder & CEO

The ESTA serves the eSports community by promoting, protecting, and advancing its interests through professional development programs, networking opportunities, industry research, and tools and resources for members.
Founded in 2018

1620 **Fantasy Sports & Gaming Association**
1818 Parmenter Street
Suite 300
Middleton, WI 53562

608-310-7540
thefsga.org
Facebook, Twitter, LinkedIn

Christina McCoy, Executive Director
Michael Fiez, Marketing
Emily Petersen, Membership

The FSGA is a national organization representing fantasy sports and gaming companies, and serving those companies and players with research and data, networking opportunities, and collective action.

1621 **Game Manufacturers Association**
240 North Fifth Street
Suite 340
Columbus, OH 43215

614-255-4500; Fax: 614-255-4499
ed@gama.org
www.gama.org
Facebook

John Stacy, Executive Director
Chris Materni, Deputy Director
Melissa Jacobs, Education Manager
Paul McGraw, Events Manager
Kelly Mignogna, Communications Manager

The Game Manufacturers Association (GAMA) is the non-profit trade organization dedicated to serving the tabletop game industry. Strengthens and supports industry professionals by advancing their interests, providing educational programs and opportunities, and promoting their form of quality social entertainment. Led by publishers and manufacturers, GAMA promotes the interests of all persons in-

volved in the commerce of games and game-related products.
450 Members
Founded in 1977

1622 **International Amusement & Leisure Defense Association**
PO Box 4563
Louisville, KY 40204
502-473-0956; Fax: 502-473-7352
info@ialda.org
www.ialda.org
LinkedIn
Michael Amaro, President
Paul Cavanaugh, Treasurer
Gaylee W. Gillim, Secretary
The International Amusement & Leisure Defense Association, Inc. is a non-profit association of lawyers and other professionals who are actively engaged in representing the interests of the amusement and leisure industries. IALDA members work closely with those in the amusement and water park industries as well as those involved in the bowling, roller skating, and other leisure industries.

1623 **International Association of Amusement Parks and Attractions**
9205 Southpark Center Loop
Suite 300
Orlando, FL 32819
321-319-7600
iaapa@iaapa.org
www.iaapa.org
Facebook, Twitter, LinkedIn
Hal McEvoy, President & CEO
David Mandt, EVP & Chief Engagement Officer
Josh Powers, EVP & Chief Financial Officer
Suzanne Pfordresher, VP, Global Marketing
Susan Storey, Director, Global Communications
International association of permanently situated amusement facilities including theme parks, museums and zoos.
5300 Members
Founded in 1918

1624 **International Association of Fairs Expositions**
3043 East Cairo St.
PO Box 985
Springfield, MO 65802
417-862-5771
800-516-0313; Fax: 417-862-0156
iafe@fairsandexpos.com
www.fairsandexpos.com
Facebook, Twitter, You Tube
Marla Calico, President/CEO
The International Association of Fairs and Expositions (IAFE) is a voluntary, non-profit corporation, serving state, provincial, regional, and county agricultural fairs, shows, exhibitions, and expositions. Its associate members include state and provincial associations of fairs, non-agricultural expositions and festivals, associations, corporations, and individuals engaged in providing products and services to its members, all of whom are interested in the improvement of fairs, and expositions.
1300 Members
Founded in 1885

1625 **International Association of Haunted Attractions**
1001 Greenbay Road
Winnetka, IL 60093
888-320-8494; Fax: 609-799-7032
Facebook
The Haunted Attraction Association assists and advances the thriving haunt industry through communication, education, and information. Our worldwide network of members exchange ideas, information, experiences and concerns via our conferences, exclusive networking events, message boards, newsletters, magazines and more. HAA members have been featured on national television shows such as Good Morning America, the Today Show, and our attractions have been featured in national publications.
400 Members
Founded in 1998

1626 **International Brotherhood of Magicians**
13 Point West Blvd
St Charles, MO 63301-4431
636-724-2400; Fax: 636-724-8566
info@magician.org
www.magician.org
Facebook, Twitter, YouTube
Stephen Bargatze, International President
Ken Scott, International Vice President
Simone Marron, International Secretary
Charles Arkin, International Treasurer
Ken Scott, International President-Elect
The International Brotherhood of Magicians is the world's largest organization dedicated to the art of magic, with members in 88 countries. Our official publication, The Linking Ring, has linked magicians throughout the world. Local branches of the I.B.M., known as Rings, meet each month in hundreds of locations. Our Annual Convention features top professional magicians in our spectacular evening shows.
12000 Members
Founded in 1922

1627 **International Festivals and Events Association (IFEA)**
2603 W. Eastover Terrace
Boise, ID 83706-2800
208-433-0950; Fax: 208-433-9812
nia@ifea.com
www.ifea.com
Facebook, Twitter, LinkedIn, YouTube
Ted Baroody, Chair
Steven Wood Schmader, CFEE, President & CEO
Nia Forster Hovde, CFEE, VP/Dir. of Marketing & Comm.
Beth Peterson, Director of Membership Services
Craig Sarton, Creative & Publications Director
The IFEA exists to serve the needs of our entire industry, who produce and support quality celebrations for the benefit of their respective 'communities' and all those who share our core values of excellence & quality; the sharing of experience, knowledge, creativity and best practices; and the importance of 'community' building both locally and globally. Our success lies in the success of those we serve through professional education, programming, products and resources, and networking.
2000 Members
Founded in 1956
Mailing list available for rent

1628 **International Game Developers Association**
#402, 150 Eglinton Avenue E.
Toronto, ON M4P 1E8
info@igda.org
www.igda.org
Facebook, Twitter, LinkedIn, YouTube, Instagram
Renee Gittins, Executive Director
Tristin Hightower, Director, Operations
The IGDA is the largest non-profit membership organization serving individuals who create video games. They are dedicated to improving developers' careers and lives through: Community, Professional Development, and Advocacy.
Founded in 1994

1629 **International Jugglers' Association**
PO Box 7307
Austin, TX 78713-7307
702-798-0099; Fax: 702-248-2550
webmaster@juggle.org
www.juggle.org
Facebook, YouTube
Mike Moore, Chair
Scott Steiskal, Operations Officer
Martin Frost, Communications Director
Erin Stephens, Marketing Director
Marilyn Sullivan, Membership Director
An organization of individuals dedicated to promoting juggling.
Founded in 1947

1630 **International Laser Display Association**
7062 Edgeworth Drive
Orlando, FL 32819-2700
407-797-7654; Fax: 503-344-3770
mail@laserist.org
www.laserist.org
Brian Gonzalez, President
Patrick Murphy, ILDA Executive Director
The International Laser Display Association (ILDA) is the world's leading organization dedicated to advancing the use of laser displays in the fields of art, entertainment and education. Promotes the use of laser displays in the international marketplace through awards programs, publications, technology standards and a code of ethics. ILDA also represents the industry on safety issues and provides forums for members to exchange ideas, forge partnerships and explore.
Founded in 1986

1631 **International Laser Tag Association: ILTA**
5351 E Thompson Road
Suite 236
Indianapolis, IN 46237
317-786-9755; Fax: 317-786-9757
Ryan McQuillen, Executive Director
Eric Gaizat, Membership Director
The International Laser Tag Association (ILTA) is the non-profit developer and operator association for the laser tag industry. Help members become better informed through our research, services, and communications with all levels of the industry. Since the creation of the ILTA, no other source has been more reliable for information about our industry. Assist members by providing them with the most accurate infor available to date.
350 Members
Founded in 1996

1632 **International Magicians Society**
581 Ellison Avenue
Westbury, NY 11590
516-333-2377; Fax: 516-333-0018
info@imsmagic.com
www.imsmagic.com
Tony Hassini, Chair/CEO
Cathy Edwards, World President
Remington Scott, Creative Director
William H. Mellhany, Magic Historian
David Ferrari, Public Relations Director
Promotes and preserves the art of magic. IMS helps create new magicians in order to pass the torch to the next generation of magicians.
37000 Members
Founded in 1968

1633 **International Ticketing Association**
5868 East 71st Street
Suite E 367
Indianapolis, IN 46220

212-629-4036; Fax: 212-628-8532
info@intix.org
www.intix.org
Facebook, Twitter, LinkedIn, YouTube

Jena Hoffman, President/CEO
Tiffany Kelham, Membership Associate
Stacey Ogren, Meeting Manager
Dorothea Heck, Business Development
Christine Payne, Marketing Manager

The International Ticketing Association is a nonprofit membership organization committed to leading the forum for the entertainment ticketing industry. INTIX represents ticketing, sales, technology, finance, and marketing professionals who work in arts, sports, and entertainment as well as a full range of public venues and institutions. Members represent organizations from across the United States, Canada and 20 countries from around the globe.
1000 Members
Founded in 1980

1634 **Major League Gaming**
Home Page: www.mlg.com
Facebook, Twitter, YouTube, Instagram, Snapchat

Steve Bornstein, Chairman
Pete Vlastelica, President & CEO
Michael Sepso, Co-Founder & SVP, Media Networks
Sundance DiGiovanni, Co-Founder & VP, Brands & Content
Pavel Murnikov, VP, Technology

A professional eSports organization. MLG.tv, its free video streaming eSports showcase, attracts 27 million users per month.
Founded in 2002

1635 **National Association of Amusement Ride Safety Officials**
PO Box 638
Brandon, FL 33509-0638

813-661-2779
800-669-9053; Fax: 813-685-5117
naarsoinfo@aol.com
www.naarso.com

Michael Wood, Chair
Len Cavalier, Executive Director
Sherrie Kontos, Office Admiistrator

NAARSO is dedicated to the advancement of amusement ride and device safety through the doctrine of Safety Through Communication. NAARSO is a non-profit organization that provides resources for amusement industry professionals dedicated to the safety of the industry and its patrons.
800 Members
Founded in 1987

1636 **National Association of Teachers of Singing**
9957 Moorings Drive
Suite 401
Jacksonville, FL 32257-2416

904-992-9101; Fax: 904-262-2587
info@nats.org
www.nats.org
Facebook, Twitter, LinkedIn, YouTube, Flickr, Pinterest

Allen Henderson, Executive Director
Deborah Guess, Director, Operations
Bob Bryan, Director, Development
Beth Buchanan, Manager, Marketing & Communications
Amandia Camahan, Coordinator, Membership Services

Encourages the highest standards of the vocal art and of ethical principals in the teaching of singing; and promote vocal education and research at all levels, both for the enrichment of the general public and for the professional advancement of the talented.
7000 Members
Founded in 1944

1637 **National Caves Association**
PO Box 625
Cobleskill, NY 12043

270-492-2228; Fax: 931-688-3988
info@cavern.com
www.cavern.com
Facebook, Twitter

Susan Berdeaux, Executive Director

Nonprofit organization of publicly and privately owned show caves and caverns - caves developed for public visitation.
Founded in 1965

1638 **National Independent Concessionaires Association, Inc.**
1043 E. Brandon Blvd.
Brandon, FL 33511

813-438-8926; Fax: 813-438-8928
nica@nicainc.org
www.nicainc.org
Facebook, RSS Feeds

Don Delahoyde, President
Rey O'Day, Executive Director
Jesse Willard, Communications & Marketing Manager
Linda Frisco, Office & Membership Manager

Striving towards better communication between fairs, festivals and independent concessionaires nationwide.
1200 Members
Founded in 1993

1639 **National Recreation and Park Association**
22377 Belmont Ridge Road
Ashburn, VA 20148-4501

703-858-0784
800-626-6772; Fax: 703-858-0794
customerservice@nrpa.org
www.nrpa.org
Facebook, Twitter, LinkedIn, YouTube, Pinterest

Kristine Stratton, President & CEO
Autumn Saxton-Ross, Chief Equity Officer/VP, Education
Gina Mullins-Cohen, Chief Marketing Officer/VP, Comm.
Brenda Camacho, Chief Financial Officer/VP, Ops.
Julie Boland, VP, Membership & Certification

NRPA is the leading advocacy organization dedicated to the advancement of public parks and recreation opportunities. Advances parks, recreation and environmental conservation efforts that enhance the quality of life.
Founded in 1965

1640 **New England Association of Amusement Parks and Attractions**
774 Portland Road
PO Box 85
Saco, ME 04072

877-999-8740; Fax: 207-283-4716
secretary@neaapa.com
www.neaapa.com
Facebook, Twitter, LinkedIn, YouTube

Eric Anderson, President
Ed Hodgdon, Secretary
Ron Gustafson, Newsletter Editor

NEAAPA is the premier regional association representing amusement parks, attractions, and their suppliers. NEAAPA works with its members on education opportunities, legislative and policy issues, as well as promotion of the Association's members.
Founded in 1912

1641 **Outdoor Amusement Business Association**
1035 S Semoran Blvd
Suite 1045A
Winter Park, FL 32792-5512

407-681-9444
800-517-6222; Fax: 407-681-9445
oaba@oaba.org
www.oaba.org
Facebook, Twitter, YouTube, Instagram

Greg Chiecko, President
Al DeRusha, Senior Vice President
Sue Gallup, Manager, Programs & Services
Tim Kwiatkowski, Director, Sales & Membership

The OABA manages and influences concerns for its members. OABA believes that all business owners and members of the trade association should continue to raise the level of safety and quality in the mobile amusement industry.
4000 Members
Founded in 1964

1642 **PLASA**
630 Ninth Avenue
Suite 609
New York, NY 10036

212-244-1505; Fax: 212-244-1502
info@plasa.org
www.plasa.org
Facebook, Twitter

Peter Heath, Managing Director
Nicky Greet, Membership, Skills & Technical Dir.
Shane McGreevy, Finance Director
Jacki Tien, PLASA Americas Director

PLASA is the lead international membership body for those who supply technologies and services to the event, entertainment and installation industries. As the worldwide voice for those who supply and service the entertainment, event and installation markets, PLASA will develop, promote, support and grow our industry.
1200+ Members

1643 **Roller Skating Association International**
6905 Corporate Dr
Indianapolis, IN 46278-1927

317-347-2626; Fax: 317-347-2636
rsa@rollerskating.com
www.rollerskating.org
Facebook, Twitter, LinkedIn, YouTube, Pinterest, Google+

Jim McMahon, Executive Director
Tonya Crenshaw, Accountant
Lynette Rowland, Director, Communications
Angela Tanner, Assistant Executive Director
Sharon McMahon, Director, Membership Services

The Roller Skating Association (RSA) is a trade association that serves commercial (for-profit) skating center owner/operators. It also serves those involved in various facets of the roller related industry such as teachers, coaches, manufacturers, distributors and other elements of the family entertainment industry. Promotes the success of members through education and advancing the roller skating business.
1000 Members
Founded in 1937

1644 **Showmen's League of America**
1023 W. Fulton Market
Chicago, IL 60607

312-733-9533
800-350-9906; Fax: 312-733-9534
office@showmensleague.org
www.showmensleague.org
Facebook, Twitter

Mary Chris Smith, President
Robert Thorson, 1st Vice President
Patrick Jamieson, 2nd Vice President
Marc Janas, 3rd Vice President
Cindy Henning, Secretary

It seeks to promote the success of our members through education and advancing the roller skating business.elp those in need through one of its many programs.
Founded in 1913

1645 **Society of Broadcast Engineers**
9102 N Meridian St
Suite 150
Indianapolis, IN 46260-1896

317-846-9000; Fax: 317-846-9120
www.sbe.org
Facebook, Twitter, LinkedIn, YouTube

John Poray, Executive Director
Chris Scherer, Member Communications Director
Cathy Orosz, Education Director
Megan Clappe, Certification Director
Debbie Hennessey, Sustaining Member Manager

Committed to serving broadcast engineers. From the studio operator to the maintenance engineer and the chief engineer to the vice president of engineering, SBE members come from commercial and non-commercial radio and television stations and cable facilities. A growing segment of members are engaging the industry on their own as consultants and contractors, field and sales engineers.
5100+ Members
Founded in 1964
Mailing list available for rent: 5700 names at $170 per M

1646 **Society of Camera Operators**
PO Box 2006
Toluca Lake, CA 91610

818-563-9110
818-382-7070; Fax: 818-563-9117
socoffice@soc.org
www.soc.org
Facebook, Twitter

Kristin Petrovich Kennedy, Business Consultant
John Bosson, Member Services & Ops. Coordinator
Jeff Victor, Sales
Kate McCallum, Camera Operator Magazine Editor
Stephanie Cameron, Camera Operator Magazine Designer

Advances the art and creative contribution of the operating cameraman in the Motion Picture and Television Industries. The Society serves the purpose of bringing into the closest confederation Industry leaders in their fields.
Founded in 1979

1647 **Society of Health and Physical Educators**
1900 Association Drive
Reston, VA 20191-1598

703-476-3400
800-213-7193; Fax: 703-476-9527
membership@shapeamerica.org
www.shapeamerica.org
Facebook, Twitter, Instagram

Stephanie A. Morris, Chief Executive Officer

Organization that provides educational programs, resources and support for professionals within the fields of health, physical education, recreation and dance. AAHPERD's mission is to promote and support leadership, research, education, and best practices in the professions that support creative, healthy, and active lifestyles.
25000 Members
Founded in 1885

1648 **Tennessee Department of Agriculture, Market Development Division**
Tennessee Department of Agriculture
440 Hogan Road
PO Box 40627
Nashville, TN 37204

615-837-5160
800-342-8206; Fax: 615-837-5194
pick.tn@tn.gov
www.picktnproducts.org
Facebook, Twitter, Pinterest

US and Canadian representatives of state/provincial agencies that are responsible for the support of educational and agricultural fairs.
35 Members
Founded in 1966

1649 **Themed Entertainment Association**
150 East Olive Avenue
Suite 306
Burbank, CA 91502-1850

818-843-8497; Fax: 818-843-8477
info@teaconnect.org
www.teaconnect.org
Facebook, Twitter, LinkedIn, YouTube

Jennie Nevin, Chief Operating Officer
Tammie Richards, Director, Events
Christy Nakada, Marketing & Communications
Judy Rubin, Publications & Social Media, PR
Sarah Barges, Coordinator

The Themed Entertainment Association (TEA) is an international non-profit association representing the world's leading creators, developers, designers and producers of compelling places and experiences.
Founded in 1991

1650 **United States eSports Federation**

Home Page: www.esportsfederation.org
Instagram

Vlad Marinescu, President
Robin Kent, General Secretary
Lance Mudd, Sport Director
Ryan Terao, VP, Education Commission
Robert Davidman, VP, Integrity Commission

USeF is the U.S. member organization of the International e-Sports Federation and official governing body of eSports in the U.S. Its goal is to promote eSports and protect athletes by uniting all facets of the industry: stakeholders, athletes, event organizers, technology producers, innovators and inventors, IP holders, parents, sponsors, and fans.
Founded in 2016

1651 **VR/AR Association**
Palo Alto, CA 94303

nathan@thevrara.com
www.thevrara.com
Facebook, Twitter, LinkedIn, YouTube

Nathan Pettyjohn, Founder & President
Kris Kolo, Global Executive Director

International organization with a mission to foster collaboration between companies and individuals in the virtual reality and augmented reality industry. It aims to accelerate growth, encourage research and education, develop industry standards, connect members, and promote their services.
Founded in 2015

1652 **Western Fairs Association**
1776 Tribute Rd
Suite 210
Sacramento, CA 95815-4495

916-927-3100; Fax: 916-927-6397
info@fairsnet.org
www.fairsnet.org
Facebook, Twitter, YouTube, Instagram

Sarah Cummings, President & CEO
Taylor Corder, Communications Manager
Cliff Munson, Chair

Western Fairs Association (WFA) serves the fair industry throughout the Western United States and Canada. Assists in maintaining the highest professional standards within the fair industry through a voluntary network of individuals and organizations. Promotes the prosperity of fairs through education and training programs.
2000 Members
Founded in 1922

1653 **World Esports Association**

info@wesa.gg
www.wesa.gg
Facebook, Twitter

Pietro Fringuelli, Executive Chair & Commissioner
Sebastian Weishaar, Board Member
Ulrich Schulze, Board Member
Ralf Reichert, Board Member
Alexander Muller, Board Member

WESA is an international body aiming to professionalize eSports by introducing elements common among traditional sports associations, including player representation, standardized regulations, & revenue shares for teams. It is a joint effort between eSports teams and eSports company ESL.

1654 **World Waterpark Association**
8826 Santa Fe Drive
Suite 310
Overland Park, KS 66212-3676

913-599-0300; Fax: 913-599-0520
wwamemberinfo@waterparks.org
www.waterparks.org
Facebook, Twitter, LinkedIn, YouTube, Instagram

Rick Root, President
Cathy Haggarty, Membership Coordinator
Kelly Harris, Dir. of Ops & Member Services
Aleatha Ezra, Director of Park Member Development
Patty Miller, Dir. of Trade Show & Advertising

The WWA is focused on providing park and supplier members with the education and networking that they need to operate safely and effectively.
1200 Members
Founded in 1982

1655 **XR Association**
1299 Pennsylvania Avenue NW
Washington, DC 20004

membership@xra.org
xra.org
Facebook, Twitter, LinkedIn

Elizabeth Hyman, Chief Executive Officer
Joan O'Hara, Senior Director, Public Policy
Laura Chadwick, Senior Director, Industry Relations
Michael Williams, Chief Operating Officer
Bethany Reitsma, Executive Assistant

Trade association for technology manufacturers in the virtual, augmented, and mixed reality industries.
Founded in 2016

Newsletters

1656 **ACE News**
American Coaster Enthusiasts
P.O. Box 540261
Grand Prairie, TX 75054-0261
469-278-6223; Fax: 740-452-2552
info@aceonline.org
www.aceonline.org
Lee Ann Draud, Publications Director
Elizabeth Ringas, Communications Director
Up-to-date information about ACE, the events, roller coasters, and amusement parks.
Frequency: Bi-Monthly

1657 **Adams Gaming Report**
Casino City Press
95 Wells Ave
Newton, MA 02459-3299
617-332-2850
800-490-1715; Fax: 617-964-2280
customerservice@casinocitypress.com
www.casinopromote.com
Michael A Corfman, CEO
Focuses on the gaming industry with nationwide coverage.
Cost: $149.00
Frequency: Monthly

1658 **Affialiate Connection**
International Festivals and Events Association
2603 W Eastover Ter
Boise, ID 83706-2800
208-433-0950; Fax: 208-433-9812
craig@ifea.com
www.ifea.com
Steven Wood Schmader, President & CEO
Nia Hovde, VP/Marketing
Craig Sarton, Director, Creative & Publications
The IFEA newsletter provides information and news 24 hours a day, 7 days a week, keeping members, suppliers and affialiates up-to-date and current.
2000 Members
Circulation: 2,700
Founded in 1956
Mailing list available for rent: 20000 names at $235 per M

1659 **Celebrity Bulletin**
Celebrity Service
252 West 37th St
Suite 1204
New York, NY 10017-3632
212-757-7979; Fax: 212-582-7701
mark@celebrityservice.com
www.celebrityservice.com
Mark Kerrigan, Manager
Nicole Bagley, COO
Nancy R. Bagley, President
Soroush Shehabi, CEO
A daily guide on the whereabouts and vital information of the famous. Includes celebrity contacts including agents, business managers, publicists, and record companies. Gives advanced notice of who's coming to town, what projects they're working on and how to get in touch with them. Features an International Page noting arrivals in cities worldwide.
Cost: $2245.00
4 Pages
Frequency: Daily
Founded in 1939

1660 **Connector**
Society of Broadcast Engineers
9102 N Meridian St
Suite 150
Indianapolis, IN 46260-1896
317-846-9000; Fax: 317-846-9120
www.sbe.org
John Poray, Executive Director
To youth members and high schools across the country that have radio or television stations. Provides students with information on careers in broadcast engineering, post-secondary education, high school student stations, scholarships and technical information.
Frequency: 3x/Year
Circulation: 300

1661 **ECA Today**
Entertainment Consumers Association
Home Page: www.theeca.com
Hal Halpin, Founder & President
Heather Ellertson, VP, Marketing
Mike Conley, Digital Marketing Coordinator
Newsletter for members only.
Frequency: Nightly

1662 **Entertainment Marketing Letter**
EPM Communications
19 W.21st St, # 303
New York, NY 10012-3208
212-941-0099
888-852-9467; Fax: 212-941-1622
www.epmcom.com
Ira Mayer, Owner
Michele Khan, Marketing
Terence Keegan, Editor
Covers marketing techniques used in the entertainment industry, and by others who link their goods and services marketing through entertainment properties.
Cost: $449.00
Frequency: 24x Year
ISSN: 1048-5112
Printed in on matte stock

1663 **INTIX e-Newsletter**
330 W 38th Street
Suite 605
New York, NY 10018
212-629-4036; Fax: 212-629-8532
info@intix.org
www.intix.org
Jena Hoffman, President/CEO
E-mail bulletin which includes news from the association, promotions, replacements, clips from industry news sources; vendor updates, conferences and exhibitions, the latest job postings, and listings of members searching for a job.
Frequency: Monthly

1664 **SBE-News**
Society of Broadcast Engineers
9102 N Meridian St
Suite 150
Indianapolis, IN 46260-1896
317-846-9000; Fax: 317-846-9120
www.sbe.org
John Poray, Executive Director
Email subscription of timely news and updates sent from the National Office.
Frequency: Semimonthly
Circulation: 4,000

1665 **Signal**
Society of Broadcast Engineers
9102 N Meridian St
Suite 150
Indianapolis, IN 46260-1896
317-846-9000; Fax: 317-846-9120
www.sbe.org
John Poray, Executive Director
Provides members with timely articles on various broadcast-related topics, information on upcoming events, recognition of members' activities and achievements and details of SBE services.
Frequency: Bimonthly
Circulation: 5,500

1666 **Theme and Museum Index Report**
Themed Entertainment Association/AECOM
150 E. Olive Ave.
Suite 306
Burbank, CA 91502-1850
818-843-8497; Fax: 818-843-8477
judy@teaconnect.org
www.aecom.com/What+We+Do/Economics/Theme+Index+Report
Judith Rubin, TEA Publications, PR & Social Media
Jennie Nevin, TEA COO
Annual attendance figures for the global attractions industry.
Frequency: Annual

Magazines & Journals

1667 **ARtillery Intelligence**
VR/AR Association
Palo Alto, CA 94303
nathan@thevrara.com
www.thevrara.com
Facebook, Twitter, LinkedIn, YouTube
Nathan Pettyjohn, Founder & President
Kris Kolo, Global Executive Director
Research and data package for VR/AR professionals.
Founded in 2015

1668 **Amusement Business**
VNU Business Media
49 Music Sq W
Suite 300
Nashville, TN 37203-3213
615-321-4251
888-900-3782; Fax: 615-327-1575
www.amusementbusiness.com
Michael Marchesano, President/CEO
Karen Oertley, Publisher
James Zoltak, Editor
Lisa Krugel, Classified Ad Manager
Serves the management of more than 10,000 mass entertainment and amusement facilities.
Cost: $129.00
Frequency: Monthly
Founded in 1894

1669 **Amusement Today**
PO Box 5427
Arlington, TX 76005-5427
817-460-7220; Fax: 817-265-6397
amusementtoday.com
Gary Slade, Publisher
Sammy Piccola, Accounting
Keeps decision makers in the amusement industry up-to-date with current events, business, international developments and new attractions at amusement parks and waterparks.
Cost: $50.00
Frequency: 14x/yr
Mailing list available for rent: 3000 names

1670 **Balloons and Parties**
PartiLife Publications
65 Sussex Street
Hackensack, NJ 07601
201-441-4224; Fax: 201-342-8118
info@balloonsandparties.com

www.balloonsandparties.com
Facebook, Twitter

Andrea P Zettler, Editor
Janet Slowik, Director

A decorating resource offering tips and suggestions for parties, special occasions, holidays, banquets and events. Targeted, informative and practical ideas for the event decorating industry. Motivates readers to produce professional, innovative party services.
Cost: $9.95
2 Members
Frequency: 4x/Year
Circulation: 7000
Founded in 1986
Printed in 4 colors on glossy stock

1671 **Bandwagon**
Circus Historical Society
3100 Parkside Lane
Williamsburg, VA 23185

757-259-0412
rfsabia@widomaker.com
circushistoricalsociety.org

Don Covington, President
Greg Parkinson, Editor

Publishes articles relating to circus history.
Cost: $5.00
Frequency: Bimonthly
Founded in 1939

1672 **Baseline**
Ziff Davis Media
28 E 28th St
Suite 1
New York, NY 10016-7914

212-503-3500; Fax: 212-503-5696
www.ziffdavis.com

Jason Young, CEO
Eileen Feretic, Editor
Stephanie McCarthy, Marketing

Publication that offers practical information and guidance on the management of information technology.
Cost: $205.00
Frequency: Monthly
Circulation: 125100

1673 **Billboard Magazine**
Prometheus Global Media
770 Broadwaye Blvd.
New York, NY 10003-9595

212-493-4100; Fax: 646-654-5368
www.prometheusgm.com
Facebook, Twitter

Richard D. Beckman, CEO
James A. Finkelstein, Chairman
Madeline Krakowsky, Vice President Circulation
Tracy Brater, Executive Director Creative Service

Packed with in-depth music and entertainment features including the latest in new media and digital music, global coverage, music and money, touring, new artists, radio news and retail reports.
Cost: $149.00
Frequency: Weekly
Founded in 1894

1674 **BoxOffice Magazine**
BoxOffice Media
9107 Wilshire Blvd.
Suite 450
Beverly Hills, CA 90210-4241

310-876-9090
www.boxoffice.com

Peter Crane, Publisher
Kenneth James Bacon, Creative Director
Phil Contrino, Editor
Amy Nicholson, Editor

The premier trade magazine covering the latest developments in the movie industry, from films in production to digital cinema and everything in between.
Founded in 1948

1675 **Camera Operator**
Society of Camera Operators
PO Box 2006
Toluca Lake, CA 91610

818-382-7070; Fax: 323-856-9155
www.soc.org

Kate McCallum, Editor
Stephanie Cameron, Designer

Features articles written by and about SOC members, presented from the camera operator's point of view. Encompassing the latest technological trends while reviewing historical productions, the Camera Operator seeks to enlighten and educate readers on the motion picture, television and commerical industries.
Cost: $20.00
Frequency: Semi-Annual
Printed in 4 colors

1676 **Carnival Magazine**
PO Box 4138
Salisbury, NC 28145-4138

704-638-0878; Fax: 704-636-1051
www.carnivalmag.com

Charles Dabbs, Publisher
Kevin Freese, Editor

Chronicles contemporary outdoor amusement history providing readers with information and news on carnivals, events, people, trade shows, manufacturers, suppliers and more.
Cost: $40.00
Frequency: Monthly

1677 **Carousel News and Trader**
11001 Peoria Street
Sun Valley, CA 91352

818-332-7944; Fax: 818-332-7944
roland@carouselnews.com
www.carouselnews.com

Dan Horenberger, Publisher
Roland Hopkins, Editor
Ted McDonald, Webmaster

Articles devoted to the collecting, restoration and selling of carousel art.
Cost: $35.00
48 Pages
Frequency: Monthly
Founded in 1985

1678 **Casino Journal**
BNP Media
2401 W Big Beaver Rd
Suite 700
Troy, MI 48084-3333

248-362-3700; Fax: 248-332-0317
www.bnp.com

Taggert Henderson, CEO
Marian Green, Editor
Lynn Davidson, Marketing

A primary information source for the key decision makers in the worldwide casino, lottery, parimutuel, bingo and emerging internet wagering markets.
Frequency: Monthly
Circulation: 13034
Founded in 1995

1679 **Connect Magazine**
8403 Colesville Rd
Suite 710
Silver Spring, MD 20910-6331

301-562-0777; Fax: 301-562-0888
membership@aza.org
www.aza.org
Facebook, Twitter

Dan Ashe, President & CEO

Your window to the professional zoo and aquarium world. Each month, the magazine features fascinating stories that explore trends, educational initiatives, member achievements and conservation efforts.
200 Members
Founded in 1924

1680 **Daily Variety**
5900 Wilshire Blvd
Suite 3100
Los Angeles, CA 90036-7209

323-617-9100; Fax: 323-965-5375
www.variety.com

Jay Penske, President
Abe Burns, Marketing
Millie Chiavelli, Managing Director
Steve Gaydos, Executive Editor
Paula Taylor, Creative Director

Focuses on film, television, video, cable, music and theater. Includes coverage of financial, regulatory and legal matters pertaining to the entertainment industry.
Cost: $329.00
Frequency: Daily
Circulation: 38248

1681 **Entertainment, Publishing and the Arts Handbook**
Thomson West Publishing
610 Opperman Dr
St Paul, MN 55123-1340

651-687-7000
800-344-5008; Fax: 651-687-5581
www.west.thomson.com

Charles B Cater, Executive VP
Laurie Zenner, VP

Provides information on the latest development in the expanding legal field of entertainment, publishing, and the arts. The articles focus on such issues as books, copyrights, right-of-publicity and more.
Cost: $538.00
Frequency: Annual

1682 **Essential Facts About the Computer and Video Game Industry**
Entertainment Software Association
601 Massachusetts Avenue NW
Suite 300
Washington, DC 20001

esa@theesa.com
www.theesa.com

Stanley Pierre-Louis, President & CEO
Gina Vetere, SVP & General Counsel
Andrew Bowins, SVP, Comm. & Public Affairs
Ana Molina, CFO

Tracks statistics about the video game industry in the US.
Frequency: Annual
Founded in 2000

1683 **Fair Dealer**
Western Fairs Association
1776 Tribute Rd
Suite 210
Sacramento, CA 95815-4495

916-927-3100; Fax: 916-927-6397
stephenc@fairsnet.org
www.fairsnet.org

Sarah Cummings, President & CEO

Offers information for fairground owners, managers and workers, fair related businesses.
Cost: $35.00
2000 Members
Frequency: Quarterly
Circulation: 1500

Founded in 1922
Printed in on glossy stock

1684 **Fairs & Expos**
International Association of Fairs & Expositions
3043 E Cairo
PO Box 985
Springfield, MO 65802

417-862-5771
800-516-0313; Fax: 417-862-0156
iafe@fairsandexpos.com
www.fairsandexpos.com

Marla Calico, President & CEO

The source for information on fair trends, innovative ideas, and association activities.
Circulation: 3250
Founded in 1885
Printed in 4 colors on glossy stock

1685 **Graphic Impressions**
Pioneer Communications
218 6th Ave
Fleming Building, Suite 610
Des Moines, IA 50309-4009

515-246-0402; Fax: 515-282-0125
www.pioncomm.net

Rick Thomas, President

Provides providing industry news and information including in-depth coverage of PIM, and PIAMS association news and events. Features cover technology, legal, environmental, niche printing, education, new products, marketing, distribution, finance and insurance.
Cost: $20.00
32 Pages
Frequency: 10 per year
Circulation: 7,000
Founded in 1995
Printed in 4 colors on glossy stock

1686 **Hollywood Reporter**
Prometheus Global Media
770 Broadway
New York, NY 10003-9595

212-493-4100; Fax: 646-654-5368
www.prometheusgm.com
Facebook, Twitter, YouTube

Richard D. Beckman, CEO
James A. Finkelstein, Chairman
Madeline Krakowsky, Vice President Circulation
Tracy Brater, Executive Director Creative Service

Gives fresh ideas for film and TV. Covers the full spectrum of craft and commerce in the entertainment industry.
Cost: $199.00
Frequency: Weekly
Circulation: 34770

1687 **Inside Arts**
Association of Performing Arts Presenters
1211 Connecticut Ave NW
Suite 200
Washington, DC 20036-2716

202-833-2787
888-820-2787; Fax: 202-833-1543
www.artspresenters.org

Mario Durham, President
Sean Handerhan, Marketing
Alicia Anstead, Editor
Margaret Stevens, Director
Laura Benson, Programme Manager

This publication explores issues critical to the performing arts, presenting and touring field.
Cost: $42.00
1900 Members
Frequency: Bi-Monthly
Founded in 1957
Printed in 4 colors

1688 **International Gaming and Wagering Business**
BNP Media
PO Box 1080
Skokie, IL 60076-9785

847-763-9534; Fax: 847-763-9538
igwb@halldata.com
www.spectrumgaming.com

James Rutherford, Editor
Lynn Davidson, Marketing
Tammie Gizicki, Director

Focuses on business strategy, legislative information, food service and promotional concerns.
Frequency: Monthly
Circulation: 25000

1689 **JUGGLE**
International Jugglers' Association
3315 E Russell Road
Suite 203
Las Vegas, NV 89120

702-798-0099; Fax: 709-248-2550
www.juggle.org

Scott Seltzer, Editor-In-Chief

Offers readers a variety of colorful articles and features on the art of juggling including interviews, a listing of jugggling clubs, upcoming events and more.
Cost: $30.00
Frequency: Quarterly
Founded in 1947

1690 **Journal of Leisure Research**
22377 Belmont Ridge Road
Ashburn, VA 20148

703-858-0784
800-626-6772; Fax: 703-858-0794
customerservice@nrpa.org
www.nrpa.org
Facebook, Twitter, LinkedIn, YouTube

Kristine Stratton, President & CEO

Advancing parks, recreation and environmental conservation efforts that enhance the quality of life for all people.
Founded in 1965

1691 **Journal of Physical Education, Recreation & Dance (JOPERD)**
Society of Health and Physical Educators
1900 Association Dr
Reston, VA 20191-1502

703-476-3400
800-213-7193; Fax: 703-476-9527
lstrecker@shapeamerica.org
www.shapeamerica.org

Stephanie A. Morris, Chief Executive Officer
Laura E. Strecker, Managing Editor

Provides a variety of information on health, physical education, recreation, and dance issues than any other publication in the field.
25000 Members
Frequency: 9/Year
Founded in 1885

1692 **Journal of Singing**
National Association of Teachers of Singing
9957 Moorings Drive
Suite 401
Jacksonville, FL 32257-2416

904-992-9101; Fax: 904-262-2587
info@nats.org
www.nats.org
Facebook, Twitter, LinkedIn

Richard Dale Sjoerdsma, Editor-in-Chief

The official journal of NATS, offering a wealth of research and insight from scholars and experts on teaching singing, with topics ranging from history and voice science to voice pedagogy.
Frequency: 5x times/year
Founded in 1944

1693 **Laserist**
International Laser Display Association
7062 Edgeworth Drive
Orlando, FL 32819

407-797-7654; Fax: 503-344-3770
www.laserist.org

Brian Gonzalez, President
Patrick Murphy, Executive Director

Providing the latest news about the art and technology of laser displays.
Frequency: Quarterly
Founded in 1986
Printed in 4 colors

1694 **Linking Ring Magazine**
International Brotherhood of Magicians
11155 S Towne Square
Suite C
St Louis, MO 63123

314-845-9200; Fax: 314-845-9220
info@magician.org
www.magician.org

Stephen Bargatze, International President

Keeps IBM members informed about what's happening in the world of magic.
13000 Members
Frequency: Monthly
Founded in 1922

1695 **Loading...**
Canadian Game Studics Assocation

jennifer.jenson@ubc.ca
gamestudies.ca

Suzanne de Catell, Editor
Jennifer Jenson, Co-Editor

Official journal of the Canadian Game Studies Association with articls on research into digital games.

1696 **Magic-Unity-Might: MUM Magazine**
Society of American Magicians
7566 John Avenue
PO Box 510260
Saint Louis, MO 63129

314-846-5659; Fax: 314-846-5659
webmaster@magicsam.com
www.magicsam.com

John Apperson, President
David Goodsell, National Secretary
Marlene Clark, National Secretary

You will find articles dealing with the business of magic, publicity, showmanship and the history of magic and the lives of famous magicians. Many of the creative minds in the business are regular contributors.
60 Pages
Frequency: Monthly
Circulation: 30,000
Founded in 1902

1697 **NRPA Express**
22377 Belmont Ridge Road
Ashburn, VA 20148

703-858-0784
800-626-6772; Fax: 703-858-0794
customerservice@nrpa.org
www.nrpa.org
Facebook, Twitter, LinkedIn, YouTube

Kristine Stratton, President & CEO

Membership publication delivering the latest news and information about upcoming events, research projects, educational opportunities, grants, and initiatives about NRPA and the parks and recreation community.
Founded in 1965

1698 **New Calliope**
Clowns of America International
PO Box C
Richeyville, PA 15358-0532

724-938-8765
888-522-5696; Fax: 724-938-8765
mycoai.com

Ruth Erkkila, Editor
Cal Olson, Editor
Tom Newton, Editor
Pat Newton, Editor
Sammy Smith, Editor

Contains informative articles regarding the art of clowning, such as make-up, costuming, props, skit development, etc. News of regional and local clown alley activities; resources for your clowning needs; information on the annual international conventions; information on the various regional conventions through the year.
Frequency: Bi-Monthly

1699 **Park & Rec Trades**
Trades Publishing Company
20 Our Way Dr
Crossville, TN 38555-5790

931-484-8819; Fax: 931-484-8825
subscribe@thetrades.com
www.parktrades.com

Tim Wilson, Owner
Kristie Irvin, Marketing

Event calendar and buying guides for amusement and recreation park professionals.
Frequency: Monthly
Circulation: 32000
Printed in 4 colors on newsprint stock

1700 **Parks and Recreation Magazine**
National Recreation and Park Association
22377 Belmont Ridge Road
Ashburn, VA 20148

703-858-0784; Fax: 703-858-0794
info@nrpa.org
www.nrpa.org

Douglas Vaira, Editor

NRPA's magazine keeps members informed about parks, recreation and envrionmental conservation efforts.
Circulation: Monthly
Founded in 1965

1701 **Play Meter**
Skybird Publishing Company
PO Box 337
Metairie, LA 70004-0337

504-488-7003
888-473-2376; Fax: 504-488-7083
news@playmeter.com
www.playmeter.com

Bonnie Theard, Editor

Trade publication that provides members with information on the coin-operated entertainment industry, including upcoming trade shows, new products, ongoing trends and more.
Cost: $60.00
Frequency: Monthly
Circulation: 60000
Founded in 1974

1702 **Pollstar: Concert Hotwire**
4697 W Jacquelyn Ave
Fresno, CA 93722-6443

559-271-7900; Fax: 559-271-7979
info@pollstar.com
www.pollstar.com

Gary Smith, COO
Shari Rice, VP
Gary Bongiovanni, CEO

Trade publication for the concert industry offering global coverage and information including concert tour schedules, ticket sales information and more.
Cost: $449.00
Frequency: Weekly
Circulation: 20000
Printed in 4 colors

1703 **Protocol**
Entertainment Services and Technology Association
630 Nonth Avenue
Suite 609
New York, NY 10036

212-244-1505; Fax: 212-244-1502
info@esta.org
www.esta.org

Beverly Inglesby, Editor
Lori Rubinstein, Executive Director
Jules Lauve, President

Featuring columns and articles of interest to professionals in the entertainment technology industry on business and technical topics, current standards issues, certification developments, and trade shows.
550 Members
Frequency: Quarterly
Printed in 4 colors

1704 **RePlay Magazine**
PO Box 572829
Tarzana, CA 91357-7004

818-776-2880; Fax: 818-776-2888
editor@replaymag.com
www.replaymag.com

Edward Adlum, Owner
Barry Zweben, Marketing

A trade publication for those within the coin-operated amusement machine industry, primarily distributors, manufacturers and operators of jukeboxes and games.
Cost: $65.00
Frequency: Monthly
Circulation: 36000
ISSN: 1534-2328
Founded in 1975
Printed in 4 colors on glossy stock

1705 **Research Quarterly for Exercise and Sport (RQES)**
1900 Association Dr
Reston, VA 20191-1502

703-476-3400
800-213-7193; Fax: 703-476-9527
www.aahperd.org
Facebook, Twitter, YouTube

Monica Mize, President
Judith C Young, VP
Paula Kun, Marketing

Publishes research in the art and science of human movement that contributes to the knowledge and development of theory either as new information, reviews, substantiation or contradiction of previous findings, or as application of new or improved techniques.
25000 Members
Founded in 1885

1706 **Rollercoaster!**
American Coaster Enthusiasts
P.O. Box 540261
Grand Prairie, TX 75054-0261

469-278-6223
info@aceonline.org
www.aceonline.org

Robert Ulrich, President
Lee Ann Draud, Publications Director
Tammy Baldwin, Editor

Magazine featuring in-depth articles of parks and coasters of the past along with profiles of today's coaster, parks, people, and places.
6000 Members
Frequency: Quarterly
Founded in 1978

1707 **Souvenirs, Gifts & Novelties Magazine**
10 E Athens Avenue
Suite 208
Ardmore, PA 19003

610-645-6940; Fax: 610-645-6943
sgnmag@kanec.com
www.sgnmag.com

Scott C Borowsky, President
Tony DeMasi, Editor

Trade magazine for the resort-gift, souvenir industry. Articles cover merchandising trends, profile successful operations, new products, trade show calendar, plus buyer's guide issue.
Cost: $40.00
Circulation: 42,362
Printed in 4 colors on glossy stock

1708 **Strategies: A Journal for Physical and Sport Educators**
Society of Health and Physical Educators
1900 Association Dr
Reston, VA 20191-1502

703-476-3400
800-213-7193; Fax: 703-476-9527
lstrecker@shapeamerica.org
www.shapeamerica.org

Stephanie A. Morris, Chief Executive Officer
Laura E. Strecker, Managing Editor

Delivers practical ideas, how-to information, and tips for sport and physical educators.
Frequency: Bimonthly

1709 **The Bulletin**
120 W Seventh Street
One City Centre, Suite 200
Bloomington, IN 47404

812-245-2284; Fax: 812-245-6710
acui@acui.org
www.acui.org
Facebook, Twitter, YouTube

Rich Steele, President
Marsha Herman-Betzen, Executive Director
Andrea Langeveld, Marketing

Features everything from research analyses to best practices to practical reports about trends in the field.
1000 Members
Founded in 1914

1710 **Therapeutic Recreation Journal**
22377 Belmont Ridge Road
Ashburn, VA 20148

703-858-0784
800-626-6772; Fax: 703-858-0794
customerservice@nrpa.org
www.nrpa.org
Facebook, Twitter, LinkedIn, YouTube

Kristine Stratton, President & CEO

Advancing parks, recreation and environmental conservation efforts that enhance the quality of life for all people.
Founded in 1965

1711 **Tourist Attractions & Parks**
10 E Athens Avenue
Suite 208
Ardmore, PA 19003

610-645-6940; Fax: 610-645-6943
tapmag@kanec.com

www.tapmag.com
Facebook, Twitter

Scott C Borosky, President/Ex Editor
Caroline Burns, Managing Editor
Larry White, Publisher
Kittey White, Account Executive
Laurie O'Malley, Account Executive

Trade magazine for amusement, national & waterparks, zoos, and aquariums, bowling, skating + family entertainment centers, forest festivals.
Cost: $49.00
28124 Members
Circulation: 31,388
Founded in 1972

1712 **Transactions of the Digital Games Research Association**
Digital Games Research Association

jose.zagal@utah.edu
todigra.org

Jose P. Zagal, Editor-in-Chief
Harald Warmelink, Support Contact

ToDiGRA is an international, open access, refereed, multidisciplinary journal for research on and practice in all aspects of digital games. It is both printed and available online.
ISSN: 2328-9422

1713 **Waterpark Development & Expansion Guide**
World Waterpark Association
8826 Santa Fe Drive
Suite 310
Overland Park, KS 66212-3676

913-599-0300; Fax: 913-599-0520
patty@waterparks.org
www.waterparks.org

Rick Root, President
Patty Miller, Dir., Trade Show & Supplier Rel's.
Aleatha Ezra, Dir., Park Member Development
Kelly Harris, Dir., Operations & Member Services

A useful reference includes vital information for someone developing a outdoor waterpark, a public sector spray park or a waterpark resort.
1000 Members
Frequency: Annual
Founded in 1981

1714 **White Tops**
Circus Fans Association of America
1515 S Butler Street
Port Angeles, WA 98363

360-452-1919
feedback@circusfan.org
www.circusfans.org

John Wells, Editor
Mardi Wells, Editor
Pete Adams, Responsible, Back Issues
Ken Sopelak, Advisory
Jan Sopelak, Advisory

Articles about the illustrious history of circus, including the greatest performers, famous acts and feats, logistical facts and figures, management and marketing, and the shows of yesteryear.
Circulation: 2000
Founded in 1926

1715 **World Waterpark Association Buyers Guide**
World Waterpark Association
8826 Santa Fe Drive
Suite 310
Overland Park, KS 66212-3676

913-599-0300; Fax: 913-599-0520
patty@waterparks.org
www.waterparks.org

Rick Root, President
Patty Miller, Dir., Trade Show & Supplier Rel's.
Aleatha Ezra, Dir., Park Member Development
Kelly Harris, Dir., Operations & Member Services

The waterpark industry's only complete listing for waterpark suppliers and vendors. Features over 200 different product categories, 1,000+ industry suppliers, and thousands upon thousands of product-category listings with the specific suppliers who offer those products and services!
1000 Members
Frequency: Annual
Founded in 1981

1716 **World Waterpark Magazine**
World Waterpark Association
8826 Santa Fe Drive
Suite 310
Overland Park, KS 66212-3676

913-599-0300; Fax: 913-599-0520
patty@waterparks.org
www.waterparks.org

Rick Root, President
Patty Miller, Dir., Trade Show & Supplier Rel's.
Aleatha Ezra, Dir., Park Member Development
Kelly Harris, Dir., Operations & Member Services

In each issue, members find profiles of waterparks around the world, business-related articles on topics such as management, safety, staff development, as well as both association and industry news. Additionally, members get product-related information to help them purchase products and supplies to make their parks run most efficiently and profitably.
1000 Members
Frequency: 10x/Year
Founded in 1981

1717 **World Waterpark Magazine Asian Edition**
World Waterpark Association
8826 Santa Fe Drive
Suite 310
Overland Park, KS 66212-3676

913-599-0300; Fax: 913-599-0520
patty@waterparks.org
www.waterparks.org

Rick Root, President
Patty Miller, Dir., Trade Show & Supplier Rel's.
Aleatha Ezra, Dir., Park Member Development
Kelly Harris, Dir., Operations & Member Services

A special edition of WWA Magazine that features waterparks currently oparting in Asia, spotlights on members, business-related articles, and association and industry news. Translated into Simplified Chinese.
1000 Members
Frequency: Biennial
Founded in 1981

Trade Shows

1718 **ACUI Conference**
Association of College Unions International
120 W 7th Street
One City Centre, Suite 200
Bloomington, IN 47404-3925

812-245-ACUI; Fax: 812-245-6710
acui@acui.org
www.acui.org

Michelle Smith, Director, Educational Prgms & Svcs
Marsha Herman, Executive Director
Tim Arth, Event and Corporate Sales Manager
Karen Keith, Financial Service Manager
Julie Sylvester, Office Administrator

Tours and outings, peer learning network, leadership meetings, orientation for new members, education sessions, seminars, networking fair, keynote speakers.
Frequency: Annual
Founded in 1914

1719 **AIMS International Safety Seminar**
Amusement Industry Manufacturers & Suppliers Intl
3026 S Orange
Santa Ana, CA 92707

714-425-5747; Fax: 714-276-9666
info@aimsintl.org
www.aimsintl.org

Holly Coston, Seminar Manager
Darlene Reese, Curriculum & Certification Manager

This AIMS event is a comprehensive week of hands-on instruction taught by today's top industry professionals, for individuals responsible for the care and safety of the amusement industry's guests. Certification testing also available.
Frequency: January

1720 **AMOA Amusement Expo International**
Amusement & Music Operators Association
380 Terra Cotta Rd
Suite F
Crystal Lake, IL 60012

815-893-6010
800-937-2662; Fax: 815-893-6248
amoa.memberclicks.net/amusement-expo-international

Lori Schneider, Executive Vice President

Coin machine industry showcase.

1721 **APAP Conference**
Association of Performing Arts Presenters
1211 Connecticut Avenue NW
Suite 200
Washington, DC 20036

202-833-2787
888-717-APAP; Fax: 202-833-1543
www.apapconference.org

Sandra Gibson, President
Sean Handerhan, Marketing
Leah Yoon, Director
Judy Moore, Conference Manager

Providing valuable networking resources and opportunities for performing arts presenters, artists and artist managers throughout the world. Hundreds of exhibitors and performances: see who is doing what in the world of performing arts. Educational tracks are offered; special events; special interests; and clinics.
1900 Members
4000 Attendees
Frequency: January
Founded in 1957

1722 **Amusement Expo**
American Amusement Machine Association
450 E. Higgins Road
Suite 201
Elk Grove Village, IL 60007-1417

847-290-9088
info@coin-op.org
www.amusementexpo.org
Facebook, Twitter, LinkedIn

Peter Gustafson, Executive Vice President
Ashley Davis, Membership Director
Tina Schwartz, Business & Finance Manager

Featuring the latest in video games, digital-jukeboxes, dartboards, redemption games,

plush toys, smart cards and more. Also offers educational programs and seminars.
140 Members
Frequency: Annual/February
Founded in 1981

1723 **Amusement Industry Expo**
I-X Center
One I-X Center Drive
Cleveland, OH 44135

216-676-6000
800-897-3942; Fax: 216-265-2621
info@ixamusementpark.com
www.ixcenter.com

John O'Brien, Director

Supplies and products for the amusement industry.
4100 Attendees
Frequency: March/April

1724 **Amusement Showcase International: ASI**
William T Glasgow Inc
10729 W 163rd Place
Orland Park, IL 60467

708-226-1300; Fax: 708-226-1310

William T Glasgow, Executive Director

Features exhibits and seminars for the coin-operated amusement industry.
4000 Attendees
Frequency: Annual/March

1725 **Augmented World Expo**
AugmentedReality.org

Home Page: www.awexr.com
Facebook, Twitter, LinkedIn, YouTube

Ori Inbar, CEO

Showcase for technologies making the world more interactive: augmented reality; virtual reality; and wearable technology.
4000 Attendees

1726 **BPAA Convention**
PO Box 4563
Louisville, KY 40204

502-473-0956; Fax: 502-473-7352
info@ialda.org
www.ialda.org

Michael Amaro, President

Nonprofit association of lawyers and other professionals who are actively engaged in representing the interests of the amusement and leisure industries.

1727 **Broadcast Engineering Conference (BEC)**
Society of Broadcast Engineers
9102 N Meridian Street
Suite 150
Indianapolis, IN 46260

317-846-9000; Fax: 317-846-9120
www.sbe.org

John Poray, Executive Director

Held in conjunction with the National Association of Broadcasters, features SBE Ennes Workshop followed by sessions covering the latest in broadcast technology.
500 Attendees
Frequency: Annual/Spring
Mailing list available for rent: 4700 names

1728 **COAI Annual Spring International Convention**
Clowns of America International
PO Box C
Richeyville, PA 15358-0532

724-938-8765
888-522-5696; Fax: 724-938-8765
mycoai.com

Adam Schill, President
Frank Bunton, Director, Conventions

The purpose of these conventions is to provide educational seminars, competitions for individuals and group skits, make up and costume competitions, as well as competitions in balloons and parade ability.
Frequency: Annual/Spring

1729 **Canadian Game Studies Association Annual Conference**
Canadian Game Studies Assocation

Home Page: gamestudies.ca

Kym Stewart, Local Arrangement Coordinator

Held in tandem with the Congress of the Humanities and Social Sciences.

1730 **CinemaCon**
National Association of Theatre Owners
750 1st St NE
Suite 1130
Washington, DC 20002-4241

202-962-0054; Fax: 202-962-0370
www.cinemacon.com
Facebook

Mitch Neuhauser, Managing Director

A gathering of cinema owners and operators.
4000 Members
3500 Attendees
Frequency: Annual/March/ Las Vegas
Founded in 2010

1731 **Comicpalooza**

Home Page: www.comicpalooza.com
Facebook, Twitter, YouTube, Instagram

Multi-genre convention on gaming, tabletop games, films, comics, literature, anime, cosplay, and more.
50K Attendees
Founded in 2008

1732 **DEXCON**
Double Exposure Inc.
Morristown, NJ

Home Page: www.dexposure.com

Gaming conference with a focus on board gaming, Larping, video gaming, and wargaming.
2200+ Attendees
Founded in 1992

1733 **Denver Pop Culture Con**

info@popcultureclassroom.org
denverpopculturecon.com
Facebook, Twitter, YouTube, Instagram

Multi-genre fan convention on comic books and web-comics, tabletop and video games, anime and manga, costplay, horros and sci-fi, movies, TV, and literature.
114K Attendees
Founded in 2012

1734 **ESTA Conference**
Esports Trade Association
541 N. Fairbanks Court
Suite 2200
Chicago, IL 60611

708-680-7133
info@esportsta.org
esportsta.org
Facebook, Twitter, LinkedIn, YouTube, Instagram

Megan Van Petten, Founder & CEO

Conference of the Esports Trade Association.
Founded in 2018

1735 **Electronic Entertainment Expo**
Entertainment Software Association
601 Massachusetts Avenue NW
Suite 300
Washington, DC 20001

Home Page: www.e3expo.com
Facebook, Twitter, YouTube, Instagram

Stanley Pierre-Louis, President & CEO
Andrew Bowins, SVP, Comm. & Public Affairs

Video game industry showcase featuring technology debuts and product launches.
50000 Attendees

1736 **FSGA Winter Conference**
Fantasy Sports & Gaming Association
1818 Parmenter Street
Suite 300
Middleton, WI 53562

608-310-7540
thefsga.org
Facebook, Twitter, LinkedIn

Christina McCoy, Executive Director
Michael Fiez, Marketing
Emily Petersen, Membership

January meeting of Fantasy Sports & Gaming Association members.

1737 **Fun Expo**
William T Glasgow
10729 W 163rd Place
Orland Park, IL 60467

708-226-1300; Fax: 708-226-1310
www.funexpo.com

William T Glasgow, Executive Director

Devoted to the family and location based entertainment industry and the trends that drive it. A focused and efficient event bringing buyers and sellers together in an atmosphere that allows industry professionals to conduct business.
Frequency: Annual/March

1738 **GAMA Trade Show**
Game Manufacturers Association
240 N.Fifth St
Suite 340
Columbus, OH 43215

614-255-4500; Fax: 614-255-4499
ops@gama.org
www.gama.org

John Stacy, Executive Director

For retailers, manufacturers, and industry professionals to network, see the newest products, and learn from others about ways to make their stores and businesses successful.
15000 Attendees

1739 **Game Developers Conference**
Informa Tech

415-947-6926
800-216-4916
gdcfeedback@ubm.com
gdconf.com
Facebook, Twitter, LinkedIn, YouTube, Instagram

The GDC provides education, inspiration, and networking opportunities to the video game development community, including programmers, artists, producers, game designers, audio professionals, and business leaders. The conference features discussions, awards ceremonies, community spaces for networking, and the GDC Expo.
Founded in 1988

1740 **Game On Expo**
Phoenix, AZ

Home Page: www.gameonexpo.com

Gaming convention with a focus on video and arcade games, board games, and tabletop games.
Frequency: Annual
Founded in 2015

1741 **GameSoundCon**
SoundCon, LLC
4735 134th Place SE
Bellevue, WA 98006

425-956-3725
brian@gamesoundcon.com
www.gamesoundcon.com
Twitter

Conference devoted to the art, technology, and business of video game audio.
350+ Attendees
Founded in 2009

1742 **GameStorm**
Red Lion Jantzen Beach
909 N. Hayden Island Drive
Portland, OR 97217

Home Page: gamestorm.org
Facebook, Twitter, Tumblr

Non-profit gaming convention with panel discussions, role-playing games, video games, and tabletop games.
Founded in 1998

1743 **Genericon**
Rensselaer Polytechnic Institute
110 Eighth Street
Troy, NY 12180

518-276-6000
chair.genericon@gmail.com
genericon.org

Convention for anime, science fiction, and gaming, featuring viewing rooms, karaoke, cosplay, video gaming and competitions, role-playing games, board games, and lectures.

1744 **IAAPA Attractions Expo**
Intl. Assn. of Amusement Parks & Attractions
9205 Southpark Center Loop
Suite 300
Orlando, FL 32819

321-319-7600
iaapa@iaapa.org
www.iaapa.org

Chris Lo, Director, Exhibitions & Conferences

Education event for entertainment facility professionals.
Frequency: Annual/Nov

1745 **IAAPA Leadership Conference**
Intl. Assn. of Amusement Parks & Attractions
9205 Southpark Center Loop
Suite 300
Orlando, FL 32819

321-319-7600
iaapa@iaapa.org
www.iaapa.org

Chris Lo, Director, Exhibitions & Conferences

New perspectives for amusement leaders.

1746 **IAAPA Tools of the Trade**
Intl. Assn. of Amusement Parks & Attractions
9205 Southpark Center Loop
Suite 300
Orlando, FL 32819

321-319-7600
iaapa@iaapa.org
www.iaapa.org

Best practices for midway, retail and food and beverage operations.

1747 **IAFE Annual Convention**
3043 East Cairo St.
PO Box 985
Springfield, MO 65802

417-862-5771
800-516-0313; Fax: 417-862-0156
iafe@fairsandexpos.com
www.fairsandexpos.com
Facebook, Twitter

Marla Calico, President & CEO

The International Association of Fairs and Expositions (IAFE) is a voluntary, non-profit corporation whose members provide services and products that promote the overall development and improvement of fairs, shows, expositions, and allied fields.
1300 Members
Founded in 1885

1748 **IFEA Annual Convention & Expo**
International Festivals and Events Association
2603 W Eastover Terrace
Boise, ID 83706

208-433-0950; Fax: 208-433-9812
schmader@ifea.com
www.ifea.com

Steven Wood Schmader, President
Nia Forster, VP/Marketing
Beth Petersen, Director Of Membership Services

Unites the world's leading festivals and events, suppliers, media, sponsors and related industry professionals to share information on every aspect of event production through in depth workshops, round table discussions and networking.
2000 Members
Frequency: Annual/Sept
Founded in 1956
Mailing list available for rent: 20000 names at $235 per M

1749 **IISF Trade Show**
1035 S Semoran Blvd
Suite 1045A
Winter Park, FL 32792-5512

407-681-9444
800-517-6222; Fax: 407-681-9445
oaba@aol.com
www.oaba.org
Facebook, Twitter, YouTube

Greg Chiecko, President

The OABA manages and influences concerns for its members. OABA believes that all business owners and members of the trade association should continue to raise the level of safety and quality in the mobile amusement industry.
4000 Members
Founded in 1964

1750 **ILDA Conference**
International Laser Display Association
7062 Edgeworth Drive
Orlando, FL 32819

407-797-7654; Fax: 503-344-3770
www.laserist.org

Brian Gonzalez, President
Patrick Murphy, Executive Director

One of the world's largest exhibitions of entertainment technology. Features international exhibitors from the fields of lighting, lasers, audio, video and staging.
70000 Attendees
Founded in 1986

1751 **INTIX Annual Conference & Exhibition**
INTIX
330 W 38th Street
Suite 605
New York, NY 10018

212-629-4036; Fax: 212-629-8532
info@intix.org
www.intix.org

Jena Hoffman, President

Combines educational workshops, committee and business meetings, networking and social events. Every major supplier serving he entertainment ticketing industry is represented at the exhibition. Launch new products and conduct user meetings for existing clients
Frequency: January

1752 **Independent Games Festival**
Informa Tech
303 Second Street
Suite 900, S. Tower
San Francisco, CA 94107

chairperson@igf.com
igf.com
Twitter

The IGF recognizes the best independent game developers, and encourages innovation in game development.
Founded in 1998

1753 **IndieCade**
Culver City, CA

central@indiecade.com
www.indiecade.com
Facebook, Twitter, YouTube, Instagram

Stephanie Barish, Chief Executive Officer
Sam Roberts, Festival Director
Celia Pearce, Festival Chair
Erin Shaver, Director, Operations
Shawn Pierre, Games Manager

The International Festival of Independent Games is dedicated to showcasing and supporting independent game development through a series of international events.
Founded in 2005

1754 **International Association of Fairs and Expositions Annual Convention**
International Association of Fairs & Expositions
3043 E Cairo
PO Box 985
Springfield, MO 65802

417-862-5771
800-516-0313; Fax: 417-862-0156
iafe@fairsandexpos.com
www.fairsandexpos.com

Marla Calico, President & CEO

Largest event serving fairs and expositions. Convention attendees are able to network and learn from each other during the intensive four days of workshops, special seminars, and round table discussions. Companies showcase themselves while serving as a one-stop shop for all of a fair's booking, product, and service needs.
5000 Attendees
Frequency: Nov

1755 **International Brotherhood of Magicians Annual Convention**
International Brotherhood of Magicians

11155 S Towne Square
Suite C
St Louis, MO 63123

314-845-9200; Fax: 314-845-9220
info@magician.org
www.magician.org

Stephen Bargatze, International President

A place where members can meet and network with others sharing an interest in the art of magic.
13000 Members
Frequency: July
Founded in 1922

1756 **International Ticketing Association Annual Conference & Exhibition**
330 W 38th Street
Suite 605
New York, NY 10018

212-629-4036; Fax: 212-628-8532
info@intix.org
www.intix.org
Facebook, Twitter, LinkedIn, YouTube

Jena Hoffman, President/CEO

Non-profit association committed to the improvement, progress and advancement of ticket management. Provides educational programs, trade shows, conducts surveys, conference proceedings, and its valuable membership directory.
1000 Members
Founded in 1979

1757 **Laser Tag Convention**
International Laser Tag Association
5351 E Thompson Road
Suite 236
Indianapolis, IN 46237

317-786-9755; Fax: 317-786-9757

Shane Zimmerman, Executive Director

The source for all things laser tag. Co-located with the Roller Skating Trade Show, this provides an opportunity to meet suppliers and manufacturers of laser tag equipment, video games, kitchen equipment and more.
Frequency: May

1758 **Laughter Works**
Laughter Works Seminars
PO Box 1220
Folsom, CA 95763-1220

916-985-6570
info@laughterworks.com
www.laughterworks.com

Jim Pelley, President

Seminars and keynote speeches on humor, create positive team environment, unleash creativity and enhance productivity in the workplace.

1759 **MAGFest**
Washington, DC

contact@magfest.org
www.magfest.org
Facebook, Twitter, YouTube, Instagram, Snapchat

Music and gaming festival to celebrate video games and video game music, running 24 hours a day for four days straight.
Founded in 2002

1760 **MidSouthCon**
Mid-South Science and Fictions Conventions, Inc.

info@midsouthcon.org
midsouthcon.org

Science-fiction-themed convention with programming that also includes comics, horror, costuming, and gaming.
2200 Attendees
Founded in 1982

1761 **Midwest Gaming Classic**
, WI

Home Page: www.midwestgamingclassic.com
Facebook, YouTube, Instagram

Trade show for all types of video game consoles, pinball machines, arcade video games, table-top games, computers, crane games, collectible card games, air hockey, and more.

1762 **Mobicon**
Renaissance Riverview Plaza Hotel
64 S. Water Street
Mobile, AL 36602

833-662-4266
president@mobilecomiccon.org
mobilecomiccon.org
Facebook, Twitter

Multi-genre convention on science fiction, fantasy, gaming, comics, anime, manga, horror, paranormal, and mass media.
1000+ Attendees
Founded in 1998

1763 **MomoCon**
Atlanta, GA

Home Page: www.momocon.com
Facebook, Twitter, YouTube, Instagram

A geek culture convention for fans of anime, gaming, comics, and animation.
39000 Attendees
Founded in 2005

1764 **NAPHA Chronicle**
Ntl. Amusement Park Historical Assn.
PO Box 871
Lombard, IL 60148-0871

Home Page: www.napha.org
Facebook, Twitter, Instagram

Only publication dedicated to the history of amusement parks.
Frequency: 6x/yr

1765 **NATS National Conference**
National Association of Teachers of Singing
9957 Moorings Drive
Suite 401
Jacksonville, FL 32257-2416

904-992-9101; Fax: 904-262-2587
info@nats.org
www.nats.org
Facebook, Twitter, LinkedIn

Allen Henderson, Executive Director
Deborah Guess, Director, Operations

Gathers professionals, scholars, and experts worldwide to share ideas and participate in lectures, workshops, and demonstrations aimed at promoting vocal arts and the teaching of singing.
Frequency: June/July
Founded in 1944

1766 **National Amusement Park Historical Association**
PO Box 871
Lombard, IL 60148-0871

Home Page: www.napha.org
Facebook, Twitter, Instagram

International educational organization dedicated to all aspects of the amusement park.
Founded in 1978

1767 **National Recreation and Park Association's Congress and Exposition**
National Recreation and Park Association
22377 Belmont Ridge Road
Ashburn, VA 20148

703-858-0784; Fax: 703-858-0794
info@nrpa.org
www.nrpa.org

Kristine Stratton, President & CEO

Education and training opportunity plus a tradeshow for the park and recreation industry.
4000 Attendees
Frequency: October
Founded in 1965

1768 **OABA Annual Meeting & Chairman's Reception**
Outdoor Amusement Business Association
1035 S Semoran Blvd
Suite 1045A
Winter Park, FL 32792-5512

407-681-9444
800-517-6222; Fax: 407-681-9445
oaba@oaba.org
www.oaba.org
Facebook, Twitter, YouTube

Debbie Powers, Chair
Andy Deggeller, 1st Vice Chair
Greg Chiecko, President

The OABA manages and influences concerns for its members. OABA believes that all business owners and members of the trade association should continue to raise the level of safety and quality in the mobile amusement industry.
4000 Members
Founded in 1965

1769 **Origins Game Fair**
280 N High Street
Suite 230
Columbus, OH 43215

614-255-4500; Fax: 614-255-4499
ops@gama.org
www.gama.org
Facebook

John Stacy, Executive Director

A non-profit trade association dedicated to the advancement of the tabletop game industry
450 Members
Founded in 1977

1770 **Penny Arcade Expo**

pax_questions@paxsite.com
www.paxsite.com

Video game expos held in cities across the States, and also in Australia. Expos feature exhibit halls, freeplay, tournaments, concerts, panels, and more.
Founded in 2004

1771 **Phoenix Fan Fusion**
Phoenix Convention Center
100 N. 3rd Street
Phoenix, AZ 85004

604-635-4306
phoenixfanfusion.com
Facebook, Twitter, YouTube, Instagram

Multi-genre convention on pop culture fandom, including comic books, sci-fi/fantasy, film and TV, anime and manga, animation, toys, card games, and video games.
57K Attendees
Founded in 2002

1772 **Pinball Expo**
Pinball Expo
3869 Niles Road SE
Warren, OH 44484

330-369-1192
800-323-3547; Fax: 330-369-6279

brkpinball@aol.com
www.pinballexpo.org

Robert Berk, Expo Chairman
Mike Pacak, Co-Expo Chairman

Annual show of manufacturers and related suppliers of pinball machines and supplies; tournaments and tours with over 50 exhibitors.
1,000 Attendees
Frequency: October

1773 **PortConMaine**
492 Main Street
Westbrook, ME 04092

331-704-0927
info@portconmaine.com
portconmaine.com
Facebook, Twitter, Instagram

Julie York, Founder

Convention dedicated to anime and gaming.

1774 **QuakeCon**
ZeniMax Media Inc.
1370 Piccard Drive
Rockville, MD 20850

questions@quakecon.org
www.quakecon.org
Facebook, Twitter, Instagram

Gaming convention to celebrate and promote video game studios owned by ZeniMax Media, with a large LAN party and other events.
Frequency: Annual
Founded in 1996

1775 **RSA Convention and Trade Show**
Roller Skating Association International
6905 Corporate Drive
Indianapolis, IN 46278

317-347-2626; Fax: 317-347-2636
rsa@rollerskating.com
www.rollerskating.org

Helping roller skating industry professionals discover ways to build strong foundations for their businesses.
1000 Members
Frequency: Annual/August
Founded in 1937

1776 **RTX**
Rooster Teeth
Austin, TX

888-512-7469
rtxevent@roosterteeth.com
rtxevent.com
Facebook, Twitter, YouTube, Instagram

Clarissa Gonzalez, Senior Events Manager
Patrick Matthews, Events Specialist
George Panga, Marketing Coordinator

Convention held to celebrate gaming and internet culture, with a focus on animation and comedy as well. Other events are held in Sydney, Australia, and London, England.
62000 Attendees
Founded in 2011

1777 **SLA Annual Meeting & Convention**
Showmen's League of America
1023 W Fulton Market
Chicago, IL 60607

312-733-9533
800-350-9906; Fax: 312-733-9534
joeb@showmensleague.org
www.showmensleague.org
Twitter

Mary Chris Smith, President
Robert Thorson, 1st Vice President

Promotes friendship and fellowship between its members and the outdoor amusement industry, and pledges to help those in need through one of its many programs.
Founded in 1913

1778 **Saferparks**
7514 Girard Ave
Suite 1322
La Jolla, CA 92037

Home Page: saferparks.org

Kathy Fackler, Founder

Amusement park safety tips for families.
Founded in 2000

1779 **TooManyGames**
Greater Philadelphia Expo Center
100 Station Avenue
Oaks, PA

info@toomanygames.com
toomanygames.com
Facebook, Twitter, YouTube, Instagram

Gaming convention with a new and used game marketplace, artists and creators, musicians, panels and demonstrations, LARPing, celebrities, an indie game showcase, and gaming arenas.
15K Members
Founded in 2004

1780 **TwitchCon**
Twitch Interactive, Inc.
San Francisco, CA

Home Page: www.twitchcon.com
Facebook, Twitter, Instagram

Convention for the video game streaming and on-demand platform Twitch, where fans can meet streamers and the online community in person, as well as play new games. The convention is hosted twice a year, once in North America and once in Europe.
50K Attendees
Frequency: Annual
Founded in 2015

1781 **VR/AR Global Summit**
VR/AR Association
Palo Alto, CA 94303

am@thevrara.com
www.thevrara.com
Facebook, Twitter, LinkedIn, YouTube

Nathan Pettyjohn, Founder & President
Kris Kolo, Global Executive Director
Anne-Marie Enns, Executive Producer

Summits bring together enterprise, hardware, software, and content providers for educational sessions and networking.
Founded in 2015

1782 **Virtual Reality Developers Conference**
Informa Tech

415-947-6926
800-216-4916
gdcfeedback@ubm.com
www.gdconf.com/vrdc
Facebook, Twitter, LinkedIn, YouTube, Instagram

The VRDC is a two-day summit for developers of Virtual Reality and Augmented Reality entertainment.

1783 **World Waterpark Association Annual Tradeshow**
World Waterpark Association
8826 Santa Fe Drive
Suite 310
Overland Park, KS 66212-3676

913-599-0300; Fax: 913-599-0520
aezra@waterparks.org
www.waterparks.org

Rick Root, President
Andy Miller, Trade Show & Advertising Manager

Exhibits include waterpark attractions, water quality equipment and apparel, with more than 300 booths. Also a great opportunity to attend all-day workshops and hour-long educational sessions, and to network with others in the industry.
1000 Members
2600 Attendees
Frequency: October
Founded in 1981

1784 **Yama-Con**
LeConte Center
2986 Teaster Lane
Pigeon Forge, TN 37863

support@www.yamacon.org
www.yamacon.org
Facebook, Instagram

Multi-genre convention on anime, comics, cosplay, and gaming.
2600 Attendees
Founded in 2012

Directories & Databases

1785 **American Casino Guide**
Casino Vacations
PO Box 703
Dania, FL 33004-0703

954-989-2766
800-741-1596; Fax: 954-966-7048
www.americancasinoguide.com

Steve Bourie, Author

A guide to every casino/resort, riverboat and Indian casino in the United States.
Cost: $16.95
448 Pages
Frequency: Annually
ISBN: 1-883768-11-X
Founded in 1992
Printed in one color

1786 **Association of Performing Arts Presenters Membership Directory**
1211 Connecticut Ave NW
Suite 200
Washington, DC 20036-2716

202-833-2787
888-820-2787; Fax: 202-833-1543
info@artspresenters.org
www.artspresenters.org

Sandra Gibson, President
Sean Handerhan, Marketing

An invaluable resource for members to keep in touch with colleagues. Puts more than 1,450 presenters, service organizations, artists, management consultants, and vendors at your fingertips. An excellent networking tool for everyone on your staff.
1900 Members
Frequency: Annual
Founded in 1957

1787 **Celebrity Access Directory**
Celebrity Access
2430 Broadway St
Suite 200
Boulder, CO 80304-4118

303-350-1700; Fax: 303-339-6877
sales@celebrityaccess.com
www.celebrityaccess.com

Peter Denholtz, President
Marc Gentilella, Editor
Keri Mullin, Marketing

Database directory of more than 35,000 performers that includes contact information for agents as well as links to websites, record companies, touring schedules, box office info and

more.
Cost: $899.00
Frequency: Annual
Founded in 1998

1788 **Data List & Membership Directory**
Western Fairs Association
1776 Tribute Rd
Suite 210
Sacramento, CA 95815-4495
916-927-3100; Fax: 916-927-6397
stephenc@fairsnet.org
www.fairsnet.org
Sarah Cummings, President & CEO
A premier source of fair industry information for the Western United States and Canada. Referred to as the Bible of the fair industry, this directory contains a complete listing of every member fair, festival, special event, fair-related business, fair association, and agriculture-related organization.
2000 Members
Frequency: Annual
Founded in 1922
Printed in on glossy stock

1789 **Dinner Theatre: A Survey and Directory**
Greenwood Publishing Group
88 Post Road W
PO Box 5007
Westport, CT 06881-5007
203-226-3571
800-225-5800; Fax: 203-222-1502
www.greenwood.com
Debra Adams, Editor
Listings of dinner theaters, including in-depth profiles are offered in this comprehensive directory.
Cost: $82.95
160 Pages
Frequency: Hardcover
ISBN: 0-313284-42-3

1790 **Directory of Historic American Theatres**
Greenwood Publishing Group
88 Post Road W
PO Box 5007
Westport, CT 06881-5007
203-226-3571
800-225-5800; Fax: 203-222-1502
www.greenwood.com
Debra Adams, Editor
Directory of theaters built before 1915.
Cost: $86.95
367 Pages
Frequency: Hardcover
ISBN: 0-313248-68-0

1791 **EPM Entertainment Marketing Sourcebook**
EPM Communications
19 W.21st St,# 303
3rd Floor
New York, NY 10012-3208
212-941-0099
888-852-9467; Fax: 212-941-1622
www.epmcom.com
Ira Mayer, Owner
Michele Khan, Marketing
Over 4,000 media companies, sponsors and retailers that provide products and services to entertainment marketers.
Cost: $95.00
278 Pages
Frequency: Annual
Printed in on matte stock

1792 **Grey House Performing Arts Directory**
Grey House Publishing
4919 Route 22
PO Box 56
Amenia, NY 12501
518-789-8700
800-562-2139; Fax: 845-373-6390
books@greyhouse.com
www.greyhouse.com
Facebook, Twitter
Leslie Mackenzie, Publisher
Richard Gottlieb, Editor
The most comprehensive resource covering the Performing Arts. This directory provides current information on over 8,500 dance companies, instrumental music programs, opera companies, choral groups, theater companies, performing arts series and performing arts facilities.
Cost: $185.00
1200 Pages
Frequency: Annual
ISBN: 1-592373-76-3
Founded in 1981

1793 **Grey House Performing Arts Directory - Online Database**
Grey House Publishing
4919 Route 22
PO Box 56
Amenia, NY 12501
518-789-8700
800-562-2139; Fax: 845-373-6390
gold@greyhouse.com
gold.greyhouse.com
Facebook, Twitter
Leslie Mackenzie, Publisher
Richard Gottlieb, President
The Grey House Performing Arts Directory - Online Database provides immediate access to dance companies, orchestras, opera companies, choral groups, theater companies, series, festivals and perfoming arts facilities across the country, or in their region, state, or in your own backyard. It offers unequaled coverage of the Performing Arts - over 8,500 listings - of the major performance organization, facilities, and information resources.
Frequency: Annual
Founded in 1981

1794 **SBE Membership Directory & Buyer's Guide**
Society of Broadcast Engineers
9102 N Meridian St
Suite 150
Indianapolis, IN 46260-1896
317-846-9000; Fax: 317-846-9120
www.sbe.org
John Poray, Executive Director
Provides a quick reference to all members and Sustaining Members' services. Offers a yellow-page guide section that contains categorical listings of all SBE Substaining Members and advertisements from leading equipment and service suppliers.
Frequency: Annually
Circulation: 5,500

1795 **Travel and Entertaiment Policies and Procedures Guide**
Institute of Management & Administration
1 Washington Park
Suite 1300
Newark, NJ 07102
973-718-4700; Fax: 973-622-0595
www.ioma.com
Joe Bremner, President
Perry Patterson, VP
Andy Dzamba, Editor
James Bell, Marketing
The report offers tips and suggestions to improve T&E operations, information on reimbursement policies and benchmark data, current trends, and more.
Cost: $329.00
Frequency: Annual
Circulation: 185,000

1796 **Who's Who in Festivals and Events Membership Directory & Buyers Guide**
International Festivals and Events Association
2603 W Eastover Terrace
Boise, ID 83706-2800
208-433-0950; Fax: 208-433-9812
craig@ifea.com
www.ifea.com
Steven Wood Schmader, President & CEO
Nia Forster, VP/Marketing
Membership directory list hundreds of festivals and vendor members.
2000 Members
2000 Pages
Founded in 1956
Mailing list available for rent: 2000 names at $235 per M

Industry Web Sites

1797 **http://gold.greyhouse.com**
G.O.L.D Grey House OnLine Databases
Grey House Publishing's online database platform, GOLD, provides Quick Search, Keyword Search and Expert Search for most business sectors, including amusement, entertainment and recreation markets. The GOLD platform makes finding the information you need quick and easy. All of Grey House's directory products are available for subscription on the GOLD platform.

1798 **www.aceonline.org**
American Coaster Enthusiasts
ACE is a non-profit organization with members across the United States that promotes the roller coaster industry through a variety of events and publications.
7000 Members
Founded in 1978

1799 **www.acui.org**
Association of College Unions International
Nonprofit educational organization. Dedicated to building community on campus through programs, services and publications with the common goal of unifying the union and activities fields.

1800 **www.amoa.com**
Amusement and Music Operators Association
Providing leadership for the amusement, music, entertainment and vending industry. AMOA works vigorously to protect and promote industry interests. Members include operators, manufacturers, suppliers, distributors, and consultants.

1801 **www.cavern.com**
National Caves Association
Nonprofit organization of publicly and privately owned show caves and caverns developed for public visitation. Provides access to a directory of caves for those seeking out adventure, fun and education.

1802 **www.circushistory.org**
Circus Historical Society

The Circus Historical Society is a not-for-profit educational organization whose mission is to record the history of the American circus. Members have the opportunity to meet and network at circus conventions where there are presentations, films and more.

1803 **www.coin-op.org**
American Amusement Machine Association
Non-profit trade association representing the manufacturers, distributors and part suppliers to the coin-operated and out of home amusement industry.

1804 **www.fairsnet.org**
Western Fairs Association
A non-profit association with members throughout the Western United States and Canada that strives to promote industry standards. Membership includes access to conventions and trade shows, educational training programs, as well as legislative advocacy support.

1805 **www.greyhouse.com**
Grey House Publishing
Reference directories for most business sectors, including amusement, entertainment and recreation markets. Users can search the online databases with varied search criteria allowing for custom searches by product category, geographic area, sales volume, keyword, subject and more. Full Grey House catalog and online ordering also available.

1806 **www.iaapa.org**
International Association of Amusement Parks &
Attractions

An international trade association that seeks to improve and support professional industry standards at permanently situated amustement facilities worldwide.
4,500 Members

1807 **www.ifea.com**
International Festivals and Events Association
A voluntary association of events, event producers, event suppliers and related professionals and organizations whose common purpose is the production and presentation of festivals, events, and civic and private celebrations.

1808 **www.intix.org**
International Ticket Association
Not-for-profit association representing 22 countries worldwide. Committed to the improvement, progress and advancement of ticket management through educational programs, trade shows, conducts surveys, conference proceedings, and produces a membership directory.
1,200 Members

1809 **www.laserist.org**
International Laser Display Association
Dedicated to advancing the use of laser displays, in art, entertainment and education. ILDA supports high industry standards, promotes safety and provides the opportunity for members to meet and network at trade shows and conventions.

1810 **www.magicsam.com**
Society of American Magicians
Promote and maintain harmonious fellowship among those interested in magic as an art, improve ethics of the magical profession, and foster, promote and improve the advancement of magical arts in the field of amusement and entertainment. Membership includes professional and amateur magicians, manufacturers of magical apparatus and collectors.

1811 **www.music-rights.com**
Ad Producer.com
Provides music rights providers with the highest quality platform to leverage the Web to market your services around the world around the clock.

1812 **www.natoonline.org**
National Association of Theatre Owners
Exhibition trade organization, representing more than 30,000 movie screens in all 50 states, and additional cinemas in 50 countries worldwide.

1813 **www.nats.org**
National Association of Teachers of Singing
Promotes and encourages the highest standards of vocal education and research at all levels, both for the enrichment of the general public and for the professional advancement of the talented.

1814 **www.oaba.org**
Outdoor Amusement Business Association
Promotes interest of the outdoor amusement industry. Provides members with public relations and safety services as well as it's monthly Show Time magazine and annual publication The Midway Marquee.
4,000 Members

1815 **www.rollerskating.org**
Roller Skating Association International
A trade association representing skating center owners, operators; teachers, coaches and judges of roller skating; and manufacturers and suppliers of roller skating equipment.

1816 **www.sbe.org**
Society of Broadcast Engineers
Professional organization of television and radio engineers and those in the related fields. SBE has members in 114 chapters across the United States and Hong Kong.

1817 **www.toyassociation.org**
Toy Industry Association
National organization for U.S. producers and importers of toys, games and children's entertainment products. Represents more than 500 member companies including designers, safety consultants, testing laboratories, licensors, communication professionals and inventors.

1818 **www.waterparks.org**
World Waterpark Association
International organization created to further safety and business effectiveness in the waterpark industry.

Associations

1819 **Accessories Council**
224 W 30th Street
Suite 201
New York, NY 10001

212-947-1135
accessoriescouncil.org
Facebook, Twitter, Instagram, Pinterest

Karen Giberson, President

International nonprofit promoting the fashion accessory industry.
280 Members
Founded in 1994

1820 **American Apparel & Footwear Association**
740 6th Street NW
3rd and 4th Floors
Washington, DC 20001

202-853-9080
www.aafaglobal.org
Facebook, Twitter, LinkedIn, YouTube, Instagram

Stephen Lemar, President & CEO
Maureen Storch, Senior Vice President, Membership
Natalie LaBella, VP, Communications & Marketing
Agata Borradori, VP, Finance
Madison Mugford, Meetings & Webinar Coordinator

The American Apparel & Footwear Association (AAFA) is the national trade association representing apparel, footwear and other sewn products companies, and their suppliers which compete in the global market. AAFA's mission is to promote and enhance its members' competitiveness, productivity and profitability in the global market by minimizing regulatory, legal, commercial, political, and trade restraints.
Founded in 2000

1821 **American Cotton Shippers Association**
88 Union Ave
Suite 1204
Memphis, TN 38103-5150

901-525-2272; Fax: 901-527-8303
bmay@acsa-cotton.org
www.acsa-cotton.org
RSS Feeds

William Barksdale, Chair
William Allen, President & CEO

ACSA members are engaged in a great enterprise, the purchasing, storing, tansporting and merchandising of America's most valuable cash crop and it's most abundant natural fiber.
Founded in 1924

1822 **American Flock Association**
PO Box 1090
Cherryville, NC 28021

617-303-6288; Fax: 704-671-2366
info@flocking.org
www.flocking.org
LinkedIn, Pinterest, YouTube

Steve Rosenthal, Managing Director

AFA members include manufacturers of roll-to-roll coated textiles, papers, and films as well as coaters of three dimensional objects and printers of apparel decoration and graphics art products. Industry suppliers are a key sector of the membership. The AFA is affiliated with the National Textile Association, a non-profit trade organization representing over 150 textile manufacturers and industry suppliers with operations in the U.S., and Canada.
Founded in 1984

1823 **American Sewing Guild**
9660 Hillcroft St
Suite 510
Houston, TX 77096-3866

713-729-3000; Fax: 713-721-9230
margo@asg.org
www.asg.org
Facebook, Twitter, YouTube

Rosemary Fajgier, Chair
Margo Martin, Executive Director
Sheryl Belson, Director
Carolyn Chen, Director

ASG is a membership organization that welcomes sewing enthusiasts of all skill levels. Chapters are located in cities all across the country and members meet monthly to learn new sewing skills, network with others who share an interest in sewing and participate in community service sewing projects.
20000 Members
Founded in 1993

1824 **Cashmere and Camel Hair Manufacturers Institute**
3 Post Office Square
8th Floor
Boston, MA 02110

617-542-7481; Fax: 617-542-2199
info@cashmere.org
www.cashmere.org

The Cashmere & Camel Hair Manufacturers Institute (CCMI) is an international trade association representing the interests of producers and manufacturers of camel hair and cashmere fiber, yarn, fabric and garments throughout the world.
25 Members
Founded in 1984

1825 **Chemical Fabrics and Film Association**
1300 Sumner Avenue
Cleveland, OH 44115-2851

216-241-7333; Fax: 216-241-0105
www.chemicalfabricsandfilm.com

International trade association representing manufacturers of polymer-based fabric and film products, used in the building and construction, automotive, fashion and many other industries.
40 Members
Founded in 1927

1826 **Color Association of the United States**
33 Whitehall Street
Suite M3
New York, NY 10004

212-947-7774; Fax: 212-594-6987
info@colorassociation.com
www.colorassociation.com
Facebook, Twitter, LinkedIn, YouTube, Pinterest, Instagram

The Color Association of The United States creates and delivers global color intelligence across industries. The Color Association serves as premier forecast agent, specialized educator, and trusted advisor to color professionals whose responsibility is to ensure marketplace success for their color decisions in the realm of brands, product and service, and spatial environments.
Founded in 1915

1827 **Costume Designers Guild**
11969 Ventura Boulevard
First Floor
Studio City, CA 91604-3570

818-752-2400; Fax: 818-752-2402
cdgia@cdgia.com
www.costumedesignersguild.com
Facebook, Twitter

Rachael Stanley, Executive Director
Brigitta Romanov, Assistant Executive Director
Suzanne Huntington, Member Services Administrator
Anna Wyckoff, Communications Director
Deme Stavrakas, Events & PR Consultant

The Costume Designers Guild (CDG) is Local 892 of the International Alliance of Theatrical and Stage Employees (I.A.T.S.E.). The Guild represents Costume Designers, Assistant Costume Designers and Costume Illustrators working at the highest levels of skill and expertise in motion pictures, television and commercials. The CDG promotes and protects the economic status of its members while improving working conditions and raising standards for our craft.
810 Members
Founded in 1953

1828 **Cotton Incorporated**
6399 Weston Pkwy
Cary, NC 27513

919-678-2220; Fax: 919-678-2230
www.cottoninc.com
Facebook, Twitter, Youtube, RSS Feeds

J. Berrye Worsham, President & CEO
Mark Messura, SVP, Global Supply Chain Marketing
Kimberley Kitchings, SVP, Consumer Marketing
John Morgans, VP, Administration
Jesse Daystar, VP, Chief Sustainability Officer

To ensure that cotton remains the first choice among consumers in apparel and home products, Cotton Incorporated helps companies manufacture, market, and sell cotton products more efficiently and more profitably.
Founded in 1970

1829 **Council of Fashion Designers of America**
65 Bleecker St
11th Floor
New York, NY 10012

212-302-1821; Fax: 212-768-0515
info@cfda.com
cfda.com
Facebook, Twitter, Instagram, Pinterest, YouTube

Tom Ford, Chair

The CFDA's goals are: to further the position of fashion design as a recognized branch of American art and culture, advance its artistic and professional standards, establish and maintain a code of ethics and practices of mutual benefit in professional, public, and trade relations, and promote and improve public understanding and appreciation of the fashion arts through leadership in quality and taste.
500 Members
Founded in 1962

1830 **Custom Tailors and Designers Association of America**
229 Forest Hills Road
Rochester, NY 14625
888-248-2832; Fax: 866-661-1240
info@ctda.com
www.ctda.com
Facebook, Twitter, LinkedIn

D-D Lazenby, Executive Director
Alan Rouleau, President
Mark Metzger, Director, Education

Established as a venue through which ideas and techniques for design, pattern making, fitting, cutting and tailoring could be shared and exchanged.
300 Members
Founded in 1880

1831 **Fashion Accessories Shippers Association**
137 West 25th Street
3rd Floor
New York, NY 10001
212-947-3424
info@fasa.nyc
www.fasa.nyc
Sara L. Mayes, President & CEO
Arlene L. Blocker, Membership Director
Anna Gorbatova-Dobran, Financial Manager
Trade association representing the interests of accessories manufacturers and importers.

1832 **Fashion Footwear Association of New York**
274 Madison Avenue
Suite 1701
New York, NY 10016
212-751-6422; Fax: 212-751-6404
info@ffany.org
www.ffany.org
Facebook, Twitter, Instagram, Pinterest
John Heron, Executive Director
FFANY's mission is to promote and assist the common business interests of its members. FFANY is committed to supporting New York City as the recognized national center of fashion trade and commerce and aims to ensure the city continues to be the best venue for both national and international footwear industry events.
300 Members
Founded in 1980

1833 **Fashion Scholarship Fund**
1501 Broadway
Suite 1810
New York, NY 10036
212-278-0008; Fax: 212-279-6241
www.ymafsf.org
Facebook, Twitter, Instagram, Pinterest, Vimeo
The YMA Fashion Scholarship Fund(FSF) is a national association dedicated to promoting education of the fashion arts and business by granting scholarships to talented students and facilitating internships, mentorships and career programs.
800+ Members
Founded in 1937

1834 **GS1 US**
300 Charles Ewing Blvd.
Ewing, NJ 08628
609-620-0200; Fax: 609-620-1200
www.gs1us.org
Facebook, Twitter, LinkedIn
Bob Carpenter, President & CEO
Yegneswaran Kumar, SVP & CFO
Melanie Nuce, SVP, Corporate Development
Siobhan O'Bara, SVP, Community Engagement
Bill Strawderman, VP, Marketing
Barcodes, eCommerce and data synchronization, to EPC/RFID and business process automation standards.
9000+ Members
Founded in 1973

1835 **Handweavers Guild of America**
1255 Buford Highway
Suite 209
Suwanee, GA 30024-8421
678-730-0010; Fax: 678-730-0836
hga@weavespindye.org
www.weavespindye.org
Facebook, Twitter, YouTube, Pinterest
Elizabeth Williamson, Executive Director
Ingrid Sciscoe, Membership/Development Coordinator
Kathi Grupp, Advertising & Marketing Manager
Whitney Young, Program Coordinator
Sally Orgren, Editor
An association that educations, supports, and inspires the fiber art community. Offers networking, education, and grants.
Founded in 1969

1836 **International Glove Association**
PO Box 146
Brookville, PA 15825
814-328-5208; Fax: 814-328-2308
internationalgloveassociation.org
Our mission is to further build an association that improves manufacturing and distribution of hand protection. Studying, clarifying, and recommending government action to help promote proper glove selection and use, and the interests of glove manufacturers and distributors, will help association members achieve success with customers and maintain a financially sound organization.
Founded in 2003

1837 **International Textile and Apparel Association**
PO Box 70687
Knoxville, TN 37938-0687
865-992-1535
info@itaaonline.org
itaaonline.org
Facebook, Twitter
Nancy Rutherford, Executive Director
Professional association for 1,000 college professors of clothing and textile studies.
Founded in 1935
Mailing list available for rent: 950 names at $80 per M

1838 **National Luggage Dealers Association**
1817 Elmdale Avenue
Glenview, IL 60026
847-998-6869; Fax: 847-998-6884
inquiry@nlda.com
www.nlda.com/stores.php
The National Luggage Dealers Association (NLDA) improves the buying power of the many stores it represents, giving the individual store owners the ability to compete with larger companies and department stores. Many of the founding members continue to be represented today by successive generations of family members.
130+ Members
Founded in 1925

1839 **National NeedleArts Association**
1100-H Brandywine Boulevard
Zanesville, OH 43701-7303
740-455-6773
800-889-8662; Fax: 740-452-2552
info@tnna.org
www.tnna.org
Facebook, Twitter, LinkedIn, Pinterest, Instagram
Janet Rapp, Executive Director
Buffy Levy, Events Director
Kelsey Kwasniak, Trade Show Senior Associate
Tom Manning, Marketing & Communications Director
Emily Marxer, Sales Director
TNNA is an international trade organization representing retailers, manufacturers, distributors, designers, manufacturers' representatives, publishers, teachers and wholesalers of products and supplies for the specialty needlearts market. These businesses create and market hand painted needlepoint canvases, hand-dyed and specialty crochet and knitting yarns, embroidery, needlepoint and cross-stitch materials, kits, tools and more.
2650 Members
Founded in 1975

1840 **North American Association of Uniform Manufacturers & Distributors**
12732 Harney Street
Omaha, NE 68154
402-639-0498
www.naumd.com
Steve Zalkin, President
Kathy Fedman-Zalkin, Chief Marketing Officer
Jackie Rosselli-Verrico, Director of Communications
Rick Levine, Director of Development
The North American Association of Uniform Manufacturers & Distributors (NAUMD) is a trade association representing the interests of all parties in the uniform & image apparel industry.
450+ Members
Founded in 1933

1841 **Private Label Manufacturers Association**
630 Third Avenue
New York, NY 10017-6506
212-972-3131; Fax: 212-983-1382
info@plma.com
www.plma.com
PLMA has steadily grown in size, reflecting the increasing importance of store brands to retailers and consumers. As you will see, PLMA member services have mirrored store brands new role in the marketplace, too.
3200+ Members
Founded in 1979

1842 **Sewn Products Equipment Suppliers Association**
9650 Strickland Rd
Suite 103-324
Raleigh, NC 27615-1902
919-872-8909
www.spesa.org
Michael McDonald, President
Maggie McDonald, VP, Communications
Marie D'Avignon, VP, Operations
Association of manufacturers and distributors that supply machinery, equipment and parts and supplies to the sewn products industry.

1843 **Sustainable Apparel Coalition**
82 Second St
San Francisco, CA 94105
Home Page: apparelcoalition.org
Facebook, Twitter, LinkedIn, Vimeo
Amina Razvi, Executive Director
Mandy Mooney, Sr. Dir., Marketing & Comm.
Wan Lee, Member Engagement Manager
Ruth Lin, Finanace & Operations Manager
Janet So, Events Manager
Alliance of the apparel, footwear and textile industries for sustainable production.

1844 **The Fashion Group International, Inc.**
8 W. 40th St.
7th Fl.
New York, NY 10018
212-302-5511; Fax: 212-302-5533
pmaffei@fgi.org
www.fgi.org
Facebook, Twitter, LinkedIn, YouTube
Maryanne Grisz, President & CEO
Charles Garone, Managing Director, Membership
Martina Lopez, Facility Coordinator
Gabriel Ayala, Graphic Design Lead & Social Media
Jazz Purewal, Special Events Manager

Global, nonprofit organization supporting the professional development of its members in the fashion and lifestyle industries.
5000 Members
Founded in 1930

1845 The Knitting Guild Association (TKGA)
1100-H Brandywine Boulevard
Zanesville, OH 43701-7303
740-452-4541; Fax: 740-452-2552
tkga@tkga.com
tkga.org
Facebook, Twitter, Pinterest
Arenda Holladay, President & Executive Director
Leslie Gonzalez, VP, Certification
Donna Estin, VP, Public Relations
Membership organization for knitters with focus on knitting education and enhancing knitters skills. TKGA seeks to advance creativity, knowledge and the quality of workmanship in knitting through education and communication.
11000 Members
Founded in 1984

1846 The Vision Council
225 Reinekers Lane
Suite 700
Alexandria, VA 22314
703-548-4560
866-826-0290; Fax: 703-548-4580
info@thevisioncouncil.org
www.thevisioncouncil.org
Facebook, Twitter, LinkedIn, YouTube
Kenneth T. Bradley, Chair
Ashley Mills, CEO
Brian Carroll, COO/CFO
Manali Patel, Controller
Maureen Beddis, VP, Marketing & Communications
Serving as the global voice for vision care products and services, The Vision Council represents the manufacturers and suppliers of the optical industry. We position our members to be successful in a competitive marketplace through education, advocacy, consumer outreach, strategic relationship building and industry forums.
263 Members
Founded in 1999

1847 Tri-State Linen Supply Association
1800 Diagonal Rd
Suite 200
Alexandria, VA 22314-2842
703-519-0029
877-770-9274; Fax: 703-519-0026
trsa@trsa.org
www.trsa.org
Facebook, Twitter, LinkedIn, YouTube, RSS Feeds
Roger Cocivera, President/CEO
George Ferencz, VP
Provides hygienic sustainable laundering services that offer cost-effective, energy-efficient solutions while protecting the environment and employing hundreds of thousands of individuals in highly safety-conscious workplaces nationwide.
1400 Members
Founded in 1913

1848 Unite Here International Union
275 Seventh Avenue
New York, NY 10001-6708
212-265-7000; Fax: 212-265-3415
ccarrera@unitehere.org
www.unitehere.org
Facebook, Twitter, Google+, RSS Feeds
D. Taylor, President
Gwen Mills, Secretary-Treasurer
Nia Winston, Gerenal VP
Rich Maroko, Recording Secretary
Annemarie Strassel, Communications
UNITE HERE represents workers throughout the U.S. and Canada who work in the hotel, gaming, food service, manufacturing, textile, distribution, laundry, and airport industries.
850k Members
Founded in 2004

1849 United States Fashion Industry Association
1717 Pennsylvania Ave NW
Suite 430
Washington, DC 20006
202-419-0444; Fax: 202-783-0727
info@usfashionindustry.com
www.usfashionindustry.com
Facebook, Twitter, LinkedIn, Google+
Julia K. Hughes, President
Shannon Brady, Communications Coordinator
Representing brands, retailers, importers and wholesalers, the association works to eliminate tariffs, quotas and other impediments to the free movement of textiles and apparel globally.
Founded in 1989

1850 Western and English Sales Association
451 E 58th Avenue
Suite 4128
Denver, CO 80216
303-295-1040
800-295-1041; Fax: 303-295-0941
info@denver-wesa.com
wesatradeshow.com
Facebook
Gerald Adame, Chair
Jay Phillips, President
Patrick Powers, Vice President
Scott Tucker, Secretary & Treasurer
WESA began under the corporate name Men's Apparel Club of Colorado. The goal was to create a forum where retailers, manufacturers, and sales representatives could conduct business in an atmosphere of fair trade and fellowship.
1200 Members
Founded in 1921

Newsletters

1851 Barbara's View/Shopping Guides
Barbara's View
PO Box 531006
Miami, FL 33153-1006
305-757-7638; Fax: 305-756-5353
barbara@barbarasview.com
www.barbarasview.com
Barbara Wexner Levy, President
Shopping guides for fashion cities around the world.
Cost: $18.00
Frequency: Monthly
Founded in 1976

1852 Clothing Manufacturers Association of the USA
Clothing Manufacturers Association of the USA
770 Broadway
10th Floor
New York, NY 10003-9559
646-654-5000; Fax: 646-654-5001
David L Calhoun, CEO
Statistical report on profit sales, production and marketing trends for the men's and boy's tailored clothing industry.
Cost: $30.00
Frequency: Annual
Circulation: 300
Founded in 1933
Mailing list available for rent: 100 names at $200 per M

1853 DNR-Daily News Record
Fairchild Publications
7 W 34th St
New York, NY 10001-8100
212-630-3880
800-360-1700; Fax: 212-630-3868
www.dnronline.com
Samuel Farrel, President/CEO
John Birmingham, Editor-in-Chief
Jim Rossi, Marketing
Don Miller, Circulation Manager
Tom Beebe, Creative Director
Supplies retail fashion, product merchandising and marketing news for men's and boys' fashion.
Cost: $85.00
Frequency: Weekly
Circulation: 15755

1854 International Association of Clothing Designers & Executives Newsletter
475 Park Avenue South
Floor 9 No. 9
New York, NY 10016-6901
212-685-6602
Joachim Hensch, President
Mina Henry, Director

1855 The Vision Voice
The Vision Council Of America
225 Reinekers Lane
Suite 700
Alexandria, VA 22314
703-548-4560
866-826-0290; Fax: 703-548-4580
info@thevisioncouncil.org
www.thevisioncouncil.org
Facebook, Twitter
Ashley Mills, CEO
Amy Applegate, Creative Director
Maureen Beddis, VP, Marketing & Membership
Newsletter for the membership of The Vision Council of America. A nonprofit association of manufacturers and distributors of sunglasses and sunglass parts.
12 Pages
Founded in 1940

1856 Uniformer
Professional Apparel Association
994 Old Eagle School Road
Suite 1019
Wayne, PA 19087-1802
610-971-4850; Fax: 610-971-4859
Sharon Tannahill, Executive Director
Seeks to enhance the growth of the professional apparel industry by educating uniform retailers.
1200+ Members
16 Pages
Frequency: Quarterly
Circulation: 500

1857 UpFront Newsletter
Embroidery Trade Association
P O Box 794534
Dallas, TX 75379-4534
888-628-2545; Fax: 972-755-2561
info@embroiderytrade.org
www.mesadist.com/trade_associations
John Swinburn, Executive Director
Dolores Cheek, Manager Of Member Services

A newsletter with advice and information on topics such as marketing, business operations and problem solving
1200 Members
Frequency: Weekly
Founded in 1990

Magazines & Journals

1858 **Accessories Magazine**
2 Penn Plaza
15th Floor
New York, NY 10121

Home Page: www.accessoriesmagazine.com
Facebook, Twitter, Instagram, Pinterest

Lauren Parker, Editor-in-Chief

Offers information on the latest in fashion, jewelry and accessories.
Founded in 1951

1859 **Apparel Magazine**
Susan S. Nichols
801 Gervais St.
Suite 101
Columbia, SC 29201

803-771-7500
800-845-8820; Fax: 803-799-1461
www.apparel.edgl.com

Susan S. Nichols, Publisher
Jordan Speer, Editor in Chief
Cindy DeBerry, Sales Manager

Trade publication for apparel/sewn products, manufacturing executives. Accepts advertising. Covers topics ranging from new products and technology to production management, sourcing, fabrics and financial news.
Cost: $48.00
180 Pages
Frequency: Monthly
Circulation: 18752
Printed in 4 colors on matte stock

1860 **California Apparel News**
MnM Publishing Corp
110 E 9th Street
Suite A-777
Los Angeles, CA 90079-1777

213-627-3737
info@apparelnews.net
www.apparelnews.net

Alison A Nieder, Executive Editor
N Jayne Seward, Fashion Editor
Deborah Belgum, Senior Editor

News and analysis on the largest manufacturing center in the country, special supplements on denim, lingerie, trade shows, textiles and more. Contains the only comprehensive coverage of Los Angeles Fashion Week.
Cost: $89.00
450 Pages
Frequency: Weekly
Founded in 1945

1861 **Children's Business**
Fairchild Publications
Po Box 5121
New York, NY 10087-5121

212-630-3880
800-932-4724; Fax: 212-630-3868
www.fairchildbooks.com

Debra Goldberg, Publisher
Tracy R Mitchell, Executive Editor
Ralph Erardy, Senior VP

Infants' and toddlers' wear, juvenile merchandise, footwear and toys.
Cost: $5.00
45 Pages
Frequency: Monthly
Circulation: 30458
ISSN: 0884-2280
Founded in 1985

1862 **Clothing and Textile Research Journal**
International Textile and Apparel Association
PO Box 70687
Knoxville, TN 37938-0687

865-992-1535
info@itaaonline.org
itaaonline.org
Facebook, Twitter

Nancy Rutherford, Executive Director

Official publication of the International Textile and Apparel Association.
Cost: $85.00
64 Pages
Frequency: Quarterly
Circulation: 1300
ISSN: 0887-3020
Founded in 1944
Printed in one color on matte stock

1863 **Costume! Business**
Gift Basket Review
815 Haines Street
Jacksonville, FL 32206-6025

904-634-1902
800-729-6338; Fax: 904-633-8764
www.festivities-pub.com

Debra Paulk, Publisher
Kathy Horak, Editor

News and current issues in the costume retailing business.
Cost: $29.95
Frequency: Quarterly
Circulation: 8,000

1864 **Dress**
Costume Society of America
390 Amwell Road
Suite 402
Hillsborough, NJ 08844

908-359-1471
800-272-9447; Fax: 908-450-1118
www.costumesocietyamerica.com/
Facebook, Twitter

Sally Halverston, Associate Editor
Rosalyn M Lester, President
Linda Welters, Editor-in-Chief
Margaret Ordonez, Managing Editor

Journal of the Costume Society of America. The Costume Society of America advances the global understanding of all aspects of dress and appearance.
ISSN: 0361-2112
Founded in 1973
Printed in on matte stock

1865 **Fashion Market Magazine**
Fashion Market Magazine Group
617 West 46th Street
New York, NY 10036

212-541-9350; Fax: 212-541-9340
www.fmmg.com
Facebook, Twitter

Victoria Monjo, Editor
Nicole Phillip, Fashion Editor

News for the apparel industry in New York, with original pictures and news in fashion, technology, finance and real estate.
Cost: $84.74
64 Pages
Frequency: Monthly
Circulation: 80000
Founded in 1985

1866 **Footwear Plus**
Symphony Publishing
36 Cooper Square
4th Floor
New York, NY 10003

646-278-1550; Fax: 646-278-1553
www.footwearplusmagazine.com
Facebook, Twitter

Greg Dutter, Editor-in-Chief
Pauline Lee, Associate Editor

Focuses on fashion, merchandising, trends and ideas in the retail footwear industry.
Cost: $50.58
Founded in 1989
Printed in on glossy stock

1867 **Hosiery News**
Home Sewing Association
105 Mall Boulevard
Po Box 369
Monroeville, PA 15146

412-372-5950; Fax: 412-372-5953
www.sewing.org

Dotty Grexa, President
Dale Sutherland, Treasurer
Jenna Sheldon, Director Trade Show/Meetings
Jenny Prevatte, Director Information Services

It covers all THA activities, industry news, personnel changes, statistics, legislative and regulatory concerns, marketing, technology, financial reports and new product information.

1868 **Impressions Magazine**
1145 Sanctuary Parkway
Suite 355
Alpharetta, GA 30009-4772

800-241-9034
impressions@bill.com
www.impressionsmag.com

Chris Casey, Publisher
Marcia Derryberry, Editor-in-Chief
Jamar Laster, Senior Editor

Offers news and information on the development or imprintable and imprinted sportswear and textiles.
Cost: $69.00
Circulation: 30000

1869 **Industrial Fabric Products Review**
U.S. Industrial Fabrics Association International
1801 County Road BW
Roseville, MN 55113-4061

651-222-2508
800-225-4324; Fax: 651-631-9334
generalinfo@ifai.com
www.ifai.com

Stephen M Warner, President
JoAnne Ferris, Director Of Marketing

Keeps individuals up to date on the information needed to keep their business growing.
Cost: $69.00
Frequency: Monthly
Founded in 1915

1870 **Juvenile Merchandising**
EW Williams Publications Company
2125 Center Ave
Suite 305
Fort Lee, NJ 07024-5898

201-592-7007; Fax: 201-592-7171

Andrew Williams, President
Phillip Russo, Publisher
Peter Berlinski, Editor-in-Chief

Offers news on the juvenile clothing, accessories and furniture industry.
Cost: $85.00
Circulation: 8000
Founded in 1938

1871 **Knit Ovations Magazine**
Woolknit Associates

267 5th Avenue
Suite 806-807
New York, NY 10016

212-683-7785; Fax: 212-683-2682

Eleanor Kairalla, Publisher

Fashions in knitwear for men and women trends in market; fashion color forecasts; guest features on knitwear by retail executives.

1872 **Made to Measure**
Halper Publishing Company
633 Skokie Blvd
Suite 490
Northbrook, IL 60062

224-406-8850; Fax: 224-406-8850
www.madetomeasuremag.com
Facebook, Twitter

Rick Levine, President

Serves the uniform and career apparel industry.
Frequency: Bi-annually
Circulation: 25000
Founded in 1930
Printed in 4 colors on glossy stock

1873 **Market Maker**
Advanstar Communications
6200 Canoga Avenue
2nd Floor
Woodland Hills, CA 91367

818-593-5000; Fax: 818-593-5020
info@advanstar.com
www.advanstar.com

Chirs DeMoulin, VP
Susannah George, Marketing Director
Joseph Loggia, President

Industry fashions
Cost: $2.00
Circulation: 14900
Founded in 1987

1874 **Menswear Retailing Magazine**
Business Journals Inc
1384 Broadway
Suite 11
New York, NY 10018-6111

212-686-4412; Fax: 212-686-6821
www.mrketplace.com

Bethany Raborn, Manager
Stuart Nifoussi, VP
Karen Alberg, Editor

Includes accurate information on the menswear retailing business, insightful analysis, bold ideas and real world fashion.
Circulation: monthly

1875 **Needle's Eye**
Union Special Corporation
1 Union Special Plz
Huntley, IL 60142-7007

847-669-5101; Fax: 847-669-4535
dkanies@unionspecial.com
www.unionspecial.com

Terence A Hitpas, President

Industry events, developments in machine-sewed products, informs about improved manufacturing methods, and promotes interest in Union Special machinery.
Frequency: Monthly
Circulation: 28595
Founded in 1881

1876 **Notions**
American Sewing Guild
9660 Hillcroft St
Suite 510
Houston, TX 77096-3866

713-729-3000; Fax: 713-729-9230
www.asg.org

Margo Martin, Executive Director

Contains articles written exclusively for us by the world's leading sewing experts, messages from the ASG Board of Directors and ASG National Headquarters, information about the latest sewing products and books.
Frequency: Quarterly

1877 **Outerwear**
Creative Marketing Plus
213-37 39th Avenue
Suite 228
Bayside, NY 11361

718-606-0767; Fax: 718-606-6345
rharrow@creativemarketingplus.com
www.creativemarketingplus.com

Richard Harrow, Presidetn/CEO
Duke Wollsoncoft, Creative Director

Focuses on outerwear buyers' needs, fashion trends, as well as leading buying offices and promotional plans.
Cost: $62.00
30 Pages
Frequency: Monthly
Circulation: 16000
Founded in 1983
Printed in 4 colors on glossy stock

1878 **Printwear Magazine**
National Business Media Inc
PO Box 1416
Broomfield, CO 80038-1416

303-469-0424
800-669-0424; Fax: 303-465-3424
pweditor@nbm.com
www.nbm.com

Bob Wieber, President
Mark Buchanan, Editor

Screen printing and embroidery equipment and technique, apparel styles and trends, heat-applied graphics, special effects printing and embroidery, business management and sales/marketing skills, digital transfers and sublimation, promotional products, embroidery digitizing, new products and the latest industry literature.
Frequency: Monthly
Circulation: 25000

1879 **Promotional Sportswear**
520 W Foothill Pkwy
Corona, CA 92882-6305

951-279-9327; Fax: 909-279-9327
www.promowear.com

Ted Taylor, Owner

Commercial direct screen printing, embroidery and complete art services on the highest quality sportswear available.

1880 **Promowear**
National Bussines Media Inc
P.O Box 1416
Broomfield, CO 80038

303-469-0424
800-669-0424; Fax: 303-469-5730
www.nbm.com/pr
Facebook, Twitter

Bob Wieber, President
Mark Buchanan, Editor

The latest style trends, detailed product and sourcing information, sales and marketing tips, industry news.
Frequency: 6 Issues/Year
Founded in 1990

1881 **Shuttle Spindle & Dyepot**
Handweavers Guild of America
1255 Buford Highway
Suite 209
Suwanee, GA 30024-8421

678-730-0010; Fax: 678-730-0836
hga@weavespindye.org
www.weavespindye.org

Sally Orgren, Editor
Elizabeth Williamson, Executive Director
Kathi Grupp, Advertising Manager

Contains articles about the fibre arts covering topics such as design, history, shows, educations, products, books, and news.
Frequency: Quarterly

1882 **Stitches**
4800 Street Road
Trevose, PA 19053

800-546-1350
800-546-1350; Fax: 215-953-3107
www.asipublications.com/stitches
Facebook, Twitter

Nicole Rollender, Editor
Ed Koehler, Advertising Director

Information and the latest technology for embroidery professionals.
Circulation: 17233
Founded in 1987

1883 **Tack N' Togs Merchandising**
The Miller Publishing Company
12400 Whitewater Dr
Suite 160
Minnetonka, MN 55343-4590

952-931-0211; Fax: 952-938-1832
www.tackntogs.com
Facebook, Twitter

Sarah Muirhead, Publisher
Julie Golson-Richards, Associate Editor
Cindy Miller-Johnson, Adverting Sales Manager
Michelle Adaway, Advertising Account Executive

Providing the latest news and information on equine retailing.
Frequency: Monthly
Circulation: 20424
Founded in 1970

1884 **Textile Rental Magazine**
Textile Rental Services Association
1800 Diagonal Rd
Suite 200
Alexandria, VA 22314-2842

703-519-0029
877-770-9274; Fax: 703-519-0026
trsa@trsa.org
www.trsa.org

Roger Cocivera, President/CEO
Jack Morgan, Editor

Packed with valuable tips and ideas.
Frequency: Monthly

1885 **Uniformer**
Professional Apparel Association
994 Old Eagle School Road
Suite 1019
Wayne, PA 19087-1866

610-971-4850; Fax: 771-261-4859

Hope Silverman, Executive Director
Frequency: Quarterly

1886 **Vows Magazine**
Peter Grimes
24 Daisy St
Ladera Ranch, CA 92694-0709

949-388-4848; Fax: 949-388-8448
www.vowsmagazine.com

Kori Grimes, Owner
Karlnon Nazarro, Director

Bridal retail, including how to survive as an independent retailer, how to merchandise and promote your business, how to effectively sell and train a sales staff, as well as identifying fashion and consumer shopping trends and preferences.
Founded in 1990

1887 **Women's Wear Daily**
Fairchild Publications
750 3rd Ave
New York, NY 10017-2703

212-630-3500
800-289-0273; Fax: 212-630-3566
www.wwd.com
Twitter

Mary G Berner, CEO
Christine Guilfoyle, Publisher
Edward Nardoza, Editor in Chief

Serves as the voice of authority, international newswire and agent of change for the fashion, beauty and retail industries
Cost: $195.00
Frequency: Daily
Circulation: 43618
Founded in 1892

Trade Shows

1888 **ASD/AMD Las Vegas Trade Show**
ASD/AMD Group
6255 W. Sunset Blvd
19th Floor
Los Angeles, CA 90028

323-817-2200
800-421-4511; Fax: 310-481-1900
www.asdonline.com

Greg Farrar, President
Mark Hosbein, Marketing

Provides a portfolio of innovative face to face, print and online products for the wholesale industry.
10000 Attendees
Frequency: BiAnnual/August/March

1889 **ASG Conference**
American Sewing Guild
9660 Hillcroft
Suite 510
Houston, TX 77096

713-729-3000; Fax: 713-729-9230
www.asg.org

Margo Martin, Executive Director

Gives all Guild members the opportunity to meet sewing professionals, industry representatives, and other sewing enthusiasts from around the country, and to participate in sewing seminars and sewing related special events and tours.
20000 Attendees
Frequency: Annual/July

1890 **AccessoriesTheShow**
UBM Fashion
50 Day Street
Norwalk, CT 06854

203-853-6015
800-358-6678; Fax: 203-852-8175
www.ubmfashion.com
F, Instagram

All accessories trade event in the fashion capital of the US attracts thousands of fine specialty buyers.
22k + Attendees

1891 **Action Sports Retailer Trade Exposition**
Miller Freeman Publications
PO Box 1899
Laguna Beach, CA 92652

847-296-6742; Fax: 847-391-9827
info@nsga.org
www.nsga.org

Matt Carlson, President & Ceo

Manufacturers, suppliers, retailers, buyers, guides, outfitters, distributors, importers, exporters, press and industry influencers have converged at Fly-Fishing Retailer to chart the future of their business.

1892 **American Flock Association Annual Meeting**
American Flock Association
6 Beacon Street
Suite 1125
Boston, MA 02108

617-303-6288; Fax: 704-671-2366
info@flocking.org
www.flocking.org

Karl Spilhaus, President
Steve Rosenthal, Managing Director

Provides positive leadership to foster a strong flock industry in North America.
60 Members
Founded in 1984

1893 **Apparel Importers Trade and Transportation Conference**
United States Fashion Industry Association (USFIA)
1140 Connecticut Ave.
Suite 950
Washington, DC 20036

202-419-0444; Fax: 202-783-0727
www.importersapparelconference.com
Facebook, Twitter, LinkedIn, Google+

Julia K. Hughes, President

Hot topics from the apparel products supply chain.
Frequency: Annual
Founded in 1989

1894 **Apparel Show of the Americas**
Bobbin Publishing/Miller Freeman
PO Box 279
Euless, TX 76039

817-215-1600
800-693-1363; Fax: 817-215-1666
www.mfi.com

Betty Webb, Trade Show Director

Conference, seminar and 329 exhibits of equipment, fabrics, accessories and services for sewn products and apparel.
Founded in 1992

1895 **Arnold Sports Festival**
Arnold Sports Festival
1215 Worthington Woods Blvd.
Worthington, OH 43805

614-431-2600; Fax: 516-625-1023
lpinney@arnoldexpo.com
www.arnoldsportsfestival.com
Facebook, Twitter

Lucy Pinneyr, Event Chair
Brent LaLonda, Media Contact

Five days of fitness equipment, sports entertainment, supplements, apparel and athletic stars, with more than 17,000 competitive athletes in 40 sporting events. Over 500 exhibitors.
150M+ Attendees
Frequency: March
Founded in 1976

1896 **Bead and Button Show**
Kalmbach Publishing Company
21027 Crossroads Circle
PO Box 1612
Waukesha, WI 53187-1612

262-796-8776
800-533-6644; Fax: 262-796-1615
www.beadandbuttonshow.com
Facebook

Gerald Boettcher, President

The biggest bead show in the country.
3500 Attendees
Frequency: Annual/May
Founded in 1985

1897 **Big and Tall Men's Apparel Needs Show**
Specialty Trade Show
3939 Hardie Road
Coconut Grove, FL 33133-6437

305-663-6635; Fax: 305-661-8118
www.spectrade.com

A gathering of buyers and vendors of apparel and accessories for tall and plus sized men. 200 Exhibitors.
1,500 Attendees
Frequency: February/August

1898 **Chicago Men's Collective: Winter**
Merchandise Mart Properties Inc
222 Merchandise Mart Plaza
Suite 470
Chicago, IL 60654

312-527-7635
800-677-6278
bschedler@mmart.com
www.mmart.com

Bruce Schedler, VP

Approximately 300 exhibitors and over 1,000 lines of product featuring men's fashion business attire.
5000 Attendees
Frequency: August

1899 **Convergence**
Handweavers Guild of America
1255 Buford Highway
Suite 209
Suwanee, GA 30024-8421

678-730-0010; Fax: 678-730-0836
hga@weavespindye.org
www.weavespindye.org

Elizabeth Williamson, Executive Director
Penny Morgan, President
Kathi Grupp, Advertising Manager
Linda Campbell, Exhibit & Editorial Assistant

Conference for everyone who loves and works in fiber.
3000 Attendees
Frequency: June, Biennial
Founded in 1969

1900 **E-Sports & Business Services Show at the Super Show**
Communications & Show Management
1450 NE 123rd Street
North Miami, FL 33161

305-893-8771; Fax: 305-893-8783
www.bizbash.com
Facebook, Twitter

Tom Cove, President

Retailers, distributors, wholesalers, importers/exporters and other buyers of sports related products come for 10,000 exhibits of sports apparel, footwear, accessories and e-commerce products and services.
100k Attendees
Frequency: Annual/January

1901 **EGA National Seminar**
Embroiderers' Guild of America

1355 Bardstown Road
Suite 157
Louisville, KY 40204

502-589-6956; Fax: 502-584-7900
www.egausa.org

Lorie Welker, President
Barbara Harrison, VP

Lectures, workshops and networking.
20000 Attendees

1902 **Eastern Men's Market/Collective**
AmericasMart Atlanta
240 Peachtree Street NW
Suite 2200
Atlanta, GA 30303-1327

404-220-3000
800-285-6278; Fax: 404-220-3030
webmaster@americasmart.com
www.americasmart.com
Facebook, Twitter

Jeff Portman, President/COO
Hank Almquist, VP

An outlet for the latest trends and designs in products and services.
500 Attendees

1903 **Embroidery Trade Association Convention**
Embroidery Trade Association
PO Box 794534
Dallas, TX 75379-4534

972-247-0415
888-628-2545; Fax: 972-755-2561
info@embroiderytrade.org

John Swinburn, Executive Director

An organization with the objective to continually strengthen the commercial embroidery business.
1200 Members
Founded in 1990

1904 **FFANY Collections**
Fashion Footwear Association of New York
274 Madison Avenue
Suite 1701
New York, NY 10016

212-751-6422; Fax: 212-751-6404
info@ffany.org
www.ffany.org
Facebook, Twitter

John Heron, Executive Director

The essential venue for fashion footwear. Held at FFANY participating show rooms.
300 Attendees
Frequency: August
Founded in 1980

1905 **Fabric Exhibition**
Advanstar Communications
2501 Colorado Avenue
Suite 280
Santa Monica, CA 90404

310-857-7500; Fax: 310-857-7500
info@advanstar.com
www.advanstar.com

Joseph Loggia, President
Chris DeMoulin, VP
Susannah George, Marketing Director

Conference and exhibition of interest to those in the fabric and garment industry.
7000 Attendees

1906 **Fitness Show at the Super Show**
Communications & Show Management
1450 NE 123rd Street
North Miami, FL 33161

305-893-8771; Fax: 305-893-8783
www.bizbash.com

Tom Cove, President

Retailers, distributors, wholesalers, importers/exporters and other buyers of sports related products come for 10,000 exhibits of sports apparel, footwear, accessories and e-commerce products and services.
100k Attendees
Frequency: Annual/January

1907 **Gatlinburg Apparel & Jewelry Market**
Norton Shows
PO Box 265
Gatlinburg, TN 37738

865-436-6151; Fax: 865-436-6152
www.nortonshows.com

Tom Norton, Show Manager/Owner
Linda Norton, Owner

Trade show that has wholesale, cash-and-carry, ladies, men's, and children's apparel, fashion jewelry, accessories, fine jewelry and gifts from around the world. There are 500-700 booths.
20000 Attendees
Frequency: March/June/Sept/Nov
Founded in 1987
Mailing list available for rent: 70,000 names

1908 **Global Leather**
American Apparel & Footwear Association
1601 N Kent Street
Suite 1200
Arlington, VA 22205

703-524-1864
800-520-2262; Fax: 847-522-6741
info@globalleathers.com
globalleathers.com

Kevin M Burke, President
Stephen E Lamar, VP
Dawn Van Dyke, Marketing

Showcases the best in new leather materials and components for footwear leather, needle and allied trades of North America. Brings together hundreds of exhibitors from the major sourcing cities around the world, showcasing thousands of products.
1500 Attendees
Frequency: February/August
Founded in 1981

1909 **Holiday Sample Sale**
San Francisco Design Center
635 8th Street
San Francisco, CA 94103

415-490-5800; Fax: 415-490-5885
www.sfdesigncenter.com

Dianne Travalini, Show Director
Aruex Dalmacio, Show Manager

Open to the public and offers jewelry, accessories and leather items, gift items, home accessories, housewares, toys and apparel.
11000 Attendees
Frequency: November

1910 **Hospitality Design Expo**
American Flock Association
6 Beacon Street
Suite 1125
Boston, MA 02108

617-303-6288; Fax: 617-542-2199
info@flocking.org
www.flocking.org

Steve Rosenthal, Director

Provides positive leadership to foster a strong flock industry in North America.
Frequency: May

1911 **IACDE Convention**
Internatl Assoc of Clothing Designers & Executives
835 NW 36th Terrace
Oklahoma City, OK 73118

405-602-8037; Fax: 405-602-8038

Joachim Hensch, President
Mina Henry, Director

Focus is on the retail link in the apparel supply chain. The students and faculty of the Fashion Institute of Technology are involved in the planning and presentation of many of the convention programs.
Frequency: Annual
Founded in 1910

1912 **ISAM: International Swimwear and Activewear Market**
California Market Center
110 E 9th Street
Los Angeles, CA 90079

213-303-3688
800-225-6278; Fax: 213-630-3708

Barbara Brady, Director

Serves the swimwear and resortwear industry.
Frequency: August/September
Founded in 1978

1913 **Imprinted Sportswear Shows (ISS)**
Imprinted Sportswear Shows (ISS)
Nielson Business Media
1145 Sanctuary Parkway, Ste 355
Alpharetta, GA 30004-4756

800-933-8735; Fax: 770-777-8700
issshows@xpressreg.net
www.issshows.com

David Loechner, President
Michael Alicea, Senior VP

Shows in: Long Beach, Orlando, Atlantic City, Atlanta and Fort Worth. Showcases the newest products, apparel, and equipment featuring new technology, sublimation, and techniques with hands-on demos. There are new conferences at every show providing learning and networking opportunities. Discuss business opportunities, best practices, artistic trends, and techniques.
Founded in 1981

1914 **International Fashion Boutique Show**
Advanstar Communications
757 3rd Ave
New York, NY 10017-2013

212-951-6600; Fax: 212-951-6793
info@advanstar.com
www.advanstar.com

Offers a variety of fashion trade shows throughout each year at the Javitz Convention Center in New York.
25000 Attendees

1915 **International Fashion Fabric Exhibition**
Advanstar Communications
641 Lexington Avenue
8th Floor
New York, NY 10022

212-951-6600; Fax: 212-951-6793
info@advanstar.com
www.advanstar.com

Joseph Loggia, CEO
Tony Calanca, Executive Vice President
Steven Sturm, Executive Vice President

Conference and exhibits of interest to those in the fabric and garment industries.
15000 Attendees

1916 **International Hosiery Exposition**
Home Sewing Association

105 Mall Boulevard
PO Box 369
Monroeville, PA 15146

412-372-5950; Fax: 412-372-5953
www.sewing.org

Dotty Grexa, President
Jenna Sheldon, Director Trade Show/Meetings
Jenny Prevatte, Director Information Services

Specialize in the latest hosiery and sewn products industries' supplies and services. 250 Exhibitors.
10000 Attendees

1917 **International Intimate Apparel Lingerie Show**
Specialty Trade Show
3939 Hardle Road
Coconut Grove, FL 33133-6437

305-663-6635; Fax: 305-661-8118

Jeff Yunis, President

Specializing in lingerie and adult products.
2,000 Attendees
Frequency: October

1918 **International Kids Fashion Show**
Advanstar Communications
641 Lexington Avenue
8th Floor
New York, NY 10022

212-951-6600; Fax: 212-951-6793
info@advanstar.com
www.advanstar.com

Joseph Loggia, CEO
Thomas Ehardt, Executive Vice President

Children's fashions, accessories, gift items, and footwear.
3500 Attendees
Frequency: Jan/March/August/October

1919 **International Show at the Super Show**
Communications & Show Management
1450 NE 123rd Street
North Miami, FL 33161

305-808-3531; Fax: 305-893-8783
www.bizbash.com

Richard Aaron, President
David Adler, CEO, Founder
Ann Keusch, COO

Retailers, distributors, wholesalers, importers/exporters and other buyers of sports related products come for 10,000 exhibits of sports apparel, footwear, accessories and e-commerce products and services.
100k Attendees
Frequency: January

1920 **International Vision Expo**
The Vision Council of America
225 Reinekers Lane
Suite 700
Alexandria, VA 22314

703-548-4560
866-826-0290; Fax: 703-548-4580
info@thevisioncouncil.org
www.thevisioncouncil.org

Ashley Mills, CEO

Learn about new market information, statistics, training and industry trends.
Frequency: Biennial
Founded in 1999

1921 **International Western Apparel and Accessories Market**
Dallas Market Center
2100 Stemmons Freeway
Dallas, TX 75207

214-655-6100
800-325-6587; Fax: 800-637-6833
www.dallasmarketcenter.com

Bill Winsor, President/CEO
Pat Zajac, Contact Home Expo

Offers array of services geared toward helping retailers expand business and increase profits.
200M Attendees
Frequency: March/August
Founded in 1957

1922 **Licensed Sports Show at the Super Show**
Communications & Show Management
1450 NE 123rd Street
North Miami, FL 33161

305-808-3531; Fax: 305-893-8783
www.bizbash.com

Richard Aaron, President
David Adler, CEO, Founder
Ann Keusch, COO

Retailers, distributors, wholesalers, importers/exporters and other buyers of sports related products come for 10,000 exhibits of sports apparel, footwear, accessories and e-commerce products and services.
100k Attendees
Frequency: January

1923 **MAGIC International Show**
MAGIC International
2501 Colorado Avenue
Suite 280
Santa Monica, CA 90404

310-857-7500; Fax: 310-593-5020
cs@MAGIConline.com
www.magiconline.com

Joe Loggia, President/CEO
Francine Rich, Womens Sales Contact
Christopher Giffin, Vice President Sales
Pam Thompson, Attendee Relations

Fashion trade show in Las Vegas. 3,000 exhibitors.
75000 Attendees
Frequency: February/August
Founded in 1933

1924 **Management Conference & Team Dealer Summit**
National Sporting Goods Association
1601 Feehanville Drive
Suite 300
Mount Prospect, IL 60056

847-296-6742
800-815-5422; Fax: 847-391-9827
info@nsga.org
www.nsga.org

Bob Dickman, Chairman of the Board
Matt Carlson, President/CEO
Dustin Dobrin, Research and Information Director

The goal is to stimulate fresh, agile thinking. How you and your company can create a culture that encourages and stimulates action, focus on the solution and fresh thinking.

1925 **Manufacturers Wholesalers Outerwear Sportswear Show**
I. Spiewak & Sons
463 7th Avenue
10th Floor
New York, NY 10018-6505

212-695-1620
800-223-6850; Fax: 212-629-4803
jerry@spiewak.com
www.spiewak.com

Gerald Spiewak, Executive Director
Roy Spiewak, President

180 booths for manufacturers and importers of outerwear and rainwear.
3M Attendees
Frequency: January

1926 **Material World**
Urban Expositions
1395 S Marietta Parkway
Building 400, Suite 210
Marietta, GA 30067

770-180-0972
800-318-2238; Fax: 678-285-7469

Doug Miller, President
Tim von Gal, Executive VP
Suzanne Pruitt, Contact

From design to delivery, Material World is the international full package, sourcing and fashion information event for the fabric related industries.
10600 Attendees
Frequency: May

1927 **Men's and Boy's Apparel Show**
Miami International Merchandise Mart
777 NW 72nd Avenue
Miami, FL 33126

305-665-5630; Fax: 305-261-3659
www.miamimart.net

Martiza Agudo, President
Glorys Covo, Administrator

This is a three-day show where wholesale buyers will find an extensive display of apparel lines including Calvin Klein, Perruzo, Supreme, just to name a few.
1000 Attendees
Frequency: April/May

1928 **National Bridal Market: Fall**
Merchandise Mart Properties Inc
222 Merchandise Mart Plaza
Suite 470
Chicago, IL 60654

312-527-4141
800-677-6278; Fax: 312-527-7971
mmailand@mmart.com
www.mmart.com

Christopher Kennedy, President
Stephanie Ambuehl, Marketing

Specializing in leading bridal and special occasion resources for department and specialty stores.
3000 Attendees
Frequency: October

1929 **National Halloween & Costume & Party Show**
Transworld Exhibits
1850 Oak Street
Northfield, IL 60093

847-784-6905
800-323-5462; Fax: 847-446-3523
www.tweshows.com

Joe Thaler, CEO
Paul O'Connor, Executive Director

Attracts people from across the US and over 50 foreign countries to see what over 700 manufacturers and distributors are showcasing as new and exciting for parties, shops and haunted houses. Free educational seminars and workshops.
10000 Attendees
Frequency: February

1930 **National Needlework Market**
The National NeedleArts Association

1100-H Brandywine Blvd
Zanesville, OH 43701

740-455-6773
800-889-8662; Fax: 740-452-2552
info@tnna.org
www.tnna.org

Enabling professionals to come together to share knowledge, products and experiences.
5M Attendees
Frequency: Annual

1931 **National Sewing Show**
Home Sewing Association
PO Box 369
Monroeville, PA 15146

412-372-5950; Fax: 412-372-5953
www.sewing.org

Dotty Grexa, President

Offers free sewing projects, guidelines and also a chat room where you can share with other about your ideas and collaborate on others.
Frequency: September

1932 **New England Apparel Club**
New England Apparel Club
75 McNeil Way
Suite 207
Dedham, MA 02026

781-326-9223; Fax: 781- 32- 689
neacrlg@aol.com
www.neacshow.com

Richard Usherwood, President
Donald Hurowitz, Vice President
Rhonda Goldberg, Executive Director

2500 regional sales reps exhibiting clothing and related equipment, supplies and services.
2000 Attendees
Frequency: October, Boston

1933 **Northstar Fashion Exhibitors**
Northstar Fashion Exhibitors
175 Kellogg Blvd West
St Paul, MN 55102

763-546-8717
800-272-6972; Fax: 763-546-9176
northstarfashion.com

Rick Siegel, President
Stanley Kaye, Show Coordinator
Debi Higgins, Manager

Trade show collections for men's, women's, Childrens apparel, accessories and textiles. 250 Booths.
1,260 Attendees
Frequency: 5/Year

1934 **Northwest Shoe Traveler's Buying Shoe Market**
Northwest Shoe Traveler's
12630 12th Street N
Lake Elmo, MN 55042

651-436-2709; Fax: 651-436-2028

Teri Tompkins, Show Manager

Trade show collections for men's, women's and Childrens.
250 Attendees
Frequency: January

1935 **Off-Price Specialist Show**
Off Price Specialist Center
16985 W Bluemound Road
Suite 210
Brookfield, WI 53005

262-782-1600; Fax: 262-782-1601
www.offpriceshow.com
Facebook, Twitter

Stephen Krogulski, President/CEO
David Lapidos, Executive Vice President
Faye Osvatic, Buyers Contact
Kevin Redlich, Product Manager

Premiere show for off-price apparel and accessories.
12000 Attendees
Frequency: May 8-10
Founded in 1995

1936 **Outdoor Retailer Summer Market**
Nielsen Sports Group
31910 Del Obispo
Suite 200
San Juan Capistrano, CA 92675

949-226-5722
www.outdoorretailer.com

Kenji Haroutunian, Director
Margle Lelvis, Marketing
Krista Dill, Account Executive
Jennifer Holcomb, Marketing Manager
Kenji Haroutunian, Show Director

The leading growth vehicle for brands that are interested in progressing and advancing into multiple channels of the outdoor marketplace.
17000 Attendees
Frequency: August

1937 **Outdoor Retailer Winter Market**
VNU Expositions
PO Box 1899
Laguna Beach, CA 92652

949-226-5722; Fax: 949-226-5625
www.outdoorretailer.com

Marisa Nicholson, National Sales Manager
Paul Dillman, Senior Account Executive
Peter Devin, Group Show Director
David Lockner, Manager

Features the most comprehensive collection of outdoor apparel, gear, equipment, climbing technology, footwear, ski mountaineering, hunting, rescue outerwear and accessory companies from which to buy products.

1938 **PGA Merchandise Show**
Reed Exhibition Companies
383 Main Avenue
Suite 3
Norwalk, CT 06851

203- 84- 562
800-840-5628; Fax: 203-840-9628
inquiry@pga.reedexpo.com
www.pgaexpo.com

Andre Smith, Director Marketing/Special Events
Marc Simon, Group Sales Director
Sherry Major, Media Contact

World's largest golf industry trade event. Open to retail buyers and golf industry professionals. Not open to the public
38500 Attendees
Frequency: January
Founded in 1954

1939 **Performance & Lifestyle Footwear Show at the Super Show**
Communications & Show Management
1450 NE 123rd Street
North Miami, FL 33161

305-893-8771; Fax: 305-893-8783
www.bizbash.com

Richard Aaron, President
David Adler, CEO/President
Chad Kaydo, Editor in Chief
Dana Price, COO

Retailers, distributors, wholesalers, importers/exporters and other buyers of sports related products come for 10,000 exhibits of sports apparel, footwear, accessories and e-commerce products and services.
100k Attendees
Frequency: January

1940 **Printwear Show**
National Business Media Inc
PO Box 1416
Broomfield, CO 80038

303-469-0424
800-669-0424; Fax: 303-465-3424
www.nbmshows.com
Twitter

Bob Wieber, President

The event for buyers involved in screen printing, embroidery, heat applied graphics, digital textile printing, sublimation and apparel.
Frequency: August

1941 **Professional Apparel Association Trade**
Professional Apparel Association
994 Old Eagle School Road
Suite 1019
Wayne, PA 19087-1866

610-971-4850; Fax: 610-971-4859

Dr. Sharon Tannahill, Executive Director

Exhibitors display health care and hospitality uniforms, shoes, and accessories, and career apparel. Workshops and seminars for uniform retailers are also available. Biennial.

1942 **Shoe Market of America**
Miami Merchandise Mart
2335 NW 107 Ave
Suite 2M31 Box 120
Miami, FL 33172

786-331-9000; Fax: 786-331-9955
info@smota.com
www.smota.com

Dianne Travalini, Executive Director
Alex Meme, Manager

Features the entire spectrum of footwear companies.
2500 Attendees
Frequency: 3x per year

1943 **Southwestern Shoe Traveler's**
Southwestern Shoe Traveler's Association
1024 Oxfordshire Dr.
Cannollton, TX 75007

972-446-4089; Fax: 214-292-9691

Mona Bennight, Executive Director

Definitive footwear trade site for footwear retailers.
1800 Attendees
Frequency: June

1944 **Syracuse Super Show**
Oncenter Complex
800 So. State Street
Syracuse, NY

315-488-4201
abc43@juno.com
www.syracusesupershow.com

Carol Sweet, Menswear Contact
Dick Pirozzolo, Footwear Contact
Rhonda Goldberg, Women's & Children's Contact

Largest assortment of fashions in Upstate New York. The show is open to the wholesale trade only - sales representatives, manufacturers and retailers.

1945 **TNNA Trade Shows**
National Needlework Association
1100-H Brandywine Boulevard
Zanesville, OH 43701

740-455-6773
800-889-8662; Fax: 740-452-2552
info@tnna.org
www.tnna.org
Facebook, Twitter

Kelsey Kwasniak, Trade Show Senior Associate

A market for serious needleart buyers and sellers learn about trends in fashion, color and design. With over 800 booths.
Frequency: 4x per year

1946 **Team Sports Show at the Super Show**
Communications & Show Management
1450 NE 123rd Street
North Miami, FL 33161

305-893-8771; Fax: 305-893-8783
www.bizbash.com

Richard Aaron, President
David Adler, CEO/founder
Chad Kaydo, Editor in Chief
Dana Price, COO

Retailers, distributors, wholesalers, importers/exporters and other buyers of sports related products come for 10,000 exhibits of sports apparel, footwear, accessories and e-commerce products and services.
100k Attendees
Frequency: January

1947 **Tennis & Golf Show at the Super Show**
Communications & Show Management
1450 NE 123rd Street
North Miami, FL 33161

305-893-8771; Fax: 305-893-8783
www.bizbash.com

Richard Aaron, President
David Adler, CEO/Founder
Chad Kaydo, Editor in Chief
Dana Price, COO

Retailers, distributors, wholesalers, importers/exporters and other buyers of sports related products come for 10,000 exhibits of sports apparel, footwear, accessories and e-commerce products and services.
100k Attendees
Frequency: January

1948 **Trend Seattle**
Pacific Northwest Apparel Association
528 North 79th Street
Seattle, WA 98103

206-767-9200; Fax: 206-588-0058
pnaa@nwtrendshow.com
www.nwtrendshow.com

Linda J. Browne, Executive Director
Judie Bartole-Ingram, President

Apparel and accessories show.
2000 Attendees
Frequency: Jan/Apr/Jun/Aug/Oct

1949 **USFIA Annual Apparel Importers Trade & Transportation Conference**
United States Fashion Industry Association
1717 Pennsylvania Ave NW
Suite 430
Washington, DC 20006

202-419-0444; Fax: 202-783-0727
info@usfashionindustry.com
www.usfashionindustry.com
Facebook, Twitter, LinkedIn, Google+

Julia Hughes, President
Shannon Brady, Communications Coordinator
John Pellegrini, Customs Counsel

Conference on the impact of global trade and transportation policy on the fashion industry.

1950 **WAM: Western Apparel Manufacturers Show**
Dallas Market Center
2300 Stemmons Freeway
Dallas, TX 75207

214-556-6100; Fax: 214-638-7221
www.dallasmarketcenter.com
Facebook, Twitter

Apparel manufacturing equipment. Held to meet the needs of the TOLA retailers who take advantage of the early fall buying opportunities.
3.2M Attendees
Frequency: April

1951 **WSA: Western Shoe Associates**
Western Shoe Associates
20281 SW Birch Street
Newport Beach, CA 92660

949-851-8451; Fax: 949-851-8523

Mitch Fisherman, President
Steve Katz, VP
Marie Mussabini, Exhibitor Coordinator
Dave Darling, Treasurer

Trade show held twice a year and featuring footwear.

1952 **WWD Magic**
MAGIC International
2501 Colorado Avenue
Suite 280
Santa Monica, CA 90404

310-857-7500; Fax: 310-857-7510
cs@magiconline.com
www.magiconline.com
Facebook, Twitter

Joe Loggia, President/CEO
Laura McConnell, VP

WWD Magic, a joint venture with Women's Wear Daily, is the recognized leader in women's apparel and accessories expositions in the world. WWD Magic offers the opportunity to discover new resources, network with industry peers, attend trend seminars and fashion shows, and meet with major manufacturers in an exciting and efficient forum. Containing over 1,000 exhibitors and 2,000 booths.
85000 Attendees
Frequency: August
Founded in 1933

1953 **Western Shoe Associates International**
Western Shoe Associates
20281 SW Birch Street
Suite 100
Newport Beach, CA 92660

949-851-8451; Fax: 949-851-8523

Mitch Fisherman, President
Marie Mussabini, Exhibitor Coordinator

Footwear trade market.

1954 **Western and English Sales Association Trade Show**
Western and English Sales Association
451 E 58th Avenue
Suite 4128
Denver, CO 80216

303-295-1040
800-295-1041; Fax: 303-295-0941
info@denver-wesa.com
wesatradeshow.com

Trade shows for Equestrian-related products; wholesalers to retailers
10000 Attendees
Frequency: 2x/Year

1955 **Women and Children's Market**
AMC Trade Shows/DMC Expositions
2140 Peachtree Street NW
Suite 2200
Atlanta, GA 30303

404-220-3000
800-285-6278; Fax: 404-220-3030

Sarah Adamson, Show Manager

Women and children's apparel.
9000 Attendees

1956 **Women's and Children's Apparel Market**
Dallas Market Center
2100 Stemmons Freeway
Dallas, TX 75207

214-556-6100
800-325-6587
www.dallasmarketcenter.com
Facebook, Twitter

Pat Zajac, Home Expo

Features the most comprehensive variety of apparel and accessories lines.
20000 Attendees
Frequency: October
Founded in 1957

1957 **Women's and Children's Fall Market**
Merchandise Mart Properties Inc
222 Merchandise Mart Plaza
Suite 470
Chicago, IL 60654

312-527-4141
800-677-6278; Fax: 312-527-7782
www.merchandisemart.com

Christopher Kennedy, President

Hundreds of designers featuring women's and children's clothing and accessories
5000 Attendees
Founded in 1950

1958 **Women's and Children's Summer/Fall Preview Market**
Merchandise Mart Properties
222 Merchandise Mart Plaza
Suite 470
Chicago, IL 60654

312-527-4141
800-677-6278; Fax: 312-527-7782
www.merchandisemart.com

H Brennen III, Executive VP

Women's and children's apparel.
5000 Attendees
Frequency: June

1959 **Wonderful World of Weddings and Occasions**
Expo Productions
510 Hartbrook Drive
Hartland, WI 53029

262-367-5500
800-367-5520; Fax: 262-367-9956
monica@epishows.com
www.weddingshowepi.com

Monica Seeger, Sales Manager

Wedding and other special occasion products, services, ideas including live and recorded music, still and video photography, cakes and catering, formal wear, gifts and much more.
6000 Attendees
Frequency: January
Founded in 1967

1960 **X-treme Sports Show at the Super Show**
Communications & Show Management

1450 NE 123rd Street
North Miami, FL 33161

305-893-8771; Fax: 305-893-8783
www.bizbash.com

Richard Aaron, President
David Adler, CEO/Founder
Chad Kaydo, Editor in Chief
Dana Price, COO

Retailers, distributors, wholesalers, importers/exporters and other buyers of sports related products come for 10,000 exhibits of sports apparel, footwear, accessories and e-commerce products and services.
100k Attendees
Frequency: January

Directories & Databases

1961 Action Sports Retailer Buyer's Guide Issue
Miller Freeman Publications
2655 Seely Avenue
San Jose, CA 95134

408-943-1234; Fax: 408-943-0513

Pat Cochran, Editor

Guide to 1,600 manufacturers and distributors of specialty watersports, beach, skateboarding, snowboarding, volleyball and bicycling equipment and clothing.
Cost: $25.00

1962 American Apparel Contractors Association Directory - American Made Apparel
4870 Nome Street
Denver, CO 80239-2728

303-373-2924; Fax: 703-522-6741

Sue C Strickland, Executive Director
Sunny Park, Owner

Over 300 listings are offered pertaining to contractors, manufacturers and suppliers to the apparel industry.
30 Members
100 Pages
Frequency: Annual
Founded in 1981

1963 Apparel Specialty Stores Directory
Chain Store Guide
3710 Corporex Park Dr
Suite 310
Tampa, FL 33619

813-627-6700
800-927-9292; Fax: 813-627-6888
webmaster@chainstoreguide.com
www.chainstoreguide.com

Mike Jarvis, Publisher
Chris Leedy, Advertising Sales
Shami Choon, Manager

The facts on more than 4,800 companies operating more than 70,700 stores all involved in the sale of women's, men's, family and children's wear. Also included are sporting goods stores that offer apparel and active wear as well as related merchandise. Includes more than 15,000 key buyers and executives.
Cost: $335.00

1964 Bobbin-Suppliers Sourcing Issue
Bobbin Blenheim Media Corporation
1110 Shop Road
PO Box 1986
Columbia, SC 29201-4743

800-845-8820; Fax: 803-799-1461

Offers information on over 8,000 suppliers to the apparel/sewn products industry.

1965 College Store Executive: Emblematics Directory Issue
Executive Business Media
825 Old Country Road
Westbury, NY 11590

516-334-3030; Fax: 516-334-3059
ebm-mail@ebmpubs.com
www.ebmpubs.com

Murry Greenwald, President

List of distributors of products with emblems or insignia; coverage includes Canada.
Cost: $5.00
Frequency: Annual, February

1966 Complete Directory of Apparel
Sutton Family Communications & Publishing Company
155 Sutton Lane
Fordsville, KY 42343

270-740-0870
www.suttoncompliance.com

Theresa Sutton, Editor
Lee Sutton, General Manager

Print-out from database of wholesalers, manufacturers, distributors, importers and close-out houses. Database is updated daily to guarantee the most current sources available.
Cost: $77.65
100+ Pages

1967 Complete Directory of Apparel Close-Outs
Sutton Family Communications & Publishing Company
155 Sutton Lane
Fordsville, KY 42343

270-740-0870
www.suttoncompliance.com

Theresa Sutton, Editor
Lee Sutton, General Manager

Print-out from database of wholesalers, manufacturers, distributors, importers and close-out houses. Database is updated daily to guarantee the most current sources available to the close-out apparel industry.
Cost: $55.20
100+ Pages

1968 Complete Directory of Baby Goods and Gifts
Sutton Family Communications & Publishing Company
155 Sutton Lane
Fordsville, KY 42343

270-740-0870
www.suttoncompliance.com

Theresa Sutton, Editor
Lee Sutton, General Manager

Print-out from database of wholesalers, manufacturers, distributors, importers and close-out houses for baby goods and gifts. Database is updated daily to guarantee the most current sources available.
Cost: $57.65
100+ Pages

1969 Complete Directory of Belts, Buckles & Boots
Sutton Family Communications & Publishing Company
155 Sutton Lane
Fordsville, KY 42343

270-740-0870
www.suttoncompliance.com

Theresa Sutton, Editor
Lee Sutton, General Manager

Print-out from database of wholesalers, manufacturers, distributors, importers and close-out houses. Database is updated daily to guarantee the most current sources available.
Cost: $55.20
100+ Pages

1970 Complete Directory of Brand New Surplus Merchandise
Sutton Family Communications & Publishing Company
155 Sutton Lane
Fordsville, KY 42343

270-740-0870
www.suttoncompliance.com

Theresa Sutton, Editor
Lee Sutton, General Manager

Print-out from database of wholesalers, manufacturers, distributors, importers and close-out houses. Database is updated daily to guarantee the most current sources available.
Cost: $92.70
100+ Pages

1971 Complete Directory of Caps & Hats
Sutton Family Communications & Publishing Company
155 Sutton Lane
Fordsville, KY 42343

270-740-0870
www.suttoncompliance.com

Theresa Sutton, Editor
Lee Sutton, General Manager

Print-out from database of wholesalers, manufacturers, distributors, importers and close-out houses. Database is updated daily to guarantee the most current sources available.
Cost: $55.20
100+ Pages

1972 Complete Directory of Clothing & Uniforms
Sutton Family Communications & Publishing Company
155 Sutton Lane
Fordsville, KY 42343

270-740-0870
www.suttoncompliance.com

Theresa Sutton, Editor
Lee Sutton, General Manager

Print-out from database of wholesalers, manufacturers, distributors, importers and close-out houses. Database is updated daily to guarantee the most current sources available.
Cost: $55.20
100+ Pages

1973 Complete Directory of Hat Pins, Feathers and Fads
Sutton Family Communications & Publishing Company
155 Sutton Lane
Fordsville, KY 42343

270-740-0870
www.suttoncompliance.com

Theresa Sutton, Editor
Lee Sutton, General Manager

Print-out from database of wholesalers, manufacturers, distributors, importers and close-out houses. Database is updated daily to guarantee the most current sources available.
Cost: $67.70
100+ Pages

1974 Complete Directory of Purses & Handbags
Sutton Family Communications & Publishing Company

155 Sutton Lane
Fordsville, KY 42343

270-740-0870
www.suttoncompliance.com

Theresa Sutton, Editor
Lee Sutton, General Manager

Print-out from database of wholesalers, manufacturers, distributors, importers and close-out houses. Database is updated daily to guarantee the most current sources available.
Cost: $55.20
100+ Pages

1975 **Complete Directory of Sunglasses & Eye Weather**
Sutton Family Communications & Publishing Company
155 Sutton Lane
Fordsville, KY 42343

270-740-0870
www.suttoncompliance.com

Theresa Sutton, Editor
Lee Sutton, General Manager

Print-out from database of wholesalers, manufacturers, distributors, importers and close-out houses. Database is updated daily to guarantee the most current sources available.
Cost: $55.20
100+ Pages

1976 **Complete Directory of T-Shirts, Heat Transfers & Supplies**
Sutton Family Communications & Publishing Company
155 Sutton Lane
Fordsville, KY 42343

270-740-0870
www.suttoncompliance.com

Theresa Sutton, Editor
Lee Sutton, General Manager

Print-out from database of wholesalers, manufacturers, distributors, importers and close-out houses. Database is updated daily to guarantee the most current sources available.
Cost: $55.20
100+ Pages

1977 **Complete Directory of Western Wear**
Sutton Family Communications & Publishing Company
155 Sutton Lane
Fordsville, KY 42343

270-740-0870
www.suttoncompliance.com

Theresa Sutton, Editor
Lee Sutton, General Manager

Print-out from database of wholesalers, manufacturers, distributors, importers and close-out houses. Database is updated daily to guarantee the most current sources available.
Cost: $55.20
100+ Pages

1978 **Complete Directory of Women's Accessories**
Sutton Family Communications & Publishing Company
155 Sutton Lane
Fordsville, KY 42343

270-740-0870
www.suttoncompliance.com

Theresa Sutton, Editor
Lee Sutton, General Manager

Print-out from database of wholesalers, manufacturers, distributors, importers and close-out houses. Database is updated daily to guarantee the most current sources available.
Cost: $55.20
100+ Pages

1979 **Directory of Active Sportswear**
Sutton Family Communications & Publishing Company
155 Sutton Lane
Fordsville, KY 42343

270-740-0870
www.suttoncompliance.com

Theresa Sutton, Editor
Lee Sutton, General Manager

Print-out from database of wholesalers, manufacturers, distributors, importers and close-out houses. Database is updated daily to guarantee the most current sources available. Approximately 740 wholesale sources in a 3-ring binder.
Cost: $67.20
100+ Pages

1980 **Directory of Apparel Specialty Stores**
AKTRIN Textile Information Center
164 S Main Street
PO Box 898
High Point, NC 27261

336-418-8583; Fax: 336-841-5435
www.textile-info.com

Information resource for people seeking in-depth, up-to-date data on the apparel specialty stores marketplace. Fully searchable database, either in form of a CD-ROM or downloadable over the Internet.
Cost: $780.00
Frequency: Annual

1981 **Directory of Mail Order Catalogs**
Grey House Publishing
4919 Route 22
PO Box 56
Amenia, NY 12501

518-789-8700
800-562-2139; Fax: 518-789-0556
books@greyhouse.com
www.greyhouse.com
Facebook, Twitter

Leslie Mackenzie, Publisher
Richard Gottlieb, President

The premier source of information on the mail order catalog industry. Covers over 13,000 consumer and business catalog companies with 44 different product chapters including clothing and sportswear.
Cost: $395.00
1900 Pages
Frequency: Annual
ISBN: 1-592373-96-8
Founded in 1981

1982 **Directory of Mail Order Catalogs - Online Database**
Grey House Publishing
4919 Route 22
PO Box 56
Amenia, NY 12501

518-789-8700
800-562-2139; Fax: 518-789-0556
gold@greyhouse.com
gold.greyhouse.com
Facebook, Twitter

Leslie Mackenzie, Publisher
Richard Gottlieb, President

Reach over 10,000 consumer catalog companies in one easy-to-use source with The Directory of Mail Order Catalogs - Online Database. Filled with business-building detail, each company profile gives you the information you need to access that organization quickly and easily. Listings provide key contacts, sales volume, employee size, printing information, circulation, list data, product descriptions and much more.
Frequency: Annual
Founded in 1981

1983 **Earnshaw's Buyer's Guide to the New York Market**
Earnshaw Publications
36 Cooper Square
4th Floor
New York, NY 10003

646-278-1550; Fax: 646- 27- 155
www.earnshaws.com

Noelle Heffernan, Publisher

A children's wear guide offering over 1,200 manufacturers and suppliers of clothing for infants, boys and girls apparel.
200 Pages
Frequency: Annual
Circulation: 10,000

1984 **Earnshaw's Infants', Girls', Boys' Wear Review: Children's Wear Directory**
Earnshaw Publications
36 Cooper Square
4th Floor
New York, NY 10003

646-278-1550; Fax: 646-278-1553
www.earnshaws.com

Noelle Heffernan, Publisher

A directory of over 1,500 children's apparel and accessory firms with offices or showrooms in the United States.
Cost: $10.00
Frequency: Annual
Circulation: 10,000

1985 **Financial Performance Profile of Public Apparel Companies**
Kurt Salmon Associates
650 Fifth Avenue
New York, NY 10019

212-319-9450
www.kurtsalmon.com

John Karonis, CEO

Information on over 60 publicly held apparel manufacturers are available.
Cost: $400.00
300 Pages
Frequency: Annual
Founded in 1935

1986 **Garment Manufacturers Index**
Klevens Publications
411 S Main Street
Suite 209
Los Angeles, CA 90013

213-625-9000; Fax: 213-625-5002
www.garmentindex.com

Herbert Schwartz, Editor

A list of over 5,000 manufacturers and suppliers of products and services such as fabrics, trimmings, factory equipment and sewing contractors used in the manufacture of apparel and other sewn products.
Cost: $105.00
264 Pages
Frequency: Annual
Circulation: 29,495
ISSN: 1065-1330
Founded in 1938
Printed in 4 colors on matte stock

1987 **Hosiery and Bodywear: Buyer's Guide to Support and Control Top Pantyhose**
Advanstar Communications

641 Lexington Ave
8th Floor
New York, NY 10022-4503

212-951-6600; Fax: 212-951-6793
info@advanstar.com
www.advanstar.com

Joseph Loggia, CEO

List of about 50 hosiery manufacturers.
Cost: $3.00
Frequency: Annual September
Circulation: 10,500

1988 **Impressions: Directory Issue**
Miller Freeman Publications
501 W. President George Bush Hwy. #150
Richardson, TX 75080
813-366-2877
800-697-8859
nimp@omeda.com
www.impressionsmag.com

Marcia Derrberry, Editor in Chief

A list of more than 1,500 suppliers of products, services and equipment used in the imprinted sportswear industry including textile screen print equipment, supplies, embroidery equipment and supplies, and all types of imprintables.
Cost: $18.00
Frequency: Annual
Circulation: 60,000

1989 **International Nonwovens Directory**
1100 Crescent Green Suite 115
PO Box 1288
Cary, NC 27518

919-233-1210; Fax: 919-233-1282
www.inda.org

Rory Holmes, President
Annette Balint, Director Finance
Ian Butler, Director Market Research/Stats

A Who's Who directory of services and supplies to the nonwovens industry.
300 Members
750 Pages
Frequency: Biennial
Circulation: 2,000

1990 **Nationwide Directory of Men's & Boys' Wear Buyers**
Reed Reference Publishing RR Bowker
630 Central Ave
New Providence, NJ 07974-1544

908-286-1090
888-269-5372; Fax: 908-464-3553
www.bowker.com

A who's who directory of services and supplies to the industry.
Cost: $147.00
700 Pages
Frequency: Annual
Circulation: 1,000

1991 **Outerwear Sourcebook: Directory Issue**
Creative Marketing Plus
213-37 39th Avenue
Suite 228
Bayside, NY 11361

718-606-0767; Fax: 718-606-6345
rharrow@creativemarketingplus.com
www.creativemarketingplus.com

Richard Harrow, President

List of more than 3,500 outerwear manufacturers in the US and Canada; 1,000 companies providing products and services to the outerwear trade.
Cost: $40.00
Frequency: Annual

1992 **WWD Buyers Guide: Womens Apparel and Accessories Manufacturers**
Fairchild Publications
750 3rd Ave
New York, NY 10017-2703

212-630-4000; Fax: 212-630-3563

Mary G Berner, Chief Executive Officer
Christine Guilfoyle, Publisher

Over 5,500 apparel and accessory manufacturers.
Founded in 1892

1993 **WWD Suppliers Guide**
Fairchild Books and Visuals
750 3rd Ave
New York, NY 10017-2700

212-630-4320; Fax: 212-630-3566

Mary G Berner, Chief Executive Officer
Christine Guilfoyle, Publisher

Over 5,500 apparel and accessory manufacturers in the US. Supplement to WWD Magazine.
Founded in 1892

Industry Web Sites

1994 **http://gold.greyhouse.com**
G.O.L.D Grey House OnLine Databases

Grey House Publishing's online database platform, GOLD, offers Quick Search, Keyword Search and Expert Search in most business sectors, including apparel and accessories markets. The GOLD platform makes finding the information you need quick and easy - whether you're a novice searcher or an experienced database user. All of Grey House's directory products are available for subscription on the GOLD platform.

1995 **www.apparelandfootwear.org**
American Apparel & Footwear Association

The national trade association for the apparel and footwear industries. Conducts seminars, compiles statistics and produces industry reports.

1996 **www.cashmere.org**
Cashmere and Camel Hair Manufacturers Institute

For cashmere and camel hair product manufacturers.

1997 **www.chemicalfabricsandfilm.com**
Chemical Fabrics and Film Association

An international trade association representing manufacturers of polymer-based fabric and film products, used in the building and construction, automotive, fashion and many other industries.

1998 **www.colorassociation.com**
Color Association of the US

Information on color/design issues; issues color charts two years in advance of selling seasons in order to profile popular American colors. Forecasts are issued in women's fashions and men's and children's clothing.

1999 **www.costumedesignersguild.com**
Costume Designers Guild

Works to promote employment and to create improved working conditions for costume designers.

2000 **www.ctda.com**
Custom Tailors and Designers Assn of America

Seeks to promote awareness of designers and makers of men's custom tailored clothing.

2001 **www.formalwear.org**
International Formalwear Association

For the formal wear industry.

2002 **www.greyhouse.com**
Grey House Publishing

Authoritative reference directories for most industries, including apparel and accessories. Users can search the online databases with varied search criteria allowing for custom searches by product category, geographic area, sales volume, keyword, subject and more. Full Grey House catalog and online ordering also available.

2003 **www.ifai.com**
Industrial Fabrics Association International

For geosynthetics, fabricators, installers, equipment manufacturers, suppliers, testing firms, consultants, and educators, who produce textiles, nets, mats, grids, and other products.

2004 **www.itaaonline.org**
Int'l Textile & Apparel Assn Membership Directory

For college professors of clothing and textile studies.

2005 **www.naumd.com**
North American Assoc. of Uniform Manufacturers

For manufacturers and distributors of uniforms and career wear.

2006 **www.sewing.org**
American Home Sewing and Craft Association

Handicraft and collectibles forum.

2007 **www.uc-council.org**
GS1 US

Members rely on the standards and services of GS1 US for the effective management and control of their supply chains. Everyday we strive to keep a leader's pace in developing, maintaining, supporting and expanding the services we offer to fulfill our mission.

2008 **www.uniteunion.org**
Union of Needletrade Industrial Textile Employees

A union fighting for working people.

2009 **www.vowsmag.com**
Grimes & Associates

Information on the business specifics necessary for today's wedding professional.

Associations

2010 Air Conditioning Contractors of America
2800 S Shirlington Road
Suite 300
Arlington, VA 22206

703-575-4477
membership@acca.org
www.acca.org
Facebook, Twitter, LinkedIn, YouTube

Barton James, President & CEO
Samuel Awotwi, Director of Finance
Christine Gibson, VP, Marketing & Partnerships
Sean Robertson, VP, Membership/Business Operations
Kimya Bailey, Director, Events & Benchmarking

ACCA is a non-profit association serving the HVACR community, working to promote professional contracting, energy efficiency, and healthy, comfortable indoor environments.
60000 Members
Founded in 1968

2011 Air-Conditioning, Heating and Refrigeration Institute
2111 Wilson Boulevard
Suite 500
Arlington, VA 22201

703-524-8800; Fax: 703-562-1942
www.ahrinet.org
Facebook, Twitter, RSS Feeds

Stephen Yurek, President & CEO
John Lanier, Chief Operating Officer
Francis Dietz, Vice President of Public Affairs
Donna Morris, Director/Accounting
James Walters, VP of International Affairs

AHRI is one of the largest trade associations in the nation, representing heating, water heating, ventilation, air conditioning and commercial refrigeration manufacturers within the global HVACR industry.
300 Members
Founded in 1953

2012 American Boiler Manufacturers Association
8221 Old Courthouse Rd
Suite 207
Vienna, VA 22182-3839

703-356-7172; Fax: 703-356-4543
www.abma.com
Facebook, Twitter, LinkedIn

Scott Lynch, President & CEO
Shaunica Jayson, Membership & Marketing Manager
Bethany Jones, Administrative Coordinator
Hugh K. Webster, General Counsel
Marissa Torres, Director of Meetings

The American Boiler Manufacturers Association (ABMA) is the national, nonprofit trade association of commercial, institutional, industrial and electricity-generating boiler system manufacturing companies (400,000 Btuh heat input), dedicated to the advancement and growth of the boiler and combustion equipment industry.
Founded in 1888

2013 American Society of Heating, Refrigeration & Air-Conditioning Engineers
1791 Tullie Cir NE
Atlanta, GA 30329-2398

404-636-8400
800-527-4723; Fax: 404-321-5478
ashrae@ashrae.org
www.ashrae.org
Facebook, Twitter, LinkedIn, YouTube

Jeff H. Littleton, Executive VP
Kim Mitchell, Chief Development Officer
Vanita Gupta, Director, Marketing
Joyce Abrams, Director, Member Services
Craig Wright, Director, Finance & Admin. Services

An international organization that fulfills its mission of advancing heating, ventilation, air conditioning and refrigeration to serve humanity and promote a sustainable world through research, standards writing, publishing and continuing education.
55000 Members
Founded in 1894

2014 American Society of Mechanical Engineers
Two Park Avenue
New York, NY 10016-5990

973-882-1170
800-843-2763
CustomerCare@asme.org
www.asme.org
Facebook, Twitter, LinkedIn, Instagram

Bryan A. Erler, President
Thomas Costabile, Executive Director & CEO
William Garofalo, Chief Financial Officer
Allian Pratt, Managing Director, Board Operations

ASME aims to promote and enhance the technical competency and professional well-being of the members, and through quality programs and activities in mechanical engineering, better enable its practitioners to contribute to the well being of human kind.
100K+ Members
Founded in 1880

2015 American Vacuum Society (AVS)
125 Maiden Lane
15th Floor
New York, NY 10038

212-248-0200; Fax: 212-248-0245
www.avs.org
Facebook, Twitter, LinkedIn, RSS Feeds

Yvonne Towse, Managing Director
Jeannette DeGennaro, Exhibition & Sales Manager
Peter Burke, Financial Administrator
Ricky Baldeo, Office Services Coordinator
Angela Klink, Member Services Administrator

As an interdisciplinary, professional Society, AVS supports networking among academic, industrial, government, and consulting professionals involved in a variety of disciplines - chemistry, physics, biology, mathematics, business, sales, etc through common interests related to the basic science, technology development and commercialization of materials, interfaces, and processing areas.
4500 Members
Founded in 1953

2016 Association of Home Appliance Manufacturers
1111 19th Street NW
Suite 402
Washington, DC 20036

202-872-5955; Fax: 202-872-9354
info@aham.org
www.aham.org

Joseph M. McGuire, President & CEO
Kathi Berge, Chief Financial Officer
Jill Notini, VP, Communications & Marketing

A not-for-profit trade association representing manufacturers of major and portable home appliance, floor care appliances and suppliers to the industry .
Founded in 1967

2017 Industrial Heating Equipment Association
5040 Old Taylor Mill Rd.
PMB 13
Taylor Mill, KY 41015

859-356-1575; Fax: 859-356-0908
ihea@ihea.org
www.ihea.org
Facebook

Anne Goyer, Executive Vice President
Andy Goyer, Accounting & Government Relations
Bruce Bryan, VP, Sales & Education
Kelly LeCount, Conference Manager & Speaker Coord.
Amanda Moore, Marketing

The Industrial Heating Equipment Association (IHEA) is a voluntary national trade association representing the major segments of the industrial heat processing equipment industry.
Founded in 1929

2018 International Housewares Association
6400 Shafer Ct
Suite 650
Rosemont, IL 60018-4929

847-292-4200; Fax: 847-292-4211
pbrandl@housewares.org
www.housewares.org
Facebook, Twitter, LinkedIn, YouTube

Derek Miller, President
Dean Kurtis, VP, Finance
Mark Adkison, VP, Member & Buyer Relations
Leana Salamah, VP, Marketing
Adrienne Tiritilli, VP, Trade Show

A full-service trade association dedicated to promoting the sales and marketing of housewares.
Founded in 1938

2019 International Institute of Ammonia Refrigeration
1001 N. Fairfax Street
Suite 503
Alexandria, VA 22314

703-312-4200; Fax: 703-312-0065
info@iiar.org
www.iiar.org
Facebook, Twitter, LinkedIn, YouTube, Google+

Gary Schrift, President
Eric Smith, VP & Technical Director
Yesenia Rector, International Director
Ben s Dawes, Membership Marketing Specialist
Eileen McKeown, VP, Marketing & Sales

IAR is an organization providing advocacy, education, standards, and information for the benefit of the ammonia refrigeration industry worldwide. IIAR's vision is to be recognized as the world's leading advocate for the safe, reliable and efficient use of ammonia and other natural refrigerants for industrial applications.
1200 Members
Founded in 1971

2020 International Kitchen Exhaust Cleaning Association
100 North 20th Street
Suite 400
Philadelphia, PA 19103

215-320-3876; Fax: 215-564-2175
information@ikeca.org
www.ikeca.org
Facebook, Twitter, LinkedIn, YouTube, Blog

Kathy DeMarco, Executive Director
April Rose, Director, Membership & Meetings
Rene Bonner, Membership Coordinator
Sara Duginske, Director, Certification &

Standards
Barb Signorelli, Senior Staff Accountant

Promotes fire safety in restaurants and professionalism in the kitchen exhaust cleaning industry. This not for profit trade association, has established stringent standards and practices for contractors engaged in kitchen exhaust cleaning, conducted a variety of educational programs, and worked with influential code setting bodies such as the National Fire Protection Association to improve existing codes and regulations.
Founded in 1989

2021 **International Microwave Power Institute**
PO Box 1140
PO Box 1140
Mechanicsville, VA 23111-5007

804-559-6667; Fax: 804-559-4087
info@impi.org
www.impi.org
Facebook, Twitter

Molly Poisant, Executive Director
Jerome Czajkowski, Executive Committee
John Gerling, Executive Committee
John Mastela, Executive Committee
Bob Schiffman, Executive Committee

The International Microwave Power Institute (IMPI) was founded in 1966 in Canada to serve the information needs of specialists working with microwave and RF heating systems. In 1977, the Institute reorganized to expand its industrial and scientific base to meet the information needs evolving in consumer microwave ovens and related products.
Founded in 1966

2022 **NSF International**
PO Box 130140
789 N Dixboro Rd
Ann Arbor, MI 48105

734-769-8010
800-673-6275; Fax: 734-769-0109
info@nsf.org
www.nsf.org

Kevan Lawlor, President & CEO
Lesley Ma, VP & Chief Information Officer
Tom Chestnut, VP & COO
Michael Walsh, VP & CFO
Colette LaForce, VP & Chief Marketing Officer

Independent standards and product testing organization.
Founded in 1944

2023 **National Air Duct Cleaners Association**
1120 Route 73
Suite 200
Mt Laurel, NJ 08054

856-380-6810; Fax: 856-439-0525
info@nadca.com
www.nadca.com
Facebook, Twitter, LinkedIn, YouTube

Jodi Araujo, Chief Executive Officer
Kristy Cohen, Executive Director
Mike Dwyer, Chief Relationship Officer
Amanda Paolini, Membership & Certification Coord.
Sarah Black, Editor, DucTales

NADCA: The HVAC Inspection, Maintenance and Restoration Association, otherwise known as the National Air Duct Cleaners Association (NADCA), was formed in 1989 as a non-profit association of companies engaged in the cleaning of HVAC systems. Its mission was to promote source removal as the only acceptable method of cleaning and to establish industry standards for the association.
1000 Members
Founded in 1989

2024 **National Kitchen and Bath Association**
687 Willow Grove Street
Hackettstown, NJ 07840-1731

800-843-6522
feedback@nkba.org
www.nkba.org
Facebook, Twitter, LinkedIn, Pinterest

Bill Darcy, CEO
Suzie Wiliford, EVP, Industry Relations & CSO
Pam Ryerson, Director, Marketplace
Nicole Young, Director, Finance & Administration

Protects the interests of members by fostering a better business climate. Offers Awards certification and conducts training schools and seminars.
14000 Members
Founded in 1963

2025 **North American Retail Dealers Association**
222 South Riverside Plaza
Suite 2100
Chicago, IL 60606

888-777-8851
nardasvc@narda.com
www.narda.com
Facebook, LinkedIn

A national organization of association members, independent retailers selling and servicing major appliances, consumer electronics products, furniture and computers. Emphasis is placed on ideas that help readers become better, more profitable businesses. Articles are featured regularly on displays, salesmanship, financial analysis and service management.
1000 Members
Founded in 1943

2026 **Professional Service Association**
1164 Marengo Ave
Marengo, IA 52301

888-777-8851; Fax: 319-642-3177
www.psaworld.com

Randy Carney, Executive Director
Mike Callahan, President
Carmine D'Alessandro, Vice President

PSA is an independent trade association dedicated to the highest standards of quality service. The purpose of PSA is to be the voice of the independent service provider and to assess and identify industry related problems and provide solutions. PSA is dedicated to providing educational training, certification, business management training, support and fairness to the independent service industry. PSA encourages professionalism and honesty identifies those techs who provide that kind of service.
1105 Members
Founded in 1989

2027 **Refrigeration Service Engineers Society**
1911 Rohlwig Road
Suite A
Rolling Meadows, IL 60008-1397

847-297-6464
800-297-5660; Fax: 847-297-5038
general@rses.org
www.rses.org
Facebook, Twitter, LinkedIn, RSS Feeds, Pinterest, Tumblr,

Roger M. Hensley, Board Chair
Michael Ralston, International President
Raymond Clary, International Vice President

To provide opportunities for enhanced technical competence by offering comprehensive, cutting-edge education and certification to our members and the HVACR industry. To advance the professionalism and proficiency of our industry through alliances with other HVACR associations. To be the definitive industry leader in all segments of the HVACR industry by providing superior educational training.
15231 Members
Founded in 1933

2028 **Silicon Valley Compucycle**
1096 Pecten Ct
Milpitas, CA 95035

408-432-1239
866-989-2970; Fax: 408-432-1249
Facebook, Twitter

Association dedicated to promote technical excellence by providing a global forum to inform, educate, and engage the members, the technical community, and the public on all aspects of vacuum coating, surface engineering and related technologies.
Founded in 2001

2029 **United Servicers Association**
3501 N. Southport Ave.
Suite 199
Chicago, IL 60657

800-683-2558; Fax: 855-290-5366
administration@unitedservicers.com
www.unitedservicers.com
Facebook, LinkedIn

Lance Kimball, President
Sarah Brown, Executive Director

Organization provides technical and service process training and education for appliance service professionals.

Newsletters

2030 **AVEM Newsletter**
Association of Vacuum Equipment Manufacturers
201 Park Washington Court
Falls Church, VA 22046-4527

703-538-3543; Fax: 703-241-5603
aveminfo@avem.org
www.avem.org

Dawn M. Shiley, Executive Director
Clay Tyeryar, Assistant Treasurer
Kim Fay, Data Analyst
Harry Buzzerd, Management Counsel

Contains news from the Association of Vacuum Equipment Manufacturers, including member company news and informational articles.
Frequency: Quarterly
Founded in 1969
Mailing list available for rent

2031 **Insights**
1791 Tullie Cir NE
Atlanta, GA 30329-2398

404-636-8400
800-527-4723; Fax: 404-321-5478
ashrae@ashrae.org
www.ashrae.org
Facebook, Twitter

Mark Owen, Director, Publications & Education
Cindy Michaels, Editor

ASHRAE Insights is the Society's newsletter with articles of interest to members, including Chapter News, Obituaries, Membership Advancement and other news.
55000 Members
Frequency: 6x/Year
Founded in 1894

2032 **SVC Bulletin**
Society of Vacuum Coaters

71 Pinon Hill Place NE
Albuquerque, NM 87122

505-856-7188; Fax: 505-856-6716
www.svc.com
Facebook, Twitter

Vivienne Harwood Mattox, Executive Director
Yvonne Swartz, Executive Manager
Beth Strong, Marketing & Communications Manager

The SVC bulletin is distributed to professionals working in the vacuum coating community and related sciences and technologies. Each issue contains contributed articles, previews, or reviews of the TechCon; SVC committee activities; technical articles from the Conference Proceedings; book reviews, Corporate Sponsor news and profiles; and Society news.
Frequency: 3x/Year
Circulation: 15000

2033 **The Buzz**
Air Conditioning Contractors of America
2800 Shirlington Rd
Suite 300
Arlington, VA 22206

703-575-4477
www.acca.org
Facebook, Twitter, LinkedIn, YouTube

Barton James, President & CEO

Roundup of latest news and interesting links for HVACR professionals.
Frequency: Weekly

2034 **Your Business**
Air Conditioning Contractors of America
2800 Shirlington Rd
Suite 300
Arlington, VA 22206

703-575-4477
www.acca.org
Facebook, Twitter, LinkedIn, YouTube

Barton James, President & CEO

Contains management advice for small business owners.
Frequency: Bi-Weekly
Founded in 1984

2035 **eSociety**
1791 Tullie Cir NE
Atlanta, GA 30329-2398

404-636-8400
800-527-4723; Fax: 404-321-5478
ashrae@ashrae.org
www.ashrae.org
Facebook, Twitter

Mark Owen, Director, Publications & Education
David Scott, Manager, E-Products & Publishing

The official electronic newsletter of ASHRAE. Contains monthly news form the society about its activities and chapters.
55000 Members
Frequency: Monthly
Founded in 1894

Magazines & Journals

2036 **ACCA Contractor Excellence**
Air Conditioning Contractors of America
2800 Shirlington Rd
Suite 300
Arlington, VA 22206

703-575-4477
www.acca.org
Facebook, Twitter, LinkedIn, YouTube

Barton James, President & CEO

Representing the HVACR contracting industry. We help our members acquire and satisfy customers while upholding the most stringent requirements for professional ethics, and advocating for improvements to the industry overall.

2037 **ACCA NOW**
Air Conditioning Contractors of America
2800 S Shirlington Road
Suite 300
Arlington, VA 22206

703-575-4477
melissa.broadus@acca.org
www.acca.org
Facebook, Twitter, LinkedIn, YouTube

Barton James, President & CEO
Melissa Broadus, Editor

ACCA Now is the leading source of Business Intelligence for Professional Contractors from HVAC and building performance, to plumbing and hydronics.

2038 **ACR Standard: Assessment, Cleaning & Restoration of HVAC Systems**
National Air Duct Cleaners Association
1518 K St NW
Suite 503
Washington, DC 20005-1203

202-737-2926; Fax: 202-347-8847
info@nadca.com
www.nadca.com

Ken Sufka, Owner

2039 **AHRI Trends Magazine**
Air Conditioning & Refrigeration Institute
2111 Wilson Boulevard
Suite 500
Arlington, VA 22201

703-524-8800; Fax: 703-562-1942
ahri@ahri.net
www.ahrinet.org
Facebook, Twitter

Stephen Yurek, President & CEO

A resource for HVAC contractors and technicians.
300+ Members

2040 **ASHRAE Journal**
American Society of Heating, Refrigeration & AC
1791 Tullie Cir NE
Atlanta, GA 30329-2398

404-636-8400
800-527-4723; Fax: 404-321-5478
ashrae@ashrae.org
www.ashrae.org

Mark Owen, Director, Publications & Education
Sarah Foster, Editor

Explores topical technical issues, such as: indoor air quality, energy management, thermal storage, alternative refrigerants, fire and life safety and more.
Cost: $59.00
Frequency: Monthly

2041 **Appliance**
Dana Chase Publications
1110 Jorie Boulevard
PO Box 90919
Oak Brook, IL 60522-9019

630-990-3484; Fax: 630-990-0078
www.appliancemagazine.com

George Shurtleff, Production Manager
Maria Nigro, Circulation Director
Dana Chase Jr, Chairman

Devoted to serving the appliance industry worldwide, producers of consumer, commercial, business and medical appliances. Editorial material serves product engineering and design, production management and supervision, purchasing, management, marketing, sales and service. Accepts advertising.
Cost: $75.00
90 Pages
Frequency: Monthly
Circulation: 34500
ISSN: 0003-6781
Founded in 1944

2042 **Appliance Design**
Business News Publishing
2401 W Big Beaver Rd
Suite 700
Troy, MI 48084-3333

248-362-3700
877-747-1625; Fax: 248-362-0317
info@asnews.com
www.bnpmedia.com
Facebook, Twitter

Mitchell Henderson, CEO
Richard Babyak, Editor-in-Chief
Amy Alef, Production Manager
Mary Lowe, Associate Editor

Devoted to providing solutions for design and engineering teams in the global, commercial, and medical appliance/durable goods industry.
Circulation: 25,000
ISSN: 0003-6803
Founded in 1955
Printed in 4 colors on glossy stock

2043 **Appliance Service News**
Gamit Enterprises
1917 S Street
PO Box 808
St Charles, IL 60174

630-845-9481
877-747-1625; Fax: 630-845-9483
info@asnews.com
www.applianceservicenews.com

William Wingstedt, Editor/Publisher
Peggy Wingstedt, Sales Representative

Published for owners, managers and technicians of appliance repair dealers. Accepts advertising.
Cost: $59.95
36 Pages
Frequency: Monthly
Circulation: 33000
ISSN: 0003-6803
Founded in 1950
Printed in 4 colors on glossy stock

2044 **Boiler Systems Engineering Magazine**
American Boiler Manufacturers Association
8221 Old Courthouse Rd
Suite 202
Vienna, VA 22182-3839

703-356-7172; Fax: 703-522-2665
randy@abma.com
www.abma.com
Facebook, Twitter, LinkedIn

Scott Lynch, President & CEO
Frequency: Monthly
Founded in 1888

2045 **Contractor Excellence**
Air Conditioning Contractors of America
2800 S Shirlington Rd
Suite 300
Arlington, VA 22206

703-575-4477
www.acca.org

Barton James, President & CEO

A quality source of business information for the HVAC industry, available to members.
Frequency: Quarterly
Founded in 2002

2046 **HPE Magazine**
American Boiler Manufacturers Association
8221 Old Courthouse Rd
Suite 202
Vienna, VA 22182-3839

703-356-7172; Fax: 703-522-2665
randy@abma.com
www.abma.com
Facebook, Twitter, LinkedIn

Scott Lynch, President & CEO
Marissa Torres, Director, Meetings
Founded in 1888

2047 **HVAC&R Research Journal**
American Society of Heating, Refrigeration & AC
1791 Tullie Circle NE
Atlanta, GA 30329-2398

404-636-8400
800-527-4723; Fax: 404-321-5478
ashrae@ashrae.org
www.ashrae.org

Offers the most comprehensive reporting of archival research in the fields of environmental control for the built environment. Also covers cooling technolgies for a wide range of applications and related processes and concepts, including underlying thermodynamics, fluid dynamics, and heat transfer.
Frequency: Bi-Monthly
ISBN: 1-883413-98-2

2048 **Indoor Comfort News Magazine**
Institute of Heating and Air Conditioning
454 W Broadway
Glendale, CA 91204-1209

818-551-1555; Fax: 818-551-1115
ihaci@ihaci.org
www.ihaci.org

Susan Evans, Senior VP

A tool for attaining the trade association's goal of educating and promoting the HVAC/R/SM industry. Readers are top buyers and decision makers. They service and install new construction and replacement/retrofit projects.
Frequency: Monthly
Founded in 1955

2049 **Journal of Microwave Power and Electromagnetic Energy**
International Microwave Power Institute
7076 Drinkard Way
P O Box 1140
Mechanicsville, VA 23111-5007

804-559-6667; Fax: 804-559-4087
info@impi.org
www.impi.org

Molly Poisant, Executive Director

Designed for the information needs of professionals specializing in the research and design of industrial and bio-medical applications, the Journal exemplifies the highest standards of scientific and technical information on the theory and application of electromagnetic power.
Cost: $250.00
Frequency: Quarterly

2050 **Mechanical Engineering Magazine**
American Society of Mechanical Engineers
Two Park Avenue
New York, NY 10016-5990

973-882-1170
800-843-2763
falcionij@asme.org
www.asme.org/network/media/mechanical-engineering-magazine

John G. Falconi, Editor-in-Chief & Publisher
Chitra Sethi, Managing Editor

Flagship publication of the American Society of Mechanical Engineering.
Frequency: Monthly
Founded in 1880

2051 **RSES Journal**
Refrigeration Service Engineers Society
1911 Rohlwing Road
Suite A
Rolling Meadows, IL 60008-1397

847-297-6464
800-297-5660; Fax: 847-297-5038
general@rses.org
www.rses.org
Facebook, Twitter, LinkedIn

Mark Lowry, Executive Vice President
Lori A Kasallis, Editor

Providing quality technical content in digital and printed forms that can be applied on the job site.
Frequency: Monthly
Circulation: 15231

2052 **Today's Boiler**
American Boiler Manufacturers Association
8221 Old Courthouse Rd
Suite 202
Vienna, VA 22182-3839

703-356-7172; Fax: 703-522-2665
www.abma.com

Scott Lynch, President & CEO

Trends, Technologies & Innovations, The Official Magazine of the American Boiler Manufacturers Association.
Founded in 1888

Trade Shows

2053 **ABMA Annual Meeting**
American Boiler Manufacturers Association
8221 Old Courthouse Road
Suite 207
Vienna, VA 22182-3839

703-356-7172; Fax: 703-356-4543
www.abma.com

Scott Lynch, President & CEO
Marissa Torres, Director, Meetings

The association's premier membership networking event where members have the opportunity to learn about developments and trends inside and outside the industry, and have the opportunity, through committee and product/market group meetings to focus on issues and concerns of specific relevance to their product and market segments.
Frequency: Bi-Annual

2054 **ABMA Manufacturers Conference**
American Boiler Manufacturers Association
8221 Old Courthouse Road
Suite 207
Vienna, VA 22182-3839

703-356-7172; Fax: 703-356-4543
www.abma.com

Scott Lynch, President & CEO
Marissa Torres, Director, Meetings

Designed to bring together manufacturing plant, office and others concerned with the design, fabrication, sales and distribution of ABMA products and services to network, discuss trends and developments, and problem solve with others in the industry and with outside experts.
Frequency: Annual/October

2055 **AHRI Annual Meeting**
Air-Conditioning, Heating & Refrigeration Inst
2111 Wilson Boulevard
Suite 500
Arlington, VA 22201

703-524-8800; Fax: 703-528-3816
www.ahrinet.org

Stephen Yurek, President & CEO
John Lanier, Chief Operating Officer

The premiere networking experience of the heating, ventillation, air conditioning and commercial refrigeration manufacturing industry addresses the topics and issues you want most. Offers opportunities to learn about the top issues facing the industry, network with industry leaders and colleagues, and participate in product section business
300+ Members
480+ Attendees
Frequency: November

2056 **ASME Annual Meeting**
American Society of Mechanical Engineers
Two Park Avenue
New York, NY 10016-5990

973-882-1170
800-843-2763
williamsk@asme.org
www.asme.org

Kim Williams, Meetings Manager

Forum for information exchange and professional growth for engineering professionals.

2057 **Air Conditioning Contractors of America Annual Conference**
Air Conditioning Contractors of America
2800 S Shirlington Road
Suite 300
Arlington, VA 22206

703-575-4477
membership@acca.org
www.acca.org
Facebook, Twitter, LinkedIn, YouTube

Barton James, President & CEO
Samuel Awotwi, Director of Finance
Kimya Bailay, Director, Events & Benchmark
Sean Robertson, VP, Membership/Business Operations

Annual meeting and exhibits of heating, air conditioning and refrigeration equipment, supplies and services. Over 140 exhibitors, plus seminar, workshop and banquet.
Frequency: Annual/March

2058 **Fall Tech Conference**
15000 Commerce Parkway
Suite C
Mt. Laurel, NJ 08054

856-380-6810; Fax: 856-439-0525
info@nadca.com
www.nadca.com

Jodi Araujo, Chief Executive Officer
Kristy Cohen, Executive Director
Taylor Check, Meeting Coordinator

One-stop shop for training and certification. Designed to help members stand out from the competition. NADCA's trainers are highly experienced and know what it takes to be ultra successful in the HVAC cleaning industry.
1000 Members
Founded in 1989

2059 **GAMA Annual Meeting**
Gas Appliance Manufacturers Association
2107 Wilson Boulevard
Suite 600
Arlington, VA 22201

703-525-7060; Fax: 703-525-6790
www.gamanet.org

Stacy Heit, Manager of Meetings/Events

National trade association whose members manufacture space and water heating appliances, components and related products.
405 Attendees
Frequency: Annual
Founded in 1935

2060 **HARDI Annual Fall Conference**
15000 Commerce Parkway
Suite C
Mt. Laurel, NJ 08054
856-380-6810; Fax: 856-439-0525
info@nadca.com
www.nadca.com
Jodi Araujo, Chief Executive Officer
Kristy Cohen, Executive Director
Taylor Check, Meetings Coordinator
Conference offers information on profitability, confidence in navigating the economic waters, and finding the most effective and efficient means to achieve the market and profit objectives.
1000 Members
Founded in 1989

2061 **IIAR**
1001 N. Fairfax Street
Suite 503
Alexandria, VA 22314
703-312-4200; Fax: 703-312-0065
iiar_request@iiar.org
www.iiar.org
Gary Schrift, President
IIAR provides advocacy, education, and standards for the benefit of the global community in the safe and sustainable installation and operation of ammonia and other natural refrigerant systems.
2086 Members
Founded in 1971

2062 **IMPI Annual Symposium**
International Microwave Power Institute
7076 Drinkard Way
P O Box 1140
Mechanicsville, VA 23111
804-596-6667; Fax: 804-559-4087
info@impi.org
www.impi.org
Molly Poisant, Executive Director
Brings together researchers from across the globe to share the latest findings related to non-communications uses of microwave energy.
Frequency: Annual/June

2063 **International Consumer Electronics Show (CES)**
Consumer Technology Association
1919 South Eads Street
Arlington, VA 22202
703-907-7600
866-858-1555; Fax: 703-907-7675
cta@cta.tech
www.cta.tech
Gary Shapiro, President & CEO
David Hagan, Chairman
World's largest consumer technology tradeshow.
Frequency: Annual

2064 **International Home & Housewares Show**
International Housewares Associaton
6400 Shafer Court
Suite 650
Rosemont, IL 60018
847-292-4200; Fax: 847-292-4211
www.housewares.org
Adrienne Tiritilli, VP, Trade Show
International housewares marketplace, showcasing thousands of new products and designs.
18500 Attendees
Frequency: March

2065 **Kitchen/Bath Industry Show and Conference**
National Kitchen & Bath Association
687 Willow Grove Street
Hackettstown, NJ 07840
800-843-6522; Fax: 908-852-1695
feedback@nkba.org
www.nkba.org
Alan Zielinski, CEO& President
Timothy Captain, PR Manager
John A Petrie, Vice President
Carolyn Cheetham, Treasurer
Bill Darcy, CEO
Showcases the latest products and cutting-edge design ideas of the kitchen and bath industry.
40000 Attendees
Frequency: May

2066 **NADCA's Annual Meeting & Exposition**
15000 Commerce Parkway
Suite C
Mt. Laurel, NJ 08054
856-380-6810; Fax: 856-439-0525
info@nadca.com
www.nadca.com
Jodi Araujo, Chief Executive Officer
Kristy Cohen, Executive Director
Taylor Check, Meeting Coordinator
Promises educational sessions, live equipment demonstrations, and opportunities to meet peers.
1000 Members
Founded in 1989

2067 **NASA Convention & Trade Show**
National Appliance Service Association
3407 Williams Drive
PO Box 2514
Kokomo, IN 46904
765-453-1820; Fax: 765-453-1895
nasahq2011@gmail.com
Scott Kopin, President
Gordon Daniels, VP/Treasurer
Carrie Giannakos, Executive Director
Mike Hanika, Director
Don Kehoe, Director
Classes on marketing, advertising, customer service, machine repair by experienced professionals in the industry. Attendees are informed about industry trends and products, and have the opportunity to take advantage of show specials offered by exhibitors.
Frequency: Annual

2068 **NCCA Annual Meeting**
National Coil Coaters Association
1300 Sumner Avenue
Cleveland, OH 44115
216-241-7333; Fax: 216-241-0105
ncca@coilcoating.org
www.coilcoating.org
Jeff Alexander, President
Jeff Widenor, Vice President
John Favilla, Treasurer
Frequency: April

2069 **National Appliance Parts Suppliers**
National Appliance Parts Suppliers Association
4015 W MARSHALL AVE
Longview, TX 75604
903- 75- 398
www.napsaweb.org
Jim Bossman, President
Sherry Harrell, Secretary, Treasurer
Jason Cunningham, Secretary
For those in the appliance parts replacement business. Containing 62 booths and 60 exhibits.

2070 **RSES Annual Conference and HVAC Technology Expo**
Refrigeration Service Engineers Society
1911 Rohlwing Road
Suite A
Rolling Meadows, IL 60008-1397
847-297-6464
800-297-5660
general@rses.org
www.rses.org
Facebook, Twitter, LinkedIn
Mark Lowry, Executive Vice President
Lori Kasallis, Publisher Editor
Jean Birch, Conference & Seminar Manager
80 booths consisting primarily of products and services.

2071 **SMACNA Annual Convention**
15000 Commerce Parkway
Suite C
Mt. Laurel, NJ 08054
856-380-6810; Fax: 856-439-0525
info@nadca.com
www.nadca.com
Jodi Araujo, Chief Executive Officer
Kristy Cohen, Executive Director
Taylor Check, Meeting Coordinator
Business and skill tips for HVAC and Contractor professionals.
1000 Members
Founded in 1989

2072 **The International Roundtable of Household Appliance Manufacturer Associations**
jnotini@aham.org
www.irhma.org
Jill A. Notini, VP, Communications & Marketing
Informal forum for discussion of issues facing global appliance manufacturer associations.
Founded in 2014

2073 **World Educational Congress for Laundering and Drycleaning (Clean Show)**
Riddle & Associates
3098 Piedmont Road NE
Suite 350
Atlanta, GA 30305
404-876-1988; Fax: 404-876-5121
info@cleanshow.com
www.cleanshow.com
Facebook, Twitter
John Riddle, Manager
Ann Howell, Communications
World's largest exposition for laundry, drycleaning and textile services industry featuring working equipment and educational program. Draws international attendance.
11000 Attendees
Frequency: Biennial, Odd Years
Founded in 1977

Directories & Databases

2074 **A Portrait of the US Appliance Industry**
UBM Canon
11444 W. Olympic Blvd.
Los Angeles, CA 90064
310-445-4200; Fax: 310-445-4299
www.appliancemagazine.com
David J Chase, President
Susan Chase Korin, CEO
Appliance companies in the US.
Cost: $45.00
Frequency: Annual
Founded in 1944

2075 **Complete Directory of Small Appliances**
Sutton Family Communications & Publishing Company
920 State Route 54 East
Elmitch, KY 42343
270-276-9500
Theresa Sutton, Publisher
Lee Sutton, Editor
Print-out from database of wholesalers, manufacturers, distributors, importers and close-out houses. Database is updated daily to guarantee the most current and up-to-date sources available.
Cost: $55.20
100 Pages

2076 **Directory of Certified Performance (Online)**
Air Conditioning & Refrigeration Institute
Ste 500
2111 Wilson Blvd
Arlington, VA 22201-3036
703-524-8800; Fax: 703-528-3816
www.ari.org
Stephen R Yurek, President
The trusted source of performace certified heating, ventilation, air-conditioning, and commercial refrigeration equipment and components.

Industry Web Sites

2077 **http://gold.greyhouse.com**
G.O.L.D Grey House OnLine Databases
Grey House Publishing's online database platform, GOLD, offers Quick Search, Keyword Search and Expert Search for most business sectors including appliances and small electroincs. The GOLD platform makes finding the information you need quick and easy. All of Grey House's directory products are available for subscription on the GOLD platform.

2078 **www.abma.com**
American Boiler Manufacturers Association
Represents companies involved in utility, industrial and commercial steam generation.

2079 **www.acca.org**
Air Conditioning Contractors of America
ACCA is a non-profit association serving the HVACR community, working to promote professional contracting, energy efficiency, and healthy, comfortable indoor environments.

2080 **www.aga.org**
American Gas Association
Represents local energy utility companies that deliver natural gas to more than 56 million homes, businesses and industries throughout the United States.

2081 **www.aham.org**
Association of Home Appliance Manufacturers
Statistical information and summaries on appliances.

2082 **www.apda.com**
Appliance Parts Distributors Association
The APDA is an association of independent businesses that aspire to provide the highest level of quality, service, support and information to its customers and suppliers in order to make its value indispensable to the parts distribution channel.

2083 **www.appliancemagazine.com**
Dana Chase Publications
Appliance industry information content focused into 20 industry zones for targeted editorial coverage.

2084 **www.ari.org**
Air Conditioning & Refrigeration Institute
Representing manufacturers of central air-conditioning and commercial refrigeration equipment.

2085 **www.ashrae.org**
American Society of Heating, Refrigeration & A/C
Serving the heating, ventilation, air conditioning and refrigeration industries.

2086 **www.bema.org**
Bakery Equipment Manufacturers Association
Serves the baking and snack food industries.

2087 **www.gamanet.org**
Gas Appliance Manufacturers Association
Serves the residential, commercial and industrial gas and oil fired appliance industries.

2088 **www.ge.com**
General Electric
Information on home appliances, lighting, home solutions, corporate trends and customer service.

2089 **www.greyhouse.com**
Grey House Publishing
Authoritative reference directories for most business sectors including appliances and small electronics markets. Users can search the online databases with varied search criteria allowing for custom searches by product category, geographic area, sales volume, keyword, subject and more. Full Grey House catalog and online ordering also available.

2090 **www.housewares.org**
International Housewares Association
Provides information on the international home & housewares industry, with search tools, consumer purchase trend data, and access to global opportunities and discount business services.

2091 **www.ihea.org**
Industrial Heating Equipment Association
A voluntary national trade association representing the major segments of the industrial heat processing equipment industry.

2092 **www.impi.org**
International Microwave Power Institute
A forum for the exchange of information on all aspects of microwave and RF heating technologies.

2093 **www.napsaweb.org**
National Appliance Parts Suppliers Association
Provides distributors of replacement parts for major home appliances with information and services.

2094 **www.narda.com**
North American Retail Dealers Association
Serves the independent retailer industry.

2095 **www.nkba.com**
National Kitchen & Bath Association
Protects the interests of members by fostering a better business climate, awarding certification, and conducting training and seminars.

2096 **www.psaworld.com**
Professional Service Association
Information for companies that service and repair electronics and appliances.

2097 **www.repairclinic.com**
RepairClinic
Installation tips and how-to information on all appliances.

2098 **www.reta.com**
Refrigerating Engineers & Technicians Association
Seeks to upgrade the skills and knowledge of experienced members. Offers home-study courses on refrigeration and air conditioning.

2099 **www.rses.org**
Refrigeration Service Engineers Society
The world's leading education, training and certification association for heating, ventilation, air conditioning and refrigeration professionals.

2100 **www.supco.com**
Sealed Unit Parts
Serves the precision electronic test and service instruments, and refrigeration & air conditioning components industries; dedicated to producing high quality, innovative products at affordable prices to a wide range of customers.

Associations

2101 **American Architectural Foundation**
740 15th Street NW
Suite 225
Washington, DC 20005

202-787-1001; Fax: 202-787-1002
www.archfoundation.org
Facebook, Twitter, RSS

G. Sandy Diehl, III, Chair
Ron Bogle, Hon. AIA, President & CEO
John Syvertsen, Vice Chair & Secretary
Thomas Paul, Content Strategist
Frances Peters, Editorial Head

The American Architectural Foundation (AAF) is dedicated to the vibrant social, economic, and environmental future of cities. In the past decade alone, AAF has worked directly with local leaders through more than 500 city engagements. During this time, AAF has served every major metropolitan region and most second-tier cities in the United States.

2102 **American Architectural Manufacturers Association**
1827 Walden Office Square
Suite 550
Schaumburg, IL 60173-4268

847-303-5664; Fax: 847-303-5774
customerservice@aamanet.org
www.aamanet.org
Facebook, Twitter, LinkedIn, YouTube, Flickr, RSS

Janice Yglesias, Executive Director
Dawn Peters, Membership Database Coordinator
Angela Dickson, Marketing & Communications Director
Florence Nicolici, Meetings Manager
Karen Allen, Accounting & HR Manager

Advocate for manufacturers and professionals in the fenestration industry with respect to product certification, standards development, education and training, legislative regulations, and building and energy codes.

2103 **American College of Healthcare Architects**
18000 W.105th St.
Olathe, KS 66061-7543

913-895-4604; Fax: 913-895-4652
www.healtharchitects.org
Twitter, YouTube

Katherine Hughey, Executive Director
Raven ÿ Hardin, Account Executive
Diane ÿ Northup, Senior Account Coordinator
Debbie Jennings, Meeting Manager

Provides certificate holders with networking, educational, and marketplace opportunities and distinguishes healthcare architects through certification, experience, and rigorous standards.

2104 **American Design Drafting Association & American Digital Design Association**
105 East Main Street
Newbern, TN 38059-1526

731-627-0802; Fax: 731-627-9321
www.adda.org
Facebook, Twitter, LinkedIn, Google+

Olen Parker, Executive Director
Donna Brenton, Administrative Manager
Pennie King, Programs Manager

The American Design Drafting Association was conceived by a dedicated and enthusiastic group of oil and gas piping drafters who were involved in various phases of design drafting. This group consisted of highly specialized industry drafters, educational instructors, piping designers, and engineering personnel.
1000+ Members
Founded in 1948

2105 **American Institute of Architects (AIA)**
1735 New York Ave Nw
Washington, DC 20006-5292

202-626-7300
800-242-3837; Fax: 202-626-7547
infocentral@aia.org
www.aia.org
Facebook, Twitter, LinkedIn, Youtube, RSS Feeds, Instagram,

Robert A. Ivy, EVP & CEO
Abigail Warnecke Gorman, Chief of Staff
Lisa Green, VP, Finance & Administration
Susan McDaid, SVP, Member & Component Services
Jay Stephens, SVP & General Counsel

Based in Washington, D.C., the AIA is the leading professional membership association for licensed architects, emerging professionals, and allied partners.
83000 Members
Founded in 1857

2106 **American Planning Association**
205 N. Michigan Ave.
Suite 1200
Chicago, IL 60601

312-431-9100; Fax: 312-786-6700
customerservice@planning.org
www.planning.org
Facebook, Twitter, LinkedIn, YouTube, Flickr, RSS, Google+

Joel Albizo, Chief Executive Officer
Ann Simms, COO & CFO
Harriet Bogdanowicz, Chief Communications Officer
Mark Ferguson, Chief Information Officer
Liz Lang, Marketing Director

An independent, nonprofit educational organization that provides leadership in the development of vital communities.
Founded in 1978

2107 **American Society for Aesthetics**
1550 Larimer Street
Suite 644
Denver, CO 80202

562-331-4424
asa@aesthetics-online.org
www.aesthetics-online.org
Facebook, Twitter

Julie Van Camp, Executive Director
Julia Minarik, Managing Editor

The American Society for Aesthetics promotes study, research, discussion, and publication in aesthetics. Aesthetics, in this connection, is understood to include all studies of the arts and related types of experience from a philosophic, scientific, or other theoretical standpoint, including those of psychology, sociology, anthropology, cultural history, art criticism, and education. The arts include the visual arts, literature, music, and theater arts.
640 Members
Founded in 1942

2108 **American Society for Healthcare Engineering**
155 N. Wacker Drive
Suite 400.
Chicago, IL 60606

312-422-3800; Fax: 312-422-4571
ashe@aha.org
www.ashe.org
Facebook, Twitter, YouTube

Deanna Martin, Executive Director
Chad E. Beebe, Deputy Executive Director
Tracy Dagnon, Director, Marketing & Communication
Charmaine Osborne, Membership Manager
Melissa Binotti Heim, Program & Conference Manager

One of the largest associations devoted to optimizing the health care built environment and is a personal membership organization of the American Hospital Association.

2109 **American Society of Architectural Illustrators**
294 Merrill Hill Road
Hebron, ME 4238

207-966-2062
HQ@asai.org
www.asai.org
Facebook

Sergei Tchoban, President
Jose Uribe, Vice President
Jon Soules, Secretary
Matthew Paquin, Treasurer
Tina Bryant, Executive Director

An international, nonprofit organization dedicated to the advancement and recognition of the art, science, and profession of architectural illustration. Through communication, education, and advocacy, this society strives to redefine and emphasize the role of illustration in the practice and appreciation of architecture.
Founded in 1986

2110 **American Society of Concrete Contractors**
2025 S. Brentwood Blvd.
Suite 105
St. Louis, MO 63144

314-962-0210
866-788-2722; Fax: 314-968-4367
questions@ascconline.org
www.ascconline.org
Facebook, LinkedIn, Pinterest

Beverly Garnant, Executive Director
Becky Finch, Director, Member Engagement
Shreya Arora, Manager, Meetings & Events
Mary Anderson, Accounting & Finance
Bruce Suprenant, Technical Director

Provides knowledge on technical production and distribution of concrete construction, educates the industry on constructability, develops business savvy members, and helps them deliver a high quality product.
500 Members

2111 **American Society of Golf Course Architects**
125 N. Executive Drive
Suite 302
Brookfield, WI 53005

262-786-5960; Fax: 262-786-5919
www.asgca.org
Facebook, Twitter, LinkedIn, Instagram

Chad Ritterbusch, Executive Director
Aileen Smith, Director, Programming
Mike Shefky, Web Master
Marc Whitney, Director, Communications

The leader in advancing the interests of golf course architects andthe profession of golf course architecture for the benefit of ASGCA members and their clients, the golf industry, and the game of golf.
Founded in 1946

2112 **American Society of Landscape Architects**
636 Eye Street NW
Washington, DC 20001-3736

202-898-2444
888-999-2752; Fax: 202-898-1185
info@asla.org
www.asla.org
Facebook, Twitter, LinkedIn, Houzz, Instagram, Pinterest

Nancy Somerville, Exec. VP & CEO
Michael O'Brien, Managing Director & CFO

Residential and commercial real estate developers, federal and state agencies, city planning commissions and individual property owners are all among the thousands of people and organizations in America and Canada that will retain the services of a landscape architect this year.
15000 Members
Founded in 1899

2113 **Applied Technology Council**
201 Redwood Shores Parkway
Suite 240
Redwood City, CA 94065

650-595-1542; Fax: 650-593-2320
atc@atcouncil.org
www.atcouncil.org

Jon A. Heintz, Executive Director
Bernadette Hadnagy, Director, Operations
Ayse Hortacsu, Director, Projects
Justin Moresco, Director, Projects
Carrie Perna, Manager, Publications & Technology

A nonprofit, tax-exempt corporation that develops and promotes state-of-the-art, user-friendly engineering resources and applications for use in mitigating the effects of natural and other hazards on the built enviroment. ATC also identifies and encourages needed research and develops consensus opinions onstructural engineering issues in a nonproprietary format.
300 Members
Founded in 1973
Mailing list available for rent: 350 names

2114 **Architectural League**
594 Broadway
Suite 607
New York, NY 10012

212-753-1722; Fax: 212-486-9173
info@archleague.org
www.archleague.org
Facebook, Twitter, YouTube, Instagram, Vimeo

Rosalie Genevro, Executive Director
Anne Rieselbach, Program Director
Mariana Mogilevich, Editor-In-Chief
Anne Carlisle, Communications Manager
Daniel Cioffi, Development & Memberhsip Manager
Founded in 1881

2115 **Architectural Precast Association**
325 John Knox Rd
Ste L103
Tallahassee, FL 32303

850-205-5637; Fax: 850-222-3019
info@archprecast.org
www.archprecast.org

Tim Michael, President
Nick Carosi, Vice President
Jesse Thompson, Secretary/Treasurer

A national trade association organized to advance the interests of architectural precast in North America.
Founded in 1966

2116 **Architectural Research Centers Consortium**

Home Page: www.arcc-arch.org
Facebook, Twitter, LinkedIn, Google+

Hazem Rashed Ali, President
Chris Jarrett, Vice President
Saif Haq, Treasurer
Philip Plowright, Editor
Richard Cottrell, Webmaster

An international association of architectural research centers committed to the expansion of the research culture and a supporting infrastructure in architecture and related design disciplines.
Founded in 1976

2117 **Association for Computer Aided Design in Architecture**

membership@acadia.org
acadia.org

Kathy Velikov, President
Jason Kelly Johnson, Vice President
Phillip Anzalone, Membership Officer
Adam Marcus, Communications Officer
Alvin Huang, Development Officer

An international network of digital design researchers and professionals that facilitate critical investigations into the role of computation in architecture, planning, and building science, encouraging innovation in design creativity, sustainability, and education.

2118 **Association for Environment Conscious Building**
PO Box 32
Llandysul, SA

845-456-9773
www.aecb.net
Facebook, Twitter

Keith Hall, Co-Founder
Sally Hall, Co-Founder & Finance Manager
Andy Simmonds, Chief Executive Officer
James Allen, Development & Communications Mngr.
Trish Andrews, Training Manager

A network of individuals, students, educational establishments, andcompanies with a common aim of promoting sustainable building. It brings together builders, architects, designers, manufacturers, housing associations, and local authorities to develop, share, and promote best practice in environmentally sustainable building.
Founded in 1989

2119 **Association for Preservation Technology International**
3085 Stevenson Drive
Suite 200
Springfield, IL 62703

217-529-9039; Fax: 888-723-4242
info@apti.org
www.apti.org
Facebook, LinkedIn

Gina Crevello, President
Natalie Feinberg Lopez, VP, Co-Chair Inclusion Advocacy
Taryn Williams, VP, Co-Chair Partnerships/Outreach
Paul Kuenstner, Executive Director

The Association for Preservation Technology (APT) is a cross-disciplinary, membership organization dedicated to promoting the best technology for conserving historic structures and their settings.
Founded in 1968

2120 **Association for Women in Architecture + Design**
1315 Storm Pkwy.
Torrance, CA 90501

310-534-8466; Fax: 310-257-1942
awaplusd.org
Facebook, Twitter, LinkedIn, Instagram, Pinterest

Meg Coffee, President
Sona Gevorkyan, Vice President
Audrey Sato, Parlimentarian
Toni Lewis, Chief Financial Officer
Yolanda Lettieri, Secretary

Organization dedicated to the professional development of women working in the fields of architecture and design.
Founded in 1915

2121 **Association of Architecture Organizations**
224 South Michigan Ave
Suite 116
Chicago, IL 60604

312-561-2143; Fax: 312-922-2607
www.aaonetwork.org
Facebook, Twitter

Michael Wood, Executive Director
Mary Fichtner, Administrator & Member Outreach
Katherine Stalker, eNews Editor

A member-based network that connects organizations around the worlddedicated to enhancing public dialogue about architecture and design.
Founded in 2005

2122 **Association of Collegiate Schools of Architecture**
1735 New York Ave NW
3rd Floor
Washington, DC 20006-5209

202-785-2324; Fax: 202-628-0448
info@acsa-arch.org
www.acsa-arch.org
Facebook, Twitter, LinkedIn, Vimeo

Michael Monti, Executive Director
Eric Wayne Ellis, Sr. Dir., Operations & Programs
Danielle Dent, Dir., Membership, Marketing & Pub.
Carol Mannix, Publications Manager & Staff Editor
Kendall Nicholson, Director, Research & Information

Nonprofit membership association founded to advance the quality of architectural education.
500 Members
Founded in 1912

2123 **Association of Licensed Architects**
One East Northwest Hwy.
Suite 200
Palatine, IL 60067

847-382-0630; Fax: 847-382-8380
ala@alatoday.org
www.alatoday.org
Facebook, Twitter, LinkedIn

Joanne Sullivan, Executive Director
Lisa Brooks, Executive Dir., Illinois Chapter

An organization open to all architects and professions related to architecture and it represents architects registered or licensed in any state, territory, or possession of the United States or foreign country.

2124 **Association of Professional Landscape Designers**
2207 Forest Hills Drive
Harrisburg, PA 17112

717-238-9780; Fax: 717-238-9985
www.apld.com
Facebook, Twitter, LinkedIn, Pinterest

Denise Calabrese, Executive Director
Jennifer Swartz, Finance Administrator
Lori Zelesko, Events Director
Michelle Keyser, Communications Director
Carolyn Kimmel, Design Online Editor

An international organization dedicated to advancing the professionof landscape design and promoting the recognition of landscape designers as qualified and dedicated professionals.
Founded in 1986

2125 **Association of University Architects**
17595 S Tamiami Trail
Fort Myers, FL 33908-4570

FAX 239-590-1010
www.theaua.org

Purpose is to achieve more effective planning in the field of higher education, improve the design and construction standards of university buildings and to develop common bonds and establish standards which will ensure clarity of communications and render effective the exchange of information.
Founded in 1955

2126 **Business Architecture Guild**

info@businessarchitectureguild.org
www.businessarchitectureguild.org

Kathy Ulrich, Executive Director
Abha Trevedi, Events
Karin Roeder, Certification
Kalena Allard, Careers/Member Support
Jeanie Clapp, Editor

A professional association that offers exclusive content to its members. Additional benefits include a private online community, opportunities to provide feedback and collaborate with them on content, a knowledge repository, newsletters, webinars, and more.

2127 **Cast Stone Institute**
813 Chestnut Street
PO Box 68
Lebanon, PA 17042-7218

717-272-3744; Fax: 717-272-5147
staff@caststone.org
www.caststone.org

Jan Boyer, Executive Director

An organization of cast stone manufacturers, associates, professional architects, engineers and concrete technologists formed for the purpose of improving the quality of cast stone and disseminating information regarding its use.
70 Members
Founded in 1927

2128 **Center for Environmental Design Research**
University of California at Berkeley
390 Wurster Hall
Suite 1839
Berkeley, CA 94720-1839

510-642-2896; Fax: 510-643-5571
earens@berkeley.edu
www.cedr.berkeley.edu
Facebook, Twitter, LinkedIn, Flickr, Youtube

Tom J. Buresh, M.Arch., Chair, Department of Architecture
Paul Waddell, M.S., Ph.D, Chair, Department of City
G. Mathias Kondolf, M.S., Ph.D., Chair, Department of Landscaping
Jennifer Wolch, Ph.D., Dean
Gary Brown, M.Arch, Associate Dean for Faculty Affairs

Mission is to foster research in environmental planning and design

2129 **Construction Sciences Research Foundation, Inc.**
Home Page: www.csrf.org

Raymond K. Best, President
Kurt T. Preston, VP Finance & Administration
Michael D. Dell'Isola, Vice President
Charles Chief Boyd, Secretary/Treasurer
Garry C. Zetterten, Executive Director

An independent, nonprofit construction industry research organization dedicated to unifying and integrating communication between programs and design/communications processes used in facilities design and construction.

2130 **Council on Tall Buildings and Urban Habitat**
SR Crown Hall, Illinois Institute of Technology
3360 S State Street
Chicago, IL 60616-3796

312-567-3487; Fax: 312-567-3820
info@ctbuh.org
www.ctbuh.org
Facebook, Twitter, YouTube

Antony Wood, Chief Executive Officer
Steve Watts, Chair

Supported by architecture, engineering, planning development and construction professionals, designed to facilitate exchanges among those involved in all aspects of the planning, design, construction and operation of tall buildings.
Founded in 1969

2131 **Environmental Design Research Association**
7918 Jones Branch Drive
Suite 300
McLean, VA 22102

703-506-2895; Fax: 703-506-3266
headquarters@edra.org
www.edra.org
Facebook, Twitter, LinkedIn, YouTube, Flickr, Instagram

Sharmin Kader, Chair
Claudia Bernasconi, Chair Elect
Deni Ruggeri, Executive Director

An organization dedicated to advancing and distributing environmental design research, thereby improving understanding of the interrelationships between people, their built and natural surroundings. EDRA's goal is also to facilitate the creation of environments that are responsive to human needs.
Founded in 1968

2132 **Green Building Alliance**
33 Terminal Way
Suite 331
Pittsburgh, PA 15219

412-431-0709
info@gbapgh.org
www.go-gba.org
Facebook, Twitter, LinkedIn, YouTube

Jenna Cramer, Executive Director
Megan Zeigler, VP, Planning & Policy
Anthony Mendicino, Communications Director
Elisabeth Udyawar, Relationships & Development Dir.
Alyssa Lyon, Sustainable Communities Director

An organization that promotes healthy, high performing places for everyone by inspiring and leading the market, demonstrating and proving value, and equipping the community with knowledge and resources.
1200 Members
Founded in 1993

2133 **Historic New England**
Soc for Preservation of New England Antiquities
141 Cambridge St
Boston, MA 02114-2702

617-227-3956; Fax: 617-227-9204
www.historicnewengland.org
Facebook, Twitter, YouTube, Tumblr, Zazzle

Vin Cipolla, President/CEO
Diane Viera, Executive Vice President/COO
Jennifer Kent, Vice President for Advancement
Wendy Gus, Director of Finance
Benjamin Haavik, Team Leader for Property Care

Focuses on buildings, landscapes and objects reflecting New England life from the 17th century to the present. Also publishes a magazine about the organizations objects, architectural holdings and activities.
6000 Members
Founded in 1910

2134 **Institute for Human Centered Design**
200 Portland St.
Boston, MA 02114

617-695-1225; Fax: 617-482-8099
info@ihcdesign.org
www.humancentereddesign.org
Facebook, Twitter, LinkedIn, YouTube

Valerie Fletcher, Executive Director
Janet Carpman, Director, Wayfinding
Kathy Gips, Director, ADA Training
Janice Majewski, Director, Inclusive Projects
Gabriela Bonome-Sims, Deputy Director

Advances the role of design in the built environment in expanding opportunity and enhancing experience for people of all ages, abilities, and cultures. Provides education, consulting, design, and research services.
Founded in 1978

2135 **Institute for Urban Design**
17 West 17th Street, 7th Floor
New York, NY 10014-3731

212-366-0780; Fax: 212-633-0125
info@ifud.org
www.ifud.org
Facebook, Twitter, LinkedIn, RSS Feeds, vimeo

Responsible for city planning.
1M Members
Founded in 1979

2136 **Insulated Cable Engineers Association**
PO Box 493
Miamitown, OH 45041

info@icea.net
www.icea.net

Professional organization dedicated to developing cable standards for electric power, control and telecommunications industries. Ensures safe, economical and efficient cable systems utilizing proven, state-of-the-art materials and concepts. ICEA documents are of interest to cable manufacturers, architects and engineers, utility and manufacturing plant personnel, telecommunication engineers, consultants and OEMs.
60+ Members
Founded in 1925

2137 **Interior Design Educators Council**
One Parkview Plaza
Suite 800
Oakbrook Terrace, IL 60181

630-544-5057
info@idec.org
www.idec.org
Facebook, Twitter, LinkedIn, YouTube, Flickr, Yahoo, Google

Lori Barker-Cummings, Executive Director
Toni Wilkerson, Coordinator
Kirsten Lew, Associate Account Executive
Darrell McCook, Events Manager

An organization dedicated to the advancement of interior design education, scholarship, and service.
Founded in 1972

2138 **International Association for Impact Assessment**
1330 23rd Street S
Suite C
Fargo, ND 58103-3705

701-297-7908; Fax: 701-297-7917
info@iaia.org
www.iaia.org
Facebook, Twitter, YouTube

David Bancroft, Executive Director
Kayla Deitch, Event Logistics Specialist
Jack Marsden, Comm. & Development Specialist
Shelli LaPlante, Membership Manager/Graphic Designer
Jennifer Howell, Resources & Conference Program Mgr.

A forum for advancing innovation, development, and communication of best practice in impact assessment. Exists to improve and better inform the decision-making of today that has environmental consequences for tomorrow.
2500 Members
Founded in 1980

2139 **International Association of Innovation Professionals**
4422 Castle Wood Street
Suite 200
Sugar Land, TX 77479

925-858-0905
800-276-1180
www.iaoip.org
Facebook, Twitter, LinkedIn, Instagram, Vimeo

Brett Trusko, President/ CEO
Lewis Archer, Webmaster
Charisma Aggarwal, Development Manager
Dana J. Landry, VP Certification Programs
Marco D. Mancin, Director

Creates events and provides resources to help professionals learn the latest innovation methodologies, and offer certification testing to help themadvance in their careers.
800 Members

2140 **International Code Council**
500 New Jersey Avenue, NW
6th Floor
Washington, DC 20001

708-799-4981
888-422-7233; Fax: 708-799-4981
members@iccsafe.org
www.iccsafe.org
Facebook, Twitter, LinkedIn, Youtube

Dominic Sims, Chief Executive Officer
John Belcik, COO & CFO
Joan O'Neil, Chief Knowledge Officer
Mark Johnson, Executive Vice President

A nonprofit membership association dedicated to preserving the public health, safety and welfare in the built environment through the promulgation of model codes suitable for adoption by governmental entities and assisting code enforcement officials, design professionals, builders, manufacturers and others involved in the design, construction and regulatory processes.
16000 Members
Founded in 1915

2141 **International Federation of Interior Archi tects/Designers**
708 3rd Ave.
6th Floor
New York, NY 10017

212-884-6275; Fax: 212-884-6247
staff@ifiworld.org
www.ifiworld.org
Facebook, Twitter, LinkedIn

Shashi Caan, Chief Executive Officer

The only international federating body for Interior Architecture/Design organizations. Connects the international community to further the knowledge, impact, influence, and application of the design of interiors, promote global social responsibility, and raise the status of the profession worldwide.
Founded in 1963

2142 **International Interior Design Association**
111 E. Wacker Dr.
Suite 222
Chicago, IL 60601

312-467-1950
888-799-4432
+01-312-467-1950
iidahq@iida.org
www.iida.org
Facebook, Twitter, LinkedIn, Instagram

Cheryl Durst, Executive VP & CEO
Lisa Taylor, Director, Finance
Lauren Haras, Director, Marketing & Communciaiton
Monae Redmond, Director, Member Services
Tracey Thomas, Director, Strategic Sales

Association that provides its members with sources, knowledge, and contacts necessary in the interior design field.

2143 **Marine Engineers' Beneficial Association**
444 N. Capitol Street, NW
Suite 800
Washington, DC 20001

202-638-5355; Fax: 202-638-5369
www.mebaunion.org
Facebook, Twitter, YouTube

Marshall Ainley, President
Bill Van Loo, Secretary/ Treasurer
Mark Gallagher, Contracts Rep
Eric C. Pittman, Comptroller

The oldest maritime trade union that represents licensed mariners, deck and engine officers and has a training plan to provide further technical training. It has worked hard in Washington, DC to ensure proper examination and licensing of engineers and the abolition of controversial license fees.
Founded in 1875

2144 **Marine Technology Society**
1100 H St., NW
Suite LL-100
Washington, DC 20005

202-717-8705; Fax: 202-347-4302
membership@mtsociety.org
www.mtsociety.org

Kathleen Herndon, Executive Director
Kristina Norman, Director, Events
Monica Ostrander, Director, Programs
Amy Morgante, Managing Editor
Judy Pagliaro, Bookkeeper

A growing organization with a membership that includes businesses, institutions, individual professionals, and students who are ocean engineers, technologists, policy makers, and educators. This group works to promote awareness, understanding, advancement, and the application of marine technology.
Founded in 1963

2145 **National Academy of Environmental Design**

A nonprofit organization that provides the public with expertise and leadership in the creation of healthier, greener, safer, and more resilient American communitites through environmental design.

2146 **National Architectural Accrediting Board**
1101 Connecticut Avn., NW
Suite 410
Washington, DC 20036

202-783-2007; Fax: 202-783-2822
info@naab.org
www.naab.org
Facebook, Twitter

Tanya Tamarkin, Executive Director
Ellen Cathey, Associate Director
Janet Runbarger, International Services
David Golden, Manager, Strategy & Communications
Nour Alhussaini, Manager, Ops. & Special Projects

Develops and maintains a system of accreditation in professional architecture education that is responsive to the needs of society and allows institutions with varying resources and circumstances to evolve according to their individual needs.

2147 **National Association of Home Builders**
1201 15th Street NW
Washington, DC 20005

202-266-8200
800-368-5242; Fax: 202-266-8400
www.nahb.org
Facebook, Twitter, LinkedIn, Google+, Pinterest

John Fowke, Chair
Gerald Howard, Chief Executive Officer
Jerry Konter, Second Vice Chair
Alicia Huey, Third Vice Chair

A trade association that helps promote the policies that make housing a national priority.
Founded in 1940

2148 **National Council of Architectural Registration Boards**
1801 K St NW
Suite 700k
Washington, DC 20006-1320

202-783-6500; Fax: 202-783-0290
www.ncarb.org
Facebook, Twitter, LinkedIn, YouTube

Michael Armstrong, Chief Executive Officer
Mary De Sousa, Chief Operating Officer
Guillermo Ortiz de Zarate, Chief Innovation & Info Officer
Roxanne Alston, VP, Customer Relations
Andy McIntyre, VP, Marketing & Communications

Committed to protecting the health, safety, and welfare of the public through effective regualtion and exemplary service.
Founded in 1919

2149 **National Organization of Minority Architects**
PO Box 3558
Washington, DC 20027

202-818-8653
info@noma.net
www.noma.net
Facebook, Twitter, LinkedIn

Bryan Hudson, President

A national organization that strives to minimize the effects of racism in the architecture profession and also battles against apathy, bigotry, and abuse of the natural environment.

2150 **Organization of Women Architects and Designers**
PO Box 10078
Berkeley, CA 94709

Home Page: www.owa-usa.org
Facebook

A nonprofit organization that is an active support network for women involved in architecture, engineering, planning, landscape architecture, interior and graphic design, and related environmental design fields.
Founded in 1970

2151 **Partners for Livable Communities**
1429 21st St Nw
Washington, DC 20036-5902

202-887-5990; Fax: 202-466-4845
livability@livable.org
www.livable.org
RSS

Robert H. McNulty, President
Penny Cuff, VP, Programs & Administration
Jessica Scheuerman, VP, Development & Marketing
Laura Lee, VP, Finance
Melanie Bourne, Communications

A non-profit leadership organization working to improve the livability of communities by promoting quality of life, economic development, and social equity.
Founded in 1977

2152 **Society for Environmental Graphic Design**
1900 L Street NW
Suite 710
Washington, DC 20036

202-638-5555; Fax: 202-478-2286
segd@segd.org
www.segd.org
Facebook, Twitter, LinkedIn, RSS Feeds

Cybelle Jones, CEO
Jennette Foreman, Director, Events
Sarah Miorelli, Graphic Design Assistant
Nadia Adona, Member Services Associate/Webmaster

The global community of people who work at the intersection of communication design and the built environment.
Founded in 1974

2153 **Society of American Registered Architects**
14 E 38th Street
11th Floor
New York, NY 10016

920-395-2330
888-385-7272; Fax: 866-668-9858
www.sara-national.org

Anthony Baker, President

A professional society that includes the participation of all architects, regardless of their roles in the architectural community, the opportunity to share information and ideas.
Founded in 1956

2154 **Society of Architectural Historians**
1365 N Astor St
Chicago, IL 60610

312-573-1365; Fax: 312-573-1141
info@sah.org
www.sah.org
Facebook, Twitter, LinkedIn, YouTube, Instagram

Pauline Saliga, Executive Director
Christopher Kirbabas, Director, Programs
Anne Bird, Director, Membership
Helena Dean, Director, Communications
Beth Eifrig, Comptroller

A not-for-profit membership organization and learned society that promotes the study and preservation of the built environment worldwide.
2400 Members
Founded in 1940

2155 **Society of Naval Architects and Marine Engineers**
99 Canal Center Plaza
Suite 310
Alexandria, VA 22314

703-997-6701
800-798-2188; Fax: 703-997-6702
www.sname.org

Valerie Hutnan, Executive Director
Kathy Hartness, VP, Events & Membership
Michael Ashman, Director, Finance
Frederick Ashcroft, Director, Technology & Education
Thais De Oliveira, Coord., Marketing & Social Media

Internationally recognized nonprofit technical, professional society of individual members serving the maritime and offshore industries and their suppliers. Dedicated to advancing the industry by recording information, sponsoring research, offering career guidance and supporting education.
10000 Members
Founded in 1893

2156 **Sustainable Buildings Industry Council**
1090 Vermont Avenue NW
Suite700
Washington, DC 20005

202-289-7800; Fax: 202- 28- 109
nibs@nibs.org
Facebook, Twitter, LinkedIn, Pinterest

Mission is to unite and inspire the building industry toward higher performance through education, outreach, advocacy and the mutual exchange of ideas.
Founded in 1980

2157 **The American Institute of Architecture Students**
1735 New York Ave NW
Washington, DC 20006

202-808-0075; Fax: 202-626-7414
mailbox@aias.org
www.aias.org
Facebook, Twitter, LinkedIn, Instagram, Snapchat, YouTube

Nick Serfass, Executive Director
Keshika De Saram, President

An independent, non-profit, student-run organization dedicated to providing unmatched programs, information, and resources on issues critical to architectural education.
Founded in 1956

2158 **The National Institute of Building Sciences**
1090 Vermont Avenue, NW
Suite 700
Washington, DC 20005-4950

202-289-7800; Fax: 202-289-1092
nibs@nibs.org
www.nibs.org
RSS

Lakisha Ann Woods, President & CEO
Rebecca Liko, VP, Finance & Controller
Sarah Swango, Sr. Dir., Membership & Development
Kristen Petersen, Managing Dir., Marketing & Comm.
Jennifer Hitzke, Manager, Executive Office

A nonprofit, non-governmental organization that brings together representatives of government, the professions, industry, labor and consumer interests, and regulatory agencies to focus on the identification and resolution of problems that hamper the contruction of safe, affordable structures for housing, commerce, and industry throughout the United States.

2159 **U.S. Green Building Council**
2101 L Street, NW
Suite 500
Washington, DC 20037

202-742-3792
800-795-1747
info@usgbc.org
www.usgbc.org
Facebook, Twitter, LinkedIn, YouTube, Instagram, Google+

Mahesh Ramanujam, President & CEO
Roger Platt, SVP, Market Transformation & Devt.
Roger Limoges, SVP, Enterprise Operations
Sarah Merricks, Chief of Staff
Susan Dorn, General Counsel

This organization is made up of tens of thousands of member organizations, chapters, and student and community volunteers that strive to transform the way buildings and communities are operated, enabling an environmentally and socially responsible, healthy, and prosperous environment that improves the quality of life.
Founded in 1973

2160 **United States Access Board**
Access Board
1331 F Street NW
Suite 1000
Washington, DC 20004-1111

202-272-0080
800-872-2253; Fax: 202-272-0081
info@access-board.gov
www.access-board.gov
Facebook, Twitter, Vimeo

Dave Yanchulis, Director, Office of Technical
David M. Capozzi, Executive Director

Independent federal agency devoted to accessibility for people with disabilities. Its key missions include developing and maintaining guidelines for the built environment, transit vehicles, telecommunications equipment and standards for electronic and information technology; providing technical assistance and training on these guidelines and standards and enforcing design standards for federally funded facilities.
Founded in 1975

2161 **Urban Design Associates**
3 PPG Place
3rd Floor
Pittsburgh, PA 15222

412-263-5200; Fax: 844-270-8374
www.urbandesignassociates.com
Facebook, Twitter, Vimeo

Designs resilient neighborhoods, towns, villages, districts, places, and buildings.
Founded in 1964

Newsletters

2162 **A/E Business Review**
6524 E Rockaway Hills Drive
PO Box 4808
Cave Creek, AZ 85331-7609

480-488-0311; Fax: 480-488-0311

Clare Ross, Publisher
The management and marketing newsletter of architects, engineers and planners.
7 Pages
Frequency: Monthly

2163 **AIA Architect**
American Institute of Architects
1735 New York Ave Nw
Washington, DC 20006-5292

202-626-7300
800-242-3837; Fax: 202-626-7547
infocentral@aia.org
www.aia.org

Robert Ivy, CEO
News of America's community of architects
Frequency: Weekly

2164 **Access Currents**
United States Access Board
1331 F Street NW
Suite 1000
Washington, DC 20004-1111

202-272-0080
800-872-2253; Fax: 202-272-0081
info@access-board.gov
www.access-board.gov

Dave Yanchulis, Director, Office of Info Services
David M. Capozzi, Executive Director

The official newsletter for the United States Access Board.

2165 **Certifier**
Nat'l Council of Architectural Registration Boards
1801 K St Nw
Suite 700K
Washington, DC 20006-1320

202-879-0520; Fax: 202-783-0290
www.ncarb.org

Michael Armstrong, CEO
Blakely Dunn, Vice President

State architectural registration boards.
Frequency: Annual
Founded in 1919

2166 **Design Drafting News**
American Design Drafting Association
105 E Main Street
Newbern, TN 38059-1526

731-627-0802; Fax: 731-627-9321
corporate@adda.org
www.adda.org

Olen Parker, Executive Director

Newsletter for the American Design Drafting Association and American Digital Design Association.
Frequency: Bi-Monthly
Circulation: 1800

2167 **Design Firm Management & Administration Report**
Institute of Management and Administration
3 Bethesda Metro Center
Suite 250
Bethesda, MD 20814-537

703-341-3500
800-372-1033; Fax: 800-253-0332
www.ioma.com

Provides practical, hands-on, timely information to design firm managers and administrators about the marketing and management aspects of operating a firm.
Cost: $429.00
Frequency: Monthly

2168 **Designline**
American Institute of Building Design
529 14th St NW
Suite 750
Washington, DC 20045

202-249-1407
800-366-2423; Fax: 866-204-0293
info@aibd.org
www.aibd.org

Dan Sater, President
Alan Kent, Vice President

Focuses on issues, education, and events as they happen in the building design industry.
Frequency: Quarterly

2169 **Direct Connection**
Nat'l Council of Architectural Registration Boards
1801 K St NW
Suite 700K
Washington, DC 20006-1301

202-870-0520; Fax: 202-782-0290
customerservice@ncarb.org
www.ncarb.org

Michael Armstrong, CEO

Offers information and news on licensing, board certification, architectural trends and more for the professional architect and intern architect.
16 Pages
Circulation: 50000
Printed in 2 colors on glossy stock

2170 **Energy Design Update**
Aspen Publishers
76 Ninth Avenue
7th Floor
New York, NY 10011

212-771-0600
800-638-8437

Mark Dorman, CEO
Gustavo Dobles, VP Operations

For professionals concerned with residential load management and energy efficient design and construction in housing.
Cost: $297.00
16 Pages
Frequency: Monthly

2171 **Guidelines Letter: New Directions and Techniques in the Design Profession**
Guidelines
PO Box 2590
Alameda, CA 94501

510-235-5174
800-634-7779; Fax: 510-523-5175
info@sfia.net
www.sfia.net

Fred Stitt, Director/Editor
Chandler Vienneau, Circulation Director

Business and technical information for design professionals including comprehensive survey information regarding fees and client costs. The Guidelines Letter is in its 28th year of publication.
Cost: $70.00
4 Pages
Frequency: Monthly
ISSN: 1089-2141
Founded in 1992

2172 **Memo**
American Institute of Architects
1735 New York Ave Nw
Washington, DC 20006-5292

202-626-7300
800-242-3837; Fax: 202-626-7547
infocentral@aia.org
www.aia.org

Robert Ivy, CEO

Architectural news and information.
Frequency: Monthly
Circulation: 85000

2173 **SARAScope**
Society of American Registered Architects
14 E 38th Street
11th Floor
New York, NY 10016

347-210-0292
www.sara-national.org/sara.scope.html

Listing society conventions, meetings and other activities. Discusses news about the Society of interest to members.
Frequency: 6X/yr
Founded in 1956

2174 **Society of Architectural Historians Newsletter**
Society of Architectural Historians
1365 N Astor St
Chicago, IL 60610

312-573-1365; Fax: 312-573-1141
info@sah.org
www.sah.org

Keeps readers informed about upcoming SAH events, conferences, tours, awards, publications and exhibitors.
Frequency: Monthly
Circulation: 12,500

2175 **The Dirt**
American Society of Landscape Architects
636 Eye Street NW
Washington, DC 20001-3736

202-898-2444
800-787-2752; Fax: 202-898-1185
info@asla.org
www.asla.org
Facebook, Twitter, LinkedIn, Pinterest, Tumblr, Reddit

Jared Green, Editor & Writer

Weekly blog of the American Society of Landscape Architects.
Frequency: Weekly

2176 **Times**
Council of Tall Buildings and Urban Habitat
Illinois Institute of Technology SR Crown
3360 S State Street
Chicago, IL 60616-3793

312-567-3487; Fax: 312-567-3820
info@ctbuh.org
www.ctbuh.org

Patti Thurmond, Operations Manager
Antony Wood, Executive Director

Tansri Muliani, News Editor
Steven Henry, Publications

Newsletter for members of CTBUH.
Cost: $75.00
Frequency: Monthly
Circulation: 1200
ISSN: 1061-5121
Founded in 1969
Printed in 2 colors on matte stock

Magazines & Journals

2177 **AI Communications**
AIAA
1735 New York Ave NW
Washington, DC 20006-5209

202-626-7300
800-242-3837; Fax: 202-626-7547
infocentral@aia.org
www.aia.org

Robert Ivy, CEO

Student programs and issues dealing with architectural education.
Founded in 1857

2178 **APT Bulletin: The Journal of Preservation Technology**
Association for Preservation Technology Int'l
3085 Stevenson Drive
Suite 200
Springfield, IL 62705

217-529-9039; Fax: 888-723-4242
info@apti.org
www.apti.org

Gina Crevello, President
Paul Kuenstner, Executive Director
Lesley Gilmore, Editor

Articles showcase cutting-edge preservation techniques, as well as innovative applications of established restoration technologies.

2179 **Adobe Magazine**
Adobe Systems
345 Park Ave
San Jose, CA 95110-2704

408-536-6000; Fax: 408-537-6000
www.adobe.com

Shantanu Narayen, CEO
Mark Garrett, SVP

Devoted to adobe and earthen architecture. Showing both old and new traditions of building the earth.
Cost: $4.00
Circulation: 4,500

2180 **American School & University**
PRIMEDIA Intertec Publication
9800 Metcalf Ave.
Overland Park, KS 66212

913-341-1300; Fax: 913-967-1898
www.penton.com

Nicola Alais, Senior VP
Gregg Herring, Publisher
David KIESELSTEIN, CEO

The industry's definitive educational facilities publication.
Cost: $50.00
508 Pages
Frequency: Monthly
Circulation: 63540
Founded in 1928
Printed in 4 colors on glossy stock

2181 **Architectural Design**
John Wiley & Sons
111 River St
Hoboken, NJ 07030-5790

201-748-6000; Fax: 201-748-6088
info@wiley.com
www.wiley.com

Matthew Kissner, CEO/President
Jean-Lou Chameau, President

Continues to publish a vigorous and wide range treatment of architectural trends of topical importance.
Cost: $145.00
Founded in 1807

2182 **Architectural Digest**
4 Times Square
Suite 15
New York, NY 10036-6518

212-286-2860; Fax: 212-286-6790
www.architecturaldigest.com

Giulio Capua, Publisher
Margaret Russell, Editor-in-Chief

For the connoisseur of interior design. The purpose is to cultivate an appreciation of excellence in the luxury world of design and furnishing.
Cost: $39.95
Frequency: Monthly
Circulation: 840,995
Founded in 1999

2183 **Architectural Record**
McGraw Hill
2 Penn Plaza
9th Floor
New York, NY 10121-2298

212-904-2594; Fax: 212-904-4256
archrecord.construction.com

William Hanley, Web Editor
Cathleen McGuigan, Editor in Chief
Ilan Kapla, Sr. Manager, Web Production
Rama Bandu, Web Producer
Elisabeth Broome, Managing Editor

Provides a compelling editorial mix of design ideas and trends, building science, business and professional strategies, exploration of key issues, news products and computer-aided practice.
Cost: $49.00
Frequency: Monthly

2184 **Architecture Magazine**
American Institute of Architects
One Thomas Circle, NW
Suite 600
Washington, DC 20005

202-452-0800; Fax: 202-785-1974
info@architecturemag.com
www.architecturemag.com

Ned Cramer, Editor-in-Chief
Greig O'Brien, Managing Editor
Katie Gerfen, Senior Editor

Evaluation of new and existing buildings and related news that affects the profession.
Frequency: Monthly
Circulation: 63449

2185 **Ballast Quarterly Review**
Ballast
2022 X Avenue
Dysart, IA 52224-9767

ballast@netins.net

Roy Behrens, Editor

Examines an eclectic assortment of publications with an emphasis on graphic design and architecture.
16 Pages
Frequency: Quarterly

2186 **Building Design & Construction**
Reed Business Information
360 Park Ave S
New York, NY 10010-1737

1 -46 -46 6; Fax: 646-756-7583
subsmail@reedbusiness.com
www.reedbusiness.com

Mark Kelsey, CEO
James Reed, President

Serves the needs of the design and construction professionals of commercial, industrial and institutional buildings that include new and retrofit projects. Geared towards the building team that includes professionals from building firms, owning firms and design firms.
Frequency: Monthly
Founded in 1946

2187 **CRIT Journal**
The American Institute of Architecture Students
1735 New York Ave NW
Washington, DC 20006

202-808-0075; Fax: 202-626-7414
mailbox@aias.org
www.aias.org
Facebook, Twitter, LinkedIn, Instagram, Snapchat, YouTube

Taylor Schaub, Editor-in-Chief

The premier source of and the only international journal of student design work.
Frequency: Bi-Annual
Circulation: 13,000
Founded in 1976

2188 **CTBUH Review Journal**
Council on Tall Buildings and Urban Habitat
S.R.Crown Hall,
3360 South State Street
Chicago, IL 60616

312-567-3487; Fax: 312-567-3820
info@ctbuh.org
www.ctbuh.org

Marshall Ali, Editor
Anthony Wood, Executive Director
Robert Lau, Associate Editor

CTBUH Review is the Professional Journal of the Council on Tall Buildings and Urban Habitat. It includes refereed papers submitted by researchers, scholars, suppliers, and practicing professionals engaged in the planning, design, construction, and operation of tall buildings and the urban environment throughout the world. Membership benefits include monthly e-updates, access to on-line buildings database, discounts on selected publications and registration at Council-sponsored activities.
Cost: $150.00
1400 Pages
Frequency: Quarterly

2189 **Classicist**
Transaction Publishing Rutgers
35 Berrue Circle
Piscataway, NJ 08854-8042

732-445-2280
888-999-6778; Fax: 732-445-3138
trans@transactionpub.com
www.transactionpub.com

Mary Curtis, President
Prof. David Shulman, Editor

Dedicated to the theory and practice of architecture and artistic classicism.
Cost: $39.95
164 Pages

2190 **Computer-Aided Engineering**
Penton Media

1300 E 9th St
Suite 316
Cleveland, OH 44114-1503

216-696-7000; Fax: 216-696-1752
information@penton.com
www.penton.com

David Kieselstein, CEO
Nicola Allais, EVP
Jasmine Alexander, Senior VP & CIO

Database applications in design and manufacturing.
Cost: $50.00
96 Pages
Founded in 1982

2191 **Concrete Masonry Designs**
13750 Sunrise Valley Drive
Herndon, VA 20171-4662

703-713-1900; Fax: 703-713-1910
ncma@ncma.org
www.ncma.org

Mary Arntson-Terrell, Director of Sales
Robert Thomas, President
Highlights concrete masonry applications, best practice tips, specifications and details. Also showcases concrete masonry landscape products.
Cost: $2.50
Frequency: Monthly
Circulation: 25000
Founded in 1918
Printed in 4 colors on glossy stock

2192 **Contemporary Stone & Tile Design**
BNP Media
210 E State Rt 4
Suite 203
Paramus, NJ 07652-5103

201-291-9001; Fax: 201-291-9002
info@stoneworld.com
www.stoneworld.com

Alex Bachrach, Publisher
Michael Reis, Editor
Jennifer Adams, Editor
Focuses on stone and ceramic tile use in interior design for architects, interior designers, specifiers and consumrs with the buying influence for stone or stone materials and a variety of architectural and construction products and services.

2193 **Design Issues**
MIT Press
55 Hayward Street
Cambridge, MA 02142-1315

617-253-5646; Fax: 617-258-6779
www.mitpress.mit.edu

Michael Sims, Managing Editor
Ellen Faran, Director
Provokes inquiry into the cultural and intellecutual issues surrounding design. Regular features include theoretical and critical articles by professional and scholarly contributions, extensive book reviews, and illustrations.
110 Pages
Frequency: Quarterly
ISSN: 0747-9360
Founded in 1984

2194 **Design Journal**
Journal Communications Group
1720 20th St #201
Santa Monica, CA 90404

310-394-4394; Fax: 310-394-0966
customer.services@benjamins.nl
designjournalmag.com

Kees Vaes, Editor
Karin Plijnaar, Marketing Manager
Focuses on the design and architecture marketplace. Includes newsbites and a calendar, as well as designer and lighting resources.
Frequency: Monthly
Circulation: 34000
Founded in 1982

2195 **Design Solutions Magazine**
Architectural Woodwork Institute
46179 Westlake Drive
Suite 120
Potomac Falls, VA 20165

571-323-3636; Fax: 571-323-3630
adsales@awinet.org
www.awinet.org

Teresa McCain, Director of Operations
Philip Duvic, Executive VP
Featuring beautiful woodwork projects manufactured by members of the Architectural Woodwork Institute (AWI). Many other related publications, including woodworking quality standards used by woodwork manufacturers and design professionals.
Cost: $25.00
Frequency: Quarterly
Circulation: 25000
Founded in 1953

2196 **Design/Build Business**
Cygnus Publishing
12735 Morris Road
Bldg. 200
Alpharetta, GA 30152-0803

770-427-5290
800-547-7377; Fax: 404-935-9290
kathy.scott@cygnusb2b.com

John French, CEO
Michael Martin, President
Serves builders, architects and designing and remodeling firms, nationwide. Edited to these professions serving the residential and light commercial marketplaces.
Cost: $24.00
72 Pages
Frequency: Monthly
Circulation: 60424
ISSN: 1068-9433
Founded in 1935

2197 **Dodge Construction News**
McGraw Hill
PO Box 182604
Columbus, OH 43272

614-866-5769
877-833-5524; Fax: 614-759-3749
www.mcgraw-hill.com

Jennifer Hayes, Editor
Harold McGraw III, President/CEO
Consists of program edition and proceedings and recap edition for the National Conventions of the American Institute of Architects and Construction Specifications Institute.
Circulation: 86400
Founded in 1958

2198 **Enquiry: A Journal for Architectural Research**
Architectural Research Centers Consortium

Home Page: www.arcc-arch.org

Hazem Rashed Ali, President
Chris Jarrett, Vice President
Saif Haq, Treasurer
Philip Plowright, Editor
Richard Cottrell, Webmaster
Frequency: Annual
ISSN: 2329-9339
Founded in 1976

2199 **Fabrics Architecture**
U.S. Industrial Fabrics Association International
1801 County Road NW
Roseville, MN 55113-4061

651-222-2508
800-225-4324; Fax: 651-631-9334
www.usifi.com

Ruth Stephens, Executive Director
Strives to inform architects, designers, landscape architects, engineers and other specifiers about architectural fabric structures, the fibers and fabrics used to make them, their design possibilities, their construction, and issues regarding their applicability and acceptance.
Cost: $39.00
Frequency: Bi-Monthly

2200 **Glass Magazine**
National Glass Association
1945 Old Gallows Rd
Suite 750
Vienna, VA 22182

703-442-4890
866-342-5642; Fax: 703-442-0630
editorialinfo@glass.org
www.glass.org

Phil James, CEO
Nicole Harris, Vice President
Offers readers experienced editorial direction and informative coverage including market segment surveys, resource guides, reader polls, industry profiles, industry states, and industry products.
Frequency: Monthly

2201 **Harvard Design Magazine**
Harvard University Graduate School of Design
48 Quincy St
Gund Hall
Cambridge, MA 02138-3000

617-495-5453; Fax: 617-495-8949
hdm@gsd.harvard.edu
www.gsd.harvard.edu
Facebook, Twitter, LinkedIn

Mohsen Mostafavi, Dean
Aims to provide a forum for thoughtful and articulate practitioners, journalists, and academics, primarily from architecture, landscape architecture and urban design and planning.
Frequency: Bi-Annual

2202 **Impact Assessment and Project Appraisal (IAPA)**
International Association for Impact Assessment
1330 23rd Street S
Suite C
Fargo, ND 58103-3705

701-297-7908; Fax: 701-297-7917
info@iaia.org
www.iaia.org

David Bancroft, Executive Director
IAPA is an international refereed journal. It welcomes papers on the environmental, social, health, technology, integrated, sustainability, etc. assessment of projects, programs, plans and policies.
Frequency: Quarterly
Circulation: 1600
ISSN: 1461-5517

2203 **Inland Architect**
Real Estate News Corporation
3500 West Peterson Avenue
Suite 403
Chicago, IL 60659

773-866-9900
888-641-3169; Fax: 773-866-9881
rencorpil@aol.com
www.inlandarchitectmag.com

Steven Polydoris, Publisher/Editor

Covers distinguished and historical buildings.
Cost: $27.00
120 Pages
Founded in 1883
Printed in 4 colors on glossy stock

2204 Journal of Architectural Education
Blackwell Publishing Inc
350 Main St
Suite 6
Malden, MA 02148-5089

781-388-8598
800-835-6770; Fax: 781-388-8210
cs-journals@wiley.com
www.blackwellpublishing.com

Vincent Marzano, VP
Stephen Smith, CEO

Enhances architectural design education, theory and practice.
Frequency: Quarterly
ISBN: 0-262753-24-3
Founded in 1947

2205 Journal of Architectural and Planning Research
Locke Science Publishing
332 S. Michigan Avenue
Suite 1032 #L221
Chicago, IL 60604

japr@lockescience.com
www.lockescience.com

Andrew Seidel, Editor-in-Chief
Ajay Garde, Editor

The major international disciplinary resource for professionals and scholars in architecture, design, and planning. Also provides a link between theory and practice for researchers and practicing professionals.

2206 Journal of Urban Technology
New York City Technical College
300 Jay St
Brooklyn, NY 11201-1909

718-260-5250; Fax: 718-260-5524
connect@citytech.cuny.edu
www.cuny.edu

Russell Hotzler, President
Miguel Cairol, VP

Covers technological developments in the architecture and transporatation fields.
Circulation: 10000
Founded in 1946

2207 Journal of the Society of Architectural Historians
Society of Architectural Historians
1365 N Astor St
Chicago, IL 60610

312-573-1365; Fax: 312-573-1141
info@sah.org
www.sah.org

Offers three to four scholarly articles on American and International topics, reviews of recently-published books, reviews of architecture exhibitions, and a variety of editorials designed to place the discipline of architectural history within a larger intellectual context.
Frequency: Quarterly
Founded in 1941

2208 Landscape Architecture Magazine
American Society of Landscape Architects
636 Eye Street NW
Washington, DC 20001-3736

202-898-2444
800-787-2752; Fax: 202-898-1185
info@asla.org
www.asla.org
Facebook, Twitter

Michael D O'Brien, Publisher
Bradford McKee, Editor
Maggie Zackowitz, Managing Editor
Sarah Strelzik, Production Manager
Daryl Brach, Senior Sales Manager

The magazine of the American Society of Landscape Architects.
Cost: $7.00
Frequency: Monthly

2209 Metal Architecture
Modern Trade Communications
7450 Skokie Blvd
Suite 200
Skokie, IL 60077-3374

847-674-2200; Fax: 847-674-3676
www.moderntrade.com
Facebook, Twitter, LinkedIn

Paul Deffenbaugh, Editorial Director
Mark Robins, Senior Editor
John S. Lawrence, CEO
John Paul Lawrence, President

Low-rise construction involving architects, engineers and specifiers.
Frequency: Monthly
Circulation: 33000
Founded in 1980

2210 Metropolis Magazine
Bellerophon Publications
61 W 23rd St
4th Floor
New York, NY 10010-4246

212-627-9977; Fax: 212-627-9988
edit@metropolismag.com
www.metropolismag.com
Facebook, Twitter, LinkedIn

Horace Havemeyer, Publisher
Susan Szenasy, Editor-in-Chief

The only magazine that covers all facets of design: architecture, interiors, furniture, preservation, urban design, graphics and crafts.
Cost: $27.95
Circulation: 61000
Founded in 1980

2211 Old House Interiors
Gloucester Publishers Corporation
10 Harbor Rd
Gloucester, MA 01930-3222

978-283-3200
800-356-9313; Fax: 978-283-4629

Regina Cole, Editor

Covers restoration techniques for the pre-1939 home.
Cost: $26.00
116 Pages
Circulation: 100000
Founded in 1995
Printed in 4 colors on glossy stock

2212 Places: A Forum of Environmental Design
Journal of Environmental Design
100 Higgans Hall
Brooklyn, NY 11205

FAX 718-399-4332

James F Fulton, Publisher

Covers architecture, landscape architecture, urban design, with a multidisciplinary view of all aspects of public and private places.
Cost: $35.00

2213 Preservation Magazine
National Trust for Historic Preservation
1785 Massachusetts Ave NW
Washington, DC 20036-2189

202-588-6000
800-944-6847; Fax: 202-588-6038
info@savingplaces.org
www.preservationnation.org

Stephanie Meeks, CEO
David Brown, EVP

Offers lively writing by the nation's best journalists on controversies, trends, accomplishments, and events of importance to cities, towns, suburbs, and rural communities.

2214 Professional Builder
Reed Business Information
360 Park Ave S
New York, NY 10010-1737

646-746-6845; Fax: 646-756-7583
corporatecommunications@reedbusiness.com
www.reedbusiness.com

Mark Kelsey, CEO
James Reed, President

New residential construction magazine with a tradition of providing builders the solutions they need to maximize profits.
Frequency: Monthly
Founded in 1936

2215 Reed Bulletin
Reed Business Informtion
30 Technology Parkway South
Suite 100
Norcross, GA 30092

800-424-3996
talisha.jackson@reedbusiness.com
www.reedconstructiondata.com

Talisha Jackson, Media Contact

Provides contractors with project news and tools suppliers.

2216 Residential Architect
Hanley-Wood
1 Thomas Circle NW
Suite 600
Washington, DC 20005-5811

202-452-0800
888-269-8410; Fax: 202-785-1974
www.residentialarchitect.com

Claire Conroy, Editorial Director
Jennifer Lash, Managing Editor
Bruce Snider, Senior Editor

It delivers substantive editorial on marketing, presentation, products, technology and business management to architects and designers.
Cost: $39.95
Frequency: 9x Yearly
Circulation: 22000
Founded in 1976

2217 Society of Architectural Administrators News Journal
Society of Architectural Administrators
15 E 7th Street NW
Cincinatti, OH 45202

513-684-3451

Patsy Frost, Publisher

Society news for professionals in the architectural community.

2218 Urban Omnibus
The Architectural League of New York
594 Broadway
Suite 607
New York, NY 10012

212-753-1722
info@urbanomnibus.net

urbanomnibus.net
Facebook, Twitter, Vimeo, YouTube

Jonathan Tarleton, Senior Editor
Emily Schmidt, Senior Editor

Online publication exploring new ideas and projects for the built environment of New York.
Frequency: Weekly
Founded in 2009

2219 World Monuments Fund
350 Fifth Avenue
Suite 2412
New York, NY 10118

646-424-9594; Fax: 646-424-9593
wmf@wmf.org
www.wmf.org

Bonnie Burnham, President
Jonathan Foyle, Chief Executive
Darlene McCloud, VP
Lisa Ackerman, Executive VP, COO

This magazine offers information on the latest architectural trends, specifically landmarks, monuments, antiquities.
Cost: $17.95
16 Pages
Frequency: Quarterly
Founded in 1965
Printed in 4 colors on glossy stock

Trade Shows

2220 AIA National Convention and Design Exposition
American Institute of Architects
1735 New York Avenue NW
Washington, DC 20006-5292

202-626-7300
800-242-3837; Fax: 202-626-7547
infocentral@aia.org
www.aia.org

Robert Ivy, CEO

Offers the chance to meet with more than 800 exhibitors and discover new products and technologies that can be used in future projects.
Frequency: Annual/April

2221 AIAS Forum
The American Institute of Architecture Students
1735 New York Ave NW
Washington, DC 20006

202-808-0075; Fax: 202-626-7414
mailbox@aias.org
www.aias.org
Facebook, Twitter, LinkedIn, Instagram, Snapchat, YouTube
Zach Dunn, Planning Chair
Michael Chang, Programming Director
Natasha Keshishian, Site Director
Hawraa Charara, Marketing Director
Esteban Armenta, Events Director

Architecture and design conference for students.
700 Attendees

2222 AIAS Grassroots Leadership Conference
The American Institute of Architecture Students
1735 New York Ave NW
Washington, DC 20006

202-808-0075; Fax: 202-626-7414
mailbox@aias.org
www.aias.org
Facebook, Twitter, LinkedIn, Instagram, Snapchat, YouTube

2223 AIAS International Conference
The American Institute of Architecture Students
1735 New York Ave NW
Washington, DC 20006

202-808-0075; Fax: 202-626-7414
mailbox@aias.org
www.aias.org
Facebook, Twitter, LinkedIn, Instagram, Snapchat, YouTube

The conference of 2018 is the first international conference of the American Institute of Architecture Students.

2224 ASLA Annual Meeting & EXPO
American Society of Landscape Architects
636 Eye Street NW
Washington, DC 20001-3736

202-988-2444
800-787-2752; Fax: 202-898-1185
info@asla.org
www.asla.org
Facebook, Twitter, LinkedIn

Kelli Bland, Manager, Meetings & Special Progs.
Lauren Martella, Marketing Manager

Landscape architect educational session and workshop plus 500 exhibits of outdoor lighting, playground and park equipment, landscape maintenance equipment, computer hardware and software and much more.

2225 American Institute of Architects Minn. Convention & Products Exhibition
American Institute of Architects, Minnesota Chap.
275 Market Street
Suite 54
Minneapolis, MN 55405

612-339-6904; Fax: 612-338-7981
infocentral@aia.org
www.aia-mn.org

Christine McEntee, CEO

175 exhibits of windows, concrete, roofing, millwork, tile and more, plus conference, seminar and dinner.
2500 Attendees
Frequency: Annual
Founded in 1934

2226 American Institute of Building Design Annual Convention
American Institute of Building Design
529 14th St NW
Suite750
Washington, DC 20045

800-366-2423; Fax: 866-204-0293
info@aibd.org
www.aibd.org

Dan Sater, President
Alan Kent, VP

A four day convention and trade show for residential design professionals
Frequency: Annual/July

2227 American Society for Aesthetics Annual Meeting
American Society for Aesthetics
1550 Larimer Street
Suite 644
Denver, CO 80202

562-331-4424
asa@aesthetics-online.org
www.aesthetics-online.org

Julie Van Camp, Executive Director

Seminar, conference, and exhibits related to the study of the arts, all disciplines.
Frequency: Annual, October
Founded in 1942

2228 Annual Technical & Educational Conference
American Design Drafting Association
105 E Main St
Newbern, TN 38059-1526

731-627-0802; Fax: 731-627-9321
www.adda.org

Olen Parker, Executive Director

Annual professional educational conference dedicated to serve the professional growth and advancement of the individuals working in the extremely fast paced, professional graphic community.
100 Members
Frequency: Annual/April

2229 Computers for Contractors and A/E/C Systems Fall
AEC Systems International/Penton Media
1300 E 9th St
Suite 316
Cleveland, OH 44114

216-696-7000; Fax: 216-696-6662
information@penton.com
www.aecsystemsibt.com

Sharon Rowlands, CEO
Nicola Allais, EVP

Computers for construction is the only tradeshow and conference dedicated exclusively to computer use by contractors. A/E/C SYSTEMS Fall is the regional technology event for the entire design and construction industry.
7000 Attendees
Frequency: Annual/November

2230 Council on Tall Buildings & Urban Habitat Congress
Lehigh University
11 East Packer Avenue
Bethlehem, PA 18015

610-583-3000; Fax: 610-758-4522
inctbuh@lehigh.edu
www.ctbuh.org

Antony Wood, Chief Executive Officer

Brings the world's leading decision makers together. For additional information visit our website or email us.
600+ Attendees
Frequency: Annual/February
Founded in 1969
Mailing list available for rent: 4500 names

2231 Design Matters Conference
Association of Architecture Organizations
224 South Michigan Ave
Suite 116
Chicago, IL 60604

312-561-2143; Fax: 312-922-2607
www.aaonetwork.org
Facebook, Twitter

Michael Wood, Executive Director

This annual event provides members with a forum for networking, sharing and learning.

2232 EDM/PDM Expo
AEC Systems International/Penton Media
1300 E 9th St
Suite 316
Cleveland, OH 44114

216-696-7000; Fax: 216-696-7000
www.aecsystems.com

Sharon Rowlands, CEO
Nicola Allais, EVP

Showcases ways to manage technical/engineering documents, product management, and drawing conversion. Over 500 exhibits are shown.
20M Attendees
Frequency: Annual/May

2233 IFI Congress
Int'l Federation of Interior Architects/Designers
708 3rd Ave.
6th Floor
New York, NY 10017
212-884-6275; Fax: 212-884-6247
staff@ifiworld.org
www.ifiworld.org
Facebook, Twitter, LinkedIn
Shashi Caan, Chief Executive Officer
Brings together professionals from around the globe. Features keynote speakers and an art exhibition.
Frequency: Biennial
Founded in 1963

2234 International Manufacturing & Engineering Technology Congress
AEC Systems International/Penton Media
1300 E 9th St
Suite 316
Cleveland, OH 44114
216-696-7000; Fax: 216-696-6662
www.aecsystems.com
Sharon Rowlands, CEO
Nicola Allais, EVP
Automotive, aeronautics, and aerospace, electrical and electronics, consumer products, industrial, heavy equipment, and process industries. 1000 exhibits.
15M Attendees
Frequency: Annual/November

2235 LightFair
AMC
120 Wall Street
17th Floor
New York, NY 10005
212-248-5000; Fax: 212-248-5017
ies@ies.org
www.iesna.org
Chip Israel, President
Daniel Salinas, Vice President
A major lighting trade show in North America featuring architectural lighting products from all spectrons of the industry. Containing 600 booths and 400 exhibits.
17M Attendees
Frequency: Annual/June
Mailing list available for rent: 10M names at $100 per M

2236 Lightfair International
Atlanta Market Center
240 Peachtree Street NW
Suite 2200
Atlanta, GA 30303-1327
404-220-3000
800-ATL-MART; Fax: 404-220-3030
webmaster@americasmart.com
www.americasmart.com
John Portman, CEO
Jeffery Portman, COO
The world's largest annual architectural/commercial lighting trade show and conference program. Lightfair International features the latest technology, products, education, information, awards and industry association events. 600 booths.
20M Attendees
Frequency: Annual/May

2237 M/Tech
AEC Systems International/Penton Media
1300 E 9th Street
Suite 316
Cleveland, OH 44114
216-696-7000; Fax: 216-696-6662
www.aecsystems.com
Sharon Rowlands, CEO
Nicola Allais, EVP
Focuses on applications to improve every phase of the product development cycle including CAD/CAM/CAE, Internet/intra/extranct, rapid prototyping and tooling, project/financial management, simulation and analysis, EDM/PDM and much more. 300 exhibits.
15M Attendees
Frequency: Annual/November

2238 M/Tech West
AEC Systems International/Penton Media
1300 E 9th St
Suite 316
Cleveland, OH 44114
216-696-7000; Fax: 216-696-6662
www.acesystems.com
Sharon Rowlands, CEO
Nicola Allais, EVP
Explores concurrent engineering practices, computer integrated manufacturing, and mechanical engineering applications. 50 exhibits.
20M Attendees
Frequency: Annual/May

2239 NOMA International Conference & Exposition
PO Box 3558
Washington, DC 20027
202-818-8653
info@noma.net
www.noma.net
Facebook, Twitter, LinkedIn
Professionl development, education and networking event.
500 Attendees

2240 National Council of Architectural Registration Boards Annual Meeting
Natl. Council of Architectural Registration Boards
1801 K Street NW
Suite 700K
Washington, DC 20006
202-783-6500; Fax: 202-783-0290
customerservice@ncarb.org
www.ncarb.org
Ronald Biltch, President
Blakely Dunn, VP
Annual meeting and exhibits of architecture equipment, supplies and services.

2241 Retail Design & Construction Conference & Expo
Primedia
3585 Engineering Drive
Suite 100
Norcross, GA 30092
678-421-3000
800-216-1423; Fax: 913-967-1898
www.primedia.com
Charles Stubbs, President
Kim Payne, SVP
Annual show of 145 exhibitors of equipment, supplies and services for retail design, construction, development, operations and maintenance, including signage, building equipment and materials, fixtures, floor coverings, furnishings, lighting, landscaping, store fronts, roofing, HVAC, maintenance materials and contractor services.
1000 Attendees

2242 SAH Annual International Conference
Society of Architectural Historians
1365 N Astor St
Chicago, IL 60610
312-573-1365; Fax: 312-573-1141
info@sah.org
www.sah.org
Sandy Isenstadt, Conference Chair
Christopher Kirbabas, Director of Programs
A presentation of new research on the history of the built environment.
Frequency: Annual

2243 SARA National Conference
Society Of American Registered Architects
14 E 38th Street
11th Floor
New York, NY 10016
920-395-2330
888-385-7272; Fax: 866-668-9858
www.sara-national.org
LinkedIn
Annual conference holding the National Board Meeting, Architecture & Design Banquet, President's Celebration Banquet & Installation of Officers, and the International & Distinguished Building Award Presentations

2244 TCAA Convention
Tile Contractors Association of America
10434 Indiana Avenue
Kansas City, MO 64137
816- 86- 930
800-655-8453; Fax: 816-767-0194
info@tcaainc.org
www.tcaainc.org
Chris Pattavina, Associate Director
Carole Damon, Executive Director
Architect/designer learning exchange, speakers, business meetings, new products and technology
Founded in 1903

2245 Technology for Construction
Hanley-Wood
6191 N State Hwy 161
Suite 500
Irving, TX 75038
972-366-6300
866-962-7469; Fax: 972-536-6301
www.technologyforconstruction.com
Rick McConnell, President
Tom Cindric, Group Director
Annual forum that showcases the technology, tools and solutions for the design, construction, maintenance and modification of commercial buildings, institutions and other structures. These tools and education are essential for the seamless collaboration and communication between all those involved throughout the asset lifecycle.
72M Attendees
Frequency: Annual
Founded in 1976

Directories & Databases

2246 Akron School Design Institute
American Architectural Foundation

1020 19th Street NW
Suite 525
Washington, DC 20036

202-787-1001; Fax: 202-78 -002
www.archfoundation.org

Ron Bogie, President/CEO
Scott Lauer, VP of Programs
Frequency: Annual

2247 **Dodge Building Stock**
DRI/McGraw-Hill
148 Princeton Heights Town Road
Height Town, NJ 08520

609- 42- 500
800-393-6343
support@construction.com
www.dodge.construction.com
Facebook, Twitter, LinkedIn

Keith Fox, President
Linda Brennan, VP of Operations

This database contains more than 18,000 historical and forecast quarterly time series on US buildings, including total square footage, number of buildings, and roof area for groups of structures in the categories of commercial, institutionals, manufacturing and residential.

2248 **Pro File/Official Directory of the American Institute of Architects**
American Institute of Architects (AIAA)
1735 New York Avenue NW
Washington, DC 20006-5292

202-783-6500
800-242-3837; Fax: 202-626-7364
infocentral@aia.org
www.aia.org

Robert Ivy, CEO

Over 18,000 architectural firms are listed. These listings have one or more principals who is a member of the American Institute of Architects.
Cost: $225.00
1800 Pages
Frequency: Annual

2249 **Progressive Architecture: Information Sources Issue**
Penton Media
1300 E 9th St
Suite 316
Cleveland, OH 44114-1503

216-696-7000; Fax: 216-696-1752
information@penton.com
www.penton.com

David Rowlands, CEO
Nicola Allais, EVP

List of trade and professional architecture associations.
Cost: $48.00

2250 **Salem Press Online Platform**
Grey House Publishing
4919 Route 22
PO Box 56
Amenia, NY 12501

800-221-1592; Fax: 201-968-0511
csr@salempress.com
online.salempress.com

The new Salem Press platform houses more than 500 titles including all of Salem's Health, Literature, History and Science titles in addition to select titles from the Grey House Publishing and H.W. Wilson product lines. Online access is free with each print purchase and includes an unlimited number of simultaneous users and remote access.

2251 **Sweets Directory**
Grey House Publishing/McGraw Hill Construction
1221 Avenue of the Americas
New York, NY 10020-1095

212-512-2000
800-442-2258; Fax: 212-512-3840
www.mcgraw-hill.com
Facebook, Twitter

Harold W McGraw III, CEO
Jack Callahan, Vice President

The leading desktop reference and preliminary research guide, featuring more than 10,000 building product manufacturers and their products.
Cost: $145.00
950 Pages
Frequency: Annual
ISBN: 1-592378-50-1
Founded in 1906

2252 **ThomasNet**
Thomas Publishing Company, LLC
User Services Department
5 Penn Plaza
New York, NY 10001

212-695-0500
800-699-9822; Fax: 212-290-7362
contact@thomaspublishing.com
www.thomasnet.com
Facebook, Twitter, LinkedIn

Carl Holst-Knudsen, President
Robert Anderson, VP, Planning
Mitchell Peipert, VP, Finance
Ivy Molofsky, VP, Human Resources

A way to reach qualified businesses that list their company information on ThomasNet.com. Detailed profiles promote their products, services, capabilities and brands carried. The ThomasNet.com web site is the most up-to-date compilation of 650,000 North American manufacturers, distributors, and service companies in 67,000 industrial categories.
Founded in 1898

2253 **Visual Merchandising and Store Design**
ST Media Group International
P.O. Box 1060
Skokie, IL 60076

847-763-4938
800-421-1321; Fax: 847-763-9030
customer@stmediagroup.com
www.stmediagroup.com

Steve Duccilli, Group Publisher
Wade Swormstedt, Editor/Publisher
Ted Swormstedt, President/CEO

Visual Merchandising and Store Design showcases the latest store designs and visual presentations, presents merchandising strategies and new products and reports on industry news and events.
Frequency: Monthly
Circulation: 27000
Founded in 1922

Industry Web Sites

2254 **http://gold.greyhouse.com**
G.O.L.D Grey House OnLine Databases

Grey House Publishing's online database platform, GOLD. offers Quick Search, Keyword Search and Expert Search for most business sectors including architecture, buidling and construction markets. The GOLD platform makes finding the information you need quick and easy. All of Grey House's directory products are available for subscription on the GOLD platform.

2255 **www.access-board.gov**
Architectural & Transportation Barriers Compliance

Devoted to accessibility for people with disabilities.

2256 **www.acsa-arch.org**
Association of Collegiate Schools of Architecture

A nonprofit, membership association founded to advance the quality of architectural education.

2257 **www.adda.org**
American Design Drafting Association

The premier professional organization for drafters, designers, engineers, architects, ilustrators, graphics artist, digital technicians, digitial imaging, visual communications and multimedia

2258 **www.aecsystems.com.au**
A/E/C Systems International/Penton Media

Focuses on Internet/Intranet for the design, engineering and construction industries.

2259 **www.aia.org**
American Institute of Architects

A professional membership association for licensed, emerging professionals, and allied partners.

2260 **www.apti.org**
Association for Preservation Technology Int'l

A cross-disciplinary, membership organization dedicated to promoting the best technology for conserving historic structures and their settings.

2261 **www.archprecast.org**
Architectural Precast Association

A national trade association organized to advance the interests of architectural precast concrete in North America.

2262 **www.asla.org**
American Society of Landscape Architects

The national professional association representing landscape architects.

2263 **www.builderspace.com**
BuilderSpace.com

An online directory for the building industry and resources created to help users find the services and information they need.

2264 **www.construction.com**
McGraw-Hill Construction

McGraw-Hill Construction (MHC), part of The McGraw-Hill Companies, connects people and projects across the design and construction industry, serving owners, architects, engineers, general contractors, subcontractors, building product manufacturers, suppliers, dealers, distributors and adjacent markets.

2265 **www.ctbuh.org**
Council on Tall Buildings and Urban Habitat

Studies and reports on all aspects of the planning, design, and construction of tall buildings.

2266 **www.greyhouse.com**
Grey House Publishing

Authoritative reference directories for most business sectors including architecture, building and construction markets. Users can search the online databases with varied search criteria allowing for custom searches by product category, geographic area, sales volume, keyword, subject and more. Full Grey House catalog and online ordering also available.

2267 **www.historicnewengland.org**
Soc. for Preservation of New England Antiquities

Focuses on buildings, landscapes and objects reflecting New England life from the 17th century to the present.

2268 **www.icea.net**
Insulated Cable Engineers Association

Professional organization dedicated to developing cable standards for the electric power, control and telecommunications industries. Ensures safe, economical and efficient cable systems utilizing proven state-of-the-art materials and concepts. ICEA documents are of interest to cable manufacturers, architects and engineers, utility and manufacturing plant personnel, telecommunication engineers, consultants and OEMs.

2269 **www.ihs.com**
International Code Council

Nonprofit membership association with more than 16,000 members who span the building community, from code enforcement officials to materials manufacturers. Dedicated to preserving the public health, safety and welfare in the built environment through the effective use and enforcement of model codes.

2270 **www.ncarb.org**
Nat'l Council of Architectural Registration Boards

For state registration boards in the United States regulating the practice of architecture.

2271 **www.reedconstructiondata.com**
Architects First Source Online

Comprehensive building products information.

2272 **www.sah.org**
Society of Architectural Historians

Provides an international forum for those who care about architecture and its related arts.

2273 **www.sara-national.org**
Society of American Registered Architects

Architects helping Architects by sharing ideas and information.

2274 **www.sarc.msstate.edu**
Small Town Center

To maintain and improve the quality of life in American small towns.

2275 **www.sbicouncil.org**
Sustainable Buildings Industry Council

Information on the design, affordability, energy performance, and enviromental soundness of residential, institutional and commercial buildings.

2276 **www.sname.org**
Society of Naval Architects and Marine Engineers

Internationally recognized nonprofit, technical, professional society of individual members serving the maritime and offshore industries and their suppliers. Dedicated to advancing the industry by recording information, sponsoring research, offering career guidance and supporting education.

2277 **www.sweets.construction.com**
McGraw Hill Construction

In depth product information that lets you find, compare, select, specify and make purchase decisions in the industrial product marketplace.

Associations

2278 **American Academy of Equine Art**
PO Box 12303
Lexington, KY 40852

859-221-3318
www.aaea.net

Booth Malone, President
Deanne Cellarosi, Vice President

The AAEA serves to educate and encourage a broad awareness and appreciation of contemporary equine art as a specific and distinctively worthy segment of fine art in America.
Founded in 1980

2279 **American Alliance of Museums**
2451 Crystal Dr
Suite 1005
Arlington, VA 22202

202-289-1818; Fax: 202-289-6578
membership@aam-us.org
www.aam-us.org
Facebook, Twitter, LinkedIn

Laura L. Lott, President & CEO
Robert J. Stein, EVP & Chief Program Officer
Arthur Affleck, VP, Development
Janet Vaughan, VP, Membership & Programs
Elizabeth Merritt, VP, Strategic Foresight

Dedicated to promoting excellence within the museum community. Through advocacy, professional education, information exchange, accreditation and guidance on current professional standards of performance, AAM assists museum staff, boards and volunteers across the country to better serve the public.
16000 Members
Founded in 1906

2280 **American Art Therapy Association**
4875 Eisenhower Ave
Suite 240
Alexandria, VA 22304

703-548-5860
888-290-0878; Fax: 703-783-8468
info@arttherapy.org
arttherapy.org
Facebook, Twitter, LinkedIn, RSS

Cynthia Woodruff, Executive Director
Christina Easterly, Coordinator, Events & Operations
Barbara Florence, Director, Events & Education
Clara Keane, Coordinator, Communication & Policy
Kat Michel, Manager, Membership

An organization of professionals dedicated to the belief that the creative process involved in art making is healing and life enhancing. Its mission is to serve its members and the general public by providing standards of professional competence, and developing and promoting knowledge in, and of, the field of art therapy.
4500 Members
Founded in 1969

2281 **American Society for Aesthetics**
1550 Larimer Street
Suite 644
Denver, CO 80202

562-331-4424
asa@aesthetics-online.org
www.aesthetics-online.org
Facebook, Twitter

Julie Van Camp, Executive Director
Julia Minarik, Managing Editor

Promotes study, research, discussion and publication in aesthetics, which includes all studies of the arts and related experience including philosophic, scientific and theoretical viewpoints.
640 Members
Founded in 1942

2282 **American Society of Bookplate Collectors & Designers**
PO Box 14964
Tucson, AZ 85732-4964

617-901-9970
info@bookplate.org
www.bookplate.org
Facebook, Twitter, LinkedIn, YouTube, Flickr, Pinterest

James P. Keenan, Director
Mark Metzger, Treasurer
Christopher Kent, Advisor
Concepcion Provenzal, Art Director

For designers, owners and collectors of bookplates.
250 Members
Founded in 1922
Mailing list available for rent: 500+ names

2283 **Antique Appraisal Association of America**
1403 Gloria Lane
Boulder City, NV 89005

702-629-4502
888-791-0033
aaaofamerica@att.net
www.antiqueappraisalassn.com

Helen Nolan, Executive Director

Members are well known for their Code of Ethics in their dealing with their customers. Our qualified professional appraisers have expertise in all types of appraisals and appraisal-related services, including insurance damage claims, estate probate, estate liquidation, estate auctions, court testimony, consultants and much more.
Founded in 1972

2284 **Antique Coin Machine Collectors Association**

diermanor@gmail.com

Association for collectors and enthusiasts of antique coin-operated devices.
Founded in 1985

2285 **Antiques & Collectibles National Association**
PO Box 4389
Davidson, NC 28036

704-895-9088
800-287-7127; Fax: 704-895-0230
www.antiqueandcollectible.com

Angie Becker, President
Mike Becker, Vice President

Association founded in 1991 for the benefit of antique dealers and collectors.
Founded in 1991

2286 **Antiques Council**
PO Box 1508
Warren, MA 01083

413-436-7064; Fax: 413-436-0448
info@antiquescouncil.com
www.antiquescouncil.com

Marty Shapiro, President
Alan Cunha, VP
John Copenhaver, Education Director
David Bernard, Facilities Director
Joel Fletcher, Communications Director

A nonprofit organization created by professional antique dealers to improve the confidence of the public in antiques and their dealers through education, service and example.
100 Members
Founded in 1990

2287 **Art Dealers Association of America**
205 Lexington Avenue
Suite 901
New York, NY 10016

212-488-5550; Fax: 646-688-6809
adaa@artdealers.org
www.artdealers.org
Facebook, Twitter, Instagram

Dorsey Waxter, President
Mary Sabbatino, Vice President
Adam Sheffer, Vice President
Laurence Shopmaker, Secretary
Mark Brady, Treasurer

Nonprofit organzation that works to improve the stature and standing of the art gallery business. Members deal primarily with paintings, sculpture, prints, drawings and photographs from the Renaissance to the present day. We have more than 160 member galleries in more than 25 US cities.
160 Members
Founded in 1962

2288 **Art Libraries Society of North America**
7044 S. 13th St.
Oak Creek, WI 53154

414-768-8000
800-817-0621; Fax: 414-768-8001
customercare@arlisna.org
www.arlisna.org
Facebook, Twitter, LinkedIn, Pinterest

Kristen Regina, President
Heather Gendron, Vice-President/President Elect
Jamie Lausch Vander Broek, Secretary
Mark Pompelia, Treasurer
Robert J. Kopchinski, Association & Conference Manager

Devoted to fostering excellence in art librarianship, visual resources and curatorship for the advancement of visual arts. See website for available publications.
1000 Members
Founded in 1972
Mailing list available for rentat $200 per M

2289 **Art and Antique Dealers League of America**
PO Box 2066
Lenox Hill Station
New York, NY 10021

212-879-7558; Fax: 212-772-7197
secretary@artantiquedealersleague.com
www.artantiquedealersleague.com

Clinton Howell, President
Robert Simon, VP
David Mayer, Secretary-Executive Director
Susan Kaplan Jacobson, Treasurer
109 Members
Founded in 1926

2290 **Art and Creative Materials Institute/ACMI**
99 Derby Street
Suite 200
Hingham, MA 02043

781-556-1044; Fax: 781-207-5550
www.acminet.org

Michael Storei, President
Joan Lilly, Vice President
Timothy Gomez, Treasurer
Debbie Gustafson, Associate Director
Debbie Munroe, Certification Director

A non-profit association of manufacturers of art, craft and other creative materials, ACMI sponsors a certification program for both children's and adult's art materials and products, certifying that these products are non-toxic and meet voluntary standards of quality and performance. ACMI

seeks to create and maintain a positive environment for art, craft and other creative materials usage, promoting safety in the materials and providing information and service resources on such products.
210 Members
Founded in 1936
Mailing list available for rent: 199 names

2291 **ArtTable**
1 E 53rd St.
5th Floor
New York, NY 10022
212-343-1735
info@attable.org
arttable.org
Jessica Porter, Executive Director
Haley Carloni, Programs Manager
Jonquil Schaller-Harris, Membership & Communications Manager
Lucia Roldan, Community Engagament Coordinator
A professional organization that strives to advance the leadership of women in visual arts. They boast an expensive network of women from diverse backgrounds and in all stages of their careers.

2292 **Arts Midwest**
2908 Hennepin Ave.
Suite 200
Minneapolis, MN 55408-1954
612-341-0755
www.artsmidwest.org
Facebook, Twitter, YouTube, Flickr
David J. Fraher, President & CEO
Peter Capell, Chair
One of six regional arts organizations established with funding from the National Endowment for the Arts, Arts Midwest provides access to performing, visual and literary arts programs in Illinois, Indiana, Iowa, Michigan, Minnesota, North Dakota, Ohio, South Dakota and Wisconsin.

2293 **Association for Preservation Technology International**
3085 Stevenson Drive
Suite 200
Springfield, IL 62703
217-529-9039; Fax: 888-723-4242
info@apti.org
www.apti.org
Facebook, LinkedIn
Gina Crevello, President
Natalie Feinberg Lopez, Vice President
Taryn Williams, Vice President
Paul Kuentsner, Executive Director
The Association for Preservation Technology (APT) is a cross-disciplinary, membership organization dedicated to promoting the best technology for conserving historic structures and their settings.
Founded in 1968

2294 **Association of Historians of American Art**
info@ahaaonline.org
www.ahaaonline.org
Facebook, LinkedIn
Ellery Foutch, Chair
Austen Barron Bailly, Co-Chair
Anna Marley, Chair Emerita
Jillian Russo, Secretary
Monica Jovanovich-Kelley, Treasurer
An association for the promotion of scholarship in American art.
Founded in 1979

2295 **Association of Restorers**
8 Medford Place
New Hartford, NY 13413
315-733-1952
800-260-1829; Fax: 315-724-7231
www.assoc-restorers.com
Andrea Daley, Founder
It is the mission of the AOR, Association of Restorers Inc, to increase the awareness of choice to consere, refurbish or restore historical works of art, household furnishings and architectural constructions
Founded in 1997

2296 **College Art Association**
TERRA Foundation
50 Broadway
21st Floor
New York, NY 10004
212-691-1051; Fax: 212-627-2381
nyoffice@collegeart.org
www.collegeart.org
Facebook, Twitter, YouTube
DeWitt Godfrey, President
John Richardson, Vice President for External Affairs
Charles A. Wright, Vice President for Committees
Doralynn Pines, Secretary
John Hyland Jr., Treasurer
Promotes excellence in scholarship and technology in the criticisim of the visual arts and in the creativity and technical skill in the teaching and practices of art.
13000 Members
Founded in 1911

2297 **Creativity Explored**
3245 16th St.
San Francisco, CA 94103
415-863-2108; Fax: 415-863-1655
info@creativityexplored.org
www.creativityexplored.org
Facebook, Twitter, YouTube, Instagram, Pinterest
Linda Johnson, Executive Director
Jamie Wong, Gallery
Megan Hover, Development & Fundraising
Michael Korcek, Marketing & Public Relations
Ann Kappes, Licensing
Supports people with developmental disabilities in becoming working artists.
Founded in 1983

2298 **Indian Arts & Crafts Association**
4010 Carlisle NE
Suite C
Albuquerque, NM 87107
505-265-9149; Fax: 505-265-8251
info@iaca.com
www.iaca.com
Facebook, Twitter
Joseph P. Zeller, President
Cliff Fragua, Vice President
Beth Hale, Secretary
Kathi Ouellet, Treasurer
Nonprofit trade association whose mission is to promote, protect and preserve Indian arts.
700 Members
Founded in 1974

2299 **International Fine Print Dealers Association (IFPDA)**
250 W 26th St
Suite 405
New York, NY 10001-6737
212-674-6095; Fax: 212-674-6783
info@ifpda.org
www.ifpda.org
Facebook, Twitter
Paula McCarthy Panczenko, President
David Cleaton-Roberts, Vice President
Barbara Krakow, Vice President
Joni Moisant Weyl, Treasurer
Armin Kunz, Secretary
A nonprofit organization that aspires to create a greater awareness and appreciation of fine prints among collectors and the general public. Povides funding for a variety of print-related educational programs, including pubications, lectures and symposia.
160 Members
Founded in 1987

2300 **International Foundation for Art Research**
500 5th Avenue
Suite 935
New York, NY 10110
212-391-6234; Fax: 212-391-8794
kferg@ifar.org
www.ifar.org
Jack A Josephson, Chairman
Sharon Flescher, Executive Director
Nonprofit educational and research organization working for the interests of art scholarship, law and the public interest.
Founded in 1969

2301 **Mid Atlantic Arts Foundation**
201 N. Charles St.
Suite 401
Baltimore, MD 21201
410-539-6656; Fax: 410-837-5517
www.midatlanticarts.org
Facebook, Twitter, YouTube, Pinterest
Alan W. Cooper, Executive Director
E. Scott Johnson, Chair
One of six regional arts organizations established with funding from the National Endowment for the Arts, Mid Atlantic Arts Foundation promotes access to and participation in the arts in Delaware, the District of Columbia, Maryland, New Jersey, New York, Pennsylvania, the US Virgin Islands, Virginia and West Virginia.
Founded in 1979

2302 **Mid-America Arts Alliance**
2018 Baltimore Ave.
Kansas City, MO 64108
816-421-1388
www.maaa.org
Facebook, Twitter, Flickr
Mary Kennedy, Chief Executive Officer
C. Kendrick Fergeson, Chair
One of six regional arts organizations established with funding from the National Endowment for the Arts, Mid-America Arts Alliance supports artists, cultural organizations and traveling exhibitions in underserved communities in Arkansas, Kansas, Missouri, Nebraska, Oklahoma and Texas.
Founded in 1972

2303 **National Antique & Collectible Association**
PO Box 4389
Davidson, NC 28036
704-895-9088
800-287-7127; Fax: 704-895-0230
info@acna.us
www.acna.us
Facebook, Twitter
Angie Becker, President
Mike Becker, Vice President
The largest trade association for antique dealers & private collectors in the country. Our association has members in all 50 states. We offer an ar-

ray of benefits including our insurance programs, merchant services, quarterly newsletter, educational seminars, travel, supply discounts and many more.
4300 Members
Founded in 1991

2304 National Antique Doll Dealers Association (NADDA)
Home Page: www.nadda.org
Facebook
Lynette Gross, President
Ed Kolibaba, Vice President
Diane Costa, Secretary
Richard K. Saxman, Treasurer
NADDA was formed to promote honesty and integrity in the increasingly popular antique doll trade.
Founded in 1986

2305 National Art Education Association
901 Prince Street
Suite 300
Alexandria, VA 22314
703-860-8000
800-299-8321; Fax: 703-860-2960
info@arteducators.org
www.arteducators.org/
Facebook, Twitter, LinkedIn
Dennis Inhulson, President
Patricia Franklin, President Elect
Deborah B Reeve, Executive Director
Promote art education through professional development, service, advancment of knowledge and leadership.
22000 Members
Founded in 1947
Mailing list available for rent: 22,000 names at $95 per M

2306 National Art Materials Trade Association
20200 Zion Ave.
Cornelius, NC 28031
704-892-6244
info@namta.org
www.namta.org
Facebook, Twitter, LinkedIn
Hayley Prendergast, President
Kevin P Lavin, Executive VP & CFO
Howard Krinsky, Vice President
Reggie Hall, Executive Director
Rick Munisteri, Director of Meetings
International association of manufacturers, importers, wholesalers and retailers of art materials.
2.1M Members

2307 National Assembly of State Arts Agencies
1200 18th St NW
Suite 1100
Washington, DC 20036
202-347-6352
202-347-5948; Fax: 202-737-0526
nasaa@nasaa-arts.org
www.nasaa-arts.org
Facebook
Gary Gibbs, President
Jonathan Katz, Chief Executive Officer
Laura S. Smith, CFRE, Chief Advancement Officer
Kelly J Barsdate, Chief Planning Officer
Sharon Gee, Director of Meetings and Events
NASAA's mission is to advance and promote a meaningful role for the arts in the lives of individuals, families and communities throughout the United States. We empower state art agencies through strategic assistance that fosters leadership, enhances planning and decision making, and increases resources. TDD 202-347-5948.
56 Members
Founded in 1968

2308 National Association of Fine Arts
1155 F Street NW
Suite 1050
Washington, DC 20004
414-332-9306; Fax: 888-884-6232
www.nafa.com
Facebook, Twitter, LinkedIn
Kim O'Brien, President & CEO
Chip Anderson, Vice Chair
S Christopher Johnson, Secretary
Nathan Zuidema, Treasurer
Seeks to provide services and networking opportunities to individuals in the arts community.
100 Members
Founded in 1986

2309 National Auctioneers Association
8880 Ballentine St
Overland Park, KS 66214
913-541-8084; Fax: 913-894-5281
support@auctioneers.org
www.auctioneers.org
Facebook, Twitter, LinkedIn, YouTube
Spanky Assiter, CAI, AARE, President
John S. Nicholls, AARE, VP
James Devin Ford, CAI, CES, Treasurer
Hannes Combest, CEO
Thomas W. Saterly, Past President
NAA promotes the auction method of marketing and enhances the professionalism of its practitioners
6,000 Members
Founded in 1948

2310 National Guild of Community Schools of the Arts
520 8th Avenue
3rd Floor, Suite 302
New York, NY 10018
212-268-3337; Fax: 212-268-3995
www.nationalguild.org
Facebook, Twitter, LinkedIn, YouTube, Instagram, RSS
Jonathan Herman, Executive Director
Ken Cole, Assosiate Director
Claire Wilmoth, Membership Associate
James Harton, Program Director
Traci Horgen, Business Manager
Arts Management in Community Institutions (AMICI) Summer Institute trains administrators to meet needs of growing and emerging arts schools. Other programs, services, guildnotes newsletter, job opportunities listings, and publications catalog available upon request on online. Mailing list $25 for non-members, free for members.
300 Members
Founded in 1937

2311 National Network for Art Placement
935 W Avenue 37
Los Angeles, CA 90065
323-222-4035
800-354-5348
NNAPnow@aol.com
www.americansforthearts.org
Facebook, Pinterest, RSS
Warren Christensen, Consultant
An organization that helps any artist with start up capital and services for small businesses.

2312 National Trust for Historic Preservation
2600 Virginia Avenue
Suite 1000
Washington, DC 20037
202-588-6000
800-944-6847; Fax: 202-588-6038
info@savingplaces.org
www.savingplaces.org
Facebook, Twitter, Pinterest, Instagram, YouTube
Stephanie K. Meeks, President &CEO
David J. Brown, Vice President & CPO
Paul Edmondson, Chief Legal Officer
Terry Richey, Chief Marketing Officer
Rosemarie Rae, Chief Financial Officer
A private, nonprofit membership organization dedicated to saving historic places and revitlizing America's communities. Also provides leadership, education, advocacy, and resources to save America's diverse historic places and revitalize the communities.
270k Members
Founded in 1949

2313 New England Foundation for the Arts
145 Tremont St.
7th Fl.
Boston, MA 02111
617-951-0010
www.nefa.org
Cathy Edwards, Executive Director
Lawrence J. Simpson, Chair
One of six regional arts organizations established with funding from the National Endowment for the Arts, New England Foundation for the Arts supports artists and their endeavours in Connecticut, Maine, Massachusetts, New Hampshire, Rhode Island and Vermont.
Founded in 1976

2314 Professional Association of Visual Artists
1240 County Road 1
Winn Dixie Plaza
Dunedin, FL 34698
Home Page: pava-artists.org
Facebook, Instagram
Linda Stump, President
Christina Paluszek-McClure, Vice President
PAVA dedicates itself to the education and advancement of visual artists while also establishing the highest professional standards of visual arts.
Founded in 1988

2315 Professional Picture Framers Association
2282 Springport Road
Suite F
Jackson, MI 49202
517-788-8100
800-762-9287; Fax: 517-788-8371
ppfa@ppfa.com
www.ppfa.com
Facebook
John Pruitt, President
Stuart M Altschuler, VP
Jim Esp, Secretary & Executive Director
Robin Gentry, Treasurer
A trade association of manufacturers, wholesalers, print publishers, importers and retailers selling art, framing and related supplies.
3000 Members
Founded in 1971

2316 **Society of Animal Artists**
5451 Sedona Hills Drive
Berthoud, CO 80513

970-532-3127; Fax: 970-532-2537
admin@societyofanimalartists.com
www.societyofanimalartists.com
Facebook

Diane Mason, President
Allen Bragden, VP
Marilyn Newmark, VP
Douglas Allen, VP
Renee Headings-Bemis, Treasurer

Devoted to promoting excellence in the portrayal of the creatures sharing our planet and to the education of the public through informative art seminars, lectures and teaching demonstrations.
360 Members
Founded in 1960

2317 **Society of Illustrators**
128 E 63rd St
New York, NY 10065

212-838-2560; Fax: 212-838-2561
info@societyillustrators.org
www.societyillustrators.org
Facebook, Twitter

Tim O'Brien, President
Karen Green, Vice President
Victor Juhasz, Executive VP
Leslie Cober-Gentry, Secretary
David Ruess, Treasurer

A professional society of illustrators and art directors.
950 Members
Founded in 1901

2318 **South Arts**
1800 Peachtree St. NW
Suite 808
Atlanta, GA 30309

404-874-7244; Fax: 404-873-2148
www.southarts.org
Facebook, Twitter, LinkedIn

Suzette M. Surkamer, Executive Director
Ted Abernathy, Chair

One of six regional arts organizations established with funding from the National Endowment for the Arts, South Arts assists state arts agencies in Alabama, Florida, Georgia, Kentucky, Louisiana, Mississippi, North Carolina, South Carolina and Tennessee with the production, promotion and presentation of southern arts and culture.
Founded in 1975

2319 **The American Institute for Conservation of Historic & Artistic Works**
1156 15th Street
Suite 320
Washington, DC 20005-1714

202-452-9545; Fax: 202-452-9328
info@conservation-us.org
www.conservation-us.org
Facebook, Twitter, YouTube, Flickr

Eryl P. Wentworth, Executive Director
Ruth Seyler, Membership & Meetings Director
Eric Pourchot, Institutional Advancement Director
Sandy T. Nguyen, Finance Director
Abigail Choudhury, Development and Education

Conservators of artistic and cultural property.
3500 Members
Founded in 1961

2320 **The Art Students League of New York**
215 W 57th Street
New York, NY 10019

212-247-4510; Fax: 212-541-7024
info@artstudentsleague.org
www.theartstudentsleague.org
Facebook, Twitter, YouTube, Pinterest, Instagram

Salvatore Barbieri, President
Susan Matz, Vice President
Howard A. Friedman, Vice President
Ira Golberg, Executive Director
Ken Park, Director of Communications

Educational organization that provides space, studios and offices to members.
Founded in 1875

2321 **The Art and Antique Dealers League of America, Inc.**
PO Box 2066
Lenox Hill Station
New York, NY 10021

212-879-7558; Fax: 212-772-7197
secretary@artantiquedealersleague.com
www.artantiquedealersleague.com

Clinton Howell, President
Robert Simon, Vice President
David Mayer, Secretary-Executive Director
Susan Kaplan Jacobson, Treasurer

Nonprofit organization promotes interests of retailers and wholesalers of antiques and art objects.
110 Members
Founded in 1926

2322 **The Association of Art Museum Curators Foundation**
174 East 80th St.
New York, NY 10075

646-405-8057
www.artcurators.org

Judith Pineiro, Executive Director
Monica Valenzuela, Program Manager
Glorimar Garcia, Administrator

The AAMC supports and promotes the work of museum curators. They provide networking opportunities, professional development and promote advancement.
Founded in 2012

2323 **The Maven Co.**
Maven Company
PO Box 937
Plandome, NY 11020-0937

51 -62 -880; Fax: 914-248-0800
fasttrack@erols.com
www.mavencompany.com

N Chittenden, VP

An innovator of new and unique programs to help antique dealers sell their merchandise and to make their shows more successful.
5,000 Attendees
Frequency: January/Annual
Founded in 1970

2324 **The National Antique & Art Dealers Association of America**
220 E 57th St
New York, NY 10022

212-826-9707; Fax: 212-832-9493
www.naadaa.org

James R McConnaughy, President
Mark Jacoby, VP
Arlie Sulka, Secretary
Steven J Chait, Treasurer

Works to promote the best interests of the antique art exhibitions and to promote just, honorable and ethical trade practices.
38 Members
Founded in 1954

2325 **The One Club For Creativity**
450 W. 31st St.
6th Floor
New York, NY 10001

212-979-1900; Fax: 212-979-5006
info@oneclub.org
www.oneclub.org
Facebook, Twitter, LinkedIn, Instagram, YouTube

Kevin Swanepoel, Chief Executive Officer
Yash Egami, VP, Content & Marketing
Lucila Lopez Travez, Director of Events & Membership
Jovanne Jerome, Inclusion & Diversity Coordinator
Crystal Ray, Financial Controller

A non-profit organization that supports and celebrates the success of the global creative community. Stimulates the intersection of art and commerce, and creates spaces for artists to grow.

2326 **The Society of Typographic Aficionados**
P.O. Box 457
Jefferson, GA 30549

info@typesociety.org
www.typesociety.org
Twitter

An international not-for-profit organization dedicated to the advancement and support of the typographic arts and design education.
Founded in 1998

2327 **Train Collectors Association**
PO Box 248
Strasburg, PA 17579-0248

717-687-8623
www.traincollectors.org

Wayne S. Sheriff, President

The worldwide organization for tinplate train collectors and enthusiasts.
30000 Members
Founded in 1954

2328 **University & College Designers Association**
199 Enon Springs Rd. W
Suite 400
Smyma, TN 37167

615-459-4559; Fax: 615-459-5229
info@ucda.com
www.ucda.com
Facebook, Twitter, Instagram, Flickr

Tadson Bussey, Executive Director
Chris Klonowski, Assistant Director

Inspires designers working in academia by delivering relevant programming and benefits. Provides for the professional and personal growth of its members, advocates for designers' and educators' roles in their institutions, and elevates the importance of design.
1000 Members
Founded in 1970

2329 **Volunteer Committees of Art Museums**
5139 Thorncroft Court
Royal Oak, MI 48073

504-488-2631; Fax: 504-484-6662
www.vcam.org
Facebook, Twitter, LinkedIn, YouTube

Peter Milne, President
Linda McGinty, Co President
Julie George, Secretary
Victoria Cather, Treasurer

An internationally recognized non-profit organization. VCAM is committed to provide a forum for information exchange, mutual

education and enhancement of services to its art museum volunteer committee members through international conferences, regional meetings, published comprehensive conference reports, resource files and the VCAM NEWS publication.
19 Members
Founded in 1952

2330 **Western States Arts Federation (WESTAF)**
1743 Wazee St.
Suite 300
Denver, CO 80202
303-629-1166
www.westaf.org
Facebook, Twitter
Anthony Radich, Executive Director
Virginia Gowski, Chair
One of six regional arts organizations established with funding from the National Endowment for the Arts, WESTAF advances the preservation and development of the arts in Alaska, Arizona, California, Colorado, Hawaii, Idaho, Montana, Nevada, New Mexico, Oregon, Utah, Washington and Wyoming.

Newsletters

2331 **ASA Newsletter**
American Society for Aesthetics
1550 Larimer Street
Suite 644
Denver, CO 80202
562-331-4424
asa@aesthetics-online.org
www.aesthetics-online.org
Facebook, Twitter
Julie Can Camp, Executive Director
Shelby Moser, Editor
Michael-Antoine Xhignesse, Editor
Promotes study, research, discussion and publication in aesthetics, which includes all studies of the arts and related experience including philosophic, scientific and theoretical viewpoints.
Frequency: 3/Year
Founded in 1942

2332 **Antique Appraisal Association of America Newsletter**
Antique Appraisal Association of America
1403 Gloria Lane
Boulder City, NV 89005
702-629-4502
888-791-0033
aaaofamerica@att.net
www.antiqueappraisalassn.com
Marge Swenson, Publisher
Supplies members with additional knowledge of antiques from research.

2333 **Art Hazards Newsletter**
New York Foundation for the Arts
155 Avenue of the Americas
14th Floor
New York, NY 10013
212-366-6900; Fax: 212-366-1778
Theodore Berger, Executive Director
Toni Lewis, Director Administration
Contains information on all hazardous materials; art materials and articles.
Cost: $24.00
Frequency: Quarterly
Founded in 1977

2334 **Art Research News**
500 5th Avenue
Suite 935
New York, NY 10110
212-391-6234; Fax: 212-391-8794
kferg@ifar.org
www.ifar.org
Sharon Flescher, Executive Director
The latest news on authenticity, ownership, theft, and other artistic, legal and ethical issues concerning art objects.
Founded in 1969

2335 **Arts & Culture Funding Report**
Capitol City Publishers
4416 East West Hwy
Suite 400
Bethesda, MD 20814-4568
301-916-1800
800-637-9915; Fax: 301-528-2497
www.capitolcitypublishers.com
A monthly newsletter on federal, state, private and nonprofit sector funding and financial assistance to arts and cultural organizations.
Cost: $198.00
Frequency: Monthly
ISSN: 1047-3297

2336 **Arts Management**
Radius Group
545 5th Ave
New York, NY 10017-3647
212-972-2929; Fax: 212-972-7581
postmaster@trflaw.com
www.trflaw.com
Leonard A Rodes, Partner
David Trachtenberg, Partner
Barry Friedberg, Partner
The national news service for those who finance, manage and communicate the arts.
Cost: $18.00
Frequency: 5 per year

2337 **Artsfocus**
Colorado Springs Fine Arts Center
30 W Dale St
Colorado Spring, CO 80903-3249
719-634-5581; Fax: 719-634-0570
info@csfineartscenter.org
www.csfineartscenter.org
Sam Gappmayer, CEO
Kari Torgerson, COO
Tom Jackson, Director of Development
Museum members publication.
Cost: $5.00
24 Pages
Frequency: Quarterly
Founded in 1936
Printed in 2 colors on matte stock

2338 **Aviso**
American Association of Museums
1575 Eye Street NW
Suite 400
Washington, DC 20005-1113
202-289-1818; Fax: 202-289-6578
membership@aam-us.org
www.aam-us.org
Ford W Bell, President
Douglas Myers, CEO Executive Director
Reports on museums in the news, federal legislation affecting museums, upcoming seminars and workshops, federal grant deadlines and AAM activities and services.
Frequency: Monthly

2339 **Bookplates in the News**
Amer. Society of Bookplate Collectors & Designers
605 N Stoneman Avenue
Suite F
Alhambra, CA 91801-1406
626-579-9147
exlibris@att.net
Audrey Spencer Arellanes, Publisher
Victor Amor, Owner
Collectors' news for designers, owners and collectors of bookplates.
Cost: $25.00
200 Pages
Frequency: Quarterly
Circulation: 250

2340 **Communique**
Association for Preservation Technology Int'l
3085 Stevenson Drive
Suite 200
Springfield, IL 62703
217-529-9039; Fax: 888-723-4242
info@apti.org
www.apti.org
Gina Crevello, President
Paul Kuenstner, Executive Director
Diana Waite, Editor
APT's electronic newsletter, enables APT members to exchange preservation information, publicize their news and awards, share project experience with colleagues, post calls for papers, and submit preservation queries to the readership.
Frequency: Quarterly

2341 **Cotton & Quail Antique Gazette**
F+W Media
38 E. 29th Street
New York, NY 10016
212-447-1400; Fax: 212-447-5231
contact_us@fwmedia.com
Greg Smith, Publisher
Linda Kunkel, Editor
Dave Paul, Marketing
Contains articles about various collecting topics, announcements of upcoming shows, reviews of shows and auctions, a Q & A column on antiques, 'how-to' articles, regular features about collecting and selling, an extensive show and auction calendar.
Cost: $20.00
Frequency: Monthly
Circulation: 25000
Founded in 1965

2342 **Encouraging Rejection**
Noforehead Press
Box 55
Kearsarge, NH 03847-0130
Home Page: www.reuben.org
Mark Heath, Editor/Publisher
To inspire and encourage artists in the face of rejection.
Cost: $19.00
Frequency: Bi-Monthly
Founded in 1994

2343 **Folk Art Finder**
Gallery Press
117 N Main Street
Essex, CT 06426-1302
860-767-0313
folkart.com
Florence Laffal, Editor/Publisher
Contains feature stories, a calendar of events, a readers exchange, news items, book reviews, and classified and display ads relating to 20th century American folk art. Other issues addressed are folk art preservation, laws affecting the arts and

funding for the arts.
Cost: $14.00
24 Pages
Frequency: Quarterly
Mailing list available for rent
Printed in one color on matte stock

2344 **IFAR Journal**
International Foundation for Art Research
500 5th Avenue
Suite 935
New York, NY 10110
212-391-6234; Fax: 212-391-8794
kferg@ifar.org
www.ifar.org
Facebook
Sharon Flescher PhD, CEO
Jack A. Josephson, Chairman
Listings of stolen art and the legal developments of articles on art recovery, art law, cultural property and art authentication.
Cost: $65.00
32 Pages
Frequency: Quarterly
ISSN: 1098-1195
Founded in 1969

2345 **Indian Arts & Crafts Association Newsletter**
4010 Carlisle NE
Suite C
Albuquerque, NM 87107
505-265-9149; Fax: 505-265-8251
info@iaca.com
www.iaca.com
Joseph Zeller, President
Don Standing Bear Forest, VP
Gail Chehak, Executive Director
Susan Pourian, Secretary
Kathi Ouellet, Treasurer

2346 **International Association of Auctioneers Newsletter**
Butterfield & Butterfield Auctioneers
220 San Bruno Ave
San Francisco, CA 94103-5018
415-861-7500
800-222-2854; Fax: 415-861-8951
appraisals.us@bonhams.com
www.butterfields.com
Melcolm Barbar, CEO
A news bulletin with descriptions of upcoming auctions around the world.
8 Pages
Frequency: Quarterly
Circulation: 6500
Founded in 1865

2347 **Kovels on Antiques and Collectibles**
Antiques
2135 N Milwaukee Ave
Chicago, IL 44122
773-360-8162; Fax: 216-752-3115
www.kovels.com
Facebook, Twitter
Terry Kovel, Co-Publisher
Ralph Kovel, Co-Publisher
Newsletter for dealers, investors and collectors.
Cost: $27.00
12 Pages
Frequency: Monthly
Founded in 1995
Printed in 4 colors on matte stock

2348 **National Association of Antiques Bulletin**
National Association of Dealers in Antiques
PO Box 421
Barrington, IL 60011-0421
847-381-3101; Fax: 815-877-4282
Shirley Kowing, Publisher
Educational and association news.

2349 **Professional Picture Framers Association Newsletter**
4305 Sarellen Road
Richmond, VA 23231-4311
804-226-0430; Fax: 804-222-2175
Rex P Boynton, Executive Director
Trade association news for manufacturers, wholesalers, print publishers, importers and retailers selling art, framing and related supplies.

2350 **Stolen Art Alert**
500 5th Avenue
Suite 935
New York, NY 10110
212-391-6234; Fax: 212-391-8794
kferg@ifar.org
www.ifar.org
Sharon Flescher, Executive Director
Reports on art thefts and recoveries and also covered major art forgery cases.
Founded in 1969

2351 **VCAM NEWS**
Volunteer Communities of Art Museums
New Orleans Museum of Art
PO Box 19123
New Orleans, LA 70179
504-488-2631; Fax: 504-484-6662
www.vcam.org
Peter Milne, President
Susan Colangelo, Secretary
Victoria Cather, Treasurer
Informs and invigorates the volunteers.
19 Members
Founded in 1952

2352 **World Fine Art**
Art Baron Management Corporation
1356 Cherry Bottom Road
Colombos, OH 43230-6771
614-476-9708
Jeffrey Coffin, Publisher
Steve Shipp, Editor
John Blackburn, Manager
Art history, values and projections regarding artists and movements.
Cost: $95.00
10 Pages
Frequency: 9 per year
Printed in one color

Magazines & Journals

2353 **A History of Art Therapy**
American Art History
4875 Eisenhower Avenew
Suite 240
Alexandria, VA 22304-3302
703-212-2238
888-290-0878
info@arttherapy.org
www.arttherapy.org
Mercedes ter Maat, President
Charlotte Boston,MA,ATR, Secretary
Joseph Jaworek ATR-BC, Treasurer
Frequency: Yearly

2354 **AIC Guide to Digital Photography and Conservation Documentation**
American Institute for Conservation
1156 15th St NW
Suite 320
Washington, DC 20005-1714
202-452-9545; Fax: 202-452-9328
www.aic-faic.org
Eryl Wentworth, Executive Director
Adam Allen, Meetings Associate
Steve Charles, Membership Assistant

2355 **Advocacy and Lobbying: Speaking up for the Arts**
National Assembly of State Arts Agencies
1029 Vermont Ave NW
2nd Floor
Washington, DC 20005-3517
202-347-6352; Fax: 202-737-0526
nasaa@nasaa-arts.org
www.nasaa-arts.org
Dennis Dewey, Manager
Arlynn Fishbaugh, President
Pam Breaux, VP
Bobby Kadis, Treasurer
John Bracey, Secretary

2356 **Airbrush Action**
3209 Atlantic Avenue
PO Box 438
Allenwood, NJ 08720
732-223-7878
800-876-2472; Fax: 732-223-2855
customerservice@airbrushaction.com
www.airbrushaction.com
Clifford S Stieglitz, President/Publisher
Offers information on the art and graphic design community. Airbrush Action's editorial includes features/coverage on: automotive customizing, hobby applications, illustration, signs, t-shirts, body art, home decorative and more.
Cost: $26.95
Circulation: 35000
Printed in 4 colors on glossy stock

2357 **Airbrush Art and Action**
Paisano Publishers
28210 Dorothy Drive
PO Box 3000
Agoura Hills, CA 91301
818-889-8740
800-247-6246; Fax: 818-889-1252
www.paisanopub.com/
Joseph Teresi, Publisher
A look at new products, step by step instruction features, profiles of professionals in the airbrushing field, and examples of airbrushed artworks.
Frequency: Bi-annually
Circulation: 68500

2358 **American Artist**
Billboard
770 Broadway
New York, NY 10003-9589
646-654-4400
800-562-2706; Fax: 646-654-5514
www.billboard.com
Jessica Letkemann, Managing Editor
Lisa Ryan Howard, Publisher
A magazine devoted to the best of the best in the art industry.
Cost: $43.45
Frequency: Monthly
Circulation: 71,435
Founded in 1894

2359 **Antique Trader**
F+W Media

38 E. 29th Street
New York, NY 10016

212-447-1400; Fax: 212-447-5231
contact_us@fwmedia.com

Jim Ogle, CFO
Sara Domville, President
Chad Phelps, Chief Digital Officer
David Nussbaum, CEO

For the antiques and collectibles hobby industry. Accepts advertising.
Cost: $38.00
100 Pages
Frequency: Weekly
Circulation: 27363
Founded in 1957

2360 Antique Week
Mayhill Publications
27 N Jefferson Street
PO Box 90
Knightstown, IN 46148

765-345-5133
800-876-5133; Fax: 800-695-8153
tony@antiqueweek.com
www.antiqueweek.com

Gary Thoe, President
David Blower, Senior Editor

Antique dealers.
Cost: $38.95
Frequency: Weekly
Circulation: 65000
Founded in 1968

2361 Aristos
Aristos Foundation
PO Box 20845
Park West Station
New York, NY 10025

212-678-8550
www.aristos.org

Louis Torres, Editor
Michelle Marder Kamhi, Editor

Independent online journal advocating objective standards in arts scholarship and criticism. Our aim is to present well-reasoned commentary on the arts and on the philosophy of art, for a broad audience of general readers and scholars.
Cost: $25.00
Frequency: Monthly
Founded in 1982

2362 Art & Antiques
Art & Antiques Worldwide Media LLC
1319-cc Military Cutoff Road #192
Wilmington, NC 28405

910-679-4402
888-350-0951; Fax: 919-869-1864
info@artandantiquesmag.com
www.artandantiquesmag.com

Jon Dorfman, Senior Editor

Magazine for collectors of the fine and decorative arts.
Frequency: Monthly

2363 Art & Auction
Art & Auction
601 West 26th Street
Suite 410
New York, NY 10001

212-447-9555
800-777-8718; Fax: 212-447-5221
info@artandauction.com
www.artinfo.com

Louise T Blouin, President/Owner
Benjamin Genocchio, Editor-in-Chief

Editorial covers the art market from antiquities to contemporary art, monthly calendar of gallery exhibitions and auction sales.
Cost: $80.00
Frequency: Monthly
Circulation: 38500
Founded in 1996

2364 Art Business News
Advanstar Communications
600 Unicorn Park Drive
Suite 400
Woburn, MA 01801

339-298-4200
800-552-4346; Fax: 781-939-2490
info@advanstar.com
www.advanstar.com/

Julie MacDonald, Editor
Joseph Loggia, CEO

Publication addressing the business aspect of art and framing. Editorial covers everything from trends and sales to new colors and the latest tax changes.
Cost: $43.00
Frequency: Monthly
ISSN: 0273-5652
Founded in 1992

2365 Art Materials Retailer
Fahy-Williams Publishing
171 Reed Street
PO Box 1080
Geneva, NY 14456-2137

315-789-0458
800-344-0559; Fax: 315-789-4263
kfahy@fwpi.com
www.fwpi.com

J Kevin Fahy, Publisher
Tina Manzer, Editorial Director
Bradley G. Gordner, Senior Editor
Frequency: Quarterly
Circulation: 12000
Printed in 4 colors on glossy stock

2366 Art Therapy: Journal of the American Art T herapy Association
American Art Therapy Association
4875 Eisenhower Avenue
Sute 240
Alexandria, VA 22304

703-548-5860
888-290-0878; Fax: 703-783-8468
info@arttherapy.org
www.arttherapy.org

Cynthia Woodruff, Executive Director
Christina Easterly, Coordinator, Events & Operations
Barbara Florence, Director, Events & Education
Clara Keane, Coordinator, Communication & Policy
Kat Michel, Manager, Membership

The leading scholarly research publication in art therapy with up-to-date professional knowledge of the field; a broad spectrum of ideas in therapy, practice, professional issues, and research; and peer-reviewed research, theory and practice papers, viewpoints, reviews of current literature, and best practices.

2367 Art in America
Brant Publications
575 Broadway
5th Floor
New York, NY 10012-3227

212-941-2900; Fax: 212-941-2885
interview_ad@brantpub.com
www.interviewmagazine.com

Sandra Brant, Publisher
Elizabeth Baker, Editor
Includes show reviews, event schedules, profiles of artists and genres and updates on literature and materials.
Cost: $24.95
Frequency: Monthly
Circulation: 64,182
Founded in 1984

2368 Arts & Health: An International Journal fo r Research, Policy and Practice
American Art Therapy Association
4875 Eisenhower Avenue
Sute 240
Alexandria, VA 22304

703-548-5860
888-290-0878; Fax: 703-783-8468
info@arttherapy.org
www.arttherapy.org

Cynthia Woodruff, Executive Director
Christina Easterly, Coordinator, Events & Operations
Barbara Florence, Director, Events & Education
Clara Keane, Coordinator, Communication & Policy
Kat Michel, Manager, Membership

An international forum for the fast-emerging field of arts and health including ways in which the arts contribute to health, wellbeing, social inclusion, and healthcare practice.

2369 Arts and Activities
Publishers' Development Corporation
12345 World Trade Dr
San Diego, CA 92128-3743

858-605-0200; Fax: 858-605-0247
promo@artsandactivities.com
www.gunsmagazine.com

Tom Von Rosen, Owner
Maryellen Bridge, Editor

Offers information and news on the latest in the visual arts.
Cost: $24.95
Frequency: Monthly
Founded in 1932

2370 Artweek
PO Box 485
Hilo, HI 96721-0485

800-733-2916
800-733-2916; Fax: 262-495-8703
info@artweek.com
www.artweek.com

Debra Koppman, Editor
Laura Richar Janku, Editor

Critical reviews of contemporary West Coast art as well as news, features, articles, interviews, special sections and opinion pieces.
Cost: $34.00
Frequency: Monthly
Founded in 1968

2371 Breakthrough Magazine
Breakthrough Magazine
2271 Old Baton Rouge Highway
PO Box 2945
Hammond, LA 70404-2945

985-345-7266
800-783-7266; Fax: 985-542-1831
info@breakthroughmagazine.com
www.breakthroughmagazine.com

Larry Blomquist, Publisher

Artist profiles, tips, previews, and a calendar of events. Incorporates similar techniques related to wildlife carvings, sculpture and photography.
Cost: $32.00
Frequency: Quarterly
Circulation: 8932

2372 CNA
F+W Media

38 E. 29th Street
New York, NY 10016

212-447-1400; Fax: 212-447-5231
contact_us@fwmedia.com

Jim Ogle, CFO
Sara Domville, President
Chad Phelps, Chief Digital Officer
David Nussbaum, CEO

A craft industry trade magazine reaching retailers and industry leaders. Readers turn to CNA each month in search of trends, innovative products, partnerships, corporate accomplishments, and retail strategies that positively impact their businesses. Regular editorial includes timely product showcases and special sections that target arts, crafts, scrapbooking, children's activities, sewing and needlework products. The editorial team has much experience in the industry.
Cost: $30.00
112 Pages
Circulation: 21777
Founded in 1945

2373 **Christie's International Magazine**
Christies Publications
20 Rockefeller Plaza
New York, NY 10020

212-636-2000
800-395-6300; Fax: 212-636-2399
info@christies.com
www.christies.com

Mark Wrey, Publisher
Victoria Tremlett, Editor
John L Vogelstein, Chairman

Devoted to the promotion of Christie's fine art auctions worldwide.
Cost: $70.00
Circulation: 60000
Founded in 1766

2374 **Craft and Needlework Age**
F+W Media
38 E. 29th Street
New York, NY 10016

212-447-1400; Fax: 212-447-5231
contact_us@fwmedia.com

Jim Ogle, CFO
Sara Domville, President
Chad Phelps, Chief Digital Officer
David Nussbaum, CEO

Trade magazine serving the crafts and needlework industry. Accepts advertising.
Cost: $20.00
Frequency: Monthly
Founded in 1952

2375 **Decorative Artist's Workbook**
F+W Media
38 E. 29th Street
New York, NY 10016

212-447-1400; Fax: 212-447-5231
contact_us@fwmedia.com

Jim Ogle, CFO
Sara Domville, President
Chad Phelps, Chief Digital Officer
David Nussbaum, CEO

The leading how-to magazine for decorative painters, because it offers detailed step-by-step instruction and illustrations for fabulous projects, plus problem-solving tips, and articles on new techniques, products and books. Readers find a full range of decorative painting subjects and styles painted in a whole range of skill levels and mediums and on a variety of surfaces...and all designed by the most well known artists and instructors in decorative painting!
Cost: $27.00
72 Pages
Frequency: Quarterly
Circulation: 111573
Founded in 1987

2376 **Folk Art**
American Folk Art Museum
2 Lincoln Square
Columbus Avenue at 66th Street
New York, NY 10023

212-595-9533; Fax: 212-265-2350
info@folkartmuseum.org
www.folkartmuseum.org

Irene Kreney, Manager
Linda Dune, Acting Director
Edward Blanchard, President, Treasurer

An award winning publication. The editorial content is geared toward collectors, scholars, and the museum community interested in traditional and contemporary American folk and decorative arts. A benefit of membership, and is delivered to a targeted national and international readership.

2377 **HOW Magazine**
F&W Publications
10151 Carver Road
Blue Ash, OH 45242

513-531-2690; Fax: 513-531-1843
contact_us@fwmedia.com
Facebook, Twitter, LinkedIn

David Nussbaum, CEO
Jim Ogle, COO/CFO
Sara Domville, President

The industry's leading creativity, business and technology magazine for graphic design professionals. Each issue provides a mix of essential business information, up-to-date technology tips, the creative whys and hows behind noteworthy projects, and profiles of professionals who are influencing design.
Cost: $27.73
140 Pages
Frequency: Monthly
Circulation: 44883
Founded in 1985

2378 **Hammer's Blow**
Artist-Blacksmith's Association of North America
259 Muddy Fork Road
Jonesborough, TN 37659

423-913-1022; Fax: 423-913-1023
hbeditor@abana.org
www.abana.org
Facebook, Twitter

Eddie Rainey, President
Tina Chisena, First VP
John Fee, Second VP
Herb Upham, Secretary
Dan Nauman, Editor

Journal of the Artist-Blacksmiths' Association of North America
4500 Members
24 Pages
Frequency: Quarterly
Founded in 1973

2379 **I.D. Magazine**
F+W Media
38 E. 29th Street
New York, NY 10016

212-447-1400; Fax: 212-447-5231
contact_us@fwmedia.com

Jim Ogle, CFO
Sara Domville, President
Chad Phelps, Chief Digital Officer
David Nussbaum, CEO
Andr,a Pellegrino, Advertising Director

The international design magazine, showcases innovative products and technologies for sophisticated readers who are at the forefront of shaping the world through design. The multi-disciplinary coverage embraces design trends, theories, experiments and innovators.
Cost: $59.96
96 Pages
Frequency: 1 Year 8 Issues
Circulation: 31,424
Founded in 1954

2380 **IFAR Journal**
500 5th Avenue
Suite 935
New York, NY 10110

212-391-6234; Fax: 212-391-8794
kferg@ifar.org
www.ifar.org

Sharon Flescher, Executive Director
Jack Josephson, Chairman

Emphasizes education and research regarding the ethical, legal and scholarly issues concerning art objects. In addition to news stories and book reviews, the Journal contains feature articles on art authenticity and attribution; forgery and fraud; art law and ethics; World War II-era art restitution issues; conserving, restoring and caring for art; and art theft.
Founded in 1969

2381 **Journal of Aesthetics and Art Criticism**
American Society for Aesthetics
1550 Larimer Street
Suite 644
Denver, CO 80202

562-331-4424
asa@aesthetics-online.org
www.aesthetics-online.org

Robert Stecker, Editor
Theodore Gracyk, Editor
Julie C. Van Camp, Executive Director

Promotes study, research, discussion and publication in aesthetics, which includes all studies of the arts and related experience including philosophic, scientific and theoretical viewpoints.
Frequency: Quarterly
Founded in 1942

2382 **Journal of the American Institute for Conservation (JAIC)**
1156 15th Street
Suite 320
Washington, DC 20005-1714

202-452-9545; Fax: 202-452-9328
info@conservation-us.org
www.conservation-us.org

Eryl Wentworth, Executive Director
Meg Loew Craft, President
Pamela Hatchfield, VP

Publication of peer-reviewed technical studies, research papers, treatment case studies and ethics and standards discussions relating to the broad field of conservation and preservation of historic and cultural works.
3500 Members
Founded in 1961

2383 **Magazine Antiques**
Brant Publications
575 Broadway
5th Floor
New York, NY 10012-3227

212-941-2900; Fax: 212-941-2885
www.interviewmagazine.com

Sandra Brant, Publisher
Allison Ledes, Editor
Donald Liebling, Circulation Manager
Jennifer Norton, Marketing Executive

Articles on American and European decorative and fine arts, architecture, historic preservation,

and collecting.
Cost: $24.95
Frequency: Monthly
Circulation: 64402
Founded in 1969

2384 Memory Makers
F+W Media
38 E. 29th Street
New York, NY 10016

212-447-1400; Fax: 212-447-5231
contact_us@fwmedia.com

Jim Ogle, CFO
Sara Domville, President
Chad Phelps, Chief Digital Officer
David Nussbaum, CEO
Buddy Redling, Editor in Chief

Entertains, informs, and inspires the burgeoning number of scrapbook enthusiasts. Features the ideas and stories of its readers - people who believe in keeping scrapbooks and the tradition of the family photo historian alive. Two special newsstand-only issues are dedicated to specific areas of interest including holidays, heritage albums, and more.
Cost: $45.00
144 Pages
Frequency: Bi-annually
Circulation: 203287
Founded in 1996

2385 Michaels Create!
F+W Media
38 E. 29th Streett
New York, NY 10016

212-447-1400; Fax: 212-447-5231
contact_us@fwmedia.com

Jim Ogle, CFO
Sara Domville, President
Chad Phelps, Chief Digital Officer
David Nussbaum, CEO

Features contemporary designs reflecting the latest trends with clear instructions. The home decorating, fashion, and gift ideas will inspire experienced crafters as well as seasonal crafters to explore new possibilities. Step-by-step instructions, tips, and techniques will engage crafters of all ages - including kids - with the creative skills of crafting to be enjoyed as a year-round activity.
Cost: $21.97
116 Pages
Frequency: Monthly
Circulation: 24991
Founded in 1975

2386 Military Trader
F+W Media
38 E. 29th Street
New York, NY 10016

212-447-1400; Fax: 212-447-5231
contact_us@fwmedia.com
Facebook, Twitter, LinkedIn

David Nussbaum, CEO
Jim Ogle, CFO/COO
Sara Domville, President

Monthly publication for collectors of military memorabilia.
Cost: $19.00
Frequency: Monthly
Founded in 1952

2387 Museum
American Association of Museums
1575 Eye Street NW
Suite 400
Washington, DC 20005-1113

202-289-1818; Fax: 202-289-6578
membership@aam-us.org
www.aam-us.org

John Strand, Publisher
Susan Breitkopf, Editor In Chief
Ford Bell, President
Frequency: Bi-Monthly

2388 Panorama
Association of Historians of American Art
Home Page: journalpanorama.org

Ross Barrett, Executive Editor
Sarah Burns, Executive Editor
Jennifer Jane Marshall, Executive Editor

The online journal of the Association of Historians of American Art.
Frequency: Biannual

2389 Pastel Journal
F+W Media
38 E. 29th Street
New York, NY 10016

212-447-1400; Fax: 212-447-5231
contact_us@fwmedia.com

Jim Ogle, CFO
Sara Domville, President
Chad Phelps, Chief Digital Officer
David Nussbaum, CEO

Written by pastel artists for pastel artists. Content is geared toward artists, amateur & professional alike, who already work in pastels and who want to further develop their skills through in-depth information on pastel painting processes and thought-provoking ideas from successful pastel artists. Also included is information on workshops and exhibitions, as well as articles providing details on the business aspects of art - creating prints, creating Web sites, framing prints, and shipping.
Cost: $27.00
84 Pages
Circulation: 19167
Founded in 1999

2390 Picture Framing Magazine
Hobby Publications
83 South Street
Unit 307
Freehold, NJ 07728

732-536-5160
800-969-7176; Fax: 732-536-5761
www.pictureframingmagazine.com

David Gherman, President
Patrick Sarver, Editor
Bruce Gherman, Executive Publisher

News and trends in the picture framing trade, marketing strategies, and economic developments.
Cost: $20.00
Frequency: Monthly
Circulation: 25000
ISSN: 1052-9977
Founded in 1955

2391 Postcard Collector
F+W Media
38 E. 29th Street
New York, NY 10016

212-447-1400; Fax: 212-447-5231
contact_us@fwmedia.com

Jim Ogle, CFO
Sara Domville, President
Chad Phelps, Chief Digital Officer
David Nussbaum, CEO

Monthly publication for postcard collectors.
Cost: $29.98
Frequency: Monthly
Founded in 1982

2392 SchoolArts
Davis Publications
50 Portland Street
Worcester, MA 01618

508-754-7201
800-533-2847; Fax: 508-753-3834
www.davisart.com
Facebook, Twitter, LinkedIn

Wyatt Wade, Owner
John Carr, Marketing

For art educators.
Cost: $23.95
60 Pages
Frequency: Monthly
Circulation: 23717
Founded in 1901
Printed in 4 colors on matte stock

2393 Sotheby's Preview Magazine
Sotheby's
1334 York Ave
New York, NY 10021-4806

212-606-7000
541-312-5682; Fax: 212-606-7107
preview@sothebys.com
www.sothebys.com

William F Ruprecht, CEO
Bruno Vinciguerra, Chief Operating Officer

Auction schedule listings, exhibition dates and catalogue pricing.
Cost: $75.00
48 Pages
Circulation: 80,000
Founded in 1976
Printed in 4 colors on newsprint stock

2394 Style: 1900
199 George Street
Lambertville, NJ 08530

609-397-4104; Fax: 609-397-4409
Facebook, Twitter, LinkedIn

Fred Albert, Editor
Jennifer Strauss, Director Advertising
David Rago, Publisher

The only publication devoted solely to the works and thoughts of the arts and crafts movement.
Cost: $6.95
88 Pages
Frequency: Quarterly
Circulation: 20000
ISSN: 1080-451X
Founded in 1987
Mailing list available for rent: 7,000 names at $250 per M
Printed in 4 colors on glossy stock

2395 The Anvil's Ring
259 Muddy Fork Road
Jonesborough, TN 37659

423-913-1022; Fax: 423-913-1023
centraloffice@abana.org
www.abana.org

Eddie Rainey, President
Tina Chisena, First VP
John Fee, Second VP
Herb Upham, Secretary

The most comprehensive overview on what's happening in the artist- blacksmithing world or the inspiration to get you out to the forge.
4500 Members
Frequency: Quarterly
Circulation: 2 Mag.
Founded in 1973

2396 The Chronicle of the Horse
American Academy of Equine Art

117 North Water Street
PO Box 1364
Georgetown, KY 40324

859-281-6031; Fax: 859-281-6043
www.aaea.net

Frances Clay Conner, Executive Director
Xochitl Barnes, AAEA President

The official magazine of the American Academy of Equine Art.
90 Members
Founded in 1980

2397 **Visual Anthropology Review**
American Anthropoligical Association
2200 Wilson Blvd
Suite 600
Arlington, VA 22201-3357

703-528-1902; Fax: 703-528-3546
www.aaanet.org

Bill Davis, Executive Director
Oona Schmid, Director of Publishing
Leith Mullings, President

Directed toward the study of visual aspects of human behavior including anthropology of art and museology and the use of media in anthropological research, representation, and teaching.
Cost: $25.00
Circulation: 1000
ISSN: 1053-7147
Founded in 1902
Mailing list available for rent
Printed in one color on glossy stock

2398 **Watercolor Magic**
F+W Media
38 E. 29th Street
New York, NY 10016

212-447-1400; Fax: 212-447-5231
contact_us@fwmedia.com

Jim Ogle, CFO
Sara Domville, President
Chad Phelps, Chief Digital Officer
David Nussbaum, CEO

Offers valuable how-to instruction and creative inspiration for artists who work in water-based media. From page after page of inspirational ideas, to illustrations of the best techniques, to must-have painting tools and materials, watercolorists will find everything they need to know to help them create art from the inside out. Plus, each issue includes special reports and tons of tips from the foremost experts in the field. The definitive source of creative inspiration and technical info.
Cost: $27.00
72 Pages
Frequency: Monthly
Circulation: 94636
Founded in 1993

Trade Shows

2399 **AAM Annual Meeting & MuseumExpo**
American Alliance of Museums
2451 Crystal Dr.
Suite 1005
Arlington, VA 22202

202-289-1818; Fax: 202-289-6578
membership@aam-us.org
www.aam-us.org

Andrea Streat, Director, Meetings & Events

The largest gathering of museum professionals in the world.
Frequency: Annual/May

2400 **ABANA International Conferences**
Artist-Blacksmith's Association of North America
259 Muddy Fork Road
Jonesborough, TN 37659

423-913-1022; Fax: 423-913-1023
conference@abana.org
www.abana.org
Facebook, Twitter

Eddie Rainey, President
Tina Chisena, First VP
John Fee, Second VP
Herb Upham, Secretary

Held biennially in the United States for members. Demonstrations, panel discussions and lectures by experts in the field from around the globe. Share knowledge of technical, aesthetic and business areas of the craft for beginners to established professionals.
1000 Attendees
Frequency: Biennial
Founded in 1975

2401 **AHAA Symposium**
Association of Historians of American Art

info@ahaaonline.org
www.ahaaonline.org/?page=Symposium
Facebook, Twitter, LinkedIn

Ellery Foutch, Chair
Austen Barron Bailly, Co-Chair
Sarah Kelly Oehler, Symposium Liaison

Biennial syposium (even-numbered years) of the Association of Historians of American Art.
Frequency: Biennial
Founded in 2010

2402 **AIGA Design Conference**
American Institute of Graphic Arts (AIGA)
233 Broadway
17th Fl.
New York, NY 10279

212-807-1990
Facebook, Twitter, Instagram

Stefan Bucher, Chair
Roman Mars, Conference Committee
Debbie Millman, Conference Committee
Nathan Shedroff, Conference Committee

Speakers, exhibitions, roundtables, professional development and a live, head-to-head design competition for up-and-comers.
Frequency: Annual

2403 **American Art Therapy Association Conference**
American Art Therapy Association
4875 Eisenhower Avenue
Sute 240
Alexandria, VA 22304

703-548-5860
888-290-0878; Fax: 703-783-8468
info@arttherapy.org
www.arttherapy.org

Cynthia Woodruff, Executive Director
Christina Easterly, Coordinator, Events & Operations
Barbara Florence, Director, Events & Education
Clara Keane, Coordinator, Communication & Policy
Kat Michel, Manager, Membership

Advanced practice courses, papers, workshops, plenary sessions, panels, exhibitors, and a town hall with the AATA board of directors.
800 Attendees
Frequency: Annual
Founded in 1969

2404 **American Institute for Conservation Annual Meeting**
Amer Institute for Conservation of Historic Works
1156 15th Street NW
Suite 320
Washington, DC 20005

202-452-9545; Fax: 202-452-9328
info@conservation-us.org
www.aic-faic.org

Eryl P Wentworth, Executive Director
Adam Allen, Meeting Manager
Meg Loew Craft, President

Annual meeting of conservators of artistic and cultural property, which includes seminars and workshops with over 1,000 members attending yearly. 50 booths.
1000 Attendees
Frequency: June
Founded in 1971

2405 **American Society for Aesthetics Annual Meeting**
American Society for Aesthetics
1550 Larimer Street
Suite 644
Denver, CO 80202

562-331-4424
asa@aesthetics-online.org
Facebook, Twitter

Susan Feagin, President
Julie C. Van Camp, Executive Director

Seminar, conference, and exhibits related to the study of the arts, all disciplines.
500 Attendees
Frequency: Annual, October
Founded in 1942

2406 **Antique Arms Show**
Beinfeld Productions
72 Sunrise Drive
Rancho Mirage, CA 92270

760-202-4489; Fax: 760-202-4793
www.antiquearmsshow.com

Wallace Beinfeld, Show Manager

Public show with 1000 booths of antiques and collectibles.
5M/6M Attendees
Frequency: January

2407 **Art Expo New York**
Advanstar Communications
641 Lexington Avenue
8th Floor
New York, NY 10022

212-951-6600; Fax: 212-951-6793
info@advanstar.com
www.advanstar.com

Joseph Loggia, CEO
Thomas Ehardt, Vice President
Tom Florio, CFO

Five hundred and eighty exhibitors of artwork including: paintings, sculpture, prints and graphics.
15000 Attendees
Frequency: Annual
Founded in 1985

2408 **Art Libraries Society of North America Annual Conference**
Art Libraries Society of North America
7044 S. 13th St.
Oak Creek, WI 53154

414-768-8000
800-817-0621; Fax: 414-768-8001
arlisna@mercury.interpath.com
www.arlisna.org

Deborah Kempe, President
Gregory Most, VP

Annual conference and show of publishers, book dealers, library suppliers and visual resources suppliers.
500 Attendees
Frequency: April
Founded in 1977

2409 **Art Miami: International Art Fair**
Advanstar Communications
641 Lexinton Avenue
8th Floor
New York, NY 10022
212-951-6600; Fax: 212-951-6793
info@advanstar.com
www.advanstar.com
Joseph Loggia, CEO
Thomas Ehardt, Vice President
Tom Florio, CFO
99 exhibits of fine arts, attended by professionals.
44500 Attendees

2410 **Art Supply Expo**
Marketing Association Services
1516 Pontius Avenue
Floor 2
Los Angeles, CA 90025-3306
310-478-0074
Randy Bauler, Executive Director
Exhibits consist of art and drafting equipment and computer graphics supplies.
10M Attendees
Frequency: October

2411 **Art and Creative Materials Institute/ACMI Annual Meeting**
99 Derby St.
Suite 200
Hingham, MA 02043
781- 55- 104; Fax: 781- 20- 555
www.acminet.org
Van Foster, President
Deborah S Gustafson, Associate Director
Debbie Munroe, Certification Director
Carol Rourke, Program Director
A non-profit association of manufacturers of art, craft and other creative materials, ACMI sponsors a certification program for both children's and adult's art materials and products, certifying that these products are non-toxic and meet voluntary standards of quality and performance. ACMI seeks to create and maintain a positive environment for art, craft and other creative materials usage, promoting safety in the materials and providing information and service resources on such products.
210 Members
Founded in 1940
Mailing list available for rent: 199 names

2412 **Conference of the Volunteer Committees of Art Museums of Canada and the US**
Volunteer Committees of Art Museums
Philbrook Museum
2727 S Rockford
Tulsa, OK 74114
FAX 918-743-4230
Grace Robin, VCAM President
Triennial conference and exhibits of art museum equipment, supplies and services.
Founded in 1952

2413 **Consumer Show**
Maven Company
PO Box 937
Plandome, NY 11030-0937
51- 62- 880
fasttrack@erols.com
www.mavencompany.com
N Chittenden, VP
Specialty show, doll, toy and teddy bear.
5,000 Attendees
Frequency: Semi-Annual
Founded in 1970

2414 **Craftsmen's Christmas Classic Arts and Crafts Festival**
Gilmore Enterprises
3514-A Drawbridge Pkwy
Greensboro, NC 27410-8584
336-282-5550; Fax: 336-274-1084
Contact@GilmoreShows.com
www.gilmoreshows.com
Jennifer Palmer, Show Manager
Clyde Gilmore, Executive Director
Features work from over 305 talented artists and craftspeople. All juried exhibitors work has been hand made by the exhibitors and must be original design and creation. Visit Christmas Tree Village to view the uniquely decorated Christmas Trees by some of our exhibitors. Something from every taste and budget with items from the most contemporary to the most traditional.
Founded in 1982

2415 **Craftsmen's Classic Arts and Crafts Festival**
Gilmore Enterprises
3514-A Drawbridge Pkwy
Greensboro, NC 27410-8584
336-282-5550; Fax: 336-274-1084
Contact@GilmoreShows.com
www.gilmoreshows.com
Jennifer Palmer, Show Manager
Clyde Gilmore, Executive Director
Features work from over 305 talented artists and craftspeople. All work has been hand made by the juried exhibitors and must be original design and creation. See the creative process in action with several exhibitors demonstrating their craft in their booths. Something from every style, taste and budget with items from the most contemporary to the most traditional.
15000 Attendees
Frequency: March/April/Aug/Sept/Oct.
Founded in 1982

2416 **Decor Expo**
Pfingsten Publishing
6000 Lombardo Center Drive
Suite 420
Seven Hills, OH 44131
216-328-8926
888-772-8926; Fax: 216-328-9452
Hugh T Tobin, Group Show Director
Rob Spademan, Marketing Director
Five hundred booths exhibiting fine art, limited edition prints, graphics, oil paintings and reproductions. Three shows a year in Orlando (January), New York City (March), and Atlanta (September).
4M Attendees
Frequency: September

2417 **Gilmore Shows**
Craftsmen's Classic Art & Craft Festivals
3514-A Drawbridge Pkwy
Greensboro, NC 27410-8584
336-282-5550; Fax: 336-274-1084
contact@gilmoreshows.com
www.gilmoreshows.com
Facebook
Jennifer Palmer, Show Manager
Clyde Gilmore, Executive Director
Jan Donovon, Marketing Manager
10 shows annually in North Carolina, South Carolina and Virginia. Each show features work from 250-450 talented artists and craftspeople from across the nationa. All juried exhibitors work has been hand made by the exhibitors and must be original design and creation. There is something from every taste and budget with items from traditional to contemporary, functional to whimsical, decorative to fun & funky. Visit Christmas Tree Village to view the trees decorated by some or our exhibitors.
20000 Attendees
Frequency: October/November
Founded in 1973

2418 **IACA Markets**
Indian Arts & Crafts Association
4010 Carlisle NE
Suite C
Albuquerque, NM 87107
505-265-9149; Fax: 505-265-8251
info@iaca.com
www.iaca.com
Joseph Zeller, President
Don Standing Bear Forest, VP
Susan Pourian, Secretary
Kathy Ouellet, Treasurer
Wholesale and retail markets of authentic, handmade Indian arts & crafts.
300 Attendees
Frequency: Semi-Annually

2419 **IFPDA Print Fair**
International Fine Print Dealers Association
250 W 26th St
Suite 405
New York, NY 10001-6737
212-674-6095; Fax: 212-674-6783
info@ifpda.org
www.ifpda.org
Michele Senecal, Executive Director
Laura Beth Gencarella, PR/Marketing Manager
Tara Reddi, President
Elizabeth Fodde-Reguer, Executive Assistant
The largest and most celebrated art fair dedicated to fine prints.

2420 **Morristown Antiques Show**
Wendy Management
PO Box 222
Harrison, NY 10528
914-316-4700; Fax: 914-698-6273
www.wendyantiquesshows.com
Meg Wendy, President
Perry Grosser, Marketing and Finance
Three day show of 85 important dealers from the Northeast. Covers the key periods of antiques for budget minded collectors.
Frequency: November/Annual
Founded in 1930

2421 **NAMTA's World of Art Materials**
National Art Materials Trade Association
20200 Zion Ave.
Cornelius, NC 28031
704-926-6244; Fax: 702-892-6247
info@namta.org
www.namta.org
Reggie Hall, Executive Director
Richard Goodban, President
Seven hundred and fifty booths including educational programs to advance the welfare of the art materials and framing industry.
5M Attendees
Frequency: May

2422 **National Art Education Association Convention**
National Art Education Association
1806 Robert Fulton Drive
Suite 300
Reston, VA 20191-1590
703-860-8000
800-299-8321; Fax: 703-860-2960
info@arteducators.org
www.naea-reston.org
Kathy Duse, Show Manager
Dr. Deborah Reeve, Executive Director
Dr. Robert Sabol, President
Annual show of 140-200 exhibitor booths displaying manufacturers, suppliers, distributors, publishing companies and universities latest art textbooks and high-tech software. Show draws approximately 4,000 or more attendees.
Frequency: April

2423 **National Guild of Community Schools of the Arts Conference**
National Guild of Community Schools of the Arts
520 Eighth Avenue, 3rd Floor
Suite 302
New York, NY 10018-8018
212-268-3337; Fax: 212-268-3995
www.nationalguild.org
Jonathan Herman, Executive Director
Kenneth Cole, Director
Exhibits of equipment, supplies and services for the advancement of education in the performing and visual arts. Arts Management in Community Institutions (AMICI) Summer Institute trains administrators to meet needs of growing and emerging arts schools. Other programs, services, guildnotes newsletter, job opportunities listings, and publications catalog available upon request on online.
350 Attendees
Frequency: Annual

2424 **New York Antiques Show**
Wendy Management
PO Box 222
Harrison, NY 10528
914-316-4700; Fax: 914-698-6273
www.wendyantiquesshows.com
Meg Wendy, President
Perry Grosser, Marketing and Finance
This unique, sophisticated show is an important convenient source for trend setting decorators. There are quality antiques for new, young, collectors as well as seasoned pros. This show is filled with 17th, 18th, and 19th Century American, English, French, Oriental and Continental furniture and decorative accessories, including rare books, clocks, silver, brass, paintings, prints, maps, porcelain, rugs, glass, lighting devices, sconces, candlesticks, garden urns, and so much more. 80/90 Dealers
Frequency: September
Founded in 1930

2425 **Professional Picture Framers Association Show**
Professional Picture Framers Association
4305 Sarellen Road
Richmond, VA 23231
517-788-8100; Fax: 517-788-8100
ppfa@ppfa.com
www.ppfa.com
Mark Klostermeyer, President
Source for manufacturers, wholesalers, print publishers, importers and retailers selling art, framing and related supplies.
Frequency: Annual
Founded in 1971

2426 **Surtex**
George Little Management
1133 Westchester Avenue
White Plains, NY 10606-3547
914-421-3200
800-272-7469; Fax: 914-948-6180
www.surtex.com
George(Jeff) Little II, President/COO
Penny Sikalis, VP, Show Manager
Rita Malek, Show Manager
In addition to providing the art and design component of this market we also include important home products.
5000 Attendees
Frequency: May/October

2427 **The AADLA Spring Show**
PO Box 2066
Lenox Hill Station
New York, NY 10021
212-879-7558; Fax: 212-772-7197
secretary@artantiquedealersleague.com
www.artantiquedealersleague.com
Clinton Howell, President
Robert Simon, VP
Susan Caplan Jacobson, Treasurer
David Mayer, Secretary/Executive Director
Ira Spanierman, Vice Chairperson
The best choice of the very best in fine art. Unique chances to view and buy paintings as well as objects reflecting excellence in the applied arts.
109 Members
Frequency: November/50 Attendees
Founded in 1926

2428 **TypeCon**
The Society of Typographic Aficionados
P.O. Box 457
Jefferson, GA 30549
info@typesociety.org
www.typesociety.org
Twitter
Features education forums, workshops, and exhibits related to typography and design.
Frequency: Annual
Founded in 1998

2429 **UCDA Design Conference**
University & College Designers Association
199 Enon Springs Rd. W
Suite 400
Smyma, TN 37167
615-459-4559; Fax: 615-459-5229
info@ucda.com
www.ucda.com
Facebook, Twitter, Instagram, Flickr
Tadson Bussey, Executive Director
Chris Klonowski, Assistant Director
A national conference for design students and professionals. Features keynotes, panels, workshops, a design show, and plenty of networking opportunities.
1000 Members
Frequency: Annual, Fall
Founded in 1970

2430 **UCDA Design Education Summit**
University & College Designers Association
199 Enon Springs Rd. W
Suite 400
Smyma, TN 37167
615-459-4559; Fax: 615-459-5229
info@ucda.com
www.ucda.com
Facebook, Twitter, Instagram, Flickr
Tadson Bussey, Executive Director
Chris Klonowski, Assistant Director
A national summit for design educators, chairs, and students that offers many opportunities for professional participation and development. Features keynotes, panels, workshops, and paper and poster presentations.
1000 Members
Frequency: Annual, Spring
Founded in 1970

2431 **UCDA Design Summit**
University & College Designers Association
199 Enon Springs Rd. W
Suite 400
Smyma, TN 37167
615-459-4559; Fax: 615-459-5229
info@ucda.com
www.ucda.com
Facebook, Twitter, Instagram, Flickr
Tadson Bussey, Executive Director
Chris Klonowski, Assistant Director
Features experienced speakers and focused sessions on key topics in design, including technologies and resources that can help your daily work flow.
1000 Members
Frequency: Annual, Spring
Founded in 1970

Directories & Databases

2432 **AADA Membership Directory**
Art Dealers Association of America
205 Lexington Avenue
Suite 901
New York, NY 10016
212-488-5550; Fax: 64- 68- 680
www.artdealers.org
Lucy Mitchell-Innes, President
Michael Findlay, Vice President
Jeffery Fraenkel, Secretary
An annual directory listing the AADA members. Published by the Art Dealers Association of America.
77 Pages
Founded in 1962

2433 **ARTWEEK Gallery Calendar Section**
Spaulding Publishing
PO Box 52100
Palo Alto, CA 94303-0751
800-733-2916; Fax: 262-495-8703
info@artweek.com
www.artweek.com
Richard J O'Brien, Chairman
John T Bourger, Vice Chairman
A screened list of galleries on the West coast and other Western states are profiled.
Cost: $34.00
Circulation: 14,500

2434 **American Art Directory**
National Register Publishing
430 Mountain Ave.
Suite 400
New Providence, NJ 07974
800-473-7020; Fax: 908-673-1189
nrpeditorial@marquiswhoswho.com
Provides important information on museums, art organizations, art schools, libraries, art editors and critics, scholarships, fellowships, exhibitions and state art countils as well as funding sources and booking agencies.

2435 **Art Index**
HW Wilson Company

10 Estes Street
Ipswich, MA 01938
800-653-2726; Fax: 978-356-6565
information@ebscohost.com
www.hwwilson.com
Tim Collins, President
Michael Gorrell, EVP of Technology, CIO
Offers more than 500,000 citations to articles and book reviews in over 300 periodicals, yearbooks and museum bulletins.
Founded in 1929

2436 **Art Museums of the World**
Greenwood Publishing Group
88 Post Road W
PO Box 5007
Westport, CT 06881-5007
203-226-3571
800-225-5800; Fax: 203-222-1502
www.greenwood.com
Debra Adams, Editor
National and international art museum list.
Cost: $259.00
1696 Pages
ISBN: 0-313213-22-4

2437 **Art in America: Guide to Galleries, Museums, and Artists**
Brant Publications
575 Broadway
New York, NY 10012-3227
212-941-2900; Fax: 212-941-2885
www.interviewmagazine.com
David Nussman, CEO
A list of over 4,000 museums, galleries and other display areas.
Cost: $15.00
Frequency: Annual
Circulation: 70,000
Founded in 1969

2438 **Arts and Humanities Search**
Institute for Scientific Information
1500 Spring Garden St
Philadelphia, PA 19130-4067
215-386-0100
800-386-4474; Fax: 215-386-2911
Offers data from more than 1100 arts and humanities journals.

2439 **Directory of MA and PhD Programs in Art and Art History**
College Art Association
50 Broadway
21 Floor
New York, NY 10004
212-691-1051; Fax: 212-627-2381
nyoffice@collegeart.org
www.collegeart.org
Facebook, Twitter, LinkedIn
Linda Downs, Executive Director
Alan Gilbert, Editor
Anne Collins Goodyear, President
Institutions are profiled that offer M.A. and Ph.D. programs in art and art history.
Cost: $12.50
152 Pages
Founded in 1911

2440 **Films and Videos on Photography**
Program for Art on Film
200 Willoughby Avenue
Brooklyn, NY 11205
718-399-4506; Fax: 718-399-4507
www.artfilm.org
Nadine Covert, Executive Director
An annotated directory of over 500 films and videos on photography, photographers, and photographic techniques.
Cost: $15.00
132 Pages
ISBN: 0-870995-75-1
Founded in 1990

2441 **IACA Directory**
Indian Arts & Crafts Association
4010 Carlisle NE
Suite C
Albuquerque, NM 87107
505-265-9149; Fax: 505-265-8251
info@iaca.com
www.iaca.com
Joseph Zeller, President
Don Standing Bear Forest, VP
Susan Pourian, Secretary
Kathy Ouellet, Treasurer
Directory of all IACA members (wholesalers, retailers, artists/craftspeople, collectors, museums and ancillary organizations)
Cost: $15.00

2442 **Illustrators Annual**
Society of Illustrators
128 E 63rd St
New York, NY 10065-7392
212-838-2560; Fax: 212-838-2561
info@societyillustrators.org
www.societyillustrators.org
Denis Dittrich, President
Tim O'Brien, Executive Vice President
Victor Juhasz, Vice President
David Reuss, Treasurer
Published by the Society of Illustrators
Cost: $49.95
320 Pages
Circulation: 7000
Founded in 1959
Mailing list available for rent: 1000 names at $600 per M
Printed in 4 colors

2443 **Key Guide to Electronic Resources: Art and Art History**
Information Today
143 Old Marlton Pike
Medford, NJ 08055-8750
609-654-6266
800-300-9868; Fax: 609-654-4309
custserv@infotoday.com
www.infotoday.com
Thomas H Hogan, President
Roger R Bilboul, Chairman of the Board
An evaluative directory of electronic reference in the fields of art and art history.
Cost: $39.50
120 Pages
ISBN: 1-573870-22-6

2444 **NAMTA International Convention & Trade Show Directory**
National Art Materials Trade Association
20200 Zion Ave.
Cornelius, NC 28031
704-892-6244; Fax: 704-892-6247
info@namta.org
www.namta.org
Facebook, Twitter, LinkedIn
Richard Fjordbotten, President
Reggie Hall, Executive Director
National Art Materials Trade Association directory.

2445 **Official Museum Directory**
National Register Publishing
430 Mountain Ave.
Suite 400
New Providence, NJ 07974
800-473-7020; Fax: 908-673-1189
nrpeditorial@marquiswhoswho.com
Comprehensive reference for those seeking information on the country's museums. Features profiles and statistics on more than 7,700 museums in the US.

2446 **The Artful Home: Furniture, Sculpture and Objects**
Kraus Sikes
931 E Main Street
Suite 106
Madison, WI 53703-2955
608-572-2590
877-223-4600; Fax: 608-257-2690
info@artfulhome.com
www.guild.com
Lisa Bayne, CEO
Bill Lathrop, Vice President
A wealth of information on craft artists working in furniture, wall decor and accessories are listed.
Cost: $29.95
256 Pages
Frequency: Annual
Circulation: 15,000

2447 **What Museum Guides Need To Know:Access For Blind & Visually Impaired Visitors**
American Foundation for the Blind
2 Penn Plaza
Suite 1102
New York, NY 10121
212-502-7600
800-232-5463; Fax: 888- 54- 833
afbinfo@afb.net
www.afb.org
Carl R Augusto, President/CEO
Paul Schroeder, Vice President, Programs
Provides practical, easy-to-use guidelines on how to greet blind and visually impaired museum goers. This handbook also covers aesthetics and visual impairment and a training outline for museum requirements for accessibility.
Cost: $16.95
64 Pages

2448 **Who's Who in Art Materials**
National Art Materials Trade Association
20200 Zion Ave.
Cornelius, NC 28031
704-892-6244; Fax: 704-892-6247
info@namta.org
www.namta.org
Facebook, Twitter, LinkedIn
Richard Fjordbotten, President
Reggie Hall, Executive Director
Membership directory of the National Art Materials Trade Association.

Industry Web Sites

2449 **http://gold.greyhouse.com**
G.O.L.D Grey House OnLine Databases
Grey House Publishing's online database platform, GOLD, offers Quick Search, Keyword Search and Expert Search for most business sectors including art, antique and renovation markets. The GOLD platform makes finding the information you need quick and easy - whether you're a novice searcher or an experienced database user. All of Grey House's directory products are available for subscription on the GOLD platform.

2450 **www.aam-us.org**
American Association of Museums
For the museum community, enhances the ability of museums to serve the public interest, works on behalf of museums in educating federal legislators, assists museums in improving technical standards.

2451 **www.acminet.org**
Art and Creative Materials Institute
For art and craft product makers who encourage safe use of materials and proper labeling through certification.

2452 **www.aristos.org/aristos2.htm**
Aristos Foundation
The Foundation's purpose is to deepen public understanding of the nature of art as well as to foster the understanding and appreciation of humanistic values in the arts. Publishes an online journal.

2453 **www.artantiquedealersleague.com**
Art and Antique Dealers League of America
Nonprofit organization promotes interests of retailers and wholesalers of antiques and art objects.

2454 **www.artdealers.org**
Art Dealers Association of America
Works to improve the stature and standing of the art gallery business. Members deal primarily in paintings, sculpture, prints, drawings and photographs from the Renaissance to the present day. We have over 160 member galleries in more than 25 US cities.

2455 **www.artnet.com**
Art Net United States
The place to buy, sell and research fine art online.

2456 **www.collegeart.org**
College Art Association
Association for institutions that offer MA and PhD programs in art and art history.

2457 **www.greyhouse.com**
Grey House Publishing
Authoritative reference directories for most business sectors, including art, antique and restoration markets. Users can search the online databases with varied search criteria allowing for custom searches by product category, geographic area, sales volume, keyword, subject and more. Full Grey House catalog and online ordering also available.

2458 **www.iaca.com**
Indian Arts & Crafts Association
Not for profit trade association. Our mission is to promote, protect and preserve Indian arts.

2459 **www.naao.net**
National Association of Artist's Organizations
For artists within nonprofit organizations. Dedicated to the presentation of alternative visual arts, media, literature, new music and performing arts.

2460 **www.naea-reston.org**
National Art Education Association
Manufacturers, suppliers, distributors, publishing companies and universities.

2461 **www.naled.com**
National Association of Limited Edition Dealers
For dealers, vendors and publishers involved with collectibles and gifts.

2462 **www.namta.org**
National Art Materials Trade Association
For manufacturers, importers, wholesalers and retailers of art materials.

2463 **www.nasaa-arts.org**
National Assembly of State Arts Agencies
For those in the arts agency field in the US.

2464 **www.societyillustrators.com**
Society of Illustrators
For professional illustrators and art directors.

2465 **www.sothebys.com**
Sotheby's
Auction schedule listings, exhibition dates and catalogue pricing.

2466 **www.ucda.org**
University & College Designers Association
Inspires designers working in academia by delivering relevant programming and benefits. Provides resources for design professionals in all aspects of design.

Associations

2467 **American Rhetoric**

owner@americanrhetoric.com
www.americanrhetoric.com

An association dedicated to rhetoric and public communication in the US.

2468 **Association for Recorded Sound Collections**

c/o Nathan Georgitis
Knoght Library, 1299 University of
Eugene, OR 97403-1299

execdir@arsc-audio.org
www.arsc-audio.org
Facebook, Twitter, YouTube

Nathan Georgitis, Executive Director

A nonprofit organization dedicated to the preservation and study of sound recordings in all genres.
Founded in 1966

2469 **Audio Engineering Society**

551 Fifth Ave
Suite 1225
New York, NY 10176

212-661-8528; Fax: 212-682-0477
www.aes.org
Facebook, Twitter, YouTube, Instagram

Colleen Harper, Executive Director
Chris Plunkett, Director, Operations
Graham Kirk, Director, Sales & Marketing
Frank Wells, Director, Communications
Ricard Cabot, Standards Manager

Worldwide professional association for professionals and students involved in the audio industry.
14000 Members
Founded in 1948

2470 **Audio Publishers Association**

100 North 20th Street, Suite 400
Philadelphia, PA 19103

215-564-2729
info@otrpr.com
www.audiopub.org

Linda Lee, President
Anthony Goff, Vice President
Beth Anderson, Director
Janet Benson, Secretary
Sean McManus, Treasurer

Association for audio publishers.
Founded in 1987

2471 **AugmentedReality.Org**

40600 Ann Arbor Road E.
Suite 201
Plymouth, MI 48170

571-293-2013
www.augmentedreality.org
Facebook, Twitter, LinkedIn, YouTube, Flickr

Ori Inbar, Co-Founder & CEO
Tish Shute, Co-Founder & Chief Content Officer
Patrick O'Shaughnessy, Chief Technology Officer

Non-profit organization seeking to advance the field of augmented reality through connecting industry professionals through events and an online platform.

2472 **BICSI**

Building Industry Consulting Service International
8610 Hidden River Pkwy
Tampa, FL 33637-1000

813-979-1991
800-242-7405; Fax: 813-971-4311
bicsi@bicsi.org
www.bicsi.org
Facebook, Twitter, LinkedIn, Youtube

Michael Collins, President
Brian Ensign, President Elect
Robert Erickson, Secretary
Mel Lesperance, RCDD, Treasurer
John D. Clark Jr., CAE, Executive Director/CEO

BICSI members include cabling contractors, manufacturers, systems integrators and other telecom professionals.
Founded in 1977

2473 **Bay Area Video Coalition**

2727 Mariposa St
2nd Floor
San Francisco, CA 94110-1468

415-861-3282; Fax: 415-861-4316
edu@bavc.org
www.bavc.org
Facebook, Twitter, LinkedIn, YouTube, Flickr, Instagram

Angela Jones, President
Dawn Valadez, VP
Andy Wasklewicz, Treasurer
Carol Varney, Executive Director
Mindy Aronoff, Director of Training

A national organization for independent video producers and artists. Advanced, noncommercial, media arts center dedicated to providing access to media, education and technology.
Founded in 1976

2474 **Canadian Game Studies Assocation**

Home Page: gamestudies.ca
Twitter

The CGSA is devoted to the interdisciplinary study of digital games, and supports the work of researchers, graduate students, artists, game designers, programmers, theorists, and others working in the industry.
Mailing list available for rent

2475 **Church Music Association of America**

12421 New Point Drive
Richmond, VA 23233

505-263-6298
contact@musicasacra.com
musicasacra.com/music/recordings
Facebook, Twitter, Google+

William P. Mahrt, President
Horst Buchholz, Vice President
Jeffrey Tucker, Director of Publications
Mary Jane Ballou, Secretary
Adam Wright, Treasurer

A nonprofit association for Catholic church musicians.
Founded in 1964

2476 **Cinema Audio Society**

827 Hollywood Way #632
Burbank, CA 91505

818-752-8624; Fax: 818-752-8624
CASAwards@CinemaAudioSociety.org
cinemaaudiosociety.org
Facebook, Twitter, YouTube

Mark Ulano, CAS, President
Phillip Palmer, CAS, Vice President
Deb Adair, Director
David J. Bondelevitch, CAS, Secretary
Peter R. Damski, CAS, Treasurer

An association celebrating the scores of movies and films.
Founded in 1964

2477 **CompTIA**

3500 Lacey Road
Suite 100
Downers Grove, IL 60515

630-678-8300
866-835-8020; Fax: 630-678-8384
www.comptia.org
Facebook, Twitter, LinkedIn, Pinterest, Google+, YouTube

Todd Thibodeaux, President & CEO
Brian Laffey, CFO
Randy Gross, CIO
Nancy Hammervik, Executive VP, Industry Relations
Kelly Ricker, Executive VP, Events & Education

A nonprofit trade association created by representatives of five microcomputer leaderships and is a provider of professional certifications for the information technology (IT) industry.

2478 **Consumer Technology Association (CTA)**

1919 S Eads Street
Arlington, VA 22202

703-907-7600
cta@cta.tech
www.cta.tech
Facebook, Twitter, LinkedIn, Google+

Gary Shapiro, President & CEO
Glenda MacMullin, COO & CFO
Jean Foster, SVP, Marketing & Communications
Brian Markwalter, SVP, Research & Standards
Tiffany Moore, SVP, Political & Industry Affairs

Formerly the Consumer Electronics Association (CEA), this organization provides valuable and innovative member-only resources including: exclusive information and unparalleled market research, networking opportunities with business advocates and leaders, up-to-date educational programs and technical training, exposure in extensive promotional programs, and representation from the voice of the industry.

2479 **Digital Games Research Association**

coordinator@digra.org
www.digra.org

William Huber, President
Hanna Wirman, Vice President
Allan Fowler, Secretary
Jussi Holopainen, Treasurer
Cody Mejeur, Diversity Officer

DiGRA is an international association of academics and professionals interested in research into digital games and related products. It features a Digital Library, Gamesnetwork mailing list, and the ToDiGRA journal.
Founded in 2003
Mailing list available for rent

2480 **Entertainment Consumers Association**

Home Page: www.theeca.com

Hal Halpin, Founder & President
Heather Ellertson, VP, Marketing
Jennifer Mercurio, VP & General Counsel
Brett Schenker, Advocacy Director
Mike Conley, Digital Marketing Coordinator

Non-profit representing the interests of consumers of digital entertainment in the US and Canada.

2481 **Entertainment Merchants Association**

16530 Ventura Blvd
Suite 400
Encino, CA 91436-4551

818-385-1500; Fax: 818-933-0911
info@entmerch.org
www.entmerch.org
Facebook, Twitter

Mark Fisher, President & CEO

A nonprofit international trade association dedicated to advancing the interests of the home entertainment industry.
80K Members
Founded in 2006

2482 **Entertainment Software Association**
601 Massachusetts Avenue NW
Suite 300
Washington, DC 20001

esa@theesa.com
www.theesa.com
Facebook, Twitter, LinkedIn

Stanley Pierre-Louis, President & CEO
Gina Vetere, SVP & General Counsel
Andrew Bowins, SVP, Comm. & Public Affairs
Ana Molina, CFO
Michael O'Leary, SVP, Government Affairs

The trade association of the video game industry.
Founded in 2000

2483 **Entertainment Software Association of Canada**
#408, 130 Spadina Avenue
Toronto, ON M5V 2L4

416-620-7171
theesa.ca
Facebook, Twitter, Instagram, YouTube

Jayson Hilchie, President & CEO
Corinne Crichlow, Director, Communications & PR
Paul Fogolin, Director, Policy & Gov. Affairs
Dylan Boyd, Digital Content Manager

The ESAC is devoted to video game developers, publishers, and distributors in Canada

2484 **Entertainment Software Rating Board**
New York, NY

marketing@esrb.org
www.esrb.org
Facebook, Twitter

Patricia E. Vance, President
David Kassack, SVP, Finance & Operations
Bill Garrity, SVP, Ratings
John Falzone, VP, ESRB Privacy Certified
Randy Walker, SVP, Marketing & Communications

Non-profit, self-regulatory body devoted to informing consumers (especially parents) about the video games they play. The ESRB established and maintains a ratings system for all video games, from E for Everyone to AO for Adults Only.
Founded in 1994

2485 **International Game Developers Association**
#402, 150 Eglinton Avenue E.
Toronto, ON M4P 1E8

info@igda.org
www.igda.org
Facebook, Twitter, LinkedIn, YouTube, Instagram

Renee Gittins, Executive Director
Tristin Hightower, Director, Operations

The IGDA is the largest non-profit membership organization serving individuals who create video games. They are dedicated to improving developers' careers and lives through: Community, Professional Development, and Advocacy.
Founded in 1994

2486 **International Society of Videographers**
8499 S. Tamiami Trail
Suite 208
Sarasota, FL 34238

941-923-5334; Fax: 941-921-3836
info@weva.com
www.weva.com
Facebook, Twitter, LinkedIn, You Tube

Exchanges information on technologies, techniques, and equipment, sponsors Hall of Fame and an international convention.
Founded in 1981

2487 **International Virtual Reality Professionals Association**
6017 Greene Street
Philadelphia, PA 19144

Home Page: ivrpa.org
Facebook, Twitter, YouTube, Instagram

Originally known as the International QuickTime VR Association, the IVRPA is a non-profit organization of professionals who create immersive experiences, namely 360-degree images and video.
Founded in 1998

2488 **International Virtual Reality Healthcare Association**
2021 L Street NW
Suite 100-242
Washington, DC 20037

202-684-6207
bob@ivrha.org
ivrha.org

Robert Fine, Executive Director
Tom Augeri, Membership Director

The organization advocates for and provides information on applications of virtual reality technology in a healthcare setting.

2489 **National Association of Record Industry Professionals**
PO Box 2446
Toluca Lake, CA 91610-2446

818-769-7007
www.narip.com
Facebook, Twitter, YouTube, Vimeo

Tess Taylor, President

Association for all professionals in the music business.
130K Members
Founded in 1998

2490 **ProductionHUB**
1806 Hammerlin Ave
Winter Park, FL 32789

877-629-4122
www.productionhub.com
Facebook, Twitter, LinkedIn, Pinterest, Instagram, YouTube

Global network of crew and vendors serving the film and video production industry.
150K Members
Founded in 1999

2491 **Professional Audio-Video Retailers Association**
10 E 22nd Street
Suite 301
Lombard, IL 60148-6191

630-268-1500
800-621-0298; Fax: 630-953-8957
webmaster@paralink.org
www.paralink.org

Rosemary Wenstrom

An organization formed to assist the owners and operators of independently owned, high-end audio/video stores to work toward the mutually compatible goal of providing services to members which would be unattainable by retailers working separately.
204 Members

2492 **Recording Industry Association of America**
Washington, DC

Home Page: www.riaa.com

Cary Sherman, Chairman & CEO
Mitch Glazier, President

A trade group that represents the U.S. recording industry whose mission is to foster a business and legal climate that supports and promotes our members' creative and financial vitality.
Founded in 1952

2493 **Special Interests**
590 Knox Run Road
PO Box 193
Lanse, PA 16849-0193

814-345-6845
800-735-6997; Fax: 814-345-5566

Vera A Lockey, Owner

Health and safety sales DVD and videos.
Founded in 1997

2494 **The Monitoring Association**
8150 Leesburg Pike
Suite 700
Vienna, VA 22182

703-242-4670; Fax: 703-242-4675
communications@tma.us
www.csaaintl.org
Facebook, Twitter, LinkedIn, RSS

Celia Trigo Besore, Executive Director

Represents companies offering security (alarm) monitoring systems through a central station. It also represents companies that provide services and products to the industry.
300+ Members
Founded in 1950

2495 **University Film and Video Association**

ufvahome@gmail.com
www.ufva.org
Facebook, Twitter, LinkedIn, Vimeo, Instagram, YouTube

Francisco Menendez, President
Jennifer Machiorlatti, Executive Vice President
Heather Addison, Conference Vice President
Joseph Brown, Editorial Vice President
Tom Sanny, Treasurer

Association for videography and film making at universities.

2496 **VR/AR Association**
Palo Alto, CA 94303

nathan@thevrara.com
www.thevrara.com
Facebook, Twitter, LinkedIn, YouTube

Nathan Pettyjohn, Founder & President
Kris Kolo, Global Executive Director

International organization with a mission to foster collaboration between companies and individuals in the virtual reality and augmented reality industry. It aims to accelerate growth, encourage research and education, develop industry standards, connect members, and promote their services.
Founded in 2015

2497 **Video Software Dealers Association**
16530 Ventura Blvd
Suite 400
Encino, CA 91436-4554

818-385-0567
800-955-8732; Fax: 818-385-0567
www.vsda.org

Crossan Andersen, President
Carrie Dieterich, VP Marketing
Mark Fisher, VP Membership/Strategic

Initiatives
Sean Bersell, VP Public Affairs
Nancy Gordon, iDEA Manager Ops & Special Projects

Nonprofit international trade association with a membership exceeding 4,500 member companies, representing more than 25,000 locations. Members include retailers, as well as manufacturers, distributors and related businesses that constitute the home video industry. Acts as a spokesperson for home video industry both internally and legislatively.
4.5M Members
Founded in 1981

2498 **Wedding and Event Videographers Association International**
8499 S. Tamiami Trail, #208
Sarasota, FL 34238

941-923-5334; Fax: 941-921-3836
www.weva.com

International association for wedding and event videographers.

2499 **Western Association of Broadcast Engineers**
8120 Beddington Boulevard NW
Suite 319
Calgary, AB T3K 2A8

403-630-4907
info@wabe.ca
wabe.ca
Facebook, Twitter, LinkedIn

Bill Stovold, President

A nonprofit organization with the objectives to promote and advance the dissemination of engineering knowledge among its members, and to represent the interests of the majority of its members to duly appointed technical, educational, and legislative institutions.

2500 **XR Association**
1299 Pennsylvania Avenue NW
Washington, DC 20004

membership@xra.org
xra.org
Facebook, Twitter, LinkedIn

Elizabeth Hyman, Chief Executive Officer
Joan O'Hara, Senior Director, Public Policy
Laura Chadwick, Senior Director, Industry Relations
Michael Williams, Chief Operating Officer
Bethany Reitsma, Executive Assistant

Trade association for technology manufacturers in the virtual, augmented, and mixed reality industries.
Founded in 2016

Newsletters

2501 **Consumer Multimedia Report**
Warren Publishing
2115 Ward Ct Nw
Washington, DC 20037-1209

202-872-9200
800-771-9202; Fax: 202-318-8350
info@warren-news.com
www.warren-news.com

Brig Easley, Manager
Daniel Warren, President/Editor
Paul Warren, Chair/Publisher

Emphasizes on emerging technologies, marketing strategies, and industry events and news.
Cost: $462.00
Frequency: BiWeekly

2502 **DVD: Laser Disc Newsletter**
PO Box 420
East Rockaway, NY 11518-420

516-594-9304; Fax: 516-594-9307
doug@dvdlaser.com
www.dvdlaser.com

Douglas Pratt, Publisher

A consumer guide to DVD's with news, reviews, ads and more.
Cost: $47.50
24 Pages
Frequency: Monthly
Circulation: 5000
ISSN: 0749-5250
Founded in 1984
Mailing list available for rent: 5000 names at $100 per M

2503 **ECA Today**
Entertainment Consumers Association

Home Page: www.theeca.com

Hal Halpin, Founder & President
Heather Ellertson, VP, Marketing
Mike Conley, Digital Marketing Coordinator

Newsletter for members only.
Frequency: Nightly

2504 **PRC News**
Corbell Publishing Company
201 S Alvarado St
Suite 410
Los Angeles, CA 90057-2353

213-483-4559; Fax: 310-258-8096
info@corbell.com
www.corbell.com

Gabriel Carabello, President
Joseph Daneshrad, Circulation Manager

A weekly newsletter for the home video industry. Covers pre-recorded video statistics, people, calendar, etc.
Cost: $577.00
8 Pages
Frequency: Monthly
Circulation: 2000
ISSN: 0898-302X
Founded in 1988
Mailing list available for rent: 7000 names at $75 per M
Printed in on newsprint stock

2505 **Production Equipment Rental Association**
1806 Hammerlin Ave
Winter Park, FL 32789

407-629-4122
877-629-4122; Fax: 407-629-8884
www.productionhub.com
Facebook, Twitter, LinkedIn, You Tube

Pat Patin, President
Mark Beasley, VP/Marketing
John Johnston, Executive Director

A worldwide trade organization that supplies production equipment to the entertainment industry. PERA promotes the commercial advancement of new technologies available from member companies to meet the ever-changing requirements of their client's artistic challenges.
180 Members

2506 **Video Business**
Reed Business Information
2000 Clearwater Dr
Oak Brook, IL 60523-8809

630-574-0825; Fax: 630-288-8781
kevin.davis@reedbusiness.com
www.reedbusiness.com

Jeff Greisch, President
Paul Sweeting, Editor-at-Large
Charles Tanner, Circulation Manager

Publication includes the retail marketplace, probes business trends and issues, reviews new and upcoming video titles, and contains information and advice for running a successful retail business, and charts top video titles.
Cost: $70.00
Frequency: Weekly
Circulation: 47807
Founded in 1983

2507 **Video Investor**
Kagan Research
1 Lower Ragsdale Dr
Building One Suite 130
Monterey, CA 93940-5749

831-624-1536
800-307-2529; Fax: 831-625-3225
www.kagan.com
Facebook, Twitter, LinkedIn

Tim Baskerville, President
Tom Johnson, Marketing Manager

Authoritative look inside the business of renting and selling video cassettes. Exclusive estimates of retail and wholesale transactions and inventories. Tracking movies into the home. Three month trial is available.
Cost: $ 795.00
Frequency: Monthly

Magazines & Journals

2508 **AES Journal**
Audio Engineering Society
551 Fifth Ave
Suite 1225
New York, NY 10176

212-661-8528; Fax: 212-682-0477
www.aes.org
Facebook, Twitter, YouTube, Instagram

Bozena Kostek, Editor-in-Chief

Journal of the Audio Engineering Society.
Cost: $310.00
Frequency: Monthly

2509 **ARtillery Intelligence**
VR/AR Association
Palo Alto, CA 94303

nathan@thevrara.com
www.thevrara.com
Facebook, Twitter, LinkedIn, YouTube

Nathan Pettyjohn, Founder & President
Kris Kolo, Global Executive Director

Research and data package for VR/AR professionals.
Founded in 2015

2510 **AudioVideo International**
Dempa Publications
275 Madison Avenue
New York, NY 10016-1101

212-682-3755; Fax: 212-682-2730
www.dempa.net/

Harry Iguchi, General Manager

Articles cover systems of home entertainment.
Cost: $48.00
100 Pages
Frequency: Quarterly
Founded in 1950

2511 **CE Pro**
EH Publishing
PO Box 989
Framingham, MA 01701-0989

508-820-1515; Fax: 508-663-1599
www.electronichouse.com

Kenneth D. Moyes, President
Jason Knott, Editor

Provides timely, top quality business, industry and product information, technical how-to articles, product comparisons, dealer profiles and marketing and management tips.
Frequency: Monthly
Circulation: 30,000

2512 **CVC Report**
Creative Video Consulting
PO Box 5195
Saratoga Springs, NY 12866-8038

212-533-9870; Fax: 212-473-3772
www.cvc.nic.in

Mitchell Rowen, Publisher

Information for music video programming and production fields, contains charts, reviews, play lists, industry dialogue and news.
Cost: $225.00
Frequency: BiMonthly
Circulation: 800

2513 **Digital Content Producer**
Prism Business Media
9800 Metcalf Avenue
Overland Park, KS 66212-2216

913-341-1300; Fax: 913-967-1905
subs@prismb2b.com
www.digitalcontentproducer.com

Scott Schwadron, Publisher
Cynthia Wisehart, Editoral Director
Kerby Asplund, Marketing
Laury Reeves, Circulation Manager

Features new product listings, updates on state of the art technology applied to new production techniques, and business industry news.
Cost: $70.00
Frequency: Monthly
Circulation: 50000
Founded in 1975

2514 **Essential Facts About the Computer and Video Game Industry**
Entertainment Software Association
601 Massachusetts Avenue NW
Suite 300
Washington, DC 20001

esa@theesa.com
www.theesa.com

Stanley Pierre-Louis, President & CEO
Gina Vetere, SVP & General Counsel
Andrew Bowins, SVP, Comm. & Public Affairs
Ana Molina, CFO

Tracks statistics about the video game industry in the US.
Frequency: Annual
Founded in 2000

2515 **Lighting & Sound America**
Professional Lighting and Sound Association
630 Ninth Ave
Suite 609
New York, NY 10036

212-244-1505; Fax: 212-244-1502
lsa@plasa.org
www.lightingandsoundamerica.com
Facebook, Twitter

Jackie Tien, Publisher
David W Barbour, Editor-in-Chief

Monthly publication dedicated to the entertainment technology industry.

2516 **Loading...**
Canadian Game Studies Assocation

jennifer.jenson@ubc.ca
gamestudies.ca

Suzanne de Catell, Editor
Jennifer Jenson, Co-Editor

Official journal of the Canadian Game Studies Assocation with articls on research into digital games.

2517 **Markee**
HJK Publications
1018 Rosetta Dr
Deltona, FL 770-341-08

386-774-8881; Fax: 386-774-8908
www.markeemag.com/
Facebook, Twitter, LinkedIn

Janet Karcher, Publisher
Jonathan T Hutchinson, Editor-In-Chief
Shirley Boone, Circulation
Shirley Boone, Circulation

For the Southeast and Southwest film industry.
Cost: $24.00
Frequency: Monthly
Circulation: 12200
Founded in 1986

2518 **PRC News**
Corbell Publishing Company
201 S Alvarado St
Suite 410
Los Angeles, CA 90057-2353

213-483-4559; Fax: 310-312-4551
info@corbell.com
www.corbell.com
Facebook, Twitter, LinkedIn

Gabriel Carabello, President
Eric Jacobson, Senior VP
Maria Arnone, Publisher
Kelly Conlin, CEO
Lori Reeves, Circulation Manager

Contains information on pre-recorded videos, software, hardware and blank cassettes, includes industry news, pricing and distribution updates, and reviews videos soon to be released.
Cost: $577.00
8 Pages
Frequency: Monthly
Circulation: 2000
ISSN: 0898-302X
Founded in 1988
Printed in one color

2519 **Professional Audio-Video Retailers**
10 E 22nd Street
Suite 301
Lombard, IL 60148-6191

630-268-1500
800-621-0298; Fax: 630-953-8957
webmaster@paralink.org
www.paralink.org

Rosemary Wenstrom

An organization formed to assist the owners and operators of independently owned, high-end audio/video stores to work toward the mutually compatible goal of providing services to members which would be unattainable by retailers working separately.
204 Members

2520 **Prosound News**
United Entertainment Media
28 East 28th Street
27th Fl
New York, NY 10016

212-378-0400; Fax: 212-378-2170
sedorusa@optonline.net
www.governmentvideo.com
Facebook, Twitter, LinkedIn

Gary Rhodes, International Ssales Manager
Frequency: Monthly
Circulation: 25500
Founded in 1978

2521 **Sound & Video Contractor**
Primedia
PO Box 12901
Shawnee Mission, KS 66282-2901

913-341-1300
866-505-7173; Fax: 913-514-6895
www.primedia.com
Facebook, Twitter, LinkedIn

Eric Jacobson, Senior VP
Maria Arnone, Publisher
Kelly Conlin, CEO
Lori Reeves, Circulation Manager
Kiby Asplund, Marketing Manager

Contains information on sound systems, video display, security, CCTV, home theater, and automation. Delivers in depth instruction and examples of successful installations, fundamental acoustical and video theory and news on new technologies affecting the systems contracting business.
Cost: $35.00
Frequency: Monthly
Circulation: 21000
Founded in 1895
Mailing list available for rent: 20,500 names at $110 per M

2522 **Television Broadcast**
Miller Freeman Publications
28 East 28th Street
Suite 4
New York, NY 10016

212-636-2700; Fax: 212-378-2170
www.governmentvideo.com
Facebook, Twitter, LinkedIn

Gary Rhodes, International Sales Manager

Television Broadcast primarily serves TV stations including commercial, public, educational, religious military TV stations or networks; teleproduction facilities including production, post-production, tape duplication, effects, audio production or independent program producer.
Frequency: Monthly
Circulation: 30,374
Founded in 1978
Printed in 4 colors on glossy stock

2523 **Transactions of the Digital Games Research Association**
Digital Games Research Association

jose.zagal@utah.edu
todigra.org

Jose P. Zagal, Editor-in-Chief
Harald Warmelink, Support Contact

ToDiGRA is an international, open access, refereed, multidisciplinary journal for research on and practice in all aspects of digital games. It is both printed and available online.
ISSN: 2328-9422

2524 **Video & Entertainment**
Fairchild Publications
2407 Timberloch Place
Suite B
New York, NY 77380

281-419-5725
877-652-5295; Fax: 281-419-5712
www.supermarketnews.com

Dan Bagan, President
David Orgal, Editor

2525 **Video Age International**
Video Age International
216 E 75th St
Suite PW
New York, NY 10021-2921

212-288-3933; Fax: 212-734-9033
sales@videoageinternational.com
www.videoageinternational.com
Facebook, Twitter, LinkedIn

Dom Serafini, Publisher

Offers information on program sales and distribution of videocassettes, discs and allied media.
Cost: $30.00
Frequency: 7x/Year
Circulation: 12000

2526 **Video Librarian**
Video Librarian
3435 NE Nine Boulder Dr
Poulsbo
Seabeck, WA 98370
360-626-1259
800-692-2270; Fax: 360-830-9346
vidlib@videolibrarian.com
www.videolibrarian.com
Randy Pitman, President
Anne Williams, Marketing Director
Jazza Williams, Associate Editor
Offers video reviews and news for public, school, academic and special libraries.
Cost: $64.00
56 Pages
Circulation: 2000
ISSN: 0887-6851
Founded in 1986

2527 **Video Store Magazine**
201 Sandpointe Ave
Suite 600
Santa Ana, CA 92707-8700
714-338-6700
800-854-3112; Fax: 714-513-8402
selliott@advanstar.com
www.homemediaretailing.com
Thomas Arnold, Editor
Don Rosenberg, Publisher
Susan Elliott, Publications Coordinator
Steven J. Apple, Director, Business Development
Renee Rosado, Online Manager
Offers market research and buying information for industry people.
Cost: $48.00
Frequency: Weekly
Circulation: 44257

2528 **Videomaker Magazine**
Videomaker
1350 East 9th Street
PO Box 4591
Chico, CA 95927-4591
530-891-8410; Fax: 530-891-8443
www.videomaker.com
Stephen Muratore, Editor-in-Chief
Jennifer O'Rourke, Managing Editor
Information about the world of camcorders, computers, tools and techniques for making video in a way that is timely, applicable, pertinent, engaging and understandable. Each month we teach production techniques, explain technology and include no less than two informative buyer's guides of products central to video. In addition, we are committed to objective analysis of videomaking products so our audience can rely on us for unbiased reporting.
Cost: $3.99
Frequency: Monthly
Circulation: 90,000
ISSN: 0889-4973
Printed in 4 colors on glossy stock

Trade Shows

2529 **Augmented World Expo**
AugmentedReality.org
Home Page: www.awexr.com
Facebook, Twitter, LinkedIn, YouTube
Ori Inbar, CEO
Showcase for technologies making the world more interactive: augmented reality; virtual reality; and wearable technology.
4000 Attendees

2530 **Canadian Game Studies Association Annual Conference**
Canadian Game Studies Assocation
Home Page: gamestudies.ca
Kym Stewart, Local Arrangement Coordinator
Held in tandem with the Congress of the Humanities and Social Sciences.

2531 **Electronic Entertainment Expo**
Entertainment Software Association
601 Massachusetts Avenue NW
Suite 300
Washington, DC 20001
Home Page: www.e3expo.com
Facebook, Twitter, YouTube, Instagram
Stanley Pierre-Louis, President & CEO
Andrew Bowins, SVP, Comm. & Public Affairs
Video game industry showcase featuring technology debuts and product launches.
50000 Attendees

2532 **Game Developers Conference**
Informa Tech
415-947-6926
800-216-4916
gdcfeedback@ubm.com
gdconf.com
Facebook, Twitter, LinkedIn, YouTube, Instagram
The GDC provides education, inspiration, and networking opportunities to the video game development community, including programmers, artists, producers, game designers, audio professionals, and business leaders. The conference features discussions, awards ceremonies, community spaces for networking, and the GDC Expo.
Founded in 1988

2533 **GameSoundCon**
SoundCon, LLC
4735 134th Place SE
Bellevue, WA 98006
425-956-3725
brian@gamesoundcon.com
www.gamesoundcon.com
Twitter
Conference devoted to the art, technology, and business of video game audio.
350+ Attendees
Founded in 2009

2534 **Independent Games Festival**
Informa Tech
303 Second Street
Suite 900, S. Tower
San Francisco, CA 94107
chairperson@igf.com
igf.com
Twitter
The IGF recognizes the best independent game developers, and encourages innovation in game development.
Founded in 1998

2535 **International Consumer Electronics Show (CES)**
Consumer Technology Association
1919 South Eads Street
3000 S. Paradise
Arlington, VA 22202
703-907-7600
866-858-1555; Fax: 703-907-7675
cta@cta.tech
www.cta.tech
Facebook, Twitter, LinkedIn
Gary Shapiro, President & CEO
David Hagan, Chairman
The CES reaches across global markets, connects the industry and enables consumer electronics to grow and thrive. International CES is owned and prroduced by the Consumer Electronics Association (CEA).
Frequency: Annual

2536 **International Society of Videographers**
PO Box 296
Sparkill, NY 10976-0296
859-624-5429; Fax: 845-359-8527
Steve Jambeck, Executive Director
Exchanges information on technologies, techniques, and equipment, sponsors Hall of Fame and an international convention.
Founded in 1981

2537 **VR/AR Global Summit**
VR/AR Association
Palo Alto, CA 94303
am@thevrara.com
www.thevrara.com
Facebook, Twitter, LinkedIn, YouTube
Nathan Pettyjohn, Founder & President
Kris Kolo, Global Executive Director
Anne-Marie Enns, Executive Producer
Summits bring together enterprise, hardware, software, and content providers for educational sessions and networking.
Founded in 2015

2538 **Virtual Reality Developers Conference**
Informa Tech
415-947-6926
800-216-4916
gdcfeedback@ubm.com
www.gdconf.com/vrdc
Facebook, Twitter, LinkedIn, YouTube, Instagram
The VRDC is a two-day summit for developers of Virtual Reality and Augmented Reality entertainment.

2539 **WABE Convention**
Western Association of Broadcast Engineers
8120 Beddington Boulevard, NW
Suite 319
Calgary, AB T3K 2A8
403-630-4907
info@wabe.ca
wabe.ca
Bill Stovold, President
An annual convention that highlights the best of radio and television technologies and provides a venue for engineers to share information and their experiences.

Directories & Databases

2540 **AV Market Place**
Information Today
143 Old Marlton Pike
Medford, NJ 08055-8750
609-654-6266
800-300-9868; Fax: 609-654-4309
custserv@infotoday.com
www.infotoday.com
Thomas H Hogan, President
Roger R Bilboul, Chairman Of The Board
The complete business directory of audio, audio visual, computer systems, film, video, and pro-

gramming with industry yellow pages. The only guide needed to find more than 7,500 companies that create, apply or distribute AV equipment and services for business, education, science, and government.
Cost: $199.95
1700 Pages
Frequency: February
ISBN: 1-573871-87-7

2541 **Orion Blue Book: Computer**
Orion Research Corporation
14555 N Scottsdale Rd
Suite 330
Scottsdale, AZ 85254-3487
480-951-1114; Fax: 480-951-1117
Roger Rohrs, Owner
A list of manufacturers of data processing hardware and products for the computer industry.
Cost: $200.00
Frequency: Annual

2542 **Orion Blue Book: Video and Television**
Orion Research Corporation
14555 N Scottsdale Rd
Suite 330
Scottsdale, AZ 85254-3487
480-951-1114
800-844-0759; Fax: 480-951-1117
www.bluebook.com
Roger Rohrs, Owner
List of more than 450 manufacturers of video and television products such as cameras, recorders, disc players, projectors, extenders, microphones, mixers, processors and color monitors.
Cost: $144.00
Frequency: Annual January

2543 **Salem Press Online Platform**
Grey House Publishing
4919 Route 22
PO Box 56
Amenia, NY 12501
800-221-1592; Fax: 201-968-0511
csr@salempress.com
online.salempress.com
The new Salem Press platform houses more than 500 titles including all of Salem's Health, Literature, History and Science titles in addition to select titles from the Grey House Publishing and H.W. Wilson product lines. Online access is free with each print purchase and includes an unlimited number of simultaneous users and remote access.

2544 **Video Networks**
Bay Area Video Coalition
1111 17th Street
San Francisco, CA 94107-2406
415-613-3282; Fax: 415-861-4316
www.bavc.com
List of over 100 film festivals for independent video producers and artists.
Cost: $3.00
Frequency: Annual

2545 **Video Source Book**
Gale/Cengage Learning
Po Box 09187
Detroit, MI 48209-0187
248-699-4253
800-877-4253; Fax: 248-699-8049
gale.galeord@cengage.com
www.gale.com
Facebook, Twitter, LinkedIn, You Tube
Patrick C Sommers, President
The Video Source Book continues its comprehensive coverage of the wide universe of video offerings with listing for more than 130,000 complete program listings, encompassing over 160,000 videos.
Frequency: Annual
ISBN: 1-414435-09-6
Mailing list available for rent

Industry Web Sites

2546 **fla-alarms.org**
Alarm Association of Florida
An association for the alarm and low voltage industry, providing information for consumers and contractors as well as training for members.

2547 **http://gold.greyhouse.com**
G.O.L.D Grey House OnLine Databases
Grey House Publishing's online database platform, GOLD, offers Quick Search, Keyword Search and Expert Search for most business sectors including video and audio markets. The GOLD platform makes finding the information you need quick and easy - whether you're a novice searcher or an experienced database user. All of Grey House's directory products are available for subscription on the GOLD platform.

2548 **www.1394ta.org**
1394 Trade Association

2549 **www.asid.org**
American Society of Interior Designers (ASID)

2550 **www.avreps.org**
Independent Professional Representatives Org

2551 **www.bavc.org**
Bay Area Video Collection

2552 **www.bicsi.org**
BICSI

2553 **www.caba.org**
Continental Automated Buildings Association (CABA)

2554 **www.cedia.org**
Custom Electronic Design & Installation Associatio

2555 **www.comptia.org**
CompTIA
A nonprofit trade association created by representatives of five microcomputer leaderships and is a provider of professional certifications for the information technology (IT) industry.

2556 **www.copper.org**
Copper Development Association (CDA)
CDA is committed to promoting the proper use of copper materials in sustainable, efficient applications for business, industry and the home.

2557 **www.csaaul.org**
Central Station Alarm Association

2558 **www.greyhouse.com**
Grey House Publishing
Authoritative reference directories for most business sectors including audio and video markets. Users can search the online databases with varied search criteria allowing for custom searches by product category, geographic area, sales volume, keyword, subject and more. Full Grey House catalog and online ordering also available.

2559 **www.nsca.org**
National Systems Contractors Association (NSCA)

2560 **www.riaa.org**
Recording Industry Association of America

2561 **www.siaonline.org**
Security Industry Association

2562 **www.soc.org**
Society of Camera Operators

2563 **www.tiaonline.org**
Telecommunications Industry Association (TIA)

2564 **www.vsda.org**
Video Software Dealers Association

Associations

2565 **Aeronautical Radio & Research Incorporated**
400 Collins Road N.E.
Cedar Rapids, IA 52498
319-295-1000
800-633-6882; Fax: 410-266-2020
corpcomm@arinc.com
www.arinc.com
Facebook, Twitter, LinkedIn, YouTube, Google+, Instagram
Stephen Timm, President
Isolde Karro, Chief Communications Officer
Christoph Feddersen, General Counsel
Provider of communications, engineering and integration solutions, we help our customers in the defense, commercial and government industries mitigate risk, improve operational and systems performance and meet program requirements.
Founded in 1929

2566 **Aeronautical Repair Station Association**
121 N Henry St
Alexandria, VA 22314-2903
703-739-9543; Fax: 703-299-0254
arsa@arsa.org
www.arsa.org
Facebook, Twitter, LinkedIn, RSS, Google+
Sarah MacLeod, Executive Director
Marshall Filler, Managing Dir. & Geberal Counsel
Christian Klein, Executive VP
Brett Levanto, VP, Operations
Kimberly Dimmick, Client Information Manager
Helps develop guidance, policy and interpretations that are clear, concise and consistent, and applied uniformly to all similarly situated companies and individuals.
700 Members
Founded in 1984

2567 **Aerospace Industries Association**
2310 E El Segundo Blvd
El Segundo, CA 90245-4609
310-336-5000; Fax: 310-336-7055
membership@aia-aerospace.org
www.aero.org
Facebook, Twitter, Youtube, Google+
Steven Isakowitz, President & CEO
Wayne Goodman, Executive Vice President
Kevin Bell, VP, Space Program Operations
Tammy Choy, VP & Chief Information Officer
David Radzanowski, VP & Chief Financial Officer
The Aerospace Industries Association shapes public policy that ensures the US aerospace, defense and homeland security industry remains preeminent and that its members are successful and profitable in a changing global market.
283 Members
Founded in 1919

2568 **Aerospace Medical Association**
320 S Henry St
Alexandria, VA 22314-3579
703-739-2240; Fax: 703-739-9652
inquiries@asma.org
www.asma.org
Facebook, Twitter, LinkedIn
Jeffery C. Sventek,MS,CASp, Executive Director
Gisselle Vargas, Operations Manager
Gloria Carter, Director, Member Services
Our mission is to apply and advance scientific knowledge to promote and enhance the health, safety and performance of those involved in aerospace and related activities.
3200 Members
Founded in 1929
Mailing list available for rent

2569 **Aerospace States Association**
107 S West St
Alexandria, VA 22314
202-257-4872; Fax: 703-548-8784
huettner@aerostates.org
www.aerostates.org
Facebook, Twitter
Will Ainsworth, National Chair
Ross Garelick Bell, Executive Director
Represents perspective of states with aerospace industries to the federal government as it defines national aerospace policy.
Founded in 1991

2570 **Air Force Association**
1501 Lee Hwy
Suite 400
Arlington, VA 22209-1198
703-247-5800
800-727-3337; Fax: 703-247-5853
membership@afa.org
www.afa.org
Facebook, Twitter, LinkedIn, Youtube, Blogger
Bruce Wright, President
Douglas Raaberg, Executive Vice President
Perry Currier, Manager, Corporate Relations
Bridget Dongu, Manager, Communications
Erika Salesses, Manager, Business Development
Independent nonprofit, civilian organization promoting public understanding of aerospace power and the pivotal role it plays in the security of the nation.
1400 Members
Founded in 1946

2571 **Air Taxi Association**
300 Galleria Parkway
Atlanta, GA 30339
770-563-7400
www.travelport.com
Twitter, LinkedIn, Youtube
Greg Webb, Chief Executive Officer
Eric Bray, Chief Financial Officer
Margaret Cassidy, Executive Vp & General Counsel
Jennifer Catto, Chief Marketing Officer
Nick Dagg, Chief Commercial Officer
Backed by leading air taxi companies, ATXA's mission is to speed the adoption of the air taxi model so that more business, individuals, and communities can enjoy the benefits of direct, personal flights.
Founded in 2006

2572 **Air Traffic Control Association**
1101 King St
Suite 300
Alexandria, VA 22314
703-299-2430; Fax: 703-299-2437
info@atca.org
www.atca.org
Facebook, Twitter, LinkedIn, RSS,YouTube
Peter Dumont, President & CEO
Kenneth Carlisle, Director, Meetings & Expositions
Abigail Glenn-Chase, Dir., Programming & Communications
Christine Oster, COO & CFO
Kristen Knott, Managing Editor & Writer
Works to establish and maintain a safe and efficient air traffic control system.
2400+ Members
Founded in 1956

2573 **Air Transport Association of America**
1301 Pennsylvania Ave NW
Suite 1100
Washington, DC 20004-1738
202-626-4000
800-497-3326; Fax: 202-626-4166
a4a@airlines.org
www.airlines.org
Facebook, Twitter, LinkedIn, YouTube, Instagram
Nicholas E. Calio, President/CEO
Paul R. Archambeault, Senior VP/CFO/COO
Patricia Vercelli, SVP/General Counsel/Secretary
Christine M. Burgeson, SVP, Global Government Affairs
John Heimlich, VP & Chief Economist
Supports and assists its members by promoting the air transport industry and the safety, cost effectiveness, and technical advancement of its operators; advocating common industry positions before state and local governments; conducting designated industry-wide programs; and assuring governmental and public understanding of all aspects of air transport.
25 Members
Founded in 1936

2574 **Aircraft Electronics Association**
3570 NE Ralph Powell Rd
Lees Summit, MO 64064
816-347-8400; Fax: 816-347-8405
info@aea.net
www.aea.net
Facebook, Twitter, LinkedIn, Youtube, Flickr
Mike Adamson, President & CEO
Debra McFarland, Executive Vice President
Linda Adams, VP, Member Services
Aaron Ward, Director, Operations
Geoff Hill, Director, Communications
Persons interested in aviation and avionics.
1200 Members

2575 **Aircraft Owners & Pilots Association**
421 Aviation Way
Frederick, MD 21701-4756
301-695-2000
800-872-2672; Fax: 301-695-2375
phil.boyer@aopa.org
www.aopa.org
Facebook, Twitter, LinkedIn, Google+, Instagram
Mark Baker, President & CEO
Jiri Marousek, SVP, Marketing
Erica Saccoia, SVP, Finance
AOPA has achieved its prominent position through effective advocacy, enlightened leadership, technical competence, and hard work. Providing member services that range from representation at the federal, state, and local levels to legal services, advice, and other assistance, we have built a service organization that far exceeds any other in the aviation community. AOPA ePilot and AOPA ePilot Flight Training Edition unique e-mail newsletters issued every Friday morning only to AOPA members.
405k Members
Founded in 1939

2576 **Airline Pilots Association International**
1625 Massachusetts Ave NW
Suite 800
Washington, DC 20036
703-689-2270; Fax: 202-797-4052
www.alpa.org
Facebook, Twitter, LinkedIn, YouTube, Instagram, Flickr
Joe DePete, President
Bob Fox, First VP
Bill Couette, VP Administration

Joseph Genovese, Jr., VP Finance
Russell Sklenka, Executive Administrator

Promotes airplane use and co-operates with government agencies and private and public flying organizations to increase general safety.
64000 Members
Founded in 1931

2577 **Airport Consultants Council**
908 King St
Suite 100
Alexandria, VA 22314

703-683-5900; Fax: 703-683-2564
info@acconline.org
www.acconline.org
Facebook, Twitter, LinkedIn, Google+

T.J. Schulz, President
Sylvia Palmer, Dir., Ops. & Regulatory Affairs
Lisa Deyo, Dir., Education & Accredation
Daniel Jagdmann, Manager, Data Services & Membership

Represents the majority of airport consulting firms in the United States.
200+ Members
Founded in 1978

2578 **Airports Association Council International**
1615 L Street NW
Suite 300
Washington, DC 20036

202-293-8500
888-424-7767; Fax: 202-331-1362
www.aci.aero
Facebook, Twitter, LinkedIn, Youtube

Luis Felipe De Oliveira, Director General
Michael Rossell, SVP, International Relations
Antoine Rostworowski, SVP, Programmes/Commercial Services
Dominic Tetu, CFO & VP, Administration
David Whitely, VP, Marketing & Communications

Members are boards, commissions, local governmental entities operating public airport facilities and more.
240 Members
Founded in 1947

2579 **Allied Pilots Association**
14600 Trinity Blvd
Suite 500
Fort Worth, TX 76155-2512

817-302-2272; Fax: 817-302-2119
public-comment@alliedpilots.org
www.alliedpilots.org
Facebook, Twitter, Youtube

Dave Ahles, Executive Director
Captian Eric Ferguson, President
Captain Patrick O'Rourke, Vice President

Provides all the traditional union representation services for its members. This includes the lobbying of airline pilots views to Congress and government agencies. In addition, it devotes more than 20 percent of its dues income to support aviation safety.
11500 Members
Founded in 1963

2580 **American Astronautical Society**
6352 Rolling Mill Place
Suite 102
Springfield, VA 22152-2370

703-866-0020; Fax: 703-866-3526
aas@astronautical.org
www.astronautical.org
Facebook, Twitter, Youtube

Jim Way, Executive Director
Sarah Robertson, Communications Coordinator
Patrick Rouin, Events Manager

Independent scientific and technical group in the United States exclusively dedicated to the advancement of space science and exploration.
1400 Members
Founded in 1954

2581 **American Bonanza Society**
Mid-Continent Airport
PO Box 12888
Wichita, KS 67277

316-945-1700; Fax: 316-945-1710
www.bonanza.org
Facebook, Twitter, LinkedIn

Whit Hickman, Executive Director
Lauren Bayless, Director, Member Services
Coy Cross, Controller
Dara Quastad, Member Services

We are nearly 10,000 owners and pilots of Bonanza, Baron and Travel Air type aircraft who have banded together to share information and experiences involving the operation and maintenance of the Beech produced aircraft. Together, we offer an underwriter recognized flight proficiency program, and service clinics scheduled throughout the year at various locations. These clinics provide members the opportunity to have their aircraft evaluated by highly experienced ABS technical personnel.
10K Members
Founded in 1967

2582 **American Helicopter Society**
2701 Prosperity Avenue
Suite 210
Fairfax, VA 22031

703-684-6777
855-247-4685; Fax: 703-739-9279
staff@vtol.org
www.vtol.org
Facebook, Twitter, LinkedIn

Mike Hirschberg, Executive Director
Valerie Sheehan, Director Of Membership
Randy Johnson, Director Of Information Resources
David Renzi, Director Of Meetings & Advertising

Promotes the interests of designers, engineers and manufacturers of the vertical flight industry. Serving as a clearinghouse for technical information, the society publishes several periodicals, organizes the largest vertical flight technology display in the world, and maintains a comprehensive library.
6000 Members
Founded in 1944

2583 **American Institute of Aeronautics and Astronautics**
1801 Alexander Bell Dr
Suite 500
Reston, VA 20191-4344

703-264-7500
800-639-2422; Fax: 703-264-7551
custserv@aiaa.org
www.aiaa.org
Facebook, Twitter, LinkedIn, YouTube, Flickr, Instagram

Basil Hassan, President
Daniel Dumbacher, Executive Director
Steve Sidorek, Dir., Public Policy/Gov. Relations
Brian Talbot, Sr. Dir., Marketing & Communication

Advancing the arts, sciences and technology of aeronautics and astronautics and promotes the professionalism of those engaged in these pursuits.
31,00 Members
Founded in 1930

2584 **Army Aviation Association of America**
593 Main Street
Monroe, CT 06468-2830

203-268-2450; Fax: 203-268-5870
aaaa@quad-a.org
www.quad-a.org
Facebook, Twitter, LinkedIn, Youtube

Bill Harris, Executive Director
Barbara McCann, Executive Assistant
Mark Albertson, Historian
Jennifer Chittem, Marketing Communications
Janis Arena, Manager

A professional force that holds the aviation community, both military and industry together.

2585 **Association of Air Medical Services**
909 N Washington Street
Suite 410
Alexandria, VA 22314

703-836-8732; Fax: 703-836-8920
jfiegel@aams.org
www.aams.org

Cameron Curtis, President & CEO
Garet Turner, VP, Member Experience
Christopher Eastlee, VP, Public Affairs
Christina Childs, Director, Special Events
Diana Lundie, Tradeshow Manager

Voluntary nonprofit organization, encourages and supports its members in maintaining a standard of performance reflecting safe operations and efficient, high quality patient care. Built on the idea that representation from a variety of medical transport services and businesses can be brought together to share information, collectively resolve problems and provide leadership in the medical transport community. We provide a e-mail newsletter called Capitol Watch for AAMS Members.
581 Members
Founded in 1980

2586 **Association of Flight Attendants-CWA**
501 3rd St NW
Suite 1
Washington, DC 20001

202-434-1300
800-424-2401; Fax: 202-434-1411
info@afacwa.org
www.afacwa.org
Facebook, Twitter, Youtube

Sara Nelson, International President
Debora Sutor, International VP
Kevin Creighan, International Secretary/Treasurer

Represents over 50,000 flight attendants at 26 airlines, serving as a voice for flight attendants at their workplace, in the industry, the media and on Capitol Hill.
55M Members
Founded in 1930

2587 **Association of Naval Aviation**
6551 Loisdale Road
Suite 222
Springfield, VA 22150

703-960-6806; Fax: 703-960-6807
anahqtr@aol.com
www.anahq.org
Facebook, Twitter, LinkedIn

Mark Fitzgerald, Chair
David L. Philman, President
Elizabeth Phillips, Secretary/Treasurer
David Kennedy, Editor
Samantha Gonzalez, Manager, Business & Membership

Professional, nonprofit, educational and fraternal society of Naval Aviation, whose main purpose is to educate the public and our national leaders on the vital roles of the Navy, Marine Corp and Coast Guard Aviation as key elements of our national defense posture. ANA continuously seeks to elucidate the key current issues impacting Naval Aviation through published writing, symposia, speeches and discussions with various interest groups.

2588 **Aviation Development Council**
141-07 20th Ave
Suite 404
Whitestone, NY 11357

718-746-0212; Fax: 718-746-1006
www.adcnynj.org

William Huisman, Executive Director

Addresses noise problems from air carriers in the New York - New Jersey region.
Founded in 1962

2589 **Aviation Distributors and Manufacturers**
Fernley & Fernley Inc
100 North 20th Street
Suite 400
Philadelphia, PA 19103-1462

215-320-3872; Fax: 215-564-2175
adma@fernley.com
www.adma.org
Facebook

Wolfgang Dillbaum, President

Promotes interests of wholesalers and manufacturers of general aviation aircraft parts and supplies.
Founded in 1943

2590 **Aviation Insurance Association**
7200 W 75th Street
Overland Park, KS 66204

913-627-9632; Fax: 913-381-2515
mandie@aiaweb.org
www.aiaweb.org
Facebook, Blog

Amanda Loroff, Executive Director
Jim Gardner, President

A not-for-profit association dedicated to expanding the knowledge of and promoting the general welfare of the aviation insurance industry through numerous educational programs and events.
900 Members
Founded in 1976

2591 **Aviation Suppliers Association**
2233 Wisconsin Ave NW
Suite 503
Washington, DC 20007

202-347-6899; Fax: 202-347-6894
info@aviationsuppliers.org
www.aviationsuppliers.org
Facebook, Twitter, LinkedIn

Michele Dickstein, President
Jason Dickstein, General Counsel & Gov. Affairs Rep.
Jeanne Meade, VP, Member Services
Tony Bringham, Program & Services Coordinator

The voice of the aviation parts supply industry on regulatory and legal matters.
604 Members
Founded in 1993

2592 **Aviation Technician Education Council**
117 North Henry Street
Alexandria, VA 22314-2903

703-548-2030
atec@atec-amt.org
www.atec-amt.org

Gary Hoyle, President
Crystal Maguire, Executive Director
Tarra Ruttman, Operations Manager

Organization of Federal Aviation Administration approved Aviation Maintenance Technician schools and supporting industries.
Founded in 1961

2593 **Cessna Owner Organization**
N7528 Aanstad Road
PO Box 5000
Iola, WI 54945

715-445-5000
888-692-3776; Fax: 715-445-4053
help@cessnaowner.org
www.cessnaowner.org
Facebook

Membership support organization for Cessna aircraft owners.
5000 Members
Founded in 1975

2594 **Civil Aviation Medical Association**
PO Box 2382
Peachtree City, GA 30269-2382

770-487-0100; Fax: 770-487-0080
civilavmed@yahoo.com
www.civilavmed.org

Gerald Saboe, President
Sherry Sandoval, Executive Vice President
Leigh Speicher, VP, Management & Planning
Edmond Feeks, VP, Communications & Representation

Aviation medical equipment, supplies and services. Working on behalf of physicians engaged in the practice of aviation medicine and dedicated to civil aviation safety.
Cost: $5.00
800+ Members
Founded in 1948

2595 **Experimental Aircraft Association**
3000 Poberezny Road
3000 Poberezny road
Oshkosh, WI 54902

920-426-4800
800-564-6322; Fax: 920-426-6761
webmaster@eaa.org
www.eaa.org
Facebook, Twitter

Jack Pelton, Chief Executive Officer & Chair
Brian Wierzbinski, Executive VP & CFO
Rick Larsen, VP, Communities & Mem. Programming
Jim Busha, VP, Publications, Marketing, Mem.
Karen Kryzaniak, VP, Risk Management & HR

Works to keep aviation history alive. Members are active restorers and enthusiasts working to keep vintage aircraft in the air and flying for the pleasure and education of themselves and the public at large. EAA's weekly electronic newsletter e-Hot Line.
170M Members
Founded in 1953

2596 **Flight Safety Foundation**
801 N Fairfax Street
Suite 400
Alexandria, VA 22314-1774

703-739-6700; Fax: 703-739-6708
wahdan@flightsafety.org
www.flightsafety.org
Facebook, Twitter, LinkedIn

Hassan Shahidi, President & CEO
Frank Jackman, VP, Communications
Kenneth Quinn, Secretary/General Counsel
Louise Martin, VP, Membership
Jerry Lederer, Founder

Supported by airlines, aerospace manufacturers, aviation professionals, corporate flight departments and others interested in flight safety.
900 Members
Founded in 1947

2597 **Forecast International**
22 Commerce Rd
Newtown, CT 06470

203-426-0800
800-451-4975; Fax: 203-426-0223
sales@forecast1.com
www.forecastinternational.com
Facebook, Twitter, LinkedIn, Google+

Raymond Jaworowski, Senior Aerospace Analyst
Richard Pettibone, Senior Government Analyst
Jim Head, Sales, Europe, Asia, Middle East
Alfred Struna, Sales, North & South America

Premier provider of market intelligence, forecasting, proprietary research and consulting services.
Founded in 1973

2598 **Future Aviation Professionals of America (FAPA)**
4959 Massachusetts Boulevard
Atlanta, GA 30337

404-997-8097; Fax: 770-997-8111
www.fapa.info

Linda Nelson, Chairman

Provides career information for those seeking careers in aviation, publications, newsletter, interview briefings and Aviation Job Bank. Also provides personal financial planning for airline pilots.
15M Members
Founded in 1974

2599 **General Aviation Manufacturers Association**
1400 K St NW
Suite 801
Washington, DC 20005-2485

202-393-1500; Fax: 202-842-4063
bforan@GAMA.aero
www.gama.aero

Pete Bunce, President & CEO
Andre Castro, Director of Communications
Lani Esparza, Director, Internal Operations
Paul H. Feldman, VP Government Affairs
Bree Foran, Dir., Meetings & Membership Service

Manufacturers of general aviation aircraft and related equipment. Members also operate fleets of aircraft, fixed based operations and pilot training facilities.
50 Members
Founded in 1970

2600 **Helicopter Association International**
1920 Ballanger Ave
Alexandria, VA 22314-2898

703-683-4646
800-435-4976; Fax: 703-683-4745
rotor@rotor.org
www.rotor.com
Facebook, Twitter, LinkedIn

James Viola, President & CEO
Roxanne Fox, Chief Of Staff
Robert Volmer, VP, Marketing Communications
Michael Hertzendorf, VP, Member Service
Kevin Cooper, Chief Financial Officer

Nonprofit organization provides members with services that directly benefit their operations and advances the civil helicopter industry by providing programs to enhance safety, encourage professionalism and promote the unique societal contributions made by the rotary flight industry.
2500 Members
Founded in 1948

2601 Helicopter Safety Advisory Conference
Marathon Oil Company
PO Box 60136
Houston, TX 77205

281-892-4088
www.hsac.org

Promotes safety and seeks to improve operations through establishment of standards of practice.
115 Members
Founded in 1978

2602 International Association of Machinists and Aerospace Workers
9000 Machinists Place
Upper Marlboro, MD 20772

301-967-4500; Fax: 301-967-4588
www.goiam.org
Facebook, Twitter, LinkedIn, YouTube, Instagram, Pinterest

Robert Martinez, Jr., President
Dora Cervantes, General Secretary, Treasurer
Sito Pantoja, VP, Transportation
Rickey Wallace, Vice President
Stan Pickthall, Vice President

Labor union whose mission is to improve job security, wages and benefits for machinists and aerospace workers.
700K+ Members
Founded in 1888

2603 International Coordinating Council of Aerospace Industries Associations
1000 Wilson Blvd.
Suite 1700
Arlington, VA 22209-3928

703-358-1064
www.iccaia.org
LinkedIn

Eric Fanning, Chair
Jim Quick, Vice Chairman
Mitchell Fox, Senior Director, Strategy
Dan Carnelly, Senior Director, Technology

The voice of the world's aerospace manufacturers in matters concerning international standards and regulations for air transport safety and security.
Founded in 1972

2604 International Council of Aircraft Owner and Pilot Associations
421 Aviation Way
Frederick, MD 21701

301-695-2220; Fax: 301-695-2375
iaopa@aopa.org
www.iaopa.org

Mark Baker, President
Craig Spence, Secretary General

Nonprofit federation of 53 autonomous, nongovernmental, national general aviation organizations. Facilitates the movement of general aviation aircraft.
40000 Members
Founded in 1962

2605 International Flight Services Association
1100 Johnson Ferry Road
Suite 300
Atlanta, GA 30342

404-252-3663; Fax: 404-252-0774
ifsanet@gmail.com
ifsa.apex.aero
Facebook, Twitter, Youtube

Joe Leader, Chief Executive Officer
Lauren Costello, Executive Director
Russell Lemieux, Chief Operating Officer
Robin Applebaum, Director, Marketing & Communication
Hannah Perkins, Coordinator, Member Services

The International Flight Services Association is a global professional association created to serve the needs and interests of airline and railway personnel, in-flight and rail caterers and suppliers responsible for providing passenger foodservice on regularly scheduled travel routes.
Founded in 1966

2606 International Society of Women Airline Pilots
6920 S Cimarron Road
Las Vegas, NV 89113

610-220-8904
chairwoman@iswap.org
www.iswap.org

Tara T. Cook, President
Maria Ziadie Haddad, Communications
Katherine Wallace, Captain's Club
Sandra Anderson, Archives/Museum
Amanda Noll, Marketing Advisor

Non-profit organization of career women airline pilots whose purpose is to: celebrate camaraderie; support informational exchange and social interaction among its members in a healthy environment; provide aviation scholarship opportunities for career-seeking women; and inspire future generations of women aviators via educational outreach.
Cost: $44.00
Founded in 1978

2607 Light Aircraft Manufacturers Association
2001 Steamboat Ridge Ct
Daytona Beach, FL 32128-6918

651-592-7565
301-693-2223; Fax: 651-226-1825
info@lama.bz
www.lama.bz

Dan Johnson, Chair/President

Promotes interests of kit-built light aircraft. Membership dues are $125 for voting members and $25 for non-voting members.
50 Members
Founded in 1984

2608 Lighter Than Air Society
Lighter Than Air Socicety
526 S. MAIN ST
Suite 406
Akron, OH 44311-3311

330-535-5827
www.blimpinfo.com

Joseph Huber, President
Ron Browning, Director Business Development

Nonprofit organization whose members are devoted to the study of the history, science and techniques of all forms of buoyant flight.
1000 Members
Founded in 1952

2609 Mount Diablo Pilots Association
PO Box 6632
Concord, CA 94524

925-370-0828
www.mdpa.org
Facebook, Twitter

Rich Cunningham, Director & President
DeWitt Hodge, Director & VP
Rod Mickels, Manager, Membership
Natasha Dotorova, Manager, Newletter & Social Media

To promote good public relations between general aviation enthusiasts and the local community; to encourage participation in fly-ins and other aviation activities; to promote safety and educational activities for pilots; to provide mutual resources of information on flying for members; to furnish information and support to the Contra Costa Airport Advisory Committee and other governmental agencies concerned with aviation; to be a proxy on aviation matters of community concern for its membership

2610 National Aeronautic Association
1 Reagan National Airport
Hangar 7, Suite 202
Washington, DC 20001-6015

703-416-4888
800-644-9777; Fax: 703-416-4877
naa@naa.aero
www.naa.aero

Greg Principato, President & CEO
Art Greenfield, Director, Contest & Records
Stephanie Berry, Director, Awards, Events & Mem.
Kit McCormick, Manager, Office Services

A non-profit association that is dedicated to the advancement of the art, sport and science of aviation in the United States.
3000 Members
Founded in 1905

2611 National Agricultural Aviation Association
1440 Duke Street
Alexandria, VA 22314

202-546-5722; Fax: 202-546-5726
information@agaviation.org
www.agaviation.org
Facebook

Andrew Moore, Chief Executive Officer
Lindsay Barber, Director, Meetings & Marketing
Marisa Beam, Registration, Membership & Programs
Deana Burke, Director, Finance & Operations
Jay Calleja, Manager, Communications

Voice of the aerial application industry, we work to preserve aerial application's place in the protection and production of America's food and fiber supply. Aerial application is one of the safest, fastest, most efficient and economical ways to apply pesticides. It is also the most environmentally friendly tool of modern agriculture.
1,300 Members
Founded in 1966

2612 National Air Traffic Controllers Association
1325 Massachusetts Ave Nw
Washington, DC 20005-4171

202-628-5451
800-266-0895; Fax: 202-628-5767
web_staff@list.natca.net
www.natca.org
Facebook, Twitter, LinkedIn, Youtube, Instagram

Dean Iacopelli, Chief Of Staff
Marguerite Graf, General Counsel

Lisa Head, Membership Services Coordinator
Preet Mohinder Singh Virk, Comptroller
Thom Metzger, Director, Public Affairs

Founded to ensure safety and longevity of air traffic controller positions around the nation. Represents over 15,000 air traffic controllers throughout the US, Puerto Rico and Guam, along with 2,508 other bargaining unit members that span all areas from engineers and architects to nurses and health care professionals to members of the accounting community.
15000 Members
Founded in 1987

2613 **National Air Transportation Association**
818 Connecticut Avenue
NW Suite 900
Washington, DC 20006

202-774-1535
800-808-6282; Fax: 202-452-0837
www.nata.aero
Facebook, Twitter, LinkedIn, RSS

Timothy Obitts, President & CEO
Jason Miller, CFO & COO
Shannon Chambers, VP, Marketing & Communications
John McGraw, VP, Regulatory Affairs
Jonathon Freye, VP, Government & Public Affairs

Aggressively promotes safety and the success of aviation service businesses through its advocacy efforts before government, the media and the public as well as by providing valuable programs and forums to further its members' prosperity.
Founded in 1940

2614 **National Association of Flight Instructors**
EAA Aviation Center
3101 E Milham Ave
Portage, MI 49002

866-806-6156; Fax: 920-426-6865
nafi@nafinet.org
www.nafinet.org
Facebook, Twitter, LinkedIn, Google+

Robert Meder, Chair
John Niehas, Director, Program Development
David Hipschman, Director & Editor, Publications
Lauretta Godbey, Director, Marketing & Communication
Matt Mathias, Director, Business Development

Dedicated exclusively to raising and maintaining the professional standing of the flight instructor in the aviation community. Maintains a benefits package available for everyone from the independent instructor to those teaching at flight schools. Every other week we'll send NAFI members with access to e-mail and electronic eMentor.
Founded in 1967

2615 **National Business Aviation Association**
1200 G Street NW
Suite 1100
Washington, DC 20005

202-783-9000; Fax: 202-331-8364
info@nbaa.org
www.nbaa.org
Facebook, Twitter, LinkedIn, instagram,youtube,itunes

Edward Bolen, President & CEO
Dan Hubbard, SVP, Communications
Chris Strong, SVP, Conventions & Membership
Marc Freeman, Chief Financial Officer
Steve Brown, Chief Operating Officer

An organization for companies that rely on general aviation aircraft to help make their businesses more efficient, productive and successful.
8000 Members
Founded in 1947

2616 **National EMS Pilots Association**
PO Box 2128
Layton, UT 84041-9128

801-436-7505
877-668-0430; Fax: 866-906-6023
www.nemspa.org
Facebook, Twitter

Miles Dunagan, President
Chris Henson, Secretary

A professional organization dedicated to serving pilots involved in the air-medical transport industry, and to improving the quality and safety of those services
Founded in 1984

2617 **Ninety-Nines**
4300 Amelia Earhart Drive
Suite A
Oklahoma City, OK 73159

405-685-7969
800-994-1929; Fax: 405-685-7985
99s@ninety-nines.org
www.ninety-nines.org
Facebook, Twitter, Google+, Skype

Laura Ohrenberg, Headquarters Manager
Corbi Bulluck, President

International organization of licensed women pilots from 35 countries. We are a nonprofit, charitable membership corporation holding 501(c)(3) US tax status. Members are professional pilots for airlines, industry and government; we are pilots who teach and pilots who fly for pleasure; we are pilots who are technicians and mechanics. First and foremost, we are women who love to fly.
5500 Members
Founded in 1929

2618 **Piper Owners Society**
N7528 Aanstad Rd
Iola, WI 54945

715-445-5000
866-697-4737; Fax: 715-445-4053
help@piperowner.org
www.piperowner.org
Facebook

Dan Weiler, Executive Director
Joe Jones, Publisher
Ryan Jones, Executive Publisher
Dennis Piotrowski, Editor
Kara Grundman, Graphic Designer

To support private owners of all models of Piper light aircraft. Members receive a full color monthly magazine which includes flying experiences, aircraft parts explained and historical features.
Founded in 1987

2619 **Popular Rotorcraft Association**
PO Box 68
Mentone, IN 46539

574-353-7227; Fax: 574-353-7021
praofficemgr@gmail.com
www.pra.org
Facebook, Youtube

Brent Drake, President
Christene Toevs, Vice President
John Rountree, Secretary & General Business Mngr.

A nonprofit organization dedicated to the advancement of knowledge, public education and safety among Rotorcraft enthusiasts worldwide.
2000 Members
Founded in 1962

2620 **Professional Aeromedical Transport**
PO Box 7519
Alexandria, VA 22307

800-541-7517

Purpose is to standardize and upgrade services of aeromedical transport operations. Membership is open to companies and individuals active in the industry.
170 Members
Founded in 1986

2621 **Professional Aviation Maintenance Association**
400 North Washington Street
Suite 300
Alexandria, VA 22314

87- 90- 541
800-356-1671; Fax: 616-527-1327
info@pama.org
www.pama.org
Facebook, Twitter, LinkedIn, Google+

John Goglia, President
Ken MacTiernan, Vice President

Enhances professionalism and recognition of the Aviation Maintenance Technician through communication, education, representation and support for continuous improvement in aviation safety.
3300 Members
Founded in 1972

2622 **Regional Airline Association**
2025 M St NW
Suite 800
Washington, DC 20036-3309

202-367-1170; Fax: 202-367-2170
raa@raa.org
www.raa.org
Facebook, Twitter, YouTube

Faye Malarkey Black, President & CEO
Nobuyo Reinsch, VP, Aviation Safety & Security
Michelle Cravez, Manager, Membership, Ops. & Events
Diana Lundie, Exhibit Sales & Sponsorship
Sara Haukap, Manager, Conventions

Membership consists of more than 70 airlines, plus 350 Associate members provide goods and services.
510 Members
Founded in 1975

2623 **Reliability Engineering & Management Institute**
University Of Arizona
1130 N Mountian Avenue
Building 119 Room N 517
Tucson, AZ 85721

520-621-6120; Fax: 520-621-8191
dimitri@u.arizona.edu

Dr Dimitri Kececioglu PE, Prof Aerospace/Mech Engineering

An institute to help provide a working knowledge in reliability engineering.
Frequency: November
Founded in 1971

2624 **Seaplane Pilots Association**
3859 Laird Blvd
Lakeland, FL 33811

863-701-7979
888-772-8923; Fax: 863-701-7588
spa@seaplanes.org
www.seaplanes.org
Facebook, Twitter, YouTube

Steven McCaughey, Executive Director
Ann Gaines, Office Manager
Peter Christie, Advertising Director
Mark Twombly, Water Flying Magazine Editor
Susie Holly, Art Director

Represents members in dozens of seaplane access issues annually and provides numerous exclusive benefits. Members who have provided SPA with a valid email address receive Water Flying Update, a bimonthly e-newsletter that provides recent news, advocacy updates, technical tips, upcoming events, and a tip for using SPA's web site.
375 Members
Founded in 1971

2625 **Soaring Society of America**
PO Box 2100
Hobbs, NM 88241-2100

505-392-1177; Fax: 505-392-8154
membership@ssa.org
www.ssa.org
Facebook, Twitter

Denise Layton, Executive Director
Eric Bick, Editor
Teresa Wilatka, Accounting Manager
Lucy Herrera, Merchandise
Melinda Hughes, Magazine Adv./Membership Services

Fosters and promote all phases of gliding and soaring, nationally and internationally.
16K Members
Founded in 1932

2626 **Society of Experimental Test Pilots**
44814 N Elm Avenue
Lancaster, CA 93534

661-942-9574; Fax: 661-940-0398
setp@setp.org
www.setp.org

Michael Wallace, President
Laurie Balderas, Executive Director
Susan Bennett, Administrator
Tammy McDonald, Membership Office

International organization that seek to promote air safety and contributes to aeronautical advancement by promoting sound aeronautical design and development; interchanging ideas, thoughts and suggestions of the members, assisting in the professional development of experimental pilots, and providing scholarships and aid to members and the families of deceased members.
2000 Members
Founded in 1955

2627 **Society of Flight Test Engineers**
44814 N Elm Avenue
Lancaster, CA 93534

661-949-2095; Fax: 661-949-2096
sfte@sfte.org
www.sfte.org
Facebook, LinkedIn, RSS

Peter Scheidler, President
Douglas Bell, Vice President

Members are engineers whose principal professional interest is the flight testing of aircraft. Purpose is to improve communications in the fields of flight test operations, analysis, instrumentation and data systems. We offer an online newsletter called SFTE Flight Test News.
900 Members
Founded in 1968

2628 **Space Foundation**
4425 Arrowswest Drive
Colorado Spring, CO 80907

719-576-8000
800-691-4000; Fax: 719-576-8801
www.spacefoundation.org
Facebook, Twitter, LinkedIn, Instagram, Google+, RSS, Pinte

Thomas Zelibor, CEO
Holly Roberts, CFO
Shelli Brunswick, COO
Richard Cooper, VP, Strategic Comm. & Outreach
Jane Rasplicka, VP, Finance & Accounting

To advance space-related endeavors to inspire, enable, and propel humanity.
- Members
Founded in 1983

2629 **Tailhook Association**
9696 Businesspark Ave
San Diego, CA 921313-164

858-689-9223
800-322-4665
www.tailhook.org
Facebook, LinkedIn, Google+

Gregory Keithley, Executive Director
Janet Warren, Office Mananger/Membership
Cyndi Deppe, Sales Manager/Convention Assistant
Chris Biggin, Web & Marketing Designer
Hill Goodspeed, Editor-In-Chief

An independent, fraternal, nonprofit organization internationally recognized as the premier supporter of the aircraft carrier and other sea-based aviation.

2630 **The Space Enterprise Council**
CompTIA
3500 Lacey Road
Suite 100
Downers Grove, IL 60515

630-678-8300
866-835-8020; Fax: 630-678-8384
dlogsodon@comptia.org
www.comptia.org
Facebook, Twitter

Todd Thibodeaux, President & CEO
Brian Laffey, CFO
Randy Gross, Chief Information Officer
Courtney Fong, Chief Legal & Privacy Officer
Colleen Hughes, Executive VP, Human Resources

Represents interests of commercial, military and civil sectors of space industry to policymakers.
Founded in 2000

2631 **Transportation-Communications International Union**
3 Research Place
Rockville, MD 20850

301-948-4910
websteward@tcunion.org
www.tcunion.org
Facebook, Twitter

Robert A Scardelletti, President
Russell C Oathout, National General Counsel

Members come from diverse transportation industries. In addition to bargaining and representation of its members, provides mortgage and bankcard programs and other services to its members.
Founded in 1899

2632 **Tripoli Rocketry Association**
PO Box 87
Bellevue, NE 68005

402-884-9530; Fax: 402-884-9531
info@tripoli.org
www.tripoli.org
Facebook, Twitter, LinkedIn, YouTube, Google+

Gerald Meux, President
Gary Dickinson, VP
Dave Rose, Treasurer
Steve Shannon, Secretary

This is a non-profit organization dedicated to the advancement and operation of non-professional high power rocketry.
Founded in 1964

2633 **United States Parachute Association**
5401 Southpoint Centre Boulevard
Fredricksburg, VA 22407

540-604-9740; Fax: 540-604-9741
uspa@uspa.org
www.uspa.org
Facebook, Twitter, LinkedIn, YouTube, Google+

Ed Scott, Executive Director
Randy Ottinger, Director, Government Relations
Stephanie Whittaker, Director, Accounting & HR
Stephanie Seidel, Director, Membership Services
Laura Sharp, Director, Publications

The USPA is a voluntary membership organization of individuals who enjoy and support the sport of skydiving. The purpose of USPA is three-fold: to promote safe skydiving through training, licensing, and instructor qualification programs; to ensure skydiving's rightful place on airports and in the airspace system; and to promote competition and record-setting programs.
33000 Members

2634 **United States Pilots Association**
1652 Indian Point Road
Branson, MO 65616

417-338-2225
jan@uspilots.org
www.uspilots.org

David Forster, President
Jan Hoynacki, Executive Director
Gustavo Rodriguez, VP, Public Relations
Mike Jesch, VP, Safety & Education

Works to promote aviation safety and pilot education and also acts as a forum for exchange of ideas.
5000 Members

2635 **United States Ultralight Association**
16192 Coastal Highway
Lewes, DE 19958

717-339-0200; Fax: 717-339-0063
usua@usua.org
www.usua.org

Dale Hooper, Executive VP
Reginald E DeLoach, President

Annual meeting and exhibits of ultralight and microlight aviation equipment, supplies and services. There will be 20 booths.
3000 Members
Founded in 1985

2636 **University Aviation Association**
2415 Moore's Mill Road
Suite 265-216
Auburn, AL 36830

901-563-0505
uaamail@uaa.aero
www.uaa.aero
Facebook, Twitter, LinkedIn, Youtube

Mary Johnson, President
Dawn Vinson, Executive Director
Laura Swanson, Member Services Coordinator
Missy Reece, Accounts Manager
Nathan Garner, Graphic Designer

The voice of collegiate aviation education to its members, the industry, government and the general public. Through the collective expertise of its members, this nonprofit organization plays a pivotal role in the advancement of degree-granting aviation programs that represent all segments of the aviation industry.
625+ Members
Founded in 1947

2637 **Vintage Aircraft Association**
P.O. Box 3086
Oshkosh, WI 54903-3086

920-426-6110; Fax: 920-426-6579
membership@eaa.org
www.vintageaircraft.org
Facebook, Twitter, LinkedIn, Instagram, Google+, Tumblr, Vi

Susan Dusenbury, President
Tim Popp, Vice President
Dan Wood, Secretary
Jerry Brown, Treasurer
Amy Lemke, Executive Assistant

Brings together people from around the world who share an interest in the aircraft of yesterday.
8000 Members
Founded in 1971

2638 **World Airline Historical Society**
P.O. Box 489
Ocoee, FL 34761

904-221-1446; Fax: 407-522-9352
Information@WAHSOnline.com
www.wahsonline.com
Facebook, Twitter, LinkedIn, Youtube, RSS

Chris Slimmer, President
Don Levine, Secretary/Treasurer

Open to all persons and groups interested in collecting airline memorabilia and the study of the airline industry, past and current.
500 Members
Founded in 1977

Newsletters

2639 **AIA Update**
Aerospace Industries Association
15049 Conference Center Drive
Suite 600
Chantilly, VA 20151-3824

571-307-0000; Fax: 571-307-1001
membership@aia-aerospace.org
www.aero.org

Steven Isakowitz, President & CEO
Frequency: 9x/Year

2640 **ATCA Bulletin**
Air Traffic Control Association
1101 King St
Suite 300
Alexandria, VA 22314-2963

703-299-2430; Fax: 703-299-2437
info@atca.org
www.atca.org
Facebook, Twitter, LinkedIn

Peter F Dumont, President & CEO

Provides information on activities of the association, important developments in the air traffic control industry.
Frequency: Monthly
ISSN: 0400-1915
Founded in 1956
Printed in on matte stock

2641 **ATXA Newsletter**
Air Taxi Association
400 Galleria Parkway
Suite 1500
Atlanta, GA 30339

678-390-0001
www.travelport.com

Offers information and association news for professionals in the aviation industry.
Frequency: Bimonthly, E-Newsletter

2642 **Accident Prevention**
Flight Safety Foundation
801 N Fairfax Street
Suite 400
Alexandria, VA 22314-1774

703-739-6700; Fax: 703-739-6708
apparao@flightsafety.org
www.flightsafety.org

J.A. Donoghue, Director Publications
Mark Lacagnina, Senior Editor
Wayne Rosenkrans, Senior Editor
Linda Werfelman, Senior Editor
Rick Darby, Associate Editor

Focuses on the flight deck, including in-depth reviews of accident reports. Authors offer tips and descriptions on pilot incapacitation, outlines techniques to prevent runway overrun and addresses a wide variety of other subjects aimed at the experienced cockpit crew. Subscription included with FSF membership. Others will be $280.00/year.
4-16 Pages
Frequency: Monthly
Circulation: 3,000
Founded in 1948
Printed in 2 colors

2643 **Aerospace Daily**
AviationNow
1200 G St Nw
Suite 900
Washington, DC 20005-3821

202-383-2378
800-525-5003; Fax: 202-383-2438
aviationdaily@aviationnow.com
www.aviationweek.com

Lee Ewing, Editor-in-Chief
Brett Davis, Managing Editor
Mark Lipowicz, Publisher
George Hamilton, President

Daily intelligence on the defense and space industries. If you're a prime or subcontractor, an aviation, defense or space official, a consultant or analyst, or an engineering or research and development manager, you'll benefit from our news on policy and programs.
8 Pages
Frequency: Daily
Founded in 1963

2644 **Air Safety Week**
Phillips Publishing
7811 Montrose Road
Potomac, MD 20854

703-522-8502
www.phillips.com

Dan Cook, Publisher

Weekly newsletter dealing with aviation safety, security, recreation, certification and accident investigation.
Cost: $695.00
10 Pages
Frequency: Monthly

2645 **Airport Consultants Council News**
Airport Consultants Council
908 King St
Suite 100
Alexandria, VA 22314-3067

703-683-5900; Fax: 703-683-2564
info@acconline.org
www.acconline.org

T.J. Schulz, President
Anthony Mavrogiannis, Editor
Sharon Brown, Operations Manager
Cassandra Lamar, Marketing Manager

Council newsletter offering information on important and relevant issues for the aviation consulting community.
Frequency: Quarterly
Circulation: 300
Founded in 1978

2646 **Airport Operations**
Flight Safety Foundation
801 N Fairfax Street
Suite 400
Alexandria, VA 22314-1774

703-396-6700; Fax: 703-739-6708
apparao@flightsafety.org
www.flightsafety.org

J.A. Donaghue, Director Publications
Mark Lacagnina, Senior Editor
Wayne Rosenkrans, Senior Editor
Linda Werfelman, Senior Editor
Rick Darby, Associate Editor

Directs attention to ground operations that involve aircraft and other equipment, airport personnel and services, air traffic control and passengers. Subscription included with FSF membership. Others will be $280.00/year.
4-8 Pages
Frequency: Bi-Monthly
Founded in 1974
Printed in 2 colors on glossy stock

2647 **Annual Conference Proceedings**
Air Traffic Control Association
1101 King St
Suite 300
Alexandria, VA 22314-2963

703-299-2430; Fax: 703-299-2437
info@atca.org
www.atca.org
Facebook, Twitter, LinkedIn

Peter F Dumont, President & CEO

A compendium of fifty or more air traffic control technical papers, covering the entire range of ATC subjects, authored by ATC experts from the full spectrum of public and private organizations engaged in advancement of the science of air traffic control.

2648 **Antique Airplane Association Newsletter**
Antique Airplance Association
22001 Bluegrass Rd
Ottumwa, IA 52501-8569

641-938-2773; Fax: 641-938-2093
antiqueairfield@sirisonline.com
www.antiqueairfield.com

Robert L Taylor, CEO
Lucinda Reis, Editor

Air museums, US and abroad historical aviation societies, for AAA chapters, flying aircraft company histories, etc. - For AAA Digest: antique and classic aircraft restorations, mystery aircraft, etc.
Founded in 1953
Printed in 4 colors on glossy stock

2649 **Aviation Accident Law & Practice**
LexisNexis Matthew Bender & Company
PO Box 933
Dayton, OH 45401-0933

212-448-2000
800-253-5624; Fax: 518-487-3584

R Kaye Esq., Publisher

Domestic and international laws.

2650 **Aviation Consumer**
Belvoir Publishers
PO Box 2626
Greenwich, CT 06836-2626

203-422-7300; Fax: 203-661-4802

Robert Englander, Publisher
Richard Weeghman, Editor

Offers valuable information to the consumer regarding airports, airlines, safety and values.

2651 **Aviation Daily**
Aviation Week

1200 G Street NW
Suite 922
Washington, DC 20005

202-383-2374
800-525-5003; Fax: 888-385-1428
aviationdaily@aviationnow.com
www.aviationweek.com

Anthony Velocci, Editor-in-Chief
James Asker, Executive Editor
Gregory Hamilton, President
Guy Norris, Senior Editor

Daily intelligence information on the commercial aviation and air transportation industry worldwide.
Cost: $1985.00
10 Pages
Frequency: Daily
Founded in 1939
Printed in on n stock

2652 **Aviation Education News Bulletin**
Aviation Distributors & Manufacturers Association
100 North 20th Street
4th-Floor
Philadelphia, PA 19103-1443

215-320-3872; Fax: 215-564-2175
adma@fernley.com
www.adma.org

F. Charles Elkins, President
Michael Shaw, VP
Kristen Olszewski, Executive Director
Meg Taft, Meeting Manager

Association news pertaining to suppliers, distributors and manufacturers of aviation materials.
Frequency: Monthly
Founded in 1943

2653 **Aviation Law Reports**
CCH
2700 Lake Cook Rd
Riverwoods, IL 60015-3867

847-940-4600
800-835-5224; Fax: 773-866-3095
www.cch.com

Mike Sabbatis, President
Douglas M Winterrose, Vice President & CFO
Jim Bryant, EVP Software Products

News covering aviation law and regulations.
Cost: $2495.00
Frequency: Weekly
Founded in 1913

2654 **Aviation Maintenance**
Professional Aviation Maintenance Association
972 E Tuttle Road
Building 204
Ionia, MI 48846

724-772-4092
800-356-1671; Fax: 616-527-1327
hq@pama.org
www.pama.org

John Goglia, President
Roger Sickler, Chairman
Jeff Gruber, Vice Chairman
John Wicht, Secretary
Richard Wellman, Treasurer

The source for information on the worldwide aviation aftermarket. Covers the latest new business trends, regulatory developments, technical advancements, and new products and services

2655 **Aviation Mechanics Bulletin**
Flight Safety Foundation
801 N Fairfax Street
Suite 400
Alexandria, VA 22314-1774

703-739-6700; Fax: 703-739-6708
apparao@flightsafety.org
www.flightsafety.org

Hassan Shadidi, President/CEO
Roger Rozelle, Publisher
Jerry Lederer, Founder

Directed to the aviation maintenance technician, with an emphasis on airline and corporate operations. Other regular sections include maintenance safety alerts, mechanical-incident reports and reviews of new products of interest to maintenance technicians.
Cost: $24.00
16 Pages
Frequency: Bi-Monthly
Founded in 1953

2656 **Aviation Medical Bulletin**
Aviation Insurance Agency
475 N Central Avenue
PO Box 20787
Atlanta, GA 30320

404-767-7501
800-241-6103; Fax: 404-761-8326
Pilot@harveywatt.com
www.harveywatt.com

Pat Hiebel, President
Sean Daigre, Claims Director

Health education for the professional airline pilot.
Cost: $13.95
Frequency: Monthly
Founded in 1951

2657 **Aviators Hot Line**
Heartland Communications
PO Box 1052
Fort Dodge, IA 50501-1052

515-955-1600
800-247-2000; Fax: 515-955-1668
www.hlipublishing.com

Gale W McKinney Ii, CEO
Joseph W Peed, Chairman
Mary Gonnerman, VP

Airline Trade Magazine.
Cost: $24.95
Frequency: Monthly
Founded in 1968

2658 **Buoyant Flight**
Lighter Than Air Society
526 S Main Street
Suite 232
Akron, OH 44311

Home Page: www.blimpinfo.com

Articles on the history, science and techniques of buoyant flight.
Founded in 1954

2659 **Cabin Crew Safety**
Flight Safety Foundation
801 N Fairfax Street
Suite 400
Alexandria, VA 22314-1774

703-739-6700; Fax: 703-739-6708
ostrega@flightsafety.org
www.flightsafety.org

Hassan Shadidi, President
Roger Rozelle, Publisher
Rick Derby, Editor
Patzy Sepezy, Circulation Manager

Focuses attention on the cabin crew, especially in airline operations, but the special requirements of corporate operations are also presented. Explanations on how to deal with hijackers, advocates of child restraints, emergency action plans and tips to reduce stress. Subscription included with FSF membership. Others will be $280.00/year.
Cost: $240.00
4 Pages
Printed in 2 colors

2660 **Command, Control, Communications and Intelligence**
American Defense Preparedness Association
22 Commerce Road
Newtown, CT 22201-3062

203-426-0800
800-451-4975; Fax: 203-426-1964
info@forecast1.com
www.forecast1.com

Ray Peterson, Vice President
Andrew Briney, Editor

Programs and funding information.
Cost: $1640.00
Founded in 1973

2661 **Federal Air Surgeons Medical Bulletin**
US Federal Aviation Administration
800 Independence Avenue SW
Washington, DC 20591

866-835-5322
www.faa.gov

Michael Huerta, Acting Administrator
David Grizzle, Chief Operating Officer
David Weingart, Chief of Staff
Victoria B. Wessmer, Assistant Administrator Of Finance

Published for aviation medical examiners and others interested in aviation safety and aviation medicine.
Frequency: Quarterly
Circulation: 8000
Founded in 1967

2662 **Flight Safety Foundation NEWS**
Flight Safety Foundation
801 N Fairfax Street
Suite 400
Alexandria, VA 22314-1774

703-396-6700; Fax: 703-739-6708
apparao@flightsafety.org
www.flightsafety.org

Hassan Shadidi, President/CEO
Roger Rozelle, Publisher
Allen Smith, Marketing Manager

A primary tool for communicating the Foundation's activities through seminars, workshops, special projects, committee actions, awards to its members.
Cost: $480.00
Frequency: Monthly

2663 **Flight Test News**
Society of Flight Test Engineers
44814 N Elm Avenue
PO Box 4037
Lancaster, CA 93539-4037

661-949-2095; Fax: 661-949-2096
sfte@sfte.org
www.sfte.org

Peter Donath, President
Michael Barrlett, Vice President
Mark Mondt, Secretary
Steve Martin, Treasurer
Barbara A. Wood, Director

Offers specific information for flight test engineers.

2664 **Flightlog**
Association of Flight Attendants

501 3rd St NW
Washington, DC 20001

202-434-1300; Fax: 202-712-9792
info@afacwa.org
www.afanet.org
Facebook, Twitter, YouTube

Elliott Kindred, Manager
Veda Shook, International President
Sara Nelson, International President

Offers updated information and news for flight attendants.
Frequency: Monthly

2665 **Helicopter News**
Phillips Business Information
1201 Seven Locks Road
Potomac, MD 20854

301-354-1400; Fax: 301-309-3847

Thomas Phillips, Publisher
Holly Yeager, Editor

Information on the rapidly changing helicopter industry.
Cost: $797.00
Frequency: 25 Issues

2666 **Helicopter Safety**
Flight Safety Foundation
801 N Fairfax Street
Suite 400
Alexandria, VA 22314-1774

703-396-6700; Fax: 703-739-6708
apparao@flightsafety.org
www.flightsafety.org

J.A. Donaghue, Director Publications
Mark Lacagnina, Senior Editor
Wayne Rosenkrans, Senior Editor
Linda Werfelman, Senior Editor
Rick Darby, Associate Editor

Highlights the broad spectrum of real-world helicopter operations. Subscription included with FSF membership. Others will be $280.00/year.
4-8 Pages
Frequency: Bi-Monthly
Founded in 1974
Printed in 2 colors

2667 **Hotline**
Aeronautical Repair Station Association
121 N Henry St
Alexandria, VA 22314-2903

703-739-9543; Fax: 703-739-9488
arsa@arsa.org
www.arsa.org
Facebook, Twitter, LinkedIn, YouTube

Sarah MacLeod, Executive Director

Devoted to regulatory compliance in aircraft design, production and maintenance.
Frequency: Monthly

2668 **Human Factors & Aviation Medicine**
Flight Safety Foundation
801 N Fairfax Street
Suite 400
Alexandria, VA 22314-1774

703-396-6700; Fax: 703-739-6708
apparao@flightsafety.org
www.flightsafety.org

J.A. Donaghue, Director Publications
Mark Lacagnina, Senior Editor
Wayne Rosenkrans, Senior Editor
Linda Werfelman, Senior Editor
Rick Darby, Associate Editor

Presents information important to the training and performance of all aviation professionals. Subscription included with FSF membership. Others will be $280.00/year.
4-8 Pages
Frequency: Bi-Monthly
Founded in 1953
Printed in 2 colors

2669 **IE News: Aerospace and Defense**
Institute of Industrial Engineers
3577 Parkway Lane
Suite 200
Norcross, GA 30092

770-449-0460
800-494-0460; Fax: 770-441-3295
boyeyemi@iienet.org

Jane Gaboury, Editorial Director
Don Greene, Vice President
Michael Hughes, Editor

Offers information and updates for industrial engineers.

2670 **Inside the Air Force**
Inside Washington Publishers
PO Box 7167
Washington, DC 20044-7167

703-685-5009
800-424-9068; Fax: 703-416-8543

Donna Haseley, Editor

An executive weekly report on Air Force programs, procurement and policymaking.
Cost: $980.00
Frequency: Weekly
Printed in one color on matte stock

2671 **Jet Fuel Intelligence**
Energy Intelligence Group
5 E 37th St
Suite 5
New York, NY 10016-2807

212-532-1112; Fax: 212-532-4479
info@energyintel.com
www.energyintel.com

Ivan Sandrea, President
Thomas Wallin, Executive Vice President and Editor
Raja W Sidawi, Chairman
Peter Kemp, Editor
Sarah Miller, Editor-at-Large

Offers the latest information on jets, fuel, cargo, safety and legislation.
Cost: $2595.00
Frequency: Weekly
Founded in 1951

2672 **Light Aircraft Manufacturers Association Newsletter**
Light Aircraft Manufacturers Association
2001 Steamboat Ridge Ct
Dayton Beach, FL 32128-6918

651-592-7565; Fax: 65- 22- 182
info@lama.bz
www.lama.bz

Larry Burke, President
Dave Martin, Editor

Manufacturers, distributors and suppliers receive the latest information and news pertaining to light aircraft, including updated news from Washington, DC.
Frequency: Quarterly
Circulation: 66
Founded in 1984
Printed in 2 colors on glossy stock

2673 **Light Plane Maintenance**
Belvoir Publishers
PO Box 5656
Norwalk, CT 06856-5656

203-422-7300
800-829-9085; Fax: 203-661-4802
www.lightplane-maintenance.com

John Likakis, Publisher

Articles of interest for light aircraft owners.
Cost: $19.97
24 Pages

2674 **Mx Newsletter**
Professional Aviation Maintenance Association
972 E Tuttle Road
Building 204
Ionia, MI 48846

724-772-4095
800-356-1671; Fax: 724-772-4064
hq@pama.org
www.pama.org
Facebook, Twitter, LinkedIn

Roger Sickler, Chairman
Jeff Gruber, Vice Chairman
John Wicht, Secretary

Features news for and about members, relevant articles and hot legislative information.
Frequency: Six/Year
Printed in one color

2675 **NAA Record**
National Aeronautic Association
1 Reagan National Airport
Hangar 7
Washington, DC 20001-6015

703-416-4888; Fax: 703-416-4877
naa@naa.aero
www.naa.aero

Greg Principato, President & CEO
Arthur W Greenfield, Contest & Records Director
Frequency: Monthly
Circulation: 3000

2676 **NBAA Management Guide**
National Business Aviation Association
1200 G Street NW
Suite 1100
Washington, DC 20005

202-783-9000; Fax: 202-331-8364
info@nbaa.org
www.nbaa.org
Facebook, Twitter, LinkedIn

Edward Bolen, President/CEO
Annemarie Oxman, Chief People Officer
Dan Hubbard, SVP, Communications
Founded in 1947

2677 **NBAA Update**
National Business Aviation Association
1200 G Street NW
Suite 1100
Washington, DC 20005

202-783-9000; Fax: 202-331-8364
info@nbaa.org
www.nbaa.org
Facebook, Twitter, LinkedIn

Edward Bolen, President & CEO
Annemarie Oxman, Chief People Officer
Dan Hubbard, SVP, Communications

Offers weekly updates on the latest in NBAA news as well as business aviation industry news.
Frequency: Weekly
Circulation: 26000
Founded in 1947

2678 **National Aeronautics**
National Aeronautic Association
1737 King Street
Suite 220
Alexandria, VA 22314

703-527-0226
800-644-9777; Fax: 703-416-4877
www.nasa.gov

Shannon Chambers, Editor
David L Ivey, Publisher
Nancy Sack, Office Manager

Information on industry events for the aviation community, also opinion articles, records and

awards, technology developments, education, and future events.
8 Pages
Circulation: 3500
Founded in 1905
Printed in 2 colors on glossy stock

2679 **National Transportation Safety Board Digest Service**
Hawkins Publishing Company
103 River Rd
Edgewater, MD 21037-3824

410-798-1098; Fax: 410-798-1098
www.ntsb.gov

Mark V Rosenker, Chairman

Loose-leafed indexed-digested-analysis of the decisions of the National Transportation Safety Board and its predecessor (the CAB), dealing with Aviation Safety Enforcement matters.
Cost: $390.00
Frequency: Monthly

2680 **News & Views**
Association of Air Medical Services
909 N Washington Street
Suite 410
Alexandria, VA 22314

703-836-8732; Fax: 703-836-8920
information@aams.org
www.aams.org

Cameron Curtis, President & CEO
David J Dries, Editor
Gloria Dow, Editor

This faxed/e-mailed newsletter contains information on association activity updates, community and member news, crew fitness and survival, member survey data, member profiles, editorials, and classifieds.
Frequency: Monthly

2681 **Ninety-Nines News**
Ninety-Nines
4300 Amelia Earhart Dr
Suite A
Oklahoma City, OK 73159-1106

405-685-7969
800-994-1929; Fax: 405-685-7985
99s@ninety-nines.org
www.ninety-nines.org

Laura Ohrenberg, Manager
Corbi Bulluck, President

News and events for licensed women pilots.
Founded in 1929

2682 **Operations Update**
Helicopter Association International
1635 Prince St
Alexandria, VA 22314-2898

703-683-4646; Fax: 703-683-4745
www.rotor.com

James Viola, President

Provides useful information to helicopter owners and operators regarding issues, events and new technologies that may effect or enhance the operator's ability to conduct business with helicopters.
Frequency: Monthly

2683 **Parachutist**
United States Parachute Association
5401 Southpoint Centre Boulevard
Fredricksburg, VA 22407

540-604-9740; Fax: 540-604-9740
uspa@uspa.org
www.uspa.org
Facebook, Twitter, LinkedIn, YouTube, RSS

Elijah Florio, Editor in Chief
Laura Sharp, Managing Editor
Guilherme Cunha, Advertising Manager, Web Developer
David Cherry, Graphic Designer

The official newsletter of the USPA.
33000 Members
Founded in 1946

2684 **Preliminary Accident Reports**
Helicopter Association International
1635 Prince St
Alexandria, VA 22314-2898

703-683-4646; Fax: 703-683-4745
www.rotor.com

James Viola, President

PARs summarize civil helicopter accident reports as received from the National Transportation Safety Board and the Transportation Safety Board of Canada. One subscription included upon request in Regular and Associate member dues.
Frequency: Quarterly

2685 **Rotor Breeze**
Bell Helicopter Textron
600 E Hurst Boulevard
PO Box 482
Hurst, TX 76053

817-280-2011; Fax: 817-280-2321
www.bellhelicopter.com

Mike Redenbaugh, Chairman/CEO
Brandon Battles, Editor

Newsletter on Bell Helicopter products and customer support.
Frequency: Quarterly
Founded in 1935

2686 **Space Calendar**
Space Age Publishing Company
65-1230 Mamalahoa Hwy
Suite D-20
Kamuela, HI 96743-7301

808-885-3473; Fax: 808-885-3475
news@spaceagepub.com
www.spaceagepub.com

Steve Durst, Owner

Publication for the space industry.
Cost: $59.00
Frequency: Weekly

2687 **Space Fax Daily**
Space Age Publishing Company
65-1230 Mamalahoa Hwy
Suite D-20
Kamuela, HI 96743-7301

808-885-3473; Fax: 808-885-3475
news@spaceagepub.com
www.spaceagepub.com

Steve Durst, Owner
Charles Bohannan, Associate Editor
Michelle Gonella, Marketing Manager

Information covering the space industry.
Cost: $59.00
Frequency: Weekly
Founded in 1988

2688 **Space Letter**
Callahan Publications
6220 Nelway Drive
PO Box 1173
Mclean, VA 22101

703-356-1925

Vincent F Callahan Jr, Editor

Information from Washington on the US multi-billion dollar National Space Program. Legislation, budgets, marketing trends and contracting.
Cost: $190.00
8 Pages
Frequency: 24/Yr
Printed in one color

2689 **Space Station News**
Phillips Publishing
7811 Montrose Road
Potomac, MD 20854-3363

301-208-6787; Fax: 301-340-0877

Tom Phillips, President/CEO/Publisher

Information pertaining to the space station program.
Founded in 1974

2690 **Speednews**
Speednews
17383 W. Sunset Boulevard
Suite A 220
Pacific Palisades, CA 90272

310-203-9603; Fax: 310-203-9352
admin@speednews.com
www.speednews.com

William Freeman III, Publisher
Stephen Costley, Editor
Joanna Speed, VP, Circulation
Stephen A. Costley, VP, Managing Editor
Pamela Leven, Subscription Sales

Market intelligence newsletter for the aviation industry.
Cost: $687.00
Frequency: Weekly
Circulation: 50000
ISSN: 0271-2598
Founded in 1979

2691 **The NAA Record**
1 Reagan National Airport
Hangar 7
Washington, DC 20001-6015

703-416-4888
800-644-9777; Fax: 703-416-4877
naa@naa.aero
www.naa.aero

Greg Principato, President & CEO
Arthur W Greenfield, Contest & Records Director

A non-profit association that is dedicated to the advancement of the art, sport and science of aviation in the United States.
3000 Members
Frequency: Monthly
Circulation: 3000
Founded in 1905

2692 **World Airline News**
Phillips Publishing
7811 Montrose Road
Potomac, MD 20854

301-354-1400; Fax: 301-340-0877
www.phillips.com

Tom Phillips, President/CEO/Publisher

Provides airline executives with news and analysis on route developments, codesharing agreements, and traffic statistics as well as aviation entertainment.
Cost: $697.00
Frequency: Weekly/Newsletter
Circulation: 1,850
Founded in 1974

2693 **World Airport Week**
Phillips Publishing
7811 Montrose Road
Potomac, MD 20854

301-354-1400; Fax: 301-340-0877
www.phillips.com

Tom Phillips, CEO

Focuses on commercialization and privatization of airports around the world.
Cost: $597.00
Frequency: Weekly
Circulation: 1800

Magazines & Journals

2694 **ABS Magazine**
American Bonanza Society
PO Box 12888
Wichita, KS 67277

316-945-1700; Fax: 316-945-1710
www.bonanza.org

Whit Hickman, Executive Director

Offers a treasury of practical information on such topics as maintenance, piloting techniques, aircraft restoration, aircraft insurance and ot her important subjects especially chosen for those with a specific interest in Bonanza, Baron, and Travel Air models of aircraft. This colorful magazine also features aircraft owned by an ABS members on its cover every month, as well as schedules of the numerous member activities which are conducted all around the nation.
Frequency: Monthly

2695 **AIAA Technical Reports**
American Institute of Aeronautics and Astronautics
1801 Alexander Bell Dr
Suite 500
Reston, VA 20191-4344

703-264-7500
800-639-2422; Fax: 703-264-7551
tammym@aiaa.org
www.aiaa.org

Basil Hassan, President

Each year AIAA sponsors approximately 25 national meetings where professionals present technical papers on subjects such as guidance and control Computers in Aerospace, etc.
Cost: $3.00
Circulation: 1925
Founded in 1963

2696 **AOPA Flight Training Magazine**
Aircraft Owners & Pilots Association
421 Aviation Way
Frederick, MD 21701-4756

301-695-2000
800-872-2672; Fax: 301-695-2375
www.aopa.org

Craig Fuller, President

Provides up-to-date aviation news and safety tips for student pilots and CFIs.

2697 **AOPA Pilot Magazine**
Aircraft Owners & Pilots Association
421 Aviation Way
Frederick, MD 21701-4756

301-695-2000
800-872-2672; Fax: 301-695-2375
www.aopa.org

Craig Fuller, President
Phil Boyer, President

Will keep you up to date on all the hottest issues in general aviation from the newest technologies in avionics to the latest safety and techniques to enhance your flying. Available only to AOPA members. Membership costs only $39.00/annually.
Frequency: Monthly
Circulation: 34,000

2698 **AUSA News**
Association of the United States Army
2425 Wilson Boulevard
Arlington, VA 22201-3326

703-841-4300
800-336-4570; Fax: 703-525-9039
ausa-info@ausa.org
www.ausa.org

Peter Murphy, Editor
Gordon R Sullivan, President

AUSA represents every American soldier by: being the voice for all components of America's army; fostering public support of the Army's role in national security; providing professional education and information programs.
Frequency: Monthly
Circulation: 10000
Founded in 1950

2699 **Aerospace Engineering**
400 Commonwealth Drive
Warrendale, PA 15096-1

724-776-4841
877-606-7323; Fax: 724-776-0790
magazines@sae.org
www.sae.org

Richard Klien, President
Mircea Gradu, Executive VP

Serves the international aerospace design and manufacturing field which consists of producers of airliners, helicopters, spacecraft, missiles; their powerplants, propulsion systems, avionics, electronic/electrical systems, parts and components.
Cost: $75.00
Frequency: 10 issues
Circulation: 28440
Founded in 1905

2700 **Agricultural Aviation**
National Agricultural Aviation Association
1005 E St SE
Washington, DC 20003-2847

202-546-5722; Fax: 202-546-5726
information@agaviation.org
www.agaviation.org

Andrew Moore, Executive Director

Official publication of the National Agricultural Aviation Association. Typical subject matter includes information on agricultural aviation business, agricultural aircraft, legislative issues, pesticides, new products and services, safety, maintenance, people profiles.
Cost: $30.00
Circulation: 5200
Founded in 1921

2701 **Air Classics**
Challenge Publications
9509 Vassar Ave
Unit A
Chatsworth, CA 91311-0883

818-700-6868
800-562-9182; Fax: 818-700-6282
customerservice@challengeweb.com
www.challengeweb.com

Edwin Schnepf, Owner

Magazine of military aviations.
Cost: $36.95
76 Pages
Frequency: Monthly
Founded in 1963

2702 **Air Force Magazine**
Air Force Association
1501 Lee Hwy
Suite 400
Arlington, VA 22209-1198

703-247-5800
800-727-3337; Fax: 703-247-5853
letters@afa.org
www.afa.org

Bruce Wright, President
Chequita Wood, Editorial Contact

Analysis of all aspects of aerospace power, from military and scientific advances to political ramifications. Includes reports on new technology and studies missile management.
Cost: $36.00
Frequency: Monthly
Circulation: 202718
Founded in 1946

2703 **Air Line Pilot**
Air Lines Pilot Association International
1625 Massachusetts Ave NW
Suite 800
Washington, DC 20036-2204

703-689-2270; Fax: 202-797-4052
www.alpa.org

Joe DePete, President
Mary Jo McPherson, Associate Editor
Bob Fox, Vice President

Emphasizes advances in air safety, flight technology, industry developments and aviation history.
Cost: $32.00
56 Pages
Frequency: Monthly
Circulation: 86,656
Founded in 1931

2704 **Air Line Pilot Magazine**
Airline Pilots Association International
1625 Massachusetts Ave NW
Suite 800
Washington, DC 20036-2204

703-689-2270; Fax: 202-797-4052
www.alpa.org

Joe DePete, President
Bob Fox, Vice President
Frequency: Monthly

2705 **Air Medical Journal**
Elsevier, Health Sciences Division
3251 Riverport Lane
Maryland Heights, MO 63043

314-447-8000
800-401-9962; Fax: 314-447-8033
elspcs@elsevier.com
www.elsevier.com

Ron Mobed, CEO
David J Dries, Editor
Adriaan Roosen, Executive Vice President

Is the industry's combined trade and research journal. Each issue contains research articles, abstracts and book reviews designed to keep you up-to-date on the latest discoveries. Membership benefits includes a complimentary subscription.
Cost: $82.00
Founded in 1986

2706 **Air Progress**
Challenge Publications
9509 Vassar Ave
Unit A
Chatsworth, CA 91311-0883

818-700-6868; Fax: 818-700-6282
customerservice@challengeweb.com
www.challengeweb.com

Edwin Schnepf, Owner
Taccy Kruger, Editor

Covers all phases of aviation.
Cost: $36.95
84 Pages
Frequency: Monthly
Founded in 1963

2707 **Air Progress - Warbirds International**
Challenge Publications
9509 Vassar Ave
Unit A
Chatsworth, CA 91311-0883

818-700-6868
800-562-9182; Fax: 818-700-6282

customerservice@challengeweb.com
www.challengeweb.com

Edwin Schnepf, Owner
Michael O'Leary, Editor
Tim Baudler, Associate Publisher

The magazine of veteran and vintage military aircraft.
Cost: $22.00
80 Pages
Frequency: Quarterly
Circulation: 3836
Founded in 1963

2708 **Air Transport World**
Penton Media
8380 Colesville Rd
Suite 700
Silver Spring, MD 20910

301-755-0200; Fax: 913-514-3909
www.atwonline.com

JA Donoghue, Editorial Director
William A Freeman III, Publisher

Lists nationwide and international information on airports, airlines and the latest technology in the aviation industry.
Cost: $65.00
85 Pages
Frequency: Monthly
Circulation: 40000
Founded in 1964
Printed in 4 colors on glossy stock

2709 **Air and Space/Smithsonian**
National Air and Space Museum
Smithsonian Institution
PO Box 37012 ,Victor Bldg 7100 MRC
Washington, DC 20013-7012

202-633-6070
800-513-3081; Fax: 202-275-1886
www.airspacemag.com/

Joseph Bonsignore, Publisher
George C Larson, Editor

Smithsonian magazine offering information on the latest developments, technology, and historical news of the aviation industry.
Cost: $24.00
124 Pages
Founded in 1986

2710 **Aircraft Maintenance Technology**
Cygnus Business Media
1233 Janesville Avenue
Fort Atkinson, WI 53538

800-547-7377; Fax: 920-563-1699
jjezo@amtonline.com

Jon Jezo, Publisher
Ronald Donner, Editor

Provides in depth coverage of the critical technical and professional issues facing today's technicians.
Cost: $90.00
98 Pages
Frequency: Monthly
Circulation: 39000
ISSN: 1072-3145
Founded in 1989
Mailing list available for rent: 41M names
Printed in 4 colors on glossy stock

2711 **Airline Pilot Careers**
Aviation Information Resources
1029 Peachtree Parkway N
Suite 352
Peachtree City, GA 30269

404-592-6500
87- 33- 293; Fax: 770-487-6617
KitDarby@gmail.com

Kit Darby, President/Publisher

Information to assist pilots in their career development as a airline pilot. Includes feature airline news, personnel announcements, aviation medical information, classifieds and calendar events.
Cost: $29.95
40 Pages
Frequency: Monthly
ISSN: 1095-4317
Founded in 1989

2712 **Airport Business**
Cygnus Business Media
1233 Janesville Avenue
Fort Atkinson, WI 53538

800-547-7377
john.infanger@cygnuspub.com

John Infanger, Editorial Director

Targets professionals who manage aitports, airport-based businesses, and corporate flight facilities in North America. Helps managers more effectively operate their operations by sharing case studies of what others are doing successfully, combined with expert analysis, industry news, and product information.
Cost: $60.00
44 Pages
Frequency: Monthly
Circulation: 14100
ISSN: 1072-1797
Founded in 1986

2713 **Airport Equipment & Technology**
8380 Colesville Rd
Suite 700
Silver Spring, MD 20910-6257

301-755-0200; Fax: 913-514-3909
www.atwonline.com

William A Freeman III, Publisher
Geoffrey Thomas, Editor-in-Chief

Related to airport and airport operations.
Cost: $65.00
Frequency: Quarterly
Circulation: 40000
Founded in 1965

2714 **Airport Journal**
Airport Journal
551 Revere Avenue
PO Box 66001
Westmont, IL 60559

630-986-8132; Fax: 630-986-5010
www.airportjournal.com

John Andrews, Editor

This journal offers news, information, statistics and reviews pertaining to airports across the globe.
Cost: $13.00
Frequency: Monthly

2715 **Airports**
Aviation Week
1200 G St NW
Suite 900
Washington, DC 20005-3821

202-383-2378
800-525-5003; Fax: 202-383-2438
aw_intelligence@aviationnow.com
www.aviationweek.com

Christopher Fotos, Editor
Kimberley Johnson, Associate Editor
Mark Lipowicz, Publisher

Airports, the weekly for airport managers, users and suppliers, gives you exclusive insider intelligence to meet business challenges with your eyes open.
Cost: $98.00
Frequency: Weekly
Founded in 1920

2716 **Airpower**
Sentry Books
Republic Press
PO Box 881526
San Diego, CA 92168

818-368-2012
support@airwingmedia.com
www.wingsairpower.com

Joseph Mizrahi, Publisher
Mike Machat, Editor/Publisher

Military and commercial aviation history, contains photos, drawings and interviews.
Cost: $44.00
56 Pages
Frequency: Monthly
Circulation: 45000
ISSN: 1067-1048
Founded in 1971

2717 **Airways**
Airways International
120 McGhee Road
PO Box 1109
Sandpoint, ID 83864

360-457-6485
800-440-5166; Fax: 208-263-5906
airways@airwaysmag.com
www.airwaysmag.com

John Wegg, Editor-in-Chief
Seija Wegg, VP Marketing

Written for airline and air travel professionals, and the consumer. Focuses on the current air transport industry: the airliner, manufacturers, the people, technologies, the airports and the airways. Plus takes a nostalgic look at the past.
Cost: $39.95
80 Pages
Frequency: Monthly
Circulation: 43000
ISSN: 1074-4320
Founded in 1994

2718 **America's Flyways**
United States Pilots Association
1652 Indian Point Road
Brandson, MO 65616

417-338-2225; Fax: 309-215-6323
jan@hoynacki.com
www.uspilots.org

David Forster, President
Jan Hoynacki, Executive Director
Frequency: Monthly

2719 **Army Aviation**
Army Aviation Publications
755 Main St
Suite 4D
Monroe, CT 06468-2830

203-268-2450; Fax: 203-268-5870
aaaa@quad-a.org
www.quad-a.org

William R Harris, Publisher
Maryann Stirling, Circulation Manager
Daniel Petrosky, President

Is a professional military publication reporting on news and developments pertinent to the field of U.S. Army Aviation and is the official publication of the Army Aviation Association of America. Each issue offers in-depth coverage of a specific development or program within U.S. Army Aviation along with dynamic, easy-to-read feature articles from key offices, agencies, and operational units worldwide.
Cost: $30.00
Frequency: Monthly
Founded in 1957
Printed in 4 colors on glossy stock

2720 **Aviation Business Journal**
National Air Transportation Association

4226 King St
Alexandria, VA 22302-1507

703-845-9000
800-808-6282; Fax: 703-845-8176
www.nata.aero
Facebook, Twitter, LinkedIn

Timothy Obitts, President & CEO
Jason Miller, CFO & COO

Authored by experienced aviation journalists and industry experts
Frequency: Quarterly

2721 Aviation Digest Associates
P.O. Box 2231
Danbury, CT 06810

203-264-3727

Robert Dorr, Publisher
Sharon Simmons, Associate Publisher

Newsmagazine/shopper distributed to owners of general aviation (private and corporate) aircraft.
Cost: $20.00
Frequency: Monthly
Circulation: 12,000

2722 Aviation Equipment Maintenance
Phillips Business Information
7811 Montrose Road
Potomac, MD 20854

301-354-1400; Fax: 301-309-3847
www.phillips.com

Richard Koulbanis, Publisher
Clif Stroud, Editor
John J. Coyle, President

Produced monthly and is the leading publication for airline and general aviation maintenance managers. AEM provides information on maintenance techniques, management procedures, new products and ground support equipment.
Frequency: Monthly
Founded in 1974

2723 Aviation International News
Convention News Company
81 Kenosia Avenue
Danbury, CT 06810

203-798-2400; Fax: 203-798-2104
jhartford@ainonline.com
www.ainonline.com

Anthony Ramodo, Publisher
Charles Alcock, Editor
Jeff Hartford, Circulation Manager
Wilson Leach, Executive Director

Update on business aviation, equipment and services, and business aviation news and events.
Cost: $74.98
116 Pages
Frequency: Monthly
Circulation: 39,000
ISSN: 0887-9877
Founded in 1972
Printed in 4 colors on glossy stock

2724 Aviation Medicine and Human Performance
Aerospace Medical Association
320 S Henry St
Alexandria, VA 22314-3579

703-739-2240; Fax: 703-739-9652
AMHPJournal@asma.org
www.asma.org

Frederick Bonato, PhD, Editor-in-Chief
Pamela C. Day, B.A., Managing Editor

A peer-reviewed journal that provides contact with physicians, life scientists, bioengineers and medical specialists working in both basic medical research and in its clinical applications.
Frequency: Monthly

2725 Aviation Safety
Belvoir Publishers
800 Connecticut Avenue
PO Box 5656
Norwalk, CT 06856

203-857-3100; Fax: 203-857-3103
customer_service@belvoir.com
www.belvoir.com

Ken Ibold, Editor-in-Chief
Robert Englander, CEO
Tom Canfield, VP

Journal on risk management and accident prevention, includes interviews with officials of the FFA.
Cost: $65.00
Frequency: Monthly
Founded in 1972

2726 Aviation Week & Space Technology
Aviation Week
1200 G St NW
Suite 900
Washington, DC 20005-3821

202-383-2378
800-525-5003; Fax: 202-383-2438
www.aviationweek.com

Anthony L Velocci Jr, Editor-in-Chief
James R Asker, Manager Editor
Jim Mathews, Publisher

Articles and features on the aviation/aerospace industry, including aircraft rockets, missiles, space vehicles, powerplants, avionics and related components and equipment.
Cost: $5.00
Frequency: Weekly
Circulation: 140000
Founded in 1884

2727 Avionics News
Aircraft Electronics Association
3570 Ne Ralph Powell Rd
Lees Summit, MO 64064-2360

816-347-8400; Fax: 816-347-8405
info@aea.net
www.aea.net
Facebook, Twitter, LinkedIn

Gregory Vall, President/Publisher

A magazine devoted exclusively to persons interested in aviation and avionics. Complimentary within North America.
Cost: $132.00
Frequency: Monthly
Circulation: 8500
Founded in 1975

2728 Avionics: The Journal of Global Airspace
PBI Media
1201 Seven Locks Road
Potomac, MD 20854

301-354-1400
847-559-7314; Fax: 301-340-0542
www.avionicsmagazine.com

Daniel E Comiskey, Publisher
Stuart Bonner, Circulation Manager
Don Pazour, CEO
David Jensen, Editor-In-Chief

Covers electronics carried aboard aircraft, ground navigational and systems for air traffic control.
Cost: $89.00
Frequency: Monthly
Founded in 1999
Printed in 4 colors on glossy stock

2729 Business & Commercial Aviation
McGraw Hill
4 International Drive
Suite 260
Rye Brook, NY 10573

914-939-0300
800-257-9402; Fax: 914-939-1184
www.aviationweek.com

William Garvey, Editor-in-Chief
Mark Lipowicz, Publisher
Richard Aarons, Safety Editor

Information for the management and executive levels of aircraft companies on improvements in operations and news of today's general aviation industry.
Cost: $60.00
Frequency: Monthly
Circulation: 52329

2730 Captain's Log
World Airline Historical Society
PO Box 489
Ocoee, FL 34761

904-221-1446; Fax: 407-522-9352
president@WAHSOnline.com
www.wahsonline.com
Facebook, Twitter

Chris Slimmer, President

The premiere magazine for collectors of airline memorabilia.
Frequency: Quarterly
Circulation: 500

2731 Cessna Owner Magazine
Cessna Owner Organization
N7450 Aanstad Rd
Iola, WI 54945-5000

715-445-5000
888-692-3776; Fax: 715-445-4053
help@cessnaowner.org
www.cessnaowner.org

Dan Weller, Executive Director
Joe Jones, Publisher

The official publication of the Cessna Owner Organization, it includes pilot tips, owner/aircraft articles, alerts, maintenance tips, new product information, SDR summaries, AD's, insurance updates, and much more.
Cost: $9.95
Frequency: Monthly
Circulation: 5000

2732 Controller
Sandhills Publishing
PO Box 82545
Lincoln, NE 68501-5310

402-479-2181
800-331-1978; Fax: 402-479-2195
human-resources@sandhills.com
www.sandhills.com

Tom Peed, Publisher

A magazine designed and edited to provide a means of communication between buyer and seller in today's general aviation marketplace.
Cost: $52.00
60 Pages
Frequency: Weekly
Circulation: 20,000 +
Founded in 1978

2733 EAA Sport Aviation
Experimental Aircraft Association
3000 Poberezny Road
PO Box 3086
Oshkosh, WI 54902

920-426-4800
800-564-6322; Fax: 920-426-6761
webmaster@eaa.org
www.eaa.org

Jack Pelton, Chief Executive Officer
Jim Busha, VP, Publications, Marketing, Mem.

For pilots, designers, and enthusiasts of sport and homebuilt aircraft.
Cost: $40.00
100 Pages
Frequency: Monthly
Circulation: 165000
ISSN: 0038-7835
Founded in 1953
Printed in 4 colors on glossy stock

2734 **EAA Sport Pilot Magazine**
Experimental Aircraft Association
3000 Poberezny Road
PO Box 3086
Oshkosh, WI 54902

920-426-4800
800-564-6322; Fax: 920-426-6761
webmaster@eaa.org
www.eaa.org

Jack Pelton, Chief Executive Officer
Jim Busha, VP, Publications, Marketing, Mem.

Dedicated to those to fly, buy, build/assemble, maintain, and have fun with light-sport aircraft, sport pilot eligible aircraft, and ultralights, as well as the full spectrum of member activities that give people the opportunity to participate in recreational aviation.

2735 **EAA Vintage Aircraft Association**
Experimental Aircraft Association
PO Box 3086
Oshkosh, WI 54903-3086

920-426-4825
800-564-6322; Fax: 920-426-6579
vintageaircraft@eaa.org
www.vintageaircraft.org

Susan Dusenbury, President

Devoted to all aspects of antique, classic and contemporary aircraft. (All aircraft cinstructed by the original manufacturer, or its licensee on or before 12/31/1970).
Cost: $36.00
6000+ Members
32 Pages
Frequency: Monthly
Circulation: 10,000
Founded in 1971

2736 **FAA Aviation News**
Government Printing Office
AFS-805 Room 832
800 Independence Avenue, S.W.
Washington, DC 20591

202-512-0000
866-835-5322
webmasteravnews@faa.gov
www.faa.gov/

Phyllis Duncan, Editor
Michael Huerta, Administrator
David Weingart, Chief of Staff
Daniel J. Mehan, Chief Information Officer

Contains regulations and approved operational techniques, also in depth accident and incident reports.
Cost: $21.00
Frequency: Bi-monthly
Circulation: 50,000
Founded in 1966

2737 **Flight Physician**
Civil Aviation Medical Association
P.O. Box 2382
Peachtree City, GA 30269-2382

770-487-0100; Fax: 770-487-0080
david.millett@yahoo.com
www.civilavmed.org

Gerald Saboe, President
Sherry Sandoval, Executive VP & Editor
Cost: $5.00
Frequency: Bi-Monthly

2738 **Flight Safety Digest**
Flight Safety Foundation
801 N Fairfax Street
Suite 400
Alexandria, VA 22314-1774

703-247-0700; Fax: 703-739-6708
Marshall@flightsafety.org
www.flightsafety.org

Hassan Shadidi, President/CEO
Roger Rozelle, Publisher
Mark Lacagnina, Senior Editor

Analyzes controversial industry issues; and authors have shared observations of important, but sometimes subtle influences that affect the airline industry. Authors have described the latest innovations in training, technology and management. Monthly sections present analyses of aviation statistics, brief accident reports and abstracts of information received at FSF Jerry Lederer Aviation Safety Library. Subscription included with FSF membership. Others will be $520.00.
Cost: $520.00
Frequency: Monthly
Circulation: 1000
Founded in 1982
Printed in one color

2739 **Flight Training**
Aircraft Owners & Pilots Association
421 Aviation Way
Frederick, MD 21701-4756

301-695-2000
800-872-2672; Fax: 301-695-2375
flighttraining@aopa.org
www.aopa.org

Craig Fuller, President
Thomas B Haines, Editor-in-Chief

Offers information to new pilots and their instructors as well as flight school managers and owners.
Cost: $21.00
Frequency: Monthly
Circulation: 40000+
Founded in 1939

2740 **Flightline Magazine**
Allied Pilots Association
14600 Trinity Blvd
Suite 500
Fort Worth, TX 76155-2559

817-302-2272; Fax: 817-302-2119
public-comment@alliedpilots.org
www.alliedpilots.org

Dave Ahles, Executive Director
Captain Eric Ferguson, President

2741 **Flying**
460 N Orlando Avenue
Suite 20
Winter Park, FL 32789

407-628-4802; Fax: 407-628-7061
www.flyingmag.com

J Mac McClellan, Editor-in-Chief
Wayne Lincourt, Associate Publisher
Rachel Goldstein, Sales Development Manager

Dedicated to general aviation and includes industry news, products, reports on every aircraft category, the latest new products, technology and photography.
Cost: $54.00
116 Pages
Frequency: Monthly
Circulation: 310321
Founded in 1918
Printed in 4 colors

2742 **Flying Magazine**
National Association of Flight Instructors
EAA Aviation Center
730 Grand Street
Allegan, MI 49010

920-426-6801
866-806-6156; Fax: 920-426-6865
nafi@eaa.org
www.nafinet.org

Robert Meder, Chair
David Hipschman, Director & Editor, Publications

Provided to all NAFI members, this highly respected general aviation magazine is a great source of information. NAFI and Flying have entered into a partnership that directly benefits you - the NAFI member! Flying is the perfect compliment to the technical flight instruction how-to's contained in NAFI Mentor.

2743 **GPS World**
Advanstar Communications
201 Sandpointe Ave
Suite 500
Santa Ana, CA 92707-8700

714-513-8400; Fax: 714-513-8680
www.gpsworld.com

Mike Weldon, Plant Manager
Alan Cameron, Editor in Chief
Tracy Cozzen, Managing Editor

Covers current news and developments in the area of GPS (global positioning system) technology.
Cost: $54.00
Frequency: Monthly
Circulation: 35010
Founded in 1987

2744 **Helicopter Association International Magazine**
1635 Prince St
Alexandria, VA 22314-2898

703-683-4646
800-435-4976; Fax: 703-683-4745
www.rotor.com

James Viola, President & CEO

Dedicated exclusively to the civil helicopter industry. It covers pertinent helicopter operational safety and regulatory issues, including FAA question and answer column, legislative and lobbying issues, and HAI committee and member activities. Accepts advertising.
Cost: $15.00
48 Pages
Frequency: Quarterly
ISSN: 0897-831X
Founded in 1988
Printed in 4 colors on matte stock

2745 **Hook Magazine**
Tailhook Association
9696 Businesspark Ave
San Diego, CA 92131

858-689-9223
800-322-4665
thookassn@aol.com
www.tailhook.org

Mark Aldrich, Senior Editor
Hill Goodspeed, Editor-In-Chief

Dedicated to telling the story of US Navy carrier aviation, both past and person. Contains a selection of carrier and squadron histories balanced with departments containing the latest news of current units and aerospace industry developments affecting carrier aviation.
Frequency: Quarterly

2746 **IAM Journal**
International Association of Machinists/Aerospace

9000 Machinists Place
Upper Marlboro, MD 20772

301-967-4500; Fax: 301-967-4588
www.goiam.org
Facebook, Twitter, LinkedIn, YouTube, Instagram, Pinterest

Robert Martinez, Jr., President
Dora Cervantes, General Secretary, Treasurer
Rickey Wallace, Vice President
Stan Pickthall, Vice President

Advocacy magazine addressing the trends and forces that affect machinists and aerospace workers. The publishing association also represents the areas of air transport, aerospace, metalworking, machinery, manufacturing and automotive industries.

2747 **Journal of Aerospace Engineering**
American Society of Civil Engineers
9000 Machinists Pl
Upper Marlboro, MD 20772-2675

301-967-4500
800-548-2723; Fax: 703-295-6222
marketing@asce.org
www.goiam.org

R Thomas Buffenbarger, President
Bill Henry, Publisher
Richard Michalski, General Vice President

Covers lunar soil mechanics, aerospace structures, and materials, extraterrestrial construction, robotics, remote sensing, applications, and real time data collection systems. Defines the role of civil engineering in space and emphasizes the practical applications of civil engineering in space and on earth.
Cost: $140.00
Frequency: Quarterly
Founded in 1852

2748 **Journal of Air Traffic Control**
Air Traffic Control Association
1101 King St
Suite 300
Alexandria, VA 22314-2963

703-299-2430; Fax: 703-299-2437
info@atca.org
www.atca.org

Peter F Dumont, President & CEO
Kenneth Carlisle, Director, Meetings & Expositions
Marion Brophy, Communications Specialist
Kristen Knott, Managing Editor & Writer

Devoted to developments in air traffic control. It contains articles on current issues involving ATC operations, innovative concepts and applications of technology to ATC, public policy debates impacting ATC, commentary by noted aviation experts and policy makers, ATC historical material, and reviews of books and videos of interest to the aviation community.
Frequency: Quarterly
Founded in 1956

2749 **Journal of Astronautical Sciences**
American Astronautical Society
6352 Rolling Mill Place
Suite 102
Springfield, VA 22152-2370

703-866-0020; Fax: 703-866-3526
aas@astronautical.org
www.astronautical.org
Facebook, Twitter

Carol S. Lane, President
Jim Way, Executive Director
Jim McAdams, Vice President, Publications
Dr. Kathleen C. Howell, Editor-in-Chief

An archival publication devoted to the sciences and technology of astronautics.
Cost: $170.00
Frequency: Quarterly
ISSN: 0021-9142

2750 **Journal of Guidance, Control & Dynamics**
American Institute of Aeronautics and Astronautics
1801 Alexander Bell Dr
Suite 500
Reston, VA 20191-4344

703-264-7500
800-639-2422; Fax: 703-264-7551
custserv@aiaa.org
www.aiaa.org

Basil Hassan, President
George T Schmidt, Editor-in-Chief

Offers information on guidance control, navigation, electronics and more related to astronautical and aeronautical systems.
Cost: $675.00
Frequency: Fortnightly
Circulation: 3000
Founded in 1930

2751 **Journal of Propulsion & Power**
American Institute of Aeronautics and Astronautics
1801 Alexander Bell Dr
Suite 500
Reston, VA 20191-4344

703-264-7500
800-639-2422; Fax: 703-264-7551
custserv@aiaa.org
www.aiaa.org

Basil Hassan, President
Vigor Yang MD, Editor

Offers information on new advances and technology in airbreathing, propulsion systems, fuels, power generation and more.
Cost: $730.00
Frequency: Fortnightly
Circulation: 1900
Founded in 1930

2752 **Journal of Rocket Motor Manufacturers and Propellant Developers**
California Rocketry Publishing
PO Box 1242
Claremont, CA 91711-1242

760-367-3393
01rocket@gte.net

Jerry Irvine, Publisher

Technical journal covering propellant formulations, motor design, performance results and methods. Back issues available.
Cost: $499.00
16 Pages
Frequency: Annual
Circulation: 500
Founded in 1994
Printed in on matte stock

2753 **Journal of the American Helicopter Society**
American Helicopter Society International
217 N Washington St
Alexandria, VA 22314-2538

703-684-6777
855-247-4685; Fax: 703-739-9279
webmaster@vtol.org
www.vtol.org

Mike Hirschberg, Executive Director
Ashis Bagai, Associate Editor

The scope of the Journal covers the full range of research, analysis, design, manufacturing, test, operations, and support. A constantly growing list of specialty areas is included within that scope. Is distributed to the AHS membership for $20.00 and is also available for subscription.
Cost: $95.00
Frequency: Quarterly

2754 **KITPLANES**
Light Aircraft Manufacturers Association
2001 Steamboat Ridge Ct
Daytona Beach, FL 94588-8233

65- 59- 756; Fax: 925-426-0771
info@lama.bz
www.lama.bz

Dan Johnson, President

Experimental-category homebuilt aircraft.
Frequency: Monthly

2755 **Maintenance Update**
Helicopter Association International
1635 Prince St
Alexandria, VA 22314-2898

703-683-4646; Fax: 703-683-4745
www.rotor.com

James Viola, President & CEO

Provides a forum for mechanics and technicians to exchange information. It includes regulatory issues, airworthiness directives, aircraft alerts and items of special interest.
Cost: $50.00
Frequency: Quarterly

2756 **Midwest Flyer Magazine**
Flyer Publications
PO Box 199
Oregon, WI 53575-199

608-835-7063; Fax: 608-835-7063
info@midwestflyer.com
www.midwestflyer.com

Dave Weinman, Publisher/Editor

Reaches all aircraft owners in the Upper Midwest. Articles include flying travel destinations, fly-in restaurants and the issues affecting general aviation in the Midwest and nationwide.
Cost: $15.00
32 Pages
Founded in 1978

2757 **NAFI Magazine**
National Association of Flight Instructors
730 Grand Street
Allegan, MI 49010

920-426-6801
866-806-6156; Fax: 920-426-6865
nafi@nafinet.org
www.nafinet.org

Robert Meder, Chair
David Hipschman, Director & Editor, Publications

A monthly magazine published by the National Association of Flight Instructors.
Cost: $39.00
18 Pages
Frequency: Monthly
Circulation: 5400
Founded in 1967

2758 **NAFI Mentor**
National Association of Flight Instructors
730 Grand Street
Allegan, MI 49010

920-426-6801
866-806-6156; Fax: 920-426-6865
nafi@nafinet.org
www.nafinet.org

Robert Meder, Chair
John Niehas, Director, Program Development

Membership includes this magazine created exclusively for flight instructors.
20 Pages
Frequency: Monthly

2759 **NASA Tech Briefs**
Associated Business Publications International

261 5th Avenue
Suite 1901
New York, NY 10016

212-490-3999; Fax: 212-986-7864
linda@techbriefs.com
www.techbriefs.com

Dominic Mucchetti, CEO
Linda Bell, Editor
Marie Claussell, Circulation Manager
Domenic Mucchetti, CEO
Zoe Wai, Manager

Features exclusive reports of innovations developed by NASA and its partners that can be applied to develop new and improved products and solve engineering or manufacturing problems.
Cost: $49.00
Frequency: Monthly
Circulation: 30000
Founded in 1985

2760 **Naval Aviation News**
Naval History and Heritage Command
805 Kidder Breese Street SE
Washington Navy Yard
Washington, DC 20374-5060

202-433-4882; Fax: 202-433-8200
navymuseum@navy.mil
www.history.navy.mil
Facebook, Twitter

Samuel Cox, Director
Jim Bruns, Director
Edward Furgol, Managing Director

Professional magazine of naval aviation.
ISSN: 0028-1417
Founded in 1917

2761 **Ninety-Nines News**
Ninety-Nines
4300 Amelia Earhart Dr
Suite A
Oklahoma City, OK 73159-1106

405-685-7969
800-994-1929; Fax: 405-685-7985
www.ninety-nines.org

Laura Ohrenberg, Manager
Corbi Bulluck, President

A bi-monthly magazine published by Ninety-Nines.
Cost: $20.00
Circulation: 6500
Founded in 1929

2762 **Northwest Airlifter**
PO Box 98801
Tacoma, WA 98498

253-584-1212
800-293-1216; Fax: 253-581-5962

Tom Swarner, CEO

Features news, mission stories and entertainment for military personnel and families of McChord AFB.
Frequency: Weekly

2763 **Overhaul & Maintenance**
McGraw Hill
1221 Avenue of the Americas
New York, NY 10020-1095

212-512-2000
800-525-5003; Fax: 212-512-3840
www.mcgraw-hill.com

Harold W McGraw III, CEO

Information for people in airlines, flight departments, maintenance operations, maintenance bases, military logistics, issues on safety, quality, and compliance in the aviation aftermarket.
Cost: $54.00
Frequency: Monthly
Circulation: 35000
ISSN: 0031-1588

2764 **PRA Rotorcraft E-Zine**
Popular Rotorcraft Association
PO Box 68
Mentone, IN 46539

574-353-7227; Fax: 574-353-7021
prahq@medt.com
www.pra.org

Igor Bensen, Founder
Brent Drake, President
Cost: $42.00
Frequency: Monthly
Circulation: 1500

2765 **Parachutist Magazine**
United States Parachute Association
5401 Southpoint Centre Blvd
Fredericksburg, VA 22407-2612

540-604-9740; Fax: 540-604-9741
uspa@uspa.org
www.uspa.org
Facebook, Twitter

Jay Stokes, President
Ed Scott, Executive Director

Supporting safe skydiving and those who enjoy it.
Cost: $4.50
112 Pages
Frequency: Monthly
Circulation: 35000
Founded in 1946

2766 **Pipers**
Pipers Owner Society
N7450 Aanstad Rd
Iola, WI 54945

715-445-5000
866-697-4737; Fax: 715-445-4053
help@piperowner.org
www.piperowner.org

Keith Mathiowetz, Editor
Daniel Weiler, Executive Director
Joe Jones, Publisher

The official magazine of the Piper Owners Society.
Cost: $9.95
55 Pages
Frequency: Monthly
Circulation: 8400
Mailing list available for rent: 2750 names
Printed in 4 colors

2767 **Plane and Pilot**
Werner Publishing
12121 Wilshire Blvd
12th Floor
Los Angeles, CA 90025-1168

310-820-1500; Fax: 310-826-5008
editors@planeandpilotmag.com
www.wernerpublishing.com

Steve Werner, Owner

Articles on general aviation from light single-engine planes to medium weight twins and related products.
Cost: $11.97
Frequency: Monthly
Founded in 1965

2768 **Powered Sport Flying Mangazine**
Popular Rotorcraft Association
PO Box 68
Mentone, IN 46539

574-353-7227; Fax: 574-353-7021
prahq@medt.com
www.pra.org

Igor Bensen, Founder
Brent Drake, President

Devoted exclusively to homebuilt rotorcraft. Also has information, technical articles, photos of autogyros and helicopters, safety tips and news of new products for rotorcraft builders and pilots.
2000 Attendees
Frequency: August

2769 **Professional Pilot**
Queensmith Communications
30 S Quaker Ln
Suite 300
Alexandria, VA 22314-4596

703-370-0606; Fax: 703-370-7082
www.propilotmag.com

Murray Smith, Owner
Anthony Herrera, General Manager
Phil Rose, Managing Editor
Ivor Tafro, Communications Manager

Offers information for career pilots.
Cost: $50.00
Frequency: Monthly
Circulation: 35000
ISSN: 0191-6238
Founded in 1966
Printed in 4 colors on glossy stock

2770 **ROTOR Magazine**
Helicopter Association International
1635 Prince St
Alexandria, VA 22314-2898

703-683-4646; Fax: 703-683-4745
www.rotor.com

James Viola, President & CEO

Dedicated to exclusively to the civil helicopter industry. It covers pertinent helicopter operations, safety and regulatory issues including an FAA question and answer column, legislative and lobbying issues, and HAI committee and member activities. Advertising space is available is this publication. Subscription included with membership.
Cost: $15.00
Frequency: Quarterly

2771 **Rotor & Wing**
Access Intelligence
4 Choke Cherry Rd
2nd Fl
Rockville, MD 20850-4024

301-354-2000; Fax: 301-340-0542
www.aviationtoday.com
Facebook, Twitter, LinkedIn

Don Pazour, CEO
Julian Clover, Managing Editor
Jim McKenna, Manager

Semitechnical information for helicopter industry, both civil and military. Includes pilot reports, features, news and product section.
Cost: $90.99
88 Pages
Frequency: Monthly
Circulation: 33,400
Founded in 1977

2772 **Rotorcraft Magazine**
Popular Rotorcraft Association
PO Box 68
Mentone, IN 46539

574-353-7227; Fax: 574-353-7021
prahq@medt.com
www.pra.org

Brent Drake, President

Devoted exclusively to homebuilt rotorcraft. Free to members.
Cost: $26.00
60 Pages
Founded in 1963

2773 **Russian Aeronautics**
Allerton Press

250 W 57th St
New York, NY 10107-2099

212-459-0535; Fax: 646-424-9695
journals@allertonpress.com
www.allertonpress.com

W Shalof, Publisher
Vyacheslav A Firsov, Editor-in-Chief

The sole scientific-technical journal in Russia publishing articles on fundamental research, application, and developments in the field of aeronautical, space, rocket science and engineering that are carried out at institutes of higher education, research institutes, design bureaus, and branch enterprises.Published in English and Russian.
Cost: $1945.00
Frequency: Quarterly
ISSN: 1068-7998
Founded in 1971

2774 **Soaring Magazine**
Soaring Society of America
5425 W Jack Gomez Boulevard
PO Box 2100
Hobbs, NM 88241-2100

505-392-1177; Fax: 505-392-8154
dlayton@ssa.org
www.ssa.org

Denise Layton, Executive Layton
Eric Bick, Editor
Melinda Hughes, Magazine Adv./Membership Services

Each issue brings you the latest developments on safety issues, delightful accounts of individual soaring accomplishments, a sharing of ideas and experiences, tips from the great soaring pilots of our times, and much more.
Cost: $26.00
60 Pages
Frequency: Monthly
Founded in 1932

2775 **Space News**
Army Times Publishing Company
6883 Commercial Dr
Springfield, VA 22151-4202

703-750-7400
800-368-5718; Fax: 703-750-8622
cust-svc@gannettgov.com
www.armytimes.com

Elaine Howard, CEO
Tobias Naegele, Editor-in-Chief
Alex Neill, Managing Editor
Judy McCoy, Publisher

For top level executives in government and industry worldwide. Devoted exclusively to issues for military government and commercial space.
Cost: $55.00
Frequency: Weekly
Circulation: 360000
Founded in 1990

2776 **Space Times**
American Astronautical Society
6352 Rolling Mill Place
Suite 102
Springfield, VA 22152-2370

703-866-0020; Fax: 703-866-3526
aas@astronautical.org
www.astronautical.org

Carol S. Lane, President
Jim Way, Executive Director
Diane Thompson, Editor & Production Manager

The voice of the AAS, presenting thought provoking ideas and opinions, features articles on salient issues in space policy and future exploration, and reviews and notes of interest to both the professional and popular community of space flight advocates.
Cost: $85.00
Frequency: Bi-Monthly
Circulation: 1300
ISSN: 1933-2793

2777 **The Airline Handbook**
Air Transport Association of America
1301 Pennsylvania Ave NW
Suite 1100
Washington, DC 20004-1738

202-626-4000
800-497-3326; Fax: 202-626-4166
a4a@airlines.org
www.airlines.org
Twitter, LinkedIn

Nicholas Calio, President
Rebecca Spicer, SVP, Communications

2778 **Trade-A-Plane**
TAP Publishing Company
174 4th St
Crossville, TN 38555-4303

931-484-5137
800-337-5263; Fax: 931-484-2532
info@trade-a-plane.com
www.trade-a-plane.com

Cosby A Stone, CEO
L Stone, Circulation Manager

World's largest advertising periodical for general aviation.
Cost: $14.95
Frequency: Monthly
Circulation: 118000
Founded in 1937

2779 **Ultralight Flying**
Glider Rider
1085 Bailey Avenue
Chattanooga, TN 37404

423-629-5375; Fax: 423-629-5379
www.ultralightflying.com

Tracy Knauss, Publisher
Sharon Hill, Editor

Conventional and motorized ultralight flying.
Cost: $36.95
48 Pages
Frequency: Monthly
Circulation: 50000+
Founded in 1973
Printed in on newsprint stock

2780 **Vertiflite**
American Helicopter Society International
217 N Washington St
Alexandria, VA 22314-2538

703-684-6777
855-247-4685; Fax: 703-739-9279
staff@vtol.org
www.vtol.org

Michael Hirschberg, Executive Director
Kim Smith, Editor

Magazine published for the vertical flight industry, pursuing excellence within the business, stimulating research, debate and expert opinion.
Cost: $80.00
72 Pages
Frequency: Monthly
Circulation: 12000
ISSN: 0042-4455
Founded in 1943
Printed in 4 colors on glossy stock

2781 **Water Flying**
Seaplane Pilots Association
3859 Laird Blvd
Lakeland, FL 33811

863-701-7979
888-772-8923; Fax: 863-701-7588
spa@seaplanes.org
www.seaplanes.org

Steve McCaughey, Executive Director
Mark Twombly, Editor
Susie Holly, Art Director

Features articles covering everything from pilot technique and safety to destinations and personalities. Each issue includes industry news and an update on regulatory issues across the country. The March/April issue is our Directory Special, with flight school and float directories.
Cost: $45.00
32 Pages
Circulation: 7500
ISSN: 0733-1754
Founded in 1972
Mailing list available for rent
Printed in on glossy stock

2782 **Western Flyer**
Northwest Flyer
PO Box 98786
Tacoma, WA 98498-0786

253-968-3422; Fax: 253-588-4005

Dave Sinclair, Publisher
Kirk Gormley, Editor

Covering general aviation, including all aspects of business and sport aviation.
Cost: $24.00
84 Pages
Frequency: BiWeekly
Circulation: 38,000

2783 **Wings**
Sentry Books
P.O. Box 881526
San Diego, CA 92168

818-368-2012
support@airwingmedia.com
www.wingsairpower.com

Mike Machat, Publisher/Editor

Historic aviation, heavy on photos, artwork, drawings, interviews with aviation designers, pilots, engineers.
Cost: $44.00
56 Pages
Frequency: Monthly
Circulation: 30000
ISSN: 1067-0637
Founded in 1971

2784 **Wings West**
Wiesner Publishing
6160 South Syracuse
Suite 300
Greenwood Village, CO 80111

303-662-5200; Fax: 303-397-7619

Babette Andre, Editor
Becky Stairs, Advertising Executive
Dan Wiesner, CEO

Information for the mountain aviation community on various facets of western flying, including travel and safety for active pilots.
Cost: $17.97
72 Pages
Frequency: Bi-Monthly

2785 **Wings of Gold Magazine**
Association of Naval Aviation
2550 Huntington Avenue
Suite 201
Alexandria, VA 22303-1400

703-960-6806; Fax: 703-960-6807
anahqtr@aol.com
www.anahq.org

David Kennedy, Editor

Articles and commentary designed to inform the public of the value of a strong maritime air posture to US national policy. Also, articles on subjects related to Navy, Marine Corps and Coast

Guard aviation, such as personnel technology, history, readiness, aircraft and weapon systems and budgetary issues within DOD and before the Congress.
Cost: $25.00

2786 World Airshow News
Flyer Publications
PO Box 975
East Troy, WI 53120-0975

262-642-2450; Fax: 262-642-4374
jeffparnau@gmail.com
www.airshowmag.com
Facebook, Twitter, LinkedIn

Jim Froneberger, Editor
Sandra Ruka, Advertising Sales
Jim Froneberger, Editor
Cost: $24.95
Frequency: Nine Times a Year
Circulation: 6000

Trade Shows

2787 AAC Annual Conference & Exposition
Airport Consultants Council
908 King Street
Suite 100
Alexandria, VA 22314-3121

703-683-5900; Fax: 703-583-2564
info@acconline.org
www.acconline.org
Facebook, Twitter, LinkedIn

T.J. Schulz, President
Emily VanderBush, Marketing & Membership Coordinator
John B Reynolds, Coordinator of Communications
Sharon Brown, Director, Programs & Finance

Enhanced networking programs; workshops; keynote speakers; exhibitors.
Frequency: July

2788 AAC/AAAE Airport Planning, Design & Construction Symposium
Airport Consultants Council
908 King Street
Suite 100
Alexandria, VA 22314-3121

703-683-5900; Fax: 703-683-2564
info@acconline.org
www.acconline.org
Facebook, Twitter, LinkedIn

T.J. Schulz, President

Planning and development, land side/terminal facilities development, airside/airfield facility development, program and construction management, and information technology are the focus of the symposium.
600 Attendees
Frequency: Spring

2789 ADMA International Fall Conference
Aviation Distributors & Manufacturers Association
100 North 20th Street
Suite 400
Philadelphia, PA 19103-1442

215-320-3872; Fax: 215-564-2175
www.adma.org

Michael Shaw, President
F Charles Elkins, Past President
Kristen Olszewski, Executive Director
Meg Taft, Meeting Manager

Educational and informational presentations, group activities, and planned networking functions, including Private Conference Sessions.
Frequency: May, November

2790 AEA International Convention & Trade Show
Aircraft Electronic Association
3570 NE Ralph Powell Road
Lee's Summit, MO 64064

816-347-8400; Fax: 816-347-8405
info@aea.net
www.aea.net
Facebook, Twitter, LinkedIn, Youtube

Mike Adamson, President & CEO
Debra McFarland, Executive Vice President
Aaron Ward, Director, Operations
Geoff Hill, Director, Communications

Workshops, training sessions, keynote speakers, and hundreds of exhibitors in the field of aviation electronics.
Frequency: April

2791 AHS International Annual Forum & Tech Display
American Helicopter Society
217 N Washington Street
Alexandria, VA 22314

703-684-6777; Fax: 703-739-9279
staff@vtol.org
www.vtol.org
Facebook, Twitter, LinkedIn, RSS, YouTube

Michael Hirschberg, Executive Director
Valerie Sheehan, Director of Membership
David Renzi, Director of Meetings & Advertising

Exhibits for technical professionals in aircraft design, engineering, government, operators and industry executives. Over 200 presentations on aerodynamics, acoustics, dynamics, operations, product support, propulsion, testing and evaluation, and other areas. Technology display is concurrent with the Forum and is presented by leading manufacturers, service providers, defense contractors, universities and r&d organizations.
Founded in 1943

2792 AIAA New Horizons Forum & Expo at the Aerospace Science Meeting
American Institute of Aeronautics & Astronautics
1801 Alexander Bell Drive
Suite 500
Reston, VA 20191-4344

703-264-7500
800-639-2422; Fax: 703-264-7551
www.aiaa.org
Facebook, Twitter, LinkedIn, Youtube

Basil Hassan, President

A forum for scientists and engineers from industry, government and academia to share and disseminate knowledge and research. New Horizons will feature speakers sharing about new technology, challenges, opportunities, and trends, as well as panel discussions. The Aerospace Expo will showcase exhibits from industry, government and small businesses with hardware and software demos, discussions, and opportunities for side meetings.
Frequency: Annual
Founded in 1930

2793 ASA Annual Conference
Aviation Suppliers Association
2233 Wisconsin Ave. NW
Suite 503
Washington, DC 20007

202-347-6899; Fax: 202-347-6894
www.aviationsuppliers.org/Annual-Conference
Facebook, Twitter

Michele Dickstein, President
Tony Brigham, Coordinator, Programs & Services

Annual event for the aviation distribution industry featuring workshops, networking opportunities and a vendor showcase.
Frequency: Annual

2794 Aerofast SAE Aerospace Automated Fastening Conference & Exposition
Society of Automotive Engineers
400 Commonwealth Drive
Warrendale, PA 15096-0001

72- 77- 484
877-606-7323; Fax: 724-776-0790
www.sae.org

Diane Applegate, Meetings/Exhibits
David Shutt, CEO

Annual show of 45 manufacturers or suppliers of fasteners, assembly systems, CNC's, tooling and fixtures, fully automated systems.
400 Attendees
Frequency: September
Founded in 1990

2795 Aerospace Atlantic
Society of Automotive Engineers
400 Commonwealth Drive
Warrendale, PA 15096-0001

724-776-4841
877-606-7323; Fax: 724-776-0790
www.sae.org

David Shutt, President

Annual show of 30 exhibitors of aircraft systems and components, engineering services, electronics, power systems and computer services.
700 Attendees
Frequency: 84,000 Members

2796 Aerospace Medical Association Annual Scien tific Meeting
Aerospace Medical Association
320 S Henry Street
Alexandria, VA 22314-3579

703-739-2240; Fax: 703-739-9652
inquiries@asma.org
www.asma.org

Jeffrey C. Sventek, MS, CAsP, Executive Director
Gisselle Vargas, Operations Manager

Provides a multi-faceted forum for all aerospace medical disciplines and concurrently provides continuing education credits for those attending the meeting. Lectures, seminars, panels, poster presentations, workshops, film reports, and technical and scientific exhibits present data on the latest results of clinical and research studies.
Frequency: Annual

2797 Aerospace Testing Expo
Society of Flight Test Engineers
44814 N Elm Avenue
Lancaster, CA 93534

661-949-2095; Fax: 661-949-2096
www.sfte.org
Facebook, Twitter, LinkedIn, Youtube

Peter Donath, President
Michael Barrlett, Vice President
Frequency: April

2798 Aerotech: Society of Automotive Engineers Aerospace Technology Congress
Society of Automotive Engineers
400 Commonwealth Drive
Warrendale, PA 15096-0001

724-776-4841
877-606-7323; Fax: 724-776-0790
advertising@sae.org
www.sae.org

David Shutt, President

Annual show of 80 suppliers to aerospace engineers and designers.
2500 Attendees
Frequency: October

2799 **Agricultural Aviation Convention**
National Agricultural Aviation Association
1440 Duke Street
Alexandria, VA 22314

202-546-5722; Fax: 202-546-5726
information@agaviation.org
www.agaviation.org

Andrew Moore, Executive Director
Marisa Beam, Registration, Membership & Programs

Information on agricultural aviation business, agricultural aircraft, legislative issues, pesticides, new products and services, safety, maintenance, people, state and regional association news. 135 booths.
1300 Attendees

2800 **Air Cargo Forum and Exposition**
The International Air Cargo Association
PO Box 661510
Miami, FL 33266-1510

786-265-7011; Fax: 786-265-7012
www.tiaca.org

Tom Davis, Deputy Director, Exhibits
Michael Steen, Chairman
Oliver Evans, Vice Chairman

This is the premier show for the Air Cargo Industry.
3000 Attendees
Frequency: September

2801 **Air Medical Transport Conference (AMTC)**
Association of Air Medical Services
909 N Washington Street
Suite 410
Alexandria, VA 22314

703-836-8732; Fax: 703-836-8920
information@aams.org
www.aams.org

Cameron Curtis, President

Provides up-to-date information on the latest techniques and innovative approaches to air medical practice from community experts, and continuing education credits opportunities; keynote speakers and educational offerings, plus technology demos and networking opportunities; and the largest trade show of the industry with exhibits from hundreds of providers.
Frequency: March

2802 **Air Show Trade Expo International**
Dayton International Airport
3800 Wright Drive
Suite A
Vandalia, OH 45377

937-898-5901
877-359-3291; Fax: 937-898-5121
info@daytonairshow.com
www.daytonairshow.com

Terry Greivous, Executive Director
Brenda Kerfoot, General Manager

One hundred and thirty three booths that encompass all aspects of the global aerospace industry. Commercial and military aircraft and equipment, plus major suppliers' products and services display.
12M Attendees
Frequency: July

2803 **Air Traffic Control Association Convention**
Air Traffic Control Association
1101 King St
Suite 300
Alexandria, VA 22314

703-299-2430; Fax: 703-299-2437
info@atca.org
www.atca.org

Peter Dumont, President & CEO
Kenneth Carlisle, Director of Meetings & Expositions

Containing over 325 booths and exhibits of air traffic control products and services.
4,500 Attendees
Frequency: 3 times per year

2804 **Aircraft Electronics Association Annual Convention & Trade Show**
Aircraft Electronics Association
3570 NE Ralph Powell Road
Lee's Summit, MO 64064

816-347-8400; Fax: 816-347-8405
info@aea.net
www.aea.net

Mike Adamson, President & CEO
Debra McFarland, Executive Vice President

Annual show of 131 exhibitors of industry related equipment and supplies.
1500 Attendees
Frequency: March/April Annual
Founded in 1980

2805 **Aircraft Owners & Pilots Association Expo**
Aircraft Owners & Pilots Association
421 Aviation Way
Frederick, MD 21701

301-695-2000
800-872-2672; Fax: 301-695-2375
aopahq@aopa.org
www.aopa.org

Mark Baker, President & CEO

From the latest technology, to tools and flight gear, you'll find today's best products. 500 Exhibit Booths.
Frequency: June

2806 **Aircraft Owners Pilots Association Expo**
Aircraft Owners & Pilots Association
421 Aviation Way
Frederick, MD 21701

301-695-2000
888-462-3976; Fax: 301-695-2375
www.aopa.org

Annual exhibits of single-engine and multi-engine aircraft, avionics, financing information and related equipment, supplies and services. Expo offers 75 seminar hours covering the latest safety, medical, proficiency, ownership, and technology issues. Over 500 booths.
Frequency: November

2807 **Airliners International**
World Airline Historical Society
PO Box 489
Ocoee, FL 34761

904-221-1446; Fax: 407-522-9352
president@WAHSOnline.com
www.wahsonline.com
Facebook, Twitter

Chris Slimmer, President
1000 Attendees
Frequency: Annual/August
Founded in 1977

2808 **Airlines Electronic Engineering Committee Conference**
Airlines Electronic Engineering Committee
2551 Riva Road
Annapolis, MD 21401-7435

410-266-4000; Fax: 410-266-2047
www.arinc.com

Stephen Timm, President
Roger S Goldberg, Show Contact

Annual show and exhibit of air transport avionics equipment and systems.
Frequency: October

2809 **Airport Systems Action Planning Meeting**
ARINC
2551 Riva Road
Annapolis, MD 21401

410-664-4000
80 -63 -688; Fax: 410-266-2329
flightops@arinc.com
www.arinc.com
Facebook, Twitter, LinkedIn

Lee Suarez, Staff VP
Stephen Timm, President
Stephen Waechter, VP Business Operations/CFO
Linda Hartwig, Sr Dir Corporate Communications

The meeting format will include organizational, technical, and project updates from the ARINC management team.
Frequency: September
Founded in 1920

2810 **Airports Council International - North America Annual Conference & Expo**
Airports Council International
1775 K Street NW
Suite 500
Washington, DC 20006

202-293-8500; Fax: 202-331-1362
www.aci.aero
Facebook, Twitter, LinkedIn, Youtube

Gregory Principato, President
Deborah McElroy, VP
Nancy Zimini, SVP Administration and Operations

Representatives from more than 100 airports around the world attend this exhibition and conference; seminars, discussions and speakers about air travel and the industry, developing legal affairs, challenges and best practices; hundreds of exhibitors.
Frequency: September
Founded in 1948

2811 **Airports Council International: North America Convention**
Airports Council International-North America
1775 K Street NW
Suite 500
Washington, DC 20006

202-293-8500; Fax: 202-331-1362
www.aci.aero

Deborah McElroy, Vice President
Nancy Zimini, SVP Administration & Operations
Juliet Wright, Senior Director Public Relations
Gregory Principato, President

Annual show and exhibit of air transportation equipment, supplies and services.
Frequency: Annual

2812 **American Bonanza Society Convention**
Midcontinent Airport

PO Box 12888
Wichita, KS 67277

316-945-1700; Fax: 316-945-1710
www.bonanza.org

Whit Hickman, Executive Director

Annual convention featuring educational seminars and 75-100 exhibits of equipment, supplies and services for the aviation industry, including aftermarket products, safety items and computer weather services.
1200 Attendees
Frequency: September
Founded in 1967

2813 Annual Repair Symposium
Aeronautical Repair Station Association
121 N Henry Street
Alexandria, VA 22314-2903

703-739-9543; Fax: 703-739-9488
arsa@arsa.org
www.arsa.org
Facebook, Twitter, LinkedIn, Youtube

Craig Fabian, VP
Daniel Fisher, VP

The Symposium will include a variety of sessions on topical subjects. Legislative Day will inform you about the issues that affect your business, and includes the opportunity for you to arrange Capitol Hill meetings with your representatives, senators and congressional staff.
Frequency: Annual/March

2814 Army Aviation Association of America Convention
Army Aviation Association of America
755 Main Street
Suite 4D
Monroe, CT 06468-2830

203-268-2450; Fax: 203-268-5870
aaaa@quad-a.org
www.quad-a.org
Facebook, Twitter, Youtube

Daniel J Petrosky, President
Howard Yellen, Senior Vice President
E.J. Sinclair, Secretary

A show of 275 or more exhibitors both military and industry displaying technology and material pertinent to the army aviation community.
6000 Attendees
Frequency: Annual/May
Founded in 1978

2815 Arnic Aviation Customer Meeting
British Telecommunications
2551 Riva Road
Annapolis, MD 21401

410-266-4000
800-633-6882; Fax: 410-266-2329
flightops@arinc.com
www.arinc.com
Facebook, Twitter, LinkedIn, Youtube

Lee Suarez, Staff VP
Stephen Timm, President
Stephen Waechter, VP Business Operations/CFO
Linda Hartwig, Sr Dir Corporate Communications

Up to date information on the current and future products and services of Arnic and its strategic partners in Asia.
Frequency: May
Founded in 1920

2816 Arnic Global Communications Workshop
British Telecommunications
2551 Riva Road
Annapolis, MD 21401

410-266-4000
800-633-6882; Fax: 410-266-2329
flightops@arinc.com
www.arinc.com
Facebook, Twitter, LinkedIn, Youtube

Lee Suarez, Staff VP
Stephen Tim, President
Stephen Waechter, VP Business Operations/CFO
Linda Hartwig, Sr Dir Corporate Communications

Concentrates on the communications needs of the airlines serving the Latin America/Caribbean region, and provides information on the benefits of implementing a data link program and associated applications.
Frequency: May
Founded in 1920

2817 Aviation Insurance Association Conference
Aviation Insurance Association
400 Admiral Blvd
Kansas City, MO 64106

816-221-8488; Fax: 816-472-7765
mandie@aiaweb.org
www.aiaweb.org
Facebook

Jim Gardner, President

Provides a forum for the biggest names and best minds in the aviation insurance industry. Offers top-notch speakers, continuing education classes, time with vendors and opportunities to network and develop relationships that last a lifetime.
Frequency: Annual
Founded in 1976

2818 Aviation Services and Suppliers Supershow
National Air Transportation Association
4226 King Street
Alexandria, VA 22302

703-845-9000
800-808-6282; Fax: 703-845-8176
www.nata.aero

Timothy Obitts, President & CEO

Workshop, conference, seminar and 700 exhibits of aviation products & services for fixed base and air charter operators.
5000 Attendees
Frequency: May/Annual

2819 Aviation Show South America
American Aerospace & Defense Industries
212 Carnegie Center
Suite 203
Princeton, NJ 08540

609-987-9050; Fax: 609-987-0277

Marianne Ferrandi, Show Contact

One hundred and seven exhibitors of areospace information.
90000 Attendees
Frequency: July

2820 Aviation Technician Education Council Conference
Aviation Technician Education Council
2090 Wexford Court
Harrisburg, PA 17112-1579

717-540-7121; Fax: 717-540-7121
www.atec-amt.org

Gary Hoyle, President
Crystal Maguire, Executive Director
Tarra Ruttman, Operations Manager

Annual conference and exhibits of aviation maintenance equipment, supplies and services.
150 Attendees
Frequency: April

2821 Business Information Technology Conference
Airports Council International - North America
1775 K Street NW
Suite 500
Washington, DC 20036-2463

202-293-8500; Fax: 202-331-1362
meetings@aci-na.org
www.aci.aero

Gregory Principato, President
Diedre Clemmons, Director, Conferences
Cassandra Jackson, Manager, Conferences

Hear from industry experts and peers on the latest way to deal with IT challenges, maximize the value of your IT infrastructure and anticipate new technologies.
Frequency: Annual

2822 Civil Air Patrol Annual Conference
Civil Air Patrol
105 S Hansell Street
Building 714
Maxwell AFB, AL 36112-6332

334-834-2236
877-227-9142; Fax: 334-953-4262
www.capmembers.com

Brig Gen Amy Courter, Interim National Commander
1.2M Attendees
Frequency: August
Founded in 1930

2823 Civil Aviation Medical Association Conference
Civil Aviation Medical Association
PO Box 2382
Peachtree City, GA 30269-2382

77- 48- 010; Fax: 77- 48- 008
david.millett@yahoo.com
www.civilavmed.org

Gerald Saboe, President
Sherry Sandoval, Executive VP

Annual conference and exhibits of aviation medical equipment, supplies and services. Containing 15 booths.
250 Attendees
Frequency: October
Founded in 1948

2824 Composites and Advanced Materials Expo (CAMX)
Soc for the Advancement of Material & Process Eng
21680 Gateway Center Drive
Suite 300
Diamond Bar, CA 91765-2454

626-521-9460
info@sampe.org
www.nasampe.org
Facebook, LinkedIn

Gregg Balko, CEO

The Society for the Advancement of Material and Process Engineering's event showcases the latest technology, applications and materials for the advanced manufacturing marketplace. Includes over 550 exhibits.
Frequency: Annual/September

2825 Defense & Security Symposium
International Society for Optical Engineering
PO Box 10
Bellingham, WA 98227-0010

360-676-3290
888-504-8171; Fax: 360-647-1445

CustomerService@SPIE.org
www.spie.org

Dr John C Carrano, Contact Person
Dr Larry B Stotts, Contact Person
Dr. Katarina Svanberg, President
William Arnold, Vice President

A large, unclassified international symposium related to sensors and sensor networks.
5700 Attendees
Frequency: March

2826 **Economic Specialty Conference**
Airports Association Council International
1775 K Street NW
Suite 500
Washington, DC 20006

202-293-8500; Fax: 202-331-1362
www.aci.aero

Gregory Principato, President
Nancy Zimini, VP
Christopher Oswald, SVP Technical Affairs
Ian A Redhead, VP Airport Services
Patricia Hahn, EVP Operations/General Counsel

Provided with information on the latest economic trends for airports and the airport industry. Attendees include executive directors and CFOs from airports throughout North America, plys representatives from insurance companies and airport concessionaires.
Frequency: May

2827 **Experimental Aircraft Association AirVenture**
Experimental Aircraft Association
3000 Poberezny Road
PO Box 3086
Oshkosh, WI 54902

920-426-4800
800-236-4800; Fax: 920-232-7772
webmaster@eaa.org
www.airventure.org

Tom Poberezny, President
David Berkley, Communications Dirctor
Adam Smith, VP Member Services

Recreational aviation event, with more than 765,000 people and 10,000 airplanes attending. Containing 900 booths and 730 exhibits.
765M Attendees
Founded in 1953

2828 **Fall Education Conference**
University Aviation Association
2415 Moore's Mill Road
Suite 265-216
Auburn, AL 36830-6444

901-563-0505
uaamail@uaa.aero
www.uaa.aero
Facebook, Twitter, LinkedIn

Dawn Vinson, Executive Director
Timm Bliss, Publications
Mary Reece, Accounts Manager
Laura. Daniel Swanson, Member Services Coordinator
Founded in 1947

2829 **GTO Annual Convention & Fly In**
Pipers Owner Society & Cessna Owner Organization
PO Box 5000
Iola, WI 54945

715-445-5000
888-692-3776; Fax: 715-445-4053
help@piperowner.org

Dan Weiler, Executive Director
Joe Jones, Publisher

Annual fly in prior to the EAA AirVenture.
150 Attendees
Frequency: Annual

2830 **Gate Way to Oshkosh**
Cessna Owner Organization
N7450 Aanstad Rd
Iola, WI 54945

715-445-5000
888-692-3776; Fax: 715-445-4053
help@cessnaowner.org
www.cessnaowner.org

Dan Weiler, Executive Director
Joe Jones, Publisher
150 Members
Frequency: Annual

2831 **Goddard Memorial Symposium**
American Astronautical Society
6352 Rolling Mill Place
Suite 102
Springfield, VA 22152-2370

703-866-0020; Fax: 703-866-3526
aas@astronautical.org
www.astronautical.org
Facebook, Twitter

Carol Lane, President
Jim Way, Executive Director

Leaders in aerospace come together to discuss the future of the space program.
350 Attendees
Frequency: Annual/ November

2832 **Heli-Expo**
Helicopter Association International
1635 Prince Street
Alexandria, VA 22314-2818

703-683-4646; Fax: 703-683-4745
heliexpo@rotor.com
www.rotor.com

James Viola, President & CEO
Roxanne Fox, Chief of Staff

The world's largest tradeshow dedicated to the international helicopter community. Attend for new ideas, business solutions, products and services, and networking. Over 550 exhibiting companies offering engines, avionics, instruments, modifications, helicopters for every mission, finance, insurance, software, uniforms and safety gear, mechanic and pilot training, parts, and accessories.
16000 Attendees
Frequency: February

2833 **IFSA Annual Conference & Exhibition**
Inflight Food Service Association
304 W Liberty Street
Suite 201
Louisville, KY 40202-3011

502-583-3783; Fax: 502-589-3602
www.ifsanet.com

Pam Chumley, Executive Administrator
Jim Fowler, Executive Director
Jacqueline Petty, Manager of Communications
Caitlin Ellery, Membership Manager

An opportunity to experience excellent educational speakers, panel discussions, culinary demos, and general sessions focused on important issues in the in-flight and onboard foodservice industry. An exhibition is held in conjunction with the conference to exhibit the latest innovations while providing network opportunities with key leaders and decision makers in in-flight and railway catering.
Frequency: Annual

2834 **International Air Cargo Forum & Exposition**
International Air Cargo Association
5600 NW 36th Street
Suite 620
Miami, FL 33266-1510

786-265-7011; Fax: 786-265-7012
secgen@tiaca.org
www.tiaca.org

Michael Steen, Chairman
George F Johnson, Treasurer
Daniel F Fernandez, Secretary General

Biennial trade show of the air cargo industry featuring services and products from aircraft manufacturers, airlines, airports, freight forwarders trade publications logistics consultants.
4,000 Attendees
Frequency: September
Founded in 1960

2835 **Joint Airports Environmental/Technical Committee Meeting**
Airports Association Council International
1615 L Street
Suite 300
Washington, DC 20006

202-293-8500
888-424-7767; Fax: 202-331-1362
memberservices@aci-na.org
www.aci.aero
Facebook, Twitter, LinkedIn

Gregory Principato, President
Nancy Zimini, VP
Christopher Oswald, SVP Technical Affairs
Frequency: May
Founded in 1948

2836 **NATA FBO Leadership Conference**
National Air Transportation Association
4226 King Street
Alexandria, VA 22302

703-845-9000
800-808-6282; Fax: 703-845-8176
www.nata.aero
Facebook, Twitter, LinkedIn

Timothy Obitts, President & CEO

An opportunity for business leaders to meet with their customers and learn about the latest challenges and opportunities facing their industry. d seminars. The Conference will focus on the changing climate of the industry and the developing environment. Opportunities to learn service and marketing techniques, network and exchange best practices.
Frequency: Annual

2837 **NBAA Annual Meeting & Convention**
National Business Aviation Association
1200 G Street NW
Suite 1100
Washington, DC 20005

202-783-9000; Fax: 202-331-8364
info@nbaa.org
www.nbaa.org

Edward M. Bolen, President & CEO
Chris Strong, SVP, Conventions & Membership
Dina Green, VP, Events
Linda Peters, VP, Exhibits

Learning sessions, networking opportunities, 1,000 exhibitors, demonstrations and displays.
32000 Attendees
Frequency: Annual/September

2838 **National Space Symposium**
Space Foundation
4425 Arrowswest Drive
Colorado Springs, CO 80907

719-768-8000
800-691-4000; Fax: 719-576-8801

www.spacefoundation.org
Facebook, Twitter, LinkedIn

Thomas Zelibor, CEO
Shelli Brunswick, COO
Holly Roberts, CFO

The National Space Symposium is the premier U.S. policy and program forum, providing an opportunity for information and interaction on all sectors of space - civil, commercial, and national security. The conference is attended by industry leaders, military and government officials and general space enthusiasts, and covered locally and nationally by broadcast, print and industry trade media.
Frequency: Annually/April

2839 Ninety Nines International Conference
International Organization of Women Pilots
4300 Amelia Earhart Road
Oklahoma City, OK 73159-1140

405-685-7969
800-994-1929; Fax: 405-685-7985
99s@ninety-nines.org
www.ninety-nines.org

Corbi Bulluck, President
Laura Ohrenberg, Headquarters Manager
Frequency: August

2840 PAMA Aviation Maintenance & Management Symposium
Professional Aviation Maintenance Association
972 E Tuttle Road
Building 204
Ionia, MI 48846

724-772-4092
800-356-1671; Fax: 616-527-1327
www.pama.org
Facebook, Twitter, LinkedIn

Roger Sickler, Chairman
Jeff Gruber, Vice Chairman
John Wicht, Secretary
Frequency: March
Founded in 1972

2841 PRA International Conference
Popular Rotorcraft Association
PO Box 68
Mentone, IN 46539

574-353-7227; Fax: 574-353-7021
prahq@medt.com
www.pra.org

Brent Drake, President
Christene Toevs, VP

Exhibits, flight demonstrations, contests, commercial exhibits, great food, forums on rotorcraft topics, and unlimited fun! There are also many other events sanctioned by PRA and its local chapters.
2000 Attendees
Frequency: August

2842 PRA International Convention Fly-In
Popular Rotorcraft Association
PO Box 68
Mentone, IN 46539

574-353-7227; Fax: 574-353-7021
www.pra.org

Igor Bensen, Founder
Brent Drake, President
Christene Toevs, VP

The largest gathering of homebuilt rotorcraft in the world. It has exhibits, flight demonstrations, contests, commercial exhibits, great food, forums on rotorcraft topics, and unlimited fun.
3500 Attendees
Frequency: Annual/Summer

2843 Professional Aviation Maintenance Symposium and Trade Show
Professional Aviation Maintenance Association
972 E Tuttle Road
Building 204
Ionia, MI 48846

202-300-0258
800-356-1671; Fax: 616-527-1327
www.pama.org

John Goglia, President

Annual show of 200 exhibitors of aviation and aerospace products for the aviation maintenance industry.
2000 Attendees
Frequency: March

2844 Regional Airline Association Convention
Regional Airline Association
2025 M Street NW
Suite 800
Washington, DC 20036

202-367-1170; Fax: 202-367-2170
raa@raa.org
www.raa.org
Facebook, Twitter

Faye Malarkey Black, President & CEO
Sara Haukap, Manager, Conventions

A forum for airport and airline professionals held twice a year in the spring and fall.
Frequency: May/October

2845 Regional Airline Association Spring Meeting
Regional Airline Association
2025 M Street NW
Suite 800
Washington, DC 20036

202-367-1170; Fax: 202-367-2170
raa@raa.org
www.raa.org
Facebook, Twitter

Faye Malarkey Black, President & CEO
Michelle Cravez, Manager, Membership, Ops. & Events

Forum for airport and airline professionals.
1.6M Attendees
Frequency: May

2846 Reliability Engineering and Management Institute Conference
Univ of Arizona, Aerospace & Mechanical Engin Dept
1130 N Mountain Avenue
Building 119 Room N 517
Tucson, AZ 85721

520-621-6120; Fax: 520-621-8191
dimitri@u.arizona.edu

Dr Dimitri B Kececioglu, Manager

Provides all engineers, and particularly Reliability Managers and Engineers, and Products Assurance Managers and Engineers in government and Industry, with a working knowledge of Reliability Engineering Theory and Practice; Mechanical Reliability Prediction; Reliability Testing and Demonstration; Failure Analysis (FAMECA); Complete Industry Product Assurance strategies; Maintainability Engineering; Reliability and Quality Management; Manufacturing Techniques, and more.
Frequency: Nov Arizona

2847 Reliability Testing Institute
University Of Arizona
1130 N Mountain Avenue
Tucson, AZ 85721

520-621-6120; Fax: 520-621-8191
dimitri@u.arizona.edu

Dr Dimitri Kececioglu PE, Prof
Aerospace/Mech Engineering

An institute to help provide a working knowledge in reliability engineering.
Frequency: May

2848 SAE AeroTech Congress & Exhibition
Society of Automotive Engineers
400 Commonwealth Drive
Warrendale, PA 15086-7511

724-776-4841
877-606-7323; Fax: 724-776-0790
www.sae.org
Facebook, Twitter, LinkedIn, Youtube

David Shutt, President

Provides a forum for the aerospace community to meet and discuss current and future challenges, opportunities and requirements of next-generation R&D, products, and systems, and to develop professional relationships among the worldwide community. Technical sessions, panel discussions, keynote speakers, presentations and demonstrations.
3M Attendees
Frequency: Annual

2849 SAE Government/Industry Event
Society of Automotive Engineers
400 Commonwealth Drive
Warrendale, PA 15086-7511

724-776-4841
877-606-7323; Fax: 724-776-0790
mjena@sae.org
www.sae.org
Facebook, Twitter, LinkedIn, Youtube

David Shutt, President

Awards and presentations, technical sessions, network receptions, and exhibits.
Frequency: Annual

2850 SAE World Congress
Society of Automotive Engineers
400 Commonwealth Drive
Warrendale, PA 15096-0001

724-776-4841
877-606-7323; Fax: 724-776-0790
agrech@sae.org
www.sae.org
Facebook, Twitter, LinkedIn, Youtube

David Shutt, President

Reinvented in 2010, the World Conference provides a highly relevant and engaging technical program, expanded and improved opportunities for networking and information exchange, and innovative exhibits.
3.5M Attendees
Frequency: Annual

2851 SAFE Symposium
SAFE Association
PO Box 130
Creswell, OR 97426

541-895-3012; Fax: 541-895-3014
safe@peak.org
www.safeassociation.com
Facebook

Robert Billings, President
Marcia Baldwin, President-Elect

The Symposium provides an internationally attended marketplace for the exchange of technical information, product and service exhibitions, and the showcasing of industry capabilities for meeting challenges in vehicular

occupant protection and personnel worn safety equipment.
Frequency: October

2852 **SAMPE Conference & Exhbition**
Soc for the Advancement of Material & Process Eng
21680 Gateway Center Drive
Suite 300
Diamond Bar, CA 91765-2454

626-521-9460
info@sampe.org
www.nasampe.org
Facebook, LinkedIn

Gregg Balko, CEO
Brian Condon, Conference Information

The Society for the Advancement of Material and Process Engineering's event showcases the latest technology, applications and materials for the advanced manufacturing marketplace; educational sessions, and exhibits. Attendees include industry leaders, academics, students, researchers, engineers, chemists and business professionals.
Frequency: Annual/May

2853 **Sea-Air-Space**
Navy League of the United States
11208 Waples Mill Road
Suite 112
Fairfax, VA 22030

703-631-6200
800-564-4220; Fax: 703-818-9177
www.jspargo.com

Paul doCarmo, Assistant Director/Exhibit Sales
Connie Shaw, Exhibit Sales Account Manager

Annual event to help promote and develop a technologically advanced naval force.
6000 Attendees
Frequency: April

2854 **Seaplane Pilots Association Conference**
Seaplane Pilots Association
3859 Laird Blvd
Lakeland, FL 33811

863-701-7979
888-772-8923; Fax: 863-701-7588
spa@seaplanes.org
www.seaplanes.org

Steve McCaughey, Executive Director

Thirty booths and conference.
1.5M Attendees
Frequency: September

2855 **Soaring Society of America Annual Convention**
Soaring Society of America
5425 W Jack Gomez Boulevard
PO Box 2100
Hobbs, NM 88241-2100

505-392-1177; Fax: 505-392-8154
merchandise@ssa.org
www.ssa.org

Denise Layton, Executive Director

Meetings, exhibits, and displays.
Frequency: Annual

2856 **Society of Automotive Engineers: Aerotech Expo**
Society of Automotive Engineers
400 Commonwealth Drive
Warrendale, PA 15096-0001

772- 77- 484
877-606-7323; Fax: 248-273-2494
advertising@sae.org
www.sae.org

David Shutt, President

Exhibits of commercial, military, business and general aviation.

2857 **Society of Experimental Test Pilots**
Society of Experimental Test Pilots
44814 Elm Avenue
Lancaster, CA 93534

661-942-9574; Fax: 661-940-0398
setp@setp.org
www.setp.org

Michael Wallace, President
Laurie Balderas, Executive Director

These conferences provide major forums for the discussion of aspects of tax, accounting, administration, statute and case law, which are of general concern to practitioners, as well as providing advance knowledge of developments affecting trusts, estates and subjects of allied subjects. Twenty Booths.
1.5M Attendees
Frequency: September

2858 **Strategic Space and Defense**
Space Foundation
4425 Arrowswest Drive
Colorado Springs, CO 80907

719-576-8000; Fax: 719-576-8801
www.spacefoundation.org

Thomas Zelibor, CEO
Shelli Brunswick, Chief Operating Officer
Holly Roberts, CFO

The definitive global security conference where the senior leadership of U.S. Strategic Command, component and supported commands, and the executive leadership of the national security industrial base gather to gain insight on the Command's mission, global activities and relationships.
Frequency: October

2859 **United States Pilots Association Meeting**
United States Pilots Association
1652 Indian Point Road
Branson, MO 65616

417-338-2225
jan@hoynacki.com
www.uspilots.org

David Forster, President
Jan Hoynacki, Executive Director

Holds two meetings a year — in the spring and fall.
Frequency: June/Septemter

2860 **United States Ultralight Association**
United States Ultralight Association
PO Box 3501
Gettysburg, PA 17325-1810

717-339-0200; Fax: 717-339-0063
www.usua.org

Steve McCaughey, Executive Director
Dale Hooper, Executive VP

Annual meeting and exhibits of ultralight and microlight aviation equipment, supplies and services. There will be 20 booths.
3000 Attendees
Frequency: February
Founded in 1998

2861 **Werner Von Braun Memorial Symposium**
American Astronautical Society
6352 Rolling Mill Place
Suite 102
Springfield, VA 22152-2370

703-866-0020; Fax: 703-866-3526
aas@astronautical.org
www.astronautical.org
Facebook, Twitter

Carol Lane, President
Jim Way, Executive Director

Features panel discussions and guess speakers from academia, government, business, and international aerospace experts.
Frequency: Annual/October

2862 **World Airline Historical Society Convention**
World Airline Historical Society
PO Box 489
Ocoee, FL 34761

904-221-1446; Fax: 407-522-9352
Information@WAHSOnline.com
www.wahsonline.com

Chris Slimmer, President
Don Levine, Secretary/Treasurer

Convention and exhibits of airline memorabilia, including airplane models, airline schedules, postcards, posters, photos and publications from airlines.
500 Members
Frequency: Annual
Founded in 1977

Directories & Databases

2863 **AAMS Resource Guide**
Association of Air Medical Services
909 N Washington Street
Suite 410
Alexandria, VA 22314

703-836-8732; Fax: 703-836-8920
information@aams.org
www.aams.org

Cameron Curtis, President & CEO
Gloria Dow, Editor

The directory contains information on the association and its products and services; pertinent details on members, including demographic and historical information; and special crew listings that help community members perform their jobs better through enhanced networking opportunities. It also provides decision makers with a buyer's guide of community vendors and suppliers and the services they supply.

2864 **ABD: Aviation Buyer's Directory**
Air Service Directory
116 Radio Circle
Suite #302
Mt Kisco, NY 10549

914-242-8700; Fax: 914-242-5422
abd@abdonline.com
abdonline.com/

Manufacturers and dealers of aviation equipment and aircraft are the focus of this directory.
Cost: $25.00
400 Pages
Frequency: Quarterly
Circulation: 17,000

2865 **AOPA's Airport Directory**
Aircraft Owners & Pilots Association
421 Aviation Way
Frederick, MD 21701-4756

301-695-2000
800-872-2672; Fax: 301-695-2375
www.aopa.org

Mark Baker, President & CEO

Includes information on over 7,400 airports, seaplane bases and heliports. Also covers more than 2,200 private use airports. In addition to basic airport information such as runways, lighting, approaches, frequencies, identifiers and lat/long, you'll also find listings of nearby hotels, transportation, restaurants, etc. Paperback.
Cost: $29.95
680 Pages
Frequency: Annual
Circulation: 300,000

Founded in 1962
Printed in one color on glossy stock

2866 Address List for Regional Airports Divisions and Airport Districts
US Federal Aviation Administration
800 Independence Avenue SW
Washington, DC 20591-0001
202-366-4000
866-835-5322; Fax: 202-493-5032
www.faa.gov
David Grizzle, COO
David Weingart, Chief of Staff
Offers district offices and airports.
20 Pages

2867 Aerospace Database
Cambridge Scientific Abstracts
Aerospace Access
59 John Street, 7th Floor
New York, NY 10038
212-349-1120; Fax: 212-349-1283
Tony Lenti, Managing Editor
Earl Spencer, Owner
Provides bibliographic coverage of basic and applied research in aeronautics, astronautics, and space sciences. The database also covers technology development and applications in complementary and supporting fields such as chemistry, geosciences, physics, communications, and electronics. In addition to periodic literature, the database also includes coverage of reports issued by NASA, other US government agencies, international institutions, universities, and private firms.

2868 Airline Handbook
Air Transport Association
1301 Pennsylvania Ave NW
Suite 1100
Washington, DC 20004
202-626-4000
800-497-3326; Fax: 301-206-9789
a4a@airlines.org
www.airlines.org
Nicholas Calio, President/CEO
Overview of the history, structure, economics and operations of the airline industry. Includes a glossary of commonly used airline terminology.
Cost: $10.00
Frequency: Hardcover
Founded in 2001

2869 Airport Operators Council International
1775 K St NW
Suite 500
Washington, DC 20006-1529
202-293-8500; Fax: 202-331-1362
webmaster@aci-na.org
www.aci.aero
Gregory Principato, President
Deborah McElroy, Executive VP External Affairs
Nancy Zimini, Senior Vice President
Contains an annual time series of aviation and airport data for more than 580 airports from the Worldwide Airport Traffic Report.
Founded in 1948

2870 Airports
CTB/McGraw Hill
20 Ryan Ranch Rd
Monterey, CA 93940-5770
831-393-0700; Fax: 831-393-6528
Ellen Haley, President
Offers information on airport management issues, including funding. Congressional and regulatory activities, legal matters, noise and capacity problems are offered as well.
Frequency: Full-text

2871 Aviation Businesses and the Service they Provide
National Air Transportation Association
4226 King St
Alexandria, VA 22302-1507
703-845-9000
800-808-6282; Fax: 703-845-8176
www.nata.aero
Facebook, Twitter, LinkedIn
Timothy Obitts, President & CEO
A detailed fact book, complete with statistical data, on the aviation services industry.

2872 Aviation Telephone Directory
Aviation Telephone Directory
6619 Tumbleweed Ridge Lane
Suite 102
Henderson, NV 89015
800-437-2962; Fax: 702-943-8982
www.aviationfinder.com
Is the leading source for General Aviation information with more than 14,000 Companies and 10,000 airports. Yellow pages, White pages, and Blue pages(by airport). Thousands of phone numbers.
Cost: $19.95
790 Pages
Frequency: BiAnnually
Circulation: 20000
ISSN: 1075-1378
Founded in 1949
Printed in 4 colors on newsprint stock

2873 Collegiate Aviation Guide
University Aviation Association
2415 Moore's Mill Road
Suite 265-216
Auburn, AL 36830-6444
901-563-0505
uaamail@uaa.aero
www.uaa.aero
Dawn Vinson, Executive Director
Timm Bliss, Publications
A comprehensive guide of regionally accredited colleges and universities with aviation offerings ranging from academic completion certificates and associate degrees to doctoral programs. Contains listings of institutions throughout the United States, with some located in Canada.
Founded in 1947

2874 Commuter Flight Statistics and Online Origin & Destination Data
US Department of Transportation
Kendall Square
Cambridge, MA 02142-1093
617-494-5906
Robin A Caldwell, Director
Covers all areas of the commuter airline flight industry, including statistical information on flights by commuter airlines.
Frequency: Statistical

2875 Flying Annual and Buyers Guide
Hachette Filipacchi Magazines
1633 Broadway
42nd Floor
New York, NY 10019-6708
212-767-6000; Fax: 212-767-5600
www.hfmnewsstand.com/index
Alain Lemarchand, CEO
Richard Collins, Editor at Large
This substantial guide lists manufacturers, dealers, suppliers and professionals in the aviation industry.
Cost: $18.00

2876 General Aviation Statistical DataBook
General Aviation Manufacturers Association
1400 K St NW
Suite 801
Washington, DC 20005-2402
202-393-1500; Fax: 202-842-4063
bforan@gama.aero
www.gama.aero
Pete Bunce, President, Chief Executive Officer
Statistics on US general aviation shipments, aircraft fleet, international trade, safety and the most current data on airport statistics and pilot population.
Cost: $10.00
Frequency: Annual

2877 Guide to Selecting Airport Consultants and Membership Directory
Airport Consultants Council
908 King Street
Suite 100
Alexandria, VA 22314-3067
703-683-5900; Fax: 703-683-2564
info@acconline.org
www.acconline.org
T.J. Schulz, President
Daniel Jagdmann, Manager, Data Services & Membership
A full nationwide listing of airport consultants and association news.
Frequency: Annual

2878 Helicopter Annual
Helicopter Association International
1635 Prince St
Alexandria, VA 22314-2898
703-683-4646; Fax: 703-683-4745
www.rotor.com
James Viola, President & CEO
A comprehensive reference guide for th civil helicopter industry. Includes specifications, industry statistics, HAI membership directories by class and geographic matrix, listings of international civil aviation contacts, key FAA personnel, association committees, and more. First copy included free with membership.
Cost: $50.00
360 Pages
Frequency: Annual
Circulation: 25,000

2879 International Aerospace Abstracts
American Institute of Aeronautics and Astronautics
1801 Alexander Bell Dr
Suite 500
Reston, VA 20191-4344
703-264-7500
800-639-2422; Fax: 703-264-7551
www.aiaa.org
Basil Hassan, President
This database contains more than 2 million references and abstracts of journal and monograph literature relating to aerospace science and technology.
Frequency: Monthly

2880 **Light Aircraft Manufacturers Association Directory**
2001 Steamboat Ridge Ct
Daytona Beach, FL 94588

651-592-7565; Fax: 925-426-0771
info@lama.bz
www.lama.bz

Dan Johnson, President

A list of over 400 member manufacturers of light and ultralight aircraft and suppliers of related products and services.

2881 **NBAA Directory of Member Companies, Aircraft & Personnel**
National Business Aviation Association
1200 G Street NW
Suite 1100
Washington, DC 20005

202-783-9000; Fax: 202-331-8364
info@nbaa.org
www.nbaa.org

Edward Bolen, President & CEO

Furnished to members only and contains a comprehensive listing of NBAA Member companies with their aircraft and flight department personnel.

2882 **Space Law**
Oceana Publications
198 Madison Avenue
New York, NY 10016

800-334-4249; Fax: 212-726-6476
custserv.us@oup.com
www.oceanalaw.com

Paul Stephen Dempsey, Editor

Provides in-depth expert coverage by today's preeminent export of the most pressing issues currently being faced by international regulators in this dynamic and growing area of the law.
Cost: $625.00
40 Pages
Frequency: 5 Volume Set
Circulation: 2,000
ISBN: 0-379012-92-8
Printed in 4 colors

2883 **United States Civil Aircraft Registry**
Insured Aircraft Title Service
PO Box 19527
Oklahoma City, OK 73144-0527

405-681-6663
800-654-4882; Fax: 405-681-9299
www.insuredaircraft.com

Matthew Kelly, Owner

This directory covers owners of over 275,000 aircraft.
Cost: $600.00
190 Pages
Frequency: Monthly
Founded in 1963

2884 **Water Landing Directory**
Seaplane Pilots Association
3859 Laird Blvd
Lakeland, FL 33811

863-701-7979
888-772-8923; Fax: 863-701-7588
spa@seaplanes.org
www.seaplanes.org

Steve McCaughey, Executive Director

Is the only publication that combines federal, state, provincial and special agency regulations affecting seaplane operators. The directory includes waterway closures and restrictions, seaplane bases listed by state and city, informative seaplane base diagrams, customs information, flight planning charts and other miscellaneous quick reference materials.

2885 **World Aviation Directory and Aerospace Database**
McGraw Hill
1200 G St NW
Suite 922
Washington, DC 20005-3821

202-343-2300; Fax: 202-383-2347

John McNicholas, Marketing Director

Aviation and the aerospace industry are covered in this global directory offering information on manufacturers, subcontractors, support services and associations.
2500 Pages

Industry Web Sites

2886 **gama.aero**
General Aviation Manufacturers Association

Association supporting manufacturers of general aviation aircraft, and related equipment.

2887 **http://gold.greyhouse.com**
G.O.L.D Grey House OnLine Databases

Grey House Publishing's online database platform, GOLD, offers Quick Search, Keyword Search and Expert Search for most business sectors including aviation and aerospace markets. The GOLD platform makes finding the information you need quick and easy - whether you're a novice searcher or an experienced database user. All of Grey House's directory products are available for subscription on the GOLD platform.

2888 **www.aams.org**
Association of Air Medical Services

Air medical transport equipment, supplies and services.

2889 **www.aci-na.org**
Airports Council International-North America

Represents local, regional and state governing bodies that own and operate commercial airports throughtout the United States and Canada.

2890 **www.aeronet.com**
Aeronet Worldwide

Specializes in urgent shipping solutions. From computer and technical supplies, to medical equipment, to odd size, one of a kind machine parts, we have always been there for our clients, one shipment at a time.

2891 **www.afa.org**
Air Force Association

Independent nonprofit, civilian organization promoting public understanding of aerospace power and the pivotal role it plays in the security of the nation.

2892 **www.afanet.org**
Association of Flight Attendants

Represents over 50,000 flight attendants at 26 airlines, serving as a voice for flight attendants at their workplace, in the industry, the media and on Capitol Hill.

2893 **www.agaviation.org**
National Agricultural Aviation Association

Voice of the aerial application industry, we work to preserve aerial application's place in the protection and production of America's food and fiber supply. Aerial application is one of the safest, fastest, most efficient and economical ways to apply pesticides. It is also the most environmentally friendly tool of modern agriculture.

2894 **www.aia-aerospace.org**
Aerospace Industries Association

The Aerospace Industries Association shapes public policy that ensures the US aerospace, defense and homeland security industry remains preeminent and that its members are successful and profitable in a changing global market.

2895 **www.aiaa.org**
American Institute of Aeronautics and Astronautics

Advances the arts, sciences, and technology of aeronautics and astronautics and promotes the professionalism of those engaged in these pursuits.

2896 **www.airlines.org**
Air Transport Association

Supports and assits its members by promoting the air transport industry and the safety, cost effectiveness, and technical advancement of its operators; advocating common industry positions before state and local governments; conducting designated industry-wide programs; and assuring governmental and public understanding of all aspects of air transport.

2897 **www.airship-association.org**
Airship Association

Circulates information on all matters affecting airships.

2898 **www.anahq.org**
Association of Naval Aviation

Professional, nonprofit, educational and fraternaL society of Naval Aviation, whose main purpose is to educte the public and our national leaders on the vital roles of the Navy, Marine Corp and Coast Guard Aviation as key elements of our national defense posture. ANA continuosly seeks to elucidate the key current issues impacting Naval Aviation through published writing, symposia, speeches and discussions with various interest groups.

2899 **www.aopa.org**
Aircraft Owners & Pilots Association

Works to make flying safer, more economical and enjoyable for private aircraft owners.

2900 **www.arinc.com**
Aeronautical Radio

Aeronautical Radio provides transportation communications and systems engineering solution for five major industries: aviation, airports, defense, government, and transportation

2901 **www.arsa.org**
Aeronautical Repair Station Association

Helps develop guidance, policy and interpretations that are clear, concise and consistent, and applied uniformly to all similarly situated companies and individuals.

2902 **www.asma.org**
Aerospace Medical Association

Our mission is to apply and advance scientific knowledge to promote and enhance the health, safety and performance of those involved in aerospace and related activities.

2903 **www.astronautical.org**
American Astronautical Society

Independent scientific and technical group in the United States exclusively dedicated to the advancement of space science and exploration.

2904 **www.atec-amt.org**
Aviation Technician Education Council

Organization of Federal Aviation Administration approved Aviation Maintenance Technician schools and supporting industries.

2905 **www.bonanza.org**
American Bonanza Society

ABS is a group of members who own, fly or have a sincere interest in Bonanza, Baron, and Travel air type aircraft. Because of this common interest we share information and experiences involving the operation and maintenance of the Beech produced aircraft.

2906 **www.cessnaowner.org**
Cessna Owner Organization
Membership support organization for Cessna aircraft owners.

2907 **www.eaa.org**
Experimental Aircraft Association
Equipment, supplies and services for sport and recreational flying.

2908 **www.goiam.org**
International Association of Machinists/Aerospace
Facebook, Twitter, LinkedIn, YouTube, Instagram, Pinterest
Labor union representing machinists and aerospace workers.

2909 **www.greyhouse.com**
Grey House Publishing
Authoritative reference directories for most business sectors including aviation and aerospace markets. Users can search the online databases with varied search criteria allowing for custom searches by product category, geographic area, sales volume, keyword, subject and more. Full Grey House catalog and online ordering also available.

2910 **www.iaopa.org**
Int'l Council of Aircraft Owner & Pilot Assns.
Nonprofit federation of 53 autonomous, nongovernmental, national general aviation organizations. Facilitates the movement of general aviation aircraft.

2911 **www.ifsanet.com**
International Inflight Food Service Association
For airline and railway personnel, caterers and suppliers responsible for providing passenger food service.

2912 **www.iswap.org**
International Society of Women Airline Pilots
Non-profit organization of career women airline pilots whose purpose is to: celebrate camaraderie; support informational exchange and social interaction among its members in a healthy environment; provide aviation scholarship opportunities for career-seeking women; and inspire future generations of women aviators via educational outreach.

2913 **www.nafinet.org**
National Association of Flight Instructors
Dedicated to raising and maintaining the professional standing of the flight instructor in the aviation community. Maintains a benefits package available for everyone from the independent instructor to those teaching at flight schools.

2914 **www.nata.aero**
National Air Transportation Association
National association of aviation business service providers.

2915 **www.natca.org**
National Air Traffic Controllers Association
Founded to ensure the safety and longevity of air traffic controller positions around the nation. Represents over 15,000 air traffic controllers throughout the US, Puerto Rico and Guam, along with 2,508 other bargaining unit members that span the areas of engineers and architects to nurses and health care professionals to members of the accounting community.

2916 **www.nbaa.org**
National Business Aviation Association
Not-for-profit, nonpartisan corporation dedicated to the success of the business aviation community.

2917 **www.ninety-nines.org**
Ninety-Nines
International organization of licensed women pilots from 35 countries. We are a nonprofit, charitable membership corporation holding 501(c)(3) US tax status. Members are professional pilots for airlines, industry, government; we are pilots who teach and pilots who fly for pleasure; we are pilots who are technicians and mechanics. First and foremost, we are women who love to fly.

2918 **www.ofainc.com.**
Organization of Flying Adjusters
Dedicated to the highest standard of professional ethics in handling aviation insurance claims, investigating causes of aircraft accidents objectively and promoting every aspect of air safety.

2919 **www.piperowner.org**
Pipers Owner Society
Independent group of Piper owners, pilots, and enthusiasts, the POS is committed to the goal of safe, fun, and affordable flying. Membership benefits include: pre-buy referral service; free STC summaries, free parts locating and a referral service. Pipers magazine is exclusively for POS members.

2920 **www.pra.org**
Popular Rotorcraft Association
A nonprofit organization dedicated to the advancement of knowledge, public education and safety among Rotorcraft enthusiasts worldwide.

2921 **www.quad-a.org**
Army Aviation Association of America
Aerospace products, helicopters, rotor blades, engines, tires, helmets and related aviation equipment. Representing membership interests to the Army and the Legislative Branch.

2922 **www.rotor.com**
Helicopter Association International
Receives and disseminates information concerning the use, operation, hiring, contracting and leasing of helicopters.

2923 **www.safeassociation.com**
SAFE Association
Website of the nonprofit organization dedicated to the preservation of human life. It provides a common meeting ground for the sharing of problems, ideas and information.

2924 **www.seaplanes.org**
Seaplane Pilots Association
Represents our members in dozens of seaplane access issues annually and provides numerous exclusive benefits.

2925 **www.ssa.org**
Soaring Society of America
Fosters and promote all phases of gliding and soaring, nationally and internationally.

2926 **www.tcunion.org**
Transportation-Communications International Union
Members come from diverse transportation industries. In addition to bargaining and representation of its members, provides mortgage and bankcard programs and other services to its members.

2927 **www.tiaca.org**
International Air Cargo Association
For air cargo industry services and products from aircraft manufacturers, airlines, airports, freight forwarders trade publications logistics consultants, etc.

2928 **www.ussf.org**
Space Foundation
Nonprofit organization advancing the exploration, development and use of space and space education for the benefit of humankind.

2929 **www.vtol.org**
AHS International
For designers, engineers and manufacturers of the vertical flight industry.

2930 **www.wahsonline.com**
World Airline Historical Society
Open to all persons and groups interested in collecting airline memorabilia and the study of the airline industry, past and current.

Associations

2931 **ARMA International**
11880 College Boulevard
Suite 450
Overland Park, KS 66210
913-444-9174
844-565-2120; Fax: 913-257-3855
headquarters@armaintl.org
www.arma.org
Facebook, Twitter, LinkedIn
Nate Hughes, Exec. Dir, Operations
Jennifer Millett, National Account Manager
Heather Lehman, Sr. Manager, Membership
ARMA International is a not-for-profit association and a source for authoritative education, the latest legislative updates, standards & best practices. The association was established in 1955. Its approximately 27,000 members include records managers, archivists, corporate librarians, imaging specialists, legal professionals, IT managers, consultants, and educators, all of whom work in a wide variety of industries.
27000 Members
Founded in 1955

2932 **Advancing Financial Crime Professionals Worldwide**
80 Southwest 8th Street
Suite 2350
Miami, FL 33130
305-373-0020
866-459-CAMS; Fax: 305-373-5229
info@acams.org
www.acams.org
Facebook, Twitter, LinkedIn
Ted Weissberg, Chief Executive Officer
Kieran Beer, Chief Analyst & Dir., Editorial
Sally Heim, VP, Global Operations & Finance
Lash Kaur, VP, Global Strategic Communications
Diana Perez Saavedra, Direcot, Global Human Resources
The largest international membership organization dedicated to enhancing the knowledge and expertise of financial crime detection and prevention professionals from a wide range of industries in both public and private sectors.

2933 **American Association of Bank Directors**
1250 24th Street NW
Suite 700
Washington, DC 20037
202-463-4888; Fax: 202-349-8080
info@aabd.org
aabd.org
Twitter, LinkedIn
David Baris, President
Richard M Whiting, Executive Director
Devoted to serving the information, education and advocacy needs of individual bank and savings institution directors. This nonprofit organization has members nationwide.
Founded in 1989

2934 **American Association of Residential Mortgage Regulators**
1025 Thomas Jefferson Street, NW
Suite 500 East
Washington, DC 20007
202-521-3999; Fax: 202-833-3636
efreundel@aarmr.org
www.aarmr.org
Kirsten Anderson, President
Clifford Charland, Vice President
Raeleen Schutte, Treasurer
Chris Romano, Secretary
David Saunders, Executive Director
Promotes the exchange of information and education concerning the licensing, supervision, and regulation of the residential mortgage industry.

2935 **American Bankers Association**
1120 Connecticut Ave NW
Washington, DC 20036
800-226-5377
custserv@aba.com
www.aba.com
Facebook, Twitter, LinkedIn, Google+, YouTube, Instagram
Rob Nichols, President & CEO
Alethia Baggett, Chief Human Resources Officer
James Edrington, Chief Member Engagement Officer
Peter Cook, Chief Communications Officer
Karin Flynn, Chief Financial Officer
Brings together all categories of banking institutions to best represent the interests of this rapidly changing industry. Its membership includes community, regional and money center banks and holding companies, as well as savings associations, trust companies and savings banks.
Founded in 1875

2936 **American Bankruptcy Institute**
66 Canal Center Plaza
Suite 600
Alexandria, VA 22314-1546
703-739-0800; Fax: 703-739-1060
info@abiworld.org
www.abi.org
Facebook, Twitter, LinkedIn, YouTube
Amy Quackenboss, Executive Director
Multidisciplinary, non-partisan organization dedicated to research and education on matters related to insolvency. Engaged in numerous educational and research activities as well as the production of a number of publications both for the insolvency practitioner and the public.
12000 Members
Founded in 1982

2937 **American Payroll Association**
660 N. Main Avenue
Suite 100
San Antonio, TX 78205
210-224-6406; Fax: 210-224-6038
www.americanpayroll.org
Facebook, Twitter, LinkedIn, YouTube, Instagram
Daniel Maddux, Executive Director
The American Payroll Association is the leading advocate for the advancement of payroll professionals and a catalyst for connecting the payroll industry with employers and government. Their vision is to create opportunities and forge a community by providing the education, skills, and resources necessary for payroll professionals to become successful leaders and strategic partners within their organizations.
20000 Members
Founded in 1982

2938 **Arab Bankers Association of North America**
150 West 28th Street
Suite 801
New York, NY 10001
212-599-3030; Fax: 212-599-3131
www.arabbankers.org
Nada Ezzat, Programs Director
MaryLisa Kinney, Office & Events Manager
Susan Peters, Senior Advisor & COO
Provides news, job listings, and resources for financial institutions in the U.S. and the Middle East.
Founded in 1983

2939 **Association For Financial Professionals**
4520 East West Highway
Suite 750
Bethesda, MD 20814
301-907-2862; Fax: 301-907-2864
www.afponline.org
Facebook, Twitter, LinkedIn, Youtube, RSS
Terry Crawford, Chair
Michael High, Vice Chair
Gaileon Thompson, Vice Chair
The Association for Financial Professionals (AFP) serves a network of more than 16,000 treasury and finance professionals. Headquartered in Bethesda, MD, AFP provides members with breaking news, economic research and data on the evolving world of treasury and finance, as well as world-class treasury certification programs, networking events, financial analytical tools, training, and public policy representation to legislators and regulators.

2940 **Association for Financial Technology**
10813 Pleasant Valley Road
Frazeysburg, OH 43822
614-895-1208; Fax: 614-895-3466
aft@aftweb.com
www.aftweb.com
Facebook, Twitter, LinkedIn
Karl Kirsch, Executive Director
Leah Allen, Association Manager
Association founded to promote high standards of professionalism in the planning, development, implementation and application of technology to the financial services industry.
Founded in 1972

2941 **Association of Independent Trust Companies**
2213 North Broadway
Ada, OK 74820
405-680-7869; Fax: 580-332-4714
ato@trustorgs.com
www.trustorgs.com
Facebook, Twitter
Somerlyn Cothran, Executive Director
Jamie Whitefield, Administration
Naomi Lemon, Communications
Janet Ranallo, Association & Meeting Manager
To provide a forum of leaders, owners and operators of trust companies and wealth management providers.
150 Members
Founded in 1989

2942 **Association of Military Banks of America (AMBA)**
PO Box 3335
Warrenton, VA 20188
540-347-3305; Fax: 540-347-5995
info@ambahq.org
www.ambahq.org
Facebook, Twitter
Steven Lepper, President & CEO
Andia Dinesen, EVP, Communications & Operations
Christiane Jacobs, Managing Dir., Admin. & Membership
AMBA is a not-for-profit association of banks operating on military installations, banks not located on military installations but serving military customers, and military banking facilities designated by the US Treasury.
130 Members
Founded in 1959

2943 Association of Residential Mortgage Compliance Professionals
167 West Hudson Street
Suite 200
Long Beach, NY 11561

516-442-3456
armcp.org
LinkedIn

The first and only national organization in the Unites States devoted exclusively to residential mortgage compliance professionals offering discussion groups, educational forums, panels, lectures, and other venues for residential mortgage compliance professionals.
Founded in 2010

2944 Bank Administration Institute
115 S LaSalle St
Suite 3300
Chicago, IL 60603-3801

312-683-2464
888-224-0037; Fax: 312-683-2373
info@bai.org
www.bai.org
Facebook, Twitter, LinkedIn, YouTube

Debbie Bianucci, President & CEO
Ann Barcroft, Chief Administrative Officer
Julie Faber, Chief Financial Officer
Karl Dahlgren, Managing Director
Holly Hughes, Chief Marketing Officer

The financial services industry's partner for breakthrough information and intelligence needed to innovate and stay relevant in an evolving marketplace. Serves a wide segment of the financial services industry, from the largest multinational banks to community-based institutions.

2945 Bank Insurance and Securities Association
2025 M Street NW
Suite 800
Washington, DC 20036

202-367-1111; Fax: 202-367-2111
bisa@BISAnet.org
www.bisanet.org
Facebook, Twitter, StumbleUpon

Jeff Hartney, Executive Director
Janet Huynh, Director, Membership & Admin.
Ellie Hurley, Director, Event Services
Nikki Bartoloni, Senior Coordinator, Marketing
Jason Myers, Managing Editor

Dedicated to serving the needs of those responsible for marketing securities, insurance and other investment and risk management products through commercial banks, trust companies, savings institutions, and credit unions.
Founded in 2002

2946 Bankers' Association for Finance & Trade
1120 Connecticut Avenue NW
Washington, DC 20036

202-663-7575; Fax: 202-663-5538
www.baft.org
Facebook, Twitter

Tod Burwell, President & CEO
Arlene Sanchez, VP, Marketing & Events
Nancy Monahan, Senior Director, Membership
Gregory Kramer, Director, Marketing & Communication
Kathryn Hoch, Director, Events & Programs

A financial services trade association headquartered in Washington, DC, whose membership primarily represents a broad range of financial institutions and service members that provide services throughout the global financial community.
180 Members
Founded in 1921

2947 Community Development Bankers Association
1444 Eye Street NW
Suite 201
Washington, DC 20005

202-689-8935
www.cdbanks.org
Facebook, Twitter, LinkedIn

Jeannine Jacokes, Chief Executive/Sr. Policy Advisor
Brian Blake, Director, Public Policy
Anna Walker, Director, Membership
Mike Bannon, Administrative/IT Manager
Hayley Roth, Special Projects Consultant

The national trade association of the community development bank sector.

2948 Conference of State Bank Supervisors
1129 20th Street, N.W.
9th Floor
Washington, DC 20036

202-296-2840; Fax: 202-296-1928
drodgers@csbs.org
www.csbs.org

John Ryan, President & CEO
Michael Stevens, Senior Executive VP
Thomas Harlow, Executive VP, Operations
Ngoc Vu, Chief Information Officer
Laura Fisher, VP, Communications

The nationwide organization of banking regulators from all 50 states, the District of Columbia, Guam, Puerto Rico, and the U.S. Virgin Islands.
Founded in 1902

2949 Consumer Bankers Association
1225 Eye St., NW
Suite 550
Washington, DC 20005

202-552-6382
rhunt@cbanet.org
www.consumerbankers.com
Facebook, Twitter, LinkedIn

Richard Hunt, President/ Chief Executive Officer
Jean Marie Bunton, Executive VP/ Chief of Staff
David Pommerehn, General Counsel/ SVP
Kevin O'Conner, VP, Corporate Membership
Joanna Beaver, SVP, Committees & Events

The recognized voice on retail banking issues in the nation's capital.

2950 Credit Union National Association
5710 Mineral Point Rd
Madison, WI 53705

800-356-8010
800-356-9655; Fax: 608-231-4333
ccsorders@cuna.coop
www.cuna.org
Facebook, Twitter, LinkedIn, YouTube

Jim Nussle, President & CEO
Greg Michlig, Membership & Engagement
Eddie Rivera, Finance
Amy Nigrelli, Marketing & Digital
Teresa Hanson, Corporate Affairs

A national trade association for both state and federally charteredcredit unions located in the United States.

2951 Electronic Funds Transfer Association
4000 Legato Road
Suite 1100
Fairfax, VA 22033

571-318-5556; Fax: 571-318-5557
www.efta.org
Twitter

Kurt Helwig, President & CEO
Melanie Renner, Meeting Coordinator

The Electronic Funds Transfer Association (EFTA) is the nation's leading inter-industry professional association promoting the adoption of electronic payment systems and commerce.
Founded in 1977

2952 Electronic Payments Association NACHA
2550 Wasser Terrace
Suite 400
Herndon, VA 20171

703-561-1100; Fax: 703-787-0996
info@nacha.org
www.nacha.org
Facebook, Twitter, LinkedIn, YouTube

Donna Schwartze, Media Contact
Joshua Maze, Sponsorship
Jane Larimer, President & CEO

NACHA manages the development, administration, and governance of the ACH Network, the backbone for the electronic movement of money and data. The ACH Network provides a safe, secure, and reliable network for direct account-to-account consumer, business, and government payments. Annually, it facilitates billions of Direct Deposit via ACH and Direct Payment via ACH transactions. Used by all types of financial institutions, the ACH Network is governed by the fair and equitable NACHA Operating Rules
Founded in 1974

2953 Electronic Transactions Association
1101 16th STREET NW #402
WASHINGTON, DC 20036

202-828-2635
800-695-5509
www.electran.org
Facebook, LinkedIn, YouTube, Flickr

Jodie Kelley, CEO
Scott Talbott, SVP, Government Affairs
Alexis Byrne, VP, Operations
Laura Hubbard, Director, Communications
Bradley Brewer, Manager, Membership

A trade organization representing independent sales organizations, merchant service providers and those help them serve their merchant clients.
Founded in 1990

2954 Environmental Bankers Association
1827 Powers Ferry Rd, Building 14
Suite 100
Atlanta, GA 30339

678-619-5045; Fax: 678-229-2777
eba@envirobank.org
www.envirobank.org
Facebook, Twitter, LinkedIn, YouTube

William Sloan, President
Lisa Kraus Gardner, Sr. Mngr. & Conference Planner
Michele Doyle, Association Coordinator
Patricia Bagley, Accounting Services

EBA voting members are banks, trust companies, credit unions, savings and loan associations, and other financial services organizations with an interest in environmental risk management and related issues. Active participants are bankers from Trust or Credit offices with responsibility for environmental liability, and financial services officers with environmental interests. Affiliate members are from law firms, consulting and insurance organizations.
Founded in 1994

2955 Financial Managers Society
1 North LaSalle Street
Suite 3100
Chicago, IL 60602-4003

312-578-1300
800-275-4367; Fax: 312-578-1308
info@fmsinc.org

www.fmsinc.org
Facebook, Twitter, LinkedIn, Instagram

John A. Carrozza, Chair
Alana Vartanian, Chief Operating Officer
Taylor Weathers, Director, Membership
Jennifer Lindberg, Director, Marketing & Communication
Mark Loehrke, Editor/Writer

A nonprofit professional society serving the financial services industry.
Founded in 1948

2956 Financial Services Roundtable
600 13th Street, NW
Suite 400
Washington, DC 20005

202-289-4322
info@fsroundtable.org
www.fsround.org
Twitter, LinkedIn, YouTube

Greg Baer, President & CEO
Ken Troshinsky, Chief Operating Officer
Bill Nelson, EVP & Chief Economist
Tracey D'Antuono, SVP, Membership & Events
Austin Anton, VP, Communcations

The leading advocacy organization for America's financial services industry. Its members include banking, insurance, asset management, finance, andcredit card companies.

2957 Financial Women International
1027 W Roselawn Avenue
Roseville, MN 55113

651-487-7632
866-807-6081; Fax: 651-489-1322
info@fwi.org

FWI is dedicated to developing leaders, accelerating careers, and generating results for professionals in the banking and financial services industry.
1000 Members
Founded in 1921

2958 Financial Women's Association
215 Park Avenue South
Suite 1712
New York, NY 10003

212-533-2141
FWAoffice@FWA.org
fwa.org
Facebook, Twitter, LinkedIn

Ria Davis, Executive Director
Lisa Buddenhagen, Chief Tech. Officer & Dir., Ops.
Robert Brown, Associate Dir., Marketing & Mem.
Michael Taylor, Educational Programs Manager
Emily Plisic, Accounting Department

A nonprofit organization established by a group of Wall Street Women to support the role and development of women in the financial services industry.
Founded in 1956

2959 Global Association of Risk Professionals
111 Town Square Place
14th Floor
Jersey City, NJ 07310

201-719-7210; Fax: 201-222-5022
info@garp.com
www.garp.com
Facebook, Twitter, LinkedIn, YouTube, Google+

Richard Apostolik, President & CEO
Ken Abbott, Chief Risk Officer
William Martin, Chief Risk Officer
Ben Golub, Chief Risk Officer
Laura Dottori, Senior Executive VP & CRO

To be the leading professional association for risk managers, managed by and for its members dedicated to the advancement of the risk profession through education, training and the promotion of best practices globally. Members come from over 100 countries.
52330 Members
Founded in 1996

2960 Impact Mortgage Management Advocacy & Advisory Group
2740 S. Newland Street
Lakewood, CO 80227

303-674-1200; Fax: 303-674-1664
bill@immaag.com
www.immaag.com

Provides thousands of state licensed mortgage loan originators the information and advocacy support necessary for the industry to deal with absorbing the results of the financial crisis being dealt with by the nation.

2961 Independent Community Bankers of America
518 Lincoln Rd.
P.O. Box 267
Sauk Centre, MN 56378

320-526-6546
800-422-7285; Fax: 320-352-5766
info@icba.org
www.icba.org
Facebook, Twitter, LinkedIn, YouTube

Rebeca Romero Rainey, President/CEO
Alex Galeano, Sr. Executive VP & CFO
Rob Birgfeld, EVP & Chief Marketing Officer
Kathy Gauger, Director, Member Relations
Julie Kulzer, Director, Conferences & Meetings

Trade association for the nation's community banks. Represents the interests of community bankers through advocacy, education, and products and services.
6000 Members

2962 Institute of International Bankers
299 Park Avenue
17th Floor
New York, NY 10171

212-421-1611; Fax: 212-421-1119
iib@iib.org
www.iib.org
Facebook, Twitter, LinkedIn

Briget Polichene, Chief Executive Officer
William Harris, Chief Administrative Officer
Meghan Milloy, Director, Strategic Communications
Paul Begey, Director, Government Relations
James Strype, Dir., Info. Tech. & Infrastructure

To help resolve the many special legislative, regulatory and tax issues confronting internationally headquartered financial institutions that engage in banking, securities and/or insurance activities in the United States.
Founded in 1966

2963 International Financial Services Association
9 Sylvan Way
Suite 130
Parsippany, NJ 07054-3817

973-656-1900; Fax: 973-656-1915

Tod Burwell, Vice President
Colleen Kennedy, Manager, Programs & Events

Represents the international operations areas of financial services providers, their customers, suppliers and partners. Dedicates itself to meeting the specific needs of those who provide, use, and support trade and payments with particular focus on documentary credits, funds transfer, treasury operations, compliance, and regulatory reporting.
Founded in 1924

2964 Investment Bankers Association
info2@investmentbankersassociation.org
www.investmentbankersassociation.org

A national organization for businesses that want to go public and raise capital to meet small regional and independent brokerage firms, investment bankers, capital sources and other capital market service providers.

2965 MasterCard Worldwide
2000 Purchase St
Purchase, NY 10577-2405

914-249-2000; Fax: 914-249-4135
www.mastercard.com/global
Facebook, Twitter, LinkedIn

Administers the MasterCard credit and other MasterCard products fo member financial institutions around the world.
25000 Members
Founded in 1940

2966 Mortgage Bankers Association
1919 M Street NW
5th Floor
Washington, DC 20036

202-557-2700
800-793-6222
www.mba.org
Facebook, Twitter

Robert Broeksmit, President & CEO
Marcia Davies, COO
Lisa Haynes, CFO/Chief of Diversity & Inclusion
Peter Grace, SVP, Strategy & Member Services
Michael Briggs, SVP, HR & General Counsel

A national association representing the entire real estate finance industry. This association develops innovative business tools and provides education and training for industry professionals.

2967 National Association of Affordable Housing Lenders
1025 Connecticut Ave NW
Suite 710
Washington, DC 20036

202-293-9850; Fax: 202-293-9852
naahl@naahl.org
www.naahl.org
Twitter, YouTube

Buzz Roberts, President & CEO
Sara Olson Spofford, Operations Director
Cherri Sinclair, Communications Director

Represents America's leaders in moving private capital to those in need. Encompasses 200 organizations committed to increasing private lending and investing in low and moderate-income communities.
Founded in 1990

2968 National Association of Bankruptcy Trustees
One Windsor Cove
Suite 305
Columbia, SC 29223

803-252-5646
800-445-8629; Fax: 803-765-0860
info@nabt.com
www.nabt.com

Jennifer Brinkley, Executive Director
Amanda Davis, Staff
Hannah Martin, Staff

A non profit association formed to address the needs of bankruptcy trustees throughout the

country and to promote the effectiveness of the bankruptcy system as a whole.
Founded in 1982

2969 **National Association of Chapter 13 Trustees**
1 Windsor Cove
Suite 305
Columbia, SC 29223
803-252-5646
800-445-8629; Fax: 803-765-0860
Info@NACTT.com
www.nactt.com
Courtney Waldrup, Executive Director
Provides a forum within which Chapter 13 Trustees will act as an information and communication resource to advance education, leadership, and continuous improvement in the administration of bankruptcy. We will provide the means to establish and implement professional standards and participate in the national legislative and administrative processes while promoting the highest ethical principles.
1000 Members
Founded in 1965

2970 **National Association of Credit Union Supervisory & Auditing Committees**
PO Box 160
Del Mar, CA 92014
800-287-5949; Fax: 858-792-3884
nacusac@nacusac.org
www.nacusac.org
Celeste Shelton, Executive Director
Lauren Clark, Associate Director
A unique organization of, by and for credit union supervisory committee members. Provides leadership, support and education to enhance the capability of credit union supervisory and auditing committee members to fulfill their responsibilities.
Founded in 1985

2971 **National Association of Federal Credit Unions**
3138 10th St N
Arlington, VA 22201-2149
703-522-4770
800-336-4644; Fax: 703-524-1082
www.nafcu.org
Facebook, Twitter, LinkedIn, YouTube
Dan Berger, President & CEO
Anthony Demangone, Executive VP & COO
Greg Johns, VP, Finance
Jacqueline Ortiz Ramsay, VP, Media Relations & Communication
Catherine Porterfield, VP, Membership
A respected and influential trade association that exclusively represents the interests of federal credit unions before the federal government and the public.
Founded in 1967

2972 **National Association of Government Guaranteed Lenders**
215 East 9th Avenue
Stillwater, OK 74074
405-377-4022; Fax: 405-377-3931
info@naggl.org
www.naggl.org
Facebook, Twitter, LinkedIn, YouTube
Tony Wilkinson, President & CEO
Tyler Adams, Marketing, Conferences & Events
Jennifer Shaklee, Marketing & Membership
Promotes professional and governmental affairs interests of financial institutions and small businesses who participate in Small Business Administration guaranteed lending and secondary market programs.
600 Members
Founded in 1984

2973 **National Association of Independent Housing Professionals**
601 Pennsylvania Ave. NW
South Building, Suite 900
Washington, DC 20004
202-587-9300; Fax: 304-267-9046
A legislative and regulatory organization comprised of all housing industry professionals.

2974 **National Association of Professional Mortgage Women**
345 North Main St
Suite 313
West Hartford, CT 06117
800-827-3034; Fax: 469-524-5121
napmw1@napmw.org
www.napmw.org
Facebook, LinkedIn, Google+, RSS
Vincent Valvo, Executive Director
Serves all mortgage professionals and employers who want to excel. Provides business, personal, and leadership development opportunities advancing women in mortgage-related professions.
4500 Members
Founded in 1964

2975 **National Association of State Credit Union Supervisors**
1655 Fort Myer Dr
Suite 650
Arlington, VA 22209
703-528-8351
800-728-7927; Fax: 703-528-3248
offices@nascus.org
www.nascus.org
Facebook, Twitter, LinkedIn
Lucy Ito, President & CEO
Brian Knight, Executive VP & General Counsel
Alicia Valencia Erb, VP, Member Relations
Shellee Mitchell, Program Specialist
Doug McGuckin, VP, Corporate Affairs
State chartered credit unions and state credit union supervisors.
900 Members
Founded in 1965

2976 **National Bankers Association**
1513 P Street NW
Washington, DC 20005
202-588-5432; Fax: 202-588-5443
mgrant@nationalbankers.org
www.nationalbankers.org
Facebook, Twitter
Michael Grant, President
Preston Pinkett III, Chairman
Neill S Wright, Treasurer
Cynthia Day, Secretary
Members are minority and women's banking institutions, minority individuals employed by majority banks and institutions.
16000 Members
Founded in 1927

2977 **National Credit Union Administration**
1775 Duke St
Suite 4206
Alexandria, VA 22314-6115
703-518-6300
800-755-1030; Fax: 703-518-6539
pacamsil@ncua.gov
www.ncua.gov
Facebook, Twitter, LinkedIn
Rodney Hood, Chair
Larry Fazio, Executive Director
Lenwood Brooks, Chief of Staff
Eugene Schied, CFO
Robert Foster, Chief Information Officer
Governed by a three member board appointed by the President and confirmed by the US Senate, this independent federal agency charters and supervises federal credit unions. NCUA, with the backing of the full faith and credit of the US government, operates the National Credit Union Share Insurance Fund, insuring the savings of 80 million account holders in all federal credit unions and many state chartered credit unions.
700 Members
Founded in 1909

2978 **National Investment Banking Association**
422 Chesterfield Rd
Bogart, GA 30622
706-208-9620; Fax: 706-993-3342
emily@nibanet.org
www.nibanet.org
Twitter
Emily Foshee, Executive Director
A national trade association of regional and independent brokerages, investment banking firms, and related capital market service providers.
Founded in 1932

2979 **National Marine Lenders Association**
1 Melvin Ave
Annapolis, MD 21401
410-980-1401; Fax: 410-268-3755
info@marinelenders.org
www.marinelenders.org
John Haymond, President
Created to educate current and prospective lenders in marine financing procedures and to promote the extension of credit to consumer and trade borrowers.
70 Members
Founded in 1979

2980 **National Mitigation Banking Association**
107 S. West Street # 573
Alexandria, VA 22314
202-457-8409
www.mitigationbanking.org
Sara Johnson, Executive Director
Seth Ginther, Executive VP
Jessica Marcus, VP, Policy & Operations
Promotes federal legislation and regulatory policy that encourages mitigation banking and conservation banking as a means of compensating for adverse impacts to America's wetlands and other natural resources.

2981 **National Reverse Mortgage Lenders Association**
1400 16th St., NW
Suite 420
Washington, DC 20036
202-939-1760; Fax: 202-265-4435
dhicks@dworbell.com
www.nrmlaonline.org
Facebook, Twitter, LinkedIn
Peter Bell, CEO
Steve Irwin, President
Darryl Hicks, VP, Communications
Violet Arthur, Manager, Financial Operations
Laura Ross, Membership Support Specialist
Trade association that serves as an educational resource, policy advocate and public affairs center for reverse mortgage lenders and related professionals.
Founded in 1997

2982 Nonprofit Risk Management Center
204 South King Street
Leesburg, VA 20175

703-777-3504; Fax: 202-785-3891
www.nonprofitrisk.org
Twitter

Melanie Lockwood Herman, Executive Director
Whitney Thomey, Project Manager
Katharine Nesslage, Project Manager
Kay Nakamura, Director, Client Solutions

Provides risk management assistance and resources for community-serving nonprofit organizations.

2983 Public Risk Management Association
700 S. Washington St.
Suite 218
Alexandria, VA 22314

703-528-7701; Fax: 703-739-0200
info@primacentral.org
www.primacentral.org

Jennifer Ackerman, Chief Executive Officer
Shaunda Ragland, Director, Education & Training
Monique Gilliam, Director, Meetings & Conferences
Melvin Bodmer, Director, Admin. & Member Services
Taquan Gilbert, Education Coordinator

Member based organization which is dedicated to providing practicaleducation, training, and information for public sector risk management practitioners.

2984 Risk Management Association
1801 Market Street
Suite 300
Philadelphia, PA 19103-1628

215-446-4000
800-677-7621; Fax: 215-446-4101
customers@rmahq.org
www.rmahq.org
Facebook, Twitter, LinkedIn, WordPress

Nancy Foster, President & CEO
William Bonnell, Chair

A not-for-profit, member driven professional association whose sole purpose is to advance the use of sound risk principles in the financial services industry.
3000 Members
Founded in 1914

2985 Securities Industry and Financial Markets Association (SIFMA)
1101 New York Ave Nw
Suite 800
Washington, DC 20005-4279

202-962-7300; Fax: 202-962-7305
www.sifma.org
Facebook, Twitter, LinkedIn

Kenneth Bentsen, President/CEO
Joseph Seidel, Chief Operating Officer
David Krasner, Chief Financial & Admin. Officer
Salvatore Chiarelli, EVP, Conferences & Events
Cheryl Crispen, EVP, Communications & Marketing

SIFMA's mission is to champion policies and practices that benefit investors and issuers, expand and perfect global capital markets, and foster the development of new products and services. SIFMA provides an enhanced member network of access and forward-looking services, as well as premiere educational resources for the professionals within the industry and the investors whom they serve.

2986 Society of Financial Examiners
12100 Sunset Hills Rd
Suite 130
Reston, VA 20190-3221

703-234-4140
800-787-7633; Fax: 888-436-8686
sofe@sofe.org
www.sofe.org

Cindy Dodson, Executive Director
Joanne Campanelli, President
Katie McRee, Assistant Executive Director
Rhenda Davis, Membership & Customer Care

Professional society for examiners of insurance companies, banks, savings and loans, and credit unions.
Founded in 1973

2987 Society of Risk Management Consultants
621 North Sherman Avenue
Madison, WI 53704

Home Page: www.srmcsociety.org

Christopher Moss, President
Roy Ivins, President-Elect
Lori Ussery, Treasurer
Peter Murdough, Secretary

An international organization of professionals engaged in risk management, insurance and employee benefits consulting.
Founded in 1984

2988 The Fiduciary and Investment Risk Management
Post Office Box 507
Stockbridge, GE 30281

678-565-6211; Fax: 678-565-8788
info@thefirma.org
www.thefirma.org
Facebook, Twitter, LinkedIn, RSS

Bruce K. Goldberg, President
Jennifer De Vries, Vice President
David Jonke, Secretary
Bradley F. Beshea, SVP, Fiduciary Compliance Officer
John L Clark, Director

Provider of current and relevant fiduciary and investment risk management education and networking opportunities to risk management professionals.

2989 The Finance, Credit & International Business Association
8840 Columbia 100 Pkwy
Columbia, MD 21045-2158

410-423-1840
888-256-3242; Fax: 410-740-5574
fcib_global@fcibglobal.com
fcibglobal.com
Twitter, LinkedIn, RSS

Noelin Hawkins, Dir., Europe, Middle East & Asia
Ron Shepherd, Dir., Membership & Bus. Dev.
Tina Mansfield, Member Services
Diana Mota, Programs & Services

The premier Association for Finance, Credit and International business professionals. The leading resource for global credit information, professional development and education.
1100 Members
Founded in 1919

2990 The First
7054 Jefferson Highway
Baton Rouge, LA 70806

225-228-7275; Fax: 225-228-7276
www.thefirstbank.com
Facebook, Twitter

Personal and commercial banking. Offers information about services,products, and locations.

2991 University Risk Management and Insurance Association
PO Box 1027
Bloomington, IN 47402

812-855-6683; Fax: 812-856-3149
urmia@urmia.org
www.urmia.org
Facebook, Twitter, LinkedIn, Flickr. YouTube

Jenny Whittington, Executive Director
Michelle Smith, Senior Director, Events
Louise Schlesinger, Communications & Community Coord.
Ronna Papesh, Website & Database Administrator
Lou Drapeau, Resource Manager

Advances the discipline of risk management in higer education.

2992 Urban Financial Services Coalition
1200 G Street NW
Suite 800
Washington, DC 20005

202-434-8970; Fax: 202-434-8707
www.ufscnet.org
Facebook, Twitter, LinkedIn, YouTube

Ola Truelove, National President
Debra Bronston, National VP

Formerly known as the National Association of Urban Bankers is an organization of minority professionals in the financial services industry and related fields.
Founded in 1974

2993 Western Independent Bankers
555 Montgomery Street
Suite 750
San Francisco, CA 94111

415-352-2323; Fax: 415-352-2314
info@wib.org
www.wib.org
Facebook, Twitter, LinkedIn, YouTube

Steve Andrews, President & CEO
Maurine Padden, EVP & Chief Operating Officer
Rich Mize, VP & Chief Financial Officer
Linda Odell, VP, HR & Administration

A trade association that informs, educates, and connects community banks with the resources and services to achieve the highest standards of personal and organizational performance.
Founded in 1937

2994 Women's World Banking
122 East 42nd Street
42nd Floor
New York, NY 10168

212-768-8513; Fax: 212-768-8519
www.womensworldbanking.org
Facebook, Twitter, LinkedIn, YouTube, Google +, Flickr

Mary Ellen Iskenderian, President & CEO
J. Thomas Jones, EVP & COO
Carlos Hornillos-Dalisme, CFO
Harsha Rodrigues, Chief Strategy Officer
Leslie Wetzel, Chief Development Officer

A global nonprofit organization devoted to giving more low-income women access to the financial tools and resources they require to build security and prosperity.

Newsletters

2995 ABA Bank Directors Briefing
American Bankers Association
1120 Connecticut Avenue NW
Washington, DC 20036

202-663-5000
800-226-5377; Fax: 202-828-4548

www.aba.com
Facebook, Twitter, LinkedIn

Rob Nichols, President/CEO

Published by the editors of ABA Banking Journal in cooperation with the American Bankers Association. Focuses on keeping bank directors informed about legislative and regulatory developments, summarizing important banking industry trends, updating all directors on the latest thinking in corporate governance, educating new directors in the basics of community bank directorship
Frequency: Monthly

2996 **ABA Bankers News**
American Bankers Association
1120 Connecticut Avenue NW
Washington, DC 20036-3902

202-635-5000
800-226-5377; Fax: 202-663-7543
custserv@aba.com
www.aba.com
Facebook, Twitter, LinkedIn

Rob Nichols, President/CEO

For everyone in the banking industry especially CEOs and compliance officers. Learn to use the internet effectively, retain your best customers, reduce risk, nurture a sales culture and more.
Cost: $450.00
Frequency: Bi-Weekly
Founded in 1875

2997 **ABI Bankruptcy Brief**
American Bankruptcy Institute
66 Canal Center Plaza
Suite 600
Alexandria, VA 22314-1546

703-739-0800; Fax: 703-739-1060
info@abiworld.org
www.abi.org

Amy Quackenboss, Executive Director

A weekly newsletter for ABI members.
Frequency: Weekly/Thursday
Founded in 1982

2998 **ABIA Insurance News**
American Bankers Association
1120 Connecticut Avenue NW
Washington, DC 20036

202-663-5163
800-226-5377; Fax: 202-828-4546
vbarton@aba.com
www.theabia.com

Paul Petrylak, President/Chairman
Neal Aton, Vice President
David Cissell, Secretary
Val Teagarden, Treasurer

The American Bankers Insurance Association (ABIA) is the insurance subsidiary of the American Bankers Association (ABA). The ABIA's mission is to develop policy and provide advocacy for banks in insurance and to support bank insurance operations through research, education, compliance assistance, and peer group networking opportunities.
300 Members
Frequency: Bi-Weekly
Founded in 2001

2999 **AITCO Advisor**
Association of Independent Trust Companies
8 S Michigan Ave
Suite 802
Chicago, IL 60603-3452

312-223-1611; Fax: 312-580-0165
www.trustorgs.com

Somerlyn Cothran, Executive Director
Jamie Whitefield, Administration
Naomi Lemon, Communications
Janet Ranallo, Association & Meeting Manager

Features professionally written articles on marketing and legislative issues as well as association updates.
Frequency: Quarterly

3000 **Access**
American Safe Deposit Association
5433 S 200 E
Franklin, IN 46131-8982

317-738-4432; Fax: 317-738-5267
jmclin@aol.com
www.tasda.com

Bill Lee, Publisher
Thomas Cullinan, President
J Wayne Merrill, First VP
Winnifred Howard-Hommack, Second Vice President
Kevin Fanning, Treasurer

A newsletter full of timely articles on safe deposit procedures, policies, problems and solutions.
Cost: $10.00

3001 **Advocacy Bulletins**
CFA Institute
Po Box 3668
Charlottesville, VA 22903-0668

434-951-5499
800-247-8132; Fax: 434-951-5262
www.cfainstitute.org

Alan Meder, Chair
John Rogers, President

To communicate time-sensitive information to interested AIMR/CFA Member Societies and members.
Frequency: Periodically

3002 **Allied News**
Allied Finance Adjusters Conference
P.O.Box 41368
Raleigh, NC 27629

800-621-3016
800-843-1232; Fax: 888-949-8520
alliedfinanceadjusters@gmail.com
www.alliedfinanceadjusters.com
Facebook, Twitter, LinkedIn

George Badeen, President

Trade Association of recovery specialists.
Cost: $200.00
Founded in 1936

3003 **American Banker**
SourceMedia
1 State Street Plaza
27th floor
New York, NY 10004-1561

212-803-8200
800-803-3424; Fax: 212-843-9608
custserv@sourcemedia.com
www.sourcemedia.com

Douglas Manoni, CEO
Richard Antoneck, CFO
Cost: $99.00
Frequency: Monthly
Founded in 2005

3004 **BNA's Banking Report**
Bureau of National Affairs
3 Bethesda Metro Center
Suite 250
Bethesda, MD 20814

800-372-1033; Fax: 800-253-0332
customercare@bna.com
www.bna.com

Josh Eastright, CEO

Legal and regulatory developments in the financial services industry.
Cost: $1780.00
Frequency: Weekly
ISSN: 1522-5984
Founded in 1929

3005 **Bank Alerts**
Consumer Bankers Association
1000 Wilson Blvd
Suite 2500
Arlington, VA 22209-3912

703-276-1750; Fax: 703-528-1290
research@cbanet.org
www.consumerbankers.com
Facebook, Twitter, LinkedIn

Richard Hunt, President & CEO

Federal legislative developments.
Frequency: Monthly
Circulation: 10,000
Founded in 1919
Printed in on newsprint stock

3006 **Bank Directors Briefing**
American Bankers Association
1120 Connecticut Avenue NW
Washington, DC 20036-3902

202-635-5000
800-226-5377; Fax: 202-663-7597
www.aba.com

Rob Nichols, President

Newsletter reporting on legislative developments and management issues affecting community banks and their boards of directors.
Frequency: Monthly
Circulation: 33130

3007 **Bank Rate Monitor**
Bank Rate
11760 US Highway 1
Suite 500
North Palm Beach, FL 33408-8888

561-630-2400; Fax: 561-625-4540
www.bankrate.com

Don Munsell, Production Director

Independent national source for the financial industry.
Cost: $499.00
4 Pages
Frequency: Weekly
Mailing list available for rent: 750 names
Printed in 3 colors

3008 **Bank Technology News**
SourceMedia
1 State Street Plaza
27th floor
New York, NY 10004-1561

212-803-8200
800-803-3424; Fax: 212-843-9608
custserv@sourcemedia.com
www.sourcemedia.com

Douglas Manoni, CEO
Richard Antoneck, CFO
Cost: $99.00
Frequency: Monthly
Founded in 2005

3009 **Bank Tellers Report**
Sheshunoff Information Services
4120 Freidrich Lane
Suite 100
Austin, TX 78744

512-305-6500
800-456-2340; Fax: 512-305-6575
customercare.sis@sheshunoff.com
www.sheshunoff.com

Bob Mate, CEO
Marge Simmons, Author

General interest publication for bank tellers.
Cost: $449.00
Frequency: Monthly
Founded in 1975

3010 **Bank and S&L Quarterly Rating Service**
Sheshunoff Information Services
4120 Freidrich Lane
Suite 100
Austin, TX 78744

512-305-6500
800-456-2340; Fax: 512-305-6575
customercare.sis@sheshunoff.com
www.sheshunoff.com

Bob Mate, CEO

Statistical reports and research on savings and loan institutions.
Cost: $580.00
Frequency: Quarterly
Circulation: 5000
Mailing list available for rent: 5000 names

3011 **Banks in Insurance Report**
John Wiley & Sons
111 River St
Hoboken, NJ 07030-5790

201-748-6000
800-225-5945; Fax: 201-748-6088
info@wiley.com
www.wiley.com

Mari Baker, CEO
Jean-Lou Chameau, President
Linda Katehi, Chancellor

Highlights the steps necessary for expansion into insurance products and services through articles that report on legislative activities, regulatory concerns, business and strategies.
Cost: $745.00
16 Pages
Frequency: Monthly
ISSN: 8756-6079
Founded in 1807
Printed in one color on matte stock

3012 **Certification News**
Independent Community Bankers of America
518 Lincoln Rd.
P.O. Box 267
Sauk Centre, MN 56378

320-526-6546
800-422-7285; Fax: 320-352-5766
info@icba.org
www.icba.org

Rebeca Romero Rainey, President/CEO
Terry J. Jorde, Sr. Executive Vice President

Contains articles written by bank peers and industry experts and case studies of challenges faced by auditors and officers.
Cost: $80.00
Frequency: Quarterly

3013 **Cheklist**
BKB Publications
98 Greenwich Avenue
1st Floor
New York, NY 10011-7743

212-807-7933; Fax: 212-807-1821
bkbpub1@ix.netcom.com

Brian Burkart, Publisher
Charlene Komar Storey, Editor

Features general news, feature articles, legislative updates, reports on trends, legal advice, marketing ideas, product information and news of state and national association activities.
Cost: $35.00
Frequency: Quarterly
Circulation: 16,000
ISSN: 1066-3029

3014 **Client Quarterly**
WPI Communications
55 Morris Ave
Suite 300
Springfield, NJ 07081-1422

973-467-8700
800-323-4995; Fax: 973-467-0368
info@wpicommunications.com
www.wpicomm.com

Steve Klinghoffer, Owner/Publisher
Lori Klinghoffer, Executive Vice President

Information and advice on financial, business and tax matters.
Frequency: Quarterly
Founded in 1952

3015 **Community Bank President**
Siefer Consultants
525 Cayuga Street
PO Box 1384
Storm Lake, IA 50588-1384

712-660-1026; Fax: 866-680-5866
info@siefer.com
www.siefer.com

Dan Siefer, Publisher

Profit making opportunities for financial institutions.
Cost: $297.00
8 Pages
Frequency: Monthly

3016 **Compliance & Management Bulletin**
American Bankers Association
1120 Connecticut Avenue NW
Washington, DC 20036-3902

202-663-5000
800-226-5377; Fax: 202-828-4540
custserv@aba.com
www.aba.com

Rob Nichols, President/CEO

Includes the information you need to keep up with and respond to the latest in new and revised laws and regulations affecting your institution's management and operations.
Cost: $375.00
Frequency: Published, As Needed
Circulation: 2000
Founded in 1992

3017 **Consumer Bankers Association**
Consumer Bankers Association
1000 Wilson Blvd
Suite 2500
Arlington, VA 22209-3912

703-276-1750; Fax: 703-528-1290
webmaster@cbanet.org

Richard Hunt, President
Janet Pike, Executive Assistant

Legislative newsletter on retail banking for association members.
Founded in 1919

3018 **Credit Card Management**
Thomson Financial Publishing
1 State St
27th Floor
New York, NY 10004-1481

212-825-8445
800-328-9378; Fax: 212-292-5216
general.info@thomson.com
www.sourcemedia.com

Douglas Manoni, CEO
Richard Antoneck, CFO

Information on the major developments in the credit card industry.
Cost: $98.00
74 Pages
Frequency: Monthly
Circulation: 19000
Printed in 4 colors on glossy stock

3019 **Credit Union Journal**
SourceMedia
1 State St
27th Floor
New York, NY 10004-1561

212-803-8200
800-803-3424; Fax: 212-843-9608
custserv@sourcemedia.com
www.sourcemedia.com

Douglas Manoni, CEO
Richard Antoneck, CFO
Cost: $99.00
Frequency: Monthly
Founded in 2005

3020 **DTCC Newsletter**
Depository Trust Company
55 Water St
New York, NY 10041-0024

212-855-1000; Fax: 212-855-2350
info@dtcc.com
www.dtcc.com

Robert Druskin, Chairman
Michael Bodson, President

Information for the banking and securities industry.
Frequency: Monthly
Circulation: 7000
Founded in 1999

3021 **Daily Treasury Statement**
Financial Management Service
3700 E West Highway
Room 502A
Hysttaville, MD 20782

202-874-9790
800-826-9434; Fax: 202-874-8447
dts.Questions@fms.treas.gov
www.fms.treas.gov

Richard L Gregg, Commissioner
Melanie Rigney, Editor

This report offers the latest news of the Treasury Department.
Frequency: Daily
Founded in 1974

3022 **Digest for Corporate & Securities Lawyers**
Bowne & Company
55 Water Street
New York, NY 10041
212-924-500
212-229-3400
www.bowne.com

Bruce Brumberg, Editor-in-Chief
Johanna McKenzie, Editor
Susan Koffman, Editor
Karen Axelrod, Managing Editor
David Shea, Chairman/CEO

Summaries of articles on corporate finance, mergers acquisitions, initial public offerings (ipos) and restructuring. Selects articles from hundreds of publications focusing on articles trends, strategies and advice on deal structuring.
2700 Members
Frequency: Monthly
Founded in 1775

3023 **Direct Deposit Authorization Forms**
NACHA: Electronic Payments Association

13450 Sunrise Valley Drive
Suite 100
Herndon, VA 20171

703-561-1100; Fax: 703-787-0996
info@nacha.org
www.nacha.org

Janet O Estep, CEO
Maurice Haitema, Chairperson

These authorizations are for companies looking for generic authorization forms that market ACH benefits to consumers.
Cost: $30.00
Frequency: Monthly

3024 **Directors & Trustees Digest**
American Bankers Association
1120 Connecticut Avenue NW
Washington, DC 20036-3902

202-663-5000; Fax: 202-828-4540
custserv@aba.com
www.aba.com

Rob Nichols, President/CEO

Provides corporate governance guidance, outlines board legal and fiduciary responsibilities and offers resourceful information on board management relations.
Frequency: Monthly

3025 **Examiner**
Conference of State Bank Supervisors
1129 20th Street, N.W.
9th Floor
Washington, DC 20036-4327

202-296-2840; Fax: 202-296-1928
www.csbs.org

Neal Milner, CEO
Thomas Harlow, CFO
Cecelia Smith, Senior Manager, Administration
John Gorman, General Counsel

Provides news, analysis and commentary on the important events affecting the state banking system.
Frequency: Weekly

3026 **FSPA Newsletter**
Financial & Security Products Association
1024 Mebane Oaks Road
Suite 273
Mebane, NC 27302

919-648-0664
800-843-6082; Fax: 919-648-0670
bj@fspa1.com
www.fspa1.com

Grant Case, Chairman
Fred Wheeler, President
B.J. Hanson, Executive Director
Bryce Good, Vice President
Dave Pepin, Secretary-Treasurer

Offers timely ideas and techniques to help you compete and run your business more effectively. Also provides low-cost opportunities for members to advertise their products and/or services within the body of the newsletter, or in an insert included with the newsletter mailing.
Frequency: Monthly

3027 **Federal Reserve Bulletin**
Board of Governors of the Federal Reserve System
20th St & Constitution Ave N
Washington, DC 20551-0001

202-452-3284; Fax: 202-452-3101
www.federalreserve.gov
Facebook, Twitter, LinkedIn

Ben S Bernanke, Chairman
Janet Yellen, Vice Chairman

Reports on analysis on economic developments, regulatory issues and new data. The quarterly version will no longer be published, however the Board will print an annual compendium.
Frequency: Annual
Founded in 1913

3028 **Federal Reserve Regulatory Service**
Federal Reserve Board Publishers
20th St & Constitution Ave N
Washington, DC 20551-0001

202-452-3000; Fax: 202-452-3819
www.federalreserve.gov
Facebook, Twitter, LinkedIn

Ben S Bernanke, Chairman
Janet Yellen, Vice Chairman

Consumer and community affairs.
Cost: $200.00
Frequency: Monthly

3029 **Financial Services Daily**
SNL Securities
One SNL Plaza
PO Box 2124
Charlottesvle, VA 22902

434-977-1600; Fax: 434-977-4466
CustomerService@snl.com
www.snl.com

Mike Chinn, President/CEO
Nick Cafferillo, COO

Comprehensive daily coverage of the financial services and technology sectors.
Cost: $795.00
40 Pages
Frequency: Monthly
Founded in 1987

3030 **Funds Transfer Report**
Bankers Research
PO Box 431
Westport, CT 06881-0431
Ted Volckhausen Sr, Publisher/Co-Editor
Ted Volckhausen Jr, Editor

Offers banking and financial information to professionals and consumers.
Cost: $324.00
Frequency: Monthly

3031 **Global Investment Technology**
Global Investment Technology
909 Third Avenue
27th Floor
New York, NY 10022

212-370-3700; Fax: 212-370-4606
info@globalinv.com
www.globalinv.com

Micheal Horton, Publisher
Paven Saeghel, Editor-in-Chief

Focuses exclusively on strategic business trends, operations, and automation issues facing US and non-US investment institutions and banks.
Cost: $695.00
Frequency: Bi-Weekly
Circulation: 1800
Founded in 1991

3032 **Global Survey of Regulatory & Market Developments in Banking**
Institute of International Bankers
299 Park Ave
17th Floor
New York, NY 10171-3896

212-421-1611; Fax: 212-421-1119
iib@iib.org
www.iib.org
Facebook, Twitter, LinkedIn

Briget Polichene, CEO
Richard Coffman, General Counsel
William Goodwin, Communications Director

The study documents the economic contributions that international banks make to the United States, and also addresses the benefits that other countries enjoy from the extensive activities of United States and other non-domestic banks in their markets.
Frequency: Annual

3033 **IBES Monthly Comments**
Lynch, Jones and Ryan
1633 Broadway
48th Floor
New York, NY 10019

212-310-9500
800-992-7526; Fax: 646-223-9081

Stanley Chamberlin, Publisher
Todd W Burns, President

Monitors changes in global earning estimates database.
Founded in 1966

3034 **ICBA Bank Director Newsletter**
Independent Community Bankers of America
518 Lincoln Rd.
P.O. Box 267
Sauk Centre, MN 56378

320-526-6546
800-422-7285; Fax: 320-352-5766
info@icba.org
www.icba.org

Rebeca Romero Rainey, President/CEO
Terry J. Jorde, Sr. Executive Vice President

Provides readers with timeley articles on developments, trends, and insights in the community banking industry.
Frequency: Bi-Monthly

3035 **IFSA Newsletter**
International Financial Services Association
1120 Connecticut Avenue, NW
Washington, DC 20036

20 -66 -757; Fax: 202-663-5538
Facebook, Twitter, LinkedIn

Tod Burwell, Vice President
250 Pages
Frequency: Quarterly
Founded in 1924

3036 **In Focus**
National Assn of Government Guaranteed Lenders
215 East 9th Avenue
Stillwater, OK 74074

405-377-4022; Fax: 405-377-3931
www.naggl.org

Tony Wilkinson, President/CEO
Jennifer Sterrett O'Neill, EVP/COO
Jenifer Brake, Assistant VP Marketing
Jennifer Sterrett-O'Neill, Assistant VP Communications

Practical tips that will help you build the little efficiencies that make a big difference.
Frequency: Monthly

3037 **Inside Mortgage Compliance**
Inside Mortgage Finance Publishers
7910 Woodmont Ave
Suite 1000
Bethesda, MD 20814-7019

301-951-1240; Fax: 301-656-1709
www.imfpubs.com

Guy Cecala, Owner/Publisher

Keeps executives on top of crucial and evolving legal and regulatory issues. Covers fair housing, predatory lending, consumer protection, RESPA, TILA, lawsuits. Features monthly CRA ratings.
Cost: $571.00
14 Pages
Frequency: Monthly
ISSN: 1093-605X

Founded in 1990
Mailing list available for rent: 750 names
Printed in 2 colors on matte stock

3038 **Inside Strategy**
Strategy Research Corporation
100 NW 37th Avenue
Miami, FL 33125

305-649-5400; Fax: 305-643-5584
strategy@canect.net
www.strategyresearch.com

Johanna Strouss, Editor
Richard Tobin, President

Inside Strategy is a newsletter that covers trends and developments in Latin America and the US Hispanic market mostly obtained from SRC, studies, products services and reports.
38511 Pages
Frequency: Monthly
Founded in 1998

3039 **Inside The GSEs**
Inside Mortgage Finance Publishers
7910 Woodmont Ave
Suite 1000
Bethesda, MD 20814-7019

301-951-1240; Fax: 301-656-1709
service@imfpubs.com
www.imfpubs.com

Guy Cecala, Owner
Greg Johnson, Editor
John Bancroft, Managing Editor
Mary L Probka, Director Marketing/Circulation

Subscribers know the latest on GSE finance, products, political contributions, their critics and supporters, and news on potential reform, controversies and regulatory activities.
Cost: $763.00
14 Pages
Frequency: Bi-Weekly
ISSN: 1093-605X
Founded in 1985
Mailing list available for rent: 400 names
Printed in 2 colors on matte stock

3040 **MSRB Manual**
Municipal Securities Rulemaking Board
1900 Duke St
Suite 600
Alexandria, VA 22314-3461

703-797-6600; Fax: 703-797-6700
MSRBsupport@msrb.org
www.msrb.org

Lynnette Hotkis, Executive Director
Marcelo Vieira, Director Research

Rules of the Municipal Rule-Making Board.
Cost: $7.00
Founded in 1975

3041 **NACHA: Electronic Payments Association Newsletter**
NACHA: The Electronic Payments Association
13450 Sunrise Valley Drive
Suite 100
Herndon, VA 20171

703-561-1100; Fax: 703-787-0996
info@nacha.org
www.nacha.org

Marcie Haitema, Chairperson
Janet O Estep, CEO

Articles on industry self regulatory organizations for automated clearing house payment systems and other electronic payments.
Cost: $120.00
Printed in 2 colors on matte stock

3042 **NAGGL News Flash**
National Assn of Government Guaranteed Lenders
215 East 9th Avenue
Stillwater, OK 74074

405-377-4022; Fax: 404-377-3931
www.naggl.org

Tony Wilkinson, President/CEO
Jennifer Sterrett O'Neill, EVP/COO
Jenifer Brake, Assistant VP Marketing
Jennifer Sterrett-O'Neill, Assistant VP Communications

This email is an at-a-glance review of recent industry news.
Frequency: Bi-Monthly

3043 **Nilson Report**
HSN Consultants
1110 Eugenia Place
Suite 100
Carpinteria, CA 930113-992

805-684-8800; Fax: 805-684-8825
info@nilsonreport.com
www.nilsonreport.com

H Spencer Nilson, Publisher

Credit card newsletter.
Cost: $945.00
12 Pages
Frequency: BiWeekly

3044 **Opportunities for Banks in Life Insurance**
American Association of Bank Directors
1250 24th Street, NW
Suite 700
Washington, DC 20037

20 -46 -488; Fax: 202-349-8080
info@aabd.org
www.aabd.org

David Baris, Executive Director

The guide reviews best insurance sales practices, distribution strategies, selling through investment brokers, using licensed branch bankers, referrals from investment specialists, referrals from licensed branch bankers, stand alone life specialists, direct sales and more.
Cost: $12.50

3045 **Origination News**
Thomson Financial
One State Street Plaza
27th floor
New York, NY 10004

212-803-8760; Fax: 212-292-5216
www.originationnews.com

Elaine Yadlon, Plant Manager
Richard J Harrington, President/CEO

Information for mortgage industry executives on mortgage brokers, mortgage bankers and mortgage executives in commercial banks, savings banks, savings and loan associations and credit unions.
Cost: $78.00
Frequency: Monthly

3046 **PayState Update**
American Payroll Association
660 N. Main Avenue
Suite 100
San Antonio, TX 78205

210-224-6406; Fax: 210-224-6038
www.americanpayroll.org

Daniel Maddux, Executive Director

Association e-newsletter offering members news on updates in state and local payroll compliance. Sold in one-year increments.
Cost: $397.00
Founded in 1982

3047 **Payments System Report**
National Automated Clearing House Association
13450 Sunrise Valley Drive
Suite 100
Herndon, VA 20171-4607

703-561-1100
800-487-9180; Fax: 703-787-0996
info@nacha.org
www.nacha.org
Facebook, Twitter, LinkedIn

Janet O Estep, CEO

Official source for Automated Clearing House (ACH) news and information. Contains reports on rule changes, legislative and regulatory developments, policy issues, market research, product developments and marketing solutions.
Frequency: Monthly

3048 **Payroll Currently**
American Payroll Association
660 N. Main Avenue
Suite 100
San Antonio, TX 78205

210-224-6406; Fax: 210-224-6038
www.americanpayroll.org

Daniel Maddux, Executive Director

Member newsletter containing information on new legislation affecting payroll, benefits, and human resources.
Frequency: Monthly
Founded in 1982

3049 **Peer News**
American Bankers Association
1120 Connecticut Avenue NW
Washington, DC 20036

202-635-5000
800-226-5377; Fax: 202-828-4540
icb@aba.com
www.aba.com/icbcertifications

Rob Nichols, President/CEO

ICB members receive a newsletter that shares program developments, member career notes, insights from ICB leadership, the latest continuing education opportunities, and more.
Frequency: Quarterly

3050 **Pratt's Bank Security Report**
AS Pratt & Sons
805 15th St. NW
Third Floor
Washington, DC 20005-2207

800-572-2797
customercare.sis@sheshunoff.com
www.aspratt.com

Peter Knopp, Editor

Security officers and consultants can keep up with the latest developments affecting bank security by subscribing to Pratt's Bank Security Report.
Cost: $455.00
Frequency: Monthly
Founded in 1867

3051 **RTC Suits Against Savings Institution Directors and Officers**
American Association of Bank Directors
1250 24th Street, NW
Suite 700
Washington, DC 20037

20 -46 -488; Fax: 202-349-8080
info@aabd.org
www.aabd.org

David Baris, Executive Director

This study reviews all 90 of the cases in the RTC's public files that were filed by the RTC against directors and officers.
Cost: $85.00

3052 **Regional Mortgage Market Report**
Mortgage Bankers Association

1717 Rhode Island Avenue, NW
Suite 400
Washington, DC 20036

202-557-2700
membership@mortgagebankers.org
www.mortgagebankers.org
Facebook, Twitter, LinkedIn

The Regional Mortgage Market Report for MSAs and/or states has been designed to provide mortgage professionals with a primary source of information to help identify mortgage lending opportunities and manage the risks associated with mortgage servicing.
Cost: $395.00
Frequency: Quarterly
Founded in 1914

3053 **Report of Task Force on Asset Freezes of Bank Directors and Officers**
American Association of Bank Directors
1250 24th Street, NW
Suite 700
Washington, DC 20037

20 -46 -488; Fax: 202-349-8080
info@aabd.org
www.aabd.org

David Baris, Executive Director
Cost: $25.00

3054 **SCOR Report**
Stewart Gordon Associates
PO Box 781992
Dallas, TX 75378-1992

972-620-2489; Fax: 972-406-0213

Tom Stewart Gordon, Publisher
C Delton Simmons, Circulation Manager
Anne D Hall, Production Manager

Capital information alternatives for small business. Target audience: small business, their lawyers and accountants.
Cost: $280.00
Founded in 1994

3055 **SNL Bank & Thrift Daily**
SNL Securities
212 7th Street NE
Charlottesville, VA 22902-2124

434-977-1600; Fax: 434-977-4466
subscriptions@snl.com
www.snl.com
Twitter, Youtube

Michael Chinn, President/CEO
Nick Cafferillo, COO

Summary of previous week's acquisition announcements, branch sales, merger conversions, FDIC transactions and deal updates and perspectives.
Cost: $1700.00
Frequency: Weekly
Founded in 1987

3056 **SNL REIT Weekly**
SNL Securities
212 7th Street NE
Charlottesvle, VA 22902

434-977-1600; Fax: 434-977-4466
subscriptions@snl.com
www.snl.com
Twitter, Youtube

Michael Chinn, President/CEO
Nick Cafferillo, COO

Fax newsletter that summarizes the previous week's activity involving REITs. Includes comprehensive articles on current industry trends, condensed news stories, recent capital offerings and the latest market information.
Cost: $496.00
15 Pages
Frequency: Weekly
Founded in 1987

3057 **Secondary Mortgage Markets**
Federal Home Loan Mortgage Corporation
8200 Jones Branch Drive
McLean, VA 22102-3110

703-903-2000
800-424-5401; Fax: 703-903-4045
www.freddiemac.com

Charles E. Haldeman, CEO
Ralph Boyd, Executive VP Community Relations

Covers buying and selling residential and commercial mortgage-backed and asset-backed loans, marketing, and risk management.
Frequency: Monthly
Circulation: 15000
Founded in 1970

3058 **Securities & Investments M&A**
SNL Securities
212 7th Street NE
Charlottesvle, VA 22902

434-977-1600; Fax: 434-977-4466
CustomerService@snl.com
www.snl.com
Twitter, Youtube

Michael Chinn, President/CEO
Nick Cafferillo, COO

Fully devoted to M&A in the securities and asset management sectors.
Cost: $795.00
40 Pages
Frequency: Monthly
Founded in 1987

3059 **Specialty Finance M&A**
SNL Securities
212 7th Street NE
Charlottesvle, VA 22902

434-977-1600; Fax: 434-977-4466
CustomerService@snl.com
www.snl.com
Twitter, Youtube

Michael Chinn, President/CEO
Nick Cafferillo, COO

A unique source dedicated exclusively to specialty finance M&A.
Cost: $795.00
40 Pages
Frequency: Monthly
Founded in 1987

3060 **Study of Leading Banks in Insurance**
American Bankers Insurance Association
1120 Connecticut Avenue NW
Washington, DC 20036

202-663-5163
800-226-5377; Fax: 202-828-4546
vbarton@aba.com
www.aba.com

Rob Nichols, President

Presents the findings from the eighth research of the current and planned insurance activities of U.S. banks. Designed as a management tool for executives who need to understand how the bank-insurance industry is developing.
300 Members
Frequency: Annual
Founded in 2001

3061 **U.S. Banker**
SourceMedia
1 State St
27th Floor
New York, NY 10004-1561

212-803-8200
800-803-3424; Fax: 212-843-9608
custserv@sourcemedia.com
www.sourcemedia.com

Douglas Manoni, CEO
Richard Antoneck, CFO
Cost: $99.00
Frequency: Monthly
Founded in 2005

3062 **World Bank News**
World Bank
1818 H St Nw
Room U11-147
Washington, DC 20433-0002

202-473-1000; Fax: 202-477-6391
www.mehr.org

Graeme Wheeler, CEO
Paul Wolfowitz, President
Cynthia Delgadillo, Production Manager

For journalists and the developing community
Frequency: Fortnightly
Circulation: 9000
Founded in 1980

Magazines & Journals

3063 **A Guide to Implementing Direct Payment**
NACHA: Electronic Payments Association
13450 Sunrise Valley Drive
Suite 100
Herndon, VA 20171

703-561-1100; Fax: 703-787-0996
info@nacha.org
www.nacha.org
Facebook, Twitter, LinkedIn

Janet O Estep, CEO

A complete overview of these popular ACH applications. Also discussed are benefits, costs, operational/implementation concerns and promotional efforts. Included are sample promotional materials and implementation checklists.

3064 **A Profile of State Chartered Banking**
1129 20th Street, N.W.
9th Floor
Washington, DC 20036-4327
202-296-2840
800-886-2727; Fax: 202-296-1928
rstromberg@csbs.org
www.csbs.org

John Ryan, President/CEO
54 Pages
Frequency: Monthly
Founded in 1902

3065 **ABA Bank Compliance**
American Bankers Association
1120 Connecticut Avenue NW
Washington, DC 20036-3971

202-635-5000
800-226-5377; Fax: 202-663-7543
custserv@aba.com
www.aba.com

Rob Nichols, President

The source for timely, authoritative analysis of the ever-changing regulatory environment. Covers all the current regulatory issues, such as Privacy and E-Commerce, and perennial Compliance focus areas, such as lending, the Community Reinvestment Act, risk management, training and technology.
Cost: $450.00
Frequency: Bi-Monthly
Founded in 1875

3066 **ABA Bank Marketing**
American Bankers Association

1120 Connecticut Avenue NW
Washington, DC 20036-3971

202-635-5000
800-226-5377; Fax: 202-828-4540
custserv@aba.com
www.aba.com

Rob Nichols, President

A designed package of marketing intelligence, featuring essential industry news, in-depth articles, award-winning columnists and opinions, useful case studies and time-saving advice.
Cost: $120.00
Frequency: Monthly
Founded in 1875

3067 **ABA Bank Marketing Survey Report**
ABA Marketing Network
1120 Connecticut Avenue NW
Washington, DC 20036-3971

202-663-5000
800-226-5377; Fax: 202-828-4540
marketingnetwork@aba.com
www.aba.com/marketingnetwork/

Rob Nichols, President

The ABA Bank Marketing Survey Report provides comprehensive detailed benchmarks of bank marketing in such areas as marketing expenditures, marketing functions, market segmentation strategies, cross-selling/sales incentives, direct marketing, Internet marketing and advertising agency use.

3068 **ABA Banking Journal**
Simmons-Boardman Publishing Corporation
345 Hudson St
12th Floor
New York, NY 10014-7123

212-620-7200; Fax: 212-633-1165
www.simmonsboardman.com

Arthur J McGinnis Jr, President

The official journal of the American Bank Association, reporting on the banking industry.
Frequency: Monthly
Circulation: 32867
Founded in 1908
Mailing list available for rent

3069 **ABA Consumer Banking Digest**
American Bankers Association
1120 Connecticut Avenue NW
Washington, DC 20036-3902

202-635-5000
800-226-5377; Fax: 202-828-4547
drhodes@aba.com
www.aba.com

Rob Nichols, President

Provides perspectives on the latest developments, shifts and changes in the e-commerce sector. The goal is to provide a comprehensive, yet concise, description of current events shaping the rapidly emerging world of e-commerce and banking.
Cost: $450.00
Frequency: Bi-Monthly
Founded in 1875

3070 **ABA Reference Guide for Regulatory Compliance**
American Bankers Association
1120 Connecticut Avenue NW
Washington, DC 20036-3200

202-635-5000
800-226-5377; Fax: 202-663-7597
www.aba.com

Rob Nichols, President

Ideal source for Compliance Managers, Department Managers and Staff, Product Managers, and Retail/Branch Managers and those preparing for the Certified Regulatory Compliance Manager Exam.
Cost: $350.00
Frequency: Annual

3071 **ABA Trust & Investments**
American Bankers Association
1120 Connecticut Avenue NW
Washington, DC 20036

202-635-5000
800-226-5377; Fax: 202-828-4540
custserv@aba.com
www.aba.com

Rob Nichols, President

Brings current, authoritative, wide-ranging coverage and updates on all aspects of the trust and investments industry
Cost: $120.00
15 Pages
Frequency: Bi-Monthly

3072 **ABI/St. Johns Law Review**
ABI/St. Johns School of Law
8000 Utopia Parkway
Queens, NY 11439

718-990-6751; Fax: 718-990-8095
abilawreview@gmail.com
www.stjohns.edu

Denise Dessel, Editor-in-Chief

A partnership between St. John's School of Law and the American Bankruptcy Institute that publishes articles and student notes on cutting edge issues of bankruptcy law and practice.
Frequency: Bi-Annual
Founded in 1993

3073 **ACH Marketing Handbook: A Guide for Financial Institutions & Companies**
NACHA: The Electronic Payments Association
13450 Sunrise Valley Drive
Suite 100
Herndon, VA 20171

703-561-1100; Fax: 703-787-0996
info@nacha.org
www.nacha.org

Marcie Haitema, Chairperson
Janet O Estep, CEO

Designed for financial institutions and companies to assist them in understanding ACH products and services-their benefits, risk management considerations, and consumer perspectives.
Cost: $70.00
Frequency: Annual+

3074 **ACH Operating Rules & Guidelines**
NACHA: Electronic Payments Association
13450 Sunrise Valley Drive
Suite 100
Herndon, VA 20171

703-561-1100; Fax: 703-787-0996
info@nacha.org
www.nacha.org

Janet O Estep, CEO
Marcie Haitema, Chairperson

Reflects the results of the Rules Simplifications initiative.
Cost: $78.00

3075 **ACH Operating Rules, Corporate Edition**
NACHA: Electronic Payments Association
13450 Sunrise Valley Drive
Suite 100
Herndon, VA 20171

703-561-1100; Fax: 703-787-0996
info@nacha.org
www.nacha.org

Janet O Estep, CEO
Marcie Haitema, Chairperson

Reflects the results of the Rules Simplification initiative. Previously organized around major topics, the simplified Rules framework is structured around the rights and responsibilities of participants in the ACH Network.
Cost: $46.00

3076 **ACH Settlement Guide**
NACHA: Electronic Payments Association
13450 Sunrise Valley Drive
Suite 100
Herndon, VA 20171

703-561-1100; Fax: 703-787-0996
info@nacha.org
www.nacha.org
Facebook, Twitter, LinkedIn

Janet O Estep, CEO

Designed to provide a thorough working knowledge of how money flows through the ACH Network and to equip financial institutions with the necessary tools to reconcile the daily ACH. Included in this publication are examples of statements, ACH advices and a sample balancing worksheet that financial institutions can use as a model for daily reconciling. This document was written as a direct result of financial institutions losing money due to the mismanagement of the ACH settlement function.

3077 **AFP Exchange**
Association for Financial Professionals
4520 East West Hwy
Suite 750
Bethesda, MD 20814-3319

301-907-2862; Fax: 301-907-2864
www.afponline.org

Terry Crawford, Chair

AFP Exchange is published for financial professionals. Editorial highlights include case studies and practical business information. Regular departments include outlook, new products and services, calendar and book reviews.
Cost: $90.00
80 Pages
Frequency: Bi-Monthly
Circulation: 12000
Founded in 1979
Printed in 4 colors on glossy stock

3078 **AITCO Membership Directory**
Association of Independent Trust Companies
8 S Michigan Ave
Suite 1000
Chicago, IL 60603-3452

312-223-1611; Fax: 312-580-0165

Douglas Nunn, President
Marcia Williams, Treasurer
Tom Blank, General Counsel/Secretary

Provides members with contact information on peers as well as industry vendors. This reference tool also include a listing of key officers as well as detailed descriptions of the company's product line and specialty areas.
50+ Pages

3079 **American Banker**
American Banker/SourceMedia

1 State St
27th Floor
New York, NY 10004-1561

212-803-8450
800-221-1809; Fax: 212-843-9600
www.sourcemedia.com

Douglas Manoni, CEO
Richard Antoneck, CFO

Focuses on the continuing changes in banking, including lending, money market shifts, developments in operations and technology, marketing, mortgages and mergers.
Cost: $945.00
Circulation: 18754
Founded in 1835

3080 American Bankruptcy Institute Journal
American Bankruptcy Institute
66 Canal Center Plaza
Suite 600
Alexandria, VA 22314-1546

703-739-0800; Fax: 703-739-1060
info@abiworld.org
www.abi.org

Amy Quackenboss, Executive Director

Benefit to ABI members. Written by experts in the insolvency community, the Journal addresses timely issues involving consumer bankruptcy, the intersection of state laws and the Bankrupcy Code, valuation, turnaround management concerns, recent legislative developments, the US trustee system and more. Available in print or online.
Frequency: Monthly
Founded in 1982

3081 BISA Magazine
Bank Insurance and Securities Association
2025 M Street NW
Suite 800
Washington, DC 20036

202-367-1111; Fax: 202-367-2111
bisa@BISAnet.org
www.bisanet.org

Jeff Hartney, Executive Director
Daniel J. McCormack, President
Andrew W. Singer, Editor-In-Chief
Jason Meyers, Managing Editor

The official publication of the Bank Insurance & Securities Association, sets the standard for in-depth industry reporting. Offers readers expert advice, exemplary editorials, in-depth articles and timely news updates.
Founded in 2002

3082 Bank Director News
American Association of Bank Directors
1250 24th Street, NW
Suite 700
Washington, DC 20037

202-463-4888; Fax: 202-349-8080
info@aabd.org
www.aabd.org

David Baris, Executive Director
Frequency: quarterly

3083 Bank News
Bank News Publications
PO Box 29156
Shawnee Mission, KS 66205-9156

913-261-7000
800-336-1120; Fax: 913-261-7010
www.banknews.com

Janet Holman, President & Publisher
Joel Holman, CEO & Publisher

News and features for banks and bankers.
Cost: $79.00
64 Pages
Frequency: Monthly
Circulation: 7000
Founded in 1901
Printed in 4 colors on glossy stock

3084 Bank Notes
510 King Street
Suite 410
Alexandria, VA 22314

703-549-0977
800-966-7475; Fax: 703-548-5945
eba@envirobank.org
www.envirobank.org

Rick Ferguson, President
Scott Beckerman, Treasurer
76 Pages
Frequency: Bi-Monthly
Founded in 1994

3085 Bank Systems & Technology
CMP Media
240 West 35th Street
New York, NY 10001

212-928-8400; Fax: 212-600-3080

David Leven, CEO
Dame Helen Alexander, Chairman

In-depth look into the new age of banking where total integration of technology is the driving force of new product business growth. Features deliver critical information on the strategic use of technology for increased profitability and productivity, in turn providing bankers with the tools to gain the competitive advantage on today's changing financial services landscape.
Cost: $52.00
Frequency: Monthly
Circulation: 23753
Founded in 1918

3086 Bank Technology News
Thomson Media
1 State St
27th Floor
New York, NY 10004-1481

212-803-8200; Fax: 212-843-9600
custserv@sourcemedia.com
www.banktechnews.com
Facebook, Twitter

Penny Crosman, Editor in Chief
Douglas J. Manoni, CEO

The leading source for financial services technology coverage, written for those individuals who are responsible for the front, middle and back office technology needs of their financial institutes.
52 Pages
Frequency: Monthly
Founded in 1987
Mailing list available for rent

3087 Bankers Digest
P.O. Box 743006
Dallas, TX 75374-3006

214-221-4544; Fax: 214-221-4546
bankersdigest@bankersdigest.com
www.bankersdigest.com

Bonnie J Blackman, Owner
R Blackman Jr, Managing Editor

A weekly news magazine devoted to the southwest banking news. Accepts advertising.
Cost: $29.00
16 Pages
Frequency: Weekly
Circulation: 3100
ISSN: 0140-1800
Founded in 1942
Printed in 2 colors on glossy stock

3088 Bankers' Magazine
Thomson Reuters
195 Broadway
Suite 4
New York, NY 10007-3124

646-822-2000
800-231-1860; Fax: 646-822-2800
trta.lei-support@thomsonreuters.com
www.ria.thomsonreuters.com

Elaine Yadlon, Plant Manager
Thomas H Glocer, CEO & Director
Robert D Daleo, Chief Financial Officer
Kelli Crane, Senior Vice President & CIO

Written by bank professionals who offer urgent information about the banking industry to the banking community.
Cost: $115.00
Frequency: Bi-Monthly
Founded in 1935

3089 Banking Strategies
Bank Administration Institute
115 S. LaSalle Street
Suite 3300
Chicago, IL 60603

312-683-2464
800-224-9889; Fax: 312-683-2373
info@bai.org
www.bai.org
Facebook, Twitter, LinkedIn, Youtube

Lewis Fischer, Chairman of the Board
Scott Peters, Vice Chairman

Includes information on finance, economics, planning, operations, regulations, retail, technology and human resources management.
Cost: $66.50
66 Pages
Circulation: 42175
ISSN: 1091-6385

3090 Banking Strategies Magazine
Bank Administration Institute
115 S LaSalle St
Suite 3300
Chicago, IL 60603

312-683-2464
888-284-4078; Fax: 312-683-2373
info@bai.org
www.bai.org
Facebook, Twitter, LinkedIn, Youtube

Lewis Fischer, Chairman of the Board
Scott Peters, Vice Chairman

To present the latest in best practices and thought leadership through high-quality, in-depth, unbiased editorial coverage of strategic and managerial issues in today's complex and dynamic financial services business.
Frequency: Annual

3091 Broker Magazine
Thomson Media
1 State St
27th floor
New York, NY 10004-1481

212-825-8445
888-501-8850; Fax: 212-292-5216
www.brokerworldmag.com

Mark Fogarty, Editorial Director
Brad Finkelstein, Editor
Timothy Murphy, Group Publisher

Features on training, motivation, technology, legislation and marketing
Cost: $60.00
Frequency: Bi-Monthly

3092 Business Credit
Assn of Executives in Finance, Credit & In'tl Bus
8840 Columbia 100 Parkway
Columbia, MD 21045-2158

410-423-1840
888-256-3242; Fax: 410-740-5574

fcib_info@fcibglobal.com
www.fcibglobal.com
Twitter, LinkedIn

Kelly Bates, Chairperson
Robin Schauseil, President
Tom Demovic, Director

For professionals responsible for extending credit and collecting receivables. Topics include business law, lien law, technology, credit management, collections, deductions, fraud, credit risk, credit scoring, outsourcing, information services, trade finance and more.
Cost: $54.00
72 Pages
Frequency: 10x/Year
Circulation: 32000
Founded in 1896
Printed in 4 colors on matte stock

3093 **Business Credit Magazine**
8840 Columbia 100 Parkway
Columbia, MD 21045-2158

410-423-1840
888-256-3242; Fax: 410-740-5574
www.fcibglobal.com
LinkedIn

Marta Chacon, Director, The Americas
Ron Shepherd, Director, Business Dev.
Noelin Hawkins, Director, Europe, Middle East

Business Credit
1000+ Members
Frequency: Monthly
Circulation: 38000
Founded in 1919

3094 **CFA Digest**
CFA Institute
PO Box 3668
Charlottesville, VA 22903-0668

434-951-5499
800-247-8132; Fax: 434-951-5262
info@cfainstitute.org
www.cfainstitute.org
Facebook, Twitter, LinkedIn

John Rogers, CEO
Daniel J Larocco, Co-Editor

Distills selected current industry research into short, easy-to-read summaries.
Frequency: Quarterly
Founded in 1971

3095 **CFA Magazine**
CFA Insitute
Po Box 3668
Charlottesville, VA 22903-0668

434-951-5499
800-247-8132; Fax: 434-951-5262
info@cfainstitute.org
www.cfainstitute.org
Facebook, Twitter, LinkedIn

John Rogers, CEO
Roger Mitchell, Associate Editor

A practice-based, professional member magazine. Created on the feedback from a series of worldwide focus groups and a member survey.
Frequency: Bi-Monthly
Founded in 2003

3096 **CMBS World**
30 Broad Street
28th Floor
New York, NY 10004

212-509-1844; Fax: 212-509-1895
info@crefc.org
www.cmbs.org
Facebook, Twitter, LinkedIn

Stephen Renna, CEO
Ed DeAngelo, VP

To inform, educate and stimulate meaningful discussions and exchanges among CMBS members on the risks and benefits of commercial mortgage-backed securities.
309 Pages
Frequency: Quarterly
Founded in 1994

3097 **Community Bank President**
Siefer Consultants
PO Box 1384
Storm Lake, IA 50588-1384

712-732-7340; Fax: 712-732-7906

Dan Siefer, Publisher

Analysis of trends, new ideas and implementation strategies, regulatory compliance, and bank profitability. Provides a glimpse at the latest deposit and loan statistics, marketing and new technology updates and bank management issues.
Frequency: Monthly
Circulation: 1800

3098 **Community Banking Advisor**
624 Grassmere Park Drive
Suite 15
Nasvhille, TN 37211

615-377-3392
800-231-2524; Fax: 615-377-7092
info@bankingcpas.com
www.bankingcpas.com

Brian Blaha, President

A publication for banking professionals that features articles on management, tax, operational, and other issues confronting community banks.
24 Pages
Frequency: Quarterly
Founded in 1995

3099 **Compliance Manual**
NACHA: The Electronic Payments Association
13450 Sunrise Valley Drive
Suite 100
Herndon, VA 20171

703-561-1100; Fax: 703-787-0996
info@nacha.org
www.nacha.org

Janet O Estep, CEO
Marcie Haitema, Chairperson

Covers authorizations, disclosures, processing, funds availability, settlement, error resolution, returns, reversals, retention, audit, all Standard Entry Class Codes and much, much more.
Cost: $90.00

3100 **Credit Union Journal**
Thomson Media
1 State St
27th Floor
New York, NY 10004-1481

212-803-8200
800-221-1809; Fax: 800-843-9600
www.cujournal.com

Frank J Diekmann, Editor/Co-Publisher
Lisa Freeman, Managing Publisher

A surging economy, combined with competitive pricing policies and regulatory changes allowing credit unions to expand their field of membership.
Cost: $119.00
Frequency: Weekly

3101 **Credit Union Management Magazine**
Credit Union Executives Society
5510 Research Park Drive
PO Box 14167
Madison, WI 53708-167

608-271-2664
800-252-2664; Fax: 608-271-2303
cues@cues.org
www.cues.org
Facebook, Twitter, LinkedIn

Fred Johnson, President/CEO
Mary Arnold, VP Publications
George Hofheimer, VP Professional Development
Barbara Kachelski, CAE, SVP/CIP

Published for credit union CEOs and senior management, the magazine focuses each month on general management, operations, marketing and human resource functions. Includes in-depth coverage of technology, facilities, finance, lending, staffing and card services, among other topics.
Cost: $129.00
11067 Members
Frequency: Monthly
Circulation: 8000
Founded in 1962

3102 **Documentary Credit World**
International Financial Services Association
1120 Connecticut Avenue NW
Washington, DC 20036

20 -66 -757; Fax: 202-663-5538

Frank Keating, President
Albert Kelly, Chairman

Published jointly by the Institute of International Banking Law and Practice and the IFSA. DCW is your source for information on LCs.
Cost: $595.00
Frequency: 10x/Year

3103 **Electronic Payments Journal**
NACHA: Electronic Payments Association
13665 Dulles Technology Dr
Suite 300
Herndon, VA 20171-4607

703-561-1100; Fax: 703-787-0996
info@nacha.org
www.nacha.org

Janet O Estep, CEO

Helps industry professionals to track the latest developments in electronic payments and provides in-depth coverage of a broad array of payment issues.
Founded in 1978

3104 **Electronic Payments Review and Buyer's Guide**
NACHA: Electronic Payments Association
13450 Sunrise Valley Drive
Suite 100
Herndon, VA 20171

703-561-1100; Fax: 703-787-0996
info@nacha.org
www.nacha.org

Janet O Estep, CEO
Marcie Haitema, Chairperson

A directory of payment services with listings for ACH Services, Authentication & Security Solutions, B2B Invoicing & Presentment Services, Card Services, Check/Electronic Check Services, Consultants & Industry Associations, Consumer-Based Bill Payment & Presentment, Electronic Government Services, Electronic Consumer Services, International Payment Resources, Payment & Processing Software & Hardware, Thrid-Party Service Providers, and Wireless Payment & Commerce
Cost: $3.50
Frequency: Annual

3105 **Federal Credit Union Magazine**
National Association of Federal Credit Unions

3138 10th St N
Suite 3
Arlington, VA 22201-2160

703-522-4770
800-336-4644; Fax: 703-524-1082
www.nafcu.org

Dan Berger, President

Written for CEOs, senior staff and volunteers of Federal Credit Unions. Offers legislative and regulatory news, as well as technology and operational issues.
Cost: $99.00
80 Pages
Frequency: Bi-Monthly
Circulation: 11136
ISSN: 1043-7789
Founded in 1967
Printed in 4 colors on glossy stock

3106 **Finance and Development**
International Monetary Fund
700 19th St NW
Washington, DC 20431-0002

202-623-7000; Fax: 202-623-6220
publicaffairs@imf.org
www.imf.org

David Lipton, First Deputy Managing Director
Christine Lagarde, Managing Director

Analysis of financial and economic developments and explanation of the policies and work of the International Monetary Fund and the World Bank.
Cost: $10.00
Frequency: Quarterly
Circulation: 130000
Founded in 1945
Mailing list available for rent: 120M names
Printed in 4 colors

3107 **Financial Analyst**
CFA Institute
PO Box 3668
Charlottesville, VA 22903-0668

434-951-5499
800-247-8132; Fax: 434-951-5262
info@cfainstitute.org
www.cfainstitute.org

John Rogers, CEO
Rodney N Sullivan, Associate Editor

Is to advance the knowledge and understanding of the practice of investment management through the publication of high-quality, practitioner-relevant research.

3108 **Financial Review**
Blackwell Publishing
350 Main St
Commerce Place
Malden, MA 02148-5089

781-388-8200; Fax: 781-388-8210
www.blackwellpublishing.com

Steven Smith, President/CEO
Vincent Marzano, Vice President, Treasurer

Publishes original empirical, theoretical and methodological research providing new insights into issues of importance in financial economics.
Frequency: Quarterly
ISSN: 0732-8516

3109 **Financial Women Today Magazine**
Financial Women International
1027 W Roselawn Avenue
Roseville, MN 55113

651-487-7632
866-807-6081; Fax: 651-489-1322
info@fwi.org

Melissa Curzon, President
Cindy Hass, VP
Carleen DeSisto, Secretary

Serves nearly 10,000 female financial service professionals, helping them to attain their economic, professional and personal goals.
Cost: $24.00
Frequency: Quarterly
Circulation: 19000
ISSN: 1059-3950
Founded in 1921
Mailing list available for rent
Printed in 4 colors on matte stock

3110 **Global Custodian**
Asset International
1055 Washington Blvd
Stamford, CT 06901

203-295-5015
888-374-3722; Fax: 203-595-3201
www.globalcustodian.com

Dominic Hobson, Editor-in-Chief
Charles Ruffel, Founder/CEO
Maredith Hughes, VP

Written for international institutional investors. Stories cover engineering markets, cross border investing, securities lending and more.
Cost: $185.00
Frequency: 5x/Year
Circulation: 20000
Founded in 1989

3111 **Government Affairs Bulletin**
Financial Services Roundtable
1001 Pennsylvania Ave NW
Suite 500 S
Washington, DC 20004-2508

202-289-4322; Fax: 202-289-1903
info@fsround.org
www.fsround.org
Facebook, Twitter

Tim Pawlenty, CEO
Richard Whiting, Executive Director

This bulletin keeps the members of the Roundtable informed on issues in the financial services industry and how the Roundtable views them.
100 Pages
Frequency: Weekly
Founded in 1993

3112 **ICBA Independent Banker Magazine**
Independent Community Bankers of America
518 Lincoln Road
P.O. Box 267
Sauk Centre, MN 56378

320-526-6546
800-422-7285; Fax: 320-352-5766
info@icba.org
www.independentbanker.org

Rebeca Romero Rainey, President/CEO
Terry J. Jorde, Sr. Executive Vice President
Matt Kusilek, Advertising Contact
Chris Lorence, Member Engagement & Strategy

Covers the news topics and trends that are important to the nation's community bank senior executives. Keeping members informed about and connected with their national association and its activities; and providing them with timely, relevant information on developments to growth their business franchise within the rapidly evolving financial services industry.
Frequency: Monthly

3113 **Independent Banker**
Inside Mortgage Finance Publishers
7910 Woodmont Ave
Suite 1000
Bethesda, MD 20814-7019

301-951-1240
800-422-8439; Fax: 301-656-1709
service@imfpubs.com
www.imfpubs.com
Twitter, LinkedIn, Youtube

John Bancroft, VP
George Brooks, Editor

Features strategies for high-performance community banks. Also includes profiles of success stories in community banks and assesses developments in legislation and regulation.
Frequency: Monthly
Circulation: 9,800
Mailing list available for rent

3114 **Information Management**
ARMA International
11880 College Boulevard
Suite 450
Overland Park, KS 66215

913-444-9174
844-565-2120; Fax: 913-257-3855
headquarters@armaintl.org
magazine.arma.org
Facebook, Twitter, LinkedIn

Nick Inglis, Exec. Dir., Content & Programming
Jeff Whited, Sr. Content Writer
Ann Snyder, Manager, Content Development

Also known as ARMA Magazine, it is a major source of information on topics and issues central to the management of records and information worldwide. Each issue features articles written by experts in the management of records and information.
61 Pages
Frequency: 6/Year
Founded in 1955

3115 **International Banking Focus**
Institute of International Bankers
299 Park Ave
17th Floor
New York, NY 10171-3896

212-421-1611; Fax: 212-421-1119
iib@iib.org
www.iib.org

Briget Polichene, Chief Executive Officer
Richard Coffman, General Counsel
Robin Wilks, Chief Administrative Officer

The Focus describes the latest legislative, regulatory and tax developments in Washington and various states, along with the Institute's efforts to address particular problems that affect international banks.
Frequency: Bi-Monthly
Founded in 1966

3116 **Mortgage Banking**
Mortgage Bankers Association
1717 Rhode Island Avenue, NW
Suite400
Washington, DC 20036

202-557-2700
membership@mortgagebankers.org
www.mortgagebankers.org

Janet Reilley Hewett, Editor-in-Chief
Michael Young, Chairman

Provides in-depth coverage of the real estate finance industry. Intelligent analysis of news and the most important issues and trends affecting the industry. Association discount available.
Cost: $60.00
120 Pages
Frequency: 14x/Year
Circulation: 6000
ISSN: 0730-0212
Founded in 1914
Mailing list available for rent: 2800 names at $100 per M
Printed in 4 colors on glossy stock

3117 **Mortgage Servicing News**
Thomson Media

1 State Street Plaza
27th Floor
New York, NY 10004-1481

212-825-8445
800-221-1809; Fax: 212-292-5216
www.mortgageservicingnews.com/

Mark Fogarty, Editor
Timothy Murphy, Group Publisher
Timothy Reifschneider, Marketing Manager
Virginia Wiese, Custom Publishing

Information on cross serving techniques, legislative decisions, management strategies, and professional profiles.
Cost: $98.00
Frequency: Monthly
Circulation: 20,000

3118 NABTalk It
National Association of Bankruptcy Trustees
One Windsor Cove
Suite 305
Columbia, SC 29223

803-252-5646
800-445-8629; Fax: 803-765-0860
info@nabt.com
www.nabt.com

Nancy H Cooper, Staff Editor
Neil Gordon, President
Frequency: Quarterly

3119 NACTT Quarterly
National Association of Chapter 13 Trustees
1 Windsor Cove
Suite 305
Columbia, SC 29223

803-252-5646
800-445-8629; Fax: 803-765-0860
info@nactt.com
www.nactt.com

Debra Miller, President
Margaret Burks, VP

The Quarterly emphasizes current local and national developments in Chapter 13. Each Quarterly provides a summary of the most recent Chapter 13 Bankruptcy court decisions.

3120 NACUSAC News
NACUSAC
PO Box 160
Del Mar, CA 92014

800-287-5949; Fax: 858-792-3884
nacusac@nacusac.org
www.nacusac.org

Celeste Shelton, Executive Director

Official magazing of the National Association of Credit Union Supervisory & Auditing Committees that keeps you up to date on the latest developments and events affecting supervisory/auditing committee members.
Frequency: Quarterly

3121 National Mortgage Broker Magazine
Banat Communications
23425 N 39th Drive
104-193
Glendale, AZ 85310

623-516-2723; Fax: 623-516-7738
www.nationalmortgagebroker.com

Mike Anderson, VP
Donald Frommeyer, President
Debbie Maxwell, Production Manager
Cost: $59.95
Frequency: Monthly
Founded in 1984

3122 New England Economic Indicators
Federal Reserve Bank of Boston
600 Atlantic Avenue
Suite 100
Boston, MA 02210-2204

617-973-3000; Fax: 617-973-5918
boston.library@bos.frb.org
www.bos.frb.org

Eric S Rosengren, President/CEO
Kenneth Montgomery, VP COO

Contains current and historical economic data for the states of CT, ME, MA, NH, RI, and VT, as well as the US data include employment, unemployment, prices and construction activity.
80 Pages
Frequency: Monthly
Circulation: 7000
Founded in 1914

3123 North Western Financial Review
NFR Communications
7400 Metro Blvd
Suite 217
Minnieapolis, MN 55439

952-835-2275; Fax: 612-831-1464
www.northwesternfinancialreview.com

Tom Bengston, Publisher

Provides useful information and useful data regarding developments without trade association bias.
Frequency: Annual+
Circulation: 9,000
Founded in 1989

3124 RMA Journal
Risk Management Association
1801 Market Street
Suite 300
Philadelphia, PA 19103-1628

215-446-4000
800-677-7621; Fax: 215-446-4101
customers@rmahq.org
www.rmahq.org
Facebook, Twitter, LinkedIn

William Githens, President/CEO
Linda O'Loughlin, Director Marketing
Dwight Overturf, CFO

Expanded both format and content to address an array of risk management issues while respecting and preserving essentials of commercial lending
Cost: $95.00
Frequency: Monthly
Founded in 1914
Printed in 4 colors on glossy stock

3125 Regional Review
Federal Reserve Bank of Boston
600 Atlantic Ave
Boston, MA 02210-2204

617-973-3000
800-409-1333; Fax: 617-973-4292
bostonlibrary@bos.frb.org
www.bos.frb.org

Erin Rosengren, President/CEO

Magazine on economics, banking, business topics, designed for the busy professional.
Frequency: Quarterly
Circulation: 15000
ISSN: 1062-1865
Founded in 1913
Printed in 5 colors on glossy stock

3126 SNL Quarterly Bank & Thrift Digest
SNL Securities
212 7th Street NE
Charlottesvle, VA 22902

434-977-1600; Fax: 434-977-4466
customerservice@snl.com
www.snl.com
Facebook, Twitter, LinkedIn, Youtube

Mike Chinn, President & CEO

Contains all relevant information on every publicly traded bank and thrift providing insight into each individual institution and allowing quick and accurate comparisons with both peer institutions and industry benchmarks.
Cost: $799.00
600 Pages
Frequency: Quarterly
Founded in 1987
Mailing list available for rent

3127 SNL Real Estate Securities Quarterly
SNL Securities
212 7th Street NE
Charlottesville, VA 22902

434-977-1600; Fax: 434-977-4466
subscriptions@snl.com
www.snl.com
Facebook, Twitter, LinkedIn, Youtube

Mike Chinn, President & CEO

This data digest provides comprehensive corporate, market, and financial information and portfolio level property data on more than 240 publicly traded and privately held real estate companies. SNL Real Estate Securities Quarterly is the industry's most comprehensive publication for evaluating real estate company performance at both a property and financial level.
Cost: $696.00
Frequency: Quarterly
Founded in 1987
Mailing list available for rent

3128 Secondary Marketing Executive Magazine
Zackin Publications
100 Willenbrock Road
Oxford, CT 06478

203-262-4670
800-325-6745; Fax: 203-262-4680
info@secondarymarketingexec.com
www.secondarymarketingexec.com
Facebook, Twitter

Michael Bates, Publisher
Patrick Barnard, Editor
Vanessa Williams, Business Development

Offers how-to information for buyers and sellers of mortgage loans.
Cost: $48.00
Frequency: Monthly
ISSN: 0891-2947
Founded in 1986

3129 Servicing Management
LDJ Corporation
100 Willenbrock Road
Oxford, CT 06478

203-755-0158
800-325-6745; Fax: 203-262-4680
www.servicingmgmt.com

Paul Zackin, Publisher
John Clapp, Editor
June Han, Marketing

Includes updates on industry and regulatory trends, and advise on operating their departments more profitably and efficiently.
Cost: $48.00
Frequency: Monthly
Circulation: 22500
Founded in 1989

3130 US Banker
Thomson Media

1 State St
27th Floor
New York, NY 10004-1481

212-803-8200
800-221-1809; Fax: 212-843-9600
www.americanbanker.com

Neil Weinberg, Editor-in-Chief
John Ceasar, Group Publisher
James Malkin, Chairman/CEO

Features on news and technological developments in the banking industry. Includes reports on companies, personalities and industry trends.
Cost: $109.00
Frequency: Monthly
Circulation: 80000
Founded in 1955

Trade Shows

3131 **ABA National Conference for Community Bankers**
American Bankers Association
1120 Connecticut Avenue NW
Washington, DC 20036

800-226-5377
800-226-5377
custserv@aba.com
www.aba.com

Rob Nichols, President

Features educational sessions, exceptional speakers, networking opportunities and world class exhibit hall.
2 mil Members
1500 Attendees
Frequency: Annual, February
Founded in 1875

3132 **ABA Sales Management Workshop**
American Bankers Association
1120 Connecticut Avenue NW
Washington, DC 20036

202-635-5000
800-226-5377
custserv@aba.com
www.salesmanagementworkshop.com

Frank Keating, President
Albert Kelly, Chairman

Workshop on creating and keeping customers, over 13 exhibitors, visited by community bank executives, managers, sales and marketing staff.
Frequency: Annual, September

3133 **ABA Wealth Management & Trust Conference**
American Bankers Association
1120 Connecticut Avenue NW
Washington, DC 20036

800-226-5377
custserv@aba.com
www.aba.com

Rob Nichols, President

Delivers practical, inventive ideas for wealth management and trust professionals.
Frequency: Annual, May

3134 **ARMA InfoCon**
ARMA International
11880 College Boulevard
Suite 450
Overland Park, KS 66210

913-444-9174
844-565-2120; Fax: 913-257-3855
headquarters@armaintl.org
www.arma.org
Facebook, Twitter, LinkedIn

Nate Hughes, Exec. Dir., Operations
Jennifer Millett, National Accounts Manager
Karen Skaggs, Sales & Events Specialist

Conference, seminar, workshop, banquet, award ceremony and 175 exhibits of micrographics, optical disk, automated document storage and retrieval systems and more technology of interest to information professionals.
3500 Attendees
Frequency: Annual
Founded in 1956

3135 **American Bankers Insurance Association Annual Conference**
American Bankers Insurance Association
1120 Connecticut Avenue NW
Washington, DC 20036

202-663-5163
800-226-5377; Fax: 202-828-4546
vbarton@aba.com
www.aba.com

Rob Nichols, President & CEO

The Conference highlights Best Practices Panel presentations as well as numerous break-out sessions with case studies by bankers and providers of insurance products and services.
300 Members
Frequency: September
Founded in 2001

3136 **American Payroll Association Annual Congress**
American Payroll Association
660 N. Main Avenue
Suite 100
San Antonio, TX 78205

210-224-6406; Fax: 210-224-6038
www.americanpayroll.org

Daniel Maddux, Executive Editor

The Annual Congress is the premier payroll event of the year. With over 190 workshops and special programs and entertainment, Congress is an excellent opportunity for payroll and other financial professionals to learn and network.
1500 Attendees
Frequency: Annual
Founded in 1982

3137 **American Payroll Association Capital Summit**
American Payroll Association
660 N. Main Avenue
Suite 100
San Antonio, TX 78205

210-224-6406; Fax: 210-224-6038
www.americanpayroll.org

Daniel Maddux, Executive Director

APA hosts the Capital Summit in Washington, D.C. This conference offers attendees the opportunity to meet with government officials and learn about the latest compliance initiatives.
Cost: $950.00
Frequency: Annual
Founded in 1982

3138 **American Payroll Association Educational Institutions Payroll Conference**
American Payroll Association
660 N. Main Avenue
Suite 100
San Antonio, TX 78205

210-224-6406; Fax: 210-224-6038
www.americanpayroll.org

Daniel Maddux, Executive Director

This conference focuses on compliance issues impacting payroll professionals working in the higher education community.
Cost: $1510.00
Frequency: Annual
Founded in 1982

3139 **American Payroll Association Payroll Leaders Conference**
American Payroll Association
660 N. Main Avenue
Suite 100
San Antonio, TX 78205

210-224-6406; Fax: 210-224-6038
www.americanpayroll.org

Daniel Maddux, Executive Director

APA's Payroll Leaders Conference offers training through four certificate programs, aimed at managers and professionals looking to become leaders.
Frequency: Annual
Founded in 1982

3140 **American Safe Deposit Association Conference**
American Safe Deposit Association
PO Box 519
Franklin, IN 46131-0519

317-738-4432; Fax: 317-738-5267
www.tasda.com

Thomas Cullinan, President
J Wayne Merrill, First VP
Winnifred Howard-Hammack, Second VP
Joyce A McLin, Executive Director
Kevin Fanning, Treasurer

Offers jam-packed sessions full of information and ideas that can be implemented immediately after conference.
200 Attendees
Frequency: June

3141 **Association for Financial Professionals Annual Conference**
Association for Financial Professionals
4520 East West Highway
Suite 750
Bethesda, MD 20814

301-907-2862; Fax: 301-907-2864
AFP@AFPonline.org
www.AFPonline.org
Facebook, Twitter, LinkedIn, Youtube

Susan Glass, Chairman
Anita Patterson, Vice Chairman

Workshop and 642 exhibits of lockboxes, check processing systems, computers, investments, pensions, foreign exchange, consulting, mergers, acquisitions and more information of interest to financial professionals.
6000 Attendees
Frequency: October
Founded in 1979

3142 **Association of Independent Trust Companies Conference**
Association of Independent Trust Companies
8 South Michigan Avenue
Suite802
Chicago, IL 60603

312-223-1611; Fax: 312-580-0615

Douglas Nunn, President
Marcia Williams, Treasurer
Tom Blank, General Counsel/Secretary

Typically attracts more than 50 financial executive to an information-packed program which addresses the practical issues and challenges of doing business within the trust and financial advisory industry.
Frequency: Annual

3143 **Association of Military Banks of America Conference**
Association of Military Banks of America(AMBA)
PO Box 3335
Warrenton, VA 20188
540-347-3305; Fax: 540-347-5995
christiane.jacobs@ambahq.org
Andrew Egeland, President
John Mitchell, Chairman
Terry Tuggle, Vice Chairman
Frequency: September

3144 **Bank Insurance and Securities Association Annual Conference**
Bank Insurance and Securities Association
2025 M Street, NW
Suite 800
Washington, DC 20036
202-367-1111; Fax: 20 -36 -211
bisa@BISAnet.org
www.bisanet.org
Jeff Hartney, Executive Director
Focus on the internal administration of the supervisory and compliance functions of the bank broker-dealer and its related activities.
Frequency: June
Founded in 2002

3145 **Bankers' Association for Finance & Trade Annual Conference**
Bankers' Association for Finance & Trade
1120 Connecticut Avenue NW
6th Floor
Washington, DC 20036-3902
202-663-7575; Fax: 202-663-5538
www.baft.org
Tod Burwell, President & CEO
Focused on the global environment and the impact of economic developments in specifications and markets including consecutive breakouts on compliance, risk mitigation and key issues.
Frequency: April

3146 **Boot Camp for BSA Professionals**
Conference of State Bank Supervisors
1129 20th Street, N.W.
9th Floor
Washington, DC 20036
202-296-2840; Fax: 202-296-1928
rstromberg@csbs.org
www.csbs.org
John Ryan, President & CEO
Will provide BSA Compliance knowledge and value to your regulatory agency, financial institution or money service business.
Frequency: May

3147 **CPSA Annual Meeting**
Check Payment Systems Association
2025 M Street NW
Suite 800
Washington, DC 20036-2422
202-671-1144; Fax: 202-367-2144
info@cpsa-checks.org
www.cpsa-checks.org
Steven Antolick, Executive Director
Renee Lurker, Senior Associate
In addition to the business meeting, there are presentations from top industry performers and innovators.
Frequency: May

3148 **CSBS Annual Meeting & Conference**
Conference of State Bank Supervisors
1129 20th Street NW
9th Floor
Washington, DC 20036
202-296-2840; Fax: 202-296-1928
mbquist@csbs.org
www.csbs.org
John Ryan, President & CEO
The largest gathering of State 7 Federal banking regulators, state bank CEOs, industry policy makers and representatives of companies who support the banking industry.
Frequency: May

3149 **Combating Payments & Check Fraud Conference**
Bank Administration Institute
115 S LaSalle St
Suite 3300
Chicago, IL 60603-3801
312-683-2464
888-224-0037; Fax: 312-683-2373
info@bai.org
www.bai.org
Facebook, Twitter, LinkedIn, Youtube
Lewis Fischer, Chairman of the Board
Scott Peters, Vice Chairman
Frequency: September

3150 **Commercial Mortgage Securities Association Conference**
Commercial Mortgage Securities Association
900 7th Street, NW
Suite 820
New York, NY 10004-2304
212-509-1844; Fax: 212-509-1895
info@crefc.org
www.cmbs.org
Facebook, Twitter, LinkedIn
Steven Renna, CEO
Intensive educational offerings and presentations on the CMBS industry's biggest challenges.
Frequency: June

3151 **Commerical Real Estate Finance/Multifamily Housing Convention & Expo**
Mortgage Bankers Association
1717 Rhode Island Avenue NW
Suite 400
Washington, DC 20036
202-557-2700
www.mortgagebankers.org
David H Stevens, President/CEO
Elaine Howard, VP Meetings/Conferences
Thousands of commerical real estate industry professionals gathered from across the country to do business with and learn the latest in industry trends, regulatory develoments and strategies to succeed in today's dynamic marketplace.
Frequency: Annual/February

3152 **Community & Regional Bank Forum**
Bank Insurance and Securities Association
2025 M Street, NW
Suite 800
Washington, DC 20036
202-367-1111; Fax: 202-367-2111
bisa@BISAnet.org
www.bisanet.org
Jeff Hartney, Executive Director
Frequency: September
Founded in 2002

3153 **Community Bank Director's Conference**
American Association of Bank Directors
1250 24th Street, NW
Suite 700
Washington, DC 20037
202-463-4888; Fax: 20 -34 -808
info@aabd.org
www.aabd.org
Keith Dalrymple, President/CEO
David Baris, Executive Director
Sponsored by the AABD and Bank CEO Network, designed to provide information community bank directors need
Frequency: Annual

3154 **Community Banking Advisory Network Super Conference**
HCAA
624 Grassmere Park Drive
Suite 15
Nasvhille, TN 37211
615-377-3392
800-231-2524; Fax: 615-377-7092
info@hcaa.com
www.hcaa.com
Helen Connolly, President

3155 **Credit Congress**
8840 Columbia 100 Parkway
Columbia, MD 21045-2158
410-423-1840
888-256-3242; Fax: 410-740-5574
www.fcibglobal.com
LinkedIn
Marta Chacon, Director, The Americas
Ron Shepherd, Director, Business Dev.
Noelin Hawkins, Director, Europe, Middle East
Business Credit
1000+ Members
1500 Attendees
Founded in 1919

3156 **Eastern Finance Association Meeting**
Eastern Finance Association
220 Holman Hall
PO Box 1848
University, MS 38677
404-498-8937; Fax: 404-498-8956
admin@easternfinance.org
www.easternfinance.org
Mark Lion, President
Jacqueline Garner, VP Local Arrangements
Annual meeting and exhibits relating to any aspect of finance, including financial management, investments and banking.
Frequency: April

3157 **Environmental Bankers Association Membership Meeting**
Environmental Bankers Association
510 King Street
Suite 410
Alexandria, VA 22314
703-549-0977
800-966-7475; Fax: 703-548-5945
eba@envirobank.org
www.envirobank.org
Rick Ferguson, President
Scott Beckerman, Treasurer
Frequency: January/June
Founded in 1994

3158 **FSPA Conference & Supplier Showcase**
Financial & Security Products Association
1024 Mebane Oaks Road
Suite 273
Mebane, NC 27302
919-648-0664
800-843-6082; Fax: 919-648-0670

bj@fspa1.com
www.fspa1.com

Grant Case, Chairman
Fred Wheeler, President
B.J. Hanson, Executive Director
Bryce Good, Vice President
Dave Pepin, Secretary-Treasurer

Annual event.
Frequency: April
Founded in 1973

3159 **Federal Reserve Board Conference**
Federal Reserve Board Publishers
20th Street & Constitution Avenue NW
Washington, DC 20551

202-452-3000; Fax: 202-728-5886
www.federalreserve.gov

Lucrezia Reichlin, Conference Organizer
Dale Henderson, Conference Organizer
Deborah Lagomarsino, Media Contact

Organized by the International Research Forum on Monetary Policy. Its purpose is to encourage research on monetary policy issues that are relevant for monetary policy making in interdependent economies.
Frequency: December

3160 **Financial Women International Annual Conference**
Financial Women International
1027 W Roselawn Avenue
Roseville, MN 55113

651-487-7632
866-807-6081; Fax: 651-489-1322
info@fwi.org

Melissa Curzon, President
Cindy Hass, VP
Carleen DeSisto, Secretary
Frequency: September

3161 **GARP Annual Risk Management Convention & Exhibit**
Global Association of Risk Professionals
111 Town Square Place
Suite 1215
Jersey City, NJ 07310

201-719-7210; Fax: 201-222-5022
rich.apostolik@garp.com
www.garp.com
Facebook, Twitter, LinkedIn

Richard Apostolik, President/CEO
Kenneth Abbott, Managing Director
Mark Wallace, Chief Operating Officer
Thomas Daula, Chief Risk Officer
Frequency: February
Founded in 1996

3162 **Global Association of Risk Professionals Annual Exhibition**
111 Town Square Place
Suite 1215
Jersey City, NJ 07310

201-719-7210; Fax: 201-222-5022
jason.mandel@garp.com
www.garp.com
Facebook, Twitter, LinkedIn

Richard Apostolik, President/CEO
Chris Donohue, Managing Director
Michael Nielsen, Chief Operating Officer

GARP's flagship event for Asia, with Keynote presentations, multi-track forum and separate workshops.
Frequency: Annual
Founded in 1996

3163 **Independent Community Bankers of America Live National Convention**
Independent Community Bankers of America
518 Lincoln Rd.
P.O. Box 267
Sauk Centre, MN 56378

320-526-6546
800-422-7285; Fax: 320-352-5766
convention@icba.org
www.icba.org

Julie Kulzer, Director, Conferences & Meetings

Only national trade show exclusively representing America's independent/community banks. Containing 200+ booths and 175+exhibitors. Offers networking, advocacy, and 60+ education sessions.
3000 Attendees
Frequency: March

3164 **Institute of International Bankers Annual Washington Conference**
Institute of International Bankers
299 Park Avenue
17th Floor
New York, NY 10171

212-421-1611; Fax: 212-421-1119
iib@iib.org
www.iib.org

Briget Polichene, CEO
Maura Christ, Executive Assistant
William Harris, Controller
Andy Lebron, Membership Associate

A two-day conference featuring senior U.S. and international government policy makers and financial industry leaders. As part of the conference, which is widely attended by general manager and other senior officers of Institute member banks, there is an evening reception for the Washington community, including Administration officials, Members of Congress, banking regulators and senior staff.
Frequency: March
Founded in 1966

3165 **International Financial Services Association Annual Conference**
International Financial Services Association
1120 Connecticut Avenue NW
Washington, DC 20036

202- 66- 757; Fax: 202-663-5538

Renee Wigfall, Manager, Meetings/Events
Todd Burwell, Vice President
Frequency: September

3166 **Legal Issues and Regulatory Compliance Conference**
Mortgage Bankers Association
1717 Rhode Island Avenue NW
Suite 400
Washington, DC 20036

202-557-2700
meetings@mortgagebankers.org
www.mortgagebankers.org

David H Stevens, President/CEO
Elaine Howard, VP Meetings/Conferences

Learn about all the legal and regulatory developments facing the industry.
Frequency: Annual/May

3167 **Microbanker**
Microbanker
PO Box 708
Lake George, NY 12061

518-745-7071; Fax: 518-745-7071
www.microbanker.com

Annual show and exhibits of microcomputer software, hardware and services for banking, savings and loans, and credit unions.
200 Attendees

3168 **Mid-Year Technical Conference**
National Assn of Government Guaranteed Lenders
424 South Squires Street
Stillwater, OK 74074

405-377-4022; Fax: 405-377-3931
www.naggl.com

Tony Wilkinson, President/CEO
Karen High, EVP/COO
Jenifer Brake, Assistant VP Marketing
Jennifer Sterrett-O'Neill, Assistant VP Communications
Cheryl Stone, VP Conferences
Frequency: May

3169 **NACUSAC Annual Conference & Exposition**
NACUSAC
PO Box 160
Del Mar, CA 92014

800-287-5949; Fax: 858-792-3884
nacusac@nacusac.org
www.nacusac.org

Celeste Shelton, Executive Director
Laura Clark, Associate Director

These events sponsored by the National Association of Credit Union Supervisory & Auditing Committees offer second-to-none networking and educational opportunities for supervisory and auditing committees.
Frequency: June

3170 **National Association of Bankruptcy Trustees Annual Convention**
National Association of Bankruptcy Trustees
One Windsor Cove
Suite 305
Columbia, SC 29223

803-252-5646
800-445-8629; Fax: 803-765-0860
info@nabt.com
www.nabt.com

Christina Hicks, President
Kelly Hagen, VP
Frequency: September

3171 **National Association of Chapter 13 Trustees Annual Seminar**
National Association of Chapter 13 Trustees
1 Windsor Cove
Suite 305
Columbia, SC 29223

803-252-5646
800-445-8629; Fax: 803-765-0860
info@nactt.com
www.nactt.com

Debra Miller, President
Margaret Burks, VP

This seminar is NAACO's educational highlight. National experts discuss complex issues and recent developments in the Chapter 13 areas.

3172 **National Association of Federal Credit Unions Conference**
National Association of Federal Credit Unions
3138 10th Street N
Suite 300
Arlington, VA 22201-2149

703-522-4770
800-336-4644; Fax: 703-524-1082
fbecker@nafcu.org
www.nafcu.org

Dan Berger, President/CEO
Anthony Demangone, Executive Vice President/COO

Stands as a national forum for the federal credit union community where new ideas, issues, con-

cerns and trends can be identified, discussed and resolved.
Frequency: July

3173 National Association of Professional Mortgage Women Annual Conference

National Assn of Professional Mortgage Women
PO Box 451718
Garland, TX 75045
425-778-6162
800-827-3034; Fax: 425-771-9588
napmw1@napmw.org
www.napmw.org
Susan Kerr, National President
Mark Jennings, President-Elect
Liz Roberts, Senior Vice President
Patricia Hull, Executive Director
Frequency: May

3174 National Fraud Issues Conference

Mortgage Bankers Association
1717 Rhode Island Avenue NW
Suite 400
Washington, DC 20036
202-557-2700
meetings@mortgagebankers.org
www.mortgagebankers.org
David H Stevens, President/CEO
Elaine Howard, VP Meetings/Conferences
Where industry professionals can learn about the issues related to the growing incidence and complexity of mortgage fraud.
Frequency: Annual/March

3175 National Investment Banking Association Annual Conference

National Investment Banking Association
PO Box 6625
Athens, GA 30604
706-208-9620; Fax: 706-993-3342
emily@nibanet.org
www.nibanet.org
James Hock, Co Chair
Gerald Alder, Director
Emily Foshee, Executive Director
D Scott Foshee, Chief Technology Officer
Vicki Barone, Treasurer/Secretary
Provides member firms with regularly scheduled forums where they are able to exchange ideas and information, evaluate presentations made by companies being underwritten or sponsored by member firms, collectively voice their positions on issues impacting their livelihood, and enhance their knowledge and expertise through ongoing educational programs designed to enable them to remain competitive.
Frequency: May

3176 National Marine Bankers Association Annual Conference

National Marine Bankers Association
231 South LaSalle Street
Suite 2050
Chicago, IL 60604
312-946-6260
bmcardle@nmma.org
www.marinebankers.org
Bernice McArdle, Associate Manager
A three-day member conference where the latest trends issues relating to the marine industry are discussed in detail.
Frequency: September

3177 National Mortgage Servicing Conference & Expo

Mortgage Bankers Association
1717 Rhode Island Avenue NW
Suite 400
Washington, DC 20036
202-557-2700
meetings@mortgagebankers.org
www.mortgagebankers.org
David H Stevens, President/CEO
Elaine Howard, VP Meetings/Conferences
Gives companies the opportunity to reach key servicing executives from residential mortgage companies. Showcase the product offerings, network with key decision makers, and obtain qualified leads.
Frequency: Annual/February

3178 National Policy Conference

Mortgage Bankers Association
1717 Rhode Island Avenue NW
Suite 400
Washington, DC 20036
202-557-2700
meetings@mortgagebankers.org
www.mortgagebankers.org
David H Stevens, President/CEO
Elaine Howard, VP Meetings/Conferences
Brings togethers key officials, cabinet members and special guest speakers to address issues of what is happening in the community as well as the practical effect proposed changes may have on the business and industry
Frequency: Annual/March

3179 National Technology in Mortgage Banking Conference

Mortgage Bankers Association
1717 Rhode Island Avenue NW
Suite 400
Washington, DC 20036
202-557-2700
meetings@mortgagebankers.org
www.mortgagebankers.org
David H Stevens, President/CEO
Elaine Howard, VP Meetings/Conferences
Forum to learn about the newest industry solutions and how they can increase the company's competitive edge. Focuses on relevant topics, including legal/regulatory updates, eMortgages, investor reporting changes adn technology advances such as mobile computing.
Frequency: Annual/March

3180 Payments

NACHA: Electronic Payments Association
13450 Sunrise Valley Drive
Suite 100
Herndon, AV 20171
703-561-1100; Fax: 703-787-0996
info@nacha.org
www.nacha.org
Marcie Haitema, Chairperson
Janet O Estep, CEO
The premier source for payments professionals from across industries and around the globe to get the most vital and actionable information needed to help address the myriad of issues and opportunities in today's rapidly changing environment.
Frequency: Annual/April-May

3181 RMA Annual Conference of Lending & Credit Risk Management

Risk Management Association
1801 Market Street
Suite 300
Philadelphia, PA 19103-1628
215-446-4000
800-677-7621; Fax: 215-446-4100
customers@rmahq.org
www.rmahq.org
William Githens, President/CEO
Sonny B Lyles, Vice Chair
Containing 31 booths and 28 exhibits.
600 Attendees
Frequency: October

3182 Retail Delivery Conference & Expo

Bank Administration Institute
115 S. LaSalle Street
Suite 3300
Chicago, IL 60603-3801
312-683-2464
888-284-4078; Fax: 312-683-2373
info@bai.org
www.bai.org
Facebook, Twitter, LinkedIn, Youtube
Lewis Fischer, Chairman of the Board
Scott Peters, Vice Chairman
2M Attendees
Frequency: November

3183 Sales Management Workshop

Bank Insurance and Securities Association
2025 M Street NW
Suite 800
Washington, DC 20036
202-367-1111; Fax: 20 -36 -211
bisa@BISAnet.org
www.bisanet.org
Jeff Hartney, Executive Director
Frequency: May/October/December
Founded in 2002

3184 Securities Industry and Financial Markets Association (SIFMA) Annual Meeting

SIFMA
1101 New York Avenue NW
8th Floor
Washington, DC 20005
202-962-7300; Fax: 202-962-7305
www.sifma.org
Timothy Ryan, President/CEO
Cheryl Crispen, Executive Vice President
The Securities Industry and Financial Markets Association/SIFMA Annual Meeting and Conference program addresses a variety of topics that may include competitiveness of the U.S. capital markets, global exchange consolidation, regulatory and legal initiatives, and trends in the fixed-income and capital markets.

3185 TransPay Conference & Expo

Bank Administration Institute
115 S LaSalle St
Suite 3300
Chicago, IL 60603
312-683-2464
800-375-5543; Fax: 312-683-2373
info@bai.org
www.bai.org
Facebook, Twitter, LinkedIn, Youtube
Lewis Fischer, Chairman of the Board
Scott Peters, Vice Chairman
Offers top solutions providers, innovators and your peers at BAY TransPay - focused on your financial institution profitability in payments.
Frequency: May

3186 Treasury & Risk Management Conference

Bank Administration Institute
115 S LaSalle St
Suite 3300
Chicago, IL 60603
312-683-2464
800-375-5443; Fax: 312-683-2373

info@bai.org
www.bai.org
Facebook, Twitter, LinkedIn, Youtube

Lewis Fischer, Chairman of the Board
Scott Peters, Vice Chairman
Frequency: May

3187 **Urban Financial Services Coalition Annual Conference**
Urban Financial Services Coalition
1200 G Street NW
Suite 800
Washington, DC 20005

202-289-8335
800-996-8335; Fax: 202-434-8707
www.ufscnet.org

Ola Truelove, National President
Debra Bronston, National VP
Frequency: June

Directories & Databases

3188 **ABA Directory of Trust Banking**
4709 Golf Road
Skokie, IL 60076

847-676-9600
800-321-3373; Fax: 847-933-8101
custserv@accuitysolutions.com
www.accuitysolutions.com

Hugh Jones, President
Kerry Hewson, VP

An official publication of the American Bankers Association. Listings include information such as national and state rankings, collective investment funds and corporate trusts.
Cost: $403.00
Circulation: 2800
ISBN: 1-563103-53-2

3189 **ABA Financial Institutions Directory**
4709 Golf Road
Skokie, IL 60076

847-676-9600
800-321-3373; Fax: 847-933-8101
custserv@accuitysolutions.com
www.accuitysolutions.com

Hugh Jones, President
Kerry Hewson, VP

This two-volume Executive Desktop Edition includes a special ABA Resource Guide with a Quick Reference Guide to Banking Regulations.
Cost: $500.00
Frequency: January/July
Circulation: 31850

3190 **ABA Key to Routing Numbers**
4709 Golf Road
Skokie, IL 60076

847-676-9600
800-321-3373; Fax: 847-933-8101
custserv@accuitysolutions.com
www.accuitysolutions.com

Hugh Jones, President
Kerry Hewson, VP
Cost: $184.00
Frequency: January/July
Circulation: 83300
Founded in 1911

3191 **ACH Participant Directory**
4709 Golf Road
Skokie, IL 60076

847-676-9600
800-321-3373; Fax: 847-933-8101
custserv@accuitysolutions.com
www.accuitysolutions.com

Hugh Jones, President
Kerry Hewson, VP
Cost: $207.00
Frequency: February/August
Circulation: 54600

3192 **ARMA International's Buyers Guide**
ARMA International
11880 College Boulevard
Suite 450
Overland Park, KS 66215

913-444-9174
844-565-2120; Fax: 913-257-3855
headquarters@armaintl.org
armabuyersguide.org
Facebook, Twitter, LinkedIn

Nick Inglis, Exec. Dir., Content & Programming
Jeff Whited, Sr. Content Writer
Ann Snyder, Manager, Content Development

75-100 companies listed. Free.
Frequency: Annual

3193 **American Financial Directory**
4709 Golf Road
Skokie, IL 60076

847-676-9600
800-321-3373; Fax: 847-933-8101
custserv@accuitysolutions.com
www.accuitysolutions.com

Hugh Jones, President
Kerry Hewson, VP
Cost: $558.00
Frequency: January/July
Circulation: 41300
ISBN: 1-563103-47-8
Founded in 1836

3194 **Annual Membership Directory & Buyers' Guide**
Financial & Security Products Association
1024 Mebane Oak Road
Suite 273
Mebane, NC 27302

919-648-0664
800-843-6082; Fax: 919-648-0670
bj@fspa1.com
www.fspa1.com

Grant Case, Chairman
Fred Wheeler, President
B.J. Hanson, Executive Director
Bryce Good, Vice President
Dave Pepin, Secretary-Treasurer

Who's Who of independent firms serving financial institutions hleps readers locate new dealers, products/service suppliers and strategic business partners. The directory is updated weekly online and available in print.
Founded in 1973

3195 **Annual Report of the Board of Governors of the Federal Reserve System**
Board of Governors
20th St & Constitution Ave N
Washington, DC 20551-0001

202-452-3284; Fax: 202-452-3101
www.federalreserve.gov

Rick McKinney, Manager
Janet Yellen, Vice Chair

Listing of directors, advisory councils and officers of banks and branches involved in mergers and acquisitions.
Frequency: Annual

3196 **Annual Software Guide**
Financial & Security Products Association
1024 Mebane Oaks Road
Suite 273
Mebane, NC 27302

919-648-0664
800-843-6082; Fax: 919-648-0670
bj@fspa1.com
www.fspa1.com

Grant Case, Chairman
Fred Wheeler, President
B.J. Hanson, Executive Director
Bryce Good, Vice President
Dave Pepin, Secretary-Treasurer

This detailed evaluation of the latest software to enhance business performance is provided by Brown Smith Wallace (BSW) only to members of participating associations, including FSPA.

3197 **BankNews Montain States Bank Directory**
BankNews Publications
PO Box 29156
Shawnee Mission, KS 66201-9156

913-261-7000
800-336-1120; Fax: 913-261-7010
www.banknews.com

Janet Holman, President & Publisher
Joel Holman, CEO & Publisher

Over 600 commercial banks, savings and loans, and holding companies are listed in this directory, state banking and regulatory agencies are also studied in the areas of Colorado, Wyoming, New Mexico, Montana and Utah.
Cost: $ 35.00
350 Pages
Frequency: Annual
Circulation: 3,500

3198 **BankRoll II**
US Federal Reserve System, Board of Governors
20th Street & Constitution Avenue NW
Washington, DC 20551-0001

Home Page: www.federalreserve.gov/
Twitter, LinkedIn

This database contains descriptive information and financial information from the Financial Report Bank Holding Companies (Y9) submitted to the Federal Reserve Board.

3199 **Bankcard Barometer**
RAM Research Corporation
1230 Avenue of the Americas
7th Floor, Rockefeller Center
New York, MD 21702-0700

301-954-4660; Fax: 301-695-0160
www.ramresearch.com

Robert B McKinley, Publisher/Editor

Database of nation's capital largest bank credit card issuers.
Cost: $1295.00
600 Pages
Frequency: Monthly
Founded in 1986
Printed in one color on matte stock

3200 **Branches of Your State: Banks, Savings & Loans, Credit Unions & Savings**
Sheshunoff Information Services
901 South Mopac
Suite 140
Austin, TX 78746-7970

512-472-4000
800-477-1772; Fax: 512-305-6575
sales@smslp.com
www.smslp.com
Facebook, Twitter, LinkedIn

Gabrielle Sheshunoff, CEO

State editions list banks, savings and loan branches and credit unions. Individual banks are listed for states without branch banking.
Cost: $345.00
Frequency: Annual

3201 **Data Book**
FDIC Public Information Center
550 17th St Nw
Washington, DC 20429-0001
202-898-3631
877-275-3342; Fax: 202-898-3984
publicinfo@fdic.gov
www.fdic.gov
Facebook, Twitter, LinkedIn
Martin Gruenberg, Chairman
Thomas Hoenig, Vice Chairman
Jeremiah Norton, Director
Offers information on bank names, locations, bank numbers and branches for each banking office, in seven volumes, divided geographically and aggregate bank deposits also known as Summary of Deposits.
Frequency: Quarterly

3202 **Directory of Minority and Women-Owned Investment Bankers**
San Francisco Redevelopment Agency
1 S Van Ness Avenue
Suite 5
San Francisco, CA 94103-5416
415-749-2400; Fax: 415-749-2565
www.sanfranciscofcu.org
Marcia Rosen, Executive Director
Erwin Tanjuaquio, Director Public Affairs
Lists 18 minority-owned investment banking firms.
Frequency: Biennial

3203 **Directory of Venture Capital & Private Equity Firms - Online Database**
Grey House Publishing
4919 Route 22
PO Box 56
Amenia, NY 12501
518-789-8700
800-562-2139; Fax: 518-789-0556
gold@greyhouse.com
gold.greyhouse.com
Facebook, Twitter
Leslie Mackenzie, Publisher
Richard Gottlieb, Editor
Packed with need-to-know information, this database offers immediate access to 2,300 VC firms, over 10,000 managing partners, and over 11,500 VC investments.
Frequency: Annual

3204 **Directory of Venture Capital and Private Equity Firms**
Grey House Publishing
4919 Route 22
PO Box 56
Amenia, NY 12501
518-789-8700
800-562-2139; Fax: 845-373-6390
books@greyhouse.com
www.greyhouse.com
Facebook, Twitter
Leslie Mackenzie, Publisher
Richard Gottlieb, Editor
Offers access to over 2,300 domestic and international venture capital and private equity firms, including detailed contact information and extensive data on investments and funds.
Cost: $685.00
1,200 Pages
Frequency: Annual
ISBN: 1-592372-72-4

3205 **Financial Institutions Directory of New England**
4709 Golf Road
Skokie, IL 60076
847-676-9600
800-321-3373; Fax: 847-933-8101
custserv@accuitysolutions.com
www.accuitysolutions.com
Hugh Jones, President
Kerry Hewson, VP
Cost: $114.00
Frequency: January/July

3206 **Financial Management**
University of South Florida COBA
3821 Holly Drive
Tampa, FL 33620-7360
813-974-4133; Fax: 813-974-5130
caminfo@arts.usf.edu
www.ira.usf.edu
Margaret Miller, Director
Alexa Favata, Associate Director
Financial management of individual firm, governmental unit or nonprofit institution, as opposed to financial structure of whole economy for practitioners and professors of financial management.
Cost: $20.00
Circulation: 11,500
Founded in 1970

3207 **National Credit Union Administration Directory**
National Credit Union Administration
1775 Duke St
Alexandria, VA 22314-6115
703-518-6300
800-755-1030; Fax: 703-518-6539
consumerassistance@ncua.gov
www.ncua.gov
J Leonard Skiles, Executive Director
Robert Fenner, Director/General Counsel
Jane Walters, Deputy Executive Director
Directory of credit unions governed by a three member board appointed by the President and confirmed by the US Senate, by the independent federal agency that charters and supervises federal credit unions. NCUA, with the backing of the full faith and credit of the US government, operates the National Credit Union Share Insurance Fund, insuring the savings of 80 million account holders in all federal credit unions and many state chartered credit unions.

3208 **North American Financial Institutions Directory**
4709 Golf Road
Skokie, IL 60076
847-676-9600
800-321-3373; Fax: 847-933-8101
custserv@accuitysolutions.com
www.accuitysolutions.com
Hugh Jones, President/CEO
Cost: $495.00
Frequency: January/July
Circulation: 31850
Founded in 1895

3209 **Ranking the Banks**
American Banker
1 State St
27th Floor
New York, NY 10004-1561
212-803-8450; Fax: 212-843-9600
www.sourcemedia.com
Douglas Manoni, President/CEO
David Longobardi, Editor-in-Chief
Richard Melville, Managing Editor
Timothy Reifschneider, Advertising Director
A comprehensive database of banking and financial services rankings, league tables, and vital statistics. Includes all tables published in the print edition of American Banker, and more. Organized by category with historical data.
Cost: $945.00
128 Pages

3210 **Salem Press Online Platform**
Grey House Publishing
4919 Route 22
PO Box 56
Amenia, NY 12501
800-221-1592; Fax: 201-968-0511
csr@salempress.com
online.salempress.com
The new Salem Press platform houses more than 500 titles including all of Salem's Health, Literature, History and Science titles in addition to select titles from the Grey House Publishing and H.W. Wilson product lines. Online access is free with each print purchase and includes an unlimited number of simultaneous users and remote access.

3211 **State and Local MBA Directory**
Mortgage Bankers Association of America
1717 Rhode Island Avenue, NW
Suite 400
Washington, DC 20036
202-557-2700
membership@mortgagebankers.org
www.mortgagebankers.org
Michael Young, Chairman
All state and local MBA officers and a calendar of significant meeting dates.
Cost: $50.00
Frequency: SemiAnnual

3212 **Thomson Bank Directory**
4709 Golf Road
Skokie, IL 60076
847-676-9600
800-321-3373; Fax: 847-933-8101
custserv@accuitysolutions.com
www.accuitysolutions.com
Hugh Jones, President
Kerry Hewson, VP
Cost: $684.00
Frequency: June/December
Circulation: 35000
ISBN: 1-563103-45-1

3213 **Thomson Credit Union Directory**
4709 Golf Road
Skokie, IL 60076-1231
847-676-9600
800-321-3373; Fax: 847-933-8101
custserv@accuitysolutions.com
www.accuitysolutions.com
Hugh Jones, President
Kerry Hewson, VP
Semi-annual directory that includes valuable industry statistics, a quick telephone lookup index of all credit unions and a resource guide featuring vendors within the credit union marketplace. Includes over 12,500 major credit unions and 5,500 branches, with asset rankings, membership totals and more. Published in partnership with the Credit Union National Association.
Cost: $247.00
Frequency: January/July
ISBN: 1-563103-24-9

3214 **Thomson Regulation CC Directory**
4709 Golf Road
Skokie, IL 60076
847-676-9600
800-321-3373; Fax: 847-933-8101

custserv@accuitysolutions.com
www.accuitysolutions.com

Hugh Jones, President
Kerry Hewson, VP
Cost: $144.00
Frequency: January/July
Circulation: 30100

3215 **Thomson Savings Directory**
4709 Golf Road
Skokie, IL 60076-1231

847-676-9600
800-321-3373; Fax: 847-933-8101
custserv@accuitysolutions.com
www.accuitysolutions.com

Hugh Jones, President
Kerry Hewson, VP

Semi-annual directory dedicated to the thrift industry. Listings include primary correspondent information, national industry statistics and breakdowns of mortgage portfolios.
Cost: $316.00
Frequency: January/July

3216 **World Bank Directory**
4709 Golf Road
Skokie, IL 60076-1231
847-676-9600
800-321-3373; Fax: 847-933-8101
custserv@accuitysolutions.com
www.accuitysolutions.com

Hugh Jones, President
Kerry Hewson, VP

Contains detailed listings for 10,000 international banks and their branches worldwide plus the top 1,000 US banks. The information in this annual directory includes world and country rankings, international and correspondent contact information, principal correspondent institutions an standard settlement instructions.
Cost: $495.00
Frequency: September
Founded in 1895

3217 **Worldwide Correspondents & Resource Guide**
4709 Golf Road
Skokie, IL 60076-1231

847-676-9600
800-321-3373; Fax: 847-933-8101
custserv@accuitysolutions.com
www.accuitysolutions.com
Hugh Jones, President
Kerry Hewson, VP

A convenient one-volume directory listing the principal correspondent relationships for banks worldwide.
Cost: $184.00
Frequency: June/December

3218 **Y-9 Report Analyzer**
Sheshunoff Information Services
901 South Mopac
Suite 140
Austin, TX 78746-7970

512-472-4000
800-477-1772; Fax: 512-305-6575
sales@smslp.com
www.smslp.com
Facebook, Twitter, LinkedIn

Gabrielle Sheshunoff, CEO

Sheshunoff Information Services provides bank holding companies (BHC) a tool to prepare and electronically file the following government forms: Y-9C, Y9-LP, Y11Q, and Y11I. Built in edit checks ensure the BHC's file the most accurate report possible.
Cost: $495.00
Frequency: Annual w/Quarterly Update

Industry Web Sites

3219 **http://gold.greyhouse.com**
G.O.L.D Grey House OnLine Databases

Grey House Publishing's online database platform, GOLD, offers Quick Search, Keyword Search and Expert Search, for most business sectors including banking and financial markets. The GOLD platform makes finding the information you need quick and easy - whether you're a novice searcher or an experienced database user. All of Grey House's directory products are available for subscription on the GOLD platform.

3220 **www.aabd.org**
American Association of Bank Directors

Devoted to serving the information, education and advocacy needs of individual bank and savings institution directors. This non-profit organization has members nationwide.

3221 **www.aba.com**
American Bankers Association

Brings together all categories of banking institutions to best represent the interests of this rapidly changing industry. It's membership — which includes community, regional and money center banks and holding companies, as well as savings associations, trust companies and savings banks makes ABA one of the largest banking trade associations in the country.

3222 **www.aba.com/ICB/default.htm**
Institute Of Certified Bankers

A national association of certified professionals in the financial services industry whose mission is to provide financial services professionals with confidence, credibility and recognition through its certifications.

3223 **www.abiworld.org**
American Bankruptcy Institute

Multidisciplinary, nonpartisan organization dedicated to research and education on matters related to insolvency. Engaged in numerous educational and research activities as well as the production of a number of publications both for the insolvency practitioner and the public.

3224 **www.aftweb.com**
Association for Financial Technology

Association founded in 1972 to promote high standards of professionalism in the planning, development, inplemtation and application of technology to the financial services industry.

3225 **www.americanpayroll.org**
American Payroll Association

Association of payroll and human resource professionals. Website furthers information exchange and meeting announcements.

3226 **www.baft.org**
Bankers' Association for Finance & Trade

Financial trade association whose membership represents a broad range of internationally active financial institutions and companies that provide important services to the global financial community. BAFT serves as a forum for analysis, discussion and action among international financial professionals on a wide range of topics affecting international trade and finace, including legislative/regulatory issues.

3227 **www.bai.org**
Bank Administration Institute

The financial services industry's partner for breakthrough information and intelligence needed to innovate and stay relevant in an evolving marketplace. Serves a wide segment of the financial services industry, from the largest multinational banks to community-based institutions.

3228 **www.bisanet.org**
Bank Insurance and Securities Association

Dedicated to serving the needs of those responsible for marketing securities, insurance and other investment and risk management products.

3229 **www.cbanet.org**
Consumer Bankers Association

Recognized voice on retail banking issues in the nation's capital. Member institutions are the leaders in consumer financial services, including auto finance, home equity lending, card products, education loans, small business services, community development, investments, deposits, and delivery.

3230 **www.cfainstitute.org**
CFA Institute

The CFA Institute is the global, non-profit professional association that administers the Chartered Financial Analyst curriculum and examination program.

3231 **www.envirobank.org**
Environmental Bankers Association

Dedicated to providing services for individuals with an interest in environmental risk management and related issues.

3232 **www.freddiemac.com**
Freddie Mac

Freddie Mac is a stockholder-owned corporation chartered by Congress to create a continuous flow of funds to mortgage lenders in support of homeownership and rental housing.

3233 **www.fwi.org**
Financial Women International

Formerly the National Association of Bank Women, the Association was founded in 1921 - one year after women won the right to vote, by a group of New York City women bankers. FWI serves women in the financial services industry that seeks to expand their personal and professional capabilities through self-directed growth in a supportive environment.

3234 **www.garp.org**
Global Association of Risk Management

This association is dedicated to being the leading professional association for risk managers, managed by and for its members.

3235 **www.greyhouse.com**
Grey House Publishing

Authoritative reference directories for most business sectors including banking and financial markets. Users can search the online databases with varied search criteria allowing for custom searches by product category, geographic area, sales volume, keyword, subject and more. Full Grey House catalog and online ordering also available.

3236 **www.icba.org**
Independent Community Bankers of America

Dedicated exclusively to enhancing the franchise value of the nation's community banks for the benefit of their customers and the communities they serve.

3237 **www.iib.org**
Institute of International Bankers

Created to help resolve the many special legislative, regulatory and tax issues confronting internationally headquartered financial institutions.

3238 **www.jpmorganchase.com**
JPMorgan Chase

A leading global financial services firm with assets of $1.3 trillion and operations in more than 50 countries.

3239 **www.marinebankers.org**
National Marine Bankers Association

Formed in 1980 in response to a request by the National Marine Manufacturers Association - NMMA - for additional sources of financing for it's members products. The purpose of the NMBA is to educate prospective lenders in marine finacing procedures, create new lenders to help finance the sales of the manufacturers products, and to create an information exchange for its members.

3240 **www.mastercardinternational.com**
MasterCard Worldwide

Administers the MasterCard credit card and other products for 25,000 member institutions around the world.

3241 **www.mbaa.org**
Mortgage Bankers Association of America

Representing the real estate finance industry, MBA serves its membership by representing their legislative and regulatory interests before the US Congress and federal agencies; by meeting their educational needs through programs and a range of periodicals and publications; and by supporting their business interests with a variety of research initiatives and other products and services.

3242 **www.mortgagebankers.org**
Mortgage Bankers Association

Seeks to improve methods of originating, servicing and marketing loans.

3243 **www.naahl.org**
National Association of Affordable Housing Lenders

For financial institutions and others with an interest in affordable housing and development lending.

3244 **www.nabt.com**
National Association of Bankruptcy Trustees

Nonprofit association formed in 1982 to address the needs of the bankruptcy trustees thoughout the country and to promote the effectiveness of the bankruptcy system as a whole. While the majority of trustees who are members of the NABT are Chapter 7 trustees who primarily liquidate nonexempt assets for the benefit of creditors, many Chapter 7 trustees also serve as Chapter 11 trustees, who operate and reorganize companies. Some of our members are also Chapter 12 or Chapter 13 trustees.

3245 **www.nacha.org**
NACHA: Electronic Payments Association

Organization developing electronic solutions to improve the payments system. Representing more than 12,000 financial institutions through direct memberships and a network of regional payments associations, and 650 organizations through its industry councils, NACHA develops operating rules and business practices for the Automated Clearing House network and for electronic payments in the areas of internet commerce, electronic bill and invoice presentment and payment and other electronic payments.

3246 **www.nactt.com**
National Association of Chapter 13 Trustees

Provides a forum within which Chapteer 13 trustees will act as an information and communication resource to advance education, leadership, and continuous imporvement in the administration of bankruptcy.

3247 **www.nacusac.org**
Nat'l Assoc. of Credit Union Super. & Audit. Comm.

A unique organization of, by and for credit union supervisory committee members.

3248 **www.nafcu.org**
National Association Of Federal Credit Unions

A respected and influential trade association that exclusively represents the interests of federal credit unions before the federal government and the public.

3249 **www.naggl.com**
Nat'l Assoc. of Government Guaranteed Lenders

Promotes professional and governmental affairs interests of financial institutions and small businesses who participate in the Small Business Administration guaranteed lending and secondary market programs.

3250 **www.namb.org**
National Association of Mortgage Brokers

Mortgage brokers who seek to increase professionalism and to foster business relationships among members.

3251 **www.napmw.org**
Nat'l Association of Professional Mortgage Women

Serves all mortgage professionals and employers who want to excel.

3252 **www.nascus.org**
Nat'l Assoc. of State Credit Union Supervisors

State chartered credit unions and state credit union supervisors.

3253 **www.nationalbankers.org**
National Bankers Association

Members are minority and women's banking institutions, minority individuals employed by majority banks and institutions.

3254 **www.ncua.gov**
National Credit Union Administration

Charters and supervises federal credit unions.

3255 **www.nibanet.org**
National Investment Banking Association

A national trade association of regional and independent brokerages, investment banking firms, and related capital market service providers.

3256 **www.rmahq.org**
Risk Management Association

Topics relating to all aspects of commercial lending, financial statement analysis and credit information exchange and managerial aspects of consumer lending.

3257 **www.sifma.org/**
Securities Industry and Financial Markets Assoc.

SIFMA's mission is to champion policies and practices that benefit investors and issuers, expand and perfect global capital markets, and foster the development of new products and services.

3258 **www.snl.com**
SNL Securities

News articles on banks and thrifts, insurance and other financial services. Also features vital company information.

3259 **www.sourcemedia.com**
SourceMedia

Provides market information, including news, analysis, and insight to the financial services and related industries.

3260 **www.ufscnet.org**
Urban Financial Services Coalition

An organization of minority professionals in the financial services industry and related fields.

3261 **www.wiley.com**
John Wiley & Sons

Wiley is a global publisher of print and electronic products, specializing in science, technical, and material books and journals, professional and consumer books and subscription services, textbooks and other educational materials for undergraduate and graduate students as well as lifelong learners. Wiley has approximately 22,700 active titles and about 400 journals, and publishes about 2000 new titles in a variety of print and electronic formats each year.

Associations

3262 Aesthetics' International Association
310 E. Interstate 30
Suite B107
Garland, TX 75043

972-203-8530
877-968-7539; Fax: 972-226-2339
iaaesthetics.org

Miodrag Suvakovic, President
Krystyna Wilkoszewska, Vice President

International professional organization for aestheticians that represents every facet of the aesthetics industry. We offer something for the student, aesthetician, make-up artist, reflexologist, aromatherapist, massage therapist, nutritionist, nurse, holistic practitioner and physician to the day spa and salon owner.
Founded in 1972

3263 American Academy of Facial Esthetics
2120 S. Green Road
South Euclid, OH 44121

800-952-0521
www.facialesthetics.org
Facebook, Twitter, LinkedIn

Rebecca Hammel, Membership

The AAFE is a multidisciplinary professional healthcare organization that teaches the best injectable techniques to professionals worldwide.

3264 American Association of Cosmetology Schools
9927 East Bell Road
Suite 110
Scottsdale, AZ 85260

480-281-0431
800-831-1086; Fax: 480-905-0993
jim@beautyschools.org
www.beautyschools.org
Facebook, Twitter

Anthony Civitano, Executive Director
Cristina Hanson, Program Associate
Allison Scudder, Program Manager

National non-profit association open to all privately owned schools of Cosmetology Arts and Sciences. AACS specializes in updating our members with information about new teaching methods, current industry events, and Washington, DC updates.
1100 Members
Founded in 1924

3265 American Beauty Association
15825 N 71st St
Suite 100
Scottsdale, AZ 85254-1521

480-281-0431
beautyassociation.org
Facebook, Twitter, LinkedIn

James Cox, Executive Director
Bruce Selan, VP
George Schaeffer, Secretary/Treasurer

ABA members are manufacturers, manufacturer reps and consultants in the professional beauty industry. Associate members are made up of trade publications, distributors and salons. The ABA's mission is to expand, serve and protect the interests of the professional beauty industry.
250 Members
Founded in 1985

3266 American Board of Certified Haircolorists
P.O. Box 9090
San Pedro, CA 90734

310-547-0814
info@haircolorist.com
Facebook, Twitter

ABCH is dedicated to the development of standardized criteria in certification, promoting credibility and consistent quality in the professional haircolorist; bringing predictability and ethical professional behavior for the well-being of the consumer and enhancing excellence in customer service; and encouraging mentors to share their knowledge with aspiring professional haircolorists.

3267 American Electrology Association
4711 Midlothian Tpk
Suite 13
Crestwood, IL 60445

708-293-1400; Fax: 708-293-1405
infoaea@electrology.com
www.electrology.com
Facebook

Pearl Warner, CPE, President
Mary Kaye Johnson, CPE, 1st Vice President
Deborah Cassin, CPE, Treasurer
Randa Thurman, Membership

The American Electrology Association (AEA), is the largest international nonprofit membership organization for permanent hair removal professionals. Promotes the highest standards in Electrology education, practice and ethics and champions state licensing and regulation of the profession to protect the public interest.
1500 Members
Founded in 1958

3268 American Hair Loss Council
30 South Main
Shenandoah, PA 17976

412-765-3666; Fax: 412-765-3669
www.ahlc.org
Facebook, Twitter, LinkedIn

Susan Kettering, Executive Director
Peggy Thornhill, President
Marsha Scott, Vice President
Joseph Ellis, Board Member
Betty Ann Bugden, Treasurer

A not-for-profit agency, dedicated to sorting through this information, discovering what works and what doesn't, and presenting findings to the consumer.

3269 American Society of Hair Restoration Surgery
225 W. Wacker Drive
Suite 650
Chicago, IL 60606

312-981-6760; Fax: 312-981-6787
info@cosmeticsurgery.org
www.cosmeticsurgery.org
Facebook, Twitter, LinkedIn

Mark Mandell-Brown, President
Kevin Duplechain, President-Elect
Rania Agha, Treasurer
Talon Maningas, Secretary
1600 Members

3270 Assn. of Cosmetology Salon Professionals
PO Box 207
Chapin, SC 29036

803-345-2909
contact@mycosmetology.org
www.mycosmetology.org
Facebook

Sandra Mullins, President
Alma Owens, Vice-President
Terry Frick, Secretary
Debbie Stabler, Treasurer

Association for the promotion of professional standards in the cosmetology, esthetics and nail industries.

3271 Associated Bodywork & Massage Professionals
25188 Genesee Trail Rd
Suite 200
Golden, CO 80401

800-458-2267; Fax: 800-667-8260
expectmore@abmp.com
www.abmp.com
Facebook, Twitter, LinkedIn

Leslie Young, VP, Communication

Practice support and liability insurance for massage/bodywork professionals.
80000 Members
Founded in 1987

3272 Associated Skin Care Professionals
25188 Genesee Trail Road
Suite 200
Golden, CO 80401

800-789-0411; Fax: 800-790-0299
getconnected@ascpskincare.com
www.ascpskincare.com

Tracy Donley, Executvie Director
Jesse Cormier, Senior Director
Mary Bathelme Abel, Editor

An association for skin care professionals, helping members build successful careers. ASCP empowers you to reach your highest potential by providing innovative business solutions, unmatched quality education, and vital professional liability insurance.
16000 Members
Founded in 2007

3273 Black Beauty Association
Home Page: blackbeautyassociation.com

Weldon Germaine Bond, Founder & President

The BBA promotes itself to the professional needs of Black Beauty professionals and students. They offer consulting, business strategies and resources.

3274 California Cosmetology Association
P.O. Box 291459
Phelan, CA 92329

800-482-3288; Fax: 760-400-2941
the-cca.com
Facebook

Madrid Johnson, President
Michael Allen, Vice President
Thelma Price, Secretary/Treasurer

The largest professional cosmetology association that promotes, represents & legislatively protects the entire cosmetology industry. CCA brings people of diverse background within the beauty industry together providing opportunities and support for its members to grow professionally and personally through leadership, education, legislation and networking.

3275 Cosmetologists Chicago
440 S LaSalle Street
Suite 2325
Chicago, IL

312-321-6809
800-883-7808; Fax: 312-673-6612
info@americasbeautyshow.com
www.americasbeautyshow.com
Facebook, Twitter, Youtube, Pinterest, WordPress

Karen Gordon, President
Robert Passage, VP
Lorrene Conino, Secretary
Chris Damolaris, Treasurer

Voice of the salon industry, a beauty authority and presenter of the Chicago Midwest Beauty Show, stylists, estheticians, color technicians, salon owners, educators and nail technicians.
35000 Members

3276 Cosmetologists and Barbers of Iowa
1425 Hawthorne Avenue
Waverly, IA 50677

Generationsalon@hotmail.com
www.cbiowa.org

Susan Charles, President
Jenni White, Secretary/Treasurer

A nonprofit association of salon professionals in Iowa. Their goal is to bring everyone in the industry into one cohesive and effective unit, in order to protect and promote with continuing education and legislative safeguards.

3277 Cosmetology Industry Association of Alabama
117 Montgomery Street
3rd Floor
Montgomery, AL 36104

334-649-8100

Steve Chew, Executive Director
Cory Brown, Membership Director

CIAA is a collection of businesses and individuals in the beauty and glamour profession, including stylists, maniscurists, estheticians, instructores, and more.

3278 Cosmoprof North America (CPNA)
15825 N 71st Street
Suite 100
Scottsdale, AZ 85254

480-281-0424
800-468-2274; Fax: 480-905-0708
info@cosmoprofnorthamerica.com
www.cosmoprofnorthamerica.com
Facebook, Twitter, LinkedIn, Pinterest, YouTube

Supports all those involved with industry related equipment, supplies and services.
Frequency: Annual
Founded in 1892

3279 Intercoiffure of America
1645 Downtown West Blvd
Suite 18
Knoxville, TN 37919

614-457-7712
800-442-3007; Fax: 614-457-7794
info@intercoiffure.com
www.intercoiffure.com
Facebook, Twitter, Google+

Sheila Zaricor-Wilson, President
Scott Buchanan, First Vice President
Adam Broderick, Second Vice Person
Terry McKee, Secretary
Salvatore Minardi, Treasurer

Sponsors semiannual hair fashion shows in New York City.
260 Members
Founded in 1933

3280 International Guild of Hair Removal Specialists
1918 Bethel Road
Columbus, OH 43220

800-830-3247

Formerly known as the International Guild of Professional Electrologists. A non-profit organization dedicated to providing the latest information about permanent and long-term hair removal to the consumer.
2000 Members
Founded in 1979

3281 International Nail Technicians Association
330 N Wabash Ave
Chicago, IL 60611

312-321-6809
800-883-7808; Fax: 312-245-1080
info@americasbeautyshow.com
Facebook, Twitter, Youtube, Pinterest, WordPress

An international organization for nail professionals. In 2001 it was acquired by Cosmetologists Chicago with the purpose of providing an association 'home' to nail care professionals that is dedicated to the needs of technicians and the industry

3282 International Salon Spa Business Network
207 E Ohio Street
#361
Chicago, IL 60611

440-846-6022
866-444-4272; Fax: 866-444-5139
margie@salonspanetwork.org
www.salonspanetwork.org
Facebook, Twitter

Scott Missad, President
Debra Penzone, Vice President
Emily Brown, Secretary
Edward Logan, Treasurer

Dedicated to helping its members grow their business, effect positive change politically, provide a forum for members to share their views and ideas and interface with the professional beauty industry on behalf of the chain salons and spas.
70 Members
Founded in 1973

3283 National Association of Barber Boards of America

870-230-0777
samdabarberman@yahoo.com
www.nationalbarberboards.com

Mark Wills, President

Association for the promotion of professional standards in the barbering industry.
110 Members
Founded in 1926

3284 National Beauty Culturists' League
25 Logan Circle NW
Washington, DC 20005-3725

202-332-2695; Fax: 202-332-0940
www.nbcl.info

Betty Herbert, Contact

Established as the National Hair System Culture League, members are black beauticians and cosmetologists who embrace diversity.
3000 Members
Founded in 1919

3285 National Cosmetology Association
15825 N. 71st Street
Suite 100
Scottsdale, AZ 85254

480-281-0424
800-468-2274; Fax: 480-905-0708
info@probeauty.org
www.probeauty.org

Membership includes salon owners, hairdressers, nail technicians, estheticians, educators, and students. Members live and work in all 50 states, and also have the option to participate in the state and local affiliate, along with national activities.
25000 Members
Founded in 1921

3286 New York State Beauty School Association
175 Fulton Avenue
Hempstead, NY 11550

888-295-8360
soressimckinley1@att.net
www.nysbsa.org

The New York State Beauty School Association serves beauty school owners, teachers and students to secure cooperation and improvement of the beauty industry.
Founded in 1993

3287 Professional Beauty Association
7766 E Gray Road
Scottsdale, AZ 85260

480-281-0424
info@probeauty.org
www.probeauty.org
Facebook, Twitter, LinkedIn, YouTube, Pinterest, Instagram

Peggy Sue Schmoldt, Chair
Sydney Berry, Vice Chair
Steve Sleeper, Executive Director
Rachel Molepske, Manager, Leadership Operations
Steve Wilkerson, Chief Financial Officer

The Professional Beauty Association (PBA) is a nonprofit trade association that represents the interests of the professional beauty industry from manufacturers and distributors to salons and spas. PBA offers business tools, education, advocacy, networking and more to improve individual businesses and the industry as a whole.

3288 Salon & Spa Professional Association
2626 E. 82nd Street
Suite 340
Bloomington, MN 55425

952-925-9731
888-213-0949; Fax: 952-925-4245
info@sspatoday.com
www.sspatoday.com
Facebook, Twitter, LinkedIn, Instagram

Susan Brinkhaus, CAE, Executive Director
Cora Barr, Administrative Coordintor
Judy Garcia, CIDESCO Diplomate/Education Coord.
Katherine Martin, Chair
Angi Cook, Vice-Chair

A community of salon professionals in the Upper Midwest connected by a common passion for learning, growing and raising the professionalism of the entire salon industry.
Founded in 1924

3289 Society of Clinical and Medical Hair Removal
2424 American Lane
Madison, WI 53704-3102

608-443-2470; Fax: 608-443-2474
homeoffice@scmhr.org
www.scmhr.org
Facebook, Twitter, Google+

Fadia Hoyek, President
Janie Simmons, Exectuive VP
Sandra Ysassi, Treasurer
Kristen Erdmann, Secretary
Lisa Nelson, Executive Secretary

An international non profit organization with members in the United States, Canada, Australia, Japan and beyond. Supports all methods of hair removal and is dedicated to the research of new technology that will keep its members at the pinnacle of their profession, offering safe, effective hair removal to their clients.
600 Members
Founded in 1985

Newsletters

3290 **ISNOW Cosmetologists Chicago**
401 N Michigan Avenue
Chicago, IL 60611-4255
312-321-6809
800-883-7808; Fax: 312-245-1080
info@americasbeautyshow.com
Represents the industries various constituencies and salon owners.
Cost: $18.95
Frequency: Monthly
Circulation: 5000
Founded in 2004

3291 **National Beauty News**
10405 E 55th Place
Suite B
Tulsa, OK 74146-6502
918-627-8000; Fax: 918-627-8660
Douglas Von Allmen, Owner
Offers news of shows, seminars, product information and columns for the professional beauty industry.
Cost: $12.00
Frequency: Monthly
Circulation: 35,500

3292 **Pink Sheet**
685 Route 202/206
Bridgewater, NJ 08807
800-332-2181
908-547-2159; Fax: 908-547-2200
custcare@elsevier.com
www.elsevierbi.com
RSS
Mike Squires, President
Cathy Kelly, Executive Editor
Brooke McManus, Managing Editor
Jim Chicca, Executive Director
Melissa Carlson, Editorial Operations Manager
Chronicles regulatory and legal news, major scientific developments and testing methodologies, and their effect on these industries. Product marketing news, new product launches, and promotions and advertising at the retail level, are also included.
Cost: $1050.00
Frequency: Weekly
Founded in 1939

Magazines & Journals

3293 **AEA Journal of Electrology**
American Electrology Association
4711 Midlothian Tpk
Suite 13
Crestwood, IL 60445
708-293-1400; Fax: 708-293-1405
infoaea@electrology.com
www.electrology.com
Pearl Warner, CPE, President
Karen Portnoff, Marketing
The Journal of Electrology is a membership news publication, published twice per year and is designed to inform and educate the professional electrologist by offering articles of interest and value by reputable authors who are well qualified in the topic area.
Cost: $42.00
1500 Members
Frequency: Semi-Annual
Circulation: 1200
Founded in 1958

3294 **Beauty Store Business**
Creative Age Publications
7628 Densmore Ave
Van Nuys, CA 91406-2042
818-782-7328
800-442-5667; Fax: 818-782-7450
webmaster@creativeage.com
www.creativeage.com
Deborah Carver, President/CEO
Mindy Rosiejka, Vice President/COO
Karie Frost, Executive Director
Industry trends and valuable tips concerning real estate, banking, insurance, product liability, advertising, merchandising, and more.
Frequency: Monthly
Circulation: 15000
ISSN: 1098-0660
Founded in 1971

3295 **BeautyLink**
American Association of Cosmetology Schools
9927 E. Bell Road
Suite 110
Scottsdale, AZ 85260
480-281-0431
800-831-1086; Fax: 480-905-0993
jim@beautyschools.org
www.beautyschools.org
Jim Cox, Executive Director
Lisa Zarda, General Manager
Quarterly magazine of the AACS, with cosmetology industry updates and features on new trends and best practices.
Frequency: Quarterly
Circulation: 7000

3296 **Cosmetic World**
Ledes Group
16 East 40th Street
Suite 700
New York, NY 10016
212-840-8800; Fax: 212-840-7246
Debra Davis, Advertising Director
Brittany Burhop, Executive Editor
Debbie Ward, Managing Editor
Current industry events, legislation, management changes and corporate activities, as well as marketing developments and financial analysis.
Cost: $175.00
Circulation: 5397
Printed in on glossy stock

3297 **DaySpa Magazine**
Creative Age Publications
7628 Densmore Ave
Van Nuys, CA 91406-2042
818-782-7328; Fax: 818-782-7450
sverba@creativeage.com
www.creativeage.com
Deborah Carver, President/CEO
Mindy Rosiejka, Vice President/COO
Karie Frost, Executive Director
DaySpa is dedicated to helping premium salon and spa owners better serve their client enhance their bottom line. Presents the most accurate, up-to-date information available on trends, products, equipment, services, and management and management tools in easy-to-read, entertaining articles.
Cost: $17.50
Frequency: Annual+
Circulation: 24,000+
Founded in 1972

3298 **Dermascope Magazine**
Aesthetics International Association
310 East I-30,
SuiteB107
Garland, TX 75043
469-429-9300
800-961-3777; Fax: 469-429-9301
press@dermascope.com
www.dermascope.com
William Strunk, Publisher
Amy McKay, Editor
Wes Wynne, Marketing Director
Provides education for skin care professionals. One of the oldest magazines in the industry.
Cost: $45.00
148 Pages
Frequency: Monthly
Circulation: 16000
ISSN: 1075-055X
Founded in 1972

3299 **Looking Fit Magazine**
Virgo Publishing LLC
3300 N Central Ave
Suite 300
Phoenix, AZ 85012-2532
48 - 9 - 11; Fax: 480-990-0819
swhitley@vpico.com
www.vpico.com
John Siefert, CEO
Kelly Ridley, Executive VP/ CFO
Educational resource for professionals in the indoor tanning industry.
Cost: $70.00
300 Pages
Frequency: Monthly
Founded in 1986

3300 **Massage & Bodywork**
Associated Bodywork & Massage Professionals
25188 Genesee Trail Rd
Suite 200
Golden, CO 80401
800-458-2267; Fax: 800-667-8260
expectmore@abmp.com
www.abmp.com
Facebook, Twitter, LinkedIn
Leslie Young, Editor-in-Chief
Magazine of the Associated Bodywork & Massage Professionals.
Cost: $26.00
Frequency: Monthly
ISSN: 1544-8827

3301 **Modern Salon**
Vance Publishing
400 Knightsbridge Pkwy
Lincolnshire, IL 60069
847-634-2600; Fax: 847-634-4379
info@vancepublishing.com
www.vancepublishing.com
William C Vance, Chairman
Peggy Walker, President
The constant leader and voice of the professional salon industry. Delivers step-by-step education for the stylist and paid circulation for the advertiser.
Frequency: Monthly
Circulation: 117000
Founded in 1924
Printed in 4 colors on glossy stock

3302 **NW Stylist and Salon**
Porter Publishing

1750 Sw Skyline Blvd
Suite 8
Portland, OR 97221-2543

503-296-4889
888-297-7010; Fax: 503-296-4893
www.portlandpsinc.com

James Pettigrove, President
Lisa Kind, Managing Editor
Joel Holland, VP
Marcy Avenson, Advertising Director

Business trade journal mailed free to every salon school and practitioner in Oregon. Accepts advertising.
Cost: $20.00
36 Pages
Frequency: Monthly
Circulation: 22000
Founded in 1983

3303 **NailPro**
Creative Age Publications
7628 Densmore Ave
Van Nuys, CA 91406-2042

818-782-7328
800-442-5667; Fax: 818-782-7450
webmaster@creativeage.com
www.creativeage.com

Deborah Carver, President/CEO
Mindy Rosiejka, Vice President/COO
Karie Frost, Executive Director

Nail care how-to's, business related articles, information on nail anatomy and pathology, as well as new products, trends, profiles and a calendar of events.
Cost: $21.95
Frequency: Monthly
Circulation: 50713
Founded in 1971

3304 **Nails Magazine**
Bobit Publishing Company
3520 Challenger St
Torrance, CA 90503-1640

310-533-2400; Fax: 310-533-2500
www.bobit.com

Edward J Bobit, CEO
Hannah Lee, Executive Editor
Uyonna Beckham, Sales Assistant
Sarah Paredes, Senior Production Manager
Ty Bobit, CEO

Offers business information on products and application techniques for professional manicurists and salon owners.
Cost: $20.00
Frequency: Monthly
Circulation: 62274
Founded in 1961

3305 **Salon News**
Fairchild Publications
750 3rd Ave
New York, NY 10017-2703

212-630-4000; Fax: 212-630-3563
www.fairchildpub.com

Mary G Berner, CEO

Profitability and stability, salon services and resale, and on motivation and education.
Frequency: Monthly
Circulation: 77,603

3306 **Salon Today**
Vance Publishing
400 Knightsbridge Pkwy
Lincolnshire, IL 60069

847-634-2600; Fax: 847-634-4379
info@vancepublishing.com
www.vancepublishing.com

William C Vance, Chairman
Peggy Walker, President

Content is modeled as a monthly exchange of ideas on how to grow salon business. Special issues include annual Salon Today 200, Salon of the Year, Technology and Spa Business.
Frequency: Monthly
Circulation: 25000

3307 **Skin Deep Magazine**
25188 Genesee Trail Road
Suite 200
Golden, CO 80401

800-789-0411; Fax: 800-790-0299
getconnected@ascpskincare.com
www.ascpskincare.com

Mary Barthelme Abel, Editor
Tracy Donley, Executive Director

Tips, talk, and techniques from some of the biggest names in the profession. ACSP members get 6 issues delivered to their door each year.
Frequency: 6x Year
Founded in 2007

3308 **Skin Magazine**
Allured Publishing Corporation
PO Box 50
Congers, NY 10920

845-267-3008
866-616-3008; Fax: 845-267-3478
skininc@cambeywest.com
www.skininc.com

Janet Ludwig, President
Lin Getner, Controller

The business magazine preferred by owners and managers of salons and spas and the official publication of the American Aestheticians Education Association. Recently awarded a Gold award for editorial from the American Business Publication editors association.
Cost: $49.00
120 Pages
Frequency: Monthly
Circulation: 16000
Founded in 1988

3309 **WWD Beauty Biz**
Fairchild Publications
7 W 34th St
New York, NY 10001-8100

212-630-3880; Fax: 212-630-3868
www.fairchildpub.com

Mary Berner, President/CEO
Patrick McCarthy, Chairman/Editorial Director
Jenny B. Fine, Editor-in-Chief
Sarah Murphy, Publisher

The premier guide to the beauty industry. Provides in-depth coverage and analysis on all aspects of the industry, including trends, brands, retailers, and personalities driving both the general consumer and insider sides of the business.
Cost: $60.00
Frequency: Monthly
Circulation: 40,056
Founded in 1892

Trade Shows

3310 **AACS Annual Convention & Expo**
American Association of Cosmetology Schools
9927 E. Bell Road
Suite 110
Scottsdale, AZ 85260

480-281-0431
800-831-1086; Fax: 480-905-0993
jim@beautyschools.org
www.beautyschools.org

Jim Cox, Executive Director
Lisa Zarda, General Manager

An opportunity to bring your professional team together to lead your school into the future. Education tracks, classes, social events, and the expo hall complete the experience.
800 Attendees
Frequency: November

3311 **ACSP Annual Meeting**
Association of Cosmetology Salon Professionals
PO Box 207
Chapin, SC 29036

803-345-2909
contact@mycosmetology.org
www.mycosmetology.org

Linda Green, President
Sandra Mullins, Vice-President
Terry Frick, Secretary

Competitions, continuing education and annual meeting.
Frequency: Annual

3312 **Aesthetics' World Expositions**
Aesthetics' International Association
2611 N Belt Line Road
Suite 140
Sunnyvale, TX 75182-9357

972-203-8530
877-968-7539; Fax: 972-226-2339
www.beautyworks.com/aia

150-250 exhibits of skin care, body therapy products make up and equipment. Salon owners, body massage therapists, and dermatologists attend.
3000 Attendees
Frequency: Biennial
Founded in 1979

3313 **American Electrology Association Annual Convention**
American Electrology Association
4711 Midlothian Tpk
Suite 13
Crestwood, IL 60445

708-293-1400; Fax: 708-293-1405
infoaea@electrology.com
www.electrology.com

Pearl G. Warner, President
Mary Kaye Johnson, 1st Vice President
Deborah Cassin, CPE, Treasurer
Donna F. Crump, Convention Committee

AEA is the largest international nonprofit membership organization for permanent hair removal. The convention features the largest number of exhibitors with the latest state of the art equipment.
1500 Members
300 Attendees
Frequency: Annual
Founded in 1958

3314 **Big Show Expo**
Big Show Expo
1841 Broadway
Room 812
New York, NY 10023-7603

212-580-1407; Fax: 212-757-3611

Bernice Calvin, President
Maggie Smallwood, Conference Coordinator

Largest group of ethnic beauty shows. 200 booths updating the skills and expertise of hairdressers with ethnic clientele and spotlighting new trends in hair fashions, with all new styles for today's fashion looks.
15M Attendees
Frequency: August, September

3315 **COSMOPROF North America**
COSMOPROF North America

15825 North 71st Street
Suite 100
Scottsdale, AZ 85254

480-281-0424
800-468-2274; Fax: 480-905-0708
cpnainfo@probeauty.org
www.cosmoprofnorthamerica.com

Eric Horn, Show Director
Ebony King, Show Manager
Wendy Forakis, Business Relations Manager

The most comprehensive and international professional beauty industry show on the continent. Attendees include manufacturers to distributors , salon owners to spa professionals, importers to retail buyers with hundreds of exhibitors.
25000 Attendees
Frequency: July
Mailing list available for rent

3316 **Hairworld**
National Cosmetology Association
15825 North 71st Street
Suite 100
Scottsdale, AZ 85254

480-281-0424
800-468-2274; Fax: 480-905-0708
info@probeauty.org

Annual show of 125 exhibitors of hair products, cosmetics and jewelry.
3000 Attendees
Frequency: July
Circulation: 30,000

3317 **International Congress of Esthetics**
Aesthetics' International Association
310 East I-30
Suite B107
Garland, TX 75043

469-429-9300
800-961-3777; Fax: 469-429-9301
press@dermascope.com
www.dermascope.com

Will Strunk, Publisher
Amy McKay, Editor

Biennial show of skin care, makeup and body therapy products and equipment.
3000 Attendees
Frequency: February
Founded in 1977

3318 **NABBA Annual Conference**
National Association of Barber Boards of America

870-230-0777
samdabarberman@yahoo.com
www.nationalbarberboards.com

Mark Wills, President
Frequency: Annual

Directories & Databases

3319 **AEA Online Directory**
American Electrology Association
4711 Midlothian Tpk
Suite 13
Crestwood, IL 60445

708-293-1400; Fax: 708-293-1405
infoaea@electrology.com
www.electrology.com

Pearl Warner, President
Randa Thurman, Referral Directory

Online directory of electrologists across the country.Available on the AEA Web site.
1500 Members
Founded in 1958

3320 **Drug Store and HBC Chains Database**
Chain Store Guide
3710 Corporex Park Dr.
Suite 310
Tampa, FL 33619-1389

813-627-6700
800-927-9292; Fax: 813-627-6888
webmaster@chainstoreguide.com
www.chainstoreguide.com

Mike Jarvis, Publisher
Arthur Sciarrotta, Senior VP

Tap into the lucrative drug industry with profiles on more than 1,700 US and Canadian companies operating two or more retail drug stores, deep discount stores, health and beauty care (HBC) stores, cosmetic stores or vitamin stores that have industry sales of at least $250,000. This powerful database empowers you to sell and market your products successfully by reaching more than 8,300 key decision-makers.
Cost: $335.00
Circulation: 8,300

3321 **Hayes Chain Drug Store Directory**
Hayes Directories
PO Box 3436
Mission Viejo, CA 92690

949-583-0537; Fax: 949-583-7419
enhayes@pacbell.net
www.hayesdir.com

James Edward Hayes, Editor

Comes in two volumes and contains information for 34,773 chain pharmacies in the United States, 8 stores or more. First volume lists the chain headquarters, and includes the total count of stores with pharmacies. The second volume groups the individual chain stores alphabetically by chain name followed by the name and address information for the headquarters of the parent company.
Cost: $250.00
Frequency: Annual,November

3322 **Hayes Drug Store Directory**
Hayes Directories
PO Box 3436
Mission Viejo, CA 92690

949-583-0537; Fax: 949-583-7419
enhayes@pacbell.net
www.hayesdir.com

James Edward Hayes, Editor

Contains information for the 53,821 retail drug stores in the United States.
Cost: $335.00
Frequency: Annual,November

3323 **Hayes Independent Drug Store Directory**
Hayes Directories
PO Box 3436
Mission Viejo, CA 92690

949-583-0537; Fax: 949-583-7419
enhayes@pacbell.net
www.hayesdir.com

James Edward Hayes, Editor

Published annually and contains information for 19,048 independent retail pharmacies in the United States. Independent stores are 7 stores or less.
Cost: $300.00
Frequency: Annual,November

Industry Web Sites

3324 **http://gold.greyhouse.com**
G.O.L.D Grey House OnLine Databases

Grey House Publishing's online database platform, GOLD, offers Quick Search, Keyword Search and Expert Search for most business sectors including beauty and cosmetics markets. The GOLD platform makes finding the information you need quick and easy - whether you're a novice searcher or an experienced database user. All of Grey House's directory products are available for subscription on the GOLD platform.

3325 **www.bbsi.org**
Beauty and Barber Supply Institute

Our members are wholesaler-distributors, manufacturers and manufacturers' representatives from around the world. Our mission is to maximize the potential of the professional salon industry.

3326 **www.beautyschools.org**
American Association of Cosmetology Schools

Serves privately owned schools of Cosmetology Arts & Sciences.

3327 **www.dermascope.com**
Aesthetics' International Association

International professional organization for aestheticians representing every facet of the aesthetics industry. From the student, aesthetician, make-up artist, reflexologist, aromatherapist, massage therapist, nutritionist, nurse, holistic practitioner and physician to the day spa/salon owner.

3328 **www.electrology.com**
American Electrology Association

Organization of professional hair removal practitioners promoting the highest standards of electrology education through our annual and state conventions with seminars following a prescribed learning standard.

3329 **www.greyhouse.com**
Grey House Publishing

Authoritative reference directories for most business sectors including beauty and cosmetics markets. Users can search the online databases with varied search criteria allowing for custom searches by product category, geographic area, sales volume, keyword, subject and more. Full Grey House catalog and online ordering also available.

3330 **www.isnow.com**
Cosmetologists Chicago

Voice of the salon industry. Presenter of the Chicago Midwest Beauty Show, we are stylists, estheticians, color technicians, salon owners, educators and nail technicians.

3331 **www.oneroof.org**
American Beauty Association

Serves the interests of the professional beauty industry.

Associations

3332 **American Association for Medical Chronobiology & Chronotherapeutics**

Home Page: www.aamcc.net

Provides a forum for the exchange and discussion of new findings, methods, and applications in medical chronobiology and chronotherapeutics.

3333 **American Association of Bioanalysts**

906 Olive Street
Suite 1200
St Louis, MO 63101

314-241-1445; Fax: 314-241-1449
aab@aab.org
www.aab.org
Facebook

Mark S Birenbaum PhD, Executive Director

AAB is committed to the pursuit of excellence in clinical laboratory services by enhancing the professional skills of each of its members; promoting more efficient and productive operations; offering external quality control programs; collaborating with other professional associations and government agencies; promoting safe laboratory practices; and educating legislators, regulators, and the general public about clinical laboratory tests and procedures.
Founded in 1956

3334 **American Association of Immunologists**

9650 Rockville Pike
Bethesda, MD 20814

301-634-7178; Fax: 301-634-7887
infoaai@aai.org
www.aai.org
Facebook

Michele Hogan, Executive Director
Bethany Coulter, Director of Communications
Maria Zavarello, Director of Finance
Jennifer Woods, Membership Manager
Gale Guerrieri, Meetings Manager

AAI is a professional organization founded to advance the knowledge of immunology and related disciplines, foster interchange of ideas and information among scientists, and promote understanding of the field of immunology.
Cost: $50.00
6500 Members
Founded in 1954

3335 **American Geophysical Union**

2000 Florida Ave Nw
Washington, DC 20009

202-462-6900
800-966-2481; Fax: 202-328-0566
service@agu.org
www.agu.org
Facebook, Twitter, LinkedIn, Youtube, RSS

Robin E Bell, President
Eric A Davidson, Past President
Jana Davis, General Secretary
Randy Fisher, Executive Director/CEO
52000 Members
Founded in 1919
Mailing list available for rent

3336 **American Institute of Biological Sciences**

1800 Alexander Bell Drive
Suite 400
Reston, VA 20191

703-674-2500
800-992-2427; Fax: 703-674-2509
www.aibs.org
Facebook, Twitter, LinkedIn, Youtube, RSS

Scott Gibson, CEO & Director, Review Services
Stephen Gallo, Chief Scientist
Scott Collins, Editor-In-Chief
Diane Bosnjak, Membership Manager
Syreeta Jones, Meetings Manager

Supports professionals involved with the biological sciences, including research, products, education; sponsors annual conference.
Mailing list available for rent

3337 **American Registry of Magnetic Resonance Imaging Technologists**

2444 NW 8th Street
Delray Beach, FL 33445

561-450-6880; Fax: 561-265-5045
armrit@msn.com
armrit.org

James F. Coffin, President & Executive Director
Thomas K. Schrack, Director
Charles G. Fiore, Senior Director & Legal Counsel
William J. Woodward, Director
Charles W. Kreines, Director

MRI schools, educational resources, certified tech resumes, practice tests, and verification of a tech's certification.
2050 Members
Founded in 1991

3338 **American Society for Biochemistry and Molecular Biology**

11200 Rockville Pike
Suite 302
Rockville, MD 20852-3110

240-283-6600; Fax: 301-881-2080
asbmb@asbmb.org
www.asbmb.org
Facebook, Twitter, LinkedIn, YouTube, Google+

Toni Antalis, President
Wei Yang, Secretary
Joan Conaway, Treasurer
Barbara Gordon, Executive Director

A professional and educational association for biochemists and molecular biologists which seeks to extend and utilize the field of biochemistry and molecular biology.
Cost: $18.50
11900 Members
Founded in 1906
Mailing list available for rent: 11000 names

3339 **American Society for Reproductive Medicine**

1209 Montgomery Highway
Birmingham, AL 35216-2809

205-978-5000; Fax: 205-978-5005
asrm@asrm.org
www.asrm.org
Facebook, Twitter, LinkedIn, Tumblr

Ricardo Azziz, Chief Executive Officer
Chevis Shannon, Chief Education & Science Officer
Sean Tipton, Chief Advocacy, Policy & Devt. Ofr.
Vickie Gamble, Chief Operations Officer
Daniel Carre, Chief Financial

Organization devoted to advancing knowledge and expertise in the study of reproduction and reproductive disorders.
Founded in 1944

3340 **American Society of Plant Biologists**

15501 Monona Drive
Rockville, MD 20855-2768

301-251-0560; Fax: 301-279-2996
info@aspb.org
my.aspb.org

Crispin Taylor, Executive and Governance
Jotee Pundu, Administrative Staff
Melanie Binder, Member Services
Susan Cato, Member Services
Annette Kessler, Publications

A professional society devoted to the advancement of the plant sciences. It publishes research and organizes conferences that are key to the advancement of plant biology.

3341 **American Soybean Association**

12125 Woodcrest Executive
Suite 100
Creve Coeur, MO 63141-5009

314-576-1770
800-688-7692; Fax: 314-576-2786
info@soy.org
soygrowers.com
Facebook, Twitter, RSS, YouTube

Steve Censky, CEO
Brian Vought, Chief Financial Officer
Wendy Brannen, Sr. Dir., Marketing & Communication
Ellen Ariston, Meetings & Conventions Coordinator
Farris Haley, Programs Coordinator

Domestic and international policy advocate for U.S. soy farmers on policy and trade.
Founded in 1920

3342 **Association for Women Geoscientists**

12000 N. Washington St.
Suite 285
Thornton, CO 80241-3134

303-412-6219; Fax: 303-253-9220
office@awg.org
www.awg.org

Noelia Beatriz Carmona, President
Michelle Sutherland, President Elect
Karen Fryer, Editor
Brianna Berg, Treasurer
Tamie Jovanelly, Communications Coordinator

A professional organization which promotes the professional development of its members, provides geoscience outreach to girls, and encourages womento become geoscientists.
Founded in 1977

3343 **Association of Biomolecular Resource Facilities**

9650 Rockville Pike
Bethesda, MD 20814

301-634-7306; Fax: 301-634-7455
abrf@abrf.org
www.abrf.org
Facebook, LinkedIn, Flickr, YouTube, Google+

Rich Cole, President
Christian Lytle, Treasurer
Ken Schoppmann, Executive Director

Dedicated to advancing core and research biotechnology laboratoriesthrough research, communication, and education.
700 Members
Founded in 1988

3344 **Association of Women Soil Scientists**

9611 S. Riverbend Ave.
Parlier, CA 93648

Suduan.Gao@ars.usda.gov
www.soils.org

Wendy Greenberg, Chair

A nonprofit organization of women and men in soil science that promotes a better understanding of the role of soil scientists and that provides assistance and encouragement for women in non-traditional fields and for women seeking employment in the field of soil science.

3345 BioSpace
10506 Justin Drive
Urbandale, IA 50322

877-277-7585; Fax: 800-595-2929
support@biospace.com
www.biospace.com
Facebook, Twitter, LinkedIn

The leading online community for industry news and careers for lifescience professionals.

3346 Biotechnology Innovation Organization
1201 Maryland Ave SW
Suite 900
Washington, DC 20024

202-962-9200; Fax: 202-488-6301
info@bio.org
www.bio.org
Facebook, Twitter, LinkedIn, YouTube

Michelle McMurray-Heath, President & CEO
Joanne Duncan, Pres., Membership & Business Ops.
Joseph Damond, EVP, International Affairs
Daniel Durham, EVP, Health Policy
Peter McHugh, General Counsel & SVP, Legal

Provides support for all those involved in biotechnology from a government, corporate, and trade viewpoint. Also represents biotechnology companies, academic institutions, biotechnology centers and related organizations in all 50 US states and 31 other nations. Researchers expand the boundaries of science to benefit mankind by providing better healthcare, enhanced agriculture, and a cleaner and safer environment.
1100+ Members
Founded in 1993
Mailing list available for rent

3347 Biotechnology Institute
1201 Maryland Avenue, SW
Suite 900
Washington, DC 20024

202-312-9269; Fax: 202-355-6706
info@biotechinstitute.org
www.biotechinstitute.org
Facebook, Twitter, LinkedIn, YouTube

Lawrence Mahan, President
Quinta Jackson, COO & CFO
Daniel Fallings, Program Assistant

An independent nonprofit organization founded to teach the public about the benefits of biotechnology.

3348 Council for Biotechnology Information
1201 Maryland Ave SW
Suite 900
Washington, DC 20024-2149

202-962-9200; Fax: 202-589-2547
www.whybiotech.com
Facebook, Twitter

James C Greenwood, CEO

A coalition of six of the world's leading biotechnology companies and two trade associations. Its mission is to improve the understanding and acceptance of biotechnology by collecting balanced, science-based information and communicating it through a variety of channels.
Founded in 2000
Mailing list available for rent

3349 Council of State Bioscience Associations
Home Page: www.bio.org

Michelle McMurray-Heath, President & CEO
Joanne Duncan, Pres., Membership & Business Ops.
Joseph Damond, EVP, International Affairs
Daniel Durham, EVP, Health Policy
Peter McHugh, General Counsel & SVP, Legal

The council is comprised of 48 state-based trade organizations. It calls for public policy to support the bioscience industry.

3350 Crop Science Society of America
5585 Guilford Rd.
Madison, WI 53711-5801

608-273-8080; Fax: 608-273-2021
membership@crops.org
www.crops.org
Facebook, Twitter, LinkedIn

Nick Goeser, Chief Executive Officer
Sara Uttech, Director, Governence
Wes Meixelsperger, CFO & Dir., Meetings
Ian Popkewitz, Director, IT & Operations
Susan Chapman, Director, Member Services

An educational and scientific organization comprised of more than 4,700 members dedicated to the advancement of crop science.
Founded in 1956

3351 CropLife America
1156 15th St. NW
Washington, DC 20005

202-296-1585; Fax: 202-463-0474
info@croplifeamerica.org
www.croplifeamerica.org
Facebook, Twitter, YouTube

Christopher Novak, President & CEO
Beau Greenwood, EVP, Gov. Relations & Pub. Affairs
Kellie Bray, Chief Of Staff
Rachel G. Lattimore, EVP, Legal & General Counsel
Genevieve O'Sullivan, VP, Communications & Marketing

U.S. trade association representing the major manufacturers, formulators, and distributors of crop protection and pest control products.
Founded in 1933

3352 Electrophoresis Society
1202 Ann Street
Madison, WI 53713

608-258-1565; Fax: 608-258-1569
matt-aes@tds.net
www.aesociety.org
Facebook, Twitter, LinkedIn

Rodrigo Martinez-Duarte, President
Chris Harrison, VP
Matt Hoelter, Executive Director
Phil Beckett, Secretary
Lawrence I Grossman, Treasurer

Unique international organization founded to improve and promote technologies necessary for biomolecular separation and detection.
200 Members
Founded in 1972
Mailing list available for rent

3353 Enzyme Technical Association
1111 Pennsylvania Avenue, NW
Washington, DC 20004-2541

202-739-5613; Fax: 202-739-3001
www.enzymeassociation.org

Ann M. Begley, Co-General Counsel & Secretary
Gary L. Yingling, Co-General Counsel
Diane Shanahan, Chair
Lori Gregg, Vice-Chair
Vince DuPont, Chair, Membership Committee

Promotes the development, preservation, maintenance and general welfare of the industry to the world of manufacturing and distributing enzyme preparations from any source for direct and indirect addition or application to foods, drugs, and other articles of use by humans or animals.
Founded in 1970

3354 Federation of American Societies for Experimental Biology
9650 Rockville Pike
Bethesda, MD 20814

301-634-7000; Fax: 301-634-7001
info@faseb.org
www.faseb.org
Facebook, Twitter, LinkedIn, YouTube

Parker B. Antin, PhD, President
Hudson H. Freeze, PhD, President-Elect
Thomas O Baldwin, Vice President for Science Policy
Mark O. Lively, PhD, Treasurer
Guy Fogleman, PhD, CFA, Federation Secretary

A nonprofit organization that is the principal umbrella organization of U.S. societies in the field of biological and medical research.
Founded in 1912

3355 International Society for Biomedical Polymeric Biomaterials
42 Broad Street
Rd # 217
Manakin Sabot, VA 23103

804-708-3010; Fax: 804-708-0603
isbppb.org
Facebook, Twitter, Google +

Mia Galijasevic, Executive Director
Munmaya Mishra, Founding Chairman
Gary L. Bowlin, President

An organization engaged in educating, networking, advocating, and advancing the field of biomedical polymers and polymeric biomaterials internationally.
Founded in 2011

3356 International Society for Chronobiology
University of Texas-Medical Branch
301 University Boulevard
Galveston, TX 77555

409-611-1011
prf@unife.it
ischronobiology.org

Ramon Hermida, President
Artemio Mojon, Secretary/Treasurer

Promotes studies on temporal parameters of biological variables and pursues related scientific and educational purposes. Encourages research centers and the establishment of chronobiology as an academic discipline in its own right.
300 Members
Founded in 1937
Mailing list available for rent

3357 International Society for Magnetic Resonance in Medicine
2300 Clayton Road
Suite 620
Concord, CA 94520

510-841-1899; Fax: 510-841-2340
info@ismrm.org
www.ismrm.org
Facebook, Twitter, LinkedIn, RSS

Roberta A Kravitz, Executive Director
Stephanie Haaf, Membership Director
Anne-Marie Kahrovic, Director of Meetings
Mariam Barzin, Finance Director
Melissa Simcox, Education Director

Nonprofit professional association devoted to furthering the development and application of magnetic resonance techniques in medicine and biology. Also holds annual scientific meeting and sponsors other major educational and scientific workshops.
5000 Members
Founded in 1994
Mailing list available for rent

3358 International Union of Biochemistry and Molecular Biology
3330 Hospital Drive N.W.
Calgary, AB T2N4N1

403-220-3021; Fax: 403-270-2211
walsh@ucalgary.ca
www.iubmb.org

Charysse Austria, General Secretary
Andrew Wang, President
Alexandra Newton, President Elect
Francesco Bonomi, Treasurer
Zengyi Chen, Member for Publications

An international non-governmental organization concerned with biochemistry and molecular biology.
Founded in 1955

3359 Massachusetts Biotechnology Council
300 Technology Sq
8th Floor
Cambridge, MA 02139

617-674-5100; Fax: 617-674-5101
www.massbio.org
Facebook, Twitter, LinkedIn, Youtube

Robert Coughlin, President & CEO
Kendalle Burlin O'Connell, Chief Operating Officer
Kristine Kelly, VP, Finance & Administration
Ben Bradford, VP, Membership & Economic Devt.
Jennifer Nason, VP, Communications & Strategy

Not for profit organization that provides services and support for the Massachusetts biotechnology industry. Committed to advancing the development of critical new science technology and medicines that benefit people worldwide.
400+ Members
Founded in 1985
Mailing list available for rent

3360 National Association of Wheat Growers
415 Second St NE
Suite 200
Washington, DC 20002

202-547-7800; Fax: 202-546-2638
wheatworld@wheatworld.org
www.wheatworld.org
Facebook, Twitter

Chandler Goule, CEO
Josh Tonsager, VP, Policy & Communications
Caitlin Eannello, Director, Communications

Represents wheat producers in Washington, D.C.
Founded in 1950

3361 National Center for Biotechnology Information
US National Library of Medicine
8600 Rockville Pike
Bethesda, MD 20894

301-496-6308
info@ncbi.nlm.nih.gov
www.ncbi.nlm.nih.gov
Facebook, Twitter, LinkedIn, YouTube, RSS, Google+

To develop new information technologies to aid in the understanding of fundamental molecular and genetic processes that control health and disease.
Founded in 1988

3362 National Corn Growers Association
632 Cepi Drive
Chesterfield, MO 63005

636-733-9004; Fax: 636-733-9005
corninfo@ncga.com
www.ncga.com
Facebook, Twitter, Pinterest. RSS

Jon Doggett, Chief Executive Officer
Fred Stemme, Chief Operating Officer
Neil Caskey, VP, Communications
Mike Shelby, Manager, Assoc. & Mem. Services
Rita Dunagan, Manager, Meetings & Events

News, facts, and information for growers, media, educators, and anyone else interested in corn.
Founded in 1957

3363 New York Biotechnology Association
205 East 42nd St
14th Floor
, NY 10017

212-433-2623; Fax: 212-433-0779
www.newyorkbio.org
Facebook, LinkedIn

Peter Robinson, Chair
Nathan Tinker, Executive Director
Donald Mazzullo, General Counsel
Robert Van Nostrand, Treasurer
Cynthia Green, Secretary

NYBA has been an active & vocal champion for New York's life science industry. Through the Association's education & advocacy efforts in both Albany and Washington DC, NYBA has focused it's resources on building a powerful innovation force in New York state by working to create an economic atmosphere that rewards entrepreneurism, expands access to capital, invests in the industry's future, and protects patient access to life saving therapies.
250 Members
Founded in 1990

3364 North Carolina Biotechnology Center
15 TW Alexander Drive
PO Box 13547
Research Triangle Park, NC 27709-3547

919-541-9366; Fax: 919-990-9544
info@ncbiotech.org
www.ncbiotech.org
Facebook, Twitter, LinkedIn, Youtube

Doug Edgeton, President & CEO
Mark Stohlman, VP, Finance
Robin Deacle, VP, Corporate Communications
Clearissa Coward, Communications & Marketing Coord.
Kelly Gangl, VP, Human Resource

To provide long-term economic and societal benefits to North Carolina through support of biotechnology research, business and education.
65 Members
Founded in 1981

3365 Pan American Marine Biotechnology Assn.

537-250-4223
pamba@cigb.edu.cu
pamba.cigb.edu.cu
Facebook, Twitter, LinkedIn, Instagram

Mario Pablo Estrada, President
Brian Dixon, Treasurer

Association for the promotion of sustainable use of marine resources in the Americas.
Founded in 1999

3366 Pennsylvania Biotechnology Association
650 East Swedesford Road
Suite 190
Wayne, PA 19087

610-947-6800; Fax: 610-947-6801
president@pennsylvaniabio.org

Christopher Molineaux, President & CEO
Vin Milano, Treasurer
Robert Bazemore, Chairman
Jeffrey Libson, Secretary
Christian Manders, COO

A catalyst to ensure Pennsylvania is a global leader in the biosciences by developing a cohesive community that unites the region's biotechnology, pharmaceutical research, and financial strategies.

3367 Protein Society
1450 S Rolling Road
Suite 3.007
Baltimore, MD 21227

443-543-5450; Fax: 443-543-5453
staff@proteinsociety.org
www.proteinsociety.org
Facebook, Twitter, LinkedIn

Raluca Cadar, Executive Director
Charney Robinson-Williams, Dir., Communications & Events
Shannan Cunniffe, Administrative Coordinator

The Protein Society is a not-for-profit scientific and educational membership organization. Our mission is to provide international forums to facilitate communication and collaboration with respect to all aspects of the study of protein molecules, the building blocks of life.
2100 Members
Founded in 1986
Mailing list available for rent: 3,000 names at $200 per M

3368 Section for Magnetic Resonance Technologists
2300 Clayton Road
Suite 620
Concord, CA 94520

510-841-1899; Fax: 510-841-2340
info@ismrm.org
www.ismrm.org
Facebook, Twitter, LinkedIn

Roberta A. Kravitz, Executive Director
Stephanie Haaf, Membership Director
Mariam Barzin, Director of Finance
Anne-Marie Kahrovic, Diretor of Meetings
Mary Day, Office Manager

A professional organization in the medical imaging community providing education, professional advice and support for magnetic resonance (MR) technologists and radiographers throughout the world.

3369 Sino-American Pharmaceutical Professionals Association
P. O. Box 282
Nanuet, NY 10954

information@sapaweb.org
www.sapaweb.org
Twitter, LinkedIn, YouTube

Dr. Weiguo Dai, President
Dr. Jiwen Chen, Director
Dr. Lei Tang, President-elect
Li Chen, Director
Baoguo Huang, Director

An independent, nonprofit and professional organization with over 4,000 members in the U.S.A., China, Hong Kong, Taiwan, and Japan. It promotes pharmaceutical science and technology.
Founded in 1993

3370 **Society For Freshwater Science**
5400 Bosque Blvd.
Suite 680
Waco, TX 76710

254-399-9636; Fax: 785-843-1274
www.freshwater-science.org

Andy Leidolf, Executive Director
Alonso Ramirez, President
Checo Colon-Gaud, Vice President

The Society for Freshwater Science (SFS) is an international scientific organization whose purpose is to promote further understanding of freshwater ecosystems (rivers, streams, lakes, reservoirs, and estuaries) and ecosystems at the interface between aquatic and terrestrial habitats. The society fosters exchange of scientific information among the membership, and with other professional societies, resource managers, policy makers, educators, and the public.
Founded in 1953

3371 **Society for Biological Engineering**
120 Wall Street
FL 23
New York, NY 10005-4020

FAX 203-775-5177
bio@aiche.org
www.aiche.org/sbe
Facebook, LinkedIn, YouTube

Monty Alger, President
Joseph Smith, Secretary
Rosemarie Wesson, Treasurer

A global organization of leading engineers and scientists dedicatedto advancing the integration of biology with engineering.

3372 **Society for Biomaterials**
1120 Route 73
Suite 200
Mt Laurel, NJ 08054

856-439-0826; Fax: 856-439-0525
info@biomaterials.org
www.biomaterials.org
Facebook, Twitter, LinkedIn

Dan Lemyre, Executive Director
Shena Seppannen, Asst. Executive Director
Anthony Celenza, Senior Meeting Manager
Jeana Hoffman, Meeting Coordinator
Lisa Howard-Fusco, Managing Editor

Promotes advances in all phases of materials, research and development by encouragement of cooperative educational programs, clinical applications, and professional standards in the biomaterials field.
1550 Members
Founded in 1969

3373 **Society for Cardiovascular Magnetic Resonance**
19 Mantua Road
Mt. Royal, NJ 8061

856-423-8955; Fax: 856-423-3420
hq@scmr.org
www.scmr.org
Facebook, Twitter

Chiara Bucciarelli-Ducci, Chief Executive Officer
Brent Schwartz, Chief Operating Officer
Lisa Colangelo, Membership Manager
Annaliese Setorie, Events Manager
Lauren Small, Program Manager

The leading international society for physicians, scientists, and technologists working in cardiovascular magnetic resonance.

3374 **Society for Industrial Microbiology and Biotechnology**
3929 Old Lee Highway
Suite 92A
Fairfax, VA 22030

703-691-3357; Fax: 703-691-7991
www.simbhq.org
Facebook, Twitter, LinkedIn, RSS

Christine Lowe, Executive Director
Jennifer Johnson, Director of Member Services
Suzannah Citrenbaum, Web Manager
Espie Montesa, Accountant
Tina Hockaday, Meeting Coordinator

A nonprofit international association dedicated to the advancement of microbiology sciences, especially as they apply to industrial products, biotechnology, materials, and processes.
Founded in 1949

3375 **Society for Laboratory Automation and Screening**
100 Illinois Street
Ste. 242
St. Charles, IL 60174

630-256-7527
877-990-7527
slas@slas.org
www.slas.org
Facebook, Twitter, LinkedIn, YouTube

Vicki Loise, CEO
Brenda Dreier, COO
Jill Hronek, Director, Marketing & Communication
Christine Diedrich, Publishing Manager
Mary Geismann, Sr. Membership Coordinator

A global community of more than 18,000 life science research and development professionals.
2000+ Members
Founded in 1994

3376 **Strategic Information for the Life Sciences**
BioAbility™
PO Box 14569
Research Triangle Park, NC 27709-4569

919-544-5111; Fax: 919-544-5401
info@bioability.com
www.bioability.com

Mark D. Dibner, President/Founder

BioAbility has provided the knowledge and experience to evaluate any area of the life sciences or biotechnology markets. Partnered with expert life science affiliates to bring a world-class level of expertise to our service offerings.
Founded in 1994

3377 **The American Society for Cell Biology**
8120 Woodmont Avenue
Suite 750
Bethesda, MD 20814

301-347-9300; Fax: 301-347-9310
ascbinfo@ascb.org
ascb.org
Facebook, Twitter, LinkedIn

Erika Shugart, Chief Executive Officer
Matthew Welch, Editor-In-Chief
Uloma Nwauche, Director, Finance
Thea Clark, Dir., Communications & Education
Azra Chughtai, Dir., Admin. & Human Resources

A professional society that provides the exchange of scientific knowledge in the area of cell biology.

3378 **Virginia Biotechnology Association**
800 E Leigh St
Suite 14
Richmond, VA 23219-1534

804-643-6360; Fax: 804-643-6361
questions@vabio.org
www.vabio.org
Facebook, Twitter

John Newby, CEO

Promotes the biotechnology industry in Virginia, to expand the knowledge and expertise of Virginia's businesses concerning biotechnology through seminars, educational publications and other means.
200 Members
Founded in 1992

3379 **Women in Cognitive Science**

Home Page: womenincogsci.org
Facebook

Laurie Feldman, Officer
Judith Kroll, Officer
Suparna Rajaram, Officer
Debra Titone, Officer
Natasha Tokowicz, Officer

Organization that works to create an environment that encourages young women to join the field of cognitive psychology/science, particularly in cognitive neuroscience and computational modeling areas.

Newsletters

3380 **AAI Newsletter**
American Association of Immunologists
9650 Rockville Pike
Bethesda, MD 20814-3999

301-634-7178; Fax: 301-634-7887
infoaai@aai.org
www.aai.org

Michele Hogan, Executive Director
Bethany Coulter, Director, Communications
Frequency: Bi-Monthly

3381 **BIOtechNOW**
Biotechnology Innovation Organization
1201 Maryland Ave SW
Suite 900
Washington, DC 20024

202-962-6655
www.biotech-now.org
Facebook, Twitter, LinkedIn, YouTube

3382 **BioPeople Magazine**
PO Box 5778
Walnut Creek, CA 94596

925-932-6364
www.biotechmedia.com

Lisa Wagner, Advertising Executive
Charlene Carpentier, Production Manager
Sukaini Virji-Jeganathan, Editor

Provides information and analysis of the international biotechnology industry, including corporate agreements, product status, financial transactions and new technologies.
Cost: $675.00
Frequency: Quarterly
Circulation: 10,000
Printed in on glossy stock

3383 **BioWorld Financial Watch**
BioWorld

3525 Piedmont Road
Building 6, Suite 400
Atlanta, GA 30305-4031

404-262-5476
800-688-2421; Fax: 404-814-0759
www.bioworld.com

Donald R Johnston, Publisher
Brady Huggett, Managing Editor
Chris Walker, Marketing Manager

Tracks public financing and portfolio performance offering expert analysis. The weekly source for biotechnology financial news.
Cost: $1197.00
Frequency: Weekly

3384 **Biotechnology News**
CTB International Publishing
PO Box 218
Maplewood, NJ 07040-218

973-966-0997; Fax: 973-966-0242
www.genengnews.com

F G Racioppi, Marketing Director

A leading biotechnology publication for executives. Provides incisive intelligence on the ever-changing biotechnology industry and includes news on research, product development and corporate doings.
Cost: $634.00
Founded in 1985
Printed in one color on newsprint stock

3385 **Biotechnology Newswatch**
McGraw Hill
1221 Avenue of the Americas
Suite C3A
New York, NY 10020-1095

212-512-2000; Fax: 212-512-3840
www.mcgraw-hill.com

Harold W McGraw III, CEO
Mara Bovsun, Editor
Kenneth M Vittor, VP

Covers the business and technical news affecting companies engaged in serving the biotechnology sciences.
Cost: $737.00
12 Pages
Frequency: Monthly
Founded in 1910

3386 **Genetic Technology News**
John Wiley & Sons
111 River St
Hoboken, NJ 07030-5790

201-748-6000; Fax: 201-748-6088
info@wiley.com
www.wiley.com

William J Pesce, CEO

Covers technical and business developments in every area of genetic engineering and related techniques, analyzing their applications in the chemical, pharmaceutical and energy industries as well as in agriculture, animal breeding and medicine.
Cost: $585.00
18 Pages
Frequency: Monthly
Founded in 1807

3387 **Industrial Bioprocessing**
John Wiley & Sons
111 River St
Hoboken, NJ 07030-5790

201-748-6000; Fax: 201-748-6088
info@wiley.com
www.wiley.com

William J Pesce, CEO

Focuses on industrial processes involving biological routes to produce chemicals/energy; the conversion of biomaterials via fermentation, process monitoring and more.
Cost: $545.00
10 Pages
Frequency: Monthly
Founded in 1807
Mailing list available for rentat $180 per M
Printed in one color on matte stock

3388 **J Biomolecular Screening**
Society for Biomolecular Screening
100 Illinois Street
Suite 242
St.Charles, IL 60174

630-256-7527; Fax: 630-741-7527
slas@slas.org
www.sbsonline.org

Michelle Palmer, President
David Dorsett, Vice President
Erik Rubin, Treasurer
Andy Zaayenga, Secretary

Biomolecular industry news and information.
Cost: $478.00
Founded in 1992

3389 **Life Sciences & Biotechnology Update**
InfoTeam
PO Box 15640
Plantation, FL 33318-5640

954-473-9560; Fax: 954-473-0544

Merton Allen, Editor

Medical and biological technology; health and disease; genetics and genetic engineering; bodily fluids, bones, tissues and organs, cancer, medical diagnoisis and treatment; medical instrumentation and procedures; medical care systems; public health; mental health; child care; medical costs; research; and more.
Frequency: Monthly

3390 **Technotrends Newsletter**
Burrus Research Associates
PO Box 47
Hartland, WI 53029-2347

262-367-0949
800-827-6770; Fax: 262-367-7163
office@burrus.com
www.burrus.com/

Dan Burrus, CEO
Patti A Thomsen, Editor
Jennifer Metcalf, Marketing

This newsletter researches the latest innovations in science and technology. Provides access to information that can give an edge on tomorrow, today and shows how you might benefit from each innovation.
Cost: $39.95
Frequency: Monthly
Circulation: 1000
Founded in 1984
Printed in 4 colors on matte stock

Magazines & Journals

3391 **American Biotechnology Laboratory**
International Scientific Communications
PO Box 870
Shelton, CT 06484-0870

203-926-9300; Fax: 203-926-9310
www.iscpubs.com

Brian Howard, Publisher
Robert G Sweeny, Publisher

American Biotechnology Laboratory serves Industry, Universities, Government and others allied to the field with special interest in life science research.
Cost: $173.12
64 Pages
Frequency: Monthly
Circulation: 60058
Mailing list available for rent: 60M names at $170 per M
Printed in 4 colors on glossy stock

3392 **Antiretroviral Resistance in Clinical Practice**
National Center for Biotechnology Information
8600 Rockville Pike
Bethesda, MD 20894

301-496-2475; Fax: 301-480-9241
www.ncbi.nlm.nih.gov

Anna Maria Geretti, Editor

3393 **Applied Biochemistry and Biotechnology**
Humana Press
999 Riverview Drive
Suite 208
Totowa, NJ 07512-1165

973-256-1699; Fax: 973-256-8341
www.humanapress.com

David Watt, Editor
Ashok Mulchandani, Editor-in-Chief
Paul Dolgert, Director
Fran Lipton, Production Manager

Reports on new techniques and original research in biotechnology and biochemistry with a focus on the application of new technologies.
Cost: $1505.00
Frequency: Monthly
Circulation: 373
Founded in 1977

3394 **BioTechniques**
52 Vanderbilt Avenue
7th Floor
New York, NY 10017

212-520-2777; Fax: 212-520-2705
webmaster@biotechniques.com
www.biotechniques.com

Nathan Blow, Editor in Chief
Bill Moran, Director of Sales
John C. Yarosh, Production Manager

Serves the biotechnical and pharmaceutical industries.
Cost: $145.00
254 Pages
Frequency: Monthly
Circulation: 85,000
Founded in 1983
Printed in 4 colors on glossy stock

3395 **Biotechnology Progress**
American Chemical Society
1155 16th St NW
Suite 600
Washington, DC 20036-4892

202-872-4600
80 - 2 - 55; Fax: 202-872-4615
service@acs.org
www.acs.org

Nancy Jackson, President

Information on new technology.
Cost: $924.00
Founded in 1876

3396 **Biotechnology and Bioengineering**
John Wiley & Sons
111 River St
Hoboken, NJ 07030-5790

201-748-6000; Fax: 201-748-6088
info@wiley.com
www.wiley.com

William J Pesce, CEO
Richard M Hochhauser, CEO

A scientific journal publishing new papers in the field of biotechnology and bioengineering.
Cost: $750.00
Frequency: 1 Year 28 Issue
Founded in 1807

3397 CleanRooms Magazine
PennWell Publishing Company
98 Spit Brook Rd
Suite L11
Nashua, NH 03062-5737
603-891-0123
80 - 2 - 05; Fax: 603-891-9294
mikel@pennwell.com
www.pennwell.com
Christine Shaw, VP
Mark A Desorbo, Associate Editor
James Enos, Publisher
Serves the contamination control and ultrapure materials and process industries. Written for readers in the microelectronics, pharmaceutical, biotech, health care, food processing and other user industries. Provides technology and business news and new product listings.
Frequency: Monthly
Circulation: 35031
Founded in 1987

3398 Engineering in Medicine and Biology
3 Park Avenue
17th Floor
New York, NY 10016
212-419-7900
800-272-6657; Fax: 212-752-4929
jenderle@bme.uconn.edu
www.ieee.org
Dr. John D Enderle, Editor
Desir,e de Myer, Managing Editor
Susan Schneiderman, Advertising Sales Manager
Focuses on up-to-date biomedical engineering applications for engineers who are at the forefront of electrotechnology innovation.
Cost: $300.00
Circulation: 7983
ISSN: 0739-5175
Founded in 1963

3399 Freshwater Science
Society for Freshwater Science
5400 Bosque Blvd.
Suite 680
Waco, TX 76710-4446
254-399-9636; Fax: 254-776-3767
www.freshwater-science.org
Pamela Silver, Editor
Rosemary J. Mackay, Managing Editor
Irwin Polls, Business Manager
Publishes timely, peer-reviewed scientific research that promotes a better understanding and environmental stewardship of biological communities living on the bottom of streams, rivers, lakes, and wetlands, with an emphasis on freshwater inland habitats. Theoretical discussions, speculative and philosophical articles, and critical appraisals of rapidly developing research fields.
Cost: $65.00
Frequency: Quarterly

3400 Journal of Biological Chemistry
American Society for Biochemistry
11200 Rockville Pike
Suite 302
Rockville, MD 20852-3110
240-283-6620; Fax: 301-881-2573
asbmb@asbmb.org
www.asbmb.org
Martha Fedor, Editor-in-Chief
Herbet Tabor, Co-Editor

3401 Journal of Biomolecular Screening
Sage Publications
2455 Teller Rd
Newbury Park, CA 91320-2234
805-499-9774
800-818-7243; Fax: 805-499-0871
journals@sagepub.com
www.sagepub.com
Blaise R Simqu, CEO
Mark Beggs, Associate Editor
Stein Roaldset, Advertising Editor
Christine Giordano, Society Updates Editor
Charles Hart, New Products Editor
An official publication of the Society for Biomolecular Sciences. Peer-reviewed publication on drug discovery sciences, with an emphasis on screening methods and technologies; Information on the latest biomolecular sciences, with regular topics including: target identification/validation assay development methods, and technologies, lead generation/optimization, virtual screening/chemo-informatics, data and image analysis, sample management, biomarkers and legal/licensing issues.
Cost: $610.00
Frequency: 10x year/Price Varies
ISSN: 1087-0571
Founded in 1994

3402 Lab Animal
Nature Publishing Group
1270 Broadway
6th Floor, Suite 807
New York, NY 10001-3224
212-278-8600; Fax: 212-564-0217
www.labanimal.com
Angelo Notaro, Partner
Rachel Burley, Publisher
Richard Charkin, CEO
A peer-reviewed journal for professionals in animal research, emphasizing proper management and care. Offers the latest on animal models, breeds, breeding practices, in vitro and computer models, lab care, nutrition, and improved animal handling techniques. Offers timely and informative material, reaching both the academic research world and applied research industries, including genetic engineering, human therapeutics and pharmaceutical companies.
Cost: $159.00
Founded in 1869

3403 Molecular Plant: Microbe Interactions
American Phytopatholgical Society
3340 Pilot Knob Road
Saint Paul, MN 55121-2097
651-454-7250
800-328-7560; Fax: 651-454-0766
aps@scisoc.org
www.apsnet.org
Dawn West, Publications - Subscriptions
Molecular biology and molecular genetics of pathological, symbiotic and associative interactions of microbes with plants, including plant response.
Frequency: Monthly
ISSN: 0894-0282
Mailing list available for rent

3404 Nature
Nature Publishing Group
1270 Broadway
Suite 807
New York, NY 10001-3224
212-278-8600
800-221-2123; Fax: 212-564-0217
nature@natureny.com
www.nature.com
Angelo Notaro, Partner
Josie Natori, CEO
A reliable source of up-to-date scientific information. Publishes papers from any area of science with great potential impact. Also publishes a broad range of informal material in the form of opinion articles, news stories, briefings and recruitment features, and contributed material.
Frequency: Monthly
Circulation: 60289

3405 Nature Biotechnology
Nature America
345 Park Avenue S
10th Floor
New York, NY 10010-1707
212-726-9200
800-221-2123; Fax: 212-696-9635
biotech@natureny.com
www.biotech.nature.com
Andrew Marshall, Editor
Richard Charkin, CEO
Annette Thomas, Managing Director
Philip Campbell, Editor-in-Chief
Peter Collins, Publishing Director
A monthly magazine of biotechnology news and research.
Cost: $178.00
550 Pages
Frequency: Monthly
Circulation: 18798
ISSN: 1054-0156
Founded in 1983
Printed in 4 colors on glossy stock

3406 Protein Science
Protein Society
9650 Rockville Pike
Bethesda, MD 20814-3999
301-634-7240
800-992-6466; Fax: 301-634-7271
www.proteinsociety.org
Cynthia A Yablonski, Executive Officer
Arthur G Palmer III, President
Jean Baum, Secretary/Treasurer
2100 Members
Founded in 1986
Mailing list available for rent: 3,000 names at $200 per M

3407 Science Illustrated
Communications Solutions
8428 Holly Leaf Drive
McLean, VA 22102-2224
703-356-1688; Fax: 202-296-1857
http://www.scienceillustrated.com/
Tod Herbers, Editor
Provides physicians with information on research and development in the fields of science related to medicine.
Cost: $18.00
Circulation: 103200
Printed in 4 colors on glossy stock

Trade Shows

3408 AAB Annual Meeting and Education Conference
American Association of Bioanalysts
906 Olive Street
Suite 1200
Saint Louis, MO 63101-1448
314-241-1445; Fax: 314-241-1449
aab@aab.org
www.aab.org
Facebook
Mark S Birenbaum PhD, Executive Director
Educational programs, abstract presentations, poster presentations and exhibits
Frequency: Annual
Founded in 1956

3409 **BIO International Convention**
Biotechnology Innovation Organization
1201 Maryland Ave SW
Suite 900
Washington, DC 20024
202-962-6655
convention@bio.org
convention.bio.org
Facebook, Twitter, LinkedIn, YouTube
John Maraganore, Co-Chair
Abbie Celniker, Co-Chair
16000 Attendees

3410 **Biometrics Technology Expo and Consortium Conference**
J Spargo & Associates
11208 Waples Mill Road
Suite 112
Fairfax, VA 22030
703-631-6200
800-564-4220; Fax: 703-654-6931
www.biometricsociety.org
Jeffrey Dunn, Chair
Fernando Podio, Chair
Co-located with the Biometric Consortium Conference, this event offers unparalleled opportunities to reach top buyers, federal and state agencies and leading industry corporations.
2000 Attendees
Frequency: September

3411 **Biophysical Society Annual Meeting**
Biophysical Society
11400 Rockville Pike
Suite 800
Bethesda, MD 20852
240-290-5600; Fax: 240-290-5555
society@biophysics.org
www.biophysics.org
Ro Kampman, Executive Officer
Harris Povich, Director of Finance and Operations
Vida Ess, Programs Coordinator
Includes 3,000 poster presentations, 200 exhibits, 20 symposias, workshops, platform sessions, and subgroup meetings. It is also the worlds largest meeting for biophysicists.
6M Attendees
Frequency: February/March
Mailing list available for rent

3412 **Biotechnology Investment Conference**
Massachusetts Biotechnology Council
One Cambridge Center
Cmabridge, MA 02142
617-674-5100; Fax: 617-674-5101
www.massbio.org
Facebook, Twitter, LinkedIn, Youtube
Robert Coughlin, President & CEO
Laura Rudberg, Director, Events
New England's largest biotechnology investor forum. Allows more than 70 local public and private companies to showcase their technologies and products in front of portfolio managers, analysts, venture capitalists and other investment professionals.
700 Attendees
Frequency: November

3413 **Int'l Conference on Strategic Business Information in Biotechnology**
Institute for Biotechnology Information
3200 Chapel Hill/Nelson Boulevard Suite 201
PO Box 14569
Research Triangle Park, NC 27709-4569
919-544-5111; Fax: 919-544-5401
info@bioability.com
www.biotechinfo.com
For strategists, company managers, information specialists, financial analysts or users of strategic business information in biotechnology.
150 Attendees
Frequency: October

Directories & Databases

3414 **BioWorld Online**
3525 Piedmont Road
Building 6, Suite 400
Atlanta, GA 30305
404-262-5476
800-688-2421; Fax: 404-814-0759
www.bioworld.com
Randy Osborne
This database contains a variety of information on biotechnology companies, products, and services.
Frequency: Full-text

3415 **Biosis/Thomson Scientific**
BIOSIS
1500 Spring Garden St
Fourth Floor
Philadelphia, PA 19130-4067
215-386-0100
800-336-4474; Fax: 215-386-2911
www.biosis.org/support; scientific.thomson.com
Facebook, Twitter, LinkedIn
Vin Caraher, President/CEO
Keith MacGregor, Executive VP
Andrea Degutis, Senior VP/Communications
A bibliographic database covering worldwide research on all biological and biomedical topics. Records contain bibliographic data, indexing information, and abstracts for most references. Biosis joined with the Thomson Corporation in early 2006 to expand its global presence.
Frequency: Updated Weekly

Industry Web Sites

3416 **http://gold.greyhouse.com**
G.O.L.D Grey House OnLine Databases
Grey House Publishing's online database platform, GOLD, offers Quick Search, Keyword Search and Expert Search for most business sectors, including scientific, technical and biotechnical markets. The GOLD platform makes finding the information you need quick and easy - whether you're a novice searcher or an experienced database user. All of Grey House's directory products are available for subscription on the GOLD platform.

3417 **www.aesociety.org**
Electrophoresis Society
International organization founded to improve and promote technologies necessary for biomolecular separation and detection.

3418 **www.asbmb.org**
American Society for Biochemistry and Molecular
Serves members who teach and conduct research at colleges and universities and in various government laboratories, nonprofit research institutions and industry.

3419 **www.asrm.org**
American Society for Reproductive Medicine
Organization devoted to advancing knowledge and expertise in reproductive medicine and biology. Members of this voluntary nonprofit organization must demonstrate the high ethical principals of the medical profession, evince an interest in reproductive medicine and biology, and adhere to the objectives of the Society.

3420 **www.benthos.org**
North American Benthological Society
International scientific organization whose purpose is to promote better understanding of the biotic communities of lake and stream bottoms and their role in aquatic ecosystems, by providing media and disseminating new investigation results, new interpetations, and other benthological information to aquatic biologists and to the scientific community at large.

3421 **www.bio.org**
Biotechnology Industry Organization
For firms involved in the use of recombinant DNA, hybridoma and immulogical technologies in a wide range of applications including human health care, animal husbandry, agriculture and specialty chemical production.

3422 **www.greyhouse.com**
Grey House Publishing
Authoritative reference directories for most business markets including science, technical and biotechnical markets. Users can search the online databases with varied search criteria allowing for custom searches by product category, geographic area, sales volume, keyword, subject and more. Full Grey House catalog and online ordering also available.

3423 **www.ismrm.org**
Int'l Society for Magnetic Resonance in Medicine
For physicians and scientists promoting the applications of magnetic resonance techniques to medicine and biology. The Society holds annual scientific meetings and sponsors other major educational and scientific workshops.

3424 **www.massbio.org**
Massachusetts Biotechnology Council
Organization that provides services and support for the Massachusets biotechnology industry.

3425 **www.proteinsociety.org**
Protein Society
Formed in 1986 to promote international interactions among investigators in order to explore all aspects of the building blocks of life, protien molecules. Members come from universities, foundations, institutes and corporations to provide leadership in this broad field of research. The Society and its members are making a strong impact on the advancements of protien science.

3426 **www.whybiotech.com**
Council for Biotechnology Information
Serves to improve understanding and acceptance of biotechnology by collecting balanced, credible and science based information, then communicating this information through a variety of channels.

Associations

3427 **American Boat Builders and Repairers Association**
1 Washington Street
Newport, RI 02840

401-236-2466; Fax: 954-239-2600
info@abbra.org
www.abbra.org
Facebook, Twitter, LinkedIn

Graham Wright, President
Kirk Ritter, VP
Peter Sabo, Treasurer
Ron Helbig, Secretary
Cathy Cope, Director

Trade association for marinas, boat builders and repairers. Also offers a monthly newsletter and training seminars.
300 Members
Founded in 1943

3428 **American Boat and Yacht Council**
613 Third Street
Suite 10
Annapolis, MD 21403

410-990-4460; Fax: 410-990-4466
info@abycinc.org
www.abycinc.org
Facebook, Twitter, LinkedIn, Youtube

John Adey, President
Kevin Scullen, Membership Director
Shannon Aronson, PR/Marketing Director

A not-for-profit membership organization that has been developing and updating the safety standards for boat building and repair.
4000+ Members
Founded in 1954

3429 **American Boatbuilders Association, Inc.**
The Brumby Building, Marietta Stn.
127 Church St., Suite 210
Marietta, GA 30060

770-792-3070; Fax: 770-792-3073
www.ababoats.com

Jay Patton, President
Gienna Stephens, Office Coordinator
Doug Alexander, Sr. Project Manager

Volume materials purchasing group for independent boat builders.
Founded in 1992

3430 **American Boating Association**
PO Box 1597
Ocean View, DE 19970

614-497-4088
admin@americanboating.org
www.americanboating.org
Facebook, RSS

Bill Condon, Founder/President

Through their membership in the American Boating Association, boaters and boating enthusiasts from across the nation share a common mission - working together to improve the safety, affordability, environmental cleanliness, growth and fun of the sport.
Cost: $10.00
30000 Members

3431 **American Power Boat Association**
17640 E. Nine Mile Road
Po Box 377
Eastpointe, MI 48021-0377

586-773-9700; Fax: 586-773-6490
www.apba-racing.com
Facebook, Twitter, LinkedIn, Youtube, RSS

Dan Wiener, Executive Director
Becky Nichols, Director, Operations
Sabrina Haudek, Membership Coordinator

The nation's authority on power boat racing which sanctions over 200 races each year.
6000 Members
Founded in 1903

3432 **American Sail Training Association**
221 3rd Street, Building 2, Ste. 101
PO Box 1459
Newport, RI 02840

401-846-1775; Fax: 401-849-5400
www.tallships.sailtraining.org
Facebook, Twitter, LinkedIn

Supports all those involved with sail training ships and programs, as well as ships under construction or renovation.
300 Members
Founded in 1973

3433 **American Society of Marine Artists**
P.O.Box 247
Smithfield, VA 23430

757-357-3785
asma1978@verizon.net
www.americansocietyofmarineartists.com
Facebook, Twitter, LinkedIn

Lisa Egeli, President
Nicolas Fox, Vice President
Mike Killelea, Secretary
Val Sandell, Administrator
Laura Cooper, Treasurer

A non-profit, tax exempt organization, whose objective is to recognize and promote marine art and history, and to encourage cooperation among artists, historians, marine enthusiasts and others in activities related to marine art and maritime history.
500+ Members
Founded in 1978

3434 **Antique & Classic Boat Society**
422 James St
Clayton, NY 13624

315-686-2628; Fax: 315-686-2680
hqs@acbs.org
www.acbs.org
Facebook, Twitter, LinkedIn

Dan Gyoerkoe, Executive Director
Stacy Dasno, Office Supervisor
Wil Vidal, Ad/Sponsor Sales

Society devoted to disseminating information on building and restoring wooden and antique boats.
12000 Members
Founded in 1975

3435 **Association of Marina Industries**
50 Water Street
Warren, RI 02885

866-367-6622; Fax: 401-247-0074
info@marinaassociation.org
www.marinaassociation.org
Facebook, Twitter, LinkedIn

Chris Petty, Chair
John Swick, Vice Chairman
Rick Chapman, Treasurer
Kevin Thompson, Secretary

The Association of Marina Industries is the international trade marine association for the marina industry.
800+ Members
Founded in 1986

3436 **Boat Owners Association of the US**
880 South Pickett Street
Alexandria, VA 22304

703-461-2878
800-395-2628; Fax: 703-461-2847
www.boatus.com
Facebook, Twitter, Youtube

Richard Schwartz, Chairman/Founder
Bill Oakerson, CEO
Margaret Podlich, President
Adam Wheeler, VP & Director of Towing
Heather Lougheed, VP, Membership

Supports all who are involved with legislation, regulations and consumer aspects of the industry.
62500 Members
Founded in 1966

3437 **Boating Writers International**
108 Ninth Street
Wilmette, IL 60091

847-736-4142
info@bwi.org
www.bwi.org
Facebook, LinkedIn

Charlie Levine, President
Chris Woodward, First Vice President
Brady Kay, Second Vice President
Zuzana Prochazka, Executive Director

A nonprofit professional organization consisting of writers, broadcasters, editors, photgraphers, public relations specialists and other media professionals in communications serving the boating industry.
Founded in 1970

3438 **Coastal Yachting Academy**
PO Box 10441
St. Petersburg, FL 33733

727-867-9466

Don Harper, Captain/Owner

To provide the recreational boater reasonably priced training equal to the training of professional mariners.
Founded in 1970

3439 **Marine Retailers Association of America**
8401 73rd Avenue N
Suite 71
Minneapolis, MN 55428

763-315-8043
matt@mraa.com
www.mraa.com
Facebook, Twitter, LinkedIn

Matt Gruhn, President
Liz Walz, Vice President
Allison Gruhn, Director, Business Development
Sherri Cuvala, Membership Manager
Sarah Korbel, Events & Operations Specialist

Raising the standards of retailing within the industry. Promotes activities for the recreational boating industry and holds seminars to improve management.
2.5M Members
Founded in 1972

3440 **Marine Safety Foundation**
5050 Industrial Rd
Suite 2
Wall Township, NJ 07727-4044

732-751-0295; Fax: 732-751-0508

Burt Thompson, Executive Director

Advances the safety of life at sea through research, education and coordination.
131 Members
Founded in 1993

3441 **National Association of Charterboat Operators**
PO Box 1070
Hurley, MS 39555

866-981-5136; Fax: 877-263-8548
info@nacocharters.org
www.nacocharters.org
Facebook

Capt. Robert F Zales II, President
Capt. Butch Smith, Vice President
Capt. Ron Maglio, Treasurer
Capt. Charlie Phillips, Secretary
Susan Mason-Yadav, Executive Director

A national association of charterboat owners and operators that represent thousands of individuals across the United States.
3600+ Members
Founded in 1991

3442 **National Association of Sailing**
15 Maritime Drive
Portsmouth, RI 02871

401-683-0800
800-877-2451; Fax: 401-683-0840
info@ussailing.org
www.ussailing.org
Facebook, Twitter, LinkedIn

Heather Monoson, Chief Financial Officer
Jill Nosach, Chief Development Officer
Peter Glass, Chief Marketing Officer
Mike Waters, Chief Technology Officer
Jack Gierhart, Executive Director

Accredits sailing schools, certifies instructors and provides teaching and management information. Publishes a newsletter and directory of American sailing schools and charter operators. Provides free consulting services for start-ups of new schools.
100 Members
Frequency: Quarterly
Founded in 1980
Mailing list available for rent

3443 **National Association of State Boating Law Administrators**
1648 McGrathiana Parkway
Suite 360
Lexington, KY 40511

859-225-9487; Fax: 859-231-6403
info@nasbla.org
www.nasbla.org
Facebook, Twitter, LinkedIn, Flickr, Foursquare, YouTube

John Johnson, Executive Director & CEO
Tom Hayward, CFO
Hannah Helsby, Deputy Executive Director, Comm.
John Fetterman, Deputy Executive Director, Advocacy
Sam Lynch, Director, Membership Services

Representing the recreational boating authorities of all 50 States and U.S. territories. To strengthen the ability of the State and territorial boating authorities to reduce death, injury and property damage associated with recreational boating.
56 Members
Founded in 1960

3444 **National Marine Bankers Association**
231 South LaSalle St
Suite 2050
Chicago, IL 60604

312-946-6260
info@marinebankers.org
LinkedIn

Created for the purpose of educating current and prospective lenders in marine financing procedures, promoting the extension of credit to consumer and trade borrowers.
81 Members
Founded in 1979

3445 **National Marine Distributors Association**
37 Pratt St
Suite 3
Essex, CT 06426-1159

860-767-7898; Fax: 860-767-7932
executivedirector@nmdaonline.com
www.nmdaonline.com

Nancy Cueroni, Executive Director
Mike Conners, President
Jim Beale, Vice President
Ryan Barber, Secretary/Treasurer

Wholesale distributors of marine accessories and hardware.
200 Members
Mailing list available for rent

3446 **National Marine Electronics Association**
7 Riggs Ave
Severna Park, MD 21146

410-975-9425
800-808-6632; Fax: 410-975-9450
info@nmea.org
www.nmea.org
Facebook

Mark Reedanauer, President & Executive Director
Mark Oslund, Director, Standards
Cindy Love, Office Manager
Steve Katz, Chair

Is the unifying force behind the entire marine electronics industry, bringing together all aspects of the industry for the betterment of all in our business.
400 Members
Founded in 1957

3447 **National Marine Manufacturers Association**
231 South LaSalle St
Suite 2050
Chicago, IL 60604

312-946-6200
www.nmma.org
Twitter, LinkedIn

Frank Hugelmeyer, President
Robert Newsome, SVP, Operations
Craig Boskey, SVP, Finance & CFO
Ellen Bradley, SVP, Marketing & Communications
Jennifer Thompson, SVP, Boat & Sport Shows

Dedicated to creating, promoting and protecting an environment where members can achieve financial success through excellence in manufacturing, selling and service for their customers.
1400+ Members
Founded in 1979

3448 **National Marine Representative Association**
PO Box 360
Gurnee, IL 60031

847-662-3167; Fax: 847-336-7126
info@nmraonline.org
www.nmraonline.org

Scott Kolodny, President
Aaron Freeman, VP
Mark Goodman, Treasurer
Craig Cochran, Secretary

A national organization serving marine industry independent sales reps and the marine manufacturers who sell through reps.
300 Members
Founded in 1960

3449 **National Safe Boating Council**
9500 Technology
Suite 104
Manassas, VA 20110

703-361-4294; Fax: 703-361-5294
www.safeboatingcouncil.org
Facebook, Twitter, LinkedIn, Youtube

Peg Phillips, Executive Director
Sandy Smith, Financial Officer
Yvonne Pentz, Communications Director
Alexis Webb, Program Coordinator

NSBC has an interest in boating safety and education to reduce accidents and enhance the boating experience.
350 Members
Founded in 1958
Mailing list available for rent

3450 **Northwest Marine Trade Association**
1900 N Northlake Way
Suite 233
Seattle, WA 98103

206-634-0911; Fax: 206-632-0078
info@nmta.net
www.nmta.net
Facebook, Twitter, LinkedIn, Youtube, Pinterest, RSS

George Harris, President
Katie Groseclose, Membership Coordinator
Jennifer Higgins, Director, Finance
Karsten McIntosh, Director, Communications
Atie McPhail, Director, Boat Shows
700+ Members
Founded in 1947

3451 **Offshoreonly**
PO Box 10868
St Petersburg, FL 33733

954-463-1101; Fax: 727-394-2451
offshoreonly@offshoreonly.com
www.offshoreonly.com
Facebook, Twitter

Kathe Walker, President
Scott Ryerson, VP

OSO is a nonprofit organization catering to fun loving boaters in the Tampa/Clearwater/St. Petersburg areas of Florida.
Mailing list available for rent

3452 **Personal Watercraft Industry Association**
650 Massachusetts Avenue NW
#520
Washington, DC 20001

202-737-9761
ddickerson@nmma.org
www.pwia.org

David Dickerson, VP, State Govt Relations

Trade association representing manufacturers of personal watercraft.
Founded in 1987

3453 **Propeller Club of the United States**
3927 Old Lee Hwy
Suite 101A
Fairfax, VA 22030

703-691-2777; Fax: 703-691-4173
shannon@propellerclubhq.com
www.propellerclubhq.com

Niels Aalund, International President
Steve Tyndal, Vice President
Pat Patrick, Secretary
Maria Conatser, Treasurer
John Cullather, Executive VP

Dedicated to the enhancement and well-being of all interests of the maritime community on a national and international basis.
10000 Members
Founded in 1927
Mailing list available for rent

3454 **Recreational Boaters of California**
925 L Street
Suite 260
Sacramento, CA 95814

916-441-4166
rboc@rboc.org
www.rboc.org
Facebook, Twitter

Cleve Hardaker, President
Otis Brock, Secretary/Treasurer
Winston Bumpus, Vice President

Monitors the proceedings in the State Capitol, reviewing each of the bills that are introduced and/or amended as to whether they would have an impact on boating.
Founded in 1968

3455 **Sail America**
50 Water St
Warren, RI 02885

401-289-2540; Fax: 401-247-0074
www.sailamerica.com
Facebook, Twitter, LinkedIn

Katie Kelly, Association Manager
Stephanie Grove, Admin Manager
Kayce Florio, Finance Manager
Sara Watson, Boat Show Sales Coordinator

Trade association for sailing segment of recreational boating industry.
200+ Members
Founded in 1990

3456 **Shipbuilders Council of America**
20 F Street, NW
Suite 500
Washington, DC 20001

202-737-3234; Fax: 202-737-0264
Facebook, Twitter, LinkedIn

Represents the U.S. shipyard industry. SCA members build, repair and service America's fleet of commercial vessels.
73 Members
Founded in 1920

3457 **Society of Accredited Marine Surveyors**
7855 Argyle Forest Blvd
Suite 203
Jacksonville, FL 32244

904-384-1494
800-344-9077; Fax: 904-388-3958
samshq@marinesurvey.org
www.marinesurvey.org

Bill Trenkle, President
Rhea Shea, Executive Director
Susan West, Admin. Assistant, Membership
Mark Shea, Admin. Assistant, Education

Dedicated to the advancement of the profession of marine surveying
1000 Members
Founded in 1986

3458 **Texas Dragon Boat Association**
PO Box 980972
Houston, TX 77098

713-205-7373
webmaster@texasdragonboat.com
www.houstondragonboat.com
Facebook, Twitter

Jim Travlos, Chair
David Mandell, President/Executive Director
Caroline Long, Secretary

Promotes the tradition and sport of dragon boating; increases the awareness of Asian and Asian-American culture; and enhances cross-cultural understanding.

3459 **Traditional Small Craft Association**
PO Box 350
Mystic, CT 06355

Home Page: www.tsca.net
Facebook

David Wyman, President
Ben Sebens, Vice President
David Fitch, Secretary
Bill Meier, Treasurer
John Weiss, Chapter & Membership Coordinator

Nonprofit, tax-exempt educational organization which works to preserve and continue the living traditions, skills, lore and legends surrounding working and pleasure watercraft whose origins predate the marine gasoline engine.

3460 **U.S. Industrial Fabrics Association International**
1801 County Road B W
Roseville, MN 55113-4061

651-222-2508
800-225-4324; Fax: 651-631-9334
generalinfo@ifai.com
www.ifai.com
Facebook, Twitter, LinkedIn, YouTube

Steve Schiffman, President & CEO
Cherie Schmit, Executive Assistant
Sheila Sumner, VP, Finance/Administration
Amy Collins, Director, Sales & Marketing
Linden Wicklund, Director, Events & Member Programs

The mission of the United States Industrial Fabrics Institute (USIFI) is to build a strong coalition of US fiber, fabric, and end product manufacturers and to serve member company interests both domestically and internationally. USIFI is part of the not-for-profit Industrial Fabrics Association International (www.ifai.com), the global association for the specialty fabrics industry.
2000 Members
Founded in 1912

3461 **United States Power Squadrons**
1504 Blue Ridge Rd
Raleigh, NC 27607

919-821-0281
888-367-8777; Fax: 888-304-0813
contactme@HQ.USPS.org
www.usps.org
Facebook, Twitter, LinkedIn, Youtube

A non-profit, educational organization dedicated to making boating safer and more enjoyable by teaching classes in seamanship, navigation and related subjects.
45000 Members
Founded in 1914

3462 **United States Rowing Association**
2 Wall Street
Princeton, NJ 08540

609-751-0700
800-314-4769; Fax: 609-924-1578
members@usrowing.org
www.usrowing.org
Facebook, Twitter, Flickr, Youtube

Amanda Kraus, CEO
Susan Smith, Chief Domestic Officer
Matt Imes, High Performance Director
Traci Stocker, Director, Member Services
Mike Zimmer, Director, National Team Programs

Non-profit membership organization, recognized by the U.S. Olympic Committee as the national governing body for the sport of rowing in the United States.
16000 Members
Founded in 1982

3463 **United States Sailing Association**
15 Maritime Drive
Portsmouth, RI 02871

401-683-0800
800-877-2451; Fax: 401-683-0840
info@ussailing.org
www.ussailing.org
Facebook, Twitter, LinkedIn, Youtube, RSS

Jack Gierhart, Executive Director
Heather Monoson, Chief Financial Officer
Jill Nosach, Chief Development Officer
Mike Waters, Chief Technology Officer
Peter Glass, Chief Marketing Officer

National governing body for the sport of sailing.
100 Members
Founded in 1897

3464 **Yacht Brokers Association of America**
105 Eastern Avenue
Suite 104
Annapolis, MD 21403

410-940-6345; Fax: 410-263-1659
info@ybaa.com
www.ybaa.com
Facebook, Twitter, LinkedIn

Jean-Pierre Skov, Executive Director
Don Smith, Chief Financial Officer
Dominique Abney, Director, Marketing & Sales
Amy Luckado, Director, Membership
Maria Koustenis, Events Coordinator

Sets the standards for professional yacht brokers throughout North America
250 Members
Founded in 1920

3465 **Yachting Club of America**
PO Box 1040
Marco Island, FL 34146

239-642-4448; Fax: 239-642-5284
bill@ycaol.com
www.ycaol.com

David Martin, Owner

A membership organization dedicated to the advancement of yachting.
30000 Members
Founded in 1963

Newsletters

3466 **ASMA News**
American Society of Marine Artists
P.O.Box 247
Smithfield, VA 23430

757-357-3785
asma1978@verizon.net
www.americansocietyofmarineartists.com

Keeps you up to date with all of the Society's activities, along with providing space where artists like yourself can share ideas, inspirations, tips and even frustrations. Provides you access to the Society's network of members, local and national marine art news and information about art exhibitions and exhibition opportunities.
Frequency: Quarterly

3467 **American Boat & Yacht Council News**
American Boat and Yacht Council

613 Third Street
Suite 10
Annapolis, MD 21403

410-990-4460; Fax: 410-990-4466
info@abycinc.org
www.abycinc.org

John Adey, President

News and technical information of interest to ABYC members.
4000+ Members
8 Pages
Frequency: Quarterly
Founded in 1954
Mailing list available for rent

3468 **American Boat Builders and Repairers Association Newsletter**
American Boat Builders and Repairers Association
50 Water Street
Warren, RI 02885

401-247-0318
866-367-6622; Fax: 401-247-0074
www.abbra.org

Jonathan Jones Haven, President
Peter Sabo, VP
Mark Amaral, Managing Director
Charles Teran, Treasurer/Secretary

Accepts advertising.
300 Members
4 Pages
Frequency: Monthly
Founded in 1943

3469 **Anchor Line Newsletter**
National Safe Boating Council
PO Box 509
Bristow, VA 20136

703-361-4294; Fax: 703-361-5294
www.safeboatingcouncil.org
Facebook, Twitter

Joyce Shaw, Chairman
Lynda Nutt, Vice Chairman
Virgil Chambers, Executive Officer
Sandy Smith, Chief Financial Officer
350 Members
Founded in 1958

3470 **BWI Newsletters**
108 Ninth Street
Wilmette, IL 60091

847-736-4142
info@bwi.org
www.bwi.org

Charlie Levine, President
Zuzana Prochazka, Executive Director

Newsletter containing content of interest to recreational boating and fishing activities and the media professionals involved in covering boating industry news.
Founded in 1970

3471 **Business of Pleasure Boats**
National Marine Bankers Association
231 South LaSalle St
Suite 2050
Chicago, IL 60604
312-946-6260
bmcardle@nmma.org
www.marinebankers.org
LinkedIn

Karen Trostle, President
Jackie Forese, Director
Mike Ryan, Vice President
Bernice McArdlen, Manager
81 Members
Frequency: Quarterly
Founded in 1979

3472 **Mainsheet**
Rhodes 19 Class Association
174 Walnut Street
Reading, MA 01867

781-944-2697
info@rhodes19.org
www.rhodes19.org
Facebook

Steve Uhl, President
Mary Kovats, Secretary
Tom Carville, Treasurer

Newsletter concerning the Rhodes 19 design sailboat. Our mission is to promote Rhodes 19 racing by encouraging and supporting local fleet development nationally, and by working to maintain the one-design integrity of the boat.
Founded in 1965

3473 **Marine Safety and Security Report**
Stamler Publishing Company
178 Thimble Islands Rd
PO Box 3367
Branford, CT 06405-1967

203-488-9808
800-422-4121; Fax: 203-488-3129

S Paul Stamler, President/CEO

Business-to-business newsletter providing information on boating and shipping safety and enforcement issues, including federal regulations and Coast Guard Actions, state safety programs, IMO activity, classification studies, vessel recalls, and safety equipment. Accepts no advertising and is solely supported by subscribers worldwide.
Cost: $77.00
4 Pages
Founded in 1973
Printed in 2 colors on matte stock

3474 **Maritime Reporter and Engineering News**
118 East 25th Street
New York, NY 10010

212-477-6700; Fax: 212-254-6271
jomalley@marinelink.com
www.marinelink.com

John O'Malley, Publisher
Greg Trauthwein, Associate Publisher
Michael Martino, Owner
Lucia M Annunziata, VP
Jennifer Rabulan, Technical Editor

Provides unparalleled coverage of the maritime industry covering the inland, Coastal and Great Lakes region.
95000 Members
Frequency: Monthly
Circulation: 50000
Founded in 1999

3475 **NACO Newsletter**
National Association of Charterboat Operators
PO Box 2990
Orange Beach, AL 36561

251-981-5136; Fax: 251-981-8191
info@nacocharters.org
www.nacocharters.org

Bob Zales II, President
Butch Smith, Vice President
Ron Maglio, Treasurer
Charlie Phillips, Secretary
Susan Mason-Yadav, Executive Director
3600+ Members
Frequency: Quarterly
Circulation: 3500
Founded in 1991

3476 **Propeller Club Newsletter**
Propeller Club of the United States
3927 Old Lee Hwy
Suite 101A
Fairfax, VA 22030-2422

703-691-2777; Fax: 703-691-4173
shannon@propellerclubhq.com
www.propellerclubhq.com

Thomas Allegretti, President/CEO
Niels Aalund, Sr. Vice President
Shannon Hendrickson-Pluta, Admin Asst
Virgil R Allen, VP Development

Features expanded coverage of Propeller Club activities, including legislative and regulatory reports, feature-length member profiles, regional news and expanded coverage of national maritime issues.
10000 Members
Frequency: Quarterly
Founded in 1927

3477 **Rudder**
Antique & Classic Boat Society
422 James St
Clayton, NY 13624-1136

315-686-2628; Fax: 315-686-2680
hqs@acbs.org
www.acbs.org
Facebook, Twitter

Jim Mersman, President
Dunc Hawkins, First VP
Teresa Hoffman, Second VP
Dick Winn, Treasurer
Brian Gagnon, Secretary

Historical news and how-to-restore wooden and antique boats.
12000 Members
Frequency: Quarterly
Founded in 1975
Printed in 4 colors

3478 **SAMS Newsletter**
Society of Accredited Marine Surveyors
7855 Argyle Forest Blvd
Suite 203
Jacksonville, FL 32244

904-384-1494
800-344-9077; Fax: 904-388-3958
samshq@marinesurvey.org
www.marinesurvey.org

Bill Trenkle, President

For members.
1000 Members
Frequency: 4/Year
Circulation: 1000
Founded in 1986

3479 **Seamanship Training**
American Boating Association
PO Box 1597
Ocean View, DE 19970

614-497-4088
admin@americanboating.org
www.americanboating.org
Facebook

Bill Condon, Founder/President

Free to all ABA (American Boating Association) members as well as all boaters. Informative content on boating skills and safety issues.
30000 Members
Frequency: Bi-Monthly

3480 **Shipyard Chronicle Newsletter**
Shipbuilders Council of America
655 Fifteenth St NW
Suite 225
Washington, DC 20005

202-347-5462; Fax: 202-347-5464
Facebook

Matt Paxton, President, Vice Chairman
Allen Walker, President
Irene Ringwood, Manager

The publication is devoted to keeping members up to date on the latest legislative and regulatory developments. It also includes a schedule of upcoming association and industry related government meetings, as well as news regarding SCA member companies.
73 Members
Founded in 1920

3481 **Soundings Trade Only**
Soundings Publications
10 Bokum Rd
Essex, CT 06426-1536

860-767-3200; Fax: 860-767-1048
info@soundingspub.com
www.soundingsonline.com
Facebook

Ian Bowen, Manager
Peter Mitchel, Publisher

Nation's boating business newspaper. Coverage of the recreational boating business; for marine dealers, marine operators, distributors and manufacturers. BPA audited.
Cost: $13.97
15500 Members
33 Pages
Frequency: Monthly
Circulation: 34,000
Founded in 1965

3482 **The ABA Beacon**
American Boating Association
PO Box 1597
Ocean View, DE 19970

614-497-4088
admin@americanboating.org
www.americanboating.org

Bill Condon, Founder & President

Free to all ABA (American Boating Association) members as well as all boaters.
30000 Members

3483 **Tidings**
National Marine Representatives Association
1333 Delany Road #500
PO Box 360
Gurnee, IL 60031

847-662-3167; Fax: 847-336-7126
info@nmraonline.org
www.nmraonline.org

Chris Kelly, President
Kathy Munzinger, VP
Ken Smaga, Treasurer
Brandon Flack, Secretary
Chris Kelly, Secretary

Contains informative articles to help manufacturers develop sound and profitable relationships with independent sales representatives and keep informed about the marine market in general.
300 Members
500+ Pages
Frequency: Quarterly
Founded in 1960

3484 **Water Life**
Northwest Marine Trade Association
1900 N Northlake Way
Suite 233
Seattle, WA 98103-9087

206-634-0911; Fax: 206-632-0078
info@nmta.net
www.nmta.net
Facebook, Twitter, LinkedIn

George Harris, President
Laura Snodgrass, Finance Director
John Thorburn, Vice President
Liz Manning, Membership Director

Provides industry information, member benefits, committee activity and new member announcements and anniversaries. Water Life continues to evolve into a valuable tool for Pacific Northwest marine leaders.
700+ Members
Founded in 1947

3485 **Yacht Broker News**
Yacht Brokers Association of America
105 Eastern Avenue
Suite 104
Annapolis, MD 21403

410-940-6345; Fax: 410-263-1659
info@ybaa.com
www.ybaa.com

Jean-Pierre Skov, Executive Director

Reports on latest business issues, industry concerns, legislation, regulatory activities and includes a member-to-member section(WayPoints), where members can report on their own company news, personnel updates and business expansion.
250 Members
Frequency: Quarterly
Founded in 1920

Magazines & Journals

3486 **American Sailor**
US Sailing Association
15 Maritime Drive
PO Box 1260
Portsmouth, RI 02871-0907

401-683-0800
800-877-2451; Fax: 401-683-0840
info@ussailing.org
www.ussailing.org
Facebook, Twitter, LinkedIn

Tom Hubbell, Us Sailing President
Jack Gierhart, Executive Director
Fred Hagedorn, Secretary
Jack Gierhart, Executive Director

Boating news.
100 Members
Frequency: Monthly
Founded in 1980

3487 **Ash Breeze**
Traditional Small Craft Association
PO Box 350
Mystic, CT 06355

drathmarine@rockisland.com
www.tsca.net

Mike Wick, Co-Editor
Ned Asplundh, Co-Editor

Devoted to topics ranging from reports from the chapters to technical details and specific designs with lines and offsets. You may find anecdotal accounts of experiences in traditional boats, and tips on how to spile a plank.
Frequency: Quarterly

3488 **Boat & Motor Dealer**
Preston Publications
6600 W Touhy Ave
PO Box 48312
Niles, IL 60714-4516

847-647-2900; Fax: 847-647-1155

Tinsley Preston, Owner
Jerome Koncel, Editorial Director

Dedicated to providing businesses in the recreational marine industry with the information, commentary and analysis needed to expand their businesses and improve profitability.
Founded in 1959
Mailing list available for rent: 30000 names at $100 per M

3489 **BoatUS Magazine**
Boat Owners Association of the US
880 South Pickett Street
Alexandria, VA 22304-4606

703-461-2864; Fax: 703-461-2845
www.boatus.com
Facebook, Twitter

Michael Vatalaro, Executive Editor
Richard Schwartz, Chairman/Founder
Chris Landers, Associate Editor

Boating magazine includes legislative, travel, safety, DIY, and consumer news of interest to recreational boat owners.
Cost: $19.00
62500 Members
Frequency: Annual/6
Circulation: 500K+
Founded in 1966

3490 **Boatbuilder**
Belvoir Publishers
PO Box 5656
Norwalk, CT 06856-5656
203-857-4880; Fax: 203-661-4802
customer_service@belvoir.com
www.belvoir.com

Robert Englander, Owner/CEO

The magazine is for those who build, modify and repair boats.
Founded in 1972

3491 **Boating Industry**
Ehlert Publishing Group
6420 Sycamore Ln N
Suite 100
Maple Grove, MN 55369-6014

763-383-4400
800-848-6247; Fax: 763-383-4499
www.boatingindustry.com
Facebook, Twitter, LinkedIn

Jonathan Sweet, Editor in Chief
Tom Kaiser, Senior Editor

Links together all sectors of the boating market from boat and motor dealers to marinas, boatyards, builders and suppliers. It also provides strategic analysis, in-depth coverage and proprietary research of the most critical issues.
Frequency: 8 Issues/2 Special Issues

3492 **Boating Magazine**
Bonnier Corporation
460 N. Orlando Ave
Suite 200
Winter Park, FL 32789

407-628-4802; Fax: 407-628-7061
editor@boatingmag.com
www.boatingmag.com
Facebook, Twitter

John McEver, Publisher
Glenn Hughes, VP
Jonas Bonnier, Chairman

Offers up-to-date information on boats, manufacturers, suppliers, distributors related to the boating industry.
Cost: $17.95
Frequency: Monthly

3493 **Canoe & Kayak Magazine**
Canoe & Kayak
12025 115th Ave. NE
Suite D200
Kirkland, WA 98034

425-827-6363
800-692-2663; Fax: 425-827-1893
letters@canoekayak.com
www.canoekayak.com
Facebook, Twitter

Jeff Moag, Editor
Dave Shively, Managing Editor

Published by the Canoe American Associates.
Cost: $17.95
Frequency: 7 Issues
Circulation: 62000
Founded in 1973
Mailing list available for rent

3494 **Dry Stack Marina Handbook**
Association of Marina Industries
50 Water Street
Warren, RI 02885

866-367-6622; Fax: 401-247-0074
info@marinaassociation.org
www.marinaassociation.org
Twitter, LinkedIn

Jim Frye, CMM, Chairman/President
Gary Groenewold, Vice Chairman
Jeff Rose, Treasurer
Keith Boulais, Secretary

This book covers: Dry stack buildings and racks, Boat handling equipment, Statistics, Site planning, Typical costs, Fire protection problems & solutions, Comparision of dry stack vs. wet slip demand, Marketing, Facility operations, Lease or purchase decision, Loss control considerations.
Cost: $90.00
800+ Members
Frequency: 61 Illustrations
Founded in 1986

3495 **Ensign**
United States Power Squadrons
1504 Blue Ridge Rd
Raleigh, NC 27607-3906

919-821-0281
888-367-8777; Fax: 888-304-0813
www.usps.org
Facebook, Twitter

Frank A. Dvorak, Executive Officer

Ensign magazine is the official magazine of United States Power Squadrons. The mission is to promote recreational boating safety through education and civic activities while providing fellowship for our members.
Cost: $10.00
45000 Members
48 Pages
Frequency: Monthly
Circulation: 35,000
Founded in 1914
Printed in 4 colors on glossy stock

3496 **Fabric Architecture**
U.S. Industrial Fabrics Association International
1801 County Road B W
Roseville, MN 55113-4061

651-222-2508
800-225-4324; Fax: 651-631-9334
generalinfo@ifai.com
www.usifi.com

Stephen Warner, CEO
JoAnne Ferris, Marketing Director

Targets architects, designers, specifiers, contractors and developers promoting the architectural advantages of fabric. Educates the industry about designing with fabric and promoting it as an environmentally-responsible choice.
Frequency: Bimonthly
Circulation: 8,000

3497 **Fabric Graphics**
Industrial Fabrics Association International
1801 County Road B W
Roseville, MN 55113-4061

651-222-2508
800-225-4324; Fax: 651-631-9334
generalinfo@ifai.com
www.ifai.com
Facebook, Twitter, LinkedIn

Mary J. Hennessy, Executive VP
JoAnne Farris, Marketing Director
Steven C. Rider, CFO, VP

Created to educate and inspire professionals to use fabric to expand their business. Promotes the use of textiles as a printing medium, showcasing the numerous applications for fabric and the technology needed to achieve good results.
Frequency: Bimonthly
Circulation: 8,000
Founded in 1912

3498 **Geosynthetics**
Industrial Fabrics Association International
1801 County Road B W
Roseville, MN 55113-4061

651-222-2508
800-225-4324; Fax: 651-631-9334
generalinfo@ifai.com
www.ifai.com
Facebook, Twitter, LinkedIn

Todd Berger, Senior Editor

Targeting those who rely on the publication for the most professional presentation of Geosynthetic products, design, and applications.
Frequency: Bimonthly
Circulation: 14,000
Founded in 1912

3499 **InTents**
Industrial Fabrics Association International
1801 County Road B W
Roseville, MN 55113-4061

651-222-2508
800-225-4324; Fax: 651-631-9334
generalinfo@ifai.com
www.ifai.com
Facebook, Twitter, LinkedIn

Sammi Jones, Editor

Focuses on tents, fabric structures, and accessories that tent renters need to operate a profitable business. The magazine and its website work together to deliver the total tent experience to readers and visitors.
Frequency: Bimonthly
Circulation: 11,000
Founded in 1912

3500 **Marina/Dock Age**
Preston Publications
6600 W Touhy Ave
Niles, IL 60714-4516

847-647-2900; Fax: 847-647-1155
atownshend@marinadockage.com
www.marinadockage.com/
Twitter, LinkedIn

Tinsley Preston, Owner
Anna Townshend, Editor

Provide marina/boatyard owners and managers with the information they need to meet ever-changing government regulations, operate more efficiently, expand their business, and improve their profitability.
Cost: $50.00
16500 Members
Frequency: Monthly
Circulation: 24000
Founded in 1989

3501 **Marinas and Small Craft Harbors**
Association of Marina Industries
50 Water Street
Warren, RI 02885

866-367-6622; Fax: 401-247-0074
info@marinaassociation.org
www.marinaassociation.org
Twitter, LinkedIn

Jim Frye, CMM, Chairman/President
Gary Groenewold, Vice Chairman
Jeff Rose, Treasurer
Keith Boulais, Secretary

The new edition includes updated and redrawn tables, charts, figures and text editing and additions, as well as newly created information on marina design characteristics of megyachts and test data, design loads, and recommendations on design and performance of dock cleats.
Cost: $89.95
800+ Members
Founded in 1986

3502 **Marine Fabricator**
Industrial Fabrics Association International
1801 County Road B W
Roseville, MN 55113-4061

651-222-2508
800-225-4324; Fax: 651-631-9334
generalinfo@ifai.com
www.ifai.com
Facebook, Twitter, LinkedIn

Elisa Bernick, Senior Editor

Educates professionals in the techniques of quality marine craftsmanship and upholstery. Marine shop professionals rely on the magazine to stay informed on the latest techniques, technologies, business management and news. .
Cost: $34.00
Frequency: Bi-Monthly
Circulation: 5,000
Founded in 1912

3503 **Marine Log**
Simmons-Boardman Publishing Corporation
345 Hudson St
12th Floor, Suite 1201
New York, NY 10014-7123

212-620-7200; Fax: 212-633-1165
www.marinelog.com
Facebook, Twitter, LinkedIn

Arthur J McGinnis Jr, President
John Snyder, Publisher/Editor in Chief

For more than 130 years, maritime executives worldwide have turned to Marine Log as the source for news and analysis on issues impacting vessel design, construction and operations.
Frequency: Monthly
Circulation: 29934
Founded in 1878

3504 **Marine News**
Maritime Activity Reports
118 East 25th Street
New York, NY 10010

212-477-6700; Fax: 212-254-6271
jomalley@marinelink.com
www.marinelink.com

John O'Malley, Publisher
Greg Trauthwein, Associate Publisher
Michael Martino, Owner
Lucia M Annunziata, VP
Jennifer Rabulan, Technical Editor

Features marine industry news and issues effecting maritime activity. Includes updates on vessel building and acquisitions as well as regular columns on research and devleopment, equipment reports and an events calendar.
95000 Members
Frequency: Monthly
Circulation: 23000
Founded in 1999

3505 **Motor Boating**
Time4 Media Marine Group

460 N. Orlando Ave
Suite 200
Winter Park, FL 32789

407-628-4802; Fax: 407-628-7061
Facebook, Twitter

Ed Baker, Associate Publisher
John McEver, Publisher
Glenn Hughes, VP

Helps its readers buy, maintain and get the most out of their powerboats. It focuses on powerboats, people, products, destinations, trends and technological developments in the boating market, as well as cruising, water sports and safety.
Frequency: Monthly
Founded in 1907
Printed in on glossy stock

3506 **National Numbering & Titling**
National Association of State Boating Law
1500 Leestown Rd
Suite 330
Lexington, KY 40511-2047

859-225-9487; Fax: 859-231-6403
info@nasbla.org
www.nasbla.org
Facebook, Twitter, LinkedIn, Flickr, Foursquare

John Johnson, Executive Director
Tom Hayward, Finance & Administration
Ron Sarver, Deputy Director

Facilitate ongoing efforts to evaluate and improve the programs' internal procedures and external interactions in the face of resource constraints and in preparation for implementing the Coast Guard's Vessel Identification System.
Cost: $14.95
56 Members
Founded in 1960
Mailing list available for rent: 56 names

3507 **Paddle Magazine**
Paddle Sport Publishing
12025 115th Ave. NE
Suite D200
Kirkland, WA 98034

970-879-1450; Fax: 970-870-1404
www.paddlermagazine.com
Facebook, Twitter

Eugene Buchanan, Publisher/Editor
Jeff Moag, Editor
Kevin Thompson, Account Manager

Information to keep the paddle sport equipment dealer up-to-date on issues that will effect their business, industry trends in boats, apparel and accessories, how to articles to assist the reader in selling boats.
Cost: $18.00
Circulation: 5527
Printed in 4 colors on glossy stock

3508 **Paddlesports Business**
Canoe & Kayak
12025 115th Ave. NE
Suite D200
Kirkland, WA 98034

425-827-6363
800-692-2663; Fax: 425-827-1893
letters@canoekayak.com
www.canoekayak.com
Facebook, Twitter

Jeff Moag, Editor
Dave Shively, Managing Editor

Trade publication for the paddlesports industry.
Founded in 1973
Mailing list available for rent

3509 **Professional BoatBuilder**
WoodenBoat Publications
41 Wooden Boat La
PO Box 78
Brooklin, ME 04616-0078

207-359-4651
800-877-5284; Fax: 207-359-8920
proboat@proboat.com
www.proboat.com
Facebook

Paul Lazarus, Sr. Editor
Aaron Porter, Editor
Carl Cramer, Co-Director

Focuses on materials, design, and construction techniques and repair solutions chosen by marine professionals. Regular technical articles provide detailed, real-world examples to improve the efficiency and quality of their work.
Cost: $35.95
76 Pages
Circulation: 27500
ISSN: 1043-2035
Founded in 1974
Printed in 4 colors on glossy stock

3510 **Propeller**
American Power Boat Association
17640 E. Nine Mile Road
PO Box 377
Eastpointe, MI 48021-0377

586-773-9700; Fax: 586-773-6490
propeller@apba-racing.com
www.apba-racing.com

Holly Jones, Editor
Tana Moore, Editor

Propeller magazine is the mouthpiece of the American Power Boat Association, the nation's leading authority on power boat racing which sanctions over 200 races each year.
Cost: $2.50
22 Pages
Frequency: Monthly
ISSN: 0194-6218
Printed in 4 colors on glossy stock

3511 **Small Craft Advisory**
National Association of State Boating Law Admnstrs
1500 Leestown Rd
Suite 330
Lexington, KY 40511-2047

859-225-9487; Fax: 859-231-6403
info@nasbla.org
www.nasbla.org
Facebook, Twitter, LinkedIn, Flickr, Foursquare

John Johnson, Executive Director
Tom Hayward, Finance & Administration
Ron Sarver, Deputy Director

Small Craft Advisory, published bimonthly, is for and about the nation's boating law administration professionals. Authoritative articles featuring practices, procedures, and research in recreational boating safety, marine law enforcement, and boating safety education are presented to enhance the efficiency and effectiveness of recreational boating safety. Each issue highlights successful recreational boating safety programs, NASBLA activities, professional news, and legislative updates
Cost: $14.00
56 Members
Frequency: Bi-Monthly
Circulation: 11000
Founded in 1960
Mailing list available for rent: 56 names

3512 **Southern Boating Magazine**
330 N Andrews Ave
Suite 200
Fort Lauderdale, FL 33301-1025

954-522-5515
888-882-6284; Fax: 954-522-2260
sboating@southernboating.com
www.southernboating.com
Facebook, Twitter

Skip Allen, Owner/Chairman/Publisher/Editor
L.J. Wallace, Executive Editor
Cathryn Allen-Zubi, VP
Rain Hernandez Rouveroy, VP of Finance
Kellie Mackenroth, Circulation Manager

Focus is on boating in the southern US, Bahamas, and Caribbean.
Cost: $22.95
Frequency: Monthly
Circulation: 42000
Founded in 1972
Printed in 4 colors on matte stock

3513 **Specialty Fabrics Review**
Industrial Fabrics Association International
1801 County Road B W
Roseville, MN 55113-4061

651-222-2508
800-225-4324; Fax: 651-631-9334
generalinfo@ifai.com
www.ifai.com
Facebook, Twitter, LinkedIn

Jill Lafferty, Editor
Elisa Bernick, Associate Editor

In print since 1915, this international publication targets specialty fabric professionals. Each issue brings timely reporting on industry topics, helpful business articles and a review of global news and market updates.
Frequency: Monthly
Circulation: 13000
Founded in 1912

3514 **The Reference Point**
American Boat and Yacht Council
613 Third Street
Suite 10
Annapolis, MD 21403

410-990-4460; Fax: 410-990-4466
info@abycinc.org
www.abycinc.org
Facebook

John Adey, President

ABYC's technical professional quarterly journal.
4000+ Members
Frequency: Quarterly
Founded in 1954

3515 **US Yacht Racing Union**
US Sailing
15 Maritime Drive
PO Box 1260
Portsmouth, RI 02871-0907

401-683-0800
800-877-2451; Fax: 401-683-0840
info@ussailing.org
www.ussailing.org
Facebook, Twitter, LinkedIn

Gary Jobson, Us Sailing President
Tom Hubbell, Vice President
Fred Hagedorn, Secretary
Jack Gierhart, Executive Director

National news of the Union, the latest in yacht racing, and dealers of yachts are covered.
100 Members
Founded in 1986

3516 **UnderWater Magazine**
Naylor, LLC
5950 NW 1st Place
Gainesville, FL 32607

800-369-6220
www.underwater.com

Jamie Williams, Publication Director
Sean Garrity, Editorial
Rebecca Roberts, Marketing Manager

It covers the entire spectrum of underwater contracting, vehicles and technology.
Cost: $50.00
500 Members
Founded in 1968

3517 **WoodenBoat**
WoodenBoat Publications
41 Wooden Boat La
PO Box 78
Brooklin, ME 04616-0078

207-359-4651
800-877-5284; Fax: 207-359-8920
www.woodenboat.com
Facebook

Tom Jackson, Sr. Editor
Carl Cramer, Publisher
Matt Murphy, Editor

Provides readers with a dynamic editorial environment that combines technologies with traditional methods of boat design, construction and repair. The magazine is about craftmanship in wood, and its active boating audience works at all levels of expertise to build, restore, and maintain their boats.
Cost: $29.95
160 Pages
Frequency: Bi-Monthly
Circulation: 98000
Founded in 1974

3518 **WorkBoat**
Diversified Business Communications
121 Free Street
Portland, ME 04101

207-842-5600; Fax: 207-842-5611
info@divcom.com
www.workboat.com
Facebook, Twitter

Mike Lodato, VP
Ken Hocke, Senior Editor
David Krapf, Editor In Chief
Jerry Fraser, Publisher

Commercial marine publication serving the North American inland and coastal waterways—the most active sector in the commercial marine market today. Consisting of captains, owners, managers, operators, chief engineers and other industry professionals, the Workboat audience represents important and influential purchasing power in the commercial marine industry.
Cost: $39.00
Frequency: Monthly
Circulation: 25000
ISSN: 0043-8014
Founded in 1949

3519 **Yachting Magazine**
Time4 Media Marine Group
PO Box 420235
Palm Coast, FL 32142-0235

386-597-4382
800-999-0869
letters@yachtingmagazine.com
www.yachtingmagazine.com
Facebook, Twitter

Ed Baker, Associate Publisher
Rich Rasor, East Coast Sales Director

Covers the finest boats, electronics and equipment, including large yachts and yacht charters. It also covers the passions, adventures and lifestyles of active, affluent boat owners.
Frequency: Monthly
Founded in 1907

3520 **Young Mariners Guide**
Yachting Club of America
PO Box 1040
Marco Island, FL 34146

239-642-4448; Fax: 239-642-5284
ycaol@hotmail.com
www.ycaol.com

David Martin, Owner

Designed to inform and teach young people about boating in simple and handy pocket book to help them on their way to becoming the future of the yachting fraternity in America.
Cost: $5.00
30000 Members
32 Pages
Frequency: Softbound
Founded in 1963
Mailing list available for rent

Trade Shows

3521 **Annual American and Canadian Sport, Travel and Outdoor Show**
Expositions, Inc.
Edgewater Branch
PO Box 550
Cleveland, OH 44107-0550

216-529-1300; Fax: 216-529-0311
showinfo@expoinc.com
www.expoinc.com

Chris Fassnacht, President
Robert Attewell, Vice President
David Rosar, CFO, VP

975 exhibits of hunting and fishing equipment, travel services, boats, recreational vehicles and related equipment, supplies and services.
300k Attendees
Frequency: March
Founded in 1937

3522 **Annual Boat & Fishing Show at the Lansing Center**
Show Span, Inc
2121 Celebration Drive NE
Grand Rapids, MI 49525

616-447-2860
800-328-6550; Fax: 616-447-2861
events@showspan.com
www.showspan.com

John Loeks, President
Henri Boucher, Vice President
Mike Wilbraham, VP, Show Producer

Held in Lansing, Michigan.
Frequency: March
Founded in 1945

3523 **Annual Boat Show**
General Sports Shows/NMMA
231 S. LaSalle St
Suite 2050
Chicago, IL 60604

312-946-6200
800-777-4766
bmcardle@nmma.org

Jennifer Thompson, Show Manager
Bonnie Schuenemann, Special Events Coordinator
Patty Gibbs, Media Contact

Enjoy 5 days of boating fun, education and one-stop shopping with hundreds of boats and exhibits and special attractions all under one roof.
Frequency: January

3524 **Annual Boat Show & Fishing Exposition**
Greenband Enterprises
3450 South Highland Drive
Suite 105
Salt Lake City, UT 84106

801-485-7399
800-657-3050; Fax: 801-485-0687
showinfo@greenband.com
www.greenband.com
Facebook

Jonathan D Greenband, Show Manager
Debra Greenband, Sales Manager

See the latest in Ski Boats, Cruisers, Fishing Boats, everything for boating fun.
45000 Attendees
Frequency: Annual, February
Founded in 1965

3525 **Annual Boat, Vacation and Outdoor Show**
Showtime Productions, Inc.
PO Box 4372
Rockford, IL 61110

815-877-8043; Fax: 815-877-9037
brenda@showtimeproduction.net
showtimeproduction.net

Tom Pellant, President
Brenda Rotoco, Event Coordinator

Boat, travel, outdoor equipment, supplies, and services plus demonstrations.
28000 Attendees
Frequency: February
Founded in 1970

3526 **Annual Conference & Educational Symposia**
Society of Accredited Marine Surveyors
7855 Argyle Forest Blvd
Suite 203
Jacksonville, FL 32244

904-384-1494
800-344-9077; Fax: 904-388-3958
samshq@marinesurvey.org
www.marinesurvey.org

Bill Trenkle, President
1000 Members
350 Attendees
Frequency: Annual/Fall
Founded in 1986

3527 **Annual Conference on Sail Training and Tall Ships**
American Sail Training Association
29 Touro Street
PO Box 1459
Newport, RI 02840

401-846-1775; Fax: 401-849-5400
asta@sailtraining.org
www.tallships.sailtraining.org
Facebook, Twitter, LinkedIn, Youtube

Mike Rauworth, Chairman
Robert Rogers, Executive Director
Caleb Pifer, Vice Chair
300 Members
Frequency: November
Founded in 1973

3528 **Annual Iowa Boat and Vacation Show**
Iowa Show Productions
PO Box 2460
Waterloo, IA 50704-2460

319-232-0218; Fax: 319-235-8932
info@iowashows.com
www.iowashows.com

John Bunge, Show Manager

Over 25 dealers, 40 brands, 100's of models. Family runabouts, fishing boats, cabin cruisers, cuddies, power boats, waterski boats, personal watercraft, jet boats, bass boats, walleye boats,

deck boats, pontoons, fish/ski boats, and marine accessories.
Frequency: January
Founded in 1975
Mailing list available for rent

3529 **Annual Lido Yacht Expo**
Duncan McIntosh Company
17782 Cowan, Ste A
Irvine, CA 92614
949-757-5959; Fax: 949-660-6172
www.lidoyachtexpo.com
Facebook
Duncan McIntosh, President
Jeff Fleming, Associate Publisher
An upscale in-the-water show of yachts and big boats. More than 2,000 feet of floating dock.
Frequency: May
Founded in 1973

3530 **Annual National Capital Boat Show**
GS Media & Events
250 Parkway Drive
Suite 270
Lincolnshire, IL 60069
800-848-6274; Fax: 270-438-4723
www.nationalcapitalboatshow.com
Ryan Reinke, Account Executive/Show Manager
Michael Alexander, Account Executive
Nearly 40 dealers form throughout Maryland and Virginia bring a wide range of boats to the National Capital Boat Show including saltware fishing boats, ski boats, runabouts, motor yachts, jet boats, jon boats, PWC, bass boats, inflatables, deck boats and pontoons.
Frequency: Annual/March

3531 **Annual Spring Boat Show**
Southern California Marine Association
1006 East Chapman Ave
Orange, CA 92866
714-633-7581; Fax: 714-633-9498
www.scma.com
Facebook, Twitter
Richard Tressler, President
Renee Acencio, Vice President
You'll find a assortment of marine accessory booths featuring the latest and newest products filled with everything that floats, affordable family runabounts, ski boats, fishing boats, cruisers, pontoons, performance sportboats and personal watercraft.
Frequency: June
Founded in 1956

3532 **Annual Spring New Products Show**
Pacific Expositions c/o Tihati Productions
3615 Harding Ave
Suite 506
Honolulu, HI 96816
808-732-6037; Fax: 808-732-6039
info@pacificexpos.com
www.pacificexpos.com
Tara Chanel-Thompson, Director/General Manager
The newest and most exciting products on land and sea with 320 exhibits for trade professionals, buyers, and the general public.
17000 Attendees
Frequency: Annual, April
Founded in 1974

3533 **Association of Marina Industries Annual Conference**
Association of Marina Industries
50 Water Street
Warren, RI 02885
866-367-6622; Fax: 401-247-0074
info@marinaassociation.org
www.marinaassociation.org
Twitter, LinkedIn
Jim Frye, CMM, Chairman/President
Gary Groenewold, Chairman
Brad Gross, Treasurer
Keith Boulais, Secretary
800+ Members
Frequency: May
Founded in 1986

3534 **Atlanta Boat Show**
National Marine Manufacturers Association
200 E Randolph Drive
Suite 1500
Chicago, IL 60601
954-441-3228
lberryman@nmma.org
www.atlantaboatshow.com
Facebook, Twitter
Larry Berryman, Show Manager
Scott Cohens, Relationship Manager
Sarah Ryser, PR Manager
Venus Berryman, Show Administrator
Debbie Harewood, Director, Shows Administration
Showcases the latest in boating products and marine technology. 225 exhibitors.
Frequency: January
Founded in 1961

3535 **Atlantic City In-Water Power Boat Show**
In-Water Power Boat Show
1650 Market St
36th Floor
Philadelphia, PA 19103
215-732-8001; Fax: 215-732-8266
info@acinwaterboatshow.com
www.acinwaterboatshow.com
Facebook, Twitter
Jerry Flaxman, Executive VP
This show provides space for over 700 boats on land and in-water and over 200 booths in the marine marketplace, including 2 tents and walkways along the piers. Showcases the new models for each coming year.
Frequency: September
Founded in 1983

3536 **Atlantic City International Power Boat Show**
National Marine Manufacturers Association
37-18 Northern Blvd
Suite 311
Long Islang City, NY 11101
718-707-0719; Fax: 888-649-7786
jpritko@nmma.org
www.acboatshow.com
Facebook, Twitter
Jon Pritko, Show Manager
Josh Rosales, Operations Manager
Showcases more than 700 all-new models of motor and express yachts, sports fisherman, cruisers and sport boats. Attracts boaters from all of the East Coast.
50000 Attendees
Frequency: February

3537 **Boat Show of Grand Rapids**
Show Span
2121 Celebration Drive NE
Grand Rapids, MI 49525
616-472-2860
800-328-6550; Fax: 616-447-2861
events@showspan.com
www.showspan.com
John Loeks, President
Henri Boucher, Vice President
Mike Wilbraham, VP, Show Producer
Over 400 exhibits of power and sail boats, accessories, clocks, dockominiums and vacation destinations. Held at the Grand Center in Grand Rapids, Michigan.
Frequency: February
Founded in 1945

3538 **Boat Show of New England**
North America Expositions Company
33 Rutherford Avenue
Boston, MA 02129-3795
617-472-1442
800-225-1577; Fax: 617-242-1817
joneal@nmma.org
www.newenglandboatshow.com
Facebook, Twitter
Joseph B O'Neal, Managing Partner
Bob McAlpine, Operations Manager
Over 600 boats on display, both power and sailboats ranging from dinghies to 45 foot yachts, along with every conceivable accessory for your new or present boat.
215M Attendees
Frequency: February

3539 **Brokerage Yacht Show**
Yachting Promotions
1115 NE 9th Avenue
Fort Lauderdale, FL 33304-2110
954-764-7642
800-940-7642; Fax: 954-462-4140
info@showmanagement.com
www.showmanagement.com
Facebook, Twitter
Steve Sheer, Director Advertising
Kaye Pearson, President
The totally in-water presentation features over 500 new and pre-owned vessels.
Frequency: February
Founded in 1976
Mailing list available for rent

3540 **Dealer Week**
Marine Retailers Association of America
8401 73rd Avenue N
Suite 71
Oak Park, IL 60304
763-315-8043
mraa@mraa.com
www.mraa.com
Facebook, Twitter, LinkedIn
Matt Gruhn, President
Liz Walz, Director

3541 **Education Under Sail Forum**
American Sail Training Association
29 Touro Street
PO Box 1459
Newport, RI 02840
401-846-1775; Fax: 401-849-5400
asta@sailtraining.org
www.tallships.sailtraining.org
Facebook, Twitter, Youtube
Mike Rauworth, Chairman
Robert Rogers, Executive Director
300 Members
Frequency: Biennial
Founded in 1973

3542 **IBEX Annual Conference**
National Marine Manufacturers Association
231 S. LaSalle St
Suite 2050
Chicago, IL 60604
312-946-6200; Fax: 312-946-0401
www.nmma.org
Frank Hugelmeyer, President
Robert Newsome, SVP, Operations
Craig Boskey, SVP, Finance & CFO

Exhibition features the products and processes now available that will streamline your boatbuilding business. See the advanced technologies ready for the upcoming model-year. Featuring 800 OEMs and suppliers, the exhibit halls offer you an opportunity to source and compare every tool available to boatbuilders.
Frequency: November
Founded in 1979

3543 **IFAI Expo Americas**
Internationl Fabrics Association International
1801 County Road B W
Roseville, MN 55113-4061

651-222-2508
800-225-4324; Fax: 651-631-9334
generalinfo@ifai.com
www.ifaiexpo.com
Facebook, Twitter, LinkedIn

Mary J. Hennessy, Executive VP
JoAnne Farris, Marketing Director
Steven C. Rider, CFO, VP

A trade event in the Americas for the technical textiles and specialty fabrics industry.
Frequency: Annual/October
Founded in 1912

3544 **International Boating and Water Safety Summit**
National Safe Boating Council
PO Box 509
Bristow, VA 20136

703-361-4294; Fax: 703-361-5294
office@safeboatingcouncil.org
www.safeboatingcouncil.org
Facebook, Twitter, Youtube

Joyce Shaw, Chair
Chris Edmonston, Vice Chair
Veronica Floyd, Past Chair
Frequency: April

3545 **International Conference of Professional Yacht Brokers**
Yacht Brokers Association of America
105 Eastern Avenue
Suite 104
Annapolis, MD 21403

410-940-6345; Fax: 410-263-1659
info@ybaa.com
www.ybaa.com
Facebook, Twitter, LinkedIn

Jean-Pierre Skov, Executive Director
Maria Koustenis, Events Coordinator
250 Members
Frequency: Annual
Founded in 1920

3546 **International Marina & Boatyard Conference**
American Boat Builders and Repairers Association
50 Water Street
Warren, RI 02885

401-247-0318
866-367-6622; Fax: 401-247-0074
info@marinaassociation.org
www.abbra.org
Twitter, LinkedIn

Jim Frye, CMM, Chairman/President
Gary Groenewold, Chairman
Brad Gross, Treasurer
Keith Boulais, Secretary

The conference is designed to meet the growing demand among those delivering the boating experience for an international forum for education and exposition.
800+ Members
Frequency: Annual
Founded in 1986

3547 **International WorkBoat Show**
The International WorkBoat Show
121 Fine Street
PO Box 7437
Portland, ME 04101-7437

207-842-5500; Fax: 207-842-5503
customerservice@divcom.com
www.workboatshow.com
Facebook, Twitter

Chris Dimmerling, Sales Director
Bob Callahan, Show Director
Denielle Christensen, Marketing Manager

The largest commercial marine tradeshow in North America, serving people in coastal, inland and offshore waters. It features 1000 exhibiting companies and is produced in partnership with WorkBoat magazine.
Frequency: Annual
Founded in 1978

3548 **MEGATEX**
Industrial Fabrics Association International
1801 County Road B W
Roseville, MN 55113-4061

651-222-2508
800-225-4324; Fax: 651-631-9334
generalinfo@ifai.com
www.ifai.com
Facebook, Twitter, LinkedIn

Mary J. Hennessy, Executive VP
JoAnne Farris, Marketing Director
Steven C. Rider, CFO, VP
Jeffrey W Kirk, President

Will be held at the Georgia World Congress Center in Atlanta, Georgia, and is anchored by the IFAI Expo and the ATMW-I shows. Together, the shows are expected to have more than 1,000 exhibitors.
20000 Attendees
Founded in 1912

3549 **Mid-America Sail & Power Boat Show**
Lake Erie Marine Trade Association
1269 Bassett Road
Cleveland, OH 44145-1116

440-899-5009; Fax: 440-899-5013
info@lemta.com
www.clevelandboatshow.com
Facebook

Norm Schultz, President Emeritus

Annual show of 325 manufacturers and suppliers of pleasure boats and related marine equipment, supplies and services.
140M Attendees
Frequency: January

3550 **Midwest Boat Show**
Lake Erie Marine Trade Association
1269 Bassett Road
Cleveland, OH 44145-1116

440-899-5009; Fax: 440-899-5013

Norm Schultz, President

Annual show and exhibits of boats, equipment, supplies and services.
23M Attendees
Frequency: August
Founded in 1980

3551 **NMBA Annual Conference**
National Marine Bankers Association
231 South LaSalle Street
Suite 2050
Chicago, IL 60604

312-812-2777
bmcardle@nmma.org
www.marinebankers.org
LinkedIn

Michael Bryant, President
Jayme Yates, Secretary
Jackie Forese, Director

NMBA hosts a three day member conference where the latest trends relating to marine industry are discussed in detail.
180 Attendees
Frequency: September

3552 **National Association of State Boating Law Administrators Annual Conference**
National Association of State Boating Law
1500 Leestown Road
Suite 330
Lexington, KY 40511

859-225-9487; Fax: 859-231-6403
info@nasbla.org
www.nasbla.org/

Toby Velasquez, President
Herb Angell, VP
Kevin Bergerson, Treasurer

Conference provides information that focuses on boating education, industry trends, workshops, and programs that discuss the history of recreational boating safety programs including an overview of state-by-state regulatory laws.
Frequency: September

3553 **National Capital Boat Show**
Royal Productions
PO Box 4197
Chester, VA 23831-8475

804-425-6556; Fax: 804-425-6563
www.royalshows.com

Serving the Washington DC and suburban Virginia/Maryland markets. 40 dealers.
Frequency: March

3554 **National Dry Stack Conference**
Association of Marina Industries
444 North Capitol Street NW
Suite 645
Washington, DC 20001

202-379-9768; Fax: 202-628-8679

Gregg Kenney, Chairman
Alex Laidlaw, Vice Chairman
Maureen Healey, Executive Director
Cris McSparen, Treasurer
Brooke Fishel, Manager Communications

The Dry Stack is a three-day hybrid school which combines an educational program along with networking among leading operations, developers and vendors.
Frequency: October

3555 **National Marine Bankers Association Annual Conference**
National Marine Bankers Association
231 South LaSalle Street
Suite 2050
Chicago, IL 60604

312-812-2777
bmcardle@nmma.org
www.marinebankers.org
LinkedIn

Michael Bryant, President
Jayme Yates, Secretary
Jackie Forese, Director

A three-day member conference where the latest trends issues relating to the marine industry are discussed in detail.
Frequency: September

3556 **North American Sail & Power Show**
Lake Erie Marine Trade Association

1269 Bassett Road
Cleveland, OH 44145-1116

440-899-5009; Fax: 440-899-5013
lemta@aol.com

Norm Schultz, President

Annual show and exhibits of marine equipment, supplies and services.
31M Attendees
Frequency: September

3557 **Portland Boat Show**
O'Loughlin Trade Shows
3600 SW Multnomah Boulevard
PO Box 80750
Portland, OR 97219-1750

503-246-8291; Fax: 503-246-1066
www.oloughlintradeshows.com

Peter O'Loughlin, Show Manager
Robert O'Loughlin Sr, President

Offers hundreds of makes and models, accessories and plenty of expert advice through seminars and hands on demonstrations.
Frequency: January

3558 **Professional Boatbuilder: International Boatbuilders Expo and Conference**
WoodenBoat Publications
86 Great Cove Drive
PO Box 78
Brooklin, ME 04616

207-359-4651; Fax: 207-359-8920
www.ibexshow.com

Carl Cramer, Publisher
Anne Dunbar, Show Director
Joanne Miller, Registration Manager

Over 450 booths offering products for boat builders, designers, repairers, surveyors, and boatyard/marina operators.
2.5M Attendees
Frequency: November
Founded in 1989

3559 **SCA Spring Safety Seminar**
Shipbuilders Council of America
655 Fifteenth St NW
Suite 225
Washington, DC 20005

202-347-5462; Fax: 202-347-5464
Facebook

Matt Paxton, President

Represents the U.S. shipyard industry. SCA members build, repair and service America's fleet of commercial vessels.
73 Members
Frequency: March
Founded in 1920

3560 **Sail America Industry Conference**
Sail America
50 Water St.
Warren, RI 02885

401-289-2540; Fax: 401-247-0074
www.sailamerica.com/events/saic

Stephanie Grove, Administration Manager

A two-day event for sailing industry professionals featuring seminars, workshops and networking events.
Frequency: Annual

3561 **Seattle Boat Show**
Northwest Marine Trade Association
1900 North Northlake Way
Suite 233
Seattle, WA 98103

206-634-0911; Fax: 206-632-0078
info@seattleboatshow.com
www.nmta.net
Facebook, Twitter, LinkedIn

George Harris, President
John Thorburn, VP

The ten-day event features more than 1,000 recreational watercraft, seminars and the latest innovations in accessories at Qwest Field Event Center, plus 200 world-class boats in their natural habitat on South Lake Union.
Frequency: January-February
Founded in 1947

3562 **St. Petersburg Boat Show**
Show Management
1115 NE 9th Avenue
Fort Lauderdale, FL 33304

954-764-7642
800-940-7642; Fax: 954-462-4140
info@showmanagement.com
www.showmanagement.com
Facebook, Twitter

Kaye Pearson, Owner/Promoter
Elise Lipoff, Director Public Relations
Steve Sheer, Director Advertising

More than 600 boats of all types and sizes, electronics, engines and a vast selection of marine accessories will be displayed on land and in water.
10000 Attendees
Frequency: December
Founded in 1977
Mailing list available for rent

3563 **Suncoast Boat Show**
Show Management
1115 NE 9th Avenue
Fort Lauderdale, FL 33304

954-764-7642
800-940-7642; Fax: 954-462-4140
info@showmanagement.com
www.showmanagement.com
Facebook, Twitter

Kaye Pearson, Owner/Promoter
Elise Lipoff, Director Public Relations
Steve Sheer, Director Advertising
Chuck Bolt, Director Sales

Annual show and exhibits of boats and marine equipment, supplies and services.
30000 Attendees
Frequency: April
Founded in 1982
Mailing list available for rent

3564 **U.S. Rowing Association Annual Convention**
United States Rowing Association
2 Wall Street
Princeton, NJ 08540

609-751-0700
800-314-4769; Fax: 609-924-1578
members@usrowing.org
www.usrowing.org
Facebook, Twitter, Youtube

James Rawson, Senior Events Manager
Sarah McAuliffe, Senior Events Managers

Coaching programs and information, referee clinics, speakers, and competitions.
Frequency: December

3565 **US Sailboat Show**
Annapolis Boatshows
100 Severn Drive
PO Box 4997
Annapolis, MD 21401-4997

410-268-8828; Fax: 410-280-3903

Dee Newman, Show Manager
Jim Barthold, General Manager

In-water sailboat show offering over 350 booths.
150M Attendees
Frequency: October

Directories & Databases

3566 **American Boat and Yacht Council**
American Boat and Yacht Council
613 Third Street
Suite 10
Annapolis, MD 21403

410-990-4466; Fax: 410-956-2737
info@abycinc.org
www.abycinc.org

John Adey, President

Marine suppliers, engineers and underwriters, as well as architects and designers for the marine industry are listed.
Frequency: Online
Founded in 1954

3567 **Boater's Source Directory**
Boat US Foundation
880 S Pickett St
Alexandria, VA 22304-4606

703-461-8952
800-336-2628; Fax: 703-461-2855
Facebook, Twitter, LinkedIn, Youtube

Richard Schwartz, President

Pocket guide for boaters containing safety and regulatory information and resources.
Cost: $5.00
Frequency: Paperback, SemiAnnual
Founded in 1966

3568 **Boating Industry: Marine Buyers' Guide Issue**
Ehlert Publishing Group
6420 Sycamore Ln N
Suite 100
Maple Grove, MN 55369-6014

763-383-4400
800-848-6247; Fax: 763-383-4499
www.bowhuntingworld.com
Facebook, Twitter, Youtube

Steven Hedlund, President
Liz Walz, Senior Editor
Jon Mohrm, Associate Editor
Tammy Galvin, Group Publisher

A who's who directory of services and supplies for the industry.
Cost: $29.95
Frequency: Annual
Circulation: 30,000
Mailing list available for rent

3569 **Confined Space Entry Video and Manual**
Shipbuilders Council of America
655 Fifteenth St NW
Suite 225
Washington, DC 20004-1166

202-347-5462; Fax: 202-347-5464
Facebook

Matt Paxton, President

This manual, in combination with the video program, covers some of the more common hazards associated with confined space entry. It also provides you with the information you will need to prevent accidents and injuries.
Cost: $ 50.00
73 Members
Founded in 1920

3570 **Consumer Protection Database**
Boat Owners Association of the US

800 South Pickett Street
Alexandria, VA 22304

703-412-2770; Fax: 703-461-2847
www.boatus.com
Facebook, Twitter, LinkedIn, Youtube

Richard Schwartz, Chairman/Founder
Jim Ellis, President/CEO

Contains consumer complaints and safety information reported by boat owners, the US Coast Guard, manufacturers, marine surveyors and marine technicians.
Founded in 1966

3571 **ISSPA Sports and Vacation Show Directory and Calendar**
International Sport Show Producers Association
PO Box 480084
Denver, CO 80248-0084

303-892-6800
800-457-2434; Fax: 303-892-6322
www.sportshow.org

Dianne Seymour, Executive Secretary

Products of outdoor recreation shows which include boating, travel, RV, hunting, and fishing.
Frequency: Annual

3572 **Marine Products Directory**
Underwriters Laboratories
12 Laboratory Drive
PO Box 13995
Research Triangle Park, NC 27709-3995

919-549-1400; Fax: 919-547-6363
Facebook, Twitter, Youtube

Keith E. Williams, President
Sanjeev Jesudas, President

UL has been testing and certifying products for marine use since 1969. With a UL Marine Mark on your product, you can show consumers, retailers, surveyors, insurers, government agencies, regulatory and ABTC, NFPA and UL Safety Standards.
Cost: $10.00
176 Pages
Frequency: Annual

3573 **Membership Directory: Boating Industry Administration**
National Association of State Boating Laws
1500 Leestown Road
Suite 300
Lexington, KY 40511-2047

859-225-9487; Fax: 859-231-6403
info@nasbla.org
www.nasbla.org

Toby Velasquez, President
Herb Angell, VP
Kevin Bergerson, Treasurer

Published by the National Association of State Boating Law Administration.

3574 **NMRA Membership Directory**
National Marine Representative Association
1333 Delany Road #500
PO Box 360
Gurnee, IL 60031

847-662-3167; Fax: 847-336-7126
info@nmraonline.org
www.nmraonline.org

Scott Kolodny, President

Provides a complete listing of all NMRA sales representatives. Includes contact information for their main and associate offices, the territories they cover, the markets they represent, and the list of companies they represent.
Cost: $10.00

3575 **National Marine Manufacturers Association Membership List**
231 S. LaSalle St
Suite 2050
Chicago, IL 60601-6539

312-946-6200; Fax: 312-946-0388
www.nmma.org

Frank Hugelmeyer, President
Robert Newsome, SVP, Operations
Craig Boskey, SVP, Finance & CFO

Directory of services and supplies to the industry.
160 Pages
Frequency: Quadrennial

3576 **Pacific Boating Almanac**
ProStar Publications
3416 Wesley Street
Suite B
Culver City, CA 90232-2901

310-280-1010
800-481-6277; Fax: 310-280-1025
www.prostarpublications.com

Peter Griffes, Owner

Consists of three regional volumes. This information includes the latest Coast Pilot, Tide & Current Tables, First Aid, Electronics, Navigation and Safety, Weather, and Yacht Club Burgees.
Cost: $26.95
Frequency: Annual
Circulation: 20,000
ISBN: 1-577857-05-4
Mailing list available for rent: 19,000 names
Printed in on matte stock

3577 **Portbook of Marine Services**
Portbook Publications
PO Box 462
Belfast, ME 04915

207-338-1619; Fax: 207-338-6025
www.portbook.net

Sandra Squire, Publisher

Marinas, yacht clubs, boatyards, dealers, marine supply stores, repair facilities, and other services for yachtsmen. For Annapolis, Maryland and Newport/Narragansett Bay, Rhode Island. Distributed free through advertisers, or four dollars by mail.
Cost: $40.00
100 Pages
Frequency: Annual
Circulation: 35M
Founded in 1982
Printed in on matte stock

3578 **Register of American Yacht Clubs**
Yachting Club of America
PO Box 1040
Marco Island, FL 34146-1040

239-642-4448; Fax: 239-642-5284
info@ycaol.com
www.ycaol.com

A reciprocity guide for yacht and sailing clubs in the United States, Hawaii, Alaska, and the Virgin Islands registered with the Yachting Club of America. 800 yacht clubs registered with the Yachting Club of America.
Cost: $35.00
200 Pages
Frequency: Softbound
Founded in 1963
Printed in on glossy stock

3579 **Sail Tall Ships: Directory of Sail Training and Adventure at Sea**
American Sail Training Association
240 Thames Street
PO Box 1459
Newport, RI 02840

401-846-1775; Fax: 401-849-5400
www.ycaol.com

Lori Aguiar, Editor
Peter A Mello, Executive Director

Offers information on sail training ships, shoreside sail training programs and ships under construction or restoration.
Cost: $50.00
400 Pages
Frequency: Annual
Circulation: 15,000
ISBN: 0-963648-36-5
Founded in 1963

3580 **Seafarers**
Admiralty Insurance
6353 Argyle Forest Boulevard
Jacksonville, FL 32244

904-777-0042
800-456-8936; Fax: 904-777-0279
www.seafarers.com

Searchable database of boating associations, yacht clubs, boating clubs and source of nautical information and links.

3581 **Ship Agents, Owners, Operators**
Maritime Association of the Port of New York
1201 Corbin St
Elizabeth, NJ 07201

212-747-1284; Fax: 212-635-9498
themaritimeassoc@erols.com
www.nymaritime.org

Andrew Saporito, President
Brian McAllister, Vice President
Edward J. Kelly, Executive Director
Phillip Moore, Operations Manager

Directory of Atlantic, Gulf and West Coasts, listing every steamship, owner, and operator in the major ports with lines that they represent and the countries that they serve.
Cost: $50.00
580 Members
Frequency: Annual
Circulation: 2,000
Founded in 1873
Mailing list available for rent

3582 **Shipyard Ergonomics Video and Workbook CD**
Shipbuilders Council of America
655 Fifteenth St NW
Suite 225
Washington, DC 20004-1166

202-347-5462; Fax: 202-347-5464
Facebook

Matt Paxton, President

Designed to instruct shipyard employees, supervisors and trainers in identifying ergonomic risks and providing tools to allow the development of creative solutions to reduce the hazards.
Cost: $75.00
73 Members
Founded in 1920

Industry Web Sites

3583 **http://gold.greyhouse.com**
G.O.L.D Grey House OnLine Databases

Grey House Publishing's online database platform, GOLD, offers Quick Search, Keyword Search and Expert Search, for most business sectors including boating manufacture and service markets. GOLD is quick and easy - whether you're a novice searcher or an experienced database user. All of Grey House's directory products are available for subscription on the GOLD platform.

3584 **www.acbs.org**
Antique & Classic Boat Society
Dedicated to the preservation and enjoyment of historic, antique and classic boats. ACBS brings people with this common interest together to share fellowship, information, experiences and ideas.

3585 **www.americanboating.org**
American Boating Association
ABA's mission is to promote boating safety, affordability, growth, and a clean environment. It provides exclusive services and benefits for boaters and boating enthusiasts.

3586 **www.apba-racing.com**
American Power Boat Association
The sole authority for UIM approved powerboat racing ine United States.

3587 **www.by-the-sea.com**
By the Sea
Everything for the boat professional and enthusiast alike. News of sales and events, message boards and contact information.

3588 **www.greyhouse.com**
Grey House Publishing
Authoritative reference directories for most business segments incluidng boat manufacturing and service markets. Users can search the online databases with varied search criteria allowing for custom searches by product category, geographic area, sales volume, keyword, subject and more. Full Grey House catalog and online ordering also available.

3589 **www.iamimarine.org**
International Association of Marine Investigators
An assocation supporting the profession of marine investigators by offering educational resources and specialized training.

3590 **www.ifai.com**
Industrial Fabrics Association International
The only trade association in the world representing the entire specialty fabrics/technical textiles industry. Member products range from fiber and fabric suppliers to manufacturers of end products, equipment and hardware.

3591 **www.lemta.com**
Lake Erie Marine Trade Association
info@lemta.com
Trade association of more than 100 recreational boat dealers, marina operators and pleasure boat service companies located across northern Ohio; also plays the key role in looking out for the consumer.

3592 **www.marinebankers.org**
National Marine Bankers Association
The purpose of the NMBA is to educate prospective lenders in marine financing procedures, create new lenders to help finance the sales of the manufacturers products, and to create an information exchange for its members.

3593 **www.mraa.com**
Marine Retailers Association of America
Manufacturers and dealers of boats, equipment, supplies and services.

3594 **www.nauticalworld.com**
Dedicated to bringing all related web sites within easy access to watersports enthusiasts, including advertiser's information. Offers sections on marine electronics and hardware, sailing, boats, dock supplies, fishing accessories, diving accessories, industry news, watersports, weather forecasting and more.

3595 **www.nauticexpo.com**
NauticExpo
This Virtual Boat Show is accessible in five languages and presents all the boats and nautical equipment available on the international market. It offers an accurate and up-to-date source of information to yachtsmen and professionals.

3596 **www.nmdaonline.com**
National Marine Distributors Association
Engages in exclusively nonprofit activities designed to promote the common business interests and improve the business conditions of wholesale distributors of marine accessories and of the marine industry in general.

3597 **www.nmraonline.org**
National Marine Representatives Association
Members are independent boat and marine accessory sales representatives national association.

3598 **www.nmta.net**
Northwest Marine Trade Association
Oldest and largest regional boating trade organization in the nation representing the interests of approximately 800 member companies. Each year it produces the Seattle Boat Show at the Stadium Exhibition Center and the Seattle Boat Show at Shilshole Bay Marina on behalf of its members.

3599 **www.propellerclubhq.com**
Propeller Club of the United States
Grassroots, nonprofit organization, whose membership resides throughout the United States and the world. It is dedicated to the enhancement and well-being of all interests of the maritime community on a national and international basis.

3600 **www.pwia.org**
Personal Watercraft Industry Association
Trade association representing manufacturers of personal watercraft.

3601 **www.rbbi.com**
Polson Enterprises
Offering research tools and papers on new product development and new product development services for boat builders, plus experience in the fields of marine drives, engine, marine vessels, propellar guards, boating safety. Industry and regulation updates are also available on this site.

3602 **www.tsca.com**
Traditional Small Craft Association
Nonprofit, tax-exempt educational organization which works to preserve and continue the living traditions, skills, lore and legends surrounding working and pleasure watercraft including construction and use of boats.

3603 **www.ussailing.org**
United States Sailing Association
Encourages participation and promotes excellence in sailing and racing in the US.

Associations

3604 American Beverage Licensees
5101 River Road
Suite 108
Bethesda, MD 20816-1560

301-656-1494; Fax: 301-656-7539
info@ablusa.org
www.ablusa.org
Facebook, Twitter

John Bodnovich, Executive Director

Trade association for retail beverage alcohol license holders.
20000 Members

3605 American Craft Spirits Association
PO Box 701414
Louisville, KY 40270

502-807-4249
www.americancraftspirits.org
Facebook, Twitter

Margie A.S. Lehrman, Executive Director
Teresa McDaniel, Membership Coordinator

Trade association of U.S. craft spirits industry.

3606 American Society for Enology and Viticulture
1784 Picasso Avenue
Suite D
Davis, CA 95618-0551

530-753-3142; Fax: 530-753-3318
pfpa@paforestproducts.org
www.asev.org

Patty Skinkis, President
Dan Howard, Executive Director
Daniel Friedlander, Publications & Tech Coordinator
Michelle Taillon, Event Coordinator
Dean Spencer, Office Coordinator

A tax exempt professional society dedicated to the interests of enologists, viticulturists, and others in the fields of wine and grape research and production throughout the world.
Founded in 1980

3607 American Society of Brewing Chemists
3340 Pilot Knob Rd
St Paul, MN 55121-2055

651-454-7250
800-328-7560; Fax: 651-454-0766
ties@rta.org
www.asbcnet.org

Jim Gauntt, Executive Director
Debbie Corallo, Association Administrator
Barbara Stacey, Committee and Website Coordinator
2500 Members
Founded in 1919

3608 Association of Winery Supplies
21 Tamal Vista Boulevard
Suite 196
Corte Madera, CA 94925-1146

415-924-2640
1983

Warner Executive Director

United States supplier of services and materials used in the winery industry.
John Members
Founded in 34

3609 Beer Institute
122 C St NW
Suite 350
Washington, DC 20001-2150

202-737-2337
800-379-2739; Fax: 202-737-7004
info@calredwood.org
www.beerinstitute.org
Youtube

Christopher Grover, President

The national trade association for the brewing industry. Representing both big and small brewers as well as importers and industry suppliers.
Founded in 1916

3610 Brewers Association
Brewers Association
1327 Spruce Street
Boulder, CO 80302

303-447-0816
888-822-6273; Fax: 303-447-2825
membership@safnet.org
www.brewersassociation.org
Facebook, Twitter, LinkedIn

A non-profit educational and trade organization for small and craft brewers. Its mission is to make quality brewing and beer knowledge accessible to all.
Founded in 1900

3611 Distilled Spirits Council of the United States
1250 Eye St NW
Suite 400
Washington, DC 20005-3998

202-628-3544; Fax: 202-682-8844
vicki@swst.org
www.discus.org
Facebook

Eric Hansen, President
Bob Smith, Vice-President
Vicki L. Herian, Executive Director
H. Michael Barnes, Editor of Wood and Fiber Science
Barb Hogan, Editorial Assistant

National trade association representing producers and marketers of liquor sold in the US.
450 Members
Founded in 1958

3612 Distillery, Wine and Allied Workers' International Union
66 Grand Avenue
Englewood, NJ 07631-3506

201-894-8444; Fax: 201-569-9216
www.ufcw.org/

Bryan Smalley, President
Alexis Sivcovich, Member Services Coordinator
Beverly Knight, Accounting Manager
Will Telligman, Government Affairs Manager

Addresses the concerns of wine makers and fellow industry workers.
350 Members
Founded in 1962

3613 Foundation for Advancing Alcohol Responsibility
2345 Crystal Dr
Suite 710
Arlington, VA 22202

202-637-0077
www.responsibility.org
Facebook, Twitter, YouTube, Pinterest, Instagram

Ralph S. Blackman, President & CEO

Promoting responsible drinking.

3614 Home Wine and Beer Trade Association
PO Box 1373
Valrico, FL 33595

813-685-4261; Fax: 813-681-5625
Facebook, Youtube

Manufacturers, wholesalers, retailers, authors and editors having a commercial interest in the beer and wine trade.
19 Members
Founded in 1905

3615 Italian Trade Commission
33 East 67th Street
New York, NY 10065

212-980-1500; Fax: 212-758-1050
mail@sfpa.org
www.italtrade.com/countries/americas/usa/new york.htm
Twitter, Youtube

Tami Kessler, Executive Director
Richard Wallace, Vice President, Communications
Vernon Barabino, Chief Financial Administrator
Rachel Elton, Admin. Assistant/Program Coor.
Eric Gee, CF, RF, Director

Developments in the Italian wine industry and market, as well as reviews of imported wines from Italy.
265 Members
Founded in 1915

3616 Italian Wine and Food Institute
Italian Wine and Food Institute
60 East 42nd Street, Suite 2214
Suite 2214
New York, NY 10165

212-867-4111; Fax: 212-867-4114
spib@spib.org

T. Furman Brodie, Chairman
Bert H. Jones, Vice Chairman
Steve Singleton, President
Shelly James, Operations & Finance Assistant
Eileen Ehrsam, Accounts Receivable Admin.

Members are producers, distributors and marketers of Italian wines and foods.
Founded in 1940

3617 National Alcohol Beverage Control Association
4401 Ford Avenue
Suite 700
Alexandria, VA 22302-1433

703-578-4200; Fax: 703-820-3551
info@forestinfo.org
www.nabca.org

Robert M Owens, Chairman
Lee F Freeman, President & CEO

Members include control jurisdictions, supplier members and industry trade associations.
Founded in 1989

3618 National Beer Wholesalers Association
1101 King Street
Suite 600
Alexandria, VA 22314

703-683-4300
800-300-6417
info@nbwa.org
www.nbwa.org

Craig Purser, President/CEO
Wendy Huerter, Executive Assistant
Lauren Kane, VP, Communications
Paul Pisano, SVP Industry Affairs & Gen. Counsel
Patti Rouzie, VP, Membership & Meetings

NBWA represents the interests of America's independent, licensed beer distributors which ser-

vice every congressional district and media market in the country.
Founded in 1938

3619 **National Wine Distribution Association**
2701 E Street
Sacramento, CA 95816-3221
916-979-3051; Fax: 916-448-9115
GM Pucilowski, Executive Director
Dedicated to promoting the interests and education of smaller wine wholesalers, importers, wineries, and others who are involved in the wine distribution business.
285 Members
Founded in 1978

3620 **Wine Institute**
425 Market Street
Suite 1000
San Francisco, CA 94105
415-512-0151
info@wineinstitute.org
www.wineinstitute.org
Facebook, Twitter, LinkedIn, YouTube, Pinterest
Robert Koch, President/CEO
Maluri Fernandez, Executive Assistant
Nancy Light, VP, Communications
Dedicated to initiating and advocating state, federal and international public policy to enhance the environment for the responsible production, promotion and enjoyment of wine.
1000 Members
Founded in 1934

3621 **Wine and Spirits Shippers Association**
11800 Sunrise Valley Dr
Reston, VA 20191-5302
703-860-2300
800-368-3167; Fax: 703-860-2422
info@tpinst.org
www.wssa.com
Michael A Cassidy, Executive Director
Provides members, importers and exporters with efficient and economical ocean transportation and other logistic services.
300 Members
Founded in 1961
Mailing list available for rent

3622 **Wine and Spirits Wholesalers of America**
805 15th Street NW
Suite 1120
Washington, DC 20005
202-371-9792; Fax: 202-789-2405
info@wswa.org
www.wswa.org
Michelle L. Korsmo, President/CEO
Jo Moak, SVP & General Counsel
Daweson Hobbs, SVP, Govt. Affairs
Heather Calio, VP, State Affairs
Ali Gormley, VP, Red. Affairs
This association is comprised of wholesale distributors of domestic and imported wine and distilled spirits.
350+ Members
Founded in 1943

Newsletters

3623 **ASBC Newsletter**
American Society of Brewing Chemists
3340 Pilot Knob Rd
Eagan, MN 55121-2055
651-454-7250
800-328-7560; Fax: 651-454-0766
asbc@scisoc.org
www.asbcnet.org
Steven C Nelson, VP
Jordana Anker, Director of Publications
Karen Cummings, Director Publications
Joan A Raumschuh, Editor
Jody Grider, Director of Operations
Cost: $20.00
Frequency: Quarterly
Founded in 1934

3624 **Alcoholic Beverage Control: From the State Capitals**
Wakeman Walworth
PO BOX 7376
Alexandria, VA 22307-7376
703-768-9600; Fax: 703-768-9690
www.statecapitals.com/alcoholbev.html
Keyes Walworth, Publisher
Covers binge drinking laws, internet sales, advertising, taxes, bottle bills, Sunday sales laws, license regulation, drunk driving laws, under-age drinking, mini-bottles and other state laws affecting beer, liquor and wine distribution.
Cost: $245.00
4 Pages
Frequency: Weekly
Printed in one color on matte stock

3625 **Beer Marketer's Insights Newsletter**
Beer Marketer's Insights
49 E Maple Ave
Suffern, NY 10901-5507
845-624-2337; Fax: 845-624-2340
www.beerinsights.com
Benj Steinman, President
Reports on the competitive battle among brewers for a share of the beer market. Analyzes recent legislation and factors that affect the industry.
Cost: $595.00
Frequency: 23/Year
Founded in 1975

3626 **Beer Statistics News**
Beer Marketer's Insights
49 E Maple Ave
Suffern, NY 10901-5507
845-624-2337; Fax: 845-624-2340
bmiexpress@aol.com
www.beerinsights.com
Benj Steinman, President
Eric Shephard, Executive Editor
Andy Leinicke, Circulation Manager
Supplies data for major brewers' shipments in 39 reporting states.
Cost: $450.00
Frequency: Monthly
Founded in 1975

3627 **Brewers Bulletin**
PO Box 677
Thiensville, WI 53092
262-242-6105; Fax: 262-242-5133
Tom Volke, President/CEO
Brewing industry newspaper.
Cost: $53.00
Frequency: Monthly
Circulation: 500
Founded in 1907

3628 **Champagne Wines Information Bureau**
KCSA
800 2nd Avenue Frnt 5
New York, NY 10017-4709
212-682-6300
800-642-4267; Fax: 212-697-0910
info@champagnes.com
www.champagnes.com
Jean-Louis Carbonnier, Editor
Representative of Comite Interprofessionnel duVinde Champagne, Epernay, France.
4 Pages
Frequency: TriAnnual
Circulation: 10,000
Printed in one color on matte stock

3629 **Impact International**
M Shanken Communications
387 Park Ave S
Suite 8
New York, NY 10016-8872
212-684-4224
800-848-7113; Fax: 212-684-5424
www.cigaraficionado.com
Marvin Shanken, Publisher
Samantha Shanken, President
Reports on the global alcoholic beverage market.
Cost: $595.00
Frequency: Annual+
Founded in 1972

3630 **Kane's Beverage Week**
Whitaker Newsletters
313 S Avenue
#340
Fanwood, NJ 07023-1364
908-889-6339
800-359-6049; Fax: 415-027-0608
Whitaker Publisher, Anne
Bittner Editor, Fred
Rossi Editor
News on marketing, economic and regulatory factors affecting the alcohol beverage industry.
Cost: $131.00
Joel Members
6 Pages
Frequency: Monthly
ISSN: 0882-2573

3631 **Notiziario**
Italian Wine and Food Institute
60 East 42nd Street, Suite 2214
Suite 1341
New York, NY 10165
212-867-4111; Fax: 212-867-4114
iwfi@aol.com
Lucio Caputo, President
Vincent Giampaoco, VP
Provides detailed information on the Italian gastronomy and wines. It distributes information materials and give press interviews for the American radio and television. It carries out an intense public relations program, participates in the most important local promotional initiatives and events and maintains contact with the American and Italian authorities in this sector.
Cost: $250.00
Founded in 1984

3632 **On Tap: Newsletter**
WBR Publishing
PO Box 71
Clemson, SC 29633
864-654-2300; Fax: 864-654-5067
Steve Johnson, Publisher
North America breweries and microbreweries.
Cost: $.95
20 Pages
Frequency: Bi-Monthly
Circulation: 1000
Printed in one color on matte stock

3633 **Spirited Living: Dave Steadman's Restaurant Scene**
5301 Towne Woods Rd
Coram, NY 11727-2808
631-736-0436; Fax: 631-736-0436
Dave Steadman, Editor
Newsletter published Bi-Weekly except January, July, and August.
Cost: $75.00

3634 **US Beer Market**
Business Trend Analysts/Industry Reports
2171 Jericho Tpke
Suite 200
Commack, NY 11725-2937
631-462-5454
800-866-4648; Fax: 631-462-1842
www.bta-ler.com
Charles J Ritchie, Executive VP
Donna Priani, Marketing Director
Profiles markets for premium, superpremium, popular and light beers.
Cost: $1495.00

3635 **Uncorked**
California Wine Club
2175 Goodyear Avenue
Suite 102
Ventura, CA 93006-3699
805-650-4330
800-777-4443; Fax: 800-700-1599
info@cawineclub.com
www.cawineclub.com
Bruce Boring, Proprietors
Judy Reynolds, Proprietors
Uncorked is an 8 page newsletter that describes the featured winery. It provides an upclose and personal look at a small 'boutique' California Winery.
Frequency: Monthly
Circulation: 10000
Founded in 1990

3636 **Vinotizie Italian Wine Newsletter**
Italian Trade Commission
33 E 67th St
New York, NY 10065-5949
212-848-0300; Fax: 212-758-1050
www.italtrade.com
Aniello Musella, President
Giovanni Mafodda, Operations Manager
This newsletter discusses developments in the Italian wine industry and market, as well as reviews of imported wines from Italy.
Frequency: Monthly
Founded in 1998

3637 **Wine & Craft Beverage News**
Lee Publications
6113 State Hwy. 5
P.O. Box 121
Palatine Bridge, NY 13428-0121
518-673-3237
888-596-5329; Fax: 518-673-2699
subscriptions@leepub.com
wineandcraftbeveragenews.com
Frederick Lee, Publisher
Joan Kark-Wren, Editor
Bruce Button, President
Larry Price, Marketing Manager
Ian Hitchener, Sales Manager
An e-newsletter containing the latest news from the craft brewing and distilling industry.
Frequency: Weekly
Circulation: Digital

3638 **Wine Investor Buyers Guide**
PGE Publications
1224 N Fairfax Avenue
Apartment 5
Los Angeles, CA 90046-5234
Paul Gillette, Publisher
JD Kronman, Editor
Reviews new releases of wines, recommends the best buys, predicts when wines will be at their peak and surveys markets for pricing trends. Accepts advertising.
Cost: $75.00
10 Pages
Frequency: Monthly

3639 **World Beer Review**
WBR Publishing
PO Box 71
Clemson, SC 29633-0071
864-654-2300
Steve Johnson, Publisher
Complete coverage of the beer and beermaking industry.

Magazines & Journals

3640 **All About Beer**
Chautauqua Inc
501 Washington St
Suite H
Durham, NC 27701-2169
919-530-8150
800-977-2337; Fax: 919-530-8160
www.allaboutbeer.com
Julie Bradford, Publisher
Natalie Abernethy, Circulation Manager
Quality beers, breweries and restaurants.
Cost: $19.99
64 Pages
Founded in 1981

3641 **Atlantic Control States Beverage Journal**
Club & Tavern
3 12th Street
Wheeling, WV 26003-3276
304-232-7620; Fax: 304-233-1236
Arnold Lazarus, Editor
A magazine for the alcoholic beverage industry. Serving bars, restaurants, clubs and industry personnel with West Virginia, Virginia, and North Carolina state editions. Includes states' liquor price lists.

3642 **Bar Business Magazine**
Simmons-Boardman Publishing Corporation
345 Hudson St
Suite 1201
New York, NY 10014-7123
212-620-7200; Fax: 212-633-1165
www.simmonsboardman.com
Arthur J McGinnis Jr, President
The premier How-To publication covering the best business practices and products for owners and managers of nightclubs, bars and lounges across the US.
Frequency: Monthly
Circulation: 8541

3643 **Bartender Magazine**
Foley Publishing Corporation
PO Box 157
Spring Lake, NJ 07762
732-449-4499; Fax: 732-974-8289
barmag@aol.com
www.bartender.com
Facebook, Twitter
Raymond Foley, Publisher
Jaclyn Wilson Foley, Editor
Serves all full service drinking establishments. Including individual restaurants, hotels, motels, bars, taverns, lounges, and all other full service on premise licenses. Subscription price is $40 for Canada, and $55 for all other foriegn countries.
Cost: $30.00
72 Pages
Frequency: Monthly
Circulation: 149044
Founded in 1979
Printed in 4 colors on glossy stock

3644 **Beer Perspectives**
National Beer Wholesalers Association
1101 King St
Suite 600
Alexandria, VA 22314-2965
703-683-4300; Fax: 703-683-8965
info@nbwa.org
www.nbwa.org
Facebook, Twitter
Craig Purser, President & CEO
Trade association for beer wholesalers. Provides government and public affairs outreach as well as education and training for its wholesaler members.
Founded in 1938

3645 **Beverage Dynamics**
The Beverage Information Group
17 High Street
2nd Floor
Norwalk, CT 06851
203-855-8499
lzimmerman@m2media360.com
www.bevinfogroup.com
Liza Zimmerman, Editor-in-Chief
Jeremy Nedelka, Managing Editor
Devoted to the needs of the off-premise beverage alcohol retailer. Covers wine, beer and spirits categories as well as beset practices for retail decision makers.
Cost: $35.00
Frequency: Bi-Monthly
Founded in 1934

3646 **Beverage Journal**
Michigan Licensed Beverage Association
920 N Fairview Ave
Lansing, MI 48912-3238
517-374-9611
800-292-2896; Fax: 517-374-1165
info@mlba.org
www.mlba.org
Lou Adado, CEO
Cathy Pavick, Executive Director
Peter Broderick, Director of Communication
Offers information on the alcoholic beverage industry/retail sales
Cost: $52.00
Frequency: Monthly
ISSN: 1050-4427
Founded in 1939
Printed in on glossy stock

3647 **Beverage Network**
Beverage Media Group
116 John St
Suite 2305
New York, NY 10038-3419
212-571-3232
800-723-8372; Fax: 212-571-4443
info@bevmedia.com
www.bevmedia.com
Jason Glasser, CEO
S Paley, Circulation Manager
Cost: $99.00
Frequency: Monthly
Circulation: 6000
Founded in 1940

3648 **Beverage Retailer Magazine**
Oxford Publishing
Ste 1
1903b University Ave
Oxford, MS 38655-4150

662-236-5510
800-247-3881; Fax: 662-236-5541
www.bevindustry.com

Brenda Owen, Editor
Ed Meek, Publisher
Stacy Clark, Production Manager
Jennifer Parsons, Marketing Director
Ruth Ann Wolfe, Circulation Director

A magazine covering the off premise market for retailers in the wine, beer and spirits business.
Cost: $30.00
Circulation: 25000
Founded in 1985
Printed in 4 colors on glossy stock

3649 **Cheers**
The Beverage Information Group
17 High St
Suite 2
Norwalk, CT 06851

203-855-8499; Fax: 203-855-9446
www.bevinfogroup.com

Charlie Forman, SVP/Group Publisher
Liza Zimmerman, Editor-In-Chief
Jeremy Nedelka, Managing Editor

Business magazine for on-premise hospitality professionals. Coverage includes trends and innovations in operations, merchandising, service and training, as well as new developments in beverage product segments.
Cost: $35.00
Frequency: Monthly
Founded in 1998

3650 **Modern Brewery Age**
Business Journals
50 Day Street
PO Box 5550
Norwalk, CT 06856-5550

203-853-6015; Fax: 203-853-8175
www.breweryage.com

Mac Brighton, Chairman/COO
Britton Jones, President/CEO
Peter V K Reid, Editor/Publisher
Arthur Heilman, Circulation Director
Diane Apicelli, Advertising Director

A magazine for the wholesale and brewing industry.
Cost: $95.00
Founded in 1933

3651 **Modern Brewery Age: Tabloid Edition**
Business Journals
50 Day Street
PO Box #5550
Norwalk, CT 06856-5550

203-853-6015; Fax: 203-853-8175
www.breweryage.com

Peter VK Reid, Editor
Peter VK Reid, Publisher
Britton Jones, President/CEO
Diane Apicelli, Advertising Director
Mac Brighton, Chairman & COO

Brewery industry tabloid.
Cost: $95.00
Frequency: Weekly
Founded in 1933

3652 **Southern Beverage Journal**
Beverage Media Group
14337 Sw 119th Ave
Miami, FL 33186-6006

305-233-7230; Fax: 305-252-2580
www.bevnetwork.com

Sharon Mijares, President
Sharon Mijares, Circulation Manager

A magazine for the alcoholic beverage industry.
Cost: $35.00
Frequency: Monthly
Circulation: 29000
Founded in 1944

3653 **StateWays**
The Beverage Information Group
17 High Street
2nd Floor
Norwalk, CT 06851

203-855-8499
lzimmerman@m2media360.com
www.bevinfogroup.com

Liza Zimmerman, Editor-In-Chief
Jeremy Nedelka, Managing Editor

Written for commissioners, board members, headquarters personnel, and retail store managers responsible for buying beverage alcohol in the eighteen control states. Covered editorial includes product knowledge, market trends, store operations, merchandising, warehousing, computerization, administration, training, and other topics.
Cost: $20.00
Frequency: Bi-Monthly
Circulation: 8500

3654 **US Beer Market: Impact Databank Review and Forecast**
M Shanken Communications
387 Park Ave S
Suite 8
New York, NY 10016-8872

212-684-4224; Fax: 212-684-5424
www.cigaraficionado.com

Marvin Shanken, Publisher
Samantha Shanken, Marketing Manager
Cost: $9.10

3655 **US Liquor Industry**
Business Trend Analysts/Industry Reports
2171 Jericho Tpke
Suite 200
Commack, NY 11725-2937

631-462-5454; Fax: 631-462-1842
www.businesstrendanalysts.com

Charles J Ritchie, Executive VP
Donna Priani, Marketing Director
Linda Sherman, Production Manager
Jennifer Wichert, Research Director

A survey summarizing the past, current and future markets and trends in the liquor industry.
Cost: $1195.00
600 Pages
Founded in 1999

3656 **US Wine Market**
Business Trend Analysts/Industry Reports
2171 Jericho Tpke
Suite 200
Commack, NY 11725-2937

631-462-5454
800- 86- 464; Fax: 631-462-1842
www.businesstrendanalysts.com

Charles J Ritchie, Executive VP
Donna Priani, Marketing Director

An analysis of the wine industry, domestic and imported.
Cost: $1995.00
470 Pages
Circulation: 2004
Founded in 1978

3657 **Vineyard and Winery Management Magazine**
Vineyard & Winery Management
421 E Street
Santa Rosa, CA 95404

707-577-7700; Fax: 707-577-7705
www.vwm-online.com

Robert Merletti, CEO/Publisher
Dennis Black, General Manager
Tina Caputo, Editor-in-Chief

A leading independent award winning wine trade magazine serving all of North America.
Cost: $37.00
100 Pages
Frequency: Bi-Monthly
Circulation: 6900
ISSN: 1047-4951
Founded in 1975
Printed in 4 colors on glossy stock

3658 **Wine Advocate**
Robert M Parker Jr
PO Box 311
Monkton, MD 21111

410-329-6477; Fax: 410-357-4504
wineadvocate@erobertparker.com
www.erobertparker.com

Robert M Parker Jr, Publisher/ Editor
Jacques Robinson, President

An independent magazine covering reviews of wine.
Cost: $60.00
64 Pages
Circulation: 40000
Founded in 1978

3659 **Wine and Spirits**
Winestate Publications
1748 Market Street
San Francisco, CA 94102-4997

415-255-7736; Fax: 415-255-9659
www.wineandspiritsmagazine.com/

Joshua Greene, Editor/Publisher
Michael Kinney, Associate Publisher
Ray Isle, Managing Editor
W. Charles Squires, Circulation Director
Gilian Handelman, Marketing Manager

A consumer magazine for wine enthusiasts.
Cost: $26.00
70 Pages
Circulation: 75000
Founded in 1987
Printed in 4 colors on glossy stock

Trade Shows

3660 **ABL Annual Meeting**
American Beverage Licensees
5101 River Road
Suite 108
Bethesda, MD 20816-1560

301-656-1494; Fax: 301-656-7539
www.ablusa.org

John Bodnovich, Executive Director

Annual show of 75 manufacturers, suppliers and distributors of alcoholic beverages.
1,000 Attendees

3661 **ASBC Annual Meeting**
American Society of Brewing Chemists

3340 Pilot Knob Road
Saint Paul, MN 55121-2055

651-454-7250
800-328-7560; Fax: 651-454-0766
bford@scisoc.org

Betty Ford, Meetings Director
Sue Casey, Meetings Coordinator
Steven Nelson, VP
300 Attendees
Frequency: June/Non-Members Fee

3662 **American Society for Enology and Viticulture Annual Meeting**
PO Box 1855
Davis, CA 95617-1855

530-753-3142; Fax: 530-753-3318
society@asev.org
www.asev.org

Michelle Taillon, Event Coordinator
Jen Smalley, Event & Tradeshow Manager

With technical sessions, research forums, symposia and a supplier showcase.
Frequency: June
Founded in 1950

3663 **American Wine Society National Conference**
American Wine Society
P.O. Box 889
Scranton, PA 18501

888-297-9070
www.americanwinesociety.org
Facebook, Twitter, LinkedIn, Instagram

David Falchek, Executive Director
Kristin Casler Kraft, President

Annual event including wine competitions and wine judge certification training.
600 Attendees
Frequency: Annual/November
Founded in 1967

3664 **Beer, Wine & Spirits Industry Trade Show**
Indiana Association of Beverage
200 S Meridian Street
Suite 350
Indianapolis, IN 46225-3418

317-847-7580; Fax: 317-673-4210

Teresa Koch

Annual show of 125 exhibitors of alcohol beverage distillers brewers that are recognized primary sources in the state of Indiana as supplies for retailers.
2500 Attendees

3665 **Craft Brewers Conference and Brew Expo America**
Brewers Association
736 Pearl Street
Boulder, CO 80302

303-447-0816
888-822-6273; Fax: 303-447-2825
info@brewersassociation.org
www.brewersassociation.org
Facebook, Twitter, Youtube

Charlie Papazian, President
Bob Pease, VP
Cindy Jones, Sales/Marketing Director
1,200 Attendees
Frequency: April

3666 **Great American Beer Festival**
Brewers Association
736 Pearl Street
Boulder, CO 80302

303-447-0816
888-822-6273; Fax: 303-447-2825
info@brewersassociation.org
www.brewersassociation.org
Facebook, Twitter, Youtube

Charlie Papazian, President
Bob Pease, VP
Cindy Jones, Sales/Marketing Director
Frequency: September

3667 **NBWA Annual Convention**
National Beer Wholesalers Association
1101 King Street
Suite 600
Alexandria, VA 22314

703-683-4300
800-300-6417
info@nbwa.org
www.nbwa.org
Facebook, Twitter

Craig Purser, President/CEO
Grace Connolly, Executive Assistant
Lauren Kane, VP, Communications
Paul Pisano, SVP Industry Affairs & Gen. Counsel
Patti Rouzie, VP, Membership & Meetings

Designed to provide valuable education programs and important networking opportunities for the beer industry. Featuring speakers and seminars on a number of topics of imprtance to beer distributors .
2500 Attendees
Frequency: Annual/Fall

3668 **National Beer Wholesalers Association Convention and Trade Show**
Corcoran Expositions
33 N Dearborn Street
Suite 505
Chicago, IL 60602-3103

312-541-0567
800-541-0359; Fax: 312-541-0573

Al Natker, Operations Manager

Biennial show of 166 manufacturers, suppliers and distributors of brewery software and hardware, trucking, beer cleaning equipment and related equipment, supplies and services.
3000 Attendees

3669 **Wineries Unlimited**
Vineyard & Winery Services
3883 Airway Drive
Suite 250
Santa Rosea, CA 95403

707-577-7700
800-535-5670; Fax: 707-577-7705

The largest, most powerful trade show and conference for the eastern wine industry.
2000 Attendees
Frequency: March

Directories & Databases

3670 **Beverage Marketing Directory**
Beverage Marketing Corporation
2670 Commercial Ave
Mingo Junction, OH 43938-1613

740-598-4133
800-332-6222; Fax: 740-598-3977
www.beveragemarketing.com

Andrew Standardi III, Director of Operations
Kathy Smurthwaite, Editor

Publication is available in Print Copy (Price-$1,465), PDF Format (Price-$1,465), CD-ROM Format (For pricing, call number listed for details or visit website), and Online.
1196 Pages

3671 **Brewers Resource Directory**
Brewers Association
736 Pearl Street
Boulder, CO 80302

303-447-0816
888-822-6273; Fax: 303-447-2825
info@brewersassociation.org
www.brewersassociation.org
Facebook, Twitter, Youtube

Charlie Papazian, President
Bob Pease, VP
Cindy Jones, Sales/Marketing Director

Various categories of listees are included that have a direct relation to the beer and liquor industry.
Mailing list available for rent

3672 **Contacts**
National Alcohol Beverage Control Association
4401 Ford Avenue, Suite 700
Alexandria, VA 22302-1507

703-578-4200; Fax: 703-820-3551
www.nabca.org
Facebook, Twitter

James M Sgueo, Executive Director
Dixie Jamieson, Executive Assistant

Members include control jurisdictions, supplier members and industry trade associations.

3673 **Directory & Products Guide**
Vineyard & Winery Services
PO Box 2358
Windsor, CA 95492

707-836-6820
800-535-5670; Fax: 707-836-6825
vwm-online.com

Jennifer Merietti, Sales/Marketing Manager
Dennis Black, General Manager
Suzanne Webb, Marketing Director

A must have reference book that belongs on the desk of every wine professional. Whether it's tracking down a particular vendor, shopping for the best deal on oak barrels or searching for out-of-state winery contacts, the DPG is a powerhouse of information. Over 2,300 supplier listings and 2,700 winery/vineyard listings, it is a reliable resource that saves time and money.
Cost: $95.00
450+ Pages
Frequency: Annually

3674 **Food & Beverage Market Place**
Grey House Publishing
4919 Route 22
PO Box 56
Amenia, NY 12501

518-789-8700
800-562-2139; Fax: 845-373-6390
books@greyhouse.com
www.greyhouse.com
Facebook, Twitter

Leslie Mackenzie, Publisher
Richard Gottlieb, Editor

This information-packed 3-volume set is the most powerful buying and marketing guide for the US food and beverage industry. Includes thousands of industry freight and transportation listings.
Cost: $595.00
2000 Pages
Frequency: Annual
ISBN: 1-592373-61-5
Founded in 1981

3675 **Food & Beverage Marketplace: Online Database**
Grey House Publishing

4919 Route 22
PO Box 56
Amenia, NY 12501

518-789-8700
800-562-2139; Fax: 518-789-0556
gold@greyhouse.com
gold.greyhouse.com
Facebook, Twitter

Richard Gottlieb, President
Leslie Mackenzie, Publisher

This complete updated Food & Beverage Market Place: Online Database is the go-to source for the food and beverage industry. Anyone involved in the food and beverage industry needs this 'industry bible' and the important contacts to develop critical research data that can make for successful business growth.
Frequency: Annual
Founded in 1981

3676 **Impact International Directory: Leading Spirits, Wine and Beer Companies**
M Shanken Communications
387 Park Ave S
8th Floor
New York, NY 10016-8872

212-684-4224; Fax: 212-684-5424
www.cigaraficionado.com

Marvin Shanken, Publisher

A directory offering information on the major players of the alcoholic beverage industry.
Cost: $295.00

3677 **Impact Yearbook: Directory of the US Wine, Spirits & Beer Industry**
M Shanken Communications
387 Park Ave S
8th Floor
New York, NY 10016-8872

212-684-4224; Fax: 212-684-5424
www.cigaraficionado.com

Marvin Shanken, Publisher

A directory offering information on the top 40 American distributors and profiles of companies.
Cost: $170.00
Frequency: Annual

3678 **US Alcohol Beverage Industry Category CD**
Beverage Marketing Corporation
2670 Commercial Ave
Mingo Junction, OH 43938-1613

740-598-4133
800-332-6222; Fax: 740-598-3977
www.beveragemarketing.com

Andrew Standardi III, Director of Operations
Kathy Smurthwaite, Editor

Contains information on approximately 3,030 companies including breweries, microbreweries, wineries, distilleries, wholesalers and importers.
Cost: $3010.00
Frequency: Annual

3679 **US Beverage Manufacturers and Filling Locations Category CD**
Beverage Marketing Corporation
850 Third Avenue, 18th Floor
New York, NY 10022

212-688-7640
800-332-6222; Fax: 212-826-1255
www.beveragemarketing.com

Andrew Standardi III, Director of Operations
Kathy Smurthwaite, Editor

Contains information on approximately 2,402 companies including breweries, microbreweries, wineries, distilleries, soft drink fillers and franchise companies, bottled water fillers, juice, sports beverages and energy drinks, soy, coffee, tea, and milk manufacturers.
Cost: $2390.00
Frequency: Annual
Mailing list available for rent

3680 **US Wine & Spirits Industry Category CD**
Beverage Marketing Corporation
2670 Commercial Ave
Mingo Junction, OH 43938-1613

740-598-4133
800-332-6222; Fax: 740-598-3977
www.beveragemarketing.com

Andrew Standardi III, Director of Operations
Kathy Smurthwaite, Editor

Contains information on approximately 1,484 companies including wineries, distilleries, wine & spirit wholesalers, and wine & spirit importers.
Cost: $1475.00
Frequency: Annual

3681 **Vineyard & Winery Management Magazine**
Vineyard & Winery Services
421 E Street
Santa Rosa, CA 95404

707-577-7700
800-535-5670; Fax: 707-577-7705
vwm-online.com

Jennifer Merletti, Sales/Marketing Manager
Robert Merletti, Chairman/Owner
George Christie, President/CEO

A leading technical trade publication serving the North American Wine Industry and designed for today's serious wine business professional.
Founded in 1975
Mailing list available for rent

3682 **Wholesale Beer Association Executives of America Directory**
Wholesale Beer Association Executives of America
2805 E Washington Avenue
Madison, WI 53704-5165

608-255-6464; Fax: 608-255-6466

7 Pages
Frequency: Annual

3683 **Wine & Spirits Industry Marketing**
Jobson Publishing Corporation
100 Avenue of the Americas
9th Floor
New York, NY 10013-1678

212-274-7000; Fax: 212-431-0500

Michael J Tansey, CEO

List of about 300 wine and liquor firms including wineries, producers, distillers and importers.
Cost: $150.00
Frequency: Annual April

3684 **Wine on Line**
Wine on Line International
400 E 59th St
Apartment 9F
New York, NY 10022-2342

212-755-4363; Fax: 212-755-7365

A database containing information including reviews about wines, production methods, serving advice, and more. Available on the Internet and worldwide web.
Frequency: Daily

3685 **Wines and Vines Directory of the Wine Industry in North America Issue**
Hiaring Company
1800 Lincoln Avenue
San Rafael, CA 94901-1221

415-453-9700; Fax: 415-453-2517
info@winesandvines.com
www.winesandvines.com

Dorthy Kubota-Cordery, Editor
Phil Hiaring, Publisher
Debbie Hennessy, Editor
Renee Skiadas, Circulation Director
Chet Klingensmith, Owner

Annual guide offering listings of wineries and wine industry suppliers in the US, Canada and Mexico.
Cost: $85.00
505 Pages
Frequency: Annual
Circulation: 5000

Industry Web Sites

3686 **http://gold.greyhouse.com**
G.O.L.D Grey House OnLine Databases

Grey House Publishing's online database platform, GOLD, offers Quick Search, Keyword Search and Expert Search for most business sectors including alcoholic beverage markets. The GOLD platform makes finding the information you need quick and easy - whether you're a novice searcher or an experienced database user. All of Grey House's directory products are available for subscription on the GOLD platform.

3687 **www.beerinstitute.org**
Beer Institute

Protects the market environment from unfair burdens imposed by government bodies. Represents members interest before Congress.

3688 **www.beertown.org**
American Homebrewers Association

Devoted to the education of home brewed beer. Publishes the only magazine devoted exclusively to education, art and science of homebrewing. Services include: Beer Judge Certification Program, Sanctioned Competitions, World's Largest Homebrew Competition.

3689 **www.cawineclub.com**
California Wine Club

A wine of the month club that features only California's small boutique wineries. Each month members receive two bottles of award-winning wine.

3690 **www.greyhouse.com**
Grey House Publishing

Authoritative reference directories for most business sectors including alcoholic beverage markets. Users can search the online databases with varied search criteria allowing for custom searches by product category, geographic area, sales volume, keyword, subject and more. Full Grey House catalog and online ordering also available

3691 **www.nbwa.org**
National Beer Wholesalers Association

Research and development, quality control and ingredients.

3692 **www.scisoc.org/asbc**
American Society of Brewing Chemists

Annual scientific meeting for professionals in the brewing industry.

3693 **www.wineinstitute.org**
Wine Institute

Dedicated to initiating and advocating state, federal and international public policy to enhance the environment for the responsible production, promotion and enjoyment of wine.

3694 **www.wssa.com**
Wine and Spirits Shippers Association
Provides members, importers and exporters with efficient and economical ocean transportation and other logistic services.

Associations

3695 Academy of Canadian Cinema & Television
411 Richmond Street E
Suite 9
Toronto, ON M5A 3S5

416-366-2227
800-644-5194; Fax: 416-366-8454
www.academy.ca
Facebook, Twitter, LinkedIn, Flickr, YouTube

John Young, Chair
Anne Marie La Traverse, Vice Chair
Anita McOuat, Treasurer
Beth Janson, President & CEO

A national non-profit, professional association dedicated to the promotion, recognition, and celebration of exceptional achievements in Candian film, television, and digital media.
Founded in 1949

3696 Academy of Television Arts and Science
5200 Lankershim Blvd
North Hollywood, CA 91601

818-754-2800; Fax: 818-761-2827
www.emmys.com
Facebook, Twitter, YouTube, Instagram, Pinterest

Jim Yeager, President
Laurel Whitcomb, Membership Events
Rose Einstein, Magazine Sales

Nonprofit corporation devoted to the advancement of telecommunications arts and sciences and to fostering creative leadership in the telecommunications industry. In addition to recognizing outstanding programming and individual achivements for Primetime and Los Angeles area programming, ATAS sponsors meetings, conferences and activities for collaboration on a variety of topics involving traditional broadcast interests, new media and emerging digital technology.
12000 Members
Founded in 1959

3697 Alaska Broadcasters Association
700 W 41st Street
Suite 102
Anchorage, AK 99503

907-258-2424; Fax: 907-258-2414
akba@gci.net
www.alaskabroadcasters.org
Facebook

DeeDee Caciari, President
Kim Williams, VP
Ed Ulman, Secretary/Treasurer
Cathy Hiebert, Executive Director

To provide assistance, which enables members to serve their communities of license through education, representation and advocacy.
Founded in 1964

3698 Alliance for Community Media
4248 Park Glen Road
Minneapolis, MN 55416

952-928-4643; Fax: 202-393-2653
info@allcommunitymedia.org
www.alliancecm.org
Facebook, Twitter, LinkedIn, Youtube, Flickr

Mike Wassenaar, President & CEO
Shelby Couch, Chief Operating Officer
Megan Dobberstein, Membership & Conference Coordinator
Katie Benson, Conference Manager

Participants include cable access television and community programmers. Individual membership dues are $70.00, organization $350.00.
1000 Members
Founded in 1976
Mailing list available for rent: 1000 names at $200 per M

3699 Alliance for Women in Media
1250 24th St NW
Suite 300
Washington, DC 20037

202-750-3664; Fax: 703-506-3266
info@allwomeninmedia.org
www.allwomeninmedia.org
Facebook, Twitter, LinkedIn, Youtube

Becky Brooks, Executive Director
LaTonya Jackson, Operations Manager
Lisa Stephenson, Events Director
Catherine Combs, PR & Marketing Manager

Leverages the promise, passion, and power of women in all forms of media carrying forth with its mission by educating, advocating, and acting as a resource to its members and the industry at large via inspired thought leadership that illuminates areas of social need.
Founded in 1951

3700 Alliance of Motion Picture and Television Producers
15301 Ventura Blvd
Building E
Sherman Oaks, CA 91403

818-995-3600; Fax: 818-382-1793
www.amptp.org

Nick Counter, President

Trade association with respect to labor issues in the motion picture and television industry. Negotiate industry wide collective bargaining agreements that cover actors, craftspersons, directors, musicians, technicians and writers.
350 Members
Founded in 1982

3701 American Auto Racing Writers and Broadcasters Association
922 North Pass Avenue
Burbank, CA 91505-2703

818-842-7005; Fax: 818-842-7020
www.aarwba.org
Facebook

Norma Brandel, President/Executive Director
Kathy Seymour, VP
Rhonda Williams, Treasurer
Patrick Reynolds, Secretary

The American Auto Racing Writers & Broadcasters Association is the oldest and largest organization devoted to auto racing coverage.
400 Members
Founded in 1955

3702 American Center for Children and Media
5400 North St Louis Avenue
Chicago, IL 60625

703-509-5510; Fax: 773-509-5303
www.childrensmediaassociation.org

Stephanie Sosa, President

Mission is to support a vibrant children's media industry by convening key constituencies to develop, implement and promote policies and practices that respect young people's well being, and are sustainable.
Founded in 1985

3703 American Disc Jockey Association
20118 N 67th Avenue
Suite 300-605
Glendale, CA 85308

888-723-5776; Fax: 866-310-4676
office@adja.org
www.adja.org
Facebook, Twitter, Youtube

Rob Snyder, Director

An association of professional mobile entertainers. Encourages success for its members through continuous education, camaraderie, and networking. The primary goal is to educate Disc Jockeys so that each member acts ethically and responsibly.

3704 American Private Radio Association (APRA)
PO Box 4221
Scottsdale, AZ 85261-4221

480-661-5000

Association members are from private radio stations.

3705 American Public Media
The Kling Public Media Center
480 Cedar St
St. Paul, MN 55101

800-562-8440
www.americanpublicmedia.org

Jon McTaggart, President & CEO
David Kansas, Exec. VP & COO
Morris Goodwin, SVP & CFO
Randi Yoder, SVP & Chief Development Officer
Tim Roesler, SVP & Chief Business Devt. Officer

Leading producer and distributor of public radio programming in the Upper Midwest, California and Florida, reaching 19 million listeners weekly.
Founded in 1967

3706 American Sportscasters Association
225 Broadway
Suite 2030
New York, NY 10007

212-227-8080; Fax: 212-571-0556
lschwa8918@aol.com
www.americansportscastersonline.com

Louis Schwartz, President/Founder
Patrick Turturro, Associate Editor

National Association of Sportscasters, radio, television and cable covering the US, Puerto Rico and Canada. Very active web site. Offers seminars, compiles statistics and operates a placement service, maintains a Hall of Fame and biographical archives and library.
500 Members
Founded in 1980

3707 Associated Press Broadcasters
1825 K Street NW
Suite 800
Washington, DC 20006-1202

212-621-1500; Fax: 202-736-1107
info@ap.org
Facebook, Twitter, LinkedIn, Youtube

Mary E Junck, Chairman
Gary Pruitt, President & CEO
Kathleen Carroll, Senior VP/Executive Editor
Jessica Bruce, VP/Director, Human Resource
Ken Dale, CFO/Senior VP

Seeks to advance journalism through radio and television, and cooperates with the AP to promote accurate and impartial news.
5.9m Members
Founded in 1846

3708 **Association for Maximum Service Television**
4100 Wisconsin Avenue NW
PO Box 9897
Washington, DC 20036-2224

202-966-1956; Fax: 202-966-9617
www.mstv.org

David Donovan, President

Assures the maintenance of an effective nationwide system of free television and seeks to meet present and future needs of the VHF and UHF system.
400+ Members
Founded in 1956

3709 **Association of Independent Commercial Producers**
3 W 18th St
5th Floor
New York, NY 10011

212-929-3000; Fax: 212-929-3359
mattm@aicp.com
www.aicp.com
Facebook, Twitter, LinkedIn, Youtube, Flickr, RSS

Matt Miller, President & CEO
Brian Doherty, Sr. Communications Manager
David Michael Gonzalez, Director, External Relations
Neal Lattner, Director, Relationships Marketing
Kristen Wilcha, VP, Operations/Chief of Staff

The national trade association of television commercial producers who account for in excess of 80% of the commercial production done in the United States annually.
500 Members
Founded in 1972

3710 **Association of Local Television Stations**
1320 19th Street NW
Washington, DC 20036

202-887-1970
www.altv.com

3711 **Association of Public Television Stations**
2100 Crystal Drive
Suite 700
Arlington, VA 22202

202-654-4200; Fax: 202-654-4236
www.apts.org
Facebook, Twitter

Patrick Butler, President & CEO
Lonna Thompson, Executive VP/COO & General Counsel
Kate Riley, VP, Government Relations
Emil Mara, VP, Finance & Administration

Nonprofit membership organization that supports the continued growth and development of a strong and financially sound noncommercial television service for the American public. Provides advocacy for public television interests at the national level, as well as consistent leadership and information in marshaling grassroots and congressional support for its members: the nation's public television stations.
153 Members
Founded in 1979

3712 **Audio Engineering Society**
551 Fifth Avenue
Room 1225
New York, NY 10176

212-661-8528; Fax: 212-682-0477
HQ@aes.org
www.aes.org
Facebook, Twitter, LinkedIn, Youtube, Google+, RSS

Colleen Harper, Executive Director
Chris Plunkett, Director, Operations
Graham Kirk, Director, Sales & Marketing
Frank Wells, Director, Communications
Richard Cabot, Standards Manager

Professional society devoted to audio technology. Membership includes leading engineers, scientists and other authorities in the field. Serves its members, the industry and the public by stimulating and facilitating advances in the constantly changing field of audio.
Founded in 1948

3713 **Broadcast Cable Credit Association**
550 W. Frontage Road
Suite 3600
Northfield, IL 60093

847-881-8757; Fax: 847-784-8059
info@bccacredit.com
www.bccacredit.com
Twitter, LinkedIn

Mary Collins, President & CEO
Jamie Grande, Director, Operations
Arcelia Pimentel, Sales/Membership
Dawn Stenstrom, Credit Investigator
Colette Pinter, Credit Investigator

BCCA, a subsidiary of Media Financial Management Association, represents credit and collection professionals from TV, radio, cable, system operators, newspaper, and magazine organizations in the U.S. and Canada. BCCA functions as a central clearinghouse for credit information on advertisers, agencies and buying services, both locally and nationally.
Founded in 1972

3714 **Broadcast Designers' Association International**
145 W 45th Street
Room 1100
New York, NY 10036-4008

212-376-6222; Fax: 212-376-6202

Association for manufacturers or suppliers of broadcast design equipment, supplies and services.

3715 **Broadcast Education Association**
1771 N St NW
Washington, DC 20036-2891

202-602-0587; Fax: 202-609-9940
help@beaweb.org
www.beaweb.org
Facebook, Twitter, LinkedIn

Tony DeMars, President
Vic Costello, VP, Academic Relations
Christine Merritt, VP, Industry Relations
Stacey Irwin, Secretary-Treasurer

Serves as a higher education association of professors and industry professionals who teach college students worldwide and prepares them to go into the broadcasting and related emerging technologies professions upon graduation from college.
1400 Members
Founded in 1955
Mailing list available for rent: 1300 names at $100 per M

3716 **Broadcast Pioneers**
7 World Trade Center
250 Greenwich Street
New York, NY 10007-0030

212-220-3000; Fax: 212-246-2163
www.bmi.com
Facebook, Twitter, YouTube, Pinterest, Google+

Michael O'Neill, President & CEO
Bruce A Esworthy, Senior Vice President & CFO
Mike West, SVP & Chief Information Officer
Nada Latto, Vice President, Human Resources
Stuart Rosen, SVP & General Counsel

Honors radio or television stations for excellence in art and community service. Maintains library documents on television broadcasting history.
1.4M Members
Founded in 1942

3717 **Broadcasters Foundation of America**
125 West 55th Street
4th Floor
New York, NY 10019

212-373-8250; Fax: 212-373-8254
info@thebfoa.org
www.broadcastersfoundation.org

James Thompson, President
Peter Doyle, Vice President
Frank Pesce, VP, Business Affairs

Provides financial assistance to radio and television broadcasters who are in financial need due to an illness, an accident, advanced age or a natural disaster.
Founded in 1960

3718 **Cable & Telecommunications Association for Marketing**
120 Waterfront Street
Suite 200
National Harbor, MD 20745

301-485-8900
info@ctam.com
www.ctam.com
Twitter, LinkedIn

Vicki Lins, President & CEO
Angie Britt, SVP, Advanced Products
Zell Murphy, SVP, Finance & Administration
Mark Snow, SVP & GM, Consumer Marketing
Ken Leonardo, VP, Marketing

Provides marketing knowledge and industry scale to help its membersmanage the future and drive business results. Also provides consumer research, industry resources, a job bank, conferences and awards.

3719 **Canadian Association of Broadcast Consultants**
130 Cree Crescent
Winnepeg, MB R3J 3W1

204-889-9202; Fax: 204-831-6650
jsadoun@yrh.com
www.cabc-accr.ca

Joseph Sadoun, Ing P Eng, President
Kerry Pelser, Secretary/Treasurer

Prepares technical briefs, coverage studies and frequencies.

3720 **Canadian Association of Broadcasters**
770-45 O'Connor St
Ottawa, ON K1P 1A4

613-233-4035; Fax: 613-233-6961
www.cab-acr.ca

Kevin Desjardins, President
Sylvie Bissonnette, VP, Finance & Administration & CFO
Latecia Lance, Controller

Serves as the eyes and ears of the private broadcasting community to advocate and lobby on its behalf and to act as a cebtral point on matters of joint interest.

3721 **Canadian Association of Ethnic Broadcasters (Radio)**
622 College Street
Toronto, ON M6G 1B6

416-531-9991; Fax: 416-531-5274
info@chinradio.com

www.chinradio.com
Facebook, Twitter

Johnny Lombardi, Founder, President

Pioneer in multicultural radio broadcasting and has lead the way for similar briadcast operations to be established.

3722 **Caribbean Broadcasting Union**
Suite 1B, Building 6A
Harbor Industrial Estate
St Michael, BB 11145

246-430-1006; Fax: 242-228-9524
patrick.cozier@caribsurf.com
www.discountdominicatravel.com

Patrick Cozier, President

Stimulates the flow of broadcast material among the radio and television systems in the Caribbean region.
Founded in 1970
Mailing list available for rent

3723 **Coalition Opposing Signal Theft**
25 Massachusetts Ave NW
Suite 100
Washington, DC 20001

202-222-2300
webmaster@ncta.com
www.ncta.com
Facebook, Twitter, LinkedIn

Michael Powell, President & CEO
James M Assey, Executive VP
K Dane Snowden, Chief Operating Officer
Mark Kulish, SVP, Finance & Admin. & CFO
William Check, SVP, Chief Technology Officer

Acts as a clearinghouse of information regarding cable signal theft.

3724 **Community Antenna Television Association**
PO Box 1005
Fairfax, VA 22030-1005

202-775-3550

An association of over 3,000 cable television systems.
3M Members

3725 **Content Delivery & Security Association**
39 N Bayles Ave
Port Washington, NY 11050

516-767-6720; Fax: 516-883-5793
info@CDSAonline.org
www.cdsaonline.org

Guy Finley, President
Don Hurley, Executive Assistant
Karen Brewer, Secretary
Garrett Randell, VP, Member Services
Chris Tribbey, Editorial Director

International trade association dealing with every facet of recording, media and related industries. Membership includes raw material providers, manufacturers, replicators, duplicators, packagers, and copyright holders.

3726 **Corporation for Public Broadcasting**
401 9th St NW
Washington, DC 20004-2129

202-879-9600
800-272-2190; Fax: 202-879-9700
oigemail@cpb.org
www.cpb.org
Facebook, Twitter

Patricia De Stacey Harrison, President & CEO
Michael Levy, EVP & COO
William Tayman Jr., CFO/Treasurer
Westwood Smithers Jr., Senior VP/General Counsel
Teresa Safon, SVP & Chief of Staff

Facilitate the development of, and ensure universal access to, non-commercial high-quality programming and telecommunications services. It does this in conjunction with non-commercial educational telecommunications licensees across the country.
Founded in 1967

3727 **Country Radio Broadcasters**
1009 16th Ave South
Nashville, TN 37212

615-327-4487; Fax: 615-329-4492
info@crb.org
www.countryradioseminar.com
Facebook, Twitter

RJ Curtis, Executive Director
Chasity Crouch, Business Manager
Heather Martin, Director, Logistics & Events
Darcie Van Etten, Director, Marketing
Ashley Bourque, Project Manager

Broadcasting forum.
Founded in 1969

3728 **Educational Broadcasting Association**
825 Eighth Ave
New York, NY 10019

212-560-1313; Fax: 212-560-1314
programming@thirteen.org
www.thirteen.org
Facebook, Twitter, Pinterest, YouTube

Neal Shapiro, President & CEO
Kellie Castruita Specter, Chief Marketing & Engagement Offr.
Caroline C Croen, VP, CFO, Treasurer
Robert A Feinberg, VP, General Counsel, Secretary
Debasish Mishra, Chief Technology Officer

Association members are producers and directors of public educational programming, channel 13, PBS.
500 Members
Mailing list available for rent

3729 **Enterprise Wireless Alliance**
2121 Cooperative Way
Suite 255
Herndon, VA 20171

703-524-1074
800-482-8282
info@EnterpriseWireless.org
www.enterprisewirelessalliance.org

Mark Crosby, President & CEO
Bill Mulholland, Executive Director, Finance
Andrea Cumpston, Director, Communications

Provides a license renewal reminder service. Maintains liaison with major radio manufacturers and mediates problems between licensees.
15 Members
Founded in 1953

3730 **Geospatial Information and Technology Association**
1360 University Ave W
Suite 455
St. Paul, MN 55104-4086

844-447-4482; Fax: 844-223-8218
bsamborski@gita.org
www.gita.org
Facebook, Twitter, LinkedIn, YouTube

Don Knox, Executive Director
Emily Dufour, Membership Specialist
Mary Fitzgerald, Conferences Director
Susan Nolte, Finance Director

Provides unbiased educational programs, forums and publications for professionals involved with geospatial information and technology.
2200 Members
Founded in 1960

3731 **Hollywood Radio and Television Society**
16530 Ventura Boulevard
Suite 411
Encino, CA 91436

818-789-1182; Fax: 818-789-1210
info@hrts.org
www.hrts.org
Facebook, Twitter, LinkedIn

Marc Korman, HRTS Board President
Melissa Grego, CEO
Elvia Gonzalez, Director of Member Services
Kira Hodge-Rochon, Director of Operations
Nicole Hancock, Coordinator, Admin. & Operations

Sponsors monthly luncheons featuring top industry and government speakers and seminars about broadcasting, maintains film and audio library.
2000 Members
Founded in 1947

3732 **Intercollegiate Broadcasting Systems**
367 Windsor Highway
New Windsor, NY 12553-7900

845-565-0003; Fax: 845-565-7446
ibs@ibsradio.org
www.collegebroadcasters.us
Facebook, Twitter

Chris Thomas, Chair
Norman Prusslin, President
Fritz Kass, CEO

Nonprofit association of student staffed radio/tv/media stations based at schools and colleges across the country. Some 1,000 member stations operate all sizes and types of facilities including Internet-Webcasting, closed circuit, AM carrier-current, cable radio and FCC-licensed FM and AM stations.
1000 Members
Founded in 1940

3733 **International Association of Broadcast Monitors**
PO Box 986
Irmo, SC 29063

803-749-9833
800-236-1741; Fax: 888-732-9004
theiabm.org

Peter White, Chief Executive
Lucinda Meek, Chief Financial Officer
Lisa Collins, Head, Membership Engagement
Ben Dales, Head, Digital
Stan Moote, Chief Technology Officer

Worldwide trade association made up of news retrieval services which monitor television, radio, internet and print news mediums. It acts as a clearinghouse or forum for discussion on topics of collective concerns and acts as a united voice for the news monitoring industry.
Founded in 1981

3734 **International Council-National Academy**
25 W 52nd Street
New York, NY 10019

212-489-6969; Fax: 212-489-6557
iemmys@iemmys.tv
www.iemmys.tv
Facebook, Twitter, LinkedIn

Fred Cohen, Chair
Bruce Paisner, President & CEO
Kevin Beggs, Treasurer

Furthers the arts and sciences by bestowing International Emmy Awards, George Movshon Fellowship and the Joan Wilson memorial scholarship.
250+ Members
Founded in 1969

3735 **International Radio and Television Society Foundation**
1697 Broadway
10th Floor
New York, NY 10019

212-867-6650; Fax: 212-867-6653
irtsfoundation.org

Joyce M. Tudrynff, President & CEO
Debra O'Connell, Chair
Karna Crawford, Vice Chair

The lines between broadcast televison and radio, cable, telephony and the computer industry may be blurring, but one thing remains clear, we all have an affinity for a business that entertains, informs, educates and serves the American public in a meaningful way. The foundation provides a unique common forum for all segments of the communication industry. Members can enjoy sharing insight and ideas with colleagues during the season's numerous events.

750 Members
Founded in 1939

3736 **International Television Academy**
25 W 52nd Street
New York, NY 10019

212-489-6969; Fax: 212-489-6557
iemmys@iemmys.tv
www.iemmys.tv
Facebook, Twitter, LinkedIn

Bruce Paisner, President & CEO
Fred Cohen, Chair
Kevin Beggs, Treasurer

Organization of global broadcasters, with representatives from over 50 countries based outside of the US, and represents the world's largest production, distribution and broadcast companies.

Founded in 1969

3737 **Jones/NCTI-National Cable Television Institute**
9697 E Mineral Ave
Centennial, CO 80112

303-792-3111
800-525-7002; Fax: 303-797-0829
www.ncti.com

Stacey Slaughter, President & CEO
Camilla Formica, Chief Revenue Officer
David Hoyt, VP, Student & Client Support
Jeff Rawson, Sr. Director, Tech. & Developmemt
Paul Eisbrener, Sr. Director, Learning & Devt.

Workforce performance products, services and education.

30 Members
Founded in 1969
Mailing list available for rent

3738 **Library of American Broadcasting**
University of Maryland
Mckeldin Library
College Park, MD 20742-7011

301-405-0800; Fax: 301-314-2634
www.lib.umd.edu
Facebook, Twitter, YouTube, Flickr

Kate Maloney, Dir., Strategic Communications
Judith Kidd, Chief of Staff
Tiffany Rogers, Director, Human Resources

Holds a wide ranging collection of audio and video recordings, books, pamphlets, periodicals, personal collections, oral histories, photographs, scripts and vertical files devoted exclusively to the history of broadcasting.

Founded in 1972

3739 **Manufacturers Radio Frequency Advisory Committee**
616 E 34th Street N
Wichita, KS 67219

316-832-9213
800-262-9206
info@mrfac.com
www.mrfac.com

Danny Hankins, President
Joe Cramer, VP
Nate Miller, Secretary
Rich Elersich, Treasurer

Representing the voice of the manufacturing industry and private land mobile radio users before the Federal Communications Commision, the responsibe federal regulatory agency for the nation's industrial communications. The leaders of the manufacturing industry, individually and collectively, have an obligation to influence the policies, plans, and procedures which govern the growth, structure and use of our national radio spectrum and telecommunications systems.

14000 Members
Founded in 1954

3740 **Media Communications Association International**
P.O.Box 5135
Madison, WI 53705-0135

608-836-0722
800-899-6224; Fax: 888-899-6224
loiswei@aol.com
iamcr.org
Facebook, Twitter, LinkedIn, Google +

Nico Carpentier, President
Bruce Girard, Executive Director

The Media Communications Association-International is a global community that provides professional development seminars and events, opportunities for networking, members-only benefits, forums for education, and information resources for media communications professionals.

Founded in 1968

3741 **Media Financial Management Association**
550 W Frontage Road
Suite 3600
Northfield, IL 60093

847-716-7000; Fax: 847-716-7004
info@mediafinance.org
www.mediafinance.org
Twitter, LinkedIn

Mary M Collins, President/CEO
Jamie Grande, Director of Operations
Arcelia Pimentel, Director of Sales
Mandy Aoieong, Admin. & Marketing Coordinator

Professional society of media's top financial, MIS Credit and HR executives, plus associates in auditing, data processing, software development, law, tax and credit and collections

1300 Members
Founded in 1961
Mailing list available for rent

3742 **Museum of Broadcast Communications**
360 North State Street
Chicago, IL 60654-5411

312-245-8200; Fax: 312-245-8207
info@museum.tv
www.museum.tv
Facebook, Twitter

Bruce DuMont, President, CEO
David Plier, VP, Secretary
Jack Weinberg, VP

Collects, preserves, and presents historic and contemporary radio and television content as well as educate, inform , and entertain the public through its archives, public programs, screenings, exhibits, publications, and online access to its resources.

3743 **National Academy of Television Arts and Sciences**
1697 Broadway
Suite 404
New York, NY 10019

212-586-8424; Fax: 212-246-8129
www.emmyonline.tv
Facebook, Twitter, LinkedIn, Google +

Adam Sharp, President & CEO
Terry O'Reilly, Chair
Paul Pillitteri, SVP, Communications & Operations

Dedicated to the advancement of the arts and sciences of television and the promotion of creative leadership for artistic, educational and technical achievements within the television industry. It recognizes excellence in television with the coveted Emmy Award.

12M Members
Founded in 1957
Printed in on glossy stock

3744 **National Alliance of State Broadcasters Associations**
2333 Wisconsin St NE
Albuquerque, NM 87110

505-881-4444
www.nasbaonline.net
Twitter

Mark Gordon, President
Bob Houghton, Vice-President
Dewey Bruce, Secretary/Treasurer

The Alliance represents the interests of the 50 state broadcast associations in Washington.

3745 **National Association of Black Owned Broadcasters (NABOB)**
1201 Connecticut Avenue NW
Suite 200
Washington, DC 20036

202-463-8970; Fax: 202-429-0657
nabobinfo@nabob.org
www.nabob.org

James Winston, President
Kathy Nickens, Executive Assistant

Largest trade organization representing the interests of African-American owners of radio and television stations across the country.

Founded in 2001

3746 **National Association of Broadcasters**
1771 N St Nw
Washington, DC 20036

202-429-5300; Fax: 202-429-4199
nab@nab.org
www.nab.org
Facebook, Twitter, LinkedIn, YouTube

Gordon Smith, President & CEO
Curtis LeGeyt, Chief Operating Officer
Tea Gennaro, EVP, Finance & CFO
Michelle Duke, Chief Diversity Officer
Sam Matheny, Chief Technology Officer

Full service trade association that represents the interests of free, over-the-air radio and television broadcasters. Offers seminars and workshops to members and holds local meetings that offer support on legal and industry issues. Sponsors the National Association of Broadcasters Educational Foundation, dedicated to serving the public interest via education and training programs, strategies to increase diverse initiatives, community support and philanthropy.

7000 Members
Founded in 1923

3747 **National Association of College Radio/TV Stations**
71 George Street
Providence, RI 02912-1824

401-863-2225; Fax: 401-863-2221
nacb@aol.com

Members are student radio/TV stations and interested individuals. Has an annual budget of approximately $300,000.
1600 Members
Founded in 1988

3748 **National Association of Farm Broadcasters**
1100 Platte Falls Road
PO Box 500
Platte City, MO 64079

816-431-4032; Fax: 816-431-4087
info@nafb.com
www.nafb.com
Facebook, Twitter

Tom Brand, Executive Director
Susan Tally, Operations Director
Mary Reder, Membership Manager
Erin Nash, Marketing & Communications Manager

Works to improve quantity and quality of farm programming and serves as a clearinghouse for new ideas in farm broadcasting.
600 Members
Founded in 1944

3749 **National Association of Television Program Executives**
3940 Laurel Canyon Blvd.
Suite 324
Studio City, CA 91604

Home Page: www.natpe.com
Facebook, Twitter, Youtube

JP Bommel, President/CEO
Wayneston Harbeson, SVP, Event Operations
Charlie Weiss, SVP, Business Development
Doug Finberg, SVP, Marketing
Shruti Shah, Digital Marketing Specialist

A global, non-profit organization dedicated to the creation, development and distribution of televised programming in all forms across all mature and emerging media platforms.
2800 Members
Founded in 1963
Mailing list available for rent

3750 **National Cable & Telecommunications Association**
25 Massachusetts Ave. NW
Suite 100
Washington, DC 20001

202-222-2300
webmaster@ncta.com
www.ncta.com
Facebook, Twitter, LinkedIn

Michael Powell, President & CEO
James Assey, Executive VP
K. Dane Snowden, Chief Operating Officer
Mark Kulish, SVP, Finance & Admin. & CFO
William Check, SVP, Chief Technology Officer

Trade association for U.S. cable industry.
200+ Members
Founded in 1940

3751 **National Council for Families & TV**
3801 Barham Boulevard
Los Angeles, CA 90068-1000

323-953-7300; Fax: 310-208-5984

Advances and promotes television awareness for family television shows.

3752 **National Federation of Community Broadcasting**
PO Box 16
1308 Clear Fork Road
Crawford, CO 81415

970-279-3411; Fax: 510-451-8208
www.nfcb.org

Sally Kane, Chief Executive Officer
Gretchen Aston-Puckett, Chief Operating Officer
Ernesto Aguilar, Program Director

A national alliance of stations, producers, and others committed to community radio. NFCB advocates for national public policy, funding, recognition, and resources on behalf of its membership while providing services to empower and strengthen community broadcasters through the core values of localism, diversity, and public service.

3753 **National Public Radio Association**
1111 North Capitol Street NW
Washington, DC 20002

202-686-0516; Fax: 202-513-3329
www.npr.org
Facebook, Twitter

John Lansing, President/CEO
Christopher Turpin, Chief of Staff
Deborah Cowan, Chief Financial Officer
Thomas Hjelm, Chief Digital Officer
Michael Smith, Chief Marketing Officer

Works in partnership with member stations to create a more informed public, one challenged and invigorated by a deeper understanding and appreciation of events, ideas, and cultures.
750 Members
Founded in 1970

3754 **National Religious Broadcasters**
9510 Technology Dr
Manassas, VA 20110

703-330-7000; Fax: 703-330-7100
info@nrb.org
www.nrb.org
Facebook, Twitter, LinkedIn, YouTube, Google+ RSS

Troy Miller, CEO
Daniel Darling, SVP, Communications
Kim Marquis, VP, Finance
Beth Wakefield, Director, Events
Lyndsey Thornton, Membership Coordinator

Represents evangelical Christian radio and television stations, program producers, multimedia developers and related organizations around the worldMembers are responsible for much of the world's Christian radio and television.
1700 Members
Founded in 1944
Mailing list available for rent

3755 **National Sports Media Association**
PO Box 5394
Winston-Salem, NC 27113

336-655-2976
nationalsportsmedia.org
Facebook, Twitter

Dave Goren, Executive Director
Dee Wilson, Local Development Director

Meet annually.
1000 Members
Founded in 1959
Mailing list available for rent

3756 **New England Cable & Telecommunications Associatoin Inc**
101 Federal Street
Suite 1900
Boston, MA 02110

781-843-3418; Fax: 781-849-6267
nectaoffice@necta.info
www.necta.info

Timothy Wilkerson, President
David Soutter, Dir., Public Policy & Reg. Affairs
Kristin Grazioso, Director, Legislative Affairs

NECTA is a six state regional trade association representing sbtstantially all private cable telecommunications companies in Connecticut, Maine, Massachusetts, New Hampshire, Rhode Island and Vermont.

3757 **North American Broadcasters Association (N ABA)**
205 Wellington Street West
Suite 6C300
Toronto, ON M5V 3G7

416-598-9877; Fax: 416-598-9774
contact@nabanet.com
www.nabanet.com

Michael McEwan, Director General
Anh Ngo, Director, Administration
Jenn Hadfield, Senior Coordinator, Committees
Ashley Lloyd Spanton, Executive Assistant & Editor
Kevin La, Web Administrator

A non-profit association of broadcasting organizations in the United States, Mexico, and Canada committed to advancing the interests of broadcasters at home and internationally.

3758 **North American Network**
5335 Wisconson Ave NW
Suite 440
Washington, DC 20015

202-243-0592
info@nanradio.com
www.nanradio.com

Tom Sweeney, Chief Client Advocate
Sherry Jones, Director, Station Services
Tom Kajubi, Dir., Finance & Administration
June Thornton, Publicist

Radio broadcasting agency that provides news and programming services to radio stations and organizations. Programming is sponsored by the corporations, government angencies, associations and nonprofit organizations who are indentified in the program notes and scripts.

3759 **Public Broadcasting Service**
2100 Crystal Dr
Arlington, VA 22202

Home Page: www.pbs.org
Facebook, Twitter, YouTube

Paula Kerger, President & CEO
Jonathan Barzilay, Chief Operating Officer
Tom Tardivo, CFO & Treasurer
Ira Rubenstein, Chief Digital & Marketing Officer
Sylvia Bugg, Chief Programming Executive

PBS is a private, nonprofit association of public TV stations providing arts content, ecucational programs for children, documentaries and non-commercial news programs to all Americans.
Founded in 1969

3760 **Public Radio in Mid-America (PRIMA)**
3651 Olive Street
St Louis, MO 63108

314-516-5968; Fax: 307-766-6184
www.wordpress.prima.org

Paul Maassen, President

Trusted source of informationa nd entertainment that opens minds and nourishes the spirit.

3761 **Radio Advertising Bureau**
1320 Greenway Dr
Suite 500
Irving, TX 75038-2547

972-753-6700
800-232-3131; Fax: 972-753-6727
jhaley@rab.com
www.rab.com
Facebook, Twitter

Erica Farber, President & CEO
Van Allen, EVP & CFO
Leah Kamon, SVP, Marketing & Communications
Brooke Williams, SVP, Membership
Madison Wright, Events & Communications Coordinator

Our mission is to lead industry initiatives and provide organizational, educational, research and advocacy programs and services that benefit the RAB membership and the Radio industry as a whole.
7000 Members

3762 **Radio Television Digital News Assn.**
529 14th Street NW
Suite 1240
Washington, DC 20045

800-807-8632; Fax: 202-223-4007
www.rtdna.org
Facebook, Twitter, LinkedIn

Dan Shelley, Executive Director & COO
Tara Puckey, Chief Staff Officer
Christen DeBard, Director, Events & Education
Karen Hansen, Dir., Mem., Marketing & Comm.

An association dedicated to setting new standards for newsgathering and reporting.

3763 **Radio Television Digital News Association Canada**
439 University Avenue
5th Floor
Toronto, ON M5G 1Y8

437-836-3088
877-257-8632; Fax: 416-364-8896
www.rtdnacanada.com
Facebook, Twitter

Fiona Conway, President
Sherry Naylor, Mem., Regional Events, Gen. Inquiry

Progressive organization offering a forum for open discussion and action in the broadcast news industry. Speaks for the leaders of Canada's radio and television news operations on the issues that impact the newsroom.

3764 **Radio and Television Research Council**
234 5th Ave
#417
New York, NY 10001

212-028-8933; Fax: 212-481-3071

Robert M Purcell, Executive Director

Members are professionals actively engaged in radio/television research.
200 Members
Founded in 1941

3765 **Satellite Broadcasting and Communication Association (SBCA)**
1100 17th Street NW
Suite 1150
Washington, DC 20036

202-349-3620
800-541-5981; Fax: 202-349-3621
info@sbca.org
www.sbca.com
Facebook, Twitter, LinkedIn

Steven Hill, President
Tracy Ann Strickland, Research Coordinator
Ali Bullis, Operations Director

National trade organization representing all segments of the satellite consumer services industry. The association is committed to expanding the utilization of satellite technology for the delivery of video, data, voice, interactive and broadband services.
1000 Members
Founded in 1986

3766 **Screen Actors Guild - American Federation of Television and Radio Artists**
5757 Wilshire Blvd
7th Floor
Los Angeles, CA 90036

323-954-1600
855-724-2387
sagaftrainfo@sagaftra.org
www.sagaftra.org
Facebook, Twitter, Instagram, YouTube, RSS

David White, National Executive Director
Arianna Ozzanto, Chief Financial Officer
Duncan Crabtree-Ireland, COO & General Counsel
Mary Cavallaro, Chief Broadcast Officer
Pam Greenwalt, Chief Communications & Marketing

Formerly the American Federation of Television and Radio Artists. Represents performers ranging from announcers, dances, journalists, recording artists, stunt performers, to actors, singers, and other media professionals.
Founded in 1952

3767 **Society of Broadcast Engineers**
9102 N Meridian St
Suite 150
Indianapolis, IN 46260

317-846-9000; Fax: 317-846-9120
mclappe@sbe.org
www.sbe.org
Facebook, Twitter, LinkedIn, YouTube

John Poray, President
Chris Scherer, Member Communications Director
Cathy Orosz, Education Director
Megan Clappe, Certification Director
Debbie Hennessey, Sustaining Member Manager

SBE provides members with the opportunity to network and share ideas and information in keeping current with the ongoing changes within the industry. Members can attend annual conferences and expositions, have access to educational opportunities and obtain professional certification.
5500 Members
Founded in 1964
Mailing list available for rent: 5700 names at $170 per M

3768 **Society of Motion Picture & Television Engineers**
3 Barker Ave
5th Floor
White Plains, NY 10601

914-761-1100; Fax: 914-761-3115
www.smpte.org
Facebook, Twitter, LinkedIn, YouTube, Flickr

Barbara Lange, Executive Director
Sally-Ann D'Amato, Director, Events
Roberta Gorman, Director, Membership
Frank Kunkle, Director, Marketing
Joyce Cataldo, Director, Business Development

The Society of Motion Picture and Television Engineers (SMPTE), is the leading technical society for the motion imaging industry. SMPTE members are spread throughout 64 countries worldwide. Sustaining (institutional) Members belong to SMPTE, allowing networking and contacts to occur on a larger scale. Touching on every discipline, our members include engineers, technical directors, cameramen, editors, technicians, manufacturers, designers, educators, consultants and field users.
6000 Members
Founded in 1916

3769 **Statenets National Association of State Radio Networks**
17911 Harwood Avenue
Homewood, IL 60430

708-799-6676
804-364-3075; Fax: 708-799-6698
www.statenets.com
Facebook, Twitter, LinkedIn, RSS

Dave Martin, Partner, East Coast Region
Carolyn Fisher, Partner, Southeast & Midwest Region
Judy Burns, Partner, West & Southwest Region
Carla Litton, Comptroller
Jason Price, Administrative Coordinator

Works with hundreds of regional and national marketers and political campaigns solve marketing challenges.

3770 **Television Bureau of Advertising**
120 Wall Street
15th Floor
New York, NY 10005-3908

212-486-1111; Fax: 212-935-5631
www.tvb.org

Steve Lanzano, President & CEO
Abby Auerbach, EVP & Chief Communications Officer
Brad Seitter, EVP, Business Development
Susan Converse, SVP, Chief Financial Officer
Hadassa Gerber, EVP, Chief Research Officer

Not-for-profit trade association of America's broadcast television industry. TVB provides a diverse variety of tools and resources to support its members and to help advertisers make the best use of local television.
600 Members
Founded in 1954

3771 **Television Bureau of Canada**
160 Bloor Street East
Suite 1005
Toronto, ON M4W 1B9

416-923-8813
800-231-0051; Fax: 416-413-3879

TVB markets the benefits and effectiveness of the TV medium in all its forms to advertisers and agencies. TVB collects, interprets, develops, identifies, and communicates information and data to be used.

3772 **Television Critics Association**
825 East Douglas Avenue
Witchita, KS 67202

316-268-6394; Fax: 316-288-6627
info@tvcritics.org
www.tvcritics.org
Facebook, Twitter

Sarah Rodman, President
Melanie McFarland, Vice President
Jacqueline Cutler, Secretary
Damian Holbrook, Treasurer

Represents journalists writing about television for print and online outlets.
220 Members

3773 **Television Operators Caucus**
1176 K Street NW
9th Floor
Washington, DC 20006

202-719-7090; Fax: 202-719-7548
Facebook, Twitter, Google+

Nate Drouin, Founder/CEO
Kurt Schneider, COO
Kevin Bedell, CTO

Non-profit group of memebers that support television issues and its impacts on the world today.

3774 **The Alliance for Community Media**
4248 Park Glen Road
Minneapolis, MN 55416

952-928-4643; Fax: 703-506-3266
info@allcommunitymedia.org
www.allcommunitymedia.org
Facebook, Twitter, RSS, YouTube, Flickr

Mike Wassenaar, President & CEO
Shelby Couch, Chief Operating Officer
Katie Benson, Conference Manager
Megan Dobberstein, Mem. & Conference Coordinator

Promotes civic engagement through community medias.
1000 Members
Founded in 1976

3775 **The Broadcasters Hall of Fame**
1240 Ashford Lane, 1A
PO Box 8247
Akron, OH 44320

330-867-3779; Fax: 330-867-4907
www.nab.org

Gordon Smith, President & CEO
Curtis LeGeyt, Chief Operating Officer
Tea Gennaro, EVP, Finance & CFO
Michelle Duke, Chief Diverity Officer
Sam Matheny, Chief Technology Officer

A wealth of memorabilia from the early days of broadcasting, clippings from newspapers and magazines, taped recorded portions of early radio shows and other gems of broadcasting history.
Founded in 1982

3776 **WGBH Educational Foundation**
One Guest Street
Boston, MA 02135

617-300-5400
www.wgbh.org
Facebook, Twitter

Jonathan C Abbott, President/CEO
Claudia Palmer, COO
Andre Alexander, CFO/VP, Finance
Amy Axelrod, Chief of Staff
Tina Cassidy, Chief Marketing Officer

Make knowledge and the creative life of the arts, sciences, and humanities available to the widest possible public
Founded in 1836

Newsletters

3777 **American Sportscasters Association Insiders Newsletter**
American Sportscasters Association
225 Broadway
Suite 2030
New York, NY 10007-3742

212-227-8080; Fax: 212-571-0556
lschwa8918@aol.com
www.americansportscastersonline.com
Facebook, Twitter

Louis O Schwartz, CEO

Newsletter keeps sportscasters up to date on important issues for the profession.
24 Pages
Frequency: Quarterly
Circulation: 2500
Founded in 1980

3778 **Bandwidth Investor**
Kagan World Media
126 Clock Tower Place
Carmel, CA 93923-8746

831-624-1536; Fax: 831-625-3225
www.kagan.com

George Niesen, Editor
Harvy Carft, Marketing Manager
Tim Baskerville, CEO/President
Harvy Carft, Circulation Manager
Cost: $945.00
Frequency: Monthly
Founded in 1969

3779 **Broadband Fixed Wireless**
Kagan World Media
126 Clock Tower Place
Carmel, CA 93923-8746

831-624-1536; Fax: 831-625-3225
www.kagan.com

George Niesen, Editor
Tom Johnson, Marketing Manager
Cost: $845.00
Frequency: Monthly

3780 **Broadband Systems & Design**
Gordon Publications
301 Gibraltar Drive
#650
Morris Plains, NJ 07950-3400

973-292-5100; Fax: 973-539-3476

Terry McCoy Jr, Publisher
Andrea Frucci, Editor

The only product tabloid serving buying influencers, engineers, corporate managers and purchasing professionals in the cable television marketplace.
Circulation: 26,400

3781 **Broadband Technology**
Kagan World Media
126 Clock Tower Place
Carmel, CA 93923-8746

831-624-1536; Fax: 831-625-3225
www.kagan.com

George Niesen, Editor
Tom Johnson, Marketing Manager
Cost: $1450.00
Frequency: Monthly
Founded in 1969

3782 **Broadcast Banker/Broker**
Kagan World Media
126 Clock Tower Place
Carmel, CA 93923-8746

831-624-1536
800-307-2529; Fax: 831-625-3225
www.kagan.com

George Niesen, Editor
Tom Johnson, Marketing Manager

A readers guide to equity deals and debt financing for radio and TV Station buying and selling analyzed. Key details on station trades with critical yardsticks of value. Three month trial is available.
Cost: $925.00
Frequency: Monthly
Founded in 1969

3783 **Broadcast Investor**
Kagan World Media
1 Lower Ragsdale Drive
Building One, Suite 130
Monterey, CA 93940-5749

831-624-1536
800-307-2529; Fax: 831-625-3225
www.kagan.com/

Tim Baskerville, President
Tom Johnson, Marketing Manager

The newsletter on investments in radio and TV stations and publicly held companies. Comprehensive analysis of cash flow multiples and trends that impact value. Three month trial available.
Cost: $1295.00
Frequency: Monthly
Founded in 1969

3784 **Broadcast Stats**
Kagan World Media
126 Clock Tower Place
Carmel, CA 93923-8746

831-624-1536
800-307-2529; Fax: 831-624-5882
www.kagan.com

George Niesen, Editor
Tom Johnson, Marketing Manager

The numbers behind the broadcast companies. Exclusive data, analysis and projections of radio and TV market billings, revenues, and cash flows, plus complete data on the buy-sell market. The industry's key reference source. Three month trial available.
Cost: $795.00
Frequency: Monthly
Founded in 1969

3785 **Business Radio**
Nt'l Association of Business & Educational Radio
500 Montgomery Street
Alexandria, VA 22314

703-548-1500; Fax: 703-836-1608

AE Goetz, Publisher

Association news for professionals, owners and consumers regarding radio stations.
Cost: $65.00
Circulation: 3,000

3786 **Cable Program Investor**
Kagan World Media
1 Lower Ragsdale Dr
Building One, Suite 130
Monterey, CA 93940-5749

831-624-1536
800-307-2529; Fax: 831-625-3225
www.kagan.com/

Tim Baskerville, President
Tom Johnson, Marketing Manager
Robin Flynn, Senior VP
Sharon Armbrust, Senior Consultant
Derek Baine, Senior Vice President

Covers the economics of basic cable programming networks. Numbers, perspective unavailable from any other source. Programmers applaud its accuracy. Three month trial available.
Cost: $1045.00
Frequency: Monthly
Founded in 1969

3787 Cable TV Advertising
Kagan World Media
126 Clock Tower Place
Carmel, CA 93923-8746

831-624-1536; Fax: 831-624-5882
www.kagan.com

George Niesen, Editor
Tom Johnson, Marketing Manager

Analysis of sales of commercial time by cable TV networks, interconnects and local systems. Detailed reports on national and local spot sales. Case studies and projections, all about the industry's upside. Three month trial available.
Cost: $795.00
Frequency: Monthly

3788 Cable TV Finance
Kagan World Media
126 Clock Tower Place
Carmel, CA 93923-8746

831-624-1536
800-307-2529; Fax: 831-624-5882
www.kagan.com

George Niesen, Editor
Tom Johnson, Marketing Manager
Larry Gerbrandt, CEO/President
Judy Pinney, Circulation Manager
Tim Baskerville, Publisher

Cable's financial bible. Analyzes sources of funding for cable TV. Selling and buying of cable systems. Financing strategies and trends. Exclusive surveys of capital sources. Three month trial available.
Cost: $795.00
Frequency: Monthly
Founded in 1969

3789 Cable TV Investor
Kagan World Media
1 Lower Ragsdale Dr
Building One, Suite 130
Monterey, CA 93940-5749

831-624-1536
800-307-2529; Fax: 831-625-3225
www.kagan.com

Tim Baskerville, President
Tom Johnson, Marketing Manager

Readers road map to cable stock trends. Chart service tracking stock price movements of 37 publicly held cable TV companies. Each graph shows two years of stock price activity. Three month trial available.
Cost: $1295.00
Frequency: Monthly
Founded in 1969

3790 Cable TV Law Reporter
Kagan World Media
1 Lower Ragsdale Dr
Building One, Suite 130
Monterey, CA 93940-5749

831-624-1536
800-307-2529; Fax: 831-625-3225
www.kagan.com

Tim Baskerville, President
Tom Johnson, Marketing Manager

The quintessential library of cable court cases, arbitrations, legal precedents. Labeled and catalogued for easy reference. Required reading for attorneys, government regulators and top executives. Three month trial available.
Cost: $995.00
Frequency: Monthly
Founded in 1969

3791 Cable TV Technology
Kagan World Media
1 Lower Ragsdale Dr
Building One, Suite 130
Monterey, CA 93940-5749

831-624-1536
800-307-2529; Fax: 831-625-3225
www.kagan.com

Tim Baskerville, President
Tom Johnson, Marketing Manager

Incisive, thorough reports on technical advances in cable TV, in terms operating executives can grasp and use to implement strategies. Analyzes growth in addressable converters, high definition TV, fiber optics and other advancements. Three month trial available.
Cost: $925.00
Frequency: Monthly
Founded in 1969

3792 Community Radio News
National Federation of Community Broadcasting
1970 Broadway
Suite 1000
Oakland, CA 94612

510-451-8200; Fax: 510-451-8208
www.nfcb.org
Facebook, Twitter

Ryan Bruce, Publications Manager

Contains calendar of events and information on public broadcasting, job listings, and legislative and regulatory updates. Annual Community Radio Conference and Community Radio Program Awards Competition.
Cost: $75.00
12-16 Pages
Frequency: Monthly
Circulation: 400
Founded in 1975
Mailing list available for rent: 300 names at $25 per M
Printed in one color on matte stock

3793 Community Television Review
National Federation of Local Cable Programmers
666 11th Street NW
Suite 806
Washington, DC 20001

202-393-2650; Fax: 202-393-2653

Andrew Lewis, Publisher

Issues of importance to community programming on cable and other areas of telecommunications.
Cost: $15.00
36 Pages

3794 DBS Report
Kagan World Media
1 Lower Ragsdale Dr
Building One, Suite 130
Monterey, CA 93940-5749

831-624-1536
800-307-2529; Fax: 831-625-3225
www.kagan.com

Tim Baskerville, President
Tom Johnson, Marketing Manager
Cost: $1045.00
Frequency: Monthly
Founded in 1969

3795 Dance on Camera Journal
Dance Films Association
48 W 21st St
Suite 907
New York, NY 10010-6989

212-727-0764; Fax: 212-727-0764
christy@dancefilms.org
www.dancefilms.org

Deidra Towers, Executive Director
Louise Spain, President

The only service organization in the world dedicated to both the dance and the film community.
ISSN: 1098-8084
Founded in 1956
Printed in on matte stock

3796 Digital Television
Kagan World Media
126 Clock Tower Place
Carmel, CA 93923-8746

831-624-1536
800-307-2529; Fax: 831-624-5882
www.kagan.com

George Niesen, Editor
Tom Johnson, Marketing Manager

News of the Digital Television. Three month trial available.
Cost: $945.00
Frequency: Monthly
Founded in 1969

3797 Hearsay
Association of Radio Reading Services
600 Forbes Ave
Pittsburgh, PA 15219-3002

412-488-3944; Fax: 412-488-3953
www.readingservice.org
Facebook, Twitter

Andy Ai, President
Erica Hacker, Vice President

Newsletter for the Radio Reading industry.

3798 Inside Sports Letter
American Sportscasters Association
225 Broadway
Suite 2030
New York, NY 10007-3742

212-227-8080; Fax: 212-571-0556
lschwa8918@aol.com
www.americansportscastersonline.com
Facebook

Louis O Schwartz, President/Editor
Patrick Turturro, Associate Editor

A quarterly newsletter published by the American Sportscasters Association.
38513 Pages
Frequency: Quarterly
Circulation: 2000
Founded in 1980

3799 Interactive Mobile Investor
Kagan World Media
1 Lower Ragsdale Dr
Building One, Suite 130
Monterey, CA 93940-5749

831-624-1536
800-307-2529; Fax: 831-625-3225
www.kagan.com

Tim Baskerville, President
Tom Johnson, Marketing Manager
Cost: $945.00
Frequency: Monthly
Founded in 1969

3800 Interactive TV Investor
Kagan World Media

1 Lower Ragsdale Dr
Building One, Suite 130
Monterey, CA 93940-5749

831-624-1536; Fax: 831-625-3225
www.kagan.com

Tim Baskerville, President
Tom Johnson, Marketing Manager
Cost: $895.00
Frequency: Monthly
Founded in 1970

3801 **Interactive Television**
Kagan World Media
1 Lower Ragsdale Dr
Building One Suite 130
Monterey, CA 93940-5749

831-624-1536
800-307-2529; Fax: 831-625-3225
www.kagan.com

Tim Baskerville, President
Tom Johnson, Marketing Manager

News of the Interactive Television. Three month trial available.
Cost: $795.00
Frequency: Monthly
Founded in 1969

3802 **Internet Media Investor**
Kagan World Media
126 Clock Tower Place
Carmel, CA 93923-8746

831-624-1536; Fax: 831-625-3225
www.kagan.com

George Niesen, Editor
Tom Johnson, Marketing Manager
Cost: $945.00
Frequency: Monthly
Founded in 1969

3803 **Interval**
Society of Cable Telecommunications Engineers
140 Philips Road
Exton, PA 19341-1318

610-363-6888
800-542-5040; Fax: 610-363-5898
scte@scte.org
www.scte.org

Howard Whitman, Senior Editor
Marci Dodd, President

A monthly member newsletter. Subscription price of $25.00 is for non-members.
Cost: $25.00
Frequency: Monthly
Circulation: 16000
Founded in 1969

3804 **Kagan Broadband**
Kagan World Media
1 Lower Ragsdale Dr
Building One, Suite 130
Monterey, CA 93940-5749

831-624-1536
800-307-2529; Fax: 831-625-3225
www.kagan.com

Tim Baskerville, President/CEO
Harvy Craft, Marketing Manager
Robert Nayoor, Circulation Manager
Sandie Borthwick, Executive Director

Daily e-mail or fax.
Cost: $1295.00
Frequency: Monthly
Founded in 1970

3805 **Kagan Media Money**
Kagan World Media
1 Lower Ragsdale Dr
Building One, Suite 130
Monterey, CA 93940-5749

831-624-1536
800- 30- 252; Fax: 831-625-3225
www.kagan.com

Tim Baskerville, President
Tom Johnson, Marketing Manager
Sandie Borthwick, Executive Director

Analysts dissect deals, anticipate trends, project revenues, track financings, and value the debt and equity of hundreds of priovately held and publicly traded advertising, broadcasting, cable TV digital TV, home video, Internet media, motion picture, newspaper, pay TV, professional sports and wireless telecommunications companies in the US and abroad.
Cost: $1245.00
Founded in 1970

3806 **Kagan Music Investor**
Kagan World Media
1 Lower Ragsdale Dr
Building One,Suite 130
Monterey, CA 93940-5749

831-624-1536
800-307-2529; Fax: 831-625-3225
www.kagan.com

Tim Baskerville, President
Tom Johnson, Marketing Manager
Sandie Borthwick, Executive Director

News and analysis of the music industry for investors.
Cost: $945.00
Frequency: Monthly
Founded in 1969

3807 **Marketing New Media**
Kagan World Media
1 Lower Ragsdale Dr
Building One, Suite 130
Monterey, CA 93940-5749

831-624-1536
800-307-2529; Fax: 831-625-3225
www.kagan.com

Tim Baskerville, President
Tom Johnson, Marketing Manager

News of the Marketing New Media. Three month trial available.
Cost: $795.00
Frequency: Monthly
Founded in 1969

3808 **Media Communications Association News**
Media Communications Association International
P.O.Box 5135
Madison, WI 53705-0135

608-836-0722; Fax: 888-899-6224
loiswei@aol.com
Facebook, Twitter, LinkedIn

Gary Shifflet, President
Lois Weiland, Executive Director
Mike Brown, Treasurer
Jim Powell, Secretary
John Coleman, Board Member

Coverage of the multimedia industry and association activities.
Frequency: Quarterly
Circulation: 3,000
Founded in 1968
Printed in on glossy stock

3809 **Media Mergers & Acquisitions**
Kagan World Media
126 Clock Tower Place
Carmel, CA 93923-8746

831-624-1536; Fax: 831-624-5882
www.kagan.com

George Niesen, Editor
Tom Johnson, Marketing Manager

Where it all comes together. Exclusive scorecard of deals done by media companies. Dollar amounts, multiples paid, trends captured in succinct summaries of complex transactions. Three month trial available.
Cost: $795.00
Frequency: Monthly

3810 **Media Sports Business**
Kagan World Media
1 Lower Ragsdale Dr
Building One, Suite 130
Monterey, CA 93940-5749

831-624-1536
800-307-2529; Fax: 831-625-3225
www.kagan.com

Tim Baskerville, President
Tom Johnson, Marketing Manager
Cost: $945.00
Frequency: Monthly
Founded in 1969

3811 **Monitoring Times**
Grove Enterprises
7540 Highway 64 W
Brasstown, NC 28902-8079

828-837-9200
800-438-8155; Fax: 828-837-2216
www.grove-ent.com

Bob Grove, President
Judy Grove, Office Manager
Belinda McDonald, Office Manager

News on radio communication, scanner monitoring, international radio broadcasts and technical advice.
Cost: $28.95
92 Pages
Frequency: Monthly
Circulation: 50000
ISSN: 0889-5341
Founded in 1970
Printed in 4 colors on glossy stock

3812 **Motion Picture Investor**
Kagan World Media
1 Lower Ragsdale Dr
Building One Suite 130
Monterey, CA 93940-5749

831-624-1536; Fax: 831-625-3225
www.kagan.com

Tim Baskerville, President
Tom Johnson, Marketing Manager
Cost: $845.00
Frequency: Monthly
Founded in 1969

3813 **Multichannel News**
360 Park Ave S
New York, NY 10010-1710

212-887-8387; Fax: 212-463-6703
www.multichannel.com

Lawrence Oliver, Publisher
Marianne Paskowski, Editorial Director
Kent Gibbons, Editor
Heather Tatrow, Production Manager
Michael Demenchuk, Managing Editor

News of the electronic media industries.
Frequency: Weekly
Circulation: 18,875
Founded in 1980

3814 **NRB Today**
National Religious Broadcasters

9510 Technology Dr
Manassas, VA 20110-4149

703-330-7100; Fax: 703-330-7100
info@nrb.org
www.nrb.org
Facebook

Frank Wright, President/CEO
Linda Smith, EVP/COO
Kenneth Chan, Director of Communications

This weekly newsletter by National Religious Broadcasters covers the latest news from the association and NRB's member organizations. The newsletter also serves as a source for tips, trends, and insights relevant to Christian communicators across the spectrum. Topics include audience building, branding, business strategy, innovation, job hunting, leadership, management, marketing, social media, and web strategy. NRB Today also features occasional columns, movie reviews, and product reviews.
Founded in 1944

3815 **Networks**
Geospatial Information & Technology Association
14456 E Evans Ave
Aurora, CO 80014-1409

303-337-0513; Fax: 303-337-1001
bsamborski@gita.org
www.gita.org

Bob Samborski, Executive Director
Lisa Connor, Membership Services Manager
Elizabeth Roberts, Marketing

A bi-monthly newsletter published by the Geospatial Information & Technology Association.
Cost: $125.00
28 Pages
Frequency: Monthly
Circulation: 2200
Founded in 1978

3816 **Pay TV Newsletter**
Kagan World Media
126 Clock Tower Place
Carmel, CA 93923-8746

831-624-1536; Fax: 831-624-5882
www.kagan.com

George Niesen, Editor
Tom Johnson, Marketing Manager

The pay TV industry's publication of record since 1973. Exclusive estimates of network subscribers and economics. The pay-per-view business, event-by-event, film-by-film. Three month trial available.
Cost: $795.00
Frequency: Monthly

3817 **Public Broadcasting Report**
Warren Communications News
2115 Ward Ct Nw
Washington, DC 20037-1209

202-872-9200
800-771-9202; Fax: 202-318-8350
info@warren-news.com
www.warren-news.com

Brig Easley, Manager
Daniel Warren, President/Editor

Industry news, personnel announcements and calendar listings for public broadcasting, digital TV, congress, FCC, and allied friends.
Cost: $575.00
Founded in 1945
Mailing list available for rent

3818 **Radio & Records**
Radio & Records
10100 Santa Monica Boulevard
3rd Floor
Los Angeles, CA 90067-4003

310-553-4330; Fax: 310-203-8450

Erica Farber, Publisher/CEO
Henry Mowry, Director Sales

A music newspaper that covers all aspects of the radio and recording industry.
Cost: $325.00
100 Pages
Frequency: Weekly
Circulation: 8006
Printed in 4 colors on n stock

3819 **Radio Business Report**
2050 Old Bridge Rd
Suite B-01
Woodbridge, VA 22192-2481

703-492-8191; Fax: 703-997-8601
www.rbr.com

Jim Carnegie, Publisher
Jack Messmer, Executive Editor
Cathy Carnegie, VP Administration
Carl Marcucci, MD/Senior Editor
June Barnes, Sales

Focuses on radio business issues, inside news on people and controversial topics.
Cost: $220.00
Frequency: Daily
Circulation: 5100
Founded in 1983
Printed in 4 colors on matte stock

3820 **Radio Ink**
Streamline Publishing
224 Datura St
Suite 1015
West Palm Beach, FL 33401-5638

561-655-8778
800-610-5771; Fax: 561-655-6164
www.radioink.com

Eric Rhoads, Owner
Reed Bunzel, Editor
Marty Sacks, Marketing
Tom Elmo, Circulation

Geared toward radio broadcast management professionals contains information on marketing trends, special reports, sales and programming issues.
Cost: $199.00
Circulation: 5000
Founded in 1992

3821 **Radio World**
Industrial Marketing Advisory Services
5827 Columbia Pike
Suite 310
Falls Church, VA 22041-2027

703-998-7600
800-336-3045; Fax: 703-998-2966

Steve Dana, President/Publisher
Lucia Cobo, Editor

A technical trade newspaper for the broadcast radio industry. Accepts advertising.
48 Pages
Circulation: 18000
Founded in 1978
Printed in 4 colors on newsprint stock

3822 **Streaming Media Investor**
Kagan World Media
126 Clock Tower Place
Carmel, CA 93923-8746

831-624-1536; Fax: 831-624-5882
www.kagan.com

George Niesen, Editor
Harvy Craft, Marketing Manager
Tim Baskerville, CEO/President

News of the Streaming Media Investor. Three month trial available.
Cost: $895.00
Frequency: Monthly
Founded in 1969

3823 **TV Program Investor**
Kagan World Media
1 Lower Ragsdale Dr
Building One, Suite 130
Monterey, CA 93940-5749

831-624-1536
800-307-2529; Fax: 831-625-3225
www.kagan.com

Tim Baskerville, President
Tom Johnson, Marketing Manager

More than just a newsletter, practically a seminar on how much programs cost and what they are worth. Exclusive spreadsheets with estimates of what goes between the commercials. Three month trial available.
Cost: $895.00
Frequency: Monthly
Founded in 1969

3824 **Television Digest with Consumer Electronics**
Warren Communications News
2115 Ward Ct Nw
Washington, DC 20037-1209

202-872-9200
800-771-9202; Fax: 202-318-8350
info@warren-news.com
www.warren-news.com

Brig Easley, Manager
Daniel Warren, President/Editor

A weekly newsletter providing continuous coverage of broadcasting, cable, consumer electronics and related industries.
Cost: $943.00
12 Pages
Frequency: Weekly
Mailing list available for rent

3825 **The Signal**
Society of Broadcast Engineers
9102 N Meridian St
Suite 150
Indianapolis, IN 46260-1896

317-846-9000; Fax: 317-846-9120
mclappe@sbe.org
www.sbe.org
Facebook, Twitter, LinkedIn

John Poray, Executive Director

Provides members with timely articles on various broadcast-related topics, information on upcoming events, recognition of members' activities and achievements and details of SBE services.
Frequency: Bi-Monthly
Circulation: 5500
Mailing list available for rent: 4700 names at $100 per M
Printed in 4 colors on glossy stock

3826 **Video Investor**
Kagan World Media
126 Clock Tower Place
Carmel, CA 93923-8746

831-624-1536; Fax: 831-624-5882
www.kagan.com

George Niesen, Editor
Harvy Craft, Marketing Manager
Tim Baskerville, CEO/President

Authoritative look inside the business of renting and selling video cassettes. Exclusive estimates of retail and wholesale transactions and inventories. Tracking movies into the home. Three

month trial is available.
Cost: $ 795.00
Frequency: Monthly
Founded in 1969

3827 **Warren Communications News**
Warren
2115 Ward Ct Nw
Washington, DC 20037-1209

202-872-9200
800-771-9202; Fax: 202-318-8350
info@warren-news.com
www.warren-news.com
Facebook, Twitter, LinkedIn

Brig Easley, Manager
Daniel Warren, President/Editor

Commercial and noncommercial television stations and networks, including educational, low-power and instructional TV stations, and translators. Lists over 11,000 operating cable systems including subscribers, channel capacities, programming, fees and personnel.
Cost: $6.45
Mailing list available for rent

3828 **Wireless Market Stats**
Kagan World Media
1 Lower Ragsdale Dr
Building One, Suite 130
Monterey, CA 93940-5749

831-624-1536
800-307-2529; Fax: 831-625-3225
www.kagan.com

Tim Baskerville, President
Tom Johnson, Marketing Manager

News of the Wireless Market Stats. Three month trial available.
Cost: $995.00
Frequency: Monthly
Founded in 1969

3829 **Wireless Telecom Investor**
Kagan World Media
1 Lower Ragsdale Dr
Building One, Suite 130
Monterey, CA 93940-5749

831-624-1536
800-307-2529; Fax: 831-625-3225
www.kagan.com

Tim Baskerville, President
Tom Johnson, Marketing Manager

Exclusive analysis of private and public values of wireless telecommunications companies, including cellular telephone, ESMR and PCS. Exclusive databases of subscribers, market penetrations, market potential, industry growth. Catching super-fast growth in a capsule. Three month trial available.
Cost: $895.00
Frequency: Monthly
Founded in 1969

3830 **Wireless/Private Cable Investor**
Kagan World Media
1 Lower Ragsdale Dr
Building One, Suite 130
Monterey, CA 93940-5749

831-624-1536
800-307-2529; Fax: 831-625-3225
www.kagan.com/

Tim Baskerville, President
Tom Johnson, Marketing Manager

The original bible of the wireless cable, multipoint distribution pay TV industry. Published continuously since 1972, this newsletter is the window on cable competition. Three month trial available.
Cost: $1095.00
Frequency: Monthly
Founded in 1969

Magazines & Journals

3831 **ARRL The National Association for Amateur Radio**
American Radio Relay League
225 Main St
Newington, CT 06111-1494

860-594-0200
800-326-3942; Fax: 860-594-0259
www.arrl.org

David Sumner, CEO
Kay Craigie, President
Bob Inderbitzen, Marketing Manager

Devoted to amateur radio information.
156M Members
Frequency: Monthly
Circulation: 146000
Founded in 1914

3832 **Album Network**
110 Spazier
Burbank, CA 91502-1852

818-842-2600; Fax: 818-972-2899
www.musicbiz.com

Steve Smith, Publisher

Editorial emphasis on chart ratings, sales performances, music reviews, and industry news.
Cost: $400.00
Frequency: Weekly
Circulation: 2,500

3833 **Alliance for Community Media**
1100 G St NW
Suite 740
Washington, DC 20005-7415

202-393-2650; Fax: 202-393-2653
info@allcommunitymedia.org
www.alliancecm.org

Mike Wassenaar, President & CEO

Participants include cable access television and community programmers. Individual membership dues are $60.00, organization $305.00.
Cost: $35.00
36 Pages
Frequency: Quarterly
Circulation: 1500
ISSN: 1074-9004
Founded in 1985

3834 **Almanac**
International Council of NATAS
888 7th Avenue
5th floor
New York, NY 10019-3300

212-489-6969; Fax: 212-489-6557
www.iemmys.tv/

Camille Bide Roizen, Executive Director
Eva Obadia, Marketing Manager
Georges Leclere, Senior VP

An annual publication with highlights of the International Emmy Program, global preference guides, articles on various facets in and around television today.
Founded in 1969

3835 **BE Radio**
Primedia
98 Metcalf Avenue
PO Box 12901
Shawnee Mission, KS 66282-2901

913-341-1300
800-441-0294; Fax: 913-514-6895
CorporateCustomerService@penton.com
www.penton.com

Eric Jacobson, Senior VP
Chriss Scherer, Editor
Kirby Asplund, Marketing Director

Provides radio station managers and engineers the information they need to make critical equipment purchase decisions. Presents need-to-know technical information to help readers solve the challenges of technology and the equipment problems they face. BE Radio serves the needs of radio engineers, managers and owners who need to make informed equipment and services buying decisions.
Cost: $30.00
Frequency: Monthly
Circulation: 12000
Founded in 1959

3836 **Broadband Advertising**
Kagan World Media
1 Lower Ragsdale Dr
Building One, Suite 130
Monterey, CA 93940-5749

831-624-1536
800-307-2529; Fax: 831-625-3225
www.kagan.com

Tim Baskerville, President

Reports and analysis of the sale of commercial time by cable TV networks, interconnects and local spot sales.
Cost: $1095.00
Frequency: Monthly
Founded in 1969
Printed in 2 colors on n stock

3837 **Broadcast Engineering**
Primedia
PO Box 12914
Overland Park, KS 66282-2914

913-341-1300
800-441-0294; Fax: 913-967-1903
www.broadcastengineering.com
Facebook, Twitter, LinkedIn

Brad Dick, Editor

Aimed at the market that includes corporate management, engineers/technicians and other management personnel at commercial and public TV stations, post-production and recording studios, broadcast networks, cable, telephone and satellite production centers and networks.
Circulation: 35000
Founded in 1960

3838 **Broadcasting**
Reed Business Information
2000 Clearwater Dr
Oak Brook, IL 60523-8809

630-574-0825
800-446-6551; Fax: 630-288-8781
webmaster@reedbusiness.com
www.reedbusiness.com

Jeff Greisch, President
Larry Dunn, Publishing Director
Jim Casella, CEO

Offers comprehensive coverage of television, radio, cable, satellite and the attendant equipment and emerging technologies. Accepts advertising.
Cost: $189.00
Founded in 1894

3839 **CQ Amateur Radio**
CQ Communications

25 Newbridge Rd
Suite 405
Hicksville, NY 11801-2887

516-681-2922; Fax: 516-681-2926
http://www.cq-amateur-radio.com

Richard Ross, CEO
Rich Moseson, Managing Editor
Gail Sheehan, Managing Editor
Mellisa Gillgan, Circulation

Information for people interested in the developments of in the field radio communications and electronics. Coverage includes reviews of new operating programs, new products and seasonal promotional ideas.
Cost: $32.00
Frequency: Monthly
Circulation: 87000
Founded in 1950

3840 **CTAM Quarterly Marketing Journal**
Cable Television Administration & Marketing
201 N Union Street
Suite 440
Alexandria, VA 22314-2642

703-549-4200; Fax: 703-684-1167
info@ctam.com
www.ctam.com/

Char Beales, President
Patrick Dougherty, Marketing Manager

A journal offering financial information to persons in the cable television management and executives.
Cost: $295.00
Frequency: Quarterly

3841 **Cable Plus/Cable TV Publications**
Cable TV Publications/TV Host
PO Box 1665
Harrisburg, PA 17105-1665

800-922-4678; Fax: 610-687-2965

Frank Dillahey, Sales Manager
Bob Newell, Marketing Director

Custom cable TV listing guides incorporating exclusive cable programming, editorial, movie reviews and TV listings that are sold to cable subscribers nationally. Circulation of this guide is over 1.75 million.
Cost: $24.00
Frequency: Monthly

3842 **Communicator**
Radio Television News Directors Association
1025 Thomas Jefferson St
7th Floor, Suite 700E
Washington, DC 20007-5214

202-625-3500
800-807-8632; Fax: 202-223-4007
Facebook

The latest information on technological breakthroughs, cutting edge newsroom practices, and contemporary management techniques.
Cost: $75.00
Frequency: 11x/yr
Circulation: 4,000

3843 **DV Digital Video Magazine**
Miller Freeman Publications
PO Box 1212
Skokie, IL 60076

888-776-7002
888-776-7002; Fax: 847-763-9614
dv@halldata.com
www.magazineline.com/digital-video-magazin e

Dominic Milano, Editorial Director
Armand DerHacobian, Associate Publisher
Jarett Cory, Sales Manager

Video production, animation and audio film, broadcast and new media. Includes discussions on training and communications.
Frequency: Monthly
Circulation: 64382
Founded in 1993

3844 **Digital TV/Television Broadcast**
United Entertainment Media
810 7th Avenue
27th Fl
New York, NY 10019

212-378-0400; Fax: 212-378-2160
sedorusa@optonline.net
www.governmentvideo.com
Facebook

Gary Rhodes, International Sales Manager

Digital TV/Television Broadcast is an in depth analysis and insider views of the business of television. It discusses the individuals, market trends, technology, products and policies that drive the television industry in the digital age.
Frequency: Monthly
Circulation: 22000
Founded in 1978
Mailing list available for rent

3845 **EQ Magazine**
Miller Freeman Publications
810 7th Ave
27th Fl, Suite 4
New York, NY 10019-5818

212-636-2700; Fax: 212-636-2750
sedorusa@optonline.net
www.governmentvideo.com
Facebook

Gary Rhodes, International Sales Manager

Articles on recording techniques and tips for musicians, producers, and engineers in the broadcast industry.
Frequency: Monthly
Circulation: 40000
Mailing list available for rent

3846 **Emmy Magazine**
Academy of Television Arts & Sciences
5200 Lankershim Blvd
North Hollywood, CA 91601-3155

818-754-2800
818-754-2860; Fax: 818-761-2827
emmymag@emmys.org
www.emmys.com/

Rose Einstein, Magazine Sales

This magazine tells of association news, EMMY information and awards for the broadcasting and media industries.
Cost: $28.00
Founded in 1995

3847 **FTTX**
Information Gatekeepers
1340 Soldiers Field Rd
Suite 302
Brighton, MA 02135-1000

617-782-5033
800-323-1088; Fax: 617-782-5735
info@igigroup.com
www.igigroup.com

Paul Polishuk, CEO
Beverly Wilson, Controller
Yesim Taskor, Controller
Brian Mark, Editor

Covers developments, products, competition, technology, and standards for the use of fiber optics and related techniques in the cable TV industry.
Cost: $695.00
Frequency: Monthly
Circulation: 2000
Founded in 1977

3848 **Financial Manager**
Broadcast Cable Credit Association
550 W. Frontage Road
Suite 3600
Northfield, IL 60093-1243

847-881-8757; Fax: 847-784-8059
info@bccacredit.com
www.bccacredit.com

Mary Collins, President & CEO
Jamie Smith, Director, Operations
Arcelia Pimentel, Sales/Membership

A bi-monthly magazine published by the Broadcast Cable Credit Association.
Frequency: Bi-Monthly

3849 **Folio**
Pacifica Foundation
1925 Martin Luther King Jr Way
Berkeley, CA 94704-1037

510-849-2590; Fax: 510-849-2617
contact@pacifica.org

Lonnie Hicks, Manager
Dan Coughlin, Executive Director

Listing of programs heard on Pacific Radio Stations.
Cost: $40.00
28 Pages
Frequency: Monthly
Founded in 1949

3850 **GBH: Member's Magazine**
WGBH Educational Foundation
PO Box 55875
Boston, MA 02205-5875

617-300-5400; Fax: 617-300-1026
feedback@wgbh.org
www.wgbh.org

Diane Dion, Editor
Jon Abbott, Owner
Mary Cotton, Owner

Offers information on station programming, personalities and more for members of WGBH, Boston's PBS and NPR station.
Cost: $50.00
Frequency: Monthly
Circulation: 175000
Founded in 1951

3851 **Hits Magazine**
Color West
3405 Pacific Avenue
Burbank, CA 91505

818-840-8881; Fax: 818-840-2753
www.colorwestprinting.com

Dennis Lavinthal, Publisher
Lynn Jensen, President
Karen Jensen, Controller

Chartmakers and hits in contemporary pop music, industry news and happenings, also includes radio news and playlists.
Cost: $300.00
Frequency: Weekly
Circulation: 10000
Founded in 1971

3852 **Inside Radio**
Inside Radio
365 Union St
Littleton, NH 03561-5619

603-444-5720
800-248-4242; Fax: 603-444-2872
www.insideradio.com

Cathy Devine, Research Director
Kelli Grisez, Operations Manager

Features issues that effect the radio industry and individuals involved in it.
Cost: $455.00
Frequency: Daily
Circulation: 7000

3853 **International Cable**
Phillips Business Information
1201 Seven Locks Road
Potomac, MD 20854-2931

301-354-1400; Fax: 301-340-0542
www.phillips.com

Nancy Umberger-Maynard, Publisher

Articles on technological advances internationally and the businesses that are making it possible.
Cost: $73.75
Frequency: Monthly
Circulation: 11,000

3854 **Journal of Broadcasting and Electronic Media**
Broadcast Education Association
1771 N St NW
Washington, DC 20036-2891

202-602-0587; Fax: 202-602-9940
help@beaweb.org
www.beaweb.org

Heather Birks, Executive Director
J D Boyle, Director, Sales & Marketing
Traci Bailey, Manager, Business Operations

Contains timely artciles about new developments, trends, and research in electronic media.
Cost: $50.00
Frequency: Quarterly
ISSN: 0883-8151
Founded in 1955
Printed in one color on matte stock

3855 **Journal of College Radio**
Intercollegiate Broadcasting System
367 Windsor Highway
New Windsor, NY 12553-7900

845-565-0003; Fax: 845-565-7446
ibshq@aol.com
www.collegebroadcasters.us

Chris Thomas, Chairman
Norman Prusslin, President & Chair Emeritus
Fritz Kass, CEO
Tom Gibson, Executive Vice President
Allen Myers, EVP, FCC Licensing

Magazine for student staffed radio stations based at schools and colleges across the US.
1000 Members
Frequency: Quarterly
Founded in 1940

3856 **Journal of Media Education**
Broadcast Education Association
1771 N St. NW
Washington, DC 20036-2891

202-602-0587; Fax: 202-602-9940
help@beaweb.org
www.beaweb.org

Craig Freeman, Editor
Heather Birks, Executive Director

Includes peer-reviewed and editor-reviewed creative and engaged scholarship. Content includes articles/essays about pedagogical issues in any aspect of media education, responsive essays such as industry analysis, scholarly papers, book reviews, and official announcements of the BEA.
Frequency: Quarterly
Circulation: Digital

3857 **Journal of Radio & Audio Media**
Broadcast Education Association
1771 N St NW
Washington, DC 20036-2891

202-602-0587; Fax: 202-609-9940
help@beaweb.org
www.beaweb.org

Heather Birks, Executive Director
Traci Bailey, Manager, Business Operations
J D Boyle, Director, Sales & Marketing

Promotes scholarly dialogues surrounding radio's modern and historical subject matter, as well as audio media that have challenged radio's traditional use.
Cost: $30.00
Frequency: Semiannually
Founded in 1955

3858 **Journal of the Audio Engineering Society**
Audio Engineering Society
60 E 42nd Street
Room 2520
New York, NY 10165-2520

212-661-8528; Fax: 212-682-0477
hq@aes.org
www.aes.org
Facebook, Twitter

Roger Furness, Executive Director
William T McQuaide, Managing Editor

The Journal contains state-of-the-art technical papers and engineering reports; feature articles covering timely topics; ore and post reports of AES conventions and society activities; news from AES sections; Standards and Education Committee work; membership news, patents, new products, and noteworthy developments. Subscriptions available in print, electronic and combination options.
Cost: $280.00
Frequency: 10/Year
Circulation: 12000
ISSN: 0004-7554
Printed in 4 colors on glossy stock

3859 **Ku-Band World Magazine**
Opportunities Publishing
305 Jackson Avenue W
Oxford, MS 38655-2154

FAX 662-236-5541

Ed Meek, Editor

Business application of developing Ku-band satellite communications systems.
Cost: $25.00
52 Pages
Frequency: Monthly
Founded in 1985

3860 **Millimeter Magazine**
2104 Harvell Circle
Bellevue, NE 68005

402-505-7100
866-505-7173; Fax: 402-293-0741
llcs@pbsub.com
www.millimeter.com

Cynthia Wisehart, Editorial Director
Gayle Grooms, Audience Marketing
Christina Heil, Marketing
Jeff Victor, Associate Editor

Authoritative resource for more than 33,000 qualified professionals in production, postproduction, animation, streaming and visual effects for motion pictures, television and commercials.
Cost: $25.00
150 Pages
Frequency: Monthly

3861 **NRB Magazine**
National Religious Broadcasters
9510 Technology Dr
Manassas, VA 20110-4149

703-330-7100; Fax: 703-330-7100
info@nrb.org
www.nrb.org
Facebook, Twitter

Frank Wright, President
Linda Smith, President Assistant

Trade publication for Christian communicators, including radio, TV, Internet and international media.
Cost: $24.00
56 Pages
Frequency: Monthly
Circulation: 9000
ISSN: 1521-1754
Founded in 1969
Printed in 4 colors on glossy stock

3862 **RPM Weekly**
Novasound Productions
PO Box 630071
Irving, TX 75063-71

972-432-8100; Fax: 972-432-8102
jv@rapmag.com
www.rapmag.com

Jerry Vigil, Publisher
Shardan Azat, Manager

Information on radio stations and independent production houses, engineering and production directors that manage these studios, industry news and latest technology information.
Cost: $115.00
Frequency: Monthly
Circulation: 7500
Founded in 1988

3863 **Radio**
1930 Century Park W
Los Angeles, CA 90067-6803

323-263-6991; Fax: 310-203-8450

Dwight Case, Editor

A magazine covering all aspects of the radio communications industry.
Cost: $215.00
Frequency: Monthly
Founded in 1973

3864 **Radio Science**
American Geophysical Union
2000 Florida Ave NW
Washington, DC 20009-1231

202-462-6900
800-966-2481; Fax: 202-328-0566
service@agu.org
www.agu.org
Facebook, Twitter

Fred Spilhaus, Executive Director

Coverage of radio propagation, communication, and upper atmospheric physics.
Cost: $10.00
Circulation: 1200
Founded in 1919

3865 **Radio-TV Interview Report**
Bradley Communications
135 E Plumstead Avenue
PO Box 1206
Lansdowne, PA 19050-8206

610-591-1070; Fax: 610-284-3704
Circ@rtir.com
www.rtir.com

Bill Harrison, President

A source for finding authors and experts to interview about a wide variety of subjects.
88 Pages
Frequency: Monthly
Circulation: 4000
Founded in 1986

3866 **SMPTE Motion Imaging Journal**
Society of Motion Picture & Television Engineers
3 Barker Ave
Floor 5
White Plains, NY 10601-1509

914-761-1100; Fax: 914-761-3115
www.smpte.org

Barbara Lange, Executive Director

The gateway to the world of motion imaging featuring industry-leading papers and standards, the Journal keeps its members on the cutting edge of this ever-changing industry.
Cost: $140.00
Frequency: Monthly

3867 **Satellite Retailer**
Triple D Publishing
1300 S Dekalb St
Shelby, NC 28152-7210

704-482-9673; Fax: 704-484-6976

Douglas G Brown Sr, President

Edited for the satellite industry.
Cost: $12.00
72 Pages
Frequency: Monthly
Founded in 1985

3868 **Satvision Magazine**
Satellite Broadcasting/Communications Association
1730 M St NW
Suite 600
Washington, DC 20036-4557

202-349-3620; Fax: 202-349-3621
info@sbca.org
www.sbca.com

Steven Hill, President

Offers information for television satellite dealers.
Cost: $35.00
Frequency: Monthly
Circulation: 10000

3869 **Teleguia USA: Novedades USA - Buscando Amor**
Echo Media
900 Circle 75 Pkwy SE
Suite 1600
Atlanta, GA 30339-6014

770-955-3346
salesinfo@echo-media.com
www.echo-media.com

Michael Puffer, CEO
Kelly Elarbee, Media Director
Frequency: Weekly
Circulation: 100,000
Founded in 1986
Mailing list available for rent
Printed in 4 colors on newsprint stock

3870 **Via Satellite**
Phillips Business Information
1201 Seven Locks Rd
Suite 300
Potomac, MD 20854

301-541-1400; Fax: 301-309-3847
www.kftv.com/company-30086.html

Scott Chase, Publisher
Richard Summers, Managing Editor

Covers voice, video and data in global commercial communications, including company profiles, market analysis and new products.
Cost: $49.00
Frequency: Monthly
Circulation: 17446

3871 **WNYC Wavelength**
1 Centre St
Suite 2453
New York, NY 10007-1699

212-669-7800; Fax: 212-669-3312
www.wnyc.org

Lori Krushefski, Marketing
Laura Walker, President

Relays broadcasting news. Accepts advertising.
16 Pages
Frequency: Monthly

3872 **Women on the Job: Careers in the Electronic Media**
American Women in Radio and Television
1760 Old Meadow Rd
Suite 800
Mc Lean, VA 22102-4306

703-506-3290; Fax: 703-506-3266
www.awrt.org

Maria Brennan, President

Association news focusing on women in the workplace, particularly media and communications industries.

3873 **World Screen News**
1123 Broadway
Suite 1201
New York, NY 10010-2007

212-924-7620; Fax: 212-924-6940
mdaswani@worldscreen.com
www.worldscreen.com

Ricardo Duise, Manager
Anna Carugati, Managing Editor
Kristin Brzoznowski, Managing Editor
Rafael Blanco, Executive Editor
Cesar Suero, Advertising Sales Director

Serves the international television cable and satellite industries including advertising agencies within the industry and others allied to the field. Also publishes the following supplements; TV Kids, TV Europe, TV Docs, TV Latina.
Cost: $50.00
Frequency: Monthly
Circulation: 4038
Founded in 1985

Trade Shows

3874 **AES Convention**
Audio Engineering Society
60 E 42nd Street
Room 2520
New York, NY 10165-2520

212-661-8528; Fax: 212-682-0477
HQ@aes.org
www.aes.org

Bob Moses, Executive Director
Roger Furness, Deputy Director
Jan Pederson, President
Frank Wells, President-Elect
Robert Breen, Vice President

An international organization that unites audio engineers, creative artists, scientists and students worldwide by promoting advances in audio and desseminating new knowledge and research.
Frequency: October

3875 **Alaska Broadcasters Association Conference**
Alaska Broadcasters Association
700 W 41st Street
Suite 102
Anchorage, AK 99503

907-258-2424; Fax: 907-258-2414
akba@gci.net
Facebook

Gary Donovan, President
Matt Wilson, Vice President

Provides assistance which enables members to serve their communities of license through education, representation and advocacy.
225 Attendees
Frequency: Annual

3876 **Annual Community Radio Conference**
National Federation of Community Broadcasters
1970 Broadway
Suite 1000
Oakland, CA 94612

510-451-8200; Fax: 510-451-8208
www.nfcb.org

Sally Kane, President & CEO

National conference for public community radio stations offering opportunities for staff development, skill building, networking, affinity group, inspiration, new ideas, discussion and exchanges; exhibit area; programming awards. Business meetings for National Federation of Community Broadcasters.
300 Attendees
Frequency: April

3877 **Annual IBS Broadcasting & Webcasting Conference**
Intercollegiate Broadcasting System
367 Windsor Highway
New Windsor, NY 12553-7900

845-565-0003; Fax: 845-565-7446
ibs@ibsradio.org
www.collegebroadcasters.us

Chris Thomas, Chairman
Norman Prusslin, President & Chair Emeritus
Fritz Kass, CEO
Tom Gibson, Executive Vice President
Allen Myers, EVP, FCC Licensing

See seminars, broadcasting professionals and student radio & webcasters from around the world.
1000 Members
Frequency: Annual
Founded in 1940

3878 **Audio Engineering Society Meeting**
Audio Engineering Society
60 E 42nd Street
Room 2520
New York, NY 10165-2520

212-661-8528; Fax: 212-682-0477
www.aes.org

Roger K Furness, Executive Director

250 booths, held in the fall and spring of each year.
5M Attendees
Frequency: October

3879 **BCCA Distance Learning Seminars**
Broadcast Cable Credit Association
550 W. Frontage Road
Suite 3600
Northfield, IL 60093

847-881-8757; Fax: 847-784-8059
info@bccacredit.com
www.bccacredit.com

Mary Collins, President & CEO
Jamie Grande, Director, Operations
Arcelia Pimentel, Sales/Membership

Teleconference and online seminars educating members on important areas of the broadcast and cable industry.
Founded in 1972

3880 **BCCA Media Credit Seminar**
Broadcast Cable Credit Association
550 W. Frontage Road
Suite 3600
Northfield, IL 60093

847-881-8757; Fax: 847-784-8059
info@bccacredit.com
www.bccacredit.com

Mary Collins, President & CEO
Jamie Grande, Director, Operations
Arcelia Pimentel, Sales/Membership

A subsidiary of the Media Financial Management Association, BCCA provides credit information, education, and networking opportunities which

enables members to efficiently manage credit risk and increase profitability.
Frequency: Annual
Founded in 1972

3881 **BEA Annual Convention**
Broadcast Education Association
1771 N St. NW
Washington, DC 20036-2891

202-602-0587; Fax: 202-602-9940
help@beaweb.org
www.beaweb.org

Heather Birks, Executive Director

Hosts over 250 sessions on media pedagogy, collaborative newtworking events, hands-on technology workshops, research and creative scholarships, and the Festival of Media Arts. It is co-located with NAB Show each April in Las Vegas.
Frequency: Annual, April

3882 **BEA Research Symposium**
Broadcast Education Association
1771 N St. NW
Washington, DC 20036-2891

202-602-0587; Fax: 202-602-9940
help@beaweb.org
www.beaweb.org

Heather Birks, Executive Director

Honours leading scholars in broadcast education and features their work alonside new and upcoming scholarship. Takes place during the BEA conference each April.
Frequency: Annual, April

3883 **Broadcast Designers' Association International Conference & Expo**
Broadcast Designers' Association International
145 W 45th Street
Room 1100
New York, NY 10036-4008

212-376-6222; Fax: 212-376-6202

Annual show and exhibits of broadcast design equipment, supplies and services.

3884 **Broadcast Engineering Conference (BEC)**
Society of Broadcast Engineers
9102 N Meridian Street
Suite 150
Indianapolis, IN 46260

317-846-9000; Fax: 317-846-9120
mclappe@sbe.org
www.sbe.org

John Poray, Executive Director

Offers broadcast engineers the opportunity to attend educational sessions, see the latest equipment and supplies, and meet with peers.
500 Attendees
Frequency: Annual/Spring

3885 **CRS - Country Radio Show**
Country Radion Broadcasters
819 18th Avenue South
Nashville, TN 37203

615-327-4487; Fax: 615-329-4492
info@crb.org
www.crb.org

Ed Salamon, Executive Director
Chasity Crouch, Business Manager

Jams, discussions, introduction of new comers, Hall of Fame presentations.
2,000 Attendees
Frequency: March

3886 **Cable Television Trade Show and Convention: East**
Convention Show Management Company
6175 Barfield Road NE
Suite 220
Atlanta, GA 30328-4327

404-252-2454; Fax: 404-252-0215

Nancy Horne, Show Manager

Nine hundred booths.
6M Attendees
Frequency: August

3887 **Cable and Satellite: European Broadcasting/Communications Show**
Reed Exhibition Companies
255 Washington Street
Newton, MA 02458-1637

617-584-4900; Fax: 617-630-2222

Elizabeth Hitchcock, International Sales

Communications forum for professionals in the broadcasting industry.
7.9M Attendees
Frequency: April

3888 **MFMA/BCCA Annual Conference: Media Finance Focus**
Broadcast Cable Credit Association
550 W. Frontage Road
Suite 3600
Northfield, IL 60093

847-881-8757; Fax: 847-784-8059
info@bccacredit.com
www.mediafinancefocus.org

Mary Collins, President & CEO
Jamie Grande, Director, Operations
Arcelia Pimenetal, Sales/Membership

Offers professional education targeting media financial and business executives; CPE opportunities; exhibitors; roundtables; and networking opportunities.
Frequency: Annual
Founded in 1972

3889 **MIP-TV: International Television Program Market**
Reed Exhibition Companies
255 Washington Street
Newton, MA 02458-1637

617-584-4900; Fax: 617-630-2222

Elizabeth Hitchcock, International Sales

Spring market for the television industry to buy, sell and distribute television programming.
9M Attendees
Frequency: April

3890 **NAB Radio Show**
National Association of Broadcasters
1771 N Street NW
Washington, DC 20036

202-429-5300
888-140-4622
301-682-7962; Fax: 202-429-4199
www.nabshow.com

David Wharton, EVP Media Relations
Jennifer Landry-Jackson, Exhibit Sales
Kelly Bryant, Event Operations

A unique networking opportunity for station professionals representing all format and market sizes, with exhibits showcasing technologies, tools and solutions for the industry.
Frequency: Annual

3891 **NAB Show**
National Association of Broadcasters
1771 N Street NW
Washington, DC 20036

202-429-5300
800-342-2460
202-429-3189; Fax: 202-429-4199
www.nabshow.com

David Wharton, EVP Media Relations
Jennifer Landry-Jackson, Exhibit Sales
Kelly Bryant, Event Operations

A global event for boradcasting news, legislation, networking, education and technology. Over 150 countries represented by 85,000+ attendees and exhibitors; conferences, and training sessions, and over 1,500 exhibitors.
85M Attendees
Frequency: April

3892 **NATPE Market & Conference**
National Association of TV Program Executives
3940 Laurel Canyon Blvd.
Suite 324
Studio City, CA 91604

Home Page: www.natpe.com

JP Bommel, President & CEO
Doug Finberg, Senior VP Marketing

The National Association of Television Program Executives (NATPE) is a global alliance of business professionals engaged in the creation, development and distribution of content as well as advertising and financial activities. NATPE is the world's largest non-profit association dedicated to facilitating the continued growth and convergence of all content across all distribution platforms.
8000 Attendees
Frequency: Annual
Founded in 1963

3893 **NATPE: The Alliance of Media Content**
National Association of TV Program Executives
6868 Wilshire Boulevard
Penthouse 10
Los Angeles, CA 90036-3681

310-453-4440
800-NAT-PEGO; Fax: 310-453-5258
info@natpe.org

Pam Silverman, Exhibition & Advertising
Linda Nichols, Exhibitor Services
Eric Low, Registration & Membership

The National Association of Television Program Executives (NATPE) is a global alliance of business professionals engaged in the creation, development and distribution of content as well as advertising and financial activities. NATPE is the world's largest non-profit association dedicated to facilitating the continued growth and convergence of all content across all distribution platforms.
1000 Attendees
Frequency: January
Founded in 1963

3894 **NECTA Convention & Exhibition**
New England Cable And Telecommunications Assn
10 Forbes Road
Suite 440W
Braintree, MA 02184-2648

781-843-3418; Fax: 781-849-6267
info@necta.info
www.necta.info

Timothy Wilkerson, President

A six state regional trade association representing substantially all private cable telecommunications companies in Connecticut, Maine, Massachusetts, New Hampshire, Rhode Island, and Vermont.
1.1M Attendees
Frequency: July

3895 **National Public Radio Association**
National Public Radio Association

635 Massachusetts Avenue NW
Washington, DC 20001-3753

202-513-2000; Fax: 202-513-3329
www.npr.org

John Lansing, President & CEO

Seventy five booths for public radio professionals and providers of resource materials for public radio.
1.2M Attendees
Frequency: April/May

3896 **National Religious Broadcasters Annual Convention and Exposition**
National Religious Broadcasters
9510 Technology Drive
Manassas, VA 20110

703-330-7000; Fax: 703-330-7100
info@nrb.org
www.nrb.org

Dr Frank Wright, President/CEO
Linda Smith, President Assistant
David Keith, VP Operations

Containing 280 exhibits. Broadcast and communications emphasis.
5,700 Attendees
Frequency: February

3897 **OAB Broadcast Engineering Conference**
Society of Broadcast Engineers
9102 N Meridian Street
Suite 150
Indianapolis, IN 46260

317-846-9000; Fax: 317-846-9120
mclappe@sbe.org
www.sbe.org

Offers broadcast engineers the opportunity to attend educational sessions, see the latest equipment and supplies, and meet with peers.
5500 Members
Frequency: Annual/November
Founded in 1964
Mailing list available for rent: 5700 names at $170 per M

3898 **RAB Conference**
Radio Advertising Bureau
1320 Greenway Drive
Suite 500
Irving, TX 75038

972-536-6700
800-232-3131; Fax: 972-753-6727
jhaley@rab.com
www.rab.com

Erica Ferber, President
Van Allen, CFO

Learn about new media opportunities from new digital platforms and monetizing streams to HD strategies that will empower you to compete at a new level and be an innovator at your station.
1600 Attendees
Frequency: Annual/March

3899 **Recruiting Conference and Expo**
Kennedy Information
1 Phoenix Mill Lane
Floor 3
Peterborough, NH 03458

603-924-1006
800-531-0007
www.recruiting2006.com

Matt Lyons, Director, Recruiting Group

Learn about the winning strategies, best practices, and tools ou will need to succeed in a challenging talent market.
Frequency: Nov New York

3900 **SCTE Cable-Tec EXPO**
Society of Cable Telecommunication Engineers
140 Philips Road
Exton, PA 19341-1318

610-363-6888
800-542-5040; Fax: 610-363-5898
scte@scte.org
www.scte.org

Lori Bower, Director
John Clark, CEO

Five hundred booths and, exhibits featuring telecommunications and programming equipment; dozens of workshops, with new technologies showcased.
12M Attendees
Frequency: Annual
Mailing list available for rent

3901 **SMPTE Annual Tech Conference & EXPO**
Society of Motion Picture & Television Engineers
3 Barker Avenue
5th Floor
White Plains, NY 10601

914-761-1100; Fax: 914-761-3115
www.smpte.org
Facebook, Twitter, LinkedIn

Barbara Lange, Executive Director
Sally-Ann D'Amato, Director, Events
Roberta Gorman, Director, Membership

The Technical Conference and Exhibition which is held in the fall. This alternates between the east and west coasts, usually in Pasadena and New York.
Frequency: Annual

3902 **Satellite Broadcasting and Communication Association (SBCA)**
Show Management & Services
900 Jorie Boulevard
Suite 200
Oak Brook, IL 60523-3835

800-654-9276; Fax: 630-990-2077

Diana Bubalo, Show Manager

Four hundred fifty booths.
2.5M Attendees

3903 **Television Bureau of Advertising Annual Meeting**
Television Bureau of Advertising
3 E 54th Street
New York, NY 10022

212-486-1111; Fax: 212-935-5631
www.tvb.org

Steve Lanzano, President
Abby Auerbach, EVP
Gary Bellis, VP/Communications

Annual show of 20-25 exhibitors of services for television stations, including research, sales and management training programs, incentives, collection agencies, advertiser contests and computer software.

3904 **Western Cable Television Conference and Expo**
Trade Associates
11820 Parklawn Drive
Suite 250
Rockville, MD 20852-2505

301-519-1610

Susan Rosenstock, Expo Director

One thousand three hundred booths featuring exhibits of programming, mobile aerial devices, video equipment and products and services for the communications and related industry fields.
10M Attendees
Frequency: November/December

3905 **Western Show**
Trade Associates
11820 Parklawn Drive
Suite 250
Rockville, MD 20852-2505

301-519-1610; Fax: 301-468-3662

Susan Rosenstock, Director

One thousand booths featuring exhibits from cable operators and suppliers to the cable industry. The California Cable Television Association and the Arizona Cable Television Association sponsor this annual event.
10M Attendees
Frequency: December

Directories & Databases

3906 **AES E-Library**
Audio Engineering Society
60 E 42nd St
Room 2520
New York, NY 10165

212-661-8528; Fax: 212-682-0477
HQ@aes.org
www.aes.org
Facebook

Bob Moses, Executive Director
Roger K Furness, Deputy Director

The library contains over 12,000 fully searchable PDF files documenting the progression of audio research from 1953 to the present, and includes every AES paper published at a convention, conference or in the Journal. Available as a subscription or pay per paper download: $135 for members, $245 for non, or $5 per paper for members or $20 for non.
Cost: $5.00
Frequency: Annual or Per-Paper

3907 **Arbitron Radio County Coverage**
Arbitron Company
142 5th Ave
New York, NY 10011-4312

212-887-1300; Fax: 212-887-1558
www.arbitron.com

Stephen Morris, CEO
Marilou Legge, Executive Vice President

This database offers access to audience listening estimates by county.
Frequency: Statistical

3908 **Audio Engineering Society: Directory of Educational Programs**
Audio Engineering Society
60 E 42nd St
Room 2520
New York, NY 10165

212-661-8528; Fax: 212-682-0477
HQ@aes.org
www.aes.org
Facebook

Bob Moses, Executive Director
Roger K Furness, Deputy Director

Institutions offering postsecondary programs and seminars in audio technology and engineering are searchable by program type or geographic area. Available free online. Educators are asked to confirm the information for their institutions.
Frequency: Free Online

3909 **Bacon's Newspaper & Magazine Directories**
Cision U.S., Inc.

322 South Michigan Avenue
Suite 900
Chicago, IL 60604

312-263-0070
866-639-5087
info.us@cision.com
us.cision.com

Joe Bernardo, President & CEO
Heidi Sullivan, VP & Publisher
Valerie Lopez, Research Director
Jessica White, Research Director
Rachel Farrell, Research Manager

Two volume set listing all daily and community newspapers, magazines and newsletters, news service and syndicates, syndicated columnists, complete editorial staff listings of each publication provided, covers U.S., Canada, Mexico, and Carribean.
Cost: $350.00
4,700 Pages
Frequency: Annual
ISSN: 1088-9639
Founded in 1951
Printed in one color on matte stock

3910 **Bacon's Radio/TV/Cable Directory**
Cision U.S., Inc.
332 South Michigan Avenue
Suite 900
Chicago, IL 60604

312-263-0070
866-639-5087
info.us@cision.com

Joe Bernardo, President & CEO
Heidi Sullivan, VP & Publisher
Valerie Lopez, Research Director
Jessica White, Research Director
Rachel Farrell, Research Manager

Includes comprehensive coverage for contact and programming information for more than 3,500 televsion networks, cable networks, television syndicators, television stations, and cable systems in the United States and Canada.
Cost: $350.00
Frequency: Annual
ISSN: 1088-9639
Printed in one color on matte stock

3911 **Broadcast Engineering Equipment Reference Manual**
Penton
249 W 17th Street
New York, NY 10011

212-204-4200
corporatecustomerservice@penton.com
www.penton.com

Sharon Rowlands, Chief Executive Officer

Offers a list of more than 1,400 manufacturers and distributors of communications equipment for radio, television and recording applications.
Cost: $20.00
Frequency: Annual
Circulation: 35,500
ISSN: 0007-1994

3912 **Burrelle's Media Directory**
BurrellesLuce
75 E Northfield Rd
Livingston, NJ 07039-4532

973-992-6600
800-631-1160; Fax: 973-992-7675
www.burrellesluce.com
Facebook, Twitter, LinkedIn

Robert C Waggoner, CEO

Offers media outreach, media monitoring and media reporting products.
Cost: $795.00

3913 **CPB Public Broadcasting Directory**
Corporation for Public Broadcasting
401 9th St NW
Suite 200
Washington, DC 20004-2129

202-879-9600; Fax: 202-879-9700
oigemail@cpb.org
www.cpb.org
Twitter

Robert T Coonrod, CEO

Offers information on public television stations, national and regional public broadcasting association and networks.
Cost: $15.00
152 Pages
Frequency: Annual
Circulation: 14,000

3914 **Cable Online Data Exchange**
Prometheus Global Media
770 Broadway
New York, NY 10003-9595

212-493-4100; Fax: 646-654-5368
www.prometheusgm.com

Richard D. Beckman, CEO
James A. Finkelstein, Chairman
Madeline Krakowsky, Vice President Circulation
Tracy Brater, Executive Director Creative Service

This database contains information on more than 10,000 US cable television system franchises.

3915 **Complete Television, Radio and Cable Industry Guide**
Grey House Publishing
4919 Route 22
PO Box 56
Amenia, NY 12501

518-789-8700
800-562-2139; Fax: 845-373-6390; Fax: new
books@greyhouse.com
www.greyhouse.com

Richard Gottlieb, President
Leslie Mackenzie, Publisher

The most comprehensive industry data on the US and Canadian Televison, Radio and Cable Industries. Can also subscibe to the database found online.
Cost: $350.00
2000 Pages
ISBN: 9-781619-25-1
Founded in 1981

3916 **Directory of Field Contacts for the Coordination of the Use of Radio**
Federal Communications Commission
445 12th Street SW
Washington, DC 20554

202-180-0450; Fax: 866-418-0232
fccinfo@fcc.gov

Radio frequency coordinating agencies are listed.
170 Pages
Frequency: Annual

3917 **Directory of Religious Media**
National Religious Broadcasters
9510 Technology Dr
Manassas, VA 20110-4149

703-330-7100; Fax: 703-330-7100
info@nrb.org
www.nrb.org

Frank Wright, President
Linda Smith, President Assistant
David Keith, VP Operations

Comprehensive guide to radio, television, music and book publishers.
Frequency: 10 per year

3918 **Editors Guild Directory**
Motion Picture Editors Guild
7715 Sunset Boulevard
Suite 200
Hollywood, CA 90046

323-876-4770; Fax: 323-876-0861
info@editorsguild.com
www.editorsguild.com

Lisa Churgin, Guild President
Dede Allen, VP
Diane Adler, Secretary
Rachel Igel, Treasurer
Tris Carpenter, Manager

An invaluable resource for producers, directors and post production professionals alike. It lists contact, credit, award and classification information for all of the Guild's active members at the time of publication, as well as a list of Oscar and Emmy winners for every year since the awards began. It also include a retirees section.
Cost: $25.00

3919 **GMRS National Repeater Guide**
Personal Radio Steering Group
PO Box 2851
Ann Arbor, MI 48106-2851

734-662-4533

Corwin Moore, Administrative Director

Lists the 3,500 GMRS repeaters nationally, along with names and addresses of station licensees.
Frequency: Monthly

3920 **Gale Directory of Publications and Broadcast Media**
Gale/Cengage Learning
PO Box 09187
Detroit, MI 48209-0187

248-699-4253
800-877-4253; Fax: 248-699-8049
gale.galeord@cengage.com
www.gale.com

Patrick C Sommers, President

This media directory contains thousands of listings for radio and television stations and cable companies.
Frequency: Annual
ISBN: 1-414434-71-5
Founded in 2008

3921 **International Motion Picture Almanac Intern Television & Video Almanac**
Quigley Publishing Company, Incorporated
64 Wintergreen Lane
Groton, MA 01450

978-448-0272; Fax: 978-448-9325
quigleypub@aol.com

William J Quigley, President/Publisher
Jayme Kulesz, Editor
Michael Quigley, Associate Editor/Ops Manager
Dee Quigley, Associate Editor

Invaluable completely updated information to the most sucscessful people in the business. Are you one of them? With thousands of corporations, 5,000 plus career profiles and the most comprehensive information available on the second largest industry in the US.
Cost: $250.00
780 Pages
Frequency: Annual
ISBN: 0-900610-74-3
ISSN: 0074-7084
Founded in 1915

3922 **Kagan Media Index**
Kagan World Media

126 Clock Tower Place
Carmel, CA 93923-8746

831-624-1536; Fax: 831-625-3225
www.kagan.com

George Niesen, Editor
Tom Johnson, Marketing Manager

The most comprehensive collection of media industry databases found anywhere. Current estimates of industry growth for a dozen different media businesses, shown on a 145-line spreadsheet, projected forward and updated monthly. Three month trial available.
Cost: $795.00
Frequency: Monthly

3923 National Radio Publicity Outlets
Volt Directory Marketing
1800 Byberry Road
Suite 800
Huntingdon Valley, PA 19006-3520

800-677-3839; Fax: 610-832-0878

Offers valuable information on over 7,000 radio stations in all major United States and Canadian markets.
Cost: $188.00
640 Pages
Frequency: SemiAnnual

3924 Radio & Records
Radio & Records
10100 Santa Monica Boulevard
5th Floor
Los Angeles, CA 90067-4003

310-553-4330; Fax: 310-203-8450
www.rronline.com

Erica Farber, Publisher/CEO
Sky Daniels, Vice President
Ron Rodriguez, Editor-in-Chief
Page Beaver, Operations Manager
Henry Mowry, Sales Executive

A music newspaper that covers all aspects of the radio and recording industry.
Cost: $299.00
Frequency: BiAnnual
Circulation: 10,000

3925 Radio Marketing Guide
Radio Advertising Bureau
1320 Greenway Dr
Suite 500
Irving, TX 75038-2547

972-753-6700
800-232-3131; Fax: 972-753-6727
jhaley@rab.com
www.rab.com

Erica Farber, President & CEO
Leah Kamon, SVP Marketing

A multi dimensional tool for Radio sales management and advertising professionals.
1600 Attendees

3926 Radio Talk Shows Need Guests
Pacesetter Publications
PO Box 101330
Denver, CO 80250-1330

303-722-7200; Fax: 303-733-2626
www.joesabah.com

Over 950 radio talk shows that interview guests over the telephone are profiled.
Cost: $198.00
Frequency: SemiAnnual
Founded in 1992

3927 SBE Members Directory
Society of Broadcast Engineers
9102 N Meridian St
Suite 150
Indianapolis, IN 46260-1896

317-846-9000; Fax: 317-846-9120
mclappe@sbe.org
www.sbe.org

John Poray, Executive Director

List of all members of SBE, Includes a history, awards earned, leadership, suppliers and other information. Free to members.
108 Pages
Mailing list available for rent: 4700 names at $170 per M

3928 Salem Press Online Platform
Grey House Publishing
4919 Route 22
PO Box 56
Amenia, NY 12501

800-221-1592; Fax: 201-968-0511
csr@salempress.com
online.salempress.com

The new Salem Press platform houses more than 500 titles including all of Salem's Health, Literature, History and Science titles in addition to select titles from the Grey House Publishing and H.W. Wilson product lines. Online access is free with each print purchase and includes an unlimited number of simultaneous users and remote access.

3929 TV Cable Publicity Guide
Volt Directory Marketing
1 Sentry Pkwy E
Blue Bell, PA 19422-2310

610-825-7720; Fax: 610-941-6874
www.volt.com

Jerry Di Pippo, CEO
Ronald Kochman, Vice President
Bruce Goodman, General Counsel

Over 5,000 cable and broadcast television stations and systems are profiled.
Cost: $188.00
545 Pages
Frequency: SemiAnnual

3930 TV Facts
Cabletelevision Advertising Bureau
830 3rd Ave
2nd Floor
New York, NY 10022-7523

212-508-1200; Fax: 212-832-3268
www.onetvworld.org

Sean Cunningham, President

An essential pocketsized media planning tool that contains 120 pages of essential data, graphs and charts highlighting the extraordinary growth and value of Cable in the changing TV landscape.
Frequency: Annual
Circulation: 20000

3931 Talk Show Selects
Broadcast Interview Source
2233 Wisconsin Ave NW
Suite 301
Washington, DC 20007-4132

202-333-5000
800-932-7266; Fax: 202-342-5411
www.expertclick.com

Mitchell Davis, Owner

More than 700 contacts at radio and television talk shows.
Cost: $185.00
240 Pages
Frequency: Annual
ISBN: 0-934333-35-1
Founded in 1984
Printed in on matte stock

3932 Television Yearbook
BIA Research
15120 Enterprise Ct
Suite 100
Chantilly, VA 20151-1275

703-818-8115
800-331-5086; Fax: 703-803-3299
www.bia.com

Tom Bruno, Owner

US television markets and their inclusive stations, television equipment manufacturers and related service providers and trade associations.
Cost: $64.00
Frequency: Annual

3933 Television and Cable Factbook
Warren Communications News
2115 Ward Ct NW
Washington, DC 20037-1209

202-872-9200
800-771-9202; Fax: 202-318-8350
info@warren-news.com
www.warren-news.com

Brig Easley, Manager
Daniel Warren, President/Editor

Commercial and noncommercial television stations and networks are profiled in this comprehensive directory. Educational and instructional stations are also included as one of the many categories of information.
Cost: $595.00
10M Pages
Frequency: 5 Volumes
Founded in 1932

3934 Top 200 National TV, News, Talk and Magazine Shows
Todd Publications
PO Box 635
Nyack, NY 10960-0635

845-358-6213
800-747-1056; Fax: 845-358-6213

B Klein, Publisher

The 200 most popular information shows on US television.
Cost: $40.00
Frequency: Annual

3935 World Broadcast News: International 500 Issue
Penton
PO Box 12901
Shawnee Mission, KS 66282-2901

913-341-1300; Fax: 913-514-6895
www.penton.com

Eric Jacobson, Senior VP

Directory of services and supplies to the industry.
Cost: $10.00
Frequency: Annual

Industry Web Sites

3936 http://gold.greyhouse.com
G.O.L.D Grey House OnLine Databases

Grey House Publishing's online database platform, GOLD, offers Quick Search, Keyword Search and Expert Search for most business sectors including broadcasting, communications and media markets. The GOLD platform makes finding the information you need quick and easy - whether you're a novice searcher or an experienced database user. All of Grey House's directory products are available for subscription on the GOLD platform.

3937 iamcr.org
International Association for Media and Comm

Professional organization serving the field of media and communication research through publications, conferences and programs.

3938 **www.aicp.com**
Association of Independent Commercial Producers

Represents exclusively, the interests of US companies that specialize in producing commercials on various media - film, video, computer- for advertisers and their agencies. AICP members account for 85 percent of all domestic commercials aired nationally, whether produced for traditional braodcast channels or nontraditional use.

3939 **www.alliancecm.org**
Alliance for Community Media

Committed to assuring everyone's access to electronic media, through public education, a progressive legislative and regulatory agenda, coalition building and grassroots organizing. A nonprofit, national membership organization founded in 1976, the Alliance represents over 1,000 Public, Educational and Govermental access organizations and community media centers.

3940 **www.americansportscasters.com**
American Sportscasters Association

Covers the U.S., Puerto Rico, and Canada. Offers seminars, compiles statistics and operates a placement service, maintains a Hall of Fame and biographical archives and library.

3941 **www.amptp.org**
Alliance of Motion Picture & Television Producers

Trade association with respect to labor issues in the motion picture and television industry. We negotiate 80 industry wide collective bargaining agreements and represents over 350 production companies and studios.

3942 **www.apts.org**
Association of Public Telecvsion Stations

Nonprofit membership organization established in 1980 to support the continued growth and development of a strong and financially sound noncommercial television service for the American public. We provide advocacy for public television interests at the national level, as well as consistent leadership and information in marshalling grassroots and congressional support.

3943 **www.bcfm.com**
Broadcast Cable Financial Management Association

A professional society of over 1,200 of television, radio and cable TV's top financial, MIS and HR executives, plus associates in auditing, data processing, software development, credit and collections.

3944 **www.collegebroadcasters.us**
Intercollegiate Broadcasting System

Facebook, Twitter

Association of student staffed radio/tv/media stations based at schools and colleges across the country.

3945 **www.ctam.com**
Cable Telecommunications Association for Marketing

Dedicated to the discipline and development of consumer marketing excellence in cable television, new media and telecommunication services. Members have the advantage of progressive research, insightful publications and forward thinking conferences.

3946 **www.emmyonline.org**
National Academy of Television Arts & Sciences

Dedicated to the advancement of the arts and sciences of television and the promotion of creative leadership for artistic, educational and technical achievements within the television industry. Bestows the Emmy Award.

3947 **www.gita.org**
Geospatial Information & Technology Association

A variety of information and useful references for your professional and technical needs, with descriptions of new programs and services, and a stable source of important member contacts, industry news and association related ongoing programs.

3948 **www.greyhouse.com**
Grey House Publishing

Authoritative reference directories for most business sectors including broadcasting, communications and media markets. Users can search the online databases with varied search criteria allowing for custom searches by product category, geographic area, sales volume, keyword, subject and more. Full Grey House catalog and online ordering also available.

3949 **www.halloffame.com**
National Sportscasters & Sportswriters Association

3950 **www.iemmys.tv**
International Television Academy

Organization of global broadcasters, with representatives from over 50 countries. Sixty percent of the 100-member board of directors come from countries outside the US, and represent the world's largest production, distribution and broadcast companies.

3951 **www.irts.org**
Int'l Radio & Television Society Foundation

For professionals in radio, broadcast and cable televison, corporate video production, collaborative communication, DVD and new media production, marketing and advertising plus related areas, as well as interested laypeople.

3952 **www.kagan.com**
Kagan World Media

For those interested in investments in radio and TV stations and publicly held companies.

3953 **www.lib.umd.edu/LAB**
Library of American Broadcasting

Devoted to television and radio broadcasting materials and archives.

3954 **www.lostremote.com**
Lost Remote

Television industry news, job listings and resources.

3955 **www.mediabistro.com**
Media Bistro

News and articles especially for those in broadcasting and publishing.

3956 **www.millimeter.com**
Millimeter Magazine

Authoritative resource for more than 33,000 qualified professionals in production, postproduction, animation, streaming and visual effects for motion pictures, television and commercials.

3957 **www.mrfac.com**
Manufacturer's Radio Frequency Advisory Committee

Representing the voice of the manufacturing industry and private land mobile radio users before the FCC.

3958 **www.nab.org**
National Association of Broadcasters

Full service trade association that represents the interests of free, over-the-air radio and television broadcasters.

3959 **www.naed.org**
National Association of Electrical Distributors

Nonprofit organization dedicated to serving and protecting the electrical distribution channel; provides networking opportunities through approximately 50 meetings and conferences a year, training, industry information and research through TED Magazine, and a marketing campaign for the industry through the NAED Advocacy Initiative.

3960 **www.nafb.org**
National Association of Farm Broadcasters

Works to improve quantity and quality of farm programming and serves as a clearinghouse for new ideas in farm broadcasting.

3961 **www.natpe.org**
Nat'l Association of Television Program Executives

Our mission is a commitment to furthering the quality and quantity of content, offering the wealth of our resources and experience to every content creator, no matter what the medium. Because the industry encompasses so much more today than ever before, NATPE too is expanding to accommodate this change and encourage progress while continuing to keep our members constantly appraised of changes.

3962 **www.ncta.com**
National Cable & Telecommunications Asssociation

National Cable and Telecommunications Association, formerly the National Cable Television Association, is the principal trade association of the cable television industry in the United States. Provides a strong national presence by providing a single, unified voice on issues affecting the cable and telecommunications industry.

3963 **www.ncti.com**
National Cable Television Institute

Independent provider of broadband communications training. Broadband cable system operators, contractors and industry vendors have turned to NCTI to train their employees who construct, operate and maintain broadband systems.

3964 **www.necta.info**
New England Cable & Telecommunications Association

NECTA is a six state regional trade association representing sbtstantially all private cable telecommunications companies in Connecticut, Maine, Massachusetts, New Hampshire, Rhode Island and Vermont.

3965 **www.nrb.org**
National Religious Broadcasters

For religious broadcasters and religious media. Hosts national convention featuring trade show and educational workshops.

3966 **www.pcia.com**
Personal Communications Industry Association

Represents companies that develop, own, manage and operate towers, commercial rooftops and other facilities for the provision of all types of wireless, broadcasting and telecommunications services. PCIA is dedicated to advancing an understanding of the benefits of wireless services and required infrastructure.

3967 www.productionhub.com
Production Hub
Television producers' news, listings, classifieds, casting notices and events.

3968 www.radiospace.com
North American Network
All information contained is provided to radio stations and networks for their free and unrestricted use.

3969 www.sbca.com
Satellite Broadcasting/Communications Association
National trade association representing all segments of the satellite consumer services industry. The association is committed to expanding the utilization of satellite technology for the delivery of video, data, voice, interactive and broadband services.

3970 www.sbe.org
Society of Broadcast Engineers
Offers a cooperative educational program intended to assist in the ongoing rollout of digital television.

3971 www.smpte.org
Society of Motion Picture & Television Engineers
Serves the needs of film and TV engineers.

3972 www.thirteen.org
Educational Broadcasting Association
For producers and directors of public educational programming, channel 13, PBS.

3973 www.tvspy.com
TVSpy
Television industry news, articles and links to other sites of interest.

Associations

3974 **ADSC: The International Association of Foundation Drilling**
8445 Freeport Parkway
Suite 325
Irving, TX 75063
469-359-6000; Fax: 469-359-6007
adsc@adsc-iafd.com
www.adsc-iafd.com
Facebook, Twitter, LinkedIn
Mike Moore, CEO
Fred Miller, Chief Financial Officer
Emily Matthews, Director, Operations
Angie Elmendorf, Director, Media Relations
Rick Marshall, Director, Safety
ADSC seeks to advance technology in the foundation of drilling and anchored earth retention industries. Represents drilled shaft, andchored earth retention, micropile contractors, civil engineers and manufacturing firms world wide.
Founded in 1972

3975 **ASM International**
9639 Kinsman Road
Materials Park, OH 44073-0002
440-338-5151
800-336-5152; Fax: 440-338-4634
memberservicecenter@asminternational.org
www.asminternational.org
Facebook, Twitter, LinkedIn
Zi-Kui Liu, President
Diana Essock, Vice President
Raymond V. Fryan, Treasurer
William T. Mahoney, Secretary & CEO
The society for materials engineers and scientists, a worldwide network dedicated to advancing industry, technology and applications of metals and materials. ASM provides information references, education, research and international events.
30K Members
Founded in 1913

3976 **Adhesive & Sealant Council**
7101 Wisconsin Avenue
Suite 990
Bethesda, MD 20814
301-986-9700; Fax: 301-986-9795
data@ascouncil.org
www.ascouncil.org
Twitter, LinkedIn, RSS
Bill Allmond, President
Steve Duran, Managing Dir., Membership
Valeryia Mikharava, Dir., Finance & Administration
Malinda Armstrong, Sr. Dir., Meetings & Expositions
Connie Howe, Sr. Director, Technical Services
A North American trade association dedicated to representing the adhesive and sealant industry. ASC is bound by the collective efforts of its members, and strives to improve the industry operating environment and strengthen its member companies.
124 Members
Founded in 1958

3977 **American Architectural Manufacturers Association**
1827 Walden Office Square
Suite 550
Schaumburg, Il 60173-4268
847-303-5664; Fax: 847-303-5774
customerservice@aamanet.org
www.aamanet.org
Facebook, Twitter, LinkedIn, YouTube, Flickr, SlideShare
Janice Yglesias, Executive Director
Dawn Peters, Membership Database Coordinator
Angela Dickson, Marketing & Communications Director
Florence Nicolici, Meetings Manager
Karen Allen, Accounting/HR Manager
Trade association that advocates for manufacturers and professionals in the fenestration industry and is dedicated to the promotion of quality window, door, curtain wall, storefront and skylight products.
Founded in 1936

3978 **American Bar Association Forum on Construction Law**
321 N Clark St
Chicago, IL 60654
Home Page:
www.americanbar.org/groups/construction_industry.html
Facebook, Twitter, LinkedIn
Arlan Lewis, Chair
An association focused on the professional development of construction lawyers and enhancing perception of the role construction lawyers perform in the broader industry.
6000 Members
Founded in 1976

3979 **American Concrete Pipe Association**
5605 N MacArthur Boulevard
Suite 340
Irving, TX 75038-2677
972-506-7216; Fax: 972-506-7682
info@concretepipe.org
www.concretepipe.org
Facebook, Twitter, LinkedIn, Youtube
Doug Dayton, President
Michael Kremer, VP, Marketing
Josh Beakley, VP, Engineering
Wanda Cochran, Member Services Director
Ginny Horrell, Controller
The American Concrete Pipe Association (ACPA) is a nonprofit organization, composed primarily of manufacturers of concrete pipe and related conveyance products located throughout the United States, Canada and in over 40 foreign countries. ACPA provides members with research, technical and marketing support to promote and advance the use of concrete pipe for drainage and pollution control applications.
286 Members
Founded in 1907

3980 **American Concrete Pressure Pipe Association**
4122 E Chapman Avenue
Suite 27
Orange, CA 92869
714-801-0298; Fax: 703-273-7230
support@acppa.org
www.acppa.org
Facebook, Twitter, LinkedIn
Jim Tully, Chair
Darren Dunker, Vice Chair
Domenico Micelli, Secretary-Treasurer
Richard Mueller, President & CEO
The American Concrete Pressure Pipe Association (ACPPA) is a nonprofit trade association representing manufacturers of concrete pressure pipe around the world. ACPPA sponsors research projects and conducts educational programs to promote and advance the use of concrete pressure pipe in water and wastewater applications. We also manage an independent audit program to certify compliance with all applicable American Water Works Association (AWWA) standards for the manufacturers.
5 Members
Founded in 1949

3981 **American Concrete Pumping Association**
606 Enterprise Drive
Lewis Center, OH 43035
614-431-5618; Fax: 614-431-6944
acpa@concretepumpers.com
www.concretepumpers.com
Facebook, Twitter, LinkedIn, Youtube, Flickr, RSS
Christi Collins, Executive Director
Janet Kasson, Member Services
Shawna Mitchell, Certification Specialist
Leah Gunther, Design & Marketing Specialist
Taylor White, Workforce Development Coordinator
The American Concrete Pumping Association promotes concrete pumping as the choice method of placing concrete, and to encourage and educate the concrete pumping industry on safe concrete pumping procedures. The ACPA Operator Certification Program is the only industry-recognized certification program for testing concrete pumping practices.
270 Members
Founded in 1974

3982 **American Congress on Surveying and Mapping**
5119 Pagasus Court
Suite Q
Frederick, MD 21704
240-439-4615; Fax: 240-439-4952
curtis.summer@acsm.net
Facebook, Twitter, Blogger
Curtis W Sumner, Executive Director
Bob Jupin, Accounting Manager
Sara Maggi, CST Program
Trish Milburn, Office Manager/Membership Services
A professional organization representing those who communicate the earth's spatial information using precisely prepared plats, charts, maps, and digital cartographic and related data systems.
7000 Members
Founded in 1941

3983 **American Council for Construction Education**
1717 N Loop 1604 East
Suite 320
San Antonio, TX 78232-1570
210-495-6161; Fax: 210-495-6168
acce@acce-hq.org
www.acce-hq.org
LinkedIn
Steve Nellis, President & CEO
The accrediting agency for postsecondary construction education programs. The mission of ACCE is to be a global advocate for programs of post-secondary construction higher education. To accomplish this mission, ACCE will develop, periodically update, and promulgate comprehensive standards for programs of construction higher education and aAccredit programs meeting these standards through a rigorous, formal process of peer review.
Cost: $150.00
115 Members
Founded in 1974

3984 **American Fence Association**
6404 International Parkway
Suite 2250-A
Plano, TX 75093

630-942-6598
800-822-4342; Fax: 314-480-7118
www.americanfenceassociation.com
Facebook, Twitter

Chris Loftus, President
Randy Ward, President Elect
Sam Williams, Secretary
Peter Williams, Treasurer

The American Fence Association benefits the fence, deck and railing industry - as well as the consumer - by promoting the highest levels of professionalism, ethics and product standards by disseminating information and educating its members. With 31 member chapters serving the association, AFA offers several educational, certification options and networking opportunities to keep its members above and beyond their competition.
Cost: $365.00
2400 Members
Founded in 1962

3985 **American Institute of Building Design**
7059 Blair Road NW
Suite 400
Washington, DC 20012

202-750-4900
800-366-2423; Fax: 866-204-0293
info@aibd.org
www.aibd.org
Facebook, Twitter, LinkedIn, RSS

Steven Mickley, Executive Director
Whit Peterson, General Manager
Karen Kassik-Michelson, President
Bernie Kim, Internal Vice President
Yu-Ngok Lo, External Vice President

AIBD provides building designers with educational resources, and has developed nationwide design standards and a code of ethics for the building design profession. Today, AIBD is a nationally recognized association with professional and associate members in 48 states, throughout Canada and in Europe, Asia, Australia and the Bahamas. Its chartered state societies are active in their respective legislative arenas and work to promote public awareness of the bldg design profession.
Founded in 1950

3986 **American Institute of Constructors**
19 Mantua Road
Mount Royal, NJ 08061

703-683-4999; Fax: 703-683-5480
info@professionalconstructor.org
www.professionalconstructor.org
Facebook, Twitter, LinkedIn

Ethan Gray, Sr. Executive Director
Nelly Flumo, Program Manager
Erin O'Leary, Meeting Planner

AIC is the organization that seeks to give Constructors the professional status they deserve. The Institute is the constructor's counterpart of professional organizations found in architecture, engineering, law and other fields. As such, the Institute serves as the national qualifying body of professional constructor. AIC membership identifies the individual as a true professional.
Founded in 1971

3987 **American Institute of Steel Construction**
One East Wacker Drive
Suite 700
Chicago, IL 60601-1802

312-670-2400; Fax: 312-670-5403
www.aisc.org

Charles Carter, President
Scott Meinick, SVP
Carly Hurd, VP, Operational Engagement
Larry Kruth, VP, Engineering & Research
Brian Raff, VP, Markert Development

The American Institute of Steel Construction (AISC), headquartered in Chicago, is a not-for-profit technical institute and trade association serving the structural steel design community and construction industry in the United States. AISC's mission is to make structural steel the material of choice by being the leader in structural-steel-related technical and market-building activities, including: specification and code development, research, education, and tech assistance.
2.7M Members
Founded in 1921

3988 **American Iron and Steel Institute**
25 Massachusetts Ave., NW
Suite 800
Washington, DC 20001

202-452-7100
www.steel.org
Facebook, Twitter

Kevin Dempsey, President & CEO
Timothy Green, Chief Economist
Lisa Harrison, SVP, Communications
John Catterall, VP, Automotive Program
Robert Wills, VP, Construction Program

An association of North American steel producers that features steel information for consumers, engineers, and other professionals.
145 Members

3989 **American Public Works Association**
1200 Main Steet
Suite 1400
Kansas City, MO 64105-2100

816-472-6100
800-848-APWA; Fax: 816-472-1610
www.apwa.net
Facebook, Twitter, Youtube

Scott Grayson, Chief Executive Officer
Mary Knollmeyer, Director of Finance
Julie Bebermeyer, Director of Operations
Lysa Byous, Meeting Planner/Exhibit Manager
Tammy Bennett, Director, Membership & Engagement

International educational and professional association of public agencies, private sector companies, and individuals dedicated to providing high quality public works goods and services. AWA provides a forum in which public works professionals' competency, increase the performance of their agencies and companies, and bring important public works-related topics to public attention in local, state, and federal areas. Mailing list for members only.
30000 Members
Founded in 1937

3990 **American Society for Nondestructive Testing**
PO Box 28518
1711 Arlingate Lane
Columbus, OH 43228-0518

614-274-6003
800-222-2768; Fax: 614-274-6899
www.asnt.org
Facebook, Twitter, LinkedIn, YouTube, Instagram

Neal Couture, Executive Director
Barry Schieferstein, Dir., Conferences & Meetings
Garra Liming, Dir., Marketing & Communications
Brad Pence, Director, Finance & Controller
Heather Cowles, Dir., Membership & Engagement

ASNT is the world's largest technical society for nondestructive tests (NDT) professionals.
15000 Members
Founded in 1941

3991 **American Society of Heating, Refrigerating and Air-Conditioning Engineers**
1791 Tullie Circle NE
Atlanta, GA 30329

404-636-8400
800-527-4723; Fax: 404-321-5478
ashrae@ashrae.org
www.ashrae.org
Facebook, Twitter

Jeff Littleton, Executive VP
Kim Mitchell, Chief Development Officer
Vanita Gupta, Director, Marketing
Joyce Abrams, Director, Member Services
Craig Wright, Director, Finance & Admin. Services

ASHRAE is a building technology society. The Society and its members focus on building systems, energy efficiency, indoor air quality and sustainability within the industry. Through research, standards writing, publishing and continuing education, ASHRAE shapes tomorrow's built environment today.
55000 Members
Founded in 1894

3992 **American Society of Professional Estimators**
2525 Perimeter Place Drive
Suite 103
Nashville, TN 37214

615-316-9200
888-378-6283; Fax: 615-316-9800
www.aspenational.org
Facebook, Twitter

Melvin Cowen, President
Chris Morton, 1st Vice President
Mike Alsgaard, 2nd Vice President

The American Society of Professional Estimators was created with dedication and commitment to the idea of providing its members with tangible benefits.
2500 Members
Founded in 1956

3993 **American Subcontractors Association, Inc.**
1004 Duke St.
Alexandria, VA 22314

703-684-3450; Fax: 703-836-3482
ASAoffice@asa-hq.com
www.asaonline.com
Facebook, Twitter, LinkedIn, YouTube, Google+, RSS

Richard Bright, Chief Operating Officer
Beth Horan, Director, Finance
Matt Levine, Director, Communications/Marketing
Mike Oscar, Director, Government Relations
Loni Warholic, Director, Membership Services

A nonprofit, national, membership trade association of constructionspecialty trade contractors, suppliers, and service providers in the United States and Canada.

3994 **Asbestos Information and Training Centers**
Georgia Institute of Real Estate
5784 Lake Forrest Drive
Atlanta, GA 30328

404-252-6768
800-633-3583; Fax: 404-257-0354
gire@learningrealestate.com
www.learningrealestate.com
Facebook, Twitter, RSS

Cherie Jolley, School Director
Shermaine Green, Membership Specialist
Jackie Townsend, Finance Director
Delaney Yellott, Finance Coordinator
Ned Kandul, Director, Art

Sponsors the Regional Asbestos Information and Training Centers. The Centers provide information and training in identification and abatement of asbestos hazards with the ultimate goal of training contractors for eventual certification. Each center offers a variety of specialized courses including identification of asbestos hazards and possible remedies of problems and solutions for those involved in the asbestos hazard abatement process.
Founded in 1959

3995 **Asphalt Emulsion Manufacturers Association**
Three Church Circle
PO Box 250
Annapolis, MD 21401

410-267-0023; Fax: 410-267-7546
www.aema.org
Facebook

Todd Ryne, President
Bob Huitt, Vice President
Dan Koeninger, Secretary/Treasurer

The Asphalt Emulsion Manufacturers Association is the International Organization representing the asphalt emulsion industry. AEMA's mission is to expand the use and applications of asphalt emulsions. Asphalt emulsions are the most environmentally sound, energy efficient and cost effective products used in pavement maintenance and construction.
150 Members
Founded in 1973

3996 **Asphalt Institute**
2696 Research Park Dr
Lexington, KY 40511-8480

859-288-4960; Fax: 859-288-4999
info@asphaltinstitute.org
www.asphaltinstitute.org
Facebook, Twitter, LinkedIn, YouTube

Peter T Grass, President
Alexander Brown, Regional Director
Bob Horan, Regional Director
Mark Blow, Senior Regional Director
Bob Humer, Senior Regional Director

The Asphalt Institute is the international trade association of petroleum asphalt producers, manufacturers and affiliated businesses. Our mission is to promote the use, benefits and quality performance of petroleum asphalt, through engineering, research, marketing and educational activities, and through the resolution of issues affecting the industry.
113 Members
Founded in 1919

3997 **Associated Builders & Contractors, Inc.**
440 1st St., N.W.
Ste., 200
Washington, DC 20001

202-595-1505
gotquestions@abc.org
www.abc.org
Facebook, Twitter, LinkedIn, YouTube

Tim Keating, Chairman
Steve Klessig, Chair-Elect
Stephanie Schmidt, Secretary
Larry May, Treasurer
Michael Bellaman, President, CEO

A national construction industry trade association representing nearly 21,000 chapter members and whose activities include government representation, legal advocacy, education, workforce development, communications, technology,etc.
21000 Members
Founded in 1950

3998 **Associated Construction Distributors**
1605 SE Deleware Avenue, Suite B
PO Box 14552
Ankeny, IA 50021

515-964-1335; Fax: 515-964-7668
acdi@acdi.net
www.acdi.net

Tom Goetz, Executive VP
Dave Hill, Director/Sales/Marketing
Jane Zieser, Controller
Mary Stoneking, Meeting Planner

Associated Construction Distributors International, Inc. (ACDI) was founded when a group of independent, entrepreneurial businessmen came together and realized they had much to offer and much to learn. Sharing business information continues today at the core of the organization. It has allowed the members to succeed individually and as group. ACDI distributors account for nearly one billion dollars in the sale of materials and equipment to the construction industry.
34 Members
Founded in 1968

3999 **Associated Construction Publications**
1200 Madison Ave
LL20
Indianapolis, IN 46225

317-423-7080
800-486-0014; Fax: 317-423-7094
www.acppubs.com
Facebook, Twitter, LinkedIn, RSS

John White, President & Publisher
Joel Bustamente, Production Designer & Coordinator
Jill White, VP, Operations
Greg Sitek, VP, Editorial
Britt Davis, Editor-In-Chief

Strives to assist the heavy construction industry with local and regional news on a nationwide basis.
14 Members
Founded in 1938

4000 **Associated Equipment Distributors**
650 E Algonquin Road
Suite 305
Schaumburg, IL 60173

630-574-0650
help@aednet.org
aednet.org
Facebook, Twitter, LinkedIn

Brian P. McGuire, President/CEO
Robert K. Henderson, EVP & Chief Operating Officer
Agnes Baczek, Director, Finance
Jon Cruthers, VP, Sales
Sara Smith, Editor-In-Chief & Marketing & Comm.

International trade association supporting companies specializing in eqipment used in construction, mining, forestry, power generation, agriculture and industrial applications.
1000 Members
Founded in 1919

4001 **Associated General Contractors of America**
2300 Wilson Blvd
Suite 300
Arlington, VA 22201

703-548-3118; Fax: 703-548-3119
info@agc.org
www.agc.org
Facebook, Twitter, LinkedIn, RSS

Robert Lanham, Jr., President
Dan Fordice, Senior Vice President
Lester Snyder, Vice President
Jeffrey DiStefano, Treasurer
Stephen E Sandherr, Chief Executive Officer

The Associated General Contractors of America (AGC) is the leading association for the construction industry. Operating in partnership with its nationwide network of 95 chartered Chapters, AGC provides a full range of services satisfying the needs and concerns of its members, thereby improving the quality of construction and protecting the public interest.
33000 Members
Founded in 1918

4002 **Association of Equipment Manufacturers**
6737 West Washington Street
Suite 2400
Milwaukee, WI 53214-5647

414-272-0943; Fax: 414-272-1170
aem@aem.org
www.aem.org
Facebook, Twitter, LinkedIn, YouTube

Jeffrey R. Reed, Chair

The international trade and business development resource for companies that offer equipment, products and services for the construction, agricultural, mining, forestry, and utility fields.
900+ Members

4003 **Association of Union Constructors (TAUC)**
1501 Lee Highway
Suite 202
Arlington, VA 22209-1109

703-524-3336; Fax: 703-524-3364
www.tauc.org

Steven Lindauer, Chief Executive Officer
David Acord, Dir., Communications & Exec. Editor
Mike Marrone, Director, Administration
Pamela Livinski, Sr. Database & Information Manager
Gwen Jackson, Meetings & Events Manager

TAUC's mission is to act as an advocate for union contractors and enhance cooperation between the three entities involved in the successful completion of construction projects: the union, the contractor and the owner-client, the company for which the work is being completed. By encouraging this tripartite dialogue, many potential issues and delays are eliminated before work even begins.
5000+ Members
Founded in 1969

4004 **Association of the Wall and Ceiling Industry**
513 West Broad Street
Suite 210
Falls Church, VA 22046

703-538-1722; Fax: 703-534-8307
info@awci.org
www.awci.org
Facebook, Twitter, LinkedIn, Youtube

Michael Stark, Chief Executive Officer
Brenton C. Stone, Associate Publisher & Sr. Director

Karen Bilak, Dir., Convention & Conferences
Laura Porinchak, Communications Director
Chris Williams, Director, Membership

Represents acoustics systems, ceiling systems, drywall systems, exterior insulation and finishing systems, fireproofing, flooring systems, insulation, and stucco contractors, suppliers and manufacturers and those in allied trades. The mission of the Association of the Wall and Ceiling Industry is to provide services and undertake activities that enhance the members' ability to operate a successful business.
2400 Members
Founded in 1918

4005 **Barre Granite Association**
PO Box 481
Barre, VT 05641

802-476-4131; Fax: 802-476-4765
BGA@barregranite.org
www.barregranite.org
Facebook, Twitter, LinkedIn, Pinterest

Doug Grahn, Executive Director

Manufacturers of cemetery monuments, mausoleums, statuary, landscape and architectural granite products. It has been estimated that one-third of the public and private monuments and mausoleums in America — and they are millions in number — are products of the Barre quarries and Barre's international community of sculptors, artisans, mechanics and laborers. All this has been largely accomplished since the closing decades of the last century.
35 Members
Founded in 1889

4006 **Brick Industry Association**
1850 Centennial Park Drive
Suite 301
Reston, VA 20191

703-620-0010; Fax: 703-620-3928
brickinfo@bia.org
www.gobrick.com
Facebook, Twitter, LinkedIn, Youtube, Pinterest

Ray Leonhard, President & CEO & CFO
Joseph Casper, Sr. VP, Gov. & Regulatory Affairs
Lisa Cyphers, Executive Assistant
Judy Grandinetti, Accounting Manager
Tricia Mauer, VP, Membership & Programs

National trade association representing distributors and manufacturers of clay brick and suppliers of related products and services. The Association is involved in a broad range of technical, research, marketing, government relations and communications activities. It is the recognized national authority on brick construction.
175 Members
Founded in 1934

4007 **Bridge Grid Flooring Manufacturers Association**
201 Castle Drive
West Mifflin, PA 15122

412-469-3985; Fax: 419-257-0332
www.abcdpittsburgh.org

Bill Ferko, President
Todd Carroll, Secretary
Jessica Saleh, Treasurer
Bill Ferko, Awards
Roxanne Podlipsky, Scholarships

Comprised of companies who manufacture steel grid flooring systems for bridges, and other companies with an interest in the steel grid market. The role of the Association is to promote the use of Grid Reinforced Concrete Bridge Decks through data collection, research/ development, and education.

4008 **Building Industry Association of Southern California**
24 Executive Park
Suite 100
Irvine, CA 92614

949-553-9500; Fax: 949-769-8943
www.biasc.org
Facebook, Twitter, LinkedIn

Tom Grable, President
Jeff Montejano, Chief Executive Officer
Craig Foster, EVP
Laura Barber, VP, Events & Human Resources

The Building Industry Association of Southern California is a nonprofit trade association representing companies involved in planning and building Southern California's communities. Our members are involved in all aspects of construction and green building - from architecture to roofing to landscape design.
1850 Members
Founded in 1923

4009 **Building Material Dealers Association**
1006 SE Grand Street
Suite 301
Portland, OR 97214

503-208-3763
888-960-6329; Fax: 971-255-0790
bmda@bmda.com
www.bmda.com

Gwyn Matras, Executive Director, Customer Servive Administrator, Research Lead, Research Department, Customer Service Associate

BMDA provides Notice of Right to a Lien service for all states and Construction Lien service for Oregon and Washington. We offer current lien law manuals for Oregon and Washington, which assists our members with all areas of the construction lien laws. At BMDA, we believe attorneys who specialize in construction lien law are your best choice for answering legal questions. Therefore, we offer attorney referrals for Oregon and Washington. BMDA will not provide legal advice at any time.
3500 Members
Founded in 1915

4010 **Building Stone Institute**
5 Riverside Drive, Bldg 2
PO Box 419
Chestertown, NY 12817

518-803-4336
866-786-6313; Fax: 518-803-4338
www.buildingstoneinstitute.org
Facebook

James Hieb, Chief Executive Officer
Jane Bennett, Executive Vice President
Sarah Gregg, Marketing Manager
Amy Oakley, Communications Manager
Gina De Nardo, Special Events Coordinator

The Building Stone Institute works on behalf of the quarries, fabricators, retailers, importers, exporters, carvers, sculptors, restorers, designers, and installers that comprise our diverse membership. BSI provides programs and services that empower our member companies to offer the highest level of quality products and services. BSI is a not-for-profit trade association dedicated to serving its member firms, and providing educational materials and continuing education.
350 Members
Founded in 1919

4011 **Building Trades Association**
6353 W. Rogers Circle
Unit 3
Boca Raton, FL 33487

800-326-7800
info@buildingtrades.com
www.buildingtrades.com
Facebook

An association made up of thousands of companies involved in all phases of the building and construction industries.

4012 **California Redwood Associates**
818 Grayson Road
Suite 201
Pleasant Hill, CA 94523

925-935-1499
888-225-7339; Fax: 925-935-1496
info@calredwood.org
www.calredwood.org
Youtube

Christopher Grover, President

A trade association for redwood lumber producers.

4013 **Cedar Shake and Shingle Bureau**
PO Box 1178
Sumas, WA 98295-1178

604-820-7700; Fax: 604-820-0266
info@cedarbureau.org
www.cedarbureau.org

Lynne Christensen, Director of Operations
Barbara Enns, Accountant
Kathy Milne, Member Services Coordinator
Christine Inglis, Administrative Coordinator

The Cedar Shake and Shingle Bureau is a non-profit organization that promotes the use of Certi-label cedar roofing and sidewall products. On June 9, 1915, at a meeting of the Trustees of the West Coast Lumber Manufacturers Association, it was agreed to establish a branch of the association to serve those members who manufactured shingles. Our influence grew, and as we survived both the Great Depression and World War II, manufacturers continued their quality commitment.
350 Members
Founded in 1915

4014 **Construction Financial Management Association**
100 Village Boulevard
Suite 200
Princeton, NJ 08540-5783

609-452-8000
888-421-9996; Fax: 609-452-0474
info@cfma.org
www.cfma.org
Facebook, Twitter, LinkedIn, YouTube

Stuart Binstock, President & CEO
Brian Summers, VP, Operations
Catherine Wasner, VP, Member Services
Samantha Lake, VP, Marketing
Stacey Scholl, Director, Finance

CFMA is the only organization dedicated to bringing together construction financial professionals and those partners serving their unique needs. CFMA has 98 chapters located throughout the US and Canada.
8600 Members
Founded in 1981

4015 **Construction Industry Service Corporation**
2000 Spring Road
Suite 110
Oak Brook, IL 60523

630-472-9411
877-562-9411; Fax: 630-472-9413
Julia@cisco.org
www.cisco.org
Facebook, Twitter, LinkedIn

David Henderson, President
Dan Allen, Executive Director
Johnetta Ryan, Education-to-Careers Director

Gary Karafiat, Comm. & Public Affairs Director
Julia Mulvey, Office Manager

The Construction Industry Service Corporation (CISCO) is a non-profit labor management association bringing union construction labor and management representatives together to work cooperatively in order to better the construction industry as a whole. CISCO currently represents union contractors and workers in Cook, DuPage, Lake, Kane, Kendall and McHenry Counties.
14800 Members
Founded in 1988

4016 Construction Owners Association of America
5000 Austell Powder Springs Rd
Suite 217
Austell, GA 30106

770-433-0820
800-994-2622; Fax: 404-577-3551
coaa@coaa.org
www.coaa.org
Facebook, Twitter, LinkedIn

Howie Ferguson, Executive Director
Lucie Castro, Manager, Membership & Chapters
Jill McKenzie, Manager, Membership & Sponsorship
LaKaya Brittian-Quander, Manager, Meetings & Events

National association dedicated to supporting project Owners' success in the design and construction of buildings and facilities through education, information and developing relationships within the industry. Comprised of public and private owners who manage facilities development and capital improvement projects.
530 Members
Founded in 1994

4017 Construction Specifications Institute
110 South Union Street
Suite 100
Alexandria, VA 22314

703-684-0300
800-689-2900; Fax: 703-236-4600
csi@csinet.org
www.csinet.org
Facebook, Twitter, LinkedIn, Youtube, Flickr

Mark Dorsey, Chief Executive Officer
Velma Hart, Chief Operating Officer
Sarah McMurdy, Dir., Marketing & Communications
Themica McBee, Manager, Membership Services
Susan Oswald, Human Resources Consultant

A national association dedicated to creating standards and formats to improve construction documents and project delivery. The organization is unique in the industry in that its members are a cross section of specifiers, architects, engineers, contractors and building materials suppliers.
15000 Members
Founded in 1948

4018 Continental Automated Buildings Association (CABA)
1173 Cyrville Road
Suite 210
Ottawa, Canada, ON K1J 7S6

613-686-1814
888-798-2222; Fax: 613-744-7833
caba@caba.org
www.caba.org
Facebook, Twitter, LinkedIn, YouTube

Ronald Zimmer, President & CEO
Conrad McCallum, Communications Director
Greg Walker, Research Director
Andrew Glennie, Member Services Coordinator
Aruna Gamage, Financial Administrator

CABA is an international, non-profit industry organization that promotes advanced technologies in homes and buildings.
380+ Members
Founded in 1988

4019 Deep Foundations Institute
326 Lafayette Avenue
Hawthorne, NJ 07506

973-423-4030; Fax: 973-423-4031
staff@dfi.org
www.dfi.org
Facebook, LinkedIn

Theresa Engler, Executive Director
Emilio Fandino, Director, Administration
Angie Gibble, Meetings & Events Specialist
KC Christie, Database & Membership Coordinator
Karol Paltsios, Managing Editor & Ad. Manager

DFI gathers professionals in the deep foundations sector of the construction industry, to create a place for discussion, inquiry and debate. In so doing, DFI brings the disciplines together where they have learned from each other, creating a better informed, more communicative foundations industry.
3000 Members
Founded in 1976

4020 Design-Build Institute of America
1331 Pennsylvania Ave., NW
4th Floor
Washington, DC 20004

202-682-0110; Fax: 202-682-5877
dbia@dbia.org
www.dbia.org
Facebook, Twitter, LinkedIn

Lisa Washington, Executive Director & CEO
Louis J. Jenny, VP, Advocacy & Outreach
Thanh Nguyen, Chief Financial Officer
Salvdor Chairez, Director, Membership Development
Kim Wright, VP, Strategic Communications

An organization that defines, teaches, and promotes best practices in design-build and represents the entire design and construction industry.
Founded in 1993

4021 Door & Access Systems Manufacturers Association International
1300 Sumner Avenue
Cleveland, OH 44115-2851

216-241-7333; Fax: 216-241-0105
www.dasma.com

Christopher Johnson ÿ, Executive Director
John Addington, Assistant Executive Director
Joseph R. Hetzelÿ, Technical Director
Rachel James, Client Services Administrator
Vicki Jones, Magazine Editor

Trade association of manufacturers of garage doors, rolling doors, high performance doors, garage door operators, vehicular gate operators, and access control products.
Founded in 1996

4022 Elberton Granite Association
1 Granite Plaza
PO Box 640
Elberton, GA 30635

706-283-2551; Fax: 706-283-6380
granite@egaonline.com
www.egaonline.com

The Elberton Granite Association, Inc. is the largest trade association of granite quarriers and manufacturers in the United States. More than 250,000 granite memorials are manufactured annually by E.G.A. firms and shipped throughout the United States.
150 Members
Founded in 1951

4023 Expanded Metal Manufacturers Association (EMMA)
800 Roosevelt Rd. Bldg. C
Suite 312
Glen Ellyn, IL 60137

630-942-6591; Fax: 630-790-3095
wlewis7@cox.net
www.naamm.org

Mike Gilboy, Division Chair
Drew Bahner, Division Vice Chair

Educational resources that promote the use of Expanded Metal which reduces scrap materials.
Founded in 1938

4024 Finishing Contractors Assn. Intl.
1 Parkview Plaza
Suite 610
Oakbrook Terrace, IL 60181

630-537-1042
866-322-3477; Fax: 630-590-5272
fca@finishingcontractors.org
www.finishingcontractors.org
Facebook, Twitter, YouTube

Anthony (Tony) Darkangelo, Chief Executive Officer
Jeremy Fitch, Director, Communications
Jon Lee, Director, Operations

The Association represents contractors performing glazing work, flooring, drywalling and painting, among other finishing trades.

4025 Florida Building Material Association
P.O. Box 65
Mount Dora, FL 32756

352-383-0366; Fax: 352-383-8756
betty@fbma.org
www.fbma.org
Facebook, Instagram

Promotes the interests of the building material industry throughout Florida.
Founded in 1920

4026 Hollow Metal Manufacturers Association (HMMA)
National Assn of Architectural Metal Manufacturer
800 Roosevelt Rd
Bldg C Suite 312
Glen Ellyn, IL 60137

630-942-6591; Fax: 630-790-3095
wlewis7@cox.net
www.naamm.org

Evan Mathews, Division Chair
Devan Stiles, Division Vice Chair

The largest of four operating divisions of the National Association of Architectural Metal Manufacturers. HMMA is a group composed of companies that manufacture, distribute and promote the use of hollow metal door and frame products.
60 Members
Founded in 1938

4027 ICC: International Code Council
500 New Jersey Avenue, NW
6th Floor
Washington, DC 20001

888-422-7233
202-370-1800; Fax: 202-783-2348
webmaster@iccsafe.org
www.iccsafe.org
Facebook, Twitter, LinkedIn, RSS, YouTube

Dominic Sims, Chief Executive Officer
John Belcik, COO & CFO
Joan O'Neil, Chief Knowledge Officer
Mark Johnson, Executive Vice President

The International Code Council is a member-focused association dedicated to helping the

building safety community and construction industry provide safe, sustainable and affordable construction through the development of codes and standards used in the design, build and compliance process. Mission: To provide the highest quality codes, standards, products and services for all concerned with the safety and performance.
Founded in 1994

4028 **Institute for Human Centered Design**
200 Portland St.
Boston, MA 02114

617-695-1225; Fax: 617-482-8099
info@ihcdesign.org
www.humancentereddesign.org
Facebook, Twitter, LinkedIn, YouTube

Valerie Fletcher, Executive Director
Janet Carpman, Director, Wayfinding
Kathy Gips, Director, ADA Training
Janice Majewski, Director, Inclusive Projects
Gabriela Bonome-Sims, Deputy Director

Advances the role of design in the built environment in expanding opportunity and enhancing experience for people of all ages, abilities, and cultures. Provides education, consulting, design, and research services.
Founded in 1978

4029 **Interlocking Concrete Pavement Institute**
14801 Murdock Stree
Suite 230
Chantilly, VA 20151

703-657-6900
800-241-3652; Fax: 703-657-6901
icpi@icpi.org
www.icpi.org
Facebook, Twitter, LinkedIn, Youtube, Pinterest

Charles McGrath, Executive Director
David Smith, Technical Director
Steven Hawkins, Director, Marketing & Membership
Alison Stern, Manager, Membership & Admin.
Erin Hobson, Manager, Meetings & Trade Shows

Self governed, self funded autonomous association representing the interlocking concrete pavement industry in North America. Membership is open to producers, contractors, suppliers, consultants and others who have an interest in the industry.
900+ Members
Founded in 1993

4030 **International Door Association**
1 Parkview Plaza
Suite 800
Oakbrook Terrace, IL 60181

202-591-2457
800-355-4432; Fax: 202-591-5442
info@doors.org
www.doors.org
Facebook, Twitter, LinkedIn, Youtube

Mike Fischer, Executive Director
Lori Barker-Cummings, Managing Director
Delia Murphy, Communications Program Director
Melanie Goff, Member Service & Engagement Manager
Monica Saunders, Meetings & Expositions Manager

The International Door Association plays an important role in the process of quality creation and control by providing helpful programs and services to those who sell, install, and service the superb products produced by the industry's list of manufacturers. Door and access systems dealers are the front line businesses that serve the customer face-to-face.
750 Members
Founded in 1995

4031 **International Living Future Institute**
1501 East Madison St.
Suite 150
Seattle, WA 98122

206-223-2028
info@living-future.org
www.living-future.org
Facebook, Twitter, LinkedIn, Instagram

KC Gauldine, Chief Executive Officer
Corinna Krauskopf, Chief Development Officer
Andrea Kristof, Chief Financial Officer
Greg Norris, Chief Scientist
Marja Williams, Chief Programs Officer

Leading and supporting the transformation toward communities that are socially just, culturally rich, and ecologically restorative. Offers green building and infrastructure solutions for single room renovations to neighborhoods and whole cities. Offices in Vancouver BC, Seattle WA, and Portland OR.

4032 **International Slurry Surfacing Association**
Three Church Circle
PO Box 250
Annapolis, MD 21401-1933

410-267-0023; Fax: 410-267-7546
www.slurry.org
Facebook, Twitter

Rusty Price, President
Carter Dabney, Vice President
Rex Eberly, Secretary
Eric Reimschiisel, Treasurer
Christine Deneuvillers, Immediate Past President

The International Slurry Surfacing Association (ISSA) is an international non-profit trade association comprised of contractors, equipment manufacturers, research personnel, consulting engineers and other industry professionals, working together to promote the concept of pavement preservation. ISSA promotes the highest standards of ethics and quality while providing its members with information, tech assistance and ongoing opportunities for networking and professional development.
Cost: $500.00
220+ Members
Founded in 1963

4033 **International Zinc Association**
1822 East NC Highway 54
Suite 120
Durham, NC 27713

919-361-4647; Fax: 919-361-1957
contact@zinc.org
www.zinc.org
Facebook, Twitter

A nonprofit global organization dedicated to the interests of zinc and its users.
Founded in 1991

4034 **Interstates Construction Services**
1520 North Main
PO Box 260
Sioux Center, IA 51250

712-722-1662; Fax: 712-722-1667
bdev@interstates.com
www.interstates.com

Scott Peterson, Chief Executive Officer
Joel Van Egdom, Chief Financial Officer
Catherine Bloom, Chief Marketing & Strategy Officer
Mike Meyers, Chief Information Officer

Combine the strengths of teams with processing industry expertise to develop the best solutions for clients' project needs. From the planning table to the plant floor, Interstates is with clients every step of the way. Assists with preliminary budgeting and help develop cost effective designs, setting the stage for a quick and efficient startup.
Founded in 1953

4035 **Manufactured Housing Institute**
1655 North Fort Myer Road
Suite 104
Arlington, VA 22209

703-558-0400; Fax: 703-558-0401
info@mfghome.org
www.manufacturedhousing.org
Facebook, Twitter

Richard Jennison, President/CEO

MHI is the national trade organization representing all segments of the factory-built housing industry. MHI serves its membership by providing industry research, promotion, education and government relations programs, and by building and facilitating consensus within the industry.

4036 **Mason Contractors Association of America: Advancing the Masonry Industry**
1481 Merchant Drive
Algonquin, IL 60102

224-678-9709
800-536-2225; Fax: 224-678-9714
www.masoncontractors.org
Facebook, Twitter, LinkedIn

Paul Oldham, Chair
Lawrence Vacala, Vice Chair
Dick Dentiger, Treasurer
Kent Huntley, Secretary

The Mason Contractors Association of America (MCAA) is the national trade association representing mason contractors. The MCAA is committed to preserving and promoting the masonry industry by providing continuing education, advocating fair codes and standards, fostering a safe work environment, recruiting future manpower, and marketing the benefits of masonry materials.
1000 Members
Founded in 1950

4037 **Masonry Society**
105 S Sunset St.
Suite Q
Longmont, CO 80501-6172

303-939-9700; Fax: 303-541-9215
info@masonrysociety.org
www.masonrysociety.org
LinkedIn

Christine Subasic, Chair

Dedicated to the advancement of scientific engineering, architectural and construction knowledge of masonry. Promotes research and education and disseminates information on masonry materials, design, construction. Publishes newsletters, codes & specifications and material on masonry design.
450 Members
Founded in 1977
Mailing list available for rent: 4200 names

4038 **Mechanical Contractors Association of America**
1385 Piccard Drive
Rockville, MD 20850

301-869-5800; Fax: 301-990-9690
www.mcaa.org

Provides high-quality educational materials and programs for 2,500 firms involved in heating, air conditioning, refrigeration, plumbing, piping, and mechanical service.

4039 **Metal Building Manufacturers Association**
1300 Sumner Avenue
Cleveland, OH 44115-2851
216-241-7333; Fax: 216-241-0105
www.mbma.com
Twitter, LinkedIn
Tony Bouquot, General Manager
W. Lee Shoemaker, Dir., Research & Engineering
Vincent Sagan, Senior Staff Engineer
Promotes the design and construction of metal building systems in the low-rise, non-residential building marketplace.

4040 **Metal Construction Association**
8735 W. Higgins Rd.
Suite 300
Chicago, IL 60631
847-375-4718; Fax: 847-375-6488
mca@metalconstruction.org
www.metalconstruction.org
Facebook, Twitter, LinkedIn
Jeff Henry, Executive Director
Peggy Doherty, Director, Operations
Jeff Irwin, Program Directoe
Bob Zabcik, Technical Director
Andy Williams, Director, Codes & Standards
An organization of manufacturers and suppliers whose metal products are used in structures.
Founded in 1983

4041 **Metal Framing Manufacturers Association**
330 N Wabash Ave
Chicago, IL 60611
312-644-6610; Fax: 312-321-4098
MFMAstats@smithbucklin.com
www.metalframingmfg.org
Mark Thorsby, Executive Director
The Members of the Metal Framing Manufacturers Association (MFMA) focus on the manufacture of ferrous and nonferrous metal framing (continuous slot metal channel systems) which consist of channels with in-turned lips and associated hardware for fastening to the channels (Strut) at random points.
Founded in 1981

4042 **Mississippi Valley Equipment Association**
11140 E Woodmen Rd
Falcon, CO 80831-8127
719-495-2283
800-388-9881; Fax: 719-495-3014
www.mvea.com
Facebook
Jim Herron, CEO
Sarah Schaefer, Public Information Officer
Amanda Hall, Administrative Manager
Randy Penn, Financil Manager
Terryl Jensen, Operations Manager
A regional affiliate of the North American Equipment Dealers Association provides members with a multitude of services designed to assist them in maintaining a profitable business operation.
165 Members
Founded in 1941

4043 **Modular Building Institute**
944 Glenwood Station Ln
Suite 204
Charlottesville, VA 22901-1480
434-296-3288
888-811-3288; Fax: 434-296-3361
info@modular.org
www.mbinet.org
Facebook, Twitter, LinkedIn, Youtube, Google+, Pinterest
Tom Hardiman, Executive Director
Steven Williams, Operations Director
Amanda Rowe, Events Director
John McMullen, Marketing Director
Jace Bower, Communications Coordinator
The Modular Building Institute (MBI) is the international non-profit trade association serving modular construction. Members are manufacturers, contractors, and dealers in two distinct segments of the industry - permanent modular construction (PMC) and relocatable buildings (RB). Associate members are companies supplying building components, services, and financing.
211 Members
Founded in 1983

4044 **National Asphalt Pavement Association**
5100 Forbes Blvd
Suite 200
Lanham, MD 20706—440
301-731-4748
888-468-6499; Fax: 301-731-4621
mcervarich@hotmix.org
www.asphaltpavement.org
Facebook, Twitter
Audrey Copeland, President & CEO
Melanie Richardson, VP, Finance & Operations
Lori Wolking, VP, Meetings & Education
Steve Shivak, Director, Membership
Kelly Kanaras, Director, Awards & Marketing
The only trade association that represents the interests of the asphalt pavement producer and paving contractor on the national level with Congress, government agencies, and other national trade and business organizations. NAPA supports an active research program designed to answer questions about environmental issues and to improve the quality of asphalt pavements and paving techniques used in the construction of roads, streets, highways, parking lots, and environmental facilities.
1200 Members
Founded in 1955

4045 **National Association of Architectural Metal Manufacturers**
800 Roosevelt Rd. Bldg. C
Suite 312
Glen Ellyn, IL 60137
630-942-6591; Fax: 630-790-3095
wlewis7@cox.net
www.naamm.org
Jeff Church, Executive Vice President
Wes Lewis, Technical Consultant
An association that represents a wide variety of architectural metal products for building construction.
Founded in 1938

4046 **National Association of Church Design Builders**
1000 Ballpark Way
Suite 306
Arlington, TX 76011
817-200-2622
866-416-2232; Fax: 817-275-4519
Facebook, Twitter
An established, board-certified, nationwide association of firms committed to focusing on the ministry needs and styles of the churches they serve.

4047 **National Association of Elevator Contractors**
1298 Wellbrook Circle NE
Suite A
Conyers, GA 30012-8031
770-760-9660
800-900-6232; Fax: 770-760-9714
info@naec.org
www.naec.org
Facebook
Rena Cozart, Executive Director
Tripp Cook, Manager, Marketing & Member Service
Britnee Irwin, Manager, Membership & Registration
Jennifer Simmons, Manager, Website Content
Kathy Bell, Manager, Education
NAEC is an association of elevator contractors and suppliers serving primarily the interests of independent elevator contractors and independent suppliers of products and services; promoting safe and reliable elevator, escalator and short-range transportation and promoting excellence in the management of member companies.
695 Members
Founded in 1950

4048 **National Association of Home Builders**
1201 15th Street NW
Washington, DC 20005
202-822-0200
800-368-5242; Fax: 202-266-8400
info@nahb.com
www.nahb.org
Facebook, Twitter, LinkedIn, Google+, Pinterest
John Fowke, Chair
Gerald Howard, Chief Executive Officer
Represents the building industry by serving its members and affiliated state and local builders associations.
2200 Members
Founded in 1942

4049 **National Association of Women in Construction**
327 S Adams Street
Fort Worth, TX 76104
817-877-5551
800-552-3506; Fax: 817-877-0324
nawic@nawic.org
www.nawic.org
Crissy Ingram, Executive Director
Amber Kohut, Membership Coordinator
Lori Wagner, Membership Manager
Kharisma Rivera, Finance Manager
Lauri McCullough, Database & Website Manager
Founded by women working in the construction industry. The founders organized NAWIC to create a support network for women in construction.
5800 Members
Founded in 1953

4050 **National Association of the Remodeling Industry**
PO Box 4250
Des Plaines, IL 60016
847-298-9200
800-611-6274; Fax: 847-298-9225
info@nari.org
www.nari.org
Facebook, Twitter, YouTube, Pinterest
David Pekel, CEO
Elsie Iturralde, Chief Operations Officer
Tracy Wright, Sr. Director, Membership & Chapters

Rob King, Director, Marketing
Kelsey Kazmierczak, Manager, Events & Communities

NARI has an inclusive, encompassing purpose to; establish and maintain a firm commitment to developing and sustaining programs that expand and unite the remodeling industry; to ensure the industry's growth and security; to encourage ethical conduct, sound business practices and professionalism in the remodeling industry; and to present NARI as the recognized authority in the remodeling industry.
Founded in 1935

4051 National Concrete Masonry Association
13750 Sunrise Valley Dr
Herndon, VA 20171-4662

703-713-1900; Fax: 703-713-1910
info@ncma.org
www.ncma.org
Facebook, Twitter, LinkedIn, Pinterest

Thomas Finch, Chair
Brittaney R. Kamhong Thompson, Executive Administrator

Consists of manufacturers of concrete masonry products and suppliers of products to the industry. Offers a variety of technical of technical services and design aids through publications, computer programs, slide presentations and technical training.
Founded in 1918

4052 National Conference of States on Building Codes & Standards
505 Huntmar Park Dr
Suite 210
Herndon, VA 20170-5103

703-437-0100; Fax: 703-481-3596

Serves as a forum for the interchange of information and provides technical services, education and training to our members to enhance the public's social, economic well-being through safe, durable, accessible and efficient buildings.
Founded in 1967

4053 National Council of Acoustical Consultants
9100 Purdue Rd
Suite 200
Indianapolis, IN 46268

317-328-0642; Fax: 317-328-4629
info@ncac.com
www.ncac.com

Eric Reuter, President
Joseph Bridger, VP Membership
Jesse Ehnert, VP, Finance
Richard Schrag, VP, Marketing & Communcations

Strives to safeguard the interests of professional acoustical consulting firms. Managing physics and psychoacoustics to provide optimum lisning environments.
130 Members
Founded in 1962

4054 National Demolition Association
2025 M Street NW
Suite 800
Washington, DC 20036

202-367-1152
800-541-2412; Fax: 202-367-2152
info@demolitionassociation.com
www.demolitionassociation.com
Facebook, Twitter, LinkedIn

Jeff Lambert, Executive Director
Natalie DeHart, Membership & Operations Manager
Linda Benck, Meetings & Events Manager
Alexa Schlosser, Demolition Magazine Editor

Represents the demolition industry including demolition contractorsto foster goodwill and the exchange of ideas with the public, governmental agencies and contractors engaged in the demolition industry, and for manufacturers or suppliers of demolition equipment, supplies and services.
900 Members
Founded in 1972

4055 National Electrical Contractors Association
3 Bethesda Metro Ctr
Suite 1100
Bethesda, MD 20814

301-657-3110; Fax: 301-215-4500
www.necanet.org
Facebook, Twitter, LinkedIn, Youtube, Flickr

Represents a segment of the construction market comprised of electrical contracting firms.
70000 Members
Founded in 1879

4056 National Environmental Balancing Bureau
8575 Grovemont Cir
Gaithersburg, MD 20877

301-977-3698
866-497-4447; Fax: 301-977-9589
jhuber@completecx.com
www.nebb.org

Tiffany Suite, Executive Vice President
Christina Spence, Office & Scheduling Coordinator
Sumayyah Milstein, Firm Certification Coordinator

NEBB is an international certification assocaition for firms that deliver high performance building systems. Members perform testing, adjusting and balancing (TAB) of heating, ventilating and air-conditioning systems, commission and retro-commission building systems commissioning, execute sound and vibration testing, and test and certify lab fume hoods and electronic and bio clean rooms. NEBB holds the highest standards in certification.
Founded in 1971

4057 National Hispanic Construction Association
1330 Locust Rd. NW
Washington, DC 20012-1319

214-566-2410
info@builtbylatinos.org
www.builtbylatinos.org
Facebook

John H. Martinez-D., Chair

Association serving the interests of Hispanic construction professionals.

4058 National Housing Endowment
1201 15th St Nw
Washington, DC 20005

202-293-9072
800-368-5242; Fax: 202-266-8177
nhe@nahb.org
www.nationalhousingendowment.org
Facebook, Twitter, LinkedIn, Pinterest

Mark Pursell, President & CEO
Karima Simmons, Director, Development & Comm.
Toris Moody, Programs & Operations Manager

Provides a permanaent source of funds to address long-term industry concerns at the national level including: supporting scholarship progams that encourage students to select home building and related fields as their life's work, assisting colleges and universities in the development of housing related curricula and activities, revitalizing the industry's labor pool and enhancing its professionalism through apprenticeship programs, seminars and continuing education.
Founded in 1987

4059 National Lumber & Building Material Dealers Association (NLBMDA)
2025 M St NW
Suite 800
Washington, DC 20036-3309

202-367-1169
800-634-8645; Fax: 202-367-2169
membersupport@dealer.org
www.dealer.org
Facebook, Twitter, LinkedIn

Jonathan M. Paine, CAE, President & CEO
Kevin McKenney, Director, Government Affairs
Alex McIntyre, Legislative & Regulatory Coord.
Allison Ward, Membership & Operations Associate
Corie Stretton, Event Manager

Promoting the industry and educating legislators and public policy personnel, assising legislative, regulatory, standard-setting and other government or private bodies in the development of laws, regulations and policies affecting lumber and building material dealers, its customers and suppliers.
6000 Members
Founded in 1917

4060 National Paint and Coatings Association
1500 Rhode Island Ave Nw
Washington, DC 20005

202-462-6272; Fax: 202-462-8549
npca@paint.org
www.paint.org
Facebook, Twitter, LinkedIn

Manufacturers of paints and industrial coatings and suppliers to the industry.
400+ Members
Founded in 1887

4061 National Railroad Construction & Maintenance Association
500 New Jersey Ave NW
Suite 400
Washington, DC 20001

202-715-1264; Fax: 202-318-0867
info@nrcma.org
www.nrcma.org
Facebook, Twitter, LinkedIn

Ashley Wieland, President
Michael McGonagle, Sr. Director, Operations
Nicole Womach, Director, Finance & Administration
James Hansen, Chief Commercial Officer
Steve Bolte, VP, Business Devt, North America

Members are railroad construction and maintenance contractors, engineering firms, manufacturing suppliers and professional associate firms.
100+ Members
Founded in 1978

4062 National Ready Mixed Concrete Association
900 Spring St
Silver Spring, MD 20910-4015

301-587-1400
888-846-7622; Fax: 301-585-4219
info@nrmca.org
www.nrmca.org
Facebook, Twitter, LinkedIn, YouTube

Michael Phillips, President
Nicole Maher, Chief Operating Officer
Joe Roche, Chief Financial Officer
Alex Land, Director, Membership Engagement
Frank Cavaliere, Director, Special Programs & Comm.

Our mission is to provide exceptional value for our members by responsibly representing and serving the entire ready mixed concrete industry through leadership, promotion, education and partnering; to ensure ready mixed concrete is the building material of choice.
1200 Members
Founded in 1930

4063 National Roofing Contractors Association
10255 W. Higgins Road
Suite 600
Rosemont, IL 60018-5607

847-299-9070; Fax: 847-299-1183
www.nrca.net
Facebook, Twitter, LinkedIn, YouTube, Instagram, Google+

Reid Ribble, Chief Executive Officer
McKay Daniels, Chief Operating Officer
Harry Ryder, Chief Financial Officer
Ambika Reid, VP, Communications
Carl Good, VP, Marketing

An association of roofing, roof deck, and waterproofing contractors; industry-related associate members; and international members worldwide.
3500 Members
Founded in 1886

4064 National Slag Association
P.O Box 1197
Pleasant Grove, UT 84062

801-785-4535; Fax: 801-785-4539
www.nationalslag.org

Charles Ochola, President

Members are processors of iron and steel slags for use as a aggregate in construction and manufacturing applications.
77 Members
Founded in 1918

4065 National Stone, Sand & Gravel Association
1605 King St
Alexandria, VA 22314

703-525-8788
800-342-1415; Fax: 703-525-7782
jwilson@nssga.org
www.nssga.org
Facebook, Twitter, LinkedIn, YouTube

Michael W Johnson, President & CEO
Jason Epstein, Director, Membership
Jennifer Dugas, VP, Meetings & Events
Chuck Fuqua, VP, Communications
Cesar Silva Orrego, VP, Finance & Adminnistration

Represents the crushed stone, sand and gravel — or aggregate — industries. Our members account for 90 percent of the crushed stone and 70 percent of the sand and gravel produced annually in the US.
570 Members
Founded in 1985

4066 National Systems Contractors Association
3950 River Ridge DR NE
Suite B
Cedar Rapids, IA 52402

319-366-6722
800-446-6722; Fax: 319-366-4164
nsca@nsca.org
www.nsca.org
Facebook, Twitter, LinkedIn, YouTube

Chuck Wilson, Executive Director
Deb Gulick, Chief Financial Officer
Leah Garris, Director, Marketing & Communication
Teresa Solorio, Director, Operations
Savannah Washburn, Events Manager

A not for profit association representing the commercial electronic systems industry. Also a powerful advocate of all who work within the low voltage industry, including systems contractors/integrators, product manufacturers, consultants, sales representatives, a growing number of architects, specifying engineers and others.
2800 Members
Founded in 1980

4067 National Terrazzo and Mosaic Association
P.O. Box 2605
Fredericksburg, TX 78624

800-323-9736; Fax: 888-362-2770
info@ntma.com
www.ntma.com

George Hardy, Executive Director

The association establishes national standards for all terrazzo floor and wall systems and provides complete specifications, color plates and general information to architects and designers at no cost.

4068 National Tile Contractors Association
626 Lakeland E Drive
PO Box 13629
Jackson, MS 39232

601-939-2071; Fax: 601-932-6117
webmaster@tile-assn.com
www.tile-assn.com
Facebook, Twitter, LinkedIn, YouTube

Bart Bettiga, Executive Director
Avia Haynes, Director, Marketing & Communication
Amber Fox, Five-Star Program Director
Trish Moss, Membership Coordinator
Lesley Goddin, Editor

Serving every segment of the industry, and is recognized as the largest and most respected tile contractors association in the world.
1000 Members
Founded in 1947
Mailing list available for rent

4069 National Utility Contractors Association
3925 Chain Bridge Road
Suite 300
Fairfax, VA 22230

703-358-9300; Fax: 703-358-9307
nuca@nuca.com
www.nuca.com
Facebook, Twitter, LinkedIn

Doug Carlson, Chief Executive Officer
Chris Barrett, Chief Operating Officer
Robert Baylor, Director, Communications
Cheryl Stratos, Director, Marketing & Sales
Zachary Jordan, Staff Editor

A national association that provides a forum for continuing education and promotes effective public policy, through its grassroots network, to protect and enhance your industry.
1400 Members
Founded in 1964

4070 North American Insulation Manufacturers Association
11 Canal Center Plaza
Suite 103
Alexandria, VA 22314-1548

703-684-0084; Fax: 703-684-0427
www.naima.org

Curt Rich, President/CEO
Stacy Fitzgerald-Redd, Dir., Marketing & Communications

Manufacturers of fiber glass, rock wool, and slag wool insulation products. NAIMA members manufacture the vast majority of fiber glass, rock and slag wool insulations produced and used in North America.
Founded in 1933

4071 Northeastern Retail Lumber Association
585 N Greenbush Rd
Rensselaer, NY 12144

518-286-1010
800-292-6752; Fax: 518-286-1755
rferris@nrla.org
www.nrla.org

Rita Ferris, President
Donna Berger, Director, Conventions & Meetings
Sandra Lacko, Dir., Finance & Administration
Melissa Stankovich, Art Director & Publisher
Tony Leone, IT Manager

A resource for industry members, consumers, and public officials independent lumber and building material suppliers and associated businesses in New York and the six New England states.
1150 Members
Founded in 1894

4072 Operative Plasterers' and Cement Masons' International Association
11720 Beltsville Dr
Suite 700
Beltsville, MD 20705

301-623-1000; Fax: 301-623-1032
opcmiaintl@opcmia.org
www.opcmia.org

Daniel Stepano, General President
Kevin Sexton, General Secretary/Treasurer
Todd Lair, EVP
Rob Mason, Vice President
Doug Taylor, Vice President

Represents and trains plasterers and cement masonsn for the purpose of protecting and promoting the quality of the industry and the livelihood of the members.
Founded in 1864

4073 Outdoor Power Equipment Institute
341 S Patrick St
Alexandria, VA 22314

703-549-7600; Fax: 703-549-7604
info@opei.org
www.opei.org
Facebook, Twitter, LinkedIn

Kris Kiser, President & CEO
Suzanne Shomers, VP, Finance & Administration
Chuck Bowen, Dir., Comm. & Member Relations
Marla Popkin, Director, Meetings

International trade association whose members are manufacturers of powered lawn and garden maintenance products, components and attachment supplies, as well as industry related services.
85 Members
Founded in 1952

4074 Painting Contractors Association
2316 Millpark Drive
Maryland Heights, MO 63043

314-514-7322
800-332-7322; Fax: 314-890-2068
www.pcapainted.org
Facebook, Twitter, LinkedIn, YouTube

Nigel Costolloe, Executive Director
Chad Schirmer, Creative Director
Marsha Bass, Operations Manager
Marcie Haselden, Member Experience Manager
Andrew Couch, Content Production Specialist

PDCA exists to lead the industry by providing quality products, programs, services, and opportunities essential to the success of our members.
5M Members
Founded in 1884

4075 **Perlite Institute**
2207 Forest Hills Drive
Suite A
Harrisburg, PA 17112
717-238-9723; Fax: 717-238-9985
info@perlite.org
www.perlite.org
Facebook, LinkedIn
Denise Calabrese, Executive Director
Michelle Keyser, Communications Director
Lori Zelesko, Events Director
Jennifer Swartz, Finance Administrator
An international trade association which establishes product standards and specifications, and which encourages the development of new product uses through research.
183 Members
Founded in 1949

4076 **Pile Driving Contractors Association**
33 Knight Boxx Road
Suite 1
Orange Park, FL 32065
904-215-4771
888-311-7322; Fax: 904-215-2977
www.piledrivers.org
Facebook, Twitter, LinkedIn
Frank Peters, Executive Director
Marian Phillips, Executive Assistant
Matt Bisbee, Director, Member Services
Kathy Harper, Manager, Education & Events
An organization of pile driving contractors that advocates the incresed use of driven piles for deep foundations and earth retention systems. Promotes the use of driven pile solutions in all cases where they are effective, support educational programs for engineers on the design and efficiency of driven piles and for contractors on improving installation procedures and give contractors a larger voice in establishing procedures and standards for pile installation and design.
450 Members
Founded in 1996

4077 **Pipe Fabrication Institute**
511 Ave Of Americas
#601
New York, NY 10011
514-634-3434
866-913-3434; Fax: 514-634-9736
pfi@pfi-institute.org
www.pfi-institute.org
Greg Howell, Chair
Steve Hinsaw, Vice Chair
Doug Barefoot, Treasurer
Guy Fortin, Executive Director
Robert B. Cottington, Legal Counsel
Members are companies producing sophisticated high temperature, high pressure piping systems that employ specialists from the United Association of Journeymen and Apprentices of the Plumbing and Pipe Fitting Industry. We exist solely for the purpose of ensuring a level of quality in the pipe fabrication industry that is without compromise.
65-70 Members
Founded in 1913

4078 **Portable Sanitation Association International**
2626 E 82nd Street
Suite 175
Bloomington, MN 55425
952-854-8300
800-822-3020; Fax: 952-854-7560
info@psai.org
www.psai.org
Facebook, Twitter, LinkedIn
Karleen Kos, Executive Director
Emily Newberg, Director, Membership & Credentials
Todd Ginter, Director, Marketing
International trade association that represents firms engaged in the leasing, renting, selling and manufacturing of portable sanitation equipment, services and supplies for construction, recreation, emergency and other uses. Devoted to the proper handling of human waste by the most modern, sanitary means, giving the greatest concern to the preservation of an unspoiled environment.
550+ Members
Founded in 1971

4079 **Portland Cement Association**
5420 Old Orchard Road
Skokie, IL 60077-1083
847-966-6200; Fax: 847-966-9781
info@cement.org
www.cement.org
Facebook, Twitter, LinkedIn, YouTube
Michael Ireland, Chief Executive Officer
Edward Sullivan, SVP & Chief Economist
Sean O'Neill, SVP, Government Affairs
Nick Ferrari, SVP, Membership & Admin. Services
Joe Roche, Chief Financial Officer
The Portland Cement Association represents cement companies in the United States and Canada. It conducts market development, engineering, research, education, and public affairs programs.
Founded in 1916

4080 **Precast Prestressed Concrete Institute**
200 W Adams St
Suite 2100
Chicago, IL 60606
312-786-0300; Fax: 312-621-1114
info@pci.org
www.pci.org
Facebook, Twitter, LinkedIn, RSS
Robert Risser PE, President & CEO
Beth Taylor, Chief Financial & Admin. Officer
Jared Brewe, VP, Technical Services
Tom Klemens, Director, Publications
Becky King, Managing Dir., Marketing & Edu.
Dedicated to fostering understanding and use of precast and prestressed concrete, maintains a full staff of techniocal and marketing specialists.
1400 Members
Founded in 1954

4081 **Professional Construction Estimators Association of America**
PO Box 680336
Charlotte, NC 28216
704-484-1494
877-521-7232; Fax: 704-489-1495
pcea@pcea.org
www.pcea.org
Facebook
Kristen Clarke, President
Adam Blalock, VP
Benjamin Carter, Treasurer
Randall Williams, Executive Director
Richard Heath, Executive Director
Promotes construction estimating as a profession by upholding the code of ethics, and expanding public awareness.
1000 Members
Founded in 1956

4082 **Resilient Floor Covering Institute**
115 Broad Street
Sutie 201
La Grange, GA 30240
301-340-8580
info@rfci.org
www.rfci.com
Facebook, Pinterest
Douglas Wiegand, Executive Director
Industry trade association of North American manufacturers who produce resilient flooring products. Associate members of RFCI supply raw materials to the industry and manufacture installation and maintenance products.
21 Members
Founded in 1975

4083 **Retail Contractors Association**
400 North Washington Street
Suite 300
Alexandria, VA 22314ÿ
800-847-5085
703-683-5637ÿ; Fax: 703-683-0018
www.retailcontractors.org
Carol Montoya, Executive Director
A national organization of retail contractors united to provide a solid foundation of ethics, quality, and professionalism within the retail construction industry.

4084 **Roof Coatings Manufacturers Association**
750 National Press Building
529 14th Street NW
Washington, DC 20045
202-207-0919; Fax: 202-223-9741
info@roofcoatings.org
www.roofcoatings.org
LinkedIn
Dan Quinonez, Executive Director
Mike Fischer, VP, Codes & Standards
Chadwick Collins, Technical Director
George Fischer, Gov. Affairs & Regulatory Director
Bill Braun, Marketing Manager
Represents the interests of manufacturers of cold applied roof coatings, cements and waterproofing agents, as well as the suppliers of products, equipment and services to and for the industry.
70+ Members
Founded in 1983

4085 **Rubber Pavements Association**
10000 N. 31st. Ave.
Suite D-408
Phoenix, AZ 85281-5738
480-517-9944
877-517-9944; Fax: 480-517-9959
mbelshe@rubberpavements.org
www.rubberpavements.org
Marc Bertsch, President
Mark Belshe, Executive Director
Guadalupe Dickerson, Office Manager
Dedicated to encouraging greater usage of high quality, cost effective asphalt pavements containing recycled tire rubber. Conducts national and international seminars.
20 Members
Founded in 1985

4086 **Safety Glazing Certification Council**
P.O. Box 730
Sackets Harbor, NY 13685
315-646-2234; Fax: 315-646-2297
erin@amscert.com
www.igcc.org
John Kent, Program Administrator
Alicia Deveau, Program Administrator
Jennifer Mackey, Meetings & Events

Administrator
Andrew Mostley, Auditor

Nonprofit corporation that provides for the certifacation of safety glazing materials, comprised of safety glazing manufacturers and other parties concerned with public safety. SGCC is managed by a board of directors comprised of representatives from the safety glazing industry and the public interest sector.
105 Members
Founded in 1977

4087 **Scaffold Industry Association**
400 Admiral Blvd
Kansas City, MO 64106-1508

602-257-1144
816-595-4860; Fax: 602-257-1166
info@scaffold.org
www.scaffold.org
Facebook, Twitter, LinkedIn

Promotes safety by developing educational and informational material, conducting educational seminars and training courses, providing audio-visual programs and codes for safe practices, and other training and safety aids; to work with state, federal and other agencies in developing more effective safety standards; to reduce accidents, thereby reducing insurance costs; and to assist members in becoming more efficient and profitable in their businesses.
1000 Members
Founded in 1972

4088 **Screen Manufacturers Association**
2850 S Ocean Boulevard
Suite 114
Palm Beach, FL 33480-6242

733-636-0672; Fax: 561-533-7466
Kathryn@SMAinfo.org
www.smainfo.org
Twitter

Alan Gray, SVP
Joe Isaacs, President
Michael White, Sales Manager

Manufacturers of insect screens, screen frames, window screens, detention screens, sliding screen doors, swinging screen doors, fiberglass insect screening and aluminum insect screening.
Cost: $1000.00
20 Members
Founded in 1955

4089 **Specialty Tools and Fasteners Distributors Association**
500 Elm Grove Rd.
Suite 210
Elm Grove, WI 53122

262-784-4774
800-352-2981; Fax: 262-784-5059
info@stafda.org
www.stafda.org
Facebook, LinkedIn

International trade association composed of distributors and manufacturers and rep agents of light construction, industrial and related products. Members also include publishers of industry press serving the construction and industrial trades.
Cost: $350.00
2603 Members
Founded in 1976

4090 **Spray Polyurethane Foam Alliance**
3827 Old Lee Hwy
Suite 101B
Fairfax, VA 22030

800-523-6154; Fax: 703-222-5816
info@sprayfoam.org
www.sprayfoam.org
Facebook, Twitter

Bryan Heidreth, President
Bonnie Strickler, Vice President
Richard Spiess, Secretary-Treasurer

A trade association representing interests associated with rigid and semi-rigid polyurethane foam products that are typically applied with spray equipment as roofing and insulation.
Founded in 1987

4091 **Steel Door Institute**
30200 Detroit Road
Westlake, OH 44145

440-899-0010; Fax: 440-892-1404
info@steeldoor.org
www.steeldoor.org

Jeff Wherry, Managing Director

A voluntary, nonprofit business association that develops quality and performance standards for steel doors and frames.
Founded in 1954

4092 **Steel Joist Institute**
234 W Cheves Street
Florence, SC 29501

843-407-4091; Fax: 843-626-5565
sji@steeljoist.org
www.steeljoist.org
Twitter, LinkedIn

J Kenneth Charles III, Managing Director

Composed of active manufacturers, the SJI cooperates with government and business agencies to establish steel joint standards.
40 Members
Founded in 1928

4093 **Steel Window Institute**
1300 Sumner Ave
Cleveland, OH 44115-2851

216-241-7333; Fax: 216-241-0105
www.steelwindows.com

John Addington, Executive Director

An association of the leading manufacturers of windows made from either solid or formed sections of steel, and such related products as casings, trim, mechanical operators, screens, and moldings when manufactured and sold by members of the industry for use in conjunction with windows.
6 Members

4094 **Structural Insulated Panel Association**
P.O. Box 39848
Fort Lauderdale, FL 33339

253-858-7472; Fax: 253-858-0272
info@sips.org
www.sips.org
Facebook, Twitter, RSS

Jack Armstrong, Executive Director & COO

A trade association representing manufacturers, suppliers, fabriators, distributors, design professionals and builders committed to providing quality structural insulated panels for all segments of the construction industry.
250 Members
Founded in 1990

4095 **Stucco Manufacturers Association**
2402 Vista Nobleza
Newport Beach, CA 92660-3545

949-640-9902; Fax: 949-701-4476
info@stuccomfgassoc.com
www.stuccomfgassoc.com
Facebook, Youtube

Michael Griffin, President
Kevin Wensel, VP
Dale Nehis, Secretary
Buzz Winchel, Treasurer

Our main purpose is to promote the advantage of 3 coat colored cementitious stucco by educating the building industry and consumers.
50 Members
Founded in 1957

4096 **Subcontractors Trade Association**
1430 Broadway
Suite 1600
New York, NY 10018

212-398-6220; Fax: 212-398-6224
www.stanyc.com
Facebook, Twitter, LinkedIn

Henry Kita, Executive Director
Samantha Sweeney, Communications Manager

Members are specialty and supply companies in the construction industry. Our goal is to improve the economic well being of our members through representation, support and assistance through the process of legislation, legal action, public relations, education and other public information programs.
350+ Members
Founded in 1966

4097 **Textile Care Allied Trades Association**
4023 N Armenia Avenue
Suite 270
Tampa, FL 33607

813-348-0075; Fax: 813-348-0077
luci@tcata.org
www.tcata.org
Facebook, Twitter, LinkedIn

Leslie Schaeffer, Chief Executive Officer
Luci Ward, Business Manager

The Textile Care Allied Trades Association (TCATA) is an international trade association representing manufacturers and distributors of dry-cleaning and laundry equipment and supplies. It is the only trade association dedicated exclusively to the interests of the allied trades.

4098 **The American Institute of Architects**
1735 New York Ave., NW
Washington, DC 20006-5292

800-AIA-3837; Fax: 202-626-7547
docstechsupport@aia.org
www.aia.org
Facebook, Twitter, LinkedIn, YouTube, RSS, Flickr

Robert A. Ivy, EVP & CEO
Abigail Warnecke Gorman, Chief Of Staff
Lisa Green, VP, Finance & Administration
Susan McDaid, SVP, Member & Component Services
Jay Stephens, SVP & General Counsel

Based in Washington D.C., the AIA is the leading professional membership association for licensed architects, emerging professionals, and allied partners.
Founded in 1857

4099 **Tile Contractors' Association of America**
9153 Tahoe Circle
Strongsville, OH 44136

800-655-8453; Fax: 216-462-0808
info@tcaainc.org
www.tcaainc.org

Lucinda Noel, Executive Director

TCAA is a trade Association representing America's finest union/BAC-signatory tile contractors and industry related suppliers. TCAA has been dedicated to promoting the ceramic tile/stone industry since 1903, and to ensuring that our members have the information skills and tools needed to ensure the highest levels of

professionalism, reliability, skilled craftsmanship and technical performance in the industry.
175 Members
Founded in 1903

4100 **Tile Roofing Institute**
23607 Highway 99
Suite 2C
Edmonds, WA 98026

425-778-6162; Fax: 425-771-9588
info@tileroofing.org
www.tileroofing.org
Facebook, Twitter, LinkedIn

Rick Olson, President
John Jensen, Director
Lisa Jensen, Director

Manufacturers of clay and concrete roof tiles. Emphasis is on technical issues and codes that involve tile.
Founded in 1971

4101 **Timber Framers Guild**
1106 Harris Ave
Suite 303
Bellingham, WA 98225

360-746-6571
855-598-1803
info@tfguild.org
www.tfguild.org
Facebook, Twitter, Pinterest

Mack Magee, Executive Director
Allison Aurand, Communications Director
Michael Cuba, Timber Framing Editor
Adam Miller, Timber Framing Editor

The Guild is dedicated to establishing training programs for dedicated timber framers, disseminating information about timber framing and timber frame building design, displaying the art of timber framing to the public, and generally serving as a center of timber framing information for the professional and general public alike.
1400 Members
Founded in 1984

4102 **Truck Mixer Manufacturers Bureau**
900 Spring St
Silver Spring, MD 20910-4015

301-587-1400
888-846-7622; Fax: 301-587-1605
nmaher@cpmb.org
www.cpmb.org

Kevin Walgenbach, Bureau Administrator
Frank Cavaliere, Bureau Coordinator
Colin Lobo, Engineer

An association of ready mixed concrete truck manufacturers who have joined together in support of the ready mixed industry. TMMB members are required to manufacture equipment in accordance to the TMMB Standards.
Founded in 1958

4103 **Western Building Material Association**
909 Lakeridge Drive SW
PO Box 1699
Olympia, WA 98507

360-943-3054
888-551-9262; Fax: 360-943-1219
wbma@wbma.org
www.wbma.org
Facebook, Twitter, LinkedIn

Casey Voorhees, Executive Director
Stephanie Masters, Office Manager

Regional trade association serving material dealers throughout the states of Alaska, Idaho, Montana, Oregon and Washington and a federated association of the National Lumber and Building Material Dealers Association.
600 Members
Founded in 1903

Newsletters

4104 **ACSM Bulletin**
American Congress on Surveying and Mapping
6 Montgomery Village Ave
Suite 403
Gaithersburg, MD 20879-3557

240-632-9716; Fax: 240-632-1321
ilse.genovese@acsm.net

Ilse Genovese, Editor

A bi-monthly professional magazine published by ACSM to inform the public about current developments taking place within the geospatial community.
Frequency: Bi-Monthly

4105 **AHW Reporter**
Duane Publishing
51 Park St
Dorchester, MA 02122-2643

617-282-4885; Fax: 617-282-0320
www.rubblemakers.com

Herb Duane, Owner
Toby Duane, Director

Asbestos and hazardous waste information.

4106 **Asbestos & Lead Abatement Report**
Business Publishers
2222 Sedwick Dr
Suite 101
Durham, NC 27713

800-223-8720; Fax: 800-508-2592
custserv@bpinews.com
www.bpinews.com

Tracks the major legislative, regulatory and technological developments in asbestos and lead abatement industries. Includes highlights of major research studies on the effect of lead and asbestos on human health.
Cost: $371.54
Frequency: BiWeekly

4107 **Brick News**
Brick Industry Association
1850 Centennial Park Drive
Suite 301
Reston, VA 20191-1542

703-620-0010; Fax: 703-620-3928
brickinfo@bia.org
www.gobrick.com

Richard Jennison, President/CEO

News, information and programs of interest to brick distributors.

4108 **Building Products News**
Palgrave Macmillan
175 5th Ave
Suite 4
New York, NY 10010-7728

212-982-3900
888-330-8477; Fax: 212-307-5035
www.macmillan.com

Winston Jeune, Director

A unique publication researching the commercial renovation and retrofit market.

4109 **Building Stone**
Building Stone Institute
5 Riverside Dr
Building 2
Chestertown, NY 12817

518-803-4336
866-786-6313; Fax: 518-803-4336
www.buildingstoneinstitute.org

Duffe Elkins, President
Rob Teel, VP

State of the industry publication for architects, designers and people in the natural stone industries: granite, marble, limestone, etc.
Cost: $65.00
Frequency: Quarterly
Circulation: 17,000
Founded in 1919

4110 **Building and Construction Market Forecast**
Reed Business Information
360 Park Ave S
New York, NY 10010-1737

646-746-6400; Fax: 646-756-7583
corporatecommunications@reedbusiness.com
www.reedbusiness.com

Mark Kelsey, CEO
Stuart Whayman, CFO

Forecasts and analysis on the construction industry.
Cost: $187.00
6 Pages
Frequency: Monthly
Founded in 1946

4111 **Concrete Pipe News**
American Concrete Pipe Association
8445 Freeport Parkway
Suite 350
Irving, TX 75063

972-506-7216; Fax: 972-506-7682
info@concrete-pipe.org
www.concrete-pipe.org

Matt Childs, President
Josh Beakley, Technical Services Director
Wanda Cochran, Events Manager

Concrete Pipe News is designed to provide information on the use and installation of precast concrete pipe products for a wide variety of applications, including drainage and pollution control systems. Industry technology, research and trends are also important subjects of the publication. Readers include engineers, specifiers, public works officials, contractors, suppliers, vendors and members of the American Concrete Pipe Association.
Cost: $3.50
16 Pages
Frequency: Quarterly
Founded in 1907

4112 **Construction Company Strategist**
Brownstone Publishers
149 5th Ave
10th Floor
New York, NY 10010

212-473-8200; Fax: 212-564-0465

Douglas Lowey, CEO
Andrew Shapiro, VP

Strategies, legal tips, and how-to advice for successfully managing a construction company in the 1990's. Features model contract language, forms, guidelines and more.
Cost: $269.00
Frequency: Monthly
Circulation: 180000
Founded in 1971
Printed in 2 colors on matte stock

4113 **Construction Contractor**
Federal Publications

1100 13th Street NW
Washington, DC 20005

202-772-8295
888-494-3696; Fax: 202-772-8298
fedpubseminars.com

Michael Canavan, Director

Bi-weekly newsletter providing in-depth legal insight and analysis for all construction professionals.
Cost: $592.00
Frequency: BiWeekly

4114 **Construction Equipment Monthly**
Heartland Communications
1003 Central Avenue
PO Box 1052
Fort Dodge, IA 50501-1052

515-955-1600
800-247-2000; Fax: 515-574-2107
www.hlipublishing.com

Patrick Van Arnam, President
Gale McKinney, CFO

Listings by category, equipment and parts for sale.
Cost: $125.00
Frequency: Annual+
Founded in 1988

4115 **Construction Labor Report**
Bureau of National Affairs
3 Bethesda Metro Center
Suite 250
Bethesda, MD 20814

800-372-1033; Fax: 800-253-0332
customercare@bna.com
www.bna.com

Josh Eastright, CEO

A weekly information service that covers union-management relations in the construction industry, reporting on significant legislative, judicial, economic, management and union developments.
Cost: $1543.00
Frequency: Weekly
Circulation: 1600
ISSN: 0010-6836

4116 **Constructor Newsletter**
Associated General Contractors of America
2300 Wilson Blvd
Suite 400
Arlington, VA 22201

703-548-3118; Fax: 703-837-5400
info@agc.org
www.agc.org

Kristine Young, President
Joe Jarboe, SVP

Reports on contractors and items of interest to the construction community.
Frequency: Monthly
Circulation: 33000
Founded in 1918

4117 **Crow's Weekly Letter**
CC Crow Publications
3635 N Farragut St
Portland, OR 97217-5954

503-241-7382; Fax: 503-646-9971
info@chadcrowe.com
www.chadcrowe.com

Chad Crowe, President

Weekly report on trends and prices in the wood products industry.
Cost: $285.00
12 Pages
Frequency: Weekly
Founded in 1921
Printed in 4 colors on matte stock

4118 **Demo-Memo**
Duane Publishing
51 Park Street
PO Box 130
Dorchester, MA 02122

617-282-4885; Fax: 617-282-0320
www.demolitionconsulting.com

Herbert Duane, President

Demolition news and information.

4119 **Dodge Report & Bulletins**
McGraw Hill
PO Box 182604
Columbus, OH 43272-1095

614-866-5769
877-833-5524; Fax: 614-759-3749
www.mcgraw-hill.com

Jennifer Hayes, Editor
Harold McGraw III, President/CEO

Dodge Reports gives you the information you need to prepare a bid or enter negotiations. The detailed project information will also enable you to sell products or services.
Frequency: Daily
Founded in 1884

4120 **E-Catalyst Industry Update**
Adhesive & Sealant Council
7101 Wisconsin Ave
Suite 990
Bethesda, MD 20814-4805

301-986-9700; Fax: 301-986-9795
data@ascouncil.org
www.ascouncil.org

Bill Allmond, President

4121 **Environmental Building News**
BuildingGreen
122 Birge St
Suite 30
Brattleboro, VT 05301-6703

802-257-7300; Fax: 802-257-7304
www.buildinggreen.com

Alex Wilson, Owner
Nadav Malin, President
Tristan Roberts, Editorial Director
Jennifer Atlee, Research Director

Featuring comprehensive, practical information on a wide range of topics related to sustainable building—from energy efficiency and recycled-content materials to land-use planning and indoor air quality.
Cost: $99.00
Frequency: Monthly
Founded in 1992

4122 **Housing Marketing Report**
CD Publications
8204 Fenton St
Silver Spring, MD 20910-4571

301-588-6380
800-666-6380; Fax: 301-588-6385
www.cdpublications.com

Michael Gerecht, President
Charles Wisniowski, Editor

Concise analysis of national and regional housing markets, materials and supplies.
Cost: $469.00
Founded in 1961
Mailing list available for rent: 2,000 names at $160 per M
Printed in on matte stock

4123 **Indoor Air Quality Update**
Aspen Publishers
76 Ninth Avenue
7th Floor
New York, NY 10011

212-771-0600
800-638-8437; Fax: 301-695-7931
www.aspenlawschool.com

Mark Dorman, CEO
Gustavo Dobles, VP Operations

A guide to the practical control of building materials.
Cost: $440.00
Circulation: 20000
ISSN: 1040-5313

4124 **Industry News**
Modular Building Institute
944 Glenwood Station Ln
Suite 204
Charlottesville, VA 22901-1480

434-296-3288
888-811-3288; Fax: 434-296-3361
info@mbinet.org
www.mbinet.org

Tom Hardiman, Executive Director
Steven Williams, Operations Director

For members only.
Circulation: 650

4125 **Machinery Outlook**
Manfredi & Associates
20934 W Lakeview Pkwy
Mundelein, IL 60060-9502

847-949-9080; Fax: 847-949-9910
frank@manfredi.com
www.machineryoutlook.com

Frank Manfredi, President
James Manfredi, Editor

A newsletter about and for the construction and mining machinery industry.
Cost: $550.00
14 Pages
Frequency: Monthly
Founded in 1984
Printed in one color on matte stock

4126 **Manufactured Structures Newsletter**
Bobbitt Group
1710 S Gilbert Rd
Ste 1167
Mesa, AZ 85204

480-982-6173
wsbobbitt@hotmail.com

William Bobbitt, Editor/Publisher
Marci Bobbitt, Associate Editor/Business Manager

Covers all aspects of the automated building industry with a monthly collection of original feature stories profiling leading and emerging companies in the industry as well as other informative information on the industry, business tips, proven sales and marketing and featured editorials.
Frequency: Monthly
ISSN: 1068-4962
Founded in 1969

4127 **NAWIC Image**
National Association of Women in Construction
327 S Adams Street
Fort Worth, TX 76104

817-877-5551
800-552-3506; Fax: 817-877-0324
nawic@nawic.org
www.nawic.org

Debra Gregoire, Presdient
Cindy Johnsen, VP

Management, trends and techniques in the construction business.
Cost: $50.00
Frequency: Bi-Monthly
Circulation: 6000

4128 **NRCMA Biweekly Email Bulletin**
National Railroad Construction & Maintenance Assoc
500 New Jersey Ave NW
Suite 400
Washington, DC 20001-2065

202-715-2919; Fax: 202-318-0867
info@nrcma.org
www.nrcma.org

Chuck Baker, President
Matt Ginsberg, Director of Operations
Frequency: Biweekly

4129 **National Commercial & Industrial Insulation Standards Manual**
National Insulation Association
516 Herndon Parkway
Suite D
Herndon, VA 20170

703-464-6422; Fax: 703-464-5896
www.insulation.org

Michele Jones, EVP/CEO
John Lamberton, President
Also known as the MICA Manual, this manual was originally developed by the Midwest Insulation Contractors Association (MICA) to serve as a resource for commercial and industrial insulation professionals.
Cost: $249.00
Frequency: 8th Edition now available

4130 **News Brief**
Granite State Designers & Installers Association
53 Regional Drive
Ste 1
Concord, NH 03301-3520

603-228-1231; Fax: 603-228-2118
info@gsdia.org
www.gsdia.org

Carl Hagstrom, Director
Randy Orvis, Director
Newsletter for members of GSD1 relative to septic system design, installation and maintenance.
Cost: $150.00
Frequency: Monthly

4131 **RCMA Newsletter**
Roof Coatings Manufacturers Association
750 National Press Building
529 14th Street NW
Washington, DC 20045

202-207-0919; Fax: 202-223-9741
info@roofcoatings.org
www.roofcoatings.org

Dan Quinonez, Executive Director
Frequency: Quarterly

4132 **Redwood Reporter**
California Redwood Association
818 Grayson Road
Suite 201
Pleasant Hill, CA 94523

925-935-1499; Fax: 925-935-1496
info@calredwood.org
www.calredwood.org

Pamela Allsebrook, Publisher
Christopher Grover, President
Information about the redwood business of interest to redwood dealers.
8 Pages
Circulation: 8000

4133 **Reed Construction Data**
700 Longwater Drive
Norwell, MA 02061

770-209-3730
800-334-3509; Fax: 800-632-6732
www.rsmeans.com

Offers statistical information for building contractors.

4134 **Road Rock Recycle**
Lee Publications
6113 Hwy. 5
P.O. Box 121
Palatine Bridge, NY 13428-0121

518-673-3237
888-596-5329; Fax: 518-673-2699
subscriptions@leepub.com
rockroadrecycle.com

Frederick Lee, Publisher
Joan Kark-Wren, Editor
Bruce Button, President
Larry Price, Marketing Manager
Ian Hitchener, Sales Manager
News resource for the aggregate, heavy construction, and recycling industries.
Frequency: Monthly

4135 **SPEC-DATA Program**
Construction Specifications Institute
110 S Union St
Ste 100
Alexandria, VA 22314-3351

703-684-0300
800-689-2900; Fax: 703-684-8436
csi@csinet.org
www.csinet.org

Walter Marlowe, CEO
Stacy Vail, Operations Director
Cost: $75.00
Frequency: Monthly

4136 **Scaffold Industry Association Newsletter**
Scaffold Industry Association
400 Admiral Blvd
Kansas City, MO 64106-1508

602-257-1144
866-687-7115; Fax: 602-257-1166
info@scaffold.org
www.scaffold.org

Steve Smith, President
Daryl Hare, Treasurer
Information on scaffold safety in the construction industry. Offers safe training programs for competent person and hazard awareness.
Cost: $65.00
Frequency: Monthly
Circulation: 1600
Founded in 1972

4137 **Scantlings**
Timber Framers Guild
1106 Harris Ave
Suite 303
Bellingham, WA 98225

360-746-6571
855-598-1803
info@tfguild.org
www.tfguild.org
Facebook, Twitter, Pinterest

Mack Magee, Executive Director
Member publication of the Timber Framers Guild.
Frequency: 6X/yr

4138 **Specialty Tools and Fasteners Distributors Association Newsletter**
Specialty Tools and Fasteners Distributors
PO Box 44
Elm Grove, WI 53122

262-784-4774
800-352-2981; Fax: 262-784-5059
info@stafda.org
www.stafda.org

Georgia Foley, President
Catherine Usher, Member Service Director
Members distribute or manufacture power equipment, anchors, fastening systems, drilling equipment and other related industrial supplies.
Circulation: 4,500
Founded in 1976

4139 **TAUC About Construction**
The Association of Union Constructors
1501 Lee Highway
Suite 202
Arlington, VA 22209-1109

703-524-3336; Fax: 703-524-3364
dacord@tauc.org
www.tauc.org

Stephen R Lindauer, CEO
Kevin J Hilton, Senior VP
E-Newsletter containing exclusive TAUC content, with the latest collective bargaining agreements, wage rates, OSHA directives, legislative activity on Capitol Hill, and much more.
Frequency: Annual/May
Founded in 1970

4140 **TIDINGS Newsletter**
Textile Care Allied Trades Association
4023 N Armenia Avenue
Suite 270
Tampa, FL 33607

813-348-0075; Fax: 813-348-0077
luci@tcata.org
www.tcata.org
LinkedIn

Luci Ward, Business Manager
Keeps members informed about relevant news in and affecting the industry, such as legislative/regulatory developments, benefits and services.

4141 **Tilt-Up eNews**
Tilt-Up Concrete Association
113 First Street W
PO Box 204
Mount Vernon, IA 52314-0204

319-895-6911; Fax: 320-213-5555
info@tilt-up.org
www.tilt-up.org

Ed Sauter, Executive Director
James Baty, Technical Director
A monthly newsletter published by the Tilt-Up Concrete Association, Tilt-Up eNews is free for members, however non-members can also sign up to receive these publications. The mission of the Tilt-Up Concrete Association is to expand and improve the use of Tilt-Up as the preferred construction method by providing education and resources that enhance quality and performance.
Cost: $25.00
Frequency: Quarterly
Circulation: 5500
Founded in 1986
Printed in 4 colors on glossy stock

4142 **Trade News**
Specialty Tools and Fasteners Distributors Assn.
500 Elm Grove Rd.
Suite 210
Elm Grove, WI 53122

262-784-4774
800-352-2981; Fax: 262-784-5059
info@stafda.org

www.stafda.org
Facebook, LinkedIn

Mike Kangas, President
Kramer Darragh, Vice President

Provides insight into the construction and industrial world, member news, Convention details, Trend Reports, and more.
4000 Attendees
Frequency: Monthly

4143 **Under Construction**
American Bar Assocation
321 N Clark St.
Chicago, IL 60654
Jayne Czik, Editor
Ridgely Jackson, Associate Editor

Current legal topics in the construction industry and highlights from the ABA's Forum on Construction Law.
Frequency: 3x/year

4144 **Western Building Material Association Newsletter**
Western Building Material Association
PO Box 1699
Olympia, WA 98507-1699

360-943-3054
888-551-9262; Fax: 360-943-1219
wbma@wbma.org
www.wbma.org

38511 Pages
Frequency: Monthly
Circulation: 700
Printed in on matte stock

4145 **World Fence News**
World Fencing Data Center
6101 W Courtyard Dr
Building 3 Suite 115
Austin, TX 78730-5031

512-349-2536
800-231-0275; Fax: 512-349-2567
editor@worldfencenews.com
www.worldfencenews.com

Roger Duke, Publisher
Rick Henderson, Editor

Includes the most up to date information on events, products, trends, and services that effect the industry.
Cost: $29.95
Frequency: Monthly
Circulation: 12500
Founded in 1983

Magazines & Journals

4146 **9300 Contractor**
Tile Contractors' Association of America
9153 Tahoe Circle
Strongsville, OH 44136

800-655-8453; Fax: 216-462-0808
info@tcaainc.org
www.tcaainc.org

Lucinda Noel, Executive Director

A free quarterly publication for signatory tile/stone contractors and architects, designers and project managers and published by TCAA for the purpose of sharing information, views and opinions related to the tile/stone industry.
Frequency: Quarterly

4147 **ABC Today**
Associated Builders and Contractors
4250 Fairfax Dr
9th Floor
Arlington, VA 22203-1665

703-812-2000; Fax: 703-812-8201
www.abc.org

Mike Bellaman, CEO
Todd Mann, COO

The purpose of this magazine is to offer industry updates on the latest trends and developments that affect general construction, labor, management, legislation, education, products and techniques for the building industry.
Cost: $36.00
Frequency: Monthly
Circulation: 25000
Founded in 1950

4148 **American Painting Contractor**
Douglas Publications
2807 N Parham Road
Suite 200
Richmond, VA 23294

703-519-2341
800-223-1797
www.douglaspublications.com

Emily Howard, Editor
Jaimy Ford, Executive Editor

Features include business management, market research, decorating trends, techniques and developments in preparation and specialty coatings. News includes association activities, personnel changes and government actions.
Frequency: Monthly
Circulation: 25000
Founded in 1985

4149 **American Public Works Magazine**
2345 Grand Blvd
Suite 700
Kansas City, MO 64108-2625

816-472-6100
800-848-2792; Fax: 816-472-1610
ddancy@apwa.net
www.apwa.net

Brian Van Norman, Director
David Dancy, Director of Marketing
Kevin Clark, Editor

International educational and professional association of public agencies, private sector companies, and individuals dedicated to providing high quality public works goods and services. The magazine is a forum for public works professionals, agencies and companies. It includes public works-related topics to public attention in local, state and federal areas.
Cost: $100.00
40 Pages
Frequency: Monthly
ISSN: 0092-4873
Founded in 1937

4150 **Architectural Record**
McGraw-Hill Construction
2 Penn Plz
9th Floor
New York, NY 10121-2298

212-904-2594; Fax: 212-904-4256
www.mcgraw-hill.com

William Hanley, Editor
Lamar Clarkson, Editor

Provides original, reliable and useful information to the architectural marketplace worldwide, setting the standards for excellence in architectural design and presenting insights and practical solutions for current challenges in the design, building construction and business practices.
Cost: $49.00
Frequency: Monthly
Circulation: 102,000
ISSN: 0003-858X

4151 **Asphalt Magazine**
Asphalt Institute
2696 Research Park Dr
Lexington, KY 40511-8480

859-288-4960; Fax: 859-288-4999
info@asphaltinstitute.org
www.asphaltinstitute.org
Facebook, Twitter, LinkedIn

Peter Grass, President
Frequency: 3x/Year
Circulation: 18000

4152 **Automated Builder**
CMN Associates
2401 Grapevine Dr
Oxnard, CA 93036

805-351-5931
800-344-2537; Fax: 805-351-5755
www.automatedbuilder.com/

Donald Carlson
Agnes Carlson, Circulation

Distributed free of charge in the US to executive and management personnel upon written request in companies that are production (big volume) site builders, panelized home manufacturers, modular home manufacturers, special unit manufacturers, component manufacturers and HUD-Code, modular, panelized and commercial building dealers.
Cost: $50.00
Frequency: Monthly
Circulation: 25000
ISSN: 0899-5540
Founded in 1964
Printed in 4 colors on glossy stock

4153 **BUILDER**
Hanley-Wood
1 Thomas Cir NW
Suite 600
Washington, DC 20005-5811

202-452-0800; Fax: 202-785-1974
www.builderonline.com

Frank Anton, CEO
Hanley Wood, Publisher
Boyce Thompson, Editoral Director

BUILDER is the leading brand in residential new construction and serves as the magazine of the National Association of Home Builders (NAHB). For more than three decades, BUILDER has provided essential news, information and resources about products, technologies, trends, regulatory requirements and best practices to help home building professionals navigate challenges for success. BUILDER is the trusted source for top builders, architects and other industry professionals across the country.
Cost: $29.95
Frequency: Monthly
Circulation: 104852
ISSN: 0744-N93
Founded in 1977
Mailing list available for rent: 100M names
Printed in 4 colors on glossy stock

4154 **Bonded Builders News**
Richard K Nicholson Enterprises
2201 Corporate Boulevard
Suite 100
Boca Raton, FL 33431-7337

561-278-6968
800-749-0381; Fax: 561-368-1781
www.bondedbuilders.com

Whit Ward, President
Howard Head, Editor-in-Chief

Provides builders and developers with information involving new technologies and changing

trends in the home building industry.
Cost: $18.00
Frequency: Quarterly
Circulation: 7000

4155 **Builder Insider**
PO Box 191125
Dallas, TX 75219-8105

214-988-9181
866-930-1950; Fax: 214-871-2931
www.builderinsider.com

Michael Anderson, Editor

Independent trade publications covering the residential and light commercial building industry.
Cost: $12.00
28 Pages
Frequency: Monthly
Circulation: 5200
Founded in 1976

4156 **Building Design & Construction**
Reed Business Information
360 Park Ave S
New York, NY 10010-1737

646-746-6400; Fax: 646-756-7583
corporatecommunications@reedbusiness.com
www.reedbusiness.com

Mark Kelsey, CEO
Stuart Whayman, CFO
James Reed, Owner

Serves the needs of the design and construction professionals of commercial, industrial and institutional buildings that include new and retrofit projects. Geared towards the building team that includes professionals from building firms, owning firms and design firms.
Frequency: Monthly
Circulation: 76,005
Founded in 1993

4157 **Building Environment Report**
IAQ Publications
7920 Norfolk Ave
Suite 900
Bethesda, MD 20814-2539

301-913-0115; Fax: 301-913-0119
www.eschoolnews.com

Robert Morrow, Owner
Nancy David, Editor

Covers information to help manage building environmental hazards, meet environmental compliance requirements, protect building occupants, conference coverage and meetings of note.
Cost: $325.00
Frequency: Monthly
Circulation: 1,500

4158 **Building Operating Management**
Trade Press Publishing Corporation
2100 W Florist Avenue
Milwaukee, WI 53209-3799

414-228-7701; Fax: 414-228-1134
www.tradepress.com

Brad Ehlert, Group Publisher
Brian Terry, Publisher

Serves the field of facilities management, encompassing commercial building: office buildings, real estate/property management firms, developers, financial institutions, insurance companies, apartment complexes, civic/convention centers, including members of the Building Owners and Managers Association
Cost: $120.00
Frequency: Monthly
Circulation: 70000
Founded in 1954
Printed in 4 colors on glossy stock

4159 **Building Products CONNECTION**
Northwestern Lumber Association
701 Decatur Avenue N
Golden Valley, MN 55427

763-544-6822
888-544-6822; Fax: 763-595-4060
info@nlassn.org
www.nlassn.org

Tim Dressen, Editor

Dedicated to providing information on issues important to the success of the lumber and building material industry in the upper Midwest.
Cost: $300.00
Frequency: Bi-Monthly
Circulation: 1900
Mailing list available for rent

4160 **Building Stone Magazine**
Building Stone Institute
5 Riverside Dr
Building 1
Chestertown, NY 12817

518-803-4336
866-786-6313; Fax: 518-803-4336
www.buildingstoneinstitute.org
Facebook

Duffe Elkins, President
Rob Teel, VP

State of the industry publication for architects, designers and people in the natural stone industries: granite, marble, limestone, etc.
Cost: $65.00
350 Members
Circulation: 18000
Founded in 1919
Printed in 4 colors on glossy stock

4161 **Building Supply Home Centers**
Reed Business Information
360 Park Ave S
New York, NY 10010-1737

646-746-6400; Fax: 646-756-7583
www.reedbusiness.com

Mark Kelsey, CEO
James Reed, Owner

For owners, manufacturers and other executives of the retail building market.
Cost: $60.00
Frequency: Monthly
Founded in 1917

4162 **Buildings: Facilities Construction & Management Magazine**
Stamats Communications
PO Box 1888
Cedar Rapids, IA 52406-1888

319-364-6167
800-553-8878; Fax: 319-365-5421
info@stamats.com
www.stamats.com

Guy Wendler, CEO
Peter Stamats, EVP/CFO

Information on construction costs, building design, space planning, fire safety, environment solutions, energy effiency, accessibilty, security, and strategic facilities planning.
Cost: $70.00
Frequency: Monthly
Circulation: 56500
Founded in 1906

4163 **CFMA Building Profits**
Construction Financial Management Association
100 Village Boulevard
Suite 200
Princeton, NJ 08540-5783

609-452-8000
888-421-9996; Fax: 609-452-0474
info@cfma.org
www.cfma.org
Facebook, Twitter, LinkedIn, YouTube

Stuart Binstock, President & CEO
Brian Summers, VP, Operations

Information for financial managers and CPAs concerned with financial management.
Frequency: Bi-Monthly
Circulation: 8,600
Founded in 1981

4164 **CIM Construction Journal**
Construction Industries of Massachusetts
1500 Providence Highway Suite 14
PO Box 667
Norwood, MA 02062

781-551-0182; Fax: 781-551-0916
info@cimass.org
www.cimass.org

Mark Drummey, Editor/Publisher
John Pourbaix, Executive Director

Digest of horizontal public works projects.
Frequency: Weekly
Circulation: 2000
Founded in 1921

4165 **Carpenter**
United Brotherhood of Carpenters & Joiners
6801 Placid St
Las Vegas, NV 89119-4205

702-938-1111; Fax: 702-938-1122
www.ubcmillwrights.com

William Irwin, Executive Director

Contains news and information on the union and its members, the craft, and the construction industry as a whole.
Founded in 1881

4166 **Catholic Cemetery**
National Catholic Cemetery Conference
1400 S Wolf Rd
Building # 3
Hillside, IL 60162

708-202-1242
888-850-8131; Fax: 708-202-1255
www.ntriplec.com

Christine Kohut, Editor
Dennis Fairbank, Executive Director

News on products and manufacturers and also gives information on cemetery maintenance and repairs.
Frequency: Monthly
Circulation: 2100
Founded in 1949

4167 **Commerical Modular Construction**
Emlen Publications/Modular Building Institute
1241 Andersen Dr
North Suite
San Rafael, CA 94901-5374

415-460-6185
800-965-8876; Fax: 415-460-6288
www.emlenmedia.com

Eli Gage, Publisher
Ahavah Revis, Managing Editor

Contains articles on modular for architects, engineering and spec writers who need building product, specification and address information.

4168 **Computer-Aided Engineering**
Penton Media
1300 E 9th St
Suite 316
Cleveland, OH 44114-1503

216-696-7000; Fax: 216-696-6662
information@penton.com
www.penton.com

Sharon Rowlands, CEO

Database applications in design and manufacturing.
Cost: $50.00
96 Pages
Founded in 1982

4169 **Concrete InFocus**
National Ready Mixed Concrete Association
900 Spring St
Silver Spring, MD 20910-4015
240-485-1139; Fax: 301-585-4219
info@nrmca.org
www.nrmca.org
Facebook, LinkedIn, YouTube
Robert Garbini, President
Deana Angelastro, Executive Administrator
The top resource for industry news, trends, research, legislative articles and company profiles.
1200 Members
Frequency: Quarterly
Circulation: 5000+
Founded in 1930

4170 **Concrete Pressure Pipe Digest**
American Concrete Pressure Pipe Association
3900 University Drive
Suite 110
Fairfax, VA 22030-2513
703-273-7227; Fax: 703-273-7230
www.acppa.org
Richard Mueller, President & CEO

4171 **Concrete Pumping Magazine**
American Concrete Pumping Association
606 Enterprise Dr
Lewis Center, OH 43035-9432
614-431-5618; Fax: 614-431-6944
www.concretepumpers.com
Christi Collins, Executive Director
Packed with articles on industry leaders, new products, and on-site examples.
Frequency: Quarterly
Circulation: 2,100

4172 **Construction Bulletin**
1200 Madison Ave
Indianapolis, IN 46225
317-423-7080; Fax: 317-422-7034
www.acppubs.com
Greg Sitek, Editor
Kenny Veach, Advertising Sales Manager
Serves heavy highway and building construction.
Cost: $199.00
Frequency: Weekly
Circulation: 4000
ISSN: 0010-6720
Founded in 1893

4173 **Construction Dimensions**
Association of the Wall and Ceiling Industry
513 W Broad St
Suite 210
Falls Church, VA 22046-3257
703-538-1600; Fax: 703-534-8307
info@awci.org
www.awci.org
Michael Stark, CEO
Brenton Stone, Assoiate Publisher & Sr. Director
A monthly magazine for manufacturers and suppliers in the wall and ceiling, and related industries. Construction Dimensions is the official publication of the Association of the Wall and Ceiling Industries International.
Cost: $ 40.00
115 Pages
Frequency: Monthly
Circulation: 23000
Founded in 1918

4174 **Construction Distribution**
Cygnus Business Media
1233 Janesville Avenue
Fort Atkinson, WI 53538
800-547-7377
nancy.terrill@cygnusb2b.com
Nancy Terrill, Publisher
Rebecca Wasieleski, Editor
Resource for product, marketing and management information for construction supply distributors and the manufacturers and reps who serve them.
Frequency: Quarterly
Circulation: 14,800
Founded in 1966

4175 **Construction Equipment Distribution (CED Magazine)**
Associated Equipment Distributors
650 E Algonquin Road
Suite 305
Schaumburg, IL 60173
630-574-0650
help@aednet.org
aednet.org
Brian P. McGuire, President/CEO
Jon Cruthers, VP, Sales
Sara Smith, Editor in Chief, CED Magazine
Offers valuable information for executives who sell and rent construction equipment.
Cost: $71.40
72 Pages
Frequency: Monthly
Circulation: 5500
Founded in 1919

4176 **Construction Equipment Operation and Maintenance**
Construction Publications
PO Box 1689
Cedar Rapids, IA 52406-1689
319-366-1597; Fax: 319-362-8808
Clark Parks, Editor
Use and maintenance of construction equipment.
Cost: $10.00
24 Pages
Frequency: Monthly
Founded in 1948

4177 **Construction Executive**
Associated Builders and Contractors
4250 Fairfax Drive
9th Floor
Arlington, VA 22203-1665
703-812-2000; Fax: 703-812-8201
www.abc.org
Lisa A Nardone, Editor-in-Chief
Lauren Pinch, Assistant Editor
Mike Bellaman, CEO
Focus on commercial and industrial construction.
Cost: $24.00
Frequency: Monthly
Circulation: 49,000

4178 **Construction Industry International**
Quarto International
10 Whirling Dun
Collinsville, CT 06022-1239
Andrew Webster, Editor
Serves the administrative construction industry.
80 Pages
Frequency: Monthly
Founded in 1975

4179 **Construction Specifier**
266 Elmwood Ave
Suite 289
Buffalo, NY 14222
716-572-5633
866-572-5633; Fax: 866-572-5677
sales@constructionspecifier.com
www.constructionspecifier.com
Jill Kaletha, Editor
The offical magazine of Construction Specifications Institute. Focused on the job functions of its core readership-professionals involved in the specification process. Offers insight and analysis on industry topics through news, product announcements, legal columns, case studies and other research as well as providing in-depth features on industry-related issues.
Frequency: Monthly
Founded in 1956
Printed in on glossy stock

4180 **Constructioneer**
Associated Construction Publication
30 Technology Pkwy S
Suite 100
Norcross, GA 30092-2925
770-209-3730
800-424-3996; Fax: 770-209-3712
rcdwebmaster@reedbusiness.com
www.reedconstructiondata.com
Iain Melville, CEO
Steve Ritchie, VP Marketing
Marco Piovesan, VP Data
Information directed to construction industry of New York, Pennsylvania, New Jersey, and Delaware.
100 Pages
Frequency: Bi-Monthly
Circulation: 18889
Founded in 1975
Printed in 4 colors on matte stock

4181 **Constructor Magazine**
Associated General Contractors of America
2300 Wilson Blvd
Suite 400
Arlington, VA 22201-5426
703-548-3118; Fax: 703-837-5400
info@agc.org
www.agc.org
Kristine Young, President
Joe Jarboe, SVP
Voice of the construction industry.
Frequency: Monthly
Circulation: 40,000
Founded in 1918

4182 **Contractors Guide**
Painting Contractors Association
1801 Park 270 Drive
Suite 220
St Louis, MO 63146-4020
314-514-7322
800-332-7322; Fax: 314-514-9417
www.pcapainted.org
Gina Koert, Chair
What every painting and decorating contractor needs to know, organized for easy use by painting and decorating contractors of all sizes.
Cost: $68.00

4183 **Custom Home**
Hanley-Wood

1 Thomas Cir NW
Suite 600
Washington, DC 20005-5811

202-452-0800; Fax: 202-785-1974
www.residentialarchitect.com

Frank Anton, CEO
Matt Flynn, CFO

Features materials, products, trends and the latest in designs for custom home construction.
Cost: $24.00
Frequency: 7 issues yearly
Circulation: 40000
Founded in 1976

4184 DBA Automated Builder Magazine
CMN Associates
2401 Grapevine Dr
Oxnard, CA 93036

805-351-5931
800-344-2537; Fax: 805-351-5755
www.automatedbuilder.com/

Don O Carlson, Editor/Publisher
Agnes Carlson, Circulation Manager

Magazine for manufacturers and suppliers who have a product line that is of interest to the factory-built housing industry. Covering all seven segments of US, Canadian and foreign housing industry, including: production builders; panelizers; component producers; modular; commercial modular; hud code; and all builder/dealers.
Frequency: Monthly
Circulation: 25000
ISSN: 0899-4450
Founded in 1964

4185 DFI Journal
Deep Foundations Institute
326 Lafayette Avenue
Hawthorne, NJ 07506

973-423-4030; Fax: 973-423-4031
staff@dfi.org
www.dfi.org

Publishes practice-oriented, high quality papers related to broad area of Deep Foundations Engineering.
Frequency: Bi-Annual

4186 Daily Construction Service
Construction Market Data
142 Arena Street
El Segundo, CA 90245

310-322-9990; Fax: 858-573-0485

Jeanne Peterson, Editor

Offers valuable information for construction workers.
Cost: $365.00
Frequency: Monthly
Founded in 1933

4187 Daily Journal of Commerce
Dolan Media Company/New Orleans Publishing Grp
111 Veterans Memorial Blvd., Suite 1440
3445 North Causeway Blvd., Suite 90
Metairie, LA 70005-3028

504-834-9292; Fax: 504-832-3435
djc@nopg.com
www.djcgulfcoast.com

Lisa Blossman, Publisher
Christian Moises, Editor
Anne Lovas, General Manager
Becky Naquin, Assistance Editor

Reports on building and engineering industries.
Cost: $456.00
Frequency: Monthly
Founded in 1922

4188 Deep Foundations Magazine
Deep Foundations Institute
326 Lafayette Avenue
Hawthorne, NJ 07506

973-423-4030; Fax: 973-423-4031
dfihq@dfi.org
www.dfi.org

Theresa Engler, Executive Director
Karol Paltsios, Managing Editor
Barbra Rodriguez, Editor

Distributed to members.
Frequency: Quarterly
Circulation: 2753

4189 Demolition
National Demolition Association
16 N Franklin St
Suite 203
Doylestown, PA 18901-3536

215-348-4949
800-541-2412; Fax: 215-348-8422
info@demolitionassociation.com
www.demolitionassociation.com

Jeff Lambert, Executive Director
Alexa Schlosser, Editor

Trade publication for the demolition industry.
Cost: $40.00
Circulation: 5000
ISSN: 1522-5690
Founded in 1972
Printed in 4 colors on matte stock

4190 Design Build
144 Lexington Street
Woburn, MA 01801

781-937-9265; Fax: 781-937-9241
www.designbuild.construction.com

Gary Merrill, Sales Director
William Angelo, Editor-in-Chief

Received by all subscribers of Engineering News Record plus 7,500 owners identified by FW Dodge as having an interest in the design-build project delivery system, and 1,000 members of the Design-Build Institute of America.
84 Pages
Frequency: Quarterly
Circulation: 20000
ISSN: 1096-7095
Founded in 1953

4191 Design Cost & Data
Rector Communications
2300 Chestnut St
Suite 340
Philadelphia, PA 19103-4398

215-963-9661; Fax: 215-963-9672
www.rector.com

Marion Rector, Owner

Cost estimating magazine for architects, builders, developers, appraisers, specifiers, insurers and construction financiers.

4192 Design Lines
American Institute of Building Design
7059 Blair Rd NW
Suite 201
Washington, DC 20012

800-366-2423; Fax: 866-204-0293
info@aibd.org
www.aibd.org
Facebook, Twitter, LinkedIn

Dan Sater, President
Alan Kent, Internal Vice President
Viki Wooster, External Vice President
Kerry Dick, Secretary/ Treasurer

Publication that focuses on issues, education, and events as they happen in the building design industry.
1500 Attendees
Frequency: Monthly
Founded in 1950

4193 Design Solutions Magazine
Architectural Woodwork Institute
46179 Westlake Dr
Suite 120
Potomac Falls, VA 20165

571-323-3636; Fax: 571-323-3630
info@awinet.org
www.awinet.org

Robert Stout, President
Mike Bell, Vice President

Each issue showcases beautiful examples of fine architectural woodwork manufactured by AWI Manufacturing Member companies. With beautiful four-color images, crisp detailed drawings and thought provoking articles, Design Solutions offers our readers a bountiful resource that's sure to inspire and delight all.
Cost: $25.00
Frequency: Quarterly
Circulation: 27,000

4194 Dodge Construction News
McGraw Hill
2 Penn Plaza
9th Floor
New York, NY 10121-1299

212-904-3507; Fax: 212-904-2820
www.mcgraw-hill.com

Jennifer Hayes, Editor
Harold McGraw, III, CEO/President

Consists of program edition and proceedings and recap edition for the National Conventions of the American Institute of Architects and Construction Specifications Institute.
Circulation: 86400
Founded in 1884

4195 Door & Window Maker
Key Communications
PO Box 569
Garrisonville, VA 22463-0569

540-720-5584; Fax: 540-720-5687
www.glass.com

Debra Levy, Owner
Brigid O'Leary, Assistant Editor
Frequency: 9 issues yearly
Circulation: 23,947
Founded in 1993

4196 Engineering News Record
McGraw Hill
2 Penn Plaza
9th Floor
New York, NY 10121-2298

212-904-3507; Fax: 212-904-2820
www.enr.com

Richard Korman, Managing Senior Editor
Ilan Kapla, Senior Manager
Keith Wallace, Production Editor

Provides the news, analysis, commentary and data that construction industry professionals need to do their jobs more effectively. ENR is the national news magazine for the construction industry.
Cost: $82.00
Frequency: Weekly
Circulation: 60000
Founded in 1874

4197 Environmental Design & Construction
Business News Publishing Company
2401 W Big Beaver Rd
Suite 700
Troy, MI 48084-3333

248-362-3700; Fax: 248-362-0317
www.edcmag.com

Derrick Teal, Editor
Diana Brown, Publisher
Laura Zielinski, Associate Editor

Magazine dedicated to integrated high-performance buildings, and efficient and sustainable design and construction.
Founded in 1926

4198 **Equipment Today**
Cygnus Business Media
1233 Janesville Avenue
Fort Atkinson, WI 53538

800-547-7377
becky.schultz@cygnuspub.com

Becky Schultz, Editor

Contractors and other users of construction machinery. Editorial is focused on the selection, application and maintenance of equipment as well as new and improved product introductions. Accepts advertising.
Cost: $60.00
54 Pages
Frequency: Monthly
Circulation: 77,000
Founded in 1966

4199 **FW Dodge Northwest Construction**
McGraw Hill
800 S Michigan St
Seattle, WA 98108-2655

206-378-4715
800-393-6343; Fax: 206-378-4741
support@construction.com
www.construction.com

Keith Fox, President
Linda Brennan, VP Operations

Project news, plans, specifications and analysis data for the construction professional.
Cost: $40.00
Frequency: Monthly
Founded in 1884

4200 **Fabric Architecture**
Industrial Fabrics Association International
1801 County Road B W
Roseville, MN 55113-4061

651-222-2508
800-225-4324; Fax: 651-631-9334
generalinfo@ifai.com
www.ifai.com

Rebecca Post, Editorial Director

Strives to inform architects, designers, landscape architects, engineers and other specifiers about architectural fabric structures, the fibers and fabrics used to make them, their design possibilities, their construction, and issues regarding their applicability and acceptance.
Cost: $39.00
Frequency: Bi-monthly

4201 **Facility Management Journal**
International Facility Management Association
1 Greenway Plz
Suite 1100
Houston, TX 77046-0194

713-623-4362; Fax: 713-623-6124
ifma@ifma.org
www.ifma.org

Andrea Sanchez, Editor-in-Chief
Laurie Steiner, Senior Associate Editor

Covers industry economic, financial trends and the industries legislative, special emphasis on developments in technology.
Cost: $75.00
Circulation: 14000
Founded in 1990

4202 **Facility News Magazines**
National Lead Abatement Council
PO Box 535
Olney, MD 20830

301-924-5490
800-590-6522; Fax: 301-924-0265

Stephen Weil, Publisher
Wendy Faxon, Editor

Information on facility maintenance management.
Cost: $36.00
20 Pages
Frequency: Monthly
Circulation: 7500
Founded in 1981

4203 **Fenestration Magazine**
Ashlee Publishing
18 E 41st Street
20th Floor
New York, NY 10017-6009

212-376-7722; Fax: 212-376-7723
www.fenestrationmagazine.com

Joel Bruinooge, Editor

Windows and door industry.
Cost: $40.00
80+ Pages
Frequency: 10x yearly
Circulation: 17,000
ISSN: 0895-450X

4204 **Fine Homebuilding**
Taunton Press
63 S Main St
Box 5506
Newtown, CT 06470-2344

203-426-8171; Fax: 203-426-3434
www.taunton.com

Harrison McCampbell, Editor
Rob Yagid, Assistant Editor

Reviews of new equipment and related building materials and guidelines to successful work techniques and general industry news.
Cost: $37.95
Circulation: 308,000
Founded in 1980

4205 **Floor Covering Installer**
Business News Publishing Company
22801 Ventura Blvd
#115
Woodland Hills, CA 91364

818-224-8035
818-224-8042
www.fcimag.com

John Moore, Editor
Jennifer Allen, Production Manager

Provides the varied information needed by those who engage in floor covering installation with how-to and skill-building articles, how-to-do-it photographic presentations, new installation product information, news of the industry, as well as how and where to get further training in various aspects of floor covering installation.
Frequency: Bi-Monthly
Circulation: 40,000

4206 **Foundation Drilling**
ADSC
8445 Freeport Parkway
Suite 325
Irving, TX 75063

469-359-6000; Fax: 469-359-6007
adsc@adsc-iafd.com
www.adsc-iafd.com

Mike Moore, CEO

Written for foundation drilling and anchored earth retention contractors and their project managers, superintendents, foremen, civil and structural engineers, soils engineers, public engineering officials, architects, manufacturers and distributors of industry related equipments.
Frequency: 8x yearly
Circulation: 5000

4207 **Frame Building News**
F+W Media
38 E. 29th Street
New York, NY 10016

212-447-1400; Fax: 212-447-5231
contact_us@fwmedia.com

David Nussbaum, CEO
Sara Domville, President

Edited for the diversified town & country builders of light-industrial, commercial, agricultural, and residential structures. The majority of the coverage is about post-frame structures. Readers look for the latest in post-frame research and techniques, building code information, equipment, and materials. Regular features include 'Builder Spotlight,' 'New Products,' 'Supplier News,' 'OSHA Updates,' 'Legal Issues,' 'Business Strategies,' and 'Calendar of Events.' Official magazine of NFBA.
56 Pages
Circulation: 19211
Founded in 1952

4208 **Glass Digest**
Ashlee Publishing
18 E 41st Street
New York, NY 10017-6009

212-376-7722; Fax: 212-376-7723

Jordan Wright, Publisher

Merchandising/technical publication for the flat glass industry.
Cost: $25.00
140 Pages
Frequency: Monthly
Founded in 1922

4209 **Hanley-Wood's Tools of the Trade**
Hanley Wood
1 Thomas Cir NW
Suite 600
Washington, DC 20005-5803

202-452-0800; Fax: 202-785-1974
www.hanleywood.com

Frank Anton, CEO
Matt Flynn, CFO

The wide array of tools and equipment in the construction and renovation industries.
Cost: $36.00
Circulation: 65,000
Founded in 1976

4210 **Home Builders Magazine**
Work-4 Projects
4819 Saint Charles Boulevard
Pierrefonds, QC H9H-3C7

514-620-2200; Fax: 514-620-6300
editor@work4.ca
www.homebuildercanada.com/

Nachmi Artzy, Publisher
Cheryl Carvery, Sales

Specializes in educating readers on the latest installation tips, building techniques and materials that can be put into on-site practice everyday.
Cost: $30.00
Frequency: Bi-Monthly
Circulation: 23265
Founded in 1988

4211 **Hot Mix Asphalt Technology**
National Asphalt Pavement Association
5100 Forbes Blvd
Suite 200
Lanham, MD 20706-4407

301-731-4748
888-468-6499; Fax: 301-731-4621

mcervarich@hotmix.org
www.hotmix.org

Mike Acott, President
Margaret Cervarich, VP Marketing/Public Affairs

The leading journal for the asphalt pavement contractor
Frequency: Bi-Monthly
Circulation: 10000

4212 **IEEE Power and Energy Magazine**
IEEE
445 Hoes Lane
Piscataway, NJ 08854

732-465-6480; Fax: - - 0
pels-staff@ieee.org
www.ieee-pels.org

Fran Zappulla, Staff Director, Publishing
Susan Hassler, Editor

Network analysis, system stability studies, fault protection and construction management.
Cost: $285.00
82 Pages
Frequency: Monthly
Circulation: 23000
ISSN: 1540-7977
Founded in 1885
Mailing list available for rent
Printed in on glossy stock

4213 **InTents**
Industrial Fabrics Association International
1801 County Road B W
Roseville, MN 55113-4061

651-222-2508
800-225-4324; Fax: 651-631-9334
generalinfo@ifai.org
www.ifai.com

Sammi Jones, Editor

Promotes the use of tents and accessories to the special-event and general-rental industries.
Cost: $39.00
Frequency: Bi-Monthly
Circulation: 12,000

4214 **Insulation Outlook**
National Insulation Association
516 Herndon Parkway
Suite D
Herndon, VA 20170

703-464-6422; Fax: 703-464-5896
editor@insulation.org
www.insulation.org

Michele Jones, EVP/CEO
John Lamberton, President

Contains information on new products, industry trends, asbestos abatement and installation practices.
Frequency: Monthly
Circulation: 7000
Founded in 1973
Printed in 4 colors on glossy stock

4215 **Interior Construction**
Ceilings & Interior Systems Construction Assn
1010 Jorie Boulevard
Suite 30
Oak Brook, IL 60223

630-584-1919; Fax: 866-560-8537
www.cisca.org

Shirley Wodynski, Executive Director
Rick Reuland, Editor

Offers information designed to keep contractors abreast of the changes in interior construction.
Cost: $35.00
Frequency: Monthly
Circulation: 10000
Founded in 1950

4216 **Interlocking Concrete Pavement Magazine**
Interlocking Concrete Pavement Institute
13921 Park Center Road
Suite 270
Herndon, VA 20171-3269

202-080-0285
800-241-3652; Fax: 202-408-0285
icpi@icpi.org
www.icpi.org

Ericka Giles, Editor
Charles McGrath, Executive Director
Cost: $5.00
32 Pages
Frequency: Quarterly
Circulation: 20,000
Founded in 1993
Printed in 4 colors

4217 **Intermountain Contractor**
McGraw Hill
1114 W 7th Avenue
Suite 100
Denver, CO 80204

303-756-9995
800-393-6343; Fax: 303-756-4465
www.intermountaincontractors.net

Seth Horositz, Publisher
Mark Shaw, Editor

For general contractors. Serves Colorado, Idaho, Montana, Utah and Wyoming.
Cost: $40.00
88 Pages
Frequency: Weekly
Circulation: 5,247

4218 **International Construction**
Primedia
3585 Engineering Drive
Suite 100
Norcross, GA 30092

678-421-3000
800-216-1423
www.primedia.com

Charles Stubbs, President
Kim Payne, SVP

Provides valuable information to help readers succeed in every aspect of their jobs, from planning strategies to targeting growth, from solving engineering problems to selecting the right equipment and materials.

4219 **Job-Site Supervisor**
FMI Corporation
5171 Glenwood Ave
Suite 200
Raleigh, NC 27612-3266

919-787-8400; Fax: 919-785-9320
www.fminet.com

Hank Harris, President

Delivers articles on safety, regulations and management; with a special section that examines a challenging construction project. Editorial is presented from a field manager's point-of-view, including charts, graphs, illustrations and industry advice.
Cost: $179.00
Circulation: 4000
Founded in 1953

4220 **Journal of Light Construction**
Hanley-Wood
186 Allen Brook Lane
Williston, VT 05495

802-879-3335
800-552-1951; Fax: 802-879-9384
www.jlconline.com

Don Jackson, Editor
Rick Strachan, Publisher

Written for builders, remodelers, contractors and architects involved in the design and construction of residential and light commercial buildings. Accepts advertising.
Cost: $39.95
150 Pages
Frequency: Monthly
Circulation: 73000
ISSN: 1040-5224
Founded in 1982
Mailing list available for rent: 70,000 names at $120 per M
Printed in 4 colors on glossy stock

4221 **Journal of Protective Coatings & Linings**
Technology Publishing Company
2100 Wharton St
Suite 310
Pittsburgh, PA 15203-1951

412-431-8300
800-837-8303; Fax: 412-431-5428
webmaster@paintsquare.com
www.paintsquare.com

Marian Welsh, Publisher
Mary Chollet, Editor-in-Chief

The right tools to help you reach the protective and marine coatings industry.
Cost: $80.00
Frequency: Monthly
Circulation: 15,000
ISSN: 8755-1985

4222 **Kitchen & Bath Design News**
Cygnus Business Media
2 University Plaza
Suite 310
Hackensack, NJ 07601

201-487-7800; Fax: 201-487-1061
kathy.scott@cygnusb2b.com

Eliot Sefrin, Editorial Director/Publisher
Scott, Director of Public Relations

Serving the kitchen and bath industry, a key niche within the residential construction and remodeling marketplace.
Frequency: Monthly
Circulation: 48667
Founded in 1966

4223 **Manufactured Home Merchandiser**
RLD Group
PO Box 269149
Suite 800
Chicago, IL 60626-9149

312-236-3529; Fax: 312-236-4024

Herb Tider, President
Wayne Beamer, Editor

Offers information for home builders and professionals in the manufactured home industry.
Cost: $36.00
Frequency: Monthly
Circulation: 18600
Founded in 1952

4224 **Masonry Magazine**
Mason Contractors Association of America
1481 Merchant Drive
Algonquin, IL 60102

224-678-9709
800-536-2225; Fax: 224-678-9714
www.masoncontractors.org

Jeff Buczkiewicz, Executive Director
Tim O'Toole, Marketing Director

This periodical covers every aspect of the mason contractor profession, not only equipment and techniques but topics such as building codes and stanards.
Cost: $29.00
Frequency: Monthly
Circulation: 17,000

4225 **Metal Roofing**
F+W Media
38 E. 29th Street
New York, NY 10016

212-447-1400; Fax: 212-447-5231
contact_us@fwmedia.com

David Nussbaum, CEO
Sara Domville, President
Circulation: 25000
ISSN: 1533-8711
Founded in 1900
Printed in 4 colors on glossy stock

4226 **Midwest Contractor**
Associated Construction Publication
1200 Madison Ave
LL20
Indianapolis, IN 46225

317-423-7080
800-486-0014; Fax: 317-423-7094
www.acppubs.com

Peter Leviton, President
Greg Sitek, Managing Editor

Annual equipment buyers' guide, a complete cross reference listing of manufacturers, area distributors and their construction equipment lines.
Cost: $96.00
Founded in 1905

4227 **Muir's Original Log Home Guide for Builders and Buyers**
Gary J Schroder
1101 SE 7th Ave
Grand Rapids, MN 55744-4087

218-326-4434
800-359-6614; Fax: 218-326-2529
www.loghelp.com

Gary Schroeder, Owner
Allan Muir, Author

Log home industry.
Cost: $12.95
Frequency: Monthly
ISBN: 0-967786-90-8
Founded in 1978

4228 **National Association of Demolition Contactors**
National Demolition Association
16 N Franklin Street
Suite 203
Doylestown, PA 18901

215-348-4949
800-541-2412; Fax: 215-348-8422
info@demolitionassociation.com
www.demolitionassociation.com

Don Rachel, President
Jeff Kroeker, VP

Bimonthly magazine.
Cost: $40.00
Circulation: 5000
ISSN: 1522-5690
Founded in 1969
Printed in 4 colors on matte stock

4229 **New England Construction**
Associated Construction Publication
1200 Madison Ave
LL20
Indianapolis, IN 46225

317-423-7080
800-486-0014; Fax: 317-423-7094
www.acppubs.com

Al Fournier, President
Greg Sitek, Managing Editor

Complete reports on contracts awarded, low bids and proposed work; features on highway construction and earthmoving, land development projects, utility construction, industrial building construction in the six-state New England region.
Cost: $96.00
Frequency: Monthly
Circulation: 10490
Founded in 1975

4230 **Northwest Construction**
McGraw Hill
800 S Michigan St
Seattle, WA 98108-2655

206-378-4715
800-393-6343; Fax: 206-378-4741
support@construction.com
www.construction.com

Jeff Greisch, President
Heather McCune, Editor-in-Chief

A regional, monthly magazine with features on Washington and design construction projects. Accepts advertising.
Cost: $60.00
64 Pages
Frequency: Monthly
Circulation: 6,200
Founded in 1997

4231 **Occupational Hazards**
Penton Media
1300 E 9th St
Suite 316
Cleveland, OH 44114-1503

216-696-7000; Fax: 216-696-6662
information@penton.com
www.penton.com

Sharon Rowlands, CEO

Analysis of qualified recipients who have indicated that they recommend, select and/or buy the safety equipment, fire protection and other occupational health products.
65 Pages
Frequency: Monthly
Circulation: 65,777
ISSN: 0029-7909
Founded in 1892
Printed in 4 colors on glossy stock

4232 **Old House Journal**
Old House Journal Group
PO Box 420235
Palm Coast, FL 32142-235

800-826-3893; Fax: 978-283-4629
daposporos@homebuyerpubs.com
www.oldhousejournal.com

Demetra Aposporos, Editor-in-Chief
Danielle Small, Advertising Manager

Covers restoration techniques for the pre-1939 home.
Cost: $27.00
Circulation: 140119
Founded in 1999

4233 **Pacific Builder & Engineer**
Associated Construction Publication
30 Technology Pkwy S
Suite 100
Norcross, GA 30092-2925

770-209-3730
800-424-3996; Fax: 770-209-3712
www.acppubs.com

Chad Dorn, President
Greg Sitek, Managing Editor

For management level personnel in the highway and heavy construction and non-residential building industries in Washington, Oregon, Idaho, Montana and Alaska. Includes notice of bid calls, low bidders, contract awards on area projects; cost cutting construction methods, unusual techniques and equipment applications, analysis of market conditions and industry trends, new products and literature, general industry news and views, personal news and legal advice. Accepts advertising.
Cost: $50.00
Circulation: 100000
Founded in 1902

4234 **Pavement**
Cygnus Business Media
1233 Janesville Avenue
Fort Atkinson, WI 53538

amy.schwandt@cygnusb2b.com

Amy Schwandt, Publisher
Allan Heydorn, Editor/Associate Publisher

Reaches contractors in the pavement maintenance and commercial paving sector. Covers the four main segments of the market in each issue: sealcoating, striping, paving and sweeping.
Circulation: 18,500
Founded in 1985

4235 **Period Homes**
Restore Media
5185 MacArthur Blvd NW
Suite 725
Washington, DC 20016

202-339-0744; Fax: 202-339-0749
info@restoremedia.com

Michael Tucker, Chairman/CEO
Paul Kitzke, EVP
Peter Miller, President/Publisher

Lists sources of products for restoration and new construction of residential architecture.
Cost: $18.00
120 Pages
Circulation: 24,600
ISSN: 0898-0284

4236 **Products Finishing**
Scott Walker/Gardner Publications
6915 Valley Ln
Cincinnati, OH 45244-3153

513-527-8800
800-950-8020; Fax: 513-527-8801
www.gardnerweb.com

Rick Kline, CEO

Serves the finishing field, including educational services, public administration and other manufacturing industries.
Cost: $89.00
Frequency: Monthly
Circulation: 42000
Founded in 1928
Printed in 4 colors on glossy stock

4237 **Professional Builder**
Reed Business Information
2000 Clearwater Dr
Oak Brook, IL 60523-8809

630-288-8000; Fax: 630-288-8781
www.reedbusiness.com

Iain Melville, CEO
Andrew Rak, SVP

New residential construction magazine with a more than 63 year tradition of providing builders the solutions they need to maximize profits.
Frequency: Monthly
Circulation: 127002
Founded in 1931

4238 **Professional Door Dealer Magazine**
Virgo Publishing LLC
3300 N Central Ave
Suite 300
Phoenix, AZ 85012-2532

480-675-9925; Fax: 480-990-0819
danielle@vpico.com
www.vpico.com

Jenny Bolton, President

Educational resource for residential and commercial door and access-control professionals.
Circulation: 20000
Founded in 1986
Printed in on glossy stock

4239 **Professional Remodeler**
Reed Business Information
360 Park Ave S
New York, NY 10010-1737

646-746-6400; Fax: 646-756-7583
corporatecommunications@reedbusiness.com
www.reedbusiness.com

Iain Melville, CEO
Andrew Rak, SVP

Designed to accomodate the needs of residential remodelers and light commercial renovators and focuses on news, features, new products, tech-takes, and management and marketing approaches.
Frequency: Monthly
Circulation: 18131
Founded in 2002

4240 **Professional Roofing**
National Roofing Contractors Association
10255 W Higgins Rd
Suite 600
Rosemont, IL 60018-5613

847-299-9070
800-323-9545; Fax: 847-299-1183
nrca@nrca.net
www.professionalroofing.net

William Good, EVP
Ambika-Punia Bailey, Editor
Chrystine Hanus, Associate Editor
Carl Good, Publisher

Articles on both technical and business aspects of professional roofing.
Cost: $35.00
3500 Members
Frequency: Monthly
Circulation: 16000
ISSN: 0896-5552
Founded in 1886

4241 **Professional Spraying**
88-11th Avenue NE
Minneapolis, MN 55413

612-623-6000; Fax: 612-623-6580
www.graco.com

Patrick McHale, President/CEO
James Graner, CFO

Targets new products, industry news, and trade literature.
Frequency: Monthly
Circulation: 40000
Founded in 1926

4242 **Qualified Remodeler**
Cygnus Publishing
1233 Janesville Avenue
Fort Atkinson, WI 53538

920-563-6388; Fax: 920-563-1704
john.huff@cygnusb2b.com

John Huff, Publisher

Serving contractors who specialize in residential and light commercial remodeling.
72 Pages
Frequency: Monthly
Circulation: 82000
Founded in 1975
Mailing list available for rent: 84,000 names
Printed in 4 colors on glossy stock

4243 **RSI**
7300 N Linder Ave
Skokie, IL 60077

847-983-2000
roofingsidinginsulation@halldata.com
www.rsimag.com

Delivers timely news, technical and business management information, including a monthly analysis of key industry trends and techniques to help roofing, siding and insulation contractors run progressive, profitable businesses
Cost: $36.00
64 Pages
Frequency: Monthly
Circulation: 23658
Founded in 1945

4244 **Reed Bulletin**
Reed Business Informtion
30 Technology Parkway South
Suite 100
Norcross, GA 30092

800-424-3996
talisha.jackson@reedbusiness.com
www.reedconstructiondata.com

Talisha Jackson, Media Contact

Provides contractors with project news and tools suppliers.

4245 **Reeves Journal**
Business News Publishing Company
23421 South Pointe Dr.
Suite 280
Laguna Hills, CA 92653

949-830-0881; Fax: 949-859-7845
www.reevesjournal.com

Souzan Azar, Production
Ellyn Fishman, Publisher/Sales
Kati Larson, Advertising Sales
Jack Sweet, Editor

Reeves Journal, has been an invaluable tool for contractors & plumbing industry professionals for the last 85 years. Their goal is to address the regional opportunities and challenges facing PHC contractors, wholesalers and engineers in the 14 western United States.
Cost: $55.00
Frequency: Monthly
Circulation: 15,535
Founded in 1922

4246 **Remodeling**
Hanley-Wood
1 Thomas Cir NW
Suite 600
Washington, DC 20005-5811

202-452-0800; Fax: 202-785-1974
rm@omeda.com
www.residentialarchitect.com

Frank Anton, CEO
Claire Conroy, Editorial Director
Jennifer Lash, Managing Editor

News on state-of-the-art in remodeling management, products, construction and techniques. Appeals to the residential and light commercial remodeling contractor.
Cost: $44.95
Frequency: Monthly
Circulation: 93612
Founded in 1955

4247 **Rental Equipment Register**
17383 W Sunset Blvd
Suite A220
Pacific Plsds, CA 90272-4187

310-230-7160; Fax: 310-230-7169
michael.roth@penton.com
rermag.com

Michael Roth, Editor
Brandey Smith, Managing Editor

Edited for owners and managers of equipment rental and sales centers.
Cost: $45.00
125 Pages
Frequency: Monthly
Circulation: 21000
Founded in 1886

4248 **Residential Architect**
Hanley-Wood
1 Thomas Cir NW
Suite 600
Washington, DC 20005-5811

202-452-0800
888-269-8410; Fax: 202-785-1974
jlash@hanleywood.com
www.residentialarchitect.com

Frank Anton, CEO
Jennifer Lash, Managing Editor
Bruce Snider, Senior Editor

An award-winning national magazine focusing exclusively on the residential architecture profession.
Cost: $39.95
Frequency: 9x Yearly
Circulation: 22000
Founded in 1976

4249 **Rock and Dirt**
174 4th St
Crossville, TN 38555-4303

931-484-5137
800-251-6776; Fax: 931-484-2532
www.rockanddirt.com

Mike Stone, Publisher

Comprehensive buy/sell publications for heavy construction. Primary target audiences worldwide are contractors and other heavy equipment buyers. A non-editorial tabloid, each issue contains display and classified ads that feature thousand of pieces of heavy machinery and related products and services. The magazine also has a large auction section.
Cost: $14.33
Circulation: 170,000
Founded in 1950
Printed in 4 colors on newsprint stock

4250 **Roofing Contractor**
BNP Media
PO Box 5125
Naperville, IL 60540

630-554-2200; Fax: 630-554-3817
mward@illinoisroofing.com
www.illinoisroofing.com

Focuses on coverage of new technology and its implementation in the field. Regular issues include equipment comparisons, new product information, safety tips and legal advice.
Frequency: Monthly
Circulation: 27205
Founded in 1926

4251 **Rural Builder**
F+W Media
38 E. 29th Street
New York, NY 10016

212-447-1400; Fax: 212-447-5231
contact_us@fwmedia.com

Scott Tappa, Editor

Focuses on the post frame and metal frame industry.
Cost: $18.94
64 Pages
Circulation: 32000
Founded in 1952
Printed in 4 colors on glossy stock

4252 **Scaffold & Access**
Scaffold Industry Association

2001 E Campbell Avenue
Suite 101
Phoenix, AZ 85016

602-257-1144
866-687-7115; Fax: 602-257-1166
www.scaffold.org

Steve Smith, President
Marty Coughlin, President Elect
Daryl Hare, Treasurer
Mike Russell, Secretary

The official publication of the SAIA. Striving to elevate the standard of practice in the scaffold and access industry by educating professionals on safety issues, better business practices and innovative solutions to difficult problems.
Frequency: Monthly

4253 **Services Magazine**
Building Service Contractors Association Int'l
401 N Michigan Avenue
22nd Floor
Chicago, IL 60611

312-321-5167
800-368-3414; Fax: 312-673-6735
info@bscai.org
www.bscai.org

Sally Schopmeyer, President
Kevin Rohan, VP

The Building Service Contractors Association International is the trade association serving the facility services industry through education, leadership, and representatiion.
Cost: $30.00
56 Pages
Frequency: Monthly
Circulation: 20,504
ISSN: 0279-0548
Founded in 1981
Printed in 4 colors on glossy stock

4254 **Shelter**
Association Publications
1168 Vickery Ln
Suite 3
Cordova, TN 38016-1664

901-843-8226

James Powell, Editor

For the national distribution and retail segments of the building products industry.
Cost: $6.00
Frequency: Monthly
Founded in 1962

4255 **Southern Building**
Southern Building Code Congress International
900 Montclair Rd
Birmingham, AL 35213-1206

205-591-1853
888-422-7233; Fax: 205-599-9871
webmaster@iccsafe.org
www.iccsafe.org

Gary Nichols, VP Operations

Publishes and maintains a set of model building codes called the Standard Codes. Also provides educational and technical support to the codes enforcement industry.
Cost: $25.00
40 Pages
Circulation: 12000
Founded in 1943

4256 **Southwest Contractor**
McGraw Hill
4747 E Elliot Rd
Suite 29-339
Phoenix, AZ 85044

602-274-2155
800-393-6343; Fax: 602-631-3073
www.southwest.construction.com

Seth Horowitz, Publisher
Scott Blair, Editor

We cover all aspects of the commercial construction industry in Arizona, Nevada and New Mexico. Our mission is to provide news about the projects, the people and the events that affect the building and highway/heavy segments market.
Cost: $40.00
48 Pages
Frequency: Monthly
Circulation: 7000
Founded in 1938

4257 **State of Seniors Housing**
American Seniors Housing Association
5225 Wisconsin Ave NW
Suite 502
Washington, DC 20015

202-237-0900; Fax: 202-237-1616
www.seniorshousing.org

David Schless, President
Doris Maultsby, VP
Frequency: Yearly

4258 **Structural Insulated Panel**
Structural Insulated Panel Association
PO Box 1699
Gig Harbor, WA 98335

253-858-7472; Fax: 253-858-0272
www.sips.org

Terry Dieken, President
Al Cobb, VP

A comprehensive, full color book on building with energy efficient SIPs.
Frequency: Quarterly
Circulation: 5000
Founded in 1990

4259 **Structures**
Business Journal of Portland
851 Sw 6th Ave
Suite 500
Portland, OR 97204-1342

503-274-8733
866-246-0424; Fax: 503-219-3450
portland@bizjournals.com
www.bizjournals.com/portland

Craig Wessel, Publisher

Special edition of The Business Journal that spotlights top construction projects and highlights the design, architecture and construction
Cost: $89.00
52 Pages
Frequency: Daily
Circulation: 400000
ISSN: 0742-6550
Printed in 4 colors on newsprint stock

4260 **Subcontractor**
Subcontractors Education Trust
1004 Duke St
Alexandria, VA 22314-3588

703-684-3450
800-221-0415; Fax: 703-836-3482
asaoffice@asa-hq.com

Colette Nelson, EVP
Franklin Davis, Director Government Relations

News from the construction industry, including up-to-date information on legislative and regulatory affairs, and business news concerning the subcontracting industry.
24 Pages
Frequency: Quarterly
Circulation: 9000
Founded in 1966
Printed in 2 colors

4261 **The Construction User**
The Association of Union Constructors
1501 Lee Highway
Suite 202
Arlington, VA 22209-1109

703-524-3336; Fax: 703-524-3364
dacord@tauc.org
www.tauc.org

Stephen R Lindauer, CEO
Kevin J Hilton, Senior VP

TAUC's official magazine, giving readers a fresh and thought-provoking perspective on union construction and the issues contractors, labor and owner-clients face on a daily basis.
Frequency: Monthly
Founded in 1970

4262 **Tileletter**
National Tile Contractors Association
626 Lakeland E Drive
PO Box 13629
Jackson, MS 39232

601-939-2071; Fax: 601-932-6117
bart@tile-assn.com
www.tile-assn.com

Bart Bettiga, Executive Director
Lesley Goddin, Editor

A trade publication to the tile industry: contractors, distributors and manufacturers.
Cost: $35.00
100 Pages
Frequency: Monthly
Circulation: 20000
Mailing list available for rent: 20,000 names at $150 per M
Printed in on matte stock

4263 **Tiling & Decorative Surfaces**
Ashlee Publishing
18 E 41st Street
New York, NY 10017

212-376-7722; Fax: 212-376-7723
www.ashlee.com

Jordan M Wright, President

Provides information about industry trends and events throughout the world including interviews with manufacturers, distributors and contractors, offering tips on successful merchandising and sales techniques. Issues include product listings and project articles.
Cost: $50.00
Frequency: Monthly
Circulation: 27181
Founded in 1950

4264 **Tilt-Up TODAY**
Tilt-Up Concrete Association
113 First Street West
PO Box 204
Mount Vernon, IA 52314-0204

319-895-6911; Fax: 320-213-5555
info@tilt-up.org
www.tilt-up.org
Facebook

Ed McGuire, President
Glenn Doncaster, President-Elect
Kimberly Corwin, Vice-President
Shane Miller, Treasurer
David Tomasula, Secretary

With continuing advancements in Tilt-Up innovation and architectural achievement, Tilt-Up TODAY highlights the wide variety of outstanding Tilt-Up construction that is taking place all across the world.
Frequency: Monthly
Founded in 2005
Printed in 4 colors on glossy stock

4265 **Timber Framing**
Timber Framers Guild
1106 Harris Ave
Suite 303
Bellingham, WA 98225

360-746-6571
855-598-1803
info@tfguild.org
www.tfguild.org
Facebook, Twitter, Pinterest

Mack Magee, Executive Director
Michael Cuba, Editor
Adam Miller, Editor

Quarterly technical journal of the Timber Framers Guild.
Cost: $45.00
Frequency: Quarterly

4266 **Timber Home Living**
Home Buyer Publications
4200 Lafayette Center Drive
Suite 100
Chantilly, VA 20151-1239

703-222-6951
800-850-7279; Fax: 703-222-3209
store@homebuyerpubs.com
www.loghomeliving.com
Facebook, LinkedIn

Lara Sloan, Publisher

For individuals wishing to plan, build, decorate, or design a log or timber frame home.
Cost: $3.99
Frequency: Bi-Monthly

4267 **Traditional Building**
Restore Media
45 Main Street
Suite 411
Brooklyn, NY 11201

718-636-0788; Fax: 718-636-0750
theditors@restoremedia.com
www.traditional-building.com

Ray Shepherd, Production Manager
Clem Labine, Editor

Lists sources of products for restoration and new construction of traditional buildings.
Cost: $19.95
Frequency: Bi-Monthly
Circulation: 29,000
ISSN: 0898-0284
Founded in 1988
Printed in on glossy stock

4268 **Underground Construction**
Oildom Publishing Company of Texas
PO Box 941669
Houston, TX 77094-8669

281-558-6930; Fax: 281-558-7029
www.oildompublishing.com

Oliver Klinger, President & Publisher
Robert Carpenter, Editor
Cost: $25.00
Frequency: Monthly
Printed in 4 colors on glossy stock

4269 **Underground Focus**
Canterbury Communications
411 South Evergreen
Manteno, IL 60950

815-468-7814; Fax: 815-468-7644
www.underspace.com

Ron Rosencrans, Editor-in-Chief
Paula Miller, Advertising Manager

People read Underground Focus magazine because it documents the importance of their work and helps them get the budgets to do the job. It powerfully dramatizes the need for underground damage prevention and excavation safety.
Cost: $25.00
46 Pages
Circulation: 18,000
ISSN: 1090-400X
Founded in 1986
Printed in 2 colors

4270 **Utility Contractor**
3925 Chain Bridge Road
Suite 300
Fairfax, VA 22030

703-358-9300; Fax: 703-358-9307
bill@nuca.com
www.nuca.com

Bill Hillman, CEO

Serves the underground utility construction industry, including contractors, manufacturers, suppliers, engineering firms, municipal/public/private utilities, and others allied to the field.
Frequency: Monthly
Circulation: 20983
ISSN: 1098-0342
Founded in 1967

4271 **Walls & Ceilings**
Business News Publishing Company
2401 West Big Beaver Road
Suite 700
Troy, MI 48084

248-362-3700; Fax: 248-362-5103
www.wconline.com

Lynette Barwin, Production Manager
John Wyatt, Editor
Mark Fowler, Editorial Directort

Information regarding management, building methods, technology, government regulations, consumer trends, and product information for the contractor involved in exterior finishes, waterproofing, insulation, metal framing, drywall, fireproofing, partitions, stucco and plaster.
Cost: $49.00
140 Pages
Frequency: Monthly
Circulation: 30000
Founded in 1938
Printed in 4 colors

4272 **Welding Journal**
American Welding Society
550 NW 42nd Ave
Miami, FL 33126-5699

305-443-9353
800-443-9353; Fax: 305-443-7559
info@aws.org
www.aws.org

Annette O'Brien, Senior Editor
Mary Ruth Johnsen, Editor

Serves the metal working field, individuals and organizations engaged in welding, cutting or related processes and equipment for the fabrication, maintenance, design or repair of metal products.
Cost: $80.00
Frequency: Monthly
Circulation: 50,000
ISSN: 0043-2296
Founded in 1919

4273 **Western Builder**
Western Builder Publishing Company
30 Technology Pkwy S
Suite 100
Norcross, GA 30092-2925

770-209-3730; Fax: 770-209-3712
www.acppubs.com

Peter Leviton, President
Greg Sitek, Editorial Director

Regional construction publication serving the heavy, highway and non-residential construction industry in Wisconsin and the Upper Peninsula of Michigan.
Cost: $53.00
Frequency: Monthly
Circulation: 100,000
Founded in 1905

4274 **Window & Door**
National Glass Association
1945 Old Gallows Rd
Suite 750
Vienna, VA 22182

703-442-4890
866-342-5642; Fax: 703-442-0630
www.glass.org

Philip James, President/CEO
Nicole Harris, VP

The focus is on technical, new product information, business management and industry issues which focus on manufacturing both new and replacement windows and doors.
Cost: $29.95
Circulation: 20000
Founded in 1948

4275 **Window Film Magazine**
Key Communications
PO Box 569
Garrisonville, VA 22463

540-720-5584; Fax: 540-720-5687
boleary@glass.com
www.windowfilmmag.com/

Debra Levy, Publisher
Penny Beverage, Assistant Editor
Katie Hodge, Editor

Provides industry news, supplier and film manufacturer profiles, technical and installation tips, as well as state-by-state legislative breakdowns and consumer marketing issues relevant to the film industry.
Cost: $35.00
Frequency: Monthly
Circulation: 7000

4276 **Window World Magazine**
Work-4 Projects
4819 St. Charles Boulevard
Pierrefonds, Quebec H9H-3C7

514-620-2200; Fax: 514-620-6300
editor@work4.ca
www.homebuildercanada.com

Nachmi Artzy, Publisher

Provides new products, announcements, calendar events, and coverage of industry news, technical and maketing information to small and medium window and door manufacturers of North America.
Cost: $30.00
Frequency: Bi-Monthly
Circulation: 9,877

4277 **Wrecking and Salvage Journal**
Duane Publishing
51 Park St
Dorchester, MA 02122-2643

617-282-4885; Fax: 617-282-0320
www.rubblemakers.com

Herb Duane, Owner
Toby Duane, Director

Business related information for those engaged in demolition and urban renewal.
Cost: $35.00
Frequency: Monthly
Circulation: 2500
Founded in 1967

Trade Shows

4278 **ACSM Annual Spring Conference**
American Congress on Surveying and Mapping
6 Montgomery Village Avenue
Suite 403
Gaithersburg, MD 20879
240-632-9716; Fax: 240-632-1321
info@acsm.net
Curtis Sumner, Executive Director
Colleen Campbell, Conference Director
Four hundred booths of products and services offered by companies involved in the aerial mapping industry.
2000 Attendees
Frequency: Annual/April

4279 **ACSM/APLS Annual Conference & Technology Exhibition**
American Congress on Surveying & Mapping
6 Montgomery Village Avenue
Gaithersburg, MD 20879
240-632-9716; Fax: 240-632-1321
curtis.sumner@acsm.net
Curtis Sumner, Executive Director
Colleen Campbell, Conference Director
The American Congress on Surveying & mapping and the Arizona Professional Land Surveyors organizations have come together to produce this exhibition with four hundred booths of products and services offered by companies involved in the aerial mapping industry.
1500 Attendees
Frequency: Annual

4280 **AED Summit**
Associated Equipment Distributors
650 E Algonquin Road
Suite 305
Schaumburg, IL 60173
630-574-0650
help@aednet.org
aednet.org
Brian P. McGuire, President/CEO
Robert K. Henderson, EVP & Chief Operating Officer
Agnes Baczek, Director, Finance
Jon Cruthers, VP, Sales
Martin Cabral, Production Manager
A place where distributors, manufacturers and suppliers of the equipment industry meet to build relationships, do business, and learn new skills.
Frequency: Annual/January

4281 **AEMA Annual Meeting**
Asphalt Emulsion Manufacturers Association
3 Church Circle
PO Box 250
Annapolis, MD 21401-1933
410-267-0023; Fax: 410-267-7546
www.aema.org
Michael Krissoff, Executive Director
Representing close to 150 of the world's leading companies in the pavement preservation and rehabilitation industry. A combined annual meeting with the International Slurry Surfacing Association and the Asphalt Recycling & Reclaiming Association.
400 Attendees
Frequency: Annual/March

4282 **AGC Building Contractors Conference**
Associated General Contractors of America
2300 Wilson Blvd
Suite 400
Arlington, VA 22201
703-548-3119; Fax: 703-837-5405
meetings@agc.org
www.agc.org
Carolyn Coker, Executive Director
Joe Jarboe, SVP
One hundred and seventy-five exhibiors of heavy and light construction equipment, trucks, building materials, management services, computer hardware and software. Contractors, subcontractors and trade professionals attend.
4500+ Attendees
Frequency: Annual

4283 **AIBD Annual Convention**
American Institute of Building Design
7059 Blair Rd NW
Suite 201
Washington, DC 20012
800-366-2423; Fax: 866-204-0293
info@aibd.org
www.aibd.org
Facebook, Twitter, LinkedIn
Dan Sater, President
Alan Kent, Internal Vice President
Viki Wooster, External Vice President
Kerry Dick, Secretary/ Treasurer
Exhibition of 25 manufacturers, suppliers, distributors and plan publishers of building products including: roofing, windows, doors, floor covering, fire places, spas/jacuzzis, lumber, intercom systems, alarm systems and appliances; computer-aid design technology, computer hardware/software and plan publishers. Containing 30 booths and 30 exhibits.
1500 Attendees
Frequency: Annual/July
Founded in 1950

4284 **AIC Annual Forum**
American Institute of Constructors
19 Mantua Road
Mount Royal, NJ 08061
703-683-4999; Fax: 703-683-5480
info@professionalconstructor.org
www.professionalconstructor.org
Facebook, Twitter, LinkedIn
Ethan Gray, Sr. Executive Director
Educational presentations from leading practitioners and educators in the world of construction, panel discussions with major voices in the industry, opportunities to network with other emerging leaders in the construction profession as they fine-tune their leadership skills.
Frequency: Annual
Founded in 1971

4285 **AISC Annual Meeting**
American Institute of Steel Construction
1 E Wacker Drive
Suite 700
Chicago, IL 60601-2000
312-670-2400; Fax: 312-670-5403
www.aisc.org
Roger Ferch, President
Katey Lenihan, Meeting Planner
One hundred booths attended by structural engineers, steel fabricators, educators and construction managers. Those interested in the design fabrication and erection of structural steel for non-residential buildings and bridges.
100 Attendees
Frequency: Annual/September

4286 **APWA North American Snow Conference**
American Public Works Association
1200 Main Street
Suite 1400
Kansas City, MO 64105-2100
816-472-6100
800-848-APWA; Fax: 816-472-1610
www.apwa.net
Scott Grayson, Executive Director
Lysa Byous, Meeting Planner & Exhibit Manager
Offers technical and hands-on education on snow and ice management.
1000 Attendees
Frequency: Annual/April
ISSN: 0092-4873

4287 **ASPE Annual Meeting and Estimators Summit**
American Society of Professional Estimators
2525 Perimeter Place Drive
Suite 103
Nashville, TN 37214
615-316-9200
888-378-6283; Fax: 615-316-9800
www.aspenational.com
Marcene N. Taylor, President
Bruce D. Schlesier, 1st Vice President
Provides two days of presentations by nationally known speakers in the construction industry. ASPE's Technical Documents Committee prepares a book for each convention attendee that contains papers submitted by the speakers at these educational sessions.
Frequency: Annual/July

4288 **AWI Annual Meeting/Convention**
Architectural Woodwork Institute
46179 Westlake Dr
Suite 120
Potomac Falls, VA 20165
571-323-3636; Fax: 571-323-2330
info@awinet.org
www.awinet.org
Kimberly Kennedy, Meeting/Conventions Director
Robert Stout, President
Seminar, workshop and woodwork products such as casework, fixtures and panelings, equipment and supplies.
Frequency: Annual/October

4289 **Adhesive and Sealant Council Fall Convention**
Adhesive & Sealant Council
7101 Wisconsin Avenue
Suite 990
Bethesda, MD 20814
301-986-9700; Fax: 301-986-9795
data@ascouncil.org
www.ascouncil.org
Malinda Armstrong, Director, Meetings & Expositions
Frequency: October

4290 **AeroMat Conference and Exposition**
ASM International
9639 Kinsman Road
Materials Park, OH 44073-0002
440-338-5151
800-336-5152; Fax: 440-338-4634
memberservicecenter@asminternational.org
www.asminternational.org
William T. Mahoney, Secretary & CEO
Lindy Good, Global Conference & Exhibit Planner
Focuses on innovative aerospace materials, fabrication and manufacturing methods that im-

prove aerospace structures, performance and durability.
30K Members
Frequency: Annual/May
Founded in 1913

4291 American Institute of Building Design Annual Convention
American Institute of Building Design
7059 Blair Road NW
Suite 201
Washington, DC 20012

202-249-1407
800-366-2423; Fax: 202-249-2473
info@aibd.org
www.aibd.org

Dan Sater, President

A four day convention and trade show for residential design professionals.
Frequency: Annual/July

4292 Annual Conference on Deep Foundations
Deep Foundations Institute
326 Lafayette Avenue
Hawthorne, NJ 07506

973-423-4030; Fax: 973-423-4031
dfihq@dfi.org
www.dfi.org

Theresa Engler, Executive Director
Angie Gibble, Events Specialist

The premier event for industry members from across the globe to gather and share experiences, exchange ideas and learn the current state-of-the-practice from various disciplines such as engineers, contractors, suppliers, manufacturers and academicians.
600 Attendees
Frequency: Annual/October
Founded in 1975

4293 Arrowhead Home and Builders Show
Shamrock Productions
14552 Judicial Rd
Suite 111
Burnsville, MN 55306

952-431-9630; Fax: 952-431-9633
info@shamrockprod.com

Randy Schauer, President/CEO

Home building, remodeling, landscaping and more.
41960 Attendees
Frequency: Annual/April

4294 Associated Builders and Contractors National Convention
Associated Builders and Contractors
4250 N Fairfax Dr
9th Floor
Arlington, VA 22203

703-812-2000; Fax: 703-812-8200
meetings@abc.org
www.abc.org

Michael Bellaman, President/CEO
Tina Schneider, Meetings/Conventions Director

Exhibits for construction contractors, subcontractors, and associated trades.

4295 Brick Show
Brick Industry Association
1850 Centennial Park Drive
Suite 301
Reston, VA 20191-1525

703-620-0100; Fax: 703-620-3928
brickinfo@bia.org
www.bia.org

Susan Ludwig, Show Manager

The only national tradeshow and conference for the clay brick industry.
950 Attendees
Frequency: Annual/March

4296 Builders Trade Show
Maryland National Capital Building Industry Assn.
1738 Elton Road
Suite 200
Silver Spring, MD 20903-5730

301-445-5400; Fax: 301-445-5499
www.mncbia.org

Jean Mathis, Events Director
Diane Swenson, EVP

Annual show and exhibits of construction equipment, supplies and services.

4297 Building Industry Show
Building Industry Assn. of Southern California
17444 Sky Park Circle
Irvine, CA 92614

949-553-9500; Fax: 949-769-8942
www.buildingindustryshow.com

Wes Keusder, President

Annual show of about 400 exhibitors of products and services for the building industry.
8000+ Attendees
Frequency: Annual/November

4298 Business Administration Conference
National Ready Mixed Concrete Association
900 Spring Street
Silver Spring, MD 20910

301-587-1400
888-846-7622; Fax: 301-585-4219
info@nrmca.org
www.nrmca.org

Robert Garbini, President
Deana Angelastro, Executive Administrator

A 3-day educational program for financial, information technology, and human resources professionals in the construction and construction materials business.
Frequency: Annual/October

4299 CABA Smart Buildings Summit
Continental Automated Buildings Association
1173 Cyrville Road
Suite 210
Ottawa, Canada, ON K1J 7S6

613-686-1814
888-798-2222; Fax: 613-744-7833
caba@caba.org
www.caba.org
Facebook, Twitter, LinkedIn, YouTube

Ronald J Zimmer, President & CEO
Conrad McCallum, Communications Director
Greg Walker, Research Director
Andrew Glennie, Member Services Coordinator
Sashien Godakandae, Business Development Officer

Current intelligent building technologies.
380+ Members
Founded in 1988

4300 CFMA Annual Conference & Exhibition
Construction Financial Management Association
100 Village Boulevard
Suite 200
Princeton, NJ 08540

609-452-8000; Fax: 609-452-0474
info@cfma.org
www.cfma.org

Stuart Binstock, President & CEO
Brian Summers, VP, Operations

A resource for construction financial professionals.
Frequency: Annual/May

4301 CONEXPO-CON/AGG
Association of Equipment Manufacturers
6737 West Washington Street
Suite 2400
Milwaukee, WI 53214-5647

414-272-0943; Fax: 414-272-1170
international@conexpoconagg.com
www.conexpoconagg.com

Jennifer Graham, Sales Director
Kathy Arnold, Account Executive
Maxx Lebiecki, Account Executive

An international gathering of those working in the construction industries, showcasing the latest equipment, products, services and technologies.
Frequency: March/Every 3 Years

4302 Composites & Polycon
American Composites Manufacturers Association
1010 North Glebe Road
Suite 450
Arlington, VA 22201

703-525-0511; Fax: 703-525-0743
info@acmanet.org
www.compositesworld.com

Lori Luchak, President

World's largest trade association serving the composites industry. Provides education and support for composites fabricators in the successful operation of businesses, and offers leading-edge services in regulatory compliance and formulation, education and training, management, and market expansion.
1.5M Attendees
Frequency: Annual/September

4303 Coverings: The Ultimate Tile & Stone Experience
NTP, Coverings Show Management
313 S Patrick Street
Alexandria, VA 22314

703-683-8500
800-687-7469; Fax: 703-836-4486
www.coverings.com

Karin Fendrich, COO

Showcasing the newest in tile and natural stone, the event provides opportunities for: continuing education, live demonstrations, networking and new business. 1200 international exhibitors, attracting 33,000+ distributors, retailers, fabricators, contractors, and design professionals.
33M Attendees
Frequency: Annual
Mailing list available for rent

4304 Design & Construction Exposition
Construction Association of Michigan
43636 Woodward
PO Box 3204
Bloomfield Hills, MI 48302

248-972-1000; Fax: 248-972-1001
marketing@cam-online.com
www.cam-online.com

Ron Riegel, Exposition Manager
Jeanny Snowden, Marketing Coordinator

Annual show of 250 manufacturers, suppliers and distributors of construction industry equipment, supplies and services.
11M Attendees
Frequency: Annual/February
Founded in 1985

4305 EdCon & Expo
Associated Builders and Contractors

4250 Fairfax Drive
9th Floor
Arlington, VA 22203-1665

703-812-2000; Fax: 703-812-8201
meetings@abc.org
www.abc.org

Michael Bellaman, CEO
Todd Mann, COO
Jason Daisey, CFO
1700 Attendees
Frequency: Annual/April

4306 Elevator Escalator Safety Awareness Annual Meeting
Elevator World
356 Morgan Avenue
Mobile, AL 36606

251-479-4514
800-730-5093; Fax: 251-479-7043

Linda Williams, Director of Administration
Patricia Cartee, Director of Operations

Meetings, discussions and exhibits on the safety of elevators.
Frequency: Annual/February

4307 Environmental Management Conference and Exposition
Environmental Information Association
6935 Wisconsin Avenue
Suite 306
Chevy Chase, MD 20815-6112

301-961-4999
888-343-4342; Fax: 301-961-3094
info@eia-usa.org
www.eia-usa.org

Kelly Rutt, Developement Manager
Brent Kynoch, Managing Director

Annual conference of 85-100 exhibitors of equipment, supplies and services for quantifying, managing or remediating environmental hazards in buildings and facilities.
1200 Attendees

4308 FENCETECH Convention & Expo
American Fence Association
800 Roosevelt Rd
Building C-312
Glen Ellyn, IL 60137-5899

630-942-6598; Fax: 630-790-3095
www.americanfenceassociation.com

Rod Wilson, President
Mike Robinson, Vice President

Four hundred and eighty booths for the fence industry. Educational opportunities that will inform you of the most up-to-date technology.
5883 Attendees
Frequency: Annual/January/February

4309 GlassBuild America: Glass, Window & Door Expo
National Glass Association
1945 Old Gallows Rd
Suite 750
Vienna, VA 22182

703-424-4890
866-342-5642; Fax: 703-442-0630
www.glass.org

Philip James, President
Nicole Harris, VP

Provides one central showcase for the class processing equipment, window and door manufacturing equipment, and the latest technology for all types of glass and fenestration products used in residential and commercial construction and related applications.
Frequency: Annual/October

4310 Great Lakes Building Products Exposition
Michigan Lumber & Building Materials Association
5815 Executive Drive
Suite B
Lansing, MI 48911

517-394-5225; Fax: 517-394-5228
www.thembsa.org

Jodi Barber, VP
Rick Seely, President

Offering new products and presentations on industry topics for the building material dealer and builders/contractors.
Frequency: Annual/January

4311 Hard Hat Expo
Lee Publications
6113 State Highway 5
P.O. Box 121
Palatine Bridge, NY 13428-0121

518-673-0103
800-218-5586; Fax: 518-673-3245
kmaring@leepub.com
www.leetradeshows.com

Ken Maring, Trade Show Manager
Larry Price, Sales Manager
Beth Snyder, Trade Show Manager

The premier showcase for heavy construction in the Northeast sharing information about the latest innovations in the construction industry!
3.5M Attendees
Frequency: Annual, April
Founded in 1989

4312 Home Improvement & Remodeling Exposition
Dmg World Media
325 Essjay Road
Suite 100
Williamsville, NY 14221

716-631-2266
800-274-6948; Fax: 716-631-2425
www.dmgevents.com

Mark Carr, President

Featuring a spectacular garden, the latest in home technology, thousands of products, celebrity appearances and over 350 exhibits where consumers can find what they need to create their own unique spaces and put their special style to work.
60000 Attendees
Frequency: Annual/March

4313 IDA Expo
International Door Association
1 Parkview Plaza
Suite 800
Oakbrook Terrace, IL 60181

202-591-2457
800-355-4432; Fax: 202-591-2445
info@doors.org
www.doors.org

Mike Fischer, Executive Director
Monica Saunders, Meetings/Exposition Manager

Workshops and Exhibits featuring the latest product innovations as well as traditional products and services in the doors and access industry. Educational programming covers sales, financing, personnel management, and marketing. Also offers a number of fun social events.
Frequency: Annual/March

4314 INTEX Expo System Construction Association
Association of the Wall and Ceiling Industry
513 W Broad Street
Suite 210
Falls Church, VA 22046

703-538-1600; Fax: 703-534-8307
info@awci.org
www.awci.org

Michael Stark, Chief Executive Officer
Karen Bilak, Dir., Convention & Conferences
Samantha Riemer, Manager, Trade Show & Meetings

The premier interior/exterior wall and ceiling commercial construction trade show. This annual show host exhibitors such as, wall and ceiling contractors, general contractors, architects, specifiers, suppliers, and distributors.
3000 Attendees
Frequency: Annual/April

4315 Independent Electrical Contractors National Convention
Independent Electrical Contractors
4401 Ford Avenue
Suite 1100
Alexandria, VA 22302

703-549-7351; Fax: 703-549-7448
info@ieci.org
www.ieci.org

Tim Welsh, Executive VP
Trayvia Watson, Meetings Manager

One hundred booths of electrical equipment, products and services.
1000 Attendees
Frequency: Annual/October

4316 International Builders Show
National Association of Home Builders
1201 15th Street NW
Washington, DC 20005

202-266-8200
800-368-5242; Fax: 202-266-8400
info@nahb.com
www.nahb.org

Gerald Howard, CEO

More than 1,600 suppliers, representing the most comprehensive showcase of home building products and services, are ready to demonstrate how their offerings can help you to corner the market.
90000 Attendees
Frequency: Annual/January

4317 International Conference Building Official
International Code Council
5360 Workman Mill Road
Whittier, CA 90601-2298

888-422-7233; Fax: 562-908-5524
www.iccsafe.org

Jay Peters, Executive Director
Mark Johnson, SVP
1,2M Attendees
Frequency: Annual/September

4318 International Construction and Utility Equipment Exposition (ICUEE)
Association of Equipment Manufacturers
6737 West Washington Street
Suite 2400
Milwaukee, WI 53214-5647

414-272-0943; Fax: 414-272-1170
aem@aem.org
www.icuee.com

Dennis Slater, President
Renee Peters, Chief Financial Officer
Nicole Hallada, VP, Marketing & Communications

Exposition for outdoor demonstrations of utility and construction equipment.
Frequency: Annual/September

4319 **International Thermal Spray Conference & Exposition**
ASM International
9639 Kinsman Road
Materials Park, OH 44073-0002

440-338-5151
800-336-5152; Fax: 440-338-4634
memberservicecenter@asminternational.org
www.asminternational.org

William T. Mahoney, Secretary & CEO
Lindy Good, Global Conference & Exhibit Planner

International annual conference for professional thermal spray technologists, researchers, manufacturers and suppliers.
30K Members
Frequency: Annual/May
Founded in 1913

4320 **Living Future Unconference**
International Living Future Institute
1501 East Madison St.
Suite 150
Seattle, WA 98122

206-223-2028
info@living-future.org
www.living-future.org
Facebook, Twitter, LinkedIn, Instagram

KC Gauldine, Chief Executive Officer
James Connelly, VP, Products & Strategic Growth
Kathleen Smith, VP, Living Building Challenge
Miranda Berger, VP, Development & Communications
Julie Tonroy, Events Director

Tours, workshops, summits, exhibits, keynote speakers, and sessions on regenerative design. Features cutting-edge products and knowledgeable professionals and activists in the field.
Frequency: Annual

4321 **Lumber and Building Material Expo**
Northeastern Retail Lumber Association
585 N Greenbush Road
Rensselaer, NY 12144

518-286-1010
800-292-6752; Fax: 518-286-1755
rferris@nrla.org
www.nrla.org

Donna Berger, Events Coordinator
Rita Ferris, President

Largest regional trade show in the lumber and building material industry. Retail lumber dealers in the Northeast are afforded the opportunity to interact with manufacturers, wholesalers, and distributors of lumber, building materials, and related technologies.
7000 Attendees
Frequency: Annual/February

4322 **MBI World of Modular Conference**
Modular Building Institute
944 Glenwood Station Ln
Suite 204
Charlottesville, VA 22901-1480

434-296-3288
888-811-3288; Fax: 434-296-3361
info@modular.org
www.modular.org

Steven Williams, Operations Director
Tom Hardiman, Executive Director

High-profile speakers, educational sessions, exhibits, discussion on trends in commercial modular, entertainment and prizes
500 Attendees
Frequency: Annual

4323 **MCAA Annual Convention & Masonry Showcase**
Mason Contractors Association of America
1481 Merchant Drive
Algonquin, IL 60102

224-678-9709
800-536-2225; Fax: 224-678-9714
www.masoncontractors.org

Tim O'Toole, Marketing Director
Jeff Buczkiewicz, Executive Director

Featuring in-depth education seminars, high-profile international skills competitions and exhibit display. Attendees includes masonry contracting firms representing all facets of masonry installation, including the largest commercial, residential, institutional, landscape, paving, retaining, glass block, and stone contractors.
Frequency: Annual/March

4324 **MIACON Construction, Mining & Waste Management Show**
Finocchiaro Enterprises
2921 Coral Way
Miami, FL 33145

305-441-2865; Fax: 305-529-9217
www.miacon.com

Michael Finocchiaro, President
Jose Garcia, VP
Justine Finocchiaro, Chief Operations

Annual show of 650 manufacturers, suppliers, distributors and exporters of equipment, machinery, supplies and services for the construction, mining and waste managment industries. There will be 600 booths.
10M Attendees
Frequency: Annual/October
Founded in 1994

4325 **Metalcon International**
PSMJ Resources
10 Midland Avenue
Newton, MA 02458-1021

617-965-0055; Fax: 617-928-1670
metalcon@psmj.com
www.metalcon.com

Claire Kilcoyne, Show Manager
Suzanne Maher, Conference Director
Paula Parker, Exhibit Sales

Architects, builders, craftspeople, designers, framers, contractors, and other industry leaders will share their expertise, hone their skills, and make connections that will help their businesses reach new heights.
8000 Attendees
Frequency: Annual/October

4326 **NCSBCS/AMCBO Annual Conference**
Int'l Conference of State Bldg Codes & Standards
505 Huntmar Park Drive
Suite 210
Herndon, VA 20170

703-437-0100; Fax: 703-481-3596
www.ncsbcs.org

Kevin Egilmez, Project Manager
Carolyn Fitch, Membership Services

Providing a wide variety of technical and administrative information of immediate value to the nation's construction and code enforcement community, trade associations, information technology firms and professional societies, academicians, students, and elected officials regarding building codes administration and public safety.
Frequency: Annual/Sept-Oct

4327 **NECA Convention**
National Electrical Contractors Association
3 Bethesda Metro Center
Suite 1100
Bethesda, MD 20814

301-657-3110; Fax: 301-215-4500
www.necanet.org

Russell Alessi, President
Katie Nolan, Convention Manager

The event brings the largest manufacturers, utilities, contractors, engineers, consultants, plant engineers, and distributors from all over North America and 31 foreign countries.
8000 Attendees
Frequency: Annual/September

4328 **NRCMA Conference**
National Railroad Construction & Maintenance Assoc
500 New Jersey Avenue NW
Suite 400
Washington, DC 20001

202-715-2919; Fax: 202-318-0867
info@nrcma.org
www.nrcma.org

Chuck Baker, President
Matt Ginsberg, Director of Operations

For railroad personnel, managers and purchasers in design, construction and maintenance. Information on breakthrough innovations in rail construction, railroad safety, new rail projects of national significance and more. 60-80 exhibitors.
750 Attendees
Frequency: Annual/January

4329 **NSSGA Dredging Seminar & Expo**
National Stone, Sand & Gravel Association
1605 King Street
Alexandria, VA 22314

703-525-8788
800-342-1415; Fax: 703-525-7782
jwilson@nssga.org
www.nssga.org

Jennifer Wilson, President/CEO
Cynthia McDowell, Conventions Director

Created to specifically meet the needs of aggregate producers who use dredges or have an interest in using dredges in the future. This seminar uses educational seminars, plant tours and manufacturer's exhibits to provide information useful to both novice and experienced dredgers.
Frequency: Annual/June

4330 **National Congress & Expo for Manufactured and Modular Housing**
Manufactured Housing Institute
2111 Wilson Boulevard
Suite 100
Arlington, VA 22201-3040

703-558-0400; Fax: 703-558-0401
info@mfghome.org
www.manufacturedhousing.org

Thayer Long, President/CEO
Lisa Quinn Brechtel, VP/Executive Director

The opportunity to network with over 1500 industry captains who make a positive difference in the modular and manufactured housing industries.
Frequency: Annual/April

4331 **National Demolition Association Conference and Trade Show**
National Demolition Association
16 North Franklin Street
Suite 203
Doylestown, PA 18901

215-348-4949
800-541-2412; Fax: 215-348-8422

info@demolitionassociation.com
www.demolitionassociation.com

Jeff Lambert, Executive Director
Linda Benck, Meetings & Events Manager
1700 Attendees
Frequency: Annual

4332 **National Hardware Show**
383 Main Avenue
Norwalk, CT 06851

203-840-5622
888-425-9377; Fax: 203-840-4824
inquiry@hardware.reedexpo.com
www.nationalhardwareshow.com
Facebook, Twitter, LinkedIn, Instagram, YouTube

Richard Russo, Event Director
Juliana Sherwood, Sales Director
Emily DeMarco, Marketing Director

The only housing after-market show, bringing together manufacturers and resellers of all products used to remodel, repair, maintain and decorate the home and its surroundings.
3M Attendees
Frequency: Annual/May

4333 **New England Home Show**
Dmg World Media
45 Braintree Hill Office Park
Suite 302
Braintree, MA 02184

781-849-0990
800-469-0990; Fax: 781-849-7544
www.newenglandhomeshow.com

Laurie Myette, Show Manager
Amy Kimball, Administrative Assistant

Annual show of 379 exhibitors of homebuilding and improvement equipment, supplies and services, including bathroom and kitchen supplies, building materials, appliances, doors and windows, swimming pools, hot tubs and spas.
100M Attendees
Frequency: Annual/February

4334 **North American Steel Construction Conference**
American Institute of Steel Construction
One East Wacker Drive
Suite 700
Chicago, IL 60601

312-670-2400; Fax: 312-670-5403
www.aisc.org

David Ratterman, General Counsel
Roger Ferch, President

A premier education event aimed at providing structural engineers, steel fabricators, erectors, and detailers with practical information and the latest design and construction techniques.
2300 Attendees
Frequency: Annual/April

4335 **Northwestern Building Products Expo**
Northwestern Lumber Association
701 Decatur Ave. N
Golden Valley, MN 55427

763-544-6822
888-644-6822; Fax: 763-595-4060
info@nlassn.org
www.nlassn.org

Jodie Fleck, Director, Conventions & Tours

Building materials and their contractors attend this trade show and conference for continuing educataion and cammeraderie
1200 Attendees
Frequency: Annual/January

4336 **PCA: Paint and Coatings Expo**
Painting Contractors Association
1801 Park 270 Drive
Suite 220
St Louis, MO 63146-4020

314-514-7322
800-332-7322; Fax: 314-514-9417
www.pcapainted.org

Nigel Costolloe, Executive Director

This mega show is the culmination of months of research and planning by members of the two professional associations (PDCA & SSPC), who joined forces in search of a 'one-stop shop' solution for convening the maximum number of industry professionals in the most cost-effective and productive way.
Frequency: Annual/January

4337 **PowerGen**
Scaffold Industry Association
2001 E Campbell Avenue
Suite 101
Phoenix, AZ 85016

602-257-1144
866-687-7115; Fax: 602-257-1166
www.scaffold.org

Steve Smith, President
Marty Coughlin, President Elect
Daryl Hare, Treasurer
Mike Russell, Secretary

Companies from all sectors of the industry exhibit and attendees come together for a look at the industry with key emphasis on new solutions and innovations for the future.
Frequency: Annual/July

4338 **Public Works Expo**
American Public Works Association
1200 Main Street
Suite 1400
Kansas City, MO 64105-2100

816-472-6100
800-848-APWA; Fax: 816-472-1610
www.apwa.net

Scott Grayson, Executive Director
Lysa Byous, Meeting Planner & Exhibit Manager

Offers the benefit of a variety of educational sessions, depth of the exhibit program and endless opportunities for networking. The latest cutting-edge technologies, managerial techniques and regulatory trends designed to keep you focused on the right solutions at the right time.
Frequency: Annual/September

4339 **RCMA Meeting**
Roof Coatings Manufacturers Association
750 National Press Building
529 14th Street NW
Washington, DC 20045

202-207-0919; Fax: 202-223-9741
info@roofcoatings.org
www.roofcoatings.org

Dan Quinonez, Executive Director

An educational program focusing on Technical, Marketing, and regulatory updates regarding roof coatings.
100 Attendees
Frequency: Annual

4340 **SIA Annual Convention & Exposition**
Scaffold Industry Association
2001 E Campbell Avenue
Suite 101
Phoenix, AZ 85016

602-257-1144
866-687-7115; Fax: 602-257-1166
www.scaffold.org

Steve Smith, President
Marty Coughlin, President Elect
Daryl Hare, Treasurer
Mike Russell, Secretary

Exhibits and classes on scaffold safety and education.
Frequency: Annual/July

4341 **SIPA Annual Meeting & Conference**
Structural Insulated Panel Association
PO Box 1699
Gig Harbor, WA 98335

253-858-7472; Fax: 253-858-0272
www.sips.org
Facebook, Twitter

Frank Baker, President

A valuable networking event for both longtime veterans and newcomers to the SIP industry. If you're a builder, architect, developer or entrepreneur interested in employing SIPs in your next commercial or residential project, you'll be interested in this conference
Frequency: Annual/April

4342 **STAFDA Annual Convention & Trade Show**
Specialty Tools and Fasteners Distributors Assn.
500 Elm Grove Rd.
Suite 210
Elm Grove, WI 53122

262-784-4774
800-352-2981; Fax: 262-784-5059
info@stafda.org
www.stafda.org
Facebook, LinkedIn

Mike Kangas, President
Kramer Darragh, Vice President

Members distribute or manufacture power equipment, anchors, fastening systems, drilling equipment and other related industrial supplies.
4000 Attendees
Frequency: Annual/November

4343 **Spray Foam Conference & EXPO**
Spray Polyurethane Foam Alliance
4400 Fair Lakes Court
Suite 105
Fairfax, VA 22033

800-523-6154; Fax: 703-222-5816
www.sprayfoam.org

Sig Hall, President
Bob Duke, Vice President
Peter Davis, Secretary/ Treasurer

Training and accreditation programs, general and breakout sessions, awards, networking receptions, and the exhibit hall
Frequency: Yearly
Founded in 1987

4344 **Spring Meeting & Legislative Conference**
National Lumber & Building Material Dealers Assn.
2025 M St NW
Suite 800
Washington, DC 20036-3309

202-367-1169
800-634-8645; Fax: 202-367-2169
membersupport@dealer.org
www.dealer.org
Facebook, Twitter, LinkedIn

Jonathan M. Paine, CAE, President & CEO
Ben Gann, VP, Legislative & Political Affairs
Frank Moore, Regulatory Counsel
Kiersten Kochanowski, Membership & Operations
Corie Stretton, Event Manager

An opportunity to meet with members of Congress and share legislative priorities and con-

cerns. Network with fellow industry partners, members of Congress and staff on Capitol Hill.
6000 Members
Frequency: Annual, Spring
Founded in 1917

4345 **TAUC Annual Meeting**
The Association of Union Constructors
1501 Lee Highway
Suite 202
Arlington, VA 22209-1109

703-524-3336; Fax: 703-524-3364
dacord@tauc.org
www.tauc.org

Stephen R Lindauer, CEO
Kevin J Hilton, Senior VP

The prime meeting of the year, bringing together our membership from around the country in a relaxed and informal setting. The meeting will provide an opportunity to network and meet our union contractors.
Frequency: Annual/May
Founded in 1970

4346 **TCA Annual Convention**
Tilt-Up Concrete Association
113 First Street West
PO Box 204
Mount Vernon, IA 52314-0204

319-895-6911; Fax: 320-213-5555
info@tilt-up.org
www.tilt-up.org
Facebook

Ed McGuire, President
Glenn Doncaster, President-Elect
Kimberly Corwin, Vice-President
Shane Miller, Treasurer
David Tomasula, Secretary

Tilt-up Concrete Association/TCA's annual convention that features intensive training and education seminars for contractors and engineers, as well as a trade show, building tour and focused sessions on marketing and architecturald design.
Frequency: Annual/October
Founded in 2005

4347 **TFG Conference East**
Timber Framers Guild
1106 Harris Ave
Suite 303
Bellingham, WA 98225

360-746-6571
855-598-1803
info@tfguild.org
www.tfguild.org
Facebook, Twitter, Pinterest

Mack Magee, Executive Director

Event dedicated to learning about the resources and skills necessary for timber-frame building.

4348 **TFG Conference West**
Timber Framers Guild
1106 Harris Ave
Suite 303
Bellingham, WA 98225

360-746-6571
855-598-1803
info@tfguild.org
www.tfguild.org
Facebook, Twitter, Pinterest

Mack Magee, Executive Director

Event dedicated to learning about the resources and skills necessary for timber-frame building.

4349 **Technology for Construction**
Hanley-Wood
8600 Freeport Parkway
Suite 200
Irving, TX 75063

972-366-6300
866-962-7469; Fax: 972-536-6402
www.technologyforconstruction.com

Tom Cindric, Show Director
Jackie James, Show Manager
Todd Gilmore, Sales Manager

International conference and tradeshow focused on the technology needs and interests of architects and interior designers; civil engineers, contractors, builders, and construction managers, facility managers, building engineers, owners, GIS, surveyors and mapping professionals for private, commercial, institutional and government sectors.
33M Attendees
Frequency: Annual/January

4350 **Utility Construction Expo**
National Utility Contractors Association
3925 Chain Bridge Road
Suite 300
Fairfax, VA 22030

703-358-9300; Fax: 703-358-9307
bill@nuca.com
www.nuca.com

Bill Hillman, CEO
Bonnie Williams, VP

The latest technologies, products, and services being offered by the leading manufacturers and suppliers in the underground utility construction industry. Next trade show is scheduled to take place in Las Vegas, Nevada.
Frequency: Annual/February

4351 **WBMA Annual Convention**
Western Building Material Association
909 Lakeridge Drive SW
PO Box 1699
Olympia, WA 98507

360-943-3054
888-551-9262; Fax: 360-943-1219
wbma@wbma.org
www.wbma.org

One hundred and fourty booths of products stocked and sold by building material dealers.
1.6M Attendees
Frequency: Annual/November

4352 **World Adhesive & Sealant Conference (WAC)**
Adhesive & Sealant Council
7101 Wisconsin Avenue
Suite 990
Bethesda, MD 20814

301-986-9700; Fax: 301-986-9795
data@ascouncil.org
www.ascouncil.org

Malinda Armstrong, Director, Meetings & Expositions

International event drawing together industry stakeholders worldwide for three days of keynote addresses, technical courses, and networking opportunities.
Frequency: Every Four Years/April

4353 **World of Asphalt Show & Conference**
National Asphalt Pavement Association
5100 Forbes Boulevard
Suite 200
Lanham, MD 20706

301-731-4748
888-468-6499; Fax: 301-731-4621
mcervarich@hotmix.org
www.hotmix.org

Mike Acott, President
Margaret Cervarich, VP Marketing/Public Affairs

The leading trade show for the asphalt pavement industry, bringing together the Asphalt Pavement Conference and the People, Plants and Paving training program.
6000 Attendees

Directories & Databases

4354 **Affirmative Action Compliance Manual for Federal Contractors**
Bureau of National Affairs
1801 S Bell St
Arlington, VA 22202-4501

703-341-3000
800-372-1033; Fax: 800-253-0332
customercare@bna.com
www.bnabooks.com

Paul N Wojcik, CEO
Gregory C McCaffery, President

Employers and attorneys can more easily monitor and measure affirmative action requirements, implement policies, and quickly access other compliance information with this complete resource guide.
Cost: $611.00
Frequency: Monthly

4355 **Automated Builder: Top Component Producers Survey Issue**
Automated Builder
2401 Grapevine Dr
Oxnard, CA 93036

805-351-5931; Fax: 805-351-5755
www.automatedbuilder.com

Don Carlson, Publisher

Over 100 leading industrialized building producers are profiled on the basis of sales. Top HUD-Code home producers, TOP pakelizers, TOP commercial modular builders. Features articles on technology, methods and machinery, sales and marketing for in-plant building.
Cost: $6.00
48 Pages
Frequency: Monthly
Circulation: 25000
ISSN: 0899-5540
Founded in 1964

4356 **Blue Book of Building and Construction**
Contractors Register
PO Box 500
Jefferson Valley, NY 10535

914-450-0200
800-431-2584; Fax: 914-243-0287
info@thebluebook.com
www.thebluebook.com
YouTube

Jeff Fandl, Editor

Regional construction directories in most major markets throughout the US. Online, thebluebook.com provides easy access to continually updated information for each of our regional editions.
4500 Pages
Frequency: Annual
Circulation: 615,000
Founded in 1913

4357 **Building & Construction Trades Department**
815 16th St NW
Suite 209
Washington, DC 20006-4101

202-347-1461; Fax: 202-628-0724
www.bctd.org
Facebook

Mark Ayers, President
Joseph Maloney, Secretary/Treasurer

Coordinates activity and provides resources to 15 affiliated trades unions in the construction industry.
386 Pages
Founded in 1908

4358 **Building Materials Directory**
Underwriters Laboratories
333 Pfingsten Rd
Northbrook, IL 60062-2096

847-412-0136
877-854-3577; Fax: 847-272-8129
cec@us.ul.com
www.ul.com

Keith E Williams, CEO
John Drengenberg, Manager Consumer Affairs

Offers information on companies that have qualified to use the UL listing mark or classification marking on products that have been found to be in compliance with UL requirements.
Cost: $30.00
512 Pages
Frequency: Annual/February

4359 **Cedar Shake and Shingle Bureau Membership Directory/Buyer's Guide**
Cedar Shake & Shingle Bureau
PO Box 1178
Sumas, WA 98295-1178

604-820-7700; Fax: 604-820-0266
www.cedarbureau.org

Jim Tuffin, Chairman
Len Taylor Jr., Vice-Chairman
Rav Dhaliwal, Secretary/Treasurer

About 102 member manufacturing mills in the Pacific Northwest and British Columbia, Canada; approximately 163 affiliated roofing applicators, builders, architects, remodelers and suppliers of related products and services.
Cost: $17.00
Frequency: SemiAnnual
Circulation: 450

4360 **Cement Americas**
Penton Media Inc
249 W 17th St
New York, NY 10011-5390

212-204-4200; Fax: 212-206-3622
steven.prokopy@penton.com
www.penton.com

Sharon Rowlands, CEO

Offers 100 cement manufacturing companies in the United States, Canada, Mexico, Central and South America.
Cost: $78.00
225 Pages
Frequency: Annual
Circulation: 300
Mailing list available for rent
Printed in on glossy stock

4361 **Construction Equipment: Construction Giants Issue**
Reed Business Information
2000 Clearwater Dr
Oak Brook, IL 60523-8809

630-574-0825; Fax: 630-288-8781
www.reedbusiness.com

Mark Kelsey, CEO
Stuart Whayman, CFO
Dan Olley, CIO

Listing of approximately 250 of the largest equipment-owning heavy construction contractors, engaged in earthmoving, paving, building and materials production owning over $10 million in equipment.
Frequency: Monthly
Circulation: 77010
Founded in 1949

4362 **Construction Specifier: Member Directory Issue**
Construction Specifications Institute
990 Canal Center Plaza
Suite 300
Alexandria, VA 22314

703-684-0300
800-689-2900; Fax: 703-684-8436
csi@csinet.org
www.csinet.org

Eugene A Valentine, President
W Richard Cooper, VP

Roster of construction specifiers certified by the institute and approximately 17,200 members.
Cost: $203.00
Frequency: Annual/January
Circulation: 19500

4363 **Constructor: AGC Directory of Membership and Services Issue**
Associated General Contractors of America
333 John Carlyle Street
Sutie 200
Alexandria, VA 22314

703-548-3118; Fax: 703-548-3119
constructinfo@riagc.org
www.agc.org

Donald Scott, Production Manager
Michael Kennedy, General Counsel
Norman Walton, Treasurer

List of more than 8,500 member firms and 24,000 national associate member firms engaged in building, highway, heavy, industrial, municipal utilities and railroad construction.
Frequency: Annual/July
Circulation: 34,000
ISSN: 0162-6191

4364 **Directory of Architectural and Construction Information Resources**
Grey House Publishing
4919 Route 22
PO Box 56
Amenia, NY 12501

518-789-8700
800-562-2139; Fax: 845-373-6390
books@greyhouse.com
www.greyhouse.com
Facebook, Twitter

Richard Gottlieb, President
Leslie Mackenzie, Publisher

The leading desktop reference and preliminary research guide, featuring more than 10,000 building product manufacturers and their products.
194 Pages
Frequency: Annual
ISBN: 1-519250-00-0

4365 **Directory of Building Codes & Regulations**
National Conference of States on Building Codes
505 Huntmar Park Dr
Herndon, VA 20170-5103

703-437-0100
800-362-2633; Fax: 703-481-3596

Robert Wible, Executive Director
Carolyn Fitch, Membership Services

This directory is a comprehensive guide to the building codes and regulations adopted and enforced in each of the 50 states, Puerto Rico, the District of Columbia, and 53 major U. S. cities in 14 different code areas - building, mechanical, plumbing, electrical, energy conservation, gas, fire prevention, life safety, accessibility, one & two family, modular, ventilation/indoor air quality, manufactured home installation, and elevator.
Cost: $78.00
Frequency: Annual

4366 **Dodge Construction Analysis System**
McGraw-Hill
1221 Avenue of the Americas
New York, NY 10020-1095

212-512-2000
800-393-6343; Fax: 212-512-3840
www.mcgraw-hill.com

Harold W McGraw III, CEO
Joseph A Scott, National Marketing Director

This database lists over 4 million time series for construction projects involving more than 200 structural types.

4367 **Dodge DataLine**
McGraw-Hill
1221 Avenue of the Americas
New York, NY 10020-1095

212-512-2000
800-393-6343; Fax: 212-512-3840
www.mcgraw-hill.com

Harold W McGraw III, CEO
Joseph A Scott, National Marketing Director

Dodge DataLine offers the most advanced searching of project leads in the industry. You can search the largest U.S. database of 500,000+ active construction projects.
Frequency: Daily

4368 **ENR Top 100 Construction Managers**
Engineering News Record/McGraw Publishing
2 Penn Plaza
9th Floor
New York, NY 10121-2298

212-512-2000
888-877-8208; Fax: 212-512-4039
support@construction.com
www.construction.com

Gary Graizzaro, Plant Manager
John J Kosowatz, Managing Editor
William G. Krizan, Assistant Managing Editor

List of the top 100 leading construction and program management firms with the largest dollar volume in new construction management contracts on a for-fee only basis and an at-risk basis in the previous year.
Cost: $250.00
Frequency: Annual/June
Circulation: 90000

4369 **ENR Top 400 Contractors Sourcebook**
Engineering News Record/McGraw Publishing
2 Penn Plaza
9th Floor
New York, NY 10121-2298

212-512-2000
888-877-8208; Fax: 212-512-4039

support@construction.com
www.construction.com

Gary Graizzaro, Plant Manager
Joann Gonchar, Associate Editor
William G. Krizan, Assistant Managing Editor
Debra K. Rubin, Managing Senior Editor

Market analysis rankings of the largest U.S.-based general contractors in eight major industry sectors: general building, transportation, manufacturing, industrial process, petroleum, power, environmental and telecommunications.
Cost: $85.00
112 Pages

4370 **ENR Top 600 Specialty Contractors Issue**
Engineering News Record/McGraw Hill
2 Penn Plaza
9th Floor
New York, NY 10121-2298

212-512-2000; Fax: 212-512-4039
support@construction.com
www.construction.com

Gary Graizzaro, Plant Manager
John J Kosowatz, Managing Editor

Lists of the 600 largest US specialty subcontractors with sub-lists of top firms in mechanical contracting, electrical, excavation-foundation, steel erection, rofing, sheet metal, demolition-wrecking, glazing curtain wall, masonry, concrete, utilities, painting, wall/ceiling and asbestos abatement.
Cost: $350.00
Frequency: Annual/September
Circulation: 90000

4371 **ENR Top Owners Sourcebook**
Engineering News Record/McGraw Hill
2 Penn Plaza
9th Floor
New York, NY 10121-2298

212-512-2000; Fax: 212-512-4039
www.construction.com

Gary Graizzaro, Plant Manager
John J Kosowatz, Managing Editor

List of 700 companies that had the largest expenditures for building construction and building acquisition in the previous year.
Cost: $300.00
Frequency: Annual/December
Circulation: 90000

4372 **Electrical Construction Materials Directory**
Underwriters Laboratories
333 Pfingsten Rd
Northbrook, IL 60062-2096

847-412-0136
877-854-3577; Fax: 847-272-8129
cec@us.ul.com
www.UL.com

Keith E Williams, CEO
John Drengenberg, Manager Consumer Affairs

Companies that have qualified to use the UL listing mark or classification marking on or in connection with products which have been found to be in compliance with UL's requirements.
Cost: $30.00
Frequency: Annual
Printed in on glossy stock

4373 **GreenSpec Directory**
BuildingGreen
122 Birge Street
Suite 30
Brattleboro, VT 05301-6703

802-257-7300; Fax: 802-257-7304
www.buildinggreen.com

Alex Wilson, Owner
Nadav Malin, Editor
Daniel Woodbury, Publisher
Charlotte Snyder, Circulation Manager

Information on more than 1,850 green building products carefully screened by the editors of Environmental Building News. Directory listings cover more than 250 categories, from access flooring to zero-VOC paints. Included are product descriptions, environmental characteristics and considerations, and manufacturer contact information with internet addresses.
Cost: $89.00
464 Pages
ISBN: 1-929884-15-X

4374 **LBM Industry Buyer's Guide**
National Lumber & Building Material Dealers Assn.
2025 M St NW
Suite 800
Washington, DC 20036-3309

202-367-1169
800-634-8645; Fax: 202-367-2169
membersupport@dealer.org
www.dealer.org
Facebook, Twitter, LinkedIn

Jonathan M. Paine, CAE, President & CEO
Ben Gann, VP, Legislative & Political Affairs
Frank Moore, Regulatory Counsel
Kiersten Kochanowski, Membership & Operations
Corie Stretton, Event Manager

A platform for dealers and consumers to search for products and services provided by NLBMDA's preferred vendors to the LBM industry.
6000 Members
Founded in 1917

4375 **Manufacturers & Services Council Directory**
National Lumber & Building Material Dealers Assn.
2025 M St NW
Suite 800
Washington, DC 20036-3309

202-367-1169
800-634-8645; Fax: 202-367-2169
membersupport@dealer.org
www.dealer.org
Facebook, Twitter, LinkedIn

Jonathan M. Paine, CAE, President & CEO
Ben Gann, VP, Legislative & Political Affairs
Frank Moore, Regulatory Counsel
Kiersten Kochanowski, Membership & Operations
Corie Stretton, Event Manager

A directory of NLBMDA preferred providers.
6000 Members
Founded in 1917

4376 **MasterFormat**
Construction Specifications Institute
110 South Union Street
Suite 100
Alexandria, VA 22314-3351

800-689-2900; Fax: 703-236-4600
csi@csinet.org
www.csinet.org
Facebook, Twitter, LinkedIn, YouTube

Paul R. Bertram Jr., President
Gregory J. Markling, President-Elect
Mitch A. Miller, Vice President
Casey F. Robb, Vice President
Lane J. Beougher, Secretary

The reengineering of this industry standard sets the present and future pace for organizing construction communication. MasterFormat 2004 Edition simplifies the process of determining where specific subject matter is located.
Cost: $159.00
516 Pages
ISBN: 0-976239-90-6
Founded in 2004

4377 **NRCMA Membership Directory**
National Railroad Construction & Maintenance Assoc
500 New Jersey Ave NW
Suite 400
Washington, DC 20001-2065

202-715-2919; Fax: 202-318-0867
info@nrcma.org
www.nrcma.org
Facebook, Twitter, LinkedIn

Chuck Baker, President
Matt Ginsberg, Director of Operations
Jim Perkins, Chairman
Terry Benton, Vice Chairman

A book of the railroad contracting industry, lists all members of the NRC, including their technical specialities ang geographic regions of operation.
Cost: $35.00
Frequency: Free to Members

4378 **Public Works Manual**
Hanley-Wood
426 S Westgate Street
Addison, IL 60101

630-543-0870
800-524-2364; Fax: 630-543-3112
www.pwmag.com

William D Palmer Jr., Editor-in-Chief
Amara Rozgus, Managing Editor
Sharon Glorioso, Associate Editor
Colette Palait, Editorial Assistant

Over 4,000 manufacturers and distributors of equipment, materials, services, computers and software used in the design, construction and maintenance of streets and highways, water systems, wastewater and solid wastes processing and recreation areas.
Cost: $30.00
Frequency: Annual
Circulation: 55000

4379 **Roofing/Siding/Insulation: Trade Directory Issue**
PO Box 1269
Skokie, IL 60076-8269

847-763-9594; Fax: 847-763-9694
roofingsidinginsulation@halldata.com
www.rsimag.com

Thomas Skernivitz, Editor
Jacke Lyttle, Publisher

Lists thousands of contractors, manufacturers and distributors of equipment and products.
Cost: $20.00
Frequency: Annual
Circulation: 22,000

4380 **STAFDA Directory**
Specialty Tools & Fasteners Distributors Assn
500 Elm Grove Rd.
Suite 210
Elm Grove, WI 53122

262-784-4774
800-352-2981; Fax: 262-784-5059
info@stafda.org
www.stafda.org
Facebook, LinkedIn

Mike Kangas, President
Kramer Darragh, Vice President

This is a Who's Who of the industry. Listings include who makes over 900 different products: nearly 2,570 member addresses and contacts; brand names; fax numbers: 800 numbers; e-mail;

www; and a recap of association services and activities.
500 Pages
Frequency: Annual
Circulation: 4500

4381 **Salem Press Online Platform**
Grey House Publishing
4919 Route 22
PO Box 56
Amenia, NY 12501

800-221-1592; Fax: 201-968-0511
csr@salempress.com
online.salempress.com

The new Salem Press platform houses more than 500 titles including all of Salem's Health, Literature, History and Science titles in addition to select titles from the Grey House Publishing and H.W. Wilson product lines. Online access is free with each print purchase and includes an unlimited number of simultaneous users and remote access.

4382 **Scaffold Industry Association Directory & Handbook**
Scaffold Industry Association
400 Admiral Blvd.
Kansas City, MO 64106-1508

816-595-4860
info@saiaonline.org
www.scaffold.org
Facebook, Twitter, LinkedIn

Steve Smith, President
Marty Coughlin, President-Elect
Daryl Hare, Treasurer
Mike Russell, Secretary

The SIA Directory and Handbook contains complete membership information, company and individual listings. It also includes federal OSHA scaffold standards for general industry, construction and maritime, scaffold plank grading rules, map and listing of OSHA regional and area offices, scaffold standards for the state of California, glossary of scaffold terms, illustrations of various types of scaffolds, and codes of safe practices.
Cost: $125.00
355 Pages
Circulation: 5000

4383 **Source: Buyer's Guide & Dealer Directory**
Northeastern Retail Lumber Association
585 N Greenbush Rd
Rensselaer, NY 12144-9615

518-286-1010
800-292-6752; Fax: 518-286-1755
rferris@nrla.org
www.nrla.org
Facebook

Rita Ferris, President
Tony Shepley, Chair
Jon Hallgren, Chair Elect
Jonas Kelly, Vice Chair

The industry's guide to names, addresses, phone numbers, fax numbers, and product lines of companies that comprise the independent retail lumber dealers of the Northeast.
Cost: $89.95
Frequency: Annual

4384 **Sourcebook**
Ray Publishing
P.O.Box 992
Morrison, CO 80465-0992

303-467-1776; Fax: 303-467-1777
www.compositesworld.com

Judith Hazen, Publisher
Mike Mussleman, Managing Editor

A comprehensive directory of composites industry suppliers, manufacturers and service companies for the entire composites industry.
60 Pages
Founded in 1993
Printed in 4 colors on glossy stock

4385 **Store Fixture Buyers' Guide and Membership Directory**
Nat'l Association of Store Fixture Manufacturers
3595 Sheridan
Suite 200
Hollywood, FL 33322

954-893-7300; Fax: 954-893-7500
nasfm@nasfm.org
www.nasfm.org
Facebook, Twitter, LinkedIn

Jo Rossman, Senior Editor
Klein Merriman, Executive Director

This buyers' guide features the products and services of some 400 store fixture manufacturers. Contact information, plant size, number of employees, and company descriptions of all member manufacturers, plant listings by location, and contact and company information on products and services of 200 supplier members is included.
Cost: $175.00
80 Pages
Frequency: Free to Members

4386 **Sweets Directory**
Grey House Publishing/McGraw Hill Construction
1221 Avenue of the Americas
New York, NY 10020-1095

212-512-2000
800-442-2258; Fax: 212-512-3840
www.mcgraw-hill.com
Facebook, Twitter

Harold W McGraw III, CEO

The leading desktop reference and preliminary research guide, featuring more than 10,000 building product manufacturers and their products.
Cost: $145.00
950 Pages
Frequency: Annual
ISBN: 1-592378-50-1
Founded in 1906

4387 **ThomasNet**
Thomas Publishing Company, LLC
User Services Department
5 Penn Plaza
New York, NY 10001

212-695-0500
800-699-9822; Fax: 212-290-7362
contact@thomaspublishing.com
www.thomasnet.com
Facebook, Twitter, LinkedIn

Carl Holst-Knudsen, President
Robert Anderson, VP, Planning
Mitchell Peipert, VP, Finance
Ivy Molofsky, VP, Human Resources

A way to reach qualified businesses that list their company information on ThomasNet.com. Detailed profiles promote their products, services, capabilities and brands carried. The ThomasNet.com web site is the most up-to-date compilation of 650,000 North American manufacturers, distributors, and service companies in 67,000 industrial categories.
Founded in 1898

Industry Web Sites

4388 **http://gold.greyhouse.com**
G.O.L.D Grey House OnLine Databases

Grey House Publishing's online database platform, GOLD, offers Quick Search, Keyword Search and Expert Search for most business sectors including architecture, building and construction markets. The GOLD platform makes finding the information you need quick and easy - whether you're a novice searcher or an experienced database user. All of Grey House's directory products are available for subscription on the GOLD platform.

4389 **www.abc.org**
Associated Builders and Contractors

National trade association representing about 23,000 contractors, subcontractors, material suppliers and related firms from across the country and from all specialties in the construction industry.

4390 **www.acdi.net**
Associated Construction Distributors International

Cooperative association of independently owned and locally opearated distributors of specialty construction products and equipment.

4391 **www.acesystems.com**
AEC Systems International/Penton Media

Focuses on Internet/Intranet for the design, engineering and construction industries.

4392 **www.aednet.org**
Associated Equipment Distributors

International trade association supporting companies specializing in eqipment used in construction, mining, forestry, power generation, agriculture and industrial applications.

4393 **www.agc.org**
Associated General Contractors of America

The voice of the construction industry, an organization of qualified construction contractors and industry related companies dedicated to skill, integrity and responsibility.

4394 **www.aibd.org**
American Institute of Building Design

Our members consist of professional building designers and architects, who have for the most part chosen residential design as the focus of their practice.

4395 **www.aisc.org**
American Institute of Steel Construction

Serving the structural steel industry in the US. Our purpose is to promote the use of structural steel through research activities, market development, education, codes and specifications, technical assistance, quality certifacation and standardization.

4396 **www.anodizing.org**
Aluminum Anodizers Council

Represents the interests of aluminum anodizers worldwide and is the principal trade organization for the anodizing industry in North America. It promotes the interests of its members through technical exchange, ongoing education, statistical data, market promotion, and industry representation.

4397 **www.apwa.net**
American Public Works Association

International educational and professional association of public agencies, private sector companies, and individuals dedicated to providing high quality public works goods and services. AWA provides a forum in which public works professionals' competency, increase the performance of their agencies and companies, and bring important public works-related topics to public attention in local, state, and federal areas. Mailing list for members only.

4398 **www.aspenational.org**
American Society of Professional Estimators
Serving the construction estimators by providing education, fellowship and opportunity for professional development. ASPE represents individual members involved in the construction industry.

4399 **www.asphaltinstitute.org**
Asphalt Institute
Conducts education, research and engineering services related to asphaltic products; conducts seminars and sells publications and videos on asphalt technology.

4400 **www.asphaltpavement.org**
National Asphalt Pavement Association
The only trade association that exclusively represents the interest s of the Hot Mix Asphalt producer and paving contractor on the national level with Congress, government agencies, and other national trade and business organizations.

4401 **www.automatedbuilder.com**
CMN Associates
Association of manufacturers and suppliers who have a product line that is of interest to the manufactured and pre-fabricated housing industry.

4402 **www.awci.org**
Association of the Wall and Ceiling Industries
Represents acoustics systems, ceiling systems, drywall systems, exterior insulation and finishing systems, fireproofing, flooring systems, insulation, and stucco contractors, suppliers and manufacturers and those in allied trades.

4403 **www.build.com**
Build.com
Providing consumers, contractors and industry professionals with a valuable resource of products, service and information related to the building and home improvement industry.

4404 **www.buildingstone.org**
Building Stone Institute
Quarries, fabricators, dealers, installers and restorers of all types of natural stone. Membership dues based on sales volume.

4405 **www.calredwood.org**
California Redwood Association
A trade association for redwood lumber producers.

4406 **www.cfma.org**
Construction Financial Management Association
Non-profit organization dedicated to serving the financial professional in the construction industry.

4407 **www.cisco.org**
Construction Industry Service Corporation
Labor management association that promotes union construction, union contractors and union apprenticeship programs throughout Northeastern Illinois.

4408 **www.coaa.org**
Construction Owners Association of America
To act as a focal point and voice for the interests of owners in construction. Comprised of a diverse group of men and women representing construction owners.

4409 **www.concretepumpers.com**
American Concrete Pumping Association
Provides education, insurance, marketing and much more to companies involved with the concrete pumping industry. Our dedication to the concrete pumping industry has led us to become a key part in the education of safety and business management to everyone involved, from the operators to the management.

4410 **www.construction.com**
McGraw-Hill Construction
McGraw-Hill Construction (MHC), part of The McGraw-Hill Companies, connects people and projects across the design and construction industry, serving owners, architects, engineers, general contractors, subcontractors, building product manufacturers, suppliers, dealers, distributors and adjacent markets.

4411 **www.csinet.org**
Construction Specifications Institute
Our mission is to continuously improve the process of creating and sustaining the built environment. We do this by facilitating communication among all those involved in that process.

4412 **www.demolitionassociation.com**
National Association of Demolition Contractors
Representing the demolition industry including demolition contractors, formed to foster goodwill and the exchange of ideas with the public, governmental agencies and contractors engaged in the demolition industry. Also for manufacturers or suppliers of demolition equipment, supplies and services.

4413 **www.dfi.org**
Deep Foundations Institute
We can best be described as being a technical association of firms and individuals in the deep foundations and related industry. DFI covers the gamut of deep foundation construction and earth retention systems.

4414 **www.ebmda.org**
Eastern Building Material Dealers Association
Established to foster, protect and promote the welfare and best interest of its members engaged in the retail lumber and building materials business.

4415 **www.floorbiz.com**
Floor Biz
Internet's leading creator and operator of a vertical business community for the flooring industry. FloorBiz leverages the interactive features and global reach of the Internet to create a multi-national, targeted business community vertically integrated from consumer to manufacturer.

4416 **www.gobrick.com**
Brick Industry Association
A national trade association representing distributors and manufacturers of clay brick and suppliers of related products and services.

4417 **www.greyhouse.com**
Grey House Publishing
Authoritative reference directories for most business sectors including architecture, building and construction markets. Users can search the online databases with varied search criteria allowing for custom searches by product category, geographic area, sales volume, keyword, subject and more. Full Grey House catalog and online ordering also available.

4418 **www.homeimprovement.com**
Hometime
Hometime is a home-improvement television show broadcast on public television, The Learning Channel and in syndication. A comprehensive online resource for your remodeling and home-improvement needs.

4419 **www.iccsafe.org**
International Code Council
Formerly known as the Building Officials and Code Administrators International, we publish codes that establish minimum performance requirements for all aspects of the construction industry.

4420 **www.icpi.org**
Interlocking Concrete Pavement Institute
Self governed, self funded, autonomous association representing the interlocking concrete pavement industry in North America. Membership is open to producers, contractors, suppliers, consultants and others who have an interest in the industry. As an industry voice, the membership represents a majority of concrete paver production in North America.

4421 **www.manufacturedhousing.org**
Manufactured Housing Institute
National trade organization representing all segments of the factory built housing industry. MHI serves its membership by providing industry research, promotion, education, and government relations programs, and by building and facilitating consensus within the industry.

4422 **www.masoncontractors.org**
Mason Contractors Association of America
Through strong programs, publications and services, the MCAA avtively promotes the interests of its members. By promoting the use of masonry, influencing resonable codes and standards, work force development and public affairs, the association advances the use of masonry.

4423 **www.masonrysociety.org**
Masonry Society
Dedicated to the advancement of scientific engineering, architechtural and construction knowledge of masonry. Promotes research and education and disseminates information on masonry materials, design, construction. Publishes a newsletter.

4424 **www.mbinet.org**
Modular Building Institute
Serving the commercial factory-built buildings industry on an international scale. Our regular members are manufacturers and dealers of commercial modular structures, while our associate members are companies supplying building components, services, and financing.

4425 **www.naamm.org**
Nat'l Assn of Architectural Metal Manufacturers
The largest of four operating divisions of the National Association of Architectural Metal Manufacturers. HMMA is a group composed of companies that manufacture, distribute and promote the use of hollow metal door and frame products.

4426 **www.nahb.org**
National Association of Home Builders
Represents the interests of concrete, log, modular, and panel manufacturers, builders, and suppliers.

4427 **www.nam.org**
National Association of Manufacturers
The nation's largest industrial trade association, representing small and large manufacturers in every industrial sector and in all 50 states.

4428 **www.nari.org**
National Association of the Remodeling Industry
A voice in the remodeling industry, NARI has an exclusive, encompassing purpose to; establish and maintain a firm commitment to developing

and sustaining programs that expand and unite the remodeling industry; to ensure the industry's growth and security; to encourage ethical conduct, sound business practices and professionalism in the remodeling industry; and to present NARI as the recognized authority in the remodeling industry.

4429 **www.nationalslag.org**
National Slag Association
Members are processors of iron and steel slags for use as a aggregate in construction and manufacturing applications.

4430 **www.nawic.org**
National Association of Women in Construction
Founded by 16 women working in the construction industry. The founders organized NAWIC to create a support network for women in construction.

4431 **www.ncac.com**
National Council of Acoustical Consultants
Strives to safeguard the interests of professional acoustical consulting firms. Managing physics and psychoacoustics to provide optimum listning environments.

4432 **www.ncma.org**
National Concrete Masonry Association
Manufacturers of concrete masonry products and suppliers of products to the industry. Offers a variety of technical services and design aids through publications, computer programs, slide presentations and technical training.

4433 **www.ncsbcs.org**
National Conference of States on Building Codes
Serving as a forum for the interchange of information and provides technical services, education and training to our members to enhance the public's social, economic well-being through safe, durable, accessible and efficient buildings.

4434 **www.necanet.org**
National Electrical Contractors Association
Represents a segment of the construction market comprised of over 70,000 electrical firms.

4435 **www.nrcma.org**
National Railroad Construction & Maintenance Assn
Railroad construction and maintenance contractors, engineering firms, manufacturing suppliers and professional associate firms.

4436 **www.nrla.org**
Northeastern Retail Lumber Association
A resource for industry members, consumers, and public officials in dependent lumber and building material suppliers and associated businesses in New York and the six New England states.

4437 **www.nrmca.org**
National Ready Mixed Concrete Association
Our mission is to provide exceptional value for our members by responsibly representing and serving the entire ready mixed concrete industry through leadership, promotion, education and partnering; to ensure ready mixed concrete is the building material of choice.

4438 **www.nssga.org**
National Stone, Sand & Gravel Association
Represents the crushed stone, sand and gravel — or aggregate — industries. Our members account for 90 percent of the crushed stone and 70 percent of the sand and gravel produced annually in the US.

4439 **www.ntma.com**
National Terrazzo and Mosaic Association
Full service nonprofit trade association headquartered in Northern Virginia. The association establishes national standards for all terrazzo floor and wall systems and provides complete specifications, color plates and general information to architects and designers at no cost.

4440 **www.nuca.com**
National Utility Contractors Association
A national association that provides a forum for continuing education and promotes effective public policy, through its grassroots network, to protect and enhance your industry.

4441 **www.oikos.com**
Oikos
Devoted to serving professionals whose work promotes sustainable design and construction. Oikos is a Greek word meaning house. Oikos serves as the root for two English words: ecology and economy.

4442 **www.opcmia.org**
Operative Plasterers' & Cement Masons' Int'l Assn
Represents and trains plasterers and cement masons for the purpose of protecting and promoting the quality of our industry and the livelihood of our members.

4443 **www.opei.org**
Outdoor Power Equipment Institute
International trade association whose members are manufacturers of powered lawn and garden maintenance products, components and attachment supplies, as well as industry related services.

4444 **www.pbmdf.com**
Composite Panel Association
The association of North American wood and agrifiber based particle board and medium density fiberboard producers, to broaden the base of participation in industry outreach programs.

4445 **www.pci.org**
Precast Prestressed Concrete Institute
Dedicated to fostering greater understanding and use of precast and prestressed concrete, maintains a full staff of technical and marketing specialists.

4446 **www.perlite.org**
Perlite Institute
International trade association which establishes product standards and specifications, and which encourages the development of new product uses through research.

4447 **www.pfi-institute.org**
Pipe Fabrication Institute
Members are companies producing sophisticated high temperature, high pressure piping systems that employ specialists from the United Association of Journeymen & Apprentices of the Plumbing & Pipe Fitting Industry. We exist solely for the purpose of ensuring a level of quality in the pipe fabrication indusrty that is without compromise.

4448 **www.piledrivers.org**
Pile Driving Contractors Association
Organization of pile driving contractors that advocates the increased use of driven piles for deep foundations and earth retention systems. To do this we promote the use of driven pile solutions in all cases where they are effective, support educational programs for engineers on the design and efficiency of driven piles and for contractors on improving installation procedures. We also give contractors a larger voice in establishing procedures and standards for pile installation and design.

4449 **www.pipefitters537.org**
American Pipe Fittings Association
Trade association for any domestic corporation, firm or individual engaged in manufacture in the US or Canada of piping components and accessories, including pipe hangers and supports.

4450 **www.psai.org**
Portable Sanitation Association International
International trade association that represents firms engaged in the leasing, renting selling and manufacturing of portable sanitation equipment, services and supplies for construction, recreation, emergency and other uses. devoted to the proper handling of human waste by the most modern, sanitary means, giving the greatest concern to the preservation of an unspoiled environment.

4451 **www.reedconstructiondata.com**
First Source Online
Provides A/E/C professionals free access to the industry's most comprehensive, up-to-date library of formatted commercial building product information, plus manufacturers' addresses, telephone numbers, trade names, and regional distributors.

4452 **www.rfci.com**
Resilient Floor Covering Institute
Industry trade association of North American manufacturers who produce resilient flooring products. Associate members of RFCI supply raw materials to the industry and manufacture installation and maintenance products.

4453 **www.roofcoatings.org**
Roof Coatings Manufacturers Association
Represents the interests for manufacturers of cold applied roof coatings, cements and waterproofing agents, as well as the suppliers of products, equipment, and services to and for the industry. Currently RCMA boasts more than 70 member companies.

4454 **www.rubberpavements.org**
Rubber Pavements Association
Dedicated to encouraging greater usage of high quality, cost effective asphalt pavements containing recycled tire rubber. Conducts national and international seminars.

4455 **www.saiaonline.org**
Scaffold Industry Association
Promotes scaffold safety and education through its publications, conventions, tradeshows and training programs. Marketing of your product is available through the monthly magazine, convention and trade show.

4456 **www.sgcc.org**
Safety Glazing Certification Council
Provides for the certification of safety glazing materials, comprised of safety glazing manufacturers and other parties concerned with public safety. SGCC is managed by a board of directors comprised of representatives from the safety glazing industry and the public interest sector.

4457 **www.sips.org**
Structural Insulated Panel Association
A trade association representing manufacturers, suppliers, fabricators, distributors, design professionals and builders committed to providing quality structural insulated panels for all segments of the construction industry.

4458 **www.spri.org**
Single Ply Roofing Institute

SPRI represents sheet membrane and related component suppliers in the commercial roofing industry.

4459 **www.stafda.org**
Specialty Tools & Fasteners Distributors Assn

International trade association composed of distributors and manufacturers and rep agents of light construction, industrial and related products. Members also include publishers of industry press serving the construction and industrial trades.

4460 **www.stanyc.com**
Subcontractors Trade Association

Members are specialty and supply companies in the construction industry. Our goal is to improve the economic well being of our members through representation, support and assistance through the process of legislation, legal action, public relations, education and other public information programs.

4461 **www.steelwindows.com**
Steel Window Institute

For United States manufacturers of windows made from hot-rolled, solid steel sections and such related products as castings, trim, mechanical operators, screens and moldings.

4462 **www.sweets.construction.com**
McGraw Hill Construction

In depth product information that lets you find, compare, select, specify and make purchase decisions in the industrial product marketplace.

4463 **www.swensongranite.com**
Swenson Granite Works

Family owned business that has been quarrying and cutting granite in New England since 1883.

4464 **www.tcaainc.org**
Tile Contractors Association of America

TCAA is an organization representing the finest union tile contractors in the United States. Founded in 1903, it is the only association which serves the needs of the union tile contractor.

4465 **www.tfguild.org**
Timber Framers Guild of North America

Dedicated to establishing training programs for dedicated timber framers, disseminating information about timber framing and timber frame building design, displaying the art of timber framing to the public, and generally serving as a center of timber framing information for the professional and general public alike.

4466 **www.thebluebook.com**
Contactors Register

Regional construction directories in most major markets throughout the US. Provides easy online access to continually updated information for each of our regional editions.

4467 **www.tile-assn.com**
National Tile Contractors Association

Serving every segment of the industry, and is recognized as the largest and most respected tile contractors association in the world.

4468 **www.tilt-up.org**
Tilt-up Concrete Association

Represents builders, engineers and suppliers involved with tilt-up concrete construction. Makes a continuing and increasingly important contribution to the success of each member through the most imaginative and efficient application of every appropriate skill, tool and service of the association.

4469 **www.wbma.org**
Western Building Material Association

Regional trade association serving building material dealers throughout the states of Alaska, Idaho, Montana, Oregon and Washington and a federated association of the National Lumber and Building Material Dealers Association.

4470 **www.wfca.org**
World Floor Covering Association

Shapes and defines public policy through agressive, national legislative advocacy on behalf of our members. Provides continuing professional educational programming through educational forums and the Regional Installation and Training Education (RITE) program.

4471 **www.windowanddoor.com**
WindowDoor.net

Anyone who is interested in window and door products can find the latest information on products, components and how-to information here.

Associations

4472 **AACC International**
3340 Pilot Knob Road
St. Paul, MN 55121

651-454-7250
800-328-7560; Fax: 651-454-0766
aacc@scisoc.org
www.aaccnet.org
Facebook, Twitter, LinkedIn, Pinterest

Robert L. Cracknell, President
Lydia Tooker Midness, Chair
Laura M. Hansen, President Elect
Dave L. Braun, Treasurer

Formerly the American Association of Cereal Chemists, a non-profit organization of members who are specialists in the use of cereal grains in foods.
Founded in 1915

4473 **AOAC International**
2275 Research Blvd
Suite 300
Rockville, MD 20850-3250

301-924-7077
800-379-2622; Fax: 301-924-7089
aoac@aoac.org
www.aoac.org
Facebook, Twitter, LinkedIn

David Schmidt, Executive Director
Palmer Orlandi, Jr., Chief Science Officer
Jonathan Goodwin, Chief Human Resources Officer
Alicia Meiklejohn, Dir., Business Dev. & Governance
Dawn Frazier, Sr. Dir., Mem., Marketing & Comm.

Serves the communities of analytical sciences by providing the tools and porcesses necessary for community stakeholders to collaborate and through, consensus building, develop fit for purpose methods and services for assuring quality measurments.
3700 Members
Founded in 1884

4474 **ASM International**
9639 Kinsman Road
Materials Park, OH 44073-0002

440-338-5151
800-336-5152; Fax: 440-338-4634
memberservicecenter@asminternational.org
www.asminternational.org
Facebook, Twitter, LinkedIn

Zi-Kui Liu, President
Diana Essock, Vice President
Raymond V. Fryan, Treasurer
William T. Mahoney, Secretary & CEO

The society for materials engineers and scientists, a worldwide network dedicated to advancing industry, technology and applications of metals and materials. ASM provides information references, education, research and international events.
30K Members
Founded in 1913

4475 **Acrylonitrile Group**
1250 Connecticut Ave NW
Suite 700
Washington, DC 20036-2657

202-419-1500; Fax: 202-659-8037
angroup@regnet.com

Robert J Fensterheim, Group Executive Director, President

Affiliated with the Synthetic Organic Chemical Manufacturers, (TAG) was formed under the Chemical manufacturers Association to do research. TAG represents producers and users of the industrial chemical used to make plastics, fibers and synthetic rubber products.
Founded in 1960

4476 **Adhesion Society**
7101 Wisconsin Avenue
Suite 990
Bethesda, MD 20814

301-986-9700; Fax: 301-986-9795
Adhesionsociety@ascouncil.org
www.adhesionsociety.org
Twitter, LinkedIn

Alfred Crosby, President
Joelle Frechette, Vice President
Chris Campbell, Treasurer
Aaron Forster, Secretary

Supports all those who are involved in adhesion's role in coatings, compostie materials, biological tissues and bonded structures.
400 Members
Founded in 1978

4477 **Alkylphenols and Ethoxylates Research Council**
1250 Connecticut Ave NW
Suite 700
Washington, DC 20036

202-419-1500
866-273-7262; Fax: 202-659-8037
info@aperc.org
www.alkylphenol.org

Robert J Fensterheim, Executive Director

Monitors regulatory developments affecting manufacturers in the chemical industry
5 Members
Founded in 1998

4478 **Alliance for Responsible Atmospheric Policy**
2111 Wilson Blvd
Suite 850
Arlington, VA 22201

703-243-0344; Fax: 703-243-2874
fay@alliancepolicy.org
www.alliancepolicy.org
Twitter

John Hurst, Chair
Nanette Lockwood, Vice Chair
Dave Calabrese, Treasurer
John Gibbons, Secretary

Made up of companies who rely on alternatives to ozone depleting chlorofluorocarbons(CFCs). Theses alternatives are HCPCs and HFCs, used primarily as refrigerants, speciality solvents, agents for foamed plastics.
300 Members
Founded in 1980

4479 **American Association Textile Chemists and Colorists**
PO Box 12215
Research Triangle Park, NC 27709-2215

919-549-8141
800-360-5380; Fax: 919-549-8933
www.aatcc.org
Facebook, Twitter, LinkedIn, Youtube

Diana Wyman, Executive VP
Debra Hibbard, Executive Assistant
Maria Thiry, Dir., Membership & Communications
Amy Holland, Director, Business Services
Angela Jabara, Director, Education

Supports all those working with colorants and chemical finishes for textile and related industries.
3000 Members

4480 **American Association for Clinical Chemistry**
900 Seventh Street, NW
Suite 400
Washington, DC 20001

202-857-0717
800-892-1400; Fax: 202-887-5093
executiveoffice@aacc.org
www.aacc.org
Facebook, Twitter, LinkedIn, YouTube

Janet B. Kreizman, Chief Executive Officer

AACC is an international scientific/medical society of clinical laboratory professionals, physicians, research scientists and other individuals involved with clinical chemistry and other clinical laboratory science related disciplines.
Founded in 1948

4481 **American Association for Crystal Growth**
10922 Main Range Trail
Littleton, CO 80127

303-539-6907
888-506-1271; Fax: 303-600-5144
AACG@comcast.net
www.crystalgrowth.org

Mariya Zhuravleva, President
Joan Redwing, VP
Luis Zepeda-Ruiz, Treasurer
Merry Koschan, Secretary

Provides support for all professionals in the field of crystal and crystal growth.

4482 **American Association of Bioanalysts**
906 Olive Street
Suite 1200
Saint Louis, MO 63101-1448

314-241-1445; Fax: 314-241-1449
aab@aab.org
www.aab.org
Facebook

Mark S Birenbaum PhD, Executive Director

Professional association whose members are clinical laboratory directors, owners, supervisors, managers, medical technologists, medical laboratory technicians, physician office laboratory technicians, and phlebotomists.
Founded in 1956

4483 **American Chemical Society**
1155 16th St NW
Washington, DC 20036

202-872-4600
800-227-5558; Fax: 202-872-4615
help@acs.org
www.acs.org
Facebook, Twitter, LinkedIn, Google+

Thomas Connelly, Jr., CEO
Kate Fryer, EVP, Membership & Society Services
John Sullivan, Chief Information Officer
Al Horvath, Chief Financial Officer
Flint Lewis, General Counsel

Self-governed individual membership organization that provides a range of opportunities for peer interaction and career development, regardless of professional or scientific interests.
15900 Members
Founded in 1876

4484 **American Chemistry Council**
700 Second St. NE
Washington, DC 20002

202-249-7000; Fax: 202-249-6100
www.americanchemistry.com
Facebook, Twitter, LinkedIn, Youtube

Chris Jahn, President & CEO
Raymond O'Bryan, CFO & CAO
Anne Womack Kolton, EVP, Communications

& Outreach
Allison Starmann, General Counsel & Corp. Secretary
Michael Walls, VP, Regulatory & Technical Affairs

Committed to improved environmental, health and safety performance through responsible care, common sense advocacy designed to address major public policy issues, health and environmental research and product testing.
190 Members

4485 American Coatings Association
1500 Rhode Island Ave Nw
Washington, DC 20005

202-462-6272; Fax: 202-462-8549
members@paint.org
www.paint.org
Facebook

Supports all those involved in the manufacturer of chemicals.
Founded in 1903

4486 American Coke & Coal Chemicals Institute
25 Massachusetts Ave NW
Suite 800
Washington, DC 20001

724-772-1167; Fax: 866-422-7794
information@accci.org
www.accci.org

David Ailor, President
Jania Deitch, Director, Administration
David Menotti, General Counsel
Formed by companies interested in establishing a forum to discuss and act upon issues of common concern to their industry. Today, ACCI represents 7 of the 8 independently owned and operated US merchant coke producers; several integrated steel companies which produce coke; and all 4 of the US and 1 Canadian coal chemical companies which refine coal tar. Nearly 50 companies contribute their knowledge and expertise to enhance the effectiveness of the Institute.
160 Members
Founded in 1944

4487 American College of Toxicology Annual Meeting
1821 Michael Faraday Drive
Suite 300
Reston, VA 20190

703-547-0875; Fax: 703-438-3113
www.actox.org
Facebook, Twitter, LinkedIn

Timothy McGovern, President
Florence Burleson, VP
Alan Brown, Treasurer
Patricia Ryan, Secretary

Multidisciplinary society composed of professionals having a common interest in toxicology. Our mission is to educate and lead professionals in industry, government and related areas of toxicology and actively promote the exchange of information and perspectives on the current status of safety assessment and the application of new developments in toxicology. Annual meeting,education courses, symposia and exhibits.
500 Members
Founded in 1979

4488 American Hydrogen Association
PO Box 4205
Mesa, AZ 85211

480-234-5070
webmaster@clean-air.org
www.clean-air.org
Facebook, YouTube

Roy McAlister, President
Kevin Kohnen, Vice President
Douglas Hawley, Secretary/Treasurer

Stimulates interest and helping to establish the renewable hydrogen energy economy.
Founded in 1966

4489 American Institute of Chemical Engineers
120 Wall Street
FL 23
New York, NY 10005-4020

212-591-7338
800-242-4363; Fax: 203-775-5177
www.aiche.org
Facebook, Twitter, LinkedIn

Monty Alger, President
Joseph Smith, Secretary
Rosemarie Wesson, Treasurer

A professional association of members that provide leadership in advancing the chemical engineering profession.
50000 Members
Founded in 1908

4490 American Institute of Chemists
315 Chestnut St
Philadelphia, PA 19106-2702

215-873-8224; Fax: 215-629-5224
info@theaic.org
www.theaic.org

David Manuta, President
E Ray McAfee, President Elect
E Gerry Meyer, Secretary
J Stephen Duerr, Treasurer
Jerry Jasinski, Chair

Supports all individual chemists and chemical engineers involved in the chemical industry.
Founded in 1923

4491 American Leather Chemists Association
1314 50th Street
Suite 103
Lubbock, TX 79412

806-744-1798; Fax: 806-744-1785
alca@leatherchemists.org
www.leatherchemists.org

Mike Bley, President
Joseph Hoefler, VP
Steven Lange, Editor
Carol Adcock, Executive Secretary

Group of leather chemists interested in the development of methods that could be utilized to standardize both the supply and application of the tanning agents utilized by the industry
500 Members
Founded in 1903

4492 American Society Biochemistry and Molecular Biology
11200 Rockville Pike
Suite 302
Rockville, MD 20852-3110

240-283-6600; Fax: 301-881-2080
asbmb@asbmb.org
www.asbmb.org
Facebook, Twitter, LinkedIn, YouTube, Google+

Barbara A Gordon, Executive Director
Toni Antalis, President
Wei Yang, Secretary
Joan Conaway, Treasurer

A professional and educational association for biochemists and molecular biologists which seeks to extend and utilize the fields of biochemistry and molecular biology.
13000 Members
Founded in 1906
Mailing list available for rent

4493 American Society for Mass Spectrometry
2019 Galisteo Street, Building I-1
Santa Fe, NM 87505

505-989-4517; Fax: 505-989-1073
www.asms.org
Facebook, Twitter, LinkedIn

Michael Easterling, Vice President
Carla Marshall-Waggett, Vicec President
Jessica Prenni, Secretary

Formed to promote and disseminate knowledge of mass spectrometry and allied topics. Members come from academic, industrial and govermental laboratories. Their interests include advancement of techniques and instrumentation in mass spectrometry, as well as fundamental research in chemistry, geology, biological sciences and physics.
3500 Members
Founded in 1969

4494 American Society for Neurochemistry
9037 Ron Den Lane
Windermere, FL 34786

407-909-9064; Fax: 407-876-0750
asnmanager@asneurochem.org
www.asneurochem.org

Sheilah Jewart, Executive Director
Karen Gottlieb, Conference Organizer

Organized by US, Canadian and Mexican members of the International Society for Neurochemistry and incorporated in the District of Columbia. Membership dues are $75/year.
1000 Members
Founded in 1969

4495 American Society of Brewing Chemists
3340 Pilot Knob Rd
St. Paul, MN 55121-2055

651-454-7250
800-328-7560; Fax: 651-454-0766
asbc@scisoc.org
www.asbcnet.org
Facebook, Twitter, LinkedIn, Pinterest

Christina Schoenberger, President
Christine S White, President-Elect
Chris D Powell, Vice President
Thomas H Shellhammer, Past President
Robert Christiansen, Secretary
700 Members
Founded in 1934

4496 Analytical, Life Science, and Diagnostics Association
500 Montgomery Street
Suite 400
Alexandria, VA 22314

703-647-6214; Fax: 703-647-6368
cstarke@alssa.org
thealda.org
Facebook, Twitter, LinkedIn

Bradley Gray, Chair
Patrick Kaltenbach, Vice Chair & Chair-Elect
Mike Copps, President & CEO

ALSSA is the primary trade association for companies that supply instruments, chemical reagents, consumables and software used for analysis and measurement in chemistry and the life sciences.

4497 **Association of Consulting Chemists and Chemical Engineers Inc.**
A C C & C E
P.O. Box 902
Murray Hill, NJ 07974-0902
908-464-3182; Fax: 908-464-3182
accce@chemconsult.org
www.chemconsult.org
J. Stephen Duerr, Executive Director
The only organization of its kind that attracts qualified technical consultants of all kinds who assist their clients in creating and using chemical knowledge and technology.
150 Members
Founded in 1928

4498 **Association of Defensive Spray Manufacturers**
906 Olive Street
Suite 1200
St Louis, MO 63101-1448
314-241-1445; Fax: 314-241-1449
Mark S Birenbaum, Executive Director
To permit manufacturers of non lethal chemical weapons to join together to promote the industry as well as to address safety, quality control, marketing and other issues relevant to the industry
6 Members
Founded in 1992

4499 **Association of Official Racing Chemists**
1021 Storrs Rd
Storrs, CT 06268
860-487-3755; Fax: 860-487-3756
www.aorc-online.org
Dennis Hill, Executive Director
The international membership consits of individuals concerned with detection of drugs in racing samples.
200 Members
Founded in 1947

4500 **Basic Acrylic Monomer Manufacturers**
17260 Vannes Court
Hamilton, VA 20158
540-751-2093; Fax: 540-751-2094
www.bamm.net
Elizabeth K Hunt, Executive Director
Addresses the issues facing the basic acrylates. Also represents manufacturers and importers of acrylic acid and its esters.
5 Members
Founded in 1986
Mailing list available for rent

4501 **Center for the Polyurethanes Industry**
700 Second St., NE
Washington, DC 20002
202-249-7000; Fax: 202-249-6100
polyurethane.americanchemistry.com
Facebook, Twitter
Chris Jahn, President/CEO
Allison Starmann, Corp. Secretary & General Counsel
Raymond J. O'Bryan, CFO/ Chief Administrative Officer
Ross Eisenberg, Vice President of Federal Affairs
Anne Womack Kolton, EVP, Communications & Outreach
CPI of the American Chemistry Council promotes the sustainable growth of the polyurethane industry, by identifying and managing issues that could impact the industry, in cooperation with user groups. Members are producers and distributors of chemicals and equipment used to make polyurethane and manufacture polyurethane products.

4502 **Chemical Coaters Association International**
5040 Old Taylor Mill Rd
PMB 13
Taylor Mill, KY 41015
859-356-1030
800-926-2848; Fax: 513-624-0601
www.ccaiweb.com
Anne Goyer, Executive Director
A technical and professional organization that provides information and training on surface coating technologies. Users and suppliers of industrial cleaners, paints, coatings, and equipment.
1000 Members
Founded in 1970
Mailing list available for rent

4503 **Chemical Development and Marketing Association (CDMA)**
330 N. Wabash Avenue
Suite 2200
Chicago, IL 60611
312-321-5145
800-232-5241; Fax: 312-673-6885
A forum for networking, learning and sharing best practices in business development and marketing for the chemical and allied industries. Keeps members informed on commercial/business development and marketing as well as industrial marketing research via its two meetings per year (spring and fall), seminars and business schools.
Founded in 1999

4504 **Chemical Fabrics and Film Association**
1300 Sumner Avenue
Cleveland, OH 44115-2851
216-241-7333; Fax: 216-241-0105
www.chemicalfabricsandfilm.com
International trade association representing manufacturers of polymer-based fabric and film products, used in the building and construction, automotive, fashion and many other industries.
40 Members
Founded in 1927

4505 **Chemical Heritage Foundation**
315 Chestnut St
Philadelphia, PA 19106
215-925-2222; Fax: 215-925-1954
info@chemheritage.org
www.chemheritage.org
Facebook, Twitter, LinkedIn, Pinterest
David Cole, President/CEO
Richard Bolte, Jr., Chair
An independent, nonprofit organization, CHF maintains major collections of instruments, fine art, photographs, papers, and books. We host conferences and lectures, support research, offer fellowships, and produce educational materials.
29 Members
Founded in 1992

4506 **Chemical Strategies Partnership**
423 Washington St
4th Floor
San Francisco, CA 94111
415-421-3405; Fax: 415-421-3304
www.chemicalstrategies.org
Jill Kauffman Johnson, Executive Director
Angeline Kung, Senior Associate
Aarthi Ananthanarayanan, Associate
Max Pike, Communications Associate
Mark Stoughton, Ph.D., Research Advisor
CSP seeks to reduce chemical use, waste, risks and cost through the transformation of the chemical supply chain by redefining the way chemicals are used and sold.
Founded in 1978
Mailing list available for rent

4507 **Chemtrec**
1300 Wilson Blvd
Arlington, VA 22209-2323
703-741-5500
800-262-8200; Fax: 703-741-6086
chemtrec@chemtrec.com
www.chemtrec.com
John Modine, Chief Executive
Daniel Chebat, Sr. Director, Sales & Marketing
Erika Palfrey, Dir., Technology & Info Management
Joe Milazzo, Director, Operations Center
Tim Oliva, Director, Financial Operations
A 24 hour emergency communication service center that helps fire fighters and emergency responders protect the public and helps shippers of hazardous materials comply with the US Department of Transportation regulations.
Founded in 1971

4508 **Chlorinated Paraffins Industry Association**
1250 Connecticut Ave NW
Suite 700
Washington, DC 20036
202-419-1500; Fax: 202-659-8037
info@regnet.com
www.regnet.com/cpia
Robert J Fensterheim, Executive Director
Composed of manufacturers, distributors, and users of chlorinated paraffins, used in lubricants, plastics and flame retardants.
Founded in 1970

4509 **Chlorine Chemistry Division of the American Chemistry Counsil**
700 Second St., NE
Washington, DC 20002
202-249-7000; Fax: 202-249-6100
chlorine.americanchemistry.com
Facebook, Twitter
Chris Jahn, President/CEO
Raymond J. O'Bryan, CFO & CAO
Anne Womack Kolton, EVP, Communications & Outreach
Allison Starmann, General Counsel & Corp. Secretary
Michael Walls, VP, Regulatory & Technical Affairs
This division represents major producers and users of chlorine in North America, working to promote and protect the sustainability of chlorine chemsitry processes, products and applications in accordance with the Responsible Care initiative.

4510 **Chlorine Free Products Association**
1304 S Main St
Algonquin, IL 60102-2757
847-658-6104; Fax: 847-658-3152
info@chlorinefreeproducts.org
www.chlorinefreeproducts.org
YouTube
Archie Beaton, Executive Director
A nonprofit association that's primary purpose is to promote total chlorine free policies, programs and technologies throughtout the world.

4511 **Chlorine Institute**
1300 Wilson Blvd
Suite 525
Arlington, VA 22209

703-894-4140; Fax: 703-894-4130
info@cl2.com
www.chlorineinstitute.org

Frank Reiner, President
Robyn Kinsley, VP, Transportation & Emergency
Robyn Brooks, VP Health, Environment & Safety
RaeAna Eiley, Coordinator, Communications
Cindy Kuranchie, Sr. Manager, Mem. Services/Outreach
Supports the chlo-alkali industry and serves the public by promoting the safe handling of chlorine and caustic materials.
204 Members
Founded in 1924

4512 **Color Pigments Manufacturers Association**
1850 M Street NW
Suite 730
Washington, DC 20036

202-465-4900; Fax: 202-296-8120
cpma@cpma.com
www.pigments.org

David Wawer, Executive Director
Tatiana Letcheva, Manager
An industry trade association representing color pigment companies in Canada, Mexico and the US. Represents small, medium, and large color pigments manufacturers accounting for 95% of the production of color pigments in North America
50 Members
Founded in 1925

4513 **Combustion Institute**
5001 Baum Blvd
Suite 644
Pittsburgh, PA 15213-1851

412-687-1366; Fax: 412-687-0340
office@combustioninstitute.org
www.combustioninstitute.org

Philippe Dagaut, President
Hai Wang, Vice President
Osamu Fujit, Vice President Section Affairs
Andreas Dreizler, Secretary
Derek Dunn-Rankin, Treasurer
International organizaton with sections in several foreign countries including Canada. A non profit, educational organization with the purpose of promoting and disseminating knowledge in the field of combustion science.
4000 Members
Founded in 1954

4514 **Consumer Specialty Products Association**
1667 K Street NW
Suite 300
Washington, DC 20006-2501

202-872-8110; Fax: 202-223-2636
Facebook, Twitter, LinkedIn, Google+

Stephen J Caldeira, President & CEO
Rick Peluso, Sr. Vice President & CFO
Nonprofit organization composed of many companies involved in the formulation, manufacture, testing and marketing of chemical specialty products. Its line includes disinfectants that kill germs in homes, hospitals and restaurants, candles and fragrances that eliminate odors, pest management products for home and garden, cleaning products and much more.
200 Members
Founded in 1914

4515 **Council for Chemical Research**
1120 Route 73
Suite 200
Mount Laurel, NJ 08054

856-439-0500; Fax: 856-439-0525
www.ccrhq.org
Facebook, LinkedIn

Dr. Jeffrey A Reimer, Chair
Dr. Eriv Lin, 1st Vice Chair
Dr. Jeff Robert, 2nd Vice Chair
Dr. Seth W. Snyder, President
Dr. Kelly O. Sullivan, Treasurer
Promotes cooperation in basic research and encourage high quality education in the chemical sciences and engineering. Membership represents industry, academia, and government.
200 Members
Founded in 1980

4516 **Council of Producers & Distributors of Agrotechnology**
1730 Rhode Island Avenue
Suite 812
Washington, DC 20036

202-386-7407; Fax: 202-386-7409
www.cpda.com

The voice of the generic pesticide, inert, adjuvant and surfactant manufacturer, as well as crop protection product formulators and distributors on federal legislative and regulatory issues affecting the crop protection industry.
56 Members
Founded in 1975

4517 **CropLife America**
1156 15th St NW
Suite 400
Washington, DC 20005-1752

202-296-1585; Fax: 202-463-0474
Info@croplifeamerica.org
www.croplifeamerica.org
Facebook, Twitter, LinkedIn, Youtube

Christopher Novak, President & CEO
Beau Greenwood, EVP, Gov. Relations & Pub. Affairs
Kellie Bray, Chief Of Staff
Genevieve O'Sullivan, VP, Communications & Marketing
Rachel Lattimore, EVP, Legal & General Counsel
A trade association of the manufacturers, formulators, and distributors of agricultural crop protection, pest control, and bitechnology products. Membership is composed of companies that produce, sell and distribute virtually all the active ingredients use in crop protection chemicals.
86 Members
Founded in 1933
Mailing list available for rent

4518 **Drug, Chemical & Associated Technologies Association**
One Union St
Suite 208
Robbinsville, NJ 08691-3162

609-208-1888
800-640-3228; Fax: 609-208-0599
info@dcat.org
www.dcat.org
Facebook, LinkedIn

Margaret Timony, Executive Director
Lauryn Kuna, Director, Membership
Miriam O'Donnell, Director, Project Integration
Patricia Van Arnum, Editorial Director
Erin Sanders, Sr. Communications/Tech. Specialist
The not for profit, member supported business development association whose membership is comprimsed of companies that manufacture, distribute or provide services to the pharmaceutical, chemical, nutritional and related industries.
350 Members
Founded in 1890

4519 **Embalming Chemical Manufacturers**
1370 Honeyspot Road Ext
Stratford, CT 06615-7115
Works to develop scientific, technological, and economic data about safety issues of the product.
Founded in 1951

4520 **Emulsion Poylmers Council**
1250 Connecticut Ave NW
Suite 700
Washington, DC 20036-2657

202-419-1500; Fax: 202-659-8037
epc@regnet.com
www.regnet.com/epc

Robert J Fensterheim, Executive Director
Represents regulatory professionals at companies which produce emulsion polymers, chemical compounds used in a variety of coating and other industril applications.
7 Members
Founded in 1995

4521 **Ethylene Oxide Sterlization Association, Inc.**
PO Box 33361
Washington, DC 20033

866-235-5030; Fax: 202-557-3836
eosainfo@eosa.org
www.eosa.org

Chris Klosen, President
Kevin Wagner, Vice President
Robert Bogart, Treasurer
Jeff Peltier, Secretary
EOSA is a non-profit organization that works to educate industry, regulators, and the public on the uses and benefits of ethylene oxide. EOSA also works to improve safety standards, foster industry communication, and provide a forum for issues related to ethylene oxide sterilization.
23 Members
Founded in 1995

4522 **Federation of Analytical Chemistry and Spectroscopy Societies**
2019 Galisteo St
Building I-1
Santa Fe, NM 87505

505-820-1653; Fax: 505-989-1073
www.facss.org
Facebook, Twitter, LinkedIn

Christopher Palmer, Governing Board Chair
Mike Carrabba, Governing Board Chair Elect
Ian Lewis, Treasurer
Glen Jackson, Secretary
Karen Esmonde-White, Marketing-Chair
Exists to combine many small meetings previously organized bythe individual societies into one joint meeting that covers the whole field of Analytical Chemistry.
12 Members
Founded in 1972

4523 **Independent Liquid Terminals Association**
1005 N Glebe Road
Suite 600
Arlington, VA 22201

703-875-2011; Fax: 703-875-2018
info@ilta.org
www.ilta.org

Kathryn Clay, President
Andy Wright, Vp, Legislative Affairs
Susan Kurdziolek, Sr. Director, Operations
Leakhena Swett, Director, Marketing &

Membership
Meredith DeZemler, Director, Meetings

Represents bulk liquid terminal companies that store commercial liquids in aboveground storage tanks (ASTs) and transfer products to and from ocean going tank ships, tank barges, pipelines, tank trucks and tank rail cars. Provides members with essential informational tools to facilitate regulatory compliance and improve operations, safety and environmental performance.
400 Members
Founded in 1974

4524 **Independent Lubricant Manufacturers Association**
400 N Columbus St
Suite 201
Alexandria, VA 22314

703-684-5574; Fax: 703-836-8503
ilma@ilma.org
www.ilma.org
Facebook, Twitter

Holly Alfano, Chief Executive Officer
Brenda Gillinson, Sr. Director, Communications
Tim Mack, Sr. Director, Member Engagement
Amber Lopez, Sr. Manager, Marketing & Digital
Meg Thaxton, Manager, Meetings

Supports all those involved in the US and international independent lubricant industry.
Founded in 1948

4525 **Institute for Polyacrylate Absorbents**
1850 M St NW
Suite 700
Washington, DC 20036

571-217-4300; Fax: 571-348-5138
www.socma.org/affiliated-organizations/ipa

Jane Wishneff, Executive Director

Represents manufacturers and users of absorbent polymers made of cross-linked polyacrylates and manufacturers and users of acrylic acid or its salts. It addreses the scientific, regulatory and related issues which are likely to impact the manufacture, use and disposal of fluid-absorbing polyacrylates.
Founded in 1985

4526 **International Cadmium Association**
168 Avenue de Tervuren BOX4
Brussels, VA 22066

202-776-0073; Fax: 202-776-0092
contact@cadmium.org
www.cadmium.org

Hugh Morrow, Consultant

Provides marketing research and promotion to the industry. Hosts seperate annual meetings in the United States and Europe.
30 Members
Mailing list available for rent

4527 **International Ozone Association: Pan American Group Branch**
PO Box 97075
Las Vegas, NV 89193

480-529-3787; Fax: 480-522-3080
infO3zone@io3a.org
www.ioa-pag.org

Robert Jarnis, Executive Director

Represents the interests of environmental and other scientific communities, application engineers, users, and manufacturers of ozone generation and contacting equipment.
810 Members
Founded in 1973

4528 **Materials Technology Institute, Inc.**
1215 Fern Ridge Pkwy
Suite 206
St Louis, MO 63141

314-576-7712; Fax: 314-576-6078
mtiadmin@mti-global.org
www.mti-global.org
Twitter, LinkedIn

Paul Whitcraft, Executive Director
Bryon Keelin, Operations Director
Lindsey Skinner, Communications & Publications

Provides leadership in materials technology for chemical processing to improve reliability, profitability and safety.
52 Members
Founded in 1977

4529 **Methanol Institute**
225 Reinekers Lane
Suite 205
Alexandria, VA 22314

703-248-3636; Fax: 703-248-3997
MI@methanol.org
www.methanol.org
Facebook, Twitter, LinkedIn

Gregory A. Dolan, CEO
Christopher D. Chatterton, COO
Lawrence Navin, Director of Gov. & Public Affairs
Eelco Dekker, Chief Representative Europe
Kai Zhao, Chief Representative China

Our mission is to expand markets for the use of methanol as a chemical commodity and an energy fuel.
35 Members
Founded in 1989

4530 **National Aerosol Association**
PO Box 5510
Fullerton, CA 92838

714-525-1518; Fax: 714-526-1295
NAA@nationalaerosol.com
www.nationalaerosol.com

Mary Metzner, Executive Director

Individuals, firms and agencies engaged in the development, manufacture, packaging, sale or distribution of aerosol products.
30 Members
Founded in 1986

4531 **National Association of Chemical Recyclers**
1900 M Street NW
Washington, DC 20036

202-296-1725; Fax: 202-296-2530

Christopher Goebel, Executive Director

Members are companies whose primary business is the reclamation of solvents and other chemicals from industrial waste streams and recycling.
Founded in 1979

4532 **National Chemical Credit Association**
500 Seneca Street
Suite 400
Buffalo, NY 14204-1963

844-462-6342; Fax: 716-878-0479
robert.gagliardi@abc-amega.com
www.abc-amega.com
Twitter, LinkedIn, YouTube, Google+

David Herer, Chief Executive Officer
Paul Catalano, President & COO
Robert States, EVP & CFO
Jason Szwed, VP, Client Services
Krista Glenn, Director, Marketing

Members are major producers of basic chemicals and allied products.
100 Members
Founded in 1938

4533 **National Pest Management Association**
10460 North Street
Fairfax, VA 22030

703-352-6762
800-678-6722; Fax: 703-352-3031
www.npmapestworld.org
Facebook, Twitter

Dominique Stumpf, Chief Executive Officer
Chris Forberg, VP, Finance & Administration
Andy Architect, Chief Operating Officer
Rachel Dittman, VP, Marketing & Communications
Kelly Harris, Director, Membership

Represents the interests of its members and the structural pest control industry.
7000 Members
Frequency: October
Founded in 1933

4534 **North American Catalysis Society**
PO Box 80262
Wilmington, DE 19880

302-695-2488; Fax: 302-695-8347
michael.b.damore@usa.dupont.com
www.nacatsoc.org

Jingguang Chen, President
Christopher Jones, Vice President
Javier Guzman, Secretary
Beata Kilos-Reaume, Treasurer

Fosters an interest in heterogeneous and homogeneous catalysis. Organizes national meetings. Members are chemists and chemical engineers engaged in the study and use of reactions involving catalysts. Publishes a newsletter.
1400 Members
Founded in 1956
Mailing list available for rent: 3400 names

4535 **Pine Chemicals Association**
PO Box 17136
Fernandina Beach, FL 32035

404-994-6267; Fax: 404-994-6267
wjones@pinechemicals.org
www.pinechemicals.org
Facebook, Twitter, LinkedIn, YouTube

Alejandro Cunningham, President/COO
Amanda Young, Executive Director
Wendi Kidd, Executive Assistant

An association of producers, processors and consumers of pine chemicals. Promotes innovative, safe and environmentally responsible practices to assure a reliable supply of high quality products.
50 Members
Founded in 1947

4536 **Polyisocyanurate Insulation Manufacturers Association**
529 14th Street NW
Suite 750
Washington, DC 20045

301-654-0000; Fax: 301-951-8401
pima@pima.org
www.polyiso.org
Facebook, Twitter

Justin Koscher, President
Renee LaMura, Sr. Director, Programs & Admin.
Marcin Pazera, Technical Director
Nathan Pobre, Program Manager

Represents the interests of polyisocyanurate manufacturers and suppliers to the industry. Efforts include education, environmental responsibility, government partnerships and energy conservation.
32 Members
Founded in 1970
Mailing list available for rent

4537 **Polyurethane Foam Association**
334 Lakeside Plz
Loudon, TN 37774

865-657-9840; Fax: 865-381-1292
rluedeka@pfa.org
www.pfa.org

Russ Batson, Executive Director
Wayne Bowman, Communications Counsel
Jim McIntyre, Legal Counsel
Kay Wright, Administrative Manager

Suppliers of raw material and equipment. Associate members are manufacturers of flexible polyurethane foam. Our mission is to educate customers and other groups about flexible polyurethane foam and promote its use in manufactured and industrial products. This includes providing facts on environmental, health and safety issues related to polyurethane foam to the membership of PFA, polyurethane foam users, regulatory officials, business leaders and the media.
63 Members
Founded in 1980

4538 **Powder Coating Institute**
5040 Old Taylor Mill Rd
PMB 13
Taylor Mill, KY 41015

859-525-9988
800-988-COAT; Fax: 859-356-0908
pci-info@powdercoating.org
www.powdercoating.org
Facebook, Twitter, LinkedIn, Pinterest

Kevin Coursin, Executive Director, Membership, Events & Operations, Training, Advertising, Sponsordhip & Exhibits

A trade association representing suppliers of powder coating materials, equipment, and related products and services in North America.
325 Members
Founded in 1981
Mailing list available for rent

4539 **Process Equipment Manufacturers Association**
201 Park Washington Ct
Falls Church, VA 22046

703-538-1796; Fax: 703-241-5603
info@pemanet.org
www.pemanet.org

Elizabeth Armstrong, Executive Director & Secretary
Harry W. Buzzerd, Management Counsel
Michelle Savoie, Meetings & Membership Manager
Dawn Shiley, Marketing & Communications Manager
Sharon Kelly, Meeting Registrar/Member Services

Manufacturers and suppliers of equipment for food, chemical, pulp and paper, water, wastewater processing.
50 Members
Founded in 1960

4540 **Society of Chemical Manufacturers and Affiliates**
1850 M St Nw
Suite 700
Washington, DC 20036-5810

202-721-4100; Fax: 202-296-8120
info@socma.com
www.socma.com
Facebook, Twitter, LinkedIn, YouTube

Jennifer Abril, President & CEO
Jenny Gaines, Sr. Dir., Comm. & Engagement
Vera Stoeva, SVP, Finance & Administration
Robert Helminiak, VP, Legal & Government
David Wawer, SVP, Association & Management

Conducts workshops and seminars. Maintains a library on cancer policies and related subjects. Its member companies have more than 2,000 manufacturing sites and 100,000 employees.
300 Members
Founded in 1921

4541 **Society of Cosmetic Chemists**
120 Wall St
Suite 2400
New York, NY 10005-4088

212-668-1500; Fax: 212-668-1504
scc@scconline.org
www.scconline.org
Facebook, Twitter, LinkedIn

Elizabeth Streland, President
Michelle Hines, Vice President
David Smith, Executive Director
Yulia Park, Secretary
Karen Chun, Treasurer

Supports all those involved in working with and developing cosmetic chemicals.
4000 Members
Founded in 1945

4542 **Society of Toxicology**
1821 Michael Faraday Drive
Suite 300
Reston, VA 20190

703-438-3115; Fax: 703-438-3113
sothq@toxicology.org
www.toxicology.org
Facebook, Twitter, LinkedIn, Pinterest, Google+

George Daston, President
Myrtle Davis, Vice President

Members are scientists concerned with the effects of chemicals on man and the environment. Promotes the acquisition and utilization of knowledge in toxicology, aids in the protection of public health and facilitates disciplines. The society has a strong commitment to education in toxicology and to the recruitment of students and new members into the profession.
5000 Members
Founded in 1961

4543 **Spray Polyurethane Foam Alliance**
3827 Old Lee Hwy.
#101B
Fairfax, VA 22030

800-523-6154; Fax: 703-222-5816
info@sprayfoam.org
www.sprayfoam.org
Facebook, Twitter

Bryan Heidreth, President
Bonnie Strickler, Vice President
Richard Spiess, Secretary/Treasurer

A trade association representing interests associated with rigid and semi-rigid polyurethane foam products that are typically applied with spray equipment as roofing and insulation.
Founded in 1987
Mailing list available for rent

4544 **The Electrochemical Society**
65 South Main St
Building D
Pennington, NJ 08534-2839

609-737-1902; Fax: 609-737-2743
www.electrochem.org
Facebook, Twitter, LinkedIn

Christopher Jannuzzi, Executive Director/CEO
Tim Gamberzky, CFO & COO
Beth Craanen, Director, Publications
John Lewis, Director, Meetings
Shannon Reed, Director, Community Engagement

An international nonprofit, educational organization concerned with a broad range of phenomena relating to electrochemical and solid-state science and technology. The Electrochemical Society has scientists and engineers in over 70 countries worldwide who hold individual membership, as well as roughly 100 corporations and laboratories that hold corporate membership.
8000 Members
Founded in 1902

Newsletters

4545 **AAB Bulletin**
American Association of Bioanalysts
906 Olive Street
Suite 1200
Saint Louis, MO 63101-1448

314-241-1445; Fax: 314-241-1449
aab@aab.org
www.aab.org

Mark S Biernbaum PhD, Executive Director

Newsletter that provides the latest information on meetings, conferences, legislative and regulatory issues and developments.
Frequency: Quarterly
Founded in 1956

4546 **AACG Newsletter**
American Association for Crystal Growth
25 4th Street
Somerville, NJ 08876-3205

908-575-0649; Fax: 908-575-0794
www.crystalgrowth.org

Candace Lynch, Chief Editor
Lara Keefer, Editor
Peter Schunemann, President
Robert Biefeld, Vice President

Technical articles and includes calendar of upcoming meetings.
Circulation: 600
ISSN: 1527-2389
Founded in 1966
Printed in 4 colors on glossy stock

4547 **AATCC News**
PO Box 12215
Research Triangle Park, NC 27709-2215

919-549-8141
800-360-5380; Fax: 919-549-8933
danielsj@aatcc.org
www.aatcc.org
Facebook, Twitter, LinkedIn

John Daniels, Executive VP
Debra Hibbard, Executive Assistant
Chris Leonard, Technical Director

Free, emailed newsletter providing up-to-date news and feature articles.
3000 Members

4548 **APE Newsletter**
Alkylphenois & Ethoxylates Research Council
1250 Connecticut Ave Nw
Suite 700
Washington, DC 20036-2657

202-419-1506
866-273-7262; Fax: 202-659-8037
angroup@regnet.com

Robert J Fensterheim, Editor

4549 **Adhesion Society Newsletter**
Adhesion Society
2 Davidson Hall
Blacksburg, VA 24061-0001

540-231-7257; Fax: 540-231-3971
adhesoc@vt.edu
www.adhesionsociety.org

Esther Brann, Manager

4550 **Advanced Coatings and Surface Technology**
John Wiley & Sons
111 River St
Hoboken, NJ 07030-5790
201-748-6000; Fax: 201-748-6088
info@wiley.com
www.wiley.com
William J Pesce, CEO
Provides intelligence service reports and puts into perspective significant developments in coatings and surface modification across a broad range of industry lines. ACT interprets developments ranging from traditional coating processes to chemical vapor deposition and iron beam methods, which offers interdisciplinary analyses of those that have true commercial potential.
Cost: $530.00
10 Pages
Frequency: Monthly
Founded in 1807

4551 **Amber-Hi-Lites**
Rohm And Haas Company
100 S Independence Mall W
Suite 1A
Philadelphia, PA 19106-2399
215-592-3000; Fax: 215-592-3377
www.rohmhaas.com
Raj L Gupta, CEO
Offers discussions of ion exchange resin use in fields of water conditioning.

4552 **Analytical Chemistry**
American Chemical Society
1155 16th St Nw
Suite 600
Washington, DC 20036-4892
202-872-4600
800-227-5558; Fax: 202-872-4615
service@acs.org
www.acs.org
Madeleine Jacobs, CEO
Elizabeth Zubritsky, Manager
Information and news on the chemical industry.
Founded in 1876

4553 **Biochemistry**
American Chemical Society
1155 16th St Nw
Suite 600
Washington, DC 20036-4892
202-872-4600
800-333-9511; Fax: 202-872-4615
service@acs.org
www.acs.org
Madeleine Jacobs, CEO
News and information for the scientific community.
Cost: $137.00
Frequency: Weekly
Founded in 1876

4554 **ChemEcology**
Chemical Manufacturers Association
1300 Wilson Boulevard
Arlington, VA 22209-2307
703-741-5502; Fax: 703-741-6807
Rebecca Swinehart, Editor
Issues on health, safety and the environment.

4555 **ChemWeek Association**
ChemWeek
110 William St
Suite 11
New York, NY 10038-3910
212-621-4900; Fax: 212-621-4800
ltattum@chemweek.com
www.chemweek.com
John Rockwell, VP
Joe Mennella, Global Sales Director
Comprehensive coverage of the latest developments, uses, production, distribution, and manufacturing of chemicals for all industries.
Cost: $159.00
Frequency: Monthly
Circulation: 20779
Founded in 1977

4556 **Chemical Bond**
American Chemical Society
1155 16th St Nw
Suite 600
Washington, DC 20036-4892
202-872-4600
800-227-5558; Fax: 202-872-4615
service@acs.org
www.acs.org
Madeleine Jacobs, CEO
Covers organization activities.

4557 **Chemical Bulletin**
American Chemical Society
Ste 312
1400 Renaissance Dr
Park Ridge, IL 60068-1336
847-647-8405; Fax: 847-647-8364
chicagoacs@ameritech.net
www.chicagoacs.org
Gail Wilkening, Office Manager
Highlights events and meetings of local chapters, profiles prominent society members, and reports on research and technological advancements in the field.
Cost: $20.00
Frequency: Monthly
Circulation: 5700

4558 **Chemical Economics Handbook Program**
SRI Consulting
4300 Bohannon Dr
Suite 200
Menlo Park, CA 94025-1042
650-384-4300; Fax: 650-330-1190
www.sriconsulting.com
John Pearson, President/CEO
Ongoing multiclient program focusing on the chemical and allied products industries. History, status and projected trends for hundreds of chemicals, chemical raw materials, and end-use products. Service includes access to on-line data base and client inquiry privileges.
Cost: $12000.00
Frequency: Monthly
Founded in 1946

4559 **Chemical Industries Newsletter**
SRI International
333 Ravenswood Ave
Menlo Park, CA 94025-3493
650-859-3711; Fax: 650-326-8916
www.srifcu.org
Steve Bowles, President
Articles discuss the activities of SRI International Chemical Industries Centers.

4560 **Chemical Industry Monitoring**
Cyrus J Lawrence
1290 Avenue of the Americas
New York, NY 10006
Don Pattison, Editor
Prices and technological developments in the industry.

4561 **Chemical Product News**
US Dept. of Commerce, Business & Defense Service
200 Constitution Ave Nw
Washington, DC 20210-0001
202-693-5000; Fax: 202-219-8822
www.dol.gov
Hilda L Solis, CEO
Offers information about chemical products and related issues.

4562 **Chemical Regulation Reporter**
Bureau of National Affairs
1801 S Bell St
Arlington, VA 22202-4501
703-341-3000
800-372-1033; Fax: 202-452-4084
customercare@bna.com
www.bnabooks.com
Paul N Wojcik, Chairman
A notification and reference service consisting of six binders that comprehensively covers federal chemical regulations.
Cost: $1103.00
Frequency: Weekly
Founded in 1929

4563 **Chemical and Engineering News**
American Chemical Society
1155 16th St Nw
Suite 600
Washington, DC 20036-4892
202-872-4600
800-227-5558; Fax: 202-872-4615
service@acs.org
www.acs.org
Madeleine Jacobs, CEO
Covers news relating to chemical engineering and technology.
Frequency: Weekly
Circulation: 137,664
ISSN: 0009-2347
Founded in 1876

4564 **Chemweek's Business Daily**
Chemical Week/Access Intelligence
110 William St
Suite 11
New York, NY 10038-3910
212-621-4900; Fax: 212-621-4800
ltattum@chemweek.com
www.chemweek.com
John Rockwell, VP
Joe Minnella, Global Sales Manager
Daily electronic newsletter covering the latest chemical industry business and financial news, including markets, pricing, regulatory and security issues, research, technologies and new services.
Cost: $1049.00
Frequency: Daily
Founded in 2002
Printed in 4 colors

4565 **Chlor-Alkali Marketwire**
Chemical Week/Access Intelligence
110 William St
Suite 11
New York, NY 10038-3910
212-621-4900; Fax: 212-621-4800
ltattum@chemweek.com
www.chemweek.com
John Rockwell, VP
Joe Mennella, Global Sales Director
Weekly electronic newsletter covering chlor-alkali market sector, including market trends in supply and demand, pricing fluctuations, pro-

duction rates in caristic soda and chlorine. Also covers vinyls, soda ash and related derivatives
Cost: $1699.00
Frequency: Weekly
Founded in 2002
Printed in 4 colors

4566 **Chlorine Institute Newsletter**
Chlorine Institute
1300 Wilson Blvd
Arlington, VA 22209-2323

703-741-5760; Fax: 703-894-4130
www.chlorineinstitute.org

Arthur Dungan, President

Articles featuring safe handling of chlorine and caustic materials.
5 Pages
Printed in 2 colors on matte stock

4567 **Clinical & Forensic Toxicology News**
1850 K St NW
Suite 625
Washington, DC 20006-2215

202-857-0717
800-892-1400; Fax: 202-887-5093
www.aacc.org
Facebook, Twitter, LinkedIn, YouTube

Greg rd Miller, President
Nancy Sasavage, Ph.D., Editor
Robert Dofour, Treasury

Online only newsletter provides practical and timely information on the clinical, forensic, technical, and regulatory issues faced by toxicology laboratories.

4568 **Clinical Laboratory Strategies**
1850 K St NW
Suite 625
Washington, DC 20006-2215

202-857-0717
800-892-1400; Fax: 202-887-5093
www.aacc.org
Facebook, Twitter, LinkedIn, YouTube

Richard Flaherty, VP
Penelope Jones, Director

Online newsletter for laboratory directors and managers gives strategic information on how to better manage the changes faced in jobs every day.

4569 **Composites and Adhesives Newsletter**
T/C Press
223 S Detroit Street
PO Box 36006
Los Angeles, CA 90036

323-938-7023; Fax: 323-938-6923
tcpress@msn.com

Mark Albert, Editor-In-Chief
Sherry Baranek, Senior Editor
Tom Beard, Senior VP
Lori Beckman, Managing Editor

News about composites and adhesives industry. Accepts very limited and selective advertising.
Cost: $190.00
20 Pages
Frequency: Quarterly
Circulation: 300
ISSN: 0888-1227
Founded in 1984

4570 **Electronic Chemicals News**
Chemical Week Associates
2 Grand Central Tower
140 E. 45th St., 40th Floor
New York, NY 10017

212-884-9528; Fax: 212-884-9514
lyn.tattum@ihs.com
www.chemweek.com

Lyn Tattum, Publisher & Director
Natasha Alperowicz, Executive Editor

Written for and about the chemicals industry and contains industry developments, environmental news, new products, and financial and corporate briefs.
Cost: $699.00

4571 **Government Affairs Update**
ASHRAE
1850 K St NW
Suite 625
Washington, DC 20006-2215

202-857-0717
800-892-1400; Fax: 202-887-5093
www.ashrae.org
Facebook, Twitter, LinkedIn, YouTube

Jeff Littleton, Executive VP

Online government affairs newsletter presents a comprehensive summary of legislative and government news that affect clinical labs and manufacturers.

4572 **ILTA Newsletter**
Independent Liquid Terminals Association
1444 I St Nw
Suite 400
Washington, DC 20005-6538

202-842-9200; Fax: 202-326-8660
info@ilta.org
www.ilta.org

E David Doane, President

International trade association representing bulk liquid terminal companies that store commercial liquids in aboveground storage tanks and transfer products to and from oceangoing tank ships, tank barges, pipelines, tank trucks, and tank rail cars.
Frequency: Monthly
Circulation: 1200
Founded in 1974
Printed in 2 colors on matte stock

4573 **Inside R&D**
John Wiley & Sons
111 River St
Hoboken, NJ 07030-5790

201-748-6000; Fax: 201-748-6088
info@wiley.com
www.wiley.com

William J Pesce, CEO

Weekly service offering information about current research and development, concentrating on new and significant developments that create new products/markets in the near-term and this are valuable to a company's bottom line.
Cost: $790.00
6 Pages
Frequency: Weekly
Founded in 1807
Mailing list available for rent

4574 **Langmuir: QTL Biosystems**
American Chemical Society
1322 Pouseo de Peralta
Santa Fe, NM 87501

505-989-1907; Fax: 505-989-1979
service@acs.org
www.pubs.acs.org

David Whitten PhD, Editor

Edited for an audience involved with high-vacuum surface chemistry and spectroscopy, heterogeneous catalysis, all aspects of interface chemistry involving fluid interfaces and disperse systems.
Frequency: BiWeekly
Circulation: 1,200

4575 **MTI Communications**
Materials Technology Institute
1215 Ferk Ridge Parkway
Suite 206
St. Louis, MO 63141

314-576-7712; Fax: 314-576-6078
mtiadmin@mti-global.org
www.mti-global.org
Twitter, LinkedIn

Paul Bancroft, Executive Director
Lindsey Skinner, Communications & Publications

Official newsletter of Materials Technology Institute, providing updates on member activities, meetings, and training announcement.
Frequency: 3x/Year
Founded in 1977

4576 **North American Catalysis Society Newsletter**
PO Box 80262
Wilmington, DE 19880-262

302-695-2488; Fax: 302-695-8347
www.nacatsoc.org

Michael B D Amore, Editor
John N Armor, President
Gary McVicker, VP

Fosters an interest in heterogeneous and homogeneous catalysis. Organizes national meetings. Members are chemists and chemical engineers engaged in the study and use of reactions involving catalysts.
Cost: $45.00
38448 Pages
Frequency: Monthly
Founded in 1956
Mailing list available for rent: 3,500 names at $160 per M

4577 **Pine Chemicals Association Newsletter**
3350 Riverwood Parkway SE
Suite 1900
Atlanta, GA 30339

770-984-5340; Fax: 404-994-6267
wjones@pinechemicals.org
www.pinechemicals.org

Walter L Jones, President/COO
Gary Reed, Chairman/Board of Directors

An association of producers, processors and consumers of pine chemicals. Promotes innovative, safe and environmentally responsible practices to assure a reliable supply of high quality products.
Frequency: Quarterly

4578 **SOCMA Newsletter**
Synthetic Organic Chemical Manufacturers Assn
1850 M St Nw
Suite 700
Washington, DC 20036-5803

202-721-4100; Fax: 202-296-8120
info@socma.com
www.socma.com

Joseph Acker, President
Vivian Diko, Executive Assistant & CEO
Liesa Brown, Editor/Marketing/Communications

Offers information on the organic chemical industry.
10 Pages
Frequency: Bi-monthly
Founded in 1921

Magazines & Journals

4579 **AATCC Review Journal**
PO Box 12215
Research Triangle Park, NC 27709-2215

919-549-8141
800-360-5380; Fax: 919-549-8933
danielsj@aatcc.org
www.aatcc.org
Facebook, Twitter, LinkedIn

John Daniels, Executive VP
Debra Hibbard, Executive Assistant
Charles E Gavin, Treasurer
Chris Shaw, Advertising Sales

Covers fibers to finished products, and chemical synthesis to retail practices.
3000 Members

4580 **AICHE Journal**
American Institute of Chemical Engineers
3 Park Ave
New York, NY 10016-5991

212-591-7338
800-242-4363; Fax: 212-591-8888
CustomerService@aiche.org
www.aiche.org
Facebook, Twitter, LinkedIn

June Wispelway, Executive Director
Steve Smith, Publications Director
Bette Lawler, Director of Operations
Neil Yeoman, Treasurer

Serves as a journal emcompassing data and results of the latest information in significant research and trends in the field.
Cost: $1250.00
Frequency: Monthly
ISSN: 0001-1541
Founded in 1908

4581 **Accounts of Chemical Research**
American Chemical Society
1155 16th St NW
Suite 600
Washington, DC 20036-4892

202-872-4600
800-227-5558; Fax: 202-872-4615
service@acs.org
www.acs.org

Madeleine Jacobs, CEO

Chemical research and statistical information.
Cost: $526.00
Frequency: Monthly
Circulation: 159,000
Founded in 1968

4582 **Advanced Coatings and Surface Technology**
605 3rd Avenue
9th Floor
New York, NY 10158

212-850-6824; Fax: 212-850-8643

4583 **American Laboratory**
International Scientific Communications
395 Oyster Pint Blvd.
#321
South San Francisco, CA 94080

650-243-5600
info@americanlaboratory.com
www.americanlaboratory.com

Brian Howard, Editor-In-Chief
Robert G Sweeny, Publisher
Donna Frankel, Direcetor Of Editorial
Susan Messinger, Managing Editor

American Laboratory serves industry, university, government, independent and foundation research laboratories.
50 Pages
Frequency: Monthly
Circulation: 91611
ISSN: 0044-7749
Founded in 1969
Printed in 4 colors on glossy stock

4584 **An Energy Efficient Solution**
Alliance for Responsible Atmoshperic Policy
2111 Wilson Blvd
Suite 850
Arlington, VA 22201-3001

703-243-0344; Fax: 703-243-2874

David Stirpe, Executive Director

4585 **Asia Pacific Chemicals**
Reed Chemical Publications
360 Park Avenue South
10th Floor
New York, NY 10010

713-525-2613
888-525-3255
jlucas@chemexpo.com
www.reedchemicals.com

Stanley F Reed
Bernard Petersen, Sales Manager
Karen Yanard, Sales Executive
Alan Taylor, Editor

4586 **Asian Chemical News**
Reed Chemical Publications
360 Park Avenue South
10th Floor
New York, NY 10010

212-791-4208
888-525-3255
csc@icis.com
www.reedchemicals.com

Stanley F Reed
Bernard Petersen, Sales Manager
Karen Yanard, Sales Executive
Alan Taylor, Editor

4587 **CPI Purchasing**
Reed Business Information
2000 Clearwater Dr
Oak Brook, IL 60523-8809

630-574-0825; Fax: 630-288-8781
k.doyle@reedbusiness.com
www.reedbusiness.com

Jeff Greisch, President
Kathy Doyle, Publisher

Trade magazine for purchasing professionals in the chemical/process industry. Accepts advertising.
Cost: $74.95
100 Pages
Circulation: 95078
Founded in 1983

4588 **Cereal Chemistry**
AACC International
3340 Pilot Knob Rd
St. Paul, MN 55121-2055

651-454-7250
800-328-7560; Fax: 651-454-0766
aacc@scisoc.org
www.aaccnet.org

Les Copeland, Editor-In-Chief
F. William Collins, Senior Editor
Ian Batey, Associate Editor

Cereal chemistry explores raw materials, processes and products utulizing cereal.
Cost: $79.00
Frequency: Bi-Monthly
ISSN: 0009-0352

4589 **Chemical Engineering**
Chemical Week Associates
2 Grand Central Tower
140 East 45th Street,40th Floor
New York, NY 10017

212-884-9528; Fax: 212-884-9514
ltattum@chemweek.com
www.chemweek.com

Lyn Tattum, Publisher/Director
Robert Westervelt, Editor-In-Chief

Highlights include a calendar of related trade shows, new products listings, operations and maintenance techniques and marketing services ideas.
Cost: $59.00
Frequency: Monthly
Circulation: 69000
ISSN: 0009-2460
Founded in 1902
Printed in 4 colors on glossy stock

4590 **Chemical Engineering Progress**
American Institute of Chemical Engineers
3 Park Ave
New York, NY 10016-5991

203-702-7660
800-242-4363; Fax: 203-775-5177
CustomerService@aiche.org
www.aiche.org

June Wispelwey, Executive Director
Marty Clancy, Director Membership/Cust. Service

Offers updated information for chemical engineers.
Cost: $245.00
Frequency: Quarterly
Founded in 1908

4591 **Chemical Equipment**
Reed Business Information
301 Gibraltar Drive
PO Box 650
Morris Plains, NJ 07950-650

973-920-7000; Fax: 973-539-3476
privacymanager@reedbusiness.com
www.reedbusiness.com

Bud Ramsey, Publisher
Geoffery Bridgman, Editor
Gerard Van de Aast, CEO/President

Chemical Equipment is for engineers, plant management personnel, maintenance engineering and others concerned with design, building, engineering, operating and maintaining chemical process plants.
Frequency: Monthly
Circulation: 106032
Founded in 1959

4592 **Chemical Equipment Literature Review**
Reed Business Information
St 600
Rockaway
New Jersey, NJ 07866

973-920-7000
800-222-0289; Fax: 973-920-7531
plundy@reedbusiness.com
www.reedbusiness.com

Geoff Bridgman, Editor
Gail Kirberger, Circulation Manager
Patrick Lundy, Publisher

Covers reviews of new catalogs and brochures on products for the chemical industry.
8 Pages
Frequency: Monthly
Circulation: 106038
Founded in 1985

4593 **Chemical Heritage**
Chemical Heritage Foundation

315 Chestnut St
Philadelphia, PA 19106-2793

215-925-2222; Fax: 215-925-1954
www.chemheritage.org

Michal Meyer, Editor

Dedicated to sharing the story chemistry and related sciences, technologies, and industries.
48 Pages
Circulation: 25000
ISSN: 0736-4555

4594 **Chemical Intelligencer**
Springer Verlag
233 Spring St
Suite 6
New York, NY 10013-1578

212-460-1500
800-777-4643; Fax: 212-460-1575
serviceny@springer.com
www.springer.com

William Curtis, President

Written for the scientist interested in the history and culture of chemistry. Includes articles and essays that develop and comment on the current directions and concerns in chemistry, new discoveries and experiments as well as present trends and opportunities in chemistry, philosophy and education.
Cost: $79.00
Frequency: Quarterly
Circulation: 1,000

4595 **Chemical Management Review**
Reed Chemical Publications
2 Wall St
26th Floor, Suite 13
New York, NY 10005-2044

212-732-3200; Fax: 212-791-4311
helga.tilton@chemicalmarketreporter.com
www.reedchemicals.com

Stanley F Reed
Helga Tilton, Editor
Keith Jones, CEO/President
Jane Burgess, Marketing

Provides information for senior managers in the chemical industry and other industrial markets.
Cost: $195.00
Frequency: Monthly
Founded in 1871
Printed in 4 colors on glossy stock

4596 **Chemical Market Reporter**
Schnell Publishing Company
2 Rector St
26th Floor
New York, NY 10006-1819

212-791-4267; Fax: 212-791-4321
editor@chemexpo.com
www.chemexpo.com

James Hannan, Publisher
Helga Tilton, Editor in Chief

Regular issue highlights include news of the week, coverage of pertinent industry trade shows/meetings, a review of new materials, and periodic insight reports on segments of the industry.
Cost: $109.00
Frequency: Weekly
Circulation: 14714

4597 **Chemical Processing**
Putman Media
1501 East Woodfield Road
Suite 400N
Schaumburg, IL 60173

630-467-1300; Fax: 630-467-0197
webmaster@putman.net
www.putmanmedia.com

John Cappelletti, President & CEO
Tony D'Avino, Vice President & Publisher
Mark Rosenzweig, Editor-In-Chief
Amanda Joshi, Managing Editor

Carries technical overview and case history articles presented in a problem-solving environment geared to operations, engineering and R&D management. Topics include instrumentation, pumping, corrosion, heat transfer, mixing and energy conservation. Accepts advertising.
60 Pages
Frequency: Monthly
Circulation: 55000
ISSN: 0009-2630
Founded in 1938
Mailing list available for rentat $130 per M
Printed in 4 colors

4598 **Chemist**
American Institute of Chemists
315 Chestnut St
Suite 420
Philadelphia, PA 19106-2702

215-873-8224; Fax: 215-925-1954
info@theaic.org
www.theaic.org

Davidah Manuta, President
Ray Mcafel, President-Elect
Jerry d Jasinski, Chair

Topics of professional, economic, social and legislative interest to individual chemists or chemical engineers.
Cost: $35.00
32 Pages
Frequency: Quarterly
Circulation: 5000
Founded in 1923

4599 **Chemistry Research in Technology**
American Chemical Society
1155 16th St NW
Suite 600
Washington, DC 20036-4892

202-872-4600
800-227-5558; Fax: 202-872-4615
service@acs.org
www.acs.org

Madeleine Jacobs, CEO/Executive Director
Elizabeth Zubritsky, Manager

Information and research summaries of the latest in the chemical industry.
Cost: $49.00
Frequency: 1 Year 3 Issues
Founded in 1876

4600 **Clinical Chemistry**
1850 K St NW
Suite 625
Washington, DC 20006-2215

202-857-0717
800-892-1400; Fax: 202-887-5093
www.aacc.org
Facebook, Twitter, LinkedIn, YouTube

Nadar Rifai, Editor-In-Chief
Tom Annesley, Deputy Editor
James Boyd, Deputy Editor

The leading forum for peer-reviewed, original research on innovative practices in today's clinical laboratory.

4601 **Clinical Laboratory News**
1850 K St NW
Suite 625
Washington, DC 20006-2215

202-857-0717
800-892-1400; Fax: 202-887-5093
www.aacc.org
Facebook, Twitter, LinkedIn, YouTube

Robert Christenson, President
Dennis Dietzen, Director
Elizabeth Frank, Secretary

News magazine that is the authoritative source for timely analysis of issues and trends affecting clinical laboratorians and clinical laboratories.
Founded in 1948

4602 **Coatings World**
Rodman Publishing
70 Hilltop Rd
3rd Floor, Suite 3000
Ramsey, NJ 07446-1150

201-825-2552; Fax: 201-825-0553
info@rodpub.com
www.nutraceuticalsworld.com

Rodman Zilenziger Jr, President
Matt Montgomery, VP

Cutting edge technical information and the most advanced and pertinent management and distribution techniques.
Frequency: 10 issues per y
Circulation: 17000
Founded in 1964

4603 **Combustion and Flame**
Combustion Institute
5001 Baum Blvd.
Suite 635
Pittsburgh, PA 15213-1851

412-687-1366; Fax: 412-687-0340
office@combustioninstitute.org
www.combustioninstitute.org

Barbara Waronek, Executive Administrator
Prof. Katherine Kohs-Hosinghaus, President
Derek Dunn-Rankin, Treasurer

A monthly publication that focuses on combustion phenomena and related topics.
6000 Members
Frequency: Monthly
Founded in 1954

4604 **Compoundings Magazine**
Independent Lubricant Manufacturers Association
651 S Washington Street
Alexandria, VA 22314

703-684-5574; Fax: 703-836-8503
ilma@ilma.org
www.ilma.org

Tom Osborne, Editor
Martha Jolkovski, Director Publications & Advertising
Carla Mangone, Managing Editor

Association and marketing news, meetings and programs, as well as employment and business opportunities to the US and international independent lubricant industry.
Cost: $150.00
Frequency: Monthly
Circulation: 2050
ISSN: 1042-508X
Founded in 1948
Printed in 4 colors on glossy stock

4605 **Energy Process**
American Institute of Chemical Engineers
3 Park Ave
New York, NY 10016-5991

212-591-7338
800-242-4363; Fax: 212-591-8888
www.aiche.org

John Sofranko, Executive Director

Offers updated information for chemical engineers.
Cost: $20.00
Frequency: Quarterly

4606 **European Chemical News**
Reed Chemical Publications

Wall St
26th Floor, Suite 13
New York, NY 10005-2044

212-732-3200; Fax: 212-791-4311
jonathan.sismey@icis.com

Stanley F Reed
Simon Platt, Director
Christopher Flook, Managing Director
Cost: $711.00
Frequency: Weekly
Circulation: 14112

4607 European Journal of Clinical Chemistry and Clinical Biochemistry
Walter De Gruyter
200 Saw Mill Road
Hawthorne, NY 1052

Home Page: journalseek.net/

Water De Gruyler, Editor

Up-to-date information on the chemistry industry.
Frequency: Monthly

4608 HAPPI Household and Personal Products Industry
Rodman Publishing
70 Hilltop Rd
3rd Floor
Ramsey, NJ 07446-1150

201-825-2552; Fax: 201-825-0553
info@rodpub.com
www.nutraceuticalsworld.com

Rodman Zilenziger Jr, President
Matt Montgomery, VP

Highlights current developments, marketing, production, formulations, technical innovations, packaging, and management problems. Includes in-depth news on developments abroad as well as in the United States.
Cost: $52.00
Frequency: Monthly
Circulation: 140000
Founded in 1964

4609 I&EC Research
American Chemical Society
1155 16th St NW
Suite 600
Washington, DC 20036-4892

202-872-4600
800-227-5558; Fax: 202-872-4615
service@acs.org
www.acs.org

Madeleine Jacobs, CEO/Executive Director

Offers information and statistical updates for chemists.
Circulation: 4600
Founded in 1876

4610 IHS Chemical Week
2 Grand Central Tower
140 E 45th St., 40th Fl.
New York, NY 10017

212-884-9528; Fax: 212-884-9514
www.chemweek.com
Facebook, Twitter, LinkedIn, YouTube

Lyn Tattum, Publisher
Robert Westervelt, Editor-in-chief

News and analysis from the chemical, petrochemical and specialty chemical industries.

4611 Industrial & Engineering Chemistry Research
American Chemical Society
1155 16th St NW
Suite 600
Washington, DC 20036-4892

202-872-4600
800-227-5558; Fax: 202-872-4615
help@acs.org
www.acs.org

Madeleine Jacobs, CEO/Executive Director
Judith Benham, Chair
Elizabeth Zubritsky, Manager

Features fundamental research, design methods, process design and development, product research and development for chemists and chemical engineers.
Circulation: 4600
Founded in 1876

4612 Inform
American Oil Chemists' Society
2710 S Boulder
Urbana, IL 61802-6996

217-359-2344; Fax: 217-351-8091
www.aocs.org

Lori Stewart, Publications Director
Kimmy Farris, Production Editor
Kethy Heine, Managing Editor
Patrick Donnelly, CEO

A member benefit that provides international news on fats, oils, surfactants, detergents, and related materials.
Cost: $175.00
100 Pages
Frequency: Monthly
Circulation: 4500
ISSN: 0897-8026
Founded in 1990
Printed in 4 colors on glossy stock

4613 International Laboratory
International Scientific Communications
PO Box 870
Shelton, CT 06484-0870

203-926-9300; Fax: 203-926-9310
www.iscpubs.com/

Brian Howard, Publisher
Robert G Sweeney, Publisher

International Laboratory serves the industry, universities, government, independent and foundation research laboratories.
50 Pages
Circulation: 50036
ISSN: 0010-2164
Founded in 1971
Printed in 4 colors on glossy stock

4614 International Laboratory Pacific Rim Edition
International Scientific Communications
PO Box 870
Shelton, CT 06484-0870

203-926-9300; Fax: 203-926-9310
www.iscpubs.com

Brian Howard, Publisher
Robert G Sweeney, Publisher

Edited for chemists and biologists throughout Far East Asia and Australia who have a professional interest in various aspects of modern laboratory practice and basic research.
40 Pages
Founded in 1986

4615 Journal of AOAC International
AOAC International
481 N Frederick Ave
Suite 500
Gaithersburg, MD 20877-2450

301-924-7078
800-379-2622; Fax: 301-924-7089
aoac@aoac.org
www.aoac.org

James Bradford, Executive Director

Publishes fully refereed contributed papers in the fields of chemical and biological analysis: on original research on new techniques and applications, collaborative studies, authentic data of composition, studies leading to method development, meeting symposia, newly adopted AOAC approved methods and invited reviews.
Cost: $98.00

4616 Journal of Analytical Toxicology
Preston Publications
6600 W Touhy Ave
PO Box 48312
Niles, IL 60714-4516

847-647-2900; Fax: 847-647-1155

Tinsley Preston, Owner
Dr. Bruce A. Goldberger, Editor
Maria Tamacho, Circulation Manager

An international publication for toxicologists, pathologists, analytical chemists, researchers, educators and others. Dedicated to the isolation, indentification, and quantification of potentially toxic substances. Emphasis is on the practical applications for use in clinical, forensic, industrial, and other toxicology laboratories, drug abuse testing, therapeutic drug monitoring, and environmental pollution. Includes new products and litrature, meetings and short courses.
Cost: $475.00
Frequency: 8 issues per ye
Circulation: 1148
Founded in 1977
Mailing list available for rent: 9939 names at $125 per M

4617 Journal of Biological Chemistry
9650 Rockville Pike
Suite 300
Bethesda, MD 20814-3999

301-530-7150; Fax: 301-634-7126
publicaffairs@asbmb.org
www.asbmb.org

Herbert Taber, Editor
Barbara Gordon, Executive Director

Features research papers on biochemistry and molecular biology and other articles of interest to the professional.
Frequency: TriAnnual

4618 Journal of Chemical Education
Division of Chemical Education
Department of Chemistry
University of Georgia
Athens, GA 30602-2556

706-542-6559; Fax: 706-542-9454
norbert-pienta@jce.acs.org
www.pubs.acs.orgorg
Facebook, Twitter

Norbert J Oienta, Editor-in-Chief
Renee S. Cole, Associate Editor

Provides information about and examples of teaching techniques for classroom and laboratory, curricular innovations, chemistry content, and chemical education research.
Cost: $45.00
136 Pages
Frequency: Monthly
ISSN: 0021-9584
Founded in 1924
Printed in on glossy stock

4619 Journal of Chemical Information & Computer Sciences
American Chemical Society
1155 16th St NW
Suite 600
Washington, DC 20036-4892

202-872-4600
800-227-5558; Fax: 202-872-4615
service@acs.org
www.acs.org

Madeleine Jacobs, CEO/Executive Director
George A. Milne, Editor

Offers the latest technological information and news directed at the chemical industry.
Cost: $27.00
Frequency: Bi-Monthly

4620 **Journal of Chemical Physics**
American Institute of Physics
2 Huntington Quadrangle
Suite 101
Melville, NY 11747-4502

516-576-2200; Fax: 516-349-7669
jcp@aip.org
www.aip.org

H. Frederick Dylia, Executive Director/CEO
Darlene Walters, Senior VP
John Haynes, VP Publishing

Targets both chemists and physicists involved in research and applications of chemical physics technology.
Frequency: Weekly
Circulation: 5,000

4621 **Journal of Chemical and Engineering Data**
American Chemical Society
180 Fitzpatrick Hall
Univerity of Notre Dame
Notre Dame, IN 46556

574-631-1149; Fax: 516-349-9704
squarles@aip.org
www.aip.org

Joan F. Brennecke, Ph.D., Editor
Marc Brodsky, CEO

Offers the latest updates and new information in the chemical industry.
Cost: $458.00
Frequency: Weekly
Circulation: 5000
Founded in 1931

4622 **Journal of Chromatographic Science**
Preston Publications
6600 W Touhy Ave
Niles, IL 60714-4516

847-647-2900; Fax: 847-647-1155
tpreston@prestonpub.com

Tinsley Preston, Owner
Kevin Bailey, Managing Editor
Janice Gordon, Director Marketing

An international publication for scientists, analytical chemists, researchers, educators, and other allied to the field. Provides in depth information about analytical techniques, applications, sample preparation methods, systems problem solving, etc. Articles cover more practical information on all types of separations—gas, liquid, thin layer, supercritical fluid, electrophoresis, spectrometry, hyphenated methods, etc. any other single source. Also problem solving/troubleshooting answers.
Cost: $405.00
Frequency: Monthly
Circulation: 1000
Founded in 1961

4623 **Journal of Colloid & Interface Science**
Academic Press
525 B St
Suite 1900
San Diego, CA 92101-4401

619-235-6336
800-321-5068; Fax: 619-699-6280
www.aceparking.com

D.T. Wasan, Editor-in-Chief
Claudia Romas, Publisher

Presents chemical and physiochemical aspects of theory and practice of colloids.
Cost: $883.00
Frequency: Monthly
Circulation: 2000
Founded in 1885

4624 **Journal of Medicinal Chemistry**
American Chemical Society
1155 16th St NW
Suite 600
Washington, DC 20036-4892

202-872-4600
800-227-5558; Fax: 202-872-4615
service@acs.org
www.acs.org

Madeleine Jacobs, CEO/Executive Director

Information on the chemistry industry, dealing with aspects directly pertaining to the medical profession.
Founded in 1876

4625 **Journal of Organic Chemistry**
American Chemical Society
1155 16th St NW
Washington, DC 20036-4892

202-872-4600
800-227-5558; Fax: 202-872-4615
service@acs.org
www.acs.org

Madeleine Jacobs, CEO/Executive Director

Areas emphasized are the multiple facets of organic reactions, natural products, studies of mechanism, theoretical organic chemistry and the various aspects of spectroscopy related to organic chemistry.
Cost: $1260.00
Frequency: BiWeekly
Circulation: 8,500

4626 **Journal of Physical Chemistry**
American Chemical Society
GA Institute of Technology
Boggs Building
Atlanta, GA 30332

404-894-0293
800-227-5558; Fax: 404-894-0294
www.pubs.acs.org

Mostafa A El-Sayed, Editor

Reports on both experimental and theoretical research dealing with the fundamental aspects of physical chemistry and chemical physics.
Frequency: Weekly
Circulation: 3774

4627 **Journal of Society of Cosmetic Chemists**
Society of Cosmetic Chemists
120 Wall St
Suite 2400
New York, NY 10005-4088

212-668-1500; Fax: 212-668-1504
www.scconline.org

Theresa Cesario, Administrator
Mindy Goldstein, Journal Editor
Doreen Scelso, Publication Coordinator

Features highlight new products, processing techniques, safety issues, and pharmacological features.
Cost: $200.00
Circulation: 4200
Founded in 1945

4628 **Journal of Surfactants and Detergents**
AOCS Press
12024 Vista Parke Drive
PO Box 200135
Austin, TX 78720-0135

512-331-2441; Fax: 512-331-2387
Michael F Cox, Editor-in-Chief

Reports on the development and performance of surfactants in all areas, from household detergents to industrial uses, as well as on the development and manufacture of other detergent ingredients and their formulation into finished products.
Cost: $85.00
Frequency: Quarterly
Circulation: 1,500

4629 **Journal of the American Chemical Society**
American Chemical Society
1155 16th St NW
Suite 600
Washington, DC 20036-4892

202-872-4600
800-227-5558; Fax: 202-872-4615
service@acs.org
www.acs.org

Madeleine Jacobs, CEO/Esecutive Director

Association news, member information and chemical industry information.
Cost: $125.00
Frequency: Weekly

4630 **Journal of the American Leather Chemists Association**
American Leather Chemists Association
1314 50th Street
Suite 103
Lubbock, TX 79412

806-744-1798; Fax: 806-744-1785
alca@leatherchemists.org
www.leatherchemists.org

Carol Adcock, Executive Secretary
Cost: $175.00
Frequency: Monthly
Circulation: 500

4631 **Journal of the Electrochemical Society**
Electrochemical Society
65 S Main St
Building D
Pennington, NJ 08534-2839

609-737-1902; Fax: 609-737-2743
ecs@electrochem.org
www.electrochem.org

Roque J. Calvo, Executive Director
Annie Goedkoop, Publications Director
Paul B. Cooper, Editorial Manager

Leader in the field of solid-state and electrochemical science and technology. This peer-reviewed journal publishes an average of 450 pages of 70 articles each month. Articles are posted online, with a monthly paper edition following electronic publication. The ECS membership benefits package includes access to the electronic edition of this journal.
450 Pages
Frequency: Monthly
ISSN: 0013-4651

4632 **LCGC North America**
Advanstar Communications
Woodbridge Corporate Plaza
485 Route 1 S, Building F
Iselin, NJ 08830

732-225-9500; Fax: 732-225-0211
www.lcgcmag.com/lcgc/
Facebook

David Esola, VP/General Manager
Michael Tessalone, Group Publisher
Tria Deibert, Marketing Director

Includes product and literature reports along with meeting and seminar listings.
Cost: $67.00
100 Pages
Frequency: Monthly

Circulation: 56000
Founded in 1987
Mailing list available for rent: 47,543 names at $155 per M
Printed in 4 colors on glossy stock

4633 **Laboratorio y Analisis**
Keller International Publishing Corporation
150 Great Neck Rd
Suite 400
Great Neck, NY 11021-3309

516-829-9210; Fax: 516-829-9306
www.supplychainbrain.com

Terry Beirne, Publisher
Bryan DeLuca, Editor
Jerry Keller, President
Mary Chavez, Director of Sales

4634 **Lipids**
American Oil Chemists' Society
2710 S Boulder
Urbana, IL 61802-6996

217-359-2344; Fax: 217-351-8091
general@aocs.org
www.aocs.org

Jody Schonfeld, Publications Director
Pam Landman, Journals Coordinator
Kimmy Farris, Production Editor
Lori Stewart, Books and Publications
Jenna Tatar, Customer Service

Scientific journal features full-length original research articles, short communications, methods papers and review articles on timely topics. All papers are meticulously peer-reviewed and edited by some of the foremost experts in their respective fields.
Cost: $461.00
Frequency: Monthly
Circulation: 2400
Founded in 1966

4635 **Nucleus**
American Chemical Society — Northeast
12 Corcoran Ave.
Burlington, MA 01803

800-872-2054
800-872-2054; Fax: 508-653-6329
webmaster@nesacs.org
www.nesacs.org

Vincent J Gale, Editor
Amy Tapper, Secretary
Anna Singer, Administrative Secretary
Liming Shao, Chair

Content includes local meeting announcements; news of members of the Northeastern Section, American Chemical Society; historical articles; book reviews; calender of events covering all chemistry disciplines in the area. No Company or product information is published. Advertising is accepted.
Frequency: Monthly
Circulation: 7500
Founded in 1888
Printed in 2 colors on matte stock

4636 **PaintSquare**
PaintSquare
2100 Wharton Street
Suite 310
Pittsburgh, PA 15203

412-431-8300
800-837-8303; Fax: 412-431-5428
webmaster@paintsquare.com
www.paintsquare.com
Facebook, Twitter

Harold Hower, Publisher

Mission is to make PaintSquare a viable and useful tool to make your job easier and more efficient.
Founded in 2002

4637 **Performance Chemicals Europe**
Reed Chemical Publications
Quadrant House, The Quadrant
Sutton, Surrey, UK SM2 5AS

212-732-3200
+44 20 8652 3335; Fax: 212-791-4311; Fax: +44 20 8652 3375
csc@icis.com
www.performancechemicals.com

Stanley F Reed
Neil Sinclair, Director
Simon Platt, Director
Christopher Flook, Managing Director
Cost: $711.00

4638 **PetroChemical News**
William F Bland Co.
709 Turmeric Ln
Durham, NC 27713-3103

919-544-1717; Fax: 919-544-1999
pcn@petrochemical-news.com
www.petrochemical-news.com

Susan Kensil, Editor
Michelle Zard, Circulation Director

Covers new plants and projects, awards of contracts, mergers and acquisitions, current technology, and related government actions.
Cost: $807.00
Frequency: Weekly
Founded in 1963

4639 **Pine Chemicals Review**
Kriedt Enterprises
3803 Cleveland Ave.
New Orleans, LA 70119

504-482-3914; Fax: 504-482-4205
info@pinechemicalsreview.com
www.pinechemicalsreview.com

Romney Richard, Publisher
Charley Richard, Editor

Pine Chemicals Review is the only trade journal covering pine and pulp chemicals within the naval stores industry. It is directed to producers and processors of pine gum and wood naval stores; pulp chemicals and pine derivative chemicals for the adhesives, coatings, printing ink, paper chemicals, flavor and fragrance.
Cost: $110.00
24 Pages
Frequency: Monthly
Circulation: 300
ISSN: 0164-4580
Founded in 1890
Printed in 4 colors on glossy stock

4640 **Polyurethane Professional Development Program**
Center for the Polyurethanes Industry
1300 Wilson Blvd
Suite 990
Arlington, VA 22209-2307

703-841-0012; Fax: 703-841-0525
www.polyurethane.org
Facebook, Twitter

Calvin Dooley, President
Frequency: Yearly

4641 **Powder and Bulk Engineering**
CSC Publishing
1155 Northland Dr
St Paul, MN 55120-1288

651-287-5600; Fax: 651-287-5650
www.cscpublishinginc.com

Richard R Cress, Publisher
Terry O'Neill, Editor
Katherine Davich, Senior Editor

Featured editorial includes technical articles, case histories, test centers, product news and literature, and industry news items.
Frequency: Monthly
Circulation: 35379
Founded in 1986

4642 **Powder/Bulk Solids**
Reed Business Information
301 Gibralter Drive
Box 650
Morris Plains, NJ 07950

973-920-7000; Fax: 973-539-3476
scrow@reedbusiness.com
www.reedbusiness.com

Mark Kelsey, CEO

Equipment and technological news for dry particulates processors.
Cost: $74.95
Frequency: Monthly
Circulation: 45,070
ISSN: 8740-6653
Founded in 1993

4643 **Proceedings of The Combustion Institute**
Combustion Institute
5001 Baum Blvd.
Suite 635
Pittsburgh, PA 15213-1851

412-687-1366; Fax: 412-687-0340
office@combustioninstitute.org
www.combustioninstitute.org

Barbara Waronek, Executive Administrator
Prof. Katharina Kohse-Hoinghaus, President
Marcus Alden, VP
Derek Dunn-Rankin, Treasurer

Contains forefront contributions in fundamentals and applications of combustion science.
6000 Members
Frequency: Biennially
Founded in 1954

4644 **Processing**
Putman Media Company
555 W Pierce Rd
Suite 301
Itasca, IL 60143-2626

630-467-1300; Fax: 630-467-0197
webmaster@putman.net
www.putman.net

John Cappelletti, CEO
Mike Bacidore, Editor-in-Chief
Tonia Becker, Publisher

Product areas covered include mechanical and pneumatic conveying, material handling, packaging, and storage. Each issue includes a specific editorial spotlight, product showcase and new literature section.
Frequency: Monthly
Circulation: 95035
ISSN: 0896-8659
Founded in 1972
Printed in 4 colors

4645 **Quimica Latinoamericana**
Reed Chemical Publications
2 Wall St
26th Floor, Suite 13
New York, NY 10005-2044

212-732-3200
888-525-3255; Fax: 212-791-4311
cnihelp@cnionline.com
www.quimicalatinoamericana.com/

Stanley F Reed
Christopher Flook, Publisher
Neil Sinclair, Managing Editor
Jeff Evans, CEO/President
Jing Huang, Project Manager

Publication of Latin American petrochemicals.

4646 **Soap/Cosmetics/Chemical Specialties**
Cygnus Publishing
445 Broad Hollow Road
Suite 21
Melville, NY 11747-3601

631-845-2700
800-308-6397; Fax: 631-845-2798
soap@erols.com

Anita Hipius Shaw, Editor-in-Chief
Paul Bonaiuto, CFO
Kathy Scott, Director of Public Relations
John French, CEO

Includes tips on general management, purchasing, as well as new products and market trends, personal care, industrial and institutional markets, especially as they affect chemical, packing and equipment suppliers and their R and D professionals.
Cost: $30.00
Frequency: Monthly
Circulation: 6,491

4647 **Spray Technology & Marketing**
Industry Publications
3621 Hill Rd
Parsippany, NJ 07054-1001

973-331-9545; Fax: 973-331-9547
www.spraytechnology.com

Cynthia Hundley, Publisher
Michael L. SanGiovanni, Executive Editor
Shirleen Dorman, Editor

Features include articles on marketers, chemical and fragrance manufacturers and components manufacturers.
Frequency: Monthly
Circulation: 6,491
ISSN: 1055-2340
Founded in 1954
Mailing list available for rent
Printed in 4 colors on glossy stock

4648 **Sulfuric Acid Today**
PO Box 3502
Covington, LA 70434

985-893-9692; Fax: 985-893-8693
www.h2so4today.com

Earl B Heard, Publisher

Editorial covers industry news, engineering, technology and upcoming events.
Cost: $39.00
Frequency: SemiAnnual
Circulation: 5,000

4649 **Today's Chemist at Work**
American Chemical Society
1155 16th St NW
Washington, DC 20036-4892

202-872-4600
800-227-5558; Fax: 202-872-4615
service@acs.org
www.acs.org

Madeleine Jacobs, CEO/Executive Director
William F Carroll, VP

Covers reports on materials, new products, chemical education, analytical chemistry and instrumentation.
Cost: $18.00
Frequency: Monthly
Circulation: 120000
Founded in 1876

Trade Shows

4650 **AACC International Annual Meeting**
3340 Pilot Knob Road
St. Paul, MN 55121-2055

651-454-7250
800-328-7560; Fax: 651-454-0766
aacc@scisoc.org
www.aaccnet.org
Facebook, Twitter, LinkedIn

Robert L. Cracknell, President
Lydia Tooker Midness, Chair
Laura M. Hansen, President-Elect
Dave L. Braun, Treasurer

Formerly the American Association of Cereal Chemists, the AACC meeting offers the chance to come together, network with peers, discuss critical issues in the science and discover the methods of others.
Frequency: Annual/October

4651 **ACOS Annual Meeting & Expo**
American Oil Chemists' Society
2710 S Boulder
Urbana, IL 61802-6996

217-693-4813; Fax: 217-351-8091
meetings@aocs.org
www.aocs.org

Greg Hatfield, General Chairperson
Doreen Berning, Registration
Jeff Newman, Meeting Management/Logistics

The premier global science and business forum on fats, oils, surfactants, lipids and related materials. Includes oral and poster presentations, short courses, and exhibit, and networking with more than 1,600 colleagues from 60 countries.
2000 Attendees
Frequency: Annual/April-May

4652 **ACS Mid-Atlantic Regional Meeting**
American Chemical Society
1155 Sixteenth Street, NW
Washington, DC 20036

202-872-4600
800-227-5558; Fax: 989-835-8356
service@acs.org
www.acs.org

Madeleine Jacobs, CEO/Executive Director

Attend poster sessions, symposia and workshops to experience the most exciting and cutting-edge research in the field of chemistry.
1M Attendees
Frequency: Annual/Spring

4653 **ACS Spring & Fall National Meeting & Expos**
American Chemical Society
1155 Sixteenth Street NW
Washington, DC 20036

202-872-4600
800-227-5558; Fax: 202-776-8044
conf_vendorrel@acs.org
www.acs.org

Madeleine Jacobs, CEO/Executive Director

Symposia, poster sessions, and workshops around cutting-edge chemistry research.
1.2M Attendees
Frequency: Biennial

4654 **ALCA Annual Meeting**
American Leather Chemists Association
1314 50th Street
Suite 103
Lubbock, TX 79412

806-744-1798; Fax: 806-744-1785
alca@leatherchemists.org
www.leatherchemists.org

Carol Adcock, Executive Secretary
100 Attendees

4655 **AOAC International Annual Meeting & Expo**
AOAC International
481 North Frederick Avenue
Suite 500
Gaithersburg, MD 20877-2417

301-924-7077
800-379-2622; Fax: 301-924-7089
aoac@aoac.org
www.aoac.org
Facebook, LinkedIn

Lauren Chelf, Director, Meetings & Exposition

The meeting offers a diverse program of symposia, workshops, and poster and scientific sessions. Specific educational tracks are offered for analytical chemists, microbiologists, laboratory managers, and other laboratory personnel.
Frequency: August

4656 **ASBC Annual Meeting**
American Society of Brewing Chemists
3340 Pilot Knob Road
Saint Paul, MN 55121

651-454-7250
800-328-7560; Fax: 651-454-0766
Facebook, Twitter

Charles F. Strachan, President
Steven Nelson, Executive Officer
Karen Cummings, Director of Publications
A. Hope, VP Operations
300 Attendees
Frequency: June/Non-Members Fee
Founded in 1934

4657 **Agricultural Retailers Association Convention and Expo**
Agricultural Retailers Association
1156 15th Street
Suite 500
Washington, DC 20005

202-457-0825
800-844-4900; Fax: 314-567-6808
www.aradc.org

Daren Coppock, President/CEO
Richard Gupton, Sr. VP, Public Policy
Melisa Augusto, Dir., Comm. & Marketing

Annual show of 120 manufacturers, suppliers and distributors of agricultural chemicals and fertilizers. Seminar, conference and banquet.
1200 Attendees
Frequency: Annual
Founded in 1993

4658 **American Assn of Textile Chemists & Colorists International Conference**
American Assn of Textile Chemists & Colorists
PO Box 12215
Research Triangle Park, NC 27709-2215

919-549-8141
800-360-5380; Fax: 919-549-8933
danielsj@aatcc.org
www.aatcc.org

John Daniels, Executive VP
Debra Hibbard, Executive Assistant
Charles E Gavin, Treasurer

Colorants and chemical finishes for the textile trade are on display.
Frequency: Annual

4659 **American Chemical Society: Southeastern Regional Conference & Exhibition**
American Chemical Society
1155 16th Street NW
Washington, DC 20036

202-872-4600
800-227-5558; Fax: 202-872-4615
service@acs.org
www.acs.org

Madeleine Jacobs, CEO/Executive Director

Booths featuring exhibits of the chemicals industry.
Frequency: Annual

4660 **American College of Toxicology Annual Meeting**
9650 Rockville Pike
Bethesda, MD 20814

301-634-7840; Fax: 301-634-7852
www.actox.org

Carol Lemire, Executive Director
Eve Gamzu Kagan, Asst. Executive Director

Education courses and scientific symposia, exhibits of contract laboratories, toxicology supplies and equipment and science journal publishing companies.
500 Attendees
Frequency: November

4661 **American Institute Chemical Engineers Petrochemical Refining Expo**
3 Park Avenue
New York, NY 10016-4363

212-591-8100
800-242-4363; Fax: 212-591-8888
www.aiche.org
Facebook, Twitter, LinkedIn

Marie Stewart, Director

A marketplace for materials used in processing chemicals.
20M Attendees
Frequency: April

4662 **American Society Biochemistry and Molecular Biology Expo**
American Society of Biochem & Molecular Biology
9650 Rockville Pike
Bethesda, MD 20814-3996

301-634-7145; Fax: 301-881-2080
asbmb@asbmb.org
www.asbmb.org

600 booths of products used in biomedical research.
8M Attendees

4663 **Annual Green Chemistry & Engineering Conference**
ACS Green Chemistry Institute
1155 16th Street NW
Washington, DC 20036

202-872-6102
800-227-5558; Fax: 202-872-4615
gci@acs.org
www.GCandE.org

Speakers, sessions, education, exhibits.
Frequency: Annual

4664 **CPMA Conference**
Color Pigments Manufacturers Association
300 N Washington St
Suite 105
Alexandria, VA 22314-2530

703-684-4044; Fax: 703-684-1795
cpma@cpma.com
www.pigments.org

J Lawrence Robinson, President

Brings together pigments manufacturers their suppliers and users, and others with an interest in color pigments including regulators, consultants, and exhibitors.
Frequency: Annual

4665 **Chem Show: Chemical Process Industries Exposition**
International Exposition Company
15 Franklin Street
Westport, CT 06880-5903

203-221-9232; Fax: 203-221-9260
info@chemshow.com
www.chemshow.com

Mark Stevens, Vice President
Jeff Stevens, Sales Vice President

Bringing together in one place major manufacturers of equipment, systems and services for the CPI. Product categories include; process equipment, fluid handling equipment and systems, solids handling equipment and sytems, engineered materials, instruments and controls, environmental and safety equipment and systems and services.
Frequency: Biennial/Oct
Founded in 1915

4666 **Chem-Distribution**
PennWell Publishing Company
1421 S Sheridan Road
Tulsa, OK 74112-6619

918-835-3161
800-331-4463; Fax: 918-831-9834
headquarters@pennwell.com
www.pennwell.com

Bill Pryor, CEO/President
Junior Isles, Publisher/Editor

Exhibits of technology for the distribution, transfer and storage of chemicals and petrochemicals.

4667 **Chem-Safe**
PennWell Conferences and Exhibitions
1421 S Sheridan Road
Tulsa, OK 74112-6619

918-835-3161
800-331-4463; Fax: 918-831-9834
headquarters@pennwell.com
www.pennwell.com

Bill Pryor, CEO/President
Junior Isles, Publisher/Editor

Exhibits of environmental, safety and health technology for the chemical and process industries.

4668 **Chlorine Institute Annual Meeting & Trade Show**
Chlorine Institute
1300 Wilson Blvd
Arlington, VA 22209-2323

703-741-5760; Fax: 703-894-4130
www.chlorineinstitute.org

Arthur Dungan, President
Frequency: Annual/Spring

4669 **Conchem Exhibition and Conference**
Reed Exhibition Companies
255 Washington Street
Newton, MA 02458-1637

617-584-4900; Fax: 617-630-2222

Elizabeth Hitchcock, International Sales

The international event featuring specialty additives and chemicals for the building industry.
Frequency: November

4670 **Eastern Analystical Symposium & Exposition**
Eastern Analytical Symposium, Inc
PO Box 633
Montchanin, DE 19710-0633

610-485-4633; Fax: 610-485-9467
easinfo@aol.com
www.eas.org

Sheree Gold, Exposition Director

The world's leading community for analytcal chemists seeking education and career advancement. Technical programs, speakers, and the expo. 240 booths.
6M Attendees
Frequency: Annual

4671 **Electrochemical Society Meetings**
Electrochemical Society
65 S Main St
Building D
Pennington, NJ 08534-2827

609-737-1902; Fax: 609-737-2743
meetings@electrochem.org
www.electrochem.org

Roque J Calvo, Executive Director
Colleen Keepser, Executive Administrator
Mary Yess, Deputy Executive Director
Corey Eberhart, Global Sales Director
Karen Baliff Ornstein, Marketing Manager

Providing a forum for exchanging information on the latest scientific and technical developments in the fields of electrochemical and solid-state science and technology. ECS meetings bring together scientists, engineers, and researchers from academia, industry, and government laboratories to share results and discuss issues on related topics through a variety of formats, such as oral presentations, poster sessions, panel discussions, and tutorial sessions.
8000 Members
Frequency: Biannual/Spring & Fall
Founded in 1902

4672 **Federation of Spectroscopy Societies**
13 N Cliffe Drive
Wilmington, DE 19809-1623

302-656-0771

Dr. Edward Brame Jr, Show Manager

120 booths of analytical chemistry.
2M Attendees
Frequency: October

4673 **GlobalChem Conference and Exhibition**
1850 M St NW
Suite 700
Washington, DC 20036-5810

202-721-4100; Fax: 202-296-8120
info@socma.com
www.socma.com

Larry Sloan, President/CEO
Alicia Massey, Senior Manager

Provides information and interaction with experts on the U.S. Toxic Substances Control Act, emerging issues and trends in the product stewardship arena and equivalent international regulations.
6 Members
Founded in 1985

4674 **ILTA Storage Tank & Bulk Liquid Terminal Int'l Operating Conf. & Trade Show**
Independent Liquid Terminals Association
1005 North Glebe Road
Suite 600
Arlington, VA 22201

703-875-2011; Fax: 703-875-2018
info@ilta.org
www.ilta.org

E David Doane, President
Melinda Whitney, Director/Government Affairs
Renita Gross, Director of Mtgs/Info. Services

Containing 202 booths and 161 exhibits.
2,700 Attendees
Frequency: June

4675 **IUPAC World Polymer Congress**
2 Davidson Hall
Blacksburg, VA 24061-0001

540-231-7257; Fax: 540-231-3971
adhesoc@vt.edu
www.adhesionsociety.org

Lynn Penn, President
Paul J Clark, Treasurer
Esther Brann, Manager

Enabling technologies for a safe, sustainable, healthy world.
400 Members
Founded in 1978

4676 **InformexUSA**
1850 M St NW
Suite 700
Washington, DC 20036-5810

202-721-4100; Fax: 202-296-8120
info@socma.com
www.socma.com

Jill Aker, President

Serving businesses across a broad range of end-use markets such as pharmaceuticals, biopharmaceuticals, agrochemicals, adhesives, electronics, paints, and plastics. Utilizing an advisory committee, made up of industry executives and decision makers from across markets to help us make decisions that come directly from the chemical industry.
6 Members
Founded in 1985

4677 **International Thermal Spray Conference & Exposition**
ASM International
9639 Kinsman Road
Materials Park, OH 44073-0002

440-338-5151
800-336-5152; Fax: 440-338-4634
memberservicecenter@asminternational.org
www.asminternational.org

William T. Mahoney, Secretary & CEO
Lindy Good, Global Conference & Exhibit Planner

International annual conference for professional thermal spray technologists, researchers, manufacturers and suppliers.
30K Members
Frequency: Annual/May
Founded in 1913

4678 **International Topical Meeting on Nuclear Applications of Accelerators**
American Nuclear Society
555 N Kensington Avenue
La Grange Park, IL 60526

708-352-6611
800-323-3044; Fax: 708-352-0499
www.ans.org
Facebook, Twitter, LinkedIn

To provide an international forum for discussing the various applications of particle accelerators.
Frequency: Annual/April
Founded in 2006

4679 **Optimizing Your Lab Automation: Lessons from the Front Line**
1850 K St NW
Suite 625
Washington, DC 20006-2215

202-857-0717
800-892-1400; Fax: 202-887-5093
www.aacc.org
Facebook, Twitter, LinkedIn, YouTube

Robert Christenson, President
Steven Wong, President-Elect
Patricia Jones, Director

The premiere event for clinical laboratorians, industry representatives, and health care executives to network and get ahead.

4680 **PCA International Conference**
Pine Chemicals Associations, Inc
3350 Riverwood Parkway SE
Suite 1900
Atlanta, GA 30339

770-984-5340; Fax: 770-984-5341
wjones@pinechemicals.org
www.pinechemicals.org

Walter L Jones, President/COO
Gary Reed, Chairman/Board of Directors
200 Attendees
Frequency: September

4681 **Powder Bulk Solids Conference and Expo**
Reed Business Information
2000 Clearwater Drive
Oak Brook, IL 60523

630-740-0825
www.reedbusiness.com

Angela Piermartini, Show Manager

1,300 booths.
11M Attendees
Frequency: May

4682 **Spray Foam Conference & EXPO**
Spray Polyurethane Foam Alliance
4400 Fair Lakes Court
Suite 105
Fairfax, VA 22033

800-523-6154; Fax: 703-222-5816
info@sprayfoam.org
www.sprayfoam.org

Sig Hall, President
Robert Duke, Vice President
Peter Davis, Secretary/Treasurer

Training and accreditation programs, general and breakout sessions, awards, networking receptions, and the exhibit hall.
Frequency: Annual/February
Founded in 1987

Directories & Databases

4683 **Adhesives Digest**
International Plastics Selector/DATA Business Pub.
15 Inverness Way E
#6510
Englewood, CO 80112-5710

303-904-0407

A who's who directory of services and supplies to the industry.
Cost: $180.00
Frequency: Biennial

4684 **Advanced Coatings and Surface Technology**
John Wiley & Sons
111 River St
Hoboken, NJ 07030-5790

201-748-6000; Fax: 201-748-6088
info@wiley.com
www.wiley.com

William J Pesce, Chief Executive Officer

Offers information on coatings and surface technology, covering breakthroughs in traditional coating processes, chemical vapor deposition and ion beam methods.
Frequency: Full-text

4685 **American Coke & Coal Chemicals Institute Directory and By-Laws**
1140 Connecticut Ave NW
Suite 705
Washington, DC 20036-4011

202-452-7177; Fax: 202-496-9702
information@accci.org
www.recycle-steel.org

Chip Foley, VP
Charles Stewart, Chairman

Represents merchant oven coke producers, integrated coke producers, tar distillers, sales agents, and industry suppliers.
75 Pages
Founded in 1944

4686 **American Laboratory Buyers Guide**
International Scientific Communications
PO Box 870
Shelton, CT 06484-0870

203-926-9300; Fax: 203-926-9310
www.iscpubs.com

Brian Howard, Editor
Robert G Sweeny, Publisher

Manufacturers of and dealers in scientifi instruments, equipment, apparatus, and chemicals worldwide.
Cost: $25.00
Frequency: Annual

4687 **Available Chemicals Directory**
MDL Information Systems
3100 Central Expressway
Santa Clara, CA 05051-6608

408-764-2000
800-635-0064; Fax: 408-748-0175

Magnetic tape, covers approximately 240,000 commercially available chemicals, including organic, and inorganic chemicals.
Frequency: Semiannual

4688 **CEH On-Line**
SRI International
333 Ravenswood Ave
Menlo Park, CA 94025-3493

650-859-3711; Fax: 650-326-8916
www.srifcu.org

Steve Bowles, President

Database containing economic data for more than 1300 major commodity and specialty chemical products.
Frequency: Full-text

4689 **CERCLIS Database of Hazardous Waste Sites**
Environmental Protection Agency
Ariel Rios Building
1200 Pennsylvania Avenue NW
Washington, DC 20460

202-272-0167
r9.info@epa.gov
www.epa.gov

Bob Zachariasiewicz, Acting Director
Shushona Hyson, Contact
Curt Spalding, Regional

Stands for Comprehensive Environmental Response, Compensation, and Liability Information System. This database contains information on more than 36,000 releases of hazardous substances reported to the US Environmental Protection Agency.
Frequency: Directory

4690 **CHEMEST**
Technical Database Services

62 W 39th Street
Rm 704
New York, NY 10018

212-245-0384; Fax: 212-556-0036

Mildred Green, Principal

This database contains information for estimating the properties of pharmaceuticals and chemicals of environmental concern.
Frequency: Properties

4691 **CLAIMS/Comprehensive Data Base**
IFI/Plenum Data Corporation
PO Box 1148
Madison, CT 06443

203-779-5301; Fax: 203-583-4521
info@ificlaims.com

Harry M Allcock, VP

This database contains enhanced indexing of the US chemical and chemically related patents included in the CLAIMS/UNITERM database.

4692 **Chem Source USA**
Chemical Sources International
PO Box 1824
Clemson, SC 29633

864-646-7840; Fax: 864-642-6168
information@chemsources.com
www.chemsources.com

Mike Desing, Editor

Book containing information on where to obtain chemicals in the US and Canada.
Cost: $495.00
1700 Pages
Frequency: Annual January
Circulation: 10000
Founded in 1958

4693 **Chem Sources International**
PO Box 1824
Clemson, SC 29633-1824

864-646-7840
800-222-4531; Fax: 864-646-6168
csinfo@chemsources.com
www.chemsources.com

Mike Desing, Editor
Dale Krohn, Owner

The most comprehensive directory ever compiled on the world's chemical industry. Includes the products of more than 8,000 chemical firms spanning 128 countries.
Cost: $750.00
Frequency: Biennial
Founded in 1958

4694 **Chemcyclopedia**
American Chemical Society
676 East Swedesford Road
Suite 202
Wayne, PA 19087-1612

610-964-8061; Fax: 610-964-8061
carroll@acs.org
www.acs.org
1

Madeleine Jacobs, Executive Director/CEO
Ken Carroll, Publisher

List of over 900 chemical manufacturers in the US.
Cost: $60.00
Frequency: Annual

4695 **Chemical Abstracts**
American Chemical Society
1155 16th St NW
Suite 600
Washington, DC 20036-4892

202-872-4600
800-227-5558; Fax: 202-872-4615
service@acs.org
www.acs.org

Madeleine Jacobs, CEO

Newsletter covering this branch of the American Chemical Society.
Frequency: Monthly

4696 **Chemical Exposure and Human Health**
McFarland & Company Publishers
PO Box 611
Jefferson, NC 28640-0611

336-246-4460
800-253-2187; Fax: 336-246-5018
info@mcfarlandpub.com
www.mcfarlandpub.com

Cynthia Wilson, Editor

A list of organizations concerned with the effects of chemical exposure. Government exposure standards on over 300 chemicals.
Cost: $55.00
ISBN: 0-899508-10-3

4697 **Chemical Regulations and Guidelines System**
Network Management CRC Systems
11242 Waples Mill Road
Fairfax, VA 22030-6079

703-219-3865

This database contains citations, with abstracts, to US government statutes and federal guidelines.

4698 **Chemical Week: Financial Survey of the 300 Largest Companies in the US**
Chemical Week Associates
110 William St
New York, NY 10038-3910

212-621-4900; Fax: 212-621-4800
www.chemweek.com

John Rockwell, Vice President

Offers information on over 300 chemical process companies in the United States.
Cost: $8.00
7 Pages
Frequency: Annual
Circulation: 50,615

4699 **DRI Chemical**
DRI/McGraw-Hill
24 Hartwell Ave
Lexington, MA 02421-3103

781-860-6060; Fax: 781-860-6002
support@construction.com
www.construction.com

Keith Fox, President
Linda Brennan, VP Operations
Bob Stuono, Senior VP And General Manager

The coverage of this database encompasses the chemical industry in the United States, including imports and exports, inventories, production, sales, shipments and uses.

4700 **DRI Chemical Forecast**
DRI/McGraw-Hill
24 Hartwell Ave
Lexington, MA 02421-3103

781-860-6060; Fax: 781-860-6002
support@construction.com
www.construction.com

Keith Fox, President

This time series contains over 700 quarterly forecasts on US supply and demand for more than 120 chemical products.

4701 **Directory of Bulk Liquid Terminal and Storage Facilities**
Independent Liquid Terminals Association
1005 North Glebe Road
Arlington, VA 22201

703-875-2011; Fax: 703-875-2018
info@ilta.org
www.ilta.org

E David Doane, President
Melinda Whitney, Director/Executive VP

Published annually in April.
Cost: $95.00

4702 **Directory of Chemical Producers: East Asia**
SRI Consulting/IHS Global
333 Ravenswood Ave
Menlo Park, CA 94025-3493

650-859-3711; Fax: 650-326-8916
www.srifcu.org

Steve Bowles, President

Over 2,000 companies producing over 14,000 chemicals in 2,600 plant locations in Indonesia, Japan, Korea, Taiwan and the Philippines.
Cost: $1800.00
800 Pages
Frequency: Annual

4703 **Directory of Chemical Producers: U.S.**
SRI Consulting/IHS Global
333 Ravenswood Ave
Menlo Park, CA 94025-3493

650-859-3711; Fax: 650-326-8916
www.srifcu.org

Steve Bowles, President

Over 1,500 United States basic chemical producers manufacturing almost 10,000 chemicals in commercial quantities at 4,500 plant locations. Providing comprehensive, accurate and timely coverage of the international chemical industry since 1961.
Cost: $1460.00
1100 Pages
Frequency: Annual

4704 **Directory of Chemical Producers: Western Europe**
SRI Consulting/IHS Global
333 Ravenswood Ave
Menlo Park, CA 94025-3493

650-859-3711; Fax: 650-326-8916
www.srifcu.org

Steve Bowles, President

Covered are over 2,500 western European chemical producers, chemicals and plant locations.
Cost: $1930.00
Frequency: Annual
Circulation: 2,100

4705 **Directory of Custom Chemical Manufacturers**
Delphi Marketing Services
400 E 89th Street
Apartment 2J
New York, NY 10128-6728
Newman Giragosian, Editor

A list of over 280 custom chemical manufacturers.
Cost: $295.00
220 Pages

4706 **Directory of Suppliers of Services**
Independent Liquid Terminals Association

1005 North Glebe Road
Arlington, VA 22201

703-875-2011; Fax: 703-875-2018
info@ilta.org
www.ilta.org

E David Doane, President
Melinda Whitney, Director/Executive VP
Cost: $25.00

4707 **Environmental Fate Data Bases**
Syracuse Research Corporation
6225 Running Ridge Rd
North Syracuse, NY 13212-2510

315-452-8000
800-724-0451; Fax: 315-452-8100

Cheryl Wolfe, President

This database, consisting of 4 interrelated files of information on the fate of organic chemicals. The files include information in physical/chemical properties, degradation and transport, and monitoring for 16,000 chemicals.

4708 **Environmental Industry Yearbook and The Gallery**
Environmental Economics
1026 Irving Street
Philadelphia, PA 19107-6707

215-877-2063; Fax: 215-440-0116

More than 80 publicly traded companies, plus Fortune 500 firms that have an impact on environmental concerns.
Cost: $75.00
250 Pages
Frequency: SemiAnnual

4709 **Fine Chemicals Database**
Chemron
PO Box 2299
Paso Robles, CA 93447

210-340-8121
800-423-1148; Fax: 210-340-8123

This large database provides supplier information for more than 27,000 chemical products available from over 50 manufacturers and distributors in North America.
Frequency: Directory

4710 **Index to Chemical Regulations**
Bureau of National Affairs
1801 S Bell St
Arlington, VA 22202-4501

703-341-3000
800-372-1033; Fax: 800-253-0332
customercare@bna.com
www.bnabooks.com

Paul N Wojcik, Chairman
Gregory C McCaffery, President

A one-binder index containing more than 80,000 citations by chemical name to the Code of Federal Regulations and the Federal Register.
Cost: $988.00
Frequency: Monthly

4711 **Information Officers of Member Companies**
Chemical Manufacturers Association
1300 Wilson Boulevard
Arlington, VA 22209-2307

703-741-5502; Fax: 703-741-6807

Thomas J Gilroy, Associate Media Director

About 180 companies.
Frequency: Biennial

4712 **International Chemical Regulatory Monitoring System**
Ariel Research Corporation
4320 East West Highway
Suite 440
Bethesda, MD 20814-3319

301-951-2500; Fax: 301-986-1681
www.3ecompany.com

John Wyatt, CEO

This database contains references to regulations and precautionary data on more than 100,000 chemical substances.
Frequency: Full-text

4713 **Kirk-Othmer Encyclopedia of Chemical Technology Online**
John Wiley & Sons
111 River St
Hoboken, NJ 07030-5790

201-748-6000
800-825-7550; Fax: 201-748-6088
info@wiley.com
www.wiley.com

Warren J Baker, President
Richard M Hochhauser, CEO

This comprehensive database offers complete text, citations, tables and abstracts of all 1,200 chapters in the 25-volume Encyclopedia of the same name. With no concurrent usage restriction, you can call up information covering the entire chemical industry and allied fields any time with a click of your mouse from the library, office or laboratory.

4714 **McCutcheons Functional Materials**
McCutcheons Division
P.O.Box 2249
New Preston Marble Dale, CT 06777-0249

201-652-2655; Fax: 201-652-3419
mcinfo@gomc.com
www.gomc.com

Michael Allured, Publisher

List of materials commonly used in conjunction with surfactants such as enzymes, lubricants, waxes, corrosion inhibitors, and other chemicals produced worldwide.
Cost: $40.00
Frequency: Monthly
Founded in 1921

4715 **Multilingual Thesaurus of Geosciences**
Information Today
143 Old Marlton Pike
Medford, NJ 08055-8750

609-654-6266
800-300-9868; Fax: 609-654-4309
custserv@infotoday.com
www.infotoday.com

Thomas H Hogan, President
Roger R Bilboul, Chairman Of The Board

Represents the state of the art use of geoscience terminology by information centers around the world.
Cost: $99.00
654 Pages
ISBN: 1-573870-09-9

4716 **OPIS/STALSBY Electric Power Industry Directory**
OPIS/STALSBY
1255 Highway 70
Suite 32-N
Lakewood, NJ 08701

732-901-8800
877-210-4287; Fax: 732-901-9632
www.opisnet.com

Karen England, Senior Editor
Karen Reng, Marketing Manager
Christine Kaniuk, Production/Advertising Coordinator

Provides detailed listings of over 1,200 companies and more than 2,700 personnel of the electric power industry. Company categories include producer, marketer, trader, broker, transmission, investor-owned, municipal, rural/co-op/fed/local government and independent. Personnel listings include sales/marketing, supply/purchasing, operations/transmissions, finance/treasury. Company listings include address, direct telephone, fax numbers and e-mails. CD-ROM $495.
Cost: $141.00

Frequency: 2 per year
Circulation: 625
Printed in 4 colors

4717 **OPIS/STALSBY Petrochemicals Directory**
OPIS/STALSBY
3349 State Route 138
Unit D
Wall Township, NJ 07719-9671

732-730-2500
877-210-4287; Fax: 732-280-0542
www.ucg.com

Ben Brockwell, Manager
Karen Reng, Marketing Manager
Christine Kaniuk, Production/Advertising Coordinator
Bruce Levenson, Co-Founder

Provides detailed listings of over 2,100 companies and more than 7,000 personnel covering all segments of the petrochemical gas industry, including manufacturing, trading and distributing of petrochemicals. Company listings include addresses, telephone, fax, TLX, personal phone/fax numbers, cell phones and home addresses, area of responsibility and job titles. Five separate indices are provided for complete cross-referencing. CD-ROM $995.
Cost: $175.00

Frequency: 2 per year
Circulation: 425
Printed in 4 colors

4718 **OPIS/STALSBY Petroleum Supply Americas Directory**
OPIS/STALSBY
1255 Highway 70
Suite 32-N
Lakewood, NJ 08701

732-901-8800
877-210-4287; Fax: 732-901-9632
www.opisnet.com

Karen England, Senior Editor
Karen Reng, Marketing Manager
Christine Kaniuk, Production/Advertising Coordinator

Helps traders, marketers and suppliers of crude oil, refined products and gas liquids to access detailed information on over 2,500 companies and 10,000 personnel in North, Central and South America. Company listings include company address, telephone, fax, TLX, personal phone/fax numbers, car phones, home addresses, area of responsibility and job title. Four separate indices are provided for complete cross-referencing. CD-ROM $995.
Cost: $235.00

Frequency: 2 per year
Circulation: 2,045
Printed in 4 colors

4719 **OPIS/STALSBY Petroleum Supply Europe Directory**
OPIS/STALSBY

1255 Highway 70
Suite 32-N
Lakewood, NJ 08701

732-901-8800
877-210-4287; Fax: 732-901-9632
www.opisnet.com

Karen England, Senior Editor
Karen Reng, Marketing Manager
Christine Kaniuk, Production/Advertising Coordinator

Helps traders, marketers and suppliers of crude oil, refined products and gas liquids to access detailed information on over 1,500 companies and 6,600 personnel in Europe, Eastern Europe, Africa and the Middle East. Listings include company address, telephone, fax, TLX, personal phone/fax numbers, car phones, home addresses, area of responsibility and job titles. Four separate indices are provided for complete cross-referencing. CD-OM $995.
Cost: $190.00
Frequency: 2 per year
Circulation: 425
Printed in 4 colors

4720 **OPIS/STALSBY Petroleum Terminal Encyclopedia**
OPIS/STALSBY
1255 Highway 70
Suite 32-N
Lakewood, NJ 08701

732-901-8800
877-210-4287; Fax: 732-901-9632
www.opisnet.com

Karen England, Senior Editor
Karen Reng, Marketing Manager
Christine Kaniuk, Production/Advertising Coordinator

Provides detailed listings of over 2,800 petroleum terminals. Information includes pipeline and rail interconnections and truck facilities for each terminal; berth, waterway and docking information for marine terminals; details on both public and private terminals for market analysis and exchange planning. Three separate indices are provided for complete cross-referencing. CD-ROM $995.
Cost: $245.00
Frequency: 2 per year
Circulation: 825
Printed in 4 colors

4721 **OPIS/STALSBY Who's Who in Natural Gas**
OPIS/STALSBY
1255 Highway 70
Suite 32-N
Lakewood, NJ 08701

732-901-8800
877-210-4287; Fax: 732-901-9632
www.opisnet.com

Karen England, Senior Editor
Karen Reng, Marketing Manager
Christine Kaniuk, Production/Advertising Coordinator

Provides detailed listings of over 2,600 companies and more than 11,000 personnel covering all segments of the natural gas industry, including producers, processors, marketers, traders, transporters, major buyers, LDCs, brokers, gas storage, regulatory, etc. Company listings include addresses, telephone, fax, TLX, personal phone/fax numbers, car phones and home addresses, area of responsibility and job titles. Four separate indices are provided for complete cross-referencing. CD-ROM $995.
Cost: $200.00
Frequency: 2 per year
Circulation: 950
Printed in 4 colors

4722 **Purchasing/CPI Edition: Chemicals Yellow Pages**
Reed Business Information
2000 Clearwater Dr
Oak Brook, IL 60523-8809

630-574-0825; Fax: 630-288-8781
www.reedbusiness.com

Jeff Greisch, President

Manufacturers and distributors of 10,000 chemicals and raw materials; manufacturers and distributors of containers and packaging.
Cost: $85.00
Frequency: Annual

4723 **Refining & Gas Processing**
Midwest Publishing Company
PO Box 4468
Suite E
Tulsa, OK 74159-0468

918-583-9999
800-829-2002; Fax: 918-587-9349
www.midwestpub.com

Will L Hammack, Owner

Over 5,200 refineries, gas processing plants, engineering contractors, equipment manufacturers and supply companies.
Cost: $145.00
Frequency: Annual, May
Founded in 1943

4724 **Regulated Chemical Directory**
Kluwer Academic Publishers
101 Philip Drive
Norwellk, MA 02061

617-871-6600; Fax: 617-871-6528
www.hcirn.com

List of major federal and selected state and international regulatory and advisory sources of information regarding chemicals in the US, Canada, Australia, Germany and Israel.
Cost: $375.00
Frequency: Annual, January

4725 **STN Easy**
Chemical Abstracts Service
PO Box 3012
Columbus, OH 43210-0012

614-473-3600
800-848-6538; Fax: 614-447-3713
help@cas.org
www.cas.org

Easy web acccess to scientific research and patents. STN Easy provides access to more than 60 databases covering all types of sci/tech information including chemistry, life sciences, buisiness, MSDS, math/computer science, engineering, medicine, pharmaceuticals, general science, food and agriculture, and regulatory information.

4726 **Soap/Cosmetics/Chemical Specialties: Blue Book Issue**
Cygnus Publishing
445 Broad Hollow Road
Suite 21
Melville, NY 11747-3601

631-845-2700; Fax: 631-845-2723

Anita Shaw, Editor-in-Chief
Shelley Colwell, CFO
Paul Bonaiuto, CFO
Kathy Scott, Director of Public Relations

Sources of raw materials, equipment and services for the chemical, soap and cosmetics industries. Includes a list of trade associations.
Cost: $15.00
Frequency: Annual, April
Circulation: 19,000

Industry Web Sites

4727 **http://gold.greyhouse.com**
G.O.L.D Grey House OnLine Databases

Grey House Publishing's online database platform, GOLD, offers Quick Search, Keyword Search and Expert Search for most business sectors including chemical and agriculture markets. The GOLD platform makes finding the information you need quick and easy - whether you're a novice searcher or an experienced database user. All of Grey House's directory products are be available for subscription on the GOLD platform.

4728 **www.aaccnet.org**
American Association of Cereal Chemists

Nonprofit international organization of nearly 4,000 members who are specialists in the use of cereal grains in foods. AACC has been an innovative leader in gathering and disseminating scientific and technical information to professionals in the grain based foods industry worldwide for over 85 years.

4729 **www.accci.org**
American Coke & Coal Chemicals Institute Directory

For merchant oven coke producers, integrated coke producers, tar distillers, sales agents, and industry suppliers.

4730 **www.actox.org**
American College of Toxicology

Multidisciplinary society composed of professionals having a common interest in toxicology. Our mission is to educate and lead professionals in industry, government and related areas of toxicology by actively promoting the exchange of information and perspectives on the current status of safety assesment and the application of new developments in toxicology.

4731 **www.aiche.org**
American Institute of Chemical Engineers

Professional association of more than 50,000 members, providing leadership in advancing the chemical engineering profession. Members develop processes and design and operate manufacturing plants, as well as research the safe and environmentally sound manufacture, use and disposal of chemical products.

4732 **www.americanchemistry.com**
American Chemistry Council

Committed to improved environmental, health and safety performance through responsible care, common sense advocacy designed to address major public policy issues, health and environmental research and product testing.

4733 **www.aoac.org**
Association of Official Analytical Communities

Calender, publications and training courses. AOAC serves as the primary resource for timely knowledge exchange, networking and high quality laboratory information for its members.

4734 **www.aocs.org**
American Oil Chemists Society

Encourages advancement of technology and research in fats, oils and other associated substances.

4735 **www.asms.org**
American Society for Mass Spectrometry

Formed to disseminate knowledge of mass spectrometry and allied topics. Members come from academic, industrial and governmental laboratories. Their interests include advancement of techniques and instrumentation in mass specrometry, as well as fundamental research in chemistry, geology, biological sciences and physics.

4736 **www.chemheritage.org**
Chemical Heritage Foundation
An independent, nonprofit organization, CHF maintains major collections of instruments, fine art, photographs, papers, and books. We host conferences and lectures, support research, offer fellowships, and produce educational materials.

4737 **www.chemistry.org**
American Chemical Society
Encourages advancement in all branches of chemistry. There are 34 ACS divisions and 188 local sections.

4738 **www.chemtrec.org**
American Chemistry Council
Serves as a referral service for non-emergency health and safety information, maintains library and speakers bureaus. Offers 24 hour emergency communication service center for hazardous materials, material data sheets, lending library, audio-visual training programs.

4739 **www.coatingstech.org**
Federation of Societies for Coatings Technology
Provides technical education and professional development to its members and to the global industry through its multi-national constituent societies and collectively as a federation.

4740 **www.combustioninstitute.org**
Combustion Institute
A non-profit, educational, scientific society whose purpose is to promote and disseminate research combustion science.

4741 **www.cspa.org**
Consumer Specialty Products Association
Nonprofit organization composed of many companies involved in the formulation, manufacture, testing and marketing of chemical specialty products. Our line includes disinfectants that kill germs in homes, hospitals and restaurants, candles that eliminate odors, pest management products for home and garden, cleaning products and much more.

4742 **www.dupont.com/nacs**
DuPont Experimental Station
For chemists and chemical engineers engaged in the study and use of reactions involving catalysts. Publishes a newsletter

4743 **www.electrochem.org**
Electrochemical Society
The society is an international nonprofit, educational organization concerned with phenomena relating to electrochemical and solid state science and technology. Members are individual scientists and engineers, as well as corporations and laboratories.

4744 **www.fibersource.com**
American Fiber Manufacturers Association
Trade association for US companies that manufacture synthetic and cellulostic fibers. The industry employs 30,000 people and produces over 9 billion pounds of fiber in the US. The association maintains close ties to other manufactured fiber trade associations worldwide.

4745 **www.greyhouse.com**
Grey House Publishing
Authoritative reference directories for most business sectors incluidng chemical and agricultural markets. Users can search the online databases with varied search criteria allowing for custom searches by product category, geographic area, sales volume, keyword, subject and more. Full Grey House catalog and online ordering also available.

4746 **www.ilta.org**
Independent Liquid Terminals Association
Representing bulk liquid terminal companies that store commercial liquids in aboveground storage tanks and transfer products to and from oceangoing tanks ships, tank barges, pipelines, tank trucks, and tank rail cars.

4747 **www.ioa-pag.org**
International Ozone Association
Nonprofit educational association providing information on ozone with a membership of scientists, engineers, systems designers, technologists, equipment manufacturers and others working with ozone and other related oxygen compounds. The association sponsors international symposia, seminars, publications, and networking among ozone specialists.

4748 **www.leatherchemists.org**
American Leather Chemists Association
Publishes the Journal of the American Leather Chemists Association where original research reports are published along with abstracts of foreign articles. A four-day technical meeting is held annually. Promotes the advancement of the knowledge of science and engineering in their application to the problems facing the leather and leather products industries.

4749 **www.methanol.org**
American Methanol Institute
Our mission is to expand markets for the use of methanol as a chemical commodity building block, a hydrogen carrier for fuel cell applications, and an alternative fuel. AMI was formed in 1989, during the height of the Clean Air Act debate, and worked to help create the highly successful reformulated gasoline program.

4750 **www.mti-link.org**
Materials Tech. Institute of the Chemical Process
MTI provides leadership in materials technology for chemical processing to improve reliability, profitability and safety.

4751 **www.nacatsoc.org**
North American Catalysis Society
Fosters an interest in heterogeneous and homogeneous catalysis. Organizes national meetings. Members are chemists and chemical engineers engaged in the study and use of reactions involving catalysts. Publishes a newsletter.

4752 **www.pemanet.org**
Process Equipment Manufacturers' Association
Organized in 1960, we represent more than 40 companies in the process equipment field. Member companies serve the liquid-solids separation, food processing, pulp and paper, waste water treatment industry and others.

4753 **www.pestworld.org**
National Pest Control Association
For over 65 years, the NPMA has represented the interests of its members and the structural pest control industry. Through the efforts of NPMA, the pest control industry is stronger, more professional, and more unified. Guiding its members and industry through legislative and regulatory initiatives on the federal and state levels, the creation of verifiable training, the changing technologies used by the industry, and public and media relations, NPMA has been a clear, positive voice.

4754 **www.pfa.org**
Polyurethane Foam Association
Educating customers and other groups about flexible polyurethane foam and to promote its use in manufactured and indutrial products. This includes providing facts on environmental, health and safety issues related to polyurethane foam to the memebership of PFA, polyurethane foam users, regulatory officials, business leaders and the media.

4755 **www.pigments.org**
Color Pigments Manufacturers Association
An industry trade association representing color pigment companies in Canada, Mexico and the US. Represents small, medium, and large color pigments manufacturers accounting for 95% of the production of color pigments in North America

4756 **www.pima.org**
Polyisocyanurate Insulation Manufacturers Assn
National association that advances the use of polyisocyanurate (polyiso) insulation. Polyiso is one of the nation's most widely used and cost-effective insulation products. PIMA's membership consiosts of manufacturers as well as suppliers to the industry.

4757 **www.pinechemicals.org**
Pine Chemicals Association
Association of producers, processors and consumers of pine chemicals. The PCA promotes innovative, safe and environmentally responsible practices to assure a reliable supply of high quality products.

4758 **www.powdercoating.org**
Powder Coating Institute
Founded in 1981 as a nonprofit organization, PCI works to advance the utilization of powder coating as an economical, non-polluting and high quality finish for industrial and consumer products.

4759 **www.scisoc.org/asbc**
American Society of Brewing Chemists
News, information, member directory and publications.

4760 **www.socma.com**
Synthetic Organic Chemical Manufacturers Assn
Trade association serving the specialty batch and custom chemical industry since 1921. Its more than 320 member companies have more than 2,000 manufacturing sites and 100,000 employees. SOCMA members encompass every segment of the industry - and manufacture 50,000 products annually that are valued at $60 billion dollars.

4761 **www.toxicology.org**
Society of Toxicology
Members are scientists concerned with the effects of chemicals on man and the environment. Promotes the aquisition and utilization of knowledge in toxicology, aids in the protection of public health and facilitates disiplines. The society has a strong commitment to education in toxicology and to the recruitment of students and new members into the profession.

Associations

4762 **American Association of Cleaning Equipment Manufacturers**
800-225-4772
aacem.org
Allison Hill, AACEM Coordinator
A subsidiary organization of ISSA that exists to serve and represent the interests of manufacturers of commercial and industrial powered cleaning equipment. AACEM promotes public awareness, professionalism, industry-wide safety standards, and education for the advancement of the cleaning equipment industry.

4763 **American Cleaning Institute**
1401 H Steet NW
Suite 700
Washington, DC 20005
202-347-2900; Fax: 202-347-4110
info@cleaninginstitute.org
www.cleaninginstitute.org
Facebook, Twitter, LinkedIn, RSS Feed, SchoolTube, YouTube
Melissa Hockstad, President & CEO
Korie Traver, CFO
Merla Zollinger, Sr. Director, Convention & Meetings
Ann Cothran, Sr. Manager, Membership
Joanne Oh, Communications & Outreach Coord.
The American Cleaning Institute (ACI) is the Home of the U.S. Cleaning Products Industry. ACI serves the growth and innocation for the U.S. cleaning products industry by advancing the health and quality of life of people and protecting the planet.
100+ Members
Founded in 1926
Mailing list available for rent

4764 **Association for Linen Management**
138 N Keeneland Dr.
Suite D
Richmond, KY 40475
859-624-0177
800-669-0863; Fax: 859-624-3580
www.almnet.org
Facebook, Twitter, Pinterest
Linda Fairbanks, Executive Director
Christina Horsley, Director, Education & Events
Anthony Carpenter, Office Manager
Nicole Morris, Marketing & Communications Manager
Fontaine Sands, Clinical Advisor
Association for the advancement of professional development in the laundry institute.
Founded in 1939

4765 **Association of Residential Cleaning Services International**
1001 Eastwind Drive
Suite 301
Westerville, OH 43081
224-534-5060
800-225-4772
847-982-0800
arcsi.org
Facebook, Twitter
ARSCI was established to assist residential cleaning service owners and professionals in starting, promoting, building and expanding their businesses. ARCSI is committed to providing valuable information to ensure the growth and development of members' businesses.
Founded in 2003

4766 **Association of Rug Care Specialists**
P.O. Box 207
Salem, OR 97308
503-949-9700; Fax: 208-977-6577
info@rugcarespecialists.org
www.rugcarespecialists.org
Facebook, Twitter
Ann Marie Thompson, Executive Director
The preeminent trade association dedicated solely to the art and science of rug care.

4767 **Building Service Contractors Association International**
330 N. Wabash Ave.
Suite 2000
Chicago, IL 60611
312-321-5167
800-368-3414; Fax: 312-673-6735
info@bscai.org
www.bscai.org
LinkedIn
Chris Mundschenk, EVP/ CEO
Paul Greenland, President
Jim Harris, Jr, Treasurer
Tom Kruse, Vice President
Michael Diamond, Director
Trade association for companies offering security, maintenance and cleaning services. The international membership now represents over 10% of the association's professional membership.
Cost: $30.00
2500 Members
Founded in 1965
Mailing list available for rentat $75 per M

4768 **California Cleaners Asssociation**
700 N. Valley Street
Suite B PMB 69559
Anaheim, CA 92801
916-239-4070; Fax: 240-295-4200
peter@calcleaners.org
www.calcleaners.com
Peter Blake, Contact
The California Cleaners Association (CCA) is the statewide, professional trade association for California's best dry cleaners and the companies who serve them.

4769 **Chlorine Free Products Association**
1304 S Main St
Algonquin, IL 60102-2757
847-658-6104; Fax: 847-658-3152
info@chlorinefreeproducts.org
www.chlorinefreeproducts.org
Archie Beaton, Executive Director
A nonprofit association that's primary purpose is to promote total chlorine free policies, programs and technologies throughtout the world.

4770 **Cleaning & Restoration Association**
3284 Ramos Circle
Sacramento, CA 95827
916-736-1100; Fax: 916-736-1134
info@crassociation.org
www.crassociation.org
Facebook, Twitter, LinkedIn
Gabe Whitney, President
Don Banister, Vice President
Jim Holland, Executive Director
Jennifer Germond, Member Services
The CRA is a nonprofit organization of Cleaning and Restoration firms from the Western United States. The association's goal is to create venues for advancing the knowledge and professionalism of the cleaning and restoration industry.

4771 **Cleaning Equipment Trade Association**
11450 U.S. Highway 380
Suite 130, #289
Cross Roads, TX 76227
800-441-0111; Fax: 704-635-7363
info@ceta.org
www.ceta.org
Debbie Murray, Managing Director
Jim Welch, President
International nonprofit association made up of manufacturers, distributors, suppliers and contractors who coordinate their efforts to promote public awareness, professionalism, industry wide safety standards, and education for the advancement of the powered cleaning equipment industry.
300 Members
Founded in 1990

4772 **Cleaning Management Institute**
125 Wolf Road Suite 112
Albany, NY 12205
800-225-4772; Fax: 847-982-1012
brant@issa.com
www.cminstitute.net
Facebook, RSS
John Barrett, Executive Director
Kim Althoff, VP, Sales, Trade Shows & Membership
Jon Adkins, VP, Divisions, Marketing & IT
CMI provides education, training and career improvement opportunities for building cleaning and maintenance professionals.
1000 Members
Founded in 1964

4773 **Coin Laundry Association**
1 S. 660 Midwest Rd.
Suite 205
Oakbrook Terrace, IL 60181
630-953-7920
800-570-5629; Fax: 630-953-7925
info@coinlaundry.org
www.coinlaundry.org
Facebook, Twitter, LinkedIn, YouTube, Google+
Brian Wallace, President & CEO
Danielle Bauer, Director, Membership
Rich Cruz, Director, Marketing & Development
Tanisha Moore, Meetings & Events Manager
Bob Nieman, Editor
Association for self-service laundry and dry cleaning industry.
2700+ Members
Founded in 1960

4774 **Drycleaning & Laundry Institute International**
14700 Sweitzer Lane
Laurel, MD 20707
301-622-1900
800-638-2627; Fax: 240-295-4200
techline@dlionline.org
www.dlionline.org
Facebook, Twitter, Flicker
Representing over ten thousand retail drycleaners in the United States alone, DLI is the world's leading professional garment care organization. Through legislative and regulatory policy development, education, professional training, information, garment analysis, and research, DLI offers solutions to help member businesses remain on the competitive edge.
Founded in 1883

4775 **Environmental Management Association**
Vickie Lewis, EMA President

38575 Mallast
Harrison Township, MI 48045

313-875-9450
866-999-4EMA; Fax: 586-463-8075
emadirector@gmail.com
www.emaweb.org
Facebook, LinkedIn

Nancy Kapral, EMA Bookkeeper
Tricia Wanamaker, Executive Director

Association for manufacturers, suppliers and distributors of sanitation maintenance supplies, products, services.
11 Members
Founded in 1994

4776 **Halogenated Solvents Industry Alliance**
3033 Wilson Boulevard
Suite 700
Arlington, VA 22201

703-875-0683
info@hsia.org
www.hsia.org

Faye Graul, Executive Director
Christopher Bevan, PhD., Director, Scientific Programs

Represents the manufacturers of trichloroethynele, perchloroethylene and methylene chloride.

4777 **ISSA**
3300 Dundee Road
Northbrook, IL 60062

847-982-0800
800-225-4772; Fax: 847-982-1012
info@issa.com
www.issa.com
Facebook, Twitter, LinkedIn

John H. Barrett, Executive Director
Kim Althoff, VP, Sales/Trade Shows/Membership
Jon Adkins, VP, Divisions/Marketing/IT

The worldwide cleaning industry association.
5700+ Members
Founded in 1923

4778 **International Drycleaners Congress**
9016 Oak Branch Dr.
Apex, NC 27502

919-363-5062; Fax: 919-387-8326
idcgroup.org
Manfred Wentz, Executive Director
Nobuyasu Igarashi, President

International organization for cleaners.
Founded in 1959

4779 **International Janitorial Cleaning Services**
260 Peachtree Street NE
Suite 2200
Atlanta, GA 30303

404-267-1830
info@ijcsa.com
www.ijcsa.org
Facebook, Twitter

An organization representing the $94.5 billion dollar janitorial industry. Membershp base is compiled of custodians, janitors, residential cleaners, small family run businesses, medium sized cleaning firms, and large cleaning and janitorial corporations with several locations.
2500+ Members

4780 **International Kitchen Exhaust Cleaning Association**
100 N. 20th St.
Suite 400
Philadelphia, PA 19103

215-320-3876; Fax: 215-564-2175
information@ikeca.org
www.ikeca.org
Facebook, Twitter, LinkedIn, YouTube

Kathy DeMarco, Executive Director
April Rose, Director, Membership & Meetings
Rene Bonner, Membership Coordinator
Sara Duginske, Director, Certification & Standards
Barb Signorelli, Senior Staff Accountant

Promotes fire safety in restaurants through stringent standards and practices for contractors engaged in kitchen exhaust cleaning. Conducts a variety of educational programs, and works with influential code setting bodies such as the National Fire Protection Association to improve existing codes and regulations.
Founded in 1989

4781 **International Maintenance Institute**
PO Box 751896
Houston, TX 77275

281-481-0869; Fax: 281-481-8337
iminst@swbell.net
Facebook, Twitter, LinkedIn

Focuses on plant workers and vendors who have products tailored to the maintenance industry. The philosophy of the organization is to professionalize the maintenance function by helping maintenance managers to work smarter through the exchange of ideas and education.
2.5M Members
Founded in 1960

4782 **International Window Cleaning Association**
7918 Jones Branch Drive
Suite 300
McLean, VA 22102

800-875-4922
www.iwca.org
Facebook, Twitter, LinkedIn, Instagram

Jennifer Hedrick, Executive Director
Kristen Hewlett, Senior Accountant
Lisa DiBenedetto, Senior Manager of Events

A group of professionals for individuals working in the window cleaning industry. The mission of the IWCA is to educate and assist its members in developing professionalism, ethics and standards of safety and to actively represent the concerns and interests of window cleaning companies.
Founded in 1989

4783 **Low Moisture Carpet Cleaners Association**
P.O. Box 342
Grandview, MO 64030

816-966-9065
info@lmcca.org
lmcca.org

The LMCCA acts as a highly visibility credible source for technological and scientific research including published research documents regarding critical issues like defining the term Low Moisture, White Paper on pH, information on chemical and equipment cleaning efficacy and viable low moisture restorative procedures.
Founded in 2001

4784 **Multi-Housing Laundry Association**
1500 Sunday Drive
Suite 102
Raleigh, NC 27607-5151

919-861-5579
800-380-3652; Fax: 919-787-4916
info@mla-online.com
mla-online.com
Facebook, Twitter, LinkedIn

John Mitchell, President
Scott Scarpato, Vice President

Furnishes information on tax and business development and promotes high business standards. Annual meetings held in June.
15M Members
Founded in 1959

4785 **National Air Duct Cleaners Association**
1120 Route 73
Suite 200
Mt. Laurel, NJ 08054

856-380-6810; Fax: 856-439-0525
nadca.com
Facebook, Twitter, LinkedIn, YouTube

Jodi Araujo, Chief Executive Officer
Kristy Cohen, Executive Director
Mike Dwyer, Chief Relationship Officer
Ashton Hald, Meeting Manager
Sarah Black, DucTales Editor

A nonprofit association of companies engaged in the cleaning of HVAC systems. NADCA supports members' success with standards, education, certification, marketing and advocacy to promote ethics and the highest quality services.
Founded in 1989

4786 **National Cleaners Association**
252 W 29th St
New York, NY 10001

212-967-3002
800-888-1622; Fax: 212-967-2240
info@nca-i.com
www.nca-i.com
Facebook, LinkedIn, Pinterest

Debra Kravet, President
Nora Nealis, Executive Director
Clint Lee, Member Services Staff
Ann Hargrove, Office Staff
Carlos Crespo, Office Staff

Professional trade association dedicated to the welfare of well groomed consumers and the professional cleaners who serve them. Elected officials, government angencies, consumer groups, fashion designers and major media outlets have recognized and responded to NCA's activities, reports and tradition of excellence.
4000 Members
Founded in 1946

4787 **North East Fabricare Association**
P.O.Box 920
Pelham, NH 03076

603-635-0322
800-442-6848; Fax: 781-942-7393
peteblke@aol.com
www.nefabricare.com

Jim Desjardins, President
John Dallas, Vice President
Yaahkov Cohn, Treasurer

Serves cleaners in the New England, New Jersey and New York with information and news about the fabricare industry.
Founded in 1992

4788 **Ohio Cleaners Association**
17 S. High Street
Suite 200
Columbus, OH 43215

614-228-4716; Fax: 614-221-1989

David W. Field, CAE, Executive Director
Nancy S. Waterhouse, Director of Services

A statewide, professional trade association for Ohio's best dry cleaners and the companies who serve them.

4789 **Pennsylvania & Delaware Cleaners Association**
P.O. Box 340
Willow Grove, PA 19090
215-830-8495
800-822-7352; Fax: 215-830-8490
executivedirector@pdclean.org
www.pdclean.org
Facebook

Carol Memberg, Executive Director
Steve Stevenson, President
Dale Kaplan, Vice President

PDCA is a non-profit organization representing dry cleaners and launders from Pennsylvania and Delaware.
Founded in 1934

4790 **Power Washers of North America**
PO Box 270634
Saint Paul, MN 55127

800-393-7962
800-393-7962; Fax: 651-213-0369
www.pwna.org

Bo Josetti, President
Ty Eubanks, Vice President
Marie Reinsel, Executive Director

Developing and communicating high standards in ethical business practices, environmental awareness and safety through continuing education and active representation of the membership. PWNA educated and trained contractors raise the level of professionalism and value to their customers.
550 Members
Founded in 1992
Mailing list available for rent: 500 names

4791 **Restoration Industry Association**
2025 M Street, NW
Suite 800
Rockville, MD 20852

202-367-1180
800-272-7012; Fax: 202-367-2180
info@restorationindustry.org
www.restorationindustry.org
Facebook, Twitter, LinkedIn

Kristy Cohen, Chief Executive Officer
Clare MacNab, Meeting Manager
Brittany Martin, Membership Coordinator
Jess Hall, Education Manager
Kristy Mahon, Sr. Marketing Manager

A trade association for cleaning and restoration professionals worldwide, and the foremost authority, trainer and educator in the industry.
1100 Members
Founded in 1946

4792 **Rocky Mountain Fabricare Association**
2110 65th Ave.
Greely, CO 80634

970-330-0124
866-964-RFMA; Fax: 303-458-0002
info@rmfa.org
www.rmfa.org
Facebook

Mary Ewing, Executive Director
Joe Blaha, President
Jim Nixon, Vice President

Enhancing the image and viability of the fabricare industry through education and development of the skills, talents and professionalism of its membership. Serves cleaners in Colorado, Utah and Wyoming.
900 Members

4793 **South Eastern Fabricare Association**
14700 Sweitzer Lane
Laurel, MD 20707

877-707-7332
877-707-7332; Fax: 912-355-3155
peter@sefa.org
www.sefa.org

Don Holecek, Chair
Rhonda Eysel, President
Peter Blake, Executive Director

Trade association that represents its members who have an interest in the dry cleaning and laundry industry.
900+ Members
Founded in 1972
Mailing list available for rent

4794 **Southwest Drycleaners Association**
5750 Balcones Dr.
Suite 201
Austin, TX 78731

512-873-8195; Fax: 512-873-7423
www.sda-dryclean.com
Facebook, Twitter

Andrew Stanley, Executive Director
Danny Bahlman, President
Kyle Nesbit, 1st Vice President
Erika Paine, 2nd Vice President
Jeff Schwarz, Sergeant at Arms

Serves cleaners in Louisiana, Mississippi, Missouri, Kansas, Arkansa, New Mexico, Oklahoma and Texas.

4795 **Sponge and Chamois Institute**
10024 Office Center Ave.
Suite 203
St. Louis, MO 63128

314-842-2230; Fax: 314-842-3999
scwaters@swbell.net

Jules Schwimmer, Executive Secretary

Members are dealers and suppliers of natural sponges and chamois leather.
Founded in 1933

4796 **Uniform and Textile Service Association**
12587 Fair Lakes Cir
Fairfax, VA 22033-3822

703-247-2600
800-486-6745; Fax: 703-841-4750

Represents textile supply and service companies. Represents 95% of the annual sales generated by the uniform service industry and 65% of the annual sales generated by the linen supply industry. UTSA members provide, clean, and maintain reusable textile products, such as uniforms, sheets, table linen, shop and print towels, floor mats, mops and other items to thousands of businesses.
100 Members
Founded in 1933

Newsletters

4797 **Bulletin**
Neighborhood Cleaners Association
252 W 29th St
New York, NY 10001-5271

212-967-3002; Fax: 212-967-2240
ncaiclean@aol.com
www.nca-i.com

Debra Kravet, President

Technical info for the dry cleaning industry. Government regulation compliance.
Frequency: Bi-Monthly

4798 **CleanFacts Newsletter**
California Cleaners Association
700 N. Valley Street
Suite B PMB 69559
Anaheim, CA 92801

916-239-4070; Fax: 240-295-4200
peter@calcleaners.org
www.calcleaners.com

Jim Douglas, President
Sassan Rahimzadeh, Vice President

The newsletter for the California Cleaners Association.

4799 **Coin Laundry Association: Journal**
Coin Laundry Association
1315 Butterfield Road
Suite 212
Downers Grove, IL 60515-5602

630-963-5547; Fax: 630-963-5864
info@coinlaundry.org
www.coinlaundry.org

Clay Pederson, Chairman
Brian Wallace, President
Bob Nieman, Editor
Laurie Moore, Circulation Manager
Bill Gilbert, Marketing Manager

Committed to offering coin-op owners the information necessary to become and remain competitive in today's changing market.
4 Pages
Frequency: Monthly
Founded in 1960

4800 **Fabricare News**
Drycleaning & Laundrey Institute International
14700 Sweitzer lane
Laurel, MD 20707

301-622-1900
800-638-2627; Fax: 240-295-4200
techline@dlionline.org
www.dlionline.org
Facebook

David MacHesny, President
Charlie Smith, Chair
Mary Scalco, CEO

Information of interest to dry cleaners and launderers.
8 Pages
Frequency: Monthly
Circulation: 5000
Founded in 1883

4801 **Maytag Commercial Newsletter**
Whirlpool Corporation
553 Benson Road
Benton Harbor, MI 49022-2692

269-923-5000
800-344-1274
www.maytag.com

Mike Klosterman, Publisher
Debbie White, Executive Director

Self-service laundry industry news.
8 Pages
Frequency: BiWeekly

4802 **Reclaimer**
South Eastern Fabricare Association

7373 Hodgson Memorial Dr
Building 3, Suite C
Savannah, GA 31406-1595

912-355-3364
877-707-7332; Fax: 912-355-3155
www.sefa.org

Rhonda Eysel, President

A monthly newsletter dedicated to the service of the drycleaning industry.
Cost: $5.00
Frequency: Monthly
Circulation: 2200

Magazines & Journals

4803 **American Coin-Op**
Crain Communications Inc
360 N Michigan Ave
Suite 7
Chicago, IL 60601-3800

312-649-5200; Fax: 312-649-7937
info@crain.com
www.crain.com

Keith Crain, CEO

Offers operators, manufacturers and suppliers in-depth coverage of the latest industry trends, new products, energy-saving methods and management strategies.
Frequency: Monthly
Circulation: 17622
Mailing list available for rent

4804 **American Drycleaner**
Crain Communications Inc
360 N Michigan Ave
Suite 7
Chicago, IL 60601-3800

312-649-5200; Fax: 312-649-7937
info@crain.com
www.crain.com

Keith Crain, CEO

Brings news, expert advice and indepth features to drycleaning businesses and suppliers nationwide every month. Stories focus on management, equipment and operations to help owners build their skills and profits.
Frequency: Monthly
Circulation: 24217

4805 **American Laundry News**
Crain Communications Inc
360 N Michigan Ave
Suite 7
Chicago, IL 60601-3800

312-649-5200; Fax: 312-649-7937
info@crain.com
www.crain.com

Keith Crain, CEO

Focuses on the widely varied issues facing the industry: productivity, technology, labor, workplace safety, the environment and more.
Frequency: Monthly
Circulation: 15350
Founded in 1974

4806 **American Window Cleaner Magazine**
12 Twelve Publishing Corporation
750-B NW Broad Street
Southern Pines, NC 28387

910-693-2644; Fax: 910-246-1681
www.awcmag.com

Norman J Finegold, President

Information on new products, add-on businesses, association and convention news and safety.
Frequency: 6x/Year
Circulation: 8000

4807 **Broom Brush & Mop**
Rankin Publishing Company
204 E Main St
PO Box 130
Arcola, IL 61910-1416

217-268-0130; Fax: 217-268-4815
DRankin125@aol.com
www.ragsmag.com

Don Rankin, Owner
Harrell Kerkhoff, Editor
Ron White, Associate Editor

Reports on import and export totals as well as updates on new products and trade show coverage, also industry trends and market conditions.
Cost: $25.00
Frequency: Monthly
Circulation: 1,700
Founded in 1912

4808 **Brushware**
Brushware
750-B NW Broad St
Southern Pines, NC 28387

910-693-2644; Fax: 910-246-1681
editors@brushwaremag.com
www.brushwaremag.com/

Karen Grinter, Publisher
Norman J Finegold, President

Information on products that apply materials, clean and polish surfaces, covers also industry news, products, methods and trends, market reports, profiles and interviews.
Cost: $45.00
Circulation: 2000
Founded in 1898

4809 **Cleaner**
COLE Publishing
1720 Maple Lake Dam Road
PO Box 220
Three Lakes, WI 54562

715-546-3346
800-257-7222; Fax: 715-546-3786
www.cleaner.com

Ted Roulphe, Editor
Geoff Bruss, CEO

The latest tools and equipment promoting safety and efficiency, employment and environmental concerns, as well as industry profiles.
Cost: $15.00
Frequency: Monthly
Circulation: 24000
Founded in 1979

4810 **Cleaner Times**
Advantage Publishing Company
1000 Nix Rd
Little Rock, AR 72211-3235

866-828-9267
800-525-7038; Fax: 501-280-9233
advpub@adpub.com
www.adpub.com

Charlene Yarbrough, Publisher
Gerry Plus, Circualtion Manager
Jim McMurry, Editor

Application, information, and productivity for persons engaged in the manufacturing, distribution, or the use of high pressure water systems and accessories. The emphasis is on safety, regulatory, which affect the industry as well as cleaning applications.
Cost: $36.00
72 Pages
Frequency: Monthly
Circulation: 25,000
ISSN: 1073-9602
Founded in 1989
Printed in 4 colors on glossy stock

4811 **Cleanfax Magazine**
National Trade Publications
19 British Amer. Blvd. West
Latham, NY 12110-2197

518-783-1281; Fax: 518-783-1386
www.cleanfax.com

Micah Ogburn, Publisher
Jeff Cross, Senio Editor
Barry Lovette, General Manager

Information on carpet cleaning, water and fire damage restoration, industry news and updates.
80 Pages
Frequency: Monthly
Circulation: 20,000
Founded in 1981
Printed in 4 colors on glossy stock

4812 **Cleaning & Restoration Magazine**
Restoration Industry Association
9810 Patuxent Woods Dr
Suite K
Columbia, MD 21046-1595

443-878-1000
800-272-7012; Fax: 443-878-1010
info@restorationindustry.org
www.restorationindustry.org

Donald E Manger, Executive Director
Patricia L Harman, Communications Director

Trade journal covering fire and water damage restoration, rug and textile cleaning, indoor air quality and business issues.
Frequency: Monthly
Circulation: 6000

4813 **Commercial Floor Care**
Business News Publishing Company
22801 Ventura Blvd
Suite 115
Woodland Hills, CA 91364-1230

818-224-8035
800-835-4398; Fax: 818-224-8042
www.bnpmedia.com

Phil Johnson, Publisher
Jeffrey Stouffer, Editor
Amy Levin, Production Manager
Jim Michaelson, Associate Publisher

Dedicated to floor care in the commercial environment.
40 Pages
Frequency: Monthly
Circulation: 26700
Founded in 1926
Printed in 4 colors on glossy stock

4814 **Fabricare**
Drycleaning & Laundry Institute International
14700 Sweitzer Lane
Laurel, MD 20707

301-622-1900
800-638-2627; Fax: 240-295-4200
DLInews@DLIonline.org
www.dlionline.org

The central publication of the International Fabricare Institute. This publication provides information, knowledge and education about drycleaning and laundry issues, the industry, as a whole, and the association.
8 Pages
Frequency: Monthly
Circulation: 8,000
Founded in 1883

4815 **ICS Cleaning Specialist**
Business News Publishing Company
2401 West Big Beaver Road
Troy, MI 48054

818-224-8035
800-835-4398; Fax: 818-224-8042
www.bnpmedia.com

Phil Johnson, Publisher
Evan Kessler, Publisher

Eric Fish, Editor
Amy Levin, Production Manager
Jim Michaelson, Associate Publisher

For carpet cleaning, restoration and floor care service providers.
68 Pages
ISSN: 1522-4708
Founded in 1928
Printed in on glossy stock

4816 **Industrial Launderer Magazine**
Uniform & Textile Service Association
1501 Lee Hwy.kes Cir
Suite 304
Arlington, VA 22209

703-247-2600
800-486-6745; Fax: 703-841-4750

George Harrinton Jr, President

The authoritative source for information for the uniform and textile service industry. It provides practical guidance and assistance for businesses that rent, lease or sell uniforms and other textiles including linen supply.
Cost: $100.00
Frequency: Monthly
Circulation: 6000

4817 **International Fabricare Institute**
12251 Tech Rd
Silver Spring, MD 20904-1901

301-622-1900
800-638-2627; Fax: 301-236-9320
techline@ifi.org

William E Fisher, Publisher

The association of Professional Dry Cleaners, wetcleaners, and launderers. With its education, research, testing and professional training, IFI offers solutions that help member businesses provide expert garment care.
Founded in 1883

4818 **Journal of the Coin Laundering and Drycleaning Industry**
Coin Laundry Association
1315 Butterfield Road
Suite 212
Downers Grove, IL 60515-5602

630-963-5547
800-570-5629; Fax: 630-963-5864
info@coinlaundry.org
www.coinlaundry.org

Brian Wallace, President
Clay Pederson, Chairman

The official voice of the coin laundry and drycleaning industry. It's the most cost effective way to reach over 28,000 small business entrepreneurs. Besides industry specific items these owners operate over 38,000 company vehicles, utilize business management materials and more. Accepts advertising.
52 Pages
Frequency: Monthly

4819 **Maintenance Sales News**
Rankin Publishing Company
204 E Main St
PO Box 130
Arcola, IL 61910-0130

217-268-4959
800-598-8083; Fax: 217-268-4815
drankin125@aol.com
www.ragsmag.com

Don Rankin, Owner
Linda Rankin, Co-Publisher
Harrell Kerkhoff, Editor
Rick Mullen, Editor

Information on selling techniques, business management, training, merchandise, and seminars.
Circulation: 18,000

4820 **Maintenance Solutions**
Trade Press Publishing Corporation
2100 W Florist Avenue
Milwaukee, WI 53209

414-228-7701; Fax: 414-228-1134
contact@facilitiesnet.com
www.facilitiesnet.com

Dick Yake, Editoridal Director
Dan Hounsell, Editor
Brad Ehlert, VP Publisher
Robert Geissler, Publisher
Stephen Bolte, Publisher

How to articles and features designed to alleviate reader problems as well as new product information and applications.
Cost: $45.00
42 Pages
Frequency: Monthly
Circulation: 35000
ISSN: 1072-3560
Founded in 1993

4821 **Maintenance Supplies**
Cygnus Publishing
3 Huntington Quadrangle
Suite 301N
Melville, NY 11747-3601

631-845-2700
800-308-6397; Fax: 720-945-2798
Rich.DiPaolo@cygnuspub.com

Tracy Rossi, Publisher
Paul Mackler, President
Rich Di Paolo, Editor
Kathy Scott, Director of Public Relations
Elise Schafer, Assistant Editor

Case histories and general industry news, also supply distributors, new methods and equipment in the field.
Cost: $66.00
Frequency: Monthly
Circulation: 16,500
Founded in 1966

4822 **Sanitary Maintenance**
Trade Press Publishing Corporation
2100 W Florist Avenue
Milwaukee, WI 53201-3799

414-228-7701; Fax: 414-228-1134
info@tradepress.com
www.tradepress.com

Dick Yake, Editorial Director
Brian Terry, Publisher
Pat Foran, Editor
Robert Wisniewski, CEO

Business management, inventory control and product trends, also includes industrial paper products, cleaning chemicals, safety supplies, janitorial supplies and packaging products.
58 Pages
Frequency: Monthly
Circulation: 16052
ISSN: 0036-4436
Founded in 1943

4823 **Services Magazine**
Building Service Contractors Association Int'l
401 N Michigan Avenue
22nd Floor
Chicago, IL 60611

312-321-5167
800-368-3414; Fax: 312-673-6735
info@bscai.org
www.bscai.org

Oliver Yandle, Executive VP/CEO
Karen Lawver, Director Membership Services

The Building Service Contractors Association International is the trade association serving the facility services industry through education, leadership, and representatiion.
Cost: $30.00
56 Pages
Frequency: Monthly
Circulation: 20064
ISSN: 0279-0548
Founded in 1981
Mailing list available for rent: 20000 names

4824 **Textile Rental Magazine**
Textile Rental Services Association
1800 Diagonal Rd
Suite 200
Alexandria, VA 22314-2842

703-519-0029
877-770-9274; Fax: 703-519-0026
trsa@trsa.org
www.trsa.org

Roger Cocivera, President/CEO
Jack Morgan, Editor
Steven Biller, Editorial Director

Packed with valuable tips and ideas.
Frequency: Monthly

4825 **Water Conditioning & Purification Magazine**
Publicom, Incorporated
2800 E. Ft. Lowell Road
Tucson, AZ 85716

520-323-6144; Fax: 520-323-7412
info@wcponline.com
www.wcponline.com

Kurt C. Peterson, Publisher
Sharon Peterson, Business Manager
Denise Roberts, Executive Editor

Water Conditioning & Purification Magazine(WC&P) has been the premier source for news, technical artticles and water science features sine 1959. We are committed to the water treatment industry. Our pro bono participation includes event and activity sponsorship, committe members, task force cahiras and association leadership.

Trade Shows

4826 **ACI Annual Meeting & Industry Convention**
American Cleaning Institute
1401 H Street NW
Suite 700
Washington, DC 20005

202-347-2900; Fax: 202-347-4110
info@cleaninginstitute.org
www.cleaninginstitute.org

Melissa Hockstad, President & CEO
Merla Zollinger, Sr. Director, Convention & Meetings

The ACI Convention provides industry professionals the opportunity to hear updates from global industry leaders, learn about new innovations in the industry, network with their peers in a variety of settings, give back to the community as they participate in charity events, and hold business-to-business meetings with suppliers and customers.
Frequency: Annaul/Jan-Feb

4827 **Association of Specialists in Cleaning & Restoration Convention**
Restoration Industry Association
9810 Patuxent Woods Drive
Suite K
Columbia, MD 21046-1595

443-878-1000
800-272-7012; Fax: 443-878-1010

info@restorationindustry.org
www.restorationindustry.org

Donald E Manger, Executive Director
Patricia L Harman, Communications Director

Annual convention and exhibits of carpet, upholstery and draperies cleaning and restoration equipment, duct cleaning supplies and services, 100+ booths.
600 Attendees
Frequency: Annual
Founded in 1945

4828 **Building Service Contractors Association International Trade Show**
401 N Michigan Avenue
22nd Floor
Chicago, IL 60611

312-321-5167
800-368-3414; Fax: 312-673-6735
info@bscai.org
www.bscai.org

Oliver Yandle, Executive VP/CEO
Karen Lawver, Director Membership Services

Containing 400 booths and 185 exhibits.
2000 Attendees
Frequency: March/April
Founded in 1965

4829 **Clean Show**
Riddle & Associates
1874 Piedmont Road
Suite 360
Atlanta, GA 30305

404-876-1988; Fax: 404-876-5121
info@cleanshow.com
www.cleanshow.com

John Riddle, Manager
Ann Howell, Communications

World's largest exposition for laundry, drycleaning and textile services industry featuring working equipment and educational program. Draws international attendance.
17000 Attendees
Frequency: Biennial, Odd Years
Founded in 1977

4830 **Educational Congress for Laundering & Drycleaning**
Coin Laundry Association
1315 Butterfield Road
Suite 212
Downers Grove, IL 60515-5602

630-963-5547
800-570-5629; Fax: 630-963-5864
info@coinlaundry.org
www.coinlaundry.org

Brian Wallace, President
Clay Pederson, Chairman

Two thousand one hundred booths of equipment and products for the cleaning industry. Service schools and other events planned.
22M Attendees
Frequency: July

4831 **IWCA Annual Convention & Trade Show**
International Window Cleaning Association
7918 Jones Branch Drive
Suite 300
McLean, VA 22102

800-875-4922
www.iwca.org

Jennifer Hedrick, Executive Director
Lisa DiBenedetto, Senior Manager of Events

The IWCA provides educational sessions to help business owners grow their business; networking opportunities; safety and equipment training; and access to the trade show with vendors dedicated to serving the window cleaning industry.
Founded in 1989

4832 **National Educational Exposition and Conference**
Environmental Management Association
Fishbones In Greektown
400 Monroe Street
Detroit, MI 48226-3333

Annual show of 15 manufacturers, suppliers and distributors of sanitation maintenance supplies, products, services.
150 Attendees

4833 **Power Clean**
Cleaning Equipment Trade Association
11450 U.S. Highway 380
Suite 130, #289
Cross Roads, TX 76227

800-441-0111; Fax: 704-635-7363
info@ceta.org
www.ceta.org

Debbie Murray, Managing Director
Jim Welch, President

Annual show of 100 manufacturers and suppliers of cleaning equipment, high pressure washers and related component accessories and products.
300 Members
Frequency: Annual/October
Founded in 1990

4834 **Southern Drycleaners Show**
South Eastern Fabricare Association
PO Box 912
Cumming, GA 30028

877-707-7332; Fax: 770-998-1441
www.sefa.org

Joel Deutsch, Manager

Trade show for the drycleaning industry with 120 exhibitors and 250 booths.
2500 Attendees
Frequency: August

4835 **Tex Care**
National Cleaners Association
252 W 29th Street
New York, NY 10001

212-967-3002; Fax: 212-967-2240
ncaiclean@aol.com
www.nca-i.com

Joseph Hallak, President
Ted Aveni, First Vice President

Containing 350 exhibits of interest to member cleaners.
5000+ Attendees
Frequency: April

Directories & Databases

4836 **Carpet Cleaners Institute of the Northwest Membership Roster**
147 SE 102nd Avenue
Portland, OR 97216-2703

503-253-9091
805-261-8222; Fax: 503-253-9172
info@ccinw.org
www.ccinw.org

Over 330 member companies involved in the carpet cleaning industry in Washington, Oregon, and Montana, USA and Alberta and British Columbia, Canada.
Frequency: Annual

4837 **Cleaning and Maintenance Management: Buyer's Guide Directory Issue**
National Trade Publications
13 Century Hill Drive
Latham, NY 12110-2197

518-783-1281; Fax: 518-783-1386
cmmonline.com

Alice J Savino, Group Publisher
Chris Sanford, Executive Editor

Over 500 manufacturers are profiled that supply equipment used in building maintenance and housekeeping.
Cost: $42.00
84 Pages
Frequency: Annual
Circulation: 42000
ISSN: 1051-5720
Founded in 1966
Mailing list available for rent: 42M names at $125 per M
Printed in 4 colors on glossy stock

4838 **Coin Laundry Association of Suppliers**
Coin Laundry Association
1315 Butterfield Road
Downers Grove, IL 60515

630-963-5547
800-570-5629; Fax: 630-963-5864
info@coinlaundry.org
www.coinlaundry.org

Brian Wallace, President
Clay Pederson, Chairman
Bob Nieman, Editor
Kathy Sherman, Director Administration
Sue Lally, Director Membership

Lists over 500 manufacturers and suppliers of products and services to the coin and dry cleaning laundry industries.
2700+ Pages
Founded in 1960

4839 **Inside Textile Service - Directories**
Uniform & Textile Service Association
12587 Fair Lakes Cir
Fairfax, VA 22033-3822

703-247-2600
800-486-6745; Fax: 703-841-4750
www.utsa.com

David Hobson, President
Jennifer Kellar, Executive Coordinator

The uniform and textile service industry's most comprehensive guide to US textile service companies. Includes contact data for UTSA's membership, and for hundreds of other textile service companies as well. Contains listings of all UTSA affiliated suppliers with catalog-like data on their products and services. Free to members.
Circulation: 3,000

4840 **Textile Rental Services Association Roster**
Textile Rental Services Association
1800 Diagonal Rd
Suite 200
Alexandria, VA 22314-2842

703-519-0029; Fax: 703-519-0026
trsa@trsa.org
www.trsa.org

Roger Cocivera, President
Scott Mallan, Finance Manager
Michael Wilson, Director Government Affairs
Jack Morgan, Editor

Offers a list of over 1,800 companies that supply linen, uniforms and other textile products to other industries.
1300 Pages
Founded in 1913

Industry Web Sites

4841 **http://gold.greyhouse.com**
G.O.L.D Grey House OnLine Databases
Grey House Publishing's online database platform, GOLD, offers Quick Search, Keyword Search and Expert Search for most business sectors inlcuding the cleaning and laundry markets. Finding the information you need quick and easy - whether you're a novice searcher or an experienced database user. All of Grey House's directory products are available for subscription on the GOLD platform.

4842 **www.ascr.org**
Assn of Specialists in Cleaning and Restoration
For professionals involved in the cleaning and restoration of interior textiles and structures, including air handling systems.

4843 **www.bscai.org**
Building Service Contractors Association Int'l
For companies offering security, maintenance and cleaning services.

4844 **www.ceta.org**
Cleaning Equipment Trade Association
For manufacturers and suppliers of cleaning equipment, high pressure washers and related component accessories and products.

4845 **www.cminstitute.net**
Cleaning Management Institute
CMI provides education, training and career improvement opportunities for building cleaning and maintenance professionals.

4846 **www.coinlaundry.org**
Coin Laundry Association
For self-service laundry and dry cleaning industry. CLA is a not for profit trade association representing the 30,000 coin laundry owners in the US and the world.

4847 **www.greyhouse.com**
Grey House Publishing
Authoritative reference directories for most business sectors including cleaning and laundry markets. Users can search the online databases with varied search criteria allowing for custom searches by product category, geographic area, sales volume, keyword, subject and more. Full Grey House catalog and online ordering also available.

4848 **www.ikeca.org**
International Kitchen Exhaust Cleaning Association
Education for members about safety, cleaning techniques and many other areas. Since its inception, IKECA, a not for profit trade association, has established stringent standards and practices for contractors engaged in kitchen exhaust clening, conducted a variety of educational programs, and worked with influential code setting bodies such as the National Fire Protection Association to improve existing codes and regulations.

4849 **www.imionline.org**
International Maintenance Institute
Focuses on plant workers and vendors who have products tailored to the maintenance industry. The philosophy of the organization is to professionalize the maintenace functiuon by helping maintenace managers to work smarter through the exchange of ideas and function.

4850 **www.jriddle.com**
Riddle & Associates
For the laundering, drycleaning and textile care industry - from single-owner coin-operated laundry and drycleaning establishments to giant industrial and institutional laundries. Our management capabilities work for any type of trade show - large or small. Our experience with heavy utility shows, and shows with highly technical requirements, gives us an expertise in these areas that is difficult to find.

4851 **www.natclo.com**
National Clothesline
News of interest to drycleaners. Links to regional and state associations, calendar of events.

4852 **www.nca-i.com**
Neighborhood Cleaners Association
Professional trade association dedicated to the welfare of well-groomed consumers and the professional cleaners and suppliers who serve them. for over 50 years, NCA has been at the vanguard of education, research and information distribution concerning garment and household fabric care. Elected officials, goverment agencies, consumer groups, fashion designers and major media outlets have recognized and responded to NCA's activities, reports and tradition of excellence.

4853 **www.pwna.org**
Power Washers of North America
Developing and communicating the highest standards in ethical business practices, environmental awareness and safety through continuing education and active representation of the membership. PWNA educated and trained contractors raise the level of professionalism and value to their customers.

4854 **www.rmfa.org**
Rocky Mountain Fabricare Association
Enhancing the image and viability of the fabricare industry through education and development of the skills, talents, and professionalism of its membership.

4855 **www.sefa.org**
South Eastern Fabricare Association
Trade association that represents its members who have an interest in the dry cleaning and laundry industry. The not for profit asscoiation provides value through education, research, legislative representation, industry specific information programs, products and services.

4856 **www.utsa.com**
Uniform & Textile Service Association
One stop place for important industry and UTSA news. It has complete information on upcoming events and activities, including online meeting brochures and secure online registration. Each department at UTSA has its own page where you will find information about committees, projects, regulations, and links to dozens of other pertinent sites such as the Clean Show or government sites.

Associations

4857 **AVIXA**
11242 Waples Mill Road
Suite 200
Fairfax, VA 22030

703-273-7200; Fax: 800-659-7469
www.avixa.org
Facebook, Twitter, LinkedIn, Google+, YouTube, Flickr

David Labuskes, Chief Executive Officer
Greg Feehan, Chief Financial Officer
Dan Goldstein, Chief Marketing Officer
Sarah Joyce, Chief Global Officer

Formerly InfoComm. Centers on the technologies, products and systems for visual display, audio reproduction, video and audio production, interfacing and signal distribution, lighting, control systems, interactive display and audio presentation systems, remote video and web conferencing.

4858 **Accuracy in Media**
4350 East West Highway
Suite 555
Bethesda, MD 20814

202-364-4401
800-787-4567; Fax: 202-364-4098
info@aim.org
www.aim.org
Facebook, Twitter, LinkedIn, YouTube

Caroline Smith, Editor-In-Chief
Christine Goss, AIM Respresentative
Adam Guillette, President
Don Irvine, Publisher

Accuracy in Media is a non-profit, grassroots citizens watchdog of the news media that critiques botched and bungled news stories and sets the record straight on important issues that have received slanted coverage.
3500 Members
Founded in 1969

4859 **Advanced Television Systems Committee**
1776 K Street NW
8th Floor
Washington, DC 20006-2304

202-872-9160; Fax: 202-872-9161
atsc@atsc.org
www.atsc.org
Facebook, Twitter

Madeleine Noland, President
Jerry Whitaker, Vice President
Daro Bruno, Director, Operations

ATSC is an international, non-profit organzation developing voluntary standards for digital television.

4860 **Agricultural Comm. Excellence in Ag., Natural Resources and Life Sciences**
University of Florida
59 College Road
Taylor Hall
Durham, NH 03824

855-657-9544; Fax: 603-862-1585
ace.info@unh.edu
www.aceweb.org
Facebook, LinkedIn, YouTube, Pinterest, RSS

Jennifer Alexander, President
Ricky Telg, VP
Matt Browning, Marketing & Membership Director
ChaNae Bradley, Member Services Director
Lulu Rodriguez, Research Director

Members are writers, editors, broadcasters and communicators who are involved in the dissemination of agricultural, food sciences and natural resource information in land-grant colleges, federal and state agencies, international agencies and other private communications work.
700+ Members
Founded in 1970

4861 **Alliance for Telecommunications Industry Solutions**
1200 G Street, NW
Suite 500
Washington, DC 20005

202-628-6380
www.atis.org
Twitter, LinkedIn

Susan Miller, President & CEO
Thomas Goode, General Counsel
Lauren Layman, VP, Marketing & Public Relations
Rich Moran, Director, Membership
Aloah Kincaid, Director, Finance

A standards organization that develops technical and operational standards and solutions for the ICT industry.

4862 **American Communication Association**
College of Business Administration
The University of Northern Iowa
1227 W 27th Street
Cedar Falls, IA 50614-0125

209-667-3374
pdecaro@csustan.edu
www.americancomm.org

Pete DeCaro, Executive Director
Aimee Roundtree, President
Vernon Humphrey, CFO
Jim Parker, CIO
Abu Naser, Managing Editor

Founded for the purposes of fostering research and scholarship in all areas of human communication behavior, promoting and improving excellence in the pedagogy of communication, providing a voice in communication law and policy, providing evaluation and certification services for academic programs in communication study.
Founded in 1993

4863 **American Public Communications Council**
625 Slaters Lane
Suite 104
Alexandria, VA 22314

703-739-1322
apcc@apcc.net

Aims to protect and expand domestic and foreign markets for public communications and provide business opportunities for members.
Founded in 1988

4864 **Armed Forces Communications & Electronics Association (AFCEA)**
4114 Legato Road
Suite 1000
Fairfax, VA 22033

703-631-6100
800-336-4583; Fax: 703-631-6169
service@afcea.org
www.afcea.org
Facebook, Twitter, LinkedIn, YouTube, Flickr

Lt. Gen. Robert Shea, USMC (Ret.), President/CEO
Pat Miorin, CPA, EVP/CFO/International Treasurer
Lt. Gen. John Wood, USA (Ret.), EVP, Defense/National Security
James Griggs, Jr., VP/CIO/CTO
Beverly Cooper, VP, Comm. & Media/CKO/Publisher

A non-profit membership association serving the military, government, industry, and academia as an ethical forum for advancing professional knowledge and relationships in the fields of communications, IT, intelligence, and global security.
31000 Members
Founded in 1946

4865 **AscdiNatd**
131 NW First Avenue
Delray Beach, FL 33444

561-266-9016; Fax: 561-431-6302
www.ascdi.com
Facebook, Twitter, LinkedIn, YouTube

Gail Goldstein, Office Manager
Joe Marion, President

An international trade association made up of companies who providetechnology solutions, technical support, and value added services to the business community.

4866 **Association Media & Publishing**
12100 Sunset Hills Road
Suite 130
Reston, VA 20190

703-234-4063; Fax: 703-435-4390
info@associationmediaandpublishing.org
associationmediaandpublishing.org
Facebook, Twitter, LinkedIn

Carla Kalogeridis, Publisher
Thomas Marcetti, Associate Editor
Weston Kalogeridis, Sponsorship & Signature Advertising

Serves the needs of association publishers, communications professionals and the media they create.
Founded in 1963

4867 **Association for Business Communication**
181 Turner St, NW
323 Shanks Hall
Blacksburg, VA 24061

540-231-8460; Fax: 646-349-5297
abcoffice@businesscommunication.org
businesscommunication.org
Facebook, Twitter

James Dubinsky, Executive Director
Geert Jacobs, President

International organization commited to fostering excellence in business communication scholarship, research, education, and practice.
1275 Members
Founded in 1935

4868 **Association for Conservation Information**
Division of Fish Game and Wildlife
Po Box 400
Trenton, NJ 08625-0400

609-984-0837; Fax: 609-984-1414
www.aci-net.org
Facebook

Jenifer Wisniewski, President
Lance Cherry, Vice-President
Sara DiRienzo, Secretary
Judy Stokes Weber, Treasurer

Works to upgrade the quality of all forms of communication in and among agencies devoted to the protection and management of natural resources and wildlife.
110 Members
Founded in 1984

4869 **Association for Education in Journalism and Mass Communication**
234 Outlet Pointe Boulevard
Suite A
Columbia, SC 29210-5667
803-798-0271; Fax: 803-772-3509
www.aejmc.org
Facebook, Twitter, LinkedIn, YouTube, Pinterest, Instagram
David Perlmutter, President
Jennifer McGill, Executive Director
Belinda Pearson, Association Business Manager
Felicia G. Brown, Assistant Executive Director
Lillian Coleman, Newsletter Editor/Project Manager
AEJMC promotes the highest possible standards for education in journalism and mass communication, encouraging the widest possible range of communication research and the implementation of a multi-cultural society in the classroom and curriculum, defending and maintaining the freedom of expression in day-to-day living.
Founded in 1912

4870 **Association for Educational Communications and Technology**
320 W. 8th Street
Suite 101
Bloomington, IN 47404-3745
812-335-7675
877-677-2328
aect@aect.org
aect.org
Facebook, Twitter
Xun Ge, President
Phillip Harris, Executive Director
Larry Vernon, Director, Electronic Services
Lois Freeland, AECT Convention Coordinator
Terri Lawson, HR & Administrative Services
A professional association of thousands of educators and others whose activities are directed towards improving instruction through technology.
Founded in 1923
Mailing list available for rentat $159 per M

4871 **Association for Information Systems**
P.O. Box 2712
Atlanta, GA 30301-2712
404-413-7445
membership@aisnet.org
aisnet.org
Facebook, Twitter, LinkedIn
Matt Nelson, Associate Executive Director
Lise Fitzpatrick, Chief Operating Officer
Robina Wahid, Conference Director
Tenez Quarles, Finance Director
Brook Pritchett, Communications Director
AIS members are academics with interest in information systems and related fields.
4300 Members
Founded in 1994

4872 **Association for Information and Image Management**
1100 Wayne Avenue
Suite 1100
Silver Spring, MD 20910
301-587-8202
800-477-2446
aiim@aiim.org
www.aiim.org
Facebook, Twitter, LinkedIn, YouTube, Google+, RSS
Peggy Winton, President & CEO
Georgina Clellend, Chief Operating Officer
Renee Martin, Director, Event Marketing
Boshia Smith, Membership Manager
A nonprofit membership organization that provides education, marketresearch, certification, and standards for information professionals.

4873 **Association for Interactive Marketing**
1430 Broadway Avenue
8th Floor
New York, NY 10018
888-337-0008; Fax: 212-391-9233
Kevin Noonan, Executive Director
AIM is a non-profit trade association for interactive marketers and service providers.

4874 **Association for Multi-Media International**
PO Box 1897
Lawrence, KS 66044
866-393-4264; Fax: 785-843-1274
hq@ami.org
www.multimedia-int.org
Vanessa Reilly, Executive Director
The professional objectives of the AMI are to promote the safety and advancement of medical illustration and allied fields of visual communication, and to promote understanding and cooperation with the medical profession and related health science professions.
1M Members
Founded in 1974

4875 **Association for Postal Commerce**
1800 Diagonal Road
Suite 600
Alexandria, VA 22314
703-524-0096; Fax: 703-997-2414
info@postcom.org
www.postcom.org
Twitter, LinkedIn
Michael Plunkett, President & CEO
Ellena Talbott, Director, Operations & Membership
Beth McConnell, Postal Consultant
Matthew Field, General Counsel
National organization representing those who use, or who support, the use of mail as a medium for communication and commerce. Publishes a weekly newsletter covering postal policy and operational issues.
231 Members
Founded in 1947

4876 **Association for Service Managers International**
11031 Via Frontera
Suite A
San Diego, CA 92127
239-275-7887
800-333-9786; Fax: 239-275-0794
J.B. Wood, President
Thomas Lah, Executive Director
A global organization dedicated to furthering the knowledge, understanding, and career development of executives, managers and professionals in the high technology service industry.
3000+ Members
Founded in 1975

4877 **Association for Women in Communications**
1717 E Republic Road
Suite A
Springfield, MO 65804
417-886-8606; Fax: 417-886-3685
chair@womcom.org
www.womcom.org
Facebook, Twitter, LinkedIn, YouTube, Google+
Anita K. Parran, Chair
Kandice Mollitiam, Data Protection Officer
Professional organization that champions the advancement of women across all communications disciplines by recognizing excellence, promoting leadership and positioning its members at the forefront of the evolving communications era. Hosts a bi-annual conference.
1000 Members
Founded in 1909
Mailing list available for rent: 1000+ names at $n/a per M

4878 **Association of Alternative Newsmedia**
116 Cass Street
Traverse City, MI 49684
703-470-2996; Fax: 866-619-9755
web@aan.org
www.altweeklies.com
Facebook, Twitter, RSS, Google+
Molly Willmott, Association Manager
Britt Ervin, Admin. & Marketing Associate
Susan Torregrossa, Events Manager
Christy Bryan, Events Manager
Amy Howarth, Accounting Manager
A trade association of alternative weekly newspapers in North America.
Founded in 1978

4879 **Association of Federal Communications Consulting Engineers**
PO Box 19333
Washington, DC 20036
941-329-6000; Fax: 703-591-0115
www.afcce.org
Facebook, Twitter, LinkedIn
John George, President
Jonathan Edwards, VP
Stephen Pumple, Secretary
Robert Weller, Treasurer
An organization of professional engineering consultants serving the telecommunications industry.
250 Members
Founded in 1948

4880 **Association of Medical Illustrators**
201 E. Main St.
Suite 1405
Lexington, KY 40507
866-393-4264; Fax: 859-514-9166
hq@ami.org
www.ami.org
RSS Feed
Whitney Wilgus, Executive Director
Sara Zach, Program Manager
Glen Ellwood, Conferences & Events Manager
Nicole Lesniewski, Association Administrator
An international organization of media professionals who promote, produce and utilize a wide range of presentation media.
1M Members
Founded in 1944

4881 **Association of Professional Communication Consultants**
211 E 28th st
Tulsa, OK 74114-3329
918-743-4793; Fax: 918-745-0932
LinkedIn
Professional community of communication consultants where members can increase their knowledge, grow their business and achieve high standards of professional practice. Services include professional development workshops, online newsletter and referral database and active listserve discussions.
200 Members
Founded in 1982

4882 **Association of Schools of Journalism & Mass Communications**
234 Outlet Pointe Boulevard
Columbia, SC 29210-5667

803-798-0271; Fax: 803-772-3509
aejmchq@aol.com
www.asjmc.org

Gracie Lawson-Boarders, President
Alan Stavitsky, President Elect
Raul Reis, Vice President
Jennifer McGill, Executive Director

Promotes excellence in journalism and mass communication education. Non-profit, educational association composed of some 190 JMC programs at the college level. Eight international journalism and communication schools have joined the association in recent years.
202 Members
Founded in 1917

4883 **Association of Teachers of Technical Writing**
Department Of Linguistics And Technical Comm.
1155 Union Circle #305298
Denton, TX 76203-5017

940-565-4458
sims@unt.edu
www.attw.org
Facebook, Twitter, LinkedIn

Angela Haas, President
Natasha Jones, Vice President
Bill Hart-Davidson, Secretary
Brian Blackburn, Treasurer

Provides communication among teachers of technical writing and develops technical communications as an academic discipline.
600 Members
Founded in 1973

4884 **BioCommunications Association**
220 Southwind Lane
Hillsborough, NC 27278

919-245-0906
office@bca.org
www.bca.org
Facebook, Twitter, LinkedIn, YouTube

Adam Cooper, President
James Hayden, Vice President
Mardell Fosse, Director, Member Services
Danielle Edwards, Director, Communications
Connie Johansen, Director, Conferences

An international association of photographers and media professionals who create and use quality images in visual communications for teaching, documentation and presentations in the life sciences and medicine.
Founded in 1931

4885 **CanWest Media Sales**
121 Bloor Street East
Suite 1500
Toronto, ON M4W 3M5

416-967-1174; Fax: 416-967-1285

Televison and newspaper advertising, marketing, and sales company.

4886 **Center for Communication**
110 East 23rd Street
Suite 900
New York, NY 10010

216-686-5005; Fax: 212-504-2632
www.cencom.org
Facebook, Twitter, Youtube

J. Max Robins, President & Executive Director
Kate Stanley, Program Director
Folade Bell, Director, Community
Erin Gromen, Director, Development

Exposes young people to the issues, the ethics, the people, and the creative product that defines the media business. Offers students interested in media careers a unique opportunity to learn about the world of communications.

4887 **Center for International Media Assistance**
1025 F Street NW
Suite 800
Washington, DC 20004

202-378-9700; Fax: 202-378-9407
CIMA@ned.org
cima.ned.org
Facebook, Twitter

Mark Nelson, Senior Director
Heather Gilberds, Associate Director & Editor
Aleksej Demjanski, Assist Program & Officer
Ann Lewandowski, Program Assistant
Daniel O'Maley, Digital Policy Specialist

Provides information, builds networks, conducts research, and highlights the role media play in the creation and development of sustainable democracies.

4888 **Center for Media Literacy**
22837 Pacific Coast Highway
#472
Malibu, CA 90265

310-804-3985
cml@medialit.org
www.medialit.org
YouTube

Tessa Jolls, President & CEO

An educational organization that provides leadership, public education, professional development and educational resources nationally and internationally.
Founded in 1977

4889 **Communication Media Management Association**
1604 Glendale Hills Drive NE
Rochester, MN 55906-8376

507-271-4307
cmma.org
Facebook, Twitter, LinkedIn, RSS

Susan Kehoe, President
Marv Mitchell, Executive Director
Chris Barry, Program Director
Jessica Ferguson, Membership Director
Casey Shannon, Marketing Director

Provides professional development and networking opportunities for communications media managers.
Founded in 1946

4890 **Communications Marketing Association**
204 S. Shaffer Drive
New Freedom, PA 17349

717-439-7391
cmaexecdirector@gmail.com
www.cma-cmc.org
Facebook, Twitter, LinkedIn, YouTube

Alex Hinerfeld, President
Carl Peek, Vice President
Rob Menees, Secretary
Cliff Peck, Treasurer
Sharon Boyle, Executive Director

Organization of manufacturers, manufacturer's representatives and distributors in the wireless communications industry.

4891 **CompTIA**
3500 Lacey Road
Suite 100
Downers Grove, IL 60515

630-678-8300
866-835-8020; Fax: 630-678-8384
www.comptia.org
Facebook, Twitter, LinkedIn, Pinterest, Google+, YouTube

Todd Thibodeaux, President & CEO
Brian Laffey, CFO
Randy Gross, CIO
Nancy Hammervik, Executive VP, Industry Relations
Kelly Ricker, Executive VP, Events & Education

A nonprofit trade association created by representatives of five microcomputer leaderships and is a provider of professional certifications for the information technology (IT) industry.

4892 **Computer and Communications Industry Association**
900 17th Street, NW
Suite 1100
Washington, DC 20006

202-783-0070; Fax: 202-783-0534
www.ccianet.org
Facebook, Twitter, RSS

Matthew Schruers, President
Daniel Johnson, Vice President & General Counsel
Mel Aldhizer, Controller
Heather Greefield, Director, Communications
Maggie Clark Brennan, Director, External Affairs

Association of computer product vendors and communications firms lobbying for free trade and open markets.

4893 **Consolidated Tape Association**
C/O New York Stock Exchange
11 Wall Street, 21st Floor
New York, NY 10005

212-656-2052; Fax: 212-656-5848
www.ctaplan.com

Members are stock exchanges and the National Association of Securities Dealers. CTA melds the reporting of transactions from the various stock exchanges.
9 Members
Founded in 1974

4894 **Consortium for School Networking**
1025 Vermont Ave NW
Suite 1010
Washington, DC 20005-3599

202-861-2676
866-267-8747; Fax: 202-393-2011
info@cosn.org
www.cosn.org
Facebook, Twitter, LinkedIn

Keith Krueger, CEO
Robert Duke, Chief Operating Officer
Susanne Bowman, Sr. Dir., Marketing & Communication
Brian Calvary, Director, Membership & Chapters
Meagan Keller, Director, Meetings & Conferences

Promotes the development and use of internet and information technologies for K-12 learning. Members are school districts, states, nonprofits and commercial organizations, all of whom share the goal of promoting the state of the art in computer networking technologies in schools.
450 Members
Founded in 1992

4895 **Cooperative Communicators Association**
174 Crestview Dr
Bellefonte, PA 16823-8516

877-326-5994; Fax: 814-355-2452
CCA@communicators.coop

www.communicators.coop
Facebook, Twitter, YouTube, Flickr

Afton Holt, President
Savannah Chandler, Vice President
Candace Croft, Secretary-Treasurer

A teaching and news tool for the Cooperative Communicators Association, CCA consists communicators, editors, photographers, graphics, designers, public relations specialists who work for cooperatives in 35 states, Canada and Poland.
350 Members
Founded in 1953

4896 **Council of Communication Management**
65 Enterprise
Aliso Viejo, CA 92656

866-463-6226; Fax: 949-715-6931
Facebook, Twitter, LinkedIn

Provides a network through which managers, consultants and educators, who work at the policy level in organizational communication can help one another advance the practice of communication in business.
270 Members
Founded in 1955

4897 **Council of Science Editors**
10200 W 44th Ave.
Suite 304
Wheat Ridge, CO 80033

720-881-6046; Fax: 703-435-4390
CSE@CouncilScienceEditors.org
www.councilscienceeditors.org
Facebook, Twitter, LinkedIn

Carissa Gilman, President
Jennifer Deyton, Vice President
Tim Bennett, Executive Director

Membership consists of individuals concerned with writing, editing and publishing in the life sciences and related fields.
1200 Members
Founded in 1957

4898 **Digital Media Association (DiMA)**
1050 17th St., NW
Suite 220
Washington, DC 20036

202-639-9509
www.digmedia.org

Garrett Levin, President & CEO
Sally Rose Larson, VP, Government Relations
Kevin Goldberg, VP, Legal

National trade organization devoted primarily to the online audio and video industries, and more generally to commercially innovative digital media opportunities.

4899 **Drug Information Association**
800 Enterprise Road
Suite 200
Horsham, PA 19044-3595

215-442-6100; Fax: 215-442-6199
DIA@diahome.org
www.diahome.org
Facebook, Twitter, LinkedIn, YouTube, Weibo, Digg, Reddit

Barbara Lopez Kunz, Global Chief Executive
Bayard Gardineer, Chief Financial Officer
Bill Allman, Chief Digital Officer

Provides a neutral global forum for the exchange and dissemination of information on the discovery, development, evaluation and utilization of medicines and related health care technologies. Through these activities the DIA provides development opportunities for its members.
20000 Members
Founded in 1964

4900 **EDUCAUSE**
1150 18th St NW
Suite 900
Washington, DC 20036

202-872-4200; Fax: 202-872-4318
info@educause.edu
www.educause.edu
Facebook, Twitter, LinkedIn, Flickr

John O'Brien, President & CEO
Stacy Ruwe, VP, Business Services & CFO
Mairead Martin, Chief Information Officer
Nicole McWhirter, Chief Planning Officer
Catherine Yang, VP, Digital Communications/Content

EDUCAUSE is a nonprofit association whose mission is to advance higher education by promoting the intelligent use of information technology.
17M Members
Founded in 1962

4901 **Eastern Communication Association**
600 Forbes Ave
340 College Hall
Pittsburgh, PA 15282

Home Page: www.ecasite.org
Facebook, Twitter

Katherine Thweatt, President
Amanda McKendree, Vice President
Stacy Smulowitz, Executive Director

A professional organization of scholars, teachers, and students of Communcation Studies.
Founded in 1910

4902 **Enterprise Wireless Alliance (EWA)**
2121 Cooperative Way
Suite 225
Herndon, VA 20171

703-528-5115
800-482-8282; Fax: 703-524-1074
customerservice@enterprisewireless.org
www.enterprisewireless.org

Mark Crosby, President/CEO
Bill Mulholland, Executive Director of Finance
Ila Dudley, EVP, Spectrum Operations
Andrea Cumpston, Communications Director
Donna Yudkin, Membership Manager

Formerly ITA and AMTA, works to preserve spectrum rights and assets for enterprise wireless customers.
1200 Members
Founded in 1953

4903 **Forest Industries Telecommunications**
1565 Oak St
Eugene, OR 97401

541-485-8441; Fax: 541-485-7556
license@landmobile.com
www.landmobile.com
Facebook, Twitter

Kevin McCarthy, President

Organized to assist the forest industry in radio matters before the FCC.
600 Members
Founded in 1947

4904 **Forestry Conservation Commuications Association**
122 Baltimore St.
Gettysburg, PA 17325

717-398-0815
844-458-0298; Fax: 717-778-4237
www.fcca-usa.org

Ralph Haller, Executive Director
Michelle Fink, National Frequency Coordinator
Bob Kimbro, Regional Frequency Coordinator
Dave Pagel, Regional Frequency Coordinator
David Warner, Regional Frequency Coordinator

Certified by the FCC as the radio frequency coordinator for the Forestry Conservation Radio Service.
200 Members
Founded in 1944

4905 **Freedom Information Center**
101 Reynolds Journalism Institute
Missouri School Of Journalism
Columbia, MO 65211

573-882-5736; Fax: 573-884-6204
www.nfoic.org
Facebook, Twitter

Maintains files documenting actions by government, media and society affecting the flow and content of information. Call or write for assistance with researching media topics or instruction in using access laws.
Founded in 1989

4906 **Geospatial Information & Technology Association**
1360 University Ave. West
Suite 455
St. Paul, MN 55104-4086

president@gita.org
www.gita.org
Facebook, Twitter, LinkedIn, YouTube

Don Knox, Executive Director
Emily Dufour, Membership Specialist
Mary Fitzgerald, Conference Director
Susan Nolte, Finance Director

A nonprofit educational association dedicated to promoting the use and benefits of geospatial information technologies.

4907 **Health Industry Business Communications Council**
2525 E Arizona Biltmore Circle
Suite 127
Phoenix, AZ 85016

602-381-1091; Fax: 602-381-1093
info@hibcc.org
www.hibcc.org

An industry-sponsored nonprofit council organized by major health care associations to develop a standard for data transfer using uniform bar code labeling, and later as the focal point for many other electronic data interchange standards.
12000 Members
Founded in 1984

4908 **IEEE Communications Society**

Home Page: www.comsoc.org
Facebook, Twitter, LinkedIn, Tumblr, Instagram, Pinterest

Harold Tepper, Executive Director
Bruce Worthman, Dir., Finance & Business Operations
David Alvarez, Dir., Info & Communication Tech.
Trish Jaraicie, Director, Marketing & Membership
Kristine Chin, Director, Conferences

A diverse group of industry professionals with a common interest inadvancing all communications technologies.
Founded in 1952

4909 **Idealliance**
1800 Diagonal Road
Suite 320
Alexandria, VA 22314

703-837-1070; Fax: 703-837-1072
info@idealliance.org
www.idealliance.org

Dick Ryan, CEO
David Steinhardt, Managing Director
Jordan Gorski, Senior Vice President

Tara Bowman, Director, Finance & Operations
Evelyn Helminen, Dir., Media, Marketing & Comm.

Idealliance, a global think tank, is a non-profit graphic communications industry organization with 12 strategically located offices around the world. Idealliance serves brands, content and media creators, manufacturers, service providers in print and packaging, fulfillment, mail delivery, marketing, material suppliers, and technology partners worldwide.
3000+ Members
Founded in 1966

4910 Information Resources Group
Ste A
2721 Industrial Dr
Jefferson City, MO 65109

573-632-6IRG
877-600- IRG; Fax: 877-295-7989
www.irginc.net
Facebook, Twitter, LinkedIn

Shyam Goel, President

A national organization that offers MIS and corporate professionals at over 150,000 companies throughout the United States.
1M Members

4911 Information Systems Consultants
4131 Idlevale Drive
Tucker, GA 30084

770-491-1500
800-832-7767

Nonprofit organization of small businesses and individuals providing consulting services to all industries and government.
350 Members
Founded in 1986

4912 Information Systems Management Benchmarking Consortium
Houston, TX

281-440-5044
Facebook, Twitter

An international resource for business process research and metrics.
Founded in 1992

4913 Information Technology Industry Council
1101 K St., NW
Suite 610
Washington, DC 20005

202-737-8888; Fax: 202-638-4922
info@itic.org
www.itic.org
Facebook, Twitter, Google+, RSS, YouTube, Blog

Jason Oxman, President, CEO
Terri O'Brien, Chief Financial Officer
Jennie Westbrook Courts, VP, Communications
Jennifer Bodie, Director, Events
Natasha Bethea, Director, Marketing & Membership

A Washington, D.C.-based trade association that represents companies from the information and communications technology (ICT) industry.
Founded in 1916

4914 Instructional Telecommunications Council
426 C St., NE
Washington, DC 20002-5839

202-293-3110; Fax: 651-450-3679
www.itcnetwork.org

Andrea Taylor, Executive Director
Maripat Traino, Meeting Manager
Renee Wolf, Program Coordinator

Members are educators and organizations involved in higher education instructional telecommunications and distance learning
500 Members
Founded in 1977

4915 Intelligent Community Foundation
250 Park Avenue
Suite 14B
New York, NY 10177

646-291-6166; Fax: 212-825-0075
icf@intelligentcommunity.org
www.intelligentcommunity.org
Facebook, Twitter, YouTube

John Jung, Co-Founder
Robert Bell, Co-Founder
Louis Zacharilla, Co-Founder
Michael Jung, Director, Business Development
Matthew Owen, Director, Operations

Promotes the understanding, development, and use of Smart Cities at a local and regional level to create Smart Communities.
606 Members
Founded in 1985

4916 Interactive Multimedia and Collaborative Communications Association
PO Box 756
Syosset, NY 11797-0756

516-818-8184; Fax: 516-922-2170
www.imcca.org
Facebook, LinkedIn, RSS Feed

Carol Zelkin, Executive Director
Michael Brandofino, Chair
Anne Hardwick, Treasurer
Mary Abram, Director, PR & Marketing
David J. Danto, Director, Emerging Technology

Provides a clearinghouse for the exchange of information between users, researchers, and providers in the field of teleconferencing.
1000 Members
Founded in 1998

4917 International Academy of Television Arts a nd Sciences
25 West 52nd Street
New York, NY 10019

212-489-6969; Fax: 212-489-1946
iemmys@iemmys.tv
www.iemmys.tv
Facebook, Twitter, YouTube

Fred Cohen, Chair
Kevin Beggs, Treasurer
Bruce Paisner, President & CEO

Member based organization comprised of leading media and entertainment figures from over 50 countries and 500 companies from all sectors of television including internet, mobile and technology.
Founded in 1969

4918 International Association for Conflict Management
1 Liberty Street
New York, NY 5006

872-302-7567
brandon@iafcm.org
iafcm.org
Facebook, Twitter

Taya Cohen, President
Brandon Charpied, Executive Director

An association for scholars and practitioners to share theories, research, and experience towards forming an understanding of conflict management in various settings.
Founded in 1970

4919 International Association of Audio Informa tion Services
1090 Don Mills Road
P.O. Box 847
Lawrence, KS 66044

416-422-4222
800-280-5325; Fax: 416-422-1622
www.iaais.org

Maryfrances Evans, President
Chuck Adkins, Director, Broadcast Operations
Amy Hatter, 1st Vice President
Andrea Pasquale, Secretary
Bekah Jerde, Treasurer

Encourages and supports the establishment and maintenance of audio information services that provide access to printed information for individuals who cannot read conventional print because of blindness or any other visual, physical, or learning disability.
Founded in 1977

4920 International Association of Audio Visual Communicators
The Cindy Competitions
57 West Palo Verde Avenue
PO Box 270779
Flower Mound, TX 75027-0779

469-464-4180; Fax: 469-464-4170
www.cindys.com
Facebook, Twitter, LinkedIn, YouTube

Sheemon Wolfe, Contact

Members are audio-visual professionals using the media of film, video, slides, filmstrips, multi-image and interactive media to communicate information
5200 Members
Founded in 1959

4921 International Association of Business Communicators
601 Montgomery St.
Suite 1900
San Francisco, CA 94111

415-544-4700
800-776-4222; Fax: 415-544-4747
service_centre@iabc.com
www.iabc.com
Twitter, LinkedIn

Peter Finn, Executive Director
Tilden Katz, Chief Communications Officer
Buffy Levy, Event Director
Jason Meyers, Content & Editorial Director
Jeff Price, Marketing & Communications Manager

International knowledge network for professionals engaged in stategic business communication management.
13,00 Members
Founded in 1970

4922 International Association of Information Technology Asset Managers
4848 Munson St. NW
Canton, OH 44718

330-628-3012
877-942-4826; Fax: 330-628-3289
info@iaitam.org
www.iaitam.org
Facebook, Twitter, LinkedIn, YouTube

Barbara Rembiesa, President, Founder, CEO

The professional association for individuals and organizations involved in any aspect of IT Asset Management (ITAM), Software Asset Management (SAM), Hardware Asset Management, and the lifecycle processes supporting IT Asset Management in organizations of every size and industry across the globe.
Founded in 2002

4923 **International Association of Medical Trans port Communication Specialists**
Birmingham, AL 35217

Home Page: www.iamtcs.org
Facebook, Twitter, LinkedIn

Aaron Bowles, President
Robert Throckmorton, President-Elect
Rickey McLester, Treasurer
Jonathan Unwin, Secretary

Professional organization whose mission is to represent the air medical communications specialist on a national level through education, standardization and recognition.
200 Members
Founded in 1989

4924 **International Communication Association**
1500 21st St NW
Washington, DC 20036

202-955-1444; Fax: 202-955-1448
icahdq@icahdq.org
www.icahdq.org
Facebook, Twitter, LinkedIn, Tumblr, Pinterest

Laura Sawyer, Executive Director
Tom Mankowski, Director, Publishing Operations
Julie Arnold, Sr. Manager, Governance
Jennifer Le, Sr. Manager, Conference Services
Kristine Rosa, Manager, Member Services/Marketing

International association for scholars interested in the study, teaching and application of all aspects of human mediated communication. ICA began as a small association of US reseachers and has matured into a international association with members in 65 countries.
3400+ Members
Founded in 1950

4925 **International Documentary Association**
3470 Wilshire Boulevard
Suite 980
Los Angeles, CA 90010

213-232-1660; Fax: 213-232-1669
michael@documentary.org
www.documentary.org
Facebook, Twitter, LinkedIn, YouTube

Simon Kilmurry, Executive Director
Dana Merwin, Program Officer
Niki Bhardwaj, Events Coordinator
Jina Chung, Director, Development
Veronica Monteyro, Membership Manager

A nonprofit membership organization dedicated to supporting the efforts of nonfiction film and video makers throughout the United States and the world; promoting the documentary form; and expanding opportunities for the production, distribution, and exhibition of documentary.
2631 Members
Founded in 1982

4926 **International Regional Magazine Association**
38 Burgess Ave.
Toronto, ON M4E 1W7

416-705-6884; Fax: 888-806-1533
www.regionalmagazines.org

Tara Flint, Executive Director
Mark Mahorsky, President
Alison Dickie, Vice President
Kelly Mero, Vice President

IRMA provides a forum for regional magazine publishers to exchange ideas with the view to improving their respective publications.
250-3 Members
Founded in 1960

4927 **International Society for Technology in Education**
621 SW Morrison Street
Suite 800
Portland, OR 97205

503-342-2848
800-336-5191; Fax: 503-882-0813
iste@iste.org
www.iste.org
Facebook, Twitter, LinkedIn, YouTube, Pinterest

Bill Bass, President
Nikole Blanchard, Treasurer
Michael McVey, Secretary
Richard Culatta, Chief Executive Officer

A large nonprofit organization serving the technology-using educator.

4928 **Internet Society**
11710 Plaza America Drive
Suite 400
Reston, VA 20190

703-439-2120
isoc@isoc.org
www.internetsociety.org
Facebook, Twitter, LinkedIn, YouTube, Instagram

Andrew Sullivan, President & CEO
Sandy Spector, CFO & SVP, Business Operations
Rinalia Abdul Rahim, SVP, Strategy, Comm. & Engagement
Jeannette Engel, Sr. Director, Global HR
Susannah Gray, Director, Communications

An international, nonprofit organization that provides leadership in Internet related standards, education, and policy.
Founded in 1992

4929 **Land Mobile Communications Council**
2121 Cooperative Way
Suite 225
Herndon, VA 20171

703-528-5114; Fax: 703-524-1074
mark.crosby@enterprisewireless.org
www.lmcc.org

Klaus Bender, President
Mark Crosby, Secretary

A nonprofit association of organizations representing land mobile radio carriers and manufacturers equipment; LMCC membership represents diverse telecommunications sectors such as public safety, industrial/land transportation, private radio, specialized mobile radion and critical infrastructure.
Founded in 1967

4930 **Media Alliance**
1904 Franklin St
Suite 818
Oakland, CA 94612

510-684-6853; Fax: 510-238-8557
information@media-alliance.org
www.media-alliance.org
Facebook, Twitter

Tracy Rosenberg, Executive Director
Eloise Rose Lee, Program Director

A nonprofit training and resource center for media workers, community organizations and political activists.
Founded in 1976

4931 **Media Communications Association Internati onal**
PO Box 5135
Madison, WI 53705-0135

888-899-MCAI; Fax: 888-862-8150
loiswei@aol.com
iamcr.org
Facebook, Twitter, LinkedIn, Google+

Nico Carpentier, President
Bruce Girard, Executive Director

Global community that provides its members opportunities for networking, learning and career advancement. Members work in video, film, collaborative communication, distance learning, web design and creation, and all forms of interactive visual communication, along with associated crafts; serving businesses, nonprofit organizations, the government, educational institutions, the medical field, and electronic media. Chapters are throughout the US, with affiliates in Asia and Europe.
Founded in 1970

4932 **Media Institute**
2300 Clarendon Blvd
Suite 602
Arlington, VA 22201

703-243-5700; Fax: 703-243-8808
info@mediainstitute.org
www.mediainstitute.org
Twitter, RSS Feed, You Tube

Richard Kaplar, President & CEO
Susanna Coto, Director, Public Events
Stuart Brotman, Distinguished Fellow

Non-profit research foundation specializing in communications policy isssues.
Founded in 1979

4933 **Media Research Center**
1900 Campus Commons Drive
Suite 600
Reston, VA 20191

571-267-3500
800-672-1423; Fax: 571-375-0099
www.mrc.org
Facebook, Twitter

A politically conservative content analysis organization.
Founded in 1987

4934 **Media Research Directors Association**
Ogilvy and Mather
309 W 49th Street
New York, NY 10019-7316

212-375-5502

Provides support for research and maintains library.

4935 **Multicultural Media, Telecom and Internet Council**
3636 16th Street NW
Suite B 366
Washington, DC 20010

202-332-0500; Fax: 202-332-0503
info@mmtconline.org
www.mmtconline.org
Twitter

Maurita Coley Flippin, President & CEO
Dorrissa Griffin, Chief of Staff & Staff Counsel
Ananda Leeke, Chief Social Media Officer

National non-profit organization dedicated to promoting and oreserving equal opportunity and civil rights in the mass media, telecommunications and broadband industries, and closing the digital divide.

4936 **NTCA-The Rural Broadband Association**
4121 Wilson Boulevard
Suite 1000
Arlington, VA 22203

703-351-2000; Fax: 703-351-2001
www.ntca.org

Shirley A. Bloomfield, CEO
Mano Koilpillai, CFO
Les Greer, SVP, Benefits, Operations & Tech
Michael Romano, SVP, Industry Affairs
April Irwin, VP, Member Engagement

A nonprofit association representing small and rural telephone cooperatives and commercial companies.

4937 **National Association for Media Literacy Education**
10 Laurel Hill Drive
Cherry Hill, NJ 8003

888-775-2652
namle.net
Facebook, Twitter, Google+, Flickr, RSS

Michelle Ciulla Lipkin, Executive Director
Donnell Probst, Associate Director
Kyle Plantz, Program Assistant

A national membership organization dedicated to media literacy as abasic life skill for the 21st century.
Founded in 1997

4938 **National Association for Multi-Ethnicity in Communications**
50 Broad Street
Suite 1801
New York, NY 10004

212-594-5985; Fax: 212-594-8391
info@namic.com
www.namic.com
Facebook, Twitter, LinkedIn, Instagram

A. Shuanise Washington, President/CEO
Anne-Marie Burton, Chief of Strategy & Programs
Sandra Girado, VP, Events & Partner Relations
Susan Waldman, Sr. Manager, Mem. & Publications
Davana O'Brien, Administrative Coordinator

Works for diversity in the telecommunications industry.
2000 Members
Founded in 1980

4939 **National Association of Broadcasters**
1771 N Street NW
Washington, DC 20036

202-429-5300
nab@nab.org
www.nab.org
Facebook, Twitter, LinkedIn, YouTube

Gordon Smith, President & CEO
Curtis LeGeyt, Chief Operating Officer
Tea Gennaro, EVP, Finance & CFO
Michelle Duke, Chief Diversity Officer
Sam Matteny, Chief Technology Officer

A trade association, workers union, and lobby group representing the interests of for-profit, over-the-air radio and television broadcasters in theUnited States.

4940 **National Association of Communication Centers**

Home Page: commcenters.org
Facebook

Carl Brown, Chair
Victoria McDermott, Vice Chair
Nick Tatum, Vice Chair Elect
Rachel Sieczkowski, Secretary

An organization devoted to the support of communication centers on college and university campuses across the country.

4941 **National Association of Hispanic Publications**
529 14th St, NW.
Suite 923
Washington, DC 20045

202-662-7250; Fax: 703-610-9005
info@nahp.org
www.nahp.org
Facebook, Twitter

Fanny Miller, President
Alvaro Gurdian, Vice President
Miriam Lira Hickerson, VP, Membership-West
Pedro De Armas, VP, Membership-East
Giancarlo Bresani, VP, Marketing

Founded in the belief that the most effective way to reach the more than 29 million Hispanic Americans in the country is through their own language.
234 Members
Founded in 1982

4942 **National Association of Independent Writers and Editors**
P.O. Box 549
Ashland, VA 23005

804-767-5961
naiwe.com
Facebook, Twitter

Janice Campbell, Director

A professional association for writers and editors, providing individual member websites and other benefits.
Founded in 2007

4943 **National Association of State Technology Directors**
PO Box 11910
Lexington, KY 40578-1910

859-244-8186; Fax: 859-244-8001
www.nastd.org

Mark McCord, Executive Director
Pamela Johnson, Meetings & Member Services Manager
Paul Czarnecki, Communications & Research Manager

Concerned with providing a forum for the exchange of ideas and practices and the development of a unified position on matters of national telecommunications policy and regulatory issues.
1000 Members
Founded in 1978

4944 **National Association of Telecommunications Officers and Advisors**
3213 Duke St.
Suite 695
Alexandria, VA 22314

703-519-8035; Fax: 703-997-7080
info@natoa.org
www.natoa.org
Facebook, Twitter, LinkedIn, RSS

Tonya Rideout, Executive Director
Jennifer Harman, Deputy Director
Nancy Werner, General Counsel
Karen Anderson, Administrative Specialist Rideout

A national association that represents the communications and interests of local governments, and those who advise local governments.
800 Members
Founded in 1980

4945 **National Association of women Business Owners**
601 Pennsylvania Avenue NW
South Building, Suite 900
Washington, DC 20004

800-556-2926; Fax: 202-403-3788
national@nawbo.org
www.nawbo.org
Facebook, Twitter, LinkedIn, Google+, YouTube

Jen Earle, National CEO
Deborah Snyder, VP, Membership & Community Outreach
Joyce Lee, VP, Operations
Elle Patout, Director, Public Relations
Lynda Bishop, Director, Programs

Sponsors studies, research and seminars to find solutions to problems and create opportunities for women. Presents annual awards.
300 Members
Founded in 1975

4946 **National Cable & Telecommunications Association**
25 Massachusetts Avenue, NW
Suite 100
Washington, DC 20001

202-222-2300; Fax: 202-222-2514
info@ncta.com
www.ncta.com
Facebook, Twitter, LinkedIn

Michael Powell, President, CEO
Mark Gulish, SVP, Finance & Admin. & CFO
William Check, SVP, Chief Technology Officer
K. Dane Snowden, Chief Operating Officer
James Assey, Executive VP

Trade association for U.S. cable industry.

4947 **National Captioning Institute**
3725 Concorde Parkway
Suite 100
Chantilly, VA 20151

703-917-7600; Fax: 703-917-9853
info@ncicap.org
www.ncicap.org
Facebook, Twitter, LinkedIn

Gene Chao, Chair & CEO
Beth Nubbe, SVP, Finance & Administration
Meredith Patterson, VP, Production
Lydy Pinzon-Dadley, Director, Sales & Marketing
Xiaochun Wang, Manager, Accounting

Non-profit organization whose primary purposes are to deliver effective captioning services and encourage, develop and fund the continuing development of captioning, subtitling, and other media access services for the benefit of peopl who require additional access to the auditory and visual information.
Founded in 1979

4948 **National Communication Association**
1765 N Street NW
Washington, DC 20036

202-464-4622; Fax: 202-464-4600
inbox@natcom.org
www.natcom.org
Facebook, Twitter, YouTube, Blog

Trevor Parry-Giles, Executive Director
Joseph Ritchie, Chief Financial Officer
Justin Danowski, Asst. Dir., Governance & Membership
LaKesha Anderson, Dir., Academic/Professional Affairs
Kristin Yednock, Asst. Dir., Conventions & Meetings

A not-for-profit membership-based scholarly society.
Founded in 1914

4949 National Council of Writing Program Administrators
Department of English
Miami University
Oxford, OH 45056

513-529-5221; Fax: 513-529-1392
www.wpacouncil.org
Facebook, Twitter, LinkedIn

Mark Blaauw-Hara, President
Susan Thomas, Vice President

National organization that fosters professional development, communication and community among college and university writing progrma administrators and other interested faculty.
700 Members
Founded in 1975

4950 National Information Standards Organization
801 Compass Way
Suite 201
Annapolis, MD 21401

443-221-2980; Fax: 443-221-2981
nisohq@niso.org
niso.org
Facebook, Twitter, LinkedIn

Todd Carpenter, Executive Director
Kimberly Graham, Office Manager
Jason Griffey, Director, Strategic Initiatives
Jill O'Neill, Director, Content
Sara Groveman, Communications & Events Coordinator

Serves those groups that aggregate, organize, and facilitate access to information. To improve member capabilities and contribute to their ongoing success. Provides opportunities for education, advocacy, and a forum to address common interests. Formerly the National Federation Abstracting & Information services (NFAIS).
60 Members
Founded in 1958
Printed in on matte stock

4951 National Newspaper Association
900 Community Drive
Springfield, IL 62703

217-241-1400; Fax: 217-241-1301
membership@nna.org
nnaweb.org
Facebook, Twitter, RSS

Lynne Lance, Executive Director
Tonda Rush, General Counsel
Carol Pierce, Director, Washington Programs
Wendy MacDonald, Director, Sales
Robert Williams, Jr., Director, Creative Resources

An association representing community newspapers, publishers, and editors. Lists resources, events, membership benefits, and jobs.
2100 Members
Founded in 1885

4952 National Newspaper Publishers Association
1816 12th Street, NW
Washington, DC 20009

202-588-8764; Fax: 202-588-8960
admin@nnpa.org
nnpa.org
Facebook, Twitter, Google+

Benjamin Chavis, President & CEO
Blexander

A trade association composed of more than 200 black newspapers in the United States and the Virgin Islands. It also created an electronic news service which enables newspapers to provide real time news and information to its national constituency.

4953 National Speakers Association
1500 S Priest Dr
Tempe, AZ 85281-6203

480-968-2552; Fax: 480-968-0911
memberservices@NSAspeaker.org
www.nsaspeaker.org
Facebook, Twitter, Google+, YouTube, Instagram

Mary Lue Peck, President & CEO
Rhette Baughman, Chief Revenue Officer
Nikki Harris, Director, Member Success
Jessi Leonardo, Director, Operations
Matt Longdon, Manager, Marketing & Communications

The leading organization for experts who speak professionally. NSA's members include experts in a variety of industries and disciplines, who reach audiences as trainers, educators, humorists, motivators, consultants, authors and more. NSA provides resources and education designed to advance the skills, integrity, and value of its members and speaking profession. NSA the voice of the speaking profession.
3500 Members
Founded in 1973
Mailing list available for rent: 3200 names

4954 National Telemedia Council
1922 University Avenue
Madison, WI 53726

608-218-1182; Fax: 608-218-1183
ntelemedia@aol.com
www.nationaltelemediacouncil.org

Marieli Rowe, Executive Director
Karen Ambrosh, President
Belinha De Abreu, Vice President

Promotes media literacy through workshops and telemediun.
Founded in 1953

4955 National Translator Association
5611 Kendall Court
Suite 2
Arvada, CO 80002

303-378-8209; Fax: 303-465-4067
stcl@comcast.net
www.nationaltranslatorassociation.org

John Terrill, President
Arnold Cruze, Vice President
Ched Keiler, Vice President, Audio
Michael Couzens, Vice President, Legal Affairs

Dedicated to the preservation of free over-the-air TV in all geographical areas. It works to improve the technology of rebroadcast translators and regulatory climate which governs them. It continously promotes the concept of universal free over-the-air TV and reprsents the ineterests of translator operators before the FCC and other government agencies such as the Forest Service and the Bureau of Land Management. Membership is open to all individuals and organizations that are interested.
Founded in 1967

4956 National Writers Association

Home Page: www.nationalwriters.com

A nonprofit organization that provides education and an ethical resource for writers at all levels of experience. It also awards scholarships and provides no or low cost workshops and seminars.

4957 Networking Institute
PO Box 650037
West Newton, MA 02465-1928

617-965-3340; Fax: 617-965-2341
info@netage.com
www.netage.com

Jessica Lipnack, Co-Founder & CEO
Jeffrey Stamps, Co-Founder
Ramana Rao, Technology Advisor
Rich Carpenter, Strategy Advisor

Promotes networks to help people work together. Offers consulting services, educational workshops and seminars. To order: The Age of the Network and The TeamNet Factor call Oliver Wright productions at 800-343-0625.
Founded in 1982

4958 News Media Alliance
4401 N. Fairfax Drive
Suite 300
Arlington, VA 22203

571-366-1000
info@newsmediaalliance.org
www.newsmediaalliance.org
Facebook, Twitter, LinkedIn, YouTube

David Chavern, President & CEO
Robert Walden, Chief Financial Officer
Rebecca Frank, VP, Research & Insights
Danielle Coffey, SVP & General Counsel
Paul Boyle, SVP, Public Policy

Formerly known as the Newspaper Association of America, the News Media Alliance represents large daily papers, non-daily/small-market publications, as well as digital and multiplatform products across North America.
2000 Members
Founded in 1992

4959 Newspaper Association Managers
32 Dunham Road
Beverly, MA

978-338-2555
www.nammembers.com

Steve Nixon, President
Thomas Silvestri, Executive Director
Monica Gilmer, Director, Member Services
Layne Bruce, Clerk

An organization of executives representing newspaper associations in the United States and Canada.

4960 North American Serials Interest Group
1902 Ridge Rd
West Seneca, NY 14224-3312

info@nasig.org
www.nasig.org

Betsy Appleton, President
Ted Westervelt, Vice President/President-Elect
Beth Ashmore, Secretary
Cris Ferguson, Treasurer

An independent organization taht promotes communication and sharing of ideas among all members of the serials information chain, anyone working with or concerned about serial publications.
1200 Members
Founded in 1985

4961 Organization for the Promotion and Advance of Small Telecommunications Co.
21 Dupont Cir NW
Suite 700
Washington, DC 20036-1109

202-833-2775; Fax: 202-659-4619
membership@ncta.org
www.opastco.org

Protects the interests of small, rural, independent commercial telephone companies and cooperatives that have less than 50,000 access lines.
675 Members
Founded in 1963

4962 **Paley Center for Media**
25 West 52nd Street
New York, NY 10019
212-621-6800; Fax: 212-621-6600
coman@paleycenter.org
www.paleycenter.org
Facebook, Twitter, YouTube, Google+, Hulu
Maureen Reidy, President, CEO
Diane Lewis, Chief Programming Officer & EVP
David Schoer, Chief Financial Officer & EVP
Joanna Scholl, SVP, Marketing & Communications
Shayne Doty, SVP, Development
Leads the discussion about the cultural, creative, and social significance of television, radio, and emerging platforms for the professional community and media-interested public.

4963 **Personal Achievement Institute**
1 Speaking Success Road
Box 6543
Kingman, AZ 86402-6543
928-753-5315
800-321-1225; Fax: 928-753-7554
Burt Dubin, President
Education that provides advice and business strategies for both novices and experts in mastering the field of professional speaking. Free monthly newsletter is accessible through Website.
Founded in 1978
Printed in one color on matte stock

4964 **Portable Computer and Communications Association**
PO Box 680
Hood River, OR 97031
541-490-5140; Fax: 413-410-8447
Gloria Kowalski, Director
Peter Rysavy, Executive Director
Represents firms, organizations, and individuals interested in moblie communications.
65 Members

4965 **Public Relations Society of America**
120 Wall St
21st Fl.
New York, NY 10005-4024
212-460-1400
www.prsa.org
Facebook, Twitter, LinkedIn, Pinterest, Tumblr
Philip Bonaventura, Chief Executive Officer
Jeneen Garcia, Executive Director
Karen Mateo, Chief Communications Officer
Maureen Walsh, Chief Marketing & Sales Officer
Jay Starr, SVP, Member Services
The PRSA is the foremost professional development and standards and ethics body in the public relations industry.
22000 Members
Founded in 1947

4966 **Railway Systems Suppliers**
13133 Professional Drive
Suite 100
Jacksonville, FL 32225
904-379-3366; Fax: 904-379-3941
rssi@rssi.org
www.rssi.org
Michael Drudy, Executive Director
Dot Frenette, Executive Assistant
A trade association serving the communication and signal segment of the rail transportation industry. Primary activity is to organize and manage a trade show for its members to exhibit their products and services.
260 Members
Founded in 1966

4967 **Real Estate Information Professionals Association**
2501 Aerial Center Parkway
Suite 103
Morrisville, NC 27560
919-459-2070
801-999-1212; Fax: 919-459-2075
Sarah Gillian, Executive Director
Supports professional information providers in the real estate industry.
110 Members
Founded in 1995

4968 **Religious Communication Association**
Department of Communication
University of Texas at Tyler
3007 North Ben Wilson
Victoria, TX 77901
903-566-7093; Fax: 903-566-7287
wardm@uhv.edu
www.relcomm.org
Janie Harden Fritz, Executive Secretary
Mark Ward, Sr., Electronic Communication Curator
An academic society of individuals interested in the study of all aspects of public religious communication, members include teachers, students, clergy, broadcasters and other scholars and professionals.
210 Members
Founded in 1973

4969 **Republican Communications Association**
PO Box 550
Washington, DC 20515
Home Page: www.joinrca.org
Facebook, Twitter, Google+
Rachel Ledbetter, President
Rachel Stephens, Vice President
Miranda Dabney, Treasurer
Sponsors professional development and networking programs. Conducts seminars, briefings, and tours.
165 Members
Founded in 1970

4970 **Satellite Broadcasting and Communications Association**
1100 17th Street NW
Suite 1150
Washington, DC 20036-4557
202-349-3620
800-541-5981; Fax: 202-349-3621
info@sbca.org
www.sbca.com
Facebook, Twitter, LinkedIn, YouTube
Steven Hill, President
Tracy Ann Strickland, Research Coordinator
Ali Bullis, Operations Director
The national trade organization representing all segments of the satellite industry. It is committed to expanding the utilization of satellite technology for the broadcast delivery of video, audio, data, music, voice, interactive and broadband services.
100 Members
Founded in 1986

4971 **Society for Technical Communication**
9401 Lee Hwy
Suite 300
Fairfax, VA 22031-1803
703-522-4114; Fax: 703-522-2075
stc@stc.org
www.stc.org
Liz Pohland, Chief Executive Officer
Erin Gallalee, Director, Membership & Community
Elaine Gilliam, Director, Meetings & Convention Op.
Sarah Black, Publications Manager
Kira Jones, Marketing Manager
Seeks to advance the theory and practice of technical communication in all media. Presents awards and sponsors high school writing contests.
19000 Members
Founded in 1953
Mailing list available for rent: 9000 names at $120 per M

4972 **Society of Satellite Professionals International**
250 Park Avenue
7th Floor
New York, NY 10177
212-809-5199; Fax: 212-825-0075
rbell@sspi.org
www.sspi.org
Facebook, Twitter, LinkedIn, YouTube
Robert Bell, Executive Director
Louis Zacharilla, Director, Development
Tamara Bond-Williams, Director, Membership
Matthew Owen, Communications Manager
Members are individuals in the fields of businesss, education, entertainment, media, science and industry who share common interests in satellite technology.
1700 Members
Founded in 1983

4973 **Society of Telecommunications Consultants**
13275 State Highway 89
PO Box 70
Old Station, CA 96071
530-335-7313
800-782-7670; Fax: 530-335-7360
stchdq@stcconsultants.org
www.sctcconsultants.org
Facebook, Twitter, Pinterest
Chuck Vondra, President
Steve Leaden, Executive Vice President
Denise Munro, Senior Vice President & Treasurer
The STC is an international organization of independent telecommunications and information technology consultants who serve clients in business and government
180 Members
Founded in 1976

4974 **Telecommunications Benchmarking International Group**
4606 Fm 1960 Rd W
Suite 250
Houston, TX 77069-4617
281-440-5044
888-739-8244; Fax: 281-440-6677
tbig@benchmarkingnetwork.com
www.benchmarkingnetwork.com
An association of contact center professionals within telecommunications companies dedicated to providing members with an opportunity to identify, document and establish best practices through benchmakring to increase value, effiencies, and profits.
3500+ Members
Founded in 1976

4975 **Telecommunications Industry Association (TIA)**
1320 N. Courthouse Rd
Suite 200
Arlington, VA 22201-3834

703-907-7700; Fax: 703-907-7727
gseiffert@tiaonline.org
www.tiaonline.org

David Stehlin, Chief Executive Officer
Ken Koffman, Chief Technology Officer & VP
Andrew Kurtzman, VP & General Counsel
Dan Brown, Director, Marketing & Communication
Alia Lawson, Membership Advisor

The Telecommunications Industry Association/TIA represents providers of communications and information technology products and services for the global marketplace through its core competencies in standards development, domestic and international advocacy, as well as market development and trade promotion programs.

4976 **The Association of Business Information and Media Companies**
675 Third Avenue
Suite 2200
New York, NY 10017-5704

212-661-6360; Fax: 212-370-0736
info@abmmail.com
www.abmassociation.com
Facebook, Twitter, LinkedIn, WordPress, YouTube

Matthew Kinsman, VP, Content & Programming

An association that focuses on the integrated business-to-business media model—which includes print publications, events, digital media and business information.
Founded in 1906

4977 **The Center for Media and Public Affairs**
933 N. Kenmore St.
Suite 405
Arlington, VA 22201

571-319-0029; Fax: 571-319-0029
rieckd@cmpa.com
www.cmpa.com
Facebook, Twitter

Robert Lichter, Founder & President
Hong Yu (Cici) Wang, Executive Director
Dan Amundson, Director, Research

A nonpartisan, nonprofit research organization in Washington, D.C.,conducting scientific studies of the news and entertainment media.
Founded in 1985

4978 **The Energy Telecommunications and Electrical Association**
5005 W Royal Lane
Suite 116
Irving, TX 75063

972-929-3169
888-503-8700; Fax: 972-915-6040
info@entelec.org
www.entelec.org
Twitter, LinkedIn

A user association focusing on communications and control technologies used by petroleum, natural gas, pipeline and electric utility companies.
Founded in 1928

4979 **The International Foundation for Information Technology**
P. O. Box 907
Summit, NJ 07901-2508

Home Page: www.if4it.com
Facebook, Twitter, LinkedIn, Google+

A global industry best practices association that promotes the interests and career development of practitioners, educators, and students who wish to extend their knowledge and understanding of IT operations, management, and leadership.

4980 **Toastmasters International**
23182 Arroyo Vista
Rancho Santa Margarita
Mission Viejo, CA 92688-2620

949-858-8255
949-835-1300; Fax: 949-858-1207
newsletters@toastmasters.org
www.toastmasters.org
Facebook, Twitter

Jim Kokocki, DTM, International President
Mike Storkey, DTM, International President-Elect
Balraj Arunasalam, DTM, First Vice President
Lark Doley, DTM, Second Vice President
Mohammed Murad, DTM, Immediate Past Intl. President

Publishes educational articles on the subjects of communication and leadership. Topics include language, listening, humor, self-improvement, goal setting, success and logical thinking.
19500 Members
Founded in 1924

4981 **United States Internet Service Providers**
700 12th St NW
Suite 700 E
Washington, DC 20005-4052

202-904-2351
www.usispa.org

John Albertine, President

Will serve both as the ISP community's representative during policy debates and as a forum in which members can share information and develop best practices for handling specific legal matters.
7 Members
Founded in 1991

4982 **United States Telecom Association**
607 14th Street, NW
Suite 400
Washington, DC 20005

202-326-7300; Fax: 202-315-3603
www.ustelecom.org
Facebook, Twitter, LinkedIn, YouTube

Jonathan Spalter, President & CEO
Allison Remsen, EVP & Chief of Staff
Sally Aman, SVP, Communications/Public Affairs
Lorna Johnson, Chief Financial Officer
Brandon Heiner, SVP, Government Affairs

A trade association that represents telecommunications-related businesses based in the United States.

4983 **Utilities Technology Council**
2550 South Clark Street
Suite 960
Arlington, VA 22202

202-872-0030; Fax: 202-872-1331
www.utc.org
Facebook, Twitter, LinkedIn

Sheryl Osiene Riggs, President/CEO
Karnel Thomas, SVP, Membership & Meetings
Daniel Thrasher, Director, Finance & Operations
Brittany Prosise, Manager, Marketing

Represents organizations using telecommunications in their operations before various federal and state legislative and regulatory agencies, particularly the FCC.
1500 Members
Founded in 1948

4984 **Utility Communicators International**
150 Mark Trai
Sandy Springs, GA 30328

970-368-2021; Fax: 512-864-7203
info@utilitycommunicators.com
www.utilitycommunicators.com
Facebook, Twitter, LinkedIn

Jerry Cargile, President
Brandy Powers, Treasurer

International organization comprimsed of advertising, public relations and marketing professionals from electric, gas and water utilities, energy companies, telephone companies, advertising and public relations agencies, and suppliers who communicate for and about the utility and energy industries.
400 Members
Founded in 1922

4985 **Wikibon**
5 Mount Royal Ave.
Suite 280
Marlborough, MA 1752

774-463-3400; Fax: 774-463-3405
inquire@wikibon.org
wikibon.org
Facebook, Twitter, LinkedIn, Blog

A professional community solving technology and business problems through an open source sharing of free advisory knowledge.
Founded in 2007

4986 **Wireless Communications Association International**
1333 H St NW
Suite 700 W
Washington, DC 20005-4754

202-452-7823; Fax: 202-452-0041
www.wcainternational.com
Facebook, Twitter, LinkedIn

Fred Campbell, President

The non-profit trade and professional association for the Wireless Broadband industry. Mission is to advance the interests of the wireless carriers that provide high-speed data, internet, voice and video services on broadband spectrum through land-based systems using reception/transmit devices in all broadband spectrum bands.
250 Members
Founded in 1987

4987 **Wireless Dealers Association**
9746 Tappenbeck Dr
Houston, TX 77055-4102

713-467-0077
800-624-6918
contact@wirelessindustry.com
www.wirelessindustry.com

Robert Hutchinson, President

Business association made up of cellular and wireless communications agents, dealers, resellers, carriers, manufacturers, distributors and importers.
2500 Members
Founded in 1986

4988 **Wireless Infrastructure Association**
2111 Wilson Blvd.
Suite 210
Arlington, VA 22201

703-739-0300; Fax: 703-836-1608
wia.org
Facebook, Twitter, LinkedIn

Jonathan Adelstein, President & CEO
Rikin Thakker, Chief Technology Officer
Tracy Ford, Executive Director, Member Services
Marta Sokol, VP, Finance & Administration
Nancy Touhill, Director, Meetings & Events

Represents companies that develop, own, manage and operate towers, commercial rooftops and other facilities for the provision of all types of wireless, broadcasting and telecommunications services.
3000 Members
Founded in 1949

4989 **Women in Cable and Telecommunications**
2000 K Street, NW
Suite 350
Washington, DC 20006

202-827-4794; Fax: 202-450-5596
membership@wict.org
www.wict.org
Facebook, Twitter, YouTube

Maria E. Brennan, CAE, President & CEO
Lesa Faris, Chief Development Officer
Rebecca Walker, Chief Financial Officer
Kathleen McNally, Director, Membership Operations
Sydney Rose, Manager, Chapters & Events

Provides opportunitites for leadership, networking, and advocacy in the industry.
4600 Members
Founded in 1979

Newsletters

4990 **411 Newsletter**
United Communications Group
11300 Rockville Pike
Suite 1100
Rockville, MD 20852-3030

301-287-2700; Fax: 301-816-8945
www.ucg.com

Benny Dicecca, President

Business newsletter for professionals in the communications industry.
Cost: $339.00
Founded in 1977

4991 **ABC Newsletter**
Association for Business Communcation
181 Turner St. NW
323 Shanks Hall
Blacksburg, VA 24061

540-231-8460; Fax: 646-349-5297
abcoffice@businesscommunication.org
www.businesscommunication.org

Sky Marsen, Editor
Jim Dubinsky, Executive Director

Content includes stories on business communication events, initiatives, awards, achievements, research, conferences, and new books. Connects members of the ABC.
Frequency: Quarterly

4992 **AEJMC News**
AEJMC
234 Outlet Pointe Boulevard
Suite A
Columbia, SC 29210-5667

803-798-0271; Fax: 803-772-3509
www.aejmc.org

Jennifer McGill, Executive Director
Lillian Coleman, Newsletter Editor/Project Manager
Newsletter of the Association for Education in Journalism and Mass Communication.
Frequency: Monthly
Circulation: 3425
Founded in 1912

4993 **ATTW Bulletin**
Association of Teachers of Technical Writing
Department of Linguistics and Technical Comm
1155 Union Circle #305298
Denton, TX 76203-5017

940-565-4458
sims@unt.edu
www.attw.org

Barbara Sims, Executive Secretary

Publishes news about members, the association, and the profession as well as bibliographic resources for teachers, teaching techniques, suggested assignments, implications of current research for the classroom, opinions on professional issues, notices and highlights of conferences, calls for papers and proposals, job announcements, and other information that will interest new and experienced teachers in undergraduate or graduate curricula.
Frequency: Semi-Annual

4994 **Bandwidth Minutes and IP Transport Markets Will Capacity Traders Succeed?**
Probe Research
3 Wing Drive
Suite 240
Cedar Knolls, NJ 07927-1000

973-285-1500; Fax: 973-285-1519
www.proberesearch.com

We look into capacity exchanges and determine how they add value, whter participants will find exchanges useful, what are the presequisites for a robust capacity market, what are the risk to telcos if they use exchanges, and what do the exchanges need to do in order to increase trading volume.

4995 **Bandwidth Pricing Trends**
Probe Research
3 Wing Drive
Suite 240
Cedar Knolls, NJ 07927-1000

973-285-1500; Fax: 973-285-1519
www.proberesearch.com

Provides an analysis of the trends in capacity pricing and the expected effects on demand. It provides a view of the drivers that determine what the bandwidth cost will be on a particular route. Also looks at how these determinants have contributes to the level of price erosion each of the routes analyzed.

4996 **Big Ideas Newsletter**
Newspaper Association of America
4401 Wilson Blvd
Suite 900
Arlington, VA 22203-4195

571-366-1000; Fax: 571-366-1195
www.naa.org

Reggie Hall, Senior VP

Designed especially for smaller market newspapers, featuring ways to increase revenues, cut costs or otherwise improve your newspaper.
Frequency: Bi-Monthly

4997 **Brandwidth Supply and Demand Analysis WIT IP Traffic Demand Update**
Probe Research
3 Wing Drive
Suite 240
Cedar Knolls, NJ 07927-1000

973-285-1500; Fax: 973-285-1519
www.proberesearch.com

Provides an analysis of the bandwidth supply and demand on number of interregional routes. Describes methodology of building up the bandwidth supply and demand picture on these routes. Analyzes what the supply and demand balance is on these routes. Concludes what the business ramifications are for ISPs and backbone providers, banks and vendors.

4998 **Broadband Wireless**
Probe Research
3 Wing Drive
Suite 240
Cedar Knolls, NJ 07927-1000

973-285-1500; Fax: 973-285-1519
www.proberesearch.com

In this bulletin, we take a look into is going on with terrestrial fixed wireless last mile solutions in the MMDS, LMDS spectrums. LMDS is emerging as the next platform for CLECs. However, these CLECs will be entering the market at the end of a long line of competitors in many cities.

4999 **Business Publisher**
JK Publishing
3105 N Newhall Street
Milwaukee, WI 53211

414-332-1625; Fax: 414-332-0916

John Kenney, Editor
Jean O'Brien, Circulation Manager

Offers information and full coverage of the magazine and business/trade publishing industry.
Cost: $335.00
8 Pages
Frequency: BiWeekly

5000 **CMA Newsletter**
College Media Advisers
University
#300
Memphis, TN 38152

512-471-5084; Fax: 901-678-4798
www.collegemedia.org

Ken Rosenauer, Publisher

Provides news and information to those who advise/supervise college media run by students (i.e. newspapers, magazines, yearbooks, radios, and TV stations).
Cost: $60.00
6 Pages
Circulation: 750
Founded in 1954

5001 **Cantu's Newsletter**
Cantu's Comedy Newsletter
PO Box 210495
San Francisco, CA 94121

415-668-2402
www.humormall.com

John Cantu, Publisher

Articles of interest to public speakers, writers, comedians, comedy writers.
Cost: $29.95
Circulation: 3000
Founded in 1999

5002 **Chamber Executive**
American Chambers of Congress Exec Communications

4875 Eisenhower Ave
Suite 250
Alexandria, VA 22304-4850

703-998-0072; Fax: 703-212-9512
webmaster@acce.org
www.acce.org

Mick Flemming, Manager

Newsletter aimed at management level communications professionals.
Cost: $99.00
12 Pages
Founded in 1914
Mailing list available for rent
Printed in 4 colors on matte stock

5003 **Circulation Update E-Newsletter**
Newspaper Association of America
4401 Wilson Blvd
Suite 900
Arlington, VA 22203-4195

571-366-1000; Fax: 571-366-1195
www.naa.org
Facebook, Twitter

Reggie Hall, Senior VP

Focused on newspaper executives with responsibility for marketing their newspapers to readers. You will find a balance of recent headline stories, consumer marketing research, information about your retailers, and regulatory information blended with success stories and resources to help you in your mission of building circulation and readership.
Frequency: Weekly

5004 **Classified Communications Newsletter**
PO Box 4242
Prescott, AZ 86302

520-778-6788

Agnes Franz, Publisher

Information and ad-writing tips for small budget advertisers. Both display and word classifieds addressed. Will also review books on advertising and marketing.
Cost: $35.00
8 Pages
Frequency: Monthly
Circulation: 2000
Founded in 1989
Printed in 2 colors on glossy stock

5005 **Communication Briefings**
Briefings Publishing Group
1101 King St
Suite 110
Alexandria, VA 22314-2944

703-548-3800; Fax: 703-684-2136
www.communicationbriefings.com

William G Dugan, Group Publisher
Susan Marshall, Executive Editor
Lois Willingham, Marketing Manager
Charles Blakeney, Owner

This newsletter provides subscribers with communications ideas and techniques to use to persuade clients, and motivate employees.
Cost: $79.00
8 Pages
Frequency: Monthly
Circulation: 55000
Founded in 1981

5006 **Communications Business Daily**
Warren Communications News
2115 Ward Ct Nw
Washington, DC 20037-1209

202-872-9200
800-771-9202; Fax: 202-318-8350
info@warren-news.com
www.warren-news.com

Brig Easley, Manager
Daniel Warren, President/Editor
Founded in 1945

5007 **Communications Concepts**
Communication Concepts
508 Mill Stone Dr
Beavercreek, OH 45434-5840

937-426-8600; Fax: 937-429-3811
cci.dayton@pobox.com
www.communication-concepts.com

Rodger L Southworth, President

Ideas and methods for professional communications.

5008 **Communiqu,**
Association for Women in Communications
1717 E Republic Road
Suite A
Springfield, MO 65804

417-886-8606; Fax: 417-886-3685
chair@womcom.org
www.womcom.org

Anita K. Parran, Chair
Allison Buehner, Vice Chair
Peggy Fleming, Secretary
Patricia Meads, Treasurer

A monthly e-newsletter for members.
Frequency: Monthly

5009 **DBS Report**
Kagan World Media
1 Lower Ragsdale Dr
Building One, Suite 130
Monterey, CA 93940-5749

831-624-1536
800-307-2529; Fax: 831-625-3225
www.kagan.com

Tim Baskerville, President
Cost: $1045.00
Frequency: Monthly
Founded in 1969

5010 **Daily Deal**
Vicki King
105 Madison Avenue
New York, NY 10016

212-313-9200
888-667-3325
customerservice@thedeal.com
www.thedeal.com

Mickey Hernandez, Advertising Sales
Elena Freed, Marketing

Reports and analyzes all the aspects of the booming, high stakes world of the deal economy. Areas of coverage include mergers and aquisitions, private equity, venture capital and bankruptcies.
Cost: $498.00
26 Pages
Frequency: Daily
Circulation: 40893
Founded in 1999

5011 **EHS News Briefs**
Newspaper Association of America
4401 Wilson Blvd
Suite 900
Arlington, VA 22203-4195

571-366-1000; Fax: 571-366-1195
www.naa.org

Reggie Hall, Senior VP

These news briefs spotlight what is happening in Congress, the Administration, Courts and around the industry.
Frequency: Weekly

5012 **Emerging Media Report**
Knight MediaCom International
2400 Kettner Boulevard
Suite 237
San Diego, CA 92101

619-338-9885; Fax: 619-338-9886
knightsmedia@hotmail.com
www.knightmedia.com

Covers VR, TV, CD, PC, and entertainment marketing.
Founded in 1978

5013 **Fusion Magazine**
Newspaper Association of America
4401 Wilson Blvd
Suite 900
Arlington, VA 22203-4195

571-366-1000; Fax: 571-366-1195
www.naa.org

Reggie Hall, Senior VP

This newsletter focuses on the business of diversity within the newspaper industry. In it you will find new strategies for making diversity work in advertising, news and editorial, circulation, marketing, production, human resources and the business office.
Frequency: Quarterly

5014 **Growing Audience E-Newsletter**
Newspaper Association of America
4401 Wilson Blvd
Suite 900
Arlington, VA 22203-4195

571-366-1000; Fax: 571-366-1195
www.naa.org

Reggie Hall, Senior VP

This newsletter provides an unparalleled array of information to keep you informed on the most current newspaper readership issues, experiments, results, ideas, successes and failures.
Frequency: Weekly

5015 **Information Broker**
Burwell Enterprises
5619 Plumtree Drive
Dallas, TX 75252

972-331-1951; Fax: 972-733-1951
www.burwellinc.com

Helen Burwell, Publisher
Jeanne Paulino, Marketing Director

Covers fee-based information services for practitioners and users of information services. Accepts advertising.
Cost: $40.00
12 Pages
Frequency: Bi-Monthly
Circulation: 500
Printed in one color on matte stock

5016 **Intercom**
Society for Technical Communication
9401 Lee Hwy
Suite 300
Fairfax, VA 22031-1803

703-522-4114; Fax: 703-522-2075
stc@stc.org
www.stc.org

Susan Burton, Executive Director
Anita Dosik, Publications Director
Maurice P. Martin, Editor
Antoinette DeSalvo, Marketing Coordinator
Suzanna Laurent, President

A monthly magazine offering Society members with information and articles on communication industry trends and activities.
Cost: $95.00
Circulation: 20000
Founded in 1957
Mailing list available for rent: 1000 names at $120 per M

5017 **Labor & Employment Law Letter**
Newspaper Association of America
4401 Wilson Blvd
Suite 900
Arlington, VA 22203-4195

571-366-1000; Fax: 571-366-1195
www.naa.org

Reggie Hall, Senior VP

This newsletter offers readers information on critical employment issues facing the newspaper industry.
Frequency: Bi-Monthly

5018 **Lifestyle Media-Relations Reporter**
InfoCom Group
5900 Hollis Street
Suite L
Emeryville, CA 94608

510-596-9300
800-959-1059
www.infocomgroup.com

This newsletter offers information on media placement in lifestyle and consumer media.
Cost: $369.00
Frequency: Monthly
Founded in 1980

5019 **MAPNetter**
Architecture Technology Corporation
9977 Valley View Rd
Suite 300
Eden Prairie, MN 55344-3586

952-829-5864; Fax: 952-829-5871
info@atcorp.com
www.atcorp.com
Facebook

Kenneth Thurber, President

Monthly newsletter covering important developments in the field of factory communication systems.
Cost: $432.00
12 Pages
Frequency: Monthly
Founded in 1981

5020 **MRC Cyberalert**
Media Research Center
325 S Patrick St
Alexandria, VA 22314-3501

703-683-9733
800-672-1423; Fax: 703-683-9736
mrc@mediaresearch.org
www.mrc.org
Facebook

Brent Bozell, CEO

A news-daily report which documents and exposes liberal media bias. MRC is the nation's leading media watchdog.
Cost: $29.00
Frequency: Monthly
Circulation: 13000
Founded in 1987

5021 **Marketing Library Services**
Information Today
143 Old Marlton Pike
Medford, NJ 08055-8750

609-654-6266
800-300-9868; Fax: 609-654-4309
custserv@infotoday.com
www.infotoday.com

Thomas H Hogan, President
Roger R Bilboul, Chairman of the Board

Provides information professional in all types of libraries with specfic ideas for marketing their services.
Cost: $79.95
Frequency: Bi Monthly
ISSN: 0896-3908

5022 **Marketing New Media**
Kagan World Media
1 Lower Ragsdale Dr
Building One, Suite 130
Monterey, CA 93940-5749

831-624-1536
800-307-2529; Fax: 831-625-3225
www.kagan.com

Tim Baskerville, President
Tom Johnson, Marketing Manager

News of the Marketing New Media. Three month trial available.
Cost: $795.00
Frequency: Monthly
Founded in 1878

5023 **Media Access**
WGBH Educational Foundation
PO Box 200
Boston, MA 02134-1008

617-300-2000; Fax: 617-300-1032
feedback@wgbh.org
www.wgbh.org

Jonathan Abbott, President
Russell Peotter, Owner
Mary Cotton, Owner

Includes information on NCAM's research and development projects, which strive to make media and technology accessible to disabled populations.
2 Pages
Circulation: 15000
Founded in 1951
Printed in 2 colors on matte stock

5024 **Media File**
Media Alliance
1904 Franklin St
Suite 500
Oakland, CA 94612-2926

510-832-9000; Fax: 510-238-8557
www.media-alliance.org

Tracy Rosenberg, Executive Director
Eloise Rose Lee, Program Director

Information about media and media workers.
8 Pages
Frequency: Quarterly

5025 **Media Law Reporter**
Bureau of National Affairs
1801 S Bell St
Arlington, VA 22202-4501

703-341-3000
800-372-1033; Fax: 800-253-0332
customercare@bna.com
www.bnabooks.com

Paul N Wojcik, CEO

A weekly reference service containing the full-text of federal and state court decisions and selected agency rulings affecting newspapers, magazines, radio, television, film and other media.
Cost: $1856.00
Frequency: Weekly
ISSN: 0148-1045
Founded in 1929

5026 **Media Mergers & Acquisitions**
Kagan World Media
1 Lower Ragsdale Dr
Building One, Suite 130
Monterey, CA 93940-5749

831-624-1536
800-307-2529; Fax: 831-625-3225
www.kagan.com

Tim Baskerville, President
Tom Johnson, Marketing Manager

Where it all comes together. Exclusive scorecard of deals done by media companies. Dollar amounts, multiples paid, trends captured in succinct summaries of complex transactions. Three month trial available.
Cost: $795.00
Frequency: Monthly
Founded in 1969

5027 **Media Sports Business**
Kagan World Media
1 Lower Ragsdale Dr
Building One, Suite 130
Monterey, CA 93940-5749

831-624-1536; Fax: 831-625-3225
www.kagan.com

Tim Baskerville, President
Tom Johnson, Marketing Manager
Cost: $945.00
Frequency: Monthly
Founded in 1969

5028 **Motion Picture Investor**
Kagan World Media
1 Lower Ragsdale Dr
Building One, Suite 130
Monterey, CA 93940-5749

831-624-1536
800-307-2529; Fax: 831-625-3225
www.kagan.com

Tim Baskerville, President
Tom Johnson, Marketing Manager
Cost: $845.00
Frequency: Monthly
Founded in 1969

5029 **NAMIC E-Newsletter**
Natl Assoc for Multi-Ethnicity in Communications
320 West 37th Street
8th Floor
New York, NY 10018

212-594-5985; Fax: 212-594-8391
info@namic.com
www.namic.com
Facebook, Twitter

A. Shuanise Washington, President & CEO
Susan Waldman, Sr. Manager, Mem. & Publications

For members only, provides timely and useful national and local information about industry-related issues, trends and events
Frequency: Bi-Monthly

5030 **Newspaper Investor**
Kagan World Media
1 Lower Ragsdale Dr
Building One, Suite 130
Monterey, CA 93940-5749

831-624-1536
800-307-2529; Fax: 831-625-3225
www.kagan.com

Tim Baskerville, President
Tom Johnson, Marketing Manager
Cost: $845.00
Frequency: Monthly
Founded in 1969

5031 **Online Publishing Update E-Newsletter**
Newspaper Association of America
4401 Wilson Blvd
Suite 900
Arlington, VA 22203-4195

571-366-1000; Fax: 571-366-1195
www.naa.org

Reggie Hall, Senior VP

A round-up of news, research, industry trends, best practices and more, focusing on items of interest to newspaper and digital media executives.

Online Publishing Update e-newsletter is published every Monday, Wednesday and Friday.
Frequency: 3x/Weekly

5032 **Pacific Dialogue**
Robert Miko
33 Ferry Ct
Stratford, CT 06615

203-378-2803
bmiko@pacificdialogue.com
www.pacificdialogue.com

Robert Miko, Publisher

Corporate communications of the Pacific Region.
Cost: $196.00
4 Pages
Frequency: Weekly
Circulation: 1,000

5033 **Party Line**
Party Line Publishing Company
35 Sutton Place
New York, NY 10022-2464

212-755-3487; Fax: 212-755-4859

Morton Yarmon, Publisher
Betty Yarmon, Editor
Betty Yarmon, Marketing

Weekly media placement newsletter with up-to-date news of the media for public relations executives in all aspects of business, hospitals, publishers and associations.
Cost: $200.00
Frequency: Weekly
Circulation: 2000
Founded in 1960
Mailing list available for rentat $100 per M
Printed in 2 colors on matte stock

5034 **Pay TV Newsletter**
Kagan World Media
126 Clock Tower Place
Carmel, CA 93923-8746

831-624-1536; Fax: 831-625-3225
www.kagan.com

George Niesen, Editor
Tom Johnson, Marketing Manager
Cost: $845.00
Frequency: Monthly

5035 **Platform News You Can Use**
Newspaper Association of America
4401 N. Fairfax Drive
Suite 300
Arlington, VA 22203

571-366-1000
info@newsmediaalliance.org
www.newsmediaalliance.org

David Chavern, President & CEO
Michael Maloon, VP, Innovation & Communications
Rebecca Frank, VP, Research & Insights
Lindsey Loving, Manager, Communications
Jennifer Peters, Reporter, Trends & Insights

Members-only e-newsletter with developments on large tech platforms and their relationships with the news industry and journalism.
Frequency: Monthly

5036 **PostCom Bulletin**
Association for Postal Commerce
1800 Diagonal Road
Suite 600
Alexandria, VA 22314

703-524-0096; Fax: 703-997-2414
info@postcom.org
www.postcom.org

Michael Plunkett, President & CEO
Ellena Talbott, Director, Operations & Membership
Beth McConnell, Postal Consultant

A source of postal news and opinion.
Founded in 1947

5037 **SIGNAL Connections**
4400 Fairfax Lakes Court
Fairfax, VA 22033

703-631-6100
800-336-4583; Fax: 703-631-6169
promo@afcea.org
www.afcea.org
Facebook, Twitter, LinkedIn

Richard K Ackerman, Editor in Chief

Bridges the gap between issues of SIGNAL by providing additional news and feature articles about the industry and the Association.
Frequency: Monthly

5038 **Satellite Week**
Warren Communications News
2115 Ward Ct Nw
Washington, DC 20037-1209

202-872-9200
800-771-9202; Fax: 202-318-8350
info@warren-news.com
www.warren-news.com

Brig Easley, Manager
Daniel Warren, President/Editor
Founded in 1945

5039 **Signal Newsletter**
International Association for Conflict Management
1 Liberty Street
New York, NY 5006

872-302-7567
brandon@iafcm.org
iafcm.org

William Bottom, President-Elect Nominee
Zoe Barsness, President-Elect Nominee
Brandon Charpied, Executive Director
Cheryl Rivers, Editor

Newsletter covering activities of the International Association for Conflict Management.
Founded in 1970

5040 **Smaller Market E-Newsletter**
Newspaper Association of America
4401 Wilson Blvd
Suite 900
Arlington, VA 22203-4195

571-366-1000; Fax: 571-366-1195
www.naa.org
Facebook, Twitter

Reggie Hall, Senior VP

Stay ahead of industry news and trends with the latest reports outlining how to improve your smaller market newspaper. Also receive a synopsis on new NAA products and services and how they can benefit smaller market newspapers.
Frequency: Monthly

5041 **Speech Technology Magazine**
2628 Wilhite Court
Suite 100
Lexington, KY 40503

859-278-2223
877-993-9767; Fax: 859-278-7364
www.speechtechmag.com/

John Kelly, Publisher & Editor
Sheila Willison, Circulation Director
Stephanie Owens, Associate Editor
Devon Taylor, Magazine Sales
Kerrie Porath, Sales Coordinator

Divided into four sections: applications, technology, new products, and a special focus section. Authors from the field contribute their expertise to this trade magazine.
73 Pages
Frequency: Fortnightly
Circulation: 25000
Founded in 1996

5042 **Telecom A.M.**
Warren Communications News
2115 Ward Ct Nw
Washington, DC 20037-1209

202-872-9200
800-771-9202; Fax: 202-318-8350
info@warren-news.com
www.warren-news.com

Brig Easley, Manager
Daniel Warren, President/Editor
Founded in 1945

5043 **Telemarketing Update: The Regulations and the Impact**
Newspaper Association of America
4401 Wilson Blvd
Suite 900
Arlington, VA 22203-4195

571-366-1000; Fax: 571-366-1195
www.naa.org
Twitter

Reggie Hall, Senior VP

Perspective on the Federal Telemarketing Regulations and an explanation of how newspapers are being impacted by the changes. What's working and what's not and what the Federal Government has in store for newspapers.

5044 **Television A.M.**
Warren Communications News
2115 Ward Ct Nw
Washington, DC 20037-1209

202-872-9200
800-771-9202; Fax: 202-318-8350
info@warren-news.com
www.warren-news.com

Brig Easley, Manager
Daniel Warren, President/Editor
Founded in 1945

5045 **The RCA News**
Grove City College
Attn: Daniel Brown
100 Campus Drive, P.O. Box 3014
Grove City, PA 16127

724-458-3793
dsbrown@gcc.edu

Daniel S Brown, Newsletter Editor
Ken Danielson, Executive Secretary
Janie Harden Fritz, President

A newsletter for the academic society of individuals interested in the study of all aspects of public religious communication, members include teachers, students, clergy, broadcasters and other scholars and professionals.
210 Members
Founded in 1973

5046 **Washington Internet Daily**
Warren Communications News
2115 Ward Ct Nw
Washington, DC 20037-1209

202-872-9200
800-771-9202; Fax: 202-318-8350
info@warren-news.com
www.warren-news.com

Brig Easley, Manager
Daniel Warren, President/Editor
Founded in 1945

5047 **dailyXchange**
Newspaper Association of America

4401 N. Fairfax Drive
Suite 300
Arlington, VA 22203

571-366-1000
info@newsmediaalliance.org
www.newsmediaalliance.org

David Chavern, President & CEO
Michael Maloon, VP, Innovation & Communications
Rebecca Frank, VP, Research & Insights
Lindsey Loving, Manager, Communications
Jennifer Peters, Reporter, Trends & Insights

Members-only e-newsletter with relevant Alliance and industry news from the past day.
Frequency: Daily

5048 **newsXchange**
Newspaper Association of America
4401 N. Fairfax Drive
Suite 300
Arlington, VA 22203

571-366-1000
info@newsmediaalliance.org
www.newsmediaalliance.org

David Chavern, President & CEO
Michael Maloon, VP, Innovation & Communications
Rebecca Frank, VP, Research & Insights
Lindsey Loving, Manager, Communications
Jennifer Peters, Reporter, Trends & Insights

News brief from the News Media Alliance with news media industry news, as well as information on digital, advertising, trends, and Alliance products and services.
Frequency: Weekly (Wed.)

Magazines & Journals

5049 **15 Minutes Magazine.Com**
7334 173rd Street
Fresh Meadows, NY 11366-1428

718-969-0404; Fax: 718-591-3660
editor@15minutesmagazine.com
www.15minutesmagazine.com

Tim Boxer, Editor/Publisher
Nina Boxer, Associate Editor
Bernie Ilson, PR Consultant
Stanley Donen, Founder
Michael Fredo, Owner

Monthly magazine online covering society benefits, with reviews of arts and entertainment, travel and new products. Targets 715,000 readers in affluent market
Cost: $50.00
Frequency: Monthly
Circulation: 4,45,000
Founded in 1999
Printed in 4 colors

5050 **AV Video and Multimedia Producer**
Knowledge Industry Publications
701 Westchester Ave
Suite 101W
West Harrison, NY 10604-3077

914-328-9157; Fax: 914-328-9093
www.kipinet.com/av_mmp/

Ollie Bieniemy, Publisher

Covers product development, graphics and animation, software and equipment, and industry news for readers involved in professional production, multimedia production, and presentation technology.
Cost: $53.00
Frequency: Monthly
Circulation: 100,000

5051 **Archive Magazine**
Luerzer's Archive Inc
410 Park Avenue
Suite 1530
New York, NY 10022-9441

212-941-2496; Fax: 212-941-5490
www.lurzersarchive.com
Twitter, LinkedIn

Walter Lurzer, Editor

Read by advertising agency executives in 35 countries, archive presents tv commercials and print ads that are currently running around the world.
Frequency: 6x a year
Circulation: 40000

5052 **Business Communications Review**
BCR Enterprises
3025 Highland Pkwy
Suite 200
Downers Grove, IL 60515-5668

630-986-1432
800-227-1234; Fax: 630-323-5324
www.bcr.com

Offers a complete package of the latest information for persons associated with the communications industry.
Cost: $46.00
80 Pages
Frequency: Monthly

5053 **Business and Professional Communication Quarterly**
Association for Business Communication
181 Turner St. NW
323 Shanks Hall
Blacksburg, VA 24061

540-231-8460; Fax: 646-349-5297
abcoffice@businesscommunication.org
www.businesscommunication.org

Melinda Knight, Editor
Jim Dubinsky, Executive Director

Publishes scholarly pieces that advance knowledge about business communication in both academic and workplace settings. Articles present a variety of theoretical, applies, and practical approaches and perspectives.
Frequency: Quarterly

5054 **Communication World**
Int'l Association of Business Communicators
601 Montgomery Street
Suite 1900
San Francisco, CA 94111

415-544-4700; Fax: 415-544-4747
cwmagazine@iabc.com
www.iabc.com

Natasha Nicholson, Executive Editor
Sue Khodarahmi, Managing Editor
Sue Cavallaro, Production Editor

Covers the leatest in communication research, technology and trends through in-depth reports and insightful interviews.
Cost: $150.00
Frequency: Bi-Monthly
Circulation: 13,000
ISSN: 0744-7612
Founded in 1982
Printed in on matte stock

5055 **Communications ASP**
Technology Marketing Corporation
1 Technology Plz
Norwalk, CT 06854-1936

203-852-6800
800-243-6002; Fax: 203-853-2845
tmc@tmcnet.com
www.tmcnet.com

Rich Tehrani, CEO

Communication solution magazine.
Cost: $2000.00
Frequency: Monthly
Founded in 1972

5056 **Communications Arts**
Coyne & Blanchard
110 Constitution Dr
Menlo Park, CA 94025-1107

650-326-6040
800-688-1971; Fax: 650-326-1648
ca@commarts.com
www.commarts.com

Patrick Coyne, Publisher/Editor

The leading professional journal in the US on graphic arts, commercial photography, illustration and interactive design. Features profile individuals, studios, and agencies with examples of their work. Accepts advertising.
Cost: $53.00
140 Pages
Frequency: 1 Year 8 Issues
Circulation: 74,834
ISSN: 0010-3519
Founded in 1959
Printed in on glossy stock

5057 **Communications Daily**
Warren Publishing
2115 Ward Ct NW
Washington, DC 20037-1209

202-872-9200
800-771-9202; Fax: 202-318-8350
info@warren-news.com
www.warren-news.com

Brig Easley, Manager
Daniel Warren, President/Editor

Covers the entire spectrum of the telephone, data communications, broadcasting, cable TV, electronic information distribution, cellulars, PCS and satellite.
Cost: $4295.00
Frequency: Daily
Founded in 1945

5058 **Computers in Libraries**
Information Today
143 Old Marlton Pike
Medford, NJ 08055-8750

609-654-6266
800-300-9868; Fax: 609-654-4309
custserv@infotoday.com
www.infotoday.com

Thomas H Hogan, President
Roger R Bilboul, Chairman of the Board

Coverage of news and issues in the field of library information technology. Focuses on practical applications of technology in community, school, academic and special libraries. Includes discussions of the impact of emerging computer technologies on library systems and services and on the library community itself.
Cost: $99.95
Frequency: 10 issues/yr
Mailing list available for rent: 4M names
Printed in 4 colors on glossy stock

5059 **Digital Magic**
PennWell Publishing Company
10 Tara Boulevard
5th Floor
Nashua, NH 03062-2800

603-891-0123; Fax: 603-891-0539

Dennis Allen, Publisher

Insights on new technology trends and techniques, covers the latest in hardware and software products to keep digital effects professional competitive and up to date.
Cost: $19.95
Frequency: Bi-Monthly
Circulation: 30,000

5060 **Documentary Magazine**
International Documentary Association
3470 Wilshire Boulevard
Suite 980
Los Angeles, CA 90010

212-232-1660; Fax: 213-232-1669
tom@documentary.org
www.documentary.org

Thomas White, Editor
Maria Elena Hewett, Account Executive
Simon Killmurry, Executive Director

Devoted exclusively to nonfiction media.
Cost: $55.00
2631 Members
Frequency: Quarterly
Founded in 1982
Mailing list available for rent: 25000 names

5061 **Extra!**
Fairness & Accuracy in Publishing
112 W 27th Street
New York, NY 10001

212-633-6700; Fax: 212-727-7668
fair@fair.org
www.fair.org

Deborah Thomas, Publisher
Jeff Cohen, Founder

Progressive media criticism.
Cost: $21.00
Frequency: Bi-monthly
Circulation: 21800
Founded in 1987

5062 **Folio: Magazine for Magazine Management**
Red 7 Media, LLC
10 Norden Place
Norwalk, CT 06855

203-854-6730; Fax: 203-854-6735
tsilber@red7media.com
www.foliomag.com

Stefanie Botelho, Associate Editor
Kerry Smith, President/CEO
Dan Trombetto, Group Creative Director
Tony Silber, General Manager
John Ellertson, Director Advertising Sales Manager

Written for the people who run the nation's magazines. Offers authoritative intelligence on the magazine market to enable industry professionals to navigate the widening range of strategic options. Every issue delivers features on the people and technologies that are transforming the magazine business, along with useful columns and departments, thought-provoking analysis and tactical advice for building successful magazines.
Cost: $96.00
Frequency: Monthly
Circulation: 11550
Founded in 1971

5063 **Government Video**
Miller Freeman Publications
810 7th Ave
27th Fl, Suite 4
New York, NY 10019-5818

212-636-2700; Fax: 212-636-2750
sedorusa@optonline.net
www.governmentvideo.com

Gary Rhodes, International Sales Manager

Articles on audio, video production and technologies, training and presentation, multimedia, video conferencing, and medical and scientific applications.
Frequency: Monthly
Circulation: 18,000

5064 **IEEE Wireless Communications**
IEEE Communications Society
3 Park Ave
17th Floor
New York, NY 10016-5997

212-705-8920; Fax: 212-705-8999
publications@comsoc.org
www.ieee.org

Laura Book, Manager
Jack Howell, Executive Director

An interdisciplinary bimonthly magazine, covers technical and policy issues relating to personal, location-independent communications in all media and at all protocol layers.
Frequency: Bi-Monthly

5065 **Information Week**
UBM LLC
600 Community Drive
Manhasset, NY 11030

516-562-5000; Fax: 516-562-5036
www.informationweek.com

Rob Preston, VP/Editor In Chief
Laurianne McLaughlin, Editor In Chief
Fritz Nelson, VP/Editorial Director

Delivers breaking news, blogs, high-impact image galleries, proprietary research as well as analysis on IT trends, a whitepaper library, video reports and interactive tools, al i a 24/7 environment.
Circulation: 440,000

5066 **International Communications Association**
1500 21st St NW
Washington, DC 20036-1000

202-955-1444; Fax: 202-955-1448
www.icahdq.org

M Haley, Executive Director
Wolfgang Donfback, Administrative Assistant
Colleen Brady, Administrative Assistant
James Danowski, Secretary

Bi-monthly newsletter that supports all students and professionals in the international communications industry.
Cost: $30.00
Circulation: 3500
Founded in 1950
Printed in on matte stock

5067 **International Journal of Business Communic ation**
Association for Business Communication
181 Turner St. NW
323 Shanks Hall
Blacksburg, VA 24061

540-231-8460; Fax: 646-349-5297
abcoffice@businesscommunication.org
www.businesscommunication.org

Jacqueline Mayfield, Editor In Chief
Milton Mayfield, Editor In Chief
Kathryn M. Rybka, Book Review Editor
Jim Dubinsky, Executive Director

Publishes pieces that contribute to knowledge and theory of business communication from the perspectives of administrative disciplines, liberal arts, and social sciences. Topics include business composition, information systems, international business communication, management communication, and organizational and corporate communication.

5068 **Journal of Advertising Education**
AEJMC
234 Outlet Pointe Boulevard
Suite A
Columbia, SC 29210-5667

803-798-0271; Fax: 803-772-3509
www.aejmc.org

Jay Newell, Editor

Peer-reviewed academic journal devoted to research and commentary on instruction, curriculum, and leadership in advertising education. Official journal of the Advertising Division of the Association for Education in Journalism and Mass Communication, and available to members of the American Academy of Advertising.

5069 **Journal of Applied Communications**
Agricultural Communicators in Education
University of Florida
PO Box 110810
Gainesville, FL 32611

352-392-9588; Fax: 352-392-8583
ace@ifas.ufl.edu
www.aceweb.org/jac/jac.html

Courtney Meyers, Managing Editor
Katie Abrams, Executive Editor

A peer-reviewed professional journal which accepts original contributions about communications, research, innovations and other pertinent information. The Journal is provided to all members, libraries and other interested people.
Cost: $75.00
Frequency: Quarterly
Circulation: 700
ISSN: 1051-0834
Founded in 1990

5070 **Journal of Open Computing**
Association for Communication Administration
1765 N Street NW
Washington, DC 20036

202-464-4622; Fax: 202-464-4600
www.natcom.org

5071 **Journal of the Association of Information Systems**
Association for Information Systems
Case Western Reserve University
P.O. Box 2712
Atlanta, GA 30301-2712

404-413-7445; Fax: 404-413-7443
publications@aisnet.org
www.aisnet.org

Suprateek Sarker, Editorn-in-Chief
Jody McGinness, Executive Director
Jason Thatcher, President

Publishes the highest quality scholarship in the field of information systems. Covers all aspects of Information Systems and Information Technology. Publishes rigorously developed and forward looking conceptual and empirical contributions.Encourages multidisciplinary and nontraditional approaches.
Frequency: Quarterly

5072 **Journal of the Relgious Communication Association**
Department of Communication & Rhetorical Studies
340 College Hall
600 Forbes Ave
Pittsburgh, PA 15282

owner@americanrhetoric.com

Kathleen Edelmayer, President
Matthew Melton, VP

The JCR addresses the concerns of the religious communicator and the communication scholar and includes reviews of current publications in the field of religious communication. The journal is semi-annual and is included with membership.
Circulation: 675

5073 **Journalism & Mass Communication Quarterly (JMCQ)**
AEJMC

234 Outlet Pointe Boulevard
Suite A
Columbia, SC 29210-5667

803-798-0271; Fax: 803-772-3509
www.aejmc.org

Jennifer McGill, Executive Director
Louisa Ha, Editor

Published by the Association for Education in Journalism and Mass Communication, the JMC Quarterly focuses on research in journalism and mass communication. Each issue features reports of original investigation, presenting the latest developments in theory and methodology of communication, international communication, journalism history, and social and legal problems. Also contains book reviews. Refereed. Four times per year. (est. 1924)
Circulation: 4800
Mailing list available for rent

5074 MAIL: Journal of Communication Distribution

Gold Key Box 2425
Milford, PA 18337

607-746-7600; Fax: 607-746-2750
mailmagazine@msn.com
www.mailomg.com

Offers updated information on electronic mail and mail messaging systems.
Cost: $6.00
105 Pages
Frequency: Monthly

5075 Managing Media Relations in a Crisis

NACHA: The Electronic Payments Association
13450 Sunrise Valley Drive
Suite 100
Herndon, VA 20171

703-561-1100; Fax: 703-787-0996
info@nacha.org
www.nacha.org

Janet O Estep, CEO
Marcie Haitema, Chairperson

Designed to assist your organization to develop, test and execute a crisis communication plan. With this guide, you will understand how to address issues, whom to call and in what order to alert them, which vendors you can count on to help and how to develop a means to track the crisis as it grows or abates.
Cost: $30.00

5076 Media Studies Journal

Columbia University, Freedom Forum Media Center
2960 Broadway
New York, NY 10027-6902

212-854-1754; Fax: 212-678-4817
www.columbia.edu

Lee C Bollinger, President

Aimed at scholars, practitioners and commentators. Offers information on mass communications issues involving the media and the public at large.
Cost: $20.00
Frequency: Quarterly
Circulation: 9000
Founded in 1754

5077 Negotiation and Conflict Management Research

International Association for Conflict Management
1 Liberty Street
New York, NY 5006

872-302-7567
cs-journals@wiley.com
iafcm.org

William Bottom, President-Elect Nominee
Zoe Barsness, President-Elect Nominee
Brandon Charpied, Executive Director
Michael A. Gross, Editor
Mallory Wallace, Editorial Assistant

Articles on theory and research related to negotiation and conflict management of all kinds, including interpersonal, intergroup, organizational, and cross-cultural conflicts.
ISSN: 1750-4716
Founded in 1970

5078 Novedades USA

Echo Media
900 Circle 75 Pkwy SE
Suite 1600
Atlanta, GA 30339-6014

770-955-3346
sales@echo-media.com
www.echo-media.com

Michael Puffer, CEO
Stacey Reece, VP

Frequency: Weekly
Circulation: 100,000
Founded in 1986
Printed in 4 colors on newsprint stock

5079 Presstime Magazine

Newspaper Association of America
4401 Wilson Blvd
Suite 900
Arlington, VA 22203-4195

571-366-1000; Fax: 571-366-1195
www.naa.org
Twitter

Reggie Hall, Senior VP

The flagship publication reaches top executives across all departments with information about the issues that affect newspaper operations today and in the future.
Frequency: Monthly
Mailing list available for rent

5080 Professional Journal: Sbusiness Publication

AFSM International
11031 Via Frontera
Suite A
San Diego, CA 92127-1709

858-673-3055
800-333-9786; Fax: 239-275-0794

JB Wood, President
Thomas Lah, Executive Director

A global organization dedicated to furthering the knowledge, understanding, and career development of executives, managers, and professionals in the high-technology services and support industry as well as to provide leadership and direction that helps our individual and corporate members expand their capabilities to meet the growing complexities and challenges of the industry. Sbusiness publication is distributed bi-monthly serving international decision makers.
Cost: $ 95.00
114 Pages
Circulation: 10000
ISSN: 1049-2135
Founded in 1975
Printed in 4 colors on matte stock

5081 Publishers Weekly

PO Box 51593
Harlan, IA 51593

800-278-2991; Fax: 712-733-8019
pwycustserv@cdsfulfillment.com
www.publishersweekly.com
Facebook, Twitter

Jim Milliot, Co-Editorial Director
Michael Coffey, Co-Editorial Director
Diane Roback, Children's Book Editor
Louisa Ermelino, Reviews Director
Calvin Reid, News Editor

PW is the international journal of book publishing and bookselling including business news, reviews and bestseller lists targeted at publishers, booksellers, librarians and literary agents.
Frequency: Weekly
Founded in 1872

5082 Red Herring: The Business of Technology

Red Herring
1900 Alameda De Las Pulgas
Suite 1
San Mateo, CA 94403-1222

650-428-2900; Fax: 650-428-2901
info@redherring.com
www.redherring.com

Alex Vieux, Publisher
Christopher Alden, Editorial Director
Joel Dreyfuss, Editor-in-Chief

Offers information on new and rising companies, as well as current industrial technology issues and topics.
Frequency: Weekly
Circulation: 45000
Founded in 1993

5083 Replication News

Miller Freeman Publications
810 7th Ave
27th Fl, Suite 4
New York, NY 10019-5818

212-636-2700; Fax: 212-636-2750
sedorusa@optonline.net
www.governmentvideo.com
Facebook, Twitter

Gary Rhodes, International Sales Manager

Information on electronic and recording media through news coverage and analysis to provide executives with the market for strategic business planning.
Frequency: Monthly
Circulation: 16,490
Mailing list available for rent

5084 SIGNAL Magazine

4400 Fair Lakes Court
Fairfax, VA 22033-3899

703-631-6100
800-336-4583; Fax: 703-631-6133
promo@afcea.org
www.afcea.org
Facebook, Twitter, LinkedIn

Robert K Ackerman, Editor in Chief

International news magazine serving the critical information needs of government, military and industry professionals active in the fields of command, control, communications, computers, intelligence, surveillance and reconnaissance (C4ISR); information security, research and development; electronics; and homeland security.
Frequency: Monthly
Circulation: 90000

5085 Signal Magazine

Armed Forces Communications & Electronics Assoc

4114 Legato Road
Suite 1000
Fairfax, VA 22033

703-631-6100
800-336-4583; Fax: 703-631-6169
service@afcea.org
www.afcea.org
Facebook, Twitter, LinkedIn

Robert K. Ackerman, Editor in Chief
George I. Seffers, Dir., Content Devel./Exec. Editor
Kimberly Underwood, Senior Editor
Cyndy Hogan, Dir., Editorial Production
Beverly Mowery Cooper, VP/Associate Publisher

SIGNAL Magazine provides news in the communications and information technology realms of the defense, intelligence and global security communities.

5086 **Speaker Magazine**
National Speakers Association
1500 S Priest Dr
Tempe, AZ 85281-6203

480-968-2552; Fax: 480-968-0911
www.nsaspeaker.org

Mary Lue Peck, President

Trends, issues and perspectives about and for the professional speaking industry.
Cost: $49.00
Frequency: 10x/Year

5087 **TV Guide**
United Video Satellite Group
1211 Avenue of the Americas
4th Floor
New York, NY 10036-8701

212-852-7500; Fax: 212-852-4914

Richard Porter, Publisher

Focuses on all aspects of network, cable and pay television programming and how it affects and reflects their audience.
Cost: $39.88
Frequency: Weekly
Circulation: 13mm

5088 **TV Technology**
IMAS Publishing
PO Box 1214
Falls Church, VA 22041

703-998-7600; Fax: 703-998-2966
www.tvtechnology.com

Steven Dana, President
Tom Butts, Editor
Eric Trabb, Publisher
Kwentin Keenan, Circulation Manager
Bob Moses, Executive Director

News of a technical nature covering topics ranging from regulatory developments through maintenance and new products.
Cost: $39.95
Frequency: Fortnightly
Circulation: 37,000
Founded in 1978

5089 **TechTrends**
Assn. for Educational Communications & Technology
320 West 8th Streete
Suite 101
Bloomington, IN 47404

812-335-7675
877-677-2328; Fax: 812-335-7678
aect@aect.org
Facebook, Twitter

Charles B. Hodges, Editor-in-Chief
Phillip Harris, Executive Editor
Brad Hokanson, President

Provides a medium of information exchange for professionals in media management programs.
Cost: $125.00
Frequency: Bi-Monthly
Circulation: 3500
ISSN: 8756-3894

5090 **Television International Magazine**
Television International Magazine
PO Box 2473
Universal City, CA 91610-8471

323-462-1099; Fax: 702-939-4725
tvi@smart90.com; www.tvimagazine.com

Josie Cory, Publisher
Mark Soval, Advertising Director

News and information regarding the television industry, includes the who's who of the business; geared toward the executives and professionals of the industry.
Cost: $129.00
Frequency: Monthly
Circulation: 16000
Founded in 1956
Printed in 4 colors on glossy stock

5091 **xchange**
Virgo Publishing LLC
3300 N Central Ave
Suite 300
Phoenix, AZ 85012-2532

480-675-9925; Fax: 480-990-0819
mikes@vpico.com; www.vpico.com
Twitter, LinkedIn

Jenny Bolton, President

Provides in-depth, executive-level news and analysis regarding strategy, technology and regulation to help communications service providers create new revenue, lower costs and achieve sustainable business models.
Cost: $75.00
Frequency: Monthly
Circulation: 35,003
Founded in 1986

Trade Shows

5092 **AEJMC Annual Conference**
AEJMC
234 Outlet Pointe Boulevard
Suite A
Columbia, SC 29210-5667

803-798-0271; Fax: 803-772-3509
www.aejmc.org

Jennifer McGill, Executive Director
Amanda Caldwell, Confernece/Meetings Manager

Annual conference of the Association for Education in Journalism and Mass Communication.
2000 Attendees
Frequency: August
Founded in 1912

5093 **AFCEA TechNet International**
Armed Forces Communications and Electronics Assn
4400 Fair Lakes Court
Fairfax, VA 22033-3899

703-631-6200
800-564-4220; Fax: 703-654-6931
technetinternational@jspargo.com
www.afcea.org
Facebook, Twitter, LinkedIn

Paul doCarmo, Sales Manager
Connie Shaw, Sales Manager

This event draws commanders and staff from every branch of the military, including warfighting integration organizations charged with the most critical responsibilities of synthesizing military power on land, at sea, and in the air.
7500 Attendees
Frequency: June

5094 **AM&AA Summer Conference**
Alliance of Merger and Acquisition Advisors
150 North Michigan Avenue
Suite 2700
Chicago, IL 60601

877-844-2535; Fax: 312-729-9800
www.amaaonline.org

Ainsley Emerson, Director

Premier international organization serving the educational and resource needs of the middle market and M&A profession.
Frequency: Annual

5095 **ATTW Conference**
Association of Teachers of Technical Writing
Department of Linguistics and Technical Comm
1155 Union Circle #305298
Denton, TX 76203-5017

940-565-4458
sims@unt.edu; www.attw.org

Bill Davidson, President
Brenda Sims, Secretary
600 Members
Frequency: Annual/April
Founded in 1973
Mailing list available for rent

5096 **American Public Communications Council Conference & Expo**
American Public Communications Council
625 Slaters Lane
Suite 104
Alexandria, VA 22314

703-739-1322; apcc@apcc.net

Conference, luncheon and 100 exhibits of public communications equipment and information including, pay phones, internet, atm, multimedia and more. Discussions include lobbying, the political climate, legal regulatory and legislative updates.
Founded in 1988

5097 **Association for Business Communication Annual Symposium**
Association for Business Communication
181 Tuerner St. NW
323 Shanks Hall
Blacksburg, VA 24061

540-231-8460; Fax: 646-349-5297
abcoffice@businesscommunication.org
www.businesscommunication.org

Geert Jacobs, First VP
D. Joel Whalen, Second VP
Marcel Robles, President
Jim Dubinsky, Executive Director
Marilyn Buerkens, Office Manager

Workshop and displays from textbook publishers, speech and business writing, technical publications and corporate communication.
400 Attendees
Frequency: Annual
Founded in 1935

5098 **Communications Marketing Association Conference**
Communications Marketing Association

204 S. Shaffer Drive
New Freedom, PA 17349

717-439-7391
cmaexecdirector@gmail.com
www.cma-cmc.org

Alex Hinerfeld, President
Carl Peek, Vice President
Rob Menees, Secretary
Cliff Peck, Treasurer
Sharon Boyle, Executive Director

Training, education, and networking conference for manufacturers, manufacturer's representatives and distributors in the wireless communications industry.

5099 DISA Customer Partnership AFCEA Technology Showcase
Armed Forces Communications and Electronics Assn
4400 Fair Lakes Court
Fairfax, VA 22033

703-631-6200
800-564-4220; Fax: 703-654-6931
www.afcea.org
Facebook, Twitter, LinkedIn

Paul doCarmo, Assistant Director/Exhibit Sales
Connie Shaw, Exhibit Sales Account Manager

This conference facilitates a continuing interface with customers and strategic partners by allowing attendees to benefit from the perspective of DoD (Department of Defense) and industry speakers. It offers information sessions that provide a forum for questions, concerns and problem resolution.
1200 Attendees
Frequency: April-May

5100 Entelec Conference & Expo
Energy Telecommunications and Electrical Assoc
5005 W Royal Lane
Suite 116
Irving, TX 75063

972-929-3169
888-503-8700; Fax: 972-915-6040
info@entelec.org; www.entelec.org

Michael Burt, President
James Coulter, VP

To bring together communications and control technology professionals from the petroleum, natural gas, pipeline, and electric utility companies for three days of quality training, seminars, exhibits and networking.
Frequency: Annual/May

5101 Getting Real Conference
International Documentary Association
3470 Wilshire Boulevard
Suite 980
Los Angeles, CA 90010

213-232-1660; Fax: 213-232-1669
michael@documentary.org
www.documentary.org
Simon Kilmurry, Executive Director

A conference for documentary professionals to network and learn from colleagues.
Frequency: Annual
Founded in 1982

5102 Graphic Communications Conference of the Int'l Brotherhood of Teamsters
1900 L Street NW
Washington, DC 20036

202-462-1400; Fax: 202-721-0600
webmessenger@gciu.org
www.gciu.org

James Hoff, President
Robert Lacey, Secretary/Treasurer

Combines three independent shows: Printing XPO, Type-X, and Art-X and gives you a complete overview of the most recently introduced technologies and the newest information in the field of graphic arts.
15000 Members
Founded in 1983

5103 IAMC Conference
International Association for Conflict Management
1 Liberty Street
New York, NY 5006

872-302-7567
brandon@iafcm.org
iafcm.org/index.php/2017-conference-philadelphia-pa

William Bottom, President-Elect Nominee
Zoe Barsness, President-Elect Nominee
Brandon Charpied, Executive Director

Conference on the topic of conflict management, welcoming scholarly papers covering conflict in religion, government, media, race and communities.
Frequency: Annual
Founded in 1970

5104 LandWarNet Conference
Armed Forces Communications and Electronics Assn
4400 Fair Lakes Court
Fairfax, VA 22033

703-631-6200
800-564-4220; Fax: 703-654-6931
www.afcea.org
Facebook, Twitter, LinkedIn

Nathan Wills, Account Manager

Thousands of key communications/information technology buyers and influencers attend the conference every year. This is an opportunity to network with the best and develop crucial relationships with some of the Army's most influential decision-makers.
3700 Attendees
Frequency: August

5105 MILCOM
Armed Forces Communications and Electronics Assn
4400 Fair Lakes Court
Fairfax, VA 22033

703-631-6200
800-564-4220; Fax: 703-654-6931
www.afcea.org
Facebook, Twitter, LinkedIn

Paul doCarmo, Assistant Director/Exhibit Sales
Connie Shaw, Exhibit Sales Account Manager

For over 20 years, MILCOM has been the premeir international conference for military communications, with over 3,000 attendees every year. It attracts decision-makers from government, military, academia and industry, including heads of multi-national forces from around the globe, all who contribute key technologies decisions and investments for their agency.
3000 Attendees
Frequency: October

5106 Mailcom
The Art & Science of Mail Communications
Po Box 7045
Philadelphia, PA 19149

732-280-8865; Fax: 732-280-7854
ljhumphries@msn.com
www.mailcom.org

Lance Humphries, Managing Director

Learn how business communications can become strategic corporate tools
9000 Attendees
Frequency: Oct Las Vegas
Mailing list available for rent

5107 NAMIC Conference
Natl Assoc for Multi-Ethnicity in Communications
320 West 37th Street
8th Floor
New York, NY 10018

212-594-5985; Fax: 212-594-8391
info@namic.com; www.namic.com
Facebook, Twitter, LinkedIn

A. Shuanise Washington, President & CEO
Sandra Girado, VP, Events & Partner Relations

Educational forum focused on leadership development, corporate diversity and inclusion, digital media and multi-ethnic content and programming. Content emphasizes diversity as a strategic business imperative
700 Attendees
Frequency: Annual

5108 NSA Convention
National Speakers Association
1500 S Priest Dr
Tempe, AZ 85281-6203

480-968-2552; Fax: 480-968-0911
www.nsaspeaker.org

Mary Lue Peck, President
1500 Attendees
Frequency: Annual

5109 National Hispanic Market Trade Show and Media Expo (Se Habla Espanol)
Hispanic Business
425 Pine Avenue
Santa Barbara, CA 93117-3709

805-964-4554; Fax: 805-964-5539
www.expomediainc.com
Facebook, Twitter, LinkedIn

John Pasini, Cfo/Coo

Annual show of 100 exhibitors of market/research, media, advertising, public relations, information services and recruitment.
1500 Attendees

5110 PRSA International Conference
Public Relations Society of America
33 Maiden Ln.
11th Fl.
New York, NY 10038

212-460-1400
Facebook, Twitter, LinkedIn, Reddit, Tumblr

Kathy Barbour, Chair

Actionable best practices are the focus of this annual event.

5111 Toastmasters Trade Show
Toastmasters International
PO Box 9052
Mission Viejo, CA 92690-9052
949-858-8255
949-835-1300; Fax: 949-858-1207
newsletters@toastmasters.org
www.toastmasters.org

Focuses on communication in general and public speaking in particular. Topics include language, listening, humor, self improvement, goal setting, success and logical thinking.
2M Attendees
Frequency: August

5112 adXchange
News Media Alliance

4401 N. Fairfax Drive
Suite 300
Vienna, VA 22203

571-366-1000
info@newsmediaalliance.org
www.newsmediaalliance.org

David Chavern, President & CEO
Rachel Fox, Event Planner & Executive Assistant

Hosted by the News Media Alliance to bring members of the news industry together with advertisers.
Frequency: Annual

Directories & Databases

5113 **ACCE Communications Council Directory**
4875 Eisenhower Ave
Suite 250
Alexandria, VA 22304-4850

703-998-0072; Fax: 703-212-9512
webmaster@acce.org
www.acce.org
Facebook, Twitter, LinkedIn

Michael Flemming, President

Offers member information on the council activities.
Frequency: Annual+
Founded in 1914

5114 **Adweek Directory**
Prometheus Global Media
770 Broadway
New York, NY 10003-9595

212-493-4100; Fax: 646-654-5368
www.prometheusgm.com

Richard D. Beckman, CEO
Jame A. Finkelstein, Chairman
Madeline Krakowsky, Vice President Circulation
Tracy Brater, Executive Director Creative Service

Adweek Directories Online is where you will find searchable databases with comprehensive information on ad agencies, brand marketers and multicultural media.
Frequency: Annual
Circulation: 800
Founded in 1981

5115 **American Showcase Illustration**
Luerzer's Archive Inc
Ste 1530
410 Park Ave
New York, NY 10022-9441

212-941-2496; Fax: 212-941-5490
www.lurzersarchive.com

Walter Lurzer, Editor

Illustrators and graphic designers.
Mailing list available for rent

5116 **Association for Educational Communications and Technology Membership Directory**
Assn. for Educational Communications & Technology
320 W. 8th Street
Suite 101
Bloomington, IN 47404-3745

812-335-7675; 877-677-2328
aect@aect.org
aect.org
Facebook, Twitter

Xun Ge, President
Phillip Harris, Executive Director

5,000 audiovisual and instructional materials specialists, educational technologists, audiovisual and television production personnel, school media specialists
Frequency: Annual

5117 **Bacon's Newspaper & Magazine Directories**
Cision U.S., Inc.
322 South Michigan Avenue
Suite 900
Chicago, IL 60604

312-263-0070
866-639-5087
info.us@cision.com
us.cision.com

Joe Bernardo, President & CEO
Heidi Sullivan, VP & Publisher
Valerie Lopez, Research Director
Jessica White, Research Director
Rachel Farrell, Research Manager

Two volume set listing all daily and community newspapers, magazines and newsletters, news service and syndicates, syndicated columnists, complete editorial staff listings of each publication provided, covers U.S., Canada, Mexico, and Carribean.
Cost: $350.00
4,700 Pages
Frequency: Annual
ISSN: 1088-9639
Founded in 1951
Printed in one color on matte stock

5118 **Bacon's Radio/TV/Cable Directory**
Cision U.S., Inc.
332 South Michigan Avenue
Suite 900
Chicago, IL 60604

312-263-0070; 866-639-5087
info.us@cision.com

Joe Bernardo, President & CEO
Heidi Sullivan, VP & Publisher
Valerie Lopez, Research Director
Jessica White, Research Director
Rachel Farrell, Research Manager

Includes comprehensive coverage for contact and programming information for more than 3,500 television networks, cable networks, television syndicators, television stations, and cable systems in the United States and Canada.
Cost: $350.00
Frequency: Annual
ISSN: 1088-9639
Printed in one color on matte stock

5119 **Burrelle's Media Directory**
BurrellesLuce
75 E Northfield Rd
Livingston, NJ 07039-4532

973-992-6600
800-631-1160; Fax: 973-992-7675
www.burrellesluce.com
Facebook, Twitter, LinkedIn

Robert C Waggoner, CEO

Approximately 60,000 media listings in North America. Listings cover newspapers, magazines (trades and consumer), broadcast, and internet outlets.
Cost: $795.00
Frequency: Annual

5120 **Corporate Yellow Book**
Leadership Directories
104 5th Ave
New York, NY 10011-6901

212-627-4140; Fax: 212-645-0931
corporate@leadershipdirectories.com
www.leadershipdirectories.com

David Hurvitz, CEO

Contact information for over 48,000 executives at over 1,000 companies and 6,000 subsidiaries and divisions, and more than 9,000 board members and their outside affiliations.
Cost: $360.00
1,400 Pages
Frequency: Quarterly
ISSN: 1058-2908
Founded in 1986
Mailing list available for rent: 50,000 names at $105 per M

5121 **Film & Video Finder**
Information Today
143 Old Marlton Pike
Medford, NJ 08055-8750

609-654-6266
800-300-9868; Fax: 609-654-4309
custserv@infotoday.com
www.infotoday.com

Thomas H Hogan, President
Roger R Bilboul, Chairman Of The Board

Contains information on 130,000 films and videos. The most comprehensive reference available to educational films and videos. A three volume hardbound set.
Cost: $295.00
6434 Pages
Frequency: Annual
ISBN: 0-937548-29-4

5122 **Gale Database of Publications and Broadcast Media**
Gale/Cengage Learning
PO Box 09187
Detroit, MI 48209-0187

248-699-4253
800-877-4253; Fax: 248-699-8049
gale.galeord@cengage.com; www.gale.com
Facebook, Twitter, LinkedIn

Patrick C Sommers, President

This media directory contains thousands of listings for radio and television stations and cable companies.
Founded in 2008

5123 **Gale's Ready Reference Shelf**
Gale/Cengage Learning
PO Box 09187
Detroit, MI 48209-0187

248-699-4253
800-877-4253; Fax: 248-699-8049
gale.galeord@cengage.com
www.gale.com
Facebook, Twitter, LinkedIn

Patrick C Sommers, President

Gale's Ready Reference Shelf allows you to search the entire database of integrated content at one time and the data updates are automatic allowing the user to access the latest information available.

5124 **Gebbie Press All-in-One Directory**
Gebbie Press
PO Box 1000
New Paltz, NY 12561-0017

845-255-7560; Fax: 845-256-1239
www.gebbieinc.com

Mark Gebbie, Editor/Publisher

TV and radio stations, daily and weekly newspapers, consumer and trade magazines, black and Hispanic media, news syndicates, networks, AP/UPI bureaus. Compact spiral bound 6x9 inches.
Cost: $140.00
500 Pages
Frequency: Also on Disk
Founded in 1970

5125 **Hudson's Washington News Media Contacts Directory**
Grey House Publishing
4919 Route 22
PO Box 56
Amenia, NY 12501

518-789-8700
800-562-2139; Fax: 845-373-6390
books@greyhouse.com; www.greyhouse.com
Facebook, Twitter

Leslie Mackenzie, Publisher
Richard Gottlieb, President

A comprehensive guide to the entire Washington, D.C. press corps, broken down into categories.
Cost: $289.00
350 Pages
ISBN: 1-592378-53-6
Printed in one color on matte stock

5126 **Hudson's Washington News Media Contacts - Online Database**
Grey House Publishing
4919 Route 22
PO Box 56
Amenia, NY 12501

518-789-8700
800-562-2139; Fax: 845-373-6390
gold@greyhouse.com; gold.greyhouse.com
Facebook, Twitter

Leslie Mackenzie, Publisher
Richard Gottlieb, President

With 100% verification of data, Hudson's is the most accurate, most up-to-date source for media contacts in our nation's capital. With the largest concentration of news media in the world, having access to Washington's news media will get your message heard by these key media outlets.

5127 **Journalism and Mass Communication Directory**
AEJMC
234 Outlet Pointe Boulevard
Suite A
Columbia, SC 29210-5667

803-798-0271; Fax: 803-772-3509
www.aejmc.org

Jennifer McGill, Executive Director

Published by the Association for Education in Journalism and Mass Communication. Features over 3,000 professionals, academics and graduate students; more than 400 journalism and mass communications schools and departments in four-year colleges and universities.
Frequency: Annual
Circulation: 5000
Founded in 1983
Mailing list available for rent

5128 **Kagan Media Index**
Kagan World Media
126 Clock Tower Place
Carmel, CA 93923-8746

831-624-1536; Fax: 831-625-3225
www.kagan.com

George Niesen, Editor
Tom Johnson, Marketing Manager

The most comprehensive collection of media industry databases found anywhere. Current estimates of industry growth for a dozen different media businesses, shown on a 145-line spreadsheet, projected forward and updated monthly. Three month trial available.
Cost: $795.00
Frequency: Monthly

5129 **M Street Radio Directory**
M Street Corporation
81 Main Street, Suite 2
PO Box 442
Littleten, NH 03561

603-444-5720
800-248-4242; Fax: 603-444-2872
www.mstreet.net

Cathy Devine, Research Director
Kelli Grisez, Operations Manager
Frank Saxe, Senior Editor

Approximately 14,000 AM and FM radio stations in the US and Canada.
Cost: $79.00
Frequency: Annual
Printed in on matte stock

5130 **News Media Directories**
PO Box 316
Mount Dora, FL 32757

352-589-9020
800-749-6399; Fax: 866-586-7020

Dean Highberger, Editor

Directory for lists, daily papers, new services, magazines, weekly papers, special publications and radio stations. We have directories covering eight states , Alabama, Florida, Georgia, Mississippi, North Carolina, Ohio, South Carolina and Tennessee. Also, we have a condensed southeast edition. Listings include address, phone, fax, e-mail, and key associates.
Frequency: Annual

5131 **News Media Yellow Book**
Leadership Directories
104 5th Ave
New York, NY 10011-6901

212-627-4140; Fax: 212-645-0931
www.leadershipdirectories.com
Facebook, Twitter

David Hurvitz, CEO
James M Petrie, Associate Publisher

Contact information for over 39,000 journalists at over 2,500 new services, networks, newspapers, television, radio stations, as well as independent journalists and syndicated columnists.
Cost: $325.00
1,200 Pages
Frequency: Quarterly
ISSN: 1071-8931
Founded in 1989
Mailing list available for rent: 32,000 names at $125 per M

5132 **O'Dwyer's Directory of Public Relations Firms**
JR O'Dwyer Company
271 Madison Ave
Suite 600
New York, NY 10016-1013

212-679-2461; Fax: 212-683-2750
jack@odwyerpr.com; www.odwyerpr.com

Jack O'Dwyer, Publisher
Kevin McCauley, Editor
Sharlene Spingler, Associate Publisher

Exclusive ranking of public relations firms and lists more than 1,700 firms in the US and 55 countries.
Cost: $125.00
400 Pages
Frequency: Annual
Founded in 1968

5133 **Pocket Media Guide**
Media Distribution Services
307 W 36th St
Department P
New York, NY 10018-6519

212-279-4800
800-637-3282; Fax: 212-643-0576
www.mdsconnect.com

Dan Cantelmo, President

Designed to fit easily into a wallet, the palm size guide includes names and addresses, with phone numbers, of more than 700 major print and media in North America, plus a calendar, annual media statistics, and a publicity primer.
40 Pages
Frequency: Annual

5134 **Power Media Selects**
Broadcast Interview Source
2233 Wisconsin Ave NW
Suite 301
Washington, DC 20007-4132

202-333-5000
800-932-7266; Fax: 202-342-5411
www.expertclick.com

Mitchell Davis, Owner
Alan Caruba, Production Manager

Approximately 3,000 media contacts throughout the US, including newswire services, syndicates, syndicated columnists, national newspapers, magazines, radio and television talk shows, etc.
Cost: $166.50
Frequency: Annual

5135 **Salem Press Online Platform**
Grey House Publishing
4919 Route 22
PO Box 56
Amenia, NY 12501

800-221-1592; Fax: 201-968-0511
csr@salempress.com; online.salempress.com

The new Salem Press platform houses more than 500 titles including all of Salem's Health, Literature, History and Science titles in addition to select titles from the Grey House Publishing and H.W. Wilson product lines. Online access is free with each print purchase and includes an unlimited number of simultaneous users and remote access.

5136 **Sound & Communications**
Testa Communications
25 Willowdale Avenue
Port Washington, NY 11050-3779

516-767-2500; Fax: 516-767-9335

David Silverman, Editor
Bob Beoder, Advertising Manager

The systems magazine for contractors and consultants who design, specify, sell, and install audio and display systems. Installation profiles, news, business and product updates, incisive theory and applications reporting.
Cost: $15.00
Frequency: Monthly
Circulation: 23,000
Founded in 1955

Industry Web Sites

5137 **http://gold.greyhouse.com**
G.O.L.D Grey House OnLine Databases

Grey House Publishing's online database platform, GOLD, offers Quick Search, Keyword Search and Expert Search for most business markets including boradcasting, communications and media markets. The GOLD platform makes finding the information you need quick and easy - whether you're a novice searcher or an experienced database user. All of Grey House's directory products are available for subscription on the GOLD platform.

5138 **iafcm.org**
International Association for Conflict Management

Facebook, Twitter

An association for scholars and practitioners to share theories, research, and experience related to conflict management.

5139 **www.acce.org**
American Chamber of Commerce Executives

National organization uniquely serving individuals involved in the management of chambers of all sizes. Chamber executives and their staffs can capitalize on a wealth of information, leadership, skill development, management techniques and innovative program offerings. Also works diligently to upgrade the economic status and professional standing of those active in the chamber field.

5140 **www.adweek.com**
Adweek

Leading decision makers in the advertising and marketing field go to Adweek.com every day for breaking news, insight, buzz, opinion, analysis, research and classifieds. The resources of all six regional editions of Adweek, as well as the national edition of Brandweek are combined with the knowledge of our editors and the multimedia-interactive capabilities of the Web to deliver vital information quickly and effectively to our target audience.

5141 **www.aim.org**
Accuracy in Media

Nonprofit, grassroots citizens watchdog of the news media that critiques botched and bungled news stories and sets the record straight on important issues that have recieved slanted coverage.

5142 **www.americomm.org**
American Communication Association

Founded for the purposes of fostering research and scholarship in all areas of human communication behavior, promoting and improving excellence in the pedagogy of communication, providing a voice in communication law and policy, and providing evaluation and certification services for academic programs in communication study.

5143 **www.amta.org**
Antenna Measurement Techniques Association

Nonprofit professional organization, open to individuals with an interest in antenna measurements. Areas of interest include: measurement facilities, unique or innovative measurement techniques, test instrumentation and systems, RCS measurements, compact range design and evaluation, near-field techniques and their applications, and the practical aspects of measurement problems problems and their solutions.

5144 **www.apco911.org**
Association of Public-Safety Communications

The world's oldest and largest professional organization dedicated to the enhancement of public safety communications and to serving its more than 15,000 members, the people who use public safety communications systems and services.

5145 **www.attw.org**
Association of Teachers of Technical Writing

Provides communication among teachers of technical writing and develops technical communications as an academic discipline.

5146 **www.bowker.com**
Reed Reference Publishing RR Bowker

Offers, in four separate volumes, syndicates, newspapers, radio and television stations, feature writers, photographers, illustrators and internal house organs.

5147 **www.consultingsuccess.org**
Assn of Professional Communication Consultants

Professional community where communication consultants increase their knowledge, grow their business, achieve high standards of professional practice. APCC's mission is to support members as they help clients reach their goals through better communication.

5148 **www.digmedia.org**
Digital Media Association

National trade organization devoted primarily to the online audio and video industries, and more generally to commercially innovative digital media opportunities.

5149 **www.drudgereport.com**

Links to international news sources and columnists.

5150 **www.entelec.org**
Energy Telecommunications and Electrical Assoc

A user association focusing on communications and control technologies used by petroleum, natural gas, pipeline and electric utility companies.

5151 **www.greyhouse.com**
Grey House Publishing

Authoritative reference directories for most business sectors including broadcasting, communications and meida markets. Users can search the online databases with varied search criteria allowing for custom searches by product category, geographic area, sales volume, keyword, subject and more. Full Grey House catalog and online ordering also available.

5152 **www.iaais.org**
Int'l Association of Audio Information Services

Formerly the National Association of Radio Reading Services, we are an organization of services that provide audio access to information for people who are print disabled. People served are blind, visually impared, learning disabled or physically disabled.

5153 **www.iabc.com**
Int'l Association of Business Communications

International knowledge network for professionals engaged in strategic business communication management. IABC links communicators in a global network that inspires, establishes and supports the highest professional standards.

5154 **www.icahdq.org**
International Communications Association

International association for scholars interested in the study, teaching and application of all aspects of human mediated communication.

5155 **www.iste.org**
International Society for Technology in Education

A large nonprofit organization serving the technology-using educator.

5156 **www.kagan.com**
Kagan World Media

For those interested in investments in radio and TV stations and publicly held companies.

5157 **www.kausfiles.com**
Kausfiles

Site for journalists and media specialists.

5158 **www.netage.com**
Networking Institute

Promotes networks to help people work together. Offers consulting services, educational workshops and seminars.

5159 **www.newsmediaalliance.org**
News Media Alliance

Formerly known as the Newspaper Association of America, the News Media Alliance represents large daily papers, non-daily/small-market publications, as well as digital and multiplatform products across North America.

5160 **www.nfais.org**
National Federation Absrtacting & Info Services

Serves those groups that aggregate, organize, and facilitate access to information. To improve member capabilities and contribute to their ongoing success. Provides opportunities for education, advocacy, and a forum to address common interests.

5161 **www.nsaspeaker.org**
National Speakers Association

The leading organization for experts who speak professionally. NSA's 4000 members include experts in a variety of industries and disciplines, who reach audiences as trainers, educators, humorists, motivators, consultants, authors and more. NSA provides resources and education designed to advance the skills, integrity, and value of its members and speaking profession. NSA the voice of the speaking profession.

5162 **www.postcom.org**
Association for Postal Commerce

National organization representing those who use, or support the use, of mail as a medium for communication and commerce. Postcom publishes a weekly newsletter covering postal policy and operational issues.

5163 **www.poynter.org**
Poynter Online

Poynter Institute is dedicated to teaching and inspiring journalists and media leaders. Promotes excellence and integrity in the practice of craft and in the practical leadership of successful businesses.

5164 **www.regionalmagazines.org**
International Regional Magazine Association

Promotes the interests of international and regional magazine professionals.

5165 **www.retailing.org**
Electronics Retailing Association

For infomercial producers, marketers, product developers, broadcasters and other industries serving the infomercial market.

5166 **www.speakingsuccess.com**
Personal Achievement Institute

5167 **www.theabc.org**
Association for Business Communication

International organization commited to fostering excellence in business communication scholarship, research, education, and practice.

5168 **www.toastmasters.org**
Toastmasters International

Publishes educational articles on the subjects of communication and leadership. Topics include language, listening, humor, self-improvement, goal setting, success and logical thinking.

5169 **www.wgbh.org**
WGBH Educational Foundation
WGBH productions are seen and heard on stations around the country.

Associations

5170 **ACM Special Interest Group on Artificial Intelligence**
Association for Computing Machinery
1601 Broadway
10th Floor
New York, NY 10019-7434
212-869-7440
800-342-6626; Fax: 212-944-1318
acmhelp@acm.org
sigai.acm.org
Sanmay Das, Chair
Nicholas Mattei, Vice Chair
John Dickerson, Secretary/Treasurer
ACM SIGAI is an offshoot of the Association for Computing Machinery, made up of academic and industrial researchers, practitioners, software developers, end users, and students.
Mailing list available for rent

5171 **AIM Global**
20399 Route 19
Suite 203
Cranberry Township, PA 16066
724-742-4470
info@aimglobal.org
www.aimglobal.org
Facebook, Twitter, LinkedIn, Pinterest
Chuck Evanhoe, President & CEO
Mary Lou Bosco, Chief Operating Officer
Michael Allen, Membership Engagement
Diana Bowser, Finance/Admin./Member Services
International trade association representing automatic identification and mobility technology solution providers.
Founded in 1972

5172 **ARMA International**
11880 College Boulevard
Suite 450
Overland Park, KS 66210
913-444-9174
844-565-2120; Fax: 913-257-3855
headquarters@armaintl.org
www.arma.org
Facebook, Twitter, LinkedIn
Nate Hughes, Exec. Dir, Operations
Jennifer Millett, National Accounts Manager
Healther Leahman, Sr. Manager, Membership
Karen Skaggs, Sales & Events Specialist
ARMA International is a not-for-profit association and a source for authoritative education, the latest legislative updates, standards & best practices. Its members include records managers, archivists, corporate librarians, imaging specialists, legal professionals, IT managers, consultants, and educators, all of whom work in a wide variety of industries.
27000 Members
Founded in 1955

5173 **Agile Alliance**
6525 Idumea Good
Corryton, TN 37721
Home Page: www.agilealliance.org
Ellen Grove, Managing Director
Pam Hughes, Marketing Chief
Ray Arell, Chief of Innovation & Business Dev.
Tarah McMaster, Membership & Registration
Rebecca Wirfs-Brock, Editor-In-Chief
A nonprofit organization committed to supporting people who explore and apply Agile values, principles, and practices to make building software solutions more effective, humane, and sustainable.
70000 Members
Founded in 2001

5174 **Allen Institute for AI**
Seattle, WA
206-548-5600
ai2-info@allenai.org
allenai.org
Twitter
Oren Etzioni, Chief Executive Officer
James Allard, Chief Operating Officer
Non-profit research instutute named after Microsoft co-founder Paul Allen, aiming to construct Artificial Intelligence systems with reasoning, learning, and reading capabilities.

5175 **Alpha Micro Users Society**
210 N Iris Avenue
Rialto, CA 92376-5727
909-874-6214; Fax: 909-874-2143
info@amus.org
www.computerhistory.org
Dan'l Lewin, President & CEO
Dave Evans, CIO & VP, Technology
George Holmes, VP & CFO
Marie Jackson, Chief Marketing Officer
Michelle Mertz, VP & Chief Development Officer
An organization supported by members to promote the uses of computers manufactured by Alpha Micro Products of Irvine, California. This basic purpose has expanded, over the years, from merely a focal point for the exchange of technical information on its use and versatility, to promotion of products (Software and Hardware) from Alpha Micro and various third party organizations having an interest in users of Alpha Micro computers.
125 Members
Founded in 1978

5176 **American Council for Technology and Industry Advisory Council (ACT-IAC)**
3040 Williams Drive
Suite 500
Fairfax, VA 22031
703-208-4800; Fax: 703-208-4805
act-iac@actiac.org
www.actiac.org
Facebook, Twitter, LinkedIn, YouTube
David Wennergren, Chief Executive Officer
Tom Scanlon, Sr. Director, Finance & Operations
Kisha Powell, Sr. Director, Meetings
April Davis, Director, Member Services
Colleen Kennedy, Director, Marketing & Events
A non-profit educational organization established to assist government in acquiring and using information technology, resources effectively and efficiently. Working with all levels of the government, ACT-IAC provides education, programming, and networking opportunities that enhance and advance the government IT profession.
50000 Members
Founded in 1978

5177 **American Medical Informatics Association**
4720 Montgomery Lane
Suite 500
Bethesda, MD 20814
301-657-1291; Fax: 301-657-1296
www.amia.org
Facebook, Twitter, LinkedIn, YouTube, Flickr
Karen Greenwood, EVP, COO & Interim CEO
Krista Martin, VP, Marketing & Communications
Lee Ann Pirrello, VP, Membership
Jasmine Casteel, Director, Finance
Dasha Cohen, Director, Meetings
Aims to lead the way in transforming healthcare through trusted science, education, and the practice of informatics. Connecting a broad community of professionals and students interested in informatics, AMIA is the bridge for knowledge and collaboration across a continuum, from basic and applied research to the consumer and public health arenas.
3200 Members
Founded in 1990
Mailing list available for rent: 2000 names

5178 **American Society for Precision Engineering**
3801 Lake Boone Trail
Suite 190
Raleigh, NC 27607
919-839-8444; Fax: 919-839-8039
www.aspe.net
Brian O'Connor, President
John Schaefer, Vice President
Members are from academia, industry and government, and include professionals in engineering, materials science, physics, chemistry, mathematics and computer science. Multidisciplinary professional and technical society concerned with precision engineering research and development, design and manufacturing of high accuracy components and systems.
Founded in 1985

5179 **Armed Forces Communications & Electronics Association (AFCEA)**
4114 Legato Road
Suite 1000
Fairfax, VA 22033
703-631-6100
800-336-4583; Fax: 703-631-6169
service@afcea.org
www.afcea.org
Facebook, Twitter, LinkedIn, Google+, YouTube
Lt. Gen. Robert Shea, USMC (Ret.), President/CEO
Pat Miorin, CPA, EVP/CFO/International Treasurer
Lt. Gen. John Wood, USA (Ret.), EVP, Defense/National Security
James Griggs, Jr., VP/CTO/CIO
Beverly Cooper, VP, Comm. & Media/CKO/Publisher
A non-profit membership association serving the military, government, industry, and academia as an ethical forum for advancing professional knowledge and relationships in the fields of communications, IT, intelligence, and global security.
31000 Members
Founded in 1946

5180 **Association for Computing Machinery**
1601 Broadway
10th Floor
New York, NY 10019-7434
212-869-7440
800-342-6626; Fax: 212-944-1318
acmhelp@acm.org
www.acm.org
Facebook, Twitter, LinkedIn, YouTube
Vicki Hanson, Chief Executive Officer
Pat Ryan, Chief Operating Officer
John Stanik, Managing Editor
Darren Ramdin, Director, Finance
Cynthia Ryan, Associate Director, Membership
Organization serving a membership of computing educators, researchers, and professionals. The association offers relevant career development, professional networking, and education opportunities.
80000 Members
Founded in 1947

5181 **Association for Educational Communications and Technology**
320 W. 8th Street
Suite 101
Bloomington, IN 47404-3745

812-335-7675
877-677-2328
aect@aect.org
aect.org
Facebook, Twitter

Xun Ge, President
Phillip Harris, Executive Director
Larry Vernon, Director, Electronic Services
Lois Freeland, AECT Convention Coordinator
Terri Lawson, HR & Administrative Services

A professional association of thousands of educators and others whose activities are directed towards improving instruction through technology.
Founded in 1923

5182 **Association for Information Science and Technology**
8555 16th Street
Suite 850
Silver Spring, MD 20910

301-495-0900; Fax: 301-495-0810
asist@asist.org
www.asist.org
Facebook, Twitter, LinkedIn

Lydia Middleton, Executive Director
Terrence Curtiss, Director of Membership
Cathy L. Nash, Director of Meetings & Events

Professional development organization for the information science and technology industry.

5183 **Association for Information and Image Management International**
8403 Colesville Road
Suite 1100
Silver Spring, MD 20910

301-587-8202
800-477-2446; Fax: 301-587-2711
aiim@aiim.org
www.aiim.org
Facebook, Twitter, LinkedIn, YouTube

Peggy Winton, President & CEO
Georgina Clelland, Chief Operating Officer
Renee Martin, Director, Event Marketing
Boshia Smith, Membership Manager

Global authority on enterprise content management (ECM). ECM Technologies are used to create, capture, customize, deliver, and manage information to support business process.
Founded in 1943

5184 **Association for Services Management International**
11031 Via Frontera
Suite A
San Diego, CA 92127

239-275-7887
800-333-9786; Fax: 239-275-0794

JB Wood, President
Thomas Lah, Executive Director

Provides the knowledge, fellowship and career connections that customer services and support managers for technology based products and solutions needed for professional and career development.
Cost: $375.00
Frequency: Membership Fee
Founded in 1975

5185 **Association for the Advancement of Computing in Education**
PO Box 719
Waynesville, NC 28786

828-246-9558; Fax: 828-246-9557
info@aace.org
www.aace.org
Facebook

Dr. Gary H. Marks, Chief Executive Officer
An international, educational and professional nonprofit organization dedicated to the advancement of the knowledge, theory and quality of learning and teaching at all levels with information technology.
Founded in 1981

5186 **Association for the Advancement of Artificial Intelligence**
2275 East Bayshore Road
Suite 160
Palo Alto, CA 94303

650-328-3123; Fax: 650-321-4457
www.aaai.org
Twitter

Carol Hamilton, Executive Director
Young Hash, Membership Coordinator
Stephanie Le, Conference Coordinator
Emma Wishmeyer, Conference Program Associate
Diane Mela, Accountant

Nonprofit society devoted to advancing the scientific understanding of the mechanisims underlying thought and intellegent behavior and their embodiment in machines.
6000 Members
Founded in 1979
Mailing list available for rent

5187 **Business Software Alliance**
20 F Street NW
Suite 800
Washington, DC 20001

202-872-5500; Fax: 202-872-5501
info@bsa.org
www.bsa.org
Facebook, Twitter, LinkedIn, YouTube

Victoria A. Espinel, President & CEO
Adam J. Coates, General Counsel & VP
Ha McNeill, Chief Operating Officer
Joe DeSalvio, Chief Financial Officer

An organization dedicated to promoting a safe and legal digital world. BSA educates consumers on software management and copyright protection, cyber security, trade, e-commerce and other internet related issues.
Founded in 1988

5188 **Business Technology Association**
12411 Wornall Road
Suite 200
Kansas City, MO 64145

800-505-2821
info@bta.org
www.bta.org
Facebook, Twitter, LinkedIn

Tim Renegar, President
Brent Hoskins, Executive Director
Valerie Briseno, Marketing Director
Elizabeth Marvel, Associate Editor
Brian Smith, Membership Sales Representative

Serving independent dealers, value-added resellers, systems integrators, manufacturers and distributors in the business equipment and systems industry. BTA helps its members profit through a wide variety of services, including free legal advice and guidance; business benchmarking studies and reports; information on the latest news, trends, and products in the industry.
Founded in 1926

5189 **CEMA: Computer Event Marketing Association**
5098 Foothills Boulevard
Suite 3-386
Roseville, CA 95747

info@cemaonline.com
www.cemaonline.com
Facebook, Twitter, LinkedIn

Kimberley Gishler, President & CEO
Olga Rosenbrook, Director of Member Services

Serving marketing professionals in the high technology industry. CEMA has grown to represent the interest of marketing communications professionals in the information technology industry.
500 Members
Frequency: $275-$775 Membership Fee
Founded in 1990

5190 **CIFAR**
MaRS Centre, West Tower
661 University Avenue
Suite 505
Toronto, ON M5G 1M1

416-971-4251
www.cifar.ca
Facebook, Twitter, LinkedIn, YouTube

Alan Bernstein, President & CEO
Pauline Yick, COO
Catherine Riddell, VP, Strategic Communications
Sharon Hainey, Event & Meetings Coordinator
Leanne Woodcock, Financial Officer

Charitable organization that looks to address important questions facing humanity, such as the risks posed by Artificial Intelligence, by gathering extraordinary individuals and allowing them to share their knowledge.
400+ Members

5191 **Canadian Artificial Intelligence Association**
Concordia University
1515 St. Catherine Street W.
Montreal, QC H3G 2W1

514-848-2424
leila.kosseim@concordia.ca
www.caiac.ca
Facebook, Twitter, LinkedIn

Leila Kosseim, President
Richard Khoury, Vice President
Xin Wang, Treasurer
Denilson Barbosa, Secretary

Formerly known as the Canadian Society for the Computational Studies of Intelligence, CAIAC seeks to further research, development and education in Canada's artificial intelligence community, through knowledge-exchange in the media and other venues.

5192 **Canadian Image Processing and Pattern Recognition Society**
Cdn. Image Processing/Pattern Recognition Society
York University
4700 Keele Street
Toronto, ON M3J 1P3

416-736-2100
jenkin@cse.yorku.ca
www.computerrobotvision.org

Helge Rhodin, Program Co-Chair
Liam Paul, Program Co-Chair

Special interest group of the Canadian Information Processing Society, and the national representative organization of the International Association of Pattern Recognition.

5193 **Carnegie Mellon University: Information Networking Institute**
4616 Henry Street
Pittsburgh, PA 15213

412-268-7195
www.cmu.edu/ini
Facebook, Twitter, LinkedIn, YouTube, Google+

Dena Haritos-Tsamitis, Director
Miroslava Angelova, Director, Business Operations
Christa Jones, Director, Marketing & Events
Jessica Shirley, Director, Strategic Communications

Established as the nation's first research and education center devoted to Information Networking. INI focuses on professional degree programs that combine technologies, economics, and policies of global communication networks and information security.
300 Members
Founded in 1989

5194 **Center for Security and Emerging Technology**
Walsh School of Foreign Service
ICC 301, 37th & O Street NW
Washington, DC 20057

202-687-0100
cset@georgetown.edu
cset.georgetown.edu

Jason Matheny, Founding Director
Tessa Baker, Director, Operations
Ben Buchanan, Director, Cybersecurity & AI
Igor Mikolic-Torreira, Director, Analysis
Dewey Murdick, Director, Data Science

CSET studies the security impacts of emerging technologies, especially Artificial Intelligence.
Founded in 2019
Mailing list available for rent

5195 **CompTIA**
3500 Lacey Road
Suite 100
Downers Grove, IL 60515

630-678-8300
866-835-8020; Fax: 630-678-8384
www.comptia.org
Facebook, Twitter, LinkedIn, Pinterest, Google+, YouTube

Todd Thibodeaux, President & CEO
Brian Laffey, CFO
Randy Gross, CIO
Nancy Hammervik, Executive VP, Industry Relations
Kelly Ricker, Executive VP, Events & Education

A nonprofit trade association created by representatives of five microcomputer leaderships and is a provider of professional certifications for the information technology (IT) industry.

5196 **Computer Assisted Language Instruction Consortium**
Texas State University
214 Centennial Hall
San Marcos, TX 78666

512-245-1417; Fax: 512-245-9089
info@calico.org
calico.org
Twitter

Esther Horn, Manager
Marta Gonzalez-Lloret, President
Bryan Smith, Journal Editor
Ana Oskoz, Journal Editor

For language teachers, linguists, courseware developers and governments who are interested in teaching languages with the use of computer assistedinstruction.
780 Members
Founded in 1983

5197 **Computer Security Institute**
350 Hudson Street
Suite 300
New York, NY 10014

415-947-6320; Fax: 415-905-2218
www.csoonline.com
Facebook, Twitter, LinkedIn

Amy Bennett, Executive Editor
Matt Egan, Editorial Director
Cost: $224.00
Frequency: Membership Fee
Founded in 1974

5198 **Computerized Medical Imaging**
National Biomedical Research Foundation
37th and O Streets, N.W
Washington, DC 20057

202-687-0100; Fax: 202-687-1662
ledley@nbrf.georgetown.edu
www.georgetown.edu
Facebook, Twitter, LinkedIn, YouTube, Flickr

Blaire V Mossman, Chief Administrator
Dr. John J. DeGioia, Ph.D, President
William J Doyle, Chair
Thomas Parkes, S.J, Vice Chair

Formerly the Computerized Radiology Society. A source for the exchange of information concerning the medical use of computerized tomography in radiological diagnosis.
Founded in 1798

5199 **Computing Research Association**
1828 L Street NW
Suite 800
Washington, DC 20036-4632

202-234-2111; Fax: 202-667-1066
info@cra.org
www.cra.org
Facebook, Twitter, YouTube

Andrew Bernat, Executive Director
Erik Russell, Director of Programs
Sandra Corbett, Program Manager

The CRA's mission is to seek to strengthen research and advanced education in computing and allied fields.
200 Members
Founded in 1972

5200 **Electronics Industries Alliance**

A national trade organization that includes a full spectrum of U.S. manufacturers. The alliance is a partnership of electronic and high-tech associations and companies whose mission is promoting the market development and competitiveness of the U.S. high-tech industry through domestic and international policy efforts.
Founded in 1952

5201 **Enterprise Computing Solutions**
26024 Acero
Mission Viejo, CA 92691

949-609-1980
info@thinkecs.com
www.thinkecs.com

Celine Blackley, President
Phil Blackley, CEO
Jen Payan, VP, Finance
Mike Suwa, Director, Technology Services

A leading provider of IT infrastructure solutions for Fortune 500 and mid-tier companies throughout California. ECS builds sophisticated IT infrastructure solutions for mission-critical applications, provides enterprise storage solutions that ensure data protection and business continuity, and delivers state-of-the-art server solutions for optimal computing capacity.
500 Members
Founded in 1995

5202 **Eta Kappa Nu**
445 Hoes Lane
Piscataway, NJ 08854

732-465-5846
800-406-2590
info@hkn.org
hkn.ieee.org

Edward Rezek, President

Eta Kappa Nu (HKN) is the electrical and computer engineering honor society of the Institute of Electrical and Electronics Engineers (IEEE).
Founded in 1904

5203 **Future of Life Institute**
Boston, MA

meia@futureoflife.org
futureoflife.org
Facebook, Twitter

Jaan Tallinn, Co-Founder
Max Tegmark, Co-Founder
Meia Chita-Termark, Co-Founder
Viktoriya Krakovna, Co-Founder
Anthony Aguirre, Co-Founder

Seeks to mitigate emerging risks facing humanity, especially from advanced artificial intelligence, but also including biotechnology, nuclear power, and climate change.

5204 **Global Association for Vision Information**
900 Victors Way
Suite 140
Ann Arbor, MI 48108

734-994-6088
www.visiononline.org
Facebook, Twitter, LinkedIn, YouTube

Jeff Burnstein, President
Alex Shikany, VP, Membership & Business
James Hamilton, Director, Sales
Robert Huschka, Director, Education Strategies
Bob McCurrach, Director, Standards Development

The AIA is dedicated to vision and imaging technologies, with members including manufacturers of vision components and systems, system integrators, distributors, OEMs, end users, consulting firms, academic institutions, and research groups.
380+ Members
Founded in 1984

5205 **IEEE Circuits and Systems Society**
Institute Of Electrical and Electronics Engineers
445 Hoes Lane
Piscataway, NJ 08854

Home Page: www.ieee-cas.org
Facebook, Twitter, LinkedIn

Amara Amara, President
Yoshifumi Nishio, VP, Membership
Myung Hoon Sunwoo, VP, Conferences
Guoxing Wang, VP, Financial Activities
Mohammad Sawan, VP, Publications

CASS fosters interdisciplinary and cross-disciplinary cooperation with regards to using circuits and systems to address humanity's greatest challenges.

5206 **IEEE Computational Intelligence Society**
445 Hoes Lane
Piscataway, NJ 08855

732-465-5892; Fax: 732-465-6435
cis-info@ieee.org
cis.ieee.org
Facebook, Twitter, LinkedIn

Bernadette Bouchon-Meunier, President
Pablo Estevez, VP, Finances
Marley Vellasco, VP, Conferences

James Keller, VP, Publications
Carlos Coello Coello, VP, Member Activities

The CIS seeks to advance computational intelligence in science and engineering.

5207 **IEEE Control Systems Society**
445 Hoes Lane
Piscataway, NJ 08854-1331

Home Page: ieeecss.org
Facebook, Twitter, LinkedIn

Anuradha Annaswamy, President
Jorge Cortes, Director, Operations

Subsidiary of the Institute of Electrical and Electronics Engineers dedicated to control system technology.

5208 **IEEE Industrial Electronics Society**
Institute Of Electrical and Electronics Engineers
445 Hoes Lane
Piscataway, NJ 08854

804-827-3999
president@ieee-ies.org
www.ieee-ies.org
Facebook, Twitter, LinkedIn, YouTube

Terry Martin, President
Thilo Sauter, VP, Publications
Juan Rodriguez-Andina, VP, Conference Activities
Kiyoshi Ohishi, VP, Workshops & Activities
Yousef Ibrahim, VP, Membership Activities

Conducts, through its members, range of technical activities dedicated to applying electronics and electrical sciences in an industrial setting, including current developments in intelligent and computer control systems, robotics, factory communications and automation, flexible manufacturing, data acquisition and signal processing, vision systems, and power electronics.

5209 **IEEE Signal Processing Society**
Institute of Electrical and Electronics Engineers
445 Hoes Lane
Piscataway, NJ 08854

732-562-3888; Fax: 732-867-9953
sp-info@ieee.org
signalprocessingsociety.org
Facebook, Twitter, LinkedIn

Rich Baseil, Executive Director
Theresa Argiropoulos, Senior Manager, Operations
Caroline Johnson, Senior Manager, Conference Services
William Colacchio, Senior Manager, Publications
Jessica Perry, Member Communications Specialist

The SPS looks to provide current scientific information and resources on signal processing, while educating professionals in the industry, and providing a venue for networking.

5210 **IEEE Society on Social Implications of Technology**
Institute of Electrical and Electronics Engineers
445 Hoes Lane
Piscataway, NJ 08854

r.dent@ieee.org
technologyandsociety.org
Facebook, Twitter, LinkedIn

Robert Dent, President
Lew Terman, Secretary
Howard Wolfman, Treasurer

The SSIT focuses on the following areas: Sustainable Development & Humanitarian Technology; Ethics, Human Values and Technology; Technology Benefits for All; Future Societal Impact of Technology Advances; and Protecting the Planet & Sustainable Technology

5211 **IEEE Solid-State Circuits Society**
Institute of Electrical and Electronics Engineers
445 Hoes Lane
Piscataway, NJ 08854

m.p.kelly@ieee.org
sscs.ieee.org
Facebook, Twitter, LinkedIn

Adam Greenberg, Executive Director
Lauren Caruso, Administrator
Abira Altvater, Technical Program Specialist
Danielle Marinese, Society Administrator

The SSCS serves members by providing them with education, communication, recognition, leadership opportunities, and networking opportunities.

5212 **IEEE Systems, Man, and Cybernetics Society**
Institute of Electrical and Electronics Engineers
445 Hoes Lane
Piscataway, NJ 08854

Home Page: www.ieeesmc.org
Facebook, Twitter, LinkedIn, Instagram

Imre Rudas, President
Sam Kwong, VP, Cybernetics
Andreas Nuernberger, VP, Conferences & Meetings
Adrian Stoica, VP, Systems Science & Engineering
Vladimir Marik, VP, Organization & Planning

Promotes all aspects of systems science and engineering, human-machine systems, and cybernetics, through conferences, publications, and other activities.

5213 **IEEE Technology & Engineering Management Society**
Institute of Electrical and Electronics Engineers
445 Hoes Lane
Piscataway, NJ 08854

Home Page: www.ieee-tems.org
Facebook, Twitter, LinkedIn

Andy Chen, President
Richard Evans, VP, Technical Activities
Sudeendra Koushik, VP, Conferences

Formerly the Engineering Management Society and the Technology Management Council, TEMS seeks to provide members with essential management and leadership knowledge and skills.
Founded in 1951

5214 **Independent Computer Consultants Association (ICCA)**
11131 S Towne Sq
Suite F
St Louis, MO 63123-7817

314-892-1675; Fax: 314-487-1345
execdirector@icca.org

Joyce Burkard, Executive Director
1000 Members
Founded in 1977

5215 **Information Management**
SourceMedia
One State Street Plaza
27th Floor
New York, NY 10004

212-803-8200
help@sourcemedia.com
www.information-management.com
Facebook, Twitter, LinkedIn, Google+

Gemma Postlethwaite, CEO, SourceMedia
Richard West, Publisher
David Weldon, Editorial-in-Chief
Eric Kavanagh, IM Live Host

A vendor independent professional organization dedicated to the advancement of data asset management concepts.
Founded in 1986

5216 **Information Resources Management Association**
701 E Chocolate Avenue
Suite 200
Hershey, PA 17033-1240

717-533-8845; Fax: 717-533-8661
member@irma-international.org
www.irma-international.org

Mehdi Khosrowpour, Executive Director
Sherif Kamel, VP, Information Management

An international professional organization dedicated to advancing the concepts and practices of information resources management in modern organizations. The primary objective of IRMA is to assist organizations and professionals in enhancing the overall knowledge and understanding of effective information resources management in the early 21st century and beyond.
Mailing list available for rent

5217 **Information Systems Audit & Control Association (ISACA)**
Rolling Meadows, IL

847-660-5505
844-472-2246
www.isaca.org
Facebook, Twitter, LinkedIn

David Samuelson, CEO
Robb Micek, Chief Financial Officer
Nader Qaimari, Chief Learning Officer
Simona Rollinson, Chief Technology Officer

With members in more than 180 countries, ISACA is a recognized worldwide leader in IT governance, control, security and assurance. Sponsors international conferences, publishes the thw ISACA Journal and develops international information systems auditing and control standards.
9000+ Members
Founded in 1967

5218 **Information Technology Management Institute**
PO Box 890
Merrifield, VA 22116

703-208-9610; Fax: 703-208-9604
www.itm-inst.com

Dr. Diane Murphy, CEO/Founder

Association for information technology organizations primarily in the US.
90 Members
Founded in 1996

5219 **Institute of Electrical & Electronics Engineers Computer Society**
2001 L Street NW
Suite 700
Washington, DC 20036-4928

202-371-0101; Fax: 202-728-9614
help@computer.org
www.computer.org
Facebook, Twitter, LinkedIn, YouTube, Google+

Melissa Russell, Executive Director
Anne Marie Kelly, Director, Governance
Eric Berkowitz, Director, Membership
Sunny Hwang, Director, Finance
Michelle Tubb, Director, Marketing & Sales

Supports all those involved in use and design of multimedia hardware, software and systems in industry, business, academia and the arts.
10000 Members
Founded in 1946

5220 **Institute of Electrical and Electronics Engineers**
3 Park Ave.
17th Fl.
New York, NY 10016-5997

212-419-7900; Fax: 212-752-4929
www.ieee.org
Facebook, Twitter, LinkedIn, YouTube, Instagram

Toshio Fukuda, President & CEO
Stephen Welby, Executive Director & COO

Supports all those involved in the field of electrical engineering, and works to nurture technological innovation and excellence for the benefit of humanity.
422K Members
Founded in 1963

5221 **International Association for Computer Systems Security**
Dix Hills, NY

Home Page: www.iacis.org

Maria Elena Corbeil, President & Director, Conferences
Kevin Floyd, Secretary & IIS Editor
Alex Koohang, Director, Technology & Operation
Daryl Nord, Executive Director
Jeretta Horn Nord, Treasurer & Director, Publications

A nonprofit association dedicated to the improvement of information systems and the education of information systems and computer professionals.
Founded in 1960

5222 **International Association of Knowledge Engineers**
973 Russell Avenue
Gaithersburg, MD 20879-3292

301-948-5390; Fax: 301-926-4243

Milton White, Owner
Julie Walker-Lowe, Executive Director

An international association of computer professionals concerned with designing reasoning machines and computer systems to receive, organize and maintain human knowledge.
Founded in 1987

5223 **International Neural Network Society**
2800 W. Higgins Road
Suite 440
Hoffman Estates, IL 60169

833-636-0351; Fax: 847-885-8393
inns@inns.org
www.inns.org
Facebook, Twitter, LinkedIn, YouTube

Irwin King, President
Marley Vellasco, Secretary
Danil Prokhorov, Treasurer
Seiichi Ozawa, VP, Membership
Richard Duro, VP, Conferences

INNS is comprised of researchers, professors, practitioners, and learners in the field of neural networks and computational science.

5224 **International Society for Technology in Education**
621 SW Morrison Street
Suite 800
Portland, OR 97205

503-342-2848
800-336-5191; Fax: 503-882-0813
iste@iste.org
www.iste.org
Facebook, Twitter, LinkedIn, YouTube, Pinterest

Bill Bass, President
Nikole Blanchard, Treasurer
Michael McVey, Secretary
Richard Culatta, Chief Executive Officer

A large nonprofit organization serving the technology-using educator.

5225 **International Technology Law Association/ ITechLaw**
7918 Jones Branch Drive
Suite 300
McLean, VA 22102

703-506-2895; Fax: 703-506-3266
memberservices@itechlaw.org
www.itechlaw.org
Facebook, Twitter, LinkedIn

Charles Morgan, Co-President
Gabriela Kennedy, Co-President
Michael Peeters, Treasurer
Peter Ruby, Secretary
Laura Liguori, Assistant Secretary

Computer Law Association changed its identity to ITechLaw to better reflect its global activities and expanded focus. Providing benefit to the worldwide community of information technology law professionals.
2000 Members
Founded in 1971

5226 **Internet Alliance**
1615 L Street NW
Suite 1100
Washington, DC 20036-5624

202-861-2407
www.internetalliance.my

Kris Larsen, Manager
Kaye Caldwell, California Policy Director

Formerly the Interactive Services Association, the Alliance has been the only consisted voice representint internet companies in the 50 states. We have a proven track record of blocking or mitigating privacy and anti-spam legislation, and a high level of expertise in the Internet state tax area.
Founded in 1999

5227 **Kestrel Institute**
3260 Hillview Avenue
Palo Alto, CA 94304

650-493-6871; Fax: 650-424-1807
info@kestrel.edu
www.kestrel.edu

Cordell Green, Director

Non-profit computer science research center.

5228 **Lifeboat Foundation**
1468 James Road
Gardnerville, NV 89460

775-409-3122; Fax: 775-409-3123
admin@lifeboat.com
lifeboat.com
Facebook, Twitter, LinkedIn, YouTube, RSS

Eric Klien, President & Founder
Chris Haley, VP & System Administrator
James Dunn, Director, Development Assistance

Non-profit, non-governmental organization encouraging scientific advancements in order to help humanity avoid existential risks from factors such as genetic engineering, nanotechnology, and robotics/AI.

5229 **Machine Intelligence Research Institute**
Berkeley, CA

contact@intelligence.org
intelligence.org
Facebook, Twitter, RSS

Nate Soares, Executive Director
Malo Bourgon, Chief Operating Officer

Uses foundational mathematics to ensure artificial intelligence systems have a positive impact.

5230 **Measurement, Control & Automation Association**
200 City Hall Avenue
Suite D
Poquoson, VA 23662

757-258-3100
automationassociation.com
Facebook, Twitter, LinkedIn, YouTube

Teresa Sebring, President
Andrea Ambrose, Director, Member Relations
Elizabeth Horton, Programs Manager
Kim Malina, Marketing Communications Manager
Rebecca Moore, Administrative Manager

The MCAA is the national trade association for manufacturers and distributors of instrumentation, systems, and software products for industrial process control and factory automation.
Founded in 1944

5231 **NaSPA: Association for Corporate Computing Technical Professionals**
NaSPA
Milwaukee, WI

262-67N-ASPA
www.naspa.com
LinkedIn

Leo A. Wrobel, President

NaSPABs mission is to serve the means to enhance the status and promote the advancement of all network and systems professionals; nurture membertechnical and managerial knowledge and skills and many more.
50000 Members
Founded in 1986

5232 **National Association of Computer Consultant Businesses**
1420 King Street
Suite 610
Alexandria, VA 22314

703-838-2050; Fax: 703-838-3610
staff@naccb.org
naccb.groupsite.com
Facebook, Twitter, LinkedIn

Members are companies providing technical support services to clients such as programming, systems analysis and software/hardware engineering.
300 Members
Founded in 1987

5233 **National BDPA**
9500 Arena Drive
Suite 106
Largo, MD 20774

301-584-3135; Fax: 301-560-8300
info@bdpa.org
www.bdpa.org
Facebook, Twitter, LinkedIn

Earl A. Pace, Founder
Terry Morris, President
Joe Blair, National Marketing Director
Eric Ejiofor, National Secretary
Karen Lipscomb, VP, Membership Services

Association for the professional advancement of African Americans and other minorities in in-

formation technology and related STEM industries.
Founded in 1975

5234 Online Audiovisual Catalogers

Home Page: www.olacinc.org
RSS

Kristi Bergland, President
Emily Creo, Vice President/Presidnet Elect
Nicole Smeltekop, Secretary
Jennifer Eustis, Treasurer/Membership Coordinator
Laura McElfresh, Newsletter Editor

To establish and maintain a group that could speak for catalogers of audiovisual materials. Provides a means for exchange of information, continuing education, and communication among catalogers of audiovisual materials and with the Library of Congress. Maintaining a voice with the bibliographic utilities that speak for catalogers of audiovisual materials, works toward common understanding of AV cataloging practices and standards.
Founded in 1980

5235 Open Applications Group
PO Box 4897
Marietta, GA 30061-4897

404-402-1962
oagi.org

A not-for-profit open standards group building process-based XML standards for both B2B and A2A integration.
Founded in 1994

5236 OpenAI
San Francisco, CA

Home Page: openai.com
Facebook, Twitter

Greg Brockman, Chair & CTO
Ilya Sutskever, Chief Scientist
Research organization dedicated to maintaining Artificial Intelligence as a benefit to humanity.

5237 Optical Society of America
2010 Massachusetts Avenue NW
Washington, DC 20036

202-223-8130; Fax: 202-223-1096
info@osa.org
www.osa.org
Facebook, Twitter, LinkedIn, YouTube

Elizabeth A. Rogan, CEO
Elizabeth Nolan, Chief Publishing Officer
Sean Bagshaw, COO/CIO
Suzanne Ffolkes, Chief Communications Officer
Genaro Montanez, Chief Employee/Membership Officer

The Optical Society of America (OSA) was organized to increase and diffuse the knowledge of optics, pure and applied; to promote the common interests of investigators of optical problems, of designers and of users of optical apparatus of all kinds; and to encourage cooperation among them. The purposes of the Society are scientific, technical and educational.
20K Members
Founded in 1916

5238 Partnership on AI
115 Sansome Street
Suite 1200
San Francisco, CA 94104

Home Page: www.partnershiponai.org
Facebook, Twitter

Terah Lyons, Founding Executive Director
Samir Goswami, Chief Operating Officer
Sasha Ramsaw, Human Resources Manager
Peter Lo, Senior Communications Manager
Hudson Hongo, Writer/Editor

Seeks to advance the understanding of AI technologies including machine perception, learning, and automated reasoning for the benefit of humanity.

5239 Personal Computer Memory Card International Association
2635 N 1st St
Suite 218
San Jose, CA 95134-2048

408-433-2273; Fax: 408-433-9558
www.pcmcia.org
Facebook

Patrick Maher, Executive Director
Ken Stufflebeam, President
Brian Ikeya, Secretary
Jim Koser, Treasurer

Created to establish standards for Integrated Circuit cards and to promote interchangeability among mobile computers where ruggedness, low power, and small size were critical.
200+ Members
Founded in 1989

5240 Polar Microsystems
Po Box 403
Huntingdon Valley, PA 19006

215-676-1590; Fax: 215-676-1596
www.polarmicro.com

Doug C Baer, Senior Systems Engineer

Provides consulting services that enable our clients to advance their businesses through full utilization of the Apple Macintosh hardware and software platform.

5241 Portable Computer and Communications Association
PO Box 680
Hood River, OR 97031

541-490-5140; Fax: 413-410-8447

Peter Rysavy, Executive Director

Represents firms, organizations and individuals interested in mobile communications. PCCA publishes information, standards, software and other materials.
Cost: $100.00
75 Members
Frequency: Individual Membership Fee
Founded in 1992

5242 Society For Modeling Simulation International
11315 Rancho Bernardo Road
Suite 139
San Diego, CA 92127

858-277-3888; Fax: 858-277-3930
scs@scs.org
www.scs.org
Facebook, LinkedIn

Oletha Darensburg, Executive Director
Carmen Ramirez, Program Assistant
Vicki Pate, Publications Manager & Editor

The only technical Society dedicated to advancing the use of modeling & simulation to solve real-world problems. SCS is the principal technical society devoted to the advancement of simulation and allied computer arts in all fields.
Cost: $55.00
Frequency: Regular Membership Dues
Founded in 1952

5243 Society for Imaging Science and Technology
7003 Kilworh Lane
Springfield, VA 22151

703-642-9090; Fax: 703-642-9094
info@imaging.org
www.imaging.org

Suzanne Grinnan, Executive Director
Marion Zoretich, Conference Program Manager
Katrina Bird, Publications Manager
Roberta Morehouse, Communications & Marketing Manager
Jennifer O'Brien, Special Projects & Website Manager

To keep members aware of the latest scientific and technological developments in the field of imaging through conferences, journals and other publications. To focus on imaging in all its aspects, with particular emphasis on silver halide, digital printing, electronic imaging, photofinishing, image preservation, image assessment, pre-press technologies and hybrid imaging systems.
2000+ Members
Founded in 1947

5244 Society for Information Display
San Jose, CA

office@sid.org
www.sid.org
Facebook, Twitter, LinkedIn, YouTube

Takatoshi Tsujimura, President
John Kymissis, Treasurer
Hrank (Qun) Yan, Secretary

Representing the international and local display communities. Offers opportunites to network, recieve information and publications and news about trade shows.
6000 Members
Founded in 1962

5245 Society for Materials Engineers and Scientists
3440 E University Drive
Phoenix, AZ 85034-7200

602-470-5700
general.inquiries@asm.com
www.asm.com
Twitter

Chuck D del Prado, CEO
Peter A.M. van Bommel, CFO

A leading supplier of semiconductor process equipment in both front and back end markets. The Company possesses a strong technological base, state-of-the-art manufacturing facilities, a competent and qualified workforce and a highly trained, strategically distributed support network.
Founded in 1968

5246 Society of Manufacturing Engineers
1000 Town Center
Suite 1910
Southfield, MI 48075

313-425-3000
service@sme.org
www.sme.org
Facebook, Twitter, LinkedIn, YouTube, Google+, Instagram

Sandra L. Bouckley, Executive Director & CEO
Craig Connop, Chief Financial Officer
Steve Prahalis, Chief Operating Officer
Erica Ciupak, Information Technology
Debbie Clark, Governance

The organization serves its members and others in the international manufacturing community by identifying, evaluating and explaining the adop-

tion and integration of emerging information technologies to create business value.
65K Members
Founded in 1932

5247 **Software Engineering Institute**
4500 Fifth Avenue
Pittsburgh, PA 15213-2612

412-268-5800
www.sei.cmu.edu
Facebook, Twitter, LinkedIn, YouTube

Paul D. Nielsen, Director & CEO
David Thompson, Deputy Director & COO
Tom Longstaff, Chief Technology Officer
Heidi Magnelia, Chief Financial Officer
Mary Catherine Ward, Chief Strategy Officer

A federally funded research and development center sponsored by the U.S. Department of Defense through the Office of the Under Secretary of Defense for Acquisition, Technology, and Logistics. Supports all those engineers involved in the software industry.
Founded in 1984

5248 **Software Management Network**
55 Madison Avenue
STE400
Morristown, CA 07960

973-285-3264; Fax: 973-538-0503
www.softwaremanagement.com

Nicholas Zvegintzov, President/Chief Technical Officer
Judith Marx Golub, VP/CFO

A publishing, consulting, and training group that serves professional software teams responsible for working, installed software systems. Its unique mission is to make available the most effective resources for managing active software.
Founded in 1996

5249 **The App Association**
1401 K Street NW
Suite 501
Washington, DC 20005

202-331-2130; Fax: 202-331-2139
actpress@actonline.org
actonline.org
Facebook, Twitter, LinkedIn, Instagram, Tumblr

Morgan Reed, President
Mike Sax, Founder & Chair
Chelsea Thomas, Executive Director
Ren, Adam, Chief Financial Officer
Alex Cooke, Director of Membership

The App Association represents app makers and connected device companies in the mobile economy across the US. The App Association is the leading industry resource on market strategy, regulated industries, privacy, and security.
5000 Members
Founded in 1998

5250 **UniForum Association**
Annapolis, MD

410-715-9500
800-333-8649; Fax: 240-465-0207
afedder@uniforum.org
www.uniforum.org

Alan Fedder, President
Deborah Murray, Managing Director & VP

Professional association for end users, developers and vendors. Promotes and exchanges information about the practices and benefits of open technologies and related hardware, software, applications and standards.
Founded in 1981

5251 **Vmebus International Trade Association**
9100 Paseo del Vita
Oklahoma City, OK 73131

info@vita.com
www.vita.com
Facebook, Twitter, LinkedIn

Jerry Gipper, Executive Director
Jing Kwok, Technical Director
Ray Alderman, Chairman of the Board

Association for manufacturers of microcomputer boards, hardware, software, military products, controllers, bus interfaces and other accessories compatible with VMEbus architecture.
150 Members
Frequency: Regular Membership Fee
Founded in 1981

Newsletters

5252 **AAR Newsletter**
School of Information Technology & Engineering
University of Ottawa
800 King Edward Avenue
Ottawa, Canada

613-562-5738; Fax: 613-562-5664
pieper@mcs.anl.gov
www-unix.mcs.anl.gov

Gail W Pieper, Editor
Mary Dzielski, Secretary
Janet Werner, Executive Secretary

Represents research notes and problem sets, discusses software advances and announces conferences and workshops.
Frequency: Quarterly

5253 **ACT-IAC Innovation Newsletter**
American Council for Technology
3040 Williams Drive
Suite 500
Fairfax, VA 22031

703-208-4800; Fax: 703-208-4805
act-iac@actiac.org
www.actiac.org

David M. Wennergren, Chief Executive Officer

The official newsletter for members of ACT-IAC.
Frequency: Monthly

5254 **ADAIC News**
Ada Information Clearinghouse
201 ILR Extension Building
Cornell University
Ithaca, NY 14853-3901

607-255-2763
800-949-4232
northeastada@cornell.edu
www.northeastada.org

Susan Carlson, Publisher
Lorrie Fessenden, Administrative Assistant

Information on Ada-an internationally standardized, general purpose computer language used in a variety of applications includes news of the Ada community.
Circulation: 20,000
Founded in 2001

5255 **AEC Automation Newsletter**
Technology Automation Services
PO Box 3593
Englewood, CO 80155-3593

303-770-1728; Fax: 303-770-3660
www.aec-me.com

Jeff Rowe, Editor
David Weisberg, Circulation Director
Randall S Newton, Editor-In-Chief
W Bradley Holtz, Group Publisher
Joel N Orr, Senior Editor

Reports on computer hardware and software issues relevant to architectural design, civil engineering, structural design, process plant design and geographic information management. Includes articles on software developments, new computer hardware, business issues, operating systems, application software, networking and technology developments.
Cost: $235.00
16 Pages
Frequency: Monthly
Founded in 1977
Printed in one color on matte stock

5256 **AI Interactions**
Academy of International Business
Michigan State University
7 Eppley Center
East Lansing, MI 48824-1121

517-432-4336; Fax: 517-432-1009
ciber@msu.edu
aib.msu.edu

G Tomas M Hult, Executive Secretary
Tunga Kiyak, Managing Director
Irem Kiyak, Treasurer

Calls for papers, meeting notices and membership news of interest to professors of international business around the world.
Circulation: 3000
Mailing list available for rent: 3000 names at $250 per M

5257 **AI Matters**
ACM SIGAI
1601 Broadway
10th Floor
New York, NY 10019-7434

212-869-7440
800-342-6626; Fax: 212-944-1318
acmhelp@acm.org
sigai.acm.org

Amy McGovern, Editor-in-Chief
Iolanda Leite, Editor-in-Chief

Official newsletter of the ACM Special Interest Group on Artificial Intelligence.
Frequency: Quarterly

5258 **AICan Bulletin**
CIFAR, MaRS Centre, West Tower
661 University Avenue
Suite 505
Toronto, ON M5G 1M1

416-971-4251
www.cifar.ca

Alan Bernstein, President & CEO

Newsletter of CIFAR, with new developments in Artificial Intelligence.
Frequency: Bi-Monthly

5259 **AIMatters**
AIM Global
One Landmark North, 20399 Route 19
Suite 203
Cranberry Township, PA 16066

724-934-4470; Fax: 724-934-4495
info@aimglobal.org
www.aimglobal.org
Facebook, Twitter, LinkedIn

Chuck Evanhoe, President & CEO
Cynthia Troup, Communciations & Marekting

Topics include AIDC, RFID, NFC, RTLS, Internet of Things, and mobile computing.
900+ Members
Frequency: Quarterly
Founded in 1972
Mailing list available for rent

5260 **Acronyms**
Computer Laboratory Michigan State University
40F Computer Ctr
East Lansing, MI 48824-1042
517-355-3600; Fax: 517-355-5176
Linda Dunn, Publisher
A listing of procedures, policies, hardware and software for computer users.
Frequency: Quarterly

5261 **Advanced Office Technologies Report**
DataTrends Publications
Po Box 4460
Leesburg, VA 20177-8541
703-779-0574
800-766-8130; Fax: 703-779-2267
info@stemcellresearchnews.com
www.stemcellresearchnews.com
Paul G Ochs, Owner
Offers information on products, technological breakthroughs and industry developments in office automation technology.
Frequency: Full-text

5262 **Alpha Forum**
Pinnacle Publishing
316 N Michigan Avenue
Suite 300
Chicago, IL 60601
312-272-2401
800-493-4867; Fax: 312-960-4106
pinpub@ragan.com
www.pinpub.com
Brent Smith, Publisher
David Stevenson, Editor
Technical newsletter for application developers and users. Hands-on articles with specific usage and programming techniques, tips and product updates.
16 Pages
Frequency: Monthly
Circulation: 8000
Founded in 1990
Mailing list available for rent
Printed in 2 colors on matte stock

5263 **Applications Software**
Thomson Media
1 State St
27th Floor
New York, NY 10004-1481
212-825-8445; Fax: 212-843-9600
James Malkin, President/CEO
William Johnson, CFO
General business management and word processing, reference services, custom services and CD-ROM services.
Frequency: Monthly

5264 **Artificial Intelligence Letter**
Kluwer Academic Publishers
101 Philip Drive
Norwell, MA 02061-1677
781-871-6600; Fax: 781-871-6528
Masoud Yazdani, Publisher
Provides a forum for the work of researchers and application developers from artificial intelligence, cognitive science and related disciplines.
Circulation: 625

5265 **Bits and Bytes Review**
Bits and Bytes Computer Resources
623 Iowa Ave
Whitefish, MT 59937-2336
406-862-7280
800-361-7280; Fax: 406-862-1124
John J Hughes, Owner
Resources and products for the academic field.
Cost: $56.90
Frequency: Monthly

5266 **Branch Automation News**
Phillips Publishing
7811 Montrose Road
Potomac, MD 20854
301-340-2100
feedback@healthydirections.com
www.healthydirections.com
Strategies for planning, implementing and managing bank technology.
Cost: $495.00
Circulation: 1000
Founded in 1974
Mailing list available for rent: 30342 names at $125 per M
Printed in 2 colors on matte stock

5267 **Business Computer Report**
Guidera Publishing Corporation
3 Myrtle Bank Road
Hilton Head Island, SC 29926-1809
Lawrence C Oakley, Editor
Hands-on review of business related software, as well as hardware, primarily for the PC world (as opposed to the MAC World). Readers are primarily owners of small to medium-sized businesses.
Cost: $95.00
8 Pages
Frequency: Monthly
Circulation: 125,000
Printed in one color on matte stock

5268 **Business Software News**
110 N Bell Avenue
Suite 300
Shawnee, OK 74801-6967
405-275-3100; Fax: 405-275-3101
www.techradar.com/news/software/business-software
Shari Bodger, Publisher
Melody Wrinkle, Editor
Shari Bodger, Marketing Manager
Offers updated information on computer software, marketing and technology news. Columnists address networks, sales and management with every issue including independent, comparative software reviews.
Cost: $40.00
8 Pages
Circulation: 1000
Founded in 1991
Printed in 4 colors on matte stock

5269 **C/C & Users Journal**
Miller Freeman Publications
2800 Campus Drive
San Mateo, CA 94403
650-513-4300
800-365-1364; Fax: 650-513-4601
www.cuj.com
Peter Westerman, Publisher
Jon Erickson, Editorial Director
Jessica Marty, Director of Marketing
Amy Stephens, Managing Editor
Information for intermediate and advanced C and C++ programmers. Includes programming techniques, tutorials and software reviews.
Cost: $29.95
Frequency: Monthly
Circulation: 39,048
Founded in 1988

5270 **C/Net News.Com**
CNET
100 Pine St
Suite 1775
San Francisco, CA 94111-5127
415-409-8900; Fax: 415-395-9254
www.ccolaw.com
Therese Cannata, Partner
John Morris, Editor
Christina Koukkos, Managing Editor
Provides information for high end audiences in the market for tech news, including the IS community, the technology business itself and the financial community.
Frequency: Daily
Founded in 1992

5271 **COM-SAC: Computer Security, Auditing & Controls-Quarterly**
Management Advisory Services & Publications
PO Box 81151
Wellesley Hills, MA 02481-0001
781-235-2895; Fax: 781-235-5446
info@masp.com
www.masp.com
A quarterly journal of in-depth tutorials in computer security, auditing and Corporate and IT Governance plus the most comprehensive digest service of all publications in the above fields.
Cost: $70.00
8 Pages
Founded in 1972
Mailing list available for rent
Printed in 2 colors on matte stock

5272 **COMDEX Show Daily**
Key 3 Media Group
795 Folsom Street
6th Floor
San Francisco, CA 94107-1243
415-905-2300; Fax: 415-905-2329
www.medialiveinternational.com
Sean Cassidy, Marketing Manager
Robert Priest-Heck, President/CEO
Tabloid newspaper of computer related exhibits.
Frequency: Daily
Circulation: 3445

5273 **CPA Technology Advisor**
Harcourt Brace Professional Publishing
9720 Carroll Centre Rd
Suite 1900
San Diego, CA 92126-4551
858-271-7390
800-831-7799
www.hbpp.com
Bruce Ta, Owner
Frank Peterson, Editor
Concise unbiased recommendations on hardware and software for CPA's.
Cost: $19.00

5274 **Client/Server Economics Letter**
Computer Economics
2082 Business Center Drive
Suite 240
Irvine, CA 92612
949-831-8700; Fax: 949-442-7688
www.computereconomics.com
Frank Scavo, President
Dan Husiak, VP
Economic look at the client/server revolution. Provides critical economic data on costs and risks of client/server computing, backed up with research and presentation-quality graphs and tables. Provides the information you need to make sound business decisions.
Cost: $395.00
Frequency: Daily
Founded in 1978

5275 **Comp-U-Fax Computer Trends Newsletter**
Microcomputers Software and Consulting
28 S 12th Avenue
Mount Vernon, NY 10550-2913
Bob James, Publisher
Corporate information resource newsletter.

5276 **Computer Aided Design Report**
CAD/CAM Publishing
7100 N Broadway
Suite 2-P
Denver, CO 80221
303-482-2813; Fax: 303-484-3610
www.cadcamnet.com
Randall Newton, Editor
Uses of computers by engineers in the manufacturing trades.
Cost: $195.00

5277 **Computer Architecture**
IEEE Computer Society
1730 Massachusetts Avenue NW
Washington, DC 20036-1992
202-371-1013; Fax: 202-728-9614
Henry Ayling, Publisher
Lee Blue, Production Manager
Current trends in computer networks, hardware description languages, performance.
Circulation: 2303

5278 **Computer Business**
Round Table Association SAB
5340 W 57th Street
Los Angeles, CA 90056-1339
310-649-2846
A Hassan, Publisher/Editor
J Hassan, Circulation Manager
Best computer/communications articles of previous month, briefly abstracted.
Cost: $20.00

5279 **Computer Economics Report**
Computer Economics
2082 Business Center Drive
Suite 240
Irvine, CA 92612
949-831-8700; Fax: 949-442-7688
www.computereconomics.com
Frank Scavo, President
Dan Husiak, VP
Written from an end-user perspective, this monthly newsletter provides analyses of new IBM technologies, plus acquisition and financial management strategies. Regular features include cost comparisons, price/performance analysis, new product forecasts, and evaluations of acquisition techniques for medium and large computer systems.
Cost: $595.00
Frequency: Monthly
Founded in 1978

5280 **Computer Industry Report**
International Data Corporation
5 Speen Street
Framingham, MA 01701
508-872-8200
leads@idc.com
www.idc.com/
Kirk Campbell, President/CEO
Research and analysis of the computer processing industry.
Founded in 1964

5281 **Computer Integrated Manufacture and Engineering**
Lionheart Publishing
2555 Cumberland Pkwy Se
Suite 299
Atlanta, GA 30339-3921
770-432-2551; Fax: 770-432-6969
Explores cutting edge developments in manufacturing systems operation management.
Circulation: 24,000

5282 **Computer Modeling and Simulation in Engineering**
Sage Science Press
2455 Teller Rd
Newbury Park, CA 91320-2234
805-499-9774
800-818-7243; Fax: 805-499-0871
info@sagepub.com
www.sagepub.com
Blaise R Simqu, CEO/President
Publishes application-oriented papers that utilize computer modeling and simulation techniques to understand and resolve industrial problems or processes that are of immediate and contemporary interest.
Frequency: Monthly

5283 **Computer Protocols**
Worldwide Videotex
PO Box 3273
Boynton Beach, FL 33424-3273
561-738-2276
markedit@juno.com
www.wvpubs.com
Mark Wright, Editor/President
Linda Dera, Marketing Manager
Linda Dera, Circulation Manager
Covers news and developments of bridges, gateway and LAN. Coverage also provided on the development of internal protocols.
Cost: $165.00
Frequency: Monthly
Circulation: 30000
Founded in 1981

5284 **Computer Reseller News**
CMP Publications
One Jericho Plaza
Jericho, NY 11753-1680
516-562-5000; Fax: 516-562-7243
shadowram@mcimail.com
www.crn.com
John Russell, Publisher
Computer news for resellers and distributors.

5285 **Computer and Communications Buyer**
Technology News of America Company
PO Box 20008
New York, NY 10025-1510
212-222-1123
www.eintelligence.com
Annotated statistical reports on capital equipment. $450.00 outside of United States.
Cost: $395.00
8 Pages
Frequency: Monthly
ISSN: 1042-4296
Founded in 1984
Mailing list available for rent

5286 **Computer and Computer Management News and Developments**
Management Advisory Services & Publications
PO Box 81151
Wellesley Hills, MA 02481-0001
781-235-2895; Fax: 781-235-5446
info@masp.com
www.masp.com
Newsletter aimed at the management level of the computer industry.

5287 **Computers & Security**
Elsevier Science
6277 Sea Harbor Drive
Orlando, FL 32887
407-345-4020
877-839-7126; Fax: 407-363-1354
usjcs@elsevier.com
www.elsevier.com
Andrew Fletcher, Publisher
E Schultz, CEO/President
Ann Dudley, Circulation Manager
Carl Lampert, Editor
International newsletter for the management of computer and information security.
Circulation: 1500

5288 **Computers, Foodservice and You**
Mike Pappas
Po Box 338
Raton, NM 87740-0338
575-445-9811; Fax: 575-445-3080
Mike Pappas, Owner
A newsletter focusing on computers for the hospitality industry.
Cost: $119.00
16 Pages
Frequency: Bi-Monthly
Circulation: 450
Printed in one color on matte stock

5289 **DM Direct**
220 Regency Court
Suite 210
Brookfield, WI 53045
262-784-0444; Fax: 262-782-9489
Tony Carrini, Associate Publisher
In this e-mail newsletter you will find articles, online columnists, news and industry events exclusive to you, the online reader. Our goal is to ensure that DM Direct provides the information you need to compete in the business intelligence, data warehousing and analytics marketplace.

5290 **DP Budget**
Computer Economics
2082 Business Center Drive
Suite 240
Irvine, CA 92612
949-831-8700; Fax: 949-442-7688
www.computereconomics.com
Frank Scavo, President
Dan Husiak, VP
Report analyzing DP expenses, salary issues and acquisition costs. Focuses on increasing productivity and improving the return on your DP investment.
Cost: $495.00
Frequency: Monthly

5291 **DPFN**
Directory & Database Publishers Forum & Network
352 Seventh Avenue
New York, NY 10001-546
212-643-5458
845-358-8034
www.dpfn.com
Barry Lee, Membership Chair
Jeff Fandl, President

Contains events, seminar information, publishers story, industry snapshots, and news pertaining to the industry. Members are large and small directory publishers, vendors to the trade and consultants. Provides networking opportunities and exposure to industry experts through their meetings and workshops.
Founded in 1990
Printed in on matte stock

5292 **Data Channels**
Phillips Publishing
7811 Montrose Road
Potomac, MD 20854

301-340-2100
feedback@healthydirections.com
www.healthydirections.com

Source of intelligence for executives making data communications decisions. Accepts advertising.
Cost: $397.00
9 Pages

5293 **Data Security Management**
Auerbach Publications
535 5th Avenue
Room 806
New York, NY 10017-3610

800-737-8034
www.auerbach-publications.com

Rich O'Hanley, Editor

Technical and management information for security managers, networks and systems administrators and data center managers.
Cost: $495.00
Frequency: Bi-Monthly
Circulation: 1,500
ISSN: 1096-7907
Printed in on matte stock

5294 **Dental Computer Newsletter**
Andent
1000 N Avenue
Waukegan, IL 60085

847-223-5077
info@andent.net
www.andent.net

For and by an international group of Dentists, Physicians and allied health professionals interested in computers. Emphasis is on the practical use of all brands of computers for the professional office.
Cost: $25.00
Frequency: Quarterly
Circulation: 3100

5295 **Digital Directions Report**
Computer Economics
2082 Business Center Drive
Suite 240
Irvine, CA 92612

949-831-8700; Fax: 949-442-7688
www.computereconomics.com

Frank Scavo, President

Provides details on the financial ramifications of future DEC products. The information is critical for decision makers involved with cost-control, strategy planning and new product analysis.
Cost: $525.00
Frequency: Monthly

5296 **Directory of Top Computer Executives**
Applied Computer Research
Po Box 41730
Phoenix, AZ 85080

602-216-9100
800-234-2227; Fax: 602-548-4800
www.acrhq.com

Computer performance and management.
Cost: $370.00
Circulation: 1000
ISSN: 0193-9920
Founded in 1972
Printed in one color on matte stock

5297 **Document Imaging Report**
Corry Publishing
5539 Peach Street
Erie, PA 16509

814-380-0025; Fax: 814-864-2037
corrypub@corrypub.com
www.corrypub.com

john Coiston, Publisher
Terry Peterson, CEO
Micole Hykes, Editor
Karrie Boocious, Marketing
Melinda Fadden, Circulation Manager

Timely and actionable information on electronic imaging applications, products and user implementation.
Frequency: Monthly
Circulation: 43000

5298 **Dvorak Developments**
Freelance Communications
PO Box 666
Ridgway, CO 81432

970-626-2255

Randy Cassingham, Publisher

Promotes the use of the Dvorak keyboard for typewriters and computers. Dvorak is more ergonomic than the common Qwerty keyboard. Accepts advertising.
8 Pages

5299 **E-News**
Patricia Seybold Group
Po Box 240565
Boston, MA 02129

617-742-5200
800-826-2424; Fax: 617-742-1028
feedback@psgroup.com
www.psgroup.com

Patricia Seybold, Founder/CEO

E-mail newsletter includes perspectives on the e-commerce industry, research and upcoming events.

5300 **EDI News**
Phillips Publishing
7811 Montrose Road
Potomac, MD 20854

301-340-2100
feedback@healthydirections.com
www.healthydirections.com

Electronic data interchange marketplace information.
Cost: $397.00
9 Pages

5301 **Education Technology News**
Business Publishers
2222 Sedwick Dr
Suite 101
Durham, NC 27713

800-223-8720; Fax: 800-508-2592
custserv@bpinews.com
www.bpinews.com

Information on educational hardware and software, trends in computer-aided teaching and computer uses in the classroom.
Cost: $217.00
Circulation: 500
Founded in 1963

5302 **Electronic Education Report**
Simba Information
60 Long Ridge Rd
Suite 300
Stamford, CT 06902-1841

203-325-8193
888-297-4622; Fax: 203-325-8915
info@simbanet.com
www.simbanet.com

Linda Kopp, Publisher

News and analysis from a business perspective on software, multimedia/CD-ROM, videodisc, distance learning, Internet/online services and educational videocassettes.
Cost: $625.00
Founded in 1989

5303 **Electronic Marketing News**
Software Assistance International
PO Box 750
Morris Plains, NJ 07950-0750

973-644-0022; Fax: 973-539-3253

George Papov, Editor

Supplier of electronic catalogs to business and industries.
Circulation: 6,000

5304 **End-User Computing Management**
Auerbach Publications
535 5th Avenue
Room 806
New York, NY 10017-3610

800-737-8034; Fax: 212-297-9176

Kim Hovan Kelly, Publisher

Technical and mangement information.
Cost: $495.00
Frequency: BiWeekly
Circulation: 1,000

5305 **Federal Computer Week**
101Communications
3141 Fairview Park Drive
#777
Falls Church, VA 22042-4507

703-876-5100; Fax: 703-876-5126
www.fcw.com

Anne Armstrong, Publisher
Jeff Calore, General Manager

The Federal Computer Week provides practical news, analysis and insight on how to buy, build and manage technology in government.
Circulation: 93000

5306 **Forestry Computer Applications**
Michaelsen's Micro Magic Publishers
PO Box 7332
Fredericksburg, VA 22404-7332
Nancy Michaelsen, Publisher

Offers news and information on computers and electronics used in the forestry services industry, including manufacturing, building, construction and architecture.
Cost: $29.95

5307 **Frontline**
Computer Security Institute
600 Harrison Street
San Francisco, CA 94107

415-947-6320; Fax: 818-487-4550

Robert Richardson, Editorial Director
Chris Keating, Director

This quarterly newsletter is to improve the security practices of your entire organization to increase end-user awareness of critical security

topics pertaining to them.
Cost: $1860.00
4 Pages
Frequency: Annual Subscription

5308 **GCN Tech Edition**
Post Newsweek Tech Media
10 G St Ne
Suite 500
Washington, DC 20002-4228

202-772-2500
866-447-6864; Fax: 202-772-2511
www.gcn.com

David Greene, President
Tom Temin, Editor-in-Chief
Kirstin Crane, Marketing Manager
Bar Blaskowsky, Circulation Manager

Evaluates performance, cost and applications of hardware, software, peripheral and communication products available to government agencies and businesses.
Cost: $95.00
Circulation: 87500
Founded in 1998
Printed in on glossy stock

5309 **Government Computer News**
Reed Business Information
2000 Clearwater Dr
Oak Brook, IL 60523-8809

630-574-0825; Fax: 630-288-8781
www.reedbusiness.com

Jeff Greisch, President

The national newspaper of government computing.
Cost: $53.00
55 Pages
Frequency: Monthly
Founded in 1982

5310 **Graphic Communications Today**
IDEA Alliance
1421 Prince Street
Suite 230
Alexandria, VA 22314-2805

703-837-1070; Fax: 703-837-1072
www.idealliance.org

Alan Kotok, Editor
David Steinhardt, CEO

Electronic commerce, direct marketing, printing and paper aspects, and graphics updates.
Frequency: Daily
Circulation: 200
Founded in 1966

5311 **HIS Insider**
United Communications Group
11300 Rockville Pike
Street 1100
Rockville, MD 20852-3030

301-287-2700; Fax: 301-816-8945
www.ucg.com

Benny Dicecca, President

News and reports on new hospital and clinical information system technologies, upcoming vendor merger acquisitions, analyses of telecommunicaiton systems used in health care.
Cost: $427.00
Frequency: Weekly
Founded in 1977

5312 **IN SYNC Magazine**
Agate Publishing
21 West 26th Street
New York, NY 10010

847-475-4457
seibold@agatepublishing.com
www.agatepublishing.com

Doug Seibold

News and how-to for distributed and cooperative applications. Particularly how to link multiple computer systems to gain best advantage from each.
Cost: $8.00
Circulation: 1000

5313 **IS Budget**
Computer Economics
2082 Business Center
Dr. Ste 240
Irvine, CA 92612

949-831-8700; Fax: 949-442-7688
www.computereconomics.com

Frank Scavo, President
Dan Husiak, VP

Tackles today's toughest IS budgeting issues head-on with exhaustively researched line-item cost comparisons by type of industry, installation size, company revenue and type of expenditure. Regular features include MIS spending comparisons, analyses of budgeting issues and inside information on vendor discounts.
Cost: $495.00
Frequency: Monthly
Founded in 1978

5314 **Independent Computer Consultants Newsletter**
Independent Computer Consultants Association
11131 S Towne Sq
Suite F
St Louis, MO 63123-7817

314-892-1675; Fax: 314-487-1345

Joyce Burkard, Executive Director

Promotes professional standards in the industry. Conducts educational programs and maintains local chapters in many major cities. Available to members only.
Circulation: 1000
Founded in 1976
Mailing list available for rent: 1200 names at $500 per M
Printed in 2 colors

5315 **Inside the Internet**
Cobb Group
115 6th Ave
Dayton, KY 41074-1111

859-291-1146
800-733-2040; Fax: 859-655-2482
tomherman@cobbinc.com
www.cobbinc.com

Tom Herman, President
Adam Browning, Production Manager

Practical advice and instructions for Internet users.

5316 **Intelligence: The Future of Computing**
Intelligence
PO Box 20008
New York, NY 10025-1510

212-222-1123
800-638-7257
www.eintelligence.com

Edward Rosenfeld, Editor/Publisher

Provides coverage of advanced computing: neutral networks, AI, genetic algorithms, fuzzy systems, wavelets, et. al., and the Net, the Web, Nanotechnologies quanteum, molecular and DNA computing.
Cost: $395.00
8 Pages
Frequency: Monthly
ISSN: 1042-4296
Founded in 1984
Printed in one color on matte stock

5317 **International Spectrum**
International Spectrum Magazine & Conferences
8956 Fox Drive
Suite 102
Thornton, CO 80260

720-259-1356; Fax: 603-250-0664
nathan@intl-spectrum.com
www.intl-spectrum.com

Nathan Rector, President
Monica Giobbi, Manager
Clif Oliver, Editor

Trade magazine for PICK/UNIX/DOS computer industry which covers hardware, software and peripherals. Company produces major trade show held annually in Southern California and regional exhibitions and conferences across the country.
88 Pages
Frequency: 6 issues/Yr
Circulation: 50,000
Founded in 1982
Mailing list available for rent: 80M names
Printed in 4 colors on glossy stock

5318 **Managing Human Resource Information Systems**
Institute of Management and Administration
1 Washington Park
Suite 1300
Newark, NJ 07102

212-244-0360; Fax: 973-622-0595
www.ioma.com

Covers management issues critical to building and maintaining state-of-the-art HRIS software, hardware, and Internet/intranet activities. It is intended to help control costs of HRIS, make better use of new technologies, migrate HRIS from mainframe, mini, and client/server systems.
Cost: $259.00
Frequency: Monthly
Circulation: 180000
Founded in 1982

5319 **Micro Publishing**
Cygnus Publishing
445 Broad Hollow Road
Melville, NY 11747

631-845-2700
800-308-6397; Fax: 631-845-2798

James Cavuoto, Publisher
Nancy Whelan, Advertising/Sales
Kenneth Spears, Production
Mark Erikson, Circulation Manager
Paul Bonaiuto, CFO

A newsletter for hardware and software vendors that examines the micro-based publishing systems market, including workstation publishing, printers, scanners, networks, technology and data-based publishing, production methods and page layout software. The editorials consists of microcomputer publishing product reviews, notes, and trend analysis, and new product announcements.
Cost: $295.00
10 Pages
Frequency: Monthly
Printed in on matte stock

5320 **Network Economics Letter**
Computer Economics
5841 Edison Place
Carlsbad, CA 92008-6500

760-438-8100
800-326-8100; Fax: 760-431-1126
www.computereconomics.com

Bruno Bassi, Publisher
Don Trevillian, Editor

Provides an executive overview for MIS and network professionals who are involved in network strategic planning and implementation. It covers such topics as comparative analysis of hardware and software systems, cost of ownership studies, analysis of emerging protocols and standards and cost-saving opportunities.
Cost: $395.00
Frequency: Monthly

5321 **News & Ideas**
CIFAR, MaRS Centre, West Tower
661 University Avenue
Suite 505
Toronto, ON M5G 1M1
416-971-4251
www.cifar.ca
Alan Bernstein, President & CEO
Newsletter of CIFAR, with association news, events, and new discoveries.

5322 **OSINetter Newsletter**
Architecture Technology Corporation
9977 Valley View Rd
Suite 300
Eden Prairie, MN 55344-3586
952-829-5864; Fax: 952-829-5871
info@atcorp.com
www.atcorp.com
Noel Schmidt, Executive VP
Covers products and company activity in the area of open systems interconnection.
Cost: $50.00
Founded in 1955

5323 **Official Memory News**
Phillips Publishing
7811 Montrose Road
Potomac, MD 20854
301-340-2100
feedback@healthydirections.com
www.healthydirections.com
Provides the latest news and analysis on OSI standards developments. Accepts advertising.
Cost: $497.00
9 Pages
Founded in 1974

5324 **Open Systems Economics Letter**
Computer Economics
2082 Business Center Drive
Suite 240
Irvine, CA 92612
949-831-8700; Fax: 949-442-7688
www.computereconomics.com/
Dan Husiak, Vo
Frank Scavo, President
Addresses the critical economic issues associated with the worldwide transformation to open systems. In a concise, monthly format, this report provides the information that you must have to successfully adopt an open systems strategy, manage your transition to open standards, and protect your corporate investment in new technology.
Cost: $395.00
Frequency: Monthly

5325 **Optical Memory News**
Phillips Publishing
7811 Montrose Road
Potomac, MD 20854
301-340-2100
feedback@healthydirections.com
www.healthydirections.com
Provides the latest news and analysis on the optical storage marketplace from vendor perspective.
Accepts advertising.
Cost: $397.00
9 Pages
Frequency: BiWeekly
Printed in one color on matte stock

5326 **Product Data Management Report**
CAD/CAM Publishing
7100 N Broadway
Suite 2-P
Denver, CO 80221
303-482-2813; Fax: 303-484-3610
www.cadcamnet.com
Randall Newton, Editor
Devoted to product data management software and systems that are used by major manufacturing firms to store, control, and distribute CAD and other engineering data.
Cost: $345.00

5327 **Public and Policy**
American Public Human Services Association
1133 19th St NW
Suite 400
Washington, DC 20036
202-682-0100; Fax: 202-204-0071
www.aphsa.org
Tracy Wareing, Executive Director
Frequency: Bimonthly

5328 **Rapid Prototyping Report**
CAD/CAM Publishing
2880 Stone Trail Dr
Bethesda, MD 20817-4556
240-425-4004; Fax: 301-365-4586
Geoff Smith-Moritz, Editor
L Wolf, Production Manager
Gives in-depth objective appraisals of strengths and weaknesses of rapid prototyping technology. Includes applications on how RP technology is used in the industry.
Cost: $295.00
Frequency: Monthly

5329 **Report on IBM**
DataTrends Publications
Po Box 4460
Leesburg, VA 20177-8541
703-779-0574; Fax: 703-779-2267
www.stemcellresearchnews.com
Paul G Ochs, Owner
For information technology professionals.
Cost: $495.00
Founded in 1983

5330 **Retail Price Week**
Personal Technology Research
63 Fountain Street
#400
Framingham, MA 01702-6262
508-875-5858
Casey Dworkin, Publisher
Product-specific advertising and pricing data on microcomputer software, perhipherals and desktop retail commodities.
Frequency: Weekly
Circulation: 300

5331 **Semiconductor Economics Report**
Relayer Group
8232 E Buckskin Trail
Scottsdale, AZ 85255-2132
Howard Dicken, Publisher
Economics in the microelectronics industry.

5332 **Small Business Systems**
Charles Moore Associates
277 Alexander Street
Suite 410
Rochester, NY 14607
585-325-5242; Fax: 585-325-5242
Charles Moore, Editor
Nancy Hannigan, Circulation Manager
Case histories which apply computers to solve small business problems.

5333 **Softletter**
Mercury Group
990 Washington Street
Suite 308 S
Dedham, MA 02026
781-518-8600
860-663-0552; Fax: 301-816-8945
customer@softletter.com
www.softletter.com
Merrill R Chapman, Publisher
Gail Wertheimer, Editor
Rick Chapman, Marketing Manager
Ruth Greenfield, Director
Trends in the microcomputer software industry.
Cost: $596.00
Frequency: Fortnightly
ISSN: 0882-3499
Founded in 1983
Printed in 2 colors

5334 **Softrader**
Amerasia Group
PO Box 53114
Indianapolis, IN 46253-0114
Ben Yanto, Publisher
Shareware public domain programs guide. Accepts advertising.
16 Pages
Frequency: BiWeekly

5335 **Software Economics Letter**
Computer Economics
5841 Edison Place
Carlsbad, CA 92008-6500
760-438-8100
800-326-8100; Fax: 760-431-1126
www.computereconomics.com
Bruno Bassi, Publisher
Don Trevillian, Editor
Devoted to management and cost control of software investments. Provides the corporate user and information systems communities with a concise analysis of software issues. Profiles the latest trends in software and software licensing and includes analysis of vendor policies and practices.
Cost: $395.00
Frequency: Daily

5336 **Step-By-Step Electronic Design**
Dynamic Graphics
6000 N Forest Park Drive
Peoria, IL 61614-3592
309-688-8851; Fax: 309-688-6579
www.dgi.com
Tom Biederbeck, Editor
Kris Elwell, Publisher
Alan Meckler, CEO/President
Mike Demilt, Marketing
Marcy Slane, Manager
For electronic designers, illustrators and prepress professionals, how-to articles with step-by-step techniques.
Cost: $36.00
Circulation: 24000
Founded in 1995

5337 **System Development**
Applied Computer Research

PO Box 41730
Phoenix, AZ 85080

602-216-9100
800-234-2227; Fax: 602-548-4800
www.acrhq.com

Philip Howard, Publisher
Allen Howard, CEO
Tara Saenz, Circulation Manager

Improvement ideas and techniques for software development.
Cost: $630.00
12 Pages
Frequency: Bi-annually
Founded in 1971
Mailing list available for rent: 20M names at $105 per M
Printed in one color on matte stock

5338 **Systems Reengineering Economics Letter**
Computer Economics
2082 Business Center Drive
Suite 240
Irvine, CA 92612

949-831-8700; Fax: 949-442-7688
www.computereconomics.com

Frank Scavo, President
Dan Husiak, VP

Economic look at the re-engineering explosion, delivering critical information on the methods, costs and risks of systems and business process re-engineering. Updates on the analyses, data, opinions, and case studies you need to make sound business decisions and capitalize on your re-engineering process.
Cost: $395.00
Frequency: Daily
Founded in 1978

5339 **TechTarget**
TechTarget
117 Kendrick St
Suite 800
Needham Heights, MA 02494-2728

781-657-1000
888-274-4111; Fax: 781-657-1100
info@techtarget.com
www.techtarget.com

Greg Strakosch, CEO
Don Hawk, President
Lisa Johnson, VP Marketing
Catherine Engelke, Director Public Relations

IBM iSeries focused media. The IBM e-Server iSeries (formerly the AS/400) is considered to be the world's most often used multi-user business computer. The installed base worldwide is huge and will get bigger, fueled by incresed Web development. The iSeries come with an integrated Web application server and all the tools needed to build internet, intranet, extranet, and e-commerce sites quickly and will figure promenently into IT strategy and implementation for years to come.
Frequency: Monthly
Founded in 1999

5340 **Technology Advertising & Branding Report**
Simba Information
60 Long Ridge Rd
Suite 300
Stamford, CT 06902-1841

203-325-8193
888-297-4622; Fax: 203-325-8915
info@simbanet.com
www.simbanet.com

Linda Kopp, Publisher

Offers news, statistics and analysis of advertising strategies in the technology industry. Provides competitive information on the advertising and marketing activities of computer hardware and software companies. Helps computer publishers target advertising sales by reporting the plans of computer advertisers. Shows computer advertisers how to get best buys.
Cost: $549.00
8 Pages

5341 **Techweek**
Metro States Media
1156 Aster Avenue
#B
Sunnyvale, CA 94086-6810

408-249-8300; Fax: 408-249-0727
www.techweek.com

John Leggett, Publisher

Provides articles for the local high technology industry programmers. Includes information about the internet, finances, job market, and new products for technology professionals.
Frequency: BiWeekly
Circulation: 100,000

5342 **The AIIM Blog**
Association for Information and Image Management
8403 Colesville Road
Suite 1100
Silver Spring, MD 20910

301-587-8202
800-477-2446; Fax: 301-587-2711
aiim@aiim.org
www.aiim.org

Peggy Winton, President & CEO
Georgina Clelland, Chief Operating Officer
June Ann Ewan, Director, Finance
Jesse Wilkins, Director, Professional Development

Provides recent industry news, trends, and practices regarding Intelligent Information Management.

5343 **The CAIAC Herald**
Canadian Artificial Intelligence Association
1515 St. Catherine Street W.
Montreal, QC H3G 2W1

514-848-2424
leila.kosseim@concordia.ca
www.caiac.ca

Leila Kosseim, President
Richard Khoury, Vice President
Xin Wang, Treasurer
Denilson Barbosa, Secretary

Official newsletter of the Canadian Artificial Intelligence Association, with new developments in artificial intelligence.

5344 **TidBITS**
TidBITS
50 Hickory Road
Ithaca, NY 14850

ace@tidbits.com
www.tidbits.com

Adam Engst, Publisher
Tonya Engst, Editor-in-Chief
Josh Centers, Managing Editor

Online newsletter and website, devoted to the person behind the most personal of personal computers, the Macintosh. TidBITS relates events and products to real life uses and concerns. New TidBITS issues go out every Monday night; breaking news and important updates appear on the website more frequently.
Frequency: Weekly
Circulation: 150000
Founded in 1990
Mailing list available for rent: 24,000 names

5345 **Wireless LAN**
Information Gatekeepers
1340 Soldiers Field Rd
Suite 3
Brighton, MA 02135-1000

617-782-5033
800-323-1088; Fax: 617-782-5735
info@igigroup.com
www.igigroup.com

Paul Polishuk, CEO
Cathey Mallen, Production Manager
Brian Mark, Newsletter Managing Editor
Bev Wilson, Managing Editor
Yesim Taskor, Controller

LAN technological trends and market opportunities.
Cost: $695.00
Frequency: Monthly
Founded in 1977

5346 **Work Process Improvement Today**
Recognition Technologies Users Association
75 Federal Street
Suite 901
Boston, MA 02110-1413

617-426-1167
800-99 -2974; Fax: 617-521-8675
www.tawpi.org

Dan Bllida, Editor
Debra Sanderson, Publisher
Frank Moran, Owner

Accepts advertising.
Cost: $60.00
Circulation: 10000

Magazines & Journals

5347 **2600 Magazine**
PO Box 752
Middle Island, NY 11953

631-751-2600; Fax: 631-474-2677
webmaster@2600.com
www.2600.com/

Emanuel Golstein, Editor

Written for computer hackers.
Cost: $20.00
Frequency: Quarterly
Founded in 1984

5348 **ACM QUEUE**
Association for Computing Machinery
1601 Broadway
10th Floor
New York, NY 10019-7434

212-869-7440
800-342-6626; Fax: 212-944-1318
acmhelp@acm.org
queue.acm.org

Jack Davidson, Co-Chair, Publications Board
Joseph A. Konstan, Co-Chair, Publications Board

Published by the Association for Computing Machinery.
Circulation: 25000
Founded in 1947

5349 **AFSM International Professional Journal and High-Technology Service Mgmt.**
AFSM International
11031 Via Frontera
Suite A
San Diego, CA 92127-1709

858-673-3055
800-333-9786; Fax: 239-275-0794

John Shoenewald, Executive Director
Jb Wood, President/Ceo

For trade association members.
Cost: $150.00
86 Pages
Frequency: Monthly
Circulation: 20000
Founded in 1975
Printed in 4 colors on glossy stock

5350 **AI Expert**
Miller Freeman Publications
2655 Seely Avenue
San Jose, CA 95134
408-943-1234; Fax: 408-943-0513
Regina Star Ridley, Editor
Practical applications of artificial intelligence in any field.
Cost: $37.00
42 Pages
Frequency: Monthly
Founded in 1986

5351 **AI Magazine**
Association for the Advancement of AT
2275 East Bayshore Road
Suite 160
Palo Alto, CA 94303
650-328-3123; Fax: 650-321-4457
www.aaai.org
David Leake, Editor Emeritus
Ashok Goel, Editor-In-Chief
Carol Hamilton, Executive Director
Quarterly issued magazine, available through AAAI membership. AI Magazine features articles regarding research in the field of artificial intelligence.
128 Pages
Frequency: Quarterly
Circulation: 7000
ISSN: 0738-4602
Founded in 1980
Printed in on matte stock

5352 **AMC Inroads**
Association for Computing Machinery
1601 Broadway
10th Floor
New York, NY 10019-7434
212-869-7440
800-342-6626; Fax: 212-944-1318
acmhelp@acm.org
dl.acm.org
Vick Hanson, Chief Executive Officer
Denis Doig, Senior Editor
Diana Crawford, Deputy Director
Scott Crawford, Director, Publications
Intended for professionals interested in advancing computing education in the world.
0 Pages

5353 **ASR News**
Voice Information Associates
P.O.Box 2861
Acton, MA 01720-6861
978-266-1966; Fax: 978-263-3461
www.asrnews.com
Walt Tetschner, Publisher and Editor
Developments in products, marketing, technology, and investments in the automatic speech recognition industry.
Cost: $345.00
Frequency: Monthly
Founded in 1990

5354 **Advanced Imaging**
Cygnus Publishing
3 Huntington Quadrangle
Suite 301N
Melville, NY 11747-3601
631-845-2700
800-308-6397; Fax: 631-845-2736
Dave Brambert, Publisher
Larry Adams, Editor-in-Chief
Paul Mackler, CEO
The only international magazine specifically designed to meet the needs of professionals using all forms of electronic imaging technologies. Offering monthly coverage of imaging application solutions for medical/diagnostic, industrial machine vision, government/security, and scientific imaging markets.
Frequency: Monthly
Circulation: 44009
Founded in 1966

5355 **Aixpert**
IBM Corporation
1133 Westchester Avenue
White Plains
New York, NY 10604-3406
914-423-3000; Fax: 866-722-9226
www.ibm.com
George Noren, Editor-in-Chief
Provides timely up-to-date technical material to help developers plot, develop, and enhance applications for IBM AIX products.
Frequency: Quarterly
Circulation: 10,000

5356 **Aldus Magazine**
Aldus Corporation
801 N 34th Street
Seattle, WA 98103-8882
Carla Noble, Publisher
Harry Edwards, Editor
Supports and educates graphics professionals using ALDUS software. Covers tips, tricks and how-to pointers for maximizing PageMaker, Freehand, PhotoStyler and Persuasion. Also covers trends in electronic publishing.
Cost: $ 24.00
68 Pages
Frequency: 8 per year
Circulation: 220,000
Founded in 1989

5357 **Algorithmica**
Springer Verlag
233 Spring St
New York, NY 10013-1578
212-460-1500; Fax: 212-460-1575
service@springer-ny.com
www.springer-ny.com
William Curtis, President
D T Lee, Managing Editor
Rubin Wang, Managing Editor
Provides an in-depth look into distributed computing, parellel processing, automated design, and software tools.
Cost: $1008.00
Frequency: Quarterly
Circulation: 1000
Founded in 1855

5358 **Analysis Solutions**
ConnectPress
2530 Camino Entrada
Santa Fe, NM 87505-4807
505-474-5000; Fax: 505-474-5001
www.isentia.com
Carolyn Mascarenas, Publisher
Design analysis and optimization for ANSYS technology users. Covers engineering simulation, acousitc analysis, model meshing, new products and case studies.
Cost: $90.00
Frequency: Quarterly
Circulation: 27,575

5359 **Application Development Trends**
600 Worcester Road
Suite 301
Framingham, MA 01702
508-875-6644; Fax: 508-875-6622
www.adtmag.com
Sheryl Katz, Publisher
Michael Alexander, Editorial-in-Chief
Tracy S. Cook, Marketing Director
Christina Schaller, Managing Editor
The number one information source on today's key application development options delivering a high powered, management-oriented editorial that covers the application development industry in greater depth and breadth than any other publication.
Frequency: Monthly
Circulation: 45000
Founded in 1998

5360 **Applied Computing Technologies**
9041 Executive Park Dr
Suite 222
Knoxville, TN 37923-4603
865-675-0508; Fax: 865-694-9096
Peyman Dehkordi, Owner

5361 **Applied Optics**
Optical Society of America
2010 Massachusetts Ave NW
Washington, DC 20036-1023
202-223-8130; Fax: 202-223-1096
info@osa.org
www.osapublishing.org
Ronald Driggers, Editor-in-Chief
Articles about applications-centered research in optics.
Frequency: 3x/mth
ISSN: 1559-128X

5362 **Automatic ID News**
Advanstar Communications
641 Lexington Ave
8th Floor
New York, NY 10022-4503
212-951-6600; Fax: 212-951-6793
info@advanstar.com
www.advanstar.com
Joseph Loggia, CEO
Information for decision-makers in all industries seeking definitive information about automatic data collection technology. The technology includes optical, magnetic, radio frequency and voice recognition systems and peripherals.
Frequency: Monthly
ISSN: 0890-9768

5363 **BAM Publications**
BAM Publications
3470 Buskirk Avenue
Pleasant Hill, CA 94523-4340
925-932-5900
Dennis Erokan, Editor
Provides regionally focused product and channel news to computer products and services.
Cost: $120.00
60 Pages
Frequency: Monthly
Founded in 1988

5364 **Better Channel**
ABCD: The Microcomputer Industry Association

450 E 22nd Street
Suite 230
Lombard, IL 60148-6158

630-268-1818; Fax: 630-268-1384

John Venator, Executive VP

A professional magazine that is exclusively dedicated to representing and serving all segments of the microcomputer industry. Accepts advertising.
Cost: $150.00
32 Pages
Frequency: Monthly

5365 **CADALYST**
Advanstar Communications
641 Lexington Ave
8th Floor
New York, NY 10022-4503

212-951-6600; Fax: 212-951-6793
info@advanstar.com
www.advanstar.com

Joseph Loggia, CEO

Expert coverage of the latest developments in auto CAD systems, their products and the various CAD applications.
Cost: $4.00
Frequency: Monthly
Circulation: 70000

5366 **CALICO Journal**
Computer Assited Language Instruction Consortium
Texas State University
214 Centennial Hall
San Marcos, TX 78666

512-245-1417; Fax: 512-245-9089
info@calico.org
calico.org

Bryan Smith, Editor
Ana Oskoz, Editor
Oksana Vorobel, Book Review Editor
Theresa Schenker, Learning Technology Reviews Editor

The official publication of the Computer Assisted Language Instruction Consortium (CALICO), this journal is devoted to the dissemination of information concerning the application of technology to language teaching and language learning.
Cost: $85.00
1983 Members
Frequency: 3x/Year
Circulation: 800
ISSN: 0742-7778

5367 **CASE Strategies**
Cutter Information Corporation
37 Broadway
Suite 1
Arlington, MA 02474-5500

781-648-1950; Fax: 781-648-1950
www.cutter.com

Verna Allee, Senior Consultant

Implementation strategies, reviews and case studies in areas of computer-aided systems engineering.
Cost: $295.00

5368 **CBT Solutions**
SB Communications
183 Whiting Street
#15
Hingham, MA 02043-3845

781-749-2151
www.cbtsolutions.com

Steve Blumberg, Publisher

Featured editorials include advanced technology in the past and future, interactive web programs, new methods to access and control information, and personal profiles.
Frequency: Bi-Monthly
Circulation: 15,000

5369 **CD-ROM Enduser**
Disc Company
6609 Rosecroft Pl
Falls Church, VA 22043-1828
Linda Helgerson, Editor

For people who use CD-ROM applications.
Cost: $3.00
Frequency: Monthly
Founded in 1989

5370 **CD-ROM Librarian**
Mecklermedia Corporation
20 Ketchum Street
Westport, CT 06880-5808

203-226-6967; Fax: 203-454-5840

Alan Meckler, Editor

A periodical intended for the library professional.
Cost: $80.00
Frequency: Monthly
Founded in 1986

5371 **CHANCE: New Directions for Statistics and Computing**
Springer Verlag
233 Spring St
New York, NY 10013-1578

212-460-1500; Fax: 212-460-1575
service@springer-ny.com
www.springer-ny.com

William Curtis, President
John E Rolph, Editor
Derk Haank, CEO
Peter Hendriks, President of Marketing
Rubin Wang, Managing Editor

Covers both statistics and computing. Designed for everyone who has an interest in the analysis of data. The informal style highlights and encourages sound statistical practice.
Cost: $7.00
Frequency: Monthly
Circulation: 4500
Founded in 1842

5372 **CRN**
UBM LLC
550 Cochituate Road
First Floor-West Wing, Suite 5
Framingham, MA 01701

508-416-1100
www.crn.com

Kelley Damore, VP/Editorial Director
Steven Burke, Editor
Jane O'Brien, Managing Editor

Delivers strategic information and useful business tools that Solution Providers and other Channel professionals
Cost: $89.00
Frequency: BiWeekly
Circulation: 95,072

5373 **Cadence**
Miller Freeman Publications
2655 Seely Avenue
San Jose, CA 95134

408-468-8603; Fax: 408-468-1902
info@gartner.com
www.gartner.com

Johanna Kleppe, Publisher
Kathleen Maher, Managing Editor
Michael Fister, CEO
Tom McCall, Senior Director Public Relations
Michael Bingle, Director

For users of Autocad - a construction/architecture program.
Cost: $6.00
Circulation: 72664

5374 **Catalyst**
Western Center for Microcomputers
1259 El Camino Real
#275
Menlo Park, CA 94025

650-855-8064

Sue Swezey, Editor
Robert Scott, Chief Information Officer

Reporting on both the increasing sophistication of technology and the increasing complexity special education. We've covered the profound changes in the lives of children and adults with special needs as they have benefited from computer use, as well as on the obstacles confronting them and those who serve them.
Cost: $18.00
Frequency: Quarterly

5375 **Christian Computing**
PO Box 319
Belton, MO 64012-0319

800-456-1868; Fax: 800-456-1868

Steve Hewitt, Editor-in-Chief
Frequency: Monthly
Founded in 1989

5376 **CircuiTree**
Business News Publishing Company
1050 IL Route 83
Suite 200
Bensenville, IL 60106-1096

630-377-5909
circuitree.com

Katie Rotella, Manager
Tom Esposito, Group Publisher
Darryl Seland, Associate Publisher/
Karl Dietz, Technical Editor
Cost: $64.00
Frequency: Monthly
Circulation: 12000
Founded in 1926

5377 **Circuits and Systems Magazine**
IEEE Circuits and Systems Society
445 Hoes Lane
Piscataway, NJ 08854

chaiwahwu@ieee.org
www.ieee-cas.org

Chai Wah Wu, Editor-in-Chief
Alyssa B. Apsel, Deputy Editor-in-Chief
Mohammad Sawan, VP, Publications

Feature articles with noteworthy results, surveys, and tutorials.

5378 **Civic.com**
FCW Government Technology Group
3141 Fairview Park Drive
Suite 777
Falls Church, VA 22042-4507

FAX 703-876-5126
www.fcw.com

Edith Holmes, President
Steve Vito, Publisher
Agnes Vanek, Circulation Director
Margo Dunn, Production Manager
Anne Armstrong, Editor

A print magazine and electronic companion designed for volume IT buyers, chief information officers and IT planners in state and local government.

5379 **CleanRooms Magazine**
PennWell Publishing Company

98 Spit Brook Rd
Suite 100
Nashua, NH 03062-5737

603-891-0123; Fax: 603-891-9294
johnh@pennwell.com
www.pennwell.com

Christine Shaw, VP
James Enos, Publisher
Angela Godwin, Managing Editor
Steve Smith, News Editor
Bob Johnson, National Sales Manager

Serves the contamination control and ultrapure materials and process industries. Written for readers in the microelectronics, pharmaceutical, biotech, health care, food processing and other user industries. Provides technology and business news and new product listings.
Cost: $97.00
Frequency: Monthly
Circulation: 35031
Founded in 1987

5380 **Com-SAC, Computer Security, Auditing & Controls**
Management Advisory Services & Publications
PO Box 81151
Wellesley Hills, MA 02481-0001

781-235-2895; Fax: 781-235-5446
info@masp.com
www.masp.com

A quarterly journal of in-depth tutorials in computer security, auditing and the most comprehensive digest service of all publications in computer security and controls.
Cost: $98.00
Frequency: Quarterly
Founded in 1973

5381 **Common Knowledge**
230 W Monroe St
Suite 220
Chicago, IL 60606-4802

312-416-3656
800-777-6734; Fax: 312-201-9588

Kris Neeley, Publisher

Features interviews with industry experts, case studies, tutorials, the latest industry news and overviews of management concerns.
Frequency: Quarterly
Circulation: 15,000

5382 **Communications of the ACM**
Association for Computing Machinery
1601 Broadway
10th Floor
New York, NY 10019-7434

212-869-7440
800-342-6626; Fax: 212-944-1318
acmhelp@acm.org
cacm.acm.org

Vicki Hanson, President
Thomas Lambert, Managing Editor
Andrew Rosenbloom, Senior Editor
Scott Delman, Director, Publications

Technical magazine covering developments in computer science for the computing and information technology fields, useful for computing professionals.
Cost: $17.00
Frequency: Monthly
Circulation: 82,867

5383 **CompactPCI Systems**
CompactPCI Systems
13253 La Montana
Dr 207
Fountain Hills, AZ 85268-5328

480-967-5581; Fax: 480-837-6466
www.compactpci-systems.com

Mike Hopper, Publisher
Joe Pavlat, Editor

Features application success stories that demonstrate how and where CompactPCI technology has provided solutions.
Circulation: 20000

5384 **Component Development Strategies**
Cutter Information Corporation
37 Broadway
Suite 1
Arlington, MA 02474-5500

781-648-1950
800-964-5118; Fax: 781-648-1950
press@cutter.com
www.cutter.com

Karen Coburn, President and CEO
Tom Welsh, Senior Consultant
Hillel Glazer, Senior Consultant
Ron Blitstein, Director

Editorial content covers the latest information and technology on object-oriented programming, databases, and analysis and design.
Cost: $2400.00
Frequency: Monthly
Founded in 1991

5385 **CompuServe Magazine**
5000 Arlington Centre Blvd
Columbus, OH 43220-5439

614-326-1002
800-848-8199
webcenters.netscape.compuserve.com/menu/

Offers updated and statistical information for computer professionals.

5386 **Computer**
IEEE Computer Society
10662 Los Vaqueros Circle
P. O. Box 3014
Los Alamitos, CA 90720-1314

714-821-8380
800-272-6657; Fax: 714-821-4010
volunteer.services@computer.org
www.computer.org/

Matt Loeb, Publisher
Doris L. Carver, Editor in Chief
Bill Schilit, Associate Editor
Judi Prow, Managing Editor
Jim Sanders, Senior Editor

Information on late breaking news, business trends, and a variety of technology specific departments.
Cost: $63.00
Frequency: Monthly
Circulation: 84340
Founded in 1988

5387 **Computer Business Review**
ComputerWire
245 5th Avenue
4th Floor
New York, NY 10016

212-770-0409; Fax: 212-686-2626
www.computerwire.com/cbr

Jake Sharp, Publisher
Micheal Danzon, CEO
Jason Stamper, Editor

Company profiles, computer market coverage and technology trends and news for investors and professionals in the computer, communications and microelectronics industries.
Cost: $195.00
Frequency: Monthly
Circulation: 20450
Founded in 1984

5388 **Computer Buyer's Guide & Handbook**
Bedford Communications
1410 Broadway
21st Floor
New York, NY 10018-5008

212-807-8220; Fax: 212-807-1098
www.techworthy.com

Ed Brown, Owner

A guide to buying peripherals and software, as well as general advice and news on the world of computing.
Cost: $36.00
128 Pages
Frequency: Monthly
Circulation: 50000
Founded in 1981

5389 **Computer Design**
PennWell Publishing Company
10 Tara Boulevard
5th Floor
Nashua, NH 03062-2800

603-891-0123; Fax: 603-891-0514

John Carroll, Group Publisher

Each issue contains in-depth articles and timely features written by experienced senior editors who concentrate on the critical technologies, components and tools needed to design microprocessor and computer based OEM products and systems.
Frequency: Monthly
Circulation: 105,028

5390 **Computer Graphics Review**
Primedia
Po Box 12901
Shawnee Mission, KS 66282-2901

913-341-1300; Fax: 913-514-6895
www.penton.com

Eric Jacobson, Senior VP

To identify and interpret significant technological and business developments.
Cost: $48.00
120 Pages
Frequency: Monthly
Founded in 1986

5391 **Computer Graphics World**
PennWell Publishing Company
98 Spit Brook Rd
Nashua, NH 03062-5737

603-891-0123
800-225-0556; Fax: 603-891-9294
phil@pennwell.com
www.pennwell.com

Christine Shaw, VP
Jenny Donelan, Managing Editor

Covers specific applications of computer graphics, written by users and vendors of equipment and services to the industry. The magazine of 3D computer graphics for engineering and animation professionals.
Frequency: Monthly
Founded in 1978
Printed in 4 colors on glossy stock

5392 **Computer Industry Almanac**
304 W White Oak
Arlington Heights, IL 60005

847-758-3687; Fax: 847-758-3686
www.c-i-a.com

Egil Juliussen, President

Annual reference book for and about the computer industry. The Almanac has ranking and awards of products, people and companies. Includes salary information, market forecasts, technology trends and directories of companies, publications, market research firms, associations and trade shows.
Cost: $45.00
Frequency: Annual

5393 **Computer Journal**
Oxford University Press
2001 Evans Rd
Cary, NC 27513-2010

919-677-0977
800-852-7323; Fax: 919-677-2673

F Leroy, Editorial Assistant:
F Murtagh, Editor-in-Chief
Julie Gribben, Special Sales Manager

Provides information on web sites, personal computers, hardware, software and online uses.
Cost: $920.00
Circulation: 18000

5394 **Computer Language**
600 Harrison Street
6th Floor
San Francisco, CA 94107

415-947-6000; Fax: 415-941-6055

Computer news and information.

5395 **Computer Link Magazine**
Millennium Publishing
100 Mobile Dr
Suite 1
Rochester, NY 14616-2145

585-797-4399

Justin Ziemniak, Editor-in-Chief

Website reviews, employment opportunities, and women's involvement in the technology age. Includes reports on the Western New York computer market.
Cost: $20.00
Frequency: Monthly
Circulation: 20000

5396 **Computer Manager**
Story Communications
116 N Camp Street
Seguin, TX 78155-5600

830-303-3328; Fax: 830-372-3011
www.storycommunications.com

James M Story, Publisher
K Wiemann, Circulation Manager

Information to help corporate end users purchase computers and communications equipment easily.
Frequency: Quarterly
Circulation: 50000

5397 **Computer Price Guide**
Computer Merchants
22 Saw Mill River Road
Hawthorne, NY 10532-1533

914-347-0290; Fax: 914-347-0292

Svend Hartmann, Publisher

Market trends and developments, prices on used IBM computer equipment.
Cost: $70.00
Frequency: Quarterly
Circulation: 3500

5398 **Computer Security Journal**
Computer Security Institute
600 Harrison Street
San Francisco, CA 94107

415-947-6320
866-271-8529; Fax: 415-947-6023

Russell Kay, Publisher
Chris Keating, Director
Robert Richardson, Editorial Director
Nancy Baer, Marketing Manager

Keeps you informed with comprehensive, practical articles, case studies, reviews and commentaries written by knowledgeable computer security professionals.
Cost: $25.00
Frequency: Quarterly
Circulation: 3000
Founded in 1974

5399 **Computer Security, Auditing and Controls (COM-SAC)**
Management Advisory Services & Publications
PO Box 81151
Wellesley Hills, MA 02481-0001

781-235-2895; Fax: 781-235-5446
www.masp.com

Indepth tutorials in computer security and auditing and the most comprehensive digest service of all publications in computer security, auditing and internal controls. Security hardware-software news.
Cost: $98.00
Frequency: Quarterly
ISSN: 0738-4262
Founded in 1973
Printed in on glossy stock

5400 **Computer Shopper**
Segal Company
1 Battery Park Plz
New York, NY 10004-1487

212-858-1000; Fax: 212-251-5490
info@segalco.com

Glenn E Siegel

A buyer's guide of sorts, listing the latest information and equipment for the world of computers.

5401 **Computer Survival Journal**
Enterprise Publishing
Po Box 328
Blair, NE 68008-0328

402-426-2121; Fax: 402-426-2227
mrhoades@enterprisepub.com
www.enterprisepub.com

Mark Rhoades, President
Dave Smith, Production Manager
Tracy Prettyman, Business Manager

Reviews and features on all areas of computer, office and home products (hardware and software). Also includes information on cellular phones, TV's and appliances, home electronics and television.
Cost: $250.00
50 Pages

5402 **Computer Technology Review**
West World Productions
420 N Camden Dr
Beverly Hills, CA 90210-4507

310-276-9500
888-889-3130; Fax: 310-276-9874
sinan@kanatsiz.com
www.wwpi.com

Yuri R Spiro, Publisher

Computer Technology Review is an all-inclusive tabloid that covers the full spectrum of new and emerging technologies vital to systems integrators, high-end VARS, and OEM.
Cost: $10.00
60 Pages
Frequency: Monthly
Circulation: 64044
ISSN: 0278-9647
Founded in 1981
Printed in 4 colors on matte stock

5403 **Computer User Magazine**
Key Professional Media
220 S 6th St
Suite 500
Minneapolis, MN 55402-4501

612-339-7571
800-788-0204; Fax: 612-333-5806
www.computeruser.com

Nat Opperman, President
Elizabeth Milllard, Associate Publisher

For small to medium-size business professionals and computer owners, ComputerUser is published in 13 markets nationally.
Cost: $14.00
60 Pages
Frequency: Monthly
Circulation: 64000
Founded in 1981
Printed in 4 colors on newsprint stock

5404 **Computer World/Focus**
PO Box 9171
Framingham, MA 01701-9171
Joe Maglitta, Feature Editor

A comprehensive magazine offering information on the computer industry.

5405 **Computer-Aided Engineering**
Penton Media
1300 E 9th St
Cleveland, OH 44114-1503

216-696-7000; Fax: 216-696-6662
caenetmaster@penton.com
www.penton.com

Jane Cooper, Marketing

Applications, news, trends and products for CAD/CAM technology as applied in manufacturing, electronics, architectural and construction industries.
Cost: $50.00
Frequency: Monthly
Circulation: 56,062

5406 **Computers & Structures**
Elsevier Science
230 Park Ave.
Suite 800
New York, NY 10169

212-989-5800
888-437-4636; Fax: 212-633-3990
www.journals.elsevier.com/computers-and-structures

K.J. Bathe, Editor
B.H.V. Topping, Editor

Publishes advances in the development and use of computational methods for the solution of problems in engineering and the sciences.
Circulation: 1500
ISSN: 0045-7949
Founded in 1971

5407 **Computers User**
220 S 6th Street
Suite 500
Minneapolis, MN 55042

612-339-7571
www.computeruser.com

David Needle, Editor
Matt Kusilek, Publisher

End user computer magazine for business and professional users of PC and Macintosh com-

puters, software and peripherals.
Cost: $24.99
Frequency: Monthly

5408 Computers and Biomedical Research
Academic Press
1901 E South Campus Drive
Suite 1195
Salt Lake City, UT 84112-9359
801-581-6461; Fax: 801-585-5414
www.aoce.utah.edu
T Allan Pryor, Editor
Liz McCoy, Executive Assistant
Brynn Roundy, Executive Secretary
Information on application of computer technology in biomedical research for medical professionals. Evaluates and discusses various techniques. Accompanied by photographs, charts, graphs and figures.
Cost: $325.00
Frequency: 6 per year
Circulation: 1,425

5409 Computers in the Schools
Taylor & Francis Group LLC
325 Chestnut St
Suite 800
Philadelphia, PA 19106-2614
215-625-8900
800-354-1420; Fax: 215-625-2940
haworthorders@taylorandfrancis.com
www.taylorandfrancis.com
Kevin Bradley, President
Articles emphasize the practical aspect of any application but also tie theory to practice, relate present accomplishments to past efforts and future trends, identify conclusions and their implications and discuss the theoretical and philosophical basis for the application.
Frequency: Quarterly

5410 Computertalk
Computertalk Associates
492 Norristown Road
Suite 160
Blue Bell, PA 19422
610-825-7686; Fax: 610-825-7641
wal@computertalk.com
www.computertalk.com
William A Lockwood Jr, President
Maggie L Lockwood, Director of Publications
Profiles on various sytems available for pharmacists purchasing and using computers.
Cost: $50.00
Frequency: Monthly
Circulation: 32,000
Founded in 1980
Printed in 4 colors on glossy stock

5411 Computerworld
CW Publishing
One Speen Street
PO Box 9171
Framingham, MA 01701-4653
508-879-0700
800-343-6474; Fax: 508-626-2705
editor@computerworld.com
www.computerworld.com
Mitch Betts, Executive Editor
Don Tennant, VP/Editor in Chief
Matt Sweeney, CEO
For computer professionals who evaluate and implement information systems.
Cost: $99.99
170 Pages
Circulation: 170000
Founded in 1967

5412 Computing Surveys
Association for Computing Machinery
1601 Broadway
10th Floor
New York, NY 10019-7434
212-869-7440
800-342-6626; Fax: 212-944-1318
acmhelp@acm.org
www.acm.org
Vicki Hanson, President
Laura Lander, Journals Manager
Scott Delman, Director, Publications
John Stanik, Managing Editor
Carefully planned and presented introductions to complex issues in computing technology, supported by exhaustive and comprehensive notations on the relevant literature. Topics covered include image understanding, software reusability, and object and relational database topics.
Cost: $170.00
Frequency: Quarterly
ISSN: 0360-0300

5413 Computing in Science & Engineering
American Institute of Physics
2 Huntington Quad
Melville, NY 11747-4502
516-576-2200; Fax: 516-349-7669
www.aip.org
Darlene Walters, Senior VP
Angela Burgess, Publisher
Georgann Carter, Marketing Manager
Computer science's interdisciplinary juncture with physics, astronomy and engineering.
Cost: $55.00

5414 Control Solutions
PennWell Publishing Company
1421 S Sheridan Rd
Tulsa, OK 74112-6619
918-831-9421
800-331-4463; Fax: 918-831-9476
www.pennwell.com
Robert Biolchini, President
Ron Kuhfeld, Editor-in-Chief
Represents control technology for engineers and engineering manage4ment.

5415 Converting Quarterly
Association of International Metallizers/Coaters
201 Springs Street
Fort Mill, SC 29715
262-697-0525; Fax: 262-697-0525
mark@aimcal.org
www.convertingquarterly.com
Mark A. Spaulding, Editor-in-Chief
Dianna Brodine, Managing Editor
Becky Arensdorf, Art Director
Janet Dunnichay, National Sales Director
Brenda Schell, Circulation Manager
Technical magazine published by the Association of International Metallizers, Coaters and Laminators. The magazine features technical content and views of industry consultants.
Frequency: Quarterly
Founded in 2010

5416 Cryptosystems Journal
Cryptosystems Journal
485 Middle Holland Road
Holland, PA 18966-2870
Tony Patti, Publisher/Editor
Unique international journal devoted to implementation of cryptographic systems on IBM-PC's and compatibles.

5417 Cyber Defense Magazine
PO Box 71748
Phoenix, AZ 85050
480-990-0407
866-487-6652; Fax: 480-990-7306
www.cyberdefensemagazine.com
John Riccio, Publisher
Curt Blakeney, Editor
Computer/Network security magazine.
Cost: $31.00
64 Pages
Frequency: 12 issues
Circulation: 64,000
Founded in 2003
Printed in 4 colors on glossy stock

5418 DBMS-Database Management Systems
Miller Freeman Publications
2655 Seely Avenue
San Jose, CA 95134
408-943-1234; Fax: 408-943-0513
Phillip Chapnick, Publisher
David Kohman, Editor
Covers the database and database applications marketplace.
Circulation: 69,029

5419 DG Review
Data Base Publications
9390 Research Blvd
Suite 300
Austin, TX 78759-7374
512-418-9590; Fax: 512-418-8165
www.bancvue.com
Gabe Krajicek, CEO
Gloria Trent, Editor
For Data General and compatible computer users.
Cost: $48.00
64 Pages
Frequency: Monthly
Founded in 1981

5420 DM Review
Powell Publishing Company
16655 W Bluemound Rd
Suite 201
Brookfield, WI 53005-5935
262-780-0202; Fax: 414-771-8058
www.b-eye-network.com
Ron Powell, Owner
Val Latzke, Editor
Jean Schauer, Editor in Chief
Mary Jo Nott, Executive Editor
Provides a wealth of knowledge through columns by top industry experts, data warehouse success stories, timely and informative articles, third-party product reviews, and executive interviews.
Frequency: Monthly
Circulation: 75012
Founded in 1994

5421 DSP Engineering
13253 La Montana Dr
Suite 207
Fountains Hills, AZ 85268
480-967-5581; Fax: 480-837-6466
Rosemary Kristoff, VP
Phyllis Thompson, Circulation Manager
Patrick Hopper, VP Marketing
Mike Hopper, Publisher

5422 Data Bus
AM Publications

PO Box 20044
Saint Petersburg, FL 33742

727-577-5500; Fax: 727-576-0622
ampubs@aol.com

Al Martino, Publisher/Editor

Contains new product reviews, trade literature and personnel announcements.
Frequency: Monthly
Circulation: 24000

5423 **Data Communications**
McGraw Hill
PO Box 182604
Columbus, OH 43272

614-866-5769; Fax: 614-759-3759
www.mcgraw-hill.com

Kevin Harold, Publisher
Steve Weiss, Production Manager

Networking magazine edited for the technical managers responsible for the implementation and integration of computer information networks.
Cost: $5.00
Circulation: 112,941

5424 **Data Sources**
Ziff Davis Publishing Company
28 E 28th St
New York, NY 10016-7940

212-503-5772
info@ziffdavis.com
www.ziffdavis.com

Steve Weitzner, CEO
Leo Greisman, General Counsel
Stephen Hicks, General Counsel
Steve Horowitz, COO
Cost: $240.00
Frequency: Monthly
Circulation: 700000
Founded in 1981

5425 **Data Storage**
PennWell Publishing Company
PO 91372
Calabasas, CA 91372

818-348-1240; Fax: 818-348-1742
www.datastorage.com

Becky Adams, Publisher
David Simpson, Editor
Kevin Komiega, Senior Editor

Features news and information on all types of systems such as magnetic disk drives, media and magnetic tape drives, CD-ROM, optical, magneto-optical, holographic and nonvolatile semiconductor storage devices.
Frequency: Monthly
Circulation: 15,140

5426 **Data to Knowledge**
Business Rule Solutions
2476 Bolsover Street
#488
Houston, TX 77005-2518

713-681-1651; Fax: 604-681-7223
www.brcommunity.com

Gladys S W Lam, Publisher
Ronald G Ross, Executive Editor
Keri Anderson Healy, Editor
Marie Yang, Director, Marketing & Business Dev
John Hall, Technology Review Editor

Provides analysis, news and tutorials for data management professionals, data administrators, DBA's and other involved in the planning, design and construction of large-scale information systems.
Circulation: 4603
Founded in 1973

5427 **Database Searcher**
Mecklermedia Corporation
11 Ferry Lane W
Westport, CT 06880-5808
Alan Meckler, Editor

Covers online and micro-computer techniques.
Cost: $95.00
Frequency: Monthly
Founded in 1985

5428 **Datamation**
Reed Business Information
2000 Clearwater Dr
Oak Brook, IL 60523-8809

630-574-0825; Fax: 630-288-8781
www.reedbusiness.com

Jeff Greisch, President
William Semich, Editor-in-Chief

The magazine that interprets products, events and technologies for computer professionals in large companies worldwide.
Cost: $4.00
Circulation: 189,101

5429 **Design Automation**
Miller Freeman Publications
2655 Seely Avenue
San Jose, CA 95134

408-943-1234; Fax: 408-943-0513

Lindsey Vereen, Editor

Targeted to computer design engineers.
Frequency: Monthly

5430 **Designfax**
NP Communications, LLC
2500 Tamiami Trail N
Nokomis, FL 34275

941-966-9521; Fax: 941-966-2590
mfoley@nelsonpub.com
www.designfax.net

Mike Foley, Editor
John W Holmes, National Sales Manager

eMagazine whose primary content focuses on the latest exciting applications and products for Electrical/Electronic, Mechanical, Motion Control, Fluid Power, and Materials engineering, including articles on powerful software programs that serve as a primary engineering tool.
Cost: $54.00
Frequency: Weekly
Circulation: 128,000
Founded in 1979
Printed in 4 colors on glossy stock

5431 **Desktop Engineering**
Helmers Publishing
174 Concord Street
PO Box 874
Peterborough, NH 03458

603-924-9631; Fax: 603-924-4004
jgooch@deskeng.com
www.deskeng.com

Brian Vaillancourt, Publisher
Anthony J Lockwood, Editorial Director
Bill Fahy, Circulation Director
Carol Laughner, Marketing Director

Magazine providing design solutions from concept throughout manufacture, focuses on hardware, software, and technologies for hands-on design engineers and engineering management in the manufacturing solutions throughout extensive product reviews, comparisions, technology updates, real-world application stories, news, product resource guides, and new product reports.
60 Pages
Frequency: Monthly
Circulation: 63000
ISSN: 1085-0422
Founded in 1995
Printed in 4 colors on glossy stock

5432 **Distributed Computing Monitor**
Patricia Seybold Group
Po Box 240565
Boston, MA 02129

617-742-5200
800-826-2424; Fax: 617-742-1028
www.psgroup.com

Patricia Seybold, Founder/CEO

The editors give advanced technologists and strategic technology architects the technical details and business perspective necessary to sell upper management on how, why and when to implement the leading edge.
Frequency: Monthly
Founded in 1978

5433 **EServer Magazine**
IBM Corporation
220 S 6th Street
Suite 500
Minneapolis, MN 55402

612-339-7571; Fax: 612-336-9220
www.eservercomputing.com

Doug Rock, Editor/Publisher
Mari Adamson-Bray, Marketing Manager
Kelly McManus, Production Manager

New products and services, technological information, and related topics that benefit the decision makers in the optimization and management of these systems are included.
80 Pages
Frequency: Monthly
Circulation: 45000
ISSN: 1074-7082
Founded in 1993
Printed in 4 colors on glossy stock

5434 **Educational Technology**
Educational Technology Publications
700 Palisade Avenue
PO Box 1564
Englewood Cliffs, NJ 07632-564

201-871-4007
800-952-2665; Fax: 201-871-4009
edtecpubs@aol.com
www.bookstoread.com/etp

Lawrence Lipsitz, Publisher/Editor

Systematic design of software and applications, and their impact on the educational community worldwide. Emphasis on computer-based instruction, the Internet, multimedia, electronic performance support, television and videoconferencing.
Cost: $139.00
Frequency: Bi-annually
ISSN: 0013-1962
Founded in 1960
Printed in on glossy stock

5435 **Educational Technology Research and Development**
Assn. of Educational Communications & Technology
320 W. 8th Street
Suite 101
Bloomington, IN 47404

812-335-7675
877-677-2328; Fax: 812-335-7678
aect@aect.org
aect.site-ym.com
Facebook, Twitter

Tristan E. Johnson, Editor-in-Chief
Brad Hokanson, President
Phillip Harris, Executive Director

Includes scholarly articles on communcations, technology and instructional development

news.
Cost: $75.00
Frequency: Bi-Monthly
ISSN: 1042-1629
Founded in 1923
Mailing list available for rent: 6000 names at $150 per M

5436 **Educational Technology Review**
AACE International
PO Box 3728
Norfolk, VA 23514
757-623-7588; Fax: 703-977-8760
info@aace.org
www.aace.org
Gary H Marks, Editor
Promotes the use of information technology in education. New products including software, hardware and related materials.
Cost: $38.00
Founded in 1981

5437 **Electronic Design**
Penton Media
1300 E 9th St
Suite 310
Cleveland, OH 44114-1503
216-696-7000; Fax: 216-696-6662
information@penton.com
www.penton.com
Jane Cooper, Marketing
David B Nussbaum, CEO
Celebrating 50 years of innovation, this authoritative magazine provides leading-edge technical information to electronic and engineering managers around the world.
Cost: $105.00
Circulation: 145000
Founded in 1890

5438 **Embedded Systems Programming**
Miller Freeman Publications
600 Harrison Street
6th Floor
San Francisco, CA 94107
415-947-6000; Fax: 415-947-6055
www.mfi.com
Frequency: Monthly
Circulation: 45,000
Founded in 1986

5439 **Empowered Learner Magazine**
International Society for Technology in Education
621 SW Morrison Street
Suite 800
Portland, OR 97205
503-342-2848
800-336-5191; Fax: 503-882-0813
iste@iste.org
www.iste.org
Richard Culatta, Chief Executive Officer
A large nonprofit organization serving the technology-using educator.

5440 **Enterprise Management Issues**
AFCOM
742 E Chapman Ave
Orange, CA 92866-1644
714-997-7966; Fax: 714-997-9743
afcom@afcom.com
www.afcom.com
Jill Eckhaus, President
Content includes an in-depth cover story and features on current developments and the impact of advancing technology. Regular departments are devoted to automation issues and data processing news.
Frequency: Bi-Monthly
Circulation: 4,000

5441 **European Sources and News**
SSC Group
3126 Woodley Road NW
Washington, DC 20008-3448
202-232-0822; Fax: 202-337-5354
www.neweurope.eu
Robert Snyder, Publisher
Steve Solomon, Editor
Provides European resellers, VAR, systems integrators and OEM with information on product sources and reseller management strategies.
Circulation: 49000

5442 **Federal Computer Week**
FCW Government Technology Group
3141 Fairview Park Drive
Suite 777
Falls Church, VA 22042-4507
703-876-5100
866-293-3194; Fax: 703-876-5126
www.fcw.com
Jeffrey Calore, General Manager, Sales & Marketing
Anne Armstrong, Publisher
John Zyskowski, Senior Editor
The markets leading newspaper for influential users and volume buyers of federal information technology.
Cost: $100.00
48 Pages
Frequency: Weekly
Circulation: 100000
Founded in 1987

5443 **Foghorn**
FOG Publications
PO Box 1030
Dixon, CA 95620-1030
Gale Rhoades, Editor
For users of 16 and 32 bit systems.
Cost: $30.00
64 Pages
Frequency: Monthly
Founded in 1985

5444 **GEOWorld**
Bel-Av Communications
359 Galahad Road
Bolingbrook, IL 60440-2108
Home Page: www.geoplace.com
Jo Treadwell, VP/Group Publisher
Todd Danielson, Editor
Offers a wealth of knowledge through features, news and commentary covering the geospatial industry. Covers local and federal government, emergency management, infrastructure, natural resource management, industry trends and onnovations and much more.
Cost: $72.00
Frequency: Monthly
Circulation: 25,000

5445 **Game Developer Magazine**
Think Services
600 Harrison Street
6th Floor
San Francisco, CA 94107
Home Page: www.gdmag.com
Simon Carless, Publisher
Brandon Sheffield, Editor-In-Chief
Jeffrey Fleming, Production Editor
Written specifically for creators of entertainment software, provides technical and industry information to professional game developers. Features articles written by professional game developers on cutting-edge game development techniques in the areas of graphics and AI programming, audio design and engineering, art and animation.
Cost: $49.95
Frequency: Monthly
Circulation: 35,000
Founded in 1971

5446 **Genealogical Computing**
Ancestry
360 W 4800 N
Provo, UT 84604-5675
801-705-7000
800-262-3787; Fax: 801-705-7001
www.myfamily.com
Timothy P Sullivan, CEO
Elizabeth Kelley Kerstens, Managing Editor
Jennifer Browning, Senior Editor
For readers who use computers and technology to organize and enhance their research into accounts of ancestries and descent.
Cost: $25.00
Frequency: Quarterly

5447 **Gilder Technology Report**
Gilder Publishing
291 Main St
Suite A
Great Barringto, MA 01230-1608
413-644-2100; Fax: 413-644-2123
www.gildertech.com
George Gilder, Editor in Chief
Focuses on the ascendence of the telecoms and the centrality of the Internet.
Cost: $195.00
Frequency: Monthly
Founded in 1995

5448 **Global Technology Business**
Global Technology Business Publishing
1157 San Antonio Road
Mountain View, CA 94043
650-934-2300; Fax: 650-934-2306
www.gtbusiness.com
Alex Vieux, Publisher
Laurence Scott, Editor
Bob Beauchamp, CEO
Emphasizes the business aspects of the global computer and communications industries through corporate strategies, financial performance, technological directions.
Frequency: Monthly
Circulation: 45000

5449 **Global Techventures Report**
Miller Freeman Publications
2655 Seely Avenue
San Jose, CA 95134
408-943-1234; Fax: 408-943-0513
Annie Feldman, Publisher
Editorial content profiles vital capital investments and start-up companies, and addresses a variety of legislation, security and communication issues as they relate to today's technology.
Frequency: SemiMonthly

5450 **Government Best Buys**
FCW Government Technology Group
3141 Fairview Park Drive
Suite 777
Falls Church, VA 22042-4507
703-876-5100
866-293-3194; Fax: 703-876-5126
www.fcw.com
Edith Holmes, President
John Stein Monroe, Editor-in-Chief
Christopher J. Dorobek, Executive Editor
Covers the hardware and software products available to government buyers on agency contracts and the General Services Administration schedule.
Founded in 1987

5451 **Hard Copy Observer**
Lyra Research
320 Nevada Street 1st Floor
PO Box 9143
Newtonville, MA 02640-9143

617-454-2600; Fax: 617-454-2601
www.lyra.com

Charles LeCompte, President
Ann Priede, Director of Marketing
Carolyn ODonnell, Director of Marketing

News on the latest products, market news, supplies, end-user reponse and product testing for the computer printer industry.
Cost: $617.00
80 Pages
Frequency: Monthly
Founded in 1991

5452 **Heller Report on Educational Technology Markets**
Nelson B Heller & Associates
810 S Alfred Street
#1
Alexandria, VA 22314

303-209-9410; Fax: 303-209-9444
info@hellerreports.com

Anne Wujcik, Publisher/Managing Editor

Information on the marketing of technology and telecommunications equipment to educators at all levels.
Cost: $395.00
Frequency: Monthly
Circulation: 1,100

5453 **Home Networking News**
111 Spleen
Suite 200
Framingham, MA 01701-2000

508-663-1500; Fax: 508-663-1599
kmoyes@ehpub.com
www.ehpub.com

Kenneth Moyes, CEO/Publisher
Cindy Tazis, Editor
Elizabeth Cruze, Marketing Manager
Christine Ayers, Circulation Manager
Cost: $14.95
Frequency: Monthly
Circulation: 100000
Founded in 1994

5454 **IEEE Computational Intelligence Magazine**
IEEE Computational Intelligence Society
445 Hoes Lane
Piscataway, NJ 08855

732-465-5892; Fax: 732-465-6435
cis-info@ieee.org
cis.ieee.org

Bernadette Bouchon-Meunier, President
Hessein Abbass, VP, Technical Activities
James Keller, VP, Publications

CIM features peer-reviewed articles with noteworthy discoveries, insights, and tutorial surveys.

5455 **IEEE Computer**
IEEE Computer Society
10662 Los Vaqueros Circle
PO Box 3014
Los Alamitos, CA 90720-1314

714-218-8380
800-272-6657; Fax: 714-821-4010
aburgess@computer.org
www.computer.org

Angela Burgess, Executive Director
Marilyn Potes, Managing Editor
Rakesh Gupta, Editor in Chief
Paul Croll, Treasurer
David Grier, VP Publications

Examines a wide range of computer-related technologies. Written and refereed by experts, it features articles on the latest developments in computer technology, applications and research in the computer field.
Cost: $37.00
Circulation: 85930
Founded in 1946

5456 **IEEE Computer Graphics and Applications**
IEEE Computer Society
10662 Los Vaqueros Circle
PO Box 3014
Los Alamitos, CA 90720-1314

714-821-8380
800-272-6657; Fax: 714-821-4010
help@computer.org
www.computer.org/

Angela Burgess, Executive Director
Sandy Brown, Marketing Director
Robin Baldwin, Managing Editor
Christine Kelly, Staff Editor
Tammi Titsworth, Staff Editor

Focuses on the design and use of computer graphics and systems. Addresses topics such as solid modeling, animation, CAD/CAM, tools for rendering graphics and graphics in medicine, science and business.
Cost: $70.00
Circulation: 10028
Founded in 1946

5457 **IEEE Computer Society of Computing Software Magazine**
Po Box 3014
Los Alamitos, CA 90720-1314

714-821-8380; Fax: 714-821-4010
volunteer.services@computer.org
www.computer.org

Angela Burgess, Executive Director
Warren Harrison, Treasurer
Paul Croll, Treasurer
David Grier, VP Publications

Offers information on the latest software programs for computer professionals.
Circulation: 10000
Founded in 1945

5458 **IEEE Expert**
IEEE Computer Society
10662 Los Vaqueros Circle
PO Box 3014
Los Alamitos, CA 90720

714-821-8380
800-272-6657; Fax: 714-821-4010
volunteer.services@computer.org
www.computer.org

Crystal Shif, Managing Editor
Angela Burgess, Executive Director
Matthew Bertholf, Advertising Manager
Sandy Brown, Senior Business Development Manager
Paul Croll, Treasurer

Accepts advertising.
Cost: $58.00
Circulation: 3,463
Founded in 1986

5459 **IEEE Industrial Electronics Magazine**
Institute Of Electrical and Electronics Engineers
445 Hoes Lane
Piscataway, NJ 08854

804-827-3999
eic-iem@ieee-ies.org
www.ieee-ies.org

Peter Palesnky, Editor-in-Chief

IEM features peer-reviewed articles presenting new trends and practices in industrial electronics research & development.

5460 **IEEE Intelligent Systems**
IEEE Computer Society
10662 Los Vaqueros Circle
PO Box 3014
Los Alamitos, CA 90720-1314

714-821-8380
800-272-6657; Fax: 714-821-4010
volunteer.services@computer.org
www.computer.org

Angela Burgess, Executive Director
Paul Croll, Treasurer
Doris L Carver, Editor-in-Chief
David Grier, VP Publications

Features emphasize advanced research that is ready to be used in the real world. Departments include interviews, books and product reviews, opinion pieces, and conference calendars.
Cost: $47.00
Circulation: 15355
Founded in 1946

5461 **IEEE Open Journal of the Computer Society**
Institute of Electrical & Electronics Engineers
2001 L Street NW
Suite 700
Washington, DC 20036-4928

202-371-0101; Fax: 202-728-9614
publications@computer.org
www.computer.org

Melissa Russell, Executive Director
Song Guo, Editor-In-Chief
Pilar Etuk, Production Manager
Robin Baldwin, Publisher
Debbie Sims, Senior Advertising Coordinator

A peer-reviewed forum for rapid publication of open access articles describing high-impact results in all areas of interest to the IEEE Computer Society.

5462 **IEEE Solid-State Circuits Magazine**
IEEE Solid-State Circuits Society
445 Hoes Lane
Piscataway, NJ 08854

rjacobbaker@gmail.com
sscs.ieee.org

R. Jacob Baker, Editor-in-Chief
Rakesh Kumar, Chair, Advisory Board

Tutorial-style articles on technical achievements, trends, and future developments in the field of Integrated Circuits.
Founded in 2009

5463 **IEEE Transactions on Computers**
IEEE Computer Society
10662 Los Vaqueros Circle
PO Box 3014
Los Alamitos, CA 90720

714-821-8380; Fax: 714-821-4010
help@computer.org
www.computer.org

Jean-Luc Gaudidt, Editor-in-Chief
Angela Burgess, Treasurer
Paul Croll, Treasurer
David Grier, VP Publications

Includes technical research reports and papers on the theory, design and applications of computer systems.
Cost: $72.00
Frequency: Monthly
Circulation: 8000
Founded in 1979

5464 **IEEE Transactions on Engineering Management**
IEEE Technology & Engineering Management Society
445 Hoes Lane
Piscataway, NJ 08854

tugrul.u.daim@pdx.edu
www.ieee-tems.org

Tugrul U. Daim, Editor-in-Chief
Alison Larkin, Peer Review Support Services
Mark Werwath, VP, Publications

Journal of the Technology and Engineering Management Society of IEEE, with peer-reviewed research on engineering, technology, and innovation management.
Frequency: Quarterly
Founded in 1954

5465 **ISACA Journal**
Information Systems Audit & Control Association
Rolling Meadows, IL

847-660-5505
844-472-2246
www.isaca.org

David Samuelson, CEO

Provides professional development information to those spearheading IT governance and those involved with information systems audit, control and security
Cost: $75.00
9000+ Members
Frequency: Bi-Monthly
Circulation: 35000
Founded in 1967

5466 **ISR: Intelligent Systems Report**
Lionheart Publishing
2555 Cumberland Pkwy SE
Suite 299
Atlanta, GA 30339-3921

770-432-2551; Fax: 770-432-6969
llewellyn@lionhrtpub.com
www.lionhrtpub.com

John Llewellyn, Publisher
Marvin Diamond, Advertising Sales Manager

Provides an in-depth look into the integration and application of advanced decision support technologies including artificial intelligence, speech recognition, neural networks, fuzzy logic, expert systems, multimedia and virtual reality, and artificial life.
Frequency: Monthly

5467 **Imaging World**
American Business Media
1300 Virginia Drive
Suite 400
Fort Washington, PA 19034-3297

215-643-8000; Fax: 215-643-8159
www.imaging-world.com

Robert Boucher Jr, President/CEO
Dan Marsh, Publisher, Eyecare Business
Stephanie De Long, Editor-in-Chief, Eyecare

Serves the needs of vendors wishing to reach the North American market for electronic imaging and document-based information management and workflow.
Frequency: Monthly
Circulation: 75000
Founded in 1997

5468 **InTech Computing Magazine**
ISA Services
67 Alexander Drive
PO Box 12277
Research Triangle Park, NC 27709
919-549-8411; Fax: 919-549-8288
info@isa.org
www.isa.org

Gregory Hale, Editor
Richard T Simpson, Publisher

Key source of information on automating manufacturing processes.
Cost: $45.00
Frequency: Monthly
Founded in 1945
Printed in 4 colors on glossy stock

5469 **Info Log Magazine**
BBS Press Service

785-286-4272; Fax: 239-992-4862

Alan Bechtold, Editor

A comprehensive magazine offering the latest information on aspects of the computer industry.
Frequency: Monthly
Founded in 1982

5470 **Information Display**
Ste 114
1475 S Bascom Ave
Campbell, CA 95008-0628

408-977-1013; Fax: 408-977-1531
office@sid.org
www.sid.org

Ken Werner, Editor
Jenny Needham, Circulation Manager
Shigeo Nikoshiba, CEO/President

A magazine published by the Society for Information Display.
Cost: $55.00
Frequency: Monthly
Circulation: 12000
Founded in 1964

5471 **Information Management**
ARMA International
11880 College Boulevard
Suite 450
Overland Park, KS 66215

913-444-9174
844-565-2120; Fax: 913-257-3855
headquarters@armaintl.org
magazine.arma.org
Facebook, Twitter, LinkedIn

Nick Inglis, Exec. Dir., Content & Programming
Jeff Whited, Sr. Content Writer
Ann Snyder, Manager, Content Development

Also known as ARMA Magazine, it is a major source of information on topics and issues central to the management of records and information worldwide. Each issue features articles written by experts in the management of records and information.
61 Pages
Frequency: 6/Year
Founded in 1955

5472 **Information Systems Management**
Auerbach Publications
3701 Algonquin Road
Suite 1010
Rolling Meadows, IL 60008

847-253-1545; Fax: 847-253-1443
publication@isaca.org
www.isaca.org

Debra Cutts, Marketing
Jen Blader, Editorial
David Samuelson, CEO

Coverage includes information technology developments and business applications, financial issues, IS staff development, and relationships with business management.
Cost: $75.00
Frequency: Bi-monthly
Circulation: 40,000
ISSN: 1058-0530
Founded in 1969

5473 **Information World Review**
143 Old Marlton Pike
Medford, NJ 08055-8750

609-654-7777; Fax: 609-654-4309

Offers a full overview of the computer industry overseas.

5474 **InformationWEEK**
CMP Publications
600 Community Dr
Manhasset, NY 11030-3810

516-562-5000; Fax: 516-562-5036

Stephanie Stahl, Editor-in-Chief
Mike Friedenberg, Publisher

For information systems management.
Frequency: Weekly
Circulation: 440,000
Founded in 1985

5475 **Infostor**
PennWell Publishing Company
98 Spit Brook Rd
Nashua, NH 03062-5737

603-891-0123; Fax: 603-891-9294
mark@pennwell.com
www.pennwell.com

Christine Shaw, VP
Jill Davis, Marketing Communications

News and information for enterprise storage professionals.
Cost: $120.00
Frequency: Monthly
Circulation: 38000
Founded in 1997

5476 **Infoworld Magazine**
Infoworld
501 Second Street
San Francisco, CA 94107

847-291-5217
feedback@infoworld.com
www.infoworld.com/

Bob Ostrow, President/Publisher
Paul Calento, VP Marketing
Kevin McKean, Chairman
Steve Fox, Editor-in-Chief
Kathy Badertscher, Executive Managing Editor

Offers information for computer professionals.
Frequency: Weekly

5477 **Inside DPMA**
Data Processing Management Association
505 Busse Highway
Park Ridge, IL 60068-3143

847-825-0880; Fax: 847-825-1693

Paul Zuziak, Editor

A monthly newspaper for the DPMA and the information management profession. Accepts advertising.
Cost: $16.00
Frequency: Monthly
Founded in 1988

5478 **Inside Technology Training**
Ziff Davis Publishing Company
500 Unicorn Park Drive
Woburn, MA 01801

781-938-2600
www.itrain.com/

Nancy J Weingarten, Publisher

Targets management level executives, technology trainers, information technology training

managers, CIO's and independent training consultants. Includes reports on new software, new media and new career paths. Also features designed to help training managers create and successfully implement strategy training and reskilling programs that anyone on any level can use.
Frequency: 10 per year
Circulation: 40,000

5479 Inside Visual Basic
ZD Journals
500 Canal View Boulevard
Rochester, NY 14623-2800
585-407-7301; Fax: 585-240-7760
Jon Pyles, Publisher
Authors discuss subjects covering the building and creating of external objects, as well as topics surrounding class development. The publication informs readers of Visual Basic online resources, and addresses real world questions reagrding controls written in the program, uses of the status bar and extending functions capabilities.
Frequency: Monthly

5480 Integrated System Design
Verecom Group
954 San Rafael Avenue
Mountain View, CA 94043-1926
650-988-9677
www.isdmag.com
James Uhl, Publisher
Richard Wallace, VP
Articles are written by designers who explain unique methods for solving design challenges. Publication supplies information on design methodologies and the use of tools and semiconductor capabilities.
Frequency: Monthly
Circulation: 58082

5481 Intelligent Enterprise
Miller Freeman Publications
411 Boral Avenue
#100
San Mateo, CA 94402-3522
650-573-3210; Fax: 650-655-4350
www.intelligententerprise.com
David Kalman, Publisher
Each issue provides detailed analyses of the products, trends and strategies that help accelerate the creation of the enterprise's information infrastructure. Topics include: business intelligence; enterprise resource planning; knowledge management; transaction processing and performance monitoring; applications and systems management.
Frequency: 18 per year
Circulation: 103,000

5482 Interactions Magazine
Association for Computing Machinery
1601 Broadway
10th Floor
New York, NY 10019-7434
212-869-7440
800-342-6626; Fax: 212-944-1318
acmhelp@acm.org
dl.acm.org
Vicki Hanson, Chief Executive Officer
Denis Doig, Senior Editor
Diane Crawford, Deputy Director
Scott Crawford, Director, Publications
Editorial content covering business, design, methods and tools, book previews, conference previews and current events pertaining to designers, developers and researchers. The focus is on human-computer interaction.
Founded in 1947

5483 International Journal of IT Standards and Standardization Research
Information Resources Management Association
701 E Chocolate Avenue
Suite 200
Hershey, PA 17033-1240
717-533-8845; Fax: 717-533-8661
members@irma-international.org
www.irma-international.org
Mehdi Khosrowpour, Executive Director
Sherif Kamel, VP, Information Management
An authoritative source and information outlet for the diverse community of IT standards researchers, publishing research findings with the goal of advancing knowledge and research in all aspects of IT standards and standardization in modern organizations.
Cost: $115.00
Frequency: Semi-Annual
ISSN: 1539-3062

5484 International Journal of Information and Communication Technology Education
Information Resources Management Association
701 E Chocolate Avenue
Suite 200
Hershey, PA 17033-1240
717-533-8845; Fax: 717-533-8861
member@irma-international.org
www.irma-international.org
Mehdi Khosrowpour, Executive Director
Sherif Kamel, VP, Information Management
Includes new applications of technology for teaching and learning, and document those practices that contribute irrefutable verification of information technology education as a discipline.
Cost: $115.00
Frequency: Quarterly
ISSN: 1550-1876
Printed in

5485 International Journal on E-Learning (IJEL)
Association for the Advancement of Computing In Ed
PO Box 719
Waynesville, NC 28786
828-246-9558; Fax: 828-246-9557
info@aace.org
www.aace.org
Gary H. Marks, Founding Editor
Provides articles on advances in technology and the growth of e-learning.

5486 Iris Universe: Magazine of Visual Computing
Silicon Graphics
1500 Crittenden Lane
Mountain View, CA 94043
650-960-1980
800-800-7441; Fax: 650-932-6102
www.sgi.com
Warren C Pratt, CEO/President
Gaye Graves, Features Editor
Anne Marie Gambelin, Publisher
Dominic Martinelli, Chief Information Officer
Written to appeal to all users of computer visualization, from the most technically oriented to the novice. Devoted to cutting edge techniques and technology used and presents the best in new products available.
Frequency: Quarterly
Founded in 1981

5487 Journal of American Society for Information Science
John Wiley & Sons
111 River St
Hoboken, NJ 07030-5790
201-748-6000; Fax: 201-748-6088
info@wiley.com
www.wiley.com
William J Pesce, CEO
Richard M Hochhauser, CEO
Communications, management, applications, economics, and other news of interest in the science field.
Cost: $95.00
72 Pages
Frequency: Bi-Monthly

5488 Journal of Computer Information Systems (JCIS)
Intl Association for Computer Systems Security
Dix Hills, NY
joanna_paliszkiewicz@sggw.pl
www.iacis.org
Kevin Floyd, Secretary & IIS Editor
Daryl Nord, Executive Director
Jeretta Horn Nord, Treasurer & Director, Publications
The Journal of Computer Information Systems (JCIS) is the forum for IACIS members and other information systems and business professionals to present their research and ideas.

5489 Journal of Computers in Mathematics and Science Teaching (JCMST)
Association for the Advancement of Computing In Ed
PO Box 719
Waynesville, NC 28786
828-246-9558; Fax: 828-246-9557
info@aace.org
www.aace.org
Dr. Gary H. Marks, Chief Executive Officer
The only periodical devoted specifically to using information technology in the teaching of mathematics and science.
Founded in 1981

5490 Journal of Educational Multimedia and Hypermedia
Association for the Advancement of Computing In Ed
PO Box 719
Waynesville, NC 28786
828-246-9558; Fax: 828-246-9557
info@aace.org
www.aace.org
Dr. Gary H. Marks, Chief Executive Officer
Designed to provide a multi-disciplinary forum to present and discuss research, development and applications of multimedia and hypermedia in education.

5491 Journal of Imaging Science and Technology
Society for Imaging Science & Technology
7003 Kilworh Lane
Springfield, VA 22151-4088
703-642-9090; Fax: 703-642-9094
info@imaging.org
www.imaging.org
George T.C. Chin, Editor
Donna Smith, Managing Editor
Provides the imaging community documentation of a broad range of research, development, and applications in imaging. The selection of papers reflects the role of IS&T as the window

on imaging, promoting communication and understanding across the boundaries of the many disciplines involved in modern imaging.
Cost: $95.00
Circulation: 2000
ISSN: 1062-3701
Founded in 1947

5492 Journal of Interactive Learning Research
AACE International
1 Morton Drive
Suite 500
Charlottesville, VA 22903

434-977-5029; Fax: 434-977-5431
info@aace.org
www.aace.org

John Self, Editor

Reports on the research, developments, applications, and integration of intelligent computer technologies in education.
Frequency: Quarterly
Circulation: 3M

5493 Journal of Object-Oriented Programming
SIGS Publications
9121 Oakdale Avenue
Chatsworth, CA 91311

818-734-1520; Fax: 818-734-1522

Richard S Weiner, Editor
Mike Valenti, Executive Vice President

Provides an international forum for research, developments, applications, and new products in the field.
Circulation: 3,50,000
Founded in 1998

5494 Journal of Technology and Teacher Education
Association for the Advancement of Computing In Ed
PO Box 719
Waynesville, NC 28786

828-246-9558; Fax: 828-246-9557
info@aace.org
www.aace.org

Dr. Gary H. Marks, Chief Executive Officer

A forum for the exchange of knowledge about the use of information technology in teacher education.

5495 Journal of the Association for Information Science and Technology
Assoc for Information Science and Technology
8555 16th Street
Suite 850
Silver Spring, MD 20910

301-495-0900; Fax: 301-495-0810
asist@asist.org
www.asist.org

Javed Mostafa, Editor

An international forum for peer-reviewed research in information science.
Frequency: Monthly

5496 Journal on Online Learning Research
Association for the Advancement of Computing In Ed
PO Box 719
Waynesville, NC 28786

828-246-9558; Fax: 828-246-9557
info@aace.org
www.aace.org

Dr. Gary H. Marks, Chief Executive Officer

A peer-reviewed, international journal devoted to the theoretical, empirical, and pragmatic understanding of technologies and their impact on primary and secondary pedagogy and policy in primary and secondary (K-12) online and blended environments.

5497 KM World
Information Today
143 Old Marlton Pike
Medford, NJ 08055-8750

609-654-6266
800-300-9868; Fax: 609-654-4309
custserv@infotoday.com
www.infotoday.com

Thomas H Hogan, President
Roger R Bilboul, Chairman of the Board

Serves the knowledge management industry by offering components and processes, including success stories, designed to improve business.
Cost: $23.95
Mailing list available for rent: 4M names
Printed in 4 colors on glossy stock

5498 LAN Magazine
Miller Freeman Publications
600 Harrison Street
6th Fl
San Francisco, CA 94107

415-947-6000; Fax: 415-947-6055
www.mfi.com

Covers Local Area Networks.
Cost: $20.00
180 Pages
Frequency: Monthly
Founded in 1986

5499 Law Office Computing
James Publishing
PO Box 25202
Santa Ana, CA 92799-5202

714-755-5450; Fax: 714-751-5508
www.jamespublishing.com

Jamie Tyo, Managing Editor
Amanda Flatten, Editor & Publisher
Jim Pawell, Marketing and Circulation

Legal software reviews, productivity enhancing tips and resources to improve law office automation.
Cost: $39.00
Founded in 1981

5500 Library Software Review
Sage Publications
Vanderbilt University
419 21st Avenue S
Nashville, TN 37240-0001

615-343-6094; Fax: 615-343-8834
info@sagepub.com
www.sagepub.com

Marshall Breeding, Editor

Provides the library professional with information necessary to make intelligent software evaluation, procurement, integration and installation decisions. Issues review software and software books and periodicals.
Cost: $52.00
Frequency: Quarterly
Circulation: 1M

5501 Link-Up Digital
Information Today
143 Old Marlton Pike
Medford, NJ 08055-8750

609-654-6266
800-300-9868; Fax: 609-654-4309
custserv@infotoday.com
www.infotoday.com

Thomas H Hogan, President
Roger R Bilboul, Chairman Of The Board

A web-only product featuring articles, reviews and more for users and producers of electronic information products and services.
Mailing list available for rent: 4M names
Printed in 4 colors on glossy stock

5502 MD Computing
Springer Verlag
175 5th Ave
New York, NY 10010-7703

212-477-8200; Fax: 212-473-6272
www.mdcomputing.com

Nhora Cortes-Comerer, Executive Editor
Kelley Suttenfield, Assistant Editor

Provides comprehensive and up-to-date information about the various segments of medical and healthcare informatics, such as clinical computing, health care information and delivery systems, telemedicine, radiology, and many others.
Cost: $69.00
74 Pages
Frequency: Bi-Monthly
Circulation: 19,771
ISSN: 0724-6811
Printed in 4 colors on glossy stock

5503 MacWeek
MacWorld Communications
501 2nd St
San Francisco, CA 94107-1496

415-243-0505; Fax: 415-442-0766

Mike Kisseberth, CEO
David Ezequelle, Publisher
Rick Lepage, President

Covers Apple's Macintosh computers. Accepts advertising.
Cost: $99.00
72 Pages
Frequency: 44 per year
Founded in 1987

5504 MacWorld Magazine
Mac Publishing
501 2nd St
San Francisco, CA 94107-1496

415-243-0505; Fax: 415-442-0766
letters@macworld.com
www.macworld.com

Mike Kisseberth, CEO
Dan Miller, Executive Editor
Scholle Sawyer McFarland, Senior Editor
Dan Frakes, Senior Writer

The ultimate resource for Mac professionals and savvy Mac users. Each issue is packed with practical how-tos, in-depth features, the latest troubleshooting tips and tricks, industry news, future trends and more.
Cost: $19.97
Frequency: Year Subscription

5505 Marketing Computers
V&U
770 Broadway
F18
New York, NY 10003-9595

646-654-5000; Fax: 646-654-5374
www.marketingcomputers.com

Donna Tapellini, Editor
Tony DiCamillo, Publisher

Edited for advertising and marketing executives in the high-tech industries. The publication covers interpretive news, timely big picture features, departments and analysis by staff editors and industry experts.
Cost: $149.00
100 Pages
Frequency: Weekly
Circulation: 15484

5506 **Mobile Office**
4845 West 111th Street
Alsip, IL 60658

708-636-5400; Fax: 708-636-8637
sales@mobileofficeinc.com
mobileofficeinc.com

Jeff Hecox, Editor

Office equipment, computer technology and information.

5507 **Motion System Distributor**
Penton Media
1300 E 9th St
Cleveland, OH 44114-1503

216-696-7000; Fax: 216-696-6662
information@penton.com
www.penton.com

Jane Cooper, Marketing
David B. Nussbaum, CEO
Larry Berardinis, Editor

Provides selling and technical information to individuals and distributors, specializing in power transmission, motion control and fluid products.
Frequency: Monthly
Circulation: 54000
Founded in 1892

5508 **NCR Connection**
Publications & Communications
505 Cypress Creek Road
Suite B
Cedar Park, TX 78613

512-250-9023; Fax: 512-331-3900

Mary Wilson, Editor

For users of NCR computer systems.
Cost: $92.00
32 Pages
Frequency: Monthly
Founded in 1983

5509 **NEWS 3X/400**
Duke Communications International
221 E 29th Street
Loveland, CO 80538-2769

970-634-4700; Fax: 970-667-2321

Tim Fixmer, Publisher
Trish Faubion, Editor

Leading technical journal for IBM Systems.
Cost: $119.00
220 Pages
Frequency: 16 per year
Circulation: 31,000
Founded in 1982

5510 **Network Support Magazine**
Technical Enterprises
7044 S 13th Street
Oak Creek, WI 53154-1429

414-768-8000; Fax: 414-768-8001
www.naspa.com

Denise Rockhill, Publisher/Advertising Sales
Rachael Zimmerman, Editor
Matthew Jossart, Art Director

The most comprehensive how to publication in the industry. Orientedtoward professionals involved with a myriad of computing technologies and discusses the topic of importance in mainframe, host based and network oriented environments.
Cost: $5.00
68 Pages
Frequency: Monthly
Circulation: 50,000
Founded in 1987

5511 **Network World**
Network World
118 Turnpike Road
Southborough, MA 01772-9108

508-756-6400
800-622-1108; Fax: 508-460-1192
www.networkworld.com

Evilee T Ebb, CEO/Publisher
John Gallant, CFO
Dylan Smith, CFO

For network IS professionals with direct responsibility for planning and managing their companies network computing environment.
Cost: $129.00
100 Pages
Frequency: Weekly
Circulation: 170,000
Founded in 1986

5512 **Neural Networks**
International Neural Network Society
2800 W. Higgins Road
Suite 440
Hoffman Estates, IL 60169

833-636-0351; Fax: 847-885-8393
inns@inns.org
www.inns.org

DeLiang Wang, Editor-in-Chief
Kenji Doya, Editor-in-Chief

Archival journal of the International Neural Network Society, the European Neural Network Society, and the Japanese Neural Network Society.

5513 **Newmedia Age**
HyperMedia Communications
PO Box 299
Brooklin, ME 04616

207-359-6573
800-935-0040; Fax: 207-359-9809

Ben Calica, Editor

Covers new products and technology trends in audio and video computing.
Cost: $24.00
Frequency: Quarterly
Circulation: 40,000

5514 **OfficeWorld News**
366 Ramtown Greenville Road
Howell, NJ 07731-2789

732-785-5976; Fax: 732-785-1347

William Urban, Publisher
Kim Chandlee McCabe, Editor-in-Chief

Provides a diverse population of business products resellers the news and information to best serve the needs of small, mid and large business customers. Provides insight into partnering with their peers in this diverse marketplace.
Frequency: Monthly
Circulation: 31,500
Printed in 4 colors on glossy stock

5515 **PC Arcade**
Softdisk Publishing
606 Common Street
Shreveport, LA 71101-3437

318-218-8718; Fax: 318-221-8870

Al Vekovius, President
Ronda Farries, Circulation Director

Publisher of software subscriptions for DOS, Windows and Macintosh computers.
Cost: $19.95
Frequency: Monthly
Founded in 1990

5516 **PC Sources**
Ziff Davis Publishing Company
500 Unicorn Park Drive
Woburn, MA 01801

781-938-2600; Fax: 781-938-2626
info@ziffdavis.com
www.ziffdavis.com

Peter McKie, Editor
Robert F Callahan, CEO
Michael J Miller, Editor-in-chief
Stephen Hicks, General Counsel

Serves experienced PC users.
Cost: $149.75
Frequency: Monthly
Founded in 1985

5517 **PC Systems and Support**
Technical Enterprises
7044 S 13th Street
Oak Creek, WI 53154

414-325-3366; Fax: 414-768-8001

Scott Sherer, President
Amy Birschbach, Editor

Offers solutions with tutorials on hardware and software implementation/upgrade techniques, workstation customization, integration and optimization. The how-to material presented each month guides those professionals in evaluating, selecting, acquiring, implementing, and supporting PC distributed resources. Presents in-depth technical information that can be applied at work.

5518 **PC Techniques**
Coriolis Group
14455 N Hyden Road
Suite 220
Scottsdale, AZ 85260

480-483-0192

Keith Weiskamp, Publisher
Jeff Duntemann, Editor

Covers information on a wide variety of computer systems and language technology.
Cost: $22.00
104 Pages
Frequency: Bi-Monthly
Founded in 1990

5519 **Pen Computing Magazine**
Aeon Publishing Group
PO Box 408
Plainview, NY 11803-0408

Home Page: www.pencomputing.com

Conrad H Blickenstorfer, Editor-in-Chief
Howard Borgen, Publisher
Wayne Laslo, Advertising Manager

In-depth coverage of pen technology, wireless communications and mobile computing.
Cost: $18.00
Frequency: Monthly
Circulation: 79515
Founded in 1993

5520 **Physicians & Computers**
Moorhead Publications
600 S Waukegan Road
#200
Lake Forest, IL 60045-2672

847-615-8333

Tom Moorhead, Publisher

Provides physicians with information on computer advances helpful in the private practice of medicine. Practice management, current medical and nonmedical software, computer diagnostics, etc.
Cost: $50.00
Frequency: Monthly

5521 **Powerbuilding Developer's Journal**
SYS-CON Publications

135 Chestnut Ridge Rd
Montvale, NJ 07645-1152

201-782-9600
800-513-7111; Fax: 201-782-9601

Fuat Kircaali, Publisher

Covers provide an advanced look at Powerbuilder techniques, new products, reader feedback and interaction, and training in the Powerbuilder language.
Frequency: Monthly
Circulation: 20000

5522 **Precision Engineering Journal**
Elsevier Science Publishing
6277 Sea Harbor Drive
Orlando, FL 32887-4800

407-345-4020
877-839-7126; Fax: 407-363-1354
usjcs@elsevier.com
www.elsevier.com

W T Estler, Editor-in-Chief
D G Chetwynd, Editor
T. Moriwaki, Co-Editor
Bill Godfrey, Chief Information Officer

Provides an integrated approach to all subjects related to the development, design, manufacture, and application of high-precision machines, systems, and components. International news, reviews, conference reports, informed comment, and a calendar of forthcoming events complete the spectrum of coverage designed to keep readers abreast with a fast-moving technology.
Cost: $1014.00
ISSN: 0141-6359
Founded in 1979

5523 **Processor**
Peed Corporation
PO Box 85518
Lincoln, NE 68501-5518

402-479-2141
800-819-9014; Fax: 402-479-2120
feedback@processor.com
www.processor.com

Susy Miller, Publisher
Rhonda Peed, CEO

Information on computer products and services.
Cost: $26.00
84 Pages
Frequency: Weekly
Founded in 1978

5524 **Products for Document Management**
Acron Publishing
1306 Gaskins Road
Richmond, VA 23233-4919

804-754-2101; Fax: 804-754-1534

Irwin Posner, Publisher

News and reviews of latest technology and applications for document management world, including hardware, software, supplies and services.
Frequency: Quarterly
Circulation: 10.963

5525 **RIS/Retail Info Systems News**
Edgell Communications
4 Middlebury Boulevard
Randolph, NJ 07869-4221

973-252-0100; Fax: 973-252-9020
www.risnews.com

Andrew Gaffney, Publisher
Jeff Zabe, Circualtion Manager
Gabriele A. Edgell, CEO
Gerald C Ryerson, President

Updates on the latest development in retail management technologies with articles that focus on the application of managerial and hi-tech advancements.
Frequency: Monthly
Founded in 1984
Printed in 4 colors on glossy stock

5526 **RTC**
RTC Group
27312 Calle Arroyo
San Juan Capistrano, CA 92675-2768

949-443-4400; Fax: 949-489-8502
johnr@rtcgroup.com
www.rtcgroup.com

John Reardo, Publisher

Provides information to answer real life questions about the open systems computer market. Also news, product updates, tech updates and standard tracking.
Frequency: Monthly
Circulation: 29,500

5527 **Real Time Graphics**
Computer Graphic Systems Development Corporation
2483 Old Middlefield Way
#140
Mountain View, CA 94043-2330

650-903-4920; Fax: 650-967-5252
www.cgsd.com

Roy Latham, Owner

In-depth information on the technology of real time graphics, VR, simulations and coverage of industry news.
Cost: $205.00
Frequency: Monthly
Circulation: 1M

5528 **Real-Time Engineering**
Micrology PBT
2618 S Shannon
Tempe, AZ 85282-2936

480-967-5581; Fax: 480-968-3446
micrology@aol.com
www.realtime-engineering.com

John Black, Editor-in-Chief

Focuses on software and operating systems.
Frequency: Quarterly
Circulation: 10,000

5529 **Red Herring: The Business of Technology**
Red Herring Communications
1550 Bryant St
Suite 450
San Francisco, CA 94103-4832

415-486-2819; Fax: 415-865-2280
info@redherring.com
www.redherring.com

5530 **Report on Healthcare Information Management**
Aspen Publishers
1101 King Street
#444
Alexandria, VA 22314

703-683-4100; Fax: 703-739-6517
www.aspenlawschool.com

Mike Brown, Publisher
H. Stephen Lieber, CEO/President
Timothy B Clark, Marketing & Business Dev

System development, clinical information systems, cost-effective clinical integration, data collection, network security and confidentiality for the health care industry.
Cost: $358.00
Frequency: Monthly

5531 **Retail Systems Alert**
Retail Systems Alert Group
377 Elliot Street
PO Box 332
Newton Upper Falls, MA 02464

617-527-4626; Fax: 617-527-8102
www.retailsystems.com

Tom Friedman, President
Hideo Funamoto, Contributing Editor

Provides updated information on automation news and trends, including decision systems, information systems implementation, in-store merchandise management, and case studies of retailers.
Cost: $295.00
8 Pages
Frequency: Monthly
Founded in 1988

5532 **Retail Systems Reseller**
Edgell Communications
4 Middlebury Boulevard
Suite 1
Randolph, NJ 07869-1111

973-252-0100; Fax: 973-252-9020

michael Kachmar, Publisher
Joe Skorupa, Editor-in-Chief
Gabriele Edgell, CEO
Gerald C. Ryerson, President
John Chiego, Vice President

Offers information to retailers, dealers, systems integraters, VARs, VADs, etc., on retail technology for small to mid-size retailers.
Cost: $190.00
Frequency: Monthly
Founded in 1984

5533 **RetailTech**
Progressive Grocer Associates
23 Old King's Highway South
Darien, CT 06820-4538

646-654-7561; Fax: 203-656-3800
www.progressivegrocer.com

John Failla, Publisher
Jenny McTaggart, Senior Editor
Stephen Dowdell, Editor-in-Chief
Joseph Tarnowski, Tech Editor, Equipment & Design

Editoral content covers software, computer peripherals, communications, electronic retailing, point-of-sale systems, networking, data warehousing, logistics/distribution systems, and the Internet.
Cost: $99.00
Frequency: Monthly

5534 **Robot Explorer**
Appropriate Solutions
85 Grove Street
PO Box 458
Peterborough, NH 03458

603-924-6079; Fax: 603-924-8668
www.appropriatesolutions.com

Raymond Cote, Editor

Targets the world of non-industrial robots. From eight-legged walking machines exploring Antarctic volcanoes, to microscopic nano-machines, Robot Explorer provides practical construction details and fascinating reviews of current technology.
Cost: $14.95
Circulation: 500

5535 **Robotics and Autonomous Systems**
Elsevier Science

230 Park Avenue
Suite 800
New York, NY 10169

212-309-8100
www.elsevier.com

K. Berns, Editor-in-Chief
M. Gini, Editor-in-Chief
J. Ota, Editor-in-Chief

Journal with articles on developments in the field of robotics, with an emphasis on autonomous systems.
Cost: $3008.00
ISSN: 0921-8890

5536 **Robotics and Computer-Intergrated Manufacturing**
Elsevier Science
230 Park Avenue
Suite 800
New York, NY 10169

212-309-8100
www.elsevier.com

Lihui Wang, Editor-in-Chief

Journal containing original papers on theoretical, applied and experimental robotics and computer-integrated manufacturing, with emphasis on flexible manufacturing systems.
Cost: $3008.00
Circulation: 2500
ISSN: 0736-5845
Founded in 1880

5537 **SCO Magazine**
600 Community Drive
Manhasset, NY 11030-3847

516-562-5836; Fax: 516-562-5466

H Newton Barrett, Publisher

5538 **SIGNAL Magazine**
4400 Fair Lakes Center
Fairfax, VA 22033-3899

703-631-6100
800-336-4583; Fax: 703-631-6169
bmowery@afcea.org
www.afcea.org

Beverly Mowery, Associate Publisher
Robert K Ackerman, Editor-in-Chief

A news magazine targeted to serve the critical information needs of government, military and industry professionals active in the fields of command, control, communications, computers, intelligence, surveillance and reconnaissance, or C4ISR; information security; research and development; electronics; and homeland security.
Cost: $56.00
Frequency: Monthly/Year Subscription
Mailing list available for rent

5539 **SMC Magazine**
IEEE Systems, Man, and Cybernetics Society
445 Hoes Lane
Piscataway, NJ 08854

smcmagazine_eic@outlook.com
www.ieeesmc.org

Saeid Nahavandi, Editor-in-Chief
Enrique Herrera Viedma, VP, Publications

Articles relevant to the research areas of the IEEE Systems, Man, and Cybernetics Society, with information on the Society's activities, and educational material as well.

5540 **SQL Forum Online**
Informant Communications Group
10519 E Stockton Boulevard
Suite 100
Elk Grove, CA 95624-9703

916-863-3700; Fax: 916-379-0610
www.informant.com

Forrest Freeman, Owner
Tom Bondur, Publisher

Written for data-base professionals to share and exchange ideas. Has papers and articles that are filled with answers to common data-base questions.
Frequency: Monthly

5541 **Sawtooth News**
Sawtooth Technologies
1500 Skokie Boulevard
Suite 510
Northbrook, IL 60062

847-239-7300; Fax: 847-239-7301
info@sawtooth.com
www.sawtooth.com

Nicole Garneau, Editor

Articles on computer aided telephone interviewing, computer interviewing, conjoint analysis, and other advanced research techniques.
Founded in 1995

5542 **Scan Tech News**
Reed Business Information
2000 Clearwater Dr
Oak Brook, IL 60523-8809

630-574-0825; Fax: 630-288-8781
www.reedbusiness.com

Jeff Greisch, President

Updates in trends in ADC technology and standards, the latest news from leading industry events, and product developments that streamline the flow of essential information in industrial settings.
Frequency: Monthly
Circulation: 82M

5543 **Scan: Data Capture Report**
Corry Publishing
5905 Beacon Hill Lane
Erie, PA 16509

814-380-0025; Fax: 814-864-2037
rickm@scandcr.com
www.rmgenterprises.com/

Larry Roberts, CEO and Publisher
(Jon) Rick Morgan, President and Editor

Developments in bar code scanning, biometric identification, electronic commerce and areas of automatic data capture.
Cost: $597.00
Frequency: Fortnightly
Founded in 1996

5544 **Scientific Computing & Automation**
Reed Business Information
2000 Clearwater Dr
Oak Brook, IL 60523-8809

630-574-0825; Fax: 630-288-8781
www.reedbusiness.com

Jeff Greisch, President

Provides the scientists working in industrial/analytical labs, clinical labs, life science labs and electronics R&D labs with information on developments in computing and automation technology for the laboratory.
Cost: $60.00
Frequency: Monthly
Circulation: 50,059

5545 **Scientific Computing & Instrumentation**
Reed Business Information
45 E 85th St
4th Floor
New York, NY 10028-0957

212-772-8300; Fax: 630-288-8686
subsmail@reedbusiness.com
www.scimag.com

Lawrence S Reed
Suzanne Tracy, Editor in Chief

5546 **Semiconductor Magazine**
Semiconductor Equipment & Materials International
3081 Zanker Road
San Jose, CA 95134

408-943-6900; Fax: 408-428-9600
semihq@semi.org
www.semi.org

T Buehler, Editor-in-Chief
Chris Bucholtz, Editor
Marie Claussell, Circulation Manager
Barbara Wietzel, Marketing Manager

Covers the technical and business information needs of inportant worldwide semiconductor manufacturers, including captive manufacturers, merchant manufacturers, research and development laboratories, equipment suppliers, government/military installations and consortiums.
Cost: $125.00
Frequency: Monthly
Founded in 1980

5547 **Sensors Magazine**
Advanstar Communications
275 Grove Street
Suite 2-130
Newton, MA 02466

603-924-5400; Fax: 603-924-5401

Barbara Goode, Group Editorial Director
Stephanie Henkel, Executive Editor
Jill Thiry, Group Publishing Director

Source among design and production engineers of information on sensor technologies and products, and topic integral to sensor-based systems and applications. Provides practical and in-depth yet accessible information on sensor operation, design, application, and implementation within systems. Covers the effective use of state-of-the-art resources and tools that enable readers to get the maximum benefit from their use of sensors.
Frequency: Monthly
Circulation: 66676
Founded in 1999

5548 **Serverworld Magazine**
Publications & Communications
11675 Jollyville Rd
Suite 150
Austin, TX 78759

512-250-9023
800-678-9724; Fax: 512-331-3900
pci@pcinews.com
www.pcinews.com

David Wohlbrueck, Editor
Gary Pittman, CEO/President
Bill Lifland, VP Operations

Dedicated to Hewlett-Packard computing.
Cost: $45.00
60 Pages
Frequency: Monthly
Founded in 1979

5549 **Signal Processing Magazine**
IEEE Signal Processing Society
445 Hoes Lane
Piscataway, NJ 08854

732-562-3888; Fax: 732-867-9953
sp-pub-info@ieee.org

signalprocessingsociety.org
Facebook, Twitter, LinkedIn

Robert Heath, Editor-in-Chief
William Colacchio, Senior Manager, Publications

Tutorials on signal processing research and applications, as well as editorial content on matters of interest.

5550 **Simulation**
Simulation Councils
PO Box 17900
San Diego, CA 92177-7900

858-277-3888; Fax: 858-277-3930
info@scs.org
www.scs.org

William Gallagher, Publisher
Richard Fujimoto, Editor-in-Chief
Steve Branch, Executive Director

Information on computer simulation including, applications, methodologies and techniques of computer simulation.
Cost: $195.00
Frequency: Monthly
Circulation: 3800
Founded in 1952

5551 **Small Business Advisor: Software News**
Software News Publishing Company
110 N Bell Avenue
Suite 300
Shawnee, OK 74801-6967

405-275-3100
800-456-0864; Fax: 405-275-3101
www.cpatechadvisor.com

Sharie Dodgen, Publisher
Melody Wrinkle, Manager
Isaac OBannon, Manager
Thomson Reuters, Executive Editor

Published for advisers to small businesses and for software installers for small businesses.
Cost: $48.00
Circulation: 50000
Founded in 1991

5552 **Smart Reseller**
Ziff Davis Publishing Company
500 Unicorn Park Drive
Woburn, MA 01801-4874

781-938-2600; Fax: 781-938-2626

Sloan Seymour, Publisher

Identifies the most lucrative new business opportunities and details how to profitably take advantage of them. In-depth business management strategies and trusted new technology solutions-based reviews.
Frequency: SemiMonthly
Circulation: 60M

5553 **Software Development**
Miller Freeman Publications
2655 Seely Avenue
San Jose, CA 95134

408-943-1234
800-227-4675; Fax: 408-943-0513

Veronica Costanza, Publisher
Nicole Freeman, Editor
Laura Merling, Executive Director

For corporate developers and technical managers involved in the development of software applications within the industries.
Circulation: 73297

5554 **Software Digest**
National Software Testing Laboratories
670 Sentry Pkwy
2nd Floor
Blue Bell, PA 19422-2325

610-832-8400; Fax: 610-941-9952
www.nstl.com

Lowrenie Goldstein, Publisher
Andrew Froning, Editor

Independent and comparative ratings on IBM PC software. All categories tested free of bias. No advertising is accepted.
Frequency: Monthly
Founded in 1983

5555 **Solid Solutions**
ConnectPress
551 W Cordova Road
Suite 701
Santa Fe, NM 87505-4100

505-474-5000; Fax: 505-474-5001
info@solidprofessor.com
www.solidmag.com

Dale Bennie, Publisher

Covers the latest market developments and tracks the growth of SolidWorks software in the CAD/CAM/CAE market. Reviews of workstations, 3D printers, and Windows NT graphic accelerators.
Cost: $99.00
Frequency: Monthly

5556 **Solutions Integrator**
International Data Group
3 Post Office Sq
4th Floor
Boston, MA 02109-3939

617-423-9030; Fax: 617-423-0240

Bob Carrigan, CEO
Joel Shore, Editor-In-Chief

Provides accessment of technology, IT buying practices and plans, business strategies and vendor technology roadmaps.
Circulation: 90000

5557 **Speech Recognition Update**
CI Publishing
PO Box 570730
Tarzana, CA 91357-730

818-708-0962
888-632-7419; Fax: 818-345-2980
info@tmaa.com
www.tmaa.com

William S Meisel, President
Bill Meisel, Editor

News and analysis of speech recognition markets, companies and technologies.
Cost: $195.00
Frequency: Monthly
Founded in 1993

5558 **Storage Management Solutions**
West World Productions
420 N Camden Dr
Beverly Hills, CA 90210-4507

310-276-9500; Fax: 310-276-9874
www.wwpi.com

Yuri R Spiro, Publisher/CEO
Steve Schone, Circulation Manager

Articles on tutorials, case studies, lab tests and new products that offer solutions to issues of data accessibility, availablity and protection and network storage.
Cost: $10.00
72 Pages
Frequency: Monthly
Circulation: 64044
ISSN: 1097-5152
Founded in 1995
Printed in 4 colors on glossy stock

5559 **Studio City**
Resource Central
4126 Pennsylvania Avenue
Suite 3
Kansas City, MO 64111-3018
Tom Weishaar, President

Information on using the multimedia package Hyper Studio, mailed on 3.5 inch disk, 6 times a year. Available in Macintosh and Apple II versions.
Frequency: Bi-Monthly

5560 **Sun Observer**
Publications & Communications
11675 Jollyville Rd
Suite 150
Austin, TX 78759

512-250-9023
800-678-9724; Fax: 512-331-3900
pci@pcinews.com
www.pcinews.com

Gary Pittman, CEO/President
Robert Martin, Editor

Journal of news and information devoted to the users of Sun Microsystems.
Cost: $14.95
80 Pages
Founded in 1980

5561 **Supply Chain Systems Magazine**
Helmers Publishing
174 Concord Street
P O Box 874
Peterborough, NH 03458-1291

603-924-9631; Fax: 603-924-7408

David Andrewso, Publisher/Editorial
Bill Fahy, Circulation Director
Paul Quinn, Editor/Senior Writer

Educates its readers about the benefits and bast practices of supply chain management in manufacturing and service industries. We educate our readers about how e-business, Enterprises Resource Planning, asset management, data capture, warehouse management and management can be integrated to create effective and efficient supply chain systems.
60 Pages
Frequency: Weekly
Circulation: 53000
Founded in 1979
Printed in 4 colors on glossy stock

5562 **Synapps**
Synergis Technologies
472 California Rd
Quakertown, PA 18951-2463

215-643-6620; Fax: 215-536-9249
marketingsupport@synergis.com
www.synergis.com

Barbara White, VP

Information for professional management of AutoCAD systems and includes application articles.
Frequency: Quarterly
Circulation: 25000

5563 **Sys Admin**
CMP Media
4601 West 6th Street
Suite B
Lawrence, KS 66046

785-841-1631; Fax: 785-841-2047
samag@neodata.com
www.sysadminmag.com

Edwin Rothrock, Publisher
Amber Ankerholz, Editor
Gary Marshall, President
Bob Cucciniello, Marketing
Deirdre Blake, Managing Editor

SYS ADMIN serves the Unix and Linux system administration market.
Cost: $43.00
100 Pages
Frequency: Monthly
Circulation: 29121
Founded in 1992
Printed in on glossy stock

5564 **Systems Development Management**
Auerbach Publications
535 5th Avenue
Room 806
New York, NY 10017-3610

800-737-8034; Fax: 212-297-9176
www.auerbach-publications.com

Rich O'Hamley, Publisher
Janet Butler, Editor

Technical and managerial information on systems development.
Cost: $495.00
Frequency: Bi-Monthly
Circulation: 1,000
ISSN: 1096-7893
Printed in on matte stock

5565 **Systems Integration**
Reed Business Information
360 Park Ave S
New York, NY 10010-1737

646-746-6400; Fax: 646-756-7583
slebris@reedbusiness.com
www.reedbusiness.com

John Poulin, CEO
Thomas Temin, Editor
James Reed, Owner
Jim Casella, CEO

Covers trade and developments for mini-micro based computer systems.
Cost: $75.00
Frequency: Monthly
Founded in 1968

5566 **TAAR: The Automated Agency Report**
Automation Management Group
4964 Sundance Square
Boulder, CO 80301-3739

303-581-0525
www.taan.com

Rick Morgan, Editor

Covers trends, developments and news, reviews new and current technology, and offers ideas and profiles on the productivity benefits.
Cost: $175.00
Frequency: Monthly

5567 **Tech Week**
1156 Aster Avenue
Suite B
Sunnyvale, CA 94086

408-249-8300; Fax: 408-249-0727

5568 **Techlinks**
3350 Riverwood Parkway
Suite 1900
Atlanta, GA 30339

678-627-8157; Fax: 678-627-8159

5569 **Technical Services Quarterly**
Taylor & Francis Group LLC
325 Chestnut St
Suite 800
Philadelphia, PA 19106-2614

215-625-8900
800-354-1420; Fax: 215-625-2940
haworthorders@taylorandfrancis.com
www.taylorandfrancis.com

Kevin Bradley, President

This journal publishes up to the minute information that technical services professionals and paraprofessionals need in order to successfully negotiate changes in the field and take full advantage of automated systems that ultimately make collections more accessible to users.
Frequency: Quarterly

5570 **Technical Support Magazine**
Technical Enterprises
7044 S 13th Street
Oak Creek, WI 53154

414-908-4945; Fax: 414-768-8001
www.naspa.com

Rachael Zimmerman, Editor
Denise Rockhill, President

Provides tips and techniques for MVS, VM and VSE mainframe operating systems and NT environments. It also examines security and system performance, product installation experiences and a host of other related enterprise concerns.
68 Pages
Frequency: Monthly
Circulation: 50,000
Founded in 1986
Printed in 4 colors on glossy stock

5571 **Technical Training**
American Society for Training & Development
1640 King St
Box 1443
Alexandria, VA 22314-2743

703-683-8100; Fax: 703-683-8103
customercare@astd.org
www.astd.org

Tony Bingham, President

Industry trends, technologies and techniques within computer, manufacturing, telecommunications and government industries.
Cost: $59.00
Frequency: Bi-Monthly
Circulation: 11M

5572 **Technology & Learning**
Tech & Learning
1111 Bayhill Drive
Suite 125
San Bruno, CA 94066

650-238-0260; Fax: 650-238-0263
www.techlearning.com

Allison Knapp, Publisher
Kevin Hogan, Editorial Director
Christine Weiser, Managing Editor

Serves the K-12 education community with practical resources and expert strategies for transforming education through integration of digital technologies. Often used as a professional development tool to help educators across the board get up to speed with the newest technologies and products in order to best prepare students for the global digital workforce.
Frequency: Monthly
Circulation: 81000
Founded in 1971
Printed in on glossy stock

5573 **Technology and Practice Guide**
ABA Publishing
321 N Clark St
Chicago, IL 60654-7598

312-988-5000
800-285-2221; Fax: 312-988-5280
askaba@abanet.org
www.abanet.org

Tommy H Wells Jr, President

Helps law professionals of general practice in making decisions about legal information management and technology.
Cost: $18.00
Frequency: SemiAnnual
Circulation: 13,477

5574 **Technology and Society**
IEEE Society on Social Implications of Technology
445 Hoes Lane
Piscataway, NJ 08854

j.pitt@imperial.ac.uk
technologyandsociety.org
Facebook, Twitter, LinkedIn

Jeremy Pitt, Editor_in-Chief
Terri A. Bookman, Managing Editor

Flagship magazine of the IEEE Society on Social Implications of Technology, with peer-reviewed articles on the impact of technology on the world.

5575 **Techscan: The Managers Guide to Technology**
Richmond Research
266 W 37th St
PO Box 537
New York, NY 10018-6609

212-594-9795
techscan@pipeline.com

Larry Richmond, President

Information and insights on how various new technologies, products and design techniques are used to solve business problems.
Cost: $87.50
Frequency: Monthly
Circulation: 2,500

5576 **Text Technology: The Journal of Computer Text Processing**
McMaster University
1280 Main Street W
Hamilton, On 0

905-525-9140; Fax: 905-577-6930
buckleyj@mcmaster.ca
texttechnology.mcmaster.ca

Joanne Buckley, Editor
Edie Rasmussen, Editor

Tips, techniques and programs for TEXT, Icon, Macintosh and other software and word-processing programs, desktop publishing and Internet as they apply to educational applications.
Cost: $45.00
Frequency: Quarterly
Circulation: 800

5577 **The Bridge**
IEEE-Eta Kappa Nu
445 Hoes Lane
Piscataway, NJ 08854

732-465-5846
800-406-2590
info@hkn.org
hkn.ieee.org/news-and-announcements/the-bridge

Sahra Sedigh Sarvestani, Editor-in-Chief
Stephen Williams, Editor-in-Chief

The award-winning digital magazine of the IEEE-HKN.
Frequency: 3x/year

5578 **Trends in Computing**
Scientific American
415 Madison Ave
New York, NY 10017-7934

212-451-8200
800-333-1199; Fax: 212-832-2998

webmaster@sciam.com
www.sciam.com

Gretchen G Teichgraeber, CEO
Elias Arnett, Owner

Targets computer managers and professionals.
Cost: $24.97
Frequency: Annual+
Founded in 1845

5579 **Unisys World/Network Computing News**
Publications & Communications
505 Cypress Creek Road
Suite B
Cedar Park, TX 78613-1868

512-250-9023; Fax: 512-331-3900

Larry Storer, Editor

Dedicated to the users and OEMs of convergent technologies products.
Cost: $48.00
24 Pages
Frequency: Monthly
Founded in 1983

5580 **Varindustry Products**
VIPublishing
30506 Palos Verdes Drive W
Rancho Palos Verdes, CA 90275-4471
Kenneth Allen, Editor

Focuses on new products and services.
Frequency: Monthly
Founded in 1990

5581 **Vision Systems Design**
PennWell Publishing Company
98 Spit Brook Rd
5th Floor
Nashua, NH 03062-5737

603-891-0123; Fax: 603-891-9294
cholton@pennwell.com
www.pennwell.com

Christine Shaw, VP
Andrew Wilson, Editor
Bonnie Heines, Managing Editor

Each issue discusses the development of leading edge industrial, scientific, medical, military, and aerospace machine vision applications.
Cost: $85.00
Frequency: Monthly
Circulation: 32000
Founded in 1910
Mailing list available for rent
Printed in 4 colors

5582 **Visual Basic Programmer's Journal**
Fawcette Technical Publications
2600 S El Camino Real
Suite 300
San Mateo, CA 94403-2381

650-378-7100
800-848-5523; Fax: 650-853-0230
www.fawcette.com/vsm/

James Fawcette, President
Tina Fontenot, Marketing
Karin Becker, Associate Publisher
Karen Koenen, Sr. Circulation Director

Provides technical news on how to increase productivity and process applications more efficiently.
Cost: $71.40
Frequency: Monthly
Circulation: 109874
Founded in 1990

5583 **WINDOWS Magazine**
CMP Publications
600 Community Dr
Manhasset, NY 11030-3810

516-562-5000; Fax: 516-562-5995

Scott Wolfe, Publisher

Offers the latest information and updates for the WINDOWS user.

5584 **Wall Street Computer Review**
Miller Freeman Publications
1199 S Belt Line Rd
Suite 100
Coppell, TX 75019-4666

972-906-6500; Fax: 972-419-7825

Elizabeth Katz, Publisher
Pavan Sahgal, Editor

For financial and investment professionals and individual investors.
Cost: $5.00
Circulation: 34,000

5585 **Waters**
Waters Information Services
270 Lafayette St
Suite 700
New York, NY 10012-3311

212-925-6990; Fax: 212-925-7585
www.watersinfo.com

Andrew Delaeny, Editor-in-Chief
Phil Albinus, Editor
John Waters, CEO
Farrell McManus, Advertising Manager

Articles on technology applications leading strategic business success, career enhancements and workplace changes.
Cost: $240.00
Frequency: Monthly
Circulation: 20000
Founded in 1993

5586 **Windows & Dot Net**
Duke Communications International
221 E 29th Street
Loveland, CO 80538

970-663-4700
800-621-1544; Fax: 970-667-2321
CorporateCustomerService@penton.com
www.penton.com

Bart Taylor, Group Publisher
Kim Paulsen, Publisher
David B. Nussbaum, CEO
Cost: $49.95
Frequency: Monthly
Circulation: 100000
Founded in 1982

5587 **Windows Developer's Journal**
600 Harrison Street
San Francisco, CA 94107

415-947-6000; Fax: 415-947-6027
www.wdj.com

John Dorsey, Editor in Chief
Kerry Gates, Publisher
Holly Vessichelli, Director of Marketing
Deirdre Blake, Managing Editor

Publication for professional Windows developers.
Founded in 1990

5588 **Windows NT Magazine**
Duke Communications International
221 E 29th Street
PO Box 447
Loveland, CO 80539-447

970-663-4700
800-621-1544; Fax: 970-203-2996
www.winntmag.com

Mark Smith, Publisher
Karen Forster, Manager
John Savill, Manager

Serves technical decision makers using the Windows NT application, and related systems.
Cost: $49.95
Frequency: Monthly
Circulation: 75000

5589 **Windows/DOS Developer's Journal**
R&D Associates
6701 W 121st Street
Suite 310
Overland Park, KS 66209

913-491-0345; Fax: 785-841-2624
www.rndassociates.com

Ron Burk, Editor

Information for professional Windows and DOS programmers.
Cost: $29.00
Frequency: Monthly
Circulation: 22000
Founded in 1996

5590 **Windowspro Magazine**
Ziff Davis Publishing Company
500 Unicorn Park Drive
Woburn, MA 01801

781-938-2600; Fax: 781-938-2626
www.windowspro.com

Jason Young, Publisher
Jacquelyn Gavron, Editor-in-Chief

Serves technology-experts responsible for Windows NT based support. Includes technologies, products, solutions, and how-to instructions.
Frequency: Monthly
Circulation: 150,000

5591 **Wired**
Wired News
520 3rd St
1st Floor
San Francisco, CA 94107-6805

415-276-8400
800-769-4733; Fax: 415-276-8500
info@wired.com
www.wired.com

Evan Hansen, Editor-in-Chief
Jeremy Barna, Production Manager
Alison Macondray, General Manager
Drew Schutte, Publisher

Focuses on people and ideas behind digital technology.
Frequency: Monthly
Circulation: 305097

5592 **Workstation News**
Data Base Publications
9390 Research Blvd
Suite 300
Austin, TX 78759-7374

512-418-9590; Fax: 512-418-8165
www.bancvue.com

Gabe Krajicek, CEO

Aimed at workstation users and volume buyers.
Frequency: Monthly
Founded in 1990

Trade Shows

5593 **AAAI National Conference**
Association for the Advancement of AT
2275 East Bayshore Road
Suite 160
Palo Alto, CA 94303

650-328-3123; Fax: 650-321-4457
www.aaai.org
Twitter

Stephanie Le, Conference Coordinator
Emma Wishmeyer, Conference Program Associate

The conference provides a forum for a broad range of topics, including knowledge representation and automated reasoning, planning, machine learning and data mining, autonomous agents, robotics and machine perception, probabilistic

inference, constraint satisfaction, search and game playing, natural language processing, neural networks, multi-agent systems, computational game theory and cognitive modeling.
1.2M Attendees
Frequency: Annual/July
Founded in 1980

5594 ACT-IAC Executive Leadership Conference
American Council for Technology
3040 Williams Drive
Suite 500
Fairfax, VA 22031

703-208-4800; Fax: 703-208-4805
act-iac@actiac.org
www.actiac.org

Kisha Powell, Sr. Director, Meetings
April Davis, Director, Member Services
David M. Wennergren, Chief Executive Officer

ACT-IAC's Executive Leadership Conference (ELC) is a collaborative and learning event in the government IT community. ELC provides a forum where senior executives from government and industry can learn from one another and collaborate on strategic and high priority issues.
850 Attendees
Founded in 1991

5595 AIIM Annual Conference
Association for Information and Image Management
8403 Colesville Road
Suite 1100
Silver Spring, MD 20910

301-587-8202
800-477-2446; Fax: 301-587-2711
aiim@aiim.org
www.aiim.org

Peggy Winton, President & CEO
Georgina Clelland, Chief Operating Officer
June Ann Ewan, Director, Finance
Jesse Wilkins, Director, Professional Development

The largest enterprise content & document management conference and exposition showcasing the technologies and solutions that provide intelligence behind information. For more than 50 years, this annual event attracts business professionals and executive management seeking the latest technologies.
Frequency: May

5596 AIM Summit
AIM Global
20399 Route 19
Suite 203
Cranberry Township, PA 16066

724-742-4470
info@aimglobal.org
www.aimglobal.org
Facebook, Twitter, LinkedIn, Pinterest

Mary Lou Bosco, Chief Operating Officer
Chuck Evanhoe, President & CEO

An opportunity for experts and professionals in automatic identification and data capture to discuss and share ideas and trends.
Frequency: Annual/October
Founded in 1972

5597 AMIA Annual Symposium
American Medical Informatics Association
4720 Montgomery Lane
Suite 500
Bethesda, MD 20814

301-657-1291; Fax: 301-657-1296
www.amia.org

Douglas B. Fridsma, MD, PhD, President & CEO
Lauren Koleszar, Sr. Meetings/Exhibits Coordinator

Features an outstanding program of scientific papers, posters, tutorials and other educational events that provide information about cutting-edge work in medical informatics.
2000 Attendees
Frequency: Annual/November

5598 ARMA InfoCon
ARMA International
11880 College Boulevard
Suite 450
Overland Park, KS 66210

913-444-9174
844-565-2120; Fax: 913-257-3855
headquarters@armaintl.org
www.arma.org
Facebook, Twitter, LinkedIn

Nate Hughes, Exec. Dir., Operations
Jennifer Millett, National Accounts Manager
Karen Skaggs, Sales & Event Specialist

Conference, seminar, workshop, banquet, award ceremony and 175 exhibits of micrographics, optical disk, automated document storage and retrieval systems and more technology of interest to information professionals.
3500 Attendees
Frequency: Annual
Founded in 1956

5599 ASIS&T Annual Meeting
Assoc for Information Science and Technology
8555 16th Street
Suite 850
Silver Spring, MD 20910

301-495-0900; Fax: 301-495-0810
asist@asist.org
www.asist.org

Lydia Middleton, Executive Director
Terrence Curtiss, Director of Membership
Cathy L. Nash, Director of Meetings & Events

Professional development organization for the information science and technology industry.

5600 ASPE Annual Meeting
American Society for Precision Engineering
3801 Lake Boone Trail
Suite 190
Raleigh, NC 27607

919-839-8444; Fax: 919-839-8039
www.aspe.net

Wendy Shearon, Meetings & Membership Manager

Offering the latest in precision engineering research through presentations from national and international speakers. Participants in the Annual Meeting have the opportunity to exchange ideas with internationally renowned experts in the field.
Frequency: Annual/Oct-Nov

5601 AWWA Annual Conference and Exposition
American Water Works Association
6666 W Quincy Ave.
Denver, CO 80235

303-794-7711
800-926-7337; Fax: 303-347-0804
www.awwa.org

Melissa Elliott, President
David B. LaFrance, Chief Executive Officer

The source of knowledge and information for water professionals who work to improve the quality and supply of drinking water in North America and beyond. Learn from industry experts in the field, hear about cutting edge research and exceptional best practices, and have the opportunity to ask questions, seek advice, and interact with other water professionals regarding both universal topics and items specifically focused to meet your needs.
Frequency: Annual/June

5602 AWWA Sustainable Water Management Conference
American Water Works Association
6666 W Quincy Ave.
Denver, CO 80235

303-794-7711
800-926-7337; Fax: 303-347-0804
www.awwa.org

Melissa Elliott, President
David B. LaFrance, Chief Executive Officer

This event brings together water sector organizations and professionals to discuss all aspects of resilient and efficient water management.

5603 Association For Services Management World Conference Expo
AFSM International
11031 Via Frontera
Suite A
San Diego, CA 92127

239-275-7887
800-333-9786; Fax: 239-275-0794

John Schoenewald, Executive Director
Jb Wood, President/Ceo

World's largest gathering of executives in the services and support industry.
Frequency: October

5604 Association of College Unions International Conference
Association of College Unions International
120 W 7th Street
One City Centre, Suite 200
Bloomington, IN 47404-3925

812-245-2284; Fax: 812-245-6710
acui@acui.org
www.acui.org

Jake Dawes, Events & Operations Coordinator
Devon Bray, Marketing Coordinator

Educational programs, speakers, and exhibits and the opportunity for attendees to connect and network.
Frequency: April
Founded in 1914

5605 Autodesk Expo
AEC Systems International/Penton Media
1300 E 9th Street
Cleveland, OH 44114

800-451-1196; Fax: 610-280-7106
sales@acesystems.com
www.acesystems.com

Philip McKay, Manager

Highlights AutoCAD and related products from Autodesk and third party developers. 500 exhibits.
20M Attendees
Frequency: May

5606 BDPA Annual Technology Conference
National BDPA
9500 Arena Drive
Suite 106
Largo, MD 20774

301-584-3135; Fax: 301-560-8300
info@bdpa.org
www.bdpa.org
Facebook, Twitter, LinkedIn

Earl A. Pace, Co-Founder
Mike Williams, President
Pamela Mathews, Vice President
Teresa Williams, Vice President, Member

Services
Monique Berry, Vice President, Finance
Founded in 1975

5607 **Bentley MicroStation Mail**
AEC Systems International/Penton Media
1300 E 9th Street
Cleveland, OH 44114

800-451-1196; Fax: 610-280-7106
sales@acesystems.com
www.acesystems.com

Philip McKay, Manager

Showcases a comprehensive line-up of intergrated design, facility management and GIS solutions built around MicroStation software. 500 exhibits.
20M Attendees
Frequency: May

5608 **CALICO Annual Conference**
Computer Assisted Language Instruction Consortium
Texas State University
214 Centennial Hall
San Marcos, TX 78666

512-245-1417; Fax: 512-245-9089
info@calico.org
calico.org

Esther Horn, Manager
Daniel Meyers, Technology Coordinator

Providing a forum for discussions of state-of-the-art educational technology and its applications to the more effective teaching and learning of languages. The symposia accommodate workshops, papers, demonstrations, panels, and special interest groups for participants at all levels of expertise.
450 Attendees
Frequency: May

5609 **CLA World Computer and Internet Law Congress Conference**
Computer Law Association
3028 Javier Road
Suite 402
Fairfax, VA 22031

703-560-7747; Fax: 703-207-7028
www.cla.org

Barbara Fieser, Executive Director

This conference will provide you with proven strategies and best practices that will enable you to effectively address your existing clients' IT-related challenges and problems and seek out clients whom you can assist with knowledge you will gain from the conference.
2000+ Attendees
Frequency: May

5610 **CSI Annual Computer Securtiy Conference & Exhibition**
CMP Media/Computer Security Institute Services
600 Community Drive
Manhasset, NY 11030

516-562-5000
866-271-8529; Fax: 818-487-4550

Jennifer Stevens, Conference Manager
Kimber Heald, Registration Manager
Annette Campo, Manager

The exhibition features 150 security vendors, from the industry leaders to the up-and coming, displaying the latest security technologies.
950 Attendees
Frequency: November

5611 **CUMREC**
Educause
4772 Walnut Street
Suite 206
Boulder, CO 80301-2538

303-449-4430; Fax: 303-440-0461
info@educause.edu
www.educause.edu

Beverly Williams, Director of Conference Activities
Lisa Gesner, Assistant Director of Marketing

Higher education administrative technology conference. The purpose of CUMREC is to provide a forum for higher education professionals to share their expertise and experiences with computer systems in our ever changing world of technology. The CUMREC annual conference, founded in 1956, is devoted to promoting the understanding and use of information technology in higher education.
3M Attendees
Frequency: May
Founded in 1956

5612 **Canadian Conference on Artificial Intelligence**
Canadian Artificial Intelligence Association
1515 St. Catherine Street W.
Montreal, QC H3G 2W1

514-848-2424
leila.kosseim@concordia.ca
www.caiac.ca

Leila Kosseim, President
Richard Khoury, Vice President
Xin Wang, Treasurer
Denilson Barbosa, Secretary

Conference on all areas of Artificial Intelligence, either theoretical or applied. Takes place with the Conference on Computer and Robot Vision.

5613 **Comdex Spring and Fall Shows**
MediaLive International
795 Folsom Street
6th Floor
San Francisco, CA 94107-1243

415-905-2300; Fax: 415-905-2FAX
www.medialiveinternational.com

Eric Faurot, VP
Marco Pardi, Exhibit Sales

COMDEX is the global marketplace for the IT industry. Buyers and sellers from around the world converge to learn how best to use technology to solve their business challenges and remain competitive. COMDEX is where hardware manufacturers, software vendors and service providers launch new products, where thought-leaders discuss industry trends, and where the media reports on the latest in the IT industry and considers its future.
100M+ Attendees
Frequency: November

5614 **Conf-IRM**
Association for Information Systems
Member Service Center
PO Box 2712
Atlanta, GA 30301-2712

404-413-7445
membership@aisnet.org
aisnet.org

Lise Fitzpatrick, Chief Operating Officer
Robina Wahid, Conference Director

Provides forums for researchers and practitioners to share leading-edge knowledge in the global resource information management area.

5615 **Conference on Computer and Robot Vision**
Cdn. Image Processing/Pattern Recognition Society
York University
4700 Keele Street
Toronto, ON M3J 1P3
416-736-2100
www.computerrobotvision.org

Liam Paull, Program Co-Chair
Michael S. Brown, Program Co-Chair

Takes place with the Canadian Conference on Artificial Intelligence.
Frequency: Annual
Founded in 2004

5616 **Design Automation Conference**
Design Automation
5405 Spine Road
Suite 102
Boulder, CO 80301

303-530-4333; Fax: 303-530-4334
feedback@dac.com
www.dac.com

Kevin Lepine, Co-President
Lee Wood, Co-President
Nannette Jordan, Registration Coordinator

The premier Electronic Design Automation (EDA) and silicon solution event. DAC features over 50 technical sessions covering the latest in design methodologies and EDA tool developments, and an Exhibition and Demo Suite area with over 250 of the leading EDA, silicon, and IP Providers.
11M+ Attendees
Frequency: June

5617 **ESRI Southwest Users Group Conference**
Southwest Users Group
18727 Nadal Street
Canyon Country, CA 91351

Home Page: www.swuggis.org

Interface with ESRI users to learn about the latest technologies and discuss ESRI software-related topics.
Frequency: Annual

5618 **Embedded Systems Conference**
CMP Media Headquarters
600 Community Drive
Manhasset, NY 11030

516-562-5000
www.esconline.com

Christian Fahlen, Senior Conference Manager
Ardis Gough, Conference Manager
Kara Pistochini, Conference Assistant
Annette Campo, Manager

The only conference to focus on the art and science of microcomptroller and microprocessor based development, covering the needs of real-time software engineers.
2.7M Attendees
Frequency: September
Mailing list available for rent

5619 **FOSE**
Post Newsweek Tech Media
10 G Street NE
Suite 500
Washington, DC 20002-4228

202-772-2500
800-791-FOSE; Fax: 202-772-2511
www.ntpshow.com

Lauri Nichols, Trade Show Operations Manager
Melanie Woodfolk, Show Marketing Manager
David Greene, President

Largest information technology exposition serving the government marketplace.
4000 Attendees
Frequency: April

5620 **Graph Expo & Convention**
Graphic Arts Show Company

1899 Preston White Drive
Reston, VA 20191

703-264-7200; Fax: 703-620-9187
info@gasc.org
www.gasc.org

Kelly Kilga, Conference/Show Operations Director
Lilly Kinney, Conference Manager

The largest, most comprehensive prepress, printing, converting and digital equipment trade show and conference in the Americas.
40000 Attendees
Frequency: October

5621 **Graphics of the Americas**
Printing Association of Florida
6275 Hazeltine National Drive
Orlando, FL 32822
407-240-8009
800-331-0461; Fax: 407-240-8333
www.flprint.org

Anne Gaither, Convention Director
Michael H Streibig, Staff Executive

We are the second largest Graphic Arts and Converting show in America. We give you two vital markets — southeast US and Latin America: Mexico, South America, Central America and the Caribbean. Our 28 year track record reflects our success with both exhibitors and show visitors.
20000 Attendees
Frequency: Feb

5622 **Healthcare Information and Management Systems Society Conference**
Healthcare Information and Management Systems
230 E Ohio
Suite 500
Chicago, IL 60611-3269

312-664-4467; Fax: 312-664-6143
kmalone@himss.org
www.himss.org

Karen Malone, Director of Meetings
John Daniels, Vice President

An opportunity to learn the latest industry intelligence, find solutions to your most pressing professional challenges, and network with your peers. Pre-conference workshops and education session, see industry newsmakers, explore the latest technologies in more than 600 exhibits and earn continuing education credit and certification.
20000 Attendees
Frequency: February

5623 **IAAP International Convention and Education Forum**
Int'l Association of Administrative Professionals
10502 NW Ambassador Drive
Kansas City, MO 16415

816-891-6600; Fax: 816-891-9118
tgoodall@iaap-hq.org
www.iaap-hq.org

Inge Hafkemeyer, Convention/Meetings/Exhibit Manager
Don Bretthauer, Executive Director

An opportunity to showcase your product or service to this important audience. Office Expo exhibitors include major office product manufacturers, publishers, software vendors, staffing firms, gift suppliers, paper companies, and many more.
2000 Attendees
Frequency: July

5624 **IAPP Privacy and Data Security Academy Expo**
Internet Alliance
1111 19th Street NW
Suite 1180
Washington, DC 20035-5782

202-284-4380; Fax: 202-955-8081
www.internetalliance.my

Emily T Hackett, Executive Director
Katy Caldwell, California Policy Director

The conference will showcase the latest thinking on important privacy issues in healthcare, financial services, technology and marketing. Attendees will gain a deeper understanding of strategies and tools required to meet today's privacy challenges.
1000 Attendees
Frequency: October
Founded in 1981

5625 **IEEE SoutheastCon**
IEEE Meeting & Conference Management (MCM)
445 Hoes Lane
Piscataway, NJ 08854

732-562-3878
800-678-4333; Fax: 732-971-1203
conference-services@ieee.org
www.ieee.org
Facebook, LinkedIn, Instagram

A student conference, technical conference, and business meeting.
800 Attendees
Frequency: Annual

5626 **IS&T/SPIE Annual Symposium Electronic Imaging**
International Society for Optical Engineering
1000 20th Street
PO Box 10
Bellingham, WA 98227-6705

360-763-3290; Fax: 360-647-1445
customerservice@spie.org
www.spie.org

Giordano B Beretta, Director
Robert L Stevenson, Co-Director
Eugene Arthurs, Executive Director
Amy Nelson, Manager

Electronic Imaging's top-notch technical program gathers the world's prominent experts to discuss and push the forefront of imaging technology and it's applications.
1200 Attendees
Frequency: Annual/January

5627 **ISACA International Conference**
Information Systems Audit & Control Association
Rolling Meadows, IL

847-660-5505
844-472-2246
conference@isaca.org
www.isaca.org

David Samuelson, CEO

The International Conference has long been recognised throughout the world for providing in-depth coverage of the leading-edge technical and managerial issues facing IT governance, control, security and assurance professionals.
Frequency: Annual/June

5628 **Industrial Virtual Reality**
Reed Exhibitions
US Consumer Show Division
225 Wyman Street
Waltham, MA 02451

781-622-8616; Fax: 781-622-8042
www.reedexpo.com

Elizabeth Hitchcock, International Sales

The first trade show focusing on industrial applications of virtual reality and tele-existence.
Frequency: June

5629 **Information Technology Week**
Information Week/CMP Media
600 Community Drive
Manhasset, NY 11030

516-562-5000; Fax: 516-562-5036
www.informationweek.com

Lisa Monvigner, Events Associate Director
Stephanie Iannuzzi, Sr. Marketing Manager
Michael Friedenberg, Publisher

A forum for computer technicians and professionals.
Frequency: May
Mailing list available for rent

5630 **International Conference on Electronics, Circuits, and Systems**
IEEE Circuits and Systems Society
445 Hoes Lane
Piscataway, NJ 08854

manager@ieee-cas.org
www.ieee-cas.org

Brittian Parkinson, Operations Manager
Myung Hoon Sunwoo, VP, Conferences
Frequency: Annual

5631 **International Conference on Methods for Surveying Hard-To-Reach Populations**
American Association for Public Opinion Research
111 Deer Lake Road
Suite 100
Deerfield, IL 60015

847-205-2651; Fax: 847-480-9282
www.aapor.org
Facebook, Twitter, LinkedIn

Delia Murphy, Executive Director

The conference will address both the statistical and survey design aspects of including hard to reach groups. Researchers will report findings from censuses and surveys and other research related to the identification, definition, measurement, and methodologies for surveying and enumerating undercounted populations.
850 Attendees
Frequency: Annual
Mailing list available for rent: 1000 names at $400 per M

5632 **International Conference on Software Engineering**
Software Engineering Institute
4500 Fifth Avenue
Pittsburgh, PA 15213-2612

412-268-5800
www.sei.cmu.edu

Paul D. Nielsen, Director & CEO

ICSE is the premier software engineering conference, providing a forum for researchers, practitioners and educators to present and discuss the most recent innovations, trends, experiences, and concerns in the field of software engineering.
800 Attendees

5633 **International Consumer Electronics Show (CES)**
Consumer Technology Association

1919 South Eads Street
Arlington, VA 22202

703-907-7600
866-858-1555; Fax: 703-907-7675
cta@cta.tech
www.cta.tech

Gary Shapiro, President & CEO
David Hagan, Chairman

The largest annual consumer technology tradeshow offering a wealth of opportunity for your business.
Frequency: Annual

5634 **International Joint Conference on Neural Networks**
International Neural Network Society
2800 W. Higgins Road
Suite 440
Hoffman Estates, IL 60169

833-636-0351; Fax: 847-885-8393
inns@inns.org
www.inns.org

Richard Duro, VP, Conference

Organized by the International Neural Network Society in cooperation with the IEEE Computational Intelligence Society, intended for researchers and other professionals in neural networks and related areas.

5635 **International Spectrum MultiValue Conference & Exhibition**
International Spectrum
715 J Street
Suite 301
San Diego, CA 92101-2478

619-515-9930; Fax: 619-515-9933
www.intl-spectrum.com

Monica Giobbi, President
Gus Giobbi, Chairman

A conference and exhibition showcasing MultiValue products and services.
6M Attendees
Frequency: March

5636 **International Symposium on Circuits and Systems**
IEEE Circuits and Systems Society
445 Hoes Lane
Piscataway, NJ 08854
manager@ieee-cas.org
www.ieee-cas.org

Brittian Parkinson, Operations Manager
Myung Hoon Sunwoo, VP, Conferences
Frequency: Annual

5637 **Interop Conference**
Interop
C/O MediaLive International
795 Folsom Street, 6th Floor
San Francisco, CA 94107-1243

415-905-2300; Fax: 415-905-2FAX
www.interop.com

Jennifer Sioteco, Sr. Operations Manager
Lenny Heymann, General Manager

Provides you an overview of the robust conference offerings, workshops and tutorials, and special programs.
60000 Attendees

5638 **Java One Conference**
Sun Microsystems
4150 Network Circle
Santa Clara, CA 95054

650-960-1300
866-382-7151

Jonathan Schwartz, President/CEO
Anil Gadre, Chief Executive Officer

Gain knowledge and Java technology education directly from Sun Microsystems, Inc. and other industry leaders. Get expert advice on solving the most common Java challenges. Benefit from four full days of content. Choose from hundreds of technical sessions and test drive real-world Java technology solutions.
5000 Attendees
Frequency: June

5639 **MCAA Industry Forum**
Measurement, Control & Automation Association
200 City Hall Avenue
Suite D
Poquoson, VA 23662

757-258-3100
automationassociation.com

Teresa Sebring, President
Andrea Ambrose, Director, Member Relations
Elizabeth Horton, Programs Manager
Kim Malina, Marketing Communications Manager
Rebecca Moore, Administrative Manager

Education and networking event for manufacturers and distributors of instrumentation, systems, and software products for industrial process control and factory automation.
Founded in 1944

5640 **MacWorld Conference & Expo**
MacWorld 2010
PO Box 3221
Boston, MA 02241

805-290-1341
800-645-EXPO; Fax: 805-654-1676
macworld2010@rcsreg.com
www.macworld.com

Annual show with hundreds of exhibitors of Mac equipment, supplies and services. Provides education, networking and thought leadership that professionals and consumers alike need to get the most from their technology investment.
65000 Attendees
Frequency: Annual

5641 **Marketechnics**
Food Marketing Institute
2345 Crystal Drive
Suite 800
Arlington, VA 22202

202-452-8444; Fax: 202-429-4519
www.fmi.org

Randy Edeker, Chair
Leslie G. Sarasin, President/CEO

Provides a once-a-year opportunity to hear, see and discuss new technologies and their impact on the supply chain, store operations and marketing/merchandising strategies.
7000 Attendees
Frequency: Jan-Feb

5642 **Measurement, Control & Automation Association**
200 City Hall Avenue
Suite D
Poquoson, VA 23662

757-258-3100
automationassociation.com
Facebook, Twitter, LinkedIn, YouTube

Teresa Sebring, President
Andrea Ambrose, Director, Member Relations
Elizabeth Horton, Programs Manager
Kim Malina, Marketing Communications Manager
Rebecca Moore, Administrative Manager

The MCAA is the national trade association for manufacturers and distributors of instrumentation, systems, and software products for industrial process control and factory automation.
Founded in 1944

5643 **NACCB Annual Conference**
National Association of Computer Consultants
1420 King Street
Suite 610
Alexandria, VA 22314

703-838-2050; Fax: 703-838-3610
staff@naccb.org
naccb.groupsite.com

The only educational, networking, and leadership event exclusively for the IT Services Industry. The NACCB conference provides a platform where IT services firms connect to address issues and solutions most affecting business today.
Frequency: Annual/November
Founded in 1987

5644 **National Ergonomics Conference and Exposition**
Continental Exhibitions
370 Lexington Avenue
Suite 1407
New York, NY 10017-6503

212-370-5005; Fax: 212-370-5699
information@ergoexpo.com
www.ergoexpo.com

Larry L Elyea, Executive Program Director
Pedro Caceres, Senior VP of Operations

The NECE maximizes your time and effort by providing direct contact with industry leaders that comprise our speaker faculty, direct contact with leading providers of ergonomics products and services, and direct contact with your peers at networking receptions during the exposition.
Frequency: Nov-Dec

5645 **Object World Conference**
Object Management Group/IDG Management
111 Speen Street
PO Box 9107
Framingham, MA 01701-9514

800-225-4698; Fax: 508-872-8237
www.omg.com

Mary DeCristoforo, Conference Director
David Elliott, Exhibit Sales Manager

An annual conference sponsored by the Object Management Group and IDG Management Group to advance object-oriented technology in commercial software development. The event features tutorials and conference sessions.
6.5M Attendees
Frequency: October

5646 **Optical Fiber Communications Conference**
Optical Society of America
2010 Massachusetts Avenue NW
Washington, DC 20036

202-238-8130; Fax: 202-416-6140
info@ofcconference.org
www.ofcnfoec.org

Colleen Morrison, Media Relations Director
Melissa Russell, Exhibit Sales Director
Colleen Morrison, Media Relations Manager
Angela Stark, Director Communications

Provides leading edge, peer reviewed educational programming along with a high powered, commerce driven exhibition. This unique combination attracts the field's most progressive professionals and exhibiting companies.
13111 Attendees
Frequency: March
Founded in 1916

5647 **PCB Design Conference West**
UP Media Group

2400 Lake Park Dr Se
Suite 440
Smyrna, GA 30080-7695

678-589-8800; Fax: 678-589-8850
askarbek@upmediagroup.com
www.pcbwest.com

Alyson Skarbek, Show Operations Manager
Andy Shaughnessy, Conference Chairperson
Brooke Anglin, Exhibit Sales Manager

The first and only conference 100% dedicated to the needs of the PCB designer.
750 Attendees
Frequency: March

5648 **PIMA Leadership Conference**
Paper Industry Management Association
4700 W Lake Avenue
Glenview, IL 60025-1485

847-375-6860
877-527-5973; Fax: 732-460-7333
www.pima-online.org

Carol Waugh, Meetings Manager
Julie Weir, Account Manager
Mary Cornell, Account Manager

Three-day conference to bring together IT and process control professionals from around the world to share their knowledge of information technology in the pulp and paper industry and to promote systems applications. The only IT conference planned for and by IT professionals.
500 Attendees
Frequency: Annual/June

5649 **Pacific Telecommunications Council Conference: PTC Conference**
Pacific Telecommunications Council
2454 S Beretania Street
3rd Floor
Honolulu, HI 96826-1596

808-941-3789; Fax: 808-944-4874
snakama@ptc.org
www.ptc.org

Sharon Nakama, Conference Director
Dolores Fung, Conference/Seminar Coordinator
Claudine Naruse, Conference/Seminar Coordinator
Justin Riel, Conference/Seminar Assistant

Provides an opportunity to learn and to analyze current issues. Registrants from the ranks of senior corporate officers and management, experts from law and consulting firms, noted analysts and scholars, and technical experts provide a wide diversity of ideas.
1500 Attendees
Frequency: January

5650 **SC: High Performance Networking & Computing**
Hall-Erickson
98 E Naperville Road
Westmont, IL 60559

630-639-9185; Fax: 630-434-1216

William Kramer, Conference General Chair
Barbara Horner-Miller, Conference Deputy Chair

The world's leading conference on high performance computing, networking and storage. Representatives from many technical communities together to exchange ideas, celebrate past successes and plan for the future.
6000 Attendees
Frequency: Annual/November
Founded in 1988

5651 **SCSC: Summer Simulation Multiconference**
Society for Modeling and Simulation International
PO Box 17900
San Diego, CA 92177-7900

858-277-3888; Fax: 858-277-3930
scs@scs.org
www.scs.org

Steve Branch, Executive Director
Mark Yen, Event Coordinator

Focusing on Innovative Technologies for Simulation this year. Modeling and Simulation is a very critical area for supporting Research and Development as well as competitiveness worldwide; new technologies are enabling new use of M&S and increasing its impact in new areas; SCSC provides an international forum for presenting the state of the art in the international simulation community.
600 Attendees
Frequency: July

5652 **SID International Symposium, Seminar and Exhibition**
Society for Information Display
San Jose, CA

office@sid.org
www.sid.org

Helge Seetzen, President
Achintya Bhowmik, Treasurer
John Kymissis, Secretary

The premier international gathering of scientists, engineers, manufacturers and users in the electronic display industry. The event provides access to a wide range of technology and applications from high-definition flat-panel displays using both emissive and liquid-crystal technology to the latest in OLED displays and large-area projection-display systems.
Frequency: May
Founded in 1962

5653 **SIGAI Career Network and Conference**
ACM SIGAI
1601 Broadway
10th Floor
New York, NY 10019-7434

212-869-7440
800-342-6626; Fax: 212-944-1318
acmhelp@acm.org
sigai.acm.org

Michael Rovatsos, Conference Coordination Officer

Conference for early-stage researchers in Artificial Intelligence.
Frequency: Quarterly

5654 **SIGGRAPH Conference**
Association for Computing Machinery
1601 Broadway
10th Floor
New York, NY 10019-7434

212-869-7440
800-342-6626; Fax: 212-944-1318
acmhelp@acm.org
www.acm.org
Facebook, Twitter, LinkedIn, Google+

Vicki Hanson, Chief Executive Officer
Irene Frawley, Prog. Mgr., Conference Operations
Hilaire Lee, Conference Financials
Diana Brantuas, Conference Budgeting

The annual conference and its year round initiatives provide a unique crossroads for a diverse community of researchers, developers, creators, educators and practitioners. The focus of the conference is the subject of computer graphics.
50000 Attendees
Frequency: July-August

5655 **SMC: Spring Simulation Multiconference**
Society for Modeling and Simulation International
PO Box 17900
San Diego, CA 92177-7900

858-277-3888; Fax: 858-277-3930
sbranch@scs.org
www.scs.org

Drew Hamilton, Conference General Chair
Steve Branch, Executive Director

Bringing together eight symposia and providing a forum for academia, industry, business and government covering a wide variety of disciplines and domains that utilize modeling and simulation to present their work in a unique setting.
400 Attendees
Frequency: April

5656 **Seybold Seminars**
MediaLive International
795 Folsom Street
6th Floor
San Francisco, CA 94107-1243

415-905-2300; Fax: 415-905-2FAX
www.medialiveinternational.com

Jackie Rees, Program Director
Cynthia Wood, Conference Content Director

Four focused conferences; Chicago, New York, San Francisco, that will deliver new solutions, emerging technologies and real world examples of businesses that have successfully implemented new digital publishing workflow and content management strategies.
21000 Attendees
Frequency: Sept, Oct, Nov

5657 **Software Architecture Conference**
O'Reilly Media
2 Avenue de Lafayette
6th Floor
Boston, MA 02111

617-354-5800; Fax: 617-661-1116
confreg@oreilly.com
conferences.oreilly.com/software-architecture

Tim O'Reilly, Founder & CEO
Gina Blaber, SVP, Conferences

Network with and learn from experts as they share their knowledge in software architecture-updating legacy systems, the impact of emergent trends, and insights on industry-specific strategies.
Frequency: Annual/February

5658 **TAWPI Annual Forum & Exposition**
Association for Work Process Improvement
185 Devonshire Street
Suite M102
Boston, MA 02110-1407
617-426-1167
800-998-2974; Fax: 617-521-8675
www.tawpi.org

Sandra Savage, Conference Planner
Jenny Star, Director Business Development
Tonya Gregoire, Director Business Development

Leading event for technology and management professionals in data capture, mail, imaging, payment/remittance, document and forms processing.
1500 Attendees
Frequency: July

5659 **TechNet International**
Armed Forces Communications and Electronics Assn

4400 Fair Lakes Court
Fairfax, VA 22033

703-631-6100
800-336-4583; Fax: 703-631-6405
www.afcea.org

Kent Schneider, President/CEO
Becky Nolan, Executive VP
John A Dubia, Executive VP

An annual event representing top government, industry and military professionals in the fields of communications, electronics, intelligence, information systems, imaging and multi-media.
Frequency: Annual/June

5660 **The Vision Show**
Global Association for Vision Information
900 Victors Way
Suite 140
Ann Arbor, MI 48108

734-994-6088
www.visiononline.org
Facebook, Twitter

Jeff Burnstein, President
Maria Kurple, Event Marketing Manager
Mandy Pawczuk, Administrator, Event Services

North America's largest display of machine vision and imaging systems.
Frequency: June

5661 **UNITE Golden Opportunities Annual Technology Conference**
UNITE
21523 Harper Avenue
St Clair Shores, MI 48080-2209

586-443-6901; Fax: 586-443-6902
cathmurphy39@hotmail.com
www.unite.org

Catherine Murphy, Conference Chair
George Gray, Conference Vice Chair

Held in mid October. Development and use of information technology. Pre-registration for full conference attendees: $1,095; daily attendees: $740.
Frequency: October

5662 **Usenix Annual Technical Conference**
Usenix
2560 9th Street
Suite 215
Berkeley, CA 94710-2573

510-528-8649; Fax: 510-548-5738
conference@usenix.org
www.usenix.org

Jennifer Joost, Conference Manager
Devon Shaw, Administrative Assistant
Andrew Gustafson, Administrative Assistant
Dan Klein, Director
John Arrasjid, Secretary

A 5 day training running alongside a 3 day conference program filled with the latest research, security breakthroughs, sessions devoted to Linux and open source software and practical approaches to the puzzles and problems you wrestle with.
3M Attendees
Frequency: June

5663 **Vue/Point Conference**
Graphic Arts Show Company
1899 Preston White Drive
Reston, VA 20191

703-264-7200; Fax: 703-620-9187
info@gasc.org
www.gasc.org

Kelly Kilga, Conference/Show Operations Director
Lilly Kinney, Administrative Assistant
Erin Omwake, Administrative Assistant
Deborah Vieder, Director of Communications

The only interactive, peer-to-peer conference event in the graphic communications industry.
Frequency: April

5664 **WMC: Western Simulation Multiconference**
Society for Modeling and Simulation International
PO Box 17900
San Diego, CA 92177-7900

858-277-3888; Fax: 858-277-3930
sbranch@scs.org
www.scs.org

Steve Branch, Executive Director
Mark Yen, Events & Publications Coordinator

15 booths of technical and scientific papers.
300+ Attendees
Frequency: January

5665 **Western Conference & Exposition**
Armed Forces Communications and Electronics Assn
4400 Fair Lakes Court
Fairfax, VA 22033

703-631-1397; Fax: 703-818-9177
gmcgovern@afcea.org
www.afcea.org

Gina McGovern, Patron/Sponsor Director
Kim Couranz, Senior Vice President
Booz Hamilton, Senior Vice President

Largest event on the West Coast for communications, electronics, intelligence, information systems, imaging, military weapon systems, aviation, shipbuilding, and more. Featuring the people you need to hear from, the products and services you need to do your job, and the critical issues of today and tomorrow.
7000 Attendees
Frequency: January

Directories & Databases

5666 **ARMA International's Buyers Guide**
ARMA International
11880 College Boulevard
Suite 450
Overland Park, KS 66215

913-444-9174
844-565-2120; Fax: 913-257-3855
headquarters@armaintl.org
armabuyersguide.org
Facebook, Twitter, LinkedIn

Nick Inglis, Exec. Dir., Content & Programming
Jeff Whited, Sr. Content Writer
Ann Snyder, Manager, Content Development

75-100 companies listed. Free.
Frequency: Annual

5667 **AV Market Place**
Information Today
143 Old Marlton Pike
Medford, NJ 08055-8750

609-654-6266
800-300-9868; Fax: 609-654-4309
custserv@infotoday.com
www.infotoday.com

Thomas H Hogan, President
Roger R Bilboul, Chairman Of The Board

The complete business directory of audio, audio visual, computer systems, film, video, and programming with industry yellow pages. The only guide needed to find more than 7,500 companies that create, apply or distribute AV equipment and services for business, education, science, and government.
Cost: $199.95
1700 Pages
Frequency: February
ISBN: 1-573871-87-7

5668 **CD-ROM Databases**
Worldwide Videotex
PO Box 3273
Boyton Beach, FL 33424

561-738-2276
markedit@juno.com
www.wvpubs.com

Contains information on currently marketed databases available on CD-ROM.
Frequency: Directory

5669 **CD-ROMs in Print**
Thomson Gale
PO Box 09187
Detroit, MI 48209-0187

248-699-4253
800-877-4253; Fax: 248-699-8049
www.galegroup.com

Patrick C Sommers, President
Rich Foley, Account Manager
Judy Roberts, Account Manager
Maria Moffre, Product Manager

International guide to CD-ROM, Cdi, 3Do, Mmcd, Cd32, Multimedia, Laserdisc and Electronic Products.
Cost: $205.00
Circulation: 13,000
ISBN: 0-787671-33-9

5670 **Computer Database**
Information Access Company
362 Lakeside Drive
Foster City, CA 94404-1171

650-378-5200
800-227-8431; Fax: 650-378-5368

Robert Howells, President

Comprehensive database offering over 500,000 citations, with abstracts, to literature from over 150 trade journals, industry newsletters and platform-specific publications covering the computer, telecommunications and electronics industries.

5671 **Computer Industry Almanac**
Computer Industry Almanac
304 W White Oak
Arlington Heights, IL 60005-3201

847-758-3687; Fax: 847-758-3686
www.c-i-a.com

Egil Juliussen, Editor
Karen Petska-Juliussen, Editor

A reference book about the computer industry.
Cost: $63.00
800 Pages
Frequency: Annual
ISBN: 0-942107-08-X

5672 **Computer Industry Market Intelligence System**
Hart-Hanks Market Intelligence
9980 Huennekens St
Suite 100
San Diego, CA 92121-2917

858-625-4800; Fax: 858-452-6857

Terry Olson, CEO
Randy Ilas, Product Management Director

Database of more than 250,000 business locations with mainframe, mini or micro computer systems.

5673 **Computer Review**
Computer Review

19 Pleasant St
Gloucester, MA 01930-5937

978-283-2100
info@computerreview.com
www.computerreview.com

George Luhowy, Owner

Your personal business tool for mining the Knowledge economy. This is a well organized hardcopy directory with a daily online monitor. It shows you what's happening in 12,000 companies from 77 technology sectors.
Cost: $495.00
750 Pages
Frequency: Annual
ISBN: 0-914730-02-9
ISSN: 0093-416X

5674 **DACS Annotated Bibliography**
Data & Analysis Center for Software
775 Daedalian Drive
Rome, NY 13441-4909

315-334-4905
800-214-7921; Fax: 315-334-4964
cust-liasn@dacs.dtic.mil

Thomas McGibbon, Director

Offers citations on over 9,000 technical reports, articles, papers and books concerned with software development and engineering.
Cost: $60.00
400 Pages

5675 **DIALOG Publications**
Dialog, Thomas Business
11000 Regency Parkway
Suite 10
Cary, NC 27511

919-462-8600
800-3DI-ALOG; Fax: 919-468-9890
www.dialog.com

Mike Eastwood, VP Finance & Administration
Al Zink, VP Human Resources
Roy Martin, CEO

Offers descriptions of DIALOG system and database publications that are available for purchase.

5676 **DP Directory**
525 Goodale Hill Rd
Glastonbury, CT 06033-4022

860-659-1065

Al Harberg, President

Offers mailing lists for the computer trade as well as information on the value and uses of press releases for marketers.

5677 **Datapro Directory of Microcomputer Hardware**
S. Karger Publishers
26 W Avon Road
PO Box 529
Farmington, CT 06085

860-675-7834
800-828-5479; Fax: 860-675-7302
www.libri.ch

Martin Buess, Managing Director
Andrea Murdoch, CEO
Monika Augstburger, Account Manager
Marianne Dill, Manager Customer Service

Offers valuable information on over 1,500 manufacturers of microcomputers and peripheral equipment.
Cost: $675.00
1000 Pages
Frequency: Monthly
ISSN: 1074-3308

5678 **Directory of Computer and High Technology Grants**
Research Grant Guides
PO Box 1214
Loxahatchee, FL 33470-1214

561-795-6129

Richard M Eckstein, Author

Offers information on over 750 foundations and corporations that award grants to nonprofit organizations for computers, computer training and software.
Cost: $52.50
200 Pages
Frequency: Biennial
ISBN: 0-945078-07-2

5679 **Directory of Library Automation Software, Systems and Services**
Information Today
143 Old Marlton Pike
Medford, NJ 08055-8750

609-654-6266
800-300-9868; Fax: 609-654-4309
custserv@infotoday.com
www.infotoday.com

Thomas H Hogan, President
Roger R Bilboul, Chairman Of The Board

Recognized as the primary reference source for software packages used in automating libraries. This entirely new expanded 2004-2005 edition provides detailed descriptions of hundreds of currently available microcomputer, minicomputer, and mainframe software packages and services.
Cost: $89.00
351 Pages
Frequency: Bi-Annually
Founded in 1983

5680 **Directory of Simulation Software**
Society for Modeling and Simulation International
4838 Ronson Ct
PO Box 17900
San Diego, CA 92177-7900

858-277-3888; Fax: 858-277-3930
info@scs.org
www.scs.org

Amy Shapiro, Publications Manager & Editor
Steve Branch, Executive Director

About 200 simulation software packages and their suppliers.
Cost: $40.00
Frequency: Annual
Circulation: 2,000
Mailing list available for rent

5681 **Directory of Top Computer Executives**
Applied Computer Research
PO Box 41730
Phoenix, AZ 85080

602-216-9100
800-234-2227; Fax: 602-548-4800
www.acrhq.com

Contains the names of more than 52,000 of the most influential information technology managers in the US and Canada. Entepreneurs and corporate executives have used this data base to build successful businesses for over 30 years.
Cost: $245.00
Frequency: Semi-Annual
Founded in 1972

5682 **Directory of US Government Software for Mainframes and Microcomputers**
US National Technical Information Service
5285 Port Royal Road
Springfield, VA 22161

703-605-6000
800-553-6847; Fax: 703-605-6900
info@ntis.gov
www.ntis.gov

Patrik Ekstr"m, Business Development Manager
Reuel Avila, Managing Director

Contains descriptions of some 550 mainframe and microcomputer programs made available from more than 100 federal agencies, or their contractors since 1984. The directory is an essential reference tool for users who wish to tap the wealth of U.S. Government software.
Cost: $65.00
174 Pages
Frequency: Annual
ISBN: 0-934213-37-2

5683 **Electronic Imaging an Image Processing: An Assessment of Technology & Products**
Richard K Mill & Associates
5880 Live Oak Parkway
Suite 270
Norcross, GA 30093-1707

770-416-0006; Fax: 770-416-0052

Richard K Miller, Editor/President
Kelli D Washington, Editor-in-Chief

List of producers and suppliers of electronic imaging computer software and hardware.
Cost: $485.00
ISBN: 0-896711-12-9

5684 **Guide to Free Films, Flimstrips and Slides**
Educators Progress Service
214 Center St
Randolph, WI 53956-1497

920-326-3126
888-951-4469; Fax: 920-326-3127

Kathy Nehmer, President

Offers sources for films, filmstrips, slide sets, audiotapes and videotapes.
Cost: $37.95
135 Pages
Frequency: Annual
ISBN: 0-877083-51-7

5685 **Hoover's Guide to Computer Companies**
Hoover's
5800 Airport Blvd
Austin, TX 78752-3826

512-374-1187
800-486-8666; Fax: 512-374-4501
customersupport@hoovers.com
www.hoovers.com

David Mather, President
Paul Pellman, Executive VP Marketing/Products

250 of the largest public and private computer industry companies in in-depth profiles.
Cost: $34.95
737 Pages
Frequency: Annual
ISBN: 1-878753-80-0

5686 **IT Computer Economics Report Journal**
Computer Economics
2082 Business Center Drive
Suite 240
Irvine, CA 92612

949-831-8700; Fax: 949-442-7688
www.computereconomics.com

Frank Scavo, President
Dan Husiak, VP

Provides decision makers throughout the world with timely insights into the management of information systems.
Frequency: Monthly
Founded in 1978

5687 **Index to AV Producers & Distributors 10th Edition**
Information Today
143 Old Marlton Pike
Medford, NJ 08055-8750

609-654-6266
800-300-9868; Fax: 609-654-4309
custserv@infotoday.com
www.infotoday.com

Thomas H Hogan, President
Roger R Bilboul, Chairman Of The Board

Contains over 23,500 producers and distributors of AV materials of all kinds. This handy softbound volume is an indispensible tool for buyers of audiovisual materials of all kinds.
Cost: $89.00
626 Pages
ISBN: 0-937548-30-8

5688 **Internet & Personal Computing Abstracts Journal**
Information Today
143 Old Marlton Pike
Medford, NJ 08055-8750

609-654-6266
800-300-9868; Fax: 609-654-4309
custserv@infotoday.com
www.infotoday.com

Thomas H Hogan, President
Roger R Bilboul, Chairman Of The Board

This comprehensive database contains over 150,000 citations, with abstracts to reviews of commentaries on the use and applications of microcomputers and software packages.
Cost: $235.00
Frequency: Quarterly
Circulation: 10,000
Founded in 1980

5689 **Inventor's Desktop Companion: A Guide to Successfully Marketing Ideas**
Visible Ink Press/Gale Research
PO Box 09187
Detroit, MI 48209-0187

248-699-4253
800-877-GALE; Fax: 248-699-8049

Patrick C Sommers, President

Offers information on agencies and organizations of interest to inventors, including regional and national associations, university innovation research centers and business incubators for the computer and desktop industries.
Cost: $24.95
470 Pages

5690 **Micro Publishing Report's Directory of Desktop Publishing Suppliers**
Cygnus Publishing
PO Box 803
Fort Atkinson, WI 53538-0803

920-000-1111
800-547-7377; Fax: 920-563-1699
rich.reiff@cygnuspub.com

John French, CEO
Tom Martin, Director of Public Relations
Kathy Scott, Director of Public Relations
Paul Bonaiuto, CFO

Offers valuable information on over 200 suppliers of microcomputer systems for desktop publishing.
Cost: $35.00
30 Pages
Frequency: Annual

5691 **Microcomputer Market Place**
Random House
202 E 50th St
New York, NY 10022

212-572-6120

Offers information on manufacturers and suppliers of computer equipment and accessories.
Cost: $29.95
795 Pages

5692 **Microprocessor Integrated Circuits**
DATA Digest
321 Inverness Drive South
Englewood, CO 80112

303-790-0600
800-525-7052
www.ihs.com

Jerre Stead, Chair/CEO
Michael Armstrong, Director

Offers a list of over 185 manufacturers and distributors of microprocessor integrated circuits.
Cost: $205.00
Frequency: SemiAnnual

5693 **Microsoft Applications and Systems Forums**
Microsoft Corporation
1 Microsoft Way
Redmond, WA 98052-8300

425-882-8080
800-426-9400; Fax: 425-936-7329
www.microsoft.com

Steve Ballmer, CEO

This database provides an exchange of information and tips on Microsoft computer systems for participants.

5694 **Modern Machine Shop's Handbook for Metalworkingi Industries on CD-ROM**
Gardner Publications
6915 Valley Ln
Cincinnati, OH 45244-3153

513-527-8800
800-950-8020; Fax: 513-527-8801
www.gardnerweb.com

Rick Kline Sr, CEO
John Campos, Manager
Brian Wertheimer, Account Manager
Eddie Kania, Sales Manager

Provides a balanced blend of traditional and modern topics. In addition to containing a wide range of reference tables covering all aspects of machining, composition of materials, and dimensions of tooling and machine components.
Cost: $55.00
2368 Pages
ISBN: 1-569903-55-7
Founded in 2002

5695 **National Directory of Bulletin Board Systems**
Penton Media
1300 E 9th St
Suite 316
Cleveland, OH 44114-1503

216-696-7000; Fax: 216-696-6662
information@penton.com
www.penton.com

Jane Cooper, Marketing

Computer bulletin board systems that display notices of special events or new products are profiled.
Cost: $45.00
400 Pages
Frequency: Annual

5696 **NetWire**
Novell
165 Nantasket Beach Avenue
Hull, MA 02045

78- 9-5 17
800-453-2167; Fax: 781-925-6545
john@netwire.com
netwire.com

This database concentrates on Novell computer software and hardware information.

5697 **Online Networks, Databases & Bulletin Boards on Assistive Technology**
ERIC Document Reproduction Service
7420 Fullerton Road
Suite 110
Springfield, VA 22153-2852

703-440-1400
800-443-ERIC; Fax: 703-440-1408

Directory of electronic networks that focus on technology-related services.

5698 **Orion Blue Book: Computer**
Orion Research Corporation
14555 N Scottsdale Rd
Suite 330
Scottsdale, AZ 85254-3487

480-951-1114
800-844-0759; Fax: 480-951-1117
orion@orionbluebook.com
www.orionbluebook.com

Roger Rohrs, Owner

63,053 products listed from 1970's to present. Over 1,000 manufacturers listed.
695 Pages
Frequency: Annual
Founded in 1985

5699 **PC-Link**
America Online
8619 Westwood Center Drive
Suite 200
Vienna, VA 22182-2238

Home Page: pclink.com.eg

Provides access to a variety of databases and computer services of interest to users of IBM and compatible computers running MS-DOS.
Frequency: Directory

5700 **ParaTechnology Directory of Systems and Network Integrators**
ParaTechnology
1215 120th Ave NE
Suite 101
Bellevue, WA 98005-2135

425-453-0676
800-377-2021; Fax: 425-453-0338
www.eside.org

One thousand computer system and network integrators in North America.
Cost: $495.00
Frequency: Annual

5701 **Personal Computing Directory**
Resources
PO Box 1067
Cambridge, MA 02238-1067

Directory of services and supplies to the industry.
Cost: $29.95
Frequency: Annual

5702 **Pocket Guides to the Internet: Telnetting**
Information Today
143 Old Marlton Pike
Medford, NJ 08055-8750

609-654-6266
800-300-9868; Fax: 609-654-4309

custserv@infotoday.com
www.infotoday.com

Thomas H Hogan, President
Roger R Bilboul, Chairman Of The Board

Logon information and resources available via telnetting.
Cost: $9.95

5703 **Q-Link**
America Online
8619 Westwood Center Drive
Suite 200
Vienna, VA 22182-2238

800-227-6364; Fax: 540-265-2135

Anne Botsford

This database consists of several files of general interest news and information for users of Commodore computers.
Frequency: Full-text

5704 **Shareware Magazine: PC SIG's Encyclopedia of Shareware Section**
Shareware Magazine
1030 E Duane Avenue
Suite D
Sunnyvale, CA 94086-2624

408-733-8900

Offers a variety of software programs for the IBM PC and its compatibles.
Cost: $19.95
Frequency: Bi-Monthly

5705 **SoftBase**
Information Resources
PO Box 8120
Berkeley, CA 94707-8120

510-525-6220; Fax: 510-525-1568

Ruth K Koolish, Editor

It produces software products, services and companies abstracted from more than 200 business, computer, technical, trade and consumer publications.
Frequency: Monthly

5706 **Software Encyclopedia**
R R Bowker LLC
630 Central Ave
New Providence, NJ 07974-1506

908-286-0288
888-269-5372; Fax: 908-464-3553
www.bowker.com

R R Bowker

A comprehensive easy to navigate guide filled with detailed information on microcomputer software. Listings of over 44,600 software programs from 4,646 publishers and distributors are fully annotated to facilitate research and acquisition.
Frequency: 2 Volume set
ISBN: 0-835249-69-0

5707 **Software Engineering Bibliography**
Kaman Sciences Corporation
258 Genesse Street
Utica, NY 13502

315-732-1955

Citation for over 15,000 technical reports, articles, theses, papers and books concerned with software technology.
Cost: $30.00
Frequency: Annual

5708 **Software Life Cycle Tools Directory**
Data & Analysis Center for Software
PO Box 1400
Rome, NY 13442-1400

315-334-4905
800-214-7921; Fax: 315-334-4964
cust-liasn@dacs.dtic.mil

Offers sources of more than 400 software packages for software engineering and maintenance.
Cost: $40.00
500 Pages

5709 **Telecom Internet Directory**
Information Gatekeepers Group
1340 Soldiers Field Rd
Suite 302
Brighton, MA 02135-1000

617-782-5033
800-323-1088; Fax: 617-782-5735
info@igigroup.com
www.igigroup.com

Paul Polishuk, CEO
Bev Wilson, Controller
Yesim Taskor, Controller

Developed to help find information in telecommunications efficiently and timely manner. A wide range of researchers, market analysts, information specialists, librarians and others will find the directory useful in finding information about telecommunications on the Internet.
Cost: $195.00

5710 **Top 100 Service Companies**
Coordinated Service
20A Court Street
Groton, MA 01450-4217

978-448-2472

100 of the largest US based independent computer service companies.

5711 **UNISYS World Software Directory**
Publications & Communications
Cypress Creek Road
Suite B
Cedar Park, TX 78613

512-250-9023

Offers valuable information on suppliers of computer software packages compatible with UNISYS Corporation computer systems.
140 Pages
Frequency: SemiAnnual
Circulation: 650

5712 **Uplink Directory**
Virginia A Ostendorf
PO Box 2896
Littleton, CO 80161-2896

303-797-3131

Directory of services and supplies to the industry.

5713 **User's Directory of Computer Networks**
Digital Press
129 Parker Street
Maynard, MA 01754-2199

978-493-1770

Offers a list of hosts, site contacts and administrative domains.
Cost: $35.95
630 Pages

Industry Web Sites

5714 **http://gold.greyhouse.com**
G.O.L.D Grey House OnLine Databases

Grey House Publishing's online database platform, GOLD, offers its Quick Search, Keyword Search and Expert Search for most business sectors including comupter and data processing markets. The GOLD platform makes finding the information you need quick and easy - whether you're a novice searcher or an experienced database user. All of Grey House's directory products are available for subscription on the GOLD platform.

5715 **www.4w.com**
Information Analytics

Dedicated to the non-profit professional development of information systems managers, directors and analysts.

5716 **www.aaai.org**
Association for the Advancement of AT

Nonprofit society devoted to advancing the scientific understanding of the mechanisms underlying thought and intelligent behavior and their embodiment in machines.

5717 **www.aace.org**
Assn for the Advancement of Computing in Education

An international, educational and professional nonprofit organization dedicated to the advancement of the knowledge, theory and quality of learning and teaching at all levels with information technology.

5718 **www.adweek.com**
Adweek

Leading decision makers in the advertising and marketing field go to Adweek.com every day for breaking news, insight, buzz, opinion, analysis, research and classifieds. The resources of all six regional editions of Adweek, as well as the national edition of Brandweek are combined with the knowledge of our online editors and the multimedia-interactive capabilities of the web to deliver vital information quickly and effectively to our target audience.

5719 **www.afsmi.de**
Association for Services Management International

Provides the knowledge, fellowship and career connections that customer services and support managers for technology based products and solutions needed for professional and career development.

5720 **www.aiim.org**
Association for Information and Image Management

Global authority on enterprise content management (ECM). ECM Technologies are used to create, capture, customize, deliver, and manage information to support business process.

5721 **www.aimglobal.org**
AIM Global

International trade association representing automatic identification and mobility technology solution providers.

5722 **www.aitp.org**
Association of Information Technology Professional

Comprised of career minded individuals who seek to expand their potential employers, employees, managers, programmers and many others. This organization seeks to provide avenues for all their members to be teachers as well as students and to make contacts with other members in the IS field, all in an effort to become more marketable in rapidly changing technological careers.

5723 **www.apple.com**
Apple

Official web site for Apple; Macintosh computers and software.

5724 **www.asm.com**
Society for Materials Engineers and Scientists
A leading supplier of semiconductor process equipment in both front and back end markets. The Company possesses a strong technological base, state-of-the-art manufacturing facilities, a competent and qualified workforce and a highly trained, strategically distributed support network.

5725 **www.bsa.org**
Business Software Alliance
An organization dedicated to promoting a safe and legal digital world. BSA educates consumers on software management and copyright protection, cyber security, trade, e-commerce and other internet related issues.

5726 **www.bta.org**
Business Technology Association
Serving independent dealers, value added resellers, system integrators, manufacturers and distributors in the business equipment and system industry. BTA helps its members profit through a wide variety of services, including free legal advice and guidance; business benchmarking studies and reports; information on the latest news, trends, and products in the industry.

5727 **www.calico.org**
Computer Assisted Language Instruction Consortium
For language teachers, linguists, courseware developers and governments who are interested in teaching languages with the use of computer assisted instruction.

5728 **www.comptia.org**
CompTIA
A nonprofit trade association created by representatives of five microcomputer leaderships and is a provider of professional certifications for the information technology (IT) industry.

5729 **www.devx.net**
DevX
The leading provider of technical and services that enable corporate application development teams to efficiently conquer development challenges and keep projects moving.

5730 **www.disa.org**
Data Interchange Standards Association
Many industries are looking to develop and implement eXtensible Markup Language (XML) specifications to eliminate paperwork, improve data accuracy, increase productivity, and reduce operating costs. This effort requires technical and administrative support. DISA can help.

5731 **www.greyhouse.com**
Grey House Publishing
Authoritative reference directories for most business sectors incluidng computer and data processing markets. Users can search the online databases with varied search criteria allowing for custom searches by product category, geographic area, sales volume, keyword, subject and more. Full Grey House catalog and online ordering also available.

5732 **www.internet.com**
Internet.Com/Mecklermedia
A leading source of global Internet news, and analyses. To learn about Internet.com's latest activities

5733 **www.intl-spectrum.com**
International Spectrum
The independent source of information for users and vendors of IBM's UniVerse and UniData; jBASE International's jBASE; Northgate information Solutions Reality; ONgroup's ONware; Raining Data's D3, mvBASE and mvEnterprise; Revelation Software's Opensight and VIA Systems UniVision Databases.

5734 **www.ioma.com**
IOMA
Supports managers involved in building and maintaining state-of-the-art HRIS software, hardware, and Internet/intranet activities. Publishes newsletter.

5735 **www.iste.org**
International Society for Technology in Education
A large nonprofit organization serving the technology-using educator.

5736 **www.openapplications.org**
Open Applications Group
A open standards group building process-based XML standards for both B2B and A2A integration.

5737 **www.pcca.org**
Portable Computer and Communications Association
A forum for disparate industries to meet, learn about each other, and collaborate on the interaction of the multiple technologies involved in wireless solutions.

5738 **www.polarmicro.com**
Polar Microsystems
Provides consulting services that enable our clients to advance their businesses through full utilization of the Apple Macintosh hardware and software platform.

5739 **www.sei.cmu.edu**
Software Engineering Institute
Works closely with defense and government organizations, industry, and academia to continually improve software-intensive systems.

5740 **www.sme.org**
Automated Systems Technical Group/SME
This group harnesses the power of information technology for advancing product development and design, manufacturing automation, enterprise integration, and communication throughout the product life cycle and supply chain.

5741 **www.spie.org**
International Society for Optical Engineering
Serves the international technical community as the premier provider of education, information, and resources covering optics, photonics, and their applications.

5742 **www.thinkecs.com**
Enterprise Computing Solutions
A leading provider of IT infrastructure solutions for Fortune 500 and mid-tier companies throughout California. ECS builds sophisticated IT infrastructure solutions for mission critical applications, provides enterprise storage solutions that ensure data protection and business continuity and delivers state of the art server solutions for optimal computing capacity.

5743 **www.unf.edu/library**
University of North Florida, Carpenter Library
For catalogers of audiovisual materials and electronic resources. Provides information exchange, continuing education, and works toward a common understanding of practices and standards.

5744 **www.vita.com**
VMEbus International Trade Association
For manufacturers of microcomputer boards, hardware, software, military products, controllers, bus interfaces and other accessories compatible with VMEbus architecture. VITA is an incorporated, nonprofit organization of vendors and users having a common market interest.

5745 **www.webdeveloper.com**
Mecklermedia/Internet.Com
Information on maintaining and growing business web sites and intranets.

5746 **www1.hp.com**
Hewlett Packard /Compaq
The official Web site for the Compaq PCs.

Associations

5747 **Association of Progressive Rental Organizations**
1540 Robinhood Trail
Austin, TX 78703-2624

512-794-0095
800-204-2776; Fax: 512-794-0097
cferguson@rtohq.org
www.rtohq.org
Facebook, Twitter, YouTube, Flickr

Jill McClure, Executive Director

Members include television, appliance and furniture dealers who rent merchandise with an option to purchase.
2000 Members
Founded in 1980

5748 **AugmentedReality.Org**
40600 Ann Arbor Road E.
Suite 201
Plymouth, MI 48170

571-293-2013
www.augmentedreality.org
Facebook, Twitter, LinkedIn, YouTube, Flickr

Ori Inbar, Co-Founder & CEO
Tish Shute, Co-Founder & Chief Content Officer
Patrick O'Shaughnessy, Chief Technology Officer

Non-profit organization seeking to advance the field of augmented reality through connecting industry professionals through events and an online platform.

5749 **Canadian Game Studies Assocation**
Home Page: gamestudies.ca
Twitter

The CGSA is devoted to the interdisciplinary study of digital games, and supports the work of researchers, graduate students, artists, game designers, programmers, theorists, and others working in the industry.
Mailing list available for rent

5750 **Consumer Technology Association (CTA)**
1919 S Eads Street
Arlington, VA 22202

703-907-7600
cta@cta.tech
www.cta.tech
Facebook, Twitter, LinkedIn, Google+

Gary Shapiro, President & CEO
Glenda MacMullin, COO & CFO
Jean Foster, SVP, Marketing & Communications
Brian Markwalter, SVP, Research & Standards
Tiffany Moore, SVP, Political & Industry Affairs

Formerly the Consumer Electronics Association (CEA), the organization provides valuable and innovative member-only resources including: exclusive information and unparalleled market research, networking opportunities with business advocates and leaders, up-to-date educational programs and technical training, exposure in extensive promotional programs, and representation from the voice of the industry.
2200 Members

5751 **Custom Electronic Design & Installation Association**
7150 Winton Dr
Suite 300
Indianapolis, IN 46268

317-328-4336
800-669-5329; Fax: 317-735-4012
www.cedia.org
Facebook, Twitter, Instagram, Houzz

Tabatha O'Connor, Acting President & CEO
Matt Nimmons, Managing Director

A global authority in the home technology industry that provides access to industry-leading education, certification, research, and consumer awareness.
3700 Members

5752 **Digital Games Research Association**
coordinator@digra.org
www.digra.org

William Huber, President
Hanna Wirman, Vice President
Allan Fowler, Secretary
Jussi Holopainen, Treasurer
Cody Mejeur, Diversity Officer

DiGRA is an international association of academics and professionals interested in research into digital games and related products. It features a Digital Library, Gamesnetwork mailing list, and the ToDiGRA journal.
Founded in 2003
Mailing list available for rent

5753 **Electronic Security Association**
6333 North State Highway 161
Suite 350
Irving, TX 75038

972-807-6800
888-447-1689; Fax: 972-807-6883
www.esaweb.orgÿ
Facebook, Twitter, LinkedIn

Marshall Marinace, President
Dee Ann Harn, Vice President
Merlin Guilbeau, Executive Director
Jon Sargent, Secretary
Steve Paley, Treasurer

A nonprofit trade association that represents, promotes, and enhances the growth and professional development of the electronic life safety, security, and integrated sytems industry.
Founded in 1948

5754 **Entertainment Consumers Association**
Home Page: www.theeca.com

Hal Halpin, Founder & President
Heather Ellertson, VP, Marketing
Jennifer Mercurio, VP & General Counsel
Brett Schenker, Advocacy Director
Mike Conley, Digital Marketing Coordinator

Non-profit representing the interests of consumers of digital entertainment in the US and Canada.

5755 **Entertainment Software Association**
601 Massachusetts Avenue NW
Suite 300
Washington, DC 20001

esa@theesa.com
www.theesa.com
Facebook, Twitter, LinkedIn

Stanley Pierre-Louis, President & CEO
Gina Vetere, SVP & General Counsel
Andrew Bowins, SVP, Comm. & Public Affairs
Ana Molina, CFO
Michael O'Leary, SVP, Government Affairs

The trade association of the video game industry.
Founded in 2000

5756 **Entertainment Software Association of Canada**
#408, 130 Spadina Avenue
Toronto, ON M5V 2L4

416-620-7171
theesa.ca
Facebook, Twitter, Instagram, YouTube

Jayson Hilchie, President & CEO
Corinne Crichlow, Director, Communications & PR
Paul Fogolin, Director, Policy & Gov. Affairs
Dylan Boyd, Digital Content Manager

The ESAC is devoted to video game developers, publishers, and distributors in Canada

5757 **Entertainment Software Rating Board**
New York, NY

marketing@esrb.org
www.esrb.org
Facebook, Twitter

Patricia E. Vance, President
David Kassack, SVP, Finance & Operations
Bill Garrity, SVP, Ratings
John Falzone, VP, ESRB Privacy Certified
Randy Walker, SVP, Marketing & Communications

Non-profit, self-regulatory body devoted to informing consumers (especially parents) about the video games they play. The ESRB established and maintains a ratings system for all video games, from E for Everyone to AO for Adults Only.
Founded in 1994

5758 **Gaming Standards Association**
51777 Brandin Court
Fremont, CA 94538

510-492-4060
www.gamingstandards.com
Facebook, Twitter, LinkedIn, YouTube

Peter DeRaedt, President
Michelle Olesiejuk, Executive Director
Mark Pace, Managing Director
Ethan Tower, Protocol Director
Oscar Salgado, Documentation Manager

International trade association that identifies, defines, develops, promotes, and implements standards in the gaming industry. It serves manufacturers, suppliers, operators, and regulators.

5759 **IEEE Consumer Electronics Society**
3 Park Ave.
17th Floor
New York, NY 10016-5997

212-419-7900; Fax: 212-752-4929
ckobert@ieee.org
cesoc.ieee.org

Charlotte Kobert, Executive Administrator

Organization for the advancement of the theory and practice of electronic engineering in consumer electronics.
5000 Members

5760 **International Age Rating Coalition**
info@globalratings.com
www.globalratings.com

The IARC unites many of the video game rating authorities around the world and provides a streamlined age classification process for digital games and mobile apps. The Entertainment Software Rating Board is the point of contact in North America.

5761 **International Game Developers Association**
#402, 150 Eglinton Avenue E.
Toronto, ON M4P 1E8
info@igda.org
www.igda.org
Facebook, Twitter, LinkedIn, YouTube, Instagram
Renee Gittins, Executive Director
Tristin Hightower, Director, Operations
The IGDA is the largest non-profit membership organization serving individuals who create video games. They are dedicated to improving developers' careers and lives through: Community, Professional Development, and Advocacy.
Founded in 1994

5762 **The Repair Association**
ggbyrne@repair.org
repair.org
Gay Gordon-Byrne, Press Contact
Advocacy group for repair industry professionals and the Right to Repair movement.
Founded in 2013

5763 **VR/AR Association**
Palo Alto, CA 94303
nathan@thevrara.com
www.thevrara.com
Facebook, Twitter, LinkedIn, YouTube
Nathan Pettyjohn, Founder & President
Kris Kolo, Global Executive Director
International organization with a mission to foster collaboration between companies and individuals in the virtual reality and augmented reality industry. It aims to accelerate growth, encourage research and education, develop industry standards, connect members, and promote their services.
Founded in 2015

5764 **Video Game Bar Association**
#2000, 222 N. Sepulveda Boulevard
El Segundo, CA 90245
818-564-7898
jolin@vgba.org
vgba.org
Twitter, LinkedIn
Patrick Sweeney, Co-Founder & President
Joseph Olin, Executive Director
Ida Ebeid, Project Manager
An international association of lawyers who specialize in the video game industry.
Founded in 2011

5765 **XR Association**
1299 Pennsylvania Avenue NW
Washington, DC 20004
membership@xra.org
xra.org
Facebook, Twitter, LinkedIn
Elizabeth Hyman, Chief Executive Officer
Joan O'Hara, Senior Director, Public Policy
Laura Chadwick, Senior Director, Industry Relations
Michael Williams, Chief Operating Officer
Bethany Reitsma, Executive Assistant
Trade association for technology manufacturers in the virtual, augmented, and mixed reality industries.
Founded in 2016

Newsletters

5766 **Consumer Electronic and Appliance News**
Kasmar Publications
41905 Boardwalk
Suite L
Palm Desert, CA 92221
800-253-9992
800-253-9992; Fax: 760-723-2876
www.kasmarpub.com
Donald Martin, Editor
Home entertainment, consumer electronics and major appliances.
28 Pages
Founded in 1970

5767 **Consumer Electronics Daily**
Warren Communications News
2115 Ward Court NW
Washington, DC 20037
800-771-9202
consumerelectronicsdaily.com
Daily coverage of the consumer electronics marketplace featuring original reporting and analysis.
Frequency: Daily

5768 **ECA Today**
Entertainment Consumers Association
Home Page: www.theeca.com
Hal Halpin, Founder & President
Heather Ellertson, VP, Marketing
Mike Conley, Digital Marketing Coordinator
Newsletter for members only.
Frequency: Nightly

5769 **Twice: This Week in Consumer Electronics**
Reed Business Information
360 Park Ave S
15th Floor
New York, NY 10010-1737
646-746-6400
800-826-6270; Fax: 646-756-7583
mgrand@reedbusiness.com
www.reedbusiness.com
John Poulin, CEO
Jeff Greisch, Editor/CEO/President
Stephen F Smith, Editor-in-Chief
James Reed, Owner
Patricia Kennedy, Production Manager
Features include industry news, statistics, financial reports and new product trends and announcements.
Cost: $94.90
Frequency: Monthly
Circulation: 41000

Magazines & Journals

5770 **ARtillery Intelligence**
VR/AR Association
Palo Alto, CA 94303
nathan@thevrara.com
www.thevrara.com
Facebook, Twitter, LinkedIn, YouTube
Nathan Pettyjohn, Founder & President
Kris Kolo, Global Executive Director
Research and data package for VR/AR professionals.
Founded in 2015

5771 **AudioXpress**
Audio Amateur Publications
PO Box 876
Peterborough, NH 03458
603-924-9464
888-924-9465; Fax: 603-924-9467
editorial@audioxpress.com
www.audioxpress.com
Edward Dell, Publisher
Focuses on the developments in sound production and enhancements in audio equipment and contains information on the construction of new and modification of existing audio equipment. Projects include schematics, parts lists and instructions necessary for completion aimed at electronic engineers and hobbyists.
Cost: $34.95
72 Pages
Frequency: Monthly
Circulation: 11000
ISSN: 1548-6028
Founded in 2001
Printed in 4 colors on glossy stock

5772 **CTA 5 Technology Trends to Watch**
Consumer Technology Association
1919 S Eads St.
Arlington, VA 22202
703-907-7600
866-858-1555; Fax: 703-907-7675
www.cta.tech
Gary Shapiro, President & CEO
Annual prediction of which products and services will transform consumers' lives.
Frequency: Annual

5773 **CTA Corporate Report**
Consumer Technology Association
1919 S Eads St.
Arlington, VA 22202
703-907-7600
866-858-1555; Fax: 703-907-7675
www.cta.tech
Gary Shapiro, President & CEO
Annual publication looking at the Association's accomplishments and goals.
Frequency: Annual

5774 **CTA Digital America**
Consumer Technology Association
1919 S Eads St.
Arlington, VA 22202
703-907-7600
866-858-1555; Fax: 703-907-7675
www.cta.tech
Gary Shapiro, President & CEO
Annual snapshot of the state of the U.S. consumer technology industry.
Cost: $995.00
Frequency: Annual

5775 **Essential Facts About the Computer and Video Game Industry**
Entertainment Software Association
601 Massachusetts Avenue NW
Suite 300
Washington, DC 20001
esa@theesa.com
www.theesa.com
Stanley Pierre-Louis, President & CEO
Gina Vetere, SVP & General Counsel
Andrew Bowins, SVP, Comm. & Public Affairs
Ana Molina, CFO
Tracks statistics about the video game industry in the US.
Frequency: Annual
Founded in 2000

5776 **IEEE Consumer Electronics Magazine**
IEEE Consumer Electronics Society
3 Park Ave.
17th Floor
New York, NY 10016-5997
212-419-7900; Fax: 212-752-4929
saraju.mohanty@unt.edu
cesoc.ieee.org/publications/ce-magazine.html
Saraju Mohanty, Editor in Chief

Magazine of IEEE Consumer Electronics Society.

5777 **Loading...**
Canadian Game Studies Assocation

jennifer.jenson@ubc.ca
gamestudies.ca

Suzanne de Catell, Editor
Jennifer Jenson, Co-Editor

Official journal of the Canadian Game Studies Assocation with articls on research into digital games.

5778 **Transactions of the Digital Games Research Association**
Digital Games Research Association

jose.zagal@utah.edu
todigra.org

Jose P. Zagal, Editor-in-Chief
Harald Warmelink, Support Contact

ToDiGRA is an international, open access, refereed, multidisciplinary journal for research on and practice in all aspects of digital games. It is both printed and available online.
ISSN: 2328-9422

Trade Shows

5779 **Augmented World Expo**
AugmentedReality.org

Home Page: www.awexr.com
Facebook, Twitter, LinkedIn, YouTube

Ori Inbar, CEO

Showcase for technologies making the world more interactive: augmented reality; virtual reality; and wearable technology.
4000 Attendees

5780 **Canadian Game Studies Association Annual Conference**
Canadian Game Studies Assocation

Home Page: gamestudies.ca

Kym Stewart, Local Arrangement Coordinator

Held in tandem with the Congress of the Humanities and Social Sciences.

5781 **Consumer Electronics Show**
Consumer Technology Association
1919 S Eads St.
Arlington, VA 22202

703-907-7600
866-858-1555; Fax: 703-907-7675
cta@cta.tech
www.cta.tech

Gary Shapiro, President & CEO

World's premier consumer technology event.
177K Attendees
Frequency: Annual

5782 **Electronic Entertainment Expo**
Entertainment Software Association
601 Massachusetts Avenue NW
Suite 300
Washington, DC 20001

Home Page: www.e3expo.com
Facebook, Twitter, YouTube, Instagram

Stanley Pierre-Louis, President & CEO
Andrew Bowins, SVP, Comm. & Public Affairs

Video game industry showcase featuring technology debuts and product launches.
50000 Attendees

5783 **Electronics Reuse Conference**
PC Rebuilders & Recyclers

773-545-7575
sc@pcrr.com
www.ereuseconference.com

Sarah Cade, Conference Director

Computer refurbishment, repair and recycling.
Founded in 2003

5784 **Game Developers Conference**
Informa Tech

415-947-6926
800-216-4916
gdcfeedback@ubm.com
gdconf.com
Facebook, Twitter, LinkedIn, YouTube, Instagram

The GDC provides education, inspiration, and networking opportunities to the video game development community, including programmers, artists, producers, game designers, audio professionals, and business leaders. The conference features discussions, awards ceremonies, community spaces for networking, and the GDC Expo.
Founded in 1988

5785 **Independent Games Festival**
Informa Tech
303 Second Street
Suite 900, S. Tower
San Francisco, CA 94107

chairperson@igf.com
igf.com
Twitter

The IGF recognizes the best independent game developers, and encourages innovation in game development.
Founded in 1998

5786 **VR/AR Global Summit**
VR/AR Association
Palo Alto, CA 94303

am@thevrara.com
www.thevrara.com
Facebook, Twitter, LinkedIn, YouTube

Nathan Pettyjohn, Founder & President
Kris Kolo, Global Executive Director
Anne-Marie Enns, Executive Producer

Summits bring together enterprise, hardware, software, and content providers for educational sessions and networking.
Founded in 2015

5787 **Virtual Reality Developers Conference**
Informa Tech

415-947-6926
800-216-4916
gdcfeedback@ubm.com
www.gdconf.com/vrdc
Facebook, Twitter, LinkedIn, YouTube, Instagram

The VRDC is a two-day summit for developers of Virtual Reality and Augmented Reality entertainment.

Industry Web Sites

5788 **repair.org**
The Repair Association

ggbyrne@repair.org
repair.org

Gay Gordon-Byrne, Press Contact

Advocacy group for repair industry professionals and the Right to Repair movement.
Founded in 2013

Associations

5789 **Aesthetics' International Association**
310 E. Interstate 30
Suite B107
Garland, TX 75043

972-203-8530
877-968-7539; Fax: 972-962-1480
iaaesthetics.org

Miodrag Suvakovic, President
Krystyna Wilkoszewska, Vice President

The association for the advancement of education and public awareness on aesthetics. Paramedical aesthetics and body spa therapy. Professionals from the medical, paramedical and beauty industries working together for the most advanced techniques for the patients and clients.
Founded in 1972

5790 **Allied Beauty Association (ABA)**
145 Traders Blvd. E.
Suites 26&27
Mississauga, ON IL4Z3L3

800-268-6644; Fax: 905-568-1581
abashows@abacanada.com
abacanada.com
Facebook, Twitter, LinkedIn

Alain Audet, Executive Director

Manufacturers and distributors of the professional beauty industry that serve Canada.
Founded in 1957

5791 **American Academy of Facial Esthetics**
2120 S. Green Road
South Euclid, OH 44121

800-952-0521
www.facialesthetics.org
Facebook, Twitter, LinkedIn

Rebecca Hammel, Membership

The AAFE is a multidisciplinary professional healthcare organization that teaches the best injectable techniques to professionals worldwide.

5792 **American Association of Cosmetology Schools**
9927 E. Bell Road
Suite 110
Scottsdale, AZ 85260

480-810-0431
800-831-1086; Fax: 480-905-0993
jim@beautyschools.org
www.beautyschools.org
Facebook, Twitter, LinkedIn, YouTube

Anthony Civitano, Executive Director
Allison Scudder, Program Manager
Cristina Hanson, Program Associate

Association open to all privately owned cosmetology schools.
1100 Members
Founded in 1924

5793 **American Beauty Association**
4330 Gaines Ranch Loop
Austin, TX 78735

512-872-2830
800-868-4265; Fax: 312-245-1080
support@beautyassociation.org
beautyassociation.org
Facebook, Twitter, YouTtbe, Google+, Instagram, P

James Cox, Executive Director
Bruce Selan, VP
George Schaeffer, Secretary

ABA members are manufacturers, manufacturer reps and consultants in the professional beauty industry. Associate members are made up of trade publications, distributors and salons. The ABA's mission is to expand, serve and protect the interests of the professional beauty industry.
200 Members
Founded in 1985

5794 **American Cosmetics Manufacturers Association**
1050 17th St. NW
Suite 600
Washington, DC 20036-4702

202-441-7500
www.acma.us
Facebook, Twitter, YouTube, Google+

An association to support the export of American-made cosmetics and personal care products.

5795 **American Hair Loss Association**
23679 Calabasas Road
#682
Calabasas, CA 91301-1502

Home Page: www.americanhairloss.org

The American Hair Loss Association is the only national, non-profit membership organization dedicated to educating the public, healthcare professionals, main stream media and legislators about the emotionaally devastating disease of hair loss (alopecia). Committed to the prevention and treatment of hair loss, the ALHA is dedicated to supporting research that will ultimately treat and cure thoses who suffer from this silent epidemic.

5796 **American Hair Loss Council**
30 South Main
Shenandoah, PA 17976

412-765-3666; Fax: 412-765-3669
info@ahlc.org
www.ahlc.org
Facebook, Twitter, LinkedIn

Susan Kettering, Executive Director

The nation's only, unbiased, not for profit agency, dedicated to sorting through this information, discovering what works and what doesn't,a nd presenting our findings to the consumer.

5797 **American Society of Hair Restoration Surgery**
225 W. Wacker Drive
Suite 650
Chicago, IL 60606

312-981-6760; Fax: 312-981-6787
info@cosmeticsurgery.org
www.cosmeticsurgery.org
Facebook, Twitter, LinkedIn

Mark Mandell-Brown, President
Kevin Duplechain, President-Elect
Raina Agha, Treasurer
Talon Maningas, Secretary

Comprised of physicians specializing in hair loss, dedicated to promulgating the highest standards of medical practice and medical ethics. Provides continuing education to physicians specializing in hair transplant surgery and gives the public the latest information on medical and surgical treatments for hair loss.
1600 Members

5798 **American Society of Perfumers**
PO Box 1256
Piscataway, NJ 08855-1256

201-500-6101; Fax: 877-732-0090
info@perfumers.org
www.perfumers.org
Facebook, Twitter, LinkedIn, Pinterest

Christopher Diienno, Chair
Vincent Kuczinski, President
Sherri Sebastian, VP
James Krivda, Secretary
James Fassold, Financial Administrator

Nonprofit organization fosters and encourages the art and science of perfumery in the US while promoting professional exchange and a high standard of professional conduct within the fragrance industry. The ASP holds yearly symposiums in the New York City area where leading members of the fragrance industry are invited to speak and present information on all aspects of the industry.
Founded in 1947

5799 **American Suntanning Association**

855-879-7678
media@americansuntanning.org
americansuntanning.org

Melinda Norton, Board President
Matt Russell, Executive Director
Joseph Levy, Scientific Advisor

The ASA is a group of professional sunbed salons committed to teaching about UV exposure and indoor tanning. They focus on scientifically supported information about UV light, sunbeds, and spray tanning through their involvment in government agencies.
Founded in 2012

5800 **Association Accredited Cosmetology Schools**
5201 Leesburg Pike
Falls Church, VA 22041-3244

Home Page: www.naccas.org

Ronald Smith, Publisher

Association for those concerned with cosmetology.
6 Members

5801 **B-cause**
PO Box 4814
Poughkeepsie, NY 12601

845-431-6670
www.bcause.org
Facebook

Rudy Sprogis, Founder/President

Non-profit organization that advances charitable causes for salon owners and beauty industry professionals.
Founded in 2000

5802 **BOBSA**
PO Box 25173
San Francisco, CA 94128

650-863-3491; Fax: 858-712-1934
bobsaone.org
Facebook, Twitter, LinkedIn

Sam Ennon, President

Representing beauty store operators in the ethnic health and beauty-care industry.

5803 **Black Beauty Association**

Home Page: blackbeautyassociation.com

Weldon Germaine Bond, Founder & President

The BBA promotes itself to the professional needs of Black Beauty professionals and students. They offer consulting, business strategies and resources.

5804 **Chain Drug Marketing Association**
43157 W Nine Mile Road
PO Box 995
Novi, MI 48376-0995

248-449-9300; Fax: 248-449-9396
support@chaindrug.com
www.chaindrug.com
Facebook, Twitter, LinkedIn, YouTube, Pinterest

Members are regional drug chains from across North ASmerica Association markets over 800

products under the name Quality Choice to its members.
101 Members
Founded in 1926

5805 **Consumer Healthcare Products Association**
1625 Eye Street, NW
Suite 600
Washington, DC 20006-2105

202-429-9260; Fax: 202-223-6835
eassey@chpa-info.org
www.chpa-info.org
Twitter, YouTube, Pinterest

Scott Melville, President & CEO
Brian Green, SVP, Finance & Operations & CFO
Mike Tringale, VP, Communications & Public Affairs
Samantha Gilson, Controller
Christopher Galczynski, Director, IT

Promotes industry growth through consumer understanding, appreciation, and acceptance of responsible self-care in America's health care system by developing and sustaining a climate that provides consumers with convenient access to safe and effective nonprescription medicines and other self-care products marketed without undue restrictions.
Founded in 1881

5806 **Cosmetic Executive Women**
159 West 25th Street
8th Floor
New York, NY 10001

212-685-5955
646-929-8000; Fax: 212-685-3334
ksweeney@cew.org
www.cew.org
Facebook, Twitter, LinkedIn, YouTube

Carlotta Jacobson, President
Claudia Flowers, COO & CFO
Lisa Klein, SVP
Nicole Cardillo, VP, Marketing & Events
Leslie Hutchings, VP, Membership & Strategy

To advance the professional growth and leadership development of women in the beauty industry.
4000 Members
Founded in 1954

5807 **Cosmetic Industry Buyers and Suppliers**
36 Lakeville Road
New Hyde Park, NY 11040

516-775-0220; Fax: 516-328-9789
cibsmail@cibsonline.com
www.cibsonline.com
LinkedIn

Jenifer Brady, President
Judy Vincenty, Vice President
Balla Murillo, Treasurer
Brenda Lily, Membership Chair
Tonilyn Bruno, Special Event Chair

Members are individuals providing and obtaining essential oils, chemicals, packaging and other goods for the cosmetic industry.
800 Members
Founded in 1948

5808 **Cosmetologists Chicago**
440 S. LaSalle Street
Suite 2325
Chicago, IL 60611-4255

312-321-6809
800-648-2505; Fax: 312-673-6612
info@americasbeautyshow.com
www.americasbeautyshow.com
Facebook, Twitter, YouTube, Pinterest

A beauty voice and presenter of cosmetology shows.

5809 **Cosmetology Advancement Foundation**
PO Box 811
FDR Station
New York, NY 10150

212-750-2412; Fax: 212-593-0862
nalcopr@aol.com

Norma A. Lee, Executive Director

Members represent the professional beauty industry's varied constituencies: cosmetologists, salon owners, cosmetology schools, distributors, manufacturers, associations and professional publications. CAF works through the All-Industry Summit to identify issues that affect the future growth and development of the industry.

5810 **Drug, Chemical & Associated Technologies Association**
One Union St
Suite 208
Robbinsville, NJ 08691-3162

609-208-1888
800-640-3228; Fax: 609-208-0599
mtimony@dcat.org
www.dcat.org

Margaret Timony, Executive Director
Lauryn Kuna, Director, Membership
Miriam O'Donnell, Director, Project Integration
Patricia Van Arnum, Editorial Director
Erin Sanders, Sr. Communications/Tech. Specialist

The premier business development association whose membership is comprised of companies that manufacture, distribute or provide services to the pharamceutical, chemical, nutritional and related industries.
Founded in 1890

5811 **Esthetics Manufacturers and Distributors Alliance**
401 N Michigan Avenue
Chicago, IL 60611

312-215-5120
800-868-4265; Fax: 312-245-1080

Paul Dykstra, Executive Director

A member of the American Beauty Association, whose members are manufacturers of specific products related to the professional beauty industry. EMDA is dedicated to meeting the needs of skin care and body care manufacturers and distributors and the salons they service. The mission of the American Beauty Association and all of its sub-groups is to expand, serve and protect the interests of the professional beauty industry.
40 Members
Founded in 1993

5812 **Fragrance Foundation**
621 2nd Avenue
2nd Floor
New York, NY 10016

212-725-2755; Fax: 646-786-3260
info@fragrance.org
www.fragrance.org
Facebook, Twitter, LinkedIn, YouTube

Linda Levy, President
Sharne Jackson, Sr. Director, Events & Education
Alissar Taremi, Director, Marketing

Nonprofit, educational arm of the international fragrance industry. Devotes its energies to creating an atmosphere of understanding and appreciation of the benefits and pleasures of fragrance in all its many forms.
160 Members
Founded in 1949

5813 **Fragrance Materials Association of the US**
1620 I St NW
Suite 925
Washington, DC 20006-4076

202-293-5800; Fax: 202-463-8998
Facebook, Twitter

Glenn Roberts, Executive Director
90 Members
Founded in 1927

5814 **Handmade Cosmetic Alliance**
Advocating for state and federal legislation that supports the growing handmade cosmetics and soap industry.
Founded in 2007

5815 **Independent Beauty Association**
21925 Field Parkway
Suite 205
Deer Park, IL 60010

847-991-4499
800-334-2623; Fax: 847-991-8161
independentbeauty.org
Facebook, Twitter, LinkedIn

Ken Marenus, President
Donna Hoye, VP
Caroline Santayana, Membership
Arnyae Neal, Marketing
Meredith Petillo, Technical/Regulatory

Represents cosmetic manufacturers, distributors and suppliers to industry. Mission: to represent, educate and foster the growth and profitability of entrepreneurial companies in the cosmetic and personal care industries worldwide.
540 Members
Founded in 1974

5816 **Indoor Tanning Association (ITA)**
2025 M St, NW
Suite 800
Washington, DC 20036

888-377-0477; Fax: 202-367-2142
Facebook, Twitter, LinkedIn

Dan Humiston, President
John Overstreet, Executive Director

Represents indoor tanning manufacturers, distributors, facility owners and members from other support industries.
1000+ Members
Founded in 1999

5817 **International Aloe Science Council**
8630 Fenton Street
Suite 918
Silver Spring, MD 20910-3818

734-476-9690; Fax: 301-588-1174
www.iasc.org

Jane Wilson, Executive Director
Rosie Ysasi, Certification Coordinator

Explores the use of aloe in cosmetic industries, hair products, herb preparations, pharmaceuticals and drinks.
300 Members
Founded in 1981

5818 **International Association of Color Manufacturers**
1101 17th Street NW
Suite 700
Washington, DC 20036

202-293-5800; Fax: 202-463-8998
info@iacmcolor.org
www.iacmcolor.org
LinkedIn

Bobby Gruber, President

Actively represents the interests of the regulated color industry by demonstrating the safety

of color additives and promotes the industry's economic growth by participating in new color approvals, regulatory and legislative issues that affect the industry worldwide.
15 Members
Founded in 1972

5819 International Fragrance Association North America
1655 Fort Myer Dr.
Suite 875
Arlington, VA 22209
571-317-1500; Fax: 571-312-8033
info@ifrana.org
ifrana.org
Facebook, Twitter, Pinterest
Farah Ahmed, President & CEO
Amanda Nguyen, VP, Government & Legal Affairs
Lia Dangelico, Director, Communications
Malory Todd, Manager, Meetings & Membership
Amy Bush, Director, Finance & Operations
Part of the International Fragrance Association network, IFRA North America advocates for the interests of companies in the fragrance manufacturing and fragrance materials supply trades.
60 Members
Founded in 2011

5820 International Perfume Bottle Association
PO Box 1299
Paradise, CA 95967
paradise@sunset.net
www.perfumebottles.org
Facebook
Terri Chappell Boyd, President
Roseann Smith, Vice President
Virginia Merrill, Membership Secretary
Worldwide non-profit organization of people who collect and deal in the variety of perfume containers.
Cost: $45.00
2000+ Members
Founded in 1988

5821 International SPA Association
2365 Harrodsburg Road
Suite A325
Lexington, KY 40504
859-226-4326
888-651-4772; Fax: 859-226-4445
ispa@ispastaff.com
www.experienceispa.com
Facebook, Twitter, LinkedIn, YouTube
Lynne McNees, President
Crystal Ducker, VP, Communications & Research
Amanda Adams, Events Manager
Nelson Lane, Marketing Manager
Samantha Smith, Project Manager
International community of spa professionals, product manufacturers and service providers.
Cost: $530.00
Founded in 1990

5822 International SalonSpa Business Network
4712 E 2nd St
#445
Belmont Shore, CA 90803
562-453-3995; Fax: 866-444-5139
salonspanetwork.org
Facebook, Twitter, Google+
Rhoda Olsen, President
Eric Bakkan, Vice President
Pat Neville, Vice President
Larry Walt, Treasurer
Charles Penzone, Secretary
The association strives to unify the industry and drive it to become more politically active. Members share information, conduct roundtables and help each other recruit, train and retain their staffs.
60+ Members

5823 Nail Manufacturers Council
Professional Beauty Association
7755 E Gray Road
Scottsdale, AZ 85260
480-281-0424
info@probeauty.org
www.probeauty.org
Facebook, Twitter, LinkedIn, YouTube, Pinterest
Beth Hickey, Chair
Sydney Berry, Vice Chair
Steve Sleeper, Executive Director
Rachel Molepske, Manager of Leadership Operations
Steve Wilkerson, Chief Financial Officer
The NMC comprises the leading manufacturers of nail care products sold to, and used in, professional salons. Members cooperate with the association to assure the dissemination of education, training, and technical information concerning nail care products. The NMC has been active in working with international, federal, and state bodies to maintain high professional standards and ensure the safety of industry professionals and their customers, as well as the communities they serve.
50 Members
Founded in 1990

5824 National Accrediting Commission of Cosmetology Arts & Sciences(NACCAS)
4401 Ford Avenue
Suite 1300
Arlington, VA 22302
703-600-7600; Fax: 703-379-2200
naccas.org
Tony Mirando, Executive Director
Eddie Broomfield, Assistant to Executive Director
To accredit post-secondary cosmetology schools and programs.
1050 Members

5825 National Beauty Culturists' League (NBCL)
25 Logan Circle N.W.
Washington, DC 20005
202-332-2695; Fax: 202-332-0940
mercedestoregano@hotmail.com
www.nbcl.info
Dr. Katie B. Catalon, President
Continuing education and higher learning degree program that serves as a unifying force and a catalyst for professionalism, excellence and growth of the beauty industry.
Founded in 1940

5826 National Coalition of Estheticians Manufacturers/Distributors Assns.
484 Spring Avenue
Ridgewood, NJ 07450-4624
201-670-4100; Fax: 201-670-4265
nceaorg@aol.com
www.ncea.tv
Susanne S Warfield, Executive Director
Represents and promotes the esthetic and related professions industry by sharing information, building consensus and providing a unified voice on behalf of the industry.
7000+ Members
Founded in 2000

5827 National Cosmetology Association
15825 N. 71st Street
#100
Scottsdale, AZ 85254-1521
480-281-0424
800-468-2274; Fax: 480-905-0708
www.probeauty.org
Facebook, Twitter, LinkedIn, YouTube, Pinterest, Instagram
Reuben Carranza, Chair
Beth Hickey, Vice Chair
Steve Sleeper, Executive Director
Rachel Molepske, Manager of Leadership Operations
Eric Z Horn, CMP, Associate Executive Director
Nationwide community of salon professionals, connected by a common passion for learning, growing and raising the professionalism of the entire salon industry. As a group we have a storng voice in our communities, our industry and with our government because ithe NCA is for everyone in the professional salon industry. Members have access to education, fashion events, community service and inurance — all the tools needed to build your career.
30000 Members

5828 National Interstate Council of State Boards of Cosmetology
7622 Briarwood Cir
Little Rock, AR 72205-4811
501-227-8262; Fax: 501-227-8212
www.nictesting.org
Kay Kendrick, President
Betty Leake, Vice President
Wayne Kindle, Secretary/ Treasurer
Merger of National Council of State Boards of Cosmetology and Interstate Council of State Boards of Cosmetology. Persons commissioned by the state governments to administer cosmetology laws and examine applicants for cosmetology licenses.
3200 Members
Founded in 1950

5829 National Latino Cosmetology Association NLCA
7925 W Russell Rd
PO Box 401044
Las Vegas, NV 89140
702-448-5020
877-658-3801; Fax: 702-448-8993
marketing@nlcamerican.org
nlcamerican.org
Facebook, Twitter, Pinterest
Julie Zepeda, President/ CEO
Gustavo Castillo, Executive Producer
Mark Sejvar, Marketing Manager
Unites beauty professionals, including salon/spa owners, licensed cosmetologists, barbers, estheticians, nail technicians, students, distributors and manufacturers representing the interests of the beauty industry on a global level.
Founded in 2006

5830 Personal Care Products Council
1620 L Street
Suite 1200
Washington, DC 20036-4702
202-331-1770; Fax: 202-331-1969
www.personalcarecouncil.org
Facebook, Twitter, LinkedIn, YouTube
Pamela Bailey, President
Mark Pollak, VP
Cheryl Mason, Secretary
The leading national trade association representing the global cosmetic and personal care products industry. Member companies manufacture,

distribute, and supply the vast majority of finished personal care products marketed in the U.S.
600 Members
Founded in 1894

5831 **Professional Beauty Association**
7755 E Gray Road
Scottsdale, AZ 85260
480-281-0424
info@probeauty.org
www.probeauty.org
Facebook, Twitter, LinkedIn, YouTube, Instagram, Pinterest
Peggy Sue Schmoldt, Chair
Sydney Berry, Vice Chair
Steve Sleeper, Executive Director
Rachel Molepske, Manager of Leadership Operations
Steve Wilkerson, Chief Financial Officer
The Professional Beauty Association (PBA) is a nonprofit trade association that represents the interests of the professional beauty industry from manufacturers and distributors to salons and spas. PBA offers business tools, education, advocacy, networking and more to improve individual businesses and the industry as a whole.

5832 **Professional Beauty Foundation**
13034 Saticoy Avenue
N Hollywood, CA 91605
800-211-4872
www.probeautyfederation.org
A nonprofit organization made up of professional beauty organizations dedicated to promote and protect the professional beauty industry as it relates to government laws and regulation.

5833 **RIFM: Research Institute for Fragrance Materials**
50 Tice Boulevard
Woodcliff Lake, NJ 07677
201-689-8089; Fax: 201-689-8090
rifm@rifm.org
www.rifm.org
Facebook, Twitter, LinkedIn, Pinterest
Sean G. Traynor, Ph.D, President (Chair)
Robert H. Bedoukian, Ph.D, President (Vice Chair)
David C. Shipman, Group Vice President (Treasurer)
Steven Hicks, Secretary
Michael Carlos, President (Fragrance Division)
Evaluates and distributes scientific data on the safety of fragrance raw materials found in cosmetics, perfumes, shampoos, acndles, air fresheners and other personal products, to encourage uniform safety standards. Membership is open to all companies that manufacture , sell, distribute or engage in business related to the fragrance industry for at least one year.
Founded in 1966

5834 **Regulatory Affairs Professionals Society**
5635 Fishers Lane
Suite 550
Rockville, MD 20852-3048
301-770-2920; Fax: 301-841-7956
raps@raps.org
www.raps.org
Facebook, Twitter, LinkedIn, YouTube, Google+, Flickr
Rainer Voelksen, Chairman of the Board
Martha A Brumfield, PhD, President
Todd Chermak, RPh, PhD, President-Elect
Salma Michor, Secretary/ Treasurer
Don Boyer, BSc, RAC, FRAPS, Director
The foremost worldwide member organization creating and upholding standards of ethica, credentialing and education for the regulatory affairs profession within the health product sector.
10000 Members
Founded in 1976

5835 **Scent Marketing Institute**
7 Fox Meadow Road
New York, NY 10583
646-236-4606; Fax: 914-470-2416
info@scentmarketing.org
Facebook, Twitter, LinkedIn, YouTube
Harald H Vogt, Founder/Chief Marketer
Avery Gilbert PhD, Chief Scientist
Provides networking, educational and marketing support to our member companies and supplies information about scent marketing to the press, marketing, advertising and branding agencies and brand owners.
Founded in 2004

5836 **Sense of Smell Institute**
621 2nd Avenue
2nd Floor
New York, NY 10016
212-725-2755; Fax: 646-786-3260
info@fragrance.org
Facebook, Twitter
Elizabeth Mushmanno, President
Provides information resources to the public, members of the media, corporate and academic sectors. Also sponsors and conducts educational and public outreach programs to increase awareness of the important role the sense of smell plays in our lives.
Founded in 1949

5837 **Society of Clinical and Medical Hair Removal**
2424 American Lane
Madison, WI 53704-3102
608-443-2470; Fax: 608-443-2474
homeoffice@scmhr.org
www.scmhr.org
Facebook, Twitter, Google+
Fadia Hoyek, President
Janie Simmons, Executive Vice President
Sandra Ysassi, Treasurer
Kristen Erdmann, Secretary
Lisa Nelson, Executive Secretary
An international non profit organization with members in the United States, Canada, Australia, Japan and beyond. Supports all methods of hair removal and is dedicated to the research of new technology that will keep its members at the pinnacle of thier professsion, offering safe, effective hair removal to their clients.
600 Members
Founded in 1985

5838 **Society of Cosmetic Chemists**
120 Wall St
Suite 2400
New York, NY 10005-4088
212-668-1500; Fax: 212-668-1504
scc@scconline.org
www.scconline.org
Facebook, Twitter, LinkedIn
Elizabeth Streland, President
Michelle Hines, Vice President
Karen Chun, Treasurer
Yulia Park, Secretary
Dedicated to the advancement of cosmetic science, the Society strives to increase and disseminate scientific information through meetings and publications. By promoting research in cosmetic science and industry, and by setting high ethical, professional and educational standards, we reach our goal of improving the qualifacations of cosmetic scientists.
4000 Members
Founded in 1945

5839 **The Day Spa Association**
2863 Hedberg Drive
Union City, NJ 07087
877-851-8998; Fax: 855-344-8990
dayspaassociation.com
Facebook, Google+
Allan Share, President & Executive Director
Open to day spas, spa salons, individuals working in the spa industry and companies supplying products and services to the industry. Its aim is to unify and support the spa industry.
900 Members

5840 **Women in Flavor & Fragrance Commerce**
55 Harristown Rd.
Suite 106
Glen Rock, NJ 07452
201-857-8955; Fax: 201-447-3831
info@wffc.org
www.wffc.org
Facebook, LinkedIn
Erica Lermond, President
Jessica Reichert Weber, Vice President
Marie Worsham, Secretary
Patricia Halle, Treasurer
This organization was borne out of a recognized need for a networking, education and support system for women in our industry. Providing a center of education, camaraderie, support, and networking.
600 Members
Founded in 1982
Mailing list available for rent: 1000 names

Newsletters

5841 **American Society of Perfumers Newsletter**
PO Box 1551
West Caldwell, NJ 07004
201-991-0040; Fax: 201-991-0073
info@perfumers.org
www.perfumers.org
Twitter
Marvel Fields, President
Information on upcoming events, industry news, fragrance related issues and special articles.
Founded in 1947

5842 **FDC Reports: Rose Sheet**
FDC Reports
5550 Friendship Boulevard
Suite 1
Chevy Chase, MD 20815-7256
301-657-9830
800-332-2181; Fax: 301-664-7238
www.fdcreports.com
Brooke Mcmanus, Editor
Susan Easton, Publisher
Mike Squires, President
Shaun Smith, Marketing
Nicole Tesschamts, Circulation Manager
For executives in the cosmetics, toiletries, fragrances and skin care industries. Provides, coverage of the regulatory and legal environment for cosmetics, major scientific developments and testing methods product marketing news, new product launches; promotions and advertising, retail weekly trademark listings, mergers and acquisitions and developments in the European community.
Cost: $1050.00
Frequency: Weekly
ISSN: 0279-1110
Founded in 1939

5843 **Perfume Bottle Quarterly**
PO Box 1299
Paradise, CA 95967

paradise@sunset.net
www.perfumebottles.org

Ed Lefkowith, President
Anne Conrad, Publications Chair

Features association news bottle photos, people, literature reviews, trade events, and classified ads. Providing a tremendous resource of knowledge about our field, PBQ is essential to staying current on information, events, and people of the field.
24 Pages
Frequency: Quarterly
Founded in 1997
Printed in 4 colors

5844 **Society of Cosmetic Chemists Newsletter**
Society of Cosmetic Chemists
120 Wall St
Suite 2400
New York, NY 10005-4088

212-668-1500; Fax: 212-668-1504
scc@scconline.org
www.scconline.org

Randy Wickett, Ph.D, President
Joseph Dallal, Vice President
Guy Padulo, Vice President-Elect
Dawn Burke-Colvin, Secretary
Tony O'Lenick, Treasurer

Issued once a month providing up-to-date information about activities within the SCC and contemporary issues in international arbitration and mediation.
3600 Members
Founded in 1945

5845 **WFFC Newsletter**
Women in Flavor & Fragrance Commerce
3301 State Route 66
Suite 205
Neptune, NJ 07753-2705

732-922-0500; Fax: 732-922-0560
info@wffc.org
www.wffc.org

Joanne Kennedy, President
Celine Roche, Vice President
Kathryn Bardsley, Secretary
Anne Marie Api, Treasurer

This organization was borne out of a recognized need for a networking, education and support system for women in our industry. Providing a center of education, camaraderie, support, and networking.
300 Members
Founded in 1982

Magazines & Journals

5846 **Beauty Fashion**
Ledes Group
286 Madison Ave
Suite 200
New York, NY 10017-6407

212-840-8800; Fax: 212-840-7246

John Ledes, Owner
Michelle Krell Kydd, Marketing

The authoritative magazine in the field of cosmetics, toiletries, fragrances and personal care.
Cost: $25.00
131 Pages
Frequency: Monthly
Circulation: 18672
ISSN: 0005-7487
Printed in 4 colors on glossy stock

5847 **Beauty Fashion: Body/Bath/Sun Issue**
Beauty Fashion
16 E 40th Street
New York, NY 10016

212-328-6789; Fax: 212-840-7246
Facebook

Offers listings of body/bath and sun products as well as manufacturers and US distributors.
Cost: $25.00
Frequency: Annual
Circulation: 17,000

5848 **Beauty Fashion: CTFA Convention Issue**
Beauty Fashion
16 E 40th Street
New York, NY 10016

212-328-6789; Fax: 212-840-7246

Offers various suppliers of goods and services to the cosmetics industry manufacturers represented at Cosmetic, Toiletry and Fragrance Association convention.
Cost: $25.00
Frequency: Annual
Circulation: 17,000

5849 **Beauty Fashion: Cosmetics Issue**
Beauty Fashion
16 E 40th Street
New York, NY 10016

212-328-6789; Fax: 212-840-7246

Offers listings of color cosmetics products for women as well as manufacturers and US distributors.
Cost: $25.00
Frequency: Annual
Circulation: 17,000

5850 **Beauty Fashion: Women's Fragrance Issue**
Beauty Fashion
16 E 40th Street
New York, NY 10016-5101

212-328-6789; Fax: 212-840-7246
www.beautyfashion.com/

Michelle Kre Kydd, Marketing
Veronica Kelly, Circulation Manager
Adelaide Farah, Editor

Offers listings of women's fragrance products including perfumes, eau de toilettes, and colognes as well as manufacturers and US distributors.
Cost: $25.00
Frequency: Monthly
Circulation: 17000

5851 **Beauty Fashion: Women's Treatment Issue**
Beauty Fashion
Ste 700
286 Madison Ave
New York, NY 10017-6407

212-840-8800; Fax: 212-840-7246
www.beautyfashion.com/

Adelaide Farah, Group Editorial Director
Veronica Kelly, Subscription
Michelle Krell Kydd, Marketing

Offers listings of products and manufacturers and US distributors of cosmetics called treatment products.
Cost: $25.00
Frequency: Monthly

5852 **Beauty Forum NAILPRO**
Creative Age Publications
7628 Densmore Ave
Van Nuys, CA 91406-2042

818-782-7560
800-442-5667; Fax: 818-782-7450
dayspa@creativeage.com
www.creativeage.com

Linda Lewis, Editor
Linda Kossoff, Marketing Manager

NAILPRO for a number of markets in Europe.
Cost: $22.00
Frequency: Monthly
Founded in 1971

5853 **Beauty Inc.**
Fairchild Publications
7 W 34th St
New York, NY 10001-8100

212-630-3880
800-289-0273; Fax: 212-630-3868
www.fairchildpub.com

Mary Berner, President
Jenny B. Fine, Editor-in-Chief
Sarah Murphy, Publisher

The ONLY resource for the global beauty supply chain-from the suppliers and manufacturers who develop the products to the retailers who influence purchase. Packed with immediate actionable information and inspiration.
Cost: $ 60.00
Frequency: Monthly
Circulation: 40056

5854 **Beauty Packaging**
Rodman Publishing
70 Hilltop Rd
3rd Floor
Ramsey, NJ 07446-1150

201-825-2552; Fax: 201-825-0553
info@rodpub.com
www.nutraceuticalsworld.com

Rodman Zilenziger Jr, President
Matt Montgomery, VP

Covering all types of packaging. Beauty Packaging is published for executives involved in the personal care, cosmetic and fragrance industry.
Cost: $40.00
Circulation: 17387
Founded in 1965

5855 **Beauty Store Business**
Creative Age Publications
7628 Densmore Ave
Van Nuys, CA 91406-2042

818-782-7560
800-442-5667; Fax: 818-782-7450
dayspa@creativeage.com
www.creativeage.com

Linda Lewis, Editor
Linda Kossoff, Marketing Manager

Products, news and trends for open-line and professional beauty stores and distributors.
Cost: $22.00
Frequency: Monthly
Founded in 1971

5856 **Cosmetic Ingredient Review**
1101 17th St NW
Suite 310
Washington, DC 20036-4720

202-331-0651; Fax: 202-331-0088
cirinfo@cir-safety.org
www.cir-safety.org

Alan Andersen, Executive Director
Wilma F. Bergfeld, Chairman

Assesses the safety of ingredients used in cosmetics in an unbiased manner and publishes the result in open, peer written literature.
Cost: $100.00
Frequency: Annual+
Founded in 1976

5857 **Cosmetic World**
Ledes Group

286 Madison Ave
Suite 200
New York, NY 10017-6407

212-840-8800; Fax: 212-840-7246

John Ledes, Owner
Dorene Kaplan, Managing Editor

Current industry events, legislation, management changes and corporate activities, as well as marketing developments and financial analysis.
Cost: $175.00
Frequency: Weekly
Circulation: 5397

5858 **Cosmetics & Toiletries**
Allured Publishing Corporation
336 Gundersen Dr
Suite A
Carol Stream, IL 60188-2403

630-653-2155; Fax: 630-653-2192
customerservice@allured.com
www.allured.com

Janet Ludwig, President
Linda Knott, Director Of Operations

This magazine presents a full range of products covering the international cosmetic technology field - including the magazine, a tradeshow, conferences, books and extensive Web sites. The magazine brings the most current technologies in formulating, research, regulations and new ingredients. It also delivers for you a devoted readership base of cosmetic chemists and scientists around the world.
Cost: $98.00
110 Pages
Frequency: Monthly
Circulation: 15,000
ISSN: 0361-4387
Printed in 4 colors on glossy stock

5859 **DaySpa Magazine**
Creative Age Publications
7628 Densmore Ave
Van Nuys, CA 91406-2042

818-782-7560
800-442-5667; Fax: 818-782-7450
dayspa@creativeage.com
www.creativeage.com

Linda Lewis, Editor
Linda Kossoff, Marketing Manager

Powerful ideas to build your spa business.
Cost: $22.00
Frequency: Monthly
Founded in 1971

5860 **Delicious Living**
New Hope Natural Media
1401 Pearl St
Suite 200
Boulder, CO 80302-5346

303-939-8440; Fax: 303-939-9886
info@newhope.com
www.newhope.com
Facebook, Twitter

Fred Linder, President
Pamela Emanoil, Advertising Manager

A trusted health and wellness resource for more than 25 years.
Cost: $12.99
Frequency: Monthly

5861 **Dermascope Magazine**
Aesthetics International Association
2611 N Belt Line Rd
Suite 101
Mesquite, TX 75182-9301

972-203-8530
800-961-3777; Fax: 972-226-2339
www.dermascope.com

William Strunk, Publisher
Rachel Valma, Circulation Director
Casey Fore, Editor

The official publication for the advancement of education and public awareness. Variety of articles on skin care, makeup, body spa therapy and paramedical articles where medical and beauty specialists interact.
Cost: $45.00
Frequency: Monthly
Circulation: 80000
Founded in 1972

5862 **Global Cosmetic Industry**
Allured Publishing Corporation
336 Gundelsen Drive
Suite A
Carol Stream, IL 60188-2755

630-653-2155; Fax: 630-597-0118
www.gcimagazine.com

Jeff Falk, Editor in Chief
Kim Jednachowski, Sales/Account Manager

The business information resource for marketers, brand managers, manufacturers and executives in the global beauty industry. Industry professionals look to GCI for the strategies, trends, analyses and market data that translate into brand impact.
Circulation: 36,500

5863 **Happi**
Rodman Publishing
70 Hilltop Rd
3rd Floor
Ramsey, NJ 07446-1150

201-825-2552; Fax: 201-825-0553
info@rodpub.com
www.nutraceuticalsworld.com

Rodman Zilenziger Jr, President
Matt Montgomery, VP

Serves the manufacturers and fillers of cosmetics, toiletries, fragrances, pharmaceuticals, detergents and chemical specialties inclusing household cleaning products and others product lines allied to the field.
Founded in 1964

5864 **Health Products Business**
Cygnus Publishing
2 Huntington Quad
Suite 301n
Melville, NY 11747-4618

631-845-2700; Fax: 631-845-2723
feedback@magazines.com
www.healthproducts.com

Susanne Alberto, Editor/Features
Bruce Leftakels, Publisher

This is a trade magazine that covers news and trends in the natural health products industry vitamins, herbs, dietary supplements and other products. Publishes annual raw materials directory and purchasing guide. Target audience, natural products retail store owners, buyers and managers. Qualified subscription only.
Founded in 1996

5865 **Inside Cosmeceuticals**
Virgo Publishing LLC
3300 N Central Ave
Suite 300
Phoenix, AZ 85012-2532

480-675-9925; Fax: 480-990-0819
peggyj@vpico.com
www.vpico.com

Jenny Bolton, President

An online information source exploring emerging product trends and scientific research designed to support the growth and development of the cosmeceuticals market. Visited by manufacturers, marketers and formulators of healthy and innovative cosmetics and personal care products.
Mailing list available for rent: 17000+ names at $var per M

5866 **Inspire**
Creative Age Publications
7628 Densmore Ave
Van Nuys, CA 91406-2042

818-782-7560
800-442-5667; Fax: 818-782-7450
dayspa@creativeage.com
www.creativeage.com

Linda Lewis, Editor
Linda Kossoff, Marketing Manager

America's most popular line of hairstyling books.
Cost: $22.00
Frequency: Monthly
Founded in 1971

5867 **Journal of Essential Oil Research/JEOR**
Allured Publishing Corporation
336 Gundersen Dr
Suite A
Carol Stream, IL 60188-2403

630-653-2155; Fax: 630-653-2192
customerservice@allured.com
www.allured.com

Janet Ludwig, President
Linda Knott, Director Of Operations

Forum for the publication of essential oil research and analysis.
Cost: $660.00
Frequency: 6x/Year

5868 **Launchpad**
Creative Age Publications
7628 Densmore Ave
Van Nuys, CA 91406-2042

818-782-7560
800-442-5667; Fax: 818-782-7450
dayspa@creativeage.com
www.creativeage.com

Linda Lewis, Editor
Linda Kossoff, Marketing Manager

News and features about new products for hair, nails, makeup, skincare and tools for beauty professionals.
Cost: $22.00
Frequency: Monthly
Founded in 1971

5869 **LiveSpa Magazine**
International Spa Association
2365 Harrodsburg Road
Suite A325
Lexington, KY 40504

888-651-4772; Fax: 859-226-4445
ispa@ispastaff.com
www.experienceispa.com
Facebook, Twitter

Lynne Walker McNees, President
Deborah Waldvogel, Chairman
Jennifer Wayland-Smith, Vice Chairman
Ella Stimpson, Secretary/ Treasurer

ISPA's consumer magazine, explores a variety of fascinating and useful spa topics and answer spa-goer questions. Insights coming straight from the experts, LiveSpa provides consumers with the practical information they need to better embrace this important aspect of their overall wellness routine. (Also available in digital format)
Cost: $530.00

5870 **MedEsthetics**
Creative Age Publications
7628 Densmore Ave
Van Nuys, CA 91406-2042
818-782-7560
800-442-5667; Fax: 818-782-7450
dayspa@creativeage.com
www.creativeage.com
Linda Lewis, Editor
Linda Kossoff, Marketing Manager
News, features and education about noninvasive cosmetic therapies, trends, products and equipment for medical professionals and spa owners/managers in the U.S.
Cost: $22.00
Frequency: Monthly
Founded in 1971

5871 **NAILPRO**
Creative Age Publications
7628 Densmore Ave
Van Nuys, CA 91406-2042
818-782-7560
800-442-5667; Fax: 818-782-7450
dayspa@creativeage.com
www.creativeage.com
Linda Lewis, Editor
Linda Kossoff, Marketing Manager
The magazine for nail professionals.
Cost: $22.00
Frequency: Monthly
Founded in 1971

5872 **Nails Magazine**
Bobit Business Media
3520 Challenger St
Torrance, CA 90503
310-533-2400; Fax: 310-533-2507
www.nailsmag.com
Dedicated to the success of nail professionals.
Cost: $34.50
Frequency: Bi-Monthly
Circulation: 4,500

5873 **Perfume 2000 Magazine**
Nathalie Publishing Corp
444 Brickell Avenue
Suite 510
Miami, FL 33131
305-669-4602; Fax: 305-669-6116
www.perfume2000.com
Bernard Pommier, Circulation Manager
Joseph P Quick, Publisher
Provides an inside look at the American and international prefume industry.
Cost: $18.00
Frequency: Bi-Monthly
ISSN: 1081-7220

5874 **Perfumer & Flavorist**
Allured Publishing Corporation
336 Gundersen Dr
Suite A
Carol Stream, IL 60188-2403
630-653-2155; Fax: 630-653-2192
customerservice@allured.com
www.allured.com
Janet Ludwig, President
Linda Knott, Director Of Operations
Helps readers to analyze global trends, discover new ingredients and innovations, and keep up-to-date with industry news and analysis.
Cost: $135.00
Frequency: 8 Issues + 3 Bonus Issues

5875 **Proud Magazine**
PO Box 19510
Chicago, IL 60619-0510
708-633-6328; Fax: 708-633-6329
www.ahbai.org
Joe Dudley, Senior President
Jory Luste, President
Nathaniel Bronner, Jr. Executive VP
AHBAI reresents leading, African American-owned companies manufacturing ethnic hair care and beauty products. Members serve African Americans through employment, scholarships and education.

5876 **Pulse Magazine**
International Spa Association
2365 Harrodsburg Road
Suite A325
Lexington, KY 40504
888-651-4772; Fax: 859-226-4445
ispa@ispastaff.com
www.experienceispa.com
Facebook, Twitter
Lynne Walker McNees, President
Deborah Waldvogel, Chairman
Jennifer Wayland-Smith, Vice Chairman
Ella Stimpson, Secretary/ Treasurer
The magazine for the spa professional. An in-depth look at the latest spa industry trends or tips on balancing your personal and professional life. At Pulse, our goal is to be a source for spa business solutions as well as a medium for personal exploration.
Cost: $530.00

5877 **Rite Aid Be Healthy & Beautiful**
Drug Store News Consumer Health Publications
425 Park Ave
New York, NY 10022-3526
212-756-5220
800-766-6999; Fax: 212-756-5250
www.drugstorenews.com
Lebhar Friedman, Publisher
Provides health and beauty tips to millions of women who visit Rite Aid stores.
Frequency: Quarterly
Circulation: 450,000
Founded in 2002

5878 **SalonOvation Magazine**
Milady Publishing Company
5 Southside Dr
Clifton Park, NY 12065-3870
518-280-9500
800-998-1498; Fax: 518-373-6200
esales@thomsonlearning.com
www.delmarlearning.com
Shannon Melldady, Owner
Donna Lewis, Executive Marketing Director
Ron Schlosser, President/CEO
Dedicated to furthering the education of new and established beauty professionals, available by paid subscription to cosmetology students, and practicing massage therapists, cosmetologists, nail technicians, barber-stylists and estheticians.
Cost: $20.00
Frequency: Monthly
Circulation: 80000
Founded in 1945

5879 **Scent Marketing Digest**
7 Fox Meadow Road
Scarsdale, NY 10583
646-236-4606; Fax: 914-470-2416
info@scentmarketing.org
Harald H Vogt, Founder/Chief Marketer
Avery Gilbert PhD, Chief Scientist
The essential blog for Scent Marketing resources, industry experts, scent developers and scent solution providers.

5880 **The Colorist**
Creative Age Publications
7628 Densmore Ave
Van Nuys, CA 91406-2042
818-782-7560
800-442-5667; Fax: 818-782-7450
dayspa@creativeage.com
www.creativeage.com
Linda Lewis, Editor
Linda Kossoff, Marketing Manager
The latest in haircolor trends, techniques, products and fashion.
Cost: $22.00
Frequency: Monthly
Founded in 1971

5881 **The Link**
30 South Main
Shenandoah, PA 17976
412-765-3666; Fax: 412-765-3669
info@ahlc.org
www.ahlc.org
Susan Kettering, Executive Director
The voice of the American Hair Loss Council.

5882 **WWD Beauty Biz**
Fairchild Publications
7 W 34th St
New York, NY 10001-8100
212-630-3880
800-289-0273; Fax: 212-630-3868
www.fairchildpub.com
Mary Berner, President
Jenny B. Fine, Editor-in-Chief
Sarah Murphy, Publisher
The premier guide to the beauty industry. Provides in-depth coverage and analysis on all aspects of the industry, including trends, brands, retailers, and personalities driving both the general comsumer and insider sides of the business.
Cost: $60.00
Frequency: Monthly
Circulation: 40056

Trade Shows

5883 **AACS Annual Convention**
9927 E. Bell Road
Suite 110
Scottsdale, AZ 85260
480-810-0431
800-831-1086; Fax: 480-905-0993
jim@beautyschools.org
www.beautyschools.org
Facebook, Twitter
Anthony Civitano, Executive Director
Cristina Hanson, Program Associate
Allison Scudder, Program Manager
Association open to all privately owned cosmetology schools.
1100 Members
Founded in 1924

5884 **AACS Annual Convention & Expo**
American Association of Cosmetology Schools

9927 E. Bell Road
Suite 110
Scottsdale, AZ 85260

480-281-0431
800-831-1086; Fax: 480-905-0993
jim@beautyschools.org
www.beautyschools.org

Anthony Civitano, Executive Director

An opportunity to bring your professional team together to lead your school into the future. Education tracks, ckasses, social events, and the expo hall complete the experience.
Frequency: Annual/Fall

5885 **AHBAI Mid-Year Conference**
American Health & Beauty Aids Institute
PO Box 19510
Chicago, IL 60619-0510

708-633-6328; Fax: 708-633-6329
www.ahbai.org

Joe Dudley, Senior President
Jory Luste, President
Nathaniel Bronner, Jr. Executive VP

AHBAI reresents leading, African American-owned companies manufacturing ethnic hair care and beauty products. Members serve African Americans through employment, scholarships and education.

5886 **Aesthetics' and Spa World Conference**
Aesthetics' International Association
2611 N Belt Line Road
Suite 140
Sunnyvale, TX 75182

972-038-8530
800-961-3777
www.dermascope.com/aia

Networking, workshops, classes, exhibitors and more for the aesthetics' and spa professionals.
2000 Attendees

5887 **America's Beauty Show**
America's Beauty Show
401 N Michigan Avenue
Chicago, IL 60611

312-321-6809
800-648-2505; Fax: 312-321-0575
info@americasbeautyshow.com
www.americasbeautyshow.com

Pat Dwyer, Tradeshow Logisitics Manager
Ingrid Qualls, Tradeshow Sr Coordinator

Evaluate new products, meet with distributors, continuing education classes on the show floor, and purchase product.
Frequency: Annual/March

5888 **America's Expo for Skin Care & Spa**
Allured Publishing Corporation
336 Gundersen Drive
Suite A
Carol Stream, IL 60188-2403

630-653-2155; Fax: 630-653-2192
customerservice@allured.com
www.allured.com

Janet Ludwig, President
Linda Knott, Director of Operations

Interactive exhibition focuses on professional skin care and spa services. Showcases the newest products, services and technologies from industry manufacturers and suppliers.
Frequency: May

5889 **American Society of Perfumers Annual Symposium**
PO Box 1551
West Caldwell, NJ 07004

201-991-0040; Fax: 201-991-0073
info@perfumers.org
www.perfumers.org
Twitter

Marvel Fields, President

All about Perfumery with special guest perfumers speaking about creativity and honors to those who help build our industry.
Founded in 1947

5890 **Annual Scientific Meeting and Technology Showcase**
Society of Cosmetic Chemists
120 Wall St
Suite 2400
New York, NY 10005-4088

212-668-1500; Fax: 212-668-1504
scc@scconline.org
www.scconline.org

Randy Wickett, Ph.D, President
Joseph Dallal, Vice President
Guy Padulo, Vice President-Elect
Dawn Burke-Colvin, Secretary
Tony O'Lenick, Treasurer

Furthering the interest and recognition of cosmetic scientists.
3600 Members
Founded in 1945

5891 **Annual Scientific Seminar**
Society of Cosmetic Chemists
120 Wall St
Suite 2400
New York, NY 10005-4088

212-668-1500; Fax: 212-668-1504
scc@scconline.org
www.scconline.org

Randy Wickett, Ph.D, President
Joseph Dallal, Vice President
Guy Padulo, Vice President-Elect
Dawn Burke-Colvin, Secretary
Tony O'Lenick, Treasurer

Providing information and forums for the exchange of ideas and new developments in cosmetic research and technology.
3600 Members
Founded in 1945

5892 **Association of Image Consultants Annual Global Conference**
Association of Image Consultants International
1000 Westgate Drive
Suite 252
Saint Paul, MN 55114

651-290-7468; Fax: 651-290-2266
info@aici.org
www.aici.org
Facebook, Twitter

Jane Seaman, President
Riet De Vlieger, President-Elect
Gail Morgan, Secretary
Chris Fulkerson, Treasurer
Eric Ewald, Executive Director

Conference and industry related exhibits.
Founded in 1991

5893 **Beacon**
Professional Beauty Association
7755 E Gray Road
Scottsdale, AZ 85260

480-281-0424
info@probeauty.org
www.probeauty.org

Beth Hickey, Chair
Sydney Berry, Vice Chair
Steve Sleeper, Executive Director
Rachel Molepske, Manager Of Leadership Operations
Steve Wilkerson, Chief Financial Officer

Beacon is held annually to provide the nation's top cosmetology students with the guidance to achieve maximum career success. Beacon students attend the most celebrated industry events during PBA Beauty Week, and benefit from specially designed educational sessions to help them embark on a successful career path.
50 Members
Founded in 1989

5894 **Beauty Exposition USA**
Beauty Expo USA
10725 Midwest Industrial Blvd
Saint Louis, MO 63132

314-426-6333; Fax: 314-426-6335
btexpo@yahoo.com
www.beautyexpousa.com

Leon Beatty, Owner
Ann Park, Marketing Director

Hair and beauty supply trade show with a mission of connecting buyers and exhibitors for concentrated business exchanges. Training for retailers in product knowledge and display methods.
2,000 Attendees
Frequency: Annual/Winter

5895 **Beauty Supply Show: West Coast**
West Coast Beauty Supply
5001 Industrial Way
Benicia, CA 94510

707-484-4800
800-233-3141; Fax: 707-748-4623

Jennifer Coleman, Director
Wayne Clark, President
Jane West, Principal

200 booths of the newest and the best beauty products for the individual and business.
15M Attendees
Frequency: March

5896 **CDMA Education & Trade Show**
Chain Drug Marketing Association
43157 W Nine Mile Road
PO Box 995
Novi, MI 48376-0995

248-499-9300; Fax: 248-449-9396
www.chaindrug.com
Facebook, Twitter, LinkedIn

James Devine, President
Judy Aspinall, VP
John Devine, VP of Store

Hundreds of exhibitors and thousands of buyers from regional chains, regional wholesalers, and independent pharmacies.
Frequency: Annual
Founded in 1926

5897 **CEA Annual Convention**
Cosmetology Educators of America
9927 E. Bell Road
Suite 110
Scottsdale, AZ 85260

480-810-0431
800-831-1086; Fax: 480-905-0993
jim@beautyschools.org
www.beautyschools.org
Facebook, Twitter

Jim Cox, Executive Director
Lisa Zarda, General Manager
Chris Cox, Member services Manager

Association open to all privately owned cosmetology schools.
1100 Members
Founded in 1924

5898 **CHPA Annual Executive Conference**
Consumer Health Care Products Association

900 19th St NW
Suite 700
Washington, DC 20006-2105
202-429-9260; Fax: 202-223-6835
eassey@chpa-info.org
www.chpa-info.org

Scott Melville, President and CEO
Katie Bernard, State Legislative Analyst
Roman Blazauskas, VP
Chelsea Crutti, Associate Director, State Gov

Join top healthcare executives from across the nation and participate in high-level education sessions focused on the industry's rapidly shifting environment.

5899 **Capitol Hill Visits**
Professional Beauty Association
15825 N. 71st Street
Suite 100
Scottsdale, AZ 85254
480-281-0424
800-468-2274; Fax: 480-905-0708
info@probeauty.org
www.probeauty.org/nmc

Max Wexler, Chair
Scott Buchanan, Vice Chair
Bruce Selan, Treasurer

PBA takes Capitol Hill by storm each year. Armed with talking points about issues such as tip-tax reform, association health plans and more, members meet with their Congressional representatives.
50 Members
Founded in 1989

5900 **Circle of Champions**
Premiere Show Group
444 Brickell Avenue
Suite 510
Miami, FL 33131
305-669-4602; Fax: 305-669-6116
www.perfume2000.com

Bernard Pommier, Circulation Manager
Joseph P Quick, Publisher

Rewarding the best of the perfume industry.
Frequency: Bi-Monthly

5901 **Cosmetic Science Symposium & Expo**
Personal Care Products Council
1101 17th Street NW
Suite 300
Washington, DC 20036-4702
202-331-1770; Fax: 202-331-1969
www.personalcarecouncil.org
Facebook, Twitter, LinkedIn, YouTube

Pamela Bailey, President
Mark Pollak, VP
Cheryl Mason, Secretary

Attracts industry leaders and decision-makers and offers personal care products industry staff one-stop shopping for information about Microbiology, Quality Assurance, Safety, and Environmental. The Science Symposium is a great opportunity to learn from the experts and meet colleagues and friends in the industry. Also features the Cosmetic Science Expo.
525 Members
Founded in 1894

5902 **Cosmoprof North America**
Professional Beauty Association
7755 E Gray Road
Scottsdale, AZ 85260
480-281-0424
800-468-2274; Fax: 480-905-0708
info@cosmoprofnorthamerica.com
www.cosmoprofnorthamerica.com
Facebook, Twitter, LinkedIn

Danica Levy, Trade Show Manager, Events

Best in hair,cosmetics,packagin and style. Attracted 25,000 professionals from 32 countries with 760 exhibitors.
10M Attendees
Frequency: July
Founded in 2002

5903 **DCAT Western Education Conference**
Drug, Chemical & Associated Technologies
1 Washington Boulevard
Suite 7
Robbinsville, NJ 08691
609-448-1000
800-640-3228; Fax: 609-448-1944
brooke@dcat.org
www.dcat.org

Mikaela Venice, Meeting Coordinator
Margaret Timony, Executive Director

Gain important insights into issues and trends that will affect the future of the nutrition and health industry. Participate in discussion on key business issues with industry experts.

5904 **Distributor Executive Conference**
Professional Beauty Association
7755 E Grat Road
Scottsdale, AZ 85260
480-281-0424
info@probeauty.org
www.probeauty.org

Steven Sleeper, Executive Director

Annual show of industry related equipment, supplies and services. Developed by industry distributors and geared towards distributors.
10M Attendees

5905 **Elements Showcase**
Skylight West
500 West 36th Street
New York, NY 10018
info@elements-showcase.com
www.elements-showcase.com
Facebook, Twitter, LinkedIn, YouTube

Showcasing diverse range of cosmetic products. Get to know the latest product range and services that will be displayed by leading and well known companies from every corner of the world.

5906 **Emerging Issues Conference**
Personal Care Products Council
1101 17th Street NW
Suite 300
Washington, DC 20036-4702
202-331-1770; Fax: 202-331-1969
www.personalcarecouncil.org
Facebook, Twitter, LinkedIn, YouTube

Pamela Bailey, President
Mark Pollak, VP
Cheryl Mason, Secretary

Regulations being considered in California have an impact on every manufacturer and consumer in the United States. Water, waste, air, packaging, ingredients, recycling, new technology, whatever the issue, the discussions often begin in this state. The Council will host an annual Emerging Issues Conference focusing on the many challenges we see on the horizon for our industry.
525 Members
Founded in 1894

5907 **Engredea**
New Hope Natural Media
1401 Pearl St
Suite 200
Boulder, CO 80302-5346
303-939-8440; Fax: 303-939-9886
info@newhope.com
www.newhope.com
Facebook, Twitter

Fred Linder, President
Pamela Emanoil, Advertising Manager

Encompassing the world of ingredients, Engredea brings together the community of leading suppliers and manufacturers to source new ingredients, packaging, technologies, equipment, and services. Cultivating innovation for tomorrow's best-selling products across food/beverage, dietary supplement and nutricosmetic categories by offering exhibits, formulation demos, networking events and education opportunities for the industry.
Frequency: Monthly

5908 **Extracts: Essentials for Spa, Home, & Travel**
George Little Management
10 Bank Street
Suite 1200
White Plains, NY 10606
914-486-6070
800-292-4560; Fax: 914-948-6289
www.extractsny.com/www.glmshows.com

Rita Malek, Show Manager
Laura Anne Woodward, Show Coordinator
George Little II, President
Paula Bertolotti, Sales Manager

EX-TRACTS: Essentials for Spa, Home and Travel is co-located with the International Hotel/Motel Restaurant Show® (IH/MRS). Presenting the finest Apparel & Accessories, Aromatherapy Products & Candles, Baby and Cildren's Spa Products, Bathrobes and Loungewear, Business Services, Cosmetics, Cosmeceuticals, Home Environment Products, Essential Oils, Frangrances, Home Spa Electrics, Massage/Reflexology, Men's Spa Products, Music & Recordings.
10000 Attendees
Frequency: Nov
Founded in 1997

5909 **Extracts: New Discoveries in Beauty and Wellness**
George Little Management
10 Bank Street
Suite 1200
White Plains, NY 10606
914-486-6070
800-292-4560; Fax: 914-948-6289
www.extractsny.com

Rita Malek, Show Manager
Laura Anne Woodward, Show Coordinator
George Little II, President
Paula Bertolotti, Sales Manager

EXTRACTS® at the NYIGF is a unique, high-quality environment, showcasing the most innovative personal care and wellness products for the gift industry: aromatherapy, bath & bodycare, cosmetics, beauty accessories, candles, home fragrances, massage oils, music & recordings, natural/organic products, perfumes, potpourri and skincare.
43M Attendees
Frequency: Jan/Aug
Founded in 1997

5910 **Face & Body Spa & Healthy Aging**
Allured Publishing
444 Brickell Avenue
Suite 510
Miami, FL 33131
305-669-4602; Fax: 305-669-6116
www.perfume2000.com

Bernard Pommier, Circulation Manager
Joseph P Quick, Publisher

Spa professionals gather at Face & Body for practical business solutions, trend information

and the latest offerings and insights from leading industry suppliers.
Frequency: Bi-Monthly
ISSN: 1081-7220

5911 **Face & Body Spa Conference & Expo**
Allured Business Media
336 Gundersen Drive
Suite A
Carol Stream, IL 60188-2403

630-653-2155; Fax: 630-653-2192
fbmw@allured.com
www.faceandbody.com
Facebook

Maureen Nolimal, Account Executive
Sandy Chapin, Group Show Director
Mary Richter, Event Coordinator
Andrew Blood, Exhibits Coordinator

Skin care professionals gather at the Face & Body Midwest for practical business solutions, education, treatments, trends, products and equipment, as well as the latest offerings and insights from leading industry suppliers.
Frequency: Annual

5912 **General Merchandise/Health and Beauty Care Conference**
Food Marketing Institute
2345 Crystal Drive
Suite 800
Arlington, VA 22202

202-452-8444; Fax: 202-429-4519
www.fmi.org
Facebook, Twitter, LinkedIn, you Tube

Randy Edeker, Chair
Leslie G. Sarasin, President/CEO

Annual show of 150 exhibitors of health and beauty care products.
3000 Attendees

5913 **HAIRCOLOR USA**
International Beauty Show Group
757 Thrid Ave
5th Floor
New York, NY 10017

212-895-8200; Fax: 212-895-8209
Facebook, Twitter, YouTube

Mike Boyce, Show Manager
Rick Rosalina, Operations
Nicole Peck, Media partnerships
0
1500 Attendees
Frequency: June

5914 **Health & Beauty America**
HBA
350 Hudson St
Ste 300
New York, NY 10014

609-759-4700; Fax: 347-962-3889
www.hbaexpo.com
Facebook, Twitter, LinkedIn

Jack Gonzalez, Director Health/Beauty Events
Caitlin Carragee, Sales Coordinator

America's largest industry-specific educational conference and exposition for cosmetics, toiletries, fragances and personal care.
16500 Attendees

5915 **ICMAD Annual Meeting**
Independent Cosmetic Manufacturers & Distributors
444 Brickell Avenue
Suite 510
Miami, FL 33131

305-669-4602; Fax: 305-669-6116
www.perfume2000.com

Bernard Pommier, Circulation Manager
Joseph P Quick, Publisher

Information about programs and services available to help companies succeed in the beauty and personal care industries.
ISSN: 1081-7220

5916 **ISPA Conference & Expo**
International Spa Association
2365 Harrodsburg Road
Suite A325
Lexington, KY 40504

888-651-4772; Fax: 859-226-4445
ispa@ispastaff.com
www.experienceispa.com
Facebook, Twitter, LinkedIn, YouTube

Lynne Walker McNees, President
Deborah Waldvogel, Chairman
Jennifer Wayland-Smith, Vice Chairman
Ella Stimpson, Secretary/ Treasurer

The largest ISPA event of the year for spa professionals. The expectation of Conference attendees is to provide spa owners, directors, managers and suppliers with cutting edge tips on where the industry is headed and how to ensure that business is sustainable. Also brings together the leading suppliers in the industry to network with spa decision makers.

5917 **ISSE Long Beach**
Professional Beauty Association
7755 E Gray Road
Scottsdale, AZ 85260

480-281-0424
info@probeauty.org
www.probeauty.org

Beth Hickey, Chair
Sydney Berry, Vice Chair
Steve Sleeper, Executive Director
Rachel Molepske, Manager of Leadership Operations
Steve Wilkerson, Chief Financial Officer

The International Salon and Spa Expo is the biggest cash-and-carry beauty show on the West Coast. ISSE Long Beach delivers valuable technical education, quality manufacturers on the exhibit floor and a professionals-only atmosphere.
50 Members
Founded in 1989

5918 **ISSE Midwest**
Professional Beauty Association
7755 E Gray Road
Scottsdale, AZ 85260

480-281-0424
info@probeauty.org
www.probeauty.org

Beth Hickey, Chair
Sydney Berry, Vice Chair
Steve Sleeper, Executive Director
Rachel Molepske, Manager of Leadership Operations
Steve Wilkerson, Chief Financial Officer

The International Salon and Spa Expo is the biggest cash-and-carry beauty show. ISSE delivers valuable technical education, quality manufacturers on the exhibit floor and a professionals-only atmosphere.
50 Members
Founded in 1989

5919 **Intercoiffure America-Canada**
Creative Age Publications
7628 Densmore Ave
Van Nuys, CA 91406-2042

818-782-7560
800-442-5667; Fax: 818-782-7450
dayspa@creativeage.com
www.creativeage.com

Deborah Carver, President and CEO
Mindy Rosiejka, VP and COO
Barbara Shepherd, Circulation Director

Creative Age Publications is the association management firm for Intercoiffure America-Canada, the premier organization for salon owners.
Frequency: Monthly
Founded in 1971

5920 **International Beauty Show**
International Beauty Show Group
757 Third Avenue
5th Floor
New York, NY 10017

212-895-8200
800-736-7170; Fax: 212-895-8209
www.ibsnewyork.com
Facebook, Twitter, LinkedIn, YouTube

Deborah Carver, Founder
Rick Rosalina, Operations

Annual exposition of hair and skin care products manufacturers and beauty technicians. Held in New York city.
75000 Attendees
Frequency: March

5921 **International Congress of Esthetics & Spa**
310 E. Interstate 30
Suite B107
Garland, TX 75043

972-203-8530
877-968-7539; Fax: 972-962-1480
iaaesthetics.org

The association for the advancement of education and public awareness on aesthetics. Paramedical aesthetics and body spa therapy. Professionals from the medical, paramedical and beauty industries working together for the most advanced techniques for the patients and clients.
Founded in 1972

5922 **International Perfume Bottle Association Annual Convention**
PO Box 1299
Paradise, CA 95967

paradise@sunset.net
www.perfumebottles.org
Facebook

Deborah Carver, Founder
Walter Jones, Vice President
Peggy Tichenor, Membership Secretary
Janet Ziffer, Treasurer
Barbara W. Miller, Recording Secretary

The most exciting event in perfume bottle collecting. A three-day extravaganza featuring the world's premiere exhibition and sale with the field's leading dealers featuring thousands of bottles and an internationally recognized auction. The convention draws together collectors and dealers from around the world.
2000+ Members

5923 **Medical Device Submission & Compliance Strategies for the U.S. Market**
5635 Fishers Lane
Suite 550
Rockville, MD 20852-3048

301-770-2920; Fax: 301-770-2924
raps@raps.org
www.raps.org
Facebook, Twitter, LinkedIn, YouTube

Susan E. James, Chairman of the Board
Cecilia Kimberlin, President
Paul Brooks, President-elect
Leigh M. Vaughan, Secretary/ Treasurer
Linda Bowen, Director

Featuring an expert panel of industry professionals and US Food and Drug Administration (FDA) regulators, this RAPS workshop will

provide critical information on navigating the medical device submission process and creating compliance strategies for products for the US market.
10000 Members
Founded in 1976

5924 **Mid American Beauty Classic**
Premiere Show Group
444 Brickell Avenue
Suite 510
Miami, FL 33131
305-669-4602; Fax: 305-669-6116
www.perfume2000.com
Bernard Pommier, Circulation Manager
Joseph P Quick, Publisher
Beauty trade show for members of the professional beauty industry. Hair Show, Nail Show, Skincare Show.
Frequency: Bi-Monthly
ISSN: 1081-7220

5925 **NAHA**
Professional Beauty Association
7755 E Gray Road
Scottsdale, AZ 85260
480-281-0424
info@probeauty.org
www.probeauty.org
Beth Hickey, Chair
Sydney Berry, Vice Chair
Steve Sleeper, Executive Director
Rachel Molepske, Manager of Leadership Operations
Steve Wilkerson, Chief Financial Officer
The North American Hairstyling Awards (NAHA) is the most prestigious photographic beauty competition in North America, celebrating the artistry and skill of the professional salon industry. Individuals are recognized in 13 categories of excellence, including the Student Hairstylist of the Year, during a star-studded Awards Ceremony.
50 Members
Founded in 1989

5926 **NAILPRO Competitions**
Creative Age Publications
7628 Densmore Ave
Van Nuys, CA 91406-2042
818-782-7560
800-442-5667; Fax: 818-782-7450
dayspa@creativeage.com
www.creativeage.com
Deborah Carver, President and CEO
Mindy Rosiejka, VP and COO
Barbara Shepherd, Circulation Director
Nail artists from all over the world compete at trade shows all over the U.S. for a chance to be the best and win the coveted annual NAILPRO Cup.
Frequency: Monthly
Founded in 1971

5927 **NAILPRO Nail Institute**
Creative Age Publications
7628 Densmore Ave
Van Nuys, CA 91406-2042
818-782-7560
800-442-5667; Fax: 818-782-7450
dayspa@creativeage.com
www.creativeage.com
Deborah Carver, President and CEO
Mindy Rosiejka, VP and COO
Barbara Shepherd, Circulation Director
Practical marketing education helps nail professionals build their businesses.
Frequency: Monthly
Founded in 1971

5928 **NAILPRO Sacramento**
Creative Age Publications
7628 Densmore Ave
Van Nuys, CA 91406-2042
818-782-7560
800-442-5667; Fax: 818-782-7450
dayspa@creativeage.com
www.creativeage.com
Deborah Carver, President and CEO
Mindy Rosiejka, VP and COO
Barbara Shepherd, Circulation Director
The industry's hottest nails-only trade show spotlights new products and innovative techniques for nail technicians from top manufacturers.
Frequency: Monthly
Founded in 1971

5929 **NBCL Annual Convention**
National Beauty Culturalists' League
25 Logan Circle NW
Washington, DC 20005-3725
202-332-2695; Fax: 202-332-0940
www.nbcl.info
Betty Herbert, Contact
One hundred booths of beauty industry associates, manufacturing companies and other businesses.
Frequency: July

5930 **NBJ Summit**
New Hope Natural Media
1401 Pearl St
Suite 200
Boulder, CO 80302-5346
303-939-8440; Fax: 303-939-9886
info@newhope.com
www.newhope.com
Facebook, Twitter
Fred Linder, President
Pamela Emanoil, Advertising Manager
The premier leadership event for progressive nutrition industry CEOs, investors and thought leaders. It has provided unparalleled education and a tremendous venue for thoughtful leaders to establish strategic relationships and grow the potential of their businesses.
Frequency: Monthly

5931 **Natural Products Association MarketPlace**
New Hope Natural Media
1401 Pearl St
Suite 200
Boulder, CO 80302-5346
303-939-8440; Fax: 303-939-9886
info@newhope.com
www.newhope.com
Facebook, Twitter
Fred Linder, President
Pamela Emanoil, Advertising Manager
An intimate trade show for the natural and healthy products industries. Topics cover advocacy, retail training and trends, standards and industry regulation, marketing, sustainability, and other relevant, timely topics direct from industry experts and business leaders.
Frequency: Monthly

5932 **Natural Products Expo**
New Hope Natural Media
1401 Pearl St
Suite 200
Boulder, CO 80302-5346
303-939-8440; Fax: 303-939-9886
info@newhope.com
www.newhope.com
Facebook, Twitter
Fred Linder, President
Pamela Emanoil, Advertising Manager
Where new products turn into record profits. Join in an experience with exhibits from different companies showcasing the newest products in natural and specialty foods, organic, health and beauty, natural living, supplements and pet products.
Frequency: Monthly

5933 **Nutracon**
New Hope Natural Media
1401 Pearl St
Suite 200
Boulder, CO 80302-5346
303-939-8440; Fax: 303-939-9886
info@newhope.com
www.newhope.com
Fred Linder, President
Pamela Emanoil, Advertising Manager
The premier education and networking conference for the health and nutrition industry. Provides relevant insights for innovation based on science and technology, case studies and market intelligence. Gain an understanding of the impact of next generation ingredients, emerging markets, consumer trend data and regulatory constraints.
Frequency: Monthly

5934 **PBA Beauty Week**
Professional Beauty Association
7755 E Gray Road
Scottsdale, AZ 85260
480-281-0424
info@probeauty.org
www.probeauty.org
Beth Hickey, Chair
Sydney Berry, Vice Chair
Steve Sleeper, Executive Director
Rachel Molepske, Manager of Leadership Operations
Steve Wilkerson, Chief Financial Officer
PBA Beauty Week is North America's largest, most inclusive beauty event, offering unlimited networking, education, and professional growth opportunities to all sectors of the beauty industry. This week of beauty also features the North American Hairstyling Awards, Best Practice Club, City of Hope and Beacon. PBA Beauty Week is produced by the Professional Beauty Association in cooperation with Cosmoprof North America.
50 Members
Founded in 1989

5935 **PBA Executive Summit**
Professional Beauty Association
7755 E Gray Road
Scottsdale, AZ 85260
480-281-0424
info@probeauty.org
www.probeauty.org
Beth Hickey, Chair
Sydney Berry, Vice Chair
Steve Sleeper, Executive Director
Rachel Molepske, Manager of Leadership Operations
Steve Wilkerson, Chief Financial Officer
PBA Executive Summit provides the upper-level business education, unlimited networking and powerful industry research. Including 300 industry leaders, this three-day educational summit will inspire and educate salon owners and licensed professionals to take their businesses and careers, as well as the entire industry, to the next level.
50 Members
Founded in 1989

5936 **Paperboard Packaging Council Annual Convention**
Independent Cosmetic Manufacturers & Distributors
444 Brickell Avenue
Suite 510
Miami, FL 33131

305-669-4602; Fax: 305-669-6116
www.perfume2000.com

Bernard Pommier, Circulation Manager
Joseph P Quick, Publisher

Industry leaders specializing in sustainability, the economy, and education will come together to impart their knowledge, experience, and business predictions.
Frequency: Bi-Monthly
ISSN: 1081-7220

5937 **Perfumers Choice Awards**
The American Society of Perfumers
444 Brickell Avenue
Suite 510
Miami, FL 33131

305-669-4602; Fax: 305-669-6116
www.perfume2000.com

Bernard Pommier, Circulation Manager
Joseph P Quick, Publisher

Excellence in fragrance creation takes center stage.
Frequency: Bi-Monthly
ISSN: 1081-7220

5938 **Personal Care Products Council Annual Meeting**
Personal Care Products Council
1101 17th Street NW
Suite 300
Washington, DC 20036-4702

202-331-1770; Fax: 202-331-1969
www.personalcarecouncil.org
Facebook

Round-tables, R&D, business strategy, and learning panels, along with companies with exhibits of supplies and raw materials for the cosmetic industry.
Frequency: Annual

5939 **Personal Care Products Council Legal & Regulatory Conference**
Personal Care Products Council
1101 17th Street NW
Suite 300
Washington, DC 20036-4702

202-331-1770; Fax: 202-331-1969
www.personalcarecouncil.org
Facebook, Twitter, LinkedIn, YouTube

Pamela Bailey, President
Mark Pollak, VP
Cheryl Mason, Secretary

The premier annual meeting for industry general counsel and legal staff, regulatory affairs staff, and outside counsel representing member companies. Held each year exclusively for Council members.
525 Members
Founded in 1894

5940 **Proud Lady Beauty Show**
PO Box 19510
Chicago, IL 60619-0510

708-633-6328; Fax: 708-633-6329
www.ahbai.org

Clyde Hammond, Senior President
Jory Luste, President
Nathaniel Bronner, Jr. Executive VP

The Beauty Professionals Marketplace
Founded in 1981

5941 **RAPS Executive Development Program at the Kellogg School of Management**
5635 Fishers Lane
Suite 550
Rockville, MD 20852-3048

301-770-2920; Fax: 301-770-2924
raps@raps.org
www.raps.org
Facebook, Twitter, LinkedIn, YouTube

Susan E. James, Chairman of the Board
Cecilia Kimberlin, President
Paul Brooks, President-elect
Leigh M. Vaughan, Secretary/ Treasurer
Linda Bowen, Director

Strong business skills are essential to your success and the ability of your company to survive in a volatile and competitive regulatory environment. This program brings the opportunity to cultivate your business management skills through vigorous discussions with some of the world's best business professors in an intimate learning environment.
10000 Members
Founded in 1976

5942 **RAPS; The Regulatory Convergence**
5635 Fishers Lane
Suite 550
Rockville, MD 20852-3048

301-770-2920; Fax: 301-770-2924
raps@raps.org
www.raps.org
Facebook, Twitter, LinkedIn, YouTube

Susan E. James, Chairman of the Board
Cecilia Kimberlin, President
Paul Brooks, President-elect
Leigh M. Vaughan, Secretary/ Treasurer
Linda Bowen, Director

Delivers the knowledge, competence development and resources you need to design effective solutions to complex challenges, seize opportunities and lead.
10000 Members
Founded in 1976

5943 **Salon Focus**
Advanstar Communications
641 Lexington Avenue
8th Floor
New York, NY 10022

212-951-6600; Fax: 212-951-6793
info@advanstar.com
www.advanstar.com

Joseph Loggia, CEO
Thomas Ehardt, EVP and CFO
Chris Demoulin, EVP

Educational and exhibiting forum for the Southwest professional salon industry. 140 booths.
6.5M Attendees
Frequency: November

5944 **Scent World Expo**
7 Fox Meadow Road
Scarsdale, NY 10583

646-236-4606; Fax: 914-470-2416
info@scentmarketing.org

Harald H Vogt, Founder/Chief Marketer
Avery Gilbert PhD, Chief Scientist

Learn about the latest scent technology, fragrance trends and success stories. Members of the scent marketing industry, executives from marketing and branding firms as well as consumer goods companies, hotels/ cruise ships, cosmetic companies and other end users of scent. A wonderful lineup of speakers, with top researchers, creative marketing & branding gurus, innovative perfumers and dynamic scent professionals. Take your business to the next level.

5945 **Spring Management and Financial Aid Conference**
9927 E. Bell Road
Suite 110
Scottsdale, AZ 85260

480-810-0431
800-831-1086; Fax: 480-905-0993
jim@beautyschools.org
www.beautyschools.org
Facebook, Twitter

Jim Cox, Executive Director
Lisa Zarda, General Manager
Chris Cox, Member services Manager

Association open to all privately owned cosmetology schools.
1100 Members
Founded in 1924

5946 **Techniques**
New Dimensions Advertising
47 W Main Street
Mechanicsburg, PA 17055-6262

717-697-4181
800-845-4694; Fax: 717-790-9441

Triennial show of 25 exhibitors of cosmetics and accessories.
1500 Attendees

5947 **The Makeup Show**

Focuses on and celebrates the art of makeup and networking. Strengthening the working capability and build a professional network for all the people from the makeup artistry community.

5948 **Welcome to Our World**
Professional Beauty Association
15825 N. 71st Street
Suite 100
Scottsdale, AZ 85254

480-281-0424
800-468-2274; Fax: 480-905-0708
info@probeauty.org
www.probeauty.org/nmc

Max Wexler, Chair
Scott Buchanan, Vice Chair
Bruce Selan, Treasurer

The professional beauty industry invites Congress for its annual makeover each year. While Congress enjoys the beauty services, members push legislative issues important to the industry.
50 Members
Founded in 1989

5949 **West Coast Spring Style and Beauty Show**
West Coast Beauty Supply
5001 Industrial Way
Benicia, CA 94510

707-484-4800
800-233-3141; Fax: 707-748-4623

Paul Eggert, Show Director
Wayne Clark, President
John Golliher, Manager

200 booths.
15M Attendees
Frequency: March

5950 **World International Nail and Beauty Association**
1221 N Lake View Ave
Anaheim, CA 92807

714-779-9892
800-541-9838; Fax: 714-779-9971
dkellenberger@inmnails.com

David Kellenberger

Represents industry, promotes effective use of products, sponsors competition and bestows

awards. Also offers world championship competitions for nails, hair and makeup.
13000 Members
Founded in 1981

Directories & Databases

5951 **Beauty Fashion: Men's Issue**
Beauty Fashion
16 E 40th Street
New York, NY 10016

212-328-6789
0; Fax: 212-840-7246
Facebook

Debra Davis, Advertising Director
Adelaide Farah, Editorial Director

Offers listings of men's fragrances, toiletries and related products as well as manufacturers and US distributors.
Cost: $25.00
Frequency: Annual
Circulation: 17,000

5952 **Complete Directory of Cosmetic Specialties**
Sutton Family Communications & Publishing Company
920 State Route 54 East
Elmitch, KY 42343

270-276-9500

Theresa Sutton, Editor
Lee Sutton, General Manager

Print-out from database of wholesalers, manufacturers, distributors, importers and close-out houses. Database is updated daily to guarantee the most current and up-to-date sources available.
Cost: $39.50
100+ Pages

5953 **Complete Directory of Personal Care Items**
Sutton Family Communications & Publishing Company
920 State Route 54 East
Elmitch, KY 42343

270-276-9500

Theresa Sutton, Editor
Lee Sutton, General Manager

Print-out from database of wholesalers, manufacturers, distributors, importers and close-out houses. Database is updated daily to guarantee the most current and up-to-date sources available.
Cost: $39.50
100+ Pages

5954 **Cosmetics & Toiletries: Cosmetic Bench Reference**
Allured Publishing Corporation
336 Gundersen Dr
Suite A
Carol Stream, IL 60188-2403

630-653-2155; Fax: 630-653-2192
customerservice@allured.com
www.allured.com

Janet Ludwig, President
Linda Knott, Director Of Operations

Offers a full list of cosmetics ingredient suppliers.
Cost: $95.00
Frequency: Biennial

5955 **Cosmetics & Toiletries: Who's Who in R&D Directory Issue**
Allured Publishing Corporation
336 Gundersen Dr
Suite A
Carol Stream, IL 60188-2403

630-653-2155; Fax: 630-653-2192
customerservice@allured.com
www.allured.com

Janet Ludwig, President
Linda Knott, Director Of Operations

Offers a list of cosmetic manufacturers and consultants for product development, legal, safety and regulatory assistance.
Cost: $25.00
Frequency: Annual
Circulation: 3,200

5956 **Fragrance Foundation Reference Guide**
Fragrance Foundation
545 5th Ave
Suite 900
New York, NY 10017-3636

212-779-9058; Fax: 212-779-9058
info@fragrance.org
www.fragrance.org

Terry Molnar, Executive Director
Mary Lapsansky, VP

Over 1100 fragrances are listed that are available in the US, with dates of introduction and description, alphabetically indexed with company name, address and phone number.
Cost: $60.00
112 Pages
Frequency: Annual

5957 **Fragrance and Olfactory Dictionary**
Fragrance Foundation
545 5th Ave
Suite 900
New York, NY 10017-3636

212-779-9058; Fax: 212-779-9058
info@fragrance.org
www.fragrance.org

Terry Molnar, Executive Director
Mary Lapsansky, VP

Definitions of ingredients, techniques, language of fragrance and olfactory references.
Cost: $7.00
32 Pages

5958 **Passion**
Milady Publishing Company
5 Southside Dr
Clifton Park, NY 12065-3870

518-280-9500
800-998-1498; Fax: 518-373-6200
www.delmarlearning.com
Twitter

Shannon Melldady, Owner
Donna Lewis, Executive Marketing Director
Ron Schlosser, President/CEO

A Salon Professionals Handbook for Building a Successful Business
Cost: $20.00
Frequency: Monthly
Circulation: 80000
Founded in 1945

5959 **Perfume 2000**
Perfume 2000
444 Brickell Avenue
Suite 510
Miami, FL 33131

305-374-6849; Fax: 305-374-6850
www.perfume2000.com

Ana Murias, Public Relations

Comprehensive database; services encourage industry networking and integration.

5960 **RIFM Database of Fragrance & Flavor Materials**
50 Tice Boulevard
Woodcliff Lake, NJ 07677

201-689-8089; Fax: 201-689-8090
rifm@rifm.org
www.rifm.org/nd

A comprehensive source offering safety evaluations and toxicology data on more than 4,500 fragrance and flavor materials. Operated in full cooperation with Flavor & Extracts Manufacturing Association (FEMA).
Founded in 1966

5961 **Who's Who: Membership Directory of the Cosmetic, Toiletry & Fragrance Assn**
Personal Care Products Council
1101 17th Street NW
Suite 300
Washington, DC 20036-4702

202-331-1770; Fax: 202-331-1969
www.personalcarecouncil.org

Gwen Hallill, Director Publications/Comm
Pamela Bailey, President

About 500 member companies of the cosmetics industry.
Cost: $75.00
Frequency: Annual, June

Industry Web Sites

5962 **http://gold.greyhouse.com**
G.O.L.D Grey House OnLine Databases

Grey House Publishing's online database platform, GOLD, offers Quick Search, Keyword Search and Expert Search for most business sectors including beauty, cosmetics, perfumes and personal care markets. The GOLD platform makes finding the information you need quick and easy - whether you're a novice searcher or an experienced database user. All of Grey House's directory products are available for subscription on the GOLD platform.

5963 **www.bbsi.org**
Beauty and Barber Supply Institute

Our members are wholesaler-distributors, manufacturers and manufacturers' representatives from around the world. Our mission is to maximize the potential of the salon industry.

5964 **www.cew.org**
Cosmetic Executive Women

Nonprofit trade organization of approximately 1,500 executives in the beauty, cosmetics, fragrance and related industries. Based in New York City, CEW has associated organizations in France and the United Kingdom. As a leading trade organization in the beauty industry, CEW helps develop the career contacts, knowledge and skills of its members so that they may advance on both professional and personal levels.

5965 **www.cosmeticindex.com**
CosmeticIndex.Com

Home Page: www.cosmeticindex.com

Online source for cosmetics, resources and services.

5966 **www.cosmeticsinfo.org**
Personal Care Products Council

1620 L St. NW
Suite 1200
Washington, DC 20036

202-331-1770; Fax: 202-331-1969
Facebook, Twitter

Lezlee Westine, President & CEO
Thia Breen, Chair

Information about safety, testing and regulation of cosmetics and personal care products. Sponsored by the Personal Care Products Council.

5967 **www.greyhouse.com**
Grey House Publishing

Authoritative reference directories for most business segments incluidng beauty, cosmetic, perfume and personal care markets. Users can search the online databases with varied search criteria allowing for custom searches by product category, geographic area, sales volume, keyword, subject and more. Full Grey House catalog and online ordering also available.

5968 **www.iacmcolor.org**
International Association of Color Manufacturers

Actively represents the interests of the regulated color industry by demonstrating the safety of color additives and to promote the industry's economic growth by participating in new color approvals, regulatory and legislative issues that affect the industry worldwide.

5969 **www.iasc.org**
International Aloe Science Council

Nonprofit trade organization for the Aloe Vera Industry world-wide. Its membership includes Aloe growers, processors, finished goods manufacturers, marketing companies, insurance companies, equipment suppliers, printers, sales organizations, physicians, scientists and researchers.

5970 **www.icmad.org**
Independent Cosmetic Manufacturers & Distributors

Information on government consumers and the media. Provides group programs for product liability.

5971 **www.inmnails.com**
World International Nail and Beauty Association

Promotes effective use of products, sponsors competition and bestows awards. Also offers world championship competitions for nails, hair and makeup.

5972 **www.isnow.com**
Cosmetologists Chicago

Voice of the salon industry. For over eight decades, we have been a beauty authority and presenter of the Chicago Midwest Beauty Show. We are stylists, estheticians, color technicians, salon owners, educators and nail technicians.

5973 **www.perfumers.org**
American Society of Perfumers

Nonprofit organization fostering and encouraging the art and science of perfumery in the US while promoting professional exchange and a high standard of professional conduct within the fragrance industry. The ASP holds symposiums in the New York City area where leading members of the fragrence community are invited to speak and present information on all aspects of the industry.

5974 **www.personalcarecouncil.org**
Personal Care Products Council

Provides a complete range of services that support the personal care products industry's needs and interests in the scientific, legal, regulatory, legislative and international fields. CTFA strives to ensure that the personal care products industry has the freedom to pursue creative product development and compete in a fair and responsible marketplace.

5975 **www.salonprofessionals.org**
National Cosmetology Association

Nationwide community of 30,000 salon professionals, connected by a common passion for learning, growing and raising the professionalim of the entire salon industry. As a group, we have a strong voice in our communities, our industry and with our government because the NCA is for everyone in the professional community. Members have access to education, fashion events, community service and insurance — all the tools needed to build your career.

Associations

5976 **ACA International**
Association of Credit and Collection Professionals
PO Box 390106
Minneapolis, MN 55439-0106
952-926-6547; Fax: 952-926-1624
aca@acainternational.org
www.acainternational.org
Facebook, Twitter, LinkedIn, YouTube
Lucia Lebens, director
International trade organization of credit and collection professionals providing a variety of accounts receivable management services to over 1,000,000 credit grantors.
5300 Members
Founded in 1995
Mailing list available for rent

5977 **Advertising Media Credit Executives Association**
PO Box 433
Louisville, KY 40201
502-582-4327; Fax: 502-582-4330
amcea@amcea.org
www.amcea.org
Facebook
Norman Taylor, President
Kimberly Archibald Russell, VP
Newt Collins, Secretary - Treasurer
Vickie Bolinger, Immediate Past President
Sandra Lawson, Directors
A non-profit organization that exists to serve the media credit manager. Directed and managed by professionals just like you, media credit managers who volunteer for various projects to benefit the industry and our association.
Founded in 1953

5978 **Affordable Housing Tax Credit Coalition**
1090 K Street NW
12th Floor
Washington, DC 20006
202-661-7698; Fax: 202-661-2299
info@taxcreditcoalition.org
www.taxcreditcoalition.org
Facebook, Twitter, LinkedIn, YouTube
Jeff Whiting, Chairman
Todd Crow, President
Tony Alfieri, First VP
Joseph Hagan, President Emeritus
Michael Novogradac, VP
Plays a major role in assuring the conitinuance of the low income housing tax credit, with the primary goal of achieving permanent extension of the low income housing tax credit program.
105 Members
Founded in 1988

5979 **American Bankruptcy Institute**
66 Canal Center Plaza
Suite 600
Alexandria, VA 22314-1546
703-739-0800; Fax: 703-739-1060
info@abiworld.org
www.abi.org
Facebook, Twitter, LinkedIn, YouTube
Amy Quackenboss, Executive Director
Multidisciplinary, nonpartisan organization dedicated to research and education on matters related to insolvency. Engaged in numerous educational and research activities as well as the production of a number of publications both for the insolvency practitioner and the public.
12000 Members
Founded in 1982

5980 **American Financial Services Association**
919 18th Street NW
Suite 300
Washington, DC 20006-5517
202-296-5544
info@afsamail.org
www.afsaonline.org
Facebook, Twitter, LinkedIn, Google+
Chris Steinebert, President/CEO
Gary L. Phillips, Chairman
Nathan D. Benson, Member
Dietmar W. Exler, VP
A national trade association for market funded providers of financial services to consumers and small businesses.
400 Members
Founded in 1916

5981 **American Recovery Association**
5525 N MacArthur Boulevard
Suite 135
Irving, TX 75038
972-755-4755; Fax: 972-870-5755
homeoffice@americanrecoveryassn.org
www.repo.org
Facebook, LinkedIn, Google+
Jerry Wilson, President
David Handschin, VP
Bennett Deese, Secretary/Treasurer
Approximately 500 offices around the US, Canada and Germany, providing repossesion services around the world.
280 Members
Founded in 1965

5982 **Broadcast Cable Credit Association**
550 W. Frontage Road
Suite 3600
Northfield, IL 60093
847-881-8757; Fax: 847-784-8059
info@bccacredit.com
www.bccacredit.com
Twitter, LinkedIn
Mary Collins, President & CEO
Jamie Grande, Director, Operations
Arcelia Pimentel, Sales/Membership
Dawn Stenstrom, Credit Investigator
Colette Pinter, Credit Investigator
BCCA, a subsidiary of Media Financial Management Association, represents credit and collection professionals from TV, radio, cable, system operators, newspaper, and magazine organizations in the U.S. and Canada. BCCA functions as a central clearinghouse for credit information on advertisers, agencies and buying services, both locally and nationally.
Founded in 1972

5983 **Business Products Credit Association**
P.O. Box 5003
St. Paul, MS 55101-7003
651-998-9609
info@bcpa.org
www.bcpa.org
Facebook, Twitter, LinkedIn
Heidi Piche, President
Sandra Sandra, Secretary
Matt Shillerstrom, Treasurer
Marie Strawser, Program Director
Bob Kunzer, Information Director
Credit Trade Association for manufacturers and wholesalers.
Founded in 1875

5984 **CDC Consumer Debt Counseling**
831 W. Morse Blvd.
Winter Park, FL 32789
314-647-9006
800-820-9232; Fax: 407-599-5954
www.consumerdebtcounselors.org
Philip Johnston, President
Melissa Towel, Advisor
Janice Diaz, Customer Care
Nonprofit provider of quality, face-to-face and telephone budget and debt counseling education.
Founded in 1998

5985 **Capital Markets Credit Analysts Society**
25 N Broadway
Tarrytown, NY 10591
914-332-0040; Fax: 914-332-1541
cmcas@cmcas.org
www.cmcas.org
Facebook
Stuart Plesser, President
Kelly Byrne, Account Manager
Bikas Tomkoria, Treasurer
Claudia Calderon, Secretary
A professional society whose membership consists primarily of managers and analysts in credit risk departments that directly support their employers' capital market activities.
500 Members
Founded in 1989
Mailing list available for rent

5986 **Coalition of Higher Education Assistance Organizations**
1101 Vermont Ave NW
Suite 400
Washington, DC 20005-3586
202-289-3910; Fax: 202-371-0197
hwadsworth@wpllc.net
www.coheao.com
Maria Livolsi, President
Carl Perry, VP
Lori Hartung, Treasurer
Tom Schmidt, Secretary
Focus is on legislative and regulatory advocacy for Federal Perkins and other campus based student loan programs.
365 Members
Founded in 1981

5987 **Commercial Finance Association**
370 7th Ave. Ste. 1801
7 Penn Plz
New York, NY 10001-3979
212-792-9390; Fax: 212-564-6053
info@cfa.com
www.cfa.com
Facebook, Twitter, LinkedIn, YouTube
Patrick Trammell, President
D. Michael Monk, Vice President - Finance
Andrea Petro, First Vice President
Robert Trojan, CEO
David Grende, VP
Trade group of the asset-based, financial services industry, with members throughout the US, Canada and around the world. Members include the asset-based lending arms of domestic and foreign commercial banks, small and large independent finance companies, floor plan financing organizations, factoring organizations and financing subsidiaries of major industrial corporations. CFA membership is by organization, not by individual.
Founded in 1944

5988 **Commercial Mortgage Securities Association**
20 Broad St
7th Floor
New York, NY 10005
212-509-1844; Fax: 646-884-7569
info@crefc.org
www.crefc.org
Facebook, Twitter, LinkedIn
Stephen Renna, CEO
Ed DeAngelo, VP
Michael Flood, VP
International trade organization for the commercial real estate capital markets. Also represents and promotes an orderly and ethical global institutional secondary market for the sale of commercial mortgage loans and equity investments.
309 Members
Founded in 1994

5989 **Consumer Credit Industry Association**
6300 Powers Ferry Road
Suite 600-286
Atlanta, GA 30339
678-858-4001
webmaster@cciaonline.com
www.cciaonline.com
Tom Keepers, Executive VP
John Euwema, VP Legislative Regulatory Counsel
Stephanie Neal, Director of Member Services
To preserve, promote and enhance the availability, utility and integrity of insurance and related products and services delivered in connection with financial transactions.
140 Members
Founded in 1951

5990 **Consumer Credit Insurance Association**
6300 Powers Ferry Road
Suite 600-286
Atlanta, GA 30339
678-858-4001; Fax: 312-939-8287
webmaster@cciaonline.com
www.cciaonline.com
Jim Pangburn, President
Dick Williams, Chairman
Michelle Dicks, General Counsel
To preserve, promote and enhance the availability, utility and integrity of insurance and related products and services delivered in connection with financial transactions.
140 Members
Founded in 1951

5991 **Credit Research Foundation**
1812 Baltimore Blvd.
Sutie H
Westminster, MD 21157
443-821-3000; Fax: 443-821-3627
crf_info@crfonline.org
www.crfonline.org
William F. Balduino, President/COO
Matthew W. Skudera, Vice Pres. Research & Education
A non-profit association dedicated to education and research in the business-to-business and procure-to-pay space.
500 Members
Founded in 1949

5992 **Credit Union National Association**
601 Penn Ave
NW South Building, Suite 600
Washington, DC 20004-2601
202-628-5777
800-356-9655; Fax: 202-638-7734
www.cuna.org
Facebook, Twitter, YouTube
Jim Nussle, President & CEO
Greg Michlig, Membership & Engagement
Eddie Rivera, Finance
Amy Nigrelli, Marketing & Digital
Teresa Hanson, Corporate Affairs
The premier trade association in the financial services arena. Supports, protects, unifies and advances the credit union movement.

5993 **FCIB**
Finance, Credit, International Business Assoc.
8840 Columbia 100 Pkwy
Columbia, MD 21045-2158
410-423-1840
888-256-3242; Fax: 410-740-5574
fcib_info@fcibglobal.com
www.fcibglobal.com
Twitter, LinkedIn
Marta Chacon-Martinez, Director
Mike Mino, CCE, Chairman
Ron Shepherd, Director, Membership & Business
FCIB enjoys an international reputation as the premier Association of executives in finance, credit and international business, providing critical export credit and collections insight, practical advice and intelligence to companies of all sizes - from Fortune 500 multi-nationals to medium and small private companies. With international credit management and trade finance professionals in 55 countries around the world, FCIB offers unique networking and educational opportunities
1200 Members
Founded in 1919

5994 **Farm Credit**
7951 East Maplewood Ave.
Suite 200
Greenwood Village, CO 80111
ask@farmcredit.com
www.farmcreditnetwork.com
Facebook, Twitter, YouTube, Pinterest, Instagram
Todd Van Hoose, President & CEO
Curtis Hancock, Chairman
Farm Credit member organizations provide credit to farmers, ranchers and rural communities for agriculture and infrastructure projects.
Founded in 1916

5995 **International Association of Commercial Collectors**
4040 W 70th Street
Minneapolis, MN 55435
952-925-0760
800-859-9526; Fax: 952-926-1624
iacc@commercialcollector.com
www.commercialcollector.com
LinkedIn
Tom Brenan, President
Greg Cohen, Vice President
Paul Eisenberg, Treasurer
Lee Vandenheuvel, Immediate Past President
Marc Bressler, Director
International trade association comprised of collection specialists and commercial attorneys, with members throughout the US and 20 international countries. IACC's mission is to promote the commercial collection profession by providing IACC members with the resources to excel in the industry.
350 Members
Founded in 1970

5996 **International Energy Credit Association**
1120 Route 73
Suite 200
Mt. Laurel, NJ 08054
856-380-6854; Fax: 856-439-0525
mbiordi@ahint.com
www.ieca.net
Facebook, Twitter, LinkedIn, RSS
Gary Nicholson, EVP
Michele Biordi, Executive Director
Zachary Starbird, President
James Hawkins, First Vice President
Amanda Kenly, Past President
The oldest international industry credit association in the United States. Membership includes companies located in the Uited States, Canada, most Western European countries, Mexico, South America and Asia.
700 Members
Founded in 1923

5997 **Jewelers Board of Trade**
95 Jefferson Blvd
Warwick, RI 02888-1046
401-467-0055; Fax: 401-467-1199
jbtinfo@jewelersboard.com
www.jewelersboard.com
Twitter
Dione Kenyen, President
A not for profit jewelry trade association whose primary function is to compile and disseminate accurate and reliable credit information among its members as to the financial standing, credit history and background of dealers of jewelry and related products.
3200 Members
Founded in 1884

5998 **Mortgage Bankers Association**
1919 M Street NW
5th Floor
Washington, DC 20036
202-557-2700
800-793-6222
www.mba.org
Facebook, Twitter
Robert Broeksmit, President & CEO
Marcia Davies, COO
Lisa Haynes, CFO/Chief of Diversity & Inclusion
Peter Grace, SVP, Strategy & Member Services
Michael Briggs, SVP, HR & General Counsel
A national association representing the entire real estate finance industry. This association develops innovative business tools and provides education and training for industry professionals.

5999 **NACUSO**
3419 Via Lido
#135
Newport Beach, CA 92663
949-645-5296
888-462-2870; Fax: 949-645-5297
info@nacuso.org
www.nacuso.org
Jack Antonini, President/CEO
Mark Zook, Chairman
Mike Atkins, Secretary
400 Members
Founded in 1984

6000 **National Association of Consumer Credit**
PO Box 20871
Columbus, OH 43220-871

614-326-1165; Fax: 614-326-1162
nacca2007@sbcglobal.net
www.naccaonline.org

Joe Mulberry, President
Mike Larsen, First VP
Brian Landis, Second VP
Carri Grube-Lybarker, Secretary/treasurer

Improving the supervision of consumer credit agencies; facilitating the administration of laws governing these agencies by providing a forum for the exchange of information, ideas and experiences among public officials having supervision of such agencies and changes with the administration of such laws; facilitating intercommunication among its members and developing standard information collection concerning consumer credit agencies in each state.
55 Members
Founded in 1935

6001 **National Association of Credit Management**
8840 Columbia 100 Pkwy
Columbia, MD 21045-2100

410-740-5560; Fax: 410-740-5574
robins@nacm.org
www.nacm.org
Facebook, Twitter, LinkedIn, Pinterest, RSS

Rocky Thomas, CCE, Chairperson
Gary Gaudette, CCE, ICCE, Chairman/elect
Kevin Quinn, Director
Jay Snyder, CCE, ICCE, Director

NACM and its network of affiliated associations are the leading resource for credit and financial management information and education, delivering products and services which improve the management of business credit and accounts receivable. Our collective voice has influenced legislative results concerning commercial business and trade credit to our nation's policy makers for more than 100 years, and continues to play an active part in legislative issues pertaining to business credit.
18000 Members
Founded in 1896

6002 **National Association of Credit Union Service Organizations**
PMB 3419 Via Lido
Suite 135
Newport Beach, CA 92663

949-645-5296
888-462-2870; Fax: 949-645-5297
info@nacuso.org
www.nacuso.org

Jack Antonini, President/CEO
Mark Zook, Chairman
Mike Atkins, Secretary

Leading professional trade association for credit unions and CUSO's seeking to provide a full aray of services, such as mortgages, business lending and business lending depository services, trust services, investments and insurance to their members and non members alike.
412 Members
Founded in 1984

6003 **National Association of Federal Credit Unions**
3138 10th St N
Arlington, VA 22201-2160

703-522-4770
800-336-4644; Fax: 703-524-1082
www.nafcu.org
Facebook, Twitter, LinkedIn, YouTube

Dan Berger, President & CEO
Anthony Demangone, Executive VP & COO
Greg Johns, VP, Finance
Jacqueline Ortiz Ramsay, VP, Media Relations & Communication
Catherine Porterfield, VP, Membership

A respected and influential trade association that exclusively represents the interest of federal credit unions before the federal government and the public.
804 Members
Founded in 1967

6004 **National Association of State Credit Union Supervisors**
1655 Fort Myer Dr
Suite 300
Arlington, VA 22209-3108

703-528-8351
800-728-7927; Fax: 703-528-3248
offices@nascus.org
www.nascus.org
Twitter

Lucy Ito, President/CEO
Brian Knight, Executive VP & General Counsel
Alicia Valencia Erb, VP, Member Relations
Shellee Mitchell, Program Specialist
Doug McGuckin, VP, Corporate Affairs

State chartered credit unions and state credit union supervisors.
900 Members
Founded in 1965

6005 **National Chemical Credit Association**
500 Seneca Street
Suite 400
Buffalo, NY 14209-1963

716-887-9527
844-937-3268; Fax: 716-878-0479
robert.gagliardi@abc-amega.com
www.nccal.org
Twitter, LinkedIn, YouTube, Google+

Glenn Lifrieri, Executive Board Chair

Members are major producers of basic chemicals and allied products.
100 Members
Founded in 1938

6006 **National Council of Postal Credit Unions**
PO Box 160
Del Mar, CA 92014-0160

858-792-3883; Fax: 858-792-3884
ncpcu@ncpcu.org
www.ncpcu.org

Kevin A Yaeger, Chairman
Rebecca Cuddy, Vice Chair
Sidney Parfait, Treasurer
Neil Crean, Secretary

Organized to represent the special interests of postal credit unions.
160 Members
Founded in 1984

6007 **National Credit Reporting Association**
701 E. Irving Park Rd
Suite 306
Roselle, IL 60712

630-539-1525; Fax: 630-539-1526
tclemans@ncrainc.org
www.ncrainc.org
Facebook, Twitter, LinkedIn

Terry W Clemans, Executive Director
Jan Gerber, Office & Members Services Manager

Purpose is to promote the general welfare of its members. Also provides leadership in education, legislation, ethics and enhanced vendor's relation
150 Members
Founded in 1992

6008 **National Credit Union Administration**
1775 Duke St
Alexandria, VA 22314-6115

703-518-6300
800-755-1030; Fax: 703-518-6539
consumerassistance@ncua.gov
www.ncua.gov
Facebook, Twitter, YouTube

Rodney Hood, Chair
Larry Fazio, Executive Director
Lenwood Brooks, Chief of Staff
Eugene Schied, CFO
Robert Foster, Chief Information Officer

Governed by a three member board appointed by the President and confirmed by the US Senate, this independent federal agency charters and supervises federal credit unions. NCUA, with the backing of the full faith and credit of the US government, operates the National Credit Union Share Insurance Fund, insuring the savings of 80 million account holders in all federal credit unions and many state chartered credit unions.
82M Members
Founded in 1970

6009 **National Federation of Community Development Credit Unions**
39 Broadway
Suite 2140
New York, NY 10006-3063

212-809-1850
800-437-8711; Fax: 212-809-3274
info@cdcu.coop
www.cdcu.coop
Facebook, Twitter, LinkedIn

Cathie Mahon, President/CEO
Eben Sheaffer, CFO/Chief Investment Officer
Pablo DeFilippi, CUDE, VP, Membership & BD
Pamela Owens, CUDE, Vice President, Programs
Ysemny (Nachi) Abood, Technical Assistance Specialist

Serve and represent financial cooperatives in low income communities. Members are community based credit unions. Provides training and management support to CDCU's and asists groups in organizing new credit unions.
200 Members
Founded in 1974

6010 **National Foundation for Credit Counseling**
2000 M Street NW
Suite 505
Washington, DC 20036

202-677-4300
800-338-2227
www.nfcc.org
Facebook, Twitter, YouTube

Susan C Keating, CEO
Paul Weiss, Chief Of Staff/CFO
Lydia Sermons-Ward, Senior VP Marketing

Sets the standard for quality credit counseling, debt reduction services and education for financial wellness.
1200 Members

6011 **National Installment Lenders Association**
PO Box 65615
Washington, DC 20035

Home Page: nilaonline.org
Facebook, Twitter, YouTube

An organization formed to educate people about the advantages of installment loans as sources of

consumer credit over credit cards, payday loans and other financial products.
Founded in 2008

6012 **National Rural Lenders Association**
2402 E 44th Place
Tulsa, OK 74105
918-430-3956; Fax: 918-550-8293
nrla-usda.org
Stephen Van Sickle, Chairman
Greg O'Donnell, Executive Director
The NRLA is an advocate for United States Department of Agriculture lending programs to support rural development.

6013 **New York Media Credit Group**
500 Seneca Street
Suite 400
Buffalo, NY 14209
716-887-9547
844-937-3268; Fax: 716-878-0479
www.ny-media.com
Twitter, LinkedIn, YouTube, Google+
Glenn Lifrieri, Executive Board Chair
One of the most active credit association for media credit proffesionals today. Many of the members are from major media including cable television, sports and news cable TV, and radio.
Founded in 1938

6014 **Risk Management Association**
One Liberty Place
1801 Market St
Suite 300
Philadelphia, PA 19103-1613
215-446-4000
800-677-7621; Fax: 215-446-4101
customers@rmahq.org
www.rmahq.org
Facebook, Twitter, LinkedIn
Nancy Foster, President & CEO
William Bonnell, Chair
Champions risk management while also monitoring emerging trends. Our strong relationship with members and regulators helps us develop new risk management techniques, innovative products and education and training programs geared to risk management professionals at different stages of their careers.
3000 Members
Founded in 1914

Newsletters

6015 **ABI Bankruptcy Brief**
American Bankruptcy Institute
66 Canal Center Plaza
Suite 600
Alexandria, VA 22314-1546
703-739-0800; Fax: 703-739-1060
info@abiworld.org
www.abi.org
Amy Quackenboss, Executive Director
A weekly newsletter for ABI members.
Frequency: Weekly/Thursday
Founded in 1982

6016 **AHTCC News**
Affordable Housing Tax Credit Coalition
401 9th Street NW
Suite 900
Washington, DC 20004
202-585-8162; Fax: 202-585-8080
info@taxcreditcoalition.org
www.taxcreditcoalition.org
Joseph Hagan, President
Frequency: Monthly

6017 **ARA News & Views**
American Recovery Association
5525 N MacArthur Boulevard
Suite 135
Irving, TX 75038
972-755-4755; Fax: 972-870-5755
homeoffice@americanrecoveryassn.org
www.repo.org/
Mary Jane Hogan, President
Paul Hallock
Provides news, information and coverage of the recovery industry. Free to members only in print. Available to all others online
28 Pages
Frequency: Quarterly
Founded in 1965

6018 **Bankcard Barometer**
RAM Research Group
320 E 72nd St
Suite 9C
New York, NY 10021
212-724-7535; Fax: 212-208-4384
www.investmenttechnologies.com
Brian Rom, Owner
Robert B McKinley, Publisher
Reports on the pricing and performance of US bank credit card portfolios. Trendline charts follow deliquency, charge-offs, attrition, payment rates, bankruptcy rates, fraud losses, interest yield, operating expenses, net interest margin and return on assets.
Cost: $1295.00
40 Pages
Frequency: Monthly
Founded in 1986
Printed in 4 colors

6019 **Bankcard Dispatch**
RAM Research Group
999 Vanderbilt Beach Road
2nd Floor
Naples, FL 34108
239-325-5300
www.cardweb.com
Robert B McKinley, Editor
Covers the entire payment card industry as it affects the US market. Comprehensive periodical is prepared for payment card executives.
Cost: $1295.00
40 Pages
Frequency: Monthly
Printed in 4 colors

6020 **Bankcard Update**
RAM Research Group
999 Vanderbilt Beach Road
2nd Floor
Naples, FL 34108
239-325-5300
www.cardweb.com
Robert B McKinley, Editor/chairman
Updated printed report and CD-ROM on quarterly statistics of the top US issuers. Covers hundreds of portfolios comprising more than 95 percent of the US market. Subscription includes both the printed version and CD-ROM.
Cost: $ 1295.00
40 Pages
Frequency: Monthly
Founded in 1986
Printed in 4 colors

6021 **Capitol Watch**
National Association of Credit Unions
3138 10th St N
Arlington, VA 22201-2149
703-522-4770
800-336-4644; Fax: 703-524-1082
www.nafcu.org
Facebook, Twitter, YouTube
Dan Berger, President
Alicia Hosmer, VP, Marketing
This members only electronic format newsletter is NAFCU's monthly communication for credit unions with assets of $50 million or less.

6022 **Collection Agency Report**
First Detroit Corporation
30033 Paul Ct
Warren, MI 48092-1805
586-573-0045
800-366-5995; Fax: 586-573-9219
www.firstdetroit.com
Albert Scace, President
Patricia Herrick, Marketing Manager
Patricia Herrick, Circulation Manager
Provides financially oriented news on the collection agency and bad debt buying industries worldwide.
Cost: $420.00
8 Pages
Frequency: Monthly
ISSN: 1052-4029
Founded in 1988
Mailing list available for rentat $110 per M

6023 **Communicator**
Consumer Data Industry Association
1090 Vermont Ave Nw
Suite 200
Washington, DC 20005-4964
202-371-0910; Fax: 202-371-0134
cdia@cdiaonline.org
www.cdiaonline.org
Norm Magnuson, VP
Alicia Payne, Contact
Comprehensive online news about the consumer reporting industry, legislation, member news and schedule of industry events. Members only benefit.
16 Pages
Frequency: Monthly
Circulation: 3000
Founded in 1906

6024 **Consumer Bankruptcy News**
LRP Publications
Po Box 24668
West Palm Beach, FL 33416-4668
561-622-6520
800-341-7874; Fax: 561-622-2423
custserv@lrp.com
www.lrp.com
Kenneth Kahn, President
Keeps readers up-to-date on the latest news and cases involving consumer bankruptcy. A must-have for every bankruptcy professional.
Cost: $290.00
Mailing list available for rent
Printed in 2 colors on matte stock

6025 **Covering Credit Newsletter**
Covering Credit
13 Calle Larspur
Rancho Santa Margarita, CA 92688
949-460-7609; Fax: 949-460-7609
newsletter@coveringcredit.com
www.coveringcredit.com
Facebook, LinkedIn
Michael C Dennis, Communications Advisor
Steve Kozack, Financial Consultant
Intended for business professionals dealing with credit risk management and/or commercial debt collection and their advsiors. Free and online.
Frequency: Monthly
Founded in 1989

6026 Credit Research Foundation News
Credit Research Foundation
1812 Baltimore Blvd.
Suite H
Westminster, MD 21157

443-821-3000; Fax: 443-821-3627
crf_info@crfonline.org
www.crfonline.org

Bill Balduino, President & COO
Matt Skudera, Vice Pres. Research & Education

Contains original articles covering finance, legal matter, process improvements, best practices, periodic survey results, and more. Offers readers thought provoking insights into topics of critical concern.
Frequency: Quarterly

6027 Credit Union News Watch
Credit Union National Association
601 Penn Ave
NW South Building, Suite 600
Washington, DC 20004

202-628-5777
800-356-9655; Fax: 202-638-7729
www.cuna.org
Facebook, Twitter

Susan Newton, Executive Director
Pat Sowick, VP
Richard Dines, Senior State and League Affairs Dir
Alicia Valencia Erb, League Relations
Shellee Mitchell, Executive Assistant

Offers news and reports on credit and lending services.
Cost: $50.00
Frequency: Weekly
Founded in 1970

6028 Credit Union Report
Callahan & Associates
1001 Connecticut Ave Nw
Suite 1001
Washington, DC 20036-5523

202-223-3920
800-446-7453; Fax: 202-223-1311
pubs@creditunions.com
www.callahan.com

Nader Moghaddam, President/CEO

Keeps an eye on the future, providing stategic vision for every level of credit union management. Each issue includes leading-edge ideas from the industry's top consultants and CEO's, as well as financial trend analysis to help credit unions operate more effectively. Available in print and electronic formats.
Cost: $149.00
Frequency: Monthly

6029 Credit Union Times
150 East 42nd Street
Mezz. Fl.
New York, NY 10017

212-457-9400
subscriptions@cutimes.com
www.cutimes.com
Facebook, Twitter, LinkedIn

Michael Ogden, Editor in Chief
Natasha Chilingerian, Managing Editor

Reports on marketing, regulation, technology and developing trends.
Cost: $120.00
Frequency: Weekly
Circulation: 9337
Printed in 4 colors on matte stock

6030 Inside MBS & ABS
Inside Mortgage Finance Publishers
7910 Woodmont Ave
Suite 1000
Bethesda, MD 20814-7019

301-951-1240; Fax: 301-656-1709
service@imfpubs.com
www.imfpubs.com
Twitter, LinkedIn, YouTube

Guy Cecala, Owner
John Bancroft, Managing Editor

If you're involved in issuing, underwriting, investing, research, rating or trading mortgage-backed securities and asset-backed securities, this publication is for you.
Cost: $1699.00
Founded in 1984

6031 Jumbo Rate News
Bauer Financial
2655 S Le Jeune Rd
Suite 1A
Coral Gables, FL 33134-5827

305-445-9500
800-388-6686; Fax: 305-445-6775
customerservice@bauerfinancial.com
www.bauerfinancial.com

Karen L Dorway, President/CEO

Each issue contains over 1,000 separate Jumbo CD rates in seven categories from over 200 creditworthy banks and thrifts nationwide. Includes star ratings, wire transfer fees, deposit requirements and financial highlights for each institution.
Cost: $4150.00
Frequency: Weekly
Founded in 1986
Printed in 2 colors on matte stock

6032 MBA Newslink
Mortgage Bankers Association
1717 Rhode Island Avenue NW
Suite 400
Washington, DC 20036

202-557-2700
www.mortgagebankers.org
Facebook, Twitter, LinkedIn, YouTube

David H Stevens, President/CEO
Marcia Davies, Chief of Staff/SVP

Learn the latest residential, commercial, and multifamily real estate finance news. Hear what's happening at MBA, read special features that provide vital facts and insight into industry trends, news from Washington, DC and more.
Cost: $69.95
Frequency: Daily
Circulation: 54,000

6033 NACM E-News
National Association of Credit Management
8840 Columbia 100 Pkwy
Columbia, MD 21045-2100

410-740-5560; Fax: 410-740-5574
robins@nacm.org
www.nacm.org
Facebook, Twitter, LinkedIn
Toni Drake, Chairperson
Chris Meyers, Chairman Elect
Kevin Quinn, Director
Jay Snyder, Director

News items of interest to credit and business professionals. Free online.

6034 National Mortgage News
Thomson Financial Publishing
1 State St
27th Floor
New York, NY 10004-1481

212-803-8333
800-221-1809; Fax: 800-235-5552
www.nationalmortgagenews.com
Facebook, Twitter, LinkedIn

Timothy Murphy, Group Publisher

Mortgage information, legislation and news.
Cost: $228.00
Frequency: Weekly
Printed in 2 colors on newsprint stock

6035 Newsbreak
First Entertainment Credit Union
PO Box 100
Hollywood, CA 90078

323-851-3673
888-800-3328; Fax: 323-874-1397
mail@firstent.org
www.firstent.org
Facebook, Twitter, You tube

Charles A Bruen, President/CEO

Provides industry, resources and investment news and information for the First Entertainment Credit Union member. Free online.
Frequency: Quarterly

6036 SNL Daily ThriftWatch
SNL Financial
212 7th Street NE
Charlottesville, VA 22902

434-977-1600
866-296-3743; Fax: 434-977-4466
www.snl.com

Mike Chin, President

Provides the information that thrift executives and investors require to stay on top of the industry. Available in print and electronic formats.
5 Pages
Frequency: Daily
Founded in 1987

6037 Scope
International Association of Commercial Collectors
4040 W 70th St
Minneapolis, MN 55435-4104

952-925-0760
800-859-9526; Fax: 952-926-1624
iacc@commercialcollector.com
www.commercialcollector.com
LinkedIn

Johon Yursha, President
Tammy Schoenberg, Executive Director
Jessica Hartman, Director
Sara Bobrowski, IACC Coordinator
Randy Frazee, Board Treasurer

Provides updates on developments in the industry, important legislative and legal issues, and IACC events and resources. Free to members only.
350 Members
Frequency: Monthly
Circulation: 350
Founded in 1970
Printed in on glossy stock

6038 Trade Vendor Quarterly
Blakeley & Blakeley
2 Park Plaza
Suite 400
Irvine, CA 92614

949-260-0611; Fax: 949-260-0613
www.vendorlaw.com

Scott Blakey, Esq.

Highlights developments in commercial, creditors' rights, e-commerce and bankruptcy law of interest to the credit and financial professional. Free online.
Frequency: Quarterly

Magazines & Journals

6039 **Affordable Housing Finance**
Hanley Wood
300 Montgomery Street
Suite 1060
San Francisco, CA 94104
415-315-1241; Fax: 415-315-1248
ahf@omeda.com
www.housingfinance.com
Facebook, Twitter
John McManus, Editorial Director
Jerry Ascierto, Editor in Chief
Offers practical information on obtaining debt and equality financing from federal, state, and local governments as well as private resources. In-depth coverage on the federal low-income housing tax credit program, tax-exempt bond financing, corporate tax credit investigation.
Cost: $83.00
88 Pages
Frequency: Monthly
Circulation: 9000
Founded in 1993
Printed in 4 colors on glossy stock

6040 **American Bankruptcy Institute Journal**
American Bankruptcy Institute
66 Canal Center Plaza
Suite 600
Alexandria, VA 22314-1546
703-739-0800; Fax: 703-739-1060
info@abiworld.org
www.abi.org
Amy Quackenboss, Executive Director
Benefit to ABI members. Written by experts in the insolvency community, the Journal addresses timely issues involving consumer bankruptcy, the intersection of state laws and the Bankrupcy Code, valuation, turnaround management concerns, recent legislative developments, the US trustee system and more. Available in print or online.
Frequency: Monthly
Founded in 1982

6041 **Apartment Finance Today Magazine**
Hanley Wood LLC
One Thomas Circle, NW
Suite 600
Washington, DC 20005
202-452-0800; Fax: 202-785-1974
www.hanleywood.com
Peter Goldston, CEO
Frank Anton, Vice Chairman
Provides in-depth and unbiased reporting and insightful analysis for owners, developers and asset managers
80 Pages
ISSN: 1097-4059
Founded in 1995
Printed in 4 colors on glossy stock

6042 **Business Credit Magazine**
National Association of Credit Management
8840 Columbia 100 Pkwy
Columbia, MD 21045-2100
410-740-5560; Fax: 410-740-5574
robins@nacm.org
www.nacm.org
Facebook, Twitter, LinkedIn
Toni Drake, Chairperson
Chris Meyers, Chairman/elect
Kevin Quinn, Director
Jay Snyder, Director
Serves those responsible for extending business and trade credit and overseeing risk management for their companies. Keeps individuals up-to-date on cutting-edge trands and important legislative, bankruptcy, business ethics, trade finance, asset protection, benchmarking and scoring issues.
Frequency: 9x/Year
Circulation: 22000

6043 **Card Technology**
Thomson Financial Publishing
Thomson Reuters
3 Times Square
New York, NY 10036
646-223-4000
general.info@thomsonreuters.com
Thomas H Glocer, Chief Executive Officer
Store-value cards, optical-memory cards, biometrics, cards on the Internet, cards for electronic data storage, and devices used with these cards in banking, government, telecommunications, transportation and education.
Cost: $ 98.00
Frequency: Monthly
Circulation: 25000
Founded in 1961
Printed in 4 colors on glossy stock

6044 **Collections & Credit Risk**
Thomson Financial Publishing
1 State St
27th Floor
New York, NY 10004-1481
212-803-8200
800-221-1809; Fax: 800-843-9600
custserv@sourcemedia.com
Darren Waggoner, Chief Editor
Melissa Buonos, National Sales Manager
Focuses on news and trends of strategic and competitive importance to collections and credit policy executives. Covers the credit risk industry's growth, diversification and technology in both commercial and consumer credit.
Cost: $98.00
66 Pages
Frequency: Monthly
Circulation: 25000
Founded in 1996

6045 **Commercial Collection Guidelines for Credit Grantors**
International Association of Commercial Collectors
4040 W 70th St
Minneapolis, MN 55435-4104
952-925-0760
800-859-9526; Fax: 952-926-1624
iacc@commercialcollector.com
www.commercialcollector.com
LinkedIn
John Yursha, President
Tammy M. Schoenberg, Executive Director
Jessica Hartman, Director
Sara Bobrowski, IACC Coordinator
Randy Frazee, Board Treasurer
Helps to assist commercial account credit managers and their staffs in evaluating receivables and collecting accounts. Topics include internal credit control, credit granting and collecting and professional commercial collection service.
Cost: $70.00
350 Members
Frequency: Monthly
Founded in 1970

6046 **Credit & Financial Management Review**
Credit Research Foundation
1812 Baltimore Blvd
Suite H
Westminster, MD 21157
443-821-3000; Fax: 443-821-3627
crf_info@crfonline.org
www.crfonline.org
Bill Balduino, President & COO
Matt Skudera, Vice Pres. Research & Education
Referred journal that publishes original material concerned with all aspects of credit, accounts receivable and customer financial relationships. It is devoted to the improvement and further development of the theory and practice of credit management.
Cost: $80.00
56 Pages
Frequency: Quarterly
Circulation: 3000
Printed in 2 colors

6047 **Credit Card Management**
Thomson Financial Publishing
Thomas Reuters
3 Times Square
New York, NY 10036
646-223-4000
800-782-5555; Fax: 646-223-8593
Thomas H Glocer, Chief Executive Officer
Information on the major developments in the credit card industry.
Cost: $98.00
74 Pages
Frequency: Monthly
Circulation: 19000
Printed in 4 colors on glossy stock

6048 **Credit Professional**
Credit Professionals International
10726 Manchester Rd
Suite B
St Louis, MO 63122-1320
314-821-9393; Fax: 314-821-7171
creditpro@creditprofessionals.org
www.creditprofessionals.org
Sue Heusing, President
Rhonda McKinney, VP
Charlotte Rancilio, Editor
A bi-annual magazine published by Credit Professionals International.
Cost: $15.00
Frequency: Bi-annually
Circulation: 550
Founded in 1989

6049 **Credit Union Magazine**
Credit Union National Association
601 Penn Ave
NW South Building, Suite 600
Washington, DC 20004
202-628-5777
800-356-9655; Fax: 202-638-7729
webservices@cuna.org
www.cuna.org
Facebook, Twitter
Jim Nussl, CEO
The role and operations of modern credit unions.
Cost: $50.00
100 Pages
Frequency: Monthly
Circulation: 34401
ISSN: 0011-1066
Printed in 4 colors on glossy stock

6050 **Federal Credit Union Magazine**
National Association of Federal Credit Unions

3138 10th St N
Arlington, VA 22201-2149

703-522-4770
800-336-4644; Fax: 703-524-1082
fbecker@nafcu.org
www.nafcu.org
Facebook, Twitter, YouTube

Dan Berger, President
Alicia Hosmer, VP, Marketing

Written for CEO's, senior staff and volunteers of Federal Credit Unions. Offers legislative and regulatory news, as well as technology and operational issues. Call for rates.
50 Pages
Circulation: 1500
ISSN: 1043-7789
Founded in 1967
Printed in 4 colors on glossy stock

6051 **Financial Manager**
Broadcast Cable Credit Association
550 W. Frontage Road
Suite 3600
Northfield, IL 60093-1243

847-881-8757; Fax: 847-784-8059
info@bccacredit.com
www.bccacredit.com

Mary Collins, President & CEO
Jamie Smith, Director, Operations
Arcelia Pimentel, Sales/Membership

A bi-monthly magazine published by the Broadcast Cable Credit Association.
Frequency: Bi-Monthly

6052 **News and Views**
Advertising Media Credit Executives Association
8840 Columbia 100 Parkway
Columbia, MD 21045-2158

410-992-7609; Fax: 410-740-5574
amcea@amcea.org
www.amcea.org

Sheila Wroten, President
Mary Younger, VP
Vickie Bolinger, Director

Our magazine reports on current trends and legal issues while offering tips on customer service, time management and collections.
Frequency: Quarterly
Founded in 1953

Trade Shows

6053 **AMCEA Conference**
Advertising Media Credit Executives Association
8840 Columbia 100 Parkway
Columbia, MD 21045-2158

410-992-7609; Fax: 410-740-5574
amcea@amcea.org
www.amcea.org

Sheila Wroten, President
Kimberly Riley, VP
Vickie Bolinger, Director

The conference encompasses four days and is a networking extravaganza. Top attorneys discuss bankruptcy and legal issues. We invite advertising agencies to discuss network buying and liability problems.
Frequency: Annual

6054 **BCCA Distance Learning Seminars**
Broadcast Cable Credit Association
550 W. Frontage Road
Suite 3600
Northfield, IL 60093

847-881-8757; Fax: 847-784-8059
info@bccacredit.com
www.bccacredit.com

Mary Collins, President & CEO
Jamie Grande, Director, Operations
Arcelia Pimentel, Sales/Membership

Teleconference and online seminars educating members on important areas of the broadcast and cable industry.
Founded in 1972

6055 **BCCA Media Credit Seminar**
Broadcast Cable Credit Association
550 W. Frontage Road
Suite 3600
Northfield, IL 60093

847-881-8757; Fax: 847-784-8059
info@bccacredit.com
www.bccacredit.com

Mary Collins, President & CEO
Jamie Grande, Director, Operations
Arcelia Pimentel, Sales/Membership

A subsidiary of the Media Financial Management Association, BCCA provides credit information, education, and networking opportunities which enables members to efficiently manage credit risk and increase profitability.
Frequency: Annual
Founded in 1972

6056 **Credit & Accounts Receivable Forum**
Credit Research Foundation
1812 Baltimore Blvd.
Suite H
Westminster, MD 21157

443-821-3000; Fax: 443-821-3627
crf_info@crfonline.org
www.crfonline.org

Bill Balduino, President/COO
Matt Skudera, Vice Pres. Research & Education

Offers attendees insight on contemporary technical, legal, and financial topics as well as the chance to network with industry peers.
Frequency: March & October

6057 **Credit & Accounts Receivable Forum & Expo**
Credit Research Foundation
1812 Baltimore Blvd.
Suite H
Westminster, MD 21157

443-821-3000; Fax: 443-821-3627
crf_info@crfonline.org
www.crfonline.org

Bill Balduino, President/COO
Matt Skudera, Vice Pres. Research & Education

Offers attendees insight on contemporary technical, legal, and financial topics as well as the chance to network with industry peers. This summer forum is also host to the largest business-to-business risk management expo in the country.
Frequency: August

6058 **Credit Union Executive Society Annual Convention: CUES**
5510 Research Park Drive
Madison, WI 53711-5377

608-712-2664
800-252-2664; Fax: 608-271-2303
cues@cues.org
www.cues.org
Facebook, Twitter, LinkedIn

Fred Johnson, CEO/President

Offers a rainbow of marketing and technology topics, as well as a supplier showcase, geared toward board members.
Frequency: June
Founded in 1962

6059 **Credit Union National Association Governmental Affairs Conference**
Credit Union National Association
601 Penn Ave
NW South Building, Suite 600
Washington, DC 20004

202-628-5777
800-356-9655; Fax: 202-638-7729
www.cuna.org
Facebook, Twitter

Susan Newton, Executive Director
Pat Sowick, VP
Richard Dines, Senior State and League Affairs Dir
Alicia Valencia Erb, League Relations
Shellee Mitchell, Executive Assistant

Annual conference held in Washington, DC, with a focus on legislative issues impacting credit unions.
Frequency: February

6060 **Credit Union National Association Future Forum**
601 Penn Ave
NW South Building, Suite 600
Washington, DC 20004

202-628-5777
800-356-9655; Fax: 202-638-7729
www.cuna.org
Facebook, Twitter

Susan Newton, Executive Director
Pat Sowick, VP
Richard Dines, Senior State and League Affairs Dir
Alicia Valencia Erb, League Relations
Shellee Mitchell, Executive Assistant

Convention and annual general meeting with exhibit hall, educational sessions, and other events.
Frequency: September

6061 **Defense Credit Union's Annual Conference**
Defense Credit Union Council
601 Pennsylvania Avenue NW
South Building, Suite 600
Washington, DC 20004

202-638-3950; Fax: 202-638-3410
admin@dcuc.org
www.dcuc.org

Conference and exhibits of equipment, supplies and services for credit unions that serve Department of Defense personnel with problems peculiar to military installations and personnel.
200 Attendees
Frequency: August

6062 **Education Credit Union Council Annual Conference**
Education Credit Union Council
PO Box 7558
Spanish Fort, AL 36577-7558

251-626-3399; Fax: 251-626-3565
www.ecuc.org

Lorraine B Zerfas, Executive Director

Any CEOs, directors, committee members and top management active in the operations of any credit union that serves the educational community who want to achieve professional excellence should attend. Interact with peers from across the US serving the fields of education, introduce executive staff and managers to credit union ideas and philosophy on a national level and discuss is-

sues important to your credit union in the coming year.
Frequency: February

6063 **Finance, Credit & International Business Global Conference**
Finance, Credit & International Business
8840 Columbia 100 Parkway
Columbia, MD 21045-2158

410-423-1840
888-256-3242; Fax: 410-423-1845
fcib_info@fciglobal.com
www.fcibglobal.com
Twitter, LinkedIn

Annual gathering of international credit and finance professionals draws upon the combined expertise of financial executives from all regions of the world to provide attendees with practical insight for managing in a rapidly evolving international environment.
Frequency: November

6064 **Fleet/Lease Remarketing**
S&A Conferences Group
Westview At Weston
301 Cascade Pointe Lane
Cary, NC 27513

800-608-7500; Fax: 919-674-6027
www.autoremarketing.com
Facebook, Twitter, LinkedIn

Ron Smith, President

Executive conference focused on remarketing strategies for manufacturer, bank, finance, commercial and rental fleet/lease vehicles.
Frequency: February

6065 **International Association of Commercial Collectors Annual Convention**
4040 W 70th Street
Minneapolis, MN 55435

952-925-0760
800-859-9526; Fax: 952-926-1624
iacc@commercialcollector.com
www.commercialcollector.com
LinkedIn

John Yursha, President
Tammy M. Schoenberg, Executive Director

International trade association comprised of more than 230 collection specialists and 140 commercial attorneys, with members throughout the US and 20 international countries. IACC's mission is to promote the commercial collection profession by providing IACC members with the resources to excel in the industry.
350 Members
Frequency: January
Founded in 1970

6066 **Legal Issues & Regulatory Compliance Conference**
Mortgage Bankers Association
1717 Rhode Island Avenue NW
Suite 400
Washington, DC 20036

202-557-2700
meetings@mortgagebankers.org
www.mortgagebankers.org
Facebook, Twitter, LinkedIn, YouTube

David H Stevens, President/CEO
Marcia Davies, Chief of Staff/SVP

Learn about all the legal and regulatory developments facing the industry.
Frequency: Annual/May

6067 **MFMA/BCCA Annual Conference: Media Finance Focus**
Broadcast Cable Credit Association
550 W. Frontage Road
Suite 3600
Northfield, IL 60093

847-881-8757; Fax: 847-784-8059
info@bccacredit.com
www.mediafinancefocus.org

Mary Collins, President & CEO
Jamie Grande, Director, Operations
Arcelia Pimenetal, Sales/Membership

Offers professional education targeting media financial and business executives; CPE opportunities; exhibitors; roundtables; and networking opportunities.
Frequency: Annual
Founded in 1972

6068 **NFCC Leaders Conference**
National Foundation for Credit Counseling
2000M Street NW
Suite 505
Washington, DC 20036

202-677-4300
800-388-2227
www.nfcc.org
Facebook, Twitter, YouTube

Susan C Keating, President/CEO
Paul Weiss, CFO/ Chief Of Staff
William Binzel, Chief Counsel

Three-day conference to discuss credit counceling industry practices, trends and issues.
300 Attendees
Frequency: Annual/Fall
Founded in 1965

6069 **NRLA Annual Conference**
National Rural Lenders Association
2402 E 44th Place
Tulsa, OK 74105

918-430-3956; Fax: 918-550-8293
media@nrla-usda.org
nrla-usda.org

Greg O'Donnell, Executive Director

Hear from, and interact with, policy makers.
Frequency: Annual
Founded in 2015

6070 **National Association of Credit Management: Annual Credit Congress**
National Association of Credit Management
8840 Columbia 100 Parkway
Columbia, MD 21045

410-740-5560; Fax: 410-740-5574
robins@nacm.org
www.nacm.org
Facebook, Twitter, LinkedIn

Toni Drake, Chairperson
Chris Meyers, Chairman/elect
Kevin Quinn, Director
Jay Snyder, Director

The event for the business credit and financial professional offering relevant, timely educational offerings, including industry specific programs, over 100 specialized service providers on the expo floor, showcasing the latest products and services, countless networking and relationship-building events to facilitate the sharing of knowlege and expertise.
18000 Members
2000 Attendees
Frequency: May/June

6071 **National Fraud Issues Conference**
Mortgage Bankers Association
1717 Rhode Island Avenue NW
Suite 400
Washington, DC 20036

202-557-2700
meetings@mortgagebankers.org
www.mortgagebankers.org
Facebook, Twitter, LinkedIn, YouTube

David H Stevens, President/CEO
Marcia Davies, Chief of Staff/SVP

The forum where industry professionals can learn about the issues related to the growing incidence and complexity of mortgage fraud.
Frequency: Annual/March

6072 **National Mortgage Servicing Conference & Expo**
Mortgage Bankers Association
1717 Rhode Island Avenue NW
Suite 400
Washington, DC 20036

202-557-2700
meetings@mortgagebankers.org
www.mortgagebankers.org
Facebook, Twitter, LinkedIn, YouTube

David H Stevens, President/CEO
Marcia Davies, Chief of Staff/SVP

Provides the opportunity to reach key servicing executives from residential mortgage companies and showcase the product offerings, network with key decision makers, and obtain qualified leads that can help reach goals.
Frequency: Annual/February

6073 **National Policy Conference**
Mortgage Bankers Association
1717 Rhode Island Avenue NW
Suite 400
Washington, DC 20036

202-557-2700
meetings@mortgagebankers.org
www.mortgagebankers.org
Facebook, Twitter, LinkedIn, YouTube

David H Stevens, President/CEO
Marcia Davies, Chief of Staff/SVP

Brings together key officials, cabinet members and special guest speakers to address these critical issues.
Frequency: Annual/March

6074 **National Technology in Mortgage Banking Conference**
Mortgage Bankers Association
1717 Rhode Island Avenue NW
Suite 400
Washington, DC 20036

202-557-2700
meetings@mortgagebankers.org
www.mortgagebankers.org
Facebook, Twitter, LinkedIn, YouTube

David H Stevens, President/CEO
Marcia Davies, Chief of Staff/SVP

Forum to learn about the newest industry solutions and how they can increase your company's competitive edge. The conference focuses on relevant topics, including legal / regulatory updates, eMortgages, investor reporting changes and technology advances such as mobile computing.
Frequency: Annual/March

6075 **Risk Management Conference**
Risk Management Association
1801 Market Street
Suite 300
Philadelphia, PA 19103-1628

215-446-4000
800-677-7621; Fax: 215-446-4100
customers@rmahq.org
www.rmahq.org

Nancy Foster, President/CEO
Beans, Public Relations Manager

Educates and helps risk management professionals develop new techniques and learn about new innovative products at different stages of

their careers. Mailing list available for exhibitors and sponsors only.
800 Attendees
Frequency: October

Directories & Databases

6076 **AMCEA Member Handbook & Roster**
Advertising Media Credit Executives Association
8840 Columbia 100 Parkway
Columbia, MD 21045-2158

410-992-7609; Fax: 410-740-5574
www.amcea.org

Sheila Wroten, President
Kimberly Riley, VP
Vickie Bolinger, Director

Inside you will find direct telephone numbers to every credit manager in our association along with numbers for credit references and fax inquiries. We also include their e-mail addresses and computer hardware and software information.

6077 **American Recovery Association Directory**
American Recovery Association
5525 N MacArthur Boulevard
Suite 135
Irving, TX 75038

972-755-4755; Fax: 972-870-5755
homeoffice@americanrecoveryassn.org
www.repo.org

Mary Jane Hogan, President
Tom Crosby, Secretary/Treasurer

Contain's listings of ARA's members, offices and services. Available in hardcopy and electronic formats.
308 Pages
Frequency: Annual
Founded in 1965

6078 **Banksearch Book**
Sheshunoff Information Services
2801 Via Fortuna
Suite 600
Austin, TX 78746-7970

512-472-4000
800-477-1772
www.smslp.com

Gabrielle Sheshunoff, CEO

Offers information on savings and loans, savings banks and credit unions with assets over 10 million. Customized for your institutution type: bank thrift, bank holding company or credit union. You buy only the data you want — by state, region or nation.
Cost: $295.00
Frequency: Annual

6079 **Business Products Credit Association**
BCPA
607 Westridge Drive
O'Fallon, MO 63366

636-924-5775; Fax: 636-754-0567
service@bpca.org
www.bpca.org

BPCA has a database of over 400,000 companies and their payment histories. This is available to members over the Internet.

6080 **Callahan's Credit Union Directory**
Callahan & Associates
1001 Connecticut Ave NW
Suite 1001
Washington, DC 20036-5523

202-223-3920
800-446-7453; Fax: 202-223-1311
www.callahan.com

Sean Hession, CEO
Charles Filson, Chairman
Jay Johnson, EVP
Alix Patterson, COO

This directory turns raw data into research, giving you the tools you need to keep up with the credit union industry. Access all the credit union information found in the print edition through the Online Edition on this website. In a special Users Area only for purchasers of the print edition, you can access updated finacials four times a year, conduct searches on key information and save those search results to return to over and over again. Real time updates directly from our database.
Cost: $135.00
Frequency: Annual

6081 **Collection Agency Directory**
First Detroit Corporation
PO Box 5025
Warren, MI 48090-5025

586-573-0045
800-366-5995; Fax: 586-573-9219
www.firstdetroit.com

Albert W Scace, Publisher

Offers information and statistics on nearly 900 collection agencies throught the world.
Cost: $347.00
301 Pages
Frequency: Annual, Paperback
ISSN: 1058-983X
Founded in 1991
Mailing list available for rent: 11,000 names at $150 per M
Printed in one color on matte stock

6082 **Credit**
American Financial Services Association
919 18th Street NW
Suite 300
Washington, DC 20006-5517

202-296-5544
www.afsaonline.org
Twitter

Chris Steinebert, President/CEO

Focuses on breaking developments on legislative and regulatory issues on the federal and state levels, as well as consumer education initiatives, industry news, news inside AFSA and information on meetings and conferences. Free online access.
1500 Pages
Frequency: Bi-Monthly

6083 **Credit Card and Check Fraud: A Stop-Loss Manual**
Fraud & Theft Information Bureau
9770 S. Military Trail
Suite 380
Boynton Beach, FL 33436

561-737-8700; Fax: 561-737-5800

Larry Schwartz, Founder and Director
Pearl Sax, Founder and Director

The Fraud And Theft Information Bureau is the leading consultant on credit card and check fraud control and loss prevention — and the publisher of related manuals and fraud-blocker data bases
Cost: $199.95
300 Pages
Founded in 1982

6084 **Credit Union Cooperatives**
Callahan & Associates
1001 Connecticut Ave NW
10th Floor
Washington, DC 20036-5523

202-223-3920
800-446-7453; Fax: 202-223-1311
www.callahan.com

Sean Hession, CEO
Charles Filson, Chairman
Jay Johnson, EVP
Alix Patterson, COO

Your source for information on credit union service organizations (CUSOs) and other cooperative providers to the credit industry. The directory has up-to-date contact names, addresses and phone numbers for more than 700 CUSOs and their associated credit unions. Use this publication to compare services offered by CUSOs or if you're looking to start or expand an existing CUSO.
Cost: $165.00

6085 **Credit Union Directory**
National Credit Union Administration
1775 Duke St
Suite 4206
Alexandria, VA 22314-6115

703-518-6300
800-755-1030; Fax: 703-518-6539
consumerassistance@ncua.gov
www.ncua.gov
Facebook, Twitter, YouTube

Rodney Hood, Chair

Federal credit and state-chartered credit unions are the focal point of this directory. Free online.
Frequency: Annual

6086 **Credit Union Financial Yearbook**
Callahan & Associates
1001 Connecticut Ave NW
Washington, DC 20036-5523

202-223-3920
800-446-7453; Fax: 202-223-1311
www.callahan.com

Sean Hession, CEO
Charles Filson, Chairman
Jay Johnson, EVP
Alix Patterson, COO

Each quarter Callahan publishes a comprehensive study on the state of the industry that includes detailed financials for all credit unions over $50 million. The third quarter edition is published in 3 volumes based on asset size. Fourth quarter edition is based on total assets for the year. Asset sizes considered are $50 to $100 million, $100 - $250 million and over $250 million.
Cost: $565.00
Frequency: Complete Year Price

6087 **Defense Credit Union Directory**
Defense Credit Union Council
601 Pennsylvania Ave NW
Suite 600
Washington, DC 20004-2601

202-638-3950; Fax: 202-638-3410
admin@dcuc.org
www.dcuc.org

Roland Arteata, President

Listing of about 360 credit unions with membership consisting wholly or partly of the military and civilian personnel of the United States and worldwide.
Cost: $150.00
60 Pages
Frequency: Biennial
Founded in 1963

6088 Directory of Venture Capital & Private Equity Firms - Online Database
Grey House Publishing
4919 Route 22
PO Box 56
Amenia, NY 12501
518-789-8700
800-562-2139; Fax: 845-373-6390
gold@greyhouse.com
gold.greyhouse.com
Facebook, Twitter
Leslie Mackenzie, Publisher
Richard Gottlieb, Editor
Packed with need-to-know information, this database offers immediate access to 2,300 VC firms, over 10,000 managing partners, and over 11,500 VC investments.
Frequency: Annual

6089 Directory of Venture Capital and Private Equity Firms
Grey House Publishing
4919 Route 22
PO Box 56
Amenia, NY 12501
518-789-8700
800-562-2139; Fax: 845-373-6390
books@greyhouse.com
www.greyhouse.com
Facebook, Twitter
Richard Gottlieb, President
Leslie Mackenzie, Publisher
Offers access to over 2,300 domestic and international venture capital and private equity firms, with detailed contact information and extensive data on investment and funds.
Cost: $685.00
1200 Pages
Frequency: Annual
ISBN: 1-592372-72-4

6090 Dun's Credit Guide
Dun & Bradstreet Information Service
103 John F Kennedy Pkwy
Short Hills, NJ 07078-2708
973-921-5500
800-234-3867; Fax: 908-665-5803
www.dnb.com
Facebook, Twitter, LinkedIn, YouTube
Sara Mathew, CEO
James Fernandez, EVP and COO
Providing a dollar-specific credit guideline on manufacturers, wholesalers and retailers, this database is updated continuously for the interested business person.

6091 National Credit Union Administration Directory
National Credit Union Administration
1775 Duke St
Suite 4206
Alexandria, VA 22314-6115
703-518-6300; Fax: 703-518-6539
ociomail@ncua.gov
www.ncua.gov
Rodney Hood, Chair
Directory of credit unions governed by a three member board appointed by the President and confirmed by the US Senate, by the independent federal agency that charters and supervises federal credit unions. NCUA, with the backing of the full faith and credit of the US government, operates the National Credit Union Share Insurance Fund, insuring the savings of 80 million account holders in all federal credit unions and many state chartered credit unions.

6092 Thomson Credit Union Directory
4709 Golf Road
Skokie, IL 60076-1231
847-676-9600
800-321-3373; Fax: 847-933-8101
custserv@accuitysolutions.com
www.accuitysolutions.com
Hugh Johnes IV, President and CEO
Kerry Hewson, EVP
Jay Ryan, Head of Sales
Semi-annual directory that includes valuable industry statistics, a quick telephone lookup index of all credit unions and a resource guide featuring vendors within the credit union marketplace. Includes over 12,500 major credit unions and 5,500 branches, with asset rankings, membership totals and more. Published in partnership with the Credit Union National Association.
Cost: $199.00
Frequency: January/July
ISBN: 1-563103-24-9

6093 Who's Who in Credit and Financial
New York Credit and Financial Management Assn
520 8th Avenue
New York, NY 10018-6507
212-695-4807
Directory of services and supplies to the industry.

6094 World Council of Credit Unions Directory
World Council of Credit Unions
5710 Mineral Point Road
Madison, WI 53705
608-395-2000; Fax: 608-395-2001
mail@woccu.org
www.woccu.org
Pepi Dougherty, Executive
Mike Muckian, Marketing & Communications
Lists over 100 World Council of Credit Union leaders and member organizations in each of seven confederations. African, Asian, Australian, Canadian, Caribbean, Latin-American and the United States.

Industry Web Sites

6095 http://gold.greyhouse.com
G.O.L.D Grey House OnLine Databases
Grey House Publishing's online database platform, GOLD, offers Quick Search, Keyword Search and Expert Search for most business sectors including banking, credid and lending service markets. The GOLD platform makes finding the information you need quick and easy - whether you're a novice searcher or an experienced database user. All of Grey House's directory products are available for subscription on the GOLD platform.

6096 www.aacul.org
American Association of Credit Union Leagues
Voluntary membership association for credit union leagues that are members of the Credit Union National Association. AACUL provides representation, products, services and programs to its members.

6097 www.abiworld.org
American Bankruptcy Institute
ABI is the largest multidiciplinary, nonpartisan organization dedicated to research and education on matters related to insolvency. The ABI membership provides a forum for the exchange of ideas and information. ABI is engaged in numerous educational and research activities, as well as the production of a number of publications both for the insolvency practitioner and the public.

6098 www.afsaonline.com
American Financial Services Association
National trade association for market funded providers of financial services to consumers and small businesses. These providers offer an array of finacial services, including unsecured personal loans, automobile loans, home equity loans and credit cards through specialized bank institutions.

6099 www.amcea.org
Advertising Media Credit Executives Association
Improving the professionalism, principles, understanding and techniques of media credit management by encouraging the exchange of ideas, methods and procedures within the membership. Providing additional education and training in the business fundamentals of media credit and credit policies and in the related areas of finance, accounting, law and economics for the purpose of enhancing the career development of members.

6100 www.bccacredit.com
Broadcast Cable Credit Association
A subsidiary of the Broadcast Cable Financial Management Association, BCCA provides industry specific credit reports on individual agencies, advertisers, or buying services (national and local).

6101 www.bpca.org
Business Products Credit Association
Nonprofit trade association for credit personnel of manufacturers, wholesalers and factors. The national credit group consists of discount stores, superstores, commercial stationers, printing and publications, business machines, computer peripherals and software, plus mass merchandisers. In addition, BPCA has groups on school supply, janitorial/sanitary supplies, fine pens/promotional products.

6102 www.cdiaonline.org
Consumer Data Industry Association
Trade association representing consumer information companies that provide fraud prevention and risk management products, credit and mortgage reports, tenant and employment screening services, check fraud and verifacation services and collection services. Sets industry standards and provides education for it's members. Provides educational materials for consumers regarding their credit rights and how consumer credit reporting agencies can better serve their needs.

6103 www.cfa.com
Commercial Finance Association
Trade group of the asset-based financial services industry, with members throughout the US, Canada and around the world. Members include the asset-based lending arms of domestic and foreign commercial banks, small and large independent finance companies, floor plan financing organizations, factoring organizations and financing subsidiaries of major industrial corporations.

6104 www.collector.com
American Collectors Association
International trade organization of credit and collection professionals that provides a variety of accounts recievable management services.

6105 www.commercialcollector.com
International Association of Commercial Collectors
International trade association comprised of more than 230 collection specialists and 140

commercial attorneys, with members throughout the US and 20 international countries. IACC's mission is to promote the commercial collection profession by providing IACC members with the resources to excel in the industry.

6106 **www.creditunions.com**
Callahan & Associates
National credit union research and consulting firm specializing in financial publications and analysis software, strategic planning and investment management.

6107 **www.crfonline.org**
Credit Research Foundation
Independent, member run organization, consisting of a dynamic community of like minded business professionals with a vested interest in improving and fostering the field of business credit — more specifically, the practices and technologies of business credit.

6108 **www.cues.org**
Credit Union Executives Society
For credit union executives, we serve to advance the professional development of CEOs, senior management and directors.

6109 **www.cuna.org**
Credit Union National Association
The premier trade association in the financial services arena. Supports, protects, unifies and advances the credit union movement.

6110 **www.ecuc.org**
Education Credit Union Council
Dedicated to providing educational and networking opportunities to credit unions who serve educational communities, industry teachers, administrators, students, support staff and others in the educational community.

6111 **www.electran.org**
Electronic Transaction Association
International trade association serving the needs of organizations offering transaction processing products and services.

6112 **www.fcibglobal.com**
FCIB
Provider of products and services to many small, medium and large size exporters as well as major multinational corporations in 30 countries around the world.

6113 **www.firstent.org**
First Entertainment Credit Union
Nonprofit institution serves as the financial resource for the entertainment community to more than 700 entertainment based companies.

6114 **www.greyhouse.com**
Grey House Publishing
Authoritative reference directories for most business sectors including banking, credit and lending service markets. Users can search the online databases with varied search criteria allowing for custom searches by product category, geographic area, sales volume, keyword, subject and more. Full Grey House catalog and online ordering also available.

6115 **www.mbaa.org**
Mortgage Bankers Association of America
Representing the real estate finance industry, MBA serves its membership by representing their legislative and regulatory interests before the US Congress and federal agencies; by meeting their educational needs through programs and a range of periodicals and publications; and by supporting their business interests with a variety of research initiatives and other products and services.

6116 **www.nacm.org**
National Association of Credit Management
Promotes honest and fair dealings in credit transactions, fosters and encourages research in the field of credit.

6117 **www.nfcc.org**
National Foundation for Credit Counceling
National nonprofit credit counseling oranization with 1,200 offices helping 1.5 million households annually. Identify NFCC members (Consumer Credit Counseling Service CCCS) by the NFCC member seal representing high standards, free and low-cost confidential services.

6118 **www.repo.org**
American Recovery Association
Approximately 500 offices throughout the US, Canada and Germany, providing repossesion services around the world.

Associations

6119 ATM Industry Association

Home Page: www.atmia.com
Facebook, Twitter, LinkedIn, YouTube

Mike Lee, CEO
David Tente, Executive Director, USA
Dana Benson, Director, Conferences/Sponsorships

Alliance promoting the proliferation of automated teller machines, ATMs and cash.
10000 Members
Founded in 1997

6120 American e-Commerce Association

Home Page: www.aeaus.com

Computer training, e-commerce education, membership, recognition, endorsement, and evaluation services.

6121 Armed Forces Communications and Electronics Association

4114 Legato Road
Fairfax, VA 22033

703-631-6100
800-336-4583; Fax: 703-631-6169
www.afcea.org
Facebook, Twitter, LinkedIn, Google+, Flickr, YouTube

Lt. Gen. Robert Shea, USMC (Ret.), President/CEO
Lt. Gen. John Wood, USA (Ret.), EVP, Defence/National Security
Pat Miorin, CPA, EVP/CFO/International Treasurer
James Griggs, Jr., VP/CIO/CTO
Beverly Cooper, VP, Comm. & Media/CKO/Publisher

A nonprofit international organization that serves its members by providing a forum for the ethical exchange of information and is dedicated to increasing knowledge through the exploration of issues relevant to information technology, communication, and electronics for the defense, homeland security and intelligence communities.
Founded in 1946

6122 Association for Executives in Healthcare Information Security (AEHIS)

710 Avis Drive
Suite 200
Ann Arbor, MI 48108

734-665-0000; Fax: 734-665-4922
staff@aehis.org
aehis.org
Twitter, LinkedIn

Russell Branzell, President & CEO
Michelle Patterson, VP, Operations
Tim Stettheimer, PhD, VP, Education

AEHIS is designed to provide an education and networking platform to healthcare's senior IT security leaders. AEHIS's mission is to advance the role of the Chief Information Security Officer (CISO) through education, collaboration and advocacy in support of secure health information for the protection of both consumers and healthcare organizations.
Founded in 2014

6123 Business Software Alliance

20 F Street NW
Suite 800
Washington, DC 20001

202-872-5500; Fax: 202-872-5501
info@bsa.org
www.bsa.org
Facebook, Twitter, LinkedIn, YouTube

Victoria A. Espinel, President & CEO
Adam J. Coates, General Counsel & VP
Ha McNeill, Chief Operating Officer
Joe DeSalvio, Chief Financial Officer

An organization dedicated to promoting a safe and legal digital world. BSA educates consumers on software management and copyright protection, cyber security, trade, e-commerce and other internet related issues.
Founded in 1988

6124 Center for Internet Security

31 Tech Valley Drive
East Greenbush, NY 12061

518-266-3460; Fax: 518-283-3216
www.cisecurity.org
Facebook, Twitter, LinkedIn, YouTube

John M. Gilligan, President & CEO
Albert Szesnat, CFO
Angelo Marcotullio, CIO
Brian Calkin, Chief HR Officer

A nonprofit organization that provides products and resources that help partners achieve security goals through expert guidance and cost-effective solutions.

6125 Cloud Security Alliance

2212 Queen Anne Avenue N
Seattle, WA 98109

info@cloudsecurityalliance.org
cloudsecurityalliance.org
Facebook, Twitter, LinkedIn, YouTube

Jim Reavis, Co-Founder & CEO
Daniele Catteddu, Chief Technology Officer
Dr. Hing Yan Lee, Executive Vice President
Jeffrey Westcott, Chief Financial Officer
Linda Strick, Managing Director

Cloud Security Alliance (CSA) is the world's leading organization dedicated to defining and raising awareness of best practices to help ensure a secure cloud computing environment.
Founded in 2009

6126 CompTIA

3500 Lacey Road
Suite 100
Downers Grove, IL 60515

630-678-8300
866-835-8020; Fax: 630-678-8384
www.comptia.org
Facebook, Twitter, LinkedIn, Pinterest, Google+, YouTube

Todd Thibodeaux, President & CEO
Brian Laffey, CFO
Randy Gross, CIO
Nancy Hammervik, Executive VP, Industry Relations
Kelly Ricker, Executive VP, Events & Education

A nonprofit trade association created by representatives of five microcomputer leaderships and is a provider of professional certifications for the information technology (IT) industry.

6127 Cyber Security Research Alliance

Home Page: www.cybersecurityresearch.org

A nonprofit organization founded by industry stakeholders as a forum develop R&D strategy to address grand challenges in cyber security, and to facilitate public-private partnerships that define a more focused, coordinated, and concerted approach to cyber security research and development.

6128 Cyber, Space, & Intelligence Association

Home Page: cyberspaceintel.org

Richard Coleman, Chairman, President & Founder
Tidal W. (Ty) McCoy, Senior Executive
Timothy J. Evans, Senior Advisor

To provide an environment for a vital flow of ideas between national security thought leaders in Government, Industry, and Congress focused Cyber, Space, and Intelligence challenges and opportunities.
Founded in 2011

6129 Cybersecurity Association

Santa Cruz, CA

info@cybersecurity.org
www.cybersecurity.org

Organization focused on testing the security capabilities and performance of firewalls, intrusion prevention systems and other similar security equipment.

6130 High Technology Crime Investigation Association

4 Lan Drive
Suite 310
Westford, MA 01886

978-364-5111; Fax: 978-250-1117
contact@htcia.org
www.htcia.org
Facebook, Twitter, LinkedIn

Anthony Reyes, President

A nonprofit professional organization devoted to the prevention, investigation, and prosecution of crimes involving advanced technologies.
Founded in 1984

6131 ISACA

847-660-5505
844-472-2246
www.isaca.org
Facebook, Twitter, LinkedIn, Google+

David Samuelson, CEO
Robb Micek, Chief Financial Officer
Nader Qaimari, Chief Learning Officer
Simona Rollinson, Chief Technology Officer

A nonprofit, independent association that advocates for professionals involved in information security, assurance, risk management and governance.
Founded in 1969

6132 Information Systems Security Association

1654 Gallows Road
Suite 310
Vienna, VA 22182

703-382-8205
www.issa.org
Facebook, Twitter, LinkedIn, Instagram, YouTube

Marc Thompson, Executive Director
Lisa O'Connell, Sales/Sponsorships

International information and professional growth organization of information security professionals.

6133 InfraGard

InfraGardTeam@fbi.gov
www.infragard.org
RSS

A nonprofit organization serving as a public-private partnership between U.S. businesses and the Federal Bureau of Investigation.

6134 Institute for Security, Technology, and Society

Dartmouth College

7 Maynard St
Sudikoff Laboratory
Hanover, NH 03755

603-646-0700; Fax: 603-646-1672
info.ists@dartmouth.edu
www.ists.dartmouth.edu
Facebook, Twitter, Flickr, YouTube

V.S. Subrahmanian, Research Director
Bill Nisen, Associate Director
Julie Gilman, Program Administrator

Organization dedicated to pursuing research and education to advance information security and privacy throughout society.
Founded in 2000

6135 **Intelligence & National Security Alliance**
Arlington, VA 22203

703-224-4672
info@insaonline.org
www.insaonline.org
Facebook, Twitter, LinkedIn, YouTube, Instagram

Suzanne Wilson Heckenberg, President
Larry Hanauer, VP for Policy
Jeff Lavine, VP for Administration/Management
Toya Cribbs, Director, Meetings/Events
Lauren Parker, Membership Manager

Public, private and academic leaders collaborate on intelligence and national security issues.
160 Members

6136 **International Association for Cryptologic Research**
Home Page: www.iacr.org
Facebook, Twitter, YouTube, Weibo

A non-profit scientific organization whose purpose is to further research in cryptology and related fields.
Founded in 1982

6137 **International Association of Security Awareness Professionals**
170 Main Street
Westhampton Beach, NY 11978

team@iasapgroup.org
iasapgroup.org
Twitter, LinkedIn

The International Association of Security Awareness Professionals is comprised of member participants who are responsible for developing and implementing the information security awareness programs for their respective organizations.
Founded in 2003

6138 **International Info System Security Certification Consortium**
311 Park Place Blvd
Suite 400
Clearwater, FL 33759

727-785-0189
866-331-4722
membersupport@isc2.org
www.isc2.org
Facebook, Twitter, LinkedIn, YouTube

David Shearer, CEO
Wesley Simpson, COO
Debra Taylor, CFO

International association of information security professionals.
125K Members
Founded in 1989

6139 **Internet Merchants Association**
info@imamerchants.org
www.imamerchants.org
Facebook

Fred Neff, President
Scott Cole, Vice President
Doyle Carver, Secretary
Andy Sollofe, Treasurer

Develops, promotes, and protects the economic vitality of internet merchants through a positive business environment and fosters a climate in whichcommerce, industry, and technology will flourish.

6140 **Internet Security Alliance**
2500 Wilson Blvd.
Suite 245
Arlington, VA 22201

703-907-7090
admin@isalliance.org
isalliance.org
Twitter, LinkedIn

Larry Clinton, President & CEO
Josh Higgins, Director, Policy & Communications

A nonprofit organization that acts as a forum for information sharing and leadership on information security, and it lobbies for corporate securityinterests.
Founded in 2001

6141 **National Council of ISACs**
Home Page: www.nationalisacs.org

Denise Anderson, Chair
Joshua Poster, Vice Chair

Coordinating body for 25 information sharing and analysis centers (ISACs).
25 Members
Founded in 2003

6142 **National Cyber Security Alliance**
1010 Vermont Avenue NW
Washington, DC 20005

info@staysafeonline.org
staysafeonline.org
Facebook, Twitter, LinkedIn, YouTube

Kelvin Coleman, Executive Director

Seeks to bring education and awareness to the forefront of cyber security; To educate and empower the global digital society to use the internet safely and securely.
Founded in 2001

6143 **National Cyber-Forensics & Training Alliance**
2000 Technology Drive
Suite 450
Pittsburgh, PA 15219

412-802-8000; Fax: 412-802-8510
info@ncfta.net
www.ncfta.net

A nonprofit corporation focused on identifying, mitigating, and neutralizing cyber crime threats through strategic alliances and partnerships with Subject Matter Experts (SME) in the public, private, and academic sectors.
Founded in 2002

6144 **National CyberWatch Center**
301 Largo Road
Room 129C
Largo, MD 20774

info@nationalcyberwatch.org
www.nationalcyberwatch.org
Facebook, Twitter, LinkedIn, YouTube

Casey W. O'Brien, Executive Director
Fran Melvin, Finance Director
Costis Toregas, Senior Advisor
Lynn Dohm, Marketing/Communications Director

An organization of higher education institutions, public and private schools, businesses, and government agencies focused on educating and supporting the national cybersecurity workforce.
300+ Members
Founded in 2008

6145 **National Cybersecurity Student Association**
301 Largo Road
Room 129C
Largo, MD 20774

414-544-4496
info@cyberstudents.org
www.cyberstudents.org
Facebook, Twitter, LinkedIn, YouTube, Snapchat

Gustavo Hinojosa, Executive Director
Vitaly Ford, Director of Chapter Development

This group supports the cybersecurity educational programs of academic institutions, inspires career awareness and encourages creative efforts to increase the number of graduates in the field.
Founded in 2016

6146 **National Cybersecurity and Communications Integration Center**
245 Murray Lane SW
Building 410
Washington, DC 20598

888-282-0870
cscexternalaffairs@hq.dhs.gov
www.us-cert.gov/nccic
Twitter, RSS

Serves as a central location where a diverse set of partners involved in cybersecurity and communications protection coordinate and synchronize their efforts. Partners include other government agencies, the private sector, and international entities.

6147 **National Initiative for Cybersecurity Careers and Studies**
NICCS@hq.dhs.gov
niccs.us-cert.gov

A national resource for cybersecurity awareness, education, careers, and training.

6148 **Women in Cybersecurity**
370 S Lowe Avenue
Cookeville, TN 38501

talywalsh@wicys.org
www.wicys.org
Facebook, Twitter, LinkedIn, Instagram, Flickr

Taly Walsh, Emeritus Executive Director
Lynn Dohm, Executive Director

WiCyS is the only non-profit membership organization with national reach that is dedicated to bringing together women in cybersecurity from academia, research and industry to share knowledge, experience, networking and mentoring.
Founded in 2012

Newsletters

6149 **ATM Industry Association Global Newsletter**
ATM Industry Association

Home Page:
www.atmia.com/media/atmia-global-newsletter

/
Facebook, Twitter, LinkedIn, YouTube

Mike Lee, CEO
David Tente, Executive Director, USAÿ
Dana Benson, Dir., Conferences & Sponsorships

Alliance promoting the proliferation of automated teller machines, ATMs and cash.
5000 Members
Founded in 1997

6150 **Dot.COM**
Business Communications Company
25 Van Zant Street
Suite 13
Norwalk, CT 06855-1713

203-853-4266; Fax: 203-853-0348
sales@bccresearch.com
www.bccresearch.com

Louis Naturman, Publisher
C Toenne, Editor

Updates readers on the commercial use of the Internet and related platforms.
Cost: $38.00

6151 **E-Healthcare Market Reporter**
Health Resources Publishing
1913 Atlantic Ave
Suite 200
Manasquan, NJ 08736-1067

732-292-1100
888-843-6242; Fax: 732-292-1111
info@themcic.com
www.hin.com/ehealth.html

Robert K Jenkins, Publisher
Judith Granel, Marketing
John Russel, Editor
Brett Powell, Regional Director
Alice Burron, Director

A bi-monthly covering strategies, new products, innovation, privacy issue, business solutions, service available, vendor news and comparative for implementing sales and marketing on the internet.
Cost: $397.00
Frequency: Fortnightly
ISSN: 1098-5654
Founded in 1988

6152 **Internet Alliance Cyberbrief**
Internet Alliance
1615 L Street NW
Suite 1100
Washington, DC 20036-5624

202-861-2407
www.internetalliance.my

Tammy Cota, Executive Director

Coverage of public policy changes in government, enhancing consumer satisfaction in interactive services, and education.
Frequency: Weekly

6153 **Internet Business**
Information Gatekeepers
1340 Soldiers Field Rd
Suite 3
Brighton, MA 02135-1000

617-782-5033
800-323-1088; Fax: 617-782-5735
info@igigroup.com
www.igigroup.com

Paul Polishuk, CEO
Hui Pan, Chief Analyst, Editor in Chief
Bev Wilson, Managing Editor

Covers the rapid developments in the industry.
Cost: $695.00
Frequency: Monthly

6154 **Internet World**
Mecklermedia Corporation
20 Ketchum Street
Westport, CT 06880

212-260-0758; Fax: 203-454-5840

Bill Besch, Publisher

Internet industry news, product reviews and technical reports, with an emphasis on Internet technology, hardware, management and security.
Cost: $160.00
Frequency: Weekly
Circulation: 98,947

6155 **Mealey's Litigation Report: Cyber Tech & E -Commerce**
LexisNexis Mealey's
555 W 5th Avenue
Los Angeles, CA 90013

213-627-1130
mealeyinfo@lexisnexis.com
www.lexisnexis.com/mealeys

Tom Hagy, VP/General Manager
Maureen McGuire, Editorial Director
Mark Rogers, Editor

The Report covers disputes arising from e-commerce. The report tracks emerging legal issues, including: Internet security, data destruction and/or alteration, defamation on the Web, software errors, hardware failure, electronic theft, e-mail trespass, online privacy, government action, shareholder lawsuits, Internet jurisdiction issues, file sharing (copyright) disputes and much more.
Cost: $999.00
100 Pages
Frequency: Monthly
Founded in 1999

6156 **National CyberWatch Communicator**
National CyberWatch Center
301 Largo Road
Room 129C
Largo, MD 20774

301-546-0452
bbelon@nationalcyberwatch.org
www.nationalcyberwatch.org

Casey W. O'Brien, Executive Director
Fran Melvin, Program Coordinator
Costis Toregas, Business Development Director
Barbara Huffman de Bel¢n, Membership Director

Newsletter published by the National CyberWatch Center featuring news on the association's events and programs.
300+ Members
Frequency: Monthly
Founded in 2008

6157 **Online Reporter**
G2 Computer Intelligence
PO Box 7
Glen Head, NY 11545-1616

516-759-7025; Fax: 516-759-7028
www.g2news.com

Maureen O'Gara, Publisher

Information on recent developments on the Internet through news briefs and a section called Chat Room. Includes information on e-commerce, Java and network security.
Cost: $695.00
Frequency: Weekly

6158 **Privacy Journal**
P.O. Box 28577
Providence, RI 02908

401-274-7861; Fax: 401-274-4747
orders@privacyjournal.net
www.privacyjournal.net

Robert Ellis Smith, Publisher

An independent monthly on privacy in a computer age.
Cost: $65.00
Frequency: Monthly
ISSN: 0145-7659
Founded in 1974
Printed in one color

6159 **The CyberSkeptic's Guide to Internet Research**
Information Today
143 Old Marlton Pike
Medford, NJ 08055-8750

609-654-6266
800-300-9868; Fax: 609-654-4309
custserv@infotoday.com
www.infotoday.com

Thomas H Hogan, President
Roger R Bilboul, Chairman Of The Board

A monthly subscription newsletter in print, that explores and evaluates free and low cost Web sites and search strategies to help you use the Internet and stay up to date.
Cost: $164.95
ISSN: 1085-2417

Magazines & Journals

6160 **Active Server Developer's Journal**
ZD Journals
500 Canal View Boulevard
Rochester, NY 14623-2800

585-407-7301; Fax: 585-214-2387
asp@zdjournals.com
www.asdj.com

Jon Pyles, Publisher
Taggard Andrews

Addresses such issues as database publishing, creating hack-proof files and getting the most out of server-side components. Special sections focus on client-side solutions, covering the basics and taking an in-depth look at more detailed techniques.
Cost: $149.00
Frequency: Monthly

6161 **CompTIA World**
CompTIA
3500 Lacey Road
Suite 100
Downers Grove, IL 60515

630-678-8300
866-835-8020; Fax: 630-678-8384
www.comptia.org
Facebook, Twitter, LinkedIn, Pinterest, Google+, YouTube

Daniel Margolis, Senior Managing Editor

Association of IT professionals offers certification programs and skills development.

6162 **Electronic Commerce Advisor**
Thomson Reuters
195 Broadway # 4
New York, NY 10007-3124

646-822-2000
800-231-1860; Fax: 646-822-2800
trta.lei-support@thomsonreuters.com
www.ria.thomsonreuters.com

Elaine Yadlon, Plant Manager
Thomas H Glocer, CEO & Director
Robert D Daleo, Chief Financial Officer
Kelli Crane, Senior Vice President & CIO

Offers the latest in electronic commerce covering what's available and how to select and employ the best technology without costly trial-and-error mistakes. Information on EDI, e-mail, fax gateways, Internet, encryption, VANs, procurement cards, imaging, voice re-

sponse, remote computering and other related information.
Cost: $155.00
Circulation: 4500
Founded in 1940

6163 ISACA Journal
3701 Algonquin Road
Suite 1010
Rolling Meadows, IL 60008ÿ
847-253-1545; Fax: 847-253-1443
www.isaca.org
Facebook, Twitter, LinkedIn
David Samuelson, CEO
Provides professional development information to those spearheading IT governance and those involved with information systems audit, control and security
Founded in 1969

6164 ISSA Journal
Information Systems Security Association
1964 Gallows Road
Suite 310
Vienna, VA 22182
703-382-8205
www.issa.org
Facebook, Twitter, LinkedIn, Instagram, YouTube
Thom Barrie, Editor
International information and professional growth organization of information security professionals.

6165 Information Security
International Computer Security Association
117 Kendrick Street
Suite 800
Needham, MA 02494
781-657-1000; Fax: 781-657-1100
lwalsh@infosecuritymag.com
www.infosecuritymag.com
Andrew Briney, VP
Lawrence Walsh, Editor
Michael S Mimoso, Senior Editor
Gabrielle DeRussy, Advertising Sales
Susan Rastellini Smith, Product Management
Articles and analysis of information-security issues such as media, entwork and virus protection, internet security and encryption reports.
Cost: $100.00
Frequency: Monthly
Circulation: 60000
Founded in 1999

6166 Innovations in Cybersecurity Education
National CyberWatch Center
301 Largo Road
Room 129C
Largo, MD 20774
301-546-0452
bbelon@nationalcyberwatch.org
www.nationalcyberwatch.org
Casey W. O'Brien, Executive Director
Fran Melvin, Program Coordinator
Costis Toregas, Business Development Director
Barbara Huffman de Bel¢n, Membership Director
Journal covering subjects of relevance to cybersecurity education.
300+ Members
Founded in 2008

Trade Shows

6167 (ISC)ý Security Congress
(ISC)ý
311 Park Place Blvd
Suite 400
Clearwater, FL 33759
727-785-0189
866-331-4722
membersupport@isc2.org
congress.isc2.org
Facebook, Twitter, LinkedIn
Jessica Hardy, Director, Customer Experience
Cybersecurity conference of the International Info System Security Certification Consortium.
1900 Attendees

6168 (ISC)ý Security Congress APAC
(ISC)ý
311 Park Place Blvd
Suite 400
Clearwater, FL 33759
727-785-0189
866-331-4722
membersupport@isc2.org
apaccongress.isc2.org
Facebook, Twitter, LinkedIn
Information security conference in Asia Pacific.
350 Attendees

6169 ATM Industry Association
ATM Industry Association
Home Page: www.atmia.com/conferences/us
Facebook, LinkedIn, YouTube
Mike Lee, CEO
David Tente, Executive Director, USA
Dana Benson, Dir., Conferences & Sponsorships
Alliance promoting the proliferation of automated teller machines, ATMs and cash.
10000 Members
Founded in 1997

6170 Community College Cyber Summit (3CS)
National CyberWatch Center
301 Largo Road
Room 129C
Largo, MD 20774
301-546-0452
info@3CS.nationalcyberwatch.org
www.my3cs.org
Facebook, Twitter, Flickr
Casey W. O'Brien, Executive Director
Fran Melvin, Program Coordinator
Costis Toregas, Business Development Director
Barbara Huffman de Bel¢n, Membership Director
Academic conference centered on the theme of cybersecurity education at community colleges, for teachers and students.
300+ Members
Founded in 2008

6171 Cyber Security Summit
Home Page: www.cybersecuritysummit.org
Facebook, Twitter, LinkedIn
Andrew Borene, Esq., Chair
Because of the scope of cyber threats, the Summit endeavors to bring together all stakeholders - industry, government and academia - to improve cyber security.
Frequency: Annual
Founded in 2011

6172 DMD New York Conference & Expo
Direct Marketing Conferences
20 Academy Street
Norwalk, CT 06850-4032
203-854-9166
800-969-6566
connecticut@dmdays.com
www.dmdays.com
Direct Marketing Days New York offers new ideas in media, creative, database, eCommerce and technology. Hundreds of exhibits showcase the newest technologies, products and services. Over 85 sessions and 25 consultation centers led by A level speakers. Network with top-level executives.
Frequency: Annual/June

6173 GovSec
National Trade Productions
313 S Patrick Street
Alexandria, VA 22314
703-838-8500; Fax: 703-836-4486
www.govsecinfo.com
Denise Medved, General Manager
Provides a full spectrum of security solutions for federal, state, and local governments tasked with developing comprehensive strategies that address physical security, information security and cyber security needs. Educational programs held in conjunction with displays of a wide variety of security products and services designed specifically for government users.
Frequency: Annual/May

6174 Intelligence and National Security Summit
Intelligence & National Security Alliance
Arlington, VA 22203
703-224-4672
info@insaonline.org
www.insaonline.org
Facebook, Twitter, LinkedIn, YouTube, Instagram
Discussion of the threats and challenges facing the Intelligence Community.

6175 WiCyS Conference
Women in CyberSecurity
370 S Lowe Avenue
Cookeville, TN 38501
Home Page: www.wicys.org
Taly Walsh, Emeritus Executive Director
Lynn Dohm, Executive Director
This event provides women students with networking opportunities within the cyber security industry.
Founded in 2012

Directories & Databases

6176 ATM Industry Association Member Directory
ATM Industry Association
Home Page: www.atmia.com/connections/members/member-directory
Facebook, Twitter, LinkedIn, YouTube
Mike Lee, CEO
Alliance promoting the proliferation of automated teller machines, ATMs and cash.
10000 Members
Founded in 1997

6177 CyberWatch Center Academic Institution Members
National CyberWatch Center

301 Largo Road
Room 129C
Largo, MD 20774

301-546-0452
bbelon@nationalcyberwatch.org
www.nationalcyberwatch.org

Casey W. O'Brien, Executive Director
Fran Melvin, Program Coordinator
Costis Toregas, Business Development Director
Barbara Huffman de Bel¢n, Membership Director

Directory listing academic institution members of the National CyberWatch Center.
300+ Members
Founded in 2008

Industry Web Sites

6178 **SANS Institute**
8120 Woodmont Ave
Suite 310
Bethesda, MD 20814

301-654-7267; Fax: 301-951-0140
info@sans.org
www.sans.org
Twitter

Research and education organization for information security professionals.
Founded in 1989

6179 **Stay Safe Online**
National Cyber Security Alliance

Home Page: www.staysafeonline.org
Facebook, Twitter, LinkedIn, Google+, YouTube
Michael Kaiser, Executive Director
Jennifer Cook, Program & Events Coordinator
Betty Hallman, Dir., Devel. & Strat. Partnerships
Tiffany Schoenike, Dir., Campaigns & Initiatives
Lisa Tumminello, Dir., Communications

A nonprofit, public-private partnership working with the Departmentof Homeland Security (DHS), private sector sponsors, and nonprofit collaboratorsto promote cyber security awareness for home users, small and medium size businesses, and primary and secondary education.

6180 **www.bsa.org**
Business Software Alliance

An organization dedicated to promoting a safe and legal digital world. BSA educates consumers on software management and copyright protection, cyber security, trade, e-commerce and other internet related issues.

6181 **www.cisecurity.org**
Center for Internet Security

Helps organizations around the world effectively manage the risks related to internet security.

6182 **www.nationalcyberwatch.org**
National CyberWatch Center

Facebook, Twitter, LinkedIn, YouTube

Association made up of education institutions, public and private schools, businesses, and government agencies engaged in educating and supporting the national cybersecurity workforce.

6183 **www.nga.org/cms/statecyber**
National Governors Association
Hall of the States
444 N Capitol St., Suite 267
Washington, DC 20001-1512

202-624-5300; Fax: 202-624-5313
www.nga.org
Facebook, Twitter

Gov. Gary Herbert, Utah, Chair
Gov. Terry McAuliffe, Virginia

Tools and resources to help states improve their cybersecurity policies and practices. Provided by the National Governors Association.

Associations

6184 **American Marketing Association**
130 E. Randolph Street
22nd Floor
Chicago, IL 60601

800-262-1150
customersupport@ama.org
www.ama.org
Facebook, Twitter, LinkedIn

Russ Klein, Chief Executive Officer
Julie Schnidman, VP, Alliances
Adara Bowen, VP, Growth
Molly Soat, VP, Professional Development
Jeremy Van Ek, Chief Operations Officer

The AMA is a professional association for individuals and organizations leading the practice, teaching and development of marketing knowledge worldwide. Their principle role is to serve as a forum to connect like-minded individuals and foster knowledge sharing, provide resources, tools and training and support marketing practice and thought leadership around the globe.
40000 Members
Founded in 1953

6185 **American Teleservices Association**
5250 E. US 36
Suite 1102B
Avon, IN 46123

317-816-9336
www.ataconnect.org
Facebook, Twitter, LinkedIn

Tim Searcy, CEO

Represents the call centers, trainers, consultants and equipment suppliers that initiate, facilitate and generate telephone, Internet and e-mail sales, service and support.
240 Members

6186 **Art Directors Club**
106 W 29th St
New York, NY 10001-5301

212-643-1440; Fax: 212-643-4266
info@adcglobal.org
www.adcglobal.org
Facebook, Twitter, LinkedIn, Pinterest

Ami Brophy, CEO
Jon Kamen, VP
Vickie Peslak, Second VP
Thomas Mueller, Secretary
Myrna Davis, Executive Director

An international nonprofit organization of leading creatives in advertising, graphic design, interactive media, broadcast design, typography, packaging, environmental design, photography, illustration and related disciplines.
1200 Members
Founded in 1920
Mailing list available for rent

6187 **Association for Postal Commerce**
1800 Diagonal Road
Suite 600
Alexandria, VA 22314

703-524-0096; Fax: 703-997-2414
info@postcom.org
www.postcom.org
Twitter, LinkedIn

Michael Plunkett, President & CEO
Ellena Talbott, Director, Operations & Membership
Beth McConnell, Postal Consultant
Matthew Field, General Counsel

National organization representing those who use, or who support, the use of mail as a medium for communication and commerce. Publishes a weekly newsletter covering postal policy and operational issues.
231 Members
Founded in 1947

6188 **Association of Direct Marketing Agencies**
Cohn & Wells
350 Hudson Street
New York, NY 10014-4504

212-192-2278; Fax: 212-302-6714

John A Greco Jr, President/CEO

Members are direct response advertising agencies.
100 Members

6189 **Association of Marketing Service Providers**
1800 Diagonal Road
Suite 320
Alexandria, VA 22314-2806

703-836-9200; Fax: 703-548-8204
kgarner@mfsanet.org
www.amsp.org

Joseph P. Truncale, President & CEO
Ken Garner, Chief Operating Officer
Dean D'Ambrosi, Chief Financial Officer
Andrew D. Paparozzi, SVP & Chief Economist
Leo Raymond, VP, Postal & Member Relations

Formerly known as the Mailing & Fulfillment Service Association, the Association of Marketing Service Providers provides educational content, networking opportunities, and legislative advocacy.

6190 **Association of National Advertisers**
Association of National Advertisers
10 Grand Central, 155 E. 44th Street
New York, NY 10017

212-697-5950; Fax: 212-687-7310
info@ana.net
www.ana.net
Facebook, Twitter, LinkedIn, Instagram

Bob Liodice, Chief Executive Officer
Christine Manna, President & COO
Brian Davidson, EVP, Membership
Mark Liebert, SVP, Marketing Training & Dev.
Kathleen Hunter, EVP, Marketing Knowledge Center

The Association of National Advertisers (ANA) is the advertising industry's oldest trade association. Currently, the ANA leads the marketing community by providing its members insights, collaboration, and advocacy. ANA's membership includes 20,000 brands that collectively spend over $400 billion in marketing communications and advertising. ANA acquired the Brand Activation Association in 2014.
1000 Members
Founded in 1910

6191 **Association of Teleservices International**
222 South Westmonte Drive
Suite 111
Altamonte Springs, FL 32714

866-896-2874; Fax: 407-774-6440
admin@atsi.org
atsi.org
Facebook, Twitter, LinkedIn

Tifani Leal, President
Jeff Rosgen, VP-Treasurer
Susan Mealer, VP-Secretary

An international trade association established by and for entrepreneurs in the TeleServices business. It provides a wide variety of services to businesses, governmental agencies, local emergency respondents and the general public.
35000 Members
Founded in 1942

6192 **Business Marketing Association: Atlanta**
13 Corporate Square
Suite 100
Atlanta, GA 30329

404-641-9417
800-664-4262; Fax: 312-822-0054
info@bmaatlanta.com
Facebook, Twitter

Ed King, President-Elect
John Wiley, Marketing & Public Relations
Barry Mirkin, Development & Research
Stacey Krizan, Membership/Education/Certification
Joe Noonan, Programs Co-Chair

The Atlanta chapter of the BMA includes marketing executives from a variety of industries and backgrounds including research, advertising, promotions, events, Web development, printing and more. The BMA offers an information-packed Web site, online skills-building, marketing certification programs, and industry surveys and papers. In addition, members have the opportunity to interact with peers at seminars, participate in chapter training programs and the BMA Annual Conference.

6193 **Business Marketing Association: Boston**
246 Hampshire Street
Cambridge, MA 02130

617-418-4000
800-664-4262; Fax: 312-822-0054
www.thebmaboston.com/

Michael Lewis, President
Will Robinson, VP Public Relations
Matthew Mamet, VP Internet Marketing
Larry Perreault, VP Finance
Chris Perkett, VP Programming

BMA Boston helps members improve their ability to manage business-to-business marketing and communications for greater productivity and profitability by providing unique access to information, ideas, and the experience of peers. The BMA offers an information-packed Website, online skills-building, marketing certification programs, and industry surveys and papers. In addition, members have the opportunity to interact with peers at seminars, chapter training programs and the BMA Annual Conference.

6194 **Cable & Telecommunications Association for Marketing**
120 Waterfront Street
Suite 200
National Harbor, MD 20745

301-485-8900
info@ctam.com
www.ctam.com
Twitter, LinkedIn

Vicki Lins, President & CEO
Angie Britt, SVP, Advanced Products
Zell Murphy, SVP, Finance & Administration
Mark Snow, SVP & GM, Consumer Marketing
Ken Leonardo, VP, Marketing

Provides marketing knowledge and industry scale to help its membersmanage the future and drive business results. Also provides consumer research, industry resources, a job bank, conferences and awards.

6195 **Color Marketing Group**
1908 Mount Vernon Avenue
3rd Floor
Alexandria, VA 22301

703-329-8500; Fax: 703-535-3190
sgriffis@colormarketing.org
www.colormarketing.org

Facebook, Twitter, LinkedIn, Pinterest, Instagram

Judith van Vliet, President
Paula Lord, VP, Marketing
Sandy Sampson, VP, Communications & PR
Peggy van Allen, VP, Color Forecasting
Sharon Griffis, Executive Director

A nonprofit international association of color designers involved in the use of color as it applies to the profitable marketing of goods and services.
1300 Members
Founded in 1962

6196 **Culture Marketing Council**
8280 Willow Oaks Corporate Drive
Suite 600
Fairfax, VA 22031

703-745-5531; Fax: 703-610-0227
info@culturemarketingcouncil.org
culturemarketingcouncil.org
Facebook, Twitter, LinkedIn, YouTube

Gonzalo Del Fa, Chair
Isabella Sanchez, Treasurer
Horacio Gavilan, Executive Director

Formerly known as the Association of Hispanic Advertising Agencies and AHAA: The Voice of Hispanic Marketing, the Culture Marketing Council represents the Hispanic marketing, communications and media industry.
45000 Members
Founded in 1996

6197 **Digital Analytics Association**
401 Edgewater Place
Suite 600
Wakefield, WA 1880

781-876-8933; Fax: 781-224-1239
info@digitalanalyticsassociation.org
www.digitalanalyticsassociation.org
Facebook, Twitter, LinkedIn

Marilee Yorchak, Executive Director
Adrienne Segundo, Education Manager
Matt Dirks, Director, Sponsorships
Catherine Hackney, Community Manager
Brooke Weldon, Membership Manager

Formerly known as the Web Analytics Association, it is a global organization of practitioners, corporations, vendors, marketing and public relations agencies, consultants, academics, and more involved in the growing digital analytics industry.
Founded in 2004

6198 **Digital Concepts for Business**
PO Box 745
Suite 102
Crystal Lake, IL 60039-0745

815-575-0089; Fax: 847-458-5134
info@dcfb.com
www.dcfb.com
Facebook, Twitter, LinkedIn, Google+, Pinterest

Mary Owens, Owner

Provides services to companies throughout the US and is dedicated to providing high-quality business communcations solutions using the latest hardware and software for both PC and Macintosh.
Founded in 1996

6199 **Direct International**
1501 3rd Avenue
New York, NY 10028-2101

212-861-4188; Fax: 212-986-3757

Alfred Goodloe, President

Offers publications and services for the international direct marketing executive.

6200 **Direct Marketing Association**
1120 Avenue of the Americas
New York, NY 10036-6700

212-768-7277; Fax: 212-302-6714
thedma.org
Facebook, Twitter, LinkedIn

Thomas J. Benton, Chief Executive Officer
Bob Greco, SVP of Operations, Finance & Events
Peggy Hudson, SVP, Government Affairs
Linsay Hutter, SVP, Communications
Xenia Boone, JD, SVP, General Counsel

Advances and protects responsible data-driven marketing.

6201 **Direct Selling Association**
1667 K St NW
Suite 1100
Washington, DC 20006-1660

202-452-8866; Fax: 202-452-9010
info@dsa.org
www.dsa.org
Facebook, Twitter, LinkedIn, Vimeo, YouTube, Instagram

Joseph N. Mariano, President & CEO
Adolfo Franco, EVP & CFO
Melissa K. Brunton, SVP, Education & Meeting Services
Brian Bennett, VP, Government Affairs & Policy
Nancy M. Burke, VP, Membership

National trade organization of the leading firms that manufacture and distribute goods and services sold directly to consumers. Members of the association are copanies including many well-known brand names. The association's mission is to protect, serve and promote the effectiveness of member companies and the independent business people they represent.
Founded in 1910

6202 **Direct-to-Direct Marketing Association Council for Hispanic Marketing**
Direct Marketing Association
1120 Avenue of the Americas
New York, NY 10036-6700

212-768-7277; Fax: 212-768-6714
thedma.org

Allison Longley, Manager

Provides education, information and networking opportunities for direct marketing professionals targeting the Hispanic market.
120 Members
Founded in 1992

6203 **EMarketing Association**
251 W. 30th Street
6th Floor
New York, NY 10001

212-678-2520
admin@emarketingassociation.com
www.emarketingassociation.com
Twitter, LinkedIn, YouTube

International association of eMarketing professionals committed to enriching the marketing community and its members through recognition, research, advocacy, education, and service.
Founded in 1997

6204 **Internet Marketing Association**
200 Spectrum Center Drive
Irvine, CA 92618

949-443-9300
info@imanetwork.org
imanetwork.org
Facebook, Twitter, LinkedIn, YouTube

Sinan Kanatsiz, Chair & Founder
Sean Conrad, CEO
Lei Lani Fera, Head Of Creative
Hall Roosevelt, General Manager
Marcus Volpe, Executive Director

Seeks to provide members with the chance to learn, network, and establish Internet Marketing best practices. Members are in fields such as sales, marketing, business ownership, programming, and creative development.
Founded in 2001

6205 **Life Insurance Direct Marketing Association**
3227 S. Cherokee Lane
Suite 1320
Woodstock, GA 30188

770-516-0207
866-890-5323
info@lidma.org
lidma.org

Robert Bland, President
Nicole Buckenmeyer, Vice President
Jeff McCauley, Secretary-Treasurer
Brian Barnes, Membership Vice Chair

A nonprofit organization dedicated specifically to supporting businesses and professionals active in direct sales of term life insurance products to consumers.

6206 **Mail Advertising Service Association**
1800 Diagonal Road
Suite 320
Alexandria, VA 22314-2862

703-836-9200; Fax: 703-548-8204
www.mfsanet.org
Facebook, Twitter, LinkedIn, YouTube, Pinterest, Google+

Ken Garner, President and CEO
Tom Saggiomo, Vice Chairman
John Rafner, Second Vice Chairman
Wayne Marshall, Treasurer

Supports all those involved in the mailing, addressing, and inserting industries.
Founded in 2014

6207 **Mailing & Fulfillment Service Association**
c/o Business Extension Bureau
4802 Travis
Houston, TX 77002

713-275-9045
joyz@bebtexas.com
themfsa.org
Facebook, Twitter, LinkedIn

Phil Gage, President
James Kelley, Second Vice President
Ron Royall, Secretary
Sandy Gaddie, Treasurer

The national trade association for the mailing and fulfillment services industry.

6208 **Midwest Direct Marketing Association**
P.O. Box 75
Suite S256
Andover, MN 55304

763-607-2943; Fax: 763-753-2240
office@mdma.org
www.mdma.org

Ed Harrington, Manager
Ben DuBois, Director

Dedicated to the advancement of professional and ethical practice of direct response marketing by members throughout the Upper Midwest.
600 Members
Founded in 1960

6209 Mobile Marketing Association
41 E. 11th Street
11th floor
New York, NY 10003
646-257-4515
mma@mmaglobal.com
www.mmaglobal.com
Facebook, Twitter, LinkedIn

Greg Stuart, CEO
Sheryl Daija, Chief Strategy Officer
Vassilis Bakopoulos, SVP, Industry Research
Andy Goldman, VP, Finance

A global nonprofit trade association comprised of more than 800 member companies that strive to accelerate the transformation and innovation of marketing through mobile technology, including emerging technologies such as 5G and artificial intelligence, driving business growth with closer and stronger consumerengagement.
800 Members

6210 Mobile Marketing Research Association
1006 Morgans Landing Drive
Atlanta, GA 30350
404-308-7173
mark@mmra-global.org
www.mmra-global.org
Facebook, Twitter, LinkedIn, YouTube

Rick West, President
Mark Michelson, Executive Director

A global trade association dedicated to the promotion and development of professional standards and ethics for conducting marketing research on mobile devices.
Founded in 2011

6211 Multi-Level Marketing International Association
119 Stanford Court
Irvine, CA 92612
949-854-0484
info@mlmia.com
www.mlmia.com
Facebook, Twitter

Doris Wood, Chair
Carrol Leclerc, President, Canada
Tony Cannuli, COO

A nonprofit professional trade organization representing all sectors of the networking marketing industry on a worldwide basis.
Founded in 1985

6212 North American Farmers' Direct Marketing Association
6161 N. Hillside Avenue
Indianapolis, IN 46220
855-623-3621
suzi@farmersinspired.com
nafdma.com

Suzi Spahr, Executive Director
Lisa Dean, Membership & Communications Manager
Jeff Winston, Education & Operations Manager

A membership association that advances the prosperity of its members and the farm direct marketing industry through networking, participation, education, and innovation.

6213 Professional Association for Customer Engagement
5250 E. US 36
Suite 1102B
Avon, IN 46123
317-816-9336
www.paceassociation.com
Facebook, Twitter, LinkedIn

Stuart Discount, CEO
Christine Haerich, SVP
Susan Burt, Director, Finance & Business Admin.

PACE is a nonprofit trade organization dedicated exclusively to the advancement of companies that utilize contact centers as an integral channel of operations.

6214 Society of Publication Designers
27 Union Square West
Suite 207
New York, NY 10003
212-223-3332; Fax: 212-223-5880
mail@spd.org
www.spd.org
Facebook, Twitter, LinkedIn, Instagram, Spotify

Jeff Glendenning, President
David Matt, Vice President
Trevett McCandliss, Vice President
Keisha Dean, Executive Director
Chelsey Lamwatt, Communications Director

An organization dedicated to promoting and encouraging excellence in editorial design. Members include art directors, designers, photo editors, editors, and graphics professionals.
Founded in 1965

6215 World Federation of Direct Selling Associations
1667 K Street NW
Suite 1100
Washington, DC 20006
202-416-6442
info@wfdsa.org
wfdsa.org
Facebook, Twitter, YouTube

Magnus Brannstrom, Chair
Tamuna Gabilaia, Executive Director & COO
Maureen Paniagua, Manager, International

International organization representing the direct selling industry around the world.
Founded in 1978

Newsletters

6216 Business Owner
Mailing & Fulfillment Service Association
1421 Prince Street
Suite 410
Alexandria, VA 22314-2806
703-836-9200; Fax: 703-548-8204
www.mfsanet.org

David L Perkins Jr, Editor

Developed specifically to communicate with owners and CEOs on issues unique to them. You'll receive a wealth of knowledge on growing your business, tax issues, insurance, estate planning, management, finance and much more.
Frequency: Bi-Monthly

6217 Career News Update
American Marketing Association
311 S Wacker Dr
Suite 5800
Chicago, IL 60606-6629
312-542-9000
800-262-1150; Fax: 312-542-9001
www.marketingpower.com

Dennis Dunlap, CEO

You'll receive the latest career and hiring advice as well as useful job resources and employment listings.
Frequency: Monthly

6218 Color Alerts
1908 Mount Vernon Avenue
3rd Floor
Alexandria, VA 22301
703-329-8500; Fax: 703-535-3190
sgriffis@colormarketing.org
www.colormarketing.org

Judith van Vliet, President
Paula Lord, VP, Marketing
Sandy Sampson, VP, Communications & PR
Peggy van Allen, VP, Color Forecasting
Sharon Griffis, Executive Director

News and relevant information for color designers involved in the use of color as it applies to the profitable marketing of goods and services.
Founded in 1962

6219 DSADigest
Direct Selling Association
1667 K St NW
Suite 1100
Washington, DC 20006-1660
202-452-8866; Fax: 202-452-9010
info@dsa.org
www.dsa.org

Joseph N. Mariano, President & CEO

Association activities and news for member companies.
Frequency: Monthly
Founded in 1910

6220 Daily News E-Mail (3D)
Direct Marketing Association
1120 Avenue of the Americas
New York, NY 10036-6700
212-768-7277; Fax: 212-302-6714
customerservice@the-dma.org
www.the-dma.org

Lawrence M Kimmel, CEO

Delivers the essential news, research, hot trends, and technological developments from the nations leading newspapers, trade publications, and the government all in an easy-to-read, time-saving format

6221 Direct Response
Direct Marketing Center
21171 S. Western Ave
Suite 260
Torrance, CA 90501
310-212-5727; Fax: 310-212-5773
www.directmarketingcenter.net

Craig Huey, President/Publisher
Kent Komae, Editor

Direct marketing information.
Cost: $79.00
Frequency: Monthly

6222 Direction
Direct Marketing Consultants
705 Franklin Tpke
Allendale, NJ 07401-1637
201-327-9213

Hugh P Curley, Publisher

How to' information on motivating buying decisions via more creative use of direct mail, sales promotion, newsletters, and other marketing tools.
Cost: $40.00
Circulation: 3800

6223 Empoyment Points
Mailing & Fulfillment Service Association

1421 Prince Street
Suite 410
Alexandria, VA 22314-2806

703-836-9200; Fax: 703-548-8204
www.mfsanet.org

The content is written for business owners and operators who want to stay informed about current employment issues. The editorial is targeted on human resource issues and employment practices in the mailing and fulfillment services industry.
Frequency: 4x/Year
Circulation: 2000

6224 Fred Goss' What's Working in Direct Marketing
United Communications Group
11300 Rockville Pike
Street 1100
Rockville, MD 20852-3030

301-287-2700; Fax: 301-816-8945
www.ucg.com/

Benny Dicecca, President

Direct response marketing-all forms.
Cost: $242.00
Founded in 1977

6225 Friday Report
Hoke Communications
224 7th Street
Garden City, NY 11530-5771

516-746-6700
800-229-6700; Fax: 516-294-8141
dmmagazine@aol.com
www.directmarketingmag.com

Henry R Hoke, Publisher
Joseph D Gatti, Editor
Stuart W Boysen, President
Edson Georges, Mailing Systems Manager

Weekly newsletter of direct marketing.
Cost: $165.00
8 Pages
Frequency: Weekly
Founded in 1951

6226 General Encouragement, Motivation and Inspirational Handbook
Economics Press
12 Daniel Road
Fairfield, NJ 07004-2565

973-227-1224; Fax: 973-227-3558
info@epinc.com
www.epinc.com

Allan Yahalen, President
Rob Gilbert, Editor
Cost: $20.00
24 Pages
Frequency: Monthly
Circulation: 200000
Mailing list available for rent: 200,000 names
Printed in 4 colors on matte stock

6227 Inside Mail Order
Mellinger Company
PO Box 956
Santa Clarita, CA 91380-9056

661-259-2303; Fax: 805-257-4840
www.tradezone.com

BL Mellinger III, Publisher

A newsletter offering the latest information to businesses on marketing and advertising through direct mail.

6228 Mail Order Digest & Washington Newsletter
National Mail Order Association
2807 Polk St Ne
Minneapolis, MN 55418-2954

612-788-1673; Fax: 612-788-1147
editor@nmoa.org
www.nmoa.org

John Schulte, President
J Bradley, Editor
Paul Muchnick, Founder Director

Contains information of interest to small to midsize mail marketers including new products available, money saving techniques, industry contacts, help for beginners, new concepts for mail order selling, and postal changes and regulations.
Cost: $99.00
Frequency: Monthly
Circulation: 7000
Founded in 1972

6229 Marketing Academics Newsletter
American Marketing Association
311 S Wacker Dr
Suite 5800
Chicago, IL 60606-6629

312-542-9000
800-262-1150; Fax: 312-542-9001
www.marketingpower.com

Dennis Dunlap, CEO

This newsletter provides news and information that affect and inform this important constituency. It reviews Academic Council activities, profiles Academic SIGS and highlights upcoming events.

6230 Marketing Matters Newsletter
American Marketing Association
311 S Wacker Dr
Suite 5800
Chicago, IL 60606-6629

312-542-9000
800-262-1150; Fax: 312-542-9001
www.marketingpower.com

Dennis Dunlap, CEO

This e-newsletter updates readers on the latest happenings in the marketing profession through news briefs, indepth features and interviews.
Frequency: 2x/Monthly

6231 Marketing Power Newsletter
American Marketing Association
311 S Wacker Dr
Suite 5800
Chicago, IL 60606-6629

312-542-9000
800-262-1150; Fax: 312-542-9001
www.marketingpower.com

Dennis Dunlap, CEO

This update of the latest news, research and trends in the marketing industry and allied fields.
Frequency: Weekly

6232 Marketing Researchers Newsletter
American Marketing Association
311 S Wacker Dr
Suite 5800
Chicago, IL 60606-6629

312-542-9000
800-262-1150; Fax: 312-542-9001
www.marketingpower.com

Dennis Dunlap, CEO

This e-newsletter provides members with content designed to educate and inform researchers or any member interested in marketing research topics.

6233 Marketing Through Leaders Newsletter
American Marketing Association
311 S Wacker Dr
Suite 5800
Chicago, IL 60606-6629

312-542-9000
800-262-1150; Fax: 312-542-9001
www.marketingpower.com

Dennis Dunlap, CEO

These articles focus on the issues and concepts that shape marketing today and tomorrow.
Frequency: Monthly

6234 Memo to Mailers
US Postal Service
475 Lenfant Plz Sw
Room 10523
Washington, DC 20260-1805

202-268-2900
800-275-8777; Fax: 202-268-6436
mmailers@usps.com
www.usps.com

Robert F Gardner, Manager

Carries information and news about the Postal Service as well as value added information about using the mail effectively and efficiently. Also offers information to mail center managers on ways to cut costs.
8 Pages
Frequency: Daily
Circulation: 100000

6235 Nonprofit Mailers Foundation
125 Michigan Avenue NE
#239
Washington, DC 20017-1004

202-628-4380

Esther Huggins, Manager

Promotes welfare of groups using nonprofit mail rates for communications and fundraising.
600 Pages
Founded in 1982

6236 PD&D Direct Mail List
Chilton Way
Radnor, PA 19089-0001

973-920-7782; Fax: 973-607-5492

Tom Lynch, Group Publisher
Christina Schmidt, Publisher
Don Grennan, Director of Marketing
Jeff Reinke, Editorial Director
David Mantey, Editor

This list is a proven response vehicle for product promotion, seminar announcements and trade show promotions.

6237 PostCom Bulletin
Association for Postal Commerce
1800 Diagonal Road
Suite 600
Alexandria, VA 22314

703-524-0096; Fax: 703-997-2414
info@postcom.org
www.postcom.org

Michael Plunkett, President & CEO
Ellena Talbott, Director, Operations & Membership
Beth McConnell, Postal Consultant

A source of postal news and opinion.
Founded in 1947

6238 PostScripts
Association of Marketing Service Providers
1800 Diagonal Road
Suite 320
Alexandria, VA 22314-2806

703-836-9200; Fax: 703-548-8204
kgarner@mfsanet.org
www.amsp.org

Joseph P. Truncale, President & CEO

Each issue of PostScripts highlights a theme relevant to mailing or fulfillment operations, such as production management or information technology.
Frequency: Monthly

6239 **Postal Points**
Mailing & Fulfillment Service Association
1421 Prince Street
Suite 410
Alexandria, VA 22314-2806

703-836-9200; Fax: 703-548-8204
www.mfsanet.org

Leo Raymond, Editor

Deals exclusively with current and pending postal and delivery issues. Here you will find the facts and analysis of developing postal issues.
Frequency: 18x/Year

6240 **SmartBrief**
Culture Marketing Council
8280 Willow Oaks Corporate Drive
Suite 600
Fairfax, VA 22031

703-745-5531; Fax: 703-610-0227
info@culturemarketingcouncil.org
culturemarketingcouncil.org

Horacio Gavilan, Executive Director

E-mail newsletter of the Culture Marketing Council (formerly the Association of Hispanic Advertising Agencies).

6241 **SupplierSource**
Direct Selling Association
1667 K St NW
Suite 1100
Washington, DC 20006-1660

202-452-8866; Fax: 202-452-9010
info@dsa.org
www.dsa.org

Joseph N. Mariano, President & CEO

Association activities and news for member companies.
Frequency: Quarterly
Founded in 1910

6242 **Target Market News**
Target Market News
228 S Wabash Ave
Suite 210
Chicago, IL 60604-2383

312-408-1867; Fax: 312-408-1867
www.targetmarketnews.com

Ken Smikle, President
Hallie Mummert, Editor

News and developments in the areas of black consumer marketing and black-oriented media.
Cost: $40.00
12 Pages
Frequency: Monthly
Founded in 1988

6243 **TeleResponse**
InfoCision Management
325 Springside Dr
Akron, OH 44333-4504

330-668-1400; Fax: 330-668-1401
www.infocision.com

Carl Albright, CEO

Specializes in making outbound sales calls for the infomercial, catalog and direct marketing industries.

6244 **Telephone Selling Report**
Business By Phone
13254 Stevens Street
Omaha, NE 68137-1728

402-455-1111
800-326-7721; Fax: 402-896-3353
arts@businessbyphone.com
www.businessbyphone.com

Art Sobczak, Production Manager

For businesses that use the phone to prospect, service and sell. How-to information on getting through screens; creating interest-grabbing openings; closes that work; overcoming tough objections; and beating call reluctance. Accepts advertising inserts.
Cost: $109.00
8 Pages
Frequency: Monthly
Mailing list available for rent: 2M names
Printed in 2 colors

6245 **Venture Views & News**
Venture Communications
60 Madison Ave
New York, NY 10010-1600

212-447-5247; Fax: 212-576-1129
sales@ven.com
www.venturedirect.com

Rachel Krasny, Editor
Richard Baumer, CEO/President
Neal Mandel, Group Division Sales Manager
Michael Platt, Founder

News and practical advice in the field of direct response marketing.
Frequency: Weekly
Founded in 1983

6246 **What's Working in DM and Fulfillment**
United Communications Group
11300 Rockville Pike
Suite 1100
Rockville, MD 20852-3030

301-816-8950
800-929-4824; Fax: 301-816-8945
www.ucg.com/

Barbara W Kaplowitz, Publisher
Monica Brown, Circulation Manager

Tested tips, tactics and techniques for direct marketers in all industries, news, legislative updates and winning (and losing) DM ideas including hard costs and how to's.
Cost: $242.00
8 Pages
Founded in 1977
Mailing list available for rentat $125 per M
Printed in 2 colors on matte stock

Magazines & Journals

6247 **ANA Magazine**
Association of National Advertisers
10 Grand Central, 155 E. 44th Street
New York, NY 10017

212-697-5950; Fax: 212-687-7310
info@ana.net
www.ana.net

Bob Liodice, Chief Executive Officer
Duke Fanelli, EVP & CMO

The latest news and insights from the Association of National Advertisers.

6248 **B-to-B Marketer**
Association of National Advertisers
10 Grand Central, 155 E. 44th Street
New York, NY 10017

212-697-5950; Fax: 212-687-7310
info@ana.net
www.ana.net

Bob Liodice, Chief Executive Officer
Duke Fanelli, EVP & CMO

Best practices, case studies and expert advice from the Association of National Advertisers.

6249 **BtoB Magazine**
Ad Age Group/ Division of Crain Communications
711 3rd Ave
New York, NY 10017-4014

212-210-0785; Fax: 212-210-0200
info@crain.com
www.crain.com

Norm Feldman, Manager

Dedicated to integrated business to business marketing. Every page is packed with substance news, reports, technologies, benchmarks, best practices served up by the most knowledgeable journalists.
Frequency: Monthly
Circulation: 45000

6250 **Chief Marketer**
Penton Media, Inc.
249 W 17th Street
New York, NY 10011

212-204-4200
www.penton.com
Facebook, Twitter, LinkedIn

Tyler T. Zachehm, Co-CEO
Anup Bagaria, Co-CEO
Nicola Allais, EVP & CFO
Jasmine Alexander, SVP & CIO

Chief Marketer provides fresh, multi-disciplined approaches to direct marketing, events, advertising research, and promotional marketing.
Frequency: Monthly
Founded in 1976

6251 **Customer Interface**
Advanstar Communications
6200 Canoga Avenue
2nd Floor
Woodland Hills, CA 91367

818-593-5000; Fax: 818-593-5020
info@advanstar.com
www.advanstar.com

Joseph Loggia, President
Chris DeMoulin, VP
Susannah George, Marketing Director

Magazine for decision-makers actively involved in planning, managing or operating a business call center.
Cost: $39.00
104 Pages
Circulation: 50000
Founded in 1992

6252 **Dateline: DMA**
Direct Marketing Association
11 W 42nd Street
New York, NY 10036-8002

212-391-9683; Fax: 212-768-4546

Offers comprehensive information on the Direct Marketing Association, trends in the industry, technological advances and more for the marketing and advertising professional.

6253 **Direct**
Chief Marketer
249 W 17th Street
New York, NY 10011

212-204-4200
www.chiefmarketer.com
Facebook, Twitter, LinkedIn

Beth Negus Viveiros, Managing Editor
Brian Quinton, Executive Editor
Patricia Odell, Managing Editor
Richard Levey, Senior Writer
Larry Riggs, Senior Editor

Information Resource for Direct Marketers.
Frequency: Monthly
Founded in 1976

6254 **Direct Marketing News**
Haymarket Media, Inc.
114 W 26th St.
4th Fl.
New York, NY 10001

646-638-6000
www.dmnews.com

Lee Maniscalco, Chairman & CEO
Ginger Conlon, Editor-in-Chief

Valuable information on the newest trends in direct marketing, catalog statistics and advertising information for persons working in the direct mail industry.
Cost: $148.00
Frequency: Monthly
ISSN: 1187-7111
Founded in 1979

6255 **Forward**
Association of National Advertisers
10 Grand Central, 155 E. 44th Street
New York, NY 10017

212-697-5950; Fax: 212-687-7310
info@ana.net
www.ana.net

Bob Liodice, Chief Executive Officer
Duke Fanelli, EVP & CMO

Thought leadership newsletter from the Association of National Advertisers.

6256 **Journal of Direct Marketing**
John Wiley & Sons
111 River St
Hoboken, NJ 07030-5790

201-748-6000
800-825-7550; Fax: 201-748-6088
info@wiley.com
www.wiley.com

William J Pesce, CEO
Richard M Hochhauser, CEO

Publication featuring research articles from some of the best minds in the field of direct marketing. Offers creative ideas for marketing products, analysis of what works, pioneering research from the nation's top universities, articles from other direct marketing publications and special reports on overseas direct marketing.
Cost: $1000.00
Frequency: Quarterly
Founded in 1807

6257 **Journal of International Marketing**
American Marketing Association
130 E. Randolph Street
22nd Floor
Chicago, IL 60601

800-262-1150
customersupport@ama.org
www.ama.org/ama-academic-journals

Kelly Hewett, Editor-in-Chief

Presents scholarly and managerially relevant articles on international marketing.
Frequency: Quarterly
ISSN: 1069-031X

6258 **Journal of Marketing**
American Marketing Association
130 E. Randolph Street
22nd Floor
Chicago, IL 60601

800-262-1150
customersupport@ama.org
www.ama.org/ama-academic-journals

Christine Moorman, Editor-in-Chief

Scholarly journal of the marketing discipline.
Frequency: Bimonthly
ISSN: 0022-2429
Founded in 1936

6259 **Journal of Marketing Research**
American Marketing Association
130 E. Randolph Street
22nd Floor
Chicago, IL 60601

800-262-1150
customersupport@ama.org
www.ama.org/ama-academic-journals

Rajdeep Grewal, Editor-in-Chief

Covers a wide range of marketing research concepts, methods and applications.
Frequency: Bimonthly
ISSN: 0022-2437
Mailing list available for rent

6260 **Journal of Public Policy & Marketing**
American Marketing Association
130 E. Randolph Street
22nd Floor
Chicago, IL 60601

800-262-1150
customersupport@ama.org
www.ama.org/ama-academic-journals

Scot Burton, Co-Editor
Pam Ellen, Co-Editor
Josh Weiner, Co-Editor

Each issue features a wide ranging forum for the research, findings and discussion of marketing subjects related to business and government.
Frequency: Semiannual
ISSN: 0743-9156

6261 **Marketing Health Services**
American Marketing Association
311 S Wacker Dr
Suite 5800
Chicago, IL 60606-6629

312-542-9000
800-262-1150; Fax: 312-542-9001
www.marketingpower.com

Dennis Dunlap, CEO

Specifically aimed at senior level healthcare marketers and managers, offers targeted information, practical strategies and thought provoking commentary to help achieve your goals and shape your vision.
Frequency: Quarterly

6262 **Marketing Management**
American Marketing Association
311 S Wacker Dr
Suite 5800
Chicago, IL 60606-6629

312-542-9000
800-262-1150; Fax: 312-542-9001
www.marketingpower.com

Dennis Dunlap, CEO

Focuses on strategic marketing issues that marketing managers face every day.
Frequency: 6x/Year

6263 **Marketing News**
American Marketing Association
311 S Wacker Dr
Suite 5800
Chicago, IL 60606-6629

312-542-9000
800-262-1150; Fax: 312-542-9001
www.marketingpower.com

Dennis Dunlap, CEO

Covers the industry's basics, the core concepts around which winning programs are built.

6264 **Marketing Research**
American Marketing Association
311 S Wacker Dr
Suite 5800
Chicago, IL 60606-6629

312-542-9000
800-262-1150; Fax: 312-542-9001
www.marketingpower.com

Dennis Dunlap, CEO

Researchers and managers count on this quarterly resource to help stay on top of current methodologies and issues, management concerns and the latest books and software.
40000 Members
Frequency: Quarterly

6265 **Multichannel Merchant**
Chief Marketer
249 W 17th Street
New York, NY 10011

212-204-4200
www.chiefmarketer.com
Facebook, Twitter, LinkedIn

Beth Negus Viveiros, Managing Editor
Brian Quinton, Executive Editor
Patricia Odell, Managing Editor
Richard Levey, Senior Writer
Larry Riggs, Senior Editor

Exclusively serves online merchants and catalog companies, as well as retailers, manufacturers and wholesale/distributors.
Frequency: Monthly
Founded in 1976

6266 **Operations & Fulfillment**
Primedia
Po Box 12901
Shawnee Mission, KS 66282-2901

913-341-1300
800-775-3777; Fax: 913-514-6895
www.penton.com

Eric Jacobson, Senior VP
Glenn Laudenslager, Marketing Manager
Leslie Bacon, Publisher
Leonard Roberto, Circulation Manager
John French, President

Provides executives information they can't get anywhere else and reach executives and managers with purchasing authority in all areas of operations management. Information on direct to customer fulfillment..
Cost: $36.00
Frequency: Monthly
Founded in 1905

6267 **Politically Direct**
Direct Marketing Association
1120 Avenue of the Americas
New York, NY 10036-6700

212-768-7277; Fax: 212-302-6714
customerservice@the-dma.org
www.the-dma.org

Lawrence M Kimmel, CEO

Published both in print and digital, this newsletter on DMA advocacy efforts keeps DMA members informed and involved in the politics and policies that impact them today and ahead of the curve on developments that will affect them tomorrow.
Frequency: Quarterly

6268 **Promo**
Chief Marketer
249 W 17th Street
New York, NY 10011

212-204-4200
www.chiefmarketer.com
Facebook, Twitter, LinkedIn

Beth Negus Viveiros, Managing Editor
Brian Quinton, Executive Editor
Patricia Odell, Managing Editor

Richard Levey, Senior Writer
Larry Riggs, Senior Editor
Promo Magazine covers the Promotions and the Promotional Marketing Industry.
Frequency: Monthly
Founded in 1976

6269 **Target**
North American Publishing Company
1500 Spring Garden St
Suite 1200
Philadelphia, PA 19130-4094
215-238-5300; Fax: 215-238-5342
www.targetmarketingmag.com
Ned S Borowsky, CEO
Peggy Hatch, Publisher
Lois Boyle, President
This monthly magazine is the authoritative information source for direct marketers with hands-on, how-to-do-it, ideas you can take to the bank.
Cost: $24.95
Frequency: Monthly
Circulation: 35000
Founded in 1977
Mailing list available for rent
Printed in 4 colors on glossy stock

6270 **Telemarketing Magazine**
Technology Marketing Corporation
1 Technology Plz
Norwalk, CT 06854-1936
203-852-6800
800-243-6002; Fax: 203-853-2845
tmc@tmcnet.com
www.tmcnet.com
Rich Tehrani, CEO
Linda Driscoll, Editor/VP
Rich Tehrani, President/Editor-in-Chief
Serves telemarketing, marketing, customer service, sales and telecommunications professionals. Features legislative updates, new product and service releases, techniques and beginner information.
Cost: $49.00
Frequency: Monthly
Founded in 1972

6271 **WFDSA Annual Publication**
World Federation of Direct Selling Associations
1667 K Street NW
Suite 1100
Washington, DC 20006
202-416-6442
info@wfdsa.org
wfdsa.org
Facebook, Twitter, YouTube
Magnus Brannstrom, Chair
Tamuna Gabilaia, Executive Director & COO
Maureen Paniagua, Manager, International
Various Federation initiatives are highlighted.
Frequency: Annual
Founded in 1978

Trade Shows

6272 **&Then**
Direct Marketing Association
1120 Avenue of the Americas
New York, NY 10036-6700
212-768-7277; Fax: 212-302-6714
thedma.org/events
The Direct Marketing Association's annual event.
Frequency: Annual

6273 **AMA Annual Conference**
American Marketing Association
130 E. Randolph Street
22nd Floor
Chicago, IL 60601
800-262-1150
customersupport@ama.org
www.ama.org
Facebook, Twitter, LinkedIn
Russ Klein, Chief Executive Officer
Jeremy Van Ek, Chief Operating Officer
Premier educational and networking event of the American Marketing Association.

6274 **AMSP Annual Conference**
Association of Marketing Service Providers
1800 Diagonal Road
Suite 320
Alexandria, VA 22314-2806
703-836-9200; Fax: 703-548-8204
kgarner@mfsanet.org
www.amsp.org
Joseph P. Truncale, President & CEO
Leo Raymond, VP, Postal & Member Relations
Opportunity for marketing professionals to network, collaborate, and learn.
Frequency: Annual

6275 **ANA Advertising Financial Management Conference**
Association of National Advertisers
10 Grand Central, 155 E. 44th Street
New York, NY 10017
212-697-5950; Fax: 212-687-7310
info@ana.net
www.ana.net
Bob Liodice, Chief Executive Officer
Kristen McDonough, SVP, Conferences
Brings together top marketing finance and procurement professionals from the client side with agency CFOs and other key industry stakeholders interested in efficiencies, cost savings, return on investment, and delivering greater value to organizations.

6276 **ANA Advertising Law & Public Policy Conference**
Association of National Advertisers
10 Grand Central, 155 E. 44th Street
New York, NY 10017
212-697-5950; Fax: 212-687-7310
info@ana.net
www.ana.net
Bob Liodice, Chief Executive Officer
Kristen McDonough, SVP, Conferences
Keeping up with the digital revolution is becoming a nearly impossible task. This conference enters the battlefield by putting together a stellar faculty, including leading regulators, top practitioners, and serious critics, capped off by a session that puts it all together led by a leading law professor.

6277 **ANA Brand Activation Marketing Conference**
Association of National Advertisers
10 Grand Central, 155 E. 44th Street
New York, NY 10017
212-697-5950; Fax: 212-687-7310
info@ana.net
www.ana.net
Bob Liodice, Chief Executive Officer
Kristen McDonough, SVP, Conferences
Coordinated brand activation strategies from top marketers.

6278 **ANA Chicago Nonprofit Conference**
Association of National Advertisers
10 Grand Central, 155 E. 44th Street
New York, NY 10017
212-697-5950; Fax: 212-687-7310
info@ana.net
www.ana.net
Bob Liodice, Chief Executive Officer
Kristen McDonough, SVP, Conferences
Marketing, fundraising, and collaborative ideas to help nonprofits expand their donor base.

6279 **ANA DC Nonprofit Conference**
Association of National Advertisers
10 Grand Central, 155 E. 44th Street
New York, NY 10017
212-697-5950; Fax: 212-687-7310
info@ana.net
www.ana.net
Bob Liodice, Chief Executive Officer
Kristen McDonough, SVP, Conferences
Marketing, fundraising, and collaborative ideas to help nonprofits expand their donor base.

6280 **ANA Data & Measurement Conference**
Association of National Advertisers
10 Grand Central, 155 E. 44th Street
New York, NY 10017
212-697-5950; Fax: 212-687-7310
info@ana.net
www.ana.net
Bob Liodice, Chief Executive Officer
Kristen McDonough, SVP, Conferences

6281 **ANA Digital & Social Media Conference**
Association of National Advertisers
10 Grand Central, 155 E. 44th Street
New York, NY 10017
212-697-5950; Fax: 212-687-7310
info@ana.net
www.ana.net
Bob Liodice, Chief Executive Officer
Kristen McDonough, SVP, Conferences
Discussing how to use social media and digital technology to impact consumer decisions and how to effectively partner with other companies to maximize social media reach and more.

6282 **ANA Email Evolution Conference**
Association of National Advertisers
10 Grand Central, 155 E. 44th Street
New York, NY 10017
212-697-5950; Fax: 212-687-7310
info@ana.net
www.ana.net
Bob Liodice, Chief Executive Officer
Kristen McDonough, SVP, Conferences
A look at regulatory changes, privacy concerns, and technical advances in email marketing.

6283 **ANA In-House Agency Conference**
Association of National Advertisers
10 Grand Central, 155 E. 44th Street
New York, NY 10017
212-697-5950; Fax: 212-687-7310
info@ana.net
www.ana.net
Bob Liodice, Chief Executive Officer
Kristen McDonough, SVP, Conferences
Conference devoted to all aspects of in-house agencies, including digital asset management, culture and talent, the evolution of in-house agencies, starting a new agency, and more.

6284 **ANA Influencer Marketing Conference**
Association of National Advertisers

10 Grand Central, 155 E. 44th Street
New York, NY 10017

212-697-5950; Fax: 212-687-7310
info@ana.net
www.ana.net

Bob Liodice, Chief Executive Officer
Kristen McDonough, SVP, Conferences

6285 ANA Masters of B2B Marketing
Association of National Advertisers
10 Grand Central, 155 E. 44th Street
New York, NY 10017

212-697-5950; Fax: 212-687-7310
info@ana.net
www.ana.net

Bo Liodice, Chief Executive Officer
Kristen McDonough, SVP, Conferences

Insights into successful B2B approaches.

6286 ANA Masters of Data & Technology
Association of National Advertisers
10 Grand Central, 155 E. 44th Street
New York, NY 10017

212-697-5950; Fax: 212-687-7310
info@ana.net
www.ana.net

Bob Liodice, Chief Executive Officer
Kristen McDonough, SVP, Conferences

Discussions on the ever-changing marketing technology ecosystem.

6287 ANA Masters of Marketing Conference
Association of National Advertisers
10 Grand Central, 155 E. 44th Street
New York, NY 10017

212-697-5950; Fax: 212-687-7310
info@ana.net
www.ana.net

Bob Liodice, Chief Executive Officer
Kristen McDonough, SVP, Conferences

The conference offers an opportunity to learn from and engage with the leaders of the industry as they build brands, leverage the expanding array of media, make marketing more accountable and improve the quality of their marketing organizations.
2500 Attendees

6288 ANA Media Conference
Association of National Advertisers
10 Grand Central, 155 E. 44th Street
New York, NY 10017

212-697-5950; Fax: 212-687-7310
info@ana.net
www.ana.net

Bob Liodice, Chief Executive Officer
Kristen McDonough, SVP, Conferences

Actionable insights into today's important issues.

6289 ANA Multicultural Marketing & Diversity Conference
Association of National Advertisers
10 Grand Central, 155 E. 44th Street
New York, NY 10017

212-697-5950; Fax: 212-687-7310
info@ana.net
www.ana.net

Bob Liodice, Chief Executive Officer
Kristen McDonough, SVP, Conferences

6290 ANA Nonprofit Federation Leadership Summit
Association of National Advertisers
10 Grand Central, 155 E. 44th Street
New York, NY 10017

212-697-5950; Fax: 212-687-7310
info@ana.net
www.ana.net

Bob Liodice, Chief Executive Officer
Kristen McDonough, SVP, Conferences

6291 ANA/BAA Marketing Law Conference
Association of National Advertisers
10 Grand Central, 155 E. 44th Street
New York, NY 10017

212-697-5950; Fax: 212-687-7310
info@ana.net
www.ana.net

Bob Liodice, Chief Executive Officer
Kristen McDonough, SVP, Conferences

6292 Annual Conference and Mailing Fulfillment Expo
Mailing & Fulfillment Service Association
1421 Prince Street
Suite 410
Alexandria, VA 22314-2806

703-836-9200; Fax: 703-548-8204
www.mfsanet.org

Ken Garner, President
Jennifer Root, Director
Bill Stevenson, Director Marketing

Quality educational sessions, industry specific exhibit hall, networking and more.
Frequency: Annual

6293 Annual Conference for Catalog and Multichannel Merchants
PRISM Business Exhibitions
11 River Bend Drive South
Stamford, CT 06907

203-358-9900
800-927-5007; Fax: 203-358-5816
registration@prismb2b.com
www.accmshow.com

Ed Berkowitz, Sales Director
Angela Eastin, Group Show Director

Co-presented by the Direct Marketing Association and Multichannel Merchant Magazine, ACCM offers the latest advances, technology and information and solutions for cataloger, retailers and multichannel merchants.
Frequency: May

6294 Association of Teleservices International Conference
Association of Teleservices International
222 South Westmonte Drive
Suite 111
Altamonte Springs, FL 32714

866-896-2874; Fax: 407-774-6440
admin@atsi.org
www.atsi.org

Tifani Leal, President

Exhibits of interest to telephone answering and voice message providers.
800+ Attendees
Founded in 1942

6295 Business-to-Business Database Marketing Conference
Interlect Events
11 Riverbend Drive S
Stamford, CT 06907

203-852-4200
http://www.importexporthelp.com/b2b-lists.htm

Robin Altman, Contact

The only database marketing conference that is focused exclusively on business-to-business marketing database strategies and tactics. 40 tabletop exhibits.
500 Attendees
Frequency: Fall

6296 CMC Annual Summit
Association of Hispanic Advertising Agencies
8280 Willow Oaks Corporate Drive
Suite 600
Fairfax, VA 22031

703-745-5531; Fax: 703-610-0227
info@culturemarketingcouncil.org
culturemarketingcouncil.org

Horacio Gavilan, Executive Director

Examines the myriad of changes facing Hispanic agencies in and beyond including shifts in approaches to communications planning, demographics and client needs.

6297 CTAM Think
Cable & Telecommunications Assn. for Marketing
120 Waterfront Street
Suite 200
National Harbor, MD 20745

301-485-8900
info@ctam.com
www.ctam.com

Vicki Lins, President & CEO
Antoinette Allen, Director, Meetings

A look at the changing nature of the cable & telecommunications industries.

6298 DAA OneConference
Digital Analytics Association
401 Edgewater Place
Suite 600
Wakefield, WA 1880

781-876-8933; Fax: 781-224-1239
info@digitalanalyticsassociation.org
www.digitalanalyticsassociation.org

Marilee Yorchak, Executive Director
Adrienne Segundo, Education Manager
Lesley Coussis, Symposia Manager

Conference of the Digital Analytics Association, which is a global organization of practitioners, corporations, vendors, marketing and public relations agencies, consultants, academics, and more involved in the growing digital analytics industry.
Founded in 2004

6299 DMA Annual Conference & Exhibition
Direct Marketing Association
1120 Avenue of Americas
New York, NY 10036-6700

212-768-7277; Fax: 212-302-6714
dmaconferences@the-dma.org
www.the-dma.org

Lawrence M Kimmel, CEO
Julie A Hogan, SVP Conferences/Events

Brings together thousands of practitioners and experts from the entire marketing continuum to discuss solutions and best practices to achieve optimal channel mix and integration that lead to measurable results and increase real-time customer engagement.
12000 Attendees
Frequency: October

6300 DMD New York Conference & Expo
Direct Marketing Conferences

20 Academy Street
Norwalk, CT 06850-4032

203-854-9166
800-969-6566
www.dmdays.com

Direct Marketing Days New York offers new ideas in media, creative, database, eCommerce and technology. Hundreds of exhibits showcase the newest technologies, products and services. Over 85 sessions and 25 consultation centers led by A level speakers. Network with top-level executives.
Frequency: Annual/June

6301 **DSA Annual Meeting**
Direct Selling Association
1667 K St NW
Suite 1100
Washington, DC 20006-1660

202-452-8866; Fax: 202-452-9010
info@dsa.org
www.dsa.org

Joseph N. Mariano, President & CEO
Melissa K. Brunton, SVP, Education & Meeting Services
Lindsay Marquardt, Sr. Manager, Education & Meetings
Eleanor Campbell, Meetings Coordinator

Education and networking sessions for direct-selling executives.
Founded in 1910

6302 **DSA Companies in Focus**
Direct Selling Association
1667 K St NW
Suite 1100
Washington, DC 20006-1660

202-452-8866; Fax: 202-452-9010
info@dsa.org
www.dsa.org

Joseph N. Mariano, President & CEO
Melissa K. Brunton, SVP, Education & Meeting Services
Lindsay Marquardt, Sr. Manager, Education & Meetings
Eleanor Campbell, Meetings Coordinator

Insider views from direct-selling companies.
Founded in 1910

6303 **DSA Legal & Regulatory Seminar**
Direct Selling Association
1667 K St NW
Suite 1100
Washington, DC 20006-1660

202-452-8866; Fax: 202-452-9010
info@dsa.org
www.dsa.org

Joseph N. Mariano, President & CEO
Melissa K. Brunton, SVP, Education & Meeting Services
Lindsay Marquardt, Sr. Manager, Education & Meetings
Eleanor Campbell, Meetings Coordinator

Policy insights lead to practical business applications.
Founded in 1910

6304 **DSA Sales & Marketing Conference**
Direct Selling Association
1667 K St NW
Suite 1100
Washington, DC 20006-1660

202-452-8866; Fax: 202-452-9010
info@dsa.org
www.dsa.org

Joseph N. Mariano, President & CEO
Melissa K. Brunton, SVP, Education & Meeting Services
Lindsay Marquardt, Sr. Manager, Education & Meetings
Eleanor Campbell, Meetings Coordinator

Discussions about the latest trends in marketing, including artificial intelligence, personalization, digital marketing, web platforms such as Amazon, and the evolution of SEO.
Founded in 1910

6305 **Direct Selling Day on Capitol Hill**
Direct Selling Association
1667 K St NW
Suite 1100
Washington, DC 20006-1660

202-452-8866; Fax: 202-452-9010
info@dsa.org
www.dsa.org

Joseph N. Mariano, President & CEO
Melissa K. Brunton, SVP, Education & Meeting Services
Lindsay Marquardt, Sr. Manager, Education & Meetings
Eleanor Campbell, Meetings Coordinator

Event in Washington, DC, aiming to preserve the freedom and flexibility of direct sellers.
Founded in 1910

6306 **Email Evolution Conference**
Direct Marketing Association
1120 Avenue of Americas
New York, NY 10036-6700

212-768-7277; Fax: 212-302-6714
dmaconferences@the-dma.org
www.the-dma.org

Julie A Hogan, SVP Conference/Events
Lawrence M Kimmel, CEO

Focuses on the ever-changing and evolving world of email marketing, providing attendees with the best ways to capitalize on the high ROI this low-cost communication tool can provide both on its own, and integrated with social, search, mobile, video and other email enhancers.
10M Attendees
Frequency: Annual/February

6307 **Internet Telephony Conference & EXPO (East or West)**
Technology Marketing Corporation (TMCnet)
One Technology Plaza
Norwalk, CT 06854

203-852-6800
800-243-6002; Fax: 203-853-2845
tmc@tmcnet.com
www.tmcnet.com

Frank Coppola, Conference Team
Lorna Lyle, Conference Team
Tim Zaccagnini, Conference Team
Kevin Lake, Exhibit Sales
Natasha Barbera, Operations Contact

The world's foremost forum on IP and VoIP, and all things telephony: workshops, training courses, focused tracks, and exhibitors.
Frequency: East/West - Winter/Fall

6308 **LIDMA Conference and Business Showcase**
Life Insurance Direct Marketing Association
3227 S. Cherokee Lane
Suite 1320
Woodstock, GA 30188

770-516-0207
866-890-5323
info@lidma.org
lidma.org

Robert Bland, President
Nicole Buckenmeyer, Vice President
Jeff McCauley, Secretary-Treasurer
Brian Barnes, Membership Vice Chair

Annual conference of the Life Insurance Direct Marketing Association.

6309 **MFSA Mailing and Fulfillment Expo**
Mailing & Fulfillment Service Association
1421 Prince Street
Suite 100
Alexandria, VA 22314-2805

703-369-9200
800-333-6272; Fax: 703-548-8204
www.mfsanet.org

Eric Casey, Manager
David Weaver, President

Annual exposition of suppliers to mailing and fulfillment companies. Containing 60 booths and 50 exhibits.
250 Attendees
Frequency: June
Mailing list available for rent

6310 **MFSA Midwinter Executive Conference**
Mailing & Fulfillment Service Association
1421 Prince Street
Suite 410
Alexandria, VA 22314-2806

703-836-9200; Fax: 703-548-8204
www.mfsanet.org

Ken Garner, President
Jennifer Root, Director
Bill Stevenson, Director Marketing

Will address financial operations and business valuation, marketing your own company, the changing world of postal regulations, technology in fulfillment, building a sales team, being strong in digital printing and the landscape of employment law.

6311 **MLMIA Convention and Expo**
Multi-Level Marketing International Association
119 Stanford Court
Irvine, CA 92612

949-854-0484
info@mlmia.com
www.mlmia.com

Doris Wood, Chair
Tony Cannuli, COO

Seeks to strengthen and improve the Direct Sales/Network Marketing/Multi-Level Marketing industry in the United States and abroad. Members are companies which market their products and services directly to consumers through independent distributors, suppliers to the industry and distributors who interface with consumers.
Founded in 1985

6312 **Mailer Strategies Conference**
Mailing & Fulfillment Service Association
1421 Prince Street
Suite 410
Alexandria, VA 22314-2806

703-836-9200; Fax: 703-548-8204
www.mfsanet.org

Ken Garner, President
Jennifer Root, Director
Bill Stevenson, Director Marketing

This conference will focus solely on postal issues that are important to your operations.

6313 **Marketing in the Millennium**
Florida Direct Marketing Association
8851 NW 10th Pl
Plantation, FL 33322-5007

954-472-6374
800-520-FDMA; Fax: 954-472-8165
www.fdma.org

Beth Kaufman, Manager

Yearly exhibit of legislative updates and more for members of the direct marketing industry.
Frequency: February
Founded in 1999

6314 **NCDM Conference**
Direct Marketing Association
1120 Avenue of Americas
New York, NY 10036-6700
212-768-7277; Fax: 212-302-6714
dmaconferences@the-dma.org
www.the-dma.org
Julie A Hogan, SVP Conference/Events
Lawrence M Kimmel, CEO
Presents industry experts and hard-hitting case studies from a variety of verticles, such as financial services, retail, automotive, publishing, non-profit and many more, who will share the latest strategies and methodologies in gathering, analyzinf, leveraging and protecting the most valuable business asset-the customer database.
10M Attendees
Frequency: Annual/December

6315 **National Catalog Operations Forum**
Primedia
9800 Metcalf Avenue
Overland Park, KS 66212
913-341-1300; Fax: 913-967-1898
www.catalogmailers.org
Robin Altman, Contact
The only major national conference devoted exclusively to the sharing of vital catalog operations information. This conference is dedicated to the crucial background of the catalog business, and brings operations management together to meet and learn; 140 booths.
1.2M+ Attendees
Frequency: April/May

6316 **National Conference on Operations & Fulfillment (NCOF)**
Direct Marketing Association
1120 Avenue of Americas
New York, NY 10036-6700
212-768-7277; Fax: 212-302-6714
dmaconferences@the-dma.org
www.the-dma.org
Julie A Hogan, SVP Conference/Events
Lawrence M Kimmel, CEO
Focuses on innovative solutions for the warehouse, distribution, operations, and ecommerce needs in the ever-changing world of operations and fulfillment.
10M Attendees
Frequency: Annual/April

6317 **New York Nonprofit Conference**
Direct Marketing Association
1120 Avenue of Americas
New York, NY 10036-6700
212-768-7277; Fax: 212-302-6714
dmaconferences@the-dma.org
www.the-dma.org
Julie Hogan, SVP Conference/Events
Discover which acknowledgement programs work best and why, increase revenue with membership options-as well as traditional fundraising appeals, learn how the Internet and e-mail campaigns can improve fundraising, lower costs and increase advocacy.
10M Attendees

6318 **PACE Convention and Expo**
Professional Association for Customer Engagement
5250 E. US 36
Suite 1102B
Avon, IN 46123
317-816-9336
www.paceassociation.com
Stuart Discount, CEO
Kayci Vincent, Director, Conventions & Events
Gathering of leaders from various industries focused on customer experience.

6319 **WFDSA World Congress**
World Federation of Direct Selling Associations
1667 K Street NW
Suite 1100
Washington, DC 20006
202-416-6442
info@wfdsa.org
wfdsa.org
Facebook, Twitter, YouTube
Magnus Brannstrom, Chair
Tamuna Gabilaia, Executive Director & COO
Maureen Paniagua, Manager, International
Event for direct-selling industry executives and external stakeholders from around the world.
Frequency: Triennial
Founded in 1978

6320 **impactSHOW**
Internet Marketing Association
200 Spectrum Center Drive
Irvine, CA 92618
949-443-9300
info@imanetwork.org
imanetwork.org
Facebook, Twitter, LinkedIn, YouTube
Sinan Kanatsiz, Chair & Founder
Sean Conrad, CEO
Lei Lani Fera, Head Of Creative
Hall Roosevelt, General Manager
Marcus Volpe, Executive Director
Conference of the Internet Marketing Association.
Founded in 2001

Directories & Databases

6321 **Adweek Directory**
Prometheus Global Media
770 Broadway
New York, NY 10003-9595
212-493-4100; Fax: 646-654-5368
www.prometheusgm.com
Richard D. Beckman, CEO
James A. Finkelstein, Chairman
Madeline Krakowsky, Vice President Circulation
Tracy Brater, Executive Director Creative Service
Adweek Directories Online is where you will find searchable databases with comprehensive information on ad agencies, brand marketers and multicultural media.
Frequency: Annual
Circulation: 800
Founded in 1981

6322 **Annual Guide to Telemarketing**
Marketing Logistics
1460 Cloverdale Avenue
Highland Park, IL 60035-2817
847-831-1575
Arnold Fishman, Editor
About 400 telemarketing services bureaus in the United States.
Cost: $475.00
Frequency: Irregular

6323 **Art Directors Annual**
Art Directors Club
106 W 29th St
New York, NY 10001-5301
212-643-1440; Fax: 212-643-4266
info@adcglobal.org
www.adcglobal.org
Ami Brophy, CEO
Myrna Davis, Executive Director
Innovative advertising, design, publishing, photography, illustration, film, video, and interactive media.
Cost: $65.00
520 Members
Circulation: 7,000
Mailing list available for rent

6324 **Associations Yellow Book**
Leadership Directories
104 5th Ave
New York, NY 10011-6901
212-627-4140; Fax: 212-645-0931
www.leadershipdirectories.com
David Hurvitz, CEO
James M Petrie, Associate Publisher
Contact information for over 41,000 officers and board members at 1,000 trade and professional associations, coalitions, PACs, and foundations.
Cost: $245.00
1,300 Pages
Frequency: SemiAnnual
ISSN: 1054-4070
Founded in 1991
Mailing list available for rent: 37,000 names at $125 per M

6325 **CMC Hispanic Market Guide**
Association of Hispanic Advertising Agencies
8400 Westpark Drive
2nd Floor
McLean, VA 22102
703-610-9014; Fax: 703-610-0227
info@culturemarketingcouncil.org
culturemarketingcouncil.org
Horacio Gavilan, President
Digital guide with advertising, media and marketing companies that specialize in the Hispanic market.

6326 **Catalog Success**
North American Publishing Company
4001 S Business Park Avenue
Marshfield, WI 54449-9027
715-387-3400; Fax: 715-486-4185
www.catalogsuccess.com
Putting marketing management to the test.
Frequency: Monthly
ISSN: 1524-2307
Printed in 4 colors

6327 **Corporate Yellow Book**
Leadership Directories
104 5th Ave
New York, NY 10011-6901
212-627-4140; Fax: 212-645-0931
corporate@leadershipdirectories.com
www.leadershipdirectories.com
David Hurvitz, CEO
Contact information for over 48,000 executives at over 1,000 companies and more than 9,000 board members and their outside affiliations.
Cost: $360.00
1,400 Pages
Frequency: Quarterly
ISSN: 1058-2098
Founded in 1986
Mailing list available for rent: 50,000 names at $105 per M

6328 **Customer Interaction Solutions**
Technology Marketing Corporation
1 Technology Plz
Norwalk, CT 06854-1936

203-852-6800
800-243-6002; Fax: 203-853-2845
www.tmcnet.com

Rich Tehrani, CEO
Tracy Schelmetic, Editor

Over 1100 domestic and foreign suppliers of equipment products and services to the telecommunications/telemarketing industry.
Cost: $25.00
Frequency: Annual/December/89 Pages
Founded in 1982
Mailing list available for rent: 63,000 names at $25 per M

6329 **D&B Million Dollar Database**
Dun & Bradstreet Information Service
3 Sylvan Way
Parsippany, NJ 07054-3822

973-605-6000
800-526-0651; Fax: 973-605-9630

160,000 public and private businesses with either a net worth of 500,000 or more, 250 emplyees at that location or 25,000,000 or more in sales volume.

6330 **D&B Million Dollar Database: International**
Dun & Bradstreet Information Service
3 Sylvan Way
Parsippany, NJ 07054-3822

973-605-6000
800-526-0651; Fax: 973-605-9630

50,000 top corporations, utilities, transportation companies, bank and trust companies, stock brolers, mutual and stock insurance companies, wholesalers, retailers, and domestic susidiaries of foreign corporations.

6331 **Direct Mail Service**
Information Resource Group
50495 Corporate Drive
Suite 112
Shelby Township, MI 48315-3132

586-726-6237

This database offers over 1,000,000 MIS and corporate professionals at over 150,000 companies throughout the United States.
Cost: $150.00

6332 **Direct Selling World Directory**
World Federation of Direct Selling Association
1776 K St NW
Suite 600
Washington, DC 20006-2304

202-546-5330; Fax: 202-463-4569
www.dsa.org

Over 50 direct selling associations and over 1,000 associated member companies are offered in this comprehensive directory.
90 Pages
Frequency: Annual

6333 **Directory of Mail Order Catalogs**
Grey House Publishing
4919 Route 22
PO Box 56
Amenia, NY 12501

518-789-8700
800-562-2139; Fax: 845-373-6390
books@greyhouse.com
www.greyhouse.com
Facebook, Twitter

Leslie Mackenzie, Publisher
Richard Gottlieb, Editor

The premier source of information on the mail order catalog industry. Covers over 13,000 consumer and business catalog companies with 44 different product chapters from Animals to Toys and Games.
Cost: $395.00
1900 Pages
Frequency: Annual
ISBN: 1-592373-96-8
Founded in 1981

6334 **Directory of Mail Order Catalogs - Online Database**
Grey House Publishing
4919 Route 22
PO Box 56
Amenia, NY 12501

518-789-8700
800-562-2139; Fax: 845-373-6390
gold@greyhouse.com
gold.greyhouse.com
Facebook, Twitter

Leslie Mackenzie, Publisher
Richard Gottlieb, Editor

Reach over 10,000 consumer catalog companies in one easy-to-use source with The Directory of Mail Order Catalogs - Online Database. Filled with business-building detail, each company profile gives you the information you need to access that organization quickly and easily. Listings provide key contacts, sales volume, employee size, printing information, circulation, list data, product descriptions and much more.
Frequency: Annual
Founded in 1981

6335 **Directory of Major Mailers**
North American Publishing Company
1500 Spring Garden St
Suite 1200
Philadelphia, PA 19130-4094

215-238-5300; Fax: 215-238-5342

Ned S Borowsky, CEO

Offers over 7,500 major direct mailers and the key players with their names, addresses, phones and fax numbers, executive contacts, types of business, and the size of the house file. The Directory also contains actual reproductions of these mailings - letters, envelopes, order cards, brochures, etc. You'll see what was mailed, what worked and what didn't.
Cost: $395.00
Frequency: Annual
Founded in 1994
Mailing list available for rent
Printed in one color on matte stock

6336 **Nonprofit Sector Yellow Book**
Leadership Directories
104 5th Ave
New York, NY 10011-6901

212-627-4140; Fax: 212-645-0931
info@leadershipdirectories.com
www.leadershipdirectories.com

David Hurvitz, CEO
James M Petrie, Associate Publisher

Contact information for over 51,000 nonprofit executives and trustees at over 1,300 nonprofit organizations, including foundations, colleges and universities, museums, performing arts group and centers, medical institutions, library systems, preparatory schools, and charitable service organizations.
Cost: $245.00
1,200 Pages
Frequency: SemiAnnual
ISSN: 1520-9148
Founded in 1999
Mailing list available for rent: 45,000 names at $125 per M

6337 **Nonprofits Job Finder: Where the Jobs are in Charities and Nonprofits**
Planning/Communications
7215 Oak Ave
River Forest, IL 60305-1935

708-366-5200
888-366-5200; Fax: 708-366-5280
dl@planningcommunications.com
www.planningcommunications.com

Daniel Lauber, President

Describes in detail over 1,500 sources of jobs in the nonprofit sectors job database online, resume banks, email job alerts, directories, salary surveys, newsletters, and magazines.
Cost: $17.95
300 Pages
Circulation: 6,000
ISBN: 1-884587-06-2
Founded in 2005
Printed in one color on matte stock

6338 **Who's Who: MASA Buyer's Guide to Blue Ribbon Mailing Services**
Mailing & Fulfillment Service Association
1421 Prince Street
Suite 410
Alexandria, VA 22314-2806

703-836-9200; Fax: 703-548-8204
www.mfsanet.org

Ken Garner, President
Bill Stevenson, Director Marketing

Offers a detailed listing of suppliers of equipment, products and services to the direct mail industry, most containing a description of the specific products they provide.
Frequency: Annual

6339 **Yellow Pages & Directory Report**
Simba Information
11200 Rockville Pike
Suite 504
Rockville, MD 20852

240-747-3096
877-352-2021; Fax: 340-747-3004
dgoddard@imslocalsearch.com
Facebook, Twitter, LinkedIn

David Goddard, EVP/Senior Analyst/Editor
Kyle Kroll, President

Covers directory publishing, advertising, printing and releases from national yellow pages accounts.
Cost: $695.00

Industry Web Sites

6340 **http://gold.greyhouse.com**
G.O.L.D Grey House OnLine Databases

Grey House Publishing's online database platform, GOLD, offers Quick Search, Keyword Search and Expert Search for most business sectors including direct marketing and public relations markets. The GOLD platform makes finding the information you need quick and easy - whether you're a novice searcher or an experienced database user. All of Grey House's directory products are available for subscription on the GOLD platform.

6341 **www.adweek.com**
Adweek

Leading decision makers in the advertising and marketing field go to Adweek.com everyday for breaking news, insight, buzz, opinion, analysis, research and classifieds. The resources of all six regional editions of Adweek, as well as the national edition of Brandweek are combined with the knowledge of our online editors and the multimedia-interactive capabilities of the web to deliver vital information quickly and effectively to our target audience.

6342 **www.amma.org**
Advertising Mail Marketing Association

Represents the interests of those who use mail for fundraising or business purposes.

6343 **www.amsp.org**
Association of Marketing Service Providers

Formerly known as the Mailing & Fulfillment Service Association, the Association of Marketing Service Providers provides educational content, networking opportunities, and legislative advocacy.

6344 **www.ataconnect.org**
American Teleservices Association

Represents the call centers, trainers, consultants and equipment suppliers that initiate, facilitate and generate telephone, Internet and e-mail sales, service and support.

6345 **www.cadm.org**
Chicago Association of Direct Marketing

Promotes the interests of Chicago's direct marketing professionals. Fosters member development through business, educational and social opportunities and provides a high-quality forum for the exchange of ideas by direct marketing professionals.

6346 **www.dmnews.com**
Haymarket Media, Inc.
114 W 26th St.
4th Fl.
New York, NY 10001

646-638-6000

Ginger Conlon, Editor-in-Chief
Al Urbanski, Senior Editor
Natasha Smith, Senior Editor

Direct Marketing News covers the latest trends, proven strategies and essential technologies.

6347 **www.dsa.org**
Direct Selling Association

National trade association of the leading firms that manufacture and distribute goods and services sold directly to consumers. More than 150 companies are members of the association, including many well-known brand names. The association's mission is to protect, serve and promote the effectiveness of member companies and the independent business people they represent.

6348 **www.greyhouse.com**
Grey House Publishing

Authoritative reference directories for most business sectors incluidng direct marketing and public relations markets. Users can search the online databases with varied search criteria allowing for custom searches by product category, geographic area, sales volume, keyword, subject and more. Full Grey House catalog and online ordering also available.

6349 **www.imanetwork.org**
Internet Marketing Association

Seeks to provide members with the chance to learn, network, and establish Internet Marketing best practices. Members are in fields such as sales, marketing, business ownership, programming, and creative development.

6350 **www.marketingpower.com**
American Marketing Association

A professional association for individuals and organizations involved in the practice, teaching and study of marketing worldwide.

6351 **www.mfsanet.org**
Mailing & Fulfillment Service Association

The national trade association for the mailing and fulfillment services industry.

6352 **www.nedma.com**
New England Direct Marketing Association

6353 **www.nmoa.org**
National Mail Order Association

Offers the stongest and lowest cost means for people to come together for the purpose of conducting business and creating sales. Small to medium sized organizations come for education, information, ideas, resources and new contacts.

6354 **www.paceassociation.com**

PACE is a nonprofit trade organization dedicated exclusively to the advancement of companies that utilize contact centers as an integral channel of operations.

6355 **www.postcom.org**
Association for Postal Commerce

National organization representing those who use, or support the use, of mail as a medium for communication and commerce. Postcom publishes a weekly newsletter covering postal policy and operational issues.

6356 **www.the-dma.org**
Direct Marketing Association

Trade association in the direct marketing field with more than 3,500 member companies from the United States and 54 foreign nations. Included are catalogers, direct marketers from consumer to business-to-business, publishers, retail stores as well as service industries that support them.

Associations

6357 **Advanced Network & Services**
1225 Eye Street NW
Suite 550
Washington, DC 20005

Home Page: consumerbankers.com
Facebook, Twitter, LinkedIn

Richard Hunt, President & CEO
Jean Marie Bunton, EVP/Chief of Staff
Melanie Duffy, Executive Administrator to the CEO
Kevin O'Connor, VP, Corporate Membership
Joanna Beaver, CMP, SVP, Committees & Events

A nonprofit corporation dedicated to advancing education by accelerating the use of computer networking applications and technology.
Mailing list available for rent

6358 **Advertising Specialty Institute**
4800 Street Road
Trevose, PA 19053

800-546-1350
customerservice@asicentral.com
www.asicentral.com
Facebook, Twitter, LinkedIn, YouTube, Instagram, Pinterest

Norman Unger Cohn, Chair
Timothy M. Andrews, President & CEO
Steve Bright, EVP & General Counsel
Nancy Carmona, SVP, Business Strategy & Analysis
Andy Cohen, SVP, Editorial

The Advertising Specialty Institute (ASI) is a membership organization for the promotional product industry, offering media, technology, marketing, and educational services to members.
26000 Members
Founded in 1950

6359 **Alliance for Public Technology**
919 18th St NW
Suite 900
Washington, DC 20006-5512

480-624-2500; Fax: 202-263-2960

Sylvia Rosenthal, Executive Director
Matthew Bennett, Policy Director

A nonprofit membership organization based in Washington, DC.

6360 **American Public Communications Council**
625 Slaters Lane
Suite 104
Alexandria, VA 22314

703-739-1322
apcc@apcc.net

Aims to protect and expand domestic and foreign markets for public communications and provide business opportunities for members.
Founded in 1988

6361 **American Registry for Internet Numbers**
PO Box 232290
Centreville, VA 20120

703-227-9840; Fax: 703-263-0417
info@arin.net
www.arin.net
Facebook, Twitter, LinkedIn, YouTube

John Curran, President & CEO
Richard Jimmerson, COO
Susan Hamlin, Sr. Director, Communications

Manage the internet numbering resources for North America focused completely on serving its members and the Internet community at large.

6362 **American e-Commerce Association**
Home Page: www.aeaus.com

Computer training, e-commerce education, membership, recognition, endorsement, and evaluation services.

6363 **Association For Women in Computing**
PO Box 2768
Oakland, CA 94602

info@awc-hq.org
www.awc-hq.org

Jill Sweeney, President
Bonnie Sherwood, Treasurer
Crista Deniz, Secretary
Gabriela Levit, Web Communications VP

AWC is dedicated to promoting the advancement of women in the computing professions. Members include many types of computer professionals, such as programmers, system analysts, operators, technical writers, Internet specialists, trainers and consultants.
Founded in 1978

6364 **Association for the Advancement of Computing in Education**
PO Box 719
Waynesville, NC 28786

282-246-9558; Fax: 828-246-9557
info@aace.org
www.aace.org

Dr. Gary H. Marks, Chief Executive Officer

An international, educational and professional nonprofit organization dedicated to the advancement of the knowledge, theory and quality of learning and teaching at all levels with information technology.
Founded in 1981

6365 **Association of Ecommerce**
1234 Hydre Street
San Francisco, CA 90043

Home Page:
www.associationofecommerce.com

The Association of Ecommerce aims to support programming purchasers and administration searchers.
Founded in 2019

6366 **Association of Internet Researchers**
910 W Van Buren Street
Suite 100, #142
Chicago, IL 60607-3636

ac@aoir.org
www.aoir.org
Facebook, Twitter

Lynn Schofield Clark, President
Tama Leaver, Vice President
Kelly Quinn, Treasurer
Kat Tiidenberg, Secretary

A learned society dedicated to the advancement of the transdisciplinary field of Internet Studies.

6367 **Association of Software Professionals**
PO Box 1522
Martinsville, IN 46151

765-349-4740
asp-software.org/www/
Facebook, LinkedIn

Jeff Gibson, President
Joel Diamond, Vice President

The ASP is a professional trade association of software developers who are creating and marketing leading-edge applications. ASP provides a platform for its members to create a community, sharing their experiences involving desktop and laptop programs, software as a service, applications, cloud computing, and mobile apps.
Cost: $100.00
Founded in 1987

6368 **Business Marketing Association: Boston**
246 Hampshire Street
Cambridge, MA 02130

617-418-4000
800-664-4262; Fax: 312-822-0054
www.thebmaboston.com/

Michael Lewis, President
Will Robinson, VP Public Relations
Matthew Mamet, VP Internet Marketing
Larry Perreault, VP Finance
Chris Perkett, VP Programming

BMA Boston helps members improve their ability to manage business-to-business marketing and communications for greater productivity and profitability by providing unique access to information, ideas, and the experience of peers. The BMA offers an information-packed Website, online skills-building, marketing certification programs, and industry surveys and papers. In addition, members have the opportunity to interact with peers at seminars, chapter training programs and the BMA Annual Conference.

6369 **Business Software Alliance**
20 F Street NW
Suite 800
Washington, DC 20001

202-872-5500; Fax: 202-872-5501
info@bsa.org
www.bsa.org
Facebook, Twitter, LinkedIn, YouTube

Victoria A. Espinel, President & CEO
Adam J. Coates, General Counsel & VP
Ha McNeill, Chief Operating Officer
Joe DeSalvio, Chief Financial Officer

An organization dedicated to promoting a safe and legal digital world. BSA educates consumers on software management and copyright protection, cyber security, trade, e-commerce and other internet related issues.
Founded in 1988

6370 **CATA Alliance**
207 Bank Street
Suite 416
Ottawa, ON K2P 2N2

613-236-6550
info@cata.ca
cata.ca

Alice Debroy, Web Master & IT Manager
Cathi Malette, Members Service Manager

CATA Alliance (Canadian Advanced Technology Alliance) lobbies for innovation in the global tech industry.

6371 **CTIA-The Wireless Association**
1400 16th Street NW
Suite 600
Washington, DC 20036

202-736-3200
www.ctia.org
Facebook, Twitter, LinkedIn

Meredith Attwell Baker, President & CEO
Brad Gillen, EVP
Scott Bergmann, SVP, Regulatory Affairs
Tom Power, SVP & General Counsel
Rocco Carlitti, SVP & CFO

An industry trade group that represents the international wireless telecommunications industry.

6372 **Consumer Technology Association (CTA)**
1919 S Eads Street
Arlington, VA 22202

703-907-7600
cta@cta.tech

www.cta.tech
Facebook, Twitter, LinkedIn, Google+

Gary Shapiro, President & CEO
Glenda MacMullin, COO & CFO
Jean Foster, SVP, Marketing & Communications
Brian Markwalter, SVP, Research & Standards
Tiffany Moore, SVP, Political & Industry Affairs

Formerly known as the Consumer Electronics Association (CEA), the association provides valuable and innovative member-only resources including: exclusive information and unparalleled market research, networking opportunities with business advocates and leaders, up-to-date educational programs and technical training, exposure in extensive promotional programs, and representation from the voice of the industry.
2000 Members

6373 **Developers Alliance**
1201 Wilson Blvd.
Arlington, VA 22209

Home Page: www.developersalliance.org
Facebook, Twitter, LinkedIn

Bruce Gustafson, President & CEO
Dakota Graves, Communications Manager

The Developers Alliance serves and supports software developers through advocacy.
70000 Members
Founded in 2012

6374 **EMarketing Association**
251 W. 30th Street
6th Floor
New York, NY 10001

212-678-2520
admin@emarketingassociation.com
www.emarketingassociation.com
Twitter, LinkedIn, YouTube

International association of eMarketing professionals committed to enriching the marketing community and its members through recognition, research, advocacy, education, and service.
Founded in 1997

6375 **GS1 US**
300 Charles Ewing Blvd.
Ewing, NJ 08628

609-620-0200; Fax: 609-620-1200
www.gs1us.org
Facebook, Twitter, LinkedIn

Bob Carpenter, President & CEO
Yegneswaran Kumar, SVP & CFO
Melanie Nuce, SVP, Corporate Development
Siobhan O'Bara, SVP, Community Engagement
Bill Strawderman, VP, Marketing

Barcodes, eCommerce and data synchronization, to EPC/RFID and business process automation standards.
9000+ Members
Founded in 1973

6376 **Hispanic Chamber of E-Commerce**
750 B Street
Suite 3308
San Diego, CA 92101

858-768-2483
info@hiscec.com
www.hiscec.com
Facebook, YouTube

Tayde Aburto, Founder, President & CEO

The Hispanic Chamber of E-Commerce is a B2B membership-based national business association focused on providing tools and solutions to members to increase their presence online.
200 Members
Founded in 2008

6377 **Information Systems Security Association**
1654 Gallows Road
Suite 310
Vienna, VA 22182

703-382-8205
www.issa.org
Facebook, Twitter, LinkedIn, Instagram, YouTube

Marc Thompson, Executive Director
Lisa O'Connell, Sales/Sponsorships

International information and professional growth organization of information security professionals.

6378 **Information Technology Association of Canada**
5090 Explorer Drive
Suite 510
Mississauga, ON L4W 4T9

905-602-8345; Fax: 905-602-8346
amondou@itac.ca
itac.ca
Twitter

Angela Mondou, President & CEO
Denise Shortt, VP, Industry Development
Janet Gibson Eichner, Director, Communications
Christine Leonard, Director, Events & Program Devel.
Mariana Kutin Morais, Director, Membership Development

ITAC is a national association providing members with advocacy, networking and professional development services.
36000 Members

6379 **International Society for Technology in Education**
621 SW Morrison Street
Suite 800
Portland, OR 97205

503-342-2848
800-336-5191; Fax: 503-882-0813
iste@iste.org
www.iste.org
Facebook, Twitter, LinkedIn, YouTube, Pinterest

Bill Bass, President
Nikole Blanchard, Treasurer
Michael McVey, Secretary
Richard Culatta, Chief Executive Officer

A large nonprofit organization serving the technology-using educator.

6380 **Internet Marketing Association**
200 Spectrum Center Drive
Irvine, CA 92618

949-443-9300
info@imanetwork.org
imanetwork.org
Facebook, Twitter, LinkedIn, YouTube

Sinan Kanatsiz, Chair & Founder
Sean Conrad, CEO
Lei Lani Fera, Head Of Creative
Hall Roosevelt, General Manager
Marcus Volpe, Executive Director

Seeks to provide members with the chance to learn, network, and establish Internet Marketing best practices. Members are in fields such as sales, marketing, business ownership, programming, and creative development.
Founded in 2001

6381 **Internet Merchants Association**

Home Page: www.imamerchants.org
Facebook

Fred Neff, President
Scott Cole, Vice President
Doyle Carver, Secretary
Andy Sollofe, Treasurer

Develops, promotes, and protects the economic vitality of internet merchants through a positive business environment and fosters a climate in whichcommerce, industry, and technology will flourish.

6382 **Internet Society**
11710 Plaza America Drive
Suite 400
Reston, VA 20190

703-439-2120
isoc@isoc.org
www.internetsociety.org
Facebook, Twitter, LinkedIn, YouTube, Instagram

Andrew Sullivan, President & CEO
Sandy Spector, CFO & SVP, Business Operations
Rinalia Abdul Rahim, SVP, Strategy, Comm. & Engagement
Jeannette Engel, Sr. Director, Global HR
Susannah Gray, Director, Communications

An international, nonprofit organization that provides leadership in Internet related standards, education, and policy.
Founded in 1992

6383 **National E-Commerce Association**
PO Box 2825
Peoria, AZ 85380

Home Page: www.ecommerceassoc.com

The National E-Commerce Association provides an ear and a voice for the E-Commerce industry at the local, state and federal level. In addition to this, we have and will continue to negotiate the most aggressive pricing on goods and services for our members.
Founded in 1980

6384 **NetSuite Ecommerce**
500 Oracle Parkway
Redwood Shores, CA 94065

650-627-1000; Fax: 650-627-1001
info@netsuite.com
www.netsuite.com
Facebook, Twitter, LinkedIn, YouTube

Evan Goldberg, EVP
Jason Maynard, SVP, Global Field Operations
David Rodman, SVP, Customer Success
Sam Levy, SVP, Sales
Gary Wiessinger, SVP, Product Management

NetSuite E-commerce provides tools needed to drive growth in the e-commerce channel and streamline and automate business operations.
10000 Members
Founded in 1998

6385 **Network Professional Association**
3517 Camino Del Rio S
Suite 215
San Diego, CA 92108-4098

888-672-6720
www.npa.org

James Belasco, Chair & Treasurer
Richard Allan Kelley, Secretary

To support the network computing professional and the ideals of an empowered, continually developing, professionally certified, educated and experienced IT practitioner. NPA provides its members with relevant articles and interviews for the IT professional, a certification program, IT job boards, and hosted events and activities.
Founded in 1993

6386 **Professional Certifications for Emerging Tech**

847-299-4227
800-843-8227

office@iccp.org
www.iccp.org

Kewal Dhariwal, Executive Director

ICCP helps organizations and their employees address the demands of today's dynamic information environment through events, education, certification, and assessments.

6387 **Technology Services Industry Association**
17065 Camino San Bernardo
Suite 200
San Diego, CA 92127

858-674-5491
www.tsia.com
Facebook, Twitter, LinkedIn, YouTube, Instagram

J.B. Wood, President & CEO
Thomas Lah, Executive Director
Tom Rich, SVP, Operations
Ren, Grossrieder, SVP, Global Membership Development

A research and advisory firm dedicated to helping technology companies optimize every service touchpoint across the engagement lifecycle, uncovering the best ways to unlock profitable growth.

6388 **The App Association**
1401 K Street NW
Suite 501
Washington, DC 20005

202-331-2130; Fax: 202-331-2139
actpress@actonline.org
actonline.org
Facebook, Twitter, LinkedIn, Instagram, Tumblr

Morgan Reed, President
Mike Sax, Founder & Chair
Chelsea Thomas, Executive Director
Ren, Adam, Chief Financial Officer
Alex Cooke, Director of Membership

The App Association represents app makers and connected device companies in the mobile economy across the US. The App Association is the leading industry resource on market strategy, regulated industries, privacy, and security.
5000 Members
Founded in 1998

6389 **The Berkman Klein Center for Internet & Society**
Harvard University
23 Everett Street
2nd Floor
Cambridge, MA 02138

617-495-7547; Fax: 617-495-7641
hello@cyber.harvard.edu
cyber.harvard.edu
Facebook, Twitter, YouTube, SoundCloud

Urs Gasser, Executive Director
Sebastian Diaz, Director of Technology
Rob Faris, Director of Research
Reuben Langevin, Manager, Events & Operations

To explore and understand cyberspace; to study its development, dynamics, norms, and standards; and to assess the need or lack thereof for laws and sanctions.
Founded in 1997

6390 **US Internet Industry Association**
Luray, VA

A nonprofit North American trade association for Internet commerce, content and connectivity.
Founded in 1994

6391 **WebGuild**

Home Page: www.webguild.org

Vicky Kreyman, Founder & Editor

WebGuild is a group of website builders, advertisers and business persons working to build better platforms and content.

6392 **WebProfessionals.org**
PO Box 584
Washington, IL 61571-0584

662-493-2776
membership@webprofessionals.org
webprofessionals.org
Facebook, Twitter, LinkedIn, Instagram, Pinterest, YouTube

Mark DuBois, Executive Director & Chair

Also known as the World Organization of Webmasters, WebProfessionals.org is a non-profit professional association dedicated to the support of individuals and organizations who create, manage or market web sites including Web designers, Web developers, Webmasters and Web administrators and Search and Content Specialist.
Founded in 1996

6393 **Women in Technology**
200 Little Falls Streets
Suite 205
Falls Church, VA 22046

703-349-1044; Fax: 703-884-9165
staff@womenintechnology.org
www.womenintechnology.org
Facebook, Twitter, LinkedIn, YouTube

Daphne Wotherspoon, President
Suzanne Porter-Kuchay, Secretary
Yolimar "Yoli" Martinez-Nadal, Treasurer
Kathryn Harris, General Counsel

Aims to promote and enable the advancement of women in the technology industry. WIT provides its members with networking and mentoring opportunities in the Washington, D.C./Maryland/Virginia metro region.
Cost: $115.00
1000+ Members
Founded in 1994

6394 **Women in eCommerce**
PO Box 550856
Fort Lauderdale, FL 33355-0856

954-625-6606
www.wecai.org
Facebook, Twitter, LinkedIn

Heidi Richards Mooney, Founder & CEO
Rosana Santos, President

The original business and social networking community for social and professional networking and business development for successful women who want to take their businesses to a new level offline and online. Offers tools, resources and networking opportunities to build a strong foundation for future growth and expansion.
5300+ Members
Founded in 2001

6395 **eCommerce Merchants Trade Association**
New York, NY 10001

LinkedIn

Brandon Dupsky, Managing Director

eCommerce Merchants is a trade association founded by a group of online retailers who realized that by working together they could enjoy the premium services and discounted pricing normally available to very large companies.
Founded in 2005

6396 **eCommerce Professionals Association**
181 Main Street
Suite 2
Westerly, RI 02891

Home Page: ecommerceprofessionals.org
LinkedIn

Anne Driscoll, Managing Director

A national membership organization that provides eCommerce professionals with a centralized community for networking, education, and career development.
Founded in 2018

Newsletters

6397 **APT News**
Alliance for Public Technology
919 18th St Nw
Suite 1000
Washington, DC 20006-5512

202-263-2970; Fax: 202-263-2960
www.apt.org

Sylvia Rosenthal, Executive Director
Frequency: Bi-Monthly

6398 **ASPects**
Association of Software Professionals
PO Box 1522
Martinsville, IN 46151

765-349-4740
asp-software.org/www/aspects/

James Greene, Editor

ASP's official newsletter provides key insights pertaining to the software development industry. The publication's entire archive of issues is available for members.
Founded in 1988

6399 **Dot.COM**
Business Communications Company
25 Van Zant Street
Suite 13
Norwalk, CT 06855-1713

203-853-4266; Fax: 203-853-0348
sales@bccresearch.com
www.bccresearch.com

Louis Naturman, Publisher
C Toenne, Editor

Updates readers on the commercial use of the Internet and related platforms.
Cost: $38.00

6400 **E-Healthcare Market Reporter**
Health Resources Publishing
1913 Atlantic Ave
Suite 200
Manasquan, NJ 08736-1067

732-292-1100
888-843-6242; Fax: 732-292-1111
info@themcic.com
www.hin.com/ehealthcare

Robert K Jenkins, Publisher
Judith Granel, Marketing
John Russel, Editor
Brett Powell, Regional Director
Alice Burron, Director

A bi-monthly covering strategies, new products, innovation, privacy issue, business solutions, service available, vendor news and comparative for implementing sales and marketing on the internet.
Cost: $397.00
Frequency: Fortnightly
ISSN: 1098-5654
Founded in 1988

6401 **E-News**
Patricia Seybold Group
Po Box 240565
Boston, MA 02129
617-742-5200
800-826-2424; Fax: 617-742-1028
www.psgroup.com
Patricia Seybold, Founder/CEO
E-mail newsletter includes perspectives on the e-commerce industry, research and upcoming events.

6402 **Ecommerce @lert**
ZD Journals
500 Canal View Boulevard
Rochester, NY 14623-2800
585-407-7301; Fax: 585-214-2387
www.ecommercealert.com
Facebook, Twitter, LinkedIn
Bob Artner, Managing Editor
Explores the emerging digital and online technology used in sales management, as well as the companies in the forefront of this change.
Cost: $495.00

6403 **Electronic Commerce News**
Phillips Publishing
PO Box 60037
Potomac, MD 20859
301-208-6787; Fax: 301-424-2098
www.ectoday.com
Heather Treat, Publisher
Stuart Zipper, Editor
Diane Schwartz, Publisher
Laurie Hofmann, Director of Marketing
Provides business strategies for the extended enterprise with the latest technological development and opportunities.
Cost: $597.00
Frequency: Weekly

6404 **Higher Education Technology News**
Business Publishers
2222 Sedwick Dr
Suite 101
Durham, NC 27713
800-223-8720; Fax: 800-508-2592
custserv@bpinews.com
www.bpinews.com
Provides timely, independent coverage of the issues surrounding technology in a higher educational setting. Offers news from federal and state government, the business world and others educators.
Cost: $307.00
8 Pages
Founded in 1963

6405 **International Cyber Centers**
Probe Research
3 Wing Drive
Suite 240
Cedar Knolls, NJ 07927-1000
973-285-1500; Fax: 973-285-1519
www.proberesearch.com
Strategic positioning and product portfolios of major domestic and international carriers in collocation, Web hosting, applications hosting, e-commerce, IP-centric data, managed services and other value added offerings. Examines the global square footage race in building or upgrading what are variously known as Internet centers, data centers or cyber centers worldwide. Profiles of several key players are included in the bulletin issue.

6406 **Internet Alliance Cyberbrief**
Internet Alliance
1615 L Street NW
Suite 1100
Washington, DC 20036-5624
202-861-2407
Tammy Cota, Executive Director
Coverage of public policy changes in government, enhancing consumer satisfaction in interactive services, and education.
Frequency: Weekly

6407 **Internet Business**
Information Gatekeepers
1340 Soldiers Field Rd
Suite 3
Brighton, MA 02135-1000
617-782-5033
800-323-1088; Fax: 617-782-5735
info@igigroup.com
www.igigroup.com
Paul Polishuk, CEO
Hui Pan, Chief Analyst, Editor in Chief
Bev Wilson, Managing Editor
Covers the rapid developments in the industry.
Cost: $695.00
Frequency: Monthly

6408 **Internet Business Advantage**
ZD Journals
500 Canal View Boulevard
Rochester, NY 14623-2800
585-407-7301; Fax: 585-214-2387
Bob Artner, Editor-in-Chief
Keeps readers up-to-date of technological advances and new services available on the Internet. Reviews new products and provides tips on businss applications.
Cost: $295.00

6409 **Internet Media Investor**
Kagan World Media
126 Clock Tower Place
Carmel, CA 93923-8746
831-624-1536
800-307-2529; Fax: 831-625-3225
www.kagan.com
Facebook, Twitter, LinkedIn, YouTube
George Niesen, Editor
Tom Johnson, Marketing Manager
Follows public stocks and private deals, analyzes publicly held interactive multimedia companies, tracks key industry subgroups through Kagan stock averages that relate companies by product lines, projects growth of new TV and data networks, programming and technology. Provides economic modeling of new corporate ventures and interprets announcements and events. Three month trial is available.
Cost: $1095.00
Frequency: Monthly
Founded in 1969

6410 **Internet World**
Mecklermedia Corporation
20 Ketchum Street
Westport, CT 06880
212-260-0758; Fax: 203-454-5840
Bill Besch, Publisher
Internet industry news, product reviews and technical reports, with an emphasis on Internet technology, hardware, management and security.
Cost: $160.00
Frequency: Weekly
Circulation: 98,947

6411 **Internetweek**
CMP Media
600 Community Drive
Manhasset, NY 11030-3847
516-562-5000; Fax: 516-562-5554
www.internetweek.com
Mike Azzara, Publisher
News and coverage of the latest trends in electronic commerce and intranet application platforms, the effects of high technology on daily production, changing regulations and operating standards, the best tools and practices, and related business and financial news.
Cost: $143.00
Frequency: Weekly
Circulation: 161264

6412 **Manufacturing Automation**
Vital Information Publications
754 Caravel Lane
Foster City, CA 94404-1712
650-345-7018
www.sensauto.com
Peter Adrian, Owner
Gary Kuba, Marketing Director
Provides market research data and vital information about key products, applications, and technologies for a wide range of industrial automation segments, such as CAD/CAM, supply chain management, e-Commerce solutions, enterprise resource planning, automation software, manufacturing technology, industrial controls, and manufacturing systems.

6413 **Mass Storage News**
Corry Publishing
2840 W 21st Street
Erie, PA 16506
814-838-0025; Fax: 814-838-0035
terryp@corrypub.com
www.corrypub.com
Terry Peterson, Publisher
News on optical disk based imaging and storage systems, new products, technical developments and industry developments.
Cost: $597.00
Frequency: BiWeekly
Circulation: 1,500

6414 **Mealey's Litigation Report: Class Actions**
LexisNexis Mealey's
555 W 5th Avenue
Los Angeles, CA 90013
213-627-1130
mealeyinfo@lexisnexis.com
www.lexisnexis.com/mealeys
Tom Hagy, VP/General Manager
Maureen McGuire, Editorial Director
David Elreth, Editor
This report will provide in-depth coverage of class action litigation involving mass torts and beyond - including consumer law, employment law, securities litigation and e-commerce disputes. Get the latest on: hard-to-find filings, notice plans, fairness hearings, class certification rulings, settlements, trial news and verdicts, attorney fee news, appeals, breaking news stories, new complaints, Supreme Court battles, and much more.
Cost: $1195.00
100 Pages
Frequency: Semi-Monthly
Founded in 1997

6415 **Mealey's Litigation Report: Cyber Tech & E -Commerce**
LexisNexis Mealey's

555 W 5th Avenue
Los Angeles, CA 90013

213-627-1130
mealeyinfo@lexisnexis.com
www.lexisnexis.com/mealeys

Tom Hagy, VP/General Manager
Maureen McGuire, Editorial Director
Mark Rogers, Editor

The Report covers disputes arising from e-commerce. The report tracks emerging legal issues, including: Internet security, data destruction and/or alteration, defamation on the Web, software errors, hardware failure, electronic theft, e-mail trespass, online privacy, government action, shareholder lawsuits, Internet jurisdiction issues, file sharing (copyright) disputes and much more.
Cost: $999.00
100 Pages
Frequency: Monthly
Founded in 1999

6416 **Mobile Internet**
Information Gatekeepers
1340 Soldiers Field Rd
Suite 3
Brighton, MA 02135-1000

617-782-5033
800-323-1088; Fax: 617-782-5735
info@igigroup.com
www.igigroup.com

Paul Polishuk, CEO
Hui Pan, Chief Analyst, Editor in Chief
Bev Wilson, Managing Editor

Covers worldwide developments in 3G wireless networks, with an emphasis on the worldwide PCS/GSM/CDMA markets.
Cost: $695.00
Frequency: Monthly
Founded in 1977

6417 **Multimedia & Internet Training Newsletter**
Brandon Hall Resources
690 W Fremont Ave
#9C
Sunnyvale, CA 94087-4200

408-736-2335
www.brandon-hall.com
Facebook, Twitter, LinkedIn

Mike Cooke, CEO
Rachel Ashkin, COO
Michael Rochelle, CSO

The latest in multimedia news, virtual clasroom reports, insight into web-based training, and technology tutorial. Job bank listings, upcoming events, seminars, and tips and techniques.
Cost: $189.00
Frequency: Monthly
Circulation: 900

6418 **Online & CD-ROM Review**
Information Today
1308 W Main
University of Illinois
Urbana, IL 61801

217-333-1074
800-248-8466; Fax: 217-762-3956
custserv@infotoday.com
www.infotoday.com/

Martha Williams, Editor
Thomas H Hogan, CEO/President
Heather Rudolph, Marketing
Inge Coffey, Circulation Manager

Covers the use and management of online and CD-ROM services, the training and education of online and CD-ROM users, creation and marketing of databases, and new development in search aids.
Cost: $115.00
Frequency: Monthly
Circulation: 4745

6419 **Online Libraries & Microcomputers**
Information Intelligence
PO Box 31098
Phoenix, AZ 31098

602-996-2283
www.phoenix-intel.com

George Machovec, Managing Editor

Examines new library online and automation applications with reviews of new software and hardware, industry news and trends, and upcoming related events.
Cost: $62.50
9 Pages
Frequency: 10 per year
ISSN: 0737-7770
Founded in 1983

6420 **Online Newsletter**
Information Intelligence
PO Box 31098
Phoenix, AZ 85046-1098

602-996-2283
www.phoenix-intel.com

Richard S Huleatt, Editor

Covers all aspects of online and CD-ROM developments throughout the world. Regular feature sections include news and events, mergers and acquisitions, people in the news, telecommunications, and networks. Editoral reflects product development and its impact on users, and provides listings of upcoming events related to this industry.
Cost: $62.50
9 Pages
Frequency: 10 per year
ISSN: 0194-0694
Founded in 1983

6421 **Online Reporter**
G2 Computer Intelligence
PO Box 7
Glen Head, NY 11545-1616

516-759-7025; Fax: 516-759-7028
www.g2news.com

Maureen O'Gara, Publisher

Information on recent developments on the Internet through news briefs and a section called Chat Room. Includes information on e-commerce, Java and network security.
Cost: $695.00
Frequency: Weekly

6422 **Privacy Journal**
P.O. Box 28577
Providence, RI 02908

401-274-7861; Fax: 401-274-4747
www.privacyjournal.net

Robert Ellis Smith, Publisher

An independent monthly on privacy in a computer age.
Cost: $65.00
Frequency: Monthly
ISSN: 0145-7659
Founded in 1974
Printed in one color

6423 **Report on Electronic Commerce**
Telecommunications Reports International
1333 H Street NW
#100 E
Washington, DC 20005-4707

202-842-3022; Fax: 202-842-1875
www.tr.com

Jerry Ashworth, Editor
Brian Hammond, Managing Editor

Provides insiths on the latest developments in EDI, EFT, EBT, digital cash, home shopping and baking, value-added networks, and transaction processing. Offers articles, analysis and case studies regarding financial and business transaction over the Internet.
Cost: $745.00
Frequency: BiWeekly

6424 **Sysop News and Cyberworld Report**
BBS Press Service
5610 SW 10th Avenue
Topeka, KS 66604-2104

785-286-4272; Fax: 785-271-0192
www.sysop.com

Alan R Bechtold, Publisher
Debbie Boos, Owner

Online industry news and updates, Web site reviews, event announcements, Web design basics, Internet-based applicaitons, business solutions and various technical articles of interest.
Cost: $59.95
Frequency: Weekly
Circulation: 18M

6425 **TechTarget**
TechTarget
117 Kendrick St
Suite 800
Needham Heights, MA 02494-2728

781-657-1000
888-274-4111; Fax: 781-657-1100
info@techtarget.com
www.techtarget.com

Greg Strakosch, CEO
Don Hawk, President
Lisa Johnson, VP Marketing
Catherine Engelke, Dieector Public Relations

IBM iSeries focused media. The IBM e-Server iSeries (formerly the AS/400) is considered to be the world's most often used multi-user business computer. The installed base worldwide is huge and will get bigger, fueled by incresed Web development. The iSeries comes with an integrated Web application server and all the tools needed to build internet, intranet, extranet, and e-commerce sites quickly and will figure prominently into IT strategy and implementation for years to come.
Frequency: Monthly
Founded in 1999

6426 **The CyberSkeptic's Guide to Internet Research**
Information Today
143 Old Marlton Pike
Medford, NJ 08055-8750

609-654-6266
800-300-9868; Fax: 609-654-4309
custserv@infotoday.com
www.infotoday.com

Thomas H Hogan, President
Roger R Bilboul, Chairman Of The Board

A monthly subscription newsletter in print, that explores and evaluates free and low cost Web sites and search strategies to help you use the Internet and stay up to date.
Cost: $164.95
ISSN: 1085-2417

6427 **Trade Vendor Quarterly**
Blakeley & Blakeley
2 Park Plaza
Suite 400
Irvine, CA 92614

949-260-0611; Fax: 949-260-0613
www.vendorlaw.com

Scott Blakey, Esq.

Highlights developments in commercial, creditors' rights, e-commerce and bankruptcy law of

interest to the credit and financial professional.
Free online.
Frequency: Quarterly

6428 **WECommerce News**
Women in eCommerce
PO Box 550856
Fort Lauderdale, FL 33355-0856

954-625-6606
heidi@wecai.org
www.wecai.org

Heidi Richards Mooney, Founder & CEO
Rosana Santos, President
Ellen Sue Burton, VP/Logistics & Hospitality
Racheli Smilovitz, VP/Professional Development
Suzannah Richards, Past President & Co-Founder

Helping women do business on the web.
Frequency: Quarterly
Founded in 2001

6429 **Web Review**
Miller Freeman Publications
600 Harrison Street
San Francisco, CA 94107

650-573-3210

Veronica Costanza, Publisher

Timely and practical information on the practice of Internet development as well as news on the latest techniques and technologies.
Frequency: BiWeekly
Circulation: 12M

6430 **Webdeveloper.com**
Mecklermedia Corporation
23 Old Kings Hwy S
Darien, CT 06820-4541

203-662-2800; Fax: 203-655-4686
info@WebMediaBrands.com
www.webmediabrands.com

Alan M Meckler, CEO
Mike Demiot, Marketing Manager

Product reviews, practical techniques, codes, tools and tips for Internet professionals who design, develop and maintain Web sites and Internet services.
Frequency: Daily

6431 **West Side Leader/Green Leader**
Leader Publications
3075 Smith Rd
Suite 204
Akron, OH 44333-4454

330-665-0909
888-945-9595; Fax: 330-665-9590
webmaster@akron.com
www.akron.com

Kathryn Core, Editor
Kathleen Collins, Managing Editor
Maria Lindsay, Assistant Editor

Weekly newspapers.
Cost: $10.00
Circulation: 53000

Magazines & Journals

6432 **Active Server Developer's Journal**
ZD Journals
500 Canal View Boulevard
Rochester, NY 14623-2800

585-407-7301; Fax: 585-214-2387

Jon Pyles, Publisher
Taggard Andrews

Addresses such issues as database publishing, creating hack-proof files and getting the most out of server-side components. Special sections focus on client-side solutions, covering the basics and taking an in-depth look at more detailed techniques.
Cost: $149.00
Frequency: Monthly

6433 **Advantages**
Advertising Specialty Institute
4800 Street Road
Trevose, PA 19053

800-546-1350
ideas@asicentral.com
www.asicentral.com

Timothy Andrews, President & CEO
Dave Vagnoni, Editor

Written especially for the promotional products sales professional, with tips and sales tactics.
Frequency: 15x/Year

6434 **Bio & Software and Internet Report**
Mary Ann Liebert
140 Huguenot St # 3
3rd Floor
New Rochelle, NY 10801-5215

914-740-2100; Fax: 914-740-2101
info@liebertpub.com
www.liebertpub.com
Facebook, Twitter, LinkedIn

Mary A Liebert, Owner
Gerry Elman, Editor-in-Chief
Robert A Bohrer, Executive Editor
Judith Gunn Bronson, Managing Editor

News and reviews of all areas of scientific computing, including software, hardware and network products.
Cost: $1554.00
ISSN: 1527-9162
Founded in 1980

6435 **Boardwatch Magazine**
Penton Media
1300 E 9th St # 316
Cleveland, OH 44114-1503

216-696-7000; Fax: 216-696-6662
www.penton.com

Jane Cooper, Marketing
David Icopf, Editorial Director

Editorial coverage for communications service providers.
Cost: $72.00
Frequency: Monthly
Circulation: 50,000
ISSN: 1054-2760
Founded in 1987
Mailing list available for rent: 50,000 names at $250 per M

6436 **BtoB Magazine**
Ad Age Group/ Division of Crain Communications
711 3rd Ave
New York, NY 10017-4014

212-210-0785; Fax: 212-210-0200
info@crain.com
www.crain.com

Norm Feldman, Manager

Dedicated to integrated business to business marketing. Every page is packed with substance news, reports, technologies, benchmarks, best practices served up by the most knowledgeable journalists.
Frequency: Monthly
Circulation: 45000

6437 **Card Technology**
Thomson Financial Publishing
1 State St
27th Floor
New York, NY 10004-1481

212-825-8445
800-221-1809; Fax: 212-843-9622

Daniel Wolfe, Editor in Chief
Austin Kilgore, Managing Editor
Ed McKinley, Independent Sales Organizations
Hope Lerman, National Sales Manager

Store-value cards, optical-memory cards, biometrics, cards on the Internet, cards for electronic data storage, and devices used with these cards in banking, government, telecommunications, transportation and education.
Cost: $ 98.00
Frequency: Monthly
Circulation: 25000
Printed in 4 colors on glossy stock

6438 **Computer & Online Industry Litigation Reporter**
Andrews Publications
175 Strafford Avenue
Building 4, Suite 140
Wayne, PA 19087-3331

610-225-0510
800-345-1101; Fax: 610-225-0501

John Backe, Publisher

Editorial covers telecommuncations and the Internet for attorneys and professionals in the legal field.
Cost: $850.00

6439 **Computer Gaming World**
Ziff Davis Publishing Company
101 2nd St # 900
8th Floor
San Francisco, CA 94105-3650

415-547-8000; Fax: 415-547-8777
info@ziffdavis.com
www.ziffdavis.com

Dale Strang, Manager
Matt Leone, Editor
Paul Fusco, Sales Director
Bobby Markowitz, Marketing Director
Stephen Hicks, General Counsel

Reviews commercially available and on-line games. Features interviews with game designers, as well as strategy tips, contests and news.
Cost: $98.88
Frequency: Monthly
Circulation: 212783

6440 **Computer Journal**
Las Vegas Computer Journal
2232 S Nellis Boulevard
#169
Las Vegas, NV 89104-6213

702-270-4656; Fax: 702-432-6204

Johanna Nezhoda, Publisher

Spotlights Web news, site reviews, interface tools and commentary on the changing face of computing.
Cost: $24.95
Frequency: Monthly
Circulation: 25M

6441 **Computer Music Journal**
MIT Press
3 Cambridge Ctr # 23
Cambridge, MA 02142-1613

617-499-3200; Fax: 617-621-0856
journals-orders@mit.edu

Miguel Suarez, Manager
Keeril Makan, Managing Editor

Tutorials and research articles, news and reviews of computer music systems, hardware and software for music sound, digital audio, sig-

nal processing and multimedia.
Cost: $82.00
120 Pages
Frequency: Quarterly
Circulation: 5000
Founded in 1926

6442 **Computer Service & Repair Magazine**
Searle Publishing Company
5511 Morning Glory Ln
#210-110
Littleton, CO 80123-2701

303-730-3006
810-797-8708; Fax: 303-797-0276
www.independentcable.com

Robert Searle, Publisher
Roderick Robles, Associate Publisher

Information on the maintenance and repair of computer systems. Reviews new products and technology.

6443 **Corporate Help Desk Solutions**
Gartner Group
Po Box 10212
Stamford, CT 06904-2212

203-964-0096; Fax: 203-316-6488
help@gartner.com
www.gartner.com
Facebook, Twitter, LinkedIn

Jean Hall, CEO
Gene Hall, CEO/President
David Godfrey, Marketing/Circulation
Robin Kranich, SVP Human Resources

Key technologies, management practices and techniques for the most cost-effective help desk solutions.
Cost: $395.00
Frequency: Monthly
Founded in 1979

6444 **Counselor**
Advertising Specialty Institute
4800 Street Road
Trevose, PA 19053

800-546-1350
ideas@asicentral.com
www.asicentral.com

Timothy Andrews, President & CEO
Andy Cohen, VP, Editorial & Marketing Services

Counselor covers marketing trends and new products, and is aimed at distributor principals.
Frequency: Monthly

6445 **Customer Interaction Solutions**
Technology Marketing Corporation
1 Technology Plz
Norwalk, CT 06854-1936

203-852-6800
800-243-6002; Fax: 203-853-2845
tmc@tmcnet.com
www.tmcnet.com

Rich Tehrani, CEO
Tracey Schelmetic, Managing Editor
Erik D Lounsbury, Editorial Director

Magazine devoted to teleservices and e-services outsourcing, marketing and consumer management issues.
Frequency: Monthly
Founded in 1982

6446 **Customer Interface**
Advanstar Communications
6200 Canoga Avenue
2nd Floor
Woodland Hills, CA 91367

818-593-5000; Fax: 818-593-5020
info@advanstar.com
www.advanstar.com

Joseph Loggia, President
Chris DeMoulin, VP
Susannah George, Marketing Director

Business management resource for senior and mid-level decision makers who are responsible for call centers, customer contact and customer service initiatives. We are stewards for the industry as we prepare it for continued transformation and growth.
Circulation: 50,000
Founded in 1988

6447 **CyberDealer**
Meister Publishing Company
37733 Euclid Ave
Willoughby, OH 44094-5992

440-942-2000
800-572-7740; Fax: 440-975-3447
www.meisternet.com

Gary Fitzgerald, President

Helps agricultural dealerships better manage their operations.
Frequency: 6 per year

6448 **Desktop Video Communications**
BCR Enterprises
950 York Road
#203
Hinsdale, IL 60521-8609

630-789-6700; Fax: 630-323-5324
www.bcr.com

Fred Knight, Publisher/Editor-in-Chief

Useful information for communications and informations systems managers, line managers, system developers and integrators, value-added resellers, and software vendors.
Frequency: Bi-Monthly
Circulation: 30M

6449 **Digital Travel**
Jupiter Communications Company
627 Broadway
2nd Floor
New York, NY 10012-2612

212-533-8885; Fax: 212-780-6075

Eva Papoutsakis, Editor
Marla Kammer, Managing Director
Ellen Daley, Managing Director
Charles Rutstein, Chief Operating Officer

Editorial includes the latest information and technology in agencies, airlines, lodging, ticketing, mapping, Web advertising, transaction processing, revenue models, demographics, and full-service sites.
Cost: $595.00
Frequency: Monthly

6450 **E-Business Advisor**
Advisor Media
P.O.Box 503350
San Diego, CA 92150-3350

858-278-5600
800-336-6060; Fax: 858-278-0300
www.e-businessadvisor.com

John L Hawkins, Editorial Director
Jane Falla, Senior Editor
Brian Dunning, Technical Editor

E-Business Advisor is the monthly magazine presenting the best innovation, strategies, and practices for e-business leaders. It is an independent guide for the team of business and technical managers within an enterprise responsible for strategic innovation, planning, design, implementation, and management of e-business and e-commerce solutions.
Cost: $49.00
68 Pages
Circulation: 60000
ISSN: 1098-8912
Founded in 1983
Mailing list available for rent: 60000 names at $175 per M

6451 **E-Content**
Information Today
143 Old Marlton Pike
Medford, NJ 08055-8750

609-654-6266
800-300-9868; Fax: 609-654-4309
custserv@infotoday.com
www.infotoday.com

Thomas H Hogan, President
Roger R Bilboul, Chairman Of The Board

Delivers essential research, reporting, news and analysis of content related issues. It is essential reading for executive and professionals involved in content creation, management, acquisition, organization and distribution in both commercial and enterprise environments.
Cost: $115.00
Frequency: 10 issues/yr
Mailing list available for rent: 4M names
Printed in 4 colors on glossy stock

6452 **ESchool News**
IAQ Publications
7920 Norfolk Ave # 900
Suite 900
Bethesda, MD 20814-2539

301-913-0115; Fax: 301-913-0119
gdowney@eschoolnews.com
www.eschoolnews.com

Robert Morrow, Owner

Guide to buying and updating classroom technology for K-12 educators. Product information listings, industry updates and related reports. Covers grant writing and funding, as well as government legislation regarding education.
Cost: $90.00

6453 **Electronic Commerce Advisor**
Thomson Reuters
195 Broadway # 4
New York, NY 10007-3124

646-822-2000
800-231-1860; Fax: 646-822-2800
trta.lei-support@thomsonreuters.com
www.ria.thomsonreuters.com

Elaine Yadlon, Plant Manager
Thomas H Glocer, CEO & Director
Robert D Daleo, Chief Financial Officer
Kelli Crane, Senior Vice President & CIO

Offers the latest in electronic commerce covering what's available and how to select and employ the best technology without costly trial-and-error mistakes. Information on EDI, e-mail, fax gateways, Internet, encryption, VANs, procurement cards, imaging, voice response, remote computering and other related information.
Cost: $155.00
Circulation: 4500
Founded in 1940

6454 **Electronic Mail & Messaging Systems**
Business Research Publications
1333 H Street NW
Suite 100 East
Washington, DC 20005-4707

202-364-6473
800-822-6338; Fax: 202-842-1875

Rod Kuckro, Editor-in-Chief

Exclusive biweekly intelligence technology applications, products and market trends in electronic mail, computer fax, wireless messaging

and the Internet.
Cost: $595.00
Frequency: BiWeekly

6455 **Electronic Publishing**
PennWell Publishing Company
98 Spit Brook Rd # Ll-1
Nashua, NH 03062-5737

603-891-0123; Fax: 603-891-9294
genepri@pennwell.com
www.pennwell.com

Christine Shaw, VP
Keith V. Hevenor, Editor

For those who communicate in print, including service bureaus, printers, prepress houses and desktop publishers, it provides latest products, news and related developments.
Cost: $59.00
Frequency: Monthly
Circulation: 68441
Founded in 1910

6456 **Electronic Retailer Magazine**
Electronic Retailing Association
7918 Jones Branch Dr
Suite 300
McLean, VA 22102

703-841-1751
800-987-6462; Fax: 703-841-1860
www.electronicretailermag.com
Facebook, Twitter, LinkedIn, YouTube

Ian P Murphy, Senior Editor
Andrew Bankert, Managing Editor
Laura Gaenzle, Account Executive

Delivers news updates, exclusives, industry research, educational features and in-depth converage of issues relating to government affairs, legal aspects, concepts and products, production, media-buying as well as all back end services.
Frequency: 6X/yr
Circulation: 10000

6457 **Emediaweekly**
Mac Publishing
501 2nd St
San Francisco, CA 94107-1496

415-243-0505
800-288-6848; Fax: 415-442-0766
sitehelp@macworld.com
www.macworld.com
Facebook, Twitter, YouTube

Mike Kisseberth, CEO

Covers the creation, technologies, applications and hardware for the publishing spectrum, including print, Web, multimedia, CD and digital video. Emphasis on hardware and software products, along with analysis, reviews, and buyer's guides.
Cost: $125.00
Frequency: Weekly

6458 **Empowered Learning Magazine**
International Society for Technology in Education
621 SW Morrison Street
Suite 800
Portland, OR 97205

503-342-2848
800-336-5191; Fax: 503-882-0813
iste@iste.org
www.iste.org

Richard Culatta, Chief Executive Officer

A large nonprofit organization serving the technology-using educator.

6459 **Explore the Net with Internet Explorer**
ZD Journals
500 Canal View Boulevard
Rochester, NY 14623-2800

585-407-7301; Fax: 585-214-2386

Joelle Martin, Publisher

Informs readers of new features and how they may be used; covering such concepts as browser upgrades, compatibility issues, authoring tools and connection utilities. Regular departments showcase the 'site of the month,' in addition to reviewing other sites that have attractive interfaces and are valaluble resources.
Cost: $49.00
Frequency: Monthly

6460 **GEOWorld**
Bel-Av Communciations
359 Galahad Rd
Bolingbrook, IL 60440-2108

Home Page: www.geoplace.com

Jo Treadwell, VP/Group Publisher
Todd Danielson, Editor

Offers a wealth of knowledge through festures, news and commentary covering the geospatial industry. Covers local and federal government, emergency management, infrastructure, natural resource management, industry trends and innovations and more.
Cost: $72.00
Frequency: Monthly
Circulation: 25000

6461 **Genealogical Computing**
Ancestry
360 W 4800 N
Provo, UT 84604-5675

801-705-7000
800-262-3787; Fax: 801-705-7001
www.myfamily.com
Facebook, Twitter

Timothy P Sullivan, CEO
Matthew Wright, Contributing Editor
David C Moon, CEO
Mary-Kay Evans, Director, Public Relations

For readers who use computers and technology to organize and enhance their research into accounts of ancestries and descent.
Cost: $25.00
Frequency: Quarterly

6462 **Geospatial Solutions**
Advanstar Communications
201 Sandpointe Ave # 600
Suite 500
Santa Ana, CA 92707-8700

714-513-8400; Fax: 714-513-8680
www.geospatial-solutions.com

Mike Weldon, Plant Manager

Practical applications of geographic information systems and technologies for planning, developing, preserving, analyzing and managing environments.
Frequency: Monthly
Circulation: 30000
Founded in 1987

6463 **Harlow Report: Geographic Information Systems**
Advanced Information Management Group
905 Thistledown Lane
Birmingham, AL 35244-3361

334-982-9203
chris@geoint.com
www.theharlowreport.com/

Chris Harlow, Publisher/Editor

Key management issues and new software highlights, service providers and users for the geographic information systems industry.
Cost: $190.00
Frequency: Monthly
Founded in 1982

6464 **Heller Report on Internet Strategies for Education Markets**
Nelson B Heller & Associates
9933 Lawler Avenue
#502
Skokie, IL 60077-3708

800-525-5811
877-435-5373; Fax: 303-209-9444
info@hellerreports.com
Facebook, Twitter

Nelson B Heller, President/Publisher
Emily Garner, Sales/Marketing Director

Covers Internet hardware, software and services for educational use. Discusses the funding and deadlines relevant to the products and services offered through the Internet.
Cost: $397.00
12 Pages
Frequency: Monthly
Circulation: 500
Founded in 1981
Printed in 2 colors

6465 **IEEE Internet Computing**
IEEE Computer Society
PO Box 3014
Los Alamitos, CA 90720-1314

714-821-8380
800-272-6657; Fax: 714-821-4010
volunteer.services@computer.org
www.computer.org/internet
Facebook, Twitter, LinkedIn, YouTube

Angela Burges, Executive Director
Davis Hennage, CEO/President
Steve Woods, Production Manager
Sandy Brown, Marketing
Steve Woods, Production Manager

Provides a technology roadmap for high-end users and application developers, as well as a venue for standards, case histories, and new ideas. Essays, interview, and roundtable discussions address the Internet's impact on engineering practice. Describes Internet tools, technologies, and application-oriented research.
Cost: $28.00
Frequency: Quarterly
Circulation: 11265
Founded in 1946

6466 **IT Cost Management Strategies**
Computer Economics
2082 Business Center Dr
Suite 240
Irvine, CA 92612

949-831-8700; Fax: 949-442-7688
www.computereconomics.com

Frank Scavo, President
Dan Husiak, VP

Covers budgeting, financial news, computer programming, marketing and management for management information systems directors as a planning assistant.
Frequency: Monthly
Founded in 1978

6467 **ITS World**
Advanstar Communications
859 Willamette Street
Eugene, OR 97401-2918

541-431-0026; Fax: 541-344-3514
www.itsworld.com

Phillip Arndt, Publisher

Articles on industry news, current issues that affect Intelligent Transportation Systems, practical advice, applications, new and existing

technology, and new product information.
Cost: $35.00
Frequency: 9 per year
Circulation: 15,124

6468 **Information Display**
Palisades Institute for Research Services
2 Shadybrook Lane
Norwalk, CT 06854

203-853-7069; Fax: 203-855-9769
office@sid.org
www.sid.org

Kenneth I Werner, Editor
Shigeol Mikoshiba, President/CEO

State-of-the-art developments in electronic, electromechanical and hardcopy display equipment; input and output technologies; storage media; human factors and display standards; entrepreneurship, marketing and management; and manufacturing.
Cost: $36.00
Frequency: Monthly
Circulation: 11000
Founded in 1962
Printed in 4 colors

6469 **Information Retrieval & Library Automation**
Lomond Publications
PO Box 88
Mount Airy, MD 21771-0088

202-362-1361; Fax: 202-362-6156

Thomas Hattery, Publisher

New technology, products and equipment that improve information systems and library services, for science, social, social science, law, medicine, academic institutions and the public.
Cost: $75.00
Frequency: Monthly

6470 **Information Security**
International Computer Security Association
117 Kendrick Street
Suite 800
Needham, MA 02494

781-657-1000; Fax: 781-657-1100
www.infosecuritymag.com

Andrew Briney, VP
Lawrence Walsh, Editor
Michael S Mimoso, Senior Editor
Gabrielle DeRussy, Advertising Sales
Susan Rastellini Smith, Product Management

Articles and analysis of information-security issues such as media, entwork and virus protection, internet security and encryption reports.
Cost: $100.00
Frequency: Monthly
Circulation: 60000
Founded in 1999

6471 **Inside the Internet**
ZD Journals
500 Canal View Boulevard
Rochester, NY 14623-2800

585-407-7301; Fax: 585-214-2387

Joelle Martin, Publisher

Information and hands-on instruction for applications along with some pictorial explanation.
Cost: $49.00
Frequency: Monthly

6472 **Internet & Intranet Business and Technology Report**
Computer Technology Research Corporation
6 N Atlantic Wharf
Charleston, SC 29401-2115

843-766-5293; Fax: 843-853-7210
www.ctrcorp.com

Edward Wagner, Publisher

Reports on international news, historical profiles of the impact of various applications, and developing standards and regulations. Topics covered include domain registration, Webcasting and the market for Internet e-mail.
Cost: $390.00
Frequency: Monthly

6473 **Internet Business**
Ziff Davis Publishing Company
28 E 28th St
New York, NY 10016-7940

212-503-5772

Steve Weitzner, CEO
Adam Gordon, VP

Provides in-depth information and analysis on Internet products, techniques and tools, based on comparative lab testing and real world experience. Feature articles address technology segments that optimize an Internet strategy such as firewalls, authoring tools, etc., and how-to columns look at technical issues surrounding Web site development.
Cost: $24.99
Frequency: Monthly

6474 **Internet Business Strategies**
Gartner Group
Po Box 10212
Stamford, CT 06904-2212

203-964-0096; Fax: 203-316-6488
info@gartner.com
www.gartner.com
Facebook, Twitter, LinkedIn

Jean Hall, CEO
Eugene Hall, CEO
David Godfrey, Senior Vice President
John Gardner, President
Robin Kranich, SVP Human Resources

Helps readers make informed decisions about how to use the Internet to deploy electronic commerce and interactive initiatives.
Cost: $395.00
Frequency: Weekly
Circulation: 10,000
Founded in 1993

6475 **Internet Reference Service Quarterly**
Taylor & Francis
325 Chestnut Street
Suite 800
Philadelphia, PA 19106

800-354-1420; Fax: 215-625-2940
www.tandf.co.uk

Brenda Reeb, Editor

Designed to function as a comprehensive information source librarians can turn to and count on for keeping up-to-date on emerging technological innovations, while emphasizing theoretical, research, and practical applications of Internet-related information services, sources and resources.
Cost: $82.00
Frequency: Quarterly
Circulation: 3000
ISSN: 1087-5301
Founded in 1978

6476 **Internet Shopper**
Mecklermedia Corporation
20 Ketchum Street
Westport, CT 06880-5908

203-662-2800; Fax: 203-454-5840
www.internetshopper.com

Susan Leiterstein, Publisher

Edited for consumers who purchas products and services direct from Interet Web sites. Covers online malls, computers and electronics, stocks, books, home furnishings, music and more. Reviews the best sites within their categoreis and includes tips on how to conduct safe and effective online transactions.
Frequency: Daily

6477 **Internet Telephony**
Technology Marketing Corporation
1 Technology Plz
Norwalk, CT 06854-1936

203-852-6800
800-243-6002; Fax: 203-853-2845
tmc@tmcnet.com
www.tmcnet.com

Rich Tehrani, CEO
Richard Tehrani, President/Group Publisher
Shirley A. Russo, Circulation Director

News and departments focus on providing readers with information they need to learn about and purchase the equipment, software and services necessary for Internet telephony, through the convergence of voice, video, fax and data.
Frequency: Monthly
Circulation: 28024
Founded in 1972

6478 **Internet World**
Mecklermedia Corporation
20 Ketchum Street
Westport, CT 06880-5908

203-226-6967; Fax: 203-454-5840

Corey Friedman, Publisher
Michael Neubarth, Editor

For noncommercial and commercial uses of Internet and the National Research and Education Network.
Cost: $5.00
Circulation: 256883
Founded in 1971

6479 **Journal of Electronic Imaging**
International Society for Optical Engineering
1000 20th Street
Bellingham, WA 98225-10

360-676-3290; Fax: 360-647-1445
customerservice@spie.org
www.spie.org

Kristin Lewotsky, Executive Editor
Winn Hardin, Senior Editor
Michael Brownell, Contributing Editors
Amy Nelson, Manager

Timely information about evolving imaging technologies, including image acquistions, image data storage, image data display, image visualization, image processing, image data communciations, hard copy output and multimedia systems.
Cost: $135.00
Frequency: Quarterly
Circulation: 1500
Founded in 1992

6480 **Journal of Internet Law**
Apen Publishers
400 Hamilton Avenue
Palo Alto, CA 94301-1809

650-328-6561; Fax: 650-327-3699
www.gcfw.com

Mark F Radcliffe, Editor-in-Chief

Discusses strategies utilized by top intellectual property, computer law and information technology industry experts.
Frequency: Monthly

6481 **Journal of Technology in Human Services**
Taylor & Francis

325 Chestnut Street
Suite 800
Philadelphia, PA 19106

800-354-1420; Fax: 215-625-2940
www.tandf.co.uk

Dick Schoech PhD, Editor

Explores the potentials of computer and telecommunciations technologies in mental health, developmental disability, welfare, addictions, education, and other human services.
Cost: $120.00
Frequency: Quarterly
ISSN: 1522-8835
Founded in 1978
Mailing list available for rent
Printed in one color on matte stock

6482 **KM World**
Information Today
18 Bayview Street
PO Box 1358
Camden, ME 04843-1358

207-236-8524; Fax: 207-236-6452
webmaster@kmworld.com
www.kmworld.com
Facebook, Twitter, LinkedIn

Hugh McKellar, Editor in Chief
Sandra Haimila, Managing Editor
Michael V Zarrello, Advertising Director
Andy Moore, Publisher
David Panara, Sales Manager

Serves content, document and knowledge of management market to help improve business performance.
Circulation: 56000

6483 **MacTech**
Xplain Corporation
PO Box 5200
Westlake Village, CA 91359-5200

805-494-9797; Fax: 805-494-9798
custservice@mactech.com
www.mactech.com
Twitter

Neil Ticktin, Publisher
Dave Mark, Executive Editor
Edward Marczak, Executive Editor
David Allen, Production Manager

Provides web developers and network administrators with the most technically advanced information for them to combat the needs of the industry. How to articles, technically oriented product reviews with a Mac focus.
Cost: $19.95
Frequency: Monthly
ISBN: 3-212874-88-7
ISSN: 1067-8360
Founded in 1984
Printed in on glossy stock

6484 **On the Internet**
Rickard Group
1775 Wiehle Ave
Suite 201
Reston, Va 20190-5108

703-439-2120
www.isoc.org
Facebook, Twitter, LinkedIn, YouTube

Wendy Rickard Bollentin, Publisher

Internet information for technologists, developers, educators, researchers, government representatives, and business people.
Cost: $22.00
Frequency: Bi-Monthly
Circulation: 9M

6485 **Optical Technology 21st Century**
Frames Data
PO Box 2141
Skokie, Il 60077

800-739-7555
847-763-9532
customerservice@framesdata.com
www.framesdata.com

Skip Johnson, President
Hunter Noell, Business Development Manager

Movement of product electronically; computerization of office functions, lab work, testing procedures and equipment; information on the Internet, optical Web sites, and onlines services.
Cost: $299.00
Frequency: Quarterly
Circulation: 19M

6486 **PCAI**
Knowledge Technology
PO Box 30130
Phoenix, AZ 85046

602-971-1869; Fax: 602-971-2321
www.pcai.com/pcai

Terry Hengl, Publisher
Daniel W Rasmus, Editorial Advisor
Don Barker, Senior Editor
Robin Okun, VP of Marketing

Information necessary to help managers, programmers, executives and other professionals understand the unfolding realm of artificial intelligence and intelligent applications.
Cost: $24.00
Founded in 1987

6487 **PDN's Pix**
VNU Business Media
30 E 23rd St # 5
New York, NY 10010-4442

212-673-1100; Fax: 212-673-7074
www.vnu.com

Penny Vane, Owner
Rob Ruijter, CFO

Covers the world of electronic digital imaging to help readers use new imaging technology and the Web, digital meda, image capture and transfer.
Cost: $19.94
Circulation: 51753
Founded in 1964

6488 **Supplier Global Resource**
Advertising Specialty Institute
4800 Street Road
Trevose, PA 19053

800-546-1350
ideas@asicentral.com
www.asicentral.com

Timothy Andrews, President & CEO
Michele Bell, Editorial Director

News on international commerce and forecasts for the promotional products industry.
Frequency: 6x/Year

6489 **Virus Bulletin**
Virus Bulletin
590 Danbury Road
Ridgefield, CT 06877-2722

203-438-7714; Fax: 203-431-8165

Richard Ford, Editor
Victoria Lammer, Production Manager

An international journal addressing computer viruses, Trojan horses and other malicious programs. Emphasis is placed on providing technical and procedural countermeasures for businesses using computers.
Cost: $35.00

6490 **WE Magazine**
Women in eCommerce
P.O. Box 550856
Fort Lauderdale, FL 33355-0856

854-625-6606
heidi@wecai.org
www.wecai.org

Heidi Richards Mooney, Founder & CEO

Features women who are making a difference in business and life. Includes interviews with women in business, articles, reviews, and more.

6491 **WWWiz Magazine**
WWWiz Corporation
8840 Warner Avenue
Suite 200
Fountain Valley, CA 92708

714-848-9600; Fax: 714-375-2493
www.wwwiz.com

Don Hamilton, Editor-in-Chief
Vivian Hamilton, Managing Editor

WWWiz is a publication focused on the internet with content aimed entrepenuers and business professionals. We interview people who have found success in internet business along with articles pertaining to legal issues, marketing, technology, travel, and other special interest areas.
Cost: $28.00
Frequency: Monthly
Circulation: 120000
Founded in 1995

6492 **Wall Street & Technology**
Miller Freeman Publications
11 West 19th Street
New York, NY 10011

212-780-0400; Fax: 212-600-3045
www.wallstreetandtech.com

Michael Friedenberg, Group Publisher
Richard Rosenblatt, CEO/President
Kerry Massaro, Editor-in-Chief
Anne Marie Miller, Senior VP/Sales & Marketing

Editoral emphasis on the automation of brokerage houses and money management firms.
Frequency: Monthly
Circulation: 21226

6493 **Wearables**
Advertising Specialty Institute
4800 Street Road
Trevose, PA 19053

800-546-1350
ideas@asicentral.com
www.asicentral.com

Timothy Andrews, President & CEO
C.J. Mittica, Editor

Serves the apparel and accessories segment of the advertising specialty industry.
Frequency: 10x/Year

6494 **Web Builder**
Fawcette Technical Publications
2600 S El Camino Real # 300
Suite 300
San Mateo, CA 94403-2381

650-378-7100
800-848-5523; Fax: 650-853-0230
www.ftponline.com

James Fawcette, President
Karen Koenen, Sr. Circulation Director
John Sutton, Executive VP
Susan Ogren, Marketing Manager
Henry Allain, President

Highly technical, code-sensitive articles that cover all that goes into designing interfaces for sophisticated Internet/Intranet applications. Features a case-study approach to finding out who is using which Web sites and how.
Cost: $32.96
Frequency: Monthly

6495 **Web Content Report**
Lawrence Ragan Communications
316 N Michigan Ave # 400
Suite 400
Chicago, IL 60601-3773

312-960-4100
800-493-4867; Fax: 312-960-4106
cservice@ragan.com
www.ragan.com

Jim Ylisela, Publisher
Mark Ragan, CEO/President
Kasia Chalko, Marketing Director Events
Frank Bleers, Marketing Director Publisher

Outlines ways to attract visitors to a Web site, and be able to then monitor and evaluate the traffic on the home page. New developments in Web technology, how products can be sold on sites, budgeting matters and communicaiton with management.
Cost: $269.00
Frequency: Monthly
Founded in 1996
Printed in 2 colors on matte stock

6496 **Web Guide Monthly**
H&S Media
430 Oak Grove Street
Suite 100
Minneapolis, MN 55403-3234

612-990-3203; Fax: 612-879-1082
wdorn@webguidemag.com
www.webguidemag.com

Dan Beaver, Publisher

Examines and evaluates useful tools that merge the Internet with everyday life, at work and at home. Sites are sorted into categories, and are referenced in an index.
Cost: $34.95
Frequency: Monthly
Circulation: 120M

6497 **Web Techniques**
Miller Freeman Publications
411 Borel Avenue
#100
San Mateo, CA 94402-3516

650-573-3210; Fax: 650-655-4250
editors@web-techniques.com
www.webtechniques.com

Manny Sawit, Publisher
Deirdre Blake, Managing Editor

Latest information, tips and techniques to Web site developers. Contains information on new products and the latest information about the ever-changing world of Web development.
Cost: $34.95
Frequency: Monthly
Circulation: 100M

6498 **Webserver Online Magazine**
Computer Publishing Group
1340 Centre Street
Newton Centre, MA 02459-2499

617-641-9101; Fax: 617-641-9102
editor@cpg.com
www.cpg.com

S Henry Sacks, CEO/President
Doug Pryor, Editorial Director
Carol Flanagan, Marketing Manager
Tina Jackson, Circulation Manager
S Sacks, Publisher

Source for information Web professionals who need to get the most ot of their Web development and deployment efforts. Technology and industry news, systems and network adminsitration issues, the latest in Web tools, and a guide to new products, services and resources.
Frequency: Monthly
Founded in 1989

6499 **WirelessWeek.com**
PO Box 266008
Highlands Ranch, CO 80163-6008

303-470-4800; Fax: 303-470-4892
subsmail@reedbusiness.com
www.wirelessweek.com

Gerard Van de Aast, CEO
Debby Denton, Publisher
Rhonda Wickham, Editor -in- Chief
Glenn Comar, Marketing Director

Trade Shows

6500 **American Public Communications Council Conference & Expo**
625 Slaters Lane
Suite 104
Alexandria, VA 22314

703-739-1322
apcc@apcc.net

Conference, luncheon and 100 exhibits of public communications equipment and information including, pay phones, internet, atm, multimedia and more.
Founded in 1988

6501 **DMD New York Conference & Expo**
Direct Marketing Conferences
20 Academy Street
Norwalk, CT 06850-4032

203-854-9166
800-969-6566
www.dmdays.com

Direct Marketing Days New York offers new ideas in media, creative, database, eCommerce and technology. Hundreds of exhibits showcase the newest technologies, products and services. Over 85 sessions and 25 consultation centers led by A level speakers. Network with top-level executives.
Frequency: Annual/June

6502 **DeveloperWeek**
Data 2.0
Oakland Convention Center
Oakland, CA 94607

Home Page: www.developerweek.com
Facebook, Twitter, LinkedIn, Instagram

Geoff Domoracki, Co-Founder & CEO
Jonathan Pasky, Co-Founder
Sara Morris, Head, Events Operations/Productions
Emily Barwig, Event Operations Coordinator
Robert Aldridge, Business Development

The world's largest developer expo and conference series bringing together developers, engineers, software architects, dev teams, managers and executives from over 70 countries to to discover the latest in developer technologies, languages, platforms, and tools.
8000 Attendees
Frequency: Annual/February
Founded in 2012

6503 **E-Sports & Business Services Show at the Super Show**
Communications & Show Management
1450 NE 123rd Street
North Miami, FL 33161

305-893-8771; Fax: 305-893-8783
www.bizbash.com
Facebook

David Adler, CEO and Founder
Richard Aaron, President
Chad Kaydo

Retailers, distributors, wholesalers, importers/exporters and other buyers of sports related products come for 10,000 exhibits of sports apparel, footwear, accessories and e-commerce products and services.
100k Attendees
Frequency: January

6504 **EcomXpo**
Wordwide Business Research
535 5th Ave
8th Floor
New York, Ny 10017

888-482-6012; Fax: 646-200-7535
www.ecomxpo.com

Rick Worden, Chairman and CEO
Steve Goldring, Managing Director

An educationally focused, online virtual trade show designed specifically for search, affiliate and interactive marketers.
Frequency: July

6505 **Info Today Conference**
Information Today
143 Old Marlton Pike
Medford, NJ 08055-8758

609-654-6266
800-300-9868; Fax: 609-654-4309
custserv@infotoday.com
www.infotoday.com

Thomas H Hogan, Publisher/President
Roger R Bilboul, Chairman Of The Board

Users of online information services, electronic databases and the Internet. 200 booths.
6M Attendees
Frequency: May
Founded in 1980
Mailing list available for rent: 5000 names

6506 **International Consumer Electronics Show (CES)**
Consumer Technology Association
1919 South Eads Street
Arlington, VA 22202

703-907-7600
866-858-1555; Fax: 703-907-7675
cta@cta.tech
www.cta.tech

Gary Shapiro, President & CEO
David Hagan, Chairman

The CES reaches across global markets, connects the industry and enables consumer electronics to grow and thrive. International CES is owned and prroduced by the Consumer Electronics Association (CEA).
Frequency: Annual

6507 **Internet Communications Exposition**
IDG Expositions
1400 Providence Highway
Norwood, MA 02062

508-879-6700

6508 **National Conference on Operations & Fulfillment (NCOF)**
Direct Marketing Association
1120 Avenue of Americas
New York, NY 10036-6700

212-768-7277; Fax: 211-302-6714
dmaconferences@the-dma.org
www.the-dma.org

Julie A Hogan, SVP Conference/Events
Lawrence M Kimmel, CEO

Focuses on innovative solutions for the warehouse, distribution, operations, and ecommerce needs in the ever-changing world of operations and fulfillment.
10M Attendees

6509 **Promote and Prosper**
Women in eCommerce

P.O. Box 550856
Fort Lauderdale, FL 33355-0856

954-625-6606
heidi@wecai.org
www.wecai.org

Heidi Richards Mooney, Founder & CEO
Rosana Santos, President
Ellen Sue Burton, VP/Logistics & Hospitality
Racheli Smilovitz, VP/Professional Development
Suzannah Richards, Past President & Co-Founder

An opportunity for women in ecommerce to learn and network. Attendess will learn tools and strategies to help their businesses, increase their online influence, and add to their bottom line.
Frequency: Annual

6510 **RTX**
Rooster Teeth
Austin, TX

888-512-7469
rtxevent@roosterteeth.com
rtxevent.com
Facebook, Twitter, YouTube, Instagram

Clarissa Gonzalez, Senior Events Manager
Patrick Matthews, Events Specialist
George Panga, Marketing Coordinator

Convention held to celebrate gaming and internet culture, with a focus on animation and comedy as well. Other events are held in Sydney, Australia, and London, England.
62000 Attendees
Founded in 2011

6511 **Sporting Goods Manufacturers Markets**
1150 17th Street NW
8th Floor
Washington, DC 20036-1604

202-775-1762; Fax: 202-296-7462
info@sgma.com

Tom Cove, President/CEO
Gregg Harrlety, VP
Kalinda Mathis, Director Marketing

Retailers, distributors, wholesalers, importers/exporters and other buyers of sports related products come for 10,000 exhibits of sports aparel, footwear, accessories and e-commerce products and services.
80000 Attendees
Frequency: Biannual/Spring/Fall

6512 **SuiteWorld User Conference**
NetSuite Ecommerce
2955 Campus Drive
Suite 100
San Mateo, CA 94403-2511

650-627-1000; Fax: 650-627-1001
info@netsuite.com
www.netsuite.com

Evan Goldberg, Co-Founder/Chief Technology Officer
Zach Nelson, President & CEO

SuiteWorld provides customers, users and partners with the opportunity to gain insights, inspiration and hands-on training to run your business smarter and faster on NetSuite.
10000 Members
Founded in 1998

6513 **VoIP 2.0**
Technology Marketing Corporation
One Technology Plaza
Norwalk, CT 06854

203-852-6800
800-243-6002; Fax: 203-853-2845
www.itexpo.com

Frequency: October, San Diego

6514 **eM Conference**
91 Point Judith Road
Suite 129
Narragansett, RI 02882

800-496-2950; Fax: 408-884-2461
www.emarketingassociation.com

Chris Baggott, CEO
Bert DuMars, C-Founder/CEO
Murray Gaylord, VP/Marketing
Jeff Hilmire, President
Simms Jenkins, Founder & Principal

The Power of eMarketing Conference offers an unparalleled experience in best practices, case histories and processes for social, email and search marketing.
Frequency: Annual/April
Founded in 1997

6515 **impactSHOW**
Internet Marketing Association
200 Spectrum Center Drive
Irvine, CA 92618

949-443-9300
info@imanetwork.org
imanetwork.org
Facebook, Twitter, LinkedIn, YouTube

Sinan Kanatsiz, Chair & Founder
Sean Conrad, CEO
Lei Lani Fera, Head Of Creative
Hall Roosevelt, General Manager
Marcus Volpe, Executive Director

Conference of the Internet Marketing Association.
Founded in 2001

Directories & Databases

6516 **Adweek Directory**
Prometheus Global Media
770 Broadway
New York, NY 10003-9595

212-493-4100; Fax: 646-654-5368
www.prometheusgm.com

Richard D. Beckman, CEO
James A. Finkelstein, Chairman
Madeline Krakowsky, Vice President Chairman
Tracy Brater, Executive Director Creative Service

Adweek Directories Online is where you will find searchable databases with comprehensive information on ad agencies, brand marketers and multicultural media.
Frequency: Annual
Circulation: 800
Founded in 1981

6517 **America Online**
8619 Westwood Center Drive
Suite 200
Vienna, VA 22182-2238

800-227-6364; Fax: 540-265-2135

Jack Daggitt, Director
Anne Botsford

This multi-faceted information service provides complete access to a variety of databases and computer services of interest to users of Macintosh and Apple II computers. Databases included in this systems range from Computing & Software to Lifestyles & Interests.
Frequency: Full-text

6518 **Boardwatch Magazine Directory of Internet Service Providers**
Penton Media
1300 E 9th St # 316
Cleveland, OH 44114-1503

216-696-7000; Fax: 216-696-6662
www.penton.com

Jane Cooper, Marketing
Bill McCarthy, Editorial Director

Reviews various Internet providers and lists different programs available through their individual companies who operate in the US and Canada.
Cost: $72.00
Frequency: Monthly
Circulation: 70,000

6519 **Fulltext Sources Online**
Information Today
143 Old Marlton Pike
Medford, NJ 08055-8750

609-654-6266
800-300-9868; Fax: 609-654-4309
custserv@infotoday.com
www.infotoday.com

Thomas H Hogan, President
Roger R Bilboul, Chairman Of The Board

A directory of periodicals accessible online in full text through 28 aggregator products. Lists over 22,000 newspapers, journals, newsletters, newswires, and transcripts.
Cost: $145.00
Frequency: Biannually Jan & July
ISBN: 1-573872-23-7

6520 **IQ Directory Adweek**
Prometheus Global Media
770 Broadway
New York, NY 10003-9595

212-493-4100; Fax: 646-654-5368
www.prometheusgm.com

Richard D. Beckman, CEO
James A. Finkelstein, Chairman
Madeine Krakowsky, Vice President Circulation
Tracy Brater, Executive Director Creative Service

Profile of companies at the leading edge of digital marketing, has the specifics you'll need to investigate, launch and/or expand your digital presence. Profiles over 2,200 interactive agencies, web developers, brand marketers, online media, CD-ROM developers, POP/Kiosk designers and multimedia creative companies
Founded in 1981

6521 **Internet Blue Pages**
Information Today
143 Old Marlton Pike
Medford, NJ 08055-8750

609-654-6266
800-300-9868; Fax: 609-654-4309
custserv@infotoday.com
www.infotoday.com

Thomas H Hogan, President
Roger R Bilboul, Chairman Of The Board

The Guide to Federal Government Web Sites is the leading guide to federal government information on the web. Includes over 1,800 annotated agency listings, arranged in the US Government Manual style to help you find the information you need.
Cost: $34.95
464 Pages
ISBN: 0-910965-43-9

6522 **Key Guide to Electronic Resources: Language and Literature**
Information Today
143 Old Marlton Pike
Medford, NJ 08055-8750

609-654-6266
800-300-9868; Fax: 609-654-4309

custserv@infotoday.com
www.infotoday.com

Thomas H Hogan, President
Roger R Bilboul, Chairman Of The Board

Part of the ongoing topic related series of reference guides is an evaluative directory of electronic reference sources in the fields of language and literature.
Cost: $39.50
120 Pages
ISBN: 1-573870-20-x

6523 **On-Line Networks, Databases & Bulletin Boards on Assistive Technology**
ERIC Document Reproduction Service
7420 Fullerton Road
Suite 110
Springfield, VA 22153-2852

703-440-1400
800-443-ERIC; Fax: 703-440-1408

Directory of electronic networks that focus on technology-related services.

6524 **Professional Trade Association Membership**
Local Hispanic Chamber of Commerce
1424 K Street NW
Suite 401
Washington, DC 20005

202-715-0494
membership@ushcc.com
www.ushcc.com

Javier Palomarez, President & CEO
DeVere Kutscher, Chief of Staff & VP of Strategy

The USHCC is a not-for-profit (501(c)6) organization founded in 1979 to foster Hispanic economic development and to create sustainable prosperity for the benefit of American society.
Founded in 1979

6525 **Trade Show News Network**
Tarsus Group plc
16985 W Bluemound Road
Suite 210
Brookfield, WI 53005

262-782-1900; Fax: 603-372-5894
rwimberly@tsnn.com
www.tsnn.com

Rachel Wimberly, Editor-in-Chief
John Rice, Sales & Business Development
Arlene Shows, Marketing Manager

The world's leading online resource for the trade show, exhibition and event industry since 1996. TSNN.com owns and operates the most widely consulted event database on the internet, containing data about more than 19,500 trade shows, exhibitions, public events and conferences.
13900 Members
Frequency: Bi-Monthly
Founded in 1196

Industry Web Sites

6526 **http://gold.greyhouse.com**
G.O.L.D Grey House OnLine Databases

Grey House Publishing's online database platform, GOLD, offers Quick Search, Keyword Search and Expert Search for most business sectors including e-commerce and internet markets. The GOLD platform makes finding the information you need quick and easy - whether you're a novice searcher or an experienced database user. All of Grey House's directory products are available for subscription on the GOLD platform.

6527 **www.aace.org**
Association for the Advancement of Computing in Ed

Promotes the use of computers and the internet in educational settings.

6528 **www.adsl.com/adsl_forum.html**
Information about ADSL, Asymmetric Digital Subscriber Line, a system that provides high-speed Internet connections

6529 **www.bsa.org**
Business Software Alliance

An organization dedicated to promoting a safe and legal digital world. BSA educates consumers on software management and copyright protection, cyber security, trade, e-commerce and other internet related issues.

6530 **www.computercpa.com**
Accountant's Home Page

Provides information on general accounting for manufacturing, contstruction, service, not-for-profit, e-commerce and more.

6531 **www.greyhouse.com**
Grey House Publishing

Authoritative reference directories for most business sectors incluidng e-commerce and internet markets. Users can search the online databases with varied search criteria allowing for custom searches by product category, geographic area, sales volume, keyword, subject and more. Full Grey House catalog and online ordering also available.

6532 **www.hayes.com/prodinfo/adsl/intro.html**
Information about ADSl, Asymmetric Digital Subscriber Line, a system that provides high-speed Internet connections

6533 **www.imanetwork.org**
Internet Marketing Association

Seeks to provide members with the chance to learn, network, and establish Internet Marketing best practices. Members are in fields such as sales, marketing, business ownership, programming, and creative development.

6534 **www.iste.org**
International Society for Technology in Education

A large nonprofit organization serving the technology-using educator.

6535 **www.sdl.com**
eMarketing Association

SDL Tridion R5, the core product, provides complete Web content management and content delivery capabilities, focusing on ease-of-use for all content contributors, site managers and power users.

6536 **www.shop.com**
Altura International

CatalogCity.com is a powerful and flexible e-commerce technology. This site includes recognized brand names such as Blair, Bombay, Chef's Catalog, Fisher-Price, Gump's by Mail, Hammacher Schlemmer, Ross-Simmons, The Sharper Image, and many more.

6537 **www.spie.org**
International Society for Optical Engineering

Serves the international technical community as the premier provider of education, information, and resources covering optics, photonics, and their applications.

6538 **www.wecai.org**
Women in eCommerce

Facebook, Twitter, LinkedIn

The original business and social networking community for social and professional networking and business development for successful women who want to take their businesses to a new level offline and online. The mission of Women in Ecommerce is to empower women with educational opportunities to enhance their businesses using the Internet and Social Media. We offer tools, resources and networking opportunities to build a strong foundation for future growth and expansion.

Associations

6539 **American Automatic Control Council**
3640 Col Glenn Hwy
Dayton, OH 45435
937-775-5062; Fax: 937-775-3936
pmisra@cs.wright.edu
www.a2c2.org
Tariq Samad, President
Glenn Y Masada, President-elect
Linda Bushnell, Treasurer
B.Wayne Bequette, Secretary
Supports all those involved in the manufacturer and distribution of automatic controls. Hosts annual trade show.

6540 **Association for High Technology Distributors**
N19 W24400 Riverwood Drive
Waukesha, WI 53188
262-696-3645
www.ahtd.org
Twitter, LinkedIn
Leigha Schatzman, Executive Director
Works to increase productivity and profitability of high technology automation solutions, providers and manufacturers.
Founded in 1984

6541 **Association of Edison Illuminating Companies**
600 18th Street N
PO Box 2641
Birmingham, AL 35291
205-257-2530; Fax: 205-257-2540
aeicdir@bellsouth.net
www.aeic.org
Terry H Waters, Executive Director/Secretary
Len Holland, Manager AEIC Services
Becky Neel, Administrative Assistant
Cindy McLeod, Administrative Assistant
Association of electric utilities concerned with generating, transmitting and distributing electricity. This organization supplies information and support to the industry.
165 Members
Founded in 1885

6542 **Contract Services Association of America**
1000 Wilson Boulevard
Suite 1800
Arlington, VA 22209
703-243-2020; Fax: 703-243-3601
info@csa-dc.org
www.pscouncil.org
Barry Cullen, President
Colleen Preston, Senior VP
Represents the government services contracting industry. Membership ranges from small businesses and corporations servicing federal and state government in numerous capacities. CSA acts to foster the effective implementation of the government's policy of reliance on the private sector for support services. Largest DOD association of service contractors.
650 Members
Founded in 1965

6543 **EOS/ESD Association, Inc. (DBA ESD Association)**
Electrostatic Discharge Association
7900 Turin Road
Building 3
Rome, NY 13440-2069
315-339-6937; Fax: 315-339-6793
info@esda.org
www.esda.org
Facebook, Twitter, LinkedIn
Terry Welsher, President
Gianluca Boselli, Sr. VP
Ginger Hansel, VP
Lisa Pimpinella, Director of Operations
EOS/ESD Association is a professional voluntary association dedicated to advancing the theory and practice of electrical overstress and electrostatice avoidance. The Association expands EOS/ESD awareness through atandards development, educational programs, local chapters, publications, tutorials, certification and symposia.
Cost: $60.00
2000+ Members
Frequency: Bi-Monthly
Founded in 1982

6544 **Edison Electric Institute**
701 Pennsylvania Avenue NW
Washington, DC 20004-2696
202-508-5000
feedback@eei.org
www.eei.org
Facebook, Twitter, YouTube
Thomas R. Kuhn, President
John S. Schlenker, CFO/Treasurer
Jim Owen, VP, Membership & Meeting Services
Emily Sanford Fisher, General Counsel & Corp. Secretary
Stephanie Voyda, VP, Communications
Advocates public policy, expands market opportunities and provides strategic business information for the shareholder-owned electric utility industry.
Founded in 1933

6545 **Electric Association**
40 Shuman Blvd
Suite 247
Naperville, IL 60563-8446
630-305-3050; Fax: 630-305-3056
cspaeth@eachicago.org
www.eachicago.org
Facebook, LinkedIn
Mark Gibson, President
Rick Jamerson, Vice President
Steven Anixter, Treasurer
Thomas Scherzer, Secretary
Provides members of the electrical industry of Chicagoland and their employees with formal educational opportunities, professional development, information exchange, and member services.
Founded in 1926

6546 **Electric Power Research Institute**
3420 Hillview Avenue
Palo Alto, CA 94304
650-855-2121
800-313-3774
askepri@epri.com
www.epri.com
Facebook, Twitter, LinkedIn
Michael W. Howard, President/CEO
Pamela J. Keefe, SVP/CFO/Treasurer
Salvador A. Casente, Jr., VP/General Counsel/CCO/Secretary
Arsha Mansoor, SVP, Research/Development
Michael A. Coleman, VP, IT/CIO
Nonprofit energy research consortium for the benefit of utility members, their customers and society. Mission is to provide science and technology-based solutions to its global energy customers by managing a far-reaching program of scientific research, technology development and product implementation.
660 Members
Founded in 1965

6547 **Electrical Apparatus Service Association**
1331 Baur Boulevard
St. Louis, MO 63132
314-993-2220; Fax: 314-993-1269
easainfo@easa.com
www.easa.com
Facebook, Twitter, LinkedIn, YouTube
Jerry Gray, Chair
Timothy Bieber, Vice Chair
Sid Seymour, Secretary/Treasurer
Linda J. Raynes, CAE, President/CEO
Dale Shuter, CMP, Manager, Meetings & Expositions
An international trade organization of electromechanical sales and service firms in 58 countries. Provides members with a means of keeping up to date on materials, equipment, and state of the art technology.
2000 Members
Founded in 1973
Mailing list available for rent

6548 **Electrical Association**
One Energy Center
40 Shuman Boulevard, Suite 247
Naperville, IL 60563
630-305-3050; Fax: 630-305-3056
cspaeth@eachicago.org
www.eachicago.org
Facebook, LinkedIn
Mark Gibson, President
Rick Jamerson, Vice President
Steven Anixter, Treasurer
Thomas Scherzer, Secretary
Provides members of the electrical industry of Chicagoland and their employees with formal educational opportunities, professional development, information exchange and member services

6549 **Electrical Equipment Representatives Association**
638 W 39th Street
Kansas City, MO 64111
816-561-5323
800-728-2272; Fax: 816-561-1991
info@eera.org
www.eera.org
Kier Cooper, President
Rob Rigsby, President Elect
Jennifer Tibbetts, VP
Bobby Cox, Secretary
Doug Softy, Treasurer
Provides technically competent, hands-on, local representation for companies providing products and services to the electric power industry.

6550 **Electrical Generating Systems Association**
1650 S Dixie Hwy
Suite 400
Boca Raton, FL 33432-7461
561-750-5575; Fax: 561-395-8557
www.egsa.org
Facebook
Ed Murphy, President
Charlie Habic, VP
David Brown, Secretary/Treasurer
A trade association made up of companies in the USA and around the world that design, manufacture, sell, distribute, rent, specify, service and use on site power equipment.
600 Members
Founded in 1965

6551 **Electrical Safety Foundation International**
1300 N 17th Street
Suite 900
Arlington, VA 22209

703-841-3229; Fax: 703-841-3329
info@esfi.org
www.esfi.org
Facebook, Twitter, LinkedIn, YouTube

Ruppert Russoniello, Chairman
Stephen Sokolow, Immediate Past Chairman
Kevin Cosgriff, Treasurer
Lorraine Carli, Secretary

The mission of the Electrical Safety Foundation International (ESFI) is to advocate electrical safety in the home and in the workplace in order to reduce electrically-related fatalities, injuries and property loss.
Founded in 1994

6552 **Electrochemical Society**
65 S Main St
Building D
Pennington, NJ 08534-2827

609-737-1902; Fax: 609-737-2743
ecs@electrochem.org
www.electrochem.org
Facebook, Twitter, LinkedIn

Christopher Jannuzzi, Executive Director/CEO
Tim Gamberzky, CFO & COO
Beth Craanen, Director, Publications
John Lewis, Director, Meetings
Shannon Reed, Director, Community Engagement

Members are electrochemists and professionals in related industries.
8000 Members
Founded in 1902

6553 **Electronic Industries Association**
2214 rock Hill Rd
Suite 170
Herndon, VA 20170

571-323-0294; Fax: 571-323-0245
www.eia.org
LinkedIn, YouTube

Ronald L Turner, Chairman
Mike Kennedy, Vice Chairman
Dave McCurdy, President
Charles Robinson, Chief Operating Officer
James Shiring, Secretary/Treasurer

Is a national trade organization that includes the full spectrum of U.S. manufacturers.
1300 Members

6554 **Electronic Technicians Association**
5 Depot St
Greencastle, IN 46135-8024

765-653-8262
800-288-3824; Fax: 765-653-4287
eta@eta-i.org
www.eta-i.org
Facebook, Twitter, LinkedIn, YouTube, Google+

Fred Weiss, Chairman
John Baldwin, Vice Chairman
Joseph LaGanga, Secretary
Ira Wiesenfeld, Treasurer
William Brinker, Communications Division Chair

Association for electronics technicians worldwide offering over 70 certifications.
5000 Members
Founded in 1978

6555 **IPC: Association Connecting Electronics**
3000 Lakeside Dr
Suite 309 S
Bannockburn, IL 60015-1249

847-615-7100; Fax: 847-615-7105
webmaster@ipc.org
www.ipc.org
Facebook, Twitter, LinkedIn, YouTube, Google+, RSS

John W. Mitchell, President & CEO
Tom Sandman, CFO
Dave Bergman, VP, International Relations
John Hassleman, VP, Government Relation
Sanjay Huprikar, VP, Member Success

A trade association for the printed circuit boards and electronics assembly industries, offering programs and resources to board manufacturers and electronic assemblers, designers, industry suppliers and original equipment manufacturers.
2700 Members
Founded in 1957

6556 **Independent Electrical Contractors Association**
4401 Ford Ave
Suite 1100
Alexandria, VA 22302-1464

703-549-7351
800-456-4324; Fax: 703-549-7448
info@ieci.org
www.ieci.org
Facebook, Twitter, LinkedIn, YouTube, Instagram, Flickr

Thayer Long, Executive Vice President/CEO
Vernice Howard, CFO
Alicia Johnson, Office Manager
Bruna Patio, Staff Accountant

The mission of IEC is to create success among independent electrical contractors by developing a professional workforce, communicating clearly with government, promoting ethical business practices, and providing leadership for the electrical industry.
73000 Members
Founded in 1957

6557 **Institute of Electrical and Electronics Engineers**
3 Park Ave.
17th Fl.
New York, NY 10016-5997

212-419-7900; Fax: 212-752-4929
www.ieee.org
Facebook, Twitter, LinkedIn, YouTube, Instagram

Toshio Fukuda, President & CEO
Stephen Welby, Executive Director & COO

Supports all those involved in the field of electrical engineering, and works to nurture technological innovation and excellence for the benefit of humanity.
422K Members
Founded in 1963

6558 **Institute of Electrical/Electronic**
3 Park Ave
17th Floor
New York, NY 10016-5997

732-562-3878; Fax: 732-562-6046
ieee-mce@ieee.org
Facebook, Twitter, LinkedIn, YouTube, Google+

Moshe Kam, President and CEO
Roger Pollard, Director and Secretary
Dr Mohamed El-Hawary, Director/Secretary
365K Members
Founded in 1963

6559 **Instrumentation and Measurement Society**
3 Park Ave
17th Floor
New York, NY 10016-5997

212-419-7900; Fax: 732-981-0225
webmaster@ieee.org
www.ieee-ims.org
Twitter, LinkedIn

Reza Zoughi, President
Ruth A. Dyer, Executive VP
Dario Petri VP Finance Committee
Dr Mohamed El-Hawary, Director/Secretary

A subsidiary of the Institute of Electrical and Electronics Engineers. Provides support to scientists and technicians who design and develop electrical and electronic measuring instruments and equipment.
36000 Members
Founded in 1980

6560 **Instrumentation, Systems, and Automation Society**
67 Alexander Drive
Box 12277
Research Triangle Park, NC 27709

919-549-8411; Fax: 919-549-8288
info@isa.org
www.isa.org
Facebook, Twitter, LinkedIn, YouTube, Flickr

Ken Baker, President
Patrick Gouhin, Executive Director
Debbie Eby, Executive Assistant
Leo Staples, Treasurer

Nonprofit, educational organization connecting people and ideas in automation. The Society fosters advancement in the theory, design, manufacture, and use of sensors, instruments, computers, and systems for automation in a wide variety of applications.
33000 Members
Founded in 1945

6561 **International Brotherhood of Electrical Workers**
900 Seventh St NW
Washington, DC 20001

202-833-7000; Fax: 202-728-7676
www.ibew.org
Facebook, Twitter, YouTube, Flickr, Vimeo

Lonnie R. Stephenson, President
Kenneth Cooper, Secretary-Treasurer

Among the largest unions in the AFL-CIO, the IBEW represents electrical workers in many fields, from railroads to telecommunications.
750K Members

6562 **International Electrical Testing Association**
3050 Old Centre Ave.
Suite 102
Portage, MI 49024

269-488-6382
888-300-6382; Fax: 269-488-6383
neta@netaworld.org
www.netaworld.org
Facebook, LinkedIn, YouTube

Melissa Richard, Finance and Business Manager
Jayne Tanz, Executive Director
Ron Widup, 1st VP
Lynn Hamrick, Secretary
John White, Treasurer

Defines the standards by which electrical equipment is deemed safe and reliable. Creates specifications, procedures, testing and requirements for commissioning new equipment and testing the reliability and performance of existing equipment.
2000 Members
Founded in 1972

6563 **International Institute of Connector and Interconnection**
3000 Lakeside Drive
Bannockburn, IL 60015
Dale Reed, Content Editor
Dedicated to the spread of technological information throughout the industry. In a time of global competition, success depends on communicating technological breakthroughs, innovations and changes in specifications to engineers, designers, specifiers, consultants and other professionals using your product or services.
2640 Members
Founded in 1958

6564 **International League of Electrical Associations**
P.O. Box 24
Mumford, NY 14511
585-538-6350; Fax: 585-538-6166
www.ileaweb.org
LinkedIn
Chris Price, President
Robert Morris, VP
Kirstie Steves, Secretary
Barbette Cejalvo, Treasurer
An organization of professional electric association and electric league managers from more than thirty US and seven Canadian cities.
Founded in 1936

6565 **International Magnetics Association**
Eight South Michigan Avenue
Suite 1000
Chicago, IL 60603-3310
312-456-5590; Fax: 312-580-0165
www.intl-magnetics.org
August Sisco, Chair
Lowell Bosley, President
George Orenchak, Secretary/Treasurer
Is the worldwide trade association representing manufacturers of magnetic materials, distributors and fabricators, suppliers to the magnetics industry and others with an interest in magnetics.
35 Members
Founded in 1959

6566 **International Microwave Power Institute**
PO Box 1140
Mechanicsville, VA 23111-5007
804-559-6667; Fax: 804-559-4087
info@impi.org
www.impi.org
Facebook, Twitter
Molly Poisant, Executive Director
Ben Schiffman, President
John Mastela, VP
John Gerling, Treasurer
Jerome Czajkowski, Secretary
To be the global organization that provides a forum for the exchange of information on all aspects of microwave and RF heating technologies.
Founded in 1966

6567 **Laser Institute of America**
13501 Ingenuity Dr
Suite 128
Orlando, FL 32826-3009
407-380-1553
800-345-2737; Fax: 407-380-5588
lia@lia.org
www.lia.org
Facebook, Twitter, LinkedIn, Google+
Robert Thomas, President
Stephen Capp, Treasurer
Paul Denny, Secretary
The Laser Institute of America is the professional membership society dedicated to fostering lasers, laser applications and safety worldwide.
1200 Members
Founded in 1968

6568 **Laser and Electro-Optic Manufacturers**
123 Kent Road
Pacifica, CA 94044-3923
650-738-1492; Fax: 650-738-1769
info@leoma.com
www.leoma.com
John Ambroseo, President
Breck Hitz, Executive Director
Lynn Strickland, Treasurer
Brian Lula, Secretary
Is the trade association for North American manufacturers of lasers and associated electro-optics equipment.
Founded in 1986

6569 **National Association of Electrical Distributors**
1181 Corporate Lake Drive
St. Louis, MO 63132
888-791-2512
www.naed.org
Facebook, Twitter, LinkedIn, YouTube
Tom Naber, President & CEO
Michelle McNamara, COO/NAED Foundation Exec. Director
Ed Orlet, SVP, Gov't Affairs
Tim Dencker, VP, Finance
The main goal of the National Association of Electrical Distributors (NAED) is to establish the electrical distributor as an essential force in the electrical industry and the economy.
Founded in 1908

6570 **National Electrical Contractors**
3 Bethesda Metro Ctr
Suite 1100
Bethesda, MD 20814-5372
301-657-3110; Fax: 301-215-4500
www.necanet.org
Facebook, Twitter, LinkedIn, YouTube
Represents a segment of the construction market comprised of over 70,000 electrical contracting firms.
65000 Members
Founded in 1901

6571 **National Electrical Manufacturers Representatives Association**
28 Deer Street
Suite 302
Portsmouth, NH 03801
914-524-8650
800-446-3672; Fax: 603-319-1667
nemra@nemra.org
www.nemra.org
Twitter, LinkedIn
Kenneth Hooper, President
Kirsty Stebbins, Manager of Marketing
Sue Todd, Office Manager
Promotes the function of the independent manufacturer's representative as the most effective way to market electrical products. Increases the income of the rep's firm employees and sales staff by increasing the value of the rep firm to owners and customers. Offers educational opportunities that help representatives strengthen the management, technical and professional capabilities of their firms. Promotes communication between independent electrical representatives and manufacturing partners.

6572 **National Electronics Service Dealers Association**
PO Box 378
Hillsboro, TX 76645
817-921-9061
info@nesda.com
nesda.wildapricot.org
Facebook
A national trade association for professionals in the business repairing consumer electronics equipment, appliances, and computers. NESDA has an e-mail group of over 600 members and manufacturers that communicate daily for information sharing.
Founded in 1950

6573 **National Rural Electric Cooperative Association**
4301 Wilson Blvd
Suite 1
Arlington, VA 22203-1860
703-907-5500; Fax: 703-907-5526
www.nreca.org
Twitter
Glenn English, CEO
Organized specifically to overcome World War II shortages of electric construction materials, to obtain insurance coverage for newly constructed rural electric cooperatives, and to mitigate wholesale power problems. Since those early days, NRECA has been an advocate for consumer owned cooperatives on energy and operational issues as well as rural community and economic development.
1000 Members
Founded in 1942

6574 **National Systems Contractors Association**
3950 River Ridge Drive NE
Cedar Rapids, IA 52402
319-366-6722
800-446-6722; Fax: 319-366-4164
nsca@nsca.org
www.nsca.org
Facebook, Twitter, LinkedIn, YouTube
Chuck Wilson, Executive Director
Deb Gulick, Chief Financial Officer
Leah Garris, Director, Marketing & Communication
Teresa Solorio, Director, Operations
Savannah Washburn, Events Manager
Represents the commercial electronic systems industry. Serves as an advocate for all those who work within the low-voltage industry, including systems contractors/integrators, product manufacturers, consultants, sales representatives and a growing number of architects, specifying engineers and others.
2800 Members
Founded in 1980

6575 **North American Electric Reliability Corporation**
3353 Peachtree Road, N.E
Suite 600 North Tower
Atlanta, GA 30326
404-446-2560
info@nerc.com
www.nerc.com
Gerry W. Cauley, President/CEO
Mark Rossi, SVP/Chief Reliability Officer
Marcus H. Sachs, SVP/Chief Security Officer
Charles A. Berardesco, SVP/General Counsel/Corp Secretary
Michael Walker, SVP/CFO/CAO/Treasurer

Principal organization for coordinating and promoting North America's electrical supplies, demands and reliability issues.
11 Members
Founded in 1968

6576 **North Central Electrical League**
2901 Metro Dr
Suite 203
Bloomington, MN 55425-8699

952-854-4405
800-925-4985; Fax: 952-854-7076
dale@ncel.org
www.ncel.org
Facebook, Twitter, LinkedIn, Flickr

Dan Paulson, Chair
Ed Studniski, Vice Chair
Dale Yohnke, Executive Director
Nikki Borgen, Manager - Membership Engagement
Eryka Pluff, Coordinator - Member Benefits

Trade association representing all segments of the electrical industry in the Upper Midwest.
1500 Members
Founded in 1936

6577 **Power Sources Manufacturers Association**
PO Box 418
Mendham, NJ 07945-0418

973-543-9660; Fax: 973-543-6207
power@psma.com
www.psma.com
LinkedIn

Ernie Parker, Chairman
Eric Persson, President
Stephen Oliver, VP
Michel Grenon, Secretary/Treasurer

The PSMA is a not-for-profit organization incorporated in the state of California. The purpose of the Association shall be to enhance the stature and reputation of its members and their products, improve their knowledge of technological and other developments related to power sources, and to educate the entire electronics industry, plus academia, as well as government and industry agencies as to the importance of, and relevant applications for, all types of power sources and conversion devices.
155 Members
Founded in 1985

6578 **Relay and Switch Industry Association**
2500 Wilson Boulevard
Arlington, VA 22201

703-907-8024; Fax: 703-875-8908
narm@ecaus.org

Robert Willis, President
James Kaplan, Chairman and CEO

Represents the electronics industry sector comprised of companies that manufacturer, produce or market relay and switch technologies and products.
Founded in 1947

6579 **SMMA: The Motor & Motion Association**
PO Box P182
South Dartmouth, MA 02748

508-979-5935; Fax: 508-979-5845
www.smma.org

Paul Murphy, President
Matt French, Vice President
Steve Herrmann, Secretary/Treasurer

Trade association for the electric motor and motion control industry in North America. The voice of the motor and motion industry providing a forum for education, communication, research and networking.
120 Members
Founded in 1975

6580 **Semiconductor Equipment and Materials International**
3081 Zanker Road
San Jose, CA 95134

408-943-6900; Fax: 408-428-9600
semihq@semi.org
www.semi.org
Twitter, LinkedIn

Yong Han Lee, Chairman
Tetsuo Tsuneishi, Vice Chairman
Mary G. Puma, Secretary/Treasurer
Denny McGuirk, President/CEO
Laith Altimime, President, SEMI Europe

Global industry association serving the manufacturing supply chains for the microelectronic, display and photovoltaic industries.
2300 Members
Founded in 1970

6581 **Semiconductor Industry Association**
1101 K Street NW
Suite 450
Washington, DC 20005

202-446-1700
866-756-0715; Fax: 202-216-9745
mailbox@sia-online.org
www.sia-online.org
Facebook, Twitter

John Neuffer, President/CEO
Latoya Arnold, Executive Assistant/Office Manager
Jimmy Goodrich, Vice President, Global Policy
Joe Pasetti, Director, Government Affairs
Dan Rosso, Communications Manager

Trade association representing the US microchip industry. Provides a forum for working collectively to enhance the competitiveness of the US chip industry.
70 Members
Founded in 1977

6582 **Society of Manufacturing Engineers**
1000 Town Center
Suite 1910
Southfield, MI 48075

313-425-3000
service@sme.org
www.sme.org
Facebook, Twitter, LinkedIn, YouTube, Google+, Instagram

Sandra L. Bouckley, Executive Director & CEO
Craig Connop, Chief Financial Officer
Steve Prahalis, Chief Operating Officer
Erica Ciupak, Information Technology
Debbie Clark, Governance

The organization serves its members and others in the international manufacturing community by identifying, evaluating and explaining the adoption and integration of emerging information technologies to create business value.
65K Members
Founded in 1932

6583 **Surface Mount Technology Association**
5200 Willson Rd
Suite 215
Edina, MN 55424-1316

952-920-7682; Fax: 952-926-1819
joann@smta.org
www.smta.org
Facebook, Twitter, LinkedIn, YouTube, Google+

Bill Barthel, President
Eileen Hibbler, VP of Membership
Raiyomand Aspandiar, Ph.D., VP Technical Programs
Michelle Ogihara, VP Communications
Richard Henrick, Secretary

Network of professionals building skills, sharing practical experience and developing solutions in electronic assembly technologies and related business operations.
3200 Members
Founded in 1984

6584 **The Bioelectromagnetics Society**
C/O Hilderbrand, Limparis & Assoc.
#200-7101 Guilford Dr.
Frederick, MD 21704

office@bems.org
www.bems.org
Facebook, Twitter

Andrew Wood, President
Alexandre Legros, Secretary

Nonprofit organization and international resource for excellence in scientific research, knowledge and understanding of the interaction of electromagnetic fields with biological systems. Members are biological and physical scientists, physicians and engineers interested in the interactions of nonionizing radiation with biological systems.
300 Members
Founded in 1978

6585 **U.S. Department of Energy**
1000 Independence Ave SW
Washington, DC 20585

202-586-5000; Fax: 202-586-4403
www.energy.gov
Facebook, Twitter, LinkedIn, YouTube, Instagram

Rick Perry, Secretary of Energy
Dan Brouillette, Deputy Secretary of Energy

The Energy Department is responsible for the transformation of the nation's energy system through the application of the latest science and technology solutions.
Founded in 1977

Newsletters

6586 **Advanced Battery Technology**
Seven Mountains Scientific
913 Tressler Street
PO Box 650
Boalsburg, PA 16827

814-466-6559; Fax: 814-466-2777
www.7ms.com

E Thomas Chesworth, Technical Editor
Josephine Chesworth, Managing Editor

The oldest, most widely read international newsletter reporting on battery technology, marketing and industry events including new products and financial news. Accepts advertising. Print and online versions available.
Cost: $ 180.00
Circulation: 1000
Printed in 4 colors on matte stock

6587 **Cleanroom Markets Newsletter**
McIlvaine Company
191 Waukegan Rd
Suite 208
Northfield, IL 60093-2743

847-784-0012; Fax: 847-784-0061
editor@mcilvainecompany.com
www.mcilvainecompany.com

Robert McIlvaine, Owner
Robert Mclvaine, President
Marilyn McIlvaine, EVP

Information on clean rooms markets worldwide.
Cost: $460.00
8 Pages
Frequency: Monthly
Printed in on newsprint stock

6588 **Cleanroom Technology Newsletter**
McIlvaine Company
191 Waukegan Rd
Suite 208
Northfield, IL 60093-2743

847-784-0012; Fax: 847-784-0061
www.mcilvainecompany.com

Robert McIlvaine, Owner
Robert McIvaine, President
Marilyn McIlvaine, EVP

Information on clean room technology.

6589 **Continuous Improvement**
James Publishing
PO Box 25202
Santa Ana, CA 92799-5202

714-755-5450
800-394-2626; Fax: 714-751-2709
customer-service@jamespublishing.com
www.jamespublishing.com

Jim Pawell, Founder and President
Stephen Sicillan, Editor

Tutorial and news on new quality assurance technologies and ISO 9000, QS 9000 and ISO 14000.
Cost: $20.00
Circulation: 2000

6590 **Currents**
Electrical Apparatus Service Association
1331 Baur Boulevard
St. Louis, MO 63132

314-993-2220; Fax: 314-993-1269
easainfo@easa.com
www.easa.com

Jerry Gray, Chair
Timothy Bieber, Vice Chair
Sid Seymour, Secretary/Treasurer
Linda J. Raynes, CAE, President/CEO
Dale Shuter, CMP, Manager, Meetings & Expositions

Provides information on EASA's programs, seminars, technical articles and industry trends and events. Members receive a copy each month.
Frequency: Monthly
Circulation: 2000+

6591 **Display Technology News**
Business Communications Company
49 Walnut Park
Building 2
Wellesley, MA 02481

781-489-7301
866-285-7215; Fax: 781-253-3933
sales@bccresearch.com
www.bccresearch.com
Facebook, Twitter

Greg Lindberg, Chairman and CEO
Bridgett Hurley, CMO
Kevin Fitzgerald, Editorial Director
Sharon Blank, Sales Director
Mark McCarthy, Operations Director

Market reports and technology updates of topics such as news materials, news applications, patents, technology transfer, processing and equipment.
Cost: $500.00
Frequency: Monthly
Founded in 1971

6592 **Document Imaging Report**
Corry Publications
5340 Fryling Road
Knowledge Park, Suite 300
Erie, PA 16510

814-897-9000; Fax: 814-899-5583
corrypub@corrypub.com
www.corrypub.com

Nicole Hykes, Editor
John Toiston, Publisher
Carry Procious, Marketing
Mindy Sadden, Circulation Manager

Presents the most timely and actionable information on electronic imaging applications, products and user implementation.
Frequency: Monthly
Circulation: 50

6593 **EA Extra**
Electrical Association of Philadelphia
527 Plymouth Road
Suite 408
Plymouth Meeeting, PA 19462-1641

610-825-1600; Fax: 610-825-1603
electric@eap.org
www.eap.org
Facebook, Twitter, YouTube

Kevin Lane, President
Joe Henry, Vice President
Kim Schneider, Treasurer
Kenneth Hull, Secretary

Carries information on industry trends, events, educational and business opportunities, economic briefings, member happening, mergers, and member benefit updates.
450 Members
Founded in 1917

6594 **Electrical Connection**
Electrical Association of Rochester
PO Box 20219
Rochester, NY 14602-0219

585-538-6350; Fax: 585-538-6166
www.eawny.com

Joe Lengen, President
Bonnie Curran, First VP
Coreg Merrill, Secretary/Treasurer
Kirstie Steves, Executive Director

Contains information on upcoming events, recaps past events, a message from the President, the current calendar and much more.
Frequency: Quarterly
Founded in 1924

6595 **Electrical Product News**
Business Marketing & Publishing
PO Box 7457
Wilton, CT 06897

203-834-9959
www.epnweb.com
Facebook

George Young, Editor/Publisher

Accepts advertising.
Cost: $39.50
20 Pages
Frequency: Monthly
Circulation: 3500
Printed in 2 colors on newsprint stock

6596 **Electro Manufacturing**
Worldwide Videotex
PO Box 3273
Boynton Beach, FL 33424-3273

561-738-2276
markedit@juno.com
www.wvpubs.com

Computer and electronic technologies used to help improve manufacturing efficiency.
Cost: $165.00

6597 **Global Electronics**
Pacific Studies Center
222B View Street
Mountain View, CA 94041-1344

650-969-1545; Fax: 650-961-9818

Leonard Siegel, Editor

News items detailing the industry throughout the world and the social, environmental and military implications of production and application.
Cost: $1.00
Circulation: 400

6598 **IEEE Transactions on Applied Superconductivity**
IEEE Instrumentation and Measurement Society
67 Alexander Drive
PO Box 12277
Research Triangle Park, NC 27709

919-549-8411; Fax: 919-549-8288
info@isa.org
www.isa.org
Facebook, Twitter, LinkedIn

Ken Baker, President
Patrick Gouhin, Executive Director
Jerry Clemons, Department VP
Leo Staples, Treasurer

Concentrates on materials and their applications to electronics and power systems where superconductivity is central to the work.

6599 **IEEE Transactions on Mobile Computing**
IEEE Instrumentation and Measurement Society
67 Alexander Drive
PO Box 12277
Research Triangle Park, NC 27709

919-549-8411; Fax: 919-549-8288
info@isa.org
www.isa.org
Facebook, Twitter, LinkedIn

Ken Baker, President
Patrick Gouhin, Executive Director
Jerry Clemons, Department VP
Leo Staples, Treasurer

Research papers are presented in this publication dealing with mobile computing, wireless networks, reliability, quality assurance, distributed systems architecture and high-level protocols.
Frequency: Quarterly

6600 **IFAC Newsletter**
American Automatic Control Council
3640 Col Glenn Hwy
Dayton, OH 45435

937-775-5062; Fax: 937-775-3936
pmisra@cs.wright.edu
www.a2c2.org

John Watkins, Editor

It contains up-to-date information about forthcoming IFAC events as well as brief announcements of other IFAC related activities. It is sent free of charge to NMO's, IFAC Affiliates and libraries.
Frequency: Bi-Monthly

6601 **Inside FERC**
McGraw Hill
PO Box 182604
Columbus, OH 43272

720-485-5000
877-833-5524; Fax: 614-759-3749
www.mcgraw-hill.com
Facebook, Twitter, LinkedIn, YouTube

Harold McGraw, President and CEO
Jack Callahan, Executive VP/CFO
John Berisford, EVP, Human Resources

Provides coverage of the Federal Energy Regulatory Commission's activities and federal regulations.
Cost: $975.00
14 Pages
Frequency: Monthly
Founded in 1884

6602 **Inside NRC**
McGraw Hill
PO Box 182604
Columbus, OH 43272
614-304-4000
877-833-5524; Fax: 614-759-3749
www.mcgraw-hill.com
Facebook, Twitter, LinkedIn, YouTube
Harold McGraw, President and CEO
Jack Callahan, Executive VP/CFO
John Berisford, EVP, Human Resources
Focuses exclusively on the US Nuclear Regulatory Commission.
Cost: $1310.00
13 Pages
Founded in 1800

6603 **SMT Trends**
New Insights
303 Vallejo Street
Crockett, CA 94525-1237
510-787-2273; Fax: 415-389-8671
Michael New, Publisher/Editor
Marketing and business news for the surface mount industry. Covers component and packaging trends, CAD, CAE, pick and place, robotics and test inspection.
Printed in one color on matte stock

6604 **SMTA News**
Surface Mount Technology Association
5200 Wilson Road
Suite 215
Minneapolis, MN 55424
952-920-7682; Fax: 952-926-1819
joann@smta.org
www.smta.org
Dan Baldwin, President
Marie Cole, VP Tech Programs
Kola Akinade, Secretary
Hal Hendrickson, Treasurer

6605 **Seven Mountain Scientific**
PO Box 650
Boalsburg, PA 16827-651
814-466-6559; Fax: 814-466-2777
www.7ms.com
E Thomas Chesworth, President
Industry news in battery and fuel cell technology, marketing and industry events including new products, electric vehicle, R&D and environmental news.
Cost: $180.00
ISSN: 0001-8627
Founded in 1965

6606 **Tech Notes**
National Technical Information Service
5301 Shawnee Rd
Alexandria, VA 22312
703-605-6000; Fax: 703-605-6900
info@ntis.gov
www.ntis.gov
Facebook, Twitter
Bruce Borzino, Director
Patrik Ekstrom, Business Development Manager
Reuel Avila, Managing Director
Describes new processes, equipment, materials and techniques developed by Federal laboratories.
Cost: $8.00

6607 **Threshold Newsletter**
Electrostatic Discharge Association
7900 Turin Road
Building 3
Rome, NY 13440-2069
315-339-6937; Fax: 315-339-6793
info@esda.org
www.esda.org
Facebook, LinkedIn, YouTube
Donn Bellmore, President
Leo G. Henry, Sr. VP
Terry Welsher, VP
Lisa Pimpinella, Director of Operations
Donn Pritchard, Treasurer
Benefits of ESD membership include a subscription to the Threshold Newsletter in addition to other Association activities and programs such as educational tutorials and seminars; the EOS/ESD Symposium; participation in local chapters; discounts on Association standards and other publications; extensive networking; membership roster, and participation in standards development.
2000+ Members
Founded in 1982

6608 **Transformers for Electronic Circuits**
Power Sources Manufacturers Association
PO Box 418
Mendham, NJ 07945-0418
973-543-9660; Fax: 973-543-6207
power@psma.com
www.psma.com
Dusty Becker, Chairman
Carl Blake, President
Jim Marinos, VP
Michel Grenon, Secretary/Treasurer
It is a complete, one-stop guide to transformer and inductor design and applications for everyone who designs, builds, or uses power magnetics components. Combines analysis and synthesis, and all theory is related to the solution of real world problems.
Cost: $100.00
155 Members
Founded in 1985

6609 **Update**
Power Sources Manufacturers Association
PO Box 418
Mendham, NJ 07945-0418
973-543-9660; Fax: 973-543-6207
power@psma.com
www.psma.com
LinkedIn
Dusty Becker, Chairman
Carl Blake, President
Jim Marinos, VP
Michel Grenon, Secretary/Treasurer
PSMA Update is published and distributed via e-mail quarterly by the Power Sources Manufacturers Association.
Frequency: Quarterly
Circulation: 2700

6610 **Wafer News Confidential**
PennWell Publishing Company
98 Spit Brook Rd
Suite Ll-1
Nashua, NH 03062-5737
603-891-0123
800-225-0556; Fax: 603-891-9294
ATD@PennWell.com
www.pennwell.com
Christine Shaw, VP
Barbara Pennwell, CEO/President
Provides semiconductor equipment industry executives with information on developments, trends, news and market insights.
Cost: $15.00
Frequency: Monthly
Founded in 1910

Magazines & Journals

6611 **Bioelectromagnetics Journal**
C/O Hildebrand, Limparis & Assoc.
#200-7101 Guilford Dr.
Frederick, MD 21704
office@bems.org
www.bems.org
James Lin, Editor in Chief
Andrew Wood, President
Alexandre Legros, Secretary
It is a peer-reviewed, internationally circulated scientific journal that specializes in reporting original data on biological effect and applications of electromagnetic fields that range in frequency from zero hertz static fields) to the terahertz undulations of visible light.
Frequency: 6x yearly

6612 **Contact**
1000 McKee Street
Batavia, IL 60510-1682
630-879-6000; Fax: 630-879-0867
Steve Wilcox, Editor
Application of electric motor controls to electrically operated machinery and equipment.
Circulation: 4,000

6613 **Control Solutions**
PennWell Publishing Company
1421 S Sheridan Rd
Tulsa, OK 74112-6619
918-835-3161
800-331-4463; Fax: 918-831-9497
Headquarters@PennWell.com
www.pennwell.com
Robert Biolchini, President
Ron Kuhfeld, Editor-in-Chief
Frequency: Monthly

6614 **Diesel & Gas Turbine Worldwide**
Diesel & Gas Turbine Publications
20855 Watertown Rd
Suite 220
Waukesha, WI 53186-1873
262-754-4100; Fax: 262-754-4175
www.dieselspec.com
Michael Osenga, President
Lynne Diefenbach, Advertising Manager
Concentrates its editorial on the design, packaging, operation and maintenance of medium and slow-speed, high output diesel, natural gas and gas turbine engine systems used in the electrical power generation, cogeneration, oil and gas, marine propulsion and railroad markets throughout the world.
Cost: $65.00
Frequency: 10x yearly
Circulation: 22,000
Founded in 1969

6615 **ECN Magazine**
Reed Business Information
360 Park Ave S
4th Floor
New York, NY 10010-1737
646-746-6400; Fax: 646-756-7583
subsmail@reedbusiness.com
www.reedbusiness.com
John Poulin, CEO
Aimee Kalnoskas, Editor
Steve Wirth, Publisher Director
James Reed, Owner

Provides product solutions for designed engineers in the electronics industry.
Cost: $96.19
Frequency: Monthly

6616 **EE Product News**
Penton Media
1166 Avenue of the Americas/10th Fl
New York, NY 10036

212-204-4200
CorporateCustomerService@penton.com
www.penton.com

David Kieselstien, CEO
Nicola Allais, CFO
Jasmine Alexander, CIO

Source of information on new products necessary to successfully design, assemble and test prototypes of commercial, industrial, military and aerospace electronic products.
Frequency: Monthly
Circulation: 111968
Founded in 1892

6617 **EE: Evaluation Engineering**
Nelson Publishing
2500 Tamiami Trl N
Nokomis, FL 34275-3476

941-966-9521
800-226-6113; Fax: 941-966-2590
www.healthmgttech.com
Facebook, Twitter

Kristine Russel, President
Phil Colpas, Managing Editor

Magazine devoted exclusively to companies that test, evaluate, design and manufacture electronic products and equipment.
Cost: $43.00
84 Pages
Frequency: Monthly
Founded in 1962
Mailing list available for rent: 65,000 names
Printed in 4 colors on glossy stock

6618 **EPRI Journal**
Electric Power Research Institute
3420 Hillview Avenue
Palo Alto, CA 94304

650-855-2121
800-313-3774
askepri@epri.com
eprijournal.com
Facebook, Twitter, LinkedIn

Michael W. Howard, President/CEO

The flagship publication of the Electric Power Research Institute. It provides in-depth reporting on electricity sector R&D, industry and technology news, EPRI thought leadership, and guest perspectives from industry leaders.

6619 **ElectriCITY**
Electric Association
40 Shuman Boulevard
Suite 247
Naperville, IL 60563

630-305-3050; Fax: 630-305-3056
www.eachicago.org

Mark Gibson, President
Rick Jamerson, Vice President
Steven Anixter, Treasurer
Thomas Scherzer, Secretary
Founded in 1925

6620 **ElectriCITY Magazine**
Electric Association
40 Shuman Boulevard
Suite 247
Naperville, IL 60563-8446

630-305-3050; Fax: 630-305-3056
admin@eachicago.org
www.eachicago.org
Facebook, LinkedIn

Mark Gibson, President
Rick Jamerson, Vice President
Steven Anixter, Treasurer
Thomas Scherzer, Secretary
Bob Porter, Secretary

Corporate news, timely articles, career announcements, product line changes, industry-dates calendars, career placement services, and government legislation updates; circulation across the Midwest.
Frequency: Quarterly

6621 **Electric Co-op Today**
National Rural Electric Cooperative Association
4301 Wilson Blvd
Suite 1
Arlington, VA 22203-1860

703-907-5500; Fax: 703-907-5526
www.nreca.org
Twitter

Glenn English, CEO

Devoted to accurate, critical coverage of electric cooperative developments and electric cooperative industry news, unavailable in any other publication. The only weekly publication covering electric cooperative industry news, legislation and regulation, and community and economic development. Each issue highlights what you need to know to understand key industry issues clearly, quickly, and easily.
Cost: $40.00
Frequency: Weekly
Founded in 1994

6622 **Electric Light & Power**
PennWell Publishing Company
1421 S Sheridan Rd
Tulsa, OK 74112-6619

918-835-3161
800-331-4463; Fax: 918-831-9497
Headquarters@PennWell.com
www.pennwell.com

Serves the North American Electric Utility Industry including electric power generation, delivery, and information technology operations in investor-owned electric utilities.
Frequency: Monthly
ISSN: 0013-4120
Founded in 1902

6623 **Electric Perspectives**
Edison Electric Institute
701 Pennsylvania Avenue NW
Washington, DC 20004-2696

202-508-5000
feedback@eei.org
www.eei.org
Facebook, Twitter, YouTube

Thomas R. Kuhn, President

The magazine for management in America's investor-owned electric utilities. Covers all areas of utility operations and concerns, providing detailed analyses and farsighted commentary on how issues and trends are shaping the industry today and the future impact.
Frequency: Bi-Monthly
Circulation: 15,000
ISSN: 0364-474X

6624 **Electrical Apparatus**
Barks Publications
400 N Michigan Ave
Suite 900
Chicago, IL 60611-4164

312-321-9440; Fax: 312-321-1288
www.barks.com

Horace Barks, Owner
Elsie Dickson, Associate Publisher
Horace Barks, CEO
Joseph Hoff, Manager

Serves the electromechanical and electronic maintenance and application industries, including manufacturing plants, institutional facilities and service companies.
Cost: $45.00
Frequency: Monthly
Circulation: 15500
Founded in 1969

6625 **Electrical Construction & Maintenance**
Primedia
1166 Avenue of the Americas/10th Fl
New York, NY 10036

212-204-4200
CorporateCustomerService@penton.com
www.penton.com

David Kieselstien, CEO
Nicola Allais, CFO
Jasmine Alexander, CIO

Owners and company officials, engineers, electrical personnel, electrical inspectors, architects and designers, purchasing and other related personnel.
Circulation: 104344

6626 **Electrical Contractor Magazine**
National Electrical Contractors Association
3 Bethesda Metro Ctr
Suite 1100
Bethesda, MD 20814-5372

301-657-3110; Fax: 301-215-4500
www.necanet.org
Facebook, Twitter, LinkedIn, YouTube

John M Grau, CEO
Dan Walter, VP and COO
Michael Thompson, Secretary/Treasurer

The magazine has been the complete information source for electrical construction professionals. Its goal is to serve all participants in the power and integrated building systems industries. It delivers the latest information in the areas of power, communications and controls in both high voltage and low voltage applications to electrical contractors who compete in residential, commercial, industrial and institutional market segments of the construction arena.
Circulation: 85,000
Founded in 1939

6627 **Electrical Distributor Magazine**
National Association of Electrical Distributors
1181 Croporate Lake Drive
St Louis, MO 63132

888-791-2512
info@naed.org
www.naed.org
Facebook, Twitter, YouTube

Tom Naber, President & CEO
Michelle McNamara, COO/NAED Foundation Exec. Director
Ed Orlet, SVP, Gov't Affairs
Tim Dencker, VP, Finance

An informative, insightful publication that offers electrical distributors the latest information affecting their business. Subscriptions are free to NAED members.

6628 **Electrical Wholesaling**
Primedia
1166 Avenue of the Americas/10th Fl
New York, NY 10036

212-204-4200
CorporateCustomerService@penton.com
www.penton.com

David Kieselstien, CEO
Nicola Allais, CFO
Jasmine Alexander, CIO

Offers information on manufacturers, suppliers, prices and marketing of electrical products.
Cost: $25.00
Frequency: Monthly
Circulation: 22,500
Founded in 1905

6629 Electricity Today
1885 Clements Road
Unit 218
Pickering, Canada, ON L1W-3V4

905-686-1040; Fax: 905-686-1078
www.electricity-today.com

Randy Hurst, Publisher

Electricity Today is a leading electrical transmission and distribution magazine distributed free of charge to North American T&D electric utility engineering, construction and maintenance personnel, and high voltage T&D consulting engineers.

6630 Electronic Design
Penton Media
1166 Avenue of the Americas/10th Fl
New York, NY 10036

212-204-4200
CorporateCustomerService@penton.com
www.penton.com

David Kieselstien, CEO
Nicola Allais, CFO
Jasmine Alexander, CIO

Celebrating 50 years of innovation, this authoritative source provides leading-edge information to electronic and engineering managers around the world.

6631 Fringe Ware Review
Fringe Ware
PO Box 49921
Austin, TX 78765-4858

512-444-2393

Paco Nathan, Co-Founder
Don Lebkowsky, Co-Founder
Monte McCarter, Art Director
Tiffany Lee Brown, Assistant Editor

Stories and review on electronic products made by smaller producers.
Cost: $4.00
Founded in 1992

6632 High Tech News
Electronic Technicians Association International
5 Depot St
Greencastle, IN 46135-8024

765-653-8262
800-288-3824; Fax: 765-653-4287
eta@eta-i.org
www.eta-i.org
Facebook, Twitter, LinkedIn

Teresa Maher, CSS, President
Cindy Reed, Financial Director
Richard Glass, CETsr, CEO Emeritus

Exclusive bi-monthly publication of ETA International, and a subscription is included with each individual membership. Each issue features information on the changing electronics industry: specialty techniques & technology, trends, qualification opportunities and educational advice.
4500 Members
Frequency: Bi-Monthly
Circulation: 10000
Founded in 1978

6633 IEEE Instrumentation and Measurement Magazine
IEEE Instrumentation and Measurement Society
67 Alexander Drive
PO Box 12277
Research Triangle Park, NC 27709

919-549-8411; Fax: 919-549-8288
info@isa.org
www.isa.org
Facebook, Twitter, LinkedIn

Kim Fowler, Editor-in-Chief

This publication is included in member dues, it contains applications-oriented articles and news nominations, awards, highlights of conferences, Technical Committee news, book reviews, tutorials and contributions from the membership.
Frequency: Quarterly

6634 IEEE Sensors Journal
IEEE Instrumentation and Measurement Society
67 Alexander Drive
PO Box 12277
Research Triangle Park, NC 27709

919-549-8411; Fax: 919-549-8288
info@isa.org
www.isa.org
Facebook, Twitter, LinkedIn

Ken Baker, President
Patrick Gouhin, Executive Director
Jerry Clemons, Department VP
Leo Staples, Treasurer

Specializes in the theory, design, fabrication, manufacturing and applications of devices for sensing and transducing physical, chemical and biological phenomena.
Frequency: Bi-Monthly

6635 IEEE Transactions on Intelligent Transportation Systems
IEEE Instrumentation and Measurement Society
67 Alexander Drive
PO Box 12277
Research Triangle Park, NC 27709

919-549-8411; Fax: 919-549-8288
info@isa.org
www.isa.org
Facebook, Twitter, LinkedIn

Ken Baker, President
Patrick Gouhin, Executive Director
Jerry Clemons, Department VP
Leo Staples, Treasurer

This journal contains basic and applied research to expand the knowledge base on transportation for improved design, management and control of future transportation systems.
Frequency: Quarterly

6636 IEEE Transactions on Nanotechnology
IEEE Instrumentation and Measurement Society
67 Alexander Drive
PO Box 12277
Research Triangle Park, NC 27709

919-549-8411; Fax: 919-549-8288
info@isa.org
www.isa.org
Facebook, Twitter, LinkedIn

Ken Baker, President
Patrick Gouhin, Executive Director
Jerry Clemons, Department VP
Leo Staples, Treasurer

The journal is devoted to the dissemination of new results and discussions related to understanding the physical basis and engineering applications of phenomena at the nanoscale level.
Frequency: Quarterly

6637 Industrial Laser Solutions
PennWell Publishing Company
98 Spit Brook Rd
Nashua, NH 03062-5737

603-891-0123
80- 2-5 05; Fax: 603-891-9294
www.pennwell.com

Christine Shaw, VP
David Belforte, Editor

For all industries that use industrial lasers.
Cost: $260.00
45 Pages
Frequency: Monthly
Circulation: 10,000
ISSN: 1523-4266
Founded in 1986

6638 Industrial Market Place
Wineberg Publications
7842 Lincoln Avenue
Skokie, IL 60077

847-676-1900
800-323-1818; Fax: 847-676-0063
info@industrialmktpl.com
www.industrialmktpl.com

Eliot Wineberg, President
Jackie Bitensky, Editor

Has advertisements on machinery, industrial and plant equipment, services and industrial auctions in each issue.
Cost: $175.00
60 Pages
Frequency: Bi-Monthly
Circulation: 14,000
Founded in 1951
Printed in 4 colors on glossy stock

6639 Interface Magazine
Electrochemical Society
65 S Main St
Building D
Pennington, NJ 08534-2827

609-737-1902; Fax: 609-737-2743
ecs@electrochem.org
www.electrochem.org

Christine Garzon, President
Tetsuya Osaka, Sr. VP
Harikila Deligianni, Secretary
Christina Bock, Treasurer

Is an authoritative accessible publication for those in the field of solid-state and electrochemical science and technology which contains technical articles about the latest developments in the field, and presents news and information about and for members of ECS.
Cost: $40.00
Frequency: Quarterly
Circulation: 9000
ISSN: 1064-8208
Founded in 1902
Printed in 4 colors

6640 Journal of Laser Applications
Laser Institute of America
13501 Ingenuity Dr
Suite 128
Orlando, FL 32826-3009

407-380-1553
800-345-2737; Fax: 407-380-5588
lia@lia.org
www.lia.org
Facebook, Twitter, LinkedIn

Klaus Loeffler, President
Stephen Capp, Treasurer
Robert Thomas, Secretary

The official journal of the Laser Institute of America and serves as the major international forum for exchanging ideas and information in disciplines that apply laser technology. Internationally known editors, reviewers, and columnists deliver the latest results of their research worldwide, dealing with the diverse, prac-

tical applications of photonic technology.
Cost: $410.00

6641 **Journal of Lightwave Technology**
IEEE Instrumentation and Measurement Society
67 Alexander Drive
PO Box 12277
Research Triangle Park, NC 27709

919-549-8411; Fax: 919-549-8288
info@isa.org
www.isa.org
Facebook, Twitter, LinkedIn

Ken Baker, President
Patrick Gouhin, Executive Director
Jerry Clemons, Department VP
Leo Staples, Treasurer

The Journal is concerned with research, applications and methods used in all aspects of lightwave technology and fiber optics.
Frequency: Monthly

6642 **Journal of Microwave Power and Electromagnetic Energy**
International Microwave Power Institute
PO Box 1140
Mechanicsville, VA 23111-5007

804-559-6667; Fax: 804-559-4087
info@impi.org
www.impi.org

Bob Schiffmann, President
Molly Poisant, Executive Director

The quarterly, technical journal of the Institute published by the Industrial, Scientific, Medical and Instrumentation (ISMI) section. Designed for the information needs of professionals specializing in the research and design of industrial and bio-medical applications, the Journal exemplifies the highest standards of scientific and technical information on the theory and application of electromagnetic power.
Cost: $250.00
Frequency: Quarterly

6643 **Journal of the Electrochemical Society**
Electrochemical Society
65 S Main St
Building D
Pennington, NJ 08534-2827

609-737-1902; Fax: 609-737-2743
ecs@electrochem.org
www.electrochem.org

Roque J Calvo, President

This peer reviewed journal publishes 60 articles each month. Articles are posted online, with a monthly paper edition following electronic publication. The ECS membership benefits package includes access to the electronic edition of this journal. Free with membership.
Cost: $110.00
Frequency: Monthly
Circulation: 8300
ISSN: 0013-4651
Founded in 1902

6644 **LIA Today**
Laser Institute of America
13501 Ingenuity Dr
Suite 128
Orlando, FL 32826-3009

407-380-1553
800-345-2737; Fax: 407-380-5588
lia@lia.org
www.lia.org
Facebook, Twitter, LinkedIn

Klaus Loeffler, President
Stephen Capp, Treasurer
Robert Thomas, Secretary

Includes articles on the latest industry news to keep members and other laser professionals current on important issues that impact the laser community. Readers of LIA TODAY consist of production managers, supervisors, safety professionals, researchers, end-users, laser physicians and nurses.
Frequency: Bi-Monthly
Circulation: 5000

6645 **Laser Tech Briefs**
Associated Business Publications International
317 Madison Avenue
New York, NY 10017

212-490-3999; Fax: 212-986-7864
www.abpi.net

Domenic Mucchetti, CEO
Josheph Pramberger, President
Luke Schnirring, Executive VP

For purchasers of laser/optical products.
Circulation: 40,000

6646 **Lighting Dimensions**
Primedia Business
249 W 17th St
New York, NY 10011-5382

212-206-1894
800-827-3322; Fax: 212-514-3719
Facebook, Twitter

Doug MacDonald, Group Publisher
David Johnson, Associate Publisher
Marian Sandberg-Dierson, Editor
Ellen Lampert-Greaux, Consulting Editor
Jennifer Hirst, Art Director

Trade publication for lighting professionals in film, theatre, television, concerts, clubs, themed environments, architectural, commercial, and industrial lighting. Sponsors of the LDI Trade Show and the Broadway Lighting Master Classes.
Cost: $34.97
Frequency: Monthly
Circulation: 14,177
Founded in 1989

6647 **Market Trends**
Electronic Industries Association
2500 Wilson Boulevard
Arlington, VA 22201-3834

703-907-7500; Fax: 703-907-7767

Statistical information and marketing trends in the electronics industry.
Cost: $195.00
Frequency: Monthly

6648 **Motion Control**
ISA Services
P.O. Box 787
Williamsport, PA 17703

570-567-1982
800-791-8699; Fax: 570-320-2079
www.douglaspublications.com

Janine Nunes, Editor
Edward Mueller, Publisher

Information for those who design and maintain motion control systems.
56 Pages
Frequency: Monthly
Circulation: 16,490
ISSN: 1058-4644
Founded in 1985
Printed in 4 colors on glossy stock

6649 **NETA World**
International Electrical Testing Association
Po Box 687
Morrison, CO 80465-0687

303-697-8441
888-300-6382; Fax: 303-697-8431
neta@netaworld.org
www.netaworld.org
Facebook, YouTube

Mose Ramieh, President
David Huffman, First VP
Ron Widup, Second VP
John White, Treasurer
Walter Cleary, Secretary

Features articles of interest to electrical testing and maintenance companies, consultants, engineers, architects, and plant personnel directly involved in electrical testing and maintenance. Free with membership.
Frequency: Quarterly

6650 **Power Conversion & Intelligent Motion**
Primedia
1166 Avenue of the Americas/10th Fl
New York, NY 10036

212-204-4200
CorporateCustomerService@penton.com
www.penton.com

David Kieselstien, CEO
Nicola Allais, CFO
Jasmine Alexander, CIO

Directed to engineers, designers and manufacturers of power electronic and electronic motion control components, subsystems and systems. Feature articles interpret trends and innovation in these subjects.
Circulation: 31,113

6651 **Power Engineering International**
PennWell Publishing Company
1421 S Sheridan Rd
Tulsa, OK 74112-6619

918-831-9421
800-331-4463; Fax: 918-831-9476
headquarters@pennwell.com
www.pennwell.com

Robert Biolchini, President

Serves the global electric power generation and transmission industry.
Frequency: Monthly
Circulation: 34000
ISSN: 1069-4994
Founded in 1896

6652 **Powerline Magazine**
Electrical Generating Systems Association
1650 S Dixie Hwy
Suite 500
Boca Raton, FL 33432-7461

561-750-5575; Fax: 561-395-8557
www.egsa.org
Facebook

Debra Laurentis, President
Edward Murphy, VP
Bob Hafich, Secretary/Treasurer

Focuses on the entire on-site power generation industry.
Cost: $5.00
Frequency: Bi-Monthly

6653 **ProService Magazine**
National Electronics Service Dealers Association
PO Box 378
Hillsboro, TX 76645

817-921-9061
info@nesda.com
nesda.wildapricot.org
Facebook

Published for members of NESDA/ISCET.
24 Pages

6654 **Process Heating**
Business News Publishing Company

155 Pfingsten Road
Suite 205
Deerfield, IL 60015

847-405-4000; Fax: 248-502-1001
PHeditors@bnpmedia.com
www.process-heating.com
Facebook, Twitter

Anne Armel, Publisher
Linda Becker, Associate Publisher & Editor
Beth McClelland, Production Manager

Magazine covers heat processing at temperatures up to 1000 degrees F at end user and OEM plants in 9 industries. Follow us at twitter.com/ProcessHeating, www.facebook.com/ProcessHeating
Circulation: 25000
Founded in 1994

6655 RE Magazine
National Rural Electric Cooperative Association
4301 Wilson Blvd
Suite 1
Arlington, VA 22203-1860

703-907-5500; Fax: 703-907-5526
www.nreca.org
Twitter

Glenn English, CEO

Editorial content covers utility operations, deployment of the latest industry products and services; a showcase of new products, services, and catalogs; online resources; safety; member(customer) services; business and management trends; marketing tools; community and economic development; local leaders and rural issues; co-op personnel news; and politics and regulatory policies impacting electric co-ops.
Cost: $43.00
Frequency: Monthly
Founded in 1942

6656 Rural Electrification
National Rural Electric Cooperative Association
4301 Wilson Blvd
Arlington, VA 22203-1860

703-907-5500; Fax: 703-907-5526
www.nreca.org
Twitter

Glenn English, CEO

Serves people involved in the rural electric cooperative industry including generation and transmission cooperatives, distribution systems and public utility district members of NRECA; electric equipment manufacturers; US Congress, state and federal regulatory agencies and commissions; and others allied to the field.
Cost: $85.00
Frequency: Monthly
Founded in 1942

6657 Service Contractor Magazine
Contract Services Association of America
1000 Wilson Boulevard
Suite 1800
Arlington, VA 22209

703-243-2020; Fax: 703-243-3601
www.pscouncil.org

Barry Cullen, President
Colleen Preston, Senior VP

Focuses on industry developments, regulatory and legislative issues, and any issues encountered in the process of competing for and securing contracts, such as changes in the acquisitions or procurement process. It tailors its content exclusively to government contractors.
Frequency: Bi-Annual

6658 Standard for Certification of Electrical Testing Technicians
International Electrical Testing Association
Po Box 687
Morrison, CO 80465-0687

303-697-8441
888-300-6382; Fax: 303-697-8431
neta@netaworld.org
www.netaworld.org
Facebook, YouTube

Mose Ramieh, President
David Huffman, First VP
Ron Widup, Second VP
John White, Treasurer
Walter Cleary, Secretary

Specifying requisite levels of training, experience, and education for the evaluator of electrical power equipment is an important test procedure itself. The requirements parallel those of the National Skill Standards Board in Washington, DC, which promulgates for various occupations.
Cost: $55.00
36 Pages

6659 Standard for Electrical Maintenance Testing of Dry-Type Transformers
International Electrical Testing Assocaition
Po Box 687
Morrison, CO 80465-0687

303-697-8441
888-300-6382; Fax: 303-697-8431
neta@netaworld.org
www.netaworld.org
Facebook, YouTube

Mose Ramieh, President
David Huffman, First VP
Ron Widup, Second VP
John White, Treasurer
Walter Cleary, Secretary

This Standard has been an individual section within the NETA document entitled Maintenance Testing Specifications for Electrical Power Distribution Equipment and Systems since 1975. The Maintenance Testing Specifications along with NETA's Acceptance Testing Specifications have long been in general use by organizations and individuals involved with testing of electrical apparatus.
Cost: $55.00
18 Pages

6660 Standard for Electrical Maintenance Testin g of Liquid-Filled Transformers
International Electrical Testing Association
PO Box 687
Morrison, CO 80465-0687

303-697-8441
888-300-6382; Fax: 303-697-8431
neta@netaworld.org
www.netaworld.org
Facebook, YouTube

Mose Ramieh, President
David Huffman, First VP
Ron Widup, Second VP
John White, Treasurer
Walter Cleary, Secretary

The Standard has been an individual section within the NETA document entitled Maintenance Testing Specifications for Electrical Power Distribution Equipment and Systems since 1975. The Maintenance Testing Specifications along with NETA's Acceptance Testing Specifications have long been in general use by organizations and individuals involved with testing of electrical apparatus.
Cost: $55.00
21 Pages

Trade Shows

6661 AHTD Spring Meeting
Association for High Technology Distributors
N19 W24400 Riverwood Drive
Waukesha, WI 53188

262-696-3645
leigha.schatzman@ahtd.org
www.ahtd.org
Twitter, LinkedIn

Leigha Schatzman, Executive Director

Works to increase productivity and profitability of high technology automation solutions, providers and manufacturers.
Frequency: Annual
Founded in 1984

6662 American Control Conference
American Automatic Control Council
2145 Sheridan Road
Evanston, IL 60208-3118

847-491-8175; Fax: 847-491-4455
aacc@ece.northwestern.edu
www.a2c2.org

R. Russell Reinehart, President
Tariq Samad, President-elect
Jordan Berg, Treasurer
B.Wayne Bequette, Secretary

Covers a broad range of topics relevant to the theory and practice of control and automation, including robotics, manufacturing, guidance and control, power systems, process control, identification and estimation, signal processing, modeling and advanced simulation.
800 Attendees
Frequency: Annual/June

6663 Annual Connector & Interconnection Technology Symposium and Trade Show
International Institute of Connector and Intercon
PO Box 20002
Sarasota, FL 34276

941-929-1806
800-854-4248; Fax: 941-929-1807

Dale Reed, Content Editor

Offers the opportunity to meet with other connector/interconnection industry users and vendors to learn about the latest advances in interconnection technology in the areas of radio frequency interconnection, quality, high speed connectors, personal computer interconnections, automotive Interconnections, materials, finishes, and platings, test methods, automation, surface mount technology, fiber optics, spaceflight connector technology, and medical applications.

6664 Annual Legislative & Regulatory Roundtable
Electronic Industries Association
2214 rock Hill Rd
Suite 170
Herndon, VA 20170

571-323-0294; Fax: 571-323-0245
www.eia.org
LinkedIn, YouTube

Gail Tannenbaum, CMP, Manager Meetings

Panel topics in the past have included Broadband, Tax, Trade, Environment, Defense, Space, and the Congressional Leadership Agenda.
Frequency: Annual/August

6665 Applied Power Electronics Conference & Exposition (APEC)
Power Sources Manufacturers Association

PO Box 418
Mendham, NJ 07945-0418

973-543-9660; Fax: 973-543-6207
power@psma.com
www.psma.com
LinkedIn

Dusty Becker, Chairman
Carol Blake, President
Jim Marinos, VP
Michel Grenon, Secretary/Treasurer

APEC continues the long-standing tradition of addressing issues of immediate and long-term interest to the practicing power electronics engineer.
1000 Attendees

6666 **Biolectromagnetics Society Meeting**
The Bioelectromagnetics Society
C/O Hildebrand, Limparis & Assoc.
#200-7101 Guilford Dr.
Frederick, MD 21704

office@bems.org
www.bems.org

Andrew Wood, President
Alexandre Legros, Secretary

This is a joint meeting of The Bioelectromagnetics Society and The European BioElectromagnetics Association. Topics will be: Electric Fields, Human Studies, Exposure Assessment, Dosimetry, In Vitro ELF, Epidemiology, Unique EMF Signals, Medical applications, Mechanisms, Electromagnetic Therapy.
400 Attendees
Frequency: Annual/June

6667 **CSA Winter Meeting**
Contract Services Association of America
1000 Wilson Boulevard
Suite 1800
Arlington, VA 22209

703-243-2020; Fax: 703-243-3601
www.pscouncil.org

Barry Cullen, President
Colleen Preston, Senior VP

This one day workshop is a free flowing exchange of information with real time interaction and information exchange.
Frequency: Annual/January

6668 **Coherence and Electromagnetic Fields in Biological Systems**
Bioelectromagnetics Society
2412 Cobblestone Way
Frederick, MD 21702-3519

301-663-4252; Fax: 301-694-4948
office@bems.org
www.bems.org

David Black, President
Gloria Parsley, Executive Director
Richard Nuccitelli, VP

Highlights of the symposium organized by the Institute of Radio Engineering and Electronics, the Academy of Sciences of the Czech Republic and others are expected to include biophysical principles of coherence, role of endogenous EMF in the organization of biological systems, biophysical mechanisms of interaction of biological systems with EMF and more.
Frequency: Annual/July

6669 **Consulting Electrical Engineers(CEE) Technical Forum & Table-Top**
Electric Association
One Energy Center,40 Shuman Boulevard
Suite 247
Naperville, IL 60563

630-305-3050; Fax: 630-305-3056
www.eachicago.org
Facebook, LinkedIn

Mark Gibson, President
Rick Jamerson, VP
Steven Anixter, Treasurer
Thomas Scherzer, Secretary

This event will feature a free technical forum for engineers, specifiers, and designers on Short Circuit analysis, Coordination, and Arc Flash Hazard analysis using conventional and computerized methods. The Table Top tradeshow will feature 45 vendors and their latest technology.
Frequency: Annual/May

6670 **EASA Annual Convention**
Electrical Apparatus Services Association
1331 Baur Boulevard
Saint Louis, MO 63132

314-993-2220; Fax: 314-993-1269
easainfo@easa.com
www.easa.com

Linda J. Raynes, CAE, President/CEO
Dale Shuter, CMO, Manager, Meetings & Expositions

Provides members with a means of keeping up to date on materials, equipment, and state-of-the-art technology. 100+ exhibitor booths.
2500 Attendees
Frequency: Annual/June
Mailing list available for rent

6671 **EDS: Where the Electronics Industry Connects**
Electronics Distributions Show Corporation
2214 Rock Hill Road
Suite 170
Herndon, VA 20170

312-648-1140; Fax: 312-648-4282
eds@edsconnects.com
www.edsconnects.com
LinkedIn

Gretchen Oie-Weghorst, Director
Gerald M Newman, Executive VP

Attendees are manufacturers of electronic components who sell their products through electronics distributors. Provides networking and meeting opportunities, and opens doors to new business. Hundreds of exhibits, thousands of attendees.
6M Attendees
Frequency: Annual/May
Founded in 1937

6672 **EEI Annual Convention**
Edison Electric Institute
701 Pennsylvania Avenue NW
Washington, DC 20004-2696

202-508-5000
lhutchinson@eei.org
www.eei.org
Facebook, Twitter, YouTube

Thomas R. Kuhn, President
Lee Hutchinson, Contact

Annual event designed for CEO and other senior-level executives from the electric industry.
1000 Attendees
Frequency: Annual/June

6673 **EEI Financial Conference**
Edison Electric Institute
701 Pennsylvania Avenue NW
Washington, DC 20004-2696

202-508-5000
feedback@eei.org
www.eei.org
Facebook, Twitter, YouTube

Thomas R. Kuhn, President

Provides a unique forum for exchange of ideas and experience; and to give you insight into emerging critical issues.
Frequency: Annual/November

6674 **EERA Annual Meeting**
Electrical Equipment Representation
638 W 39th Street
Kansas City, MO 64111

816-561-5323
800-728-2272; Fax: 816-561-1249
info2005@eera.org
www.eera.org

Vince Brown III, President
Brad Cahoon, President Elect
Don Shirk, VP
Kier Cooper, Secretary
Rob Rigsby, Treasurer
Frequency: Annual/April

6675 **EGSA Annual Spring Convention**
Electrical Generating Systems Association
1650 S Dixie Highway
Suite 500
Boca Raton, FL 33432

561-750-5575; Fax: 561-398-8557
www.egsa.org
Facebook

Cara Clark, Director Conventions/Meetings
Bob Breese, Director of Education

Offers educational sessions covering a broad range of issues effecting the on-site power industry.
Frequency: Annual/March

6676 **EIA's Congressional Technology Forum**
Electronic Industries Association
2214 rock Hill Rd
Suite 170
Herndon, VA 20170

571-323-0294; Fax: 571-323-0245
www.eia.org
LinkedIn, YouTube

Gail Tannenbaum, CMP, Manager Meetings

Discusses the issues most relevant for the electronics and high-tech industries.
Frequency: Annual/October

6677 **Electri...FYI**
Electrical Association of Rochester
PO Box 20219
Rochester, NY 14602-0219

585-538-6350; Fax: 585-538-6166
www.eawny.com

Ed Langschwager, President
Joe Lengen, First VP
Rich Monroe, Secretary/Treasurer
Kirstie Steves, Executive Director

Upstate Electrical Show. 120+ exhibitors. Free entry.
2000 Attendees
Frequency: Tri-Annual

6678 **Electric West Conference**
PRIMEDIA Business Exhibitions
11 River Bend Drive S
PO Box 4232
Stamford, CT 06907-0232

203-358-9900; Fax: 203-358-5816

David Small, Show Director
Tara Keating-Magee, Show Coordinator

Educational sessions attract electrical professionals from contracting companies, industrial plants, consulting engineering firms, datacom installers and electricians. Presentations focus

on such topics as power quality, lighting, the NEC, project management, claims management and fiber optics. Also provides in-depth coverage of National Electrical Code changes that directly impact the work of electrical professionals. 250 Exhibitors.
6000 Attendees
Frequency: Annual/March

6679 **Energy - Exhibit Promotions Plus**
US Department of Energy/US Dept. of Defense/GSA
11620 Vixens Path
Ellicott City, MD 21042

301-596-3028; Fax: 410-997-0764
www.epponline.com

Harve Horowitz, President
Kevin Horowitz, Senior Association Manager

Energy is an exclusive Federal Grant sponsored annual educational forum and exhibition.
1000+ Attendees
Frequency: Annual/August

6680 **Fall Technical and Marketing Conference**
Electrical Generating Systems Association
1650 S Dixie Highway
Suite 500
Boca Raton, FL 33432

561-750-5575; Fax: 561-395-8557
www.egsa.org
Facebook

Cara Clark, Director Conventions/Meetings
Bob Breese, Director of Education

Will focus on technical presentations and marketing efforts.
Frequency: Annual/September

6681 **IETA Annual Technical Conference**
International Electrical Testing Association
106 Stone Street
Morrison, CO 80465

303-697-8441
888-300-6382; Fax: 303-697-8431
neta@netaworld.org
www.netaworld.org
Facebook, YouTube

Mose Ramieh, President
David Huffman, First VP
Ron Widup, Second VP
John White, Treasurer
Walter Cleary, Secretary

Targets the electrical testing industry.
Frequency: Annual/March

6682 **IFAC World Congress**
American Automatic Control Council
3640 Col Glenn Hwy
Dayton, OH 45435

937-775-5062; Fax: 937-775-3936
pmisra@cs.wright.edu
www.a2c2.org

R. Russell Reinehart, President
Tariq Samad, President-elect
Jordan Berg, Treasurer
B.Wayne Bequette, Secretary

You will have the opportunity to take part in the wide spectrum of categories for technical presentations, including plenary lectures, survey papers, regular papers of both lecture and poster session types, panel discussions and case studies.
Frequency: Annual/July

6683 **ILEA Annual Conference**
International League of Electrical Association
12165 West Center Road
Suite 59
Omaha, NE 68144

402-330-7227; Fax: 402-330-7283
www.ileaweb.org
LinkedIn

Monique DeBoer, President
Chris Price, VP
Kirstie Steves, Secretary
Barbette Cejalvo, Treasurer

Provides a venue through which information and ideas exchanged and by encouraging all members to attend and share ideas.
Frequency: Annual/July

6684 **IMA Spring Meeting**
International Magnetics Association
8 S Michigan Avenue
Suite 1000
Chicago, IL 60603-3310

312-456-5590; Fax: 312-580-0165
www.intl-magnetics.org

August Sisco, Chair
Lowell Bosleyeo, President
George Orenchak, Secretary/Treasurer

Promote the worldwide growth, development, and use of magnetic materials through: collection and dissemination of global trade statistics, publication of industry standards and user and industry education.
Frequency: Annual/May

6685 **IMAPS International Symposium on Microelectronics**
International Microelectronics & Packaging Society
611 2nd Street NE
Washington, DC 20002

202-548-4001
888-464-6277; Fax: 202-548-6115
http://www.imaps.org

Michael O'Donoghue, Executive Director
Ann Bell, Manager Marketing/Communications

Symposium for the microelectronics and electronics packaging industries. Features a powerful technical program, progressive professional development courses and many forums to share the latest developments in microelectronics. Comprehensive exhibition of materials and equipment for the industry.
3000 Attendees
Frequency: Annual/September

6686 **IMPI Annual Symposium**
International Microwave Power Institute
PO Box 1140
Mechanicsville, VA 23111

804-596-6667; Fax: 804-559-4087
info@impi.org
www.impi.org

Bob Schiffman, President
Molly Poisant, Executive Director

Brings together researchers from across the globe to share the latest findings related to non-communications uses of microwave energy.
Frequency: Annual/June

6687 **IPC Printed Circuits Expo**
IPC: Association Connecting Electronics
3000 Lakeside Drive
Suite 309 S
Bannockburn, IL 60015

847-615-7100; Fax: 847-615-7105
www.ipc.org
Facebook, Twitter, LinkedIn, YouTube

Robert Ferguson, Chairman
Stephen Pudles, Vice Chairman
Don Schroeder, Secretary/Treasurer

Meet with everyone who designs, manufactures, and assembles printed circuit boards and electronics assemblies.
Frequency: Annual/February

6688 **ISA Expo**
ISA
67 Alexander Drive
Box 12277
Research Triangle Park, NC 27709

919-549-8411; Fax: 919-549-8288
info@isa.org
www.isa.org
Facebook, Twitter, LinkedIn

Tracey Berrett-Noble, Event Manager
Rodney Jones, Conference Coordinator
Cyrus Taft, Program Chair
Dale Lee, Director Convention Services
Tracey Berrett, Manager Convention Services

Features the latest and most extensive products and services exhibition, a strategically relevant technical conference, and a prominent continuing education and training program. With practitioners from over 70 countries. Offers the most complete automation and control experience in today's marketplace.
15000 Attendees
Frequency: Annual/October

6689 **ISA Fugitive Emissions LDAR Symposium and Training**
Instrumentation, Systems, and Automation Society
67 Alexander Drive
Box 12277
Research Triangle Park, NC 27709

919-549-8411; Fax: 919-549-8288
info@isa.org
www.isa.org
Facebook, Twitter, LinkedIn

Dale Lee, Director Convention Services
Tracey Berrett, Manager Convention Services

Covers topics including, but not limited to leak detection repair methods and fugitive emissions management systems. Industry experts in leak detection and repair will discuss implementations and improvements in LDAR programs in plant facilities.
Frequency: Annual/May

6690 **Innovation in Power Generation Measurement & Control Conference**
Instrumentation, Systems, and Automation Society
67 Alexander Drive
Box 12277
Research Triangle Park, NC 27709

919-549-8411; Fax: 919-549-8288
info@isa.org
www.isa.org
Facebook, Twitter, LinkedIn

Denny Younie, Conference General Chair
Rodney Jones, Conference Coordinator
Cyrus Taft, Program Chair
Dale Lee, Director Convention Services
Tracey Berrett, Manager Convention Services

Dedicated to instrumentation and control in the fossil and nuclear power generation industry. This year's conference includes approximately 50 technical papers presented in 8 sessions over two and a half days, a vendor exhibition area, 5 training courses, several ISA committee meetings, and the EPRI I&C Interest Group meeting and a Sunday evening welcome reception.
Frequency: Annual/June

6691 **International Conference and Exhibition on Device Packaging**
International Microelectronics & Packaging Society

611 2nd Street NE
Washington, DC 20002

202-548-4001
888-464-6277; Fax: 202-548-6115
www.imaps.org

Jim Drehle, President
Michael O'Donoghue, Executive Director
Steve Capp, Treasurer
Lawrence J Rexing, Secretary

Will provide a comprehensive technical program addressing the challenges of applications, and the latest developments in packaging for emerging devices, circuits, MEMS, sensors as well as materials and processes.
Frequency: Annual/March

6692 International Congress Applications of Lasers and Electro-Optics
Laser Institute of America
13501 Ingenuity Drive
Suite 128
Orlando, FL 32826-3204

407-380-1553
800-345-2737; Fax: 407-380-5588
icaleo@laserinstitute.org
www.laserinstitute.org
Facebook, Twitter, LinkedIn

Klaus Loeffler, President
Yongfeng Lu, President Elect
Stephen Capp, Treasurer
Robert Thomas, Secretary

Provides an international forum for the exchange of technical information between the people in the industrial, government and academic communities who apply laser/electro-optic technologies and the scientists, engineers and technicians engaged in developing these technologies. Accepts advertising.
5M Attendees
Frequency: Annual/October

6693 International Instrumentation Symposium
Instrumentation, Systems, and Automation Society
67 Alexander Drive
Box 12277
Research Triangle Park, NC 27709

919-549-8411; Fax: 919-549-8288
info@isa.org
www.isa.org
Facebook, Twitter, LinkedIn

Denny Younie, Conference General Chair
Rodney Jones, Conference Coordinator
Cyrus Taft, Program Chair
Dale Lee, Director Convention Services
Tracey Berrett, Manager Convention Services

Provides an outstanding opportunity to gain valuable technical information and training in the traditional areas of measurements/sensors, instrumentation systems, data and advanced system/sensor technology as well as innovative papers in many other state of the art areas.
Frequency: Annual/May

6694 International Laser Safety Conference
Laser Institute of America
13501 Ingenuity Drive
Suite 128
Orlando, FL 32826

407-380-1553
800-345-2737; Fax: 407-380-5588
lia@laserinstitute.org
www.laserinstitute.org
Facebook, Twitter, LinkedIn

Klaus Loeffler, President
Yongfeng Lu, President Elect
Stephen Capp, Treasurer
Robert Thomas, Secretary

A comprehensive four-day conference covering all aspects of laser safety practice and hazard control. Technical sessions and workshops will address developments in regulatory, mandatory and voluntary safety standards for laser products and laser use.
Frequency: Annual/March

6695 International Symposium on Bioenergetics and Bioelectrochemistry
Bioelectromagnetics Society
2412 Cobblestone Way
Frederick, MD 21702-3519

301-663-4252; Fax: 301-694-4948
office@bems.org
www.bems.org

David Black, President
Gloria Parsley, Executive Director
Richard Nuccitelli, VP
Phil Chadwick, Treasurer
Jonna Wilen, Secretary

Covers analytical chemistry.
Frequency: Annual/June

6696 Joint Conference on Decision and Control & European Control Conference
American Automatic Control Council
3640 Col Glenn Hwy
Dayton, OH 45435

937-775-5062; Fax: 937-775-3936
pmisra@cs.wright.edu
www.a2c2.org

R. Russell Reinehart, President
Tariq Samad, President-elect
Jordan Berg, Treasurer
B.Wayne Bequette, Secretary

Dedicated to the advancement of the theory and practice of systems and control. It brings together an international community of experts to discuss the state-of-the-art, new research results, perspectives of future developments, and innovative applications relevant to decision making, control, automation, and related areas.
Frequency: Annual/December

6697 Laser Institute of America
Laser Institute of America
13501 Ingenuity Drive
Suite 128
Orlando, FL 32826

407-380-1553; Fax: 407-380-5588
lia@lia.org
www.lia.org
Facebook, Twitter, LinkedIn

Klaus Loeffler, President
Stephen Capp, Treasurer
Robert Thomas, Secretary

Devoted to the field of laser applications and laser safety in both medical and industrial fields.

6698 Magnetism Conference: Institute of Electrical/Electronics Engineers
Courtesy Associates
2000 L Street NW
Suite 710
Washington, DC 20036

202-331-2000; Fax: 202-331-0111
www.magnetism.org

Paul Crowell, Chair
Yumi Ljiri, Treasurer
Brian Maranville, Publicity

Conference brings together scientists and engineers interested in recent developments in all branches of fundamental and applied magnetism. Emphasis is placed on experimental and theoretical research in magnetism, the properties and synthesis of new magnetic materials and advances in magnetic technology. Program consists of invited and contributed papers.
1.1M Attendees
Frequency: Annual/October

6699 Meeting of the Electrochemical Society
Appliance Manufacturer
65 South Main Street
Building D
Pennington, NJ 08534

609-737-1902; Fax: 609-737-2743
ecs@electrochem.org
www.electrochem.org

Christine Garzon, President
Tetsuya Osaka, Sr. VP
Harikila Deligianni, Secretary
Christina Bock, Treasurer

Has become the leading society for solid-state and electrochemical science and technology. ECS has 8000 scientists and engineers in over 75 countries worldwide who hold individual membership, as well as roughly 100 corporations and laboratories who hold corporate membership.
Frequency: Annual/May
Founded in 1902

6700 Mid-Atlantic Electrical Exposition
S&L Productions
1916 Crain Highway S
Suite 16
Glen Burnie, MD 21061-5572

410-863-1180
888-532-3669; Fax: 410-863-1187

Triennial show and 150 exhibits with 200 booths of electrical supplies, hardware and services.
3000 Attendees
Frequency: Annual/October
Founded in 2000

6701 NAED Annual Meeting
National Association of Electrical Distributors
1181 Corporate Lake Drive
St. Louis, MO 63132

888-791-2512
www.naed.org
Facebook, Twitter

Tom Naber, President & CEO
Michelle McNamara, COO/NAED Foundation Exec. Director
Ed Orlet, SVP, Gov't Affairs
Tim Dencker, VP, Finance

The only event to bring the entire industry together in the same place at the same time. In addition to offering strong topical and informational programming, the NAED Annual Meeting provides distributors access to the top management of more than 225 electrical product suppliers.

6702 NECA
National Electrical Contractors Association
3 Bethesda Metro Center
Suite 1100
Bethesda, MD 20814

301-657-3110; Fax: 301-215-4500
www.necanet.org
Facebook, Twitter, LinkedIn, YouTube

Russell Alessi, President
John Grau, CEO
Dan Walter, VP and COO
Michael Thompson, Secretary/Treasurer

Brings the largest manufacturers, utilities, contractors, engineers, consultants, plant engineers, and distributors from all over North America and 31 foreign countries.
8000 Attendees
Frequency: Annual/September

6703 **NEMA Annual Meeting**
National Electrical Manufacturers Association
1300 North 17th Street
Suite 1752
Rosslyn, VA 22209
703-841-3200; Fax: 703-841-5900
www.nema.org
Facebook, Twitter, LinkedIn, You tube
Evan Gaddis, President
Provides a forum for the standardization of electrical equipment, enabling consumers to select from a range of safe, effective and compatible electrical products.
Frequency: Annual/November
Founded in 1926

6704 **NEMRA Annual Conference**
Nat'l Electrical Mfgs Representatives Association
28 Deer Street
Suite 302
Portsmouth, NH 03801
914-524-8650
800-446-3672; Fax: 603-319-1667
nemra@nemra.org
www.nemra.org
Twitter, LinkedIn
Mark Gibson, Chairman
Greg reynolds, Chairman Elect
Greg Baker, Secretary/Treasurer
Provides a forum for the standardization of electrical equipment, enabling consumers to select from a range of safe, effective, and compatible electrical products.
Frequency: Annual/March

6705 **NORTHCON**
Electronic Conventions
8110 Airport Boulevard
Los Angeles, CA 90045-3119
800-877-2668; Fax: 310-641-5117
Donna Ybarra, Show Manager
400 booths featuring exhibits of components and microelectronics instrumentation.
6057 Attendees
Frequency: Annual/October

6706 **NOx Emissions & Source Monitoring Technical Conference and Training**
Instrumentation, Systems, and Automation Society
67 Alexander Drive
Box 12277
Research Triangle Park, NC 27709
919-549-8411; Fax: 919-549-8288
info@isa.org
www.isa.org
Facebook, Twitter, LinkedIn
Denny Younie, Conference General Chair
Rodney Jones, Conference Coordinator
Cyrus Taft, Program Chair
Dale Lee, Director Convention Services
Tracey Berrett, Manager Convention Services
Will present experiences with the measurement and control of low level NOx emissions, new concepts for NOx reduction techniques, and innovative monitoring systems. Presenters will participate in Q&A sessions, panel discussions, and be accessible throughout the two days to answer your questions.
Frequency: Annual/August

6707 **NRECA's Annual Meeting**
National Rural Electric Cooperative Association
4301 Wilson Boulevard
Suite 1
Arlington, VA 22203-1860
703-907-5500; Fax: 703-907-5514
www.electric.coop
Glenn L English, CEO
The national service organization dedicated to representing the national interests of cooperative electric utilities and the consumers they serve. An advocate for consumer-owned cooperatives on energy and operational issues as well as rural community and economic development.
Frequency: Annual/February
Founded in 1942

6708 **NSCA Systems Integration Expo**
National Systems Contractors Assocaition
3950 River Ridge Drive NE
Cedar Rapids, IA 52402
319-366-6722
800-446-6722; Fax: 319-366-4164
nsca@nsca.org
www.nsca.org
Facebook, Twitter, LinkedIn, YouTube
Chuck Wilson, Executive Director
Savannah Washburn, Events Manager
Dedicated to building connections between the people, knowledge and new ideas of the commercial electronic systems industry. A leading not-for-profit association representing the commercial electronic systems industry. A powerful advocate of all who work within the low-voltage industry, including systems contractors/integrators, product manufacturers, consultants, sales representatives, a growing number of architects, engineers and others. 600 exhibitors
11000 Attendees
Frequency: Annual/March

6709 **National Electrical Equipment Show**
Reed Exhibition Companies
255 Washington Street
Suite 275
Newton, MA 02458-1649
617-584-4900; Fax: 617-630-2222
Mike Rusbridge, Chairman/CEO
Serves the electrical and electronic industries.
7.5M Attendees
Frequency: Annual/March

6710 **National Electrical Wire Processing Technology Expo**
Expo Productions
510 Hartbrook Drive
Hartland, WI 53029
262-367-5500
800-367-5520; Fax: 262-367-9956
cheryl@epishows.com
www.electricalwireshow.com
Facebook
Cheryl L Luck, Sales Manager
Jay Partington, Show Manager
Only trade show tailored expressly to the electrical wire cable processing industry.
2000 Attendees
Frequency: Annual/May

6711 **National Lighting Fair**
Dallas Market Center
2100 N Stemmons Freeway
Suite 1000
Dallas, TX 75207-3009
214-556-6100; Fax: 214-655-6100
Charlie Sullivan, Executive Director
Cindy Morris, Chief Operating Officer
250 booths.
5M Attendees
Frequency: Annual/February

6712 **National Professional Service Convention**
National Electronics Service Dealers Association
PO Box 378
Hillsboro, TX 76645
817-921-9061
info@nesda.com
nesda.wildapricot.org
Facebook
Annual show of manufactures, suppliers and distributor of electronics, receivers, recorders, and supplies, software, telecommunications equipment, computers, videocassette recorders, parts and accessories, business forms, warranty companies and magazines/associations.
950 Attendees
Frequency: Annual/June
Founded in 1964

6713 **Pacific International Conference on Applications of Lasers and Optics**
Laser Institute of America
13501 Ingenuity Drive
Suite 128
Orlando, FL 32826
407-380-1553; Fax: 407-380-5588
lia@laserinstitute.org
www.laserinstitute.org
Facebook, Twitter, LinkedIn
Milan Brandt, Conference General Chair
Will focus on growth and application of lasers and optics in the Pacific region.
Frequency: Annual/April

6714 **Power-Gen International Trade Show**
Electrical Generating Systems Association
1650 S Dixie Highway
Suite 500
Boca Raton, FL 33432
561-750-5575; Fax: 561-395-8557
www.egsa.org
Cara Clark, Director Conventions/Meetings
Bob Breese, Director of Education
This is a special section of a larger show where we concentrate booths of firms that make, sell, and distribute on-site power products.
Frequency: Annual/December

6715 **Product Safety and Liability Conference**
National Electrical Manufacturers Association
1300 North 17th Street
Suite 1752
Rosslyn, VA 22209
703-841-3200; Fax: 703-841-5900
www.nema.org
Facebook, Twitter, LinkedIn, YouTube
Evan Gaddis, President
Tom Hixon, Vice President
Provides a forum for the standardization of electrical equipment, enabling consumers to select from a range of safe, effective and compatible electrical products.
Frequency: Annual/September

6716 **Reliability and Maintenance Symposium**
Consulting Services
1768 Lark Lane
Cherry Hill, NJ 08003-3215
856-428-2342; Fax: 856-616-9315
vrmonshaw@ieee.org
www.rams.org
V R Monshaw, Administrator
Raymond Sears, Treasurer
Patrick Dallosta, Secretary, Treasurer

The symposium offers the opportunity to explore and learn more about this and other related R&M subjects. 50 booths.
1M Attendees
Frequency: Annual/January

6717 **Rocky Mountain Electronics Expo**
Conference and Management Specialists
138 Garfield St
Denver, CO 80206-5517
303-568-8028; Fax: 303-799-0678
Karen Hone, Executive Director
Annual show and exhibits of products and services related to the hi-tech electronics industry.

6718 **SESHA Annual Symposium**
Semiconductor Environmental, Safety & Health Assn
1313 Dolly Madison Boulevard
Suite 402
McLean, VA 22101
703-790-1745; Fax: 703-790-2672
sesha@burkinc.com
seshaonline.org
John D Cox, President
Brett Burk, Co-Founder
Glenn Tom, Co-Founder
For individuals employed within the electronics and related high technology industries with an interest in environmental, health and safety issues.
1235 Attendees
Frequency: Annual/May
Founded in 1978

6719 **SMMA: Fall Technical Conference**
SMMA: The Motor & Motion Association
PO Box P182
South Dartmouth, MA 02748
508-979-5935; Fax: 508-979-5845
www.smma.org
Elizabeth B Chambers, Executive Director
William Chambers, Operations Director
Provide members and prospective members the opportunity to interact with industry colleagues. Attendees learn about industry trends and technologies, identify new supplier partners and network with other motor and drives professionals.
120 Attendees
Frequency: Annual/November

6720 **SMMA: Spring Management Conference**
SMMA: The Motor & Motion Association
PO Box P182
S Dartmouth, MA 02748
508-979-5935; Fax: 508-979-5845
www.smma.org
Elizabeth B Chambers, Executive Director
William Chambers, Operations Director
Provide members and prospective members the opportunity to interact with industry colleagues. Attendees learn about industry trends and technologies, identify new supplier partners and network with other motor and drives professionals.
80 Attendees
Frequency: Annual/May

6721 **SMTA International**
Surface Mount Technology Association
5200 Wilson Road
Suite 215
Minneapolis, MN 55424
952-920-7682; Fax: 952-926-1819
joann@smta.org
www.smta.org
Dan Baldwin, President
Marie Cole, VP Technical Programs
Kola Akinade, Secretary
Hal Hendrickson, Treasurer
A network of professionals who build skills, share practical experience and develop solutions in electronics assembly technologies and related business operations.
1200 Attendees
Frequency: Annual/October

6722 **SOUTHCON**
Electronic Conventions
12340 Rosecrans Avenue
Suite 100
Manhattan Beach, CA 90266
310-524-4100
800-877-2668; Fax: 310-643-7328
Donna Ybarra, Show Manager
Companies attending represent a major cross-section of the electronics industry including consumer, computer, medical, automotive and others. Offers conference sessions, in-depth technical sessions, product demonstrations and exhibits by vendors.
10M Attendees
Frequency: Annual/March

6723 **TechAdvantage Conference**
National Rural Electric Cooperative Association
4301 Wilson Boulevard
Suite 1
Arlington, VA 2203-1860
703-907-5500; Fax: 703-907-5514
Glenn L English, CEO
The only utility industry trade show exclusively for electric cooperative network management; engineering and operations; information services and technology; and purchasing employees.

6724 **Upper Midwest Electrical Expo**
North Central Electrical League
2901 Metro Drive
Suite 203
Bloomington, MN 55425
952-854-4405
800-925-4985; Fax: 952-854-7076
dale@ncel.org
www.ncel.org
Jeff Keljik, Chair
Chuck Healy, Vice Chair
Dan Paulson, Treasurer
Dale Yohnke, Secretary
Unites our electrical industry by providing vital industry commerce, educational discussion forums and offering various outlets for peer interaction. NCEL is the bridge between industry sectors and our electrical industry joins together to develop, expand and to protect all stakeholder interests in our Upper MIdwest Electrical Industry.
10213 Attendees
Frequency: Every 2 Years

Directories & Databases

6725 **Buyer's Guide and Member Services Directory**
Diesel & Gas Turbine Publications
1650 S Dixie Highway
Suite 500
Boca Raton, FL 33432
561-750-5575; Fax: 561-395-8557
www.egsa.org
Donald M Ferreira, Director Publications
George Rowley, Director of Education
It is the ultimate gen-set industry buyer's guide, because the members are listed in one or more of 23 different product categories. Each member's listing also shows whether they sell, rent, and/or service equipment.
Cost: $6.00
Frequency: Annual

6726 **Circuits Assembly: Buyers' Guide Issue**
Miller Freeman Publications
600 Harrison Street
Suite 400
San Francisco, CA 94107-1391
FAX 415-905-2239
Ron Daniels, Editor-in-Chief
List of suppliers of products and services to the surface mount industry; representatives and distributors.
Cost: $7.00
Frequency: Annual, November
Circulation: 40,500

6727 **Compressor Tech Two**
Diesel & Gas Turbine Publications
20855 Watertown Rd
Suite 220
Waukesha, WI 53186-1873
262-754-4100; Fax: 262-832-5075
www.dieselspec.com
Michael Osenga, President
Phil Burnside, Editor-in-Chief
Brent Haight, Managing Editor
Kara Kane, Advertising Manager
Sheila Lizdas, Circulation Manager
Covers the operation, application and design of gas compression systems, as used in the gas gathering, transportation, storage, processing and related industries worldwide. Featured are new products, new technologies and interesting new applications related to gas compression systems and components.
Cost: $45.00
Frequency: 6 per year
Circulation: 13,000
Founded in 1996

6728 **Diesel Progress: International Edition**
Diesel & Gas Turbine Publications
20855 Watertown Rd
Suite 220
Waukesha, WI 53186-1873
262-754-4100; Fax: 262-832-5075
www.dieselspec.com
Michael Osenga, President
Michael J Brezonick, Editor-in-Chief
Katie Evans, Advertising Sales Manager
Covers the design of engine-powered equipment manufactured outside of North America. This includes various types of mobile on-and-off-highway equipment including construction, mining, forestry, agricultural and turf maintenance vehicles, trucks and buses; specialty vehicles; pleasure boats; and generator, pump and compressor set manufacturers. Editorial focus is on new products and technology for these markets.
Cost: $40.00
Frequency: 6 per year
Circulation: 12,000
ISSN: 1091-3696
Founded in 1981

6729 **Diesel Progress: North American Edition**
Diesel & Gas Turbine Publications
20855 Watertown Rd
Suite 220
Waukesha, WI 53186-1873
262-754-4100; Fax: 262-832-5075
www.dieselspec.com
Michael Osenga, President
Patricia May, Advertising Sales Manager

Published for those concerned with the design, distribution and service of equipment powered by diesel, gasoline, or alternatively fueled engines. This includes all types of mobile on-and-off-highway equipment and stationary equipment. Markets covered include: construction, mining, forestry, agricultural and turf maintenance equipment; trucks and buses; pleasure boats; and generator, pump and compressor sets. Editorial focus is on new products and technology for these markets.
Cost: $75.00
Frequency: Monthly
Circulation: 30,000
ISSN: 1091-370X
Founded in 1935

6730 **Directory of Electrical Wholesale Distributors**
Penton
249 W. 17th Street
New York, NY 10011

212-204-4200
www.penton.com

Sharon Reynolds, CEO

Features a full search and download capabilities, you can easily assess your current distributor network and look for new distributors for your products. Search by MSA market, location square footage, employee count and many other critical variables. The handy main house and branch cross-reference brings the ever-changing electrical distribution market into focus. Using the simple search functions, you can build and download highly targeted lists in just seconds.
Frequency: Cd-Rom

6731 **EASA Yearbook**
Electrical Apparatus Services Association
1331 Baur Boulevard
Saint Louis, MO 63132

314-993-2220; Fax: 314-993-1269
easainfo@easa.com
www.easa.com

Linda J. Raynes, CAE, President
Cost: $100.00
267 Pages
Mailing list available for rent

6732 **Electrical Construction Materials Directory**
Underwriters Laboratories
2600 N.W. Lake Rd
Camas, WA 98607

877-854-3577; Fax: 360-817-6278
cec@us.ul.com
www.UL.com

Keith E Williams, CEO
John Drengenberg, Manager Consumer Affairs

Offers information on companies that have qualified to use the UL listing mark or classification marking with products that have been found to be in compliance with UL regulations.
Cost: $40.00
912 Pages
Frequency: Annual
Printed in on glossy stock

6733 **Electrical Distributor**
National Association of Electrical Distributors
1181 Corporate Lake Drive
St. Louis, MO 63132

888-791-2512
info@naed.org
www.naed.org

Tom Naber, President & CEO
Michelle McNamara, COO/NAED Foundation Exec. Director
Ed Orlet, SVP, Gov't Affairs
Tim Dencker, VP, Finance

List of manufacturers and distributors of electrical components, supplies and equipment.
Cost: $295.00
Frequency: Biennial
Circulation: 3,500

6734 **Electrical Equipment Representatives Association Membership Directory**
Electrical Equipment Representatives Association
638 W 39th Street
Kansas City, MO 64111

816-561-5323
800-728-2272; Fax: 816-561-1249
www.eera.org

Scott Whitehead, President
Vince Brown, President Elect
Brad Cahoon, Vice-President
Don Shirk, Secretary
Kier Cooper, Treasurer

More than 105 manufacturers representatives of electrical equipment companies.
Frequency: Annual, October
Founded in 1948

6735 **Engineers Relay Handbook**
Relay and Switch Industry Association
2500 Wilson Boulevard
Arlington, VA 22201

703-907-8025; Fax: 703-875-8908
narm@ecaus.org

Dave Baicjaome, Chairman
Jeffrey Boyce, Director Business Development
Rodd Ruland, Director Business Development
Steve Lane, General Manager

In summary, special effort has been made by the editors to cover specification parameters in sufficient detail to provide systems and product design engineers with all the information they need to obtain the correct types of relays for their applications.
Cost: $60.00
Frequency: Annual

6736 **Global Sourcing Guide**
Diesel & Gas Turbine Publications
20855 Watertown Rd
Suite 220
Waukesha, WI 53186-1873

262-754-4100; Fax: 262-832-5075
www.dieselspec.com

Michael Osenga, President
Michael J Mercer, Managing Editor
Kara Kane, Publication Manager
Christa Stern, Production Manager
Sheila Lizdas, Circulation Manager

The Global Sourcing Guide is one of the premier references and purchasing guides for the power systems and components industry. Covering products and systems used across the mobile and stationary engine-powered equipment industries, this guide incorporates information in a wide range of classifications.
Cost: $110.00
Frequency: Annual
Founded in 1935

6737 **High-Performance Composites Directory**
Ray Publishing
PO Box 992
Morrison, CO 80465-0992

303-467-1776; Fax: 303-467-1777
www.compositesworld.com

Judith Hazen, Publisher
Mike Mussleman, Managing Editor

The publisher of High-Performance Composites and Composites Technology magazines and well as the Sourcebook Industry directory and special design and application guides.
60 Pages
Founded in 1993
Printed in 4 colors on glossy stock

6738 **Indoor Electrical Safety Check Booklet**
Electrical Safety Foundation International
1300 N 17th Street
Suite 900
Arlington, VA 22209

703-841-3229; Fax: 703-841-3329
info@esfi.org
www.esfi.org

Ruppert Russoniello, Chair
Kevin Cosgriff, Treasurer
Lorraine Carli, Secretary

Instructions on running an electrical safety audit of your home and at the same time learn about electrical inspections, circuit maps, power audits, and potential electrical hazards and safety tips from your circuit breaker or fuse panel to your outlets, power cords and extension cords, light bulbs, space heaters, ground fault circuit interrupters (GFCIs), arc fault circuit interrupters (AFCIs), batteries, and much more.

6739 **NEMA Database**
National Electrical Manufacturers Association
1300 17th St N
Suite 1752
Rosslyn, VA 22209-3806

703-841-3200; Fax: 703-841-5900
www.nema.org

Evan R Gaddis, CEO
Tom Hixon, VP

This database offers time series on orders, shipments and unfilled orders for 6 major segments of the electrical manufacturing industry.

6740 **National Electrical Manufacturers Representatives Association Locator**
National Electrical Manufacturers Rep Assoc
28 Deer Street
Suite 302
Portsmouth, NH 03801

914-524-8650
800-446-3672; Fax: 603-319-1667
nemra@nemra.org
www.nemra.org

Michael Gorin, Chairman
Mark Gibson, Chair Elect
Greg Reynolds, Secretary/Treasurer

Approximately 1,000 electrical manufacturers representative companies.
Cost: $200.00
Frequency: Annual

6741 **National Electronic Distributors Association Membership Directory**
National Electronic Distributors Association
1111 Alderman Dr
Suite 400
Alpharetta, GA 30005-4175

678-393-9990; Fax: 678-393-9998

Brian McNally, President
Michael Knight, President Elect
Robin Gray, Executive VP

Approximately 300 member distributors and 180 member manufacturers of electronics products, plus 1,100 branch offices.

6742 **On-Site Power Generation: A Reference Book**
Electrical Generating Systems Association

1650 S Dixie Hwy
Suite 400
Boca Raton, FL 33432-7461

561-750-5575; Fax: 561-395-8557
www.egsa.org

Jalane Kellough, Executive Director
George Rowley, Director of Education

This book contains the most complete and up-to-date technical information covering on-site electrical power generation.
Cost: $95.00
600 Pages

6743 Outdoor Electrical Safety Check Booklet
Electrical Safety Foundation International
1300 N 17th Street
Suite 900
Arlington, VA 22209

703-841-3229; Fax: 703-841-3329
info@esfi.org
www.esfi.org

Ruppert Russoniello, Chairman
Kevin Cosgriff, Treasurer
Lorraine Carli, Secretary

A reference guide book that highlights important tips and advice for the safe outdoor use of electricity, and explains how you can use electrical safety devices to help protect against conditions that can cause electrical shock and fire hazards. It includes safety tips for dealing with power tools, downed power lines, floods and electricity, and portable generator use.

6744 Product and Supplier Information
Electrical Generating Systems Association
1650 S Dixie Hwy
Suite 400
Boca Raton, FL 33432-7461

561-750-5575; Fax: 561-395-8557
www.egsa.org

Jalane Kellough, Executive Director
George Rowley, Director of Education

EGSA publishes a new Buyer's Guide and Member Services Directory listing every member.

6745 SMMA: Directory
SMMA: Small Motors & Motion Association
PO Box P182
S Dartmouth, MA 02748

508-979-5935; Fax: 508-979-5845
www.smma.org

Elizabeth Chambers, Executive Director
William Chambers, Operations Director

Manufacturers, suppliers and users of fractional and subfractional horsepower electric motors.
Founded in 1975

6746 Transmission and Distribution: Specifiers and Buyers Guide Issue
Penton
249 W. 17th Street
New York, NY 10011

212-204-4200
CorporateCustomerService@penton.com
www.penton.com

Sharon Rowlands, CEO

List of manufacturers and distributors of equipment for electric power transmission and distribution.
Cost: $20.00
Frequency: Annual, September
Circulation: 49,000

6747 Wholesale Source Directory of Electrical Products, Supplies & Accessories
Sutton Family Communications & Publishing Company
155 Sutton Lane
Fordsville, KY 42343

270-740-0870
www.suttoncompliance.com

Theresa Sutton, Editor
Lee Sutton, General Manager

Listings include names, addresses, phone/fax numbers and product descriptions for wholesale distributors, importers, manufacturers, close-out houses and liquidators. Every item needed to become an electrical contractor, open an electrical store or sell this type of merchandise in a hardware store, flea market or other market. Daily updated laser printed copy. Price includes shipping and handling.
Cost: $57.20
100+ Pages
Founded in 1977

Industry Web Sites

6748 http://gold.greyhouse.com
G.O.L.D Grey House OnLine Databases

Grey House Publishing's online database platform, GOLD, offers Quick Search, Keyword Search and Expert Search for most business sectors including electrical markets. The GOLD platform makes finding the information you need quick and easy - whether you're a novice searcher or an experienced database user. All of Grey House's directory products are available for subscription on the GOLD platform.

6749 www.7ms.com
Seven Mountains Scientific

Industry news in battery technology, marketing and industry events including new products, electric vehicles, R&D and environmental news.

6750 www.ahtd.org
Association for High Technology Distributors

The Association for High Technology Distribution has worked to increase the productivity and profitability of the high technology Automation Solutions Providers and Manufacturers who satisfy the automation needs of general industry and OEM manufacturers.

6751 www.bems.org
Bioelectromagnetics Society

International resource for excellence in scientific research, knowledge and understanding of the interaction of electromagnetic fields with biological systems. Members of the society are biological and physical scientists, physicians and engineers interested in the interactions of nonionizing radiation with biological systems.

6752 www.construction.com
McGraw-Hill Construction

McGraw-Hill Construction (MHC), part of The McGraw-Hill Companies, connects people and projects across the design and construction industry, serving owners, architects, engineers, general contractors, subcontractors, building product manufacturers, suppliers, dealers, distributors and adjacent markets.

6753 www.csa-dc.org
Contract Services Association of America

Represents the government services contracting industry in Washington, DC. Members range from small businesses to large corporations servicing federal and state government in numerous capacities. CSA acts to foster effective implementation of the government's policy of reliance on the private sector for support services.

6754 www.eachicago.org
Electric Association

Its purpose is to serve as the umbrella organization for the various electrical disciplines in the Chicagoland area.

6755 www.easa.com
Electrical Apparatus Service Association

An international trade organization of electromechanical sales and service firms in 58 countries. Provides members with a means of keeping up to date on materials, equipment, and state of the art technology.

6756 www.eei.org
Edison Electric Institute

Advocates public policy, expands market opportunities and provides strategic business information for the shareholder-owned electric utility industry.

6757 www.eera.org
Electrical Equipment Representatives Association

Sales agents for manufacturers of electrical equipment used by utilities. Mission is to advance the quality and increase effectiveness of manufacturer's representatives in the electrical equipment industry.

6758 www.electric-find.com
Electric Find

A directory/search engine for the electrical construction industry. Search results have been screened by electrical professionals.

6759 www.electrochem.org
Electrochemical Society

The society is an international nonprofit, educational organization concerned with phenomena relating to electrochemical and solid state science and technology. Members are individual scientists and engineers, as well as corporations and laboratories.

6760 www.epri.com
Electric Power Research Institute

Nonprofit energy research consortium for the benefit of utility members, their customers and society. Mission is to provide science and technology-based solutions to its global energy customers by managing a far-reaching program of scientific research, technology development and product implementation.

6761 www.esda.org
Electrostatic Discharge Association

Dedicated to advancing the theory and practice of electrostatic discharge avoidance.

6762 www.ewh.ieee.org
Instrumentation and Measurement Society

A subsidiary of the Institute of Electrical and Electronics Engineers. Provides support to scientists and technicians who design and develop electrical and electronic measuring instruments and equipment.

6763 www.greyhouse.com
Grey House Publishing

Authoritative reference directories for most business sectors incluidng electrical markets. Users can search the online databases with varied search criteria allowing for custom searches by product category, geographic area, sales volume, keyword, subject and more. Full Grey House catalog and online ordering also available.

6764 **www.icea.net**
Insulated Cable Engineers Association
Professional organization dedicated to developing cable standards for the electric power, control and telecommunications industries. Ensures safe, economical and efficient cable systems utilizing proven state-of-the-art materials and concepts. ICEA documents are of interest to cable manufacturers, architects and engineers, utility and manufacturing plant personnel, telecommunication engineers, consultants and OEMs.

6765 **www.imaps.org**
International Microelectronics & Packaging Society
Dedicated to the advancement and growth of the use of microelectronics and electronic packaging through public and professional education, dissemination of information by means of symposia, workshops and conferences and promotion of the Society's portfolio of technologies.

6766 **www.impi.org**
International Microwave Power Institute
IMPI's members include scientists, researchers, lab technicians, product developers, marketing managers and a variety of other professionals in the microwave industry. The Institute serves the information needs of all specialists working with dielectric (microwave and RF) heating sytems, and was expanded in 1977 to meet the information needs relating to consumer microwave ovens and related products.

6767 **www.ipc.org**
IPC:Association Connecting Electronics
Works to develop standards in circuit board assembly equipment. Brings together all players in the electronic interconnection industry, including designers, board manufacturers, assembly companies, suppliers and original equipment manufacturers. Offers workshops, conferences, meetings and online communications.

6768 **www.ncel.org**
North Central Electrical League
Trade association representing all segments of the electrical industry in the Upper Midwest.

6769 **www.necanet.org**
National Electrical Contractors Association
Represents a segment of the construction market comprised of over 70,000 electrical firms.

6770 **www.nerc.com**
North American Electric Reliability Council
Voluntary organization promoting bulk electric system reliability and security.

6771 **www.netaworld.org**
International Electrical Testing Association
Defines the standards by which electrical equipment is deemed safe and reliable. Creates specifications, procedures, testing and requirements for commissioning new equipment and testing the reliability and performance of existing equipment.

6772 **www.nsca.org**
National Systems Contractors Association
Not-for-profit association representing the commercial electronic systems industry. Serves as an advocate for all those who work within the low-voltage industry including systems contractors/integrators, product manufacturers, consultants, sales representatives and a growing number of architects, specifying engineers and others.

6773 **www.platts.com**
Electrical World
The latest trends in utility engineering and IT, equipment and services, best business practices and critical industry thinking. For managers, engineers and technicians who plan, design, build, maintain and upgrade electric T&D systems around the world.

6774 **www.psma.com**
Power Sources Manufacturers Association
Worldwide membership consists of manufacturers of power sources and conversion equipment. Nonprofit association strives to integrate the resources of the power sources industry to more effectively and profitably serve the needs of the power sources users, providers and PSMA members. Educates the electronics industry and others on the relevant applications for power sources and conversion devices.

6775 **www.semi.org**
Semiconductor Equipment & Materials International
Strengthens the performance of member companies through lobbying, promotion, education and statistical research.

6776 **www.seshaonline.org**
Semiconductor Environmental, Safety & Health Assn
Members are individuals employed within the electronics and related high technology industries with an interest in environmental, health and safety issues.

6777 **www.sia-online.org**
Semiconductor Industry Association
Trade association representing the US microchip industry.

6778 **www.smma.org**
SMMA: Small Motors & Motion Association
Trade association for the electric motor and motion control industry in Northern America. The voice of the motor and motion industry providing a forum for education, communication, research and networking.

6779 **www.smta.org**
Surface Mount Technology Association
A network of professionals building skills, sharing practical experience and developing solutions in electronic assembly technologies and related business operations.

6780 **www.sweets.construction.com**
McGraw Hill Construction
In depth product information that lets you find, compare, select, specify and make purchase decisions in the industrial product marketplace.

Associations

6781 **AG Electronic Association**
10 S Riverside Plaza
Suite 1220
Chicago, IL 60606-3710

312-321-1470; Fax: 312-321-1480

Darrin Dollinger, Marketing Manager

Identifies, develops & or facilitates appropriate action aimed at furthering the compatibility & interchangeability of electronics and information systems used in agriculture.

6782 **ASM International**
9639 Kinsman Road
Materials Park, OH 44073-0002

440-338-5151
800-336-5152; Fax: 440-338-4634
memberservicecenter@asminternational.org
www.asminternational.org
Facebook, Twitter, LinkedIn

Zi-Kui Liu, President
Diana Essock, Vice President
Raymond V. Fryan, Treasurer
William T. Mahoney, Secretary & CEO

The society for materials engineers and scientists, a worldwide network dedicated to advancing industry, technology and applications of metals and materials. ASM provides information references, education, research and international events.
30K Members
Founded in 1913

6783 **AVS Science & Technology Society**
125 Maiden Ln
15th Floor
New York, NY 10038

212-248-0200; Fax: 212-248-0245
ricky@avs.org
www.avs.org
Facebook, Twitter, LinkedIn

Yvonne Towse, Managing Director
Jeannette DeGennaro, Exhibition & Salesmanager
Ricky Baldea, Office Services Coordinator
Angela Klink, Member Services Administrator
Peter Burke, Financial Administrator

Supports all those involved with all aspects of science and technology through research, education, new products, publications and conferences.
5500 Members
Founded in 1953

6784 **Aircraft Electronics Association**
3570 Ne Ralph Powell Rd
Lees Summit, MO 64064-2360

816-347-8400; Fax: 816-347-8405
info@aea.net
www.aea.net
Facebook, Twitter, LinkedIn, Flickr, YouTube

Mike Adamson, President & CEO
Debra McFarland, Executive Vice President
Linda Adams, VP, Member Services
Geoff Hill, Director, Communications
Aaron Ward, Director, Operations

AEA represents aviation businesses, including repair stations that specialize in maintenance, repair and installation of avionics and electronic systems in general aviation aircraft.
1250 Members
Founded in 1957
Mailing list available for rent

6785 **American Association of Electronic Reporters and Transcribers**
P.O. Box 9826
Wilmington, DE 19809

302-765-3510
800-233-5306; Fax: 302-241-2177
www.aaert.org
Facebook, Twitter, LinkedIn

Geoffrey Hunt, President
Steve Townsend, Vice President
Richard Russell, Treasurer
K.C. Corbin, Secretary
Michael F. Tannen, CSEP, Executive Director

A national professional association that deals with the electronic court reporting.

6786 **American Electronics Association**
5201 Great America Parkway
Santa Clara, CA 95054

408-987-4200
800-284-4232; Fax: 408-987-4298
www.aeanet.org

John V Harker, Chairman
William T Archey, President/CEO
Samuel J Block, VP/Controller
Tim Bennett, COO/EVP

Works to foster a healthy business climate by providing services, education and research programs.
3500 Members
Founded in 1943

6787 **Armed Forces Communications and Electronics Association (AFCEA)**
4400 Fair Lakes Ct
Fairfax, VA 22033-3899

703-631-6100
800-336-4583; Fax: 703-631-6169
www.afcea.org
Facebook, Twitter, LinkedIn, Flickr, YouTube, Google+, Slid

Lt. Gen. Robert Shea, USMC (Ret.), President/CEO
Lt. Gen. John Wood, USA (Ret.), EVP, Defense/National Security
Pat Miorin, CPA, EVP/CFO/International Treasurer
James L. Griggs Jr., VP/CIO/CTO
Beverly Cooper, VP, Comm. & Media/CKO/Publisher

A non-profit membership association serving the military, government, industry, and academia as an ethical forum for advancing professional knowledge and relationships in the fields of communications, IT, intelligence, and global security.
30000 Members
Founded in 1946

6788 **Association for Electronics Manufacturing**
1 SME Drive
PO Box 930
Dearborn, MI 48121

313-425-3000
800-733-4763; Fax: 313-425-3400
service@sme.org
www.sme.org
Facebook, Twitter, LinkedIn, YouTube, Google+

Wayne F. Frost, CMfgE, President
Jeffrey M. Krause, Chief Executive Officer
Kathleen Borgula, Human Resources
Erica Ciupak, Information Technology
Debbie Clark, Governance

Represents the electrical manufacturers.
3.6M Members
Founded in 1932

6789 **Augmented Reality for Enterprise Alliance**
401 Edgewater Place
Suite 600
Wakefield, MA 01880

info@theAREA.org
thearea.org
Facebook, Twitter, LinkedIn, Vimeo

Mark Sage, Executive Director
James Cassidy, Editor & Content Manager
Michael Rygol, Researcher
Angela Lang, Event & Media Partnerships
Benjamin Buse, New Members Facilitator

AREA seeks to help companies across all industries adopt augmented reality systems into their day-to-day activities.

6790 **AugmentedReality.Org**
40600 Ann Arbor Road E.
Suite 201
Plymouth, MI 48170

571-293-2013
www.augmentedreality.org
Facebook, Twitter, LinkedIn, YouTube, Flickr

Ori Inbar, Co-Founder & CEO
Tish Shute, Co-Founder & Chief Content Officer
Patrick O'Shaughnessy, Chief Technology Officer

Non-profit organization seeking to advance the field of augmented reality through connecting industry professionals through events and an online platform.

6791 **Electrical Apparatus Service Association**
1331 Baur Boulevard
St. Louis, MO 63132

314-993-2220; Fax: 314-993-1269
easainfo@easa.com
www.easa.com
Facebook, Twitter, LinkedIn, YouTube

Jerry Gray, Chair
Timothy Bieber, Vice Chair
Sid Seymour, Secretary/Treasurer
Linda J. Raynes, CAE, President/CEO
Dale Shuter, CMP, Manager, Meetings & Expositions

An international trade organization of electromechanical sales and service firms in 58 countries. Provides members with a means of keeping up to date on materials, equipment, and state of the art technology.

6792 **Electronic Components Industry Association**
1111 Alderman Drive
Suite 400
Alpharetta, GA 30005

678-393-9990; Fax: 678-393-9998
www.ecianow.org
Facebook, Twitter, LinkedIn, YouTube

Blair Haas, Chair
Ed Smith, Chair Elect
John Denslinger, President and CEO
Victor Meijers, VP, Marketing & Comm.
Barney Martin, VP, Industry Practices

Organization made up of electronic component manufacturers, their manufacturer representatives and authorized distributors that provides resources and opportunities for members to improve their business performance while enhancing the industry's overall capacity for growth and profitability.

6793 Electronic Industries Alliance
2500 Wilson Boulevard
Arlington, VA 22201-3834

703-907-7500; Fax: 703-907-7500
www.eia.org

Ronald L Turner, Chairman
Mike Kennedy, Vice Chairman
Dave McCurdy, President/CEO
Neal McDonald, Senior Coordinator
James Shiring, Secretary/Treasurer

Trade organization representing the entire spectrum of manufacturers and consumer manufacturers involved in electronic products.
1.5M Members
Founded in 1924

6794 Electronic Security Association
6333 North State Highway 161
Suite 350
Irving, TX 75038

972-807-6800
888-447-1689; Fax: 972-807-6883
www.esaweb.orgÿ
Facebook, Twitter, LinkedIn

Marshall Marinace, President
Dee Ann Harn, Vice President
Merlin Guilbeau, Executive Director
Jon Sargent, Secretary
Steve Paley, Treasurer

A nonprofit trade association that represents, promotes, and enhances the growth and professional development of the electronic life safety, security, and integrated sytems industry.
Founded in 1948

6795 Electronic Transactions Association
1101 16th Street NW
Suite 402
Washington, DC 20036

202-828-2635
800-695-5509; Fax: 202-828-2639
meghan.cieslak@electran.org
www.electran.org
Facebook, LinkedIn, YouTube, Flickr

Jodie Kelley, CEO
Scott Talbott, SVP, Government Affairs
Alexis Byrne, VP, Operations
Laura Hubbard, Director, Communications
Bradley Brewer, Manager, Membership

ETA is the international trade association serving the needs of organizations offering transaction processing products/services.
400M Members
Founded in 1990

6796 Electronics Representatives Association
1325 S. Arlington Heights Road
Suite 204
Elk Grove Village, IL 60007

312-419-1432; Fax: 312-419-1660
info@era.org
www.era.org

Chuck Tanzola, CPMR, President
Dave Norris, Chairman

Provides services and benefits to electronic industry manufacturers' representatives, manufacturers and distributors.
600 Members
Founded in 1935

6797 Electronics Technicians Association International
5 Depot Street
Greencastle, IN 46135

765-653-8262
800-288-3824; Fax: 765-653-4287
eta@eta-i.org
www.eta-i.org
Facebook, Twitter, LinkedIn, YouTube, Google+

Teresa Maher, CSS, President
Bryan Allen, CSM, CSS, Vice President
Richard Glass, CETsr, CEO Emeritus
Delores Andrews, Staff Support
Emily Hatfield, Research & Development

Association for electronic technicians worldwide offering over 70 certifications.
4500 Members
Founded in 1978

6798 Eta Kappa Nu
445 Hoes Lane
Piscataway, NJ 08854

732-465-5846
800-406-2590
info@hkn.org
hkn.ieee.org

Edward Rezek, President

Eta Kappa Nu (HKN) is the electrical and computer engineering honor society of the Institute of Electrical and Electronics Engineers (IEEE).
Founded in 1904

6799 Federated Rural Electric
77100 US Highway 71
PO Box 69
Jackson, MN 56143-0069

507-728-8366
800-321-3520; Fax: 507-728-8366
info@federatedrea.coop
www.federatedrea.coop

David A. Hansen, President
Dave Meschke, Vice-President
Darvin Voss, Secretary
Bruce Brockmann, Director
Glenn Dicks, Director

A distribution electric utility.
Founded in 1935

6800 IEEE Circuits and Systems Society
Institute Of Electrical and Electronics Engineers
445 Hoes Lane
Piscataway, NJ 08854

Home Page: www.ieee-cas.org
Facebook, Twitter, LinkedIn

Amara Amara, President
Yoshifumi Nishio, VP, Membership
Myung Hoon Sunwoo, VP, Conferences
Guoxing Wang, VP, Financial Activities
Mohammad Sawan, VP, Publications

CASS fosters interdisciplinary and cross-disciplinary cooperation with regards to using circuits and systems to address humanity's greatest challenges.

6801 IEEE Computational Intelligence Society
445 Hoes Lane
Piscataway, NJ 08855

732-465-5892; Fax: 732-465-6435
cis-info@ieee.org
cis.ieee.org
Facebook, Twitter, LinkedIn

Bernadette Bouchon-Meunier, President
Pablo Estevez, VP, Finance
Marley Vellasco, VP, Conferences
James Keller, VP, Publications
Carlos Coello Coello, VP, Member Activities

The CIS seeks to advance computational intelligence in science and engineering.

6802 IEEE Control Systems Society
445 Hoes Lane
Piscataway, NJ 08854-1331

Home Page: ieeecss.org
Facebook, Twitter, LinkedIn

Anuradha Annaswamy, President
Jorge Cortes, Director, Operations

Subsidiary of the Institute of Electrical and Electronics Engineers dedicated to control system technology.

6803 IEEE Industrial Electronics Society
Institute Of Electrical and Electronics Engineers
445 Hoes Lane
Piscataway, NJ 08854

804-827-3999
president@ieee-ies.org
www.ieee-ies.org
Facebook, Twitter, LinkedIn, YouTube

Terry Martin, President
Thilo Sauter, VP, Publications
Juan Rodriguez-Andina, VP, Conference Activities
Kiyoshi Ohishi, VP, Workshops & Activities
Yousef Ibrahim, VP, Membership Activities

Conducts, through its members, range of technical activities dedicated to applying electronics and electrical sciences in an industrial setting, including current developments in intelligent and computer control systems, robotics, factory communications and automation, flexible manufacturing, data acquisition and signal processing, vision systems, and power electronics.

6804 IEEE Industry Applications Society
Institute Of Electrical and Electronics Engineers
445 Hoes Lane
Piscataway, NJ 08854

732-562-2663
p.mccarren@ieee.org
ias.ieee.org
Facebook, Twitter, LinkedIn

Patrick McCarren, Executive Director
Lynda Bernstein, IAS Program Specialist

Seeks to link theory and practice by advancing science and technology in the electrical and electronic systems.

6805 IEEE Intelligent Transportation Systems Society
Institute Of Electrical and Electronics Engineers
445 Hoes Lane
Piscataway, NJ 08854

Home Page: www.ieee-itss.org
Facebook, Twitter, LinkedIn

Wei-Bin Zhang, President
Lingxi Li, VP, Administrative Activities
Nobuyuki Ozaki, VP, Standards
Javier Sanchez Medina, VP, Technical Activities

ITSS seeks to advance electrical engineering & information technology as applied to intelligent transportation systems.

6806 IEEE Photonics Society
445 Hoes Lane
Piscataway, NJ 08855-1331

732-562-3926; Fax: 732-562-8434
C.Jannuzzi@ieee.org
www.photonicssociety.org

Dalma Novak, President
Paul Juodawlkis, VP Membership
Catrina Coleman, VP Publications
Christopher Jannuzzi, Executive Director
Douglas Razzano, Associate Executive Director

A leading professional network of 7,000+ members that provide access to technical information.
Founded in 1965

6807 **IEEE Power Electronics Society**

m.p.kelly@ieee.org
www.ieee-pels.org
Twitter, LinkedIn

Philip Krein, History Chair
Michael P. Kelly, Executive Director
Donna Florek, Tech Community Program Specialist
Michael Markowycz, Tech Community Program Specialist
Jo-Ellen Snyder, Tech Community Program Specialist

A society of the Institute of Electrical and Electronics Engineers (IEEE) that focuses on the developmnet of power electronics technology.
7000 Members

6808 **IEEE Signal Processing Society**
Institute of Electrical and Electronics Engineers
445 Hoes Lane
Piscataway, NJ 08854

732-562-3888; Fax: 732-867-9953
sp-info@ieee.org
signalprocessingsociety.org
Facebook, Twitter, LinkedIn

Rich Baseil, Executive Director
Theresa Argiropoulos, Senior Manager, Operations
Caroline Johnson, Senior Manager, Conference Services
William Colacchio, Senior Manager, Publications
Jessica Perry, Member Communications Specialist

The SPS looks to provide current scientific information and resources on signal processing, while educating professionals in the industry, and providing a venue for networking.

6809 **IEEE Society on Social Implications of Technology**
Institute of Electrical and Electronics Engineers
445 Hoes Lane
Piscataway, NJ 08854

r.dent@ieee.org
technologyandsociety.org
Facebook, Twitter, LinkedIn

Robert Dent, President
Lew Terman, Secretary
Howard Wolfman, Treasurer

The SSIT focuses on the following areas: Sustainable Development & Humanitarian Technology; Ethics, Human Values and Technology; Technology Benefits for All; Future Societal Impact of Technology Advances; and Protecting the Planet & Sustainable Technology

6810 **IEEE Solid-State Circuits Society**
Institute of Electrical and Electronics Engineers
445 Hoes Lane
Piscataway, NJ 08854

m.p.kelly@ieee.org
sscs.ieee.org
Facebook, Twitter, LinkedIn

Adam Greenberg, Executive Director
Lauren Caruso, Administrator
Abira Altvater, Technical Program Specialist
Danielle Marinese, Society Administrator

The SSCS serves members by providing them with education, communication, recognition, leadership opportunities, and networking opportunities.

6811 **IEEE Systems, Man, and Cybernetics Society**
Institute of Electrical and Electronics Engineers
445 Hoes Lane
Piscataway, NJ 08854

Home Page: www.ieeesmc.org
Facebook, Twitter, LinkedIn, Instagram

Imre Rudas, President
Sam Kwong, VP, Cybernetics
Andreas Nuernberger, VP, Conferences & Meetings
Adrian Stoica, VP, Systems Science & Engineering
Vladimir Marik, VP, Organization & Planning

Promotes all aspects of systems science and engineering, human-machine systems, and cybernetics, through conferences, publications, and other activities.

6812 **IEEE Technology & Engineering Management Society**
Institute of Electrical and Electronics Engineers
445 Hoes Lane
Piscataway, NJ 08854

Home Page: www.ieee-tems.org
Facebook, Twitter, LinkedIn

Andy Chen, President
Richard Evans, VP, Technical Activities
Sudeendra Koushik, VP, Conferences

Formerly the Engineering Management Society and the Technology Management Council, TEMS seeks to provide members with essential management and leadership knowledge and skills.
Founded in 1951

6813 **IEEE Vehicular Technology Society**
3 Parl Avenue
17th Floor
New York, NY 10016-5997

212-419-7900
oliver.holland@ieee.org
vtsociety.org
Facebook, Twitter, LinkedIn

Oliver Holland, Chapter Coordinator & Developer

VTS focuses on the theory and practice of electrical engineering with regards to land transportation, railroad and mass transit, mobile communications, vehicular electrotechnology equipment and systems, and land, airborne and maritime mobile Services.

6814 **IPC Association**
3000 Lakeside Drive
105 N
Bannockburn, IL 60015

847-615-7100; Fax: 847-615-7105
answers@ipc.org
www.ipc.org
Facebook, Twitter, LinkedIn, YouTube, Google+, RSS

Marc Peo, Chairman
Joseph Joe O'Neil, Vice Chairman
John W. Mitchell, President/ CEO
Mikel H. Williams, Secretary/ Treasurer
Stephen Steve Pudles, Immediate Past Chairman

A trade association that standardizes the assembly and production requirements of electronic equipment and assemblies.

6815 **IPC: Association Connecting Electronics**
3000 Lakeside Drive
105 N
Bannockburn, IL 60015

847-615-7100; Fax: 847-615-7105
webmaster@ipc.org
www.ipc.org
Facebook, Twitter, LinkedIn, YouTube, Google+, RSS

Marc Peo, Chairman
Joseph Joe O'Neil, Vice Chairman
John W. Mitchell, President/ CEO
Mikel H. Williams, Secretary/ Treasurer
Jennifer Sandahl, Controller

A trade association for the printed circuit boards and electronics assembly industries, offering programs and resources to board manufacturers and electronic assemblers, designers, industry suppliers and original equipment manufacturers.
2000 Members
Founded in 1957

6816 **Independent Distributors of Electronics Association**
116 Helen Highway
#2900
Cleveland, GA 30528

714-670-0200; Fax: 714-670-0201
info@IDofEA.org
www.idofea.org
Facebook, Twitter, LinkedIn

Paul Romano, President
Dan Ellsworth, Vice President
Homey Shorooghi, Secretary/ Treasurer
Brian Wilson, Executive Board member
Jason Jowers, Executive Board member

A global trade association comprised of organizations for independent distributors to find relevant information and to participate in advancing industry ethics, ensuring customer satisfaction, establishing standards, and promoting education.

6817 **Independent Electrical Contractors**
4401 Ford Avenue
Suite 1100
Alexandria, VA 22302

703-549-7351
800-456-4324; Fax: 703-549-7448
info@ieci.org
www.ieci.org
Facebook, Twitter, LinkedIn, YouTube, Flickr, Instagram

Mark Gillespie, National President
Bruce Seilhammer, National Senior Vice President
Thayer Long, Executive Vice President/CEO
Vernice Howard, Chief Financial Officer
Bruna Patio, Staff Accountant

A national trade association for merit shop electrical and systems contractors.
Founded in 1957

6818 **Institute of Electrical and Electronics Engineers**
3 Park Ave.
17th Fl.
New York, NY 10016-5997

212-419-7900; Fax: 212-752-4929
www.ieee.org
Facebook, Twitter, LinkedIn, YouTube, Instagram

Toshio Fukuda, President & CEO
Stephen Welby, Executive Director & COO

Supports all those involved in the field of electrical engineering, and works to nurture techno-

logical innovation and excellence for the benefit of humanity.
422K Members
Founded in 1963

6819 **Instrumentation & Measurement Society**

Home Page: www.ieee-ims.org
Facebook, Twitter, LinkedIn

Reza Zoughi, President
Ruth A Dyer, Executive VP
Dario Petri, VP Finance
Alessandra Flammini, VP Conferences
Mark Yeary, VP Publications

A professional society of the IEEE whose field of interest is the science, technology, and application of instrumentation and measurement.

6820 **Instrumentation and Measurement Society**
799 N Beverly Glen
Los Angeles, CA 90077

310-446-8280; Fax: 732-981-0225
bob.myers@ieee.org
www.ewh.ieee.org

Robert Myers, Executive Director
Lee Myers, Assistant Director
Robert Rassa, President
Barry Oakes, VP Finance

A subsidiary of the Institute of Electrical and Electronics Engineers. Provides support to scientists and technicians who design and develop electrical and electronic measuring instruments and equipment.
6500+ Members
Founded in 1950

6821 **International Electrical Testing Association**
3050 Old Centre Ave.
Suite 102
Portage, MI 49024

269-488-6382; Fax: 269-488-6383
mrichard@netaworld.org
www.netaworld.org
Facebook, LinkedIn, YouTube

Dave Huffman, President
Ron Widup, 1st Vice President
Jim Cialdea, 2nd Vice President
Jayne Tanz, Executive Director
Melissa Richard, Finance and Business Manager

Establishes standards, publishes specifications, accredits independent, third-party, electrical testing companies, certifies test technicians, and promotes the services of association members.

6822 **International Federation of Air Traffic Safety Electronics Associations**

info@ifatsea.org
www.ifatsea.org

Daniel Boulet, President
Theodore Kiritsis, Vice-President

Federation represents the interests of air traffic safety electronics personnel.
50 Members
Founded in 1972

6823 **International Microelectronics and Electronic Packaging**
611 2nd Street NE
Washington, DC 20002

202-548-4001
888-464-6277; Fax: 919-287-2339
www.imaps.org

Michael O'Donoghue, Executive Director
Jennifer Davis, Office Assistant
Brian Schieman, Director Information Technology
Ann Bell, Manager Marketing/Communications
Brianne Lamm, Membership & Events Manager

Promotes interaction among technologies of ceramics, thin and thick films, semiconductor packaging, surface mount technology, multichip modules, semiconductor devices and monolithic circuits. Dedicated to the advancement and growth of the use of microelectronics and electronic packaging through education. Disseminates information through symposia, workshops and conferences.

11000 Members
Founded in 1967

6824 **International SEMATECH**
257 Fuller Road
Albany, NY 12203

518-437-8686; Fax: 512-356-3135
rcollier@sunypoly.edu
www.sunycnse.com

Alain Kaloyeros, Founding President/CEO
Walter Gerald Barber, President/Chief Admin Officer
Scott Bateman, CFO
Patricia Bucklin, Vice President for Administration
Richard Collier, Director for Student Affairs

A global consortium of leading semiconductor manufacturers who engage in cooperative precompetitive efforts to improve semiconductor manufacturing technology through the support of their members.

Founded in 2004

6825 **International Society of Certified Electronic Technicians**
3000-A Landers St.,
Fort Worth, TX 76107-5642

817-921-9101
800-946-0201; Fax: 817-921-3741
info@iscet.org
www.iscet.org

Pete Founding PresidentCEO, President
Daniel Champion, Vice President
Mack Blakely, Executive Director
Rich Reid, Secretary
John Wilkins, Treasurer

Helps train, prepare, and test technicians in the electronics and appliance service industry.

Founded in 1965

6826 **International Society of Certified Electronic Technicians**
3000-A Landers St.,
Fort Worth, TX 76107-5642

817-921-9101
800-946-0201; Fax: 817-921-3741
info@iscet.org
www.iscet.org

Pete Rattigan, President
Daniel Champion, Vice President
Mack Blakely, Executive Director
Rich Reid, Secretary
John Wilkins, Treasurer

Seeks to provide awareness of and services to certified electronics technicians. Provides educational materials in electronics training to schools, technical institutes and junior colleges. Offers certification programs for electronics technicians in associate and journeyman levels.

46000 Members
Founded in 1965

6827 **International Virtual Reality Healthcare Association**
2021 L Street NW
Suite 100-242
Washington, DC 20037

202-684-6207
bob@ivrha.org
ivrha.org

Robert Fine, Executive Director
Tom Augeri, Membership Director
The organization advocates for and provides information on applications of virtual reality technology in a healthcare setting.

6828 **Measurement, Control & Automation Association**
200 City Hall Avenue
Suite D
Poquoson, VA 23662

757-258-3100
automationassociation.com
Facebook, Twitter, LinkedIn, YouTube

Teresa Sebring, President
Andrea Ambrose, Director, Member Relations
Elizabeth Horton, Programs Manager
Kim Malina, Marketing Communications Manager
Rebecca Moore, Administrative Manager

The MCAA is the national trade association for manufacturers and distributors of instrumentation, systems, and software products for industrial process control and factory automation.
Founded in 1944

6829 **Minerals, Metals & Materials Society**
184 Thorn Hill Road
Warrendale, PA 15086-7514

724-776-9000
800-759-4867; Fax: 724-776-3770
webmaster@tms.org
www.tms.org
Facebook, LinkedIn, YouTube

James Robinson, Executive Director
Adrianne Carolla, Deputy Executive Director
Nancy Lesko, Executive & Board Administrator
Marleen Schrader, Accounting & HR Specialist
Paul Zappas, Information Technology Manager

Supports all those in the minerals, metals and materials industries with education, publications, trade shows and conferences.
Founded in 1971

6830 **Mobile Electronics Retailers Association**
85 Flagship Drive
Suite F
North Andover, MA 1845

800-949-6372

Mike Anderson, Chairman
Chris Cook, President
Mike Bartells, Advisory Board
Tony Dehnke, Advisory Board
Joe Forcella, Advisory Board

Focuses on education and networking opportunities designed to advance the professionalism and profitability of the mobile electronics industry.
Founded in 1992

6831 **National Electrical Manufacturers Association**
1300 North 17th Street
Suite 900
Arlington, VI 22209

703-841-3200
www.nema.org
Facebook, Twitter, LinkedIn, YouTube, Google+, Instagram

Donald J. Hendler, Chairman
Maryrose Sylvester, Vice Chairman

Kevin J. Cosgriff, President
Donald R. Leavens, PhD., Vice President and Chief Economist
John Caskey, Assistant VP, Operations

Develops standards for the electrical manufacturing industry.
Founded in 1926

6832 **National Electronic Distributors Association**
2211 South 47th Street
Suite 400
Phoenix, AZ 85034

678-393-9990
800-408-8353; Fax: 678-393-9998
avnetexpress.avnet.com
Facebook, Twitter, LinkedIn, YouTube

Ed Smith, President
Rick Hamada, CEO
Debbie Conyers, Director Marketing
Barney Martin, VP Industry Practices

Conducts research and offers educational programs for wholesale distributors of electronic components.
Founded in 1921
Mailing list available for rent

6833 **National Electronics Service Dealers Association**
PO Box 378
Hillsboro, TX 76645

817-921-9061
info@nesda.com
nesda.wildapricot.org

A national trade association for professionals in the business repairing consumer electronics equipment, appliances, and computers. NESDA has an e-mail group of over 600 members and manufacturers that communicate daily for information sharing.
600 Members
Founded in 1950

6834 **National Marine Electronics Association**
692 Ritchie Highway
Suite 104
Severna Park, MD 21146

410-975-9425; Fax: 410-975-9450
info@nmea.org
www.nmea.org
Facebook

Steve Katz, Chair
Mark Reedanauer, President & Executive Director

Is the unifying force behind the entire marine electronics industry, bringing together all aspects of the industry for the betterment of all in our business.
400 Members
Founded in 1957

6835 **National Rural Electric Cooperative Association**
4301 Wilson Blvd.
Arlington, VA 22203

703-907-5500
www.nreca.coop
Facebook, Twitter, LinkedIn, YouTube

Jo Ann Emerson, Chief Executive Officer
Kirk Johnson, SVP of Government Relations
Peter Baxter, SVP
Marc Breslaw, Executive Director
Jeffrey Connor, Chief of Staff and COO

An organization that represents the interests of over 900 electric cooperatives in the United States to various legislatures.
Founded in 1933

6836 **Optical Society of America**
2010 Massachusetts Avenue NW
Washington, DC 20036

202-223-8130; Fax: 202-223-1096
info@osa.org
www.osa.org
Facebook, Twitter, LinkedIn, YouTube

Elizabeth A. Rogan, CEO
Elizabeth Nolan, Chief Publishing Officer
Sean Bagshaw, COO/CIO
Suzanne Ffolkes, Chief Communications Officer
Genaro Montanez, Chief Employee/Membership Officer

The Optical Society of America (OSA) was organized to increase and diffuse the knowledge of optics, pure and applied; to promote the common interests of investigators of optical problems, of designers and of users of optical apparatus of all kinds; and to encourage cooperation among them. The purposes of the Society are scientific, technical and educational.
20K Members
Founded in 1916

6837 **Power Electronics Society**
799 N Beverly Glen
Los Angeles, CA 90077

310-446-8280; Fax: 310-446-8390
bob.myers@ieee.org

Michael P. Kelly, Executive Director
Donna Florek, Program Specialist
Michael Markowycz, Program Specialist
Jo-Ellen Snyder, Tech Community Program Specialist
Grant Pitel, Volunteer PELS Webmaster

A subsidiary of the Institute of Electrical & Electronics Engineers. Supports professionals working in the field of power electronics technology.
5000 Members
Founded in 1987

6838 **Power Sources Manufacturers Association**
PO Box 418
Mendham, NJ 07945-0418

973-543-9660; Fax: 973-543-6207
power@psma.com
www.psma.com
LinkedIn

Ernie Parker, Chairman
Eric Persson, President
Stephen Oliver, VP
Michel Grenon, Secretary/ Treasurer

The PSMA is a not-for-profit organization incorporated in the state of California. The purpose of the Association shall be to enhance the stature and reputation of its members and their products, improve their knowledge of technological and other developments related to power sources, and to educate the entire electronics industry, plus academia, as well as government and industry agencies as to the importance of, and relevant applications for, all types of power sources and conversion devices.
155 Members
Founded in 1985

6839 **SPIE**
1000 20th St.
Bellingham, WA 98225-6705

360-676-3290
888-504-8171; Fax: 360-647-1445
CustomerService@SPIE.org
www.spie.org
Facebook, Twitter, LinkedIn, RSS, YouTube, Blogspot

Dr. H. Philip Stahl, President
Mr. William Arnold, Immediate Past President
Prof Toyohiko Yatagai, President Elect
Dr. Robert A Lieberman, Vice President
Brian Lula, Secretary/ Treasurer

A nonprofit international professional society for optics and photonics technology.
Founded in 1955

6840 **Semiconductor Environmental, Safety & Health Association**
1313 Dolly Madison Boulevard
Suite 420
McLean, VA 22101

703-790-1745; Fax: 703-790-2672
sesha@burkinc.com
www.seshaonline.org

Hilary Matthews, President
Raymond McDaid, Secretary
Brian Sherin, Treasurer
Karl Albrecht, Secretary

Members are individuals employed within the electronics and related high technology industries with an interest in environmental, health and safety issues.
1500 Members
Founded in 1978

6841 **Semiconductor Equipment and Materials International**
3081 Zanker Road
San Jose, CA 95134

408-943-6900; Fax: 408-428-9600
semihq@semi.org
www.semi.org

Yong Han Lee, Chairman
Tetsuo Tsuneishi, Vice Chairman
Denny McGuirk, President/CEO
Richard Salsman, CFO/VP, Operations
Peter Gillespie, Chief Marketing Officer

An international trade association representing firms supplying equipment, materials and services to the semiconductor industry. Strengthens the performance of members through promotion, lobbying, education and statistical research.
2300 Members
Founded in 1970

6842 **Semiconductor Industry Association**
1101 K Street NW
Suite 450
Washington, CA 20005
202-446-1700
866-756-0715; Fax: 202-216-9745
mailbox@sia-online.org

John Neuffer, President and CEO
Jimmy Goodrich, Vice President, Global Policy
Mike Williams, Chief Financial Officer
Joe Pasetti, Director, Government Affairs
Dan Rosso, Communications Manager

Trade association representing the US microchip industry. Provides a forum for working collectively to enhance the competitiveness of the US chip industry.
70 Members
Founded in 1977

6843 **Society of Manufacturing Engineers**
1000 Town Center
Suite 1910
Southfield, MI 48075

313-425-3000
service@sme.org
www.sme.org
Facebook, Twitter, LinkedIn, YouTube, Google+, Instagram

Sandra L. Bouckley, Executive Director & CEO
Craig Connop, Chief Financial Officer
Steve Prahalis, Chief Operating Officer
Erica Ciupak, Information Technology
Debbie Clark, Governance

The organization serves its members and others in the international manufacturing community by identifying, evaluating and explaining the

adoption and integration of emerging information technologies to create business value.
65K Members
Founded in 1932

6844 **Surface Mount Technology Association**
5200 Willson Rd
Suite 215
Minneapolis, MN 55424-1316

952-920-7682; Fax: 952-926-1819
joann@smta.org
www.smta.org
Facebook, Twitter, LinkedIn

Bill Barthel, President
JoAnn Stromberg, Executive Administrator
Eileen Hibbler, VP Membership
Raiyomand Aspandiar, Ph.D., VP Technical Programs
Debbie Carboni, VP Expos

Network of professionals building skills, sharing practical experience and developing solutions in electronic assembly technologies and related business operations.
3200 Members
Founded in 1984

6845 **Tobacco Vapor Electronic Cigarette Association**
1005 Union Center Dr.
Suite F
Alpharetta, GA 30004

888-998-8322
info@tveca.com
www.tveca.com
Facebook, Twitter, LinkedIn, Google+

Ray Story, CEO
Keith Nelson, US Chief Political Officer
Thomas R. Kiklas, CFO
Chrissy Keheley, Secretary
Christopher Fowler, CTO/Web Development

A nonprofit organization dedicated to create a sensible and responsible electronic cigarette market by providing the media, legislative bodies, andconsumers with education, communication, and research.

6846 **Universal Association of Computer and Electronics Engineers**
42 Broadway
Suite 12-217
New York, NY 10004

212-901-3781; Fax: 212-901-3786

A registered nonprofit society to promote research.

6847 **VR/AR Association**
Palo Alto, CA 94303

nathan@thevrara.com
www.thevrara.com
Facebook, Twitter, LinkedIn, YouTube

Nathan Pettyjohn, Founder & President
Kris Kolo, Global Executive Director

International organization with a mission to foster collaboration between companies and individuals in the virtual reality and augmented reality industry. It aims to accelerate growth, encourage research and education, develop industry standards, connect members, and promote their services.
Founded in 2015

6848 **Video Electronics Standards Association**
1754 Technology Dr.
Suite 238
San Jose, CA 95110

408-982-3850; Fax: 408-669-0976
moderator@vesa.org
www.vesa.org
Twitter, YouTube

Alan Kobayashi, Chairman
Syed Athar Hussain, Vice Chairman
Richard Hubbard, Secretary/ Treasurer
Bill Lempesis, Executive Director
Joan White, Membership Services Manager

An international nonprofit corporation standards body for computer graphics.

6849 **Wheatland Rural Electric Association**
P. O. Box 1209
Wheatland, WY 82201

307-322-2125
800-344-3351; Fax: 307-322-5340
www.wheatlandrea.com
Facebook

Robert Brockman, President
Bill Teter, Vice-President
Britt Wilson, Secretary/ Treasurer
Sandra Hranchak, Director
Jack Finnerty, Director

Home power usage calculations, product and new service information,and youth scholarships.
Founded in 1936

6850 **XR Association**
1299 Pennsylvania Avenue NW
Washington, DC 20004

membership@xra.org
xra.org
Facebook, Twitter, LinkedIn

Elizabeth Hyman, Chief Executive Officer
Joan O'Hara, Senior Director, Public Policy
Laura Chadwick, Senior Director, Industry Relations
Michael Williams, Chief Operating Officer
Bethany Reitsma, Executive Assistant

Trade association for technology manufacturers in the virtual, augmented, and mixed reality industries.
Founded in 2016

Newsletters

6851 **AEA Monthly News**
American Electronics Association
5201 Great America Parkway
Santa Clara, CA 95054

408-987-4200
800-284-4232; Fax: 408-987-4298
www.aeanet.org

John V Harker, Chairman
William T Archey, President/CEO
Samuel J Block, VP/Controller
Tim Bennett, COO/EVP

AEA Advancing the Business of Technology, Access to Investors, State, Federal & International Lobbying, Insurance Services, Government Procurement, Business Networking, Foreign Market Access, Select Business Services, Executive Education.
Frequency: Monthly

6852 **AEA by the Bay**
American Electronics Association
5201 Great America Parkway
Santa Clara, CA 95054

408-987-4200
800-284-4232; Fax: 408-987-4298
www.aeanet.org

John V Harker, Chairman
William T Archey, President/CEO
Samuel J Block, VP/Controller
Tim Bennett, COO/EVP

Newsletter for the AEA Bay Area Council.
Frequency: Monthly

6853 **AEA's Californica Monday Morning Report**
American Electronics Association
5201 Great America Parkway
Santa Clara, CA 95054

408-987-4200
800-284-4232; Fax: 408-987-4298
www.aeanet.org

John V Harker, Chairman
William T Archey, President/CEO
Samuel J Block, VP/Controller
Tim Bennett, COO/EVP

A weekly report of what is going on in Californica policy relating to the high-tech industry, and how to change it.
Frequency: Weekly

6854 **American Electronics Association Impact**
American Electronics Association
5201 Great America Parkway
Santa Clara, CA 95054-1122

408-987-4200; Fax: 408-970-8565
www.aeanet.org

William Archey, President

Representing the electronics software and information technology industries. Covers business and management issues for electronics executives.
Frequency: Monthly
Circulation: 25000
Founded in 1945

6855 **Currents**
Electrical Apparatus Service Association
1331 Baur Boulevard
St. Louis, MO 63132

314-993-2220; Fax: 314-993-1269
easainfo@easa.com
www.easa.com
Facebook, Twitter, LinkedIn

Jerry Gray, Chair
Timothy Bieber, Vice Chair
Sid Seymour, Secretary/Treasurer
Linda J. Raynes, CAE, President/CEO
Dale Shuter, CMP, Manager, Meetings & Expositions

Provides information on EASAprograms, seminars, technical articles and industry trends and events. Members receive a copy each month.
Frequency: Monthly
Circulation: 2000+

6856 **Electronic Advertising Marketplace Report**
Simba Information
PO Box 4234
Stamford, CT 06907-0234

203-258-8193; Fax: 203-358-5825
simbainfo@simbanet.com
www.simbanet.com

Linda Kopp, Editor
Donna Devall, Marketing Director
Joyce Brigish, Circulation Manager

Provides news, analysis and opinion for the emerging business of electronic advertising and shopping and commerce. Discover how publishers, telephone companies, distributors, and retailers are now using information technologies to build the information infrastructure that will reach new customers and match buyers with sellers. Covers electronic marketing, new electronic classified and transactional services, the role of the Internet, electronic yellow pages, etc.
Cost: $499.00
Frequency: BiWeekly

6857 **Electronic Education Report**
Simba Information

PO Box 4234
Stamford, CT 06907-0234

203-258-8193; Fax: 203-358-5825
simbainfo@simbanet.com
www.simbanet.com

Megan St. John, Manager
Patrick Quinn, Editor

Provides information on the multi-billion dollar market for electronic instructional materials. Includes company rankings, financial profiles, sales and distrbution trends, funding and adoptions, enrollement and demographics, trademark and copyright issues, strategic alliances and mergers.
Cost: $445.00
Frequency: BiWeekly

6858 **Electronic Imaging Report**
Phillips Publishing
7811 Montrose Road
Potomac, MD 20854

301-340-2100
feedback@healthydirections.com
www.healthydirections.com

Written for top-level executives interested in learning how imaging technology can streamline their operations, cut their overhead costs and boost their competitiveness. Accepts advertising.
Cost: $397.00
9 Pages
Frequency: BiWeekly

6859 **Electronic Information Report**
Simba Information
PO Box 4234
Stamford, CT 06907-234

203-258-8193; Fax: 203-358-5825
simbainfo@simbanet.com
www.simbanet.com

Linda Kopp, Editor
Charlie Friscia, Marketing Director

The original information industry newsletter. Every week, this report monitors, analyzes, and reports on trends and developments in information services. It covers new storage and distribution media, databases, electronic publishing, value-added fax, online, multimedia and voice services. Readers will receive up-to-the-minute news written from a product, financial and marketing viewpoint.
Cost: $685.00
Frequency: 46 Issues Per Y
Founded in 1989

6860 **Electronic Materials Technology News**
Business Communications Company
25 Van Zant Street
Suite 13
Norwalk, CT 06855-1713

203-853-4266; Fax: 203-853-0348
sales@bccresearch.com
www.bccresearch.com

Louis Naturman, President
Marc Favrean, Editor
Alan Hall, Editorial Director
Thomas Abraham, VP Research
Marc Favreau, VP Development

Reports on electronic materials and processes, patents, companies involved, trends and business opportunities.
Cost: $35.00
Founded in 1971

6861 **IEEE All-Society Periodicals Package(ASPP)**
Power Electronics Society
799 N Beverly Glen
Los Angeles, CA 90077

310-446-8280; Fax: 310-446-8390
bob.myers@ieee.org

Jerry Hudgins, President
Robert Myers, Executive Director
Steven Leeb, Treasurer
Ronald Harley, VP Operations

Provides access to our core collection of engineering, electronics, and computer science periodicals.

6862 **ISCET Update**
Int'l Society of Certified Electronics Technicians
3608 Pershing Ave
Fort Worth, TX 76107-4527

817-921-9101
800-946-0201; Fax: 817-921-3741
info@iscet.org
www.iset.org

Ed Clingman, Administrator
Sheila Fred, Editor
Brian Gibbson, Circulation Manager

News and information for the electronics community.
Frequency: Monthly
Circulation: 1300

6863 **Integrated Circuit Manufacturing Synopsis**
Semiconductor Equipment & Materials International
3081 Zanker Road
San Jose, CA 95134

408-943-6900; Fax: 408-428-9600
semihq@semi.org
www.semi.org

Maggie Hershey, Manager
Anne Miller, Author
Victoria Hadfield, Executive VP/President, N America

An illustrated booklet that provides an excellent introduction to the semiconductor industry and makes a great handout for new employee orientation or as a resource for industry suppliers. It is easy to understand and free of technical terminology.
Cost: $15.75
35 Pages

6864 **Manufacturing Market Insider**
JBT Communications
PO Box 782
Needham Heights, MA 02494-0006

781-444-2154; Fax: 781-455-8409
www.mfgmkt.com

John B Tuck, Publisher/Editor
Ann Connors, Circulation Manager

Specializes in contract manufacturing of electronics. Includes acquisitions, expansions, financial results and contract awards announced by contract manufacturers of electronics.
Cost: $420.00
8 Pages
Frequency: Monthly
ISSN: 1072-8651
Founded in 1991
Printed in one color on matte stock

6865 **Military & Aerospace Electronics**
PennWell Publishing Company
98 Spit Brook Rd
Suite Ll-1
Nashua, NH 03062-5737

603-891-0123; Fax: 603-891-9294
ATD@PennWell.com
www.pennwell.com

Christine Shaw, VP
Tobias Naegele, Editor

Engineering newspaper written exclusively for military-aeronautical electronic systems designers, buyers and project managers.
Cost: $10.00
Frequency: Monthly
Circulation: 48,100
Founded in 1910

6866 **Optics & Photonics News**
Optical Society of America
2010 Massachusetts Ave NW
Washington, DC 20036-1023

202-223-8130; Fax: 202-223-1096
info@osa.org
www.osa-opn.org

Stewart Wills, Editor & Content Director
Alessia Kirkland, Creative Director

Optics & Photonics/OPN is a monthly magazine that keeps members up to date on technical innovations, industry news, OSA activities and much more. OPN promotes the generation application, archiving and worldwide dissemination of knowledge in optics and photonics.
Frequency: Monthly
Circulation: 17000
Mailing list available for rent

6867 **Quick Connections**
Electronic Representatives Association
1325 S. Arlington Heights Road
Suite 204
Elk Grove Village, IL 60007

312-419-1432; Fax: 312-419-1660
info@era.org
www.era.org

Chuck Tanzola, CPMR, President
Dave Norris, Chairman

ERA's Quick Connections is an e-newsletter for the association's members.
Frequency: Bi-Weekly

6868 **SITE**
American Electronics Association
5201 Great America Parkway
Santa Clara, CA 95054

408-987-4200
800-284-4232; Fax: 408-987-4298
www.aeanet.org

John V Harker, Chairman
William T Archey, President/CEO
Samuel J Block, VP/Controller
Tim Bennett, COO/EVP

Brings High-Tech HR professionals important information about compensation and benefits, employment law, relevant legislation, education and training.
Frequency: Bi-Monthly

6869 **SouthWest Technology Report**
Communications
PO Box 23899
Tempe, AZ 85285-3899

480-345-1118; Fax: 480-345-1119

Walter J Schuch, Publisher

Focused on business and technology news related to high tech and electronics companies and organizations based in the Southwestern United States.
Cost: $69.00
8 Pages
Frequency: Monthly
Printed in one color on matte stock

6870 **Technician Association News**
Electronic Technicians Association International
5 Depot St
Greencastle, IN 46135-8024

765-653-8262
800-288-3824; Fax: 765-653-4287

eta@eta-i.org
www.eta-i.org

Dick Glass, President
Brianna Pinson, Office Manager

A professional and trade journal servicing electronic technicians nationwide. Lists new certified electronics technicians, technical repair services, upcoming seminars and satellite training sessions.
Frequency: Monthly
ISSN: 1092-9592
Founded in 1978
Printed in 2 colors

6871 **Technology News Today**
American Electronics Association
5201 Great America Parkway
Santa Clara, CA 95054

408-987-4200
800-284-4232; Fax: 408-987-4298
www.aeanet.org

John V Harker, Chairman
William T Archey, President/CEO
Samuel J Block, VP/Controller
Tim Bennett, COO/EVP
Melissa La vigna, Contact

Aims to benefit investors with exclusive information on high-tech industry trends available only through AEA's extensive research, legislative monitoring and high-leveled networking capabilities.
Frequency: Quarterly

Magazines & Journals

6872 **ARtillery Intelligence**
VR/AR Association
Palo Alto, CA 94303

nathan@thevrara.com
www.thevrara.com
Facebook, Twitter, LinkedIn, YouTube

Nathan Pettyjohn, Founder & President
Kris Kolo, Global Executive Director

Research and data package for VR/AR professionals.
Founded in 2015

6873 **Advancing Microelectronics**
ISHM-Microelectronics Society
611 2nd street NE
Washington Dc, DC 20002

202-548-4001
888-464-6277; Fax: 202-548-6115
www.imaps.org

For the Microelectronics Society.
Circulation: 4010

6874 **Applied Microwave & Wireless**
Noble Publishing Corporation
1334 Meridian Rd
Thomasville, GA 31792

229-377-0587; Fax: 229-377-0589
www.noblepub.com

Joseph White, Publisher
Randy W Rhea, CEO

Edited for the RF and microwave professional.
Cost: $30.00
Frequency: Monthly
Circulation: 26287
ISSN: 1075-0207
Founded in 1994

6875 **Avionics News Magazine**
Aircraft Electronics Association
3570 Ne Ralph Powell Rd
Lees Summit, MO 64064-2360

816-347-8400; Fax: 816-478-3100
info@aea.net
www.aea.net

Mike Adamson, President & CEO
Tracy Lykins, Editor
Linda Adams, Managing Editor

This publication is the voice of the general aviation electronics industry. It is recognized as one of the leading publications for the latest information in avionics technology. Subscriptions are complimentary within North America, however, subscribers must be employed within the aviation industry to receive the magazine.
Cost: $132.00
Frequency: Monthly
Mailing list available for rent

6876 **Channel Magazine**
Semiconductor Equipment & Materials International
3081 Zanker Road
San Jose, CA 95134-4080

408-943-6900; Fax: 408-428-9600
semihq@semi.org
www.semi.org

Karen Savala, Publisher
Steve Buehler, Editor

A forum for equipment and material suppliers committed to the environment, health and safety as a Global Care member.
Founded in 1970

6877 **Circuits Assembly**
Circuit Assembly
18 Thomas Street
Irvine, CA 92618-2777

949-855-7887; Fax: 949-855-4298
sales@circuitassembly.com
www.circuitassembly.com

Laura Brown Sims, Associate Publisher

Devoted to the global electronics assembly industry.
Frequency: Monthly

6878 **Circuits and Systems Magazine**
IEEE Circuits and Systems Society
445 Hoes Lane
Piscataway, NJ 08854

chaiwahwu@ieee.org
www.ieee-cas.org

Chai Wah Wu, Editor-in-Chief
Alyssa B. Apsel, Deputy Editor-in-Chief
Mohammad Sawan, VP, Publications

Feature articles with noteworthy results, surveys, and tutorials.

6879 **CleanRooms Magazine**
PennWell Publishing Company
98 Spit Brook Rd
Nashua, NH 03062-5737

603-891-0123
800-225-0556; Fax: 603-891-9294
jhaystead@pennwell.com
www.pennwell.com

Christine Shaw, VP
Angela Godwin, Managing Editor
Heidi Barns, Circulation Manager
Lisa Bergevin, Marketing
James Enos, Publisher

Serves the contamination control and ultrapure materials and process industries. Written for readers in the microelectronics, pharmaceutical, biotech, health care, food processing and other user industries. Provides technology and business news and new product listings.
Frequency: Monthly
Circulation: 35031
Founded in 1987

6880 **CommVerge**
Reed Business Information
2000 Clearwater Dr
Oak Brook, IL 60523-8809

630-574-0825; Fax: 630-288-8781
www.reedbusiness.com

Jeff Greisch, President

The world leading publisher and information provider. Provides a range of communication and information channels, magazines, exhibitions, directories, online media, marketing services across five continents. Prestige brands in leading positions in key business sectors we deliver unrivalled access to business professionals across a diverse range of industries.

6881 **Computer Business Review**
ComputerWire
150 Post Street
#520
San Francisco, CA 94108-4707

415-274-8290; Fax: 415-274-8281
www.computerwire.com/cbr

Tim Langford, Publisher

Company profiles, computer market coverage and technology trends and news for investors and professionals in the computer, communications and microelectronics industries.
Cost: $195.00
Frequency: Monthly
Circulation: 23M

6882 **Computer-Aided Engineering**
Penton Media
1300 E 9th St
Cleveland, OH 44114-1503

216-696-7000; Fax: 216-696-6662
www.penton.com

Jane Cooper, Marketing

Applications, news, trends and products for CAD/CAM technology as applied in manufacturing, electronics, architectural and construction industries.
Cost: $50.00
Frequency: Monthly
Circulation: 56,062

6883 **Control Solutions**
PennWell Publishing Company
1421 S Sheridan Rd
Tulsa, OK 74112-6619

918-831-9421
800-331-4463; Fax: 918-831-9476
headquarters@pennwell.com
www.pennwell.com

Robert Biolchini, President
Ron Kuhfeld, Editor-in-Chief
Frequency: Monthly
Founded in 1910

6884 **Dealerscope**
North American Publishing Company
1500 Spring Garden St
Suite 1200
Philadelphia, PA 19130-4094

215-238-5300
800-627-2689; Fax: 215-238-5342
webmaster@napco.com
www.napco.com

Ned S Borowsky, CEO
Rhoda Dixon, Circulation Manager
Eric Schwartz, President/Publishing Dir

Dedicated to delivering peer-based knowledge and experience, Dealerscope is the ultimate vehicle for presenting product and service solutions to the consumer.
Frequency: Monthly
Founded in 1958

6885 **Digital America**
Consumer Technology Association (CTA)
1919 South Eads Street
Arlington, VA 22202
703-907-7600
866-858-1555; Fax: 703-907-7675
cta@cta.tech
www.cta.tech
Cindy Stevens, Senior Director, Publications
Gary Shapiro, President & CEO
David Hagan, Chairman
Mike Fasulo, Vice Chairman
Glenda MacMullin, Treasurer
Annual publication covering state of the industry analysis, including market research, data and analysis.
Cost: $995.00
Frequency: Annual
Circulation: 1000

6886 **ECN Magazine**
Reed Business Information
360 Park Ave S
4th Floor
New York, NY 10010-1737
646-746-6400; Fax: 646-756-7583
subsmail@reedbusiness.com
www.reedbusiness.com
John Poulin, CEO
James Reed, Owner
Provides product solutions for design engineers in the electronics industry.
Circulation: 117923
Founded in 1957

6887 **EDN Asia**
Reed Business Information
45 E 85th St
4th Floor
New York, NY 10028-0957
212-772-8300; Fax: 630-288-8686
www.edn.com/
Lawrence S Reed
Mike Pan, Editor
Robin Peter Lange, Managing Editor
Raymond Wong, Publishing Director
Chen Wai Chun, Publisher
A source for all the design features, technology trends, design ideas, hands-on applications and product updates.
Frequency: Monthly
Circulation: 30000
Founded in 1990

6888 **EDN China**
Reed Business Information
45 E 85th St
4th Floor
New York, NY 10028-0957
212-772-8300; Fax: 630-288-8686
john.dodge@reedbusiness.com
www.reedbusiness.com
Lawrence S Reed
William Zhang, Publisher Director
John Mu, Executive Editor
Stephen D. Moylan, President
A source for design, development, & applications information foe electronics engineers & managers.
Frequency: Monthly
Circulation: 30018
Founded in 1946

6889 **EDN Europe**
Reed Business Information
45 E 85th St
4th Floor
New York, NY 10028-0957
212-772-8300; Fax: 630-288-8686
gprophet@reedbusiness.com
www.edninteractive.com
Lawrence S Reed
Martin Savery, Publisher
Graham Prophet, Editor
A focused product specific to, and unique in, its own region, that draws on a unique international network of editorial expertise. EDN serves design engineers, providing exactly the information they need to conceive and create tomorrow's electronic products.
Circulation: 35,024

6890 **EE Product News**
Penton Media
1300 E 9th St
Cleveland, OH 44114-1503
216-696-7000; Fax: 216-696-6662
information@penton.com
www.penton.com
Jane Cooper, Marketing
David B. Nussbaum, CEO
Source of information in new products necessary to successfully design, assemble and test prototypes of commerical, industrial, military and aerospace electronic products.
Frequency: Monthly
Circulation: 111968
Founded in 1892

6891 **EE: Evaluation Engineering**
Nelson Publishing
2500 Tamiami Trl N
Nokomis, FL 34275-3476
941-966-9521
800-226-6113; Fax: 941-966-2590
www.healthmgttech.com
A Verner Nelson, Owner
Michael Hughes, Sales
Magazine devoted exclusively to companies that test, evaluate, design and manufacture electronic products and equipment.
Cost: $43.00
84 Pages
Frequency: Monthly
Founded in 1962
Mailing list available for rent: 65,000 names
Printed in 4 colors on glossy stock

6892 **Electromagnetic News Report**
Seven Mountains Scientific
913 Tressler Street
PO Box 650
Boalsburg, PA 16827
814-466-6559; Fax: 814-466-2777
www.7ms.com
Josephine Chesworth, Managing Editor
E Thomas Chesworth, Technical Editor
Patrick D. Elliott, Production Manager
Offers industry news and technical articles of interest to readers as well as a calendar of events, product news and EMI publications.
Cost: $90.00
40 Pages
Circulation: 1000
ISSN: 0270-4935
Founded in 1972
Printed in 4 colors on matte stock

6893 **Electronic Business**
Reed Business Information
5525 Sierra Rd
Building N
San Jose, CA 95132-3421
408-926-6340; Fax: 408-345-4400
subsmail@reedbusiness.com
www.reedbusiness.com
Donald Reed, Owner
Kathleen Doler, Editor-in-Chief
James A Casella, CEO
Shahrokh Rad, Owner
Salina Le Bris, Corporate Communications/PR
Frequency: Monthly
Circulation: 65732
Founded in 1975

6894 **Electronic Components**
Global Sources
7341 Washington Avenue
Suite C
Whittier, CA 90602
562-945-4612; Fax: 562-945-4192
www.globalsources.com
Anna Maria Anguiano, Account Manager
Mark Sanderson, Publisher
Dan Katz, Managing Director
Cost: $75.00
Frequency: Monthly
Founded in 1971

6895 **Electronic Design**
Penton Media
1300 E 9th St
Cleveland, OH 44114-1503
216-696-7000; Fax: 216-696-6662
information@penton.com
www.penton.com
Jane Cooper, Marketing
Mark David, Editor in Chief
Janet Connors, Marketing
Celebrating 50 years of innovation, this authoritative source provides leading-edge technical information to electronic and engineering managers around the world.
Frequency: Monthly
Circulation: 145000
Founded in 1892

6896 **Electronic Packaging & Production**
Reed Business Information
1350 E Touhy Avenue
Des Plaines, IL 60018
630-320-7000; Fax: 630-288-8686
www.reedbusiness.com
Vicky Steen, Publisher
Michael Sweeney, Editorial Director
Edited for engineers and managers who are involved in packaging designed, printed circuit board fabrication and assembly, and production testing of electronic circuits, systems, products and equipment.

6897 **Electronic Products**
Hearst Business Communications
645 Stewart Ave
Garden City, NY 11530-4769
516-227-1300; Fax: 516-227-1342
ralphr@electronicproducts.com
www.elecprod2.com
Todd Christenson, Publisher
Gail Meyer, Production Manager
R Pell, Editor-in-Chief
News about developments in electronic components and equipment.
Frequency: Monthly
Circulation: 123767
Founded in 1958
Mailing list available for rent: 123767 names
Printed in 4 colors on glossy stock

6898 Electronic Products Magazine
Home Page: www.electronicproducts.com
Electronic products and product technology news from an engineering standpoint.

6899 High Density Interconnect
CMP Media
600 Community Drive
Manhasset, NY 11030
516-562-5000; Fax: 415-947-6090

6900 High Tech News
Electronic Technicians Association International
5 Depot St
Greencastle, IN 46135-8024
765-653-8262
800-288-3824; Fax: 765-653-4287
eta@eta-i.org
www.eta-i.org
Facebook, Twitter, LinkedIn
Teresa Maher, CSS, President
Chrissy Baker, Marketing Coordinator
Richard Glass, CETsr, CEO Emeritus
Exclusive bi-monthly publication of ETA International, and a subscription is included with each individual membership. Each issue features information on the changing electronics industry: specialty techniques & technology, trends, qualification opportunities and educational advice.
4500 Members
Frequency: Bi-Monthly
Circulation: 10000
Founded in 1978

6901 IEEE Computational Intelligence Magazine
IEEE Computational Intelligence Society
445 Hoes Lane
Piscataway, NJ 08855
732-465-5892; Fax: 732-465-6435
cis-info@ieee.org
cis.ieee.org
Bernadette Bouchon-Meunier, President
Hessein Abbass, VP, Technical Activities
James Keller, VP, Publications
CIM features peer-reviewed articles with noteworthy discoveries, insights, and tutorial surveys.

6902 IEEE Control Systems Magazine
IEEE Control Systems Society (CSS)
445 Hoes Lane
Piscataway, NJ 08854-1331
732-562-3937
m.david@ieee.org
www.ieee.org
Jonathan How, Editor-in-Chief
Rodolphe Sepulchre, Deputy Editor-in-Chief
Focuses on applications of technical knowledge and concentrates on industrial implementations, design tools, technology review, control education and applied research. Geared towards readers with many different responsibilities including applied research, device design, product development and design including software and semiconductor components.
Cost: $210.00
Founded in 1973
Mailing list available for rent

6903 IEEE Industrial Electronics Magazine
Institute Of Electrical and Electronics Engineers
445 Hoes Lane
Piscataway, NJ 08854
804-827-3999
eic-iem@ieee-ies.org
www.ieee-ies.org
Peter Palesnky, Editor-in-Chief
IEM features peer-reviewed articles presenting new trends and practices in industrial electronics research & development.

6904 IEEE Solid-State Circuits Magazine
IEEE Solid-State Circuits Society
445 Hoes Lane
Piscataway, NJ 08854
rjacobbaker@gmail.com
sscs.ieee.org
R. Jacob Baker, Editor-in-Chief
Rakesh Kumar, Chair, Advisory Board
Tutorial-style articles on technical achievements, trends, and future developments in the field of Integrated Circuits.
Founded in 2009

6905 IEEE Transactions on Engineering Management
IEEE Technology & Engineering Management Society
445 Hoes Lane
Piscataway, NJ 08854
tugrul.u.daim@pdx.edu
www.ieee-tems.org
Tugrul U. Daim, Editor-in-Chief
Alison Larkin, Peer Review Support Services
Mark Werwath, VP, Publications
Journal of the Technology and Engineering Management Society of IEEE, with peer-reviewed research on engineering, technology, and innovation management.
Frequency: Quarterly
Founded in 1954

6906 IEEE Transactions on Industry Applications
Institute Of Electrical and Electronics Engineers
445 Hoes Lane
Piscataway, NJ 08854
732-562-2663
t.nondahl@ieee.org
www.ieee.org
Thomas A. Nondahl, Editor-in-Chief
The development and applications of electrical systems, apparatus, devices and controls to the processes and equipment of industry and commerce.
Circulation: 5100
Founded in 1980

6907 IEEE Vehicular Technology Magazine
IEEE Vehicular Technology Society
3 Parl Avenue
17th Floor
New York, NY 10016-5997
212-419-7900
david@uni-kassel.de
vtsociety.org
Klaus David, Editor-in-Chief
Focus is on mobile radio, connected and automated vehicles, automotive electronics, and transportation systems.
Frequency: Quarterly

6908 ITS Magazine
IEEE Intelligent Transportation Systems Society
445 Hoes Lane
Piscataway, NJ 08854
Home Page: www.ieee-itss.org
Wei-Bin Zhang, President
Petros A. Ioannou, VP, Publications Activities
Ljubo Vlacic, Magazine Editor
Features peer-reviewed articles on research and applications, with case studies and examinations of challenges in the intelligent transportation system industry.

6909 Journal of Microelectronics & Electronic Packaging
International Microelectronics & Electronic Pack.
611 2nd Street NE
Washington, DC 20002
202-548-4001
888-464-6277; Fax: 202-548-6115
www.imaps.org
Fred D Barlow III PhD, Editor-in-Chief

6910 Journal of Microelectronics and Electronic Packaging
International Microelectronics & Electronics
611 2nd Street NE
Washington, DC 20002
202-548-4001
888-464-6277; Fax: 202-548-6115
www.imaps.org
Michael O'Donoghue, Executive Director
Rick Mohn, Operations Manager
Brian Schieman, Director Information Technology
Ann Bell, Manager Marketing/Communications
Dedicated to publishing peer-reviewed papers in microelectronics, multichip module technologies, electronic packaging, electronic materials, surface mount and other related technologies, interconnections, RF and microwaves, wireless communications, manufacturing, design, test, and reliability.
Cost: $35.00

6911 Journal of Microwave Power and Electromagnetic Energy
International Microwave Power Institute
PO Box 1140
Mechanicsville, VA 23111-5007
804-559-6667; Fax: 804-559-4087
info@impi.org
www.impi.org
Facebook, Twitter
Molly Poisant, Executive Director
The quarterly, technical journal of the Institute published by the Industrial, Scientific, Medical and Instrumentation (ISMI) section. Designed for the information needs of professionals specializing in the research and design of industrial and bio-medical applications, the Journal exemplifies the highest standards of scientific and technical information on the theory and application of electromagnetic power.
Cost: $250.00
Frequency: Quarterly

6912 Laser Focus World
PennWell Publishing Company
98 Spit Brook Rd
Nashua, NH 03062-5737
603-891-0123; Fax: 603-891-9294
allisono@pennwell.com
www.pennwell.com
Christine Shaw, Publisher
Carol Settino, Managing Editor
The world of optoelectronics.
Cost: $150.00
173 Pages
Frequency: Monthly

Circulation: 70004
Founded in 1965
Printed in 4 colors on glossy stock

6913 **Modeling Power Devices and Model Validation**
Power Sources Manufacturers Association
PO Box 418
Mendham, NJ 07945-0418

973-543-9660; Fax: 973-543-6207
power@psma.com
www.psma.com

Dusty Becker, Chairman
Carl Blake, President
Jim Marinos, VP

This report consists of two parts, one devoted to modeling, and the other, model validation. The first article in the report reviews commonly used device models used in circuit simulations, and applies these to simulation designed power converters and rectifers. The second article establishes processes by which the features and accuracy of a model are determined by simulating the results of test circuits containing power devices and comparing these results with the results of actual measurements
Cost: $20.00
155 Members
Founded in 1985

6914 **Optics Letters**
Optical Society of America
2010 Massachusetts Ave NW
Washington, DC 20036-1023

202-223-8130; Fax: 202-223-1096
info@osa.org
www.osapublishing.org/ol/home.cfm

Xi-Cheng Zhang, Editor-in-Chief

Offers rapid dissemination of new results in all areas of optics with short, original, peer-reviewed communications. Optics Letters covers the latest research in optical science, including atmospheric optics, quantum electronics, Fourier optics, integrated optics, and fiber optics.
Frequency: 2x/mth
ISSN: 0146-9592

6915 **Power Conversion & Intelligent Motion**
Primedia
Po Box 12901
Shawnee Mission, KS 66282-2901

913-341-1300; Fax: 913-514-6895
www.penton.com

Eric Jacobson, Senior VP
Sam Davis, Editor

Directed to engineers, designers and manufacturers of power electronic and electronic motion control components, subsystems and systems. Feature articles interpret trends and innovation in these subjects.
Circulation: 31,113

6916 **Power Electronics Technology**
Penton Media, Inc
249 W 17th Street
New York, NY 10011

212-204-4200
www.powerelectronics.com

Bill Baumann, Group Publisher
Sam Davis, Editor-in-Chief

Formerly PCIM Power Electronic Systems, delivers timely information to professionals in the power electronic industry.
Frequency: Monthly
Circulation: 36,000
Founded in 1975

6917 **Printed Circuit Fabrication**
CMP Media
600 Community Drive
Manhasset, NY 11030

516-562-5000; Fax: 415-947-6090

6918 **ProService**
Int'l Society of Certified Electronics Technicians
3608 Pershing Ave
Fort Worth, TX 76107-4527

817-921-9101
800-946-0201; Fax: 817-921-3741
info@iscet.org
www.iset.org

Ed Clingman, Administrator
Shiela Fredrickson, Publisher

A bi-monthly magazine published by the International Society of Certified Electronics Technicians.
24 Pages
Founded in 1965

6919 **ProService Magazine**
National Electronics Service Dealers Association
PO Box 378
Hillsboro, TX 76645

817-921-9061
info@nesda.com
nesda.wildapricot.org

Published for members of NESDA/ISCET.
24 Pages

6920 **RTOHQ: The Magazine**
Association of Progressive Rental Merchandise
1540 Robinhood Trail
Austin, TX 78703-2624

512-794-0095
800-204-APRO; Fax: 512-794-0097
cferguson@rtohq.org
www.rtohq.org

Bill Keese, Executive Director
John C Cleek, President
Bill Kelly, Secretary
Frequency: Bi-Monthly
Circulation: 11000

6921 **Representor Magazine**
Electronics Representatives Association
300 W Adams St
Suite 617
Chicago, IL 60606-5109

312-527-3050
800-776-7377; Fax: 312-527-3783
info@era.org
www.era.org

Tom Shanahan, Executive VP
Bob Walsh, President

Devoted to fulfilling the management, informational, educational and communications needs of representatives and manufacturers in the electronics industry.
Cost: $15.00
450 Members
Frequency: Quarterly
Founded in 1935

6922 **Review of the Electronic and Industrial Distribution Industries**
National Electronic Distributors Association
1111 Alderman Dr
Suite 400
Alpharetta, GA 30005-4175

678-393-9990; Fax: 678-393-9998
admin@nedassoc.org

Robin B Gray Jr, Executive VP
Debbie Conyers, Director Marketing
Barney Martin, VP Industry Practices

Contains academic articles on topics pertinent to our members' business. Leading electronic and industrial distribution academicians provides the content. Offers insightful articles aimed at improving industry practices. $12.00 per volume or $20.00 for an annual subscription.
Cost: $20.00
Frequency: Bi-Annually

6923 **Robotics and Autonomous Systems**
Elsevier Science
230 Park Avenue
Suite 800
New York, NY 10169

212-309-8100
www.elsevier.com

K. Berns, Editor-in-Chief
M. Gini, Editor-in-Chief
J. Ota, Editor-in-Chief

Journal with articles on developments in the field of robotics, with an emphasis on autonomous systems.
Cost: $3008.00
ISSN: 0921-8890

6924 **Robotics and Computer-Intergrated Manufacturing**
Elsevier Science
230 Park Avenue
Suite 800
New York, NY 10169

212-309-8100
www.elsevier.com

Lihui Wang, Editor-in-Chief

Journal containing original papers on theoretical, applied and experimental robotics and computer-integrated manufacturing, with emphasis on flexible manufacturing systems.
Cost: $3008.00
Circulation: 2500
ISSN: 0736-5845
Founded in 1880

6925 **SIGNAL Magazine**
Armed Forces Communications and Electronics Assn
4400 Fair Lakes Ct
Fairfax, VA 22033-3899

703-631-1397
800-336-4583; Fax: 703-631-4693
www.afcea.org

Kent Schneider, President/CEO
Becky Nolan, Executive VP
John A Dubia, Executive VP

Is a international news magazine serving the critical information needs of government, military and industry professionals active in the fields of command, control, communications, computers, intelligence, surveillance and reconnaissance (C4ISR); information security; research and development; electronics; and homeland security.
Frequency: Monthly

6926 **SMC Magazine**
IEEE Systems, Man, and Cybernetics Society
445 Hoes Lane
Piscataway, NJ 08854

smcmagazine_eic@outlook.com
www.ieeesmc.org

Saeid Nahavandi, Editor-in-Chief
Enrique Herrera Viedma, VP, Publications

Articles relevant to the research areas of the IEEE Systems, Man, and Cybernetics Society, with information on the Society's activities, and educational material as well.

6927 **Science Robotics**
American Assn for the Advancement of Science
1200 New York Avenue NW
Washington, DC 20005-3941

202-326-6490; Fax: 202-789-4669
sciroboteditors@aaas.org
robotics.sciencemag.org

Alan I. Leshner, Interim Executive Publisher
Jeremy Berg PhD, Editor-in-Chief
Monica M. Bradford, Executive Editor

Publishes original, peer-reviewed, science- or engineering-based research articles that advance the field of robotics. The journal also features editor-commissioned reviews.
Frequency: Monthly

6928 **Sensors Magazine**
Questex Media
275 Grove St
Suite 2-130
Auburndale, MA 02466-2275

617-219-8300
888-552-4346; Fax: 617-219-8310
jmcmahon@questex.com
www.questex.com

Kerry C Gumas, CEO
Stephanie Henkel, Executive Editor

Source among design and production engineers of information on sensor technologies and products, and topic integral to sensor-based systems and applications. Provides practical and in-depth yet accessible information on sensor operation, design, application, and implementation within systems. Covers the effective use of state-of-the-art resources and tools that enable readers to get the maximum benefit from their use of sensors.
Cost: $99.00
Frequency: Monthly
Circulation: 75000
Founded in 1984

6929 **Signal Processing Magazine**
IEEE Signal Processing Society
445 Hoes Lane
Piscataway, NJ 08854

732-562-3888; Fax: 732-867-9953
sp-pub-info@ieee.org
signalprocessingsociety.org
Facebook, Twitter, LinkedIn

Robert Heath, Editor-in-Chief
William Colacchio, Senior Manager, Publications

Tutorials on signal processing research and applications, as well as editorial content on matters of interest.

6930 **Tech Briefs**
Associated Business Publications International
1466 Broadway
Suite. 910
New York, NY 10036-7309

212-490-3999; Fax: 212-986-7864
alfredo@abpi.net
www.techbriefs.com

Dominic Mucchetti, CEO
Hugh Dowling, Circualtion Manager
Linda Bell, Chief Editor

Serves design engineers, managers and scientists in the industries of electronics, industrial equipment, computers, communications, bio-medical, transportation/automotive, power and energy, materials, chemicals and many more related fields.
Cost: $75.00
Frequency: Monthly
Founded in 1958

6931 **Technology and Society**
IEEE Society on Social Implications of Technology
445 Hoes Lane
Piscataway, NJ 08854

j.pitt@imperial.ac.uk
technologyandsociety.org
Facebook, Twitter, LinkedIn

Jeremy Pitt, Editor_in-Chief
Terri A. Bookman, Managing Editor

Flagship magazine of the IEEE Society on Social Implications of Technology, with peer-reviewed articles on the impact of technology on the world.

6932 **Test & Measurement World**
Reed Business Information
275 Washington St
Suite 275
Newton, MA 02458-1611

617-964-3030; Fax: 617-558-4470
www.designnews.com

Rick Nelson, Chief Editor
Deborah M Sargent, Managing Editor
Russ Pratt, Publisher

The magazine on test, measurement and inspection in the electronics industry
Frequency: Monthly
Circulation: 65000
Founded in 1981
Mailing list available for rent

6933 **The Bridge**
IEEE-Eta Kappa Nu
445 Hoes Lane
Piscataway, NJ 08854

732-465-5846
800-406-2590
info@hkn.org
hkn.ieee.org/news-and-announcements/the-bridge

Sahra Sedigh Sarvestani, Editor-in-Chief
Stephen Williams, Editor-in-Chief

The award-winning digital magazine of the IEEE-HKN.
Frequency: 3x/year

6934 **The Minerals, Metals & Materials Society/ Journal of Electronic Materials**
Minerals, Metals & Materials Society
184 Thorn Hill Road
Warrendale, PA 15086-7528

724-776-9000
800-759-4867; Fax: 724-776-3770
www.tms.org

Suzanne Mohney, Editor-In-Chief

Reports on the science and technology of electronic materials, while examining new applications for semiconductors, magnetic alloys, insulators, optical and display materials.
Cost: $131.00
11000 Members
Frequency: Monthly
Circulation: 1400
ISSN: 0361-5235
Founded in 1957
Printed in 2 colors on glossy stock

6935 **The Representor**
Electronic Representatives Association
1325 S Arlington Heights Road
Suite 204
Elk Grove Village, IL 60007

312-419-1432; Fax: 312-419-1660
info@era.org
www.era.org

Chuck Tanzola, CPMR, President
Dace Norris, Chairman

Provides services and benefits to electronic industry manufacturers' representatives, manufacturers and distributors.
Frequency: Quarterly

6936 **Wideband**
Advanstar Communications
641 Lexington Ave
8th Floor
New York, NY 10022-4503

212-951-6600; Fax: 212-951-6793
info@advanstar.com
www.advanstar.com

Joseph Loggia, CEO

Covers accessories, equipment, services, products, and an anlysis of major market trends, industry news, statistics, new products, and personnel changes are featured in every issue.
Frequency: SemiMonthly
Circulation: 26,000

Trade Shows

6937 **AEA Annual Convention & Trade Show**
Aircraft Electronics Association
4217 S Hocker
Independence, MO 64055

816-373-6565; Fax: 816-478-3100
info@aea.net
www.aea.net

Mike Adamson, President & CEO
Debra McFarland, Executive Vice President
Geoff Hill, Director, Communications

Annual show of 131 exhibitors of industry related equipment and supplies.
1500 Attendees
Frequency: Annual
Founded in 1957

6938 **AFCEA Sponsored Conferences/Symposia**
Armed Forces Communications and Electronics Assn
4400 Fair Lakes Court
Fairfax, VA 22033-3899

703-631-6100
800-336-4583; Fax: 703-631-6405
www.afcea.org

Kent Schneider, President/CEO
Becky Nolan, Executive VP
John A Dubia, Executive VP

Offers problem solving and networking opportunities through exhibits, technical panels, and featured speakers. Decision-makers from around the world attend AFCEA conferences for hands-on demonstrations, question-and-answer sessions and system solutions.

6939 **AFCEA TechNet Asia-Pacific**
Armed Forces Communications and Electronics Assn
4400 Fair Lakes Court
Fairfax, VA 22033-3899

703-631-6200
800-654-4220; Fax: 703-654-6931
technet@jspargo.com
www.afcea.org

Paul doCarmo, Assistant Director/Exhibit Sales
Connie Shaw, Exhibit Sales Account Manager

Military, government and industry communications and electronics professionals gather to see exhibits of communications and electronics equipment, supplies and services. Seminar, con-

ference, dinner and luncheon. Co-sponsored by AFCEA International and AFCEA Hawaii.
2000 Attendees
Frequency: Nov 7-9
Founded in 1985

6940 AFCEA TechNet International
Armed Forces Communications and Electronics Assn
4400 Fair Lakes Court
Fairfax, VA 22033-3899

703-631-6200
800-564-4220; Fax: 703-654-6931
www.afcea.org

Paul doCarmo, Sales Manager
Connie Shaw, Sales Manager

This event draws commanders and staff from every branch of the military, including warfighting integration organizations charged with the most critical responsibilities of synthesizing military power on land, at sea, and in the air.
7500 Attendees
Frequency: June

6941 AFCEA/USNI West Conference & Exposition
Armed Forces Communications and Electronics Assn
4400 Fair Lakes Court
Fairfax, VA 22033

703-631-6200
800-564-4220; Fax: 703-654-6931
www.afcea.org

Paul doCarmo, Assistant Direct/Exhibit Sales
Connie Shaw, Exhibit Sales Account Manager

Over 350 of the industry's most recognized defense and technology organizations showcase their technology products and services to top decision-makers from the US Pacific Fleet, Naval Station San Diego, Space & Warfare Command, Naval Base Coronado, Camp Pendleton Marine Corps Base and many other west coast military and government facilities.
6000 Attendees
Frequency: January
Founded in 1980

6942 APRO Rent-To-Own Convention & Trade Show
1504 Robin Hood Trail
Austin, TX 78703

512-794-0095
800-204-APRO; Fax: 512-794-0097
www.rtohq.org

Shannon Strunkec, President
John C Cleek, First VP
Jeannie Hutchison, Program Coordinator
Bill Keese, Manager

Seminar, reception and tours, plus 280 exhibits of products and services of interest to rent to own dealers: stereos, televisions, furniture, fabric protection and more.
1400 Attendees
Frequency: Annual

6943 ASM/TMS Spring Symposium
Minerals, Metals & Materials Society
184 Thorn Hill Road
Warrendale, PA 15086-7514

724-776-9000; Fax: 724-776-3770
foundation@tms.org
www.tms.org

Tresa Pollock, President
Brajendra Mishra, VP
Alexander Scott, Executive Director
John Parsey, Financial Planning Officer
Marc DeGraef, Director Information Technology

This symposium, organized by the local chapters of TMS and ASM, will focus on materials for extreme environments, with sessions on materials characterization in three dimensions, structural materials for high temperature, materials for space applications, and materials by design.
Frequency: May

6944 ATE and Instrumentation West
Miller Freeman Publications
600 Harrison Street
Suite 400
San Francisco, CA 94107-1391

415-905-2354; Fax: 415-905-2232

Steve Schulderfrei, Trade Show Director

Geared to the test and measurement of electronics.
5.8M Attendees
Frequency: January

6945 AVS Annual Symposium & Exhibition
AVS Science & Technology Society
125 Maiden Lane
15th Floor
New York, NY 10038

212-248-0200; Fax: 212-248-0245
www.avs.org

Christie R Marrian, President
John Coburn, Treasurer
Joseph E Greene, Clerk/Secretary
Yvonne Towse, Executive Director

Promotes communication, dissemination of knowledge, recommended practices, research, and education in the use of vacuum and other controlled environments to develop new materials, process technology, devices, and related understanding of material properties for the betterment of humanity.
Frequency: Annual/February

6946 AVS International Symposium and Exhibition
AVS Science & Technology Society
120 Wall Street
32nd Floor
New York, NY 10005-3993

212-248-0200; Fax: 212-248-0245
angela@avs.org
www.avs.org

Christie R Marrian, President
John Coburn, Office Manager
Nancy Schultheis, Office Manager
Joseph E Greene, Clerk/Secretary
Yvonne Towse, Executive Director

This conference has been developed to address cutting edge issues associated with vacuum science and technology in both the research and manufacturing communities. The equipment exhibition is one of the largest in the world and provides an excellent opportunity to view the latest products and services offered by over 200 participating companies.
3000 Attendees

6947 All-Service Convention
Electronic Technicians Association International
5 Depot Street
Greencastle, IN 46135

765-653-4301
800-288-3824; Fax: 765-653-4287
eta@eta-i.org
www.eta-i.org

Teresa Maher, President
Chrissy Baker, Marketing Coordinator

Appliances and electronic service products and services. Third party administrators. Certification exams and study materials. Tools and test equipment. Containing 40 booths and 50 exhibits.

6948 Annual Legislative & Regulatory Roundtable
Electronic Industries Alliance
2500 Wilson Boulevard
Arlington, VA 22201-3834

703-907-7500
703-907-7500
www.eia.org

Gail Tannenbaum, CMP, Manager Meetings/Industry Relations
Frequency: Annual/August

6949 Asia Card Technology Exhibition
Reed Exhibition Companies
383 Main Avenue Suite 3
PO Box 6059
Norwalk, CT 06851

203-840-4800; Fax: 203-840-9628

Emily Hackett, Executive Director
Peter DiLeo, Marketing Director
Deborah Luongo, Conference Manager

Trade professionals see exhibits on computers and electronics.
Frequency: Annual

6950 Assembly Northeast Exhibition
Reed Exhibition Companies
383 Main Avenue Suite 3
PO Box 6059
Norwalk, CT 06851

203-840-4800; Fax: 203-840-9628

Emily Hackett, Executive Director
Peter DiLeo, Marketing Director
Deborah Luongo, Conference Manager
Gregg Vautrin, CEO

Assembly industry equipment, supplies and services for engineers and managers from electronic and automated assembly operations.
1365 Attendees
Frequency: Annual
Founded in 1999

6951 Assembly Technology Exposition
Reed Exhibition Companies
383 Main Avenue Suite 3
PO Box 6059
Norwalk, CT 06851

203-840-4800
800-267-3796; Fax: 203-840-9686
www.atexpo.com

Emily Hackett, Executive Director
Peter DiLeo, Marketing Director
Deborah Luongo, Conference Manager

525 exhibitors with robotics, vision systems, electronics and production machinery of interest to engineers and managers from automated assembly plants.
14000 Attendees
Frequency: Annual
Founded in 1979

6952 Assembly West Exhibition
Reed Exhibition Companies
383 Main Avenue Suite 3
PO Box 6059
Norwalk, CT 06851

203-840-4800; Fax: 203-840-9628

Emily Hackett, Executive Director
Peter DiLeo, Marketing Director
Deborah Luongo, Conference Manager
Gregg Vautrin, CEO

Assembly industry equipment, supplies and services for engineers and managers from electronic and automated assembly operations.
3000 Attendees
Frequency: Annual

6953 **Augmented World Expo**
AugmentedReality.org
Home Page: www.awexr.com
Facebook, Twitter, LinkedIn, YouTube
Ori Inbar, CEO
Showcase for technologies making the world more interactive: augmented reality; virtual reality; and wearable technology.
4000 Attendees

6954 **Automated Manufacturing Exposition: New England**
TEC
2001 Assembly Street
Suite 204
Columbia, SC 29201
803-779-7123
Tony Smith, Founder
Rafael Pastor, Chairman/CEO
Richard Carr, President/Vice Chairman
Jerry Schneider, Chief Financial Officer
In addition to the exhibits, the conference will feature seminars that focus on topics such as continuous improvement and lean manufacturing.

6955 **CEO Summit**
Consumer Technology Association (CTA)
1919 S Eads Street
Arlington, VA 22202
703-907-7600
866-858-1555; Fax: 703-907-7675
cesreg@cta.tech
www.ces.tech
Gary Shapiro, President & CEO
David Hagan, Chairman
An invite-only event that presents a rare opportunity to network in a qualified, executive-only environment, to gather insight helpful to your business and to focus on the issues most critical to the industry.
Frequency: Annual

6956 **CES Unveiled**
Consumer Technology Association
1919 South Eads Street
Arlington, VA 22202
703-907-7600
866-858-1555; Fax: 703-907-7675
cta@cta.tech
www.cta.org
Gary Shapiro, President & CEO
David Hagan, Chairman
Held in major tech cities around the world, this event brings together industry experts, tech startups and electronics professionals for a chance to network with peers and showcase ideas.
Frequency: Annual

6957 **COM Conference of Metallurgists**
Minerals, Metals & Materials Society
184 Thorn Hill Road
Warrendale, PA 15086-7514
724-776-9000; Fax: 724-776-3770
foundation@tms.org
www.tms.org
Tresa Polloc, President
Brajendra Mishra, VP
Alexander Scott, Executive Director
John Parsey, Financial Planning Officer
Marc DeGraef, Director Information Technology
Topic: Challenges for the Metals and Materials Industry. This conference will feature symposia on computational analysis in hydrometallurgy; nickel and cobalt; pipelines for the 21st century; materials degradation: innovation, inspection, control, and rehabilitation; light metals; fuel cell and hydrogen technologies; recruitment and early career development programs; and the treatment of gold ores.
Frequency: August

6958 **CONNECTIONS - The Digital Living Conference and Showcase**
Parks Associates
5310 Harvest Hill Road
Suite 235, Lock Box 162
Dallas, TX 75230-5805
972-490-1113
800-727-5711
info@parksassociates.com
www.connectionsconference.com
Tricia Parks, Founder and CEO
Stuart Sikes, President
Farhan Abid, Research Analyst
Bill Ablondi, Director, Home Systems Research
John Barrett, Director of Research
This conference attracts over 500 executives focused on innovative consumer technology solutions. The unique conference and showcase highlights consumer and industry research from Parks Associates, showcases key players and new technologies, and delivers insight and recommendations for new business models and opportunities in digital media/content, mobile applications and services, connected consumer electronics, broadband and value-added services, and home systems.
Frequency: Annual
Founded in 1986
Mailing list available for rent

6959 **Ceramic Interconnect and Ceramic Microsystems**
International Microelectronics & Electronics
611 2nd Street
Washington, DC 20002
202-548-4001
888-464-6277; Fax: 202-548-6115
www.imaps.org
Michael O'Donoghue, Executive Director
Rick Mohn, Operations Manager
Brian Schieman, Director Information Technology
Ann Bell, Manager Marketing/Communications
Frequency: April

6960 **DistribuTech Conference**
PennWell Conferences and Exhibitions
350 Post Oak Blouevard
Suite 205
Houston, TX 77056
713-621-8833; Fax: 713-963-6284
www.pennwell.com
Bob Biolchini, CEO
Is the leading automation and information technology conference and exhibition in the utility industry; and provides the best resources, tools and networking opportunities relating to electric utility automation and control systems, IT, T&D engineering, power and delivery equipment, and water utility technology.
3000 Attendees
Frequency: January

6961 **EASA Convention**
Electrical Apparatus Service Association
1331 Baur Boulevard
St. Louis, MO 63132
314-993-2220; Fax: 314-993-1269
easainfo@easa.com
www.easa.com
Facebook, Twitter, LinkedIn
Jerry Gray, Chair
Timothy Bieber, Vice Chair
Sid Seymour, Secretary/Treasurer
Linda J. Raynes, CAE, President/CEO
Dale Shuter, CMP, Manager, Meetings & Expositions
An international trade organization of electromechanical sales and service firms in 58 countries. Provides members with a means of keeping up to date on materials, equipment, and state of the art technology.
2000+ Attendees
Frequency: Annual, June

6962 **EIA's Congressional Technology Forum**
Electronic Industries Alliance
2500 Wilson Boulevard
Arlington, VA 22201-3834
703-907-7500; Fax: 703-907-7500
www.eia.org
Gail Tannenbaum, CMP, Manager Meetings/Industry Relations
Frequency: October

6963 **EOS/ESD Symposium & Exhibits**
Electrostatic Discharge Association
7900 Turin Road
Building 3
Rome, NY 13440-2069
315-339-6937; Fax: 315-339-6793
info@esda.org
www.esda.org
Facebook, LinkedIn
Donn Bellmore, President
Leo G. Henry, Sr. VP
Terry Welsher, VP
Lisa Pimpinella, Director of Operations
Donn Pritchard, Treasurer
International technical forum on electrical overstress and electrostatic discharge that features research, technology, and solutions to increase understanding, enhance quality and reliability, reduce and control costs, and improve yields and productivity.
2000+ Members
1M Attendees
Frequency: September
Founded in 1982

6964 **ERA Management & Marketing Conference**
Electronics Representatives Association
1325 S. Arlington Heights Road
Suite 204
Elk Grove Village, IL 60007
312-419-1432; Fax: 312-419-1660
info@era.org
www.era.org
Chuck Tanzola, CPMR, President
Dave Norris, Chairman
Provides services and benefits to electronic industry manufacturersrepresentatives, manufacturers and distributors.
Frequency: Annual/February

6965 **ETA Annual Meeting and Expo**
Electronic Transactions Association
1101 16th Street NW
Suite 402
Washington, DC 20036
202-828-2635
800-695-5509; Fax: 202-828-2639
www.electran.org
Jennifer Leo, Meetings Manager
Kurt Strawhecker, Managing Director
Steve Carnevale, Senior Vice President
Featuring valuable networking opportunities, outstanding speakers and educational seminars.
Frequency: April, Las Vegas

6966 **ETA Expo Network**
Electronic Transactions Association

1101 16th Street NW
Suite 402
Washington, DC 20036

202-828-2635
800-695-5509; Fax: 202-828-2639
www.electran.org

Jennifer Leo, Meetings Manager
Kurt Strawhecker, Managing Director
Steve Carnevale, Senior Vice President

Offers conference events that focus specifically on delivering need to know education to ISOs and sales agents. ETA created these meetings to increase educational and business development opportunities for the industry. These affordable and easily accessible conferences are the ideal opportunity to increase your knowledge and meet new business partners.

6967 **East Coast Video Show**
Expocon Management Associates
363 Reef Road
PO Box 915
Fairfield, CT 06430-0915

203-882-1300; Fax: 203-256-4730

Diane Stone, Show Director
8000 Attendees

6968 **Electronic Distribution Show and Conference**
Electronic Distribution Show Corporation
222 S Riverside Plaza
Suite 2160
Chicago, IL 60606-6160

312-648-1140; Fax: 312-648-4282
eds@edsc.org
www.edsc.org

Gretchen Oie-Weghorst, Show Manager
Gretchen Oie, Manager

Annual conference and exhibits of 500 manufacturers of electronic components who sell through distribution. Containing 700 booiths and 500 exhibits.
10M Attendees
Frequency: May

6969 **Electronic Imaging East**
Miller Freeman Publications
600 Harrison Street
Suite 400
San Francisco, CA 94107-1391

415-905-2354; Fax: 415-905-2232

Stephen Schuldenfrei, Trade Show Director

300 booths consisting of electrical equipment and services.
5.3M Attendees
Frequency: October

6970 **Electronic Imaging West**
Miller Freeman Publications
600 Harrison Street
Suite 400
San Francisco, CA 94107-1391

415-905-2534; Fax: 415-905-2232

Stephen Schuldenfrei, Trade Show Director

Exhibits of equipment, supplies and services for the computer and electronics industries.
3M Attendees

6971 **Electronic Materials Conference**
Minerals, Metals & Materials Society
184 Thorn Hill Road
Warrendale, PA 15086-7514

724-776-9000; Fax: 724-776-3770
foundation@tms.org
www.tms.org

Tresa Pollock, President
Brajendra Mishra, VP
Alexander Scott, Executive Director
John Parsey, Financial Planning Officer
Marc DeGraef, Director Information Technology

This conference will provide a forum for topics of current interest and significance related to the preparation and characterization of electronic materials. Individuals actively engaged or interested in electronic materials research and development are encouraged to submit an abstract or attend the meeting. A technological exhibition will also be held.
Frequency: June

6972 **Electronic West: Annual Western Electrical Exposition Conference**
Continental Exhibitions
370 Lexington Avenue
Suite 1401
New York, NY 10017

212-370-5005; Fax: 212-370-5699

10000 Attendees

6973 **Embedded Systems Conference - West**
Miller Freeman Publications
600 Harrison Street
Suite 400
San Francisco, CA 94107

415-905-2354; Fax: 415-905-2220
www.esconline.com

Lisa Ostrom, Electronics Show Director
Christian Fahlen, CEO

This is an ideal forum to learn relevant new skills, and about the latest technologies and products; to network with industry experts, vendors and your peers; and to discover an exhibits floor featuring leading companies showcasing cutting edge products.
13000 Attendees
Frequency: March

6974 **Executive Leadership Forum & Board of Governors Meeting**
Electronic Industries Alliance
2500 Wilson Boulevard
Arlington, VA 22201-3834

703-907-7500; Fax: 703-907-7500
www.eia.org

Gail Tannenbaum, CMP, Manager Meetings/Industry Relations
Frequency: February, California

6975 **IMPI Annual Symposium**
International Microwave Power Institute
7076 Drinkard Way
PO Box 1140
Mechanicsville, VA 23111

804-596-6667; Fax: 804-559-4087
info@impi.org
www.impi.org
Facebook, Twitter

Bob Schiffmann, President
Molly Poisant, Executive Director

Brings together researchers from across the globe to share the latest findings related to non-communications uses of microwave energy.
Frequency: Annual/June

6976 **IS&T/SPIE's Electronic Imaging**
International Society for Optical Engineering
1000 20th Street
PO Box 10
Bellingham, WA 98227-0010

360-763-3290; Fax: 360-647-1445
meetinginfo@spie.org
www.spie.org

Electronic Imaging's top-notch technical program gathers the world's most prominent experts to discuss and push the forefront of imaging technology and it's applications.
1200 Attendees
Frequency: Annual/January

6977 **Industry Wide Service and Retail Convention**
Electronic Technicians Association International
5 Depot Street
Greencastle, IN 46135

765-653-4301
800-288-3824; Fax: 765-653-4287
eta@eta-i.org
www.eta-i.org

Teresa Maher, President
Brianna Pinson, Office Manager

Three groups united to offer the largest schedule of business management and technical seminars and trade show for educators, servicers and retailers. Thirty booths.
200 Attendees
Frequency: February

6978 **Innovate! and Celebrate**
Consumer Technology Association (CTA)
1919 South Eads Street
Arlington, VA 22202

703-907-7600
866-858-1555; Fax: 703-907-7675
cta@cta.tech
www.cta.org

Gary Shapiro, President & CEO
David Hagan, Chairman

Bringing together CTA members, industry thought leaders, and industry professionals for networking and learning opportunities.

6979 **International Conference on Electronics, Circuits, and Systems**
IEEE Circuits and Systems Society
445 Hoes Lane
Piscataway, NJ 08854

manager@ieee-cas.org
www.ieee-cas.org

Brittian Parkinson, Operations Manager
Myung Hoon Sunwoo, VP, Conferences
Frequency: Annual

6980 **International Conference on Trends in Welding Research**
Minerals, Metals & Materials Society
184 Thorn Hill Road
Warrendale, PA 15086-7514

724-776-9000; Fax: 724-776-3770
foundation@tms.org
www.tms.org

Tresa Pollock, President
Brajendra Mishra, VP
Alexander Scott, Executive Director
John Parsey, Financial Planning Officer
Marc DeGraef, Director Information Technology

This conference will feature five days of technically intensive programming focusing on both fundamental and applied topics related to welding and joining. Top researchers from industry, government, and academia will present the latest in experimental and modeling developments.
Frequency: May

6981 **International Symposium for Testing & Failure Analysis**
ASM International
9639 Kinsman Road
Materials Park, OH 44073-0002

440-338-5151
800-336-5152; Fax: 440-338-4634

memberservicecenter@asminternational.org
www.asminternational.org

William T. Mahoney, Secretary & CEO
Lindy Good, Global Conference & Exhibit Planner
Annual event focusing on failure analysis and makers of tools such as microscopes, stress and measurement analytical tools, etchants and chemicals, ESD protective materials and other products used for this purpose.
30K Members
Frequency: Annual/Oct/Nov
Founded in 1913

6982 International Symposium on Circuits and Systems
IEEE Circuits and Systems Society
445 Hoes Lane
Piscataway, NJ 08854

manager@ieee-cas.org
www.ieee-cas.org

Brittian Parkinson, Operations Manager
Myung Hoon Sunwoo, VP, Conferences
Frequency: Annual

6983 MCAA Industry Forum
Measurement, Control & Automation Association
200 City Hall Avenue
Suite D
Poquoson, VA 23662

757-258-3100
automationassociation.com

Teresa Sebring, President
Andrea Ambrose, Director, Member Relations
Elizabeth Horton, Programs Manager
Kim Malina, Marketing Communications Manager
Rebecca Moore, Administrative Manager
Education and networking event for manufacturers and distributors of instrumentation, systems, and software products for industrial process control and factory automation.
Founded in 1944

6984 Materials, Science & Technology
Minerals, Metals & Materials Society
184 Thorn Hill Road
Warrendale, PA 15086-7514

724-776-9000; Fax: 724-776-3770
www.tms.org

Tresa Pollock, President
Brajendra Mishra, VP
Alexander Scott, Executive Director
John Parsey, Financial Planning Officer
Marc DeGraef, Director Information Technology
Offers a materials science and applied technology event unlike any other.
Frequency: September

6985 NCSLI Workshop & Symposium
NCSL
1800 30th Street
Suite 305 B
Boulder, CO 80301

303-440-3339; Fax: 303-440-3384
info@ncsli.org
www.ncsli.org

Harry J Moody, President
William T Pound, Executive Director
Will provide a forum to discuss the impact of these advances have had on metrology, as well as other related issues. Please join us as we reflect on how far and fast metrology has progressed over the past quarter of a century and to discuss its future needs and directions.
1200 Attendees
Frequency: August, Washington

6986 NEDA Executive Conference
National Electronic Distributors Association
1111 Alderman Drive
Suite 400
Alpharetta, GA 30005-4175

678-393-9990; Fax: 678-393-9998
admin@nedassoc.org

Francis Flynn Jr, President
Robin B Gray Jr, Executive VP
Debbie Conyers, Director Marketing
Barney Martin, VP Industry Practices
Frequency: November

6987 NMEA Convention & Expo
National Marine Electronics Association
Seven Riggs Avenue
Severna Park, MD 21146

410-975-9425; Fax: 410-975-9450
info@nmea.org
www.nmea.org

Mark Reedanauer, President & Executive Director
Steve Katz, Chair
Frequency: October

6988 NPSC Meeting
National Electronics Service Dealers Association
3608 Pershing Avenue
Fort Worth, TX 76107-4527

817-921-9061
800-797-9197; Fax: 817-921-3741
webmaster@nesda.com
www.nesda.com

Brian Gibson, President
Don Cressin, VP
Mack Blakely, Executive Director
Fred Paradis, CSM, Treasurer
Wayne Markman, Secretary
Featuring Training, Sponsored Meal Events, Meetings, and Opportunities to Network with other service professionals as well as key service industry representatives.
Frequency: July

6989 Northwest Electronics Technology Conference
Electronic Conventions Management
8110 Airport Boulevard
Los Angeles, CA 90045-3119

310-215-3976
800-877-2668; Fax: 310-641-5117
northcon@ieee.org
www.nedme.com

James Lipman, PhD, Conference Director
Sue Kingston, Trade Show Manager
Offers a concentrated technical conference with complimenting exhibits. It provides a venue where those involved with the design, production and marketing of electronics-related products can converge in a real time, interactive atmosphere.
7000 Attendees
Frequency: May

6990 OEMBoston
Canon Communications
11444 W Olympic Boulevard
Suite 900
Los Angeles, CA 90064-1549

310-445-4200; Fax: 310-445-4299
www.oemboston.com

William F Cobert, President/CEO
Diane O'Conner, Trade Show Director
Dan Cutrone, Show Marketing Director
The creation of two seperate shows, OEM Electronics and OEMed, the OEMBoston is accessible to thousands of electronics and medical OEMs, who can benefit from the combination of the two shows. The different product classification found at this show include Contract Manufacturing, Electronics Components, Component Fabrication, Production/Assembly Equipment, Packaging Equipment & Supplies, Tubing and more. Held at the Bayside Expo Center in Boston, Massachusetts.
1604 Attendees
Frequency: September

6991 SEMI Expo CIS
Semiconductor Equipment & Materials International
3081 Zanker Road
San Jose, CA 95134

408-943-6900; Fax: 408-428-9600
semihq@semi.org
www.semi.org

Scott Smith, Public Relations Manager
Will highlight CIS as a region with huge potential and a new developing market for the world semiconductor equipment and materials manufacturers.
Frequency: September

6992 SESHA Annual Symposium
Semiconductor Environmental, Safety & Health Assn
1313 Dolly Madison Boulevard
Suite 402
McLean, VA 22101

703-790-1745; Fax: 703-790-2672
sesha@burkinc.com
seshaonline.org

Bernie First, President
Brett Burk, Co-Founder
Glenn Tom, Co-Founder
Brian Sherin, Treasurer
Karl Albrecht, Secretary
For individuals employed within the electronics and related high technology industries with an interest in environmental, health and safety issues.
1235 Attendees
Frequency: May
Founded in 1978

6993 SOUTHCON
Electronic Conventions
12340 Rosecrans Avenue
Suite 100
Manhattan Beach, CA 90266

310-524-4100
800-877-2668; Fax: 310-643-7328

Susan Kingston, Show Manager
Companies attending represent a major cross-section of the electronics industry including consumer, computer, medical, automotive and others. Offers conference sessions, in-depth technical sessions, product demonstrations and exhibits by vendors.
10M Attendees
Frequency: March

6994 Semiconductor
Semiconductor Equipment & Materials International
3081 Zankeer Road
San Jose, CA 95134

408-943-6900; Fax: 408-428-9600
semihq@semi.org
www.semi.org

Scott Smith, Public Relations Manager
The future of the European Semiconductor Industry.
Frequency: June

6995 Service & Retail Convention
Electronic Technicians Association International

5 Depot Street
Greencastle, IN 46135

765-653-4301
800-288-3824; Fax: 765-653-4287
eta@eta-i.org
www.eta-i.org

Teresa Maher, President
Brianna Pinson, Office Manager

6996 **Southeastern Technology Week**
TEC
2001 Assembly Street
Suite 204
Columbia, SC 29201

803-779-7123; Fax: 803-772-9964

6997 **Strategic Leadership and Networking Forum**
Electronic Transactions Association
1101 16th Street NW
Suite 402
Washington, DC 20036

202-828-2635
800-695-5509; Fax: 202-828-2639
www.electran.org

Jennifer Leo, Meetings Manager
Kurt Strawhecker, Managing Director
Steve Carnevale, Senior Vice President

A unique event designed to help executives thrive in the new payments industry. The Forum goes far beyond fundamental education to tackle the strategic, big-picture issues that today's payment executives and CEOs deal with each day. ETA takes a distinct approach to executive education and has adopted interactive formats conducive to peer-to-peer learning and business-to-business networking.

6998 **Strategic Materials Conference**
Semiconductor Equipment & Materials International
3081 Zanker Road
San Jose, CA 95134

408-943-7805; Fax: 408-428-9600
www.semi.org

Anna Morais, Conference Contact

Hear about new business models, emerging players, green requirements and the the diverse partnerships in the semiconductor materials sector; the latest market trends, forecasts, best-practices, and discussions.
12000 Attendees
Frequency: May, Singapore

6999 **TABES Technical Business Exhibition & Symposium**
Huntsville Association of Technical Societies
3414 Governors Dr SW
PO Box 1964
Huntsville, AL 35805

256-882-1234; Fax: 205-837-4275
www.hats.org/society

J Tardy, Manager
John Young, Treasurer

Brings new business into the community.
10000 Attendees
Founded in 1969

7000 **Tech Advantage Exposition**
National Rural Electric Cooperative Association
4301 Wilson Blouevard
Arlington, VA 22203

703-907-5500; Fax: 703-907-5528
www.nreca.org

Gary Pfann, Conference Contact
Barbara Christiana, Expo Contact
11000 Attendees

7001 **Technology & Standards Forum**
Consumer Technology Association (CTA)
1919 S Eads Street
Arlington, VA 22202

703-907-7600
866-858-1555; Fax: 703-907-7675
cta@cta.tech
www.cta.tech

Gary Shapiro, President & CEO
David Hagan, Chairman

Focus on development of emerging industry standard, contribute your company's viewpoint, and gain networking opportunities. Take advantage of valuable opportunities to interface with industry technical leaders as they consider, develop, and finalize, crucial CE standards.

7002 **VR/AR Global Summit**
VR/AR Association
Palo Alto, CA 94303

am@thevrara.com
www.thevrara.com
Facebook, Twitter, LinkedIn, YouTube

Nathan Pettyjohn, Founder & President
Kris Kolo, Global Executive Director
Anne-Marie Enns, Executive Producer

Summits bring together enterprise, hardware, software, and content providers for educational sessions and networking.
Founded in 2015

7003 **Winter Break**
Consumer Technology Association (CTA)
1919 South Eads Street
Arlington, VA 22202

703-907-7600
866-858-1555; Fax: 703-907-7675
cta@cta.tech
www.cta.tech

Gary Shapiro, President & CEO
David Hagan, Chairman

Attendees can focus on the development of emerging industry standards, contribute their company's viewpoints, and gain networking opportunities. Interface with industry technical leaders as they consider, develop, and finalize crucial CE standards.

Directories & Databases

7004 **Antenna Book**
Electronic Technicians Association International
5 Depot St
Greencastle, IN 46135-8024

765-653-8262
800-288-3824; Fax: 765-653-4287
eta@eta-i.org
www.eta-i.org

Dick Glass, President
Brianna Pinson, Office Manager

Written by professional technicians who have worked closely with antennas, this two book series is the ultimate study guide for technicians seeking certification through ETA-I's Video Distribution, Certified Satellite Installer and TVRO programs. It can also serve as study materials for electronics classes, employee training, or as a quick reference guide your whole shop can use. Includes shipping & handling.
Cost: $33.00
ISBN: 1-891749-14-5
Printed in on matte stock

7005 **Battery Report**
Power Sources Manufacturers Association
PO Box 418
Mendham, NJ 07945-0418

973-543-9660; Fax: 973-543-6207
power@psma.com
www.psma.com

Dusty Becker, Chairman
Carl Blake, President
Jim Marinos, VP

Is a comprehensive report describing the state-of-the-art, current problems and R&D needs for numerous battery systems. The report also includes battery global market trends, status of electric/hybrid vehicle battery development and UN requirements for shipping lithium.
Cost: $125.00
155 Members
Founded in 1985

7006 **ERA Rep Locator**
Electronics Representatives Association
444 N Michigan Avenue
Suite 1960
Chicago, IL 60611

312-527-3050
800-776-7377; Fax: 312-527-3783
info@era.org
www.era.org

Mark Motsinger, Chairman
Dave Rossi, Vice Chairman
Mike Kunz, President
Raymond J Hall, EVP/CEO
William R Warfield, Director Finance/Operations

Manufacturers match your products and territories with qualified, professional representatievs firms. The Locator lists ERA member companies with informtion on size of firm, territories covered, type of products represented and customer bases.
Cost: $90.00
Frequency: Annually

7007 **Electronic Buyers News: Specialized and Local/Regional Directory**
CMP Publications
600 Community Dr
Manhasset, NY 11030-3810

516-562-5000; Fax: 516-562-5123

Hailey McKeefry, Editor

List of about 325 distributors of electronic products and supplies operating on less than national scale, or offering only one or a few produst nationwide.

7008 **Electronic Buyers News: Top 50 Distributors Issue**
CMP Publications
600 Community Dr
Manhasset, NY 11030-3810

516-562-5000; Fax: 516-562-5123

David Gabel, Editor

List of electronic distributors ranked by annual gross sales.

7009 **Electronic Distribution Directory**
Electronic Distribution Show Corporation

222 S Riverside Plz
Suite 2160
Chicago, IL 60606-6112

312-648-1140; Fax: 312-648-4282
eds@edsc.org
www.edsconnects.com

Gretchen Oie, Manager

7010 **Electronic Industries Association: Trade Directory and Membership List**
Electronic Industries Alliance
2500 Wilson Boulevard
Arlington, VA 22201-3834

703-907-7500; Fax: 703-907-7501
www.eia.org

Dave McCurdy, President/CEO
Charles L Robinson, Chief Operating Officer

More than 1,200 member companies in the electronic manufacturing industry.
Frequency: Annual

7011 **Electronic Materials & Process Handbook**
International Microelectronics & Electronics
611 2nd Street NE
Washington, DC 20002

202-548-4001
888-464-6277; Fax: 202-548-6115
www.imaps.org

Charles A Harper, Editor
Ronald M Sampson, Editor

Offers guidance on insulations, conductors, and semiconductor materials, defines critical manufacturing parameters, and shows how these parameters can be combined to create successful electronic devices.
Cost: $80.00
ISBN: 0-070542-99-6

7012 **Electronic Representatives Directory**
Harris Publishing Company
360 B Street
Idaho Falls, ID 83402-1938

208-524-4217; Fax: 208-522-5241
customerservice@harrispublishing.com
www.harrispublishing.com

Directory of services and supplies to the industry.
Cost: $25.00
320 Pages
Frequency: Annual
Circulation: 7,500

7013 **Electronics Manufacturers Directory on Diskette**
Harris InfoSource International
2057 E Aurora Rd
Twinsburg, OH 44087-1938

330-425-4481
800-888-5900; Fax: 330-487-5368
www.harrisinfo.com

David Wilkof, VP

Diskette. Covers approximately 1,000,000 manufacturers of electronic equipment and products.
Cost: $329.00
Frequency: Annual

7014 **North American Directory of Contract Electronic Manufacturers**
Miller Freeman Publications
600 Harrison Street
Suite 400
San Francisco, CA 94107-1391

FAX 415-905-2239
www.cassembly.com

Kimberly Cassidy, Editor

Over 1,350 electronics manufacturers facilities in the United States, Canada, and Mexico.
Cost: $295.00
Frequency: Annual

7015 **ProService Directory and Yearbook**
National Electronics Service Dealers Association
3608 Pershing Ave
Fort Worth, TX 76107-4527
817-921-9061
800-797-9197; Fax: 817-921-3741
webmaster@nesda.com
www.nesda.com

Clyde Nabors, Publisher
Wallace Harrison, Editor
Mary Margaret Merill, Production Manager

The yearbook is an annual resource listing for servicers. This directory is sent each January to current members.
Frequency: Annual

7016 **Product Source Guide for Electronic Devices**
Reed Business Information
275 Washington St
Newton, MA 02458-1611

617-964-3030; Fax: 617-558-4470
www.designnews.com

Donald Swanson, Editor

List of over 4,000 manufacturers and suppliers of equipment and materials used in the production, testing, and packaging of electronic devices and systems.
Cost: $25.00
Frequency: Annual

7017 **Source Book**
Armed Forces Communications and Electronics Assn
4400 Fair Lakes Ct
Suite 100
Fairfax, VA 22033-3899

703-631-1397
800-336-4583; Fax: 703-631-4693
www.afcea.org

Kent Schneider, President/CEO
Becky Nolan, Executive VP
John A Dubia, Executive VP

The Source Book published in the January issue, contains the company profiles and contacts of AFCEA's corporate members. It is the who's who of C$ISR and homeland secuity organizations. The annual Security Directory, published in the February issue, focuses on security solutions and the organizations that provide them.
31000 Members
Founded in 1946

7018 **Who's Who in Electronics Buyer's Guide**
Harris Publishing Company
360 B Street
Idaho Falls, ID 83402-1938

208-524-4217; Fax: 208-522-5241
customerservice@harrispublishing.com
www.harrispublishing.com

A list of over 15,000 manufacturers and distributors of electronics products in five regional volumes.
Cost: $65.00
Frequency: Annual
Circulation: 60,000

Industry Web Sites

7019 **Nesda.Wildapricot.Org**
National Electronics Service Dealers Association

A national trade association for professionals in the business repairing consumer electronics equipment, appliances, and computers. NESDA has an e-mail group of over 600 members and manufacturers that communicate daily for information sharing.

7020 **http://gold.greyhouse.com**
G.O.L.D Grey House OnLine Databases

Grey House Publishing's online database platform, GOLD, offers Quick Search, Keyword Search and Expert Search for most business sectors including electronics markets. The GOLD platform makes finding the information you need quick and easy - whether you're a novice searcher or an experienced database user. All of Grey House's directory products are available for subscription on the GOLD platform.

7021 **www.afcea.org**
Armed Forces Communications and Electronics Assn

An association that represents the professional communications, electronics, intelligence and information systems community.

7022 **www.aprovision.org**
Association of Progressive Rental Organizations

Members include television, appliance and furniture dealers who rent merchandise with an option to purchase.

7023 **www.cta.tech**
Consumer Technology Association (CTA)

7024 **www.era.org**
Electronics Representatives Association

Provides services and benefits to electronic industry manufacturers representatives.

7025 **www.eta-i.org**
Electronic Technicians Association International

A worldwide professional association founded by electronics technicians and servicing dealers.

7026 **www.ewh.ieee.org**
Instrumentation and Measurement Society

A subsidiary of the Institute of Electrical and Electronics Engineers. Provides support to scientists and technicians who design and develop electrical and electronic measuring instruments and equipment.

7027 **www.greyhouse.com**
Grey House Publishing

Authoritative reference directories for most business sectors including electronic markets. Users can search the online databases with varied search criteria allowing for custom searches by product category, geographic area, sales volume, keyword, subject and more. Full Grey House catalog and online ordering also available.

7028 **www.imaps.org**
International Microelectronics & Packaging Society

Dedicated to the advancement and growth of the use of microelectronics and electronic packaging through public and professional education, dissemination of information by means of symposia, workshops and conferences and promotion of the Society's portfolio of technologies.

7029 **www.ipc.org**
IPC-Association Connecting Electronics Industries

Works to develop standards in circuit board assembly equipment. Brings together all players in the electronic interconnection industry, including designers, board manufacturers, assembly companies, suppliers and original equipment manufacturers. Offers workshops, conferences, meetings and online communications.

7030 **www.iscet.org**
Int'l Society of Certified Electronics Technicians

Designed to measure the degree of theoretical knowledge and technical proficiency of practicing technicians.

7031 **www.nmea.org**
National Marine Electronics Association

The unifying force behind the entire marine electronics industry, bringing together all aspects of the industry for the betterment of all in the business.

7032 **www.psma.com**
Power Sources Manufacturers Association

Worldwide membership consists of manufacturers of power sources and conversion equipment. Nonprofit association strives to integrate the resources of the power sources industry to more effectively and profitably serve the needs of the power sources users, providers and PSMA members. Educates the electronics industry and others on the relevant applications for power sources and conversion devices.

7033 **www.semi.org**
Semiconductor Equipment & Materials International

Strengthens the performance of member companies through lobbying, promotion, education and statistical research.

7034 **www.seshaonline.org**
Semiconductor Environmental, Safety & Health Assn

Members are individuals employed within the electronics and related high technology industries with an interest in environmental, health and safety issues.

7035 **www.sia-online.org**
Semiconductor Industry Association

Trade association representing the US microchip industry.

7036 **www.sme.org**
Society of Manufacturing Engineers

Facebook, Twitter, LinkedIn, YouTube, Google+, Instagram

Association representing electrical manufacturers.

7037 **www.smta.org**
Surface Mount Technology Association

A network of professionals building skills, sharing practical experience and developing solutions in electronic assembly technologies and related business operations.

Associations

7038 **ASM International**
9639 Kinsman Road
Materials Park, OH 44073-0002
440-338-5151
800-336-5152; Fax: 440-338-4634
memberservicecenter@asminternational.org
www.asminternational.org
Facebook, Twitter, LinkedIn
Zi-Kui Liu, President
Diana Essock, Vice President
Raymond V. Fryan, Treasurer
William T. Mahoney, Secretary & CEO
The society for materials engineers and scientists, a worldwide network dedicated to advancing industry, technology and applications of metals and materials. ASM provides information references, education, research and international events.
30K Members
Founded in 1913

7039 **ASTM International**
100 Barr Harbor Drive
PO Box C700
W Conshohocken, PA 19428-2959
610-832-9500; Fax: 610-832-9555
service@astm.org
www.astm.org
Facebook, Twitter, LinkedIn, RSS, Youtube
Ronald J. Ebelhar, Chairman
D. Thomas Marsh, Vice Chairman
James A. Thomas, President
Not-for-profit organization that provides a global forum for the development and publication of voluntary consensus standards for materials, products, systems and services. Members are users, producers, consumers and representatives of academia and government. Formerly known as the American Society for Testing and Materials.
30000 Members
Founded in 1898

7040 **AVS Science & Technology Society**
125 Maiden Ln
15th Floor
New York, NY 10038-4714
212-248-0200; Fax: 212-248-0245
ricky@avs.org
www.avs.org
Yvonne Towse, Managing Director
Peter Burke, Financial Administrator
Angela Klink, Member Services Administrator
Jeannette DeGennaro, Exhibition & Sales Manager
Ricky Baldeo, Office Services Coordinator
AVS is a resource for scientists, engineers, industrialists, students and educators.
6000 Members
Founded in 1963

7041 **Abrasive Engineering Society**
144 Moore Road
Butler, PA 16001-1312
724-282-6210
aes@abrasiveengineering.com
www.abrasiveengineering.com
Ted Giese, Executive Director
Dedicated to promoting technical information about abrasives minerals and their uses including abrasives grains and products such as grinding wheels, coated abrasives and thousands of other related tools and products that serve manufacturing and the consumer.
500 Members
Founded in 1957

7042 **Accreditation Board for Engineering and Technology**
415 North Charles Street
Baltimore, MD 21201
410-347-7700; Fax: 443-522-3644
comms@abet.org
www.abet.org
Michael Milligan, Executive Director, CEO
Joe Sussman, PhD, F.ASME, Chief Accreditation Officer, CIO
Jessica Silwick, CPA, CAE, CFO/COO
Dan Losapio, Senior Manager
ABET is a nonprofit, non-governmental organization that accredits college and university programs in applied and natural science, computing, engineering and engineering technology.
36 Members
Founded in 1932
Mailing list available for rent: 16000 names

7043 **Acoustical Society of America**
2 Huntington Quad
Suite 1N01
Melville, NY 11747-4505
516-576-2360; Fax: 516-576-2377
asa@aip.org
acousticalsociety.org
Christy K. Holland, President
Lily M. Wang, VP
Susan E. Fox, Executive Director
James F. Lynch, Editor-in-Chief
Christopher J. Struck, Standards Director
Supports all those involved with the acoustics industry.
7000 Members
Founded in 1929

7044 **Adhesive & Sealant Council**
7101 Wisconsin Ave
Suite 990
Bethesda, MD 20814-4805
301-986-9700; Fax: 301-986-9795
data@ascouncil.org
www.ascouncil.org
Twitter, LinkedIn, RSS
William Allmond, President
Valeryia Mikharava, Director, Finance and Admin.
Malinda Armstrong, Director, Meetings & Expositions
Mark Collatz, Director, Regulatory Affairs
Steve Duren, Senior Director, Member Services
A North American trade association dedicated to representing the adhesive and sealant industry. ASC is bound by the collective efforts of its members, and strives to improve the industry operating environment and strengthen its member companies.
124 Members
Founded in 1958

7045 **Air and Waste Management Association**
436 7th Avenue
Suite 2100
Pittsburgh, PA 15219
412-232-3444
800-270-3444; Fax: 412-232-3450
info@awma.org
www.awma.org
Facebook, Twitter, LinkedIn
Stephanie Glyptis, Executive Director
Gerald Armstrong, Customer Service & Membership
Tracy Fedkoe, Director, Marketing/Project Mgmt.
Jeff Schurman, Manager, Exhibits & Sponsorship
Lisa Bucher, Managing Editor
Professional organization that provides training, information, and networking opportunities to environmental professionals.
5000 Members
Founded in 1907

7046 **Alpha Pi Mu**
3005 Lancaster Drive
Blacksburg, VA 24060
540-553-2043
office@alphapimu.com
www.alphapimu.com
Dr. Wafik H Iskander, President
Sarah Lam, Executive Vice President
Dr. C. Patrick Koelling, Executive Director
Dr. Wafik H Iskander, Vice President
Dr. S. Balachandran, Treasurer
An honor society for Industrial and Systems Engineering students.
Founded in 1949

7047 **American Academy of Environmental Engineers & Scientists**
147 Old Solomons Island Road
Suite 303
Annapolis, MD 21401-7003
410-266-3311; Fax: 410-266-7653
www.aaees.org
Facebook, Twitter, LinkedIn, Youtube, Flickr
Burk Kalweit, Executive Director
Howard B. LaFever, President
Dr. Robert Williams, President-Elect
C. Hunter Nolen, Vice President
Joyce Dowen, Executive Assistant
Periodical for environmental engineers, environmental engineer professionals, as well as environmental engineering services, and scientists in the environmental field.
2500 Members
Founded in 1955

7048 **American Association for the Advancement of Science**
1200 New York Ave NW
Washington, DC 20005
202-326-6400
www.aaas.org
Facebook, Twitter, LinkedIn, YouTube, Instagram
Alan I. Leshner, Interim Chief Executive Officer
Andrew Black, Chief of Staff & External Affairs
Michael Savelli, Chief Operating Officer
Maureen Kearney, Chief Program Officer
Tiffany Lohwater, Chief Communications Officer
A nonprofit organization that has research news, issue papers, educational programs, etc.
Founded in 1848

7049 **American Association of Engineering Societies**
1801 Alexander Bell Drive
Reston, VA 20191
202-296-2237
888-400-2237; Fax: 202-296-1151
dbateson@aaes.org
www.aaes.org
Dr. James L. Melsa, Chairman
Alyse Stofer, Vice Chair
Wendy Cowan, CAE, Executive Director/Secretary
Mark W. Woodson, P.E., Treasurer
Association for national, U.S. organizations concerned with engineering and related fields.
14 Members
Founded in 1979

7050 **American Automatic Control Council**
Northwestern University

3640 Col Glenn Highway
Dayton, OH 45435

937-775-5062; Fax: 937-775-3936
pmisra@cs.wright.edu
www.a2c2.org

Tariq Samad, President
Linda Bushnell, Treasurer
B. Wayne Bequette, Secretary
Pradeep Misra, Secretary

Supports industry of automatic controls producers.
1M Members
Founded in 1960

7051 **American Council of Engineering Companies**
1015 15th St
8th floor NW
Washington, DC 20005-2605

202-347-7474; Fax: 202-898-0068
acec@acec.org
www.acec.org
Facebook, Twitter, Pinterest

Ralph W. Christie, Chairman
Harvey M. Floyd, Senior Vice Chair and Treasurer
David A. Raymond, President and CEO
Mary Ann Emely, VP, Operations & Membership
Steven Hall, Vice President, Government Affairs

Membership includes US firms engaged in a range of engineering works. Mission is to contribute to the nation's prosperity through advancing the interests of member firms.
55000 Members
Founded in 1905

7052 **American Crystallographic Association**
Ellicott Station
PO Box 96
Buffalo, NY 14205-0096

716-898-8690; Fax: 716-898-8695
aca@hwi.buffalo.edu
www.amercrystalassn.org
Twitter

Christopher Cahill, President
Tom Terwilliger, Vice President
William L. Duax, Chief Executive Officer
S.N. Rao, Chief Financial Officer
Kristina Vitale, Membership Secretary

Supports all those involved with hardware, software, and x-ray equipment for the crystal industry.
2200 Members
Founded in 1949

7053 **American Design Drafting Association**
105 East Main Street
Newbern, TE 38059

731-627-0802; Fax: 731-627-9321
okparker@adda.org
www.adda.org
Facebook, Twitter, LinkedIn, Google+

Olen Parker, Executive Director
Donna Brenton, Administrative Manager
Pennie King, Programs Manager

An individual membership society for the design drafting community across all industries.
Founded in 1948

7054 **American Engineering Association, Inc.**
533 Waterside Blvd.
Monroe Township, NJ 08831

201-664-6954
aea@aea.org
www.aea.org

Richard F. Tax, President
Charles Fischer, Vice President
Jenny Blackford, Marketing Director
Laurie Johnson, Office Assistant

As a national nonprofit professional association the AEA is a voice for engineers. The AEA, Inc. is dedicated to the enhancement of the engineering profession and U.S. Engineering capabilities. AEA is a strong advocate for providing opportunities for US engineers and is involved in issues of utilization, skill enhancement, loss of jobs, offshore manufacturing, layoffs, and many others that affect the lives and professional welfare of our engineers.
Founded in 1979

7055 **American Helicopter Society**
2701 Prosperity Avenue
Suite 210
Fairfax, VA 22031

703-684-6777
855-247-4685; Fax: 703-739-9279
staff@vtol.org
www.vtol.org
Facebook, Twitter, LinkedIn, YouTube, RSS

Mick Hirschberg, Executive Director
Valerie Sheehan, Director, Membership
Randy Johnson, Director, Information Resources
David Renzi, Director, Meetings & Advertising

The professional society for the advancement of vertical flight technology and its useful application throughout the world.
Founded in 1943

7056 **American Indian Science and Engineering Society**
2305 Renard SE
Suite 200
Albuquerque, NM 87106

505-765-1052; Fax: 505-765-5608
www.aises.org
Facebook, Twitter, LinkedIn, YouTube, Instagram

Richard Stephens, Chair
Dr. Twyla Baker-Demaray, Vice-Chair
Marlene Watson, Secretary
Dr. James May, Treasurer
Sarah Echohawk, Chief Executive Officer

A nonprofit professional association with the goal of increasing American Indian and Alaskan Native representation in the fields of engineering, science, and other related technology disciplines.
3500 Members
Founded in 1977

7057 **American Institute of Chemical Engineers**
120 Wall Street
FL 23
New York, NY 10005-4020

203-702-7660
800-242-4363; Fax: 203-775-5177
www.aiche.org
Facebook, Twitter, LinkedIn, YouTube, Flickr, Slideshare

Monty Alger, President
Joseph Smith, Secretary
Rosemarie Wesson, Treasurer

Professional association providing leadership in advancing the chemical engineering profession. Members are those who develop processes and design and operate manufacturing plants, as well as researchers who assure the safe and environmentally sound manufacture, use and disposal of chemical products.
50000 Members
Founded in 1908

7058 **American Institute of Physics**
1 Physics Ellipse
College Park, MD 20740-3841

301-209-3100; Fax: 301-209-0843
dylla@aip.org
www.aip.org

Louis J. Lanzerotti, Chair
Robert G. W. Brown, Chief Executive Officer
Gigi Swartz, Chief Financial Officer
Margaret Wiley, Senior Executive Secretary
Liz Dart Caron, Senior Director

Presents original research in high performance polymer science and technology. Primarily applications-driven, with a major focus on the molecular structure/processability/property relationship with regard to the specified applications.
1931 Members
Founded in 1931

7059 **American Iron and Steel Institute**
25 Massachusetts Avenue, NW
Suite 800
Washington, DC 20001

202-452-7100
www.steel.org
Facebook, Twitter, YouTube

Kevin Dempsey, President & CEO
Timothy Green, Chief Economist
Lisa Harrison, SVP, Communications
John Catterall, VP, Automotive Program
Robert Wills, VP, Construction Program

Steel information for consumers, engineers, and other professionals.
125 Members
Founded in 1855

7060 **American Nuclear Society**
555 N Kensington Ave
La Grange Park, IL 60526

708-352-6611
800-323-3044; Fax: 708-352-0499
www.ans.org
Facebook, Twitter, LinkedIn

Serves its members in their efforts to develop and safely apply nuclear science and technology for public benefit through knowledge exchange, professional development, and enhanced public understanding.
Founded in 1954

7061 **American Oil Chemists Society**
2710 S. Boulder
Urbana, IL 61802

217-359-2344; Fax: 217-351-8091
general@aocs.org
www.aocs.org
Facebook, Twitter, LinkedIn, Blogger

M. Trautmann, President
B. Hendrix, VP
Patrick J. Donnelly, Chief Executive Officer
Jamie Lourash, Data Services Coordinator
Jeffry L. Newman, Senior Director, Programs

A global forum to promote the exchange of ideas, information, and experience, to enhance personal excellence, and to provide high standards of quality among those with a professional interest in the science and technology of fats, oil, surfactants, and related materials.
5400+ Members
Founded in 1909

7062 **American Oil Chemists' Society (AOCS)**
2710 S Boulder Drive
PO Box 17190
Urbana, IL 61803-6996

217-359-2344; Fax: 217-351-8091
general@aocs.org
www.aocs.org
Facebook, Twitter, LinkedIn, Blogger

M. Trautmann, President
B. Hendrix, VP
Patrick J. Donnelly, Chief Executive Officer
Jamie Lourash, Data Services Coordinator
Jeffry L. Newman, Senior Director, Programs

AOCS is a global scientific society open to all individuals and corporations who are interested in fats, oils, surfactants, detergents and related materials. AOCS is a trusted source of information for its members and thousands of non-members from more than 90 countries worldwide.
4500 Members
Founded in 1909
Mailing list available for rent

7063 **American Society for Engineering Education**
1818 N St NW
Suite 600
Washington, DC 20036-2476

202-331-3500; Fax: 202-265-8504
prism@asee.org
www.asee.org

Norman Fortenberry, Executive Director
Joe Dillon, Managing Director, Finance/CFO
Keith Mounts, Chief Information Officer (CIO)
Ashok Agrawal, Managing Director
Patti Greenawalt, Managing Director, Member Services

Supports all those educators in the engineering technology fields.
12000 Members
Founded in 1893

7064 **American Society for Nondestructive Testing**
PO Box 28518
1711 Arlingate Lane
Columbus, OH 43228-0518

614-274-6003
800-222-2768; Fax: 614-274-6899
www.asnt.org
Facebook, Twitter, LinkedIn, YouTube, Instagram

Neal Couture, Executive Director
Barry Schieferstein, Dir., Conferences & Meetings
Garra Liming, Dir., Marketing & Communications
Brad Pence, Director, Finance & Controller
Heather Cowles, Dir., Membership & Engagement

ASNT is the world's largest technical society for nondestructive tests (NDT) professionals.
15000 Members
Founded in 1941

7065 **American Society for Precision Engineering**
3801 Lake Boone Trail
Suite 190
Raleigh, NC 27607

919-839-8444; Fax: 919-839-8039
www.aspe.net

Brian O'Connor, President
John Schaefer, Vice President

Members are from academia, industry and government, and include professionals in engineering, materials science, physics, chemistry, mathematics and computer science. Multidisciplinary professional and technical society concerned with precision engineering research and development, design and manufacturing of high accuracy components and systems.
Founded in 1985

7066 **American Society for Quality**
600 N Plankinton Avenue
Milwaukee, WI 53203

414-272-8575
800-248-1946; Fax: 414-272-1734
help@asq.org
asq.org
Facebook, Twitter, LinkedIn

Elmer Corbin, Chair
Bill Troy, CEO
Brian Savoie, Chief Financial Officer
Andrew Baines, Managing Director, Global
Ann Jordan, General Counsel

The association's mission is to facilitate continuous improvement and customer satisfaction in manufacturing by sharing ideas, tools, standards and expertise on quality management.
80K Members
Founded in 1946

7067 **American Society of Agricultural and Biological Engineers**
2950 Niles Rd
St Joseph, MI 49085-8607

269-429-0300
800-371-2723; Fax: 269-429-3852
hq@asabe.org
www.asabe.org

Candice Engler, President
Darrin Drollinger, Executive Director
Joann McQuone, Executive Assistant
Mark Zielke, Senior Director
Dolores Landeck, Director of Public Affairs

Holds annual meetings and conferences and publishes journals related to agricultural engineering, biological engineering and food process engineering.
8500 Members
Founded in 1907

7068 **American Society of Certified Engineering**
PO Box 1348
Flowery Branch, GA 30542

770-967-9173; Fax: 770-967-8049
www.ascet.org

Russell E Freier, Chairman
Leo Saenz, CET, President
Kurt Schuler, Secretary/Treasurer

Strives to obtain recognition of engineering technicians as essential to the engineering scientific team. Provides a forum for discussion of employment issues and improvement of the professional status of engineering technicians.
2000 Members
Founded in 1964

7069 **American Society of Civil Engineers**
1801 Alexander Bell Dr
Reston, VA 20191-4382

703-295-6300
800-548-2723; Fax: 703-295-6222
cybrarian@asce.org
www.asce.org/
Facebook, Twitter, LinkedIn, YouTube, Google+

Robert D. Stevens, President
Dennis D. Truax, Ph.D., P.E., Treasurer
Randall M. Perkinson, P.E., Assistant Treasurer
Thomas W. Smith III, ENV SP, CAE, Secretary

Professional association of engineers and scientists working in civil and structural engineering, applied mechanics and engineering science, aeronautics and astronautics.
Founded in 1852

7070 **American Society of Gas Engineers**
P.O. Box 66
Artesia, CA 90702

562-455-9417
asgecge@aol.com
www.asge-national.org

Jerry Moore, Executive Director
Ray Maddock, President
Eric Bruton, Vice President
Chad Johnson, Treasurer

Supports all engineers in the gas industry.
300 Members
Founded in 1954

7071 **American Society of Heating, Refrigeration & Air-Conditioning Engineers**
1791 Tullie Cir Ne
Atlanta, GA 30329-2398

404-636-8400
800-527-4723; Fax: 404-321-5478
ashrae@ashrae.org
www.ashrae.org

Jeff H. Littleton, Executive VP
Kim Mitchell, Chief Development Officer
Vanita Gupta, Director, Marketing
Joyce Abrams, Director, Member Services
Craig Wright, Director, Finance & Admin. Services

An international organization that fulfills its mission of advancing heating, ventilation, air conditioning and refrigeration to serve humanity and promote a sustainable world through research, standards writing, publishing and continuing education.
55000 Members
Founded in 1894

7072 **American Society of Mechanical Engineers**
Two Park Avenue
New York, NY 10016-5990

973-882-1170
800-843-2763
CustomerCare@asme.org
www.asme.org
Facebook, Twitter, LinkedIn, Instagram

Bryan A. Erler, President
Thomas Costabile, Executive Director & CEO
William Garofalo, Chief Financial Officer
Allian Pratt, Managing Director, Board Operations

ASME aims to promote and enhance the technical competency and professional well-being of the members, and through quality programs and activities in mechanical engineering, better enable its practitioners to contribute to the well being of human kind.
100K+ Members
Founded in 1880

7073 **American Society of Naval Engineers**
1452 Duke Street
Alexandria, VA 22314-3458

703-836-6727; Fax: 703-836-7491
asnehq@navalengineers.org
www.navalengineers.org

Anthony W. Lengerich, USN, President
Mr. Mike D'Amato, Vice President
Dr. William H. Luebke, Vice President
VADM Paul E. Sullivan, USN (Ret.), Vice President
Dr. Leigh McCue, Executive Dir/Secretary/Treasurer

Naval engineering includes all arts construction and sciences as applied in research, development design, construction, operation, maintenance, and logistic support of: surface/sub-surface ships and marine craft.
Founded in 1888

7074 American Society of Petroleum Operations Engineers
301 East Culpeper Street
Culpeper, VA 22701

703-768-4159
800-918-8962
www.aspoe.org
Facebook, Twitter, LinkedIn, YouTube, Google+, Instagram, P

John B Stanley, President
Gerald Holton, VP
Harry Lyon, Executive VP
Coles Marsh, Treasurer
Cheryl George, Secretary

Works to stimulate interest from the academic world in the qualifications necessary to become a Petroleum Operations Engineer.
Founded in 1976

7075 American Society of Plumbing Engineers
6400 Shafer Ct.
Suite 350
Rosemont, IL 60018-4914

847-296-0002; Fax: 773-695-9007
info@aspe.org
www.aspe.org

Mitch Clemente, CPD, President
Billy Smith, FASPE Executive Director / CEO
Donald Thurner, Director of Finance & Admin.
Stacey A. Kidd, Director of Membership & Meetings
Richard Albrecht, Director of Information Technology

Supports all those engineers in the plumbing industry.
7500 Members
Founded in 1964

7076 American Society of Safety Engineers
520 N. Northwest Hwy
Park Ridge, IL 60068

847-699-2929; Fax: 847-768-3434
customerservice@asse.org
www.asse.org

Michael Belcher, CSP, President
James D. Smith, M.S., CSP, Senior VP
Stephanie A. Helgerman, CSP, VP of Finance
Fred J. Fortman, Secretary and Executive Director

The oldest and largest professional safety organization. Its members manage, supervise and consult son safety, health, and environmental issues in industry, insurance, government and education.
30000 Members
Founded in 1911

7077 American Society of Sanitary Engineering
18927 Hickory Creek Drive
Suite 220
Mokena, IL 60448

708-995-3019; Fax: 708-479-6139
www.asse-plumbing.org

Douglas A. Marian, President
Dana Colombo, Vice President
Scott Hamilton, Executive Director
Conrad Jahrling, Staff Engineering Supervisor
Benjamin Ryan, Communications Editor

Members are from all segments of the plumbing industry, including contractors, engineers, inspectors, journeymen, apprentices and others who are involved in various segments of the industry. Provides information, an opportunity to exchange ideas, solve problems and offers a forum where all sides can express their views.
300 Members

7078 American Water Works Association
6666 W Quincy Ave.
Denver, CO 80235

303-794-7711
800-926-7337; Fax: 303-347-0804
www.awwa.org
Facebook, Twitter, LinkedIn, YouTube

Melissa Elliott, President
Aurel Arndt, Treasurer
David B. LaFrance, Chief Executive Officer

The professional society of North American drinking water experts. Develop standards and support research programs in waterworks design, construction, operation, and management. Conducts in-service training schools and offers placement service.
50000 Members
Founded in 1881

7079 Applied Technology Council
201 Redwood Shores Parkway
Suite 240
Redwood City, CA 94065

650-595-1542; Fax: 650-593-2320
atc@atcouncil.org
www.atcouncil.org

Jon A. Heintz, Executive Director
Bernadette Hadnagy, Director, Operations
Ayse Hortacsu, Director, Projects
Justin Moresco, Director, Projects
Carrie Perna, Manager, Publications & Technology

Nonprofit, tax-exempt corporation established through the efforts of the Structural Engineers Association of California. ATC's mission is to develop and promote state-of-the-art, user-friendly, engineering resources and applications for use in mitigating the effects of natural and other hazards on the built environment.
300 Members
Founded in 1973

7080 Association for Advancing Automation
900 Victors Way
Suite 140
Ann Arbor, MI 48108

734-994-6088; Fax: 734-994-3338
info@a3automate.org
www.a3automate.org
Facebook, Twitter, LinkedIn, YouTube

Jeff Burnstein, President
Dana Whalls, Vice President
Bob Doyle, Vice President, RIA & A3 Mexico
Robert Huschka, Director, Education Strategies
James Hamilton, Director, Sales

A3 is the umbrella association for the Robotic Industries Association, representing automation manufacturers, component suppliers, system integrators, end users, research groups, and consulting firms internationally.
1000 Members

7081 Association for Computing Machinery
1601 Broadway
10th Floor
New York, NY 10019-7434

212-869-7440
800-342-6626; Fax: 212-944-1318
acmhelp@acm.org
www.acm.org
Facebook, Twitter, LinkedIn, YouTube, Google+

Vicki Hanson, Chief Executive Officer
Pat Ryan, Chief Operating Officer
John Stanik, Managing Editor
Darren Ramdin, Director, Finance
Cynthia Ryan, Associate Director, Membership

Organization serving a membership of computing educators, researchers, and professionals. The association offers relevant career development, professional networking, and education opportunities.
80000 Members
Founded in 1947

7082 Association for Facilities Engineering
1000 Potomac Street NW
Suite 500
Washington, DC 20007

202-791-9080; Fax: 571-766-2142
grodriguez@afe.org
www.afe.org
Facebook, Twitter, LinkedIn, Instagram

Gabriella Rodriguez, Senior Manager, Membership
Joshua Watkins, Manager, Professional Development

Provides education, certification, technical information and other relevant information for plant and facility engineering operations and maintenance professionals worldwide.

7083 Association for Iron & Steel Technology (AIST)
186 Thorn Hill Rd
Warrendale, PA 15086-7528

724-814-3000; Fax: 724-814-3001
memberservices@aist.org
www.aist.org
Facebook, Twitter, LinkedIn, YouTube

George J. Koenig, President
Wendell L. Carter, First Vice President
Randy C. Skagen, Second Vice President
Joseph Dzierzawski, Treasurer
Ronald E. Ashburn, Secretary

The Association for Iron & Steel Technology (AIST) is an international technical association representing iron and steel producers, their allied suppliers and related academia. The association is dedicated to advancing the technical development, production, processing and application of iron and steel.
13800 Members
Founded in 2004

7084 Association for Women in Science
1667 K Street NW
Suite 800
Washington, DC 20006

202-588-8175
awis@awis.org
www.awis.org
Facebook, Twitter, LinkedIn

Bahija Jallal, President
Robert Powell, Secretary
Pamela Marrone, Treasurer
Janet Bandows Koster, Executive Director & CEO
Meredith Gibson, Chief Operations Officer

Provides support for female scientists and bioengineers. Also dedicated to achieving equity and full participation for women in science, mathematics, engineering and technology.
5000 Members
Founded in 1971
Mailing list available for rent

7085 Association for the Advancement of Cost Engineering
1265 Suncrest Towne Centre Drive
Suite 100
Morgantown, WV 26505-1876

304-296-8444
800-858-2678; Fax: 304-291-5728
info@aacei.org
web.aacei.org
Facebook, Twitter, LinkedIn

Ms Julie K Owen, President
Charity A. Golden, MBA CIA CCT, Executive Director

Penny Whoolery, Manager, Certification
Jennie Amos, Director
Amanda Bliss, Certification Administrator

Leading-edge society for cost estimators, cost engineers, schedulers project managers, and project control specialists.
7000 Members
Founded in 1956

7086 Association of Building Officials and Code Administrators
500 New Jersey Ave
6th Floor
Washington, DC 20001-2070

202-370-1800
888-422-7233; Fax: 202-783-2348
webmaster@iccsafe.org
www.iccsafe.org
Facebook, Twitter, LinkedIn

Dominic Sims, Chief Executive Officer
John Belcik, COO & CFO
Joan O'Neil, Chief Knowledge Officer
Mark Johnson, Executive Vice President

An independent nonprofit organization which conducts a voluntary program of evaluation of both traditional and innovative building materials, products and systems for compliance with BOCA National Codes.
14000 Members
Founded in 1994

7087 Association of Energy Engineers
3168 Mercer University Drive
Atlanta, GA 30341

770-447-5083
www.aeecenter.org

Lary Good, Dir., International Member Devel.
Stephen A. Roosa, Dir., Sustainable & Local Programs
Timothy B. Janos, Dir., Special Projects
Eric Oliver, Dir., Governmental Affairs
Albert Thumann, Executive Director

Promotes energy certification, management and education.
17500 Members
Founded in 1977

7088 Association of Environmental & Engineering Geologists
1100-H Brandywine Blvd.
Suite 575
Zanesville, OH 43701

303-757-2926
844-331-7867; Fax: 740-452-2552
aeg@aegweb.org
www.aegweb.org

Dale C. Andrews, President
Kathy Troost, Vice President
Kevin Richards, Treasurer
Cynthia Palomares, Secretary

Meets the professional needs of geologists who are applying their scientific training and experience to the broad field of civil and environmental engineering. Mission is to provide leadership in the development and application of geologic principles and knowledge to serve engineering, environmental and public needs.
Founded in 1957

7089 Association of Printing and Data Solutions Professionals
P.O. Box 13347
Chicago, IL 60613

708-218-7755
ed.avis@apdsp.org
www.apdsp.org
LinkedIn

Kyle Batsford, President
Camille Vieux, Vendor Director
Ed Avis, Managing Director
Michael Shaw, Director
Joe Williamson, Director

Represents entrepreneurial businesses serving the wide-format imaging needs of graphic arts, architectural, engineering, manufacturing, corporate, legal, retail, and POP industries.
Founded in 1927

7090 Association of State Dam Safety Officials
239 S. Limestone
Lexington, KY 40508

859-550-2788
info@damsafety.org
www.damsafety.org
Facebook, Twitter, LinkedIn, YouTube

Jim Pawloski, President
Jon Garton, Secretary
Roger Adams, P.E, Secretary
Jon Garton, Secretary
Dusty Myers, Treasurer

Provides outreach programs and a forum for the exchange of information to advance and improve the safety of dams.
Founded in 1983

7091 Association of Technology, Management, and Applied Engineering
3801 Lake Boone Trail
Suite 190
Raleigh, NC 27607

919-635-8335
admin@atmae.org
www.atmae.org
Facebook, Twitter, LinkedIn

Jim Thompson, Executive Director
Melissa Smith, Director of Programs
Caitlin Schwab-Falzone, Director of Accreditation

Provides support to all those involved in the industrial technology industry. Hosts trade shows and publishes various materials.
1000+ Members
Founded in 1967
Mailing list available for rent

7092 Audio Engineering Societyÿ
551 Fifth Ave.
Suite 1225
New York, NY 10176

212-661-8528; Fax: 212-682-0477
www.aes.org
Facebook, Twitter, LinkedIn, YouTube, Google+

Colleen Harper, Executive Director
Chris Plunkett, Director, Operations
Graham Kirk, Director, Sales & Marketing
Frank Wells, Director, Communications
Richard Cabot, Standards Manager

Worldwide professional association for professionals and students involved in the audio industry.

7093 Biomedical Engineering Society
8201 Corporate Dr
Suite 1125
Landover, MD 20785-2224

301-459-1999
877-871-2637; Fax: 301-459-2444
info@bmes.org
www.bmes.org
Facebook, Twitter, LinkedIn

Richard T. Hart, PhD, President
Edward L. Schilling, III, Executive Director
Doug Beizer, Communications Director
Michele Surricchio Ciapa, Education Director
Terry Young, BMES Career Connections Director

Supports all those involved in the biomedical engineering industry.
3800 Members
Founded in 1968

7094 Carnegie Mellon University: Information Networking Institute
Carnegie Mellon University
Electrical & Computer Engineering Department
4616 Henry Street
Pittsburgh, PA 15213

412-268-7195; Fax: 412-268-7196
ini@cmu.edu
www.ini.cmu.edu
Facebook, Twitter, LinkedIn, YouTube, Instagram, Google+, F

Dr. Dena Haritos Tsamitis, Director
Mike Niederberger, Business/Finance Administrator
Donald Shields, Director Development
Dean Haritos Tsamitis, Director Information Networking
Sean O'Leary, Manager

Focusing on professional degrees programs combining economics, technologies and global communication networks - information security policies.
Founded in 1989

7095 Cold Regions Research and Engineering Laboratory
US Army Corps of Engineers
72 Lyme Road
Hanover, NH 03755-1290

603-646-4100; Fax: 603-646-4278
info@crrel.usace.army.mil

James L Wuebben, PE, Director
Dr Mary Albert, Research Mechanical Engineer

The mission of this Laboratory is to understand the characteristics of the cold regions of the world and to apply this knowledge to make it easier for people to live and work in those regions. For example, CRREL engineers have conducted a long-term program on the correct design of roofs in heavy snowfall areas.

7096 Cold-Formed Steel Engineers Institute
25 Massachusetts Avenue, N.W.
Suite 800
Washington, DC 20001

202-263-4488
866-465-4732; Fax: 202-452-1039
info@cfsei.org
www.cfsei.org

Jennifer Zabik, P.E., S.E, Chairman
Robert Warr, P.E, Vice Chairman
Jennifer Zabik, Vice Chairman

Produces safe and efficient designs for commercial and residential structures with cold-formed steel.
Founded in 1849

7097 Construction Financial Management Association
100 Village Boulevard
Suite 200
Princeton, NJ 08540-5783

609-452-8000
888-421-9996; Fax: 609-452-0474
info@cfma.org
www.cfma.org
Facebook, Twitter, LinkedIn, YouTube

Stuart Binstock, President & CEO
Brian Summers, VP, Operations
Catherine Wasner, VP, Member Services
Samantha Lake, VP, Marketing
Stacey Scholl, Director, Finance

CFMA is the only organization dedicated to bringing together construction financial professionals and those partners serving their unique needs. CFMA has 98 chapters located throughout the US and Canada.
8600 Members
Founded in 1981

7098 **Construction Management Association of America**
7926 Jones Branch Drive
Suite 800
McLean, VA 22102-3303
703-356-2622; Fax: 703-356-6388
info@cmaanet.org
www.cmaanet.org
Facebook, Twitter, LinkedIn, YouTube
Rebecca Jones, Chair
Sandy Hamby, AIA, CCM, Vice Chair
Tim Murchison, JD, CCM, Vice Chair
Brian Ott, CCM, Vice Chair
Tim Murchison, JD, CCM, Vice Chair
A nonprofit and non-governmental professional association serving the construction management industry.
11000 Members
Founded in 1982

7099 **Construction Owners Association of America**
5000 Austell Powder Springs Road
Suite 217
Austell, GA 30106
770-433-0820
800-994-2622; Fax: 404-577-3551
coaa@coaa.org
www.coaa.org
Facebook, Twitter, LinkedIn
Howie Ferguson, Executive Director
Lucie Castro, Manager, Membership & Chapters
Jill McKenzie, Manager, Membership & Sponsorship
LaKaya Brittian-Quander, Manager, Meetings & Events
A national organization of public and private owners who manage facilities development and capital improvement projects.

7100 **Continental Automated Buildings Association (CABA)**
1173 Cyrville Road
Suite 210
Ottawa, Canada, ON K1J 7S6
613-686-1814
888-798-2222; Fax: 613-744-7833
caba@caba.org
www.caba.org
Facebook, Twitter, LinkedIn, YouTube
Ronald J Zimmer, President & CEO
Conrad McCallum, Communications Director
Greg Walker, Research Director
Andrew Glennie, Member Services Coordinator
Aruna Gamage, Financial Administrator
CABA is an international, non-profit industry organization that promotes advanced technologies in homes and buildings.
380+ Members
Founded in 1988

7101 **CorrConnecty̆**
GSG Inc
Home Page: www.gsgsystems.com
Joshua Bane, Project Manager
An online resource center for training modules on corrosion.
Founded in 2007

7102 **Council of Engineer and Scientific Specialty Board**
PO Box 1448
Annapolis, MD 21401-1448
410-266-3766; Fax: 410-721-1746
wanderson@cesb.org
www.cesb.org
William C Anderson PE DEE, Executive Director
Accredits engineering, science and technology certification programs from professional to technician certificates.
Founded in 1990
Mailing list available for rent

7103 **Electric Power Research Institute**
3420 Hillview Avenue
Palo Alto, CA 94304
650-855-2121
800-313-3774
askepri@epri.com
www.epri.com
Facebook, Twitter, LinkedIn
Michael W. Howard, President/CEO
Pamela J. Keefe, SVP/CFO/Treasurer
Salvador A. Casente, Jr., VP/General Counsel/CCO/Secretary
Arshad Mansoor, SVP, Research/Development
Michael A. Coleman, VP, IT/CIO
Nonprofit energy research consortium for the benefit of utility members, their customers and society. Mission is to provide science and technology-based solutions to its global energy customers by managing a far-reaching program of scientific research, technology development and product implementation.
660 Members
Founded in 1965

7104 **Engineering Workforce Commission**
1801 Alexander Bell Drive
Reston, VA 20191
202-296-2237
888-400-2237; Fax: 202-296-1151
dbateson@aaes.org
www.ewc-online.org
Dan Batson, Director
AAES's Engineering Workforce Commission monitors engineering job stats that help universities, corporations, and government set salary, hiring, enrollment, and degree trends in the marketplace. It publishes three major surveys per year that are regarded as the most accurate, objective and timely reports about the engineering workforce: Degrees, Enrollments, and Salaries.
35 Members
Founded in 1950

7105 **Environmental Information Association**
6935 Wisconsin Ave
Suite 306
Chevy Chase, MD 20815-6112
301-961-4999
888-343-4342; Fax: 301-961-3094
info@eia-usa.org
www.eia-usa.org
Kevin Cannan, President
Steve Fulford, Vice President
Brent Kynoch, Managing Director
Kim Goodman, Membership and Marketing Manager
Kelly Rutt, Development and Comm. Manager
Nonprofit organization dedicated to providing environmental information to individuals, members and industry. Disseminates information on the abatement of asbestos and lead-based paint, indoor air quality, safety and health issues, analytical issues and environmental site assessments.

7106 **Ergosyst Associates**
4840 W 15th Street
Suite 1012
Lawrence, KS 66049
785-842-7334; Fax: 785-842-7348
John Burch, Publisher
Association for those interested in economics/human factors.

7107 **Eta Kappa Nu**
445 Hoes Lane
Piscataway, NJ 08854
732-465-5846
800-406-2590
info@hkn.org
hkn.ieee.org
Edward Rezek, President
Eta Kappa Nu (HKN) is the electrical and computer engineering honor society of the Institute of Electrical and Electronics Engineers (IEEE).
Founded in 1904

7108 **Federation of Materials Societies**
910 17th St NW
Suite 800
Washington, DC 20006-2606
202-296-9282; Fax: 202-833-3014
Betsy Houston, Executive Director
Petr Vanysek, President
Promotes cooperation among societies concerned with the understanding, development and application of materials and processes.
700K Members
Founded in 1972

7109 **Geoprofessional Business Association (GBA)**
15800 Crabbs Branch Way
Suite 300
Rockville, MD 20855
301-565-2733
info@geoprofessional.org
www.geoprofessional.org
Facebook, Twitter, LinkedIn, YouTube, RSS, Vimeo
Not-for-profit trade association that supports all employees of engineering companies.
Founded in 1969

7110 **Global Association for Vision Information**
900 Victors Way
Suite 140
Ann Arbor, MI 48108
734-994-6088
www.visiononline.org
Facebook, Twitter, LinkedIn, YouTube
Jeff Burnstein, President
Alex Shikany, VP, Membership & Business
James Hamilton, Director, Sales
Robert Huschka, Director, Education Strategies
Bob McCurrach, Director, Standards Development
The AIA is dedicated to vision and imaging technologies, with members including manufacturers of vision components and systems, system integrators, distributors, OEMs, end users, consulting firms, academic institutions, and research groups.
380+ Members
Founded in 1984

7111 **ICC Evaluation Service**
3060 Saturn Street
Suite 100
Whittier, CA 92821
562-699-0541
800-423-6587; Fax: 562-695-4694
es@icc-es.org

www.iccsafe.org
Facebook, Twitter, LinkedIn

Dominic Sims, Chief Executive Officer
John Belcik, COO & CFO
Joan O'Neil, Chief Knowledge Officer
Mark Johnson, Executive Vice President

An independent, nonprofit organization that conducts a voluntary program of evaluation of both traditional and innovative building materials, products and systems for compliance with the three major model codes in the United States.
Founded in 2003

7112 **IEEE Circuits and Systems Society**
Institute Of Electrical and Electronics Engineers
445 Hoes Lane
Piscataway, NJ 08854

Home Page: www.ieee-cas.org
Facebook, Twitter, LinkedIn

Amara Amara, President
Yoshifumi Nishio, VP, Membership
Myung Hoon Sunwoo, VP, Conferences
Guoxing Wang, VP, Financial Activities
Mohammad Sawan, VP, Publications

CASS fosters interdisciplinary and cross-disciplinary cooperation with regards to using circuits and systems to address humanity's greatest challenges.

7113 **IEEE Computational Intelligence Society**
445 Hoes Lane
Piscataway, NJ 08855

732-465-5892; Fax: 732-465-6435
cis-info@ieee.org
cis.ieee.org
Facebook, Twitter, LinkedIn

Bernadette Bouchon-Meunier, President
Pablo Estevez, VP, Finance
Marley Vellasco, VP, Conferences
James Keller, VP, Publications
Carlos Coello Coello, VP, Member Activities

The CIS seeks to advance computational intelligence in science and engineering.

7114 **IEEE Control Systems Society**
445 Hoes Lane
Piscataway, NJ 08854-1331

Home Page: ieeecss.org
Facebook, Twitter, LinkedIn

Anuradha Annaswamy, President
Jorge Cortes, Director, Operations

Subsidiary of the Institute of Electrical and Electronics Engineers dedicated to control system technology.

7115 **IEEE Industrial Electronics Society**
Institute Of Electrical and Electronics Engineers
445 Hoes Lane
Piscataway, NJ 08854

804-827-3999
president@ieee-ies.org
www.ieee-ies.org
Facebook, Twitter, LinkedIn, YouTube

Terry Martin, President
Thilo Sauter, VP, Publications
Juan Rodriguez-Andina, VP, Conference Activities
Kiyoshi Ohishi, VP, Workshops & Activities
Yousef Ibrahim, VP, Membership Activities

Conducts, through its members, range of technical activities dedicated to applying electronics and electrical sciences in an industrial setting, including current developments in intelligent and computer control systems, robotics, factory communications and automation, flexible manufacturing, data acquisition and signal processing, vision systems, and power electronics.

7116 **IEEE Industry Applications Society**
Institute Of Electrical and Electronics Engineers
445 Hoes Lane
Piscataway, NJ 08854

732-562-2663
p.mccarren@ieee.org
ias.ieee.org
Facebook, Twitter, LinkedIn

Patrick McCarren, Executive Director
Lynda Bernstein, IAS Program Specialist

Seeks to link theory and practice by advancing science and technology in the electrical and electronic systems.

7117 **IEEE Intelligent Transportation Systems Society**
Institute Of Electrical and Electronics Engineers
445 Hoes Lane
Piscataway, NJ 08854

Home Page: www.ieee-itss.org
Facebook, Twitter, LinkedIn

Wei-Bin Zhang, President
Lingxi Li, VP, Administrative Activities
Nobuyuki Ozaki, VP, Standards
Javier Sanchez Medina, VP, Technical Activities

ITSS seeks to advance electrical engineering & information technology as applied to intelligent transportation systems.

7118 **IEEE Robotics and Automation Society**
445 Hoes Lane
Piscataway, NJ

732-562-3906
ras@ieee.org
www.ieee-ras.org
Facebook, Twitter, LinkedIn, YouTube

Kathy Colabaugh, Society Operations Manager
Amy Reeder, Society Program Specialist
Alexis Simoes, Society Program Coordinator

A scientific, literary and educational society of the Institute of Electrical and Electronics Engineers, seeking to facilitate scientific and technological knowledge exchange in robotics and automation.

7119 **IEEE Signal Processing Society**
Institute of Electrical and Electronics Engineers
445 Hoes Lane
Piscataway, NJ 08854

732-562-3888; Fax: 732-867-9953
sp-info@ieee.org
signalprocessingsociety.org
Facebook, Twitter, LinkedIn

Rich Baseil, Executive Director
Theresa Argiropoulos, Senior Manager, Operations
Caroline Johnson, Senior Manager, Conference Services
William Colacchio, Senior Manager, Publications
Jessica Perry, Member Communications Specialist

The SPS looks to provide current scientific information and resources on signal processing, while educating professionals in the industry, and providing a venue for networking.

7120 **IEEE Society on Social Implications of Technology**
Institute of Electrical and Electronics Engineers
445 Hoes Lane
Piscataway, NJ 08854

r.dent@ieee.org
technologyandsociety.org
Facebook, Twitter, LinkedIn

Robert Dent, President
Lew Terman, Secretary
Howard Wolfman, Treasurer

The SSIT focuses on the following areas: Sustainable Development & Humanitarian Technology; Ethics, Human Values and Technology; Technology Benefits for All; Future Societal Impact of Technology Advances; and Protecting the Planet & Sustainable Technology

7121 **IEEE Solid-State Circuits Society**
Institute of Electrical and Electronics Engineers
445 Hoes Lane
Piscataway, NJ 08854

m.p.kelly@ieee.org
sscs.ieee.org
Facebook, Twitter, LinkedIn

Adam Greenberg, Executive Director
Lauren Caruso, Administrator
Abira Altvater, Technical Program Specialist
Danielle Marinese, Society Administrator

The SSCS serves members by providing them with education, communication, recognition, leadership opportunities, and networking opportunities.

7122 **IEEE Systems, Man, and Cybernetics Society**
Institute of Electrical and Electronics Engineers
445 Hoes Lane
Piscataway, NJ 08854

Home Page: www.ieeesmc.org
Facebook, Twitter, LinkedIn, Instagram

Imre Rudas, President
Sam Kwong, VP, Cybernetics
Andreas Nuernberger, VP, Conferences & Meetings
Adrian Stoica, VP, Systems Science & Engineering
Vladimir Marik, VP, Organization & Planning

Promotes all aspects of systems science and engineering, human-machine systems, and cybernetics, through conferences, publications, and other activities.

7123 **IEEE Technology & Engineering Management Society**
Institute of Electrical and Electronics Engineers
445 Hoes Lane
Piscataway, NJ 08854

Home Page: www.ieee-tems.org
Facebook, Twitter, LinkedIn

Andy Chen, President
Richard Evans, VP, Technical Activities
Sudeendra Koushik, VP, Conferences

Formerly the Engineering Management Society and the Technology Management Council, TEMS seeks to provide members with essential management and leadership knowledge and skills.
Founded in 1951

7124 **IEEE Vehicular Technology Society**
3 Parl Avenue
17th Floor
New York, NY 10016-5997

212-419-7900
oliver.holland@ieee.org

vtsociety.org
Facebook, Twitter, LinkedIn

Oliver Holland, Chapter Coordinator & Developer

VTS focuses on the theory and practice of electrical engineering with regards to land transportation, railroad and mass transit, mobile communications, vehicular electrotechnology equipment and systems, and land, airborne and maritime mobile Services.

7125 Illuminating Engineering Society of North America

120 Wall Street
17th Floor
New York, NY 10005

212-248-5000; Fax: 212-248-5018
ies@ies.org
www.ies.org

Clayton Gordon, Marketing Manager
Nicole DeGirolamo, Executive Assistant
Samuel Fontanez, Senior Art Director
Robert Horner, Director of Public Policy
Samantha Schwirck, Senior Associate Editor, LD+A

To advance knowledge and disseminate information for the improvement of the lighted environment to the benefit of society. Publishes a monthly magazine; Lighting Design & Applications.
7000 Members
Founded in 1906

7126 Industrial Designers Society of America

555 Grove St.
Suite 200
Herndon, VA 20170

703-707-6000; Fax: 703-787-8501
idsa@idsa.org
www.idsa.org
Facebook, Twitter, LinkedIn, Pinterest, Vimeo Flickr

John Barratt, Chairman
Daniel Martinage, CAE, Executive Director
Karen Berube, Senior Creative Director
Lisa Brenner, CPA, Director of Finance & Accounting
Jordan Fleger, Member Relations Coordinator

The IDSA is the world's oldest, largest, member-driven society for product design, industrial design, interaction designs, human factors, ergonomics, design research, design management, university design and related fields.

7127 Industrial Fabrics Association International

1801 County Road B W
Roseville, MN 55113-4061

651-222-2508
800-225-4324; Fax: 651-631-9334
generalinfo@ifai.com
www.ifai.com
Facebook, Twitter, LinkedIn, YouTube

Steve Schiffman, President & CEO
Cheria Schmit, Executive Assistant
Sheila Sumner, VP, Finance & Administration
Amy Collins, Director, Sales & Marketing
Linden Wicklund, Director, Events & Member Programs

A not-for-profit trade association whose member companies represent the international specialty fabrics marketplace, who facilitates the development, application and promotion of products manufactures by the diverse membership.
2000 Members

7128 Industrial Research Institute

2200 Clarendon Boulevard
Suite 1102
Arlington, VA 22201

703-647-2580; Fax: 703-647-2581
www.iriweb.org

Tom Kavassalis, Chairman
Edward Bernstein, President
Ana Escobar, Associate, Executive & Publications
Lee Green, Vice President, Knowledge Creation
Pamela R. Hanner, Manager, Web & IT

The mission is to enhance the effectiveness of technological innovation industry.
200 Members
Founded in 1938

7129 Institute of Biological Engineering

3493 Lansdowne Drive
Suite 2
Lexington, KE 40517

859-977-7450; Fax: 859-271-0607
info@ibe.org
www.ibe.org
Facebook, LinkedIn

Jeong Yeol Yoon, President
Prem Parajuli, Secretary
Melanie Correll, Treasurer

A nonprofit professional organization which encourages inquiry and interest in the field of biological engineering.

7130 Institute of Electrical and Electronics Engineers

3 Park Ave.
17th Fl.
New York, NY 10016-5997

212-419-7900; Fax: 212-752-4929
www.ieee.org
Facebook, Twitter, LinkedIn, YouTube, Instagram

Toshio Fukuda, President & CEO
Stephen Welby, Executive Director & COO

Supports all those involved in the field of electrical engineering, and works to nurture technological innovation and excellence for the benefit of humanity.
422K Members
Founded in 1963

7131 Institute of Industrial Engineers

3577 Parkway Lane
Suite 200
Norcross, GA 30092

770-449-0460
800-494-0460; Fax: 770-441-3295
cs@iienet.org
Facebook, Twitter, LinkedIn, YouTube, Google+

Don Greene, CEO
Donna Calvert, COO
Nancy LaJoice, Director of Membership
Pam Patterson, Membership Administrator
Elaine Schwartz, Membership Administrator

Supports all industrial engineers with training, education, publications, conferences, etc.
15000 Members
Founded in 1948

7132 Institute of Noise Control Engineering

12100 Sunset Hills Rd.
Suite 130
Reston, VA 20190

703-234-4073; Fax: 703-435-4390
ibo@inceusa.org
www.inceusa.org

Gordon Ebbitt, President
Joseph M. Cuschieri, Executive Director
George C. Maling, Jr., Managing Director Emeritus
Deane Jaeger, Treasurer
Karl B. Washburn, Secretary

Supports those involved with hearing protection, modal analysis, and signal processing.
1200 Members

7133 Institute of Transportation Engineers

1627 Eye Street, NW
Suite 600
Washington, DC 20006

202-785-0060; Fax: 202-785-0609
ite_staff@ite.org
www.ite.org
Facebook, Twitter, LinkedIn, YouTube, Instagram, Google+

W. Hibbett Neel, International President
John J Kennedy, International Vice President
Zaki Mustafa, Immediate Past President
Colleen L Hill-Stramsak, International Director
Dean J Kaiser, International Director

An international educational and scientific association of transportation professionals who are responsible for meeting mobility and safety needs.
13199 Members
Founded in 1930

7134 Institution of Engineering and Technology

379 Thornall Street
Edison, NJ 08837

732-321-5575
ietusa@theiet.org
theiet.org
Facebook, Twitter, LinkedIn, Instagram, Pinterest, YouTube

Nigel Fine, Chief Executive & Secretary
Michelle Richmond, MBE, Director of Membership
Ed Almond, Director of Finance and Planning
Richard Best, Director of IT & Digital Services

To inspire, inform and influence the global engineering community, supporting technology innovation to meet the needs of society.
9000+ Members
Founded in 2006

7135 Instrument Society of America

67 T.W. Alexander Drive
PO Box 12277
Research Triangle Park, NC 27709

919-549-8411; Fax: 919-549-8288
info@isa.org
www.isa.org
Facebook, Twitter, LinkedIn, YouTube, Flickr, Google+

Richard W. Roop, President
Michelle Anderson, Human Resources Manager
Eugenia Bell, Production Coordinator
Patrick J Gouhin, Executive Director/CEO
James W Keaveney, Treasurer

A nonprofit technical society for engineers, technicians, businesspeople, educators and students who work, study or are interested in industrial automation and pursuits related to it, such as instrumentation.
30000 Members
Founded in 1945

7136 Instrumentation and Measurement Society

799 N Beverly Glen
Los Angeles, CA 90077

310-446-8280; Fax: 732-981-0225
bob.myers@ieee.org
http://sites.ieee.org/

Michael P. Kelly, Executive Director
Donna Florek, Program Specialist

Michael Markowycz, Program Specialist
Jo-Ellen Snyder, Tech Community Program Specialist
Grant Pitel, Volunteer PELS Webmaster

A subsidiary of the Institute of Electrical and Electronics Engineers. Provides support to scientists and technicians who design and develop electrical and electronic measuring instruments and equipment.

6500 Members
Founded in 1950

7137 **Insulated Cable Engineers Association**
PO Box 2694
Alpharetta, GA 30023

770-830-0369
info@icea.net
www.icea.net

Professional organization dedicated to developing cable standards for the electric power, control and telecommunications industries. Ensures safe, economical and efficient cable systems utilizing proven, state-of-the-art materials and concepts. ICEA documents are of interest to cable manufacturers, architects and engineers, utility and manufacturing plant personnel, telecommunication engineers, consultants and OEMs.

Founded in 1925

7138 **International Association for Radio, Telec ommunications and Electromagnets**
600 N. PLANKINTON AVE
Suite 301
Milwaukee, WI 53201

888-722-2440
888-722-2440; Fax: 414-765-8661
info@exemplarglobal.org
Facebook, Twitter, LinkedIn, YouTube, Google+

Peter Holtmann, President & Chief Executive Officer
Sal Agnello, General Manager, iNARTE

A worldwide, nonprofit, professional association which certifies qualified engineers and technicians in the fields of Telecommunications, Electromagnetic Compatibility/Interference (EMC/EMI), Product Safety (PS), Electrostatic Discharge control (ESD) and Wireless Systems Installation.

7139 **International Facility Management Association**
800 Gessner Rd.
Ste. 900
Houston, TX 77024-4257

713-623-4362; Fax: 713-623-6124
ifma@ifma.org
www.ifma.org
Facebook, Twitter, LinkedIn, YouTube, Flickr, RSS

Michael D. Feldman, FMP, CM, Chair
Maureen Ehrenberg, FRICS, CRE, First Vice Chair
Tony Keane, CAE, President/CEO
John Perry, Chief Operating Officer
Aaron Clark, Vice President, Corporate Services

International association for facility management professionals.

22659 Members
Founded in 1978

7140 **International Society Weighing/Measurement**
13017 Wisteria Drive
#341
Germantown, MD 20874

240-753-4397; Fax: 866-285-3512
staff@iswm.org
www.iswm.org

James Baxter, President
Jerry Finnegan, Vice President
Jamie Notter, Executive Director

Supports all those involved in the weighing and measurement industry.

7141 **International Society for Optical Engineering**
1000 20th Street
P O Box 10
Bellingham, WA 98225-6705

360-676-3290
888-504-8171; Fax: 360-647-1445
spie@spie.org
www.spie.org
Facebook, Twitter, LinkedIn, RSS, YouTube, Blogspot

Katerina Svanberg, President
William Arnold, Vice President
Brian Lula, Ssecretary/Treasurer
Eugene Arthurs, CEO

Serves the international, technical community as the premier provider of education, information, and resources covering optics, photonics, and their applications.

16000 Members
Founded in 1955

7142 **Investigative Engineers Association**
10001 W Oakland Park Blvd.
Suite 301
Sunrise, FL 33351

954-530-0715
844-217-6975; Fax: 954-537-4942
jhogge@ienga.net
www.ienga.net
Facebook, Twitter, LinkedIn

Lewis W Ernest, Advisor
James R Hogge, CEO
Tom Hogge, President
Nancy Pashkoff, Marketing Director
Tammy Lane, National Director

Consists of independent forensic engineering firms nationwide and abroad.

7143 **Materials Research Society**
506 Keystone Dr
Warrendale, PA 15086-7573

724-779-3003; Fax: 724-779-8313
info@mrs.org
www.mrs.org

Oliver Kraft, President
Kristi S. Anseth, Vice President
Sean J. Hearne, Secretary
Michael R. Fitzsimmons, Treasurer
Todd M. Osman, Executive Director

The Materials Research Society is a not-for-profit organization that brings together scientists, engineers and research managers from industry, government, academia and research laboratories to share findings in the research and development of new materials of technological importance. The Materials Research Society promotes communication for the advancement of interdisciplinary materials research to improve the quality of life.

16000 Members
Founded in 1973

7144 **Measurement, Control & Automation Association**
200 City Hall Avenue
Suite D
Poquoson, VA 23662

757-258-3100
automationassociation.com
Facebook, Twitter, LinkedIn, YouTube

Teresa Sebring, President
Andrea Ambrose, Director, Member Relations
Elizabeth Horton, Programs Manager
Kim Malina, Marketing Communications Manager
Rebecca Moore, Administrative Manager

The MCAA is the national trade association for manufacturers and distributors of instrumentation, systems, and software products for industrial process control and factory automation.

Founded in 1944

7145 **Motion Control & Motor Association**
900 Victors Way
Suite 140
Ann Arbor, MI 48108

734-994-6088
info@motioncontrolonline.org
www.motioncontrolonline.org
Facebook, Twitter, LinkedIn, YouTube

Matt French, Chair
Gunnar Block, Vice Chair
Paul Horvat, Vice Chair

The MCMA seeks to advance motion control and related automation technologies, and to help members and the industry grow.

Founded in 2006

7146 **NACE International**
1440 S Creek Drive
Houston, TX 77084-4906

281-228-6200
800-797-6223; Fax: 281-228-6300
firstservice@nace.org
www.nace.org
Facebook, Twitter, LinkedIn, YouTube, Google+, Instagram

Jim Feather, President
A. I. Sandy Williamson, Vice President
D. Terry Greenfield, Treasurer
Bob Chalker, CEO

Advances the knowledge of corrosion engineering and science in all major industries through education, certification, standards, publications, and public awareness.

21000 Members
Founded in 1943

7147 **National Academy of Engineering**
500 5th Street NW
Washington, DC 20001

202-334-3200; Fax: 202-334-2290
www.nae.edu
Twitter, LinkedIn, YouTube

C. D. Mote, Jr., President
Alton D. Romig, Jr., Executive Officer
Mary Lee Berger-Hughes, Membership Director
Joan Zaorski, Director of Finance
Randy Atkins, Senior Program Officer

Promotes public understanding of the role that engineering plays in the technical fields. Sponsors programs aimed at meeting national needs in the field. Encourages research.

2000 Members
Founded in 1964

7148 **National Association of Fire Equipment Distributors**
180 N. Wabash Avenue
Suite 401
Chicago, IL 60601

312-461-9600; Fax: 312-461-0777
dharris@nafed.org
www.nafed.org
LinkedIn, YouTube

Ed Hugill, President
Danny Harris, Executive Director/CEO
Norbert Makowka, Vice President, Technical
Tamara Matthews, Communications Manager
Socorro Garcia, Office Manager

Improves the economic environment, business performance, and technical competence in the fire protection industry.
Founded in 1963

7149 **National Association of Minority Engineers**
701 West Stadium Ave.
Suite 130
West Lafayette, IN 47907

765-494-4936; Fax: 407-629-2502
namepa@namepa.org
www.namepa.org

Virginia Booth Womack, President and Executive Director
Darryl A. Dickerson, Treasurer
Alaine M. Allen, Secretary
Jahi Sauk Simbai, Treasurer
Ivan Favila, Secretary

Provides a communication network among college-level administrators of minority engineering programs.
575 Members

7150 **National Board of Boiler and Pressure Vessel Inspectors**
1055 Crupper Ave
Columbus, OH 43229-1108

614-888-8320; Fax: 614-888-0750
information@nationalboard.org
www.nationalboard.org

Don Tanner, Executive Director
Connie Homer, Senior Executive Secretary

Membership is composed of chief boiler inspectors of states, major US cities and Canadian provinces having boiler laws.
55 Members
Founded in 1919

7151 **National Council of Examiners for Engineering and Surveying**
280 Seneca Creek Road
Seneca, SC 29678

864-654-6824
800-250-3196; Fax: 864-654-6033
www.ncees.org
Facebook, Twitter, LinkedIn, YouTube, RSS, Google+

Michael Conzett, P.E., President
Jerry Carter, Chief Executive Officer
Davy McDowell, P.E., Chief Operating Officer
Tim Miller, P.E., Director of Exam Services
Donna Moss, SHRM-CP, PHR, Director of Human Resources

Promotes uniform standards of registration and coordinates interstate registration of engineers and surveyors.
68 Members
Founded in 1920

7152 **National Electrical Contractors Association**
3 Bethesda Metro Center
Suite 1100
Bethesda, MD 20814

301-657-3110; Fax: 301-215-4500
www.necanet.org
Facebook, Twitter, LinkedIn, YouTube, Flickr

A trade association in the United States that represents the electrical industry.
Founded in 1901

7153 **National Environmental Balancing Bureau**
8575 Grovemont Cir
Gaithersburg, MD 20877-4121

301-977-3698
866-497-4447; Fax: 301-977-9589
www.nebb.org

Tiffany Suite, Executive Vice President
Christina Spence, Office & Scheduling Coordinator
Sumayyah Milstein, Firm Certification Coordinator

NEBB is an international certification association for firms that deliver high performance building systems. Members perform testing, adjusting and balancing (TAB) of heating, ventilating and air-conditioning systems, commission and retro-commission building systems commissioning, execute sound and vibration testing, and test and certify lab fume hoods and electronic and bio clean rooms. NEBB holds the highest standards in certification.
Founded in 1971

7154 **National Fire Protection Association**
1 Batterymarch Park
Quincy, MA 02169-7471

617-770-3000
800-844-6058; Fax: 617-770-0700
www.nfpa.org
Facebook, Twitter, LinkedIn, YouTube, Flickr, Google+

Ernest J Grant, Chair
Randolph W Tucker, First Vice Chair
Jim Pauley, President/ CEO
Julie Lynch, Vice President, Talent & Culture
Bruce H. Mullen, Executive Vice President and CFO

Publishes fire and building safety standards including the NationalElectrical Code.
Founded in 1896

7155 **National Institute for Certification in Technologies**
1420 King St
Alexandria, VA 22314-2750

703-548-1518
888-476-4238; Fax: 703-682-2756
certify@nicet.org
www.nicet.org
Facebook, LinkedIn

Greg Cagle, SET, Chair
Thomas J. Frericks, Jr., CT, Vice-Chair
Michael A. Clark, Chief Operating Executive
Regina L. Stevenson, Director, Administrative Services
Gloria Mathson, Manager, General Services

Issues certification to engineering technicians and technologists who voluntarily apply for certification and satisfy competency criteria through examinations and verification of work experience.
113K Members
Founded in 1961

7156 **National Society of Black Engineers**
205 Daingerfield Road
Alexandria, VA 22314

703-549-2207; Fax: 703-683-5312
info@nsbe.org
www.nsbe.org
Facebook, Twitter, LinkedIn, Pinterest, Google+

Neville Green, National Chair
Candice M Dixon, Vice Chairperson
Justin Brown, National Parliamentarian
Jennifer Jasper, National Secretary
Carl Mack, Executive Director

Supports all black technical professionals involved in the manufacturing engineering industry.
15000 Members
Founded in 1971

7157 **National Society of Professional Engineers**
1420 King St
Alexandria, VA 22314-2794

703-684-2800; Fax: 703-836-4875
www.nspe.org
Facebook, Twitter, LinkedIn

Tim Austin, P.E., F.NSPE, President
Thomas C. Roberts, P.E., F.NSPE, Vice President
Julia M. Harrod, P.E., F.NSPE, Treasurer
Mark Golden, FASAE, CAE, Executive Director and Secretary

The mission of the Society is to promote the ethical, competent and licensed practice of engineering and to enhance the professional, social and economic well-being of its members.
60000 Members
Founded in 1934

7158 **North American Die Casting Association**
3250 N. Arlington Heights Rd
Ste 101
Arlington Heights, IL 60004

847-279-0001; Fax: 847-279-0002
nadca@diecasting.org
www.diecasting.org

Daniel Twarog, President

The organization serves as the voice of the industry, promoting growth and enhancing member's ability to compete domestically in the global marketplace.
3700 Members
Founded in 1989

7159 **North American Manufacturing Research Institute**
1 SME Drive
Dearborn, MI 48128

313-425-3000
800-733-4763; Fax: 313-425-3400
service@sme.org
www.sme.org
Facebook, Twitter, LinkedIn, Google+, RSS

Wayne F. Frost, President
Jeffrey M. Krause, Chief Executive Officer
Kathleen Borgula, Human Resources
Erica Ciupak, Information Technology
Julie Duff, Finance

Members are engaged in manufacturing, research and technology development.
180 Members
Founded in 1973

7160 **Order Of The Engineer**
PO Box 25473
Scottsdale, AZ 85255-0107

866-364-7464; Fax: 480-585-6418
orderofeng@gmail.com
www.order-of-the-engineer.org

Paula Ostaff, Executive Director

An association for graduate and professional engineers in the United States that emphasizes pride and responsibility in the engineering profession.

7161 **Pi Tau Sigma**
Home Page: www.pitausigma.net

Dr. Mun Young Choi, President
Dr. Gloria J Wiens, Eastern Region Vice-President
Dr. Alex Moutsoglou, National Secretary-Treasurer
Dr. Chris Wilson, Central Region Vice-President
Dr. Darryl James, Western Region Vice-President

An International Mechanical Engineering Honor Society.
Founded in 1947

7162 **Professional Engineers in Private Practice**
1420 King Street
Alexandria, VA 22314-2750

703-684-2800; Fax: 703-836-4875
www.nspe.org
Facebook, Twitter, LinkedIn

Terrance N Glunt, Chair
Larry L Britt, PE, Chair-Elect
Steve M Theno, PE, Secretary

Addresses the concerns of individual engineers in private practice, primarily working in design for construction. Offers resources, standard contracts, newsletters and management guidance in the forms of videos, books, and newsletters.
24M Members
Founded in 1956

7163 **Railway Engineering: Maintenance Suppliers Association**
500 New Jersey Ave. NW
Suite 400
Washington, DC 20001

202-715-2921; Fax: 202-204-5753
info@remsa.org
www.remsa.org

Trent Marshall, President
Bruce R. Wise, Vice President
Alan D. Reynolds, Secretary/Treasurer
David Tennent, Executive Director, REMSA
C. David Soule, CEM, Director of Trade Shows, REMSA

Members are distributors and manufacturers of railway machinery supplies and services.
225 Members
Founded in 1965

7164 **Refrigeration Service Engineers Society**
1911 Rohlwing Road
Suite A
Rolling Meadows, IL 60008-1397

847-297-6464
800-297-5660; Fax: 847-297-5038
general@rses.org
www.rses.org
Facebook, Twitter, LinkedIn, RSS

Michael Ralton, International President
Raymond Clary, International Vice President

A leading education, training and certification association for heating, ventilation, air conditioning and refrigeration professionals. RSES credentials include the SM/CM/CMS exam series as well as one of the largest EPA Section 608 certification programs in the industry.
15231 Members
Founded in 1933

7165 **Reliability Engineering and Management Institute**
1077 N Highland
Tucson, AZ 85721

520-626-8324; Fax: 520-621-8191
dimitri@u.arizona.edu
www.u.arizona.edu

Michele Norin, VP for IT/CIO
Christian Schreiber, Chief Information Security Officer
Derek Masseth, Deputy Chief Info Officer/CTO
Thomas C Bourgeois, Executive Director
Kay Stevens Beasock, Director, Communications/Marketing

Supports all engineers and managers who deal with the issue of Reliability Engineering. Provides publications, training, education, new techniques and product forums and two annual conference.
Founded in 1963
Mailing list available for rent: 44000 names

7166 **Research Council on Structural Connections**
Sargent & Lundy
55 E Monroe Street
Chicago, IL 60603-5780

312-269-2000; Fax: 312-269-3681
rshaw@steelstructures.com
www.boltcouncil.org

Ray Tide, Chairman Executive Committee
Geoff Kulak, Vice Chairman
Charles Carter, Chairman Membership/Funding
Emile Troup, Secretary/Treasurer

Researches the effects of stress on bolted and riveted joints for its member companies and institutions.
45 Members
Founded in 1946

7167 **Robotic Industries Association**
900 Victors Way
Suite 140
Ann Arbor, MI 48108

734-994-6088; Fax: 734-994-3338
info@robotics.org
www.robotics.org
Facebook, Twitter, LinkedIn, YouTube

Jeff Burnstein, President
Dana Whalls, Vice President, A3
Clarissa Carvalho, Marketing Specialist
James Hamilton, Sales Director
Bob Doyle, Vice President

Trade group serving the robotics industry. Members include robot manufacturers, users, system integrators, component suppliers, research groups, and consulting firms. The Robotic Industries Association offers educational resources, events and news for its members.
Founded in 1974
Mailing list available for rent

7168 **Sigma Phi Delta**
3010 Saint Joseph Drive
Mansfield, TX 76063

214-686-2240
execsecr@sigmaphidelta.org
www.sigmaphidelta.org
Facebook, Twitter, LinkedIn

Alixandre R. Minden PE, PMP, Grand President
Eric J. Pew, Grand VP
Tyler S. Condon, Treasurer
Seth F. Huy, Director of Alumni Relations
Aaren Salido, Director of Chapter Development

A professional and social fraternity in engineering.
10420 Members
Founded in 1924

7169 **Society for Experimental Mechanics**
7 School St
Bethel, CT 06801-1855

203-790-6373; Fax: 203-790-4472
sem@sem1.com
www.sem.org
Facebook, Twitter, YouTube

Peter Ifgu, President
Emmanuel Gdoutos, Vice President
Jon Rogers, Treasurer
Tom Proulx, Executive Director

Supports all those involved with general experimental mechanics and the measurement of stresses and strains in metals and other materials.
Founded in 1943

7170 **Society for the Advancement of Material and Process Engineering**
21680 Gateway Center Drive
Suite 300
Diamond Bar, CA 91765-2454

626-521-9460
info@sampe.org
www.nasampe.org
Facebook, Twitter, LinkedIn

Gregg Balko, CEO
Mike Keilty, Director of Finance
Dr. Scott Beckwith, Technical Director/Journal Editor

An international professional member society, provides information on new materials and processing technology either via technical forums, journal publications, or books in which professionals in this field can exchange ideas and air their views.
Founded in 1944

7171 **Society of Allied Weight Engineers**
5734 E. Lucia Walk
Long Beach, CA 90803-4015

562-596-2873; Fax: 562-596-2874
exdirector@sawe.org
www.sawe.org

Anthony Primozich, President
Robert Hundl, Executive VP
Rick Watkins, Senior VP
Jerry L. Pierson, VP Training
Ronald Fox, Executive Director

Consists of engineers in the aerospace, shipbuilding, land vehicles, offshore and allied industries.
800 Members
Founded in 1941

7172 **Society of American Military Engineers**
607 Prince St
Alexandria, VA 22314-3117

703-549-3800
800-336-3097; Fax: 703-684-0231
webmanager@same.org
www.same.org

Jane C. Penny, President
Col. Kurt Ubbelohde, F.SAME, Vice President
Gen. Joseph Schroedel, P.E.,, Executive Director
Desyre, Jones, Senior Operations & Admin Manager
Belle Febbraro, Program Manager

Brings together professional engineers and those in engineering related fields to improve and increase the engineering capabilities of the nation and to exchange and advance the knowledge of

engineering technologies, applications and practices.
20000 Members
Founded in 1920

7173 **Society of Automotive Engineers**
1200 G St., NW
Suite 800
Washington, DC 20005

202-463-7318; Fax: 202-463-7319
www.sae.org
Facebook, Twitter, LinkedIn, Google+

Frank Menchaca, Chief Product Officer
Dana M Pless, Chief Financial Officer
David L Schutt, Chief Executive Officer
George Bradley, Esq., General Counsel
Sandra L. Dillner, Director of Human Resources

Advances mobility in land, sea, air, and space.
Founded in 1905

7174 **Society of Broadcast Engineers**
9102 North Meridian Street
Suite 150
Indianapolis, IN 46260

317-846-9000
www.sbe.org
Facebook, Twitter, LinkedIn, YouTube, Blogger

John Poray, Executive Director
Chris Scherer, Member Communications Director
Cathy Orosz, Education Director
Megan Clappe, Certification Director
Debbie Hennessey, Sustaining Member Manager

A professional organization for engineers in broadcast radio and television.
5500 Members

7175 **Society of Fire Protection Engineers**
9711 Washingtonian Blvd
Suite 380
Gaithersburg, MD 20878

301-718-2910; Fax: 240-328-6225
foundation@sfpe.org
www.sfpe.org
Facebook, Twitter, LinkedIn, YouTube, RSS

Michael Madden, P.E., FSFPE, President
Milosh Puchovsky, P.E., FSFPE, President Elect
Jack Poole, P.E., FSFPE, Secretary-Treasurer
Nicole Testa Boston, CAE, Ex-Officio
David Barber, Director

The largest professional society for fire safety engineers.
4500 Members
Founded in 1971

7176 **Society of Hispanic Professional Engineers**

323-725-3970
703-373-7930
shpenational@shpe.org
shpe.org
Facebook, Twitter, LinkedIn, YouTube, Instagram

Barry Cordero, Chair
Miguel Alemany, Vice Chair
Yuliana Porras Mendoza, Secretary
Ernesto Felix, Treasurer
Rodrigo T. Garcia, President

A national organization of professional engineers to serve as rolemodels in the Hispanic community.
Founded in 1974

7177 **Society of Manufacturing Engineers**
1000 Town Center
Suite 1910
Southfield, MI 48075

313-425-3000
service@sme.org
www.sme.org
Facebook, Twitter, LinkedIn, YouTube, Google+, Instagram

Sandra L. Bouckley, Executive Director & CEO
Craig Connop, Chief Financial Officer
Steve Prahalis, Chief Operating Officer
Erica Ciupak, Information Technology
Debbie Clark, Governance

The organization serves its members and others in the international manufacturing community by identifying, evaluating and explaining the adoption and integration of emerging information technologies to create business value.
65K Members
Founded in 1932

7178 **Society of Naval Architects and Marine Engineers**
99 Canal Center Plaza
Suite 310
Alexandria, VA 22314

703-997-6701; Fax: 703-997-6702
www.sname.org

Valerie Hutnan, Executive Director
Kathy Hartness, VP, Events & Membership
Michael Ashman, Director, Finance
Frederick Ashcroft, Director, Technology & Education
Thais De Oliveira, Coord., Marketing & Social Media

A global professional society that provides a forum for the advancement of the engineering profession as applied to the marine field.
8500 Members
Founded in 1893

7179 **Society of Petroleum Engineers**
222 Palisades Creek Dr.
Richardson, TX 75080

972-952-9393
800-456-6863; Fax: 972-952-9435
spedal@spe.org
www.spe.org
Facebook, Twitter, LinkedIn, Instagram, YouTube

Helge Hove Haldorsan Statoil, President
Roland Moreau, Vice President, Finance
Dan Hill, Director For Academia
David Curry, Technical Director
Trey Shaffer, Technical Director

To provide the means for collection, dissemination and exchange of technical information concerning the development of oil and gas resources, subsurface fluid flow and production of other materials through well bores for the public benefit.
64000 Members
Founded in 1957

7180 **Society of Rheology**
American Institute of Physics
2 Huntington Quadrangle
Suite 1N01
Meville, NY 11747-4502

516-576-2471; Fax: 516-576-2223
rheology@aip.org
www.rheology.org

Greg McKenna, President
Gareth H. McKinley, Vice President
Albert Co, Secretary
Montgomery T. Shaw, Treasurer
Ralph H. Colby, Editor

Composed of physicists, chemists, biologists, engineers, and mathematicians interested in advancing and applying rheology, which is defined as the science of deformation and flow of matter.
1700 Members

7181 **Society of Tribologists and Lubrication Engineers**
840 Busse Hwy
Park Ridge, IL 60068-2376

847-825-5536; Fax: 847-825-1456
information@stle.org
www.stle.org

Dr. Martin N. Webster, President
Dr. Eli Erdemir, Vice President
Mr. Michael Anderson, Secretary
Mr. Greg Croce, Treasurer
Mr. James Arner, Director

Strives to advance the science of lubrication tribology and related arts and sciences. Sponsors courses and an annual meeting.
4400 Members
Founded in 1960

7182 **Society of Women Engineers**
203 N La Salle Street
Suite 1675
Chicago, IL 60601

877-793-4636
hq@swe.org
societyofwomenengineers.swe.org
Facebook, Twitter, LinkedIn, YouTube, Instagram, Google+

Colleen M. Layman, President
Jessica Rannow, President Elect
Stephanie Loete, Secretary
Cindy Hoover, Treasurer
Mary Perkinson, Director Of Advocacy

An organization that stimulates women to achieve full potential in careers as engineers.

7183 **Tau Beta Pi Association**
PO Box 2697
Knoxville, TN 37901-2697

865-546-4578; Fax: 865-546-4579
www.tbp.org
Facebook, Twitter, WordPress

Joseph P. Blackford, President
Norman Pih, Vice President
Curtis D. Gomulinski, Exec. Dir./Sec-Treasurer & Editor
James D. Froula, Secretary-Treasurer Emeritus
Susan L. R. Holl, Councillor

The National Engineering honor society recognizes engineering students of superior scholarship and exemplary character and practitioners of engineering. The organization includes 230 collegiate chapters and 16 alumnus chapters.
525K Members
Founded in 1885

7184 **The American Association for Wind Engineers**
1415 Blue Spruce Drive
Suite 3
Fort Collins, CO 80524

970-498-2334; Fax: 970-221-3124
aawe@aawe.org
www.aawe.org

Dr. Partha Sarkar, President
Dr. Greg Kopp, President Elect
Dr. Steve C. S. Cai, Secretary/ Treasurer
Dr. David O Prevatt, Board of Directors
Dr. Anne Cope, Board of Directors

A nonprofit professional organization that promotes and disseminates technical information in the research community.
Founded in 1995

7185 **The Associated General Contractors of America**
2300 Wilson Blvd.
Suite 300
Arlington, VA 22201
703-548-3118
800-242-1767; Fax: 703-837-5405
info@agc.org
www.agc.org
Facebook, Twitter, LinkedIn
Robert Lanham, President
Dan Fordice, Senior Vice President
Lester Snyder, Vice President
Jeffrey DiStefano, Treasurer
Stephen E. Sandherr, Executive Director
Trade association for the construction industry.
26000 Members

7186 **The Order of the Engineer, Inc.**
PO Box 25473
Scottsdale, AZ 85255-0107
866-364-7464; Fax: 480-585-6418
www.order-of-the-engineer.org
Paula Ostaff, Executive Director
Association for graduate and professional engineers emphasizing pride and responsibility.
Founded in 1970

7187 **The Tire Society**
810 E. 10th St.
Lawrence, KS 66044
785-865-9403
800-627-0326; Fax: 785-843-6153
tst@allenpress.com
www.tiresociety.org
Saied Taheri, President
Randy Jenniges, Vice President
Ric Mousseau, Past President
Michell Hoo Fatt, Secretary
Rusty Adams, Treasurer
A professional engineering society that increases and disseminates knowledge as it pertains to the science and technology of tires.

7188 **Theta Tau**
1011 San Jacinto
Suite 205
Austin, TX 78701
512-482-1904
800-264-1904; Fax: 512-472-4820
central.office@thetatau.org
www.thetatau.org
Facebook, Twitter, LinkedIn
Michael Livingston, Grand Regent
Justin Wisemen, Grand Vice Regent
Rachael Stensrud, Grand Scribe
J. Matthew Clark, Grand Treasurer
A professional fraternity in engineering. Founded at the University of Minnesota. Purpose of the fraternity is to develop and maintain a high standard of professional interest among its members, and to unite them in a strong bond of fraternal fellowship.
30000 Members
Founded in 1904

7189 **United Engineering Foundation**
16 Copper Penny Road
Flemington, NJ 08822-5540
engfnd@aol.com
www.uefoundation.org
Ian Sadler, President
Patrick J. Natale, Executive Director
Supports research in engineering science and seeks to advance the profession of engineering.
19 Members
Founded in 1904

7190 **United Engineering Trustees**
16 Copper Penny Road
Flemington, NJ 08822-5540
Home Page: www.uefoundation.org
Ian Sadler, President
Patrick J. Natale, Executive Director
Aims to advance engineering arts and sciences.
Founded in 1904

Newsletters

7191 **AEG News**
Assn. of Environmental & Engineering Geologists
1100-H Brandywine Boulevard
Suite 575
Zanesville, OH 43701
303-757-2926
844-331-7867; Fax: 740-452-2552
aeg@aegweb.org
www.aegweb.org
Dale C. Andrews, President
Kathy Troost, Vice President
Kevin Richards, Treasurer
Cynthia Palomares, Secretary
Includes reports of committee activities, section news, and other news items of interest to the profession.
Frequency: Quarterly

7192 **AIP History Newsletter**
American Institute of Physics
1 Physics Ellipse
College Park, MD 20740-3841
301-209-3100; Fax: 301-209-0843
dylla@aip.org
www.aip.org
Marc Brodsky, CEO
Margaret Wiley, Senior Executive Secretary
Benjamin Snavely, AIP Corporate Secretary
Melissa Poleski, Assistant To Corporate Secretary
Our Newsletter reports on work in the history of physics (and allied fields such as astronomy and geophysics), carried out at the American Institute of Physics and elsewhere. It includes lists of recent publications in the history of modern physics, and reports on papers deposited in archives worldwide.

7193 **ANS News**
American Nuclear Society
555 N Kensington Avenue
La Grange Park, IL 60526
708-352-6611
800-323-3044; Fax: 708-352-0499
www.ans.org
For personnel involved in nuclear power operation and development. Coverage includes power, plant operations and maintenance, fuel cycle, legislation, international employment and more.
Frequency: Monthly

7194 **ASFE Newslog**
ASFE/The Geoprofessional Business Association
8811 Colesville Rd
Suite G106
Silver Spring, MD 20910-4343
301-565-2733; Fax: 301-589-2017
info@asfe.org
www.asfe.org
David Gaboury, President
Information on geo professional, environmental, and civil engineering firms. Past issues are available through the online store. Electronic copies are always free to members.

7195 **ASGE Newsletter**
American Society of Gas Engineers
P.O. Box 66
Artesia, CA 90702
562-455-9417
asgecge@aol.com
www.asge-national.org
Jerry Moore, Executive Director
Ray Maddock, President
Eric Bruton, Vice President
Chad Johnson, Treasurer
Keeps members current on events and issues facing the Gas Appliance Industry. Features articles that address new technologies and trends.
Founded in 1954

7196 **ASTM International Business Link**
ASTM International
PO Box C700
W Conshohocken, PA 19428-0700
610-832-9500; Fax: 610-832-9555
service@astm.org
www.astm.org
James A Thomas, President
Provides information on the topics connecting the business and technical communities.
Frequency: Semi-Annual

7197 **Access ASTM International**
ASTM International
PO Box C700
W Conshohocken, PA 19428-0700
610-832-9500; Fax: 610-832-9555
service@astm.org
www.astm.org
James A Thomas, President
John Pace, Manager
Jeff Adkins, Manager
Fran Dougherty, Administrative Assistant
Periodic update for ASTM's global customers.
Frequency: Semi-Annual

7198 **American Automatic Control Council Newsletter**
AACC Secretariat
2145 Sheridan Road
Evanston, IL 60208-3118
847-491-8175; Fax: 847-491-4455
aacc@ece.northwestern.edu
www.a2c2.org
Bonnie Heck, Publisher
William Levine, President
A Ulsoy, Vice-President
Automatic control council information.
4 Pages
Frequency: Quarterly
Founded in 1961

7199 **BMES Bulletin**
Biomedical Engineering Society
8401 Corporate Dr
Suite 140
Hyattsville, MD 20785-2263
301-459-1999; Fax: 301-459-2444
info@bmes.org
www.bmes.org
Barbara Dunlevy, Executive Director
Heather Comstock, Meeting Manager
The Bulletin presents bioengineering science articles, student chapter news, Society and public policy announcements, employment opportunities, and a calendar of conference and events. It is also a forum for member opinions through editorials and letters.
Cost: $30.00
Frequency: Monthly
Circulation: 3500
Founded in 1969
Printed in 2 colors on matte stock

7200 **Bot Brief**
Robotic Industries Association
900 Victors Way
Suite 140
Ann Arbor, MI 48108

734-994-6088; Fax: 734-994-3338
info@robotics.org
www.robotics.org

Jeff Burnstein, President
Dana Whalls, Vice President, A3
Clarissa Carvalho, Marketing Specialist
Bob Doyle, Vice President

Weekly newsletter from the Robotic Industries Association with the latest industry news.
Frequency: Weekly
Founded in 1974

7201 **Bulletin of Tau Beta Pi**
Tau Beta Pi Association
PO Box 2697
Knoxville, TN 37901-2697

865-546-4578; Fax: 865-546-4579
www.tbp.org

R E Hawks, Editor

The purpose of The Bulletin is to disseminate news and information about Tau Beta Pi of special interest to the collegiate chapters. It is an important vehicle for the annual repetition of instructions from the Executive Council and national headquarters to the chapters on election and initiation procedures and for the exchange of chapter project ideas and experience.
Frequency: 3x Annually
Founded in 1925

7202 **Computer Integrated Manufacture and Engineering**
Lionheart Publishing
506 Roswell St Se
Suite 220
Marietta, GA 30060-4101

770-422-3139; Fax: 770-432-6969
lpi@lionhrtpub.com
www.lionhrtpub.com/

Marvin Diamond, Advertising Sales Manager

Explores cutting edge developments in manufacturing systems operation management.
Circulation: 24000

7203 **Cross Connection Protection Devices**
American Society of Sanitary Engineering
901 Canterbury Rd
Suite A
Westlake, OH 44145-1480

440-835-3040; Fax: 440-835-3488
www.asse-plumbing.org

James Bickford, President
Donald Summers, First VP
John Flader, Treasurer

Summary of backflow conditions and method of eliminating or minimizing their possible dangers.
Cost: $15.00

7204 **E-Catalyst Industry Update**
Adhesive & Sealant Council
7101 Wisconsin Ave
Suite 990
Bethesda, MD 20814-4805

301-986-9700; Fax: 301-986-9795
data@ascouncil.org
www.ascouncil.org

William Allmond, President

7205 **Echoes Newsletter**
Acoustical Society of America
2 Huntington Quad
Suite 1N01
Melville, NY 11747-4505

516-576-2360; Fax: 516-576-2377
asa@aip.org
www.acousticalsociety.org

Charles E Schmid, President

Covers current and topical happenings of general interest and features articles about current research and personalities. Distributed free to members.
Frequency: Quarterly

7206 **Engineering Department Management and Administration Report**
Institute of Management and Administration
3 Bethesda Metro Center
Suite 250
Bethesda, MD 20814

703-341-3500; Fax: 800-253-0332
www.ioma.com

Focuses on improving efficiency and productivity.
Cost: $245.00
16 Pages
Frequency: Monthly

7207 **Engineering Times**
National Society of Professional Engineers
1420 King St
Alexandria, VA 22314-2794

703-684-2800; Fax: 703-836-4875
webmaster@nspe.org
www.nspe.org

Larry Jacobson, Executive Director/Secretary
Robert Grey, President

Reports on issues affecting the engineering profession; featured monthly series on ethics. Free to members.
Cost: $30.00
24 Pages

7208 **High-Tech Materials Alert**
Technical Insights
605 3rd Avenue
New York, NY 10158

212-850-6824
800-245-6217; Fax: 212-850-8643

Kenneth Kovaly, Publisher

Opportunities in advanced materials.
Cost: $867.00
12 Pages

7209 **Highpoints Newsletter**
American Academy of Environmental Engineers
147 Old Solomons Island Road
Suite 303
Annapolis, MD 21401-7003

410-266-3311; Fax: 410-266-7653
www.aaees.org

Newsletter providing news and updates on Academy activities, as well as general industry information and news.
Frequency: Monthly

7210 **Hufact Quarterly: A Current Awareness Resource**
Ergosyst Associates
123 W 8th Street
Suite 210
Lawrence, KS 66044-2687

FAX 785-842-7348

John Burch, Publisher

Covers economics/human factors.
Cost: $100.00

7211 **IE News: Ergonomics**
Institute of Industrial Engineers
3577 Parkway Lane
Suite 200
Norcross, GA 30092

770-449-0460
800-494-0460; Fax: 770-441-3295
cs@iienet.org

Don Greene, CEO
Donna Calvert, COO

Newsletter for Ergonomics Division.
4 Pages
Frequency: Quarterly
Founded in 1948

7212 **IE News: Facilities Planning and Design**
Institute of Industrial Engineers
25 Technology Pkwy S
Suite 150
Norcross, GA 30092-2946

770-449-0461; Fax: 770-263-8532

Dona Brown, Publisher

Accepts advertising.
4 Pages

7213 **IE News: Operations Research**
Institute of Industrial Engineers
25 Technology Pkwy S
Suite 150
Norcross, GA 30092-2946

770-449-0461; Fax: 770-263-8532

Dona Brown, Publisher

News for industrial engineers. Accepts advertising.
4 Pages

7214 **IE News: Quality Control and Reliability Engineering**
Institute of Industrial Engineers
25 Technology Pkwy S
Suite 150
Norcross, GA 30092-2946

770-449-0461; Fax: 770-263-8532

Dona Brown, Publisher

Association news.
4 Pages

7215 **Innovators Digest**
InfoTeam
PO Box 15640
Plantation, FL 33318-5640

954-473-9560; Fax: 954-473-0544

Merton Allen, Editor

A multidisciplinary publication covering developments in science, engineering, products, markets, business development, manufacturing and other technological developments having industrial or commercial significance.
Frequency: Bi-Annual

7216 **Instrumentation Newsletter**
National Instruments
6504 Bridge Point Parkway
Austin, TX 78730-5017

512-389-9119
888-280-7645; Fax: 512-794-8411
info@natinst.com
www.natinst.com

Gail Folkins, Managing Editor
John Graff, Vice President of Sales
James Truchard, President
Frequency: Quarterly
Circulation: 150000
Founded in 1976

7217 **Last Word**
American Council of Engineering Companies
1015 15th St
8th Floor NW
Washington, DC 20005-2605

202-347-7474; Fax: 202-898-0068
acec@acec.org
www.acec.org
Facebook, Twitter

Dave Raymond, President
Ann Randstapter, Editor
Sheila Mahoutchian, Marketing Manager
Mary Jaffe, Director, Publications
Alan Crockett, Director, Public Relations

Independent private practice engineering companies.
Cost: $90.00
2 Pages
Frequency: Monthly
Circulation: 5800
Founded in 1905
Printed in on glossy stock

7218 **Leadership and Management in Engineering**
American Society of Civil Engineers
1801 Alexander Bell Dr
Suite 100
Reston, VA 20191-4382

703-295-6300
800-548-2723; Fax: 703-295-6222
cybrarian@asce.org
www.asce.org

D Wayne Klotz, President

A cutting-edge periodical focusing on the art and practice of management and leadership in the civil engineering community.
Frequency: Quarterly

7219 **Licensure Exchange**
National Council of Examiners for Engineering
280 Seneca Creek Road
PO Box 1686
Clemson, SC 29633

864-654-6824
800-250-3196; Fax: 864-654-6033
www.ncees.org

Keri Anderson, Editor
Ashley Cheney, Treasurer
David Widmer, Treasurer
Theodore Sack, Vice President

Provides information, opinion, and ideas regarding the licensure of engineers and land surveyors.
Frequency: Bi-Monthly

7220 **Motion Control Market Report**
Motion Control & Motor Association
900 Victors Way
Suite 140
Ann Arbor, MI 48108

734-994-6088
info@motioncontrolonline.org
www.motioncontrolonline.org

Matt French, Chair
Gunnar Block, Vice Chair
Paul Horvat, Vice Chair

Quarterly release for members.
Founded in 2006

7221 **Plumbing Systems & Design**
American Society Of Plumbing Engineers
2980 S River Rd
Des Plaines, IL 60018-4203

773-693-2773; Fax: 773-695-9007
www.psdmagazine.org/

Tom Govedarica, Executive Publisher
Gretchen Pienta, Managing Editor
Maria Barriga, Circulation Manager
Jill Dirksen, Technical Director
David Ropinski, Graphic Designer

Industry leading technical publication with ASPE news and features. Free to ASPE members and subscribers.
Cost: $150.00
Circulation: 25500
Printed in 4 colors on glossy stock

7222 **Power**
McGraw Hill
PO Box 182604
Columbus, OH 43272-1095

720-485-5000
877-833-5524; Fax: 614-759-3749
www.mcgraw-hill.com

Harold McGraw, Chairman and President
Jack Callahan, Executive VP

Published for engineers who design, construct, operate and maintain power operating facilities in cogeneration and independent power plants in electric utilities. Accepts advertising.
Cost: $50.00
Frequency: Monthly
Founded in 1888

7223 **Rheology Bulletin**
Society of Rheology
2 Huntington Quadrangle
Suite 1N01
Meville, NY 11747-4502

516-576-2471; Fax: 516-576-2223
rheology@aip.org
www.rheology.org

Faith Morrison, President
Jeffrey Giacomin, Vice President
Albert Co, Secretary
Montgomery Shaw, Treasurer

To inform members of the Society affairs and matters of general interest to rheologists.
Frequency: 2x yearly

7224 **SAWE Technical Papers**
Society of Allied Weight Engineers
5734 E. Lucia Walk
Long Beach, CA 90803-4015

562-596-2873; Fax: 562-596-2874
exdirector@sawe.org
www.sawe.org

Patrick Brown, President
Jeffrey Cerro, Executive VP
Ronald Fox, Executive Director

The Technical Paper Index.
Frequency: Every 3 Years

7225 **Systems**
Institute of Industrial Engineers
25 Technology Pkwy S
Suite 150
Norcross, GA 30092-2946

770-449-0461; Fax: 770-263-8532

SL Browder, Publisher

Newsletter for IIE's society.
4 Pages
Frequency: Quarterly

7226 **The AOCS Newsletter**
American Oil Chemists' Society
2710 S Boulder Drive
P.O. Box 17190
Urbana, IL 61803-6996

217-359-2344; Fax: 217-351-8091
general@aocs.org
www.aocs.org
Facebook, Twitter, LinkedIn

Gloria Cook, Senior Director, Finance
Jeffry L. Newman, Senior Director, Programs

The AOCS Newsletter is sent electronically each month to approximately 4,200 AOCS members and 10,000 other related industry professionals. It contains the latest AOCS news, including discounted offers, upcoming meeting information and registration details, AOCS press releases, and technical services updates.
4500 Members
Frequency: Annual/April-May
Founded in 1909

7227 **The Star**
Sigma Phi Delta
3010 Saint Joseph Drive
Mansfield, TX 76063

214-686-2240
execsecr@sigmaphidelta.org
www.sigmaphidelta.org

Alixandre R. Minden PE, PMP, Grand President
Eric J. Pew, Grand VP
Tyler S. Condon, Treasurer
Seth F. Huy, Director of Alumni Relations
Aaren Salido, Director of Chapter Development

A newsletter for Sigma Phi Delta members.
Founded in 1924

7228 **Tribology Letters**
Kluwer Academic/Plenum Publishers
840 Busse Highway
Park Ridge, IL 60068-2376

847-825-5536; Fax: 847-825-1456
information@stle.org
www.stle.org

Karl Phipps, Associate Managing Editor

Devoted to the development of the science of Tribology and to its applications. It also serves as the depository for new information on the mechanical properties of surfaces.
Frequency: 95x Yearly

7229 **Velocitus Officers Newsletter**
Theta Tau
815 Brazos
Suite 710
Austin, TX 78701

512-482-1904
800-264-1904; Fax: 512-472-4820
central.office@thetatau.org
www.thetatau.org

Michael T Abraham, Executive Director
Dana Wortman, Grand Treasurer
Brandon J Satterwhite, Western Regional Director
Matthew Clark, Treasurer

Available by request via email or calling our 800 number.

Magazines & Journals

7230 **ASEE Prism**
American Society for Engineering Education
1818 N St NW
#600
Washington, DC 20036-2476

202-331-3500; Fax: 202-265-8504
pubsinfo@asee.org
www.asee.org

Frank L Huband, Executive Director
Mary Dalheim, Editor
Sherra E. Kerns, President

Geared towards educators in the engineering technology fields.
Frequency: Monthly
Circulation: 12000
Founded in 1893

7231 **ASTM Standardization News**
ASTM International

100 Barr Harbor Drive
PO Box C700
W Conshohocken, PA 19428-2959

610-832-9500
610-832-9500; Fax: 610-832-9555
service@astm.org
www.astm.org

James A Thomas, President
Jeff Grove, Vice President

The official magazine of ASTM International, SATM Standardization news reports events in materials research and standardization.
Cost: $18.00
88 Pages
Frequency: Monthly
Circulation: 35000
Founded in 1898

7232 **AWIS Magazine**
Association for Women in Science
1667 K Street NW
Suite 800
Washington, DC 20006

202-588-8175
awis@awis.org
www.awis.org
Facebook, Twitter, LinkedIn

Janet Bandows Koster, Executive Director

Focuses on issues relevant to women scientists. Contains articles about current events, career advancement, financial planning, work-life balance, and creating a diverse work environment.
Frequency: Quarterly
Circulation: 3500

7233 **Advanced Materials & Processes**
ASM International
9639 Kinsman Road
Materials Park, OH 44073-0002

440-338-5151
800-336-5152; Fax: 440-338-4634
magazines@asminternational.org
www.asminternational.org

William T. Mahoney, Secretary & CEO
Joanne Miller, Editor
Vicki Burt, Managing Editor

AM&P is the monthly technical magazine from ASM International, designed to keep readers aware of leading-edge developments and trends in engineering materials - metals and alloys, engineering polymers, advanced ceramics, and composites - and the methods used to select, process, fabricate, test, and characterize them.
30K Members
Frequency: Monthly
Circulation: 23000
Founded in 1913

7234 **Aerospace Engineering**
400 Commonwealth Drive
Warrendale, PA 15096-1

724-776-4841; Fax: 724-776-9765
www.sae.org

JE Robertson PE, President
Robert E Spitzer, VP Aerospace
Raymond Morris, Executive Vice President
Richard Schaum, VP Automotive
Andrew Brown, Treasurer

Serves the international aerospace design and manufacturing field which consists of producers of airliners, helicopters, spacecraft, missiles, and power plants, propulsion systems, avionics, electronic/electrical systems, parts and components.
Cost: $75.00
Circulation: 28440
Founded in 1905

7235 **American Consulting Engineer**
American Council of Engineering Companies
1015 15th St
8th Floor NW
Washington, DC 20005-2605

202-347-7474; Fax: 202-898-0068
acec@acec.org
www.acec.org
Facebook, Twitter

David A Raymond, President

American Consulting Engineer serves engineers and surveyors who are employed by Consulting Engineering Firms, Architectural & Engineering Firms, and Surveying Firms.
Cost: $45.00
42 Pages
Frequency: Monthly
Circulation: 15841
ISSN: 1050-2203
Founded in 1905
Printed in 4 colors on glossy stock

7236 **Annals of Biomedical Engineering**
Biomedical Engineering Society
8201 Corporate Dr
Suite 1125
Landover, MD 20785-2224

301-459-1999
877-871-2637; Fax: 301-459-1999
info@bmes.org
www.bmes.org

Edward L. Schilling, Executive Director
Barbara Colburn, Membership Director
Heather Comstock, Meeting Manager

Presents original research in the following areas: tissue and cellular engineering and biotechnology; biomaterials and biological interfaces; biological signal processing and instrumentation; biomechanics, rheology, and molecular motion; dynamical, regulatory, and integrative biology; transport phenomena, systems analysis and electrophysiology; imaging.
Frequency: Monthly

7237 **Automotive Engineering International**
Society of Automotive Engineers
400 Commonwealth Dr
Warrendale, PA 15086-7511

724-776-4841
877-606-7323; Fax: 724-776-5760
magazines@sae.org

Richard O Schaum, President
Kevin Jost, Editor
J Robertson, President

For engineers involved in the auto design industry.
Cost: $120.00
125 Pages
Frequency: Monthly
Circulation: 124451
Founded in 1905

7238 **Biomedical Engineering Society**
8401 Corporate Dr
Suite 140
Hyattsville, MD 20785-2263

301-459-1999; Fax: 301-459-2444
info@bmes.org
www.bmes.org

Barbara Dunlevy, Executive Director
Heather Comstock, Meeting Manager

Of interest to those in the biomedical engineering field. To promote the increase of biomedical engineering knowledge and its utilization.
Cost: $175.00
Frequency: Monthly
Founded in 1968
Printed in 8 colors on matte stock

7239 **Bridge**
National Academy of Engineering
500 5th Street NW
Washington, DC 20001

202-334-3200; Fax: 202-334-2290
www.nae.edu

Charles M. Vest, President
Laura Mersky, Senior Executive Assistant

Solicited articles only. News related to the organization
Frequency: Quarterly
Circulation: 6500
Founded in 1954

7240 **CET Magazine**
American Society of Certified Engineering
PO Box 1348
Flowery Branch, GA 30542-0023

770-967-9173; Fax: 770-967-8049
www.ascet.org

Russell E Freier, Chairman
Leo Saenz, CET, President
Kurt Schuler, Secretary/Treasurer

It contains technical, educational, notices of upcoming events, employment opportunities, legislative and informational articles. Also included are national, regional and local society news, reports and activities.
32 Pages
Frequency: Bi-Monthly
Founded in 1964
Printed in one color

7241 **CFMA Building Profits**
Construction Financial Management Association
100 Village Boulevard
Suite 200
Princeton, NJ 08540-5783

609-452-8000
888-421-9996; Fax: 609-452-0474
info@cfma.org
www.cfma.org
Facebook, Twitter, LinkedIn, YouTube

Stuart Binstock, President & CEO
Brian Summers, VP, Operations

Information for financial managers and CPAs concerned with financial management.
Frequency: Bi-Monthly
Circulation: 8,600
Founded in 1981

7242 **Chemical & Engineering News**
American Chemical Society
1155 16th St Nw
Suite 600
Washington, DC 20036-4892

202-872-4600
800-227-5558; Fax: 202-872-4615
service@acs.org
www.acs.org

Madeleine Jacobs, CEO

Professional magazine which covers all areas of interest to the chemical community, including business, science and government.
Frequency: Weekly
Founded in 1934

7243 **Circuits and Systems Magazine**
IEEE Circuits and Systems Society
445 Hoes Lane
Piscataway, NJ 08854

chaiwahwu@ieee.org
www.ieee-cas.org

Chai Wah Wu, Editor-in-Chief
Alyssa B. Apsel, Deputy Editor-in-Chief
Mohammad Sawan, VP, Publications

Feature articles with noteworthy results, surveys, and tutorials.

7244 **Civil Engineering**
American Society of Civil Engineers

1801 Alexander Bell Dr
Reston, VA 20191-4382

703-295-6300
800-548-2723
703-295-6300; Fax: 703-295-6222
member@asce.org
www.asce.org

D Wayne Klotz, President
Virginia Fairweather, Editor-in-Chief
Anne Powell, Editor

Comprised of news, information and updates for the civil engineering industry.
Cost: $180.00
Frequency: Monthly
Circulation: 107,000
Founded in 1855
Printed in 4 colors

7245 **Clientship**
American Council of Engineering Companies
1015 15th St
8th Floor NW
Washington, DC 20005-2605

202-347-7474; Fax: 202-898-0068
acec@acec.org
www.acec.org
Facebook, Twitter

Dave Raymond, President
Frequency: Monthly

7246 **Community Matters**
Accreditation Board for Engineering & Technology
111 Market Place
Suite 1050
Baltimore, MD 21202-4012

410-347-7700; Fax: 410-625-2238
info@abet.org
www.abet.org

Phillip E. Borrowman, President
Larry A. Kaye, President-Elect/VP
Frequency: Monthly
Founded in 1932

7247 **Composites Technology**
Ray Publishing
P.O.Box 992
Morrison, CO 80465-0992

303-467-1776; Fax: 303-467-1777
www.raypubs.com

Judith Ray Hazen, Publisher/Editor
Michael Musselman, Managing Editor
Donna K. Dawson, Senior Editor
Susan Rush, Copy Editor
Dirk Weed, Global Sales Manager

To provide comprehensive coverage of the composites industry by focusing on the design, engineering, manufacture and performance of products made from this type of material. Particular attention is given to the transfer of technology from traditional end-use markets into high-volume commercial and industrial arenas.
Cost: $15.00
44 Pages
Circulation: 24000
ISSN: 1083-4117
Founded in 1993
Printed in 4 colors on glossy stock

7248 **Computer-Aided Engineering**
Penton Media
249 W. 17th Street
New York, NY 10011

216-696-7000; Fax: 216-696-6662
information@penton.com
www.penton.com

Sharon Rowlands, CEO

Database applications in design and manufacturing.
Cost: $50.00
96 Pages
Founded in 1982

7249 **Computing in Science & Engineering**
American Institute of Physics
2 Huntington Quad
Suite 1NO1
Melville, NY 11747-4502

516-576-2200; Fax: 516-349-7669
www.aip.org

Darlene Walters, Senior VP
Angela Dombroski, CEO
Randolph Nanna, Publisher

Computer science's interdisciplinary juncture with physics, astronomy and engineering.
Cost: $42.00
Frequency: Monthly
Founded in 1931

7250 **Consulting-Specifying Engineer**
Reed Business Information
360 Park Avenue South
New York, NY 10010

646-746-6400
877-422-4637; Fax: 630-288-8781
e-letters@reedbusiness.com
www.reedbusiness.com

Jeff Greisch, President
Jim Crockett, Chief Editor
Scott Siddens, Senior Editor

Serves engineering management and engineering personnel who perform mechanical and/or electrical engineering activities.
100 Pages
Frequency: Monthly
Circulation: 46,157
ISSN: 0892-5046
Founded in 1958
Printed in 4 colors on glossy stock

7251 **Control Solutions**
PennWell Publishing Company
1421 S Sheridan Rd
Tulsa, OK 74112-6619

918-831-9421
800-331-4463; Fax: 918-831-9476
www.pennwell.com

Robert Biolchini, President
Ron Kuhfeld, Editor-in-Chief

A highly diversified, business-to-business media company providing authoritative print and online publications, conferences and exhibitions, research, databases, online exchanges and information products to strategic global markets.
Founded in 1910

7252 **Corrosion Journal**
NACE International
1440 S Creek Dr
Houston, TX 77084-4906

281-492-0535; Fax: 281-228-6300
www.nace.org

Angela Jarrell, Managing Editor
Suzanne Moreno, Editorial Assistant

Recognized internationally as the world's leading research journal devoted exclusively to furthering corrosion science and engineering
Cost: $150.00
Frequency: Monthly
Circulation: 7800

7253 **Cost Engineering Journal**
AACE International
1265 Suncrest Towne Centre Drive
Morgantown, WV 26501-1876

304-296-8444
800-858-2678; Fax: 304-291-5728
info@aacei.org
www.aacei.org

Michael R. Nosbisch, President
Marlene Hyde, President-Elect

International journal of cost estimation, cost/schedule control, and project management read by cost professionals around the world to get the most up-to-date information about the profession.
Frequency: Monthly

7254 **Cutting Tool Engineering**
CTE Publications
40 Skokie Blvd
Suite 395
Northbrook, IL 60062-1698

847-498-9100; Fax: 847-559-4444
alanr@jwr.com
www.ctemag.com

John W Roberts, CEO
Don Nelson, CEO
Alan Rooks, Director

Serves manufacturing plants in the metal working industries.
Cost: $65.00
72 Pages
Frequency: Monthly
Circulation: 34871
ISSN: 0011-4189
Founded in 1955
Printed in 4 colors on glossy stock

7255 **Design News**
Reed Business Information
225 Wyman St
Waltham, MA 02451-1216

781-734-8000; Fax: 781-290-3178
www.reedbusiness.com

Mark Finklestein, President
Karen Auguston Field, CFO
Stuart Whayman, CFO
Tracey Farina, Marketing,
Reck Allis, Circulation Manager

A magazine devoted exclusively to engineering design.
Frequency: Monthly
Circulation: 170114
Founded in 1958
Printed in 4 colors on glossy stock

7256 **EE: Evaluation Engineering**
Nelson Publishing
2500 Tamiami Trl N
Nokomis, FL 34275-3476

941-966-9521
800-226-6113; Fax: 941-966-2590
www.healthmgttech.com

Kristine Russel, President
Phil Colpas, Managing Editor

Magazine devoted exclusively to companies that test, evaluate, design and manufacture electronic products and equipment.
Cost: $43.00
84 Pages
Frequency: Monthly
Circulation: 80000
Founded in 1962
Mailing list available for rent: 65,000 names
Printed in 4 colors on glossy stock

7257 **Energy Engineering Journal**
The Fairmont Press, Association of Energy Engineer

4025 Pleasantdale Road
Suite 420
Atlanta, GA 30340

770-447-5083; Fax: 770-446-3969
info@aeecenter.org
www.aeecenter.org

Jennifer Vendola, Accountant
Ruth Whitlock, Executive Admin

Engineering solutions to cost efficiency problems and mechanical contractors who design, specify, install, maintain, and purchase non-residential heating, ventilating, air conditioning and refrigeration equipment and components.
Cost: $160.00
Circulation: 8000

7258 Energy Services Marketing Institute News

Association of Energy Engineers
3168 Mercer University Drive
Atlanta, GA 30341

770-447-5083
www.aeecenter.org

Albert Thumann, Executive Director

Subjects addressed include IPMVP Management and Verification Standard; Performance Contracting; Energy Project Financing and Energy Procurement.
Frequency: 3x Yearly

7259 Engineering Automation Report

Technology Automation Services
PO Box 3593
Englewood, CO 80155-3593

303-689-9099; Fax: 303-770-3660

David Weisberg, Publisher
Steve Weisberg, Editor
Dave White, President

Internet/intranet technologies for use in engineering design are covered along with software news.
Cost: $235.00
Frequency: Monthly

7260 Engineering News Record

McGraw Hill
2 Penn Plaza
9th Floor
New York, NY 10121-2298

212-904-3507; Fax: 212-904-2820
www.enr.com

Richard Korman, Managing Senior Editor
Ilan Kapla, Senior Manager
Keith Wallace, Production Editor

Provides the news, analysis, commentary and data that construction industry professionals need to do their jobs more effectively. ENR is the national news magazine for the construction industry.
Cost: $82.00
Frequency: Weekly
Circulation: 60000
Founded in 1874

7261 Engineering and Mining Journal

Primedia Business
29 N Wacker Drive
10th Floor
Chicago, IL 60606-2802

312-726-2802; Fax: 312-726-2574
www.mining-media.com

Peter Johnson, Publisher
Steve Fiscor, Managing Editor
Russ Carter, Managing Editor
Victor Matteucci, National Sales Manager

Serves the field of mining including exploration, development, milling, smelting, refining of metals and nonmetallics.
Cost: $79.00
Circulation: 20589
Founded in 1989
Mailing list available for rent
Printed in 4 colors

7262 Engineering in Medicine and Biology

445 Hoes Lane
Piscataway, NJ 08854-1331

732-981-0060
800-678-4333; Fax: 732-981-1721
customer-service@ieee.org

DesirTe de Myer, Managing Editor
John Enderle, Editor
Susan Schneiderman, Business Development

Focuses on up-to-date biomedical engineering applications for engineers who are at the forefront of electrotechnology innovation.
Cost: $300.00
Circulation: 7983
ISSN: 0739-5175
Founded in 1988

7263 Environmental Engineer and Scientist

American Academy of Environmental Engineers
147 Old Solomons Island Road
Suite 303
Annapolis, MD 21401-7003

410-266-3311; Fax: 410-266-7653
www.aaees.org

Burk Kalweit, Executive Director
J. Sammi Olmo, Manager, Special Projects

Articles dealing with environmental engineering practice issues and history.
Cost: $10.00
Frequency: Quarterly
Circulation: 12000
Founded in 1955
Mailing list available for rent

7264 Environmental and Engineering Geosciences

Assn. of Environmental & Engineering Geologists
1100-H Brandywine Boulevard
Suite 575
Zanesville, OH 43701

303-757-2926
844-331-7867; Fax: 740-452-2552
aeg@aegweb.org
www.aegweb.org

Dale C, Andrews, President
Kathy Troost, Vice President
Kevin Richards, Treasurer
Cynthia Palomares, Secretary

Presents reviewed technical papers and discussions and book reviews related to the general field of engineering geology.
Frequency: Quarterly

7265 Experimental Mechanics

Society for Experimental Mechanics
2455 Teller Road
Thousand Oaks, CA 91320-1855

800-818-7243; Fax: 805-499-0871
info@sagepub.com
www.sagepub.com

Thomas W Proulx, Publisher
N R Sottos, Editor
Hugh Bruck, Associate Tech Editor

Concentrates on advanced research and development. EM is the archival publication of the Society and is recognized as one of the many journals in engineering mechanics. Members receive free electronic access.
Cost: $767.04
Frequency: Quarterly
Circulation: 4500
Founded in 1965

7266 Experimental Techniques

Society for Experimental Mechanics
7 School St
Bethel, CT 06801-1855

203-790-6373; Fax: 203-790-4472
sem@sem1.com
www.sem.org

Kathy Ramsey, Manager
Thomas Proulx, Execetive Director

Focused on the techniques utilized in experimental mechanics. ET includes Society news, peer-reviewed technical articles and notes, new product information and much more. All members receive a printed copy of the journal and free electronic access.
Cost: $145.00
48 Pages
Circulation: 4000
Founded in 1943
Printed in 4 colors on glossy stock

7267 Exponent

Iowa Engineering Society
100 Court Ave
#102
Des Moines, IA 50309-2257

515-284-7055; Fax: 515-284-7301
ies@iaengr.org
www.iaengr.org

David Scott, Executive Director
Brian E Roth, President

Supplies the Iowa engineering society members with vital information on issues and activities such as state legislation, education, ethics.
Cost: $6.00
26 Pages
Frequency: Quarterly
Circulation: 1000

7268 Facilities Engineering Journal

Association for Facilities Engineering
1000 Potomac Street NW
Suite 500
Washington, DC 20007

202-791-9080; Fax: 571-766-2142
grodriguez@afe.org
www.afe.org

Gabriella Rodriguez, Senior Manager, Membership
Joshua Watkins, Manager, Professional Development

Provides practical, in-depth information on the key issues faced by facilities engineers on the job every day.
Frequency: Quarterly

7269 Fiberoptic Product News

Reed Business Information
100 Enterprise Drive
Suite 600
Rockaway, NJ 07866-912

973-920-7000; Fax: 973-920-7534
www.fpnmag.com

Steve Wirth, VP/Group Publisher
Diane Himes, Editor
Kim Potts, Managing Editor
Ernest Worthman, Technical Editorial Director
R Reed, Owner

Edited for designers, engineers, researchers and management personnel who design, install and the buy the products and services that make up the fiberoptic marketplace.
Frequency: Monthly
Circulation: 35000
Founded in 1986
Printed in 4 colors on glossy stock

7270 Fusion Science and Technology

American Nuclear Society

555 N Kensington Avenue
La Grange Park, IL 60526

708-352-6611
800-323-3044; Fax: 708-352-0499
www.ans.org

Rick Michal, Director, Publications
Leigh Winfrey, Editor

The source of information on fusion plasma physics and plasma engineering, fusion plasma enabling science and technology, fusion nuclear technology and material science, fusion applications, fusion design and system studies.
Frequency: 8x Yearly

7271 Geosynthetics
Industrial Fabrics Association International
1801 County Road B W
Roseville, MN 55113-4061

651-222-2508
800-225-4324; Fax: 651-631-9334
generalinfo@ifai.com
www.ifai.com

Todd Berger, Senior Editor

Peer reviewed technical journal for civil engineers using geosynthetics in road construction, erosion control, hazardous waste, drainage, containment and reinforcement.
Cost: $49.00
Circulation: 16000
ISSN: 0882-4983
Founded in 1982
Printed in 4 colors on glossy stock

7272 Geotechnical Testing Journal
ASTM International
PO Box C700
W Conshohocken, PA 19428-0700

610-832-9500; Fax: 610-832-9555
service@astm.org
www.astm.org

James A Thomas, President
Jeff Adkins, Manager
Fran Dougherty, Administrative Assistant

Provides a high quality publication that informs the profession of new developments in soil and rock testing and related fields; provides a forum for the exchange of information, particularly that which leads to the development of new test procedures; and to stimulate active participation of the profession in the work of ASTM International Committee D18 on Soil and Rock and related information.
Cost: $229.00
Frequency: Bi-Monthly

7273 Global Design News
Reed Business Information
360 Park Avenue South
New York, NY 10010

646-746-6400
877-422-4637; Fax: 630-288-8781
e-letters@reedbusiness.com
www.reedbusiness.com

Jeff Greisch, President
Jim Crockett, Chief Editor
Scott Siddens, Senior Editor

Publication includes articles that cover the key product areas necessary for product development; reports on new technologies in the OEM industries, developments in the field of engineering design; and regular features on European product listings, technique and system updates.
Circulation: 30173
Founded in 1958

7274 Heat Transfer Engineering
Taylor & Francis Group Ltd
2 Park Square
Milton Park
Abingdon Oxford UK OX14 4RN

4.40207E+12; Fax: 4.40207E+12
taylorandfrancis.com

James Edward, Publisher
Afshin Ghajar, Editor-in-Chief
Jack Taylor, Owner

Information on refereed papers of original work, state-of-the-art reviews, articles on new developments in equipment and practices and news items on people and companies in the field.

7275 Hispanic Engineer & Information Technology
Career Communications Group
729 E Pratt St
Suite 504
Baltimore, MD 21202-3302

410-244-7101; Fax: 410-752-1837
www.ccgmag.com

Jean Hamilton, Chief Financial Officer
Vishal Thakkar, Director of Marketing
Diane Jones, Director of Marketing
Christy Flemming, Director

Devoted to science and technology and to promoting opportunities in those fields for Hispanic Americans.
Cost: $13.00
56 Pages
ISSN: 1088-3452
Founded in 1982
Printed in 4 colors on glossy stock

7276 Hydraulics & Pneumatics
Penton Media
249 W. 17th Street
New York, NY 10011

212-204-4200; Fax: 216-696-6662
www.penton.com

Sharon Rowlands, CEO
Nicola Allais, Executive VP

Issues highlight the application of new hydraulic and pneumatic components, new equipment research and listings, new design and literature innovations in fluid power and motion control systems.
Cost: $65.00
Frequency: Monthly
Circulation: 49,878
Founded in 1892

7277 ID International Design
F&W Publications
38 E 29th St
Floor 3
New York, NY 10016-7911

212-447-1400; Fax: 212-447-5231
www.printmag.com

Joyce Rutter Kaye, VP
Julie Lasky, Editor - in - chief
Nicole Martin, Circualtion Manager
Barbara Schmitz, VP

The issues include news and features on computers, new technologies, case studies, design management, materials, aesthetics, new components and design trends. They also cover new sources, a calendar of events, personnel news, book reviews and products.
Cost: $30.00
Circulation: 19852
Founded in 1954

7278 IEEE Computational Intelligence Magazine
IEEE Computational Intelligence Society
445 Hoes Lane
Piscataway, NJ 08855

732-465-5892; Fax: 732-465-6435
cis-info@ieee.org
cis.ieee.org

Bernadette Bouchon-Meunier, President
Hessein Abbass, VP, Technical Activities
James Keller, VP, Publications

CIM features peer-reviewed articles with noteworthy discoveries, insights, and tutorial surveys.

7279 IEEE Control Systems Magazine
IEEE Control Systems Society (CSS)
445 Hoes Lane
Piscataway, NJ 08854-1331

732-562-3937
m.david@ieee.org
www.ieee.org

Jonathan How, Editor-in-Chief
Rodolphe Sepulchre, Deputy Editor-in-Chief

Focuses on applications of technical knowledge and concentrates on industrial implementations, design tools, technology review, control education and applied research. Geared towards readers with many different responsibilities including applied research, device design, product development and design including software and semiconductor components.
Cost: $210.00
Founded in 1973
Mailing list available for rent

7280 IEEE Industrial Electronics Magazine
Institute Of Electrical and Electronics Engineers
445 Hoes Lane
Piscataway, NJ 08854

804-827-3999
eic-iem@ieee-ies.org
www.ieee-ies.org

Peter Palesnky, Editor-in-Chief

IEM features peer-reviewed articles presenting new trends and practices in industrial electronics research & development.

7281 IEEE Solid-State Circuits Magazine
IEEE Solid-State Circuits Society
445 Hoes Lane
Piscataway, NJ 08854

rjacobbaker@gmail.com
sscs.ieee.org

R. Jacob Baker, Editor-in-Chief
Rakesh Kumar, Chair, Advisory Board

Tutorial-style articles on technical achievements, trends, and future developments in the field of Integrated Circuits.
Founded in 2009

7282 IEEE Transactions on Engineering Management
IEEE Technology & Engineering Management Society
445 Hoes Lane
Piscataway, NJ 08854

tugrul.u.daim@pdx.edu
www.ieee-tems.org

Tugrul U. Daim, Editor-in-Chief
Alison Larkin, Peer Review Support Services
Mark Werwath, VP, Publications

Journal of the Technology and Engineering Management Society of IEEE, with peer-reviewed research on engineering, technology, and innovation management.
Frequency: Quarterly
Founded in 1954

7283 **IEEE Transactions on Industry Applications**
Institute Of Electrical and Electronics Engineers
445 Hoes Lane
Piscataway, NJ 08854

732-562-2663
t.nondahl@ieee.org
www.ieee.org

Thomas A. Nondahl, Editor-in-Chief

The development and applications of electrical systems, apparatus, devices and controls to the processes and equipment of industry and commerce.
Circulation: 5100
Founded in 1980

7284 **IEEE Vehicular Technology Magazine**
IEEE Vehicular Technology Society
3 Parl Avenue
17th Floor
New York, NY 10016-5997

212-419-7900
david@uni-kassel.de
vtsociety.org

Klaus David, Editor-in-Chief

Focus is on mobile radio, connected and automated vehicles, automotive electronics, and transportation systems.
Frequency: Quarterly

7285 **IIE Solutions**
Institute of Industrial Engineers
3577 Parkway Lane
Suite 200
Norcross, GA 30092

770-449-0460
800-494-0460; Fax: 770-441-3295
cs@iienet.org

Don Greene, CEO
Donna Calvert, Chief Operating Officer

Listings, literature and news for executive engineers.
Cost: $66.00
Frequency: Monthly
Circulation: 26276
Founded in 1948

7286 **ITS Magazine**
IEEE Intelligent Transportation Systems Society
445 Hoes Lane
Piscataway, NJ 08854

Home Page: www.ieee-itss.org

Wei-Bin Zhang, President
Petros A. Ioannou, VP, Publications Activities
Ljubo Vlacic, Magazine Editor

Features peer-reviewed articles on research and applications, with case studies and examinations of challenges in the intelligent transportation system industry.

7287 **InTents**
Industrial Fabrics Association International
1801 Country Road BW
Roseville, MN 55113

651-222-2508
800-225-4324; Fax: 651-631-9334
www.ifai.com

Sammi Jones, Editor

Promotes the use of tents and accessories to the special-event and general rental industries.
Cost: $39.00
Frequency: Bi-Monthly
Circulation: 12,000

7288 **Industrial Equipment News**
TCC Media Group
90 W Aftan Avenue
#117
Yardley, PA 19067

267-519-1705
800-733-1127
todd@ien.com
www.ien.com

Todd Baker, President

Serves the industrial field including manufacturing, mining, utilities, construction, transportation,governmental establishments, and educational services.
Frequency: Monthly
Circulation: 205000
ISSN: 0019-8258
Founded in 1933

7289 **Inform**
American Oil Chemists' Society
2710 S Boulder Drive
P.O. Box 17190
Urbana, IL 61803-6996

217-359-2344; Fax: 217-351-8091
general@aocs.org
www.aocs.org
Facebook, Twitter, LinkedIn

Gloria Cook, Senior Director, Finance & Operatio
Jeffry L. Newman, Senior Director, Programs

Inform magazine is an AOCS member benefit providing international news on fats, oils, surfactants, detergents, and related materials.
4500 Members
Frequency: Annual/April-May
Founded in 1909

7290 **Innovation**
Industrial Designers Society of America
45195 Business Court
Suite 250
Dulles, VA 20166-6717

703-707-6000; Fax: 703-787-8501
idsa@idsa.org
www.idsa.org

Clive Roux, CEO
Annette Butler, Executive Assistant
Kaycee Childress, Marketing
Roxann Henze, Press, Media & Public Relations

IDSA is the world's oldest, largest, member-driven society for product design, industrial design, interaction design, human factors, ergonomics, design research, design management, universal design and related design fields. IDSA publishes Innovation, a quarterly on design. IDSA's charitable arm, the Design Foundation, supports the dissemination of undergraduate scholarships annually to further industrial design education.
Cost: $50.00
Frequency: Quarterly
Circulation: 3500
Founded in 1965

7291 **Interface Magazine**
Electrochemical Society
65 S Main St
Building D
Pennington, NJ 08534-2827

609-737-1902; Fax: 609-737-2743
interface@electrochem.org
www.electrochem.org

Roque J Calvo, Executive Director
Mary E. Yess, Deputy Executive Director

Editorial material contains news, reviews, advertisements and articles on technical matters in the fields of electrochemical and solid state science and technology.
Cost: $61.97
Frequency: Quarterly
Circulation: 8000
Founded in 1902

7292 **International Dredging Review**
PO Box 1487
Fort Collins, CO 80522-1487

970-416-1903; Fax: 970-416-1878
editor@dredgemag.com
www.dredgemag.com

Judith Powers, Publisher/Editor
Leonard F Cors, Business Manager
Nelson Spencer, Business Manager
Julia Leach, Production Manager

Targeted to dredging company executives, project managers and dredge crew members, suppliers and service people such as pump manufacturers, hydrographic surveyors, consulting engineers, etc.
Cost: $85.00
Circulation: 3300
ISSN: 0737-8181
Founded in 1981
Mailing list available for rent
Printed in 4 colors on glossy stock

7293 **Iron & Steel Technology**
Association for Iron & Steel Technolgy (AIST)
186 Thorn Hill Rd
Warrendale, PA 15086-7528

724-814-3000; Fax: 724-814-3001
memberservices@aist.org
www.aist.org
Facebook, Twitter, LinkedIn

Ron Ashburn, Executive Director
Lori Wharrey, Board Administrator
Chris McKelvey, Assistant Board Administrator

The official monthly publication of AIST, this is the premier technical journal for metallurgical, engineering, operating and maintenance personnel in the global iron and steel industry.
Cost: $20.00
Frequency: Monthly
Circulation: 9500

7294 **Journal of Construction Engineering and Management**
American Society of Civil Engineers
1801 Alexander Bell Dr
Reston, VA 20191-4382

703-295-6300
800-548-2723; Fax: 703-295-6222
cybrarian@asce.org
www.asce.org

D Wayne Klotz, President

Quality papers that aim to advance the science of construction engineering, to harmonize construction practices with design theories, and to further education and research in construction engineering and management.

7295 **Journal of Engineering Education**
American Society for Engineering Education
1818 N St NW
Suite 600
Washington, DC 20036-2476

202-331-3500; Fax: 202-265-8504
pubsinfo@asee.org
www.asee.org

Frank L Huband, Executive Director

It serves as an archival record of scholarly research in engineering education.
Frequency: Quarterly
ISSN: 1069-4730

7296 **Journal of Management in Engineering**
American Society of Civil Engineers

1801 Alexander Bell Dr
Reston, VA 20191-4382

703-295-6300
800-548-2723; Fax: 703-295-6222
cybrarian@asce.org
www.asce.org

D Wayne Klotz, President

Examines contemporary issues associated with leadership and management for the twenty-first century civil engineer.

7297 **Journal of Materials Engineering and Performance**
ASM International
9639 Kinsman Road
Materials Park, OH 44073-0002

440-338-5151
800-336-5152; Fax: 440-338-4634
memberservicecenter@asminternational.org
www.asminternational.org

William T. Mahoney, Secretary & CEO
Rajiv Asthana, Editor

Peer-reviewed journal that publishes contributions on all aspects of materials selection, design, characterization, processing and performance testing. The journal is useful for solving day-to-day engineering challenges - especially those involving components for larger systems.
30K Members
Frequency: Bi-Monthly
Founded in 1913

7298 **Journal of Petroleum Technology**
Society of Petroleum Engineers
PO Box 833836
Richardson, TX 75083-3836

972-529-9300
800-456-6863; Fax: 972-952-9435
spedal@spe.org
www.spe.org

Giovanni Paccaloni, President
Bill Cobb, VP Finance
John E Bethancourt, Director Management/Information
Ian Gorman, Director Production/Operations
Niki Bradbury, Managing Director

A suite of peer-reviewed, discipline-centered journals; books written by the industry's most honored professionals; and an online, 35,000-paper library.
Cost: $15.00
Frequency: Monthly

7299 **Journal of Phase Equilibria & Diffusion**
ASM International
9639 Kinsman Road
Materials Park, OH 44073-0002

440-338-5151
800-336-5152; Fax: 440-338-4634
memberservicecenter@asminternational.org
www.asminternational.org

William T. Mahoney, Secretary & CEO
John Morral, Editor
Ursula R. Kattner, Editor
H. Okamoto, Editor

Peer-reviewed journal containing basic and applied research results, evaluated phase diagrams, a survey of current literature, and comments or other material pertinent to the previous three areas. The aim of the journal is to provide a broad spectrum of information concerning phase equilibria for the materials community.
30K Members
Frequency: Bi-Monthly
Founded in 1913

7300 **Journal of Process Control**
Butterworth Heinemann
313 Washington Street
Suite 302
Newton, MA 02458-1626

617-928-5460; Fax: 617-928-5494

JD Perkins, Editor
T McAvoy, Regional Editor

Covers the application of control theory, operations research, computer science and engineering principles to the solution of process control problems.

7301 **Journal of Quality Technology**
American Society for Quality
600 N Plankinton Avenue
Milwaukee, WI 53203

414-272-8575
800-248-1946; Fax: 414-272-1734
help@asq.org
asq.org/pub/jqt/index.html

Elmer Corbin, Chair
Bill Troy, CEO
Brian Savoie, Chief Financial Officer
Andrew Baines, Managing Director, Global
Ann Jordan, General Counsel

Published by the American Society for Quality, the Journal of Quality Technology is a quarterly, peer-reviewed journal that focuses on the subject of quality control and the related areas of reliability and similar disciplines.
80K Members
Frequency: Quarterly
Founded in 1946

7302 **Journal of Rheology**
Society of Rheology
2 Huntington Quadrangle
Suite 1N01
Meville, NY 11747-4502

516-576-2471; Fax: 516-576-2223
rheology@aip.org
www.rheology.org

Faith A. Morrison, President
A. Jeffrey Giacomin, Vice President
Frequency: Bi-Monthly

7303 **Journal of Surfactants and Detergents (JSD)**
American Oil Chemists' Society
2710 S Boulder Drive
P.O. Box 17190
Urbana, IL 61803-6996

217-359-2344; Fax: 217-351-8091
general@aocs.org
www.aocs.org
Facebook, Twitter, LinkedIn

Gloria Cook, Senior Director, Finance
Jeffry L. Newman, Senior Director, Programs

Since 1998, JSD has remained dedicated to the practical and theoretical aspects of oleochemical and petrochemical surfactants, soaps and detergents. This growing quarterly scientific journal publishes peer-reviewed research papers, and reviews related to surfactants and detergents technologies.
4500 Members
Frequency: Annual/April-May
Founded in 1909

7304 **Journal of Technology, Management, and Applied Engineering**
Assn. of Technology, Management & Applied Eng.
3801 Lake Boone Trail
Suite 190
Raleigh, NC 27607

919-635-8335
admin@atmae.org
www.atmae.org

Jim Thompson, Executive Director
Melissa Smith, Director of Programs
Caitlin Schwab-Falzone, Director of Accreditation

ATMAE's on-line peer-refereed scholarly journal that publishes peer-refereed scholarly articles involving research and applications, along with non-refereed informational articles.
1000+ Members
Founded in 1967

7305 **Journal of Testing and Evaluation**
ASTM International
PO Box C700
W Conshohocken, PA 19428-0700

610-832-9500; Fax: 610-832-9555
service@astm.org
www.astm.org

James A Thomas, President
Jeff Adkins, Manager
Fran Dougherty, Administrative Assistant

Provides a multidisciplinary forum for applied sciences and engineering.
Cost: $249.00
Frequency: Bi-Monthly

7306 **Journal of Thermal Spray Technology**
ASM International
9639 Kinsman Road
Materials Park, OH 44073-0002

440-338-5151
800-336-5152; Fax: 440-338-4634
memberservicecenter@asminternational.org
www.asminternational.org

William T. Mahoney, Secretary & CEO
Armelle Vardelle, Editor-in-Chief
Andre McDonald, Lead Editor

Peer-reviewed journal which publishes contributions on all aspects, fundamental and practical, of thermal spray science, including processes, feedstock manufacture, testing and characterization. As the primary vehicle for thermal spray information transfer, its mission is to synergize the rapidly advancing thermal spray industry and related industries by presenting research and development efforts leading to advancements in implementable engineering applications of the technology.
30K Members
Frequency: Bi-Monthly
Founded in 1913

7307 **Journal of the Acoustical Society of America**
Acoustical Society of America
2 Huntington Quad
Suite 1N01
Melville, NY 11747-4505

516-576-2360; Fax: 516-576-2377
asa@aip.org
www.acousticalsociety.org

Charles E Schmid, President

Distributed free to members.
Cost: $1545.00
7000 Pages
Frequency: Monthly

7308 **Journal of the American Oil Chemists' Society (JAOCS)**
American Oil Chemists' Society
2710 S Boulder Drive
P.O. Box 17190
Urbana, IL 61803-6996

217-359-2344; Fax: 217-351-8091
general@aocs.org
www.aocs.org
Facebook, Twitter, LinkedIn

Gloria Cook, Senior Director, Finance
Jeffry L. Newman, Senior Director, Programs

Since 1947, the Journal of the American Oil Chemists' Society has been the leading source for technical papers related to the fats and oils indus-

tries. JAOCS is a monthly, peer-reviewed journal devoted to fundamental and practical research, production, processing, packaging and distribution in the growing field of fats, oils, proteins and other related substances.
4500 Members
Frequency: Annual/April-May
Founded in 1909

7309 **Journal of the Electrochemical Society**
Electrochemical Society
65 S Main St
Building D
Pennington, NJ 08534-2827

609-737-1902; Fax: 609-737-2743
ecs@electrochem.org
www.electrochem.org

Roque J Calvo, Executive Director
Mary E. Yess, Deputy Executive Director
Roque Calvo, Manager

Contains technical papers covering basic research and technology.
Cost: $63.00
Circulation: 8300
Founded in 1902

7310 **LD&A**
Illuminating Engineering Society of North America
120 Wall Street
17th Floor
New York, NY 10005

212-248-5000; Fax: 212-248-5017
ies@ies.org
www.ies.org

Denis Lavoie, President
Chip Israel, Vice President

A magazine for professionals involved in the art, science, study, manufacture, teaching and implementation of lighting. LD&A is designed to enhance and improve the practice of lighting. Free to members.
Cost: $44.00
Frequency: Monthly
Circulation: 7000
ISSN: 0360-6325
Mailing list available for rent: 8000 names

7311 **LEUKOS, The Journal Of IES**
Illuminating Engineering Society of North America
120 Wall Street
17th Floor
New York, NY 10005

212-248-5000; Fax: 212-248-5017
ies@ies.org
www.ies.org

Denis Lavoie, President
Chip Israel, Vice President

LEUKOS serves members of the IES, the lighting community, and the public. The journal contains international technical developments of current interest and lasting importance relating to illuminating engineering and lighting design. Free to members, online.
Cost: $250.00
Frequency: Quarterly
ISSN: 1550-2729
Mailing list available for rent: 8000 names

7312 **Lighting Design & Application**
Illuminating Engineering Society of North America
120 Wall St
17th Floor
New York, NY 10005-4001

212-248-5000; Fax: 212-248-5017
iesna@iesna.org
www.ies.org

Denis Lavoie, President
Chip Israel, Vice President

Is a magazine for professionals involved in the art, science, study, manufacture, teaching and implementation of lighting. LD+A is designed to enhance and improve the practice of lighting. Every issue of LD+A includes feature articles on design projects, technical articles on the science of illumination, new product developments, industry trends, news of the Illuminating Engineering Society and vital information about the illuminating profession.
Cost: $32.00
Frequency: Monthly
Circulation: 8000
ISSN: 0360-6325

7313 **Lipids**
American Oil Chemists' Society
2710 S Boulder Drive
P.O. Box 17190
Urbana, IL 61803-6996

217-359-2344; Fax: 217-351-8091
general@aocs.org
www.aocs.org
Facebook, Twitter, LinkedIn

Gloria Cook, Senior Director, Finance
Jeffry L. Newman, Senior Director, Programs

Introduced in 1966, Lipids is a premier journal published in the lipid field today. This monthly scientific journal features full-length original research articles, short communications, methods papers and review articles on timely topics. All papers are meticulously peer-reviewed and edited by some of the foremost experts in their respective fields.
4500 Members
Frequency: Annual/April-May
Founded in 1909

7314 **Low Temperature Physics**
200 Huntington Quadrangle
Suite 1N01
Melville, NY 11747-4502

516-516-2270; Fax: 516-349-9704

7315 **Machine Design**
1300 E 9 Street
Cleveland, OH 44114-2518

216-696-7000
847-763-9670; Fax: 216-696-0177
mdeditor@penton.com
www.machinedesign.com

Leland Teschler, Editor
Ken Korane, Managing Editor
Bobbie Macy, Circulation Manager

The only magazine for applied technology for design engineering edited for design engineers and engineering managers. It covers new products and design practices in the fields of mechanical, electromechanical, electronics, motion control and process engineering.
Circulation: 180000
Founded in 1929

7316 **Maintenance Solutions**
Trade Press Publishing Corporation
2100 W Florist Avenue
Milwaukee, WI 53209

414-228-7701; Fax: 414-228-1134
contact@facilitiesnet.com
www.facilitiesnet.com/

Dick Yake, Editorial Director
Dan Hounsell, Editor
Brad R. Ehlert, VP
Brian Terry, Publisher
Renee Gryzkewicz, Associate Editor

How to articles and features designed to alleviate reader problems as well as new product information and applications.
Cost: $45.00
42 Pages
Frequency: Monthly
Circulation: 35000
ISSN: 1072-3560
Founded in 1993

7317 **Maintenance Technology**
Applied Technology Publications
1300 S Grove Ave
Suite 105
Barrington, IL 60010-5246

847-382-8100; Fax: 847-304-8603
www.mt-online.com

Jane Alexander, Editor-in-Chief
Rick Carter, Executive Editor
Randy Buttstadt, Director of Creative Services

Maintenance Technology magazine serves the business and technical information needs of managers and engineers responsible for assuring availability of plant equipment and systems. It provides readers with articles on advanced technologies, strategies, tools, and services for the life-cycle management of capital assets.
Frequency: Monthly
Circulation: 50,827
Mailing list available for rent: 35,263 names at $$15 per M

7318 **Manufacturing Engineering Magazine**
Society of Manufacturing Engineers
1 SME Drive
Dearborn, MI 48128

313-425-3000
800-733-4763; Fax: 313-425-3400
editorial@sme.org
advancedmanufacturing.org

Jeffrey M. Krause, CEO
Alan Rooks, Editor-in-Chief
James A. Lorincz, Senior Editor
Patrick Waurzyniak, Senior Editor

Magazine covering a range of manufacturing technologies for engineering professionals.
65K Members
Frequency: Monthly
Circulation: 90000
Founded in 1932

7319 **Marine Fabricator**
Industrial Fabrics Association International
1801 County Road B W
Roseville, MN 55113-4061

651-222-2508
800-225-4324; Fax: 651-631-9334
generalinfo@ifai.com
www.ifai.com

Elisa Bernick, Senior Editor

Educates and informs 5,000 marine shop professionals and also provides reportage that reflects the innovations and trends of the industry.
Cost: $34.00
Frequency: Bi-Monthly

7320 **Material Handling Business**
Penton Media

249 W. 17th Street
New York, NY 10011

212-204-4200; Fax: 216-696-6662
information@penton.com
www.penton.com

Sharon Rowlands, CEO
Nicola Allais, Executive VP
Antoinette Sanchez Perkins, Circulation Manager

Journal written for design engineering managers, system integrates, material handling distributors and manufacturing sales executives.
86 Pages
Circulation: 92836
Founded in 1892
Printed in 4 colors on glossy stock

7321 **Materials Performance**
NACE International
1440 S Creek Dr
Houston, TX 77084-4906

281-492-0535
800-797-6223; Fax: 281-228-6300
www.nace.org

Oliver Moghissi, President
Kevin Garrity, Vice President

Provides current news and features, practical data, and information on new products and services in the corrosion industry.
Frequency: Monthly
Circulation: 22000
Founded in 1943

7322 **Materials at High Temperatures**
Butterworth Heinemann
313 Washington Street
Newton, MA 02458-1626

617-928-5460; Fax: 781-933-6333

T Suzuki, Co-Editor
TB Gibbons, Co-Editor

Serves the needs of those developing and using materials for high temperature applications in the power, chemical, engine, processing and furnace industries.

7323 **Measurements and Control News**
Measurements and Data Corporation
100 Wallace Avenue
Suite 100
Sarasota, FL 34237

941-954-8405; Fax: 941-366-5743

Ken Kemski, Editor-in-Chief
Kristine Burmester, Associate Editor

Serves engineers, technichians, scientists, and other professionals involved in the recommendation and specification, of instuments and devices for measurement, inspection, testing, analysis, computing, and control.
Frequency: Bi-Monthly

7324 **Mechanical Engineering Magazine**
American Society of Mechanical Engineers
Two Park Avenue
New York, NY 10016-5990

973-882-1170
800-843-2763
falconij@asme.org
www.asme.org/network/media/mechanical-engineering-magazine

John G. Falconi, Editor-in-Chief & Publisher
Chitra Sethi, Managing Editor

Flagship publication of the American Society of Mechanical Engineering.
Frequency: Monthly
Founded in 1880

7325 **Medical Equipment Designer**
Adams Business Media
6001 Cuchran Road
Suite 300
Cleveland, OH 44139

216-249-9444; Fax: 440-248-0187
www.medicaldesigner.com

Terry Person, Publisher
Steve Wafalosky, Publisher

Published for the design function as it relates specifically to medical manufacturing and design of materials, components and complete systems.
1004 Pages
Frequency: Bi-Monthly
Circulation: 15,000
Founded in 1985
Printed in 4 colors on glossy stock

7326 **Medical Physics**
2 Huntington Quadrangle
Suite 1N01
Melville, NY 11747

516-576-2200; Fax: 516-576-2481
www.aip.org

Bill Hendee, Editor
Founded in 1931

7327 **Microwave and RF**
Penton Media
45 Eisenhower Drive
5th Floor
Paramus, NJ 07652

201-452-2400
800-829-9028; Fax: 201-845-2493
www.mwrf.com

Jack Browne, Publisher/Editor
Dawn Prior, Editorial Assistant

Dedicated to educating senior level design engineers, engineering managers, both domestic and foreign, who work all types of microwave systems, subsystems and components.
Cost: $81.00
Frequency: Monthly
Circulation: 47000
Founded in 1967
Mailing list available for rent
Printed in on glossy stock

7328 **Modern Materials Handling**
Reed Business Information
275 Washington St
Newton, MA 02458-1611

617-964-3030; Fax: 617-630-3925
www.designnews.com

Peter Boniface, Publisher
Raymond Kulwiec, Editor
James A Casella, CEO
Jason Cassidy, VP
Greg Flores, Senior Vice President

The magazine for managers and engineers responsible for handling materials and managing inventories in manufacturing, warehousing and distribution.
Frequency: 14x Yearly
Founded in 1977
Printed in 4 colors on glossy stock

7329 **Motion Control**
ISA Services
Po Box 12277
Resrch Trngle P, NC 27709-2277

919-549-8411; Fax: 919-549-8288
info@isa.org
www.isa.org

Pat Gouhin, Executive Director

Information for those who design and maintain motion control systems.
Cost: $54.00
56 Pages
Circulation: 41000
ISSN: 1058-4644
Founded in 1945
Printed in 4 colors on glossy stock

7330 **Motion System Distributor**
Penton Media
249 W. 17th Street
New York, NY 10011

212-204-4200
800-249-9365; Fax: 216-696-6662
information@penton.com
www.penton.com

Sharon Rowlands, CEO
Nicola Allais, Executive VP
Larry Berardinis, Editor

Provides selling and technical information to individuals and distributors specializing in power transmission, motion control and fluid products.
Cost: $65.00
Frequency: Monthly
Circulation: 54,000
Founded in 1892

7331 **NSBE Magazine**
National Society of Black Engineers
1454 Duke Street
Alexandria, VA 22314-3403

703-549-2207; Fax: 703-683-5312
office@nsbe.org
www.nsbe.org

Pamela D Sharif, Publisher
Carl Mack, Manager
George Bowman, Manager

Coverage of all aspects of manufacturing engineering, geared towards black technical professionals.
Cost: $30.00
Circulation: 100000
Printed in 4 colors on glossy stock

7332 **Naval Engineers Journal**
American Society of Naval Engineers
1452 Duke Street
Alexandria, VA 22314-3458

703-836-6727; Fax: 703-836-7491
asnehq@navalengineers.org
www.navalengineers.org

Susan King, Editor

It contains technical papers authored by professionals engaged in naval and related engineering fields. Its high quality content is sought by those with an interest in topics of importance to the advancement of naval engineering.
Frequency: Quarterly

7333 **New Equipment Digest**
Penton Media
1300 E 9th St
Cleveland, OH 44114-1503

216-696-7000; Fax: 216-696-1752
information@penton.com
www.penton.com

Sharon Rowlands, CEO
Dave Madonia, Publisher
Robert.F King, Editor
Nicola Allais, Executive VP & CEO

New Equipment Digest serves the general industrial field which includes manufacturing, processing, engineering services, construction, transportation, mining, public utilities, wholesale distributors, educational services, libraries and governmental establishments.
Cost: $65.00
Frequency: Monthly
Circulation: 206006
Founded in 1936

7334 **Noise Control Engineering Journal**
Institute of Noise Control Engineering

62 Timberline Drive, Arlington Branch
PO Box 3206
Poughkeepsie, NY 12603-0206

845-462-4006; Fax: 845-463-0201
www.ince.org

Alan Marsh, Editor

Includes articles on hearing protection, modal analysis, and signal processing. Information is refereed, authoritative, and technical.
Cost: $110.00
Frequency: Bi-Monthly
Circulation: 2,000
ISSN: 0736-2501

7335 **Noise/News International**
Institute of Noise Control Engineering
9100 Purdue Road
Suite 200
Indianapolis, IN 46268

317-735-4063
ibo@inceusa.org
www.inceusa.org

James K Thompson, President
Rich Peppin, Advertising/Expo Manager

Contains not only news items but also feature articles on a wide variety of topics of broad interest in noise control engineering.
Cost: $60.00
Frequency: Quarterly
ISSN: 1021-643X

7336 **Nuclear Science and Engineering**
American Nuclear Society
555 N Kensington Avenue
La Grange Park, IL 60526

708-352-6611
800-323-3044; Fax: 708-352-0499
www.ans.org

Rick Michal, Director, Publications
Dan G. Cacuci, Editor

A source of information on research in all scientific areas related to the peaceful use of nuclear energy and radiation. Technical papers, notes, critical reviews, and computer code abstracts are presented.
Frequency: Monthly
Founded in 1956

7337 **Nuclear Technology**
American Nuclear Society
555 N Kensington Avenue
La Grange Park, IL 60526

708-352-6611
800-323-3044; Fax: 708-352-0499
www.ans.org

Rick Michal, Director, Publications
Andrew C. Klein

Leading international publication reporting on new information in all areas of the practical application of nuclear science. Topics include all aspects of reactor technology: operations, safety materials, instrumentation, fuel, and waste management. Also covered are medical uses, radiation detection, production of radiation, health physics, and computer applications.
Frequency: Monthly

7338 **Off-Highway Engineering**
SAE
400 Commonwealth Dr
Warrendale, PA 15086-7511

724-776-4841; Fax: 724-776-5760

Richard O Schaum, President
Mark Davies, Editor-In-Chief

Off-Highway Engineering serves the international off highway design and manufacturing field which consists of producers of construction, lawn and garden, agricultural equipment, and industrial vehicles. Also served are makers of engines and parts and components and others allied to the field.
Cost: $70.00
66 Pages
Circulation: 16308
ISSN: 1074-6919
Founded in 1905
Printed in 4 colors on glossy stock

7339 **PM Engineer**
Business News Publishing Company
2401 W Big Beaver Road
Suite 700
Troy, MI 48084

248-362-3700
www.bnpmedia.com

Katie Rotella, Manager

Provides technical sheets, manufacturer product brochures, news features and analysis of useful industry information on the engineering and design of plumbing, piping, hydronics, cooling/heating, and fire protection/sprinkler systems. Free to trade engineers.
Cost: $64.00
80 Pages
Frequency: Monthly
Circulation: 25000
Founded in 1970
Printed in 4 colors on glossy stock

7340 **PT Design**
Penton Media
1300 E 9th St
Cleveland, OH 44114-1503

216-696-7000; Fax: 216-696-1752
information@penton.com
www.penton.com

Sharon Rowlands, CEO
David Madonia, Publisher

Blends state-of-the-art motion system designs with traditional electrical and mechanical technology for the system designer. Also features articles on new products and technology, industry trends and application ideas.
Cost: $ 65.00
Frequency: Monthly
Circulation: 54000
Founded in 1892

7341 **PT Distributor**
Reed Business Information
2000 Clearwater Dr
Oak Brook, IL 60523-8809

630-288-8000; Fax: 630-288-8781
www.reedbusiness.com

Mark Kelsey, Global CEO
Jeff DeBalko, President, Media Division

provides information on selling techniques, fiscal and personnel management, purchasing, improving profits, training, and inventory and warehousing control.
Cost: $30.00
Frequency: Bi-Monthly
Circulation: 10,000

7342 **Pharmaceutical Engineering**
Int'l Society for Pharmaceutical Engineering
600 N Westshore Blvd.
Suite 900
Tampa, FL 33609

813-960-2105; Fax: 813-264-2816
ask@ispe.org
www.ispe.org

Charles DiMarco, Director of Marketing
Danielle Hould, Communications Manager
Angie Brumley, Publications Coordinator
Valerie Adams, Advertising Sales Coordinator

Journal is published bi-monthly for members only and is considered by ISPE members to be the number one member benefit. Feature articles provide practical application and specification information on the design, construction, supervision and maintenance of process equipment, plant systems, instrumentation and facilities.
Circulation: 13138

7343 **Plant Engineering**
Reed Business Information
8878 Barrons Blvd
Littleton, CO 80129-2345

303-470-4000
800-446-6551; Fax: 303-470-4691
subsmail@reedbusiness.com
www.reedbusiness.com

Tim Myers, Executive
Bobbie Wisniewski, Advertising Production Manager
Rick Ellis, Circulation Manager
Rick Dunn, Editor
Jim Silvestri, Managing Editor

Provides a constant reminder of engineering products and services and helps keep your company at the top of your customers' minds.
Frequency: Monthly
Circulation: 100034
Founded in 1947

7344 **Plant Services**
Putman Media
555 W Pierce Rd
Suite 301
Itasca, IL 60143-2626

630-467-1301
800-984-7644; Fax: 630-467-0197
www.putman.net

John Cappelletti, CEO
Mike Bacidore, Editor-in-Chief
Mike Brenner, Group Publisher
Keith Larson, VP Content

The newsletters reach a monthly world wide audience of more than 150,000 professionals responsible for optimizing the productivity and insuring the reliability of manufacturing plants, facilities and utilities in North America and across the globe.
Cost: $96.00
Frequency: Monthly
Circulation: 80100
ISSN: 0199-8013
Founded in 1938
Mailing list available for rent: 10,000 names
Printed in 4 colors on glossy stock

7345 **Plastics Engineering**
Society of Plastics Engineers
13 Church Hill Rd
Newtown, CT 06470

203-775-0471; Fax: 203-775-8490
info@4spe.org
www.4spe.org

Susan Oderwald, Executive Director

A communication to SPE's global audience of plastics professionals about current developments in the industry, technology, and activities of the Society.
Frequency: Monthly

7346 **Plumbing Engineer**
Delta Communications
1167 W Bluemound Road
Wauwatosa, WI 53226

262-542-8820; Fax: 262-542-9111
delta@deltacommunications.com
www.deltairaq.net

Edwin Scott, Editor

Offers news and updates to plumbing engineers and manufacturers.
Cost: $35.00
Frequency: Monthly
Founded in 1973

7347 **Plumbing Standard Magazine**
American Society of Sanitary Engineering

901 Canterbury Rd
Suite A
Cleveland, OH 44145-1480

440-835-3040; Fax: 440-835-3488
www.asse-plumbing.org

Ken Van Wagnen, Manager
Donald Summers, First VP
Steve Silber, Second VP
Scott Hamilton, Third VP
Shannon Corcoran, Executive Director

This magazine includes technical articles, current information on codes, standards, and other developments in the plumbing industry and related fields. Free with membership.
Cost: $12.00
Frequency: Quarterly

7348 Powder Diffraction
International Center for Diffraction Data
12 Campus Boulevard
Newton Square, PA 19073-3200

610-325-9814; Fax: 610-325-9823
info@icdd.com
www.icdd.com

Timothy Fawcett, Executive Director
Cathyann Colaiezzi, Managing Editor
Theresa Kahmer, Publication Manager

A quarterly journal devoted to the use of the powder method for material characterization is available on annual subscription. The journal focus is on materials. Characterization employing x-ray powder diffraction and related techniques.
Cost: $90.00
Frequency: Quarterly
Founded in 1941

7349 Powder and Bulk Engineering
CSC Publishing
1155 Northland Dr
St Paul, MN 55120-1288

651-287-5600; Fax: 651-287-5650
www.cscpublishinginc.com

Richard R Cress, Publisher
Terry O' Neill, Editor

Featured editorial includes technical articles, case histories, test centers, product news and literature, and industry news items.
Cost: $100.00
Frequency: Monthly

7350 Power Engineering International
PennWell Publishing Company
1421 S Sheridan Rd
Tulsa, OK 74112-6619

918-835-3161
800-331-4463; Fax: 918-831-9497
candiced@pennwell.com
www.pennwell.com

Robert Biolchini, President
Brian Schimmoller, Managing Editor

Serves the global electric power generation and transmission industry.
Cost: $180.00
Frequency: Monthly
ISSN: 1069-4994
Founded in 1896

7351 Precision Engineering
Elsevier Science
PO Box 10826
Raleigh, NC 27605-0826

919-839-8444; Fax: 919-839-8039
www.aspe.net

W T Estler, Editor-in-Chief

Is the foremost international journal devoted to the study of ultra-high precision engineering and metrology.

7352 Printed Circuit Design
CMP Media
240 West 35th Street
New York, NY 10001

516-562-5000; Fax: 415-947-6090

David Levin, CEO

7353 Process Heating
Business News Publishing Company
155 Pfingsten Road
Suite 205
Deerfield, IL 60015

847-405-4000; Fax: 248-502-1001
PHeditors@bnpmedia.com
www.process-heating.com
Facebook, Twitter

Anne Armel, Publisher
Linda Becker, Associate Publisher & Editor
Beth McClelland, Production Manager

Magazine covers heat processing at temperatures up to 1000 degrees F at end user and OEM plants in 9 industries. Follow us at twitter.com/ProcessHeating, www.facebook.com/ProcessHeating
Circulation: 25000
Founded in 1994

7354 Processing
Putman Media
PO Box 698
Birmingham, AL 35243

888-431-2877; Fax: 205-408-3797
webmaster@grandviewmedia.com
www.grandviewmedia.com

Dennis Van Milligen, Editor in Chief
Mike Wasson, Publisher

Offers information on printing, publishing and processing. Information is given on the latest technology in these and other desktop industries.
Cost: $15.00
53 Pages
Frequency: Monthly
Founded in 1960

7355 Product Design and Development
Reed Business Information
301 Gibraltar Drive
Box 650
Morris Plains, NJ 07950

973-292-5100; Fax: 630-288-8686
www.reedbusiness.com

Stuart Whayman, CFO

7356 Product Development Best Practices Report
Management Roundtable
92 Crescent St
Waltham, MA 02453-4315

781-891-8080; Fax: 781-398-1889
www.pharmcentric.com

Stewart Maws, Owner

The goal of this publication is to help firms market, manufacture and design better products at a lower rate.
Cost: $219.00
Frequency: Monthly

7357 Professional Safety Journal
American Society of Safety Engineering
1800 E Oakton Street
Des Plaines, IL 60018

847-699-2929; Fax: 847-768-3434
customerservice@asse.org
www.asse.org
Facebook, Twitter, LinkedIn

Fred Fortman, Executive Director
Bruce Sufranski, Finance/Controller Director
Diane Hurns, Manager Public Relations Department
Sally Madden, Human Resources Manager

The American Society of Safety Engineers (ASSE) is the oldest professional safety society committed to protecting people, property and the environment. ASSE has more than 32,000 occupational safety, health and environmental (SH&E) professional members who manage, supervise, research and consult on safety, health, transportation and the environment in all industries, government, labor and education.
34000 Members
Frequency: Monthly
Circulation: 40,000
Founded in 1911

7358 Quality Engineering
American Society for Quality
600 N Plankinton Avenue
Milwaukee, WI 53203

414-272-8575
800-248-1946; Fax: 414-272-1734
help@asq.org
asq.org/pub/qe/index.html

Elmer Corbin, Chair
Bill Troy, CEO
Brian Savoie, Chief Financial Officer
Andrew Baines, Managing Director, Global
Ann Jordan, General Counsel

Co-published by Taylor and Francis, this journal is for professional practitioners and researchers in quality engineering improvement and solutions. Subjects include quality assurance management, physical technology, statistical tools and more.
80K Members
Frequency: Quarterly
Founded in 1946

7359 Quality Management Journal
American Society for Quality
600 N Plankinton Avenue
Milwaukee, WI 53203

414-272-8575
800-248-1946; Fax: 414-272-1734
help@asq.org
asq.org/pub/qmj/index.html

Elmer Corbin, Chair
Bill Troy, CEO
Brian Savoie, Chief Financial Officer
Andrew Baines, Managing Director, Global
Ann Jordan, General Counsel

Quarterly, peer-reviewed journal focusing on research on the subject of quality management practice. The journal provides a discussion forum for both practitioners and academics.
80K Members
Frequency: Quarterly
Founded in 1946

7360 Quality Progress
American Society for Quality
600 N Plankinton Avenue
Milwaukee, WI 53203

414-272-8575
800-248-1946; Fax: 414-272-1734
help@asq.org
asq.org/qualityprogress

Elmer Corbin, Chair
Bill Troy, CEO
Brian Savoie, Chief Financial Officer
Andrew Baines, Managing Director, Global
Ann Jordan, General Counsel

Peer-reviewed journal exploring the subject of quality control, discussing the usage and implementation of quality principles. Topics include customer satisfaction, trends and developments.
80K Members
Founded in 1946

7361 RIA Tech Papers
Robotic Industries Association

900 Victors Way
Suite 140
Ann Arbor, MI 48108

734-994-6088; Fax: 734-994-3338
info@robotics.org
www.robotics.org/Tech-Papers

Jeff Burnstein, President
Dana Whalls, Vice President, A3
Clarissa Carvalho, Marketing Specialist
Bob Doyle, Vice President

Technical papers on various subjects relating to the robotics industry, including manufacturing challenges, software and safety concerns.
Frequency: Monthly
Founded in 1974

7362 **RSES Journal**
Refrigeration Service Engineers Society
1666 Rand Rd
Des Plaines, IL 60016-3552

847-297-6464
800-297-5660; Fax: 847-297-5038
general@rses.org
www.rses.org
Facebook, Twitter, LinkedIn

Robert Sherman, President
Lawrence Donaldson, Vice President
Wes Maxfield, Secretary Treasurer

Providing quality technical content in digital and printed forms that can be applied on the job site.
Frequency: Monthly
Circulation: 15231

7363 **Radwaste Solutions**
American Nuclear Society
555 N Kensington Avenue
La Grange Park, IL 60526

708-352-6611
800-323-3044; Fax: 708-352-0499
www.asn.org

Rick Michal, Director, Publications

The magazine of radioactive waste management and facility remediation. Serving the nuclear waste management and cleanup business segments of the industry. Also included are articles on radwaste management programs and practices outside the US, as well as guest editorials and letters to the editor, shorter thought-pieces, and articles on recent academic/technical advances detailing their immediate or planned practical applications.
Circulation: 2000
Founded in 1994

7364 **Reliability Engineering and Management Proceedings**
7340 N La Oesta Ave
Tucson, AZ 85704-3119

520-621-6120; Fax: 520-621-8191
dimitri@u.arizona.edu
www.u.arizona.edu

Dimitri B Kececioglu, Owner

Proceedings where over 15 leading corporations present their latest techniques in this field.
Cost: $50.00
Frequency: Annual+
Circulation: 50
Founded in 1963
Mailing list available for rent: 43000 names at $152 per M

7365 **Research-Technology Management**
Industrial Research Institute
2300 Clarendon Boulevard
Suite 400
Arlington, VA 22201-3331

703-647-2580; Fax: 703-647-2581
information@iriweb.org
www.iriweb.org

Martha Collins, Chairman
Daniel Abramowicz, Chairman-Elect
Edward Bernstein, President
James Euchner, Editor-in-Chief
Maryanne Gobble, Managing Editor

As the official journal of IRI, Research-Technology Management, is the bi-monthly, peer-reviewed journal, providing authoritative, practitioner-oriented articles for technology leaders.
200 Members
Frequency: 6x Yearly
Circulation: 1800
ISSN: 0895-6308
Founded in 1938

7366 **Resource**
American Society of Agricultural Engineers
2950 Niles Rd
St Joseph, MI 49085-8607

269-429-0300
800-371-2723; Fax: 269-429-3852
hq@asabe.org
www.asabe.org

Ronald McAllister, President
Donna Hull, Publication Director

Accepts advertising.
Cost: $75.00
Circulation: 9000
ISSN: 1076-3333
Founded in 1907
Printed in on matte stock

7367 **Review of Scientific Instruments**
American Institute of Physics
2 Huntington Quadrangle
Melville, NY 11747-4502

516-576-2200; Fax: 516-349-7669
rsi@aip.org
www.aip.org

Darlene Walters, Senior VP
Douglas LaFrenier, Marketing Director

Presents original articles on new principles, devices and techniques in scientific instrumentation.
Cost: $90.00
Frequency: Monthly
Circulation: 3100
Founded in 1931

7368 **Robotics and Autonomous Systems**
Elsevier Science
230 Park Avenue
Suite 800
New York, NY 10169

212-309-8100
www.elsevier.com

K. Berns, Editor-in-Chief
M. Gini, Editor-in-Chief
J. Ota, Editor-in-Chief

Journal with articles on developments in the field of robotics, with an emphasis on autonomous systems.
Cost: $3008.00
ISSN: 0921-8890

7369 **Robotics and Computer-Intergrated Manufacturing**
Elsevier Science
230 Park Avenue
Suite 800
New York, NY 10169

212-309-8100
www.elsevier.com

Lihui Wang, Editor-in-Chief

Journal containing original papers on theoretical, applied and experimental robotics and computer-integrated manufacturing, with emphasis on flexible manufacturing systems.
Cost: $3008.00
Circulation: 2500
ISSN: 0736-5845
Founded in 1880

7370 **SAMPE Journal**
Soc for the Advancement of Material & Process Eng
21680 Gateway Center Drive
Suite 300
Diamond Bar, CA 91765-2454

626-521-9460
swbeckwith@aol.com
www.nasampe.org
Facebook, LinkedIn

Dr. Scott Beckwith, Editor/Technical Director

An informative and acclaimed publication provides a steady stream of technical articles, industry and international technical news, product and new literature announcements, book reviews, technical events calendars, and local SAMPE information. This publication is mailed complimentary to all SAMPE members.
Cost: $125.00
Frequency: Bi-Monthly

7371 **SAWE Weight Engineers Handbook**
Society of Allied Weight Engineers
5734 E. Lucia Walk
Long Beach, CA 90803-4015

562-596-2873; Fax: 562-596-2874
exdirector@sawe.org
www.sawe.org

Patrick Brown, President
Jeffery Cerro, Executive VP
Ronald Fox, Executive Director
Robert Ridenour, VP Publications
Clint Bower, Executive VP

Contains technical information on materials, engineering formulas as well as other reference materials.
Cost: $100.00
348 Pages
Frequency: Periodic

7372 **SMC Magazine**
IEEE Systems, Man, and Cybernetics Society
445 Hoes Lane
Piscataway, NJ 08854

smcmagazine_eic@outlook.com
www.ieeesmc.org

Saeid Nahavandi, Editor-in-Chief
Enrique Herrera Viedma, VP, Publications

Articles relevant to the research areas of the IEEE Systems, Man, and Cybernetics Society, with information on the Society's activities, and educational material as well.

7373 **SPE Drilling & Completion**
Society of Petroleum Engineers
PO Box 833836
Richardson, TX 75083-3836

972-529-9300
800-456-6863; Fax: 972-952-9435
spedal@spe.org
www.spe.org

Giovanni Paccaloni, President
Bill Cobb, VP Finance
John E Bethancourt, Director

Management/Information
Ian Gorman, Director Production/Operations
Niki Bradbury, Managing Director

Features papers covering bit technology, completions, drilling fluids and operations, equipment and instrumentation, perforation and sand control, simulations tubulars, well control, and work over well construction related topics.
Cost: $30.00
Frequency: Quarterly

7374 **SPE Journal**
Society of Petroleum Engineers
PO Box 833836
Richardson, TX 75083-3836

972-529-9300
800-456-6863; Fax: 972-952-9435
spedal@spe.org
www.spe.org

Giovanni Paccaloni, President
Bill Cobb, VP Finance
John E Bethancourt, Director Management/Inforamtion
Ian Gorman, Director Production/Operations
Niki Bradbury, Managing Director

Includes full length technical papers covering all aspects of petroleum technology. SPE Journal covers the theories and emerging concepts that will become the new technologies of tomorrow.
Cost: $60.00
Frequency: Quarterly

7375 **SPE Production & Facilities**
Society of Petroleum Engineers
PO Box 833836
Richardson, TX 75083-3836

972-529-9300
800-456-6863; Fax: 972-952-9435
spedal@spe.org
www.spe.org

Giovanni Paccaloni, President
Bill Cobb, VP Finance
John E Bethancourt, Director Management/Information
Ian Gorman, Director Production/Operations
Niki Bradbury, Managing Director

It includes papers on artificial lift, chemical treatments, design and operation of surface facilities and downhole equipment, formation damage control, fracturing, gas production and storage, offshore operations, production logging and optimization systems, sand control, separation and processing, and work over-production improvement.
Cost: $30.00
Frequency: Quarterly

7376 **SPE Reservoir Evaluation & Engineering**
Society of Petroleum Engineers
PO Box 833836
Richardson, TX 75083-3836

972-529-9300
800-456-6863; Fax: 972-952-9435
spedal@spe.org
www.spe.org

Giovanni Paccaloni, President
Bill Cobb, VP Finance
John E Bethancourt, Director Management/Information
Ian Gorman, Director Production/Operations
Niki Bradbury, Managing Director

The journal covers a wide range of topics, including the following: Reservoir Engineering.
Cost: $40.00
Frequency: Bi-Monthly

7377 **Science Robotics**
American Assn for the Advancement of Science
1200 New York Avenue NW
Washington, DC 20005-3941

202-326-6490; Fax: 202-789-4669
sciroboteditors@aaas.org
robotics.sciencemag.org

Alan I. Leshner, Interim Executive Publisher
Jeremy Berg PhD, Editor-in-Chief
Monica M. Bradford, Executive Editor

Publishes original, peer-reviewed, science- or engineering-based research articles that advance the field of robotics. The journal also features editor-commissioned reviews.
Frequency: Monthly

7378 **Sea Technology Magazine**
Compass Publications, Inc.
4600 N. Fairfax Drive
Suite 304
Arlington, VA 22203-1553

703-524-3136; Fax: 703-841-0852
seatechads@sea-technology.com
www.sea-technology.com
Facebook, Twitter

Amos Bussmann, President/Publisher
Leslie Carr, Circulation Manager
Aileen Torres-Bennett, Managing Editor

Worldwide information leader for marine/offshore business, science and engineering. Read in more than 110 countries by management, engineers, scientists and technical personnel working in industry, government and education.
Cost: $40.00
Frequency: Monthly
Circulation: 16304
ISSN: 0093-3651
Founded in 1960
Mailing list available for rentat $80 per M
Printed in 4 colors

7379 **Signal Processing Magazine**
IEEE Signal Processing Society
445 Hoes Lane
Piscataway, NJ 08854

732-562-3888; Fax: 732-867-9953
sp-pub-info@ieee.org
signalprocessingsociety.org
Facebook, Twitter, LinkedIn

Robert Heath, Editor-in-Chief
William Colacchio, Senior Manager, Publications

Tutorials on signal processing research and applications, as well as editorial content on matters of interest.

7380 **Software Quality Professional**
American Society for Quality
600 N Plankinton Avenue
Milwaukee, WI 53203

414-272-8575
800-248-1946; Fax: 414-272-1734
help@asq.org
asq.org/pub/sqp/index.html

Elmer Corbin, Chair
Bill Troy, CEO
Brian Savoie, Chief Financial Officer
Andrew Baines, Managing Director, Global
Ann Jordan, General Counsel

Quarterly, peer-reviewed journal for software development professionals that focuses on the subject of quality practice principles in the implementation of software and the development of software systems.
80K Members
Frequency: Quarterly
Founded in 1946

7381 **TEST Engineering & Management**
Mattingley Publishing Company
3756 Grand Ave
#205
Oakland, CA 94610-1545

510-839-0909; Fax: 510-839-2950
www.mattingley-publ.com

Eve Mattingley, Owner
Nora Archambeau, Advertising Sales Manager

Includes mechanical testing, environmental simulation, and related technologies in industry, government, testing labs, and universities.
Cost: $45.00
Frequency: Monthly
Circulation: 9500
ISSN: 0193-4120
Founded in 1959
Printed in 4 colors on glossy stock

7382 **Technology and Society**
IEEE Society on Social Implications of Technology
445 Hoes Lane
Piscataway, NJ 08854

j.pitt@imperial.ac.uk
technologyandsociety.org
Facebook, Twitter, LinkedIn

Jeremy Pitt, Editor_in-Chief
Terri A. Bookman, Managing Editor

Flagship magazine of the IEEE Society on Social Implications of Technology, with peer-reviewed articles on the impact of technology on the world.

7383 **The Bent**
Tau Beta Pi Association
PO Box 2697
Knoxville, TN 37901-2697

865-546-4578
800-250-3196; Fax: 865-546-4579
www.tbp.org
Facebook

James D Froula, Executive Director/Editor
Dr. Larry Simonson, President

The official publication of the Tau Beta Pi Association - the engineering honor society and the world's largest engineering organization.
Cost: $10.00
Frequency: Quarterly
Circulation: 87000
ISSN: 0005-884x

7384 **The Bridge**
IEEE-Eta Kappa Nu
445 Hoes Lane
Piscataway, NJ 08854

732-465-5846
800-406-2590
info@hkn.org
hkn.ieee.org/news-and-announcements/the-bridge

Sahra Sedigh Sarvestani, Editor-in-Chief
Stephen Williams, Editor-in-Chief

The award-winning digital magazine of the IEEE-HKN.
Frequency: 3x/year

7385 **The Castle**
Sigma Phi Delta
3010 Saint Joseph Drive
Mansfield, TX 76063

214-686-2240
execsecr@sigmaphidelta.org
www.sigmaphidelta.org

Alixandre R. Minden PE, PMP, Grand President
Eric J. Pew, Grand VP
Tyler S. Condon, Treasurer
Seth F. Huy, Director of Alumni Relations
Aaren Salido, Director of Chapter Development

A magazine for Sigma Phi Delta members that details organization news and updates, member profiles, and more.
Frequency: Quarterly
Founded in 1924

7386 **Tribology & Lubrication Technology**
Society of Tribologists & Lubrication
840 Busse Hwy
Park Ridge, IL 60068-2376

847-825-5536; Fax: 847-825-1456
information@stle.org
www.stle.org

Ed Salek, Executive Director
Karl Phipps, Associate Editor
Dr Neil Canter, Contributing Editor

Technical magazine that serves an audience of interdisciplinary professionals from industry, academic institutions and government. Included in this group are scientists, engineers, corporate leaders, researchers and product developers, plant managers and maintenance professionals, sales and marketing people and more.
Frequency: Monthly
Circulation: 7,000

7387 **Tribology Transaction**
Society of Tribologists & Lubrication
840 Busse Hwy
Park Ridge, IL 60068-2376

847-825-5536; Fax: 847-825-1456
information@stle.org
www.stle.org

Ed Salek, Executive Director

Provides you with new and useful reports and analysis of every aspect of tribology and lubrication presented by renowned authors from around the globe. Available online as well.
Frequency: Quarterly

7388 **US Black Engineer & Information Technology**
Career Communications Group
729 E Pratt St
Suite 504
Baltimore, MD 21202-3302

410-244-7101; Fax: 410-752-1837
www.ccgmag.com

Jean Hamilton, Chief Financial Officer
Lango Deen, Technology Editor
Antonio Watson, VP Sales
Guy Madison, Publisher
Diane Jones, Director of Marketing

Devoted to engineering, science, and technology and to promoting opportunities in those fields for Black Americans.
Cost: $26.00
84 Pages
Frequency: Quarterly
Circulation: 100,000
ISSN: 1088-3444
Printed in 4 colors on glossy stock

7389 **VXI Journal**
30233 Jefferson Avenue
Saint Clair Shores, MI 48282

586-415-6500; Fax: 586-415-4882

Magazine is geared towards test engineers who are using or considering VXI bus systems and equipment.
Frequency: Quarterly
Circulation: 8000

7390 **Way Ahead Magazine**
Society of Petroleum Engineers
PO Box 833836
Richardson, TX 75083-3836

972-529-9300
800-456-6863; Fax: 972-952-9435
spedal@spe.org
www.spe.org

Giovanni Paccaloni, President
Bill Cobb, VP Finance
John E Bethancourt, Director Management/Information
Ian Gorman, Director Production/Operations
Niki Bradbury, Managing Director

Designed for and written by young professionals in the oil and gas industry. In it, you will find items of particular interest to the younger members of our industry, including articles on the current state of the job market, how to improve communication skills, and what SPE young professionals are doing will be.
Frequency: 3x Yearly

7391 **Weighing & Measurement**
Key Markets Publishing Company
4729 Charles Street
PO Box 5867
Rockford, IL 61125-0867

815-636-7739

David M Mathieu, Publisher

Articles on new products, industry news, previews and reviews of events, and technical approaches to measurement.
Frequency: Bi-Monthly
Circulation: 12,000

7392 **Wireless Design & Development**
Reed Business Information
301 Gibraltar Drive
PO Box 650
Morris Plains, NJ 07950-0650

973-292-5100; Fax: 973-292-0783
www.wirelessdesignmag.com

Wayne Curtis, Group Publisher
Kim Stokes, Editor

Edited for wireless component and system design engineers in the commercial RF and microwave market.
Frequency: Monthly

Trade Shows

7393 **A3 Business Forum**
Association for Advancing Automation
900 Victors Way
Suite 140
Ann Arbor, MI 48108

734-994-6088; Fax: 734-994-3338
info@a3automate.org
www.a3automate.org

Jeff Burnstein, President
Maria Kurple, Event Marketing Manager
Mandy Pawczuk, Administrator, Event Services

Conference for professionals working in robotics, vision & imaging, motion control, and motors industries.
550+ Attendees
Frequency: Annual/January

7394 **AACE Annual Meeting**
Association of Cost Engineering
1265 Suncrest Towne Centre Drive
Morgantown, WV 26505-1876

304-296-8444
800-858-2678; Fax: 304-291-5728
info@aacei.org
www.aacei.org

Jennie Amos, Marketing/Meetings Manager

See and hear outstanding technical presentations, panel discussions, workshops, tours, and guest speakers
Frequency: Annual/June

7395 **ACA Annual Meeting & Exhibition**
American Crystallographic Association
Ellicott Station
PO Box 96
Buffalo, NY 14205-0096

716-898-8690; Fax: 716-898-8695
aca@hwi.buffalo.edu
www.AmerCrystalAssn.org

Thomas Koetzle, President
George Philip, Vice President

75 manufacturers exhibits of commercial hardware and software, and x-ray equipment. In addition to the exhibition, take advantage of workshops, and scientific and poster sessions.
1000 Attendees
Frequency: Annual
Founded in 1955

7396 **AEG Annual Meeting**
Assn. of Environmental & Engineering Geologists
1100-H Brandywine Boulevard
Suite 575
Zanesville, OH 43701

303-757-2926
844-331-7867; Fax: 740-452-2552
aeg@aegweb.org
www.aegweb.org

Dale C. Andrews, President
Frequency: Annual

7397 **AHR Expo**
Refrigeration Service Engineers Society
1666 Rand Road
Des Plaines, IL 60016-3552

847-297-6464
800-297-5660
webmaster@rses.org
www.rses.org

Robert Sherman, Intl President
Lawrence Donaldson, Intl Vice President

Attracts thousands of attendees from all facets of the industry, including contractors, engineers, dealers, distributors, wholesalers, OEM's, architects and builders, industrial plant operators, facility owners and managers, agents and reps.
Frequency: Annual/January

7398 **AISTech Conference & Exposition**
Association for Iron & Steel Technology
186 Thorn Hill Rd
Warrendale, PA 15086-7528

724-814-3000; Fax: 724-814-3001
info@aist.org
www.aist.org

Ronald E Ashburn, Executive Director
Brian Bliss, Technology Programs Manager
Karen Hickey, Publications Manager/Editor
Mark Didiano, Finance & Administration Manager
Stacy Varmecky, Membership Services Manager

Featuring technologies from across the globe, allowing steel producers to compete in today's global market. Submit technical papers for presentation at the event. 300 exhibitors. Registration starts at $425.
7000 Attendees
Frequency: Annual/Spring

7399 **ANS Annual Meeting**
American Nuclear Society
555 North Kensington Avenue
La Grange Park, IL 60526

708-352-6611
800-323-3044; Fax: 708-352-0499
www.ans.org

Serves its members in their efforts to develop and safely apply nuclear science and technology

for public benefit through knowledge exchange, professional development, and enhanced public understanding.
Frequency: Annual/June

7400 **AOCS Annual Meeting & Expo**
American Oil Chemists Society
2710 S Boulder
Urbana, IL 61802-6996
217-359-2344; Fax: 217-351-8091
general@aocs.org
www.aocs.org
Joy McClaugherty, Conference Contact
Jodey Schonfeld, Publications
Frequency: Annual/April-May

7401 **APPA Annual Conference & Exposition**
Association of Higher Education Facilities
1643 Prince Street
Alexandria, VA 22314-2818
703-684-1446; Fax: 703-549-2772
katy@appa.org
www.appa.org
E. Lander Medlin, Executive VP
Anita Dosik, Publications Manager
Ted Weidner, CAPPA Event Contact
Discussions and programs centered around today's educational facilities professionals: gain insight on current trends and conditions, identify challenges and solutions being implemented by industry experts, CEU and networking opportunities, and the innovative showcase of exhibitors.
Frequency: Annual

7402 **ASA Annual Meeting & Noise-Con**
Acoustical Society of America
2 Huntington Quadrable
Suite 1NO1
Melville, NY 11747
516-576-2360; Fax: 516-576-2377
asa@aip.org
www.acousticalsociety.org
Charles E Schmid, Executive Director
Elaine Moran, ASA Office Manager
Mardi Hastings, President
700 Attendees
Frequency: Annual/Spring

7403 **ASA: Drive Systems-Control Units-Automation**
Stygar Associates
1202 Allanson Road
Mundelein, IL 60060
847-566-4566; Fax: 847-566-4580
estygariii@aol.com
376 exhibitors of hydraulic and pneumatic elements, compressed air systems, automation components, openloop and measuring controls.
40000 Attendees
Frequency: Biennial

7404 **ASCE Annual Civil Engineering Conference & Exposition**
American Society of Civil Engineers
1801 Alexander Bell Drive
Reston, VA 20191-4400
703-295-6000
800-548-2723; Fax: 703-295-6144
conf@asce.org
www.asce.org
Mark Geiger, Sr Coor, Exhibits & Meeting Svcs
Heather Doughlin, Sr Mgr, Conferences & Meeting Svcs
Kathy Caldwell, President
175 exhibits of industry related products and services, seminars, workshops and banquet plus continuing education classes.
3000 Attendees
Frequency: Annual/Fall
Founded in 1879

7405 **ASCE Annual Meeting**
American Society of Certified Engineering
PO Box 1348
Flowery Branch, GA 30542-0023
770-967-9173; Fax: 770-967-8049
www.ascet.org
Russell E Freier, Chairman
Leo Saenz, CET, President
Kurt Schuler, Secretary/Treasurer
Frequency: Annual/June

7406 **ASCE's Annual Civil Engineers Conference**
American Society of Civil Engineers
1801 Alexander Bell Drive
Reston, VA 20191-4400
703-295-6000
800-548-2723; Fax: 703-295-6144
www.asce.org
Phil Gaughan, President
Focus on the challenges faced by companies and agencies already implementing the next generation of infrastructure in Water (e.g. dams, desalination, and recycling) and Transportation (e.g. seaports, rail, and roads). 100 booths.
24M Attendees
Frequency: Annual/October

7407 **ASEE Annual Conference & Exposition**
American Society for Engineering Education
1818 N Street NW
Suite 600
Washington, DC 20036-2476
202-331-3500; Fax: 202-265-8504
pubsinfo@asee.org
www.asee.org
Patti Greenawalt, Director Meetings/Conventions
Frank Huband, Executive Director
Frequency: Annual/June

7408 **ASFE Fall Meeting**
ASFE/The Geoprofessional Business Association
8811 Colesville Road
Suite G106
Silver Springs, MD 20910
301-565-2733; Fax: 301-589-2017
info@asfe.org
www.asfe.org
John P Bachner, Executive VP
David Gaboury, President
Frequency: Annual/Fall

7409 **ASFE Spring Meeting**
ASFE/The Geoprofessional Business Association
8811 Colesville Road
Suite G106
Silver Springs, MD 20910
301-565-2733; Fax: 301-589-2017
info@asfe.org
www.asfe.org
John P Bachner, Executive VP
David Gaboury, President
Frequency: Annual/Spring

7410 **ASFE Winter Leadership Conference**
ASFE/The Geoprofessional Business Association
8811 Colesville Road
Suite G106
Silver Springs, MD 20910
301-565-2733; Fax: 301-589-2017
info@asfe.org
www.asfe.org
John Bachner, Executive VP
David Gaboury, President
Frequency: Annual/January

7411 **ASGE National Conference**
American Society of Gas Engineers
P.O. Box 66
Artesia, CA 90702
562-455-9417
asgecge@aol.com
www.asge-national.org
Jerry Moore, Executive Director
Ray Maddock, President
Eric Bruton, Vice President
Chad Johnson, Treasurer
Where members meet to discuss the most current events and issues facing the Gas Appliance industry. Allows individuals to learn about new technology and to network with other Gas Industry Professionals.
300 Members
Frequency: Annual
Founded in 1954

7412 **ASME Annual Meeting**
American Society of Mechanical Engineers
Two Park Avenue
New York, NY 10016-5990
973-882-1170
800-843-2763
williamsk@asme.org
www.asme.org
Kim Williams, Meetings Manager
Forum for information exchange and professional growth for engineering professionals.

7413 **ASNT Annual Conference**
American Society for Nondestructive Testing
1711 Arlingate Lane
PO Box 28518
Columbus, OH 43228-0518
614-274-6003
800-222-2768; Fax: 614-274-6899
www.asnt.org
Arnold Bereson, Executive Director
Scott Cargill, President
Seminar, conference and 150 exhibits of nondestructive testing equipment, services, supplies and laboratory representatives. Holds a smaller conference in the spring.
3000 Attendees
Frequency: Annual

7414 **ASPE Annual Meeting**
American Society for Precision Engineering
3801 Lake Boone Trail
Suite 190
Raleigh, NC 27607
919-839-8444; Fax: 919-839-8039
www.aspe.net
Wendy Shearon, Meetings & Membership Manager
Offering the latest in precision engineering research through presentations from national and international speakers. Participants in the Annual Meeting have the opportunity to exchange ideas with internationally renowned experts in the field.
Frequency: Annual/Oct-Nov

7415 **ASPE Technical Symposium**
American Society of Plumbing Engineers

8614 Catalpa Avenue
Suite 1007
Chicago, IL 60656-1116

773-693-2773; Fax: 773-695-9007
info@aspe.org
www.aspe.org

Pat Delaney, Convention/Symposium Information
Stan Wolson, Executive Director

For professional plumbing engineers, designers and contractors to improve their skills, learn original design concepts and make important networking contacts to help them stay abreast of current trends, codes and technologies.
Frequency: Annual/October

7416 **ATCE**
Society of Petroleum Engineers
PO Box 833836
Richardson, TX 75083-3836

972-529-9300
800-456-6863; Fax: 972-952-9435
spedal@spe.org
www.spe.org

Giovanni Paccaloni, President
Bill Cobb, VP Finance
John E Bethancourt, Director Management/Information
Ian Gorman, Director Production/Operations
Niki Bradbury, Managing Director
40482 Attendees
Frequency: Annual/October

7417 **ATMAE Annual Conference**
Association of Technology, Management, and AE
3801 Lake Boone Trail
Suite 190
Raleigh, NC 27607

919-635-8335
admin@atmae.org
www.atmae.org

Jim Thompson, Executive Director
Cost: $550.00

7418 **AVS International Symposium & Exhibition**
American Vacuum Society
125 Maiden Lane
15th Floor
New York, NY 10038

212-248-0200; Fax: 212-248-0245
jeannette@avs.org
www.avs.org

Jeannette DeGennaro, Exhibition & Sales Coordinator
Angela Klink, Membership Services Coordinator
Heather Korff, Events/Office Coordinator AVS West
Yvonne Towse, Managing Director
Angus Rockett, President

The Symposium and Exhibition has been developed to address cutting-edge issues associated with the vacuum science and technology in both the research and manufacturing communities. It offers a week long forum for exchange, topical conferences, courses, training, career workshops and networking. Over 200 booths of the latest products and services around vacuum science and technology.
3000 Attendees
Frequency: Annual

7419 **AVS International Symposium and Exhibition**
AVS Science & Technology Society
120 Wall Street
32nd Floor
New York, NY 10005-3993

212-248-0200; Fax: 212-248-0245
david_aspnes@avs.org
www.avs.org

David E Aspnes, President
Christie R Marrian, President-Elect
John Coburn, Treasurer
Joseph J Greene, Clerk/Secretary
Yvonne Towse, Executive Director

This has been developed to address cutting-edge issues associated with vacuum science and technology in both the research and manufacturing communities. The Symposium is a week long forum for science and technology exchange featuring papers from technical divisions and technology groups, and topical conferences on emerging technologies.
3000 Attendees
Founded in 1953

7420 **AVS New Mexico Chapter Annual Symposium Short Courses/Vendor Show**
AVS Science & Technology Society
120 Wall Street
32nd Floor
New York, NY 10005-3993

212-248-0200; Fax: 212-248-0245
david_aspnes@avs.org
www.avs.org

David E Aspnes, President
Christie R Marrian, President-Elect
John Coburn, Treasurer
Joseph J Greene, Clerk/Secretary
Yvonne Towse, Executive Director
Frequency: Annual/May

7421 **Adhesion Society Annual Meeting**
Adhesion Society
2 Davidson Hall-0201
Blacksburg, VA 24061

540-231-7257; Fax: 540-231-3971
www.adhesionsociety.org

Ken Shull, Program Chair
Leonardo Lopez, Exhibition Chair
Esther Brann, Office Manager

Engineers, chemists, biologists, mathematicians, physicists, physicians and dentists visit exhibits relating to the study of adhesion's role in coatings, composite materials, the function of biological tissues, and the performance of bonded structures.
400 Attendees
Frequency: Annual/February

7422 **Adhesive & Sealant Fall Convention**
Adhesive & Sealant Council
7101 Wisconsin Avenue
Suite 990
Bethesda, MD 20814

301-986-9700; Fax: 301-986-9795
data@ascouncil.org
www.ascouncil.org

Malinda Armstrong, Director, Meetings & Expositions
William Allmond, President
Frequency: Annual/October

7423 **Airlines Engineering Committee**
Aeronautical Radio
2551 Riva Road
Annapolis, MD 21401-7435

410-266-4000; Fax: 410-266-4040

Daniel Martinec, Director Avionics

Commercial airline and other transport aircraft avionics engineers.
800 Attendees
Frequency: October

7424 **American Association for the Advancement of Science Annual Meeting**
American Assn for the Advancement of Science
1200 New York Ave NW
Washington, DC 20005

202-326-6400
www.aaas.org

Alan I. Leshner, Interim Chief Executive Officer
Founded in 1848

7425 **American Society for Engineering Education Conference and Exposition**
American Society for Engineering Education
1818 N State Street
Suite 600
Washington, DC 20036

202-331-3500; Fax: 202-265-8504
conferences@asee.org
www.asee.org

Patti Greenawalt, Director Conventions/Meetings
Jennifer Atkinson, Meetings Assistant
Kathi J Springer, Manager Exhibits/Sponsorships
Frank Huband, Executive Director

Annual conference of 150 publishers, manufacturers, producers, suppliers, designers of scientific instrumentation and distributors. Exhibits include publications, engineering supplies and equipment, computers, software and research companies all products and services related to engineering education.
1700 Attendees
Frequency: Annual/June

7426 **American Society of Plumbing Engineers Meeting**
American Society of Plumbing Engineers
2980 S River Road
Des Plaines, IL 60018

847-296-0002; Fax: 773-695-9007
info@aspe.org
www.aspe.org

Cliff Reis, Managing Director of Education
Jim Kendzel, Executive Director

Biennial meeting and exhibits for the plumbing engineering industry. 600 booths.
7000 Attendees
Founded in 1964

7427 **American Society of Safety Engineers Professional Development Conference**
American Society of Safety Engineers
1800 E Oakton Street
Des Plaines, IL 60018

847-699-2929; Fax: 847-768-3434
customerservice@asse.org
www.asse.org

Terri Norris, President
James Smith, Vice President/ Finance
Diane Hurns, Manager Public Relations Department

Annual conference and expo of 250 manufacturers and suppliers of safety equipment and health products.
3500 Attendees
Frequency: Annual/June

7428 **Annual Applied Reliability Engineering and Product Assurance**
The University of Arizona

Aerospace and Mechanical Engineering Department
Building 119, PO Box 210119
Tucson, AZ 85721-0119

520-215-5511; Fax: 520-621-8191

Dimitri B Kececioglu PE, Professor Aerospace/Mechanical Eng.
Frequency: Annual/July

7429 **Annual Canadian Conference on Intelligent Systems**
Robotics Industris Association
900 Victors Way
PO Box 3724
Ann Arbor, MI 48106

734-994-6088; Fax: 734-994-3338
webmaster@robotics.org
www.robotics.org

Don Vincent, Executive VP
Brian Huse, Director Marketing/PR
Jim Adams, Manager of Public Relations
Sharon Adams, Accounting Manager

Canada's leading showcase of research excellence and breakthroughs in robotics and intelligent systems, featuring technology displays, demonstrations, presentations and workshops.
Frequency: Annual/June

7430 **Annual Lean Management Solutions Conference**
Institute of Industrial Engineers
3577 Parkway Lane
Suite 200
Norcross, GA 30092

770-449-0460
800-494-0460; Fax: 770-441-3295
cs@iienet.org

Gregg Griffith, Marketing Director
Don Greene, CEO

Will enable you to significantly improve performance, reduce costs, and increase customer satisfaction. With over 60 presentations and new tracks in MRO, Food Processing, Aviation, Healthcare, and Product Design, you will find what you need.
Frequency: Annual/December

7431 **Annual Meeting of the Society of Rheology**
Socieety of Rheology
2 Huntington Quadrangle
Suite 1N01
Meville, NY 11747-4502

516-576-2471; Fax: 516-576-2223
rheology@aip.org
www.rheology.org

A. Jeffrey Giacomin, VP
Faith Morrison, President
Frequency: Annual/October

7432 **Annual Physical Electronics Conference**
AVS Science & Technology Society
120 Wall Street
32nd Floor
New York, NY 10005-3993

212-248-0200; Fax: 212-248-0245
david_aspnes@avs.org
www.avs.org

David E Aspnes, President
Christie R Marrian, President-Elect
John Coburn, Treasurer
Joseph J Greene, Clerk/Secretary
Nancy Schultheis, Office Manager

Will provide a forum for the dissemination and discussion of new research results in the physics and chemistry of surfaces and interfaces. The conference will continue to emphasize fundamental science in materials systems, including metals, semiconductors, insulators and biomaterials.
Frequency: Annual/June

7433 **Annual RSES Conference & Expo**
Refrigeration Service Engineers Society
1666 Rand Road
Des Plaines, IL 60016-3552

847-297-6464
800-297-5660
webmaster@rses.org
www.rses.org

Robert Sherman, Intl President
Lawrence Donaldson, Intl Vice President
Frequency: Annual/September

7434 **Annual Simulation Solutions Conference**
Institute of Industrial Engineers
3577 Parkway Lane
Suite 200
Norcross, GA 30092

770-449-0460
800-494-0460; Fax: 770-441-3295
cs@iienet.org

Greg Griffith, Marketing Director
Don Greene, CEO

You will have a rich menu of over forty presentations by successful practitioners of simulation in transportation and military applications; management strategies; manufacturing; lean scheduling and operations; healthcare; simulation skills; supply chain, material handling, and distribution; and service and business processes.
Frequency: Annual/May

7435 **Atlantic Design & Manufacturing**
Canon Communications
11444 W Olympic Boulevard
Suite 900
Los Angeles, CA 90064-1549

310-445-4200; Fax: 310-445-4299
www.cancom.com

Diane O'Conner, Trade Show Director
Dan Cutrone, Show Marketing Manager

Serves the East Coast's dynamic design, process, and manufacturing marketplace. This exposition, recently acquired by Canon Communications, is now co-located with Medical Design and Manufacturing East. Product classifications include: Coatings and Finishes, Composites, Computer Aided Design/Computer Aided Manufacturing, Electrical/Electronic, Electric Optical Components and Equipment, Engineered Safety Products, Engineering Management and Tools, Fasteners, Fluid Media, Fluid Power and Control.
Frequency: Annual/May

7436 **Atomic Layer Deposition**
AVS Science & Technology Society
120 Wall Street
32nd Street
New York, NY 10005-3993

212-248-0200; Fax: 212-248-0245
david_aspnes@avs.org
www.avs.org

David E Aspnes, President
Chrisitie R Marrian, President-Elect
John Coburn, Treasurer
Joseph J Greene, Clerk/Secretary
Nancy Schultheis, Office Manager

Conference will be a three-day meeting, dedicated to the science and technology of atomic layer controlled deposition of thin films, in particular atomic layer deposition.
Frequency: Annual/August

7437 **Automate**
Motion Control & Motor Association
900 Victors Way
Suite 140
Ann Arbor, MI 48108

734-994-6088
info@motioncontrolonline.org
www.motioncontrolonline.org

Matt French, Chair
Gunnar Block, Vice Chair
Paul Horvat, Vice Chair

Trade show and conference on automation technologies.
20K Attendees

7438 **BMES Annual Fall Meeting**
Biomedical Engineering Society
8201Corporate Drive
Suite 1125
Landover, MD 20785-2224

301-459-1999
877-871-BMES; Fax: 301-459-2444
info@bmes.org
www.bmes.org

Richard Waugh, President
Edward Schilling, Executive Director
Debra Tucker, Meetings Director
Frequency: Annual/September

7439 **CABA Smart Buildings Summit**
Continental Automated Buildings Association
1173 Cyrville Road
Suite 210
Ottawa, Canada, ON K1J 7S6

613-686-1814
888-798-2222; Fax: 613-744-7833
caba@caba.org
www.caba.org
Facebook, Twitter, LinkedIn, YouTube

Ronald J Zimmer, President & CEO
Conrad McCallum, Communications Director
Greg Walker, Research Director
Andrew Glennie, Member Services Coordinator
Sashien Godakandae, Business Development Officer

Current intelligent building technologies.
380+ Members
Founded in 1988

7440 **CFMA Annual Conference & Exhibition**
Construction Financial Management Association
100 Village Boulevard
Suite 200
Princeton, NJ 08540

609-452-8000; Fax: 609-452-0474
info@cfma.org
www.cfma.org

Stuart Binstock, President & CEO
Brian Summers, VP, Operations

A resource for construction financial professionals.
Frequency: Annual/May

7441 **Design Part Show**
Job Shop Company
16 Waterbury Road
Prospect, CT 06712-1215

800-317-0474
www.jobshoptechnology.com

Gerald Schmidt, President
Jennifer Bryda, Production Manager

The show is designed to attract the highest caliber engineers and buyers from your major DEM product manufacturers.
2000 Attendees
Frequency: Annual/April
Founded in 1999

7442 **EASTEC Exposition**
Society of Manufacturing Engineers
1 SME Drive
Dearborn, MI 48128

313-425-3000
800-733-4763; Fax: 313-425-3400
service@sme.org
www.easteconline.com/about/about-eastec

Jeffrey M. Krause, CEO
Nancy Totten, Conference Management
Kim Farrugia, CEM, Event Management
Chris Moody, Event Operations
Patti Miller, EASTEC Marketing

Exposition with over 500 exhibitors presenting information on technologies and manufacturing.
65K Members
Frequency: Annual/May
Founded in 1932

7443 **ESTECH, IEST's Annual Technical Meeting and Exposition**
American Institute of Physics
One Physics Ellispe
College Park, MD 20740-3843

301-209-3100
dylla@aip.org
www.aip.org

H. Frederick Dylia, Executive Director/CEO
John Haynes, Vice President Publishing
Benjamin Snavely, AIP Corporate Secretary
Melissa Poleski, Assistant To Corporate Secretary

Will feature a cutting-edge technical program, hot-topic tutorials, must attend Working Group meetings, and a state-of-the-art exposition.
Frequency: Annual/May

7444 **Earth and Space**
American Society of Civil Engineers
1801 Alexander Bell Drive
Reston, VA 20191

703-295-6000
800-548-2723; Fax: 703-295-6222
webmaster@asce.org
www.asce.org

Patricia Galloway, President
Lawrence Roth, Deputy Executive Director
Patrick Natale, Secretary/Treasurer

You will be among experts from a variety of disciplines and have ample, enjoyable opportunities to discuss exploration, engineering, construction, and operations in challenging environments on Planet Earth, in Space, and on other planetary bodies such as the Moon and Mars.
Frequency: Annual/March

7445 **East Energy Conference & Expo**
Association of Energy Engineers
3168 Mercer University Drive
Atlanta, GA 30341

770-447-5083
www.aeecenter.org
Facebook, Twitter, LinkedIn, YouTube

Albert Thumann, Executive Director

Learn about the latest developments from business, industry and government sectors.
17500 Members
Founded in 1977

7446 **Electric West**
PRIMEDIA Business Exhibitions
11 River Bend Drive S
PO Box 4949
Stamford, CT 06907-0949

203-358-9900; Fax: 203-358-5816

Liza Wylie, Show Director
Mandy Ferreira-Nunez, Operations Manager

Educational sessions attract electrical professionals from contracting companies, industrial plants, consulting engineering firms, datacom installers and electricians. Presentations focus on such topics as power quality, lighting, the NEC, project management, claims management and fiber optics. Also provides in-depth coverage of National Electrical Code changes that directly impact the work of electrical professionals.
Frequency: Annual/March

7447 **European Symposium of the Protein Society**
American Institute of Physics
One Physics Ellipse
College Park, MD 20740-3843

301-209-3100
dylla@aip.org
www.aip.org

H. Frederick Dylla, Executive Director/CEO
John Haynes, Vice President Publishing
Benjamin Snavely, AIP Corporate Secretary
Melissa Poleski, Assistant To Corporate Secretary

The meeting features sessions on nanotechnology, biosensors and proteins as materials, proteomics, protein networks and systems biology. membrane proteins and diseases, protein folding and diseases, protein flexibility, and molecular recognition.
Frequency: Annual/May

7448 **GBA Fall Conference**
Geoprofessional Business Association
15800 Crabbs Branch Way
Suite 300
Rockville, MD 20855

301-565-2733
info@geoprofessional.org
www.geoprofessional.org

Joel G. Carson, Executive Director
Sara Menase, Program Manager/Membership Services
Barb Nappy, Director of Events

A conference where members of the GBA can network, collaborate, and learn from fellow colleagues and experts about geoprofessional business issues.
Frequency: Annual/Fall
Founded in 1969

7449 **GBA Spring Conference**
Geoprofessional Business Association
15800 Crabbs Branch Way
Suite 300
Rockville, MD 20855

301-565-2733
info@geoprofessional.org
www.geoprofessional.org

Joel G. Carson, Executive Director
Sara Menase, Program Manager/Membership Services
Barb Nappy, Director of Events

A conference where geoprofessionals can network, collaborate, and learn from colleagues and experts about geoprofessional business issues.
Frequency: Annual/Spring
Founded in 1969

7450 **GeoFlorida**
Geo-Institute, American Society of Civil Engineers
1801 Alexander Bell Drive
Reston, VA 20191-4400

703-295-6350; Fax: 703-295-6351
stacey.gardiner@tggroup.com

Stacey Gardiner, Conference Director
Greory DiLoreto, President- Elect
Mark Rusnica, Deputy Executive Director

The annual geo-conference of the Geo-Institute of ASCE. Presents developments in geotechnical engineering analysis, modeling and design; opportunities to share knowledge, learn about innovations and emerging technologies; panel discussions, technical sessions, lectures, short courses, workshops and student competition; and an extensive exhibit hall.
Frequency: Annual

7451 **Government Affairs Briefing**
North American Die Casting Association
241 Holbrook Drive
Wheeling, IL 60090-5809

847-279-0001; Fax: 847-279-0002
twarog@diecasting.org
www.diecasting.org

Daniel Twarog, President

Will provide you with important information in the following informative sessions, state of US manufacturing, trade and global competition, metalcasting research programs, health care & other worker issues, new air standards & other environmental issues.
Frequency: Annual/June

7452 **Heat Treating Society Conference & Expo**
ASM International
9639 Kinsman Road
Materials Park, OH 44073-0002

440-338-5151
800-336-5152; Fax: 440-338-4634
memberservicecenter@asminternational.org
www.asminternational.org

William T. Mahoney, Secretary & CEO
Lindy Good, Global Conference & Exhibit Planner

Conference and expo for heat treating equipment and supplies as well as information of interest to metallurgists, maintenance supervisors and production engineering staff.
30K Members
Frequency: October
Founded in 1913

7453 **IDSA National Conference**
Industrial Designers Society of America
45195 Business Court
Suite 250
Sterling, VA 20166-6717

703-707-6000; Fax: 703-787-8501
idsa@idsa.org
www.idsa.org

Clive Roux, CEO
Bob Swartz, Executive Director
Kaycee Childress, Marketing
Roxann Henze, Press, Media & Public Relations

IDSA is the world's oldest, largest, member-driven society for product design, industrial design, interaction design, human factors, ergonomics, design research, design management, universal design and related design fields. IDSA organizes the renowned International Design Excellence Award competition annually; hosts the International Design Conference and five regional conferences each year.
800 Attendees
Frequency: Annual/August

7454 **IEEE SoutheastCon**
IEEE Meeting & Conference Management (MCM)
445 Hoes Lane
Piscataway, NJ 08854

732-562-3878
800-678-4333; Fax: 732-971-1203
conference-services@ieee.org
www.ieee.org
Facebook, LinkedIn, Instagram

A student conference, technical conference, and business meeting.
800 Attendees
Frequency: Annual

7455 **IES Annual Meeting**
Illuminating Engineering Society of North America
120 Wall Street
17th Floor
New York, NY 10005

212-248-5000; Fax: 212-248-5018
ies@ies.org
www.ies.org

William Hanley, Executive VP
Marianne Conrad, Director Member Services
400 Attendees
Frequency: Annual

7456 **IFAI Annual Expo**
Industrial Fabrics Association International
1801 Country Road BW
Roseville, MN 55113

651-222-2508
800-225-4324; Fax: 651-631-9334
generalinfo@ifai.com
www.ifai.com

Aaron Monson, Education & Events Manager
Christian Welland, Marketing & Communicaitons Manager

A trade event in the Americas for the technical textiles and specialty fabrics industry.
Frequency: Annual/September

7457 **IFAI Outlook**
Industrial Fabrics Association International
1801 Country Road BW
Roseville, MN 55113

651-222-2508
800-225-4324; Fax: 651-631-9334
generalinfo@ifai.com
www.usifi.com

Todd Lindemann, VP Conference Manger
Stephen Warner, President

Will bring industry leaders together to discuss important issues and challenges faced by the United States textile industry.
Frequency: Annual/May

7458 **IIE Annual Conference**
Institute of Industrial Engineers
3577 Parkway Lane
Suite 200
Norcross, GA 30092

770-449-0460
800-494-0460; Fax: 770-441-3295
cs@iienet.org

Greg Griffith, Marketing Director
Don Greene, CEO

With over 600 content filled presentations and expert speakers, it is the productivity event of the year. Discover the latest tools, techniques and solutions from top professionals in the field. Network with peers, decision makers, and leaders during the conference.
1,100 Attendees
Frequency: Annual/May

7459 **IPTC**
Society of Petroleum Engineers
PO Box 833836
Richardson, TX 75083-3836

972-529-9300
800-456-6863; Fax: 972-952-9435
spedal@spe.org
www.spe.org

Giovanni Paccaloni, President
Bill Cobbs, VP Finance
John E Berthancourt, Director Management/Information
Ian Gorman, Director Production/Operations
Niki Bradbury, Managing Director

The theme for the conference is Sustaining World Growth - Technology and People. A new meeting brought to you by four leading industry societies (AAPG, EAGE, SEG, and SPE). Natural gas will be a major focus of this meeting.
Frequency: Annual/November

7460 **IRI Annual Meeting**
Industrial Research Institute
2200 Clarendon Boulevard
Suite 1102
Arlington, VA 22201

703-647-2580; Fax: 703-647-2581
www.iriweb.org

Robert Kumpf, Chairman
Ryan Dirkx, Chairman-Elect
Edward Bernstein, President
Frequency: Annual/May

7461 **ISWM Annual Conference & Expo**
International Society of Weighing & Measurement
1801 Alexander Bell Avenue
Reston, VA 20191

703-295-6350; Fax: 703-295-6351
staff@iswm.org

Kate Fitzgerald CMP, Director of Meetings

150 booths; presentations from industry leaders; workshops, panels, and discussions.
1.8M Attendees

7462 **International Code Council Annual Conference**
BOCA Evaluation Services
500 New Jersey Avenue
6th Fl
Washington, DC 20001-2070

888-422-7233; Fax: 202-783-2348
webmaster@iccsafe.org
www.iccsafe.org

James Brothers, President
William Dupler, Vice President

The conference features the Final Action Hearings, the Education Program, the Annual Business Meeting, the International Code Council Expo and networking opportunities with your peers in the building safety and fire prevention fields.
Frequency: Annual/September

7463 **International Conference on Automation Science and Engineering**
IEEE Robotics and Automation Society
445 Hoes Lane
Piscataway, NJ

732-562-3906
ras@ieee.org
www.ieee-ras.org

Kathy Colabaugh, Society Operations Manager
Amy Reeder, Society Program Specialist
Alexis Simoes, Society Program Coordinator

CASE is the flagship conference of the IEEE Robotics and Automation Society.

7464 **International Conference on Construction Engineering/Management**
American Society for Civil Engineers
1801 Alexander Bell Drive
Reston, VA 20191

703-295-6000
800-548-2723; Fax: 703-295-6222
webmaster@asce.org
www.asce.org

Patricia Galloway, President
Lawrence Roth, Deputy Executive Director
Patrick Natale, Secretary/Treasurer
Frequency: Annual/October

7465 **International Conference on Electronics, Circuits, and Systems**
IEEE Circuits and Systems Society
445 Hoes Lane
Piscataway, NJ 08854

manager@ieee-cas.org
www.ieee-cas.org

Brittian Parkinson, Operations Manager
Myung Hoon Sunwoo, VP, Conferences
Frequency: Annual

7466 **International Conference on Intelligent Robots and Systems**
Robotics and Automation Society
445 Hoes Lane
Piscataway, NJ

732-562-3906
ras@ieee.org
www.ieee-ras.org

Kathy Colabaugh, Society Operations Manager
Amy Reeder, Society Program Specialist
Alexis Simoes, Society Program Coordinator

7467 **International Conference on Metallurgical Coatings and Thin Films**
AVS Science & Technology Society
120 Wall Street
32nd Floor
New York, NY 10005-3993

212-248-0200; Fax: 212-248-0245
david_aspnes@avs.org
www.avs.com

David E Aspnes, President
Christie R Marrian, President-Elect
John Coburn, Treasurer
Joseph J Greene, Clerk/Secretary
Steve Sukman, Executive Vice President

Internationally recognized as a vibrant technical conference that integrates fundamentals and applied research focused on thin film deposition, characterization, and advanced surface modification techniques leading-edge technology.
Frequency: Annual/May

7468 **International Conference on Robotics and Automation**
Robotics and Automation Society
445 Hoes Lane
Piscataway, NJ

732-562-3906
ras@ieee.org
www.ieee-ras.org

Kathy Colabaugh, Society Operations Manager
Amy Reeder, Society Program Specialist
Alexis Simoes, Society Program Coordinator

7469 **International Conference on Shape Memory and Superelastic Technologies**
ASM International
9639 Kinsman Road
Materials Park, OH 44073-0002

440-338-5151
800-336-5152; Fax: 440-338-4634
memberservicecenter@asminternational.org
www.asminternational.org/web/smst

William T. Mahoney, Secretary & CEO
Lindy Good, Global Conference & Exhibit Planner

A forum for the discussion of SMA design in Irish Biotechnology.
30K Members
Frequency: May
Founded in 1913

7470 **International Symposium for Testing & Failure Analysis**
ASM International

9639 Kinsman Road
Materials Park, OH 44073-0002

440-338-5151
800-336-5152; Fax: 440-338-4634
memberservicecenter@asminternational.org
www.asminternational.org

William T. Mahoney, Secretary & CEO
Lindy Good, Global Conference & Exhibit Planner

Annual event focusing on failure analysis and makers of tools such as microscopes, stress and measurement analytical tools, etchants and chemicals, ESD protective materials and other products used for this purpose.
30K Members
Frequency: Annual/Oct/Nov
Founded in 1913

7471 **International Symposium on Advances in Abrasives Technology**
Abrasive Engineering Society
141 Moore Road
Butler, PA 16001

724-826-6210; Fax: 742-234-2376
aes@abrasiveengineering.com
www.abrasiveengineering.com

Doug Haynes, President
Ted Giese, Executive Director

Jointly sponsored by the International Committee for Abrasives Technology and the Japan Society for Abrasive Technology, which has conducted eight international conferences on abrasives technologies. Topics including abrasive machining, finishing, assessment of grinding performance, machine tools and systems, coolant and other topics.
Frequency: Annual/November

7472 **International Symposium on Circuits and Systems**
IEEE Circuits and Systems Society
445 Hoes Lane
Piscataway, NJ 08854

manager@ieee-cas.org
www.ieee-cas.org

Brittian Parkinson, Operations Manager
Myung Hoon Sunwoo, VP, Conferences
Frequency: Annual

7473 **International Thermal Spray Conference & Exposition**
ASM International
9639 Kinsman Road
Materials Park, OH 44073-0002

440-338-5151
800-336-5152; Fax: 440-338-4634
memberservicecenter@asminternational.org
www.asminternational.org

William T. Mahoney, Secretary & CEO
Lindy Good, Global Conference & Exhibit Planner

International annual conference for professional thermal spray technologists, researchers, manufacturers and suppliers.
30K Members
Frequency: Annual/May
Founded in 1913

7474 **International Workshop on Deep Inelastic Scattering - DIS05**
American Institute of Physics
One Physics Ellipse
College Park, MD 20740-3843

301-209-3100
dylla@aip.org
www.aip.org

H. Frederick Dylla, Executive Director/CEO
Benjamin Snavely, Senior Executive Secretary
Benjamin Snavely, AIP Corporate Secretary
Melissa Poleski, Assistant to Corporate Secretary

The aim of these workshops is to review the progress in the field of DIS and QCD and to discuss and lay the groundwork for the future. DIS 2005 will bring together about 250 experimentalists and theorists. The workshop format will involve plenary sessions with review talks and parallel working group sessions with shorter contributions.
Frequency: Annual/April

7475 **LIGHTFAIR International Trade Show**
Illuminating Engineering Society of North America
120 Wall Street
17th Floor
New York, NY 10005

212-248-5000; Fax: 212-248-5018
ies@ies.org
www.ies.org

William Hanley, Executive VP
Marianne Conrad, Director Member Services
Denis Lavoie, President
23000 Attendees
Frequency: Annual

7476 **Lean and Six Sigma Conference**
American Society for Quality
600 N Plankinton Avenue
Milwaukee, WI 53203

414-272-8575
800-248-1946; Fax: 414-272-1734
help@asq.org
asq.org/conferences/six-sigma

Elmer Corbin, Chair
Bill Troy, CEO
Brian Savoie, Chief Financial Officer
Andrew Baines, Managing Director, Global
Ann Jordan, General Counsel

Networking event for practitioners in the Lean Six Sigma community. Industries addressed will include operations, manufacturing, transactional, healthcare, financial, service and government.
80K Members
Frequency: Annual/February
Founded in 1946

7477 **MCAA Annual Conference**
Mechanical Contractors Association of America
1385 Piccard Drive
Rockville, MD 20850-4340

301-869-5800; Fax: 301-990-9690
www.mcaa.org

Lonnie Coleman, MCAA President

Containing 100 booths and 95 exhibits. Education sessions, leadership and keynote presentations, exhibitions.

7478 **MCAA Industry Forum**
Measurement, Control & Automation Association
200 City Hall Avenue
Suite D
Poquoson, VA 23662

757-258-3100
automationassociation.com

Teresa Sebring, President
Andrea Ambrose, Director, Member Relations
Elizabeth Horton, Programs Manager
Kim Malina, Marketing Communications Manager
Rebecca Moore, Administrative Manager

Education and networking event for manufacturers and distributors of instrumentation, systems, and software products for industrial process control and factory automation.
Founded in 1944

7479 **MCMA TechCon**
Motion Control & Motor Association
900 Victors Way
Suite 140
Ann Arbor, MI 48108

734-994-6088
info@motioncontrolonline.org
www.motioncontrolonline.org

Matt French, Chair
Gunnar Block, Vice Chair
Paul Horvat, Vice Chair

The Motion Control & Motor Association Technical Conference provides attendees with recent updates on motion control and automation.

7480 **MIACON Construction, Mining & Waste Management Show**
Finocchiaro Enterprises
2921 Coral Way
Miami, FL 33145

305-441-2865; Fax: 305-529-9217
www.miacon.com

Michael Finocchiaro, President
Jose Garcia, VP
Justine Finocchiaro, Chief Operations

Annual show of 650 manufacturers, suppliers, distributors and exporters of equipment, machinery, supplies and services for the construction, mining and waste managment industries. There will be 600 booths.
10M Attendees
Frequency: Annual/October
Founded in 1994

7481 **Meeting of the Acoustical Society of America**
Acoustical Society of America
2 Huntington Quandrangle
Suite 1N01
Melville, NY 11747-4502

516-576-2360; Fax: 516-576-2377
asa@aip.org
www.acousticalsociety.org

William A Kuperman, President
William A Yost, President-Elect
Mark F Hamilton, VP
Donna L Neff, VP Elect
Charles E Schmid, Executive Director
Frequency: Annual/May

7482 **Metalcasting Congress**
North American Die Casting Association
241 Holbrook Drive
Wheeling, IL 60090-5809

847-279-0001; Fax: 847-279-0002
twarog@diecasting.org
www.diecasting.org

Daniel Twarog, President

With the wide range of opportunities for technology transfer, it promises to be the industry's premier show. The American Foundry Society and the North American Die Casting Association are joining together.
Frequency: Annual/April

7483 **Mid-Atlantic Job Shop Show**
Edward Publishing
16 Waterbury Road
Prospect, CT 06712-1215

203-758-6658; Fax: 203-758-4476
www.jobshoptechnology.com

Jennifer Bryda, Production Manager

The show is designed to attract the highest caliber engineers and buyers from your major DEM product manufacturers. There will be 260 exhibitors and booths.
2500 Attendees
Frequency: Annual/May
Founded in 1999

7484 **NACE International Annual Conference & Expo (CORROSION)**
NACE International
1440 S Creek Drive
Houston, TX 77084-4906

281-228-6200
800-797-6223; Fax: 281-228-6300
firstservice@nace.org
www.nace.org

Oliver Moghissi, President
Bob Chalker, Executive Director

World's largest conference dedicated to Corrosion control and prevention
5000 Attendees
Frequency: Annual

7485 **NADCA Sales Training**
North American Die Casting Association
241 Holbrook Drive
Wheeling, IL 60090-5809

847-279-0001; Fax: 847-279-0002
twarog@diecasting.org
www.diecasting.org

Daniel Twarog, President

NADCA will be providing a one day seminar to address the challenges we face in today's marketplace.
Frequency: Annual/June

7486 **NSPE Annual Convention and Expo**
National Society of Professional Engineers
1420 King Street
Alexandria, VA 22314-2794

703-684-2800
888-285-2853; Fax: 703-836-4875
webmaster@nspe.org
www.nspe.org

Katrina Robinson, Marketing Manager

The National Society of Professional Engineers is the only engineering society that represents individual engineering professionals and licensed engineers across all disciplines. Founded in 1934, NSPE serves some 60,000 members and the public through 53 state and territorial societies and more than 500 chapters nationally and internationally. The conference brings together the decision makers of engineering companies and business owners nationwide to network and discuss issues of importance.
700 Attendees
Frequency: Annual/July
Mailing list available for rent: 50,000+ names at $130 per M

7487 **National Industrial Automation, Integration & Control Show**
Reed Exhibition Companies
383 Main Avenue Suite 3
PO Box 6059
Norwalk, CT 06851-1543

203-840-4800; Fax: 203-840-5805
inquiry@reedexpo.com
www.reedexpo.com

Peter DiLeo, Marketing Director
Mike Rusbridge, CEO
Domonic Shine, Chief Information Officer

Annual show of 200 exhibitors of chemical engineering and processing, electronics, machinery equipment, supplies and services.
19M Attendees

7488 **Northern American Material Handling Show & Forum**
Appliance Manufacturer
5900 Harper Road
Suite 105
Solon, OH 44139-1935

440-349-3060
800-345-1815; Fax: 440-498-9121
cmiller@mhia.org

Carol Miller, Senior Director Marketing
Frequency: Bi-Annual

7489 **Northwest Plant Engineering & Maintenance Show and Conference (NWPE)**
Cygnus Expositions
3167 Skyway Court
Fremont, CA 94539

510-543-3131; Fax: 510-354-3159
facilitiesexpo.com

Erin Sparks, Marketing Manager
Paul Bonaiuto, CFO
Kathy Scott, Director of Public Relations

Annual show of 233 exhibitors of low-tech cleaning systems, high-tech computerized maintenance management systems, diagnostic problem software, indoor air quality controllers and related products and services.
5000 Attendees
Frequency: Annual/May

7490 **Nuclear and Emerging Technologies for Space**
555 N Kensington Ave
La Grange Park, IL 60526-5592

708-352-6611
800-323-3044; Fax: 708-352-0499
advertising@ans.org
www.ans.org
Facebook, Twitter, LinkedIn

Jack Tuohy, Executive Director
James S Tulenko, VP
William F Naughton, Treasurer

Positive collaborative environment and series of discussion forums and technical showcasing.
10500 Members
Founded in 1954

7491 **OTC Expo**
Society of Petroleum Engineers
PO Box 833836
Richardson, TX 75083-3836
972-529-9300
800-456-6863; Fax: 972-952-9435
spedal@spe.org
www.spe.org

Giovanni Paccaloni, President
Bill Cobbs, VP Finance
John E Bethancourt, Director Management/Information
Ian Gorman, Director Production/Operations
Niki Bradbury, Managing Director
51300 Attendees

7492 **Pacific Design & Manufacturing**
Canon Communications
11444 W Olympic Boulevard
Suite 900
Los Angeles, CA 90064-1549

310-445-4200; Fax: 310-445-4299
www.pacdesignshow.com

Diane O'Conner, Trade Show Director
Dan Cutrone, Show Marketing Manager

The Pacific Design Engineering show is the most comprehensive event serving the West Coast's design, process and manufacturing marketplace. Product classifications include Coatings & Finishes, Composites, Computer Aided Design/Computer Aided Manufacturing, Electrical/Electronic, ElectroOptical Components & Equipment, Engineered Safety products, Engineering Management & Tools and more. Held at the Anaheim Convention Center in Anaheim, California.
35970 Attendees
Frequency: Annual/January

7493 **Plant & Facilities Expo (PFE)**
Association of Energy Engineers
3168 Mercer University Drive
Atlanta, GA 30341

770-447-5083
www.aeecenter.org

Albert Thumann, Executive Director

Seek solutions for plant and facility needs. Vendors have an opportunity to meet prospective customers, reacquaint themselves with existing customers, and network with other vendors.

7494 **ProMat**
Material Handling Industry of America
8720 Red Oak Blvd
Suite 201
Charlotte, NC 28217

704-676-1190
800-345-1815; Fax: 704-676-1199
www.mhia.org

Tom Carbott, Exhibiting Information
Terri Heisey, Educational Conference & Seminar

You can compare the latest solutions essential to the productivity of your manufacturing, warehousing, and distribution operations. The material handling & logistics solutions you discover at ProMat will help you differentiate your product, improve customer service and increase overall corporate profitability. 700 exhibits.
Frequency: Annual

7495 **Professional Development Conference & Exposition**
1800 E Oakton Street
Des Plaines, IL 60018

847-699-2929; Fax: 847-768-3434
customerservice@asse.org
www.asse.org
Facebook, Twitter, LinkedIn

Fred Fortman, Executive Director
Bruce Sufranski, Finance/Controller Director
Diane Hurns, Manager Public Relations Department
Sally Madden, Human Resources Manager

The American Society of Safety Engineers (ASSE) is the oldest professional safety society committed to protecting people, property and the environment. ASSE has more than 32,000 occupational safety, health and environmental (SH&E) professional members who manage, supervise, research and consult on safety, health, transportation and the environment in all industries, government, labor and education.
34000 Members
4,000 Attendees
Founded in 1911

7496 **REMSA and AREMA Meeting**
Railway Engineering: Maintenance Supplies Assn
500 New Jersey Avenue
Suite 400
Washington, DC 20001

202-715-2921; Fax: 202-204-5753
home@remsa.org
www.remsa.org

Philip Hoffman, President
John Fox, VP
David Soule, Executive Director
Ronald C Olds, Secretary/Treasurer

Holding the exhibits and technical conference simultaneously in Louisville give added benefit to REMSA members.
Frequency: Annual/September

7497 **REMSA and NRC: Synergy in Action**
Railway Engineering: Maintenance Supplies Assn
500 New Jersey Avenue
Suite 400
Washington, DC 20001
202-715-2921; Fax: 202-204-5753
home@remsa.org
www.remsa.org
Philip Hoffman, President
John Fox, VP
David Soule, Executive Director
Ronald C Olds, Secretary/Treasurer
Members and other industry suppliers discuss their products, services and equipment with attendees representing a broad spectrum of railroaders: transits, short lines, commuter and Class I railroads. There were 56 exhibiting companies.
Frequency: Annual/January

7498 **RSES Annual Conference and HVAC Technology Expo**
Refrigeration Service Engineers Society
1666 Rand Road
Des Plaines, IL 60016-3552
847-297-6464
800-297-5660
general@rses.org
www.rses.org
Facebook, Twitter, LinkedIn
Lawrence Donaldson, Intl. Executive Vice President
Josh Flaim, Operations Manager
Jean Birch, Conference & Seminar Manager
80 booths consisting primarily of products and services.

7499 **RoboBusiness Conference and Exposition**
American Institute of Physics
One Physics Ellipse
College Park, MD 20740-3843
301-209-3100
dylla@aip.org
www.aip.org
H. Frederick Dylla, Executive Director/CEO
John Haynes, Vice President Publishing
Benjamin Snavely, AIP Corporate Secretary
Melissa Poleski, Assistant To Corporate Secretary
Focuses on the business development and technical issues involved with the commercial application of mobile robotics and intelligent systems technology to develop entirely new markets and product categories, open additional lines of business and enhance existing product lines.
Frequency: Annual/May

7500 **SAFETY Expo**
American Society of Safety Engineers
1800 E Oakton Street
Des Plaines, IL 60018
847-699-2929; Fax: 847-768-3434
info@asse.org
www.asse.org
Terri Norris, President
Kathy Seabrook, Senior Vice President
Diane Hurns, Manager Public Relations Department
A full 3-day conference featuring more than 200 sessions, an exposition with 300 exhibitors, special pre- and post-conference seminars, conference proceedings on CD, numerous networking events and more.
Frequency: Annual/July

7501 **SAMPE Conference & Exhibit**
Soc for the Advancement of Material & Process Eng
21680 Gateway Center Drive
Suite 300
Diamond Bar, CA 91765-2454
626-521-9460
info@sampe.org
www.nasampe.org
Facebook, LinkedIn
Gregg Balko, CEO
Briana Condon, Conference Information
The Society for the Advancement of Material and Process Engineering's event showcases the latest technology, applications and materials for the advanced manufacturing marketplace; educational sessions, and exhibits. Attendees include industry leaders, academics, students, researchers, engineers, chemists and business professionals.
Frequency: Annual/May

7502 **STL Annual Meeting**
Society of Tribologists & Lubrication
840 Busse Highway
Park Ridge, IL 60068-2376
847-825-5536; Fax: 847-825-1456
information@stle.org
www.stle.org
Merle Hedland, Meetings Manager
Expect more than 300 technical and practical presentations will be selected for the Calgary program.
Frequency: Annual/May

7503 **Street & Area Lighting Conference**
Illuminating Engineering Society of North America
120 Wall Street
17th Floor
New York, NY 10005
212-248-5000; Fax: 212-248-5018
ies@ies.org
www.ies.org
William Hanley, Executive VP
Valerie Landers, Director Member Services
500 Attendees
Frequency: Annual

7504 **TBP Annual Convention**
Tau Beta Pi Association
PO Box 2697
Knoxville, TN 37904-2697
865-546-4578; Fax: 865-546-4579
www.tbp.org
Facebook, LinkedIn
James D Froula, Executive Director
Larry Simonson, President
James Froula, Executive Director
A convention at which members conduct the official business of the Association, network with engineers from around the country, and participate in a recruiting fair.
500+ Attendees

7505 **Texoma Regional Education & Training Conference**
Society of American Military Engineers
607 Prince Street
Alexandria, VA 22314-3117
703-549-3800
800-336-3097; Fax: 703-684-0231
webmanager@same.org
www.same.org
Dr Robert D Wolff, Executive Director
Ann McLeod, Director of Meetings
Jenni Ford, CPA, Director Finance/Accounting
Will provide opportunities to attend SAME sponsored sessions as well as TSPE sponsored training sessions. This diversity of training venues is intended to provide the attendee with exposure to a wide variety of topics and will provide a beneficial learning experience.
Frequency: Annual/June

7506 **The Vision Show**
Global Association for Vision Information
900 Victors Way
Suite 140
Ann Arbor, MI 48108
734-994-6088
www.visiononline.org
Facebook, Twitter
Jeff Burnstein, President
Maria Kurple, Event Marketing Manager
Mandy Pawczuk, Administrator, Event Services
North America's largest display of machine vision and imaging systems.
Frequency: June

7507 **Total Product Development**
American Supplier Institute
17333 Federal Drive
Suite 220
Allen Park, MI 48101-3614
313-336-8877
800-462-4500; Fax: 313-336-3187
Dr Genichi Taguchi, Executive Director
Annual show and exhibits relating to the encouragement of change in US industry through development and implementation of advanced manufacturing and engineering technologies.
200 Attendees

7508 **UNYVAC's Co-Sponsored Symposium**
AVS Science & Technology Society
120 Wall Street
32nd Floor
New York, NY 10005-3993
212-248-0200; Fax: 212-248-0245
david_aspnes@avs.org
www.avs.org
Yvonne Towse, Managing Director
Topic: Functional Coatings and Surface Engineering. Will provide a forum for training and discussion of the physics and chemistry of functional coatings and surfaces.
Frequency: Bi-Annual

7509 **West Energy Conference & Expo**
Association of Energy Engineers
3168 Mercer University Drive
Atlanta, GA 30341
770-447-5083
www.aeecenter.org
Albert Thumann, Executive Director
Bringing together commercial, industrial, and governmental energy professionals from the West Coast and Northwest regions of the United States to discuss key energy issues, energy-efficient solutions, new energy initiatives, and developments in clean energy technologies.
Frequency: Annual/June

7510 **Winter Meeting and Nuclear Technology Expo**
American Nuclear Society
555 North Kensington Avenue
La Grange Park, IL 60526
708-352-6611
800-323-3044; Fax: 708-352-0499
www.ans.org
Serves its members in their efforts to develop and safely apply nuclear science and technology for public benefit through knowledge exchange, professional development, and enhanced public understanding.
Frequency: Annual/November

7511 **World Conference on Quality and Improvement**
American Society for Quality

600 N Plankinton Avenue
Milwaukee, WI 53203

414-272-8575
800-248-1946; Fax: 414-272-1734
help@asq.org
asq.org/conferences/wcqi

Elmer Corbin, Chair
Bill Troy, CEO
Brian Savoie, Chief Financial Officer
Andrew Baines, Managing Director, Global
Ann Jordan, General Counsel

Conference on quality and improvement exploring quality tools, techniques and methodologies.
80K Members
Frequency: Annual
Founded in 1946

7512 **World Energy Conference & Expo**
Association of Energy Engineers
3168 Mercer University Drive
Atlanta, GA 30341

770-447-5083
www.aeecenter.org

Albert Thumann, Executive Director

A comprehensive forum where participants can fully assess the big picture and see exactly how the economic and market forces, new technologies, regulatory developments and industry trends all merge to shape their critical decisions on their organizations' energy and economic future.
Frequency: Annual/September

Directories & Databases

7513 **AEG Annual Directory**
Assn. of Environmental & Engineering Geologists
1100-H Brandywine Boulevard
Suite 575
Zanesville, OH 43701

303-757-2926
844-331-7867; Fax: 740-452-2552
aeg@aegweb.org
www.aegweb.org

Dale C. Andrews, President
Kathy Troost, Vice President

Contains member and Association information.

7514 **ANS Buyers Guide**
American Nuclear Society
555 N Kensington Avenue
La Grange Park, IL 60526

708-352-6611
800-323-3044; Fax: 708-352-0499
www.ans.org

Rick Michal, Director, Publications

Buyer's Guide Directory lists approximately 1150 suppliers of products and services to the nuclear industry. This comprehensive listing contains approximately 500 categories representing the wide range of nuclear components and services available today.
Cost: $110.00
Frequency: Annual

7515 **ASM Handbooks Online**
ASM International
9639 Kinsman Road
Materials Park, OH 44073-0002

440-338-5151
800-336-5152; Fax: 440-338-4634
sales@asminternational.org
www.asminternational.org

William T. Mahoney, Secretary & CEO
Madrid Tramble, eDocument Production Manager

Contains information on ferrous and non-ferrous metals and materials technology presented through articles, illustrations, tables, graphs and practical examples.
30K Members
25000 Pages
Founded in 1913

7516 **AWWA Buyer's Guide**
American Water Works Association
6666 W Quincy Ave
Denver, CO 80235

303-794-7711
800-926-7337; Fax: 303-347-0804
www.awwa.org

Melissa Elliott, President
David B. LaFrance, Chief Executive Officer

The official resource guide to water industry products and services.

7517 **Advanced Energy Design Guide for Small Office Buildings**
Illuminating Engineering Society of North America
120 Wall St
17th Floor
New York, NY 10005-4001

212-248-5000; Fax: 212-248-5017
ies@ies.org
www.ies.org

William Hanley, Executive VP
Valerie Landers, Director Member Services

Provides a sensible approach by including practical products and readily-available, off-the-shelf technology. The Guide offers you all the tools you need to create an energy-efficient building where the owners will see a 30 percent energy savings compared to buildings that only meet the minimum requirements of Standard 90.1.
Cost: $47.00
390 Pages
Founded in 2004

7518 **American Association of Cost Engineers Membership Directory**
Association for Total Cost Management
209 Prairie Avenue
#100
Morgantown, WV 26501-5949

FAX 304-291-5728

Andy Dowd, Executive Director

Member directory.
Cost: $35.00
100 Pages
Frequency: Annual

7519 **American Society for Engineering Education Membership Directory**
1818 N St NW
Suite 600
Washington, DC 20036-2476

202-331-3500; Fax: 202-265-8504
www.asee.org

Frank L Huband, Executive Director

Offers information on over 10,000 colleges and university engineering professors and personnel, practicing engineers and industry executives who are members of the ASEE.
200 Pages
Frequency: Annual
Circulation: 10,000

7520 **American Society of Civil Engineers Official Register**
1801 Alexander Bell Dr
Suite 100
Reston, VA 20191-4382

703-295-6300
800-548-2723; Fax: 703-295-6222
conf@asce.org
http://www.asce.org

D Wayne Klotz, President

Provides ready access to governing documents, statistics, and general information about ASCE for leadership, members, and staff.
Cost: $24.00
640 Pages
Frequency: Annual
ISBN: 0-784407-73-8
Founded in 2005

7521 **BMES Membership Directory**
Biomedical Engineering Society
8201 Corporate Dr
Suite 1125
Landover, MD 20785-2224

301-459-1999
888-871-BMES; Fax: 301-459-2444
www.bmes.org

Richard Waugh, President
Debra Tucker, Meeting Manager
Edward Schilling, Executive Director

A directory listing members' names, mailing addresses, telephone numbers, e-mail addresses, areas of specialization, as well as indexes of professional interest and geographic location.
Frequency: Annual

7522 **Basics of Code Division Multiple Access (CDMA)**
International Society for Optical Engineering
PO Box 10
Bellingham, WA 98227-0010

360-676-3290; Fax: 360-647-1445
customerservice@spie.org
www.spie.org

Raghuveer Rao, Editor
Sohail Dianat, President
Amy Nelson, Manager

This text, aimed at the reader with a basic background in electrical or optical engineering, covers CDMA fundamentals: from the basics of the communication process and digital data transmission, to the concepts of code division multiplexing, direct sequence spreading, diversity techniques, the near-far effect, and the IS-95 CDMA standard form.
Cost: $35.00
120 Pages
ISBN: 0-819458-69-4

7523 **CED Directory of Engineering and Engineering Technology Programs**
Mississippi State University
PO Box 6046
Mississippi State, MS 39762-6046

662-258-8122; Fax: 662-325-8733

Mike Mathews, Editor

Over 150 colleges and universities with cooperative education programs in engineering and engineering technology are listed.
Cost: $50.00
250 Pages
Frequency: Biennial

7524 **CRC Press**
2000 NW Corporate Boulevard
Boca Raton, FL 33431

561-994-0555
800-272-7737; Fax: 772-998-0876
techsupport@crcpress.com
www.crcpress.com

Eleanor Riemer, Publisher
Emmett Dages, CEO

Publisher in science, medicine, environmental science, forensic, engineering, business, technology, mathematics, and statistics. Our food science and nutrition books and our journal, Critical

Reviews in Food and Nutrition, are well established and respected publications in the food science industry.

7525 **CSA Engineering**
Cambridge Scientific Abstracts
7200 Wisconsin Ave
Suite 601
Bethesda, MD 20814-4890
301-961-6700; Fax: 301-961-6790
www.csa.com
Andrew M Snyder, President
Martin Nowicki, Editor, Engineering
This database offers information on more than 500,000 citations, with abstracts, to international periodical and other research literature covering all fields of engineering and science.
Cost: $945.00
Frequency: Monthly

7526 **Coolant Filtration-Additional Technologies**
Society of Tribologists & Lubrication
840 Busse Hwy
Park Ridge, IL 60068-2376
847-825-5536; Fax: 847-825-1456
information@stle.org
www.stle.org
Ed Salek, Executive Director
The text covers coolant cleaning and handling for metalworking operations where coolants are used as part of the process. The publication also provides the latest thinking on specific metalworking applications with some comprehensive guidelines. 76 illustrations.
Cost: $56.00
223 Pages

7527 **Design-Build Project Delivery (ACEC)**
American Council of Engineering Companies
1015 15th St
8th Floor NW
Washington, DC 20005-2605
202-347-7474; Fax: 202-898-0068
acec@acec.org
www.acec.org
Facebook, Twitter
Dave Raymond, President
Howard Messner, Executive Director
Guide for firms considering design/build projects. Analyzes risks, steps and milestones necessary for successful completion of design/build projects.

7528 **Directory of Accredited Engineering & Technology Certification Programs**
Council of Engineer and Scientific Specialty Board
PO Box 1448
Annapolis, MD 21404-1488
410-266-3766; Fax: 410-721-1746
www.cesb.org
Ronald Council, Owner
William C Anderson PE DEE, Executive Director
Provides a description of existing programs for persons interested in being certified and for those seeking an objective assessment of an expert's capability and competence.

7529 **Directory of Engineering Document Sources**
Global Engineering Documents
15 Inverness Way E
Englewood, CO 80112-5710
303-900-0600
800-854-7179; Fax: 303-397-2740
CustomerCare@ihs.com
www.global.ihs.com
Charles Picasso, CEO
Offers over 10,000 document initialisms and acronyms for governmental, military and industry specifications and related publications.
Cost: $145.00
274 Pages
Frequency: Annual

7530 **Directory of Engineers in Private Practice**
National Society of Professional Engineers
1420 King St
Suite 500
Alexandria, VA 22314-2794
703-684-2800; Fax: 703-836-4875
webmaster@nspe.org
www.nspe.org
Larry Jacobson, Executive Director
Consulting engineering firms and individuals who are members of the Society's Professional Engineers in Private Practice division.
Cost: $85.00
260 Pages
Frequency: Annual

7531 **Directory of Iron and Steel Plants**
186 Thorn Hill Rd
Warrendale, PA 15086-7528
724-814-3000; Fax: 724-814-3001
memberservices@aist.org
www.aist.org
Ronald E Ashburn, Executive Director
William A Albaugh, Technology Programs Manager
Joann Cantrell, Publications Manager/Editor
Mark Didiano, Finance & Administration Manager
Stacy Varmecky, Membership Communications Manager
The Directory lists more than 2,000 companies and 17,500 individuals. Featuring data on essentially ever steel producer in the USA, Canada and Mexico, including names and titles of executive, engineering, maintenance and operating personnel. Also includes an alpha listing of all major equipment, product and service providers to the international iron and steel industry, and a listing of associations affiliated with the industry, with complete geo-indexing. Softbound book with CD.
Cost: $95.00
ISBN: 1-935117-00-1

7532 **EI Page One**
Engineering Information
1 Castle Point Ter
Hoboken, NJ 07030-5906
201-356-6800
800-221-1044; Fax: 201-356-6801
eicustomersupport@elsevier.com
www.ei.org
This database contains a table of contents listing citations to more than 350,000 journal articles and conference papers and proceedings in all fields of engineering.

7533 **ENR: Top International Design Firms Issue**
McGraw Hill
1221 Avenue of the Americas
47th Floor
New York, NY 10020-1095
212-512-2000; Fax: 212-512-3840
www.mcgraw-hill.com
Harold W McGraw III, CEO
Offers a list of over 200 design firms competing outside their own national borders who received largest dollar volumes in foreign contracts.
Cost: $270.00
Frequency: Annual
Circulation: 900,000

7534 **Energy Engineering: Directory of Software for Energy Managers and Engineers**
Fairmont Press
700 Indian Trail Lilburn Rd NW
Lilburn, GA 30047-6862
770-925-9388; Fax: 770-381-9865
www.fairmontpress.com
Brian Douglas, President
Directory of services and supplies to the industry.
Cost: $15.00
Circulation: 8,500
ISSN: 0199-8895

7535 **Manufacturer and Repair Directory**
National Board of Boiler & Pressure Vessel
1055 Crupper Ave
Columbus, OH 43229-1108
614-888-0750; Fax: 614-888-0750
information@nationalboard.org
www.nationalboard.org
Don Tanner, Manager
Connie Homer, Senior Executive Secretary
Manufacturers of boilers, pressure vessels, or other pressure-retaining items who are authorized to register these items with the National Board, Repair organizations holding National Board certificates of authorization for use of either the R, VR, or NR stamps.

7536 **Mechanical Contractor Directory Marketing**
Mechanical Contractors Association America
1385 Piccard Dr
Rockville, MD 20850-4329
301-869-5800; Fax: 301-990-9690
webmaster@mcaa.org
www.mcaa.org
John Gentille, Executive VP
John Gentille, Executive VP

7537 **Plumbing Directory**
American Society of Sanitary Engineering
901 Canterbury Rd
Suite A
Cleveland, OH 44145-1480
440-835-3040; Fax: 440-835-3488
www.asse-plumbing.org
Ken Van Wagnen, Manager
Sara Marxen, Compliance Coordinator
Steven Hazzard, Staff Engineer
Contains more than 4,000 plumbing words and terms, abbreviations, cross references, helpful charts and illustrations, solar energy terms. A great teaching tool for plumbing and related fields.
Cost: $21.00

7538 **Research, Training, Test, and Production Reactor Directory**
American Nuclear Society
555 N Kensington Avenue
La Grange Park, IL 60526
708-352-6611
800-323-3044; Fax: 708-352-0499
www.asn.org
Rick Michal, Director, Publications
This comprehensive directory includes administrative, operational, and technical data for all

nonpower reactors in the United States.
Cost: $420.00
876 Pages
ISBN: 0-894485-12-1
Founded in 1988

7539 **Salem Press Online Platform**
Grey House Publishing
4919 Route 22
PO Box 56
Amenia, NY 12501

800-221-1592; Fax: 201-968-0511
csr@salempress.com
online.salempress.com

The new Salem Press platform houses more than 500 titles including all of Salem's Health, Literature, History and Science titles in addition to select titles from the Grey House Publishing and H.W. Wilson product lines. Online access is free with each print purchase and includes an unlimited number of simultaneous users and remote access.

7540 **Tau Beta Pi Information Book**
Tau Beta Pi Association
PO Box 2697
Knoxville, TN 37901-2697

865-546-4578; Fax: 865-546-4579
www.tbp.org
Facebook, LinkedIn

Larry Simonson, President
Solange Dao, VP
Curtis D. Gomulinski, Executive Director/Treasurer

The book also serves as a reference to membership and alumni giving statistics as well as names of past and present officers, fellows, scholars, and other award winners.
Frequency: Yearly

7541 **US Abrasives Industry Directory**
Abrasive Engineering Society
144 Moore Rd
Butler, PA 16001-1312

724-282-6210; Fax: 724-234-2376
aes@abrasiveengineering.com
www.abrasiveengineering.com

Ted Giese, Owner

Though the scene for industrial abrasive manufacturers has changed significantly over the last decade, the US continues as one of the world's largest manufacturers of abrasive products developing new abrasive grains and products that set international standards for quality and performance.

7542 **Wage & Benefit Survey**
North American Die Casting Association
241 Holbrook Drive
Wheeling, IL 60090-5809

847-279-0001; Fax: 847-279-0002
twarog@diecasting.org
www.diecasting.org

Daniel Twarog, President

This survey provides a comprehensive look at 13 different job classifications of hourly wage earners, how they are compensated, what benefits they receive and how practices vary by company size and location.
Cost: $200.00
42 Pages
Founded in 2004

7543 **Who's Who in Environmental Engineering**
American Academy of Environmental Engineers
147 Old Solomons Island Road
Suite 303
Annapolis, MD 21401-7003

410-266-3311; Fax: 410-266-7653
www.aaees.org

Burk Kalweit, Executive Director
Howard B. LaFever, President
Dr. Robert Williams, President-Elect

A recognized reference for industry, consultants, recruiters, attorneys and health professionals who need to identify and locate experts in the environmental engineering profession.
Cost: $75.00
Frequency: Annual
Mailing list available for rent

7544 **World Directory of Nuclear Utility Management**
American Nuclear Society
555 N Kensington Avenue
La Grange Park, IL 60526

708-352-6611; Fax: 708-352-0499
www.ans.org

Rick Michal, Director, Publications

Is a handy desk reference listing key personnel at nuclear utility headquarters and nuclear plant sites, including plant managers, maintenance superintendents, radwaste managers, contacts for purchasing and public relations, and more.
249 Pages
Founded in 2005

Industry Web Sites

7545 **http://gold.greyhouse.com**
G.O.L.D Grey House OnLine Databases

Grey House Publishing's online database platform, GOLD, offers Quick Search, Keyword Search and Expert Search for most business sectors including engineering markets. The GOLD platform makes finding the information you need quick and easy - whether you're a novice searcher or an experienced database user. All of Grey House's directory products are available for subscription on the GOLD platform.

7546 **www.aacei.org**
Association for Advancement of Cost Engineering

Individuals interested in applying scientific principals to the solution of problems.

7547 **www.aaee.org**
American Association for Employment in Education

Provides information and other resources to assist colleges and universities in the employment of education.

7548 **www.aaees.org**
American Academy of Environmental Engineers

Improves the standards of environmental engineering. Certifies those with the special knowledge of environmental engineering and supplies a list of certified engineers to the public. Publishes reference books and other matters of interest for the profession.

7549 **www.aaes.org**
American Association of Engineering Societies

A multidisciplinary organization dedicated to advancing the knowledge, understanding and practice of engineering in the public interest.

7550 **www.abet.org**
Accreditation Board for Engineering and Technology

Accreditation of engineering, technology and applied science educational programs.

7551 **www.acec.org**
American Council of Engineering

Membership includes more than 5,800 US firms engaged in a range of engineering works. Mission is to contribute to the nation's prosperity through advancement of the business interests of member firms.

7552 **www.acesystems.com**
AEC Systems International/Penton Media

Focuses on Internet/Intranet for the design, engineering and construction industries.

7553 **www.aea.org**
American Engineering Association, Inc.

Dedicated to the enhancement of the engineering profession and U.S. Engineering capabilities.

7554 **www.aeecenter.org**
Association of Energy Engineers

Promotes energy certification, management and education.

7555 **www.aegweb.org**
Association of Engineering Geologists

Meets the professional needs of geologists who are applying their scientific training and experience to the broad field of civil and environmental engineering. Mission is to provide leadership in the development and application of geologic principles and knowledge to serve engineering, environmental and public needs.

7556 **www.aes.org**
Audio Engineering Society

Professional society devoted to audio technology. Membership includes leading engineers, scientists and other authorities in the field. Serves its members, the industry and the public by stimulating and facilitating advances in the constantly changing field of audio.

7557 **www.aiche.org**
American Institute of Chemical Engineers

Professional association of more than 50,000 members, providing leadership in advancing the chemical engineering profession. Members are those who develop processes and design and operate manufacturing plants, as well as researchers who assure the safe and environmentally sound manufacture, use and disposal of chemical products.

7558 **www.aocs.org**
American Oil Chemists Society

Largest international society focused on the science and technology of fats, oils, lipids, and related substances.

7559 **www.ascet.org**
American Society of Certified Engineering

Strives to obtain recognition of engineering technicians as essential to the engineering scientific team. Provides a forum for discussion of employment issues and improvement of the professional status of engineering technicians.

7560 **www.asem.org**
American Society for Engineering Management

Strives to promote the profession of engineering management as well as assisting its members in developing and improving their skills as practicing managers of engineering and technology. Members are from academic, field, industrial and governmental organizations.

7561 **www.asfe.org**
ASFE

Not-for-profit trade association. Helps geoprofessional, environmental and civil engineering firms profit through professionalism.

7562 **www.asme.org**
American Society of Mechanical Engineers
Focuses on technical, educational and research issues of the engineering and technology community.

7563 **www.asnt.org**
American Society for Nondestructive Testing
Helps create a safer world by serving the nondestructive testing professions and promoting NDT technologies through publishing, certification, research and conferencing.

7564 **www.aspe.net**
American Society for Precision Engineering
Members are from academia, industry and government, and include professionals in engineering, materials science, physics, chemistry, mathematics and computer science. Multidisciplinary professional and technical society concerned with precision engineering research and development, design and manufacturing of high accuracy components and systems.

7565 **www.asq.org**
American Society for Quality
Facebook, Twitter, LinkedIn
Associaion with the mission to promote quality principles concepts and technologies through information, contacts and development opportunities for management professionals in various industries.

7566 **www.asse-plumbing.org**
American Society of Sanitary Engineering
Members are from all segments of the plumbing industry, including contractors, engineers, inspectors, journeymen, apprentices and others involved in the industry. Provides information, the opportunity to exchange ideas, solve problems and offers forum where all sides can express their views.

7567 **www.astm.org**
ASTM International
Not-for-profit organization providing a global forum for development and publication of voluntary consensus standards for materials, products, systems and services. Over 30,000 members from 100 nations include producers, users, consumers and representatives of academia and government. Formerly known as the American Society for Testing and Materials.

7568 **www.atcouncil.org**
Applied Technology Council
A nonprofit, tax-exempt corporation established through the efforts of the Structural Engineers Association of California. ATC's mission is to develop and promote state-of-the-art, user-friendly engineering resources and applications for use in mitigating the effects of natural and other hazards on the built environment.

7569 **www.construction.com**
McGraw-Hill Construction
McGraw-Hill Construction (MHC), part of The McGraw-Hill Companies, connects people and projects across the design and construction industry, serving owners, architects, engineers, general contractors, subcontractors, building product manufacturers, suppliers, dealers, distributors and adjacent markets.

7570 **www.eia-usa.org**
Environmental Information Association
Nonprofit organization dedicated to providing environmental information to individuals, members and the industry. Disseminates information on the abatement of asbestos and lead-based paint, indoor air quality, safety and health issues, analytical issues and environmental site assessments.

7571 **www.electrochem.org**
Electrochemical Society
The society is an international nonprofit, educational organization concerned with phenomena relating to electrochemical and solid state science and technology. Members are individual scientists and engineers, as well as corporations and laboratories.

7572 **www.ewh.ieee.org**
Instrumentation and Measurement Society
A subsidiary of the Institute of Electrical and Electronics Engineers. Provides support to scientists and technicians who design and develop electrical and electronic measuring instruments and equipment.

7573 **www.greyhouse.com**
Grey House Publishing
Authoritative reference directories for most business sectors incluidng engineering markets. Users can search the online databases with varied search criteria allowing for custom searches by product category, geographic area, sales volume, keyword, subject and more. Full Grey House catalog and online ordering also available.

7574 **www.icc-es.org**
ICC Evaluation Service
An independent, nonprofit organization that conducts a voluntary program of evaluation of both traditional and innovative building materials, products and systems for compliance with the three major model codes in the United States.

7575 **www.iccsafe.org**
International Code Council
Nonprofit membership association with more than 16,000 members who span the building community, from code enforcement officials to materials manufacturers. Dedicated to preserving the public health, safety and welfare in the built environment through the effective use and enforcement of model codes.

7576 **www.icea.net**
Insulated Cable Engineers Association
Professional organization dedicated to developing cable standards for the electric power, control and telecommunications industries. Ensures safe, economical and efficient cable systems utilizing proven state-of-the-art materials and concepts. ICEA documents are of interest to cable manufacturers, architects and engineers, utility and manufacturing plant personnel, telecommunication engineers, consultants and OEMs.

7577 **www.manufacturing.net**
Manufacturing Marketplace
Manufacturing industry news and resources for the engineering, design, purchasing, logistics and distribution professional.

7578 **www.mt-online.com**
Applied Technology Publications
MT-online.com is the premier source of capacity assurance and best practice solutions for manufacturing, process and service operations worldwide. Online home of Maintenance Technology magazie, the dynamic MT-online.com portal serves the critical technical, business and professional-development needs of engineers, managers and technicians from across all industrial, institutional and commercial sectors.

7579 **www.nace.org**
National Association of Corrosion Engineers
Conducts research on corrosion control. Sponsors short courses annually at universities.

7580 **www.nationalboard.org**
National Board of Boiler & Pressure Vessel Inspec.
Membership is composed of chief boiler inspectors of states, major US cities and Canadian provinces having boiler laws.

7581 **www.ncees.org**
Natl Council of Examiners for Engineering & Survey
Promotes uniform standards of registration and to coordinate interstate registration of engineers and surveyors.

7582 **www.nspe.org**
National Society of Professional Engineers
The mission of the Society is to promote the ethical, competent and licensed practice of engineering and to enhance the professional, social and economic well-being of its members.

7583 **www.remsa.org**
Railway Engineering-Maintenance Suppliers Assn
Members are distributors and manufacturers of railway track machinery supplies and services.

7584 **www.reta.com**
Refrigerating Engineers & Technicians Association
Seeks to upgrade the skills and knowledge of experienced members. Offers home-study courses on refrigeration and air conditioning.

7585 **www.robotics.org**
Robotic Industries Association
Trade group serving the robotics industry through educational resources, events and news. Members include robot manufacturers, users, system integrators, component suppliers and more.

7586 **www.rses.org**
Refrigeration Service Engineers Society
RSES is the leading training and education association for heating, ventilation, air conditioning and refrigeration professionals. It is a non-profit organization of 25,000 members in 421 chapters in the US and Canada, as well as affiliate organizations in other countries.

7587 **www.same.org**
Society of American Military Engineers
Brings together professional engineers and those in engineering-related fields to improve and increase the engineering capabilities of the nation, and to exchange and advance the knowledge of engineering technologies, applications, and practices.

7588 **www.sawe.org**
Society of Allied Weight Engineers
Consists of engineers in the aerospace industry.

7589 **www.sme.org**
Society of Manufacturing Engineers
Facebook, Twitter, LinkedIn, YouTube, Google+, Instagram
Association representing manufacturers, researchers and those working in technology development.

7590 **www.spe.org**
Society of Petroleum Engineers
To provide the means for collection, dissemination and exchange of technical information con-

cerning the development of oil and gas resources, subsurface fluid flow and production of other materials through well bores for the public benefit. To provide opportunities through its programs for interested individuals to maintain and upgrade their individual technical competence in the aforementioned areas for the public benefit.

7591 **www.steelnews.com**
Association for Iron and Steel Technology (AIST)
SteelNews.com is a publication created by the Association for Iron and Steel Technology (AIST) for the steel community. The site features daily updates of the latest global headlines.

7592 **www.sweets.construction.com**
McGraw Hill Construction
In depth product information that lets you find, compare, select, specify and make purchase decisions in the industrial product marketplace.

7593 **www.tbp.org**
Tau Beta Pi Association
The National Engineering honor society recognizes engineering students of superior scholarship and exemplary character and practitioners of engineering. Founded in 1885, the world's largest engineering organization includes 218 collegiate chapters and 220 alumnus chapters.

7594 **www.thetatau.org**
Theta Tau
A professional fraternity in engineering. Founded at the Univerity of Minnesota. Purpose of the fraternity is to develop and maintain a high standard of professional interest among its members, and to unite them in a strong bond of fraternal fellowship.

7595 **www.u.arizona.edu/n aimitril**
Reliability Engineering and Management Institute
This is an annual conference on Reliability Engineering and Management of all types of products. Over 15 leading corporations present their latest techniques in this field, and the proceedings thereof are published.

7596 **www.uefoundation.org**
United Engineering Foundation
Aims to advance engineering arts and sciences.

7597 **www.usace.army.mil**
US Army Corps of Engineers
Information on flood control, environmental protection, disaster response, military construction and support of others through the sharing of engineering expertise with other agencies, state and local governments, academia and foreign nations.

Associations

7598 **ASFE/The Geoprofessional Business Association**
8811 Colesville Rd
Suite G106
Silver Springs, MD 20910-4343
301-565-2733; Fax: 301-589-2017
info@geoprofessional.org
www.geoprofessional.org
Facebook, Twitter, LinkedIn, YouYube, RSS
Gordon M. Matheson, President
Laura R. Reinbold, P.E., President-Elect
John P. Bachner, Executive Vice President
Charles L. Head, P.E., P.G., Secretary/Treasurer
Joel G. Carson, Executive Director
Not-for-profit trade association. Supports all employess of engineering companies.
300 Members
Founded in 1969

7599 **Academy for Educational Development**
1825 Connecticut Ave Nw
Washington, DC 20009-5728
202-884-8978; Fax: 202-884-8997
rjohn@aed.org
www.pciaonline.org/academy-educational-development-aed
Facebook, Twitter, YouTube
Edward W. Russell, Chairman of the Board
Roberta N. Clarke, Vice Chairman of the Board
Rebecca Logan, President and CEO
A nonprofit organization working globally to improve education, health, civil society and economic development-the foundation of thriving societies.
Founded in 1961

7600 **Adirondack Council**
103 Hand Ave, Suite 3
PO Box D-2
Elizabethtown, NY 12932-0640
877-873-2240; Fax: 518-873-6675
info@adirondackcouncil.org
www.adirondackcouncil.org
Facebook, Twitter, YouTube, Flickr
Robert K. Kafin, Chair
Lee Keet, Vice-Chair
Meredith Prime, Vice-Chair
Curt R. Welling, Treasurer
Virginia M. Lawrence, Secretary
Research, education and advocacy to protect the natural character and communities of the Adirondack Park. Also publishes an annual State of Park Report and quarterly newsletters.
Founded in 1975
Mailing list available for rent

7601 **African American Environmentalist Association**
1629 K Street, NW
Suite 300
Washington, DC 20006
443-569-5102
africanamericanenvironmentalist@msn.com
aaenvironment.Blogspot.com
Facebook, Twitter, LinkedIn, YouTube, RSS
Norris McDonald, President
Derry Bigby, Vice President
Dedicated to providing energy and environmental information and educating the African American community.

7602 **Agricultural Research Institute**
1034 Miner Farm Road
PO Box 90
Chazy, NY 12921
518-846-7121; Fax: 518-846-8445
www.whminer.com
Facebook, Google +
Richard J. Grant, President
Kirk E. Beattie, VP, Administration & Finance
Rachel Dutil, Public Relations & Marketing Coord.
Catherine Ballard, Director, Research
Wanda Emerich, Dairy Outreach Coordinator
Institutions concerned with environmental issues, pest control, agricultural meteorology, biotechnology, food irradiation, agricultural policy, research and development, food safety, technology transfer and remote sensing.
125 Members

7603 **Air Pollution Control Association**
420 Fort Duquesne Boulevard
One Gateway Center, 3rd Floor
Pittsburgh, PA 15222-1435
412-232-3444
800-270-3444; Fax: 412-232-3450
info@awma.org
www.awma.org
Facebook, Twitter, LinkedIn
Dallas Baker, President
Brad Waldron, QEP, CHMM, President Elect
Michael Miller, Immediate Past President
Nancy Meilahn Fowler, Treasurer
Stephanie Glyptis, Secretary/ Executive Director
Association for the environment and conservation industry.
9000 Members
Founded in 1907

7604 **Air and Waste Management Association**
436 7th Avenue
Suite 2100
Pittsburgh, PA 15219
412-232-3444
800-270-3444; Fax: 412-232-3450
info@awma.org
www.awma.org
Facebook, Twitter, LinkedIn
Stephanie Glyptis, Executive Director
Gerald Armstrong, Customer Service & Membership
Tracy Fedkoe, Director, Marketing/Project Mgmt.
Jeff Schurman, Manager. Exhibits & Sponsorship
Lisa Bucher, Managing Editor
Professional organization that provides training, information, and networking opportunities to environmental professionals.
5000 Members
Founded in 1907

7605 **Alliance for Bio-Integrity**
54 North Park Street
Fairfield, IA 52556
206-888-4852
www.biointegrity.org
Steven M Druker, Executive Director
A nonprofit organization dedicated to the advancement of human and environmental health through sustainable and safe technologies.

7606 **Alliance to Save Energy**
1850 M Street NW
Suite 610
Washington, DC 20036
202-857-0666
www.ase.org
Facebook, Twitter, LinkedIn, Google+, Flickr, YouTube
Jason Hartke, President
Kara O'Connell, Chief Operating Officer
Ross Robinson, Chief Financial Officer
Susanna Silvan, Manager, Events/Executive Affairs
Ben Somberg, Manager, Communications
Organization that leads worldwide energy efficiency initiatives in policy advocacy, research, education and technology deployment.
Founded in 1977

7607 **America the Beautiful Fund**
P.O. Box 6007
Indianapolis, IN 46206-6007
202-638-1649
800-421-4225; Fax: 888-421-4351
www.americanfunds.com
Nanine Bilski, President
Kathleen Rehicaldt, Program Director
Daniel Schneider, Secretary
Groups and private citizens that improve the quality of the environment.
1M Members
Founded in 1965

7608 **American Association for Aerosol Research (AAAR)**
12100 Sunset Hills Road
Suite 130
Reston, VA 20190
703-437-4377
800-485-3106; Fax: 856-439-0525
info@aaar.org
Jay Turner, President
Sheryl Ehrman, Vice President
Allen Robinson, Vice President Elect
Linsey Marr, Treasurer
Suresh Dhaniyala, Secretary
AAAR is a nonprofit professional organization for scientists and engineers who wish to promote and communicate technical advances in the field of aerosol research. The Association fosters the exchange of information among members and with other disciplines through conferences, symposia and publication of a professional journal. Committed to the development of aerosol and its application to important social issues, AAAR offers an international forum for education, communication and networking.
1000 Members
Founded in 1982

7609 **American Association for the Advancement of Science**
1200 New York Ave NW
Washington, DC 20005
202-326-6400
www.aaas.org
Facebook, Twitter, LinkedIn, YouTube, Instagram
Alan I. Leshner, Interim Chief Executive Officer
Andrew Black, Chief of Staff & External Affairs
Michael Savelli, Chief Operating Officer
Maureen Kearney, Chief Program Officer
Tiffany Lohwater, Chief Communications Officer
A nonprofit organization that has research news, issue papers, educational programs, etc.
Founded in 1848

7610 **American Bird Conservancy**
4249 Loudoun Ave.
P.O. Box 249
The Plains, VA 20198-2237
540-253-5780
888-247-3624; Fax: 540-253-5782
www.abcbirds.org
Warren F. Cooke, Chair
V Richard Eales, Treasurer & Vice Chair
William H. Leighty, Vice Chair
William F. Sheehan, Vice Chair
George H. Fenwick, President
A nonprofit membership organization dedicated to the conservation of wild birds and their habitats in the Americas.
Founded in 1980

7611 **American Council on Science and Health**
1995 Broadway
Suite 202
New York, NY 10023-5882
212-362-7044
866-905-2694; Fax: 212-362-4919
acsh@acsh.org
www.acsh.org
Facebook, Twitter, YouTube
Hank Campbell, President
Cheryl Martin, Director Of Development
Dr. Gilbert Ross, M.D., Medical Director
Ruth Kava Ph.D, Senior Nutrition Fellow
Lila Abassi M.D., Director Of Medicine
A consumer education organization providing the public with scientifically accurate evaluations of food, chemicals, the environment and health.
Founded in 1978

7612 **American Farmland Trust**
1150 Connecticut Avenue
Suite 600
The Plains, VA 20036
800-431-1499; Fax: 202-659-8339
halthouse@farmland.org
www.farmland.org
Facebook, Twitter, LinkedIn, Pinterest
Barton H. Thompson, Jr., Chair
John Hardin Jr., Vice Chair
William Cohan, Treasurer
Ralph Grossi, Interim President
Susan Sink, VP, Dev. & Ext. Affair
An organization that protects farmland and ranch land in the UnitedStates, promotes environmentally sound farming practices and keeps farmers on the land.
Founded in 1980

7613 **American Fisheries Society**
425 Barlow Place
Suite 110
Bethesda, MD 20814-2144
301-897-8616; Fax: 301-897-8096
main@fisheries.org
fisheries.org
Facebook, Twitter, vimeo, flickr
Douglas Austen, Executive Director
Erin Del Collo, Membership Coordinator
Katrina Dunn, Director of Development
Laura Hendee, Journals Production Manager
Shawn Johnston, Meetings Manager
Organization dedicated to strengthening the fisheries profession and advancing fisheries.
Founded in 1870

7614 **American Forests**
1220 L Street NW
Suite 750
Washington, DC 20005
202-737-1944
info@americanforests.org
www.americanforests.org
Facebook, Twitter
Ann Nichols, Chair
Bruce Lisman, Vice Chair
Roderick DeArment, Treasurer
Scott Steen, President & CEO
Peter Hutchins, Vice President/ COO
The oldest national nonprofit conservation organization in the U.S.that advocates for the protection and expansion of forests.
Founded in 1990

7615 **American Institute of Hydrology**
PO Box 3948
Parker, CO 80134
303-339-0523; Fax: 720-496-4974
admin@aihydrology.org
www.aihydrology.org
John L. Nieber. P.H., P.E., President
Dr. Faisal Hossain, VP for Academic Affairs
Jul, Rizzardo, VP for Institute Development
Dr/ Zhuping Sheng, VP for International Affairs
Rahul Ranade, VP for Communication
Registers and certifies hydrologists and hydrogeologists, provides a forum to discuss national and international issues, and provides educational courses.
Founded in 1981

7616 **American Nuclear Society**
555 N Kensington Avenue
La Grange Park, IL 60526
708-352-6611
800-323-3044; Fax: 708-352-0499
www.ans.org
Facebook, Twitter, LinkedIn
Serves its members in their efforts to develop and safely apply nuclear science and technology for public benefit through knowledge exchange, professional development, and enhanced public understanding.
Founded in 1954

7617 **American Phytopathological Society**
3340 Pilot Knob Road
Saint Paul, MN 55121-2097
651-454-7250
800-328-7560; Fax: 651-454-0766
aps@scisoc.org
www.apsnet.org
Facebook, Twitter, LinkedIn, Pinterest
Amy Hope, Executive VP
Carol Ericson, Director, Operations
Kim Davis, Director, Finance
Greg Grahek, Director, Publications
Linda Schmitt, Dir., Foundation, Award Program
Scientific organization that studies plant diseases and their control.
4500 Members
Founded in 1908

7618 **American Public Works Association**
1200 Main Street
Suite 1400
Kansas City, MO 64105-2100
816-472-6100
800-848-APWA; Fax: 816-472-1610
www.apwa.net
Facebook, Twitter, YouTube
Scott Grayson, Chief Executive Officer
Mary Knollmeyer, Director of Finance
Julie Bebermeyer, Director of Operations
Lysa Byous, Meeting Planner/Exhibit Manager
Tammy Bennett, Director, Membership & Engagement
International educational and professional association of public agencies, private sector companies, and individuals dedicated to providing high quality public works goods and services. AWA provides a forum in which public works professionals' competency, increase the performance of their agencies and companies, and bring important public works-related topics to public attention in local, state, and federal areas. Mailing list for members only.
30000 Members
Founded in 1937

7619 **American Shore and Beach Preservation Association**
5460 Beaujolais Lane
Fort Myers, FL 33919
239-489-2616; Fax: 239-362-9771
managing@asbpa.org
www.asbpa.org
Facebook, Twitter
Anthony P. Pratt, President
Russell Boudreau, Vice President
Nicole Elko Ph.D, Vice President
Phillip Roehrs, Vice President
Brad Pickel, Treasurer
Federal, state and local government agencies and individuals interested in conservation, development and restoration of beaches and shorefronts.
1M Members
Founded in 1926

7620 **American Society for Environmental History**
UW Interdisciplinary Arts and Sciences Program
1900 Commerce Street
Tacoma, WA 98402
206-343-0226; Fax: 206-343-0249
info.aseh@gmail.com
www.aseh.net
Kathleen Brosnan, President
Graeme Wynn, Vice President/ President Elect
Jay Tylor, Secretary
Mark Madison, Treasurer
Emily Greenwald, Executive Committee
ASEH members are techers and researchers with an interest in human ecology and environmental history.
1200 Members
Founded in 1976

7621 **American Society for Photogammetry and Remote Sensing (ASPRS)**
5410 Grosvenor Lane
Suite 210
Bethesda, MD 20814-2160
301-493-0290; Fax: 301-493-0208
asprs@asprs.org
www.asprs.org
Facebook, Twitter
Dr. E. Lynn Usery, President
Dr. Charles K. Toth, CP, President-Elect
Ms. Rebecca A. Morton, CP, Vice President
Dr. A. Stewart Walker, CP, Immediate Past President
Mr. Gregory Brunner, National Director
Supports all those involved in mapping, photogrammetry, environmental management, remote sensing, geographic infromation, and natural resources.
6000 Members
Founded in 1934

7622 **American Society of Agronomy**
5585 Guilford Rd.
Madison, WI 53711-1086
608-273-8080; Fax: 608-273-2021
headquarters@sciencesocieties.org
www.agronomy.org
Facebook, Twitter, LinkedIn
Nick Goeser, Chief Executive Officer
Wes Meixelsperger, CFO & Director, Meetings
Sara Uttech, Director, Governance

Susan Chapman, Director, Member Services
Ian Popkewitz, Director, IT & Operations

Supports educators and scientists interested in the impacts of environmental perturbations on the biological and physical sciences.
10000 Members
Founded in 1907

7623 **American Society of Mining and Reclamation**
American Society of Mining and Reclamation
1800 South Oak Street
Suite 100
Champaign, IL 61820

217-333-9489
217-493-7847; Fax: 859-335-6529
rdarmody@illinois.edu
www.asmr.us
Facebook

Robert Darmody, Executive Secretary
Pete Stahl, President
Kimery Vories, President Elect

Dissemination of technical information relating to the reclamation of lands disturbed by mineral extraction. Members yearly issue is paid out of proceeding. Membership dues $50 regular $10 students.
Founded in 1973

7624 **American Society of Safety Engineers**
520 N. Northwest Hwy
Park Ridge, IL 60068

847-699-2929; Fax: 847-768-3434
info@asse.org
www.asse.org
Facebook, Twitter, LinkedIn, Instagram

Michael Belcher, CSP, President
Thomas F. Cecich, CSP, CIH, President-Elect
James Smith, M.S., CSP, Senior Vice President
Fred J. Fortman, Jr., Secretary and Executive Director
Stephanie A. Helgerman, CSP, Vice President, Finance

The oldest and largest professional safety organization. Its members manage, supervise and consult on safety, health, and environmental issues in industry, insurance, government and education.
30000 Members
Founded in 1911

7625 **American Solar Energy Society**
2525 Arapahoe Ave
Ste E4-253
Boulder, CO 80302

303-443-3130; Fax: 303-443-3212
info@ases.org
www.ases.org
Facebook, Twitter, LinkedIn, Instagram

Carly Rixham, Executive Director

The nation's leading association of solar professionals & advocates. Mission is to inspire an era of energy innovation and speed the transition to a sustainable energy economy. Advancing education, research and policy.
Founded in 1954

7626 **American Wind Energy Association**
1501 M Street NW
Suite 900
Washington, DC 20005

202-383-2500
engage.awea.org
Facebook, Twitter, LinkedIn, YouTube, Instagram

Tom Kiernan, Chief Executive Officer
Heather Graving, Manager, Executive Services
Joshua DeShong, Public Affairs Coordinator
Mark Bakke, Manager, Member Relations/Exhibits
Angela Bell, Manager, Member Relations

Promotes wind energy as a clean source of electricity for consumers around the world. Representing wind power project developers, equipment suppliers, services providers, parts manufacturers, utilities, researchers, and others involved in the wind industry.

7627 **Animal Protection and Rescue League**
302 Washington St.
#404
San Diego, CA 92103

858-999-2343
info@aprl.org
www.aprl.org
Facebook, Twitter, YouTube

A nonprofit organization that influences animal protection legislation, conducts rescues of abused factory farmed animals and educates people abouthumane eating.
Founded in 2003

7628 **Aquatic Plant Management Society**
7922 NW
71st Street
Gainesville, FL 32653

FAX 601-634-5502
dpetty@ndrsite.com
www.apms.org
Facebook, LinkedIn

An international organization of scientists, educators, students, commercial pesticide applicators, administrators, and concerned individuals interested in the management and study of aquatic plants.
Founded in 1961

7629 **Association for Environmental Health and Sciences (AEHS) Foundation, Inc.**
150 Fearing Street
Amherst, MA 01002

413-549-5170; Fax: 413-549-0579
www.aehsfoundation.org

Paul T Kostecki, PhD, Executive Director
Brenna Lockwood, Managing Director
Sierra Pelletier, Program Assistant
Ed Calabrese, Editor-In-Chief
Denise Leonard, Managing Editor

AEHS Foundation is a multi-disciplinary association providing a forum for individual professionals concerned with soil protection and cleanup. Fields represented include chemistry, geology, hydrogeology, law, engineering, modeling, toxicology, regulatory science, public health and public policy.
600 Members
Founded in 1989

7630 **Association for Population/Family Planning Libraries & Information Conference**
Family Health International Library
PO Box 13950
Research Triangle Park, NC 27709

919-447-7040
www.aplici.org

Yan Fu, President
Alli Buehler, Vice-President
Jill Leonard, Treasurer
Liz Nugent, Recording Secretary
Debra Dickson, Past President

Offers support for all those involved in issues concerning population and family planning, including publications, training and conferences.
Frequency: Annual

7631 **Association of Environmental & Engineering Geologists**
1100-H Brandywine Blvd.
Suite 575
Zanesville, OH 43701
303-757-2926
844-331-7867; Fax: 740-452-2552
aeg@aegweb.org
www.aegweb.org
Facebook, Twitter

Dale C. Andrews, President
Kathy Troost, Vice Rpesident
Kevin Richards, Treasurer
Cynthia Palomares, Secretary

Meets the professional needs of geologists who are applying their scientific training and experience to the broad field of civil and environmental engineering. Mission is to provide leadership in the development and application of geologic principles and knowledge to serve engineering, environmental and public needs.
3000 Members
Founded in 1957
Mailing list available for rent: 3000 names at $100 per M

7632 **Association of Environmental Engineering and Science Professors**
1211 Connecticut Ave NW,
Suite 650
Washington, DC 20036

202-640-6591; Fax: 217-355-9232
bschorr@aeesp.org
www.aeesp.org

Gregory W. Characklis, President
Peter J. Vikesland, President-Elect
Linda K. Weavers, Vice President
Ching Hua Huang, Secretary
Andrea Ferro, Treasurer

Individuals working or teaching in the field of environmental engineering, including water quality and treatment, air quality, air pollution control and solid and hazardous waste management.
700 Members
Founded in 1963

7633 **Association of Environmental and Resource Economists**
13006 Peaceful Terrace
Silver Spring, MD 20904

202-559-8998; Fax: 202-559-8998
info@aere.org
www.aere.org

W.L (Vic) Adamowicz, President
Dr. Richard G. Newell, Vice President
Prof. Sarah West, Secretary
Dr. Dallas Burtraw, Treasurer
Prof. Elena G. Irwin, Board Of Director

AERE serves as an information resource for economists involved in natural resources policy planning and research. It was estabilshed as a way to exchange ideas, stimulate research, and promote graducate research in environmental economics.
900 Members
Founded in 1979

7634 **Association of Fish & Wildlife Agencies**
1100 First Street NE
Suite 825
Washington, DC 20002

202-838-3474; Fax: 202-350-9869
info@fishwildlife.org
www.fishwildlife.org
Facebook, Twitter

Ron Regan, Executive Director
Dave Chanda, President
Nick Wiley, Vice President

Carol Bambrey, Association Council
Glenn Normandeau, Secretary/Treasurer

The organization that represents all of North America's fish and wildlife agencies that promotes sound management and conservation, and speaks with a unified voice on important fish and wildlife issues.
Founded in 1902

7635 **Association of State Floodplain Managers**
575 D'Onofrio Drive
Suite 200
Madison, WI 53719

608-828-3000; Fax: 608-828-6319
Larry@floods.org
www.floods.org
Facebook, Twitter, Google+

Larry Larson, Director Emeritus
Maria Cox Lamm, Vice Chair
Leslie Durham, Secretary
Karen McHugh, Treasurer
Ingrid Danler, Deputy Director

Promotes common interest in flood damage abatement, supports environmental protection for floodplain areas, provides education on floodplain management practices and policy and urges incorporating multi-objective management approaches to solve local flooding problems.
6500 Members
Founded in 1977

7636 **Association of Zoos and Aquariums**
8403 Colesville Rd
Suite 710
Silver Spring, MD 20910-6331

301-562-0777; Fax: 301-562-0888
membership@aza.org
www.aza.org
Facebook, Twitter

Dan Ashe, President & CEO
Craig Hoover, Executive Vice President
Jack Keeney, Jr., General Counsel
Phil Wagner, Chief Financial Officer
Melissa Howerton, SVP, Member Services

A nonprofit organization dedicated to the advancement of accredited zoos and aquariums in the areas of animal care, wildlife conservation, education and science.
200 Members
Founded in 1924

7637 **Celebrate Planet Earth**
PO Box 1536
Santa Fe, MN 87504-1536

505-986-6040
800-698-4438; Fax: 505-395-9410
kids@celebrateplanetearth.org
www.celebrateplanetearth.org
Facebook, Twitter

Clifford Ross, Executive Director

A 30-year-old U.S. based educational nonprofit organization that inspires wonder, learning, and care of the natural world in children, teachers, and parents. Celebrate Planet Earth ships live painted lady butterfly caterpillars, giant sunflower seeds, and pollinator finger puppets knit by women in protected areas of Latin America, to educators nationally.
Founded in 1989

7638 **Center for Biological Diversity**
P.O. Box 710
Tucson, AZ 85702-0710

520-623-5252
866-357-3349; Fax: 520-623-9797
center@biologicaldiversity.org
www.biologicaldiversity.org
Facebook, Twitter, YouTube, Instagram

Marcey Olajos, Board Chair
Stephanie Zill, Treasurer
Robin Silver, Secretary
Paula Simmonds, Director, Development
Mike Stark, Communications Director

National U.S. group using science, law, and creative media to protect the lands, waters, and climate that species need to survive.

7639 **Center for Environmental Philosophy**
1155 Union Circle
#310980
Denton, TX 76203-5017

940-565-2727; Fax: 940-565-4439
cep@unt.edu
www.cep.unt.edu

Graduate program in environmental ethics at the University of NorthTexas.

7640 **Center for Food Safety**
660 Pennsylvania Ave, SE
#302
Washington, DC 20003

202-547-9359; Fax: 202-547-9429
office@centerforfoodsafety.org
www.centerforfoodsafety.org
Facebook, Twitter, Pinterest, YouTube

Andrew Kimbrell, Executive Director
Rebecca Spector, West Coast Director
Adam Keats, Senior Attorney
Cristina Stella, Staff Attorney
Amy Van Saun, Legal Fellow

A U.S. environmental, nonprofit organization based in Washington, D.C.

7641 **Center for a New American Dream**
PO Box 797
Charlottesville, VA 22902

301-891-3683
newdream@newdream.org
www.newdream.org
Facebook, Twitter, YouTube, Pinterest

Casey Williams, Interim Executive Director
Edna Rienzi, Program Director
Guinevere Higgins, Director Of Development
Lisa Mastny, Publications Director

A nonprofit organization that helps Americans reduce and shift their consumption to improve quality of life, protect the environment, and promote social justice.
Founded in 1997

7642 **Citizens Campaign for the Environment**
225-A Main Street
Farmingdale, NY 11735

516-390-7150; Fax: 516-390-7160
farmingdale@citizenscampaign.org
www.citizenscampaign.org
Facebook, Twitter, YouTube, RSS, Blog

Adrienne Esposito, Executive Director
Brian Smith, Associate Exe. Dir.
Mary Ellen Dour, Education & Financial Director
Sarah Eckel, Policy Director
Jacob McCaffery, Outreach Dir.

Works to protect the environment and public health with the supportof members in New York and Connecticut.
Founded in 1985

7643 **Citizens' Climate Lobby**
1330 Orange Ave
#300
Coronado, CA 92118

619-437-7142
ccl@citizensclimatelobby.org
citizensclimatelobby.org
Facebook, Twitter, Instagram, YouTube, Google+

Marshall Saunders, Founder/ President
Mark Reynolds, Executive Director
Steve Valk, Communications Director
Amy Bennett, Director, Operations
Danny Richter, Legislative Director

An international grassroots environmental group that trains and supports volunteers to build relationships with their Members of Congress in order to influence climate policy.

7644 **Coastal Conservation Association**
6919 Portwest Dr
Suite 100
Houston, TX 77024-8049

713-626-4234
800-201-FISH; Fax: 713-626-5852
ccantl@joincca.org
www.joincca.org
Facebook, Twitter, RSS

Degraaf Adams, Executive Board, Texas
Bill Bird, Executive Board, Florida
Stan Brogdon, Executive Board, Washington
Robert Donlin, Executive Board, South Carolina
Jim Flannery, Executive Board , Maryland

Seeks to advance protection and conservation of all marine life. Conducts seminars and bestows awards.
85000 Members
Founded in 1977

7645 **Committee for a Constructive Tomorrow**
P.O. Box 65722
Washington, DC 20035

202-429-2737
www.cfact.org
Facebook, Twitter, RSS, YouTube

David Rothbard, President/ Co-Founder
Craig Rucker, Executive Director, Co-Founder
Marc Morano, Director of Communications
Duggan Flanakin, Director of Policy Research
Christina Wilson Norman, Development Officer

A conservative Washington, D.C.-based nonprofit organization that promotes a positive voice on environment and development issues.

7646 **Community Alliance with Family Farmers**
PO Box 363
Davis, CA 95617-363

530-756-8518; Fax: 530-756-7857
info@caff.org
www.caff.org
Facebook, Twitter, YouTube

Paul Towers, Executive Director
David Runsten, Policy Director
Holly Markham, Development & Admin. Director
Ben Thomas, Program Director, Farm To Market
Evan Wiig, Dir., Membership & Communications

Non-profit organization that advocates for California's family farmers and sustainable agriculture. Strives to build on shared values around food and agriculture, and work together in practical, on-the-ground programs. Parterships create locally based economic vitality, improved human and environmental health, and long-term sustainability of family farms.
Cost: $47.95

7647 **Conservation Education Association**
Department of Conservation

PO Box 180
Jefferson City, MO 65102-0180

573-751-4115; Fax: 573-751-4467
www.aheia.com

John Hoskins, Director
Lorna Domke, Outreach/Education
Tom Cwyner, Editor

Focuses on conservation and the importance of protecting the environment.
Founded in 1937

7648 **Conservation Fund**
1655 N. Fort Myer Drive
Suite 1300
Arlington, VA 22209-3199

703-525-6300; Fax: 703-525-4610
webmaster@conservationfund.org
www.conservationfund.org
Facebook, Twitter, LinkedIn, YouTube

J. Rutherford Seydel II, Chairman
R. Michael Leonard, Vice Chairman
Lawrence A. Selzer, President and CEO
Richard L. Erdmann, Executive VP and General Counsel
David K. Phillips, Jr., Treasurer, Executive VP & CFO

Works with private and public agencies and organizations to protect wildlife habitats, historic sites and parks.
Founded in 1985

7649 **Conservation International**
2011 Crystal Dr
Suite 500
Arlington, VA 22202-3787

703-341-2400
800-429-5660
community@conservation.org
www.conservation.org
Facebook, Twitter, YouTube, Instagram, RSS

Peter Seligmann, Chairman of the Board & CEO
Rob Walton, Chairman Of Executive Committee
Harrison Ford, Vice Chair
Andr, Esteves, Vice Chair
Dawn Arnall, Board Member

Mission is to conserve the Earth's living heritage-our global biodiversity-and to demonstrate that human societies are able to live harmoniously with nature.
60M Members
Founded in 1987

7650 **Conservation Law Foundation**
62 Summer Street
Boston, MA 02110-1016

617-350-0990
e-info@clf.org
www.clf.org
Facebook, Twitter, LinkedIn, RSS, Instagram, Pinterest, Goo

Sara Molyneaux, Chair
Gordan Hall III, Vice Chair
Peter Nessen, Vice Chair
Eugene H. Clapp, Treasurer
Bradley Campbell, President

An environmental advocacy organization based in New England that advocates on behalf of the region's environment and its communities.
Founded in 1966

7651 **Conservation Treaty Support Fund**
3705 Cardiff Road
Chevy Chase, MD 20815

301-654-3150
800-654-3150; Fax: 301-652-6390
www.conservationagreementfund.org

George A Furness Jr, President
Frederick E. Morris
John C. Goldsmith

Promotes awareness, understanding and support of conservation treaties and their goals. Through the International Endangered Species Treaty, the Wetlands Convention, and other conservation agreements, more than 150 nations are committed to work together to preserve the wildlife and habitats that are our shared natural heritage.
Founded in 1986

7652 **Conservation and Preservation Charities of America**
1100 Larkspur Landing Circle
Suite 340
Larkspur, CA 94939

800-626-6685
www.conservenow.org

Patrick Mcguire, President

CPCA is a consortium of environmental stewardship organizations. CPCA acts as a central focus for charitable giving dedicated to the protection of the natural habitat and historic treasures. Sponsors workplace giving campaigns in support of its member organizations.

7653 **Defenders of Wildlife**
1130 17th Street, NW
Washington, DC 20036

202-682-9400
800-385-9712
defenders@mail.defenders.org
www.defenders.org
Facebook, Twitter, RSS, YouTube, Flickr

Winsome Dunn McIntosh, Chair
Susan Wallace, Vice Chair
Mark Caylor, Treasurer
Caroline Gabel, Secretary
Jamie Rappaport Clark, President, CEO

A nonprofit conservation organization based in the United States that protects all animals and plants native to North America in their natural communities.
Founded in 1947

7654 **Earth Island Institute**
2150 Allston Way
Suite 460
Berkeley, CA 94704-1375

510-859-9100; Fax: 510-859-9091
www.earthisland.org
Facebook, Twitter, YouTube

Michael Mitrani, President
Martha Davis, Vice President
Kenneth Brower, Vice President
Jennifer Snyder, Secretary
Alex Giedt, Treasurer

Seeks to prevent destruction of environment and sponsors fund drives and activist projects to protect wildlife.
33M Members
Founded in 1985

7655 **Earth Policy Institute**
1350 Connecticut Avenue NW
Suite 403
Washington, DC 20036

202-496-9290; Fax: 202-496-9325
www.earth-policy.org
Facebook, Twitter, RSS

Judith Gradwohl, Chairman
Lester R. Brown, Founder, President
Reah Janise Kauffman, Co-Founder, VP
Janet Larsen, Director of Research
J. Matthew Roney, Research Associate

An independent nonprofit environmental organization based in Washington D.C. in the United States.
Founded in 2001

7656 **Earth Regeneration Society**
1442A Walnut Street
#57
Berkeley, CA 94709-1405

510-527-9716; Fax: 510-559-8410

Alden Bryant, President
Cynthia Johnson, Secretary
Glen A. Frendel, Executive Director
Alden Bryant, Acting Treasurer
Dolores Huerta, Board Of Director

Organized to develop and study scientific and practical solutions to environmental issues.

7657 **Earth Society Foundation**
238 East 58th Street
Suite 2400
New York, NY 10022

212-832-3659
800-3EA-THDA
earthsociety1@hotmail.com
www.earthsocietyfoundation.org
Facebook

Helen Garland, Chairperson
Thomas C. Dowd, President
Tom Dowd, VP

News of interest in environmental and sociological issues. Purpose is to promote Earth Day and the Earth Trustee agenda; Every individual and institution should seek choices in ecology, economics, and ethics that will eliminate pollution, poverty, and violence.

7658 **Earthjustice**
50 California St
Suite 500
San Francisco, CA 94111

800-584-6460; Fax: 415-217-2040
headquarters@earthjustice.org
earthjustice.org
Facebook, Twitter

Trip Van Noppen, President
Drew Caputo, VP, Litig., Lands/Wildlife/Oceans
Abigail Dillen, VP, Litigation, Climate & Energy
Lisa Garcia, VP, Litigation, Healthy Communities
Patrice Simms, VP, Litigation

Non-profit environmental law organization.
Founded in 1971

7659 **Ecological and Toxicological Association of Dyes**
Stadthausgasse 18
4051 Basel
Switzerland

616-909-966; Fax: 616-914-278
www.etad.com

Jill Aker, President

Represents the interests of manufacturers and formulators of dyes in the region with regard to environmental and health hazards in the manufacture, processing, shipment, use and disposal of thier products.
Founded in 1974

7660 **Energy & Environmental Research Center**
University of North Dakota
15 North 23rd St., Stop 9018
Grand Forks, ND 58202-9018

701-777-5000; Fax: 701-777-5181
www.eerc.und.nodak.edu
Facebook, Twitter, LinkedIn, Google+, YouTube, Flickr

Thomas A. Erickson, CEO
John A. Harju, VP, Strategic Relationships
Erin M. O'Leary, CFFO
Edward N. Steadman, VP, Research

The EERC conducts research on fossil, renewable and altenative fuels, as well as pollution prevention and environmental cleanup.
Founded in 1951

7661 **Energy Action Coalition**
Home Page: www.energyactioncoalition.org
Facebook, Twitter, RSS, Flickr, YouTube, Vimeo
Lydia Avila, Executive Director
Kristina Banks, Operations Coordinator
Sean Estelle, National Divestment Campaigner
Tina Johnson, Sr. Dir of Env. Justice & Programs
Kendall Mackey, National Tar Sands Organizer
A North American nonprofit organization made up of 50 partner organizations in the U.S. and Canada that runs campaigns to build the youth and student clean energy movement and advocate for changes on local, state, national, andinternational levels in North America.

7662 **Environmental & Energy Study Institute**
1112 16th Street, NW
Suite 300
Washington, DC 20036
202-628-1400; Fax: 202-204-5244
alaporte@eesi.org
www.eesi.org
Facebook, Twitter, YouTube, Google+
Jared Blum, Board Chair
Shelley Fidler, Board Secretary/Treasurer
Richard L. Ottinger, Board Chair Emeritus
Quincalee Brown, Executive Director
Frances S. Buchholzer, Director
A non-profit organization dedicated to promoting environmentally sustainable societies.
Founded in 1984

7663 **Environmental Alliance for Senior Involvement**
PO Box 250
Milford, CT 06460
203-779-0024; Fax: 203-779-0025
easi@easi.org
www.easi.org
Thomas Benjamin, President
Roy Geiger, VP Administration
Peggy Knight, VP Programs
Engaging senior volunteers to use their experience in the restoration and maintenance of environmentally sound environments. International network.
Founded in 1990

7664 **Environmental Assessment Association**
PO Box 879
Palm Springs, CA 92263
877-743-6806
877-810-5643; Fax: 760-327-5631
info@eaa-assoc.org
www.eaa-assoc.org
LinkedIn
Bill C. Merrell Ph.D , CEI, National Education Director
Supports all those involved in environmental assessment, including training and education, publications, conferences and research resources.

7665 **Environmental Bankers Association**
1827 Powers Ferry Rd.
Building 14, Suite 100
Atlanta, GA 30339
678-619-5045
800-966-7475; Fax: 678-229-2777
eba@envirobank.org
www.envirobank.org
William Sloan, President
Lisa Kraus Gardner, Sr. Mngr. & Conference Planner
Michele Doyle, Association Coordinator
Patricia Bagley, Accounting Services
EBA voting members are banks, trust companies, credit unions, savings and loan associations, and other financial services organizations with an interest in environmental risk management and related issues. Active participants are bankers from Trust or Credit offices with responsibility for environmental liability, and financial services officers with environmental interests. Affiliate members are from law firms, consulting and insurance organizations.
Founded in 1994

7666 **Environmental Business Association**
126 State Street
3rd Floor
Albany, NY 12207-1637
518-432-6400; Fax: 518-432-1383
John L. Cusack, President
Linda R. Shaw, Vice President
Martha M. Holstein, Secretary
Ronald J. Beruta, Treasurer
Robert Hall, Director
EBA members represent all segments of the environmental industry—consultants, labaoratories, remediation companies, disposal firms, recyclers and technology innovators. EBA facilitates arrangements and information exchange among members to develop business opportunities. Services include sponsoring seminars, monthly meetings, industry trends, changes in technology and legislation.
Founded in 1989

7667 **Environmental Compliance Institute**
165 Sherwood Ave
Farmingdale, NY 11735
631-414-7757
866-670-5366; Fax: 631-843-6331
pbany@c2g.us
www.c2g.us
Attorneys and corporations interested in environmental law and federal regulations governing waste disposal and other matters related to the environment.

7668 **Environmental Council of the States(ECOS)**
50 F Street NW
Suite 350
Washington, DC 20001
202-266-4920; Fax: 202-266-4937
ecos@ecos.org
www.ecos.org
Martha Rudolf, President
John Linc Stine, Vice President
Elizabeth Dieck, Secretary-Treasurer
John Stine, Committe Chair, Air
Sara Parker Pauley, Committe Chair, Water
Improving the capability of State environmental agencies and their leaders to protect and improve human health and the environment of the United States of America.

7669 **Environmental Design Research Association**
1760 Old Meadow Road
Suite 500
McLean, VA 22102
703-506-2895; Fax: 703-506-3266
www.edra.org
Facebook, Twitter, LinkedIn
Sharmin Kader, Chair
Claudia Bernasconi, Chair-Elect
Deni Ruggeri, Executive Director
Is to advance the art and science of environmental design research, to improve understanding of the interrelationships between people and their built and natural surroundings, and to help create environments responsive to human needs. EDRA members are designers and other professionals with an interest in environmental design research.
700 Members
Founded in 1968

7670 **Environmental Industry Association**
4301 Connecticut Ave Nw
Suite 300
Washington, DC 20008-2304
202-244-4700
800-424-2869; Fax: 202-966-4824
www.oneia.ca
Facebook
Bruce Parker, President
Supports all those involved with technology of recycling, resource recovery and sanitary landfills. Publishes magazine.

7671 **Environmental Information Association**
6935 Wisconsin Ave
Suite 306
Chevy Chase, MD 20815-6112
301-961-4999
888-343-4342; Fax: 301-961-3094
info@eia-usa.org
www.eia-usa.org
Kevin Cannan, President
Chris Gates, President Elect
Steve Fulford, Vice President
Robert De Malo, Secretary
Kyle Burroughs, Treasurer
Nonprofit organization dedicated to providing environmental information to individuals, members and industry. Disseminates information on the abatement of asbestos and lead-based paint, indoor air quality, safety and health issues, analytical issues and environmental site assessments.

7672 **Environmental Law Institute**
1730 M Street NW
Suite 700
Washington, DC 20036-4919
202-939-3800
800-433-5120; Fax: 202-939-3868
law@eli.org
www.eli.org
Facebook, Twitter, LinkedIn
Scott Fulton, President
Scott Schang, Executive Vice President
Martin Dickinson, VP Development
John V. Pendergrass, Acting VP, Research & Policy
Loretta Reinersmann, VP, Finance & Administration
Supports all those involved in environmental issues from a legal perspective, fostering the exchange of ideas and solutions for pressing environmental issues.

7673 **Environmental Mutagen Society**
1821 Michael Faraday Drive
Suite 300
Reston, VA 20190
703-438-8220; Fax: 703-438-3113
emshq@ems-us.org
www.emgs-us.org
Suzanne M. Morris, President
Bevin P. Engelward, Vice President
Barbara L. Parsons, Secretary
Barbara S. Shane, Treasurer
Marguerite Leishman, Executive Director
Members are scientists of diverse backgrounds and varied interests working in the field of molecular genetics and mutagenesis, whether in academia, industry or government. Focus is to encourage the study mutagens in the human environment particularly as they affect public health.
1500 Members
Founded in 1969

7674 **Environmental and Energy Study Instituteÿ**
1112 16th Street, NW
Suite 300
Washington, DC 20036
202-628-1400; Fax: 202-204-5244
www.eesi.org
Facebook, Twitter, YouTube, Google+
Jared Blum, Board Chair
Richard L. Ottinger, Chaise-Emeritus
Shelley Fidler, Board Secretary/Treasurer
Quincalee Brown, Executive Director
Frances S. Buchholzer, Director
Educating Congress on energy efficiency and renewable energy; advancing innovative policy solutions.
Founded in 1984

7675 **Federation of Environmental Technologists**
W175 N11081 Stonewood Dr.
Ste 203
Germantown, WI 53022-4771
262-437-1700; Fax: 262-437-1702
info@fetinc.org
www.fetinc.org
Facebook, LinkedIn
Jeff Nettesheim, Board Chair
Cheryl Moran, President
Patrick Rego, Vice President
Anthony Montemurro, Treasurer
Barbara Hurula, Executive Director
Educational Seminars and Courses on Environmental, Health and Safety topics throughout the year around the state of Wisconsin for business and industry. Annual conference and exhibition held each October in Wisconsin.
700 Members
Founded in 1981

7676 **Floodplain Management Association**
PO Box 712080
Santee, CA 92072-2080
760-936-3676; Fax: 619-749-9524
admin@floodplain.org
www.floodplain.org
Facebook, LinkedIn, YouTube
Mark Seits, Chair
Maria Lorenzo Lee, Vice Chair
John Powderly, Secretary
George Booth, Treasurer
Andrew Trelease, Director
A nonprofit educational association established to promote the reduction of flood losses and to encourage the protection and enhancement of nautral floodplain values through the use of effective wetland management strategies and engineering technolgies.
Founded in 1990

7677 **Forest History Society**
701 William Vickers Ave
Durham, NC 27701-3162
919-682-9319; Fax: 919-682-2349
recluce2@duke.edu
www.foresthistory.org
Facebook, Twitter, LinkedIn, Flickr
Hayes Brown, Chairman
Kent Gilges, Co-Vice Chairman
Chris Zinkhan, Co-Vice Chairman
Henry I. Barclay III, Treasurer
Steven Anderson, Secretary & President
Nonprofit, educational institution that explores the history of the environment, forestry and conservation.
2000 Members
Founded in 1946

7678 **Forestry, Conservation Communications Association**
122 Baltimore Street
Gettysburg, PA 17325
717-778-4237
844-458-0298; Fax: 717-398-0815
david.steinour@frequencycoordination.org
www.fcca.info
Chief Paul M. Leary (ret.), President
Roy Mott, Vice President
John McIntosh, Secretary/Treasurer
Ralph Haller, Executive Director
Janet Muncy, Financial Assistant
Association for manufacturers or suppliers of forestry and conservation communications equipment, systems and procedures.

7679 **Friends of the Earth USA**
1100 15th Street NW
11th Fl.
Washington, DC 20005
202-783-7400
877-843-8687; Fax: 202-783-0444
foe.org
Facebook, Twitter, Instagram, YouTube
Erich Pica, President
Michelle Chan, VP, Programs
Peter Stocker, VP, Membership & Development
Julie Dyer, Operations Director
Global organization of environmental activists.

7680 **Friends of the Trees Society**
PO Box 165
Hot Springs, MT 59845
406-741-5809
friendsofthetrees@yahoo.com
www.friendsofthetrees.net
Michael Pilarski, Founder & Director
Nonprofit organization helping tree lovers worldwide.
Founded in 1978

7681 **GREENGUARD Environmental Institute**
2211 Newmarket Parkway
Suite 110
Marietta, GA 30067
888-485-4733; Fax: 770-980-0072
environment@ul.com
www.greenguard.org
An industry-independent organization that aims to protect human health and improve quality of life by enhancing indoor air quality and reducing people's exposure to chemicals and other pollutants.

7682 **Global Water Policy Project**
info@globalwaterpolicy.org
www.globalwaterpolicy.org
Promotes the preservation and sustainable use of Earth's fresh water through research, writing, outreach, and public speaking.

7683 **Green Zionist Alliance**
PO Box 1176
Long Beach, NY 11561
347-559-4492
info@aytzim.org
www.aytzim.org
Rabbi Michael Cohen, Co-founder
David Krantz, Board of Director
Susan Levine, Board of Director
Netta Schmeidler, Board of Director
Pesach Stadlin, Board of Director
A North America-based nonprofit organization that works to educate and mobilize people around the world for Israel's environment, to protect Israel's environment and support its environmental movement.
Founded in 2001

7684 **GreenBlue**
600 E. Water St.
Suite C
Charlottesville, VA 22902
434-817-1424
info@greenblue.org
www.greenblue.org
Facebook, Twitter
Nina Goodrich, Executive Director
Michael Brann, Director of Operations
James Ewell, Sr. Director, Sustainable Materials
Anne Elsea, Communications Manager
An environmental nonprofit organization dedicated to the sustainable use of materials in society. Encourages innovation and best practices to promote the creation of a more sustainble materials economy.

7685 **Greenpeace USA**
702 H St NW
Suite 300
Washington, DC 20001-3876
202-462-1177
800-722-6995; Fax: 202-462-4507
goa@wdc.greenpeace.org
www.greenpeaceusa.org
Facebook, Twitter, YouTube
John Passacantando, CEO
Ellen McPeake, COO
Leading independent campaigning organization that uses non-violent direct action and creative communication to expose global environmental problems and to promote solutions that are essential to a green and peaceful future.
2.5M Members
Founded in 1971

7686 **Honor The Earth**
PO Box 63
607 Main Ave,
Callaway, MN 56521
218-375-3200
info@honorearth.org
www.honorearth.org
Facebook, Twitter
A nonprofit organization founded to raise awareness and financial support for Indigenous environmental justice.
Founded in 1993

7687 **Institute for Energy and Environmental Research**
6935 Laurel Ave.
Suite 201
Takoma Park, MD 20912

301-270-5500; Fax: 301-270-3029
info@ieer.org
ieer.org
Facebook, Twitter, RSS

Arjun Makhijani, President, Senior Engineer
Sadaf Rassoul Cameron, Vice President
David Close, Ph.D., Treasurer, Secretary
Annie Makhijani, Project Scientist
Christina Mills, Staff Scientist

Focuses on the environmental safety of nuclear weapons production, ozone layer depletion, and other issues relating to energy.
Founded in 1987

7688 **Institute for Environmental Auditing**
City Office Park
Tritton Road
Lincoln LNS7AS

152-254-0069; Fax: 152-254-0090
info@iema.net
www.iema.net
Twitter, LinkedIn, Google+

Dr Diana Montgomery FIEMA, Chairman
Richard Powell OBE, Executive Director
Tim Balcon, Chief Executive
Martin Baxter FIEMA, CEnv, Executive Director Policy
Dave Stanley. FIEMA, Cenv, Director

A professional organization of environmental auditors.
100 Members

7689 **Institute for World Resource Research**
PO Box 50303
Palo Alto, CA 94303-0303

630-910-1551; Fax: 202-729-7610
www.globalwarming.net

BJ Jefferson, Advertising/Sales

Supports those involved in all phases of developments in forestry and reforestation of northern nations including the US, Canada, Russia, Sweden, Finland, Norway, China, Japan and others. Its goal is to increase the worldwide understanding of the ecological and economic roles of the northern forest regions of the world.

7690 **Institute of Environmental Sciences and Technology**
1827 Walden Office Square
Suite 400
Schaumburg, IL 60173

847-981-0100; Fax: 847-981-4130
information@iest.org
www.iest.org
Facebook, Twitter, LinkedIn

David Sgro, President
Nick Clinkinbeard, President-Elect

The Institute of Environmental Sciences and Technology (IEST) is the leading technical, nonprofit membership association that connects professionals who deal with controlled environments. IEST provides technical guidance through International Standards, Recommended Practices, and education programs developed by experts in the fields of contamination control, environmental test and reliability, and nanotechnology facilities.
750 Members
Founded in 1953

7691 **Institute of Gas Technology**
1700 S Mount Prospect Rd
Des Plaines, IL 60018-1804

847-768-0500; Fax: 847-768-0501
publicrelations@gastechnology.org
www.gastechnology.org
Twitter, LinkedIn, YouTube

David Carroll, President & CEO
Ronald Snedic, Vice President/ Corporate Devel.
Jim Ingold, Vice President, Finance
Edward Johnston, VP, Research Operations
Paul Armstrong, Director

Supports all those involved in the gas industry worldwide, including energy industry production, consumption, reserves, imports and prices.

7692 **Institute of Scrap Recycling Industries**
1615 L St NW
Suite 600
Washington, DC 20036-5664

202-662-8500; Fax: 202-626-0900
isri@isri.org
www.isri.org
Facebook, Twitter, LinkedIn, Instagram

Doug Kramer, Chairman
Mark Lewon, Chair Elect
Brian Shine, Vice Chair
Gary Champlin, Secretary Treasurer
Robin K. Wiener, President

Supports all those involved in the scrap processing and recycling industry.
165 Members
1987 Attendees

7693 **International Association for Food Protection**
6200 Aurora Ave
Suite 200W
Des Moines, IA 50322-2864

515-276-3344
800-369-6337; Fax: 515-276-8655
info@foodprotection.org
www.foodprotection.org
Facebook, Twitter, LinkedIn

Timothy C. Jackson, President
Kalmia E. Kniel, President-Elect
Roger L. Cook, Vice President
Ruth Petran, Secretary
David W. Tharp, Executive Director

Nonprofit, educational association of food protection professionals. The association is dedicated to the education and service of its members, specifically, as well as industry personnel.
4200 Members
Founded in 1911

7694 **International Association of Wildland Fire**
1418 Washburn Street
Missoula, MT 59801

406-531-8264
888-440-4293
www.iawfonline.org
Facebook, Twitter, LinkedIn

Tom Zimmerman, President
Alan Goodwin, Vice President
David Moore, Treasurer
Kathy Clay, Secretary
Timothy Brown, Board Member

IWAF members are academics and professionals with an interest in wildland fires.
800 Members
Founded in 1990

7695 **International Council on Nanotechnology - ICON**
214-494-2071

Vicki Colvin, Executive Director
Kristen Kulinowski, Director

A portal for information about the environmental, health, and safety aspects of nanotechnology.

7696 **International Ecotourism Society**
427 North Tatnall Street
Wilmington, DE 19801-2230

202-506-5033; Fax: 202-789-7279
info@ecotourism.org
www.ecotourism.org
Facebook, Twitter, YouTube

Kelly Bricker, Chair
Tony Charters, Vice Chair
Neal Inamdar, Director Finance/Administration

Society members include park managers, tour operators, conservation professionals, and others with an interest in the development of ecology-centered tourism.
900 Members
Founded in 1990

7697 **International Lead Zinc Research Organization**
1822 NC Highway 54 East
Suite 120
Durham, NC 27713

919-361-4647; Fax: 919-361-1957
www.ilzro.org

Stephen Wilkinson, President
Frank Goodwin, VP Materials Sciences
Scott Mooneyham, Treasurer
Rob Putnam, Director Communications

ILZRO members are miners and refiners of lead and zinc. Trade association of the lead and zinc industry worldwide. Focus on research and development to detect new uses for the metals and refine existing uses.
Founded in 1958

7698 **International Living Future Institute**
1501 East Madison St.
Suite 150
Seattle, WA 98122

206-223-2028
info@living-future.org
www.living-future.org
Facebook, Twitter, LinkedIn, Instagram

KC Gauldine, Chief Executive Officer
Corinna Krauskopf, Chief Development Officer
Andrea Kristof, Chief Financial Officer
Greg Norris, Chief Scientist
Marja Williams, Chief Program Officer

Leading and supporting the transformation toward communities that are socially just, culturally rich, and ecologically restorative. Offers green building and infrastructure solutions for single room renovations to neighborhoods and whole cities. Offices in Vancouver BC, Seattle WA, and Portland OR.

7699 **International Society for Ecological Economics**
15 River Street
#204
Boston, MA 02108

703-790-1745; Fax: 703-790-2672
http://www.isecoeco.org/
Facebook, Twitter, LinkedIn, Google+, Pinterest

Dr. Marina Fischer-Kowalski, President
Sabine O'Hara, President-Elect
Anne Carter Aitken, Treasurer
Bina Agarwal, Past President
Rashid Hassan, Board of Director

Members are researchers, academics, and other professionals who study the impact of economic models and policies on the environment.
750 Members
Founded in 1989

7700 **Isaak Walton League**
707 Conservation Lane
Gaithersburg, MD 20878
301-548-0150
800-453-5463; Fax: 301-548-0146
info@iwla.org
www.iwla.org
Facebook, Twitter, LinkedIn, Google+, Pinterest
Jodi Arndt Labs, Chair
Shawn Gallagher, President
Jeff Deschamps, Vice President
Jim Storer, Secretary
Walter Lynn Jr., Treasurer
Protects America's outdoors through education, community-based conservation, and promoting outdoor recreation.
37000 Members
Founded in 1922

7701 **Keep America Beautiful**
1010 Washington Boulevard
Stamford, CT 6901
203-659-3000; Fax: 203-659-3001
info@kab.org
www.kab.org
Facebook, Twitter, Tumblr, YouTube, Pinterest
Howard Ungerleider, Chairman
Tom Waldeck, Treasurer
Thomas H. Tamoney, Jr., Secretary
Shannon Reiter, President
Gregory H. Ray, Senior Vice President
Nonprofit organization that builds and sustains vibrant communities.
Founded in 1953

7702 **League of Conservation Votersÿ**
1920 L Street, NW
Suite 800
Washington, DC 20036
202-785-8683; Fax: 202-835-0491
www.lcv.org
Facebook, Twitter, YouTube, Flickr
Carol Browner, Chair
Sherwood Boehlert, Vice Chair
Trip Van Noppen, Treasurer
Carrie Clark, Secretary
Gene Karpinski, President
A political advocacy organization that advocates for sound environmental policies and elects pro-environmental candidates who will adopt and implement such policies.

7703 **Marine Technology Society**
1100 H St., Nw
Suite LL-100
Washington, DC 20005
202-717-8705; Fax: 202-347-4302
membership@mtsociety.org
www.mtsociety.org
Facebook, Twitter, LinkedIn, YouTube
Kathleen Herndon, Executive Director
Kristina Norman, Director, Events
Monica Ostrander, Director, Programs
Amy Morgante, Managing Editor
Judy Pagliaro, Bookkeeper
Addresses coastal zone management, marine, mineral and energy resources, marine environmental protection, and ocean engineering issues.
2M Members
Founded in 1963

7704 **Midwest for Environmental Science and Public Policy**
1845 N Farwell Avenue
Suite 100
Milwaukee, WI 53202
414-271-7280; Fax: 414-273-7293
www.mcespp.org
Patrice Ann Morrow, Chair
Jeffery A Foran, President/CEO
For citizens concerned with environmental protection.

7705 **NORA: Association of Responsible Recyclers**
7250 Heritage Village Plaza,
Suite 201
Gainesville, VA 20155
703-753-4277; Fax: 703-753-2445
sparker@noranews.org
www.noranews.org
Bill Hinton, President
Chris Bergstrom, Executive Vice President
Roy Schumacher, Vice President
Brandon Velek, Past President
Ellie Bruce, Board Of Director
Is a trade association representing the interests of companies in the United States engaged in the safe recycling of used oil, antifreeze, waste water and oil filters.
Founded in 1984

7706 **National Association for Environmental Management**
1612 K St NW
1002
Washington, DC 20006-2830
202-986-6616
800-391-6236; Fax: 202-530-4408
programs@naem.org
www.naem.org
Facebook, Twitter, LinkedIn
Rick Taylor, President
Kris Morico, 1st Vice President
Mark Hause, 2nd Vice President
Alan Leibowitz, Treasurer
Stephen Evanoff, Ex-Officio Member - Past President
Dedicated to advancing the profession of environmental management and supports the professional corporate and facility environmental manager.
1000+ Members
Founded in 1990

7707 **National Association for PET Containers**
7310 Turfway Road
Suite 550
Florence, KY 41042
859-372-6635; Fax: 707-935-1998
n4mayshun@napcor.com
www.napcor.com
Facebook
Rick Moore, Executive Director
Resa Dimino, Director Of Public Policy
Kate Eagles, Project Director
National association for the PET plastic industry. Promotes the use of PET plastic packaging and facilitates the recycling of PET containers.
Frequency: Bi-Monthly
Founded in 1987

7708 **National Association of Environmental Professionals**
PO Box 460
Collingswood, NJ 08108
856-283-7816; Fax: 856-210-1619
naep@bowermanagementservices.com
www.naep.org
Facebook, LinkedIn
Brock Hoegh, CEP, President
David Dickson, Vice President
Courtney Arena, Treasurer
Kristin Bennett, Secretary
Harold Draper,ÿD.Sc., CEP, Immediate Past President
Our mission is to be the interdisciplinary organization dedicated to developing the highest standards of ethics and proficiency in the environmental professions. Our members are public and private sector professionals who promote excellence in decision-making in light of the environmental, social, and economic impacts of those decisions.

7709 **National Association of Local Government Environmental Professionals**
1001 Connecticut Avenue
Suite 405
Washington, DC 20036-1532
202-337-4503; Fax: 202-429-5290
Facebook
Ellen Walkowiak, Chair
John Stufflebean, Vice Chair
Douglas MacCourt, Treasurer
Lee Ilan, Secretary
Chris Bird, Director
Is a national organization representing local government professionals responsible for environmental compliance and the development of local environmental policy. NALGEP brings together local environmental officials to share information on practices, conduct policy projects, promote environmental training and education, and communicate the view of local officials on national environmental issues.
150 Members
Founded in 1993

7710 **National Audubon Society**
225 Varick Street
New York, NY 10014
212-979-3000
webmaster@audubon.org
www.audubon.org
Facebook, Twitter, YouTube
Conserves and restores natural ecosystems, focusing on birds, other wildlife, and their habitats for the benefit of humanity and the earth's biological diversity.
50000 Members
Founded in 1992

7711 **National Center for Appropriate Technology**
3040 Continental Drive
Butte, MT 59702
406-494-4572
800-275-6228; Fax: 406-494-2905
www.ncat.org
Facebook, Twitter, LinkedIn, RSS, Pinterest
Gene Brady, Chairman
Randall Chapman, Vice Chairman
Jeannie Jertson, Secretary
Brian Castelli, Treasurer
John Colgan, Commissioner
Their mission is to help people by championing small-scale, local, and sustainable solutions to reduce poverty, promote healthy communities, and protect natural resources.
Founded in 1976

7712 **National Conference of Local Environmental Health Administrators**
1010 South Third Street
Dayton, WA 99328

509-382-2181; Fax: 360-382-2942
David_Riggs@co.columbia.wa.us

A professional association for supervisors, administrators and managers of environmental health programs in local agencies.

7713 **National Council for Science and the Environment**
1101 17th Street NW
Suite 250
Washington, DC 20036

202-530-5810; Fax: 202-628-4311
www.ncseonline.org
Facebook, Twitter, LinkedIn, YouTube, Flickr

Peter Saundry, Ph.D., Executive Director
Andi Glashow, Director, Finance
Sudeep Vyapari, Ph.D., Associate Executive Director
Jessica Soule, Director, EnvironMentors
David Blockstein, Ph.D., Senior Scientist, Dr. Education

A U.S. based nonprofit organization that improves the scientific basis for environmental decision-making.

7714 **National Environmental Balancing Bureau**
8575 Grovemont Circle
Gaithersburg, MD 20877-4121

301-977-3698
866-497-4447; Fax: 301-977-9589
www.nebb.org

Tiffany Suite, Executive Vice President
Christina Spence, Office & Scheduling Coordinator
Sumyyah Milstein, Firm Certification Coordinator

NEBB is an international certification assocaition for firms that deliver high performance building systems. Members perform testing, adjusting and balancing (TAB) of heating, ventilating and air-conditioning systems, commission and retro-commission building systems commissioning, execute sound and vibration testing, and test and certify lab fume hoods and electronic and bio clean rooms. NEBB holds the highest standards in certification.
Founded in 1971

7715 **National Environmental Development Association**
One Thomas Circle NW
10th Floor
Washington, DC 20006

202-332-2933; Fax: 202-530-0659
www.nedacap.org

Phil Clapp, President
Steve Hellem, Executive Director

NEDA members are companies and other organizations concerned with balancing environmental and economic interests to obtain both a clean environment and a strong economy.
Founded in 1973

7716 **National Environmental, Safety and Health Training Association**
2700 N. Central Avenue
Suite 900
Phoenix, AZ 85004-1147

602-956-6099; Fax: 602-234-1867
neshta@neshta.org
www.neshta.org
Facebook, Twitter, LinkedIn, Google+, Pinterest, Tumblr

Myrtle I. Turner-Harris, President
Jeffery K. Dennis, CET, CSP, CHMM, Vice President
Dave Owings, CET, General Manager
Bruce V. Guiliani, CET, CSP, Dir. Of Saftey Loss & Prevention
David L. Galt, Managing Editor for Safety

A non-profit educational society for environmental, safety, health and other technical training and adult education professionals. Mission is to promote trainer competency through trainer skills training, continuing education, voluntary certification, peer networking and the adoption of national and international training and trainer standards.
Founded in 1977

7717 **National Institutes for Water Resources**
47 Harkness Road
Pelham, MA 10002

413-253-5686; Fax: 413-253-1309
tracy@uidaho.edu
niwr.net

Jeffery Allen, President
Reagan Waskom, President-Elect
John Tracy, Secretary-Treasurer

NIWRD represents state and territorial Water Research Institutes and Centers in collective activities to implement the provisions of the Water Resources Act of 1984, and subsequesnt federal legislation. NIWR networks these separate institutes into a coordinated unit, represented by 8 regional groupings, and facilitates the response of the Water Research Institutes and its membership to other mutual concerns and interests in water resources.
54 Members
Founded in 1974

7718 **National Parks Conservation Association**
777 6th Street NW
Suite 700
Washington, DC 20001-3723

202-223-6722
800-628-7275; Fax: 202-454-3333
npca@npca.org
www.npca.org
Facebook, Twitter

Theresa Pierno, President & CEO
Robin Martin McKenna, Executive Vice President
Tim Moyer, CFO
Elizabeth Fayad, VP & General Counsel

Advocates for the preservation of America's national parks and historical sites.
Founded in 1919

7719 **National Registry of Environmental Professionals**
PO Box 2099
Glenview, IL 60025

847-724-6631; Fax: 847-724-4223
nrep@nrep.org
www.nrep.org
Facebook, Twitter, LinkedIn, YouTube

Scott Spear, Executive Chairperson
Richard Young, PhD, REM, P, Executive Director
Edward C. Beck, PhD, REM, PE,, Director
Charles J. McAfee, REM, CEA,, Director
Marie Hunter , REM, Director

To promote legal and professional recognition of individuals possessing education, training and experience as environmental managers, engineers, technologists, scientists and technicians-and to consolidate that recognition in one centralized source-so that the public, government, employers and insurers can justify the importance and acceptance of such individuals to carry out operations and management of environmental activities.
17000 Members
Founded in 1983
Mailing list available for rent

7720 **National Society of Environmental Consultants**
PO Box 460
Collingswood, NJ 08108

856-283-7816; Fax: 856-210-1619
naep@bowermanagementservices.com
www.naep.org

Brock Hoegh, CEP, President
David Dickson, Vice President
Courtney Arena, Treasurer
Kristin Bennett, Secretary
Harold Draper, D.Sc., CEP, Immediate Past President

Supports all activities of environmental consultants.
600 Members
Founded in 1992

7721 **National Solid Wastes Management Association**
4301 Connecticut Ave NW
Suite 300
Washington, DC 20008-2304

202-244-4700
800-424-2869; Fax: 202-966-4824
www.wasterecycling.org
Facebook, Twitter, Google +

Sharon H. Kneiss, President
Kevin Kraushaar, Esq., CAE, VP, Gov. Affairs & Chapters
Christopher Doherty, VP, Communications
Sheila R. Alkire, Director, Education
Tiffany Jones, Director, Certification

Supports all those involved in the environment industry, especially the handling, transportation and disposal of infectious wastes.

7722 **National Wildlife Federation**
PO Box 1583
Merrifield, VA 22116-1583

703-438-6000
800-822-9919; Fax: 703-438-3570
www.nwf.org
Facebook, Twitter, LinkedIn, YouTube

Bruce Wallace, Chair
Paul Beaudette, Eastern Vice Chair
Clark Bullard, Central Vice Chair
Kent Salazar, Western Vice Chair
Brian Bashore, Director

Encourages management of natural resources. Gives financial aid to local groups and graduate studies. Conducts guided nature trail tours, produces programs and sponsors competitions.
4.5MM Members
Founded in 1936

7723 **National Wildlife Refuge Association**
1001 Connecticut Ave. NW
Suite 905
Washington, DC 20036

202-417-3803
nwra@refugeassociation.org
refugeassociation.org
Facebook, Twitter, LinkedIn, RSS

Rebecca Rubin, Chair
Donal O'Brien, Vice Chair
David Houghton, President
Anne Truslow, VP, Chief Operating Officer
Desiree Sorenson-Groves, VP, Government Affairs

An independent membership organization that works to conserve American wildlife.

7724 **National Woodland Owners Association**
374 Maple Avenue East
Suite 310
Vienna, VA 22180-4718
703-255-2700
800-470-8733; Fax: 703-281-9200
www.woodlandowners.org

Keith A. Argow, President
Dick Courter, Chairman
Phil Gramelspacher, Vice Chairman

Provides timely information about forestry and forest practices with news from Washington,DC and state capitals. Written for non-industrial land owners. Includes state landowner association news.
39M Members
Founded in 1983

7725 **Native Forest Council**
PO Box 2190
Eugene, OR 97402

541-688-2600; Fax: 541-461-2156
info@forestcouncil.org
Facebook, Twitter, Vimeo, YouTube

Bill Barton, Board of Director
Allan Branscomb, Board of Director
Calvin Hececta, Board of Director
Timothy Hermach, Board of Director
Timothy Moxley, Board of Director

Provides news and resources for the protection of publicly owned lands from logging, mining, grazing, drilling, and off-road vehicles.
Founded in 1987

7726 **Natural Resources Defense Council**
40 W 20th St
New York, NY 10011-4231

212-727-2700; Fax: 212-727-1773
nrdcinfo@nrdc.org
www.nrdc.org
Facebook, Twitter, YouTube, Tumblr, RSS

Daniel R. Tishman, Chair
Frederick A.O. Schwarz Jr., Chair Emeritus
Wendy K. Neu, Vice Chair
Alan F. Horn, Vice Chair
Patricia Bauman, Vice Chair

Dedicated to the wise management of natural resources through research, public education and the development of effective public policies.
50000 Members
Founded in 1970

7727 **Nature's Classroom**
19 Harrington Rd.
Charlton, MA 1507

508-248-2741
800-433-8375; Fax: 508-248-2745
info@naturesclassroom.org
www.naturesclassroom.org
Facebook

A nonprofit outdoor environmental education program.

7728 **NatureServe**
4600 N. Fairfax Dr.
7th Floor
Arlington, VA 22203

703-908-1800; Fax: 703-229-1670
info@natureserve.org
www.natureserve.org
Facebook, Twitter, LinkedIn, YouTube, Vimeo, Flickr, RSS

Mary Klein, President/ CEO
Lori Scott, Chief Information Officer
Ravi Shankar, CFO/ COO
Leslie Honey, VP, Conservation Services
Don Kent, Director of Network Relations

A nonprofit organization that provides proprietary wildlife conservation-related data, tools, and services to private and government clients, partner organizations, and the public.
Founded in 1974

7729 **Negative Population Growth**
2861 Duke St.
Suite 36
Alexandria, VA 22314

703-370-9510; Fax: 703-370-9514
www.npg.org
Facebook, Twitter, LinkedIn, RSS, YouTube

Donald Mann, President
Craig Lewis, Executive Vice President
Tracy Canada, Deputy Director
Dianeÿ Saco, Board of Director
Sharon Marks, Board of Director

A membership organization in the United States that works on overpopulation issues and advocates a gradual reduction in U.S. and world population.
Founded in 1972

7730 **North American Association for Environmental Education**
2000 P Street NW
Suite 540
Washington, DC 20036

202-419-0412; Fax: 202-419-0415
info@naaee.org
www.naaee.org
Facebook

Jose Pepe Marcos-Iga, President
Judy Braus, Executive Director
Susan McGuire, Secretary
Mary Ford, Treasurer
Flisa Stevenson, At-Large Board Member

Purpose is to assist and support the work of individuals and groups engaged in environmental education, research and service.
1500 Members
Founded in 1971

7731 **North American Chapter - International Society for Ecological Modelling**
550 M Ritchie Highway
PMB 255
Severna Park, MD 21146

webmaster@isemna.org
www.isemna.org

Sven E. Jorgensen, President
Tarzan Legovic, Secretary-General
David A. Mauriello, Treasurer
Brian D. Faith, President, North America
Guy Larocque,, Secretary, North America

Promotes the international exchange of general knowledge, ideas and scientific results in the area of the application of systems analysis and simulation to ecology, environmental science and natural resource management using mathematical and computer modelling of ecological systems.
150 Members
Founded in 1983

7732 **North American Lake Management Society**
PO Box 5443
Madison, WI 53705-443

608-233-2836; Fax: 608-233-3186
info@nalms.org
www.nalms.org
Facebook, LinkedIn, Flickr

Reed Green, President
Julie Chambers, President-Elect
Sara Peel, Secretary
Mike Perry, Treasurer
Terry McNabb, CLM, Past President

Members are academics, lake managers and others interested in furthering the understanding of lake ecology. The North American Lake Management Society's mission is to forge partnerships among citizens, scientists and professionals to foster the management and protection of lakes and reservoirs for today and tomorrow. Please call for rate information.
1700 Members
Founded in 1980

7733 **Oceana**
1350 Connecticut Ave. NW
5th Fl.
Washington, DC 20036

202-833-3900
877-762-3262; Fax: 202-833-2070
info@oceana.org
oceana.org
Facebook, Twitter, Instagram, YouTube, Google+

Andrew Sharpless, Chief Executive Officer

Environmental organization focused solely on the protection and restoration of the world's oceans.
Founded in 2001

7734 **Organic Seed Alliance**
PO Box 772
Port Townsend, WA 98368-0772

360-385-7192; Fax: 360-385-7455
info@seedalliance.org
www.seedalliance.org
Facebook, Twitter

Cara Loriz, Executive Director
Micaela Colley, Program Director
Kiki Hubbard, Advocacy & Communications Director
Cathleen McCluskey, Outreach Director
Jennifer Turney, Financial Manager

Organic Seed Alliance suppports the ethical development and stewardship of the genetic resources of agricultural seed.
25M Members
Founded in 1975

7735 **Plant Growth Regulation Society of America**
Rhone-Poulenc, Ag Company
1018 Duke Street
Alexandria, VA 22314
703-836-4606; Fax: 706-883-8215
www.pgrsa.org
Facebook, Twitter, RSS

Dr. Carl Sams, President
Dr. Holly Little, 1st Vice President
Mr. Michael Rethwisch, 2nd Vice President
Dr. Tim Spann, Past President
Dr. Chris Gunter, Secretary

Functions as a nonprofit educational and scientific organization.
325 Members
Founded in 1973

7736 **Rachel Carson Council**
8600 Irvington Ave
Bethesda, MD 20817

301-214-2400
office@rachelcarsoncouncil.org
rachelcarsoncouncil.org
Facebook, Twitter, Instagram

Dr. Robert K Musil, President & CEO
Roger Christie, Chairman
Martha Hayne Talbot, Vice President
Richard J Mandel, Treasurer
John H More, Esq., Secretary

Non-profit educates on environmental, peace, and justice issues.
Founded in 1965

7737 **Rainforest Action Network**
425 Bush St.
Suite 300
San Francisco, CA 94108
415-398-4404
800-989-7246
ran@ran.org
www.ran.org
Facebook, Twitter, Instagram, YouTube
Lindsey Allen, Executive Director
Environmental organization focused on forest systems.

7738 **Renewable Fuels Association**
425 Third Street, SW
Suite 1150
Washington, DC 20024
202-289-3835; Fax: 202-289-7519
www.ethanolrfa.org
Facebook, Twitter, LinkedIn, YouTube, Google+, Instagram
Randall Doyal,, Chairman
Mick Henderson, Vice Chairman
Jim Seurer, Treasurer
Bob Dinneen, President
Geoff Cooper, Senior Vice President
Members are companies and individuals involved in the production and use of ethanol.
55 Members
Founded in 1981

7739 **Renewable Natural Resources Foundation**
6010 Executive Boulevard
5th Floor
Bethesda, MD 20852-3827
301-493-9101; Fax: 301-770-9104
info@rnrf.org
www.rnrf.org
Facebook, Twitter
Richard A. Engberg, Chairman
John E. Durrant, Vice-Chairman
Robert D. Day, Executive Director
Sarah Gerould, Director
Erik Hankin, Director
A consortium of professional and scientific societies whose members are concerned with the advancement of research, education, scientific practice and policy formulation for the conservation, replenishment and use of the earth's renewable natural resources.
14 Members
Founded in 1972

7740 **Resource Policy Institute**
1525 Selby Avenue
Ste. 304
Los Angeles, CA 90024-5796
310-470-9711
www.bu.edu/hrpi
Dr Arthur Purcell, Director/Founder
Education, and consulting research group concerned with environmental policies, technologies, and management strategies..
Founded in 1975

7741 **SPC Advance**
Sustainable Packaging Coalition
600 E. Water St.
Suite C
Charlottesville, VA 22902
434-817-1424
anne.elsea@greenblue.org
www.sustainablepackaging.org
Twitter, LinkedIn
Nina Goodrich, GreenBlue CEO & SPC Director
Adam Gendell, Associate Director, SPC
Anne Elsea, Communications Manager
The Sustainable Packaging Coalition's annual members-only Fall event. Features tours, workshops, masterclasses, committee meetings, exhibitors, speakers, and more.
Frequency: Annual, Fall

7742 **SPC Impact**
Sustainable Packaging Coalition
600 E. Water St.
Suite C
Charlottesville, VA 22902
434-817-1424
anne.elsea@greenblue.org
www.sustainablepackaging.org
Twitter, LinkedIn
Nina Goodrich, GreenBlue CEO & SPC Director
Adam Gendell, Associate Director, SPC
Anne Elsea, Communications Manager
The Sustainable Packaging Coalition's annual Spring event is open to both members and non-members. Features tours, panels, committee meetings, deep dive sessions, workshops, keynote speakers, exhibitors, and more.
Frequency: Annual, Spring

7743 **Safe Buildings Alliance**
Metropolitan Square
655 15th Street NW
Suite 1200
Washington, DC 20005-5701
202-879-5120; Fax: 202-638-2103
sba.lfpc.org
Association of building products companies that formerly manufactured asbestos-containing materials for building construction. Its main focus is to provide public information on issues relating to asbestos in building. SBA promotes a reasonable, safe response to the problem of asbestos in buildings, including the development of uniform, objective Federal and State standards for asbestos identification and abatement, nonremoval alternatives and the regulation of inspectors.
Founded in 1984

7744 **Sagamore Institute of the Adirondacks Inc**
Great Camp Sagamore
PO Box 40
Raquette Lake, NY 13436-0040
315-354-5311; Fax: 315-354-5851
info@greatcampsagamore.org
www.greatcampsagamore.org
Facebook, YouTube
Garet Livermore, Executive Director
Bob Henisler, Superintendant
Dr. Jeffery Flagg, Program Director
Hannah Gibbons, Program Manager
Andrew Gillcrist, Director Of Family Programs
Non-profit 501c3 National Historic Landmark, former retreat of the Vanderbilts, offering educational programs on history, ecology and culture of the Adirondack Park.

7745 **Sierra Club**
2101 Webster St
Suite 1300
Oakland, CA 94612
415-977-5500; Fax: 510-208-3140
information@sierraclub.org
www.sierraclub.org
Facebook, Twitter, Instagram
Michael Brune, Executive Director
Lou Barnes, Chief Financial Officer
Bruce Hamilton, Deputy Executive Director
Sarah Hodgdon, National Program Director
Founded in 1892, the largest environmental organization in the United States campaigns for the protection of endangered species, habitat conservation, environmental protection and an end to the use of fossil fuels.
3MM Members
Founded in 1892

7746 **Silicones Environmental Health and Safety**
700 Second St., NE
Washington, DC 20002
202-249-7000; Fax: 202-249-6100
www.sehsc.com
Facebook, Twitter
Calvin M. Dooley, President
Dell Perelman, Chief Of Staff & General Counsel
Raymond J. O'Bryan, Chief Financial Officer
Nacole B. Hinton, Managing Director
Anne Womack Kolton, VP Of Communications
A not-for-profit trade association comprised of North American silicone chemical producers and importers.
6 Members
Founded in 1971

7747 **Society for Ecological Restoration International**
1017 O Street NW
Washington, DC 20001
202-299-9518; Fax: 270-626-5485
info@ser.org
www.ser.org
Facebook, Twitter, LinkedIn
Alan Unwin, Chair
Cara R. Nelson, Vice Chair
Stuart Allison, Secretary
Jim Hallet, Treasurer
James Aronson, Representative - At- Large
SER members are academics, scientists, environmental consultants, government agencies and others with an interest in ecological restoration.
2300 Members
Founded in 1988

7748 **Society for Human Ecology**
College of the Atlantic
105 Eden Street
Bar Harbor, ME 04609-0180
207-801-5630; Fax: 207-288-3780
info@societyforhumanecology.org
www.societyforhumanecology.org
Facebook, Twitter
Rob Dyball, President
Lee Cerveny, Second Vice President
Chiho Watanabe, Third Vice President-International
Rob Lilieholm, Treasurer
Barbara Carter, Secretary
SHE members are academics, scientists, health professionals and others with an interest in studying the interrelationship of man's actions and his environment.
150 Members
Founded in 1981

7749 **Society for Occupational and Environmental Health**
111 North Bridge Road
#21-01 Peninsula Plaza
Singapore 179098
oehsadmin@gmail.com
www.oehs.org.sg
Dr. Lee Lay Tin, President
Mr. Eric Ng, Vice President
Kam Wai Kuen, Honorary Secretary
Dr. Lucy Leong, Honorary Treasurer
Dr. Gregory Chan, Committee Members
Members include physicians, hygienists, economists, laboratory scientists, academicians, labor and industry representatives, or anyone interested in occupational and/or environmental health. Serves as a forum for the presentation of

scientific data and the exchange of information among members; sponsors conferences and meetings which address specific problem areas and policy questions.
300 Members
Founded in 1972

7750 **Society of Environmental Toxicology and Chemistry**
229 South Baylen Street
2nd Floor
Pensacola, FL 32502

850-469-1500; Fax: 888-296-4136
setac@setac.org
www.setac.org
Facebook, Twitter, LinkedIn

Paul van den Brink, President
Tim Canfield, Vice President
Fred Heimbach, Treasurer

Is a professional society established to promote the use of multidisciplinary approaches to solving problems of the impact of chemicals and technology on the environment. SETA members are professionals in the fields of chemistry, toxicology, biology, ecology, atmospheric sciences, health sciences, earth sciences, and environmental engineering.
4000 Members
Founded in 1979

7751 **Society of Exploration Geophysicists**
8801 South Yale
Suite 500
Tulsa, OK 74137-3575

918-497-5500
877-778-5463; Fax: 918-497-5557
web@seg.org
www.seg.org
Facebook, Twitter, LinkedIn

Mary Fleming, Executive Director
Vladimir Grechka, Editor

The Society of Exploration Geophysicists/SEG is a not-for-profit organization that promotes the science of geophysics and the education of applied geophysicists. SEG fosters the expert and ethical practice of geophysics in the exploration and development of natural resources, in characterizing the near surface, and in mitigating earth hazards.
Founded in 1930

7752 **Soil and Plant Analysis Council**
347 North Shores Circle
Windsor, CO 80550

970-686-5702
rmiller@lamar.colostate.edu
www.spcouncil.org

Supports all those involved in the analysis of soil and plants.

7753 **Soil and Water Conservation Society**
945 SW Ankeny Rd
Ankeny, IA 50023-9764

515-289-2331
800-843-7645; Fax: 515-289-1227
swcs@swcs.org
www.swcs.org
Facebook, Twitter, LinkedIn

Mark Berkland, President
Jon Scholl, Vice-President
Mike Collins, Secretary
Susan Meadows, Treasurer
Wendi Goldsmith, NE Region Director

SWCS is a nonprofit scientific and educational organization that serves as an advocate for conservation professionals and for science-based conservation practice, programs, and policy.
5000+ Members
Founded in 1943

7754 **Southeastern Association of Fish and Wildlife Agencies**
27 Sylwood Place
Jackson, MS 39209

601-668-6916; Fax: 850-893-6204
crayhopkins@bellsouth.netÿ
www.seafwa.org

Bob Ziehmer, President
Gordon Myers, Vice President
Robert Barham, Secretary/Treasurer
Nick Wiley, Past President
Ed Carter, At Larger Executive Board Member

An organization whose members are the state agencies with primary responsibility for management and protection of the fish and wildlife resources in 16 states, Puerto Rico and the US Virgin Islands.
18 Members
Founded in 1947

7755 **Steel Recycling Institute**
680 Andersen Drive
Pittsburgh, PA 15220-2700

412-922-2772
800-876-7274; Fax: 412-922-3213
www.recycle-steel.org
Facebook, Twitter, YouTube, Google+

William H Heenan Jr, President

Promotes steel recycling and works to forge a coalition of steelmakers, can manufacturers, legislators, government officials, solid waste managers, business and consumer groups.
Founded in 1988

7756 **Student Conservation Association**
4245 North Fairfax Drive
Suite 825
Arlington, VA 22203

703-524-2441; Fax: 603-543-1828
www.thesca.org
Facebook, Twitter, YouTube

Jamie Berman Matyas, President and CEO
Karen Davis, SVP & Chief Advancement Officer
Aimee Dobrzeniecki, Chief Financial Officer
Barbara Gonzalez-McIntosh, Chief Counsel
Laura Herrin, Senior VP, Programs

To build the next generation of conservation leaders and inspire lifelong stewardship of our environment and communities by engaging young people in hands-on service to the land.
35000 Members
Founded in 1957

7757 **Surfaces in Biomaterials Foundation**
1000 Westgate Drive
Suite 252
St Paul, MN 55114-8679

651-290-6267; Fax: 651-290-2266
memberservices@surfaces.org
www.surfaces.org
Twitter, LinkedIn

Dr. Aylvin A. Dias, President
Chander Chawla, President-Elect
Bill Theilacker, Vice President
Mark Smith PhD, Treasurer
Joe McGonigle, Secretary

Dedicated to exploring creative solutions to technical challenges at the BioInterface by fostering education and multidisciplinary cooperation among industrial, academic, clinical and regulatory communities.
250 Members

7758 **Sustainable Packaging Coalition**
600 E. Water St.
Suite C
Charlottesville, VA 22902

434-817-1424
anne.elsea@greenblue.org
www.sustainablepackaging.org
Twitter, LinkedIn

Nina Goodrich, GreenBlue CEO & SPC Director
Adam Gendell, Associate Director, SPC
Anne Elsea, Communications Manager

The leading voice on sustainable packaging with a membership that encompasses the entire supply chain. A child organization of GreenBlue.

7759 **Test Boring Association**
181 Beagle Club Road
Washington, PA 15301

722- 22- 299
888-267-4647; Fax: 724-228-2992
jrselvoski@testboringservices.com
www.testboring.com

Patrizia Zita, Management Executive

Contractors engaged in test boring and core drilling.
Founded in 1941

7760 **The African Wild Dog Conservancyÿ**
208 N California Ave.
Silver City, NM 88061

lycaonpictus@awdconservancy.org
www.awdconservancy.org

A nonprofit, non-governmental organization working with local communities, and national and international stakeholders to conserve the African wilddog through scientific research and education.
Founded in 2001

7761 **The Center for International Environmental Law**
1350 Connecticut Avenue NW
Suite #1100
Washington, DC 20036

202-785-8700; Fax: 202-785-8701
info@ciel.org
www.ciel.org
Facebook, Twitter, LinkedIn, RSS

Carroll Muffett, President/ CEO
Jeffrey Wanha, Dir., Finance & Admin.
Marcos A. Orellana, Director, Human Rights
Cameron Aishton, Administrator
Kevin Parker, Development Directorÿ

Nonprofit organization that provides environmental legal services in international and comparative environmental law.

7762 **The Indoor Air Institute**
2548 Empire Grade
Santa Cruz, CA 95060

831-426-0148; Fax: 831-426-6522
info@IndAir.org
indair.org

Hal Levin, President
William Fisk, Vice President
William Nazaroff, Vice President

Supports all those involved with indoor air quality and climate with training, education, resource materials and an annual conference.

7763 **The Marine Mammal Center**
2000 Bunker Road
Fort Cronkhite
Sausalito, CA 94965-2619

415-289-7325
415-289-SEAL
info@tmmc.org
www.marinemammalcenter.org
Facebook, Twitter, RSS, Pinterest, YouTube

Marci Davis, Chief Financial Officer
Dr. Jeff Boehm, Executive Director
Nancy Sackson, Dir., Marketing & Development

Rachel Bergren, Education Director
Heather Groninger, Human Resources Director

A private, nonprofit U.S. organization established for the purpose of rescuing, rehabilitating, and releasing marine mammals who are injured, ill, or abandoned.
Founded in 1975

7764 The Nature Conservancy
4245 North Fairfax Drive
Suite 100
Arlington, VA 22203-1606

703-841-5300
800-628-6860
members@tnc.org
www.nature.org
Facebook, Twitter, LinkedIn, Google+, Flickr

Craig O. McCaw, Chairman
James E. Rogers, Vice Chair
Frank e. Loy, Secretary
Mark R. Tercek, President & CEO
Muneer A. Satter, Treasurer

The leading conservation organization working around the world to protect ecologically important lands and waters for nature and people. Addresses the most pressing conservation threats at the largest scale.
Founded in 1984

7765 The School for Field Studies
100 Cummings Center
Suite 534-G
Beverly, MA 1915

978-741-3567
800-989-4418; Fax: 978-922-3835
jcramer@fieldstudies.org
www.fieldstudies.org
Facebook, Twitter, LinkedIn, YouTube, Google+, Flickr

Terry Andreas, Chairman Of Board
James A. Cramer, President
Leslie Granese, B.A, Vice President
Carrie Camp, B.S, Chief Finance Officer
Yizette Colon, M.B.A, Accounting Manager

Creates transformative study abroad experiences through field-basedlearning and research.
Founded in 1980

7766 The Wilderness Society
1615 M St NW
Washington, DC 20036-3258

202-833-2300
800-843-9453; Fax: 202-429-3945
member@tws.org
wilderness.org
Facebook, Twitter, LinkedIn, Pinterest, YouTube

Jamie Williams, President
Thomas Tepper, VP, Finance & Administration
Melyssa Watson, Vice President, Conservation
Kitty Thomas, VP, Communications & Marketing
Ame Hellman, VP, Philanthropy

An American nonprofit organization that is dedicated to protecting wilderness areas as national public lands in the United States.
200M Members
Founded in 1935

7767 Union of Concerned Scientists
Two Brattle Sq.
Cambridge, MA 02138-3780

617-547-5552; Fax: 617-864-9405
www.ucsusa.org
Facebook, Twitter, Google+

James J. McCarthyÿ, Chair
Peter A. Bradford, Vice Chair
James S. Hoyte, Treasurer
Thomas H. Stone, Secretary
Kenneth Kimmell, President

A nonprofit science advocacy organization based in the United States.

7768 United Association of Used Oil Services
318 Newman Road
Sebring, FL 33870-6702

941-655-3880
800-877-4356

Established to be an effective presence in dealing with regulations and to provide a network for those with an interest in the collection and proper disposition of used lubricating oils.
Founded in 1987

7769 Water Environment Federation
601 Wythe St
Alexandria, VA 22314-1994

703-684-2400
800-666-0206; Fax: 703-684-2492
inquiry@wef.org
www.wef.org
Facebook, Twitter

Paul Bowen, President
Rick Warner, President-Elect
Jenny Hartfelder, Vice President
Ed McCormick, Immediate Past President
Ralph Exton, Treasurer

Supports those involved in issues that affect the international water environment.
79 Members
ISSN: 1044-9943
Founded in 1928

7770 Water Quality Association
4151 Naperville Rd.
Lisle, IL 60532-3696

630-505-0160; Fax: 630-505-9637
www.wqa.org
Facebook, Twitter, YouTube

Pauli Undesser, Executive Director
Tom Buursema, Assc. Exec. Dir., Member Engagement
Wesley Bleed, Director, Marketing/Communications
LyNae Schleyer, Director, Meeting Services
Scott Freeman, Chief Financial Officer

An international, nonprofit trade association representing retail/dealers and manufacturer/suppliers in the point of use/entry water quality improvement industry. Membership benefits and services include technical and scientific information, educational seminars and home correspondence course books, professional certification and discount services.
2700+ Members
Founded in 1974

7771 Wilderness Society
1615 M St NW
Washington, DC 20036-3258

202-833-2300
800-843-9453; Fax: 202-429-3945
member@tws.org
www.wilderness.org
Facebook, Twitter, LinkedIn, Pinterest, YouTube

Jamie Williams, President
Thomas Tepper, VP, Finance & Administration
Melyssa Watson, Vice President, Conservation
Kitty Thomas, VP, Communications & Marketing
Ame Hellman, VP, Philanthropy

Establishes the land ethic as a basic element of the American culture and educates people on the importance of wilderness preservation and land protection.
200M Members
Founded in 1935
Mailing list available for rent: 178000 names at $90 per M

7772 Wildlife Conservation Society
2300 Southern Boulevard
Bronx, NY 10460

718-220-5100; Fax: 718-584-2625
membership@wcs.org
Facebook, Twitter, YouTube, Google+, Instagram

Ward W. Woods, Chair
Edith McBean, Vice Chair
Gordon B. Pattee, Vice Chair
Brian J. Heidtke, Treasurer
Andrew H. Tisch, Secretary

Supports all those involved in the conservation of wildlife, especially the most rare and endangered species.

7773 Wildlife Habitat Council
8737 Colesville Road
Suite 800
Silver Spring, MD 20910

301-588-8994; Fax: 301-588-4629
whc@wildlifehc.org
www.wildlifehc.org
Facebook, Twitter, LinkedIn, YouTube, Flickr

Margaret O'Gorman, President
Josiane Bonneau, Sr. Director
Linda Duvall, Director, Finance & HR
Monica Keller, Director, Marketing & Comm.
Thelma Redick, Sr. Director

Supports corporate, government and conservation leaders from around the globe involved in environmental stewardship.
120+ Members
Founded in 1988

7774 Wildlife Management Institute
4426 VT Route 215N
Cabot, VT 05647

802-563-2087; Fax: 802-563-2157
www.wildlifemanagementinstitute.org

Richard E McCabe, Executive VP
Scot J Williamson, VP
Carol J Peddicord, Finance Manager
Robert L Byrne, Wildlife Program Coordinator
Ronald R Helinski, Conservation Policy Specialist

Supports all those involved with the challenges of modern conservation.

7775 Wildlife Society
5410 Grosvenor Ln
Suite 200
Bethesda, MD 20814-2144

301-897-9770; Fax: 301-530-2471
tws@wildlife.org
www.wildlife.org
Facebook, Twitter, LinkedIn

Michael Hutchins, Executive Director
Laura Bies, Director, Government Affairs
Jane Jorgensen, Office and Finance Manager
Yanin Walker, Operations Manager

Supports all those involved in wildlife conservation, including wildlife artists, environmental consultants, conservation groups, scientific associations and natural resource companies, industry groups and government agencies.
9000 Members
Founded in 1937

7776 Women's Council on Energy and the Environment
PO Box 33211
Washington, DC 20033-0211

202-997-4512; Fax: 202-478-2098
www.wcee.org
Facebook, Twitter, Pinterest

Robin Cantor, President
Mary Brosnan-Sell, Vice President
Alice Grabowski, Secretary

Barbara Tyran, Treasurer
Joyce Chandran, Executive Director

Supports women involved in the environmental community with education, research, new trend information and several publications.

7777 **World Research Foundation**
PO Box 20828
Sedona, AZ 86341

928-284-3300; Fax: 928-284-3530
info@wrf.org
www.wrf.org
Facebook, Twitter, Google+

Steven A Ross, President

A unique, international, health information network, so that people could be informed of all available treatments around the world, and so that they could have the freedom to choose, based on complete and in-depth information.
41000 Members
Founded in 1984

7778 **World Resources Institute**
10 G St NE
Suite 800
Washington, DC 20002-4252

202-729-7600; Fax: 202-729-7686
front@wri.org
wri.org
Facebook, Twitter, LinkedIn, YouTube, RSS

James A. Harmon, Chairman
Harriet C. Babbitt, Vice Chair
Susan Tierney, Vice Chair
Afsaneh M. Beschloss, President & CEO
Frances Beinecke, Former President

Compiles information, conducts research, publishes the Environmental Almanac and more.
Founded in 1982

7779 **World Society for the Protection of Animals**
Nelson Tower Building
450 Seventh Avenue, 31st Floor
New York, NY 10123

646-783-2200; Fax: 212-564-4250
info@worldanimalprotection.us.org
www.worldanimalprotection.org
Facebook, Twitter, YouTube

Robert S. Cummings, President
John Bowen, Secretary
Carter Luke, Treasurer

International animal protection news reports. Lobbies for effective animal welfare laws and provides educational material.
12 Members

7780 **World Wildlife Fund**
1250 24th Street, NW
Washington, DC 20037

800-963-0993
membership@wwfus.org
www.worldwildlife.org
Facebook, Twitter, YouTube, Instagram, Google+

Neville Isdell, Chair
Carter Roberts, President & CEO
Margaret Ackerley, Senior VP & general Counsel
Brad Ack, Senior VP, Oceans
Suzanne Apple, Senior VP, Pvt Sector Engagement

Supports all those involved in maintaining wildlife and their environment. Monitors human development, and seeks to influence public opinion and policy makers in favor of ecologically sound practices.
4M Members
Founded in 1961

7781 **Worldwatch Institute**
1400 16th Street NW
Suite 430
Washington, DC 20036

202-745-8092; Fax: 202-478-2534
worldwatch@worldwatch.org
www.worldwatch.org
Facebook, Twitter, LinkedIn, RSS, YouTube, Flickr

Ed Groarkÿ, Chair
Robert Charles Friese, Vice Chair
John Robbins, Treasurer
Nancy Hitzÿ, Secretary
Barbara Fallin, Dir., Finance & Administration

Analyzes interdisciplinary environmental data from around the world, providing information on how to build a sustainable society.
Founded in 1974

Newsletters

7782 **AEESP Newsletter**
2303 Naples Court
Champaign, IL 61822

217-398-6969; Fax: 217-355-9232
www.aeesp.org

Joanne Fetzner, Business Secretary

Official newsletter of the Association of Environmental Engineering and Science Professors. Topics cover the scope and diversity of challenges faced in environmental engineering and science.
Frequency: Quarterly

7783 **AEG News**
Assn. of Environmental & Engineering Geologists
1100-H Brandywine Boulevard
Suite 575
Zanesville, OH 43701

303-757-2926
844-331-7867; Fax: 740-452-2552
www.aegweb.org
Facebook, Twitter

Dale C. Andrews, President
Kathy Troost, Vice President
Kevin Richard, Treasurer
Cynthia Palomares, Secretary

Connecting Professionals, Practice and the Public.
3000 Members
Founded in 1957
Mailing list available for rent: 3000 names at $100 per M

7784 **AERE Newsletter**
Association of Environmental and Resource
1616 P St Nw
Suite 400
Washington, DC 20036-1434

202-328-5157; Fax: 202-939-3460
voigt@rff.org
www.aere.org

Marilyn Voigt, Executive Secretary
Ralph Metts, President

Includes policy essays, meeting announcements, calls for papers, new publications, research reports, position announcements and other information of interest to AERE members and environmental economists in general.
Frequency: Semi-Annual

7785 **AIH Bulletin**
American Institute of Hydrology
PO Box 3948
Parker, CO 80134

303-339-0523; Fax: 720-496-4974
admin@aihydrology.org
www.aihydrology.org

John L. Nieber, P.H., P.E., President
Dr. Faisal Hossain, VP for Academic Affairs
Jul, Rizzardo, VP for Institute Development
Dr. Zhuping Sheng, VP for International Affairs
Rahul Ranade, VP for Communication

Newsletter for the American Institute of Hydrology, providing information designed to improve professional skills and abilities of its members, the professional community and the public at large.
Frequency: Quarterly

7786 **APLIC Communicator**
Family Health International Library
PO Box 13950
Research Triangle Park, NC 27709

919-447-7040
www.aplici.org

Claire Twose, President
Lori Rosman, Vice-President
Joann Donatiello, Treasurer

Read by population and reproductive health information specialists, librarians, and documentalists.
Frequency: Annual

7787 **ASBPA Newsletter**
American Shore & Beach Preservation Association
5460 Beaujolais ch Road
Fort Myers, FL 33919

239-489-2616; Fax: 239-362-9771
exdir@asbpa.org
www.asbpa.org
Facebook, Twitter

Harry Simmons, President
Nicole Elko, Secretary
Brad Pickel, Treasurer
Kate Gooderham, Editor

Federal, state and local government agencies and individuals interested in conservation, development and restoration of beaches and shorefronts.
1M Members
Founded in 1926

7788 **ASEH News**
American Society for Environmental History
UW Interdisciplinary Arts and Sciences Program
1900 Commerce Street
Tacoma, WA 98402

206-343-0226; Fax: 206-343-0249
director@aseh.net
www.aseh.net

John McNeill, President
Gregg Mitman, Vice President/ President Elect
Ellen Stroud, Secretary
Mark Madison, Treasurer

Updated and timely information on current environmental issues and their historical background, as well as Society news and events.
1200 Members
Founded in 1976

7789 **ASFE Newslog**
ASFE/The Geoprofessional Business Association

8811 Colesville Rd
Suite G106
Silver Springs, MD 20910-4343
301-565-2733; Fax: 301-589-2017
info@asfe.org
www.asfe.org
John P Bachner, Executive VP
Information on geo professional, environmental, and civil engineering firms. Past issues are available through the online store. Electronic copies are always free to members.
Cost: $240.00
16 Pages
Frequency: 6/Year
Circulation: 5000

7790 **ATTRAnews**
National Center for Appropriate Technology
3040 Continental Drive
PO Box 3838
Butte, MT 59702
406-494-4572
800-275-6228; Fax: 406-494-2905
www.ncat.org
Facebook, Twitter, LinkedIn
Eugene Brady, Chairman
Kathleen Hadley, Executive Director
ATTRAnews brings you up to date on the latest developments in sustainable agriculture, what's happening at the USDA and with Sustainable Agriculture Working Groups around the country. ATTRAnews features events and opportunities in sustainable agriculture, information on funding and financing, and it keeps you current on programs and policies that can affect your future.
Frequency: 6x/Year
Founded in 1976

7791 **Advisor**
Great Lakes Commission
2805 S Industrial Hwy
Suite 100
Ann Arbor, MI 48104-6791
734-971-9135; Fax: 734-971-9150
www.glc.org
Tim Eder, Executive Director
Cook Havtrkamp, Author
Covers economic and environmental issues of the Great Lakes region with a special focus on activities of the Great Lakes Commission.
12 Pages
Frequency: Quarterly
Founded in 1955
Printed in one color on matte stock

7792 **Air Water Pollution Report's Environment Week**
Business Publishers
8737 Colesville Road
Suite 1100
Silver Spring, MD 20910-3928
301-876-6300
800-274-6737; Fax: 301-589-8493
custserv@bpinews.com
www.bpinews.com
Leonard A Eiserer, Publisher
Beth Early, Operations Director
David Goeller, Editor
Provides a balanced, insightful update on the week's most important environmental news from Washington, D.C.
Cost: $595.00
Frequency: Weekly
Founded in 1963

7793 **Annual Research Program Report**
National Institutes for Water Resources
Home Page: niwr.net
Paul Joseph Godfrey, PhD, Executive Director

7794 **Aquatic Plant News**
Aquatic Plant Management Society
PO Box 821265
Vicksburg, MS 39182-1265
FAX 601-634-5502
dpetty@ndrsite.com
www.apms.org
Facebook, LinkedIn
Linda Nelson, President
Terry Goldsby, VP
Sherry Whitaker, Treasurer
Aquatic Plant News is produced 3 times each year, and is distributed primarily by email.
Frequency: 3x/Year
Founded in 1961

7795 **Asbestos & Lead Abatement Report**
Business Publishers
8737 Colesville Road
Suite 1100
Silver Spring, MD 20910-3928
301-876-6300
800-274-6737; Fax: 301-589-8493
custserv@bpinews.com
www.bpinews.com
Leonard Eiserer, Publisher
Contains articles on regulation compliance, environmental trends, and business opportunities.
Cost: $382.00
Frequency: Monthly
Founded in 1963

7796 **BNA's Environmental Compliance Bulletin**
Bureau of National Affairs
1801 S Bell St
Arlington, VA 22202-4501
703-341-3000
800-372-1033; Fax: 800-253-0332
customercare@bna.com
www.bnabooks.com
Paul N Wojcik, CEO
Gregory C McCaffery, President
Water and air pollution, waste management and regulatory updates, as well as a summary of selected regulatory actions and a list of key environmental compliance dates.
Cost: $649.00
Frequency: Annual+
Founded in 1929

7797 **BankNotes**
Environmental Bankers Association
510 King St
Suite 410
Alexandria, VA 22314-3212
703-549-0977; Fax: 703-548-5945
eba@envirobank.org
www.envirobank.org
Rick Ferguson, President
Sharon Valverde, Vice President
Scott Beckerman, Treasurer
Stephen Richardson, Secretary
Timely information on the EBA, read by bank and non-bank financial institutions, insurers, asset management firms and those who provide services to them. Covers environmental risk issues, risk management, development, and due diligence policies and procedures.
Frequency: Bi-Monthly

7798 **Bulletins**
World Research Foundation
41 Bell Rock Plz
Sedona, AZ 86351-8804
928-284-3300; Fax: 928-284-3530
laverne@wrf.org
www.wrf.org
Steven A Ross, President
Updates on recent research including topics involving health information pertinent to the World Research Foundation.
Frequency: Quarterly

7799 **CCA Newsletter**
Coastal Conservation Association
6919 Portwest Dr
Suite 100
Houston, TX 77024-8049
713-626-4234
800-201-FISH; Fax: 713-626-5852
ccantl@joincca.org
www.joincca.org
Twitter
David Cummins, President
Contains timely updates from CCA state chapters and bulletins on developing fisheries issues.
85000 Members
Founded in 1977

7800 **CCHEST Newsletter**
Council on Certification of Health, Environmental
2301 W. Bradley Avenue
Champaign, IL 61821
217-359-9263; Fax: 217-359-0055
cchest@cchest.org
www.cchest.org
Facebook, Twitter, LinkedIn
Margaret M. Carroll, President
Carl W. Heinlein, Vice President
Emory E. Knowles III, Treasurer
Keeps members up to date on events, OSHA news and the latest safety courses.
Frequency: Annual
Mailing list available for rent: 20,000 names

7801 **Capitol Connect**
Society of Chemical Manufacturers & Affiliates
1850 M St Nw
Suite 700
Washington, DC 20036-5803
202-721-4100; Fax: 202-296-8120
info@socma.org
www.socma.org
Larry Brotherton, Ph.D., Chair
Dave Hurder, Vice Chair
Davide DeCuir, Treasurer
J. Steel Hutchinson, Secretary
Government relations newsletter covering a range of environmental, safety, security, chemicals management and trade topics.
10 Pages
Frequency: Bi-Weekly

7802 **ChemStewards**
Society of Chemical Manufacturers & Affiliates
1850 M St Nw
Suite 700
Washington, DC 20036-5803
202-721-4100; Fax: 202-296-8120
info@socma.org
www.socma.org
Larry Brotherton, Ph.D., Chair
Dave Hurder, Vice Chair
Davide DeCuir, Treasurer
J. Steel Hutchinson, Secretary
e-Newsletter focusing on ChemStewards Training Opportunities, upcoming events, and the latest program news.
10 Pages
Frequency: Bi-Weekly

7803 **Clean Water Report**
CJE Associates

Silver Spring, MD 20910-3928

301-589-5103
800-274-6737; Fax: 301-589-8493
custserv@bpinews.com
www.bpinews.com

Follows the latest news from the EPA, Congress, the states, the courts, and private industry. A key information source for environmental professionals, covering the important issues of ground and drinking water, wastewater treatment, wetlands, drought, coastal protection, non-point source pollution, agrichemical contamination and more.
8 Pages

7804 **Climate Change News**
Environmental & Energy Study Institute
122 C Street NW
Suite 630
Washington, DC 20001

202-628-1400; Fax: 202-628-1825
eesi@eesi.org
www.eesi.org
Facebook, Twitter, YouTube

Jared Blum, Board Chair
Shelley Fidler, Board Treasurer
Richard L. Ottinger, Board Chair Emeritus

Recounts the top climate science, business, and politics stories of the week and includes a list of upcoming events and pending federal legislation.
Founded in 1984

7805 **Composting News**
McEntee Media Corporation
9815 Hazelwood Ave
Strongsville, OH 44149-2305

440-238-6603; Fax: 440-238-6712
ken@recycle.cc
www.recycle.cc

Ken Mc Entee, Owner

The latest in composting, wood waste recycling and organics management in a monthly newsletter.
Cost: $83.00
Frequency: Monthly
Circulation: 2000
Founded in 1990

7806 **Conservation Commission News**
New Hampshire Association of Conservation Comm.
54 Portsmouth Street
Concord, NH 03301-5486

603-225-3431; Fax: 603-228-0423

Marjory Swope, Publisher

Encourage conservation and appropriate use of New Hampshire's natural resources by providing assistance to New Hampshire's municipal conservation commissions and by facilitating communication among commissions and between commissions and other public and private agencies involved in conservation.
Cost: $5.00
8 Pages
Frequency: Quarterly
Circulation: 1,650
Printed in one color on matte stock

7807 **Convention Proceedings**
Society for Human Ecology
College of the Atlantic
105 Eden Street
Bar Harbor, ME 04609-0180

207-288-5015; Fax: 207-288-3780
www.societyforhumanecology.org

Barbara Carter, Assistant to Executive Director

7808 **Cosecha Mensual**
National Center for Appropriate Technology
3040 Continental Drive
PO Box 3838
Butte, MT 59702

406-494-4572
800-275-6228; Fax: 406-494-2905
www.ncat.org
Facebook, Twitter, LinkedIn

Eugene Brady, Chairman
Kathleen Hadley, Executive Director

NCAT's Spanish-language electronic newsletter on sustainable agriculture. Subscribers enjoy news items and reviews of Spanish-language resources.
Frequency: Monthly
Founded in 1976

7809 **Council on Women in Energy and Environmental Leadership Newsletter**
Association of Energy Engineers
3168 Mercer University Drive
Atlanta, GA 30341

770-447-5083
www.aeecenter.org
Facebook, Twitter, LinkedIn, YouTube

Albert Thumann, Executive Director

Addressing the high cost of energy, present and future sources of energy, and the impact of energy on the environment.
17500 Members
Founded in 1977

7810 **Daily Environment Report**
Bureau of National Affairs
1801 S Bell St
Arlington, VA 22202-4501

703-341-3000
800-372-1033; Fax: 800-253-0332
customercare@bna.com
www.bnabooks.com

Paul N Wojcik, CEO
Gregory C McCaffery, President

A 40-page daily report providing comprehensive, in-depth coverage of national and international environmental news. Each issue contains summaries of the top news stories, articles, and in-brief items, and a journal of meetings, agency activities, hearings and legal proceedings. Coverage includes air and water pollution, hazardous substances, and hazardous waste, solid waste, oil spills, gas drilling, pollution prevention, impact statements and budget matters.
Cost: $ 3537.00
40 Pages
Frequency: Daily
ISSN: 1060-2976

7811 **Digital Traveler**
International Ecotourism Society
733 15th Street NW
Suite 1000
Washington, DC 20005

202-547-9203; Fax: 202-387-7915
www.ecotourism.org

Martha Honey, Executive Director
Amos Bien, Director International Programs
Neal Inamdar, Director Finance/Administration

Regular updates about TIES work and programs.
Frequency: Monthly

7812 **E&P Environment**
Pasha Publications
1616 N Fort Myer Dr
Suite 1000
Arlington, VA 22209-3107

703-528-1244
800-424-2908; Fax: 703-528-1253
www.newsletteraccess.com

Harry Baisden, Group Publisher
Jerry Grisham, Editor

Reports on environmental regulations, advances in technology and litigation aimed specifically at the exploration and production segments of the oil and gas industry.
Cost: $395.00

7813 **E-Scrap News**
Resource Recycling
PO Box 42270
Portland, OR 97242-270

503-233-1305; Fax: 503-233-1356
info@resource-recycling.com
www.resource-recycling.com

Jerry Powell, Publisher/Editor
Andrew Santosusso, Managing Editor
Betsy Loncar, Circulation Director

Monthly newsletter covering all aspects of recovering, recycling, and managing electronics scrap. Coverage includes market prices and trends, collection events, product stewardship developments and global trends.
Cost: $99.00
6 Pages
Frequency: Monthly
Circulation: 1000
ISSN: 1536-3856
Founded in 1983
Mailing list available for rent: 40,000 names at $100 per M
Printed in 2 colors on matte stock

7814 **ECOMOD Newsletter**
International Society for Ecological Modelling
University of California, Animal Sciences Dept
One Shields Avenue
Davis, CA 95616-8521

530-752-5362; Fax: 530-752-0175
www.isemna.org

Wolfgang Pittroff, Secretary-General

Information on conferences, workshops and symposia that promote the systems philosophy in ecological research and teaching. Members frequently contribute articles.
Frequency: Quarterly

7815 **EH&S Software News Online**
Donley Technology
PO Box 152
Colonial Beach, VA 22443-152

804-224-9427
800-201-1595; Fax: 804-224-7958
www.ehssoftwarenews.com

John Donley, Editor

Reports on news and upgraded software products, database, and on-line systems from commercial developers and government resources.
Cost: $125.00
Founded in 1988

7816 **EMS Newsletter**
Environmental Mutagen Society
1821 Michael Faraday Drive
Suite 300
Reston, VA 20190
703-438-8220; Fax: 703-438-3113
emshq@ems-us.org
www.ems-ph.org

Kathleen Hill, Editor
Barbara Parsons, Editor
Cathy Klein, Editor

Current scientific research, policies, and guidelines for the causes and consequences of damage to the genome and epigenome.
Frequency: Bi-Annual

7817 **Economic Opportunity Report**
Business Publishers

2222 Sedwick Dr
Suite 101
Durham, NC 27713

800-223-8720; Fax: 800-508-2592
custserv@bpinews.com
www.bpinews.com

Antipoverty news coverage and analysis which gives insight into developments that affect social programs.
Cost: $383.00
Frequency: Weekly

7818 **Environment Reporter**
Bureau of National Affairs
1801 S Bell St
Arlington, VA 22202-4501

703-341-3000
800-372-1033; Fax: 800-253-0332
customercare@bna.com
www.bnabooks.com

Paul N Wojcik, CEO
Gregory C McCaffery, President

A weekly notification and reference service covering the full-spectrum of legislative, administrative, judicial, industrial and technological developments affecting pollution control and environmental protection.
Cost: $3776.00
Frequency: Weekly
ISSN: 0013-9211
Founded in 1929

7819 **Environmental Design Research Association Newsletter**
Environmental Design Research Association
PO Box 7146
Edmond, OK 73083-7146

405-330-4863; Fax: 405-330-4150
www.edra.org

Deni Ruggeri, Executive Director

Document collection includes pdfs of full papers that have appeared in the annual EDRA conference proceedings.
Frequency: Annual

7820 **Environmental Engineers and Managers Institute Newsletter**
Association of Energy Engineers
3168 Mercer University Drive
Atlanta, GA 30341

770-447-5083
www.aeecenter.org
Facebook, Twitter, LinkedIn

Albert Thumann, Executive Director

Keeps members ahead on trends, upcoming conferences, industry leaders, jobs, relevant publications and more.
17500 Members
Founded in 1977

7821 **Environmental Health Newsletter**
International Lead Zinc Research Organization
2525 Meridian Parkway, Suite 100
PO Box 12036
Durham, NC 27713

919-361-4647; Fax: 919-361-1957
www.ilzro.org

Stephen Wilkinson, President
Frank Goodwin, VP Materials Sciences
Scott Mooneyham, Treasurer
Rob Putnam, Director Communications

Information on environmental health sciences, use of technology, rules, and public education.
Frequency: Quarterly

7822 **Environmental Nutrition**
52 Riverside Drive
Suite 15A
New York, NY 10024

212-362-0424
800-424-7887; Fax: 212-362-2066
betty@environmentalnutrition.com
www.environmentalnutrition.com

Betty Goldblatt, Publisher
Susan Male Smith, Editor

Monthly nutrition newsletter on nutrition and health. Written and edited by registered dietitians.
Cost: $24.00
Frequency: Monthly
Circulation: 50000
Founded in 1977
Printed in 2 colors on matte stock

7823 **Environmental Policy Alert**
Inside Washington Publishers
1919 S Eads St
Suite 201
Arlington, VA 22202-3028

703-418-3981
800-424-9068; Fax: 703-416-8543
www.iwpnews.com

Alan Sosenko, Owner

Adresses the legislative news and provides reports on the federal environmental policy process.
Cost: $560.00
Founded in 1980

7824 **Environmental Problems & Remediation**
InfoTeam
PO Box 15640
Plantation, FL 33318-5640

954-473-9560; Fax: 954-473-0544

Merton Allen, Editor

Concerned with environmental problems and effects, the methods and approaches for mitigation and remediation. Covers air pollution; surface and ground water pollution; wastewater; soil contamination; waste recycling; medical wastes; landfills and waste sites; stack gases; combustion and incineration; earth warming and more.

7825 **Environmental Regulatory Advisor**
JJ Keller
3003 W Breezewood Lane
Neenah, WI 54956-368

920-722-2848
800-327-6868; Fax: 800-727-7516
sales@jjkeller.com
www.jjkeller.com

Webb Shaw, Editor
Robert Keller, CEO

Covers developments at the EPA.
Founded in 1953

7826 **Environotes Newsletter**
Federation of Environmental Technologists
PO Box 624
Slinger, WI 53086-0624

414-540-0070; Fax: 262-644-7106
info@fetinc.org
www.fetinc.org

Triese Haase, Administrator

Educating and Developing Excellence in Environmental Professionals
Frequency: Monthly

7827 **Facility Managers Institute Newsletter**
Association of Energy Engineers
3168 Mercer University Drive
Atlanta, GA 30341

770-447-5083
www.aeecenter.org
Facebook, Twitter, LinkedIn, YouTube

Albert Thumann, Executive Director

Online newsletter addresses subjects such as the Integrated Approach to plant management, security and safety issues, and overall facility management.
17500 Members
Founded in 1977

7828 **Fibre Market News**
GIE Media
4012 Bridge Avenue
Cleveland, OH 44113-3320

216-961-4130
800-456-0707; Fax: 216-961-0364

Richard Foster, Publisher
Daniel Sandoval, Editor

Covers the international paper recycling industry. Trends, markets, expansions, economics covered in an in-depth fashion. Also have weekly fax update covering late-breaking news.
Cost: $115.00
16 Pages
Frequency: BiWeekly

7829 **ForeFront**
National Registry of Environmental Professionals
PO Box 2099
Glenview, IL 60025

847-724-6631; Fax: 847-724-4223
nrep@nrep.org
www.nrep.org
Facebook, Twitter, LinkedIn

Richard A Young, PhD, Executive Director
Edward Beck, PhD, Senior Director
Carol Schellinger, Director
Christopher Young, Director of Operation
Marie Hunter, Director

Information on continuing education, certification, and recognition for the professionals who help understand and study the environment.
20000 Members
Frequency: Bi-Monthly
Founded in 1987

7830 **Forest History Society**
Forest History Society
701 William Vickers Ave
Durham, NC 27701-3162

919-682-9319; Fax: 919-682-2349
recluce2@duke.edu
www.foresthistory.org

Steven Anderson, President
R Scott Wallinger, Chairman
Yvan Hardy, Co-Vice Chairman
Mark Wilde, Co Vice-Chairman

Nonprofit educational institution that explores the history of the environment, forestry and conservation.

7831 **From the Ground Up**
Ecology Center
117 Division Street
Ann Arbor, MI 48104-1523

734-761-3186; Fax: 734-663-2414
www.ecocenter.org

Ted Sylvester, Editor
Mike Wallad, President
Michael Garfield, Director

Progressive environmental news from southeast Michigan.
Cost: $30.00
32 Pages
Frequency: Monthly
Circulation: 5000

Founded in 1970
Printed in 4 colors on newsprint stock

7832 GRAS Flavoring Substances 25
Flavor & Extract Manufacturers Association
1620 I Street NW
Suite 925
Washington, DC 20006
202-293-5800; Fax: 202-462-8998
www.femaflavor.org
YouTube, RSS Feed
Ed R. Hays, Ph.D., President
George C. Robinson, III, President Elect
Mark Scott, Treasurer
Arthur Schick, VP & Secretary
John Cox, Executive Director
The 25th publication by the Expert Panel of the Flavor and Extract Manufacturers Association provides an update on recent progress in the consideration of flavoring ingredients generally recognized as safe under the Food Additive Amendment.
123 Members
Frequency: Biennial
Founded in 1909

7833 Global Environmental Change Report
Aspen Publishers
76 Ninth Avenue
7th Floor
New York, NY 10011
212-771-0600
800-638-8437
www.aspenlawschool.com
Mark Dorman, CEO
Gustavo Dobles, VP Operations
News and analysis of policy, science and industry developments in the areas of global warming and acid rain.
Cost: $447.00
Frequency: BiWeekly

7834 HazTECH News
Haztech News
14120 Huckleberry Lane
Silver Spring, MD 20906
301-871-3289; Fax: 301-460-5859
Cathy Dombrowski, Editor/Publisher
Describes technologies for hazardous waste management, site remediation, industrial wastewater treatment and VOC control.
Cost: $385.00
8 Pages
Frequency: Bi-Weekly
Printed in one color

7835 Hazardous Materials Intelligence Report
World Information Systems
PO Box 535
Cambridge, MA 02238-535
617-492-3312; Fax: 617-492-3312
members.aol.com/socejp/hmir.html
Richard S Golob, Publisher
Roger B Wilson Jr, Editor
Provides news analysis on environmental business, hazardous materials, waste management, pollution prevention and control. Covers regulations, legislation and court decisions, new technology, contract opportunities and awards and conference notices.
Cost: $375.00
Frequency: Weekly
Circulation: 50000

7836 Hazardous Materials Transportation
Bureau of National Affairs
1801 S Bell St
Arlington, VA 22202-4501
703-341-3000
800-372-1033
customercare@bna.com
www.bnabooks.com
Gregory C McCaffery, President
Paul N Wojcik, Chairman
A two-binder service containing the full-text of rules and regulations governing shipment of hazardous material by rail, air, ship, highway and pipeline, including DOT's Hazardous Materials Tables and EPA's rules for its hazardous waste tracking system.
Cost: $933.00
Frequency: Monthly

7837 Hazardous Waste Report
Aspen Publishers
7201 McKinney Cir
Frederick, MD 21704-8356
301-698-7100
800-638-8437; Fax: 212-597-0335
www.aspenlawschool.com
Paul Gibson, Publisher
Sally Almeria, Editor
Bruce Becker, CEO/President
Tom Ceodi, Marketing
Provides information on industry news.
Cost: $875.00
8 Pages
Founded in 1958

7838 Health Facts and Fears.com
American Council on Science and Health
1995 Broadway
2nd Floor
New York, NY 10023-5882
212-362-7044; Fax: 212-362-4919
acsh@acsh.org
www.acsh.org
Dr Elizabeth Whelan, President
Jeff Stier, Associate Director
Daily e-mail blast on the latest public health news and junk science scares.
Frequency: Weekly

7839 IES Quarterly Newsletter
International Ecotourism Society
733 15th Street NW
Suite 1000
Washington, DC 20005
202-547-9203; Fax: 202-387-7915
www.ecotourism.org
Martha Honey, Executive Director
Amos Bien, Director International Programs
Neal Inamdar, Director Finance/Administration
Offering information on advocacy uniting communities, conservation, and sustainable travel.
Frequency: Quarterly

7840 Industrial Health & Hazards Update
InfoTeam
PO Box 15640
Plantation, FL 33318-5640
954-473-9560; Fax: 954-473-0544
Merton Allen, Editor
Covers occupational safety, health, hazards, and disease, mitigatioin and control of hazardous situations; waste recycling and treatment; environmental pollution and control; product safety and liability; fires and explosions; plant and computer security,; air pollution; surface and ground water; wastewater; soil gases; combustion and incineration; earth warming; ozone layer depletion; electromagnetic radiation; toxic materials; and many other related topics.

7841 Infectious Wastes News
National Solid Wastes Management Association
4301 Connecticut Ave Nw
Suite 300
Washington, DC 20008-2304
202-966-4701; Fax: 202-966-4818
www.wasterecycling.org
Bruce Parker, President
A publication by the Environmental industry association geared toward providing readers with timely news and information about the handling, transportation and disposal of infectious wastes.
Frequency: BiWeekly

7842 Integrated Environmental Assessment and Management
Society of Environmental Toxicology and Chemistry
1013 N 12th Ave
Pensacola, FL 32501-3306
850-437-1901; Fax: 850-469-9778
rparrish@setac.org
www.edwardjones.com
Rodney Parrish, Executive Director
Focuses on the application of science in environmental decision-making, regulation, and management, including aspects of policy and law, and the development of scientifically sound approaches to environmental problem solving.
Frequency: Quarterly

7843 Integrated Waste Management
1801 S Bell Street
Arlington, VA 22202
212-512-3916
800-372-1033; Fax: 212-512-2723
www.bna.com
Josh Eastright, CEO
Articles geared toward integration of solid waste management.
Cost: $745.00
8 Pages
Frequency: BiWeekly

7844 International Environment Reporter
Bureau of National Affairs
1801 S Bell St
Arlington, VA 22202-4501
703-341-3000
800-372-1033; Fax: 800-253-0332
customercare@bna.com
www.bnabooks.com
Gregory C McCaffrey, President
Paul N Wojcik, Chairman
A four-binder information and reference service covering international environmental law and developing policy in the major industrial nations.
Cost: $2555.00

7845 Journal of Science and Sustainability
National Registry of Environmental Professionals
PO Box 2099
Glenview, IL 60025
847-724-6631; Fax: 847-724-4223
nrep@nrep.org
www.nrep.org
Facebook, Twitter, LinkedIn
Richard A Young, PhD, Executive Director
Edward Beck, PhD, Senior Director
Carol Schellinger, Director
Christopher Young, Director of Operation
Marie Hunter, Director

Digital journal serving sustainability professionals worldwide.
20000 Members
Frequency: Semi-Annual
Circulation: 50,000
Founded in 1987

7846 **Marine Conservation News**
Center for Marine Conservation
2029 K Street
Washington, NW 20006
202-750-0574
800-519-1541; Fax: 202-872-0619
www.cmc-ocean.org

Rose Bierce, Publisher
Roger Rufe, President
Stephanie Drea, VP Commun
Matt Schatzle, VP Membership & Development
Wanda Cantrell, Manager

Updates members of CMC on the organization projects and activities.
24 Pages
Frequency: Quarterly
Circulation: 100000
Printed in 2 colors on matte stock

7847 **McCoy's Hazardous Waste Regulatory Update**
McCoy & Associates
25107 Genesee Trail Road
Suite 200
Golden, CO 80228-4173

303-526-2674; Fax: 303-526-5471
info@mccoyseminars.com
www.mccoyseminars.com/contact.cfm

Offers a complete text of the federal hazardous waste regulations, summaries, interpretations and indexes.
Founded in 1983

7848 **McCoy's Regulatory Analysis Service**
McCoy & Associates
25107 Genesee Trail Road
Golden, CO 80401-5708

303-526-2674; Fax: 303-526-5471
info@mccoyseminars.com
www.mccoyseminars.com

Provides timely, in-depth analyses of hazardous waste regulations within 10 working days after their publication in the Federal Register.
Cost: $550.00
Founded in 1983

7849 **Mealey's Litigation Report: Insurance**
LexisNexis Mealey's
555 W 5th Avenue
Los Angeles, CA 90013

213-627-1130
mealeyinfo@lexisnexis.com
www.lexisnexis.com/mealeys

Tom Hagy, VP/General Manager
Maureen McGuire, Editorial Director
Vivi Gorman, Editor
Shawn Rice, Co-Editor

The report tracks declaratory judgment actions regarding coverage for litigation arising from long-tail claims, including environmental contamination and latent damage and injury allegedly caused by asbestos, tox chemicals and fumes, lead, breast implants, medical devices, construction defects, and more. Key issues: allocation, occurrence, policy exclusion, choice of law, discovery, duty to defend, notice, trigger of coverage and known loss.
Founded in 1984

7850 **Montana Green Power Update**
National Center for Appropriate Technology
3040 Continental Drive
PO Box 3838
Butte, MT 59702

406-494-4572
800-275-6228; Fax: 406-494-2905
www.ncat.org
Facebook, Twitter, LinkedIn

Eugene Brady, Chairman
Kathleen Hadley, Executive Director

This free monthly electronic newsletter contains the latest success stories in renewable energy development in the state of Montana, hot tips, information on financing and tax incentives, upcoming events, and links to stories from regional and national sources as featured on the Montana Green Power web site.
Frequency: Monthly
Founded in 1976

7851 **Motor Carrier Safety Report, HAZMAT Transp ortation Report**
J.J. Keller & Associates, Inc.
3003 Breezewood Lane
PO Box 368
Neenah, WI 54957-0368

920-722-2848
800-327-6868; Fax: 800-727-7516
sales@jjkeller.com
www.jjkeller.com

Stephanie Hallman, Business Development

The nation's leader in risk and regulatory management solutions, including printed publications, videos, and online training for workplace safety, hazardous materials, transportation, human resources, and environmental safety.
Cost: $90.00
12 Pages
Frequency: Monthly
ISSN: 1056-3164
Founded in 1953

7852 **NAESCO Newsletter**
National Association of Energy Service Companies
1615 M St NW
Suite 800
Washington, DC 20036-3213

202-822-0950; Fax: 202-822-0955
info@naesco.org
www.naesco.org

Terry E Singer, Executive Editor
Michael Hamilton, Marketing Manager
Mary Lee Berger-Hughes, Publisher

Targets energy service companies, electric and gas utilities amd other energy providers. Highlights industry news and features energy conservation.
Circulation: 200
Founded in 1985

7853 **NCAT Action**
National Center for Appropriate Technology
3040 Continental Drive
PO Box 3838
Butte, MT 59702

406-494-4572
800-275-6228; Fax: 406-494-2905
www.ncat.org
Facebook, Twitter, LinkedIn

Eugene Brady, Chairman
Kathleen Hadley, Executive Director

Action is a quarterly newsletter featuring local solutions for a sustainable future. Each issue focuses on a different topic, providing information that will help you move toward a more sustainable lifesytle in your home and in your community. Action features thought-provoking commentary, informative news stories, and extensive resource lists compiled by NCAT's expert professional staff.
Frequency: Quarterly
Founded in 1976

7854 **NORA News**
NORA: an Association of Responsible Recyclers
5965 Amber Ridge Rd
Haymarket, VA 20169-2623

703-753-4277; Fax: 703-753-2445
sparker@noranews.org
www.noranews.org

Scott Parker, Executive Director

7855 **National Association of Conservation Districts**
National Association of Conservation Districts
509 Capitol Ct. NE
Washington, DC 20002-4937

202-547-6223; Fax: 202-547-6450
www.nacdnet.org

Krysta Harden, CEO
Bob Cordova, Second Vice President

Highlights forestry issues of importance to districts and to showcase district-related forestry projects and success stories. Funded through a cooperative agreement between NACD and the U.S. Forest Service.
Cost: $35.00
12 Pages
Frequency: Monthly
Circulation: 25000
Founded in 1937

7856 **Nature's Voice**
National Resources Defense Council
40 W 20th St
New York, NY 10011-4231

212-727-2700; Fax: 212-727-1773
nrdcinfo@nrdc.org
www.nrdc.org
Facebook, Twitter, YouTube

Frances Beinecke, President
Daniel R. Tishman, Chair
Frederick A.O. Schwarz Jr., Chair Emeritus
Adam Albright, Vice Chair
Patricia Bauman, Vice Chair

Environmental news and activism, using law, science and the support of more than 1 million members and online activists to protect the plante's wildlife and wild places and to ensure a healthy environment for all living things.
50000 Members
Founded in 1970

7857 **Networker**
National Center for Appropriate Technology
3040 Continental Drive
PO Box 3838
Butte, MT 59702

406-494-4572
800-275-6228; Fax: 406-494-2905
www.ncat.org
Facebook, Twitter, LinkedIn

Eugene Brady, Chairman
Kathleen Hadley, Executive Director

The newsletter is compiled by the LIHEAP Clearinghouse, and NCAT project. Stories highlight state energy assistance program and low-income energy news.
Frequency: Quarterly
Founded in 1976

7858 **News Flash**
National Association of Local Government

1333 New Hampshire Ave Nw
Suite 400
Washington, DC 20036-1532

202-887-4107; Fax: 202-393-2866
nalgep@spiegelmcd.com

Kenneth E Brown, Executive Director
David Dickson, Projects Manager

Brings together noteworthy funding opportunities, conferences, legislative tracking on climate change and highlights projects completed on the federal or local level.
Frequency: Bi-Weekly

7859 **Noise Regulation Report**
Business Publishers
2222 Sedwick Dr
Suite 101
Durham, NC 27713

800-223-8720; Fax: 800-508-2592
custserv@bpinews.com
www.bpinews.com

Exclusive coverage of airport, highway, occupational and open space noise, noise control and mitigation issues.
Cost: $511.00
10 Pages
Frequency: 12 per year
Printed in on matte stock

7860 **Nuclear Monitor**
Nuclear Information & Resource Services
1424 16th Street NW
Suite 404
Washington, DC 20036-2239

202-328-0002; Fax: 202-462-2183
nirsnet@nirs.org
www.nirs.org
Twitter, YouTube

Michael Mariotte, Editor
Linda Gunder, Media Manager

NIRS and WISE merged the Nuclear Monitor and WISE News Communique into a new Nuclear Monitor. Now available as an international edition.
Cost: $250.00
12 Pages
Frequency: 18 issues per y
Circulation: 1200
Founded in 1978
Printed in one color on matte stock

7861 **Nuclear Waste News**
Business Publishers
2222 Sedwick Dr
Suite 101
Durham, NC 27713

800-223-8720; Fax: 800-508-2592
custserv@bpinews.com
www.bpinews.com

Worldwide coverage of the nuclear waste management industry including waste generation, packaging, transport, processing and disposal.
Cost: $697.00
10 Pages
Frequency: 25 per year
Mailing list available for rent
Printed in 2 colors on matte stock

7862 **Outdoor News Bulletin**
Wildlife Management Institute
4426 VT Route 215N
Cabot, VT 05647

802-563-2087; Fax: 802-563-2157
www.wildlifemanagementinstitute.org

Richard E McCabe, Executive VP
Scot J Williamson, VP
Carol J Peddicord, Finance Manager
Robert L Byrne, Wildlife Program Coordinator
Ronald R Helinski, Conservation Policy Specialist

Reports on select, significant issues, circumstances and other information that bear on the professional management of wildlife and related natural resources.

7863 **RESTORE**
Society for Ecological Restoration
1017 O Street NW
Washington, DC 20001

202-299-9518; Fax: 270-626-5485
info@ser.org
www.ser.org

Steve Whisenant, Chair
Cara R. Nelson, Vice Chair
Mary Travaglini, Treasurer
Alan Unwin, Secretary

Weekly e-bulletin. Contains articles of interest to people in the field of restoration ecology, and is an indispensable way to keep up with what's happening in the world of ecological restoration, rounding up all the latest, breaking news from around the world on a wide variety of restoration-related issues. Available in electronic form only.
Frequency: Semi-Annual

7864 **Recycling Markets**
NV Business Publishers Corporation
43 Main St
Avon By the Sea, NJ 07717-1051

732-502-0500; Fax: 732-502-9606
www.nvpublications.com

Ted Vilardi, Owner
Anna Dutko, Managing Editor
Tom Vilardi, President/Publisher
Ted Vilardi Jr., Co-Publisher

Contains profiles on recycling mills, as well as large users and generators of recycled materials for the broker, dealers and processors of paper stock, scrap metal, plastics and glass.
Cost: $180.00
Frequency: Weekly
Circulation: 3315
Printed in 4 colors on newsprint stock

7865 **Resource Conservation & Recovery Act: A Guide to Compliance**
McCoy & Associates
13701 W Jewell Avenue
Suite 202
Lakewood, CO 80228-4173

303-870-0835; Fax: 303-989-7917

Drew McCoy, Publisher
Deborah McCoy, President

Land disposal restrictions for hazardous waste.
300 Pages
Frequency: Annual

7866 **Resource Development Newsletter**
University of Tennessee
PO Box 1071
Knoxville, TN 37996-1071

865-974-1000; Fax: 865-974-7448
rpdavis@utk.edu

Alan Barefield, Publisher

Community development information.
4 Pages
Frequency: Quarterly
Circulation: 2000
Founded in 1794
Printed in one color on matte stock

7867 **Resource Recovery Report**
PO Box 3356
Warrenton, VA 20188-1956

540-347-4500
800-627-8913; Fax: 540-349-4540
www.alexandriava.gov/resourcerecovery

Richard Will, Production Manager

Covers all alternatives to landfills, i.e., recycling, energy recovery, composting in North America, Government, industry, associations, universities, etc. are included.
Cost: $227.00
12 Pages
Frequency: Monthly
Mailing list available for rent: 12M names
Printed in one color on matte stock

7868 **SEG Extra**
Society of Exploration Geophysicists
8801 South Yale
Suite 500
Tulsa, OK 74137-3575

918-497-5500; Fax: 918-497-5557
web@seg.org
www.seg.org
Facebook, Twitter, LinkedIn

Mary Fleming, Executive Director
Vladimir Grechka, Editor

eNewsletter, delivering the most relevant, up-to-date information pertaining directly to SEG members and stakeholders.
Founded in 1930

7869 **SOCMA Newsletter**
Society of Chemical Manufacturers & Affiliates
1850 M St Nw
Suite 700
Washington, DC 20036-5803

202-721-4100; Fax: 202-296-8120
info@socma.org
www.socma.org

Larry Brotherton, Ph.D., Chair
Dave Hurder, Vice Chair
Davide DeCuir, Treasurer
J. Steel Hutchinson, Secretary

Provides the specialty, batch and custom chemical industry with the latest regulatory, legislative and commerce news in a convenient newsletter exclusively compiled for members.
10 Pages
Frequency: Bi-Weekly

7870 **Salt & Highway Deicing Newsletter**
Salt Institute
700 N Fairfax St
Suite 600
Alexandria, VA 22314-2085

703-549-4648; Fax: 703-548-2194
info@saltinstitute.org
www.saltinstitute.org

Richard L Hanneman, President
Tammy Goodwin, Director
Mark OKeefe, Director of Communications

A quarterly e-newsletter published by the Salt Institute that focuses on highway uses of salt.
Frequency: Quarterly
Circulation: 77000
Founded in 1914
Printed in on glossy stock

7871 **Salt and Trace Minerals Newsletter**
Salt Institute
700 N Fairfax St
Suite 600
Alexandria, VA 22314-2085

703-549-4648; Fax: 703-548-2194
info@saltinstitute.org
www.saltinstitute.org

Richard L Hanneman, President

E-Newsletter containing information on animal nutrition.
Frequency: Quarterly
Circulation: 77000
Founded in 1914
Printed in on glossy stock

7872 **Society Update**
American Society of Safety Engineers
1800 E Oakton Street
Des Plaines, IL 60018

847-699-2929; Fax: 847-768-3434
customerservice@asse.org
www.asse.org
Facebook

Terrie S. Norris, President
Richard A. Pollock, President Elect
Kathy Seabrook, Senior Vice President
Fred J. Fortman, Jr., Secretary & Executive Director
James D. Smith, Vice President, Finance

Highlights the latest Society news, activities, upcoming events and notable member achievements.
30000 Members
Founded in 1911

7873 **Society of Chemical Manufacturers & Affiliates Newsletter**
1850 M St NW
Suite 700
Washington, DC 20036-5803

202-721-4100; Fax: 202-296-8120
info@socma.org
www.socma.org

Larry Brotherton, Ph.D., Chair
Dave Hurder, Vice Chair
Davide DeCuir, Treasurer
J. Steel Hutchinson, Secretary

Newsletter tailored to provide industry executives with the most up-to-date information on events hosted or sponsored by SOCMA.
10 Pages
Frequency: Bi-Weekly

7874 **State Recycling Laws Update**
Raymond Communications
5111 Berwin Road
Suite no#115
College Park, MD 20740

301-345-4237; Fax: 301-345-4768
www.raymond.com

Lorah utter, Editor
Bruce Popka, Vice President of Communications
Allyn Weet, Circulation Manager

Contains analysis and reports, provides coverage of recycling legislation affecting business, as well as the outlook on future legislation across the states and Canada. Also publishes special reports on related topics, for example, Transportation Packaging and the Environment.
Cost: $367.00
Frequency: Monthly
Circulation: 200
Founded in 1991

7875 **Superfund Week**
Pasha Publications
8737 Colesville Road
Suite 1100
Silver Spring, MD 20910-3928

301-589-5103
800-274-6737; Fax: 301-589-8493
custserv@bpinews.com
www.bpinews.com

Harry Baisden, Group Publisher
Michael Hopps, Editor

Reporting the most recent developments in Congress, the EPA, and other government offices affecting hazardous waste investigations and cleanups in the federal Superfund and RCRA programs. Contains progress reports on specific cleanup sites in federal and state programs.
Cost: $525.00
Frequency: Weekly
Founded in 1963

7876 **SurFACTS in Biomaterials**
Surfaces in Biomaterials Foundation
1000 Westgate Drive
Suite 252
St Paul, MN 55114-8679

651-290-7487; Fax: 651-290-2266
memberservices@surfaces.org
www.surfaces.org

Steven Goodman, Executive Editor
Janeyy Duntley, Managing Editor

Dedicated to exploring creative solutions to technical challenges at the BioInterface by fostering education and multidisciplinary cooperation among industrial, academic, clinical and regulatory communities.
Frequency: Bimonthly

7877 **The Current**
Women's Council on Energy and the Environment
PO Box 33211
Washington, DC 20033-0211

202-997-4512; Fax: 202-478-2098
www.wcee.org
Facebook, Twitter

Ronke Luke, President
Mary Brosnan-Sell, Secretary
Robin Cantor, Vice President
Alice Grabowski, Treasurer
Joyce Chandran, Executive Director

Keeps members up to date on energy and environmental issues to foster the professional development.

7878 **The Dirt**
Land and Water
Po Box 1197
Fort Dodge, IA 50501-1197

515-576-3191; Fax: 515-576-2606
www.landandwater.com
Facebook

Amy Dencklau, Publisher
Shanza Dencklau, Assistant Editor
Rasch M. Kenneth, President

eNewsletter including information relating to the erosion control and water management industry such as: feature stories, industry news, conferences, expert tips and video clips, new products and more. Striving to keep readers up-to-date on all current happenings and relevant information beyond the pages of Land and Water Magazine.
Cost: $20.00
72 Pages
Circulation: 20000
Founded in 1959
Mailing list available for rent: 20M names
Printed in 4 colors on glossy stock

7879 **The Forest Timeline**
Forest History Society
701 William Vickers Ave
Durham, NC 27701-3162

919-682-9319; Fax: 919-682-2349
recluce2@duke.edu
www.foresthistory.org
Facebook, Twitter

L. Michael Kelly, Chairman
Robert Healy, Co-Vice Chairman
Mark Wilde, Co-Vice Chairman
Henry I. Barclay III, Treasurer
Steven Anderson, Secretary & President

E-newsletter to keep the public informed of FHS news and activities.
2000 Members
Founded in 1946

7880 **The Networker**
National Center for Appropriate Technology
3040 Continental Drive
PO Box 3838
Butte, MT 59702

406-494-4572
800-275-6228; Fax: 406-494-2905
www.ncat.org
Facebook, Twitter, LinkedIn

Gene Brady, Chairman
Randall Chapman, Vice Chairman
George Ortiz, Chairman Emeritus
Jeannie Jertson, Secretary
Brian Castelli, Treasurer

Compiled by the LIHEAP Clearinghouse, an NCAT project. Stories highlight state energy assistanc program and low-income energy news.
Founded in 1976

7881 **The Resource**
National Association of Conservation Districts
509 Capitol Ct. NE
Washington, DC 20002-4937

202-547-6223; Fax: 202-547-6450
www.nacdnet.org

Krysta Harden, CEO
Bob Cordova, Second Vice President

NACD's print publication provides in depth coverage of the association's recent activities and features columns by the NACD CEO and President, in addition to guest and partnership columns.
Cost: $35.00
12 Pages
Frequency: Monthly
Circulation: 25000
Founded in 1937

7882 **The Soil Plant Analyst**
Soil and Plant Analysis Council
347 North Shores Circle
Windsor, CO 80550

970-686-5702
www.spcouncil.org

Quarterly newsletter dedicated to the Agricultural Laboratory Industry.
Cost: $80.00
Circulation: 250

7883 **The Stormwater Report**
Water Environment Federation
601 Wythe St.
Alexandria, VA 22314

800-666-0206; Fax: 703-684-2492
inquiry@wef.org
www.wef.org
Facebook, Twitter

Walt Marlowe, Executive Director
Tim Williams, Deputy Executive Director
Penny Young, Chief Financial Officer

Monthly e-newsletter covering advanced practices, local programs, and case studies as well as policy updates, grant opportunities, and financing options.
79 Members
ISSN: 1044-9943
Founded in 1928

7884 **WEF Highlights**
Water Environment Federation
601 Wythe St.
Alexandria, VA 22314

800-666-0206; Fax: 703-684-2400
inquiry@wef.org
www.wef.org
Facebook, Twitter

Walt Marlowe, Executive Director
Tim Williams, Deputy Executive Director
Penny Young, Chief Financial Officer

Covers current Federation activities, Member Association news, and items of concern to the water quality field.
79 Members
ISSN: 1044-9943
Founded in 1928

7885 WEF SmartBrief
Water Environment Federation
601 Wythe St.
Alexandria, VA 22314

800-666-0206; Fax: 703-684-2400
inquiry@wef.org
www.wef.org
Facebook, Twitter

Walt Marlowe, Executive Director
Tim Williams, Deputy Executive Director
Penny Young, Chief Financial Officer

Daily e-newsletter designed for water sector professionals.
79 Members
ISSN: 1044-9943
Founded in 1928

7886 Washington Environmental Protection Report
Callahan Publications
PO Box 1173
Mc Lean, VA 22101-1173

703-356-1925; Fax: 703-356-9614
sue@newsletteraccess.com
www.newsletteraccess.com

Vincent Callahan, Editor

Twice-monthly letter on contracting opportunities, legislation, research and development, and rules and regulations for the nation's environmental programs. The war on pollution, in all its forms, is coming to the forefront of federal priorities and could be the answer to the many economic problems facing America.
Cost: $190.00
8 Pages
Frequency: Bi-monthly
Founded in 1990
Printed in one color

7887 Waste News
Crain Communications
1155 Gratiot Ave.
Detroit, MI 48207-2997

313-446-6000
www.crain.com

Keith Crain, Chairman
Rance Crain, President
Mary Kay Crain, Treasurer/Assistant Secretary
Merrilee P. Crain, Secretary/Assistant Treasurer

Trade publication covering the solid waste industry.
Frequency: Bi-Weekly
Circulation: 52838
Founded in 1995

7888 Waste Recovery Report
Icon: Information Concepts
211 S 45th St
Philadelphia, PA 19104-2995

215-349-6500; Fax: 215-349-6502
wasterec@aol.com
www.wrr.icodat.com

Alan Krigman, Publisher/Editor

Contains information on waste-to-energy, recycling, composting and other technologies.
Cost: $60.00
6 Pages
Frequency: Monthly
Circulation: 500
ISSN: 0889-0072
Founded in 1975

7889 Water Environment Regulation Watch
Water Environment Federation
601 Wythe St
Alexandria, VA 22314-1994

800-666-0206; Fax: 703-684-2492
www.wef.org
Facebook, Twitter

Matt Bond, President
Cordell Samuels, President-Elect
Sandra Ralston, Vice President
Chris Browning, Treasurer
Jeff Eger, Secretary and Executive Director

Monthly snapshot of Washington's water quality activities. Provides concise reports of related bills, regulations, legal decisions, congressional hearings, and other federal government actions, following key issues from introduction to final determination.
79 Members
ISSN: 1044-9943
Founded in 1928

7890 Weather & Climate Report
Nautilus Press
1056 National Press Building
Washington, DC 20045-2001

202-347-6643

John R Botzum, Editor

Reports on federal actions which impact weather, climate research and global changes in climate.

7891 Weekly Harvest
National Center for Appropriate Technology
3040 Continental Drive
PO Box 3838
Butte, MT 59702

406-494-4572
800-275-6228; Fax: 406-494-2905
www.ncat.org
Facebook, Twitter, LinkedIn

Eugene Brady, Chairman
Kathleen Hadley, Executive Director

This e-newsletter is a Web digest of sustainable agriculture news, resources, events and funding opportunities gleaned from the Internet and featured on the website.
Frequency: Weekly
Founded in 1976

7892 World Research News
World Research Foundation
41 Bell Rock Plz
Sedona, AZ 86351-8804

928-284-3300; Fax: 928-284-3530
laverne@wrf.org
www.wrf.org

LaVerne Boeckman, Co-Founder
Steven Ross, Co-Founder

Health information that is collected, categorized and disseminated in an independent and unbiased manner. Including allopathic medicine alongside complementary and alternative medicine... ancient and traditional techniques and healing therapies as well as the latest medical technology.
Frequency: Quarterly

7893 World Wildlife Fund: Focus
World Wildlife
PO Box 97180
Washington, DC 20090-7180

202-293-4800; Fax: 202-293-9211
www.worldwildlife.org

Kathryn S Fuller, CEO
Jennifer Seeger, Chief Financial Officer
Michael Bauer, Chief Financial Officer
Marcia Marsh, Chief Operating Officer

WWF projects are highlighted around the world in 450 national parks and nature reserves, with emphasis on coverage of programs and activities in the US.
8 Pages
Frequency: Monthly
Founded in 1960

7894 eNotes
National Association of Conservation Districts
509 Capitol Ct. NE
Washington, DC 20002-4937

202-547-6223; Fax: 202-547-6450
www.nacdnet.org

Krysta Harden, CEO
Bob Cordova, Second Vice President

NACD's weekly news briefs.
Cost: $35.00
12 Pages
Frequency: Monthly
Circulation: 25000
Founded in 1937

Magazines & Journals

7895 ACCA Now
Air Conditioning Contractors of America
2800 S Shirlington Road
Suite 300
Arlington, VA 22206

703-575-4477
melissa.broadus@acca.org
www.acca.org
Facebook, Twitter, LinkedIn, YouTube

Barton James, President & CEO
Melissa Broadus, Editor

ACCA Now is the leading source of Business Intelligence for Professional Contractors from HVAC and building performance, to plumbing and hydronics.

7896 ANS News
American Nuclear Society
555 N Kensington Avenue
La Grange Park, IL 60526

708-352-6611
800-323-3044; Fax: 708-352-0499
www.ans.org
Facebook, Twitter, LinkedIn

For personnel involved in nuclear power operation and development. Coverage includes power, plant operations and maintenance, fuel cycle, legislation, international employment and more.
Founded in 1954

7897 Aerosol Science and Technology (AS&T)
American Association for Aerosol Research
15000 Commerce Parkway
Suite C
Mount Laurel, NJ 08054

856-439-9080; Fax: 856-439-0525
info@aaar.org

Peter McMurry, Editor-In-Chief
Tami C Bond, Editor
Warren H Finlay, Editor

AS&T is the offficial journal of AAAR. It publishes the results of theoretical and experimental investigations into aerosol phenomena and closely related material as well as high-quality reports on fundamental and applied topics.
Cost: $1214.00

7898 Agronomy Journal
American Society of Agronomy

5585 Guilford Rd.
Madison, WI 53711-1086

608-273-8080; Fax: 608-273-2021
headquarters@sciencesocieties.org
www.agronomy.org
Facebook, Twitter, LinkedIn

Emily Mueller, Managing Editor

Journal of agriculture and natural resource sciences. Articles convey original research in soil science, crop science, agroclimatology, agronomic modeling, production agriculture, instrumentation, and more.
10000 Members
Founded in 1907

7899 **American Environmental Laboratory**
International Scientific Communications
30 Controls Drive
PO Box 870
Shelton, CT 06484-0870

203-926-9300
www.iscpubs.com

Brian Howard, Editor
Robert G Sweeny, Publisher

Laboratory activities, new equipment, and analysis and collection of samples are the main topics.
Cost: $282.42
Frequency: Monthly
Circulation: 185000

7900 **American Forests**
Po Box 2000
Suite 800
Washington, DC 20013-2000

202-737-1944; Fax: 202-955-4588
info@amfor.org
www.americanforests.org

Deborah Gangloff, Executive Director

A publication that offers our members the best in conservation news. Articles include different perspectives on current environmental issues, stories on wildlife restoration projects, updates on forest management practices, and ways to engage the conservation movement in your community.
Cost: $25.00
Frequency: Quarterly
Founded in 1875

7901 **American Waste Digest**
Charles G Moody
226 King St
Pottstown, PA 19464-9105
610-326-9480
800-442-4215; Fax: 610-326-9752
awd@americanwastedigest.com

Carasue Moody, Publisher
Shannon Costa, Circulation Manager
J. Robert Tagert, Sales Manager

Provides reviews on new products, profiles on sucessful waste removal businesses, and provides discussion on legislation on municipal regulations on recycling.
Cost: $24.00
86 Pages
Frequency: Monthly
Circulation: 33000
Printed in 4 colors on glossy stock

7902 **Archives of Environmental Health**
Society for Occupational and Environmental Health
111 North Bridge Road #21-01
Peninsula Plaza
Singapore 179098

703-556-9222; Fax: 703-556-8729
www.oehs.org

Laura Degnon, Manager

Publishing new research based on the most rigorous methods and discussion to put this work in perspective for public health, public policy, and sustainability, the Archives addresses such topics of current concern as health significance of chemical exposure, toxic waste, new and old energy technologies, industrial processes, and the environmental causation of disease.
Frequency: Bi-Monthly

7903 **Bio-Mineral Times**
Allen C Forter & Son
3450 W Central Avenue
#328
Toledo, OH 43606-1418

419-535-6374; Fax: 419-535-7008

Bonnie Hunter, Publisher
James McHugh, Chief Financial Officer

Issues focus on environmental legislation efforts, regulation compliance, and finding answers to the mechanics and practical applications of the distribution and management of biosolids derived products.
Frequency: Quarterly
Circulation: 25,000

7904 **CONNECT Magazine**
Association of Zoos and Aquariums
8403 Colesville Rd
Suite 710
Silver Spring, MD 20910-6331

301-562-0777; Fax: 301-562-0888
www.aza.org
Facebook, Twitter

Dan Ashe, President & CEO

Window to the professional zoo and aquarium world. Magazine features fascinating stories that explore trends, educational initiatives, member achievements and conservation efforts.
200 Members
Founded in 1924

7905 **CSA News**
American Society of Agronomy
5585 Guilford Rd.
Madison, WI 53711-1086

608-273-8080; Fax: 608-273-2021
headquarters@sciencesocieties.org
www.agronomy.org
Facebook, Twitter, LinkedIn

Matt Nilsson, Managing Editor

The official magazine for members of the American Society of Agronomy, Crop Science Society of America, and Soil Science Society of America.
10000 Members
Founded in 1907

7906 **Crop Science**
American Society of Agronomy
5585 Guilford Rd.
Madison, WI 53711-1086

608-273-8080; Fax: 608-273-2021
headquarters@sciencesocieties.org
www.agronomy.org
Facebook, Twitter, LinkedIn

Liz Gebhardt, Managing Editor

Publishes original research in crops and turfgrass science.
10000 Members
Founded in 1907

7907 **Crops & Soils**
American Society of Agronomy
5585 Guilford Rd.
Madison, WI 53711-1086

608-273-8080; Fax: 608-273-2021
headquarters@sciencesocieties.org
www.agronomy.org
Facebook, Twitter, LinkedIn

Matt Nilsson, Managing Editor

The magazine for certified crop advisors, agronomists, and soil scientists. Focuses on solutions to the daily challenges facing those working in the field and features information on new technology and products, company strategies, CEU articles and quizzes, and regulatory and industry news.
10000 Members
Founded in 1907

7908 **E/Environmental Magazine**
28 Knight St
Norwalk, CT 06851-4719

203-854-5559
800-967-6572; Fax: 203-866-0602
www.emagazine.com

Jim Motavalli, Editor
Karen Soucy, Associate Publisher
Doug Moss, Publisher & Executive Dir
Brita Belli, Director
Trudy Hodenfield, Operations Manager

Providing information about environmental issues and sharing ideas and resources so that readers can live more sustainable lives and connect with ongoing efforts for change. Covers everything environmental, from big issues like climate change, renewable energy and toxins and health, to the topics that directly impact our readers' daily lives; how to eat right and stay healthy, where to invest responsibly and how to save energy at home.
Cost: $19.95
Circulation: 185,000
Founded in 1988

7909 **EI Digest: Hazardous Waste Marketplace**
Environmental Information
PO Box 390266
Minneapolis, MN 55439

952-831-2473; Fax: 952-831-6550
www.envirobiz.com

Cary Perket, President

Focused on serving the market information needs of the commercial hazardous waste management sector. Included those involved in recycling and re-use, energy recovery, waste treatment, and waste disposal. Provides compilations and analysis of the commercial markets for hazardous waste energy recovery, fuel blending, incineration, landfill and solvent recovery. Also undertakes special reports on chemical distributors, RCRA metal recyclers and wastewater treatment.
ISSN: 1042-251X
Founded in 1983
Printed in 2 colors

7910 **EM Magazine**
Air and Waste Management Association
436 7th Avenue
Suite 2100
Pittsburgh, PA 15219

412-323-3444
800-270-3444; Fax: 412-232-3450
info@awma.org
www.awma.org
Facebook, Twitter, LinkedIn

Lisa Bucher, Managing Editor

EM Magazine is a monthly publication for environmental managers. It explores a range of issues affecting the industry with provocative articles and regular columns written by leaders in the field.
5000 Members
Founded in 1907

7911 **Earth First! Journal**
PO Box 964
Lake Worth, FL 33460

561-320-3840
collective@earthfirstjournal.org

earthfirstjournal.org
Facebook, Twitter, Google+, Reddit

Quarterly voice of the radical environmental movement.
Frequency: Quarterly
Founded in 1979

7912 **Earth Island Journal**
2150 Allston Way
Suite 460
Berkeley, CA 94704-1375

510-859-9100; Fax: 510-859-9091
www.earthisland.org
Facebook, Twitter, YouTube

Martha Davis, President
Kenneth Brower, Vice President
Michael Hathaway, Vice President
Jennifer Snyder, Secretary
Alex Giedt, Treasurer

Combines investigative journalism and thought-provoking essays that make the subtle but profound connections between the environment and other contemporary issues. The Journal's unique brand of environmental journalism is a key resource for anyone eager to help protect our shared planet.
33M Members
Founded in 1985

7913 **Ecological Economics, The ISEE Journal**
International Society for Ecological Economics
15 River Street
#204
Boston, MA 02108

703-790-1745; Fax: 703-790-2672
www.ecoeco.org
Facebook, Twitter

John Gowdy, President
Bina Agarwal, President-Elect
Anne Aitken, Managing Editor

Concerned with extending and integrating the study and management of ecology and economics. This integration is necessary because conceptual and professional isolation have led to economic and environmental policies which are mutually destructive rather than reinforcing in the long term.
750 Members
Founded in 1989

7914 **Ecological Management & Restoration**
Society for Ecological Restoration International
1017 O Street NW
Washington, DC 20001

202-299-9518; Fax: 270-626-5485
info@ser.org
www.ser.org
Facebook

Steve Whisenant, Chair
Cara R. Nelson, Vice Chair
Mary Travaglini, Treasurer
Alan Unwin, Secretary

Aims to bridge the gap between the ecologist's perspective and field manager's experience. Answers the growing need among land managers for reliable, relevant information and acknowledges the need for two-way communication in devising new hypotheses, sound experimentation, effective treatments and reliable monitoring.
2300 Members
Frequency: Quarterly
Founded in 1988

7915 **Economics of Energy and Environmental Policy (EEEP)**
International Association for Energy Economics
28790 Chagrin Blvd
Suite 350
Cleveland, OH 44122-4642

216-464-5365; Fax: 216-464-2737
www.iaee.org
Facebook, LinkedIn

Mine Yucel, President
Lars Bergman, President-Elect
David L. Williams, Executive Director

Policy oriented, focusing on all policy issues in the interface between energy and environmental economics. Provides a research-based, scholarly, yet easily read and accessible source of information on contemporary economic thinking and analysis of energy and environmental policy.
3400 Members
Founded in 1977

7916 **Environ: A Magazine for Ecologic Living and Health**
Environ
1616 Seventeenth Street
Suite 468
Denver, CO 80202

303-285-5543; Fax: 303-628-5597

Suzanne Randegger, Publisher/Editor
Ed Randegger, Co-Publisher/Ad Director
John Haasbeek, Senior Manager
Chris Keller, Managing Director

Designed to keep health and ecology conscious readers aware of circumstances hazardous to human health, and provide alternatives - practical, political, and global. Coverage of environmental legislation, ecologic food-growing practices and certification, geographically and climatically safe and hazardous locations, and a view of today's health problems with active solutions. Supported by screened advertisers.
Cost: $15.00
40 Pages
Frequency: Quarterly

7917 **Environment**
Helen Dwight Reid Educational Foundation
1319 18th Street NW
Washington, DC 20036-1802

202-296-6267; Fax: 202-296-5149
brichman@heldref.org
www.heldref.org

Douglas Kirkpatrick, Publisher
Barbara Richman, Editor
Fred Huber, Circulation Manager
Emily Tawlowski, Marketing Manager
Steve Hellem, Executive Director

Analyzes the problems, places, and people where environment and development come together, illuminating concerns from the local to the global. Articles and commentaries from researchers and practitioners who provide a broad range of international perspectives. Also features in-depth reviews of major policy reports, conferences, and environmental education initiatives, as well as guides to the best Web sites, journal articles, and books.
Cost: $51.00
Frequency: Monthly
Circulation: 11,408
Founded in 1956

7918 **Environmental & Engineering Geoscience**
Assn. oF Environmental & Engineering Geologists
1100-H Brandywine Boulevard
Suite 575
Zanesville, OH 43701

303-757-2926
844-331-7867; Fax: 740-452-2552
www.aegweb.org
Facebook, Twitter

Dale C. Andrews, President
Kathy Troost, Vice President

Publishes peer reviewed manuscripts that address issues relating to the interaction of people with hydrologic and geologic systems. Theoretical and applied contributions are appropriate, and the primary criteria for acceptance are scientific and technical merit.
3000 Members
Founded in 1957
Mailing list available for rent: 3000 names at $100 per M

7919 **Environmental Business Journal**
Environmental Business International
4452 Park Boulevard Suite 306
PO Box 371769
San Diego, CA 92116-1769

619-295-7685; Fax: 619-295-5743
www.ebiusa.com

Grant Ferrier, Publisher
Dan Johnson, Manager

An overview piece, segment analysis by country, profiles of domestic and foreign firms, financial data on listed environmental companies in the region, the latest developments on government initiatives and regulations, company news and projects are included in the features of this publications.
Cost: $495.00
Founded in 1988
Printed in 2 colors

7920 **Environmental Communicator**
North American Association for Environmental
2000 P St NW
Suite 540
Washington, DC 20036-6921

202-419-0412; Fax: 202-419-0415
www.naaee.org

Brian Day, Executive Director

A publication of the North American Association for EE. Feature articles, association news, affiliate news, op-ed pieces, announcements on new EE resources, available jobs, and future events and opportunities.
Frequency: Bi-Monthly

7921 **Environmental Engineering Science**
Mary Ann Liebert
140 Huguenot St
New Rochelle, NY 10801-5215

914-740-2100; Fax: 914-740-2101
info@liebertpub.com
www.liebertpub.com

Mary A Liebert, Owner
Dumpnico Grosso, Editor-in-Chief
Stephanie Paul, Production Editor
Lisa Cohen, Associate Editors

Publishing studies of innovative solutions to problems in air, wter, and land contamination and waste disposal. Features applications of environmental engineering and scientific discoveries, policy issues, environmental economics, and sustainable development.
Cost: $330.00
Frequency: Monthly
Circulation: 1800
ISSN: 1092-8758
Founded in 1980

7922 **Environmental Forensics**
AEHS Foundation Inc

150 Fearing Street
Amherst, MA 01002

413-549-5170; Fax: 413-549-0579
www.aehsfoundation.org

Paul T Kostecki, PhD, Executive Director

An international publication offering scientific studies that explore source, fate, transport and ecological effects of environmental contamination, with contamination being delineated in terms of chemical characterization, biological influence, responsible parties and legal consequences.
600 Members
Founded in 1989

7923 **Environmental History (EH)**
UW Interdisciplinary Arts and Sciences Program
1900 Commerce Street
Tacoma, WA 98402

206-343-0226; Fax: 206-343-0249
www.aseh.net

John McNeill, President
Gregg Mitman, Vice President/ President Elect
Ellen Stroud, Secretary
Mark Madison, Treasurer

The world's leading scholarly journal in environmental history. Brings together scholars, scientists, and practitioners from a wide array of disciplines to explore changing relationships between humans and the environment over time.
1200 Members
Founded in 1976

7924 **Environmental Practice**
National Association of Environmental Professional
PO Box 2086
Bowie, MD 20718-2086

888-251-9902; Fax: 301-860-1141
www.naep.org

John Perkins, Editor

Incorporates original research articles, news of issues and of the NAEP, and opinion pieces. Of interest to private consultants, academics, and professionals in federal, state, local, and tribal governments, as well as in corporations and non-governmental organizations. Reports on historic and contemporary environmental issues that help inform current practices.
Frequency: Quarterly

7925 **Environmental Protection**
Stevens Publishing Corporation
5151 Belt Line Rd
10th Floor
Dallas, TX 75254-7507

972-687-6700; Fax: 972-687-6767
www.eponline.com

Craig S Stevens, President
Dana Cornett, President/COO
Randy Dye, Publisher
Sherleen Mahoney, Editor
Margaret Perry, Circulation Director

The comprehensive online information resource for environmental professionals.
Circulation: 63000
Founded in 1925

7926 **Environmental Science and Technology**
American Chemical Society
1155 16th St Nw
Washington, DC 20036-4892

202-872-4600
800-227-5558; Fax: 202-872-4615
service@acs.org
www.acs.org

Madeleine Jacobs, CEO/Executive Director

Publishes news and research in diverse areas of environmental science and engineering.
Cost: $156.00
110 Pages
Frequency: Monthly
Circulation: 13000
Founded in 1966

7927 **Environmental Times**
Environmental Assessment Association
1224 N Nokomis NE
Alexandria, MN 56308

320-763-4320
info@eaa-assoc.org
www.iami.org/eaa.html

Robert Johnson, Executive Director

This publications contents contain environment conferences and expos, industry trends, federal regulations related to the environment and industry assessments.
Cost: $19.95
24 Pages
Circulation: 7000
Founded in 1972
Printed in 4 colors on newsprint stock

7928 **Environmental Toxicology and Chemistry**
Society of Environmental Toxicology and Chemistry
1013 N 12th Ave
Pensacola, FL 32501-3306

850-437-1901; Fax: 850-469-9778
rparrish@setac.org
www.edwardjones.com

Chad Stacy, Manager

Dedicated to furthering scientific knowledge and disseminating information on environmental toxicology and chemistry, including the application of these sciences to risk management. Provides a forum for professionals in academia, business, and government.

7929 **Environmental and Molecular Mutagenesis**
Environmental Mutagen Society
1821 Michael Faraday Drive
Suite 300
Reston, VA 20190

703-438-8220; Fax: 703-438-3113
emshq@ems-us.org
www.ems-ph.org

Publishes original research articles on environmental mutagenesis. Manuscripts published in the six general areas of mechanisms of mutagenesis, genomics, DNA damage, replication, recombination and repair, public health, and DNA technology.
Frequency: 8/year

7930 **ExecutiveBrief**
Synthetic Organic Chemical Manufacturers Assn
1850 M St Nw
Suite 700
Washington, DC 20036-5803

202-721-4100; Fax: 202-296-8120
info@socma.org
www.socma.org

Joseph Acker, President
Vivian Diko, Executive Assistant & CEO
Charlene Patterson, Editor

Provides quality content on software development, outsourcing, project and risk management.

7931 **Fisheries**
American Fisheries Society
425 Barlow Place
Suite 110
Bethesda, MD 20814-2144

301-897-8616; Fax: 301-897-8096
main@fisheries.org
fisheries.org

Douglas Austen, Executive Director
Erin Del Collo, Membership Coordinator
Laura Hendee, Journals Production Manager

Peer reviewed articles that address contemporary issues and problems, techniques, philosophies and other areas of interest to the general fisheries profession. Monthly features include letters, meeting notices, book listings and reviews, environmental essays and organization profiles.
Cost: $76.00
50 Pages
Frequency: Monthly
Founded in 1870
Mailing list available for rent

7932 **Forest History Today**
Forest History Society
701 William Vickers Ave
Durham, NC 27701-3162

919-682-9319; Fax: 919-682-2349
recluce2@duke.edu
www.foresthistory.org
Facebook, Twitter

L. Michael Kelly, Chairman
Robert Healy, Co-Vice Chairman
Mark Wilde, Co-Vice Chairman
Henry I. Barclay III, Treasurer
Steven Anderson, Secretary & President

Providing members of FHS with engaging writings in forest history and staying updated with current FHS activities.
2000 Members
Founded in 1946

7933 **Fusion Science and Technology**
American Nuclear Society
555 N Kensington Avenue
La Grange Park, IL 60526

708-352-6611
800-323-3044; Fax: 708-352-0499
www.ans.org
Facebook, Twitter, LinkedIn

Rick Michal, Director, Publications
Leigh Winfrey, Editor

The source of information on fusion plasma physics and plasma engineering, fusion plasma enabling science and technology, fusion nuclear technology and material science, fusion applications, fusion design and system studies.
Founded in 1954

7934 **Geophysics**
Society of Exploration Geophysicists
8801 South Yale
Suite 500
Tulsa, OK 74137-3575

918-497-5500; Fax: 918-497-5557
web@seg.org
www.seg.org
Facebook, Twitter, LinkedIn

Mary Fleming, Executive Director
Vladimir Grechka, Editor

An archival journal encompassing all aspects of research, exploration, and education in applied geophysics.
Founded in 1930

7935 **Hauler**
Hauler Magazine
166 S Main Street
PO Box 508
New Hope, PA 18938

800-220-6029
800-220-6029; Fax: 215-862-3455

mag@thehauler.com
www.thehauler.com

Thomas N Smith, Publisher/Editor
Barbara Gibney, Circulation Manager
Leslie T Smith, Marketing Director

Dedicated to the refuse and solid waste industry. It is the acknowledged leader in the new and used refuse truck and equipment marketplace, and now lists hundreds of new and used trash trucks, trailers, containers, services, plus parts and accessories from the best suppliers in the industry.
Cost: $12.00
Frequency: Monthly
Circulation: 18630
Founded in 1978

7936 **Hazardous Management**
Ecolog
1450 Don Mills Road
Don Mills, Ontario M3B-2X7

416-442-2292
888-702-1111; Fax: 416-442-2204
www.hazmatmag.com

Lynda Reilly, Publisher

The latest environmental regulations and programs as well as the evolving technology and equipment needed to achieve compliance.
Cost: $39.50
Frequency: Bi-Monthly
Circulation: 16,000
ISSN: 0843-9303
Founded in 1989
Mailing list available for rentat $250 per M
Printed in 4 colors on glossy stock

7937 **Hazardous Waste Consultant**
Aspen Publishers
8400 east cresent parkway
6 floor greenwood village
Lakewood, CO 80111

720-528-4270
800-638-8437; Fax: 212-597-0335

A unique approach to hazardous waste issues. It is written by engineers and regulatory specialists who have an extensive background in the field and understand the problems that industry, consultants, and regulators face.
Cost: $475.00

7938 **Human Ecology Review**
Society for Human Ecology
College of the Atlantic
105 Eden Street
Bar Harbor, ME 04609-0180

207-288-5015; Fax: 207-288-3780
www.societyforhumanecology.org

Barbara Carter, Assistant to Executive Director

Publishes peer-reviewed research and theory on the interaction between humans and the environment and other links between culture and nature, essays and applications relevant to human ecology, book reviews, and relevant commentary, announcements, and awards.
Frequency: Semi-Annual

7939 **Human and Ecological Risk Assessment**
AEHS Foundation Inc
150 Fearing Street
Amherst, MA 01002

413-549-5170; Fax: 413-549-0579
www.aehsfoundation.org

Paul T Kostecki, PhD, Executive Director

Devoted to providing a framework for professionals researching and assessing developments in both human and ecological risk assessment.
600 Members
Founded in 1989

7940 **Hydrological Science and Technology**
American Institute Of Hydrology
300 Village Green Circle
Suite 201
Smyrna, GA 30080

770-269-9388
www.aihydro.org

Cathy Lipsett, Owner
Cathryn Seaburn, Manager

Peer-reviewed international journal covering research and practical studies on hydrological science, technology, water resources and related topics including water, air and soil pollution and hazardous waste issues. Communicating ideas, findings, methods, techniques and summaries of interesting projects or investigations in the area of hydrology.
Frequency: Quarterly

7941 **IEEE Power and Energy Magazine**
IEEE
PO Box 1331
Piscataway, NJ 08855

732-981-0061; Fax: 732-981-9667
society-info@ieee.org
www.ieee.org

Mel Olken, Editor
Susan Schneiderman, Business Development

Dedicated to disseminating information on all matters of interest to electric power engineers and other professionals involved in the electric power industry. Feature articles focus on advanced concepts, technologies, and practices associated with all aspects of electric power from a technical perspective in synergy with nontechnical areas such as business, environmental, and social concerns.
Cost: $260.00
82 Pages
Frequency: Monthly
Circulation: 23000
ISSN: 1540-7977
Founded in 2003
Mailing list available for rent
Printed in on glossy stock

7942 **Identifying Business Risks & Opportunities**
World Resources Institute
10 G St NE
Suite 800
Washington, DC 20002-4252

202-729-7600; Fax: 202-729-7610
front@wri.org
www.wcdassessment.org

Jonathan Lash, President

7943 **Indoor Air Journal**
The Indoor Air Institute
2548 Empire Grade
Santa Cruz, CA 95060

831-426-0148; Fax: 831-426-6522
info@IndAir.org
indair.org

Hal Levin, President
William Fisk, Vice President
William Nazaroff, Vice President

Providing a location for reporting original research results in the broad area defined by the indoor environment of non-industrial buildings. The results will provide the information to allow designers, builders, owners and operators to provide a healthy and comfortable environment for building occupants. Health effects, monitoring and modelling, source characterization, ventilation and other environmental control techniques, thermal comfort, and public policy.

7944 **Indoor Environment Review**
IAQ Publications
7920 Norfolk Ave
#900
Bethesda, MD 20814-2539

301-913-0115; Fax: 301-913-0119
www.eschoolnews.com

Robert Morrow, Owner

New technology, research and legislation concerning all indoor air and water quality issues.
Frequency: Monthly
Circulation: 10000

7945 **Industrial Safety & Hygiene**
Business News Publishing Company
2401 W. Big Beaver Road
Suite 700
Troy, MI 48084

847-763-9534; Fax: 847-763-9538
ishn@halldata.com
www.ishn.com

Randy Green, Publisher/ West Coast Manager
Dave Johnsen, Editor
Maureen Brady, Managing Editor/Project Editor
Vince Miconi, Production Manager
Lydia Stewart, Inside Sales/Classifides

A business-to-business trade publication targeted at key safety, health and industrial hygiene buying influencers at manufacturing facilities of all sizes. Designed for the busy professionals with early mail dates and short articles backed by dynamite graphics. Each issue is packed with vital editorial on OSHA and EPA regulations, ho-to features, safety and health management topics, and the latest product news. For safety and health managers at high-hazard worksites.

7946 **Industrial Wastewater**
Water Environment Federation
601 Wythe St
Alexandria, VA 22314-1994

800-666-0206; Fax: 703-684-2492
www.wef.org
Facebook, Twitter

Matt Bond, President
Cordell Samuels, President-Elect
Sandra Ralston, Vice President
Chris Browning, Treasurer
Jeff Eger, Secretary and Executive Director

Discusses relevant regulatory and legal issues, provides examples of real-world treatment options, and offers suggestions on minimizing waste and preventing pollution.
79 Members
ISSN: 1044-9943
Founded in 1928

7947 **Inside EPA**
Inside Washington Publishers
1919 S Eads St
Arlington, VA 22202-3028

703-418-3981
800-424-9068; Fax: 703-416-8543
support@iwpnews.com
www.iwpnews.com

Alan Sosenko, Owner

Gives timely information on all facets of waste, water, air, and other environmental regulatory programs.
Frequency: Weekly
Founded in 1980

7948 **Inside Waste**
John Cupps Associates
2757 13th Street
Sacramento, CA 95818-2907

916-448-5272; Fax: 916-448-7862

John A Cupps, Publisher/Editor

The waste trade spans a diverse range of activities, from waste collection to resource recovery

to landfilling. The operating environment varies from state to state, between urban and rural areas, and even among different councils. Inside Waste brings this all together, covering all the news, projects, contracts and issues that matter to the waste trade.
Frequency: Monthly

7949 Integrated Environmenal Assessment and Management

SETAC
1013 N 12th Ave
Pensacola, FL 32501-3306

850-437-1901; Fax: 850-469-9778
setac@setac.org
www.setac.org
Facebook, Twitter, LinkedIn

Paul van den Brink, President
Tim Canfield, Vice President
Fred Heimbach, Treasurer

Bridges the gap between scientific research and its application in environmental decision-making, regulation, and management.
4000 Members
Founded in 1979

7950 International Dredging Review

PO Box 1487
Fort Collins, CO 80522-1487

970-416-1903; Fax: 970-416-1878
editor@dredgemag.com
www.dredgemag.com

Judith Powers, Publisher
Julia Leach, Business Manager
Nelson Spencer, Business Manager

Targeted to dredging company executives, project managers and dredge crew members, suppliers and service people such as pump manufacturers, hydrographic surveyors, consulting engineers, etc.
Cost: $85.00
Frequency: Monthly
Circulation: 3300
ISSN: 0737-8181
Founded in 1967

7951 International Environmental Systems Update

CEEM
3975 University Drive
Suite 230
Fairfax, VA 22030-3223

703-437-9000
800-745-5565; Fax: 703-437-9001

Paul Scicchitano, Publisher
Suzanne Leonard, Senior Editor

Provides information covering the emerging environmental issues that affect business and industry around the globe including competitive advantages, global updates, strategies, management systems and company profiles.
Cost: $ 390.00
24 Pages
Frequency: Monthly
Circulation: 50000
ISSN: 1079-0837
Founded in 1994
Mailing list available for rent
Printed in 2 colors on matte stock

7952 International Journal of Energy Management

Association of Energy Engineers
3168 Mercer University Drive
Atlanta, GA 30341

770-447-5083
info@aeecenter.org
www.aeecenter.org

Albert Thumann, Executive Director
Steven Parker, Editor

Exclusively written for engineers, energy managers, facility managers, utility professionals, VP's of operations, governmental energy managers and plant engineers involved in the design and application of energy management and facility improvement technologies.
17500 Members
Circulation: 8000
Founded in 1976

7953 International Journal of Phytoremediation

AEHS Foundation Inc.
150 Fearing Street
Amherst, MA 01002

413-549-5170
888-540-2347
www.aehsfoundation.org

Paul T Kostecki, PhD, Executive Director

Devoted to the publication of current laboratory and field research describing the use of plant systems to remediate contaminated environments. Designed to link professionals in the many environmental disciplines involved in the development, application, management, and regulation of emerging phytoremediation technologies.
600 Members
Frequency: Quarterly
Founded in 1989

7954 International Journal of Wildland Fire

International Association of Wildland Fire
4025 Fair Ridge Drive
Fairfax, VA 22033

785-423-1818; Fax: 785-542-3511
www.iawfonline.org
Facebook, Twitter

Sacha Dick, Programs Manager
Mikel Robinson, Executive Director

Online journal publishing new and significant papers that advance basic and applied research concerning wildland fire. Aims to publish quality papers on a broad range of wildland fire issues, and has an international perspective, since wildland fire plays a major social, economic, and ecological role around the globe.
Frequency: Quarterly

7955 Journal of Air & Waste Management Association

Air and Waste Management Association
436 7th Avenue
Suite 2100
Pittsburgh, PA 15219

412-323-3444
800-270-3444; Fax: 412-232-3450
info@awma.org
www.awma.org
Facebook, Twitter, LinkedIn

Lisa Bucher, Managing Editor
S. Trivikrama Rao, Technical Editor-in-Chief

Intended to serve those occupationally involved in air pollution control and waste management through the publication of timely and reliable information. Descriptions of contemporary advances in air quality and waste management science and technology for use in improving environmental protection.
Cost: $330.00
Frequency: Monthly
Circulation: 3500
ISSN: 1047-3289
Founded in 1951

7956 Journal of Environmental Economics and Management

Association of Environmental and Resource
1616 P St Nw
Suite 400
Washington, DC 20036-1434

202-328-5125; Fax: 202-939-3460
info@aere.org
www.aere.org

Devoted to the publication of theoretical and empirical papers concerned with the linkage between economic systems and environmental and natural resources systems. The top journal in natural resources and environmental economics, it concentrates on the management and/or social control of the economy in its relationship with the management and use of natural resources and the natural environment.
Frequency: Bi-Monthly

7957 Journal of Environmental Education

Heldref Publications
1319 18th St Nw
Washington, DC 20036-1802

202-296-6267; Fax: 202-296-5149
jee@heldref.org
www.heldref.org

James Denton, Executive Director
J. Heldref, Editor

Details how best to present environmental issues and how to evaluate programs already in place for primary through university level and adult students. Publishes material that advances the instruction, theory, methods, and practice of environmental education and communication. Subject areas include the sciences, social sciences, and humanities.
Cost: $58.00
Frequency: Quarterly
Circulation: 1250
Founded in 1970

7958 Journal of Environmental Engineering

American Society of Civil Engineers
1801 Alexander Bell Dr
Reston, VA 20191-4382

703-295-6300
800-548-2723
703-295-6300; Fax: 703-295-6222
webmaster@asce.org
www.asce.org

D Wayne Klotz, President
M. Kathy Banks, Editor

Emphasizes on the implementaion of effective and safe methods for handling, transporting, and treating waste materials.
Cost: $308.00
Frequency: Monthly
Circulation: 2,500
Founded in 1852

7959 Journal of Environmental Health

National Environmental Health Association
720 S Colorado Blvd
Suite 970S
Denver, CO 80246-1926

303-756-9090; Fax: 303-691-9490
staff@neha.org
www.neha.org
Facebook, Twitter, LinkedIn

Nelson Fabian, Executive Director
Julie Collins, Research
Kim Brandow, Marketing/Sales Manager
Larry Marcum, Managing Director
Bob Custard, Manager

A practical journal containing information on a variety of environmental health issues.
Cost: $90.00
5000 Members
70 Pages
Frequency: 10 per year
Circulation: 20,000
ISSN: 0022-0892

Founded in 1937
Printed in 4 colors on glossy stock

7960 Journal of Environmental Quality
American Society of Agronomy
5585 Guilford Rd.
Madison, WI 53711-1086

608-273-8080; Fax: 608-273-2021
headquarters@sciencesocieties.org
www.agronomy.org
Facebook, Twitter, LinkedIn

Ann Edahl, Manging Editor

Papers are grouped by subject matter and cover water, soil, and atmospheric research as it relates to agriculture and the environment.
10000 Members
Founded in 1907

7961 Journal of Food Protection
International Association for Food Protection
6200 Aurora Ave
Suite 200W
Des Moines, IA 50322-2864

515-276-3344
800-369-6337; Fax: 515-276-8655
info@foodprotection.org
www.foodprotection.org
Facebook, Twitter, LinkedIn

Timothy C. Jackson, President

Each issue contains scientific research and authoritative review articles reporting on a variety of topics in food science pertaining to food safety and quality.
4200 Members
Founded in 1911

7962 Journal of Intelligent Material Systems and Structures
Sage Journals Online

Home Page: journals.sagepub.com

Dan Inman, Editor-In-Chief

An international peer reviewed journal that publishes the highest quality original research. JIMSS reports on the results of experimental or theoretical work on any aspect of intelligent materials systems and/or structures research also called smart structure, smart materials, active materials, adaptive structures and adaptive materials.
Cost: $995.00
80 Pages
Frequency: Monthly
ISSN: 1045-389X
Printed in 2 colors on matte stock

7963 Journal of Natural Resources & Life Sciences Education
American Society of Agronomy
5585 Guilford Rd.
Madison, WI 53711-1086

608-273-8080; Fax: 608-273-2021
headquarters@sciencesocieties.org
www.agronomy.org
Facebook, Twitter, LinkedIn

Susan Ernst, Managing Editor

Today's educators look here for the latest teaching ideas in the life sciences, natural resources, and agriculture.
10000 Members
Founded in 1907

7964 Journal of Plant Registrations
American Society of Agronomy
5585 Guilford Rd.
Madison, WI 53711-1086

608-273-8080; Fax: 608-273-2021
headquarters@sciencesocieties.org
www.agronomy.org
Facebook, Twitter, LinkedIn

Ann Edahl, Managing Editor

Publishes cultivar, germplasm, parental line, genetic stock, and mapping population registration manuscripts.
10000 Members
Founded in 1907

7965 Journal of Soil and Water Conservation
Soil and Water Conservation Society
945 SW Ankeny Rd.
Ankeny, IA 50023

515-289-2331; Fax: 515-289-1227
pubs@swcs.org
www.swcs.org

Annie Binder, Director of Publications/Editor
Jorge A. Delgado, Research Editor
Jody Thompson, Editorial Assistant

A multidisciplinary journal of natural resource conservation research, practice, policy, and perspectives. The journal has two sections: the A Section containing various departments and features and the Research Section containing peer-reviewed research papers.
Cost: $99.00
Frequency: Bimonthly
Circulation: 2000
ISSN: 0022-4561
Founded in 1945

7966 Journal of Wildlife Management
Wildlife Society
5410 Grosvenor Ln
Suite 200
Bethesda, MD 20814-2197

301-897-9770; Fax: 301-530-2471
tws@wildlife.org
www.wildlife.org
Facebook, Twitter, LinkedIn

Michael Hutchins, Executive Director

One of the world's leading scientific journals covering wildlife science, management and conservation.
Founded in 1937

7967 Journal of the Air Pollution Control Association
Air Pollution Control Association
1 Gateway Center 3rd Floor
420 Fort Duquesne Blvd.
Pittsburgh, PA 15222-1435

412-232-3444
800-270-3444; Fax: 412-232-3450
info@awma.org
www.awma.org/
Facebook, Twitter, LinkedIn

Tim Keener, Technical Editor-in-Chief
George Hidy, Co-Editor
Jeffrey Brook, Associate Editor

A comprehensive journal offering information to the environment and conservation industry.
Cost: $95.00
Frequency: Monthly
Circulation: 700
Founded in 1907

7968 Journal of the American Society of Mining and Reclamation
American Society of Mining and Reclamation
1800 South Oak Street
Suite 100
Champaign, IL 61820

217-333-9489; Fax: 859-335-6529
rdarmody@illinois.edu
www.asmr.us

Robert Darmody, Executive Secretary
Pete Stahl, President
Kimery Vories, President Elect
Richard Barnhisel, Editor-in-Chief

The official journal of the ASMR, offering professional insights and trends on reclamation.
Founded in 1973

7969 Journal of the IEST
Institute of Environmental Sciences and Technology
1827 Walden Office Square
Suite 400
Schaumburg, IL 60173

847-981-0100; Fax: 847-981-4130
information@iest.org
www.iest.org

David Sgro, President
Nick Clinkinbeard, President-Elect

Official publication of the Institute of Environmental Sciences and Technology.
Frequency: Annual

7970 Lake & Reservoir Management
North American Lake Management Society
PO Box 5443
Madison, WI 53705

608-233-2836; Fax: 608-233-3186
info@nalms.org
www.nalms.org
Facebook, LinkedIn, Flickr

Bev Clark, President
Reesa Evans, Secretary

Publishes original studies relevant to lake and reservoir management. Papers address the management of lakes and reservoirs, their watersheds and tributaries, along with limnology and ecology needed for sound supervision of these systems.
Frequency: Quarterly

7971 LakeLine Magazine
North American Lake Management Society
PO Box 5443
Madison, WI 53705-443

608-233-2836; Fax: 608-233-3186
info@nalms.org
www.nalms.org

Bev Clark, President
Reesa Evans, Secretary
Linda Green, Treasurer

Contains news, commentary and articles on topics affecting lakes, reservoirs and watersheds. Organized around a theme, like control of invasive species or resolving recreational conflicts, each issue becomes a valued resource for lake users and advocates.
Frequency: Quarterly

7972 Land and Water Magazine
Land and Water
Po Box 1197
Fort Dodge, IA 50501-1197

515-576-3191; Fax: 515-576-2606
www.landandwater.com
Facebook

Amy Dencklau, Publisher
Shanza Dencklau, Assistant Editor
Rasch M. Kenneth, President

Edited for contractors, engineers, architects, government officials and those working in the field of natural resource management and restoration from idea stage through project completion and maintenance.
Cost: $20.00
72 Pages
Circulation: 20000
Founded in 1959
Mailing list available for rent: 20M names
Printed in 4 colors on glossy stock

7973 MSW Management
Forester Communications

2946 De La Vina street
Santa Barbara, CA 93105

805-682-1300; Fax: 805-682-0200
customerservice@forester.net
www.foresterpress.com

Daniel Waldman, Publisher/President
John Trotti, Group Editor

Provides municipal solid waste professionals with general news on facility construction, financing, new equipment and revenue issues.
Cost: $94.95
Circulation: 25000
Founded in 1990

7974 **Marine Technology Society Journal**
Marine Technology Society
1100 H St., Nw
Suite LL-100
Washington, DC 20005

202-717-8705; Fax: 202-347-4302
membership@mtsociety.org
www.mtsociety.org
Facebook, Twitter, LinkedIn

Jerry Boatman, President
Drew Michel, President-Elect
Jerry Wilson, VP of Industry and Technology
Jill Zande, VP of Education and Research
Amy Morgante, Managing Editor

Publishes the highest caliber, peer-reviewed papers on subjects of interest to the society; marine technology, ocean science, marine policy and education. Dedicated to publishing timely special issues on emerging ocean community concers while also showcasing general interest and student-authored works.
2M Members
Founded in 1963

7975 **National Woodlands Magazine**
National Woodland Owners Association
374 Maple Avenue East
Suite 310
Vienna, VA 22180-4718

703-255-2700
800-470-8733; Fax: 703-281-9200
www.woodlandowners.org
Facebook

Keith A. Argow, President
Dick Courter, Chairman
Eric Johnson, National Woodlands Editor

7976 **Natural History Magazine**
American Museum of Natural History
79th St & Central Park W
New York, NY 10024

212-769-5400; Fax: 212-769-5009
communications@amnh.org
www.library.amnh.org

Michael J Novacek, CEO
Victor W Fazio, Editor

Chronicled the major expeditions and research findings by curators at the American Museum of Natural History and at other natural history museums and science centers. Mission of this magazine is to promote public understanding and appreciation of nature and science.
Cost: $55.00

7977 **Natural Resources & Environment**
American Bar Association
321 N Clark St
Chicago, IL 60654-7598

312-988-5000
800-285-2221; Fax: 312-988-5280
askaba@abanet.org
www.abanet.org
Facebook, Twitter

Lori Lyons, Staff Editor
Christine LeBel, Executive Editor

Practical magazine on the latest developments in the field of natural resources law for the ABA Section of Environment, Energy, and Resources.
Cost: $80.00
64 Pages
Frequency: Quarterly
ISSN: 0822-3812
Printed in 4 colors

7978 **North American Elk: Ecology & Management**
Wildlife Management Institute
1146 19th St NW
Suite 700
Washington, DC 20036-3727

202-973-7710; Fax: 202-785-1348
www.wildlifemanagementinstitute.org

Dale E Toweill, Editor

7979 **Northeast Sun**
NE Sustainable Energy Association
50 Miles St
Greenfield, MA 01301-3255

413-774-6051; Fax: 413-774-6053
nesea@nesea.org
www.nesea.org

David Barclay, Executive Director
Paul Horowitz, Chairman

Includes articles by leading authorities on sustainable energy practices, energy efficiency and renewable energy.
Frequency: Quarterly
Circulation: 5000
Founded in 1974

7980 **Nuclear Science and Engineering**
American Nuclear Society
555 N Kensington Avenue
La Grange Park, IL 60526

708-352-6611
800-323-3044; Fax: 708-352-0499
www.ans.org
Facebook, Twitter, LinkedIn
Rick Michal, Director, Publications
Dan G. Cacuci, Editor

A source of information on research in all scientific areas related to the peaceful use of nuclear energy and radiation. Technical papers, notes, critical reviews, and computer code abstracts are presented.
Founded in 1954

7981 **Nuclear Technology**
American Nuclear Society
555 N Kensington Avenue
La Grange Park, IL 60526

708-352-6611
800-323-3044; Fax: 708-352-0499
www.ans.org
Facebook, Twitter, LinkedIn

Rick Michal, Director, Publications
Andrew C. Klein, Editor

Leading international publication reporting on new information in all areas of the practical application of nuclear science. Topics include all aspects of reactor technology: operations, safety materials, instrumentation, fuel, and waste management. Also covered are medical uses, radiation detection, production of radiation, health physics, and computer applications.
Founded in 1954

7982 **Occupational Health and Safety**
Stevens Publishing Corporation
5151 Belt Line Rd
10th Floor
Dallas, TX 75254-7507

972-687-6700; Fax: 972-687-6767
www.ohsonline.com

Craig S Stevens, President
Dana Cornett, President/COO
Randy Dye, Publisher
Jerry Laws, Editor
Margaret Perry, Circulation Director

Practical advice on how to keep the workplace safe from hazards and in full compliance with ever-changing laws and regulations. Delivering the most up-to-date info for professionals in the health, safety, industrial hygiene, environmental, security and fire protection fields with in-depth features, new product releases and more!
Circulation: 63000
Founded in 1925

7983 **Oceana**
1350 Connecticut Ave.
5th Fl.
Washington, DC 20036

202-833-3900
oceana.org/publications/magazine

Suzannah Evans, Interim Editor
Brianna Elliott, Online Content Editor

The magazine of Oceana, the largest environmental organization focused solely on ocean conservation.

7984 **OnEarth**
National Resources Defense Council
40 W 20th St
New York, NY 10011-4231

212-727-2700; Fax: 212-727-1773
nrdcinfo@nrdc.org
www.nrdc.org
Facebook, Twitter, YouTube

Frances Beinecke, President
Daniel R. Tishman, Chair
Frederick A.O. Schwarz Jr., Chair Emeritus
Adam Albright, Vice Chair
Patricia Bauman, Vice Chair

Publication exploring the challenges that confront our world, the solutions that promise to heal it, and the way we can use those solutions to improve our homes, our health, our communities, and our future.
50000 Members
Founded in 1970

7985 **Outdoor America**
Isaak Walton League
707 Conservation Lane
Gaithersburg, MD 20878

301-548-0150; Fax: 301-548-0146
general@iwla.org
www.iwla.org

David Hoskins, Executive Director

Entertaining and educational articles about the conservation work of IWLA members. Also provides in-depth coverage of broader conservation issues such as national energy policy, urban sprawl, and wetland loss.
Cost: $36.00
Frequency: Quarterly
Circulation: 37000
ISSN: 0021-3314

7986 **Photogrammetric Engineering & Remote Sensing (PE&RS)**
ASPRS
5410 Grosvenor Lane
Suite 210
Bethesda, MD 20814-2160

301-493-0290; Fax: 301-493-0208
asprs@asprs.org

www.asprs.org
Facebook, Twitter

Jaws Plasker, Exec. Director

The official journal for imaging and geospation information science and technology.
6000 Members
Founded in 1934

7987 **Phytopathology**
American Phytopatholgical Society
3340 Pilot Knob Road
Saint Paul, MN 55121-2097

651-454-7250
800-328-7560; Fax: 651-454-0766
aps@scisoc.org
www.apsnet.org

Dawn West, Journal Subscriptions

The premier international journal for publication of articles on fundamental research that advances understanding of the nature of plant diseases, the agents that cause them, their spread, the losses they cause, and measures that can be used to control them.
Frequency: Monthly
Circulation: 1200
ISSN: 0031-949X
Printed in 4 colors

7988 **Plant Disease**
American Phytopatholgical Society
3340 Pilot Know Road
Saint Paul, MN 55121-2097

651-454-7250
800-328-7560; Fax: 651-454-0766
aps@scisoc.org
www.apsnet.org

Brian Simdars, Publications - Submissions
Dawn West, Publications - Subscriptions

Leading international journal for rapid reporting of research on new diseases, epidemics, and methods of disease control. Covers basic and applied research, which focuses on practical aspects of disease diagnosis and treatment.The popular Disease Notes section contains brief and timely reports of new diseases, new disease outbreaks, new hosts, and pertinent new observations of plant diseases and pathogens worldwide.
Frequency: Monthly
Circulation: 1200
ISSN: 0191-2917

7989 **Plastics Recycling Update**
Resource Recycling
PO Box 42270
Portland, OR 97242-270

503-233-1305; Fax: 503-233-1356
pru@resource-recycling.com
www.resource-recycling.com

Jerry Powell, Publisher

The only magazine in North America focusing exclusively on polymer recovery efforts. A superb source for marketing recycling equipment and services and offers an excellent means of sourcing new suppliers of recovered plastics. The authority in plastic recycling market analysis, coverage of the latest legislation, industry news and views, and technical specs on the latest equipment.
Cost: $59.00
6 Pages
Frequency: Monthly
Circulation: 1000
ISSN: 1052-4908
Founded in 1981
Mailing list available for rent: 40,000 names at $100 per M
Printed in one color on matte stock

7990 **Pollution Engineering**
Business News Publishing Company
2401 W Big Beaver Rd
Suite 700
Troy, MI 48084-3333

248-362-3700; Fax: 248-362-0317
www.bnpmedia.com
Facebook, Twitter

Mitchell Henderson, CEO
Roy Bigham, Managing Editor
Seth Fisher, Products Editor

Providing must read information for today's Engineers and Consulting Engineers in Pollution Control for; Air, Wastewater, and Remediation Hazardous Solid Waste. Up-to-date information on regulatory requirements, coverage of economic benefits of environmental control techniques, and up-to-date information on innovative and cost-effective environmental equipment, products, technology and services.
Frequency: Monthly
ISSN: 0032-3640
Founded in 1969

7991 **Pollution Equipment News**
Rimbach Publishing
8650 Babcock Blvd
Suite 1
Pittsburgh, PA 15237-5010

412-364-5366
800-245-3182; Fax: 412-369-9720
info@rimbach.com
www.rimbach.com
Facebook, Twitter

Norberta Rimbach, President
Karen Galante, Circulation Manager
Paul Henderson, VP of Sales and Marketing

Provides information to those responsible for selecting products and services for air, water, wastewater and hazardous waste pollution abatement.
Frequency: Bi-Annually
Circulation: 91000
Founded in 1968

7992 **Pollution Prevention Northwest**
US EPA
Ariel Rios Building
1200 Pennsylvania Avenue NW
Washington, DC 20460

202-272-0167
www.epa.gov

Bob Zachariasiewicz, Acting Director

Articles include recent information on source reduction and sustainable technologies in industry, transportation, consumer, agriculture, energy, and the international sector.
Frequency: Monthly
Circulation: 12000
Founded in 1970

7993 **Popular Science**
2 Park Ave
9th Floor
New York, NY 10016-5614

212-779-5000; Fax: 212-986-2656
letters@popsci.com
www.popsci.com

Greg Hano, Publisher
Robert Novick, General Manager

A leading source of science and technology news, with insightful commentary on the new innovations, and even scientific takes on the hottest Hollywood stories.
Cost: $48.00
Frequency: Monthly
Founded in 1964

7994 **Pumper**
COLE Publishing
PO Box 220
Three Lakes, WI 54562-220

715-546-3346; Fax: 715-546-3786
info@pumper.com
www.pumper.com
Facebook, Twitter, YouTube

Ted Rulseh, Editor
Jeff Bruss, President

Emphasis on companies, individuals and industry events while focusing on customer service, environmental issues and employment trends.
Cost: $16.00
Frequency: Monthly
Circulation: 20,740
Founded in 1978

7995 **Radwaste Solutions**
American Nuclear Society
555 N Kensington Avenue
La Grange Park, IL 60526

708-352-6611
800-323-044; Fax: 708-352-0499
www.ans.org

Rick Michal, Director, Publications

The magazine of radioactive waste management and facility remediation. Serving the nuclear waste management and cleanup business segments of the industry. Also included are articles on radwaste management programs and practices outside the US, as well as guest editorials and letters to the editor, shorter thought-pieces, and articles on recent academic/technical advances detailing their immediate or planned practical applications.
Circulation: 2000
Founded in 1994
Printed in on matte stock

7996 **Recharger Magazine**
1050 E Flamingo Rd
Suite 237
Las Vegas, NV 89119-7427

702-438-5557; Fax: 702-873-9671
info@rechargermag.com
www.rechargermag.com
Facebook, Twitter

Phyllis Gurgeview, Publisher
Amy Turner, Managing Editor
Brenda Potts, Circulation Manager
Becky Fenton, Manager
Amy Weiss, Director

Information on remanufacturing imaging supplies including articles that cover business and marketing, technical updates, association and industry news, and company profiles. Related features focus on supply sales and equipment service.
Cost: $45.00
250 Pages
Frequency: Monthly
Circulation: 8000
ISSN: 1053-7503
Printed in 4 colors

7997 **Reclamation Matters**
American Society of Mining and Reclamation
1800 South Oak Street
Suite 100
Champaign, IL 61820

217-333-9489; Fax: 859-335-6529
asmr@insightbb.com
www.asmr.us
Facebook

Robert Darmody, Executive Secretary
Pete Stahl, President
Kimery Vories, President Elect
Richard Barnhisel, Editor-in-Chief

The official magazine of ASMR.
500 Members
ISSN: 2328-8744
Founded in 1973

7998 Recycling Laws International
Raymond Communications
P.O.Box 4311
Silver Spring, MD 20914-4311
301-345-4237; Fax: 301-345-4768
circulation@raymond.com
www.raymond.com
Lorah Utter, Editor
Allyn Sweet, Circulation Manager
Michele Raymond, President
Covers recycling, takeback, green labeling policy for business in 35 countries. Also contains a country page document that is updated annually.
Cost: $485.00
200 Pages
Circulation: 150
Founded in 1991

7999 Recycling Product News
Baum Publications
2323 Boundary Road
#201
Vancouver, BC 0
604-291-9900; Fax: 604-291-1906
www.baumpub.com
Engelbert J Baum, Publisher
Keith Barker, Editor
Published for the recycling center operators and other waste mangers, articles discuss technology and new products.
Circulation: 14000

8000 Recycling Today
GIE Media
4012 Bridge Avenue
Cleveland, OH 44113-3320
216-961-4130
800-456-0707; Fax: 216-961-0364
www.recyclingtoday.com/
Facebook, Twitter
James R Keefe, Group Publisher
Brian Taylor, Editor
Richard Foster, CEO
Debbie Kean, Manager
Published for the secondary commodity processing/recycling market.
Cost: $30.00
Frequency: Monthly
Circulation: 15000

8001 Renewable Resources Journal
Renewable Natural Resources Foundation
5430 Grosvenor Ln
Suite 220
Bethesda, MD 20814-2193
301-493-9101; Fax: 301-493-6148
info@rnrf.org
www.rnrf.org
Robert D Day, Executive Director
Ryan M Colker, Programs Director
Chandru Krishna, Circulation
Provides information of general interest concerning public policy issues related to natural resources management. Comprised of contributed and solicited articles on a wide range of natural resource issues, news items about RNRF's members, notices of significant meetings, editorials, and commentaries.
Cost: $25.00
32 Pages
Frequency: Quarterly
Circulation: 1800
ISSN: 0738-6532
Founded in 1975
Printed in 2 colors on matte stock

8002 Resource Recycling
Resource Recycling
PO Box 42270
Portland, OR 97242-270
503-233-1305; Fax: 503-233-1356
info@resource-recycling.com
www.resource-recycling.com
Jerry Powell, Editor/Publisher
Rick Downing, Graphic Designer
Suzette Ducharme, Graphic Designer
Mary Lynch, Executive Editor
The nation's leading recycling and composting magazine. This monthly journal focuses on efforts in the US and Canada to recover materials from homes and businesses for recycling. Accepts advertising.
Cost: $52.00
64 Pages
Frequency: Monthly
Circulation: 14000+
ISSN: 0744-4710
Founded in 1982
Printed in 4 colors on glossy stock

8003 Restoration Ecology
Blackwell Science
350 Main St
Malden, MA 02148-5089
781-388-8250; Fax: 781-388-8210
www.blackwellpublishing.com
Amy Yodaniss, VP
Richard Hobbs, Editor
Provides the most recent developments in the ecological and biological restoration field for both the fundamental and practical implications of restorations.
Cost: $200.00
Frequency: Quarterly
Circulation: 2000
Founded in 1897

8004 Restoration Ecology Journal
Society for Ecological Restoration International
1017 O Street NW
Washington, DC 20001
202-299-9518; Fax: 270-626-5485
info@ser.org
www.ser.org
Facebook
Steve Whisenant, Chair
Cara R. Nelson, Vice Chair
Mary Travaglini, Treasurer
Alan Unwin, Secretary
Primary emphases are: research on restoration and ecological principles that help explain restoration processes, descriptions of techniques that the authors have pioneered and that are likely to be of use to other practicing restorationists, desriptions of setbacks and surprises encountered during restoration and the lessons learnt, analytical opinions, and reviews of articles that summarize literature on specialized aspects of restoration.
2300 Members
Frequency: Bi-Monthly
Founded in 1988

8005 Review of Environmental Economics and Policy (REEP)
Association of Environmental and Resource Economis
13006 Peaceful Terrace
Silver Spring, MD 20904
202-559-8998; Fax: 202-559-8998
info@aere.org
www.aere.org
Catherine L. Kling, President
Sarah L. Stafford, Secretary
Juha Siikamaki, Treasurer
Wiktor L. Adamowicz, Vice President
Designed for broad appeal to economists and others in academia, government, the private sector, and the advocacy world who share a common interest in environmental and natural resource policy. Rather than focusing on technical and methodological aspects of research, articles will focus on the broad lessons that can be learned, for environmental and resource economics or for public policy, from broader lines of research.
900 Members
Founded in 1979

8006 Risk Policy Report
Inside Washington Publishers
1919 S Eads St
Suite 1400
Arlington, VA 22202-3028
703-418-3981; Fax: 703-415-8543
support@iwpnews.com
www.iwpnews.com
Alan Sosenko, Owner
David Clarke, Editor
Contains analysis, great perspectives, industry news, policymaking profiles and a calendar of events.
Cost: $295.00
Frequency: Monthly
Founded in 1980

8007 SETAC Globe
Society of Environmental Toxicology and Chemistry
1013 N 12th Ave
Pensacola, FL 32501-3306
850-437-1901; Fax: 850-469-9778
www.edwardjones.com
Chad Stacy, Manager
Greg Schifer, Manager
Stay up to date on the latest firm news, and learn about the companies followed with Edward Jones.
Frequency: Bi-Monthly

8008 Science Advances
American Assn for the Advancement of Science
1200 New York Avenue NW
Washington, DC 20005-3941
202-326-6550; Fax: 202-326-6483
membership@aaas.org
advances.sciencemag.org
Alan I. Leshner, Interim Executive Publisher
Jeremy Berg PhD, Editor-in-Chief
An open access multidisciplinary journal, publishing impactful research papers and reviews in any area of science, in both disciplinary-specific and broad, interdisciplinary areas.

8009 Science Immunology
American Assn for the Advancement of Science
1200 New York Avenue NW
Washington, DC 20005-3941
202-326-6550; Fax: 202-326-6483
membership@aaas.org
immunology.sciencemag.org
Alan I. Leshner, Interim Executive Publisher
Jeremy Berg PhD, Editor-in-Chief
Publishes original, peer-reviewed, science-based research articles that report critical advances in all areas of immunological research, including important new tools and techniques.
Frequency: Monthly

8010 Science Magazine
American Assn for the Advancement of Science

1200 New York Avenue NW
Washington, DC 20005-3941

202-326-6550; Fax: 202-326-6483
membership@aaas.org
www.sciencemag.org
Facebook, Twitter, Google+

Alan I. Leshner, Interim Executive Publisher
Jeremy Berg, Editor-in-Chief

The world's leading outlet for scientific news, commentary, and cutting-edge research. Available online and in print, Science Magazine continues to publish the very best in scientific research, news, and opinion.
Frequency: Weekly

8011 **Science Signaling**
American Assn for the Advancement of Science
1200 New York Avenue NW
Washington, DC 20005-3941

202-326-6550; Fax: 202-326-6483
membership@aaas.org
stke.sciencemag.org

Alan I. Leshner, Interim Executive Publisher
Michael B. Yaffe, MD, PhD, Chief Scientific Editor
Jeremy Berg, PhD, Editor-in-Chief

Offers researchers the most up-to-date resource for groundbreaking research and commentary in the dynamic field of cellular signaling.
Frequency: Weekly

8012 **Science Translational Medicine**
American Assn for the Advancement of Science
1200 New York Avenue NW
Washington, DC 20005-3941

202-326-6550; Fax: 202-326-6483
membership@aaas.org
stm.sciencemag.org

Alan I. Leshner, Interim Executive Publisher
Jeremy Berg PhD, Editor-in-Chief

Devoted to research and issues of strong interest to the translational medicine community.
Frequency: Weekly

8013 **Scrap Magazine**
Institute of Scrap Recycling Industries
1615 L St NW
Suite 600
Washington, DC 20036-5664

202-662-8500; Fax: 202-626-0900
isri@isri.org
www.isri.org

John Sacco, Chairman
Jerry I. Simms, Chair Elect
Douglas Kramer, Vice Chair
Mark R. Lewon, Secretary Treasurer

Providing practical and useful information to scrap professionals through articles and columns that will increase the profitability of their businesses. The editorial content is designed to stimulate- to help scrap professionals manage all aspects of their businesses more successfully.
165 Members
1987 Attendees

8014 **Security Products**
Stevens Publishing Corporation
5151 Belt Line Rd
10th Floor
Dallas, TX 75254-7507

972-687-6700; Fax: 972-687-6767
www.secprodonline.com

Craig S Stevens, President
Dana Cornett, President/COO
Randy Dye, Publisher
Ralph Jensen, Editor-In-Chief
Margaret Perry, Circulation Director

Leading new product and technology resource for security dealers, integrators and end users seeking comprehensive product-related information.
Circulation: 63000
Founded in 1925

8015 **Shore & Beach**
American Shore and Beach Preservation Association
5460 Beaujolais Lane
Fort Myers, FL 33919

239-489-2616; Fax: 239-362-9771
exdir@asbpa.org
www.asbpa.org
Facebook, Twitter

Harry Simmons, President
Kate Gooderham, Executive Director
Lesley Ewing, Editor
Beth Sciaudone, Managing Editor
Ken Gooderham, Production

Information and articles regarding management of shores and beaches.
1M Members
Founded in 1926

8016 **Sierra**
85 Second St.
2nd Fl.
San Francisco, CA 94105-3459

sierra.magazine@sierraclub.org
www.sierraclub.org/sierra
Facebook, Twitter, Pinterest, Instagram

Jason Mark, Editor-in-Chief
Tracy Cox, Art Director

The official magazine of the Sierra Club.
Cost: $3.95
Frequency: Bimonthly
Circulation: 1000000
ISSN: 0161-7362

8017 **Soil Science Society of America Journal**
American Society of Agronomy
5585 Guilford Rd.
Madison, WI 53711-1086

608-273-8080; Fax: 608-273-2021
headquarters@sciencesocieties.org
www.agronomy.org
Facebook, Twitter, LinkedIn

Rebecca Funck, Managing Editor

Publishes basic and applied soil research in agricultural, forest, wetlands, urban settings and more.
10000 Members
Founded in 1907

8018 **Soil Survey Horizons**
American Society of Agronomy
5585 Guilford Rd.
Madison, WI 53711-1086

608-273-8080; Fax: 608-273-2021
headquarters@sciencesocieties.org
www.agronomy.org
Facebook, Twitter, LinkedIn

Rebecca Funck, Managing Editor

Informs and entertains with research updates, soil problems and solutions, history of soil survey, and personal essays from the lives of soil scientists in the field.
10000 Members
Founded in 1907

8019 **Soil and Sediment Contamination**
AEHS Foundation Inc.
150 Fearing Street
Suite 21
Amherst, MA 01002

413-549-5170
888-540-2347
www.aehs.com

Paul T Kostecki, PhD, Executive Director

Focuses on soil and sediment contamination from; sludges, petroleum, petrochemicals, chlorinated hydrocarbons, pesticides, and lead and other heavy metals. Offers detailed descriptions of all the latest and most efficient offsite and in situ remediation techniques, strategies for assessing health effects and hazards, and tips for dealing with everyday regulatory and legal issues. Assess, mitigate, and solve rural and urban soil contamination problems.
Frequency: Bi-Monthly

8020 **Solar Today**
American Solar Energy Society
2525 Arapahoe Ave
Suite E4-253
Boulder, CO 80302

303-443-3130; Fax: 303-443-3212
www.ases.org
Facebook, Twitter

With the renewable energy industry changing at an unprecedented pace, Solar Today helps readers understand the changes, where the industry is headed, and how it's affecting the country.
Frequency: 6 issues/yr

8021 **Solid Waste & Recycling**
Southam Environment Group
1450 Don Mills Road
Don Mills, ON 0

905-305-6155
888-702-1111; Fax: 416-442-2026
bobrien@solidwastemag.com
www.solidwastemag.com

Brad O'Brien, Publisher
Bibi Khan, Circualtion Manager
Guy Crittenden, Editor-in-Chief

Emphasizes municipal and commercial aspects of collection, handling, transportation, hauling, disposal and treatment of solid waste , including incineration, recycling and landfill technology.
Cost: $29.95
Frequency: Weekly
Circulation: 10000

8022 **Solid Waste Report**
Business Publishers
2222 Sedwick Dr
Suite 101
Durham, NC 27713

800-223-8720; Fax: 800-508-2592
custserv@bpinews.com
www.bpinews.com

Comprehensive news and analysis of legislation, regulation and litigation in solid waste management including resource recovery, recycling, collection and disposal. Regularly features international news, state updates and business trends.
Cost: $567.00
Founded in 1963

8023 **TIDE**
Coastal Conservation Association
6919 Portwest Dr
Suite 100
Houston, TX 77024-8049

713-626-4234
800-201-FISH; Fax: 713-626-5852
ccantl@joincca.org
www.joincca.org
Twitter

David Cummins, President

The official magazine of the CCA.
85000 Members
Founded in 1977

8024 The Leading Edge
Society of Exploration Geophysicists
8801 South Yale
Suite 500
Tulsa, OK 74137-3575

918-497-5500; Fax: 918-497-5557
web@seg.org
www.seg.org
Facebook, Twitter, LinkedIn

Mary Fleming, Executive Director
Vladimir Grechka, Editor

A gateway publication, introducing new geophysical theory, instrumentation, and established practices to scientists in a wide range of geoscience disciplines. Most material is presented in a semitechnical manner that minimizes mathematical theory and emphasizes practical application. Also serves as SEG's publication venue for official society business.

8025 The Plant Genome
American Society of Agronomy
5585 Guilford Rd.
Madison, WI 53711-1086

608-273-8080; Fax: 608-273-2021
headquarters@sciencesocieties.org
www.agronomy.org
Facebook, Twitter, LinkedIn

Liz Gebhardt, Managing Editor

Electronic journal providing leadership of the latest advances and breakthroughs in plant genomics research.
10000 Members
Founded in 1907

8026 Tree Farmer Magazine, the Guide to Sustaining America's Family Forests
American Forest Foundation
1111 19th St NW
Suite 780
Washington, DC 20036

202-463-2700; Fax: 202-463-2785
info@forestfoundation.org
www.forestfoundation.org

Tom Martin, President & CEO
Brigitte Johnson APR, Director Communications, Editor

The official magazine of ATFS, this periodical provides practical, how-to and hands-on information and techniques, and services to help private fore landowners to become better stewards, save money and time, and add to the enjoyment of their land.

8027 Vadose Zone Journal
American Society of Agronomy
5585 Guilford Rd.
Madison, WI 53711-1086

608-273-8080; Fax: 608-273-2021
headquarters@sciencesocieties.org
www.agronomy.org
Facebook, Twitter, LinkedIn

Richard Easby, Managing Editor
Kaitlin Miller, Assistant Managing Editor

Focuses on multidisciplinary research in the unsaturated zone appealing to a diverse group of scientists and engineers.
10000 Members
Founded in 1907

8028 Washington Environmental Compliance Update
M Lee Smith Publishers
PO Box 5094
Bentwood, TN 37024-5094

615-737-7517
800-274-6774

F Lee Smith, Publisher
Douglas S Little, Editor

Review of environmental laws.
Cost: $225.00
8 Pages
Frequency: Daily
Mailing list available for rent
Printed in 2 colors on matte stock

8029 Waste Age
Environmental Industry Association
4301 Connecticut Ave NW
#300
Washington, DC 20008-2304

202-966-4701; Fax: 202-966-4818
www.wasterecycling.org
Facebook, Twitter, YouTube

Bruce Parker, President
Patricia-Ann Tom, Editor
Laura Magliola, Marketing Manager
Christine Hutcherson, Director Member Services
Alice Jacobsohn, Director Education

Contents focus on new system technologies, recycling, resource recovery and sanitary landfills with regular features on updates in the status of government regulations, new products, guides, company profiles, exclusive survey information, legislative implications and news.
Frequency: Monthly
Circulation: 38000

8030 Waste Age's Recycling Times
Environmental Industry Association
4301 Connecticut Ave NW
#300
Washington, DC 20008-2304

202-966-4701; Fax: 202-966-4818
www.wasteage.com

Bruce Parker, President
Wendy Angel, Assistant Editor
Gregg Herring, Group Publisher

Features municipalities, recycling goals and rates, program innovations, waste habits, and new materials being recycled.
Cost: $99.00
Frequency: Monthly
Circulation: 5000

8031 Water & Wastes Digest
Scranton Gillette Communications
3030 W Salt Creek Lane
Suite 201
Arlington Heights, IL 60005-5025

847-391-1000; Fax: 847-390-0408
www.scrantongillette.com
Facebook, Twitter, LinkedIn

Neda Simeonova, Editorial Director
Caitlin Cunningham, Managing Editor

Serves readers in the water and/or wastewater industries. These people work for municipalities, in industry, or as engineers. They design, specify, buy, operate and maintain equipment, chemicals, software and wastewater treatment services.
Cost: $40.00
128 Pages
Frequency: Monthly
Circulation: 101000
ISSN: 0043-1181
Founded in 1961

8032 Water Environment & Technology (WE&T)
Water Environment Federation
601 Wythe St.
Alexandria, VA 22314

800-666-0206; Fax: 703-684-2492
inquiry@wef.org
www.wef.org
Facebook, Twitter

Walt Marlowe, Executive Director
Tim Williams, Deputy Executive Director
Penny Young, Chief Financial Officer

Premier magazine for the water quality field. Provides information on what professionals demand; cutting-edge technologies, innovative solutions, regulatory and legislative impacts, and professional development.
79 Members
ISSN: 1044-9943
Founded in 1928

8033 Water Environment Research (WER)
Water Environment Federation
601 Wythe St
Alexandria, VA 22314-1994

800-666-0206; Fax: 703-684-2492
www.wef.org
Facebook, Twitter

Matt Bond, President
Cordell Samuels, President-Elect
Sandra Ralston, Vice President
Chris Browning, Treasurer
Jeff Eger, Secretary and Executive Director

Original, fundamental and applied research in all scientific and technical areas related to water quality, pollution contro, and management.
79 Members
ISSN: 1044-9943
Founded in 1928

8034 Water Quality Products
Scranton Gillette Communications
3030 W Salt Creek Lane
Suite 201
Arlington Heights, IL 60005

847-391-1000; Fax: 847-390-0408
www.wqpmag.com
Facebook, Twitter

Neda Simeonova, Editorial Director
Dennis Martyka, VP/Group Publisher
Kate Cline, Managing Editor

Provides balanced editorial content including developments in water conditioning, filtration and disinfection for residential, commercial and industrial systeme.
Cost: $40.00
68 Pages
Frequency: Monthly
Circulation: 19000
ISSN: 1092-0978
Founded in 1995

8035 Water Resources IMPACT
American Water Resources Association
4 W. Federal Street
P.O. Box 1626
Middleburg, VA 20118-1626

540-687-8390; Fax: 540-387-8395
info@awra.org
www.awra.org

Christine McCrehin, Membership & Marketing Director
Kenneth D. Reid, CAE, Executive VP
Michael J. Kowalski, CAE, Director of Operations

A practical, solution-oriented magazine containing diverse and timely articles written for water resources professionals at all levels of the profession.
Frequency: Bi-Monthly
Founded in 1964
Printed in 4 colors

8036 Wildfire Magazine
International Association of Wildland Fire
4025 Fair Ridge Drive
Fairfax, VA 22033

785-423-1818; Fax: 785-542-3511
www.iawfonline.org

Sacha Dick, Programs Manager
Mikel Robinson, Executive Director

Addresses the needs of chiefs and wildland forestry managers by providing a unique international prospective. Each issue focuses on the demand of leaders responsible for managing and controlling wildland fires. Readers are the top decision makers and leaders who have influence over purchasing equipment, supplies and contracted services. Readership includes fire chiefs, governmental agencies, private sector professionals, consultants and contractors.
Frequency: Monthly

8037 Wildlife Conservation Magazine
2300 S Boulevard
Bronx, NY 10460

718-220-5121
800-786-8226; Fax: 718-584-2625
magazine@wcs.org
www.wildlifeconservation.org/

Debby Bahler, Editor
Diana Warren, Advertising Director
4teve Sanderson, President

A national nature and science magazine. Contains stunning photography, conservation news and special updates on endangered species. Learn how to help protect local wildlife, and the secrets of the world's rarest and most mysterious animals.
Cost: $19.95
96 Pages
Circulation: 150000
Founded in 1895

8038 Word Water: Stormwater Management
Water Environment Federation
601 Wythe St.
Alexandria, VA 22314

800-666-0206; Fax: 703-684-2492
inquiry@wef.org
www.wef.org
Facebook, Twitter

Walt Marlowe, Executive Director
Tim Williams, Deputy Executive Director
Penny Young, Chief Financial Officer

A quarterly magazine that focuses on current solutions that will help manage runoff and stormwater flows on municipal, industrial, and commercial lands.
79 Members
ISSN: 1044-9943
Founded in 1928

8039 World Resource Review
SUPCON International
International Headquarters 2W381
75th Street
Naperville, IL 60565-9245

630-910-1551; Fax: 630-910-1561
syshen@megsinet.net
www.globalwarming.net

Dr. Sinyan Shen, Production Manager

For business and government readers, provides expert worldwide reviews of global warming and extreme events in relation to the management of natural, mineral and material resources. Subjects include global warming impacts on agriculture, energy, and infrastructure, monitoring of changes in resources using remote sensing, actions of national and international bodies, global carbon budget, greenhouse budget and more.
Cost: $72.00
Frequency: Quarterly
Circulation: 12000
ISSN: 1042-8011

8040 World Wastes: The Independent Voice
Communication Channels
6151 Powers Ferry Road NW
Atlanta, GA 30339-2959

770-953-4805; Fax: 770-618-0348

Bill Wolpin, Editor
Jerrold France, President Argus Business

Reaches individuals and firms engaged in the removal and disposal of solid wastes.
Cost: $48.00
Frequency: Monthly
Circulation: 36,000

8041 World Water
Water Environment Federation
601 Wythe St.
Alexandria, VA 22314

800-666-0206; Fax: 703-684-2492
inquiry@wef.org
www.wef.org
Facebook, Twitter

Walt Marlowe, Executive Director
Tim Williams, Deputy Executive Director
Penny Young, Chief Financial Officer

International magazine for the water quality industry. Provides the most cutting-edge and helpful information on global water issues.
79 Members
ISSN: 1044-9943
Founded in 1928

8042 World Water Reuse & Desalination
Water Environment Federation
601 Wythe St.
Alexandria, VA 22314

800-666-0206; Fax: 703-684-2492
inquiry@wef.org
www.wef.org
Facebook, Twitter

Walt Marlowe, Executive Director
Tim Williams, Deputy Executive Director
Penny Young, Chief Financial Officer

Becoming the global news and information resource for the water reuse and quality industries. Provides the most up-to-date and innovative information on all facets of global water reuse and desalination issues.
79 Members
ISSN: 1044-9943
Founded in 1928

Trade Shows

8043 AAAR Annual Conference
American Association for Aerosol Research
15000 Commerce Parkway
Suite C
Mount Laurel, NJ 08054

856-439-9080
877-777-6753; Fax: 856-439-0525
info@aaar.org

William Nazaroff, President
Barbara Turpin, Vice President
Barbara Wyslouzil, Vice President Elect
Murray Johnston, Treasurer
CY Wu, Secretary

Benefit from learning about the latest advances across the full frontier of aerosol science and technology. An excellent opportunity to renew old acquaintances and to meet new colleagues.
1000 Members
Founded in 1982

8044 AAAR Annual Meeting
American Association for Aerosol Research
15000 Commerce Parkway
Suite C
Mount Laurel, NJ 08054

856-439-9080; Fax: 856-439-0525
dbright@ahint.com

Lynn Russell, Program Chair
Melissa Baldwin, Executive Director

Exibits related to aerosol research in areas including industrial process, air pollution, and industrial hygiene. Over 600 professionals attend.
600 Attendees
Frequency: Annual, October

8045 AAAS Annual Meeting
Renewable Natural Resources Foundation
5430 Grosvenor Ln
Bethesda, MD 20814-2193

301-493-9101; Fax: 301-493-6148
info@rnrf.org
www.rnrf.org

Howard N. Rosen, Chairman
Richard A. Engberg, Vice-Chairman
Robert D. Day, Executive Director

The most important general science venue for a growing segment of scientists and engineers.
14 Members
Founded in 1972

8046 ACE Annual Conference
Air and Waste Management Association
436 7th Avenue
Suite 2100
Pittsburgh, PA 15219

412-323-3444; Fax: 412-232-3450
info@awma.org
www.awma.org
Facebook, Twitter, LinkedIn

Stephanie Glyptis, Executive Director
Jeff Schurman, Manager, Exhibits & Sponsorship

Environmental professionals from around the world to the outstanding technical program, exhibits of the latest products and services, and networking and professional development opportunities.
5000 Members
Founded in 1907

8047 AEESP Annual Meeting
Association of Environmental Engineering and
2303 Naples Court
Champaign, IL 61822

217-398-6969; Fax: 217-355-9232
joanne@aeesp.org
www.aeesp.org

Joanne Fetzner, Business Secretary

With the Water Environment Federation
Frequency: Fall

8048 AERE Summer Conference
Association of Environmental and Resource
1616 P Street NW
Suite 600
Washington, DC 20036

202-328-5125; Fax: 202-939-3460
voigt@rff.org
www.aere.org

Marilyn Voigt, Executive Director

nonprofit international professional association for economists working on the environment and natural resources.
850 Members
350 Attendees
Frequency: January
Founded in 1979

8049 **APLIC Annual Conference**
Family Health International Library
PO Box 13950
Research Triangle Park, NC 27709
919-447-7040
www.aplici.org
Claire Twose, President
Lori Rosman, Vice-President
Joann Donatiello, Treasurer
Focuses on current issues in communication, information, and resource technology and management.
Frequency: Annual

8050 **ASAS Annual Meeting**
American Society of Animal Science
1111 N Dunlap Avenue
Savoy, IL 61874
217-356-9050; Fax: 217-398-4119
www.asas.org
This meeting serves as an international forum to gather vital information for the future of the animal agriculture industry. A cutting-edge scientific program in food science, animal health, dairy production, beef nutrition, swine nutrition, reproduction, companion animals, and many other diverse interests.
3500 Attendees
Frequency: July/Non-Members Fee
Founded in 1908

8051 **ASBPA Coastal Summit**
American Shore & Beach Preservation Association
5460 Beaujolais Lane
Fort Myers, FL 33919
239-489-2616; Fax: 239-362-9771
www.asbpa.org
Facebook, Twitter
Tony Pratt, President
Nicole Elko, Vice President
Cameron Perry, Treasurer
Derek Brockbank, Executive Director
information and articles regarding management of shores and beaches.
1M Members
Founded in 1926

8052 **ASBPA National Coastal Conference**
American Shore and Beach Preservation Association
5460 Beaujolais Lane
Fort Myers, FL 33919
239-489-2616; Fax: 239-362-9771
www.asbpa.org
Facebook, Twitter
Tony Pratt, President
Kate Gooderham, Executive Director
Nicole Elko, Secretary
Russell Boudreau, VP
Brad Pickel, Treasurer
Federal, state and local coastal policy and legal issues, shoreline processes and coastal management, shoreline projects and global coastal issues are discussed.
1M Members
Founded in 1926

8053 **ASEH Annual Meeting**
American Society for Environmental History
119 Pine Street
Suite 301
Seattle, WA 98101
206-343-0226; Fax: 206-343-0249
www.aseh.net
Lisa Mighetto, Acting Executive Director
Individuals and groups all over the world will attend to collaborate on ways to live better with nature, and to make a better world for all outside of traditional political structures and older models of environmentalism.
Frequency: Spring, Texas

8054 **ASFE Fall Meeting**
ASFE/The Geoprofessional Business Association
8811 Colesville Road
Suite G106
Silver Springs, MD 20910
301-565-2733; Fax: 301-589-2017
info@asfe.org
www.asfe.org
John P Bachner, Executive VP
Providing geotechnical, geologic, environmental, construction materials engineering and testing, and related professional services information and education.
Frequency: Annual/Fall

8055 **ASFE Spring Meeting**
ASFE
8811 Colesville Road
Suite G106
Silver Springs, MD 20910
301-565-2733; Fax: 301-589-2017
info@asfe.org
www.asfe.org
John P Bachner, Executive VP
Provides geotechnical, geologic, environmental, construction materials engineering and testing, and related professional services information and education.
Frequency: Annual/Spring

8056 **ASFE Winter Leadership Conference**
ASFE/The Geoprofessional Business Association
8811 Colesville Road
Suite G106
Silver Springs, MD 20910
301-565-2733; Fax: 301-589-2014
info@asfe.org
www.asfe.org
John Bachner, Executive VP
ASFE's leaders meet to finish priorities for the current year and determine the direction of ASFE for the coming year.
Frequency: Annual/January

8057 **ASFPM Annual Conference**
Association of State Floodplain Managers
2809 Fish Hatchery Road
Suite 204
Madison, WI 53713
608-274-0123; Fax: 608-274-0696
memberhelp@floods.org
www.floods.org
Larry Larson, Executive Director
Alison Stierli, Manager
Diane Brown, Manager
Focus on floodproofing techniques, materials, floodproofing and elevation contractors, current issues and programs, new federal tax impications and the various means of funding floodproofing projects. implications.
Frequency: Annual

8058 **ASFPM Annual National Conference**
Association of State Floodplain Managers
2809 Fish Hatchery Rd
Suite 204
Madison, WI 53713-5020
608-274-0123; Fax: 608-274-0696
Larry@floods.org
www.floods.org
Facebook
Sally McConkey, Chair
William Nechamen, Vice Chair
Alan J. Giles, Secretary
John V. Crofts, Treasurer
The national conferences all community, state and federal floodplain managers plan to attend. Many of the most important consulting firms and product vendors associated with floodplain management attend.
6500 Members
Founded in 1977

8059 **ASMA Annual Meeting**
American Society of Mining and Reclamation
1800 South Oak Street
Suite 100
Champaign, IL 61820
217-333-9489; Fax: 859-335-6529
asmr@insightbb.com
www.asmr.us
Facebook
Robert Darmody, Executive Secretary
Pete Stahl, President
Kimery Vories, President Elect
Approximately 30 exhibitors.
Frequency: Annual
Founded in 1973

8060 **ASMR Meeting & Conference**
American Society of Mining and Reclamation
1800 South Oak Street
Suite 100
Champaign, IL 61820-6974
859-335-6529
asmr@insightbb.com
www.asmr.us
Robert Darmody, Executive Secretary
Pete Stahl, President
Kimery Vories, President Elect
Promoting the advancement of basic and applied reclamation science through research and technology transfer.
Founded in 1973

8061 **ASNT Annual Conference**
American Society for Nondestructive Testing
1711 Arlingate Lane
PO Box 28518
Columbus, OH 43228-0518
614-274-6003
800-222-2768; Fax: 614-274-6899
www.asnt.org
Neal Couture, Executive Director
Barry Schieferstein, Dir., Conferences & Meetings
Seminar, conference and 150 exhibits of nondestructive testing equipment, services, supplies and laboratory representatives. Holds a smaller conference in the spring.
3000 Attendees
Frequency: Annual

8062 **ASPRS Annual Conference**
American Society for Photogammetry/Remote Sensing

5410 Grosvenor Lane
Suite 210
Bethesda, MD 20814-2160

301-493-0290; Fax: 301-493-0208
asprs@asprs.org
www.asprs.org

Dr. Carolyn J. Merry, Ph.D., President
Roberta Lenczowski, VP
Dr. Donald Laurer, Treasurer
James Plasker, Executive Director

One hundred exhibits of mapping, photogrammetry, environmental management, remote sensing, geographic information, natural resources and much more.
6000 Members
2000 Attendees
Founded in 1934

8063 AWEA CLEANPOWER
American Wind Energy Association
1501 M Street NW
Suite 900
Washington, DC 20005

202-383-2500
conference@awea.org
engage.awea.org/events
Facebook, Twitter, LinkedIn

Tom Kiernan, Chief Executive Officer
Mark Bakke, Manager, Member Relations/Exhibits

Bringing together attendees and exhibitors from every aspect of the industry. Exhibitors display the latest industry products and services from manufacturing leaders, component suppliers, and other wind energy organizations. This conference combines education, exhibition, and networking creating a perfect venue for business development.
7000 Attendees
Frequency: Annual/June

8064 AWEA Offshore WINDPOWER
American Wind Energy Association
1501 M Street NW
Suite 900
Washington, DC 20005

202-383-2500
engage.awea.org/events
Facebook, Twitter, LinkedIn, YouTube, Instagram

Tom Kiernan, Chief Executive Officer
Mark Bakke, Manager, Member Relations/Exhibits

Brings together exhibitors and attendees from all over the world who are interested in becoming players in this new and highly promising market.
Frequency: Annual/October

8065 AWRA Spring Conference
American Water Resources Association
4 W. Federal Street
P.O. Box 1626
Middleburg, VA 20118-1626

540-687-8390; Fax: 540-387-8395
info@awra.org
www.awra.org

Christine McCrehin, Membership & Marketing Director
Kenneth D. Reid, CAE, Executive VP
Michael J. Kowalski, CAE, Director of Operations

Brings together a diverse group of water resource professionals from across the state and allows them to interact together.
2000 Members
Frequency: Annual/Spring
Founded in 1964

8066 AWRA Summer Conference
American Water Resources Association
4 W. Federal Stret
P.O. Box 1626
Middleburg, VA 20118-1626

540-687-8390; Fax: 540-387-8395
info@awra.org
www.awra.org

Christine McCrehin, Membership & Marketing Director
Kenneth D. Reid, CAE, Executive VP
Michael J. Kowalski, CAE, Director of Operations

Brings together a diverse group of water resource professionals from across the state and allows them to gather and interact together.
2000 Members
Frequency: Annual/Summer
Founded in 1964

8067 Aerosol/ Atmospheric Optics: Visibility and Air Pollution
A&WMA
420 Fort Duquesne Boulevard
One Gateway Center, 3rd Floor
Pittsburgh, PA 15222-1435

412-652-2458; Fax: 412-232-3450
info@awma.org
www.awma.org
Facebook, Twitter, LinkedIn

Jeffry Muffat, President
Merlyn L. Hough, President Elect
Mike Kelly, Secretary/ Executive Director
Amy Gilligan, Treasurer
Dallas Baker, Vice President

Provide a technical forum on advances in the scientific understanding of the effects of aerosols.
9000 Members
Founded in 1907

8068 Air Conditioning Contractors of America Annual Conference
Air Conditioning Contractors of America
2800 S Shirlington Road
Suite 300
Arlington, VA 22206

703-575-4477
membership@acca.org
www.acca.org
Facebook, Twitter, LinkedIn, YouTube

Barton James, President & CEO
Samuel Awotwi, Director of Finance
Kimya Bailey, Director, Events & Benchmarking
Sean Robertson, VP, Membership/Business Operations

Annual meeting and exhibits of heating, air conditioning and refrigeration equipment, supplies and services. Over 140 exhibitors, plus seminar, workshop and banquet.
Frequency: March

8069 Air Quality Measurement Methods and Technology
A&WMA
420 Fort Duquesne Boulevard
One Gateway Center, 3rd Floor
Pittsburgh, PA 15222-1435

412-652-2458; Fax: 412-232-3450
info@awma.org
www.awma.org
Facebook, Twitter, LinkedIn

Jeffry Muffat, President
Merlyn L. Hough, President Elect
Mike Kelly, Secretary/ Executive Director
Amy Gilligan, Treasurer
Dallas Baker, Vice President

Explore advances in measurement technology, data quality assurance, and data uses.
9000 Members
Founded in 1907

8070 Air and Waste Management Association Annual Conference and Exhibition
Air and Waste Management Association
436 7th Avenue
Suite 2100
Pittsburgh, PA 15219

412-232-3444
800-270-3444; Fax: 412-232-3450
info@awma.org
www.awma.org
Facebook, Twitter, LinkedIn

Stephanie Glyptis, Executive Director
Jeff Schurman, Manager, Exhibits & Sponsorship

Environmental professionals from all sectors of the economy including colleges, universities, natural resource manufacturing and process industries, consultants, local state, provincial, regional and federal governments, construction, utilities industries. Over 300 exhibits of envirnomental control products.
6000 Attendees

8071 American Association for the Advancement of Science Annual Meeting
American Assn for the Advancement of Science
1200 New York Ave NW
Washington, DC 20005

202-326-6400
www.aaas.org

Alan I. Leshner, Interim Chief Executive Officer
Founded in 1848

8072 American Meteorological Society Annual Meeting
Renewable Natural Resources Foundation
5430 Grosvenor Ln
Bethesda, MD 20814-2193

301-493-9101; Fax: 301-493-6148
info@rnrf.org
www.rnrf.org

Howard N. Rosen, Chairman
Richard A. Engberg, Vice-Chairman
Robert D. Day, Executive Director

Technology in research and operations, how we got here and where we're going.
14 Members
Founded in 1972

8073 American Occupational Health Conference & Exhibits
Slack
4930 Del Ray Avenue
Bethesda, MD 20814

301-654-2055; Fax: 301-654-5920
member@gastro.org
www.gastro.org

Robert Greenberg, Executive Vp
Michael Stolar, Senior Vp

400 exhibits of pharmaceuticals, equipment, software and supplies for health professionals, offices and labs.
4500 Attendees

8074 American Society of Safety Engineers Professional Development Conference
American Society of Safety Engineers

1800 E Oakton Street
Des Plaines, IL 60018

847-699-2929; Fax: 847-768-3434
customerservice@asse.org
www.asse.org

Fred Fortman, Executive Director
Jim Drzewiecki, Finance/Controller Director
Diane Hurns, Manager Public Relations Department

Annual conference and expo of 250 manufacturers and suppliers of safety equipment and health products.
3500 Attendees
Frequency: June

8075 American Water Resources Association Annual Water Resource Conference
American Water Resources Association
4 W. Federal Street
P.O. Box 1626
Middleburg, VA 20118-1626

540-687-8390; Fax: 540-387-8395
info@awra.org
www.awra.org

Christine McCrehin, Membership & Marketing Director
Kenneth D. Reid, CAE, Executive VP
Michael J. Kowalski, CAE, Director of Operations

Brings together a diverse group of water resource professionals from across the state. Presenting a unique opportunity for water resource practitioners from diverse disciplines to gather and interact together.
2000 Members
Frequency: Annual/November
Founded in 1964

8076 Annual EcoFarm Conference
Community Alliance with Family Farmers
PO Box 363
Davis, CA 95617-363

530-756-8518; Fax: 530-756-7857
info@caff.org
www.caff.org
Facebook, Twitter, YouTube

Oldest and largest ecological agricultural gathering in the West, meets every year to create, maintain, and promote healthy, safe, and just food farming systems. Myriad opportunities for networking with colleagues, discovering the newest ecological agricultural delvelopment and techniques, and building skills for individuals and together as a community.

8077 Annual International Conference on Soil, Water, Energy, and Air
AEHS Foundation Inc
150 Fearing Street
Amherst, MA 01002

413-549-5170; Fax: 413-549-0579
www.aehsfoundation.org

Paul T Kostecki, PhD, Executive Director

Live equipment demonstrations augment the exhibition hall, bringing real world application to the technical theory presented in the sessions. An exciting opportunity for all those concerned with the challenge of developing creative, cost-effective assessments and solutions that can withstand the demands of regulatory requirements.
600 Members
Founded in 1989

8078 Annual International Conference on Soils, Sediments, Water and Energy
AEHS Foundation Inc
150 Fearing Street
Amherst, MA 01002

413-549-5170; Fax: 413-549-0579
www.aehsfoundation.org

Paul T Kostecki, PhD, Executive Director

Live equipment demonstrations augment the exhibition hall, bringing real world application to the technical theory presented in the sessions. An exciting opportunity for all those concerned with the challenge of developing creative, cost-effective assessments and solutions that can withstand the demands of regulatory requirements.
600 Members
Founded in 1989

8079 Annual National Ethanol Conference
Renewable Fuels Association
425 Third Street, SW
Suite 1150
Washington, DC 20024

202-289-3835; Fax: 202-289-7519
www.ethanolrfa.org
Facebook, Twitter

Chuck Woodside, Chairman
Neill McKinstray, Vice Chairman
Randall Doyal, Treasurer
Walter Wendland, Secretary

Delivers accurate, timely information on marketing, legislative and regulatory issues facing the ethanol industry. Industry leaders and experts address accelerating innovation in technology, marketing, logistics and feedstocks for the production of advanced ethanol.
55 Members
Founded in 1981

8080 Annual Odors and Air Pollutants Conference
Water Environment Federation
601 Wythe St.
Alexandria, VA 22314

800-666-0206; Fax: 703-684-2492
inquiry@wef.org
www.wef.org
Facebook, Twitter

Walt Marlowe, Executive Director
Tim Williams, Deputy Executive Director
Penny Young, Chief Financial Officer

Topics covered include; odor and emission Control Systems, Biological odor control, innovative technologies, design of odor control systems, collection systems tunnel ventilation, emission from biosolids, fate and odor modeling, and many more.
79 Members
ISSN: 1044-9943
Founded in 1928

8081 Annual SWCS International Conference
Soil and Water Conservation Society
945 SW Ankeny Rd.
Ankeny, IA 50023

515-289-2331; Fax: 515-289-1227
www.swcs.org

Clare Lindahl, Chief Executive Officer
Courtney Allen, Event/Professional Development Dir.
Catherine DeLong, Special Projects/Policy Director

SWCS is a nonprofit scientific and educational organization that serves as an advocate for conservation professionals and for science-based conservation practice, programs, and policy.
5000+ Members
Founded in 1943

8082 Aquatic Plant Management Society Annual Meeting
Aquatic Plant Management Society
PO Box 821265
Vicksburg, MS 39182-1265

FAX 601-634-2398
dpetty@ndrsite.com
www.apms.org
Facebook, LinkedIn

Linda Nelson, President
Terry Goldsby, VP
Sherry Whitaker, Treasurer
Jeff Schardt, Secretary
Greg Aguillard, Director

An international organization of educators, scientists, commercial pesticide applicators, administrators and individuals interested in aquatic plant species and plant management.
Founded in 1961

8083 Biennial International Conference on Petroleum Geophysics
Society of Exploration Geophysicists
8801 South Yale
Suite 500
Tulsa, OK 74137-3575

918-497-5500; Fax: 918-497-5557
web@seg.org
www.seg.org
Facebook, Twitter, LinkedIn

Mary Fleming, Executive Director
Vladimir Grechka, Editor

Continuing education courses, exhibitions and networking.
Founded in 1930

8084 BioInterface
Surfaces in Biomaterials Foundation
1000 Westgate Drive
Suite 252
Saint Paul, MN 55114

651-290-6295; Fax: 651-290-2266
memberservices@surfaces.org
www.surfaces.org

Bill Monn, Executive Director
Larry Salvati, President

One of the best technical and most stimulating conferences in the field of biomaterials science. Connect, share and learn by relaxed contact with fellow attendees. Be enriched by the science, and the high quality of interaction that is fostered by the unique blend of industry, academic, regulatory and clinical attendees.
150 Attendees
Frequency: Annual/Fall

8085 CONTE Conference on Nuclear Training and Education
555 N Kensington Ave
La Grange Park, IL 60526-5592

708-352-6611
800-323-3044; Fax: 708-352-0499
advertising@ans.org
www.ans.org
Facebook, Twitter, LinkedIn

Jack Tuohy, Executive Director
James S Tulenko, VP
William F Naughton, Treasurer

Topics of interest include knowledge retention, industry training practices, workforce development, government support, partnerships with colleges and universities, applications of technology to training, and training for next generation of nuclear plants.
10500 Members
Founded in 1954

8086 Collection Systems Conference
Water Environment Federation
601 Wythe St.
Alexandria, VA 22314

800-666-0206; Fax: 703-684-2492
inquiry@wef.org

www.wef.org
Facebook, Twitter

Walt Marlowe, Executive Director
Tim Williams, Deputy Executive Directors
Penny Young, Chief Financial Officer

Highlighting continued advances in the wastewater collection systems sector.
79 Members
ISSN: 1044-9943
Founded in 1928

8087 Conference of the Brazilian Association for Aerosol Research
American Association for Aerosol Research
15000 Commerce Parkway
Suite C
Mount Laurel, NJ 08054

856-439-9080
877-777-6753; Fax: 856-439-0525
info@aaar.org

William Nazaroff, President
Barbara Turpin, Vice President
Barbara Wyslouzil, Vice President Elect
Murray Johnston, Treasurer
CY Wu, Secretary

Opportunity to meet with other aerosol scientists and learn of the latest advances in all frontiers of aerosol science and technology. Meet new colleagues, and network with academia, government, and industry researchers.
1000 Members
Founded in 1982

8088 Conference on the Applications of Air Pollution Meteorology
A&WMA
420 Fort Duquesne Boulevard
One Gateway Center, 3rd Floor
Pittsburgh, PA 15222-1435

412-652-2458; Fax: 412-232-3450
info@awma.org
www.awma.org
Facebook, Twitter, LinkedIn

Jeffry Muffat, President
Merlyn L. Hough, President Elect
Mike Kelly, Secretary/ Executive Director
Amy Gilligan, Treasurer
Dallas Baker, Vice President

Topics dealing with ALL aspects of air pollution meteorology ranging from the microscale to the global scale and including field and laboratory measurements, instrumentation, theoretical studies, numerical modeling, evaluation studies and applications. Also on transport and dispersion modeling systems, urban meteorology and dispersion, and regional to global scale transport and dispersion.
9000 Members
Founded in 1907

8089 Downscaling Climate Models for Planning
A&WMA
420 Fort Duquesne Boulevard
One Gateway Center, 3rd Floor
Pittsburgh, PA 15222-1435

412-652-2458; Fax: 412-232-3450
info@awma.org
www.awma.org
Facebook, Twitter, LinkedIn

Jeffry Muffat, President
Merlyn L. Hough, President Elect
Mike Kelly, Secretary/ Executive Director
Amy Gilligan, Treasurer
Dallas Baker, Vice President
9000 Members
Founded in 1907

8090 EBA Annual Meeting
Environmental Business Association
1150 Connecticut Avenue NW
9th Floor
Washington, DC 20036-4129

202-624-4363; Fax: 202-828-4130
wbode@bode.com

William H Bode, President

Learn more about the research, development and demonstration activities in fuel cells, hydrogen production delivery and storage technologies.
Frequency: June

8091 EBA Semi-Annual Meeting
Environmental Bankers Association
510 King Street
Suite 410
Alexandria, VA 22314

703-549-0977
800-966-7475; Fax: 703-548-5945
www.envirobank.org

D J Telego, Executive Co-Director

Network with peers in the bank and non-bank financial institutions, insurers, asset management firms and those who provide services to them. Learn more about environmental risk management, sustainable development, and due diligence policies and procedures in financial institutions.
Frequency: January, June

8092 EDRA Annual Meeting
Environmental Design Research Association
PO Box 7146
Edmond, OK 73083-7146

405-304-4863; Fax: 403-330-4150
www.edra.org

Deni Ruggeri, Executive Director

Providing information about the advancement and dissemination of environmental design research, improving understanding of the interrelationships between people, their built and natural surroundings, and creating environments responsive to human needs.
Frequency: Spring-Summer

8093 EHS Management Forum
National Assoc. for Environmental Management
1612 K St NW
Suite 1102
Washington, DC 20006-2830

202-986-6616
800-391-6236; Fax: 202-530-4408
programs@naem.org
www.naem.org
Facebook, Twitter, LinkedIn

Kelvin Roth, President
Stephen Evanoff, 1st Vice President
Debbie Hammond, 2nd Vice President
Frank Macielak, Secretary and Treasurer

The largest annual gathering of EHS and sustainability decision-makers. Three days of interactive breakout sessions and keynote presentations, the Forum is the best opportunity for professional networking, benchmarking, and best-practice sharing available to EHS and sustainability practitioners today.
1000+ Members
Founded in 1990

8094 EIA's National Conference & Exposition
Environmental Information Association
6935 Wisconsin Ave
Suite 306
Chevy Chase, MD 20815-6112

301-961-4999
888-343-4342; Fax: 301-961-3094
info@eia-usa.org
www.eia-usa.org

Dana Hudson, President
Mike Schrum, President Elect
Kevin Cannan, Vice President
Joy Finch, Secretary
Chris Gates, Treasurer

Providing the environmental industry with the information needed to remain knowledgeable, responsible, and competitive in the environmental health and safety industry.

8095 EMS Annual Meeting
Environmental Mutagen Society
1821 Michael Faraday Drive
Suite 300
Reston, VA 20190

703-438-8220; Fax: 703-438-3113
emshq@ems-us.org
www.ems-ph.org

Tonia Masson, Executive Director
Suzanne Morris, Secretary
Barbara Shane, Treasurer

Environmental Impacts on the Genome and Epigenome; Mechanisms and Risks.
Frequency: Spring

8096 EPRI-A&WMA Workshop on Future Air Quality Model Development Needs
American Association for Aerosol Research
15000 Commerce Parkway
Suite C
Mount Laurel, NJ 08054

856-439-9080
877-777-6753; Fax: 856-439-0525
info@aaar.org

William Nazaroff, President
Barbara Turpin, Vice President
Barbara Wyslouzil, Vice President Elect
Murray Johnston, Treasurer
CY Wu, Secretary

Designed to bring together researchers from academia, government and private institutions, industry, and other stakeholders to brainstorm on various air quality model development needs and to develop a comprehensive research agenda that can be used by the community to help guide research plans and to promote collaboration amongst researchers.
1000 Members
Founded in 1982

8097 ESTC Annual Convention
International Ecotourism Society
PO Box 96503 #34145
Washington, DC 20090-6503

202-506-5033; Fax: 202-789-7279
info@ecotourism.org
www.ecotourism.org
Facebook, Twitter, YouTube

Kelly Bricker, Chair
Tony Charters, Vice Chair
Neal Inamdar, Director Finance/Administration

Highlighting global challenges and local opportunities, supporting sustainable development of tourism and promoting solutions that balance conservation, communities and sustainable travel.
900 Members
Founded in 1990

8098 ESTECH
Institute of Environmental Sciences and Technology

1827 Waldon Office Square
Suite 400
Schaumburg, IL 60173

847-981-0100; Fax: 847-981-4130
information@iest.org
www.iest.org

David Sgro, President
Nick Clinkinbeard, President-Elect

Single source of contamination control knowledge for the industry. Participate in exceptional continuing education training courses and interactive working group meetings.
Frequency: Spring
Founded in 1953

8099 **ETAD Annual Meeting**
Ecological and Toxicological Association of Dyes
1850 M Street NW
Suite 700
Washington, DC 20036

202-721-4154; Fax: 202-296-8120
www.etad.com

Dr C Tucker Helmes, Executive Director

Cooperate with ETAD member companies and value chain for the benefit of health and the environment. Learn more about environmental regulations.
Frequency: Spring

8100 **East Energy Conference & Expo**
Association of Energy Engineers
3168 Mercer University Drive
Atlanta, GA 30341

770-447-5083
www.aeecenter.org
Facebook, Twitter, LinkedIn, YouTube

Albert Thumann, Executive Director

Learn about the latest developments from business, industry and government sectors.
Frequency: Annual/April
Founded in 1977

8101 **Effective Cover Cropping in the Midwest**
Soil and Water Conservation Society
945 SW Ankeny Rd
Ankeny, IA 50023-9764

515-289-2331
800-843-7645; Fax: 515-289-1227
swcs@swcs.org
www.swcs.org

Bill Boyer, President
Dan Towery, Vice-President
Clark Gantzer, Secretary
Jerry Pearce, Treasurer

Targeted to farmers and cover crop service providers. Provides a forum for farmers to exchange information, discuss opportunities for collaboration, and learn about new and successful practices related to cover crops. Goal of this conference is to get farmers together to learn how to effectively manage cover crops in a way that enhances soil quality, keeps nutrients in the fields, and increases the bottom line.
5000+ Members
Founded in 1943

8102 **Enviro Expo**
Industrial Shows Northeast
333 Trapelo Road
Belmont, MA 02478-1856

617-489-2302
800-543-5259; Fax: 781-489-5534
www.enviroexpo.com
Facebook, Twitter, LinkedIn

Russ Ryan, President
Diane Fisher, Show Manager

A single stop responsible family-oriented event, designed to educate and entertain. Variety of products and services that specialize in; health & wellness, transportation, home & garden, renewable energy, and Eco fashions.
5,000 Attendees
Frequency: May
Founded in 1987

8103 **FET Annual Meeting**
Federation of Environmental Technologists
PO Box 624
Slinger, WI 53086-0624

414-540-0070; Fax: 262-644-7106
info@fetinc.org
www.fetinc.org

Triese Haase, Administrator

Attend the program, visit the exhibitions and hear from keynote speakers on relevant environmental topics.
Frequency: March

8104 **FET-Federation Of Environmental Technologist, Inc.**
Federation of Environmental Technologists
W175 N11081 Stonewood Dr.
Ste 203
Germantown, WI 53022-4771

262-437-1700; Fax: 262-437-1702
info@fetinc.org
www.fetinc.org

Dan Brady, Board Chair
Mark Steinberg, President
Dave Seitz, Vice President
Anthony Montemurro, Treasurer
Jeffrey Nettesheim, Secretary

Educational Seminars and Courses on Environmental, Health and Safety topics throughout the year around the state of Wisconsin for business and industry.
700 Members
Founded in 1982

8105 **Fish Wildlife Agencies Association Southeast**
8005 Freshwater Farms Road
Tallahassee, FL 32309

850-893-1204; Fax: 850-893-6204
seafwa@aol.com
www.seafwa.org

Robert Brently, Executive Secretary

Fifteen booths.
1,000 Attendees
Frequency: October

8106 **Forestry, Conservation Communications Association Annual Meeting**
Forestry, Conservation Communications Association
Hall of the States
444 N Capitol
Washington, DC 20001

202-624-5416; Fax: 202-751-9099

Joe Friend, Executive Director

Annual meeting and exhibits of forestry and conservation communications equipment, systems and procedures.

8107 **Global Warming International Conference & Expo**
SUPCON International
PO Box 5275
Woodridge, IL 60517-0275

630-910-1551; Fax: 630-910-1561
syshen@megsinet.net
www.globalwarming.net

Environmental and energy technology, global warming mitigation, journals, publications and software, greenhouse gas measurements, alternative vehicles and alternative energy. Containing 100 booths and exhibits.
2000 Attendees
Frequency: April Boston

8108 **Green Industry Conference - GIC**
Professional Lawncare Network, Inc (PLANET)
950 Herndon Parkway
Suite 450
Herndon, VA 20170

703-736-9666
800-395-2522; Fax: 703-736-9668
info@gie-expo.com
www.landscapeprofessionals.org

Held in conjunction with the GIE+EXPO, the conference offers leadership series, workshops, educational opportunities, events, and new member orientation.
Frequency: Annual

8109 **Healthy Buildings Conference & Exhibition**
The Indoor Air Institute
2548 Empire Grade
Santa Cruz, CA 95060

831-426-0148; Fax: 831-426-6522
info@IndAir.org
indair.org

Hal Levin, President
William Fisk, Vice President
William Nazaroff, Vice President

Issues addressed relate to indoor air quality and its impact on health. The main focus is on buildings as confined spaces where we spend around 90% of our life.

8110 **Heating with Biomass;**
Environmental & Energy Study Institute
122 C Street NW
Suite 630
Washington, DC 20001

202-628-1400; Fax: 202-628-1825
eesi@eesi.org
www.eesi.org
Facebook, Twitter, YouTube

Jared Blum, Board Chair
Shelley Fidler, Board Treasurer
Richard L. Ottinger, Board Chair Emeritus

Win-Win for Households, Economic Development, Energy Security. Learn about how clean, renewable, efficient biomass heating can contribute to job creation, economic development, and energy security in communities across the country, as well as ways in which policies can help overcome some of the existing challenges and barriers to biomass use in the residential, commercial, and institutional sectors.
Founded in 1984

8111 **HydroVision**
HCI Publications
410 Archibald Street
Kansas City, MO 64111-3001

816-931-1311; Fax: 816-931-2015
www.hcipub.com

Leslie Eden, Manager

Focusing on asset management, civil works and dam safety, new development, ocean/ tidal/ stream power, operations and maintenance, policies and regulations, and water resources.
1,600 Attendees
Frequency: July-August

8112 **IAWF Annual Meetings**
International Association of Wildland Fire

4025 Fair Ridge Drive
Fairfax, VA 22033

785-423-1818; Fax: 785-542-3511
www.iawfonline.org
Facebook, Twitter

Sacha Dick, Programs Manager
Mikel Robinson, Executive Director

Participants represent a wide range of organizations, disciplines, and countries. Conference program includes workshops, invited speakers, oral and poster presentations, panels, and vendor displays.

8113 **ILZRO Annual Meeting**
International Lead Zinc Research Organization
2525 Meridian Parkway, Suite 100
PO Box 12036
Durham, NC 27713-2036

919-361-4647; Fax: 919-361-1957
www.ilzro.org

Stephen Wilkinson, President
Frank Goodwin, VP Materials Sciences
Scott Mooneyham, Treasurer
Rob Putnam, Director Communications

Focused on new technology and its role in managing risks in the production and use of lead, the drivers for health and environmental legislation and their likely future direction, trends, threats and opportunities in the global lead/zinc market, in particular those arising from the increasing desire for more low emission vehicles. Enabling delegates to meet a wide cross-section of key players in the lead producing and consuming countries.
Frequency: November

8114 **ISEE Annual Meetings**
International Society for Ecological Economics
1313 Dolley Madison Boulevard
Suite 402
McLean, VA 22101

703-790-1745; Fax: 703-790-2672
www.iseepi.org
Facebook, Twitter, LinkedIn

Heide Scheiter-Rohland, Director Membership

Provides an excellent opportunity for members to meet other ecological economists, test their ideas by presenting papers, and participate in the governance of the Society.
Frequency: Summer or Fall

8115 **ISEMNA Annual Meeting**
International Society for Ecological Modelling
University of California, Animal Sciences Dept
One Shields Avenue
Davis, CA 95616-8521

530-752-5362; Fax: 530-752-0175
webmaster@isemna.org
www.isemna.org

Wolfgang Pittroff, Secretary-General
David Mauriello, Treasurer

Providing a forum for scientists from around the world to exchange ideas, theories, concepts, methodologies, and results from ecological modelling that address these important issues.
Frequency: August

8116 **IWLA National Convention**
Izaak Walton League
707 Conservation Lane
Gaithersburg, MD 20878

301-548-0150
800-453-5463; Fax: 301-548-0146
general@iwla.org
www.iwla.org
Facebook, Twitter

Jim A. Madsen, President
Robert Chapman, Vice President
Marj Striegel, Secretary
Walter Lynn Jr., Treasurer

Explore how Izaak Walton League members can make a difference for the future of America's great rivers, and the people and wildlife that depend on them.
37000 Members
Founded in 1922

8117 **Instructional Technology for Occupational Safety and Health Professionals**
Nat. Environmental, Safety & Health Training Assoc
2700 N. Central Avenue
Suite 900
Phoenix, AZ 85004-1147

602-956-6099; Fax: 602-956-6399
neshta@neshta.org
www.neshta.org

Design, develop, deliver, evaluate and manage workplace safety and health training programs. Prepare and give a 15-minute presentation on a relevant workplace health and safety topic. The presentation will include skills and techniques learned in the course; however you will be encouraged to also bring materials that you are currently working on to use as a reference.
Founded in 1977

8118 **Int'l Conference on Southern Hemisphere Meteorology & Oceanography**
Renewable Natural Resources Foundation
5430 Grosvenor Ln
Bethesda, MD 20814-2193

301-493-9101; Fax: 301-493-6148
info@rnrf.org
www.rnrf.org

Howard N. Rosen, Chairman
Richard A. Engberg, Vice-Chairman
Robert D. Day, Executive Director

An interdisciplinary forum for presentations of our current state of knowledge, as well as motivating new research and applications within the variety of disciplines related to weather and climate of the ocean and atmosphere.
14 Members
Founded in 1972

8119 **International Association for Energy Economics Conference**
International Association for Energy Economics
28790 Chagrin Boulevard
Suite 350
Cleveland, OH 44122-4630

216-464-5365; Fax: 216-464-2737
www.iaee.org

David Williams, Executive Director
John Jimison, Managing Director

Semi-annual conference and exhibits relating to energy economics including publications, consultants, energy database software.
325 Attendees

8120 **International Conference & Exhibition on Liquefied Natural Gas (LNG)**
Institute of Gas Technology
1700 S Mount Prospect Rd
Des Plaines, IL 60018-1804

847-768-0664; Fax: 847-768-0669
www.gastechnology.org
Facebook, Twitter, LinkedIn, YouTube

David Carroll, President & CEO
Ronald Snedic, Vice President/ Corporate Dev
Paul Chromek, General Counsel & Secretary

A landmark strategic, technical and commercial event for leaders, experts and committed professionals of the worldwide LNG Industry.

8121 **International Conference On Air Quality- Science and Application**
A&WMA
420 Fort Duquesne Boulevard
One Gateway Center, 3rd Floor
Pittsburgh, PA 15222-1435

412-652-2458; Fax: 412-232-3450
info@awma.org
www.awma.org
Facebook, Twitter, LinkedIn

Jeffry Muffat, President
Merlyn L. Hough, President Elect
Mike Kelly, Secretary/ Executive Director
Amy Gilligan, Treasurer
Dallas Baker, Vice President

One of the most prominent forums for discussing the latest scientific developments, applications and implications for policy and other uses. An important feature it that it brings together scientists and other stakeholders from the air pollution, climate change, policy and health communities.
9000 Members
Founded in 1907

8122 **International Conference on Facility Operations-Safeguards Interface**
555 N Kensington Ave
La Grange Park, IL 60526-5592

708-352-6611
800-323-3044; Fax: 708-352-0499
advertising@ans.org
www.ans.org
Facebook, Twitter, LinkedIn

Jack Tuohy, Executive Director
James S Tulenko, VP
William F Naughton, Treasurer

New methods, products, instructions and ideas for the nuclear science and technology safety field.
10500 Members
Founded in 1954

8123 **International Conference on Ground Penetrating Rador GPR**
Society of Exploration Geophysicists
8801 South Yale
Suite 500
Tulsa, OK 74137-3575

918-497-5500; Fax: 918-497-5557
web@seg.org
www.seg.org
Facebook, Twitter, LinkedIn

Mary Fleming, Executive Director
Vladimir Grechka, Editor

Devoted to the development of ground penetrating radar. Presents the most recent technical information and case studies on ground penetrating radar for engineers, scientists, and end users.
Founded in 1930

8124 **International Conference on Indoor Air Quality and Climate**
International Academy of Indoor Air Sciences

343 Soquel Avenue
PMB 312
Santa Cruz, CA 95062

831-426-0148; Fax: 831-426-6522
www.indoorair2002.org

Multidisciplinary event involving participants from medicine, engineering, architecture and related fields. The conference will cover all aspects of Indoor Air Quality and Climate and the effects on human health, comfort and productivity. Cutting-edge research results will be presented, including ways to achieve an optimal indoor environment in a sustainable manner. Will address a variety of indoor environments, residential, office, school, industrial, commercial and transport.
Frequency: June-July

8125 International Hazardous Materials Response Teams Conference
International Association of Fire Chiefs
4025 Fair Ridge Drive
Suite 300
Fairfax, VA 22033-2868

703-273-0911; Fax: 703-273-9363
thicks@iafc.org
www.iafc.org
Facebook, Twitter, LinkedIn

Mark Light, Executive Director & CEO
Lisa Yonkers, Director, Conferences & Education
Jason Nauman, Education & Learning Manager
Leanne Shroeder, Conference Manager

Also known as the IAFC Hazmat Conference. One of the largest gatherings of hazmat responders, facilitating new ideas. Dedicated exhibit hours and events, and indoor and outdoor exhibits.
Frequency: Annual

8126 International High-Level Radioactive Waste Management
555 N Kensington Ave
La Grange Park, IL 60526-5592

708-352-6611
800-323-3044; Fax: 708-352-0499
advertising@ans.org
www.ans.org
Facebook, Twitter, LinkedIn

Jack Tuohy, Executive Director
James S Tulenko, VP
William F Naughton, Treasurer

Subject coverage includes site characterization, analogue studies, geochemical studies, disruptive events, spent fuel and high-level-waste transportation, engineered barrier systems, design and testing, disposal containers, and waste form. Performance assessment and regulatory issues are also addressed.
10500 Members
Founded in 1954

8127 International Society for Environmental Epidemiology Meeting
American Association for Aerosol Research
15000 Commerce Parkway
Suite C
Mount Laurel, NJ 08054

856-439-9080
877-777-6753; Fax: 856-439-0525
info@aaar.org

William Nazaroff, President
Barbara Turpin, Vice President
Barbara Wyslouzil, Vice President Elect
Murray Johnston, Treasurer
CY Wu, Secretary

Discussion of problems unique to the study of health and the environment.
1000 Members
Founded in 1982

8128 International Topical Meeting on Nuclear Plant Instrumentation
555 N Kensington Ave
La Grange Park, IL 60526-5592

708-352-6611
800-323-3044; Fax: 708-352-0499
advertising@ans.org
www.ans.org
Facebook, Twitter, LinkedIn

Jack Tuohy, Executive Director
James S Tulenko, VP
William F Naughton, Treasurer

Control and Human Machine Interface Technologies
10500 Members
Founded in 1954

8129 International Workshop on Seismic Anisotropy
Society of Exploration Geophysicists
8801 South Yale
Suite 500
Tulsa, OK 74137-3575

918-497-5500; Fax: 918-497-5557
web@seg.org
www.seg.org
Facebook, Twitter, LinkedIn

Mary Fleming, Executive Director
Vladimir Grechka, Editor

Cover both theoretical and applied aspects of seismic anisotropy in earth sciences. Focusing on applications of anisotropic models and methods in exploration & development of both conventional and unconventional Oil & Gas reservoirs, earthquake seismology, and reservoir monitoring using seismic anisotropy and microseismic.
Founded in 1930

8130 Living Future Unconference
International Living Future Institute
1501 East Madison St.
Suite 150
Seattle, WA 98122

206-223-2028
info@living-future.org
www.living-future.org
Facebook, Twitter, LinkedIn, Instagram

KC Gauldine, Chief Executive Officer
James Connelly, VP, Products & Strategic Growth
Kathleen Smith, VP, Living Building Challenge
Miranda Berger, VP, Development & Communications
Julie Tonroy, Events Director

Tours, workshops, summits, exhibits, keynote speakers, and sessions on regenerative design. Features cutting-edge products and knowledgeable professionals and activists in the field.
Frequency: Annual

8131 Living Product Expo
International Living Future Institute
1501 East Madison St.
Suite 150
Seattle, WA 98122

206-223-2028
info@living-future.org
www.living-future.org
Facebook, Twitter, LinkedIn, Instagram

KC Gauldine, Chief Executive Officer
James Connelly, VP, Products & Strategic Growth
Kathleen Smith, VP, Living Building Challenge
Miranda Berger, VP, Development & Communications
Julie Tonroy, Events Director

Connect with industry leaders who are part of the movement to create beautiful, healthy and sustainable products. Features educational sessions, speakers, workshops, networking opportunities, and a trade show.
Frequency: Annual

8132 MEGA Symposium
A&WMA
420 Fort Duquesne Boulevard
One Gateway Center, 3rd Floor
Pittsburgh, PA 15222-1435

412-652-2458; Fax: 412-232-3450
info@awma.org
www.awma.org
Facebook, Twitter, LinkedIn

Jeffry Muffat, President
Merlyn L. Hough, President Elect
Mike Kelly, Secretary/ Executive Director
Amy Gilligan, Treasurer
Dallas Baker, Vice President

Addresses issues related to power plant air emissions through the combined efforts of four key industry payers. Update seasoned professionals and provide an excellent learning experience for early career engineers.
9000 Members
Founded in 1907

8133 MTS TechSurge, Oceans in Action
Marine Technology Society
1100 H St., Nw
Suite LL-100
Washington, DC 20005

202-717-8705; Fax: 202-347-4302
membership@mtsociety.org
www.mtsociety.org
Facebook, Twitter, LinkedIn

Jerry Boatman, President
Drew Michel, President-Elect
Jerry Wilson, VP of Industry and Technology
Jill Zande, VP of Education and Research
Justin Manley, VP of Gov. & Public Affairs

Learn how government agencies and universities are supporting both current and emerging oceanographic operations worldwide. Discover how marine science, technology, engineering, products and services come together to support real-world issues around the globe, including piracy, disaster monitoring and recovery, prediction and forecast of ocean properties, coastal restoration, hypoxia, harmful algal blooms, fisheries and much more.
2M Members
Founded in 1963

8134 Middle East Geosciences Conference & Exhibition
Society of Exploration Geophysicists
8801 South Yale
Suite 500
Tulsa, OK 74137-3575

918-497-5500; Fax: 918-497-5557
web@seg.org
www.seg.org
Facebook, Twitter, LinkedIn

Mary Fleming, Executive Director
Vladimir Grechka, Editor
Founded in 1930

8135 NAAEE Annual Meeting
North American Association for Environmental
2000 P Street NW
Suite 540
Washington, DC 20036

202-419-0412; Fax: 202-419-0415
www.naaee.org

William H Dent, Jr, Executive Director
Barbara Eager, Conference Coordinator
Paul Werth, Owner

Concurrent sessions, plenary sessions and networking, as well as workshops, field experiences and special events.
Frequency: Fall

8136 **NAEP Annual Meeting**
National Association of Environmental Professional
PO Box 2086
Bowie, MD 20718-2086
301-860-1140
888-251-9902; Fax: 301-860-1141
www.naep.org
Sandi Worthman, Administrator
Learn unbiased information on environmental practices.
Frequency: Spring

8137 **NALGEP Annual Meetings**
National Association of Local Government
1333 New Hampshire Avenue NW
Washington, DC 20036
202-638-6254; Fax: 202-393-2866
nalgep@spiegelmcd.com
Kenneth Brown, Executive Director
David Dickson, Project Manager
Discussion of congressional issues
Frequency: Regional Workshops

8138 **NALMS Symposium**
North American Lake Management Society
4513 Vernon Boulevard, Suite 100
PO Box 5443
Madison, WI 53705-443
608-233-2836; Fax: 608-233-3186
www.nalms.org
Bev Clark, President
Reesa Evans, Secretary
Linda Green, Treasurer
A collection of professional presentations, general workshops and non-stop discussions on managing lakes and reservoirs. Vendors are present with the latest lake management tools displayed. Scientific and environmental minds will offer a variety of relevant topical subject matter to be covered in breakout educational sessions, and networking opportunities will allow for collaboration with lake property association members and other interested parties.
1700 Members
Frequency: Annual/October
Founded in 1980

8139 **NAPE**
Society of Exploration Geophysicists
8801 South Yale
Suite 500
Tulsa, OK 74137-3575
918-497-5500; Fax: 918-497-5557
www.napeexpo.com
Facebook, Twitter, LinkedIn
Mary Fleming, Executive Director
Vladimir Grechka, Editor
Provides a marketplace for the buying, selling and trading of oil and gas products and producing properties via exhibit booths. Brings prospects and producing properties, capital formation, services and technologies all together in one location, creating an environment to establish strategic alliances for doing business and initiating purchases and trades.
Founded in 1930

8140 **NEHA Annual Educational Conference and Exhibition**
National Environmental Health Association
720 S Colorado Boulevard
Suite 970-S
Denver, CO 80246-1925
303-756-9090; Fax: 303-691-9490
staff@neha.org
www.neha.org
Toni Roland, Conference Coordinator
Kim Brandow, Managing Director
Larry Marcum, Managing Director
Bob Custard, Manager
Jill Cruickshank, Communications Manager
The National Environmental Health Association (NEHA) is a unique organization representing all professionals in environmental health. NEHA offers credentials, publications, training, Journal of Environmental Health, and discounts for members. Each year NEHA conducts the Annual Educational Conference and Exhibition, this year it will be at the Minneapolis Hilton in Minneapolis, MN.
2000 Attendees
Frequency: June-July

8141 **NEHA Annual Meeting**
National Conference of Local Environmental Health
c/o NEHA, 720 S Colorado Boulevard
South Tower, Suite 970
Denver, CO 80246-1925
303-756-9090; Fax: 303-691-9490
nfabian@neha.org
http://www.neha.org
Nelson E Fabian, Executive Director
Held with the National Environmental Health Association.
Frequency: June

8142 **NESHTA Annual Meetings**
National Environmental, Safety and Health Training
PO Box 10321
Phoenix, AZ 85064-0321
602-956-6099; Fax: 602-956-6399
info@neshta.org
www.neshta.org
Charles L Richardson, Executive Director
Joan J Jennings, Manager Association Services
Suzanne Lanctot, Manager Certification/Membership
The network for academic, government, industrial, utility and consulting trainers and training managers responsible for protecting public health, workers, and our physical environment.
Frequency: June

8143 **NGWA Ground Water Summit & GWPC Spring Meeting**
Renewable Natural Resources Foundation
5430 Grosvenor Ln
Bethesda, MD 20814-2193
301-493-9101; Fax: 301-493-6148
info@rnrf.org
www.rnrf.org
Howard N. Rosen, Chairman
Richard A. Engberg, Vice-Chairman
Robert D. Day, Executive Director
Innovate and Integrate.
14 Members
Founded in 1972

8144 **NIWR Annual Conference**
National Institutes for Water Resources
47 Harkness Road
Pelham, MA 10002
413-253-5686; Fax: 413-253-1309
tracy@uidaho.edu
Jeffery Allen, President
Reagan Waskom, President-Elect
John Tracy, Secretary-Treasurer
Water Resource Institute directors and associate directors are invited to join for the annual meeting.
54 Members
Founded in 1974

8145 **NORA Semi-Annual Meetings**
NORA: Association of Responsible Recyclers
5965 Amber Ridge Road
Haymarket, VA 20169
703-753-4277; Fax: 703-753-2445
sparker@noranews.org
www.noranews.org
Scott D Parker, Executive Director
Jim Letteney, Vice President
The liquid recycling industry's premier networking and education event.
Frequency: May, November

8146 **NREP Annual Meetings**
National Registry of Environmental Professionals
PO Box 2099
Glenview, IL 60025
847-724-6631; Fax: 847-724-4223
nrep@nrep.org
www.nrep.org
Richard A Young, PhD, Executive Director
Certification preparatory workshops, technical papers and special seminars.
1000 Attendees
Frequency: Semi-Annual
Mailing list available for rent

8147 **National Environmental Balancing Bureau Meeting**
National Environmental Balancing Bureau
8575 Grovemont Circle
Gaithersburg, MD 20877-4121
301-977-3698; Fax: 301-977-9589
Michael Dolim, VP
Annual meeting and exhibits of testing and balancing equipment, supplies and services.

8148 **National Fish & Wildlife Conservation Congress**
Association of Fish & Wildlife Agencies
444 N Capitol St NW
Suite 725
Washington, DC 20001-1553
202-624-7890; Fax: 202-624-7891
info@fishwildlife.org
www.fishwildlife.org
Facebook, Twitter
Jon Gassett, President
Jeff Vonk, Vice President
Dave Chanda, Secretary/ Treasurer
Curtis Taylor, Past President
Bring together leading fish and wildlife scientists, government leaders, federal, provincial, state and local fish and wildlife agencies, conservation organizations and anglers and hunters to participate in discussions and debates about the future of fish and wildlife resources in North America.
Founded in 1902

8149 **National Flood Risk Management; Flood Risk Summit**
Association of State Floodplain Managers
2809 Fish Hatchery Rd
Suite 204
Madison, WI 53713-5020
608-274-0123; Fax: 608-274-0696
Larry@floods.org

www.floods.org
Facebook

Sally McConkey, Chair
William Nechamen, Vice Chair
Alan J. Giles, Secretary
John V. Crofts, Treasurer

Invitation-only. Soliciting feedback and providing updates to local, state, regional, and federal officials and the private sector on vital national policies currently under construction at the Federal level.
6500 Members
Founded in 1977

8150 National FloodProofing Conference and Exposition Levees and Beyond
Association of State Floodplain Managers
2809 Fish Hatchery Rd
Suite 204
Madison, WI 53713-5020

608-274-0123; Fax: 608-274-0696
Larry@floods.org
www.floods.org
Facebook

Sally McConkey, Chair
William Nechamen, Vice Chair
Alan J. Giles, Secretary
John V. Crofts, Treasurer

Making Wise Choices Highlighting the various floodproofing methods, products, techniques, programs, funding sources, and issues that have developed. Showcasing the state-of-the-art in materials, services, equipment, accessories and techniques.
6500 Members
Founded in 1977

8151 National Planning Conference
Renewable Natural Resources Foundation
5430 Grosvenor Ln
Bethesda, MD 20814-2193

301-493-9101; Fax: 301-493-6148
info@rnrf.org
www.rnrf.org

Howard N. Rosen, Chairman
Richard A. Engberg, Vice-Chairman
Robert D. Day, Executive Director

Hosted by the American Planning Association.
14 Members
Founded in 1972

8152 National Quail Symposium
Wildlife Habitat Council
8737 Colesville Road
Suite 800
Silver Spring, MD 20910

301-588-8994; Fax: 301-588-4629
whc@wildlifehc.org
www.wildlifehc.org
Facebook, YouTube

Greg Cekander, Chairman
Lawrence A Selzer, Vice Chairman
Kevin Butt, Secretary-Treasurer

Highlight the diversity in conservation of quails. Serve as an excellent venue to publish current research and advance quail conservation.
120+ Members
Founded in 1988

8153 National Real Estate Environmental Conference
National Society of Environmental Consultants
PO Box 12528
San Antonio, TX 78212-0528

210-225-2897
800-486-3676; Fax: 956-225-8450

Annual conference and exhibits related to the environmentally responsible use of real estate.

8154 National Stormwater Symposium
Water Environment Federation
601 Wythe St.
Alexandria, VA 22314

800-666-0206; Fax: 703-684-2492
inquiry@wef.org
www.wef.org
Facebook, Twitter

Walt Marlowe, Executive Director
Tim Williams, Deputy Executive Director
Penny Young, Chief Financial Officer

Designed to expand technical knowledge of professionals involved with stormwater management.
79 Members
ISSN: 1044-9943
Founded in 1928

8155 National Water Monitoring Conference
Renewable Natural Resources Foundation
5430 Grosvenor Ln
Bethesda, MD 20814-2193

301-493-9101; Fax: 301-493-6148
info@rnrf.org
www.rnrf.org

Howard N. Rosen, Chairman
Richard A. Engberg, Vice-Chairman
Robert D. Day, Executive Director

National forum provides an exceptional opportunity for federal, state, local, tribal, volunteer, academic, private, and other water stakeholders to exchange information and technology related to water monitoring, assessment, research, protection, restoration, and management, as well as to develop new skills and professional networks.
14 Members
Founded in 1972

8156 North American Environmental Field Conferences & Expositions
1230 Lincoln Drive
Carbondale, IL 62901

618-453-7809
aih@engr.siu.edu
www.aihydrology.org

Emitt C. Witt, III, President
Marzi Sharfaei, Secretary
T. Allen J. Gookin, Treasurer

Interactive indoor workshops, presented by some of the world's foremost authorities in the field, discussing cutting-edge field-based technologies and methods for environmental site characterization, sampling monitoring and remediation. Hands-on interactive outdoor workshops and equipment demos featuring the latest environmental field methods and equipment.
1000 Members
Founded in 1981

8157 North American Wildlife and Natural Resources Conference
Wildlife Management Institute
1101 14th Street NW
Suite 801
Washington, DC 20005

202-371-1808; Fax: 202-408-5059
www.wildlifemanagementinstitute.org

Meeting the challenges of modern conservation. Industry leaders dedicated to the conservation, enhancement and management of North America's wildlife and other natural resources.

8158 Ocean Sciences Meeting
Renewable Natural Resources Foundation
5430 Grosvenor Ln
Bethesda, MD 20814-2193

301-493-9101; Fax: 301-493-6148
info@rnrf.org
www.rnrf.org

Howard N. Rosen, Chairman
Richard A. Engberg, Vice-Chairman
Robert D. Day, Executive Director

Largest worldwide conference in the geophysical sciences, attracting Earth and space scientists, educators, students and policy makers. Meeting showcases current scientific theory focused on discoveries that will benefit humanity and ensure a sustainable future for our planet.
14 Members
Founded in 1972

8159 Oceans MTS/IEEE Conference
Marine Technology Society
1100 H St., Nw
Suite LL-100
Washington, DC 20005

202-717-8705; Fax: 202-347-4302
membership@mtsociety.org
www.mtsociety.org
Facebook, Twitter, LinkedIn

Jerry Boatman, President
Drew Michel, President-Elect
Jerry Wilson, VP of Industry and Technology
Jill Zande, VP of Education and Research
Justin Manley, VP of Gov. & Public Affairs

The major international forum for scientists, engineers, and responsible ocean users to present the latest research results, ideas, developments, and applications in Oceanic Engineering and Marine Technology.
2M Members
Founded in 1963

8160 Offshore Technology Conference
Marine Technology Society
1100 H St., Nw
Suite LL-100
Washington, DC 20005

202-717-8705; Fax: 202-347-4302
membership@mtsociety.org
www.mtsociety.org
Facebook, Twitter, LinkedIn

Jerry Boatman, President
Drew Michel, President-Elect
Jerry Wilson, VP of Industry and Technology
Jill Zande, VP of Education and Research
Justin Manley, VP of Gov. & Public Affairs

The world's foremost event for the development of offshore resources in the fields of drilling, exploration, production and environmental protection. A worldwide forum for the exchange of technical information vital to exploration and development of ocean resources.
2M Members
Founded in 1963

8161 Plant Growth Regulation Society of America Annual Conference
Rhone-Poulenc, Ag Company
1018 Duke Street
Alexandria, VA 22314

703-836-4606; Fax: 706-883-8215
Facebook, Twitter

Dr Eric A Curry, President
Dr Louise Ferguson, VP
Dr Ed Stover, Secretary

Highlights the latest in basic and applied research in plant growth regulation including hormone binding, stress physiology and plant growth regulator application.
325 Members
Founded in 1973

8162 Public Works Expo
American Public Works Association

1200 Main Street
Suite 1400
Kansas City, MO 64105-2100

816-472-6100
800-848-APWA; Fax: 816-472-1610
www.apwa.net

Scott Grayson, Executive Director
Lysa Byous, Meeting Planner & Exhibit Manager

Offers the benefit of a variety of educational sessions, depth of the exhibit program and endless opportunities for networking. The latest cutting-edge technologies, managerial techniques and regulatory trends designed to keep you focused on the right solutions at the right time.
Frequency: Annual/September
ISSN: 0092-4873

8163 **Residuals and Biosolids Conference**
Water Environment Federation
601 Wythe St.
Alexandria, VA 22314

800-666-0206; Fax: 703-684-2492
inquiry@wef.org
www.wef.org
Facebook, Twitter

Walt Marlowe, Executive Director
Tim Williams, Deputy Executive Director
Penny Young, Chief Financial Officer

Highlights beneficial reuse options, science, and technologies currently available to leverage biosolids as a valuable resource.
79 Members
ISSN: 1044-9943
Founded in 1928

8164 **SEG Annual Meeting**
Society of Exploration Geophysicists
PO Box 702740
Tulsa, OK 74170-2740

918-497-5500; Fax: 918-497-5557
web@seg.org
www.seg.org

Mary Fleming, Executive Director
Vladimir Grechka, Editor

The world's largest oil, energy and mineral exposition showcasing cutting-edge technology for use in exploration and associated industries. It is the premier venue for individuals to meet and discuss new geophysical technologies and their uses.
9300 Attendees
Frequency: October

8165 **SER Annual Meeting**
Society for Ecological Restoration
285 West 18th Street #1
Tucson, AZ 85701

520-622-5485; Fax: 520-622-5491
info@ser.org
www.ser.org

Mary Kay C LeFevour, Executive Director
Jane Cripps, Membership
Julie St John, Communications
Dennis Martinez, Founder
Val Schaefer, Secretary

Provides members (and non-members) with the opportunity to exchange ideas and information, participate in activities such as workshops and field trips, reconnect with friends and colleagues, and make new acquaintances.
Frequency: Fall

8166 **SER World Conference on Ecological Restoration**
Society for Ecological Restoration
1017 O Street NW
Washington, DC 20001

202-299-9518; Fax: 270-626-5485
info@ser.org
www.ser.org

Steve Whisenant, Chair
Cara R. Nelson, Vice Chair
Mary Travaglini, Treasurer
Alan Unwin, Secretary

Provide members and non-members with the opportunity to exchange ideas and information, participate in activities such as workshops and field trips, reconnect with friends and colleeagues, and make new acquaintances.
Frequency: Semi-Annual

8167 **SETAC Annual Meeting**
Society of Environmental Toxicology and Chemistry
1010 N 12th Street
Pensacola, FL 32501-3367

850-469-1500; Fax: 850-469-9778
www.setac.org

Rodney Parrish, Executive Director
Greg Schifer, Manager

Information and collaboration on environmental toxicology and chemistry.
Frequency: Fall

8168 **SHE Bi-Ennial Meetings**
Society for Human Ecology
College of the Atlantic
105 Eden Street
Bar Harbor, ME 04609-0180

207-288-5015; Fax: 207-288-3780
www.societyforhumanecology.org

Barbara Carter, Assistant to Executive Director

Brings together scholars and practitioners associated with the study and practice of human ecology because of the importance of the disciplines' philosophy and applications in developing mutually beneficial solutions for society and the environment. A platform for sharing knowledge on present status and approaches for sustainable development.

8169 **SOCMA Annual Meeting**
Synthetic Organic Chemical Manufacturers Assn
1850 M Street NW
Suite 700
Washington, DC 20036

202-721-4100; Fax: 202-296-8120
info@socma.com
www.socma.com

Joseph Acker, President
Vivian Diko, Executive Assistant & CEO
Charlene Patterson, Director Human Resources

Industry leaders come together.
Frequency: Early Spring

8170 **SOEH Annual Meeting**
Society for Occupational and Environmental Health
6728 Old McLean Village Drive
McLean, VA 22101

703-556-9222; Fax: 703-556-8729

George K Degnon, CAE, Executive Director

Topic will be international aspects of pesticide exposure and health, and key interest areas for presentations and posters will be; chronic health effects from pesticide exposure, agricultural worker surveillance and biomonitoring studies, good models of integrated pesticide management and involvement of community members, and much more.
Frequency: Spring

8171 **Science, Politics, and Policy: Environmental Nexus**
National Association of Environmental Professional
PO Box 460
Collingswood, NJ 08108

856-283-7816; Fax: 856-210-1619
naep@bowermanagementservices.com
www.naep.org
Facebook, LinkedIn

Paul Looney, President
Harold Draper, Vice President
Joseph F. Musil Jr., Treasurer
Robert P. Morris Jr., Secretary

NEPA and Decision Making, program on what happens after NEPA documents are prepared, and how that information is useful to their preparation. Also a program on Advance Topics in Visual Resource Impact Assessment.

8172 **SeminarFest**
American Society of Safety Engineers
1800 E Oakton Street
Des Plaines, IL 60018

847-699-2929; Fax: 847-768-3434
customerservice@asse.org
www.asse.org
Facebook

Terrie S. Norris, President
Richard A. Pollock, President Elect
Kathy Seabrook, Senior Vice President
Fred J. Fortman, Jr., Secretary & Executive Director
James D. Smith, Vice President, Finance

Pass your ASP, CSP, OHST and CHST exams with confidence by taking our certification preparation workshops. Earn a certificate of completion in Safety Management & the Executive Program in Safety Management. Develop business acument, leadership and training skills. Measure safety effectiveness and review safety management approaches. Also participate in technical and topical seminars.
30000 Members
Founded in 1911

8173 **Smart Energy Summit**
Parks Associates
5310 Harvest Hill Road
Suite 235, Lock Box 162
Dallas, TX 75230-5805

972-490-1113
800-727-5711
info@parksassociates.com
www.parksassociates.com

Tricia Parks, Founder and CEO
Stuart Sikes, President
Farhan Abid, Research Analyst
Bill Ablondi, Director, Home Systems Research
John Barrett, Director of Research

Smart Energy Summit is an annual three-day event that examines the opportunities and technical business requirements inherent in the consumer programs and advanced systems and services made possible by Smart Grids and Residential Energy Management solutions.
Frequency: Annual
Founded in 1986

8174 **Soil and Water Conservation Society Annual International Conference**
Soil and Water Conservation Society
945 SW Ankeny Rd.
Ankeny, IA 50021

515-289-2331; Fax: 515-289-1227
www.swsc.org

Clare Lindahl, Chief Executive Officer
Courtney Allen, Event/Professional Development Dir.

Catherine DeLong, Special Projects/Policy Director

Explores ways to improve the linkages among conservation science, policy and application at local, national, and international scales. The conference will provide participants an opportunity to teach skills, learn techniques, compare successes, and improve understanding.
Frequency: Annual/July

8175 **Spatial Cognition for Architectural Design Symposium**
Environmental Design Research Association
1760 Old Meadow Road
Suite 500
McLean, VA 22102

703-506-2895; Fax: 703-506-3266
www.edra.org
Facebook, Twitter, LinkedIn

Nick Watkins, Chair
Mallika Bose, Chair-Elect
Vikki Chanse, Secretary
Shauna Mallory-Hill, Treasurer
Deni Ruggeri, Executive Director

Addresses the theoretical and methodological achievements of the cognitive and computational disciplines in the domain of architectural design. A dialogue between scientists from design research and educational disciplines is sought with the aim to identify how such application of knowledge may provide real benefit for the theory and professional practice of architectural design.
700 Members
Founded in 1968

8176 **Sustainability in Public Works Conference**
2345 Grand Blvd
Suite 700
Kansas City, MO 64108-2625

816-472-6100
800-848-2792; Fax: 816-472-1610
www.apwa.net
Facebook, Twitter, YouTube

Diane M. Linderman, President
Elizabeth Treadway, President Elect
Richard F. Stinson, Director, Region I
Edward A. Gottko, Director, Region II
William Barney Mills, Jr., Director, Region III

International educational and professional association of public agencies, private sector companies, and individuals dedicated to providing high quality public works, goods and services. APWA provides a forum brings important public works-related topics to public attention in local, state, and federal areas. Mailing list for members only.
26000 Members
Founded in 1937

8177 **Take It Back**
Raymond Communications
5111 Berwin Road
#115
College Park, MD 20740

301-345-4237; Fax: 301-345-4768
www.raymond.com

Michele Raymond, Publisher/Editor

The conference brings in the top recycling policy experts from around the world to brief customers. We also have practical sessions with case histories on such issues as packaging design, design for environment in electronics, and lifecycle issues.
150 Attendees
Frequency: March
Founded in 1996

8178 **Teaming With Wildlife Fly-In Day**
Association of Fish & Wildlife Agencies
444 N Capitol St NW
Suite 725
Washington, DC 20001-1553

202-624-7890; Fax: 202-624-7891
info@fishwildlife.org
www.fishwildlife.org
Facebook, Twitter

Jon Gassett, President
Jeff Vonk, Vice President
Dave Chanda, Secretary/ Treasurer
Curtis Taylor, Past President

Join in supporting funding for the State & Tribal Wildlife Grants Program, the nation's CORE program for preventing fish and wildlife from becoming endangered in every state and territory.
Founded in 1902

8179 **The Utility Management Conference**
Water Environment Federation
601 Wythe St.
Alexandria, VA 22314

800-666-0206; Fax: 703-684-2492
inquiry@wef.org
www.wef.org
Facebook, Twitter

Walt Marlowe, Executive Director
Tim Williams, Deputy Executive Director
Penny Young, Chief Financial Officer

Water and wastewater managers and professionals will gather to be part of the latest approaches, practices, and techniques in all aspects of utility management.
79 Members
ISSN: 1044-9943
Founded in 1928

8180 **Thermal Treatment Technologies/ Hazardous Waste Combustors**
A&WMA
420 Fort Duquesne Boulevard
One Gateway Center, 3rd Floor
Pittsburgh, PA 15222-1435

412-652-2458; Fax: 412-232-3450
info@awma.org
www.awma.org
Facebook, Twitter, LinkedIn

Jeffry Muffat, President
Merlyn L. Hough, President Elect
Mike Kelly, Secretary/ Executive Director
Amy Gilligan, Treasurer
Dallas Baker, Vice President

Brings together industry experts from around the world to share experiences, lessons learned and new ideas on how to best operate thermal treatment facilities.
9000 Members
Founded in 1907

8181 **Topical Meeting on the Technology of Fusion Energy (TOFE)**
555 N Kensington Ave
La Grange Park, IL 60526-5592

708-352-6611
800-323-3044; Fax: 708-352-0499
advertising@ans.org
www.ans.org
Facebook, Twitter, LinkedIn

Jack Tuohy, Executive Director
James S Tulenko, VP
William F Naughton, Treasurer

Providing a forum for sharing the exciting new progress that has been made in fusion research as well as presenting the future of national and worldwide fusion programs. Draws together scientists, engineers, and students from various countries.
10500 Members
Founded in 1954

8182 **Underwater Intervention Conference**
Marine Technology Society
1100 H St., Nw
Suite LL-100
Washington, DC 20005

202-717-8705; Fax: 202-347-4302
membership@mtsociety.org
www.mtsociety.org
Facebook, Twitter, LinkedIn

Jerry Boatman, President
Drew Michel, President-Elect
Jerry Wilson, VP of Industry and Technology
Jill Zande, VP of Education and Research
Justin Manley, VP of Gov. & Public Affairs

The conference is of interest to a number of diverse marine industries, including offshore oil and gas, marine construction, shipwreck exploration, ocean mining and marine salvage. Presentation tracks include cable, remote intervention, commercial diving, and shipwreck salvage, among others.
2M Members
Founded in 1963

8183 **Utility Working Conference and Vendor Technology Expo**
555 N Kensington Ave
La Grange Park, IL 60526-5592

708-352-6611
800-323-3044; Fax: 708-352-0499
advertising@ans.org
www.ans.org
Facebook, Twitter, LinkedIn

Jack Tuohy, Executive Director
James S Tulenko, VP
William F Naughton, Treasurer

Dedicated to identifying innovations in all areas of nuclear power plant operations. The functional area tracks/ sessions bring together professionals with different perspectives focusing on current issues and innovations.
10500 Members
Founded in 1954

8184 **WSSA Annual Meeting**
Weed Science Society of America
PO Box 7050
Lawrence, KS 66044

785-429-9622
800-627-0629; Fax: 785-843-1274
www.wssa.net

Rhonda Green, Registration Coordinator

Usually held during the first full week of February in the United States or Canada. These Meetings provide a venue for the exchange of research and educational ideas and for discussion and activity on society business.
1M Attendees
Frequency: February
Founded in 1956

8185 **Water Innovation Summit**
Water Environment Federation
601 Wythe St.
Alexandria, VA 22314

800-666-0206; Fax: 703-684-2492
inquiry@wef.org
www.wef.org
Facebook, Twitter

Walt Marlowe, Executive Director
Tim Williams, Deputy Executive Director
Penny Young, Chief Financial Officer

Summit is formed of industry leaders, entrepreneurs, investors, philanthropic partners, and government officials.
79 Members
ISSN: 1044-9943
Founded in 1928

8186 **Waterpower XIII**
HCI Publications
410 Archibald Street
Kansas City, MO 64111-3001

816-931-1311; Fax: 816-931-2015
www.hcipub.com

Leslie Eden, Manager

The conference offers industry professionals a forum in which to share new ideas and approaches to move hydropower forward as the world's leading source of renewable energy. Containing 120 booths.
1,000 Attendees
Frequency: July-August

8187 **West Energy Conference & Expo**
Association of Energy Engineers
3168 Mercer University Drive
Atlanta, GA 30341

770-447-5083
www.aeecenter.org

Albert Thumann, Executive Director

Bringing together commercial, industrial, and governmental energy professionals from the West Coast and Northwest regions of the United States to discuss key energy issues, energy-efficient solutions, new energy initiatives, and developments in clean energy technologies.
Frequency: Annual/June

8188 **Wildlife Habitat Council Annual Symposium**
Wildlife Habitat Council
8737 Colesville Road
Suite 800
Silver Spring, MD 20910

301-588-8994; Fax: 301-588-4629
whc@wildlifehc.org
www.wildlifehc.org

Bill Howard, President
Martha Gruelle, Program Manager
Linda Duvall, Accounting Manager
Tiffany Msonthi, Executive Assistant

The annual symposium brings together corporate, government and conservation leaders from around the globe for informative sessions, exhibits and field trips on environmental stewardship.
400 Attendees
Frequency: November

8189 **Wildlife Society Annual Conference**
Wildlife Society
5410 Grosvenor Lane
Suite 200
Bethesda, MD 20814-2144

301-897-9770; Fax: 301-530-2471
tws@wildlife.org
www.wildlife.org

Lisa Moll, Program Assistant/Membership

Hear from industry leaders to discuss new and evolving trends and innovations in wildlife management and conservation, learn about the latest research from original research and techniques presented by wildlife professionals, connect with colleagues at the largest gathering of wildlife professionals in North America.
1200 Attendees
Frequency: September
Founded in 1994

8190 **World Energy Conference & Expo**
Association of Energy Engineers
3168 Mercer University Drive
Atlanta, GA 30341

770-447-5083
www.aeecenter.org

Albert Thumann, Executive Director

A comprehensive forum where participants can fully assess the big picture and see exactly how the economic and market forces, new technologies, regulatory developments and industry trends all merge to shape their critical decisions on their organizations' energy and economic future.
Mailing list available for rent

Directories & Databases

8191 **ACCA Membership Directory**
Air Conditioning Contractors of America
2800 S Shirlington Road
Suite 300
Arlington, VA 22206

703-575-4477
membership@acca.org
www.acca.org
Facebook, Twitter, LinkedIn, YouTube

Barton James, President & CEO
Samuel Awotwi, Director of Finance
Christine Gibson, VP, Marketing & Partnerships
Sean Robertson, VP, Membership/Business Operations

ACCA is a non-profit association serving the HVACR community, working to promote professional contracting, energy efficiency, and healthy, comfortable indoor environments.

8192 **ACSH Media Update**
American Council on Science and Health
1995 Broadway
2nd Floor
New York, NY 10023-5882

212-362-7044; Fax: 212-362-4919
acsh@acsh.org
www.acsh.org

Elizabeth Whelan, President
Jeff Stier, Director of Publications
Alyssa Pelish, Director of Publications
Gilbert Ross, Executive Director
Frequency: Semi-Annual

8193 **Aboveground Storage Tank Management and SP CC Guide**
ABS Group
PO Box 846304
Dallas, TX 75284-6304

FAX 301-921-0264

8194 **Acid Rain**
Watts, Franklin
90 Sherman Turnpike
Danbury, CT 06816

203-797-3500
800-621-1115; Fax: 203-797-3657

Lists over 4,000 citations, with abstracts, to the worldwide literature on the sources of acid rain and its effects on the environment.

8195 **Alternative Energy Network Online**
Environmental Information Networks
119 S Fairfax Street
Alexandria, VA 22314-3301

703-548-1202

Reports on news of all energy sources designed as alternatives to conventional fossil fuels, including wind, solar and alcohol fuels.
Frequency: Full-text

8196 **American Recycling Market: Directory/Reference Manual**
Recycling Data Management Corporation
PO Box 577
Ogdensburg, NY 13669-0577

315-785-9072

Offers information, in three volumes, encompassing over 15,000 recycling companies and centers.
Cost: $175.00
1000 Pages
Frequency: Annual
ISSN: 0885-2537

8197 **Business and the Environment: A Resource Guide**
Island Press
1718 Connecticut Ave NW
Suite 300
Washington, DC 20009-1148

202-232-7933; Fax: 202-234-1328
info@islandpress.org
www.islandpress.org

Chuck Savitt, President
Allison Pennell, Editor

List of approximately 185 business and environmental educators working to integrate environmental issues into management, research, education and practices.
Cost: $60.00

8198 **Canadian Environmental Directory**
Grey House Publishing
4919 Route 22
PO Box 56
Amenia, NY 12501

518-789-8700
800-562-2139; Fax: 845-373-6390
books@greyhouse.com
www.greyhouse.com
Facebook, Twitter

Leslie Mackenzie, Publisher
Tannys Williams, Managing Editor

Canada's most complete national listing of environmental associations and organizations, government regulators and purchasing groups, product and service companies, special libraries, and more.
Cost: $315.00
900 Pages
ISBN: 1-592372-24-9
Founded in 1981

8199 **Carcinogenicity Information Database of Environmental Substances**
Technical Database Services
10 Columbus Circle
New York, NY 10019-1203

212-556-0001; Fax: 212-556-0036

This database contains test results on the carcinogenic and mutagenic effects of approximately 1000 substances of environmental or health concerns.

8200 **Conservation Directory**
National Wildlife Federation
11100 Wildlife Center Dr
Reston, VA 20190-5362

703-438-6000
800-822-9919; Fax: 703-438-3570
info@nwf.org
www.nwf.org

Mark Van Putten, CEO

Federal agencies, national and international organizations and state government agencies.
Cost: $20.00
500 Pages
Frequency: Annual

8201 Department of Energy Annual Procurement and Financial Assistance Report
US Department of Energy
1000 Independence Ave SW
Washington, DC 20585-0001

202-586-5000; Fax: 202-586-0573
www.energy.gov

Mary Lein, Manager

Offers a list of universities, research centers and laboratories that represent the Department of Energy.
Frequency: Annual

8202 Directory of Environmental Websites: Online Micro Edition
US Environmental Directories
PO Box 65156
Saint Paul, MN 55165-0156

612-331-6050
www.geocities.com/usenvironmentaldirectories

Roger N McGrath, Publisher
John C Brainard, Editor

The Directory is a complete guide to the environmental movement on the Internet, provides a concise, practical listing of over 190 of the major Internet addresses of the Environmental Movement. A clear, understandable and comprehensive guide to national and international environmental organizations, directories, networks and services on the Internet.
Cost: $25.75
48 Pages
ISSN: 1096-3316
Founded in 1998

8203 Directory of International Periodicals & Newsletters on Built Environments
Division of Mineral Resources
PO Box 3667
Charlottesville, VA 22903-0667

434-951-6341; Fax: 434-951-6365
www.ulrichsweb.com

Scott Richeson, Programs Director

More than 1,400 international periodicals and newsletters that cover architectural design and the building industry, and the aspects of the environment that deal with the industry are covered.
Cost: $6.00
29 Pages

8204 EDOCKET
Environmental Protection Agency
1200 Pennsylvania Avenue NW
Mail Code 3213A
Washington, DC 20460

202-260-2090; Fax: 202-566-0545
r9.info@epa.gov
www.epa.gov

An electronic public docket and on-line comment system designed to expand access to documents in EPA's major dockets.
Frequency: Full-text

8205 EH&S Compliance Auditing & Teaching Software Report
Donley Technology
PO Box 152
Colonial Beach, VA 22443-0152

804-224-9427
800-201-1595; Fax: 804-224-7958
donleytech@donleytech.com
www.donleytech.com

Elizabeth Donley, Editor

Profiles 25 software packages for achieving and maintaining compliance, including detailed product descriptions, tables comparing system features, and contact information.
Cost: $195.00
240 Pages
Frequency: Every 2 Years
ISBN: 1-891682-08-3
Founded in 1997
Printed in on matte stock

8206 EMS Membership Roster
Environmental Mutagen Society
1821 Michael Faraday Drive
Suite 300
Reston, VA 20190

703-438-8220; Fax: 703-438-3113
emshq@ems-us.org
www.ems-ph.org

Tonia Masson, Executive Director
Suzanne Morris, Secretary
Barbara Shane, Treasurer
Frequency: Irregular

8207 Ecology Abstracts
Cambridge Scientific Abstracts
7200 Wisconsin Ave
Suite 601
Bethesda, MD 20814-4890

301-961-6700
800-843-7751; Fax: 301-961-6790
www.csa.com

Andrew M Snyder, President
Theodore Caris, Publisher
Robert Hilton, Editor
Mark Furneaux, VP Marketing
Angela Hitti, Production Manager

This large database updated continuously, offers over 150,000 citations, with abstracts, to the worldwide literature available on ecology and the environment.
Cost: $945.00
Frequency: Monthly

8208 Education for the Earth: A Guide to Top Environmental Studies Programs
Peterson's Guides
202 Carnegie Center
#2123
Princeton, NJ 08540-6239

800-338-3282; Fax: 609-869-4531

Colleges and universities that offer programs in environment and conservation are listed.
Cost: $10.95
192 Pages

8209 Educational Communications
PO Box 351419
Los Angeles, CA 90035-9119

310-559-9160
ecnp@aol.com
www.ecoprojects.org

Nancy Pearlman, Editor/Executive Director
Environmental and humanitarian projects include: ECONEWS tv (over 600 documentaries available on dvd); Environmental Directions radio (over 2100 programs available on mp3); Ecology Center of Southern California Resources Library; Compendium Newsletter (bi-monthly); Humanity and the Planet (orphanage in Kenya); Earth Cultures (ethnic dance programs to schools, libraries and retirement homes); Project Ecotourism includes sustainability consultations.
Cost: $20.00
244 Pages
Frequency: Annual Paperback
Founded in 1957
Mailing list available for rent

8210 El Environmental Services Directory
Environmental Information Networks
7301 Ohms Lane
Suite 460
Eding, MN 55439

952-831-2473; Fax: 952-831-6550
customerservice@envirobiz.com
www.envirobiz.com

Cary Perket
James Rue, Secretary
Marshall Sanders, Manager
Bruce McGranahan, Director

Waste-handling facilities, transportation and spill response firms, laboratories and the broad scope of environmental services. Online versions are also available.
Cost: $1250.00
Frequency: Biennial
ISSN: 1053-475N
Founded in 1984

8211 Emergency Response Directory for Hazardous Materials Accidents
Odin Press
PO Box 536
New York, NY 10021-0011

212-605-0338

Pamela Lawrence, Editor

Over 1,000 federal, state and local governmental agencies, chemical manufacturers and transporters, hotlines and strike teams, burn care centers, civil defense and disaster centers and other organizations concerned with the containment and cleanup of chemical spills and other hazardous materials accidents.
Cost: $36.00
Frequency: Biennial

8212 Energy Statistics Spreadsheets
Institute of Gas Technology
1700 S Mount Prospect Rd
Des Plaines, IL 60018-1804

847-768-0664; Fax: 847-768-0669
www.gastechnology.org

Carol L Worster, Manager
Edward Johnston, Managing Director

The coverage of this database encompasses worldwide energy industry statistics, including production, consumption, reserves, imports and prices.

8213 Energy User News: Energy Technology Buyers Guide
Chilton Company
300 Park Ave
Suite 19
New York, NY 10022-7409

212-751-3596; Fax: 212-443-7701
www.chiltonfunds.com

Richard L Chilton Jr, Owner
Lisa Czachor, Director
Mary Morse, Senior Vice President

A list of about 1,500 manufacturers, dealers and distributors of energy conservation and used equipment.
Cost: $10.00
Frequency: Annual
Circulation: 40,000

8214 Environmental Bibliography
International Academy at Santa Barbara
5385 Hollister Avenue
#210
Santa Barbara, CA 93111

805-683-8889; Fax: 805-965-6071
info@iasb.org

Gloria Lindfield, Executive Assistant
Hilary Eastman, Manager
Tom Seidenstein, Chief Operating Officer

Over 615,000 citations are offered in this database, aimed at scientific, technical and popular

periodical literature dealing with the environment.
Cost: $1750.00
ISSN: 1053-1440
Founded in 1972

8215 **Environmental Cost Estimating Software Report**
Donley Technology
PO Box 152
Colonial Beach, VA 22443-0152
804-224-9427
800-201-1595; Fax: 804-224-7958
donleytech@donleytech.com
www.donleytech.com
Elizabeth Donley, Editor
John Donley, Editor
Profiles 20 software packages for estimating the cost of environmental projects, including detailed product descriptions, tables comparing system features, and contact information.
Cost: $195.00
162 Pages
ISBN: 1-891682-05-9
Founded in 1996
Printed in on matte stock

8216 **Environmental Health & Safety Dictionary**
ABS Group
PO Box 846304
Dallas, TX 75284-6304
FAX 301-921-0264
Lydia Simpson, Manager

8217 **Environmental Law Handbook**
ABS Group
PO Box 846304
Dallas, TX 75284-6304
FAX 301-921-0264

8218 **Environmental Protection Agency Headquarters Telephone Directory**
Environmental Protection Agency
1200 Pennsylvania Avenue NW
Pittsburgh, PA 15250-7954
412-442-4000; Fax: 202-512-2250
www.epa.gov/customerservice/phonebook
Ken Bowman, Executive Director
Directory of services and supplies to the industry.
Cost: $15.00
400 Pages

8219 **Environmental Resource Handbook**
Grey House Publishing
4919 Route 22
PO Box 56
Amenia, NY 12501
518-789-8700
800-562-2139; Fax: 845-373-6390
books@greyhouse.com
www.greyhouse.com
Facebook, Twitter
Leslie Mackenzie, Publisher
Richard Gottlieb, Editor
The most up-to-date and comprehensive source for Environmental Resources and Statistics. Included is contact information for resource listings in addition to statistics and rankings on hundreds of important topics such as recycling, air and water quality, climate, toxic chemicals and more.
Cost: $155.00
1200 Pages
ISBN: 1-592371-95-7
Founded in 1981

8220 **Environmental Resource Handbook - Online Database**
Grey House Publishing
4919 Route 22
PO Box 56
Amenia, NY 12501
518-789-8700
800-562-2139; Fax: 845-373-6390
gold@greyhouse.com
gold.greyhouse.com
Facebook, Twitter
Leslie Mackenzie, Publisher
Richard Gottlieb, Editor
With a subscription to Environmental Resource Handbook - Online Database, you'll have immediate access to over 7,000 associations, organizations & government agencies, awards & honors, conferences & trade shows, foundations & charities, national parks & wildlife refuges, research centers & educational programs, legal resources and much more.
Founded in 1981

8221 **Environmental Statutes**
Government Institutes
4 Research Place
Suite 200
Rockville, MD 20850-3226
301-921-2323; Fax: 301-921-0264
www.govinst.com
Two-volume set. Complete and exact text of the statues and amendments made by Congress concerning environmental law.
Cost: $125.00
1678 Pages
Frequency: Paperback
ISBN: 0-865879-33-8

8222 **Fibre Market News: Paper Recycling Markets Directory**
Recycling Media Group GIE Publishers
4012 Bridge Avenue
Cleveland, OH 44113-3320
216-961-4130
800-456-0707; Fax: 216-961-0364
www.giemedia.com
Dan Moreland, Executive Vice President
A list of over 2,000 dealers, brokers, packers and graders of paper stock in the United States and Canada.
Cost: $28.00
Frequency: Annual
Circulation: 3,000

8223 **Floodplain Management: State & Local Programs**
Association of State Floodplain Managers
2809 Fish Hatchery Rd
Suite 204
Fitchburg, WI 53713-5020
608-274-0123; Fax: 608-274-0696
memberhelp@floods.org
www.floods.org
Larry A Larson, Executive Director
Alison Stierli, Member Services Coordinator
Anita Larson, Member Services
Mark Riebau, Project Manager
Diane Brown, Manager
The most comprehensive source assembled to date, this report summarizes and analyzes various state and local programs and activities.
Cost: $25.00

8224 **Geothermal Progress Monitor**
Office of Geothermal Technologies EE-12
1000 Independence Avenue SW
Washington, DC 20585-0001
202-586-1361; Fax: 202-586-8185
Allan J Jelacic, Director
Lists of operating, planned and under construction geothermal electric generating plants; geothermal articles and publications; federal and state government employees active in geothermal energy development.
Frequency: Annual

8225 **Grey House Safety & Security Directory**
Grey House Publishing
4919 Route 22
PO Box 56
Amenia, NY 12501
518-789-8700
800-562-2139; Fax: 845-373-6390
books@greyhouse.com
www.greyhouse.com
Facebook, Twitter
Leslie Mackenzie, Publisher
Richard Gottlieb, Editor
Kristen Thatcher, Production Manager
Comprehensive guide to the safety and security industry, including articles, checklists, OSHA regulations and product listings. Focuses on creating and maintaining a safe and secure enviroment, and dealing specifically with hazardous materials, noise and vibration, workplace preparation and maintenance, electrical and lighting safety, fire and rescue and more.
Cost: $165.00
1600 Pages
ISBN: 1-592373-75-5
Founded in 1981

8226 **Handling Dyes Safely - A Guide for the Protection of Workers Handling Dyes**
ETAD North America
1850 M St NW
Suite 700
Washington, DC 20036-5810
202-721-4100; Fax: 202-296-8120
www.etad.com
Jill Aker, President

8227 **Hazardous Materials Guide**
JJ Keller
PO Box 368
Neenah, WI 54957-0368
920-722-2848
800-327-6868; Fax: 800-727-7516
contactus@jjkeller.com
www.jjkeller.com
Webb Shaw, Editor
A complete reference guide of hazardous materials regulations.

8228 **Hazardous Materials Information Resource System**
One Church Street
Suite 200
Rockville, MD 20850
301-577-1842; Fax: 301-738-2330
CAPT Michael J. Macinski, Commanding Officer
CAPT Robert W. Farr, Executive Officer
HMCM Robert E. Searles, II, Command Master Chief
The Hazardous Materials Information Resource System is a Department of Defense (DOD) automated system developed and maintained by the Defense Logistics Agency. HMIRS is the central repository for Material Safety Data Sheets (MSDS) for the United States Government military services and civil agencies.

8229 **Hazardous Waste Guide**
JJ Keller

PO Box 368
Neenah, WI 54957-0368
920-722-2848
800-327-6868; Fax: 800-727-7516
contactus@jjkeller.com
www.jjkeller.com

Webb Shaw, Editor

Contains word-for-word regulations.

8230 **Hydro Review: Industry Sourcebook Issue**
HCI Publications
410 Archibald St
Kansas City, MO 64111-3288
816-931-1311; Fax: 816-931-2015
www.hcipub.com

Leslie Eden, President

List of over 800 manufacturers and suppliers of products and services to the hydroelectric industry in the US and Canada.
Cost: $20.00
180 Pages
Frequency: Annual December
Circulation: 5000
Founded in 1984
Printed in 4 colors on glossy stock

8231 **IES Membership Directory**
International Ecotourism Society
733 15th Street NW
Suite 1000
Washington, DC 20005
202-547-9203; Fax: 202-387-7915
www.ecotourism.org

Martha Honey, Executive Director
Amos Bien, Director International Programs
Neal Inamdar, Director Finance/Administration
Frequency: Annual

8232 **International Directory of Human Ecologists**
Society for Human Ecology
College of the Atlantic
105 Eden Street
Bar Harbor, ME 04609-0180
207-288-5015; Fax: 207-288-3780
www.societyforhumanecology.org

Barbara Carter, Assistant to Executive Director
Frequency: Irregular

8233 **LEXIS Environmental Law Library**
Mead Data Central
9443 Springboro Pike
Dayton, OH 45401
888-223-6337; Fax: 518-487-3584
www.lexis-nexis.com

Andrew Prozes, CEO
Rebecca Schmitt, Chief Financial Officer

This database contains decisions related to environmental law from the Supreme Court and other legislative bodies.
Frequency: Full-text

8234 **NIWR Member Directory**
National Institutes for Water Resources
47 Harkness Road
Pelham, MA 10002
413-253-5686; Fax: 413-253-1309
godfrey@tei.umass.edu

Paul Joseph Godfrey, PhD, Executive Director

8235 **National Directory of Conservation Land Trusts**
Land Trust Alliance
1319 F Street NW
Suite 501
Washington, DC 20004-1106
202-638-4725; Fax: 202-638-4730
info@lta.org
www.lta.org

More than 1,200 nonprofit land conservation organizations at the local and regional levels are profiled.
Cost: $12.00
210 Pages
Frequency: Biennial

8236 **National Environmental Data Referral Service**
US National Environmental Data Referral Service
1825 Connecticut Avenue NW
Washington, DC 20235-0003
202-606-4089

More than 22,200 data resources that have available data on climatology and meteorology, ecology and pollution, geography, geophysics and geology, hydrology and limnology, oceanography and transmissions from remote sensing satellites.
Frequency: Quarterly

8237 **National Organic Directory**
Community Alliance with Family Farmers
PO Box 363
Davis, CA 95617-0363
530-756-8518
800-892-3832; Fax: 530-756-7857
info@caff.org
www.caff.org

Wriiten for all sectors of the booming organic food and fiber industry. Offers international listing with full contact information and extensive, cross-referenced index - Also provides regulatory updates, essays by industry leaders and other ressources.
Cost: $47.95
324 Pages
Frequency: Annual
Circulation: 2,500
ISBN: 1-891894-04-8
Founded in 1983

8238 **POWER**
US Department of Energy
Forrestal Building
5H - 021
Washington, DC 20585-0001
202-646-5095; Fax: 202-586-1605
www.eren.doe.gov

Timothy Unruh, Program Manager

A large database offering information on all forms of energy, including fossil, nuclear, solar, geothermal and electrical.

8239 **Pollution Abstracts**
Cambridge Scientific Abstracts
7200 Wisconsin Ave
Suite 601
Bethesda, MD 20814-4890
301-961-6700; Fax: 301-961-6790
www.csa.com

Andrew M Snyder, President
Ted Caris, Publisher
Evelyn Beck, Editor
Mark Furneaux, VP Marketing
Angela Hitti, Production Manager

This database offers information on environmental pollution research and related engineering studies.
Cost: $985.00
Frequency: Monthly

8240 **Public Citizen Organizations**
Public Citizen
215 Pennsylvania Ave SE
Suite 3
Washington, DC 20003-1188
202-544-4985; Fax: 202-547-7392

Bob Ritter, Manager
Patricia Lovera, Organizer
Ronald Taylor, Manager

We provide many publications regarding nuclear safety, nuclear waste, water, food, and energy deregulation.
Frequency: Annual

8241 **RIFM/FEMA Fragrance and Flavor Database**
Flavor & Extract Manufacturers Association
1620 I Street NW
Suite 925
Washington, DC 20006
202-293-5800; Fax: 202-462-8998
www.femaflavor.org
YouTube, RSS Feed

Ed R. Hays, Ph.D., President
George C. Robinson, III, President Elect
Mark Scott, Treasurer
Arthur Schick, VP & Secretary
John Cox, Executive Director

The Database currently contains over 50,000 references and more than 103,000 human health and environmental studies.
Frequency: Annual
Founded in 1909

8242 **Recycling Today: Recycling Products & Services Buyers Guide**
Recycling Today GIE Publishers
4012 Bridge Avenue
Cleveland, OH 44113-3320
216-961-4130; Fax: 216-961-0364
http://www.recyclingtoday.com

Richard Foster, President
James Keefe, Publisher
Mark Phillips, Editor
Rosalie Slusher, Circulation Director
Jami Childs, Production Manager

Directory of services and supplies to the industry.
Cost: $19.95
Frequency: Annual
Circulation: 22,000

8243 **Salem Press Online Platform**
Grey House Publishing
4919 Route 22
PO Box 56
Amenia, NY 12501
800-221-1592; Fax: 201-968-0511
csr@salempress.com
online.salempress.com

The new Salem Press platform houses more than 500 titles including all of Salem's Health, Literature, History and Science titles in addition to select titles from the Grey House Publishing and H.W. Wilson product lines. Online access is free with each print purchase and includes an unlimited number of simultaneous users and remote access.

8244 **Using Multiobjective Management to Reduce Flood Losses in Your Watershed**
Association of State Floodplain Managers

2809 Fish Hatchery Rd
Suite 204
Fitchburg, WI 53713-5020

608-274-0123; Fax: 608-274-0696
memberhelp@floods.org
www.floods.org

Larry A Larson, Executive Director
Alison Stierli, Manager
Diane Brown, Manager

Introduction to multiobjective management and planning process that helps a community select suitable flood loss reduction measures.
Cost: $15.00

8245 **Waste Manifest Software Report**
Donley Technology
PO Box 152
Colonial Beach, VA 22443-0152

804-224-9427
800-201-1595; Fax: 804-224-7958
donleytech@donleytech.com
www.donleytech.com

Elizabeth Donley, Editor

Profiles 30 software packages for solid and hazardous waste management, including detailed product descriptions, tables comparing system features, and contact information.
Cost: $97.50
118 Pages
ISBN: 1-891682-01-6
Founded in 1996
Printed in on matte stock

8246 **Water Environment and Technology Buyers Guide**
Water Environment Federation
601 Wythe St.
Alexandria, VA 22314

800-666-0206; Fax: 703-684-2400
inquiry@wef.org
www.wef.org

Walt Marlowe, Executive Director
Tim Williams, Deputy Executive Director
Penny Young, Chief Financial Officer

Offers listings of the Water Environment Federation and consultant members.
Cost: $28.00
Frequency: Annual
ISSN: 1044-9943

8247 **Weather America**
Grey House Publishing
4919 Route 22
PO Box 56
Amenia, NY 12501

518-789-8700
800-562-2139; Fax: 845-373-6390
books@greyhouse.com
www.greyhouse.com
Facebook, Twitter

Leslie Mackenzie, Publisher
Richard Gottlieb, Editor

Provides extensive climatological data for over 4,000 places throughout the United States - states, counties, cities, and towns. Included are rankings across the US for precipitation, snowfall, fog, humidity, wind speed and more.
Cost: $175.00
2020 Pages
ISBN: 1-891482-29-7
Founded in 1981

8248 **Who's Who in Training**
National Environmental, Safety and Health Training
5320 N 16th Street
Suite 114
Phoenix, AZ 85016-3241

602-956-6099; Fax: 602-956-6399
info@neshta.org
www.neshta.org

Charles L Richardson, Executive Director
Joan J Jennings, Manager Association Services
Suzanne Lanctot, Manager Certification/Membership
Frequency: Annual

8249 **Wilderness Preservation: A Reference Handbook**
ABC-CLIO
PO Box 1911
Santa Barbara, CA 93116-1911

805-705-9339

Offers a list of agencies and organizations concerned with wilderness preservation.

8250 **World Directory of Environmental Organizations**
California Institute of Public Affairs
PO Box 189040
Sacramento, CA 95818-9040

916-442-2472; Fax: 916-442-2478
www.interenvironment.org

Over 2,500 governmental, intergovernmental and United Nations organizations are covered.
Cost: $47.00
232 Pages

8251 **Your Resource Guide to Environmental Organizations**
Smiling Dolphin Press
4 Segura
Irvine, CA 92612-1726

Information is offered, in three separate sections, on non-governmental organizations, federal agencies and state agencies that address environmental concerns.
Cost: $15.95
514 Pages

Industry Web Sites

8252 **The Environmental Literacy Council**
1625 K St. NW
Suite 1020
Washington, DC 20006

202-296-0390; Fax: 202-822-0991
enviroliteracy.org
Facebook, LinkedIn

Roger A. Sedjo, Chairman
Kathleen Berry, President

The Council provides resources on environmental topics for teachers and students.

8253 **http://gold.greyhouse.com**
G.O.L.D Grey House OnLine Databases

Grey House Publishing's online database platform, GOLD, offers Quick Search, Keyword Search and Expert Search for most business sectors including environment and conservation markets. The GOLD platform makes finding the information you need quick and easy - whether you're a novice searcher or an experienced database user. All of Grey House's directory products are available for subscription on the GOLD platform.

8254 **www.adirondackcouncil.org**
Adirondack Council

Research, education and advocacy to protect the natural character and communities of the Adirondack Park. Also publishes an annual State of Park Report and quarterly newsletters.

8255 **www.aeecenter.org**
Association of Energy Engineers

Promotes energy certification, management and education.

8256 **www.aga.org**
American Gas Association

Association for the natural gas industry.

8257 **www.apwa.net**
American Public Works Association

International educational and professional association of public agencies, private sector companies, and individuals dedicated to providing high quality public works goods and services. AWA provides a forum in which public works professionals' competency, increase the performance of their agencies and companies, and bring important public works-related topics to public attention in local, state, and federal areas. Mailing list for members only.

8258 **www.ases.org**
American Solar Energy Society

Individuals and professionals working in the field of solar energy and conservation.

8259 **www.asfe.org**
ASFE

Not-for-profit trade association. Helps geoprofessional, environmental and civil engineering firms profit through professionalism.

8260 **www.bisoncentral.com**
National Bison Association

The National Bison Association was formed to promote the production, marketing, and preservation of bison.

8261 **www.blr.com**
Business & Legal Reports

Provides essential tools for safety and environmental compliance and training needs

8262 **www.cbemw.org**
Citizens for a Better Environment

For citizens concerned with environmental protection. Maintains library.

8263 **www.conservationfund.org**
Conservation Fund

Works with private and public agencies and organizations to protect wildlife habitats, historic sites and parks.

8264 **www.construction.com**
McGraw-Hill Construction

McGraw-Hill Construction (MHC), part of The McGraw-Hill Companies, connects people and projects across the design and construction industry, serving owners, architects, engineers, general contractors, subcontractors, building product manufacturers, suppliers, dealers, distributors and adjacent markets.

8265 **www.earthsite.org**
Earth Society Foundation

News of interest in environmental and sociological issues. Purpose is to promote Earth Day and the Earth Trustee agenda.

8266 **www.eia-usa.org**
Environmental Information Association

Nonprofit organization dedicated to providing environmental information to individuals, members and the industry. Disseminates information on the abatement of asbestos and lead-based paint, indoor air quality, safety and health issues, analytical issues and environmental site assessments.

8267 **www.epa.gov**
US Environmental Protection Agency

8268 **www.femaflavor.org**
Flavor & Extract Manufacturers Assn of the US
1620 I Street NW
Suite 925
Washington, DC 210006
202-293-5800; Fax: 202-463-8998
Ed R. Hayes, President
George C. Robinson III, President Elect
Mark Scott, Treasurer
Arthur Schick, Vice President & Secretary
FEMA is comprised of flavor manufacturers, flavor users, flavor ingredient suppliers, and others with an interest in the U.S. flavor industry. FEMA works with legislators and regulators to assure that the needs of members and consuemr are continuously addressed and is committed to assuring a substantial supply of safe flavoring substances.

8269 **www.floods.org**
Association of State Floodplain Managers
Promotes common interest in flood damage abatement, supports environmental protection for floodplain areas, provides education on floodplain management practices and policy, and urges incorporating multi-objective management, approaches to solve local flooding problems.

8270 **www.greyhouse.com**
Grey House Publishing
Authoritative reference directories for most business sectors including environment and conservation markets. Users can search the online databases with varied search criteria allowing for custom searches by product category, geographic area, sales volume, keyword, subject and more. Full Grey House catalog and online ordering also available.

8271 **www.ia-usa.org**
National BioEnergy Industries Association

8272 **www.iaee.org**
International Association for Energy Economics
Association for those involved in energy economics including publications, consultants, energy database software.

8273 **www.iaia.org**
International Association for Impact Assessment
IAIA provides a forum for the exchange of the ideas and experiences to stimulate innovation in assessing, managing and mitigating the consequences of development.

8274 **www.iwla.org**
Isaak Walton League
Conducts research and education on river ecosystems and healthy fisheries.

8275 **www.joincca.org**
Coastal Conservation Association
Seeks to advance protection and conservation of all marine life. Conducts seminars and bestows awards.

8276 **www.lib.duke.edu/forest/**
Forest History Society
Non-profit educational institution that explores the history of the environment, forestry, and conservation.

8277 **www.members.aol.com/rccouncil**
Rachael Carson Council
Seeks to promote awareness of the problems of environmental contamination and by serving as an information clearing house on chemical contaminates, especially pesticides.

8278 **www.mtsociety.org**
Marine Technology Society
Addresses coastal zone management, marine mineral and energy resources, marine environmental protection, and ocean engineering issues.

8279 **www.nacdnet.org**
National Association of Conservation Districts
Association for those interested in the environment.

8280 **www.naem.org**
National Association for Environmental Management
Dedicated to advancing the profession of environmental management and supports the professional corporate and facility environmental manager.

8281 **www.nalms.org**
North American Lake Management Society
Members are academics, lake managers and others interested in furthering the understanding of lake ecology.

8282 **www.napcor.com**
National Association for Pet Container Resources
National trade association which promotes the recycling of food containers made from PET plastic (containers with recycle code #1).

8283 **www.nationalwoodlands.org**
National Woodland Owners Association
Provides timely information about forestry and forest practices with news from washington,Dc and state capitals. written for non-industrial land owners. Includes state landowner association news.

8284 **www.ncat.org**
National Center for Appropriate Technology
A resource center for information and expertise on methods of promoting conservation and energy self sufficiency. The term, appropriate technology, is defined as a small-scale, environmentally sound, low-cost, locally based approach to problems with an emphasis on self help.

8285 **www.neha.org**
National Environmental Health Association
Association for suppliers of environmental educational materials.

8286 **www.noaa.gov**
National Oceanic and Atmospheric Administration
National weather forecasts, statistics, searchable databases, agency directory and links to related agencies and sites.

8287 **www.pollutiononline.com**
Pollution Online
For vendors and professionals in pollution equipment and control industries. News, product information, links to related web sites and business information.

8288 **www.purezone.com**
PureZone
Devoted to indoor air quality. Discussion forum moderated by industry experts on topics such as sensors and transducers technology.

8289 **www.rnrf.org**
Renewable Natural Resources Foundation
A consortium of professional and scientific societies whose members are concerned with the advancement of research, education, scientific practice and policy formulation for the conservation, replenishment and use of the earth's renewable natural resources.

8290 **www.socma.com**
Silicone Health Council
Coordinates health, environmental and safety programs. Conveys scientifically sound information about silicones.

8291 **www.sweets.construction.com**
McGraw Hill Construction
In depth product information that lets you find, compare, select, specify and make purchase decisions in the industrial product marketplace.

8292 **www.techknow.org**
TechKnow
Lists environmentally friendly remediation and ozone-depleting substance management resources.

8293 **www.usace.army.mil**
US Army Corps of Engineers
Information on flood control, environmental protection, disaster response, military construction and support of others through the sharing of engineering expertise with other agencies, state and local governments, academia and foreign nations.

8294 **www.woodlandowners.org**
National Woodland Owners Association
Provides timely information about forestry and forest practices with news from washington,Dc and state capitals. written for non-industrial land owners. Includes state landowner association news.

8295 **www.wqa.org**
Water Quality Association
An international nonprofit trade association representing retail/dealers and manufacturer/suppliers in the point of use/entry water quality improvement industry. Membership benefits and services include technical and scientific information, educational seminars and home correspondence course books, professional certification and discount services.

Associations

8296 **AMC Institute**
1940 Duke Street
Suite 200
Alexandria, VA 22314

703-570-8954; Fax: 856-439-0525
info@amcinstitute.org
www.amcinstitute.org

Tina Wehmeir, Chief Executive Officer
Greg Schultz, Chair
Fred Stringfellow, Chair-Elect
Michael Payne, Treasurer
Jeanne Sheehy, Secretary

AMCs are professional service firms that provide executive, administrative, and financial management; strategic counsel planning; membership development; public affairs and lobbying; education and professional development; statistical research; meetings management; and marketing and communication services.
175 Members
Founded in 2006

8297 **American Business Media**
675 Third Avenue
Suite 2200
New York, NY 10017-5704

212-661-6360; Fax: 212-370-0736
www.siia.net
Facebook, Twitter, LinkedIn

Doug Manoni, Chair
Marion Minor, Secretary
Edward Keating, Treasurer
Ethan Eisner, Immediate Past Chair
Ty Bobit, Board Member

An association for business-to-business information providers, including producers of print publications, Web sites, trade shows and other media.
200+ Members
Founded in 1906

8298 **American Society of Association Executives**
1575 I Street NW
Washington, DC 20005

202-626-2723
888-950-2723; Fax: 202-371-8315
ASAEservice@asaecenter.org
www.asaecenter.org
Facebook, Twitter, LinkedIn, YouTube, Instagram

John Graham, President & CEO
Francine Alestock, Executive Coordinator
Shaniece Brown, Member Relations Coordinator
Laura Gaske, Marketing Manager
Sabrina Kidwai, Senior Manager, Public Relations

Association providing advocacy and future-oriented research for member organizations in support of the association and nonprofit profession.
39K Members
Founded in 1920

8299 **Association of Collegiate Conference and Special Events**
Colorado State University
S. College Avenue
Suite 3B
Fort Collins, CO 80525

970-449-4960; Fax: 970-449-4965
info@acced-i.org
www.acced-i.org
Facebook, Twitter, LinkedIn

Trish Carlson, President
Lisa Beringer Salazar, CCEP, President-Elect
Daniel L. Dykstra, Immediate Past President
Jim Hodges, Treasurer
Mary Kay Baker, CCEP, Director

Members are college and university conference and special events directors, professionals and others who design, market and coordinate conferences and special events.
1400 Members
Founded in 1980

8300 **Association of International Meeting Planners**
2547 Monroe Street
Dearborn, MI 48124-3013

313-563-0360; Fax: 972-702-3070

Meeting planners.
40 Members
Founded in 1986

8301 **Association of Science-Technology Centers**
818 Connecticut Avenue, NW
7th Floor
Washington, DC 20006-2734

202-783-7200; Fax: 202-783-7207
info@astc.org
www.astc.org
Facebook, Twitter, LinkedIn

Chevy Humphrey, Chair
Linda Conlon, Chair-Elect
Joanna Haas, Secretary
David Chesebrough, Treasurer
Kate Bennett, Director

Organization of science centers and museums dedicated to futhering the public understanding of science among increasingly diverse audiences. Encourges excellence and innovation in informal science learning by serving and linking its members worldwide and advancing their common goals.
550 Members
Founded in 1973

8302 **CEMA**
1512 Weiskopf Loop
Round Rock, TX 78664-6128

512-310-8330; Fax: 510-682-0555
www.cemaonline.com

Kimberley Gishler, President & CEO
Olga Rosenbrook, Director, Member Services

Professionals from the event, trade show and marketing communications industry. Striving to be the definitive resource for event marketing professionals in the information technology industry.
250 Members
Founded in 1990

8303 **Center for Exhibition Industry Research**
12700 Park Central Dr
Suite 750
Dallas, TX 75251-1526

972-687-9242; Fax: 972-692-6020
info@ceir.com
www.ceir.org
Facebook, LinkedIn

Britton Jones, Chair
Aaron Bludworth, Vice Chair
Dennis Slater, immediate Past Chair
Steve Moster, Secretary/Treasurer
David Audrain, Director

The Center for Exhibition Industry Research is an apolitical, nonprofit orgnization with the dual mission of producing research that supports the unique features and value of exhibitors; then, using that research and other tools to promote the image and growth of the exhibition industry

8304 **Connected International Meeting**
9200 Bayard Place
Fairfax, VA 22032

512-684-0889; Fax: 267-390-5193
susan2@cimpa.org
www.cimpa.org

Andrea Sigler, President/CEO

Members are conference and convention planners with a certificate in convention management. Specializes in planning meetings events, incentives, using the internet.
8000 Members
Founded in 1982

8305 **Convention Industry Council**
700 N Fairfax Street
Alexandria, VA 22314

571-527-3116; Fax: 571-527-3105
www.conventionindustry.org
Facebook, Twitter, LinkedIn, YouTube

David Dubois, CMP, CAE, Chair
Bonnie Fedchock, CAE, Vice Chair
Bob Gilbert, CHME CHBA, Immediate Past Chair
Vicki Hawarden, CMP, Board Member At-Large
Kimberly Miles, CMP, Board Member At-Large

An organization that represents individuals as well as 15,000 firms and properties involved in the meetings, conventions and exhibitions industries.
98000 Members
Founded in 1949

8306 **Convention Liaison Council**
10200 W 44th Avenue
Suite 310
Wheat Ridge, CO 80033-2840

303-420-2902; Fax: 303-422-8894
www.clc.org

Francine Butler, Executive VP

Members are associations which are directly involved in the convention, exposition, trade show and meeting industry.

8307 **Display Distributors Association**
Modern Display
424 S 700 E
Salt Lake City, UT 84102-2864

801-355-7427; Fax: 801-521-3040

Members are distributors of display equipment.
16 Members
Founded in 1950

8308 **Event Service Professionals Association**
191 Clarksville Road
Princeton Junction, NJ 08550

609-799-3712; Fax: 609-799-7032
info@espaonline.org
www.espaonline.org
Facebook, Twitter, LinkedIn

Denise I. Suttle,CMP, President
Madonna Carr, CMP, President-Elect
Paul Ruby, CMP, 1st Vice President
Kathy Denkenberger, 2nd Vice President
Amy Cabe, Treasurer

Dedicated to elevating the event and convention service profession and to preparing members, through education and networking, for their pivotal role in innovating and successful event execution.
400 Members
Founded in 1988

8309 Exhibit Designers & Producers Association
10 Norden Place
Norwalk, CT 06855

203-852-5698; Fax: 203-854-6735
www.edpa.com

Robert Campbell, President
Kelli Glasser, VP, Finance & Administration
Gwen Hill, VP, Education
Donna Shultz, VP, Member Services
Dave Flory, VP, Member Development

Internationally recognized, national trade association with corporate members from 18 countries that are engaged in the design, manufacture, transport, installation and service of displays and exhibits primarily for the trade show industry. EDPA's purpose is to champion the prosperity of member businesses.
400+ Members
Founded in 1956

8310 Exhibit and Event Marketers Association
2214 NW 5th St.
Bend, OR 97701

541-317-8768; Fax: 541-317-8749
tsea@tsea.org

Amanda Helgemoe, President
Michael Mulry, Vice President
Glenda Brundgardt, Treasurer
Chris Griffin, Secretary
Jim Wurm, Executive Director

Supports marketing and management professionals.

8311 Exposition Service Contractors Association
5068 West Plano Parkway
Suite 300
Plano, TX 75093

972-447-8212
877-792-3722; Fax: 972-447-8209
www.esca.org

Jay Atherton, President
Lenny Servedio, President-Elect
Julia Smith, Vice President
Richard P. Curran, Secretary/Treasurer
Bruce Nable, Immediate Past President

Annual guide to exposition service is distributed annually and lists safety regulations and building rules in major US convention centers.
120 Members
Founded in 1970

8312 Healthcare Convention & Exhibitors Association
1100 Johnson Ferry Rd NE
Suite 300
Atlanta, GA 30342-1733

678-298-1183; Fax: 404-385-5595
hcea@kellencompany.com
www.hcea.org
Facebook, Twitter, LinkedIn

Christine Farmer, President
Don Schmid, MBA, CME/H, President-Elect
Kyle Wood, Vice President
Sue Huff, Secretary/Treasurer
Diane Benson, CTSM, Immediate Past President

Trade association of organizations involved in health care exhibiting or providing services to health care conventions, exhibitions, and/or meetings.
600 Members
Founded in 1930

8313 Hospitality Sales & Marketing Association International
7918 Jones Branch Drive
Suite 300
McLean, VA 22102

703-506-3280; Fax: 703-506-3266
info@hsmai.org
www.hsmai.org
Facebook, Twitter, LinkedIn, Flicker

Robert A. Gilbert, President & CEO
Fran Brasseux, EVP
Jason Smith, VP, Marketing & Communications
Juli Jones, Vice President
Chris Durso, VP, Content Development

Global organization of sales, marketing, and revenue management professionals involved in the hospitality industry.
5000 Members
Founded in 1927

8314 International Association for Exhibition Management
12700 Park Central Dr
Suite 308
Dallas, TX 75251-1313

972-458-8002; Fax: 972-458-8119
info@iaee.com
www.iaee.com
Facebook, Twitter, LinkedIn, YouTube

Megan Tanel, CEM, Chairperson
Julia Smith, CEM, CTA, Chair-Elect
Daniel McKinnon, CEM, Secretary/Treasurer
Jonathan Skip Cox, Immediate Past Chairperson
Vicki Bedi, Director

Members are managers of shows, exhibits and expositions; associate members are industry suppliers.
3500 Members
Founded in 1928

8315 International Association for Modular Exhibitry
155 W Street
Suite 3
Wilmington, MA 01887-3064

978-988-1200

Irving Sacks, Executive Director

Members are companies that promote the use of modular exhibits for trade shows and museums.
47 Members
Founded in 1987

8316 International Association of Exhibitions and Events
12700 Park Central Dr.
Suite 308
Dallas, TX 75251

972-458-8002; Fax: 972-458-8119
info@iaee.com
www.iaee.com
Facebook, Twitter, LinkedIn, Instagram, YouTube

Daniel McKinnon, Chairperson

Represents the interests of both those who produce trade shows and exhibitions, and those who provide the exhibition industry with products and services.
9000 Members
Founded in 1928

8317 International Association of Assembly Management
635 Fritz Dr
Suite 100
Coppell, TX 75019-4462

972-906-7441
800-935-4226; Fax: 972-906-7418
www.iaam.org

Dexter King, Executive Director
Robyn Williams, First Vice President

Members are managers of auditoriums, arenas, convention centers, stadiums and performing arts centers.
400 Members
Founded in 1924

8318 International Association of Conference Centers
35 East Wacker Drive
Suite 850
Chicago, IL 60601

312-224-2580; Fax: 312-644-8557
http://www.iacconline.org/
Facebook, Twitter, LinkedIn

Alex Caba□as, President
Rachael Bartlett, Vice President, UK
TJ Fimmano, Vice President, USA
Sean Anderson, Director
Lotta Boman, Director

Facilities-based organization which advances the understanding and awareness of conference centers as distinct within the training, education, hospitality and travel fields.
377 Members
Founded in 1981

8319 International Association of Fairs and Expositions
3043 E Cairo
PO Box 985
Springfield, MO 65802

417-862-5771
800-516-0313; Fax: 417-862-0156
iafe@fairsandexpos.com
www.fairsandexpos.com
Facebook, Twitter, YouTube

Marla Calico, President & CEO

The International Association of Fairs and Expositions (IAFE) is a voluntary, non-profit corporation whose members provide services and products that promote the overall development and improvement of fairs, shows, expositions, and allied fields.
Founded in 1885

8320 International Congress and Convention Association
PO Box 6833
Freehold, NJ 07728-6833

732-851-6603; Fax: 732-851-6584
www.iccaworld.com

Joanne Joham, Regional Director, North America
Monica Pataki, Membership Dev. Mgr., North America

Representing events specialists in more than 90 countries.
1000+ Members
Founded in 1963

8321 International Festivals and Events Association
2603 W Eastover Ter
Boise, ID 83706-2800

208-433-0950; Fax: 208-433-9812
nia@ifea.com
www.ifea.com

Ted Baroody, Chair
Steven Wood Schmader, President & CEO

Nia Forster Hovde, VP & Dir., Marketing & Comm.
Beth Peterson, Director, Membership Services
Craig Sarton, Director, Creative & Publications

A voluntary association of events, event producers, event suppliers, and related professionals and organizations whose common purpose is the production and presentation of festivals, events, and civic and private celebrations.
2000 Members
Founded in 1956

8322 **International Laser Display Association**
7062 Edgeworth Drive
Orlando, FL 32819

407-797-7654; Fax: 503-344-3770
mail@laserist.org
www.laserist.org

Brian Gonzalez, President
Patrick Murphy, Executive Director

ILDA members are individuals involved in the laser entertainment and display industry.
Founded in 1986

8323 **International Special Events Society**
330 M Wabash Ave.
Suite 2000
Chicago, IL 60611-4267

312-321-6853
800-688-4737; Fax: 312-673-6953
info@ises.com
www.ises.com

Jodi Collen, CSEP, President
Judy Brillhart, President-Elect
Ingrid Nagy, CSEP, Treasurer
Sara Hunt, CSEP, Secretary
Kevin White, CSEP, Immediate Past President

Professionals in over a dozen countries representing special event producers, caterers, decorators, florists, destination management companies, rental companies, special effects experts, tent suppliers, audio-visual technicians, party and convention coordinators, ballon artists, educators, journalists, hotel sales managers, specialty entertainers, convention center managers and more.
4000 Members
Founded in 1987

8324 **Meeting Professionals International**
3030 LBJ Fwy
Suite 1700
Dallas, TX 75234-2759

972-702-3000; Fax: 972-702-3065
feedback@mpiweb.org
www.mpiweb.org
Facebook, Twitter, LinkedIn

Paul Van DeVenter, President & CEO
Michael Woody, Chief Operating Officer
Daniel Gilmartin, Chief Financial Officer
Darren Temple, Chief Business Dev Officer

MPI members manage meetings and related activities for association, corporations, and educational institutions, or provide goods and services to the meetings industry.
1900 Members
Founded in 1972

8325 **National Association for Campus Activities**
13 Harbison Way
Columbia, SC 29212

803-732-6222
800-845-2338; Fax: 803-749-1047
info@naca.org
www.naca.org
Facebook, Twitter, Instagram, YouTtube, Pinterest

Steve Westbrook, Director Student Affairs
Alan Davis, Executive Director
Gordon Schell, Manager/Member Services
Dawn Thomas, Director/Educational/Events
Erin Wilson, Manager Communications

Largest collegiate organization for campus activities. Purpose is to assist in marketing entertainment services to educational institutions and providing student leadership development programs and services.
1100 Members
Founded in 1960

8326 **National Association of Agricultural Fair Agencies**
MI State Department of Agriculture
PO box 40627
Nashville, TN 37204

615-837-5081; Fax: 517-373-9146
www.nasda.org

Barb Glenn, Chief Executive Officer
Martha Dale, Chief Financial & Strategy Officer
Amanda Culp, Communications & Event Director
Elizabeth Rowland, Human Resources Director
Lisa Benson, NASDA Foundation Executive Director

U.S. and Canadian representatives of state/provincial agencies that are responsible for the support of education and agricultural fairs.
Founded in 1966

8327 **National Association of Consumer Shows**
147 Se 102nd Ave
Portland, OR 97216-2703

503-253-0832
800-728-6227; Fax: 503-253-9172
www.publicshows.com
Facebook, Twitter

Mark Adams, President
Marc McIntosh, Treasurer
Mark Concilla, Secretary
Carolyn Alt, Director
Jim Fricke, Director

Nonprofit organization dedicated to furthering the interests of consumer show producers and suppliers.
265 Members
Founded in 1987

8328 **National Association of Display Industries**
4651 Sheridan Street
Suite 200
Hollywood, FL 33021

954-893-7300; Fax: 954-893-7500
www.nadi-global.com

Klein Merriman, Executive Director
Tracy Dillon, Director Communications

Sponsors seminars and annual contests. Conducts research programs and maintains placement services.
400 Members
Founded in 1937

8329 **National Association of Professional Organizers**
1120 Route 73
Suite 200
Mount Laurel, NJ 08054-2212

856-380-6828; Fax: 856-439-0525
napo@napo.net
www.napo.net
Facebook, Twitter, Pinterest, Flickr, YouTube

Ellen Faye , CPO, COC, President
Susie Hayman, Secretary
Lisa Mark , CPO, Treasurer
Danielle Liu, MPA, CPO, Director
Elizabeth Dodson, Corp Associate Members Director

Members are time, productivity and organization management consultants.
1800 Members
Founded in 1985

8330 **National Catholic Educational Exhibitors**
2621 Dryden Road
Suite 300
Dayton, OH 45439

937-293-1415
888-555-8512; Fax: 937-293-1310
cynpleg@aol.com
www.ncee.org

Peter Li, Executive Director

A group for companies that provide products or services for Catholoc education.
500 Members
Founded in 1950

8331 **National Coalition of Black Meeting Planners**
700N Fairfax Street
Suite 510
Alexandria, VA 22314

571-527-3110; Fax: 301-860-0500
info@ncbmp.org
www.ncbmp.com

Ana Aponte-Curtis, Chair
Kevin J. Johnson, President
JoAnn S. Brown, Vice President
Stephanie Marshall, CMP, Secretary
Myron L. Hardiman, Treasurer

Nonprofit organization dedicated to the training needs of African American meeting planners.
Founded in 1983

8332 **North American Farm Show Council**
590 Woody Hayes Drive
Room 232
Columbus, OH 43210

614-292-4278; Fax: 614-292-9448
gamble.19@osu.edu
www.farmshowcouncil.org

Matt Jungmann, President
Jerry Sinift, First Vice President
Marti Smith, Executive Coordinator

Strives to improve the value of its member shows through education, communication and evaluation. The overall goal is to provide the beest possible marketing showcase for exhibitors for agricultural equipment and related products to the farmer/rancher/producer customer.
37 Members
Founded in 1972

8333 **Professional Convention Management Association**
35 East Wacker Drive
Suite 500
Chicago, IL 60601-2105

312-423-7262
877-827-7262; Fax: 312-423-7222
communications@pcma.org
www.pcma.org
Facebook, Twitter, LinkedIn

Ray Kopcinski, CMP, Chair
William Reed , FASAE, CMP, Chair-Elect
Mary Pat Heftman, Secretary-Treasurer
Christopher Wehking, CMP, Immediate Past Chair
Martin Balogh, Director

PCMA delivers superior and innovative education, to promote the value of professional convention management.
6100 Members
Founded in 1957

8334 **Professional Show Managers Association**
41 Applewood Lane
Avon, CT 06001

860-677-0094; Fax: 860-286-0787
info@rdpgroup.com
www.psmashows.org
Facebook, LinkedIn

Dordy Fontinel, President
Christine Palmer, Vice President
Frank Gaglio, Secretary/Treasurer
Nancy Johnson, Immediate Past President
Bart Caple, Director
Founded in 1987

8335 **Religious Conference Management Association**
7702 Woodland Dr
Suite 120
Indianapolis, IN 46278

317-632-1888; Fax: 317-632-7909
rcma@rcmaweb.org
www.rcmaweb.org
Facebook, Twitter, Vimeo

Harry R. Schmidt, President & CEO
Dean Jones, Director of Conferences & Events
Judy Valenta, Special Projects Coordinator
Debbie Hochstetler, Director of Finance & Admin.
David Wright, VP, Partner Relations
Provides members with a wealth of resources designed specifically to enhance their professionalism and overall effectiveness as religious leaders.
3200 Members
Founded in 1972

8336 **Society of Government Meeting Professionals**
PO Box 321025
Alexandria, VA 22320

703-549-0892; Fax: 703-549-0708
www.sgmp.org
LinkedIn, YouTube

Maggie McGowan, CGMP, CMP, President
Michelle Milligan, First Vice President
James Lynton, CGMP, 2nd Vice President
Brett Sterenson, Treasurer
Maurine Hill, Secretary
Trade association for government meeting planners and exhibitors.
3100 Members
Founded in 1981

8337 **Society of Independent Show Organizers**
2601 Ocean Park Blvd
Suite 200
Santa Monica, CA 90405-5250

310-450-8831
877-937-7476; Fax: 310-450-9305
www.shomex.com
Facebook, Twitter, LinkedIn

David Audrain, Chairman
Rick McConnell, Vice Chair
Charles McCurdy, Treasurer
Tony Calanca, Secretary
Lewis R. Shomer, Executive Director
200 Members
Founded in 1990

8338 **Visitor Studies Association**
2885 Sanford Ave SW
Suite 18100
Grandville, MI 49418

740-872-0566; Fax: 301-637-3312
info@visitorstudies.org
www.visitorstudies.org
Facebook, Twitter, LinkedIn

Joe Heimlich, President
Kimberly Kiehl, President-elect
Dave Ucko, Vice President, Organizational Dev
Bob Breck, Vice President, Outreach
Jessica Luke, Vice President, Professional Dev
Members are professionals at various institutions interested in studying audience experiences at museums, zoos, parks, etc. Promotes research in visitor participation and application of such research to programming and policy.
365 Members
Founded in 1990

Newsletters

8339 **ACOMmodate**
Association for Convention Operations Management
191 Clarksville Road
Princeton Junction, NJ 08550

609-799-3712; Fax: 609-799-7032
www.espaonline.org

Lynn McCullough, Executive Director
Includes news, networking ideas, and articles of professional interest.
Frequency: Quarterly

8340 **Affiliate Connection**
International Festivals and Events Association
2603 W Eastover Ter
Boise, ID 83706-2800

208-433-0950; Fax: 208-433-9812
craig@ifea.com
www.ifea.com

Steven Wood Schmader, President & CEO
The IFEA newsletter provides information and news 24 hours a day, 7 days a week, keeping members, suppliers and affialiates up-to-date and current.
2000 Members
Frequency: Monthly
Founded in 1956

8341 **Annual Conference Abstracts**
Visitor Studies Association
8175-A Sheridan Boulevard
Suite 362
Arvada, CO 80003-1928

303-467-2200; Fax: 303-467-0064
info@visitorstudies.org
www.visitorstudies.org

Alan Friedman, President
Ellen Cox, Treasurer
Jessica Luke, Treasurer
Frequency: Annual

8342 **Aviso**
American Association of Museums
1575 Eye Street NW
Suite 400
Washington, DC 20005-1113

202-289-1818; Fax: 202-289-6578
membership@aam-us.org
www.aam-us.org

Ford Bell, President
Kim Igone, VP Policy & Program
Reports on musuems in the news, federal legislation affecting museums, upcoming seminars and workshops, fedel grant deadlines and AAM activities and services.
Frequency: Monthly
Mailing list available for rent

8343 **CEMA E-Newsletter**
Computer Event Marketing Association
5098 Foothills Boulevard
Suite 3-386
Roseville, CA 95747

info@cemaonline.com
www.cemaonline.com

Kimberly Gishler, President & CEO
Olga Rosenbrook, Director of Member Services
Stacey Z. Diemer, Membership Manager
The e-newsletter for members of the Computer Event Marketing Association.
Frequency: Monthly
Founded in 1990

8344 **ESCA Voice Newsletter**
Exhibition Services and Contractors Association
2260 Corporate Circle
Suite 400
Henderson, NV 80914

702-319-9561
877-792-3722; Fax: 702-450-7732
askus@esca.org
www.esca.org

Susan L Schwartz, Director Communications
Cynthia Kelly, Accounting Manager
Frequency: Quarterly

8345 **Exhibition Perspectives**
American Academy of Equine Art
c/o Kentucky Horse Park
4089 Iron Works Parkway
Lexington, KY 40511

859-281-6031; Fax: 859-281-6043
www.aaea.net

Julie Buchanan, Director
Frequency: Annual

8346 **HCEA Edge**
Healthcare Convention & Exhibitors Association
5775 Peachtree Dnwdy Rd
Building G, Suite 500
Atlanta, GA 30342-1556

404-252-3663; Fax: 404-252-0774
hcea@kellencompany.com
www.hcea.org

Eric Allen, Executive Vice President
News and events of the trade association of over 600 organizations involved in healthcare exhibiting or providing services to healthcare conventions, exhibitions and/or meetings.
Frequency: Monthly, Members Only

8347 **IEG Endorsement Insider**
IEG
640 N La Salle Dr
Suite 600
Chicago, IL 60654-3186

312-944-1727
800-834-4850; Fax: 312-944-1897
www.sponsorship.com

Lesa Ukman, CEO
John Ukman, Publisher
A newsletter covering the use of sports and entertainment personalities for endorsements, appearances and other marketing purposes.
Cost: $295.00
Frequency: Monthly

8348 **IEG Sponsorship Report**
IEG

640 N La Salle Dr
Suite 600
Chicago, IL 60654-3186

312-944-1727
800-834-4850; Fax: 312-944-1897
ieg@sponsorship.com
www.sponsorship.com

Lesa Ukman, CEO
John Ukman, Publisher
Bart Zautcke, CEO
Brad Smith, Marketing

Newsletter on sports, arts, event, entertainment and cause marketing.
Cost: $415.00
8 Pages
Frequency: Biweekly
Circulation: 15000
Founded in 1982

8349 **NAAFA Newsletter**
National Association of Agricultural Fair Agencies
MI State Department of Agriculture
PO Box 30017
Lansing, MI 48909

517-373-9766; Fax: 517-373-9146

Carol Carlson, Secretary/Treasurer
Frequency: Annual

8350 **NAFSC Brochure**
North American Farm Show Council
590 Woody Hayes Drive
Columbus, OH 43210-6131

614-292-4278; Fax: 614-292-9448
gamble19@osu.edu
www.worldagexpo.com

Dennis Alford, First VP
Chuck Gamble, Secretary-Treasurer

The North American Farm Show Council strives to improve the value of its member shows through education, communication and evaluation. The goal of the Council is to provide the best possible marketing showcase for the exhibitors of agricultural equipment & related products.
Frequency: Bi-Ennial
Founded in 1972

8351 **NCEE News**
National Catholic Educational Exhibitors
2621 Dryden Road
Suite 300
Dayton, OH 45439

937-293-1415
888-555-8512; Fax: 937-293-1310
cynpleg@aol.com
www.ncee.org

Peter Li, Executive Director

A regular newsletter for the exclusive use of NCEE members. Each issue brings messages from the NCEE president and the NCEA Convention and Exposition Director; market and association updates, and the Exhibition Planning Calendar

8352 **Newsbytes**
Meeting Professionals International
3030 Lbj Fwy
Suite 1700
Dallas, TX 75234-2759

972-702-3000; Fax: 972-702-3070
feedback@mpiweb.org
www.mpiweb.org

Bruce Mac Millan, President
Frequency: Weekly

8353 **Newsletter**
American Academy of Equine Art
c/o Kentucky Horse Park
4089 Iron Works Parkway
Lexington, KY 40511

859-281-6031; Fax: 859-281-6043
www.aaea.net

Julie Buchanan, Director
Frequency: Semi-Annual

8354 **Workshop Brochure**
American Academy of Equine Art
c/o Kentucky Horse Park
4089 Iron Works Parkway
Lexington, KY 40511

859-281-6031; Fax: 859-281-6043
www.aaea.net

Julie Buchanan, Director
Frequency: Annual

Magazines & Journals

8355 **American Speaker**
Briefings Publishing Group
1101 King St
Suite 110
Alexandria, VA 22314-2944

703-548-3800
800-722-9221; Fax: 703-684-2136
www.briefings.com

Aram Bakshian Jr, Editor-in-Chief
Alan Douglas, President

An updateable loose leaf product geared to amateur and polished public speakers. The product has tips on speaking, model speeches, and filler material for all speaking needs.
Cost: $395.00
Frequency: Monthly
Founded in 1992
Mailing list available for rent: 14000 names at $125 per M
Printed in 2 colors on matte stock

8356 **Association Conventions & Facilities**
Coastal Communications Corporation
2700 N Military Trail
Suite 120
Boca Raton, FL 33431

561-989-0600; Fax: 561-989-9509
www.themeetingmagazines.com

Harvey Grotsky, Publisher/Editor-In-Chief
Susan Wycoff Fell, Managing Editor
Susan Gregg, Managing Editor

Edited for association meeting planners with the responsibility for staging and planning meetings, conferences and conventions, for site selection, specifying accommodations and transportation. Issues provide in-depth focus on sites and transportation, current legislation, seminar and training oprtions, budget and cost controls, and destination reports.
Cost: $60.00
Frequency: BiMonthly
Circulation: 20,500
ISSN: 2162-8831
Founded in 2008

8357 **Association Meetings**
Primedia
Po Box 12901
Shawnee Mission, KS 66282-2901

913-341-1300; Fax: 913-514-6895
www.penton.com

Eric Jacobson, Senior VP
Larry Keltto, Editor

Directed to association executive directors and meeting planners with the objective of aiding the planning, site selection, and organization of meetings and conventions.
Cost: $223.65
Circulation: 20065
Printed in 4 colors

8358 **Convene Magazine**
Professional Convention Management Association
2301 S Lake Shore Dr
Suite 1001
Chicago, IL 60616-1419

312-423-7262
877-827-7262; Fax: 312-423-7222
communications@pcma.org
www.pcma.org

Deborah Sexton, President/CEO
Kati S Quigley CMP, Chairman of Board
Barry L Smith, Chair Board of Trustees

The leading meetings industry trade publication for education content and timely, relevant information from the Professional Convention Management Association
Frequency: Monthly
Circulation: 35000

8359 **Convention South**
2001 W First Street
2001 West First Street
Gulf Shores, AL 36542

251-968-5300; Fax: 251-968-4532
info@conventionsouth.com
www.conventionsouth.com

J Talty O'Connor, Editor/Publisher
Kristen S McIntosh, VP/Executive Editor
Pamela Redden, Marketing Services Manager
Suzanne Kellams, Manager, Circulation Development

For planners of meetings, conferences, seminars and similar events that are held in the South
Frequency: Monthly
Circulation: 18000
ISSN: 1074-0627
Founded in 1983
Printed in 4 colors on glossy stock

8360 **Corporate & Incentive Travel**
Coastal Communications Corporation
2700 N Military Trail
Suite 120
Boca Raton, FL 33431

561-989-0600; Fax: 561-989-9509
ccceditor1@att.net
www.themeetingmagazines.com

Harvey Grotsky, Publisher/Editor-In-Chief
Susan Wyckoff Fell, Managing Editor
Susan Gregg, Managing Editor

The magazine for corporate meetings and incentive travel planners. In-depth editorial focus on site selection, accommodations and transportation, current legislation, conference, seminar and training facilities, budget and cost controls, and destination reports. Regular features highlight industry news and developments, trends and personalities, meeting values, facilities, and destinations.
Frequency: Monthly
Circulation: 40,000
Founded in 1983

8361 **Corporate Meetings & Incentives**
Primedia
Po Box 12901
Shawnee Mission, KS 66282-2901

913-341-1300; Fax: 913-514-6895
www.penton.com

Eric Jacobson, Senior VP
Melissa Fromento, Publisher

Senior executives guide to decision-making.
138 Pages
Frequency: Monthly
Circulation: 34246

Founded in 1980
Printed in 4 colors on glossy stock

8362 **ESCA Extra Magazine**
Exhibition Services and Contractors Association
2260 Corporate Circle
Suite 400
Henderson, NV 80914

702-319-9561
877-792-3722; Fax: 702-450-7732
askus@esca.org
www.esca.org

Susan L Schwartz, CEM, Executive Director
Heather Geldner, Accounting Manager
Cynthia Kelly, Accounting Manager
Frequency: Monthly

8363 **EXPO Magazine**
Expo Magazine
7015 College Blvd
Overland Park, KS 66211-1579

913-469-1185
800-444-4388; Fax: 913-469-0806
expo@halldata.com
www.expoweb.com

Cam Bishop, President
Donna Sanford, Publisher
Danica Tormohlen, Editor-in-Chief

Magazine for exposition managment.
Cost: $48.00
134 Pages
Circulation: 7500
ISSN: 1046-3925
Founded in 1989
Printed in 4 colors on glossy stock

8364 **Event Solutions**
Virgo Publishing LLC
3300 N Central Ave
Suite 300
Phoenix, AZ 85012-2532

480-675-9925; Fax: 480-990-0819
mikes@vpico.com
www.vpico.com

Jenny Bolton, President

Topics featured include decor, themes, high tech support, indoor facility equipment, food and beverage ideas, special effects, new products, and financial issues and regulations. Provides corporate, product and even profiles with suggestions from experts in the field.
Cost: $45.00
Frequency: Monthly
Circulation: 25,000

8365 **Events World**
International Special Events Society: Indiana
401 North Michigan Avenue
Chicago, IL 60611-4267

312-321-6853
800-688-4737; Fax: 312-673-6953
www.ises.com

Kevin Hacke, Executive Director
Kristin Prine, Operations Director

Editorial contents include practical information on each of the seven disciplines, news on promotions, job banks, people in the industry, ISES activities and events, technology trends, and global vision information about environmental, legal and political issues relating to the special events industry.
Frequency: Monthly
Circulation: 20000
Founded in 1987

8366 **Exhibit Builder**
Exhibit Builder
22900 Ventura Boulevard #245
PO Box 4144
Woodland Hills, CA 91365

818-225-0100
800-356-4451; Fax: 818-225-0138
www.exhibitbuilder.net

Jill Brookman, CEO/President
Judy Pomerantz, Managing Editor
Jollen Ryan, Circulation Manager
Scott Gray, Editors

Devoted to the business and technical interest of the designers and fabricators of exhibits for trade shows, museums and point of purchase displays, includes application articles, new products, and new technology for creating booths.
Cost: $40.00
72 Pages
Frequency: Annual+
Circulation: 15000
ISSN: 0887-6878
Founded in 1983
Printed in 4 colors on glossy stock

8367 **Exhibit Marketing Magazine**
Eaton Hall Publishing
256 Columbia Turnpike
Florham Park, NJ 07932-1231

973-514-5900
800-746-9646; Fax: 973-514-5977
info@eatonhall.com
www.eatonhall.com

Scott Goldman, Publisher

Eaton Hall is a publishing and trade show firm which specializes in bringing buyers and sellers together.
Cost: $5.00
52 Pages
Frequency: Quarterly
Circulation: 31000
Founded in 1990
Printed in 4 colors on glossy stock

8368 **Exhibitor**
Exhibitor Magazine Group
Po Box 368
Suite 745
Rochester, MN 55903-0368

507-289-6556
888-235-6155; Fax: 507-289-5253
webmaster@exhibitoronline.com
www.exhibitoronline.com

Lee Knight, Owner
John Pavek, VP Publishing
Cara Schulz, National Sales Manager
Nicole Brudos Ferrara, Managing Editor
Whitney Archibald, Editor

The magazine for trade show and event marketing management.
Cost: $78.00
122 Pages
Frequency: Monthly
Circulation: 30000
ISSN: 0739-6821
Founded in 1982
Printed in 4 colors on glossy stock

8369 **Facilities & Destinations**
Bedrock Communications
650 1st Ave
7th Floor
New York, NY 10016-3240

212-532-7088; Fax: 212-213-6382
mikecaffin@aol.com
www.facilitiesonline.com

Stella Johnson, Senior Executive Editor
Timothy Herrick, Director

Serves the association meeting industry defined as finance, banking, health, education,religious, trade, labor, fraternal, manufacturing, civic, social, professional, government/military, association management companies, independent meeting planners, destination management companies, trade show/event production companies and other groups who use the facilities industry for meetings, conferences, exhibitions, trade shows and conventions.
45 Pages
Circulation: 34000+
Founded in 1988

8370 **Facilities & Event Management**
Bedrock Communications
650 1st Ave
7th Floor
New York, NY 10016-3240

212-532-7088; Fax: 212-213-6382
mikecaffin@aol.com
www.facilitiesonline.com/

Michael Caffin, Managing Editor
Glen O'Grady, Director
Timothy Herrick, Director

Editorial articles solve problems based on industry facts and statistics and coverage encompasses various segments of the facilities industry, including: convention centers, exhibition halls, hotel/conference centers, civic centers, arenas, stadiums, arts centers, etc. Monthly features detail facility business activity and provide coverage of the products and services available.
Subscription, $48.00
Cost: $4.95
52 Pages
Frequency: Monthly
Circulation: 30000
ISSN: 1524-0258

8371 **Fairs and Expositions**
International Association of Fairs & Expositions
3043 E Cairo
PO Box 985
Springfield, MO 65802

417-862-5771
800-516-0313; Fax: 417-862-0156
www.fairsandexpos.com

Marla Calico, President & CEO

The source of information for fair trends, innovative ideas and association activities.
Frequency: 10/year
Founded in 1885

8372 **Feed and Grain**
Cygnus Business Media
1233 Janesville Avenue
Fort Atkinson, WI 53538

920-563-6388; Fax: 920-563-1702
www.feedandgrain.com

Arlette Sambs, Publisher
Jackie Roembke, Editor

Committed to providing targeted editorial that addresses the specific needs of its readers. Subscribers consist of feed manufacturers, integrated livestock operators, pet food manufacturers, soybean processors, builders, designers and millwrights, as well as businesses such as rice mills, country and terminal elevators, flour mills, breweries and distilleries.
Cost: $48.00
Frequency: Bi-Monthly
Circulation: 15700
Founded in 1966
Mailing list available for rent: 16,505 names at $100 per M
Printed in 4 colors on glossy stock

8373 **IE - Business of International Events Magazine**
International Festivals and Events Association

2603 W Eastover Ter
Boise, ID 83706-2800

208-433-0950; Fax: 208-433-9812
craig@ifea.com
www.ifea.com

Steven Wood Schmader, President & CEO

IFEA'S quarterly magazine that provides members with the latest news and features focusing on current trends and topics, events, resources and more.
2000 Members
Founded in 1956

8374 **Inside Events**
Trio Communications
8899 Beverly Boulevard
#408
Los Angeles, CA 90048-2431

310-888-8566; Fax: 310-888-1866

Elisabeth Familian, Publisher

Articles include area listings of sites and vendors for any type of gathering. Profiles the creative ideas of industry professionals.
Frequency: Quarterly
Circulation: 20,000

8375 **Insurance & Financial Meetings Management**
Coastal Communications Corporation
2700 N Military Trail
Suite 120
Boca Raton, FL 33431-6394

561-989-0600; Fax: 561-989-9509
www.themeetingmagazines.com

Harvey Grotsky, Publisher/Editor-In-Chief
Susan Wyckoff Fell, Managing Editor
Susan Gregg, Managing Editor

The executive source for planning meetings and incentives for the financial and insurance sectors. With regular features and special focus on site selection, destinations, industry-related studies and activities, motivational and incentive programs, program and event planning.
Frequency: Monthly
Circulation: 40,000
Founded in 1983

8376 **Insurance Conference Planner**
Primedia
Po Box 12901
Shawnee Mission, KS 66282-2901

913-341-1300
866-505-7173; Fax: 913-514-6895
www.penton.com

Eric Jacobson, Senior VP
Melissa Fromento, Publisher

Meeting and incentive strategies for the financial services industry.
148 Pages
Frequency: Monthly
Circulation: 8005
Founded in 1965
Printed in 4 colors on glossy stock

8377 **Laserist**
International Laser Display Association
7062 Edgeworth Drive
Orlando, FL 32819

407-797-7654; Fax: 503-344-3770
www.laserist.org

Brian Gonzalez, President
Patrick Murphy, Executive Director

Providing the latest news about the art and technology of laser displays
Frequency: Quarterly
Founded in 1986

8378 **Medical Meetings**
Primedia
11 Riverbend Dr S
Stamford, CT 06907-2524

203-316-8178; Fax: 203-358-5812
www.meetingsnet.com

Betsy Bair, Editor Director
Melissa Framento, Publisher

International guide for health care and meeting planners.
106 Pages
Frequency: Monthly
Circulation: 10,823
Founded in 1973
Printed in 4 colors on glossy stock

8379 **Meeting Professionals**
Meeting Professionals International
3030 LBJ Fwy
Suite 1700
Dallas, TX 75234-2759

972-702-3000; Fax: 972-702-3070
feedback@mpiweb.org
www.mpiweb.org

Bruce MacMillan, President
Eric Rozenberg CMP,CMM, Vice Chairman Administration

Furthers the professional development and education of all those who participate in the meetings industry.
Cost: $99.00
Frequency: Monthly
Circulation: 28,000
Founded in 1972

8380 **Meetings & Conventions**
Reed Business Information
500 Plaza Drive
Secaucus, NJ 07094

201-021-1960; Fax: 201-902-2053
lcioffi@ntmllc.com
www.meetings-conventions.com

Bernard Lynch, Associate Editor
Lori Cioffi, Editor in Chief
Loren G. Edelstein, Executive Editor
Allen Sheinman, Managing Editor
Lisa Grimaldi, Senior Editor

Serves the corporate and independent travel and meeting planner with features on meeting facilities, hotels/airports/car rental, incentive travel options, trade show coverage, entertainment/leisure options and industry news.
Cost: $70.00
Frequency: Monthly
Circulation: 70013
Founded in 1965

8381 **Meetings Industry**
Dunn Enterprises
513 Commerce Dr
Upper Marlboro, MD 20774-7434

301-249-4600; Fax: 301-249-9100
www.jtdunn.com

Barbara Cox, Owner
Robert Lantang, Graphic Designer

Profiles meetings sites and accomodations for meetings of all sizes. Includes personnel appointments of other meeting planners.
Circulation: 35000

8382 **Programming Magazine**
National Association for Campus Activities
13 Harbison Way
Columbia, SC 29212-3401

803-732-6222
800-845-2338; Fax: 803-749-1047
info@naca.org
www.naca.org

Glenn Farr, Editor
Erin Wilson, Circulation

Features cover facilities and financial management, promotions, and student development to help plan a wide range of events.
Cost: $70.00
Circulation: 4300
Founded in 1960

8383 **Religious Conference Manager**
Religious Conference Management Association
7702 Woodland Drive
Suite 120
Indianapolis, IN 46228-6150

317-632-1888; Fax: 317-632-7909
www.rcmaweb.org

Eric Allen, Executive Director

Presents timely information for the meeting professional. Content focuses on current trends and features educational articles and news within this specialized field.
Frequency: Bi-Monthly

8384 **Resorts, Hotels, Meetings & Incentives**
Publishing Group
PO Box 318
Trumbull, CT 06611-0318

860-279-0149

John Mortimer, Publisher

Editorial contents include in-depth articles on industry trends, budgeting, planning tips, and profiles of the top meeting facilities in the world.
Frequency: Monthly
Circulation: 58,601

8385 **Special Events Magazine**
Primedia Publication
17383 W Sunset Blvd
Suite A220
Pacific Plsds, CA 90272-4187

310-230-7160
800-543-4116; Fax: 310-230-7168
lhurley@specialevents.com
www.specialevents.com

Lisa Hurley, Editor
Lisa Perrin, President, Chief Executive Officer
Wanda McKnight, Sales Manager

Resource for event professionals who design and produce special events (including social, corporate and public events) in hotels, resorts, banquet facilities and other venues.
Cost: $48.43
Frequency: Monthly
Circulation: 2000+
Founded in 1982

8386 **Tradeshow & Exhibit Manager**
Goldstein & Associates
2117 Highland Avenue
Louisville, KY 40204

502-548-3188; Fax: 502-742-8749
www.goldsteinandassociates.com

Steve Goldstein, Publisher

Featured articles focus on the issues, trends and products of interest connected to the tradeshow industry. Topics include security, boothmanship, legislation and shipping.
Cost: $80.00
Circulation: 14600

8387 **Tradeshow Week**
Reed Business Information
5700 Wilshire Boulevard
Suite 120
Los Angeles, CA 90036-5804

323-576-6600; Fax: 323-965-2407
www.tradeshowweek.com

Amy Lacey, Marketing Director
Adam Schaffer, Publisher
Michael Hart, Editor-in-Chief

Carlos Lopez, Production Director
Heidi Genoist, Senior Associate Editor

For corporate exhibit managers, independent show managers, special event and meeting planners, association show managers and industry suppliers. Focuses on changing trends, new ideas and issues shaping the exposition industry in the US/Canada and abroad. Each issue contains a national and international show calendar.
Cost: $439.00
Frequency: Weekly
Circulation: 2394
Founded in 1971
Printed in 4 colors on matte stock

8388 **Visitor Studies Today**
Visitor Studies Association
8175-A Sheridan Boulevard
Suite 362
Arvada, CO 80003-1928

303-467-2200; Fax: 303-467-0064
info@visitorstudies.org
www.visitorstudies.org

Alan Friedman, President
Ellen Cox, Treasurer
Jessica Luke, Treasurer
Frequency: 3/year

Trade Shows

8389 **AAEA Annual Meetings**
American Academy of Equine Art
c/o Kentucky Horse Park
4089 Iron Works Parkway
Lexington, KY 40511

859-281-6031; Fax: 859-281-6043
www.aaea.net

Shelley Hunter, Executive Director
Julie Buchanan, President
Frequency: April, September

8390 **AAM Annual Meeting & MuseumExpo**
American Alliance of Museums
2451 Crystal Dr.
Suite 1005
Arlington, VA 22202

202-289-1818; Fax: 202-289-6578
membership@aam-us.org
www.aam-us.org

Andrea Streat, Director, Meetings & Events

The largest gathering of museum professionals in the world.
Frequency: Annual/May

8391 **ASTC Annual Conference & Exhibit Hall**
Association of Science/Technology Centers
1025 Vermont Avenue NW
Suite 500
Washington, DC 20005-6310

202-783-7200; Fax: 202-783-7207
conference@astc.org
www.astc.org

Cindy Kong, Director, Meetings & Conferences
Wendy Pollock, Dir, Research, Pubs, Exhibitions
Sheryl Thorpe, Manager, Conference & Exhibit Hall

Provides science center professionals from across the world a forum to exchange ideas and discuss the field's leading issues. With over 100 conference sessions, participants are challenged to explore ways of making science centers more essential to their communities.
1500 Attendees
Founded in 1973

8392 **Affordable Meetings Exposition and Conference**
George Little Management
10 Bank Street
Suite 1200
White Plains, NY 10606-1954

914-486-6070
800-272-7469; Fax: 914-948-6180

Susan Sloan, Show Manager
George Little II, President

Focuses on the needs of meeting planners from all types and sizes of organizations who are responsible for producing successful yet cost effective meetings. 430 booths.
3M Attendees
Frequency: September

8393 **Association of Collegiate Conference & Events Directors Conference**
Assn of Collegiate Conference & Events Directors
1301 S College Avenue
Fort Collins, CO 80523-8037

877-502-2233; Fax: 970-491-0667

Deborah Blom, Executive Director
Monica Nesbit Schultz, Marketing/Sales Manager

Workshop, conference, banquet and luncheon plus exhibits of conference and special event planning supplies, equipment and service information.
1300 Attendees
Frequency: March
Founded in 1980

8394 **Business to Business Exposition**
Trade Shows West
2880 S Main
Suite 110
Salt Lake City, UT 84115

801-485-0176; Fax: 801-485-0241

16000 Attendees

8395 **Conventions and Expositions**
American Society of Association Executives
1575 I Street NW
Washington, DC 20005-1105

202-262-2723; Fax: 202-626-8825

Judy Comeaux, Advertising
John Young, Production

Exposition planners trade show; 500-700 booths.
2-5M Attendees
Frequency: March

8396 **ESC Semi-Annual Meetings**
Exhibition Services and Contractors Association
2260 Corporate Circle
Suite 400
Henderson, NV 80914

702-319-9561
877-792-3722; Fax: 702-450-7732
askus@esca.org
www.esca.org

Susan L Schwartz, CEM, Executive Director
Heather Geldner, Accounting Manager
Cynthia Kelly, Accounting Manager

December Meeting with International Association for Exposition Management and Summer Educational Conference.
Frequency: December, Summer

8397 **ESCA's Summer Educational Conference**
Exhibition Services & Contractors Association
2340 E Trinity Mills Road
Suite 100
Carrollton, TX 75006

469-574-0698
877-792-ESCA; Fax: 469-574-0697
www.esca.org

Designed to give attendees the opportunity to advance their knowledge and to have an impact on the shape of the exhibition industry's future, as well as to network. Three session tracks, interactive forums and roundtables, speakers, and exhibits.
Frequency: Annual

8398 **ESPA Annual Conference**
Event Service Professionals Association
191 Clarksville Road
Princeton Junction, NJ 08550

609-799-3712; Fax: 609-799-7032
info@espaonline.org
www.espaonline.org
Facebook, Twitter, LinkedIn

Lynn McCullough, Executive Director
Diane Galante, Meeting Planner
Elizabeth Roe, Association Coordinator
Meghan Higgins, Public Relations Manager

Conference geared specifically to the event and convention services industry.
Frequency: Annual

8399 **Exhibit Ideas Show**
Exhibit Builder
1600 Golf Road
Suite 550
Rolling Meadows, IL 60008-4273

800-638-6396; Fax: 847-280-0771

Russ Eisenhardt, Show Manager
Jill Brookman, Publisher

Marketplace for products, services and technologies for exhibit builders and buyers. Elements included in trade show, museum and point of purchase booth construction are displayed, as are portable, modular and custom exhibit systems. 700 booths.
20M Attendees
Frequency: April

8400 **Exhibit Industry Conference & Exposition**
Trade Show Exhibitors Association
McCormick Place, 2301 S Lake Shore Drive
Suite 1005
Chicago, IL 60616

312-842-8732; Fax: 312-842-8744
tsea@tsea.org

Stephen Schuldenfrei, President
Emily Burger, Sales Manager
Frequency: July

8401 **Exhibitor Conference**
Exhibitor Magazine Group
98 E Naperville Road
Westmont, IL 60559

630-434-7779
800-752-6312; Fax: 630-434-1216
www.exhibitorshow.com

Carol Fojtik, Managing Director/Sr VP

Conference program combined with exhibit hall featuring latest products and resources shaping the future of exhibiting and corporate event programs. Anyone responsible for planning, managing or implementing trade show or corporate event marketing functions should attend. Conference is held annually in Las Vegas, NV.
5M Attendees
Frequency: March
Founded in 1989

8402 **HCEA Annual Meeting**
Healthcare Convention & Exhibitors Association
1100 Johnson Ferry Rd NE
Suite 300
Atlanta, GA 30342-1733
404-252-3663; Fax: 404-252-0774
hcea@kellencompany.com
www.hcea.org
Eric Allen, Executive Vice President
Jackie Beaulieu, Associate Director
Cost varies; approximately 50 booths; 800 attendees.
200 Attendees
Frequency: Annual

8403 **HCEA Marketing Summit**
Healthcare Convention & Exhibitors Association
1100 Johnson Ferry Rd NE
Suite 300
Atlanta, GA 30342-1733
404-252-3663; Fax: 404-252-0774
hcea@kellencompany.com
www.hcea.org
Eric Allen, Executive Vice President
Jackie Beaulieu, Associate Director
Cost varies; no exhibits; 200-250 attendees.
200 Attendees
Frequency: Annual

8404 **IAAM Annual Conference & Trade Show**
International Association of Assembly Managers
635 Fritz Drive
Suite 100
Coppell, TX 75019-4442
972-906-7441
800-935-4226; Fax: 972-906-7418
www.iaam.org
Kristie Todd, Membership & Exposition Coordinator
JoAnn Ramsey, Exhibition Manager
Members are managers of auditoriums, arenas, convention centers, stadiums and performing arts centers, coming together for education and networking opportunities, expert speakers, and exhibits.
3000 Attendees
Frequency: Annual/
Founded in 1925
Mailing list available for rent: 2800 names at $300 per M

8405 **IAEE Expo! Expo!**
International Assn of Exhibitions and Events
12700 Park Central Drive
Suite 308
Dallas, TX 75251
972-458-8002; Fax: 972-458-8119
news@iaee.com
www.iaee.com
Annual show of 250 exhibitors of conventions and visitor bureaus, hotels, travel airlines, car rental, shippers, insurance, computer hardware and software, service contractors, printing products, specialty advertisement products, photography equipment and audio-visual equipment.
2500 Attendees
Frequency: Annual/December
Founded in 1928

8406 **IAEM Semi-Annual Meetings**
International Association for Exhibition Mgmt
8111 LBJ Freeway, Suite 750
PO Box 802425
Dallas, TX 75251-1313
972-458-8002; Fax: 972-458-8119
www.iaee.com
Steven G Hacker, CAE, President
Cathy Breden, CAE CMP, SVP
Susan Brower, Director Marketing/Communications
Annual show of 250 exhibitors of conventions and visitor bureaus, hotels, travel airlines, car rental, shippers, insurance, computer hardware and software, service contractors, printing products, specialty advertisement products, photography equipment and audio-visual equipment.
2200 Attendees
Frequency: June, December

8407 **IAFE Annual Meeting**
International Association of Fairs & Expositions
3043 E Cairo
PO Box 985
Springfield, MO 65802
417-862-5771
800-516-0313; Fax: 417-862-0156
iafe@fairsandexpos.com
www.fairsandexpos.com
Many branch divisions of the IAFE within the United States and Canada have their own annual meetings where members can meet, have access to resources, programs and workshops.
5000 Attendees
Frequency: Fall, Neveda
Founded in 1885

8408 **IBTM America**
800-417-8646
203-840-5636
ibtmamerica@reedexpo.com
www.ibtmamerica.com
Facebook, Twitter, LinkedIn, Instagram, Pinterest, YouTube
Jaime McAuley, Event Director
IBTM's 8 global and regional events are showcases for the meetings and events industry.

8409 **IFEA Annual Convention and Expo**
International Festivals and Events Associations
2603 W Eastover Terrace
Boise, ID 83706
208-433-0950; Fax: 208-433-9812
www.ifea.com
Steve Wood Scmader, President & CEO
Unites hundreds of the world's leading festivals and events, suppliers, media, sponsors and related industry professionals to share information on every aspect of event production through in-depth workshops, round-table discussions and networking.
2000 Members
800 Attendees
Frequency: Fall
Founded in 1956

8410 **ILDA Conference**
International Laser Display Association
7062 Edgeworth Drive
Orlando, FL 32819
407-797-7654; Fax: 503-344-3770
www.laserist.org
Brian Gonzalez, President
Patrick Murphy, Executive Director
One of the world's largest exhibitions of entertainment technology. Features international exhibitors from the fields of lighting, lasers, audio, video and staging.
70000 Attendees
Founded in 1986

8411 **International Technology Meetings & Incentives Conference**
Techno-Savvy Meeting Professional
9200 Bayard Place
Fairfax, VA 22032-2103
703-978-6287; Fax: 703-978-5524
cimpa@cimpa.org
www.cimpa.org
Andrea Sigler, President
Containing 100 booths and 100 exhibits.
Frequency: November

8412 **MPI Semi-Annual Meetings**
Meeting Professionals International
3030 LBJ Freeway
Suite 1700
Dallas, TX 75234
972-023-3000; Fax: 972-702-3070
feedback@mpiweb.org
www.mpiweb.org
Colin C Rorrie, Jr PhD CAE, President/CEO
Frequency: Summer, Winter

8413 **NAAFA Semi-Annual Meetings**
National Association of Agricultural Fair Agencies
MI State Department of Agriculture
PO Box 30017
Lansing, MI 48909
517-373-9766; Fax: 517-373-9146
Carol Carlson, Secretary/Treasurer
Frequency: Summer, Winter

8414 **NAFSC Annual Meeting**
North American Farm Show Council
590 Woody Hayes Drive
Columbus, OH 43210-6131
614-292-4278; Fax: 614-292-9448
gamble19@osu.edu
www.worldagexpo.com
Dennis Alford, First VP
Chuck Gamble, Secretary/Treasurer
Frequency: May
Founded in 1972

8415 **NCEE Annual Meeting**
National Catholic Educational Exhibitors
2621 Dryden Road
Suite 300
Dayton, OH 45439
937-293-1415
888-555-8512; Fax: 937-293-1310
bthomas@peterli.com
Bret Thomas, Executive Director
In conjunction with the National Catholic Educational Association.
Frequency: March

8416 **PCMA Annual Meeting**
Professional Convention Management Association
2301 S Lake Shore Dr
Suite 1001
Chicago, IL 60616-1419
312-423-7262
877-827-7262; Fax: 312-423-7222
communications@pcma.org
www.pcma.org
Deborah Sexton, President/CEO
Kati S Quigley CMP, Chairman of Board
Barry L Smith, Chair Board of Trustees
3000 Members

8417 **RCMA Conference & Exposition**
Religious Conference Management Association

7702 Woodland Drive
Suite 120
Indianapolis, IN 46228-6150

317-632-1888; Fax: 317-632-7909
www.rcmaweb.org

Eric Allen, Executive Director
Frequency: Annual

8418 **The Special Event Annual Conference & Exhibition**
Special Event Magazine
PO Box 8987
Malibu, CA 90265-8987

708-486-0731
866-486-0731; Fax: 310-317-0264
registration@penton.com
www.specialevents.com

Sharon Morabito, Group Show Director
Tara Melingonis, Conference Manager
Kim Romano, Special Events Manager
Wanda McKnight, Sales Manager
Dacia Coppola, Show Coordinator

Brings together those in the special events industry for new product displays, education, networking and learning. 275 booths.
3M Attendees
Frequency: Annual/January

8419 **VSA Annual Meeting**
Visitor Studies Association
8175-A Sheridan Boulevard
Suite 362
Arvada, CO 80003-1928

303-467-2200; Fax: 303-467-0064
info@visitorstudies.org
www.visitorstudies.org

Alan Friedman, President
Ellen Cox, Treasurer
Jessica Luke, Treasurer
Frequency: Summer

Directories & Databases

8420 **Association Management: Convention Bureau and Convention Hall Issue**
American Society of Association Executives
1575 Eye St NW
Washington, DC 20005-1103

202-626-2700; Fax: 202-371-8825
publicpolicy@asaenet.org
www.asaenet.org

A list of halls, centers, auditoriums, arenas and visitors bureaus in the United States and Canada.
Cost: $4.00
Circulation: 20,000

8421 **Audarena International Guide & Facility Buyers Guide**
VNU Business Publications
49 Music Sq W
4th Floor
Nashville, TN 37203-3213

615-321-4251; Fax: 615-320-0454
Research@billboard.com
www.billboard.com

Ken Schlager, Executive Editor
Mitch Tebo, Directory Marketing Director
George Van, President
Monica Herrera, Manager
Bill Werde, Director
Cost: $99.00
310 Pages
Frequency: October

8422 **CEMA Member Directory**
Computer Event Marketing Association
5098 Foothills Boulevard
Suite 3-386
Roseville, CA 95747

info@cemaonline.com
www.cemaonline.com

Kimberly Gishler, President & CEO
Olga Rosenbrook, Director of Member Services
Stacey Z. Diemer, Membership Manager

All event managers and primary IA members.
500 Pages
Founded in 1990

8423 **Constitution and Membership Roster**
National Association of Agricultural Fair Agencies
MI State Department of Agriculture
PO Box 30017
Lansing, MI 48909

517-373-9766; Fax: 517-373-9146

Carol Carlson, Secretary/Treasurer
Frequency: Annual

8424 **Corporate and Incentive Travel: Official**
2700 N Military Trl
Suite 120
Boca Raton, FL 33431-6394

561-989-0600; Fax: 561-989-9509
www.themeetingmagazines.com/corporate-incentive-travel

Harvey Grotsky, President

8425 **HCEA Directory of Healthcare Meetings and Conventions**
Healthcare Convention & Exhibitors Association
5775 Peachtree Dnwdy Rd
Building G, Suite 500
Atlanta, GA 30342-1556

404-252-3663; Fax: 404-252-0774
hcea@kellencompany.com
www.hcea.org

Eric Allen, Executive Director
Carol Wilson, Director Meetings

Information on 6,000 health care meetings, available to members only.
500 Pages
Founded in 1930

8426 **IAFE Directory**
International Association of Fairs & Expositions
3043 E Cairo
PO Box 985
Springfield, MO 65802

417-862-5771
800-516-0313; Fax: 417-862-0156
iafe@fairsandexpos.com
www.fairsandexpos.com

A annual reference guide giving members access to their associate members' products, services, and business activities.
1300 Members
Frequency: Annual
Founded in 1885

8427 **IEG Sponsorship Sourcebook**
IEG
640 N La Salle Dr
Suite 450
Chicago, IL 60654-3186

312-944-1727
800-834-4850; Fax: 312-944-1897
ieg@sponsorship.com
www.sponsorship.com

Lesa Ukman, CEO
John Ukman, Publisher
Alicia Fidler, Product Manager

A directory of sponsors, properties, agencies and suppliers from th most active sponsors to the hottest sponsorship opportunities. Contains the critical data you need to make smart sponsorship connections.
Cost: $299.00
468 Pages
Frequency: Annual
ISBN: 0-944807-43-7
Printed in on glossy stock

8428 **MPI Membership Directory**
Meeting Professionals International
3030 Lbj Fwy
Suite 1700
Dallas, TX 75234-2759

972-702-3000; Fax: 972-702-3070
feedback@mpiweb.org
www.mpiweb.org

Bruce Mac Millan, President
Frequency: Annual

8429 **Meetings and Conventions: Gavel International Directory Issue**
Reed Travel Group
500 Plaza Dr
Suite C
Secaucus, NJ 07094-3619

201-902-1800; Fax: 207-319-1628

Alina Dalmau, Editor
Lori Cioffi, Manager

Lists over 4,000 convention halls and hotels in the United States, suitable for meetings.
Cost: $35.00
Frequency: Annual
Circulation: 80,000

8430 **NCEE Membership Directory**
National Catholic Educational Exhibitors
2621 Dryden Road
Suite 300
Dayton, OH 45439

937-293-1415
888-555-8512; Fax: 937-293-1310

Bret Thomas, Executive Director
Frequency: Annual

8431 **Nationwide Directory of Corporate Meeting Planners**
Reed Reference Publishing RR Bowker
121 Chanlon Road
New Providence, NJ 07974-1541

908-665-2834; Fax: 908-464-3553
www.bowker.com

Offers valuable information on over 12,000 corporations that hold regular, off-site meetings arranged by over 18,000 corporate meeting planners.
Cost: $297.00
1140 Pages
Frequency: Annual

8432 **Official Meeting Facilities Guide**
Reed Travel Group
500 Plaza Dr
Suite C
Secaucus, NJ 07094-3619

201-902-1800; Fax: 201-902-2053

Virginia Nonneman, Editor
Lori Cioffi, Manager

One thousand national and international meeting facilities, primarily hotels in the US.
Cost: $45.00
Frequency: SemiAnnual
Circulation: 18,500

8433 **Protocol**
Protocol Directory

101 W 12th St
Suite PH-H
New York, NY 10011-8142

212-633-6934; Fax: 212-633-6934
noemail@councilofprotocolexecutives.org
www.councilofprotocolexecutives.org

Edna Greenbaum, Editor

Approximately 4,000 suppliers of products and services used by planners of executive meetings, special events and other entertainment.
Cost: $60.00
Frequency: 1 issue
Founded in 1989
Printed in on matte stock

8434 **Sports Market Place Directory - Online Database**
Grey House Publishing
4919 Route 22
PO Box 56
Amenia, NY 12501

518-789-8700
800-562-2139; Fax: 845-373-6390
gold@greyhouse.com
gold.greyhouse.com
Facebook, Twitter

Leslie Mackenzie, Publisher
Richard Gottlieb, Editor

For over 20 years, this comprehensive, up-to-date directory provides current key information about the people, organizations and events involving the sports industry including, contact information and key executives for single sports organizations, multi-sport organizations, media, sponsors, college sports, manufacturers, trade shows and more.
Founded in 1981

8435 **Trade Show Exhibitors Association: Membership Directory**
Trade Show Exhibitors Association
2301 S Lake Shore Dr
Suite 1005
Chicago, IL 60616-1419

312-842-8732; Fax: 541-317-8749
tsea@tsea.org

Steve Schuldenfrei, President
Emily Burger, Sales Manager

About 1,900 members of the Trade Show Exhibitors Association.
Cost: $55.00
Frequency: Annual February

8436 **Trade Show News Network**
Tarsus Group plc
16985 W Bluemound Road
Suite 210
Brookfield, WI 53005

262-782-1900; Fax: 603-372-5894
rwimberly@tsnn.com
www.tsnn.com

Rachel Wimberly, Editor-in-Chief
John Rice, Sales & Business Development
Arlene Shows, Marketing Manager

The world's leading online resource for the trade show, exhibition and event industry since 1996. TSNN.com owns and operates the most widely consulted event database on the internet, containing data about more than 19,500 trade shows, exhibitions, public events and conferences.
13900 Members
Frequency: Bi-Monthly
Founded in 1196

8437 **TradeShow & Exhibit Manager's Buyer's Guide**
2117 Highland Avenue
Louisville, KY 40204

502-548-3188; Fax: 502-742-8749
www.goldsteinandassociates.com

Steve Goldstein, Publisher

Over 1,000 suppliers of products and services to the trade show industry are profiled.
Cost: $60.00
150 Pages
Frequency: Annual
Circulation: 12,000

8438 **Tradeshow Week Exhibit Manager**
Goldstein & Associates
2117 Highland Avenue
Louisville, KY 40204

502-548-3188; Fax: 502-742-8749
www.goldsteinandassociates.com

Steve Goldstein, Publisher

For exhibit managers.
Cost: $80.00
Frequency: Bi-Monthly
Founded in 1983

8439 **Tradeshow Week's Tradeshow Services Directory**
Business Information Publication
5700 Wilshire Blvd
Suite 120
Los Angeles, CA 90036-7209

323-549-4100; Fax: 323-965-2407
www.tradeshowweek.com

Tina George-Reyes, Editor
Adam Schaffer, Publisher

Offers information on designers, builders, carriers and decorators involved in tradeshow and convention industries.
Cost: $95.00
300 Pages
Frequency: Annual

8440 **VSA Membership Directory**
Visitor Studies Association
8175-A Sheridan Boulevard
Suite 362
Arvada, CO 80003-1928

303-467-2200; Fax: 303-467-0064
info@visitorstudies.org
www.visitorstudies.org

Alan Friedman, President
Ellen Cox, Treasurer
Jessica Luke, Treasurer
Frequency: Annual

8441 **Who's Who in Exposition Management**
International Assn for Exhibition Management
PO Box 802425
Dallas, TX 75380-2425

972-216-1511; Fax: 972-458-8119

Over 1,500 show manager members and 1,500 associate members.
Cost: $225.00
Frequency: Annual June

8442 **Worldwide Tradeshow Schedule**
1700 K Street NW
Suite 403
Washington, DC 20006-3810

202-463-4088

Over 110 international trade fairs are listed in all major industrial sectors.
10 Pages

Industry Web Sites

8443 **http://gold.greyhouse.com**
G.O.L.D Grey House OnLine Databases

Grey House Publishing's online database platform, GOLD, offers Quick Search, Keyword Search and Expert Search for most business sectors including exhibit and meeting planning markets. The GOLD platform makes finding the information you need quick and easy - whether you're a novice searcher or an experienced database user. All of Grey House's directory products are available for subscription on the GOLD platform.

8444 **www.aacei.org**
Association for Advancement of Cost Engineering

Association for Advancement of Cost Engineering provides its members with the resources they need to enhance their performance and ensure continued grouth and success. Serves cost management professionals: cost management and engineers, project managers, planners and schedulers, estimators and bidders, and value engineers.

8445 **www.acmenet.org**
Association for Convention Marketing Executives

Annual meetings for marketing and sales executives.

8446 **www.acomonline.org**
Association for Convention Operations Management

Dedicated to advancing the practice of convention services management in the meetings industry, and to preparing CSM professionals for their critical role in the growth and success of their organizations.

8447 **www.cimpa.org**
Connected Int'l Meeting Professionals Association

Members are conference and convention planners with a certificate in convention management. Specializes in planning meetings events, incentives, using the internet.

8448 **www.clc.org**
Convention Liaison Council

Members are associations which are directly involved in the convention, exposition, trade show and meeting industry.

8449 **www.edpa.com**
Exhibit Designers & Producers Association

Exhibit Designers and Producers Association is an internationally recognized national trade association with more than 370 corporate members from 18 countries that are engaged in the design, manufacture, transport, installation and service of display and exhibits primarily for the trade show industry

8450 **www.edsc.org**
Electronic Distribution Show Corporation

Attendees are manufacturers of electronic components who sell their products through electronics distributors.

8451 **www.esca.org**
Exposition Service Contractors Association

Guide to exposition service is distributed annually and lists safety regulations and building rules in major US convention centers.

8452 **www.greyhouse.com**
Grey House Publishing

Authoritative reference directories for most business sectors including exhibit and meeting planning markets. Users can search the online databases with varied search criteria allowing for custom searches by product category, geographic area, sales volume, keyword, subject and more. Full Grey House catalog and online ordering also available.

8453 **www.hcea.org**
Healthcare Convention & Exhibitors Association

Trade association of over 700 organizations involved in health care exhibiting or providing services to health care conventions, exhibitions and/or meetings.

8454 **www.iaam.org**
International Association of Assembly Managers

Members are managers of auditoriums, arenas, convention centers, stadiums and performing arts centers.

8455 **www.iacc.online.org**
International Association of Conference Centers

A facilities-based organization which advances the understanding and awareness of conference centers as distinct within the training, education, hospitality and travel fields.

8456 **www.moderndisplay.com**
Modern Display

Members are distributors of display equipment.

8457 **www.mpiweb.org**
Meeting Planners International

Meeting industry professionals who plan and/or manage meetings, trade shows and conferences for corporations, educational institutions and associations.

8458 **www.naca.org**
National Association for Campus Activities

Largest collegiate organization for campus activities.

8459 **www.pcma.org**
Professional Convention Management Association

Features emphasize solutions of practical and logistical problems concerning business travel, the hospitality/hotel industry, and related event planning topics

8460 **www.publicshows.com**
National Association of Consumer Shows

Non-profit organization dedicated to furthering the interests of consumer show producers and suppliers.

8461 **www.rcmaweb.org**
Religious Conference Management Association

Provides members with a wealth of resources designed specifically to enhance their professionalism and overall effectiveness as religious leaders.

8462 **www.sgmp.org**
Society of Government Meeting Planners

Trade association for government meeting planners and exhibitors.

Associations

8463 **ACA International**
Association of Credit and Collection Professionals
4040W 70th Street
Minneapolis, MN 55435
952-926-6547; Fax: 952-926-1624
aca@acainternational.org
www.acainternational.org
Facebook, Twitter, LinkedIn, YouTube, The Hub
Mark Neeb, President
International trade organization of over 5,300 credit and collection professionals providing a variety of accounts receivable management services to over 1,000,000 credit grantors.

8464 **About US Association for Financial Counseling and Planning Education**
1940 Duke Street
Suite 200
Alexandria, VA 22314
703-684-4484; Fax: 703-684-4485
rwiggins@afcpe.org
www.afcpe.org
Facebook, Twitter, LinkedIn
Michael Gutter, President
Barry Wilkinson, Past President
Jinhee Kim, President-Elect
Brenda Vaughn, Secretary
Leslie Green-Pimentel, Treasurer
AFCPE is a non-profit professional organization created to promote the education and training of the professional in financial management.
810 Members
Founded in 1983

8465 **Alliance of Merger & Acquisition Advisors**
222 North LaSalle Avenue
Suite 300
Chicago, IL 60601
312-856-9590
877-844-2535; Fax: 312-729-9800
info@amaaonline.org
www.amaaonline.com
Facebook, Twitter, LinkedIn, Google+
Michael Nall, CM&AA, CGMA, Founder and Managing Director
Diane Niederman, VP Business Development
Amie Schneider, Director of Operations
Dylan Whitcher, CM&AA, Business Development Manager
Maxie Gallegos, Social Media & Marketing Specialist
AM&AA is the premier International Organization serving the educational and resource needs of the middle market M&A profession.
Founded in 1998

8466 **Alliance of Merger and Acquisition Advisors**
222 North LaSalle Avenue
Suite 300
Chicago, IL 60601
312-856-9590
877-844-2535; Fax: 312-729-9800
info@amaaonline.org
www.amaaonline.com
Facebook, Twitter, LinkedIn, Google+
Michael Nall, CM&AA, CGMA, Founder and Managing Director
Diane Niederman, VP Business Development
Amie Schneider, Director of Operations
Dylan Whitcher, CM&AA, Business Development Manager
Maxie Gallegos, Social Media & Marketing Specialist
A national organization serving the educational and resource needs of the M&A profession.
200 Members
Founded in 1999

8467 **Allied Financial Adjusters Conference**
956 S. Bartlett Road
Suite 321
Bartlett, IL 60103
800-843-1232; Fax: 888-949-8520
alliedfinanceadjusters@gmail.com
www.alliedfinanceadjusters.com
Facebook, LinkedIn, YouTube
George Badeen, President
Jamie Hernandez, First Vice President
James Osselburn, Second Vice President
Elisa Schmid, Executive Secretary
Bryan Finn, Treasurer
Membership is composed of professsional liquidators, repossessors and skip tracers. Membership fee varies with size of populations of the city served.
200 Members
Founded in 1936

8468 **American Association of Commercial Finance Brokers**
326 E Main Street
Louisville, KY 40202
800-996-2352; Fax: 502-589-3602
info@aacfb.org
www.aacfb.org
Facebook, Twitter, LinkedIn, YouTube
Monica Harper, Executive Director
Natasha Pitcock, Director, Membership & Programs
Broker-oriented association.
500 Members
Founded in 1990
Mailing list available for rent

8469 **American Association of Individual Investors**
625 N Michigan Ave
Suite 1900
Chicago, IL 60611
312-280-0170
800-428-2244; Fax: 312-280-9883
members@aaii.com
www.aaii.com
James B Cloonan, Ph.D., Founder
John Bajkowski, President
Wayne Thorp, Sr. Financial Analyst
An independent, nonprofit corporation formed in 1978 for the purpose of assisting individuals in becoming effective managers of their own assets through programs of education, information and research.
100M+ Members
Founded in 1978

8470 **American Association of Residential Mortgage Regulators**
1025 Thomas Jefferson Street NW
Suite 500 East
Washington, DC 20007
202-521-3999; Fax: 202-833-3636
efreundel@aarmr.org
www.aarmr.org
Kirsten Anderson, President
Clifford Charland, Vice President
Raeleen Schutte, Treasurer
Chris Romano, Secretary
David A. Saunders, Executive Director
Members are state employees responsible for administration or residential mortgage oversight. Primary members include model legislation and best practics.
100 Members
Founded in 1989

8471 **American Bankers Association**
1120 Connecticut Avenue NW
Washington, DC 20036-3902
202-663-5000
800-226-5377; Fax: 202-828-4540
custserv@aba.com
www.aba.com
Facebook, Twitter, LinkedIn, YouTube, Google+, Instagram
Rob Nichols, President & CEO
Alethia Baggett, Chief Human Resources Officer
James Edrington, Chief Member Engagement Officer
Peter Cook, Chief Communications Officer
Karin Flynn, Chief Financial Officer
Brings together all categories of banking institutions to best represent the interests of this rapidly changing industry. It's membership — which includes community, regional and money center banks and holding companies, as well as savings associations, trust companies and savings banks, makes ABA one of the largest banking trade associations in the country.
Founded in 1875

8472 **American Bankruptcy Institute**
66 Canal Center Plaza
Suite 600
Alexandria, VA 22314-1546
703-739-0800; Fax: 703-739-1060
info@abiworld.org
www.abi.org
Facebook, Twitter, LinkedIn, YouTube
Amy Quackenboss, Executive Director
Multidisciplinary, nonpartisan organization dedicated to research and education on matters related to insolvency. Engaged in numerous educational and research activities as well as the production of a number of publications both for the insolvency practitioner and the public.
12000 Members
Founded in 1982

8473 **American Benefits Council**
1501 M Street NW
Suite 600
Washington, DC 20005
202-289-6700; Fax: 202-289-4582
info@abcstaff.org
www.americanbenefitscouncil.org
James A. Klein, President
Lynn D. Dudley, SVP, Global Retirement & Comp. Pol.
Kathryn Spangler, Senior Advisor, Health Policy
Diann Howland, Vice President, Legislative Affairs
On behalf of its members - benefit plan sponsors or service providers - advocates for employer-sponsored benefit programs in Washington.

8474 **American Council of Life Insurers**
101 Constitution Avenue NW.
Suite 700
Washington, DC 20001-2133
202-624-2000
webadmin@acli.com
www.acli.com
Facebook, Twitter, LinkedIn
Daniel Houston, Chair
Susan K. Neely, President & CEO
David C. Turner, EVP & Corporate Secretary
Joyce Y. Meyer, EVP, Government Relations
Jill Kozeny, SVP, Comm. & Public Affairs
Trade association advocating federal, state, and international forums for public policy that supports the industry marketplace. ACLI members offer life insurance, annuities, retirement plans,

long-term care, disability income insurance, and reinsurance.
290 Members
Founded in 1976

8475 **American Education Finance Association**
8365 S Armadillo Trail
Evergreen, CO 80439

303-674-0857; Fax: 303-670-8986
www.aefa.cc

Ed Steinbecher, Executive Director

AEFA encourages communications among groups and individuals in the education finance field, including academicians, researchers, policy makers and practitioners. Serving as a forum for a broad range of issues and concerns, AEFA concerns include traditional school finance concepts, issues of public policy, and teaching school finance.
650 Members
Founded in 1975
Mailing list available for rent

8476 **American Finance Association**
350 Main Street
Malden, MA 02148

781-388-8599
800-835-6770; Fax: 781-388-8232
cs-membership@wiley.com
www.afajof.org
Facebook, Twitter

Patrick Bolton, President
Campbell R. Harvey, President Elect
David Scharfstein, Vice President
James (Jim) Schallheim, Executive Secretary and Treasurer
Kenneth J. Singleton, Editor of the Journal of Finance

Seeks to improve public understanding of financial problems and to provide for exchange of ideas.
11500 Members
Founded in 1939

8477 **American Financial Services Association**
919 18th Street NW
Suite 300
Washington, DC 20006-5517

202-296-5544
info@afsamail.org
www.afsaonline.org
Facebook, Twitter, LinkedIn, Google+

Andrew Stuart, Chair
Nathan D. Benson, Chair-Elect
Gary Phillips, Immediate Past Chair
Chris Stinebert, President & CEO
Jeffery D. Adams, Executive Vice President

The American Financial Services Association is the national trade association for market funded providers of financial services to consumers and small business. These providers offer an array of financial services, including unsecured personal loans, automotive loans, home equity loans and credit cards through specialized bank institutions
400 Members
Founded in 1916

8478 **American Society of Appraisers**
11107 Sunset Hills Road
Suite 310
Reston, VA 20190

703-478-2228
800-272-8258; Fax: 703-742-8471
asainfo@appraisers.org
www.appraisers.org
Facebook, Twitter, YouTube

Johnnie White, Chief Executive Officer
Bonny Price, Chief Operating Officer
Joseph Noselli, Chief Financial Officer
Todd Paradis, Chief Marketing Officer
Sarah Sebastian, Director of Membership Development

Organization provides education and accreditation for appraisers.
Founded in 1939

8479 **American Society of Military Comptrollers**
415 N. Alfred Street
Alexandria, VA 22314

703-549-0360
800-462-5637; Fax: 703-549-3181
www.asmconline.org
Facebook, Twitter, LinkedIn

Ed Gardiner, President
Leslie Ferguson, Vice President
Al Runnels, Executive Director
Nancy A. Phillips, Treasurer
Tery L. Elling, General Counsel

A non-profit educational and professional organization for persons, military and civilian, involved in the overall field of military comptrollership. ASMC promotes the education and training of its members, and supports the development and advancement of the profession of military comptrollership. The society provides professional programs to keep members abreast of current issues and encourages the exchange of information, techniques and approaches.
20000 Members
Founded in 1948

8480 **American Trucking Association**
950 North Glebe Road
Suite 210
Arlington, VA 22203-4181

703-838-1700
nafc@trucking.org
www.truckline.com
Facebook, Twitter, YouTube

Pat Thomas, Chairman
Kevin Burch, First Vice Chairman
David Manning, Second Vice Chairman
Bill Graves, President & CEO
John M. Smith, Secretary

ATA's mission is to serve and represent the trucking industry with a single, united voice to influence policies beneficial to the industry; promote safety on America's highways; improve the industry's image, efficiency, and competitiveness; educate the public about the critical role trucking plays in the economy
1000 Members
Founded in 1933

8481 **Association for Financial Professionals**
4520 East West Hwy
Suite 750
Bethesda, MD 20814-3319

301-907-2862; Fax: 301-907-2864
www.afponline.org
Facebook, Twitter, LinkedIn, YouTube

Terry Crawford, Chair
Michael High, Vice Chair
Gaileon Thompson, Vice Chair

Association of 12,000 financial professionals. Please call for our publication listings or visit us online.
14000 Members
Founded in 1979

8482 **Association for Financial Technology**
10813 Pleasant Valley Road
Frazeysburg, OH 43822

614-895-1208; Fax: 614-895-3466
aft@aftweb.com
www.aftweb.com
Twitter, LinkedIn

Karl Kirsch, Executive Director
Leah Allen, Association Manager

Trade association for companies providing services to the financial industry. Our members provide systems, applications and outsourcing services to 90% of America's banks. Vendors of computer hardware, software and ancilliary products and services are also welcome.
52 Members
Founded in 1975

8483 **Association for the Advancement of Cost Engineering**
1265 Suncrest Towne Centre Drive
Morgantown, WV 26505-1876

304-296-8444; Fax: 304-291-5728
info@aacei.org
www.aacei.org
Twitter, LinkedIn

Ms Julie K. Owen, CCP, PSP, President
Mr John C. Livengood, President-Elect
Mr James E. Krebs, PE, CCP, VP - Administration
Mr. Joseph W. Wallwork. PE, CCP,CFCC, VP - Finance
Dr. Dan Melamed CCP, EVP, VP -TEC

The leading-edge professional society for cost estimators, cost engineers, schedulers project managers, and project control specialists.
7000 Members
Founded in 1956

8484 **Association of Commercial Finance Attorneys**
Kennedy Covington Lobdell & Hickman, LLP
214 N Tryon St
22nd Floor
Charlotte, NC 28202-2367

704-350-7721
www.acfalaw.org

Alison Manzer, President
R. Marshall Grodner, Vice President
Janet Nadile, Vice President
Paul Ricotta, Treasurer
Kenneth Lewis, Secretary

ACF members are attorneys specializing in commercial finance and bankruptcy law. ACFA provides continuing education and publishes material relevant to the field for its members.
350 Members
Founded in 1958

8485 **Association of Finance and Insurance Professionals**
4104 Felps Drive
Suite H
Colleyville, TX 76034-5868

817-428-2434; Fax: 817-428-2534
info@afip.com
www.afip.com
Facebook, Twitter, LinkedIn

Deb Hankins, Manager
Linda J Robertson, Senior Vice President

A nonprofit educational foundation that serves the needs of in-dealership finance and insurance personnel for the automobile, RV, commercial truck and equipment, motorcycle, and motorized sports industries while assisting the lenders, vendors and independent general agents who support the F&I function.
Founded in 1989
Mailing list available for rent

8486 **Association of Government Accountants**
2208 Mount Vernon Avenue
Alexandria, VA 22301-1314
703-684-6931
800-242-7211; Fax: 703-519-0039
communications@agacgfm.org
www.agacgfm.org
Facebook, Twitter, LinkedIn, Flickr
Ann M. Ebberts, Chief Executive Officer
Susan Fritzlen, Chief Operating Officer
Cristina Barbudo, Dir., Finance & Administration
Katya Silver, Dir., Professional Certification
AGA supports the careers and professional development of government finance professionals working in federal, state and local governments as well as the private sector and academia. Through education, research, publications, certification and conferences, AGA reaches thousands of professionals and offers more than 100,000 continuing professional education (CPE) hours annually.
14K+ Members
Founded in 1950

8487 **Association of Latino Professionals in Finance and Accounting**
1717 W. 6th Street
Suite 410
Austin, TX 78703
855-692-5732
carlos.perez@national.alpfa.org
www.alpfa.org
Facebook, Twitter, LinkedIn, YouTube, Instagram
Damian Rivera, Chief Executive Officer
Selene Benavides, Chief Financial Officer
Justin Lopez, Chief Operating Officer
Ann Marquez, Chief of Staff
ALPFA is the leading professsional association dedicated to enhancing opportunities for Latinos in the accounting, finance and related professions. ALPFA is a nonprofit entity registered with the IRS.
72000 Members
Founded in 1972

8488 **Bond Market Foundation**
360 Madison Avenue
New York, NY 10017-7111
646-637-9067; Fax: 646-637-9120
Micah Green
The Bond Market Foundation is a charitable and educational not for profit (501-c-3) association. The Foundation develops and enhances the public's access to quality saving and investor education in addition to providing credible non-proprietary research capacity and expert discussion on public issues relevant to the bond markets. The Bond Market Foundation is partner to the Securities Industry and Financial Markets Association (SIFMA).

8489 **Broadcast Cable Credit Association**
550 W. Frontage Road
Suite 3600
Northfield, IL 60093
847-881-8757; Fax: 847-784-8059
info@bccacredit.com
www.bccacredit.com
Twitter, LinkedIn
Mary Collins, President & CEO
Jamie Grande, Director, Operations
Arcelia Pimentel, Sales/Membership
Dawn Stenstrom, Credit Investigator
Colette Pinter, Credit Investigator
BCCA, a subsidiary of Media Financial Management Association, represents credit and collection professionals from TV, radio, cable, system operators, newspaper, and magazine organizations in the U.S. and Canada. BCCA functions as a central clearinghouse for credit information on advertisers, agencies and buying services, both locally and nationally.
Founded in 1972

8490 **CFA Institute**
560 Ray C. Hunt Drive
PO Box 3668
Charlottesville, VA 22903
434-951-5499
800-247-8132; Fax: 434-951-5262
info@cfainstitute.org
www.cfainstitute.org
Facebook, Twitter, LinkedIn, YouTube, Google+, Instagram
Beth Hamilton- Keen, CFA, Chair, Board of Governors
Frederic P. Lebel, CFA, Vice Chair
Aaron Low, CFA, Immediate Past Chair
Paul Smith, CFA, President & CEO
John L. Bowman , CFA, Managing Director
CFA Institute is the global, non-profit professional association that administers the Chartered Financial Analyst curriculum and examination program worldwide and sets voluntary, ethics-based professional and performance-reporting standards for the investment industry.
70000 Members
Founded in 1990

8491 **CRE Finance Council**
20 Broad St
7th Ffloor
New York, NY 10005
FAX 646-884-7569
info@crefc.org
www.crefc.org
Facebook, Twitter, LinkedIn
Gregory Michaud, Chairman
Matthew Borstein, Chairman-Elect
Nik Chillar, Membership Committee Chair
Daniel E. Bober, Treasurer
Stephen M. Renna, President & CEO
International trade organization for the commercial real estate capital markets. Also represents and promotes an orderly ans ethical global institutional secondary market for the sale of commercial mortgage loans and equity investments.
309 Members
Founded in 1994

8492 **Coalition of Higher Education Assistance Organizations**
1101 Vermont Ave NW
Suite 400
Washington, DC 20005-3586
202-289-3910; Fax: 202-371-0197
hwadsworth@wpllc.net
www.coheao.com
Maria Livolsi, President
Carl Perry, Vice President
Tom Schmidt, Secretary
Lori Hartung, Treasurer
Robert Perrin, Past President
Focus is on legislative and regulatory advocacy for Federal Perkins and other campus based student loan programs.
365 Members
Founded in 1981

8493 **Commercial Finance Association**
370 7th Avenue
Suite 1801
New York, NY 10001
212-792-9390; Fax: 212-564-6053
info@cfa.com
www.cfa.com
Facebook, Twitter, LinkedIn, YouTube
Michael Coiley, Chairman of the Board
Patrick Trammel, President
Andrea Petro, First Vice President
D. Michael Monk, Vice President - Finance
David Grende, Vice President
Trade group of the asset based financial services industry, with members throughout the US, Canada and around the world. Members include the asset based lending arms of domestic and foreign commercial banks, small and large independent finance companies, floor plan financing organizations, factoring organizations and financing subsidiaries of major industrial corporations. CFA membership is by organization, not by individual.
300 Members
Founded in 1944

8494 **Construction Financial Management Association**
100 Village Boulevard
Suite 200
Princeton, NJ 08540-5783
609-452-8000
888-421-9996; Fax: 609-452-0474
info@cfma.org
www.cfma.org
Facebook, Twitter, LinkedIn, YouTube
Stuart Binstock, President & CEO
Brian Summers, VP, Operations
Catherine Wasner, VP, Member Services
Samantha Lake, VP, Marketing
Stacey Scholl, Director, Finance
CFMA is the only organization dedicated to bringing together construction financial professionals and those partners serving their unique needs. CFMA has 98 chapters located throughout the US and Canada.
8600 Members
Founded in 1981

8495 **Defense Credit Union Council**
601 Pennsylvania Ave NW
South Building, Suite 600
Washington, DC 20004-2601
202-638-3950; Fax: 202-638-3410
admin@dcuc.org
www.dcuc.org
Facebook, Twitter
Denise Floyd, Chairman & At Large Representative
Gordon A. Simmons, 1st Vice Chair
Frank Padak, 2nd Vice Chair
Michael Kloiber, Secretary & Air Force Rep.
Craig Chamberlin, Treasurer & Marine Corps Rep
Organizations of credit unions whose membership consists wholly or in part of personnel of the US Department of Defense, both military and civilians.
14 m Members
Founded in 1963

8496 **EMTA - Emerging Markets Trade Association**
360 Madison Avenue
17th Floor
New York, NY 10017
646-289-5410; Fax: 646-289-5429
awerner@emta.org
www.emta.org
Mark L. Coombs, Co-Chair
Robert H. Milam, J.P, Co-Chair
Brian Weinstein, Vice Chair
Alberto Agrest, Vice Chair
Marcel Naime, Vice Chair
EMTA is the principal trade group for the Emerging Markets trading and investment community and is dedicated to promoting the or-

derly development of fair, efficient, and transparent trading markets for Emerging Markets into the global capital markets.
Founded in 1990

8497 **Emerging Markets Private Equity Association**
Watergate Office Building
2600 Virginia Ave. NW, Suite 500
Washington, DC 20037-1905
202-333-8171
support@empea.net
www.empea.org
Facebook, Twitter, LinkedIn
Shannon Stroud, VP, Programs & Business Development
Randy Mitchell, VP, Strategic Development
Ann Marie Plubell, VP, Regulatory Affairs
Holly Radel, VP, Marketing & Communications
Kyoko Terada, VP, Membership & Industry Partners
A nonprofit organization that supports private equity investors in emerging markets with data and market intelligence.
300 Members

8498 **Equipment Leasing and Finance Association**
1625 Eye St. NW
Suite 850
Washington, DC 20006
202-238-3400; Fax: 202-238-3401
rpetta@elfaonline.org
www.elfaonline.org
Facebook, Twitter, LinkedIn, RSS, YouTube
Ralph Petta, President and CEO
Paul Stilp, Chief Financial & Operating Officer
Amy Vogt, VP, Communications
Julie Benson, VP, Membership Marketing
Andy Fishburn, VP, Federal Government Relations
Represents financial services companies and manufacturers involved in the dynamic equipment finance sector to the business community, government and media.
700+ Members
Founded in 1961
Mailing list available for rent

8499 **Evangelical Council for Financial Accountability**
440 W Jubal Early Dr
Auite 100
Winchester, VA 22601-6319
540-535-0103
800-323-9473; Fax: 540-535-0533
info@ecfa.org
www.ecfa.org
Facebook, Twitter, LinkedIn, YouTube
Michael Little, Chair
Michael Batts, Vice Chair
Kenneth Larson, Secretary
Richard A. Alvis, Treasurer
Thomas Addington, Board Member
Helps organizations earn the public's trust through developing and maintaining standards of accountability that convey ethical practices.
1500 Members
Founded in 1979

8500 **FSC/DISC Tax Association**
3 Bethesda Metro Center
Suite 250
Bethesda, MD 20814-5377
703-341-3500
800-372-1033; Fax: 914-328-5757
blawhelp@bna.com
www.bna.com
Facebook, Twitter
Josh Eastright, CEO
Mike McCarty, Chief Financial Officer
Christina Correira, Chief Human Resources Officer
Cesca Antonelli, Editor-In-Chief
The only organization operating on a national level devoted to educational interests of companies that have set up a foreign sales corporation.
300 Members
Founded in 1982

8501 **Financial & Security Products Association**
1024 Mebane Oaks Road
Suite 273
Mebane, NC 27302
919-648-0664
800-843-6082; Fax: 919-648-0670
www.fspa1.com
Grant Case, Chairman
Fred Wheeler, President
B.J. Hanson, Executive Director
Bryce Good, Vice President
Dave Pepin, Secretary-Treasurer
Independent dealers, manufacturers and associates whose outstanding products and services give financial institutions a crucial edge in performance, efficiency and economy.
Founded in 1973

8502 **Financial Executives International**
1250 Headquarters Plaza
West Tower, 7th Floor
Morristown, NJ 07960
973-765-1000; Fax: 973-765-1018
membership@financialexecutives.org
www.financialexecutives.org
Facebook, Twitter, LinkedIn, Instagram
Andreas Rothe, National Chair
Andrej Suskavcevic, President/CEO
Kevin McBride, National Vice Chair
Alice Jolla, National Secretary
Bret Lawson, National Treasurer
FEI strives to be recognized globally as the leading organization for senior-level financial executives. Connects members through: interaction: providing local and international forums for connecting with peers, information: providing insight to assist with informed business decisions, influence: providing authoritative representation for members' interests, and integrity: providing the tools to advance the profession through ethical leadership.
10000 Members
Founded in 1931

8503 **Financial Management Association International**
University of South Florida
4202 E. Fowler Avenue
BSN 3403
Tampa, FL 33620-5500
813-974-2084; Fax: 813-974-3318
fma@coba.usf.edu
www.fma.org
Facebook, Twitter, LinkedIn, YouTube
Michelle Lui, Executive Director
Dawn Appleby, Program Assistant
Linda Grimm, Manager, Admin. & Membership
Kieara Nunez, Manager, Marketing & Communications
Shannon Tompkins, Director, Student Programs
Serving the global finance community by: Promoting the development of high-quality research that extends the frontier of financial knowledge; Promoting the understanding of basic and applied research and of sound financial practices; Enhancing the quality and relevance of education in finance; Providing opportunities for professional interaction between and among academics, practitioners, and students.
Founded in 1970

8504 **Financial Managers Society**
1 North LaSalle Street
Suite 3100
Chicago, IL 60602-4003
312-578-1300
800-275-4367; Fax: 312-578-1308
info@fmsinc.org
www.fmsinc.org/cms
John A. Carrozza, Chair
Alana Vartanian, Chief Operating Officer
Taylor Weathers, Director, Membership
Jennifer Lindberg, Director, Marketing & Communication
Mark Loehrke, Editor/Writer
Is the only individual membership society exclusively serving the technical and professional needs of today's bank, thrift and credit union financial officers.
1600 Members
Founded in 1948

8505 **Financial Markets Association**
333 Second Street NE
#104
Washington, DC 20002
202-547-6327
www.fmaweb.org
Peter Wadkins, President
Geoffrey Gowey, Vice President
Robert J Tum-Suden, Treasurer
Carlene Crnkovich, Secretary
A world-class organization of Foreign Exchange, Money Market, and Derivative traders, salespersons, brokers, vendors, and corporate participants organized for the purpose of education, promotion, fellowship, and advancement of the wholesale market within the United States.
300 Members
Founded in 1958

8506 **Financial Planning Association**
7535 E. Hampden Avenue
Suite 600
Denver, CO 80231
303-759-4900
800-322-4237; Fax: 303-759-0749
info@onefpa.org
www.plannersearch.org
Facebook, Twitter, LinkedIn
Marv Tuttle, Executive Director
Ian McKenzie, Managing Director/Publishing
Lauren Schadle CAE, Associate Executive Director/COO
FPA is the professional membership association that represents the financial planning community.
29000 Members
Founded in 2000

8507 **Financial Services Technology Consortium**
600 13th Street NW
Suite 400
Washington, DC 20005
202-289-4322; Fax: 202-628-2558
bits@fsround.org
www.bits.org
Christopher F. Feeney, President
Nancy Guglielmo, Vice President
Andrew Kennedy, Senior Program Manager
Josh Magri, Regulatory Counsel
Denise Miller, Executive & Comm. Assistant
Association of leading North American-based financial institutions, technology vendors, independent research organizations and government agencies. Goal is to promote interoperable,

open-standard technologies that provide critical infrastructures for the finacial services industry.
Founded in 1993

8508 Financial Services Roundtable
600 13th Street NW
Suite 400
Washington, DC 20005

202-289-4322; Fax: 202-628-2558
info@fsroundtable.org
www.fsroundtable.org
Twitter, LinkedIn, YouTube

Frederick H Waddel, Chairman
Ajaypal S. Banga, Chairman-Elect
Larry Zimpleman, Immediate Past Chairman
Kessel Stelling, Treasurer
Richard K. Davis, Director

Mission is to be the premier executive forum for the leaders of the financial services industry; to provide powerful legislative and regulatory advocacy; to enhance the industry's public reputation; and led by BITS, to promote best practices and a strong infrastrucutre in technology.
Founded in 1993

8509 Financial Services Technology Consortium
600 13th Street NW
Suite 400
Washington, DC 20005

202-289-4322; Fax: 202-628-2558
www.bits.org

Christopher F. Feeney, President
Nancy Guglielmo, Vice President
Andrew Kennedy, Senior Program Manager
Josh Magri, Regulatory Counsel
Denise Miller, Executive & Comm. Assistant

FSTC sponsors product testing, development programs, and other projects to ensure the continued viability of new technologies in the financial sector.
Founded in 1993

8510 Financial Services Technology Network
411 Borel Ave
Ste 620
San Mateo, CA 94402

312-782-4951; Fax: 312-580-0165
fstn@gss.net
www.fsnweb.com
Facebook, Twitter, LinkedIn

Kathleen Luleasile, Executive Director
Dale Smith, President
Kathy Johnson, Secretary/Treasurer

8511 Financial Women International
1027 W Roselawn Avenue
Roseville, MN 55113

651-487-7632
866-807-6081; Fax: 651-489-1322
info@fwi.org

FWI is dedicated to developing leaders, accelerating careers, and generating results for professionals in the banking and financial services industry.
1000 Members
Founded in 1921

8512 Fraud & Theft Information Bureau
9770 S Military Trail
Suite 380
Boynton Beach, FL 33436

561-737-8700; Fax: 561-737-5800

Larry Schwartz, Founder/Director
Pearl Sax, Founder/Director

A leading consultant on credit card and check fraud control and loss prevention, and the publisher of related manuals and fraud-blocker data bases.
Founded in 1982

8513 Futures Industry Association
2001 Pennsylvania Ave NW
Suite 600
Washington, DC 20006-1823

202-446-5460; Fax: 202-296-3184
info@fia.org
www.fia.org
Facebook, Twitter, LinkedIn, Flickr

Gerald Corcoran, Chairman & CEO
M. Clark Hutchison, Treasurer
Emily Portney, Secretary
Craig Abruzzo, Managing Director
Antoine Babule, Managing Director

Representative of all organizations that have an interest in the futures market.
180 Members
Founded in 1955

8514 Global Association of Risk Professionals
111 Town Square Place
14th Floor
Jersey City, NJ 07310-2778

201-719-7210; Fax: 201-222-5022
Memberservices@garp.com
www.garp.com
Facebook, Twitter, LinkedIn, Google+, YouTube

Richard Apostolik, President & CEO
Ken Abbott, Chief Risk Officer
William Martin, Chief Risk Officer
Ben Golub, Chief Risk Officer
Laura Dottori, Senior Executive VP & CRO

GARP's international membership includes a varity of professionals from the finance industry who share a common interest in financial risk management practice and research.
52330 Members
Founded in 2000

8515 Government Finance Officers Association
203 N La Salle St
Suite 2700
Chicago, IL 60601-1216

312-977-9700; Fax: 312-977-4806
inquiry@gfoa.org
www.gfoa.org
Facebook, Twitter, LinkedIn, YouTube

Marion M. Gee, President
Chris Morrill, Executive Director
Mike Mucha, Deputy Executive Director
John Jurkash, Chief Financial Officer

The purpose of the Government Finance Officers Association is to enhance and promote the professional management of governments for the public benefit by identifying and developing financial policies and practices and promoting them through education, training and leadership.
17300 Members
Founded in 1906

8516 Healthcare Billing and Management Association
2025 M Street NW
Suite 800
Washington, DC 20036

877-640-4262; Fax: 202-367-2177
info@hbma.org
www.hbma.org
Facebook, Twitter, LinkedIn, YouTube

Andre Williams, Executive Director
Zoe Fuller, Operations & Administration
Caroline Fabacher, Program Coordinator
Ellie Hurley, Event Services
David Merli, Advertising/ Sales

Members are companies providing third-party medical billing services.
500 Members
Founded in 1993
Mailing list available for rent

8517 Healthcare Financial Management Association
3 Westbrook Corporate Center
Suite 600
Westchester, IL 60154

708-531-9600
800-252-4362; Fax: 708-531-0032
webmaster@hfma.org
www.hfma.org
Facebook, Twitter, LinkedIn, YouTube

Joseph J. Fifer, FHFMA, CPA, CEO & President
Joyce Zimowski, FHFMA, CPA, Executive Vice President & CFO
Susan Brenkus, Vice President, Human Resources
Richard L Gundling, Vice President, Healthcare

Brings perspective and clarity to the industry's complex issues for the purpose of preparing our members to succeed. Through our programs, publications and partnerships we enhance the capabilities that strengthen not only individual careers, but also the organizations from which our members come.
40000 Members

8518 Initiatives of Change, USA
2201 West Broad Street
Suite 200
Richmond, VA 23220-2022

804-305- 176; Fax: 804-358-1769
www.us.iofc.org
Facebook, Twitter

H. Alexander Wise, Chairman
Patrick T. Mcnamara, Executive Vice Chairman
William S. Elliott, Executive Director
Valerie Lemmie, Treasurer
Anjum A. Ali, Secretary

Is the national voice for lenders and investors engaged in the reverse mortgage business.
Founded in 1997
Mailing list available for rent

8519 Institute for Divorce Financial Analysts
1005 Slater Road
Suite 101
Durham, NC 27703

800-875-1760
info@institutedfa.com
www.institutedfa.com
Twitter, LinkedIn

Carol Lee Roberts, President

The Institute for Divorce Financial Analysts (IDFAT) is the premier national organization dedicated to the certification, education and promotion of the use of financial professionals in the divorce arena.
5000 Members
Founded in 1993

8520 Institute of Internal Auditors
247 Maitland Ave
Altamonte Springs, FL 32701-4201

407-937-1111; Fax: 407-937-1101
customerrelations@theiia.org
www.theiia.org
Facebook, Twitter, LinkedIn

Lawrence J. Harrington, Chairman of the Board
J. Michael Joyce Jr. CIA , CRMA, Chairman of North American Board
Richard F. Chambers, CIA, CGAP, C, President and CEO

Independent, objective assurance and consulting activity designed to add value to an organization's operations. It helps an organization accomplish its objectives by bringing a systematic, disciplined approach to evaluate and improve the effectiveness of risk management, control and governance processes. Representation from more than 100 countries.

10000 Members
Founded in 1941

8521 Institute of International Finance
1333 H St NW
Suite 800 E
Washington, DC 20005-4770

202-857-3600; Fax: 202-775-1430
info@iif.com
www.iif.com
Facebook, YouTube

Douglas J. Flint, Chairman
Roberto E Setubal, Vice Chairman
Walter Kielholz, Vice Chairman
Marcus Wallenberg, Vice Chairman and Treasurer
Timothy D. Adams, President and CEO

Members are primarily international, commercial banks that focus on middle-income countries by communicating with the debtor countries, international financial institutions and regulatory agencies in order to improve the process of international lending.

450 Members
Founded in 1983

8522 Institute of Management & Administration
3 Bethesda Metro Center
Suite 250
Bethesda, MD 20814-5377

800-372-1033
703-341-3500; Fax: 800-253-0332
blawhelp@bna.com
www.ioma.com
Facebook, Twitter, YouTube

Gregory C. McCaffery, President & CEO
Sue Martin, Chief Operating Officer
Paul Albergo, Bureau Chief
Joe Breda, Executive Vice President - Product
Daniel M. Fine, Executive Vice President-Strategy

An independent source of exclusive business management information for experienced senior and middle management professionals.

8523 Institute of Management Accountants
10 Paragon Dr
Suite 1
Montvale, NJ 07645-1760

201-573-9000
800-638-4427; Fax: 201-474-1600
ima@imanet.org
www.imanet.org
Facebook, Twitter, LinkedIn, YouTube

Paul E. Juras, Chair
Jeffrey C. Thomson, President & CEO

To provide a dynamic forum for management accounting and finance professionals to develop and advance their careers through certification, research and practice development, education, networking, and the advocacy of the highest ethical and professional practices.

90K Members
Founded in 1919

8524 Institutional Shareholder Services
101 Federal St.
Suite 2105
Boston, MA 02110

646-680-6350; Fax: 301-556-0491
www.issgovernance.com

Gary Retelny, President & CEO
Stephen Harvey, Chief Revenue Officer
Nancy Adler, Head of Marketing
Chris Cernich, Deputy Director Of Global Research
Mark Brockway, Head of the ISS Corporate Services

Leading provider of independent and impartial research on coporations and their shareholders.
500 Members
Founded in 1972

8525 International Association of Financial Engineers
555 Eight Avenue
Suite 1902
New York, NY 10018

646-736-0705; Fax: 646-417-6378
www.iaqf.org

David Jaffe, Executive Director

The IAFE is a not-for-profit, professional society dedicated to fostering the profession of quantitative finance by providing platforms to discuss cutting-edge and pivotal issues in the field. Its composed of individual academic and practioners from banks, broker dealers, hedge funds, pension funds, asset managers, technology firms, regulators, accounting, consulting and law firms and universities worldwide.
Founded in 1992

8526 International Association of Purchasing
45 Woodside W
Patchogue, NY 11772

631-654-2384; Fax: 516-475-2754

A professional organization dedicated to the advancement of world trade. Membership is open to buyers, purchasing managers, executives and all individuals that may be involved or have an interest in the important function of buying goods and services on the global market. A nonprofit organization.
1600 Members
Founded in 1985

8527 International Society of Financiers
64 Brookside Drive
Hendersonville, NC 28792-9207

828-698-7805; Fax: 828-698-7806

Ronald I Gershen, Chairman/President

A professional society of brokers, consultants, investors and corporate lenders active in financial projects and transactions. ISF provides an exclusive and confidential forum for member-to-member exchange and business networking.
300 Members
Founded in 1979

8528 International Swaps and Derivatives Association
360 Madison Ave
16th Floor
New York, NY 10017

212-901-6000; Fax: 212-901-6001
isda@isda.org
www.isda.org

Eric Litvack, Chairman
Richard Prager, Vice Chairman
Keith Bailey, Secretary
Dianeÿ Genova, Treasurer
Yasunobu Arima, Director

Represents firms, primarily financial institutions, corporations and government entities who deal in privately-negoiated derivatives, as well as firms who provide services to such institutions. ISDA's, mission is to encourage the productive development of interest rate, currency, commodity, and equity swaps as financial products.
Founded in 1985

8529 International Union of Housing Finance
Rue Jacques de Lalaing 28
B-1040 Brussels
Belgium

322-231-0371; Fax: 322-230-8245
info@housingfinance.org

Dale Bottom, Secretary General

Disseminates information in housing finance policies and techniques worldwide.
107 Members
Founded in 1914

8530 Investment Company Institute
1401 H St NW
Suite 1200
Washington, DC 20005

202-326-5800
webmaster@ici.org
www.ici.org
Facebook, Twitter, LinkedIn, vimeo.com

F.William McNabb III, Chairman
Gregory E. Johnson, Vice Chairman
Paul Schott Stevens, President & CEO
Peter H Gallary, Chief Operating Officer
Donald C Auerbach, Chief Government Affairs Officer

Acts to represent members in matters of legislation, taxation, regulation, economic research and marketing and public information regarding investments and mutual funds.
9400+ Members
Founded in 1940

8531 Investment Recovery Association
638 W 39th Street
Kansas City, MO 64111

816-561-5323
800-728-2272; Fax: 816-561-1991
www.invrecovery.org

Barry Street, President
Sean Byro, Senior Vice President
Kelly May, Secretary
Todd Thompson, Treasurer
Paul Hoffman, Director

Helps fulfill an important role by bringing people together from disparate industries...all focused on sharing best IR practices and improving the knowledge and skills necessary to properly perform the wide-ranging responsibilities required of investment recovery practitioners.

8532 Latin American Private Equity and Venture Capital Association
589 Eighth Ave
18th Fl.
New York, NY 10018

646-315-6735; Fax: 646-349-1047
lavca.org
Twitter, LinkedIn

Cate Ambrose, President & Executive Director
Ivonne Cuello, Director, Bus. Dev. & Strategy

A nonprofit organization that supports the growth of the private equity and venture capital industry in Latin America.
170+ Members

8533 **Media Financial Management Association**
550 W. Frontage Road
Suite 3600
Northfield, IL 60093
847-716-7000; Fax: 847-716-7004
info@mediafinance.org
www.mediafinance.org
Twitter, LinkedIn
Mary M. Collins, President & CEO
Jamie Grande, Director of Operations
Arcelia Pimentel, Director of Sales
Mandy Aioeong, Admin. & Marketing Coordinator
Professional society of more than 1,300 of media's top financial, MIS Credit and HR executives, plus associates in auditing, data processing, software development, law, tax and credit and collections.
1200 Members
Founded in 1961

8534 **Mutual Fund Education Alliance**
100 NW Englewood Rd
Suite 130
Kansas City, MO 64118-4076
816-454-9422; Fax: 816-454-9322
mfea@mfea.com
www.mfea.com
Facebook, Twitter
Michelle Smith, Executive Director
Conducts public education and public relation activities in an effort to acquaint investors, industry organizations and government agencies with direct market funds.
Founded in 1971

8535 **Mutual Fund Investors Association**
85 Wells Avenue
Suite 109
Newton, MA 02459
617-321-2200
800-492-6868; Fax: 61 -32 -221
info@adviserinvestments.com
www.kobren.com
Daniel P Weiner, Chair & CEO
David Thorne, President
James H. Lowell, Chief Investment Officer
Chris Keith, Senior Vice President
Jeffrey DeMaso, Director Of Research
Association for those interested in information and rates for mutual funds, investments, stocks and bonds.
Founded in 1994

8536 **NACHA - Electronic Payments Association**
2550 Wasser Terrace
Suite 400
Herndon, VA 20171
703-561-1100; Fax: 703-787-0996
www.nacha.org
Facebook, Twitter, LinkedIn
Jane Larimer, CEO
Deb Evans-Doyle, Sr Director Conference Marketing
Julie Hedlund, Sr Director Electronic Commerce
Michael Herd, Director Public Relations
NACHA is a trade association that forms the cooperative foundation for the automated clearing house (ACH) payments system through a network of 21 ACH associations nationwide. It also provides marketing and educational members through direct memberships and a network of regional payment associations.
Founded in 1974

8537 **Nat'l Institute of Pension Administrators**
330 N Wabash Ave
Suite 2000
Chicago, IL 60611-7621
800-999-6472
800-999-6272; Fax: 312-673-6609
nipa@nipa.org
www.nipa.org
LinkedIn
Patrick M. Shelton, President
Michelle Marsh, President Elect and CFO
Joseph Burt, Chief financial Officer
Robert Chin, Director
Ralph DelSesto, Director
The Institute is responsible for the formation Of professional standards, an ongoing education program consisting of workshops and home study courses, and awards of the APA and the APR designations by examination and experience.
1000 Members
Founded in 1983

8538 **National Aircraft Finance Association**
PO Box 1570
Edgewater, MD 21037
410-571-1740; Fax: 410-571-1780
info@nafa.aero
www.nafa.aero
Facebook, Twitter, LinkedIn
David Jarvis, President
Chris Miller, Vice President
Ford Von Weise, Vice President
Karen Griggs, Executive Director
Anthony Kioussis, Secretary
A non-profit corporation dedicated to promoting the general welfare of individual and organization providing aircraft financing and loans secured by aircraft; to improve the industry's service to the public; to work with government agencies to foster a greater understanding of our member's needs.
95 Members
Founded in 1969

8539 **National Association of Affordable Housing Lenders**
1667 K St NW
Suite 210
Washington, DC 20006
202-293-9850; Fax: 202-293-9852
naahl@naahl.org
www.naahl.org
Buzz Roberts, President & CEO
Sara Olson Spofford, Operations Director
Cherri Sinclair, Communications Director
Is the only association devoted to increasing private capital lending and investment in low and moderate income communities.
800 Members
Founded in 1977

8540 **National Association of Bankruptcy Trustees**
One Windsor Cove
Suite 305
Columbia, SC 29223
803-252-5646
800-445-8629; Fax: 803-765-0860
info@nabt.com
www.nabt.com
Jennifer Brinkley, Executive Director
Amanda Davis, Staff
Hannah Martin, Staff
The majority of the members of the NABT are Chapter 7 trustees who primarily liquidate non-exempt assets for the benefit of creditors.
1200 Members
Founded in 1982

8541 **National Association of Certified Valuators and Analysts**
5217 South State Street
Suite 400
Salt Lake City, UT 84107
801-486-0600
800-677-2009; Fax: 801-486-7500
nacva1@nacva.com
www.nacva.com
Alina Rivera, Chair, Executive Advisory Board
Parnell Black, CEO
Brien K. Jones, Executive VP & COO
Jonathan Jackson, Executive Director
Global, professional association that supports the business valuation and litigation consulting disciplines within the CPA and professional communities. Along with its training and certification programs, NACVA offers a range of support services, reference materials, software, and customized databases to enhance the professional capabilities and capacities of its members.
6500 Members
Founded in 1990

8542 **National Association of Corporate Treasurers**
12100 Sunset Hills Road
Suite 130
Reston, VA 20190-3221
703-437-4377; Fax: 703-435-4390
nact@nact.org
www.nact.org
LinkedIn
Ramon Yi, Chairman
Mary Dean Hall, President
Joseph C. Sullivan, Vice-President
Ruud Roggekamp, Secretary/Treasurer
Thomas C. Deas, Immediate Past Chairman
Members are corporate chief financial officers, treasurers or assistant treasurers.
825 Members
Founded in 1982

8543 **National Association of Development Companies**
1725 Desales St NW
Suite 504
Washington, DC 20036
202-349-0070; Fax: 202-349-0071
www.nadco.org
Facebook, Twitter, Stumbleupon
Sally Robertson, Chairman
Mary Mansfield, Vice Chair
Randy Griffin, Treasurer
Pat MacKrell, Secretary
Barbara Vohryxek, President & CEO
Provides long term, fixed asset financing to small businesses.
135 Members
Founded in 1981

8544 **National Association of Division Order Analysts**
PO Box 2300
Less Summit, MO 64063
972-715-4489
administrator@nadoa.org
www.nadoa.org
Facebook, Twitter, LinkedIn
Jason Lucas, President
Mary Sons, Vice President
Nancy Cemino, CDOA, 2nd Vice President
Angela Korthauer, Treasurer
Kim Henderson, CDOA, Corresponding Secretary
Division order analysts are petroleum and gas company employees or independent consultants responsible for royalty working interest and overiding royalty payments. Offers a certif-

ication program providing education, training and testing for qualified applicants desiring to attain Certified Divison Order Analyst credentials.

900 Members
Frequency: 4
Founded in 1974

8545 **National Association of Federal Credit Unions**

3138 10th St N
Arlington, VA 22201-2149

703-522-4770
800-336-4644; Fax: 703-524-1082
www.nafcu.org
Facebook, Twitter

B. Dan Berger, President & CEO
Anthony W. Demangone, Executive VP & COO
Greg Johns, VP, Finance
Jacqueline Ortiz Ramsay, VP, Media Relations & Communication
Catherine Porterfield, VP, Membership

Trade association exclusively represents the interests of federal credit unions before the federal government and the public. Provides members with representation, information, education and assistance to meet the challenges that cooperative financial institutions face in today's economic environment. Stands as a national forum for the federal credit union community where new ideas, issues, concerns and trends can be identified, discussed and resolved.

Founded in 1967

8546 **National Association of Independent Public Finance Advisors**

19900 MacArthur Boulevard
Suite 1100
Irvine, CA 92612

630-896-1292
844-770-6262; Fax: 209-633-6265

Jeanine Rogers Caruso, President
Terri Heaton, Vice President
Bruce A. Kimmel, CIPFA, Secretary
Micheal Sudsina, CIPFA, Treasurer
Shelly Aronson,CIPFA, Director at large

A professional organization limited to firms that specialize in providing financial advice on bond sales and financial planning on public projects of public agencies. Promotes the common interests of independent advisory firm members.

48 Members
Founded in 1989

8547 **National Association of Investors Corporation**

711 W 13mile Road
Suite 900
Madison Heights, MI 48071

248-654-3047
877-275-6242; Fax: 248-583-4880
webmaster@betterinvesting.org
www.betterinvesting.org
Facebook, Twitter

Roger H Ganser, Chairman
Kamie Zaracki, CEO
Stephen Sanborn, Treasurer
Gary Ball, Director
Robert Brooker, Director

Strives to counsel and teach investing techniques and sound investment procedures to interested people.

23000 Members
Founded in 1951

8548 **National Association of Local Housing Finance Agencies**

2025 M St NW
Suite 800
Washington, DC 20036

202-367-1197; Fax: 202-367-2197
info@nalhfa.org
www.nalhfa.org

Ron Williams, President
W.D Morris, Vice President
Vivian Benjamin, Treasurer
Tom Cummings, Secretary
Kurt Creager, Director

The National Association of Local Housing Finance Agencies, founded in 1982, is the national association of professionals working to finance affordable housing in the broader community development context at the local level. As a non-profit association, NALHFA is an advocate before Congress and federal agencies on legislative and regulatory issues affecting affordable housing and provides technical assistance and educational opportunities to its members and the public.

Founded in 1982

8549 **National Association of Personal Financial Advisors**

8700 W. Bryn Mawr Avenue
Suite 700 N
Chicago, IL 60631

847-483-5400
888-333-6659; Fax: 847-483-5415
info@napfa.org
www.napfa.org

Geoffrey Brown, CEO
Mardi Lee, Assistant to CEO
Heidi Tennant, Sr. Coordinator, Membership

Members are financial planners who are compensated only by fees. NAPFA members are prohibited from receiving any type of product-related compensation, such as sales commissions. Members do not sell products nor do they direct sales to parties with whom they have financial interests.

2400 Members
Founded in 1983

8550 **National Association of Publicly Traded Partnerships**

1200 19th Street, NW
Suite 700
Washington, DC 20036

202-973-2400
800-621-8390; Fax: 202-973-2401
inquiries@navigant.com
www.mlpassociation.org
LinkedIn, YouTube

William M Goodyear, Chairman And CEO
Thomas A. Glidehaus, Director
Cynthia A. Glassman, Phd, Director
Julie M. Howard, Director & Navigant CEO
Stephan A. James, Director

A trade association representing publicly traded limited partnerships (and publicly traded LLCs taxed partnerships) and those who work with them.

Founded in 1983
Mailing list available for rent

8551 **National Association of Review Appraisers & Mortgage Underwriters**

810 N Farrell Drive
Palm Springs, CA 92262

760-327-5284
877-743-6805; Fax: 760-327-5631
support@assoc-hdqts.org
www.naramu.org
LinkedIn

Jerry M. Green, Owner
Gary R. Vermaat, President
Robert e. Runyan, Vice President

Association for professionals who review real estate appraisals and underwrite real estate mortgages. The association offers the CRA, Certified Review Appraiser and RMU, Registered Mortgage Underwriter, professional designation.

2852 Members
Founded in 1975
Mailing list available for rent: 3500 names at $75 per M

8552 **National Association of Sales Professionals**

555 Friendly Street
Bloomfield Hills, MI 48341

480-596-6634
866-365-1520; Fax: 248-254-6757
www.nasp.com
Facebook, Twitter, LinkedIn

Rod Hairston, CEO & Chairman
Idris Grant, President and COO
Tonia Revere, Director
Sabine Grant, Vice President
Amanda Ritz, Membership, director & advisor

Members are companies who purchase structured settlements, lottery annuities, and similar periodic payment plans from their beneficiaries.

Founded in 1991

8553 **National Association of State Budget Officers**

444 N Capitol St NW
Suite 642
Washington, DC 20001

202-624-5382; Fax: 202-624-7745
spattison@nasbo.org
www.nasbo.org
Facebook, Twitter, LinkedIn

Shelby Kerns, Executive Director
Keely Martin Bosler, Director, Finance
Kate Nass, President

Membership limited to three budget officers per state. Affiliated with the National Governors Association.

160 Members
Founded in 1945

8554 **National Association of Tax Professionals**

PO Box 8002
Appleton, WI 54912-8002

800-558-3402
800-558-3402; Fax: 800-747-0001
natp@natptax.com
www.natptax.com

Brett Rosser, EA, President
Jaimee Hammer, Vice-President
Melissa Bowman, Treasurer
Sherri Hoskisson, Secretary

The National Association of Tax Professionals (NATP) is a nonprofit professional association founded in 1979 and is committed to excellence in the tax profession. Our national headquarters is located in Appleton, Wisconsin and employs 42 professionals and 25 instructors. NATP was formed to serve professionals who work in all areas of tax practice and has more than 19,500 members nationwide.

24000 Members
Founded in 1979

8555 National Association of Trade Exchanges
926 easterm Avenue
Malden, MA 02148

617-763-3311
bartertrainer@aol.com
www.natebarter.com
Facebook, LinkedIn

Anne Weiser, President
Ric Zampatti, Vice President
Rolf Wilkin, Director
Maurya Lane, Director
Kim Ames, Secretary

NATE offers their members additional benefits such national and regional meetings and accreditation opportunities.
80 Members
Founded in 1984

8556 National Automotive Finance Association
7037 Ridge Road
Suite 300
Hanover, MD 21076-1343

410-712-4036
800-463-8955; Fax: 410-712-4038
inquire@nafassociation.com
www.nafassociation.com
LinkedIn

Steve Hall, Chairman
Mark Floyd, President
Scot Seagrave, Vice President
Ian Anderson, Vice President
Gary Schultz, Secretary

NAF Association serves companies and professionals in the non-prime auto lending industry.
85 Members
Founded in 1996

8557 National Bankers Association
1513 P St Nw
Washington, DC 20005

202-588-5432; Fax: 202-588-5443
eholliday@nationalbankers.org
www.nationalbankers.org

Preston Pinkett III, Chairman
B. Doyle Mitchell, Immediate Past Chairman
Michael A. Grant, President
Cynthia N. Day, Secretary
Neill S. Wright, Treasurer

Association for banks owned or controlled by minority group persons or women.
15000 Members
Founded in 1927

8558 National Community Capital Association
Public Ledger Building, 620 Chestnut Street
Suite 572
Philadelphia, PA 19106

215-923-4754; Fax: 215-923-4755
info@opportunityfinance.net
www.ofn.org
Facebook, Twitter, LinkedIn, www.vimeo.com

Trinita Logue, Chair President
Eric Belsky, Executive Director
John Berdes, President/CEO
Keith Bisson, Program Management & Development
Lori Chatman, Vice Chair

Provides support for nonprofit, revolving loan funds that lend capital and offer technical assistance in distressed and disenfranchised communities.
52 Members
Founded in 1986

8559 National Credit Union Administration
1775 Duke St
Alexandria, VA 22314-6115

703-518-6300; Fax: 703-518-6539
ociomail@ncua.gov
www.ncua.gov

Rodney Hood, Chair
Larry Fazio, Executive Director
Lenwood Brooks, Chief of Staff
Eugene Schied, CFO
Robert Foster, Chief Information Officer

Governed by a three member board appointed by the President and confirmed by the US Senate, this independent federal agency charters and supervises federal credit unions. NCUA, with the backing of the full faith and credit of the US government, operates the National Credit Union Share Insurance Fund, insuring the savings of 80 million account holders in all federal credit unions and many state chartered credit unions.

8560 National Defined Contribution Council
307 Waverley Oaks Rd.
Waltham, MA 02452

781-693-7500; Fax: 866-904-9666
www.zoominfo.com
Facebook, Twitter, LinkedIn

Yonaton Stern, CEO & Chief Scientist
Eugenia Gillan, Vice President of Engineering
Steve Hill, Chief Financial Officer
Hila Nir, Vice President of Production Mgt.
Philip Garlick, VP, Corporate Development

NDCC is dedicated to the promotion and protection of the defined contribution industry and the public it serves. The Council specifically addresses the legislative needs of the defined contribution industry's plan service providers.
300 Members
Founded in 1995

8561 National Federation of Municipal Analysts
PO Box 14893
Pittsburgh, PA 15234

412-341-4898; Fax: 412-341-4894
lgood@nfma.org
www.nfma.org
Twitter, LinkedIn

Jeffery Burger, Chairman
Susan Dushock, Vice Chairman
Jennifer Johnston, Treasurer
Lisa Washburn, Secretary
Lisa Good, Executive Director

Promotes the profession of municipal credit analysts through educational programs, industry, communications and related programming.
1000 Members
Founded in 1997

8562 National Finance Adjusters
PO Box 2652
Glenville, NY 12325

623-516-1018; Fax: 410-728-2528
www.nfacoop.com

Burton Greenwood Jr, Secretary/Treasurer
Jack S Barnes, Executive Director

Members are collateral recovery specialists.

8563 National Futures Association
300 S. Riverside Plaza
#1800
Chicago, IL 60606-6615

312-781-1300; Fax: 312-781-1467
information@nfa.futures.org
www.nfa.futures.org

Christopher K. Hehmeyer, Chairman
Michael C. Dawley, Vice Chair
Leo Melamed, Chaise & CEO
Scott A. Cordes, President
Gerald F. Corcoran, Chief Executive Officer

Association for corporations and firms that are registered with the Commodity Futures Trading Commission.

8564 National Home Equity Mortgage Association
42484 Bellagio Drive
Bermuda Dunes, CA 92203

760-772-5806

Jeffrey Zeltzer, Principal

Mission is to promote the growth and recognition of the home equity lending industry.
300 Members
Founded in 1974

8565 National Institute of Pension Administrators
330 N Wabash Ave
Suite 2000
Chicago, IL 60611-7621

800-999-6472; Fax: 312-673-6609
nipa@nipa.org
www.nipa.org
LinkedIn

Patrick M. Shelton, GBA, President
Michelle Marsh, QKA, President Elect and CFO
Joseph Burt, Chief Financial Officer
Darren Holsy, Executive Committee Member-at-Large
Laura Rudzinski, Executive Director

The mission is to enhance professionalism in the retirement plan industry
1000 Members
Founded in 1983

8566 National Investment Company Service Association
8400 Westpark Drive
2nd Floor
McLean, VA 22102

508-485-1500; Fax: 508-488-1560
info@nicsa.org
www.nicsa.org
Facebook, Twitter, LinkedIn, Google+

George Batejan, Chairman
Dan Houlihan, Vice Chairman
Barry Benjamin, Treasurer
Steve Avera, Co-Chair
Jim Fitzpatrick, President

NICSA works to facilitate and promote leadership and innovation within the operations sector of the mutual fund industry.
10000 Members
Founded in 1962

8567 National Pawnbrokers Association
891 Keller parkway
Suite 220
Keller, TX 76248

817-337-8830; Fax: 817-337-8875
info@nationalpawnbrokers.org
www.nationalpawnbrokers.org
Facebook, Twitter, Youtube

Larry Nuckols, President
Tim Collier, Vice President
Robert Anderson, Treasurer
Kathleen barbee, Secretary
Edward Bean, Director

NPA was founded to unite all pawnbrokers in their common efforts to improve the image of the industry, educate the public, adn disseminate professional information and assistance.
2000 Members
Founded in 1987

8568 National Vehicle Leasing Association
N83 W13410 leon road
Menomonee Falls, WI 53051
414-533-3300
800-225-6852; Fax: 410-712-4038
info@nvla.org
www.nvla.org
LinkedIn

Ben Carfrae, CVLE, Past President
PJ McMahon, CVLE, President/Treasurer
Terry L. Bowlder, 1st Vice president
David Blassingame, 2nd Vice President
Scott Crawford, CVLE, Director

Fosters education, publishing, conferences, legal services, advancement and industry relations certification.
500 Members
Founded in 1968

8569 National Venture Capital Association
25 Massachusetts Avenue NW
Suite 730
Washington, DC 20001

202-864-5920; Fax: 202-864-5930
info@nvca.org
www.nvca.org
Facebook, Twitter, LinkedIn, Youtube

Jon Callaghan, Chairman
Venky Ganesan, Chair-Elect
Scott Kupar, Treasurer
John Backus, Secretary
Maria Cirino, At Large

National trade association that represents venture capital firms. Activities include advocacy, professional development, networking and research.
450 Members
Founded in 1973

8570 Neighborhood Reinvestment Corporation
5111 North Scottsdale Road
Suite 201
Scottsdale, AZ 85250

800-808-3372; Fax: 480-994-4456
sales@federalregister.com
www.federalregister.com

Supplies training, grants, developmental assistance, and a range of other technical services designed to help the local partnerships achieve substantially self-reliant neighborhoods. The goal is to improve a neighborhood's housing and physical conditions, build a positive community image, and establish a healthy real estate market and a core of neighbors capable of managing the continued health of their neighborhood.
Founded in 1978

8571 Partnership for Philanthropic Planning
233 McCrea St
Suite 300
Indianapolis, IN 46225

317-269-6274; Fax: 317-269-6268
info@pppnet.org
www.charitablegiftplanners.org
Facebook, Twitter, LinkedIn, YouTube, flickr

Gregory Sharkey, Chair
Melanie Norton, Chair-elect
Alexandra Brovey, Treasurer
Thomas H. Armstrong, Secretary
Michael Kenyon, President and CEO

Members are professionals involved in the process of planning and cultivating charitable gifts.
11500 Members
Founded in 1988

8572 RMA - Risk Management Association
1801 Market Street
Suite 300
Philadelphia, PA 19103-1628

215-446-4137
800-677-7621; Fax: 215-446-4100
customers@rmahq.org
www.rmahq.org

Nancy Foster, President & CEO
William Bonnell, Chair

Seeks to improve the risk management capabilities and principles of commercial lending and credit functions, loan administration and asset management in commercial banks and other financial industries.
17500 Members
Founded in 1914

8573 Retirement Industry Trust Association
4251 Pasadena Circle
Sarasota, FL 34233

941-724-0900; Fax: 301-577-6476
www.ritaus.org

Mary L. Mohr, Executive Director

8574 Securities Industry and Financial Markets Association (SIFMA)
1101 New York Ave NW
8th Floor
Washington, DC 20005

202-962-7300; Fax: 202-962-7305
webmaster@sifma.org
www.sifma.org
Twitter, LinkedIn, Youtube, Google+

Kenneth Bentsen, President & CEO
Joseph Seidel, Chief Operating Officer
David Krasner, Chief Financial & Admin. Officer
Salvatore Chiarelli, EVP, Conferences & Events
Cheryl Crispen, EVP, Communications & Marketing

SIFMA's mission is to champion policies and practices that benefit investors and issuers, expand and perfect global capital markets, and foster the development of new products and services. SIFMA provides an enhanced member network of access and forward-looking services, as well as premiere educational resources for the professionals within the industry and the investors whom they serve.

8575 Security Traders Association
1115 Broadway
Suite 1110
New York, NY 10010

646-699-5996; Fax: 212-321-3449
sta@securitytraders.org
www.securitytraders.org
Facebook, Twitter, LinkedIn, Instagram

Rory O'Kane, Chairman
Jim Toes, President & CEO
John Russell, Vice Chairman
Jon Schneider, Treasurer
Doug Clark, Secretary

Members involved in the securities industry.
7000 Members
Founded in 1934

8576 Small Business Investor Alliance
1100 H Street NW
Suite 1200
Washington, DC 20005

202-628-5055; Fax: 202-628-5080
info@sbia.org
www.sbia.org
Twitter, LinkedIn

Mike Blackburn, Chairman
JD White, Chair-Elect
Jeri Harman, Vice Chairman
Carolyn Galiette, Secretary
Brett Palmer, President

Trade association representing federally licensed venture capital firms and small private equity firms.
400 Members
Founded in 1958

8577 Society for Information Management
1120 Royte73
Ste 200
Mount Laurel, NJ 08054-5113

800-387-9746
800-387-9746; Fax: 856-439-0525
sim@simnet.org
www.simnet.org
Facebook, Twitter, LinkedIn, www.multiview.com

Eric Gorham, Chairman
Kevin More, Vice Chairman
Caren Shiozaki, Treasurer/Secretary
Jim Knight, Chair Emeritus
Kevin Sauer, Director, Chapter Representative

SIM was formed to enhance international recognition of information as a basic organizational resource and to promote the effective utilization and management of this resource towards the improvement of management performance. It attempts to enhance communications between IS executives and the senior executives responsible for management of the business enterprise.
3000 Members
Founded in 1969

8578 Society of Financial Examiners
12100 Sunset Hills Rd
Suite 130
Reston, VA 20190-3221

703-234-4140
800-787-7633; Fax: 888-436-8686
sofe@sofe.org
www.sofe.org
Facebook, LinkedIn

Joanne Campanelli, President
Cindy Dodson, Executive Director

Is a professional society for examiners of insurance companies, banks, savings and loans, and credit unions.
1600 Members
Founded in 1973

8579 Society of Quantitative Analysts
1450 Western avenue
Suite 101
Albany, NY 12203

518-694-3157
800-918-7930
www.sqa-us.org
Facebook, LinkedIn

Peg DioRio, President
Inna Okounkova, Vice President
Kennith N. Hightower, Secretary
Randy O' Toole, Treasurer
Indrani De, CFA PRM, Past President

SQA is concerned with the application of new and innovative techniques for finance, with particular emphasis on the use of quantitative techniques in investment management.
350 Members
Founded in 1989

8580 Stable Value Investment Association
1025 Connecticut Avenue NW
Suite 1000
Washington, DC 20036

202-580-7620
800-327-2270; Fax: 202-580-7621
info@StableValue.org

www.stablevalue.org
Twitter, LinkedIn

Marc Magnoli, Chair

Members are firms and individuals with a professional interest in savings for retirement.
Founded in 1990

8581 State Debt Management Networking
2760 Research Park Drive
Lexington, KY 40511

859-244-8175; Fax: 859-244-8053
www.sdmn.org

Hon. Manju Ganeriwala, Chair
Steve Wisloski, Vice-chair
Laura Lockwood-Mccall, Director, Debt Management
Ellen Evans, Deputy Treasurer Debt Management
Robert L. Watson, Assistant Director

SDMN members are state officials concerned with the insurance or management of state debt. The purpose is to enhance debt management practices throough training, development of educational materials, and data collection and dissemination
50 Members
Founded in 1991

8582 State Risk and Insurance Management Association
PO Box 13777
Austin, TX 78711

304-766-2646
robert.a.fisher@wv.gov
www.strima.org

Robert Fischer, President

STRIMA members are state government risk and insurance managers.
50 Members
Founded in 1974

8583 Tax Executives Institute
1200 G St NW
Suite 300
Washington, DC 20005

202-638-5601; Fax: 202-638-5607
www.tei.org

Timothy Mc Cormally, Executive Director
Deborah K Gaffney, Director Conference Planning
Deborah C Giesey, Director Administration

A professional organization of corporate tax executives. Membership is open to corporate officers and employees chargesd with administering their company's tax affairs.
7000 Members
Founded in 1944

8584 The Fiduciary & Investment Risk Management Association
P.O.Box 507
Stockbridge, GA 30281-0507

678-565-6211; Fax: 678-565-8788
info@thefirma.org
www.thefirma.org
Facebook, Twitter, LinkedIn

Bruce K Goldberg, CTA, CPA, President
Jennifer De Vries, CTA, Vice President
David Jonke CTA, CPA, Secretary
John L. Clark, Director
Daniele G Nicotra, Director-Compliance

Members are audit and compliance professionals.
820 Members
Founded in 1989

8585 The Resource Centre for Religious Institutes
8824 Cameron Street
Silver Spring, MD 20910

301-589-8143; Fax: 301-589-2897
www.trcri.org
Facebook, Twitter, www.blogspot.com

Fr. Thomas Carkhuff, OSC, President
Sr. Lynn McKenzie, OSB, Vice-President
Daniel J. Ward, OSB, JCL, JD, Executive Director
Sr. Margaret Ma Cosgrove, BVM, Treasurer
Sr. Margaret Perron, RJM, Secretary

The leading resource and provider of education, services, and information to meet the current and emerging stewardship needs of all religious institutes throughout the Unted States.
Founded in 1981

8586 Urban Homesteading Assistance Board
120 Wall St.
20th Fl.
New York, NY 10005

212-479-3300; Fax: 212-344-6457
info@uhab.org
www.uhab.org
Facebook, Twitter, YouTube

Andrew Reicher, Executive Director
Anya Irons, Director of Operations
Charles Laven, President
Carolina Prado, Chief Financial Officer
Rania Dalloul, Director of Comm. & Fundraising

UHAB is an affordable housing services nonprofit that empowers low- to moderate-income residents to take control of their housing and strengthens communities by creating and supporting tenant associations and affordable co-ops.
Founded in 1973

8587 Wall Street Technology Association
620 Shrewsbury Ave
Suite C
Tinton Falls, NJ 07701

732-530-8808; Fax: 732-530-0020
info@wsta.org
www.wsta.org
Facebook, Twitter, LinkedIn

John Killeen, President
Chris Randazzo, 1st Vice President
Joseph Weitekamp, 2nd Vice President
Ronald F. Ries, Treasurer
Michael Maffattone, Secretary

Nonprofit educational organization that focuses on technologies, operational approaches, and business issues for the global financial community.
2600+ Members
Founded in 1967

8588 Wall Street Technology Association (WSTA)
620 Shrewsbury Ave
Suite C
Tinton Falls, NJ 07701

732-530-8808; Fax: 732-530-0020
info@wsta.org
www.wsta.org
Facebook, Twitter, LinkedIn

John Killeen, President
Chris Randazzo, 1st Vice President
Joseph Weitekamp, 2nd Vice President
Ronald F. Ries, Treasurer
Michael Maffattone, Secretary

Nonprofit educational organization that focuses on technologies, operational approaches, and business issues for the global financial community.
2800+ Members
Founded in 1967

8589 Washington Municipal Treasurers Associaion
2601 Fourth Avenue
Suite 800
Seattle, WA 98121-1280

206-625-1300
www.wmta-online.com

Stpehanie McKanzie, President
Elizabeth Alba, President-Elect
Philip Steffan, Secretary
Gwen Pilo, Treasurer
Cheryl Grant, Director

Mission is to promote the profession of municipal treasurers through education, mutual support, professional recognition, and legislative advocacy.
Founded in Was

Newsletters

8590 AAII Dividend Investing Newsletter
American Association of Individual Investors
625 N. Michigan Ave.
Suite 1900
Chicago, IL 60611

312-280-0170
888-428-2244; Fax: 312-280-9883
members@aaii.com
www.aaiidividendinvesting.com

James Cloonan, Founder
John Bajkowski, President
Wayne Thorp, Sr. Financial Analyst

In-depth analysis and education to help the reader become a successful dividend investor.
Cost: $169.00
Frequency: Monthly

8591 AARMR Newsletter
American Association of Residential Mortgage
1025 Thomas Jefferson Street NW
Suite 500 East
Washington, DC 20007

202-521-3999; Fax: 202-833-3636
www.aarmr.org

David A Saunders, Executive Director
Erika Freundel, Manager Of Member Services
Frequency: Quarterly

8592 ABI Bankruptcy Brief
American Bakruptcy Institute
66 Canal Center Plaza
Suite 600
Alexandria, VA 22314-1546

703-739-0800; Fax: 703-739-1060
info@abiworld.org
www.abi.org

Amy Quackenboss, Executive Director

A weekly newsletter for ABI members.
Frequency: Weekly/Thursdays
Founded in 1982

8593 AEFA Newsletter
American Education Finance Association
8365 S Armadillo Trail
Evergreen, CO 80439

303-674-0857; Fax: 303-670-8986
www.aefa.cc

Ed Steinbacher, Executive Director
Frequency: Quarterly

8594 **AFCPE Newsletter**
Association for Financial Counseling and Planning
2112 Arlington Avenue
Suite H
Upper Arlington, OH 43221
614-485-9650; Fax: 614-485-9621
www.afcpe.org
Sharon Burns, PhD, Executive Director
Frequency: Quarterly

8595 **Airline Financial News**
PBI Media
1201 Seven Locks Road
Suite 300
Potomac, MD 20854-2931
301-354-1400
800-777-5006; Fax: 301-309-3847
www.aviationtoday.com
Richard Koulbanis, Publisher
Provides information for CEO's financial directors, operations managers, engine aircraft manufacturers and suppliers on financial, market development, buying, leasing and aircraft transactions.
Cost: $697.00
Frequency: Weekly
Circulation: 1850

8596 **Annual Statement Studies**
RMA - Risk Management Association
6147 Ridge Ave
Suite 2300
Philadelphia, PA 19128-2627
215-482-3222
800-677-7621; Fax: 215-446-4101
customers@rmahq.org
www.rmahq.org
Angelo Roma, Owner
William F Githens, Director Member Relations
Dwight Overturf, CFO/Information Technology Officer
Florence J Wetzel, COO/Administrative Officer
John Rumm, Executive Director
Frequency: Annual

8597 **Asset-Backed Alert**
Harrison Scott Publications
5 Marine View Plz
Suite 301
Hoboken, NJ 07030-5722
201-386-1491; Fax: 201-659-4141
info@hspnews.com
www.hspnews.com
Andy Albert, Owner
Tom Ferris, Editor
Daniel Cowles, CEO/President
Barbara Bannace, Marketing
Joan Tassie, Operations Director
A weekly newsletter on the securitization of consumer and corporate receivables.
Cost: $2297.00
10 Pages
Frequency: Weekly
Circulation: 2178
ISSN: 1520-3700
Founded in 1988
Printed in 4 colors on matte stock

8598 **BNA Pension & Benefits Reporter**
Bureau of National Affairs
1801 S Bell St
Arlington, VA 22202-4501
703-341-3000
800-372-1033; Fax: 800-253-0332
customercare@bna.com
www.bnabooks.com
Gregory C McCaffrey, President
Paul N Wojcik, Chairman
Covers latest pension developments stemming from the passage of ERISA and its amendments, plus pension and welfare benefit regulations, standards, enforcement actions, court decisions, legislative and administrative actions, agency options, and employee benefit trust fund requirements.
Cost: $1448.00
Frequency: Weekly
Founded in 1929
Printed in on matte stock

8599 **Back-Office Bulletin**
United Communications Group
Two Washingtonian Center
9737 Washingtonian Blvd Suite 100
Gaithersburg, MD 20878-7364
301-287-2700; Fax: 301-287-2039
www.ucg.com
Daniel Brown, Publisher
For financial operations professionals.
Founded in 1970

8600 **Bandwidth Investor**
Kagan World Media
1 Lower Ragsdale Dr
Building 1, Suite 130
Monterey, CA 93940-5749
831-624-1536; Fax: 831-625-3225
www.kagan.com
Tim Baskerville, President/CEO
Harvey Kraft, Circulation/Marketing Manager
Cost: $1195.00
Frequency: Monthly
Founded in 1969

8601 **Bank 13D Dictionary**
SNL Securities
PO Box 2124
Charlottesvle, VA 22902-2124
434-977-1600; Fax: 434-977-4466
isales@snl.com
www.snl.com
Todd Davenport, Editor
Reid Nagle, Chief Operating Officer
Nick Cafferillo, Chief Operating Officer
Adam Hall, Managing Director
For banks, thrifts, investors, investment bankers, law firms, consultants and regulatory agencies. Contains all active 13D filings and related filings for every public traded bank in the country, including those which trade on the 'pink sheets.'
Frequency: Quarterly
Founded in 1987

8602 **Benefax**
SNL Securities
PO Box 2124
Charlottesvle, VA 22902-2124
434-977-1600; Fax: 434-977-4466
isales@snl.com
www.snl.com
Keith Davis, Editor
Reid Nagle, Chief Operating Officer
Nick Cafferillo, Chief Operating Officer
Adam Hall, Managing Director
For bank and thrift executives. Contains only summaries of available information.
1 Pages
Frequency: Monthly
Founded in 1987

8603 **Bollinger Bands Letter**
Bollinger Capital Management
P.O. Box 3358
Manhattan Beach, CA 90266-1358
310-798-8855
bbands@bollingerbands.com
www.bollingerbands.com
Dorit Kehr, Marketing Director
The Bollinger Bands Letter provides John Bollinger's current analysis of the markets covering stocks, inerest rates, precious metals, commodities, currencies and the international markets. Each issue provides charts, analysis, and commentary on the markets plus timely investment recommendations. Included is a weekly update with commentary and any portfolio changes including the ETF portfolio, a Market Timing Report, the Ice Breaker trading system and the Value Line Plan signals.
Cost: $300.00
12 Pages
Frequency: Monthly
Circulation: 500
Founded in 1980
Printed in 2 colors

8604 **Bondweek**
Institutional Investor
225 Park Ave S
7th Floor
New York, NY 10003-1605
212-224-3300; Fax: 212-224-3197
iieditor@institutionalinvestor.com
www.institutionalinvestor.com
Christopher Brown, CEO
Erik Kolk, Publisher
Deirdre Brennan, Managing Editor
Nick Ferris, Group Marketing Director
Coverage of stocks, bonds and investments for the financial professional and consumer, information includes rates.
Cost: $2245.00
Frequency: 51 issues per y
Founded in 1967

8605 **Broadcast Banker/Broker**
Kagan World Media
1 Lower Ragsdale Dr
Building One,Suite 130
Monterey, CA 93940-5749
831-624-1536
800-307-2529; Fax: 831-625-3225
www.kagan.com
Tim Baskerville, President
Tom Johnson, Marketing Manager
A readers guide to equity deals and debt financing for radio and TV Station buying and selling analyzed. Key details on station trades with critical yardsticks of value. Three month trial is available.
Cost: $925.00
Frequency: Monthly

8606 **Broadcast Investor**
Kagan World Media
126 Clock Tower Place
Carmel, CA 93923-8746
831-624-1536; Fax: 831-624-5882
www.kagan.com
George Niesen, Editor
Tom Johnson, Marketing Manager
The newsletter on investments in radio and TV stations and publicly held companies. Comprehensive analysis of cash flow multiples and trends that impact value. Three month trial available.
Cost: $895.00
Frequency: Monthly

8607 **Broker Magazine**
Thomson Media

1 State St
27th Floor
New York, NY 10004-1481

212-825-8445
800-221-1809; Fax: 800-235-5552
www.sourcemedia.com

Timothy Murphy, Publisher
James Malkin, Director of Sales
Melissa Sefic, Director of Sales

Features on training, motivation, technology, legislation and marketing
Frequency: Monthly
Circulation: 750000

8608 Budget Processors in the States
National Association of State Budge Officers
444 N Capitol St NW
Suite 642
Washington, DC 20001-1512

202-624-5382; Fax: 202-624-7745
spattison@nasbo.org
www.nasbo.org

Frequency: Bi-Ennial

8609 Bull & Bear Financial Report
PO Bo 917179
Longwood, FL 32791

954-781-3455
800-336-2855; Fax: 954-781-5865
www.thebullandbear.com

David J Robinson, Publisher/Editor

Dozens of original articles by leading investment pros with investment information on precious metals, commodities, mutual funds, currencies, economic trends and monetary survival.
Circulation: 55000

8610 Bulletin Newsletter
EMTA - Trade Association for the Emerging Markets
360 Madison Avenue
17th Floor
New York, NY 10017

646-289-5410; Fax: 646-289-5429
awerner@emta.org
www.emta.org

Michael M Chamberlin, Executive Director
Aviva Werner, General Counsel
Jonathan Murno, Managing Director
Suzette Ortiz, Office Manager
Monika Forbes, Administrative Assistant
Frequency: Quarterly

8611 CIPFA Newsletter
National Association of Independent Public Finance
PO Box 304
Montgomery, IL 60538-0304

630-896-1292
800-624-7321; Fax: 209-633-6265

Roseanne M Hoban, Executive Director
Frequency: Quarterly

8612 Cable Program Investor
Kagan World Media
126 Clock Tower Place
Carmel, CA 93923-8746

831-624-1536; Fax: 831-624-5882
www.kagan.com

George Niesen, Editor
Tom Johnson, Marketing Manager

Covers the economics of basic cable programming networks. Numbers, perspective unavailable from any other source. Programmers applaud its accuracy. Three month trial available.
Cost: $845.00
Frequency: Monthly

8613 Cable TV Finance
Kagan World Media
126 Clock Tower Place
Carmel, CA 93923-8746

831-624-1536
800-307-2529; Fax: 831-624-5882
www.kagan.com

George Niesen, Editor
Tom Johnson, Marketing Manager
Tim Baskerville, CEO/President

Cable's financial bible. Analyzes sources of funding for cable TV. Selling and buying of cable systems. Financing strategies and trends. Exclusive surveys of capital sources. Three month trial available.
Cost: $995.00
Frequency: Monthly
Founded in 1969

8614 Cable TV Investor
Kagan World Media
1 Lower Ragsdale Dr
Building One, Suite 130
Monterey, CA 93940-5749

831-624-1536
800-307-2529; Fax: 831-625-3225
www.kagan.com

Tim Baskerville, President
Tom Johnson, Marketing Manager

Readers road map to cable stock trends. Chart service tracking stock price movements of 37 publicly held cable TV companies. Each graph shows two years of stock price activity. Three month trial available.
Cost: $945.00
Frequency: Monthly

8615 Card News
Phillips Publishing
7811 Montrose Road
Potomac, MD 20854

301-340-2100
feedback@healthydirections.com
www.healthydirections.com

Covering the financial card marketplace.

8616 Client Information Bulletin
WPI Communications
55 Morris Ave
Suite 300
Springfield, NJ 07081-1422

973-467-8700; Fax: 973-467-0368
info@wpicomm.com
www.wpicomm.com

Steve Klinghoffer, Owner
Marilyn Lang, Chairman

Bulletin for lawyers and CPAs to distribute to clients to keep them informed on tax matters. This original publication which has been helping accountants build their practices since 1952, has been redesigned. Covers important new tax developments, general business principals, financial planning, estate planning and other related topics.

8617 Collection Agency Report
First Detroit Corporation
PO Box 5025
Warren, MI 48090-5025

586-573-0045
800-366-5995; Fax: 586-573-9219
www.firstdetroit.com

Albert Scace, President
Petricia Herrick, Marketing Manager

Provides financially oriented news on the collection agency and bad debt buying industries worldwide.
Cost: $289.00
8 Pages
Frequency: Monthly
ISSN: 1052-4029
Mailing list available for rent: 5000 names at $110 per M

8618 Commercial Mortgage Alert
Harrison Scott Publications
5 Marine View Plz
Suite 301
Hoboken, NJ 07030-5722

201-386-1491; Fax: 201-659-4141
info@hspnews.com
www.hspnews.com

Andy Albert, Owner
Tom Ferris, Director
Michelle Lebowitz, Director

A weekly newsletter on the securitization of consumer and corporate receivables.
Cost: $1497.00
10 Pages
Frequency: Weekly
Circulation: 500
ISSN: 1520-3700
Printed in 4 colors on matte stock

8619 Conference Executive Summaries
Society for Information Management
401 N Michigan Avenue
Chicago, IL 60611

312-215-5190; Fax: 312-245-1081
www.simnet.org

Jim Luisi, Executive Director
Frequency: Semi-Annual

8620 Conversion Candidates List
SNL Securities
PO Box 2124
Charlottesvle, VA 22902-2124

434-977-1600; Fax: 434-977-4466
isales@snl.com
www.snl.com

Chris Smith, Editor
Reid Nagle, Chief Operating Officer
Nick Cafferillo, Chief Operating Officer
Adam Hall, Managing Director

For thrift executives, individual investors and institutional investors. Lists mutual thrifts that are in a position to convert to stock ownership by offering shares for sale.
Frequency: Monthly
Founded in 1987

8621 Conversion Watch
SNL Securities
PO Box 2124
Charlottesvle, VA 22902-2124

434-977-1600; Fax: 434-977-4466
isales@snl.com
www.snl.com

Chris Smith, Editor
Nick Cafferillo, Chief Operating Officer
Adam Hall, Managing Director

Delivered via fax whenever new activity is announced, including rumored, pending, announced and completed activity. Provides relevant data from conversion-related filings, including eligible record dates, offering size, Pro Formas, opening and closing dates for the subscription, asset size, net worth and rating of the thrift.
Cost: $1200.00
5 Pages
Frequency: Annual+
Founded in 1987

8622 Cost Control News
Siefer Consultants

PO Box 1384
Storm Lake, IA 50588-1384

712-732-7340; Fax: 712-732-7906
info@siefer.com
www.siefer.com/

Dan Siefer, Publisher

Cost cutting opportunities for financial institutions.
Cost: $297.00
8 Pages
Founded in 1981

8623 Credit Collections News
SourceMedia
550 W Van Buren
Suite 1100
Chicago, IL 60607-6680

312-913-1334; Fax: 312-913-1340
www.sourcemedia.com

John Stewart, Publisher
Melissa Sefic, Director of Sales

Analysis of the global economy, current industry trends and policies, as well as problems commonly encountered in credit collections.
Frequency: Monthly

8624 Credit Union Journal
SourceMedia
224 Datura Street
Suite 615
West Palm Beach, FL 33401

561-832-2929; Fax: 561-832-2939
www.cujournal.com

Frank J Dierkmann, Publisher/Editor
Tim O'Hara, Co-Publisher

JournalScan to review recent credit union developments, industry news articles, an agenda of upcoming meetings, deadlines and events and Washington Watch covering the latest news in Washington DC.
Frequency: Weekly
Circulation: 5300

8625 Credit Union Management
Credit Union Executives Society
PO Box 14167
Madison, WI 53714-167

608-271-2664
800-252-2664; Fax: 608-271-2303
cues@cues.org
www.cues.org

Mary Arnold, Publisher
Theresa Sweeney, Editor
Fred Johnson, CEO/President
Cost: $93.00
Frequency: Monthly
Printed in 4 colors on glossy stock

8626 Credit and Collection Manager's Letter
Bureau of Business Practice
76 Ninth Avenue
7th Floor
New York, NY 10011

212-771-0600; Fax: 212-771-0885
www.aspenlawschool.com
Facebook, Twitter, LinkedIn

Mark Dorman, CEO
Gustavo Dobles, VP Operations

Hands-on information for improving the credit and collection departments in both commercial and consumer markets.
Frequency: SemiMonthly
Circulation: 9380

8627 Daily Tax Report
Bureau of National Affairs
1801 S Bell St
Arlington, VA 22202-4501

703-341-3000
800-372-1033; Fax: 800-253-0332
customercare@bna.com
www.bnabooks.com

Paul N Wojcik, CEO

A daily tax notification service that covers legislative, regulatory, judicial and policy developments on a national basis, designed to give tax professionals rapid notification and comprehensive coverage of those developments.
Cost: $3215.00
Frequency: Daily
ISSN: 0092-6884

8628 Debit Card News
SourceMedia
224 Datura Street
Suite 615
West Palm Beach, FL 33401

561-832-2929; Fax: 561-832-2939
www.cujournal.com

Don Davis, Editor

Marketing, pricing, different card applications, smart cards, point-of-sale and other electronic banking activities.
Frequency: SemiMonthly

8629 Declined Contribution Market Insights
National Defined Contribution Council
9101 E Kenyon
Suite 300
Denver, CO 80237-0467

303-770-5353; Fax: 303-770-1812

Al Brust, Executive VP
Frequency: Annual

8630 ELFA QuickBrief
Equipment Leasing And Finance Association
1625 Eye St. NW
Suite 850
Washington, DC 20006

202-238-3400; Fax: 202-238-3401
avogt@elfaonline.org
www.elfaonline.org

Amy Vogt, Managing Editor

A weekly newsletter for equipment finance professionals. Features compelling, industry-focused content.
Frequency: Weekly
Founded in 1961
Printed in 4 colors on glossy stock

8631 Executive Brief
Society for Information Management
401 N Michigan Avenue
Chicago, IL 60611

312-215-5190; Fax: 312-245-1081
www.simnet.org

Jim Luisi, Executive Director
Frequency: Quarterly

8632 Executive Compensation Review for Commercial Banks
SNL Securities
PO Box 2124
Charlottesvle, VA 22902-2124

434-977-1600; Fax: 434-977-4466
www.snlnet.com

Keith Davis, Editor
Nick Cafferillo, Chief Operating Officer
Reid Nagle, Publisher
Mark Outlaw, Advertising Director
Adam Hall, Managing Director

For banks, regulatory agencies and executive recruiters. Includes detailed compensation and benefit information for the top 5 officers of all publicly traded banks, thrifts, REITs and insurance companies.
550 Pages
Frequency: Annual
Founded in 1988

8633 Executive Compensation Review for Insurance Companies
SNL Securities
PO Box 2124
Charlottesvle, VA 22902-2124

434-977-1600; Fax: 434-977-4466
www.snlnet.com

Keith Davis, Editor
Nick Cafferillo, Chief Operating Officer
Reid Nagle, Publisher
Mark Outlaw, Advertising Director
Pat LaBua, Subscription Manager

For insurance companies, investment analysts, service providers to the insurance industry and regulators. Includes detailed compensation and benefit information for the top 5 officers of all publicly traded banks, thrifts, REITs and insurance companies.
200 Pages
Frequency: Annual
Founded in 1997

8634 Executive Compensation Review for REITs
SNL Securities
PO Box 2124
Charlottesvle, VA 22902-2124

434-977-1600; Fax: 434-977-4466
isales@snl.com
www.snl.com

Keith Davis, Editor
Chandler Spears, Chief Operating Officer
Nick Cafferillo, Chief Operating Officer
Adam Hall, Managing Director

For REITs, REIT service providers, investment companies, executive recruiters and regulators. Annual data digests that include detailed compensation and benefit information for the top 5 officers of all publicly traded banks, thrifts, REITs and insurance companies.
Cost: $495.00
Frequency: Monthly
Founded in 1987

8635 Executive Compensation Review for Thrift Institutions
SNL Securities
PO Box 2124
Charlottesvle, VA 22902-2124

434-977-1600; Fax: 434-977-4466
isales@snl.com
www.snl.com

Keith Davis, Editor
Nick Cafferillo, Chief Operating Officer
Adam Hall, Managing Director

For thrifts, regulatory agencies and executive recruiters. Annual data digests that include detailed compensation and benefit information for the top 5 officers of all publicly traded banks, thrifts, REITs and insurance companies.
Cost: $495.00
Frequency: Monthly
Founded in 1987

8636 Export Finance Letter
International Business Affairs Corporation
5523 Brite Dr
#346
Bethesda, MD 20817-6304

301-907-8647; Fax: 301-907-8650
www.internationalrelationsedu.org

Richard Barovick, Owner

A report on government and private resources in US Export & Import Finance, Payments and Risk Management.
Founded in 1979

8637 FEI Briefing
Financial Executives Institute
200 Campus Drive
PO Box 674
Forham Park, NJ 07932

973-360-0177; Fax: 973-765-1023
www.fei.org

P Norman Roy, Publisher
Christopher Allen, Editor
Colleen Sayther Cunningham, CEO/President
Christopher Allen, Marketing
Lucinda Arsenio, Secretary

Up-to-date news for treasurers and controllers of large corporations.
Circulation: 14000
Founded in 1931

8638 FSR Newsletter
Financial Services Roundtable
1001 Pennsylvania Ave Nw
Suite 500 S
Washington, DC 20004-2508

202-628-2455; Fax: 202-289-1903
info@fsround.org
www.fsround.org

Greg Baer, CEO
Frequency: Monthly

8639 Federal Securities Act
Matthew Bender and Company
744 Broad St
Newark, NJ 07102-3885

973-820-2000
800-227-9597; Fax: 937-865-1284
info.in@lexisnexis.com
www.lexisnexis.com

Kent Frankstone, Manager
Rebecca Schmitt, Chief Financial Officer

A comprehensive, up-to-date treatise on the Securities Act of 1933 and all amendments thereto, as well as the application of the Trust Indenture Act of 1939.

8640 Fee Income Report
Siefer Consultants
PO Box 1384
Storm Lake, IA 50588-1384

712-732-7340; Fax: 712-732-7906
www.siefer.com

Dan Siefer, Publisher

Fee income news and opportunities for financial institutions.
Cost: $297.00
8 Pages
Frequency: Monthly
Founded in 1981

8641 Fidelity Insight
Mutual Fund Investors Association
20 William St
Suite 200
Wellesley, MA 02481-4138

781-235-1560
800-586-4727
www.kobren.com

Eric Kobren, President
Chris Keith, Senior Vice President
Todd Peters, Senior Vice President

Offers information and rates for mutual funds, investments, stocks and bonds.
Cost: $127.00
8 Pages
Frequency: Monthly
Founded in 1985

8642 Finance Company Weekly
SNL Securities
PO Box 2124
Charlottesvle, VA 22902-2124

434-977-1600; Fax: 434-977-4466
isales@snl.com
www.snl.com

David Meadors, Editor
Nick Cafferillo, Chief Operating Officer
Adam Hall, Managing Director

Weekly news on publicly and privately traded finance companies. Includes consumer, commercial, credit card companies, pawn shops and leasing companies. Summarizes recent industry earnings announcement, trends, registration statements and performance rankings.
Cost: $396.00
10 Pages
Frequency: Weekly
Founded in 1987

8643 Financial Management Association International (FMA)
University of South Florida
4202 E Fowler Ave
Tampa, FL 33620-9951

813-974-2011; Fax: 813-974-5530
www.usf.edu

Judy L Genshaft, President
William Christie, Financial Management Editor
Keith M Howe, Journal of Applied Finance Editor
James Schallheim, FMA Survey Synthesis Series Editor
John Finnerty, Editor FMA Online

Financial books, textbooks, databases, newspapers, research services, software and related products and services.
Frequency: Quarterly
Founded in 1970

8644 Financial Managers Update
Financial Managers Society
100 W Monroe
Suite 810
Chicago, IL 60603

312-578-1300
800-275-4367; Fax: 312-578-1308
info@fmsinc.org
www.fmsinc.org/cms

John A. Carrozza, Chair
Alana Vartanian, Chief Operating Officer
Jennifer Lindberg, Director, Marketing & Communication

The latest accounting and regulatory information related to financial institutions, as well as news and trends. Includes a regulatory check list.
8 Pages
Circulation: 1400
Mailing list available for rent
Printed in one color

8645 Financial NetNews
Institutional Investor
488 Madison Ave
15th Floor
New York, NY 10022-5701

212-303-3100
800-115-9196; Fax: 212-224-3491
iieditor@institutionalinvestor.com
www.institutionalinvestor.com

Dahlia Weinman, Publisher
Deirdre Brennan, Editor
Nick Ferris, Marketing Manager
Chris Brown, CEO/President

Businesses and their Web sites, providing up-to-date information on networkings and assessment of industry trends and mistakes.
Frequency: Weekly

8646 Financial News
Financial News Corporation
PO Box 1769
Jacksonville, FL 32201-1769

904-356-2466; Fax: 904-353-2628
editorial@jaxdailyrecord.com
www.jaxdailyrecord.com

James F Bailey Jr, Publisher
Angie Campbell, Business Manager
Karen Mathis, Managing Editor

Business and legal information for financial institutions.
Cost: $89.00
Frequency: Daily

8647 Financial Planning Advisory
WPI Communications
55 Morris Ave
Suite 300
Springfield, NJ 07081-1422

973-467-8700
800-323-4995; Fax: 973-467-0368
info@wpicomm.com
www.wpicomm.com

Steve Klinghoffer, Owner
Marilyn Lang, Chairman

Offers institutions and businesses information on financial planning and campaigns.
Founded in 1952

8648 Financial Services
8180 Corporate Park Drive
Suite 305
Cincinnati, OH 45242-3309

513-591-0149; Fax: 513-527-3141

Linda Niesz, Publisher

National and regional news for members.
Cost: $7.00
6 Pages
Frequency: Monthly

8649 Financial Services Daily
SNL Securities
PO Box 2124
Charlottesvle, VA 22902-2124

434-977-1600; Fax: 434-977-4466
isales@snl.com
www.snl.com

David Meadors, Editor
Nick Cafferillo, Chief Operating Officer
Adam Hall, Managing Director

Daily fax of news headlines on finance companies, mortgage banks, investment advisors and brokers/dealers, plus divident and earnings announcements, stock highlights and index values, registration statements and ownership filings.
6 Pages
Frequency: Daily
Founded in 1987

8650 Financial Services M&A Insider
SNL Securities
PO Box 2124
Charlottesvle, VA 22902-2124

434-977-1600; Fax: 434-977-4466
isales@snl.com
www.snl.com

L Vencil, Editor
Reid Nagle, Chief Operating Officer
Nick Cafferillo, Chief Operating Officer
Adam Hall, Managing Director

Fax newsletter featuring in-depth articles and the latest financial information on financial services M&A activity. Covers mortgage banks, finance companies, investment advisors and broker/dealers. Analyzes industry trends and specific market and ownership changes to iden-

tify potential consolidation activity.
Cost: $695.00
10 Pages
Frequency: Monthly
Founded in 1987

8651 **Financial Women Today**
Financial Women International
1027 W Roselawn Avenue
Roseville, MN 55113
651-487-7632
866-807-6081; Fax: 651-489-1322
info@fwi.org
Melissa Curzon, President
Cindy Hass, VP
Carleen DeSisto, Secretary
Covers financial services industry trends, as well as women's issues and association news.
1000 Members
Circulation: 10,000
Founded in 1921

8652 **First Friday**
ASCU
PO Box 5488
Madison, WI 53705-0488
608-238-2646; Fax: 608-238-2646
C Barle, Publisher
Market research and statistics.
Cost: $35.00
6 Pages
Frequency: Monthly
Founded in 1973
Mailing list available for rent: 11,000 names at $60 per M
Printed in on matte stock

8653 **Fiscal Survey of the States**
National Association of State Budget Officers
444 N Capitol St Nw
Suite 642
Washington, DC 20001-1556
202-624-8020; Fax: 202-624-7745
spattison@nasbo.org
www.nasbo.org
Shelby Kerns, Executive Director
Frequency: Semi-Annual

8654 **Focus on Accountability**
Evangelical Council for Financial Accountability
440 W Jubal Early Dr
Suite 130
Winchester, VA 22601
540-535-0103
800-323-9473; Fax: 540-535-0533
info@ecfa.org
www.ecfa.org
Dan Busby, President
Kim Sandretzky, Vice President, Communications
2250 Members
Frequency: Quarterly
Circulation: 30000
Founded in 1979

8655 **Forecaster**
Forecaster Publishing Company
19623 Ventura Blvd
Tarzana, CA 91356-2918
818-345-4421; Fax: 818-345-0468
John Kamin, Owner
Brian Kamin, CEO/President
Analyzes lucrative speculations in unusual areas. Researches gold, silver, coins, gems, property, antiques, interest rates, business cycles, economic advice, tax strategies, wine, guns, collector cars and more.
Cost: $180.00
8 Pages
Frequency: Weekly
ISSN: 0095-294X
Founded in 1962
Mailing list available for rentat $170 per M
Printed in 2 colors on matte stock

8656 **Fund Directions**
Financial Communications Company
225 Park Avenue S
New York, NY 10003
212-953-3500
800-715-9195; Fax: 212-224-3699
customerservice@iinews.com
www.funddirections.com
Colin Minnihan, Publisher
Wendy Connett, Executive Editor
Amy Cohen, Managing Editor
Kevin Francella, Plant Manager
Kim Lemmonds, Marketing Director
Trends in the rapidly changing fund environment and analysis of key issues in fund governance.
Frequency: Monthly
Circulation: 2500

8657 **Futures Market Alert**
Robbins Trading Company
8700 W Bryn Mawr Ave
Seventh Floor, S Tower
Chicago, IL 60631-3530
773-380-9700
800-453-4444; Fax: 773-380-9701
info@robbinstrading.com
www.rabjohnsnef.com
Reginold Rabjohns, Partner
Covers futures trading.

8658 **Global Money Management**
Institutional Investor
225 Park Ave S
7th Floor
New York, NY 10003-1605
212-224-3300
800-543-4444; Fax: 212-224-3197
iieditor@institutionalinvestor.com
www.institutionalinvestor.com
Christopher Brown, President/CEO
Deirdre Brennan, Managing Editor
Stuart Wise, Senior Editor
Nick t Ferris, Group Marketing Director
Money management news. Accepts advertising.
Cost: $11.95
Frequency: Fortnightly
Founded in 1967

8659 **Gold Newsletter**
Blanchard and Company
2400 Jefferson Hwy
Suite 600
New Orleans, LA 70121-3838
504-835-0029
800-877-8847; Fax: 504-837-4884
gnlmail@jeffersoncompanies.com
www.neworleansconference.com
James Blanchard, President
Brien Lundin, CEO
Offers information and news for the financial community on stocks, bonds and investment opportunities.
Cost: $198.00
Frequency: Monthly
Founded in 1971

8660 **Government Affairs Bulletin**
Financial Services Roundtable
1001 Pennsylvania Ave Nw
Suite 500 S
Washington, DC 20004-2508
202-628-2455; Fax: 202-289-1903
info@fsround.org
www.fsround.org
Greg Baer, CEO
Frequency: Monthly

8661 **Government Finance Officers Association Newsletter**
Government Finance Officers Association
203 N La Salle St
Suite 2700
Chicago, IL 60601-1216
312-977-9700; Fax: 312-977-4806
inquiry@gfoa.org
www.gfoa.org
Chris Morrill, Executive Director
Marcy Boggs, Managing Editor
John Jurkash, Chief Financial Officer
The purpose of the Government Finance Officers Association is to enhance and promote the professional management of governments for the public benefit by identifying and developing financial policies and practices and promoting them through education, training and leadership. Membership includes a twice-monthly newsletter in addition to specialty newsletters on cash management, accounting, auditing, and financial reporting.
17300 Pages
Founded in 1906

8662 **HBMA Newsletter**
Healthcare Billing and Management Association
1540 South Coast Highway
Suite 203
Laguna Beach, CA 92651
877-640-4262
http://www.hbma.org
Bradley Lund, Executive Director
Paul Myers, Director of Education
Frequency: Monthly

8663 **HFMA's Leadership E-Newsletter**
Healthcare Financial Management Association
Two Westbrook Corporate Center
Suite 700
Westchester, IL 60154-5700
708-319-9600
800-252-4362; Fax: 708-531-0032
www.hfma.org/leadership
Robert Fromberg, Editor-in-Chief
Maggie Van Dyke, Product Manager & Editor
Chris Burke, Advertising Manager
Kurt Belisle, Sponsorhip Manager
Showcases examples of how leading healthcare organizations are driving down costs, enhancing quality, and collaborating across disciplines and care sites. The initiative highlightes innovative providers. Subscription includes a twice-yearly print publication, monthly e-newsletter, webcasts, and exclusive invites.
Frequency: Monthly
Circulation: 32900

8664 **HFMA's The Business of Caring**
Healthcare Financial Management Association
Two Westbrook Corporate Center
Suite 700
Westchester, IL 60154-5700
708-319-9600
800-252-4362; Fax: 708-531-0032
www.hfma.org/boc
Robert Fromberg, Editor-in-Chief
Maggie Van Dyke, Product Manager & Editor

Chris Burke, Advertising Manager
Kurt Belisle, Sponsorhip Manager

Helps nurse managers navigate the business side of health care to become successful hospital leaders. Topics discussed include: budgeting, workforce management, cost containment, and IT implementation. Available Free Online.
Frequency: Quarterly

8665 Hedge Fund Alert
Harrison Scott Publications
5 Marine View Plz
Suite 301
Hoboken, NJ 07030-5722

201-386-1491; Fax: 201-659-4141
info@hspnews.com
www.hspnews.com

Andy Albert, Owner
Tom Ferris, Editor
Howard Kapiloff, Managing Editor
Barbara Eannace, Advertising Director
Michelle Lebowitz, Director

A weekly newsletter on the securitization of consumer and corporate receivables.
Cost: $2097.00
10 Pages
Frequency: Weekly
Circulation: 500
ISSN: 1520-3700
Printed in 4 colors on matte stock

8666 High Yield Report
American Banker-Bond Buyer
1 State St
27th Floor
New York, NY 10004-1561

212-803-8450
800-367-3989; Fax: 212-843-9624
www.sourcemedia.com

Jim Malkin, CEO
Mario DiUbaldi, Director of Sales
Melissa Sefic, Director of Sales

The only financial publication dealing exclusively with high yield corporate debt and distressed bank debt.
Cost: $795.00
Frequency: Weekly
Circulation: 350

8667 Housing Finance Report
National Assn. of Local Housing Finance Agencies
2025 M St Nw
Suite 800
Washington, DC 20036-2422

202-367-1197; Fax: 202-367-2197
www.noca.org

Greg Brown, Editor
Karen Thompson, Production Manager

This newsletter covers major developments in housing finance in the Congress, federal agencies and private sector. It also gives highlights new and innovative activities of ALHFA members.
Circulation: 450
Founded in 1982

8668 IBC's Money Fund Report
IBC Financial Data
1 Research Dr
Westborough, MA 01581-3922

508-616-5567; Fax: 508-616-5511
info@imoneynet.com
www.imoneynet.com/

Kenneth Bohlin, Publisher
Peter Crane, Editor
Randy Wood, CEO
Claudia Missert, marketin

Compiles yield, average maturity and portfolio data for each money fund along with summary information for more than a dozen categories.
Cost: $3125.00
Frequency: Weekly
Circulation: 200
Founded in 1975
Printed in 2 colors on matte stock

8669 IE News: Financial Services
Institute of Industrial Engineers
25 Technology Pkwy S
Suite 150
Norcross, GA 30092-2946

770-449-0461; Fax: 770-263-8532

Offers full coverage of the financial community pertaining to engineering and industrial corporations.

8670 IHS Haystack Standard Standards
Information Handling Services
15 Inverness Way E
Englewood, CO 80112-5710

303-790-0600
800-525-7052; Fax: 303-754-3940
www.ihs.com

Jerre L Stead, CEO
Michael Armstrong, Director
Frequency: Daily

8671 IPO Reporter
Securities Data Publishing
1290 6th Avenue
36th Floor
New York, NY 10104-0101

212-765-5311; Fax: 212-957-0420

Ted Weissberg, Group Publisher

Reliable news, data and analysis. Provides the most comprehensive coverage available, including a detailed calendar of upcoming deals; new IPOs filled with the SEC; valuation information; comaparison data; company name and locationas well as names of underwriters, auditors and counsels.
Frequency: Weekly

8672 IRA Reporter
Universal Pensions
PO Box 979
Brainerd, MN 56401-0979

218-855-0565
800-346-3860; Fax: 218-829-4814

Thomas G Anderson, President
Jennifer M Norquist, Editor

Discusses IRS rulings, regulations, legislation and other industry news and trends relating to IRA's.
Cost: $115.00
8 Pages
Frequency: Monthly
Printed in on glossy stock

8673 ISDA Newsletter
International Swaps and Derivatives Association
360 Madison Ave
16th Floor
New York, NY 10017-7126

212-901-6000; Fax: 212-901-6001
isda@isda.org
www.isda.org

Robert Pickel, CEO
Ruth Ainslie, Director Communications
Corrine Gerasley, Director Administration
Frequency: 5/year

8674 Insurance M&A Newsletter
SNL Securities
One SNL Plaza
PO Box 2124
Charlottesville, VA 22902

434-977-1600; Fax: 434-977-4466
subscriptions@snl.com
www.snl.com

L Todd Vencil, Editor
Reid Nagle, Chief Operating Officer
Nick Cafferillo, Chief Operating Officer
Adam Hall, Managing Director

For investment bankers, analysts, insurance investors, insurance company executives and insurance regulators. Features in-depth articles and the latest financial information on insurance mergers and acquisitions activity.
Cost: $998.00
15 Pages
Frequency: Fortnightly
Founded in 1987

8675 Interactive Mobile Investor
Kagan World Media
126 Clock Tower Place
Carmel, CA 93923-8746

831-624-1536; Fax: 831-625-3225
www.kagan.com

George Niesen, Editor
Tom Johnson, Marketing Manager
Cost: $945.00
Frequency: Monthly

8676 Interactive TV Investor
Kagan World Media
126 Clock Tower Place
Carmel, CA 93923-8746

831-624-1536; Fax: 831-625-3225
www.kagan.com

George Niesen, Editor
Tom Johnson, Marketing Manager
Cost: $895.00
Frequency: Monthly

8677 International Financier Newsletter
International Society of Financiers
PO Box 398
Naples, NC 28760

828-698-7805; Fax: 828-698-7806

Ronald I Gershen, Chairman/President
Frequency: Monthly

8678 International Securitization & Structured Finance
WorldTrade Executive
2250 Main Street Suite 100
PO Box 761
Concord, MA 01742-761

978-287-0301; Fax: 978-287-0302
www.wtexec.com

Jill McKenna, Production Manager
Gary Brown, CEO
Scott stutbar, Editor
John Margel, Marketing
Heather Margel, Circulation Manager

A twice monthly report devoted exclusively to asset-backed securities in international markets. Covers all aspects of international asset-backed securitization, including innovative product trends, issuer considerations, regulatory matters, and tax and accounting considerations. Examines what is working in emerging markets and spotlights unique US transactions.
Cost: $1333.00

8679 International Wealth Success
PO Box 1866
Merrick, NY 11566

516-378-3922
800-323-0548; Fax: 516-766-5919

Tyler G Hicks, Publisher

Monthly newsletter giving sources and techniques for financing a variety of small businesses - import-export, mail order, real estate, home-based activities, etc. Gives specific, hands-on methods for beginners to start and own a successful business of their own.
Cost: $24.00
16 Pages
Frequency: Monthly
Mailing list available for rent: 100 M names at $75 per M
Printed in 2 colors on matte stock

8680 **Internet Media Investor**
Kagan World Media
126 Clock Tower Place
Carmel, CA 93923-8746
831-624-1536; Fax: 831-625-3225
www.kagan.com
George Niesen, Editor
Tom Johnson, Marketing Manager
Cost: $945.00
Frequency: Monthly

8681 **Investing in Crisis**
KCI Communications
1750 Old Meadow Road
Suite 301
McLean, VA 22102
703-905-8000
800-832-2330; Fax: 703-905-8100
service@kci-com.com
www.kcicommunications.com
Allie Ash Jr, Publisher
Offers information on investments, low-risk bonds, stocks and campaigns for businesses in times of economic survival.
Cost: $195.00
80 Pages

8682 **Investment Dealers' Digest**
Thomson Financial Publishing
195 Broadway
Suite 4
New York, NY 10007-3124
646-822-2000; Fax: 646-822-2800
www.thomson.com
Elaine Yadlon, Plant Manager
James Smith, Chief Operating Officer
Corporation financing, market conditions, financial techniques and organizational strategies.
Frequency: Weekly
Circulation: 6255

8683 **Investment News**
Crain Communications Inc
711 3rd Ave
Suite 3
New York, NY 10017-9214
212-210-0171; Fax: 212-210-0237
info@crain.com
www.investmentnews.com
Rance Crain, President
Provides news vital to their businesses, including news affecting their clients investments and reports about the growing financial advisory industry and the companies that serve it.
Frequency: Weekly
Circulation: 61000
Founded in 1916

8684 **Investment Quality Trends**
IQ Trends
2888 Loker Avenue East
Suite 116
Carlsbad, CA 92010
866-927-5250; Fax: 866-927-5251
info@iqtrends.com
www.iqtrends.com
Michael Minney, Publisher
Kelley Wright, Managing Editor
Geraldine Weiss, Publisher Emeritus
Investment newsletter specializing in high-quality, divident-paying blue chip stocks, macro-economics, and market outlook.
Cost: $310.00
12 Pages
Frequency: Bi-monthly
Founded in 1966

8685 **Investment Recovery Association**
638 W 39th Street
Kansas City, MO 64111
816-561-5323
800-728-2272; Fax: 816-561-1991
www.invrecovery.org
David Rupert CMIR, President
Al Kidney CMIR, VP
Helps fulfill an important role by bringing people together from disparate industries...all focused on sharing best IR practices and improving the knowledge and skills necessary to properly perform the wide-ranging responsibilities required of investment recovery practitioners.
Cost: $300.00
16 Pages
Frequency: Monthly
Circulation: 900

8686 **Investor Relations Newsletter**
Kennedy Information
1 Pheonix Mill Lane
Floor 3
Petersborough, NH 03458
603-924-1006
800-531-0007
www.kennedyinfo.com
Gerald Murray, Editor
Provides practical, hands on strategy and tactics for the investor relations professional.
Cost: $295.00
Frequency: Monthly
ISSN: 1535-5802
Founded in 1970

8687 **Jumbo Rate News**
Bauer Financial
Gables International Plaza
PO Box 143520
Coral Gables, FL 33114
800-388-6686; Fax: 800-230-9569
customerservice@bauerfinancial.com
www.bauerfinancial.com
Karen L Dorway, President/CEO
Caroline Jervey, Editor
Each issue contains over 1,000 separate Jumbo CD rates in seven categories from over 200 creditworthy banks and thrifts nationwide. Includes star ratings, wire transfer fees, deposit requirements and financial highlights for each institution.
Cost: $445.00
Frequency: Weekly
Founded in 1983
Printed in 2 colors on matte stock

8688 **Kagan Media Investor**
Kagan World Media
126 Clock Tower Place
Carmel, CA 93923-8746
831-624-1536
800-307-2529; Fax: 831-625-3225
www.kagan.com
George Niesen, Editor
Tom Johnson, Marketing Manager
Robin Flynn, Senior VP
News of the Kagan Media Investor. Three month trial available.
Cost: $1195.00
Frequency: Monthly
Founded in 1969

8689 **Kagan Media Money**
Kagan World Media
1 Lower Ragsdale Dr
Bldg 1 Suite 130
Monterey, CA 93940-5749
831-624-1536; Fax: 831-625-3225
www.kagan.com
George Niesen, Editor
Harvey Kraft, Marketing Manager
Tim Baskerville, CEO
Harvey Kraft, Circulation Manager
Sandy Borthwick, Communications Manager
Analysts dissect deals, anticipate trends, project revenues, track financings and value the debt and equity of hundreds of privately held and publicly traded advertising, broadcasting, cable TV, digital TV, home video, Internet media, motion picture, newspaper, pay TV, professional sports and wireless telecommunications companies in the US and abroad.
Cost: $1245.00
Frequency: Monthly
Founded in 1969

8690 **Kagan Music Investor**
Kagan World Media
126 Clock Tower Place
Carmel, CA 93923-8746
831-624-1536; Fax: 831-625-3225
www.kagan.com
George Niesen, Editor
Tom Johnson, Marketing Manager
News and analysis for investors in the music industry.
Cost: $945.00
Frequency: Monthly

8691 **Kiplinger Tax Letter**
Kiplinger Washington Editors
1729 H St Nw
Washington, DC 20006-3924
202-887-6400
800-544-0155; Fax: 202-778-8976
sub.services@kiplinger.com
www.kiplinger.com
Knight Kiplinger, VP
Steven D Ivins, Editor
Biweekly tax letter for investors, business owners and managers. Covers current developments in Congress, IRS and the courts.
Cost: $54.00
4 Pages
Circulation: 125000
Mailing list available for rent
Printed in one color

8692 **Latin American Finance & Capital Markets**
WorldTrade Executive
PO Box 761
Concord, MA 01742-0761
978-287-0301; Fax: 978-287-0302
www.wtexec.com
Alison French, Production Manager

An action-oriented report on treasury management, tax, legal, accounting and other operational issues that impact doing business in Latin America. Provides an independent assessment of local capital markets.
Cost: $595.00
Frequency: Twice monthly

8693 **Limelight eNewsletter**
Wall Street Teechnology Association
521 Newman Springs Road
Suite 12
Lincroft, NJ 07738
732-530-8808; Fax: 732-530-0020
info@wsta.org
www.wsta.org
Phyllis Lampell, Executive Director
JoAnn Cooper, Executive Director
Frequency: Monthly
Circulation: 14000

8694 **Long Term Investing**
Concept Publishing
5202 Humphreys Road
Lake Park, GA 31636
229-257-0367; Fax: 229-219-1097
www.newconceptspublishing.com
Jim Dovan, Publisher
David Coleman, Editor
Madris Gutierrez, Editor-in-Chief
Andrea DePasture, Senior Editor
Offers full coverage of long term stocks, bonds and investments.
Cost: $98.00
12 Pages
Frequency: Monthly
Circulation: 600
Founded in 1998
Printed in one color on matte stock

8695 **MAR/Hedge**
Managed Account Reports
1250 Broadway
26th Floor
New York, NY 10001
212-213-6202
800-638-2525; Fax: 212-213-1870
subs@marhedge.com
Greg Newton, Publisher
Randall Devere, Editor-in-Chief
Lisa McErlane, Director of Marketing
Gary Lynch, President/Publisher
The first newsletter to cover the field of hedge funds in its entirety with industry news, in-depth articles and reviews of hedge fund managers and fund of funds and rankings of these managers and fund of funds.
Cost: $1195.00
16 Pages
Frequency: Monthly
Circulation: 300
Founded in 1994
Printed in 2 colors on matte stock

8696 **Managing 401(k) Plans**
Institute of Management and Administration
1 Washington Park
Suite 1300
Newark, NJ 07102
212-244-0360; Fax: 973-622-0595
www.ioma.com
The definitive resource for HR and Financial Department managers looking to run the best plan for their company.
Cost: $429.00

8697 **Managing Credit, Receivable & Collections**
Institute of Management and Administration
1 Washington Park
Suite 1300
Newark, NJ 07102
212-244-0360; Fax: 973-622-0595
www.ioma.com
Accelerate receivables and learn what technology and techniques are working best.
Cost: $269.00
Frequency: Monthly

8698 **Media Mergers & Acquisitions**
Kagan World Media
126 Clock Tower Place
Carmel, CA 93923-8746
831-624-1536; Fax: 831-624-5882
www.kagan.com
George Niesen, Editor
Tom Johnson, Marketing Manager
Where it all comes together. Exclusive scorecard of deals done by media companies. Dollar amounts, multiples paid, trends captured in succinct summaries of complex transactions. Three month trial available.
Cost: $795.00
Frequency: Monthly

8699 **Merger Strategy Report**
SNL Securities
PO Box 2124
Charlottesvle, VA 22902-2124
434-977-1600; Fax: 434-977-4466
www.snlnet.com
Erik Winthrow, Editor
John Minor, Editor
Reid Nagle, Publisher
Mark Outlaw, Advertising Director
Nick Cafferillo, Chief Operating Officer
For bank and thrift executives, with a regional M&A recap; list of deals; ranking of advisors and lawyers.
5 Pages
Frequency: Quarterly
Founded in 1995

8700 **Mergers & Acquisitions Executive Compensation Review**
SNL Securities
One SNL Plaza
PO Box 2124
Charlottesvle, VA 22902-2124
434-977-1600; Fax: 434-977-4466
isales@snl.com
www.snl.com
John Minor, Editor
Michael Spears, Advertising
Mike Scott, Mergers/Acquisitions
Nick Cafferillo, Chief Operating Officer
Adam Hall, Managing Director
For banks, thrifts, investment banks, law firms that advise on mergers, executives at banks expecting to merge and personnel and compensation specialists. Provides compensation information on the executives of banks that have entered into agreements to be acquired.
Cost: $495.00
10 Pages
Frequency: Monthly
Founded in 1987

8701 **Micro Ticker Report**
Waters Information Services
PO Box 2248
Binghamton, NY 13902-2248
607-770-8535; Fax: 607-723-7151
Dennis Waters, Publisher
Andrew Delaney, Editor
Covers the financial quotation industry.

8702 **Money Management Letter**
Institutional Investor
225 Park Ave S
12th Floor
New York, NY 10003-1605
212-224-3300; Fax: 212-224-3197
iieditor@institutionalinvestor.com
www.institutionalinvestor.com
Christopher Brown, CEO
Tom Lamont, Editor
This newsletter offers businesses information on investments, stocks, bonds, low-risk campaigns and financial planning opportunities.

8703 **Mortgaged Backed Securities Letter**
American Banker-Bond Buyer
1 State St
26th Floor
New York, NY 10004-1483
212-803-8350; Fax: 212-843-9600
John Del Mauro, VP
Tom Steinert-Threlkeld, Director
Provides coverage of structured finance and includes comprehensive listings of asset backed securities.
Frequency: Weekly
Circulation: 4200

8704 **Motion Picture Investor**
Kagan World Media
126 Clock Tower Place
Carmel, CA 93923-8746
831-624-1536; Fax: 831-625-3225
www.kagan.com/
George Niesen, Editor
Tom Johnson, Marketing Manager
Cost: $845.00
Frequency: Monthly
Founded in 1969

8705 **NACHA Operating Rules & Guidelines**
NACHA: The Electronic Payments Association
13450 Sunrise Valley Drive
Suite 100
Herndon, VA 20171
703-561-1100; Fax: 703-787-0996
info@nacha.org
www.nacha.org
Jane Larimer, CEO
Marcie Haitema, Chairperson
Reflects the results of the Rules Simplification initiative. PReviously organized around major topics, the simplified Rules framework is structured around the rights and responsibilities of participants in the ACH Network.
Cost: $78.00
Frequency: Annual

8706 **NADOA Newsletter**
National Association of Division Order Analysts
2805 Oak Trail Court
Suite 6312
Arlington, TX 76016
972-715-4489
administrator@nadoa.org
www.nadoa.org
Lynn S McCord, Administrator
Frequency: Bi-Monthly

8707 **NALHFA Newsletter**
National Association of Local Housing Finance

2025 M St Nw
Suite 800
Washington, DC 20036-2422

202-367-1197; Fax: 202-367-2197
www.noca.org

John C Murphy, Executive Director
Scott Lynch, Association Manager
Kim McKinon, Coordinator Membership
Frequency: Bi-Monthly

8708 **NAPFA Newslink**
National Association of Personal Financial Advisor
3250 N Arlington Heights Road
Suite 109
Arlington Heights, IL 60004

847-483-5400
800-366-2732; Fax: 847-483-5415
info@napfa.org
www.napfa.org

Geoffrey Brown, CEO
Susan Weiner, Managing Editor
Frequency: Quarterly

8709 **NASDAQ Subscriber Bulletin**
National Association of Securities Dealers
1212newyork anenue
suite950
Washington, DC 20005-1516

202-371-5535; Fax: 202-371-5536

Margo Porter, Publisher
Richard DeLouise, Editor
Pamela Anderson, Executive

Developments in the NASDAQ market.

8710 **NATRI Newsletter**
National Association for Treasurers of Religious
8824 Cameron Street
Silver Springs, MD 20910

301-587-7776; Fax: 301-589-2897
www.natri.org

Laura Reicks, Publisher
Lorelle Elcock, Associate Director Finance
Frequency: Bi-Monthly

8711 **NICSA News**
National Investment Company Service Association
36 Washington Street
Suite 70
Wellesley Hills, MA 02481

781-416-7200; Fax: 781-416-7065
info@nicsa.org
www.nicsa.org

Barbara V Weidlich, President
Keith Dropkin, Director Operations
Doris Jaimes, Registrar
Sheila Kobaly, Events Manager
Chris Ludent, IT Manager
Frequency: Quarterly

8712 **National Mortgage News**
Thomson Financial Publishing
1 State St
27th Floor
New York, NY 10004-1481

212-825-8445
800-235-5552; Fax: 212-292-5216
www.nationalmortgagenews.com/

Timothy Murphy, Group Publisher
Mark Fogarty, Editorial Director
Paul Muolo, M&A/Data Editor
Timothy Reifschneider, Advertising Director
Jose Thomas, Manager

Mortgage information, legislation and news.
Cost: $228.00
Frequency: Weekly
Circulation: 5000
Printed in 2 colors on newsprint stock

8713 **Network Newsletter**
Society for Information Management
401 N Michigan Avenue
Chicago, IL 60611

312-215-5190; Fax: 312-245-1081
www.simnet.org

Jim Luisi, Executive Director
Frequency: Bi-Monthly

8714 **Newspaper Investor**
Kagan World Media
1 Lower Ragsdale Dr
Building One, Suite 130
Monterey, CA 93940-5749

831-624-1536
831-625-3225; Fax: 831-625-3225
www.kagan.com

Tim Baskerville, President
Tom Johnson, Marketing Manager
Cost: $845.00
Frequency: Monthly
Founded in 1969

8715 **OTC Chart Manual**
Standard & Poor's Corporation
55 Water St
New York, NY 10041-0003

212-438-1000; Fax: 212-438-0299
www.standardandpoors.com

Deven Sharma, President

Charts on over 800 OTC stocks.

8716 **Origination News**
4709 Golf Road
Skokie, IL 60076

847-676-9600
800-321-3373; Fax: 847-933-8101
custserv@accuitysolutions.com
www.accuitysolutions.com

Timothy Murphy, Group Publisher
Mark Fogarty, Editorial Director
Jose Thomas, Manager
Malcolm Taylor, Managing Director

Information for mortgage industry executives on mortgage brokers, mortgage bankers and mortgage executives in commercial banks, savings banks, savings and loan associations and credit unions.
Cost: $78.00
Frequency: Monthly

8717 **Pawnbroker News**
National Pawnbrokers Association
P.O.Box 508
Keller, TX 76244-0508
817-491-4554; Fax: 817-491-8770
info@NationalPawnbrokers.org
www.nationalpawnbrokers.org

Bob Benedict, CAE, Executive Director
Emmett Murphy, Director
Teresa Congleton, Administrative Assistant
Frequency: 8/year

8718 **Pink Comparison Report**
SNL Securities
PO Box 2124
Charlottesvle, VA 22902-2124

434-977-1600; Fax: 434-977-4466
www.snlnet.com

Maria Moyer, Editor
Reid Nagle, Publisher
Mark LaBua, Subscription Manager
Mark Outlaw, Advertising Director
Nick Cafferillo, Chief Operating Officer

For CEOs, CFOs and IRCs of banks. Compares a subscribing bank or thrift's consolidated financial and market performance to other banks and thrifts chosen by the subscriber and banks and thrifts of similar asset size and location.
40 Pages
Frequency: Quarterly

8719 **Private Equity Week**
Securities Data Publishing
40 W 57th St
New York, NY 10019-4001

212-484-4701; Fax: 212-956-0112

Jennifer Reed, Editor-in-Chief
Edward Cortese, Marketing Executive

News of the past week and forecast of the weeks to come for investors.
Cost: $780.00
Frequency: Weekly

8720 **Private Placement Letter**
Securities Data Publishing
1290 6th Avenue
36th Floor
New York, NY 10104-101

212-765-5311; Fax: 212-957-0420
custserv@sourcemedia.com
www.privateplacementletter.com/

John Toth, Publisher
Ronald Cooper, Editor-in-Chief
Lauren Klopacs, Marketing Manager
Mark Cialdella, Circulation Manager
David Harkey, Advertising Manager

Highly sophisticated information on the debt private placement market including senior and mezzanine level debt.
Cost: $1395.00

8721 **Proceedings of the National Conference on Planned Giving**
National Committee on Planned Giving
233 S McCrea St
Suite 400
Indianapolis, IN 46225-1068

317-269-6274; Fax: 317-269-6276

Tanya Howe Johnson, President
Sandra Kerr, Director Government Education
Barbara Owens, Director Membership
Kathryn J Ramsey, Director Meetings
Kurt Reusze, Manager Education/Technology
Frequency: Annual

8722 **Quality Performance Report**
Managed Account Reports
220 5th Avenue
19th Floor
New York, NY 10001-7708

212-213-6202
800-638-2525; Fax: 212-213-6273

Randall Devere, Editor-in-Chief
Lois Peltz, Editor
Gary Lynch, President
Lisa McErlane, Marketing

The pre-eminent source of qualitative and quantitative information on global managed derivatives. Delivers in-depth analysis on the performance of the trading advisors in MAR's qualified database. Now covering over 500 trading advisors and programs.
Cost: $299.00
Frequency: Quarterly
Circulation: 400
Founded in 1913
Printed in 2 colors on matte stock

8723 **Quarterly Low-Load Mutual Fund Update**
American Association of Individual Investors
625 N. Michigan Ave.
Chicago, IL 60611

312-280-0170
800-428-2244; Fax: 312-280-9883
members@aaii.com
www.aaii.com

John Bajkowski, President
Charles Rotblut, Vice President
James Cloonan, Founder
Wayne Thorp, Sr. Financial Analyst

An editorial by the vice-president of AAII that provides an overview of the quarter and a summary of the markets behavior. Covers over 900 no-load and low-load mutual funds, as well as major stock and bond index returns.
Cost: $ 30.00
Frequency: Quarterly

8724 **REIT Daily Fax**
SNL Securities
One SNL Plaza
PO Box 2124
Charlottesvle, VA 22902-2124

434-977-1600; Fax: 434-293-0407
isales@snl.com
www.snl.com

Amy Woolard, Editor
Nick Cafferillo, Chief Operating Officer
Alan Zimmerman, Publisher
Pat LaBua, Customer Service Director
Adam Hall, Managing Director

Newsletter designed specifically for REIT industry professionals and investors. Features important industry events, condensed news stories, recent capital offerings and the latest market information.
4 Pages
Frequency: Daily
Founded in 1987

8725 **REIT Performance Graph**
SNL Securities
One SNL Plaza
PO Box 2124
Charlottesvle, VA 22902-2124

434-977-1600; Fax: 434-977-4466
subscriptions@snl.com
www.snl.com

Steve Arnold, Vice Chairman, CFO
Chandler Spears, Editor
Keven Lindemann, Real Estate
Gregg Amonette, General Media
Nick Cafferillo, Chief Operating Officer

For publicly traded REITs and REIT service providers. Compares the investment performance of a publicly traded REIT to a specific SNL index or to a selected peer group and the appropriate broad multi-industry index. Covers a 5-year period or the period beginning with the IPO date.
Cost: $399.00
1 Pages
Founded in 1987

8726 **Real Estate Alert**
Harrison Scott Publications
5 Marine View Plz
#301
Hoboken, NJ 07030-5722

201-386-1491; Fax: 201-659-4141
info@hspnews.com
www.hspnews.com

Andy Albert, Owner
Bob Mura, Editor
Barbara Eannaci, Marketing Manager
Michelle Lebowitz, Director

Information on investment opportunities in institutional grade commercial real estate, includes sales acquisitions and personnel changes.
Cost: $1597.00
Frequency: Weekly
Circulation: 650
Founded in 1989

8727 **Real Estate Finance Today**
Mortgage Bankers Association of America
1919 Pennsylvania Avenue NW
Washington, DC 20006-3404

202-557-2700
www.mortgagebankers.org

Information on anticipating industry trends, regulatory changes, economic outlook, federal and state legislation and trends in the secondary mortgage industry.
Cost: $100.00
Frequency: Monthly
Circulation: 1500
Founded in 1939

8728 **Real-Estate Alert**
Harrison Scott Publications
5 Marine View Plz
Suite 301
Hoboken, NJ 07030-5722

201-386-1491; Fax: 201-659-4141
info@hspnews.com
www.hspnews.com

Andy Albert, Owner
Tom Ferris, Director
Michelle Lebowitz, Director

A weekly newsletter on the securitization of consumer and corporate receivables.
Cost: $1497.00
10 Pages
Frequency: Weekly
Circulation: 600
ISSN: 1520-3700
Printed in 4 colors on matte stock

8729 **Reducing Benefits Costs**
Institute of Management and Administration
1 Washington Park
Suite 1300
Newark, NJ 07102

212-244-0360; Fax: 973-622-0595
www.ioma.com

Provides information on controlling benefit costs.
Cost: $245.00
16 Pages
Frequency: Monthly

8730 **Regional Economic Digest**
Federal Reserve Bank of Kansas City
925 Grand Avenue
Kansas City, MO 64198-0001

816-881-2970
800-333-1010; Fax: 816-881-2569
http://ideas.repec.org

Thomas Davis, Publisher
Bob Regan, Editor

A review of financial and economic conditions in the Tenth District. Includes articles of regional interest, statistics on District commercial banks and the area economy and results of a survey of agricultural credit conditions.
32 Pages

8731 **Regulatory Risk Monitor**
United Communications Group
11300 Rockville Pike
Street 1100
Rockville, MD 20852-3030

301-287-2700; Fax: 301-816-8945
www.ucg.com

Benny Dicecca, President

Updates banking officials, credit union, compliance officers, attorneys and auditors with current independent news and guidance.
Founded in 1970

8732 **Report on Financial Analysis, Planning & Reporting**
Institute of Management and Administration
1 Washington Park
Suite 1300
Newark, NJ 07102

212-244-0360; Fax: 973-622-0595
www.ioma.com

FARP regularly covers performance measurements effective use of new FASB, IRS and SEC financial and accounting requirements for all industries, shows managers the best way to evaluate business opportunities, how to read and evaluate capital budgets, earbug reports and analysts see the big picture through the use of new financial tools such as Economic Value Assets and Shareholder Valuations models.
Cost: $269.00
Frequency: Monthly

8733 **Retirement Plans Bulletin**
Universal Pensions
PO Box 979
Brainerd, MN 56401

218-855-0565
800-346-3860; Fax: 218-829-4814

Thomas G Anderson, President
Jennifer M Norquist, Editor

Digests IRS technical jargon on IRA's and qualified plans and translates it into understandable articles and advice for financial organizations.
Cost: $89.00
10 Pages
Frequency: Monthly
Printed in 2 colors on glossy stock

8734 **SNL Bank M&A DataSource**
SNL Securities
One SNL Plaza
PO Box 2124
Charlottesvle, VA 22902-2124

434-977-1600; Fax: 434-977-4466
subscriptions@snl.com
www.snl.com

John Minor, Publisher
Eric Hoffer, Editor
John McCune, Banks/Thrifts Manager
Michael Spears, Advertising
Nick Cafferillo, Chief Operating Officer

For investment bankers, investment companies, banks, thrifts, consultants and broker/dealers. Includes all merger and acquisition activity involving a bank or thrift as a buyer or seller.
Founded in 1987

8735 **SNL Branch Migration DataSource**
SNL Securities
PO Box 2124
Charlottesvle, VA 22902-2124

434-977-1600; Fax: 434-977-4466
www.snlnet.com

Melissa Hobson, Editor
John Minor, Editor
Reid Nagle, Publisher
Mark Outlaw, Advertising Director
Nick Cafferillo, Chief Operating Officer

For investment bankers, investment companies, banks, thrifts, consultants and regulatory agencies. Re-assigns bank and thrift branch deposits to account for all M&A activity that has occurred since the last regulatory release.
Frequency: Annual
Founded in 1991

8736 **SNL Corporate Performance Graphs for Banks**
SNL Securities
One SNL Plaza
PO Box 2124
Charlottesvle, VA 22902-2124

434-977-1600; Fax: 434-977-4466
subscriptions@snl.com
www.snl.com

Will Wick, Editor
James Record, Editor
John McCune, Banks/Thrifts Manager
Michael Spears, Advertising
Nick Cafferillo, Chief Operating Officer

For publicly traded banks, law firms, accountants and consulting firms. Includes a 5-year comparison of an institution's stock to both a selected peer group index and a broad multi-industry index.
1 Pages
Founded in 1987

8737 **SNL Financial DataSource**
SNL Securities
One SNL Plaza
PO Box 2124
Charlottesvle, VA 22902-2124

434-977-1600; Fax: 434-977-4466
subscriptions@snl.com
www.snl.com

Steve Tomasi, Editor
Steve Ferguson, Editor
Edward Metz, Financial
Michael Spears, Advertising
Nick Cafferillo, Chief Operating Officer

For investment bankers, investment companies, banks, thrifts, institutional investors, consultants and broker/dealers. Available in six separate interactive modules that contain data for equity research, industry trend analysis, peer group comparisons and identification of investment and acquisition opportunities.
Founded in 1987

8738 **SNL Mutual Thrift Conversion Investors Kit**
SNL Securities
One SNL Plaza
PO Box 2124
Charlottesvle, VA 22902-2124

434-977-1600; Fax: 434-977-4466
subscriptions@snl.com
www.snl.com

Chris Smith, Editor
Reid Nagle, Publisher
John McCune, Banks/Thrifts Manager
Michael Spears, Advertising
Nick Cafferillo, Chief Operating Officer

For thrift executives, individual investors and institutional investors. Contains a set of articles explaining the mechanics of mutual-to-stock conversion and the 'how-to' of investing, reviewing profitability of conversion investments and outlining regulatory issues that affect conversions.
Cost: $495.00
100 Pages
Frequency: Monthly
Founded in 1987

8739 **SNL Pink Quarterly**
SNL Securities
PO Box 2124
Charlottesvle, VA 22902-2124

434-977-1600; Fax: 434-977-4466
www.snlnet.com

Maria Moyer, Editor
Reid Nagle, Publisher
Mark Outlaw, Advertising Director
Pat LaBua, Subscription Manager
Nick Cafferillo, Chief Operating Officer

For investment companies, banks and thrifts, broker/dealers and individual investors. Contains detailed financial and market information on all banks and thrifts traded on the OTC bulletin boards and by market makers, as well as in-depth analysis of this sector.
240 Pages
Frequency: Quarterly
Founded in 1995

8740 **SNL Securities Thrift Performance Graph**
SNL Financial
PO Box 2124
Charlottesvle, VA 22902-2124

434-977-1600; Fax: 434-977-4466
www.snlnet.com

Reid Nagle, Publisher
John Racine, Editor
Mark Outlaw, Advertising Director
Pat Labua, Subscription Manager
Jeff Sternberg, Production Editor

SNL Securities is a research and publishing company that focuses on banks, thrifts, REITs insurance companies, and specialized, financial service companies. Founded in 1987, SNL securities has become the authority for information on financial institutions.

8741 **SNL Securities Bank Comparison Report**
SNL Securities
PO Box 2124
Charlottesvle, VA 22902-2124

434-977-1600; Fax: 434-977-4466
www.snlnet.com

Mona Thompson, Editor
Dan Oakey, Editor
Keith Davis, Editor
Reid Nagle, Publisher
Nick Cafferillo, Chief Operating Officer

For CEOs, CFOs and IRCs of banks. Compares a subscribing bank's consolidated financial and market performance to that of banks and thrifts of similar asset size and location.
40 Pages
Frequency: Quarterly
Founded in 1987

8742 **SNL Securities Thrift Comparison Report**
SNL Securities
PO Box 2124
Charlottesvle, VA 22902-2124

434-977-1600; Fax: 434-977-4466
www.snlnet.com

Dave Spence, Editor
Reid Nagle, Publisher
Mark Outlaw, Advertising Director
Pat LaBua, Subscripton Manager
Nick Cafferillo, Chief Operating Officer

Report for CEOs, CFOs and IRCs of thrifts and major corporate stockholders. Illustrates and compares a subscribing thrift's consolidated financial and market performance to thrifts of similar asset size and location.
40 Pages
Frequency: Quarterly
Founded in 1988

8743 **Secured Leader**
Commercial Finance Association
Ste 1801
7 Penn Plz
New York, NY 10001-3979

212-594-3490; Fax: 212-564-6053
info@cfa.com
www.cfa.com

Bruce H Jones, Executive Director
Theodore Kompa, President

Only publication devoted exclusively to the asset-based financial services industry. Editorial matter is directed toward practitioners of asset-based financing. Accepts advertising.
Cost: $56.00
76 Pages
Circulation: 5000
Founded in 1944

8744 **Securities Industry News**
Source Media
1 State St
27th floor
New York, NY 10004-1561

212-803-8200
800-221-1809; Fax: 212-843-9608
custserv@sourcemedia.com
www.sourcemedia.com

James M Malkin, CEO
Michael Eggebrecht, Managing Editor
Edward Hanasik, Marketing Director
Omar Asmar, Art Director
David Greenough, VP/Business Technology Group

Securities Industry News is a weekly newspaper in the global securities and financial markets that delivers original, time-critical news and analysis to senior decision-makers in charge of operations, technology, processing services, and compliance in the global securities and financial markets.
Cost: $575.00
Frequency: 42 Issues Annually

8745 **Securities Week**
McGraw Hill
PO Box 182604
Columbus, OH 43272

614-304-4000
877-833-5524; Fax: 614-759-3759
www.mcgraw-hill.com

Michael Ocrant, Managing Editor
Harold McGraw, CEO

Information on firms and exchanges strategy plans, new hires, events and issues, as well as legislation and legal rulings impacting the securities industry.
Frequency: Weekly
Founded in 1884

8746 **Shareholder Satisfaction Survey**
National Investment Company Service
36 Washington Avenue
Suite 70
Wellesley Hills, MA 02481

781-416-7200; Fax: 781-416-7065
info@nicsa.org
www.nicsa.org

Barbara V Weidlich, President
Keith Dropkin, Director Operations
Doris Jaimes, Registrar
Sheila Kobaly, Events Manager
Chris Ludent, IT Manager
Frequency: Annual

8747 **Special Stock Report**
Wall Street Transcript
67 Wall Street
9th Floor
New York, NY 10005-3701

212-952-7400
800-246-7673; Fax: 212-668-9842

twsteditor@twst.com
www.twst.com

Andrew Pickup, President/CEO
Doug Estadt, Online Editor
Andrew Pickup, Publisher
Jason Flatt, Marketing

Monthly stock pick based on research, interviews, and data contained in the wall st. transcript.
Cost: $399.00
Frequency: Monthly
Circulation: 7274
Founded in 1963

8748 **Specialty Lender**
SNL Securities
PO Box 2124
Charlottesvle, VA 22902-2124

434-977-1600; Fax: 434-977-4466
www.snlnet.com

Dave Meadors, Editor
Jim Allen, Editor
L Todd Vencil, Editor
Reid Nagle, Publisher
Nick Cafferillo, Chief Operating Officer

For executives of specialty lending companies, banks and thrifts which have specialty lending operations, heads of captive finance companies, investors, investment bankers and equity analysts. Provides news, analysis and financial and market information about specialty lenders, focusing on credit management and access to capital.
40 Pages
Frequency: Monthly
Founded in 1996

8749 **Specialty Lender Performance Graph**
SNL Securities
PO Box 2124
Charlottesvle, VA 22902-2124

434-977-1600; Fax: 434-977-4466
www.snlnet.com

David Meadors, Editor
Reid Nagle, Publisher
Mark Outlaw, Advertising Director
Pat LaBua, Subscription Manager
Nick Cafferillo, Chief Operating Officer

For publicly traded specialty lenders and specialty lender service providers. Compares the investment performance of a specialty lender to a specific SNL index or to a selected peer group and the appropriate broad multi-industry index. Covers a 5-year period or the period beginning with the IPO date.
Frequency: By request
Founded in 1997

8750 **Stock Superstars Report**
American Association of Individual Investors
625 N. Michigan Ave.
Suite 1900
Chicago, IL 60611

312-280-0170
888-428-2244; Fax: 312-280-9883
members@aaii.com
www.stocksuperstars.com

James Cloonan, Founder
John Bajkowski, President
Wayne Thorp, Sr. Financial Analyst

Information to help the reader build a successful investment portfolio by combining investment research with risk-reduction strategies.
Cost: $149.00
Frequency: Monthly

8751 **Streaming Media Investor**
Kagan World Media
126 Clock Tower Place
Carmel, CA 93923-8746

831-624-1536; Fax: 831-624-5882
www.kagan.com

George Niesen, Editor
Tom Johnson, Marketing Manager

News of the Streaming Media Investor. Three month trial available.
Cost: $895.00
Frequency: Monthly

8752 **TV Program Investor**
Kagan World Media
126 Clock Tower Place
Carmel, CA 93923-8746

831-624-1536
800-307-2529; Fax: 831-625-3225
www.kagan.com

George Niesen, Editor
Harvy Kraft, Marketing Manager
Tim Baerville, CEO/President
Robert Naylor, Circulation Manager
Cost: $895.00
Frequency: Monthly
Founded in 1969

8753 **Tax Management Compensation Planning**
1250 23rd Street NW
Washington, DC 20037-1164

202-337-7240
800-223-7270; Fax: 202-496-6013

David McFarland, President
Glenn Davis, Managing Editor

Nearly 40 portfolios, each focusing on specific tax, labor and other aspects of qualified and non-qualified retirement plans, employee welfare benefit plans, executive compensation, employment taxes and accounting for deferred compensation. Offers practitioner-authored articles, analysis of recent developments and decisions, and insightful comments from leading practitioners on the latest planning strategies.
Cost: $837.00
Frequency: Monthly

8754 **Taxpractice**
Tax Analysts
6830 North
Fairfax Drive
Arlington, VA 22213-1001

703-533-4400
800-955-2444; Fax: 703-533-4444
webmaster@tax.org
www.tax.org

Thomas F Field, Publisher
Jill Biden, Vice President

Contains comprehensive coverage of IRS rulings, court decisions, tax law changes and other topics of interest.
Cost: $749.00
Frequency: Weekly
Circulation: 2200
Founded in 1970

8755 **TheStreet Ratings, Inc.**
14 Wall Street
15th Floor
New York, NY 10005

212-321-5000
800-289-9222; Fax: 212-321-5016
letters@thestreet.com
www.thestreet.com

Dave Kansas, Editor-in-Chief

Information on what is happening on Wall Street, along with mutual fund and economic news, stock quotes, market summaries, and analyses of key indicators.
Cost: $69.95
Frequency: Daily

8756 **Thrift 13D Dictionary**
SNL Securities
PO Box 2124
Charlottesvle, VA 22902-2124

434-977-1600; Fax: 434-977-4466
www.snlnet.com

Todd L Davenport, Editor
Reid Nagle, Publisher
Mark Outlaw, Advertising Director
Pat LaBua, Subscription Manager
Nick Cafferillo, Chief Operating Officer

Contains all active 13D filings and related filings for every publicly traded bank in the country, including those which trade on the pink sheets.
250 Pages
Frequency: Quarterly

8757 **Thrift Performance Graph**
SNL Securities
One SNL Plaza
PO Box 2124
Charlottesvle, VA 22902-2124

434-977-1600; Fax: 434-977-4466
subscriptions@snl.com
www.snl.com

Will Wick, Editor
James Record, Editor
John McCune, Banks/Thrifts Manager
Michael Spears, Advertising
Nick Cafferillo, Chief Operating Officer

Compares investment performance of a publicly traded Thrift company to a specific SNL index or to a selected peer group and the appropriate broad multi-industry index. Graph covers a 5-year period or the period beginning with the IPO date. For publicly traded thrifts, law firms, accountants and consulting firms.
1 Pages
Founded in 1987

8758 **Topics Newsletter**
Association of Government Accountants
2208 Mount Vernon Avenue
Alexandria, VA 22301-1314

703-684-6931
800-242-7211; Fax: 703-519-0039
communications@agacgfm.org
www.agacgfm.org

Ann M. Ebberts, Chief Executive Officer
Mary Margaret Yodzis, Editor/Copywriter

Designed to give national exposure to chapter events, community service projects and member accomplishments while offering the most up-to-date Association news, released every other Monday morning by e-mail to members.
Frequency: Weekly
Founded in 1950

8759 **Trading Technology Week**
Waters Information Services
270 Lafayette St
Suite 700
New York, NY 10012-3311

212-925-6990; Fax: 212-925-7585
www.dealingwithtechnology.com

Tim Weller, CEO
Eugene Grygo, Editor
Adrian Goulbourn, Publisher
Lillian Lopez, Production Manager
Melissa Jao, Business Development Manager

Information covering the latest applications, platforms and strategies in trading room systems and proprietary execution.
Cost: $2025.00
Frequency: Weekly
Founded in 2000

8760 **Transactions**
AACE International

209 Prairie Ave
Suite 100
Morgantown, WV 26501-5934

304-296-8444
800-858-2678; Fax: 304-291-5728
info@aacei.org
www.aacei.org

Andrew Dowd, Executive Director
Megan McCulla, Asst Manager
Jenny Alms, Marketing Manager
Cost: $65.00
Frequency: Monthly
Circulation: 5000
Founded in 1956

8761 **Turning Points**
Concept Publishing
PO Box 500
York, NY 14592-500

800-836-4575
800-836-4575; Fax: 585-243-3148
publishing@conceptpub.com
www.conceptpub.com

Jim Dovan, Publisher
David Coleman, Editor

Economic news.
Cost: $198.00
2 Pages
Circulation: 600
Founded in 1974
Printed in one color on matte stock

8762 **VMQ Stocks**
American Association of Individual Investors
625 N. Michigan Ave.
Chicago, IL 60611

312-280-0170
800-428-2244; Fax: 312-280-9883
members@aaii.com
www.aaii.com

John Bajkowski, President
Charles Rotblut, Vice President
James Cloonan, Founder
Wayne Thorp, Sr. Financial Analyst

The VMQ strategy analyzes stock on their Value, Momentum, and Quality. A subscription to VMQ Stocks includes a weekly newsletter, a model portfolio, and a stock analyzer tool.
Cost: $279.00
Frequency: Weekly

8763 **VOD Investor**
Kagan World Media
126 Clock Tower Place
Carmel, CA 93923-8746

831-624-1536
800-307-2529; Fax: 831-625-3225
www.kagan.com

George Niesen, Editor
Tom Johnson, Marketing Manager
Robin Flynn, Senior VP

News of the VOD Investor. Three month trial available.
Cost: $1045.00
Frequency: Monthly
Founded in 1969

8764 **Video Investor**
Kagan World Media
126 Clock Tower Place
Carmel, CA 93923-8746

831-624-1536; Fax: 831-624-5882
www.kagan.com

George Niesen, Editor
Tom Johnson, Marketing Manager

Authoritative look inside the business of renting and selling video cassettes. Exclusive estimates of retail and wholesale transactions and inventories. Tracking movies into the home. Three month trial is available.
Cost: $ 795.00
Frequency: Monthly

8765 **Wall Street Technology Association Enewsletter**
620 Shrewsbury Ave
Suite C2
Tinton Falls, NJ 07701

732-530-8808; Fax: 732-530-0020
info@wsta.org
www.wsta.org
Facebook, Twitter, LinkedIn

John Killeen, President
Phyllis Lampell, Executive Director
JoAnn Cooper, Executive Director

Nonprofit educational organization that focuses on technologies, operational approaches, and business issues for the global financial community.
2000+ Members
Frequency: Monthly
Circulation: 14000+
Founded in 1967

8766 **Water Investment Newsletter**
US Water News
230 Main St
Halstead, KS 67056-1913

316-835-2222
800-251-0046; Fax: 316-835-2223
www.uswaternews.com

Thomas Bell, Owner
Toni Young, Chairman

News, features and profiles of shareholder owned water supply and treatment companies. General news on water-related investment opportunities with stock portfolio.
Cost: $140.00
8 Pages
Frequency: Monthly
ISSN: 1049-443X
Printed in one color on matte stock

8767 **Wireless Market Stats**
Kagan World Media
1 Lower Ragsdale Dr
Building One, Suite 130
Monterey, CA 93940-5749

831-624-1536
800-307-2529; Fax: 831-625-3225
www.kagan.com

Tim Baskerville, President
Tom Johnson, Marketing Manager

News of the Wireless Market Stats. Three month trial available.
Cost: $1095.00
Frequency: Monthly
Founded in 1969

8768 **Wireless Telecom Investor**
Kagan World Media
1 Lower Ragsdale Dr
Bldg 1, Suite 130
Monterey, CA 93940-5749

831-624-1536
800-307-2529; Fax: 831-625-3225
www.kagan.com

Tim Baskerville, President
Harvey Kraft, Director of Marketing
George Niesen, Editor
Robert Naylor, Circulation Manager
Sandie Borthwick, Publisher

Exclusive analysis of private and public values of wireless telecommunications companies, including cellular telephone, ESMR and PCS. Exclusive databases of subscribers, market penetrations, market potential, industry growth. Catching super-fast growth in a capsule. Three month trial available.
Cost: $1095.00
Frequency: Monthly
Founded in 1970

8769 **Wireless/Private Cable Investor**
Kagan World Media
126 Clock Tower Place
Carmel, CA 93923-8746

831-624-1536; Fax: 831-624-5882
www.kagan.com

George Niesen, Editor
Tom Johnson, Marketing Manager

The original bible of the wireless cable, multipoint distribution pay TV industry. Published continuously since 1972, this newsletter is the window on cable competition. Three month trial available.

Magazines & Journals

8770 **AAII Journal**
American Association of Individual Investors
625 N Michigan Avenue
Chicago, IL 60611

312-280-0170
800-428-2244; Fax: 312-280-9883
members@aaii.com
www.aaii.com

John Bajkowski, President
James Cloonan, Founder
Charles Rotblut, Editor, AAII Journal

Journal focusing on personal finance, specifically investing in stocks and mutual funds and portfolio management.
Cost: $29.00
40 Pages
Circulation: 170000
ISSN: 0192-3315
Founded in 1978

8771 **ABI/St. John's Law Review**
ABI/St. Johns School of Law
8000 Utopia Parkway
Queens, NY 11439

718-990-6751; Fax: 718-990-8095
abilawreview@gmail.com
www.stjohns.edu

Denise Dessel, Editor-in-Chief

A partnership between St. John's School of Law and the American Bankruptcy Institute that publishes articles and student notes on cutting edge issues of bankruptcy law and practice.
Frequency: Bi-Annual
Founded in 1993

8772 **AG Lender**
Food 360/Vance Media
10901 W 84th Ter
Lenexa, KS 66214-1631

913-438-5721
800-808-2623; Fax: 913-438-0697
rkeller@vancepublishing.com
www.vancepublishing.com

Cliff Becker, VP

AG Lender magazine reaches key agricultural financial leaders with editorial material geared to their business success.
Frequency: Monthly
Circulation: 1700
Founded in 1923

8773 **Accounting and Business Review World**
Scientific Publishing Company

1060 Main Street
River Edge, NJ 07661-2013

201-487-9655; Fax: 201-487-9656

Ed Yang Hoong Pang

Aims to provide a forum for the publication of accounting and business research papers which are of interest to educators, students and practitioners.
Cost: $60.00

8774 **Affiliate Forum**
NACHA: Electronic Payments Association
13665 Dulles Technology Dr
Suite 300
Herndon, VA 20171-4607

703-561-1100; Fax: 703-787-0996
info@nacha.org
www.nacha.org

Jane Larimer, CEO

8775 **Alert**
Defense Credit Union Council
601 Pennsylvania Ave NW
South Building, Suite 600
Washington, DC 20004-2601

202-638-3950; Fax: 202-638-3410
www.dcuc.org

Roland Arteata, President
Frequency: Monthly

8776 **American Bankruptcy Institute Journal**
American Bankruptcy Institute
66 Canal Center Plaza
Suite 600
Alexandria, VA 22314-1546

703-739-0800; Fax: 703-739-1060
info@abiworld.org
www.abi.org

Amy Quackenboss, Executive Director

Benefit to ABI members. Written by experts in the insolvency community, the Journal addresses timely issues involving consumer bankruptcy, the intersection of state laws and the Bankrupcy Code, valuation, turnaround management concerns, recent legislative developments, the US trustee system and more. Available in print or online.
Frequency: Monthly
Founded in 1982

8777 **Annual Institute Journal**
National Association of Division Order Analysts
2805 Oak Trail Court
Suite 6312
Arlington, TX 76016

972-715-4489
administrator@nadoa.org
www.nadoa.org

Lynn S McCord, Administrator
Frequency: Annual

8778 **Armed Forces Comptroller**
American Society of Military Comptrollers
415 N. Alfred Street
Alexandria, VA 22314

703-549-0360
800-462-5637; Fax: 703-549-3181
www.asmconline.org
Facebook, Twitter, LinkedIn

Al Runnels, Executive Director
Catherine Kenol, Associate Director, Communications

Leading industry journal from the American Society of Military Comptrollers, being one of the Society's means of sharing professional information. Articles are received from a variety of sources, such as academia, the government, and our members.
Founded in 1948

8779 **Asset Management**
ASMC
170 Avenue at the Common
PO Box 7930
Shrewsbury, NJ 07702-4803

732-389-8700; Fax: 732-389-8701
www.djassetmanagement.com

Barry Vinocur, Publisher

Departments include a mutual fund snapshot, a variable annuity databank, asset allocation, a journal watch and much more. Also offering topical features of interest to industry professionals.
Frequency: Bi-Monthly
Circulation: 30,000

8780 **Asset Protection: Offshore Tax Reports**
Offshore Press
4500 W 72nd Ter
Shawnee Mission, KS 66208-2824

913-362-9667; Fax: 913-432-7174

Vernon K Jacobs, President
Cost: $120.00
Frequency: Weekly
Founded in 1981

8781 **BCCA Credit and Collection Survey**
Broadcast Cable Credit Association
550 W. Frontage Road
Suite 3600
Northfield, IL 60093-1243

847-881-8757; Fax: 847-784-8059
info@bccacredit.com
www.bccacredit.com

Mary Collins, President & CEO
Jamie Smith, Director, Operations
Arcelia Pimentel, Sales/Membership
Frequency: Bi-Annual

8782 **Barter News**
PO Box 3024
Mission Viejo, CA 92690-1024

949-831-0607; Fax: 949-831-9378
www.barternews.com

Bob Meyer, Publisher/Editor
Michael Mercier, VP
Fredrick Fuest, COO
Julia Homer, CFO

Industry news is covered including listings of CEO's and CFO's and editorials. An in-depth look into the changes and evolution of barter, and shows how-to profitability use barter to increase the bottom line.
Cost: $40.00
96 Pages
Frequency: Quarterly
Circulation: 30,000
Founded in 1980
Printed in 4 colors on glossy stock

8783 **Business Credit**
National Association of Credit Management
8840 Columbia 100 Pkwy
Columbia, MD 21045-2100

410-740-5560; Fax: 410-740-5574
robins@nacm.org
www.nacm.org

Robin Schauseil, President
Jim Vanghel, Vice President

For professionals responsible for extending credit and collecting receivables. Topics include business law, lein law, technology, credit management, collections, deductions, fraud, credit risk, credit scoring, outsourcing, information services, trade finance and more.
Cost: $54.00
72 Pages
Circulation: 32000
Founded in 1896
Printed in 4 colors on matte stock

8784 **Business Finance**
Duke Communications International
221 E 29th Street
PO Box 3438
Loveland, CO 80539-3438

970-634-4700; Fax: 970-593-1050
info@businessfinancemag.com
www.businessfinancemag.com

David Blansfield, Publisher
Laurie Brannen, Editor-in-Chief
Meg Waters, Managing Editor
Matthew Weiner, Associate Publisher
Bruce Lynn, Managing Partner

Articles cover a broad range of topics from accounting to the Internet, from benchmarking to best practices, and cost management to career management.
Frequency: Monthly
Circulation: 50000

8785 **CEIR - Quarterly National Economic Reports**
National Association of Certified Valuation
1111 Brickyard Road
Suite 200
Salt Lake City, UT 84106-5401

303-698-1883
800-677-2009
sherril@nacva.com

Pamela R Bailey, Executive Director
Parnell Black, MBA CPA CVA, CEO
Roberto Castro, Director Business Development
Dean Dinas, Director Economic Research
Brien K Jones, General Manager Conferences
Frequency: Quarterly

8786 **CFMA Building Profits**
Construction Financial Management Association
100 Village Boulevard
Suite 200
Princeton, NJ 08540-5783

609-452-8000
888-421-9996; Fax: 609-452-0474
info@cfma.org
www.cfma.org
Facebook, Twitter, LinkedIn, YouTube

Stuart Binstock, President & CEO
Brian Summers, VP, Operations

Information for financial managers and CPAs concerned with financial management.
Frequency: Bi-Monthly
Circulation: 8,600
Founded in 1981

8787 **CMBA World**
Commerical Mortgage Securities Association
30 Broad St
28th Floor
New York, NY 10004-4119

212-509-1844; Fax: 212-509-1895
info1@cmbs.org
www.cmbs.org

Dottie Cunningham, CEO
Frequency: Quarterly

8788 **Collections & Credit Risk**
Thomson Financial Publishing

1 State St
27th Floor
New York, NY 10004-1481

212-825-8445
800-221-1809; Fax: 212-803-1592

Sharon Rowlands, President/CEO
Louis Eccleston, Marketing Director
Catherine Ladwig, Editor
Darren Waggoner, Executive Editor
Jose Thomas, Manager

Focuses on news and trends of strategic and competitive importance to collections and credit policy executives. Covers the credit risk industry's growth, diversification and technology in both commercial and consumer credit.
Cost: $98.00
66 Pages
Frequency: Monthly
Circulation: 25000
ISSN: 1093-1260
Founded in 1961
Printed in 4 colors on glossy stock

8789 Collector Magazine
ACA International
PO Box 390106
Minneapolis, MN 55439-106

952-926-6547; Fax: 952-926-1624
aca@acainternational.org
www.acainternational.org

Timothy Dressen, Editor/Director Comm
Gary Rippentrop, CEO
Anne Rosso, Associate Editor

Brings you vital, up to the minute information on industry trends, regulations and legislation each month.
Cost: $70.00
Frequency: Monthly
Circulation: 6000
Founded in 1939

8790 Computerized Investing
American Association of Individual Investors
625 N Michigan Avenue
Chicago, IL 60611

312-280-0170
800-428-2244; Fax: 312-280-9883
members@aaii.com
www.aaii.com

James Cloonan, Chairman

Offers information on computed investing, stocks and bonds.
Cost: $40.00
Founded in 1978

8791 Consumer Finance Law Quarterly Report
Conference on Consumer Finance Law
Oklahoma City University School of Law
2501 N Blackwelder
Oklahoma City, OK 73106

405-208-5363; Fax: 405-208-5089
www.ccfonline.org

Alvin C Harrell, Executive Director
Frequency: Quarterly

8792 Contingency Planning & Management
Witter Publishing Corporation
84 Park Avenue
Flemington, NJ 08822

908-788-0343; Fax: 908-788-3782
www.WitterPublishing.com

Steve Biggers, Publisher
Andy Hagg, Editor
Andrew Witter, President

Serves the fields of financial/banking, manufacturing industrial, transportation, utilities, telecommunications, health care, government, insurance and other allied fields.
Founded in 1996

8793 Controller's Quarterly
Institute of Management Accountants
10 Paragon Dr
Suite 1
Montvale, NJ 07645-1774

201-573-9000
800-638-4427; Fax: 201-474-1600
ima@imanet.org
www.imanet.org

Paul Juras, Chair
Jeffrey C. Thomson, President & CEO
Frequency: Monthly

8794 Corporate Controller
Thomson Reuters
195 Broadway
New York, NY 10007-3124

646-822-2000
800-231-1860; Fax: 646-822-2800
trta.lei-support@thomsonreuters.com
www.ria.thomsonreuters.com

Elaine Yadlon, Plant Manager
Thomas H Glocer, CEO & Director
Robert D Daleo, Chief Financial Officer
Kelli Crane, Senior Vice President & CIO

Includes health care costs, cash management, executive compensation and environmental insurance as well as regular columns on tax planning, technology advances, and innovative business trends.
Frequency: Bi-Monthly
Circulation: 3500

8795 Corporate Risk Management
Oster Communications
219 Main St
Cedar Falls, IA 50613-2742

319-277-1271; Fax: 319-277-7481

Merrill Oster, President

Written for financial decision makers.
48 Pages
Frequency: Monthly
Founded in 1989

8796 Cost Engineering Journal
AACE International
209 Prairie Avenue
Suite 100
Morgantown, WV 26501-5934
304-296-8444
800-858-2678; Fax: 304-291-5728
info@aacei.org
www.aacei.org

Marvin Gelhausen, Managing Editor
Noah Kinderknecht, Editor

International journal of cost estimation, cost/schedule control, and project management read by cost professionals around the world to get the most up-to-date information about the profession.
Frequency: Monthly

8797 Cost Management Update
Institute of Management Accountants
10 Paragon Dr
Suite 1
Montvale, NJ 07645-1774

201-573-9000
800-638-4427; Fax: 201-474-1600
ima@imanet.org
www.imanet.org

Jeffrey C. Thomson, President & CEO
Paul E. Juras, Chair
Frequency: Monthly

8798 Credit Card Management
Thomson Financial Publishing
1 State St
27th Floor
New York, NY 10004-1481

212-825-8445
800-535-8403; Fax: 800-235-5552
custserv@sourcemedia.com
www.cardforum.com

James Daly, Editor
Sharon Rowlands, President/CEO
Louis Eccleston, Marketing Director
Jose Thomas, Manager

Information on the major developments in the credit card industry.
Cost: $98.00
74 Pages
Frequency: Monthly
Circulation: 19000
Founded in 1962
Printed in 4 colors on glossy stock

8799 Credit Union Executive Journal
Credit Union National Association
Po Box 431
Madison, WI 53701-0431

608-231-4000
800-356-9655; Fax: 608-231-1869
dorothy@cuna.org
www.cuna.org

Jim Nussle, CEO

Techniques and concepts available in management, finance, marketing, lending, human resources and technology for credit unions.
Cost: $202.00
Circulation: 2400
Founded in 1930

8800 Credit Union Magazine
Credit Union National Association
5710 Mineral Point Road
Madison, WI 53705-4454

800-356-9655; Fax: 608-231-4263
dorothy@cuna.org
www.cuna.org

Jim Nussle, CEO

The role and operations of modern credit unions.
Cost: $50.00
100 Pages
Frequency: Monthly
Circulation: 32776
ISSN: 0011-1066
Founded in 1981
Printed in 4 colors on glossy stock

8801 Credit Union Technology
Credit Union Technology
110-64 Queens Boulevard
#106
Forest Hills, NY 11375-6347

718-793-9400; Fax: 718-793-9414
www.cutmag.com

Andrew Mallon, Publisher

Information on improving customer service through technological advances.
Cost: $36.00
24 Pages
Frequency: Bi-Monthly
Circulation: 6000
ISSN: 1054-7304
Founded in 1991
Printed in 4 colors on glossy stock

8802 DC Advocate
National Defined Contribution Council

9101 E Kenyon
Suite 300
Denver, CO 80237-0467

303-770-5353; Fax: 303-770-1812

Al Brust, Executive VP
Frequency: Quarterly

8803 Disclosure Record
Newsfeatures
8511 249th Street
Jamaica, NY 11426-2105
Jack Lotto, Editor

Full texts of corporate and financial news reports.
Cost: $50.00
8 Pages
Frequency: Monthly
Founded in 1973

8804 Electronics Payment Journal
NACHA: Electronic Payments Association
13665 Dulles Technology Dr
Suite 300
Herndon, VA 20171-4607

703-561-1100; Fax: 703-787-0996
info@nacha.org
www.nacha.org

Jane Larimer, CEO
Deb Evans-Doyle, Senior Director Conference Mktg
Julie Hedlund, Senior Director Electronic Commerce
Michael Herd, Director Public Relations
Priscilla Holland, AAP, Senior Director Corporate Pymts

8805 Equipment Leasing & Finance
Equipment Leasing And Finance Association
1625 Eye St. NW
Suite 850
Washington, DC 20006

202-238-3400; Fax: 202-238-3401
avogt@elfaonline.org
www.elfaonline.org

Amy Vogt, Managing Editor

As the flagship publication of the Equipment Leasing and Finance Association, Equipment Leasing & Finance is the trusted leader, bringing readers unrivaled coverage of the people, trends and issues that have an impact on the $628 billion equipment finance industry. Information of funding sources, portfolio management, sales and marketing strategy, large ticket leasing, transportation leasing, the computer leasing market, remarketing equipment, and the role of the equipment manager.
Frequency: 6x/Year
Circulation: 10000
Founded in 1961
Printed in 4 colors on glossy stock

8806 Estate Planning Review
2700 Lake Cook Road
Riverwoods, IL 60015-3867

847-267-7000
800-224-8299; Fax: 800-224-8299
www.support.cch.com

Robert Becker, President and CEO
Cost: $275.00
Frequency: Monthly
Founded in 1913

8807 Examiner
Society of Financial Examiners
174 Grace Blvd
Altamonte Spgs, FL 32714-3210

407-682-4930
800-787-7633; Fax: 407-382-3175
www.sofe.org

Pauline Keyes, Owner
Stephen J Szypula, Financial Administrator
Frequency: Quarterly

8808 F & I Management Technology
Association of Finance and Insurance Professionals
4112 Southwood E
Colleyville, TX 76034

817-428-2434; Fax: 817-428-2534
www.afip.com

David N Robertson, Executive Director

8809 Federal Credit Union Magazine
National Association of Federal Credit Unions
3138 10th St N
Arlington, VA 22201-2160

703-522-4770
800-336-4644; Fax: 703-524-1082
www.nafcu.org

Dan Berger, President

Written for CEO's, senior staff and volunteers of Federal Credit Unions. Offers legislative and regulatory news, as well as technology and operational issues. Call for rates.
50 Pages
Circulation: 1500
ISSN: 1043-7789
Founded in 1967
Printed in 4 colors on glossy stock

8810 Financial Analysts Journal
CFA Institiure
Po Box 3668
Charlottesville, VA 22903-0668

434-951-5499
800-247-8132; Fax: 434-951-5262
info@cfainstitute.org
www.cfainstitute.org

John Rogers, CEO
Rodney N Sullivan, Associate Editor

To advance the knowledge and understanding of the practice of investment management through the publication of high-quality, practitioner-relevant research
Founded in 1945

8811 Financial Executive
Financial Executives International
200 Campus Dr
Suite 8
Florham Park, NJ 07932-1007

973-236-0177
800-336-0773; Fax: 973-765-1018
www.financialexecutives.com

Jim Abel, President
Ellen Heffes, Managing Editor
Colleen S Cunningham, President
Maria O'Grady, Marketing Manager

Addresses accounting and treasury subjects, as well as overall strategies in corporate financial mangement.
Cost: $74.39
72 Pages
Frequency: Monthly
Circulation: 16500
ISSN: 0895-4186
Founded in 1931
Printed in 4 colors on glossy stock

8812 Financial Executive Magazine
Financial Executives International
1250 Headquarters Plaza
West Tower, 7th Floor
Morristown, NJ 07960

973-765-1000; Fax: 973-765-1018
membership@financialexecutives.org
www.financialexecutives.org

Andrej Suskavcevic, President & CEO

Addresses accounting and treasury subjects, as well as overall strategies in corporate financial management.
72 Pages
Frequency: 10x/yr
Circulation: 17000
ISSN: 0895-4186
Founded in 1931
Printed in 4 colors on glossy stock

8813 Financial Management
Financial Management Association International
University of South Florida
4202 E. Fowler Avenue, BSN 3403
Tampa, FL 33620-5500

813-974-2084; Fax: 813-974-3318
fma@coba.usf.edu
www.fma.org

Utpal Bhattacharya, Executive Editor

Financial Management serves the profession by publishing significant new scholarly research in finance that is of the highest quality. The principal criteria for publishability are originality, rigor, timeliness, practical relevance and clarity.
Frequency: Quarterly

8814 Financial Manager
Broadcast Cable Credit Association
550 W. Frontage Road
Suite 3600
Northfield, IL 60093-1243

847-881-8757; Fax: 847-784-8059
info@bccacredit.com
www.bccacredit.com

Mary Collins, President & CEO
Jamie Smith, Director, Operations
Arcelia Pimentel, Sales/Membership

A bi-monthly magazine published by the Broadcast Cable Credit Association.
Frequency: Bi-Monthly

8815 Financial Planning & Counseling Journal
Association for Financial Counseling and Planning
2112 Arlington Avenue
Suite H
Upper Arlington, OH 43221

614-485-9650; Fax: 614-485-9621
www.afcpe.org

Sharon Burns, PhD, Executive Director
Frequency: Semi-Annual

8816 Financial Planning Digest
Harcourt Brace Professional Publishing
6277 Sea Harbor Drive
Orlando, FL 32887

407-345-2000; Fax: 407-345-3016
www.smartbrief.com

Angelita Streeter, Editor
Paul Amidei, Managing Editor

Estate, retirement, insurance planning tips and strategies, practice management insight, book reviews and legislation updates.
Cost: $99.00
Frequency: Monthly

8817 Financial Review Magazine
NFR Communications

4948 Washburn Avenue S
Minneapolis, MN 55410

612-929-8110; Fax: 612-929-8146
www.nfrcom.com

Tom Bengtson, Editor
Jackie Hilgert, Production Manager

Trade publication covering the commercial banking industry in the upper midwest. Designed for the decision-maker in the bank.
Frequency: 25 per year

8818 Financial Services Quarterly
SNL Securities
One SNL Plaza
PO Box 2124
Charlottesvle, VA 22902-2124

434-977-1600; Fax: 434-977-4466
subscriptions@snl.com
www.snl.com

Pam Askea, Editor
Dan Oakey, Editor
Michael Spears, Advertising
Edward Metz, Financial Services
Nick Cafferillo, Chief Operating Officer

Comprehensive reference guide available on finance companies, mortgage banks, investment advisors and securities brokers/dealers. In-depth company profiles and financial data on these publicly traded companies and summary financials on thousands of non-public financial services companies.
Cost: $696.00
400 Pages
Frequency: Quarterly
Founded in 1987

8819 Financier
Bank Administration Institute
1 N Franklin St
Chicago, IL 60606-3598

312-553-4600; Fax: 312-683-2373
info@bai.org
www.bai.org

Deborah Bianucci, President & CEO
Ann Barcroft, Chief Administrative Officer
Julie Faber, Chief Financial Officer
Karl Dahlgren, Managing Director
Holly Hughes, Chief Marketing Officer

Forum of ideas for the private sector.
Cost: $5.00
Circulation: 32,000

8820 Forbes Global
Forbes Media LLC.
60 5th Ave
New York, NY 10011-8868

212-620-2200; Fax: 212-620-1857
readers@forbes.com
www.forbes.com

Malcolm S Forbes Jr, CEO
Bruce Rogers, VP Marketing
Paul Maidment, Executive Editor
Michael Smith Maidment, VP, GM Operations

A magazine giving detailed information about business and finance.
Frequency: Monthly

8821 Forbes Magazine
Forbes Media LLC.
60 5th Ave
11th Floor
New York, NY 10011-8868

212-620-2200; Fax: 212-620-1857
customerservice@forbes.com
www.forbes.com

Malcolm S Forbes Jr, CEO
Bruce Rogers, VP Marketing
Paul Maidment, Executive Director
Micheal Smith Maidment, VP, GM Operations

A magazine giving detailed information about business and finance.
Cost: $4.95
304 Pages
Founded in 1917

8822 Futures Industry
Futures Industry Association
2001 Pennsylvania Ave NW
#600
Washington, DC 20006-1823

202-223-1528; Fax: 202-296-3184
info@futuresindustry.org
www.futuresindustry.org

John Damgard, President/CEO
Erin Kairys, Manager
Will Acworth, Editor
Roselia Marmolejos, Administrative Assistant

Front and back office operations, marketing, research, money management, regulatory and brokerage issues from a domestic and international perspective.
Circulation: 15000
Founded in 1955

8823 Futures Magazine
Oster Communications
219 Main St
Suite 6
Cedar Falls, IA 50613-2742

319-277-1271; Fax: 319-277-7481
www.futuresmag.com

Merrill Oster, President
Ginger Szala, Publisher

News, analysis, and strategies for futures, options and derivatives traders. Descriptions include annual sourcebook directory of exchange, contract, company and product information.
Cost: $39.00
Frequency: Monthly
Circulation: 60000
Founded in 1972

8824 Global Custodian
Asset International
125 Greenwich Avenue
Greenwich, CT 06830

203-295-5015; Fax: 203-629-5024
www.globalcustodian.com

Dominic Hobson, Editor-in-Chief
Charles Ruffel, Executive Editor
Meredith Hughes, Publisher
Alix Hughes, Sales Director

An in-depth perspective on the business of international investing, custody and clearing, and directory-type data on industry participants and trends. Provides investment professionals with an analysis of the strength and weaknessed of the players and systems that underlie international investing.
Cost: $185.00
Circulation: 30,488
Founded in 1989

8825 Global Finance
7 E 20th St.
New York, NY 10003

Home Page: www.gfmag.com
Facebook, Twitter, LinkedIn

Joseph Giarraputo, Publisher & Editorial Director

The magazine offers analysis, articles and data to help corporate leaders, bankers and investors make decisions.
Frequency: Monthly
Circulation: 50,050
Founded in 1987

8826 Global Investment Magazine
Global Investment Technology
820 2nd Ave
4th Floor
New York, NY 10017-4504

212-370-3700; Fax: 212-370-4606
www.globalinv.com

Micheal Horton, Publisher
Pierre-Yves Sacchi, Managing Director

Portfolio management, trading and global asset services, and a wide range of issues pertaining to institutional portfolio management strategies and decision making in the US and cross-border markets.
Frequency: Quarterly
Circulation: 15000

8827 Global Investment Technology
Global Investment Technology
820 2nd Ave
4th Floor
New York, NY 10017-4504

212-370-3700; Fax: 212-370-4606
www.globalinv.com

Micheal Horton, Publisher
Pavan Sehgal, Managing Director
Pierre-Yves Sacchi, Managing Director

The strategic business interests of top-level decision makers as well as their operations and systems professionals.
Cost: $695.00
Circulation: 1800
Founded in 1990

8828 Healthcare Financial Management
2 Westbrook Corporate Ctr #700
Westchester, IL 60154-5723

708-531-9614; Fax: 708-531-0032
www.hfma.org

Richard L Clarke, President

8829 IBIS Review
Charles D Spencer
250 S Wacker Drive
#600
Chicago, IL 60606-5800

312-993-7900; Fax: 312-993-7910

Charles D Spencer, Publisher
Celia Cruz, Owner

For the individual responsible for the compensation and benefits of employees working abroad. Topics include pensions and profit-sharing plans, stock purchase and savings plans, death and disability benefits, health care coverage, termination indemnities, executive renumeration plans, investments, and expatriate plans.
Frequency: Monthly
Circulation: 1500

8830 IMA Focus
Institute of Management Accountants
10 Paragon Dr
Suite 1
Montvale, NJ 07645-1774

201-573-9000
800-638-4427; Fax: 201-474-1600
ima@imanet.org
www.imanet.org

Jeffrey C. Thomson, President & CEO
Frequency: Bi-Monthly

8831 INSIGHT
Society of Financial Examiners
174 Grace Blvd
Altamonte Spgs, FL 32714-3210

407-682-4930
800-787-7633; Fax: 407-682-3175
www.sofe.org

Pauline Keyes, Owner
Stephen J Szypula, Financial Administrator
Frequency: Monthly

8832 **ISM Info Edge**
Institute for Supply Management
2055 E Centennial Circle
PO Box 22160
Tempe, AZ 85285-2160

480-752-6276
800-888-6276; Fax: 480-752-7890
infocenter@ism.ws
www.ism.ws

Paul Novak, CPM, CEO
Holly LaCroix Johnson, Senior Vice President
Deborah Webber, SVP
Jean McHale, Manager
Frequency: Quarterly

8833 **Inside Mortgage Finance**
Inside Mortgage Finance Publishers
7910 Woodmont Ave
Suite 1010
Bethesda, MD 20814-7019

301-951-1240
800-570-5744; Fax: 301-656-1709
service@imfpubs.com
www.insidemortgagefinance.com

John Bancroft, CEO & Publisher
John Bancroft, Vice President & Executive Editor
Paul Muolo, Managing Editor
Mari Mullane, Director, Marketing
Tony Cecala, Production Manager

Residential finance industry news and related trade literature. Includes extensive rankings from top originators to the leading private mortgage insurers.
Cost: $889.00
12 Pages
Frequency: Weekly
ISSN: 8756-0003
Founded in 1984
Printed in 2 colors on matte stock

8834 **Inside Supply Management**
Insitute for Supply Management
2055 E Centennial Circle
PO Box 22160
Tempe, AZ 85285-2160

480-752-6276
800-888-6276; Fax: 480-752-7890
infocenter@ism.ws
www.ism.ws

Paul Novak, CPM, CEO
Holly LaCroix Johnson, Senior Vice President
Deborah Webber, SVP
Jean McHale, Manager
Frequency: Monthly

8835 **Institute of Management & Administration Newsletter**
Institute of Management and Administration
1 Washington Park
Suite 1300
Newark, NJ 07102

212-244-0360; Fax: 973-622-0595
www.ioma.com

Information for those involved in international sales. Regular monthly features.

8836 **Institutional Investor**
225 Park Ave. S
New York, NY 10003

212-224-3300
info@institutionalinvestor.com
www.institutionalinvestor.com
Facebook, Twitter, LinkedIn, Google+, StockTwits

Diane Alfano, Chairman
David E. Antin, Chief Executive Officer
Allison Adams, Publisher

Authoritative financial news for institutional investors.

8837 **Insurance & Financial Meetings Managment**
Coastal Communications Corporation
2700 N Military Trail
Suite 120
Boca Raton, FL 33431

561-989-0600; Fax: 561-989-9509
www.themeetingmagazines.com

Harvey Grotsky, Publisher/Editor-In-Chief
Susan Wycoff Fell, Managing Editor
Susan Gregg, Managing Editor

The executive source for planning meetings and incentives for the financial and insurance sectors. With regular features and special focus on site selection, destinations, industry-related studies and activities, motivational and incentive programs, program and event planning.
Frequency: Monthly
Circulation: 40,000
Founded in 1983

8838 **International Journal of Supply Chain Management**
Institute for Supply Management
2055 E Centennial Circle
PO Box 22160
Tempe, AZ 85285-2160

480-752-6276
800-888-6276; Fax: 480-752-7890
infocenter@ism.ws
www.ism.ws

Paul Nocak, CPM, CEO
Holly LaCroix Johnson, Senior Vice President
Deborah Webber, SVP
Jean McHale, Manager
Frequency: Quarterly

8839 **Investor Relations Business**
Securities Data Publishing
40 W 57th St
New York, NY 10019-4001

212-484-4701; Fax: 212-956-0112
sdp@tfn.com

Matthew Greco, Editor
Edward Cortese, Marketing Executive

News updates, career opportunities and personnel announcements for CEO's, CFO's, treasurers and directors of corporations.
Cost: $415.00
Frequency: Bi-Monthly

8840 **Journal of Applied Corporate Finance**
Financial Management Association International
University of South Florida
4202 E. Fowler Avenue, BSN 3403
Tampa, FL 33620-5500

813-974-2084; Fax: 813-974-3318
fma@coba.usf.edu
www.fma.org

Matt Staton, Managing Editor

The Journal of Applied Corporate Finance's goal is to be the leading bridging journal between practitioners and academics. The mission is to publish well-crafted papers of interest to practitioners and of use to academics in stimulating research and in their teaching function.
Frequency: 2 Times/Year

8841 **Journal of Asset Protection**
Thomson Reuters
195 Broadway
New York, NY 10007-3124

646-822-2000
800-231-1860; Fax: 646-822-2800
trta.lei-support@thomsonreuters.com
www.ria.thomsonreuters.com

Elaine Yadlon, Plant Manager
Thomas H Glocer, CEO & Director
Robert D Daleo, Chief Financial Officer
Kelli Crane, Senior Vice President & CIO

Information on shielding personal and business assets from creditors, third party attachments and government claims.
Cost: $195.00
Frequency: Bi-Monthly
Circulation: 2,000

8842 **Journal of Cost Management**
Thomson Reuters
195 Broadway
New York, NY 10007-3124

646-822-2000
800-231-1860; Fax: 646-822-2800
trta.lei-support@thomsonreuters.com
www.ria.thomsonreuters.com

Elaine Yadlon, Plant Manager
Thomas H Glocer, CEO & Director
Robert D Daleo, Chief Financial Officer
Kelli Crane, Senior Vice President & CIO

Information on cost management techniques and manufacturing technology. Provides essays and or research papers by professionals and educators.
Cost: $210.00
Frequency: Monthly
Circulation: 5000
Founded in 1940

8843 **Journal of Education Finance**
American Education Finance Association
5249 Cape Leyte Drive
Sarasota, FL 34242-1805

941-349-7580

Information and news to educational organizations on financial investing and prospecting.
150 Pages
Frequency: Quarterly
Circulation: 700
Founded in 1978

8844 **Journal of Finance**
American Finance Association
Haas School of Business
Berkley, CA 94720-1900

510-642-2397; Fax: 510-525-6246
pyle@haas.berkley.edu
www.afajof.org

Robert F Stambaugh, Editor
Anat R Admati, Associate Editors
Wendy Washburn, Editorial Assistant
David H Pyle, Business Manager

Covers theory and practice in the field of finance.
Frequency: Bi-Monthly
Circulation: 10000+
Founded in 1939

8845 **Journal of Financial Planning**
4100 E Mississippi Avenue
Suite 400
Denver, CO 80246

303-759-4900
800-322-4237; Fax: 303-759-0749
journal@fpanet.org
www.fpanet.org

Marvin W Tuttle CAE, Executive Director/CEO
Ian McKenzie, Managing Director/Publishing

A comprehensive financial publication offering information and news on financial planning, investing and prospecting.
Cost: $90.00
Frequency: Monthly
Circulation: 50,000
Founded in 1979

8846 **Journal of Fixed Income**
Institutional Investor

488 Madison Ave
16th Floor
New York, NY 10022-5701

212-303-3100
800-945-2034; Fax: 212-224-3491
iieditor@institutionalinvestor.com
www.institutionalinvestor.com/

Allison Adams, Publisher
Brian Bruce, Editor
Anne O'Brien, Marketing

Reporting on analysis of theories and ideas involving fixed income.
Cost: $370.00
Frequency: Quarterly
Circulation: 2500
Founded in 1967

8847 **Journal of Gift Planning**
National Committee on Planned Giving
233 S McCrea St
Suite 400
Indianapolis, IN 46225-1068

317-269-6274; Fax: 317-269-6276

Tanya Howe Johnson, President
Sandra Kerr, Director Government Education
Barbara Owens, Director Membership Manager
Kathryn J Ramsey, Director Meetings
Kurt Reusze, Manager Education/Technology
Frequency: Quarterly

8848 **Journal of Government Financial Management**
Association of Government Accountants
2208 Mount Vernon Avenue
Alexandria, VA 22301-1314

703-684-6931
800-242-7211; Fax: 703-519-0039
communications@agacgfm.org
www.agacgfm.org

Ann M. Ebberts, Chief Executive Officer
Mary Margaret Yodzis, Editor/Copywriter

Provides valuable information for governmental decision makers. Examines budgeting, accounting, auditing and data process developments.
Cost: $33.00
Frequency: Quarterly
Circulation: 14,250
Founded in 1950

8849 **Journal of Healthcare Administrative Management**
American Association of Healthcare Administrative
11240 Waples Mill Rd
Suite 200
Fairfax, VA 22030-6078

703-281-4043; Fax: 703-359-7562
info@aaham.org
www.aaham.org

Sharon R. Geller, CMP, Executive Director
Moayad Zahralddin, Operations & Membership Director
Matthew Hundley, Certification Director
Danielle Burns, Conference & Meetings Manager
Julia Tiffany, Certification Manager

The primary source of information for individuals in the field of healthcare administrative management.
Frequency: Quarterly

8850 **Journal of Investing**
Institutional Investor
1900 Preston Road
#267-310
Plano, TX 75093-5175

214-495-9533; Fax: 212-224-3491
www.iijournals.com

Brian Bruce, Editor-in-Chief
Allison Adams, Publisher
Anne O'Brien, Director of Marketing

Features equity investments, fixed income investing, security valuation and related investment vehicles.
Cost: $360.00
Frequency: Quarterly
Circulation: 2500
Founded in 1967

8851 **Journal of Mutual Fund Services**
Securities Data Publishing
600 Atlantic Avenue
Boston, MA 02210-2211

617-723-6400; Fax: 617-624-7200
www.dalbar.com

Ken Heath, Publisher
Kathleen Whalen, Managing Director

Focuses on backroom operations of the mutual fund industry, with directories featuring transfer assets, fund accountants, custodians, attorneys and other service personnel.
Cost: $795.00
Frequency: 8 per year

8852 **Journal of Portfolio Management**
Institutional Investor
488 Madison Ave
16th Floor
New York, NY 10022-5701

212-303-3100
800-437-9997; Fax: 212-224-3491
iieditor@institutionalinvestor.com
www.institutionalinvestor.com/

Allison Adams, Publisher
Peter Bernstein, Editor
Anne O'Brien, Marketing Manager

Ideas and concepts in the practice and theory of portfolio management.
Cost: $430.00
Frequency: Quarterly
Circulation: 5000
Founded in 1975

8853 **Journal of Taxation**
Thomson Reuters
195 Broadway
New York, NY 10007-3124

646-822-2000
800-231-1860; Fax: 646-822-2800
trta.lei-support@thomsonreuters.com
www.ria.thomsonreuters.com

Elaine Yadlon, Plant Manager
Thomas H Glocer, CEO & Director
Robert D Daleo, Chief Financial Officer
Kelli Crane, Senior Vice President & CIO

Information on tax developments and trends, revenue rulings, court decisions and legislative and administrative actions of significance to the sophisticated tax professional.
Cost: $315.00
Frequency: Monthly
Circulation: 12000
ISSN: 0022-4863
Founded in 1984
Printed in on glossy stock

8854 **Legislative Currents**
American Association of Healthcare Administrative
11240 Waples Mill Rd
Suite 200
Fairfax, VA 22030-6078

703-281-4043; Fax: 703-359-7562
info@aaham.org
www.aaham.org

Sharon Geller, Executive Director
Moayad Zahralddin, Operations & Membership Director
Matthew Hundley

Members-only blog posts.
Frequency: Bi-Monthly

8855 **MS Quarterly Journal**
Society for Information Management
401 N Michigan Avenue
Chicago, IL 60611

312-215-5190; Fax: 312-245-1081
www.simnet.org

Jim Luisi, Executive Director
Frequency: Quarterly

8856 **Management and Technology**
Association of Finance and Insurance Professionals
412 Southwood E
Colleyville, TX 76034

817-428-2434; Fax: 817-428-2534
www.afip.com

David N Robertson, Executive Director

8857 **Market Survey**
International Swaps and Derivatives Association
360 Madison Ave
16th Floor
New York, NY 10017-7126

212-901-6000; Fax: 212-901-6001
isda@isda.org
www.isda.org

Robert Pickel, CEO
Ruth Ainslie, Director Communications
Corrine Greasley, Director Administration
Frequency: Semi-Annual

8858 **Money**
1271 Avenue of the Americas
32nd Floor
New York, NY 10020-1300

212-759-4094; Fax: 212-522-0773

8859 **Mortgage Originator**
Pfingsten Publishing
3990 Oldtown Avenue
Suite A203
San Diego, CA 92110

619-223-9989
800-995-2090; Fax: 619-223-9943
www.mortgageoriginator.com

Chuck Hirsch, Publisher
David Robinson, Editor
Andy Strasser, Marketing Manager
Sue Burns, Circulation Director

Information on sales and marketing issues, correspondent management, retail mortgage, bankers and wholesale originators.
Cost: $58.00
Circulation: 19,500
ISSN: 1070-5708
Founded in 1998
Printed in 4 colors on glossy stock

8860 **Mortgage Servicing News**
Thomson Financial Publishing

1 State St
27th floor
New York, NY 10004-1481

212-825-8445
800-221-1809; Fax: 212-292-5216
www.mortgageservicingnews.com

Timothy Murphy, Publisher
Mark Fogarty, Editorial Director
Robert Cullen, CEO

Information on cross serving techniques, legislative decisions, management strategies, and professional profiles.
Cost: $98.00
Frequency: Monthly
Circulation: 20000

8861 **NABTalk**
National Association of Bankruptcy Trustees
One Windsor Cove
Suite 305
Columbia, SC 29233

803-252-5646
800-445-8629; Fax: 803-765-0860
info@nabt.com
www.nabt.com

Jennifer Brinkley, Executive Director
Frequency: Quarterly

8862 **NAPFA Advisor Magazine**
National Association of Personal Financial Advisor
3250 N Arlington Heights Road
Suite 109
Arlington Heights, IL 60004

847-483-5400
800-366-2732; Fax: 847-483-5415
info@napfa.org
www.napfa.org

Geoffrey Brown, CEO
Susan Weiner, Managing Editor
Frequency: Monthly

8863 **NATE Update**
National Association of Trade Exchange
8836 Tyler Road
Mentor, OH 44060

440-205-5378; Fax: 440-205-5379
www.nate.org

Thomas H McDowell, Executive Director

8864 **Natinal Pawnbroker Magazine**
National Pawnbrokers Association
P.O.Box 508
Keller, TX 76244-0508

817-491-4554; Fax: 817-481-8770
info@NationalPawnbrokers.org
www.nationalpawnbrokers.org

Bob Benedict, CAE, Executive Director
Emmett Murphy, Director
Teresa Congleton, Administrative Assistant
Frequency: Quarterly

8865 **National Association of Investors Corporation**
Po Box 220
Royal Oak, MI 48068-0220

248-583-6242
887-ASK-NAIC; Fax: 248-583-4880

Kathleen Zaracki, CEO
Adam Ritt, Editor

Articles on counseling and teaching investing techniques. Magazine is included with membership.
100 Pages
Frequency: Monthly
Circulation: 250,000
Founded in 1951
Printed in 4 colors on glossy stock

8866 **Nelson's World's Best Money Managers**
Nelson Publishing
2500 Tamiami Trl N
Nokomis, FL 34275-3476

941-966-9521; Fax: 941-966-2590
www.healthmgttech.com

A Verner Nelson, Owner
George G Lindsey, COO
Kevin T Black, VP Database

A special quarterly report extracted from the Nelson Investment Manager Database which ranks the top investment managers by performance results in each of 200 categories.
Cost: $245.00
200 Pages
Frequency: Quarterly

8867 **OCC Quarterly Journal**
Comptroller of the Currency
250 E St Sw
250 E Street SW
Washington, DC 20219-0001

202-874-5000
800-613-6743; Fax: 202-874-4490
Webmaster@occ.treas.gov
www.occ.treas.gov

John C Dugan, CEO
Nancy K Jones, Administrative Assistant
Ruth Montgomery, Administrative Assistant
Teri Pote, Program Manager

Significant actions and policies of the Office of Comptroller of the Currency, the agency that regulates national banks. Legal interpretations, merger decisions, speeches and testimony and statistical and structural data on national banks are included.
Cost: $100.00
132 Pages
Frequency: Quarterly
Circulation: 6500
Founded in 1863

8868 **Pensions & Investments**
Crain Communications
360 N Michigan Ave
Chicago, IL 60601-3800

312-649-5200; Fax: 312-649-7937
info@crain.com
www.crain.com

Keith Crain, CEO

Delivers critical financial news to executives responsible for the investment of large institutional assets such as pension funds, endowments and foundations.
Frequency: Monthly
Circulation: 52000

8869 **Plan Horizons**
National Institute of Pension Administrators
401 N Michigan Avenue
Suite 2200
Chicago, IL 60611-4267

800-999-6472
nipa@nipa.org
www.nipa.org

Laura J Rudzinski, Executive Director
Frequency: Quarterly

8870 **Professional Collector**
Pohly & Partners
27 Melcher Street
2nd Floor
Boston, MA 02210

617-451-1700; Fax: 617-338-7767

Karen English, Editor
Piania Pohly, CEO/President
Annie Swearingven, Marketing Manager

Information on the latest technology, legislation and other issues affecting the debt collections industry.
Cost: $24.95
Frequency: Quarterly
Circulation: 148000
Printed in 4 colors

8871 **Purchasing**
Reed Business Information
225 Wyman St
Waltham, MA 02451-1216

781-734-8000
800-446-6551; Fax: 781-290-3201
subsmail@reedbusiness.com
www.reedbusiness.com

Mark Finklestein, President
Kathy Doyle, CFO
Stuart Whayman, CFO

Information for purchasing personnel in industry.
Frequency: bi-monthly
Circulation: 95,078
Founded in 1915
Printed in 4 colors on glossy stock

8872 **REIT Securities Monthly**
SNL Securities
PO Box 2124
Charlottesvle, VA 22902-2124

434-977-1600; Fax: 434-977-4466
www.snlnet.com

Eden Rood, Editor
Reid Naglews, Chief Operating Officer
Nick Cafferillo, Chief Operating Officer
Adam Hall, Managing Director

Features sector analysis and interviews with industry leaders, as well as coverage of REIT investing and capital raising. The source for REIT and real estate investors, analysts and executives.
50 Pages
Frequency: Monthly

8873 **RMA Journal**
RMA - Risk Management Association
6147 Ridge Ave
Suite 2300
Philadelphia, PA 19128-2627

215-482-3222
800-677-7621; Fax: 215-446-4101
customers@rmahq.org
www.rmahq.org

Angelo Roma, Owner
William F Githens, Director Member Relations
Dwightce J Overturf, CFO/Information Technology Officer
Florence J Wetzel, COO/Administrative Officer
Dom DiBernardi, Associate Director
Frequency: Monthly

8874 **Regional Review**
Federal Reserve Bank of Boston
600 Atlantic Ave
Boston, MA 02210-2204

617-973-3397
800-248-0168; Fax: 617-973-4292
boston.library@bos.frb.org
www.bos.frb.org

Joyce Hannan, Manager
Cathy E Minehan, President/CEO
Jane Katz, Editor

Reliable and balanced discussions of economic issues. It is addressed to the opinion leaders of New England's business and government community.
Frequency: Quarterly
Circulation: 21000
Founded in 1913

8875 **Registered Representative**
Primedia
Po Box 12901
Shawnee Mission, KS 66282-2901
913-341-1300
866-505-7173; Fax: 913-514-6895
rgcs@pbsub.com
www.penton.com
Eric Jacobson, Senior VP
Rich Santos, Group Publisher
Magazine for retail stockbrokers that presents highly focused career-oriented editorials. Accepts advertising.
Cost: $59.00
Frequency: Monthly
Circulation: 108067
Founded in 1976
Printed in 4 colors on glossy stock

8876 **Report on Business**
Institute for Supply Management
2055 E Centennial Circle
PO Box 22160
Tempe, AZ 85285-2160
480-752-6276
800-888-6276; Fax: 480-752-7890
infocenter@ism.ws
www.ism.ws
Paul Novak, CFM, CEO
Holly LaCroix Johnson, Senior Vice President
Deborah Webber, SVP
Jean McHale, Manager
Frequency: Monthly

8877 **Research**
Financial Communications Company
PO Box 7588
San Francisco, CA 94120
415-621-0220; Fax: 415-621-0735
www.researchmag.com
Robert Tyndall, Publisher
Bill Nieder, Managing Director
Joseph Geraci, Managing Director
Corporate profiles, investment information, and reports on building and keeping client base.
Cost: $35.00
Frequency: Monthly
Circulation: 65,227

8878 **Responsible Owner**
Institute for Responsible Housing Preservation
401 9th St NW
Suite 900
Washington, DC 20004-2145
202-585-8000; Fax: 202-457-5355
info@housingpreservation.org
Kathryn Holmes, VP
Frequency: Monthly

8879 **Reverse Mortgage Advisor**
National Reverse Mortgage Lenders Association
1625 Massachusetts Ave Nw
Suite 601
Washington, DC 20036-2212
202-939-1780; Fax: 202-265-4435
www.nrmlaonline.org
Peter H Bell, Executive Director
Glenn Petherick, Director Communications
Frequency: Quarterly

8880 **Secondary Marketing Executive Magazine**
Zackin Publications
100 Willenbrock Road
Oxford, CT 06478
203-262-4670
800-325-6745; Fax: 203-262-4680
info@secondarymarketingexec.com
www.secondarymarketingexec.com
Facebook, Twitter
Michael Bates, Publisher
Patrick Barnard, Editor
Vanessa Williams, Business Development
Delivers news, analysis and how-to advice to people involved in the buying and selling of mortgage loans and servicing rights nationwide.
Frequency: Monthly
Founded in 1986

8881 **Secured Lender**
Commercial Finance Association
Ste 1801
7 Penn Plz
New York, NY 10001-3979
212-594-3490; Fax: 212-564-6053
info@cfa.com
www.cfa.com
Bruce H Jones, Executive Director
Theodore Kompa, President
Eileen M. Wubbe, Assistant Editor
Edward R. Fallon, Editorial Consultant
Linda C. Mohr, Production Manager
Provides in-depth reporting on federal and state legislation affecting the industry, legal notes on a wide range of issues, a full caladar year of industry workshops, meetings and seminars, personnel shifts, industry news and reviews of publications covering the industry. Discouted subscription rates for members.
Cost: $56.00
Frequency: 6 issues per ye
Circulation: 27000
Founded in 1944
Printed in 4 colors on glossy stock

8882 **Small Business Update**
Institute of Management Accountants
10 Paragon Dr
Suite 1
Montvale, NJ 07645-1774
201-573-9000
800-638-4427; Fax: 201-474-1600
ima@imanet.org
www.imanet.org
Jeffrey C. Thomson, President & CEO
Frequency: Monthly

8883 **Stable Times**
Stable Value Investment Association
2121 K St Nw
Suite 800
Washington, DC 20037-1801
202-261-6530
800-327-2270; Fax: 202-261-6527
info@StableValue.org
www.stablevalue.org
Andrew Cohen, Editor
Frequency: Quarterly

8884 **Strategic Finance**
Institute of Management Accountants
10 Paragon Dr
Suite 1
Montvale, NJ 07645-1774
201-573-9000
800-638-4427; Fax: 201-474-1600
ima@imanet.org
www.imanet.org
Jeffrey C. Thomson, President & CEO
Paul E. Juras, Chair
IMA's award winning magazine that provides the latest information about practices and trends in finance, accounting, and information management that will impact members and their jobs.
Cost: $195.00
Frequency: Monthly
Printed in 4 colors on glossy stock

8885 **Tax Executive**
Tax Executives Institute
1200 G St NW
Suite 300
Washington, DC 20005-3833
202-638-5601; Fax: 202-638-5607
www.tei.org
Timothy Mc Cormally, Executive Director
Deborah K Gaffney, Director Conference Planning
Deborah C Giesey, Director Administration
Karina Horesky, Coordinator Membership
Fred F Murray, General Counsel
Frequency: Bi-Monthly

8886 **Tax Lawyer**
American Bar Association Section of Taxation
321 N Clark St
Chicago, IL 60654-7598
312-988-5000
800-285-2221; Fax: 312-988-6281
askaba@abanet.org
www.abanet.org
Louis A. Mezzullo, Editor-in-Chief
William H. Lyons, Managing Editor
Journal of scholarly articles written by highly respected tax attorneys and professors. It provides key reports by Section committees and task forces, and student notes and comments on timely topics.
Frequency: Quarterly

8887 **Taxes: the Tax Magazine**
CCH
2700 Lake Cook Rd
Riverwoods, IL 60015-3867
847-940-4600
800-835-5224; Fax: 773-866-3095
taxes@cch.com
www.cch.com
Mike Sabbatis, President
Douglas M Winterrose, Vice President & CFO
Jim Bryant, EVP Software Products
Information on legal, accounting and economic aspects of federal and state taxes.
Cost: $245.00
Frequency: Monthly
Circulation: 10000
Founded in 1913

8888 **The Financial Manager**
Broadcast Cable Financial Management Association
550 W Frontage Rd
Suite 3600
Northfield, IL 60093-1243
847-716-7000; Fax: 847-784-8059
info@bccacredit.com
www.bcfm.com
Mary Collins, President
Jamie Smith, Director of Operations
Rachelle Brooks, BCCA Sales
A bi-monthly magazine published by the Broadcast Cable Credit Association.
Cost: $69.00
36 Pages
Circulation: 300
Mailing list available for rent: 1100 names at $495 per M

8889 **The Wall Street Journal**
Home Page: www.wsj.com
Facebook, Twitter, LinkedIn, Google+, YouTube
Gerard Baker, Editor-in-Chief

International English-language business newspaper.
Circulation: 2.4m
ISSN: 0099-9660
Founded in 1889

8890 **ThriftInvestor**
SNL Securities
One SNL Plaza
PO Box 2124
Charlottesvle, VA 22902
434-977-1600; Fax: 434-977-4466
isales@snl.com
www.snl.com
Mark Saunders, Editor
Pat LaBua, Customer Service
Michael Spears, Advertising Director
Nick Cafferillo, Chief Operating Officer
Adam Hall, Managing Director
Timely articles by industry experts on topics such as conversions, investment opportunities and government regulations. Source for important financial news, investor filings, conversion data and current financial and market information on all publicly traded thrifts.
Cost: $495.00
80 Pages
Frequency: Monthly
Founded in 1987

8891 **Ticker Magazine**
Wall Street Teechnology Association
521 Newman Springs Road
Suite 12
Lincroft, NJ 07738
732-530-8808; Fax: 732-530-0020
info@wsta.org
www.wsta.org
JoAnn Cooper, Managing Editor
Features articles that provide practical suggestions for technology professionals in the financial community, evaluate costs and benefits of alternate technologies, and disseminate news about the association
Frequency: Quarterly
Circulation: 14000

8892 **Trader's World Magazine**
Halliker's
2508 W Grayrock St
Springfield, MO 65810-2165
417-882-9697; Fax: 417-886-5180
publisher@tradersworld.com
www.tradersworld.com
Lawrence Jacobs, Owner
Information on stock indexes, techniques of trading, exchange activities and current developments.
Cost: $19.95
64 Pages
Frequency: Quarterly
Circulation: 12000
ISSN: 1045-7690
Founded in 1989
Printed in 4 colors on glossy stock

8893 **Traders Magazine**
Securities Data Publishing
40 W 57th St
11th Floor
New York, NY 10019-4001
212-484-4701; Fax: 212-956-0112
Ken Heath, Publisher
Edward Cortese, Marketing Executive
Focuses on industry news, market and regulatory trends and the firms and individuals who shape the equities market.
Frequency: Monthly
Circulation: 6,000

8894 **Trusts and Estates**
PRIMEDIA Intertec-Marketing & Professional Service
Po Box 12901
Shawnee Mission, KS 66282-2901
913-341-1300; Fax: 913-514-6895
www.penton.com
Eric Jacobson, Senior VP
Rorie Sherman, Editor in Chief
Thrupthi Reddy, Editor
Rich Santos, Group Publisher
Features updates on trust department operations, estates and life insurance, wills, federal tax notes and current literature.
Cost: $199.00
Frequency: Monthly
Circulation: 14730
Founded in 1886

8895 **Value Examiner**
National Association of Certified Valuation
1111 Brickyard Road
Suite 200
Salt Lake City, UT 84106-5401
801-486-0600
800-677-2009; Fax: 801-486-7500
nacva1@nacva.com
www.nacva.com
Parnell Black, CEO
Frequency: Bi-Monthly

8896 **Venture Capital Journal**
Securities Data Publishing
40 W 57th St
New York, NY 10019-4001
212-484-4701; Fax: 212-956-0112
sdp@tfn.com
Merry Logan, Associate Publisher
Edward Cortese, Marketing Executive
Provides information on recent issues, monitors current companies and looks at companies who have recently gone public.
Cost: $1025.00
Frequency: Monthly
Circulation: 1500

8897 **Wall Street Computer Review**
Miller Freeman Publications
1199 S Belt Line Rd
Suite 100
Coppell, TX 75019-4666
972-906-6500; Fax: 972-419-7825
Elizabeth Katz, Publisher
Pavan Sahgal, Editor
For financial and investment professionals and individual investors.
Cost: $5.00
Circulation: 34,000

8898 **Washington Alert**
Institute for Responsible Housing Preservation
401 9th St NW
Suite 900
Washington, DC 20004-2145
202-585-8000; Fax: 202-457-5355
info@housingpreservation.org
www.nixonpeabody.com
Kathryn Holmes, VP
Brian Moynihan, Communications Manager
Frequency: Irregular

8899 **Washington Update**
National Association of Affordable Housing Lenders
1667 K St NW
Suite 905
Washington, DC 20006-1612
202-293-9850; Fax: 202-293-9852
naahl@naahl.org
www.naahl.org
Judy Kennedy, President
Frequency: Monthly

Trade Shows

8900 **AACE Annual Meeting**
AACE International
209 Prairie Avenue
Suite 100
Morgantown, WV 26501-5934
304-296-8444
800-858-2678; Fax: 304-291-5728
info@aacei.org
www.aacei.org
Andrew S Dowd Jr, Executive Director
Jennie Amos la, Marketing/Meetings Manager
Frequency: June

8901 **AACFB Annual Conference**
American Association of Commercial Finance Brokers
326 E Main Street
Louisville, KY 40202
800-996-2352; Fax: 502-589-3602
info@aacfb.org
www.aacfb.org
Monica Harper, Executive Director
Natasha Pitcock, Director, Membership & Programs
Broker-oriented association.
Frequency: Annual/May

8902 **AACFB Commercial Financing Expo**
American Association of Commercial Finance Brokers
326 E Main Street
Lousville, KY 40202
800-996-2352; Fax: 502-589-3602
info@aacfb.org
www.aacfb.org
Monica Harper, Executive Director
Natasha Pitcock, Director, Membership & Programs
Broker-oriented association.
Frequency: Annual/September

8903 **AAHAM Annual National Institute**
American Association of Healthcare Administrative
11240 Waples Mill Road
Suite 200
Fairfax, VA 22030
703-281-4043; Fax: 703-359-7562
moayad@aaham.org
www.aaham.org
Sharon R. Galler, CMP, Executive Director
Moayad Zahralddin, Operations & Membership Director
Matthew Hundley, Certification Director
Danielle Burns, Conference & Meetings Manager
Julia Tiffany, Certification Manager
Attended by nearly 500 National members and over 75 exhibitors who come together to share ideas, network with colleagues, and further their knowledge and education in the field of Patient Account Management.
Frequency: Annual

8904 **AAII Investor Conference**
American Association of Individual Investors

625 N Michigan Ave.
Suite 1900
Chicago, IL 60611

312-280-0170
800-428-2244; Fax: 312-580-9883
members@aaii.com
www.aaii.com

James Cloonan, Founder
John Bajkowski, President
Wayne Thorp, Sr. Financial Analyst

Provides attendees with education, information, tools, and innovation to succeed in the investment marketplace. Features over 25 speakers and 30 investor workshops.
Frequency: Annual

8905 **AARMR Annual Meeting**
American Association of Residential Mortgage
1255 23rd Street NW
Suite 200
Washington, DC 20037

202-521-3999; Fax: 202-883-3636
www.aarmr.org

David Saunders, Executive Director
Frequency: Fall

8906 **ABA Annual Convention, Business Expo & Director' Forum**
American Bankers Association
1120 Connecticut Avenue NW
Washington, DC 20036

202-635-5000
800-BAN-KERS
custserv@aba.com
www.aba.com

Gail Kolakowski, VP Bus Development & Show Manager

Event for CEOs, presidents and other C-level executives from financial services firms across the nation, offering a products and services showcases, lanches and announcements, sessions focused on strategies and tactics for success, regulatory updates, effective leadership, and more.
Frequency: Annual

8907 **ACA Annual International Convention & Exposition**
American Credit Association International
PO Box 390106
Minneapolis, MN 55439

952-926-6547; Fax: 952-926-1624
aca@acainternational.org
www.acainternational.com

Gary D Rippentorp CAE, CEO
Cathy Berg, Director Meetings

Annual international convention and exposition for credit and collection professionals.
Frequency: July

8908 **AEFA Annual Meeting**
American Education Finance Association
8365 S Armadillo Trail
Evergreen, CO 80439

303-674-0857; Fax: 303-670-8986
www.aefa.cc

Ed Steinbecher, Executive Director
Frequency: March

8909 **AGA National Leadership Training**
Association of Government Accountants
2208 Mount Vernon Avenue
Alexandria, VA 22301-1314

703-684-6931
800-242-7211; Fax: 703-519-0039
communications@agacgfm.org
www.agacgfm.org

Ann M. Ebberts, Chief Executive Officer
Susan Fritzlen, Chief Operating Officer
Jerome Bruce, Director, Meetings & Expositions

Presents new tools, innovations and insights from financial management and accountability leaders, as well as their strategies, mistakes, and new management techniques; and the most current standards and regulations updates. The event is worth up to 14 CPE hours.
Cost: $800.00
Frequency: Annual/February
Founded in 1950

8910 **AGA Professional Development Training**
Association of Government Accountants
2208 Mount Vernon Avenue
Alexandria, VA 22301-1314

703-684-6931
800-242-7211; Fax: 703-519-0039
communications@agacgfm.org
www.agacgfm.org

Ann M. Ebberts, Chief Executive Officer
Susan Fritzler, Chief Operating Officer
Jerome Bruce, Director, Meetings & Expositions

Worth 25 CPE hours, the conference covers the latest research and information about the American Recovery Act, the constantly changing rules and standards, new management techniques, technological advances and practical tips for bringing greater efficiency to government operations.
Cost: $1075.00
Frequency: Annual
Founded in 1950

8911 **ALPFA Convention**
ALPFA
1717 W. 6th Street
Suite 410
Austin, TX 78703

855-692-5732
carlos.perez@national.alpfa.org
www.alpfa.org
Facebook, Twitter, LinkedIn, YouTube, Instagram

Damian Rivera, Chief Executive Officer
Selene Benavides, Chief Financial Officer
Justin Lopez, Chief Operating Officer
Ann Marquez, Chief of Staff

Conference of the Association of Latino Professionals in Finance and Accounting, dedicated to enhancing opportunities for Latinos in the accounting, finance and related professions.
Frequency: Annual
Founded in 1972

8912 **American Bankers Association Annual Convention & Banking Industry Forum**
American Bankers Association
1120 Connecticut Avenue NW
Washington, DC 20036-3902

202-635-5000; Fax: 202-663-5210
http://www.aba.com

Edward Yingling, President/CEO

Annual convention and 200 exhibitors of systems and products for the banking industry.
5000 Attendees

8913 **American Bankers Association National Agricultural Bankers Conference**
1120 Connecticut Avenue NW
Washington, DC 20036-3902

800-226-5377
custserv@aba.com
www.aba.com

Edward Yingling, President/CEO
Diane M Casey-Landry, COO/Senior Executive VP
1M Attendees
Frequency: Novembe

8914 **American Bankers Association: Bank Operations & Technology Conference**
American Bankers Association
1120 Connecticut Avenue NW
Washington, DC 20036-3902

202-635-5000; Fax: 202-663-5210

Edward Yingling, President/CEO
Diane M Casey-Landry, COO/Senior Executive VP

Designed to address hot topics for bank operations professinals, covers critical issues and provides insights into the practical applications of bank technology
2600 Attendees
Frequency: April

8915 **American Bankers Association: National Bank Card Conference**
American Bankers Association
1120 Connecticut Avenue NW
Washington, DC 20036-3902

202-635-5000; Fax: 202-663-5210
http://www.aba.com
Edward Yingling

8916 **Appraisers Association of America National Conference**
Appraisers Association of America
212 W. 35th Street
11th Floor South
New York, NY 10001

212-889-5404; Fax: 212-889-5503
referrals@appraisersassociation.org
www.appraisersassociation.org

Linda Selvin, Executive Director
Yasemin Yeldener, Communications Coordinator

Exhibits of interest to appraisers, workshops, and presentations.
Founded in 1949

8917 **Association for Financial Professionals Annual Conference**
Association for Financial Professionals
4520 East West Highway
Suite 750
Bethesda, MD 20814

301-907-2862; Fax: 301-907-2864
www.AFPonline.org

Loren Starr, Chairman
James Gilligan, Vice Chairman
Karen E Ball, Marketing Director

Workshop and 642 exhibits of lockboxes, check processing systems, computers, investments, pensions, foreign exchange, consulting, mergers, aquistions and more information of interest to finacial professionals.
6000 Attendees
Frequency: November
Founded in 1979

8918 **BCCA Distance Learning Seminars**
Broadcast Cable Credit Association

550 W. Frontage Road
Suite 3600
Northfield, IL 60093

847-881-8757; Fax: 847-784-8059
info@bccacredit.com
www.bccacredit.com

Mary Collins, President & CEO
Jamie Grande, Director, Operations
Arcelia Pimentel, Sales/Membership

Teleconference and online seminars educating members on important areas of the broadcast and cable industry.
Founded in 1972

8919 **BCCA Media Credit Seminar**
Broadcast Cable Credit Association
550 W. Frontage Road
Suite 3600
Northfield, IL 60093

847-881-8757; Fax: 847-784-8059
info@bccacredit.com
www.bccacredit.com

Mary Collins, President & CEO
Jamie Grande, Director, Operations
Arcelia Pimentel, Sales/Membership

A subsidiary of the Media Financial Management Association, BCCA provides credit information, education, and networking opportunities which enables members to efficiently manage credit risk and increase profitability.
Frequency: Annual
Founded in 1972

8920 **CCFL Semi-Annual Meetings**
Conference on Consumer Finance Law
Oklahoma City University School of Law
2501 N Blackwelder
Oklahoma City, OK 73106

405-521-5363; Fax: 405-521-5089
www.theccfl.com

Alvin C Harrell, Executive Director

Held with American Bar Association.
Frequency: Spring, Summer

8921 **CDFA Annual Meeting**
Council of Development Finance Agencies
301 NW 63rd Avenue
Suite 500
Oklahoma City, OK 73116

405-848-6059; Fax: 405-842-3299
info@cdfa.net
www.cdfa.net

Stan Provus, Training Director
Don Conkle, Manager
Frequency: Fall

8922 **CDVCA Annual Conference**
Community Development Venture Capital Alliance
330 Seventh Avenue
19th Floor
New York, NY 10001

212-594-6747; Fax: 212-594-6717
info@cdvca.org
www.cdvca.org

Kerwin Tesdell, President
Gary Brooks, Managing Director

Attended by management of social venture capital funds; those thinking of starting funds; investors in social venture capital funds; economic development professionals; banking and investment professionals; foundation representatives and policy makers and government professionals.
Frequency: March

8923 **CFA Institute Annual Conference**
CFA Institute
560 Ray C Hunt Drive
Charlottesville, VA

434-951-5499
800-247-8132; Fax: 434-951-5262
info@cfainstitute.org
www.cfainstitute.org

Jeffrey Diermeier, President/CEO

Provides an unparalleled look at the trends and investment issues critical to success in today's global marketplace
Frequency: April

8924 **CFMA Annual Conference & Exhibition**
Construction Financial Management Association
100 Village Boulevard
Suite 200
Princeton, NJ 08540

609-452-8000; Fax: 609-452-0474
info@cfma.org
www.cfma.org

Stuart Binstock, President & CEO
Brian Summers, VP, Operations

A resource for construction financial professionals.
Frequency: Annual/May

8925 **CIFA Semi-Annual Meetings**
Council of Infrastructure Financing Authorities
805 15th Street NW
Suite 500
Washington, DC 20005

202-371-9694; Fax: 202-371-6601
www.cifanet.org

Richard T Farrell, Executive Director
Richard T Farrell, Executive Director
Letitia Chambers, Owner

Legislative Conference, Spring & Workshop, Fall

8926 **CMSA Annual Meeting**
Commercial Mortgage Securities Association
30 Broad Street
28th Floor
New York, NY 10004

212-509-1844; Fax: 212-509-1895
info1@cmbs.org

Dottie Cunningham, CEO
Frequency: Winter

8927 **CORFAC Semi-Annual Meetings**
Corporate Facility Advisors
2000 N 15th Street
Suite 101
Arlington, VA 22201

703-528-3500; Fax: 703-528-0113
info@corfac.com
www.corfac.com

Thomas P Bennett, Executive Director
Bill Hawkins, Treasurer
Robert Tillsley, Secretary
Frequency: February, September

8928 **California Accounting & Business Show**
Flagg Management
353 Lexington Avenue
New York, NY 10016

212-286-0333; Fax: 212-286-0086
flaggmgmnt@msn.com
www.flaggmgmt.com

Russell Flagg, President

150 exhibitors of investment management systems, databases, real-time and on-line systems. Global and US markets, Windows, PC and client/server systems. New income opportunities for CPAs in California with the change to commissionable financial services. The show is free; the conference is $40 per day and offers CPE sessions. Sponsored by the California CPA Education Foundation.
Frequency: Annual

8929 **Credit Union Executives Expo**
Credit Union Executives Society
Po Box 14167
Madison, WI 53708-0167

608-712-2664
800-252-2664; Fax: 608-271-2303
www.cues.org

Fred Johnson, President/CEO

Expo is held in conjunction with CUES Marketing, Operations and Technology Conference, where the top marketers and operations professionals in the industry gather.
500 Attendees
Frequency: May
Founded in 1962

8930 **Current Financial Reporting Issues Conference**
Financial Executives International
1250 Headquarters Plaza
West Tower, 7th Floor
Morristown, NJ 07960

973-765-1000; Fax: 973-765-1018
membership@financialexecutives.org
www.financialexecutives.org

Andrej Suskavcevic, President & CEO

The conference focuses on FASB/IASB technical accounting, revenue recognition, accounting for leases by lessors and lessees, financial instruments-recognition, measurement, hedging and expected loss model, Washington tax update, and the latest SEC happenings.
Founded in 1931

8931 **DCUC Annual Meeting**
Defense Credit Union Council
601 Pennsylvania Avenue NW
South Building, Suite 600
Washington, DC 20004-2601

202-638-3950; Fax: 202-638-3410
www.dcuc.org

Frequency: August

8932 **Detecting & Deterring Financial Reporting Fraud**
200 Campus Drive
PO Box 674
Florham Park, NJ 07932

973-360-0177; Fax: 973-898-4649
www.financialexecutives.org

Andrej Suskavcevic, President & CEO

Executive workshop for exploring strategies for building an ethical philosophy that deters fraud, employs skepticism-an enemy of fraud- in management's attitude and developing a culture of collaboration and knowledge sharing to deter and detect fraud.
15M Members
Frequency: 10x/Year
Founded in 1931

8933 **EMTA Annual Meeting**
EMTA - Trade Association for the Emerging Markets
360 Madison Avenue
18th Floor
New York, NY 10017

646-637-9100; Fax: 646-637-9128
awerner@emta.org
www.emta.org

Michael M Chamberlin, President
Aviva Werner, Managing Director

Jonathan Murno, Managing Director
Suzette Ortiz, Office Manager
Monika Forbes, Administrative Assistant
Frequency: December

8934 **Equipment Leasing & Finance Association An nual Convention**
Equipment Leasing and Finance Association
1625 Eye St. NW
Suite 850
Washington, DC 20006

202-238-3400; Fax: 202-238-3401
hstaverman@elfaonline.org
www.elfaonline.org

Heather Staverman, Director, Meetings & Exhibits
Ralph Petta, President & CEO
Kelli J. Nienaber, Executive Director
1,200 Attendees
Frequency: October

8935 **FCS Race for Kids**
Financial Communications Society
368 Ninth Avenue
9th Floor
New York, NY 10001

908-858-0427
admin@thefcs.org
thefcs.org

Tim Hart, Chair
Tom Jago, Vice Chair
Katherine Divney, Secretary
Kevin Windorf, CEO

Charity event and marketing summit held by the Financial Communications Society.
Founded in 1967

8936 **FMA Annual Meeting**
Financial Management Association International
University of South Florida
4202 E. Fowler Avenue, BSN 3403
Tampa, FL 33620-9951

813-974-2084; Fax: 813-974-3318
fma@coba.usf.edu
www.fma.org

Michelle Lui, Executive Director
Dawn Appleby, Program Assistant
Karen Wright, Special Events Coordinator

The Financial Management Association International (FMA) is the global leader in developing and disseminating knowledge about financial decision making. FMA's members include adademicians and practitioners worldwide.
Founded in 1970

8937 **FMS Annual Meeting**
Financial Managers Society
100 W Monroe Street
Suite 810
Chicago, IL 60603-1959

312-781-1300
800-275-4367; Fax: 312-578-1308
diane@fmsinc.org
www.fmsinc.org

John A. Carrozza, Chair
Jennifer Lindberg, Director, Marketing & Communication
Frequency: June

8938 **FPA Annual Meeting**
Financial Planning Association
4100 E Mississippi Avenue
Suite 400
Denver, CO 80246

303-759-4900
800-322-4237; Fax: 303-759-0749
info@fpanet.org
www.fpanet.org

Martin W Tuttle CAE, Executive Director/CEO
Ian McKenzie, Managing Director Publishing
Frequency: Fall

8939 **FPA Experience: The Annual Conference of the Financial Planning Community**
Financial Planning Association
7535 East Hampden Avenue
Suite 600
Denver, CO 80231

303-759-4900
800-322-4237; Fax: 303-759-0749
www.fpaannualconference.org
Facebook, Twitter, LinkedIn, FPA Connect

The event provides networking and professional development opportunities, as well as exhibits.
24000 Members
3000 Attendees
Frequency: Annual/Fall
Founded in 2000

8940 **FSR Semi-Annual Meetings**
Financial Services Roundtable
1001 Pennsylvania Avenue NW
Suite 500 S
Washington, DC 20004

202-289-4322; Fax: 202-628-2507
www.fsround.org

Greg Baer, President/CEO
Frequency: Spring, Fall

8941 **FSTC Annual Meeting**
Financial Services Technology
44 Wall Street
12th Floor
New York, NY 10005

212-711-1400; Fax: 646-349-3629
www.fstc.org

Zachary Tumin, Executive Director
Frequency: Spring

8942 **Fiduciary and Risk Management Association Annual Meeting**
Fiduciary and Risk Management Association
PO Box 48297
Athens, GA 30604

706-354-0083; Fax: 706-353-3994
info@thefirma.org
www.thefirma.org

Hale Mast, Executive Director
Deborah A Austin, VP

To educate, support and promote risk management professionals and improve the effectiveness of risk management for the fiduciary and investment service industry.
Frequency: Spring

8943 **FinEXPO**
Miller Freeman Publications
1975 W El Camino Real
Suite 307
Mountain View, CA 94040-2218

FAX 650-966-8934

Sixty exhibitors of full range of systems, software, service and solutions that financial and information system decision makers need to meet the challenges of today and the future.
2000 Attendees

8944 **Financial Leadership Summit**
Financial Executives International
1250 Headquarters Plaza
West Tower, 7th Floor
Morristown, NJ 07960

973-765-1000; Fax: 973-765-1018
membership@financialexecutives.org
www.financialexecutives.org

Andrej Suskavcevic, President & CEO

Forum to help advance the success of senior-level financial executives.
Founded in 1931

8945 **Financial Women International Annual Conference**
Financial Women International
1027 W Roselawn Avenue
Roseville, MN 55113

651-487-7632
866-807-6081; Fax: 651-489-1322
info@fwi.org

Melissa Curzon, President
Cindy Hass, VP
Carleen DeSisto, Secretary
Frequency: September

8946 **HBMA Annual Meeting**
Healthcare Billing and Management Association
1540 South Coast Highway
Suite 203
Laguna Beach, CA 92651

877-640-4262
http://www.hbma.org

Bradley Lund, Executive Director
Paul Myers, Director of Education
Frequency: March

8947 **HMFA's ANI: The Healthcare Finance Conference**
Healthcare Finance Management Association
100 W Monroe Street
Suite 1001
Chicago, IL 60603

312-541-0567; Fax: 312-541-0573
www.hfma.org/events/ani

Access to education programs, speaker sessions and hundreds of vendors, as well as networking and best practices sharing opportunities.

8948 **HMFA's Virtual Healthcare Finance Conference & Career Fair**
Healthcare Finance Management Association
100 W Monroe Street
Suite 1001
Chicago, IL 60603

312-541-0567; Fax: 312-541-0573
virtualhcfc@hfma.org
www.hfma.org

Access live education programs and on-demand sessions from your office. Keynote speakers and presenters, and a virtual exhibit hall and career fair.

8949 **Hall of Fame Gala**
Financial Executives International
1250 Headquarters Plaza
West Tower, 7th Floor
Morristown, NJ 07960

973-765-1000; Fax: 973-765-1018
membership@financialexecutives.org
www.financialexecutives.org

Andrej Suskavcevic, President & CEO

Providing recognition to senior-level financial executives who have epitomized the performance, leadership and integrity of the most exemplary financial professionals throughout their careers and in doing so, have made significant contributions to the betterment of their respec-

tive organizations and to the profession as a whole.
Founded in 1931

8950 **IMA Annual Meeting**
Institute of Management Accountants
10 Paragon Drive
Suite 1
Montvale, NJ 07645-1718
201-573-9000
800-638-4427; Fax: 201-474-1600
ima@imanet.org
www.imanet.org
Paul E. Juras, Chair
Jeffrey Thomson, President & CEO
1500 Attendees
Frequency: July

8951 **IRHP Meeting/Conference**
Institute for Responsible Housing Preservation
401 Ninth Street NW
Suite 900
Washington, DC 20004
202-858-8000; Fax: 202-585-8080
info@housingpreservation.org
www.housingpreservation.org
Linda D Kirk, Executive Director
Frequency: January

8952 **ISM Annual Meeting**
Institute for Supply Management
2055 E Centennial Circle
PO Box 22160
Tempe, AZ 85285-2160
480-752-6276
800-888-6276; Fax: 480-752-7890
infocenter@ism.ws
www.ism.ws
Paul Novak, CPM, CEO
Holly LaCroix Johnson, Senior Vice President
Deborah Webber, SVP
Jean McHale, Manager
3000 Attendees
Frequency: May

8953 **NAAHL Annual Meetings**
National Association of Affordable Housing Lenders
1300 Connecticut Avenue NW
Suite 905
Washington, DC 20036
202-293-9850; Fax: 202-293-9852
naahl@naahl.org
Judith A Kennedy, President/CEO
Frequency: Winter, Spring

8954 **NABT Semi-Annual Meetings**
National Association of Bankruptcy Trustees
One Windsor Cove
Suite 305
Columbia, SC 29233
803-252-5646
800-445-8629; Fax: 803-765-0860
info@nabt.com
www.nabt.com
Jennifer Brinkley, Executive Director
Frequency: August

8955 **NACM's Credit Congress and Exposition**
National Association of Credit Management
8840 Columbia 100 Parkway
Columbia, MD 21045-2282
410-740-5560; Fax: 410-740-5574
robins@nacm.org
www.nacm.org
Jim Vanghel, Vice President
Robin Schauseil, President
Annual exhibits of relevance to credit and financial executives.
2500 Attendees
Frequency: June

8956 **NACVA Annual Consultants' Conference**
Nat'l Association of Certified Valuation Analysts
1111 Brickyard Road
Suite 200
Salt Lake City, UT 84106-5401
801-486-0600
800-677-2009; Fax: 801-486-7500
nacva1@nacva.com
www.nacva.com
Parnell Black, CEO
750 Attendees
Frequency: June

8957 **NADOA Annual Meeting**
National Association of Division Order Analyst
2805 Oak Trail Court
Suite 6312
Arlington, TX 76016
972-715-4489
administrator@nadoa.org
www.nadoa.org
Lynn S McCord, Administrator
Frequency: September

8958 **NAFC Annual Meeting**
National Accounting and Finance Council
2200 Mill Road
Alexandria, VA 22314
703-838-1915
nafc@trucking.org
www.truckline.com
David Hershey, Executive Director
500 Attendees
Frequency: June

8959 **NAFCU Annual Conference and Exhibition**
National Association of Federal Credit Unions
3138 10th Street N
Suite 300
Arlington, VA 22201-2149
703-224-4770
800-336-4644; Fax: 703-524-1082
http://www.nafcu.org
Jerome Bruce, Exhibits/Advertising Manager
Fred Becker, President
Annual show of 150 manufacturers and suppliers of complete range of financial products and services. 175 booths.

8960 **NALHFA Semi-Annual Meetings**
National Association of Local Housing Finance
2025 M Street NW
Suite 800
Washington, DC 20036-3309
202-367-1197; Fax: 202-367-2197
www.nalhfa.org
John C Murphy, Executive Director
Scott Lynch, Association Manager
Kim McKinon, Coordinator Membership
Frequency: Spring, Fall

8961 **NAPFA Annual Meeting**
National Association of Personal Financial Advisor
3250 N Arlington Heights Road
Suite 109
Arlington Heights, IL 60004
847-483-5400
800-366-2732; Fax: 847-483-5415
info@napfa.org
www.napfa.org
Geoffrey Brown, CEO
800 Attendees
Frequency: May

8962 **NAPTP Meeting/Conference**
Nat'l Assoc of Publicly Traded Partnerships
805 15th Street NW
Suite 500
Washington, DC 20005
202-973-4515; Fax: 202-973-3101
Mary Lyman, Executive Director
Frequency: February

8963 **NASBO Annual Meeting**
National Association of State Budget Officers
444 North Capitol Street NW
Suite 642
Washington, DC 20001
202-624-5382; Fax: 202-624-7745
spattison@nasbo.org
www.nasbo.org
Shelby Kerns, Executive Director
Frequency: Summer

8964 **NATP National Conference & Expo**
National Association of Tax Professionals
PO Box 8002
Appleton, WI 54912
920-749-1040
800-558-3402; Fax: 800-747-0001
natp@natptax.com
www.natptax.com
Annual conference and exhibits of computer hardware, tax accounting and planning software, tax research information, tax forms, one-write accounting, financial planning information, office products and business equipment.
Frequency: Annual

8965 **NATRI National Conference**
National Association for Treasurers of Religious
8824 Cameron Street
Silver Springs, MD 20910
301-587-7776; Fax: 301-589-2897
www.natri.org
Barbara Matteson, Executive Director
Helen Burke, Associate Director
Frequency: November

8966 **NCPG Annual Meeting**
National Committee on Planned Giving
233 McCre Street
Suite 400
Indianapolis, IN 46225-1030
317-269-6274; Fax: 317-269-6276
Tanya Howe Johnson, President/CEO
Sandra Kerr, Director Government Education
Barbara Owens, Director Membership/Manager HR
Kathryn J Ramsey, Director Meetings
Kurt Reusze, Manager Education/Technology
1700 Attendees

8967 **NDCC Semi-Annual Meetings**
National Defined Contribution Council
9101 E Kenyon
Suite 300
Denver, CO 80237-0467
303-770-5353; Fax: 303-770-1812
Al Brust, Executive VP
Frequency: Spring, Fall

8968 **NICSA Annual Meeting**
National Investment Company Service Association
36 Washingtn Street
Suite 70
Wessesley Hills, MA 02481
781-416-7200; Fax: 781-416-7065
www.nisca.org
Barbara V Weidlich, President
Keith Dropkin, Director Operations
Doris Jaimes, Registrar
Sheila Kobaly, Events Manager
Chris Ludent, IT Manager
Frequency: February

8969 **NIPA Semi-Annual Meetings**
National Institute of Pension Administrators
401 N Michigan Avenue
Suite 2200
Chicago, IL 60611-4267
800-999-6472
nipa@nipa.org
www.nipa.org
Laura J Rudzinski, Executive Director
Frequency: Winter, Spring

8970 **NPA Annual Meeting**
National Pawnbrokers Association
PO Box 1040
Roanoke, TX 76262
817-491-4554; Fax: 817-491-8770
info@NationalPawnbrokers.org
www.nationalpawnbrokers.org
Bob Benedict, CAE, Executive Director
Emmett Murphy, Director
Teresa Congleton, Administrative Assistant
1000 Attendees
Frequency: Summer

8971 **National Association of Review Appraisers & Mortgage Underwriters Convention**
National Assn of Review Appraisers/Mortgage Under.
1224 N Nokomis NE
Alexandria, MN 56308
320-763-7626; Fax: 320-763-9290
nara@iami.org
www.iami.org
Robert G Johnson, Executive Director
Annual convention of real estate related information and services. Containing 50-75 booths, as well as environmental, home inspection, and construction inspection.
450 Attendees
Frequency: October
Founded in 1962
Mailing list available for rent: 2500 names at $75 per M

8972 **Payments**
NACHA: Electronic Payments Association
13450 Sunrise Valley Drive
Suite 100
Herndon, VA 20171
703-561-1100; Fax: 703-787-0996
info@nacha.org
www.nacha.org
Marcie Haitema, Chairperson
Jane Larimer, CEO
The premier source for payments professionals from across industries and around the globe to get the most vital and actionable information needed to help address the myraid of issues and opportunities in today's rapidly changing environment.
1000 Attendees
Frequency: Annual/April-May

8973 **Private Equity Analyst Global Investing Conference**
Asset Alternatives
170 Linden Street
2nd Floor
Wellesley, MA 02482-7919
781-235-4565; Fax: 781-304-1440
www.assetalt.com
Lisa Hughs, Production Manager
Hundreds of institutional investors, private equity managers, and deal sources to debate the merits of funds of funds and regional funds for investing in Western and Eastern Europe, Latin America, Asia, the Middle East, and elsewhere.

8974 **Risk Management Association's Annual Conference**
Risk Management Association
1801 Market St
Suite 300
Philadelphia, PA 19103-1628
215-446-4000
800-677-7621; Fax: 215-446-4100
customers@rmahq.org
www.rmahq.org
Nancy Foster, President/CEO
Educates and helps risk management professionals develop new techniques and learn about new innovative products at different stages of their careers.
800 Attendees
Frequency: September/October

8975 **SFE Annual Meeting**
Society of Financial Examiners
174 Grace Boulevard
Altamonte Springs, FL 32714
407-682-4930
800-787-7633; Fax: 407-682-3175
www.sofe.org
Cindy Dodson, Executive Director
Stephen J Szypula, Financial Administrator
500 Attendees

8976 **SIM Annual Meeting**
Society for Information Management
401 N Michigan Avenue
Chicago, IL
312-215-5190; Fax: 312-245-1081
www.simnet.org
Jim Luisi, Executive Director
Frequency: Fall

8977 **SQA Annual Meeting**
Society of Quantitative Analysts
25 North Broadway
Tarry Town, NY 10591
914-332-0040; Fax: 914-332-1541
cmcas@cmcas.org
Stuart Ganes, President
Frequency: May

8978 **STA's Annual Conference & Business Meeting**
Security Traders Association
777 Post Road
Suite 200
Darien, CT 06820
203-202-7680; Fax: 203-202-7681
www.securitytraders.org
John C Giesea, President & CEO
Keynote speakers, discussions on trading issues, regulatory updates, exchange topics, and exhibits.
1700 Attendees
Frequency: Annual

8979 **Securities Industry and Financial Markets Association (SIFMA) Annual Meeting**
1101 New York Avenue NW
8th Floor
Washington, DC 20005
202-962-7300; Fax: 202-962-7305
www.sifma.org
T Timothy Ryan Jr, President/CEO
Randy Snook, Senior Managing Director/EVP
Donald D Kittell, CFO
The Securities Industry and Financial Markets Association/SIFMA Annual Meeting and Conference program addresses a variety of topics that may include competitiveness of the U.S. capital markets, global exchange consolidation, regulatory and legal initiatives, and trends in the fixed-income and capital markets.

8980 **Southern Finance Association**
University of Florida
Mowry Road, Building 116
PO Box 110811
Gainesville, FL 32611-0811
352-392-5930; Fax: 352-392-7902
www.aceweb.org
Dr. Robert Radcliffe, Show Manager
Twenty five ooths.
1.4M Attendees
Frequency: November

8981 **Success Forum**
International Association for Financial Planning
2 Concourse Parkway NE
Suite 800
Atlanta, GA 30328-5588
770-351-9600
800-945-IAFP; Fax: 770-668-7758
J Patrick Tinley, CEO
Annual show and exhibits of financial services equipment, supplies and services.
2500 Attendees

8982 **TEI Annual Meeting**
Tax Executives Institute
1200 G Street NW
Suite 300
Washington, DC 20005-3814
202-638-5601; Fax: 202-638-5607
dgaffney@tei.org
www.tei.org
Timothy J McNormally, Executive Director
Deborah K Gaffney, Director Conference Planning
Deborah C Giesey, Director Administration
Karina Horesky, Coordinator Membership
Fred F Murray, General Counsel/Dir Tax Affairs
Frequency: April

8983 **Venture Capital & Health Care Conference**
Asset Alternatives
170 Linden Street
2nd Floor
Wellesley, MA 02482-7919
781-235-4565; Fax: 781-304-1440
Lisa Hughs, Production Manager
This annual gathering of top investors, deal sources, entrepreneurs, Wall Street analysts, and senior health care executives explores the latest trends in health care services, devices, and medical information systems.
Circulation: 0

Directories & Databases

8984 AACE Directory
Assoc. for the Advancement of Cost Engineering
209 Prairie Ave
Suite 100
Morgantown, WV 26501-5934
304-296-8444
800-858-2678; Fax: 304-291-5728
info@aacei.org
www.aacei.org
Andrew Dowd, Executive Director
Megan McCulla, Asst Manager
Charla Miller, Staff Director Education
Carol S Rogers, Manager Finance
Frequency: Annual

8985 AEFA Membership Directory
American Education Finance Association
8365 S Armadillo Trail
Evergreen, CO 80439
303-674-0857; Fax: 303-670-8986
www.aefpweb.org
Ed Steinbecher, Executive Director
Frequency: Annual

8986 ALERT
AuTex Systems
11 Farnsworth Street
Boston, MA 02210-1210
617-345-2000
A database offering all available information on securities and securities trading information.

8987 ATLAS
Technical Data
11 Farnsworth Street
Boston, MA 02210-1210
617-345-2000
Contains a variety of financial data and analyses of 7 major government bond markets.

8988 All-Quotes
545 Madison Avenue
Suite 1400
New York, NY 10022-4219
FAX 212-425-6895
Offers real-time and delayed quotes, and price and volume history for about 100,000 stocks, options and commodities.

8989 Almanac of Business and Industrial Financial Ratios
Pearson Education
1 Lake St
Upper Saddle Rv, NJ 07458-1813
201-236-7000
800-947-7700; Fax: 201-236-7696
www.prenhall.com
Will Ethridge, President
Profiles corporate performance in two analytical tables for a variety of industries.
Cost: $69.95
Frequency: Annual

8990 American Banker On-Line
American Banker-Bond Buyer
1 State St
27th Floor
New York, NY 10004-1561
212-803-8450
207-581-3042; Fax: 207-581-3015
www.sourcemedia.com
Jim Malkin, CEO
Mario DiUbaldi, Publisher
Phil Roosevelt, Editor
Carole Lambert, Sales/Marketing Director
Stacy Weinstein, Production Director
World wide web edition of daily financial services newspaper. Journal available.

8991 American Financial Directory
4709 Golf Road
Skokie, IL 60076
847-676-9600
800-321-3373; Fax: 847-933-8101
custserv@accuitysolutions.com
www.accuitysolutions.com
Marideth Johnson, Manager, Marketing/Communications
Malcolm Taylor, Managing Director
Cost: $523.00
Frequency: January/July
Circulation: 41300
ISBN: 1-563103-47-8

8992 American Society of Appraisers Directory
American Society of Appraisers
11107 Sunset Hills Road
Suite 310
Reston, VA 20190
703-478-2228
800-272-8258; Fax: 703-742-8471
asainfo@appraisers.org
www.appraisers.org
Facebook, Twitter, LinkedIn, YouTube
Johnnie White, Chief Executive Officer
Todd Paradis, Chief Marketing Officer
Sarah Sebastian, Director of Membership Development
Directory of association members who are accredited appraisers.
Circulation: 7
Founded in 1939

8993 American Stock Exchange Fact Book
Publications Department
86 Trinity Pl
New York, NY 10006-1817
212-308-0046; Fax: 212-306-2160
Neal Wolkoff, CEO
Lists addresses, telephone and fax numbers and ticker symbols of every listed company. Historical statistics and all-time trading records for equities, with a list of every stock option, index option and derivative security traded on the American Stock Exchange.
Cost: $20.00
Frequency: Annual
Circulation: 10,000
Founded in 1994

8994 American Stock Exchange Guide
CCH
2700 Lake Cook Rd
Riverwoods, IL 60015-3867
847-940-4600
800-835-5224; Fax: 773-866-3095
www.cch.com
Mike Sabbatis, President
Douglas M Winterrose, Vice President & CFO
Jim Bryant, EVP Software Products
Volume 1 lists a directory of officials, members, organizations and securities; Volume 2 lists by-laws and rules of the exchange.
Cost: $570.00

8995 Asia Pacific Securities Handbook
Reference Press
6448 E Highway 290
Suite E104
Austin, TX 78723-1041
512-331-1815; Fax: 512-374-4501
Dan Capper, President
Offers stock information on the exchanges in Australia, Bangladesh, China, Hong Kong, India, Indonesia, Japan, Malaysia, Nepal, New Zealand, Pakistan, Taiwan, Sri Lanka, and Thailand.
Cost: $99.95
250 Pages
Founded in 1993

8996 Bank Mergers & Acquisitions Yearbook
SNL Securities
PO Box 2124
Charlottesvle, VA 22902-2124
434-977-1600; Fax: 434-977-4466
www.snlnet.com
John Minor, Editor
Nick Cafferillo, Chief Operating Officer
Christie Atkinson, Editor
Reid Nagle, Publisher
Mark Outlaw, Advertising Director
For bank and thrift CEOs, CFOs, investment banks, merger and acquisition advisors, law firms, accounting firms and individual investors. Covers all bank and thrift merger activity from the previous year, state-by-state reviews of all private sector whole-bank and whole-thrift transactions, branch sales, merger conversions and government-assisted transactions announced in that year.
150 Pages
Frequency: Annual
Founded in 1994

8997 Bank Securities Monthly
SNL Securities
212 7th Street NE
Charlottesville, VA 22902
434-977-1600; Fax: 434-977-4466
www.snlnet.com
Mike Chinn, President
Steve Tomasi, Editor
Reid Nagle, Publisher
Mark Outlaw, Senior Vice President
Provides current financial, market and merger information on publicly traded banks. News highlights of the past month and comprehensive industry articles addressing topics such as bank investment opportunities, capital structure and earnings prospects.
70 Pages
Frequency: Monthly

8998 Bloomberg Business News
499 Park Ave
New York, NY 10022-1240
212-893-5555; Fax: 212-369-5966
www.bloomberg.com
Kim Bang, Manager
Matthew Winkler, Editor
A 24-hour global news service available exclusively on The Bloomberg. All stories are fully integrated into The Bloomberg's newsminder which instantly alerts you to developments in all stock and bond markets.

8999 **Bloomberg Financial Markets Commodities News**
PO Box 888
Princeton, NJ 08542-0888

609-279-3000; Fax: 609-279-2028

Michael Bloomberg, Publisher
Matthew Winkler, Editor
Beth Mazzeo, Global Products

A leading multimedia distributor of news, information, data and analysis, providing information on everything from capital markets and airline schedules to employment opportunities and luxury goods.
Cost: $795.00
Frequency: Monthly

9000 **Bond Buyer's Municipal Marketplace**
Thomson Financial Publishing
4709 Golf Road
6th Floor
Skokie, IL 60076-1231

847-778-8037

James L Nowell, Editor

Offers information on firms and personnel in the municipal bond industry, including municipal bond dealers, chief finance officers of municipalities which issue bonds, and attorneys specializing in the field of municipal finance.
Cost: $185.00
937 Pages
Frequency: Semiannual

9001 **Bonds Data Base**
ADP Data Services
42 Broadway
Suite 1730
New York, NY 10004-1617

212-406-2820

This database, update daily, contains historical prices and trading volumes for more than 33,000 corporate, government and agency bonds.

9002 **Bowser Directory of Small Stocks**
Bowser Report
PO Box 6278
Newport News, VA 23606-0278

757-877-5979; Fax: 757-595-0622
Ministocks@aol.com
thebowserreport.com

Cindy Bowser, Editor

Lists 14 fields of information on over 700 low-priced stocks.
Cost: $89.00
35 Pages
Frequency: Monthly
ISSN: 1053-0908

9003 **Bridge Information System**
717 Office Parkway
Saint Louis, MO 63141-7115

314-567-8100
800-325-3282; Fax: 314-432-5391

Tony Bridge, Manager

This large database contains real-time, last sale and quote data on all listed and unlisted stocks, options, futures and foreign securities.

9004 **Bull and Bear's Directory of Investment Advisory Newsletters**
Bull & Bear Financial Report
PO Box 917179
Longwood, FL 32791-7179

407-682-6170
www.thebullandbear.com

David J Robinson, President

Advice from investment advisory newsletters on various investment areas, small-cap stocks, global and domestic stock markets, mutual funds, precious metals and economy.
Cost: $29.00
48 Pages
Frequency: Annual
Circulation: 55,000
Founded in 1974

9005 **Business and Financial News Media**
Larriston Communications
PO Box 20229
New York, NY 10025-1518

310-871-0563

Sheila Gordon, Editor

Lists over 300 daily newspapers with at least 50,000 in circulation and a business or finance correspondent; television stations and all-news radio stations in the largest 40 markets.
Cost: $89.00
175 Pages
Frequency: Annual

9006 **CDA/Wiesenberger Investment Companies Service**
CDA Investment
1355 Piccard Drive
Suite 200
Rockville, MD 20850-4300
Jay Nadler, Editor

Lists 5,000 open and closed mutual funds, unit trusts and investment companies listing policies and objectives, history, and statistical information of the company.
1500 Pages
Frequency: Annual

9007 **CIN: Corporation Index System**
Office of Applications & Reports Services
450 5th Street NW
Washington, DC 20001-2739

202-942-0020

David Weiss, Manager

Lists 1,580 active companies registered under the Investment Company Act of 1940. Information is extend to include related underwriters and advisers and 800 number.
Cost: $90.00
Frequency: Monthly

9008 **CISCO**
CISCO
170 W Tasman Dr
San Jose, CA 95134-1706

408-526-4000
805-553-6387; Fax: 408-853-3683
www.cisco.com

Frank A Calderoni, Executive VP

Contains technical analyses and prices of commodities futures, and currencies.

9009 **CUSIP Master Directory**
Standard & Poor's Corporation
55 Water St
New York, NY 10041-0003

212-438-1000; Fax: 212-438-0299

Deven Sharma, President

Official listings of numbers and descriptions for more than 1,500,000 stocks, bonds and warrants of 100,000 issuers, including corporations and municipalities of the United States and Canada.
Cost: $1900.00
Frequency: Annual

9010 **Commodity Futures Trading Commission Geographic Directory**
Three Lafayette Centre
1155 21st Street NW
Washington, DC 20581

202-418-5000; Fax: 202-418-5521
www.cftc.org

Offers information on corporations and firms that are registered with the Commodity Futures Trading Commission.
Cost: $25.00

9011 **Corporate Finance Sourcebook**
National Register Publishing
430 Mountain Ave.
Suite 400
New Providence, NJ 07974

800-473-7020; Fax: 908-673-1189
NRPeditorial@marquiswhoswho.com
www.financesourcebook.com

Contains a variety of information on the financial services industry. Listings include securities research analysts, major private lenders, mergers and acquisitions, commercial finance firms, pension managers and leasing companies.
Cost: $425.00
1600 Pages
Frequency: Annual

9012 **Corporate Venturing Directory & Yearbook**
Asset Alternatives
170 Linden Street
Wellesley, MA 02482

781-304-1400; Fax: 781-304-1440
www.corporateventuring.com

Dave Barry, Senior Editor
Barbara Bissonnette, VP Marketink/Sales

Features the most comprehensive data ever essembled on corporations participating in venture-backet deals, and the young companies they're financing.
Cost: $495.00
Frequency: Annual
Printed in on matte stock

9013 **Cost Engineers Notebook**
AACE International
209 Prairie Ave
Suite 100
Morgantown, WV 26501-5934

304-296-8444
800-858-2678; Fax: 304-291-5728
info@aacei.org
www.aacei.org

Andrew Dowd, Executive Director
Megan McCulla, Asst Manager
Charla Miller, Staff Director Education
Carol S Rogers, Manager Finance
Frequency: Irregular

9014 **Current Market Snapshot**
CompuServe Information Service
5000 Arlington Centre Blvd
Columbus, OH 43220-5439

614-326-1002
800-848-8199

Offers information on up-to-date stock prices foreign currency data, and general market statistics.

9015 **DIAL/DATA**
Track Data Corporation
95 Rockwell Pl
Brooklyn, NY 11217-1105

718-522-7373; Fax: 718-260-4324

Martin Kaye, CEO
Stan Stern, Senior Vice President

This database contains current and historical data on securities, options and commodities.

9016 DRI Commodities
DRI/McGraw-Hill
11000 Regency Parkway
Suite 400
Cary, NC 27511

919-462-8600; Fax: 919-468-9890
www.profound.com

This database contains more than 51,000 daily time series of price and trading data for major commodities traded on makrets in the US, Canada, London and Singapore.

9017 DRI Transportation
DRI/McGraw-Hill
11000 Regency Parkway
Suite 400
Cary, NC 27511

919-462-8600; Fax: 919-468-9890
www.profound.com

This large database contains over 15,000 weekly, monthly, and annual time series on commodity traffic by mode, carrier operations and financial data.

9018 DRI US Bonds
DRI/McGraw-Hill
11000 Regency Parkway
Suite 400
Cary, NC 27511

919-462-8600; Fax: 919-468-9890
www.profound.com

This financial database contains daily time series of current and historical prices, yields and fundamental financial information for more than 60,000 dealer-priced debt issues.

9019 Daily Foreign Exchange Analysis & Updates
Technical Data
11 Farnsworth Street
Boston, MA 02210-1210

617-345-2000

This database offers daily reports from major world financial centers including, currency forecasts, analysis of the US bond and money markets, currency reports and the trends of the New York foreign exchange market.
Frequency: Full-text

9020 Dick Davis Digest
Dick Davis Publishing
P.O.Box 2049
Salem, MA 01970-6249

954-733-3996; Fax: 954-733-8559

Steven Halpern, Publisher/Editor
Lorianne Kiesl, Marketing Director
Donald Hanrahan, Owner

The digest excerpts over 400 newsletters and the research reports from leading Wall Street analysts and compiles this information into a 12 page compendium of what leading financial advisors currently recommend.
Cost: $165.00
Frequency: BiWeekly

9021 Directory of Buyout Financing Sources
Securities Data Publishing
40 W 57th St
New York, NY 10019-4001

212-484-4701; Fax: 212-956-0112
sdp@tfn.com

Ted Weissberg, Editor-in-Chief
Deborah Chieglis, Advertising Manager
Edward Cortese, Marketing Executive

Over 700 sources of financing, including senior lenders, equity and mezzanine providers in the United States and international avenues, with detailed information on industry, geographic and invetment size preferances and recent activity for each firm.

9022 Directory of Defense Credit Union
Defense Credit Union Council
601 Pennsylvania Ave NW
Suite 600
Washington, DC 20004-2601

202-638-3950; Fax: 202-638-3410
www.dcuc.org

Roland Arteata, President
Frequency: Bi-Ennial

9023 Directory of Manufacturers' Sales
Manufacturers' Agents National Association
PO Box 3467
Laguna Hills, CA 92654-3467

949-859-4040; Fax: 949-855-2973
www.manaonline.org

Joseph Miller, President
Susan Strouse, Secretary, Treasurer
Alane LaPlante, Director

Association for independent agents and firms representing manufacturers and other businesses in specified territories on a commission basis, including consultants and associate member firms interested in the manufacturer/agency method of marketing.
Cost: $129.00
Frequency: Annual
Circulation: 25,000

9024 Directory of Mastercard and Visa Credit Cards
Todd Publications
PO Box 635
Nyack, NY 10960-0635

845-358-6213; Fax: 845-358-1059
toddpublications.com

Barry Klein, Editor

Offers information on 500 credit cards from 200 banks across the country.
Cost: $50.00
1000 Pages
Frequency: Biennial
Circulation: 5,000
Founded in 1994
Mailing list available for rent: 200 names at $50 per M

9025 Directory of Mutual Funds
Investment Company Institute
100 F Street
Washington, DC 20549

202-942-8088

Sue Duncan, Editor
Cost: $5.00
247 Pages
Frequency: Annual

9026 Directory of Venture Capital & Private Equity Firms - Online Database
Grey House Publishing
4919 Route 22
PO Box 56
Amenia, NY 12501

518-789-8700
800-562-2139; Fax: 845-373-6390
gold@greyhouse.com
gold.greyhouse.com
Facebook, Twitter

Leslie Mackenzie, Publisher
Richard Gottlieb, Editor

Packed with need-to-know information, this database offers immediate access to 2,300 VC firms, over 10,000 managing partners, and over 11,500 VC investments.
Frequency: Annual

9027 Directory of Venture Capital and Private Equity Firms
Grey House Publishing
4919 Route 22
PO Box 56
Amenia, NY 12501

518-789-8700
800-562-2139; Fax: 845-373-6390
books@greyhouse.com
www.greyhouse.com
Facebook, Twitter

Leslie Mackenzie, Publisher
Richard Gottlieb, Editor

Offers access to over 2,300 domestic and international venture capital and private equity firms, including detailed contact information and extensive data on investments and funds.
Cost: $685.00
1200 Pages
Frequency: Annual
ISBN: 1-592372-72-4

9028 Dow Jones Business and Finance Report
Dow Jones & Company
PO Box 300
Princeton, NJ 08543-0300

609-520-4000
http://www.dowjones.com

This large database offers financial news and information on developments in business and industry, domestic and international economies, and the stock market.
Frequency: Full-text

9029 Dow Jones Futures and Index Quotes
Dow Jones & Company
PO Box 300
Princeton, NJ 08543-0300

609-520-4000

This database, updated continuously, offers current and historical stock quotations for more than 80 contracts from major North American stock exchanges.

9030 Dow Jones Text Library
Dow Jones & Company
PO Box 300
Princeton, NJ 08543-0300

609-520-4000
http://www.dowjones.com

This large database offers business and financial news covering more than 6,000 US companies, 700 Canadian companies and 50 industries.
Frequency: Full-text

9031 E-Z Telephone Directory of Brokers and Banks
106 7th Street
Garden City, NY 11530-5796

516-294-0350; Fax: 516-294-0356

MJ Gentile, Editor

Security brokers, banks, and financial organizations in the New York area are listed in this directory.
Cost: $90.00
200 Pages
Frequency: SemiAnnual
Circulation: 10,000
Printed in on matte stock

9032 ECFA Member List
Evangelical Council for Financial Accountability

440 W Jubal Early Dr
Suite 130
Winchester, VA 22601

540-535-0103
800-323-9473; Fax: 540-535-0533
dan@ecfa.org
www.ecfa.org

Dan Busby, President
John Van Drunen, Executive Vice President
Kim Sandretzky, Vice President, Communications

ECFA is an accrediting organization whose mission is enhancing trust in christ-centered churches and ministries.
2250 Members
Founded in 1979

9033 **EMARKET**
International Financial Corporation
1818 H St NW
Washington, DC 20433-0001

202-473-1000; Fax: 202-974-4384
www.ifc.org

Robert Zoellich, President

This database offers over 1,000 weekly, annual and monthly time series on company stocks from over 18 developing countries.

9034 **Evans Economics Analysis and Commentary**
Evans Economics
1660 L Street NW
Suite 207
Washington, DC 20036-5603

This database reports on changes in economic activity to all major financial markets. Over 20 files are listed that provide the forecasts and reports on the effect of economic variables on debt and equity markets.
Frequency: Full-text

9035 **Financial Ratios for Manufacturing Corporations Database**
US Department of Commerce
Herbert Rm 4885
Washington, DC 20230-0001

202-690-7650; Fax: 202-482-0325
www.access.gpo.gov

Pam Nacci

This database provides 20 quarterly seasonally adjusted financial and operating ratios for selected two- and three-digit SIC groups in the manufacturing sector.
Cost: $85.00
Frequency: Series

9036 **Financial Services Canada**
Grey House Publishing
4919 Route 22
PO Box 56
Amenia, NY 12501

518-789-8700
800-562-2139; Fax: 845-373-6390
books@greyhouse.com
www.greyhouse.com
Facebook, Twitter

Leslie Mackenzie, Publisher
Richard Gottlieb, Editor

With over 18,000 organizations and hard-to-find business information, Financial Services Canada is the most up-to-date source for names and contact information of industry professionals, senior executives, portfolio managers, financial advisors, agency bureaucrats and elected representatives.
Cost: $325.00
900 Pages
ISBN: 1-592372-78-3
Founded in 1981

9037 **Financial Yellow Book**
Leadership Directories
104 5th Ave
New York, NY 10011-6901

212-627-4140; Fax: 212-645-0931
www.leadershipdirectories.com

David Hurvitz, CEO
James M Petrie, Associate Publisher

Contact information for over 26,000 executives at public and private financial institutions, and over 5,000 board members and their outside affiliations.
Cost: $245.00
900 Pages
Frequency: Semiannual
ISSN: 1058-2878
Founded in 1987
Mailing list available for rent: 20,000 names at $95 per M

9038 **Financing Your Business in Eastern Europe**
WorldTrade Executive
PO Box 761
Concord, MA 01742-0761

978-287-0301; Fax: 978-287-0302
www.wtexec.com

Alison French, Production Manager

Provides reliable information on financing sources, including local and international banks, capital markets, venture capital funds, and government sources
Cost: $135.00

9039 **FirstList**
Vision Quest Publishing
37308 12th Street
Phoenix, AZ 86086

928-451-4445
http://www.firstlist.com

A Robert Weicherding, President

Information is offered in this directory covering companies that are candidates for merger or acquisition, buyers seeking acquisitions, sources of financinf, equity or debt financing and joint venture and licensing opportunities. Also available on-line and the Internet.
Cost: $350.00
120 Pages
Frequency: 8 per year

9040 **Ford Data Base**
Ford Investor Services
11722 Sorrento Valley Rd
Suite 1
San Diego, CA 92121-1021

858-755-1327; Fax: 858-455-6316
info@fordequity.com
www.fordequity.com

Tim Alward, President

This database offers 80 financial data items for each of 2,000 leading common stocks.

9041 **Futures Magazine Sourcebook**
Oster Communications
5081 Olympic Boulevard
Erlanger, KT 41018

319-277-1271

Ginger Szala, Group Publisher/Editorial Director
Daniel P Collins, Managing Editor
Christine Birkner, Associate Editor

This issue deals with exchanges in futures and options contracts, including commodities, foreign currencies, stock indexes and international financial coverage.
Cost: $22.00
130 Pages
Frequency: Annual
Circulation: 60,000

9042 **Hulbert Guide to Financial Newsletters**
Dearborn Financial Publishing
155 Wacker Avenue
Chicago, IL 60606

312-836-4400

Matt Schiff, Owner
Kathleen A Welton, VP

Lists over 100 financial newsletters offering descriptions and evaluation of model portfolios.
Cost: $27.95
574 Pages
Frequency: Biennial

9043 **IBC/Donoghue's Money Fund Report/ Electronic**
290 Eliot Street
#9104
Ashland, MA 01721-2351

This valuable database offers information and analyses of trends and developments in the money market mutual funds industry.
Frequency: Full-text

9044 **IBC/Donoghue's Mutual Funds Almanac**
290 Eliot Street
#9104
Ashland, MA 01721-2351
Ann V Needle, Editor

Over 2,400 load and no load mutual funds, including equity, bond and municipal funds.
Cost: $39.95
Circulation: 25,000

9045 **Insider Trading Monitor Database**
CDA Investment
3265 Meridian Parkway
Suite 130
Fort Lauderdale, FL 33331-3506

954-384-1500

More than 12,500 companies and all insider security transactions reported to the US Securities and Exchange Commission, FDIC, Toronto Stock Exchange and OTS.
Frequency: Daily

9046 **Insiders' Chronicle**
CDA Investment
3265 Meridian Parkway
Suite 130
Fort Lauderdale, FL 33331-3506

954-384-1500

Robert Gabele, Editor

Publicly held companies in whose securities there has been significant buying or selling by executive officers, directors, and those who hold 10% or more of its shares.
15 Pages

9047 **International Financial Statistics**
International Monetary Fund
700 19th St NW
Washington, DC 20431-0002

202-623-7000; Fax: 202-623-4661
publications@imf.org
www.imf.org

Masood Ahmed, VP
Kathleen Tilmans, Secretary
Olivier Blanchard, Secretary
Christine Lagarde, Managing Director

Offers informaiton on more than 23,000 annual, quarterly and monthly time series of economic and dinancial statistics on over 200 countries.

9048 **International Investor's Directory**
Asset International
125 Greenwich Avenue
Suite 5
Greenwich, CT 06830-5512

203-629-5015; Fax: 203-629-5024

Eric Laursen, Editor

Directory of services and supplies to the industry.
Cost: $235.00
735 Pages
Frequency: Annual

9049 **Investment Blue Book**
Securities Investigations
PO Box 888
Woodstock, NY 12498-0888

845-679-2300

Lists over 6,000 brokers and dealers in tax shelter plans; 2,000 sponsors of tax shelter products and suppliers of service to the industry and mutual funds information.
Cost: $145.00
350 Pages
Frequency: Irergular
Circulation: 10,000

9050 **Investment Recovery Association Directory**
Investment Recovery Association
5800 Foxridge Drive
Suite 115
Mission, KS 66202-2338

913-624-4597; Fax: 913-262-0174

Jane Male, Editor

Directory of services and supplies to the industry.
Cost: $250.00
Frequency: Annual
Circulation: 400

9051 **Investor Relations Resource Guide**
National Investor Relations Institute
8045 Leesburg Pike
Suite 600
Vienna, VA 22182

571-633-0532; Fax: 703-506-3571
info@niri.org
www.niri.org

Melissa Jones, Editor
Ariel Finno, Director Research

Lists about 110 investment counseling firms, 50 financial investment associations and 40 financial investment service firms such as publishers of magazines and newsletters.
Cost: $50.00
83 Pages
Frequency: Annual

9052 **Japanese Investment in the Midwest**
Japan-America Society of Greater Cincinnati
441 Vine Street
Cincinnati, OH 45202-2821

513-579-3114; Fax: 513-579-3101
www.patent-pros.com

Jack Adams, Executive Director

A list of more than 400 Japanese manufacturing firms in the states of Illinois, Indiana, Kentucky, Michigan, Ohio, and Tennessee.
Cost: $40.00
30 Pages
Frequency: Annual

9053 **Lipper Marketplace**
Lipper, A Thomson Reuters Company
3 Times Square
New York, NY 10036

646-223-4000
800-782-5555
salesinquiries@thomsonreuters.com

James C Smith, Chief Executive Officer
Stephane Bello, Chief Financial Officer
David W Craig, President, Finance
Robert D Daleo, Vice Chairman
Susan Taylor Martin, President, Reuters Media

This powerful web-based solution opens the door to highly targeted prospects by putting the tools to identify your market at your fingertips. Designed with the input of institutional investment professionals, MarketPlace not only helps you qualify your prospects, it also gives you the cutting-edge competitive intelligence you need to transform your prospects into clients.

9054 **Loan Broker: Annual Directory**
Ben Campbell, Publisher
917 S Park Street
Owosso, MI 48867-4422

Lists approximately 800 loan brokers, private funding sources and business financing services operating in the continental United States.
Cost: $59.95
Frequency: Annual
Circulation: 3,000

9055 **MJK Commodities Database**
MJK Associates
1289 S Park Victoria Drive
Suite 205
Milpitas, CA 95035-6974

FAX 408-941-3404

Offers information on United States and Canadian commodities; international monetary markets; futures indexes and stock index futures.

9056 **Mentor Support Group Directory**
National Association of Certified Valuation
1111 Brickyard Road
Suite 200
Salt Lake City, UT 84106-5401

801-486-0600
800-677-2009; Fax: 801-486-7500
nacva1@nacva.com
www.nacva.com

Parnell Black, CEO
Frequency: Annual

9057 **Merger & Acquisition Sourcebook Edition**
Quality Services Company
5290 Overpass Road
Suite 126
Santa Barbara, CA 93111-3009

805-964-7841; Fax: 805-964-1073

Walter Jurek, Editor
Nancy Rothlein, Production Manager

Contains complete information on the previous years' merger and acquisitions actuary.
Cost: $350.00

9058 **Merger Yearbook**
Securities Data Publishing
40 W 57th St
11th Floor
New York, NY 10019-4001

212-484-4701; Fax: 212-956-0112
sdp@tfn.com

Ted Weissberg, Editor-in-Chief
Deborah Chieglis, Advertising Manager
Edward Cortese, Marketing Executive

Information on tens of thousands of announces and completed deals plus charts giving awards information on industry rankings and transactions.

9059 **Merger and Corporate Transactions Database**
Securities Data Publishing
1180 Raymond Boulevard
Suite 5
Newark, NJ 07102-4107

This database contains more than 85,000 records on transactions involving mergers, acquisitions, divestitures leveraged buyouts and stock repurchases.
Frequency: Full-text

9060 **Mergers & Acquisitions Yearbook**
American Banker-Bond Buyer
1 State St
27th Floor
New York, NY 10004-1561

212-803-8450
800-367-3989; Fax: 212-843-9624
www.sourcemedia.com

Jim Malkin, CEO
Mario DiUbaldi, Publisher
Phil Roosevelt, Editor
Carole Lambert, Sales/Marketing Director
Stacy Weinstein, Production Director

Annual yearbook detailing all bank merger and acquisition activity for the previous year. Includes sale price, financial and legal advisors and governmental information.
Cost: $175.00
Frequency: Annual

9061 **Mergers and Acquisitions Handbook**
National Association of Division Order Analysts
2805 Oak Trail Court
Suite 6312
Arlington, TX 76016

972-715-4489
administrator@nadoa.org
www.nadoa.org

Lynn S McCord, Administrator
Frequency: Annual

9062 **Money Market Directory of Pension Funds and their Investment Managers**
Money Market Directories
PO Box 1608
Charlottesville, VA 22902-1608

434-977-1450
800-446-2810; Fax: 434-979-9962
www.mmdaccess.com

Tom Lupo, Manager
John Martin, Production Manager
Dennis Thurston, Publications

Over 44,000 tax-exempt funds with over $1,000,000 in assets, and about 1,800 investment management services including bank trust departments and insurance companies, each handling at least $25,000,000 in tax-exempt funds.
Cost: $1150.00
2000 Pages
Frequency: Annual January
Circulation: 8,500
ISBN: 0-939712-31-8
ISSN: 0736-6051
Founded in 1970

9063 **Money Source Book**
Business Information Network
15851 Dallas Parkway
Suite 600
Dallas, TX 75248

972-982-8686

Over 1,500 traditional and non-traditional sources of business capital with an emphasis on

the south-central United States.
Cost: $24.95
200 Pages
Frequency: Annual
Circulation: 20,000

9064 **MoneyData**
Technical Data
11 Farnsworth Street
Boston, MA 02210-1210

617-345-2000

This database offers a full line of information on money markets.

9065 **MoneyWatch**
McCarthy, Crisanti & Maffei
71 Broadway
New York, NY 10006-2601

212-675-5880; Fax: 212-509-7389

This database offers valuable information on the money market, including economic indicators.
Frequency: Full-text

9066 **Morningstar**
Morningstar
225 W Washington Street
Chicago, IL 60602

312-384-4000; Fax: 312-696-6001
productinfo@morningstar.com
www.morningstar.com

Joe Mansueto, Chairman & CEO
Chris Boruff, President, Software Division
Peng Chen, President, Global Investment Div.
Bevin Desmond, President, International Operations
Scott Cooley, Chief Financial Officer

Morningstar provides data on approximately 330,000 investment offerings, including stocks, mutual funds, and similar vehicles, along with real-time global market data on more than 5 million equities, indexes, futures, options, commodities, and precious metals, in addition to foreign exchange and Treasury markets. Morningstar also offers investment management services and has more than $167 billion in assets under advisement and management.

9067 **Mutual Fund Encyclopedia**
Dearborn Financial Publishing
155 Wacker Drive
Chicago, IL 60606

312-836-4400

Gerald W Perritt, Author

Directory of services and supplies to the industry.
Cost: $35.95
600 Pages
Frequency: Annual

9068 **Mutual Fund/Municipal Bond**
Interactive Data Corporation
10 Post Office Sq
39th Floor
Boston, MA 02109-4695

617-428-1600
info@interactivedata.com
www.interactivedata.com

James Murawski, Manager

This database contains over 3,000 time series of price data for municipal bonds held in the portfolios of selected mutual funds.

9069 **NADOA Directory**
National Association of Division Order Analysts
2805 Oak Trail Court
Suite 6312
Arlington, TX 76016

972-715-4489
administrator@nadoa.org
www.nadoa.org

Lynn S McCord, Administrator
Frequency: Annual

9070 **NALHFA Membership Directory**
National Associatin of Local Housing Finance
2025 M St NW
Suite 800
Washington, DC 20036-2422

202-367-1197; Fax: 202-367-2197
www.noca.org

John C Murphy, Executive Director
Scott Lynch, Association Manager
Kim McKinon, Coordinator Membership
Frequency: Annual

9071 **NASBO Newsletter**
National Association of State Budget Officers
444 N Capitol St NW
Suite 642
Washington, DC 20001-1556

202-624-8020; Fax: 202-624-7745
spattison@nasbo.org
www.nasbo.org

Shelby Kerns, Executive Director

9072 **NASD Manual**
CCH
2700 Lake Cook Rd
Riverwoods, IL 60015-3867

847-940-4600
800-835-5224; Fax: 773-866-3095
www.cch.com

Mike Sabbatis, President
Douglas M Winterrose, Vice President & CFO
Jim Bryant, EVP Software Products

Officials, members, by-laws and rules of NASD.
Founded in 1913

9073 **NATRI Membership Directory**
National Association for Treasurers of Religious
8824 Cameron Street
Silver Springs, MD 20910

301-587-7776; Fax: 301-589-2897
www.natri.org

Laura Reicks, Executive Director
Lorelle Elcock, Associate Director Finance
Frequency: Annual

9074 **National Bankers Association: Roster of Minority Banking Institutions**
National Bankers Association
1513 P St NW
Washington, DC 20005-1909

202-588-5432; Fax: 202-588-5443
webmaster@nationalbankers.org
www.nationalbankers.org

Michael Grant, President
Floyd Weekes, Chairman

About 140 banks owned or controlled by minority group persons or women.
Cost: $5.00
Frequency: Annual October

9075 **National Credit Union Administration Directory**
National Credit Union Administration
1775 Duke St
Suite 4206
Alexandria, VA 22314-6115

703-518-6300; Fax: 703-518-6539
ociomail@ncua.gov
www.ncua.gov

Rodney Hood, Chair
Sarah Vega, Executive Director

Directory of credit unions governed by a three member board appointed by the President and confirmed by the US Senate, by the independent federal agency that charters and supervises federal credit unions. NCUA, with the backing of the full faith and credit of the US government, operates the National Credit Union Share Insurance Fund, insuring the savings of 80 million account holders in all federal credit unions and many state chartered credit unions.

9076 **National Directory of Investment Newsletters**
GPS
PO Box 372
Morrisville, PA 19067-8372

215-295-8700
www.investmentnewsletterdirectory.com

George T Scilieber, Editor

Lists over 800 newsletters dealing with investments and financial planning and their publishers.
Cost: $49.95
60 Pages
Frequency: Biennial

9077 **North American Financial Institutions Directory**
4709 Golf Road
Skokie, IL 60076

847-676-9600
800-321-3373; Fax: 847-933-8101
custserv@accuitysolutions.com
www.accuitysolutions.com

Marideth Johnson, Manager, Marketing/Communications
Malcolm Taylor, Managing Director
Cost: $460.00
Circulation: 31850

9078 **PC Bridge**
Bridge Information Systems
717 Office Parkway
Saint Louis, MO 63141-7115

314-567-8100; Fax: 314-432-5391

Tony Bridge, Manager

This database delivers real-time market information, monitoring up to 100 symbols per page on 10 available pages.

9079 **Pacific Stock Exchange Guide**
CCH
2700 Lake Cook Rd
Riverwoods, IL 60015-3867

847-940-4600
800-835-5224; Fax: 773-866-3095
www.cch.com

Mike Sabbatis, President
Douglas M Winterrose, Vice President & CFO
Jim Bryant, EVP Software Products

Lists officials, members, member organizations; by-laws and rules of the Pacific Stock Exchange.
Cost: $405.00

9080 **Pensions & Investments: Investment Managers**
Crain Communications

711 3rd Ave
New York, NY 10017-4014

212-210-0785; Fax: 212-210-0465
jmurphy@crain.com

Norm Feldman, Manager
Chris Battaglia, Publisher

List of over 1,050 banks, insurance companies, investment advisors and other investment management organizations.
Cost: $40.00
Frequency: Annual May
Circulation: 41,000

9081 **Pensions & Investments: Master Trust, Custody and Global Custody Banks**
Crain Communications
711 3rd Ave
New York, NY 10017-4014

212-210-0785; Fax: 212-210-0465
jmurphy@crain.com

Norm Feldman, Manager
Chris Battaglia, Publisher

List of banks with master trust/master custodial assets and global custody assets.
Cost: $10.00
Frequency: Annual October
Circulation: 41,000

9082 **Philadelphia Stock Exchange Guide**
CCH
2700 Lake Cook Rd
Riverwoods, IL 60015-3867

847-940-4600
800-835-5224; Fax: 773-866-3095
www.cch.com

Mike Sabbatis, President
Douglas M Winterrose, Vice President & CFO
Jim Bryant, EVP Software Products

Lists officials, members, member organizations, securities, by-laws and rules of the Exchange.
Cost: $350.00
Frequency: Monthly

9083 **Pratt's Guide to Private Equity & Venture Capital Sources**
Thomson Reuters
3 Times Square
New York, NY 10036

646-223-4431
800-782-5555
rpp.americas@thomsonreuters.com
www.thomsonreuters.com

James C Smith, Chief Executive Officer
Stephane Bello, Chief Financial Officer
David W Craig, President, Finance
Robert D Daleo, Vice Chairman
Susan Taylor Martin, President, Reuters Media

This is the definitive reference source to actively investing private equity and venture capital firms operating around the world. Pratt's Guide is available in both hard copy and online format - the latter being continually updated with new fund-raising data, new investment and exit data and new contact information.

9084 **Professional Investor Report**
Dow Jones & Company
PO Box 300
Princeton, NJ 08543-0300

609-520-4000

Offers information on unusual stock trading activity taking place on the New York and American stock exchanges and the National Market System portion of the OTC market.

9085 **Quarterly Financial Report**
GE Information Services
401 N Washington Street
Rockville, MD 20850-1707

301-388-8284; Fax: 301-294-5501

Cathy Ge, Owner

This unique database offers information on financial estimates for US enterprises within 31 industry classifications.

9086 **RSP Funding for Nursing Students and Nurses**
Reference Service Press
5000 Windplay Dr
Suite 4
El Dorado Hills, CA 95762-9319

916-939-9620; Fax: 916-939-9626
info@rspfunding.com
www.rspfunding.com

Gail Schlachter, Owner
R David Weber, Manager
Martin Sklar, Manager

You can find out about the more than 600 scholarships, fellowships, loans, loan repayment programs, forgivable loans, grants, awards, prizes and interships set aside specifically to support study, research, creative activities, past accomplishments, future projects, professional development and traineeships. This is more than twice the number of nursing related funding programs covered in any other source.
Cost: $30.00
210 Pages
Frequency: Biennial
ISBN: 1-588410-95-1
Founded in 1998

9087 **Registry of Financial Planning Practitioners**
International Association for Financial Planning
1580 W. El Camino Real
Suite 10
Mountain View, CA 94040

877-794-9511
650-390-6400; Fax: 650-989-2131
customer.service@trademarkia.com
www.trademarkia.com

J Patrick Tinley, CEO
Alexander Esq, Owner

Directory of services and supplies to the industry.
80 Pages
Frequency: Annual

9088 **Research Reports**
National Committee on Planned Giving
233 S McCrea St
Suite 400
Indianapolis, IN 46225-1068

317-269-6274; Fax: 317-269-6276

Tanya Howe Johnson, President
Sandra Kerr, Director Government Education
Barbara Owens, Director Membership/Manager HR
Kathryn J Ramsey, Director Meetings
Kurt Reusze, Manager Education/Technology
Frequency: Irregular

9089 **Roster of Minority Financial Institutions**
US Department of the Treasury
401 14th Street SW
Room 523C
Washington, DC 20024-2106

202-874-5740; Fax: 202-874-6907

Robert Jones, Editor

About 170 commercial, minority-owned and controlled financial institutions participating in the Department of the Treasury's Minority Bank Deposit program.
Frequency: Biennial

9090 **S&P MarketScope Database**
Standard & Poor's Corporation
55 Water St
New York, NY 10041-0003

212-438-1000; Fax: 212-438-0299

Deven Sharma, President

Over 5,000 companies are listed in the Reference Section of Standard and Poors database offering names, addresses, background information and current and historical financial information.

9091 **Secondary Marketing Executive Directory of Mortgage Technology**
LDJ Corporation
P.O.Box 2180
Waterbury, CT 06722-2180

203-755-0158; Fax: 203-755-3480

David Zackin, Publisher
John Florian, Editor

A who's who directory of technology products and services to the real estate finance industry.
Cost: $5.00
Frequency: Annual
Circulation: 21,000

9092 **Service Directory**
National Association for Treasurers of Religious
8824 Cameron Street
Silver Springs, MD 20910

301-587-7776; Fax: 301-589-2897

Laura Reicks, Executive Director
Lorelle Elcock, Associate Director Finance
Frequency: Annual

9093 **Sheshunoff Bank & S&L Quarterly**
Sheshunoff Information Services
2801 Via Fortuna
Suite 600
Austin, TX 78746-7970

512-472-4000
800-477-1772; Fax: 512-305-6575
sales@smslp.com
www.smslp.com

Gabrielle Sheshunoff, CEO

Overview of the financial health of the banking industry and of every bank and S&L in the nation. Information includes CAMEL, fachois, asset quality, earnings, and rotation.
Cost: $543.00
Frequency: Quarterly

9094 **Sheshunoff Banking Organization Quarterly**
Sheshunoff Information Services
2801 Via Fortuna
Suite 600
Austin, TX 78746-7970

512-472-4000
800-456-2340; Fax: 512-305-6575
gsheshunoff@smslp.com
www.smslp.com

Gabrielle Sheshunoff, CEO

Offers ownership structure for all bank holding companies and overview and ratings for bank holding companies and their brinking subs.
Cost: $499.00
Frequency: Quarterly

9095 **Small Business Investment Company Directory and Handbook**
International Wealth Success
PO Box 186
Merrick, NY 11566-0186

516-766-5850
800-323-0548; Fax: 516-766-5919
admin@iwsmoney.com

www.iwsmoney.com
Facebook, LinkedIn

Tyler G Hicks, President

Lists more than 400 small business investment companies that invest in small businesses to help them prosper. Also gives tips on financial management in business.
Cost: $20.00
135 Pages
Frequency: Annual
ISBN: 1-561503-12-6
Founded in 1975

9096 Speakers Bureau Directory
National Association of Certified Valuation
1111 Brickyard Road
Suite 200
Salt Lake City, UT 84106-5401

801-486-0600
800-677-2009; Fax: 801-486-7500
nacva1@nacva.com
www.nacva.com

Parnell Black, CEO
Frequency: Annual

9097 Standard & Poor's Directory of Bond Agents
Standard & Poor's Corporation
55 Water St
New York, NY 10041-0003

212-438-1000; Fax: 212-438-0299

Deven Sharma, President

A list of paying agents, registrars, co-registrars and conversion agents for 30,000 corporate and municipal bonds are included.
Cost: $1250.00

9098 Standard & Poor's Security Dealers of North America
Standard & Poor's Financial Services, LLC
401 East Market Street
PO Box 1608
Charlottesville, VA 22902

434-977-1450
800-446-2810; Fax: 434-979-9962
marketintelligence.spglobal.com

Deven Sharma, President

The most comprehensive guide to brokerage and investment banking firms in the US and Canada. The directory contains all the facts you need for conveniently locating firms and facilitating transactions.
Cost: $498.00
Frequency: 2x/Year

9099 State Expenditure Report
National Association of State Budget Officers
444 N Capitol St NW
Suite 642
Washington, DC 20001-1556

202-624-8020; Fax: 202-624-7745
www.nasbo.org

Shelby Kerns, Executive Director
Lauren Cummings, Manager Member Relations
Frequency: Annual

9100 TA Guide & Checklist
National Investment Company Service Association
36 Washington Street
Suite 70
Wellesley Hills, MA 02481

781-416-7200; Fax: 781-416-7065
www.nisca.org

Barbara V Weidlich, President
Keith Dropkin, Director Operations
Doris Jaimes, Registrar
Sheila Kobaly, Events Manager
Chris Ludent, IT Manager
Frequency: Annual

9101 TRW Trade Payment Guide
TRW Business Credit Services
500 City Pkwy W
Orange, CA 92868-2913

714-385-7000
800-344-0603; Fax: 714-938-2586

Approximately 2,500,000 credit active business locations.
Frequency: Quarterly

9102 Tax Directory
Tax Analysts
6830 N Fairfax Drive
Arlington, VA 22213-1001

703-533-4400
800-955-3444; Fax: 703-533-4664
taxdir@tax.org
www.tax.org

Amie Chant, Editor
Thomas F Field, Vice President
Jill Biden, Vice President

A reference tool that provides users with comprehensive listings of federal, state and private sector tax professionals. Now in three sections - Government Officials, Corporate Tax Managers and International Officials.
Cost: $ 399.00
960 Pages
Frequency: Quarterly
Circulation: 2,000
ISSN: 0888-1243

9103 Tax Free Trade Zones of the World
Matthew Bender and Company
11 Penn Plz
Suite 5101
New York, NY 10001-2006

212-000-1111

Eric Blood, Data Processing

Covers over 450 free trade zones, transit zones, free perimeters and free ports. The emphasis is placed on tax advantages of each.
Cost: $280.00
1000 Pages

9104 Technical Resources Handbook
National Association of Certified Valuation
1111 Brickyard Road
Suite 200
Salt Lake City, UT 84106-5401

801-486-0600
800-677-2009; Fax: 801-486-7500
nacva1@nacva.com
www.nacva.com

Parnell Black, CEO
Frequency: Annual

9105 TheStreet Ratings Guide to Bond & Money Market Mutual Funds
Grey House Publishing
4919 Route 22
PO Box 56
Amenia, NY 12501

518-789-8700
800-562-2139; Fax: 845-373-6390
books@greyhouse.com
www.greyhouse.com
Facebook, Twitter

Leslie Mackenzie, Publisher
Richard Gottlieb, Editor

Each quarterly edition provides ratings and analyses of more than 4,200 fixed income funds, more than any other publication, including corporate bond funds, municipal bond funds, mortgage security funds, money market funds, global bond funds, and government bond funds.
Cost: $249.00
600 Pages
Frequency: Quarterly
Founded in 1981

9106 TheStreet Ratings Guide to Common Stocks
Grey House Publishing
4919 Route 22
PO Box 56
Amenia, NY 12501

518-789-8700
800-562-2139; Fax: 845-373-6390
books@greyhouse.com
www.greyhouse.com
Facebook, Twitter

Leslie Mackenzie, Publisher
Richard Gottlieb, Editor

Each quarterly edition provides reliable insight into the risk-adjusted performance of over 7,500 common stocks listed on the NYSE, AMEX, and NASDAQ, more than any other publication. This user-friendly guide offers step-by-step guidance for users to find out which type of stocks are best for them, and quickly and easily points the user to the best performing stocks in that category.
Cost: $249.00
600 Pages
Frequency: Quarterly
Founded in 1981

9107 TheStreet Ratings Guide to Exchange-Traded Funds
Grey House Publishing
4919 Route 22
PO Box 56
Amenia, NY 12501

518-789-8700
800-562-2139; Fax: 845-373-6390
books@greyhouse.com
www.greyhouse.com
Facebook, Twitter

Leslie Mackenzie, Publisher
Richard Gottlieb, Editor

The intuitive, consumer-friendly ratings allow investors to instantly identify those funds that have historically done well and those that have under-performed the market. Identifies top-performing exchange-traded funds based on risk category, type of fund, and overall risk-adjusted performance.
Cost: $249.00
600 Pages
Frequency: Quarterly
Founded in 1981

9108 TheStreet Ratings Guide to Stock Mutual Funds
Grey House Publishing
4919 Route 22
PO Box 56
Amenia, NY 12501

518-789-8700
800-562-2139; Fax: 845-373-6390
books@greyhouse.com
www.greyhouse.com
Facebook, Twitter

Leslie Mackenzie, Publisher
Richard Gottlieb, Editor

Offers ratings and analyses on more than 8,000 equity mutual funds, including growth funds, index funds, balanced funds and sector or international funds - more than any other publication.
Cost: $249.00
600 Pages
Frequency: Quarterly
Founded in 1981

9109 **TheStreet Ratings Ultimate Guided Tour of Stock Investing**
Grey House Publishing
4919 Route 22
PO Box 56
Amenia, NY 12501
518-789-8700
800-562-2139; Fax: 845-373-6390
books@greyhouse.com
www.greyhouse.com
Facebook, Twitter
Leslie Mackenzie, Publisher
Richard Gottlieb, Editor
This user-friendly guide provides a step-by-step introduction to stock investing designed for the beginning to intermediate investor. Starting with the basics of stock investing and ending with an evaluation of the user's risk tolerance and the identification of the types of stocks that best match their needs, this easy-to-navigate guide pulls together all of the information necessary to educate the consumer on how to get the best start in investing.
Cost: $249.00
600 Pages
Frequency: Quarterly
Founded in 1981

9110 **Trading Volume Survey**
EMTA - Trade Association for the Emerging Markets
360 Madison Avenue
18th Floor
New York, NY 10017
646-637-9100; Fax: 646-637-9128
awerner@emta.org
www.emta.org
Michael M Chamberlin, Executive Director
Aviva Werner, Managing Director
Jonathan Murno, Managing Director
Suzette Ortiz, Office Manager
Monika Forbes, Administrative Assistant
Frequency: Quarterly

9111 **Trusts & Estates: Directory of Trust Institutions Issue**
Primedia
PO Box 12901
Shawnee Mission, KS 66282-2901
913-341-1300; Fax: 913-514-6895
www.penton.com
Eric Jacobson, Senior VP
Offers a list of about 5,000 trust departments in the United States and Canadian banks.
Cost: $82.00
Frequency: Annual January
Circulation: 12,200

9112 **Valuation Compilation**
National Association of Certified Valuation
1111 Brickyard Road
Suite 200
Salt Lake City, UT 84106-5401
801-486-0600
800-677-2009; Fax: 801-486-7500
nacva1@nacva.com
www.nacva.com
Parnell Black, CEO
Frequency: Bi-Ennial

9113 **Venture Capital: Where to Find it**
National Association of Small Business Investment
1199 N Fairfax Street
Suite 200
Alexandria, VA 22314-1437
703-549-2100
Jeanette D Smith, Editor
Directory of services and supplies to the industry.
Frequency: Annual

9114 **Weiss Ratings Consumer Box Set**
Grey House Publishing
4919 Route 22
PO Box 56
Amenia, NY 12501
518-789-8700
800-562-2139; Fax: 845-373-6390
books@greyhouse.com
www.greyhouse.com
Facebook, Twitter
Leslie Mackenzie, Publisher
Richard Gottlieb, Editor
Each guide in the Weiss Ratings Consumer Box Set is packed with accurate, unbiased information, including helpful, step-by-step Worksheets & Planners. The set consists of Consumer Guides to Variable Annuities, Elder Care Choices, Medicare Supplement Insurance, Medicare Prescription Drug Coverage, Homeowners Insurance, Automobile Insurance, Long-Term Care Insurance, and Term Life Insurance.
Cost: $249.00
600 Pages
Frequency: Quarterly
Founded in 1981

9115 **Weiss Ratings Guide to Banks & Thrifts**
Grey House Publishing
4919 Route 22
PO Box 56
Amenia, NY 12501
518-789-8700
800-562-2139; Fax: 845-373-6390
books@greyhouse.com
www.greyhouse.com
Facebook, Twitter
Leslie Mackenzie, Publisher
Richard Gottlieb, Editor
Offers accurate, intuitive safety ratings your patrons can trust; supporting ratios and analyses that show an institution's strong & weak points; identification of the Weiss Recommended Companies with branches in your area and more.
Cost: $249.00
600 Pages
Frequency: Quarterly
Founded in 1981

9116 **Weiss Ratings Guide to Credit Unions**
Grey House Publishing
4919 Route 22
PO Box 56
Amenia, NY 12501
518-789-8700
800-562-2139; Fax: 845-373-6390
books@greyhouse.com
www.greyhouse.com
Facebook, Twitter
Leslie Mackenzie, Publisher
Richard Gottlieb, Editor
This new reference tool provides accurate financial strength ratings of the 7,800 credit unions in the United States.
Cost: $249.00
600 Pages
Frequency: Quarterly
Founded in 1981

9117 **Weiss Ratings Guide to Health Insurers**
Grey House Publishing
4919 Route 22
PO Box 56
Amenia, NY 12501
518-789-8700
800-562-2139; Fax: 845-373-6390
books@greyhouse.com
www.greyhouse.com
Facebook, Twitter
Leslie Mackenzie, Publisher
Richard Gottlieb, Editor
Weiss Ratings Guide to Health Insurers is the first and only source to cover the financial stability of the nation's health care system, rating the financial safety of more than 6,000 health maintenance organizations (HMOs) and all of the Blue Cross Blue Shield plans - updated quarterly to ensure the most accurate, up-to-date informations.
Cost: $249.00
600 Pages
Frequency: Quarterly
Founded in 1981

9118 **Weiss Ratings Guide to Life & Annuity Insurers**
Grey House Publishing
4919 Route 22
PO Box 56
Amenia, NY 12501
518-789-8700
800-562-2139; Fax: 845-373-6390
books@greyhouse.com
www.greyhouse.com
Facebook, Twitter
Leslie Mackenzie, Publisher
Richard Gottlieb, Edtior
Each easy-to-use edition provides independent, unbiased ratings on the financial strength of 1,000 life and annuity insurers, including companies providing life insurance, annuities, guaranteed investment contracts (GICs) and other pension products.
Cost: $249.00
600 Pages
Frequency: Quarterly
Founded in 1981

9119 **Weiss Ratings Guide to Property & Casualty Insurers**
Grey House Publishing
4919 Route 22
PO Box 56
Amenia, NY 12501
518-789-8700
800-562-2139; Fax: 845-373-6390
books@greyhouse.com
www.greyhouse.com
Facebook, Twitter
Leslie Mackenzie, Publisher
Richard Gottlieb, Editor
Updated quarterly, this publication is the only resource that provides independent, unbiased ratings and analyses on the 2,400 insurers offering auto & homeowners, business, worker's compensation, product liability, medical malpractice and other professional liability insurance in the United States.
Cost: $249.00
600 Pages
Frequency: Quarterly
Founded in 1981

9120 **Who's Who in Economic Development Directory**
International Economic Development Council (IEDC)
734 15th St NW
Suite 900
Washington, DC 20005-1013
202-223-7800; Fax: 202-223-4745
www.iedconline.org
Jeffrey Finkle, CEO
Jon Roberts, Managing Director
Jackie Gibson, Project Manager
Charles Stein, Founder

A listing of over 2,500 Council members and other certified individuals. Directory is limited to international coverage.
200 Pages
Frequency: Annual

9121 **Who's Who in Venture Capital**
Grey House Publishing
4919 Route 22
PO Box 56
Amenia, NY 12501
518-789-8700
800-562-2139; Fax: 845-373-6390
books@greyhouse.com
www.greyhouse.com
Facebook, Twitter

Leslie Mackenzie, Publisher
Richard Gottlieb, Editor

Provides immediate access to nearly 10,000 principals, partners and managing directors heading the world's Venture Capital and Private Equity firms. The listings contain comprehensive profile information including partner and firm names, titles, education, professional background, directorships and full contact information.
Cost: $295.00
643 Pages
Founded in 1981

9122 **World Emerging Stock Markets**
Probus Publishing Company
1333 Burbridge Parkway
Burbridge, IL 60521

Directories of stock markets in Central and South America, Middle East and Europe.
Cost: $59.95

9123 **Yearbook of Education Finance**
American Education Finance Association
8365 S Armadillo Trail
Evergreen, CO 80439
303-674-0857; Fax: 303-670-8986
www.aefa.cc

Ed Steinbecher, Executive Director

Information and updates for educational institutions and organizations regarding financial investing, prospecting and fundraising.
Frequency: Annual

Industry Web Sites

9124 **http://gold.greyhouse.com**
G.O.L.D Grey House OnLine Databases

Grey House Publishing's online database platform, GOLD, offers Quick Search, Keyword Search and Expert Search for most business sectors including financial services and banking markets. The GOLD platform makes finding the information you need quick and easy - whether you're a novice searcher or an experienced database user. All of Grey House's directory products are available for subscription on the GOLD platform.

9125 **www.aacei.org**
Association for Advancement of Cost Engineering

Association for those interested in the financial aspects of engineering all aspects of cost management.

9126 **www.aaii.com**
American Association of Individual Investors

An independent nonprofit corporation formed in 1978 for the purpose of assisting individuals in becoming effective managers of their own assets through programs of education, information and research.

9127 **www.abiworld.org**
American Bankruptcy Institute

A multidisiplinary, nonpartisan organization dedicated to research and education on matters related to insolvency. Provides a forum for the exchange of ideas and information. ABI is engaged in numerous educational and research activities, as well as the production of a number of publications both for the insolvency practitioner and the public.

9128 **www.aefa.org**
American Education Finance Association

Encourages communications among groups and individuals in education financial fields.

9129 **www.afponline.org**
Association for Financial Professionals

Association of 12,000 financial professionals.

9130 **www.afsaonline.com**
American Financial Services Association

National trade association for market funded providers of financial services to consumers and small businesses. These providers offer an array of finacial services, including unsecured personal loans, automobile loans, home equity loans and credit cards through specialized bank institutions.

9131 **www.agacgfm.org**
Association of Government Accountants

AGA is an educational association dedicated to enhancing public financial management by serving the professional interests of governmental managers and public accounting firms.

9132 **www.appraisalinstitute.org**
Appraisal Institute

Promotes a code of ethics and uniform standards of the real estate appraisal practice. Publishes periodicals, books and appraisal-related materials, and sponsors courses and seminars.

9133 **www.appraisers.org**
American Society of Appraisers

Organization provides education and accreditation for appraisers.

9134 **www.bcfm.com**
Broadcast Cable Financial Management Association

Professional association for TV, radio and cable CEOs, bueinss managers, HR, MIS controllers and financial personnel, as well as associate members in legal, audit and related fields.

9135 **www.ecfa.org**
Evangelical Council for Financial Accountability

Helps Christ-centered organizations earn the public's trust through developing and maintaining standards of accountability that convey God-honoring ethical practices.

9136 **www.financialratingsseries.com**
Grey House Publishing

Financial Ratings Series Online combines the strength of Weiss Ratings and TheStreet Ratings to offer the library community with a single source for financial strength ratings and financial planning tools covering Banks, Insurers, Mutual Funds and Stocks. This powerful database will provide the accurate, independent information consumers need to make informed decisions about their financial planning.

9137 **www.fma.org**
Financial Management Association International

Strives to facilitate exchanges of ideas among persons in financial management.

9138 **www.fmsinc.org**
Financial Managers Society

Provides technical information and education to financial officers in banks, thrifts and credit unions.

9139 **www.globalpurchasing.org**
International Association of Purchasing Managers

A professional organization dedicated to the advancement of world trade, membership is open to buyers, purchasing managers, executives and all individuals that may be involved or have an interest in the important function of buying goods and services on the global market. A NON-PROFIT organization..

9140 **www.greenwood.com**
Greenwood Publishing Group

Business and professional publishing, academic books in Business, Finance, Business Law, and Applied Economics management.

9141 **www.greyhouse.com**
Grey House Publishing

Authoritative reference directories for most business sectors including financial services and banking markets. Users can search the online databases with varied search criteria allowing for custom searches by product category, geographic area, sales volume, keyword, subject and more. Full Grey House catalog and online ordering also available.

9142 **www.iami.org**
National Association of Review Appraisers

Association for professionals who review real estate appraisals and underwrite real estate mortgagers. The association offers the CRA, Certified Review Appraiser and RMU, Registered Mortgage Underwriter, professional designation.

9143 **www.ici.org**
Investment Company Institute

Acts to represent members in matters of legislation, taxation, regulation, economic research and marketing and public information regarding investments and mutual funds.

9144 **www.invrecovery.org**
Investment Recovery Association

Association for manufacturers of services and supplies to the industry.

9145 **www.irrc.org**
Investor Responsibility Research Center

Acts to publish reports and analyses of social issues and public policy affecting corporation and investors.

9146 **www.kobren.com**
Mutual Fund Investors Association

Association for those interested in information and rates for mutual funds, investments, stocks and bonds.

9147 **www.marketresearch.com**
Research Reports

Search financial services reports from over 350 sources. Updated daily.

9148 **www.mfea.com**
Mutual Fund Education Alliance

Conducts public education and public relation activities in an effort to acquaint industry, organizations and government agencies with direct market funds.

9149 **www.mortgagepress.com**
National Mortgage Professional

Information on new products, industry news, personnel announcements and calendar of events.

9150 **www.nact.org**
National Association of Corporate Treasurers
Members are corporate chief financial officers, treasurers or assistant treasurers.

9151 **www.nadco.org**
National Association of Development Companies
Provides long-term fixed asset financing to small businesses.

9152 **www.nafa-us.org**
National Aircraft Finance Association
Members are lending institutions involved in aircraft financing.

9153 **www.nasbic.org**
Nat'l Assn of Small Business Investment Companies
Trade Association representing federally licensed ventures capital firms, Email, and business investment companies.

9154 **www.natptax.com**
National Association of Tax Professionals
The National Association of Tax Professionals (NATP) is a nonprofit association dedicated to excellence in taxation and related financial services. NATP was formed to serve professionals who work in all areas of tax practice. Members include Enrolled Agents, Certified Public Accountants, individual practitioners, accountants, attorneys, and financial planners.

9155 **www.nchffa.com**
National Council of Health Facilities Finance
To serve the common interests and enhance the effectiveness of member Authorities through communication, education and advocacy.

9156 **www.nfa.future.org**
National Futures Association
Association for corporations and firms that are registered with the Commodity Futures Trading Commission.

9157 **www.nfa.org**
National Finance Adjusters
Serves collateral recovery specialists.

9158 **www.nfma.org**
National Federation of Municipal Analysts
Promotes the profession of municipal credit analysts through educational programs, industry, communications and related programming.

9159 **www.nipa.org**
National Institute of Pension Administrators
Enhancing professionalism in the retirement plan industry through education.

9160 **www.nvca.org**
National Venture Capital Association
Corporations, corporate financiers and private individuals who invest private capital in young companies on a professional basis.

9161 **www.nvla.org**
National Vehicle Leasing Association
Fosters education, publishing, conferences, legal services, advancement and industry relations certification.

9162 **www.securitytraders.org**
Security Traders Association
Serves the securities industry.

9163 **www.snl.com**
SNL Securities
News articles on banks and thrifts, insurance and other financial services. Also features vital company information.

9164 **www.thefcs.org**
Financial Communications Society
The FCS is devoted to improving professional standards in financial marketing communications, with a membership comprised of managers in advertising, marketing, PR, IR, corporate communications, and social and digital media.

9165 **www.theiia.org**
Institute of Internal Auditors
International organization composed of internal auditors, corporate executives and board members. Contact and current development information.

9166 **www.thestreet.com**
TheStreet Ratings, Inc.
Publisher of ratings guides.

9167 **www.uhab.org**
Urban Homesteading Assistance Board
Information on affordable housing and self reliance. Activities include advocacy, organizing, classroom and on-site training, direct technical assistance, development consulting, development and sponsorship of new co-ops and services to member co-ops that include bookkeeping, insurance, legal services, bulk purchasing, newsletters and IT services.

9168 **www.wsta.org**
Wall Street Technology Association
White papers on the latest in technology for IT professionals working in the finacial field. Resource guide for industry products and services and information on seminars and conferences included.

Associations

9169 **American Albacore Fishing Association**
4364 Bonita Rd., Box 311
Bonita, CA 91902

619-941-2307; Fax: 619-863-5046
nataliewebster@americanalbacore.com
americanalbacore.com

Tim Thomas, President
Carl Nish, Vice President
Jack Vantress, Treasurer
Jack Webster, Secretary

A nonprofit representing commercial pole and line vessels that advocates for a sustainable tuna fishery.

9170 **American Crappie Association**
125 Ruth Avenue
Benton, KY 42025

270-395-4204; Fax: 270-395-4381
office@crappieusa.com
www.crappieusa.com
Facebook

Darrell VanVactor, President
Charles Rogers, VP
Larry Crecelius, Public Relations Director
Jim Perry, Secretary/Treasurer
Dan Wagoner, Member

For all crappie anglers, from weekend fishermen to tournament pros. Influencing national manufacturers to produce more and better crappie fishing products, establishing a voice and lobby for crappie anglers everywhere and elevating the sport of crappie fishing to its rightful place in the limelight.
Cost: $20.00
Frequency: Individual Membership

9171 **American Fisheries Society**
425 Barlow Place
Suite 110
Bethesda, MD 20814-2144

301-897-8616; Fax: 301-897-8096
main@fisheries.org
fisheries.org
Facebook, Twitter, LinkedIn, Pinterest, Google+, Vimeo

Douglas Austen, Executive Director
Erin Del Collo, Membership Coordinator
Katrina Dunn, Director of Development
Laura Hendee, Journals Production Manager
Shawn Johnston, Meetings Manager

Organization dedicated to strengthening the fisheries profession and advancing fisheries.
Cost: $100.00
8500 Members
Frequency: Membership Fee
Founded in 1870
Mailing list available for rent: 8500 names

9172 **American Fly Fishing Trade Association**
321 East Main St.
Suite 300
Bozeman, MO 59715

406-522-1556; Fax: 406-522-1557
www.affta.com
Facebook

Ben Bulis, President
Tucker Ladd, Chairman

A sole trade organization for the fly fishing industry. The mission is to promote the sustained growth of the fly fishing industry.
400 Members
Founded in 2003
Mailing list available for rent

9173 **American Institute of Fishery Research Biologists**
205 Blades Road
Havelock, NC 28532

Home Page: www.aifrb.org
Facebook, Twitter, LinkedIn, Stumbleupon, www.digg.com

Tom Keegan, President
Allen Shimada, Treasurer
Barbara Warkentine, Secretary
Sarah Fox, Executive Editor
Linda Jones, Past President

A professional organization founded to promote conservation and proper utilization of fishery resources through application of fishery science and related sciences.
1000 Members
Founded in 1956

9174 **American Littoral Society**
18 Hartshorne Drive
Suite #1
Highlands, NJ 07732

732-291-0055; Fax: 732-291-3551
www.littoralsociety.org
Facebook, Twitter, Stumbleupon

Tim Dillingham, Executive Director
Kathleen Gasienica, President
Peter Hetzler, Vice President
Gregory Quirk, Treasurer
Sameul Huber, Secretary

Dedicated to the environmental well-being of coastal habitat.
5000+ Members
Frequency: Membership Fee: $30-$35
Founded in 1961
Mailing list available for rent

9175 **American Shrimp Processors Association**
PO Box 4867
EIN #72-6029637
Biloxi, MS 39535

857-445-4165; Fax: 228-385-2565
info@fundraise.com
www.fundraise.com
Facebook, Twitter

Nate Drouin, CEO
Kurt Schneider, Chief Operating Officer
Kevin Bedell, Chief Technical Officer
Ivan Sifrim, UX Developer
Nick Alekhine, Developer

A non-profit trade organization designed to represent U.S. shrimp processors in all aspects of business. Allowing processors and related industries to work together to foster a business and technological climate in which its members can prosper while providing the highest quality product to its customers.
Founded in 1964

9176 **American Sportfishing Association**
1001 North Fairfax St.
Suite 501
Alexandria, VA 22314

703-519-9691; Fax: 703-519-1872
info@asafishing.org
asafishing.org
Facebook, Twitter

Mike Nussman, President & CEO
Scott Gudes, VP, Government Affairs
Diane Carpenter, VP, Operations & CFO
Glenn Hughes, VP, Industry Relations
Mary Jane Williamson, Communications Director

The Association advocates for fish, anglers and the sportfishing industry.
Founded in 1933

9177 **Association of Fish and Wildlife Agencies**
1100 First Street NE
Suite 825
Washington, DC 20002

202-838-3474; Fax: 202-350-9869
info@fishwildlife.org
www.fishwildlife.org
Facebook, Twitter

Ron Regan, Executive Director
Dave Chanda, President
Nick Wiley, Vice President
Carol Bambrey, Association Council
Glenn Normandeau, Secretary/Treasurer

The organization that represents all of North America's fish and wildlife agencies that promotes sound management ans conservation, and speaks with a unified voice on important fish and wildlife issues.
Founded in 1902

9178 **Association of Smoked Fish Processors**
c/o Shuster Labs
85 John Road
Canton, MA 02120

781-821-2200
800-444-8705; Fax: 781-821-9266

Members are food processors with an interest in smoked fish.
Founded in 1963

9179 **Association of Zoos and Aquariums**
8403 Colesville Rd
Suite 710
Silver Spring, MD 20910-3314

301-562-0777; Fax: 301-562-0888
membership@aza.org
www.aza.org
Facebook, Twitter

Dan Ashe, President & CEO
Craig Hoover, Executive Vice President
Jack Keeney, Jr., General Counsel
Phil Wagner, Chief Financial Officer
Melissa Howerton, SVP. Member Services

A nonprofit organization dedicated to the advancement of accredited zoos and aquariums in the areas of animal care, wildlife conservation, education and science.
200 Members
Founded in 1924

9180 **At-Sea Processors Association**
4039 21st Ave W
Suite 400
Seattle, WA 98199

206-285-5139; Fax: 206-285-1841
jgilmore@atsea.org
www.atsea.org

Stephanie Madsen, Executive Director
Paul MacGregor, General Counsel
Jim Gilmore, Public Affairs Director
Ed Richardson, PhD., Resource Economist
Melinda Madson Schmidt, Program Coordinator

A trade association representing seven copmanies that own and operate 19 U.S. flag cathcer/processor vessels that participate principally in the Alaska pollack fishery and west coast Pacific whiting fishery.
Cost: $500.00
7 Members
Frequency: Membership Fees Vary
Founded in 1985

9181 **Atlantic States Marine Fisheries Commission**
1050 N Highland Street
Suite 200 A-N
Arlington, VA 22201

703-842-0740; Fax: 703-842-0741
info@asmfc.org
www.asmfc.org
Facebook, Twitter

Patrick C. Keliher, Chair
A.G. "Spud" Woodward, Vice Chair
Robert E. Beal, Executive Director
Tina L. Berger, Director of Communications

The commission was formed by the fifteen Atlantic coast states. It serves as a deliberative body, coordinating the conservation and management of the states shared near shore fishery resources.
45 Members
Founded in 1942

9182 **Bass Anglers Sportsman Society**
3500 Blue Lake Drive
Suite 330
Birmingham, AL 35243

334-272-9530
877-227-7872; Fax: 334-279-7148
bassmaster@emailcustomerservice.com
www.bassmaster.com
Facebook, Twitter

Dean Kassel, President
Chris Horton, Associate Director

A service organization for bass fishermen. It protects and preserves the fishing environment, reports on the newest products and techniques, and provides an arena for professional and amateur fishing competitions.
Cost: $14.95
600M Members
Frequency: Annual Membership Fee
Founded in 1972

9183 **Blue Water Fishermen's Association**
PO Box 779
Forked River, NJ 08731-0779

609-891-8672; Fax: 732-279-4522
bwfa@usa.net
Facebook, Twitter, LinkedIn, Stumbleupon

Nelson R Beideman, Executive Director

Non-profit organization of companies and individuals representing fishermen, Captains, vessel owners, docks, dealers, suppliers and related service businesses.
Founded in 1990

9184 **California Fisheries & Seafood Institute**
1521 I St
Sacramento, CA 95814

916-441-5560; Fax: 916-446-1063
Info@calseafood.net
www.calseafood.net

Kevin Joyce, President
Dave Rudie, 1st Vice President
Steve Foltz, Treasurer
Sal Balestrieri, Vice President-Legislative
Kathleen Halson, Vice President-Promotion

Regional trade organization representing members of the consumer seafood supply industry.
130+ Members
Founded in 1954

9185 **California Salmon Council**
PO Box 2255
Folsom, CA 95763-2255

916-933-7050; Fax: 916-933-7055
info@calkingsalmon.org
www.calkingsalmon.org

Greg Ambiel, Chairman
Bill Dawson, Vice-Chairman

Represents the marketing interests of California's commercial salmon fishermen. It creates consumer awareness and demand for California King Salmon.
Founded in 1989

9186 **Catfish Farmers of America**
1100 Highway 82 E
Suite 202
Indianola, MS 38751

662-887-2699; Fax: 662-887-6857
www.catfishfarmersofamerica.com
Facebook, Twitter

Hugh Warren, President

Represents the largest aquaculture industry in the United States. Represents the interests of farm-raised catfish industry of farmers, processors, feed mills, researchers and supplier industries.
Cost: $40.00
Frequency: Membership Fee
Founded in 1968

9187 **FishAmerica Foundation**
1001 North Fairfax St.
Suite 501
Alexandria, VA 22314

703-519-9691; Fax: 703-519-1872
fafgrants@asafishing.org
www.fishamerica.org
Facebook, Twitter, Youtube

Gregg Walner, Chairman
Dave Bulthuis, Vice Chairman
Donn Schaible, Secretary
Jim Hubbard, Treasurer
Jeff Marble, Immediate Past President

The sportfishing industry's trade association, committed to looking out for the interests of the entire sportfishing community.
650+ Members
Founded in 1962

9188 **Fishermen's Marketing Association**
1585 Heartwood Drive
Suite E
McKinleyville, CA 95519

707-840-0182; Fax: 707-840-0539
fma@trawl.org
www.trawl.org

Peter Leipzig, Executive Director

Represents commercial groundfish and shrimp fishermen from San Pedro, California to Bellingham, Washington. The mission is to engage in activities which promote stable prices and an orderly flow of wholesome seafood to the consumer
60 Members
Founded in 1952

9189 **Fishing Vessel Owners Association**
4005 20th Ave W
Room 232
Seattle, WA 98199

206-284-4720; Fax: 206-283-3341
www.fvoa.org

Per Odegaard, President
Paul Clampitt, Vice-President
John Crowley, Secretary/Treasurer
Robert D. Alverson, Manager
Miachel Offerman, Trustee

Trade association of longline vessel operators which promotes safety at sea, habitat-friendly gear with minimum bycatch and ensures competitive pricing.
Founded in 1914

9190 **Garden State Seafood Association**
212 W State St
Trenton, NJ 08608

609-898-1100; Fax: 609-898-6070
www.gardenstateseafood.org
Facebook, Twitter

Ernie Panacek, President
Jeffrey Reichel, Vice-President
Greg DiDomenico, Executive Director
Rick Marks, Washington D.C. Representative
Scot Mackey, Trenton Representative

Dedicated to assure that New Jersey's marine resources are managed responsibly and are able to be enjoyed by anglers and seafood consumers for generations.
Founded in 1999

9191 **Great Lakes Fishery Commission**
2100 Commonwealth Blvd
Suite 100
Ann Arbor, MI 48105

734-662-3209; Fax: 734-741-2010
info@glfc.org
www.glfc.int
Facebook, Twitter

Michael Hansen, Chairman
Dale Burkett, Director
Steve Domeracki, Manager
Robert (Bob) Lambe, Executive Secretary
Ted Treska, Information Manager

The commission has two major responsibilities; to develop coordinated programs of research on the Great Lakes and to formulate and implement a program to eradicate or minimize sea lamprey populations in the Great Lakes.
Founded in 1955
Mailing list available for rent

9192 **Gulf and Caribbean Fisheries Institute (GCFI)**
2796 Overseas Highway
Suite 119
Marathon, FL 33050

305-289-2330; Fax: 305-289-2334
bob.glazer@gcfi.org
www.gcfi.org
Facebook

Gracia Garcia-Moliner, Chairman
Nancy Brown-Peterson, Vice Chair
LeRoy Cresswel, Executive Secretary
Mel Goodwin, PhD, Treasurer
Bob Glazer, Executive Director

Provides information exchange among governmental, non-governmental, academic and commerical users of marine resources in the Gulf and Carribean Region
950 Members
Founded in 1947

9193 **Gulf of Mexico Fishery Management Council**
2203 N Lois Avenue
Suite 1100
Tampa, FL 33607

813-348-1630
888-833-1844; Fax: 813-348-1711
gulfcouncil@gulfcouncil.org
www.gulfcouncil.org
Facebook

Doug Gregory, Executive Director
Carrie Simons, Deputy Executive Director
Charlene Ponce, Public Information Officer
Cathy Readinger, Administrative Officer
Beth Hager, Financial Assistant

The council preserves fishery plans which are designed to manage fishery resources from where state waters end out to the 200 mile limit of the Gulf of Mexico.
Founded in 1976

9194 **ICFA-USA**
Home Page: internationalcarpfishingassociation.com
David Moore, ICFA USA Representative
The International Carp Fishing Association promotes carp angling worldwide.
Founded in 2004

9195 **International Institute of Fisheries Economics and Trade**
Dept of Agricultural & Resource Economic
Oregon State University
Corvallis, OR 97331-3601
541-737-1416; Fax: 541-737-2563
iifet@oregonstate.edu
www.oregonstate.edu/dept/iifet
Ann L Shriver, Executive Director
Dr. Rebecca Metzner, President
Dr. Ralph Townsend, President-Elect
Kara Keenan, Assistant
An international group of economists, government managers, private industry members, and others interested in the exchange of research and information on marine resource issues. Founded to promote interaction and exchange between people from all countries and professional disciplines about marine resource economics and trade issues.
Founded in 1982

9196 **National Fisheries Institute**
7918 Jones Branch Dr
Suite 700
Mc Lean, VA 22102-3319
703-752-8890; Fax: 703-752-7583
www.sirfonline.org
Facebook, Twitter, LinkedIn
Russ Mentzer, Chairman
Eric Bloom, Director
Jim Bonnvie, Director
Pete Cardone, Director
Dan DiDonato, Director
Members are farmers, food processors and food distributors with an interest in aquaculture.
Founded in 1964

9197 **National Seafood Educators**
PO Box 93
Shamokawa, WA 98647
206-546-6410; Fax: 206-546-6411
Evie Hansen, Founder
The goal is to educate and inform the public about the many health benefits of a seafood diet. National Seafood Educators has also consulted with many seafood retail businesses on how to sell, store and prepare wholesome seafood.
Founded in 1977

9198 **National Shellfisheries Association**
c/o US EPA, Atlantic Ecology Division
27 Tazewell Drive
Narragansett, RI 02880
631-653-6327; Fax: 631-653-6327
webmaster@shellfish.org
www.shellfish.org
Karolyn Mueller Hansen, President
Steven M. Allen, President-Elect
Shirley Baker, Vice-President
Lisa Milke, Secretary
John Scarpa, Treasurer
An international organization of scientists, management officials and members of industry, all deeply concerned with the biology, ecology, production, economics and management of shellfish resources-clams, oysters, mussels, scallops, snails, shrimp, lobsters, crabs, among many other species of commercial importance.
Cost: $85.00
1000 Members
Frequency: Membership Fee
Founded in 1908

9199 **North Carolina Fisheries Association**
PO Box 335
Bayboro, NC 28515-0335
252-745-0225; Fax: 252-745-0258
peggy@ncfish.org
www.ncfish.org
Brent Fulcher, Chairman
Karolyn Mueller Hansen, President
Leslie Daniel, Treasurer
Peggy C. Page, Accounting Manager
Lauren Morris, Membership and Operations Manager
Non-profit trade organization created to facilitate the promotion of North Carolina families, heritage and seafood through accessible data about the commercial fishing industry. NCFA lobbies Local, State, and Federal legislators and engages in a wide scope of public awareness projects.
Founded in 1952

9200 **Pacific Coast Federation of Fishermen's Association**
Building 991, Marine Drive, Crissy Field
PO Box 29370
San Francisco, CA 94129-0370
415-561-5080; Fax: 415-561-5464
fish1ifr@aol.com
www.pcffa.org
Zeke Grader, Executive Director
David Bitts, President
Vivian Helliwell, Watershed Conservation Director
Glen Spain, Northwest Regional Director
Mitch Farro, Fishey Enhancement Director
Commercial fishermen's organizations from California to Alaska. Works to prevent and improve the resources of the commercial fishing industry, protect rivers from herbicide and pesticide applications that may threaten salmon populations, maintain activity within the industry, regain local control over fisheries management.
22 Members
Founded in 1976

9201 **Pacific Seafood Processors Association**
1900 West Emerson Place
Suite 205
Seattle, WA 98119
206-281-1667; Fax: 206-283-2387
info@pspafish.net
www.pspafish.net
Glenn Reed, President
Nancy Diaz, Administrative Assistant
Trade association to foster a better public understanding of the seafood industry and its value to the regional and national economies.
25 Members
Founded in 1914

9202 **Recreational Fishing Alliance**
Po Box 3080
New Gretna, NJ 08224
609-404-1060
888-564-6732; Fax: 609-294-3812
www.joinrfa.org
Jim Donofrio, Executive Director
John DePersenaire, Researcher
Jim Martin, West Coast Regional Director
Gary Caputi, Corporate Relations Director
An organization that supports and fights back against federal government state legislatures impose unreasonable restrictions on our ability to enjoy recreational fishing.
Frequency: $35/Membership

9203 **Southeastern Fisheries Association**
1118-B Thomasville Rd.
Tallahassee, FL 32303
850-224-0612; Fax: 850-222-3663
www.seafoodsustainability.us
Bob Jones, Executive Director
To defend, preserve and enhance the commercial fishing industry in the southeastern United States for present participants as well as future generations through all legal means.
Founded in 1952

9204 **The International Game Fish Association**
300 Gulf Stream Way
3rd Fl.
Dania Beach, FL 33004
954-927-2628; Fax: 954-924-4299
www.igfa.org
Rob Kramer, President
Michael J. Myatt, Chief Operating Officer
A nonprofit organization that advocates for a sustainable game fishing industry.

9205 **West Coast Seafood Processors Association**
650 NE Holladay St.
Suite 1600
Portland, OR 97232
503-227-5076; Fax: 503-296-2824
lori.wcseafood@gmail.com
www.wcspa.com
Lori Steele, Executive Director
Susan Chambers, Deputy Director
Kim Lowman, Executive Assistant
Serves the needs of the shore-based seafood processors in California, Oregon and Washington, helping them to face and survive economic, environmental and regulatory challenges.
13 Members

9206 **Women's Fisheries Network**
2442 NW Market Street
#243
Seattle, WA 98107
206-789-1987; Fax: 206-789-1987
www.fis.com/wfn
Nancy Munro, President
Men and women dedicated to education of issues confronting the fishing and seafood industry.
2000 Members
Founded in 1993

Newsletters

9207 **American Sportfishing**
American Sportfishing Association
1001 North Fairfax Street
Suite 501
Alexandria, VA 22314
703-519-9691; Fax: 703-519-1872
info@asafishing.org
www.asafishing.org
Facebook
Mike Nussman, President/CEO
Joyce Anderson-Logan, Executive Assistant
Gordon Robertson, Vice President
Diane Carpenter, Chief Financial Officer
Provides a broader view of the activities of ASA and our partners. Includes information about in-

dustry news, events, perspectives and trends that affect the sportfishing community.
Frequency: Bi-Monthly

9208 **Aquaculture North America**
Capamara Communications
815 1st Ave
#301
Seattle, WA 98104
250-474-3982
800-936-2266; Fax: 250-478-3979
www.naqua.com
Peter Chetteburgh, Editor-in-Chief
Jeremy Thain, Sales Manager
James Lewis, Production Department
Follows the trends, issues, people and events that have set the pace for the fastest growing agribusiness sector on the continent. Coverage is relevant to all finfish and shellfish species grown in North America plus special reports from other regions around the world.
Cost: $27.95
Frequency: Bi-monthly
Circulation: 4000
Founded in 1985

9209 **Briefs**
American Institute of Fishery Research Biologists
205 Blades Road
Havelock, NC 28532
Home Page: www.aifrb.org
John Butler, Editor
John Merriner, Production Editor
It is intended to communicate the professional activities and accomplishments of the Institute, its District, and Members; the results of research; the effects of management; unusual biological events; matters affecting the profession; political problems and other matters of importance to the fishery community.
Frequency: Bi-Monthly

9210 **Commercial Fisheries News**
Compass Publications
Deer Isle, ME
800-989-5253; Fax: 207-348-1059
comfish@fish-news.com
www.fish-news.com
Richard W Martin, Publisher
Susan Jones, Editor
Provides the latest waterfront news along with coverage of the state and federal rules and regulations affecting the harvest of all the region's major species. Regular features include lobster and fish market reports, a safety column, new boats, the enforcement report, and the popular and effective classifieds section.
Cost: $21.95
72 Pages
Frequency: Monthly
Circulation: 9223
ISSN: 0273-6713
Founded in 1978
Printed in 4 colors on n stock

9211 **Crow's Nest**
Casamar Group/Holdings
8082 Firethorn Lane
Las Vegas, NV 89123
702-792-6868; Fax: 702-792-6668
www.casamargroup.com
Malu Marigomen, Executive Director
An in-depth report on the status of the Tuna Industry
Frequency: Monthly

9212 **Currents**
Women's Fisheries Network
2422 NW Market Square
Seattle, WA 98107
206-789-1987; Fax: 206-789-1987
www.fis.com/wfn
Debbie Slotivg, Editor
Ron Gawith, Owner
Features current topics in fisheries, members'activities, upcoming events and chapter reports.
Frequency: Monthly

9213 **Fish Farming News**
Compass Publications
Deer Isle, ME
800-989-5253; Fax: 207-348-1059
comfish@fish-news.com
www.fish-news.com
Richard W Martin, Publisher
Susan Jones, Editor
The business newspaper for the U.S. aquaculture industry. Readers are aquaculture professionals who are directly or indirectly involved in the business of growing fish and seafood products. Encompassing all major farm raised species (finfish, shellfish and aquatic plants) both marine (saltwater) and fresh water aquaculture.
Cost: $21.95
72 Pages
Frequency: Monthly
Circulation: 9223
ISSN: 0273-6713
Founded in 1978
Printed in 4 colors on n stock

9214 **Fisheries Focus**
Atlantic States Marine Fisheries Commission
1050 N Highland Street
Suite 200 A-N
Arlington, VA 22201
703-842-0740; Fax: 703-842-0741
info@asmfc.org
www.asmfc.org
Robert E. Beal, Executive Director
Tina L. Berger, Director of Communications
A monthly newsletter.
Frequency: Monthly

9215 **Fishermen's News**
PCFFA
Building 991, Marine Drive
PO Box 29370
San Francisco, CA 94129-0370
415-561-5080; Fax: 415-561-5464
fish1ifr@aol.com
www.pcffa.org
Zeke Grader, Executive Director
Chuck Wise, President
Oldest publication in the west coast commercial fishing industry. Deals with resource protection and policy issues of great importance to the fishing industry, as well as with critical Congressional issues which affect us all.
22 Members
Founded in 1976

9216 **Habitat Hotline Atlantic**
Atlantic States Marine Fisheries Commission
1050 N Highland Street
Suite 200 A-N
Arlington, VA 22201
703-842-0740; Fax: 703-842-0741
info@asmfc.org
www.asmfc.org
Robert E. Beal, Executive Director
Tina L. Berger, Director of Communications
An annual newsletter.
Frequency: Annually

9217 **IIFET Newsletter**
International Institute of Fisheries Economics
Dept of Agricultural & Resource Economic
Oregon State University
Corvallis, OR 97331-3601
541-737-1439; Fax: 541-737-2563
iifet@oregonstate.edu
www.oregonstate.edu/dept/iifet
Provides conference listings, news items, and information on new publications and the activities of members.
20 Pages
Frequency: Semi-Annual
ISSN: 1048-9509

9218 **Littorally Speaking**
American Littoral Society Northeast Chapter
28 W 9th Rd
Broad Channel, NY 11693-1112
718-318-9344; Fax: 718-318-9345
www.alsnyc.org
Don Riepe, Executive Director
A digest of environmental concerns

9219 **Makin' Waves Quarterly Newsletter**
Recreational Fishing Alliance
PO Box 3080
New Gretna, NJ 08224
609-404-1060
888-564-6732; Fax: 609-294-3812
www.joinrfa.org
James Donofrio, Executive Director
Gary Caputi, Corporate Relations Director
Courtney Howell Thompson, Marketing Coordinator/PR
This RFA paper has proven that fish and fishermen are not the only variables in the equation of fisheries management.
Frequency: $35/Membership

9220 **NSA Newsletter**
National Shellfisheries Association
c/o US EPA, Atlantic Ecology Division
27 Tazewell Drive
Narragansett, RI 02880
401-782-3155; Fax: 401-782-3030
news@shellfish.org
www.shellfish.org
Dr Evan Ward, Editor
Current issues and concerns in shellfish research and in the shellfish industry, including details regarding upcoming meetings, employment listings, and gossip items for our Metamorphoses column.

9221 **National Shellfisheries Association Quarterly Newsletter**
National Shellfisheries Association
C/O US EPA, Atlantic Ecology Division
27 Tazewell Drive
Narragansett, RI 02880
631-653-6327; Fax: 631-653-6327
www.shellfish.org
R. LeRoy Creswell, President
Christopher V. Davis, President-Elect
George E. Flimlin, VP & Program Chair
Marta Gomez-Chiarri, Secretary
An informative newsletter for the shellfish industry, shellfish managers and shellfish researchers.
Cost: $85.00
1000 Members
Frequency: Membership Fee
Founded in 1908

9222 **PSPA Update**
Pacific Seafood Processors Association

1900 W Emerson Pl
Suite 205
Seattle, WA 98119-1649

206-281-1667; Fax: 206-283-2387
info@pspafish.net
www.pspafish.net

Glenn Reed, President

Daily news update for major seafood processing companies with operations in Alaska and Washington.
25 Members
Founded in 1914

9223 **Tradewinds**
North Carolina Fisheries Association
PO Box 12303
New Bern, NC 28561

252-633-2288; Fax: 252-633-9616
peggy@ncfish.org
www.ncfish.org

Sean McKeon, President
Peggy C Page, Bookkeeper

Members only newspaper, which includes special bulletins regarding legislative issues and various articles concerning fisheries issues.
24 Pages
Frequency: Bi-Monthly

9224 **Wheel Watch**
Fishing Vessel Owners Association
4005 20th Ave W
Room 232, West Wall Bldg
Seattle, WA 98199-1273

206-284-4720; Fax: 206-283-3341
www.fvoa.org

Robert D. Alverson, Manager
Carol M. Batteen, Executive Assistant

Brings you up-to-date with regards to action of the Halibut Commission, North Pacific Council, Pacific Council, and market information.
Frequency: Quarterly

Magazines & Journals

9225 **Aquaculture North America**
Capamara Communications
PO Box 1409
Arden, NC 28704

250-474-3982
877-687-0011; Fax: 250-478-3979
aquaculturenorthamerica.com

Gregory J Gallagher, Editor/Publisher
Rebekah Craig, Circulation Manager
Brenda Jo McManama, Advertising/Sales

Earning the respect of aquaculture industry professionals throughout the world who hold its trade publications in high regard.
Cost: $24.00
96 Pages
Frequency: Annually/Summer
Circulation: 5000
ISSN: 0199-1388
Founded in 1968

9226 **Atlantic Fisherman**
Advocate Media Publishing
181 Brown's Point Road
Nova Scotia B0K-1H0

902-485-1990
800-236-9526; Fax: 902-485-6353
www.atlanticfisherman.com
Twitter

Susan Purdy, Publications Manager

Provides news for the commercial fisherman in the four Atlantic provinces of Canada. Includes prespectives from the unions, the government and the fishermen themselves.
Cost: $16.00
Frequency: Monthly
Circulation: 9950

9227 **Bass Times**
Bass Anglers Sportsman Society
3500 Blue Lake Drive
Suite 330
Birmingham, AL 35243

334-272-9530
877-227-7872; Fax: 334-279-7148
www.bassmaster.com
Facebook, Twitter

Dean Kassel, President
Chris Horton, Associate Director

Each issue includes; detailed, in-depth tips & techniques, bass biology, conservation news, BASS Federation Nation news, Bassmaster Tournament Trail coverage, and Legislation coverage.
Cost: $14.95
600M Members
Frequency: Annual Membership Fee
Founded in 1972

9228 **Catfish Journal**
Catfish Farmers of America
6311 Ridgewood Road
Suite W404
Jackson, MS 39211

601-977-9559; Fax: 601-977-9632
www.uscatfish.com
Facebook, Twitter

Mike McCall, Editor
Sandra Goff, Production Manager

News on catfish production, processing, feed manufacturing and research.
Frequency: Monthly

9229 **Connect Magazine**
American Zoo and Aquarium Association
8403 Colesville Rd
Suite 710
Silver Spring, MD 20910-6331

301-562-0777; Fax: 301-562-0888
www.aza.org

Dan Ashe, President & CEO

For the professional zoo and aquarium world. This magazine features fascinating stories that explore trends, educational initiatives, member achievements and conservation efforts.
200 Members
Frequency: Monthly
Circulation: 6000

9230 **Esox Angler**
Esox Angler
PO Box 895
Hayward, WI 54843

715-638-2311

Jack Burns, Senior Editor
Rob Kimm, Editor

A muskie and pike magazine for the world's muskie and pike anglers. Articles focusing on proven techniques and new ideas from top name anglers, as well as regular guys who are catching lots of fish.

9231 **Fish Sniffer**
3201 Eastwood Road
Sacramento, CA 95821

916-685-2245; Fax: 916-685-1498
danielbacher@fishsniffer.com
www.fishsniffer.com
Facebook

Dan Bacher, Editor
Cal Kellogg, Associate Editor

Current fishing reports, weather conditions, fishing news, photos, boats for sale, what and where to fish and much more.
Cost: $29.00
Frequency: Bi-Weekly

9232 **Fisheries**
American Fisheries Society
425 Barlow Place
Suite 110
Bethesda, MD 20814-2144

301-897-8616; Fax: 301-897-8096
main@fisheries.org
fisheries.org
Facebook, Twitter, LinkedIn

Douglas Austen, Executive Director
Erin Del Collo, Membership Coordinator
Laura Hendee, Journals Production Manager

Peer reviewed articles that address contemporary issues and problems, techniques, philosophies and other areas of interest to the general fisheries profession. Monthly features include letters, meeting notices, book listings and reviews, environmental essays and organization profiles.
Cost: $76.00
50 Pages
Frequency: Monthly
Founded in 1870
Mailing list available for rent

9233 **Fishermen's News**
Philips Publishing Group
2201 W Commodore Way
Seattle, WA 98199-1298

206-284-8285; Fax: 206-284-0391
circulation@rhppublishing.com
www.pacmar.com

Peter Philips, Publisher
Lisa Albers, Editor
Maggie Cheung, Circulatiom Manager

Covers commercial fishing activity, market trends, gear and boat building news, political news and financial matters related to the industry.
Founded in 1945

9234 **Fly Fisherman**
InterMedia Outdoors Inc
PO Box 420235
Palm Coast, FL 32142-0235

212-852-6600
www.flyfisherman.com
Facebook, Twitter

Jeff Paro, President

From the deepest bass ponds, wildest rivers or abundant saltwater flats, America's fishing sportsmen rely on this magazine to provide them with the newest techniques, tools and tips whenever and wherever they need this information.
Cost: $19.95
Frequency: Annually
Founded in 1969

9235 **IAFWA Proceedings**
International Association of Fish and Wildlife
444 N Capitol St NW
Suite 725
Washington, DC 20001-1553

202-638-7999; Fax: 202-638-7291
www.statenet.com

Wayne Muhlstein, VP
Eric Schwaab, Resource Director

Reports on the business transacted by the Association at its March meeting held in conjunction with the North American Wildlife and Natural Resources Conference and at its September annual conference.

9236 **In-Fisherman**
InterMedia Outdoors Inc

PO Box 420235
Palm Coast, FL 420235

218-829-1648
ross.purnell@imoutdoors.com
www.in-fisherman.com
Facebook, Twitter

Ross Purnell, Editor

Written for the avid freshwater angler. In each issue, you'll find detailed instructions and demonstrations on catching, cleaning, and eating your favorite species of fish, and reports on the latest scientific studies concerning fish and habitat conservation.
Cost: $12.00
Frequency: 8x/year
Founded in 1975

9237 **Island Fisherman**
610 Azalea Place
Campbell River
BC Canada V9W 7H2

250-923-0939
www.islandfishermanmagazine.com

Larry E Stefanyk, Founder/Publisher
Bob Jones, Editor

Covering the west coast of British Columbia from the Queen Charlottes to Victoria on Vancouver Island. Covering saltwater and freshwater fishing with how to and where to tips to help you find the big one or just experience what the west coast of British Columbia has to offer.
Cost: $40.00
Frequency: Monthly
Founded in 2001

9238 **Journal of Aquatic Animal Health**
American Fisheries Society
425 Barlow Place
Suite 110
Bethesda, MD 20814-2144

301-897-8616; Fax: 301-897-8096
main@fisheries.org
fisheries.org
Facebook, Twitter

Douglas Austen, Executive Director
Erin Del Collo, Membership Coordinator
Laura Hendee, Journals Production Manager

International journal publishing original research on diseases affecting aquatic life, including effects, treatments and prevention.
Cost: $100.00
Frequency: Membership Fee

9239 **Marine and Coastal Fisheries**
American Fisheries Society
425 Barlow Place
Suite 110
Bethesda, MD 20814-2144

301-897-8616; Fax: 301-897-8096
main@fisheries.org
fisheries.org
Facebook, Twitter

Douglas Austen, Executive Director
Erin Del Collo, Membership Coordinator
Laura Hendee, Journals Production Manager

Online publication focusing on marine, coastal, and estuarine fisheries.
Cost: $100.00
Frequency: Membership Fee

9240 **Marlin**
World Publications
460 N Orlando Avenue
Suite 200
Winter Park, FL 32789

407-628-4802; Fax: 407-628-7061
www.marlinmag.com/www.worldpub.net

Dave Ferrell, Editor
Glen Hughes, Group Publisher
Terry Snow, Owner

The bible for big-game fishermen. It is written for the most affluent anglers who need to know what is happening around the world regarding offshore fishing. It is the who's who of the sport, written in the voice of the sportfisherman, one-on-one to a peer, as a member of this elite fraternity. Marlin magazine will continue to be the No. 1 buy in big-game fishing by delivering the best targeted edit to the wealthiest boat-owning saltwater fishermen in the world.
Cost: $24.95
Frequency: 8x/year
Circulation: 40,000

9241 **National Fisherman**
Diversified Business Communications
Po Box 7437
Portland, ME 04112-7437

207-842-5600; Fax: 207-842-5503
editor@nationalfisherman.com
www.nationalfisherman.com
Facebook, Twitter

Nancy Hasselback, President/CEO
Lincoln Bedrosian, Senior Editor

Regional coverage of boats, fishing gear, environmental developments, technology, new products, and fishery resource information
Cost: $19.95
Frequency: Monthly
Circulation: 38,000
Founded in 1903

9242 **North American Journal of Aquaculture**
American Fisheries Society
425 Barlow Place
Suite 110
Bethesda, MD 20814-2144

301-897-8616; Fax: 301-897-8096
main@fisheries.org
fisheries.org
Facebook, Twitter

Douglas Austen, Executive Director
Erin Del Collo, Membership Coordinator
Laura Hendee, Journals Production Manager

Publishes research in all areas of fish culture.
Cost: $38.00
Frequency: Quarterly
ISSN: 1548-8454

9243 **North American Journal of Fisheries Management**
American Fisheries Society
425 Barlow Place
Suite 110
Bethesda, MD 20814-2144

301-897-8616; Fax: 301-897-8096
main@fisheries.org
fisheries.org
Facebook, Twitter

Douglas Austen, Executive Director
Erin Del Collo, Membership Coordinator
Laura Hendee, Journals Production Manager

Promotes communication among managers. Published with a focus on maintenance, enhancement, and allocation of resources.
Cost: $100.00
8500 Members
Frequency: Membership Fee
Founded in 1870

9244 **Outdoor Journal**
American Crappie Association
125 Ruth Avenue
Benton, KY 42025

270-395-4204; Fax: 270-395-4381
office@crappieusa.com
www.crappieusa.com

Darrell VanVactor, President
Larry Crecelius, Public Relations Director

Features news and updates on memberships, events, tournaments, and more for crappie anglers from amateurs to professionals.
Frequency: Annually
Circulation: 60000

9245 **Pacific Fishing**
Pacific Fishing
1000 Andover Park E
Seattle, WA 98188-7632

206-324-5644; Fax: 206-324-8939
www.pacificfishing.com

Michael Daigle, Owner
Jon Holland, Editor
Duane Brady, es & Marketing Manager

Serving owners and operators of commercial fishing boats throughout the world's most productive ocean, from Alaska to the tropical Pacific. Our readers also include crew members, processors, fisheries managers, suppliers, seafood brokers and distributors, educators, and others who want serious information about the business of hauling up food from the Pacific.
Cost: $15.00
Frequency: Monthly
Circulation: 7160
Founded in 1980

9246 **SaltWater**
Time, Inc.
2 Park Avenue
New York, NY 10016

212-221-1212; Fax: 212-779-5999
editor@saltwatersportsman.com
www.saltwatersportsman.com

David DiBenedetto, Editor
Gerald Bethge, Executive Editor
Jason Y Wood, Managing Editor
Karl Anderson, Senior Editor

A publication on salt-water sport fishing. Each monthly issue contains exciting feature stories, columns, award-winning color photos covering both big- and small-game fishing, the newest techniques, tackle, boats and equipment, and the latest developments in conservation and fishery management.
Founded in 1939

9247 **Saltwater Sportsman**
World Publications
460 N Orlando Avenue
Suite 200
Winter Park, FL 32789

407-628-4802; Fax: 407-628-7061
www.marlinmag.com/www.worldpub.net
Facebook, Twitter

Dave Ferrell, Editor
Glen Hughes, Group Publisher
Terry Snow, Owner

Designed for serious recreational salt water fishermen who demand the most accurate and detailed information available on inshore and offshore fishing from boats. Articles cover the entire spectrum of boat and tackle rigging, tactics and methods for catching game fish, travel, boat and equipment reviews, U.S. regional/ local coverage, and fisheries management and conservation.
Cost: $24.95
Frequency: 8x/year
Circulation: 40,000

9248 **Sea Technology Magazine**
Compass Publications, Inc.
4600 N. Fairfax Drive
Suite 304
Arlington, VA 22203-1553

703-524-3136; Fax: 703-841-0852
oceanbiz@sea-technology.com

www.sea-technology.com
Twitter

Amos Bussmann, President/Publisher
Leslie Carr, Circulation Manager
Aileen Torres-Bennett, Managing Editor

Worldwide information leader for marine/offshore business, science and engineering. Read in more than 110 countries by management, engineers, scientists and technical personnel working in industry, government and education.
Cost: $40.00
Frequency: Monthly
Circulation: 16304
ISSN: 0093-3651
Founded in 1960
Mailing list available for rentat $80 per M
Printed in 4 colors

9249 **Seafood Business**
Diversified Business Communications
121 Free Street
PO Box 7438
Portland, ME 04112-7437

207-842-5542
mlarkin@divcom.com
Facebook, Twitter, LinkedIn

Mary Larkin, Publisher
Fiona Robinson, Associate Publisher, Editor
James Wright, Associate Editor
Melissa Wood, Assistant Editor

Focuses on the business of buying and selling seafood and provides seafood buyers with the tools and analysis they need to make educated safood buying decisions.
Frequency: Monthly
Circulation: 15,000
Founded in 1982

9250 **Sport Fishing**
World Publications
460 N Orlando Avenue
Winter Park, FL 32789

407-628-4802; Fax: 407-628-7061
editor@sportfishingmag.com
www.sportfishingmag.com
Facebook, Twitter

Glenn Hughes, Group Publisher
Bruce Miller, Circulation VP
Terry Snow, Owner

Written for the passionate angler who must have in-depth, cutting-edge information on the latest techniques, the hottest locations and the newest equipment to maximize his day on the water, Sport Fishing magazine is the source for saltwater fishing information.
Cost: $19.97
Frequency: 10x/year
Circulation: 150,000
Founded in 2001

9251 **The Fisherman**
326 12th Street
1st Floor
New Westminster, BC V3M-4H6

604-669-5569; Fax: 604-688-1142
fisherman@ufawu.org
Facebook, Twitter, YouTube

Sean Griffin, Editor
Suzanne Thomson, Advertising Manager

Covering saltwater and freshwater fishing from Maine through Delaware Bay. Local fishing reports.
Frequency: Monthly
Circulation: 8000

9252 **Transactions of the American Fisheries Society**
American Fisheries Society
425 Barlow Place
Suite 110
Bethesda, MD 20814-2144

301-897-8616; Fax: 301-897-8096
main@fisheries.org
fisheries.org

Douglas Austen, Executive Director
Erin Del Collo, Membership Coordinator
Laura Hendee, Journals Production Manager

Features results of basic and applied research in genetics, physiology, biology, ecology, population dynamics, economics, health, culture, and other topics germane to marine and freshwater finfish and shellfish and their respective fisheries and environments.
Cost: $43.00
Frequency: Bi-Monthly
ISSN: 0002-8487
Founded in 1872

Trade Shows

9253 **ASA Sportfishing Summit**
American Sportfishing Association
225 Reinekers Lane
Suite 420
Alexandria, VA 22314

703-519-9691; Fax: 703-519-1872
info@asafishing.org
www.asafishing.org

Mary Jane Williamson, Communications Director
Amy Yohanes, Administrative Services Manager

Membership meeting and premier networking event. From special sessions, to busiess workshops to association committee meeting, the Summit provides a wide-range of opportunities to gain information on the most relevant issues facing the sportfishing industry.
Frequency: October

9254 **ASA/Eastern Fishing & Outdoor Exposition**
American Sportfishing Association
1001 North Fairfax Street
Suite 501
Alexandria, VA 22314

703-519-9691; Fax: 703-519-1872
info@asafishing.org
www.asafishing.org
Facebook

Mike Nussman, President/CEO
Joyce Anderson-Logan, Executive Assistant
Gordon Robertson, Vice President
Diane Carpenter, Chief Financial Officer

The finest sportsmen's expos on the East Coast. The best outdoor gear, accessories and resources for fishing, boating, hunting, adventure and travel are available at these shows. The only sport shows where 100 percent of the proceeds go to safeguarding and promoting the enduring social, economic and conservation values of America's outdoor heritage.
Frequency: Bi-Monthly

9255 **AZA Regional Conference**
American Zoo and Aquarium Association
8403 Colesville Road
Suite 710
Silver Spring, MD 20910-3314

301-562-0777; Fax: 301-562-0888
www.aza.org

Dan Ashe, President & CEO

Exhibits, workshops and discussions about the industry.
200 Members
Founded in 1924

9256 **Annual Fish Baron's Ball**
North Carolina Fisheries Association
PO Box 12303
New Bern, NC 28561

252-745-0225; Fax: 252-633-9616
www.ncfish.org

Billy Carl Tillett, Chairman
Sherrill Styron, Vice Chairman
Sean McKeon, President
Janice Smith, Treasurer

Attendees getting together for an evening of great seafood and fun, and participate in the silent auction. Program proceeds go toward Association-related activities.
Founded in 1952

9257 **CFA Fish Farming Trade Show**
Catfish Farmers of America
1100 Highway 82 E
Suite 202
Indianola, MS 38751

662-887-2699; Fax: 662-887-6857

America's largest fish farming equipment expo.
Frequency: February

9258 **Catfish Farmers of America Annual Convention & Research Symposium**
Catfish Farmers of America
1100 Highway 82 E
Suite 202
Indianola, MS 38751-2251

662-887-2699; Fax: 662-887-6857
www.catfishfarmersofamerica.org

Hugh Warren, President

Opportunity to launch new products, meet new buyers, learn emerging trends and access the North American seafood market.
Frequency: Membership Fee
Founded in 1968

9259 **Eastern Fishing & Outdoor Expo**
Eastern Fishing & Outdoor Expositions
PO Box 4720
Portsmouth, NH 00380

603-431-4315; Fax: 603-431-1971
info@sportshows.com
www.sportshows.com

Paul Fuller, President/Show Director
Judy L Chapman, Assistant Show Director

Partnership with American Sportfishing Association. Exhibitors representing the entire spectrum of saltwater sportfishing. This includes inshore to offshore, light tackle to big-game tackle, and everything in between. Fishermen will see and touch the latest from major tackle manufacturers and buy the latest tackle from local retailers at special show prices.

9260 **Fish Expo Workboat Atlantic**
National Fisherman/Diversified Bus. Communications
121 Free Street
PO Box 7437
Portland, ME 04112

207-425-5608; Fax: 207-842-5509

Bob Callahan, Show Director
Heather Palmeter, Show Coordinator

Newest products and technology, attend free seminars and workshops, talk to technical experts, and find the best deals on equipment and gear.
6,000 Attendees
Frequency: April

9261 **Fly-Fishing Retailer World Trade Expo**
VNU Expositions/Business Media

770 Broadway
New York, NY 10003

646-545-5100
nielsen.com/us/en.html

Andy Tompkins, Show Director
Peter Devin, Group Show Director

Where brands are launched, innovations are unveiled and connections are made. Designed for the specialty fly-fishing industry, Fly-Fishing Retailer World Trade Expo connects a targeted audience to conduct business in a professional yet friendly atmosphere.
Frequency: August
Founded in 1998

9262 **IAFWA Annual Meeting**
International Association of Fish and Wildlife
444 North Capitol Street NW
Suite 725
Washington, DC 20001

202-624-7890; Fax: 202-624-7891
www.fishwildlife.org

Gary T Myers, Executive Director
Cindy Delaney, Meetings Coordinator
Wayne Muhlstein, VP

Providing many opportunities to hear from our nation's wildlife conservation leaders, partners, and management experts. The meeting is our response to the need for national consensus on state-by-state fish and wildlife management issues.
250 Attendees
Frequency: September

9263 **ICAST**
American Sportfishing Association
225 Reinekers Lane
Suite 420
Alexandria, VA 22314

703-519-9691; Fax: 703-519-1872
mdelvalle@asafishing.org
www.asafishing.org

Maria del Valle, ICAST Director
Kenneth Andres, ICAST Associate

The sportfishing industry's largest trade event is a major catalyst for sales and a terrific networking opportunity for the sportfishing community.

9264 **IIFET Biennial International Conference**
IIFET
Dept of Agricultural & Resource Economic
Oregon State University
Corvallis, OR 97331-3601

541-737-1416; Fax: 541-737-2563
iifet@oregonstate.edu
www.oregonstate.edu/dept/iifet

Ann L Shriver, Executive Director
Dr. Rebecca Metzner, President
Dr. Ralph Townsend, President-Elect

An important forum for members and others to learn about important research developments in seafood trade, aquaculture, and fisheries management issues. Attended by fisheries social scientists, managers, and industry members from all of the world's fishing areas. Provides participants with unparalleled opportunities to interact with the world's foremost fisheries economists in both formal and informal settings. Learn more about fishing and aquaculture activities across the globe.
Founded in 1982

9265 **IPHC Annual Meeting**
Pacific Seafood Processors Association
1900 West Emerson Place
Suite 205
Seattle, WA 98119-1649

206-281-1667; Fax: 206-283-2387
www.pspafish.net

Glenn Reed, President

Annual members meeting to discuss catch limits each year.
25 Members
Founded in 1914

9266 **International Boston Seafood Show**
Diversified Business Communications
PO Box 7437
Portland, ME 04112-7437

207-842-5504; Fax: 207-842-5505
customerservice@divcom.com

Diane Vassar, Promotions Director
David Lowell, President

This event attracts top-tier buyers and sellers of seafood. You will find exhibit categories representing every aspect of seafood including; seafood, seafood equipment, services and organizations and seafood packaging.
20M Attendees
Frequency: March/Silver Pkg $250

9267 **International Convention of Allied Sportfishing Trades (ICAST)**
American Sportfishing Association
1001 North Fairfax Street
Suite 501
Alexandria, VA 22314

703-519-9691; Fax: 703-519-1872
info@asafishing.org
www.asafishing.org
Facebook

Mike Nussman, President/CEO
Joyce Anderson-Logan, Executive Assistant
Gordon Robertson, Vice President
Diane Carpenter, Chief Financial Officer

World's largest sportfishing trade show, representing the cornerstone of the sportfishing industry, driving sportfishing companies' product sales year round and is the showcase for the latest innovations in gear and accessories.
Frequency: Bi-Monthly

9268 **International Fly Tackle Dealer Show**
American Fly Fishing Trade Association
901 Front St.
Suite B-125
Louisville, CO 80027

303-604-6132; Fax: 303-604-6162
www.affta.com

Randi Swisher, President
Gary Berlin, Business Manager
Jim Klug, Chairman

The largest international gathering of fly fishing manufacturers, retailers, sales reps, media and fly fishing organizations in the world. Best venue to meet with the industry, people, products, innovations, emerging trends and the leading brand presentations, latest gear, equipment, waders, fly like, tippet and accessories for the upcoming season.
400 Members
Founded in 2003

9269 **International West Coast Seafood Show**
Diversified Business Communications
PO Box 7437
Portland, ME 04112-7437

207-842-5500; Fax: 207-842-5503
mlarkin@divcom.com
www.westcoastseafood.com

Mary Larkin, VP Seafood Expositions

A total resource for seafood industry leaders; showcases the latest seafood products and equipment from the US, Pacific Rim and beyond.
Frequency: October
Founded in 1996

9270 **NSA Annual Meeting**
National Shellfisheries Association
c/o US EPA, Atlantic Ecology Division
27 Tazewell Drive
Narragansett, RI 02880

401-782-3155; Fax: 401-782-3030
news@shellfish.org
www.shellfish.org

Dr Lou D'Abramo, President
Christopher Davis, Treasurer

A time and place to interact with other associations and industry people.
Frequency: Spring

9271 **National River Rally**
American Sportfishing Association
225 Reinekers Ln
Suite 420
Alexandria, VA 22314-2875

703-519-9691; Fax: 703-519-1872
info@asafishing.org
www.fishamerica.org

Mike Nussman, President/CEO
Diane Carpenter, CFO
Gordon Robertson, Vice President

The premier national event to come together to learn, inspire and celebrate the passionate work of all things rivers and watersheds. Trainings, field trips and a deeply moving River Heroes awards banquet honoring incredible River leaders.
650+ Members
Founded in 1962

9272 **Pacific Marine Expo**
Diversified Business Communications
121 Free Street
PO Box 7437
Portland, ME 04112

207-425-5608; Fax: 207-842-5509
www.pacificmarineexpo.com

Bob Callahan, Show Director
Heather Palmeter, Show Coordinator

A trade show dedicated to the pacific maritime industry that provides a gathering of marine products and services. With nearly 500 manufacturers and distributors showcasing the latest technologies and thousands of products for all commercial vessels, tugs, barges, boat building, marine construction, passenger vessels, seafood processing plants and more, PME is the best source for all marine business needs.
6,000 Attendees
Frequency: November

9273 **Seafood Processing America**
Catfish Farmers of America
1100 Highway 82 E
Suite 202
Indianola, MS 38751-2251

662-887-2699; Fax: 662-887-6857
www.catfishfarmersofamerica.org

Hugh Warren, President

Opportunity to launch new products, meet new buyers, learn emerging trends and access the North American seafood market.
Frequency: Membership Fee
Founded in 1968

9274 **Sportfishing Summit**
American Sportfishing Association

1001 North Fairfax Street
Suite 501
Alexandria, VA 22314

703-519-9691; Fax: 703-519-1872
info@asafishing.org
www.asafishing.org
Facebook

Mike Nussman, President/CEO
Joyce Anderson-Logan, Executive Assistant
Gordon Robertson, Vice President
Diane Carpenter, Chief Financial Officer

Where industry leaders met to discuss the issues impacting recreational fishing.
Frequency: Bi-Monthly

Directories & Databases

9275 **AZA Membership Directory**
American Zoo and Aquarium Association
8403 Colesville Rd
Suite 710
Silver Spring, MD 20910-3314

301-562-0777; Fax: 301-562-0888
membership@aza.org
www.aza.org
Facebook, Twitter

Melissa Howerton, SVP, Membership Services

Accredited institutions, professional affiliates, professional fellows, commercial members, related facilities and conservation partners receive one complimentary copy as a membership benefit.
Cost: $50.00
200 Members
Frequency: Annual
Founded in 1924

9276 **Angling America Database**
PO Box 22567
Alexandria, VA 22304
Home Page: www.anglingamerica.com

Stephen Aaron, Director
Austin Ducworth, Director

The most searchable database for fishing charters and guides across America.

9277 **Commercial Marine Directory & Fish Farmers Phone Book/ Directory**
Compass Publications
Deer Isle, ME

800-989-5253; Fax: 207-348-1059
comfish@fish-news.com
www.fish-news.com

Richard W Martin, Publisher
Susan Jones, Editor

Go-to-reference tools for commercial fishermen and fish farmers. Comprehensive listing of suppliers providing essential goods and services and convenient industry yellow pages.
Cost: $21.95
72 Pages
Frequency: Monthly
Circulation: 9223
ISSN: 0273-6713
Founded in 1978
Printed in 4 colors on n stock

9278 **IIFET Membership Directory**
International Institute of Fisheries Economics
Dept of Agricultural & Resource Economic
Oregon State University
Corvallis, OR 97331-3601

541-737-1416; Fax: 541-737-2563
iifet@oregonstate.edu
www.orst.edu/dept/iifet
Facebook, Twitter, LinkedIn, YouTube, Flickr

Ann L Shriver, Executive Director
Kara Kennan, Assistant Executive Director

This handbook lists all members with complete contact information, including an e-mail directory, plus areas of interest. Regular updates are provided with the newsletter.
Frequency: Biennial

9279 **Who's Who in the Fish Industry**
Urner Barry Publications
PO Box 389
Toms River, NJ 08754-0389

732-240-5330
800-932-0617; Fax: 732-341-0891
sales@urnerbarry.com
www.urnerbarry.com

Jay Bailey, Sales Manager
Janice Brown, Advertising Manager

The source for buying and selling contacts in the North American Seafood Industry. This 2006-2007 edition is fully updated and verified, boasting over 6,000 listings of seafood companies in the US and Canada. The directory boasts detailed information about each company listed such as products handled, contact names, product forms, product origin, sales volume, company website and much more.
Cost: $199.00
800 Pages
Frequency: Annual
ISSN: 0270-1600
Founded in 1979

Industry Web Sites

9280 **http://gold.greyhouse.com**
G.O.L.D Grey House OnLine Databases

Grey House Publishing's online database platform, GOLD, offers Quick Search, Keyword Search and Expert Search for most business sectors including fishing and food markets. The GOLD platform makes finding the information you need quick and easy - whether you're a novice searcher or an experienced database user. All of Grey House's directory products are available for subscription on the GOLD platform.

9281 **www.asafishing.org**
American Sportfishing Association

Manufacturers and importers of fishing tackle and allied products. Promotes fishing for children and adults. Compiles statistics. Sponsors National Fishing Week.

9282 **www.greyhouse.com**
Grey House Publishing

Authoritative reference directories for most businsee sectors including fishing and food markets. Users can search the online databases with varied search criteria allowing for custom searches by product category, geographic area, sales volume, keyword, subject and more. Full Grey House catalog and online ordering also available.

9283 **www.nauticalworld.com**

Dedicated to bringing all related web sites within easy access to watersports enthusiasts. This search engine has been designed to locate advertiser's information within Nautical World but will also offer access to other watersport related web sites as well. Offers sections on marine electronics and hardware, sailing, boats, dock supplies, fishing accessories, diving accessories, industry news, watersports, weather forecasting and more.

9284 **www.nfi.org**
National Fishing Institute

Promotes the shipping and production of fishery products in international trade.

9285 **www.pcffa.org**
Pacific Coast Federation of Fishermen's Assoc

Commercial fishermen's organizations from California to Alaska. Works to prevent and improve the resources of the commercial fishing industry, protect rivers from herbicide and pesticide applications that may threaten salmon populations, maintain activity within the industry, regain local control over fisheries management.

Associations

9286 **AACC International**
3340 Pilot Knob Road
St. Paul, MN 55121
651-454-7250
800-328-7560; Fax: 651-454-0766
aacc@scisoc.org
www.aaccnet.org
Facebook, Twitter, LinkedIn
Robert L. Cracknell, President
Lydia Tooker Midness, Chair
Laura M. Hansen, President-Elect
Dave L. Braun, Treasurer
Formerly the American Association of Cereal Chemists, a non-profit organization of members who are specialists in the use of cereal grains in foods.
Founded in 1915

9287 **ASI Food Safety Consultants**
7625 Page Avenue
St. Louis, MO 63133
314-725-2555
800-477-0778; Fax: 314-727-2563
www.asifood.com
Facebook, Twitter, LinkedIn
Tom Huge, President
Gary Huge, Vice President
Jane Griffith, Technical Director
Jeff Capell, GMP, Technical Director
Jeanette Huge, Director
A full service provider of food safety audits, GMP audits, seminars and HACCP setups, as well as HACCP verification. Thoroughly addresses every vital concern of your valuable facility including food safety, pest control, employee practices and facility conditions.
Founded in 1930

9288 **Academy of Nutrition and Dietetics**
120 S Riverside Plaza
Suite 2190
Chicago, IL 60606-6995
312-899-0040
800-877-1600
info@eatright.org
www.eatright.org
Facebook, Twitter, LinkedIn, Youtube
The American Dieteric Association is the World's largest organization of food and nutrition professionals. ADA is committed to improving the nation's health and advancing the profession of dietetics through research, education and advocacy.
75000 Members
Founded in 1917
Mailing list available for rent

9289 **Agribusiness Council**
P.O. Box 5565
Washington, DC 20016
202-296-4563; Fax: 202-244-4694
info@agribusinesscouncil.org
www.agribusinesscouncil.org
Nicholas E. Hollis, President/CEO
Organization dedicated to strengthening US agro-industrial competitiveness through programs which highlight international trade and development potentials as well as broad issues which encompass several individual agribusiness sectors and require a food systems approach.
Founded in 1967

9290 **Agricultural & Applied Economics Association**
555 E Wells Street
Suite 1100
Milwaukee, WI 53202-6600
414-918-3190; Fax: 414-276-3349
info@aaea.org
www.aaea.org
Facebook, Twitter, LinkedIn, Blogger, Google+
Dawn Thilmany McFadden, President
Madhu Khanna, President-Elect
The Agricultural & Applied Economics Association (AAEA) is a not-for-profit association serving the professional interests of members working in agricultural and broadly related fields of applied economics. Members of the AAEA are employed by academic or government institutions, as well as in industry and not-for-profit organizations, and engage in a variety of teaching, research, and extension/outreach activities.
3000 Members
Founded in 1910

9291 **Agricultural Retailers Association**
1156 15th St NW
Suite 500
Washington, DC 20005
202-457-0825
800-844-4900; Fax: 202-457-0864
ara@aradc.org
www.aradc.org
Facebook, Twitter
Daren Coppock, President & CEO
Richard Gupton, Senior Vice President
Donnie Taylor, Vice President
Melisa Augusto, Director of Comm. and Marketing
Nonprofit trade organization representing the interests of retailers across the United States on legislative and regulatory issues on Capitol Hill.
1200 Members
Frequency: Membership Dues Vary
Founded in 1993

9292 **Allied Purchasing**
PO Box 1249
Mason City, IA 50402-1249
800-247-5956; Fax: 800-635-3775
kbamrick@alliedpurchasing.com
www.alliedpurchasing.com
Facebook, LinkedIn
Brian Janssen, President/CFO
Steve Husome, Executive Vice President
Kari Mondt, Senior Account Manager
Nicole Reisdorfer, Senior Account Manager
Kim Bamrick, Account Manager
A member owned not-for-profit buying organization established to negotiate favorable purchasing programs in part because we offer quantity purchases and prompt payment to suppliers. Purchases equipment, supplies, ingredients, and services for, dairy, soft drink, bottled water, water treatment and brewery industries.
Cost: $50.00
1200 Members
Frequency: Membership: 1 Share Stock
Founded in 1937

9293 **Allied Trades of the Baking Industry**
c/o Cereal Food Processors
2001 Shawnee Mission Parkway
Mission Woods, KS 66205
913-890-6300
t.miller@cerealfood.com
www.atbi.org
Rick McGrath, President
Tom McCurry, First Vice President
John Hellman, Second Vice President
Tom McCurry, Secretary/Treasurer
An organization which exists to serve the grain-based food industry through cooperation between a large cross-section of suppliers to the wholesale manufacturers that each day provide our country with bread, rolls, cereals, cakes, cookies, crackers, tortillas and any number of other items that incorporate grains as their base. Values the relationships which have been built between the supplier and the manufacturer over the nearly 90 years since its inception.
Cost: $50.00
Frequency: Annual Dues
Founded in 1920

9294 **Aluminum Foil Container Manufacturers Association**
10 Vecilla Lane
Hot Springs Village, AR 71909
440-781-5819; Fax: 440-247-9053
info@afcma.org
www.afcma.org
Coke Williams, Executive Secretary
Represents leading manufacturers of aluminum foil containers in the United States and Canada. The Association has worked to promote aluminum foil as a superior packaging material since the beginning.
13 Members
Founded in 1955

9295 **American Agricultural Law Association**
American Agricultural Economics Association
PO Box 5861
Columbia, SC 29250
803-728-3200; Fax: 360-423-2287
ellenberg@aglaw-assn.org
www.aglaw-assn.org
Mike Traxinger, President
Scott Heidner, Executive Director
The only national professional organization focusing on the legal needs of the agricultural community. Crossing traditional barriers, it offers an independent forum for investigation of innovative and workable solutions to complex agricultural law problems. This role has taken on greater importance in the midst of the current international and environmental issues reshaping agriculture and the impending technological advances which promise equally dramatic changes.
600 Members
Founded in 1980

9296 **American Angus Association**
3201 Frederick Ave
St Joseph, MO 64506
816-383-5100; Fax: 816-233-9703
angus@angus.org
www.angus.org
Facebook, Twitter
David A. Dal Porto, President
Jerry Connealy, Vice President
Mark McCully, CEO
Chuck Grove, Treasurer
To provide programs, services, technology and leadership to enhance the genetics of the Angus breed, broaden its influence within the beef industry, and expand the market for superior tasting, high-quality Angus beef worldwide. Achieve Angus excellence through information, increase beef demand with Angus equity, identify and implement relevant technologies, optimize resources, and create opportunities.
Cost: $80.00
30+M Members
Frequency: Membership Fees Vary
Founded in 1883

9297 **American Association of Candy Technologist**
711 W Water St.
PO Box 266
Princeton, WI 54968
920-295-6959; Fax: 920-295-6843
aactinfo@gomc.com
www.aactcandy.org
LinkedIn
Judy Cooley, President
Adam Lechter, First Vice President
Mike Gordon, Second Vice President
Lynn Wieland, Secretary
Mike Allured, Treasurer
A premier professional group of individual technologists, operations personnel, educators, students, business staff and others dedicated to the advancement of the confectionery industry.
Cost: $60.00
Frequency: Membership Fee
Founded in 1947

9298 **American Association of Crop Insurers**
1 Massachusetts Ave NW
Suite 800
Washington, DC 20001-1401
202-789-4100; Fax: 202-408-7763
www.cropinsurers.com
Michael Davenport, President
AACI is widely recognized on Capitol Hill as the leading source of crop insurance information and advice on legislative and administrative proposals. AACI is a member of a coalition of groups in Washington working together to improve the risk management options for America's farmers.
15 Members
Frequency: Membership Fee

9299 **American Association of Grain Inspection and Weighing Agencies**
PO Box 26426
Kansas City, MO 64196
816-569-4020; Fax: 816-221-8189
www.aagiwa.org
David Ayers, President
Tom Dahl, Vice President
David Reeder, Secretary/ Treasurer
Established to provide a liaison between the Federal Grain Inspection Service and designated agencies.
50 Members
Founded in 1964

9300 **American Association of Meat Processors**
One Meating Place
Elizabethtown, PA 17022
717-367-1168
aamp@aamp.com
www.aamp.com
Facebook, Twitter, YouTube, Google+
Rick Reams, President
Chris Young, Executive Director
Diana Dietz, Communications Manager
Niki Cloud, Convention Manager
Jane Frey, Accounting Manager
Membership consists of small to medium sized meat, poultry and food businesses including, slaughterers, processors, wholesalers, home food service businesses, deli and catering operators and suppliers to the industry. AAMP is affiliated with 28 state, regional and provincial associations.
1300+ Members
Founded in 1939

9301 **American Association of Nutritional Consultants**
220 Parker St.
Warsaw, IN 46580
574-269-6165
888-828-2262; Fax: 574-268-2120
registrar@aanc.net
www.aanc.net
Facebook, Twitter, Pinterest
Wendell Whitman, Owner
Promotes ethical standards in the field of nutrition consultants, and those who hold bachelor's degrees in the health related fields.
Cost: $60.00
Frequency: Annual Membership Fee
Founded in 1985

9302 **American Bakers Association**
1300 I St NW
Suite 700 West
Washington, DC 20005
202-789-0300; Fax: 202-898-1164
info@americanbakers.org
www.americanbakers.org
Twitter, LinkedIn, Youtube, Stationerswidows
Rich Scalise, Chairman of the Board
Fred Penny, First Vice Chairman
Bradley K. Alexander, Second Vice Chairman
Robb MacKie, President & CEO
Lee Sanders, Secretary
A long and dedicated history of representing the interests of the wholesale baking industry before the U.S. Congress, federal agencies, state legislatures and agencies, and international regulatory authorities.
300 Members
Frequency: Membership Dues Vary
Founded in 1897

9303 **American Beekeeping Federation**
3525 Piedmont Rd
Bldg 5 Suite 300
Atlanta, GA 30305
404-760-2875; Fax: 404-240-0998
info@abfnet.org
www.abfnet.org
Molly Sausaman, Executive Director
A national organization that continually works in the interest of all beekeepers, large or small, and those associated with the industry to ensure the future of the honey bee. Members share a common interest to work toward better education and information for all segments of the industry in the hope of increasing chances for survival in today's competitive world.
4700 Members
Frequency: Membership Fees Vary
Founded in 1943

9304 **American Berkshire Association**
2637 Yeager Road
West Lafayette, IN 47906
765-497-3618; Fax: 765-497-2959
berkshire@nationalswine.com
www.americanberkshire.com
Facebook
Lorraine Hoffman, President
John Baker, Vice President
Merrill Smith, Secretary
Steve Brown, Treasurer
The official national registry for the Berkshire breed of pigs. The ABA promotes the Berkshire breed of hogs, and maintains breed purity through registration of purebred Berkshires. Dedicated Berkshire breeders focus on delivering the superior meat quality that drives the popularity of Berkshire pork among discerning culinary experts.
300+ Members
Founded in 1998

9305 **American Beverage Association**
1101 Sixteenth Street NW
Washington, DC 20036
202-463-6732; Fax: 202-659-5349
info@ameribev.org
www.ameribev.org
Facebook, Twitter, YouTUBE
Rodger L. Collins, Chair
Jeffrey Honickman, Vice Chair
Susan Neely, President
Mark Hammond, Chief Financial Officer
Ralph D. Crowley Jr., Treasurer
The national voice for the non-alcoholic refreshment beverage industry, providing a neutral forum in which members convene to discuss common issues while maintaining their tradition of spirited competition in the American marketplace. Also serving as liaison between the industry, government and the public, and providing a unified voice in legislative and regulatory matters.
Founded in 1919

9306 **American Beverage Licensees**
5101 River Road
Suite 108
Bethesda, MD 20816-1560
301-656-1494; Fax: 301-656-7539
info@ablusa.org
www.ablusa.org
Facebook, Twitter
John Bodnovich, Executive Director
Trade association for retail beverage alcohol license holders.
20000 Members

9307 **American Brahman Breeders Association**
3003 S Loop W
Suite 520
Houston, TX 77054
713-349-0854; Fax: 713-349-9795
abba@brahman.org
www.brahman.org
Facebook, Twitter, YouTube, Instagram
Craig Fontenot, President
Mike England, Vice President
Pasquale Swaner, Secretary/Treasurer
American Brahman is a beef crossbreeding organization that plays a big role in the United States and beyond.
Founded in 1924

9308 **American Center for Wine, Food & the Arts**
500 First Street
Napa, CA 94559
707-259-1600
888-512-6742; Fax: 707-257-8601
www.copia.org
Arthur Jacobus, President
Kurt Nystrom, COO
Larry Tsai, Chief Marketing Officer
A non-profit discovery center whose mission is to explore and celebrate the cultural significance of wine, food and the arts.

9309 **American Cheese Society**
2696 S. Colorado Blvd
Suite 570
Denver, CO 80222-5954
720-328-2788; Fax: 720-328-2786
info@cheesesociety.org
www.cheesesociety.org
Facebook, Twitter, LinkedIn, YouTube
Peggy Smith, Chair
Dick Roe, President
Jeff Jirik, Vice President

Nora Weiser, Executive Director
Jane Bauer, Education & Outreach Manager

The Society's membership includes farmstead, artisanal and specialty cheesemakers; academicians and enthusiasts; marketing and distribution specialists; food writers and cookbook authors and specialty foods retailers from the United States, Canada and Europe.
800 Members
Founded in 1983

9310 **American Council on Science and Health**
1995 Broadway
Suite 202
New York, NY 10023-5882

212-362-7044
866-905-2694; Fax: 212-362-4919
acsh@acsh.org
www.acsh.org
Facebook, Twitter, Youtube

Nigel Bark, M.D., Chairman
Hank Campbell, President
Josh Bloom, Director of Chemical Science
Gilbert Ross, Senior Director
Josh Bloom, Ph.D., Director

A consumer education organization providing the public with scientifically accurate evaluations of food, chemicals, the environment and health.
Founded in 1978

9311 **American Culinary Federation**
180 Center Place Way
St. Augustine, FL 32095

904-824-4468
800-624-9458; Fax: 904-940-0741
acf@acfchefs.net
www.acfchefs.org
Facebook, Twitter, LinkedIn, Flickr, Instagram

Heidi Cramb, Executive Director

Professional organization for chefs and cooks.
Founded in 1929

9312 **American Dairy Association Mideast**
5950 Sharon Woods Blvd
Columbus, OH 43229

614-890-1800
800-292-MILK; Fax: 614-890-1636
info@drink-milk.com
www.drink-milk.com
Facebook, Twitter, Youtube, Pinterest

Scott Higgins, CEO
Jenny Hubble, Vice President of Communication

We represent dairy farmers and serve as the local affiliate for the American Dairy Association and the National Dairy Council. We work closely with Dairy Management Inc. and the Milk Processors Education Program to extend national dairy promotion programs to the local level.
3800 Members
Founded in 1915

9313 **American Dairy Council**
Interstate Place II
100 Elwood Davis Road
North Syracuse, NY 13212

315-472-9143; Fax: 315-472-0506
dairyinfo@adadc.com
www.adadc.com
Facebook, Twitter, YouTube, Instagram

Richard Naczi, Director

To economically benefit diary farmers by encouraging the consumption of milk and diary products through advertising, education and promotion, to reach consumers with product benefits and advantages.
Founded in 1915
Mailing list available for rent

9314 **American Dairy Products Institute**
126 N. Addison Avenue
Elmhurst, IL 60126

630-530-8700; Fax: 630-530-8707
info@adpi.org
www.adpi.org

Doug Wilke, President
Jerry O'Dea, Vice President
David Thomas, Chief Executive Officer
Dan Meyer, Director of Technical Services
Beth Holcomb, Director of Member Communications

An association for manufactured dairy products, including dry milks, whey, lactose, evaporated and condensed milk. ADPI's main purpose is to effectively communicate the many positive attributes and benefits of our members' products. Additionally, we serve our membership by offering the most current industry information available and by collaborating with dairy associations to represent members' interests before state and federal regulatory agencies.
150 Members
Founded in 1986

9315 **American Dairy Science Association**
1800 S. Oak Street
Suite 100
Champaign, IL 61820-6974

217-356-5146; Fax: 217-398-4119
adsa@assochq.org
www.adsa.org

Rich Erdman, President
Paul Kindstedt, Vice President
Catharine Kuber Perry, Executive Director
Paul Kononoff, Editor-In-Chief

Organization of professional researchers. Publishes journals and holds annual member meetings.
4000 Members
Founded in 1896

9316 **American Dry Bean Boardÿ**

Home Page: www.americanbean.org

Health benefits of beans, bean salad recipes, healthy bean soup recipes, and bean facts.

9317 **American Egg Board**
1460 Renaissance Drive - Ste 301
PO Box 738
Park Ridge, IL 60068

847-296-7043; Fax: 847-296-7007
aeb@aeb.org
www.aeb.org
Twitter

Joanne Ivy, CEO
Elisa Maloberti, Consumer Information Coordinator

U.S. egg producer's link to the consumer in communicating the value of the incredible egg. As the egg industry's promotion arm, AEB's foremost challenge is to convince the American public that the egg is still one of nature's most nearly perfect foods. AEB's basic task is to improve the demand for shell eggs, egg products, as well as spent fowl throughout the United States.
300 Members
Founded in 1976

9318 **American Emu Association**
510 W Madison Street
Suite 2
Ottawa, IL 61350

541-332-0675
info@aea-emu.org
www.aea-emu.org
Facebook

Tony Citrhyn, President
Terry Turner, Vice President
Joylene Reavis, Secretary
Susan Wright, Treasurer
Richard Merrow, Parliamentarian

A national, member driven, non-profit agricultural association dedicated to the emu industry. AEA promotes public awareness of emu products, fosters research and publishes a bi-monthly newsletter and several industry brochures. Represents an alternative agricultural industry, dominated by the small farmer, who is committed to humane and environmentally positive practices that produce high quality, beneficial products.
Cost: $100.00
1,700 Members
Frequency: Membership Fee
Founded in 1989

9319 **American Farm Bureau Federation**
600 Maryland Ave SW
Suite 1000 W
Washington, DC 20024

202-406-3600
www.fb.org
Facebook, Twitter, Instagram, YouTube

Zippy Duvall, President
Julie Anna Potts, Exec. VP
Christy Lilja, Executive Director, Administration
Mace Thornton, Executive Director, Communications

Federation of state Farm Bureaus with 6 million member families.
Founded in 1919

9320 **American Forage and Grassland Council**
PO Box 867
Berea, KY 40403

800-944-2342; Fax: 859-623-8694
info@afgc.org
www.afgc.org
Facebook, Twitter, YouTube

An international organization with the primary objective to promote the profitable production and sustainable utilization of quality forage and grasslands.
Cost: $30.00
3,000 Members
Frequency: Annual Dues
Mailing list available for rent: 2400+ names

9321 **American Frozen Food Institute**
2000 Corporate Ridge, Blvd.
Suite 1000
McLean, VA 22102

703-821-0770; Fax: 703-821-1350
info@affi.com
www.affi.com

Joseph Clayton, Interim President
Kraig R. Naasz, CEO
Kathleen R. Greco, Chief Administrative Officer
Tom Kearney, Chief Financial Officer
Karim Kadrie, Director of Finance

AFFI is the national trade association the promotes and represents the interests of all segments of the frozen food industry.
500 Members
Founded in 1942

9322 **American Guernsey Association**
1224 Alton Darby Creek Road
Suite G
Columbus, OH 43228

614-864-2409; Fax: 614-864-5614
info@usguernsey.com
www.usguernsey.com
Facebook

David Coon, President
Chris Lang, 1st Vice President
Brian Dinderman, 2nd Vice President

Robin Alden, Executive Secretary
Victoria L. Baker, Purebred Publishing President

Promotes programs and services to the dairy industry.
36 Members
Founded in 1877

9323 **American Herb Association**
PO Box 1673
Nevada City, CA 95959

530-265-9552; Fax: 530-274-3140
www.ahaherb.com

Kathi Keville, Director
Robert Brucia, Co-Director
Marion Wyckoff, Secretary

An association of Medical Herbalists. Membership is open to anyone interested in herbs and includes the AHA Quarterly. The goals of the AHA are to promote the understanding, acceptance and ecological use of herbs.
Cost: $20.00
Frequency: Membership Fee
Founded in 1981

9324 **American Herbal Products Association**
8630 Fenton St
Suite 918
Silver Spring, MD 20910

301-588-1171; Fax: 301-588-1174
ahpa@ahpa.org
www.ahpa.org

Graham Rigby, Chair
Michael McGuffin, President
Maged Sharaf, Chief Science Officer
Merle Zimmermann, PhD, Chief Information Analyst
Monica Kendrick, Office and Finance Administrator

The national trade association which represents manufacturers, importers and distributors of herbs and herbal products. AHPA seeks self-regulation, establishment of standards and rules of ethical conduct, member enrichment and public outreach.
Cost: $1000.00
300 Members
Frequency: Membership Fees Vary
Founded in 1983

9325 **American Hereford Association**
PO Box 014059
Kansas City, MO 64101

816-842-3757; Fax: 816-842-6931
aha@hereford.org
www.hereford.org
Facebook

Jack Ward, Executive VP
Shane Bedwell, Chief Operating Officer
Leslie Mathews, Chief Financial Officer
Diane Meyer, Director of Communications
Amy Cowen, Youth Activities Director

Association for people in the Hereford cattle industry.
8M Members
Founded in 1986

9326 **American Honey Producers Association**
PO Box 435
Mendon, UT 84325

281-900-9740; Fax: 403-463-2583
cassie@AHPAnet.com
www.americanhoneyproducers.org

Randy Verhoek, President
Darren Cox, VP
Cassie Cox, Executive Secretary
Kelvin Adee, Treasurer

Represents the interests of major US honey producers and pollinators.
Cost: $150.00
700 Members
Frequency: Membership Fees Vary
Founded in 1969

9327 **American Institute for Cancer Research**
1759 R Street, NW
Washington, DC 20009

202-328-7744
800-843-8114; Fax: 202-328-7226
aicrweb@aicr.org
www.aicr.org
Facebook, Twitter, Pinterest

Melvin Hutson, Chairman
Lawrence Pratt, Vice Chairman
Marilyn Gentry, President
Kelly B. Browning, Chief Executive Officer
Susan Pepper, Secretary/Treasurer

First organization to focus research on the link between diet and cancer and translating the results into practical information for the public. AICR helps people make choices that reduce their chances of developing cancer.
Founded in 1982

9328 **American Institute of Baking**
1213 Bakers Way
Manhattan, KS 66505-3999

785-537-4750
800-633-5137; Fax: 785-537-1493
sales@aibonline.org
www.aibonline.org
Facebook, Twitter, LinkedIn

Andre Biane, President & CEO

Committed to protecting the safety of the food supply chain worldwide and providing high value technical programs.
Founded in 1919

9329 **American Institute of Food Distribution**
10 Mountain View Road
Suite S125
Upper Saddle River, NJ 07458

201-791-5570; Fax: 201-791-5222
questions@foodinstitute.com
www.foodinstitute.com
Facebook, Twitter, LinkedIn

Dean Erstad, Chairman
Brian Todd, President/CEO
Donna L. George, President and COO
Susan T. Borra, Senior Vice President
Peter R. Lavoy, Former President & CEO

The best source for timely, current, and relevant information about the food industry. A nonprofit organization for providing information on the hottest topics and latest trends, reports and studies, and industry analysts to answer member inquiries.
Cost: $725.00
2700 Members
Frequency: Annual Membership Fee
Founded in 1928

9330 **American Institute of Wine & Food**
P.O. Box 973
Belmont, CA 94002-0973

415-508-6790
info@aiwf.org
www.aiwf.org
Facebook

Frank Giaimo, National Chair
Mary Chamberlin, National Vice Chair
Drew Jaglom, National Secretary
Joyce Kucharvy, National Treasurer

The American Institute of Wine & Food is one of the few national organizations with the unique combination membership of dedicated wine and food enthusiasts and professionals. Wine and food enthusiasts get to meet and learn from reowned chefs, winemakers, authors, culinary historians, and food producers, while industry professionals have the opportunity to know and understand their core consumers
Cost: $75.00
6000+ Members
Founded in 1981

9331 **American International Charolais Association**
11700 NW Plaza Circle
Kansas City, MO 64153

816-464-5977; Fax: 816-464-5759
north@charolaisusa.com
www.charolaisusa.com

Larry Lehman, President
Bill Nottke, Vice President
Robb Creasey, Treasurer
John Chism, Secretary
J. Neil Orth, Executive VP

The official registry of Charolais and Charbray cattle in the United States.
2,900 Members

9332 **American Jersey Cattle Association**
6486 E Main Street
Reynoldsburg, OH 43068-2362

614-861-3636; Fax: 614-861-8040
www.usjersey.com
Facebook, Twitter

Neal Smith, Executive Secretary & CEO
Vickie White, Treasurer
Kimberly Billman, Director, Communications
Cari Wolfe, Director, Research
Kristin Paul, Director, Field Service

They improve and promote the Jersey cattle breed.
Founded in 1868

9333 **American Livestock Conservancy**
33 Hillsboro St
PO Box 477
Pittsboro, NC 27312

919-542-5704; Fax: 919-545-0022
albc@albc-usa.org
www.livestockconservancy.org
Facebook, Blogger, Youtube

Alison Martin, Executive Director
Brittany Sweeney, Communications Manager
Michele Brane, Information Manager
Charlene Couch, Program Manager
Angelique Thompson, Operations Director

Ensuring the future of agriculture through genetic conservation and the promotion of endangered breeds of livestock and poultry. A non profit membership organization working to protect over 180 breeds of livestock and poultry from extinction.
Cost: $30.00
Frequency: Membership Fee
ISSN: 1064-1599
Founded in 1977

9334 **American Meat Institute**
1150 Connecticut Ave NW
12th Floor
Washington, DC 20036

202-587-4200; Fax: 202-587-4300
Facebook, Twitter, LinkedIn

Barry Carpenter, President & CEO
Ron Nunnery, Chief Financial Officer
Eric Mittenthal, Vice President, Public Affairs
Scott Goltry, Vice President, Regulatory Affairs
Susan Backus, Executive Director

AMI keeps its fingers on the pulse of legislation, regulation and media activity that impacts the meat and poultry industry and provides rapid updates and analyses to its members to help them

stay informed. Also conducts scientific research through its Foundation designed to help meat and poultry companies improve their plants and their products.
300 Members
Frequency: Membership Fees Vary
Founded in 1906

9335 **American Meat Science Association**
201 W Springfield Ave
Suite 1202
Champaign, IL 61820
217-356-5370
800-517-AMSA; Fax: 888-205-5834; Fax: 217-356-5370
information@meatscience.org
www.meatscience.org
Facebook, Twitter, LinkedIn, Vimeo
Dean Pringle, President
Collette Kaster, Chief Executive Officer
Deidrea Mabry, Chief Operating Officer
Morgan Pfeiffer, Membership & Marketing Manager
Rachel Adams, Youth Programs Coordinator
AMSA fosters community and professional development among individuals who create and apply science to efficiently provide safe and high quality meat.

9336 **American Mushroom Institute**
1284 Gap Newport Pike
Suite 800
Avondale, PA 19311
610-268-7483; Fax: 610-268-8015
ami@mwmlaw.com
www.americanmushroom.org
Joseph G. Poppiti, Chairman
Don Needham, Chairman Elect
Curtis Jurgensmeyer, Vice Chair/ Treasurer
Stephen Anania, Secretary
Laura Phelps, President
This organization is comprised of mushroom growers, associate businesses and suppliers who represent growers and coordinate industry research.
Founded in 1955

9337 **American Oil Chemists' Society**
2710 S. Boulder
Urbana, IL 61802-6996
217-359-2344; Fax: 217-351-8091
general@aocs.org
www.aocs.org
Facebook, Twitter, LinkedIn, Blogger
M. Trautmann, President
B. Hendrix, Vice President
N. Widlak, Secretary
D. Bibus, Treasurer
P. Donnelly, Chief Executive Officer
Largest international society focused on the science and technology of fats, oils, lipids and related substances.
Cost: $10.00
5400 Members
Frequency: Membership Dues Vary
Founded in 1909

9338 **American Ostrich Association**
PO Box 166
Ranger, TX 75158
972-968-8546; Fax: 936-333-6142
aoa@ostriches.org
www.ostriches.org
Joel Brust, President
Boyd Clark, Vice President
Sharon Birmingham, Secretary/ Treasurer
Carol Garnett, Director at large
Organization that provides leadership for the ostrich industry and its future through the promotion of ostrich products.
Cost: $150.00
Frequency: Membership Fee
Founded in 1988

9339 **American Peanut Council**
1500 King St
Suite 301
Alexandria, VA 22314
703-838-9500; Fax: 703-838-9508
www.peanutsusa.com
Facebook, Twitter
Patrick Archer, President
The council was formed through a merger of the National Peanut Council and the National Peanut Council of America. Serving as a forum for all segments of the peanut industry to discuss issues which impact the production, utilization and marketing of peanuts and peanut products worldwide.
Founded in 1997

9340 **American Peanut Research and Education Society**
2360 Rainwater Road
UGA/NESPAL Building
Tifton, GA 31793
229-329-2949; Fax: 229-386-7371
kim.cutchins@apresinc.com
www.apresinc.com
Naveen Puppala, President
Kimberly J. Cutchins, Executive Officer
Kimberly J. Cutchins, Executive Officer
Jeffrey Pope, Board Representative
Howard Valentine, Director of Science & Technology
The purpose of this Society is to instruct and educate the public on the properties, production, and use of the peanut through the organization and promotion of public discussion groups, forums, lectures, and other programs or presentations to the interested public.
Cost: $80.00
550 Members
Frequency: Organizational Fee: $100
Founded in 1968

9341 **American Pie Council**
PO Box 368
Lake Forest, IL 60045
Home Page: www.piecouncil.org
Facebook, Twitter, Pinterest, YouTube
The Pie Council is dedicated to preserving America's pie heritage.

9342 **American Pomological Society**
102 Tyson Building
University Park, PA 16802
814-863-6163; Fax: 814-237-3407
www.americanpomological.org
Peter Hirst, President
Michele Warmund, 1st Vice-President
Marvin Pritts, 2nd Vice-President
Richard Marini, Secretary
Robert Crassweller, Treasurer/ Business Manager
The oldest fruit organization in North America, to foster the science and practice of fruit growing and variety development.
Cost: $40.00
1000 Members
Frequency: Annual Membership Fee
Founded in 1848

9343 **American Seafood Institute**
25 Fairway Circle
Hope Valley, RI 02832
401-491-9017; Fax: 401-491-9024
www.americanseafood.org
Colleen Coyne, Director

9344 **American Seed Trade Association**
1701 Duke Street
Suite 275
Alexandria, VA 22314
703-837-8140; Fax: 703-837-9365
infi@amseed.org
www.amseed.com
Facebook, Twitter, Youtube, Googleplus
Andy Lavigna, President & CEO
Bernice Slutsky, Senior Vice President
Jane Demarchi, Vice President
Rick Dunkle, Senior Director
Michelle Kohn, Director
Producers of seeds for planting purposes. Consists of companies involved in seed production and distribution, plant breeding and related industries in North America.
850 Members
Frequency: Membership Fees Vary
Founded in 1883

9345 **American Sheep Industry Association**
9785 Maroon Circle
Suite 360
Englewood, CO 80112
303-771-3500; Fax: 303-771-8200
eatlamb@wildblue.net
www.sheepusa.org
Facebook, Twitter
Benny Cox, President
Susan Shultz, Vice President
Peter Orwick, Executive Director
Larry Kincaid, Chief Financial Officer
Rita Kourlis Samuelson, Deputy Dir. & Dir., Wool Marketing
A federation of state associations dedicated to the welfare and profitability of the sheep industry.
8000+ Members
Founded in 1865

9346 **American Shrimp Processors Association**
PO Box 4867
EIN #72-6029637
Biloxi, MS 39535
228-806-9600; Fax: 228-385-2565
director@americanshrimp.com
www.americanshrimp.com
Facebook, Twitter, Pinterest, YouTube, Instagram
Andrew Blanchard, President
Jonathan McLendon, Vice President
Scott Young, Secretary/Treasurer
Ivan Sifrim, UX Developer
Nick Alekhine, Developer
A non-profit trade organization designed to represent U.S. shrimp processors in all aspects of business. Allowing processors and related industries to work together to foster a business and technological climate in which its members can prosper while providing the highest quality product to its customers.
Founded in 1964

9347 **American Society for Enology and Viticulture**
PO Box 1855
Davis, CA 95617-1855
530-753-3142; Fax: 530-753-3318
society@asev.org
www.asev.org
Twitter, LinkedIn
Patty Skinkis, President
Dan Howard, Executive Director
Daniel Friedlander, Publications & Tech Coordinator
Dean Spencer, Officer Coordinator
Michelle Taillon, Event Coordinator

A tax exempt professional society dedicated to the interests of enologists, viticulturists, and others in the fields of wine and grape research and production throughout the world.
2400+ Members
Founded in 1950

9348 **American Society for Horticultural Science**
1018 Duke Street
Alexandria, VA 22314
703-836-4606; Fax: 703-836-2024
webmaster@ashs.org
www.ashs.org
Facebook, Twitter, LinkedIn, Pinterest
Louise Ferguson, President
Michael W. Neff, Executive Director
Heather Hilko, Member Services & Subscriptions
Negar Mehdavian, Conferences
Sylvia DeMar, Publication Submissions
A cornerstone of research and education in horticulture and an agent for active promotion of horticultural science.
2500+ Members
Frequency: Membership Fees Vary
Founded in 1903

9349 **American Society for Parenteral and Enteral Nutrition**
8630 Fenton Street
Suite 412
Silver Spring, MD 20910
301-587-6315; Fax: 301-587-2365
aspen@nutritioncare.org
www.nutritioncare.org
Facebook, Twitter, LinkedIn, YouTube
Gordon Sacks, President
Charlene W. Compher, President-Elect
M. Molly McMahon, Vice President
Phil Ayers, Secretary/Treasurer
Albert Barrocas, Director
Advancing the science and practice of clinical nutrition and metabolism. An interdisciplinary organization whose members are involved in the provision of clinical nutrition therapies, including parenteral and enteral nutrition.
6400+ Members
Founded in 1976

9350 **American Society of Agricultural Consultants**
605 Columbus Ave South
New Prague, MN 56071
952-758-5811; Fax: 952-758-5813
www.agconsultants.org
Facebook, Twitter, LinkedIn, YouTube
Amy Keith McDonald, Executive Vice President
An association representing the full range of agricultural consultants which serves as an information, resource, and networking base for its members.
181 Members
Founded in 1963

9351 **American Society of Agronomy**
5585 Guilford Road
Madison, WI 53711-5801
608-273-8080; Fax: 608-273-2021
membership@agronomy.org
www.agronomy.org
Facebook, Twitter, LinkedIn
Nick Goeser, Chief Executive Officer
Wes Meixelsperger, CFO & Director, Meetings
Sara Uttech, Director, Governance
Susan Chapman, Director, Member Services
Ian Popkewitz, Director, IT & Operations
Society members are dedicated to the conservation and wise use of natural resources to produce food, feed, and fiber crops while maintaining and improving the environment. Membership is tax deductible. ASA is seen as a progressive, scientific society.
11000 Members
Founded in 1907

9352 **American Society of Animal Science**
PO Box 7410
Champaign, IL 61826-7410
217-356-9050; Fax: 217-568-6070
asas@asas.org
www.asas.org
Facebook, Twitter, Youtube
Glenn C. Duff, President
Meghan C. Wulster-Radcliffe, Chief Executive Officer
Justin E. Bartlett, Director, Programming & Operations
A professional organization for animal scientists designed to help members provide effective leadership through research, extension, teaching and service for the dynamic and rapidly changing livestock and meat industries.
5000+ Members
ISSN: 0021-8812
Founded in 1908

9353 **American Society of Baking**
7809 N Chestnut Avenue
Kansas City, MO 64119
800-713-0462; Fax: 888-315-2612
info@asbe.org
www.asbe.org
Facebook, Twitter, Google+
Kent Van Amburg, Executive Director
Promoting the advancement of baking science and technology through the exchange of information and interaction among baking industry professionals.
Founded in 1924

9354 **American Society of Brewing Chemists**
3340 Pilot Knob Rd
St. Paul, MN 55121
651-454-7250; Fax: 651-454-0766
asbc@scisoc.org
www.asbcnet.org
Facebook, Twitter, LinkedIn
Christina Schoenberger, President
Christine S. White, President-Elect
Chris D. Powell, Vice President
Robert Christiansen, Secretary
Kelly A. Tretter, Treasurer-Elect
ASBC is dedicated to ensuring the highest quality, consistency and safety of malt-based beverages and their ingredients. Analytical, scientific process control methods, problem solving on industry-wide issues, scientific support to evaluate raw materials for optimum performance, and professional development opportunities.
Cost: $233.00
750+ Members
Frequency: Membership Fee
Founded in 1934

9355 **American Society of Farm Managers and Rural Appraisers**
720 S. Colorado Boulevard
Suite 360-S
Glendale, CO 80246
303-758-3513; Fax: 303-758-0190
info@asfmra.org
www.asfmra.org
Facebook, Twitter, LinkedIn, Plaxo
Brian Stockman, Ecevutive VP/CEO
Alex Clark, Dir., Membership/Marketing/Comm.
Mya Sadler, Dir., Education/Accreditation
Brian Sheppelmen, Dir., Finance/Administration
Protects and promotes the interests of members before government, regulatory bodies, and other organizations; enhances member opportunities for professional development and integration with peers; improves ethics, standards and quality of service offered by members; promotes awareness and confidence; and recruits and maintains a highly qualified, professional membership.
2100+ Members
Founded in 1929

9356 **American Society of Sugar Cane Technologists**
LSU AgCenter
Sturgis Hall #112
Baton Rouge, LA 70803
225-324-7211; Fax: 225-642-0224
assct@assct.org
www.assct.org
Manuel Lezcano, President, Florida
Stephen Savoie, President, Louisiana
With branches in Florida and Louisiana, the Society is dedicated to the study and advancement of the cane sugar industry in the United States.

9357 **American Soybean Association**
12125 Woodcrest Executive
Suite 100
Crece Coeur, MO 63141-5009
314-576-1770
800-688-7692; Fax: 314-576-2786
info@soy.org
www.soygrowers.com
Facebook, Twitter, Youtube, RSS
Steve Censky, CEO
Vickie Wilks, COO
Brian Vaught, CFO
Christy Seyfert, Exec. Director, Government Affairs
Bill Schuermann, Exec. Director, Industry Relations
A primary focus of the American Association is policy development and implementation and to advocate for U.S. soy farmers on policy and trade.
22000 Members
Founded in 1920

9358 **American Spice Trade Association**
1101 17th St NW
Suite 700
Washington, DC 20036
202-331-2460; Fax: 202-463-8998
info@astaspice.org
www.astaspice.org
Greg Lightfood, President
Vinayak Narin, Vice President/ Secretary
Matt Meilander, Treasurer
Frank Collette, Associate Group Director
Cheryl Deem, Executive Director
ASTA, The voice of the US spice industry, works to ensure the supply of clean, safe spice, shape public policy on behalf of the global industry and advance the business interests of its members.
Frequency: Membership Dues Vary
Founded in 1907

9359 **American Sugar Alliance**
2111 Wilson Blvd
Suite 700
Arlington, VA 22201
703-351-5055; Fax: 703-351-6698
info@sugaralliance.org
www.sugaralliance.org
Facebook, Twitter, YouTube, Pinterest
Don Phillips, Trade Adviser
Vickie Meyer, Executive Director
Jack Roney, Dir.Economics & Policy Analysis
Phillip W. Hayes, Director of Media Relations
Laura Gouge, Special Projects Coordinator

The American Sugar Aliance is a national coalition of sugarcane and sugarbett farmers, processors, refiners, suppliers, workers and others dedicated to preserving a strong domestic sugar industry.
Frequency: Membership Fee
Founded in 1983

9360 American Sugar Beet Growers Association
1156 15th St NW
Suite 1101
Washington, DC 20005

202-833-2398; Fax: 240-235-4291
info@americansugarbeet.org
www.americansugarbeet.org
Facebook

John Snyder, President
Ruthann Geib, Vice President
Luther Markwart, Executive Vice President
Galen Lee, Vice President
Mark Olson, Treasurer

The purpose of the organization is to unite sugarbeet growers in the United States and promote the common interest of state and regional beet grower associations, which include legislative and international representation and public relations.
10000 Members

9361 American Sugar Cane League
PO Drawer 938
206 E Bayou Rd.
Thibodaux, LA 70301

985-448-3707; Fax: 985-448-3722
www.amscl.org
Facebook, Twitter, LinkedIn, YouTube, Pinterest

Michael Melancon, President
James H. Simon, General Manager

A Louisiana nonprofit involved in research, promotion and education in support of the state's sugar industry.
Founded in 1922

9362 American Veal Association
2900 NE Brooktree Lane
Suite 200
Gladstone, MO 64119

816-556-3169
www.americanveal.com
Facebook, Twitter, Digg, Stumbleupon,Reddit

Jurian Bartelse, President
Dr. Adnan Aydin, Vice President
Chris Landwehr, Treasurer
Dale Bakke, Secretary

Provides information on veal production practices, industry facts, a tour of a modern veal barn and educational materials. Promoting the American veal industry, and encouraging communications and distributing information pertinent to the veal industry.
1300 Members
Founded in 1984

9363 American Wholesale Marketers Association
11311 Sunset Hills Road
Reston, VA 20190

703-208-3358
800-482-2962; Fax: 703-573-5738
info@cdaweb.net
www.cdaweb.net
Facebook, Twitter

Scott Ramminger, President & CEO
Robert Pignato, IOM, Senior Vice President & COO
Anne Holloway, Vice President Government Affairs
Jane Berzan, Vice President of Strategy
Bob Gatty, Vice President, Communications

International trade organization working on behalf of convenience distributors in the U.S. Associate members include manufacturers, brokers, retailers and others allied to the convenience product industry. Typical products purchased and sold by convenience distributors include candy, tobacco, snacks, beverages, health and beauty care items, general merchandise, foodservice and groceries.
530 Members
Frequency: Membership Dues
Founded in 1942

9364 American Wine Society
P.O. Box 889
Scranton, PA 18501

888-297-9070
www.americanwinesociety.org
Facebook, Twitter, LinkedIn

Kristin Casler Kraft, President
Joseph Broski, Vice President
David Falchuk, Executive Director
Jay Bileti, Director, Member Services

The oldest and largest consumer based wine education organization in North America. A non-profit, educational, consumer-oriented organization for those interested in learning more about all aspects of wine.
5000 Members
Frequency: Membership Dues Vary
Founded in 1967

9365 Animal Agriculture Alliance
2101 Wilson Blvd
Suite 916-B
Arlington, VA 22201

703-562-5160; Fax: 703-524-1921
info@animalagalliance.org
www.animalagalliance.org
Facebook, Twitter

Sarah Novak, Chair
Kay Johnson Smith, Pesident & CEO
Hannah Thompson, VP, Communications
Casey Kinler, Director, Membership & Marketing
Emily Solis, Communications Specialist

The animal Agriculture Alliance is a 501 (c)(3) education foundation. The alliance's mission is to support and promote animal agricultural practices that provide for farm animal well-being through sound science and public education.
3000 Members
Founded in 1987

9366 Apple Processors Association
1701 K Street NW
Suite 650
Washington, DC 20006

202-785-6715; Fax: 202-331-4212
pweller@agriwashington.org
www.appleprocessors.org
Facebook

Andrea Ball, President
Paul S. Weller Jr., EVP Communications
Elizabeth Johnson, VP, Food & Nutrition Policy
Jacquie Ball, Director of Administration

A national association of companies that manufacture quality apple products from whole apples. Members are either apple grower/processor cooperatives, or proprietary firms.
25 Members
Founded in 1987

9367 Apple Products Research & Education Council
1100 Johnson Ferry Road
Suite 300
Atlanta, GA 30342

404-252-3663; Fax: 404-252-0774

Formerly known as The Processed Apples Institute. We are producers of processed apple products; suppliers of equipment, packaging or ingredients to the industry and brokers and concentrate manufacturers.
80 Members
Founded in 1951

9368 Association for Dressings & Sauces
1100 Johnson Ferry Road
Suite 300
Atlanta, GA 30342

678-298-1181; Fax: 404-252-0774
ads@kellencompany.com
www.dressings-sauces.org
Facebook, Twitter, YouTube, Pinterest

Pam Chumley, President
Jeannie Milewski, Executive Director
Jacque Knight, Membership/Administration Manager

This association is comprised of manufacturers of mayonnaise, salad dressings and condiment sauces, as well as industry suppliers. Its purpose is to serve the best interests of industry members, its customers, and consumers of its products.
184 Members
Founded in 1926
Mailing list available for rent

9369 Association of American Feed Control Officials
Purdue University
1800 S. Oak Street
Suite 100
Champaign, IL 61820-6974

217-356-4221; Fax: 217-398-4119
aafco@aafco.org
www.aafco.org
Facebook

A voluntary membership association of local, state and federal agencies charged by law to regulate the sale and distribution of animal feeds and animal drug remedies.
54 Members
Founded in 1909

9370 Association of American Seed Control Officials
Utah Department of Agriculture and Food
350 N Redwood Road
PO Box 146500
Salt Lake City, UT 84114-6500

801-538-7182; Fax: 801-538-7189
walshm@purdue.edu
www.seedcontrol.org

Jason Goltz, President
Jeff Claxton, 1st Vice President
Jan Morawski, 2nd Vice President
Greg Helmbrecht, Treasurer
Don Robison, Secretary

The AASCO's purpose is to promote and establish basic requirements of a state seed law which shall serve as guidelines for member states, to promote and foster uniformity of procedures and policies by member states, to exchange problems and solutions or ideas and suggestions, to coordinate action and cooperate, and to impress and create a sense of mutual understanding between members and other organizations that are concerned with orderly legal merchandising of high quality seed.
Founded in 1949

9371 Association of Correctional Food Service Affiliates
PO Box 10065
Burbank, CA 91510

818-843-6608; Fax: 818-843-7423
www.acfsa.org
Facebook, Twitter, LinkedIn, Instagram

Jon Nichols, Executive Director

An organization dedicated to advancing all aspects of food service in correctional facilities.
Founded in 1969

9372 **Association of Food Industries**
3301 State Route 66
Building C, Suite 205
Neptune, NJ 07753

732-922-3008; Fax: 732-922-3590
info@afius.org
www.afius.org
Facebook

Fred Mortati, Chair
Stephen O'Mara, 1st Vice Chair
James Libby, 2nd Vice Chair
John Sessler, Treasurer
Joe Fragola, Secretary

Promotes free trade and commerce in the food industry. Offers information and education on customs and usage of trade in the food markets and represents member interests in government.
Cost: $1040.00
800 Members
Frequency: Membership Dues Vary
Founded in 1906

9373 **Association of Food and Drug Officials**
2550 Kingston Rd
Suite 311
York, PA 17402

717-757-2888; Fax: 717-650-3650
afdo@afdo.org
www.afdo.org
Twitter

Stephen Stich, President
Stan Stromberg, President-elect
Steven Mandernach, Vice-President
Steven Moris, Secretary/Treasurer
Joseph Corby, Executive Director

Promotes the enforcement of laws and regulations at all levels of government. Fosters understanding and cooperation between industry and regulators. Develops model laws and regulations and seeks their adoption.
800 Members
Frequency: Membership Dues Vary
Founded in 1896

9374 **Association of Fruit and Vegetable Inspection**
PO Box 588
Williamston, NC 27892

252-792-1672; Fax: 252-792-4787
ronnie.wynn@ncagr.gov
www.afvisa.org

Russell Beamsley, President
Carrie Porterfield, Vice President
Laura Thomas, Second Vice President
Dennis Clary, Treasurer
Gregory Hoggard, Secretary

An organization of shipping point inspection programs that advocates for more uniformity between states.
Founded in 1986

9375 **Association of Seafood Importers**
Empress International
10 Harbor Park Drive
Port Washington, NY 11050-4681

516-621-5900
800-645-6244; Fax: 516-621-8318

Burt C Faure

Membership is comprised of seafood importers focusing on problems facing the industry.

9376 **Association of Smoked Fish Processors**
85 John Road
Canton, MA 02021

781-821-2200
800-444-8705; Fax: 781-821-9266

This association provides technical consulation and services to the smoked fish and seafood industry. Services include recall manuals, plant audits, product evaluations, process evaluation, process evaluation, microbiological testing, analytical testing. HACCP plan development and plan ventilation.

9377 **At-Sea Processors Association**
4039 21st Ave W
Suite 400
Seattle, WA 98199

206-285-5139; Fax: 206-285-1841
www.atsea.org

Stephanie Madsen, Executive Director
Paul MacGregor, General Counsel
Jim Gilmore, Public Affairs Director

A trade association representing seven copmanies that own and operate 19 U.S. flag cathcer/processor vessels that participate principally in the Alaska pollack fishery and west coast Pacific whiting fishery.
Cost: $500.00
7 Members
Frequency: Membership Varies
Founded in 1985

9378 **Bakery Equipment Manufacturers and Allieds (BEMA)**
10740 Nall Avenue
Suite 230
Overland Park, KS 66211

913-338-1300; Fax: 913-338-1327
info@bema.org
www.bema.org
Facebook, Twitter

KERWIN BROWN, President & CEO
Terry Bartsch, Chairman
Allen Wright, 1st Vice Chairman
Don Osborne, 2nd Vice Chairman
Paul Lattan, 3rd Vice Chairman

Through the exchange of information, active involvement on committees and participation in educational seminars, BEMA members are continually able to increase the efficiency and sophistication of their equipment while keeping design in adherence with Baking Industry Standarts Committee (BISSC) codes. Continually improving the efficiency of production and establishing sanitation standards.
208 Members
Frequency: Annual Membership Dues
Founded in 1918

9379 **Baking Industry Sanitation Standards Committee**
PO Box 3999
Manhattan, KS 66505-3999

866-342-4772
785-537-4750; Fax: 785-537-1493
bissc@bissc.org
www.bissc.org

James Munyon, President
Jon Anderson, Board Member

Develops and promotes sanitation standards for the design and construction of bakery equipment. Offers certification and third party verification programs for the member companies whose equipment conforms to the BISSC standards.
125 Members
Founded in 1949

9380 **Beef Industry Food Safety Council**
Attn: Deb Cole
9110 E. Nichols Ave
Centennial, CO 80112

303-850-3320; Fax: 303-770-6921
dcole@beef.org
www.bifsco.org

Deborah Cole, Administrative Coordinator
Gary Voogt, President
Forrest Roberts, CEO
Luisa Munsee, Treasurer
Bill Donald, VP

BIFSCo brings together representatives from all segments of the beef industry to develop industry-wide, science-based strategies to solve the problem of food borne pathogens.

9381 **Beef and Lamb New Zealand**
PO Box 121
Wellington, NZ 6140

644-473-9150
800-233-352; Fax: 644-474-0800
enquiries@beeflambnz.com
www.beeflambnz.com
Facebook, Twitter, LinkedIn, Youtube, Pinterest

Dr. Scott Champion, Chief Executive Officer
Cros Spooner, Chief Operating Officer
Andrew Morrison, Director
Anne Munro, Director
Kirsten Bryant, Director

Funded by livestock producers through levies on all beef, sheep and goats slaughtered and on all wool sold. This income is used primarily to market New Zealand wool and meat worldwide, to maintain and extend trade access for New Zealand wool and meat, to provide solutions that will help improve New Zealand farm returns, and to provide technology to the wool industry.

9382 **Beer Institute**
Beer Institute
440 First Street NW
Suite 350
Washington, DC 20001

202-737-2337
800-379-2739; Fax: 202-737-7004
info@beerinstitute.org
www.beerinstitute.org
Facebook, Twitter

James A. McGreevy III, President & CEO
Sandra Castro, Manager, Administration
Joy Dubost, Senior Director
Denise A. Dunckel, Vice President, Public Affairs
Susan Haney, Vice President of Operations

The national trade association for the brewing industry. Representing both big and small brewers as well as importers and industry suppliers.
Founded in 1986

9383 **Beet Sugar Development Foundation**
800 Grant Street
Suite 300
Denver, CO 80203

303-832-4460; Fax: 303-832-4468
Tom@bsdf-assbt.org
www.bsdf-assbt.org

J.W. Schorr, President
T.D. Knudsen, First Vice President
J. Dean, Second VP
T.K. Schwartz, Executive Vice President/Secretary
Aimee Dokes, Administrative Assistant

Association specializing in beet sugar research and the advertisement of seed companies.
Cost: $100.00
13 Members
Frequency: Membership Fee/Max. $450

9384 Biodynamic Farming & Gardening Association
1661 N Water Streetў
Suite 307
Milwaukeeў, WI 53202

262-649-9212; Fax: 262-649-9213
info@biodynamics.com
www.biodynamics.com
Facebook

Thea Maria Carlson, Executive Director
Kaitlin Downs, Community Outreach Coordinator
Anna McAvoy-Emerick, Director, Operations & Finance
Rebecca Briggs, Communications Coordinator
Raphael Guzman, Special Events Organizer

A non-profit, membership organization open to the public with a purpose to foster knowledge of the practices and principles of the biodynamic method of agriculture, horticulture, and forestry in the North American continent and to advance the applications of this method through educational activities such as research, lectures, conferences; publishing literature on the biodynamic methods, and supporting consultation and extension services to farmers, gardeners, and foresters.
Cost: $45.00
Frequency: 6 per year
Circulation: 1000+
Founded in 1938

9385 Biscuit & Cracker Manufacturers' Association
6325 Woodside Court
Suite 125
Columbia, MD 21046

443-545-1645; Fax: 410-290-8585
www.thebcma.org
Facebook, Twitter, Googel+

Dave Van Laar, President
Vanessa Vial, Comm. & eLearning Manager
Kathy Kinter Phelps, Member & Edu. Services Mgr
Todd Wallin, Treasurer
Kathy Kinter Phelps, Secretary

An international trade organization representing the entire spectrum of companies in the manufacturing of cookies and crackers and suppliers to theindustry.
Founded in 1901

9386 Blue Diamond Growers
1701 C Street
Sacramento, CA 95811

916-442-0771
800-987-2329; Fax: 916-446-8461
feedback@bdgrowers.com
www.bluediamondgrowers.com
Facebook, Twitter, Youtube, Pinterest

Dan Cummings, Chairman of the Board
Dale Van Groningen, Vice Chairman
Mark Jansen, President & CEO
Don Yee, Director-at-large
Mel Machado, Director, Member relations

The world's largest tree nut processing and marketing company. Building markets and creating new products, uses, and opportunities for members.

9387 Board of Trade of Wholesale Seafood
7 Dey Street
Room 801
New York, NY 10007-3223

212-732-4340; Fax: 212-732-6644
www.aboutseafood.com
Facebook, Twitter, Googelplus

John Connelly, President/Administrator

Credit exchange and collection agency for wholesale seafood merchants and producers, in the US and Canada.
Founded in 1931

9388 Bread Bakers Guild of America
1129 Industrial Avenue
Suite 206
Petaluma, CA 94952

707-935-1468; Fax: 707-935-1672
info@bbga.org
www.bbga.org
Facebook, Twitter

Jeff Yankellow, Board Chair
Phyllis Enloe, Board Vice Chair
Neale Creamer, Treasurer
Cathy Wayne, Director of Operations
Jill Valavanis, Administrative Assistant

Well known in the baking community as the go-to educational resource for substantive, accurate information on the craft of making bread. The definitive resource on all aspects of artisan baking in America, supporting and fostering the growth of the artisan baking community. Defining and upholding the highest professional standarts, and celebrating the craft and the passion of the artisan baker.
1300 Members
Founded in 1993

9389 Brewers Association
1327 Spruce Street
Boulder, CO 80302

303-447-0816
888-822-6273; Fax: 303-447-2825
info@brewersassociation.org
www.homebrewersassociation.org
Facebook, Twitter

Sam Calagione, Chair
Gary Fish, Vice Chair
Mark Edelson, Treasurer/Secretary
Katie Brown, Finance Assistant
Tom Clark, Finance Director

The goal of the BA is to promote and protect small and independent American brewers, their craft beers and the community of brewing enthusiasts.
43000 Members
Founded in 1978

9390 Brown Swiss Association
800 Pleasant St
Beloit, WI 53511-5456

608-365-4474; Fax: 608-365-5577
info@brownswissusa.com
www.brownswissusa.com
Facebook

Lee Barber, President
Tome Portner, Vice President
David Wallace, Executive Secretary
David Gunter, Director
Annissa Jones, Bookkeeper

Membership is comprised of key dairy industry leaders and dairy producers who are on the cutting edge of the world's latest agricultural technology.
800 Members
Founded in 1880

9391 Brown Swiss Cattle Breeder's Association
800 Pleasant Street
Beloit, WI 53511

608-365-4474; Fax: 608-365-5577
info@brownswissusa.com
www.brownswissusa.com
Facebook

Lee Barber, President
Tom Portner, Vice President
David Wallace, Exec. Secretary
David Gunter, Director
Annissa Jones, Bookkeeper

Registers about 10,000 animals per year and promotes and expands the Brown Swiss breed with programs that assist the membership and industry to compete favorably in the market place.
800 Members
Founded in 1880

9392 Calaveras Winegrape Alliance
P.O. Box 2492
Murphys, CA

209-728-9467
866-806-9463
calaveraswines@att.net
www.calaveraswines.org
Facebook, Twitter, Pinterest

Dedicated to increasing the awareness of all wines produced in Calaveras County and/or produced from Calaveras grapes.

9393 California Walnuts
101 Parkshore Dr.
Ste. 2503
Folsom, CA 95630

916-932-7070; Fax: 916-932-7071
info@walnuts.org
www.walnuts.org
Facebook, Twitter, YouTube, Pinterest

Dennis A. Balint, Executive Director

Established to represent walnut growers and handlers. The board promotes usage of walnuts in the U.S. through publicity, product promotions and production research and education programs.
Founded in 1948
Mailing list available for rent

9394 Calorie Control Council
2611 Winslow Dr Ne
Atlanta, GA 30305-3777

678-608-3200; Fax: 404-252-0774
webmaster@caloriecontrol.org
www.caloriecontrol.org

An international non-profit association representing the low-calorie food and beverage industry. The Council seeks to provide an effective channel of communication among its members, the public and government officials, and to assure that scientific, medical and other pertinent research and information is developed and made available to all interested parties.
60 Members
Founded in 1966

9395 Can Manufacturers Institute
1730 Rhode Island Ave NW
Suite 1000
Washington, DC 20036

202-232-4677; Fax: 202-232-5756
www.cancentral.com
Facebook, Twitter, LinkedIn

Robert Budway, President

Serves as the voice of the metal can making industry, providing a forum for members to advocate common industry problems to legislative and regulatory agencies whose activities impact the metal can market, to address issues of common concern, and to promote cost-effectively the benefits of the can to protect and grow the market.
35 Members
Founded in 1939

9396 **Canned Foods**
PO Box 5258
Madison, WI 53705-0000
608-231-2250; Fax: 608-231-6952
www.cannedveggies.org
Gene Kroupa, Executive Director
An educational and promotional organization of vegetable canners whose goals are to raise the awareness of consumer and food service buyers regarding canned vegetables.
80 Members
Founded in 1977

9397 **Canola Council of Canada**
167 Lombard Avenue Suite 400
Winnipeg, Manitoba
Canada R3B 0T6
204-982-2100
866-834-4378; Fax: 204-942-1841
admin@canola-council.org
www.canolacouncil.org
Patti Miller, President
Jim Everson, Vice President, Gov Relations
Bruce Jowett, Vice President, Market Development
Curtis Rempel, Vice President, Crop Production
Cari Mell, Comptroller
Representing canola growers, input suppliers, researchers, processors and marketers of canola and its products.

9398 **Cape Cod Cranberry Growers Association**
1 Carver Square Boulevard
PO Box 97
Carver, MA 02330
508-866-7878; Fax: 508-866-4220
info@cranberries.org
www.cranberries.org
Steve Ward, President
Brian Wick, Executive Director
Bonnie Soule, Special Projects Coordinator
Patti Silvia, Membership & Office Coordinator
Dawn Gates, Dir., Member & Financial Services
Established to standardize the measure with which cranberries are sold, the CCCGA is one of the country's oldest farmers' organizations. Giving growers both a single voice and a collective strength in promoting the cranberry industry, and working to ensure that cranberry farming can survive urbanization and the open space and clean water, vital to growing, will be preserved.
Founded in 1888

9399 **Carneros Wine Alliance**
PO Box 189
Vineburg, CA 95487
707-812-1919
info@carneros.com
www.carneros.com
Facebook, Twitter
Anne Moller-Racke, Chair
Heidi Soldinger, Vice Chair
T. J. Evans, Treasurer
Alison Crowe, Board of Director
Carla Bosco, Secretary
A nonprofit association of wineries and grape-owners in the Carneros American Viticultural Area (AVA).

9400 **Center for Food Safety & Applied Nutrition**
5100 Paint Branch Parkway
College Park, MD 20740
888-723-3366
http://www.fda.gov/AboutFDA/CentersOffices/OfficeofFoods/CFSAN/
Provides services to consumers, domestic and foreign industry and other outside groups regarding field programs; agency administrative tasks; scientific analysis and support; and policy, planning and handling of critical issues related to food and cosmetics.

9401 **Cheese Importers Association of America**
204 E Street NE
Washington, DC 20002
202-547-0899; Fax: 202-547-6348
info@theciaa.org
www.theciaa.org
Thomas Gellert, President
Dominique Delugeau, First Vice President
Ken Olsson, 2nd Vice President
Philip Marfuggi, Treasurer
Daniel Schnyder, Secretary
Helps facilitate the efficient import of dairy products from around thw world into the United States. The CIAA endeavors to support dairy trade, within the context of compliance with international trade agreements and all applicable US regulations, and maintains active contacts with government officials worldwide in order to further the objectives of the organization and its members.
150 Members
Founded in 1942

9402 **Cherry Marketing Institute**
12800 Escanaba Drive
Suite A
Dewitt, MI 48820
925-838-5454; Fax: 925-838-2311
info@choosecherries.com
www.choosecherries.com
Facebook, Twitter
Philip Korson II, President
Fred Tubbs, Chairman
Chris Dunkel, Manager
Association representing the cherry industry. Provides promotional material to food service operators, brokers, retailers and manufacturers.
Founded in 1988
Mailing list available for rent

9403 **Chocolate Manufacturers Association**
1101 30th Street NW
Suite 200
Washington, DC 20007
202-534-1440; Fax: 202-337-0637
info@candyUSA.com
www.thestoryofchocolate.com
Dennis Whalen, Chairman
Louise Hilsen, Vice Chairman
Alison Bodor, Executive Vice President
Susan S. Smith, SVP, Communications
Liz Clark, VP Government Affairs
The trade group for manufacturers and distributors of cocoa and chocolate products in the United States. The association was founded to fund and administer research, promote chocolate to the general public and serve as an advocate of the industry before Congress and government agencies.
9 Members
Founded in 1884

9404 **Citrus Industry Magazine**
5053 NW Hwy 225-A
Ocala, FL 34482
352-671-1909; Fax: 888-957-2226
www.citrusindustry.net
Facebook
Ernie Ness, Editor
Association for citrus grower organizations and other trade associations within the industry.
Founded in 1920
Mailing list available for rent

9405 **Coca-Cola Bottlers Association**
3282 Northside Parkway
Suite 200
Atlanta, GA 30327
404-872-2258; Fax: 404-872-2869
ccba.atl@gmail.com
www.ccbanet.com
Hank Flint, President
M. Trevor Messinger, Vice President
Mark Francouer, Treasurer
Ann Burton, CFO
John Gould, Executive Director & CEO
Assisting members in reducing costs and improving efficiency, the Association acts as a servicing arm and agent on behalf of participating Bottlers to meet their needs in numerous areas, including procurement, employee benefits, insurance programs and retirement plans. Also serves as a primary mechanism for fostering the exchange of ideas and information within the Coca-Cola system.
Founded in 1913

9406 **Coffee, Sugar and Cocoa Exchange**
New York Board of Trade
1 N End Avenue
New York, NY 10282-1101
212-748-4000; Fax: 212-748-4039
www.csce.com
Acts as a financial exchange where futures and options are traded, the CSCE provides hedging and investing, opportunities in the coffee, sugar, cocoa and dairy markets.

9407 **Colombia Coffee Federation**
140 E 57th Street
New York, NY 10022
212-421-8300; Fax: 212-758-3816
www.cafedecolombia.com/en/familia
John Boden, Manager
Founded in 1964

9408 **Commercial Food Equipment Service Association**
3605 Centre Circle
Fort Mill, SC 29715
336-346-4700; Fax: 336-346-4745
asidders@cfesa.com
www.cfesa.com
Facebook, LinkedIn, MySpace, YouTube
Paul Toukatly, President
John Schwindt, Vice President
Gary Potvin, Vice President
Wayne Stoutner, Treasurer
David Hahn, Secretary
The trade association of professional service and parts distributors. Helps members meet the challenges of the industry and ensure customer satisfaction.
450 Members
Founded in 1963
Mailing list available for rent

9409 **Communicating for America**
112 E Lincoln Avenue
Fergus Falls, MN 56537
218-739-3241
800-432-3276; Fax: 218-739-3832
memberbenefits@cainc.org
www.communicatingforamerica.org
Stephen Ruder, Chair & General Council
Patty Strickland, President & COO
Angela Nelson, Chief Financial Officer
Milt Smedsrud, Founder & Chair Emeritus
Strives to promote health, well-being and advancement of people in agriculture and agribusiness.
40M Members
Founded in 1972

9410 **Communication and Agricultural Education**
Oklahoma State University
301 Umberger Hall
Manhattan, KS 66506

785-532-5804; Fax: 785-532-5633
commdept@ksu.edu
www.communications.ksu.edu
Facebook, Twitter, Youtube, Foursquare

Beth Holz, President
Wyatt Betchel, First VP
Megan Brouk, Second VP
Amanda Spoo, Secretary
Brittney Machado, Treasurer

The Mission of National ACT is to build relationships among agricultural communication professionals and college students and faculty, to provide professional and academic development for members and to promote agriculture through communications efforts.
Founded in 1970

9411 **Composite Can and Tube Institute**
50 S Pickett Street
Suite 110
Alexandria, VA 22304-7206

703-823-7234; Fax: 703-823-7237
ccti@cctiwdc.org
www.cctiwdc.org

Kristine Garland, Executive VP
Janine Marczak, Associate Manager, Events
Wayne Vance, Association Counsel

CCTI is an international nonprofit trade association representing the interests of manufacturers of composite paperboard cans, containers, canisters, tubes, cores, edgeboard and related or similar composite products and suppliers to those manufacturers of such items as paper, machinery, adhesives, labels and other services and materials.
Founded in 1933

9412 **Concord Grape Association**
1 Cliffstar Avenue
Dunkirk, NY 14048

716-366-6100
www.concordgrape.org

Pam Chumley, Executive Director
Linda Whitley, Contact

The Concord Grape Association represents processors of Concord grapes and manufacturers of products derived from them. The organization operates as the Concord Grape Section under the umbrella of the Juice Products Association (JPA), which represents the juice and juice products industry in the U.S. and overseas. Members handle more than the majority of the Concord grapes processed annually in the United States.
Founded in 1956

9413 **Consultants Association for the Natural Products Industry (CANI)**
PO Box 4014
Clovis, CA 93613

559-325-7192; Fax: 559-325-7195
info@cani-consultants.org
www.cani-consultants.org
LinkedIn

Karena K. Dillon, President
Robert Forbes, Vice President
Ginni Garner, Treasurer
Sheldon Baker, Director
Kathy Francis, SECRETARY

Committed to working individually and collectively, to enhance the growth and integrity of the natural products industry by providing professional expertise and objective counsel to our clients. These specialized services contribute to the prosperity and values of the individual business as well as the industry as a whole.
Founded in 1991

9414 **Cookware Manufacturers Association**
PO Box 531335
Birminghan, AL 35253-1335

205-592-0389; Fax: 205-599-5598
hrushing@usit.net
www.cookware.org

Jay Zilinskas, President
Gene Karlson, VP
Hugh J Rushing, Executive VP

Represents manufactures of cookware and bakeware in the US and Canada. Publishes consumer guides to cookware and engineering standards for industry.
21 Members
Founded in 1922

9415 **Corn Refiners Association**
1701 Pennsylvania Avenue N.W.
Suite 950
Washington, DC 20006

202-331-1634; Fax: 202-331-2054
comments@corn.org
www.corn.org
Facebook, Twitter, Stumbleupon, Digg

Rob Ritchie, Chair
John Bode, President & CEO
Steve Gardner, Chief Operating Officer
Keniece Barbee, Director, Member Serivices
Johnelle Brown, Director, Operations

Supports carbohydrate research programs through grants to colleges, government laboratories and private research centers.
8 Members
Founded in 1913

9416 **Council for Agricultural Science and Technology**
4420 West Lincoln Way
Ames, IA 50014-3447

515-292-2125
cast@cast-science.org
www.cast-science.org
Facebook, Twitter, LinkedIn, YouTube, Blogspot, Schooltube

Kent G. Schescke, Executive Vice President
Melissa Sly, Director, Council Operations
Dan Gogerty, Managing Communications Editor
Megan Wickham, Scientific Editor
Gale Osborne, Office Manager/Events Coordinator

CAST, through its network of experts, assembles, interprets, and communicates science-based information to policymakers, the media, the private sector, and the public. Its primary work is the publication of task force reports, commentaries, special publications, and issue papers written by volunteer experts-economists, legal experts and scientists from many disciplines. These documents cover issues related to food sciences, agricultural technology, animal sciences, and plant and soil sciences.
700+ Members
Founded in 1972

9417 **Council for Responsible Nutrition**
1828 L St NW
Suite 510
Washington, DC 20036-5114

202-204-7700; Fax: 202-204-7701
webmaster@crnusa.org
www.crnusa.org
Twitter, Googleplus

Steve Mister, President & CEO
Judy Blatman, Senior Vice President
Mike Greene, Vice President, Gov Relations
James C. Griffiths, Vice President, Scientific
Andrea Wong, Ph.D., Vice President, Science

The leading trade association representing dietary supplement manufacturers and ingredient suppliers. Member companies manufacture popular national brands as well as the store brands marketed by major supermarkets, drug store and discount chains. All members also agree to adhere to voluntary guidelines for manufacturing, marketing and CRN's Code of Ethics.
70 Members
Founded in 1973

9418 **Council of Supply Chain Management Professionals**
333 E Butterfield Rd
Suite 140
Lombard, IL 60148

630-574-0985; Fax: 630-574-0989
www.cscmp.org
Facebook, Twitter, LinkedIn, YouTube

Heather Sheehan, Chair
Theodore Stank, Chair-Elect
Kevin Smith, Vice Chair
Mary Long, Secretary & Treasurer

CSCMP's mission is to lead the evolving supply chain management profession by developing, advancing, and disseminating supply chain knowledge and research.
10000 Members
Founded in 1963

9419 **Crop Insurance and Reinsurance Bureau**
440 First St NW
Suite 500
Washington, DC 20001

202-544-0067; Fax: 202-330-5255
mtorrey@cropinsurance.org
www.cropinsurance.org

Zane Vaughn, Chair
Mike Torrey, Executive Vice President
Tara Smith, Federal Affairs Vice President
Barbara Patterson, Director Of Government Relations
Perry Harlow, Manager Of Membership & Events

National trade association made up of insurance providers and related organizations that provide a variety of insurance products for our nation's farmers.
Founded in 1964

9420 **Crop Science Society of America**
5585 Guilford Rd.
Madison, WI 53711-5801

608-273-8080; Fax: 608-273-2021
membership@sciencesocieties.org
www.crops.org
Facebook, Twitter, LinkedIn

Nick Goeser, Chief Executive Officer
Sara Uttech, Director, Governance
Wes Meixelsperger, CFO & Dir., Meetings
Ian Popkewitz, Director, IT & Operations
Susan Chapman, Director, Member Services

Dedicated to the conservation and wise use of natural resources to produce food, feed, and fiber crops while maintaining and improving the environment. Continuously evolving and modifying it's educational offerings to support the changing needs of its members.
5000+ Members
Founded in 1956

9421 **CropLife America**
1156 15th St NW
Washington, DC 20005

202-296-1585; Fax: 202-463-0474
info@croplifeamerica.org

www.croplifeamerica.org
Facebook, Twitter, LinkedIn, YouTube

Christopher Novakk, President & CEO
Kellie Bray, Chief Of Staff
Beau Greenwood, EVP, Legal & General Counsel
Rachel Lattimore, EVP, Legal & General Counsel
Genevieve O'Sullivan, VP, Communications & Marketing

A trade association of manufacturers and distributors of agriculture crop protection and pest control products.
74 Members
Founded in 1933

9422 **Dairy Farmers of America**
10220 N Ambassador Dr
Kansas City, MO 64153

816-801-6455
888-332-6455; Fax: 816-801-6456
webmail@dfamilk.com
www.dfamilk.com
Facebook, Twitter, LinkedIn, YouTube

Rick Smith, President & CEO
John McDaniel, Senior Vice President
Alex Bachelor, Senior Vice President
Randy McGinnis, Senior Vice President & COO
David Meyer, Senior Vice President, Finance

A milk marketing cooperative and dairy food processor dedicated to delivering value to members through secure markets, competitive pricing and increasing value throughout the entire diary chain.
Founded in 1998

9423 **Dairy Management, Inc.**
O'Hare International Center
10255 W Higgins Rd
Suite 900
Rosemont, IL 60018-5616

847-803-2000
800-853-2479; Fax: 847-803-2077
www.dairy.org

James Ahlem, Chair
Skip Hardie, Secretary
Thomas P. Gallagher, Chief Executive Officer
Barbara O'Brien, President
Mollie Waller, Chief Communication Officer

This association aims to provide the sale and consumption of milk and milk products in the US.
Founded in 1980

9424 **Dairy and Food Industries Supply Association**
1451 Dolley Madison Boulevard
McLean, VA 22101-3879

703-883-0515; Fax: 703-761-4334

John Martin, President
Burce D'Agostino, Vice President
Mary O'Dea, Communications Manager

Trade association of almost 800 suppliers to the food, beverage, dairy, pharmaceutical and related sanitary processing industries.

9425 **Diamond of California**
1050 S Diamond Street
Stockton, CA 95205

209-467-6000; Fax: 209-467-6788
www.diamondnuts.com

Brian J. Discoll, President & CEO
Ray Silcock, Executive Vice President & CFO
Lloyd J. Jhonson, Executive Vice President
David Colo, Executive Vice President & COO
Stephen Kim, Senior Vice President

Walnut growers' association with Diamond guarantees a market for their crops and provides the company with high quality walnuts. Diamond provides information and resources to help growers to produce the best nuts in the world.
1900 Members
Founded in 1912

9426 **Distillers Grains Technology Council**
University of Louisville
3327 Elings Hall
Ames, IA 50011

515-294-4019
800-759-3448; Fax: 502-852-1577
karosent@iastate.edu
www.distillersgrains.org

Dr. Kurt Rosentrater, Executive Director/CEO

A non-profit organization that stresses the importance of utilization of distillers co-products in animal feeds. We address the production and product quality issues that are known to impact the market acceptability and production costs of these products.
7 Members
Founded in 1945

9427 **Dr. Pepper Bottlers Association**
PO Box 906
Rowlett, TX 75030-0906

972-475-7397; Fax: 972-475-5290
Facebook, Twitter, Googleplus

Bill Elmore Jr, President
James Lee, Vice President
Scott Chase, Secretary/ Director
Bill Yarbrough, Treasurer/ Director

Represents 430 bottlers for the Dr. Pepper Company.

9428 **Drug, Chemical & Associated Technologies Association**
One Union St.
Suite 208
Robbinsville, NJ 08691

609-208-1888
800-640-3228; Fax: 609-208-0599
mtimony@dcat.org
www.dcat.org

Margaret Timony, Executive Director
Lauryn Kuna, Director, Membership
Miriam O'Donnell, Director, Project Integration
Patricia Van Arnum, Editorial Director
Erin Sanders, Sr. Communications/Tech. Specialist

The premier business development association whose membership is comprised of companies that manufacture, distribute or provide services to the pharamceutical, chemical, nutritional and related industries.
Founded in 1890

9429 **Eastern Frosted and Refrigerated Foods Association**
17 Park St
Wanaque, NJ 07465

973-835-1710; Fax: 973-835-1708
efra@efraweb.org
www.efraweb.org

Hans Ketels, President
Paul Raguso, 1st Vice President
Ken Atkinson, 2nd Vice President
Jody Avallone, Director
Mike Ryan, Executive Director

Brings together all related segments of the frozen food industry; brokers, warehousing, manufacturers, transportation, distributors, packaging/labeling and retailers. Constantly gathering information for members from authoritative national and regional sources, other members, and publication editorials affecting the industry.
65 Members
Founded in 1937

9430 **Electric Foodservice Council**
180 Raymond Court
PO Box 142156
Fayetteville, GA 30214

770-461-3870; Fax: 770-461-7799
krhutchinson1@msn.com

Billy Griffis, President
Jim Wixson, Senior Vice President
Roshena Ham, Secretary
Mitzi Shanks, Treasurer

Unique organization designed to bring together utilities, equipment manufacturers, trade allies, and foodservice operators who are committed to the advancement of the foodservice industry.
Founded in 1987

9431 **Farmer Direct Foods Inc.**
511 Commercial
PO Box 326
Atchison, KS 66002

913-367-4422
800-372-4422; Fax: 913-367-4443
www.farmerdirectfoods.com

Mark Fowler, President / Chief Executive Officer
Marcia Walters, Accounting Manager
Justin Howie, Plant Operations Manager

A producer owned cooperative marketing corporation formed in 1988 with the mission to develop white wheat markets for wheat producers.
125 Members
Founded in 1988

9432 **Fermenters International Trade Association**
PO Box 1373
Valrico, FL 33595

813-685-4261; Fax: 813-681-5625
Facebook, Twitter

Dee Roberson, Executive Director
Bill Metzger, Editor

Manufacturers, wholesalers, retailers, authors and editors having a commercial interest in the beer and wine trade. Offers publications to members only.
200+ Members
Founded in 1976

9433 **Fertilizer Institute**
425 Third Street, SW
Suite 950
Washington, DC 20024

202-962-0490; Fax: 202-962-0577
information@tfi.org
www.tfi.org
Facebook, Twitter, LinkedIn

Corey Rosebusch, President & CEO
Bradley Cheng, Director, Accounting
Mariana Gallo, Senior Director, Conferences
Christopher Glen, Director, Communications
Roberta Rosenberg, Senior Director, Marketing

Members include brokers, producers, importers, dealers and manufacturers of fertilizer and fertilizer-related equipment.
325 Members
Founded in 1969

9434 **Fishermens Marketing Association**
1585 Heartwood Drive
Suite E
McKinleyville, CA 95519

707-840-0182; Fax: 707-840-0539
fma@trawl.org
trawl.org

Peter Leipzig, Executive Director

An organization made up of fishermen which promotes stable prices and an orderly flow of wholesome seafood to the consumer.
Founded in 1952

9435 **Flavor & Extract Manufacturers Association (FEMA)**
1101 17th St NW
Suite 700
Washington, DC 20036
202-293-5800; Fax: 202-463-8998
www.femaflavor.org
YouTube, RSS Feed
Kevin Renskers, President
Timothy Webster, President Elect
John Cavallo, Vice President & Secretary
John Cox, Executive Director
Gary Smith, Treasurer
Comprised of flavor manufacturers, flavor users, flavor ingredient suppliers, and others with an interest in the U.S. flavor industry. Working with legislators and regulators to assure that the needs of members and consumers are continuously addressed. FEMA is committed to assuring a substantial supply of safe flavoring substances.
123 Members
Founded in 1909

9436 **Food & Nutrition Service**
3101 Park Center Drive
Alexandria, VA 22302
703-305-2062; Fax: 703-305-2312
www.fns.usda.gov
Facebook, Twitter, Flickr, YouTube
Audrey Rowe, Administrator
Kevin Concannon, Under Secretary
Dr. Janey Thronton, Deputy under Secretary
Telora Dean, Associate Administrator & COO
Rich Lucas, Deputy Administrator
Provides children and needy families better access to food and a more healthful diet through its food assistance programs and comprehensive nutrition education efforts. FNS also works to empower program participants with knowledge of the link between diet and health.
Founded in 1969
Mailing list available for rent

9437 **Food Allergy Research & Education**
7925 Jones Branch Dr.
Suite 1100
McLean, VA 22102
703-691-3179
800-924-4040; Fax: 703-691-2713
www.foodallergy.org
Facebook, Twitter, Youtube, Flickr, Pinterest
Janet Atwater, Chairman
Elliot S. Jaffe, Chairman Emeritus
Robert Nichols, Vice Chair
James R. Baker, Jr., Chief Executive Officer
Michael Lade, Treasurer
The only nonprofit organization in the United States devoted solelyto patient education for food allergies. Mission is to create public awareness about food allergies and anaphylaxis, to provide education, and to advance research on behalf of all those affected by food allergy.
Cost: $30.00
22000 Members
Frequency: 6 per year
Founded in 1991

9438 **Food Distribution Research Society**
PO Box 441110
Fort Washington, MD 20749-1110
301-292-1970; Fax: 706-542-0739
Jonathan_baros@ncsu.edu
www.fdrsinc.org
Dawn Thilmany, President
Kynda Curtis, President-Elect
Randall D. Little, Vice President Communication
Alba J. Collart, Vice President Education
Ronald L. Rainey, Vice President Logistics & Outreach
Food distribution research society encourages research, serves as an information clearinghouse and encourages implementation of research. The Society organizes conferences and meetings for industry, academic and government leaders within the food industry sector.
Founded in 1967

9439 **Food Export Association of the Midwest USA**
309 West Washington
Suite 600
Chicago, IL 60606
312-334-9200; Fax: 312-334-9230
info@foodexportusa.org
www.foodexport.org
Facebook
Tim F Hamilton, Executive Director
Lauren Swartz, Deputy Director
John Belmont, Communications Manager
Suzanne Milshaw, International Marketing Program
A non-profit organization that promotes the export of food and agricultural products from the northeast region of the United States. The organization has been helping exporters of northeast food and agricultural products sell their products overseas since it was first organized.
Founded in 1973

9440 **Food Industry Association Executives**
664 Sandpiper Bay Dr., SW
Sunset Beach, NC 28468
910-575-3423; Fax: 815-550-1731
bev@mgmt57.com
www.fiae.net
Jamie Pfhul, Chairwoman
Ellie Taylor, Vice Chairwoman
Bev Lynch, President
Pat Davis, Vice President, State Government
Brian Jordan, Secretary/Treasurer
Sponsors meetings, activities, publications and services to advance the knowledge and professionalism of the food industry association executive, and serves as a vehicle for the advancement of the food industry's agenda.
125 Members
Founded in 1927

9441 **Food Industry Suppliers Association**
1207 Sunset Drive
Greensboro, NC 27408
336-274-6311; Fax: 336-691-1839
stella@fisanet.org
www.fisanet.org
Jason Ryan, President
Eric Perkins, VP
Rob Clark, Past President
Trade association dedicated to promoting distribution in serving high purity industries. Membership includes independent distributors and manufacturers who go to market through distribution. Members serve customers in food, beverage, personal care, pharmaceutical, Bio-Pharm and other high purity industries.
245 Members
Founded in 1968
Mailing list available for rent

9442 **Food Information Service Center**
21050 SW 93rd Lane Road
Dunnellon, FL 34431
352-489-8919
800-443-5820; Fax: 352-489-8919
James Allen Mixon, President
Publishes technical assistance manuals for operating congregate feeding food service programs. Reaches market through direct mail and publicity.
Founded in 1957

9443 **Food Marketing Institute**
2345 Crystal Drive
Suite 800
Arlington, VA 22202
202-452-8444; Fax: 202-429-4519
www.fmi.org
Facebook, Twitter, LinkedIn, YouTube
Randy Edeker, Chair
Leslie G. Sarasin, President/CEO
FMI conducts programs in public affairs, food safety, research, education and industry relations on behalf of its 1,500 member companies in the United States and around the world.
1500 Members

9444 **Food Processing Suppliers Association (FPSA)**
1451 Dolley Madison Boulevard
Suite 101
McLean, VA 22101-3850
703-761-2600; Fax: 703-761-4334
info@fpsa.org
www.fpsa.org
Facebook, Twitter, LinkedIn, Google+
David Seckman, President & CEO
Robyn Roche, Chief Financial Officer
Dolores Alonso, VP, Membership & Business Dev
Andy Drennan, International Market Development
Grace A. Cular Yee, Vice President, Sales
Trade association for food and beverage processing suppliers and those working in the packaging industry. The association offers advocacy, business solutions and trade shows. The five main industry areas covered are bakery, beverage, dairy, prepared foods and meat.
400+ Members
Founded in 1983

9445 **Food Processors Suppliers Association**
1451 Dolly Madison Boulevard
Suite 101
McLean, VA 22101-3850
703-761-2600; Fax: 703-761-4334
info@fpsa.org
www.fpsa.org
Facebook, Twitter, LinkedIn
Gil Williams, Chairman, Vice Chair
David Seckman, President & CEO
Robyn Roche, CFO
Scott Gregory, Treasurer
MISA offers its members an opportunity to project a common and uniform stance on important industry issues, particularly in the regulatory and machinery safety and hygienic standards area.
500+ Members
Founded in 1983

9446 **Foodservice & Packaging Institute**
7700 Leesburg Pike
Suite 421
Falls Church, VA 22043
703-592-9889; Fax: 703-592-9864
www.fpi.org
Facebook, Twitter, LinkedIn
Lynn Dyer, President
Natha Dempsey, Vice President
Jennifer Goldman, Membership & Meetings Manager
A national association comprised of manufacturers and suppliers of single-use foodservice packaging products.
25 Members
Founded in 1933

9447 **Foodservice Consultants Society International**
PO Box 4961
Louisville, KY 40204

502-379-4122
info@fcsi.org
www.fcsi.org
Facebook, Twitter, LinkedIn

Martin Rahmann, President

A foodservice association with members in over 30 countries.
1000+ Members
Founded in 1955

9448 **Foodservice Sales & Marketing Association**
5225 Wisonsin Avenue NW
Suite 316
Washington, DC 20015-2055

202-596-8112; Fax: 202-293-1702
info@fsmaonline.com
www.fsmaonline.com
Twitter, LinkedIn, Youtube

Jerry Campbell, Chair & President
Barry Maloney, General Counsel, CFO & Exec. Dir.
John Krattenmaker, Operations Manager
Arlene Murphy, Director, Member Development

Specializes in selling food and related products to foodservice companies.
150 Members
Founded in 2003
Mailing list available for rent

9449 **Fresh Mushrooms - Nature's Hidden Treasure**
2880 Zanker Road
Suite 203
San Jose, CA 95134

408-432-7210; Fax: 408-432-7213
info@mushroomcouncil.org
www.mushroomcouncil.org
Facebook, Twitter, YouTube, Pinterest, Google+, R

Carla Blackwell-Mckinney, Vice Chair
Robert Crouch, Secretary

Plays an important role in the national promotion of fresh mushrooms through consumer public relations, foodservice communications and retail communications.
Founded in 1993
Mailing list available for rent

9450 **Fresh Produce Association of the Americas**
590 East Frontage Road
PO Box 848
Nogales, AZ 85621

520-287-2707; Fax: 520-287-2948
info@freshfrommexico.com
www.freshfrommexico.com

Lance Jungmeyer, President
Allison Moore, Vice President
Emmis Yubeta, Director, Membership Programs
Georgina Feliz Burrueto, Director, Operations
Conchita Singh, Dir., Accounting & Human Resources

Represents more than 125 member companies involved in growing, harvesting, marketing and importing of Mexican produce entering the US at Nogales, Arizona.
125 Members
Founded in 1944

9451 **Fresh Produce and Floral Council**
2400 E. Katella Ave.
Ste. 330
Anaheim, CA 92806

714-739-0177; Fax: 714-739-0226
info@fpfc.org
www.fpfc.org

Don Gann, Interim Executive Director
Emma McBride-Taylor, Event & Communication Specialist

Provides unique networking and business growth opportunities for professionals in the produce and floral industries in California. Members include growers, snippers, shippers, wholesalers, brokers, distributors and retailers of produce and/or floral items.
500 Members
Founded in 1965

9452 **Frozen & Refrigerated Association of the North East**
PO Box 6377
Wolcott, CT 06716-0377

203-597-7215; Fax: 203-879-0594
frane@frane.org
www.frane.org
Facebook

Jim Wright, Chair
Donna Maglio, Executive Chair
Jason Adams, Director
Sal Marrocco, Vice-President
John Powers, Director

Non-profit regional trade association, representing the ever changing frozen and refrigerated industries throughout the Northeast. It remains one of the largest and most active associations in the United States and is affiliated with the National Frozen & Refrigerated Association (NFRA).
135 Members
Founded in 1955

9453 **Future Food**
101 Finsbury Pavement
London, UK EC2A 1RS

203-002-3002; Fax: 203-003-3003
prteam@marcusevans.com
www.marcusevans.com
Facebook, Twitter, LinkedIn, Googleplus, vimeo

European events and publications for food industry.
Founded in 1983

9454 **Ginseng Board of Wisconsin**
668 Maratech Avenue
Suite E
Marathon, WI 54448

715-443-2444; Fax: 715-443-2444
ginseng@ginsengboard.com
www.ginsengboard.com

Joe Heil, President

Representing Wisconsin Ginseng producers as the worldwide leader of the American Ginseng industry, committed to the advertising, promotion and the sale of Wisconsin Ginseng, the purest ginseng in the world. Working to improve the health and wellness of consumers while suporting the sustainability of the industry and the rural economy associated with it.
Founded in 1986

9455 **Glass Packaging Institute**
1220 North Fillmore Street
Suite 400
Arlington, VA 22201

703-684-6359; Fax: 703-546-0588
info@gpi.org
www.gpi.org
Facebook, Twitter

Andres Lopez, Chairman
Lynn M. Bragg, President
John Riordan, Director
Sanjay Gandhi, Director
John Gallo, Director

Represents the North American glass container industry. Through GPI, glass container manufacturers speak with one voice to advocate industry standards, promote sound environmental policies and educate packaging professionals. Member companies manufacture glass containers for food, beverage, cosmetic and many other products.
Founded in 1919

9456 **Global Cold Chain Alliance**
241 18th St. S
Suite 620
Alexandria, VA 22202

703-373-4300; Fax: 703-373-4301
email@gcca.org
www.gcca.org
Facebook, Twitter, LinkedIn

Corey Rosenbuch, President & CEO

The Global Cold Chain Alliance (GCCA) is committed to building and strengthening the temperature-controlled supply chain around the world. As part of that mission, GCCA provides specialized cold chain advisory services to government agencies, organizations, and associations through its core partner, the World Food Logistics Organization (WFLO).
1300+ Members
Frequency: Membership Dues Vary
Founded in 2007

9457 **Glutamate Association: US**
1010 Wiconsin Ave. NW
Ste. 350
Washington, DC 20007

202-384-1840; Fax: 202-384-1850
info@watsongreenllc.com
www.msgfacts.com
Facebook, Twitter, LinkedIn

Lisa Watson, Executive Director

(TGA) ia an association of manufacturers,national marketers,and processed food users of glutamic acid and its salts, principally the flavor enhancer, monosodium glutamat (MSG). TGA seeks to povide an effective channel of communcation among its members, the public,the media,the scientific community, foof professionals and government officials about the use and safety of glutamates.
12 Members
Founded in 1977

9458 **Golden Gold Chain Alliance**
1500 King Street
Suite 201
Alexandria, VA 22314-2730

703-373-4300; Fax: 703-373-4301
email@gcca.org
www.gcca.org
Facebook, Twitter, LinkedIn

Corey Rosenbuch, President & COO
Megan Costello, Vice President of Member & Industry
Rita Haley, Executive Assistant and Manager
Richard Tracy, Vice President
Tori Miller Liu, Director of Information Systems

The Global Cold Chain Alliance (GCCA) is committed to building and strengthening the temperature-controlled supply chain around the world. As part of that mission, GCCA provides specialized cold chain advisory services to government agencies, organizations, and associations through its core partner, the World Food Logistics Organization (WFLO)
900 Members
Founded in 1891

9459 **Grocery Manufacturers Association**
1350 Eye (I) Street NW
Suite 300
Washington, DC 20005

202-639-5900; Fax: 202-639-5932
info@gmaonline.org
www.gmaonline.org
Facebook, Twitter, RSS

Advances the interests of the food, beverage and consumer products industry on key issues that affect the ability of brand manufacturers to market their products profitably and deliver superior value to the consumer.
Founded in 1908

9460 **Hand in Hand Foundation**
PO Box 67351
Scott's Valley, CA 95067

831-438-3736; Fax: 831-535-6331
adoptions@handinhand.us
www.handinhandfoundation.com

David Boschen, Director
Melissa Thomas, Case Worker
April Pao, Case Worker
Kristi VanPykren, Case Worker
Katie Garcia, Office Administrator

Not for profit that solicits food and donations for the needy.
Founded in 1971

9461 **Healthy Water Association**
PO Box 1417
Patterson, CA 95363

408-897-3023; Fax: 408-897-3028
paulmason@mgwater.com
www.mgwater.com/hwa.shtml

Paul Mason, President

Serves the bottled water industry.

9462 **Herb Growing and Marketing Network**
PO Box 245
Silver Spring, PA 17575-0245

717-393-3295; Fax: 717-393-9261
herbworld@aol.com
www.herbworld.com

Maureen Rogers, Director

The largest trade association for the herb industry.
Cost: $48.00
1000+ Members
Founded in 1990

9463 **Herb Research Foundation**
5589 Arapahoe Ave
Suite 205
Boulder, CO 80303

303-449-2265; Fax: 303-449-7849
info@herbs.org
www.herbs.org

Rob McCaleb, President

Provides scientific based and traditional information about use and safety of herbs for health. Fee based hotline, information packs and literature are available to all.
Founded in 1983
Mailing list available for rent

9464 **Herb Society of America**
9019 Kirtland Chardon Rd
Kirtland, OH 44094

440-256-0514; Fax: 440-256-0541
herbs@herbsociety.org
www.herbsociety.org
YouTube, Wordpress

Katrinka Morgan, Executive Director
Amy Rogers, Administrative Assistant
Robin Siktberg, Editor/Horticulturist
Brent DeWitt, Editor/Graphic Designer
Karen Frandanisa, Accountant

An organization that focuses on educating its members and the public on the cultivation of herbs and the study of their history and uses, both past and present.
Founded in 1933

9465 **Holstein Association USA**
1 Holstein Place
PO Box 808
Brattleboro, VT 05302-0808

802-254-4551
800-952-5200; Fax: 802-254-8251
www.holsteinusa.com
Facebook, Twitter, YouTube

Corey Geiger, President
Jonathan Lamb, Vice President
Barbara Casna, Treasurer
John M. Meyer, Executive Secretary

The world's largest dairy cattle breed organization offering information services to all dairy producers.
Founded in 1903

9466 **Home Baking Association**
2931 SW Gainsboro Road
Topeka, KS 66614-4413

785-478-3283; Fax: 785-478-3024
hbapatton@aol.com
www.homebaking.org
Facebook, Twitter, Flickr

Eric Wall, President

National organization promoting scratch baking education and practice.
Founded in 1951

9467 **Hospitality Link**
866 SE 14th Terrace
Suite 128
Deerfield Beach, FL 33441

954-579-1802; Fax: 954-421-1046
LinkedIn

Provides consulting for food technology.

9468 **Hydroponic Society of America**
PO Box 1183
El Cerrito, CA 94530

510-926-2908
www.lisarein.com/hydroponics

Joseph O Brien, President

The scientific and educational arm of the hydroponic community. The H.S.A. is rooted in science and physics, plant physiology and photo-biology and the other 16 disciplines required to understand the complexity of the science known as hydroponics. The H.S.A. separates the fiction from the fact, and the truth from the mythology.
Founded in 1976

9469 **Independent Bakers Association**
PO Box 3731
Washington, DC 20027-0231

202-333-8190; Fax: 202-337-3809
independentbaker@yahoo.com
www.independentbaker.net
Twitter, LinkedIn

Ron Cardey, Chairman
Joe Davis, First Vice Chair
Scott Barth, Second Vice Chair
Brian Stevenson, Secretary
Heidi Brenner, Treasurer

National trade association of mostly family owned wholesale bakeries and allied industry trades. Protects the interests of independent wholesale bakers from antitrust and anti-competitive mergers and acquisitions; pressures Congress to support market-oriented farm commodity programs, seeking representation to consider federal labor, tax and environmental law.
400 Members
Founded in 1968

9470 **Indian River Citrus League**
7925 20th Street
Vero Beach, FL 32966

772-562-2728; Fax: 772-562-2577
info@ircitrusleague.org
ircitrusleague.org

Rusty Varn, Board of Director
Trey Smith, Board of Director
Scott Lambeth, Board of Director
Daniel R. Richey, Board of Director
Daniel Scott, Board of Directors

Organization of growers in the area. Newsletters, links and contactinformation.
Founded in 1807

9471 **Institute of Food Science and Engineering**
2650 North Young Avenue
Fayetteville, AR 72704

479-575-4040; Fax: 479-575-2165
www.uark.edu/depts/ifse

Steve Brooks, President & CEO
Dr. Jean Francois Meullent, Director
Dr. Donald Freeman, Advisory Board
Dr. Patti Landers, Advisory Board
Don McCaskill, Advisory Board

Serves as the primary entity in Arkansas for research, graduate education and extension to help ensure that; food supply is high quality, wholesome, safe and nutritious, value is added to raw agricultural products to enhance economic development of the state, region and nation, and the nutritional needs of society are understood, communicated and met.

9472 **Institute of Food Technologists**
525 W Van Buren
Suite 1000
Chicago, IL 60607

312-782-8424
800-438-3663; Fax: 312-782-8348
info@ift.org
www.ift.org
Facebook, Twitter, LinkedIn, Youtube

Robert Gravani, Chairman
Colin Dennis, President
John Neil Coupland, President-Elect
Christie Tarantino, Executive Vice President
Robert Gravani, Treasurer

A nonprofit scientific society working in food science, food technology, and related professions in industry, academia and government.
18000 Members
Founded in 1939

9473 **Institute of Food and Agricultural Sciences**
University of Florida
PO Box 110180
Gainesville, FL 32611-0180

352-392-1971
ifas.ufl.edu
Facebook, Twitter

Ruth Borger, Asst. Vice President

A federal-state-county partnership throughout Florida, dedicated to improving your life by developing and providing knowledge in agriculture, natural resources, and life sciences.
Founded in 1964

9474 **Institute of Packaging Professionals**
One Parkview Plaza
Suite 800
Oakbrook Terrace, IL 60181

630-544-5050
800-432-4085; Fax: 630-544-5055
info@iopp.org
www.iopp.org
Facebook, Twitter, LinkedIn, YouTube

Jane Chase, Chair
Toby Wingfield, Treasurer
Dan Alexander, Vice Chair
Robert Meisner, EVP - Education & Certification
Suzanne Simmons, Executive VP-Membership

Information regarding the packaging industry internationally.

9475 **Institute of Shortening & Edible Oils**
1319 F Street NW
Suite 600
Washington, DC 20004

202-783-7960; Fax: 202-393-1367
contactus@iseo.org
www.iseo.org

Robert L. Collette, President
Diana L. Stare, Office Administrator

A trade association representing the refiners of edible fats and oils in the United States. Members represent approximately 90-95 percent of the edible fats and oils produced domestically that are used in baking and frying fats (shortening), cooking and salad oils, margarines, spreads, confections and toppings, and ingredients in a wide variety of foods.
Founded in 1936

9476 **International Dairy-Deli-Bakery Association (IDDBA)**
636 Science Drive
Madison, WI 53711-1073

608-310-5000; Fax: 608-238-6330
iddba@iddba.orgÿ
www.iddba.org

A nonprofit trade association providing education, training, and marketing resources for food retailers, manufacturers, brokers, distributors, and other interested professionals.
Founded in 1964

9477 **International Association for Color Manufacturers**
1101 17th Street NW
Suite 700
Washington, DC 20036

202-293-5800; Fax: 202-463-8998
info@iacmcolor.org
www.iacmcolor.org
LinkedIn

Bobby Gruber, President

The IACM is a trade association that represents the manufacturers and end-users of coloring substances that are used in foods. Members include producers and users of both certified and exempt colors.
Founded in 1972

9478 **International Association of Culinary Professionals**
1221 Avenue of the Americas
42nd Floor
New York, NY 10020

646-358-4957
866-358-4951; Fax: 866-358-2524
info@iacp.com
www.iacp.com
Facebook, Twitter, Youtube, Vimeo

Martha Holmberg, Chief Executive Officer
Shani Phelan, Member Progams and Ops Manager
Glenn Mack, Chair
Kendra McMurray, CMP, Director, Conferences and Events

IACP connects culinary professionals with the people, places, and knowledge they need to succeed. IACP is a worldwide forum for the development and exchange of information, knowledge, and inspiration within the professional food and beverage community. This organization of creative and talented professionals is engaged in and committed to excellence in the food industry.
3000+ Members
Founded in 1978

9479 **International Association of Ice Cream and Vendors**
3601 East Joppa Road
Baltimore, MD 21234

410-931-8100; Fax: 410-931-8111
info@iaicdv.org
www.iaicdv.org
Facebook, Twitter, Stumbleupon, Gmail

Hoss Rafaty, President
Taylor Dubord, Executive Director
Michelle Franklin, Vice President
Nick Nikbakht, Secretary-Treasurer

Members are manufacturers and distributors of ice cream novelties and street vendors.
Founded in 1969

9480 **International Association of Milk Control Agencies**
Department of Agriculture
Division of Dairy Industry Services
Albany, NY 12235-0001

518-457-3880; Fax: 518-485-5816

Charles Huff, Secretary/Treasurer

Founded to improve the effectiveness and uniformity of regulation among the economic regulatory agencies and to provide a forum for exchange of information.
Founded in 1935

9481 **International Association of Operative Millers**
12351 W. 96th Terrace
Suite 100
Lenexa, KS 66215

913-338-3377; Fax: 913-338-3553
info@iaom.info
www.iaom.info/about/
Facebook, Twitter, LinkedIn

Melinda Farris, CEO
Annette Peterson, Office Coordinator
Cynthia Malone, Director, Meetings & Exhibitions

An international organization, comprised of flour millers, cereal grain and seed processors and allied trades representatives and companies devoted to the advancement of technology in the flour milling, cereal grain processing industries.
1500 Members
Founded in 1896

9482 **International Banana Society**
1901 Pennsylvania Ave NW
Suite 1100
Washington, DC 20006-3412

202-303-3400; Fax: 202-303-3433
www.bananas.org
Facebook, LinkedIn, Youtube

A trade organizatoin consisting of members engaged in teh business of importing bananas into the United States. Provides a forum for members to discuss common and technical issues pertaining to banana production, distribution, and marketing.
Founded in 1982

9483 **International Beverage Dispensing Equipment Association**
PO Box 248
Reisterstown, MD 21136

410-602-0616
877-404-2332; Fax: 410-486-6799
ibdea@cornerstoneassoc.com
www.ibdea.org
Facebook, LinkedIn, Youtube

An international non-profit trade association representing companies that sell, lease, rent, manufacture and service beverage dispensing equipment and supplies. Members are companies that provide equipment, related products and services to restaurants, bars, taverns, hospitals, schools and other institutions.
250+ Members
Founded in 1971

9484 **International Bottled Water Association**
1700 Diagonal Rd
Suite 650
Alexandria, VA 22314

703-683-5213
800-928-3711; Fax: 703-683-4074
info@bottledwater.org
www.bottledwater.org
Facebook, Twitter, YouTube

Bryan Shinn, Chairman
Joe Bell, Vice Chairman
Joseph Doss, President
Robert R. Hirst, Vice President
Shayron Barnes-Selby, Treasurer

The leading voice of the bottled water industry and serves to protect the interests of bottled water bottlers, distributors and suppliers.
Founded in 1958

9485 **International Chewing Gum Association**
1001 G Street NW
Suite 500 West
Washington, DC 20001

information@gumassociation.org
www.gumassociation.org

Andy Pharoah, President

The leading voice of the chewing gum industry. ICGA continues to gain recognition and credibility among decision-makers across the globe.

9486 **International Council on Hotel, Restaurant and Institutional Education**
2810 N Parham Road
Suite 230
Richmond, VA 23294

804-346-4800; Fax: 804-346-5009
info@chrie.org
www.chrie.org
Facebook, Twitter, LinkedIn

Maureen Brookes, President
Margaret Steiskal, Vice President
Kathy McCarty, Chief Executive Officer
Wanda Costen, Secretary
Stephanie Hein, Treasurer

A marketplace for facilitating exchanges of information, ideas, research, products and services related to education, training and resource development for the hospitality and tourism industry (food, lodging, recreation and travel services). Serving as the hospitality and tourism education network, striving to unite educators, industry executives and associations.
1400 Members
Founded in 1946

9487 **International Dairy Foods Association**
1250 H Street NW
Suite 900
Washington, DC 20005

202-737-4332; Fax: 202-331-7820
membership@idfa.org
www.idfa.org
Facebook, Twitter, YouTube, Blog, Smartbrief

Patricia Stroup, Chair
Jeffery Kaneb, Vice Chair
Michael Walls, Secretary
Mike Reidy, Treasurer
Connie Tipton, President and CEO

Represents the nation's dairy manufacturing and marketing industries and their suppliers. IDFA is composed of three constituent organizations; Milk Industry Foundation, National Cheese Institute, and the International Ice Cream Association.
550 Members

9488 **International Dairy-Deli-Bakery Association**
636 Science Drive
PO Box 5528
Madison, WI 53705-0528

608-310-5000; Fax: 608-238-6330
iddba@iddba.org

William J. Klump, Chairman
David Leonhardi, Executive Vice Chairman
John Cheesman, Vice Chairman
Jewel Hunt, Treasurer

IDDBA members meet the challenges of today's business world by exchanging information and ideas, participating in educational programs and networking.
Founded in 1964

9489 **International Flight Services Association**
1100 Johnson Ferry Road
Suite 300
Atlanta, GA 30342

404-252-3663; Fax: 404-252-0774
ifsa@kellencompany.com
www.ifsanet.com
Facebook, Twitter, LinkedIn, YouTube

David Loft, Chairperson
Pam Suder Smith, President
Jane Bernier -Tran, Vice President
Paul Platamone, Treasurer
Denise Poole, Secretary

Represents the $14 billion inflight and travel catering industry. Activities include annual conferences, trade shows, seminars and training events around the world.
400 Members
Founded in 1965

9490 **International Food Additives Council**
1100 Johnson Ferry Road
Suite 300
Atlanta, GA 30342

404-252-3663; Fax: 404-252-0774
jrogers@kellencompany.com
www.foodadditives.org

An international trade association of food additives manufacturers and businesses having interest in food additives.

9491 **International Food Information Council Foundation**
1100 Connecticut Ave NW
Suite 430
Washington, DC 20036

202-296-6540; Fax: 202-296-6547
info@foodinsight.org
www.foodinsight.org
Facebook, Twitter, LinkedIn

David B. Schmidt, President & CEO
Geraldine McCann, COO
Marianne Smith Edge, Senior VP, Nutrition & Food Safety
Andy Benson, VP, International Relations
Kimberly Reed, President

Dedicated to the mission of effectively communicating science-based information on health, nutrition and food safety for the public good. Independent and non-profit, bringing together, working with, and providing information to consumers, health and nutrition professionals, educators, government officials, and food, beverage, and agricultural industry professionals.
33 Members
Founded in 1985

9492 **International Food Processors Association**
200 Daingerfield Road
Suite 100
Alexandria, VA 22314-2884

703-684-1080; Fax: 703-548-6563

9493 **International Food Service Brokers Association**
1101 Pennsylvania Avenue
Washington, DC 20004

Home Page: www.foodbrokers.org

1500 Members
ISSN: 0884-7185
Founded in 1956

9494 **International Food Service Editorial Council**
7 Point Place
PO Box 491
Hyde Park, NY 12538

845-229-6973; Fax: 845-229-6973
ifec@ifeconline.com
www.ifeconline.com
Facebook, Twitter

Sam Oches, President
Cathy Holley, Vice President
Bill Schreiber, Secretary
Rachel Tracy, Treasurer
Carol Lally, Executive Director

A networking association that fosters the open exchange of information and the building of productive working relationships among foodservice editor and publicist members. Conferences and other activities offer professional development as well as opportunities to make new contacts and gain hands-on-experience of the food cultures and personalities in cities where conferences are held.
265 Members
Founded in 1956

9495 **International Food Service Executives Association**
PO Box 1125
Placitas, NM 87043

855-268-1367
www.ifsea.org
Facebook

Richard Weil, Chairman

Provides education and community service to the foodservice industry.
3,000 Members
Founded in 1901

9496 **International FoodService Manufacturers Association**
180 North Stetson Avenue
Suite 850
Chicago, IL 60601

312-540-4400; Fax: 312-540-4401
ifma@ifmaworld.com
www.ifmaworld.com
Facebook, LinkedIn, YouTube

Richard Ferranti, Chairman
Joe Bybel, First Vice Chairman
Kevin Delahunt, Vice Chairman
Ben Shanley, Vice Chairman
Don Davis, Treasurer

Member companies of the IFMA can capitalize on opportunities, tackle challenges, as well as gain new customer contact and networking opportunities, education and training that helps company sales force build market share, and leadership roles in such initiatives as GS1.
650 Members
Founded in 1952

9497 **International Foodservice Distributors Association**
1660 International Drive
Suite 550
McLean, VA 22102

703-532-9400; Fax: 703-880-7117
www.ifdaonline.org
Twitter, LinkedIn

John Tracy, Chairman
Craig Hoskins, Vice Chairman
Mark Harman, Treasurer
Mark S. Allen, President/CEO

Trade association comprised of food distribution companies that supply independent grocers and food service operations throughout the US, Canada and 19 other countries.
135 Members
Founded in 2003

9498 **International Glutamate Technical Committee**
5775 Peachtree Dunwoody Rd NE
Atlanta, GA 30342

404-252-3663; Fax: 404-252-3663
www.aspartame.org

Andrew Ebert PhD, Chairman
Judy Rogers, Contact

Members are associations that are engaged in the manufacture, sale and commercial use of glutamates.
8 Members
Founded in 1965

9499 **International HACCP Alliance**
120 Rosenthal Center
2471 TAMU
College Station, TX 77843-2471

979-862-3643; Fax: 979-862-3075
kharris@tamu.edu
www.haccpalliance.org

Ranzell Nickelson, Chairman
Rosemary Mucklow, Vice Chairman
Robert Hibbert, Treasurer/ Secretary
Rafael Rivera, Past Chairman
Rena Pietrami, Board of Directors

Provides a uniform program to assure safer meat and poultry products.
Founded in 1994

9500 **International Herb Association**
PO Box 5667
Jacksonville, FL 32247-5667

904-399-3241; Fax: 904-396-9467
www.iherb.org

Matthias Reisen, President
Dianna Nance, Vice President

Karen O'Brien, Secretary
Marge Powell, Treasurer
Davy Dabney, Chairman

Supports herb businesses and educates the public.
Founded in 1986

9501 **International Institute of Fisheries Economics & Trade**
213 Ballard Hall
Corvallis, OR 97331-3601

541-737-2942; Fax: 541-737-2563
osuweb@lists.orst.edu
www.oregonstate.edu/dept/IIFET

Dr. Dan Holland, President
Dr. Claire Armstrong, President-elect
Ann L. Shriver, Executive Director
Kara Keenan, Assistant

Promotes discussion, research projects and sponsors educational courses. Publications available.
400 Members
Founded in 1982

9502 **International Maple Syrup Institute**
5072 Rock St. RR#4
Spencerville, ON K0E 1X0

613-658-2329; Fax: 877-683-7241
agrofor@ripnet.com
www.internationalmaplesyrupinstitute.com

Pam Greene, President
Tom Zaffis, Vice President
David Campbell, Treasurer
Jean Lamontagne, Executive Director

Members are producers, processors, industry suppliers and others interested in promoting the industry.
15M Members
Founded in 1975

9503 **International Natural Sausage Casing Association**
12100 Sunset Hills Road
Suite 130
Reston, VA 20190

703-234-4112; Fax: 703-435-4390
www.insca.org

David Blanga, Chairman
Elliot Simon, Vice Chairman
Michael Mayo, Treasurer

The only international association for the natural sausage casing industry. Members include producers, suppliers and brokers of natural casing products.
265+ Members
Founded in 1965

9504 **International Olive Council**
Principe de Vergara
154
Spain, MD 28002

491-590-3638; Fax: 491-563-1263
iooc@internationaloliveoil.org
www.internationaloliveoil.org

Jean Louis Barjol, Executive Director

The world's only international intergovernmental organization in the field of olive oil and table olives. The Council is a decisive player in contributing to the sustainable and responsible development of olive growing and serves as a world forum for discussing policymaking issues and tackling present and future challenges.
Founded in 1959

9505 **International Organization of the Flavor Industry (IOFI)**
Flavor & Extract Manufacturers Association
1101, 17th Street NW
Suite 700
Washington, DC 20036

202-293-5800; Fax: 202-462-8998
www.femaflavor.org

Kevin Renskers, President
Timothy Webster, President Elect
John Cavallo, Vice President & Secretary
John Cox, Executive Director
Gary Smith, Treasurer

FEMA staff monitors regulations that impact flavor and extracts all around the world.
Frequency: Annual
Founded in 1909
Mailing list available for rent

9506 **International Packaged Ice Association**
238 East Davis Blvd.
Suite 213
Tampa, FL 33606

813-258-1690
800-742-0627; Fax: 919-251-2783
jane@packagedice.com
www.packagedice.com

John Smibert, Chairman
Tommy Sedler, Vice Chairman/ Treasurer
Dann Ades, Secretary/ Assistant Treasurer
Mike Ringstaff, Conference Chairman
Bo Russell, Immediate Past Chairman

A trade association representing manufacturers and distributors of packaged ice and manufacturers of ice making equipment.
400 Members
Frequency: Call For Membership Info
Founded in 1917

9507 **International Society of Beverage Technologists(ISBT)**
14070 Proton Rd
Suite 100, LB 9
Dallas, TX 75244-3601

972-233-9107; Fax: 972-490-4219
office@bevtech.org
www.bevtech.org

Brian Stegmann, President
Cloeann Durham, 1st Vice President
Sieg Mueller, 2nd Vice President
Larry Hobbs, Executive Director
Jessica Anacker, Director

Enhance promotione, development and dissemination of knowledge relating to art and science of beverage technology. Focus ares include beverage formulation, production, packaging and more. We provide forums, stimulate the uise of science in the industry, encourage and foster research.

9508 **International Warehouse Logistics Association**
2800 S River Road
Suite 260
Des Plaines, IL 60018

847-813-4699; Fax: 847-813-0115
mail@iwla.com
www.iwla.com
Facebook, Twitter, LinkedIn, YouTube

Steve W. Dehaan, President & CEO
Jay D. Strother, Vice Chairman
Jennifer Director, Membership Director
Hank Vaughan, Education & Meetings Director
Robert Budo, Finance & Accounting Manager

The unified voice of the global logistics outsourcing industry, representing third party warehousing, transportation and logistics service providers. Our member companies provide the most timely and cost-effective global logistics solutions for their customers and are committed to protecting the free flow of products across international borders.
500 Members
Founded in 1997

9509 **Interstate Professional Applicators Association**
PO Box 1420
Milton, WA 98354-1420

253-922-9437; Fax: 253-922-3788

Provides education and information for the professional horticultural applicator. Legislative work involves the states of Washington, Oregon, Idaho in the area of laws and regulations.

9510 **Iowa Meat Processors Association**
PO Box 334
Clarence, IA 52216

563-452-3329; Fax: 563-452-2141
execdirector@iowameatprocessors.org
www.iowameatprocessors.org

Tom Taylor, President
Merrill Angell, 1st Vice President
Dave Burma, 2nd Vice President
Jason Ludwig, 3rd Vice President
Marcia Richmann, Executive Directors

An organization comprised of beef, pork, wild game, and poultry processors and allied businesses from throughout the state of Iowa. Members include slaughterers, food service companies, packers, locker operators, butcher shops, ham manufacturers, smokehouse owners, wholesalers, custom operations, retail operations, and companies that supply goods and services to the meat industry.

9511 **Islamic Food and Nutrition Council of America (IFANCA)**
777 Busse Hwy
Park Ridge, IL 60068

847-993-0034; Fax: 847-993-0038
www.ifanca.org
Facebook, Twitter, LinkedIn, Youtube,stumbleupon,digg,frien

Zeshan Sadek, Director International Services
Mujahid Masood, Ph.D., Senior Food Scientist

A non-profit Islamic organization dedicated to promote halel food and the institution of halel.
Founded in 1982

9512 **Italian Trade Agency**
Italian Trade Commission
33 E 67th St
New York, NY 10065-5949
212-980-1500; Fax: 212-758-1050
newyork@ice.it
www.italtrade.com

Pace Marisa, Executive Secretary
Augusta Smargiassi, Senior Deputy Trade Commissioner
Antonio Lucarelli, Senior Trade Commission

The Italian government agency entrusted with the promotion of trade, business opportunities and industrial cooperation between Italian and foreign companies. It supports the internationalisation of Italian firms and their consolidation in foreign markets.

9513 **Italian Wine and Food Institute**
One Grand Central Place
60 East 42nd St. Suite 2214
New York, NY 10165

212-867-4111; Fax: 212-867-4114
iwfi@aol.com

Lucio Caputo, President
Vincent Giampaolo, VP

Members are producers, distributors and marketers of Italian wines and foods.
Founded in 1983

9514 **Juice Products Association**
750 National Press Building
529 14th Street NW
Washington, DC 20045

202-785-3232; Fax: 202-223-9741
jpa@kellencompany.com
www.juiceproducts.org

Richard E Cristol, President
Carol Freysinger, Executive Director
Patricia Faison, Technical Director
Darrell McCook, Meetings Manager
Jim Wolters, Account Coordinator

The trade association for the fruit and juice products industry, including juice processors, packers, extractors, brokers as well as marketers of fruit juices and vegetable juices, juice beverages, fruit jams, jellies and preserves and similar products. JPA also represents juice industry suppliers and food testing laboratories and includes firms engaged in the trading of frozen concentrated orange juice futures and/or options on behalf of JPA processor members.
135 Members
Founded in 1957

9515 **LaSalle Food Processing Association**
108 S Broadway
PO Box 97
La Salle, MN 56056-0097

507-375-3408; Fax: 507-642-3077

Pat Thiner, Manager

A meat packers trade association.

9516 **Leafy Greens Council**
PO Box 143
Waterport, NY 14571

716-517-0248
www.leafy-greens.org

Ray Clark, Executive Director
Robert Strube, President

Purpose is to improve the marketing and increase consumption through national promotions, to educate consumers about the nutritional values of leafy greens through media campaigns, to represent member interests to government, and to provide networking opportunities for members. Members represent growers, shippers, brokers, terminal market operators, and suppliers.
117 Members
Founded in 1974

9517 **Les Amis d'Escoffier Society of New York, Inc.**
787 Ridgewood Road
Millburn, NJ 07041

212-414-5820; Fax: 973-379-3117
www.escoffier-society.com

Mark Arnao, President
George McNeill, First Vice President
Jay Jones, Secretary
Kurt Keller, TREASURER

Providing opportunitites for members' delight and edification and also generate gains in the perfection of the art of fine dining. Membership consists of chefs de cuisine, hotel executives, restaurateurs and business executives.
Founded in 1936

9518 **Livestock Marketing Association**
10510 NW Ambassador Drive
Kansas City, MO 64153

816-891-0502
800-821-2048; Fax: 816-891-0552
lmainfo@lmaweb.com
www.lmaweb.com
Facebook, Twitter

Mark Mackey, Chief Executive Officer
Sheri Crist, Chief Financial Officer
Jennifer Aiman, Vice President, Operations
Chelsea Good, VP, Government & Industry Affairs
Kristen Parman, Vice President, Membership Services

Committed to the support and protection of the local livestock auction markets. LMA is the voice for the auction markets on legislative and regulatory issues and in providing member services to maintain successful, viable marketing businesses and better service to all of the livestock producers who sell at auction.

9519 **Machalek Communications, Inc.**
Machalek Communications
12550 W Frontage Road
Suite 220
Burnsville, MN 55337

952-736-8000
800-846-5520; Fax: 866-490-8834
info@machalek.com
www.machalek.com
Facebook, LinkedIn

Andrea McChalek, President/CEO
Deanna Morin, Vice Pres. of Business Development
Krista Gardner, Office Manager
Maria Palmer, Lead Graphic and Web Designer

Includes over 20 employees and publishes seven nationwide postcard advertising decks. Distributes more then 100 million postcards per year to over 800,000 qualified buyers. Company has furthermore evolved to include additional sales lead generation services including list rental, mail, and internet marketing.
25 Members
Founded in 1987
Mailing list available for rent

9520 **Maraschino Cherry and Glace Fruit Processors**
3301 State Route 66
Neptune, NJ 07753

732-922-3008

Richard Sullivan, Executive VP

9521 **Material Handling Industry of America**
8720 Red Oak Blvd
Suite 201
Charlotte, NC 28217-3996

704-676-1190; Fax: 704-676-1199
dvarner@mhi.org
www.mhi.org
Facebook, Twitter, LinkedIn, YouTube

Dave Young, Executive Chairman
John Paxton, President
Gregg E. Goodner, Vice President
George Prest, CEO
Donna Varner, Executive Administrator

The complexity of managing supply chains that span continents and dominate markets demands strategies, equipment and systems that are agile, adaptable, and aligned. With product lifescycles shortening and worldwide competition increasing, success depends on effective material handling and logistics solutions for the global supply chain. Being able to deliver the right product to the right market at the right time.

9522 **Meat & Livestock Australia**
Level 1, 40 Mount Street
Locked Bag 991
North Sydney, NS 2060

294-639-333; Fax: 294-639-393
info@mla.com.au
www.mla.com.au
Facebook, Twitter, YouTube

Michele Allan, Chairman
Richard Norton, Managing Director
Lucinda Corrigan, Director
Geoffrey Maynard, Director
John McKillop, Director

Providing marketing and research and development services to cattle, sheep and goat producer members and the broader red meat industry to help them meet community and consumer expectations. MLA is committed to fostering world leadership for the Australian red meat and livestock industry for creating opportunities for its stakeholders, the environment, red meat consumers and the community.
30000 Members
Founded in 1998

9523 **Meat & Livestock Australia, North American Region**
1401 K Street NW
Suite 602
Washington, DC 20005

202-521-2551; Fax: 202-521-2699
info@mlana.com
www.australian-meat.com
Facebook, Twitter, YouTube

David Pietsch, Regional Manager, North America
Scott Hansen, Managing Director

Providing marketing and research and development services to cattle, sheep and goat producer members and the broader red meat industry to help them meet community and consumer expectations. MLA is committed to fostering world leadership for the Australian red meat and livestock industry for creating opportunities for its stakeholders, the environment, red meat consumers and the community.
30000 Members
Founded in 1998

9524 **Meat Import Council of America**
1901 Fort Myer Dr
Suite 1110
Arlington, VA 22209

703-522-1910
800-522-1910; Fax: 703-524-6039
lauriebryant@micausa.org
www.micausa.org

Kim Holzner, Chairman
David Rind, Vice Chairman
Donald E. Stewart, Treasurer
Laurie I. Bryant, Executive Director & Secretary

To foster the trade, commerce and interests of importers and exporters of fresh and/or frozen and/or cured and/or cooked and/or canned meats.
130 Members
Founded in 1962

9525 **Meat Trade Institute**
213 South Avenue East
Spencer Savings Bank Building
Cranford, NJ 07016

908-276-5111; Fax: 212-279-4016
www.spcnetwork.com/mti/

John J. Calcangno, President

A full-time fully-staffed trade association serving meat and poultry industries in the northeast. The Institute seeks to build and strengthen the relationships of its members with government, labor, and all other segments of the meat and poultry industry.

9526 **Mid-Atlantic Canners Association**
316 S Front Street
Hamburg, PA 19526

610-562-3061; Fax: 610-562-0281

Robert Crosswell, Crosswell
D Seibert, VP Finance

Mid Atlantic Canners Association is a cooperative soft drink canning facility for the

Coca-Cola system. All of the national Coca-Cola Company brands are canned, packaged and shipped by truck to various Coca-Cola franchised distributors located throughout the northeast United States.

9527 **Mid-Atlantic Dairy Association**
325 Chestnut St
Suite 600
Philadelphia, PA 19106

215-627-8800; Fax: 215-627-8887
dairyspot@milk4u.org
www.dairyspot.com
Facebook, Twitter, LinkedIn, Youtube, Pinterest, Googleplus

Patty Purcell, CEO

Mid-Atlantic Dairy Association is one of 19 state and regional promotion organizations working under the umbrella of the United Dairy Industry Association. Working to bring a fully integrated national promotion program to the Mid-Atlantic region.
Mailing list available for rent

9528 **Mid-States Meat Association**
1335 Dublin Rd
Suite 10
Columbus, OH 43215-1000

614-459-5188; Fax: 614-442-5516
www.midstatesmeat.org

Kristin Mullins, Executive Director
100 Members

9529 **Midwest Dairy Association**
2015 Rice St
St Paul, MN 55113

651-488-0261
800-642-3895; Fax: 651-488-0265
www.midwestdairy.com
Facebook, Twitter, Youtube, Pinterest

Mike Kruger, CEO

Works on behalf of dairy farmers to increase dairy sales, foster innovation and inspire consumer confidence in dairy products and practices.
210M Members
Founded in 1940

9530 **Midwest Food Processors Association**
4600 American Pkwy
Suite 210
Madison, WI 53718-8334

608-255-9946; Fax: 608-255-9838
info@mwfpa.org
www.mwfpa.org
Facebook, Twitter, LinkedIn

Nick George, President
Brian Elliot, Director of Communications
Robin Fanshaw, Manager
Brian Deschane, Director of Operations

Trade association that advocates on behalf of food processing companies and affiliated industries in Illinois, Minnesota, and Wisconsin. Influencing public policy and making the Midwest a great place for food processors to do business. Advocating, educating, communicating, and facilitating.
Founded in 1905

9531 **Missouri Grocers Association**
315 North Ken Avenue
Springfield, MO 65802

417-831-6667; Fax: 417-831-3907
cmcmillian@missourigrocers.com
www.missourigrocers.com
Facebook

Erick Taylor, Chairman
John Porter, President
Mike Beal, Vice President
Chuck Murfin, III, Treasurer
Dan Shaul, State Director

Committed to the growth and profitability of its members by providing proactive state and federal legislative and regulatory representation, effective communication, beneficial member services, and education of industry innovations.

9532 **Mushroom Council**
2880 Zanker Road
Suite 203
San Jose, CA 95134

408-432-7210; Fax: 408-432-7213
info@mushroomcouncil.org
www.mushroomcouncil.org
Facebook, Twitter, YouTube, Pinterest, Google+, R

Carla Blackwell-Mckinney, Vice Chair
Robert Crouch, Secretary

Plays an important role in the national promotion of fresh mushrooms through consumer public relations, foodservice communications and retail communications.
Founded in 1993

9533 **National Advisory Group**
200 Ponte Vedra Blvd.
Ponte Vedra Beach, FL 32082

440-250-1583
nagconvenience.com
Facebook

John Lofstock, Executive Director

This association represents senior level management of retail companies organized to enhance buying power, merchandising programs and an exchange of ideas.
500 Members
Founded in 1983

9534 **National Agri-Marketing Association**
11020 King Street
Suite 205
Overland Park, KS 66210

913-491-6500; Fax: 913-491-6502
agrimktg@nama.org
www.nama.org
Facebook, Twitter, LinkedIn, YouTube, Flickr

Jennifer Pickett, Executive VP & CEO
Sherry Pfaff, Chief Operating Officer
Janae Prewitt, Manager, Information Services
Debbie Brummel, Student Coordinator

The nation's largest association for professionals in marketing and agribusiness.
Cost: $170.00
3500 Members
Frequency: Membership Dues
Founded in 1957

9535 **National Agriculture Day**
11020 King St
Suite 205
Overland Park, KS 66210

913-491-1895; Fax: 913-491-6502
www.agday.org
Facebook, Twitter, YouTube, Flickr

Greg Horstmeier, Chair
Jonathon Ebert, Vice Chair
Amy Bradford, Secretary/Treasurer

An organization uniquely composed of leaders in the agriculture, food and fiber communities dedicated to increasing the public awareness of agriculture's vital role in our society.
Founded in 1973

9536 **National Alcohol Beverage Control Association**
4401 Ford Avenue
Suite 700
Alexandria, VA 22302-1433

703-578-4200; Fax: 703-820-3551
nabca.info@nabca.org
www.nabca.org
Facebook, Twitter, Youtube, Google

Stephen Larson, Chairman
Stephanie O'Brien, Chairman-Elect
James M. Sgueo, President & CEO
Jeffrey R. Anderson, Board of Director
Andrew J. Deloney, Board of Director

It is the mission of the National Alcohol Beverage Control Association to support and benefit alcohol control systems by providing research, fostering relationships, and managing resources to address policy for the responsible sale and consumption of alcohol beverages. Members include control jurisdictions, supplier members and industry trade associations.
175 Members
Frequency: Membership Dues Vary
Founded in 1938

9537 **National Aquaculture Association**
PO Box 12759
Tallahassee, FL 32317

850-216-2400; Fax: 850-216-2480
naa@thenaa.net
thenaa.net

Jim Parsons, President
Sebastian Belle, Vice President
Adam Hater, Secretary
Rick Martin, Treasurer

A producer-based, non-profit trade association dedicated to advocacy for U.S. aquaculture.

9538 **National Association for the Specialty Food Trade**
Home Page: www.specialtyfood.com
Facebook, Twitter, LinkedIn, YouTube, Pinterest

Nonprofit business trade association established to foster trade, commerce, and interest in the specialty food industry.
Founded in 1952

9539 **National Association of Agricultural Educators**
University of Kentucky
300 Garrigus Building
Lexington, KY 40546-0215

859-257-2224
800-509-0204; Fax: 859-323-3919
naae@uky.edu
www.naae.org
Facebook, Twitter

Alissa Smith, Chief Executive Officer
Wm. Jay Jackman, Executive Director
Olivia Thomas, Specialist, Marketing & Comm.
Ashley Hood, Membership Coordinator
Sarah Warren, Meeting Planner & Program Assistant

A federation of 50 affiliated state vocational agricultural teacher associations. The mission is to provide agricultural education for the global community through visionary leadership, advocacy and service.
7600 Members
Founded in 1948

9540 **National Association of Animal Breeders**
PO Box 1033
Columbia, MO 65205
573-445-4406; Fax: 573-446-2279
naab-css@naab-css.org
www.naab-css.org
Paul Hunt, Chair
Christopher England, Director
Bobby Fair, Director
Earl Souva, Director
Roy Wilson, Director
Unite those individuals and organizations engaged in the artificial insemination of cattle and other livestock into an affiliated federation operating under self-imposed standards of performance and to conduct and promote the mutual interest and ideals of its members. Members are farmer co-ops and others interested in livestock improvement.
Founded in 1946

9541 **National Association of Beverage Importers Inc.**
529 14th St NW
Suite 1183
Washington, DC 20045
202-393-6224; Fax: 202-393-6595
www.bevimporters.org
John F. Beaudette, Chairman
Michael J. Rudy, Chairman of the Committee
Stacey M. Tank, Vice Chairman
William T. Earle, President
Marc P. Goodrich, Treasurer
Trade association representing US importers of alcohol beverages, representing the interests of importers of alcohol beverages on issues that have a principal impact on importers, and cooperating with other trade associations on issues that impact all alcohol beverages whether imported or domestic.
Founded in 1934

9542 **National Association of Concessionaires**
180 N. MICHIGAN AVENUE
Suite 2215
Chicago, IL 60601
312-236-3858; Fax: 312-236-7809
info@naconline.org
www.naconline.org
Facebook, LinkedIn
John Evans Jr., Chairman
Jeff Scudillo, Presdient
Terry Conlon, President-Elect
Dan Borschke, Executive Vice President
Andrew Cretors, Treasurer
Trade association for the recreation and leisure-time food and beverage concessions industry. Providing members with information and services that maintain and enhance the standards of excellence and professionalism within the recreation and leisure time food, beverage and related services industry.
800 Members
Founded in 1944

9543 **National Association of Convenience Stores**
1600 Duke Street
Alexandria, VA 22314
703-684-3600
800-966-6227; Fax: 703-836-4564
www.convenience.org
Facebook, Twitter, LinkedIn, YouTube, Instagram
Sandy Smith, National Sales Manager
Association supporting convenience and fuel retailing companies.
2.3M Members
Founded in 1961
Mailing list available for rent

9544 **National Association of Flavors and Food Ingredient Systems**
3301 State Route 66
Building C, Suite 205
Neptune, NJ 07753
732-922-3218; Fax: 732-922-3590
info@naffs.org
www.naffs.org
Dave Adams, Chair
Christine Daley, President
Pia Henzi, President-Elect
Cynthia Astrack, Vice President
Chris Williams, Vice Presdient
A broad-based trade association of manufacturers, processors and suppliers of fruits, flavors, syrups, stabilizers, emulsifiers, colors, sweeteners, cocoa and related food ingredients. Its associate membership is open to all companies that provide products and services to the food industry.
120 Members
Founded in 1917

9545 **National Association of Margarine Manufacturers**
NAMM@kellencompany.com
www.iheartbutterytaste.com
Facebook, Twitter, Pinterest
Information and recipes about buttery soft spread margarines.

9546 **National Association of Pizzeria Operators**
909 S 8th Street
Suite 200
Louisville, KY 40203
502-736-9532; Fax: 502-736-9502
dwyatt@pizzatoday.com
www.napo.com
Facebook, Twitter, Youtube
Joe Straughan, President
Mary Sullivan, Membership Coordinator
Mission is to create and foster a community of independent and small chain pizzeria operators and their industry suppliers where doing business with another is mutually beneficial.
1100+ Members
Founded in 1984
Mailing list available for rent: 25000 names

9547 **National Association of State Departments of Agriculture**
4350 North Fairfax Drive
Suite 910
Arlington, VA 22203
202-296-9680; Fax: 703-880-0509
nasda@nasda.org
www.nasda.org
Facebook, Twitter
Barb Glenn, Chief Executive Officer
Martha Dale, Chief Financial & Strategy Officer
Amanda Culp, Communications & Events Director
Elizabeth Rowland, Human Resources Director
Lisa Benson, NASDA Foundation Executive Director
Mission is to represent the state departments of agriculture in the development, implementation, and communication of sound public policy and programs which support and promote the American agricultural industry, while protecting consumers and the environment.
Founded in 1915

9548 **National Association of Wheat Growers**
415 Second St NE
Suite 200
Washington, DC 20002
202-547-7800; Fax: 202-546-2638
wheatworld@wheatworld.org
www.wheatworld.org
Facebook, Twitter
Chandler Goule, CEO
Caitlin Eanello, Director, Communications
Josh Tonsager, VP, Policy & Communications
Represents wheat producers in Washington, D.C.
Founded in 1950

9549 **National Association of Wholesaler - Distributors**
1325 G Street NW
Suite 1000
Washington, DC 20005-3100
202-872-0885; Fax: 202-785-0586
naw@naw.org
www.naw.org
Facebook, Twitter, YouTube
Eric Hoplin, President & CEO
The NAW provides members with the opportunity for networking and benchmarking within the entire wholesale distribution industry. NAW also represents the wholesale distribution industry before Congress, the White House, and the judiciary on issues that cross the industry's many lines of trade.

9550 **National Automatic Merchandising Association**
20 N Wacker Dr.
Suite 3500
Chicago, IL 60606
312-346-0370
800-331-8816; Fax: 312-704-4140
www.namanow.org
Facebook, Twitter, x, YouTube, Instagram
Carla Balakgie, President & CEO
Association serving the convenience services industry.
1250+ Members
Founded in 1936

9551 **National Bar and Restaurant Association**
307 W Jackson Avenue
Oxford, MS 38655
662-236-5510; Fax: 202-331-2429
www.bar-restaurant.com
Jennifer Robinson, COO
Laura Speakes, Financial Affairs VP
Founded by Nightclub and Bar magazine, the association's mission is to provide discounts, services and networking opportunities enabling restaurant, bar and hospitality professionals to increase revenues and profits through innovative promotions, marketing and management.
Founded in 1924

9552 **National Barbecue & Grilling Association**
PO Box 782
Kirkland, WA 98083
360-670-0194
info@nbbqa.org
www.nbbqa.org
Facebook, Twitter, LinkedIn, Youtube
Patrick Murty, President
Barbara Latimer, President-Elect
Ken Phillips, Treasurer
Joey Machado, Secretary
Saffron Hodgson, Executive Director

Mission is to provide the barbeque community with a visionary, beneficial, and responsive association. NBBQA goals are to promote the art and enjoyment of barbecue, facilitate the effective networking of industry resources and to foster new business opportunities.
735 Members
Founded in 1991

9553 **National Beer Wholesalers Association**
1101 King Street
Suite 600
Alexandria, VA 22314

703-683-4300
800-300-6417
info@nbwa.org
www.nbwa.org
Facebook, Twitter, YouTube, Flickr

Craig Purser, President/CEO
Grace Connolly, Executive Assistant
Lauren Kane, VP, Communications
Paul Pisano, SVP Industry Affairs & Gen. Counsel
Patti Rouzie, VP, Membership & Meetings

NBWA represents the interests of America's 2,850 independent, licensed beer distributors which service every congressional district and media market in the country.
Founded in 1938
Mailing list available for rent

9554 **National Bison Association**
8690 Wolff Ct
200
Westminster, CO 80031

303-292-2833; Fax: 303-845-9081
david@bisoncentral.com
www.bisoncentral.com
Facebook

Dave Carter, Executive Director
Jim Matheson, Assistant Director
Barb Dowdy, Bookkeeper
Karen Conley, Communications Director
Anita Shaver, Design & Production Manager

Bringing together stakeholders to celebrate the heritage of American bison/buffalo, educating, and creating a sustainable future for our industry.
900 Members
Founded in 1975

9555 **National Bulk Vendors Association**
1202 East Maryland Avenue
Suite 1k
Phoenix, AZ 85014

888-628-2872; Fax: 480-302-5108
admin@nbva.org
www.nbva.org
Facebook

Judi Heston, President
Shawn Dumphy, Vice President
Carl Morcate, Treasurer
John P. Winters, Secretary
George Wells, Membership Chair

A national, not-for-profit trade association comprised of the manufacturers, distributors and operators of bulk vending machines and products.
Founded in 1950

9556 **National Cattlemen's Beef Association**
9110 E. Nichols Ave.
#300
Centennial, CO 80112

303-694-0305; Fax: 303-694-2851
customerservice@beef.org
www.beef.org
Facebook, Twitter

Forrest Roberts, CEO
John Queen III, President
Thad Larson, Director

Consumer focused, producer directed organization representing the largest segment of the nation's food and fiber industry.
28000 Members
Founded in 1898
Mailing list available for rent

9557 **National Cherry Growers and Industries Foundation (NCGIF)**
2667 Reed Road
Hood River, OR 97031

541-386-5761; Fax: 541-386-3191
maraschinocherries.org
Facebook, LinkedIn, YouTube, Pinterest

B J Thurlby, President
Idell Dunn, Assessment Supervisor
Andrew Willis, Promotion Director
Cheryl Kroupa, Marketing Director

Formed for the purpose of having a unified effort from the processed cherry industry to lobby against excessive cherry imports. The foundation compiles and distributes to members a yearly statistical publication of information regarding cherry production, utilization, and sales, both import and export.
Founded in 1948

9558 **National Coffee Association**
45 Broadway
Suite 1140
New York, NY 10006

212-766-4007; Fax: 212-766-5815
info@ncausa.org
www.ncausa.org
Facebook, Twitter, LinkedIn

Bruce Goldsmith, Chairman
John DeMuria, Vice Chairman
William (Bill) Murray, President & CEO
William M. Cortner, Secretary
Thrisha Andrews, Administrative Assistant

Established on behalf of the coffee companies in the United States. Respond to external issues and represent the coffee industry before the legislative and executive branches of government.
200 Members
Founded in 1911

9559 **National Confectioners Association**
1101 30th Street NW
Suite 200
Washington, DC 20007

202-534-1440; Fax: 202-337-0637
info@candyUSA.com
www.candyusa.com
Facebook, Twitter, LinkedIn, YouTube, Pinterest, Instagram

Peter W. Blommer, Chairman
Michael G. Rosenberg, Vice Chairman
John H. Downs, Jr., President
Martino Caretto, Vice President
John E. Brooks, Jr., Treasurer

Representing the entire confection industry, offering education and leadership in manufacturing, technical research, public relations, retailing practices, government relations, and statistical analyses.
Founded in 1884

9560 **National Confectionery Sales Association**
Spitfire House
3135 Berea Road
Cleveland, OH 44111

216-631-8200; Fax: 216-631-8210
info@candyhalloffame.org
candyhalloffame.org/NCSA/contact.shtml
Facebook, Twitter

Joe Muck, Chairman
John A. Leipold Jr., President
Russell Berg, Director
David Fleischer, Director
Anthony P. Cognetti, Treasurer

Dedicated to furthering positive growth and acceptance of confectionery and allied products by education, open and frank dialogue, and recognition of peers' notable accomplishments. The Associations' responsibility to principals, customers, members and the community is to represent their products and services professionally and ethically in all relationships.
375 Members
Founded in 1899

9561 **National Conference of State Liquor Administrators**
543 Long Hill Road
Gurnee, IL 60031

847-721-6410
www.ncsla.org

Jerry W. Waters, Sr, President
Matthew D. Botting, 1st Vice President
Richard Haymaker, 2nd Vice President
A. Keith Burt, 3rd Vice President
Pamela Frantz, Executive Director

Promoting the enactment of the most effective and equitable types of state alcoholic beverage control laws, to devise and promote the use of methods which provide the best enforcement of the particular alcoholic beverage control laws in each state, to work for the adoption of uniform laws, and to promote harmony with the federal government in its administration.

9562 **National Conference on Interstate Milk Shipments**
PO Box 108
Monticello, IL 61856

217-762-2656
ncims.bordson@gmail.com
www.ncims.org

Dr. Stephen Beam, Chair
David E. Latten, Vice Chair
Marlena G. Bordson, Executive Secretary
Beth Briczinski, Board Member
Ken Anderson, Board Member

The goal is to assure the safest possible milk supply for all the people. The NCIMS is governed by an executive board comprised of representatives from state and local regulatory agencies from three geographical regions; FDA, USDA, industry and laboratories and academia.
Founded in 1940

9563 **National Corn Growers Association**
632 Cepi Drive
Chesterfield, MO 63005

636-733-9004; Fax: 636-733-9005
corninfo@ncga.com
www.ncga.com
Facebook, Twitter, Pinterest

Jon Doggett, Chief Executive Officer
Fred Stemme, Chief Operating Officer
Neil Caskey, VP, Communications
Mike Shelby, Manager, Assoc. & Mem. Services
Rita Dunagan, Manager, Meetings & Events

Mission is to create and increase opportunities for corn growers. The Association will continue to be the recognized leader working in cooperation with its suppliers and customers to maintain sustainability and to achieve new business and profit opportunities for those it represents.
32300 Members
Founded in 1957
Mailing list available for rent

9564 National Council of Chain Restaurants
1101 New York Ave. NW
Suite 1200
Washington, DC 20005
202-783-7971
800-673-4692; Fax: 202-737-2849
nrf.com
Facebook, Twitter, LinkedIn, YouTube, Instagram
Matthew R. Shay, President & CEO
The leading trade association exclusively representing chain restaurant companies. Working to advance sound public policy that best serves the interests of restaurant businesses and the millions of people they employ.
Founded in 1965

9565 National Council of Farmer Cooperatives
50 F Street NW
Suite 900
Washington, DC 20001
202-626-8700; Fax: 202-626-8722
www.ncfc.org
Facebook, Twitter, Flickr
Charles Conner, President/ CEO
Marlis Carson, SVP, Legal, Tax
Justin Darisse, Vice President, Communications
Lisa Van Doren, Vice President & Chief of Staff
Kevin Natz, Vice President
Regional and national farmer cooperatives.
Founded in 1929

9566 National Country Ham Association
PO Box 948
Conover, NC 28616
828-466-2760
800-820-4426; Fax: 828-466-2770
eatham@countryham.org
www.countryham.org
Allan Benton, President
Encourages promotion, development and improvement of the businesses of country ham carvers and encourages the use of country carved meats through co-operative methods of production, promotion, education and advertisement.
53 Members
Founded in 1992

9567 National Dairy Council
Interstate Place II
100 Elwood Davis Road
North Syracuse, NY 13212
315-472-9143; Fax: 315-472-0506
ndc@dairyinformation.com
www.nationaldairycouncil.org
Facebook, Twitter, Pinterest
This association operates under the auspices of the United Dairy Industry Association. NDC provides timely, scientifically sound nutrition information to the media, physicians, dietitians, nurses, educators, consumers and others concerned about fostering a healthier society.
Founded in 1915
Mailing list available for rent

9568 National Farmers Organization
528 Billy Sunday Road
Suite 100, P.O. Box 2508
Ames, IA 50010ÿ
800-247-2110
nfo@nfo.org
www.nfo.org
Facebook, YouTube
Paul Olson, President, Chair
Bruce Shultz, Vice President
Members represent a cross-section of both conventional and organic production—grain growers, cattle and hog producers and dairymen and women.

9569 National Farmers Union
20 F Street NW
Suite 300
Washington, DC 20001
202-554-1600
800-347-1961; Fax: 202-554-1654
nfu.org
Facebook, Twitter, YouTube, Instagram
Rob Larew, President
Patty Edelburg, Vice President
Dave Velde, General Counsel
Ethan Whitmore, Vice President, Operations
Martha Van Dale, Director, Finance
Farmers Union helped shape national policy, organized cooperative businesses that thrive today, delivered educational programs designed to build rural leaders, and provided farmers and ranchers with opportunities to be at the table.
Founded in 1902

9570 National Federation of Coffee Growers of Colombia
140 E 57th St
New York, NY 10022-2765
212-271-8802
www.federaciondecafeteros.org
This organization is comprised of coffee growers from Colombia whose goal is to promote Colombian coffee in the US.

9571 National Frozen & Refrigerated Foods Association Inc.
4755 Linglestown Road
Suite 300
Harrisburg, PA 17112
717-657-8601; Fax: 717-657-9862
nfra@nfraweb.org
www.nfraweb.org
Facebook, Twitter, LinkedIn, YouTube, Pinterest
H.V. Skip Shaw Jr., President/CEO
Jeff Rumachik, EVP/COO
Julie W. Henderson, VP, Communications
Jessica Scott, VP, Finance
Natalie Limm, Member Communications Manager
NFRA is a non-profit trade association representing all segments of the frozen and refrigerated foods industry.
450 Members
Founded in 1945

9572 National Frozen Dessert and Fast Food Association
9614 Tomstown Road
Waynesboro, PA 17268
800-535-7748
This association is made up of small, independent owners and operators of ice cream and fast food establishments.

9573 National Grape Co-Operative/Welch's
2 South Portage Street
Westfield, NY 14787
716-326-5200; Fax: 716-326-5494
www.welchs.com
Facebook, Twitter
Joseph C Falcone, President
More than just an organization of grape growers, stringent quality growing and harvesting standards, viticultural research, and aggressively funding new product development, manufacturing and marketing programs of Welch's.
Founded in 1897

9574 National Honey Board
11409 Business Park Circle
Suite 210
Firestone, CO 80504-9200
303-776-2337; Fax: 303-776-1177
honey@nhb.org
www.honey.com
Facebook, Twitter, YouTube, Pinterest, Google+, I
Jill Clark, Chairperson
Mark Mammen, Vice Chairperson
Margaret Lombard, Chief Executive Officer
Eric S. Wenger, Secretary/Treasurer
Douglas Hauke, Producers
Conducts research, advertising and promotion programs to help maintain and expand domestic and foreign markets for honey.
Founded in 1987
Mailing list available for rent

9575 National Honey Packers & Dealers Association
3301 Route 66
Suite 205, Building C
Neptune, NJ 07753
732-922-3008; Fax: 732-922-3590
info@nhpda.org
www.nhpda.org
Bob Bauer, Executive Vice President
Comprised of US packers, importers and foreign exporters.

9576 National Hot Dog and Sausage Council
1150 Connecticut Avenue, NW
12th Floor
Washington, DC
202-587-4200
www.hot-dog.org
Facebook, YouTube, Pinterest
Janet Riley, President
Eric Mittenthal, Vice President, Public Affairs
Conducts scientific research to benefit hot dog and sausage manufacturers.
Founded in 1994

9577 National Hot Pepper Association
400 NW 20th Street
Fort Lauderdale, FL 33311-3818
954-565-4972; Fax: 954-566-2208
Networking among industry and private members. Education and information sharing.

9578 National Ice Cream Mix Association
2101 Wilson Blvd
Suite 400
Arlington, VA 22201
703-243-5630; Fax: 703-841-9328
nicma@nmpf.org
www.icecreammix.org
Joe Duscher, President
Pat Galloway, Vice President
Jamie Jonker, Vice President, Scientific Regs
Bob Kmetz, Treasurer
Tom Balmer, Executive Director
This group is made up of manufacturers of soft-serve ice cream, ice milk, shakes and other dessert mixes.
Founded in 1926

9579 National Mango Board
3101 Maguire Blvd
Suite 111
Orlando, FL 32803
407-629-7318
877-MAN-OS 1

www.mango.org
Facebook, Twitter, Pinterest, YouTube

Lucy Keith, Consumer Media
Susan Hughes, Foodservice
Kristine Concepcion, Mango Industry Contact
Katie Ola, Trade Media
Wendy McManus, Retail Contact

A national promotion and research organization which is supported by assessments from domestic and imported mangos.

9580 **National Meat Canners Association**
1150 Connecticut Avenue, NW
12th Floor
Washington, DC 20036

202-587-4200; Fax: 202-587-4300
webmaster@meatami.com
www.meatami.org
Facebook, Twitter, LinkedIn

Nick Merigolli, Chairman
Greg Benedict, Vice-Chairman
Barry Carpenter, President & CEO
J. Michael Townsley, Treasurer
John Vatri, Secretary

AMI is the national trade association representing companies that process 70 percent of U.S. meat and their suppliers throughout America.

9581 **National Milk Producers Federation**
2101 Wilson Blvd
Suite 400
Arlington, VA 22201

703-243-6111; Fax: 703-841-9328
info@nmpf.org
www.nmpf.org
Facebook, Twitter, Flickr, YouTube

Randy Mooney, Chairman
Ken Nobis, 1st Vice Chairman
Adrian Boer, 2nd Vice Chairman
Mike McCloskey, 3rd Vice Chairman
Pete Kappelman, Treasurer

Develops and carries out policies that advance the well being of dairy producers and the cooperatives they own. Provides a forum through which dairy farmers and their cooperatives formulate policy on national issues that affect milk production and marketing.
Founded in 1916
Mailing list available for rent

9582 **National Oilseed Processors Association**
1300 L St NW
Suite 1020
Washington, DC 20005

202-842-0463; Fax: 202-842-9126
www.nopa.org

Thomas A. Hammer, President
David J. Hovermale, Executive Vice President
Katie Vassalli, Director, Regulatory Affairs
Jeanne L. Seibert, Office Administrator
Steve O'Nan, Chair

Represents firms engaged in the actual processing of oilseeds, and associate firms who are consumers of vegetable oil or oilseed meal, including some refiners and mixed feed manufacturers.
Founded in 1929

9583 **National Onion Association**
822 7th St
Suite 510
Greeley, CO 80631

970-353-5895; Fax: 970-353-5897
www.onions-usa.org
Twitter, Pinterest

Greg Yielding, Executive Vice President
Doug Bulgrin, President
Rene Hardwick, Dir., Public & Industry Relations
Courtney Herbst, Admin. Assistant & Accounting

Represents interests of US onion producers. Informational lobbying and generic promotional headquarters for fresh dry bulb onion growers. Provides connections for networking and education exchange.
600 Members
Founded in 1913
Mailing list available for rent

9584 **National Pasta Association**
750 National Press Building
529 14th Street NW
Washington, DC 20045

202-591-2459; Fax: 202-591-2445
info@ilovepasta.org
www.ilovepasta.org

Greg Pearson, Chairman
Bastiaan DeZeeuw, Vice Chairman
Jim Meyer, Treasurer
Peter Bisaccia, Board Member
Randy Gilbertson, Board Member

To increase the consumption of pasta, to promote the development of sound public policy and, act as a center of knowledge for the industry.
Founded in 1904

9585 **National Peanut Board**
3350 Riverwood Parkway
Suite 1150
Atlanta, GA 30339

678-424-5750
866-825-7946; Fax: 678-424-5751
peanuts@nationalpeanutboard.org
www.nationalpeanutboard.org
Facebook, Twitter, Pinterest

Bob H. White, Chairman
Monty Rast, Vice Chairman
Gayle White, Treasurer
Ed White, Secretary
Gregory Gill, Board Member

A farmer-funded national research, promotion and education check-off program. Through NPB, growers from across the United States come together to contribute to the research and promotion of USA-grown peanuts.

9586 **National Pecan Shellers Association**
1100 Johnson Ferry Road
Suite 300
Atlanta, GA 30342

678-298-1189; Fax: 404-591-6811
npsa@kellencompany.com
www.ilovepecans.org
Facebook, Twitter, Pinterest

The NPSA is the trade association for the pecan shelling and processing industry. The association is dedicated to educating culinary and health professionals, food technologists, educators and the general public about the health benefits, nutritional value, variety of uses and all-around great taste of pecans.

9587 **National Pork Board**
1776 NW 114th St.
Des Moines, IA 50325

515-223-2600
800-456-7675
info@pork.org
www.pork.org

Bill Even, CEO
John Johnson, COO

Uniting pork producers for the future of the pork industry.

9588 **National Pork Producers Council**
122 C Street NW
Suite 875
Washington, DC 20001

202-347-3600; Fax: 202-347-5265
warnerd@nppc.org
www.nppc.org
Facebook, Twitter, LinkedIn, Swinecast, Pinterest, Flickr

Neil Dierks, Chief Executive Officer
Jeff Smouse, Chief Financial Officer
Liz Wagstrom, Chief Vetrinarian
Nick Giordano, VP & Counsel, Global Gov. Affairs
Dallas Hockman, VP, Industry Relations

Conducts public-policy outreach on behalf of its 43 affiliated state associations, enhancing opportunities for the success of US pork producers and other industry stakeholders by establishing the US pork industry as a consistent and responsible supplier of high-quality pork to the domestic and world markets.

9589 **National Potato Council**
1300 L St NW
Suite 910
Washington, DC 20005

202-682-9456; Fax: 202-682-0333
spudinfo@nationalpotatocouncil.org
www.nationalpotatocouncil.org
Facebook, Twitter, Youtube

Kam Quarles, Chief Executive Officer
Mike Wenkel, Chief Operating Officer
Hollee Alexander, VP, Industry Relations & Events
Hillary Hutchins, Dir., Member Outreach & Programs
Mark Szymanski, Director, Public Relations

Represents US potato growers on federal legislative and regulatory issues.
6000 Members
Founded in 1948

9590 **National Poultry & Food Distributors Association**
2014 Osborne Road
Saint Marys, GA 31558

770-535-9901; Fax: 770-535-7385
cece@npfda.org
www.npfda.org
Facebook, Twitter, LinkedIn

Cece Corbin, President
Carol Lanham, Member Services & Development Dir.
Alina Cooper, Membership Relations & Comm. Dir.

To promote the poultry and food distributors, processors and allied industries by bringing them together and providing a forum to foster long term business relationships.
210 Members
Founded in 1967

9591 **National Renderers Association**
500 Montgomery Street
Suite 310
Alexandria, VA 22314

703-683-0155; Fax: 571-970-2279
renderers@nationalrenderers.com
www.nationalrenderers.org
Twitter

Gerald F. Smith Jr., Chairman
Ross Hamilton, First Vice Chairman
Tim Guzek, Second Vice Chairman
Nancy Foster, President
Marty Covert, Convention Coordinator

Representing members' interests to regulatory and other governmental agencies, promoting the greater use of animal by-products and fostering

the opening and expansion of trade between foreign buyers and North American exporters.
Founded in 1933

9592 **National Restaurant Association**
2055 L Street NW
Suite 700
Washington, DC 20036
202-331-5900
800-424-5156; Fax: 202-331-2429
restaurant.org
Facebook, Twitter, YouTube
Dawn Sweeney, President & CEO
Foodservice trade association
500M Members
Founded in 1919

9593 **National Seafood Educators**
PO Box 93
Skamokawa, WA 98647
206-546-6410; Fax: 206-546-6411
information@seafoodeducators.com
Evie Hansen, Founder
Goal is to educate and inform the public about the many health benefits of a seafood diet. Also has consulted with many seafood retail businesses on how to sell, store, and prepare wholesome seafood.
Founded in 1977

9594 **National Seasoning Manufacturers Association Inc**
8905 Maxwell Dr
Suite 200
Potomac, MD 20854
301-765-9675; Fax: 301-299-7523
alsmeyerfood@isp.com
Dick Alsmeyer PhD, Executive Director
Food seasoning manufacturers, producers of meat curing compounds, flavors, supplies, services, and equipment used for the seasoning and preserving of food.
23 Members
Founded in 1972

9595 **National Shellfisheries Association**
National Marine Fisheries Service Laboratory
Oxford, MD 21654
631-653-6327; Fax: 631-653-6327
webmaster@shellfish.org
www.shellfish.org
Karolyn Mueller Hansen, President
Steven Allen, President-Elect
Shirley Baker, Vice President
Lisa Milke, Secretary
John Scarpa, Treasurer
Organization comprised of scientists, public health workers, shellfish producers and fishery administrators to promote and advance shellfisheries research and the application of results to the shellfish industry.
1M Members
Founded in 1908

9596 **National Society on Healthcare Foodservice**
455 S. 4th Street
Suite 650
Louisville, KY 40202
888-528-9552; Fax: 502-589-3602
info@healthcarefoodservice.org
www.healthcarefoodservice.org
Facebook, Twitter, LinkedIn, YouTube
Laura Watson, President
Lisette Coston, President-Elect
Jacqueline Sikoski, Secretary
Robert Darrah, Treasurer
Julie Jones, Treasurer-Elect
The only professional society dedicated to professionals and suppliers in the self-operated healthcare foodservice industry- those facilities who choose to keep their foodservice departments on staff, instead of outsourcing them to third-party contractors.

9597 **National Sunflower Association**
2401 46th Avenue SE
Suite 206
Mandan, ND 58554-4829
701-328-5100
888-718-7033; Fax: 701-328-5101
larryk@sunflowernsa.com
www.sunflowernsa.com
Facebook, YouTube
John Sandbakken, Executive Director
Tina Mittlesteadt, Business & Office Manager
A non-profit commodity organization working on problems and opportunities for the improvement of all members. Members include growers and the support industry.
20000 Members
Founded in 1981

9598 **National Turkey Federation**
1225 New York Avenue NW
Suite 400
Washington, DC 20005
202-898-0100; Fax: 202-898-0203
info@turkeyfed.org
www.eatturkey.com
Facebook, Twitter, Youtube, Pinterest
Joel Brandenberger, President
Beth Breeding, VP, Communications & Marketing
Hayden Demos, Coordinator, Member Services
Shelby Shaw, Manager, Communications
(NTF) is the national Advocate for all segments of the $8 billion turkey industry, providing services and conducting activities that increase demand for its members' products. The federation also protects and enhances its members' ability to effectively and profitably provide wholesome, high quality, nutritious turkey products.
264 Members
Founded in 1939

9599 **National WIC Association**
2001 S St NW
Suite 580
Washington, DC 20009
202-232-5492; Fax: 202-387-5281
douglasg@nwica.org
www.nwica.org
Facebook, Twitter, Pinterest
Douglas Greenaway, President & CEO
Cecilia Richardson, VP, Nutrition Program & Admin
Emily Gilcher, Membership Engagement
Stephen Padre, Communications, Media, Marketing
Rita Arni, Chair
The National WIC Association (NWA) is the non-profit education arm and advocacy voice of the Special Supplemental Nutrition Program for Women, Infants and Children (WIC), the over 7 million mothers and young children served by WIC and the 12,000 service provider Agencies who are the front lines of WIC's public health nutrition services for the nation's nutritionally at-risk mothers and young children.
1389 Members
Founded in 1983

9600 **National Watermelon Promotion Board**
1321 Sundial Point
Winter Springs, FL 32708
407-657-0261
877-599-9595; Fax: 407-657-2213
info@watermelon.org
www.watermelon.org
Facebook, Twitter, RSS, YouTube, Instagram
Mark Arney, Executive Director
Rebekah Dossett, Director of Operationsÿ
Megan McKenna, Dir., Marketing
Stephanie Barlow, Director of Communications
Andrea Smith, Industry Affairs Manager
Increase consumer demand for fresh watermelon through promotion, research, and educational programs.
Founded in 1989

9601 **National Yogurt Association**
Washington, DC
703-245-7698
info@aboutyogurt.com
aboutyogurt.com
Mariano Lozano, Chair
Alison Bodor, President
Non-profit representing the nation's yogurt manufacturers and marketers.

9602 **Natural Marketing Institute**
272 Ruth Road
Harleysville, PA 19438
215-513-7300; Fax: 215-513-1713
Michael.Molyneaux@NMIsolutions.com
www.NMIsolutions.com
Facebook, Twitter, LinkedIn
Maryellen Molyneaux, President
George Ward, Vice President Strategic Consulting
John Devries, Vice President Strategic Consulting
Diane Ray, Vice President of Strategy
Kathryn Schulte, Director Project Management
NMI is an international strategic marketing consultancy specializing in health, wellness, sustainability and healthy aging with full-service consulting and market research services.
Founded in 1989

9603 **Natural Products Association**
1773 T Street, NW
Washington, DC 20009
202-223-0101
800-966-6632; Fax: 202-223-0250
natural@NPAinfo.org
www.npainfo.org
Facebook, Twitter, LinkedIn, Pinterest, Googleplus
Jon Fiume, President Elect
Jain Drinkwalter, Chair
Roxanne Green, President
Daniel Fabricant, Executive Director & CEO
Mark LeDoux, Treasurer
The nation's largest and oldest non-profit organization dedicated to the natural products industry. NPA unites a diverse membership, from the smallest health food store to the largest dietary supplement manufacturer.
1900+ Members
Founded in 1936

9604 **New York Apple Association**
7645 Main Street
PO Box 350
Fishers, NY 14453-0350
585-924-2171; Fax: 585-924-1629
www.nyapplecountry.com
Facebook, Twitter
Jim Allen, President
Julia Stewart, Communications
Molly Golden, Director of Marketing
Linda Quinn, Media Representative
Ellen Mykins, Accounting
The New York Apple Association is a non-profit trade association representing over 600 commercial apple growers in New York

State. The apple industry produces about 25 million bushels each year at a value of approximately $137 million, making it one of the largest sectors in New York agriculture.
600 Members
Founded in 1950

9605 **North American Association of Food Equipment Manufacturers**
161 N Clark Street
Suite 2020
Chicago, IL 60601

312-821-0201; Fax: 312-821-0202
info@nafem.org
www.nafem.org
Facebook

Michael L. Whiteley, President
Kevin Fink, President-Elect
Joseph Carlson, CFSP, Secretary/Treasurer
Deirdre Flynn, Executive Vice President
Genny Bertalmio, Office Manager

The North American Association of Food Equipment Manactuers (NAFEM) is a trade association of more than 625 foodservice equipment and supplies manufacturers that provide products for food preparation, cooking, storage and table service providers. NAFEM's biennial trade show attracts approximately 20,000 foodservice professionals and features more than 600 North American manufacturers.
625 Members

9606 **North American Blueberry Council**
80 Iron Point Circle
Suite 114
Folsom, CA 95630

916-983-2279; Fax: 916-983-9370
www.nabcblues.org

Bob Carini, President
Tom Bodtke, First Vice President
Tom Avinelis, Second Vice President
Art Galletta, Treasurer
Ken Patterson, Secretary

A non-profit association with the important role of acting as a voice for the highbush blueberry industry.
Founded in 1965

9607 **North American Farm Show Council**
590 Woody Hayes Drive
Columbus, OH 43210

614-292-4278; Fax: 614-292-9448
gamble.19@osu.edu
www.worldexpo.com

Dennis Alford, President
Chip Blalock, 1st Vice President
David Zimmerman, 2nd Vice President
Chuck Gamble, Secretary/Treasurer

Strives to improve the value of its member shows through education, communication and evaluation. The overall goal is to provide the best possible marketing showcase for exhibitors of agricultural equipment and related products to the farmer/rancher/producer customer.
Founded in 1972

9608 **North American Limousin Foundation**
6 Inverness Court East
Suite 260
Englewood, CO 80112-5595

303-220-1693; Fax: 303-220-1884
limousin@nalf.org
www.nalf.org
Facebook, Twitter

Chad Settje, President
Bret Begert, Vice President
Jim Bob Hendrickson, Secretary
Dexter Edwards, Treasurer
Mark Anderson, Executive Director

Register, promote and research on Limousin beef cattle.
4000 Members
Founded in 1968

9609 **North American Meat Institute**
1150 Connecticut Avenue, NW
12th Floor
Washington, DC 20036

202-640-5333; Fax: 202-318-4078
info@meatinstitute.org
www.meatinstitute.org
Twitter, LinkedIn

Warren Panico, Chairman
Julie Anna Potts, President & CEO
Christl McCarthy, Executive Administrator
Rosemary Mucklow, Director Emeritus Consultant
William Sessions, Director, Product Marketing

Provides its members unique one-on-one assistance resolving regulatory issues. Mission is to be proactive and responsive in serving members both individually and collectively.
400 Members
Founded in 2012

9610 **North American Millers' Association**
600 Maryland Ave SW
Suite 825 West
Washington, DC 20024

202-484-2200; Fax: 202-488-7416
generalinfo@namamillers.org
www.namamillers.org
Facebook

Jane DeMarchi, President
Dale Nellor, VP, Government & Technical Affairs
Christopher Clark, VP, Communications & Administration
Kim Cooper, Manager, Government Affairs
Holly Wiedemann, Administrative Coordinator

Trade association representing the wheat, corn, oat and rye milling industry. NAMA members operate one hundred and seventy mills in thrirty-eight states and Canada. Their aggregate production of more than one hundred and sixty million pounds per day is approximately ninety-five percent of the industry capacity in the U.S.
Founded in 1902

9611 **North American Natural Casing Association**
494 Eighth Avenue
Suite 805
New York, NY 10001

212-695-4980; Fax: 212-695-7153
nanca18hq@yahoo.com
www.nanca.org

Barbara Negron, President
Phil Schwartz, Vice President
Mike Wallace, Secretary
Eric Svendsen, Treasurer

To obtain legislation favorable to the industry's interests and prevent or change legistation deemed harmful at the local, state and federal levels, including protection from unfair trade practices by foreign countries, and working with member governments to ease trade. Also addresses common industry problems encountered by management in the production, distribution and financial function of the naturasl casing industry.

9612 **North American Olive Oil Association**
3301 Route 66
Suite 205, Building C
Neptune, NJ 07753

732-922-3008; Fax: 732-922-3590
info@naooa.org
www.naooa.org
Facebook, Twitter

Eryn Balch, Executive Vice President

Committed to supplying North American consumers with quality products in a fair and competitive environment; to fostering a clear understanding of the different grades of olive oil; and to expounding the benefits of olive oil in nutrition, health, and the culinary arts.
Founded in 1989

9613 **Northeast Fresh Foods Alliance**
1189R N Main Street
Randolph, MA 02368

781-963-9726; Fax: 781-963-5829

Brian Long, President
Bob Ogan, Executive VP
Chris Bruhn, First VP
Paul Sullivan, Secretary
Paul Palumbo, Treasurer
350 Members
Founded in 1979

9614 **Northern Nut Growers Association, Inc.**
Home Page: nutgrowing.org

Tim Ford, President
Shawn Mehlenbacher, Vice President
Jeanne Romero-Severson, Treasurer
Tom Molnar, Secretary

The Association brings together people interested in growing nut trees, from amateurs to tree breeders.
Founded in 1910

9615 **Northwest Cherry Briners Association Inc.**
2667 Reed Rd
Hood River, OR 97031

director.orgcouncil@gmail.com
www.orgcouncil.com

Carl Payne, VP Tech Services

Association of briners of sweet cherries in the northwestern US. The organization works to inform briners of regulatory decisions and current practices affecting brining operations.
8 Members
Founded in 1936

9616 **Northwest Food Processors Association**
8338 NE. Alderwood Road
Suite 160
Portland, OR 97220

503-327-2200; Fax: 503-327-2201
www.nwfpa.org
Facebook, Twitter, LinkedIn

Kurt McKnight, Chair
Debbie Radie, Chair Elect
Steven Rowe, Vice Chair
David McGiverin, President
Greg Satrum, Director

NWFPA is an advocate for members interests and a resource for enhancing the food processing industry in Oregon, Washington and Idaho.
350 Members
Founded in 1914

9617 **Northwest Meat Processors Association**
2380 NW Roosevelt St
Portland, OR 97210-2323

503-226-2758; Fax: 503-224-0947
haysmgmt@pipeline.com

Dennis Hays, Executive Director
250 Members
Founded in 1962

9618 **Organic Alliance**
Organic Alliance International
Asheville, NC 28804

828-337-6114
www.organicalliance.org

An alliance of people, businesses and organizations working together to promote the goodness of organics and help to make it available to all.

9619 **Organic Crop Improvement Association International (OCIA)**
1340 North Cotner Boulevard
Lincoln, NR 68505-1838

402-477-2323; Fax: 402-477-4325
info@ocia.org
www.ocia.org

Amanda Brewster, Executive Director
Deana McKinstry, Director, Finance
Angie Tunink, Director, Marketing
Cindy Elder, Director, Accredation
Shelby Workman, Officer Clerk

An accredited world leader in the certified organic industry, provides certification, education and research services to thousands of organic farmers, processors and handlers from 20 countries in North, Central and South America and Asia.
3500 Members
Founded in 1985

9620 **Organic Trade Association**
28 Vernon St
Suite 413
Brattleboro, VT 05301

202-403-8520
info@ota.com
www.ota.com
Facebook, Twitter, LinkedIn

Danielle Cote, Membership Manager

The Organic Trade Association is a membership-based business association representing the organic industry in North America.
1400 Members
Founded in 1985

9621 **Ozark Food Processors Association**
2650 N Young Avenue
Fayetteville, AR 72704

479-575-4607; Fax: 479-575-2165
ofpa@uark.edu
ofpa.uark.edu

Jason Hayward, President
Andrea Dunigan, Vice President
Dr. Renee Threlfall, Secretary
Steve Crider, Board Member
Jared Brooks, Board Member

This association is comprised of regional food processors and national suppliers for the food service industry.
90 Members
Founded in 1906

9622 **Pacific Coast Shellfish Growers Association**
120 State Ave NE
#142
Olympia, WA 98501

360-754-2744; Fax: 360-754-2743
www.pcsga.net
Facebook, Flickr

Margaret Pilaro Barrette, Executive Director
Connie Smith, Projects Manager
Mary Middleton, Executive Assistant

Members grow a wide variety of healthy, sustainable shellfish including oysters, clams, mussels, scallops and geoduck. PCSGA works on behalf of its members on a broad spectrum of issues, including environmental protection, shellfish safety, regulations, technology, and marketing.
Founded in 1930

9623 **Packaging Machinery Manufacturers Institute**
11911 Freedom Drive
Suite 600
Reston, VA 20190

571-612-3200; Fax: 703-243-8556
info@pmmi.org
www.pmmi.org
Facebook, Twitter, LinkedIn, YouTube, Instagram

Charles D. Yuska, President & CEO
Corinne G. Mulligan, Executive Assistant
Caroline Abromavage, Operations Director
Jeremy Adams, Marketing & Communications
Heather Harvey, Membership Manager

The association's vision is to be the leading global resource for manufacturers of packaging and packaging-related converting equipment, components and materials.
800+ Members
Founded in 1933

9624 **Paperboard Packaging Council**
1350 Main Street
Suite 1508
Springfield, MA 01103-1670

413-686-9191; Fax: 413-747-7777
www.ppcnet.org
Facebook, Twitter, LinkedIn, YouTube

Kyle Eldred, Chair
Charles Johnson, Vice Chair
Ben Markens, President
Lou Kornet, Vice President
Steven Levkoff, Treasurer

Trade association serving converters and suppliers of all forms of paperboard packaging, including folding cartons, rigid boxes, paper cylinders, and laminated small flute containers.
Founded in 1929

9625 **Peanut and Tree Nut Processors Association**
PO Box 2660
Alexandria, VA 22301

301-365-2521; Fax: 301-365-7705
ptnpa.org
Twitter

Brian Ezell, Chairman
JOEL PERKINS, Vice Chairman
Michael J. Valentine, Secretary/Treasurer
Jeannie Shaughnessy, Executive Director
Trish Schechtman, Oepratiions/Membership Manager

Representing the owners and operators of companies (large and small) who shell, process, salt and/or roast peanuts and tree nuts. In addition, our members also supply equipment and services that are critical to our industry.
Founded in 1939

9626 **Pear Bureau Northwest**
4382 SE International Way
Suite A
Milwaukie, OR 97222-4635

503-652-9720; Fax: 503-652-9721
info@usapears.com
www.usapears.com
Facebook, Twitter, LinkedIn, YouTube, Pinterest

Kevin D. Moffitt, President & CEO
Linda Bailey, VP of Operations
Kathy Stephenson, Director Marketing Communications

A non-profit marketing organization that promotes, advertises and develops markets for fresh pears grown in Oregon and Washington. Through professional representatives in the U.S. and around the world, the Bureau coordinates activities designed to increase awareness and consumption of fresh USA Pears, facilitating research on behalf of the Northwest pear industry relative to consumer awareness and preferences, nutritional benefits and emerging global markets.
1600 Members
Founded in 1931

9627 **Pickle Packers International Inc.**
1101 17th Street NW
Suite 700
Washington, DC 20036

202-331-2465; Fax: 202-463-8998
www.ilovepickles.org
Facebook

Sponsors research, represents industry before government agencies, produces educational materials, and provides superior networking opportunities to members. Members inlude processors, salters, green shippers, brokers, growers, seed companies, ingredient and equipment manufacturers, packaging suppliers, and those providing goods and services to the industry.
Founded in 1896

9628 **Popcorn Board**
330 N Wabash Avenue
Suite 2000
Chicago, IL 60611

312-644-6610; Fax: 312-527-6783
info@popcorn.org
www.popcorn.org
Facebook, Twitter, Blog

A non-profit organization funded by US popcorn processors to raise awareness of popcorn as a versatile, whole-grain snack.
Founded in 1943

9629 **Printing Industries of America**
301 Brush Creek Road
Warrendale, PA 15086

412-741-6860
800-910-4283; Fax: 412-741-2311
www.printing.org
Facebook, Twitter, LinkedIn, Pinterest, Googleplus

David A. Olberding, Chairman
Bradley L. Thompson II, 1st Vice Chairman
MR CURT KREISLER, 2nd Vice Chairman
Michael L. Wurst, Treasurer
BRYAN T. HALL, Secretary

Members are companies printing labels for food or consumer products.
40 Members
Founded in 1887

9630 **Produce Marketing Association**
1500 Casho Mill Road
PO Box 6036
Newark, DE 19711

302-738-7100; Fax: 302-731-2409
solutionctr@pma.com
www.pma.com
Facebook, Twitter, Flickr, YouTube, Xchange

Cathy Burns, CEO
Doug Bohr, Executive Director
Lauren Scott, Chief Marketing Officer
Yvonne Bull, Chief Financial Officer
Max Teplitski, Chief Science Officer

Providing business solutions that strengthen and lead the global produce community, PMA has set the standard for quality events with the annual convention and continues to revolutionize one of the world's most vibrant industries.
100 Members
Founded in 1949

9631 **Professional Farmers of America**
6612 Chancellor Dr.
Cedar Falls, IA 50613
319-277-1278
800-772-0023; Fax: 319-827-1792
editors@profarmer.com
www.profarmer.com

Mike Walsten, VP
Merrill Oster, Executive Director
Rich Posson, Editor
Provides farmers with marketing strategies and market-trend data, as well as seminars and home study courses.
25M Members
Founded in 1972

9632 **Quality Bakers of America Cooperative**
1275 Glenlivet Drive
Suite 100
Allentown, PA 18106-3107
info@qba.com
www.qba.com

Don Cummings, VP, Finance
Marc Knox, EVP & COO
Jonathan J. Fink, Counsel
R. Jack Lewis, Jr., Chairman
J.R. Paterakis, President
Providing members with access to sources of appropriate services in order to maintain the highest product quality and sanitation standards.
35 Members
Founded in 1922

9633 **Quality Chekd Dairies**
901 Warrenville Rd
Suite 405
Lisle, IL 60532

800-222-6455; Fax: 630-717-1126
qchekd@qchekd.com
www.qchekd.com

Peter Horvath, President
Mary DeMarco, Accounting & Admin Manager
Steve Drabek, Human Resource & Training Director
Laura Moehs, Training & Admin Coordinator
Chuck Yarris, Quality & Food Safety Director
A cooperative of dairy foods processors who use the Quality Checked trademark on their products and engage in group purchasing of ingredients and supplies.
Founded in 1944

9634 **Raisin Administration Committee**
2445 Capitol Street
Suite 200
Fresno, CA 93721-2236

559-225-0520; Fax: 559-225-0652
info@raisins.org
www.raisins.org

Gary Schulz, President
Debbie Powell, Sr. Vice President of Operations
Larry Blagg, Sr. Vice President of Marketing
Ron Degiuli, Vice President of Accounting
Administrative board of growers and packers of raisins.

9635 **Red Angus Association of America**
4201 N Interstate 35
Denton, TX 76207-3415

940-387-3502; Fax: 888-829-6069
info@redangus.org
www.redangus.org
Facebook

Kim Ford, President
Twig Marston, CEO
Jeanene McCuistion, Accounting Director
Kevin Miller, 1st Vice President
Bob Morton, 2nd Vice President
Dedicated to providing its members with excellence and innovation in leadership, service, information and education. An association for breeders of Red Angus cattle.
2000 Members
Founded in 1954

9636 **Refrigerated Foods Association**
3823 Roswell Road
Suite 208
Marietta, GA 30062

678-426-8175; Fax: 678-550-4504
info@refrigeratedfoods.org
www.refrigeratedfoods.org

Josh Knott, President
Lauren Edmonds, Vice President
Karen Bishop Carbone, Secretary
Tom Davis, Treasurer
Megan Levin, Executive Director
An organization of manufacturers and suppliers of refrigerated prepared foods united by a common interest; to advance and safeguard the industry. Members include manufacturers and suppliers of wet salads, refrigerated entrees and side dishes, dips, desserts, soups, and ethnic foods, as well as companies engaged in business operations related to the refrigerated foods industry.
200+ Members
Founded in 1980

9637 **Research and Development Associates for Military Food and Packaging Systems**
16607 Blanco Rd
Suite 501
San Antonio, TX 78232

210-493-8024; Fax: 210-493-8036
hqs@militaryfood.org
www.militaryfood.org
Facebook

Bill McCreary, Chairman
Daniel Weil, Vice Chairman
John Q. McNulty, Executive Director
Jan Cook, Director of Administration
Kimberly Addison Sanford, Marketing Events Coordinator
To provide the safest and highest food service to the US Armed Forces by linking industry, government and academics.
700 Members
Founded in 1946

9638 **Retail Bakers of America**
15941 Harlem Ave
Suite 347
Tinley Park, IL 60477

800-638-0924
www.retailbakersofamerica.org
Facebook, Twitter

Bernadette Shanahan-Haas, Director of Operations
Paul Sapienza, Director of Finance
Lynn Schurman, Education Director
Comprised of retail bakeries, allied suppliers and other industry members. The purpose is to offer our members knowledge and resources to enhance business operations through learning opportunities, shared best practices, networking and industry communication.
2000 Members
Founded in 1918

9639 **Retail Confectioners International**
2053 S. Waverly
Ste. C
Springfield, MO 65804

417-883-2775
800-545-5381; Fax: 417-883-1108
info@retailconfectioners.org
www.retailconfectioners.org
Facebook, Twitter, YouTube

Brian Pelletier, President
Judith Hilliard McCarthy, 1st Vice President
Steve Vande Walle, 2nd Vice President
John Asher, III, 3rd Vice President
Angie Burlison, Secretary/Treasurer
Providing education, promotion and legislative services to our members who are manufacturing retailers of quality boxed chocolate and other confectionery products throughout the U.S., Canada and overseas.
600 Members
Founded in 1917

9640 **Rocky Mountain Bean Dealers Association**
PO Box 1285
Elizabeth, CO 80107

303-646-8883; Fax: 720-306-2878

Vickie Root, Executive Director
This organization is dedicated to advancing the general interest of its members and the industry.

9641 **Rocky Mountain Food Industry Association**
PO Box 1083
Arvada, CO 80001-1083

303-830-7001; Fax: 303-424-7114
www.rmfia.org

Mary Lou Chapman, President/CEO
The trade organization for the Colorado and Wyoming grocery industry, representing retail grocers, convenience stores, and their wholesale suppliers. The association serves as a voice for its members with state legislatures, US Congress and the various governmental agencies that regulate the food industry.
500 Members
Founded in 1917

9642 **Roundtable of Food Professionals**
4363 Larwin Avenue
Cypress, CA 90630

714-562-5088; Fax: 714-670-2965

Barb Colucci, President
Jenny Rosoff, President-Emeritus
David Stennes, VP
Stephany Rosenthal, Membership Co-Chair
Provide opportunities for development and career expansion within the whole spectrum of the food industry.
50 Members
Founded in 2002

9643 **Royal Crown Bottlers Association**
515 Eline Ave
St Matthews, KY 40207-3655

502-896-0861; Fax: 502-896-0861

Stephanie Garling, Executive Director
Represents franchised Royal Crown bottlers.
100 Members
Founded in 1964

9644 **Salt Institute**
405 5th Ave. South
Suite 7C
Naples, FL 34102-6515

239-231-3305; Fax: 239-330-1492
jorge@saltinstitute.org
www.saltinstitute.org
Facebook, Twitter, YouTube

Lori Roman, President
Morton Satin, Vice President
Jorge Amselle, Director of Communication
Wilfrid Nixon, VP Science and the Environment
A source of authoritative information about salt and its more than 14,000 known users. Provides

public information and advocates on behalf of its members, including use of the website.
Founded in 1914

9645 **Santa Gertrudis Breeders International**
PO Box 1257
Kingsville, TX 78364
361-592-9357; Fax: 361-592-8572
sgbi@sbcglobal.net
www.santagertrudis.com
Facebook, Twitter, Googleplus
Curtis Salter, President
Deanna Parker, Secretary/Treasurer
John E. Ford, Executive Director
The original American beef breed. Custom built for the range and market, these cattle have proven themselves worldwide to be a hardy and profitable breed from the mountains of Montana and Mexico to the tropics and deserts of Argentina and Australia. Worldwide, cattlemen are getting results using Santa Gertrudis genetics.
Founded in 1950

9646 **School Nutrition Association**
120 Waterfront St
Suite 300
National Harbor, MD 20745
301-686-3100
800-877-8822; Fax: 301-686-3115
servicecenter@schoolnutrition.org
www.schoolnutrition.org
Digg
Jean Ronnei, President
Becky Domokos-Bays, President-Elect
Lynn Harvey, Vice President
Linda Eichenberger, Secretary/Treasurer
Patricia Montague, CEO
This is a national, nonprofit professional organization representing members who provide high quality, low-cost meals to students across the country.
55000 Members
Founded in 1946

9647 **Sioux Honey Association**
301 Lewis Boulevard
PO Box 388
Sioux City, IA 51101
712-258-0638; Fax: 712-258-1332
Facebook, Twitter, Pinterest
David Allibone, President/CEO
Established by five beekeepers so that they could market their honey at greater profit through sharing services and equipment, processing and packing facilities and complete marketing and sales organizations.
315 Members
Founded in 1921

9648 **Small Farm Resource**
Home Page: www.farminfo.org
Contains a wide variety of information useful to those with small farms and rural property.
Founded in 1995

9649 **Snack Food Association**
1600 Wilson Blvd
Suite 650
Arlington, VA 22209
703-836-4500
800-628-1334; Fax: 703-836-8262
www.sfa.org
Facebook, Twitter, LinkedIn, Youtube, Flickr
Tom Dempsey, CEO
Liz Wells, Vice President, Meetings & Events
Paul Downey, Director of Finance and Admin
David Walsh, Director, Government Affairs
Meegan Smith, Director, Communications & Marketin
Representing snack manufacturers and suppliers worldwide. Serving as the voice for the snack industry before government, researches and compiles annual snack sales and consumer data, educates manufacturers on technological advances in equipment and raw ingredients and provides technical support to its members through direct assistance, videos, seminars and publications.
800 Members
Founded in 1937

9650 **Society for Laboratory Automatic and Screening**
100 Illinois Street
Suite 242
St. Charles, IL 60174
630-256-7527
877-990-7527; Fax: 630-741-7527
slas@slas.org
www.slas.org
Facebook, Twitter, LinkedIn, YouTube
Vicki Loise, CEO
Brenda Dreier, COO
Jill Hronek, Director, Marketing & Communication
Christine Diedrich, Publishing Manager
Mary Geismann, Sr. Membership Coordinator
Supports research and discovery in pharmaceutical biotechnology and the agrichemical industry that utilize biomolecular screening procedures.
2000+ Members
Founded in 1994

9651 **Society of Commercial Seed Technologists**
653 Constitution Avenue NE
Washington, DC 200002
202-870-2412; Fax: 607-273-1638
scst@seedtechnology.net
www.analyzeseeds.com
Jess Peterson, Executive Director
Kelly Polzin, Director, Membership Services
Kelly Fogarty, Annual Meeting Director
Kristen Albers, Finance
Lia Biondo, Communications
A organization comprised of commercial, independent and government seed technologists. Developed over the years into a progressive organization that trains and provides accreditation of technologists, conducts research studies and proposes rule changes, and serves as an important resource to the seed industry.
Founded in 1922

9652 **Southeast United Dairy Industry Association**
5340 W Fayetteville Rd
Atlanta, GA 30349-5416
678-833-0580
800-343-4693; Fax: 770-996-6925
www.southeastdairy.org
Facebook, Twitter, YouTube, Pinterest
Amanda Trice, Director of IR & Communications
Rebecca Egseiker, Assistant Director of Communication
Provides a wealth of information for milk and dairy consumers, media, school and health professionals and dairy farmers.
6000 Members
Founded in 1971
Mailing list available for rent

9653 **Southeastern Dairy Foods Research Center**
NCSU Department of Food Science
PO Box 7624
Raleigh, NC 27695
919-515-4197; Fax: 919-513-0014
fbns.ncsu.edu/
Facebook, Twitter, YouTube
Chris Daubert, Department Head
One of six National Centers funded and managed by Dairy Management Incorporated. The mission is to conduct research to develop and apply new technologies for value-added processing of fluid milk and its components into dairy products and ingredients with improved safety, quality or expanded functionalities.
Founded in 1988

9654 **Southern Peanut Farmers Federation**
1025 Sugar Pike Way
Canton, GA 30115
770-751-6615
lpwagner@comcast.net
www.southernpeanutfarmers.org
Formed to educate American consumers about the US peanut industry and its products.
Founded in 1998

9655 **Southern Peanut Growers**
1025 Sugar Pike Way
Canton, GA 30115
770-751-6615
lpwagner@comcast.net
www.peanutbutterlovers.com
Facebook, Twitter, YouTube, Pinterest
Leslie Wagner, Executive Director
A nonprofit trade association representing peanut farmers in Georgia, Alabama, Florida and Mississippi. Formed to educate American consumers about the US peanut industry and its products.
6000 Members
Founded in 1980
Mailing list available for rent

9656 **Southern US Trade Association**
701 Poydras Street
Suite 3845
New Orleans, LA 70139
504-568-5986; Fax: 504-568-6010
susta@susta.org
www.susta.org
Facebook
Bernadette Wiltz, Executive Director
Danielle Viguerie, Marketing Director
Missie Lindsey, Marketing Coordinator
Tina Meshell, Office Manager
Troy Rosamond, Deputy Director & Financial Directo
A non-profit agricultural export trade development association comprised of the Departments of Agriculture of the 15 southern states and the Commonwealth of Puerto Rico.
Founded in 1973

9657 **Soy Protein Council**
1255 23rd Street NW
Washington, DC 20037
202-467-6610; Fax: 202-833-3636
www.spcouncil.org
Facebook, Twitter
Primary purpose is to promote the growth and interests of the soy protein industry and broaden the acceptance of soy products as key components of the worldwide food system.
Founded in 1971

9658 Soyfoods Association of North America
1050 17th Street, NW
Suite 600
Washington, DC 20036
202-659-3520
info@soyfoods.org
www.soyfoods.org
Facebook, Twitter, YouTube, Pinterest
Kate Leavltt, President
Helen Kor, Vice President
Kate Leavitt, Treasurer
Nancy Chapman, Executive Director
A trusted advocate in providing information about the health benefits and nutritional advantages of soy consumption. Encouraging sustainability, integrity and growth of the soyfoods industry through members.
50+ Members
Founded in 1978

9659 Specialty Coffee Association of America
117 W. 4th St,
Suite 300
Santa Ana, CA 92701
562-624-4100; Fax: 562-624-4101
info@scaa.org
www.scaa.org
Facebook, Twitter, YouTube
Tracy Allen, President
Ben Pitts, Vice President
Heather Perry, 2nd Vice President
Guy Burdett, Secretary/Treasurer
Colleen Anunu, Director
One of the primary functions is to set the industry's standards for growing, roasting and brewing. Members of the SCAA include coffee retailers, roasters, producers, exporters and importers, as well as manufacturers of coffee equipment and related products.
2500+ Members
Founded in 1982
Mailing list available for rent

9660 Specialty Food Association and Fancy Food Show
136 Madison Avenue
12th Floor
New York, NY 10016
646-878-0301; Fax: 212-482-6459
www.specialtyfood.com
Facebook, Twitter, LinkedIn, YouTube
Mike Silver, Chair
Shawn McBride, Vice Chair
Ann Daw, President
Becky Renfro Borbolla, Treasurer
Matt Neilsen, Secretary
A business trade association to foster trade, commerce and interest in the specialty food industry. Composed of domestic and foreign manufacturers, importers, distributors, brokers, retailers, restaurateurs, caterers and others in the specialty foods business.
3000+ Members
Founded in 1952

9661 Sugar Association
1300 L Street NW
Suite 1001
Washington, DC 20005
202-785-1122; Fax: 202-785-5019
sugar@sugar.org
www.sugar.org
Facebook, Twitter, Pinterest
Andrew Briscoe, President/CEO
P. Courtney Gaine, VP, Scientific Affairs
Cheryl Digges, VP Public Policy & Education
Lisa Swanson, Administrative Assistant
Promoting the consumption of sugar through sound scientific principles while maintaining an understanding of the benefits that sugar contributes to the quality of wholesome foods and beverages.
Founded in 1943

9662 Switzerland Cheese Association
704 Executive Blvd
Suite I
Valley Cottage, NY 10989-2010
845-268-2460; Fax: 845-268-9991
Paul U Schilt, CEO

9663 Tea Association of the USA
362 Fifth Avenue
Suite 1002
New York, NY 10001
212-986-9415; Fax: 212-697-8658
info@teausa.com
www.teausa.com
Facebook, Twitter
Peter F. Goggi, President
Association of companies dedicated to the interests and growth of the US tea industry.
100 Members
Founded in 1899
Mailing list available for rent

9664 Tea Board of India
14 B.T.M. Sarani
Kolkata, KO 700001
332-235-1331; Fax: 332-221-5715
www.teaboard.gov.in
Santosh Sarangi, Chairman
A.K Das, Deputy Chairman
Sumita Lahiri, Personal Secretary to Chairman
A. Rajan, Secretary
Joydip Biswas, Deputy Director
This association promotes Indian tea and develops new markets for tea in the US and Canada.
Founded in 1953

9665 The American Dairy Association Indiana, Inc.
9360 Castlegate Drive
Indianapolis, IN 46256
317-842-3060
800-225-6455; Fax: 317-842-3065
osza@winnersdrinkmilk.comÿ
Facebook, Twitter, LinkedIn, YouTube, Pinterest, Instagram
Donald Gurtner, President
Paul Mills, Vice President
Steve Phares, Treasurer
Anita Schmitt, Secretary
A not-for-profit organization which promotes the sale and consumption of diary foods.
Founded in 1915

9666 The Biscuit & Cracker Manufacturers' Association
6325 Woodside Court
Suite 125
Columbia, MD 21046
443-545-1645; Fax: 410-290-8585
www.thebcma.org
Facebook, LinkedIn
David Van Laar, President
Kathy Kinter Phelps, Membership & Education Manager
Vickie Clancy, Meetings Assistant
Dennis Loalbo, Technical Advisor
Blake Hutzley, Technical Advisor
International trade organization representing the entire spectrum of companies involved in the manufacturing of biscuits and crackers and the suppliers to the baking industry. Our mission is to bring unparalled educational training programs and networking opportunities to members of the cookie and cracker industry.
250 Members
Founded in 1901

9667 The Catfish Institute
6311 Ridgewood Road
Suite W404
Jackson, MS 39211
601-977-9559; Fax: 662-887-6857
catfishinfo@uscatfish.com
www.uscatfish.com
Facebook, Twitter, Youtube, Pinterest
Butch Wilson, President
Roger Barlow, Executive Vice-President
Represents the largest aquaculture industry in the United States. Represents the interests of the farm-raised catfish industry of farmers, processors, feed mills, researchers, and supplier industries. Promotes the many healthy, great tasting uses for genuine U.S. Farm-Raised Catfish.
Cost: $40.00
Frequency: Membership Fees
Founded in 1986
Mailing list available for rent

9668 The Cranberry Institute
PO Box 497
Carver, MA 02330
508-866-1118; Fax: 774-843-5641
cinews@cranberryinstitute.org
www.cranberryinstitute.org
Bob Wilson, Chairman
Todd May, Vice Chairman
Steve Berlyn, Secretary/Treasurer
A nonprofit that supports cranberry growers and the cranberry industry.
Founded in 1951

9669 The Food and Beverage Association of America
111 East 14th Street
Suite 390
New York, NY 10003
212-344-8252; Fax: 212-504-9536
office@fbassoc.com
www.fbassoc.com
Facebook, LinkedIn, YouTube
Steven V. Gattullo, President
Sean Cassidy, First Vice President
Gus Montesantos, Second Vice President
Guy Salisch, Secretary
Daniel Saalman, Treasurer
A nonprofit, philanthropic, trade organization for executives of the food and beverage industries of the New York metropolitan area.
Founded in 1956

9670 The Industry Council for Research on Packaging and the Environment
SoanePoint, 6-8 Market Place
Reading
Berkshire RG1 2EG
118-925-5991; Fax: 202-833-3636
www.incpen.org
Facebook, Twitter
Steve Young, President
A research organization, which draws together an influential group of companies who share a vision of the future where all production, distribution, and consumption are sustainable. Aiming to ensure policies on packaging makes a positive contribution to sustainability, encourages the industry to minimize the environmental impact of packaging and continuously improve packaging, and explain the role of packaging in society.
Founded in 1974

9671 The National Chicken Council
1152 15th Street NW
Suite 430
Washington, DC 20005-2622

202-296-2622; Fax: 202-293-4005
ncc@chickenusa.org
www.nationalchickencouncil.org
Facebook, Twitter

Michael J. Brown, President
Ashley Peterson, Senior Vice President
Mary M. Colville, VP of Government Affairs
Tom Super, Vice President of Communications
Margaret A. Ernst,, Senior Director

National, non-profit trade association representing the US chicken industry. Promoting and protecting the interests of the chicken industry and acts as the industry's voice before Congress and federal agencies. Members include chicken producer/processors, poultry distributors, and allied industry firms.
150+ Members
Founded in 1954

9672 The National Confectioners' Association
1101 30th Street, NW
Suite 200
Washington, DC 20007

202-534-1440; Fax: 202-337-0637
info@CandyUSA.com
www.candyusa.com
Facebook, Twitter, LinkedIn, Flickr, Pinterest, YouTube

Robert M. Simpson, Jr., Chairman
Peter W. Blommer, Vice Chairman
John H. Downs, Jr., President/ CEO
Joseph Vittoria, Treasurer
Martino Caretto, Vice President

Advances, protects, and promotes the confectionery industry.
Founded in 1884

9673 The National Grange
1616 H Street NW
Suite 10
Washington, DC 20006

202-628-3507
888-447-2643; Fax: 202-347-1091
www.nationalgrange.org
Facebook, Twitter, YouTube, RSS Feeds

Betsy Huber, National President
Samantha Wilkins, Operations Coordinator
Joseph Stefenoni, Leadership & Membership Director
Amanda Leigh Brozana-Rios, Communications Director
Loretta Washington, Sales, Benefits & Programs Director

Non-partisan fraternal organization with its roots in rural agriculture.
160K Members
Founded in 1867

9674 The Peanut Institute
PO Box 70157
Albany, GA 31708-0157

229-888-0216
888-873-2688; Fax: 229-888-5150
www.peanut-institute.org
Facebook, Twitter, Instagram, Pinterest

A nonprofit that supports nutrition research and advocates for the peanut's place in healthful lifestyles.

9675 Today's Market Prices
Home Page: www.todaymarket.com

A user friendly information center that provides within its market prices service, daily price information on more than 200 fruit, vegetables, and herbs from the most important wholesale markets of the USA, Canada, Mexico, and Europe.
Founded in 1996

9676 Tortilla Industry Association
1600 Wlison Blvd
Suite 650
Arlington, VA 22209

800-944-6099; Fax: 800-944-6177
info@tortilla-info.com
www.tortilla-info.com

Criss Cruz, Chairman
Jim Kabbani, Executive Director
Dana Beall, Secretary

Members include companies engaged in manufacturing tortillas and suppliers, food brokers and Mexican restaurant owners.
175 Members
Founded in 1886

9677 U.S. Meat Export Federationÿ
1855 Blake Street
Suite 200
Denver, CO 80202

303-623-6328; Fax: 303-623-0297
migoe@usmef.org
www.usmef.org
Facebook, Twitter, YouTube

Leann Saunders, Chair
Roel Andriessen, Chair-elect
Bruce Schmoll, Vice Chair
Dennis Stiffler, Treasurer/ Secretary
Philip M. Seng, President, CEO

A nonprofit trade association working to create new opportunities and develop existing international markets for U.S. beef, pork, lamb, and veal.

9678 U.S. Poultry & Egg Associationÿ
1530 Cooledge Road
Tucker, GA 30084-7303

770-493-9401; Fax: 770-493-9257
info@uspoultry.org
www.uspoultry.org
Facebook, Twitter, LinkedIn, Google+, YouTube

John Starkey, President
Charles Olentine, PhD, Executive Vice President
Gwen Venable, Vice President of Communications
Jason Rivera, Vice President, IT
Barbara Jenkins, Vice President - Education Programs

Represents producers and processors of broilers, turkeys, eggs and breeding stock, as well as allied companies.
Founded in 1947

9679 U.S. Wheat Associates
3103 10th Street, North
Suite 300
Arlington, VA 22201

202-463-0999; Fax: 703-524-4399
www.uswheat.org
Facebook, Twitter, YouTube, Flickr

Brian O'Toole, Chairman
Jason Scott, Vice Chairman
Roy Motter, Past Chairman
Alan Tracy, President
Mike Miller, Secretary-Treasurer

Supports the sale of wheat by offering education for overseas buyers, onsite training services, promotes trade policies, and consumer promotion.

9680 US Animal Health Association
4221 Mitchelle Ave.
Saint Joseph, MO 64507

816-671-1144; Fax: 816-671-1201
usaha@usaha.org
www.usaha.org
Facebook, Twitter

Marty Zaluski, President
Ben Richey, Executive Director
Kelly Janicek, Executive Assistant

Seeks to prevent, control and eliminate livestock diseases.
1400 Members
Founded in 1897

9681 US Apple Association
8233 Old Courthouse Rd
Suite 200
Vienna, VA 22182

703-442-8850; Fax: 703-790-0845
info@usapple.org
www.usapple.org
Facebook, Twitter, Youtube

Jim Bair, President & CEO
Diane Kurrle, Senior Vice President
Jessa Allen, Director,Membership&Communicatons
Wendy Brannen, Director,Consumer Health
Niza Strike, Office manager

Providing all segments of the US apple industry the means to profitably produce and market apples and apple products. Committed to serving the entire US apple industry by representing the industry on national issues, increasing the demand for apples and apple products, and providing information on matters pertaining to the apple industry.
440 Members
Founded in 1970

9682 US Beet Sugar Association
1156 15th St NW
Suite 1019
Washington, DC 20005

202-296-4820
800-872-0127; Fax: 202-331-2065
www.beetsugar.org

James Johnson, President
Elin Peltz, VP
Claudia Tidwell, Director of Administration
Hillary Fabrico, Government Affairs Assistant
Cassie Bladow, Director of Government Affairs

Beet sugar processing companies make up the membership of this association.
Founded in 1911

9683 US Canola Association
600 Pennsylvania Ave SE
Suite 320
Washington, DC 20003

202-969-8113; Fax: 202-969-7036
info@uscanola.com
www.uscanola.com
Facebook, Twitter, YouTube

John Gordley, Executive Director
Dale Thorenson, Assistant Director
Angela Dansby, Communications Director
Blair Elias, Advertising Sales Representative

Works to support and advance US canola production, marketing, processing and use through government and industry relations. Striving to develop and implement agricultural policies, promote efficient production of the crop, and develop markets for US canola products.
Founded in 1989

9684 US Grains Council
20 F Street, NW
Suite 600
Washington, DC 20001

202-789-0789; Fax: 202-898-0522
grains@grains.org

www.grains.org
Facebook, Twitter, Youtube, Flickr

Jim Raben, Chair
Chad Willis, Vice Chair
Ryan LeGrand, President & CEO
Josh Miller, Secretary/Treasurer
Greg Hibner, Agribusiness Sector Director

Develops export markets for US barley, corn, grain sorghum and related products. Members include producer organizations and agribusinesses with a common interest in developing export markets.
100 Members
Founded in 1960

9685 **US Meat Export Federation**
1855 Blake St
Suite 200
Denver, CO 80202

303-623-6328; Fax: 303-623-0297
www.usmef.org

Leann Saunders, Chair
Roel Andriessen, Chair-elect
Bruce Schmoll, Vice Chair
Dennis Stiffler, Treasurer/ Secretary
Philip M. Seng, President, CEO

A trade association working to create new opportunities and develop existing international markets for U.S. beef, pork, lamb and veal.
160 Members
Founded in 1996

9686 **US Poultry & Egg Association**
1530 Cooledge Rd
Tucker, GA 30084-7303

770-938-6915; Fax: 770-493-9257
www.poultryegg.org
Facebook

Gary Cooper, Chairman
John Starkey, President
Carol 9anson, Executive Assistant

Representing the entire industry as an All Feather association. Membership includes producers and processors of broilers, turkeys, ducks, eggs, and breeding stock, as well as allied companies.
Cost: $300.00
600 Members
Frequency: Membership Dues
Founded in 1947

9687 **USA Hops**
Liberty Building
32 N 3rd Street, Suite 408
Yakima, WA 98901

509-453-4749; Fax: 509-457-8561
info@usahops.org
www.usahops.org
Facebook, YouTube

Supports commercial hop producers in US Pacific Northwest.

9688 **USA Rice Federation**
2101 Wilson Boulevard
Suite 610
Arlington, VA 22201ÿÿ

703-236-2300; Fax: 703-236-2301
riceinfo@usarice.com
www.usarice.com
Facebook, Twitter, RSS, YouTube, Pinterest

Betsy Ward, President & CEO
Rebecca Greenway, Chief Financial Officer
Michael Klein, VP, Communications & Domestic Promo
Ben Mosely, VP, Government Affairs
Jeanette Davis, Sr. Dir., Meetings & Member Service

A national association representing producers, millers and allied businesses advancing the use and consumption of U.S. grown rice.

9689 **United Agribusiness League**
54 Corporate Park
Irvine, CA 92606

800-223-4590; Fax: 949-975-1671
membership@unitedag.org
www.unitedag.org
Facebook

Brian Edmonds, Chairman
Anthony Vollering, Vice Chairman
A.J. Cisney, Treasurer
Les Graulich, Director
Jerry Pogorzelski, Director

Creating a community for agribusiness—networking and education.
Founded in 1983

9690 **United Braford Breeders**

Home Page: www.brafords.org

Organization that registers Braford cattle in the United States.

9691 **United Egg Producers**
1720 Windward Concourse
Alpharetta, GA 30005

770-360-9220; Fax: 770-360-7058
www.unitedegg.org
Facebook, Twitter

Chad Gregory, President & CEO
Oscar Garrison, SVP, Food Safety
Sherry Shedd, VP, Finance
Larry Sadler, VP, Animal Welfare
Kathy Bryan, Director, Communications

UEP is a Capper-Volstead cooperative of egg farmers from all across the United States and representing the ownership of all the nation's egg-laying hens.
Founded in 1968

9692 **United Food and Commercial Workers International Union**
1775 K St Nw
Washington, DC 20006

202-223-3111; Fax: 202-466-1562
ssmith@ufcw.org
www.ufcw.org
Facebook, Twitter, YouTube, Flickr

Anthony Marc Perrone, President
Patrick J O'Neill, Secretary/Treasurer
Paul Meinema, Executive VP
Esther lopez, Executive VP
Wayne E. Hanley, Executive VP

UFCW is North America's neighborhood union, members standing together to improve the lives and livelihoods of workers, families and communities.
1.4 M Members
Founded in 1979

9693 **United Fresh Produce Association**
1901 Pennsylvania Ave NW
Suite 1100
Washington, DC 20006

202-303-3400; Fax: 202-303-3433
united@unitedfresh.org
www.unitedfresh.org
Facebook, Twitter, LinkedIn

Thomas Stenzel, President & CEO
Robert Guenther, SVP, Public Policy
Mary Coppola, VP, Marketing & Communications
Julian Gamez, VP, Finance & Operations
Miriam Wolk, VP, Member Services

A trade association committed to driving the growth and success of produce companies ans their partners. Represents the interests of member companies throughout the global, fresh produce supply chain, including family-owned, private and publicly trade businesses as well as regional, national and international companies.
Founded in 1987

9694 **United Soybean Board**
16305 Swingley Ridge Rd
Suite 150
Chesterfield, MO 63017

636-530-1777
800-989-8721; Fax: 636-530-1560
ydock@unitedsoybean.com
www.unitedsoybean.org
Facebook, Twitter, YouTube

Jim Stillman, Chairman
Jim Call, Vice Chair
John Becherer, CEO
Lewis Brainbridge, Secretary
Bob Haselwood, Treasurer

Mission is to ensure that US soy is of the highest quality and the most competitive in a global marketplace.
Founded in 1972
Mailing list available for rent

9695 **United States Cane Sugar Refiners**
1730 Rhode Island Ave NW
#608
Washington, DC 20036-3101

202-331-1458

Joseph Cox, President

9696 **United States Potato Board**
4949 S. Syracuse St.
#400
Denver, CO 80237

303-369-7783; Fax: 303-369-7718
potatoesusa.com
Facebook, Twitter, LinkedIn, YouTube, Pinterest, Instagram

Blair Richardson, President & CEO
Carrie Connelly, Exec. Admin. & Human Resources Dir.
Monica Heath, VP, Finance & Policy
John Toaspern, Chief Marketing Officer
Chelsea Gray, Meetings & Events Manager

The nation's potato marketing organization. The central organizing force in implementing programs that will increase demand for potatoes, providing the ideas, information, tools and inspiration for the industry to unite in achieving common goals.
Founded in 1971

9697 **United States Tuna Foundation**
1101 17th St NW
Suite 609
Washington, DC 20036-4718

202-857-0610
www.tunafacts.com

Desiree Filippone, Manager

Serves as an umbrella organization representing the various interests of the U.S. canned tuna industry. Representing the internationaln and domestic interests to federal and state regulations, to national legislation, to domestic marketing.
Founded in 1976

9698 **Vegetarian Awareness Network/VEGANET**
4041G Hadley Road,
Suite 101
South Plainfield, NJ 07080

908-769-1160
800-872-8343; Fax: 908-769-1171
www.wholefoodsmagazine.com
Facebook, Twitter, LinkedIn

Howard V. Wainer, President

Networks to promote healthful living, environmental healing, and respect for all life; to advance public awareness of the advantages of the increasingly popular vegetarian lifestyle; to enhance the visibility and accessibility of vegetarian products and services; and to facilitate the

formation and expansion of local vegetarian organizations.
Founded in 1980

9699 **Vegetarian Resource Group**
PO Box 1463
Baltimore, MD 21203

410-366-8343; Fax: 410-366-8804
vrg@vrg.org
www.vrg.org
Facebook, Twitter, LinkedIn

Debra Wasserman, Director
Jeanne Yacoubou, Research Director

An organization dedicated to educating the public on vegetarianism and veganism and related issues such as health, nutrition, ecology, ethics, and world hunger. Members of the group include health professionals, activists, and educators.
10000 Members
Founded in 1982
Mailing list available for rent

9700 **Vidalia Onion Committee**
100 Vidalia Sweet Onion Drive
PO Box 1609
Vidalia, GA 30474

912-537-1918; Fax: 912-537-2166
info@vidaliaonion.org
www.vidaliaonion.org
Facebook, Twitter, YouTube, Pinterest

Aries Haygood, Chairman
Michael E. Hively, Vice Chairman
Myrtle S. Jones, Secretary

Promote growth, distribution and awareness of this one of a kind crop.
225 Members
Founded in 1931

9701 **Vinegar Institute**
1100 Johnson Ferry Road
Suite 300
Atlanta, GA 30342

404-252-3663; Fax: 404-252-0774
vidsmith@kellencompany.com
www.versatilevinegar.org
Facebook

Pamela A Chumley, President
Jeannie Milewski, Executive Director

Manufacturers and bottlers of vinegar and suppliers to the industry are the members of this association. Publications available only to members.
Founded in 1967

9702 **Walnut Council**
1007 N 725 W
West Lafayette, IN 47906-9431

765-583-3501; Fax: 765-583-3512
walnutcouncil@walnutcouncil.org
www.walnutcouncil.org

Bill Hammitt, President
John Katzke, Quartermaster
Liz Jackson, Executive Director
Bill Hoover, Treasurer

Representing woodland owners, foresters, forest scientists and wood producing industry representatives. The purpose is to assist in the technical transfer of forest research to field applications, help build and maintain bettermarkets for wood products and nut crops.
1000 Members
Founded in 1970

9703 **Western Dairy Association**
12000 Washington
Suite 175
Thornton, CO 80241

303-451-7711
800-274-6455; Fax: 303-451-0411
www.westerndairyassociation.org
Facebook, Twitter, YouTube

Rick Podtburg, Chairman
Jim Webb, Vice-Chairman
Ron Shelton, Secretary
Tim Bernhardt, Treasurer
Cindy Haren, Chief Executive Officer

Leading dairy farmer members and the industry in a world class direction of partnerships and business resulting in economic viability, new innovations in dairy products and building stronger community commitment to dairy farms and dairy families.
Founded in 1936

9704 **Western Growers Association**
17620 Fitch Street
Irvine, CA 92614

949-863-1000
800-333-4942; Fax: 949-863-9028
info@wga.com
www.wga.com

Stephen J. Barnard, Chairman
Bruce C. Taylor, Senior Vice Chairman
Victor Smith, Vice Chairman
John S. Manfre, Secretary
Mark J. Teixeria, Treasurer

Association for growers, shippers, packers, brokers and distributors of fruits and vegetables in California and Arizona.
3000 Members
Founded in 1926

9705 **Western United States Agricultural Trade Association**
4601 NE 77th Avenue
Suite 240
Vancouver, WA 98662

360-693-3373; Fax: 360-693-3464
export@wusata.org
www.wusata.org

Andy Anderson, Executive Director
Rebecca Roberts, Executive Administrator
Tricia Walker, FundMatch Manager
Terri Curtis, Office Coordinator
Monica Quenette, Outreach & Communications Coord.

This organization offers information and support to increase exports of US agricultural products.
200 Members
Founded in 1980

9706 **Wheat Foods Council**
51 Red Fox Lane
Unit D
Ridgway, CO 81432

970-626-9828; Fax: 303-840-6877
wfc@wheatfoods.org
www.wheatfoods.org
Facebook, Twitter

Don Brown, Chair
Debi Rogers, Vice Chair
Tim O'Connor, President
Gayle Veum, Vice President
Reid Christopherson, Treasurer/Secretary

An industry-wide partnership dedicated to increasing wheat and other grain foods consumption through nutrition information, education, research and promotional programs.
Founded in 1972

9707 **Wild Blueberry Association of North America**
PO Box 100
Old Town, ME 04468

207-570-3535; Fax: 207-581-3499
wildblueberries@gwi.net
www.wildblueberries.com
Facebook, Twitter, Youtube, Pinterest, Googleplus

Ragnar Kamp, President
Mike Collins, Marketing Manager

Represents processors and growers of wild blueberries in Eastern Canada and Maine. The Association is focused on the generic promotion of wild blueberries around the world. It offers promotional materials, joint funding, product development, assistance, seminars, newsletters, supplier lists and ongoing support to users of wild blueberries in all retail, manufacturing, food service and bakery trade segments.
Founded in 1981

9708 **Wine Appreciation Guild**
360 Swift Ave
Unit 30-40
S San Francisco, CA 94080

650-866-3020
800-239-9463; Fax: 650-866-3029
info@wineappreciation.com
www.wineappreciation.com

James Mackey, Manager
Jason Simon, Manager
Jeff Szczesney, Contact
Hamlin Endicott, Contact
Amy Decker, Contact

Formed as the official successor in the distribution of wine accessories, and the publication and distribution of books and educational materials.
1500 Members
Founded in 1973

9709 **Wine Institute**
425 Market Street
Suite 1000
San Francisco, CA 94105

415-512-0151
info@wineinstitute.org
www.wineinstitute.org
Facebook, Twitter, LinkedIn, YouTube, Pinterest

Robert Koch, President/CEO
Maluri Fernandez, Executive Assistant
Nancy Light, VP, Communications

Dedicated to initiating and advocating state, federal and international public policy to enhance the environment for the responsible production, promotion and enjoyment of wine.
1000 Members
Founded in 1934

9710 **Wine and Spirits Shippers Association**
11800 Sunrise Valley Dr
Suite 332
Reston, VA 20191

703-860-2300
800-368-3167; Fax: 703-860-2422
info@wssa.com
www.wssa.com
Facebook, Twitter, LinkedIn

V. James Andretta, Jr., Chairman Emeritus
Louis Healey, President
Howard Jacobs, Vice President
Alison Leavitt, Managing Director
Heather Randolph, Director of Operations

A non-profit shippers association composed of importers and exporters of beverages and allied products. Provides members, importers and exporters with efficient and economical ocean transportation and other logestic services.
400 Members
Founded in 1976

9711 **Wine and Spirits Wholesalers of America**
805 15th Street NW
Suite 1120
Washington, DC 20005
202-371-9792; Fax: 202-789-2405
Info@wswa.org
www.wswa.org
Facebook, Twitter, YouTube, RSS
Michelle L. Korsmo, President/CEO
Jo Moak, SVP & General Counsel
Dawson Hobbs, SVP, Govt. Affairs
Heather Calio, VP, State Affairs
Ali Gormley, VP, Fed. Affairs
This association is comprised of wholesale distributors of domestic and imported wine and distilled spirits.
350+ Members
Founded in 1943

9712 **Wine and Spirits Wholesalers of America, Inc.**
805 15th Street, NW
Suite 430
Washington, DC 20036
202-371-9792; Fax: 202-789-2405
Info@wswa.org
www.wswa.org
Facebook, Twitter, YouTube, RSS
Brien Fox, Chairman
Alan Dreeben, Immediate Past Chairman
Doug Epstein, Vice Chairman
Carmine Martignetti, Senior VP
Sydney Ross, Treasurer
National trade organization representing the wholesale branch of the wine and spirits industry.
450 Members
Founded in 1943

Newsletters

9713 **AAMPlifier Newsletter**
American Association of Meat Processors
One Meating Place
Elizabethtown, PA 17022
717-367-1168
aamp@aamp.com
www.aamp.com
Rick Reams, President
Chris Young, Executive Director
Contains a wealth of information on industry trends, important national news, Association activities, and operational information to keep members fully informed about events affecting their business.
1300+ Members
Frequency: Bi-Monthly
Founded in 1939

9714 **ABL Insider**
American Beverage Licensees
5101 River Rd
Suite 108
Bethesda, MD 20816-1560
301-656-1494; Fax: 301-656-7539
info@ablusa.org
www.ablusa.org
Lyle Fitzsimmons, Editor
The voice of America's beer, wine & spirits retailers.
Frequency: Monthly

9715 **ADPI Weekly Newsletter**
American Dairy Products Institute
116 N York Street
Suite 200
Elmhurst, IL 60126
630-530-8700; Fax: 630-530-8707
info@adpi.org
www.adpi.org
Electronic communication of industry news, regulatory developments, and association matters.
Frequency: Weekly
Circulation: 1000

9716 **AFFI Newsletter**
American Frozen Food Institute
2000 Corporate Ridge
Suite 1000
McLean, VA 22102-7862
703-821-0770; Fax: 703-821-1350
info@affi.com
www.affi.com
Kraig R Naasz, President/CEO
Jason Bassett, Director Legislative Affairs
Chuck Fuqua, VP Communications
Robert L Garfield, SVP Public Policy/Intl Affairs
Frequency: Weekly

9717 **AHA Quarterly**
American Herb Association
PO Box 1673
Nevada City, CA 95959-1673
530-265-9552; Fax: 530-274-3140
www.ahaherb.com
Kathi Keville, Director
Robert Brucia, Co-Director
Marion Wyckoff, Secretary
Reports on the latest scientific studies, new herb, aromatherapy, cooking and gardening books, international herb news, legal and environmental issues, herb-related events and conferences.
Cost: $20.00
20 Pages
Frequency: w/Membership
Founded in 1981

9718 **AICR Newsletter**
American Institute for Cancer Research
1759 R St NW
Washington, DC 20009-2570
202-328-7744
800-843-8114; Fax: 202-328-7226
aicrweb@aicr.org
www.aicr.org
Marilyn Gentry, President
Explains current cancer research, provides recipes and menu ideas for healthy eating, and offers practical advice to lower cancer risk.
Frequency: Quarterly
Circulation: 1.6MM
Founded in 1982

9719 **ALBC News**
American Livestock Breeds Conservancy
15 Hillsboro Street
PO Box 477
Pittsboro, NC 27312
919-542-5704; Fax: 919-545-0022
albc@albc-usa.org
www.albc-usa.org
Marjorie Bender, Prog. Coord./Research
Don Schrider, Communication Director
Charles Bassett, Executive Director
Angelique Thompson, Operations Manager
Jennifer Kendall, Communications Director
Breeders directory; annual conference; catalog of publications available.
Cost: $30.00
20 Pages
Circulation: 3000
ISSN: 1064-1599
Founded in 1977
Printed in one color on matte stock

9720 **AMSA eNews**
American Meat Science Association
2441 Village Green Pl
Champaign, IL 61822-7676
800-517-AMSA; Fax: 888-205-5834; Fax: 217-356-5370
information@meatscience.org
www.meatscience.org
Dean Pringle, President
Collette Kaster, Chief Executive Officer
Published for all AMSA members every other week, including member news and meat science information updates.

9721 **APIS**
CITA International
3464 W Earll Drive
Suites E & F
Phoenix, AZ 85017
602-447-0480; Fax: 602-447-0305
esam@citainternational.com
EM Morsy, Editor
PE Pederson, Advertising/Sales
The international bulletin for specialty livestock, pet animal and ag-chem product developments.
Frequency: Quarterly
Founded in 1988

9722 **ASBC Newsletter**
American Society of Brewing Chemists
3340 Pilot Knob Rd
Eagan, MN 55121-2055
651-454-7250; Fax: 651-454-0766
asbc@scisoc.org
www.asbcnet.org
Steven C Nelson, VP
Contains the annual meeting program, lists of ASBC committees and reports, and local section news.
Frequency: Quarterly
Circulation: 800+
Founded in 1934

9723 **ASTA Advocate**
American Spice Trade Association
2025 M St NW
Suite 800
Washington, DC 20036-2422
202-367-1127; Fax: 202-367-2127
info@astaspice.org
www.astaspice.org
Donna Tainter, President
Roger Clarke, Vice President/ Secretary
Gaspare Colletti, Treasurer
David Howe, Associate Group Director
Electronic newsletter designed to keep members informed about the spice industry, events impacting the industry and ASTA activities. ASTA Advocate is ASTA's regulatory newsletter.
Frequency: Membership Dues Vary
Founded in 1907

9724 **Agri Times Northwest**
Sterling Ag
PO Box 189
Pendleton, OR 97801
541-276-7845; Fax: 541-276-7964
www.agritimes.com/
Virgil Rupp, CEO/President
Sterling Allen, Publisher/Marketing Director
Regional agricultural newspaper.
Cost: $20.00
16 Pages
Circulation: 3700
Printed in 4 colors on newsprint stock

9725 **Agri-Pulse**
International Dairy Foods Association

1250 H Street NW
Suite 900
Washington, DC 20005

202-737-4332; Fax: 202-331-7820
membership@idfa.org
www.idfa.org
Facebook, Twitter, YouTube, Blog

Connie Tipton, President & CEO
Mike Nosewicz, Chair
Brian Perry, Vice Chair
Jon Davis, Secretary
Ed Mullins, Treasurer

The latest information and news in agricultural information. Investigating several aspects of the food, fuel, feed and fiber industries, looking at the economic, statistical and financial trends and evaluate the changes impacting businesses.
550 Members
Frequency: Weekly

9726 **Alcoholic Beverage Control Fast: From the State Capitals**
Wakeman Walworth
PO Box 7376
Alexandria, VA 22307-7376

703-768-9600; Fax: 703-768-9690
www.statecapitals.com/alcoholbev.html

Keyes Walworth, Publisher

Covers binge drinking laws, internet sales, advertising, taxes, bottle bills, Sunday sales laws, license regulation, drunk driving laws, under-age drinking, mini-bottles and other state laws affecting beer, liquor and wine distribution.
4 Pages
Frequency: Weekly
Founded in 1962
Printed in one color on matte stock

9727 **Alcoholic Beverage Executives' Newsletter International**
Patricia Kennedy
PO Box 3188
Omaha, NE 68103-1088

402-397-5514; Fax: 402-397-3843

Patricia Kennedy, Editor

Current news of the wine, beer, and distilled spirits marketplace, and provides information and ideas for the marketing and advertising campaigns of these beverages.
Cost: $275.00
Frequency: Weekly
ISSN: 0889-3510

9728 **American Agriculturist**
Farm Progress Companies
255 38th Avenue
Suite P
St Charles, IL 60174-5410

630-462-2224
800-441-1410
jvogel@farmprogress.com
www.farmprogress.com/american-agriculturist/

John Vogel, Editor
Willie Vogt, Cororate Editorial Director
Dan Crummett, Executive Editor

Serves Northeast producers with information to help them maximize their productivity and profitability. Each issue is packed with information, ideas, news and analysis.
Cost: $29.65
Frequency: Monthly
Founded in 1842

9729 **American Bakers Association Bulletin**
American Bakers Association
1350 I Street NW
Suite 1290
Washington, DC 20005-3305

202-789-0300; Fax: 202-898-1164
kkotche@americanbakers.org
www.americanbakers.org

Kelly Kotche, Communications/Membership Manager
Paul Abenante, President/CEO

The association's newsletter that covers the conventions.
Frequency: Semi-Annual

9730 **American Beekeeping Federation Newsletter**
American Beekeeping Federation
3525 Piedmont Rd
Bldg 5 Suite 300
Atlanta, GA 30305-1509

404-760-2875; Fax: 404-240-0998
info@abfnet.org
www.abfnet.org

Molly Sausaman, Executive Director

ABF-member benefit to inform members about ABF activities and happenings in the beekeeping industry.
24 Pages
Frequency: Bi-Monthly
Circulation: 1,200
Founded in 1943

9731 **American Herb Association Quarterly Newsletter**
American Herb Association
PO Box 1673
Nevada City, CA 95959-1673

530-265-9552; Fax: 530-274-3140
www.ahaherb.com

Kathi Keville, Director
Robert Brucia, Co-Director
Marion Wyckoff, Secretary

Updates and news on the herbal industry, such as; new scientific herbal and aromatherapy studies, plants interaction with ecology, reports on legal issues about herbs, a calendar of herbal and aromatherapy events, and a media report listing the herbal stories in the media.
Cost: $20.00
Frequency: Membership Fee
Founded in 1981

9732 **American Institute of Baking Technical Bulletin**
American Institute of Baking
PO Box 3999
Manhattan, KS 66505-3999

785-537-4750
866-342-4772; Fax: 785-565-6060
bissc@bissc.org
www.bissc.org

James Munyon, President

Developed to keep the baking and allied trades apprised of current trends in ingredients, products, equipment, processing, packaging, nutrition and research.
Frequency: Monthly

9733 **American Meat Institute: Newsletter**
American Meat Institute
1150 Connecticut Ave Nw
Suite 1200
Washington, DC 20036-4126

202-587-4200; Fax: 202-587-4300

J Patrick Boyle, CEO
Janet Riley, Editor
Ayoka Blandford, Marketing Manager

Subscription includes news of legislative and government regulations and actions relevant to the meat industry.
Frequency: Quarterly
Circulation: 3000
Founded in 1906

9734 **American Society of Agricultural Consultants News**
American Society of Agricultural Consultants
950 S Cherry Street
Suite 508
Denver, CO 80246-2664

303-758-3514; Fax: 303-758-0190
www.agconsultants.org

Deborah Wiig, Editor

Informs ASAC members of news regarding members, events, education and government issues.
8-12 Pages
Frequency: Quarterly
Circulation: 200
Founded in 1963
Printed in on newsprint stock

9735 **American Soybean Association Newsletter**
American Soybean Association
12125 Woodcrest Executive
Suite 100
Creve Coeur, MO 63141-5009

314-576-1770
800-688-7692; Fax: 314-576-2786
info@soy.org
www.soygrowers.com

Steve Censky, CEO

Their mission is to advocate for U.S. soy farmers on policy and trade.
Frequency: Monthly
Founded in 1920

9736 **Angus Beef Bulletin**
American Angus Association
3201 Frederick Ave
St Joseph, MO 64506-2997

816-383-5100; Fax: 816-233-9703
angus@angus.org
www.angus.org
Facebook, Twitter

David A. Dal Porto, President

To provide programs, services, technology and leadership to enhance the genetics of the Angus breed, broaden its influence within the beef industry, and expand the market for superior tasting, high-quality Angus beef worldwide. Achieve Angus excellence through information.
Cost: $80.00
30+M Members
Frequency: Membership Fees Vary
Founded in 1883

9737 **Association of American Seed Control Officials Bulletin**
Utah Department of Agriculture
801 Summit Crossing Place
Suite C
Gastonia, NC 28054

704-810-8877; Fax: 704-853-4109
www.seedcontrol.org

Seed laws in the US and Canada.
Frequency: Annual

9738 **Association of Food Industries Newsletter**
Association of Food Industries

3301 State Route 66
Suite 205, Building C
Neptune, NJ 07753-2705

732-922-3008; Fax: 732-922-3590
info@naooa.org
www.naooa.org

Robert Bauer, President

Offers information & education on customs and usage of trade in the food industry and current events in the business.
Founded in 1906

9739 **BEMA Newsletter**
Bakery Equipment Manufacturers Association
10740 Nall Avenue
Suite 230
Overland Park, KS 66211

913-338-1300; Fax: 913-338-1327
info@bema.org
www.bema.org

Published by BEMA, to keep members informed about the latest baking and food industry news.
Frequency: Quarterly

9740 **Bakers Band Together to Demand Relief-ABA Calls for March on Washington**
American Bakers Association
1120 Connecticut Avenue NW
Washington, DC 200036

800-226-5377
www.aba.com

Rob Nichols, President & CEO
Frequency: Monthly

9741 **Bakery Insider**
Retail Bakers of America
15941 Harlem Ave
Suite 347
Tinley Park, IL 60477

800-638-0924
www.retailbakersofamerica.org
Facebook, Twitter

Bernadette Shanahan-Haas, Director of Operations
Paul Sapienza, Director of Finance
Lynn Schurman, Education Director

Updates, education and info from Retail Bakers of America.
Frequency: Weekly

9742 **Beer Marketer's Insights Newsletter**
Beer Marketer's Insights
49 E Maple Ave
Suffern, NY 10901-5507

845-624-2337; Fax: 845-624-2340
www.beerinsights.com

Benj Steinman, President

Reports on the competitive battle among brewers for a share of the beer market. Analyzes recent legislation and factors that affect the industry.
Frequency: Monthly

9743 **Beer Statistics News**
Beer Marketer's Insights
49 E Maple Ave
Suffern, NY 10901-5507

845-624-2337; Fax: 845-624-2340
www.beerinsights.com

Benj Steinnan, CEO/President
Jerry Curley, Circulation Manager

Supplies data for major brewers' shipments in 39 reporting states.
Cost: $450.00
Frequency: Annual+

9744 **Beverage Digest**
Beverage Digest
PO Box 621
Bedford Hills, NY 10507-0621

914-244-0700; Fax: 914-244-0774
order@beverage-digest.com
www.beverage-digest.com

John Sicher, Editor/Publisher
Tom Fine, Managing Editor

Authoritative publication covering the non-alcoholic beverages industry.
Cost: $675.00
Frequency: 22 issues per y
Founded in 1982

9745 **Beverage World Periscope**
Keller International Publishing Corporation
150 Great Neck Rd
Suite 400
Great Neck, NY 11021-3309

516-829-9722; Fax: 516-829-9306
www.supplychainbrain.com

Terry Beirne, Publisher
Bryan DeLuca, Editor
Jerry Keller, President
Mary Chavez, Director of Sales

Analysis of developments as they occur in the beverage marketplace, presented in a tightly-written, four-color tabloid format, makes this a unique newsletter. This publication limits advertising to tabloid or standard pages.
Frequency: Monthly
Circulation: 33000
Founded in 1882

9746 **Bottled Water Reporter**
Bottled Water Association
1700 Diagonal Road
Suite 650
Alexandria, VA 22314-2844

703-683-5213; Fax: 703-683-4074
mbusetti@bottledwater.org
www.bottledwater.org

Sabrina Hicks, Editor

Trade news.

9747 **Brewers Bulletin**
PO Box 677
Thiensville, WI 53092

262-242-6105; Fax: 262-242-5133

Thomas Volke, President

Brewing industry newspaper.
Cost: $53.00
Circulation: 550
Founded in 1907

9748 **Brown Swiss Bulletin**
Brown Swiss Cattle Breeder's Assoc of the USA
800 Pleasant St
Beloit, WI 53511-5456

608-365-4474; Fax: 608-365-5577
info@brownswissusa.com
www.brownswissusa.com

David Wallace, Executive Secretary
Charlotte Muenzenberg, Sup't of Records
Leonard Johnson, Genetic Programs/Show Manager
Cost: $25.00
Frequency: Monthly
ISSN: 0007-2516

9749 **BuSiness of Herbs**
Herb Growing and Marketing Network
PO Box 245
Silver Spring, PA 17575-0245

717-393-3295; Fax: 717-393-9261
herbworld@aol.com
www.herbworld.com

Finds a wide variety of articles that will help with marketing, growing and genergal business issues. Has profiles of herb businesses and how they've created a business that allows them to support themselves with their passion.
Cost: $48.00
Frequency: Monthly

9750 **Calorie Control Commentary**
Calorie Control Council
2611 Winslow Dr Ne
Atlanta, GA 30305-3777

678-608-3200; Fax: 404-252-0774
webmaster@caloriecontrol.org
www.caloriecontrol.org

Timely information on low-calorie and reduced-fat foods and beverages, weight management, physical activity and healthy eating.
60 Members
Founded in 1966

9751 **Cameron's Foodservice Marketing Reporter**
Cameron's Publications
5423 Sheridan Drive
PO Box 676
Williamsville, NY 14231

519-586-8785; Fax: 519-586-8816
www.cameronpub.com

Successful promotion and advertising case histories for the restaurant and hotel industry.

9752 **Can Shipments Report**
Can Manufacturers Institute
1730 Rhode Island Ave Nw
Suite 1000
Washington, DC 20036-3112

202-232-4677; Fax: 202-232-5756
www.cancentral.com

Robert Budway, President
Shawn Relly, Editor/Publisher

Provides a summary of the past year's accomplishments, as well as a look at the strategy to fulfill goals in the coming year.
Frequency: Annual
Founded in 1938

9753 **Capitol Lineup Newsletter**
American Association of Meat Processors
One Meating Place
Elizabethtown, PA 17022

717-367-1168
aamp@aamp.com
www.aamp.com

Rick Reams, President
Chris Young, Executive Director

Deals strictly with governmental affairs in the industry. Keeps AAMP members up to date with the latest news about government affairs from Congress and key agencies in Washington, as well as state legislatures and state regulatory bodies.
Frequency: 26x Yearly

9754 **Catering Service Idea Newsletter**
Prosperity & Profits Unlimited
PO Box 416
Denver, CO 80201

303-573-5564

A Doyle, Editor

Catering service business ideas and possibilities.

9755 **Cereal Foods World**
AACC International
3340 Pilot Knob Rd
Eagan, MN 55121-2055

651-454-7250
800-328-7560; Fax: 651-454-0766

aacc@scisoc.org
www.aaccnet.org

Amy Hope, Publisher
Jody Grider, Executive Editor
Jordana Anker, Managing Editor
Greg Grahek, Director, Publications

Covers grain-based food science, technology, and new product development. Includes articles that focus on advances in grain-based food science and the application of these advances to product development and food production practices.
Frequency: Bimonthly
ISSN: 0146-6283

9756 **Champagne Wines Information Bureau**
KCSA
800 2nd Avenue
5th Floor
New York, NY 10017-4709

212-682-6300
800-642-4267; Fax: 212-697-0910
info@champagnes.com
www.champagnes.com

Jean-Louis Carbonnier, Editor
Herbert L Corbin, President/CEO

Representative of Comite Interprofessionnel duVinde Champagne, Epernay, France.
4 Pages
Circulation: 10000
Printed in one color on matte stock

9757 **Cheese Reporter**
Cheese Reporter Publishing Company
2810 Crossroads Dr
Suite 3000
Madison, WI 53718-7972

608-246-8430; Fax: 608-246-8431
info@cheesereporter.com
www.cheesereporter.com

Dick Groves, Publisher/Editor
Kevin Thome, Marketing Director
Betty Mertes, Circulation Manager

Leading weekly publication serving manufacturers and marketers of cheese, butter, ice cream, yogurt and other fermented milk foods, whey and other dairy processors.
Cost: $150.00
16 Pages
Frequency: Weekly
Circulation: 2000
ISSN: 0009-2142
Founded in 1876
Printed in 4 colors on n stock

9758 **Coffee Reporter**
National Coffee Association
15 Maiden Ln
Suite 1405
New York, NY 10038-5113

212-766-4007; Fax: 212-766-5815
info@ncausa.org
www.ncausa.org

Robert F Nelson, President
Joseph F DeRupo, Communications/PR Director

Contains news of NCA activities and programs, new product development and market trends in both the U.S. and global coffee industry, regulatory action affecting the U.S. coffee industry and statistical data on ICO prices and U.S. retail prices. A single copy subscription is supplied free of charge to members, non-eligible parties for membership the cost is $40.00
Cost: $65.00
Frequency: Quarterly

9759 **Coffee, Sugar and Cocoa Exchange Daily Market Report**
New York Board of Trade
1 North End Avenue
New York, NY 10282-1101

212-748-4000
877-877-8890; Fax: 212-748-4039
webmaster@nybot.com
www.nybot.com

Leonel Fern ndez, President

Offers market reports on the stock market exchange covering foods and specific food investing.

9760 **Communique**
CHRIE
2810 N Parham Road
Suite 230
Richmond, VA 23294

804-346-4800; Fax: 804-346-5009
info@chrie.org
www.chrie.org
Facebook, Twitter, LinkedIn

Susan Fournier, President
Josette Katz, Vice President
Chris Roberts, Secretary
John Drysdale, Treasurer
Kathy McCarty, CEO

Council on Hotel, Restaurant, and Institutional Educations informational newsletter.
Cost: $45.00
Frequency: Monthly

9761 **Concessionworks Newsletter**
National Association of Concessionaires
35 E Wacker Dr
Suite 1816
Chicago, IL 60601-2270

312-236-3858; Fax: 312-236-7809
scross@naconline.org
www.naconline.org

Charles A Winans, Executive Director

For members with updates on association happenings, feature articles, new member listings, product news and industry updates.
Founded in 1944

9762 **Country World Newspaper**
Echo Publishing Company
401 Church Street
PO Box 596
Sulphur Springs, TX 75483

903-885-8663
800-245-2149; Fax: 903-885-8768

Scott Keys, Publisher
Lori Cope, Editor
Jim Horton, Advertising Manager

A newspaper offering agricultural information to farmers, ranchers, dairyfarmers, and agribusinesses.
Cost: $24.00
36 Pages
Frequency: Weekly
Circulation: 16200
Founded in 1981
Printed in 4 colors on newsprint stock

9763 **Crop Protection Management**
2892 Crescent Avenue
Eugene, OR 97408

541-343-5641
800-874-3276; Fax: 541-686-0248

Jeff Powell, Publisher

This newsletter covers all aspects of crop management and protection, including pesticides, agricultural chemicals and legislation.
Frequency: 5 per year

9764 **Daily Advocate**
Thomson Newspapers
PO Box 220
Greenville, OH 45331-220

937-548-3151; Fax: 937-548-3913
webmaster@dailyadvocate.com
www.dailyadvocate.com

Gary Lamberg, Publisher
Bob Robinson, Editor
Ken Bowen, Circulation Manager
Ashley Fritz, Graphic Designer
Barb Wilson, Business Manager

Farming interests, grain, livestock. Sections on senior citizens, farmers, builders, religion, sports, as well as special sections on agriculture and home improvement.
Cost: $117.00
Frequency: Daily
Founded in 1883

9765 **Dairy Council Digest**
National Dairy Council
Interstate Place II
100 Elwood Davis Road
North Syracuse, NY 13212

315-472-9143; Fax: 315-472-0506
ndc@dairyinformation.com
www.nationaldairycouncil.org
Facebook, Twitter

Provides a comprehensive review of research on topics ranging from the benefits of dairy foods in child nutrition, to dairy's potential protective role for metabolic syndrome and type 2 diabetes.
Frequency: Bi-Monthly
Founded in 1915

9766 **Dairy Industry Newsletter**
Eden Publishing Company
10255 W Higgins Road
Suite 900
Rosemont, IL 60018-4924

312-240-2880
www.dairyindustrynewsletter.com

Resource serving all sectors of the dairy industry. Reports on commercial, trade, political and market information.
8 Pages
Frequency: 25x Yearly
Printed in 2 colors on glossy stock

9767 **Dairy Market Report**
American Butter Institute
2101 Wilson Boulevard
Suite 400
Arlington, VA 22201

703-243-5630; Fax: 703-841-9328
AMiner@nmpf.org
www.nmpf.org/ABI

Peter Vitaliano, Editor

9768 **Dairy Profit Weekly**
DairyBusiness Communications
6437 Collamer Road
East Syracuse, NY 13057-1031

315-703-7979
800-334-1904; Fax: 315-703-7988
www.dairybusiness.com

Dave Natzke, Editorial Director
Joel Hastings, Publisher
Eleanor Jacobs, Regional Editor

Latest information, tips, and trends.
Cost: $179.00
4 Pages
Frequency: Weekly
Circulation: 1700
Printed in 2 colors on newsprint stock

9769 **Dairy-Deli-Bake Digest**
International Dairy-Deli-Bakery Association

636 Science Drive
PO Box 5528
Madison, WI 53705-0528

608-310-5000; Fax: 608-238-6330
IDDBA@iddba.org

Carol Christison, Executive Director

Packed with practical how-to information to help readers run a successful business. Features new management trends, new products, reports, reviews, association news, features, and consumer attitudes and trends.
Frequency: Monthly
Founded in 1964

9770 Dairy-Deli-Bake Wrap-Up
International Dairy-Deli-Bakery Association
636 Science Drive
PO Box 5528
Madison, WI 53705-0528

608-310-5000; Fax: 608-238-6330
IDDBA@iddba.org

Carol Christison, Executive Director

Covers IDDBA's seminars, expositions, member news, awards, and programs and services.
Frequency: Quarterly
Founded in 1964

9771 Distributor News
Food Industry Suppliers Association
1207 Sunset Drive
Greensboro, NC 27408

336-274-6311; Fax: 336-691-1839
stella@fisanet.org
www.fisanet.org

Jason Ryan, President
Eric Perkins, VP
Rob Clark, Past President

FISA's official newsletter, publishing industry happenings and business management information.
245 Members
Frequency: Quarterly
Founded in 1968

9772 Doane's Agricultural Report
Doane Agricultural Services
77 Westport Plz
Suite 250
St Louis, MO 63146-3121

314-569-2700
866-647-0918; Fax: 314-569-1083
www.doane.com

Dan Manternach, Editor

Provides information to US farmers and agricultural professionals. Doane keeps you up to date on factors affecting your farm program benefits and production costs too.
Frequency: Weekly

9773 FDRS Newsletter
Food Distribution Research Society
PO Box 441110
Fort Washington, MD 20749

301-292-1970; Fax: 301-292-1787
Jonathan_baros@ncsu.edu

John Park, President
Ron Rainey, President-Elect
Kellie Raper, Secretary/ Treasurer
Jennifer Dennis, Director
Stan Ernst, Director

Reports on Society events and happenings as well as related news from the industry and abroad.
Frequency: Quarterly

9774 FPA Update
Flexible Packaging Association
971 Corporate Blvd
Suite 403
Linthicum, MD 21090-2253

410-694-0800; Fax: 410-694-0900
fpa@flexpack.org
www.flexpack.org

Marla Donahue, President

Updating membership as well as the industry on FPA activities, events and accomplishments throughthe FPA Update, which is included within Flexible Packaging magazine.
Frequency: Monthly

9775 FSC Newsletter
Food Safety Consortium
110 Agriculture Building
University of Arkansas
Fayetteville, AR 72701

479-575-5647; Fax: 479-575-7531
www.fsconsortium.net

Dave Edmark, Communications Manager

A production of the three member schools of the consortium; University of Arkansas, Iowa State University and Kansas State University.
Frequency: Monthly
Founded in 1988

9776 FYI ASTA
American Spice Trade Association
2025 M St NW
Suite 800
Washington, DC 20036-2422

202-367-1127; Fax: 202-367-2127
info@astaspice.org
www.astaspice.org

Donna Tainter, President
Roger Clarke, Vice President/ Secretary
Gaspare Colletti, Treasurer
David Howe, Associate Group Director

Electronic newsletter designed to keep members informed about the spice industry, events impacting the industry and ASTA activities. The resource for members looking for information about ASTA, our programs and services.
Frequency: Membership Dues Vary
Founded in 1907

9777 Federal Focus
Natural Products Association
2112 E 4th St
Suite 200
Santa Ana, CA 92705-3816

714-460-7732
800-966-6632; Fax: 714-460-7444
www.npainfo.org
Facebook, Twitter, LinkedIn

John F. Gay, Executive Director & CEO
Jeffrey Wright, President

Provides information and alerts from the federal and state agencies that affect the industry.
1900+ Members
Frequency: Monthly
Founded in 1936

9778 Fence Post
423 Main Street
Windsor, CO 80550-5129

970-686-5691
800-275-5646; Fax: 970-686-5694
www.thefencepost.com

Jim Eisberry, President
Gary Sweeney, Publisher
Luke Gonzales, Business Manager
Tom Vilsack, Secretary

Farming news and reports.
Cost: $39.00
Frequency: Weekly

9779 Food Allergy News
Food Allergy & Anaphlaxis Network
11781 Lee Jackson Mem Hwy
Suite 160
Fairfax, VA 22033-3309

703-691-3179
800-929-4040; Fax: 703-691-2713
www.foodallergy.org

Anne Munoz-Furlong, President
Andreia Miller, Editor

Allergy newsletter with two pages of allergy-free recipes, coping strategies, research and studies.
Cost: $30.00
12 Pages
Circulation: 28000
ISSN: 1075-4318
Founded in 1991
Printed in 2 colors on glossy stock

9780 Food Industry Futures: A Strategy Service
CRS
PO Box 430
Fayetteville, NC 28302

910-486-9059; Fax: 910-486-9058

Ian Cuthill, Publisher, Editor

Includes new developments concerning management or marketing practices, mergers and acquisitions, economics, trade policies, etc. It covers the industry from farm and retail stores, mostly in the US but also internationally. Accepts advertising.
Cost: $150.00
4 Pages

9781 Food Industry Newsletter
Newsletters
PO Box 342730
Bethesda, MD 20827-2730

301-469-8507; Fax: 301-469-7271

Ellis Meredith, Publisher
Ray Marsili, Editor
Alice Corcoran, Circulation Manager

Concise, objective report for busy food executives, covering major food industry developments, including mergers and acquisitions, new trends and products, corporate and marketing strategies, etc. In addition to 22 regular issues a year, subscription also includes Special Food Marketing Reports on timely matters.
Cost: $245.00
Frequency: twice monthly except Aug.
Founded in 1972

9782 Food Insight
International Food Information Council
1100 Connecticut Ave Nw
Suite 430
Washington, DC 20036-4120

202-296-6540; Fax: 202-296-6547
foodinfo@ific.org

Dave Schmidt, President
Nick Alexander, Associate Editor
Michael Hayes, Copy Editor
8 Pages
Frequency: 6 issues per ye
Circulation: 45000
Printed in 4 colors on glossy stock

9783 Food Institute Report
American Institute of Food Distribution
1 Broadway
2nd Floor
Elmwood Park, NJ 07407-1844

201-791-5570; Fax: 201-791-5222
www.foodinstitute.com

Brian Todd, President
Mike Slattery, Chairman
Michael Sansolo, Senior Vice President
Joe Crocker, Vice Chairman
Donna George, Treasurer

Membership includes a subscription to The Food Institute Report, an in-depth weekly digest that delivers insights on new products, crop markets, legislation, customer demographics, mergers, food industry statistics, competitors and market trends.
Frequency: Weekly
Circulation: 3000
Founded in 1928

9784 **Food Merchants Advocate**
New York State Food Merchant
130 Washington Ave
Albany, NY 12210-2220
518-463-0300; Fax: 518-462-5474
www.nyscar.org
Christopher Pellnat, Editor
A tabloid newspaper for food retailers.
Cost: $10.00
Frequency: Monthly

9785 **Food Safety Professional**
Carpe Diem
208 Floral Vale Boulevard
Yardley, PA 19067
215-860-7800; Fax: 215-860-7900
www.foodquality.com
Paul Juestrich, Production Manager
Ken Potuznik, Director
Lisa Dionne, Creative Director
The Food Safety Professional is a quarterly publication of The antional Registry of Food Safety Professionals. Practical hands on article and advice form the experts will keep you informed of the latest technique an technologies in food safety.'
Cost: $20.00
Frequency: Quarterly
Circulation: 30,000

9786 **Food Trade News**
Best-Met Publishing
5537 Twin Knolls Rd
Suite 438
Columbia, MD 21045-3270
410-730-5013; Fax: 410-740-4680
office@best-met.com
www.best-met.com
Jeff Metzger, Publisher
Terri Maloney, Editor
Beth Pripstein, Office Manager
Cost: $63.00
Frequency: Monthly
Printed in one color on matte stock

9787 **Food World Information Services**
Best-Met Publishing Company
5537 Twin Knolls Rd
Suite 438
Columbia, MD 21045-3270
410-730-5013; Fax: 410-740-4680
tmaloney@best-met.com
www.best-met.com
Jeff Metzger, Publisher
Terri Maloney, Editor
Beth Pripstein, Office Manager
Richard J. Bestany, President
Provides market data for Baltimore, Washington, Central Pennsylvania and Philadelphia
Frequency: Monthly
Printed in on newsprint stock

9788 **Food for Thought**
D/FW Grocers Association
3044 Old Denton Rd
Suite 111, PMB 323
Carrollton, TX 75007
214-731-3132
800-791-6590; Fax: 469-574-5252
info@dfwga.net
www.dfwga.net
Offers information on grocery retailing and items of interest to members of the Grocers Association.
Frequency: Quarterly
Circulation: 1,000
Founded in 1947

9789 **FoodTalk**
Pike & Fischer
PO Box 25277
Alexandria, VA 22313
703-548-3146; Fax: 703-548-3017
Declan Couroy, Editor/Publisher
Sanitation tips for food workers.
Cost: $120.00
Frequency: Quarterly
Circulation: 5000
Founded in 1987
Printed in 2 colors on matte stock

9790 **Friday Notes**
Council For Agricultural Science and Technology
4420 West Lincoln Way
Ames, IA 50014-3447
515-292-2125
cast@cast-science.org
www.cast-science.org
Kent G. Schescke, Executive Vice President
Dan Gogerty, Managing Communications Editor
E-Newsletter featuring lead articles on current topics being discussed in agriculture, congressional updates, announcements of upcoming CAST publications and activities, and information about CAST's scientific society, company, and nonprofit members.
Frequency: Weekly
Circulation: 4000
Founded in 1972

9791 **GRAS Flavoring Substances 25**
Flavor & Extract Manufacturers Association
1620 I Street NW
Suite 925
Washington, DC 20006
202-293-5800; Fax: 202-462-8998
www.femaflavor.org
YouTube, RSS Feed
Ed R. Hays, Ph.D., President
George C. Robinson, III, President Elect
Mark Scott, Treasurer
Arthur Schick, VP & Secretary
John Cox, Executive Director
The 25th publication by the Expert Panel of the Flavor and Extract Manufacturers Association provides an update on recent progress in the consideration of flavoring ingredients generally recognized as safe under the Food Additive Amendment.
Frequency: Biennial
Founded in 1909

9792 **Global Food Marketer**
Food Export USA
309 West Washington
Suite 600
Chicago, IL 60606
312-334-9200; Fax: 312-334-9230
info@foodexportusa.org
Tim F Hamilton, Executive Director
Daleen D Richmond, Deputy Director
Newsletter for US exporters, containing useful articles, updates on overseas market conditions and trends, marketing tips, a column by a food export helpline counselor, and calendar of upcoming events.
Frequency: Bi-Monthly
Founded in 1973

9793 **Gourmet News**
Oser Communications Group
1877 N Kolb Road
Tuscon, AZ 85715
520-721-1300
www.gourmetnews.com
Rocelle Aragon, Editor
Kate Seymour, Senior Associate Publisher
The authoritative voice, and publication of choice for thousands of professionals in the gourmet and specialty food business. Reports timely and trustworty stories about events, issues, trends and other happenings within the trade.
Cost: $65.00
Frequency: Monthly
Circulation: 23100
Founded in 1991

9794 **Grayson Report**
Grayson Associates
30728 Paseo Elegancia
San Juan Cpstrn, CA 92675-5426
949-487-9970; Fax: 949-487-9975
www.graysonassociates.com
Suzanne Grayson, President
Robert Grayson, Director
Marketing analysis of the packaged goods industry.
Founded in 1970

9795 **Grocery Manufacturers of America:**
Grocery Manufacturers Association of America
1350 I St Nw
Suite 300
Washington, DC 20005-3377
202-337-9400; Fax: 202-639-5932
info@gmaonline.org
Pamela G Bailey, CEO
Jeff Nedelman, VP Communications
Focuses on the productivity and public policy issues affecting our industry.
Founded in 1908

9796 **Herd on the Hill**
National Meat Association
1970 Broadway
Suite 825
Oakland, CA 94612
510-763-1533; Fax: 510-763-6186
staff@nmaonline.org
www.nmaonline.org
Robert Rebholtz, Chairman
Larry Vad, President
Marty Evanson, Vice President
Mike Hesse, Secretary
Brian Coelho, Treasurer
Provides up-to-date information on what's happening in Washington in relation to the meat and poultry industry.
600 Members
Frequency: Weekly
Founded in 1946

9797 **Hot Sheet**
Fresh-Cut Produce Association
1600 Duke Street
Suite 440
Alexandria, VA 22314
530-756-8900; Fax: 530-756-8901
www.fresh-cuts.org
Jerry Gorny, President
Sean Handerhan, Marketing Director
A newsletter containing technical information, marketing news and exhibit information on the

produce trade. Serves over 500 members.
Cost: $35.00
Frequency: Monthly
Circulation: 23,000
Founded in 1987

9798 **Hotel, Restaurant, Institutional Buyers Guide**
Urner Barry Publications
PO Box 389
Toms River, NJ 08754

732-240-5330
800-932-0617; Fax: 732-341-0891
help@urnerbarry.com
www.urnerbarry.com/

Paul B Brown Jr, President
Sheila M Deane, Marketing Manager
Richard A. Brown, VP

Reports on perishable food prices, meat, seafood, fruits, vegetables and others compiled for the metropolitan New York, New Jersey and Connecticut markets.
Cost: $86.00
4 Pages
Frequency: Weekly
Circulation: 120
ISSN: 0270-4161
Founded in 1858

9799 **Hotel, Restaurant, Institutional Meat Price Report**
Urner Barry Publications
PO Box 389
Toms River, NJ 08754-2741

732-240-5330
800-932-0617; Fax: 732-341-0891
help@urnerbarry.com
www.urnerbarry.com

Paul B Brown Jr, President
Karen Mick, Circulation Director

Current meat and poultry pricing for the hotel, restaurant and institutional buyers.
Cost: $174.00
Frequency: Weekly
Circulation: 200
ISSN: 1067-3962
Founded in 1858

9800 **IAFIS Global Food MegaTrends**
International Assn of Food Industry Suppliers
1451 Dolley Madison Boulevard
Suite 101
McLean, VA 22101

703-761-2600; Fax: 703-761-4334
info@fpsa.org
www.fpsa.org

George Melnykovich, President
Andrew Drennan, VP

A quarterly bulletin covering international news and its effect on the food processing and packaging industries.

9801 **IBDEA Report**
International Beverage Dispensing Association
3837 Naylors Lane
Baltimore, MD 21208

410-602-0616
877-404-2332; Fax: 410-486-6799
ibdea@cornerstoneassoc.com
www.ibdea.org

Official newsletter of the International Beverage Dispensing Association, offering the latest news and technologies in the industry.
Frequency: Quarterly

9802 **IDDBA & YOU**
International Dairy-Deli-Bakery Association
636 Science Drive
PO Box 5528
Madison, WI 53705-0528

608-310-5000; Fax: 608-238-6330
IDDBA@iddba.org

Carol Christison, Executive Director

E-Newsletter designed for deli and bakery supermarket management and in-store staff teams. A fact-filled relevant resource on deli and bakery trends, timely sales data, merchandising ideas, training, new products, seminars, experts, news, and programs.
Frequency: Monthly
Founded in 1964

9803 **IDDBA Legis-Letter**
International Dairy-Deli-Bakery Association
636 Science Drive
PO Box 5528
Madison, WI 53705-0528

608-310-5000; Fax: 608-238-6330
IDDBA@iddba.org

Carol Christison, Executive Director

Formerly IDDA UPDATE, a membership benefit. Highlights recent legislative bills and reports, FDA activities, and topical issues such as state action on bst, NLEA, and HACCP.
Frequency: Monthly
Founded in 1964

9804 **IFSEA News**
International Food Service Executives Association
PO Box 1125
Placitas, NM 87043

855-268-1367
www.ifsea.org
Facebook

Richard Weil, Chairman

Newsletter of the IFSEA focusing on the happenings and news, as well as industry tips and recipes.
Frequency: Monthly

9805 **INsight**
Southern US Trade Association
701 Poydras St
Suite 3725
New Orleans, LA 70139-4596

504-568-5986; Fax: 504-568-6010
susta@susta.org
www.susta.org

Troy Rosamond, Financial Director
Bernadette Wiltz, Deputy Director

Providing the latest exporting information.
Frequency: Quarterly
Founded in 1973

9806 **Ice Cream Reporter**
Ice Cream Reporter
Hilton Terrace
Willsboro, NY 12996

518-963-4333; Fax: 518-963-4999

Howard Waxman, Publisher/Editor

News for ice cream executives.
Cost: $395.00
Frequency: Monthly
Founded in 1987

9807 **Independent Bakers Association Newsletter**
Independent Bakers Association
Georgetown Station
PO Box 3731
Washington, DC 20027-0231

202-333-8190; Fax: 202-337-3809
independentbaker@yahoo.com
www.independentbaker.net

Updating Washington legislative and regulatory actions and analyzing pro-business positions impacting on wholesale baking, allied industry operations.
Frequency: Monthly

9808 **International Association of Food**
1451 Dolley Madison Boulevard
Suite 101
McLean, VA 22101

703-761-2600; Fax: 703-761-4334
info@fpsa.org
www.fpsa.org

George Melnykovich, President
Andrew Drennan, VP

Dairy food and beverage industries, and related sanitary processing industries addressing the marketing and business information needs of the food supply channel.
Founded in 1983
Mailing list available for rent

9809 **IoPP update**
Institute of Packaging Professionals
Ste 123
1833 Centre Point Cir
Naperville, IL 60563-4848

630-544-5050
800-432-4085; Fax: 630-544-5005
info@iopp.org
www.iopp.org
Facebook, Twitter, LinkedIn, YouTube

Edwin Landon, Executive Director
Patrick Farrey, General Manager
Stan Zelesnik, Director Education
Robert DePauw, Finance Manager
Kelly Staley, Member Services Manager

Emailed newsletter of the Institute of Packaging Professionals.
Frequency: Bi-Weekly

9810 **Kane's Beverage Week**
Whitaker Newsletters
313 S Avenue
#340
Fanwood, NJ 07023-1364

800-359-6049; Fax: 908-889-6339

Joel Whitaker, Publisher

News on marketing, economic and regulatory factors affecting the alcohol beverage industry.
Cost: $499.00
6 Pages
Frequency: Quarterly
ISSN: 0882-2573

9811 **Kashrus Magazine**
Yeshiva Birkas Revuen
PO Box 204
Brooklyn, NY 11230

718-336-8544; Fax: 718-336-8550
webmaster@kashrusmagazine.com
www.kashrusmagazine.com

Rabbi Yosef Wikler, Editor
Vaad Hakashrut, Director
Rabbi Levin, Executive Director

Regular, complete update on Kosher food mislabelings, dairy/nondairy status, kosher supervision standards, newly certified products and food technology, travel and Jewish life.
Cost: $18.00
88 Pages
Circulation: 10000
Founded in 1980
Printed in 4 colors on glossy stock

9812 **Kettle Talk**
Retail Confectioners International
2053 S Waverly Ave
Suite 204
Springfield, MO 65804-2414

417-883-2775
800-545-5381; Fax: 847-724-2719
info@retailconfectioners.org
www.retailconfectioners.org

Terry Craft, President
Terry Hickling, Chairman of Marketing
Dan Malley, VP

Membership newsletter, including confection recipes. Also regional meetings.
Frequency: Monthly
Circulation: 550
Founded in 1917
Printed in on matte stock

9813 **Kiplinger Agricultural Letter**
Kiplinger Washington Editors
1729 H St Nw
Washington, DC 20006-3924

202-887-6400
800-544-0155; Fax: 202-778-8976
sub.services@kiplinger.com
www.kiplinger.com

Knight Kiplinger, VP
Kevin McCormally, Editorial Director
Fred Frailey, Editor
David Harrison, Manager

Forecasts and judgments on wages, income, food packaging, processing and marketing techniques.
Cost: $56.00
Founded in 1923

9814 **Kitchen Times**
Howard Wilson and Company
PO Box 290
Waukegan, IL 60079-0290

708-339-5111
800-245-7224; Fax: 708-210-2069
www.hwilson.com

Howard Wilson, Publisher/Editor

News on food and cooking.
Cost: $33.00
8 Pages
Frequency: Monthly
Founded in 1959

9815 **Lean Trimmings**
National Meat Association
1970 Broadway
Suite 825
Oakland, CA 94612-2299

510-763-1533; Fax: 510-763-6186
staff@nmaonline.org
www.nmaonline.org

Barry Carpenter, CEO
Jen Kempis, Operations Manager

Covers industry regulations, new technology and export news, as well as labor issues and business strategy.
Frequency: Weekly
Founded in 1946
Printed in one color on matte stock

9816 **Legislative Onion Outlet**
Legislative Onion Outlet
822 7th St
Suite 510
Greeley, CO 80631-3941

970-353-5895; Fax: 970-353-5897
info@onions-usa.org
www.onions-usa.org

Greg Yielding, Executive Vice President
Doug Bulgrin, President

An annual bulletin published by the National Onion Association.
Circulation: 600
Founded in 1913
Mailing list available for rent: 600 names

9817 **Link Newsletter**
R&D Associates
16607 Blanco Road
Suite 1506
San Antonio, TX 78232-1940

210-493-8024; Fax: 210-493-8036
www.militaryfood.org

David Dee, Editor

Food packaging, food processing and foodservice industry.
300 Pages
Frequency: Quarterly

9818 **Loan Trimmings & Herd on the Hill**
1970 Broadway Avenue
Suite 825
Oakland, CA 94612-2299

510-763-1533; Fax: 510-763-6186
www.nmaonline.org

Barry Carpenter, Executive Director
Jen Kempis, Associate Director
Frequency: Weekly
Circulation: 600

9819 **Make It Tasty**
Prosperity & Profits Unlimited
PO Box 416
Denver, CO 80201-0416

303-573-5564

AC Doyle, Publisher

Spice company blends food business newsletter with salt-free, herb and spice blend recipes.
Founded in 1996

9820 **Market News**
Meat & Livestock Australia
1401 K Street NW
Suite 602
Washington, DC 20005

202-521-2551; Fax: 202-521-2699
info@mla.com.au
www.mla.com.au
Facebook, Twitter, YouTube

Don Heatley, Chairman
David Palmer, Managing Director
Bernie Bindon, Director
Chris Hudson, Director

eNewsletter presents the latest market news from Australia and key international markets.
30000 Members
Frequency: Weekly
Founded in 1998

9821 **Meat & Poultry**
Meat Trade Institute
213 South Avenue East
Spencer Savings Bank Building
Cranford, NJ 07016

908-276-5111; Fax: 212-279-4016
www.spcnetwork.com/mti/

John Calcangno, President

A respected newsletter which keeps readers abreast of membership information and all news pertinent to Institute members. Available online.
Frequency: Monthly

9822 **Meat and Livestock Weekly**
Meat & Livestock Australia
1401 K Street NW
Suite 602
Washington, DC 20005

202-521-2551; Fax: 202-521-2699
info@mla.com.au
www.mla.com.au
Facebook, Twitter, YouTube

Don Heatley, Chairman
David Palmer, Managing Director
Bernie Bindon, Director
Chris Hudson, Director

eNewsletter providing the latest news, analysis and trends for domestic and export markets, including information on buyer and competitor activity and trends.
30000 Members
Frequency: Weekly
Founded in 1998

9823 **More Beef from Pastures**
Meat & Livestock Australia
1401 K Street NW
Suite 602
Washington, DC 20005

202-521-2551; Fax: 202-521-2699
info@mla.com.au
www.mla.com.au
Facebook, Twitter, YouTube

Don Heatley, Chairman
David Palmer, Managing Director
Bernie Bindon, Director
Chris Hudson, Director

eNewsletter designed to keep readers up-to-date with the latest developments in the MLA More Beef from Pastures program.
30000 Members
Frequency: Quarterly
Founded in 1998

9824 **NAFEM online**
N. American Assn. of Food Equipment Manufacturing
161 N Clark Street
Suite 2020
Chicago, IL 60601

312-821-0201; Fax: 312-821-0202
info@nafem.org
www.nafem.org

Steven R. Follett, President
Thomas R. Campion, President-Elect
Michael L. Whiteley, Secretary/Treasurer
Deirdre Flynn, Executive Vice President

The latest and greatest NAFEM and industry news to all NAFEM members. e-Newsletter.
Frequency: Monthly

9825 **NAMA Newsletter**
North American Millers' Association
600 Maryland Ave SW
Suite 825 W
Washington, DC 20024

202-484-2200; Fax: 202-488-7416
generalinfo@namamillers.org
www.namamillers.org

Jane DeMarchi, President
Christopher Clark, VP, Communications & Administration

Trade association representing the wheat, corn, oat and rye milling industry. NAMA members operate one hundred and seventy mills in thrirty-eight states and Canada. Their aggregate production of more than one hundred and sixty million pounds per day is approximately ninety-five percent of the industry capacity in the U.S.
Frequency: Monthly
Circulation: 250

9826 **NBBQA News**
National Barbecue & Grilling Association

PO Box 782
Kirkland, WA 98083

360-670-0194
info@nbbqa.org
www.nbbqa.org

Patrick Murty, President
Saffron Hodgson, Executive Director

The official e-newsletter for members of the National Barbecue & Grilling Association.

9827 **NCA Annual Convention**
National Coffee Association
15 Maiden Ln
Suite 1405
New York, NY 10038-5113

212-766-4007; Fax: 212-766-5815
info@ncausa.org
www.ncausa.org

Robert F Nelson, President
Steven M Wolfe, Membership/Marketing Director

The coffee event of the year, industry executives from all over the world get together to learn from the most current educational sessions, see old friends and meet new ones.
Frequency: Annual/March
Founded in 1911

9828 **NFRA What's Hot and New**
National Frozen & Refrigerated Foods Association
4755 Linglestown Road
Suite 300
Harrisburg, PA 17112

717-657-8601; Fax: 717-657-9862
nfra@nfraweb.org
www.nfraweb.org

H.V. Skip Shaw Jr., President/CEO
Jeff Romachik, EVP/COO
Julie W. Henderson, VP, Communications
Jessica Scott, VP, Finance
Natalie Limm, Member Communications Manager

NFRA's main communication tool in keeping members informed of upcoming frozen and refrigerated food promotions and Association meetings and resources. Also covers local associations, members' personnel changes and member news such as the introduction of new products and facility expansions.
Frequency: Quarterly
Circulation: 2300

9829 **NPA Fact of the Week**
Natural Products Association
2112 E 4th St
Suite 200
Santa Ana, CA 92705-3816

714-460-7732
800-966-6632; Fax: 714-460-7444
www.npainfo.org
Facebook, Twitter, LinkedIn

John F. Gay, Executive Director & CEO
Jeffrey Wright, President

Emailed to Congressional staffers who handle health issues for their representative or senator. Highlights the latest news, research and trends in dietary supplements and the natural products industry.
1900+ Members
Frequency: Weekly
Founded in 1936

9830 **NPA NOW**
Natural Products Association
2112 E 4th St
Suite 200
Santa Ana, CA 92705-3816

714-460-7732
800-966-6632; Fax: 714-460-7444
www.npainfo.org
Facebook, Twitter, LinkedIn

John F. Gay, Executive Director & CEO
Jeffrey Wright, President

Provides members with important association and industry news on a timely basis.
1900+ Members
Frequency: 6x Yearly
Founded in 1936

9831 **NPFDA NEWS**
National Poultry & Food Distributors
2014 Osborne Road
Saint Marys, GA 31558

770-535-9901; Fax: 770-535-7385
www.npfda.org

Cece Corbin, President
Carol Lanham, Member Services & Development Dir.
Alina Cooper, Membership Relations & Comm. Dir.

Brings the latest information about NPFDA members- featuring Member Spotlights, government regulations and upcoming industry events.
Frequency: Monthly
Founded in 1967

9832 **NSA Newsletter**
National Shellfisheries Association
National Marine Fisheries Service Laboratory
Oxford, MD 21654

631-653-6327; Fax: 631-653-6327
webmaster@shellfish.org
www.shellfish.org

R. LeRoy Creswell, President
Christopher V. Davis, President-Elect
George E. Flimlin, VP & Program Chair
Marta Gomez-Chiarri, Secretary
Sandra E. Shumway, Editor

Current issues and concerns in shellfish research and in the shellfish industry, including details regarding upcoming meetings, employment listings, and column.
1M Members
Frequency: Quarterly
Founded in 1908

9833 **National Conference on Interstate Milk Shipments**
National Conference on Interstate Milk
123 Buena Vista Drive
Frankfort, KY 40601-8770

502-695-0253; Fax: 502-695-0253
www.ncims.org

Leon Townsend, Executive Secretary
Marlena Bordson, Chair
Founded in 1946

9834 **National Fertilizer Solutions Association Newsletter**
339 Consort Drive
Manchester, MO 63011-4439

636-256-6650; Fax: 636-256-4901

Kelly O'Brien-Wray, Publisher
Fred Speckmann, Editor

Accepts advertising.
90 Pages

9835 **National Honey Market News**
US Department of Agriculture
21 N 1st Avenue
#224
Yakima, WA 98902-2663

509-575-2494; Fax: 509-457-7132
FVInfo@ams.usda.gov
www.ams.usda.gov/fv/mncs

Linda Verstrate, Publisher
Michael Jarvis, Director

Current honey market information and colony conditions in the US.
Cost: $24.00
10-12 Pages
Frequency: Monthly

9836 **National Hot Pepper Association**
400 NW 20th Street
Fort Lauderdale, FL 33311-3818

954-565-4972; Fax: 954-566-2208
www.peppergal.com

Robert J Payton, Publisher
Betty Payton, Editor

Networking among industry and private members. Education and information sharing.
Cost: $20.00
28 Pages
Frequency: Quarterly
Printed in on matte stock

9837 **National Nutritional Foods Association Today**
National Nutritional Foods Association
2112 E 4th St
Suite 200
Santa Ana, CA 92705-3816

949-622-6272
800-966-6632; Fax: 949-622-6266
www.nnfa.org

Amanda Thomason, Editor/Publications Manager
Paul Bennett, CEO/President

Nonprofit trade organization dedicated to protecting and advancing the natural products industry for both retailers and suppliers.
Cost: $48.00
Frequency: Monthly
Circulation: 8000
Founded in 1936

9838 **National Onion Association Newsletter**
National Onion Association
822 7th St
Suite 510
Greeley, CO 80631-3941

970-353-5895; Fax: 970-353-5897
info@onions-usa.org
www.onions-usa.org

Greg Yielding, Executive Vice President
Doug Bulgrin, President

Newsletter published by and only for the National Onion Association.
Frequency: Monthly
Circulation: 600
Founded in 1913
Mailing list available for rent: 600 names

9839 **National Seasoning Manufacturers Newsletter**
National Seasoning Manufacturers Association
2527 Mill Race Road
Frederick, MD 21701-6812

301-694-0419; Fax: 301-299-7523

Dick Alsmeyer PhD, Executive Director
Frequency: Quarterly

9840 **National Shellfisheries Association News**
Long Island University/Southampton College
Natural Sciences Division
Southampton, NY 11968

631-283-4000; Fax: 631-287-8054

Sandra Shumway, Production Manager
Eric Lang, Owner

Newsletter focusing on information for public health workers, shellfish producers and fishery

administrators.
Cost: $125.00
Circulation: 1000
Mailing list available for rent: 1M names
Printed in one color on matte stock

9841 Natural News Update
Natural Products Association
2112 E 4th St
Suite 200
Santa Ana, CA 92705-3816

714-460-7732
800-966-6632; Fax: 714-460-7444
www.npainfo.org
Facebook, Twitter, LinkedIn

John F. Gay, Executive Director & CEO
Jeffrey Wright, President

A weekly news and information resource, offering the latest news, federal activity, association announcements and research.
1900+ Members
Frequency: Weekly
Founded in 1936

9842 Nebraska Alfalfa Dehydrators Bulletin
Nebraska Alfalfa Dehydrators Association
8810 Craig Dr
Shawnee Mission, KS 66212-2916

913-648-6800; Fax: 913-648-2648
www.nebada.org

Carlton Bert, President

Market Information on Alfalfa Pellets, Meal, Cubes, and Hay.
Frequency: Weekly
Founded in 1941

9843 News in a Nutshell
National Peanut Board
2839 Paces Ferry Road
Suite 210
Atlanta, GA 30339-5769

678-424-5750
866-825-7946; Fax: 678-424-5751
peanuts@nationalpeanutboard.org
www.nationalpeanutboard.org
Facebook, Twitter, YouTube, Flickr

George Jeffcoat, Chairman
Cindy Belch, Vice Chairman
John Harrell, Secretary
Vic Jordan, Treasurer

e-Newlsetter from the National Peanut Board with news about everything peanut.
Frequency: Bi-Weekly

9844 No-Till Farmer
Lessiter Media
PO Box 624
Brookfield, WI 53008-0624

262-782-4480
800-645-8455; Fax: 262-782-1252
info@no-tillfarmer.com
www.no-tillfarmer.com

Frank Lessiter, Owner
Darrell Bruggnik, Executive Editor/Publisher
John Dobberstein, Senior Editor
Mark McNeely, Managing Editor

Management information for farmers interested in conservation tillage.
Cost: $37.95
16 Pages
Frequency: Monthly
Circulation: 5500
ISSN: 0091-9993
Founded in 1984
Printed in 2 colors on glossy stock

9845 Organic Business News
Hotline Printing & Publishing
PO Box 161132
Atamonte Springs, FL 32716-1132

407-628-1377; Fax: 407-628-9935
www.hotlineprinting.com/obn.html

Dennis Blank, Publisher/Editor
Christine Blank, Senior Editor

Leading industry publication that tracks the latest government actions, policy trends and financial development in development in the organic food business.
Cost: $110.00
12 Pages
Printed in 2 colors

9846 Organic Trade Association Newsletter
Organic Trade Association
60 Wells Street
PO Box 547
Greenfield, MA 01302

413-774-7511; Fax: 413-774-6432
info@ota.com
www.ota.com

Christine Bushway, Executive Director/CEO
Linda Lutz, Membership Manager
Laura Batcha, Marketing/Public Relations Director

Members are businesses involved in the organic agriculture and products industry. Seeks to promote the industry and establish production and marketing standards. Also publishes The Organic Page: North American Resource Directory

9847 Packer
Vance Publishing
400 Knightsbridge Parkway
Lincolnshire, IL 60069

847-634-2600; Fax: 847-634-4379
info@vancepublishing.com
www.vancepublishing.com

William C Vance, Chairman
Peggy Walker, President

News and information on fresh fruit and vegetable marketing.

9848 Pear Newsletter
Pear Bureau Northwest
4382 SE International Way
Suite A
Milwaukie, OR 97222-4627

503-652-9720; Fax: 503-652-9721
info@usapears.com
www.usapears.com

Kevin Moffitt, President/CEO
Cristie Mather, Communciations Manager
Frequency: Monthly

9849 Peterson Patriot
Peterson Patriot Printers-Publishers
202 Main Street
Peterson, IA 51047

712-295-7711; Fax: 712-295-7711

Roger Stoner, Publisher
Jane Stoner, Editor

Agricultural news.
Cost: $18.00
12 Pages
Frequency: Weekly
Circulation: 549

9850 Practical Gourmet
Linick Group
Gourmet Building 7 Putter Lane
PO Box 102
Middle Island, NY 11953-0102

631-924-3888
www.practicalgourmet.com

Gaylen Andrews, Publisher/Editor
Roger Dextor, VP/Director of PR
Barbara Deal, Marketing Manager
Andrew Linick, Manager
Bill Bruzy, Contributing Editor

Since 1982, the focus of this upscale monthly publication is on providing 'healthy dining trends for the affluent traveler' 45 plus; includes feature articles and in-depth interviews with award winning chefs, wineries/tastings, honoring 2-5 star restaurants with PG's Gold Taste Dining Awards, upscale hotels, properties, resorts, spas, cruises/yachting, airlines, ground operators, food festivals/contests, cooking schools and worldwide culinary events.
Cost: $48.00
36 Pages
Frequency: Monthly
Circulation: 210,000
Founded in 1975
Mailing list available for rent: 210 M names at $110 per M
Printed in 4 colors on glossy stock

9851 Produce Merchandiser
United Fresh Fruit & Vegetable Association
1901 Pennsylvania Ave Nw
Suite 1100
Washington, DC 20006-3412

202-862-4989; Fax: 202-303-3433
united@uffva.org
www.uffva.org

Thomas E Stenzel, CEO

Information on promotion and consumer issues.

9852 Product Alert
Marketing Intelligence Service
482 N Main St
Canandaigua, NY 14424-1049

585-374-6326
800-836-5710; Fax: 585-374-5217

Christine Dengler, Marketing/Sales Manager

A twice-monthly briefing on new packaged goods introduced in North America. Featuring product pictures and descriptions with indexing provided in two convenient formats. Also available in a twice monthly, international version.
Cost: $795.00
Frequency: Fortnightly

9853 Regulatory Register
American Butter Institute
2101 Wilson Boulevard
Suite 400
Arlington, VA 22201

703-243-5630; Fax: 703-841-9328
AMiner@nmpf.org
www.nmpf.org/ABI

Randy Mooney, Chairman
Dave Fuhrmann, Secretary
Clyde Rutherford, 1st Vice Chairman
Cornell Kasbergen, 2nd Vice Chairman
Ken Nobis, Treasurer

A publication for dairy cooperatives and producers which details recent regulatory activity directly impacting the operation of their farms and manufacturing facilities. Highlights the following areas of regulatory affairs; animal health, food safety, nutrition, standards and labeling, and environment and energy.
31 Members
Founded in 1908

9854 Research Report for Foodservice
1 Bridge St
Irvington, NY 10533-1550

914-591-4297
www.restaurantchains.net

James Santo, President

Market research company that provides contact information for companies in the foodservice industry. Our two primary brands are

RestaurantChains.net, a directory of company profiles and sales leads for US restaurant chains, and FoodserviceReport.com; a weekly bulletin on new US restaurant openings and changes of ownership.
3600 Members
Founded in 1996
Mailing list available for rent: 80000 names

9855 **Restaurant Chain Growth**
Research Report for Foodservice
1 Bridge St
Irvington, NY 10533-1550

914-591-4297
www.restaurantchains.net

James Santo, President

Providing the reader with proprietary information.
3600 Members
Frequency: Weekly
Founded in 1996
Mailing list available for rent: 80000 names

9856 **Restaurants and Institutions**
Reed Business Information
125 Park Avenue
23rd Floor
New York, NY 10017

212-309-8100; Fax: 212-309-8187

A magazine for restaurant professionals faced with fast-paced consumer demands, government regulations, health concerns and evolving food trends in a variety of market segments. R&I keeps these professionals informed and offers menu advice to prepare for new customers and business growth.

9857 **Salad Special**
Refrigerated Foods Association
2971 Flowers Rd S
Suite 266
Chamblee, GA 30341-5403

770-452-0660; Fax: 770-455-3879
info@refrigeratedfoods.org
www.refrigeratedfoods.org

Terry Dougherty, Executive Director

A newsletters covering technical and marketing aspects of the industry, including news of projects, conventions and expositions.
Frequency: Monthly
Founded in 1980

9858 **Salt & Trace Mineral Newsletter**
Salt Institute
700 N Fairfax St
Suite 600
Alexandria, VA 22314-2085

703-549-4648; Fax: 703-548-2194
info@saltinstitute.org
www.saltinstitute.org

Richard L Hanneman, President
Martina Moran, Director
Tammy Goodwin, Director
Mark OKeefe, Director of Communications

Information on animal nutrition.
Circulation: 3000
Founded in 1940
Printed in on glossy stock

9859 **Seafood Price-Current**
Urner Barry Publications
PO Box 389
Toms River, NJ 08754-389

732-240-5330
800-932-0617; Fax: 732-341-0891
help@urnerbarry.com
www.urnerbarry.com

Paul B Brown Jr, President
Karen Mick, Circulation Director

Spot market prices of the most widely traded fresh and frozen fin and shellfish items.
Cost: $383.00
8 Pages
Frequency: Weekly
Circulation: 1500
ISSN: 0270-4170
Founded in 1858

9860 **Seafood Trend Newsletter**
Seafood Trend
8227 Ashworth Ave N
Seattle, WA 98103-4434

206-523-2280; Fax: 206-526-8719
seafoodtrend@aol.com

Ken Talley, Editor/Publisher

Provides information, statistics and economic facts and figures pertaining to the seafood market.
Cost: $235.00
4 Pages
Circulation: 400
ISSN: 1057-2708
Founded in 1984
Printed in 2 colors on matte stock

9861 **Shelby Report of the Southeast**
Shelby Publishing Company
517 Green St Nw
Gainesville, GA 30501-3300

770-534-8380; Fax: 770-535-0110
www.shelbypublishing.com

Ron Johnston, President
Chuck Gilmer, Editor
Carol Tomaseski, Circulation Manager
Ileen Bloch, VP Publishing

A newsletter offering information on the retail and wholesale food trade.
Cost: $36.00
Frequency: Monthly
Circulation: 25,201
Founded in 1966
Printed in on newsprint stock

9862 **Shrimp News International**
Aquaculture Digest
9450 Mira Mesa Boulevard
#B562
San Diego, CA 92126-4850

FAX 858-271-0324

Robert Rosenberry, Editor

Publishes reports and directories on the world's shrimp industry.
Cost: $95.00
24 Pages
Frequency: Biweekly
Mailing list available for rent
Printed in one color on matte stock

9863 **Signals Newsletter**
Association for Communications Excellence
University of Florida
PO Box 110811
Gainesville, FL 32611-0811

FAX 352-392-8583
ace@ifas.ufl.edu
www.aceweb.org

Features news of interest to members. Includes articles with a professional development focus; updates from special interest groups, states and regions; announcements about upcoming workshops and conferences; and write-ups about members' awards and accomplishments, job changes and more.

9864 **Soft Drink Letter**
Whitaker Newsletters
313 S Avenue
#203
Fanwood, NJ 07023-1364

908-889-6336
800-359-6049; Fax: 908-889-6339
www.att.net

Joel Whitaker, Editor

For managers and owners of bottling and soft drink and water companies.
Cost: $349.00
Printed in one color

9865 **Speedy Bee**
Fore's Honey Farms
PO Box 998
Jesup, GA 31598

912-427-4018; Fax: 912-427-8447

Troy Fore, Editor

Honey and beekeeping industry news.
Cost: $17.25
16 Pages
Frequency: Monthly
Circulation: 4000
ISSN: 0190-6798
Founded in 1972
Printed in on newsprint stock

9866 **Spiceletter**
American Spice Trade Association
2025 M St Nw
Suite 800
Washington, DC 20036-2422

202-367-1127; Fax: 202-367-2127

Cheryl Deem, Executive Director
Frequency: Bi-Monthly

9867 **Spirited Living: Dave Steadman's Restaurant Scene**
5301 Towne Woods Rd
Coram, NY 11727-2808

631-736-0436; Fax: 631-736-0436

Dave Steadman, Editor

Newsletter published biweekly except January, July, and August.
Cost: $75.00

9868 **Sunflower Week in Review**
National Sunflower Association
2401 46th Avenue SE
Suite 206
Mandan, ND 58554-4829

701-328-5100
888-718-7033; Fax: 701-328-5101
larryk@sunflowernsa.com
www.sunflowernsa.com
Facebook, YouTube

John Sandbakken, Executive Director

Provides the latest news regarding sunflower information, conveniently summarized with highlights and data to keep you informed.
Frequency: Weekly
Founded in 1981

9869 **Supermarket News**
Fairchild Publications
750 3rd Ave
New York, NY 10017-2703

212-630-4000
877-652-5295; Fax: 212-630-3563

Mary G Berner, CEO
David Merrefield, VP, Editorial Director
David Orgel, Editor-in-Chief
Dan Bagan, Publishing Director

A weekly guide aimed at retailers, wholesalers, manufacturers and others in the food industry.
Cost: $23.00
Frequency: Weekly
Circulation: 36346
Founded in 1892

9870 **THE LINK**
R & D Associates for Military Food & Packaging
16607 Blanco Rd
Suite 501
San Antonio, TX 78232-1940

210-493-8024; Fax: 210-493-8036
www.militaryfood.org

Barney Guarino, Chairman
Jim Merryman, Vice Chairman
Tim Zimmerman, President
Bill McCreary, Executive Vice President
Jim Fagan, Executive Director

Provides pertinent data available and will keep readers informed of the activities of major government agencies.
Frequency: Quarterly
Founded in 1946

9871 **TecAgri News**
Clark Consulting International
PO Box 68
Park Ridge, IL 60068-0068

847-836-5100; Fax: 847-792-7565
warren.clark@ccimarketing.com
www.tecagrinews.com

Warren E Clark, President

News on new technology in agriculture reaching large computerized family farmers.
Cost: $1200.00
Frequency: Weekly
Circulation: 100,000
Founded in 1986
Mailing list available for rent: 2.1M names at $250 per M

9872 **Technical E-News**
Refrigerated Foods Association
1640 Powers Ferry Road
Bldg. 2, Suite 200A
Marietta, GA 30067

770-303-9905; Fax: 770-303-9906
info@refrigeratedfoods.org
www.refrigeratedfoods.org

Brian Edmonds, President
George Bradford, Vice President
Steve Loehndorf, Secretary
Wes Thaller, Treasurer

Contains the latest technical and regulatory news affecting the industry.
200+ Members
Frequency: Bi-Monthly
Founded in 1980

9873 **The Business of Herbs**
Herb Growing and Marketing Network
PO Box 245
Silver Spring, PA 17575-0245

FAX 717-393-9261
herbworld@aol.com
www.herbnet.com

Maureena Rogers, Editor

Information on commercial cultivation of herbs and marketing. Also regulatory information, calender of events, business notes.
40 Pages
Frequency: Monthly
Circulation: 2,000
Founded in 1990

9874 **The Coffee Reporter**
National Coffee Association
45 Broadway
Suite 1140
New York, NY 10006

212-766-4007; Fax: 212-766-5815
info@ncausa.org
www.ncausa.org
Facebook, Twitter, LinkedIn

Dub Hay, Chairman
John E. Boyle, Vice Chairman
Richard Emanuele, Secretary
Robert F. Nelson, President & CEO

National Coffee Association's official online newsletter.
Frequency: Weekly

9875 **The Culinary Insider**
American Culinary Federation
180 Center Place Way
St. Augustine, FL 32095

904-824-4468
800-624-9458; Fax: 904-940-0741
www.acfchefs.org

Heidi Cramb, Executive Director
Edward G Leonard, President
Brent T. Frei, Director of Marketing
Kay Orde, Editor
Michael Feierstein, Administrative Assistant

The official membership newsletter of the American Culinary Federation.
Frequency: Monthly
Circulation: 21000
Founded in 1929
Printed in 2 colors on matte stock

9876 **The Exchange**
Agricultural & Applied Economics Association
555 E Wells Street
Suite 1100
Milwaukee, WI 53202-6600

414-918-3190; Fax: 414-276-3349
jsaunders@aaea.org
www.aaea.org

Dawn Thilmany McFadden, President

Electronic newsletter for members of the American Agricultural Economics Association featuring association announcements, membership news, and updates from the profession.
3000 Members
Frequency: Bi-Monthly
Founded in 1910

9877 **Today's Grocer**
Florida Grocer Publications
PO Box 430760
S Miami, FL 33243

305-661-0792
800-440-3067; Fax: 305-661-6720
www.todaysgrocer.com

Jack Nobles, Publisher
Dennis Kane, Editor

Provides the latest food industry news and trends to Florida, Georgia, Alabama, Louisiana, Mississippi and the Carolinas.
Cost: $29.00
24 Pages
Frequency: Monthly
Circulation: 19500
ISSN: 1529-4420
Founded in 1968
Printed in 4 colors on newsprint stock

9878 **US Beer Market**
Business Trend Analysts/Industry Reports
2171 Jericho Tpke
Suite 200
Commack, NY 11725-2937

631-462-5454
800-866-4648; Fax: 631-462-1842
www.bta-ler.com

Charles J Ritchie, Executive VP
Donna Priani, Marketing Director

Profiles markets for premium, superpremium, popular and light beers.
Cost: $1495.00
Founded in 1978

9879 **USA Rice Daily**
USA Rice Federation
4301 N Fairfax Drive
Suite 425
Arlington, VA 22203

703-226-2300; Fax: 703-236-2301
riceinfo@usarice.com
www.usarice.com

Betsy Ward, President & CEO

The latest news on issues and activities for the U.S. rice industry.

9880 **Uncorked**
California Wine Club
2175 Goodyear Ave Suite 102
PO Box 3699
Ventura, CA 93006-3699

805-504-4330
800-777-4443; Fax: 800-700-1599
info@cawineclub.com
www.cawineclub.com

Bruce Boring, Publisher
Judy Reynolds, Editor

8 page newsletter that describes featured winery. It provides an upclose and personal look at a small boutique California winery.
Circulation: 10000
Founded in 1990

9881 **Urner Barry's Price-Current**
Urner Barry Publications
PO Box 389
Toms River, NJ 08754-0389

732-240-5330
800-932-0617; Fax: 732-341-0891
help@urnerbarry.com
www.urnerbarry.com

Paul B Brown Jr, President
Sheila M Deane, Marketing Manager

Daily market price report serving the poultry and egg industries.
Cost: $415.00
8 Pages
Frequency: Daily
Circulation: 3,000
ISSN: 0273-9992

9882 **Urner Barry's Price-Current West Coast Edition**
Urner Barry Publications
PO Box 389
Toms River, NJ 08754

732-240-5330
800-932-0617; Fax: 732-341-0891
help@urnerbarry.com
www.urnerbarry.com/

Paul Brown Jr, President
Sheila M Deane, Marketing Manager
Richard A. Brown, VP

Reports changes in price and market conditions of poultry and eggs on the West Coast.
Cost: $444.00
8 Pages
Frequency: Daily
Circulation: 3000

ISSN: 0273-5016
Founded in 1858

9883 Urner Barry's Yellow Sheet
Urner Barry Publications
PO Box 389
Toms River, NJ 08754
732-240-5330
800-932-0617; Fax: 732-341-0891
help@urnerbarry.com
www.urnerbarry.com
Paul B Brown Jr, President
Richard A Brown, VP/Treasurer
Market price report of timely unbiased meat quotes to help pinpoint the latest trading levels of beef, pork, lamb, veal, meat by-products, carcasses and boxed cuts.
Cost: $559.00
8 Pages
Frequency: Daily
Circulation: 1500
ISSN: 1066-8195
Founded in 1858

9884 Vegetarian Times
Active Interest Media
300 Continental Blvd
Suite 650
El Segundo, CA 90245-5067
310-356-4100; Fax: 310-356-4110
www.amedia.com
Efrem Zymbalist III, CEO
John Robles, Marketing Manager
Inspiring everyone to eat healthier, live greener, and be happier.
Cost: $19.95
Frequency: Monthly
Founded in 1999

9885 Vinotizie Italian Wine Newsletter
Italian Trade Commission
499 Park Ave
6th Floor
New York, NY 10022-1240
212-980-1500; Fax: 212-758-1050
www.italtrade.com/ice
Michelle Jones, Editor
This newsletter discusses developments in the Italian wine industry and market, as well as reviews of imported wines from Italy.
Frequency: Bi-Monthly

9886 WSSA Newsletter
Weed Science Society of America
P.O.Box 7065
Lawrence, KS 66044-7065
785-429-9622
800-627-0629; Fax: 785-843-1274
wssa@allenpress.com
www.wssa.net
David Shaw, Editor
Michael E Foley, Publications Director
Subscription is included in the annual dues.
Cost: $5.00
Frequency: Quarterly/Non-Member Fee

9887 Washington Association of Wine Grape Growers
PO Box 716
Cashmere, WA 98815
509-782-8234; Fax: 509-782-1203
info@wawgg.org
www.wawgg.org
Vicky Scharlau, Executive Director
Paul Champoux, Business Manager
Debbie Sands, Business Manager
Janet Heath, Office Manager
Julie Lindholm, Director
Guidance in research and education, and maintaining leadership in local, state and national wine grape issues.
Cost: $115.00
Founded in 1983

9888 Washington Report Newsletter
National Chicken Council
1015 15th Street NW
Suite 930
Washington, DC 20005-2622
202-081-1339; Fax: 202-293-4005
ncc@chickenusa.org
www.nationalchickencouncil.org
George Watts, President
William P Roenigk, Senior VP
Richard L Lobb, Communications Director
Margaret Ernst, Director Meetings/Membership Comm.
NCC's weekly, member's only newsletter provides information on current statistics, as well as information on economic, trade, and marketing developments, updates on regulatory, legislative, technology, and other industry issues and news
Frequency: Weekly
Circulation: 5000
Founded in 1954

9889 Webster Agricultural Letter
Webster Communications Corporation
1530 Key Blvd
Suite 401W
Arlington, VA 22209-1531
703-525-4512; Fax: 703-852-3534
James C Webster, Editor/CEO
Agricultural politics and policy issues.
Cost: $397.00
6 Pages
Frequency: Fortnightly
ISSN: 1073-4813
Founded in 1980
Printed in one color on matte stock

9890 Weekly Insiders Dairy & Egg Letter
Urner Barry Publications
PO Box 389
Toms River, NJ 08754
732-240-5330
800-932-0617; Fax: 732-341-0891
help@urnerbarry.com
www.urnerbarry.com
Paul B Brown Jr, President
Randy Pesciotta, Editor
Janice Brown, Advertising
Statistical newsletter of storage stocks of whole, liquid and dried eggs, slaughter and consumption figures and retail selling prices as well as critical data on butter, margarine and cheese.
Cost: $24.00
4 Pages
Frequency: Weekly
Circulation: 10000
ISSN: 0270-4153
Founded in 1858

9891 Weekly Insiders Poultry Report
Urner Barry Publications
PO Box 389
Toms River, NJ 08754-389
732-240-5330
800-932-0617; Fax: 732-341-0891
help@urnerbarry.com
www.urnerbarry.com
Paul B Brown Jr, President
Sheila M Deane, Marketing Manager
Statistical news of broiler eggs set and hatched, current chicken and fowl slaughter, storage holdings and competing red meat availability.
Cost: $190.00
4 Pages
Frequency: Weekly
Circulation: 230
ISSN: 0160-4910
Founded in 1858

9892 Weekly Insiders Turkey Report
Urner Barry Publications
PO Box 389
Toms River, NJ 08754-389
732-240-5330
800-932-0617; Fax: 732-341-0891
help@urnerbarry.com
www.urnerbarry.com
Paul B Brown Jr, President
Sheila M Deane, Marketing Manager
Richard A. Brown, VP Treasurer
Michael W. O'Shaughnessy, Secretary
Statistical report containing slaughter figures, consumption patterns, US Storage Stock Estimates and comparative weekly prices.
Cost: $173.00
4 Pages
Frequency: Weekly
Circulation: 230
ISSN: 0160-4910
Founded in 1858

9893 Weekly Livestock Reporter
Weekly Livestock
PO Box 7655
Fort Worth, TX 76111-0655
817-838-0106; Fax: 817-831-3117
service@weeklylivestock.com
www.weeklylivestock.com
Ted Gouldy, Publisher
Phil Stoll, Editor
Offers comprehensive weekly information for cattle farmers and livestock agricultural professionals.
Cost: $18.00
Frequency: Weekly
Circulation: 10000
Founded in 1897

9894 Weekly Weather and Crop Bulletin
NOAA/USDA Joint Agricultural Weather Facility
1400 Independence Ave SW
Washington, DC 20250
202-720-2791
www.noaa.gov
Robert Keeney, Administrator
David Miscus, Managing Editor
Provides a vital source of information on weather, climate and agricultural developments worldwide, along with detailed charts and tables of agrometeorological information that is appropriate for the season.
Frequency: Weekly
Circulation: 1500
Founded in 1807

9895 Western Hemisphere Agriculture and Trade Report
US Department of Agriculture
Room 112-A
US Department of Agriculture
Washington, DC 20250-3810
202-012-2000; Fax: 202-690-4915
webmaster@usda.gov
www.usda.gov
Miriam Stuart, Publisher
Abraham Lincoln, Chief Information Officer
Chris Smith, Chief Information Officer
Matt Paul, Director of Communications
Ramona Romero, General Counsel
Information on current and projected agricultural production and trade trends for North, Central, South America and the Caribbean. Includes information on trade agreements and blocks in the Hemisphere.
Founded in 1862

9896 **What's News in Organic**
Organic Trade Association
60 Wells Street
PO Box 547
Greenfield, MA 01302
413-774-7511; Fax: 413-774-6432
info@ota.com
www.ota.com
Facebook, Twitter, LinkedIn
Matt McLean, President
Sarah Bird, Vice President
Todd Linsky, Secretary
Kristen Holt, Treasurer
Includes a feature focusing on a hot topic for the industry, a pertinent quotation, and a world of news section outlining brief news related to the industry. Electronic publication.
Frequency: Quarterly
Founded in 1985

9897 **Wine on Line Food and Wine Review**
Enterprise Publishing
PO Box 328
Blair, NE 68008-0328
402-426-2121; Fax: 402-426-2227
mrhoades@enterprisepub.com
www.enterprisepub.com
Mark Rhoades, President
Dave Smith, Production Manager
Tracy Prettyman, Business Manager
Reviews, feature articles and information on all areas of food and wine, including restaurants, hotels, trains and airlines. Accepts advertising.
Cost: $100.00
10 Pages
Frequency: Monthly

9898 **fridayfeedback**
Meat & Livestock Australia
1401 K Street NW
Suite 602
Washington, DC 20005
202-521-2551; Fax: 202-521-2699
info@mla.com.au
www.mla.com.au
Facebook, Twitter, YouTube
Don Heatley, Chairman
David Palmer, Managing Director
Bernie Bindon, Director
Chris Hudson, Director
Providing a weekly wrap-up of market information, industry news and updates, and on-farm information including tools and calculators, and producer case studies.
30000 Members
Frequency: Weekly
Founded in 1998

Magazines & Journals

9899 **ABF E-Buzz**
American Beekeeping Federation
3525 Piedmont Rd
Bldg 5 Suite 300
Atlanta, GA 30305-1509
404-760-2875; Fax: 404-240-0998
info@abfnet.org
www.abfnet.org
Molly Sausaman, Executive Director
A member benefit published electronically to inform members about ABF activities and happenings in the beekeeping industry.
Cost: $35.00
Frequency: Membership Fees Vary
Founded in 1943

9900 **AHA Quarterly**
American Herb Association
PO Box 1673
Nevada City, CA 9595-1673
530-265-9552; Fax: 530-274-3140
www.ahaherb.com
Kathi Keville, Editor/Director
Mindy Green, Associate Editor
Contains news bulletins, scientific studies, book reviews, research in the field and networking between members. Also offers directories of herb education and mail order sources of herbs.
Cost: $20.00
20 Pages
Frequency: Quarterly
Circulation: 1000
Founded in 1981
Printed in on matte stock

9901 **AWS Wine Journal**
American Wine Society
P.O. Box 889
Scranton, PA 18501
888-297-9070
www.americanwinesociety.org
Facebook, Twitter, LinkedIn
David Falchek, Executive Director
Kristin Casler Kraft, President
Contains articles on all aspects of wine appreciation, wine making, wine destinations, and wine & food. Articles provide a wide range of exciting stories and educational information.
Frequency: Quarterly
Founded in 1967
Mailing list available for rent: 3000 names

9902 **AgProfessional Magazine**
Agricultural Retailers Association
1156 15th St NW
Suite 500
Washington, DC 20005-1745
202-457-0825
800-844-4900; Fax: 202-457-0864
Twitter, YouTube
Provides editorial and advertising for agronomic and business management solutions specifically to agricultural retailers/distributors, professional farm managers and crop consultants.
1200 Members
Frequency: Membership Dues Vary
Founded in 1993

9903 **Agri Marketing Magazine**
Henderson Communications LLC
1422 Elbridge Payne Rd
Suite 250
Chesterfield, MO 63017-8544
636-728-1428; Fax: 636-777-4178
info@agrimarketing.com
www.agrimarketing.com
Lynn Henderson, Owner
Covers the unique interests of corporate agribusiness executives, their marketing communications agencies, the agricultural media, ag trade associations and other ag related professionals.
Frequency: Monthly
Circulation: 8000
Founded in 1962

9904 **Agribusiness Fieldman**
Western Agricultural Publishing Company
4969 E Clinton Way
Suite 104
Fresno, CA 93727-1549
559-252-7000
888-382-9772; Fax: 559-252-7387
Paul Baltimore, Publisher
Randy Bailey, Editor
Robert Fujimoto, Assistant Director
For the professional agricultural consultant, featuring the latest information on chemical regulation, pest control techniques and feature stories on PCA and PCO community.

9905 **Airline Catering International**
International Inflight Food Service Association
5775 Peachtree-Dunwoody Road, Building G
Suite 500
Atlanta, GA 30342
404-252-3663; Fax: 404-252-0774
ifsa@kellencompany.com
www.ifsanet.com
Facebook, Twitter, LinkedIn, YouTube
Sandra Pineau, President
Ken Samara, VP
A review of inflight catering and galley equipment. Provides expert coverage and analysis of next-generation galley technology through to the latest menu development trends and eco-friendly food packaging initiatives. Offers a fresh take on the fast-moving and specialized inflight catering market.
400 Members
Frequency: Bi-Annually
Founded in 1965

9906 **Alaska Fisherman's Journal**
Diversified Business Communications
PO Box 7437
Portland, ME 04112-7437
207-842-5600; Fax: 207-842-5503
www.divbusiness.com
Nancy Hasselback, CEO
Randy Le Shane, Production Manager
Mike Lodato, Publisher
Neil Casey, Advertising Coordinator
Stephanie Wendel, Audience Development Manager
Primary publication serving the North Pacific commercial fishing fleet in the world's healthiest and most lucrative commercial fishing region.
Cost: $21.00
Frequency: Monthly
Circulation: 10,000
ISSN: 0164-8330

9907 **Alimentos Balanceados Para Animales**
WATT Publishing Company
122 S Wesley Ave
Mt Morris, IL 61054-1451
815-734-7937; Fax: 815-734-4201
www.wattnet.com
Clayton Gill, Editorial Director
James Watt, Owner
For feed industry professionals in Latin America.
Cost: $42.00
Circulation: 9471
ISSN: 0274-5571
Founded in 1917
Printed in 4 colors on glossy stock

9908 **All About Beer**
501 Washington St
Suite H
Durham, NC 27701-2169
919-530-8150
800-999-9718; Fax: 919-530-8160
www.allaboutbeer.com
Julie Bradford, Publisher
Natalie Abernethy, Circulation Manager
Quality beers, breweries and restaurants.
Cost: $19.99

9909 **Allied Tradesman**
Allied Trades of the Baking Industry

2001 Shawnee Mission Pkwy
Mission Woods, KS 62205

707-935-0103; Fax: 707-935-0174
www.atbi.org

Gary Cain, President
Tim Miller, Secretary, Treasurer
Brad Hahn, Secretary, Treasurer
Matt Ungashick, Secretary
Bruce Criss, Vice President
Frequency: Monthly
Circulation: 500
Founded in 1920

9910 **Almond Facts**
Blue Diamond Growers
1802 C Street
PO Box 1768
Sacramento, CA 95811

916-442-0771; Fax: 916-325-2880
www.bluediamond.com

Robert Donovan, CFO
Douglas D Youngdahl, CEO/President

The latest news affecting Blue Diamond and the almond industry with Almond Facts magazine. Service to Blue Diamond's grower-owners, also available online.
Cost: $25.00
Frequency: Bi-Monthly
Founded in 1910
Printed in 4 colors

9911 **American Beefalo World Registry**
30 Stevenson Road
#5
Laramie, WY 82070

307-745-3505
866-374-2297; Fax: 307-745-3505
www.abwr.org

Offers information for beef and cattle farmers.

9912 **American Brewer**
1049 B Street
PO Box 510
Hayward, CA 94543-510

510-886-7418; Fax: 510-538-7644
www.ambrew.com

Bill Owens, Publisher
Greg Kitsock, Editor

A magazine covering the business of beer.
Cost: $50.00
Frequency: Quarterly
Founded in 1979

9913 **American Fruit Grower**
Meister Publishing Company
37733 Euclid Ave
Willoughby, OH 44094-5992

440-942-2000
800-572-7740; Fax: 440-975-3447
www.meisternet.com

Gary Fitzgerald, President
Joe Monahan, Group Publisher
Fran Mihalik, Circulation Manager

Specialized production and marketing information and industry-wide support for fruit growers.
Cost: $19.95
66 Pages
Frequency: Monthly
Circulation: 37,000
Founded in 1931

9914 **American Journal of Enology and Viticulture**
American Society for Enology and Vinticulture
1784 Picasso Avenue Suite D
PO Box 2160
Davis, CA 95617-2160

530-753-3142; Fax: 530-753-3318
www.ajevonline.org

Judith McKibben, Managing Editor

Full-length research papers, literature reviews, research notes and technical briefs on various aspects of enology and viticulture, including wine chemistry, sensory science, process engineering, wine quality assessments, microbiology, methods development, plant pathogenesis, diseases and pests of grape, rootstock and clonal evaluation, effect of field practices and grape genetics and breeding.
Frequency: Quarterly
Mailing list available for rent

9915 **American Red Angus Magazine**
Red Angus Association of America
4201 N Interstate 35
Denton, TX 76207-3415

940-387-3502; Fax: 888-829-5573
info@redangus.org
www.redangus.org
Facebook

Joe Mushrush, President
Greg Comstock, CEO

The most comprehensive resource guide to the Red Angus breed. Keep informed about a breed that is focused on economic value, efficiency and quality.
2000 Members
Founded in 1954

9916 **American Small Farm Magazine**
560 Sunbury Rd
Suite 6
Delaware, OH 43015-8692

740-363-2395; Fax: 740-369-9526
www.smallfarm.com

Marti Smith, Information
Andy Stevens, Editor

Published for the owner/operator of farms from five to three hundred acres. Focuses on production agriculture including alternative and sustainable farming ideas and technology, case studies, small farm lifestyle and tradition.
Cost: $18.00
ISSN: 1064-7473

9917 **American Vegetable Grower**
Meister Media Worldwide
37733 Euclid Ave
Willoughby, OH 44094-5992

440-942-2000
800-572-7740; Fax: 440-975-3447
www.meisternet.com

Gary Fitzgerald, President
Ken Hall, Communications Manager
Josep W Monahan, Publisher
Fran Mihalik, Circulation manager

Information source for commercial vegetable growers.
Cost: $19.95
Frequency: Monthly
Circulation: 34772
Founded in 1931

9918 **American Wholesale Marketers Association/ Convenience Distribution**
American Wholesale Marketers Association
2750 Prosperity Ave
Suite 530
Fairfax, VA 22031-4338

703-208-3358
800-482-2962; Fax: 703-573-5738
info@awmanet.org
www.cdaweb.net

Scott Ramminger, Publisher Executive Editor
Joan Fay, Editor + Associate Publisher

A magazine specifically targeted toward convenience distributors. Our readers are involved in the purchase and sale of candy, tobacco, snacks, beverages, health and beauty care items, general merchandise, foodservice, groceries and more.
Cost: $36.00
Frequency: Monthly/Non-Members Fee
Circulation: 11,000
ISSN: 1083-9313
Printed in 4 colors on glossy stock

9919 **Angus Journal**
American Angus Association
3201 Frederick Ave
St Joseph, MO 64506-2997

816-383-5100; Fax: 816-233-9703
angus@angus.org
www.angus.org
Facebook, Twitter

David A. Dal Porto, President

To provide programs, services, technology and leadership to enhance the genetics of the Angus breed, broaden its influence within the beef industry, and expand the market for superior tasting, high-quality Angus beef worldwide. Achieve Angus excellence through information.
Cost: $80.00
30+M Members
Frequency: Membership Fees Vary
Founded in 1883

9920 **Applied Economic Perspectives and Policy**
Agricultural & Applied Economics Association
555 E Wells Street
Suite 1100
Milwaukee, WI 53202-6600

414-918-3190; Fax: 414-276-3349
cggunder@illinois.edu
www.aaea.org/publications/aepp

Dawn Thilmany McFadden, President
Craig Gundersen, Managing Editor
Roderick Rejesus, Submitted Article Editor
Christopher McIntosh, Editor

Publishes research articles for an audience of agricultural and applied economists as well as a general audience.
3000 Members
Founded in 1910

9921 **Applied Engineering in Agriculture**
American Society of Agricultural Engineers
2950 Niles Rd
St Joseph, MI 49085-8607

269-429-0300
800-371-2723; Fax: 269-429-3852
hq@asabe.org
www.asabe.org

Mark D Zielke, CEO
Donna Hull, Pubilcation Director

Focus is on agricultural equipment, farm buildings, electrification, soil conservation, irrigation and food engineering.
26 Pages
Frequency: Monthly
Circulation: 9000
Founded in 1907

9922 **Aquaculture Magazine**
Achill River Corporation

PO Box 2329
Asheville, NC 28802-2329

828-687-0011; Fax: 828-681-0601
www.aquaculturemag.com

Gregory J Gallagher, Editor/Publisher
Doinita Cociovei, Circulation Manager
Joseph Strickland, Advertisement Manager

Focus emphasizes the production, processing, and marketing of aquatic organisms and plant life.
Founded in 1968

9923 **Arbor Age**
Green Media
1030 W Higgins Road
Suite 230
Park Ridge, IL 60068

847-720-5600; Fax: 847-720-5601
www.arborage.com

John Kmitta, Senior Editor

Targets arborists in the commercial, municipal and utility sectors. Content is provided by a wide range of green industry experts, including professional arborists, academicians, instructors, consultants, government bodies and research organizations.
43 Pages
Frequency: 9x Yearly
Circulation: 16,500
Founded in 1981
Printed in 4 colors on glossy stock

9924 **Atlantic Control States Beverage Journal**
Club & Tavern
3 12th Street
Wheeling, WV 26003-3276

304-232-7620; Fax: 304-233-1236

Arnold Lazarus, Editor

A magazine for the alcoholic beverage industry. Serving bars, restaurants, clubs and industry personnel with West Virginia, Virginia, and North Carolina state editions. Includes states' liquor price lists.

9925 **Bake Magazine**
Sosland Publishing Company
4801 Main St
Suite 100
Kansas City, MO 64112-2513

816-756-1000; Fax: 816-756-0494
www.sosland.com

John Unrein, Editor
John Sonderegger, Publisher
Troy Ashby, Associate Publisher

Focuses on wholesale baking, specialty bakeries, and retail bakeries.
Cost: $25.00
Frequency: Annual

9926 **Bakery Production and Marketing**
245 W 17th Street
1350 E Toughy Avenue
New York, NY 10011

212-414-1160; Fax: 212-337-7198

Doug Krumrei, Editor
Stuart Whayman, CFO

Dedicated to delivering sensible ideas for profitable baking with editorial that addresses solutions and opportunities found within retail, instore, food service and intermediate wholesale bakeries.
Cost: $70.00
Frequency: Monthly
Circulation: 31,000

9927 **Baking & Snack**
Sosland Publishing Company
4801 Main St
Suite 100
Kansas City, MO 64112-2513

816-756-1000; Fax: 816-756-0494
www.sosland.com

Dan Malovany, Editorial Director
Lauri Gorton, Executive Editor
Joanie Spences, Managing Editor
Mike Gude, Director, Publishing

Magazine published with a focus on food processing & in-plant operations.
Circulation: 31000
Founded in 1922

9928 **Baking and Snack**
Paul Lattan
4800 Main Street
Suite 100
Kansas City, MO 64112-2504

816-756-1000; Fax: 816-756-0494
bbcservice@sosland.com
www.bakingbusiness.com

Steve Barne, Editor
Laurie Gorton, Executive Editor

A magazine offering information on baking equipment and ingredients for the commercial baker.
Frequency: Monthly
Circulation: 12,494
Founded in 1922

9929 **Bar & Beverage Business Magazine**
Mercury Publications
1839 Inkster Boulevard
Winnipeg, Ma 0

204-954-2085; Fax: 204-954-2057
webmaster@mercury.mb.ca
www.mercury.mb.ca/

Frank Yeo, Publisher
Robert Thompson, National Account Manager
Kelly Gray, Editor
Angie Finnbogason, Circulation Manager
Carly Peters, Editorial Production Manager

The buying and selling of beverages, operator profiles, new products, product merchandising and trends.
Cost: $35.00
Frequency: Quarterly
Circulation: 16923
Founded in 1948
Mailing list available for rent

9930 **Bartender Magazine**
Foley Publishing Corporation
PO Box 157
Spring Lake, NJ 07762

732-449-4499; Fax: 732-974-8289
barmag@aol.com
www.bartender.com
Facebook, Twitter

Raymond Foley, Publisher
Jaclyn Wilson Foley, Editor

Serves all full-service drinking establishments, including individual restaurants, hotels, motels, bars, taverns, lounges and all other full service on premise licenses.
76 Pages
Frequency: Quarterly
Circulation: 104000
Founded in 1979
Printed in 4 colors on glossy stock

9931 **Bee Culture**
AI Root Company
PO Box 706
Medina, OH 44258-0706

330-725-6677
800-289-7668; Fax: 330-725-5624
weboptout@rootcandles.com
www.rootcandles.com

John Root, President
Kathy Summers, Production Manager

Honey bees and their keeping for beginners and experienced apiculturists. Accepts advertising, press releases, new products, and book reviews.
Cost: $21.50
64 Pages
Circulation: 12000
ISSN: 1071-3190
Founded in 1863
Printed in 4 colors on matte stock

9932 **Beverage Dynamics**
The Beverage Information Group
17 High Street
2nd Floor
Norwalk, CT 06851

203-855-8499
www.bevinfogroup.com

Liza Zimmerman, Editor-in-Chief
Jeremy Nedelka, Managing Editor

Provides a unique and essential communciations link between suppliers and chain and independent retailers in the off-premise market (liquor stores, supermarkets, beverage outlets, etc)
Cost: $35.00
Frequency: Bi-Monthly
Founded in 1934

9933 **Beverage Industry**
Stagnito Communications
2401 W Big Beaver Road
Suite 700
Troy, MI 48084

847-763-9534; Fax: 847-763-9538
bi@halldata.com
www.bevindustry.com
Facebook, Twitter, LinkedIn

Steve Pintarelli, Publisher
Jessica Jacobsen, Editor
Stephanie Cernivec, Managing Editor

Provides the most in-depth information about the beverage market including production, technology and distribution. The changing industry demands a change leader and BI fills that role by reporting behind the scenes of the gigantic 65 billion market.
Cost: $40.00
Frequency: Monthly
Circulation: 28000
Founded in 1946

9934 **Beverage Journal**
Michigan Licensed Beverage Association
920 N Fairview Ave
Lansing, MI 48912-3238

517-374-9611
877-292-2896; Fax: 517-374-1165
info@mlba.org
www.mlba.org

Lou Adado, CEO
Catherine Pavick, Executive Director

Offers information on the alcoholic beverage industry/retail sales
Cost: $52.00
Frequency: Monthly
ISSN: 1050-4427
Printed in on glossy stock

9935 **Beverage Media**
Beverage Media Group

152 Madison Avenue
Suite 600
New York, NY 10016

212-571-3232; Fax: 212-571-4443
www.bevnetwork.com

Journal offering information on the liquor, wine and beer trade. New products & promotions, industry news and current trends.
Cost: $119.00
Frequency: Monthly

9936 Beverage Network
4437 Concord Lane
Skokie, IL 60076-2605

617-497-0062; Fax: 617-812-7740
sales@bevnet.com
www.bevnet.com

Organization of beverage distributors dealing with specialty, nonalcoholic products.

9937 Beverage Retailer Magazine
Oxford Publishing
Ste 1
1903b University Ave
Oxford, MS 38655-4150

662-236-5510
800-247-3881; Fax: 662-236-5541
www.bevindustry.com

Ed Meek, Publisher
Brenda Owen, Editor
Ruth Ann Wolfe, Circualtion Manager

A magazine covering the off-premise market for retailers in the wine, beer and spirits business.
Cost: $30.00
Frequency: Monthly
Circulation: 25000
Founded in 1920
Printed in 4 colors on glossy stock

9938 Biodynamics
Biodynamic Farming & Gardening Association
PO Box 944
East Troy, WI 53120-0944

262-649-9212
info@biodynamics.com
www.biodynamics.com
Facebook

Charles Beedy, Contact

A membership publication providing a thoughtful collection of original articles centered on a theme of interest to the biodynamic community. Voices from the community, discussion of the biodynamic preparations, regional, national, and international news and updates, event overviews, book and film reviews, organizational updates, seasonal recipes, columns and more.
Cost: $45.00
Frequency: 6 per year
Circulation: 1000+

9939 Bison World Magazine
National Bison Association
8690 Wolff Ct
200
Westminster, CO 80234

303-292-2833; Fax: 303-845-9081
david@bisoncentral.com
www.bisoncentral.com

Dave Carter, Executive Editor
Anita Shaver, Design & Production Manager

Featured articles and regular departments cover all aspects of raising bison and what's happening in this exciting industry. Available with all levels of membership with the association.
Frequency: Quarterly
Circulation: 1000

9940 Body, Mind & Spirit Magazine
PO Box 95
Dogsland, SK

306-356-4634; Fax: 306-356-4634
www.saskworld.com/bodymindspirit

Jeni Mayer, Publisher
Adele Azar-Rucquoi, Contributing Writers
Frequency: Quarterly

9941 Bottled Water Reporter
International Bottled Water Association
1700 Diagonal Rd
Suite 650
Alexandria, VA 22314-2870

703-683-5213
817-719-6197; Fax: 703-683-4074
ibwainfo@bottledwater.org
www.bottledwater.org

Joseph Doss, Publisher/President

Covers IBWA events and programs while highlighting new technologies and equipment within the industry, taking notice of personnel changes and reporting on the latest industry statistical data. It also features useful articles on management, operations and marketing specific to the bottled water industry.
Cost: $50.00
74 Pages
Circulation: 2500
Founded in 1958
Printed in 4 colors on glossy stock

9942 Brahman Journal
American Brahman Breeders Association
915 12th Street
Suite 520
Houston, TX 77054

979-826-4347; Fax: 979-826-2007
info@brahmanjournal.com
www.brahmanjournal.com
Facebook

Victoria Lambert, Editor
Brandy Barnes, Field Representative
Mandy Chambers, Assistant Editor

Provides timely, useful information about one of the largest. most dynamic and most influential breeds of beef cattle in the world. Each issue reports on American Brahman and International Brahman shows, American Brahman and international Brahman events, Brahman sales and Brahman history, as well as pertinent cattle industry news, technical articles and the latest research as it pertains to the Brahman Breed and its followers.
Cost: $25.00
Frequency: Monthly
Circulation: 7000
Founded in 1971

9943 Brandpackaging
Independent Publishing Company
P.O.Box 3116
Saint George, UT 84771-3116

435-656-1555
800-808-7449; Fax: 435-656-1511
www.independentpublishing.com

Josh Warburton, President/Publisher
Circulation: 5500
Founded in 1996

9944 Brewers Digest
Siebel Publishing Company
Business Office
PO Box 677
Thiensville, WI 53092-6026

915-877-3319; Fax: 915-877-3319

Thomas Volke, Publisher
Dori Whitney, Editor

The gamut of operational, production, buying, engineering, and packaging issues affecting brewing companies and enterprises.
Cost: $20.00
70 Pages
Frequency: Monthly
Circulation: 3000
ISSN: 0006-971X
Founded in 1926
Printed in 4 colors on glossy stock

9945 Business of Herbs
Northwind Farm Publications
439 Ponderosa Way
Jemez Springs, NM 87025-8036

505-829-3448; Fax: 505-829-3449
www.herbworld.com/businessofherbs.htm

Paula Oliver, Publisher
David Oliver, Editor

Primarily for herb businesses and those keenly interested in herbs and botanicals.
Cost: $4.00

9946 Calf News (Cattle Feeder Magazine)
1531 Kensington Boulevard
Garden City, KS 67846

620-276-7844; Fax: 620-275-7333
www.calfnews.net

Betty Jo Gigot, Editor & Publisher
Patti Wilson, Sales Manager
Larisa Willrett, Copy Editor/Circulation
Kathie Bedolli, Director

This magazine offers the latest information to cattle breeders and feeders.
Cost: $33.00
Circulation: 6,352
Founded in 1964

9947 Candy Industry
Stagnito Communications
155 Pfingsten Road
Suite 205
Deerfield, IL 60015

847-205-5660; Fax: 847-205-5680
www.stagnito.com

Harry Stagnito, President
Korry Stagnito, Publishing Director
Sue Ravenscraft, VP Circulation

Magazine serving chocolate and confectionary manufacturers.
Cost: $59.00
Frequency: Monthly
Founded in 1944
Printed in 4 colors on glossy stock

9948 Capital Press
Press Publishing Company
PO Box 2048
Salem, OR 97308-2048

503-364-4431
800-882-6789; Fax: 503-370-4383
www.capitalpress.com

Carl Sampson, Managing Editor
Elaine Shein, Editor/Publisher
Mike O'Brien, Circulation/General Manager

For the agricultural and forest community of the Pacific Northwest.
Cost: $44.00
60 Pages
Frequency: Weekly
Circulation: 37000
Founded in 1928
Printed in 4 colors on newsprint stock

9949 Carnetec
1415 N Dayton
Chicago, IL 60622

312-266-3311; Fax: 312-266-3363
annica@meatingplace.com
www.carnetec.com

Ryan Pfister, Product Manager

Spanish language magazine reaching executives in the Latin American meat and poultry processing industry. Helps improve the manufacturing process, equipment, sanitation, safety and technology.

9950 Carrot Country
Columbia Publishing
8405 Ahtanum Rd
Yakima, WA 98903-9432

509-248-2452
800-900-2452; Fax: 509-248-4056
www.carrotcountry.com

Brent Clement, Editor/Publisher
Mike Stoker, Publisher

Includes information on carrot production, grower and shipper feature stories, carrot research, new varieties, market reports, spot reports on overseas production and marketing and other key issues and trends of interest to US and Canadian carrot growers.
Cost: $10.00
Frequency: Quarterly
Circulation: 2700
Founded in 1975
Printed in 4 colors on glossy stock

9951 Cereal Chemistry
AACC International
3340 Pilot Knob Rd
St. Paul, MN 55121-2055

651-454-7250
800-328-7560; Fax: 651-454-0766
aacc@scisoc.org
www.aaccnet.org

Les Copeland, Editor-In-Chief
F. William Collins, Senior Editors
Ian Batey, Associate Editors

The premier international archival journal in cereal science. Juried, original research exploring topics that range from raw materials, processes, products utilizing cereal, to oilseeds, pulses, as well as analytical procedures, technological tests and fundamental research in the cereals area.
Cost: $79.00
Frequency: Bi-Monthly
Circulation: 3539
ISSN: 0009-0352
Founded in 1915

9952 Cereal Foods World
AACC International
3340 Pilot Knob Rd
Eagan, MN 55121-2055

651-454-7250
800-328-7560; Fax: 651-454-0766
www.scientificsocieties.org

Steven Nelson, VP
Bernie Bruinsma, Chair of Board
Laura Hansen, Treasurer

A leading source of information on grain-based food science, technology, and new product development. Includes articles that focus on advances in grain-based food science and the application of these advances to product development and current food production practices.
Cost: $48.00
Frequency: Bi-Monthly
Circulation: 4500
ISSN: 0146-6283
Founded in 1956

9953 Cheers
Jobson Publishing Corporation
100 Avenue of the Americas
Suite 9
New York, NY 10013-1678

212-274-7000; Fax: 212-431-0500
www.jobson.com

Michael J Tansey, CEO

Every issue is designed to help on-premise operators enhance the profitability of their beverage operations.

9954 Cheese Market News
Quarne Publishing
PO Box 620244
Middleton, WI 53562

608-831-6002; Fax: 608-831-1004
www.cheesemarketnews.com

Susan Quarne, Publisher
Kate Sander, Editorial Director

Weekly trade news for the nation's cheese and dairy/deli business
Cost: $105.00
16 Pages
Frequency: Weekly
Circulation: 2200
ISSN: 0891-1509
Founded in 1981
Mailing list available for rent: 2200 names at $500 per M
Printed in 4 colors on newsprint stock

9955 Chef
Talcott Communications Corporation
20 W Kinzie St
Suite 1200
Chicago, IL 60654-5827

312-849-2220
800-229-1967; Fax: 312-849-2174
www.talcott.com

Daniel Von Rabenau, Executive Director
Robert S Benes, Senior Editor

Information on food production and presentation, includes chef profiles, trend studies, marketing information and restaurant profiles.
Cost: $32.00
Circulation: 40,000
ISSN: 1087-061X
Founded in 1956
Printed in 4 colors on glossy stock

9956 Chemical and Pharmaceutical Press
C&P Press
90 william strret
5th Floor
New York, NY 10106-2899

212-326-6760
800-544-7377; Fax: 646-733-6010
www.pharmpress.com

Dr. Mary Conway, Executive Editor
Bron Zienkiewicz, Sales/Marketing
Sonia Tighe, Publisher

Supplies chemical information to professionals involved with the sale, application, storage or regulations of agricultural or ornamental and turf pesticides. Information is available in either reference book form or on computer disc. Complete product labels, MSDS's and indexes are included.
Founded in 1984

9957 Choices
Agricultural & Applied Economics Association
555 E Wells Street
Suite 1100
Milwaukee, WI 53202-6600

414-918-3190; Fax: 414-276-3349
Alison.Davis@uky.edu
www.choicesmagazine.org
Twitter

Jill McCluskey, President
Janet Perry, Editor
Kynda Curtis, Editor
Alison Davis, Co-Editor
Amy Bekkerman, Technical Editor

Provides current coverage on economic implications of food, farm, resource or rural community issues. Subjects covered include agriculture and trade, resources and the environment, consumers and markets, agribusiness and finance.
3000 Members
Frequency: Quarterly
Founded in 1910

9958 Citograph
Western Agricultural Publishing Company
4969 E Clinton Way
#104
Fresno, CA 93727-1549

559-252-7000; Fax: 559-252-7387

Paul Baltimore, Publisher

The oldest continuous citrus-specific publication in the world. Stories centering on all aspects of citrus production from planting to harvest and all maintenance in between. Lemons, limes, oranges, avocados — all citrus is included.

9959 Citrus & Vegetable Magazine
Vance Publishing
400 Knightsbridge Parkway
Lincolnshire, IL 60069

847-634-2600; Fax: 847-634-4379
info@vancepublishing.com
www.vancepublishing.com

William C Vance, Chairman
Peggy Walker, President

Delivers profitable production and management strategies to commerical citrus and vegetable growers in Florida.
Cost: $45.00
Frequency: Monthly
Circulation: 12004

9960 CleanRooms Magazine
PennWell Publishing Company
98 Spit Brook Rd
Suite 100
Nashua, NH 03062-5737

603-891-0123; Fax: 603-891-9294
info@pennwell.com
www.pennwell.com

Christine Shaw, VP
James Enos, Publisher
Adam Japker, CEO

Serves the contamination control and ultrapure materials and process industries. Written for readers in the microelectronics, pharmaceutical, biotech, health care, food processing and other user industries. Provides technology and business news and new product listings.
Founded in 1987

9961 Communications in Soil Science and Plant Analysis
Marcel Dekker
270 Madison Avenue
New York, NY 10016

212-696-9000
800-228-1160; Fax: 212-685-4540
www.dekker.com

Harry A Mills, Editor
Marcel Dekker, President

All aspects of soil science and crop production in all climates.
Cost: $567.00
120 Pages
Circulation: 23500
ISSN: 0010-3624
Founded in 1963

9962 Concession Profession
National Association of Concessoinaires
35 East Wacker Drive
Suite 1816
Chicago, IL 60601-2270

312-236-3858; Fax: 312-236-7809
info@naconline.org

www.naconline.org
Facebook, LinkedIn

Charles A Winans, Executive Director
Susan M Cross, Communications Director
Barbara Aslan, Membership Services Manager

The NAC member magazine devoted to the recreational and leisuretime food and beverage concessions industry, featuring news briefs, feature articles, association news and advertising opportunities.
800 Members
Founded in 1944

9963 **Concession Professsion**
National Association of Concessionaires
35 E Wacker Dr
Suite 1816
Chicago, IL 60601-2270

312-236-3858; Fax: 312-236-7809
scross@NAConline.org
www.naconline.org
Facebook, LinkedIn

John Evans, Jr., President
Jeff Scudillo, President-Elect
Ron Krueger II, Board Chairman

Devoted to the recreational and leisuretime food and beverage concessions industry, featuring news briefs, feature articles, association news and advertising opportunities.
Frequency: Bi-Annual
Printed in 4 colors

9964 **Convenience Store Decisions**
Harbor Communications
19111 Detroit Road
Suite 201
Rocky River, OH 44116

440-250-1538; Fax: 440-333-1892
www.csdecisions.com

Jeff Donohoe, Owner
Jay Gordon, Editor

For buyers, directors, field managers, owners and executives in the convenience store business. Free to qualified subscribers.
180 Pages
Frequency: Monthly
Circulation: 40000+
Founded in 1892

9965 **Cooking for Profit**
CP Publishing
PO Box 267
Fond du Lac, WI 54936

920-923-3700; Fax: 920-923-6805
comments@cookingforprofit.com
www.cookingforprofit.com

Colleen Phalen, Editor-in-Chief/Publisher

Paid subscription trade magazine targeted to foodservice owners, managers and chefs. Each month features current trends in food preparation with step-by-step recipes and photographs; effective management techniques; and the latest in foodservice equipment — all written by industry experts. Also features in-depth profiles of a successful foodservice operation.
Cost: $26.00
28 Pages
Frequency: Monthly
Circulation: 75000
Founded in 1932
Printed in 4 colors on glossy stock

9966 **Cooperative Grocer**
361 East College Street
Iowa City, IA 52240-267

319-466-9029; Fax: 866-600-4588
cooperativegrocer.coop

Dave Gutknecht, Editor
Dan Nordley, Publisher
Don McLemore, CEO

Trade magazine by and for people working with consumer cooperative grocery stores.
Founded in 1999

9967 **Cotton Farming**
One Grower Publishing
5118 Park Avenue
Suite 111
Memphis, TN 38117-5710

901-767-4020; Fax: 901-767-4026
www.cottonfarming.com
Twitter, Flickr

Lia Guthrie, Publisher/VP
Tommy Horton, Editor

Serving the industry, providing the latest news and technology information.
Frequency: Monthly
Founded in 1937

9968 **Country Folks**
Lee Publications
6113 State Highway 5
PO Box 121
Palatine Bridge, NY 13428-121

518-673-3237
888-596-5329; Fax: 518-673-2699
subscriptions@leepub.com
www.countryfolks.com

Frederick Lee, Publisher
Joan Kark-Wren, Editor
Bruce Button, President
Larry Price, Marketing Manager
Ian Hitchener, Sales Manager

Agricultural news from national, state and local levels. Some features on farm and agricultural industry, rural interest, etc.
Cost: $12.00
75 Pages
Frequency: Weekly
Circulation: 27000

9969 **Country Living**
Arens Corporation
PO Box 69
Covington, OH 45318-0069

937-473-2020; Fax: 937-473-2500
garyg@arenspub.com
www.arenspub.com

Gary Godfrey, Publisher/President
Don Selanders, Sales Manager
Connie Didier, Circulation Manager

Current news and features devoted to the agricultural industry.
Cost: $1395.00
Frequency: Monthly
Circulation: 17500
Founded in 1950

9970 **Country Woman**
Reiman Publications
5400 S 60th St
Greendale, WI 53129-1404

414-423-0100
800-344-6913; Fax: 414-423-1143
editors@countrywomanmagazine.com
www.countrywomanmagazine.com

Barbara Newton, President
Ann Kaiser, Editor

Offers recipes, stories, profiles and articles pertaining to the country woman.
Cost: $14.98
68 Pages
Founded in 1965

9971 **Critical Reviews in Food and Nutrition**
CRC Press
6000 Broken Sound Pkwy NW
Suite 300
Boca Raton, FL 33487-5704

561-994-0555
800-272-7737; Fax: 561-989-9732
techsupport@crcpress.com
www.crcpress.com

Emmett Dages, CEO
Susan Lee, Editor
Founded in 1913

9972 **Culinary Trends**
Culinary Trends Publications
6285 Spring St
Number 107
Long Beach, CA 90808

714-826-9188; Fax: 714-826-0333
www.culinarytrends.net

Fred Mensigna, Publisher
Jean Hutchins, Director

Information for food and beverage managers along with managers of hotels and restaurants.
Cost: $21.00
Frequency: Quarterly
Circulation: 10000
Founded in 1993

9973 **DDBC News**
Dairy, Deli, Bakery Council of Southern California
PO Box 1872
Whittier, CA 90609

562-947-7016; Fax: 562-947-7872
www.ddbcformation.org

Bob Dreffler, CEO
Dave Daniel, Editor
Susan Steele, Circulation Manager

Serves the deli, dairy, bakery and meat industry.
Cost: $25.00
Frequency: Monthly
Circulation: 5000
ISSN: 0011-7862
Founded in 1960
Printed in 4 colors on glossy stock

9974 **DFA Leader**
Dairy Farmers of America
10220 N Ambassador Dr
Kansas City, MO 64153-1367

816-801-6455
888-332-6455; Fax: 816-801-6456
webmail@dfamilk.com
www.dfamilk.com
Facebook, Twitter, LinkedIn, YouTube

Randy Mooney, Chairman of the Board
George Mertens, Vice Chairman
Tom Croner, Secretary/ Treasurer

Provides members with information about DFA and the dairy industry, along with features on members whose innovative ideas are worth emulating.
Frequency: Quarterly
Founded in 1998

9975 **Dairy Foods Magazine**
Business News Publishing
1050 IL Route 83
Suite 200
Bensenville, IL 60106-1096

630-377-5909; Fax: 630-227-0527
www.dairyfoods.com

Katie Rotella, Manager
David Phillips, Executive Editor
Marina Mayer, Executive Editor
Scott Wolters, Director
Barb Szatko, Regional Sales Manager

Dairy Foods serves the dairy industry by analyzing and reporting on technologies trends and issues and how they affest North America's processors of milk, cheese, frozen deserts and

cultured products. Current issues and qualification forms for free subsciptions will be available to attendees. Dairy Foods is part of BNP Food Group.
Frequency: Weekly
Circulation: 20000
Founded in 1926
Printed in 4 colors on glossy stock

9976 Dairy Today
AgWeb
30 S 15th Street
Suite 900
Philadelphia, PA 19102-4826

215-557-8900; Fax: 215-568-4436
jdickrell@farmjournal.com
www.agweb.com

Bill Newham, Publisher
Jim Dickrell, Editor

A trusted source of dairy information for its subscriber base of US dairy producers.
Frequency: Monthly
Circulation: 65000
Founded in 1989

9977 Dairy, Food and Environmental Sanitation
International Association for Food Protection
6200 Aurora Ave
Suite 200W
Des Moines, IA 50322-2864

515-276-3344
800-369-6337; Fax: 515-276-8655
info@foodprotection.org
www.foodprotection.org

David W. Tharp, Executive Director

Published as the general membership publication by the International Association for Food Protection, each issue contains referred articles on applied research, applications of current technology and general interest subjects for food safety professionals. Regular features include industry and association news, an industry related product section and a calendar of meetings, seminars and workshops.Updates of government regulations and sanitary design is also featured. All members receive DFES.
Cost: $227.00
Frequency: Monthly
Circulation: 3000
ISSN: 1043-3546
Mailing list available for rent: 3000+ names at $150 per M
Printed in 4 colors

9978 Dietitian's Edge
Rodman Publishing
70 Hilltop Rd
3rd Floor
Ramsey, NJ 07446-1150

201-825-2552; Fax: 201-825-0553
info@rodpub.com
www.nutraceuticalsworld.com

Rodman Zilenziger Jr, President
Matt Montgomery, VP

9979 Drovers Journal
Vance Publishing
400 Knightsbridge Parkway
Lincolnshire, IL 60069

847-634-2600; Fax: 847-634-4379
info@vancepublishing.com
www.vancepublishing.com

William C Vance, Chairman
Peggy Walker, President

Recognized as the beef industry leader for more than 30 years, valued for its management, production and marketing information.
Cost: $60.00
Frequency: Monthly
Circulation: 91715
Founded in 1937

9980 Eastern Milk Producer
Eastern Milk Producers Cooperative Association
PO Box 6966
Syracuse, NY 13217-6966

315-437-1225

Bob Stronach, Editor
Trish Stokes, Production Manager

Communicates to members of the association dairy issues, farm issues, association events and policy.
Cost: $13.00
20 Pages
Frequency: Monthly

9981 Egg Industry
WATT Publishing Company
303 N Main Street
Suite 500
Rockford, IL 61101

815-966-5400; Fax: 815-966-6416
tokeefe@wattnet.net
www.wattnet.com

James Watt, Chairman/CEO
Greg Watt, President/COO
Terrence O'Keefe, Editor

Reports on trends, production practices, processing, marketing and economics, and is regarded as the standard for information on current issues, personalities and emerging technology. A pivotal source of news, data and information for innovators and decision-makers in the buying centers of companies producing eggs and further-processed products.
Cost: $36.00
Frequency: Monthly
Circulation: 1553
Founded in 1917

9982 El Restaurante Mexicano
Maiden Name Press
PO Box 2249
Oak Park, IL 60303

708-267-0023
kfurore@restmex.com
www.restmex.com
Facebook

A quarterly magazine featuring industry specific food news, features restaurant profiles and new product information for personnel of restaurants serving mexican/southwestern menu items nationwide.
Cost: $108.00
Circulation: 27000
ISSN: 1091-5885
Founded in 1997
Printed in 4 colors on glossy stock

9983 Europe Agriculture and Trade Report
USDA Economic Research Service
1800 M Street NW
Washington, DC 20036-5831

202-203-3935
800-999-6779
www.ers.usda.gov

Susan Offutt, Administrator
Leslee Lowstuter, Central Operations Staff Director
Thomas McDonald, Publishing/Communications
Suchada Langley, Global Agricultural Markets Branch
Ron Bianchi, Associate Director

An important resource for agribusiness and researchers.
Circulation: 2000

9984 Executive Guide to World Poultry Trends
WATT Publishing Company
303 N Main Street
Suite 500
Rockford, IL 61101

815-966-5400; Fax: 815-966-6416
www.wattnet.com

James Watt, Chairman/CEO
Greg Watt, President/COO
Jeff Swanson, Publishing Director

Packed with facts and figures that give a full overview of the world poultry market.
Frequency: Annual

9985 FFA New Horizons
National FFA Organization
6060 FFA Drive
Indianapolis, IN 46268

317-802-4235
800-772-0939
newhorizons@ffa.org
www.ffanewhorizons.org

Jessy Yancey, Association Editor
Christina Carden, Associate Production Director
Julie Woodard, FFA Publications Manager

The official member magazine of the FFA is published bimonthly and mailed to more than 525,000 readers. Each issue contains information about agricultural education, career possibilities, chapter and individual accomplishments and news on FFA. Now available online.
100 Pages
ISSN: 1069-806x
Founded in 1928
Printed in 4 colors

9986 Fancy Foods & Culinary Products
Talcott Communications Corporation
20 W Kinzie St
12th Floor
Chicago, IL 60654-5827

312-849-2220
888-545-3676; Fax: 312-849-2174
www.talcott.com

Daniel Von Rabenau, Executive Director
Natalie Hamm Noblitt, Editor

Specialty food stores, department store specialty food departments, gift departments, confection stores, independent groceries and supermarket chains, gift basket retailers, cookware and kitchen stores, cooking school gift stores, cheese stores, coffee and tea stores brokers/represenatives/manufacturers/importers/wholesalers/distributors and others allied to the field.
Cost: $26.00
Frequency: Monthly
Circulation: 23,000
ISSN: 1521-5156
Founded in 1983

9987 Fastline Catalog
Fastline Media Group
4900 Fox Run Road
P.O. Box 248
Buckner, KY 40010-0248

502-222-0146
800-626-6409; Fax: 502-222-0615
www.fastline.com
Facebook, Twitter, YouTube, Flickr

William G Howard, President
Susan Arterburn, Marketing Director
Pat Higgins, Vice President, Sales

Nationwide and regional picture buying guides for the farming industry.
Frequency: Monthly
Founded in 1978

9988 **Feedback**
Meat & Livestock Australia
1401 K Street NW
Suite 602
Washington, DC 20005
202-521-2551; Fax: 202-521-2699
info@mla.com.au
www.mla.com.au
Facebook, Twitter, YouTube
Don Heatley, Chairman
David Palmer, Managing Director
Bernie Bindon, Director
Chris Hudson, Director
The red meat and livestock industry journal, featuring on-farm updates and market information for the north, south-east and south-west areas of Australia.
30000 Members
Frequency: 9x Yearly
Founded in 1998

9989 **Fine Foods Magazine**
Griffin Publishing Group
201 Oak Street
Suite A
Pembroke, MA 02359
781-294-4700; Fax: 781-829-0134
www.griffinpublishinginc.com
Stephen Griffin, President
A magazine offering information on the Northeast specialty, ethnic and prepared foods business.
Frequency: Monthly

9990 **Fisheries**
American Fisheries Society
425 Barlow Place
Suite 110
Bethesda, MD 20814-2144
301-897-8616; Fax: 301-897-8096
main@fisheries.org
fisheries.org
Douglas Austen, Executive Director
Erin Del Collo, Membership Coordinator
Laura Hendee, Journals Production Manager
Peer reviewed articles that address contemporary issues and problems, techniques, philosophies and other areas of interest to the general fisheries profession. Monthly features include letters, meeting notices, book listings and reviews, environmental essays and organization profiles.
Cost: $106.00
50 Pages
Frequency: Monthly
Circulation: 9800
Founded in 1870
Mailing list available for rent: 8500 names at $250 per M

9991 **Food & Drug Packaging**
Stagnito Communications
210 S 5th Street
Suite 202
Saint Charles, IL 60174
847-205-5660; Fax: 630-377-1678
www.fdp.com
Edwin Landon, Publisher
Vince Miconi, Advertising Production Manager
George Misko, Regional Sales Manager
Catherine Wynn, Sales Manager
Food and Drug Packaging serves industries engaged in packaging food, beverages, pharmaceuticals, cosmetics and consulting/engineering firms.
Frequency: Monthly
Circulation: 75140
Founded in 1959

9992 **Food Aid Needs Assessment**
US Department of Agriculture
200 Independence Ave SW
Washington, DC 20201-0007
202-690-7650; Fax: 202-219-0942
Gene Mathia, Branch Chief
This annual report assesses the food situation in 60 developing countries. Most of the data are presented by region; crisis countries are covered individually.

9993 **Food Arts Magazine**
M Shanken Communications
387 Park Ave S
8th Floor
New York, NY 10016-8872
212-684-4224; Fax: 212-684-5424
www.cigaraficionado.com
Marvin Shanken, Publisher
Julie Mautner, President
A publication serving the fine food service industry is edited for restauranteurs, chefs, food and beverage directors and caterers.
Frequency: Monthly
Circulation: 50000
Founded in 1972
Printed in 4 colors on glossy stock

9994 **Food Channel Trend Wire**
Noble & Associates
2155 W Chesterfield Blvd
Springfield, MO 65807-8650
417-875-5000
800-545-4087; Fax: 417-875-5051
www.noble.net
Robert Noble, CEO
Designed to make the food industry professionals food trend experts. Encapsulates trend information from more than 125 food and consumer publications each month. Provides insights into emerging food trends.
Cost: $195.00
Circulation: 2000

9995 **Food Distribution Research Society News**
Silesia Companies
PO Box 441110
Fort Washington, MD 20749-1110
301-292-1970; Fax: 706-542-0739
www.fdrsinc.org
John Strovinsky, Publisher
Wojciech Florkowski, Editor
Food distribution research society encourages research, serves as an information clearinghouse and encourages implementation of research. The Society organizes conferences, and meetings for industry, academic and government leaders within the food industry sector.
Cost: $65.00
16 Pages
Circulation: 150
Founded in 1960
Mailing list available for rent: 150 names

9996 **Food Engineering**
Business News Publishing Company
1050 IL Route 83
Suite 200
Bensenville, IL 60106-1096
630-377-5909; Fax: 947-763-9538
www.foodengineering.com
Facebook, Twitter
Patrick Young, Publisher & District Sales Manager
Paul Kelly, District Sales Manager
Brian Gronowski, District Sales Manager
Wayne Wiggins Jr, District Sales Manager
Carolyn Dress, Inside & Online Sales Manager
A publication offering information on all facets of the food industry, from ingredients to food packaging and processing.
Cost: $64.00
Frequency: Monthly
Circulation: 15000
Founded in 1926

9997 **Food Management**
Penton Publishing Company
1300 E 9th St
Suite 1020
Cleveland, OH 44114-1514
216-861-0360; Fax: 216-696-0836
information@penton.com
www.food-management.com
Preston L Vice, CFO
Adrian Meredith, CFO
David Brodowski, General Manager
Denise Walde, Senior Production Manager
Combines the industry's most comprehensive circulation package with an editorial mix that emphasizes business management strategies and ideas, food trends and recipes and in-depth news analysis in a contemporary feature magazine.
90 Pages
Frequency: Monthly
Circulation: 47899
ISSN: 0091-018X
Founded in 1892
Printed in 4 colors on glossy stock

9998 **Food Processing**
555 W Pierce Road
Suite 301
Itasca, IL 60143
630-467-1300; Fax: 630-467-1124
www.foodprocessing.com
Lily Modjeski, Sales Manager
Patricia Donatiu, Circulation Manager
Dave Fusaro, Editor-in-Chief
Steve Slankis, Group Publisher
Anetta Gauthier, Production Manager
Information on food equipment, packaging material and other supplies and services.
Frequency: Monthly
Circulation: 65000
Founded in 1938

9999 **Food Product Design**
Virgo Publishing LLC
3300 N Central Ave
Suite 300
Phoenix, AZ 85012-2532
480-675-9925; Fax: 480-990-0819
peggyj@vpico.com
www.foodproductdesign.com
Jenny Bolton, President
Publication distributed to product development professionals and corporate management executives at food and beverage manufacturing and foodservice companies.
Circulation: 20000
Founded in 1986
Printed in on glossy stock

10000 **Food Production/Management Magazine**
CTI Publications

2823 Benson Mill Rd
Sparks Glencoe, MD 21152-9575

410-308-2080; Fax: 410-308-2079
www.ctipubs.com

Randy Gerstmyer, Publisher/Editor

Serves those in the canning, glasspacking, freezing and aseptic packaged food industries. Readers include corporate executives and staff personnel responsible for direction of management, operations, production, engineering, packaging, research and development. Accepts advertising.
Cost: $40.00
32 Pages
Frequency: Monthly
Circulation: 4482
ISSN: 0191-6181
Founded in 1878
Mailing list available for rent: 4500 names at $675 per M
Printed in 4 colors on glossy stock

10001 **Food Protection Trends**
International Association for Food Protection
6200 Aurora Ave
Suite 200W
Des Moines, IA 50322-2864

515-276-3344
800-369-6337; Fax: 515-276-8655
info@foodprotection.org
www.foodprotection.org

David W. Tharp, Executive Director

Each issue contains articles on applied research, applications of current technology and general interest subjects for food safety professionals. Regular features include industry and association news, and industy-related products section and a calendar of meetings, seminars and workshops. Updates of government regulations and sanitary design are also featured.
Cost: $227.00
Frequency: Monthly
Circulation: 9000
ISBN: 0-362028-X -
Founded in 1911
Mailing list available for rent
Printed in 4 colors on glossy stock

10002 **Food Quality**
Wiley-Blackwell
111 River Street
Hoboken, NJ 07030-5774

856-380-4117
800-322-9373
www.foodquality.com

The established authority in the market as the science-based news magazinw focused on quality, assurance, safety, and security in the food and beverage industry.
Cost: $195.00
66 Pages
Frequency: Monthly
Circulation: 21000
ISSN: 1092-7514
Founded in 1994
Mailing list available for rent: 15,000 names at $195 per M
Printed in 4 colors on glossy stock

10003 **Food Safety Magazine**
Target Group
1945 W Mountain St
Glendale, CA 91201-1258

818-842-4777; Fax: 818-769-2939
info@foodsafetymagazine.com
www.foodsafetymagazine.com
Facebook, Twitter, LinkedIn

Don Meeker, Owner/CEO
Andrea Karges, Circulation Manager
Barbara VanRenterghem, Editorial Director

Publicaton is for food safety and quality assurance/control professionals at food and beverage processors, food service companies and agri-food laboratories worldwide. These decision makers implement science-based food safety strategies and systems to prevent, control, test and verify that chemical, microbiological and physical hazards do not enter the food supply.
Cost: $19.00
Frequency: Monthly
Circulation: 20,000
Founded in 1980

10004 **Food Service Equipment & Supplies Specialist**
Reed Business Information
2000 Clearwater Dr
Oak Brook, IL 60523-8809

630-574-0825; Fax: 630-288-8781
www.reedbusiness.com

Jeff Greisch, President
Maureen Slocum, Publisher
Judy Erickson, Group Circulation Manager
Stuart Whayman, CFO

Magazine for professionals who specify, sell and distribute food service equipment, supplies and furnishings.
Cost: $69.95
Frequency: Monthly
Circulation: 22,740
Founded in 1948
Printed in 4 colors on glossy stock

10005 **Food Technology**
Institute of Food Technologists
525 W Van Buren
Suite 1000
Chicago, IL 60607-3842

312-782-8424; Fax: 312-782-8348
info@ift.org
www.ift.org

Bob Swientek, Editor-in-Chief

The leading publication addressing all facets of food science and technology. Its in-depth and balance coverage includes the latest research developments, industry news, consumer product innovations, and professional opportunities.
Cost: $190.00
Frequency: Monthly
Circulation: 18000
ISSN: 0015-6639

10006 **Food Trade News**
Best-Met Publishing
5537 Twin Knolls Rd
Suite 438
Columbia, MD 21045-3270

410-730-5013; Fax: 410-740-4680
jmetzger@best-met.com
www.best-met.com

Jeff Metzger, Publisher
Terri Maloney, Editor
Nina Weiland, VP
Beth Pripstein, Office Manager
Richard J Bestany, Advertising Director

A magazine aimed at the players in the food distribution industry.

10007 **Food World**
Best-Met Publishing Company
5537 Twin Knolls Rd
Suite 438
Columbia, MD 21045-3270

410-730-5013; Fax: 410-740-4680
jmetzger@best-met.com
www.best-met.com

Jeff Metzger, Publisher
Jeffrey W. Metzger, Publisher
Beth Pripstein, Office Manager
Richard J. Bestany, President

Regional food trade newspaper covering the Mid-Atlantic market
Frequency: Monthly
Printed in on newsprint stock

10008 **FoodService and Hospitality**
Kostuch Publications
Two City Place Drive
Suite 200 PMB 2004
Saint Louis ario, MO 63141-3P6

314-812-2565; Fax: 314-835-0044
wgilchri@ix.netcom.com
www.foodserviceworld.com

Mitch Kostuch, President
Rosanna Caira, Publisher/Editor
Wendy Gilchrist, Director Business Development
Phoebe Fung, Owner
Owen Knowlton, Director

Canada's only national specialty business magazine reaching owners,managers and buyers in all sections of the foodservice industry.
Cost: $50.00
Frequency: Monthly
Circulation: 25,000
Printed in on glossy stock

10009 **FoodTalk**
Pike & Fischer
PO Box 25277
Alexandria, VA 22313

703-548-3146; Fax: 703-548-3017

Declan Couroy, Editor/Publisher

Sanitation tips for food workers.
Cost: $120.00
Frequency: Quarterly
Circulation: 5000
Founded in 1987
Printed in 2 colors

10010 **Foodservice Consultant**
Foodservice Consultants Society International

editorial@foodserviceconsultant.org
www.fcsi.org/foodservice-consultant

Stuart Charlton, Publisher

Professional publication for FCSI members and the food service industry.
Cost: $40.00
150 Pages
Frequency: Quarterly
Circulation: 4500
Printed in 4 colors on glossy stock

10011 **Foodservice Equipment & Supplies**
Reed Europe
2000 Clearwter Drive
Oak Brook, IL 60523

630-320-7000
800-446-6551; Fax: 630-288-8282
www.fesmag.com

Maureen Slocum, Publisher
Mitchell Schechter, Editor-in-Chief

Edited for readers outside the US who are employed in firms that manufacture food and beverage products.
Frequency: Monthly
Founded in 1948

10012 **For Fish Farmers**
Mississippi Cooperative Extension Service
PO Box 9690
Mississippi State, MS 39762-9690

662-325-3174; Fax: 601-857-2358

Martin W Bunson, Editor

A magazine offering information that addresses the concerns of fish farmers.
Frequency: Quarterly

10013 **Fresh Cup Magazine**
Fresh Cup Publishing Company
537 SE Ash Street Suite 300
PO Box 14827
Portland, OR 97293

503-236-2587
800-868-5866; Fax: 503-236-3165
www.freshcup.com

Ward Barbee, Publisher
Jan Weigel, President
Julie Beals, Marketing
Bill Berninger, Circulation Manager
Natalie Caceres, Marketing Coordinator
Cost: $60.00
80 Pages
Frequency: Monthly
Circulation: 15000
Founded in 1992
Printed in 4 colors on glossy stock

10014 **Fresh Cut Magazine**
Great American Publishing
75 Applewood Drive, Suite A
PO Box 128
Sparta, MI 49345

616-887-9008; Fax: 616-887-2666
www.freshcut.com

Matt McCallum, Publisher
Scott Christie, Managing Editor

The only publication covering all sectors of the international value-added produce industry. Growers, processors, retailers and foodservice professionals all find information relating to their day-to-day operations in the pages of Fresh Cut magazine.
Cost: $15.00
40 Pages
Frequency: Monthly
ISSN: 1072-2831
Founded in 1993
Printed in 4 colors on glossy stock

10015 **Frozen Food Digest, Inc.**
271 Madison Ave
Suite 1402-A
New York, NY 10016-1014

212-557-8600; Fax: 212-986-9868

Saul Beck, President/Hall of Fame Member
Cost: $45.00
Circulation: 16000
Founded in 1985

10016 **Fruit Country**
Clintron Publishing
PO Box 30998
Spokane, WA 99223-3016

509-248-2452
800-869-7923; Fax: 509-458-3547

Clintke Withers, Publisher
John M Dahlin, Editor
Tyson Graff, Circualtion Manager

Written for and about growers, their operations and their needs. Stories on growers and shippers, developments and trends in the fruit industry, human interest stories and politics, new products, chemicals and supplies, avant garde management techniques, cultural practices and tips on profitability. Advertising equipment and services to the fruit industry and distribution system.
Cost: $12.00
Frequency: Monthly
Circulation: 11500
Founded in 1976

10017 **Futures Magazine**
Futures Magazine
111 W Jackson Blvd
7th Floor
Chicago, IL 60604-4139

312-977-0999; Fax: 312-846-4638
dcollins@futuresmag.com
www.aip.com

Steve Lown, Manager
Daniel P Collins, Editor
Gabby Mouizerh, Production Manager
Steve Lown, Manager

Agriculture commodities charted by various technical studies, plus analysis.
Cost: $39.00
24 Pages
Frequency: Monthly
Circulation: 60,000
Founded in 1972

10018 **Game Bird Gazette**
Allen Publishing
970 East
3300 South
Salt Lake City, UT 84106

801-485-1299

George Allen, Editor

All about keeping, breeding and raising pheasants, quails, partridges, peacocks, doves, pigeons, waterfowl and gamebirds of all kinds.
Cost: $23.95
45 Pages
Frequency: Monthly
Founded in 1940

10019 **Gourmet Retailer Magazine**
3301 Ponce De Leon Blvd
Suite 300
Coral Gables, FL 33134-7273

305-273-0437
800-765-9797; Fax: 305-446-2868

Edward Loeb, Publisher
Michael Keighley, Editorial Director
Laura Everage, Managing Editor
Shari Levenson, Marketing Manager
Kathy Colwell, Advertising Production Manager
Frequency: Monthly
Circulation: 25000
Founded in 1979

10020 **Grape Grower**
Western Agricultural Publishing Company
4969 E Clinton Way
#104
Fresno, CA 93727-1549

559-252-7000
888-382-9772; Fax: 559-252-7387

Paul Baltimore, Publisher
Randy Bailey, Editor
Robert Fujimoto, Assistant Editor

The West's most widely read authority on the cultivation of table grapes, raising grapes and wine grapes. All aspects of production are covered with the most current university, government and private research.
Mailing list available for rent

10021 **Greenhouse Product News**
Scranton Gillette Communications
3030 W Salt Creek Lane
Suite 201
Arlington Heights, IL 60005-5025

847-391-1000; Fax: 847-390-0408
www.gpnmag.com

Bob Bellew, VP/Group Publisher
Tim Hodson, Editorial Director
Jasmina Radjevic, Managing Editor

Features the industry's leading Buyer's Guide directory, the PGR table and the bookstore are just a few of the reasons the industry's buyers keep coming back.
Cost: $30.00
Frequency: Monthly
Circulation: 19000
Mailing list available for rent: 19,000 names

10022 **Griffin Report: Market Studies**
Griffin Publishing Company
201 Oak Street
Pembroke, MA 02359

781-829-4700; Fax: 781-829-0134
www.griffinreport.com

Mike Berger, Editor
Kevin Griffin, Vice President
Karen Harty, Vice President
Julie Mignosa, Office Manager

This report offers statistics on the leading chain and multi-store independent grocers in the northeast.
Cost: $42.00
Frequency: Monthly
Founded in 1966
Mailing list available for rent: 10,000 names at $350 per M
Printed in on newsprint stock

10023 **Grocers Report**
Super Markets Productions
PO Box 6124
San Rafael, CA 94903-124

415-479-0211; Fax: 415-479-0211

Lori Abrams, CEO
JM Adlman, Publisher
Joan Adams, Circulation Manager

Offers information on the retail grocery industry.
Cost: $10.00
Frequency: Quarterly
Circulation: 18000
Founded in 1978
Printed in 4 colors on glossy stock

10024 **Growertalks Magazine**
Ball Publishing
622 Town Road
PO Box 1660
West Chicago, IL 60186

630-231-3675
888-888-0013; Fax: 630-231-5254
info@ballpublishing.com
www.growertalks.com

Chris Beytes, Editor/Publisher
Jennifer Zurko, Associate Editor

Specializes in the publishing of horticulture information, primarily related to floriculture production and marketing.
Frequency: Monthly
Circulation: 12000
Founded in 1937

10025 **Growing for Market**
Fairplain Publications
PO Box 3747
Lawrence, KS 66046

785-748-0605
800-307-8949; Fax: 785-748-0609
www.growingformarket.com

Lynn Byczynski, Editor/Publisher
Roger Yepsen, Author

A monthly periodical for small-scale farmers, market gardeners, and grower of vegetables, fruits, herbs and flowers. Offers news and ideas about organic production, pest control, tools and equipment and direct marketing.
Cost: $ 30.00
20 Pages
Frequency: Monthly
Circulation: 4000
ISSN: 1060-9296
Founded in 1992

10026 **Guernsey Breeders' Journal**
Purebred Publishing Inc
7616 Slate Ridge Blvd
Reynoldsburg, OH 43068-3126

614-575-4620; Fax: 614-864-5614
khenson@usguernsey.com
www.usguernsey.com

Katie Henson, Editor

The oldest dairy breed magazine published by a US breed organization. Contents range across current management trends, breeder stories and events withing the Guernsey industry in the US and worldwide.
Cost: $20.00
Frequency: 10x Yearly

10027 **Health Products Business**
Cygnus Publishing
445 Braod Hollow Road
Melville, NY 11747-3669

631-845-2700
800-308-6397; Fax: 631-845-2723
micheal.schiavitz@cygnuspub.com
www.healthproducts.com

Bruce Ceftakes, Publisher/Sales
Micheal Schiavetta, Editor
Christian Biscuiti, Assistant Editor

This is a trade magazine that covers news and trends in the natural health products industry including vitamins, herbs, dietary supplements and other products. Publishes annual raw materials directory and purchasing guide, as well as other speciality issues. Targets natural products retail store owners, buyers and managers. Qualified subsciption only.
ISSN: 0149-9602

10028 **Herb Quarterly**
EGW Publishing Company
4075 Papazian Way
Suite 204
Fremont, CA 94538-4372

510-668-0268; Fax: 510-668-0280
www.herbquarterly.com

Chris Slaughter, VP
Jennifer Barrett, Editor

Each issue introduces readers to new herbs and fascinating herbal lore; provides tips on hard to grow varieties and medicinals; showcases gardens from around the world; and tempts the palate with seasonal menus and tantalizing recipes built around herbs and edible flowers.
Cost: $19.97
68 Pages
Frequency: Quarterly
Circulation: 36753
Founded in 1978
Printed in 4 colors on matte stock

10029 **Hereford World**
American Hereford Association
PO Box 014059
Kansas City, MO 64101

816-842-3757; Fax: 816-842-6931
aha@hereford.org
www.hereford.org

Jack Ward, Executive VP

Trade magazine for breeders of registered Hereford cattle. Articles and columns provide in-depth information about the beef industry.
Frequency: Monthly
Circulation: 9500
Founded in 1742

10030 **Honey Producer**
American Honey Producers Association
PO Box 162
Power, MT 59468

406-463-2227; Fax: 406-463-2583
beeguy4jensen@yahoo.com
www.americanhoneyproducers.org

Lyle Johnston, Editor

Highlights current industry news, publishes submitted articles from the scientific community, informs of legal battles being fought in Washington,'DC, provides cmoplete AHPA convention schedules.
Cost: $20.00
Frequency: Quarterly
ISSN: 1091-3394

10031 **Hospitality News Featuring Coffee Talk**
PO Box 21027
Salem, OR 97307-1027

503-390-8343
800-685-1932; Fax: 503-390-8344
www.hospnews.com

Kerri R Goodman-Small, Publisher
Miles Small, Editor-in-Chief

Serves restaurants, lodges, health care facilities, schools, clubs,casinos, caterers, and culinary and beverage marketplaces nationally.
Circulation: 30000
ISSN: 1084-2551
Founded in 1988
Printed in on newsprint stock

10032 **IAFIS Reporter**
International Assn of Food Industry Suppliers
1451 Dolley Madison Boulevard
Suite 101
McLean, VA 22101

703-761-2600; Fax: 703-761-4334
info@fpsa.org
www.fpsa.org

George Melnykovich, President
Andrew Drennan, VP

Happenings and trends in the food and dairy industry.
Founded in 1983

10033 **IGA Grocergram**
Pace Communications
PO Box 13607
Greensboro, NC 27415-3607

336-378-6065; Fax: 336-275-2864
info@pacecommunications.com
www.pacecommunications.com

Bonnie McElveen, CEO
Wes Isley, Chief Financial Officer
Leigh Klee, Chief Financial Officer
Ed Calfo, Executive Vice President

Edited for IGA retailers and wholesalers throughout the US. Focuses on training, merchandising, display, promotion, and advertising and marketing techniques. Also addresses financial and personnel management and innovations in store engineering and development.
Cost: $24.00
Frequency: Monthly

10034 **Import Statistics**
Association of Food Industries
3301 State Route 66
Suite 205, Building C
Neptune, NJ 07753-2705

732-922-3008; Fax: 732-922-3590
info@afius.org
www.naooa.org

Robert Bauer, President
Cost: $40.00
Frequency: Annual+
Circulation: 1200
Founded in 1906

10035 **In Good Taste**
Specialty Coffee Association of America
302 5th Avenue
5th Floor
New York, NY 10001

646-733-6000
800-544-7377; Fax: 646-733-6010
www.pharmpress.com

Ted R Lingle, Editor

This periodical offers business, promotional and educational advice in the areas of cultivation, processing, preparation and marketing of specialty coffee.
Frequency: Monthly

10036 **Industria Alimenticia**
Stagnito Communications
155 Pfingster Road
Suite 205
Deerfield, IL 60015

847-205-5660; Fax: 847-205-5680
www.stagnito.com

Harry Stagnito, President
Elsa Rico, Director/Editor
Mary Mazur, Circulation

Information source for Latin American food and beverage processors
Cost: $85.00
Printed in 4 colors on glossy stock

10037 **Inform**
American Oil Chemists' Society
2710 S. Boulder
PO Box 17190
Urbana, IL 61802-6996

217-359-2344; Fax: 217-351-8091
general@aocs.org
www.aocs.org
Facebook, Twitter

E. Dumelin, President
D. Myers, Vice President
S. Erhan, Secretary
T. Kemper, Treasurer

The monthly business and scientific magazine of AOCS, providing international news on fats, oils, surfectants, detergents, and related materials.
Cost: $10.00
5400 Members
Frequency: Membership Dues Vary
Founded in 1909

10038 **Insider Magazine**
Assn. of Correctional Food Service Affiliates
PO Box 10065
Burbank, CA 91510

818-843-6608; Fax: 818-843-7423
www.acfsa.org

Jon Nichols, Executive Director

Contains news pertaining to correctional foodservice activities of the Association and fellow members, as well as industry-specific educational articles.
56 Pages
Frequency: Quarterly
Circulation: 1500
Founded in 1969
Mailing list available for rent: 900 names at $200 per M
Printed in 4 colors on glossy stock

10039 **Institute of Food and Nutrition**
HealthComm International
9770 44th Avenue
N.W. Suite 100
Gig Harbor, WA 98332

253-851-3943
800-692-9400; Fax: 253-851-9749

info@metagenics.com
www.metagenics.com

Jeffrey Bland, President/Chief Science Officer
Jeffrey Katke, Chairman of the Board/CEO
Carl Mickey Moore, Co-Chief Operating Officer
Janice Moore, Co-Chief Operating Officer
Matthew Tripp, VP of Research & Development
Founded in 1983

10040 **Intermountain Retailer**
Utah Food Industry Association
1578 W 1700 S
Suite 100
Salt Lake City, UT 84104-3489

801-973-9517
800-423-6636; Fax: 801-972-8712
www.utfood.com

James Olsen, President
Meik Rapp, Editor

This annual guide offers information on brokers in Utah that are serving the retail food industry.
Cost: $25.00
48 Pages
Frequency: Annual+
Circulation: 1200
Founded in 1896

10041 **International Journal of Food Engineering**
Reed Business Information
360 Park Ave S
New York, NY 10010-1737

646-746-6400; Fax: 646-756-7583
corporatecommunications@reedbusiness.com
www.reedbusiness.com

John Poulin, CEO
Peter Havens, Publisher
James Reed, Owner

Devoted to engineering disciplines related to processing foods. The areas of interest include heat, mass transfer and fluid flow in food processing; food microstructure development and characterization; application of artificial intelligence in food research; food biotechnology, and more.
Frequency: Annual
Circulation: 15,000

10042 **International Product Alert**
Marketing Intelligence Service
482 N Main St
Canandaigua, NY 14424-1049

585-374-6326
800-836-5710; Fax: 585-374-5217

Tom Vierhile, Executive Editor
Sherry Meeker-Barton, Editor-in-Chief

Reports the introduction of new food, beverage, health & beauty aides, household & pet products outside of North America. Reports include full product descriptions and selected illustrations of products and advertising backup.
Cost: $700.00

10043 **Italian Cooking and Living**
Italian Culinary Institute
302 5th Avenue
9th Floor
New York, NY 10001

212-899-9057
888-742-2373; Fax: 212-889-3907
irene@italiancookingandliving.com

Paolo Villoresi, Publisher
Irene De Gasparis, Associate Publisher
Charles Pennino, Owner

American magazine devoted to Italian cuisine/culture/travel
Founded in 2001

10044 **JAOCS**
American Oil Chemists' Society
2710 S. Boulder
PO Box 17190
Urbana, IL 61802-6996

217-359-2344; Fax: 217-351-8091
general@aocs.org
www.aocs.org
Facebook, Twitter

E. Dumelin, President
D. Myers, Vice President
S. Erhan, Secretary
T. Kemper, Treasurer

The leading source for technical papers related to the fats and oils industries. A peer-reviewed journal devoted to fundamental and practical research, production, processing, packaging and distribution in the growing field of fats, oils, proteins and other related substances.
Cost: $10.00
5400 Members
Frequency: Membership Dues Vary
Founded in 1909

10045 **Journal of Animal Science**
American Society of Animal Science
2441 Village Green Pl
Champaign, IL 61822-7676

217-356-9050; Fax: 217-398-4119
susanp@assochq.org
www.asas.org

Meghan Wulster-Radcli, Executive Director
Susan Pollack, Managing Editor/Editorial Director

The official journal of the American Society of Animal Science, JAS publishes results of original research in Genetics, Growth and Physiology, Nutrition, Production, Products, and Special Topics. JAS consistently ranks in the top tier in the category of Agriculture, Dairy, and Animal Sciences
Frequency: Monthly
Circulation: 3500
ISSN: 0021-8812
Founded in 1908
Printed in on glossy stock

10046 **Journal of Business Logistics**
Council of Supply Chain Management Professionals
333 E Butterfield Rd
Suite 140
Lombard, IL 60148-5617

630-574-0985; Fax: 630-574-0989
www.cscmp.org
Facebook, Twitter, LinkedIn, YouTube

Rick Blasgen, President & CEO
Sue Paulson, Executive Assistant
Nancy Nix, Chair
Rick J. Jackson, Chair-Elect
Theodore Stank, Secretary & Treasurer

Provides a forum for the dissemination of original thoughts, research, and best practices within the logistics and supply chain arenas. Provides readers with new and helpful information, new supply chain management theory or techniques, research generalizations, creative views and sytheses of dispersed concepts, and articles in subject areas which have significant current impact on thought and practice in logistics and supply chain management.
10000 Members
Founded in 1963

10047 **Journal of Child Nutrition & Management**
School Nutrition Association
120 Waterfront St
Suite 300
National Harbor, MD 20745-1142

301-686-3100
800-877-8822; Fax: 301-686-3115
servicecenter@schoolnutrition.org
www.schoolnutrition.org

Helen Phillips, President
Sandy Ford, President-Elect
Leah Schmidt, Vice President
Beth Taylor, Secretary/Treasurer

Features up-to-date research articles on significant issues affecting child nutrition and school foodservice management. Provides timely and relevant insights into the many challenges and opportunities surrounding child nutrition programs. Information facilitates decision-making and serves as evidence of how effective child nutrition programs are.
55000 Members
Frequency: Monthly
Founded in 1946

10048 **Journal of Dairy Science**
American Dairy Science Association
2441 Village Green Pl
Champaign, IL 61822-7676

217-356-5146; Fax: 217-398-4119
adsa@assochq.org
www.adsa.org

Michael Mangino, Senior Editor
Sharon Frick, Secretary
Diane Hekken, Secretary
Richard Pursley, Secretary, Treasurer

Research in dairy cattle production and dairy food products.
Cost: $110.00
Frequency: Monthly
Founded in 1990

10049 **Journal of Environmental Quality**
American Society of Agronomy
5585 Guilford Road
Madison, WI 53711-1086

608-273-8080; Fax: 608-273-2021
headquarters@agronomy.org
www.agronomy.org
Facebook, Twitter, LinkedIn

Ann Edahl, Managing Editor

Papers are grouped by subject matter and cover water, soil, and atmospheric research as it relates to agriculture and the environment.
11000 Members
Founded in 1907

10050 **Journal of Food Distribution Research**
Food Distribution Research Society
PO Box 441110
Fort Washington, MD 20749

301-292-1970; Fax: 301-292-1787
Jonathan_baros@ncsu.edu

John Park, President
Ron Rainey, President-Elect
Kellie Raper, Secretary/ Treasurer
Jennifer Dennis, Director
Stan Ernst, Director

Publishes articles that cover every aspect of our modern food system. JFDR is a peer reviewed journal published exlusively online.
Frequency: 3x Yearly

10051 **Journal of Food Protection**
International Association for Food Protection
6200 Aurora Ave
Suite 200W
Des Moines, IA 50322-2864

515-276-3344
800-369-6337; Fax: 515-276-8655
info@foodprotection.org
www.foodprotection.org
Facebook, Twitter, LinkedIn

Timothy C. Jackson, President
David W. Tharp, Executive Director

Each issue contains scientific research and authoritative review articles reporting on a variety of topics in food science pertaining to food safety and quality.
4200 Members
Founded in 1911

10052 **Journal of Food Science**
Institute of Food Technologists
525 W Van Buren St
Suite 1000
Chicago, IL 60607-3842

312-782-8424; Fax: 312-782-8348
info@ift.org
www.ift.org

Barbara Byrd Keenan, Executive VP
Daryl B Lund, Editor-in-Chief

IFT's premier science journal, containing peer-reviewed reports of original research and critical reviews of all aspects of food science.
Frequency: 9x Yearly
Founded in 1936

10053 **Journal of Foodservice Business Research**
Taylor & Francis Group LLC
325 Chestnut St
Suite 800
Philadelphia, PA 19106-2614

215-625-8900
800-354-1420; Fax: 215-625-2940
www.taylorandfrancis.com

Kevin Bradley, President

Features articles from international experts in various disciplines, including management, marketing, finance, law, food technology, nutrition, psychology, information systems, anthropology, human resources, and more.
Frequency: Quarterly

10054 **Journal of Hospitality & Tourism Research**
CHRIE
2810 N Parham Road
Suite 230
Richmond, VA 23294

804-346-4800; Fax: 804-346-5009
info@chrie.org
www.chrie.org
Facebook, Twitter, LinkedIn

Susan Fournier, President
Josette Katz, Vice President
Chris Roberts, Secretary
John Drysdale, Treasurer
Kathy McCarty, CEO

Offers high quality refereed articles which advance the knowledge base of the hospitality field. Articles on empirical research, theoretical developments and innovative methodologies are guided by an editor and a review board consisting of leading hospitality and tourism researchers.
Frequency: Quarterly

10055 **Journal of Hospitality and Tourism Education**
CHRIE
2810 N Parham Road
Suite 230
Richmond, VA 23294

804-346-4800; Fax: 804-346-5009
info@chrie.org
www.chrie.org
Facebook, Twitter, LinkedIn

Susan Fournier, President
Josette Katz, Vice President
Chris Roberts, Secretary
John Drysdale, Treasurer
Kathy McCarty, CEO

A refereed, interdisciplinary quarterly magazine designed to serve the needs of all levels of hospitality and tourism education through the presentation of issues and opinions pertinent to the field.
Frequency: Quarterly

10056 **Journal of Natural Resources & Life Sciences Education**
American Society of Agronomy
5585 Guilford Road
Madison, WI 53711-1086

608-273-8080; Fax: 608-273-2021
headquarters@agronomy.org
www.agronomy.org
Facebook, Twitter, LinkedIn

Susan Ernst, Managing Editor

Today's educators look here for the latest teaching ideas in the life sciences, natural resources, and agriculture. Articles are written by and for educators in extension, universities, industry, administration, and grades k-12.
11000 Members
Founded in 1907

10057 **Journal of Packaging**
Institute of Packaging Professionals
Ste 123
1833 Centre Point Cir
Naperville, IL 60563-4848

630-544-5050
800-432-4085; Fax: 630-544-5005
info@iopp.org
www.iopp.org
Facebook, Twitter, LinkedIn, YouTube

Edwin Landon, Executive Director
Patrick Farrey, General Manager
Stan Zelesnik, Director Education
Robert DePauw, Finance Manager
Kelly Staley, Member Services Manager

Serves the entire packaging community's educational needs. The Journal is a resource for professional analysis of all packaging issues. Available online only, it is a forum that covers issues in depth.
Frequency: Daily

10058 **Journal of Plant Registrations**
Crop Science Society of America
5585 Guilford Rd.
Madison, WI 53711-1086

608-273-8080; Fax: 608-273-2021
www.crops.org
Facebook, Twitter, LinkedIn

Maria Gallo, President
Jeffrey Volenec, President-Elect
Ellen G.M. Bergfeld, CEO

Publishes cultivar, germplasm, parental line, genetic stock, and mapping population registration manuscripts.
4700 Members
Frequency: Monthly
Founded in 1955

10059 **Journal of Shellfish Research**
National Shellfisheries Association
National Marine Fisheries Service Laboratory
Oxford, MD 21654

631-653-6327; Fax: 631-653-6327
webmaster@shellfish.org
www.shellfish.org

R. LeRoy Creswell, President
Christopher V. Davis, President-Elect
George E. Flimlin, VP & Program Chair
Marta Gomez-Chiarri, Secretary
Sandra E. Shumway, Editor

The international journal promoting all aspects of shellfish research.
1M Members
Frequency: Monthly
Founded in 1908

10060 **Journal of Sugar Beet Research**
Beet Sugar Development Foundation
800 Grant Street
Suite 300
Denver, CO 80203

303-832-4460; Fax: 303-832-4468
aa@bsdf-assbt.org
www.bsdf-assbt.org

Fosters all phases of sugarbeet and beet sugar research, promotes the dissemination of relevant scientific knowledge, and strives to maintain high standards of ethics, and to cooperate with other organizations having objectives beneficial to the beet sugar industry.
Frequency: Quarterly
ISSN: 0899-1502

10061 **Journal of Surfactants and Detergents (JSD)**
American Oil Chemists' Society
2710 S. Boulder
PO Box 17190
Urbana, IL 61802-6996

217-359-2344; Fax: 217-351-8091
general@aocs.org
www.aocs.org
Facebook, Twitter

E. Dumelin, President
D. Myers, Vice President
S. Erhan, Secretary
T. Kemper, Treasurer

A scientific journal dedicated to the practical and theoretical aspects of oleochemical and petrochemical surfectants, soaps, and detergents.
Cost: $10.00
5400 Members
Frequency: Membership Dues Vary
Founded in 1909

10062 **Journal of the American Dietetic Association**
Elsevier Health Publishing
1600 John F Kennedy Blvd
Suite 1800
Philadelphia, PA 19103-2398

215-239-3900; Fax: 215-239-3990
www.elsevier.com

Michael Hansen, CEO
Jason Swift, Editor
Ryan Lipscomb, Department Editor
Linda Van Horn, Editor-in-Chief

A premier source for the practice and science of food, nutrition, and dietetics. The Journal focuses on advancing professional knowledge across the range of research and practice issues such as: nutritional science, medical nutrition therapy, public health nutrition, food science and biotechnology, foodservice systems, leadership and management and dietetics education.
Cost: $229.00
Frequency: Monthly/Subscription
ISSN: 0002-8223

10063 **Journal of the American Oil Chemists' Society**
American Oil Chemists' Society
2710 S Boulder
Urbana, IL 61802-6996

217-359-2344; Fax: 217-351-8091
general@aocs.org
www.aocs.org

Jody Schonfeld, Publications Director
Pam Landman, Journals Coordinator
Kimmy Farris, Production Editor

The leading source for technical papers related to the fats and oils industries. A peer-reviewed journal devoted to fundamental and practical research, production, processing, packaging and

distribution in the growing field of fats, oils, proteins and other related substances
Frequency: Monthly
Founded in 1947

10064 Journal of the American Pomological Society
103 Tyson Building
University Park, PA 16802-4200
814-863-6163; Fax: 814-237-3407
bardenja@vt.edu
www.americanpomological.org

Dr John Barden, Editor

The Journal contains refereed technical articles and a wide variety of applied articles relating to fruit varieties.
Frequency: Quarterly/Free to Members

10065 Journal of the American Society for Horticultural Science
American Society for Horticultural Science
1018 Duke Street
Alexandria, VA 22314
703-836-4606; Fax: 703-836-2024
journal@ashs.org
www.ashs.org

Michael Neff, Executive Director

A peer-reviewed publication of results of orginal research on horticultural plants and their products or directly related research areas. Its prime function is communication of mission-oriented, fundamental research to other researchers.
Cost: $85.00
Frequency: Bi-Monthly
ISSN: 0003-1062
Founded in 1903
Mailing list available for rent: 2500 names at $100 per M

10066 Journal of the Association of Food and Dru g Officials
Association of Food and Drug Officials
2550 Kingston Rd
Suite 311
York, PA 17402-3734
717-757-2888; Fax: 717-755-8089
afdo@afdo.org
www.afdo.org

Denise Rooney, Executive Director

News and the latest legislation for the Food and Drug Association.
Founded in 1937

10067 Kosher Today
1428 36th street
219
Brooklyn, NY 11218
718-854-4460; Fax: 718-854-4474
info@koshertoday.com
www.koshertoday.com/

Menachem Lubinsky, CEO
Bill Springer, Account Executive
Christine Salmon, Account Executive
Karyn Gilbert, Marketing Manager

Covers the kosher food industry.
28 Pages
Frequency: Weekly
Circulation: 20000
Founded in 1984
Printed in 4 colors on newsprint stock

10068 Lean Trimmings Prime
National Meat Association
1970 Broadway
Suite 825
Oakland, CA 94612
510-763-1533; Fax: 510-763-6186
staff@nmaonline.org
www.nmaonline.org

Robert Rebholtz, Chairman
Larry Vad, President
Marty Evanson, Vice President
Mike Hesse, Secretary
Brian Coelho, Treasurer

Brings a broad range of topics and essential association information to the membership and beyond.
600 Members
Frequency: Weekly
Founded in 1946

10069 Lipids
American Oil Chemists' Society
2710 S. Boulder
PO Box 17190
Urbana, IL 61802-6996
217-359-2344; Fax: 217-351-8091
general@aocs.org
www.aocs.org
Facebook, Twitter

E. Dumelin, President
D. Myers, Vice President
S. Erhan, Secretary
T. Kemper, Treasurer

A premier journal in the lipid field, published monthly, featuring full-length original research articles, short communications, methods papers, and review articles on timely topics.
Cost: $10.00
5400 Members
Frequency: Membership Dues Vary
Founded in 1909

10070 Logistics Journal
Transportation Intermediaries Association
1625 Prince St
Suite 200
Alexandria, VA 22314-2883
703-299-5700; Fax: 703-836-0123
info@tianet.org
www.tianet.org

Robert Voltmann, President
Nancy King, Marketing Manager

Education and policy organization for North American transportation intermediaries. The only national association representing the interests of all third party transportation service providers. Members include logistics management firms, property brokers, perishable commodities brokers, freight forwarders, intermodal marketers and ocean and air forwarders.
Frequency: Monthly
Circulation: 1000
Founded in 1978

10071 Manufacturing Confectioner
MC Publishing
711 W Water Street
PO Box 266
Princeton, WI 54968
920-295-6969; Fax: 920-295-6843
mcinfo@gomc.com
www.gomc.com

Eric Schmoyer, President
Michael Allured, Publisher/Editor-in-Chief

The worldwide business, marketing and technology journal of the candy, chocolate, confectionery, cough drop, and sweet baked goods industry. Provides in-depth coverage of news, industry statistics, sales and marketing, ingredients, equipment and services.
Cost: $65.00
Frequency: Monthly
Founded in 1921

10072 Meat & Poultry
Sosland Publishing Company
4801 Main St
Suite 100
Kansas City, MO 64112-2513
816-756-1000; Fax: 816-756-0494
www.sosland.com

Joel Crews, Editorn-in-Chief
Kimberlie Clyma, Managing Editor
Dave Crost, Publisher

Serves meat, poultry and seafood processors, wholesalers-distrubuters, slaughterers, fabricators, cutters, meat buyers, and rendering and pet food manufacturers.
Frequency: Monthly
Circulation: 21,000
Founded in 1955
Printed in 4 colors on glossy stock

10073 Meat Marketing and Technology
Marketing & Technology Group
1415 N Dayton St
Suite 115
Chicago, IL 60642-7033
312-266-3311; Fax: 312-266-3363
webinars@meatingplace.com
www.meatingplace.com

Mark Lefens, Owner
Dan Allen, Editor-at-Large
Jim Goldberg, VP Sales/Marketing
John Gregerson, Editor
Deborah Silver, Managing Editor

Provides information on meat processing, retail, slaughtering and fabricating and rendering.
Cost: $40.00
Frequency: Monthly
Circulation: 20,009
Founded in 1993
Printed in 4 colors on glossy stock

10074 Meat Science
American Meat Science Association
2441 Village Green Pl
Champaign, IL 61822-7676
800-517-AMSA; Fax: 888-205-5834; Fax: 217-356-5370
information@meatscience.org
www.meatscience.org

Dean Pringle, President
Collette Kaster, Chief Executive Officer

The official journal of AMSA. Peer-reviewed resource is the best way to stay current on the latest research in meat science across all meat products and in all aspects of meat production and processing. Available online or in print.

10075 Midwest Food Service News
Pinnacle Publishing
316 N Michigan Avenue
Suite 300
Chicago, IL 60601
312-272-2401
800-493-4867; Fax: 312-960-4106

Keith Hadley, Publisher
Joanne Cooper, Editor

Communicates directly and exclusively with restaurant and food service operations in Indiana, Kentucky, Michigan, Ohio, Pennsylvania and West Virginia.
52 Pages
Frequency: Bi-Monthly
Circulation: 40,000
Founded in 1982
Printed in 4 colors on newsprint stock

10076 Military Grocer
Downey Communications

4800 Montgomery Lane
Suite 710
Bethesda, MD 20814-3461

301-718-7600; Fax: 301-718-7604

Richard T Carroll, Publisher
Loretta M Downey, CEO

Serves defense commissary employees worldwide.
Frequency: 5 per year
ISSN: 1058-8620
Printed in 4 colors on glossy stock

10077 **Milk and Liquid Food Transporter**
Glen Street Publications
W4652 Glen Street
Appletone, WI 54913

920-749-4880; Fax: 920-749-4877

Jane Plout, Publisher

Information for owners, operators and managers of companies that haul milk or other liquid foods in sanitary or food grade tankers. Publication covers maintenance, association news, state of the industry, business management, and activities of independent haulers.
16 Pages
Frequency: Monthly
Circulation: 4768
Founded in 1960
Printed in 4 colors on glossy stock

10078 **Milling & Baking News**
Sosland Publishing Company
4801 Main St
Suite 100
Kansas City, MO 64112-2513

816-756-1000; Fax: 816-756-0494
www.sosland.com

Morton Sosland, Editor-in-Chief
Josh Sosland, Editor
Neil N Sosland, Executive Editor
Eric Schroeder, Managing Editor
Jeff Gelski, Associate Editor

This magazine is aimed at baking, milling and food processing industries.
Cost: $135.00
Frequency: Monthly
Circulation: 4032

10079 **Milling Journal**
3065 Pershing Court
Decatur, IL 62526

217-877-9660
800-728-7511; Fax: 217-877-6647
webmaster@grainnet.com
www.grainnet.com

Jim Camillo, Editor
Mark Avery, Publisher
Kay Merryfield, Circulation Manager
Jody Sexton, Editorial Assistant
Deb Coontz, Sales Manager

Mailed to all active AOM members in the US, Canada, and internationally, including wheat flour/corn mills and corn/oilseed processors in US and Canada.
Frequency: Quarterly
Circulation: 1217

10080 **Missouri Grocer**
Missouri Grocers Association
315 North Ken Avenue
Springfield, MO 65802-6213

417-831-6667; Fax: 417-831-3907
cmcmillian@missourigrocers.com
www.missourigrocers.com
Facebook

Erick Taylor, President
John Porter, Vice President
Mike Beal, Treasurer
Linda Ryan, Chairperson

Referred to as the pre-convention issue. Highlights the exhibitors, sponsors, awardees and events that will be taking place during the Annual Convention and Merchandising Show.

10081 **Modern Baking**
Penton Media
330 N Wabash
Suite 2300
Chicago, IL 60611

katie.martin@penton.com
modern-baking.com

Jerry Rymont, VP Penton Food Group
Katie Martin, Chief Editor
Matt Reynolds, Group Managing Editor

Provides the latest product and service information to the $20 billion in-store and $14.9 billion retail baking and foodservice markets.
Cost: $75.00
112 Pages
Frequency: Monthly
Circulation: 27000
ISSN: 0897-6201
Founded in 1987
Mailing list available for rent: 27,000 names
Printed in 4 colors on glossy stock

10082 **Modern Brewery Age**
Business Journals
50 Day Street
S Norwalk, CT 06854-3100

203-853-6015; Fax: 203-852-8175

Peter VK Reid, Editor
Britton Jones, President
Arthur Heilman, Circulation Manager

A magazine for the wholesale and brewing industry.
Cost: $95.00
Frequency: Quarterly
Founded in 1933

10083 **Modern Brewery Age: Tabloid Edition**
Business Journals
50 Day Street
#5550
Norwalk, CT 06854-3100

203-853-6015; Fax: 203-852-8175

Peter VK Reid, Editor

Brewery industry tabloid.
Cost: $85.00
Frequency: Weekly

10084 **Monthly Price Review**
Urner Barry Publications
PO Box 389
Toms River, NJ 08754

732-240-5330
800-932-0617; Fax: 732-341-0891
help@urnerbarry.com
www.urnerbarry.com

Paul B Brown Jr, President
Karen Mick, Circulation Director

Lists price of eggs, turkeys, chickens, fowl, butter, margarine, cheese and concentrated milk products for the month and compares the monthly average to the previous year.
Cost: $149.00
Frequency: Monthly
Circulation: 310
ISSN: 0566-3628
Founded in 1858

10085 **Mushroom News**
American Mushroom Institute
1284 Gap Newport Pike
Suite 2
Avondale, PA 19311-9503

610-268-7483; Fax: 610-268-8015
www.americanmushroom.org

Sara Manning, Manager
Mark Wach, Chairman
Laura Phelps, President
Bill Barber, Publisher

For growers and scientists in mushroom production.
Cost: $275.00
Frequency: Monthly
Founded in 1956

10086 **NACS Magazine**
National Association of Convenience Stores
1600 Duke St.
Alexandria, VA 22314

703-684-3600
800-966-6227; Fax: 703-836-4564
nacsmagazine@convenience.org
www.convenience.org

Erin Pressley, Vice President, Education & Media

Delivered to all members, this magazine reaches a majority of the convenience and petroleum marketing channel of trade.
Frequency: Monthly
Circulation: 27,632

10087 **NWAC News: Thad Cochran National Warmwater Aquaculture Center**
127 Experiment Station Road
Stoneville, MS 38776-197

662-686-3273; Fax: 662-686-3320
javery@drec.msstate.edu
www.msstate.edu/dept/tcnwac

Jimmy Avery, Editor
J Lee, CEO/President
Frequency: Monthly
Circulation: 1200
Founded in 1998
Printed in 3 colors on matte stock

10088 **Nation's Restaurant News**
Informa USA Inc.
101 Arthur Andersen Pkwy.
Sarasota, FL 34232-6323

508-616-6600
800-944-4676; Fax: 508-616-5522
jenna.telesca@knect365.com
www.nrn.com

Jenna Telesca, Editor-in-Chief
Kent Scholla, Director, Sales
Laura Viscusi, VP, Market Leader

Serves commercial and onsite food service and lodging establishments including restaurants, schools, universities, hospitals, nursing homes and other health and welfare facilities, hotels and motels with food service, government installations, clubs and other related firms.
Cost: $44.95
Circulation: 85999
Founded in 1925
Mailing list available for rent: 100,000 names at $100 per M
Printed in 4 colors on matte stock

10089 National Confectionery Sales Association Annual Journal
Teresa Tarantino
10225 Berea Road, Suite B
Cleveland, OH 44102

216-631-8200; Fax: 216-631-8210
ttarantino@mail.propressinc.com
www.candyhalloffame.com

Tony Rufrano, President
Steve Foster, Executive Director

Annual membership listing and biographies of Candy Hall of Fame industees.
Cost: $25.00
76 Pages
Founded in 1997
Printed in 4 colors on matte stock

10090 National Fisherman
Diversified Business Communications
PO Box 7437
Portland, ME 04112-7437

207-842-5600; Fax: 207-842-5503
info@divcom.com
www.divbusiness.com

Nancy Hasselback, President/CEO
Randy Le Shane, VP Operations
Nancy Gelette, VP Operations
Stephnie Wendel, Circulation Manager

The most widely read commercial fishing magazine and the only commercial fishing publication providing national coverage and national circulation.
Cost: $22.95
Frequency: Monthly
Circulation: 38000
ISSN: 0027-9250
Founded in 1949

10091 National Food Processors Association State Legislative Report
National Food Processors Association
1350 Eye St NW
Suite 300
Washington, DC 20005-3377

202-393-0890
800-355-0983; Fax: 202-639-5932
www.nfpa-food.org

Cal Dooley, CEO
Lisa Weddig, Executive Director
Tammy Morgan, Contact
Frequency: Monthly
Circulation: 345
Founded in 1901

10092 National Hog Farmer
7900 International Dr
Suite 300
Minneapolis, MN 55425-2562

952-851-4710; Fax: 952-851-4601
nationalhogfarmer.com/

Dale Miller, Editor
Tom Vilsack, Secretary
JoAnn DeSmet, Marketing
Robert Moraczewski, Senior Vice President

Offers production information for hog farming business managers.
Frequency: Monthly
Circulation: 84000
Founded in 1960
Mailing list available for rent: 84M names
Printed in 4 colors on glossy stock

10093 National Provisioner
Stagnito Communications
155 Pfingster Road
Suite 205
Deerfield, IL 60015

847-205-5660; Fax: 847-205-5680
www.nationalprovisioner.com

Ned Bardic, Publisher
Barbara Young, Editor
Tommy Howell, Marketing
Vito Laudati, Business Development Manager
Diana Rotman, Sales Manager

Magazine for meat, poultry, prepared food processors.
Cost: $85.00
Frequency: Monthly
Circulation: 25000
Founded in 1912

10094 Natural Foods Merchandiser
New Hope Natural Media
1401 Pearl St
Suite 200
Boulder, CO 80302-5346

303-939-8440
800-431-1255; Fax: 303-939-9886
info@newhope.com
www.newhope.com

Fred Linder, President
Marty Traynor, Editor
Lynne Brenner, Human Resources Executive

Natural Foods Merchandiser features a comprehensive overview of the industry, the latest reports on new ingredients and formulations, market news, new product releases and many other features specifically designed for the retailmarket. It offers the information and the products retailers require to succeed in the competitive natural products marketplace.
65 Pages
Frequency: Monthly
Circulation: 15,000
ISSN: 0164-335x
Founded in 1979
Printed in 4 colors on glossy stock

10095 Natural Products INSIDER
Virgo Publishing LLC
3300 N Central Ave
Suite 300
Phoenix, AZ 85012-2532

480-675-9925; Fax: 480-990-0819
www.naturalproductsinsider.com

Jenny Bolton, President

Official magazine for SupplySide. Provides timely information and news for marketers, manufacturers and formulators of dietary supplements, functional foods and personal care. The website also offers exclusive resources and offers, free weekly e-newsletters and a searchable news archive.
Mailing list available for rent: 15000+ names at $var per M

10096 Natural Products Marketplace
Virgo Publishing LLC
3300 N Central Ave
Suite 300
Phoenix, AZ 85012-2532

480-675-9925; Fax: 480-990-0819
peggyj@vpico.com
www.vpico.com

Jenny Bolton, President

Publication discussing the dietary supplement, food and personal care industries, focusing on the latest news, products and trend analysis to keep retailers informed and ahead of the competition.
Mailing list available for rent: 15000+ names at $var per M

10097 North Africa and Middle East International Agricultural and Trade Report
US Department of Agriculture
1301 New York Avenue NW
#612
Washington, DC 20005-4701

202-219-0724; Fax: 202-219-0942

Michael Kurrzig, Editor

Information on current and projected agriculture production and trade in North Africa and the Middle East. Reports include trade and production data and highlight US and European trade with the region.
Frequency: Annual

10098 North American Deer Farmers Magazine
North American Deer Farmers Association
104 S Lakeshore Dr
Lake City, MN 55041-1641

651-345-5600; Fax: 651-345-5603
info@nadefa.org
www.nadefa.org

Shawn Schafer, Executive Director
Dave McQuaig, First VP
Glenn Dice Jr, Second VP

National association of deer farming and ranching. Membership dues are $75-195 which include this quarterly magazine.
Frequency: Quarterly
Circulation: 1000
ISSN: 1084-0583
Founded in 1983
Mailing list available for rent
Printed in on glossy stock

10099 North American Journal of Aquaculture
American Fisheries Society
425 Barlow Place
Suite 110
Bethesda, MD 20814-2144

301-897-8616; Fax: 301-897-8096
main@fisheries.org
fisheries.org

Douglas Austen, Executive Director
Erin Del Collo, Membership Coordinator
Laura Hendee, Journals Production Manager

Formerly published as The Progressive Fish-Culturist. The focus is on culture of all aquatic organisms that are of importance to North American culturists. Topics include, but are not limited to, nutrition and feeding, broodstock selection and spawning, drugs and chemicals, health and water quality, and testing new techniques and equipment for the management and rearing of aquatic species
Cost: $38.00
Frequency: Quarterly
ISSN: 1548-8454

10100 Northeast DairyBusiness
DairyBusiness Communications
6437 Collamer Road
East Syracuse, NY 13057-1031

315-703-7979
800-334-1904; Fax: 315-703-7988
www.dairybusiness.com

Eleanor Jacobs, Editor
Susan Harlow, Managing Editor

Business resource for successful milk producers. Devoted exclusively to the business and dairy management needs of milk producers in the 12 northeastern states.
Cost: $38.95
51 Pages
Frequency: Monthly
Circulation: 17,500
ISSN: 1523-7095

Founded in 1904
Printed in 4 colors on glossy stock

10101 **Northwest Palate Magazine**
Pacifica Publishing
PO Box 10860
Portland, OR 97296

503-224-6039
800-398-7842; Fax: 503-222-5312
http://www.northwestpalate.com

Cameron Nagel, Publisher/Editor
Angie Jabine, Owner
Ericka Burke, Owner

Regional magazine that focuses on food, wine and travel. Coverage includes restaurants, destinations and the wines of the Pacific Northwest states and British Columbia.
Cost: $15.00
56 Pages
Frequency: 6 issues per ye
Circulation: 45000
ISSN: 0892-8363
Founded in 1987
Printed in 4 colors on glossy stock

10102 **Nut Grower**
Western Agricultural Publishing Company
4969 E Clinton Way
Suite 104
Fresno, CA 93727-1549

559-252-7000
888-382-9772; Fax: 559-252-7387

Paul Baltimore, Publisher
Randy Bailey, Editor
Robert Fujimoto, Assistant Editor

Covers production topics, the latest in research developments, and crop news on almonds, walnuts, pistachios, pecans and chestnuts.

10103 **Nutraceuticals World**
Rodman Publishing
70 Hilltop Rd
3rd Floor
Ramsey, NJ 07446-1150

201-825-2552; Fax: 201-825-0553
info@rodpub.com
www.nutraceuticalsworld.com

Rodman Zilenziger Jr, President
Matt Montgomery, VP

Articles about many aspects of the market, from dietary supplements to functional foods to nutritional beverages, and everything in between.
Frequency: Monthly
Circulation: 12010

10104 **Nutrition Action Healthletter**
Center for Science in the Public Interest
1875 Connecticut Avenue NW
Suite 300
Washington, DC 20009

202-332-9110; Fax: 202-265-4954
cspi@cspinet.org
www.cspinet.org

Stephen B Schmidt, Editor-in-Chief
Chris Schmidt, Customer Service Manager
Michael Jacobson, Executive Director
Jamie Jonker, Director Regulatory Affairs

A magazine covering food and nutrition, the food industry, and relevant government regulations.
Cost: $32.00
16 Pages
Circulation: 800000
Founded in 1971
Mailing list available for rent: 700,000 names at $90 per M
Printed in 4 colors on matte stock

10105 **On-Campus Hospitality**
Executive Business Media
825 Old Country Road
PO Box 1500
Westbury, NY 11590

516-334-3030; Fax: 516-334-8959
ebm-mail@ebmpubs.com
www.ebmpubs.com

Murry H Greenwald, President/Publisher
Paul Ragusa, Managing Editor

College and university food service operations and outlets and related purchasing and administrative offices.
Cost: $30.00
Circulation: 9,445
ISSN: 0887-431X
Founded in 1979
Printed in 4 colors

10106 **Onboard Services**
International Publishing Company of America
664 La Villa Dr
Miami Springs, FL 33166-6030

305-887-1700
800-525-2015; Fax: 305-885-1923

Alexander Morton, Owner
George Hulcher, Contributing Editor

Keeps airline, cruise ships, railroad, and terminal concessions management and purchasing departments up-to-date on all phases of passenger services.
Cost: $25.00
24 Pages
ISSN: 0892-4236
Founded in 1968
Printed in 4 colors on glossy stock

10107 **Organic WORLD**
John Pappenheimer
3939 Leary Way NW
Seattle, WA 98107-5043

206-781-3347; Fax: 206-632-7055

Covers the news of organic gardening.
Cost: $15.00
Frequency: Quarterly

10108 **PMMI ProFood World**
Packaging Machinery Manufacturers Institute (PMMI)
11911 Freedom Drive
Suite 600
Reston, VA 20190

571-612-3200; Fax: 703-243-8556
info@pmmi.org
www.pmmimediagroup.com/pfw/profood-world

Patrick Young, Publisher
Carolyn Dress, Business Development
Joyce Fassl, Editor-In-Chief
Maya Norris, Managing Editor
Brian Gronowski, Sales Manager

Magazine published by PMMI Media Group, featuring information, news, products and technologies related to the food and beverage processing industry for the benefit of professionals working in manufacturing, engineering, operations and supply chain/logistics.
800+ Members
Founded in 1933

10109 **Pacific Farmer-Stockman**
999 West Riverside Avenue
PO Box 2160
Spokane, WA 99201-1006

509-595-5385
800-624-6618; Fax: 509-459-3929
www.nmv.pointshop.com

Barry Roach, Ad Director
Shaun Higgins, President
Colleen Striegel, Operations Manager
Mike Craigen, Marketing Executive

Offers farming news and information for farmers and herdsmen located in the Pacific states.
Cost: $29.95
Frequency: Monthly

10110 **Packer**
Vance Publishing
400 Knightsbridge Parkway
Lincolnshire, IL 60069

847-634-2600; Fax: 847-634-4379
info@vancepublishing.com
www.vancepublishing.com

William C Vance, Chairman
Peggy Walker, President

Leading source of news and information on fresh fruit and vegetable marketing.
Frequency: Weekly
Circulation: 12434
Founded in 1937
Printed in on glossy stock

10111 **Peanut Farmer**
Specialized Agricultural Publications
5808 Faringdon Place
Suite 200
Raleigh, NC 27609

919-872-5040; Fax: 919-876-6531
www.peanutfarmer.com

Dayton H Matlick, President
Mary Evans, Publisher
Mary Cornwall, Chief Copy Editor
Jeanne Sherman, Director of Circulation

Offers peanut farmers profitable methods of raising, marketing and promoting peanuts, plus key related issues.
Cost: $15.00
24 Pages
Frequency: Monthly
Circulation: 18500
Founded in 1965
Printed in 4 colors on glossy stock

10112 **Peanut Grower**
Vance Publishing
38 Peace Drive
Bronson, FL 32621

352-486-7006; Fax: 352-486-7009
ahuber@svic.net
www.peanutgrower.com

Amanda Huber, Editor
Lia Guthrie, Sales

Written for the largest 24,000 US peanut farmers. Covers disease, weed and insect control, legislation, farm equipment, marketing and new research.
Founded in 1937

10113 **Peanut Science**
American Peanut Research and Education Society
Oklahoma State University
376 Ag Hall
Stillwater, OK 74078-6025

405-372-3052; Fax: 405-624-6718
www.peanutscience.com

Dr J Ronald Sholar, Executive Officer

A professional journal with current research results.
Cost: $9.00
Frequency: Bi-Annual
Founded in 1979

10114 **Pig International**
WATT Publishing Company

303 N Main Street
Suite 500
Rockford, IL 61101

815-966-5400; Fax: 815-966-6416
www.wattnet.com

James Watt, Chairman/CEO
Greg Watt, President/COO
Roger Abbott, Editor

Covers nutrition, animal health issues, feed procurement, and how producers can be profitable in the world pork market.
Cost: $50.00
Frequency: Monthly
Circulation: 17642
ISSN: 0191-8834
Founded in 1971
Printed in 4 colors on glossy stock

10115 **Pizza Today**
National Association of Pizzeria Operators
908 S 8th Street
Suite 200
Louisville, KY 40203

502-736-9500
800-489-8324; Fax: 502-736-9502
plachapelle@pizzatoday.com
www.pizzatoday.com
Facebook, Twitter

Pete Lachapelle, Publisher/President
Jeremy White, Editor-in-Chief
Mandy Detwiler, Managing Editor
Pat Cravens, Editorial Coordinator

Up-to-date information on pizza restaurant management, pizza equipment for sale, a vendor directory and more.
130 Pages
Frequency: Monthly
Circulation: 47,000
Founded in 1983
Printed in 4 colors on glossy stock

10116 **Pork**
10901 W 84th Ter
Suite 200
Lenexa, KS 66214-1631

913-438-8700
800-255-5113; Fax: 913-438-0695
info@vancepublishing.com
www.vancepublishing.com

Cliff Becker, Publisher
Jane Messenger, Chief Financial Officer
Lori Eppel, Chief Financial Officer
Bill Raufer, Contributing Editor

A magazine specifically designed for the professional pork producer.
Cost: $59.88
Frequency: Monthly
Circulation: 21,464
Founded in 1981
Mailing list available for rent

10117 **Potato Country**
Columbia Publishing
8405 Ahtanum Rd
Yakima, WA 98903-9432

509-248-2452
800-900-2452; Fax: 509-248-4056
www.potatocountry.com

Brent Clement, Editor/Publisher
Mike Stoker, Publisher

Edited for potato growers and allied industry people throughout the Western fall-production states. Editorial material covers production, seed, disease forecast, equipment, fertilizer, irrigation, pest/weed management, crop reports and annual buyers guide.
Cost: $18.00
32 Pages
Circulation: 6300
ISSN: 0886-4780
Founded in 1975
Printed in 4 colors on glossy stock

10118 **Potato Grower**
Harris Publishing Company
360 B Street
Idaho Falls, ID 83402

208-524-4217; Fax: 208-522-5241
www.potatogrower.com

Jason Harris, Publisher
Gary Rawlings, Editor
Nancy Butler, Staff Writer
Rob Erickson, Marketing
Eula Endecott, Circulation

Current news on growing potatoes, market trends, technology.
Cost: $20.95
48 Pages
Frequency: Monthly
ISBN: m-ountai-n -w
Founded in 1965
Printed in 4 colors on glossy stock

10119 **Poultry**
Marketing and Technology Group
1415 N Dayton St
Suite 115
Chicago, IL 60642-7033

312-266-3311; Fax: 312-266-3363
webinars@meatingplace.com
www.meatingplace.com

Mark Lefens, Owner
Tom Cosgrove, Editor

Serves companies who deal with poultry slaughter, rendering or processing.
Frequency: Monthly
Circulation: 20,000
Founded in 1993
Printed in 4 colors on glossy stock

10120 **Poultry Digest**
WATT Publishing Company
122 S Wesley Ave
Mt Morris, IL 61054-1451

815-734-7937; Fax: 815-734-4201
www.wattnet.com

James W Watt, President
Charles G Olentine Jr, PhD, Publisher

A magazine serving the production side of the entire poultry industry.
Founded in 1917

10121 **Poultry International**
WATT Publishing Company
303 N Main Street
Suite 500
Rockford, IL 61101

815-966-5400; Fax: 815-966-6416
mclements@wattnet.net
www.wattnet.com

James Watt, Chairman/CEO
Greg Watt, President/COO
Mark Clements, Editor

Viewed by commercial poultry integrators as the leading international source of news, data and information for their businesses. Serves commercial broiler, turkey, duck and egg producers.
Cost: $63.00
68 Pages
Frequency: Monthly
Circulation: 20000
ISSN: 0032-5767
Founded in 1962
Printed in 4 colors

10122 **Poultry Times**
Poultry & Egg News
PO Box 1338
Gainesville, GA 30503-1338

770-536-2476; Fax: 770-532-4894
www.poultrytimes.net
Facebook

Cindy Wellborn, Manager
Chris Hill, CEO
Barbara L Olejnik, Associate Editor
Kyle Hatcher, National Sales Representative

The only newspaper in the poultry industry. Provides the most up to date news for the poultry industry.
Cost: $12.00
Frequency: 26 X a year
Circulation: 13000
ISSN: 0885-3371
Founded in 1954
Printed in on glossy stock

10123 **Poultry USA**
WATT Publishing Company
303 N Main Street
Suite 500
Rockford, IL 61101

815-966-5400; Fax: 815-966-6416
www.wattnet.com

James Watt, Chairman/CEO
Greg Watt, President/COO
Jeff Swanson, Publishing Director

Poultry USA serves individuals and firms engaged in the production, processing and marketing of broilers.
60 Pages
Frequency: Monthly
Circulation: 15,092
ISSN: 0007-2176
Founded in 1917
Printed in 4 colors on glossy stock

10124 **Practical Winery & Vineyard**
58 Paul Dr
Suite D
San Rafael, CA 94903-2054

415-479-5819; Fax: 415-492-9325
Office@practicalwinery.com
www.practicalwinery.com

Don Neel, Owner
Tina L Vierra, Associate Publisher

Journal of grape grown and wine production in North America.
Cost: $33.86
Frequency: 6 issues per ye
Circulation: 7,500
Founded in 1985

10125 **Prepared Foods**
Business News Publishing
2401 W Big Beaver Rd
Suite 700
Troy, MI 48084-3333

248-362-3700; Fax: 248-362-0317
www.bnpmedia.com

Mitchell Henderson, CEO
Kathy Travis, Art Director

About 600 food and beverage companies.
Cost: $95.00
109 Pages
Circulation: 70100
Founded in 1926
Printed in 4 colors on glossy stock

10126 **Private Label Buyer**
Stagnito Communications
155 Pfingsten Road
Suite 205
Deerfield, IL 60015

847-205-5660; Fax: 847-205-5680
www.stagnito.com

Steven T Lichtenstein, Publisher
Jill Bruss, Editor

Serves the private label industry, including retailers, voluntaries, wholesalers, manufacturers and others allied to the field.
Frequency: Monthly
Circulation: 30021
Founded in 1986

10127 Process Cooling & Equipment
BNP Publications
1050 IL Route 83
Suite 200
Bensenville, IL 60106-1096

630-377-5909; Fax: 630-694-4002
www.process-cooling.com

Katie Rotella, Manager
Doug Glenn, Publishing Director

Written for manufacturing engineers who use cooling equipment, components, materials and supplies. refrigerated engineers and technicians assoc

10128 Prograzier
Meat & Livestock Australia
1401 K Street NW
Suite 602
Washington, DC 20005

202-521-2551; Fax: 202-521-2699
info@mla.com.au
www.mla.com.au
Facebook, Twitter, YouTube

Don Heatley, Chairman
David Palmer, Managing Director
Bernie Bindon, Director
Chris Hudson, Director

Companion publication to feedback magazine. Highlights how individual producers have succesfully introduced best management practices into their farming enterprise and the benefits that have been achieved.
30000 Members
Frequency: Quarterly
Founded in 1998

10129 Progressive Farmer
2100 Lakeshore Drive
Birmingham, AL 35209-6721

205-877-6333
800-357-4466; Fax: 205-877-6860
ProgressiveFarmer@timeinc.com
www.progressivefarmer.com

Ed Dickinsen, Publisher
Jack Odle, Editor

Farming news with regional focus on the midwest, midsouth and southwest.
Cost: $84.00
106 Pages
Frequency: Monthly
Circulation: 610000
ISSN: 0033-0760

10130 Progressive Grocer's Marketing Guidebook
Trade Dimensions
770 Broadway
New York, NY 10003

847-763-9050; Fax: 203-563-3131
www.progressivegrocer.com

Jenny McTaggart, Senior Editor
Olivia Wilson, Publisher

Over 800 retailer chains and wholesalers in the US and Canada. Also includes over 20,000 key executives. Plus, over 1,700 speciality distributors including C-Store and smaller food store wholesalers, food brokers, and candy, tobacco, and media distributors.
Cost: $380.00
Founded in 1970

10131 QSR Magazine
101 Europa Drive
Suite 150
Chapel Hill, NC 27517

919-945-0705; Fax: 919-945-0701
www.qsrmagazine.com

Sam Oches, Editor
Eugene Drezner, National Sales Director
Webb Howell, President
Frequency: Monthly
Founded in 1997

10132 RCI Magazine
Retail Confectioners International
2053 S Waverly Ave
Suite 204
Springfield, MO 65804-2414

417-883-2775
800-545-5381; Fax: 847-724-2719
info@retailconfectioners.org
www.retailconfectioners.org

Evans Billington, Executive Director

Covers the retail confection industry.
Frequency: Monthly
Circulation: 800
Founded in 1917

10133 RF Design
131 E Main Street
Bellevue, OH 44811-1449

419- 48- 741; Fax: 419-483-3617
www.rfdesign.com/

David Morrison, Editor
Pete May, President

Comprehensive source of rural agricultural news and information for farmers and the general public.
Frequency: Monthly
Founded in 2000

10134 Reciprocation
American Meat Science Association
2441 Village Green Pl
Champaign, IL 61822-7676

800-517-AMSA; Fax: 888-205-5834; Fax: 217-356-5370
information@meatscience.org
www.meatscience.org

Dean Pringle, President
Collette Kaster, Chief Executive Officer
Deidrea Mabry, Chief Operating Officer

Published twice a year for all AMSA members, this magazine features articles on current meat science issues facing the industry.

10135 Refrigerated & Frozen Foods
Stagnito Communications
155 Pfingsten Road
Suite 205
Deerfield, IL 60015

847-205-5660; Fax: 847-205-5680
www.refrigeratedfrozenfood.com

Jeff Plaster, Publisher
Geneine Esquibel, Marketing Manager
Katie Gutierrez, Marketing Manager

Features on leading refrigerated and frozen food processors. Current and future trends in processing, packaging, new product development, food safety and logistics. Serves the dairy, meat, vegetable, fruit, bakery, deli, ingredient, snack, ethnic and other food industry related organizations. Free to qualified subscribers.
Cost: $65.00
64 Pages
Frequency: Monthly
Circulation: 20500
ISSN: 1061-6152
Founded in 1919
Printed in 4 colors on glossy stock

10136 Render
National Renderers Association
801 N Fairfax St
Suite 205
Alexandria, VA 22314-1776

703-683-0155; Fax: 703-683-2626
www.nationalrenderers.org

Thomas M Cook, President

Keeping members abreast of advancements and trends taking place within the industry.
Frequency: Monthly

10137 Restaurant Business
National Council of Chain Restaurants
325 7th St NW
Suite 1100
Washington, DC 20004

202-783-7971
800-673-4692; Fax: 202-737-2849
info@nrf.com
www.nccr.net

Mike Starnes, Chairman
Rob Green, Executive Director
Scott Vinson, Vice President
Chip Kunde, Treasurer
Mary Schell, Secretary

The only publication that is all about and only about the restaurant entrepreneur, serving regional and emerging chains, multi-concept operators and high-volume independents with ideas to innovate and grow. Features include growth strategies, innovations, the restaurant life, and more.
Frequency: Monthly
Founded in 1965

10138 Restaurant Digest
Panagos Publishing
7913 Westpark Drive
Suite 305
McLean, VA 22102

703-917-6420; Fax: 703-917-6408
www.restaurantdigest.com

Bruce Panagos, Publisher

Developments and news of interest to owners, managers, and operators of dining and entertainment establishments in the region.

10139 Restaurant Hospitality
Penton Media
1300 E 9th St
Suite 316
Cleveland, OH 44114-1503

216-696-7000; Fax: 216-696-6662
information@penton.com
www.penton.com

Jane Cooper, Marketing
Mike Sanson, Editor-in-Chief

A national trade publication that covers the full-service restaurant industry. It offers cover story features, an extensive food section with recipes, a multi-page news section and a variety of one page profiles on rising stars, equipment, food safety, beverages, design and more.
Cost: $70.00
130 Pages
Frequency: Monthly
Circulation: 117,721
ISSN: 0147-9989
Founded in 1892
Mailing list available for rentat $165 per M
Printed in 4 colors on glossy stock

10140 Restaurant Wine
Wine Profits

PO Box 222
Napa, CA 94559-222

707-224-4777; Fax: 707-224-6740
www.restaurantwine.com

Zelma Long, President
Ronn R Wiegand, Publisher
Sandy Flanders, Director of Marketing
Paul Grieco, Co-Owner

Information on the marketing of wine in restaurants, hotels and clubs, wine and food pairing ideas and review of wines.
Cost: $99.00
Circulation: 3000
ISSN: 1040-7030
Printed in 2 colors on matte stock

10141 **Restaurants & Institutions**
Reed Business Information
2000 Clearwater Dr
Oak Brook, IL 60523-8809

630-574-0825
800-446-6551; Fax: 630-288-8781

Jeff Greisch, President
Scott Hume, Managing Editor

For restaurant professionals faced with fast-paced consumer demands, government regulations, health concerns and evolving food trends in a variety of market segments.
Frequency: Monthly
Circulation: 154110
Founded in 1937
Printed in 4 colors on glossy stock

10142 **Rice Farming**
Vance Publishing
5050 Poplar Avenue
Suite 200
Memphis, TN 38157-2099

901-767-4020
800-888-9784; Fax: 901-767-4026
vlboyd@worldnet.att.net
www.ricefarming.com

John Sowell, Publisher
Marci Deshores, Editor
Barbara Johnson, Manager

Profitable production strategies for commercial rice growers.
Founded in 1937

10143 **Rice Journal**
Specialized Agricultural Publications
3000 Highwoods Boulevard
Suite 300
Raleigh, NC 27604-1029

919-878-0540; Fax: 919-876-6531
www.ricejournal.com

Dayton H Matlick, President
Mary Evans, Publisher

Offers rice growers profitable methods of producing, marketing and promoting rice, plus key related issues.
Cost: $15.00
24 Pages
Frequency: Monthly January-July
Circulation: 11,600
Founded in 1897
Printed in 4 colors on glossy stock

10144 **Ristorante|**
1010 Lake St
Suite 604
Oak Park, IL 60301-1136

708-848-3200; Fax: 708-445-9477
www.ristorantemag.com

Joe Madden, Owner

10145 **Rural Heritage**
Allan Damerow
281 Dean Ridge Ln
Gainesboro, TN 38562-5039

931-268-0655; Fax: 931-268-5884
info@ruralheritage.com
www.ruralheritage.com

Gail Damerow, Owner
Allan Damerow, Publisher

Publication for people who farm and log with horses and other draft animals.
Cost: $28.00
100 Pages
ISSN: 0889-2970
Founded in 1976
Printed in 4 colors on glossy stock

10146 **Rural Living**
Michigan Farm Bureau
7373 W Saginaw Highway
PO Box 30960
Lansing, MI 48909-8460

517-237-7000
800-292-2680; Fax: 517-323-6793
www.michiganfarmbureau.com

Dennis Rudat, Editor
Sue Snyder, President
Brigette Leach, Director
Earl Butz, Secretary

Editorial emphasis on consumer food news, travel information and issue analysis.
24 Pages
Frequency: Quarterly

10147 **S.O. Connected**
National Society on Healthcare Foodservice
455 S. 4th Street
Suite 650
Louisville, KY 40202

888-528-9552; Fax: 502-589-3602
info@healthcarefoodservice.org
www.healthcarefoodservice.org
Facebook, LinkedIn, YouTube

Patti Oliver, President
Beth Yesford, President-Elect
Laura Watson, Secretary
Randy Sparrow, Treasurer
Robert Darrah, Treasurer-Elect

An important resource for news and recognition.

10148 **School Foodservice & Nutrition**
School Nutrition Association
120 Waterfront St
Suite 300
Oxon Hill, MD 20745-1142

301-749-1481
800-877-8822; Fax: 301-739-3915
servicecenter@schoolnutrition.org
www.schoolnutrition.org

Mary Hill, Director
Dora Rivas SNS, President-Elect
Nancy Rice SNS, VP

This is the official publication of the School Nutrition Association which contains the latest information on a host of items that affect the successful operation of a school foodservice program.
Cost: $75.00
Frequency: Monthly
Circulation: 57,000

10149 **School Nutrition Magazine**
School Nutrition Association
120 Waterfront St
Suite 300
National Harbor, MD 20745-1142

301-686-3100
800-877-8822; Fax: 301-686-3115
servicecenter@schoolnutrition.org
www.schoolnutrition.org

Helen Phillips, President
Sandy Ford, President-Elect
Leah Schmidt, Vice President
Beth Taylor, Secretary/Treasurer

The latest information on a host of items that affect the successful operation of a school foodservice program.
55000 Members
Frequency: Monthly
Founded in 1946

10150 **Science Matters**
Natural Products Association
2112 E 4th St
Suite 200
Santa Ana, CA 92705-3816

714-460-7732
800-966-6632; Fax: 714-460-7444
www.npainfo.org
Facebook, Twitter, LinkedIn

John F. Gay, Executive Director & CEO
Jeffrey Wright, President

Dedicated to providing timely information and advancing the understanding of natural products from a scientific perspective.
1900+ Members
Frequency: Monthly
Founded in 1936

10151 **Seafood Business**
Diversified Business Communications
121 Free Street
PO Box 7437
Portland, ME 04112-7437

207-842-5500; Fax: 207-842-5503
bspringer@divcom.com

Fiona Robinson, Editor
Bill Springer, Publisher
Nancy Hasselback, CEO
Linda Skinner, Managing Editor
Wendy Jalbert, Production Director

Current, comprehensive news on the rapidly expanding seafood industry.
Frequency: Monthly
Circulation: 15,000
Founded in 1949

10152 **Sheep!**
145 Industrial Drive
Medford, WI 54451

715-785-7979
800-551-5691; Fax: 715-785-7414
www.sheepmagazine.com

Dave Belanger, Publisher
Nathan Griffith, Editor

Explores a wide range of sheep-related topics of interest to sheep growers and sheep product marketers at all levels of experience.
Cost: $21.00
Frequency: 6x Yearly

10153 **Shorthorn Country**
Durham Management Company
5830 S 142nd St
Suite A
Omaha, NE 68137-2894

402-827-8003; Fax: 402-827-8006
www.durhamstaffingsolutions.com

Machael Durham, President
Pat Cloutier, Production Manager

Magazine published for cattle producers who breed and sell registered Shorthorn and Polled Shorthorn cattle.
Cost: $24.00
Frequency: 11 per year
Circulation: 3,000
ISSN: 0149-9319

10154 **Simply Seafood**
Sea Fare Group

2360 W Commodore Way
Suite 210
Seattle, WA 98199

206-829-2323; Fax: 206-789-0504
peter@seafare.com
www.simplyseafood.com

Peter Redmayne, Editor

Articles on today's seafood, with cooking ideas, tips & techniques and recipes for healthy meal. Editor's Letter provides all the latest news and insights on seafood products and consumer issues as well as a Market Report with each seasons best buys.
Frequency: Quarterly
Circulation: 131,257

10155 **Sizzle**
American Culinary Federation
180 Center Place Way
St. Augustine, FL 32095

904-824-4468
800-624-9458; Fax: 904-940-0741
sizzlemagazine@acfchefs.net
www.acfchefs.org/sizzle
Facebook, Twitter

Jocelyn Tolbert, Editor

The American Culinary Federation quarterly for culinary, baking, and pastry students. Includes articles on emerging job markets, mentoring, continuing education, culinary trends and product application, as well as scholarship information and culinary/ pastry techniques. Digital publication.
19000 Members
Founded in 1929
Mailing list available for rent: 19,000 names at $150 per M

10156 **Snack Food & Wholesale Bakery**
Stagnito Communications
155 Pfingster Road
Suite 205
Deerfield, IL 60015

847-205-5660; Fax: 847-205-5680
www.stagnito.com

Ron Bean, Publisher
Harry Stagnito, Publishing Director
Dan Malovany, Editor
Bernard Pacyniak, Editorial Director
Andy Hanacek, Managing Editor

Covers topics and products in the snack and wholesale bakery market
Cost: $85.00
Frequency: Monthly
Circulation: 14,854
Founded in 1912
Printed in 4 colors on glossy stock

10157 **Snack World**
Snack Food Association
1233 Janesville Avenue
Fort Atkinson, WI 53538-2738

703-836-4500
800-547-7377; Fax: 920-563-1702

Gloria Cosby, Publisher
Tracey McMahon, Editor

The official international publication of the Snack Food Association covering trends in the snack food industry, including new products and services, industry news and supplier services.
Frequency: 10 per year
Circulation: 14,000

10158 **Southeastern Peanut Farmer**
Southern Peanut Farmer's Federation
110 E 4th Street
PO Box 706
Tifton, GA 31794

229-386-3470; Fax: 229-386-3501
info@gapeanuts.com
www.gapeanuts.com/

Joy Carter, Editor

Offers information to peanut farmers.
Cost: $25.00
20 Pages
Frequency: 5x/Year
Circulation: 9000
ISSN: 0038-3694
Founded in 1961
Printed in 4 colors on glossy stock

10159 **Southern Beverage Journal**
14337 Sw 119th Ave
Miami, FL 33186-6006

305-233-7230; Fax: 305-252-2580
info@bevmedia.com
www.bevmedia.com

Sharon Mijares, Manager
William Slone, Publisher

A magazine for the alcoholic beverage industry.
Cost: $35.00
Frequency: Monthly
Circulation: 10000

10160 **Soybean Digest**
Primedia Business
7900 International Dr
Suite 300
Minneapolis, MN 55425-2562

952-851-9329
800-722-5334; Fax: 952-851-4601
www.penton.com

Robert Moraczewski, Executive VP
Ron Sorensen, Chairman
Kelly Conlin Conlin, President/CEO

Leading publication in the soybean market. Offers in-depth coverage for wise management decisions dealing with production of soybeans, corn, wheat, sorghum and cotton.
Cost: $25.00
Frequency: Monthly
Circulation: 147000
Founded in 1940

10161 **Soybean South**
6263 Poplar Avenue
Suite 540
Memphis, TN 38119-4736

901-385-0595; Fax: 901-767-4026

John Sowell, Publisher
Jeff Kehl, Circulation Director

Profitable prediction strategies for soybean farmers.
Frequency: 5 per year
Printed in 4 colors on glossy stock

10162 **Specialty Food Magazine**
National Association for the Specialty Food Trade
120 Wall St
27th Floor
New York, NY 10005-4011

212-482-6440; Fax: 212-482-6459
www.fancyfoodshows.com

Ann Daw, President

Provides comprehensive planning information for each Show and aggressive on-site bonus distribution, as well as the industry's most in-depth pre-Show, on-site, and post-Show coverage.
Cost: $30.00
Frequency: Monthly
Circulation: 30100
Founded in 1952

10163 **Spudman Magazine**
75 Applewood Drive
Sparta, MI 49435

616-887-9008; Fax: 616-887-2666
www.spudman.com

Matt McCallum, Publisher
Greg Brown, Managing Editor
Erica Bernard, Circulation Manager
Marnie Draper, Advertising Manager
Jill Peck, Creative Director

Information for potato farming and marketing.
Frequency: 9 issues per ye
Circulation: 15500
Founded in 1964

10164 **StateWays**
The Beverage Information Group
17 High St
2nd Floor
Norwalk, CT 06851

203-855-8499
www.bevinfogroup.com

Liza Zimmerman, Editor-in-Chief
Jeremy Nedelka, Managing Editor

Written for commissioners, board members, headquarters personnel, and retail store managers responsible for buying beverage alcohol in the eighteen control states. Covered editorial product knowledge, market trends, store operations, merchandising, warehousing, comoputerization, administration, training and other topics.
Cost: $20.00
Frequency: Bi-Monthly
Circulation: 8500

10165 **Stores Magazine**
National Council of Chain Restaurants
325 7th St NW
Suite 1100
Washington, DC 20004

202-783-7971
800-673-4692; Fax: 202-737-2849
info@nrf.com
www.nccr.net

Mike Starnes, Chairman
Rob Green, Executive Director
Scott Vinson, Vice President
Chip Kunde, Treasurer
Mary Schell, Secretary

Offers an insider's view of the entire retail industry by featuring the latest trends, hottest ideas, current technologies and consumer attitudes.
Frequency: Monthly
Founded in 1965

10166 **Sugar: The Sugar Producer Magazine**
Idaho Golf Harris Publishing
520 Park Avenue
Idaho Falls, ID 83402

208-523-1500
800-638-0135; Fax: 208-522-5241
customerservice@harrispublishing.com
www.sugarproducer.com

Jason Harris, Publisher
David FairBourn, Editor
Eula Endecott, Circulation Manager
Rob Erickson, Marketing Manager

Sugar beet industry information.
Cost: $15.95
Frequency: Monthly
Circulation: 16000
Founded in 1975

10167 **Sunbelt Food Service**
Shelby Publishing Company

517 Green St Nw
Gainesville, GA 30501-3300

770-534-8380; Fax: 770-535-0110
www.shelbypublishing.com

Ron Johnston, President
Penny Smith, Account Manager

Sales and promotion of products and services sold through food service establishments across the sunbelt.
Cost: $36.00
Frequency: Monthly
Circulation: 30090
Founded in 1965
Printed in on newsprint stock

10168 **Sunflower Magazine**
National Sunflower Association
Ste 206
2401 46th Ave SE
Mandan, ND 58554-4829

701-328-5100
888-718-7033; Fax: 701-328-5101
www.sunflowernsa.com

John Sandbakken, Executive Director
Tina Mittelsteadt, Business & Office Manager

Magazine geared to sunflower products.
Cost: $9.00
Frequency: Monthly
Circulation: 29,300
Founded in 1981
Printed in 4 colors

10169 **Sunflower and Grain Marketing Magazine**
Sunflower World Publishers
3307 Northland Drive
Suite 130
Austin, TX 78731-4964

512-407-3434; Fax: 512-323-5118

Ed Randall Allen

Offers news and information on the sunflower and grain industries.
Circulation: 15,000

10170 **Supermarket News: Center Store**
Penton Media Inc
249 W 17th St
Suite 6
New York, NY 10011-5390

212-204-4200; Fax: 212-206-3622
julie.gallagher@penton.com
www.penton.com

Sharon Rowlands, CEO
Jerry Rymont, Publisher

A nationally circulated weekly trade magazine for the food distribution industry.

10171 **Supermarket News: Retail/Financial**
Penton Media Inc
249 W 17th St
Suite 6
New York, NY 10011-5390

212-204-4200; Fax: 212-206-3622
mark.hamstra@penton.com
www.penton.com

Sharon Rowlands, CEO

A nationally circulated weekly trade magazine for the food distribution industry
Frequency: Monthly
Circulation: 36346
ISSN: 0039-5803
Founded in 1892

10172 **Supermarket News: Technology & Logistics**
Penton Media Inc
249 W 17th St
Suite 6
New York, NY 10011-5390

212-204-4200; Fax: 212-206-3622
michael.garry@penton.com
www.penton.com

Sharon Rowlands, CEO

A nationally circulated weekly trade magazine for the food distribution industry
Cost: $45.00
ISSN: 0039-5803
Founded in 1892

10173 **Swine Practitioner**
Vance Publishing
10901 W 84th Terrace
3 Pine Ridge Plaza
Lenexa, KS 66214-1649

913-438-8700
800-255-5113; Fax: 913-438-0695
cbecker@vancepublishing.com
www.vancepublishing.com

Jim Carlton, Editor
Cliff Becker, Group Publisher
William C Vance, Chairman

Offers technical information, primarily on swine health and related production areas, to veterinarians and related industry professionals.
Founded in 1937
Mailing list available for rent

10174 **Tea & Coffee Trade Journal**
Lockwood Publications
26 Broadway
Floor 9M
New York, NY 10004-1704

212-391-2060
845-267-3489; Fax: 212-391-2060
www.lockwoodpublications.com

Robert Lockwood Sr, President

Premiere magazine for tea and coffee industry.
Cost: $49.00
Frequency: Monthly
Circulation: 12
Founded in 1901
Printed in 4 colors on glossy stock

10175 **The American Journal of Agricultural Economics (AJAE)**
Agricultural & Applied Economics Association
555 E Wells Street
Suite 1100
Milwaukee, WI 53202-6600

414-918-3190; Fax: 414-276-3349
junjie.wu@oregonstate.edu
www.aaea.org/publications/ajae

Dawn Thilmany McFadden, President
JunJie Wu, Editor
James A. Vercammen, Editor
Timothy Beatty, Editor

Journal presenting research and policy articles about agricultural economics. The journal contains scholarly materials on the economics of agriculture and food, natural resources and the environment, and rural and community development.
3000 Members
Frequency: 5x Yearly
Founded in 1910

10176 **The County Agent**
National Association of County Agricultural Agents
6584 W Duroc Road
Maroa, IL 61756

217-794-3700; Fax: 217-794-5901
exec-dir@nacaa.com
www.nacaa.com

J. Craig Williams, President

Members receive professional improvement, news of association activities, shared education efforts from other states and reports from NACAA leadership and member states.
Frequency: Monthly
Circulation: 5000
Founded in 1916

10177 **The National Culinary Review**
American Culinary Federation
180 Center Place Way
St. Augustine, FL 32095

904-824-4468
800-624-9458; Fax: 904-940-0741
www.acfchefs.org

Heidi Cramb, Executive Director
Edward G Leonard, President
Brent T. Frei, Director of Marketing
Kay Orde, Editor
Michael Feierstein, Administrative Assistant

Flagship publication of the American Culinary Federation.
Frequency: 6x/yr
Circulation: 21000
Founded in 1932

10178 **The New Brewer**
Brewers Association
736 Pearl Street
Boulder, CO 80302

303-447-0816
888-822-6273; Fax: 303-447-2825
webmaster@brewersassociation.org
www.beertown.org
Facebook, Twitter

Chris P. Frey, Chair
Jake Keeler, Vice Chair
Roxanne Westendorf, Secretary

Offers practical insights and advice for breweries of all sizes. Features on topics like brewing technology and problem solving, pub and restaurant management, and packaged beer sales and distribution. Also important industry news, sales charts and market share performance. The annual Industry Review tallies production for every craft brewery in America, producing both regional and national lists of the biggest players in every sector.
1900 Members
Founded in 1978

10179 **Today's Grocers**
Florida Grocer Publications
PO Box 430760
S Miami, FL 33246

305-661-0792
800-440-3067; Fax: 305-661-6720

Jack Nobles, Publisher
Dennis Kane, Editor

Provides the latest food industry news and trends to Florida, Georgia, Alabama, Louisiana, Mississippi and the Carolinas.
Cost: $29.00
24 Pages
Frequency: Monthly
Circulation: 19,000
ISSN: 1529-4420
Founded in 1956
Printed in on newsprint stock

10180 **Tomato Country**
Columbia Publishing
8405 Ahtanum Rd
Yakima, WA 98903-9432

509-248-2452
800-900-2452; Fax: 509-248-4056
www.tomatomagazine.com

Brent Clement, Editor/Publisher
Mike Stoker, Publisher

Includes information on tomato production and marketing, grower and shipper feature stories, to-

mato research, from herbicide and pesticide studies to new varieties, market reports, feedback from major tomato meetings and conventions, along with other key issues and points of interest for US and Canada tomato growers.
Cost: $12.00
Frequency: Annually
Founded in 1993

10181 Trading Rules
National Oilseed Processors Association
1300 L St NW
Suite 1020
Washington, DC 20005-4168

202-842-0463; Fax: 202-842-9126
www.nopa.org

Thomas Hammer, President
David Hovermale, EVP, Government Relations
Cost: $50.00
Founded in 1929

10182 Transactions of the American Fisheries Society
American Fisheries Society
425 Barlow Place
Suite 110
Bethesda, MD 20814-2144

301-897-8616; Fax: 301-897-8096
main@fisheries.org
fisheries.org

Douglas Austen, Executive Director
Erin Del Collo, Membership Coordinator
Laura Hendee, Journals Production Manager

Features results of basic and applied research in genetics, physiology, biology, ecology, population dynamics, economics, health, culture, and other topics germane to marine and freshwater finfish and shellfish and their respective fisheries and environments.
Cost: $43.00
Frequency: Bi-Monthly
ISSN: 0002-8487
Founded in 1872

10183 Tree Fruit
Western Agricultural Publishing Company
4969 E Clinton Way
#104
Fresno, CA 93727-1546

559-252-7000
888-382-9772; Fax: 559-252-7387

Paul Baltimore, Publisher
Randy Bailey, Editor
Robert Fujimoto, Assistant Editor

For tree fruit growers in California.

10184 Truth About Organic Foods
Henderson Communications LLC
1422 Elbridge Payne Rd
Suite 250
Chesterfield, MO 63017-8544

636-728-1428; Fax: 636-777-4178
info@agrimarketing.com
www.agrimarketing.com

Lynn Henderson, Owner

This 231-page book provides a fair and balanced look from a scientific standpoint about the heritage, production and nutritive value of organic foods.

10185 US Beer Market: Impact Databank Review and Forecast
M Shanken Communications
387 Park Ave S
8th Floor
New York, NY 10016-8872

212-684-4224; Fax: 212-684-5424
impact@mshanken.com
www.cigaraficionado.com

Marvin Shanken, Publisher
Cost: $895.00
Frequency: Annual+
Founded in 1972

10186 US Fast Food and Multi-Unit Restaurants
Business Trend Analysts/Industry Reports
2171 Jericho Tpke
Suite 200
Commack, NY 11725-2937

631-462-5454
800-866-4648; Fax: 631-462-1842
www.businesstrendanalysts.com

Charles J Ritchie, Executive VP
Donna Priani, General Manager

This survey offers information on the fast food industry, including chains and franchises.
Cost: $1995.00
Founded in 1986

10187 US Liquor Industry
Business Trend Analysts/Industry Reports
2171 Jericho Tpke
Suite 200
Commack, NY 11725-2937

631-462-5454; Fax: 631-462-1842
www.businesstrendanalysts.com

Charles J Ritchie, Executive VP
Donna Priani, Marketing Director

A survey summarizing the past, current and future markets and trends in the liquor industry.
Cost: $1495.00
Founded in 1999

10188 US Market for Bakery Products
Business Trend Analysts/Industry Reports
2171 Jericho Tpke
Suite 200
Commack, NY 11725-2937

631-462-5454
800-866-4648; Fax: 631-462-1842
www.businesstrendanalysts.com/

Charles J Ritchie, Executive VP
Donna Priani, General Manager

Profiles markets for bread, rolls, cakes, pies, cookies, crackers, other sweets and pretzels; provides information on consumption patterns, distribution trends, pricing, new products, and advertising strategies.
Cost: $1495.00
Frequency: Annual+
Founded in 1978

10189 Valley Potato Grower
Ola Highway 2 E
East Grand Forks, MN 56721

218-773-7783; Fax: 218-773-6227
communication@nppga.org
www.rrvpotatoes.org

Duane W Maatz, President
Ted Kreis, Marketing

Information on potato farming.
Cost: $17.95
Frequency: Monthly
Founded in 1946

10190 Vegetable
US Department of Agriculture
PO Box 1258
Sacramento, CA 95812-1258

Home Page: www.usda.gov

Chris Smith, Chief Information Officer
Matt Paul, Director of Communications
Ramona Romero, General Counsel

Historic information relating to various types of vegetable crops.

10191 Vegetable Growers News
Great American Publishing
75 Applewood Drive Suite A
PO Box 128
Sparta, MI 49345-1531

616-887-9008; Fax: 616-887-2666
www.vegetablegrowersnews.com

Kimberly Warren, Managing Editor
Matt McCallum, Executive Publisher
Erica Bernard, Circulation Manager
Jill Peck, Creative Director
Greg Ryan, Graphic Designer

Market and marketing news.
Cost: $12.00
Frequency: Monthly
Circulation: 14000
Founded in 1970

10192 Vegetables
Western Agricultural Publishing Company
4969 E Clinton Way
#104
Fresno, CA 93727-1549

559-252-7000
888-382-9772; Fax: 559-252-7387

Paul Baltimore, Publisher
Randy Bailey, Editor
Robert Fujimoto, Assistant Editor

The definitive source for information on all aspects of western vegetable production.

10193 Vegetarian Journal
Vegetarian Resource Group
PO Box 1463
Baltimore, MD 21203

410-366-8343; Fax: 410-366-8804
vrg@vrg.org
www.vrg.org

Debra Wasserman, Director
Jeanne Yacoubou, Research Director

A magazine for those interested in vegetarian and vegan health, ecology, and ethics.
10000 Members
Frequency: Quarterly
Founded in 1982

10194 Veggie Life Magazine
EGW
4075 Papazian Way
Suite 204
Fremont, CA 94538-4372

510-668-0268; Fax: 510-668-0280
www.veggielife.net

Chris Slaughter, VP
Shanna Masters, Editor

The modem voice on seasonal vegetarian cooking, optimum nutrition, and natural healing for today's health-conscious consumer features vaulable tips techniques, recipes, and remedies from dieticians, herbalists, doctors and other health experts on new ways to prpare creative plant-based cuisine, implement diet programs, and use natural remedies for an improved and vibrant lifestyle.
Cost: $19.96
68 Pages
Frequency: Quarterly
Circulation: 80000
Founded in 1980

10195 Vineyard and Winery Management
Vineyard & Winery Management
421 E Street
P.O. Box 14459
Santa Rosa, CA 95404
707-577-7700
800-535-5670; Fax: 707-577-7705
www.vwmmedia.com
Robert Merletti, CEO/Publisher
Jason Thomas, Business Manager
Tina Caputo, Editor-in-Chief
Ethan Simon, Director of Sales
Suzanne Webb, Marketing Director
Leading independent and award-winning wine trade magazine serving all of North America.
Cost: $37.00
100 Pages
Frequency: Bi-monthly
Circulation: 6900
ISSN: 1047-4951
Founded in 1975
Printed in 4 colors on glossy stock

10196 WATT Poultry Magazine
WATT Poultry USA
122 S Wesley Ave
Mt Morris, IL 61054-1451
815-734-7937; Fax: 815-734-4201
www.wattnet.com
James Watt, President
Charles Olentine, Publisher
Gary Thornton, Editor
Dedicated to supporting every phase of the turkey industry by providing information for decision-makers on breeding, production, management, processing and marketing.

10197 Wallaces Farmer
Farm Progress Companies
255 38th Avenue
Suite P
St Charles, IL 60174-5410
630-462-2224
800-441-1410
rswoboda@farmprogress.com
www.farmprogress.com
Rod Swoboda, Editor
Willie Vogt, Corporate Editorial Director
Frank Holdmeyer, Executive Editor
Serves Iowa farmers and ranchers with information to help them maximize their productivity and profitability. Each issue is packed with information, ideas, news and analysis.
Cost: $26.95
Frequency: Monthly
Founded in 1855

10198 Western Dairy Business
DairyBusiness Communications
6437 Collamer Road
East Syracuse, NY 13057-1031
315-703-7979
866-520-2880; Fax: 315-703-7988
circ@dairybusiness.com
www.dairybusiness.com
Ron Goble, Associate Publisher
Cecilia Parsons, Associate Editor
Scott A Smith, CEO
Business resource for successful milk producers. Covers 13 Western states. Provides information and news that is helpful in the daily operations of dairymen.
Cost: $38.95
67 Pages
Frequency: Monthly
Circulation: 14000
ISSN: 1528-4360
Founded in 1904
Printed in 4 colors on glossy stock

10199 Western Farm Press
Primedia
2104 Harvell Circle
Bellevue, NE 68005
913-341-1300
866-505-7173; Fax: 913-967-1898
wfcs@pbsub.com
www.westernfarmpress.com
Facebook, Twitter
Robert Fraser, Managing Editor
Harry Cline, Editor
Greg Frey, Publisher
Darrah Parker, Marketing Director
Timely reliable information for western agriculture.
Circulation: 16,000
Founded in 1989

10200 Western Fruit Grower
Meister Media Worldwide
37733 Euclid Ave
Willoughby, OH 44094-5992
440-942-2000
800-572-7740; Fax: 440-975-3447
www.meisternet.com
Gary Fitzgerald, President
Brian Sparks, Editor
Terry Doak, Circulation Manager
Edited for commercial growers of deciduous crops and citrus fruit, nut grape crops in the Western US.
Cost: $20.00
66 Pages
Frequency: Monthly
Circulation: 36,000

10201 Western Grocery News
80 Willow Road
Menlo Park, CA 94025-3661
650-321-3600
800-227-7346; Fax: 650-327-7537
Frequency: Bi-Monthly
Circulation: 9,187

10202 Western Growers & Shippers
Western Growers Association
PO Box 2130
Newport Beach, CA 92658-8944
949-863-1000; Fax: 949-863-9028
www.wga.com
Tom Nassif, President
Tim Linden, Editor
Listing over 3,000 growers, shippers, packers, brokers and distributors of fruits and vegetables in California and Arizona.
32 Pages
Frequency: Monthly
Circulation: 5000
ISSN: 0043-3799
Founded in 1926
Printed in 4 colors on glossy stock

10203 Western Livestock Journal
Crow Publications
7355 E Orchard Road
Suite 300
Greenwood Village, CO 80111
303-722-7600
800-850-2769; Fax: 303-722-0155
editorial@wlj.net
www.wlj.net
Pete Crow, Publisher
Offers its readers the best coverage of timely, necessary news and information that affects the livestock industry, particularly cattle.
Cost: $45.00
Frequency: Weekly
Founded in 1922

10204 Whole Foods Magazine
WFC
4041g Hadley Rd
Suite 101
South Plainfiel, NJ 07080-1120
908-769-1160; Fax: 908-769-1171
info@wfcinc.com
www.wfcinc.com
Facebook, Twitter, LinkedIn
Howard Wainer, President
Kaylynn Ebner, Editor
Ronda Collins, Circulation Manager
Tim Person, Assistant Editor
Serves the natural/health products industry.
Cost: $70.00
Frequency: Monthly
Founded in 1979
Printed in on glossy stock

10205 Wine Advocate
Robert M Parker Jr
PO Box 311
Monkton, MD 21111
410-329-6477; Fax: 410-357-4504
wineadvocate@erobertparker.com
www.erobertparker.com
Robert M Parker Jr, Editor/CEO
Daniel Thomases, Partner
An independent magazine covering reviews of wine.
Cost: $60.00
64 Pages
Frequency: Bi-monthly
Circulation: 40000
Founded in 1978

10206 Wine World
Wine World Publishing
6433 Topanga Canyon Boulevard
#412
Canoga Park, CA 91303-2621
Dee Snidt, Editor
For the wine consumer and industry.
Cost: $16.00
48 Pages
Frequency: Monthly
Founded in 1971

10207 Wines & Vines
1800 Lincoln Ave
San Rafael, CA 94901-1298
415-453-9700; Fax: 415-453-2517
info@winesandvines.com
www.winesandvines.com
Chet Klingensmith, Publisher
Kendra Campbell, Director of Sales and Marketing
Tina Caputo, Editor
Jacques Brix, Vice President
Voice of the grape and wine industry.
Cost: $32.50
Frequency: Monthly
Circulation: 3200
Founded in 1919
Printed in 4 colors on matte stock

10208 Yankee Food Service
201 Oak Street
Suite A
Pembroke, MA 02359
781-829-4700
866-677-4700; Fax: 781-829-0134
info@griffinpublishing.net
www.griffinpublishing.net
Stephen M Griffin, President
Jack Walsh, Vice President
Karen Harty, Vice President
Julie Mignosa, Office Manager

Reports news and happenings of the food service industry in New England.
Cost: $47.00
48 Pages
Frequency: Monthly
Circulation: 22,111
Founded in 1970

Trade Shows

10209 A Year of Enchantment
Int'l Council on Hotel, Restaurant Institute Edu.
1200 17th Street NW
Washington, DC 20036-3006
202-467-6300
publications@chrie.org
www.chrie.org
Susan Gould, Manager
Joseph Bradley, Treasurer
Containing over 70 booths and over 50 exhibits.
750 Attendees
Frequency: August
Founded in 1946

10210 AACC International Annual Meeting
3340 Pilot Knob Road
St. Paul, MN 55121-2055
651-454-7250
800-328-7560; Fax: 651-454-0766
aacc@scisoc.org
www.aaccnet.org
Facebook, Twitter, LinkedIn
Robert L. Cracknell, President
Lydia Tooker Midness, Chair
Laura M. Hansen, President-Elect
Dave L. Braun, Treasurer
Formerly the American Association of Cereal Chemists, the AACC meeting offers the chance to come together, network with peers, discuss critical issues in the science and discover the methods of others.
Frequency: Annual/October

10211 AACT Technical Conference
American Association of Candy Technologists
711 W. Water St.
PO Box 266
Princeton, WI 54968
920-295-6969; Fax: 920-295-6843
aactinfo@gomc.com
www.aactcandy.org
Bob Huzinec, President
Bill Dyer, First VP
Approximately 20 papers are presented to an audience of technologists in the sweet goods industry. These talks range from basics to innovations, provising the industry with practical information to help in understanding processes and ingredients used by their companies.
300 Attendees
Frequency: Annual/October

10212 AAEA Annual Meeting
Agricultural & Applied Economics Association
555 E Wells Street
Suite 1100
Milwaukee, WI 53202-6600
414-918-3190; Fax: 414-276-3349
www.aaea.org
Dawn Thilmany McFadden, President
Annual meeting and trade show for those interested in the fields of agricultural and applied economics.
3000 Members
Frequency: Annual/August
Founded in 1910

10213 AAW Annual Convention
American Agri-Women
2103 Zeandale Road
Manhattan, KS 66502
785-537-6171; Fax: 785-537-9727
www.americanagriwomen.org
Marcie Williams, President
Tradeshow consisting of products of interest to women in agriculture.
350 Attendees
Frequency: Annual/November

10214 ABI/ADPI Joint Annual Meeting
American Butter Institute
2101 Wilson Boulevard
Suite 400
Arlington, VA 22201
703-243-6111; Fax: 703-841-9328
AMiner@nmpf.org
Jerome J Kozak, Executive Director
Chris Galen, Communications VP
This event is co-sponsored by The American Dairy Products Institute for manufacturers, marketers and suppliers of manufactured dairy products. 35 exhibitors.
700 Attendees
Frequency: Annual

10215 ABL Annual Meeting
American Beverage Licensees
5101 River Road
Suite 108
Bethesda, MD 20816-1560
301-656-1494; Fax: 301-656-7539
www.ablusa.org
John Bodnovich, Executive Director
Annual show of 75 manufacturers, suppliers and distributors of alcoholic beverages.
1,000 Attendees

10216 ACF National Convention
American Culinary Federation
180 Center Place Way
St. Augustine, FL 32095
904-824-4468
800-624-9458; Fax: 904-940-0741
acf@acfchefs.net
www.acfchefs.org
Brent Frei, Director Marketing
Michael Baskette, Administrative Assistant
Michael Feierstein, Administrative Assistant
Bryan Hunt, Graphic Designer
Patricia Carroll, Director of Communications
200 booths of products and foodstuffs for the food service industry. Seminars, workshops, cooking demos, more.

10217 ACFSA Conference
Assn. of Correctional Food Service Sffiliates
PO Box 10065en Road
Burbank, CA 91510
818-843-6608; Fax: 818-843-7423
www.acfsa.org
Jon Nichols, Executive Director
Annual exhibit of 200 exhibitors of food products, kitchen equipment, food processing equipment, dining facility equipment, tableware and related food service equipment.
450 Attendees
Founded in 1999
Mailing list available for rentat $200 per M

10218 ACS Annual Conference and Competition
American Cheese Society
304 W Liberty Street
Suite 201
Louisville, KY 40202
502-583-3783; Fax: 502-589-3602
mwilson@hqtrs.com
www.cheesesociety.org
Marci Wilson, Executive Director
Carlos Scrivener, Manager
This Conference and Competition offers a unique opportunity to learn the latest about cheese in America and indulge your cheese fantasies by tasting more than 700 American artisan and specialty cheeses.
Frequency: Associate Fee

10219 ADPI/ABI Annual Conference
American Dairy Products Institute
126 N Addison St
Elmhurst, IL 60126
630-530-8700; Fax: 630-530-8707
info@adpi.org
www.adpi.org
Dale Kleber, CEO
Held in Chicago, this event attracts programs, the annual meeting, and the exhibition hall. Fifty exhibits of equipment and supplies for condensed milk, dry and evaporated milk and whey products, plus conference, seminar, workshop and banquet.
650 Attendees
Frequency: Annual/April

10220 AEA National Convention
American Emu Association
PO Box 2502
San Angelo, TX 76902
541-332-0675
info@aea-emu.org
www.aea-emu.org
Charles Ramey, President
Martha Hendricks, VP
This convention provides a chance for the AEA Board of Directors (AEA-BOD) to meet, face to face, during the week prior to the actual convention. It is a place for members to gather to learn the latest information and research about the emu industry, see the latest new products and network with other emu growers from across the U.S. and around the world.
Frequency: July/Non-Member $230

10221 AFBF Annual Convention & Trade Show
600 Maryland Ave SW
Suite 1000 W
Washington, DC 20024
202-406-3600
www.fb.org/events/afbf-annual-convention
Exhibits of farm equipment, chemical fertilizers and agricultural equipment and supplies.
Frequency: Annual/January

10222 AFBF Young Farmers & Ranchers Conference
600 Maryland Ave SW
Suite 1000 W
Washington, DC 20024
202-406-3600
yfr@fb.org
www.fb.org/events/2018-young-farmers-ranchers-conference
Development event for young farmers and ranchers.

10223 AFFI Frozen Food Convention
American Frozen Food Institute

2000 Corporate Ridge, Blvd.
Suite 1000
McLean, VA 22102-7862

703-821-0770; Fax: 703-821-1350
info@affi.com
www.affi.com

Kraig R Naasz, President/CEO
Thomas Bradshaw, Manager Legislative Affairs
Corey Henry, VP Communications
Robert L Garfield, SVP Public Policy/Intl Affairs

Learn more about the frozen food industry, network with peers, see new research, and get higher education.
500 Members
Founded in 1942

10224 **AFFI-Con**
American Frozen Food Institute
2000 Corporate Ridge Blvd
Suite 1000
McLean, VA 22102

703-821-0770; Fax: 703-821-1350
info@affi.com
www.affi.com

Mary Becton, Conference Director

Helping you make connections and helping you be better informed about industry issues.
1500 Attendees
Frequency: Annual/February

10225 **AFS Annual Meeting**
American Fisheries Society
425 Barlow Place
Suite 110
Bethesda, MD 20814-2144

301-897-8616; Fax: 301-897-8096
sjohnston@fisheries.org
afsannualmeeting.fisheries.org
Facebook, Twitter, LinkedIn, Pinterest, Google+, Vimeo

Douglas Austen, Executive Director
Erin Del Collo, Membership Coordinator
Katrina Dunn, Director of Development
Shawn Johnston, Meetings Manager
Steven Kambouris, Meetings & Program Coordinator

Held in conjunction with American Institute of Fishery Research Biologists. Explore the interrelation between fish, aquatic habitats and man; highlight challenges facing aquatic resource professionals and the methods that have been employed to resolve conflicts between those that use or have an interest in our aquatic resources.
Frequency: Annual/September

10226 **AMI International Meat, Poultry & Seafood Convention and Exposition**
Convention Mangement Group
10472 Armstrong Street
Fairfax, VA 22031

703-934-4700; Fax: 703-934-4899
www.amiexpo.com
Facebook, Twitter, LinkedIn

Anne Halal, Convention/Member Services VP
Anne Nuttall, Convention/Members Director
Katie Brannan, Convention/Members Sr. Manager

Sponsored by the American Meat Institute it features exhibits featuring the latest innovations in processing and packaging equipment, business and processing software systems, supplies, services and formulations.
25000 Attendees
Frequency: Annual/April

10227 **AMSA Reciprocal Meat Conference**
American Meat Science Association
2441 Village Green Place
Champaign, IL 61822

217-356-5370
800-517-AMSA; Fax: 888-205-5834; Fax: 217-356-5370
information@meatscience.org
www.meatscience.org\rmc

Dean Pringle, President
Collette Kaster, Chief Executive Officer

RMC is the annual meeting for AMSA, featuring an interactive program tailored to bring attendees the very best and inspiring educational experience. Attendees are professionals in academia, government and industry, as well as students in the meat, food and animal science fields.
Frequency: Annual

10228 **AOCS Annual Meeting & Exposition**
American Oil Chemists' Society
2710 S Boulder
Urbana, IL 61802-6996

217-359-2344; Fax: 217-359-8091
meetings@aocs.org
www.aocs.org

Nurhan Dunford, General Chairperson
Mindy Cain, Meetings Specialist

The premier global science and business forum on fats, oils, surfactants, lipids, and related materials. Includes oral and poster presentations, short courses, and exhibit, and networking with more than 1,600 colleagues from 60 countries.
2000 Attendees
Frequency: Annual/April

10229 **APA Annual Meeting**
Apple Processors Association
1701 K Street NW
Suite 650
Washington, DC 20006

202-785-6715; Fax: 202-331-4212
pweller@agriwashington.org
www.appleprocessors.org
Facebook

Andrea Ball, President
Paul S. Weller, Jr., EVP, Communications
Elizabeth Johnson, VP, Food & Nutrition Policy
Jacquie Ball, Director, Administration

A three-day meeting which brings top industry and consumer experts together for a dialogue on timely issues. These include marketing tips, packaging trends, consumer research, and media reports and reaction to industry initiatives.
Frequency: Annual/June

10230 **APS/CPS/MSA Annual Joint Meeting**
American Phytopathological Society
3340 Pilot Knob Road
Saint Paul, MN 55121-2097

651-454-7250
800-328-7560; Fax: 651-454-0766
aps@scisoc.org
www.apsnet.org
Facebook, Twitter, LinkedIn, YouTube

Megan Boatman, Meetings - Programs
Tori Clark, Meetings - Registration
Brianna Plank, Meetings - Exhibits, Sponsorship

Featuring over 18 state-of-the-art education sessions daily, over 700 poster presentations, one-of-a-kind preconvention tours and workshops and exhibits from leading suppliers.
Frequency: Annual/Summer

10231 **ASA/CSSA/SSSA International Annual Meeting**
American Society of Agronomy
677 S Segoe Road
Madison, WI 53711

608-273-8080; Fax: 608-273-2021
www.agronomy.org

Wes Meixelsperger, Director, Meetings
Stacey Giesen, Meetings Manager
Jeanne Pluemer, Senior Meetings Manager

Co-sponsored with Crop Science Society of America and with the Soil Science Society of America. This event is a unique convergence of the leading agronomy, crops, soils and environmental sciences professionals from around the world. A blend of technical sessions, poster sessions, social functions, career networking and exhibits draw a growing number of prominent professionals and students.
3,500 Attendees
Frequency: November
Founded in 1907

10232 **ASABE Annual International Meeting**
American Society of Agricultural & Biological Eng.
950 S Cherry Street
Suite 508
Denver, CO 80246-2664

303-759-5091; Fax: 303-758-0190
chesser@asabe.org
www.asabe.org

Michael Chesser, Meetings/Conference Director
Sharon McKnight, Meetings Support Staff

100 and more diverse technical sessions, 11 continuing professional development sessions, 5 technical tours, an industry exhibit hall and a keynote address from Dr. Lowell B. Catlett; this year's meeting is full of must attend events.
Frequency: July

10233 **ASBC Annual Meeting**
American Society of Brewing Chemists
3340 Pilot Knob Road
Saint Paul, MN 55121-2055

651-454-7250; Fax: 651-454-0766
bford@scisoc.org

Betty Ford, Meetings Director
Sue Casey, Meetings Coordinator
Steven Nelson, VP

Network with peers and learn about the latest technologies available to brewers.
300 Attendees
Frequency: Annual/June

10234 **ASHS Annual Conference**
American Society for Horticultural Science
1018 Duke Street
Alexandria, VA 22314

703-836-4606; Fax: 703-836-2024
www.ashs.org
Facebook, Twitter, LinkedIn

Michael W. Neff, Executive Director
Negar Mahdavian, Conference Manager
Angie Lower, Conference Manager

A place to meet with colleagues, talk with exhibitors and view over 400 posters.
Cost: $560.00
Frequency: Annual

10235 **ASTA/CSTA Joint Annual Convention**
American Seed Trade Association
225 Reinekers Lane
Suite 650
Alexandria, VA 22314-2875

703-837-8140; Fax: 703-837-9365
www.amseed.com

Jennifer Lord, Meetings Director
Jason Laney, Meetings Associate Director

Includes meetings of all divisions of ASTA and CSTA and several joint meetings of both organizations, exhibits, prominent keynote speakers relevant to both associations, sessions that include representatives discussing how seed moves through the pipelines of our industry to the end user and those whose roles affect the regulation and administration of the framework.
800 Attendees
Frequency: July/Fee $129-$799

10236 **AWMA Real Deal Expo**
American Wholesale Marketers Association
2750 Prosperity Avenue
Suite 530
Fairfax, VA 22031

703-208-3358; Fax: 703-573-5738
www.cdaweb.net

Marcia Barker, Public Affairs Manager
Nate Wills, Exhibit Information

The only trade show geared to convenience distributors. Exhibitors include purveyors of tobacco products, candy, beverages, snacks, foodservice, health and beauty care items, general merchandise, warehouse equipment, computer systems and much more.
2,500 Attendees
Frequency: Annual/February

10237 **AWS National Conference**
American Wine Society
P.O. Box 889
Scranton, PA 18501

888-297-9070
www.americanwinesociety.org

David Falchuk, Executive Director
Kristin Casler Kraft, President

The annual conference brings professional, serious amateurs and novices together to discover what is new in wine. Seminars and lectures on all aspects of wine appreciation, wine production, grape growing and cuisine. Attendees must be a member of the society.
Frequency: Annual/November
Founded in 1967

10238 **Ag Progress Days**
Penn State University Agricultural Sciences
420 Agricultural Administration Building
University Park, PA 16802

814-865-2081; Fax: 814-865-1677

Bob Oberheim, Manager

Agricultural trade show focusing on the innovations and progress made in the agricultural industry.
50M Attendees
Frequency: Annual/August

10239 **Agri News Farm Show**
Agri News
18 1st Avenue SE
Rochester, MN 55904-3722

507-857-7707
800-633-1727; Fax: 507-281-7474
www.agrinews.com

Rosie Allen, Advertising Manager
John Losness, President
Todd Heroff, Manager

Annual show of 160 exhibitors of farming equipment, supplies and services.
8000 Attendees
Frequency: March

10240 **Agri-Marketing Conference**
National Agri-Marketing Association
11020 King Street
Suite 205
Overland Park, KS 66210-1201

913-491-6500; Fax: 913-491-6502
agrimktg@nama.org
www.nama.org
Facebook, Twitter, LinkedIn, YouTube, Flickr

Jennifer Pickett, Executive VP & CEO

Learn more about customer behaviors, market shares, and other top industry tips.
3500 Members
Frequency: Annual/April
Founded in 1957

10241 **Agricultural Retailers Association Convention and Expo**
Agricultural Retailers Association
1156 15th Street
Suite 500
Washington, DC 20005

202-457-0825
800-844-4900; Fax: 314-567-6888
www.aradc.org

Daren Coppock, President/CEO
Richard Gupton, Sr. VP., Public Policy
Michelle Hummel, Dir., Comm. & Marketing

Annual show of 120 manufacturers, suppliers and distributors of agricultural chemicals and fertilizers. Seminar, conference and banquet.
1200 Attendees
Frequency: December, St. Louis

10242 **Agro-International Trade Fair for Agricultural Machinery & Equipment**
Glahe International
PO Box 2460
Germantown, MD 20875-2460

301-515-0012; Fax: 301-515-0016

Biennial show of agricultural machinery and equipment.

10243 **All Candy Expo**
National Confectioners Association
110 30th Street NW
Suite 200
Washington, DC 20007

202-534-1440
allcandyexpo.com

Theresa Delaney, Expo/Membership Director
Daria Moore, Exhibits Manager

A trade show offering exhibits of confectionery industry supplies.
5000+ Attendees
Frequency: Annual/June

10244 **All Things Organic Conference and Trade Show**
Organic Trade Association
28 Vernon St.
Suite 413
Brattleboro, VT 05301

802-275-3800; Fax: 802-275-3801
info@ota.com
www.ota.com

Christine Bushway, Executive Director
Linda Lutz, Membership Manager
Laura Batcha, Marketing/Public Relations Director

Join OTA members, Board and staff for association business, member meetings, and social and networking events.
Frequency: Annual/June

10245 **America's Supermarket Showcase**
National Grocer's Association
1825 Samuel Morse Drive
Reston, VA 20190

703-437-5300; Fax: 703-437-7768

Dan Rudt

350 exhibits of food and non food consumer goods and services, fixtures and equipment for supermarket operations. Workshop, conference, banquet, luncheon and tours.
5000 Attendees
Frequency: Annual
Founded in 1983

10246 **American Bakery Expo**
5 Executive Court
Suite 2
South Barrington, IL 60010

610-667-9600; Fax: 610-667-1475
www.americanbakers.org
Facebook, Twitter

Mark Gedris, Membership Manager

Sponsored by Retail Bakers of America and New York/New Jersey Bakers Association. A trade show, creative decorating competition, bakery arts and cakes display, industry chats, tips and trends demonstrations and seminars.
8000 Attendees
Frequency: Annual/October

10247 **American Butter Institute Annual Conference**
American Butter Institute
2101 Wilson Boulevard
Suite 400
Arlington, VA 22201

703-243-5630; Fax: 703-841-9328
AMiner@nmpf.org

The annual conference and meeting is a joint project between the American Butter Institute and the American Diary Products Institute. Over 600 manufacturers, marketers and suppliers of butter and dairy products are represented at the convention which offers the opportunity to network with industry professionals.
Frequency: Annual/November

10248 **American Convention of Meat Processors**
American Association of Meat Processors
One Meating Place
Elizabethtown, PA 17022

717-367-1168
aamp@aamp.com
www.aamp.com

Rick Reams, President
Chris Young, Executive Director
Diana Dietz, Communications Manager
Niki Cloud, Convention Manager
Jane Frey, Accounting Manager

This annual event features an educational program for operators, exhibits and displays by leading industry manufacturers and suppliers.
Frequency: Annual

10249 **American Convention of Meat Processors & Suppliers' Exhibit**
American Association of Meat Processors
One Meating Place
Elizabethtown, PA 17022

717-367-1168
aamp@aamp.com
www.aamp.com

Rick Reams, President
Chris Young, Executive Director
Diana Dietz, Communications Manager
Niki Cloud, Convention Manager
Jane Frey, Accounting Manager

Geared toward U.S., Canadian, and Foreign operators of small and very small firms in the meat, poultry & food business: packers, processors, wholesalers, HRI, retailers, caterers, deli operators, home food service dealers, and catalog marketers. Both members and non-members of the Association attend this event looking for a vast array of ideas, supplies, and services.
1400 Members
Founded in 1939

10250 **American Craft Beer Week**
Brewers Association
736 Pearl Street
Boulder, CO 80302

303-447-0816
888-822-6273; Fax: 303-447-2825
webmaster@brewersassociation.org
www.beertown.org
Facebook, Twitter

Chris P. Frey, Chair
Jake Keeler, Vice Chair
Roxanne Westendorf, Secretary

Celebrates craft brewers and craft beer culture in the US.
1900 Members
Founded in 1978

10251 **American Cured Meat Championships**
American Association of Meat Processors
One Meating Place
Elizabethtown, PA 17022

717-367-1168
aamp@aamp.com
www.aamp.com

Rick Reams, President
Chris Young, Executive Director
Diana Manager, Communications Manager
Niki Cloud, Convention Manager
Jane Frey, Accounting Manager

This competition is the only national event of its kind in North America. Meat processors enter their products for evaluation by judges who are meat scientists and specialists in the meat industry. This evaluation provides information for product enhancement that could result in greater sales and business opportunities.
1300+ Members
Founded in 1939

10252 **American Mushroom Institute**
North American Mushroom Conference
1 Massachusetts Avenue, Suite 800
Washington, DC 20001

202-842-4344; Fax: 202-408-7763

Laura Phelps, President

10253 **American Peanut Research and Education Society Annual Meeting**
American Peanut Research and Education Society
Oklahoma State University
376 Ag Hall
Stillwater, OK 74078

405-372-3052; Fax: 405-624-6718
www.apresinc.com/meetings/annual-meeting/

Ron Sholar, Executive Officer

Annual meetings of the Society are held for the presentation of papers and/or discussion, and for the transaction of business. At least one general business session will be held during regular annual meetings at which reports from the executive officer and all standing committees will be given to such other matters as the Board of Directors may determine.
Frequency: Annual/July

10254 **American Society for Enology and Viticulture Annual Meeting**
American Society for Enology and Vinticulture
PO Box 1855
Davis, CA 95617

530-753-3142; Fax: 530-753-3318
society@asev.org
www.asev.org

Michelle Taillon, Event Coordinator
Jen Smalley, Event & Trade Show Manager

With technical sessions, research forums, symposia and a supplier shocasw.
Frequency: June
Founded in 1951
Mailing list available for rent

10255 **American Spice Trade Association Annual Meeting**
2025 M Street NW
Washington, DC 20036

202-367-1127; Fax: 202-367-2127
info@astaspice.org
www.astaspice.org

Cheryl Deem, Executive Director

10256 **American Sugarbeet Growers Asscociation Annual Meeting**
American SugarBeet
1156 15th Street NW
Suite 101
Washington, DC 20005-1704

202-833-2398; Fax: 202-833-2962
www.americansugarbeet.org

Ruthann Geib, Meetings Director/VP
Luther Markwart, Executive VP
James Creek, Executive Assistant
Pam Alther, Office/Financial Manager

Attendees are primarily the officers and board members of these local associations and their spouses, as well as representatives of seed, chemical, and other supplier companies. The purpose of the Annual Meeting is to bring members up-to-date on legislative and international issues that affect the domestic sugar industry, and to determine future policy and strategies.
350 Attendees
Frequency: July/November
Founded in 1983

10257 **Animal Transportation Association**
PO Box 797095
Dallas, TX 75379-7095

FAX 214-769-2867

Cherie Derouin, Administrator
Sherry Lynne Boone, Administrative Assistant

An international association promoting the humane handling and transportation of animals.
10-15 booths.
150 Attendees
Frequency: Spring

10258 **Annual Chicken Marketing Seminar**
National Poultry & Food Distributors
2014 Osborne Road
Saint Marys, GA 31558

770-535-9901; Fax: 770-535-7385
www.npfda.org

Cece Corbin, President
Carol Lanham, Member Services & Development Dir.
Alina Cooper, Membership Relations & Comm. Dir.

Features a very informative program, great networking opportunities, and golf. Learn new techniques for greater marketing success.
Frequency: Annual/July
Founded in 1967

10259 **Annual Conference of the Food Distribution Research Society**
Food Distribution Research Society
PO Box 441110
Fort Washington, MD 20749

301-292-1970; Fax: 301-292-1787
Jonathan_baros@ncsu.edu

John Park, President
Ron Rainey, President-Elect
Kellie Raper, Secretary/ Treasurer
Jennifer Dennis, Director
Stan Ernst, Director

Meeting the quality demands of food buyers. Discuss how the industry is meeting these specific aspects of quality demands, and how these factors impact trade success, how members of the food chain are incorporating them in food production and handling, and how sensory examination is incorporated into food quality assurance, design and product development.
Frequency: Annual/October

10260 **Annual Food Manufacturing & Packaging Expo and Conference**
The Foodservice Group, Inc
PO Box 681864
Marietta, GA 30068-0032

770-971-8116; Fax: 770-971-1094
www.fsgroup.com

Chris Bresler, President
Brad Johnson, Vice President
Bob Sheridan, Secretary
Bryan Lewis, Treasurer

This event attracts a diverse range of professionals including CEO's, plant managers, puchasing managers, production and quality assurance managers, engineers, and sales/marketing managers as well as mechanics on the production floor. See and experience the latest technology, systems and related information to improve business operations.
Frequency: Annual/January

10261 **Annual Hotel, Motel and Restaurant Supply Show of the Southeast**
Leisure Time Unlimited
PO Box 332
Myrtle Beach, SC 29577

843-448-9483
800-261-5991; Fax: 843-626-1513
hmrss@sc.rr.com
www.hmrsss.com
Facebook, Twitter

Trade show for the hospitality industry.
23000 Attendees
Frequency: Annual/January

10262 **Annual Meat Conference**
American Meat Institute
1150 Connecticut Ave NW
12th Floor
Washington, DC 20036-4126

202-587-4200; Fax: 202-587-4300
Facebook, Twitter

Dennis Vignieri, Chairman
Larry Odom, Vice Chairman
Nick Meriggioli, Treasurer
Greg Benedict, Secretary
J. Patrick Boyle, President & CEO

The educational format of this conference includes a variety of ways to explore the latest developments in meat retailing today. Gain tools, insights, inspiration and new ideas to differentiate unique products and services, fortify marketing ROI, increase sales, and build customer loyalty.
300 Members
Frequency: Membership Fees Vary
Founded in 1906

10263 **Annual Sugar Outlook**
1300 L Street NW
Suite 1001
Washington, DC 20005

202-785-1122; Fax: 202-785-5019
sugar@sugar.org
www.sugar.org
Facebook, Twitter

Andrew Briscoe, President/CEO
Charles W Baker, Executive VP/Chief Science Officer
Melanie Miller, VP Public Relations
Cheryl Digges, VP Public Publicy & Education

To discuss sugar consumption and demand issues and initiatives.
Frequency: Annual/April

10264 Asia Food Processing & Packaging Technology Exhibition
Reed Exhibition Companies
383 Main Avenue
PO Box 6059
Norwalk, CT 06851
203-840-4800; Fax: 203-840-9628
One hundred and seventy four exhibitors for an audience of manufacturers, packaging design and development professionals.
Frequency: Biennial

10265 Associated Food Dealers Annual Trade Show
Associated Food Dealers of Michigan
18470 W Ten Mile
Southfield, MI 48075
248-557-9600; Fax: 248-557-9610
www.afpdonline.org
Ginny Bennett, Show Manager
Frequency: September

10266 Association for Dressing and Sauces Annual Meeting
1100 Johnson Ferry Road
Atlanta, GA 30342
404-252-3663; Fax: 404-252-0774
ads@kellencompany.com
www.dressings-sauces.org
Facebook
Pam Chumley, President
Jeannie Milewski, Executive Director
Jacque Knight, Membership/Administration Manager
Learn about the most up-to-date technologies and guidelines for packaging, food safety, emulsions and quality.
Frequency: Annual/October

10267 Association of College Unions International Conference
One City Centre, 120 W. 7th St.
Suite 200
Bloomington, IN 47404
812-245-2284; Fax: 812-245-6710
acui@acui.org
www.acui.org
Devon Bray, Marketing Coordinator
Jake Dawes, Events & Operations Coordinator
International conference with 100 exhibits of graphic supplies, recreation equipment, computer hardware & software, furnishings, entertainment and speaker bureau information, food service equipment, and more related information and supplies.
1000 Attendees
Frequency: Annual

10268 Atlantic Coast Exposition: Showcasing the Vending and Food Service Industry
InfoMarketing
2501 Aerial Center Parkway
Suite 103
Morrisville, NC 27560
919-459-2070; Fax: 919-459-2075
www.atlanticcoastexpo.com
Facebook
Sarah Gillian, Executive Director
This convention offers exhibits of vending machines, office coffee service products, commissary equipment, food and beverage products for the institututional market, as well as accountability systems and security devices.
3M Attendees
Frequency: Annual/May

10269 B&CMA Convention
Biscuit & Cracker Manufacturer's Association
6325 Woodside Court
Suite 125
Columbia, MD 21046
443-545-1645; Fax: 410-290-8585
www.thebcma.org
Stacey Sharpless, President
Kerry Kurowski, Education/Meetings Manager
Provides members an invaluable opportunity to network with fellow executives.
Founded in 1901

10270 BIF Annual Meeting and Research Symposium
Red Angus Association of America
4201 N Interstate 35
Denton, TX 76207-3415
940-387-3502; Fax: 888-829-5573
info@redangus.org
www.redangus.org
Facebook
Joe Mushrush, President
Greg Comstock, CEO
Seedstock and commercial cow-calf producers, university specialists and breed association leaders will gather to explore innovative technologies and management practices to improve beef production for the benefit of seedstock and commercial producers.
2000 Members
Founded in 1954

10271 BakingTech
American Society of Baking
7809 N Chestnut Avenue
Kansas City, MO 64119
800-713-0462; Fax: 888-315-2612
info@asbe.org
www.asbe.org
Leading baking industry technology conference and exposition.
1300 Attendees
Frequency: Annual

10272 Beer, Wine & Spirits Industry Trade Show
Indiana Association of Beverage
200 S Meridian Street
Suite 350
Indianapolis, IN 46225
317-684-7580; Fax: 317-673-4210
Teresa Koch, Show Manager
Annual show of 125 exhibitors of alcohol beverage distillers brewers that are recognized primary sources in the state of Indiana as supplies for retailers.
2500 Attendees

10273 Beltwide Cotton Conference
National Cotton Council of America
7193 Goodlett Farms Parkway
Cordova, TN 38016
901-274-9030; Fax: 901-725-0510
www.cotton.org/beltwide/
Gary Adams, President/CEO
Offers a forum for agricultural professionals.
Frequency: Annual/January

10274 Branding ID: Strategies to Drive Sales
Association of Sales & Marketing Companies
1010 Wisconsin Avenue NW #900
Washington, DC 20007
202-337-9351; Fax: 202-337-4508
Mark Baum, President
Karen Connell, Executive VP
Rick Abraham, VP/COO Foodservice
Jamie DeSimone, Director Marketing/Member Services
Frequency: March

10275 CMAA's World Conference on Club Management & Club Business Expo
Club Managers Association of America
1733 King Street
Alexandria, VA 22314
703-739-9500; Fax: 703-739-0124
cmaa@cmaa.org
www.cmaa.org
Guy Doria, Show Manager
Jim Singerling, Executive VP
Provides a variety of unique education opportunities that reflect the latest trends in the club industry.
5000 Attendees
Frequency: Annual/February

10276 California League of Food Processors Expo & Showcase of Processed Foods
980 Ninth Street
Sacremento, CA 95814
916-444-9260; Fax: 916-444-2746
www.clfp.com
Robert Graf, President/CEO
Ed Yates, Senior VP
Nora Basrai, Meetings/Members Services
Rob Neenan, Senior Vice President
Amy Alcorn, Marketing Manager
Information, networking and displays of processed food from apricots to zucchini in every package type imaginable.
Frequency: January
Founded in 1905

10277 Candy Hall of Fame
National Confectionery Sales Association
Spitfire House
3135 Berea Road
Cleveland, OH 44111
216-631-8200; Fax: 216-631-8210
info@candyhalloffame.org
Facebook, Twitter
Michael F. Gilmore, Chairman
Alastair Northway, President
Mark Antonucci, 1st Vice President
Joe Muck, 2nd Vice President
Morton B. Gleit, Treasurer
Recognizes the achievements of industry leaders drawn from across the world. Inductees are selected from numerous nominations of candy brokers, sales personnel, manufacturers, retail buyers, wholesalers, industry suppliers, retail confectioners and others allied to the industry.
375 Members
Founded in 1899

10278 CaterSource
PO Box 14776
Chicago, IL 60614
773-525-6800
800-932-3632; Fax: 800-387-4744
info@catersource.com
www.catersource.com
Micheal Roman, President
Jean Blackmer, Creative Director
Laurie Scheel, Advertising Director

10279 Cattle Industry Convention
Red Angus Association of America

4201 N Interstate 35
Denton, TX 76207-3415
940-387-3502; Fax: 888-829-5573
info@redangus.org
www.redangus.org
Facebook
Joe Mushrush, President
Greg Comstock, CEO
The oldest and largest convention for the cattle business. The convention and trade show create a unique, fun environment for cattle industry members to come together to network, create policy for the industry and to have some fun.
2000 Members
Founded in 1954

10280 **Chicken Marketing Seminar**
National Chicken Council
1015 15th Street NW
Suite 930
Washington, DC 20005-2622
202-296-2622; Fax: 202-293-4005
ncc@chickenusa.org
www.nationalchickencouncil.org
Facebook
Michael J. Brown, President
William P. Roenigk, Senior Vice President
Mary M. Colville, VP of Government Affairs
Dr. Ashley Peterson, VP of Science & Technology
Brings together poultry marketing and sales managers, distributors, supermarket and foodservice buyers, further processors, traders and brokers, and other executives working in the chicken industry. Informative general sessions, social networking events, and recreational opportunities.
Frequency: Annual/July
Founded in 1954

10281 **Commodity Classic**
American Soybean Association
12125 Woodcrest Executive Drive
Suite 100
Saint Louis, MO 63141-5009
314-576-1770
800-688-7692; Fax: 314-576-2786
registration@commodityclassic.com
www.commodityclassic.com
Meeting and exhibits of soybean industry related equipment and information.
4000 Attendees
Frequency: Annual/March

10282 **Conference on New Food & Beverage Concepts Innovators**
NorthStar Conference
1211 Avenue of the Americas
New York, NY 10036
212-596-6006; Fax: 212-596-6092
www.northstarconference.com
Cheryl Callahan, Marketing Director

10283 **Council of Food Processors Association Annual Convention**
1401 New York Avenue NW
Suite 400
Washington, DC 20005-2124
202-471-1835; Fax: 202-639-5932
John Cady, President
Barbara Arnwine, Executive Director

10284 **Craft Brewers Conference and Brew Expo America**
Brewers Association
736 Pearl Street
Boulder, CO 80302
303-447-0816
888-822-6273; Fax: 303-447-2825
www.craftbrewersconference.com
Charlie Papazian, President
Bob Pease, VP
Cindy Jones, Sales/Marketing Director
For professional brewers, CBC is the number one environment in North America for concentrated, affordable brewing education and idea sharing to improve brewery quality and performance.
2600 Attendees
Frequency: Annual/May

10285 **Crop Life America & RISE Spring Conference**
Crop Life America
1156 15th St NW
Washington, DC 20005-1752
202-296-1585; Fax: 202-463-0474
webmaster@croplifeamerica.org
www.croplifeamerica.org
Facebook, Twitter, LinkedIn, YouTube
Christopher Novak, President & CEO
Discuss the most up-to-date science and regulatory issues impacting the crop protection and specialty pesticide industries.
Frequency: Annual/April

10286 **Crop Science Society of America Meeting and Exhibits**
Crop Science Society of America
677 S Segoe Road
Madison, WI 53711-1048
608-273-8086; Fax: 608-273-2021
tmoeller@agronomy.org
www.crops.org
John Nicholiadis, Managing Editor
David M Kral, Associate Executive VP
Ellen Bergfeld, Executive VP
Annual exhibits of agricultural equipment, supplies and services.
Frequency: October

10287 **Dairy-Deli-Bake Seminar & Expo**
International Dairy-Deli-Bakery Association
636 Science Drive
Madison, WI 53711-1073
608-310-5000; Fax: 608-238-6330
iddba@iddba.org
www.iddba.org
Judy Valaskey, Membership Coordinator
The largest show in the world serving these categories. Also the most focused show because it only targets the serious buyers, merchandisers, and executives who have a shared passion for food.
7000 Attendees
Frequency: Annual/June

10288 **Distribution Solutions Conference**
International Foodservice Distributors Association
1660 International Drive
Suite 550
McLean, VA 22102
703-532-9400; Fax: 703-880-7117
www.ifdaonline.org
Mark Allen, President & CEO
Includes a robust operations agenda that incorporates warehouse and transportation issues, plus a powerful executive track, people issues in an HR track, and special sessions on convenience distribution and supply chain issues.
Frequency: Annual/October

10289 **Dixie Classic Fair**
City of Winston-Salem
PO Box 7525
Winston-Salem, NC 27109
336-727-2236; Fax: 336-727-2236
David Sparks, Executive Director

10290 **EMDA Industry Showcase**
Equipment Marketing & Distribution Association
PO Box 1347
Iowa City, IA 52244
319-354-5156
pat@emda.net
www.emda.net
Patricia A. Collins, Executive Vice President
Annual convention and 130 exhibits of equipments, supplies and services for wholesaler-distributor and independent manufacturer's representatives of shortline and specialty farm equipment, light industrial, lawn and garden, turf care equipment, eestate and park maintenance equipment.
600 Attendees
Frequency: Annual/November

10291 **EastPack**
Cannon Communications
11444 W Olympic Boulevard
Los Angeles, CA 90064-1549
323-755-7646; Fax: 310-996-9499
www.eastpackshow.com

10292 **El Foro**
WATT Publishing Company
122 S Wesley Avenue
Mount Morris, IL 61054-1497
815-734-4171; Fax: 815-734-7727
www.wattnet.com
James Watt, Owner
A trade show and technical symposium for the Latin American poultry, pig and feed industries. Containing 50 booths and 150 exhibits.
275 Attendees
Frequency: July

10293 **Executive Conference**
Association of Sales & Marketing Companies
1010 Wisconsin Avenue NW
#900
Washington, DC 20007
202-337-9351; Fax: 202-337-4508
Mark Baum, President
Karen Connell, Executive VP
Rick Abraham, VP/COO Foodservice
Jamie DeSimone, Director Marketing/Member Services
Frequency: July

10294 **Executive Leadership Forum**
Snack Food Association
1600 Wilson Blvd
Suite 650
Arlington, VA 22209-2510
703-836-4500
800-628-1334; Fax: 703-836-8262
www.sfa.org
James A McCarthy, President/CEO
An invitation only event for CEO's and senior level executives in the international snack food industry.
800 Members
Frequency: Annual/September
Founded in 1937

10295 **Expo Carnes**
Consejo Mexicano de la Carne

Ave. Parque Fundidora
#505 Loc. 88, P.N. Col. Obrera
Monterrey N.L. Mexico

52(81)8369 6660; Fax: 52(81)8369 6732
lsierra@apex.org.mx
www.expocarnes.com

The every other year Meat Industry International Exposition and Convention that brings together meat suppliers, meat packers and other sectors of the meat industry, facilitating meat specialists from around the world to do business in Latin America. This event takes place in February 2011.
150 Members

10296 **Expo of the Americas**
EJ Krause & Associates
6550 Rock Spring Drive
Suite 500
Bethesda, MD 20817-1126

301-493-5500; Fax: 301-493-5705
www.ejkrause.com

Ned Krause, President

Annual show and exhibits of hotel and restaurant food and beverages.

10297 **FEDA Annual Conference**
Foodservice Equipment Distributors Association
5600 N River Road
Suite 740
Rosemont, IL 60018

224-293-6500
info@feda.com
www.feda.com

Tracy Mulqueen, CEO
George Maul, Director, Finance & Operations
Tim O'Connor, Communications Manager

Dealers and distributors of foodservice equipment and supplies.

10298 **FEMA Annual Convention**
FEMA
1620 I Street NW
Suite 925
Washington, DC 20006

202-293-5800; Fax: 202-462-8998
www.femaflavor.org
YouTube

Ed R. Hays, Ph.D., President
George C. Robinson, III, President Elect
Mark Scott, Treasurer
Arthur Schick, VP & Secretary
John Cox, Executive Director

FEMA is comprised of flavor manufacturers, flavor users, flavor ingredient suppliers and others with an interest in the U.S. flavor industry.
Founded in 1909

10299 **FEMA Winter Committee Meetings**
FEMA
1620 I Street NW
Suite 925
Washington, DC 20006

202-293-5800; Fax: 202-462-8998
www.femaflavor.org
YouTube

Ed R. Hays, Ph.D., President
George C. Robinson, III, President Elect
Mark Scott, Treasurer
Arthur Schick, VP & Secretary
John Cox, Executive Director

FEMA is comprised of flavor manufacturers, flavor users, flavor ingredient suppliers and others with an interest in the U.S. flavor industry.
Founded in 1909

10300 **FIAE Annual Convention**
Food Industry Association Executives
5657 W. 10770 North
Highland, UT 84003-2711

801-599-1095; Fax: 815-550-1731
www.fiae.net

Jim Olsen, President

Format of the convention continues to provide valuable information and networking opportunities.
125 Members
Frequency: Annual/November
Founded in 1927

10301 **FMI/AMI Annual Meat Conference**
American Meat Institute
1150 Connecticut Avenue NW
Washington, DC 20036

202-587-4200; Fax: 202-587-4223
www.meatconference.com

Eric Zito, Manager, Convention & Member Svcs

400 booths for equipment, supplies and services to the meat-packaging industry.
12M Attendees
Frequency: Annual/Spring

10302 **FPSA Annual Conference**
Food Processing Suppliers Association
1451 Dolley Madison Blvd
Suite 101
Mc Lean, VA 22101-3850

703-761-2600; Fax: 703-761-4334
info@fpsa.org
www.fpsa.org
Facebook, Twitter, LinkedIn

David Seckman, President
George Melnykovich, Senior Advisor
Robyn Roche, CFO

Where suppliers to the food and beverage industry connet and network. Ample opportunity is given to network with peers as participants expand their industry knowledge through educational business sessions and research roundtables.
510 Members
Frequency: Annual/November
Founded in 2005

10303 **Farm Progress Show**
Farm Progress Companies
255 38th Avenue
Suite P
St Charles, IL 60174-5410

630-462-2224
800-441-1410
drovner@farmprogress.com
www.farmprogressshow.com
Facebook, Twitter

Matt Jungmann, National Shows Manager

Annual farm show of 400 exhibitors representing various types of agricultural products and services for farmers and agribusiness, including small operations to top producers.
Frequency: Annual/August

10304 **Farm Science Review**
Ohio State University
590 Woody Hayes Drive
Agricultural Engr. Building- Rm 232
Columbus, OH 43210

614-292-3671
800-644-6377; Fax: 614-292-9448
fendrick.1@osu.edu
fsr.osu.edu
Facebook, Twitter, YouTube, Flickr

Craig Fendrick, Manager

Annual show of 625 exhibitors of agricultural equipment, supplies and services.
140M Attendees
Frequency: Annual/September

10305 **Farmfest**
Farm Fairs
PO Box 731
Lake Crystal, MN 56055-0731

507-726-6863
800-347-5863; Fax: 507-726-6750

Annual show of 450 manufacturers, suppliers and distributors of farm equipment and machinery, computers and software products, chemicals, seeds and crops, and techniques of planting, tillage and harvesting.
50M Attendees

10306 **Fertilizer Outlook and Technology Conference**
Fertilizer Institute
425 Third Street, SW
Suite 950
Washington, DC 20024

202-962-0490; Fax: 202-962-0577
information@tfi.org
www.tfi.org
Facebook, Twitter, LinkedIn

Mariana Gallo, Senior Director, Conferences

Geared towards industry members, financial analysts, business consultants, trade press representatives, agricultural retailers, agronomists, engineers and government economists. Key topics of discussion include new technology and issues that impact plant nutrition.
Frequency: Annual/November

10307 **Fish Expo Workboat Northwest**
National Fisherman Magazine
121 Free Street
PO Box 7437
Portland, ME 04112

207-842-5608; Fax: 207-842-5509
cmmarketing@divcom.com
www.pacificmarineexpo.com

Jane Bogual, Director

West Coast trade show attracting thousands of visitors from the fields of commercial fishing, workboat, port/harbor, boatbuilding, seafood processing, and other marine industries.
6,000 Attendees
Frequency: November

10308 **Food & Nutrition Conference & Expo**
American Dietetic Association
120 South Riverside Plaza
Suite 2000
Chicago, IL 60606

312-899-0040
800-877-1600
info@eatright.org
www.eatright.org
Facebook, Twitter

Katie Roski, Exhibits Manager

The premiere event for food and nutrition professionals. Features the latest nutrition science information, foodservice trends and access to the top experts.
Frequency: Annual/October

10309 **Food Marketing Institute Conferences**
Food Marketing Institute
2345 Crystal Drive
Suite 800
Arlington, VA 22202

202-452-8444; Fax: 202-429-4519
www.fmi.org

Randy Edeker, Chair
Leslie G. Sarasin, President/CEO

Hosts shows that cover a number of different topics.

10310 **Food Processing Suppliers Association Annual Conference**
Food Processing Suppliers Association
1451 Dolley Madison Boulevard
Suite 101
McLean, VA 22101-3850
703-761-2600; Fax: 703-761-4334
info@fpsa.org
www.fpsa.org/annual-conference
Facebook, Twitter, LinkedIn, Google+
David Seckman, President & CEO
Robyn Roche, Chief Financial Officer
Dolores Alonso, VP, Membership & Business Dev
Alaina Herrera, Exhibit Sales Associate
Gathering of equipment suppliers, distributors and processors working in the food and beverage industry. The conference will provide insights into the business of food processing and production, as well as networking opportunities.
Frequency: Annual/March

10311 **Food Product Design**
Virgo Publishing LLC
3300 N Central Avenue
Suite 300
Phoenix, AZ 85012
480-990-1101; Fax: 480-675-8154
peggyj@vpico.com
www.foodproductdesign.com
Peggy Jackson, Publishing Director
Publication distributed to product development professionals and corporate management executives at food and beverage manufacturing and foodservice companies.

10312 **Food Safety Summit**
ASI Food Safety Consultants
7625 Page Boulevard
St. Louis, MO 63133
314-725-2555
800-477-0778; Fax: 314-727-2563
www.asifood.com
Facebook, Twitter, LinkedIn
Dr. W. Ernest McCullough, Vice President of Operations
Tom Huge, President, Food Safety Consultant
Gary Huge, VP, Food Safety Consultants
Provides useful food safety information and solutions to those responsible for assuring food safety across the food supply chain thereby keeping the food safety platform current and relevant for today and tomorrow.
Founded in 1930

10313 **Food Safety Summit: Chicago**
Eaton Hall Exhibitions
256 Columbia Turnpike
Florham Park, NJ 07932
973-514-5900
800-746-9646; Fax: 973-514-5977
sgoldman@eatonhall.com
www.foodsafetysummit.com
Scott Goldman, President
Michael Pesick, Exhibits/Sponsors
Amy Reimer, Registration
Food safety, quality assurance, microbiology and plant sanitation.
1500 Attendees
Frequency: October

10314 **Food Safety Summit: Washington**
Eaton Hall Exhibitions
256 Columbia Turnpike
Florham Park, NJ 07932
973-514-5900
800-746-9646; Fax: 973-514-5977
sgoldman@eatonhall.com
www.foodsafetysummit.com
Scott Goldman, President
Michael Pesick, Exhibits/Sponsors
Amy Reimer, Registration
Held in Washington DC. Food safety, quality assurance, microbiology and plant sanitation.
1500 Attendees
Frequency: March

10315 **Food System Summit: Food Choices, Challenges and Realities**
Crop Life America
1156 15th St NW
Washington, DC 20005-1752
202-296-1585; Fax: 202-463-0474
webmaster@croplifeamerica.org
www.croplifeamerica.org
Facebook, Twitter, LinkedIn, YouTube
Christopher Novak, President & CEO
Hosts speakers sharing a wide range of perspectives on key food and health issues focusing on four significant topic areas: food animal well-being, nutrition and health, food safety, and technology and innovation.
Frequency: Annual/October

10316 **Food Tech**
Glahe International
PO Box 6009
Sun City Center, FL 33571
813-633-6335; Fax: 813-633-6355
Iye Boyd, President
Annual exhibits of food technology.

10317 **Global Minor Use Summit**
Crop Life America
1156 15th St NW
Washington, DC 20005-1752
202-296-1585; Fax: 202-463-0474
webmaster@croplifeamerica.org
www.croplifeamerica.org
Facebook, Twitter, LinkedIn, YouTube
Christopher Novak, President & CEO
Brings regulators, growers, and representatives of the crop protection industry from around the world together to explore options and incentives for improving the availability of crop protection tools for production of minor crops.
Frequency: Annual/December

10318 **Gourmet Products Show**
George Little Management
577 Airport Boulevard
Suite 440
Burlingame, CA 94010
650-344-5171
800-272-SHOW; Fax: 650-344-5270
www.thegourmetshow.com
Susan Corwin, VP
Cookware, tabletop, gadgets, cutlery, specialtry electric appliances, home textiles, contemporary lifestyle, furnishings, garden and travel accessories, home storage items, personal care, coffee and teas and specialty foods. Contains 950 exhibitors. 2700 booths
9000 Attendees
Frequency: April

10319 **Government Action Summit**
American Frozen Food Institute
2000 Corporate Ridge Blvd.
Suite 1000
McLean, VA 22102-7844
703-821-0770; Fax: 703-821-1350
info@affi.com
www.affi.com
Kraig R. Naasz, President & CEO
National trade association representing the interests of the frozen food industry for more than 60 years. Its 540 corporate members account for more than 90 percent of the frozen food production in the US.
Frequency: Annual/September

10320 **Government Affairs Conference**
USA Rice Federation
4301 N Fairfax Drive
Suite 425
Arlington, VA 22203
703-226-2300; Fax: 703-236-2301
riceinfo@usarice.com
www.usarice.com
Ben Mosely, VP, Government Affairs
Jeannette Davis, Sr. Dir., Meetings & Member Service
Jamison Cruce, Director, Government Affairs
Discuss issues and activities for the U.S. rice industry, legislation, training, and seminars.
Frequency: Annual

10321 **Grape Grower Magazine Farm Show**
Western Agricultural Publishing Company
4974 E Clinton Way
Suite 123
Fresno, CA 93727-1520
559-261-0396; Fax: 559-252-7387
Phill Rhoads, Manager
Seminars, exhibits and prizes for grape growers. Contianing 80 booths and exhibits.

10322 **Great American Beer Festival**
Brewers Association
736 Pearl Street
Boulder, CO 80302
303-447-0816
888-822-6273; Fax: 303-447-2825
www.greatamericanbeerfestival.com
Facebook, Twitter
Charlie Papazian, President
Bob Pease, VP
Cindy Jones, Sales/Marketing Director
Don't miss the largest gathering of beer enthusiasts.
Frequency: Annual/September

10323 **GrowerExpo**
Ball Publishing
PO Box 9
Batavia, IL 60510-0009
630-208-9080
800-456-5380; Fax: 630-456-0132
John Martens, President
A trade show devoted to horticulture and floriculture production and marketing. 175 booths.
2M Attendees
Frequency: January

10324 **HMAA Food & New Products Show**
Pacific Expositions
1580 Makaola Street
Suite 1200
Honolulu, HI 92814
808-945-3594; Fax: 808-946-6399
Pat Shine, General Sales Manager
Kimalar K Carroll, Show Director/Coordinator
This popular event, featuring the Food Show in the arena and New Products Show in the exhibition hall, is the original new products expo. Local and mainland exhibitors gather each year to present electronic, household, recreational and food products and service— often unvailed for the first time in Hawaii.
96000 Attendees

10325 **Hawkeye Farm Show**
Midwest Shows

PO Box 737
Austin, MN 55912

507-437-7969; Fax: 507-437-7752
www.farmshowsusa.com

Penny Swank, Show Manager
18000 Attendees
Frequency: March

10326 **Health & Nutrition Product Development Start to Finish**
New Hope Natural Media
1401 Pearl Street
Suite 200
Boulder, CO 80302

303-998-9399
rdebarros@newhope.com

Rob DeBarros, Marketing Manager
Frequency: March, Anaheim

10327 **Heart of America Hospitality Expo**
Bartle Hall Convention & Entertainment Center
301 W 13th Street, Suite 100
Kansas City, MO 64105

816-513-5000
800-821-7060; Fax: 816-513-5001
www.kcconvention.com

Charles Hart II, President
Pat Bergaur, Regional Director

10328 **Hospitality Food Service Expo**
Reed Business Information
275 Washington Street
Boston, MA 02458

617-261-1166; Fax: 630-288-8686
www.reedbusiness.com

Patrick Paleno, Show Manager
Barry Reed Jr, CFO
Stuart Whayman, CFO

Four hundred booths featuring educational seminars, culinary salon, and exhibits of products and services.
12M Attendees
Frequency: October

10329 **Hydroponic Society of America**
PO Box 6067
Concord, CA 94524-1067

FAX 510-232-2323

Gene Brisbon, Executive Director

Thirty five booths featuring the latest in hydroponic equipment.
500 Attendees
Frequency: April

10330 **IACP Annual Conference**
International Association of Culinary Professional
1221 Avenue of the Americas
42nd Floor
New York, NY 10020

646-358-4957
866-358-4951; Fax: 866-358-2524
info@iacp.com
www.iacp.com
Facebook, Twitter, Flickr

Martha Holmberg, Cheif Executive Officer
Shani Phelan, Member Programs And Ops Manager
Glenn Mack, Chair
Margaret Crable, Communications & Marketing Manager

Go behind the scenes with key industry players, getting access to the style-makers, tasting the latest culinary trends.
3000+ Members
Frequency: Annual/March
Founded in 1978

10331 **IBA Messe Duesseldorf North America**
150 N Michigan Avenue
Suite 2920
Chicago, IL 60601

312-621-5800; Fax: 312-781-5188
info@mdna.com
www.mdna.com

Frank Thorwirth, President
Pyon Klemon, Vice President
Eva Rowe, Vice President
Justin Kesselring, Project Manager
100 T Attendees
Frequency: October

10332 **IBIE Bakery Expo**
BEMA: Baking Industry Suppliers Association
7101 College Boulevard
Suite 1505
Overland Park, KS 66210

913-338-1300; Fax: 913-338-1327
info@bema.org

Matt Zielsdorf, Convention Chairman

Co-sponsored with the American Bakers Association. event that offers complete equipment, ingredient and supply solutions to serious baking professionals. Directors and managers from every segment of the grain-based food industry count on IBIE for the new technology, products, strategies and information they need to stay competitive in all aspects of their operation.
20000 Attendees
Frequency: October

10333 **IBWA Convention & Trade Show International Bottled Water Assn**
International Bottled Water Association
1700 Diagonal Road
Suite 650
Alexandria, VA 22314
703-683-5213
800-WAT-ER11; Fax: 703-683-4074
ibwainfo@bottledwater.org
www.bottledwater.org

Trade association representing the bottled water industry. IBWA's member companies produce and distribute 80 percent of the bottled water sold in the US. Our membership includes US and international bottlers, distributors and suppliers.
3250 Attendees
Frequency: Annual/October

10334 **IFDA Distribution Solutions Conference**
1660 International Drive
Suite 550
McLean, VA 22102

703-532-9400; Fax: 703-880-7117
www.ifdaonline.org

John Tracy, Chairman
Craig Hoskins, Vice Chairman
Mark Harman, Treasurer
Mark S. Allen, President/CEO

Workshops, assemblies, facility tours and an exposition are featured. Educational programming features many practitioners who sahre knowledge to be applied to various operations. Practical information for transportation, information technology, human resources and more.
Frequency: October
Founded in 2003

10335 **IFDA Executive Leadership Summit**
International Foodservice Distributors Association
1660 International Drive
Suite 550
McLean, VA 22102

703-532-9400; Fax: 703-880-7117
www.ifdaonline.org

John Tracy, Chairman
Craig Hoskins, Vice Chairman
Mark Harman, Treasurer
Mark S. Allen, President/CEO

An invitation-only program for foodservice distribution owners, CEOs, and presidents to address industry opportunities and challenges.
Frequency: Annual/October

10336 **IFDA SMart Conference**
International Foodservice Distributors Association
1660 International Drive
Suite 550
McLean, VA 22102

703-532-9400; Fax: 703-880-7117
www.ifdaonline.org

John Tracy, Chairman
Craig Hoskins, Vice Chairman
Mark Harman, Treasurer
Mark S. Allen, President/CEO

Designed to explore innovations in sales and marketing. SMart includes industry insights, leadership development, peer interaction, and networking with trading partners.
Frequency: Annual/July

10337 **IFEC Annual Conference**
International Food Service Editorial Council
7 Point Place
PO Box 491
Hyde Park, NY 12538-491

845-229-6973; Fax: 845-229-6973
ifec@ifeconline.com
www.ifeconline.com
Facebook, Twitter

Megan McKenna, President
Jeffrey Yarbrough, Vice President
Amelia Levin, Secretary
John Scroggins, Treasurer

Sessions with government and industry leaders, top chefs, and food tour hosts, gain new insights into the complex role that government plays in shaping America's diet, the growing impact that food environmentalism is having on foodservice, and the confluence of the two.
Frequency: Annual/November

10338 **IFT Annual Meeting & Food Expo**
Institute of Food Technologists
525 W Van Buren St
Suite 1000
Chicago, IL 60607-3842

312-782-8424; Fax: 312-782-8348
www.ift.org

Barbara Byrd Keenan, EVP
Marianne Gillette, President

Brings together the most repected food professionals in industry, government and academia.
20000 Attendees
Frequency: June

10339 **IHA Educational Conference & Meeting of Members**
International Herb Association
PO Box 5667
Jacksonville, FL 32247-5667

904-399-3241; Fax: 904-396-9467
www.iherb.org

Nancy Momsen, President
Kathryn Clayton, Vice President
Karen O'Brien, Secretary
Marge Powell, Treasurer

Conference offers tours, herb information and recipes, as well as leading industry news.
Frequency: Annual/July
Founded in 1986

10340 IMPA Convention & Trade Show
Iowa Meat Processors Association
PO Box 334
Clarence, IA 52216-0334
563-452-3329; Fax: 563-452-2141
execdirector@iowameatprocessors.org
www.iowameatprocessors.org
David L. Walter, President
Kent Stricker, 1st Vice President
Kevin Hastings, 2nd Vice President
Andy Thesing, 3rd Vice President
IMPA, leading the way in innovations, marketing, profits and adaptations. Also featuring a cured meat competition and product show.

10341 IS/LD Conference
1350 I Street NW
Suite 300
Washington, DC 20005
202-639-5900; Fax: 202-639-5932
info@gmaonline.org
Cindy Baker, Meetings/Conference Sr. Manager
A place where senior logistics and information technology executives from CPG manufacturers and leading retailers come together to study and seek solutions to the pressing issues affecting today's global supply chain.
Frequency: Annual/April

10342 IWLA Convention & Expo
International Warehouse Logistics Association
2800 S River Road
Suite 260
Des Plaines, IL 60018
847-813-4699; Fax: 847-813-0115
mail@iwla.com
www.iwla.com
Steve W. Dehaan, President & CEO
Jay D. Strother, Vice President
Jennifer Rezny, Membership Director
Hank Vaughan, Education & Meetings Director
Robert Budo, Finance & Accounting Manager
Promoting professional development and expose attendees to newer and better ways of doing business.
Founded in 1997

10343 Independent Bakers Association Annual Convention
Independent Bakers Association
Georgetown Station
PO Box 3731
Washington, DC 20027-0231
202-333-8190; Fax: 202-337-3809
independentbaker@yahoo.com
www.independentbaker.net
Enables bakers and allied industry representatives to tackle vital issues and develop strategies to enhance industry interests.
Frequency: Annual/June

10344 Institute of Food Technologists Annual Meeting & Food Expo
Institute of Food Technologists
525 W Van Buren
Suite 1000
Chicago, IL 60607-3814
312-782-8424; Fax: 312-782-8348
info@ift.org
www.ift.org
Roger Clemens, President
John Ruff, President-Elect
Bruce Stillings, Treasurer
Barbara Byrd Keenan, Executive VP
Technical exposition directed to the $302 billion food industry. Offering person-to-person marketplace and technical forum for suppliers of food ingredients. 2,400 booths.
24M Attendees
Frequency: Annual/June

10345 International Air Conditioning, Heating & Refrigerating Expo
ASHRAE
1791 Tullie Circle NE
Atlanta, GA 30329
404-636-8400
800-527-4723; Fax: 404-321-5478
ashrae@ashrae.org
www.ashrae.org
Jeff H. Littleton, Executive VP
The largest HVAC&R event in America featuring over 1,600 exhibiting companies. Held in conjunction with the ASHRAE Winter Meeting
30000 Attendees
Frequency: Annual/January

10346 International Assoc of Operative Millers Technical Conference/Trade Show
International Association of Operative Millers
10100 W 87th Street
Suite 306
Overland Park, KS 66212
913-338-3377; Fax: 913-338-3553
info@iaom.info
www.iaom.info
Facebook, LinkedIn
Melinda Farris, CEO
Annette Peterson, Office Coordinator
Cynthia Malone, Director, Meetings & Exhibitions
Conference, banquet and over 100 exhibits of cereal milling equipment, ancillary equipment, supplies and information.
Frequency: Annual/May

10347 International Beverage Industry Exposition
1101 16th Street NW
Washington, DC 20036-4803
202-857-4722
Lisa Feldman, Show Manager
450 booths.
16M Attendees
Frequency: October

10348 International Boston Seafood Show
National Fishermans Expositions
PO Box 7437
Portland, ME 04112-7437
207-842-5500; Fax: 207-842-5505
Diane Vassar, Promotions Director
David Lowell, President
Nine hundred and seventy booths. Annual trade show for the seafood industry.
20M Attendees
Frequency: March

10349 International Dairy Foods Show
International Dairy Foods Association
1250 H St NW
Suite 900
Washington, DC 20005-5902
202-737-4332; Fax: 202-331-7820
membership@idfa.org
www.idfa.org
Constance Tipton, President
Neil Moran, Sr. VP, Finance/Tradeshow/Admin.
Peggy Armstrong, VP, Communications
Diana Carmenates, VP, Meetings & Educational Services
Cindy Cavallo, Director, Membership
The International Dairy Foods Association, the Milk Industry Foundation and the International Ice Cream Association work to represent the best interests of manufacturers, distributors and marketers of ice cream, frozen yogurt, frozen desserts, fluid milk, cultured dairy products, dips and other milk products.
Frequency: Annual

10350 International Exposition for Food Processors
Food Processing Machinery Association
1451 Dolly Madison Boulevard
Suite 200
McLean, VA 22101
703-761-2600
800-331-8816; Fax: 703-548-6563
www.ippexpo.com
Nancy Janssen, Show Manager
Show with more than 1,600 exhibitors, up-to-the-minute technology, fast-track educational sessions. Great source for solutions and networking with industry peers. Colocated with Pack Expo International. McCormick Place, Chicago, IL.
50M Attendees
Frequency: Annual/September

10351 International Food Processors Association Expo
200 Daingerfield Road
Suite 100
Alexandria, VA 22314-2884
703-299-5001; Fax: 703-299-5100
George Melnykozich, Show Manager
Four hundred and twenty five booths of food processing and supplies.
16M Attendees
Frequency: January

10352 International Food Service Exposition
Florida Restaurant Association
230 S Adams Street
Tallahassee, FL 32301
850-224-2250; Fax: 850-224-9213
Hosting the third largest food service show in the country with over 1,200 booths and over 23,000 qualified buyers and attendees.
22000 Attendees

10353 International Fundraising Conference
Association of Fundraising Professionals
4300 Wilson Blvd.
Suite 300
Arlington, VA 22203
703-684-0410
800-666-3863; Fax: 703-684-0540
afpfc.com
Facebook, Twitter, LinkedIn, Instagram, YouTube
Andrew Watt, President & CEO
Terry Rauh, Chief Operating Officer
Skills building and thought leaders in international fundraising and philanthropy.
Founded in 2006

10354 International Institute of Foods and Family Living Annual Meeting
225 W Ohio Street
Chicago, IL 60610-4198
312-527-3860; Fax: 312-670-0824
Phyllis Favelman, President

10355 International Marketing Conference & Annual Membership Meeting
US Grains Council

1400 K St NW
Suite 1200
Washington, DC 20005-2449

202-789-0789; Fax: 202-898-0522
grains@grains.org
www.grains.org

Ryan LeGrand, President/CEO
Jim Raben, Chair
Chad Willis, Vice Chair
Josh Miller, Secretary & Treasurer

Join Council members and guests to kick off this special meeting with a welcome reception. Great opportunity to network with industry colleagues, get acquainted with new Council members and talk with the Council's international directors and staff.
Frequency: Annual/February
Founded in 1960

10356 **International Pizza Expo**
MacFadden Protech
137 E Market Street
New Albany, IN 47150

812-949-0909
800-489-8324; Fax: 812-949-1867
boakley@pizzatoday.com
www.pizzaexpo.com

William T Oakley, Senior VP Expositions
Linda Keith, Manager
Patty Crone, Manager

One thousand booths featuring exhibits of equipment for pizza industry and restaurants.
6000 Attendees
Frequency: February/March

10357 **International Poultry Expo**
US Poultry & Egg Association/American Feed Assoc.
1530 Cooledge Road
Tucker, GA 30084-7303

770-493-9401; Fax: 770-493-9257
Facebook, Twitter, LinkedIn

Charles Olentine, Executive VP
Pennie Stathes, Logistics Manager

A world large trade show for the poultry and feed sectors.
15000 Attendees
Frequency: January

10358 **International Whey Conference**
American Dairy Products Institute
126 N Addison St
Elmhurst, IL 60126

630-530-8700; Fax: 630-530-8707
www.internationalwheyconference.org

Dale Kleber, CEO

Offers an unparalleled opportunity to learn about the latest research, cutting-edge product innovations, technical developments and marketing strategies relating to this intriguing, value-added ingredient.
500 Attendees
Frequency: September

10359 **Interpack**
150 N Michigan Avenue
Suite 2920
Chicago, IL 60601

312-781-5180; Fax: 312-781-5188
info@mdna.com
www.mdna.com

Ryan Klemm, Senior Project Manager
Eva Rowe, Vice President
Justin Kesselring, Project Manager
Frequency: April

10360 **JPA Annual Meeting**
Juice Products Association
750 National Press Building
529 14th Street NW
Washington, DC 20045

202-785-3232; Fax: 202-223-9741
jpa@kellencompany.com
www.juiceproducts.org

Richard E Cristol, President
Carol Freysinger, Executive Director

Includes presentations of current interest, such as crop estimates and conditions, transportation and export problems, packaging and marketing concepts, advertising trends and government and regulatory reporting.
Frequency: Annual/Spring

10361 **KFYR Radio Agri International Stock & Trade Show**
KFYR Radio
PO Box 1658
Bismarck, ND 58502-1738

701-224-9393
800-472-2170; Fax: 701-255-8155
mwall@clearchannel.com
www.kfyr.com

Syd Stewart, General Manager
Michelle J Wall, Manager
Jim Lowe, Manager

Annual show of 250 exhibitors of agricultural equipment, supplies, livestock and services.
15000 Attendees
Frequency: February

10362 **Keystone Farm Show**
Lee Publications
PO Box 121
Palatine Bridge, NY 13428-0121

518-673-2445
800-218-5586; Fax: 518-673-3245
kmaring@leepub.com
www.leetradeshows.com

Ken Maning, Show Manager
Tom Mahoney, Sales Manager

The largest commercial farm equipment & service provider trade show in Pennsylvania.
Frequency: Annual, January

10363 **MEATXPO**
National Meat Association
1970 Broadway
Suite 825
Oakland, CA 94612

510-763-1533; Fax: 510-763-6186

Barry Carpenter, CEO
Jen Kempis, Operations Manager

Biennial suppliers' exposition that brings together consultants, equipment manufacturers and other professionals in the industry, to give a first-hand view of the newest industry equipment, packaging and related services.
Frequency: Annual/February
Founded in 1948

10364 **MWR Expo**
American Logistics Association
1133 15th Street NW
Suite 640
Washington, DC 20005-2708

202-466-2520; Fax: 202-296-4419
membership@ala-national.org
www.ala-national.org

Cologne Hunter, Meetings/Expo Director
Maurice Branch, Operations VP

A gathering of MWR professionals and brings together the many components of the Morale, Welfare and Recreation industry. The event features products and services that are sold to military and government agencies for use in community support activities on military installations throughout the world.
Frequency: Biennial/August
Founded in 1972

10365 **Maraschino Cherry and Glace Fruit Processors Annual Convention**
5 Ravine Drive
#776
Matawan, NJ 07747-3106

FAX 732-583-0798

Richard Sullivan, Executive VP
Frequency: April/May

10366 **Marketechnics**
Food Marketing Institute
800 Connecticut Avenue NW
Washington, DC 20006

202-220-0600; Fax: 202-429-4519

Beth Watt, Contact
6000 Attendees

10367 **Meat Industry Research Conference**
American Meat Science Association
2441 Village Green Pl
Champaign, IL 61822-7676

800-517-AMSA; Fax: 888-205-5834; Fax: 217-356-5370
information@meatscience.org
www.meatscience.org

Dean Pringle, President
Collette Kaster, Chief Executive Officer

Cosponsored by the American Meat Institute Foundation and the American Meat Science Association. A forum for presenting the latest research in terms of direct application for the meat industry.

10368 **Mid-America Farm Show**
Salina Area Chamber of Commerce
120 W Ash Street
PO Box 586
Salina, KS 67401

785-827-9301; Fax: 785-827-9758
www.salinakansas.org

Don Weiser, Show Manager

Annual show of 325 exhibitors of agricultural equipment, supplies and services, including irrigation equipment, fertilizer, farm implements, hybrid seed, agricultural chemicals, tractors, feed, farrowing crates and equipment, silos and bins, storage equipment and farm buildings.
13M Attendees
Frequency: Annual/March

10369 **Mid-America Horticultural Trade Show**
1000 N Rand Road
Suite 214
Wauconda, IL 60084-1188

847-526-2010; Fax: 847-526-3993
mail@midam.org
www.midam.org

Rand A Baldwin CAE, Managing Director
Suzanne Spohr, President
Jim Melka, Secretary

Mid-Am is the premier event featuring more than 650 leading suppliers offering countless products, equipment, and services for the horticulture industry. Mid-Am also offers a variety of educational seminars featuring the best and the brightest in the horticultural and business communities to help keep you informed of the latest trends.
Frequency: January

10370 **Mid-America Resturant, Soft Serve & Pizza Exposition**
Exhibition Productions

PO Box 81845
Wellesley, MA 02481

800-909-7469; Fax: 617-431-2662

17000 Attendees

10371 Mid-Atlantic Food, Beverage & Lodging Expo
Restaurant Association of Maryland
6301 Hillside Court
Columbia, MD 21046

410-290-6800
800-874-1313; Fax: 410-290-7898
dimbessi@marylandrestaurants.com
www.midatlanticexpo.com

Dennis Imbessi, Director Expo/Membership Sales
Licia Spinelli, Director Marketing/Special Events
Valerie Maione, Owner

Annual Mid-Atlantic regional trade show of products and services for the restaurant and hospitality industry. Exhibitors include food manufacturers, equipment, beverages and services providers. Open to food service professionals, taking place annually during the month of September with 500 exhibitors and 600 booths.
15M Attendees
Frequency: Annual/October

10372 Midway USA Food Service and Hospitality Exposition
Kansas Restaurant and Hospitality Association
359 S Hydraulic Street
Wichita, KS 67211-1908

316-267-8383; Fax: 316-267-8400

Dennis Carpenter, CEO

Annual show of 35 food service, beverage, suppliers.
6000 Attendees

10373 Midwest Expo: IL
Illinois Fertilizer & Chemical Association
130 W Dixie Highway
PO Box 186
Saint Anne, IL 60964-0186

815-939-1566
800-892-7122; Fax: 815-427-6573

Jean Trobec, President

Annual show of 130 manufacturers, suppliers and distributors of agricultural chemical and fertilizer application equipment, supplies and services.
2500 Attendees
Frequency: August, Danville

10374 Midwest Farm Show
North Country Enterprises
5322 250th Street
Cadott, WI 54727

715-289-4632
nceinfo@yahoo.com
www.northcountryenterprises.com

Steve Henry, President

Top farm show exhibiting dairy and Wisconsin's tillage equipment, feed and seed. 20 booths.
11M+ Attendees
Frequency: January
Founded in 1975

10375 Midwest Food Processors Association Convention/Trade Show
4600 American Pkwy
Suite 110
Madison, WI 53718-8334

608-255-9946; Fax: 608-255-9838
info@mwfpa.org
www.mwfpa.org

Nick George, President
Robin Fanshaw, Office Manager/Event Planner
Brian Elliott, Director of Communications
Bruce Jacobson, Chair

Processing industry members come together at the convention to learn, network and gain insight to improve their company's course.
1M Attendees
Frequency: Annual/November
Founded in 1905

10376 Midwest Gourmet Exposition
Fairchild Urban Expositions
1395 S Marietta Parkway
Building 400, Suite 210
Marietta, GA 30067

678-901-1700; Fax: 770-956-9644

Robert Collins, President

10377 Midwest Leadership Conference
Indiana Retail Grocers Association
115 W Washington Street
Suite 1364
Indianapolis, IN 46204

317-220-0033; Fax: 317-231-7858

10378 Midwest Regional Grape & Wine Conference
Missouri Grape and Wine Board
1616 Missouri Boulevard
Jefferson City, MO 65109-0630

573-751-3374
800-392-WINE; Fax: 573-751-2868
sue.berendzen@mda.mo.gov
www.missouriwine.org
Facebook, Twitter, YouTube, Flickr

Jim Anderson, Executive Director
Denise Kottwitz, Assistant

A major national conference for hundreds of vintners, growers and wine industry executives throughout the US Conference includes speakers, trade show, workshops and wine dinners. Over 45 booths.
400+ Attendees
Frequency: Annual/February
Founded in 1985

10379 Midwestern Food Service and Equipment Exposition
Missouri Restaurant Association
9233 Ward Parkway
Suite 123
Kansas City, MO 64114

816-753-5222; Fax: 816-753-6993
www.morestaurants.org

Chad Treaster, President

Annual show of 200 suppliers of food service and hospitality industries equipment, supplies and services.
12M Attendees

10380 NAAB Annual Convention
National Association of Animal Breeders
PO Box 1033
Columbia, MO 65205
573-445-4406; Fax: 573-446-2279
naab-css@naab-css.org
www.naab-css.org

Paul Hunt, Chair

A welcomer reception, election of directors, consideration of Bylaw Amendments, resolutions and other association business and a award recognitions presentation.
Frequency: Annual/September

10381 NAAE Annual Convention
National Association of Agricultural Educators
University of Kentucky
300 Garrigus Building
Lexington, KY 40546-215

859-257-2224
800-509-0204; Fax: 859-323-3919
JJackman.NAAE@uky.edu
www.naae.org

Alissa Smith, CEO
Wm. Jay Jackman, Executive Director

Featuring a meet and greet, professional development workshops, meetings, tours and a career tech expo.
Frequency: Nov/Fees Vary
Founded in 1948
Mailing list available for rent

10382 NABCA Annual Conference
National Alcohol Beverage Control Association
4401 Ford Avenue
Suite 700
Alexandria, VA 22302

703-784-4200; Fax: 703-820-3551
jsgueo@nabca.org
www.nabca.org
Facebook, Twitter

James M Sgueo, President/CEO

An event to provides its members opportunities to interact and conduct business. Featuring nationally known speakers, informative seminars, interact workshops and suppliers and vendors demonstrating their products.
Frequency: Annual

10383 NAC Annual Convention & Trade Show
35 E Wacker Drive
Suite 1816
Chicago, IL 60601-2103

312-236-3858; Fax: 312-236-7809
www.naconline.org
Facebook, LinkedIn

John Evans Jr., President
Ron Krueger II, Board Chairman
Jeff Scudillo, President-Elect
Andrew Cretors, Treasurer

Bringing together the top food and beverage concession leaders in the recreation and leisure-time industry at this annual event.
3M Attendees
Frequency: Annual/August
Founded in 1982

10384 NACD Annual Meeting
National Association of Conservation Districts
509 Capitol Court NE
Washington, DC 20002-4937

202-547-6223; Fax: 202-547-6450
www.nacdnet.org
Facebook, Flickr

Krysta Harden, CEO
Bob Cordova, Second Vice President

Discussions with agency leaders on priorities for the coming years, training sessions, key leaders in agricultural, conservation and wildlife discussing their perspectives on the future Farm Bill, highlighted challenges and addressing areas of common interest.
Frequency: Annual/February
Founded in 1946

10385 NAFEM Annual Meeting & Management Workshop
NAFEM
161 N Clark Street
Suite 2020
Chicago, IL 60601

312-821-0201; Fax: 312-821-0202
info@nafem.org
www.nafem.org

Steven R. Follett, President
Thomas R. Campion, President-Elect
Michael L. Whiteley, Secretary/Treasurer
Deirdre Flynn, Executive Vice President

Workshop geared toward CEOs, CFOs, COOs and directors of member companies. Education is offered on a wide range of topics designed to inspire you personally and professionally. Plenty of networking time with industry peers is built in to encourage the exchange of ideas and expertise.
625 Members
Frequency: Biennial/February

10386 NAFEM Show
North American Assoc of Food Equipment Manufacture
161 N Clark Street
Suite 2020
Chicago, IL 60601

312-245-1054; Fax: 312-821-0202
info@nafem.org
www.nafem.org

Deirdre Flynn, Executive VP

Attracts approximately 20,000 foodservice professionals and features 500+ exhibitors displaying products for food preparation, cooking, storage and table service.
Frequency: Biennial/February

10387 NAG Conference
National Convenience Store Advisory Group
3331 Street Road
Suite 410
Bensalem, PA 19020

215-245-4555; Fax: 215-245-4060
www.nag-net.com

Joseph Howton, Executive VP/COO

Promoting relationships, networking, and executable ideas and takeaways.
Frequency: Annual/September

10388 NAMP PROCESS EXPO
NAMP
1910 Association Drive
Reston, VA 20191-1545

703-758-1900
800-368-3043; Fax: 703-758-8001
www.myprocessexpo.com

Sabrina Moore, Accounting/Meeting Manager
Philip Kimball, Executive Director

Delivering the most valuable tradeshow experience to food industry suppliers and processors at the lowest possible cost.
250 Attendees
Frequency: Annual/November

10389 NAPO International Pizza Expo
National Association of Pizzeria Operators
908 S 8th Street
Suite 200
Louisville, KY 40203

502-736-9500
800-489-8324; Fax: 502-736-9501
bmacintosh@pizzatoday.com
www.pizzatoday.com

Bobbie MacIntosh, Booth/Sponsorship Sales Director

The trade show for the pizza industry that includes; pizzeria owners, operators, managers, distributors and food brokers. Workshops, seminars and exhibits.
5400 Attendees
Frequency: March

10390 NASFT Fancy Food Shows
National Association for the Specialty Food Trade
136 Madison Avenue
12th Floor
New York, NY 10016

212-482-6440; Fax: 212-482-6459
www.fancyfoodshows.com
Facebook

Dennis Deschaine, Chairman
Mike Silver, Vice Chairman
Shawn McBride, Treasurer
Becky Renfro Borbolla, Secretary

Held three times a year; winter, spring and summer time. Over 350 domestic exhibitors from around the country, presentations of exotic new specialty foods from all over the world, tastings, seminars and workshops. These shows are a chance to learn about each product first-hand and do business directly with the decision makers onsite.
30M Attendees
Frequency: 3x Yearly

10391 NBBQA Annual Convention
National Barbecue & Grilling Association
PO Box 782
Kirkland, WA 98083

360-670-0194
info@nbbqa.org
www.nbbqa.org

Patrick Murty, President
Barbara Latimer, President-Elect
Ken Phillips, Treasurer
Joey Machado, Secretary
Saffron Hodgson, Executive Director

Learn and network with a group of BBQ folks on how to better prepare and utilize grills, smokers, fuels, sauces, marinades, rubs and all the necessary utensils. Barbeque presentations, programming, demonstrations, contests, sampling and contacts and leads.
Frequency: Annual/April

10392 NBVA Annual Convention
National Bulk Vendors Association
1202 East Maryland Avenue
Suite 1K
Phoenix, AZ 85014

888-628-2872
www.nbva.org
Facebook

Bernie Schwarzli, President
Lauri Logue, Vice President
Steve Schnecher, Secretary
Andy Belsky, Treasurer & CPA

Each spring the leading manufacturers and suppliers of bulk vending machines and products display their merchandise. Featuring workshops and seminars to discuss current industry problems and interchange ideas.
530 Attendees
Frequency: Annual/Spring

10393 NBVA Conference
National Bulk Vendors Association
1202 East Maryland Avenue
Suite 1k
Phoenix, AZ 85014

888-628-2872
www.nbva.org
Facebook

Bernie Schwarzli, President
Lauri Logue, Vice President
Steve Schnecher, Secretary
Andy Belsky, Treasurer & CPA

Brings together suppliers, manufacturers, distributors and operators to see the newest products and innovations. Seminars are created to familiarize attendees with the latest bulk vending innovations and legal issues.
Frequency: Annual/April
Founded in 1950

10394 NBWA Annual Convention
National Beer Wholesalers Association
1101 King Street
Suite 600
Alexandria, VA 22314

703-683-4300
800-300-6417
info@nbwa.org
www.nbwa.org
Facebook, Twitter

Craig Purser, President/CEO
Grace Connolly, Executive Assistant
Lauren Kane, VP, Communications
Paul Pisano, SVP Industry Affairs & Gen. Counsel
Patti Rouzie, VP, Memmbership & Meetings

Designed to provide valuable education programs and important networking opportunities for the beer industry. Featuring speakers and seminars on a number of topics of importance to beer distributors.
2500 Attendees
Frequency: Annual/Fall

10395 NBWA Legislative Conference
National Beer Wholesalers Association
1101 King Street
Suite 600
Alexandria, VA 22314

703-683-4300
800-300-6417
info@nbwa.org
www.nbwa.org
Facebook, Twitter, YouTube, Flickr

Craig Purser, President/CEO
Grace Connolly, Executive Assistant
Lauren Kane, VP, Communications
Paul Pisano, SVP Industry Affairs & Gen. Counsel
Patti Rouzie, VP, Membership & Meetings

Industry leaders meet in Washington, D.C. to discuss the industry's legislative goals and priorities with members of Congress and their staffs.
Frequency: Annual/April

10396 NBWA Next Generation Conference
National Beer Wholesalers Association
1101 King Street
Suite 600
Alexandria, VA 22314

703-683-4300
800-300-6417
info@nbwa.org
www.nbwa.org
Facebook, Twitter, YouTube, Flickr

Craig Purser, President/CEO
Grace Connolly, Executive Assistant
Lauren Kane, VP, Communications
Paul Pisano, SVP Industry Affairs & Gen. Counsel
Patti Rouzie, VP, Membership & Meetings

Gives beer distributors an opportunity to interact with brewers and vendors and make valuable contacts for future business needs. Introduces distributors to new brewers as well as new products, innovative technologies and vendors who supply the materials needed to run their operations.
Frequency: Biennial
Founded in 1938

10397 NCA Annual Convention
National Coffee Association

45 Broadway
Suite 1140
New York, NY 10006

212-766-4007; Fax: 212-766-5815
info@ncausa.org
www.ncausa.org
Facebook, Twitter, LinkedIn

Dub Hay, Chairman
John E. Boyle, Vice Chairman
Richard Emanuele, Secretary
Robert F. Nelson, President & CEO

Meet a worldwide mix of leadership in the industry in one location, get educational as well as social interaction that cannot be matched at any other convention.
Frequency: Annual/March

10398 **NCA Coffee Summit**
National Coffee Association
45 Broadway
Suite 1140
New York, NY 10006

212-766-4007; Fax: 212-766-5815
info@ncausa.org
www.ncausa.org
Facebook, Twitter, LinkedIn

Dub Hay, Chairman
John E. Boyle, Vice Chairman
Richard Emanuele, Secretary
Robert F. Nelson, President & CEO

Bringing together industry knowledge and expertise, for the best available education, networking and product knowledge.
Frequency: Annual/March

10399 **NCBA Annual Convention & Trade Show**
National Cattlemen's Beef Association
9110 E Nichols Avenue
Suite 300
Centennial, CO 80112

303-694-0305; Fax: 303-694-2851
dkaylor@beef.org
www.beefusa.org
Facebook, Twitter

Debbie Kaylor, Convention/Meetings Executive Dir.
Valerie Proni, Registration Manager
Kristin Torres, Trade Show Coordinator
Forest Roberts, CEO

The meeting features joint and individual meetings by five industry organizations. Over 250 companies will offer attendees a chance to see the latest products and services while networking with other cattle producers.
28000 Members
6000 Attendees
Frequency: Annual
Founded in 1898

10400 **NCC's Annual Conference**
National Chicken Council
1015 15th Street NW
Suite 930
Washington, DC 20005-2622

202-296-2622; Fax: 202-293-4005
ncc@chickenusa.org
www.nationalchickencouncil.org
Facebook

Michael J. Brown, President
William P. Roenigk, Senior Vice President
Mary M. Colville, VP of Government Affairs
Dr. Ashley Peterson, VP of Science & Technology

Brings together senior executives from US chicken processing companies and allied industries to address current agricultural, public affiars, legislative, regulatory, political, economic, and world trade issues affecting the chicken industry.
Frequency: Annual/October
Founded in 1954

10401 **NCIMS Conference**
National Conference on Interstate Milk Shipments
585 County Farm Road
Monticello, IL 61856

217-762-2656
ncims.bordson@gmail.com
www.ncims.org

Leon Townsend, Executive Secretary

Bringing together the people in the dairy industry to discuss laws that directly involve the dairy industry.
Frequency: Biennially/May
Founded in 1950

10402 **NCPA's Annual Convention**
National Cottonseed Products Association
866 Willow Tree Circle
Cordova, TN 38018-6376

901-682-0800; Fax: 901-682-2856
info@cottonseed.com
www.cottonseed.com
Twitter, Flickr, YouTube

Featuring a board of directors meeting, committee meeting, luncheons, and discussion on the latest trends in the industry.
Founded in 1897

10403 **NCSLA Annual Conference**
National Conference of State Liquor Administrators
C/O Massachusetts ABCC
239 Causeway Street, 1st Floor
Boston, MA 02114

617-727-3040; Fax: 617-727-1510
www.ncsla.org

Cheryl Marshall, Conference Coordinator

Provide opportunities for state-licensed administrators to meet and exchange ideas and information and to formulate uniform regulations, statue and laws affecting the sales of alcholic beverages.
Frequency: June/Fee Varies

10404 **NICRA Convention**
National Ice Cream Retailers Association
743 Spirit 40 Park Dr.
Suite 121
Chesterfield, MO 63005

636-778-1822
866-303-6960; Fax: 636-898-4326
info@nicra.org
www.nicra.org

Steve Christensen, Executive Director

Offers educational seminars, exhibits, networking and social opportunities
325 Attendees
Frequency: Annual
Founded in 1933

10405 **NPFDA Annual Convention**
National Poultry & Food Distributors
2014 Osborne Road
Saint Marys, GA 31558

770-535-9901; Fax: 770-535-7385
www.npfda.org

Cece Corbin, President
Carol Lanham, Member Services & Development Dir.
Alina Cooper, Membership Relations & Comm. Dir.

Features the Poultry Suppliers Showcase and many opportunities to network with other industry representatives. Participating in this convention provides access to the latest industry trends, presents ways to improve business operations, and increases number of industry contacts.
Frequency: Annual/January
Founded in 1967

10406 **NW Food Manufacturing & Packaging Expo**
Northwest Food Processors Association
9700 SW Capitol Highway
Suuite 250
Portland, OR 97219

503-327-2200; Fax: 503-327-2201
www.nwfpa.org

Teonna Embelton, Events Coordinator
Stephanie Kennedy, Events Consultant

Provides comprehensive programs encompassing topics ranging from food sciences and technologies to energy efficiencies.
Frequency: Jan Oregon

10407 **NW Food Manufacturing and Packaging Expo**
8338 NE. Alderwood Road
Suite 160
Portland, OR 97220

503-327-2200; Fax: 503-327-2201
www.nwfpa.org
Facebook, Twitter, LinkedIn

David Zepponi, President
David C Klick, Cluster Outreach Executive
Craig Smith, VP
Connie Kirby, Scientific & Technical Director
Pam Barrow, Energy Affairs Manager

NWFPA is an advocate for members interests and a resource for enhancing the food processing industry in Oregon, Washington and Idaho.
350 Members
4000 Attendees
Founded in 1914

10408 **NWA Annual Education and Networking Conference & Exhibits**
National WIC Association
2001 S St NW
Suite 580
Washington, DC 20009-1165

202-232-5492; Fax: 202-387-5281
www.nwica.org
Facebook, Twitter

Douglas Greenaway, President & CEO
Emily Gilcher, Membership Engagement

Offers a terrific opportunity to learn new skills and to network with more than 1200 colleagues and peers, public health professionals, technical experts and nationally recognized speakers from a variety of fields who will engage participants during plenary and concurrent sessions.
1389 Members
Frequency: Annual, April
Founded in 1983

10409 **NWA Technology Conference**
National WIC Association
2001 S St NW
Suite 580
Washington, DC 20009-1165

202-232-5492; Fax: 202-387-5281
www.nwica.org
Facebook, Twitter

Douglas Greenaway, President & CEO
Emily Gilcher, Membership Engagement

The future is now! Learn about the latest technologies available and used in all the WIC programs.
1389 Members
Frequency: Biennial, September
Founded in 1983

10410 **NWA Washington Leadership Conference**
National WIC Association

2001 S St NW
Suite 580
Washington, DC 20009-1165

202-232-5492; Fax: 202-387-5281
www.nwica.org
Facebook, Twitter

Douglas Greenaway, President & CEO
Emily Gilcher, Membership Engagement

The conference will provide a forum to discuss Federal initiatives affecting the health and nutritional wellbeing of WIC mothers and young children, WIC's role as a preventative public health nutrition program, as well as service delivery and the effective management of the Program.
1389 Members
Frequency: Annual/March
Founded in 1983

10411 National Agri-Marketing Association Conference
National Agri-Marketing Association
11020 King Street
Suite 205
Overland Park, KS 66210-1201

913-491-6500; Fax: 913-492-6502
agrimktg@nama.org
www.nama.org
Facebook, Twitter, LinkedIn, YouTube, Flickr

Jennifer Pickett, Executive VP & CEO

Annual show of 60 exhibitors of marketing and communication suppliers, including trade publications, radio and television broadcast sales organizations, premium/incentive manufacturers, printers, marketing research firms and photographers.
1100 Attendees
Frequency: Annual

10412 National Agricultural Plastics Congress
American Society for Plasticulture
526 Brittany Drive
State College, PA 16803-1420

814-238-7045; Fax: 814-238-7051
www.plasticulture.org

Patricia Heuser, Executive Director

Congress of research presentations, with exhibit area of equipment, supplies and services relating to greenhouse production and mulch film production of agricultural and horticultural crops.
225 Attendees
Frequency: September

10413 National Association Extension 4-H Agents Convention
University of Georgia
Hoke Smith Annex
Athens, GA 30602

706-542-3000; Fax: 706-542-2115

Peggy Adkins, Show Manager

Fifty booths for young people, youth staff and volunteers involved in 4-H.
1.2M Attendees
Frequency: November

10414 National Association of College and University Food Services Convention
Michigan State University-Manly Miles Building
1405 S Harrison Road
Suite 305
East Lansing, MI 48823-5245

517-332-2494; Fax: 517-332-8144
jspina@nacufs.org

Joseph Spina, Executive Director
Donna Addy, Administrative Assistant
Nancy Lane, Director

Annual convention and exhibits of equipment, supplies and services for food preparation and service on college and university campuses.

10415 National Association of County Agricultural Agents Conference
National Association of County Agricultural Agents
Courthouse-Room 217
5th & Main Street
Ellensburg, WA 98926

FAX 509-627-74

Annual conference and exhibits for county agricultural agents and extension workers.

10416 National Association of Fruits, Flavors and Syrups Annual Convention
5 Ravine Drive
#776
Matawan, NJ 07747-3106

732-988-4800; Fax: 732-583-0798

Bob Bauer, Director
Frequency: September

10417 National Chicken Council Conference
1015 15th Street NW
Suite 930
Washington, DC 20005-2622

202-296-2622; Fax: 202-293-4005
www.nationalchickencouncil.org

Michael J. Brown, President
William P. Roenigk, Senior VP

NCC's Annual Conference brings together senior executives from U.S. chicken processing companies and allied industries to address current agricultural, public affairs, legislative, regulatory, political, economic, and world trade issues affecting the chicken industry.
Frequency: Annual
Founded in 1954

10418 National Confectioners Association Education Exposition
National Confectioners Association
7900 Westpar Drive
Suite A-320
McLean, VA 22102

703-790-5750; Fax: 730-790-5752

Linda Jamie, Finance Executive
600 Attendees

10419 National Confectioners Association Expo
8320 Old Courthouse Road
Suite 300
Vienna, VA 22182

703-790-5750; Fax: 703-790-5752
info@candyusa.org
www.allcandyexpo.com

Larry Graham, President
Libby Taylor, VP

Confectionery trade show featuring more chocolate, candy and gum than one can imagine. Held annually in June at Chicago's McCormick Place.
1200 booths.
15 M Attendees
Frequency: June

10420 National Conservation Association District Annual Convention
9150 W Jewell Avenue
Suite 113
Lakewood, CO 80232-6469

303-839-1852

Robert Raschke, Regional Representative

Eighty booths including companies who manufacture, service or who are otherwise involved with equipment used in agricultural production.
2M Attendees
Frequency: February

10421 National Convenience Store Advisory Group Convention
2063 Oak Street
Jacksonville, FL 32204

904-845-5989; Fax: 904-387-3362
www.nag-net.com

Joseph Howton, Executive VP/COO

One-hundred booths.
500 Attendees
Frequency: January

10422 National Corn Growers Association
1000 Executive Parkway Drive
Suite 105
Creve Cocur, MO 63141-6397

314-275-9915; Fax: 314-275-7061

Peggy Findley, Director of Conventions

Five hundred and fifty booths of equipment, seed and chemicals.
4000 Attendees
Frequency: February

10423 National Country Ham Association Annual Meeting
PO Box 948
Conover, NC 28613

828-466-2760
800-820-4426; Fax: 828-466-2770
eatham@countryham.org
www.countryham.org

Candace Cansler, Executive Director

Providing an array of speakers, discussion topics and activities.
Frequency: Non-Members:$300

10424 National Farm Machinery Show and Championship Tractor Pull
Kentucky Fair and Exposition Center
PO Box 37130
Louisville, KY 40233

502-367-5000; Fax: 502-367-5299
www.farmmachineryshow.org

Harold Workman, Show Manager

Annual show of 800 plus exhibitors of agricultural products, equipment, supplies and services.
280M Attendees
Frequency: February

10425 National Food Processors Association Convention
National Food Processors Association
1350 I Street NW
Suite 300
Washington, DC 20005-3377

202-930-0890; Fax: 202-639-5932

John Cady, President
Lisa Weddig, Executive Director

Annual convention and exhibits of equipment, supplies and services for food processing quality control measures, spoilage prevention, frozen food technology, sanitation techniques and waste treatment techniques.

10426 National Frozen and Refrigerated Foods Convention
National Frozen & Refrigerated Foods Association

4755 Linglestown Road
Suite 300
Harrisburg, PA 17112

717-657-8601; Fax: 717-657-9862
nfra@nfraweb.org
nfraconvention.org

H.V. Skip Shaw Jr., President/CEO
Jeff Rumachik, EVP/COO
Julie W. Henderson, VP, Communications
Jessica Scott, VP, Finance
Natalie Limm, Member Communications Coordinator

The National Frozen and Refrigerated Foods Convention is an opportunity to meet with hundreds of frozen and refrigerated food decision-makers. This premier business event brings representatives from all segments of the industry together to conduct business and build relationships. It is structured around one-on-one business appointments, with networking opportunities.
1,200 Attendees
Frequency: Annual/October

10427 **National Grocers Association Annual Convenience & Supermarket Showcase**
National Grocers Association
1825 Samuel Morse Drive
Reston, VA 22090

703-437-5300; Fax: 703-437-7768

2800 Attendees

10428 **National Homebrewers Conference and National Homebrew Competition**
Brewers Association
736 Pearl Street
Boulder, CO 80302

303-447-0816
888-822-6273; Fax: 303-447-2825
webmaster@brewersassociation.org
www.beertown.org
Facebook, Twitter

Chris P. Frey, Chair
Jake Keeler, Vice Chair
Roxanne Westendorf, Secretary

Education and fun combine for a great experience at the national conference for amateur brewers.
1900 Members
Founded in 1978

10429 **National Ice Cream Retailers Association Annual Convention**
1028 West Devon Avenue
Elk Grove Village, IL 60007

847-301-7500
866-303-6960; Fax: 847-301-8402
info@nicra.org
www.nicra.org

Dan Messer, President
David Zimmerman, President-Elect
Nanette Frey, Vice President
Carl Chaney, Secretary/Treasurer
Lynda Utterback, Executive Director

A major national convention for those in the retail ice ceam and frozen dessert business. Attendees are mostly independent operators/owners and vendors that sell to the retail/wholesale trade. Thirty-five to forty booths.
Frequency: Annual/November

10430 **National Nutritional Foods Association**
1773 T Street, NW
Washington, DC 20009

202-223-0101
800-966-6632; Fax: 202-223-0250
natural@NPAinfo.org
www.npainfo.org
Facebook, Twitter, LinkedIn

John F. Gay, Executive Director & CEO
Jeffrey Wright, President

Six hundred booths including educational seminars and exhibits of health and natural foods.
7.5M Attendees
Frequency: Annual/June

10431 **National Orange Show**
PO Box 5749
San Bernardino, CA 92412-5749

909-888-6788; Fax: 909-889-7666

Esther Armstrong, Executive Director
Brad Randall, Manager

Agricultural forum.
262M Attendees
Frequency: May

10432 **National Pest Management Association Annual Eastern Conference**
10460 North Street
Fairfax, VA 22030

703-352-6762
800-678-6722; Fax: 703-352-3031
www.npmapestworld.org
Facebook, Twitter

Alexis Wirtz, SVP, Meetings & Management Services
Megan Moloney, Director, Meetings & Exhibitions

Two hundred forty booths.
7000 Members
3500 Attendees
Frequency: Annual/October
Founded in 1933

10433 **National Policy Conference**
Crop Life America
1156 15th St NW
Washington, DC 20005-1752

202-296-1585; Fax: 202-463-0474
webmaster@croplifeamerica.org
www.croplifeamerica.org
Facebook, Twitter, LinkedIn, YouTube

Christopher Novak, President & CEO

Brings together leading experts, academics and politicos to engage in a debate on the development of the Farm Bill. How does Congress design a Farm Bill that addresses human, social, economic, research and environmental needs while taking into account farmers, consumers and the natural systems that give us the food and fiber we need to live?
Frequency: Annual/May

10434 **National Potato Council's Annual Meeting**
National Potato Council
5690 Dtc Boulevard
Greenwood Village, CO 80111-3232

303-773-9295; Fax: 303-773-9296
www.npcspud.com

Annual meeting and exhibits of potato growing equipment, supplies and services.

10435 **National ProStart Invitational**
NRAEF
175 W Jackson Boulevard
Suite 1500
Chicago, IL 60604-2814

312-715-1010
800-765-2122; Fax: 312-583-9767
www.nraef.org

Culinary and management competition attracts top high school ProStart students from around the country. Winning teams secure scholarships from the NRAEF and The Coca-Cola Company, along with colleges and universities.
Frequency: Annual/April
Founded in 1987

10436 **National Soft Drink Association Show**
1101 16th Street NW
Suite 700
Washington, DC 20036-4877

202-463-6732; Fax: 202-463-8178

Susan K Neely, President
Patricia M Vaughan, Secretary
Jim L Turner, Treasurer

Annual show of 300 members of soft drink makers and their suppliers.
25M Attendees
Frequency: Annual Fall
Founded in 1919

10437 **National Turkey Federation Annual Meeting**
National Turkey Federation
1225 New York Avenue NW
Suite 400
Washington, DC 20005-6404

202-898-0100; Fax: 202-898-0203
info@turkeyfed.org
www.eatturkey.com
Facebook, Twitter, YouTube

Joel Brandenberger, President
Beth Breeding, VP, Communications & Marketing
Hayden Demos, Coordinator, Member Services
Shelby Shaw, Manager, Communications

Advocates for all segments of the US turkey industry, providing services and conducting activities that increase demand for its members' products. The federation also protects and enhances its members' ability to effectively and profitably provide wholesome, high quality, nutritious turkey products.
Frequency: Annual

10438 **National Watermelon Association**
Annual Meeting
406 Railroad Street
Morven, GA 31638

229-775-2130; Fax: 229-775-2344

Nacy Childers, Contact

10439 **National Wheat Growers Association Convention**
415 2nd Street NE
Suite 300
Washington, DC 20002-4900

202-547-7800; Fax: 202-546-2638
wheatworld@wheatworld.org
www.wheatworld.org
Facebook, Twitter, YouTube

Chandler Goule, Chief Executive Officer

Major agri business exhibits including farm equipment and services. 100 booths.
Frequency: Annual/January

10440 **Natural Products Exposition East**
New Hope Natural Media
1301 Spruce Street
Boulder, CO 80302

303-939-8440; Fax: 303-939-9559

20000 Attendees

10441 **Natural Products Exposition West**
New Hope Communications
1301 Spruce Street
Boulder, CO 80302

303-939-8440; Fax: 303-939-9559

31000 Attendees

10442 **New England Equipment Dealers Association**
PO Box 895
Concord, NH 03302-0895

603-225-5510; Fax: 603-225-5510

George M Becker, Managing Director

Annual convention and trade show held the first weekend in December for farm, industrial and outdoor equipment dealers in the six New England states. 95 booths.
300 Attendees
Frequency: December

10443 **Nightclub & Bar Show**
Questex LLC
3 Speen St.
Framingham, MA 01701

nightclubbarshow@xpressreg.net
www.ncbshow.com
Facebook, Twitter, Instagram, Vimeo

Jeremiah Batucan, Group Conference Director
Jillian Blauvelt, Conference Coordinator

Annual gathering of bar, nightlife, hospitality and beverage professionals.

10444 **Nightclub and Bar/Beverage Retailer Convention and Trade Show**
National Bar and Restaurant Association
307 Jackson Avenue W
Oxford, MS 38655

662-236-5510
800-247-3881; Fax: 662-236-5541
www.bevindustry.com

Jennifer Robinson, Senior VP
Hollis Green, Trade Show Director
Kaytee Hazlewood, VP Marketing

The industry's first national conference and trade show devoted to business basics, promotions and marketing for liquor stores, nightclubs and bars. More than 2,500 exhibits.
38800 Attendees
Frequency: March

10445 **North American Deer Farmers Association Annual Conference & Exhibit**
North American Deer Farmers Association
104 S Lakeshore Drive
Lake City, MN 55041-1266

651-345-5600; Fax: 651-345-5603
info@nadefa.org
www.nadefa.org
Facebook

Carolyn Laughlin, President
R.Ray Burdette, First VP
Will Ainsworth, Second VP
Bill Pittenger, Third VP
Dr. Hank Dimuzio, Treasurer

Annual show of more than 30 exhibitors of deer farming equipment, supplies and services.
550+ Attendees
Frequency: Annual/Summer
Founded in 1984

10446 **North American Farm and Power Show**
Tradexpos
811 W Oakland Avenue
PO Box 1067
Austin, MN 55912

507-437-4697
800-949-3976; Fax: 507-437-8917
steve@tradexpos.com
www.tradexpos.com

Steve Guenthner, Show Director

Agri-business farm show for the 5-state region. Free admission and parking.
32M Attendees
Frequency: Annual/March

10447 **North American Fertilizer Transportation Conference**
Fertilizer Institute
425 Third Street, SW
Suite 950
Washington, DC 20024

202-962-0490; Fax: 202-962-0577
information@tfi.org
www.tfi.org
Facebook, Twitter, LinkedIn

Mariana Gallo, Senior Director, Conferences

Provides an opportunity for shippers and carriers to discuss issues of concern and work to reach mutually-beneficial solutions to logistical problems.
Frequency: Annual/October

10448 **North American Olive Oil Association Mid- Year Meeting**
North American Olive Oil Association
3301 Route 66
Suite 205, Building C
Neptune, NJ 07753

732-922-0500; Fax: 732-922-3590
www.aboutoliveoil.org

Bob Bauer, President

Olive growers and oil processors group for legislative advocacy and trade networking.

10449 **North American Specialty Coffee Retailers' Expo**
PO Box 14827
Portland, OR 97293

503-236-2587
800-548-0551; Fax: 503-236-3165

Jan Weigel, Director
Founded in 1995

10450 **Northeast Food Service and Lodging Expo and Conference**
Reed Exhibition Companies
383 Main Avenue
Norwalk, CT 06851

203-840-4800; Fax: 203-840-4824

Linda Karpowich, Customer Service Manager

Annual show of 600 exhibitors of food services, operating equipment and services for the hospitality and institutional foodservice industry.
29000 Attendees

10451 **Northeast Pizza Expo**
MacFadden Protech
137 E Market Street
New Albany, IN 47150

812-949-0909
800-489-8324; Fax: 812-949-1867
lkeith@pizzatoday.com
www.pizzaexpo.com

William T Oakley, Senior VP Expositions
Linda F Keith, Manager
Patty Crone, Manager

Manufacturers, food purveyors and service representatives from pizza or related industries.

10452 **Northwest Agricultural Congress**
4991 Drift Creek Rd SE
Sublimity, OR 97385-9764

503-769-8940; Fax: 503-769-8946
www.nwagshow.com

Jim Heater, Show Manager

Second largest agricultural show on the west coast. Show is produced by the Northwest Horticultural Congress which is a partnership between Oregon Horticultural Society, the Oregon Association of Nurseries and Northwest Nut Growers Association. Show held in conjunction with annual meetings and seminars by all three of the horticultural groups.
21000 Members

10453 **Northwest Food Manufacturing & Packaging Association**
Northwest Food Processors Association
6950 SW Hampton Street
Suite 340
Portland, OR 98223-8332

503-639-7676; Fax: 503-639-7007

Stephanie Green, Show Manager
Mindy Todd, Marketing Coordinator

Containing 450 booths.
3000 Attendees
Frequency: Janurary

10454 **Nut Grower Magazine Farm Show**
Western Agricultural Publishing Company
4974 E Clinton Way
Suite 123
Fresno, CA 93727-1520

559-261-0396; Fax: 559-252-7387

Phill Rhoads, Manager

Productions seminars, guest speakers, prizes and exhibits for nut growers. Containing 80 booths and exhibits.

10455 **OFPA Annual Convention and Exposition**
Ozark Food Processors Association
2650 N Young Avenue
Fayetteville, AR 72704

479-575-4607; Fax: 479-575-2165
ofpa@uark.edu
ofpa.uark.edu

Cindy Stricklaw, President
Roure Threfall, Director

OFPA members and registered guests learn about new trends in the food industry during technical sessions and the exposition. The location for the 2012 meeting is Springfield, AR.
500 Attendees
Frequency: Annual/ April
Founded in 1906

10456 **Oklahoma Restaurant Convention & Expo**
Oklahoma Restaurant Association
3800 N Portland Avenue
Oklahoma City, OK 73112-2948

405-942-8181
800-375-8181; Fax: 405-942-0541
www.okrestaurants.com

Lori Culver, Convention Manager

Annual show of 450 manufacturers, suppliers and distributors. Exhibits of providers of food service and hospitality products, services and equipment. Held at the Myriad Convention Center in Oklahoma City, Oklahoma.
9M Attendees
Frequency: April
Founded in 1938

10457 **PACK International Expo**
Packaging Machinery Manufacturers Institute
11911 Freedom Drive
Suite 600
Reston, VA 20190

571-612-3200; Fax: 703-243-8556
jbrown@pmmi.org
www.packexpointernational.com

Charles D. Yuska, President & CEO
Carolyn Dress, Business Development Manager
Jessie Brown, Exhibit Sales Contact
Beth Murray, Exhibit Sales Contact
Merideth Newman, Exhibit Sales Contact

The event will feature more than 2,400 packaging and processing exhibitors covering a wide range of the packaging supply chain. It will offer opportunities to network with others in the industry, specialized education sessions led by industry experts and hands on demonstrations of the latest technologies in the industry.
800+ Members
50K Attendees
Frequency: October
Founded in 1933

10458 **PACex International**
Packaging, Food Process and Logistics Exhibition
2255 Sheppard Avenue E
Suite E330
Toronto Ontario M2J-4YI
416-490-7860; Fax: 416-490-7844
www.pacexinternational.com
Maria Tavares, Expositions Manager
15000 Attendees
Frequency: September-October

10459 **PLMA Trade Show**
Private Label Manufacturers Association
630 Third Avenue
New York, NY 10017-6506
212-972-3131; Fax: 212-983-1382
info@plma.com
www.plma.com
Brian Sharoff, President
Myra Rosen, VP
Tom Prendergast, Director, Research Services
The best place for private label networking.
3200+ Members
10000 Attendees
Frequency: Annual/November
Founded in 1979

10460 **PMA Foodservice Conference & Exposition**
Produce Marketing Association
1500 Casho Mill Road
Newark, DE 19711-3547
302-738-7100; Fax: 302-731-2409
showmanagement@pma.com
www.pma.com
Twitter, YouTube, Flickr
Cathy Burns, CEO
Dan Stark, Chief Content Officer
Join the who's-who of chefs, menu developers, restaurant operators, grower-shippers, distributors and foodservice suppliers to see and sample the newest products and services, learn about the latest consumer trends and tastes, see old colleagues or make new contacts.
Frequency: Annual/July
Founded in 1981

10461 **PMA Fresh Summit International Convention & Exposition**
Produce Marketing Association
1500 Casho Mill Road
PO Box 6036
Newark, DE 19711-3547
302-387-7100; Fax: 302-731-2409
showmanagement@pma.com
www.pma.com/freshsummit
Facebook, Twitter, YouTube
Cathy Burns, CEO
Dan Stark, Chief Content Officer
An event that attracts buyers and suppliers from the produce and floral industries; from the retail and foodservice channels and from more than 70 counties.
17M Attendees
Frequency: Annual/October

10462 **PTNPA Annual Convention**
Peanut & Tree Nut Processors Association
PO Box 2660
Alexandria, VA 22301
301-365-2521; Fax: 301-365-7705
ptnpa.org
Twitter
General meeting sessions, keynote speakers, exhibitors from the industry.
400 Attendees
Frequency: Annual/January

10463 **Pan-American International Livestock Exposition**
State Fair of Texas
PO Box 150009
Dallas, TX 75315-0009
214-565-9931; Fax: 214-421-8792
livestock@greatstatefair.com
www.bigtex.com
Benny Clark, Director
Elvis Presley, Vice President
Annual show and exhibits of livestock, livestock equipment, agricultural technology and consumer products.
3.5M Attendees
Frequency: September/October

10464 **Pickle Packers International Pickle Fair**
1620 i St Nw
Suite 925
Washington, DC 20006-4035
202-312-2859; Fax: 630-584-0759
Richard Hentschell, Executive VP
Fifty booths, seminars and programs held in odd numbered years.
300+ Attendees
Frequency: October

10465 **Poultry Supplier Showcase**
National Poultry & Food Distributors
2014 Osborne Rd
Saint Marys, GA 31558
770-535-9901
877-845-1545; Fax: 770-535-7385
info@npfda.org
www.npfda.org
Cece Corbin, President
Carol Lanham, Member Services & Development Dir.
Alina Cooper, Membership Relations & Comm. Dir.
Annual convention and poultry suppliers showcase. Three day convention and trade show.
900 Attendees
Frequency: Annual/January
Founded in 1967

10466 **Pre-Harvest Food Safety Conference**
North American Meat Processors Association
1910 Association Drive
Reston, VA 20191-1500
703-758-1900
800-368-3043; Fax: 703-758-8001
Philip Kimball, Executive Director
Sabrina Moore, Accounting/Meetings Manager
Ann Wells, Director Scientific Affairs
Jane Jacobs, Communications Director
Brings regulators and researchers together with experts from the poultry industry, and the allied industries that serve them, to discuss the known and unknown issues associated with the control of food borne pathogens in pre-harvest operations. Conference will be one of the most thorough explorations into the poultry pre-harvest arena that has ever been conducted.
Frequency: Annual/January

10467 **Presidents Conference**
International Foodservice Distributors Association
1660 International Drive
Suite 550
McLean, VA 22102
703-532-9400; Fax: 703-880-7117
www.ifdaonline.org
John Tracy, Chairman
Craig Hoskins, Vice Chairman
Mark Harman, Treasurer
Mark S. Allen, President/CEO
Gain breakthrough insights and take away high value solutions. Collaborate with fellow leaders in an information rich learning environment with plenty of networking opportunities. All-industry forum addressing issues impacting the foodservice supply chain.
Frequency: Annual/October

10468 **Private Label Manufacturers Association Trade Show**
630 Third Avenue
New York, NY 10017
212-972-3131; Fax: 212-983-1382
info@plma.com
www.plma.com
Brian Sharoff, President
Myra Rosen, Vice President
A private label trade show.
3200+ Members
Frequency: Annual/November
Founded in 1979

10469 **ProMat**
Material Handling Industry of America
8720 Red Oak Boulevard
Suite 201
Charlotte, NC 28217-3992
704-676-1190; Fax: 704-676-1199
gbaer@mhia.org
www.mhia.org
Greg Baer, Senior Sales Associate
Jennifer Breadling, Manager Of Communications
The premier showcase of material handling and logistics solutions in North America. The show is designed to offer productivity solutions and information by showcasing the products and services of over 700 leading material handling and logistics providers.
Frequency: Annual

10470 **Process Expo**
Food Processing Suppliers Association
1451 Dolley Madison Blvd
Suite 101
Mc Lean, VA 22101-3850
703-761-2600; Fax: 703-761-4334
info@fpsa.org
www.fpsa.org
Facebook, Twitter, LinkedIn
David Seckman, President
George Melnykovich, Senior Advisor
Robyn Roche, CFO
Tradeshow where qualified buyers representing every market of the food industry meet face to face with suppliers showcasing the newest developments in processing technology. Exhibitors are able to demonstrate state-of-the-art food processing equipment in baking, beverage, dairy, fruit and vegetable, and meat/poultry industries.
510 Members
Frequency: Annual/November
Founded in 2005

10471 **R&DA Annual Spring & Fall Meeting and Exhibition**
R&D Associates

16607 Blanco Road
Suite 305
San Antonio, TX 78232-1940

210-682-4302; Fax: 830-493-8036

Jim Fagan, Meeting Coordinator

Hear presentations by key officials, network with decision makers, get updates on key issues and gain a competitive edge within the industry.
300 Attendees
Frequency: Apr/Oct/Non-Members:$1099

10472 **RFA Annual Conference**
Refrigerated Foods Association
1640 Powers Ferry Road
Bldg. 2, Suite 200A
Marietta, GA 30067

770-303-9905; Fax: 770-303-9906
info@refrigeratedfoods.org
www.refrigeratedfoods.org

Brian Edmonds, President
George Bradford, Vice President
Steve Loehndorf, Secretary
Wes Thaller, Treasurer

The RFA Conference is a great way to network and gain important new information affecting the industry, including technical innovations, sales and marketing tips, consumer trends, distribution solutions, new product and package development, and food safety issues.
200+ Members
Frequency: Annual/February
Founded in 1980

10473 **RFA Annual Conference & Exhibition**
Refrigerated Foods Association
2971 Flowers Road S
Suite 266
Atlanta, GA 30341-5403

770-452-0660; Fax: 770-455-3879
info@refrigeratedfoods.org
www.refrigeratedfoods.org

Brian Edmonds, President
George Bradford, Vice President
Steve Loehndorf, Secretary
Wes Thaller, Treasurer

Suppliers displaying the latest offerings in equipment, packaging, ingredients and services for the industry. A great way to network and gain important new information affecting the industry, including technical innovations, sales and marketing tips, consumer trends, distribution solutions, new product and packaging development and food safety issues.
Frequency: Annual/April

10474 **Restaurants Rock**
NRAEF
175 W Jackson Boulevard
Suite 1500
Chicago, IL 60604-2814

312-715-1010
800-765-2122; Fax: 312-583-9767
www.nraef.org

The only official party of the NRA Show, Restaurants Rock brings together the restaurant and hospitality industry in a night of networking and celebration.
Frequency: Annual/May
Founded in 1987

10475 **Retail Confectioners International Annual Convention and Exposition**
Retail Confectioners International
1807 Glenview Road
Suite 204
Glenview, IL 60025-2968

847-724-6120; Fax: 847-724-2719

Van Billington, Director
Michelle May, Contact

Annual exhibition offering exhibits of confectionery equipment, supplies, finished products and packaging materials.
1.5M Attendees
Frequency: Annual

10476 **SANA/USB Annual Soy Symposium**
Soyfoods Association of North America
1001 Connecticut Avenue NW
Suite 1120
Washington, DC 20036

202-659-3520
www.soyfoods.org

Nancy Chapman, Executive Director
Anne Chambers, Membership Coordinator

Co-sponsored with United Soybean Board, see the latest innovative designs and products from industry representatives.
Frequency: Apr/Non-Members:$995
Founded in 1978

10477 **SAVOR, An American Craft Beer & Food Experience**
Brewers Association
736 Pearl Street
Boulder, CO 80302

303-447-0816
888-822-6273; Fax: 303-447-2825
webmaster@brewersassociation.org
www.beertown.org
Facebook, Twitter

Chris P. Frey, Chair
Jake Keeler, Vice Chair
Roxanne Westendorf, Secretary

The main beer and food pairing event in the US. Where beer enthusiasts and foodies can interact directly with some of the greatest brewers and brewery owners in the world.
1900 Members
Founded in 1978

10478 **SBS Annual Conference & Exhibition**
Society for Biomolecular Sciences
36 Tamarack Avenue
Suite 348
Danbury, CT 06811

203-788-8828; Fax: 203-748-7557
www.sbsonline.org

Agnes Amos, Exhibitions/Meetings Director
Marietta Manoni, Exhibitions/Meetings Manager

This event brings together leaders in the pharmaceutical, biotech and agrochemical industries from around the world. Highlighting the impact of screening and technology applications on drug discovery.
Frequency: Sept/Non-Members $1,445
Founded in 1995

10479 **SCAA Annual Conference & Exhibition**
Specialty Coffee Association of America
330 Golden Shore
Suite 50
Long Beach, CA 90802

562-624-4100; Fax: 562-624-4101
coffee@scaa.org
www.scaa.org

Ted Lingle, Executive Director
Scott Welker, Administrative Director

The country's premier coffee event, attracting coffee professionals from more than 40 countries. Attendees include coffee producers, exporters and importers, roasters, manufacturers, brew masters, and consumer enthusiasts.
8000 Attendees
Frequency: April/Non-Members:$585
Founded in 1982

10480 **SCAA Annual Exposition**
Specialty Coffee Association of America
330 Golden Shore
Suite 50
Long Beach, CA 90802-4246

562-624-4100; Fax: 562-624-4101
info@scaa.org
www.scaa.org
Facebook, Twitter, YouTube

Ric Rhinehart, Executive Director
Tracy Ging, Deputy Executive Director
Ted Lingle, Senior Advisor

Roasters & retailers attend and have the opportunity to exhibit products on the show floor, network with industry's decision makers, and further their professional careers by participating in the SCAA's numerous lectures, labs or certification programs.
2500+ Members
Frequency: Annual/April
Founded in 1982

10481 **SCST Annual Meeting**
Society of Commerical Seed Technologists
101 E State Street
Suite 214
Ithaca, NY 14850

607-256-3313; Fax: 607-256-3313
www.analyzeseeds.com

Jess Peterson, Executive Director
Kelly Polzin, Annual Meeting Coordinator

A joint meeting with the Association of Official Seed Analysts and the Association of Official Seed Certifying Agencies. Workshops, Exhibits, speakers and more regarding the seed industry.
Frequency: June
Founded in 1922

10482 **SEAFWA Annual Convention**
Southeast Association of Fish & Wildlife Agencies
8005 Freshwater Farms Road
Tallahassee, FL 32309-9009

850-893-1204; Fax: 850-893-6204
www.seafwa.org

Robert M Brantly, Executive Secretary
Dianne Waller, Conference Coordinator

Providing a forum for presentation of information and exchange of ideas regarding the management and protection of fish and wildlife resources throughout the nation but emphasis on the southeast.
Frequency: Oct/Nov
Founded in 1947

10483 **SFA's Legislative Summit**
Snack Food Association
1600 Wilson Blvd
Suite 650
Arlington, VA 22209-2510

703-836-4500
800-628-1334; Fax: 703-836-8262
www.sfa.org

James A McCarthy, President/CEO

Discuss many of the most important legislative issues which will impact the snack food industry.
800 Members
Frequency: Annual/May
Founded in 1937

10484 **SNAXPO**
Snack Food Association

1600 Wilson Blvd
Suite 650
Arlington, VA 22209-2510

703-836-4500
800-628-1334; Fax: 703-836-8262
www.sfa.org

James A McCarthy, President/CEO

The world's largest, most comprehensive trade show devoted exclusively to the international snack food industry. Owners, executives and buyers from every segment of the industry around the globe come together for this premier event.
800 Members
Frequency: Annual/March
Founded in 1937

10485 SNAXPO: Snack Food Association
1600 Wilson Boulevard
Suite 650
Arlington, VA 22209-2510

703-836-4500
800-628-1334; Fax: 703-836-8262
www.sfa.org

Judi Barth, VP Marketing
Ann Wilkes, VP Communications
2000 Attendees
Frequency: February/March
Founded in 1938

10486 School Nutrition Association Annual National Conference
School Nutrition Association
120 Waterfront Street
Suite 300
National Harbor, MD 20745

301-686-3100
800-877-8822; Fax: 301-686-3115
servicecenter@schoolnutrition.org
www.schoolnutrition.org

Helen Phillips, President
Sandy Ford, President-Elect
Leah Schmidt, VP
Beth Taylor, Secretary/Treasurer

Learn, grow and exchange ideas with others committed to the healthful feeding of our children. With over 400 exhibitors and more than 90 quality education sessions, ANC gives you the opportunity to learn about the top trends and issues in school nutrition.
Frequency: Annual/July

10487 Southern Convenience Store & Petroleum Show
GA Ass'n of Convenience Stores/Petroleum Retailers
168 North Johnston Street
Suite 209
Dallas, GA 30132-4744

770-736-9723
877-294-1885; Fax: 770-736-9725
jtudor@aol.com
www.gacs.com
Facebook

Jim Tudor, President
Angela Holland, Vice President

Targeted to reach key individuals in the convenience store and petroleum industry from throughout the South. Attendees will include board members and key representatives from the Georgia Association of Convenience Stores and will be open to retailers from throughout the southern US.
2000 Attendees
Frequency: Annual/October

10488 Southwest Foodservice Exposition
Texas Restaurant Association
PO Box 1429
Austin, TX 78767

512-472-8990; Fax: 512-472-2777

31000 Attendees

10489 Special Event
Special Event Corporation
PO Box 8987
Malibu, CA 90265-8987

310-317-4522; Fax: 310-317-9644

4300 Attendees

10490 Sunbelt Agricultural Exposition
PO Box 28
Tifton, GA 31793-0028

229-985-1968; Fax: 229-387-7503

Dr. Edward White, Director

The latest agricultural technology in products and equipment plus harvesting and tillage demonstrations in the field. Largest farm show in North America. 4,000 booths.
Frequency: October

10491 Supermarket Industry Convention and Educational Exposition
Food Marketing Institute
2345 Crystal Drive
Suite 800
Arlington, VA 22202

202-452-8444; Fax: 202-429-4519
www.fmi.org
Facebook, Twitter, LinkedIn, YouTube

Leslie G. Sarasin, President/CEO

Features over 1,500 exhibitors, over 30 educational workshops and unique pavilions as well as the presentation of the Food Marketing Institute's annual state of the industry research. Attended by a worldwide audience of professionals with an interest in the food distribution industry from CEOs through store level management.
36000 Attendees
Frequency: Annual/May

10492 SupplySide East
Virgo Publishing LLC
3300 N Central Avenue
Suite 300
Phoenix, AZ 85012

480-990-1101; Fax: 480-675-8154
peggyj@vpico.com
www.supplysideshow.com
Facebook, Twitter, LinkedIn

Tradeshow that brings global dietary supplement, food and personal care companies together with healthy and innovative ingredient suppliers. Meadowlands Exposition Center, Secaucus New Jersey. More than 340 booths.
Frequency: Annual/May

10493 SupplySide West
Virgo Publishing LLC
3300 N Central Avenue
Suite 300
Phoenix, AZ 85012

480-990-1101; Fax: 480-675-8154
peggyj@vpico.com
www.supplysideshow.com

Tradeshow that brings global dietary supplement, food and personal care companies together with healthy and innovative ingredient supplier. More than 1100 booths.
Frequency: Annual/October

10494 TFI Fertilizer Marketing & Business Meeting
Fertilizer Institute
425 Third Street, SW
Suite 950
Washington, DC 20024

202-962-0490; Fax: 202-962-0577
information@tfi.org
www.tfi.org
Facebook, Twitter, LinkedIn

Roberta Rosenberg, Senior Director, Marketing

Brings together members from each sector of the fertilizer industry for two days of networking and conducting business leading up the the spring planting season.
Frequency: Annual/February

10495 TFI World Fertilizer Conference
Fertilizer Institute
425 Third Street, SW
Suite 950
Washington, DC 20024

202-962-0490; Fax: 202-962-0577
information@tfi.org
www.tfi.org
Facebook, Twitter, LinkedIn

Mariana Gallo, Senior Director, Conferences

Providing two days of networking and conducting business with industry leaders. Agenda includes two breakfast sessions with high profile speakers focusing on the global challenges facing the fertilizer industry.
Frequency: Annual/September

10496 The NAFEM Show
NAFEM
161 N Clark Street
Suite 2020
Chicago, IL 60601

312-821-0201; Fax: 312-821-0202
info@nafem.org
www.nafem.org

Steven R. Follett, President
Thomas R. Campion, President-Elect
Michael L. Whiteley, Secretary/Treasurer
Deirdre Flynn, Executive Vice President

Attracts foodservice professionals and features exhibitors displaying products for food preparation, cooking, storage and table service. Connecting buyers and sellers of foodservice equipment and supplies, The NAFEM Show provides a showcase for the hottest and coolest products available and features education sessions and social events with big-name entertainment.
625 Members
Frequency: Biennial/February

10497 The NAMA Show
National Automatic Merchandising Association
20 N Wacker Dr.
Suite 3500
Chicago, IL 60606

312-346-0370
800-331-8816; Fax: 312-704-4140
members@namanow.org
www.namanow.org/events/thenamashow
Facebook, Twitter, YouTube

Carla Balakgie, President & CEO

This event features an impressive array of the industry's newest products and hottest technology, educational sessions and unmatched networking opportunities.
4500 Attendees
Founded in 1936

10498 The NGA Show
National Grocers Association
1005 N Glebe Road
Suite 250
Arlington, VA 22201

703-516-0700; Fax: 703-516-0115
thefoodshows@clarionevents.com

www.thengashow.com
Facebook, Twitter, LinkedIn, YouTube

Peter J. Larkin, President & CEO

Providing an unparalleled opportunity to network, learn, and advance business. Guaranteed a convention experience that is informational, motivational, and enjoyable.
Frequency: Annual/February

10499 Top-to-Top Conference
Association of Sales & Marketing Companies
1010 Wisconsin Avenue NW
#900
Washington, DC 20007

202-337-9351; Fax: 202-337-4508

Mark Baum, President
Karen Connell, Executive VP
Rick Abraham, VP/COO Foodservice
Jamie DeSimone, Director Marketing/Member Services
Frequency: February

10500 Top2Top Nexgen
5225 Wisonsin Avenue NW
Suite 316
Washington, DC 20015-2055

202-596-8112; Fax: 202-293-1702
info@fsmaonline.com
www.fsmaonline.com

Jerry Campbell, Chair & President

Annual conference of the Foodservice Sales & Marketing Association.
Founded in 2003

10501 Tortilla Industry Annual Convention and Trade Exposition
Tortilla Industry Association
1600 Wilson Blvd
Suite 650
Arlington, VA 22209

800-944-6099; Fax: 800-944-6177
info@tortilla-info.com
www.tortilla-info.com

Nathan W. Fisher, Chairman
Joseph F. Riley, Chairman-Elect
Nick Scheurer, 2nd Vice President
Sam Tamayo, Treasurer

A growing event for tortilla producers and suppliers that provides the only annual trade show featuring materials, equipment, and services exclusively for the Tortilla industry, plus business lectures to assist in improving your business and personal knowledge.
900 Attendees
Frequency: Annual/September

10502 Tree Fruit Expo
Western Agricultural Publishing Company
4974 E Clinton Way
Suite 123
Fresno, CA 93727-1520

559-261-0396; Fax: 559-252-7387

Phill Rhoads, Manager

Productions seminars, dessert contest, guest speakers, prizes and exhibits for tree fruit growers. Containing 80 booths and exhibits.

10503 US Apple Association Annual Apple Crop Outlook & Marketing Conference
8233 Old Courthouse Road
Suite 200
Vienna, VA 22182

703-442-8850; Fax: 703-790-0845
info@usapple.org
www.usapple.org
Facebook, Twitter, YouTube

Provides up to the minute apple market analysis and premier networking opportunities.
300+ Attendees
Frequency: Annual/April

10504 US Meat Export Federation
1050 17th Street
Suite 2200
Denver, CO 80265-2077

303-623-6328; Fax: 303-623-0297
www.usmef.org

Jackie Boubin, Director of Services
Phil Seng, President

A convention of meat packers, grain, cattle and hog producers, trade officials and agribusiness and a trade show offering exhibits of beef, pork, veal, lamb products and more for foreign buyers. Trade show in May, convention in November.
300 Attendees

10505 USA Rice Millers' Association Convention
USA Rice Millers Association/Federation
4301 N Fairfax Drive
Suite 425
Arlington, VA 22203-1616

703-226-2300; Fax: 703-236-2301
riceinfo@usarice.com
Facebook, Twitter, YouTube

Jeanette Davis, Convention Coordinator
Betsy Ward, President/CEO
Linda Sieh, Vice President Finance
Johnny Broussard, Legislative Affairs Director
Lauren Echols, Government Affairs Coordinator

Exhibits, seminars on the advances in products, technologies and services, keynote speakers from the industry. The convention is recognized as the annual gathering for the U.S. rice milling industry. It is an opportunity to strengthen business ties and make new connections.
Frequency: Annual/June
Founded in 1900

10506 Unified Wine and Grape Symposium
PO Box 1855
Davis, CA 95617-1855

530-753-3142; Fax: 530-753-3318
info@unifiedsymposium.org
unifiedsymposium.org

Bill Mead, Event/Tradeshow Coordinator

One of the industry's premier gatherings, presents a vital platform to focus on the issues shaping today, while interfacing the topics and trends shaping the future of grapegrowing and winemaking.
Frequency: Annual/January

10507 Unipro Food Service Companies Association
Unipro Food Service
PO Box 724945
Atlanta, GA 31139-1945

770-952-0871; Fax: 770-952-0872

Donna Campbell, Show Manager
Roger Toomey, CEO

250 tables.
1.3M Attendees

10508 United Produce Show
United Fresh Fruit & Vegetable Association
1901 Pennsylvania Avenue NW
Suite 1100
Washington, DC 20006

202-303-3400; Fax: 202-303-3433
united@unitedfresh.org
www.uffva.org
Facebook, Twitter, YouTube

Access to the best and newest products from the entire retail supply continuum, make new contacts, learn what your competition is bringing to the table and much more.
30M Attendees
Frequency: Annual/May

10509 Upper Midwest Hospitality Restaurant & Lodging Show
Corcoran Expositions
100 W. Monroe
Suite 1001
Chicago, IL 60603

312-541-0567; Fax: 312-541-0573
www.corcexpo.com

Tom Corcoran, President
33000 Attendees
Founded in 1990

10510 Vinegar Institute Annual Meeting
1100 Johnson Ferry Road
Suite 300
Atlanta, GA 30342

404-252-3663; Fax: 404-252-0774
vi@kellencompany.com
www.versatilevinegar.org

Pamela A Chumley, President
Jeannie Milewski, Executive Director

Presentations regarding possible health claims for vinegar, an economic update and a world wine and grape supply update. Other topics include from green to greenwashing; how food companies are succeeding (and failing) at market sustainability and best practices in energy & carbon management. Also numerous networking opportunities available for all attendees.
Frequency: Annual/March

10511 WFLO/IARW Annual Convention & Trade Show
World Food Logistics Organization

703-373-4300; Fax: 707-373-4301

Megan Kalaski, Trade Show Coordinator
Lorien Onderdonk, Member Services Coordinator

offers a singular opportunity to present product and service information to the largest concentration of public refrigerated warehouse executives in the world.
Frequency: Annual/April

10512 WSWA Annual Convention
Wine and Spirits Wholesalers of America
805 15th Street NW
Suite 1120
Washington, DC 20005

202-371-9792; Fax: 202-789-2405
www.wswaconvention.org

Kristi Hepner, Coordinator, Meetings & Conventions
Kari Langerman, Sr. Director, Conventions

Get the latest information for wholesale wine distributors, exhibits and speakers from the industry.
Frequency: April-May
Founded in 1943

10513 WSWA Convention & Exposition
Wine and Spirits Wholesalers of America
805 15th Street NW
Suite 1120
Washington, DC 20005

202-371-9792; Fax: 202-789-2405
www.wswa.org

Michelle L. Korsmo, President/CEO
Kristi Hepner, Coordinator, Meetings &

Conventions
Kari Langerman, Sr. Director, Conventions

Where distributors seek out new and exciting beverage products for US consumers, meet with existing portfolio partners and look for services to enhance internal operations. Providing the opportunities needed to introduce new products or grow brands, products, or services in the US marketplace.
450 Members
Frequency: Annual/April
Founded in 1943

10514 **WSWA Executive Committee Meeting**
Wine and Spirits Wholesalers of America
805 15th Street NW
Suite 1120
Washington, DC 20005

202-371-9792; Fax: 202-789-2405
www.wswa.org

Sydney Ross, Chairman
Barkley Stuart, Vice Chairman
Danny Wirtz, Vice Chairman
Chris Underwood, Senior Vice President
Tom Cole, Vice President

The Executive Committee, Committee Chairs and Vice Chairs and past chairmen are invited to attend.
450 Members
Frequency: Annual/January
Founded in 1943

10515 **Waldbaum International Food Nutrition Show**
80 Town Line Road
Rocky Hill, CT 06067-1249

860-529-1416; Fax: 860-721-6258

John Masterson, Manager

A wide variety of new and existing food products and services. 225 booths.
25M Attendees
Frequency: March

10516 **Walnut Council Annual Meeting**
Walnut Council
Wright Forestry Center
1011 N 725 West
West Lafayette, IN 47906-9431

765-583-3501; Fax: 765-583-3512
www.walnutcouncil.org

Liz Jackson, Executive Director

Exhibits of equipment, supplies and services for walnut growing.
Frequency: Annual/July

10517 **Washington Insight & Advocacy Conference**
International Foodservice Distributors Association
1660 International Drive
Suite 550
McLean, VA 22102

703-532-9400; Fax: 703-880-7117
www.ifdaonline.org

John Tracy, Chairman
Craig Hoskins, Vice Chairman
Mark Harman, Treasurer
Mark S. Allen, President/CEO

IFDA members from coast-to-coast converge on the capitol to gain insight from congressional leaders and federal regulators and let them know how their decisions affect the foodservice distribution idustry.
Frequency: Annual/April

10518 **West Coast Seafood Show**
Diversified Expositions
121 Free Street
Portland, ME 04112

207-842-5500; Fax: 207-842-5505
food@divcom.com
www.westcoastseafood.com

Karen Butland, Show Manager
Brian Perkins, Executive Director
Frequency: November

10519 **Western Food Industry Exposition**
555 Capitol Mall
Suite 235
Sacramento, CA 95814-4557

FAX 703-876-0904

Keith Biersner, Account Executive

Retailers from 13 western states and suppliers from around the world. Relevant education sessions, vibrant exhibits and excellent social events are all designed to create the best form to enhance your companies bottom line. 400 booths.
3500 Attendees
Frequency: October
Founded in 1998

10520 **Western Food Service and Hospitality Expo**
California Restaurant Association
383 Main Avenue
PO Box 6059
Norwalk, CT 06851

203-840-5612
800-840-5612; Fax: 203-840-9612
www.westernfoodexpo.com

Chris Tatulli, Sales Manager
Steve Kalman, Industry VP

Showcases food products, food service equipment and allied services for the restaurant, food service and hospitality industries, as well as gourmet and prepared foods. Located on the West Coast, the show alternates annually between the Moscone Center in San Francisco and the LA Convention Center.
20M Attendees
Frequency: August

10521 **Western Restaurant Show**
California Restaurant Association
1011 10th St
Sacramento, CA 95814-3501

916-447-5793; Fax: 213-384-1723

A trade show of food service equipment, supplies and services. 2,000 booths.
35M Attendees
Frequency: August

10522 **Wine and Spirits Wholesalers of America**
805 15th Street NW
Suite 430
Washington, DC 20005

202-371-9792; Fax: 202-789-2405
wswa@wswa.org
www.wswa.org

Craig Wolf, President/CEO
Megan McIntire, Director Convention/Meetings
Karen Gravois, VP Public Relations/Communications

Suppliers of alcoholic beverages from around the world. 300 booths plus educational sessions.
3M Attendees
Frequency: April

10523 **Wineries Unlimited**
Vineyard & Winery Management
3883 Airway Drive
Suite 250
Santa Rosa, CA 95403

707-577-7700; Fax: 707-577-7705
Facebook, Twitter

The largest, longest running, and most powerful wine industry event in the eastern US.
2000 Attendees
Frequency: Annual/February

10524 **Winter State Policy Conference**
Wine and Spirits Wholesalers of America
805 15th Street NW
Suite 1120
Washington, DC 20005

202-371-9792; Fax: 202-789-2405
www.wswa.org

Michelle L. Korsmo, President & CEO
Kristi Hepner, Coordinator, Conventions
Kari Langerman, Sr. Director, Conventions

Provides an opportunity for wholesaler state association leaders to discuss the political and legal issues facing wholesalers across the country.
450 Members
Frequency: Annual/December
Founded in 1943

10525 **Wisconsin Restaurant Expo**
Wisconsin Restaurant Association
2801 Fish Hatchery Road
Madison, WI 53703-3197

608-270-9950
800-589-3211; Fax: 608-270-9960
dfaris@wirestaurant.org
www.wirestaurant.org

Dawn Renz-Faris, Exposition Director
Carrie Douglas, Executive Assistant
Gail Parr, Executive Vice President

Comprehensive foodservice trade show featuring hundreds of exhibits, free educational seminars and exciting floor show events.
10000 Attendees
Frequency: March
Founded in 1933
Mailing list available for rent

10526 **World Conference & Exhibition on Oil Seed and Vegetable Oil Utilization**
American Oil Chemists Society
2710 S. Boulder
Urbana, IL 61802-6996

217-359-2344; Fax: 217-351-8091
general@aocs.org
www.aocs.org
Facebook, Twitter

Sevim Erhan, Committee Chairperson

Attendees are interested in learning the latest information on currint and emerging technologies from all areas in oilseed and vegetable oil utilization.
Frequency: Annual/August

10527 **World Dairy Expo**
3310 Latham
Madison, WI 53713

608-224-6455; Fax: 608-224-0300
wde@wdexpo.com
www.worlddairyexpo.com

Tom McKittrick, Manager
Lisa Behnke, Marketing Manager
65M Attendees
Frequency: October, Annually
Founded in 1966

10528 **World Pork Exposition**
National Pork Producers Council

PO Box 10383
Des Moines, IA 50306-9960

515-788-8012; Fax: 847-838-1941
wrigleyj@nppc.org
www.worldpork.org

John Wrigley, General Manager
Alice Vinsand, Trade Show Manager

More than 450 companies show the newest technology, information, products and services for pork producers. Activities include breed shows and sales, business district, environmental education center, pork product showcase, big grill, pork 101, educational seminars and activities.
40000 Attendees
Frequency: June

10529 World Wine Market
775 E Blithedale Avenue
#370
Mill Valley, CA 94941

415-383-1226; Fax: 415-383-0858
sclarke@world-wine-market.com
www.world-wine-market.com

Stephanie Clarke, VP Sales/Marketing

10530 World of Food and Fuel EXPO
Tennessee Grocers Association
1838 Elm Hill Pike
Suite 136
Nashville, TN 37210-3726

615-889-0136
800-238-8742; Fax: 615-889-2877
www.tngrocer.org

Jarron Springer, President
Cyndi Randle, Chairman
John Wampler, Treasurer
8000 Attendees
Frequency: April

10531 Worldwide Food Expo
Dairy and Food Industries Supply Association
1451 Dolley Madison Boulevard
Suite 101
McLean, VA 22101

703-761-2600; Fax: 703-761-4334
www.worldwidefoodexpo.com

Trade show and education forum for the food, dairy, beverage and technologically related industries, featuring equipment, services and ingredients that highlight new development and technologies in processing and packaging.
350,000 square feet.
Frequency: Annual/October

Directories & Databases

10532 AGRICOLA
US National Agricultural Library
10301 Baltimore Ave
Room 13
Beltsville, MD 20705-2351

301-504-5755; Fax: 301-504-5675
www.nal.usda.gov

Gary K McCone, Associate Director

A database containing more than 3.2 million citations to journal literature, government reports, proceedings, books, periodicals, theses, patents, audiovisuals, electronic information, and other materials related to agriculture and its allied sciences.

10533 ARI Network
330 E Kilbourn Ave
Suite 565
Milwaukee, WI 53202-3144

414-220-9100
800-558-9044; Fax: 414-283-4357

Lawrence Shindell, Owner
John Kermath, Director

Offers current information on agricultural business, financial and weather information as well as statistical information for farmers.

10534 Ag Ed Network
ARI Network Services
330 E Kilbourn Ave
Suite 565
Milwaukee, WI 53202-3144

414-220-9100
800-558-9044; Fax: 414-283-4357

Lawrence Shindell, Owner
John Kermath, Director

Offers access to more than 1,500 educational agriculture lessons covering farm business management and farm production.
Frequency: Full-text

10535 AgriMarketing Services Guide
Henderson Communications LLC
1422 Elbridge Payne Rd
Suite 250
Chesterfield, MO 63017-8544

636-728-1428; Fax: 636-777-4178
www.agrimarketing.com

Lynn Henderson, Owner

AgriMarketing Services Guide is published each December and is commonly referred to as the Who's Who in the North American ag industry sector.
Frequency: Annual

10536 Agribusiness Worldwide International Buyer's Guide Issue
Keller International Publishing Corporation
150 Great Neck Rd
Great Neck, NY 11021-3309

516-829-9722; Fax: 516-829-9306
www.supplychainbrain.com

Jerry Keller, President
Mary Chavez, Director of Sales

A list of companies that supply, manufacture or distribute agricultural products and services.
Cost: $42.00
Frequency: Annual

10537 Agricultural Research Institute: Membership Directory
Agricultural Research Institute
9650 Rockville Pike
Bethesda, MD 20814-3998

301-530-7122; Fax: 301-530-7007

Richard A Herrett, Executive Director

One hundred and twenty-five member institutions; also lists study panels and committees interested in environmental issues, pest control, agricultural meteorology, biotechnology, food irradiation, agricultural policy, research and development, food safety, technology transfer and remote sensing.
Cost: $50.00
Frequency: Annual

10538 Airline, Ship & Catering: Onboard Service Buyer's Guide & Directory
International Publishing Company of America
664 La Villa Dr
Miami Springs, FL 33166-6030

305-887-1700; Fax: 305-885-1923

Alexander Morton, Owner

Offers information on over 6,000 airlines, railroads, ship lines and terminal restaurants.
Cost: $125.00
Frequency: Annual
Circulation: 6,000

10539 Almanac of Food Regulations and Statistical Information
Edward E Judge & Sons
PO Box 866
Westminster, MD 21158-0866

410-876-2052
800-729-5517; Fax: 410-848-2034
www.eejudge.com

Includes labeling law and FDA regulations, HACCP requirements for seafood, FDA current good manufacturing practice regulations, USDA canning regulations, frozen food handling code, FDA standards of identity, quality and fill of container, USDA quality grade standards, frozen fruit and vegetable pack statistics, agricultural statistics, and census of manufacturing.
Cost: $71.00
824 Pages
Frequency: Annual
Circulation: 3,000
ISBN: 1-880821-19-2
Founded in 1916

10540 American Butter Institute: Membership Directory
American Butter Institute
2101 Wilson Boulevard
Suite 400
Arlington, VA 22201

703-243-5630; Fax: 703-841-9328

Cindy Cazallo, Editor

This directory offers a comprehensive list of over 35 processors, distributors and packagers of butter in the US and suppliers to the industry. Members only.
Cost: $250.00
25 Pages
Frequency: Annual

10541 American Fruit Grower
Meister Media Worldwide
37733 Euclid Ave
Willoughby, OH 44094-5992

440-942-2000
800-572-7740; Fax: 440-975-3447
jwmonahan@meistermedia.com
www.meisternet.com

Gary Fitzgerald, President
Sue Stearns, Assistant Circulation Manager
JoAnne Mauer, Sales Assistant

Offers a list of manufacturers and distributors of equipment and supplies for the commercial fruit growing industry.
Cost: $19.95
66 Pages
Frequency: 10x
Circulation: 35,849
Founded in 1880

10542 American Meat Science Association Directory of Members
American Meat Science Association
2441 Village Green Pl
Champaign, IL 61822-7676

217-356-5370
800-517-AMSA; Fax: 888-205-5834; Fax: 217-356-5370

information@meatscience.org
www.meatscience.org

Dean Pringle, President
Collette Kaster, Chief Executive Officer
Morgan Pfeiffer, Membership & Marketing Manager

Directory for American Meat Science members only.
Cost: $20.00
230 Pages
Frequency: Biennial

10543 American Red Angus: Breeders Directory
Red Angus Association of America
4201 N Interstate 35
Denton, TX 76207-3415

940-387-3502; Fax: 940-383-4036
info@redangus.org
www.redangus.org
Facebook

Judy Edwards, Manager
Betty Grimshaw, Association Admin Director
Clint Berry, Commercial Marketing Director

This directory is a list of over 1,800 breeders of Red Angus cattle.
Frequency: Annual
Circulation: 8,000

10544 American Society of Consulting Arborists: Membership Directory
American Society of Consulting Arborists
15245 Shady Grove Road
Rockville, MD 20850-3222

301-947-0483

Beth Palys, Executive Director
Steven Geist, President

About 270 persons specializing in the growth and care of urban shade and ornamental trees; includes expert witnesses and monetary appraisals.
Frequency: Annual March

10545 American Spice Trade Association Membership Roster
American Spice Trade Association
2025 M St NW
Suite 800
Washington, DC 20036-2422

202-367-1127; Fax: 202-367-2127

Cheryl Deem, Executive Director
Frequency: Annual

10546 Automatic Merchandiser Blue Book Buyer's Guide Issue
Cygnus Publishing
PO Box 803
Fort Atkinson, WI 53538-0803

920-000-1111
800-547-7377; Fax: 920-563-1699

John French, CEO
Kathy Scott, Director of Public Relations
Paul Bonaiuto, CFO

Thousands of suppliers are profiled that offer products, services and equipment to the merchandise vending, food service and office coffee service industries.
Cost: $35.00
Frequency: Annual

10547 BEMA Equipment & Suppliers Datebase
BEMA
10740 Nall Avenue
Suite 230
Overland Park, KS 66211

913-338-1300; Fax: 913-338-1327
info@bema.org
www.bema.org

Find the baking industry's leading suppliers.
220 Pages
Founded in 1918

10548 Bakery Materials and Methods
Elsevier Science
655 Avenue of the Americas
New York, NY 10010-5107

212-633-3800; Fax: 212-633-3850
www.elsevier.com

Young Suk Chi, Chairman
Bill Godfrey, Chief Information Officer
David Clark, Senior Vice President
Cost: $41.50
Founded in 1978

10549 Bakery Production and Marketing Buyers Guide Issue
Delta Communications
11617 W Bluemound Road
Wauwatosa, WI 53226

414-774-7270; Fax: 414-777-7277
delta@deltacommunications.com

Pat Reynolds, Editor

This publication offers a list of over 1,800 manufacturers of equipment, ingredients, and supplies for bakeries. Enteries offer company names, addresses, phones, faxes and name and title of contract.

10550 Bakery Production and Marketing Red Book Issue
Delta Communications
Ste 300
20900 Swenson Dr
Waukesha, WI 53186-4050

262-542-9111; Fax: 262-542-8820
delta@deltacommunications.com
www.deltairaq.net

Offers a list of over 2,500 wholesale, multi-unit retail, grocery chain and co-op bakery companies and plants in the US and Canada that manufacture bread, cakes, cookies, crackers, pretzels, snack foods, and frozen bakery products.
Cost: $255.00
Frequency: Annual

10551 Baking & Snack Directory and Buyers Guide
Sosland Publishing Company
4800 Main St
Suite 100
Kansas City, MO 64112-2513

816-756-1000; Fax: 816-756-0494
www.sosland.com

Wholesalers of bread and baked goods, as well as snacks and frozen dough are listed in this directory.
Cost: $205.00
Frequency: Annual
Circulation: 8,000

10552 Beef Sire Directory
American Breeders Service/Customer Service
PO Box 459
De Forest, WI 53532-0459

608-846-3721; Fax: 608-846-6392
www.absglobal.com

Ian Biggs, CEO

A directory listing beef cattle associations in the US and Canada.
Frequency: Annual

10553 Beverage Digest Fact Book
Beverage Digest
PO Box 621
Bedford Hills, NY 10507-0621

914-244-0700; Fax: 914-244-0774
order@beverage-digest.com
www.beverage-digest.com

John Sicher, Owner

This book is a complete portrait of the global non-alcoholic beverage business.

10554 Beverage Digest Soft Drink Atlas
Beverage Digest
PO Box 621
Bedford Hills, NY 10507-0621

914-244-0700; Fax: 914-244-0774
www.beverage-digest.com

John Sicher, Owner

Book of US maps related to soft drink bottler territories. This book offers a geographic portrait of the US carbonated beverage bottling business.

10555 Beverage Marketing Directory
Beverage Marketing Corporation
2670 Commercial Ave
Mingo Junction, OH 43938-1613

740-598-4133
800-332-6222; Fax: 740-598-3977
www.beveragemarketing.com

Andrew Standardi III, Director of Operations
Kathy Smurthwaite, Editor

Publication is available in Print Copy (Price-$1,465), PDF Format (Price-$1,465), CD-ROM Format (For pricing, call number listed for details or visit website), and Online.
1196 Pages

10556 Biological & Agricultural Index
HW Wilson Company
950 Dr Martin L King Jr Blvd
Bronx, NY 10452-4297

718-588-8405
800-367-6770; Fax: 718-590-1617
www.hwwilson.com

Harold Regan, CEO
Kathleen McEvoy, Director of Public Relations

Provides fast access to core literature. In addition to citations to research and feature articles, users finding indexing of reports of symposia and conferences, and citations to current book reviews. Available on Web and disc.

10557 Blue Book Buyer's Guide
Food Processing Machinery Association
1451 Dolley Madison Blvd
Suite 101
McLean, VA 22101-3850

703-761-2600; Fax: 703-761-4334
info@fpsa.org
www.fpsa.org

A buyers guide offering information on over 500 member food and beverage industry firms. Entries are cross-referenced with both a product and commodity locator.
Cost: $50.00
200 Pages
Circulation: 30,000

10558 Blue Book: Fruit and Vegetable Credit and Marketing Service
Produce Reporter Company
845 E Geneva Rd
Carol Stream, IL 60188-3520

630-668-3500; Fax: 630-668-0303
www.bluebookprco.com

C James Carr, President

A directory offering information on over 15,000 produce growers, wholesalers, shippers and re-

tailers in the US.
Cost: $575.00
1275 Pages
Frequency: Semiannual
Founded in 1901

10559 **Bottled Water Market**
MarketResearch.com
641 Avenue of the Americas
3rd Floor
New York, NY 10011

212-807-2629
800-298-6699; Fax: 212-807-2676

The report provides descriptions and coverage of market size and growth, market comppsition, leading marketers, the competitive situation, new product trends, advertising and promotion, and more.
Cost: $2750.00
139 Pages

10560 **Brand Directory**
Vance Publishing
10901 W 84th Ter
Suite 200
Lenexa, KS 66214-1631

913-438-5721
800-255-5113; Fax: 913-438-0697
info@vancepublishing.com
www.vancepublishing.com

Cliff Becker, Vice President, Director
Dan Woods, Chief Financial Officer
Lori Eppel, Chief Financial Officer

A composite of major fresh fruit and vegetable brands and suppliers. It is divided into three sections and contains 66 commodities.
Cost: $10.00

10561 **Brewers Digest: Buyers Guide and Brewery Directory**
Ammark Publishing
4049 W Peterson Avenue
Chicago, IL 60646-6001
Lists all breweries in the Western Hemisphere, suppliers, associations and importers.
Cost: $30.00
Frequency: Annual
Circulation: 3,000

10562 **Brewers Resource Directory**
Brewers Association
736 Pearl Street
Boulder, CO 80302

303-447-0816
888-822-6273; Fax: 303-447-2825
www.beertown.org
Facebook, Twitter

Various categories of listees are included that have a direct relation to the beer and liquor industry.
Mailing list available for rent

10563 **Brown Swiss Cattle Breeders' Association Directory**
Brown Swiss Cattle Breeders' Association
800 Pleasant St
Beloit, WI 53511-5456

608-365-4474; Fax: 608-365-5577
info@brownswissusa.com
www.brownswissusa.com

Roger Neitzel, Manager
David Kendall, Secretary

10564 **CID Service**
US Department of Agriculture
200 Independence Ave SW
Washington, DC 20201-0007

202-690-7650

This database contains 467 categories of information prepared by the US Department of Agriculture and its agencies.
Frequency: Full-text

10565 **CRC Press**
2000 NW Corporate Boulevard
Boca Raton, FL 33431

561-994-0555
800-272-7737; Fax: 561-998-0876
techsupport@crcpress.com
www.crcpress.com

Eleanor Riemer, Publisher
Emmett Dages, CEO

Publisher in science, medicine, environmental science, forensic, engineering, business, technology, mathematics, and statistics. Our food science and nutrition books and our journal, Critical Reviews in Food and Nutrition, are well established and respected publications in the food science industry.

10566 **CRIS/USDA Database**
Current Research Information System
1400 Independence Avenue SW
Suite 2270
Washington, DC 20250

202-690-0119; Fax: 202-690-0634

Ellen A Terpstra, CEO
Don Tilmon, Director

Offers over 35,000 ongoing and recently completed agricultural, food and nutrition and forestry research projects sponsored by the US Department of Agriculture.

10567 **California League of Food Processors Annual Directory of Members**
980 Ninth Street
Sacremento, CA 95814

916-444-9260; Fax: 916-444-2746
www.clfp.com

Robert Graf, President/CEO
Ed Yates, Senior VP
Nora Basrai, Meetings/Members Services
Rob Neenan, Senior Vice President
Amy Alcorn, Marketing Manager

Contains listings of all members, including plant locations and products produced. Over 800 industry leaders are listed.
200 Pages
Founded in 1905

10568 **Candy Marketer: Candy, Snack and Tobacco Buyers' Guide**
Stagnito Communications
155 Pfingster Road
Suite 205
Deerfield, IL 60015

847-205-5660; Fax: 847-205-5680

Linda Stagnito, President

A publication that includes a list of suppliers to the confectionery, snack and tobacco products industries. Entries include company names, addresses, key personnel, warehouse locations and firms represented.
Cost: $25.00
Frequency: Annual

10569 **Cheese Market News: Annual**
Quarne Publishing
PO 628254
Middleton, WI 53562

608-831-6002; Fax: 608-831-1004
www.cheesemarketnews.com

Susan Quarne, Publisher

Comprehensive listings include the companies that manufacture the latest styles and varieties of cheese as well as the industry's key suppliers of cheese equipment, packaging equipment, materials and supplies and services.
Cost: $30.00
Frequency: Annual
Circulation: 3,000

10570 **Citrus & Vegetable Magazine: Farm Equipment Directory Issue**
Vance Publishing
10901 W 84th Ter
Suite 200
Lenexa, KS 66214-1631

913-438-5721; Fax: 913-438-0697
info@vancepublishing.com
www.vancepublishing.com

Cliff Becker, Vice President, Director
Lori Eppel, Chief Financial Officer

Offers information on a list of manufacturers of produce and citrus growing, handling, picking and packaging equipment.
Cost: $25.00
48 Pages
Frequency: Annual
Circulation: 12,000
ISSN: 0009-7586
Founded in 1938

10571 **Coffee Anyone???**
9616 Thunderbird Drive
Suite 215
San Ramon, CA 94583

925-829-4022
800-347-9687; Fax: 925-829-4025
coffee@coffee-anyone.com
http://www.coffeeanyone.com

This database contains descriptions of gourmet, regular, decaffenated and flavored coffees, including a chart summarizing the strength and taste of each coffee.

10572 **Coffee, Sugar and Cocoa Exchange Guide**
Commerce Clearing House
2700 Lake Cook Rd
Riverwoods, IL 60015-3867

847-940-4600; Fax: 847-779-1535
mediahelp@cch.com
www.cch.com

Mike Sabbatis, President

Offers information on member and member organizations of the Exchange.
Cost: $240.00
170 Pages
Frequency: Monthly

10573 **Complete Directory of Concessions & Equipment**
Sutton Family Communications & Publishing Company
920 State Route 54 East
Elmitch, KY 42343

270-276-9500

Theresa Sutton, Editor
Lee Sutton, General Manager

Printout from database of wholesalers, manufacturers, distributors, importers and close-out houses; updated daily to guarantee the most current and up-to-date sources available.
Cost: $27.90
100+ Pages

10574 **Complete Directory of Food Products**
Sutton Family Communications & Publishing Company

920 State Route 54 East
Elmitch, KY 42343

270-276-9500

Theresa Sutton, Editor
Lee Sutton, General Manager

Printout from database of wholesalers, manufacturers, distributors, importers and close-out houses. Database is updated daily to guarantee the most current and up-to-date sources available.
Cost: $27.90
100+ Pages

10575 **Consumer's Guide to Fruits & Vegetables & Other Farm Fresh Products**
Missouri Cooperative Extension Service
PO Box 29
Jefferson City, MO 65102-0029

573-681-5301; Fax: 573-635-2314

David N Sasseville, Editor

A directory covering over 400 fruit and vegetable farm markets in Missouri.
124 Pages
Frequency: Annual

10576 **Contemporary World Issues: Agricultural Crisis in America**
ABC-CLIO
PO Box 1911
Santa Barbara, CA 93116-1911

805-705-9339
800-422-2546; Fax: 805-685-9685

Barbara McEwan, Editor

List of agencies and organizations in the US concerned with agricultural issues.
Cost: $39.50

10577 **Convenience Store Decisions Sales Tracking Study**
Harbor Communications
19111 Detroit Road
Suite 201
Rocky River, OH 44116

440-250-1583; Fax: 440-333-1892
www.csdecisions.com

Joseph Howton, Executive VP/COO

Survey of convenience store chain buyers that tracks the effectiveness of supplier promotional programs. It reports on how manufacturers call on retail chains and how those chains are responding to suppliers' merchandising efforts.
Frequency: Annual

10578 **Cookies Market**
MarketResearch.com
641 Avenue of the Americas
3rd Floor
New York, NY 10011

212-807-2629
800-298-6699; Fax: 212-807-2676

This report uncovers trends in its in-depth investigation of US retail sales of packaged and fresh-baked cookies. The analysis covers packaged cookie retail sales by distribution channel, marketer, and product line. The leading marketers are profiled in order to review growth-and-profit-oriented strategies. The data information is analyzed in order for users to uncover growing product lines, target key demographics, pinpoint distribution channel sales opportunities, and profitable strategies.
Cost: $2250.00
169 Pages

10579 **Corn Annual**
Corn Refiners Association
1701 Pennsylvania Ave NW
Suite 950
Washington, DC 20006-5806

202-331-1634; Fax: 202-331-2054
www.corn.org

Report featuring articles on the state of the industry. Includes statistical report on corn shipments, supply and consumption in the US and abroad.
Frequency: Annually
Circulation: 8,000

10580 **Crop Protection Reference**
C&P Press
565 5th Ave
5th Floor
New York, NY 10017-2413

212-587-8620; Fax: 646-733-6010
www.pharmpress.com

A single comprehensive source of up-to-date label information of crop protection products marketed in the US by basic manufacturers and formulators. Extensive product indexing helps to locate products by brand name, manufacturer, crop site, mode of action, disease, insect, week, product category, common name and tank mix.
Cost: $170.00
Frequency: Annual

10581 **Culinary Collection Directory**
International Association/Culinary Professionals
304 W Liberty Street
Suite 201
Louisville, KY 40202

502-587-7953
800-928-4227; Fax: 502-589-3602
info@iacp.com
www.iacp.com

Kerry Edwards, Sr Member Services Representative
Trina Gribbins, Manager

Teachers, cooking school owners, caterers, writers, chefs, media cooking personalities, editors, publishers, food stylists, food photographers, restauranteurs, leaders of major food corporations and vintners. Literally a who's who of the food world.

10582 **Dairy Foods Market Guide**
Delta Communications
455 N Cityfront Plaza Drive
Chicago, IL 60611-5503

312-836-2000; Fax: 312-222-2026

A guide including a list of 1,600 manufacturers of dairy processing equipment and over 900 distributors of dairy processing equipment.
Cost: $99.00
Frequency: Annual

10583 **Developing Successful New Products for Foodservice Markets**
International Food Service Manufacturers
180 North Stetson Avenue
Suite 4400
Chicago, IL 60601-6766

312-540-4400; Fax: 312-540-4401
ifma@ifmaworld.com
www.ifmaworld.com
Facebook, LinkedIn, YouTube

Larry Oberkfell, President & CEO
Jennifer Tarulis, CFO
Michael Hickey, Chairman
Mark Bendix, 1st Vice Chairman
Loren Kimura, Treasurer

Handbook on new product development offers sound advice on the critical success factors confronting new product managers. Up-to-date information on new products and practices and an expanded section on market research.
Cost: $ 495.00
Frequency: Annual

10584 **Directory & Products Guide**
Vineyard & Winery Services
PO Box 2358
Windsor, CA 95492

707-836-6820
800-535-5670; Fax: 707-836-6825
vwm-online.com

Jennifer Merietti, Sales/Marketing Manager
Dennis Black, General Manager
Suzanne Webb, Marketing Director

A must have reference book that belongs on the desk of every wine professional. Whether it's tracking down a particular vendor, shopping for the best deal on oak barrels or searching for out-of-state winery contacts, the DPG is a powerhouse of information. Over 2,300 supplier listings and 2,700 winery/vineyard listings, it is a reliable resource that saves time and money.
Cost: $95.00
450+ Pages
Frequency: Annually

10585 **Directory of AFFI Member Companies**
American Frozen Food Institute
2000 Corporate Ridge
Suite 1000
McLean, VA 22102-7862

703-821-0770; Fax: 703-821-1350
info@affi.com

Robert L Garfield, President
Jason Bassett, Director Legislative Affairs
Chuck Fuqua, VP Communications
Cost: $100.00
Frequency: Annual
Circulation: 5000

10586 **Directory of American Agriculture**
Agricultural Resources & Communications
301 Broadway
Belvue, KS 66407

785-456-9705; Fax: 785-456-1654
chris@agresources.com
www.agresources.com

Christina Wilson, President

This directory lists over 7,000 state and national associations involved in providing products and services related to food and fiber industries, in 27 categories. There are categorical indexes as well. Includes guide to Washington, DC offices, USDA listings, and guide to ag commodity commissions. Available on CD for $99.
Cost: $64.95
350 Pages
ISSN: 0897-1919
Founded in 1988
Printed in on matte stock

10587 **Directory of Convenience Stores**
Trade Dimensions
45 Danbury Rd
Wilton, CT 06897-4445

203-563-3000; Fax: 860-563-3131
www.tradedimensions.com

Jennifer Gillbert, Editor
Lynda Guticulez, Managing Editor

The directory comprises nearly 1,500 detailed profiles on the companies you need to do business with. Extensive dependable information on the grocery industry's most volatile segment.
Cost: $245.00
Frequency: Annual

10588 **Directory of Custom Food Processors and Formulators**
Delphi Marketing Services

400 E 89th Street
Apartment 2J
New York, NY 10128-6728

Covers formulators and processors of custom food products.
Cost: $260.00
Frequency: Annual

10589 Directory of State Departments of Agriculture
US Department of Agriculture
200 Independence Ave SW
Room 3964
Washington, DC 20201-0007

202-690-7650
www.usda.gov

Chris Smith, Chief Information Officer
Matt Paul, Director of Communications
Ramona Romero, General Counsel

Offer valuable information on all the state departments of agriculture, including their officials.
73 Pages
Frequency: Biennial

10590 Directory of the Canning, Freezing, Preserving Industries
Edward E Judge & Sons
PO Box 866
Westminster, MD 21158-0866

410-876-2052; Fax: 410-848-2034
www.eejudge.com

Daniel P Judge, Publisher

This directory offers extensive company profiles including over 10,000 managers, over 3,000 North American Food plants that are involved in canning, freezing and preserving fruits, vegetables, dinners, specialties and more. Published in standard edition, 768 pages, and special deluxe edition 1,408 pages.
Cost: $175.00
768 Pages
Frequency: Biennial
ISBN: 1-880821-20-6
Founded in 1966

10591 Diversified Business Communications
PO Box 7437
Portland, ME 04112-7437

207-842-5600; Fax: 207-842-5503
www.divbusiness.com

Nancy Hasselback, CEO
Nancy Gelette, VP Operations

A producer of international trade expositions for the seafood and commercial marine industries.

10592 EMDA Membership Directory
Equipment Marketing & Distribution Association
PO Box 1347
Iowa City, IA 52244

319-354-5156
pat@emda.net
www.emda.net

Patricia A. Collins, Executive Vice President

Annual directory of FEWA-AIMRA members, includes address, phone, fax, web, e-mail, territory covered (with map) product descriptions, key personnel, and a descriptive paragraph.
Cost: $50.00

10593 Electronic Pesticide Reference: EPR II
C&P Press
New York, NY 10001

212-326-6760; Fax: 646-733-6010
www.pharmpress.com

Complete electronic reference to our 1,500 crop protection products; a full range of product information: full text labels and supplemental labels, full text MSDS's, product summaries, list of labeled tank mixes, worker protection information, DOT shipping information, SARA Title III reporting information. Search by brand name, manufacturer, common name crop, plant, site, weed, disease, insect plus much more. All versions of EPR II are provided on CD-ROM for windows.

10594 Essential Rendering
National Renderers Association
801 N Fairfax St
Suite 205
Alexandria, VA 22314-1776

703-683-0155; Fax: 703-683-2626
www.nationalrenderers.org

Thomas M Cook, President

An in-depth guide that covers the various aspects of rendering.
Frequency: Monthly

10595 FPSA Membership Directory
Food Processing Suppliers Association
1451 Dolley Madison Boulevard
Suite 101
McLean, VA 22101-3850

703-761-2600; Fax: 703-761-4334
info@fpsa.org
mx.fpsa.org/Member-List

David Seckman, President & CEO
Robyn Roche, Chief Financial Officer
Dolores Alonso, VP, Membership & Business Dev
Ann Marie Penaranda, Membership & Outreach Associate

Directory listing all the member organizations of the Food Processing Suppliers Association (FPSA).

10596 Feed Additive Compendium
The Miller Publishing Company
12400 Whitewater Dr
Suite 160
Hopkins, MN 55343-4590

952-931-0211; Fax: 952-938-1832

Sarah Muirhead, Publisher

Provides the latest information on which medicated additives can be used at what inclusion levels for what puposes. Also provides information on regulation, compliance and quality control, product specimen labels, and a directory of state and FDA contacts.
Cost: $52.00
Frequency: Weekly
Founded in 1931

10597 Food & Beverage Marketplace Directory
Grey House Publishing
4919 Route 22
PO Box 56
Amenia, NY 12501
518-789-8700
800-562-2139; Fax: 845-373-6390
books@greyhouse.com
www.greyhouse.com
Facebook, Twitter

Richard Gottlieb, President
Leslie Mackenzie, Publisher

A three-volume set that is the most comprehensive resource in the food and beverage industry. Available in print, a subscription-based online database, as well as a mailing list and database formats.
Cost: $595.00
2000 Pages
Frequency: Annual

10598 Food & Beverage Marketplace: Online Database
Grey House Publishing
4919 Route 22
PO Box 56
Amenia, NY 12501

518-789-8700
800-562-2139; Fax: 845-373-6390
gold@greyhouse.com
gold.greyhouse.com
Facebook, Twitter

Richard Gottlieb, President
Leslie Mackenzie, Publisher

This complete updated Food & Beverage Market Place: Online Database is the go-to source for the food and beverage industry. Anyone involved in the food and beverage industry needs this 'industry bible' and the important contacts to develop critical research data that can make for successful business growth.
Frequency: Annual
Founded in 1981

10599 Food Businesses: Snack Shops, Specialty Food Restaurants & Other Ideas
Prosperity & Profits Unlimited
PO Box 416
Denver, CO 80201

303-573-5564

A Doyle, Editor

Ideas and possibilities for food businesses, snack shops, restaurants.
Cost: $29.95
82 Pages
Circulation: 8000
ISBN: 0-911569-69-3
Founded in 1990
Printed in on matte stock

10600 Food Channel Database
Noble Communications
500 N Michigan Avenue
Chicago, IL 60611-3764

312-670-4470; Fax: 312-670-7410

This database reports industry news and developments of interest to decision-makers in food processing, grocery, and c-store retailing distribution.

10601 Food Engineering Directory
Business News Publishing
3817 Timothy Lane
Bethlehem, PA 18020

610-317-6180; Fax: 610-317-0378

George Misko

Hardbound reference book listing of all food and beverage companies with 20 or more employees throughout the US.
Cost: $395.00

10602 Food Master
BNP Media
45 Beacon St
Sommerville, MA 02143

617-660-1322
www.foodmasterinc.com

Bob Iannaccone, Manager
Founded in 1947

10603 Food Processing Guide & Directory
555 W Pierce Road
Suite 301
Itasca, IL 60143

773-252-7891; Fax: 630-467-1108

Lily Modjeski, Sales Manager

Presents advertising opportunities that will generate quality sales leads, incerase market share,

identify market opportunities and increase exposure through our website.
Frequency: Annual

10604 **Food Production Management: Advertisers Buyers Guide Issue**
CTI Publications
2823 Benson Mill Rd
Sparks Glencoe, MD 21152-9575
410-308-2080; Fax: 410-308-2079
www.ctipubs.com
W Randall Gerstmyer, Publisher
Cost: $15.00
48 Pages
Frequency: Annual
Circulation: 5,000
ISSN: 0191-6181
Founded in 1878

10605 **Food Service Industry**
MarketResearch.com
641 Avenue of the Americas
3rd Floor
New York, NY 10011
212-807-2629
800-298-6699; Fax: 212-807-2676
The report analyzes sales and profit trends of full-service restaurants, limited-service restaurants, cafeterias, snack bars, in-plant contractors, caterers, mobile food services and drinking places.
Cost: $2250.00
240 Pages

10606 **Food and Agricultural Export Directory**
US Department of Agriculture
PO Box 2022
Washington, DC 20250-0001
202-690-7650; Fax: 202-512-2250
www.access.gpo.gov
Offers valuable information on federal and state agencies, trade associations and others willing to assist the US firms that wish to export food and agricultural products overseas.
100 Pages
Frequency: Annual

10607 **Food, Beverages & Tobacco in US Industrial Outlook**
Superintendent of Documents
US Government Printing Office
Washington, DC 20402-0001
FAX 202-512-2250
Contains industry reviews and forecasts; coverage includes bakery products.
Cost: $34.00
Frequency: Annual

10608 **Food, Hunger, Agribusiness: A Directory of Resources**
Third World Resources
218 E 21st Street
Oakland, CA 94606
510-533-7583; Fax: 510-533-0923
Offers information on organizations and publishers of books and other materials on food, hunger and agribusiness overseas.
Cost: $12.95
160 Pages

10609 **FoodService Distributors Database**
Chain Store Guide
3710 Corporex Park Dr.
Suite 310
Tampa, FL 33619-1389
813-627-6700
800-927-9292; Fax: 813-627-6888
webmaster@chainstoreguide.com
www.chainstoreguide.com
Mike Jarvis, Publisher
Shami Choon, Manager
Over 4,900 distributors of food, equipment and supplies to restaurants and institutions are reviewed in this directory for the food service industry. The names of more than 23,000 key executives are included, along with each company's distribution centers.
Cost: $575.00
800 Pages
Frequency: Annual

10610 **Foods ADLIBRA**
Foods ADLIBRA Publications
9000 Plymouth Avenue N
Minneapolis, MN 55427-3870
763-764-4759; Fax: 763-764-3166
Judith O'Connell, Editor
This database offers over 287,000 citations, with abstracts to journal literature on research and development in food technology and packaging. Seafood, food service, snacks and beverage monthly current awareness are also available.
Cost: $200.00
ISSN: 0146-9304

10611 **Foodservice Yearbook International/Global Foodservice**
150 Great Neck Road
Great Neck, NY 11021
516-829-9210; Fax: 516-829-5414

10612 **Foreign Countries and Plants Certified to Export Meat and Poultry to the US**
US Department of Agriculture
Food Safety & Inspection Services
Washington, DC 20250-0001
202-690-7650
800-535-4555
A comprehensive list of over 1,000 meat and poultry plants in foreign countries.
150 Pages
Frequency: Annual

10613 **Fortified Foods Market**
MarketResearch.com
641 Avenue of the Americas
3rd Floor
New York, NY 10011
212-807-2629
800-298-6699; Fax: 212-807-2676
This new study examines the regulatory environment, analyzes the growth and product trends shaping the fortified foods market and inspects the changing retail picture. It also unveils the marketing and promotional strategies of major players such as Kellogg's, General Mills, PepsiCo, Coca-Cola, Novartis, Heinz and many others. Finally, the study takes a look at differences and commonalities among consumers of fortified cereals, breads, juice drinks, baby foods and snacks.
Cost: $2750.00
234 Pages

10614 **Frozen Dinners and Entrees**
Leading Edge Reports/Industry Reports
2171 Jericho Turnpike
Suite 200
Commack, NY 11725-2937
631-462-5454; Fax: 631-462-1842
www.businesstrendanalysts.com
Charles J Ritchie, Executive VP
Donna Priani, Marketing Director
Linda Sherman, Production Manager
Jennifer Wichert, Research Director
A product-by-product analysis of the markets for frozen dinners and entrees, including traditional as well as low-calorie and health oriented products.
Cost: $1995.00
170 Pages
Founded in 1996

10615 **Getaways for Gourmets in the Northeast**
Wood Pond Press
365 Ridgewood Rd
West Hartford, CT 06107-3517
860-521-0389; Fax: 860-313-0185
www.green-cuisine.com
Richard M Woodworth, Owner
Directory of services and supplies to the industry.
Cost: $14.95
514 Pages

10616 **Gold Book: AAMP**
American Association of Meat Processors
One Meating Place
Elizabethtown, PA 17022
717-367-1168
aamp@aamp.com
www.aamp.com
Rick Reams, President
Chris Young, Executive Director
Consists of AAMP members, including: honorary members, associates, operators/wholesalers, home food service companies, suppliers, distributors, allied and affiliated state/regional/provincial associations. A powerful source for meat business buyers seeking products/services.
Cost: $300.00
170 Pages
Frequency: Every 2 Years
Circulation: 2,000

10617 **Grain & Milling Annual**
Sosland Publishing Company
4801 Main St
Suite 100
Kansas City, MO 64112-2513
816-756-1000; Fax: 816-756-0494
www.sosland.com
Offers a list of milling companies, mills, grain companies and cooperatives.
Cost: $100.00
Frequency: Annual
Circulation: 6,000

10618 **Grain Journal**
Country Journal Publishing Company
2490 N Water Street
Decatur, IL 62526-4251
217-877-9660
800-728-7511; Fax: 217-877-6647
webmaster@grainnet.com
www.grainnet.com
Mark Avery, Publisher
Ed Zdrojewski, Editor
Deb Coontz, Advertising Sales
Jeff Miller, Advertising Sales
Provides a list of over 700 equipment manufacturers, suppliers and system designers, as well as offering useful information on governmental agencies relevant to the grain industry.
Cost: $40.00
254 Pages
Frequency: Bi-Monthly
Circulation: 13,000
ISSN: 0274-7138
Founded in 1972
Mailing list available for rent: 10,000 names at $600 per M
Printed in 4 colors on glossy stock

10619 **Great Lakes Vegetable Growers News**
PO Box 128
Sparta, MI 49345-0128
616-887-9008; Fax: 616-887-2666
Barry Brand, Editor

10620 **Guernsey Breeders' Journal: Convention Directory Issue**
Purebred Publishing Inc
7616 Slate Ridge Blvd
Reynoldsburg, OH 43068-3126
614-575-4620; Fax: 614-864-5614
sjohnson@usguernsey.com
www.usguernsey.com
Victoria L. Baker, Purebred Publishing President
David Coon, President
A convention directory offering a list of officers and national members of the American Guernsey Cattle Association.
Cost: $15.00
Frequency: Annual

10621 **Guide to Poultry Associations**
Poultry & Egg News
PO Box 1338
Gainesville, GA 30503-1338
770-536-2476; Fax: 770-532-4894
Randall Smalladod, Publisher
Chris Hill, Editor
This directory offers information on national, regional and state poultry associations.
Cost: $25.00
24 Pages
Frequency: Annual
Circulation: 11,500

10622 **Health and Natural Foods Market**
MarketResearch.com
641 Avenue of the Americas
3rd Floor
New York, NY 10011
212-807-2629
800-298-6699; Fax: 212-807-2676
The report covers six product categories: packaged groceries, bulk groceries, frozen, refrigerated, produce and other/miscellaneous. The major players in the market are profiled, including Gardenburger, Hain Food Group, Horizon Organic Dairy, Small Planet Foods and others. The report details which types of new products have been recently introduced and reports on consumer attitudes and behavior.
Cost: $2750.00
289 Pages

10623 **Health and Natural Foods Market: Past Performance, Current Trends & More**
Business Trend Analysts/Industry Reports
2171 Jericho Tpke
Suite 200
Commack, NY 11725-2937
631-462-5454; Fax: 631-462-1842
www.businesstrendanalysts.com
Charles J Ritchie, Executive VP
Vincent Seeno, Editor
Donna Priani, General Manager
Linda Holm, Production Manager
A statistical summary and analysis offering historical, current and projected sales data for the natural foods market.
Cost: $2195.00
335 Pages
Founded in 1986

10624 **Herbal Green Pages**
Herb Growing and Marketing Network
PO Box 245
Silver Spring, PA 17575-0245
FAX 717-393-9261
herbworld@aol.com
www.herbnet.com
Maureen Rogers, Editor
This annual guide offers information on 5,000 companies involved in herbal marketing and growing.
Cost: $25.00
Frequency: Annual
Printed in one color on matte stock

10625 **High Volume Independent Restaurants Database**
Chain Store Guide
3710 Corporex Park Dr.
Suite 310
Tampa, FL 33619-1389
813-627-6700
800-927-9292; Fax: 813-627-6888
webmaster@chainstoreguide.com
www.chainstoreguide.com
Mike Jarvis, Publisher
Shami Choon, Manager
Covers this growing niche through its nearly 5,900 listings featuring casual dining, family restaurants and fine dining establishments. Plus, access to over 15,000 key personnel names puts you in contact with key decision makers.
Cost: $575.00
1,000 Pages
Frequency: Annual

10626 **Hort Expo Northwest**
Mt Adams Publishing and Design
14161 Fort Road
White Swan, WA 98552-9786
509-948-2706
800-554-0860; Fax: 509-848-3896
Vee Graves, Editor
Julie LaForge, Advertising Manager
Besides being mailed to it's family of subscribers it is also available complimentary at horticulture shows in the Northwest.
32 Pages
Frequency: Annually
Circulation: 11,000
Founded in 1989
Printed in 4 colors on glossy stock

10627 **IGWB Buyer's Guide**
BNP Media
PO Box 1080
Skokie, IL 60076-9785
847-763-9534; Fax: 847-763-9538
igwb@halldata.com
James Rutherford, Editor
Lynn Davidson, Marketing
Nikki Smith, Director
A comprehensive resource listing over 1000 gaming products and services suppliers.
Frequency: Annual
ISSN: 0 -

10628 **Ice Cream and Frozen Desserts**
Business Trend Analysts/Industry Reports
2171 Jericho Tpke
Commack, NY 11725-2937
631-462-5454; Fax: 631-462-1842
www.businesstrendanalysts.com
Charles J Ritchie, Executive VP
Donna Priani, Marketing Director
Linda Sherman, Production Manager
Jennifer Wichert, Research Director
A survey of the ice cream and frozen dessert market, including low-calorie, low-fat and gourmet ice creams and frozen desserts.
Cost: $1295.00
Founded in 2000

10629 **Impact International Directory: Leading Spirits, Wine and Beer Companies**
M Shanken Communications
387 Park Ave S
8th Floor
New York, NY 10016-8872
212-684-4224; Fax: 212-684-5424
www.cigaraficionado.com
Marvin Shanken, Publisher
A directory offering information on the major players of the alcoholic beverage industry.
Cost: $295.00

10630 **Impact Yearbook: Directory of the US Wine, Spirits & Beer Industry**
M Shanken Communications
387 Park Ave S
8th Floor
New York, NY 10016-8872
212-684-4224; Fax: 212-684-5424
www.cigaraficionado.com
Marvin Shanken, Publisher
A directory offering information on the top 40 American distributors and profiles of companies.
Cost: $170.00
Frequency: Annual

10631 **International Association of Food Industry Suppliers**
1451 Dolley Madison Boulevard
Suite 101
McLean, VA 22101
703-761-2600; Fax: 703-761-4334
info@fpsa.org
www.fpsa.org
George Melnykovich, President/CEO
A directory offering information on member manufacturers and suppliers of equipment, ingredients and services to the food and dairy industry.
700 Pages
Founded in 1911

10632 **International Dairy Foods Association: IDFA Membership Directory**
IDFA Membership Directory
1250 H St NW
Suite 900
Washington, DC 20005-5902
202-737-4332; Fax: 202-331-7820
membership@idfa.org
www.idfa.org
Constance Tipton, President
Miriam Brown, Advisory Committee
The directory provides a complete listing of IDFA's members— over 500 companies— representing approximately 83 percent of all dairy foods processed in the US, as well as the industry's leading supplier companies. Information about locations, products and contacts is included.
Cost: $495.00
250 Pages

10633 **International Directory of Refrigerated Warehouse & Distribution Centers**
Int'l Association of Refrigerated Warehouses

1500 King Street
Suite 201
Alexandria, VA 22314

301-652-5674; Fax: 703-373-4301
email@iarw.org
www.iarw.org

Corey Rosenbusch, Vice President
Nikki Duncan, Programs Manager
Margot Dersal, Controller

A complete listing of public refrigerated warehouses available to the food industry.
Cost: $18.00

10634 **International Green Front Report**
Friends of the Trees
PO Box 1064
Tonasket, WA 98855-1064

FAX 509-485-2705
michael@friendsofthetrees.net

Michael Pilarski, Editor

Organizations and periodicals concerned with sustainable forestry and agriculture and related fields.
Cost: $7.00
Frequency: Irregular

10635 **International Soil Tillage Research Organization**
International Soil Tillage Research
1680 Madison Avenue
Wooster, OH 44691-4114

330-263-3700; Fax: 330-263-3658

More than 750 individuals and institutions in 72 countries involved in the research or application of soil tilage and related subjects.
Cost: $100.00
Frequency: Semiannual

10636 **Kosher Directory: Directory of Kosher Products & Services**
Union of Orthodox Jewish Congregations of America
333 7th Avenue
18th Floor
New York, NY 10001-5004

212-563-4122; Fax: 212-564-9058

Shelly Sharf, Editor

A directory covering over 10,000 consumer, institutional and industrial products and services.

10637 **Landscape & Irrigation: Product Source Guide**
Adams Business Media
Suite J
Cathedral City, CA 92234

760-322-9878; Fax: 312-846-4638
www.americanbusinessmedia.com

Leslee Adams, Owner

Offers information on suppliers, distributors and manufacturers serving the professional agriculture and landscaping community.
Cost: $6.00
Circulation: 37,000

10638 **LifeWise Ingredients**
3540 N 126th Street
Suite D
Brookfield, WI 53005

262-788-9141; Fax: 262-788-9143
info@lifewise1.com
www.lifewise1.com

Dean Antczak, Manager
Carol Bender, Manager

Manufactures industrial food ingredients.

10639 **MISA Buyer's Guide on CD**
Meat Industry Suppliers Alliance
1451 Dolly Madison Boulevard
McLean, VA 22101

703-761-2600
800-331-8816; Fax: 703-548-6563
info@fpsa.org

George O Melnkovich, PhD, President
Cheryl Clark, Director Member Services
Frequency: Annual

10640 **Manufacturing Confectioner: Directory of Ingredients, Equipment & Packaging**
Manufacturing Confectioner Publishing Company
P.O.Box 2249
New Preston Marble Dale, CT 06777-0249

201-652-2655; Fax: 201-652-3419
mcinfo@gomc.com
www.gomc.com

Kate Allured, Editor

Publication offers suppliers of machinery, equipment, raw materials, and supplies to the confectionery industry.
Cost: $25.00
Frequency: Annual

10641 **Market for Nutraceutical Foods & Beverages**
Frost & Sullivan Market Intelligence
2525 Charleston Road
Mountain View, CA 94043-1626

650-961-1000; Fax: 650-961-5042

Analyzes the nutraceutical market and offers information on ongoing laboratory research and forecasts for this particular industry.
Cost: $1850.00

10642 **Material Safety Data Sheet Reference**
C&P Press
565 5th Ave
5th Floor
New York, NY 10017-2413

212-587-8620; Fax: 646-733-6010
www.pharmpress.com

Regulatory and product safety requirements. Contains full text MSDS's for products listed in the 1999 15th Edition Crop Protection Reference plus additional safety information such as DOT shipping information, SARA Title III regulations, Hazardous Chemical inventory reporting information plus much more.

10643 **Meat Buyer's Guide**
North American Meat Processors Association
1920 Association Dr
Suite 400
Reston, VA 20191-1500

703-758-8001
800-368-3043; Fax: 703-758-8001

Sabrina Moore, Accounting/Meeting Manager
Philip Kimball, Executive Director

A pictorial directory depicting the food service cuts of beef, lamb, pork, and veal, along with their corresponding IMPS numbers (Institutional Meat Purchase Specification) numbers, instituted by USDA. The Guide is used by chefs, meat processors, and purveyors, food service personnel in institutions, hotels and restaurants.

10644 **Meat Price Book**
Urner Barry Publications
PO Box 389
Toms River, NJ 08754-0389

732-240-5330
800-932-0617; Fax: 732-341-0891
help@urnerbarry.com
www.urnerbarry.com

Paul B Brown Jr, President
Sheila M Deane, Marketing Manager

Seven year price history of selected beef, lamb and veal cuts as quoted in Urner Barry's Yellow Sheet.
Cost: $95.00
Frequency: Annual
Circulation: 400

10645 **Meat and Poultry Inspection Directory**
US Department of Agriculture
Administration Building
Room 344
Washington, DC 20250-0001

202-690-7650; Fax: 202-512-2250
www.access.gpo.gov

Offers valuable information on all meat and poultry plants that ship meat interstate and therefore come under the US Department of Agriculture inspection.
Cost: $16.00
600 Pages
Frequency: Semiannual

10646 **Membership Directory of the Retail Confectioners International**
1807 Glenview Rd
Suite 104
Glenview, IL 60025-2961

847-657-7400; Fax: 847-724-2719
www.retailconfectioners.org

Frequency: Annual

10647 **Mid-Atlantic Retail Food Industry Buyers' Guide**
Mid-Atlantic Food Dealers Services
19 Hamill Rd # E
Baltimore, MD 21210-1754

410-522-6924; Fax: 410-377-7137

Robert Mead, Executive Director

Offers extensive coverage of retail food stores and suppliers to the food industry in the states of Delaware, Maryland, New Jersey, Virginia and Washington, DC.
Cost: $15.00
130 Pages
Frequency: Annual
Circulation: 5,000

10648 **Missouri Grocers Association Annual Convention & Food Trade Show**
Missouri Grocers Association
PO Box 10223
Springfield, MO 65808

417-831-6667; Fax: 417-831-3907
http://www.missourigrocers.com

1300 Pages

10649 **NASDA Directory**
National Association of State Dept of Agriculture
1156 15th St NW
Suite 1020
Washington, DC 20005-1711

202-296-9680; Fax: 202-296-9686
www.nasda.org

Barb Glenn, Chief Executive Officer

Top agricultural officials in 50 states and four territories.
Cost: $100.00
Frequency: Annual

10650 **National Agri-Marketing Association Directory**
11020 King St
Suite 205
Overland Park, KS 66210-1201
913-491-6500; Fax: 913-491-6502
agrimktg@nama.org
www.nama.org
Jennifer Pickett, CEO
Janae Prewitt, Manager, Information Services
Cost: $150.00
2500 Pages
Frequency: Annual Spring
Founded in 1956

10651 **National Association of Specialty Food and Confection Brokers**
11004 Wood Elves Way
Columbia, MD 21044-1085
410-969-3663; Fax: 410-740-2958
Judi Epstein, Secretary
Lists members by state of residence and by states covered. Code of ethics and articles describing the function of a 'specialty' food broker in the marketplace.
86 Pages

10652 **National Coffee Service Association: Membership Directory**
8201 Greensboro Drive
Suite 300
McLean, VA 22102-3814
703-610-9000
800-221-3196; Fax: 703-273-9011
A directory covering over 800 member operators and suppliers of office coffee service products.
Frequency: Annual

10653 **National Meat Association: Membership Directory**
1970 Broadway
Suite 825
Oakland, CA 94612-2299
510-763-1533; Fax: 510-763-6186
www.nmaonline.org
Barry Carpenter, CEO
Jen Kempis, Associate Director
This annual guide offers information on over 250 meat packers, processors and jobbers in 19 western states.
100 Pages
Frequency: Annual

10654 **National Organic Directory**
Community Alliance with Family Farmers
PO Box 464
Davis, CA 95617-0464
916-786-5155
800-852-3832; Fax: 530-756-7857
Annual directory offering information on over 1,000 growers and wholesalers of organically grown produce and organic products. The new edition includes information on regulations and resources for the industry.
Cost: $34.95
288 Pages
Frequency: Annual
Circulation: 2,500

10655 **New Product News**
Avtex
N6w23673 Bluemound Rd
Waukesha, WI 53188-1741
262-542-9111; Fax: 262-542-8820
info@avtex.com
www.avtex.com
Spencer Thomason, President
Martin Friedman, Editor
Diane McBride, Circulation Manager
Chris Kumsher, Chief Financial Officer
Offers food and drug manufacturers up-to-date information on products sold in supermarkets, drug stores, gourmet stores and natural food stores. Includes in-depth analysis of new product trends.
Cost: $359.00
65 Pages
Frequency: Monthly
Mailing list available for rentat $300 per M
Printed in one color on matte stock

10656 **Organic Food Mail Order Suppliers**
Center for Science in the Public Interest
1875 Connecticut Avenue NW
Suite 300
Washington, DC 20009-5736
202-332-9110; Fax: 202-265-4954
www.cspinet.org
Michael Jacobson, Executive Director
Jamie Jonker, Director Regulatory Affairs
A directory of organic-food growers and suppliers who make their products available by mail-order.
Founded in 1992

10657 **Organic Pages Online**
Organic Trade Association
60 Wells Street
PO Box 547
Greenfield, MA 01302
413-774-7511; Fax: 413-774-6432
www.theorganicpages.com
Christine Bushway, Executive Director/CEO
Linda Lutz, Membership Manager
Laura Batcha, Marketing/Public Relations Manager
Online searchable directory
Founded in 1984

10658 **PMMI Packaging Machinery Directory**
Packaging Machinery Manufacturers Institute (PMMI)
11911 Freedom Drive
Suite 600
Reston, VA 20190
571-612-3200; Fax: 703-243-8556
info@pmmi.org
www.pmmi.org
Charles D. Yuska, President & CEO
Corinne G. Mulligan, Executive Assistant
Caroline Abromavage, Operations Director
Heather Harvey, Membership Manager
Fred Hayes, Technical Services Director
Contains listings of packaging and processing companies that make up the membership of the Packaging Machinery Manufacturers Institute (PMMI).
800+ Members
Founded in 1933

10659 **Packer: Produce Availability and Merchandising Guide**
Vance Publishing
10901 W 84th Ter
Suite 200
Lenexa, KS 66214-1631
913-438-5721
800-255-5113; Fax: 913-438-0697
info@vancepublishing.com
www.vancepublishing.com
Cliff Becker, Vice President, Director
Ben Wood, Editor
Lance Jungmeyer, Managing Editor
Leanne Ball, Manager
Lori Eppel, Chief Financial Officer
Publication of about 6,000 fruit and vegetable suppliers and sales agents.
Cost: $35.00
Frequency: Annual

10660 **Parity Corp**
11812 N Creek Pkwy N
Suite 204
Bothell, WA 98011-8202
425-487-0997; Fax: 425-487-2317
info@paritycorp.com
www.paritycorp.com
Arvid Tellevik, Owner
Integrated business information system and services designed specifically for the food industry.
Founded in 1985

10661 **Pasta Industry Directory**
National Pasta Association
1156 15th St NW
Suite 900
Washington, DC 20005-1717
202-367-1861; Fax: 202-367-1865
info@ilovepasta.org
www.civilwar.org
Jim Lighthizer, President
Lists by category pasta manufacturers and industry suppliers, including contact names.
Cost: $25.00
Frequency: Annual
Circulation: 1,000

10662 **Pickle Packers International Directory**
1620 Eye St NW
Suite 925
Washington, DC 20006-4076
202-293-5800; Fax: 202-463-8998
www.hazmatshippers.org
Glenn Roberts, President
Frequency: Annual

10663 **Pioneers of the Hospitality Industry**
CHRIE
2810 N Parham Road
Suite 230
Richmond, VA 23294
804-346-4800; Fax: 804-346-5009
info@chrie.org
www.chrie.org
Facebook, Twitter, LinkedIn
Susan Fournier, President
Josette Katz, Vice President
Chris Roberts, Secretary
John Drysdale, Treasurer
Kathy McCarty, CEO
Lessons from Leaders, Innovators and Visionaries. A tribute to those dedicated individuals who have shaped the hospitality industry through their colorful lives, their foresight, and their leadership. These profiles offer readers the opportunity to analyze successful leadership and entrepreneurial characteristics, and to evaluate the significance of their contributions.
Cost: $45.00

10664 **Pizza Today: Pizza Industry Buyer's Guide**
National Association of Pizzeria Operators (NAPO)
908 S 8th Street
Suite 200
Louisville, KY 40203
502-736-9530
800-489-8324; Fax: 502-736-9531
www.pizzatoday.com
Pete Lachapelle, Publisher
Joe Straughan, Association Executive Director

A directory listing over 3,000 manufacturers and suppliers of products, equipment and services to the pizza industry.
Cost: $25.00
Frequency: Annual
Circulation: 40000
Founded in 1984

10665 Pork Guide to Hero Health Issue
Vance Publishing
10901 W 84th Ter
Suite 200
Lenexa, KS 66214-1631

913-438-5721; Fax: 913-438-0697
info@vancepublishing.com
www.vancepublishing.com

Cliff Becker, Vice President, Director
Lori Eppel, Chief Financial Officer

This comprehensive directory offers a list of manufacturers of swine health products.
Cost: $25.00
Frequency: Annual
Circulation: 77,000

10666 Poultry Digest: Buyer's Guide Issue
WATT Publishing Company
122 S Wesley Ave
Mt Morris, IL 61054-1451

815-734-7937; Fax: 815-734-4201
www.wattnet.com

Charles Perry, Editor
James Watt, Owner

A list of suppliers to the poultry industry of the US and Canada are listed.
Cost: $6.00
Frequency: Annual
Circulation: 20,000

10667 Poultry International: Who's Who International
WATT Publishing Company
303 N Main Street
Suite 500
Rockford, IL 61101

815-966-5400; Fax: 815-966-6416
www.wattnet.com

James Watt, Chairman/CEO
Greg Watt, President/COO
Jeff Swanson, Publishing Director

A guide offering information on over 2,500 manufacturers and suppliers of poultry equipment, services and products.
Cost: $15.00
Frequency: Annual
Circulation: 20,000
ISSN: 0032-5767

10668 Poultry Price Book
Urner Barry Publications
PO Box 389
Toms River, NJ 08754-0389

732-240-5330
800-932-0617; Fax: 732-341-0891
help@urnerbarry.com
www.urnerbarry.com

Paul B Brown Jr, President
Sheila M Deane, Marketing Manager

Seven year price history of selected turkey and chicken items as quoted in Urner Barry's Price—Current.
Cost: $55.00
Frequency: Annual
Circulation: 400

10669 Poultry Processing: Buyer's Guide Issue
WATT Publishing Company
122 S Wesley Ave
Mt Morris, IL 61054-1451

815-734-7937; Fax: 815-734-4201
www.wattnet.com

Virginia Lazar, Editor
James Watt, Owner

Annual reference offering information on over 800 manufacturers and suppliers of equipment, machinery and raw materials for the poultry packing industry.

10670 Prepared Foods
Delta Communications
455 N Cityfront Plaza Drive
Chicago, IL 60611-5503

312-836-2000; Fax: 312-222-2026

This database offers information of interest to the processed food industry.
Frequency: Full-text

10671 Proceedings
Flavor & Extract Manufacturers Assn of the US
1620 Eye St NW
Suite 925
Washington, DC 20006-4076

202-293-5800; Fax: 202-463-8998
www.hazmatshippers.org

Glenn Roberts, President
Kim Earle, Contact

Updates and reports on the proceedings of the association.
Frequency: Annual

10672 Produce Marketing Association Membership Directory & Buyer's Guide
Produce Marketing Association
1500 Casho Mill Road
PO Box 6036
Newark, DE 19711-3547

302-738-7100; Fax: 302-731-2409

Kathy Means, VP Membership
Dan Henderson, Marketing
Bryan Silbermann, President

A directory offering information on over 2,000 members involved in retail grocery and food service marketing.
Cost: $70.00
280 Pages
Frequency: Annual

10673 Produce Services Sourcebook
Vance Publishing
10901 W 84th Ter
Suite 200
Lenexa, KS 66214-1631

913-438-5721
800-255-5113; Fax: 913-438-0697
info@vancepublishing.com
www.vancepublishing.com
Cliff Becker, Vice President, Director
Lori Eppel, Chief Financial Officer

The produce industry's directory of allied services and products. Content is a balance between practical reference information, allied trends and supplier or source listings.
Cost: $20.00

10674 Professional Workers in State Agricultural Experiment Stations
US Department of Agriculture
PO Box 2022
Washington, DC 20250-0001

202-690-7650; Fax: 202-512-2250

This directory offers information on academic and research personnel in all agricultural, forestry, aquaculture and home economics industries.
Cost: $15.00
289 Pages
Frequency: Annual

10675 Purebred Picture: Breeders Directory Issue
American Berkshire Association
PO Box 2346
W Lafayette, IN 47996-2346

765-497-3618; Fax: 765-497-2959

Lois Wall, Managing Editor

Annual guide offering information on cattle and hog breeders in the US.
Cost: $12.00
Frequency: Annual
Circulation: 4,000

10676 Quick Frozen Foods Annual Processors Directory & Buyer's Guide
Frozen Food Digest, Saul Beck Publications
271 Madison Ave
Suite 1402a
New York, NY 10016-1014

212-557-8600; Fax: 212-986-9868

Saul Beck, Owner
Audrey Beck, General Manager

A buyer's guide listing over 10,000 frozen food processors, associations, equipment manufacturers and suppliers, and public refrigerated warehouses, transportation, freezing & refrigerated equipment, manufacturers, packagers and railroad lines, brokers, etc.
Cost: $140.00
400 Pages
Frequency: Annual
Circulation: 5,000

10677 RIFM/FEMA Fragrance and Flavor Database
Flavor & Extract Manufacturers Association
1620 I Street NW
Suite 925
Washington, DC 20006

202-293-5800; Fax: 202-462-8998
www.femaflavor.org
YouTube, RSS Feed

Ed R. Hays, Ph.D., President
George C. Robinson, III, President Elect
Mark Scott, Treasurer
Arthur Schick, VP & Secretary
John Cox, Executive Director

The Database currently contains over 50,000 references and more than 103,000 human health and environmental studies.
Frequency: Annual
Founded in 1909

10678 Refrigerated Transporter: Warehouse Directory Issue
Penton
PO Box 66010
Houston, TX 77266

713-523-8124
800-880-0368; Fax: 713-523-8384
refrigeratedtransporter.com

Ray Anderson, Publisher

Listing of approximately 265 refrigerated warehouses in the US and Canada.

10679 Restaurant Hospitality: Hospitality 500 Issue
Penton Media

1300 E 9th St
Suite 316
Cleveland, OH 44114-1503

216-696-7000; Fax: 216-696-6662
information@penton.com
www.penton.com

Jane Cooper, Marketing

500 independent restaurants selected on basis of sales.
Cost: $25.00
Frequency: Annual June
Circulation: 123,000

10680 Restaurants and Institutions: Annual Issue
Reed Business Information
1350 E Touhy Avenue
Suite 200E
Des Plaines, IL 60018-3358

847-962-2200; Fax: 630-288-8686
www.reedbusiness.com

Roland Dietz, CEO
Stuart Whayman, CFO
Cost: $25.00
Frequency: Annual
Circulation: 16,000

10681 Santa Gertrudis Breeders International Membership Directory
PO Box 1257
Kingsville, TX 78364-1257

361-592-9357; Fax: 361-592-8572
http://www.santagertrudis.com

Ervin Kaatz, Executive Director

Annual guide offering information on over 4,5000 producers of Santa Gertrudis beef and cattle throughout the world.

10682 Santa Gertrudis USA
Santa Gertrudis Breeders International
PO Box 1257
Kingsville, TX 78364-1257

361-592-9357; Fax: 361-592-8572
http://www.santagertrudis.com

Ervin Kaatz, Executive Director

Monthly publication offering information on over 1,000 producers of Santa Gertrudis beef cattle throughout the United States.
Cost: $30.00
125 Pages
Frequency: Monthly
Circulation: 2,500
Founded in 1998
Printed in on glossy stock

10683 Sauces and Gravies
MarketResearch.com
641 Avenue of the Americas
3rd Floor
New York, NY 10011

212-807-2629
800-298-6699; Fax: 212-807-2676

This market profile analyzes US shipments, retail sales, consumer demographics, and food service and food processor purchases for 22 product lines. Also analyzes the sauce and gravy product line, retail sales, brand share, and customer demographics for 16 major marketers.
Cost: $2250.00
250 Pages

10684 Seafood Buyer's Handbook
Diversified Business Communications
PO Box 7438
Portland, ME 04112-7438

207-842-5500; Fax: 207-842-5505
www.divbusiness.com

Nancy Gelette, VP Operations

This comprehensive directory lists about 1,200 North American fish and shellfish suppliers, distributors and suppliers of related services and equipment to the seafood industry.
Cost: $18.00
250 Pages
Frequency: Annual
Circulation: 15,000

10685 Seafood Price Book
Urner Barry Publications
PO Box 389
Toms River, NJ 08754-0389

732-240-5330
800-932-0617; Fax: 732-341-0891
help@urnerbarry.com
www.urnerbarry.com

Paul B Brown Jr, President
Sheila M Deane, Marketing Manager

Seven year price history of selected fresh/frozen seafood items as quoted in Urner Barry's Seafood Price— Current.
Cost: $95.00
Frequency: Annual
Circulation: 400

10686 Seafood Shippers' Guide
American Seafood Institute
25 Fairway Circle
Hope Valley, RI 02832

401-491-9017; Fax: 401-491-9024
www.americanseafood.org

Trucking, freight and cold storage companies that directly affect the seafood packing and shipping industry.
Cost: $29.95
100 Pages
Circulation: 2,000

10687 Seed Technologist Training Manual
Society of Commercial Seed Technologists
101 E State Street
Suite 214
Ithaca, NY 14850

607-256-3313; Fax: 607-256-3313
www.analyzeseeds.com

Jess Peterson, Executive Director

This manual represents the most comprehensive treatment of seed testing technology anywhere.
Cost: $175.00
450 Pages
Frequency: Bi-Annually
Circulation: 500
Founded in 1922

10688 Single Unit Supermarkets Operators Directory
Chain Store Guide
3710 Corporex Park Dr.
Suite 310
Tampa, FL 33619-1389

813-627-6700
800-927-9292; Fax: 813-627-6888
webmaster@chainstoreguide.com
www.chainstoreguide.com

Mike Jarvis, Publisher
Shami Choon, Manager

Discover more than 7,100 single-unit supermarkets with annual sales topping $500,000 dollars. This comprehensive desktop reference makes it easy to reach our compiled list of 21,000 key executives and buyers, plus their primary wholesalers.
Cost: $575.00
725 Pages
Frequency: Annual

10689 Soya & Oilseed Bluebook
Soyatech Inc
P.O.Box 1307
Southwest Harbor, ME 04679-1307
207-288-4969
800-424-7692; Fax: 207-288-5264
www.soyatech.com

Provides the world with information on the processing industry that supports development and value creation along each step of the supply chain.

10690 Supermarket News Distribution Study of Grocery Store Sales
Fairchild Publications
7 W 34th St
3rd Floor
New York, NY 10001-8100

212-630-3880; Fax: 212-630-3868

Directory of services and supplies to the industry.
Cost: $75.00
Frequency: Annual

10691 Supermarket News Retailers & Wholesalers Directory
Fairchild Publications
7 W 34th St
New York, NY 10001-8100

212-630-3880
800-360-1700; Fax: 212-630-3868

Over 2,200 US and Canadian retailers, including supermarkets, discount department stores, membership clubs, drug stores, plus voluntary, cooperative and nonsponsoring wholesalers.

10692 Supermarket, Grocery & Convenience Store Chains
Lebhar-Friedman
425 Park Ave
New York, NY 10022-3526

212-756-5088; Fax: 212-838-9487
www.nrn.com

Heather Martin, Manager

Directory of US and Canadian supermarket chains.
Cost: $335.00

10693 Supermarket, Grocery & Convenience Stores
Chain Store Guide
3710 Corporex Park Dr.
Suite 310
Tampa, FL 33619-1389

813-627-6700
800-927-9292; Fax: 813-627-6888
webmaster@chainstoreguide.com
www.chainstoreguide.com

Mike Jarvis, Publisher
Shami Choon, Manager

Contains information on close to 3,400 U.S. and Canadian supermarket chains, each with at least $2 million in annual sales - one of the most profitable segments in this sector of the economy. The companies in this database operate over 41,000 individual supermarket, superstore, club store, gourmet supermarkets and combo-store units. A special convenience store section profiles 1,700 convenience store chains operating over 85,000 stores.
Cost: $575.00
Frequency: Annual

10694 Trade Dimensions
45 Danbury Rd
Wilton, CT 06897-4445

203-563-3000; Fax: 203-563-3131
www.tradedimensions.com

Hal Clark, Owner

Trade Dimensions has over 30 years of experience and innovation in developing some of the most sophisticated, reliable and widely used directories and retail site data bases available.

10695 **US Agriculture**
WEFA Group
800 Baldwin Tower Boulevard
Eddystone, PA 19022-1368

610-490-4000; Fax: 610-490-2770
info@wefa.com
www.wefa.com

Harry Baurnes

This large database offers information on US macroeconomic farm crop and related agricultural data.

10696 **US Alcohol Beverage Industry Category CD**
Beverage Marketing Corporation
2670 Commercial Ave
Mingo Junction, OH 43938-1613

740-598-4133
800-332-6222; Fax: 740-598-3977
www.beveragemarketing.com

Andrew Standardi III, Director of Operations
Kathy Smurthwaite, Editor

Contains information on approximately 3,030 companies including breweries, microbreweries, wineries, distilleries, wholesalers and importers.
Cost: $3010.00
Frequency: Annual

10697 **US Bagel Industry**
Leading Edge Reports/Industry Reports
2171 Jericho Turnpike
Suite 200
Commack, NY 11725-2937

631-462-5454; Fax: 631-462-1842
www.businesstrendanalysts.com

Charles J Ritchie, Executive VP
Donna Priani, Marketing Director
Linda Sherman, Production Manager
Vincent Seeno, Research Director

A comprehensive investigation of the dynamics of the US Bagel Industry. Both historical and current market data is presented.
Cost: $1995.00
150 Pages
Founded in 2000

10698 **US Beer Industry Category CD**
Beverage Marketing Corporation
2670 Commercial Ave
Mingo Junction, OH 43938-1613

740-598-4133
800-332-6222; Fax: 740-598-3977
www.beveragemarketing.com

Andrew Standardi III, Director of Operations
Kathy Smurthwaite, Editor

Contains information on approximately 2,084 companies including breweries, microbreweries, beer wholesalers and beer importers.
Cost: $2070.00
Frequency: Annual

10699 **US Beverage Distribution Landscape Category CD**
Beverage Marketing Corporation
2670 Commercial Ave
Mingo Junction, OH 43938-1613

740-598-4133
800-332-6222; Fax: 740-598-3977
www.beveragemarketing.com

Andrew Standardi III, Director of Operations
Kathy Smurthwaite, Editor

Contains information on approximately 3,340 companies distributing soft drinks, bottled water, beer, wine and spirits.
Cost: $3320.00
Frequency: Annual

10700 **US Beverage Manufacturers and Filling Locations Category CD**
Beverage Marketing Corporation
2670 Commercial Ave
Mingo Junction, OH 43938-1613

740-598-4133
800-332-6222; Fax: 740-598-3977
www.beveragemarketing.com

Andrew Standardi III, Director of Operations
Kathy Smurthwaite, Editor

Contains information on approximately 2,402 companies including breweries, microbreweries, wineries, distilleries, soft drink fillers and franchise companies, bottled water fillers, juice, sports beverages and energy drinks, soy, coffee, tea, and milk manufacturers.
Cost: $2390.00
Frequency: Annual

10701 **US Bottled Water Industry**
Business Trend Analysts/Industry Reports
2171 Jericho Tpke
Suite 200
Commack, NY 11725-2937

631-462-5454; Fax: 631-462-1842
www.businesstrendanalysts.com

Charles J Ritchie, Executive VP
Donna Priani, Marketing Director
Linda Sherman, Production Manager
Vincent Seeno, Research Director

BTA continues its pioneering coverage of the bottled water industry with this updated and dramatically expanded edition.
Cost: $1550.00
Founded in 1997

10702 **US Bottled Water Operations Category CD**
Beverage Marketing Corporation
2670 Commercial Ave
Mingo Junction, OH 43938-1613

740-598-4133
800-332-6222; Fax: 740-598-3977
www.beveragemarketing.com

Andrew Standardi III, Director of Operations
Kathy Smurthwaite, Editor

Contains information on approximately 3,010 companies including bottled water fillers and distributors.
Cost: $2995.00
Frequency: Annual

10703 **US Bread Market**
MarketResearch.com
641 Avenue of the Americas
3rd Floor
New York, NY 10011

212-807-2629
800-298-6699; Fax: 212-807-2676

This study covers packaged, fresh and frozen bread products, including a growing number of specialty bread products. Major marketing, retailing and demographic trends are all explored in-depth. Special attention is given to the in-store bakery phenomenon.
Cost: $2750.00
197 Pages

10704 **US Candy and Gum Market**
MarketResearch.com
641 Avenue of the Americas
3rd Floor
New York, NY 10011

212-807-2629
800-298-6699; Fax: 212-807-2676

This report dissects the 23.5 billion market for chocolate candy, hard candy, soft candy, mints and gum, covering both the mass-market and gourmet levels. Market size, growth and composition are tabulated, with sales projections through 2004. Competition at the retail level as a major impetus to market growth is covered in full, as are consumer demographics by product type, brand and usage levels.
Cost: $2750.00
351 Pages

10705 **US Carbonated Soft Drink Operations Category CD**
Beverage Marketing Corporation
2670 Commercial Ave
Mingo Junction, OH 43938-1613

740-598-4133
800-332-6222; Fax: 740-598-3977
www.beveragemarketing.com

Andrew Standardi III, Director of Operations
Kathy Smurthwaite, Editor

Contains information on approximately 2,713 companies including CSD bottlers, canners, franchise companies and distributors.
Cost: $2700.00
Frequency: Annual

10706 **US Cheese Market**
Business Trend Analysts/Industry Reports
2171 Jericho Tpke
Suite 200
Commack, NY 11725-2937

631-462-5454
800-866-4648; Fax: 631-462-1842
www.bta-ler.com

Charles J Ritchie, Executive VP
Donna Priani, Marketing Director
Linda Holm, Production Manager
Jennifer Wichert, Research Director

Survey offering the size and growth of markets for natural, process, cottage and substitute cheeses.
Cost: $1395.00
480 Pages
Founded in 2001

10707 **US Confectionary Market**
Business Trend Analysts/Industry Reports
2171 Jericho Tpke
Suite 200
Commack, NY 11725-2937

631-462-5454; Fax: 631-462-1842
www.businesstrendanalysts.com

Charles J Ritchie, Executive VP
Donna Priani, Marketing Director
Linda Sherman, Production Manager
Vincent Seeno, Research Director

Profiles markets for chocolate and nonchocolate candies, gum, snack nuts, and seeds, as well as providing information on distribution, trends and future opportunities.
Cost: $1250.00
760 Pages
Founded in 1996

10708 **US Date Code Directory for Product Labeling**
Danis Research
1 Gothic Plaza
Fairfield, NJ 07004-2411

973-575-3509; Fax: 973-575-5366

Over 500 companies using date code labeling on their food products; over 500 quality control managers and consumer affairs managers from

companies that produce snack foods, baked goods, confectioneries and other food products.
Cost: $295.00

10709 **US Ethnic Foods Market**
Business Trend Analysts/Industry Reports
2171 Jericho Tpke
Suite 200
Commack, NY 11725-2937

631-462-5454; Fax: 631-462-1842
www.businesstrendanalysts.com

Charles J Ritchie, Executive VP
Donna Priani, Marketing Director
Linda Sherman, Production Manager
Vincent Seeno, Research Director

A detailed analysis of the expanding US markets for Italian, Hispanic/Mexican, Oriental, Indian and Kosher foods.
Cost: $995.00
Founded in 1995

10710 **US Hot Beverage Market**
Business Trend Analysts/Industry Reports
2171 Jericho Tpke
Suite 200
Commack, NY 11725-2937

631-462-5454; Fax: 631-462-1842
www.businesstrendanalysts.com

Charles J Ritchie, Executive VP
Donna Priani, Marketing Director
Linda Sherman, Production Manager
Vincent Seeno, Research Director

A survey offering profiles of the coffee, tea and cocoa products market.
Cost: $1995.00
330 Pages
Founded in 1998

10711 **US Market for Cereal & Other Breakfast Foods**
Business Trend Analysts/Industry Reports
2171 Jericho Tpke
Suite 200
Commack, NY 11725-2937

631-462-5454
800-866-4648; Fax: 631-462-1842
www.businesstrendanalysts.com

Charles J Ritchie, Executive VP
Donna Praini, General Manager
Linda Sherman, Production Manager
Jennifer Wichert, Research Director

Provides up-to-date information on consumer attitudes and buying patterns, new product development, marketing strategies and current and projected sales trends for all types of hot and cold cereals, baked breakfast foods and frozen breakfast products.
Cost: $1495.00
396 Pages
Founded in 1986

10712 **US Market for Fats & Oils**
Business Trend Analysts/Industry Reports
2171 Jericho Tpke
Suite 200
Commack, NY 11725-2937

631-462-5454; Fax: 631-462-1842
www.businesstrendanalysts.com

Charles J Ritchie, Executive VP
Donna Priani, Marketing Director
Linda Sherman, Production Manager
Vincent Seeno, Research Director

Analyzes the markets for different oils (corn, soybean, peanut, canola, linseed, cottonseed, fish and others), edible and inedible tallow, grease and lard.
Cost: $1295.00
540 Pages
Founded in 1998

10713 **US Market for Fruit and Vegetable Based Beverages**
MarketResearch.com
641 Avenue of the Americas
3rd Floor
New York, NY 10011

212-807-2629
800-298-6699; Fax: 212-807-2676

This new study covers refrigerated juices and juice drinks, aseptic juices, frozen and unfrozen concentrates, shelf-stable juices and juice drinks in bottles and cans. It provides the latest available sales and volume by category and retail outlet, as well as detailed marketer/brand shares. The report unveils the competitive strategies, advertising and promotional campaigns and new product launches of major players; tracks trends in packaging, flavor-blending, health drinks, and other niches.
Cost: $2750.00
258 Pages

10714 **US Market for Juices, Aides & Noncarbonated Drinks**
Business Trend Analysts/Industry Reports
2171 Jericho Tpke
Suite 200
Commack, NY 11725-2937

631-462-5454; Fax: 631-462-1842
www.businesstrendanalysts.com

Charles J Ritchie, Executive VP
Donna Priani, Marketing Director
Linda Sherman, Production Manager
Vincent Seeno, Research Director

A comprehensive market analysis covering all types of fresh and frozen fruit juices, fruit drinks, vegetable juices and canned ades.
Cost: $1195.00
810 Pages
Founded in 1998

10715 **US Market for Pizza**
Leading Edge Reports/Industry Reports
2171 Jericho Turnpike
Suite 200
Commack, NY 11725-2937

631-462-5454; Fax: 631-462-1842
www.businesstrendanalysts.com

Charles J Ritchie, Executive VP
Donna Priani, Marketing Director
Linda Sherman, Production Manager
Vincent Seeno, Research Director

This report examines the size and growth of the US Pizza market through all channels.
Cost: $1995.00
225 Pages
Founded in 1999

10716 **US Market for Salted Snacks**
MarketResearch.com
641 Avenue of the Americas
3rd Floor
New York, NY 10011

212-807-2629
800-298-6699; Fax: 212-807-2676

This new study provides a coherent view of the market as well as its individual segments: potato chips, tortilla chips, corn chips, pretzels, popcorn, snack nuts and extruded snacks. It explains not only what the industry does, but how it works: how shelf life shapes the entire industry; how hundreds of smaller companies manage to thrive in a market dominated by Frito-Lay. This study profiles the giant companies and regional players.
Cost: $2750.00
263 Pages

10717 **US Non-Alcoholic Beverage Industry Category CD**
Beverage Marketing Corporation
2670 Commercial Ave
Mingo Junction, OH 43938-1613

740-598-4133
800-332-6222; Fax: 740-598-3977
www.beveragemarketing.com

Andrew Standardi III, Director of Operations
Kathy Smurthwaite, Editor

Contains information on approximately 4,206 companies including CSD and bottled water operations, sports beverages and energy drinks, juice, soy, coffee, tea, and milk manufacturers.
Cost: $4185.00
Frequency: Annual

10718 **US Organic Food Market**
MarketResearch.com
641 Avenue of the Americas
3rd Floor
New York, NY 10011

212-807-2629
800-298-6699; Fax: 212-807-2676

This report covers the booming organic market as it expands into mainstream and gains increased public awareness. The report covers the market size and composition, important trends, and projections for future growth. The information contained in this report will help players in the organic arena make informed decisions to complete successfully in this exciting market.
Cost: $2750.00
275 Pages

10719 **US Pasta Market**
Business Trend Analysts/Industry Reports
2171 Jericho Tpke
Suite 200
Commack, NY 11725-2937

631-462-5454; Fax: 631-462-1842
www.businesstrendanalysts.com

Charles J Ritchie, Executive VP
Donna Priani, Marketing Director
Linda Sherman, Production Manager
Vincent Seeno, Research Director

Quantifies historial, current and projected sales trends in the ever-expanding market for pasta products. Covers all typed of dry, canned, frozen and fresh pasta, as well as shelf-stable noodle dishes and pasta meals.
Cost: $ 1395.00
380 Pages
Founded in 2000

10720 **US Poultry and Small Game Market**
Business Trend Analysts/Industry Reports
2171 Jericho Tpke
Suite 200
Commack, NY 11725-2937

631-462-5454; Fax: 631-462-1842
www.businesstrendanalysts.com

Charles J Ritchie, Executive VP
Donna Priani, Marketing Director
Linda Sherman, Production Manager
Vincent Seeno, Research Director

Profiles market for poultry and small game products and provides information on pricing, foreign trade, and advertising and promotion.
Cost: $1995.00
280 Pages
Founded in 1999

10721 **US Processed Fruits & Vegetables Market**
Business Trend Analysts/Industry Reports

2171 Jericho Tpke
Suite 200
Commack, NY 11725-2937

631-462-5454; Fax: 631-462-1842
www.businesstrendanalysts.com

Charles J Ritchie, Executive VP
Donna Priani, Marketing Director
Linda Sherman, Production Manager
Vincent Seeno, Research Director

A comprehensive marketing, economic and financial analysis of the processed fruits and vegetables industry, covering all types of canned, frozen, dried and dehydrated fruits and vegetables.
Cost: $1195.00
815 Pages
Founded in 1997

10722 US Processed Meat Market
Business Trend Analysts/Industry Reports
2171 Jericho Tpke
Suite 200
Commack, NY 11725-2937

631-462-5454; Fax: 631-462-1842
www.businesstrendanalysts.com

Charles J Ritchie, Executive VP
Donna Priani, Marketing Director
Linda Sherman, Production Manager
Vincent Seeno, Research Director

Profiles markets for processed meat products, including sausage, processed pork products, canned meats, and meat snacks.
Cost: $1295.00
800 Pages
Founded in 2000

10723 US Snack Food Market
Business Trend Analysts/Industry Reports
2171 Jericho Tpke
Suite 200
Commack, NY 11725-2937

631-462-5454; Fax: 631-462-1842
www.businesstrendanalysts.com

Charles J Ritchie, Executive VP
Donna Priani, Marketing Director
Linda Sherman, Production Manager
Vincent Seeno, Research Director

A product-by-product analysis of the intensely competitive US snack food industry.
Cost: $1495.00
860 Pages
Founded in 1999

10724 US Soyfoods Market
MarketResearch.com
641 Avenue of the Americas
3rd Floor
New York, NY 10011

212-807-2629
800-298-6699; Fax: 212-807-2676

This report covers five product categories: meat alternatives, dairy alternatives, snacks, cereals, breads, bulk soybeans, meal replacements/protein powders and other soyfoods including soy sauce and miso. It profiles leading soyfoods producers such as Kellog's, White Wave and Lightlife Foods. The report projects sales trends through 2005 and provides insight into the factors shaping this market. Distributor trends and consumer attitudes and behaviors are also covered in detail.
Cost: $2750.00
150 Pages

10725 US Sweeteners Market
Business Trend Analysts/Industry Reports
2171 Jericho Tpke
Suite 200
Commack, NY 11725-2937

631-462-5454; Fax: 631-462-1842
www.businesstrendanalysts.com

Charles J Ritchie, Executive VP
Donna Priani, Marketing Director
Linda Sherman, Production Manager
Vincent Seeno, Research Director

In-depth coverage of the continually evolving sweetener industry, providing up-to-date information on the latest product developments.
Cost: $1995.00
375 Pages
Founded in 1998

10726 US Vitamins & Nutrients Market
Business Trend Analysts/Industry Reports
2171 Jericho Tpke
Suite 200
Commack, NY 11725-2937

631-462-5454; Fax: 631-462-1842
www.businesstrendanalysts.com

Charles J Ritchie, Executive VP
Donna Priani, Marketing Director
Linda Sherman, Production Manager
Vincent Seeno, Research Director

Statistical report on the vitamin and health food industries.
Cost: $1995.00
410 Pages
Founded in 1999

10727 US Wine & Spirits Industry Category CD
Beverage Marketing Corporation
2670 Commercial Ave
Mingo Junction, OH 43938-1613

740-598-4133
800-332-6222; Fax: 740-598-3977
www.beveragemarketing.com

Andrew Standardi III, Director of Operations
Kathy Smurthwaite, Editor

Contains information on approximately 1,484 companies including wineries, distilleries, wine & spirit wholesalers, and wine & spirit importers.
Cost: $1475.00
Frequency: Annual

10728 US Wine Market
Business Trend Analysts/Industry Reports
2171 Jericho Tpke
Suite 200
Commack, NY 11725-2937

631-462-5454; Fax: 631-462-1842
www.businesstrendanalysts.com

Charles J Ritchie, Executive VP
Donna Priani, Marketing Director
Linda Sherman, Production Manager
Jennifer Wichert, Research Director

An analysis of the wine industry, domestic and imported.
Cost: $1295.00
470 Pages
Founded in 1996

10729 Uker's International Tea and Coffee Buyer's Guide & Directory
Lockwood Trade Journal
26 Broadway
Suite 1050
New York, NY 10004-1777

212-269-7053; Fax: 212-827-0945
teacof@aol.com
www.lockwoodpublications.com

Robert Lockwood, CEO
Jane McCabe, Editor

A directory covering firms that are involved in importing and exporting coffee and tea; manufacturers, suppliers and retailers to the industry; and specialty roasters and their suppliers.
Cost: $48.00
Frequency: Annual
Printed in 4 colors on glossy stock

10730 Urner Barry's Meat & Poultry Directory
Urner Barry Publications
PO Box 389
Toms River, NJ 08754-0389

732-240-5330
800-932-0617; Fax: 732-341-0891
help@urnerbarry.com
www.urnerbarry.com

Paul B Brown Jr, President
Karen Mick, Circulation Director

National business directory of traders in the meat and poultry industry.
Cost: $95.00
760 Pages
Frequency: Annual
Circulation: 2,000
ISSN: 0738-6745

10731 Vinegar Institute Directory
1100 Johnson Ferry Road
Suite 300
Atlanta, GA 30342

404-252-3663; Fax: 404-252-0774
vi@kellencompany.com
www.versatilevinegar.org

Pamela A Chumley, President
Jeannie Milewski, Executive Director

Online membership directory for members only

10732 Vinegar Institute: Basic Reference Manual
Vinegar Institute
1100 Johnson Ferry Road
Suite 300
Atlanta, GA 30342

404-252-3663; Fax: 404-252-0774
vi@kellencompany.com
versatilevinegar.org

Looseleaf service guide to vinegar products for technical personnel such as shop foremen and production managers.
Cost: $250.00

10733 Vineyard & Winery Management Magazine
Vineyard & Winery Services
PO Box 2358
Windsor, CA 95492

707-836-6820
800-535-5670; Fax: 707-836-6825

Robert Merletti, President
Jennifer Merletti, Sales/Marketing Manager

A leading technical trade publication serving the North American Wine Industry and designed for today's serious wine business professional.
Founded in 1975

10734 Warehouses Licensed Under US Warehouse Act
Farm Service Agency-US Dept. of Agriculture
PO Box 2415
Washington, DC 20013-2415

FAX 202-690-0014

Agricultural warehouses voluntarily licensed under the US Warehouse Act governing public storage facilities.
Frequency: Annual

10735 Western Fruit Grower: Source Book Issue Agriculture
Meister Publishing Company

37733 Euclid Ave
Willoughby, OH 44094-5992

440-942-2000
800-572-7740; Fax: 440-975-3447
www.meisternet.com

Gary Fitzgerald, President

This annual resource offers information on manufacturers and distributors of suppliers and supplies for the fruit growing industry.
Cost: $5.00
Frequency: Annual
Circulation: 57,000

10736 **Western Growers Export Dirctory**
Western Growers Association
PO Box 2130
Newport Beach, CA 92658-8944

949-863-1000; Fax: 949-863-9028
www.wga.com

Heather Flower, Editor

A directory offering information on shippers of fresh produce and fruit in the states of California and Arizona.
32 Pages
Frequency: Annual

10737 **Who is Who: A Directory of Agricultural Engineers Available for Work**
American Society of Agricultural Engineers
2950 Niles Rd
St Joseph, MI 49085-8607

269-429-0300
800-371-2723; Fax: 269-429-3852
www.asabe.org

Mark D Zielke, CEO
Donna Hukk, Publication Director

This directory pertains to the availability of agricultural engineers to work in developing countries. The directory lists over 650 individuals from 60 countries, primarily engineers, available for work in land or water management, farm structures and other aspects of the field.
Cost: $27.50
210 Pages

10738 **Who's Who International**
WATT Publishing Company
303 N Main Street
Suite 500
Rockford, IL 61101

815-966-5400; Fax: 815-966-6416
www.wattnet.com

James Watt, Chairman/CEO
Greg Watt, President/COO
Jeff Swanson, Publishing Director
Founded in 1917

10739 **Who's Who in the Egg & Poultry Industries in the USA & Canada**
WATT Publishing Company
303 N Main Street
Suite 500
Rockford, IL 61101

815-966-5400; Fax: 815-966-6416
www.wattnet.com

James Watt, Chairman/CEO
Greg Watt, President/COO
Jeff Swanson, Publishing Director

Annual directory offering information on producers, processors, and distributors of poultry meat and eggs in the US and Canada.
Cost: $75.00
170 Pages
Frequency: Annual
Circulation: 10,000

10740 **Who's Who in the Egg & Poultry Industry**
WATT Publishing Company
303 N Main Street
Suite 500
Rockford, IL 61101

815-966-5400; Fax: 815-966-6416
www.wattnet.com

James Watt, Chairman/CEO
Greg Watt, President/COO
Jeff Swanson, Publishing Director

10741 **Who's Who in the Fish Industry**
Urner Barry Publications
PO Box 389
Toms River, NJ 08754-0389

732-240-5330
800-932-0617; Fax: 732-341-0891
help@urnerbarry.com
www.urnerbarry.com

Paul B Brown Jr, President
Sheila M Deane, Marketing Manager

A business directory of Canadian traders in the seafood industry.
Cost: $125.00
Frequency: Annual
Circulation: 2,000

10742 **Whole Foods Annual Source Book**
Wainer Finest Communications
3000 Hadley Road
2nd Floor
South Plainfield, NJ 07080-1183

908-769-1160; Fax: 908-769-1171
info@wfcinc.com
www.wfcinc.com

Howard Wainer, Publisher
Alan Richman, Editor
Heather Wainer, Associate Publisher
Cost: $75.00
135 Pages
Frequency: Monthly
Circulation: 16,000
Founded in 1979
Mailing list available for rent: 16000 names at $125 per M

10743 **Wholesale Beer Association Executives of America Directory**
Wholesale Beer Association Executives of America
2805 E Washington Avenue
Madison, WI 53704-5165

608-255-6464; Fax: 608-255-6466

7 Pages
Frequency: Annual

10744 **Wholesale Grocers Directory**
Chain Store Guide
3710 Corporex Park Dr.
Suite 310
Tampa, FL 33619-1389

813-627-6700
800-972-0292; Fax: 813-627-6888
webmaster@chainstoreguide.com
www.chainstoreguide.com

Mike Jarvis, Publisher
Shami Choon, Manager

We have uncovered the facts on more than 1,900 grocery suppliers in the U.S. and Canada in this database. This targeted database allows you to reach food wholesalers, cooperatives and voluntary group wholesalers, non-sponsoring wholesalers, and cash and carry operators who serve grocery, convenience, discount and drug stores. You will also find information regarding company headquarters, divisions, branches, and over 11,000 key executives and buyers.
Cost: $575.00
Frequency: Annual

10745 **Wine & Spirits Industry Marketing**
Jobson Publishing Corporation
100 Avenue of the Americas
9th Floor
New York, NY 10013-1678

212-274-7000; Fax: 212-431-0500

Michael J Tansey, CEO

List of about 300 wine and liquor firms including wineries, producers, distillers and importers.
Cost: $150.00
Frequency: Annual April

10746 **Wines and Vines Directory of the Wine Industry in North America Issue**
Hiaring Company
1800 Lincoln Avenue
San Rafael, CA 94901-1221

415-453-9700; Fax: 415-453-2517
info@winesandvines.com
www.winesandvines.com

Dorthy Kubota-Cordery, Editor
Phil Hiaring, Publisher
Debbie Hennessy, Editor
Renee Skiadas, Circulation Director
Chet Klingensmith, Owner

Annual guide offering listings of wineries and wine industry suppliers in the US, Canada and Mexico.
Cost: $85.00
505 Pages
Frequency: Annual
Circulation: 5000

10747 **Yogurt Market**
MarketResearch.com
641 Avenue of the Americas
3rd Floor
New York, NY 10011

212-807-2629
800-298-6699; Fax: 212-807-2676

Brand share and brand consumer profiles are supplemented with profiles of major US manufacturers and new product information in order to provide the reader with competitor intelligence.
Cost: $2250.00
140 Pages

10748 **Zagat.Com Restaurant Guides**
Zagat Survey
4 Columbus Cir
3rd Floor
New York, NY 10019-1180

212-977-6000; Fax: 212-977-9760
customerservice@zagat.com
www.zagat.com

Tim Zagat, CEO

Zagat.com was launched in May of 1999 and contains the most trusted and authoritive dining information online for over 20,000 restaurants in dozens of cities worldwide. Based in New York City, the Zagat survey was founded in 1979 by Tim and Nina Zagat.

Industry Web Sites

10749 **calclingpeach.com**
California Cling Peach Board

10750 **cfesa.com/directory**
Commercial Food Equipment Service Association

3605 Centre Circle
Fort Mill, SC 29715

336-346-4700; Fax: 336-346-4745
cfesa.com

Directory of commercial food equipment repair companies.

10751 cscmp.org
Council of Supply Chain Management Professionals

Association serving supply chain management professionals through education, networking opportunities, research and more.

10752 frozenandrefrigeratedfoods.com
Frozen & Refrigerated Food Council of Northern CA

Nonprofit dedicated to educating the public on the benefits of frozen and refrigerated food, as well as supporting manufacturers and retailers in the industry.

10753 http://gold.greyhouse.com
G.O.L.D Grey House OnLine Databases

Grey House Publishing's online database platform, GOLD, offers Quick Search, Keyword Search and Expert Search for most business sectors including food, beverage and agriculture markets. The GOLD platform makes finding the information you need quick and easy - whether you're a novice searcher or an experienced database user. All of Grey House's directory products are available for subscription on the GOLD platform.

10754 juiceproducts.org
Juice Products Association

Association made up of processors, packers, extractors, brokers and marketers working in the juice products industry. The purpose of the orgnization is to offer resources, networking opportunties, news and best practices to its members.

10755 nightclub.com
Questex LLC
3 Speen St.
Framingham, MA 01701

Home Page: www.nightclub.com
Facebook, Twitter, Instagram

Bob Stewart, Publisher
David Klemt, Online Content Editor

Authoritative resource on the bar industry for independent operators.

10756 scaa.org
Specialty Coffee Association of America

Association offering business, professional, promotional and educational assistance in the areas of cultivation, processing, and marketing of specialty coffees. The association also hosts the largest event in the world dedicated to coffee, the SCAA Annual Conference and exhibition.

10757 www.aaccnet.org
American Association of Cereal Chemists

Non profit international organization of nearly 4,000 members who are specialists in the use of cereal grains in foods. AACC has been an innovative leader in gathering and disseminating scientific and technical information to professionals in the grain-based foods indusrty wordwide for over 85 years. We know it's hard to keep up with the latest technology, that's why AACC is here to help you. We're a tool unlike any other in your lab or office. Industry leaders turn to and trust AACC.

10758 www.aaea.org
Agricultural & Applied Economics Association

Facebook, Twitter, LinkedIn, Blogger, Google+

A nonprofit association serving the professional interests of those working in agricultural and broadly related fields of applied economics.

10759 www.aaicc.org
National Alliance of Independent Crop Consultants

Represents individual crop consultants and contract researchers.

10760 www.aamp.com
American Association of Meat Processors

Membership consists of small to medium sized meat, poultry and food businesses including, slaughterers, processors, wholesalers, home food service businesses, deli and catering operators and suppliers to the industry. AAMP is affiliated with 28 state, regional and provincial associations.

10761 www.aanc.net
American Association of Nutritional Consultants

An association combating public ignorance and adverse legislation.

10762 www.aapausa.org
American Alfalfa Processors Association

Information for the processors and suppliers in the alfalfa industry.

10763 www.abfnet.org
American Beekeeping Federation

For honey producers, packers, suppliers and shippers of honey products.

10764 www.aceweb.org
Agricultural Communicators in Education

For writers, editors, broadcasters and communicators who are involved in the dissemination of agricultural, food sciences and natural resource information in land-grant colleges, federal and state agencies, international agencies and other private communications work.

10765 www.acfsa.org
American Correctional Food Service Affiliates

International, professional association created to serve the needs and interests of food service personnel in the correctional environments. The association brings together highly skilled food service workers and their vendors who are interested in the common goal of providing nutritious, cost-efficient meal service for confined populations.

10766 www.acri-cocoa.org
American Cocoa Research Institute

Nonprofit organization dedicated to scientific research on the subject of cocoa and chocolate. Its membership includes chocolate manufacturers as well as researchers.

10767 www.acsh.org
American Council on Science and Health

A nonprofit, consumer education organization concerned with issues related to food, nutrition, chemicals, pharmaceuticals, lifestyles, the environment and health.

10768 www.adpi.org
American Dairy Products Institute

An association for manufactured dairy products, including dry milks, whey, lactose, evaporated and condensed milk. ADPI's main purpose is to effectively communicate the many positive attributes and benefits of our members' products. Additionally, we serve our membership by offering the most current industry information available and by collaborating with dairy associations to represent members' interests before state and federal regulatory agencies.

10769 www.aeb.org
American Egg Board

Facts, recipes, industry and nutrition information.

10770 www.afco.org
Association of American Feed Control Officials

Officials of government agencies at the state and federal levels engaged in the regulation and distribution of products, animal feeds and livestock remedies.

10771 www.affi.com
American Frozen Food Institute

News and events, facts, tips, and recipes, etc.

10772 www.afia.org
Animal Industry Foundation

Works to improve animal production practices in the US, to dispel misconceptions that a diet containing meat, milk and eggs is unhealthy and that animals raised for foods in the US are mistreated.

10773 www.afius.org
Association of Food Industries

The association is a trade association serving the food import trade.

10774 www.agnic.org/

Access to experts in various fields of agriculture as well as links to agricultural databases. Find out about conferences, meetings and seminars in your area.

10775 www.agview.com/

All aspects of agriculture: Usenet groups, Web resources, archives, mailing lists, etc.

10776 www.ahpa.org
American Herbal Products Association

For manufacturers, importers and distributors of herbs and herbal products. AHPA seeks self-regulation, establishment of standards and rules of ethical conduct, member enrichment and public outreach.

10777 www.aibonline.org
American Institute of Baking Technical Bulletin

This organization provides research, education, training and consulting for the baking and food industries worldwide.

10778 www.aiccbox.org
International Corrugated Packaging Foundation

Videos, promotional materials, demonstrating support of the corrugated packaging industry worldwide. Place corrugated equipment into universities and technical colleges to provide students with corrugated industry skills.

10779 www.aicr.org
American Institute for Cancer Research

Third largest cancer charity in the US, focusing exclusively on research and education in regard to diet and cancer.

10780 www.aiwf.org
American Institute of Wine & Food

A non-profit educational organization devoted to improving the appreciation, understanding and accessibility of food and drink.

10781 www.ala-national.org
American Logistics Association
A nonprofit trade organization supporting the Military Resale and Morale, Welfare & Recreation industry.

10782 www.alaskaseafood.org
Alaska Seafood Marketing Institute
Organization of private industry and government fishing. Markets only Alaskan seafood. This association also offers educational and promotional materials on fresh and frozen seafood.

10783 www.americanbakers.org
American Bakers Association
Association comprised of wholesale bakers.

10784 www.americanberkshire.com
American Berkshire Association
Association for cattle and hog breeders in the US.

10785 www.americandairyproducts.com
American Dairy Products Institute
A national trade association representing the processed dairy products industry.

10786 www.americanhoneyproducers.org
American Honey Producers Association
Represents the interests of major USA honey producers and pollinators.

10787 www.americanwineries.org
American Vintners Association

10788 www.amif.org
American Meat Institute Foundation

10789 www.amseed.com
American Seed Trade Association
Producers of seeds for planting purposes.

10790 www.angus.org
American Angus Association
Industry and member links, information, etc.

10791 www.animalagriculture.org
National Institute for Animal Agriculture

10792 www.aob.org
Association of Brewers
Membership, publications, news, events, etc.

10793 www.apics.org
APICS Association for Operations Management
The primary purpose of this specific industry group is to educate food and beverage manufacturers on effective marketing strategies, market trends and material management.

10794 www.appleprocessors.org
Apple Processors Association
A national association of companies that manufacture quality apple products from whole apples. Members are either apple grower/processor cooperatives, or proprietary firms.

10795 www.apricotproducers.com
Apricot Producers of California

10796 www.asac.org
American Society of Agricultural Consultants
For agricultural consultants acting as an information base for members.

10797 www.asas.org
American Society of Animal Society
For professional researchers, publishes journals and holds seminars in the Animal Science field.

10798 www.asbe.org
American Society of Baking
Research and development of machinery for baking applications.

10799 www.asfsa.org
American School Food Service Association
An association focused on good nutrition for all children.

10800 www.ashrae.org
American Society of Heating, Refrigerating and
Air Conditioning

An international membership organization of engineers who create the worlds we live in.

10801 www.asifood.com
ASI Food Safety Consultants
ASI Food Safety Consultants is a full service provider of food safety audits, seminars and HACCP programs.

10802 www.astaspice.org
American Spice Trade Association
United States based organization whose worldwide membership is comprised of the leading firms in the spice industry.

10803 www.atsea.org
AT-SEA Processors Association
The At-sea Association represents US flag catcher/processor vessels that participate in the healthy and abundant ground fish fisheries of the Bering Sea.

10804 www.australian-beef.com
Meat & Livestock Australia
Promotes comsumption of Australian beef, lamb, mutton and goat in Canada, US and Mexico. The company is funded by Australian producers. They key focus is to increase access for Australian meat producers to the North American market and to raise awareness of its nutritional value, quality and safety.

10805 www.australian-lamb.com
Meat & Livestock Australia
Promotes comsumption of Australian beef, lamb, mutton and goat in Canada, US and Mexico. The company is funded by Australian producers. They key focus is to increase access for Australian meat producers to the North American market and to raise awareness of its nutritional value, quality and safety.

10806 www.avocado.org
California Avacado Commission
A resource for the California avocado industry.

10807 www.bakeryonline.com
Bakery Online
A database for bakers, food scientists, food engineers, process engineers, plant managers, business managers, executives and other professionals involved in the bakery industry. Features a comprehensive buyer's guide, interactive discussion forums and daily news updates and reports on business, regulatory and technology trends vital to the industry.

10808 www.bbga.org
Bread Bakers Guild of America
Links to member sites.

10809 www.beef.org
National Cattlemen's Beef Association
Related industry information.

10810 www.beerinstitute.org
Beer Institute
National trade association for the malt beverage industry. Represents the diversity of brewers and suppliers.

10811 www.beertown.org
American Homebrewers Association
Devoted to the education of home-brewed beer. Publishes magazine devoted exclusively to education, art and science of homebrewing. Services include: Beer Judge Certification Program, Sanctioned Competitions, World's Largest Homebrew Competition.

10812 www.bema.org
Bakery Equipment Manufacturers Association
An international nonprofit association representing leading bakery and food equipment manufacturers and suppliers whose combined efforts in research and development have led to the continual improvement of the baking and food industries.

10813 www.bestapples.com
Washington Apple Commission
Marketing professionals promote apples through retail marketing, advertising, public relations, health and food communications.

10814 www.beverageonline.com
Beverage Online
A database for beverage chemists, food scientists, food technologists, process engineers, plant managers, business managers, executives and other professionals involved in the beverage processing industry.

10815 www.biodynamics.com
Bio-Dynamic Farming and Gardening Association
Supporting biodynamic growers and processors in North America and acts to safeguard and promote the biodynamic method of agriculture.

10816 www.bisoncentral.com
National Bison Association
The National Bison Association was formed to promote the production, marketing and preservation of bison.

10817 www.bissc.org
Baking Industry Sanitation Standards Committee
Develops and promotes sanitation standards for the design and construction of bakery equipment. Offers self certification and third party certification programs for member companies whose equipment conforms to the BISSC standards.

10818 www.blueberry.org
North American Blueberry Council
History, crop information, products, international markets and berry sites.

10819 www.bottledwater.org
Bottled Water Association

10820 www.brownswissusa.com
Brown Swiss Cattle Breeders Associ of the USA

10821 www.bsdf-assbt.org
Beet Sugar Development Foundation
Association specializing in beet sugar research and the advertisement of seed companies.

10822 www.ca-seafood.org
California Seafood Council

10823 www.calbeef.org
California Beef Council

10824 **www.californiafigs.com**
California Fig Advisory Board
History and facts, nutritional information, recipes and contests.

10825 **www.calolive.org**
California Olive Committee

10826 **www.caloriecontrol.org**
Calorie Control Council

10827 **www.calpear.com**
California Pear Association
Consumer information, research reports, marketing and promo information.

10828 **www.calstrawberry.com**
California Strawberry Commission
Health and nutrition, contests, recipes, news, etc.

10829 **www.cancentral.com**
Can Manufacturers Institute
Serves can manufacturers and can industry suppliers

10830 **www.candyhalloffame.com**
National Confectionery Sales Association
Association of salespersons, brokers, sales managers, wholesalers and manufacturers in the confectionery industry.

10831 **www.candyusa.org**
National Confectioners Association
Association news, candy stats, health information, and candy history.

10832 **www.canonline.org**
Composite Can & Tube Institute
Serving the composite cans and tube industry.

10833 **www.cast-science.org**
Council for Agricultural Science and Technology
Identifies food, fiber, environmental and other agricultural issues for all stake holders.

10834 **www.cawineclub.com**
California Wine Club
A wine of the month club that features only California's small boutique wineries. Each month members receive two bottles of award-winning wine.

10835 **www.cdfa.ca.gov**
North American Agricultural Marketing
For state and provincial officials responsible for agricultural products marketing programs in the US, Canada and ultimately Mexico.

10836 **www.cemanet.org**
Conveyor Equipment Manufacturers Association
Facebook, Twitter, LinkedIn, YouTube

10837 **www.cheesesociety.org**
American Cheese Society
Promotes cheese industry. Holds cheese tasting and workshops on cheesemaking. Sponsors competition.

10838 **www.chicagomidwestmeatasso.com**
Chicago-Midwest Meat Association
The CMMA conducts its activities as a not-for-profit trade association for meat companies in the midwest. Its purpose is to support and promote the meat industry

10839 **www.choosecherries.com**
Cherry Marketing Institute
Association representing the cherry industry. Provides promotional material to food service operators, brokers, retailers and manufacturers.

10840 **www.chowbaby.com**
This web site is a search engine for restaurants. Provides help in finding the perfect eatery close to your home or travel destination. Online reservations, maps, menus and more. Can be searched by International Location, US Location, US Map or Cuisine type.

10841 **www.chrie.org**
Int'l Council on Hotel, Restaurant Institute Edu.
To enhance professionalism at all levels of the hospitality and tourism industry through education and training.

10842 **www.christree.org**
National Christmas Tree Association
Provides industry leaders a chance to work directly with their suppliers and distributors.

10843 **www.ciachef.edu**
Culinary Institute of America

10844 **www.colborne.com/apc/home.htm**
American Pie Council
Membership, recipes, coupons, etc.

10845 **www.corn.org**
Corn Refiners Association
Stats, career opportunities, publications and newsbriefs.

10846 **www.cosmos.com.mx:80**
Index of Food
Manufacturers indexed by industry, company name, products and brands.

10847 **www.cottonseed.com**
National Cottonseed Products Association
National association of cottonseed products.

10848 **www.countryham.org**
National Country Ham Association
The NCHA encourages promotion, development, and improvement at the businesses of country ham carvers and encourages the use of country carved meats through cooperative methods of production, promotion, education and advertisement.

10849 **www.cpif.org**
California Poultry Industry Federation
Links to other associations.

10850 **www.cpma.ca**
Canadian Produce Marketing Association
Profile and services, links, technical resources, etc.

10851 **www.cranberries.org**
Cranberry Institute
Association which gathers and disseminates information about cranberry growing, horticultural and environmental issues to cranberry growers and handlers in the US and Canada.

10852 **www.crnusa.org**
Council for Responsible Nutrition
Vitamin manufacturers.

10853 **www.cropinsurance.org**
Crop Insurance Research Bureau
Crop insurance trade organization.

10854 **www.croplifeamerica.org**
CropLife America
Information on protecting crops and environmentally fragile agriculture.

10855 **www.crops.org**
Crop Science Society of America
Seeks to advance research, extension and teaching of all basic and applied phases of the crop sciences.

10856 **www.csce.com**
Coffee, Sugar and Cocoa Exchange
Acts as a financial exchange where futures and options are traded, the CSCE provides hedging and investing, opportunities in the coffee, sugar, cocoa and dairy markets.

10857 **www.culinary.com**
Louisiana Sweet Potato Commission
Links to member sites.

10858 **www.dairyinfo.com**
Dairy Management
Links to related associations.

10859 **www.dairynetwork.com**
Dairy Network
Searchable database of food industry related items.

10860 **www.ddbcsocal.org**
Dairy Deli Bakery Council of Southern California
An association of retailers, brokers, suppliers, distributors and manufacturers working in the perishable food industry.

10861 **www.delianet.com**
Deli Associates
Association for manufacturers or suppliers of confectionary, candy and bakery products.

10862 **www.dhia.org**
National Dairy Herd Improvement Association
Sets policies, holds meetings and offers seminars for dairymen.

10863 **www.doitwithdairy.com**
Dairy Management — American Dairy Association, National Dairy Council, US Dairy Export Council

10864 **www.dressings-sauces.org**
Association for Dressings and Sauces
This association is comprised of manufacturers of mayonnaise, salad dressings and condiment sauces, as well as industry suppliers.

10865 **www.drink-milk.com**
American Dairy Association Mideast
We represent dairy farmers and serve as the local affiliate for the American Dairy Association and the National Dairy Council. We work closely with Dairy Management Inc. and the Milk Processors Education Program to extend national dairy promotion programs to the local level.

10866 **www.duckling.org**
Duckling Council
Consortium of duckling producers located coast-to-coast, whose goal is to increase consumption of duckling nationwide and increase awareness of duckling's nutritionally improved profile.

10867 **www.eatchicken.com**
National Broiler Council
Recipes, industry information and statistics.

10868 **www.eatright.org**
American Dietetic Association
Nutrition resources, hot topics, FAQ's.

10869 **www.eatturkey.com**
National Turkey Federation
Advocate for all segments of the US turkey industry, providing services and conducting activi-

ties that increase demand for its members' products. The federation also protects and enhances its members' ability to effectively and profitably provide wholesome, high quality, nutritious turkey products.

10870 www.eggs.org
Egg Clearing House
Links to related members and associations.

10871 www.ejkrause.com
EJ Krause & Associates
Association for suppliers of hotel and restaurant food and beverages.

10872 www.elettric80.com
Electric 80
Supports automated material handling systems, robotic palletizers and laser-guided vehicles.

10873 www.eppainc.org
Eastern Dairy Perishable Products Association
This association encourages growth and education regarding perishable products. It promotes the sales of perishable products through supermarkets and specialty stores and acts as a resource and information center for the industry.

10874 www.fancyfoodshows.com
Nat'l Association for the Specialty Food Trade
Members are manufacturers, importers, distributors and retailers of specialty gourmet and fancy foods. Has an annual budget of approximately $15 million.

10875 www.farmshowcouncil.org
Farm Show Council
Agriculture trade shows and suppliers of services to these shows. Strives to improve education, communication and evaluation and provide the best possible marketing showcase for exhibitors and related products to the farmer/rancher/producer customer.

10876 www.fb.com
American Farm Bureau Federation
For state Farm Bureaus in the 50 states and Puerto Rico.

10877 www.fbminet.ca/agnews.htm
Agricultural news releases.

10878 www.fcsi.org
Food Service Consultants Society International
Membership, publications, industry links etc.

10879 www.fda.gov
Food and Drug Administration
The official website of FDA.

10880 www.fdi.org
Food Service Distributors International

10881 www.feda.com
Food Service Equipment Distributors Association
Dealers and distributors of foodservice equipment and supplies.

10882 www.femaflavor.org
Flavor & Extract Manufacturers Assn of the US
1620 I Street NW
Suite 925
Washington, DC 210006
202-293-5800; Fax: 202-463-8998
Ed R. Hayes, President
George C. Robinson III, President Elect
Mark Scott, Treasurer
Arthur Schick, Vice President & Secretary
FEMA is comprised of flavor manufacturers, flavor users, flavor ingredient suppliers, and others with an interest in the U.S. flavor industry. FEMA workds with legislators and regulators to assure that the needs of members and consumers are continuously addressed and is committed to assuring a substantial supply of safe flavoring substances.

10883 www.fewa.org
Farm Equipment Wholesalers Association
For wholesale/distributors of ag equipment and related products.

10884 www.fiae.com
Food Industry Association Executives

10885 www.fightbac.org
Fight Bac
Sound advice for better food safety.

10886 www.foodallergy.org
Food Allergy & Anaphylaxis Network
The only nonprofit organization in the US devoted solely to patient education for food allergies. Mission is to create public awareness about food allergies and anaphylaxis to provide education, and to advance research on behalf of all those affected by food allergy.

10887 www.foodcontact.com
Food Contact
Searchable directory of food and beverage processors and exporters.

10888 www.foodexplorer.com
Food Explorer
Database of industry related materials.

10889 www.foodfront.com
Internet Foodfront
Searchable database of food industry related items and resources.

10890 www.foodindustry.com
Industry Guides.net
Link directory for related industry.

10891 www.foodingredientsonline.com
Food Ingredients Online
International forum where buyers and sellers connect. Highly targeted and focused site offers original material, daily news updates, a product showcase, projects for bid, employment opportunities, downloadbale software, and a free interactive buyers guide which produces instant leads.

10892 www.foodinsight.org
International Food Information Council
Organization offering food safety and nutritional information, press releases and publications.

10893 www.foodinstitute.com
American Institute of Food Distribution
Serves as a central information service for food trades. Issues, reports, studies and statistical data and maintains a library. Member companies throughout the US and over 40 foreign countries.

10894 www.foodonline.com
Food Online
Searchable database of food industry related items.

10895 www.foodproductdesign.com
Food product design magazine

10896 www.foodprotection.org
International Association for Food Protection
The International Association for Food Protection, founded in 1911, is a nonprofit educational association with a mission to provide food safety professional worldwide with a forum to exchange information on protecting the food supply. The Association is comprised of over 3,000 members from 50 nations. Affiliate chapters are located in the US, Canada, Mexico and South Korea.

10897 www.foodserviceworld.com
Food Service World
Food associations, suppliers and events.

10898 www.foodweb.com
Foodweb
Links to suppliers of food and equipment, distributors, unions, etc.

10899 www.foodwine.com/digest
Netfood Directory (The BLUE Directory)
List of relevant food and food service internet sites.

10900 www.fourhcouncil.edu
National 4-H Council
Focuses on diverse groups of young people in a variety of urban and suburban locales while continuing to serve youth in rural areas. Helps provide hands-on co-educational programs and activities to young people nationwide.

10901 www.fpaota.org
Fresh Produce Association of the Americas
Trade association for Mexican produce. Formerly known as West Mexico Vegetable Distributors Association.

10902 www.fpfc.org
Fresh Produce and Floral Council
Promotes through communication and education, fresh fruit, vegetable and floral products.

10903 www.fpi.org
Food Service & Packaging Institute
A national association comprised of manufacturers and suppliers of disposables for the food service industry.

10904 www.fpsa.org
Food Processing Suppliers Association
Facebook, Twitter, LinkedIn, Google+
An association for food and beverage processing suppliers and those working in the packaging industry.

10905 www.fresh-cuts.org
International Fresh-Cut Produce Association
IFPA advances the fresh-cut produce industry by supporting members with technical information, representation, and knowledge to provide convenient safe and wholesome food. Members are processor companies, suppliers and researchers.

10906 www.freshcut.com
Columbia Publishing
Information on carrot production, growers and shippers.

10907 www.fsgroup.com
Food Service Group
This organization is comprised of food service brokerage companies meeting the needs and offering a national exchange of ideas and information of food service sales professionals.

10908 www.fspronet.com
Food Service Professionals Network
Database of food industry related items including directories, etc.

10909 **www.gcca.org**
International Assn. of Refridgerated Warehouses
Trade association of public refrigerated warehouse storing of all types of perishable products.

10910 **www.gcca.org/wflo**
World Food Logistics Organization
Sponsors graduate-level scientific research on the refrigeration of perishable commodities. Offers annual training institute for public refrigerated warehouse personnel. Formerly known as the Refrigeration Research and Education Foundation.

10911 **www.georgiapecans.org**
Georgia Pecan Commission

10912 **www.gmaonline.org**
The Grocery Manufacturers Association
Represents food, beverage and consumer product companies by offering them advocacy, industry information, news, research and other useful resources.

10913 **www.gpi.org**
Glass Packaging Institute
Serves the glass container suppliers for the beer, juice, RTD tea, liquor, wine and dairy businesses.

10914 **www.grains.org**
US Feed Grains Council
For grain sorghum, barley and corn producer associations and representatives of the agricultural community. Provides commodity export market development.

10915 **www.greyhouse.com**
Grey House Publishing
Authoritative reference directories for most business sectors including food, beverage and agriculture markets. Users can search the online databases with varied search criteria allowing for custom searches by product category, geographic area, sales volume, keyword, subject and more. Full Grey House catalog and online ordering also available.

10916 **www.hazelnut.com**
Hazelnut Growers of Oregon
Recipes, health and ingredient information, etc.

10917 **www.hazelnutcouncil.org**
Hazelnut Council
Promotion to commercial information exhibiting ingredient users and recipies, formulas and food service

10918 **www.healthfinder.gov**
Association of Food and Drug Officials
Promotes the enforcement of laws and regulations at all levels of government. Fosters understanding and cooperation between industry and regulators. Develops model laws and regulations and seeks their adoption.

10919 **www.herbnet.com**
Herb Growing and Marketing Network
Trade assocation information services for herb related businesses. Hosts national conference for those in the herb industry with seminars covering commercial production, medicinal herbs and general business topics.

10920 **www.herbs.org**
Herb Research Foundation
Provides scientific-based and traditional information about use and safety of herbs for health. Fee-based hotline, information packs and literature are available to members.

10921 **www.herbsociety.org**
Herb Society of America
Educates its members and the public on the cultivation of herbs, as well as the history and uses of herbs.

10922 **www.hereford.org**
American Hereford Association
For people in the Hereford cattle industry.

10923 **www.holsteinusa.com**
Holstein Association
For people with strong interests in breeding, raising and milking Holstein cattle.

10924 **www.iacp.com**
International Association of Culinary Professional
A not-for-profit organization whose members represent virtually every profession in the culinary universe: teachers, cooking school owners, caterers, writers, chefs, media cooking personalities, editors, publishers, food stylists, food photographers, restauranteurs, leaders of major food corporations and vintners. Literally a who's who of the food world. Founded in 1978.

10925 **www.iacsc.org**
International Association of Cold Storage

10926 **www.iaff.ttu.edu/aals**
Association for Arid Land Studies

10927 **www.iafis.org**
Int'l Association of Food Industry Suppliers
Serves the dairy food and beverage industries, and related sanitary processing industries addressing the marketing and business information needs of the food supply channel.

10928 **www.iaicv.org**
International Association of Ice Cream Vendors
Members are manufacturers and distributors of ice cream novelties and street vendors.

10929 **www.ibabaker.com**
Independent Bakers Association
Trade association supporting family-owned wholesale bakeries through advocacy, programs and networking.

10930 **www.ibdea.org**
International Beverage Dispensing Equipment
Serves independent purveyors of equipment, service and products for the food and beverage industry.

10931 **www.iddba.org**
International Dairy-Deli-Bakery Association
Furthers relationship between manufacturing, production, marketing used in delivery of goods to marketplace. Presents awards and maintains a hall of fame.

10932 **www.idfa.org**
International Dairy Foods Association
IDFA represents the best interests of the U.S. dairy processing and manufacturing industry, as well as its supplier members and industry's leading suppliers companies.

10933 **www.ifas.ufl.edu**
Agricultural Communicators of Tomorrow
For college students professionally interested in communications related to agriculture, food, natural resources and allied fields.

10934 **www.ifmaworld.com**
International Foodservice Manufacturers
Trade association for food, beverage, equipment and supply manufacturers and ancillary service companies serving the food service industry.

10935 **www.ifsea.org**
International Food Service Executives
Provides education and community service to the foodservice industry.

10936 **www.ift.org**
Institute of Food Technologists
Member information, publications, calender of expos and meetings.

10937 **www.iherb.org**
International Herb Association
Supports the herb businesses and educates the public.

10938 **www.iiar.org**
International Institute of Ammonia Refrigeration
Promotes the safe use of ammonia as a refrigerant. Offers educational, promotional and standards development programs and legislative/regulatory support to manufacturers, contractors, consulting engineers, wholesalers and end users.

10939 **www.ilovepasta.org**
National Pasta Association
List of members, FAQ's, pasta nutrition and recipes.

10940 **www.ilovepickles.org**
Pickle Packers International
Addresses the concerns of pickle packers, shippers and manufacturers.

10941 **www.ilsi.org**
International Life Sciences Institute
Scientific institution that supports research on nutrition, food safety and toxicology.

10942 **www.insca.org**
International Natural Sausage Casing Association

10943 **www.iopp.org**
Institute of Packaging Professionals

10944 **www.irrigation.org**
Irrigation Association
Membership organization for irrigation equipment and system manufacturers, dealers, distributors, designers, consultants, contractors and end users.

10945 **www.iseo.org**
Institute of Shortening & Edible Oils

10946 **www.iwla.com**
International Warehouse Logistics Association
The unified voice of the global logistics outsourcing industry, representing third party warehousing, transportation and logistics service providers. Our member companies provide the most timely and cost-effective global logistics solutions for their customers and are committed to protecting the free flow of products across international borders.

10947 **www.juanvaldez.com**
National Federation of Coffee Growers of Colombia
This organization is comprised of coffee growers from Colombia whose goal is to promote Colombian coffee in the US.

10948 **www.kab.org**
Keep America Beautiful
National nonprofit education organization whose corporate members include packagers, retailers, bottlers, and makers of chemical, steel, glass, paper and aluminum products.

10949 **www.kiwifruit.org**
California Kiwifruit Commission
News, recipes, export information, etc.

10950 **www.kla.org**
Kansas Livestock Association

10951 **www.lambchef.com**
American Lamb Council

10952 **www.leafy-greens.org**
Leafy Greens Council
Made up of growers and shippers. This association promotes the consumption of leafy greens and vegetables for battling diseases like cancer.

10953 **www.mainelobsterpromo.com**
Maine Lobster Promotion Council

10954 **www.meatandpoultryonline.com**
Meat and Poultry Online
Searchable database of food industry related items.

10955 **www.meatpoultry.com**
Meat and poultry magazine

10956 **www.mhia.org**
Material Handling Industry

10957 **www.micausa.org**
Meat Importers Council of America

10958 **www.militaryfood.org**
Research and Development Associates for Military
Founded as a forum for the interchange of technical data on food products, feeding systems, food and feeding equipment and food packaging between industry and professors of Food Science and Technology and the US Armed Forces and Government.

10959 **www.msgfacts.com**
Glutamate Association— US
Members are manufacturers, distributors and processed food users of glutamate, glutamate acid and its salts in the food industry.

10960 **www.mushroomcouncil.com**
Mushroom Council

10961 **www.mwfpa.org**
Midwest Food Processors Association
This association offers member companies information on legislation and industry matters.

10962 **www.naab-css.org**
National Association of Animal Breeders
For farmer co-ops and others interested in livestock improvement.

10963 **www.nacaa.com**
National Association County Agricultural Agents
For agents focusing on educational programs for the youth of the community.

10964 **www.naconline.org**
National Association of Concessionaires
This association works to professionalize the concession industry by providing information services and training programs for concession managers and employees. Holds conventions, seminars, trade shows, and certification programs for the leisure time food and beverage industry. Produces newsletters and magazines for its international membership.

10965 **www.nacufs.org**
National Assn of College & University Food Service
Educational programs, conferences, publications, etc.

10966 **www.nadefa.org**
North American Deer Farmers Association
A nonprofit organization that offers representation of US and Canadian breeders and producers of venison. Velvet and trophy stock.

10967 **www.nafem.org**
Food Equipment Manufacturers Association
A trade association of foodservice equipment and supplies manufacturers, that provide products for food preparation, cooking, storage and table service.

10968 **www.naffs.org**
National Association of Fruits, Flavors & Syrups
Industry information, member directory and links to member sites.

10969 **www.nama.org**
National Agri-Marketing Association
Marketing and communication suppliers, including trade publications, radio and television broadcast sales organizations, premium/incentive manufacturers, printers, marketing research firms, photographers and related professionals.

10970 **www.namamillers.org**
North American Millers' Association

10971 **www.nanca.org**
North American Natural Casing Association
The NANCA responds to issues and service needs that are unique to the North American segment of the industry.

10972 **www.nas.edu**
National Research Council/National Academy

10973 **www.nasda-hq.org**
National Association of State Departments of
Agriculture

10974 **www.nationalgrange.org**
National Grange
Promotes general welfare and agriculture through local organizations. Presides over the advancement and promotion of the farming and agriculture industry.

10975 **www.nationalgrocers.org**
National Grocers of America
This association services as the information network to the National Grocers Association. Purposes of this organization: handling government affairs regarding the operation of retail groceries; developing educational programs and literature regarding the industry; and supports women in the retail distribution industry.

10976 **www.nbva.org**
National Bulk Vendors Association
An organization comprised of manufacturers, distributors and operators of bulk vending merchandise and equipment.

10977 **www.nbwa.org**
National Beer Wholesalers Association
Research and development, quality control and ingredients.

10978 **www.ncausa.org**
National Coffee Association of USA
This association promotes business relations among members of the trade. Also collects and publishes information on the coffee industry, maintaining a library of 1000 science and medical books and literature about coffee and caffeine.

10979 **www.ncga.com**
National Corn Growers Association

10980 **www.nfi.org**
National Aquaculture Council
For farmers, food processors and food distributors with an interest in aquaculture.

10981 **www.nfo.org**
National Farmers Union
Promotes educational, cooperative and legislative activities of farm families in 44 states.

10982 **www.nfpa-food.org**
National Food Processors Association
A leading food industry trade association.

10983 **www.nfraweb.org**
National Frozen & Refrigerated Foods Association
Nonprofit trade association comprised of 650 member companies representing all segments of the frozen and refrigerated food industry. NFRA has been serving the frozen food industry since 1945 and just recently in 2001 began serving the refrigerated foods industry. The mission of NFRA is to promote the sales and consumption of frozen and refrigerated foods through: educations, training, research, sales planning and menu development and providing a forum for industry dialogue.

10984 **www.nhb.org**
National Honey Board
This organization offers information and support to members in the honey producing industry.

10985 **www.nicra.org**
National Ice Cream Retailers Association
A trade organization whose members are in the retail ice cream; frozen custard; gelato; frozen yogurt and water ice business. Members are located all across the United States, Canada and several other countries.

10986 **www.nims.com**
Network of Ingredient Marketing Specialists
This organization has established a network of ingredient manufacturers' representatives that offers ingredient manufacturers the most cost effective access to US, Canadian and European markets.

10987 **www.nmaonline.org**
National Meat Association
Provides it members unique one-on-one assistance resolving regulatory issues. Mission is to be proactive and responsive in serving members both individually and collectively.

10988 **www.nmpf.org**
National Milk Producers Federation

10989 **www.noble.net**
Noble & Associates
Advertising agency for food industry professionals.

10990 **www.nopa.org**
National Oilseed Processors Association

10991 **www.npcspud.com**
National Potato Council
Represents US potato growers on federal legislative and regulatory issues.

10992 **www.nppc.org**
National Pork Producers Council

Nutrition information, educational resources and research results.

10993 **www.nwcherries.com**
Northwest Cherry Growers

10994 **www.nwfpa.com**
Northwest Food Processors Association
Conventions and exhibits, member listings and links.

10995 **www.nwfpa.org**
Northwest Food Processors Association
An organization that aims to develop and promote the food processing industry located in Oregon, Idaho, and Washington.

10996 **www.nwica.org**
National WIC Association
Association whose mission is to provide members with the tools and resources to help them develop nutrition services for mothers and young children.

10997 **www.oamp.org**
Ohio Association of Meat Processors

10998 **www.ocia.org**
Organic Crop Improvement Association
For farmers, processors, manufacturers and traders of organic crops.

10999 **www.oilseeds.org**
American Soybean Association
Consumption statistics, related associations.

11000 **www.onions-usa.org**
National Onion Association
Recipes, member information and allied industry and export information.

11001 **www.opensecrets.org**
Cheese Association of America
The Center for Responsive Politics is a nonpartisan, nonprofit research group based in Washington, DC that tracks money in politics, and its effect on campaign finance issues for the news media, academics, activists and the public at large.

11002 **www.oregon-berries.com**
Oregon Rasberry & Blackberry Commission
Supports the rasberries, blackberries, marionberries and boysenberries industries.

11003 **www.oregonhazelnuts.org**
Hazelnut Marketing Board
This organization was established to promote and provide for the Oregon hazelnut industry.

11004 **www.organic.org**
Organic Alliance

11005 **www.ostriches.org**
American Ostrich Association
Organization that provides leadership for the ostrich industry and its future through the promotion of ostrich products.

11006 **www.osu.orst.edu/dept/iifet**
International Institute of Fisheries Economics
Promotes discussion, research projects and sponsors educational courses. Publications available.

11007 **www.ota.org**
Organic Trade Association
For businesses involved in the organic agriculture and products industry. Seeks to promote the industry and establish production and marketing standards.

11008 **www.ou.org**
Orthodox Union

11009 **www.pabeef.org**
Pennsylvania Cattlemen's Association

11010 **www.packagingnetwork.com**
Packaging Network
Searchable database of food industry related items.

11011 **www.packexpo.com**
Packging Machinery Manufacturers Institute
Members are manufacturers of packaging and packaging related coconverting machinery in the US and Canada. PMMI offers meetings, an inquiry service, statistics and surveys and a business to business service on it's website. PMMI also sponsors several Pack Expos (packaging related tradeshows).

11012 **www.packinfo-world.com**
World Packaging Organization
Information regarding the packaging industry internationally.

11013 **www.packinfo-world.org**
Contract Packaging and Manufacturing Association
Information on major packaging associations.

11014 **www.peanutbutterlovers.com**
Peanut Advisory Board
This organization conducts the marketing and promotion of peanut and peanut butter products.

11015 **www.peanutsusa.com**
American Peanut Council
Association members include growers and manufacturers of peanuts and peanut products.

11016 **www.pigglywiggly.com**
National Piggly Wiggly Operators Association
An association of independent grocers operating under Piggly Wiggly franchises in 24 states. Includes both small operators of one to five supermarkets as well as multiple store organizations of as many as 90 or more supermarkets.

11017 **www.pizzatoday.com**
National Association of Pizza Operators
The membership of this organization is independent and franchised pizza operators, manufacturers and suppliers of pizza equipment.

11018 **www.plma.com**
Private Label Manufacturers Association (PLMA)
Trade Association promoting the private label industry.

11019 **www.pma.com**
Produce Marketing Association
For those who market fresh fruits, vegetables, and floral products worldwide; involved in the production, distribution, retail, and food service sectors of the industry.

11020 **www.popcorn.org**
Popcorn Institute
A trade association representing the popcorn industry. Institute activites include projects to improve popcorn growing and processing technology, serving as a liasion with several government regulatory agencies and a generic marketing program to promote product awareness and consumption.

11021 **www.poultryegg.org**
US Poultry & Egg Association

11022 **www.ptnpa.org**
Peanut and Tree Nut Processors Association

11023 **www.qba.com**
Quality Bakers of America Cooperative
Members are independent wholesale bakeries and their suppliers.

11024 **www.qchekd.com**
Quality Checked Dairies
A cooperative of Dairy foods processors who use the Quality Checked trademark on their products and engage in group purchasing of ingredients and supplies.

11025 **www.raisins.org**
California Raisin Marketing Food Tech. Program

11026 **www.rbanet.com**
Retail Bakers Association
Links to other associations.

11027 **www.realbutter.com**
American Dairy Association
Recipes, media information, celebrity chefs and industry news.

11028 **www.redraspberry.com**
Washington Red Raspberry Commisson

11029 **www.refrigeratedfoods.com**
Refrigerated Foods Association
Formerly called the Salad Manufacturers Association, the Refrigerated Foods Association is an international organization comprised of manufacturers and suppliers of prepared, refrigerated, ready-to-eat food products.

11030 **www.renderers.org**
National Renderers Association
Members recycle animal by-products only, also provide services to renderers.

11031 **www.restaurant.org**
National Restaurant Association
Trends, government affairs, training, research, dining guides and links.

11032 **www.reta.com**
Refrigerating Engineers & Technicians Association

11033 **www.retailconfectioners.org**
Retail Confectioners International
Provides education, promotion and legislative services. Holds courses and bestows awards.

11034 **www.saltinstitute.org**
Salt Institute
Industry information and member businesses.

11035 **www.sbsonline.org**
Society for Biomolecular Screening
Supports research and discovery in pharmaceutical biotechnology and the agrichemical industry that utilize biomolecular screening procedures.

11036 **www.scisoc.org/asbc**
American Society of Brewing Chemists
Annual scientific meeting for professionals in the brewing industry.

11037 **www.seafwa.org**
Southeastern Association of Fish and Wildlife
The Southeastern Association of Fish and Wildlife Agencies is an organization whose members are the state agencies with primary responsibility for management and protection of the fish and wildlife resources in 16 states, Puerto Rico and the US Virgin Islands.

11038 **www.seedtechnology.net**
Society of Commercial Seed Technologists
Professionals involved in the testing and analysis of seeds, including research, production and handling based on botanical and agricultural sciences.

11039 **www.sheepusa.org**
American Sheep Industry Association
For state associations dedicated to the welfare and profitability of the sheep industry.

11040 **www.shellfish.org**
National Shellfisheries Association
Organization comprised of scientists, public health workers, shellfish producers and fishery administrators. To promote and advance shellfisheries research and the application of results to the shellfish industry

11041 **www.snax.com**
Snack Food Association
Facts, stats and trivia about snack food industry.

11042 **www.southeastdairy.org**
Southeast United Dairy Industry Association
Promotes milk and milk products in the southeastern states.

11043 **www.southerncottonginners.org**
Southern Cotton Ginners Association
Operates in a five state area as an information center covering safety and governmental regulations.

11044 **www.soyfoods.com**
US Soy Food Directory
Searchable database of soy food processors, suppliers, and industry information.

11045 **www.soyfoods.org**
Soyfoods Association of North America
Sponsors April as soy foods month. Conducts annual seminar on soy foods in fall.

11046 **www.spcouncil.org**
Soy Protein Council
Members of this association include persons, firms and corporations regularly engaged within the US in the processing and sale of vegetable proteins or vegetable protein products derived from agricultural services.

11047 **www.state.id.us/bean**
Idaho Bean Commission
Directory of dealers, recipes, nutritional values and research.

11048 **www.steel.org**
American Iron and Steel Institute
Develops and implements market development programs for appropriate food and beverage packaging applications.

11049 **www.sugar.org**
Sugar Association
Represents processors and refiners of beet and cane sugar in nutrition and health matters.

11050 **www.sugaralliance.org**
American Sugar Alliance
For domestic producers, processors, suppliers and labor organizations in the sugar and sugarcane industry.

11051 **www.sunflowernsa.com**
National Sunflower Association
For companies associated with sunflower products.

11052 **www.sunmaid.com**
Sun-Maid Growers of California

11053 **www.susta.org**
Southern US Trade Association
A non-profit agricultural export trade development association comprised of the Departments of Agriculture of the 15 southern states and the Commonwealth of Puerto Rico.

11054 **www.teausa.com**
Tea Council of the USA
International companies and governments interested in cultivating and expanding the demand for the sale and consumption of tea in the US.

11055 **www.tfi.org**
Fertilizer Institute
For brokers, producers, importers, dealers and manufacturers of fertilizer and fertilizer-related equipment.

11056 **www.theamericancenter.org**
American Center for Wine, Food & the Arts

11057 **www.thebcma.org**
Biscuit & Cracker Manufacturers Association
An organization that represents and promotes the cookie and cracker manufacturing industry.

11058 **www.therestaurantfinder.com**
This search engine help to find restaurants by type or location.

11059 **www.tianet.org**
Transportation Intermediaries Association
Education and policy organization for North American transportation intermediaries representing the interests of all third party transportation service providers. Members include logistics management firms, property brokers, perishable commodities brokers, freight forwarders, intermodal marketers, ocean and air forwarders, and NVOCC's.

11060 **www.tortilla-info.com**
Tortilla Industry Association
News, trade information, 'where to buy' and recipes.

11061 **www.turkeyfed.org**
National Turkey Federation
Member site links and industry information.

11062 **www.txbeef.com**
Texas Beef Council
Recipes, ranching information, tips and links.

11063 **www.uark.edu/depts/ifse/ofpa**
Ozark Food Processors Association
This association is comprised of regional food processors and national suppliers for the food service industry. Hosts an annual convention in the spring which includes at attendence of over 700 and over 100 exhibitors.

11064 **www.uffva.org**
United Fresh Fruit & Vegetable Association
Equipment, supplies, cartons, packaging machinery, computers, sorting and sizing equipment, harvesting equipment, film wrap manufacturing and commodity organizations.

11065 **www.usapears.com**
Pear Bureau Northwest
Promotes fresh pears grown in the Pacific Northwest area.

11066 **www.usapple.org**
US Apple Association
Members are US and foreign firms, other than retailers, that handle apples.

11067 **www.usarice.com**
USA Rice Federation

11068 **www.usda.gov**
US Department of Agriculture
The official website of USDA.

11069 **www.usguernsey.com**
American Guernsey Association
Register and deliver guernsey cattle throughout the US.

11070 **www.usmef.org**
US Meat Export Federation

11071 **www.uspastry.org**
US Pastry Alliance

11072 **www.uspotatoes.com**
National Potato Promotion Board
Also known as the potato board. Organized to operate a national promotion plan to position potatoes as low calorie, nutritious vegetables and to facilitate market expansion into domestic and export sales.

11073 **www.vealfarm.com**
American Veal Association
For veal producers and processors.

11074 **www.vending.org**
National Automatic Merchandising Association
Serves merchandising, vending, contract foodservice management and office coffee service industries.

11075 **www.versatilevinegar.org**
Vinegar Institute
Manufacturers and bottlers of vinegar and suppliers to the industry are the members of this association. Publications available only to members.

11076 **www.vrg.org**
Vegetarian Resource Group
Facebook, Twitter, LinkedIn
An association of health professionals, activists, and educators working together to educate the public about vegetarianism and veganism.

11077 **www.vtcheese.com**
Vermont Cheese Council

11078 **www.watermelon.org**
National Watermelon Promotional Board

11079 **www.wawgg.org**
Washington Association of Wine Grape Growers
Guidance in research and education, and maintaining leadership in local, state and national wine grape issues.

11080 **www.wdairycouncil.com**
Western Dairyfarmers' Promotion Association
Promotes dairy products for the dairy farmer.

11081 **www.wflo.com**
World Food Logistics Organization
The activities of the WFLO include improving the application of refrigeration technology for the preservation and distribution of food and other commodities, stimulating and supporting research in the science of food refrigeration through grants, training and educating industry personnel, growing its bank of scientific information on the storage and distribution of perishable goods, and developing and supporting national associations.

11082 **www.wga.com**
Western Growers Association
Links and news, safety and legal information.

11083 **www.wheatfoods.org**
Wheat Foods Council
Links, nutrition and product information, news and tips.

11084 **www.wheatworld.org**
National Association of Wheat Growers
Member information, government agencies, research information, etc.

11085 **www.wildblueberries.com**
Wild Blueberry Association of North America
Sources, recipes, news and product ideas.

11086 **www.wineinstitute.org**
Wine Institute
Dedicated to initiating and advocating state, federal and international public policy to enhance the environment for the responsible production, promotion and enjoyment of wine.

11087 **www.wssa.com**
Wine and Spirits Shippers Association
Provides members, importers and exporters with efficient and economical ocean transportation and other logistic services.

11088 **www.wusata.org**
Western US Agricultural Trade Association
This organization offers information and support to increase exports of US agricultural products.

Associations

11089 American Apparel & Footwear Association
740 6th Street NW
3rd and 4th Floors
Washington, DC 20001

202-853-9080
www.aafaglobal.org
Facebook, Twitter, LinkedIn, YouTube, Instagram

Stephen Lemar, President & CEO
Maureen Storch, Senior Vice President, Membership
Natalie LaBella, VP, Communications & Marketing
Agata Borradori, VP, Finance
Madison Mugford, Meetings & Webinar Coordinator

The American Apparel & Footwear Association (AAFA) is the national trade association representing apparel, footwear and other sewn products companies, and their suppliers which compete in the global market. AAFA's mission is to promote and enhance its members' competitiveness, productivity and profitability in the global market by minimizing regulatory, legal, commercial, political, and trade restraints.
Founded in 2000

11090 Association of Footwear Distributors
1319 F St Nw
Suite 700
Washington, DC 20004

202-737-5660; Fax: 202-645-0789
info@fdra.org
fdra.org
Facebook, Twitter, LinkedIn, Flickr, Instagram

Matt Priest, President
Andy Polk, Vice President
Thomas Crockett, Director of Gov. & Reg. Affairs
Christie Horan, Marketing & Comm. Coordinator
Sue Myrick, Strategic Policy Advisor

Major distributors of footwear.
130+ Members
Founded in 1944

11091 Fashion Footwear Association of New York
274 Madison Avenue
Suite 1701
New York, NY 10016

212-751-6422; Fax: 212-751-6404
Facebook, Twitter, Pinterest, Youtube

Ronald Fromm, President
Diane Sullivan, Secretary
Debbie King, Vice Chairman
Jim Issler, Chairman
Wayne Kulkin, Treasurer

4 International Trade Shows per year.
300 Members
Founded in 1980

11092 Footwear Distributors and Retailers of America
1319 F St Nw
Suite 700
Washington, DC 20004

202-737-5660; Fax: 202-645-0789
info@fdra.org
Facebook, Twitter, LinkedIn, Flickr, Instagram

Andy Polk, Vice President
Rick Muskat, Chairman
Edward Rosenfeld, Vice Chair
Mike Jeppesen, Treasurer
Matt Priest, President

Trade association for footwear distributors and volume retailers.
130+ Members
Founded in 1944

11093 National Shoe Retailers Association
7386 N. La Cholla Boulevard
Tuscon, AZ 85741

520-209-1710
800-673-8446
www.nsra.org
Facebook, Twitter

Chuck Schuyler, President
Lenny Comeras, Esq., Chairman
Roger Brooks, Vice Chair

A nonprofit organization representing independent shoe store owners throughout the United States and Canada.
Founded in 1912

11094 Pedorthic Footwear Association
1610 East Forsyth Street
Suite D
Americus, GA 31709

229-389-3440; Fax: 888-563-0945
pedorthicsusa@gmail.com
www.pedorthics.org
Facebook, Twitter, LinkedIn, Google+, Pinterest

Matt Almeida, Secretary
Jay Zaffater, Past President
Robert Sobel, President
Dean Mason, Vice President
Christopher J. Costantini, Treasurer

Membership organization for individuals and companies involved in the design, manufacture, modification and fit of therapeutic footwear. Provides educational programs, publications, legislative monitoring, marketing materials, professional liason and business operations services.
Cost: $55.00
2000 Members
Founded in 1958

11095 Sports & Fitness Industry Association
962 Wayne Ave
Suite 300
Silver Spring, MD 20910

301-495-6321; Fax: 301-495-6322
info@sfia.org
www.sfia.org
Facebook, Twitter, LinkedIn

Tom Cove, President & CEO
Jackie Murray, CFO

Our purpose is to support our member companies and promote a healthy environment for the sporting goods industry. SGMA enhances industry vitality and fosters sports, fitness and active lifestyle participation.
1000 Members
Founded in 1906

11096 Two Ten Footwear Foundation
1466 Main St
Waltham, MA 02451

800-346-3210; Fax: 781-736-1555
info@twoten.org
www.twoten.org
Facebook, Twitter, LinkedIn, Flickr, YouTube

Michael Atmore, Editorial Director
Robert McHugh, Treasurer
Blake Krueger, Chairman
Diane Sullivan, Vice Chair
Lawrence Siff, Secretary

Mission is to take action and create change for those in need. Built upon a foundation of caring, serving our community through social services and educational programs.
Founded in 1939

11097 United Shoe Retailers Association
28015 Smyth Dr
Valencia, CA 91355

661-367-4816; Fax: 866-929-6068
linda@usraonline.org
usraonline.org

Linda Hauss, Executive Director

The Association helps independent shoe retailers be profitable.
Founded in 1977

Newsletters

11098 Footwear News
Fairchild Publications
750 3rd Ave
Suite 7
New York, NY 10017-2700

212-630-4320
800-360-1700
www.wwd.com/footwear-news

Jay Spaleta, Publisher
Katie Abel, Editor

Weekly publication covering the international footwear industry's fashion trends, news developments, finances and market data.
Cost: $72.00
Frequency: Weekly
Circulation: 17892
Founded in 1892

11099 WSA Today
Show Dailies International
460 Richmond Street West
Suite 701
Toronto, ON 90049-5103

416-730-8488
800-360-3234; Fax: 416-730-1878
www.ingle-international.com

Rich DiGiacomo, Publisher
Robin Ingle, Chairman/CEO

Features products and industry news, conference information and interviews. Published daily during the semiannual Western Shoe Show.
Founded in 1946

Magazines & Journals

11100 Current Pedorthics
Pedorthic Footwear Association
7150 Columbia Gateway Drive
Suite G
Columbia, MD 21046-1151

410-381-8282
800-673-8447; Fax: 410-381-1167
www.pedorthics.org

Ed Habre, Board Chairman
Chuck Schuyler, President
Tanya Allain, Communicaton Coordinator

Covers pedorthics; the design, manufacture, modification and fit of shoes and foot orthoses to alleviate foot problems caused by disease, overuse or injury.
Cost: $35.00
44 Pages
Frequency: Quarterly
Circulation: 5000
Founded in 1958

11101 **Footwear Market Guide**
307 West 38th Street
Suite 1005
New York, NY 10018

212-398-5505; Fax: 212-398-5504
www.infomat.com
Facebook, Twitter, LinkedIn

Provides a broad industry overview, including key press, manufacturing and sales contacts in one superb, value-prived package.
Cost: $165.00

11102 **Pedorthic Footwear Magazine**
7150 Columbia Gateway Drive
Suite G
Columbia, MD 21046-1151

410-381-7278
800-673-8447; Fax: 410-381-1167
info@pedorthics.org
www.pedorthics.org

Nancy Hultquist, Director Communications
Brian Lagana, Executive Director
Kalin Wilburn, Sales Coordinator
Mike Forgrave, Publisher
Amy Bloom, Membership Manager

Provides educational articles, marketing materials and professional information.
Cost: $55.00
44 Pages
Circulation: 5000
Founded in 1958
Printed in 2 colors on glossy stock

11103 **Runner's World**
Runner's World Magazine Company
135 N 6th Street
Emmaus, PA 18098

610-967-5171
800-845-8050; Fax: 610-967-8883
www.runnersworld.com

Andrew R Hersam, Publisher
David Willey, Editor
Steven Pleshette Murphy, CEO/President
Charles DeLana, Marketing
Richard Alleger, Vice President of Finance

A magazine dedicated to the lifestyle fitness activity of running. Aims to inform, advise, educate and motivate runners of all ages and abilities.
Cost: $21.00
Frequency: Monthly
Circulation: 530511
Founded in 1966
Mailing list available for rent: 370,000 names
Printed in on glossy stock

11104 **Shoestats**
Footwear Industries of America
1420 K St NW
Suite 600
Washington, DC 20005-2506

202-962-0380; Fax: 202-789-7257
shoes@shoeinfonet.com
www.shoeinfonet.com

Maria L Abrantes, President
Ivo Geidl, office Manager

Complete statistical coverage of the footwear industry.
Cost: $40.00
210 Pages
Frequency: Bi-annually

Trade Shows

11105 **Annual Symposium**
Pedorthic Footwear Association
7150 Columbia Gateway Drive
Columbia, MD 21046-2972

800-673-8447; Fax: 410-381-1167
info@pedorthics.org
www.pedorthics.org

Jeanne Williams, Manager
Brian Lagana, Executive Director

The Annual Symposium is a combination education event and trade show expo. Containing 100+ booths and exhibits.
600+ Attendees
Frequency: November
Founded in 1958

11106 **Metropolitan Shoe Show New York**
50 W 34th Street
Apartment 8A6
New York, NY 10001-3057

212-564-1069

Mary Stanton, Show Manager

225 booths.
2M Attendees
Frequency: March/September

11107 **Northwest Show Travelers Buying Show Market**
2720 W 43rd Street
Minneapolis, MN 55410-1643

612-920-5005

Dona Merchant, Show Manager

100 booths of shoe retailers and specialty store personnel from Minnesota, Iowa, North Dakota, Maryland and South Dakota.
1.5M Attendees
Frequency: January

11108 **PFA Annual Symposium & Exhibition**
Pedorthic Footwear Association
1610 E Forsyth St.
Suite D
Americus, GA 31709

229-389-3440; Fax: 888-563-0945
pedorthicsusa@gmail.com
www.pedorthics.org

Jeanne Williams, Show Manager
Brian Lagana, Executive Director
Nancy Hultquist, Director Communications

One hundred fifty booths plus educational sessions regarding the design, manufacture or modification and fit of shoes and foot orthoses to alleviate foot problems caused by disease, congenital condition, overuse or injury.
1000 Attendees
Frequency: November

11109 **World Shoe Associates: Shoe Show**
15821 Ventura Boulevard
Suite 415
Encino, CA 91436-2974

818-799-9400; Fax: 949-851-8523
www.wsashow.com

Chris Aiken, Show Manager

One million square feet of exhibition space. Features thousands of footwear styles, accesories, handbags and foot care products.
12M Attendees
Frequency: August/February

Directories & Databases

11110 **American Shoemaking**
Shoe Trades Publishing Company
61 Massachusetts Avenue
PO Box 1530
East Arlington, MA 02174-8160

781-648-8160; Fax: 781-646-9832
www.shoetrades.com

John J Moynihan, Publisher

Brings the shoe manufacturer the news he needs to know.
Cost: $55.00
30 Pages
Frequency: Monthly

11111 **Complete Directory of Socks & Shoes**
Sutton Family Communications & Publishing Company
155 Sutton Lane
Fordsville, KY 42343

270-740-0870
www.suttoncompliance.com

Theresa Sutton, Editor
Lee Sutton, General Manager

Print-out from database of wholesalers, manufacturers, distributors, importers and close-out houses. Database is updated daily to guarantee the most current and up-to-date sources available.
Cost: $44.50
100+ Pages

11112 **Directory of Mail Order Catalogs**
Grey House Publishing
4919 Route 22
PO Box 56
Amenia, NY 12501

518-789-8700
800-562-2139; Fax: 845-373-6390
books@greyhouse.com
www.greyhouse.com
Facebook, Twitter

Leslie Mackenzie, Publisher
Richard Gottlieb, Editor

The premier source of information on the mail order catalog industry. Covers over 13,000 consumer and business catalog companies with 44 different product chapters from Animals to Toys and Games.
Cost: $395.00
1900 Pages
Frequency: Annual
ISBN: 1-592373-96-8
Founded in 1981

11113 **Directory of Mail Order Catalogs - Online Database**
Grey House Publishing
4919 Route 22
PO Box 56
Amenia, NY 12501

518-789-8700
800-562-2139; Fax: 845-373-6390
gold@greyhouse.com
gold.greyhouse.com
Facebook, Twitter

Leslie Mackenzie, Publisher
Richard Gottlieb, Editor

Reach over 10,000 consumer catalog companies in one easy-to-use source with The Directory of Mail Order Catalogs - Online Database. Filled with business-building detail, each company profile gives you the information you need to access that organization quickly and easily. Listings provide key contacts, sales volume, employee size, printing information, circulation, list data, product descriptions and much more.
Frequency: Annual
Founded in 1981

11114 **Financial Performance Profile of Public Consumer Products Manufacturers**
Kurt Salmon Associates
1355 Peachtree St NE
Suite 900
Atlanta, GA 30309-3257

404-892-0321; Fax: 404-898-9590
www.kurtsalmon.com

William B Pace, CEO

About 23 publicly held footwear manufacturers.
Frequency: Annual June

11115 **Footwear Distributors and Retailers of America: Membership Directory**
Footwear Distributors and Retailers of America
1319 F Street NW
Washington, DC 20004-1106

202-628-1838; Fax: 202-638-2615
http://www.fdra.org

Peter Mangione, President

About 65 American footwear importers and retailers.

11116 **Shoe Factory Buyer's Guide**
Shoe Trades Publishing Company
323 Cornelia Street
Suite 274
Plattsburgh, NY 12901

514-457-8787; Fax: 514-457-5832
sfbg@shoetrades.com
www.shoetrades.com

George McLeash, Publisher

Over 750 suppliers and their representatives to the shoe manufacturing industries in the US and Canada.
Cost: $59.00
Frequency: Annual
Circulation: 1,000

Industry Web Sites

11117 **http://gold.greyhouse.com**
G.O.L.D Grey House OnLine Databases

Grey House Publishing's online database platform, GOLD, offers Quick Search, Keyword Search and Expert Search for most business sectors including shoe and accessory markets. The GOLD platform makes finding the information you need quick and easy - whether you're a novice searcher or an experienced database user. All of Grey House's directory products are available for subscription on the GOLD platform.

11118 **www.apparelandfootwear.org**
American Apparel & Footwear Association

National trade association representing apparel, footwear and other sewn products companies and their suppliers. Our mission is to promote and enhance our members competitiveness, productivity and profitability in the global market.

11119 **www.greyhouse.com**
Grey House Publishing

Authoritative reference directories for most business sectors including shoe and accessory makrets. Users can search the online databases with varied search criteria allowing for custom searches by product category, geographic area, sales volume, keyword, subject and more. Full Grey House catalog and online ordering also available.

11120 **www.ssia.info**
Shoe Service Institute of America

Shop to shop chat room, links and listings of manufacturers and wholesalers plus shoe care tips.

Associations

11121 A Philanthropic Partnership for Black Communities
333 Seventh Avenue
14th Floor
New York, NY 10001

646-230-0306; Fax: 646-230-0310
info@abfe.org
www.abfe.org
Facebook

Gary Cunningham, Chair
Samuel Cargile, PH.D., Vice Chair
Kenneth Jones, Treasurer
Towalame Austin, Secretary
Susan TAYLOR BATTEN, President

Encourages blacks in the grantmaking field and helps members improve their job effectiveness.
Founded in 1971

11122 American Society of Association Executives
1575 I Street NW
Washington, DC 20005

202-626-2723
888-950-2723; Fax: 202-371-8315
ASAEservice@asaecenter.org
www.asaecenter.org
Facebook, Twitter, LinkedIn, YouTube, Instagram

John Graham, President & CEO
Francine Alestock, Executive Coordinator
Shaniece Brown, Member Relations Coordinator
Laura Gaske, Marketing Manager
Sabrina Kidwai, Senior Manager, Public Relations

Association providing advocacy and future-oriented research for member organizations in support of the association and nonprofit profession.
39K Members
Founded in 1920

11123 Arthritis Foundation
1355 Peachtree St. NE
Suite 600
Atlanta, GA 30309

404-872-7100
800-283-7800
www.arthritis.org
Facebook, Twitter, LinkedIn, Instagram

Ann M. Palmer, President & CEO
Rowland W. Chang, Chair

The Arthritis Foundation is the voice of the arthritis community.

11124 Association for Healthcare Philanthropy
313 Park Avenue
Suite 400
Falls Church, VA 22046

703-532-6243; Fax: 703-532-7170
ahp@ahp.org
www.ahp.org
Facebook, LinkedIn

David L. Flood, Chair
Jory Pritchard-Kerr, Vice Chair
Steven W. Churchill, MNA, President & CEO
Randy A. Varju, Secretary/Treasurer
Norman Flores, Finance Director

Represents health care fundraising professionals through education and eventually bestows the credentials upon them.
4100 Members
Founded in 1967

11125 Association of Fund-Raising Professionals
4300 Wilson Blvd.
Suite 300
Arlington, VA 22203

703-684-0410
800-666-3863; Fax: 703-684-0540
mbrship@afpnet.org
www.afpnet.org
Facebook, Twitter, LinkedIn, YouTube, Pinterest, Instagram

Patrick J. Feeley, Chair
Ann M. Hale, Chair-Elect
Susan Earl Hosback, Vice Chair,Resource Dev.
Joshua R. Newton, Secretary
Joseph Goepfrich, Treasurer

Supports all involved in the fundraising profession. Publishes monthly newsletter.
26000 Members
Founded in 1965

11126 Association of Fundraising Professionals
4300 Wilson Blvd.
Suite 300
Arlington, VA 22203

703-684-0410
800-666-3863; Fax: 703-684-0540
www.afpnet.org

Jason Lee, Interim President & CEO
Terry Rauh, Chief Operating Officer

The Association promotes the professional development of fundraising professionals and advocates for high ethical standards in the industry.
30000 Members
Founded in 1960

11127 Association of Small Foundations/ASF
1720 N St NW
Washington, DC 20036

202-580-6560
888-212-9922; Fax: 202-580-6579
info@exponentphilanthropy.org
www.exponentphilanthropy.org
Twitter

Christopher Petermann, Chair
Jean Buckley, Vice Chair
Shirish Dayal, Officer-at-Large
Megan McTiernan, Secretary
Janis A. Reischmann, Treasurer

ASF enhances the power of small foundation giving by providing the donors, trustees, and staff of member foundations with peer learning opportunities, targeted tools and resources, and a collective voice in and beyond the philanthropic community.
3000 Members

11128 BoardSource
750 9th Street, NW
Suite 650
Washington, DC 20001-4793

202-349-2500
877-892-6873; Fax: 202-349-2599
www.boardsource.org

John Griswold, Chair
Philip Henderson, Vice Chair
Anne Wallestad, President & CEO
Sharon Rossmark, Treasurer
Kimberly Roberson, Secretary

Formerly the National Center for Nonprofit Boards, is the premier resource for practical information, tools and best practices, training, and leadership development for board members of nonprofit organizations worldwide.
7000 Members
Founded in 1988

11129 Bond Market Foundation
360 Madison Avenue
New York, NY 10017-7111

646-637-9200; Fax: 646-637-9120

Michael D McCarthy, Chairman
Kathryn L Edmundon, Executive Director
Robert E Foran, Vice Chairman
Hugh Moore, Treasurer
Brian Macwilliams, Assistant Secretary

The Bond Market Foundation is a charitable and educational not for profit (501-c-3) association. The Foundation develops and enhances the public's access to quality saving and investor education in addition to providing credible non-proprietary research capacity and expert discussion on public issues relevant to the bond markets. The Bond Market Foundation is partner to the Securities Industry and Financial Markets Association (SIFMA).

11130 Center for Effective Philanthropy
675 Massachusetts Avenue
7th Floor
Cambridge, MA 02139

617-492-0800; Fax: 617-492-0888
addya@effectivephilanthropy.org
www.effectivephilanthropy.org
Facebook, Twitter, LinkedIn, Youtube, Flickr

Phil Buchanan, President
Latia King, Executive Assistant to President
Ellie Beteau, Vice President, Research
Kevin Bolduc, Vice President, Assessment Tools
Grant Oliphant, Chair

To provide management and governance tools to define, assess, and improve overall foundation performance
Mailing list available for rent

11131 Council for Advancement & Support of Education
1307 New York Ave NW
Suite 1000
Washington, DC 20005

202-328-2273; Fax: 202-387-4973
memberservicecenter@case.org
www.case.org
Facebook, Twitter, LinkedIn, Blog

Sue Cunningham, President/CEO
Brett Chambers, Executive Director of Volunteers
Donald Falkenstein, VP business and finance
Ron Mattocks, VP marketing, membership
Norma Walker, VP advancement programs

Supports all those involved in campus fund raising, public relations,and alumni administration. Publishes monthly magazine.
Founded in 1974

11132 Council on Foundations
2121 Crystal Drive
Suite 700
Arlington, VA 22202

800-673-9036
MEMBERSHIP@COF.ORG
www.cof.org
Facebook, Twitter

Sherry P. Magill, Chair
JAVIER SOTO, Vice Chair
Vikki Spruill, President & CEO
SHERRY ELISE RISTAU, Secretary
EUGENE W. COCHRANE JR., Treasurer

Supports all those involved in the foundation business. Publishes monthly magazine. We provide leadership expertise, legal services and networking opportunities among other services to our members and to the general public.
2000 Members
Founded in 1949

11133 **Foundation Center**
32 Old Slip
24th Floor
New York, NY 10005
212-620-4230
800-424-9836; Fax: 212-807-3677
feedback@foundationcenter.org
www.foundationcenter.org
Facebook, Twitter, YouTube, Flickr, Googleplus, Fo
Bradford K. Smith, President
Lisa Philip, VP for Strategic Philantropy
Lawrence T. McGill, VP for Research
Jeffery Falkenstein, VP for Data Architecture
R. Nancy Albilal, VP Development
A national association for those interested in fund raising related to government agencies. The leading source on philanthropy worldwide.
Founded in 1956

11134 **Freelancers Union**
help@freelancersunion.org
www.freelancersunion.org
Facebook, Twitter, Youtube, Instagram, Google+
Caitlin Pearce, Executive Director
Represents independent workers and offers benefits, such as health and dental, community, advocacy for policy change, and resources.
375M Members
Founded in 1995

11135 **Giving Institute**
225 W. Wacker Drive
Chicago, IL 60606-3396
312-981-6794
800-462-2372; Fax: 312-265-2908
info@givinginstitute.org
www.givinginstitute.org
Facebook, Twitter
Jeffrey D. Byrne, Chair
Rachel Hutchison, 1st Vice Chair
Sarah J. Howard, 2nd Vice Chair
Derek Alley, Secretary
Peter J. Fissinger, Treasurer
Formerly the American Association of Fundraising Counsel (AAFRC). Mission is to educate and engage members in the ethical delivery of counsel and related services to non-profits through research, advocacy, and best practices.
Founded in 1935
Mailing list available for rent

11136 **Independent Sector**
1602 L St NW
Suite 900
Washington, DC 20036
202-467-6100
888-860-8118; Fax: 202-467-6101
info@independentsector.org
www.independentsector.org
Facebook, Twitter
Stephen B. Heintz, Chair
Ralph B. Everett, Vice Chair
Diana Aviv, President & CEO
Lorie A. Slutsky, Treasurer
Kelvin H. Taketa, Secretary
The leadership forum for charities, foundations, and corporate giving programs committed to advancing the common good in America and around the world.
700 Members
Founded in 1980

11137 **MacArthur Foundation**
140 S Dearborn Street
Chicago, IL 60603-5285
312-726-8000; Fax: 312-920-6258
4answers@macfound.org
www.macfound.org/site/htm
Facebook, Twitter, YouTube, RSS
Majorie M. Scardino, Chair
Julia M. Stasch, President
Marc P. Yanchura, Vice President & CFO
Elizabeth Kane, Secretary
Angela Abbott, Communications Assistant
Private, independent grant-making institution dedicated to helping groups and individuals foster lasting improvement in the human condition. Through the support it provides, the Foundation fosters the development of knowledge, nurtures individual creativity, strengthens institutions, helps improve public policy, and provides information to the public, primarily through support for public interest media.
Founded in 1978

11138 **Music Performance Trust Fund**
1501 Broadway
Suite 600
New York, NY 10036
212-391-3950; Fax: 212-221-2604
sramos@musicpf.org
www.musicpf.org
Facebook
Dan Beck, Trustee
Vidrey Blackburn, Contact
Al Elvin, Director of Finance
Samantha Ramos, Contact
Foundation allocates money for the promotion of live music for the general public. The concerts must be free of charge and have no admittance restrictions.
Founded in 1948

11139 **National Catholic Development Conference Inc.**
734 15th St NW
Suite 700
Washington, DC 20005-1013
202-637-0470
888-879-6232; Fax: 202-637-0471
www.ncdc.org
Facebook, Twitter, LinkedIn
Chad McEachern, Chair
Greg Griffin, Vice-Chair
Georgette Lehmuth, President & CEO
Daniel McCormack, Treasurer
Dolly Sokol, Ph.D., Secretary
Members include development officers and key fund raisers of charitable institutions and agencies.
400 Members
Founded in 1968
Mailing list available for rent

11140 **National Committee for Responsive Philanthropy**
1331 H Street NW
Suite 200
Washington, DC 20005
202-387-9177; Fax: 202-332-5084
info@ncrp.org
www.ncrp.org
Facebook, Twitter, RSS
Sherece Y. West-Scantlebury, Chair
Gara LaMarche, Vice Chair
Judy Hatcher, Treasurer
Priscilla Hung, Secretary
Aaron Dorfman, Executive Director
Supports all those involved in the philanthropy field. Publishes quarterly newsletter.
Founded in 1976

11141 **National Council of Nonprofits**
1001 G St. NW
Suite 700E
Washington, DC 20001
202-962-0322; Fax: 202-962-0321
www.councilofnonprofits.org
Tim Delaney, President & CEO
Kyle Caldwell, Chair
The Council is a resource for the nation's nonprofits, identifying trends, sharing best practices and promoting solutions.

11142 **National School Foundation Association (NSFA)**
509 Aurora Ave
Ste 406
Naperville, IL 60540
516-971-2324
866-824-8513; Fax: 813-280-4820
bill@billhoffmanandassociates.com
www.schoolfoundations.org
Facebook, Twitter
Bill Hoffman, Board Chair
Nina Menis, Executive Director
David Else, Vice Chair
Shanon Solava, Membership Director
Jennifer Nihart, Accounting & Website Updates
The mission of the National School Foundation Association is to encourage K-12 school and school foundation personnel in the very rewarding and important process of establishing, developing and maintaining school foundations.
Founded in 2001

11143 **Northwest Development Officers Association**
2150 N 107th Street
Suite 205
Seattle, WA 98133-9009
206-971-3605; Fax: 206-367-8777
office@afpadvancementnw.org
www.ndoa.org
Facebook, Twitter, LinkedIn
Anne Marie MacPherson, Co President
Jodie Miner, Co President
Ray Li, President Elect
Kirk Laughlin, Secretary
Linda Hunt, Treasurer
To provide its members and other fundraising professionals with collegial peer support, networking, and comprehensive training opportunities to advance philanthropy and strengthen community. Provides fellowship,. targeted training, and a sounding board for development officers, volunteers, board members, students, nonprofit managers and others who are committed to fundraising and philanthropy.
800+ Members
Founded in 1978

11144 **Partnership for Philanthropic Planning**
233 S McCrea St
Suite 300
Indianapolis, IN 46225
317-269-6274; Fax: 317-269-6268
info@pppnet.org
www.charitablegiftplanners.org
Facebook, Twitter, LinkedIn, YouTube, Flickr, Googleplus
Gregory Sharkey, Chair
Melanie J. Norton, Chair Elect
Michael Kenyon, President & CEO
Alexandra Brovey, Treasurer
Thomas Armstrong, Secretary
Serving people and organizations that work together to make charitable giving most meaningful.
112 Members
Founded in 1988

11145 **Society for Non-Profits**
P.O.Box 510354
Livonia, MI 48151

734-451-3582; Fax: 734-451-5935
www.snpo.org
Facebook, Twitter, LinkedIn, Yahoo

Katie Burnham Laverty, President

Provides busy nonprofit leaders with concise and practical articles whose advice can be easily implemented .
Cost: $69.00
6000 Members
Frequency: Bi-Monthly
Circulation: 7000
ISSN: 8755-7614
Founded in 1983

11146 **Society for Nonprofit Organizations**
PO Box 510354
Livonia, MI 48151

734-451-3582; Fax: 734-451-5935
www.snpo.org
Facebook, Twitter, LinkedIn, Yahoo

Katie Burnham Laverty, President

Dedicated to bringing together those who serve in the nonprofit world in order to build a strong network of professionals throughout the country. Publishes Nonprofit World Magazine and has an on-line certificate in Nonprofit Management in partnership with Michigan State University.
6000 Members
Founded in 1983

11147 **The Association of Fund-Raising Distributors & Suppliers**
1100 Johnson Ferry Rd
Suite 300
Atlanta, GA 30342

404-252-3663; Fax: 404-252-0774
afrds@kellencompany.com
www.afrds.org
Facebook

Kurt Koehler, President
Russ Colombo, Vice President Distributor Affairs
Mark Van Wyk, Vice President Supplier Affairs
Paul Mahler, Treasurer
Lisa Dieltz, Secretary

Association for manufacturers or suppliers of fundraising products, supplies and services. Its members manufacturer, supply or distribute products that are resold by not-for-profit organizations for fundraising purposes.
700+ Members

11148 **The Grantsmanship Center**
350 South Bixel St.
Suite 110
Los Angeles, CA 90017

213-482-9860
800-421-9512; Fax: 213-482-9863
info@tgci.com
www.tgci.com
Facebook, Twitter, YouTube, Pinterest, Google+

Cathleen Kiritz, President, CEO & Publisher
Barbara Floersch, Director of Training & Curriculum
Roger Stephenson, Alumni Manager
Areli Arellano, Creative & Brand Manager
Gail Brauner, Training Program Coordinator

In-person and online classes on how to secure grant funding for nonprofit, academic, and government agencies. Publisher of textbook: Grantsmanship: Program Planning & Proposal Writing. Free info on website, including state grant resources.
14000 Members
Founded in 1972

Newsletters

11149 **AFP eWire**
Association of Fund-Raising Professionals
4300 Wilson Blvd.
Suite 300
Arlington, VA 22203

703-684-0410
800-666-3863; Fax: 703-684-0540
mbrship@afpnet.org
www.afpnet.org
Facebook, Twitter, LinkedIn, YouTube

Andrew Watt, President & CEO
Tom Clark, COO
Rebecca A. Knight, Director
Mike Eason, CFO

Delivers the latest fundraising news and information.
26000 Members
Frequency: Weekly
Founded in 1965

11150 **AHP E-Connect**
Association for Healthcare Philanthropy
313 Park Avenue
Suite 400
Falls Church, VA 22046

703-532-6243; Fax: 703-532-7170
ahp@ahp.org
www.ahp.org
Facebook, LinkedIn

Susan J. Doliner, Chair
William S. Littlejohn, Chair Elect
Merv D. Webb, Secretary/Treasurer

Provides updates on industry news and research, educational and professional opportunities, book reviews and articles related to health care philanthropy.
Cost: $60.00
4100 Members
Frequency: 8x Yearly
Founded in 1967

11151 **AID for Education**
CD Publications
8204 Fenton St
Silver Spring, MD 20910-4571

301-588-6380
800-666-6380; Fax: 301-588-6385
www.cdpublications.com

Michael Gerecht, President
Frank Kalimko, Editor

Private and federal funding opportunities and news for all levels of education including grants for bilingual education, special education, literacy, minorities and more.
Cost: $419.00
18 Pages
Founded in 1991
Mailing list available for rent: 2,000 names at $160 per M

11152 **Board Source**
Board Source
1828 L St Nw
Suite 900
Washington, DC 20036-5114

202-452-6262
800-883-6262; Fax: 202-452-6299
www.boardsource.org

Linda Crompton, CEO
Betsy Rosenblatt, Senior Editor

National newsletter for board members and staff leaders of nonprofit organizations includes strategies for building effective nonprofit boards. Comentaries from nonprofit leaders, case studies, and nonprofit governance news.
Cost: $139.00
Founded in 1988

11153 **BoardSource E-Newsletter**
BoardSource
750 9th Street, NW
Suite 650
Washington, DC 20001-4590

202-349-2500
877-892-6873; Fax: 202-349-2599
www.boardsource.org

Linda C. Crompton, President & CEO
Fred Sherman, CFO
Anne Wallestad, COO
David J. Nygren, Ph.D, Chair
Roxanne Spillett, Vice Chair

Members-only benefit, offering timely news and information on nonprofit governance issues and trends affecting nonprofit boards.
7000 Members
Frequency: Monthly
Founded in 1988

11154 **CEO Connection**
Association for Healthcare Philanthropy
313 Park Avenue
Suite 400
Falls Church, VA 22046

703-532-6243; Fax: 703-532-7170
ahp@ahp.org
www.ahp.org
Facebook, LinkedIn

Susan J. Doliner, Chair
William S. Littlejohn, Chair Elect
Merv D. Webb, Secretary/Treasurer

From AHP President to health care organization CEOs discussing issues affecting health care philanthropy.
4100 Members
Frequency: Quarterly
Founded in 1967

11155 **Chronicle of Philanthropy**
1255 23rd St Nw
Suite 700
Washington, DC 20037-1146

202-466-1200
800-728-2819; Fax: 202-452-1033
www.philanthropy.com

Robin Ross, Publisher
Phil Semas, Editor
Michael Solomon, Manager of External Communications

A newspaper providing news and information for executives of nonprofit, tax-exempt organizations in health, education, religion, the arts, social services and other fields, as well as fund raisers, professional employees of foundation, and corporate grant makers. Features news, lists of grants, fundraising ideas and techniques, statistics, updates on regulations, reports on tax and court rulings, book summaries, calendar of events.
Cost: $72.00
Frequency: Fortnightly
Circulation: 100000
Founded in 1997

11156 **Community Health Funding Report**
CD Publications
8204 Fenton St
Silver Spring, MD 20910-4571

301-588-6380
800-666-6380; Fax: 301-588-6385
www.cdpublications.com

Michael Gerecht, President
Amy Bernstein, Editor
Jessica Cha, Owner

Highlights sources of funding for healthcare ranging from AIDS education to teen pregnancy

to minority health care. Plus national and local community health news.
Cost: $339.00
Mailing list available for rent: 2,000 names at $160 per M

11157 Connections
Foundation Center
79 5th Ave
New York, NY 10003-3076

212-620-4230
800-424-9836; Fax: 212-807-3677
feedback@foundationcenter.org
www.foundationcenter.org
Facebook, Twitter, YouTube, Flickr

Melissa Berman, President & CEO

The best philanthropy-related content the Web has to offer.
Frequency: Bi-Weekly
Founded in 1956

11158 Corporate Giving Directory
Information Today Inc
143 Old Marlton Pike
Medford, NJ 08055-8750

609-654-6266; Fax: 609-654-4309
custserv@infotoday.com
www.infotoday.com

Thomas H Hogan, President

Delivers the latest information on program priorities, giving preferences, evaluation criteria, corporate and foundation officers and directors, and all the other data you need to help your nonprofit organization gain a crucial edge as corporate philanthropy budgets tighten.

11159 Corporate Philanthropy Report
LRP Publications
PO Box 24668
West Palm Beach, FL 33416-4668

561-622-6520; Fax: 561-622-0757
webmaster@lrp.com
www.lrp.com

Kenneth Kahn, President
Eileen Banashek, Editor

A report for both the corporate and nonprofit communities, spotlighting a different field or industry in each issue.
Cost: $235.00
Frequency: Monthly
Founded in 1977

11160 Development and Alumni Relations Report
LRP Publications
747 Dresher Road Suite 500
PO Box 980
Horsham, PA 19044-980

215-784-0912
800-341-7874; Fax: 215-784-9639
webmaster@lrp.com
www.lrp.com

Anne Checkosky, Editor
Dionne Ellis, Marketing

Gives innovative ideas for improving annual giving, endowment and capital campaigns, planned giving, and alumni relations. Offers suggestions on new ways to spur participation and increase total contributions from alumni, corporate donors and foundations.
Cost: $185.00
Frequency: Monthly
Founded in 1977

11161 Dimensions
National Catholic Development Conference
86 Front St
Hempstead, NY 11550-3667

516-481-6000
888-879-6232; Fax: 516-489-9287
www.ncdc.org

Rachel Donofrio, Editor
Richard Reale, Director Membership
Georgette Lehmuth, CEO
Patricia Newman, Manager

Offers information on development and fund raising including direct mail, planned giving and major gifts and capitol campaigns.
Cost: $1000.00
16 Pages
Circulation: 550
Founded in 1968
Printed in 2 colors on matte stock

11162 Disability Funding News
CD Publications
8204 Fenton St
Silver Spring, MD 20910-4571

301-588-6380
800-666-6380; Fax: 301-588-6385
www.cdpublications.com

Michael Gerecht, President
Martha McPartlin, Editor

Alerts the reader to funding for programs for the disabled, including housing, transportation, rehabilitation, research and special education. Plus advice on successful grantseeking and news updated on national and local developments.
Cost: $419.00
Founded in 1993
Mailing list available for rent: 2,000 names at $160 per M

11163 E-ssentials
National Catholic Development Conference
86 Front St
Hempstead, NY 11550-3667

516-481-6000
888-879-6232; Fax: 516-489-9287
www.ncdc.org

Mark Melia, Chair
Curtis Yarlott, Vice-Chair
Keith Zekind, Treasurer

Connects NCDC members together by providing news about upcoming NCDC events, workshops, and webinars; membership committee news; member success stories; award notifications; fundraising white papers and quick tips; and CFRE exam information.
400 Members
Frequency: Weekly
Founded in 1968

11164 Funding Alert Newsletter
Society for Nonprofit Organizations
PO Box 510354
Livonia, MI 48151

734-451-3582; Fax: 734-451-5935
www.snpo.org
Facebook, Twitter, LinkedIn

Katherine Burnham Leverty, Co-Founder/President/CEO

The leading e-newsletter for current grant and funding opportunities.
7000 Members
Founded in 1983

11165 Giving USA Update
American Association of Fund-Raising Counsel
4700 W Lake Avenue
Glenview, IL 60025

847-375-4709
800-462-2372; Fax: 866-263-2491
info@aafrc.org
www.aafrc.org

Ann Kaplan, Publisher
John J Glier, Chair

Contains analysis, data and comments on charitable giving.
Cost: $125.00
Frequency: Quarterly
Founded in 1935

11166 Health Grants Funding Alert
Health Resources Publishing
1913 Atlantic Ave
Suite 200
Manasquan, NJ 08736-1067

732-292-1100
888-843-6242; Fax: 732-292-1111
info@healthresourcesonline.com
www.hin.com/ehealthcare

Robert K Jenkins, Publisher
Barbara Brown, Regional Director
Brett Powell, Regional Director
Alice Burron, Director

Monthly report sharing news of critical federal and foundation funding opportunities and trends, read by development directors and grants officers.
Cost: $495.00
8 Pages
Frequency: Monthly
ISSN: 0193-7928
Founded in 1978

11167 Kaleidoscope
Association of Fund-Raising Professionals
4300 Wilson Blvd.
Suite 300
Arlington, VA 22203

703-684-0410
800-666-3863; Fax: 703-684-0540
mbrship@afpnet.org
www.afpnet.org
Facebook, Twitter, LinkedIn, YouTube

Andrew Watt, President & CEO
Tom Clark, COO
Rebecca A. Knight, Director
Mike Eason, CFO

Supports AFP's strategic goal of connecting communities around the world by promoting diversity to donors, boards and fundraisers.
26000 Members
Frequency: Quarterly
Founded in 1965

11168 National Center for Nonprofit Boards: Board Member Newsletter
1828 L Street NW
Washington, DC 20036

202-452-6262
800-883-6262; Fax: 202-452-6299
www.ncnb.org

Monthly newsletter for board members and staff leaders of nonprofit organizations includes news updates, case studies, checklists, interviews and opinion pieces to increase the effectiveness of nonprofit boards.
Cost: $99.00
Frequency: Monthly
Circulation: 6800
Printed in 2 colors on matte stock

11169 Philanthropy News Digest
Foundation Center
79 5th Ave
New York, NY 10003-3076

212-620-4230
800-424-9836; Fax: 212-807-3677
feedback@foundationcenter.org

www.foundationcenter.org
Facebook, Twitter, YouTube, Flickr

Melissa Berman, President & CEO

Long-running, award-winning news digest of the Foundation Center.
Frequency: Weekly
Founded in 1956

11170 RFP Bulletin
Foundation Center
79 5th Ave
New York, NY 10003-3076

212-620-4230
800-424-9836; Fax: 212-807-3677
feedback@foundationcenter.org
www.foundationcenter.org
Facebook, Twitter, YouTube, Flickr

Melissa Berman, President & CEO

A roundup of recently announced Requests for Proposals (RFPs) from private, corporate, and government funding sources.
Frequency: Weekly
Founded in 1956

11171 Responsive Philanthropy
National Committee for Responsive Philanthropy
2001 S St Nw
Suite 620
Washington, DC 20009-1165

202-387-9177; Fax: 202-332-5084
info@ncrp.org
www.ncrp.org

Aaron Dorfman, Executive Director
Naomi Tacuyan, Editor

With news and feature articles about philanthropy, fund raising and social justice, covering issues often unreported in mainstream philanthropic publications.
Cost: $25.00
16 Pages
Frequency: Quarterly
Circulation: 5000
Founded in 1976
Mailing list available for rent: 10000 names
Printed in 2 colors on matte stock

11172 Smith Funding Report
SFR
20 O'Neill Circle
Monroe, NY 10950-3210

914-774-4449

Melanie Smith, President

Quarterly guide to private foundation research/project grant opportunities for education and health institutions.
Cost: $195.00
40 Pages
Frequency: Quarterly
Printed in one color on matte stock

11173 Substance Abuse Funding News
CD Publications
8204 Fenton St
Silver Spring, MD 20910-4571

301-588-6380
800-666-6380; Fax: 301-588-6385
www.cdpublications.com

Michael Gerecht, President
Joseph Smith, Editor

Detailed coverage of private and federal funding opportunities nationwide for alcohol and substance abuse programs. Advice on successful grantmaking strategies and roundup of national news.
Cost: $419.00
Founded in 1992
Mailing list available for rent: 2,000 names at $160 per M

11174 Te Informa
Association of Fund-Raising Professionals
4300 Wilson Blvd.
Suite 300
Arlington, VA 22203

703-684-0410
800-666-3863; Fax: 703-684-0540
mbrship@afpnet.org
www.afpnet.org
Facebook, Twitter, LinkedIn, YouTube

Andrew Watt, President & CEO
Tom Clark, COO
Rebecca A. Knight, Director
Mike Eason, CFO

AFP's Spanish-language e-newsletter covering issues of fundraising pertinent to Mexico and other Latin American countries.
26000 Members
Frequency: Quarterly
Founded in 1965

Magazines & Journals

11175 Advancing Philanthropy
Association of Fund-Raising Professionals
4300 Wilson Blvd.
Suite 300
Arlington, VA 22203

703-684-0410
800-666-3863; Fax: 703-684-0540
mbrship@afpnet.org
www.afpnet.org
Facebook, Twitter, LinkedIn, YouTube

Andrew Watt, President & CEO
Tom Clark, COO
Rebecca A. Knight, Director
Mike Eason, CFO

Provides practical information, useful tools and other resources to help members succeed and advance.
26000 Members
Frequency: Bi-Monthly
Founded in 1965

11176 Association Management
American Society of Association Executives
1575 I St NW
Washington, DC 20005-1103

202-626-2700; Fax: 202-408-9635
publicpolicy@asaenet.org
www.asaenet.org

Keith C Skillman, Editor
Karl Ely, Publisher

Association Management strives to provide timely, practical information to help association executives succeed in their dual role as manager and visionary.
Cost: $50.00
106 Pages
Frequency: Monthly
Circulation: 24678
ISSN: 0004-5578
Founded in 1920
Printed in 4 colors on glossy stock

11177 Association for Healthcare Philanthropy
313 Park Avenue
Suite 400
Falls Church, VA 22046-3303

703-532-6243; Fax: 703-532-7170
ahp@ahp.org
www.ahp.org

Kathy Renzetti, Marketing Manager/Editor
William C McGinly, CEO/President
Yvette Banks, Membership Manager
Alison Shaffer, Administrative Assistant

Written for development professionals, fundraisers, trustees, public relations professionals and executives in health care fundraising. Provides timely information on fundraising, career enhancement, planned giving, donor relations, organizational strategies and the effect of health care reform on philanthropy.
Founded in 1967
Mailing list available for rent: 3000 names at $200 per M

11178 BBB Wise Giving Guide
BBB Wise Giving Alliance
4200 Wilson Boulevard
Suite 800
Arlington, VA 22203-1838

703-276-0100; Fax: 703-525-8277
give.org/wise-giving-guide

Includes a summary of the latest results of the BBB Wise Giving Alliance's national charity evaluations along with a cover story about giving tips and or charity accountability issues.
Frequency: 3x Yearly
Circulation: 35000

11179 Currents
Council for Advancement & Support of Education
1307 New York Ave NW
Suite 1000
Washington, DC 20005-4726

202-393-1301; Fax: 202-387-4973
memberservicecenter@case.org
www.case.org

John Lippincott, President
Deborah Bangiorno, Editor-in-Chief
Andrea Gabrick, Senior Editor
Toni Lewis-Bennett, Director of Membership
Anne Brown, Executive Director

Offers information on campus fund raising, public relations,and alumni administration.
Cost: $115.00
Circulation: 15,000
Founded in 1994

11180 Essentials
Association of Small Foundations/ASF
1720 N St NW
Washington, DC 20036-2907

202-580-6560
888-212-9922; Fax: 202-580-6579
asf@smallfoundations.org
Twitter

Henry L. Berman, CEO
Floyd S. Keene, Chair

Provides practical articles on a range of information in one easy read.
3000 Members
Frequency: Quarterly

11181 Foundation News & Commentary
Council on Foundations
2121 Crystal Drive
Suite 700
Arlington, VA 22202
8006739036

Offers news and information for foundations, legislation news and fundraising campaign reviews.
Cost: $24.00
Frequency: Monthly

11182 Freelancing in America Study
Freelancers Union

help@freelancersunion.org
www.freelancersunion.org
Facebook, Twitter, Youtube, Instagram, Google+

Caitlin Pearce, Executive Director

An annual report on the state of freelancing in America.
375M Members
Frequency: Annual
Founded in 1995

11183 **Fundraising EDGE**
Association of Fund-Raising Distributors
1100 Johnson Ferry Rd
Suite 300
Atlanta, GA 30342-1733

404-252-3663; Fax: 404-252-0774
afrds@kellencompany.com
www.afrds.org
Facebook

Kurt Koehler, President
Leslie Lawrence, Secretary
Steve Wienkers, Treasurer

Published by the Association of Fund-Raising distributors and suppliers, offers the latest information about product fundraising.
700+ Members

11184 **Fundraising: Hands on Tactics for Nonprofit Groups**
McGraw-Hill Trade
2 Penn Plz
New York, NY 10121-0101

212-904-4450
877-833-5524; Fax: 212-904-2348

L Peter Edles, Editor
Philip Ruppel, VP & Group Publisher
Jeffrey Krames, Publisher & Editor-in-Chief
William Garvey, Managing Editor
Iain Blackhall, Managing Director

This hands-on operations manual remedies the funding crisis by showing nonprofit professionals and volunteers how to design and run successful fundraising campaigns for their organizations. Combines sound, cost-effective strategies for building better organizational, management, sales, and marketing practices.
Cost: $19.95
288 Pages
ISBN: 0-070189-28-5
Founded in 1992

11185 **Giving USA**
American Association of Fund-Raising Counsel
4700 W Lake Avenue
Glenview, IL 60025-7406

847-375-4709
800-462-2372; Fax: 866-263-2491
www.aafrc.org/

Ann Kaplan, Editor

An annual report on charitable giving in the United States, tracking total charitable giving from four categories of sources to seven kinds of organizations.
Cost: $125.00
Frequency: Quarterly
Circulation: 9000
Founded in 1935

11186 **Grant Funding for Elderly Health Services**
Health Resources Publishing
1913 Atlantic Ave
Suite 200
Manasquan, NJ 08736-1067

732-292-1100
888-843-6242; Fax: 732-292-1111
info@healthresourcesonline.com
www.hin.com/ehealthcare

Robert K Jenkins, Publisher
Lisa Mansfield, Marketing Assistant
Caroline Pense, Editor
Brett Powell, Regional Director
Alice Burron, Director

This report will give insight into which proposals will get funds for which organization. Lists the organizations that will recieve the most funds from grantmakers during this decade and beyond. Also studies different case histories of successful grant proposals.
Cost: $95.00
Frequency: Monthly
ISBN: 1-882364-46-5
Founded in 1978

11187 **Grants Magazine**
Plenum Publishing Corporation
233 Spring St
New York, NY 10013-1522

212-242-1490; Fax: 212-463-0742
info@plenum.com
www.plenum.com

Ricot Paillent, Manager

A magazine listing sources for grants, offering legislative news for the fundraising community, and foundation listings.
Founded in 1946

11188 **Healthcare Philanthropy**
Association for Healthcare Philanthropy
313 Park Avenue
Suite 400
Falls Church, VA 22046

703-532-6243; Fax: 703-532-7170
ahp@ahp.org
www.ahp.org
Facebook, LinkedIn

Susan J. Doliner, Chair
William S. Littlejohn, Chair Elect
Merv D. Webb, Secretary/Treasurer

Previously called the AHP Journal. Contains articles on health care fundraising and development, including ideas and methods for creating successful development programs, analyses of the current health care environment and projections of future trends.
Cost: $50.00
4100 Members
Frequency: Bi-Annually
Founded in 1967

11189 **International Journal of Educational Advancement**
Association of Fundraising Professionals
Henry Stewart Publications
PO Box 10812
Birmingham, AL 35202-0812

205-995-1567
800-633-4931; Fax: 205-995-1588
brenda@hspublications.co.uk
www.afpnet.org

Joyce O'Brien, VP of Communications & Marketing
Brenda Rouse, Publisher

Features new ideas, shares examples of best practices and develops a body of knowledge in educational advancement.
Cost: $250.00
Frequency: 4x/year

11190 **Journal of Gift Planning**
National Committee on Planned Giving
233 S McCrea St
Suite 400
Indianapolis, IN 46225-1068

317-269-6274; Fax: 317-269-6276

Tanya Howe Johnson, President

Provides in-depth analysis of issues of daily concern to both nonprofit planners and for-profit donor advisors. Each issue provides an orientation to national issues and trends affecting the profession, such as the release of major research related to planned gift fundraising or the debate over professional certification for gift planners.
Cost: $45.00
Frequency: Quarterly

11191 **Nonprofit World**
Society for Nonprofit Organizations
PO Box 510354
Livonia, MI 48151

734-451-3582; Fax: 734-451-5935
info@snpo.org
www.snpo.org
Facebook, Twitter, LinkedIn

Katherine Burnham Laverty, President
Jason Chmura, Membership Director
Jill Muehrcke, Editor

Contains original articles and departments on all aspects of running an effective nonprofit organization. Accepts advertising. Now includes the Directory of Service and Product Providers and the Resource Center Catalog with discounted resources for nonprofit organizations.
Cost: $79.00
40 Pages
Frequency: Bi-Monthly
Circulation: 4000
ISSN: 8755-7614
Founded in 1983
Printed in 2 colors

11192 **Philanthropy Monthly**
Non-Profit Report
PO Box 989
New Milford, CT 06776

860-354-7132
860-354-7132; Fax: 860-354-7132

Henry Suhrke, Publisher

Editorial range covers concerns of nonprofits; legislative, economic, fund raising, nonprofit accounting, litigation, etc.
Cost: $84.00
Circulation: 6208

11193 **Responsive Philanthropy**
National Committee for Responsive Philanthropy
1331 H Street NW
Suite 200
Washington, DC 20005

202-387-9177; Fax: 202-332-5084
info@ncrp.org
www.ncrp.org
Facebook, Twitter

Diane Feeney, Chair
Dave Beckwith, Vice Chair
Cynthia Guyer, Secretary
Robert Edgar, Treasurer

Looks at ending homelessness, funding direct services, supporting re0enfranchisement efforts and more.
Frequency: Quarterly
Founded in 1976

Trade Shows

11194 **AFP International Conference on Fundraising**
Association of Fundraising Professionals
1101 King Street
Suite 700
Alexandria, VA 22314-2944

703-684-0410
800-666-3863; Fax: 703-684-0540
webmaster@afpnet.org
www.afpnet.org

Shannon Watson, Director Meetings & Expositions
Myrlin Young, Conferences Coordinator
Paulette Maehara, President
Michael Nilsen, senior Director public affairs

The largest gathering of fundraisers in the profession. The Conference has become the premier resource for fundraisers to network, learn, and discover new products and services.
Frequency: April
Founded in 1962

11195 ASF Annual National Conference
Association of Small Foundations/ASF
1720 N St NW
Washington, DC 20036-2907

202-580-6560
888-212-9922; Fax: 202-580-6579
asf@smallfoundations.org
Twitter

Henry L. Berman, CEO
Floyd S. Keene, Chair

Dozens of educational sessions, preconference workshops, networking opportunities, and inspiring site visits and service projects.
3000 Members
Frequency: Biennial

11196 Annual AFRDS Convention & Trade Show
Association of Fund-Raising Distributors
1100 Johnson Ferry Rd
Suite 300
Atlanta, GA 30342-1733

404-252-3663; Fax: 404-252-0774
afrds@kellencompany.com
www.afrds.org
Facebook

Kurt Koehler, President
Leslie Lawrence, Secretary
Steve Wienkers, Treasurer

The biggest event in product fundraising.
700+ Members
1000+ Attendees
Frequency: Annual/January

11197 Annual NCDC Conference and Exposition
National Catholic Development Conference
86 Front St
Hempstead, NY 11550-3667

516-481-6000
888-879-6232; Fax: 516-489-9287
www.ncdc.org

Mark Melia, Chair
Curtis Yarlott, Vice-Chair
Keith Zekind, Treasurer

Network, learn and be inspired by the amazing community gathered in the spirit of the ministry of fundraising.
400 Members
Frequency: Weekly
Founded in 1968

11198 Annual Winter & Spring Conferences
Northwest Development Officers Association
2150 N 107th Street
Suite 205
Seattle, WA 98133

206-367-8704; Fax: 206-367-8777
www.ndoa.org

Lara Littlefield, President
Louise S. Miller, Executive Director
Jenny Poast, Secretary

Educational meetings focusing on fundraising issues, skills, and best practices. 30 exhibitions.
400 Attendees
Frequency: Annual Winter & Spring

11199 CEP Bi-Annual Conference
Center for Effective Philanthropy
675 Massachusetts Avenue
7th Floor
Cambridge, MA 02139

617-492-0800; Fax: 617-492-0888
addya@effectivephilanthropy.org
www.effectivephilanthropy.org

Phil Buchanan, President

To provide management and governance tools to define, assess, and improve overall foundation performance.
Frequency: Bi-Annual

11200 Council on Foundations Annual Conference
Council on Foundations
1828 L Street NW
Washington, DC 20036-5104

202-466-6512; Fax: 202-785-3926
jonee@cof.org
www.cof.org

Edward Jones, Program Director
Heidi Lyn Capati, Conference Logistics
Michelle Dunston, Registration
Dorothy Ridings, President

Annual conference and exhibits relating to trends and legislation in the field of philanthropy.
Frequency: April

11201 Fall Conference for Community Foundations
Council on Foundations
2121 Crystal Drive
Suite 700
Arlington, VA 22202

800-673-9036
info@cof.org
www.cof.org
Facebook, Twitter

Carol Larson, Chair
Kevin Murphy, Vice Chair
Sherece West, Secretary
Will Ginsberg, Treasurer

Three days of bold steps, original ideas, and new solutions for community foundations.
2000 Members
Frequency: Annual/September

11202 Independent Sector Annual Conference
Independent Sector
1602 L Street NW
Suite 900
Washington, DC 20036

202-467-6100
888-860-8118; Fax: 202-467-6101
info@independentsector.org
www.independentsector.org
Facebook, Twitter

Stephen B. Heintz, Chair
Ralph B. Everett, Vice Chair
Kelvin H. Taketa, Treasurer
Lorie A. Slutsky

The conference focuses on the social compact of the charitable community's role.
1000 Attendees
Frequency: Annual/November

11203 National Conference on Planned Giving
National Committee on Planned Giving
233 McCrea Street
Suite 400
Indianapolis, IN 46225-1030

317-269-6274; Fax: 317-269-6276

Shana McMahon, Meetings Manager
Kathryn J Ramsey, Meetings Director
Tanya Howe Johnson, President

Annual conference and exhibits of fundraising equipment, supplies and services.
Frequency: September-October

11204 Rural Philanthropy Conference
Council on Foundations
2121 Crystal Drive
Suite 700
Arlington, VA 22202

800-673-9036
info@cof.org
www.cof.org
Facebook, Twitter

Carol Larson, Chair
Kevin Murphy, Vice Chair
Sherece West, Secretary
Will Ginsberg, Treasurer

Each session encourages defining rural philanthropy's role, focusing on successful case studies, providing the tools needed to replicate them in the communities.
2000 Members
Frequency: Annual/July

11205 Windows Annual Conference
Council on Foundations
2121 Crystal Drive
Suite 700
Arlington, VA 22202

800-673-9036
info@cof.org
www.cof.org
Facebook, Twitter

Carol Larson, Chair
Kevin Murphy, Vice Chair
Sherece West, Secretary
Will Ginsberg, Treasurer

Features three days of transparency, honesty, and candor in the field of philanthropy.
2000 Members
Frequency: Annual/April

Directories & Databases

11206 Annual Register of Grant Support: A Directory of Funding Services
Information Today
143 Old Marlton Pike
Medford, NJ 08055-8750

609-654-6266
800-300-9868; Fax: 609-654-4309
custserv@infotoday.com
www.infotoday.com

Beverley McDonough, Editor
Daniel Bazikian, Editor

Contains more that 3,500 grant giving organziations. IS also the definitive resource for researching and uncovering a full range of available grant sources.Also directs you to traditional corporate, private, and public funding programs, it also shows you the way to little known, nontraditional grant sources such as educational associations and unions.
Cost: $240.00
1476 Pages
Frequency: Annual
ISBN: 1-573872-04-0

11207 Charitable Trust Directory
Office of the Secretary of State
Charitable Trust Program
801 Capitol Way South
Olympia, WA 98504-0234

360-753-0863
800-332-GIVE
www.secstate.wa.gov/charities

Sam Reed, Chairman/Secretary of State
Linda Vallegos Bremer, Director of General Administration

Directory of charitable trusts regulations in the State of Washington.
Cost: $27.00
290 Pages
Frequency: CD-ROM Available

11208 **Corporate Giving Directory**
Information Today Inc
143 Old Marlton Pike
Medford, NJ 08055-8750

609-654-6266; Fax: 609-654-4309
custserv@infotoday.com
www.infotoday.com

Thomas H Hogan, President

Delivers the latest information on program priorities, giving preferences, evaluation criteria, corporate and foundation officers and directors, and all the other data you need to help your nonprofit organization gain a crucial edge as corporate philanthropy budgets tighten.
1610 Pages
Frequency: Biennial
ISBN: 1-573872-93-5

11209 **Directory of Research Grants**
Greenwood Publishing Group
130 Cremona Drive
PO Box 1911
Santa Barbara, CA 93117

800-368-6868; Fax: 866-270-3856
CustomerService@abc-clio.com
www.abc-clio.com

Directory containing information for more than 5,100 programs being offered through 1,880 sponsors. Includes contact info for grants and examples of past grants awarded, all of which is divided by subject, program, location, and sponsoring organization.
Cost: $151.95
1208 Pages
ISBN: 9-780897-74-9

11210 **Environmental Grantmaking Foundations Directory**
Resources for Global Sustainability
PO Box 3665
Cary North, NC 27519-3665

800-724-1857; Fax: 919-363-9841
www.environmentalgrants.com

Corrine Szymko, President

Over 900 private foundations, community foundations and corporate giving programs that provide funding for environmental interests.
Cost: $115.00
Frequency: Annual
ISBN: 0-976788-00-4

11211 **Financial Aid for African Americans**
Reference Service Press
5000 Windplay Dr
Suite 4
El Dorado Hills, CA 95762-9319

916-939-9620; Fax: 916-939-9626
info@rspfunding.com
www.rspfunding.com

Gail Schlachter, Editor
Martin Sklar, Manager

This directory describes nearly 1,450 scholarships, fellowships, loans, grants, awards and internships for African Americans
Cost: $40.00
522 Pages
Frequency: Biennial
ISBN: 1-588410-68-5
Founded in 1997

11212 **Financial Aid for Asian Americans**
Reference Service Press
5000 Windplay Dr
Suite4
El Dorado Hills, CA 95762-9319

916-939-9620; Fax: 916-939-9626
info@rspfunding.com
www.rspfunding.com

Gail Schlachter, Editor
Martin Sklar, Manager

Use this source to find funding for Americans of Chinese, Japanese, Korean, Vietnamese, Filipino, or other Asian origins. Nearly 1,000 funding opportunities are described.
Cost: $37.50
346 Pages
Frequency: Biennial
ISBN: 1-588410-69-2
Founded in 1997
Printed in on matte stock

11213 **Financial Aid for Hispanic Americans**
Reference Service Press
5000 Windplay Dr
Suite 4
El Dorado Hills, CA 95762-9319

916-939-9620; Fax: 916-939-9626
info@rspfunding.com
www.rspfunding.com

Gail Schlachter, Editor
Martin Sklar, Manager

This directory describes nearly 1,300 funding opportunities open to Americans of Mexican, Puerto Rican, Central American, or other Latin American heritage.
Cost: $30.00
402 Pages
Frequency: Biennial
ISBN: 1-588410-70-6
Founded in 1997
Printed in on matte stock

11214 **Financial Aid for Native Americans**
Reference Service Press
5000 Windplay Dr
Suite 4
El Dorado Hills, CA 95762-9319

916-939-9620; Fax: 916-939-9626
info@rspfunding.com
www.rspfunding.com

Gail Schlachter, Editor
Martin Sklar, Manager

In this directory you will find 1,500 funding opportunities set aside just for American Indians, Native Alaskans, and Native Pacific Islanders.
Cost: $40.00
546 Pages
ISBN: 1-588410-71-4
Founded in 1997

11215 **Financial Aid for Veterans, Military Personnel and their Dependents**
Reference Service Press
5000 Windplay Dr
Suite 4
El Dorado Hills, CA 95762-9319

916-939-9620; Fax: 916-939-9626
info@rspfunding.com
www.rspfunding.com

Gail Schlachter, Editor
Martin Sklar, Manager

This one-stop directory identifies 1,200 scholarships, fellowships, loans, awards, grants and internships.
Cost: $40.00
418 Pages
Frequency: Biennial
ISBN: 1-588410-97-8
Founded in 1988
Printed in on matte stock

11216 **Financial Aid for the Disabled and their Families**
Reference Service Press
5000 Windplay Dr
Suite 4
El Dorado Hills, CA 95762-9319

916-939-9620; Fax: 916-939-9626
info@rspfunding.com
www.rspfunding.com

Gail Schlachter, Editor
Martin Sklar, Manager

A comprehensive directory identifies 1,200 scholarships, fellowships, loans, internships, awards, and grants for these groups.
Cost: $40.00
502 Pages
Frequency: Biennial
ISBN: 0-918276-65-9

11217 **Foundation Directory**
Foundation Center
79 5th Ave
New York, NY 10003-3076

212-620-4230
800-424-9836; Fax: 212-807-3677
feedback@foundationcenter.org
www.foundationcenter.org

Bradford K Smith, President
Laura Cascio, Chief Information Officer
Patrick Collins, Chief Information Officer
Nancy Kami, Executive Director

Key facts on the nation's top 10,000 foundations by total giving. And, with over 46,000 descriptions of selected grants, the Directory provides fundraisers with unique insight into foundation giving priorities.
Cost: $215.00
2,533 Pages
ISBN: 1-595420-18-5

11218 **Foundation Directory Online Database**
Foundation Center
79 5th Ave
New York, NY 10003-3076

212-620-4230
800-424-9836; Fax: 212-807-3677
feedback@foundationcenter.org
www.foundationcenter.org

Bradford K Smith, President
Laura Cascio, Chief Information Officer
Patrick Collins, Chief Information Officer
Nancy Kami, Executive Director

Search our databases online to get detailed information on up to nearly 80,000 foundations, links to current foundation 990-PF returns, crucial facts on more than half a million grants, including the purpose of grants.
Cost: $ 19.95
Frequency: Monthly

11219 **Foundation Directory Supplement**
Foundation Center
79 5th Ave
New York, NY 10003-3076

212-620-4230
800-424-9836; Fax: 212-807-3677
feedback@foundationcenter.org
www.foundationcenter.org

Bradford K Smith, President
Laura Cascio, Chief Information Officer
Patrick Collins, Chief Information Officer
Nancy Kami, Executive Director

Provides revised entries for hundreds of foundations in The Foundation Directory and The Foundation Directory Part 2. Any alterations in giving interests, or updates on staff, financial data, contact information, and more, will be re-

flected in the Supplement.
Cost: $125.00
1000 Pages
ISBN: 1-931923-89-2

11220 Foundation Grants Index
Foundation Center
79 5th Ave
New York, NY 10003-3076

212-620-4230
800-424-9836; Fax: 212-807-3677
feedback@foundationcenter.org
www.foundationcenter.org

Bradford K Smith, President
Laura Cascio, Fulfillment Manager
Michael Seltver, President
Patrick Collins, Chief Information Officer
Nancy Kami, Executive Director

Covers the grants of over 1,000 of the largest independent, corporate, and community foundations in the U.S. and features approximately 125,000 grant descriptions in all.
Cost: $175.00
Frequency: CD-ROM
ISBN: 1-595420-09-6

11221 Foundation Grants to Individuals
Foundation Center
79 5th Ave
New York, NY 10003-3076

212-620-4230
800-424-9836; Fax: 212-807-3677
feedback@foundationcenter.org
www.foundationcenter.org

Bradford K Smith, President
Laura Cascio, Fulfillment Manager
Michael Seltver, President
Patrick Collins, Chief Information Officer
Nancy Kami, Executive Director

Featuring over 6,200 entries packed with current information for individual grantseekers.
Cost: $65.00
1,117 Pages
Frequency: Biennial
ISBN: 1-595420-42-8

11222 Foundation Operations and Management Report
Association of Small Foundations/ASF
1720 N St NW
Washington, DC 20036-2907

202-580-6560
888-212-9922; Fax: 202-580-6579
asf@smallfoundations.org
Twitter

Henry L. Berman, CEO
Floyd S. Keene, Chair

The tool for small foundation benchmarking. Easy-to-read data and commentary on small foundation administration, boards, grantmaking and investments.
3000 Members
50+ Pages
Frequency: Annual

11223 Foundation Salary & Benefits Report
Association of Small Foundations/ASF
1720 N St NW
Washington, DC 20036-2907

202-580-6560
888-212-9922; Fax: 202-580-6579
asf@smallfoundations.org
Twitter

Henry L. Berman, CEO
Floyd S. Keene, Chair

Small foundations use this annual report to benchmark base salaries by region, gender, experience, asset size, and more. Data includes information on health insurance premiums, retirement contributions, paid leave, and more.
3000 Members
50+ Pages
Frequency: Annual

11224 Funding for Persons with Visual Impairments
Reference Service Press
5000 Windplay Dr
Suite 4
El Dorado Hills, CA 95762-9319

916-939-9620; Fax: 916-939-9626
www.rspfunding.com

Gail Schlachter, Editor
Martin Sklar, Manager

For low-vision readers, we have prepared a large-print listing of the scholarships, fellowships, loans, grants-in-aid, awards, and internships that are set aside just for persons with visual impairments (from high school seniors through professionals and others). Nearly 270 funding opportunities are described in detail here.
Cost: $30.00
274 Pages
Frequency: Annual
ISBN: 1-588411-29-X
Founded in 1997

11225 Grants for Foreign and International Programs
Foundation Center
79 5th Ave
New York, NY 10003-3076

212-620-4230
800-424-9836; Fax: 212-807-3677
feedback@foundationcenter.org
www.foundationcenter.org

Bradford K Smith, President
Michael Seltver, Chief Information Officer
Patrick Collins, Chief Information Officer
Nancy Kami, Executive Director

A customized list of thousands of recent grants of $10,000 or more that have been awarded to organizations in foreign countries and to domestic recipients for international activities in such areas as: development and relief, peace and security, arms control, human rights, conferences and research, and more.
Cost: $75.00
436 Pages
ISBN: 1-595420-23-1

11226 Guide to Funding for International and Foreign Programs
Foundation Center
79 5th Ave
New York, NY 10003-3076

212-620-4230
800-424-9836; Fax: 212-807-3677
feedback@foundationcenter.org
www.foundationcenter.org

Bradford K Smith, President
Patrick Collins, Chief Information Officer
Nancy Kami, Executive Director

Includes up-to-date information on over 1,000 foundations and corporate givers that have supported a wide range of projects with an international focus both in the U.S. and in foreign countries.
Cost: $125.00
358 Pages
ISBN: 1-931923-95-7

11227 Guide to US Foundations, Their Trustees, Officers and Donors
Foundation Center
79 5th Ave
New York, NY 10003-3076

212-620-4230
800-424-9836; Fax: 212-807-3677
feedback@foundationcenter.org
www.foundationcenter.org

Bradford K Smith, President
Patrick Collins, Chief Information Officer
Nancy Kami, Executive Director

The only published source of data on all active grantmaking foundations and the individuals who run them, provides current information on over 68,000 foundations. Featuring a master list of the decision-makers who direct America's foundations, the Guide is a powerful fundraising reference tool.
Cost: $350.00
4,235 Pages
Frequency: Annual
ISBN: 1-595420-35-5

11228 Matching Gift Details
Council for Advancement & Support of Education
1307 New York Ave NW
Suite 1000
Washington, DC 20005-4726

202-393-1301; Fax: 202-387-4973
memberservicecenter@case.org
www.case.org

Silvia France, Matching Gifts Coordinator

Compiled and maintained by the Matching Gifts Clearinghouse, a comprehensive annual directory of more than 8,600 companies that match employee charitable gifts.
Cost: $100.00
286 Pages
ISBN: 0-899643-83-3

11229 National Directory of Corporate Giving
Foundation Center
79 5th Ave
New York, NY 10003-3076

212-620-4230
800-424-9836; Fax: 212-807-3677
www.foundationcenter.org

Bradford K Smith, President
Patrick Collins, Chief Information Officer
Nancy Kami, Executive Director

This comprehensive directory features up-to-date information that helps fundraisers tap into their share of grant money earmarked by companies for nonprofit support. Detailed portraits of close to 2,500 corporate foundations and some 1,400 direct giving programs feature essential information.
Cost: $195.00
1,165 Pages
Frequency: Annual
ISBN: 1-595420-04-5

11230 New Foundation Guidebook
Association of Small Foundation
4905 Del Ray Avenue
Suite 200
Bethesda, MD 20814

301-073-3337
888-212-9922; Fax: 301-907-0980
asf@smallfoundations.org

Carmen Wong, Director of Communications
Deborah Brody Hamilton, CEO
Hanh Le, Director Member Services
Kathryn Petrillo-Smith, Managing Director

Contains articles and advice from over 40 foundation representatives and experts included in the Association of Small Foundations' newsletters and publications.
Cost: $40.00
86 Pages

11231 New Nonprofit Almanac & Desk Reference
Independent Sector

1602 L St NW
Suite 900
Washington, DC 20036-5682

202-467-6100
888-860-8118; Fax: 202-467-6101
info@independentsector.org
www.independentsector.org

Provides managers, researchers, volunteers, and the press with the essential facts and figures needed to understand the size, scope, and nature of the nonprofit sector and its contributions to American society.
Cost: $42.00
288 Pages
ISBN: 9-780787-95-7

11232 **The Complete Guide to Grantmaking Basics: A Field Guide for Funders**
Council on Foundations
2121 Crystal Drive
Suite 700
Arlington, VA 22202

800-673-9036
info@cof.org
www.cof.org
Facebook, Twitter

Carol Larson, Chair
Kevin Murphy, Vice Chair
Sherece West, Secretary
Will Ginsberg, Treasurer

A practical guide to honing your grantmaking effectiveness and adapting to the changing nonprofit world.
Cost: $65.00
2000 Members

11233 **The Foundation Guidebook**
Association of Small Foundations/ASF
1720 N St NW
Washington, DC 20036-2907

202-580-6560
888-212-9922; Fax: 202-580-6579
asf@smallfoundations.org
Twitter

Henry L. Berman, CEO
Floyd S. Keene, Chair

Gain the baseline knowledge to operate your foundation smoothly and effectively.
Cost: $69.00
3000 Members

Industry Web Sites

11234 **http://gold.greyhouse.com**
G.O.L.D Grey House OnLine Databases

Grey House Publishing's online database platform, GOLD, offers Quick Search, Keyword Search and Expert Search for most business sectors including foundation and fund raising markets. The GOLD platform makes finding the information you need quick and easy - whether you're a novice searcher or an experienced database user. All of Grey House's directory products are available for subscription on the GOLD platform.

11235 **www.ahp.org**
Association for Healthcare Philanthropy

Represents health care fundraising professionals through education and eventually bestows the credentials upon them.

11236 **www.cof.org**
Council on Foundations

Supports all those involved in the foundation business. Publishes monthly magazine. We provide leadership expertise, legal services and networking opportunities among other services to our members and to the general public.

11237 **www.grantsmart.org**
Grantsmart

An online resource database that contains 96,337 private foundations and charitable trusts.

11238 **www.greyhouse.com**
Grey House Publishing

Authoritative reference directories for most business sectors including foundation and fund raising markets. Users can search the online databases with varied search criteria allowing for custom searches by product category, geographic area, sales volume, keyword, subject and more. Full Grey House catalog and online ordering also available.

11239 **www.guidestar.org**
GuideStar

A database of more than 1 million nonprofit organizations in the United States. It's the world's most comprehensive source of information about American nonprofit organizations.

11240 **www.idealist.org**
Action Without Borders

Over 45,000 nonprofit and community organizations in 165 countries, which you can search or browse by name, location or mission.

11241 **www.independentsector.org**
Independent Sector

The leadership forum for charities, foundations, and corporate giving programs committed to advancing the common good in America and around the world.

11242 **www.naspl.org**
North American Assn of State & Provincial Lottery

Represents 47 lottery organizations throughout North America. Provides information and benefits of state and provincial lottery organizations.

11243 **www.ncdcusa.org**
National Catholic Development Conference

Members include development officers and key fund raisers of charitable institutions and agencies.

11244 **www.tgci.com**
The Grantsmanship Center

Launched the world's first training program for grantseekers in 1972 and continues to set the standard in the field.

11245 **www.uwex.edu/li**
Learning Institute

The Center provides you with a number of resources on the web that could provide you with assistance in a variety of nonprofit management and leadership issues. In the nonprofit web sites section you will find a number of useful annotated resources organized by topic.

Associations

11246 **Adhesive and Sealant Council**
7101 Wisconsin Avenue
Suite 990
Bethesda, MD 20814

301-986-9700; Fax: 301-986-9795
data@ascouncil.org
www.ascouncil.org
Twitter, LinkedIn

William Allmond, President
Valeryia Mikharava, Dir., Finance & Administration
Connie Howe, Sr. Director, Technical Services
Steve Duren, Senior Director, Member Services
Malinda Armstrong, Director, Meetings & Expositions

ASC is a North American trade association dedicated to representing the adhesive and sealant industry. ASC is bound by the collective efforts of its members, and strives to improve the industry operating environment and strengthen its member companies.

11247 **American Chemistry Council**
700 Second St, NE
Washington, DC 20002

202-249-7000; Fax: 202-249-6100
plastics.americanchemistry.com/pfpg
Facebook, Twitter

Calvin M. Dooley, President
Raymond J. O Bryan, CFO & Chief Administrative Officer
Rudy Underwood, Vice President, State Affairs
Bryan Zumwalt, Vice President of Federal Affairs
Anne Womack Kolton, Vice President of Communications

Promotes effective use of recycling of polystyrene. Works to provide effective information about waste disposal and offers technical assistance.
Founded in 1988

11248 **American Trucking Association**
950 North Glebe Road
Suite 210
Arlington, VA 22203-4181

703-838-1700
nafc@trucking.org
www.trucking.org

Pat Thomas, Chairman
Bill Graves, President & CEO
Kevin Burch, First Vice Chairman
Karla Hulett, Secretary
G. Tommy Hodges, Treasurer

Largest national trade association for the trucking industry.
1000 Members
Founded in 1933

11249 **Association of Marketing Service Providers**
1800 Diagonal Road
Suite 320
Alexandria, VA 22314-2806

703-836-9200; Fax: 703-548-8204
kgarner@mfsanet.org
www.amsp.org

Joseph P. Truncale, President & CEO
Ken Garner, Chief Operating Officer
Dean D'Ambrosi, Chief Financial Officer
Andrew D. Paparozzi, SVP & Chief Economist
Leo Raymond, VP, Postal & Member Relations

Formerly known as the Mailing & Fulfillment Service Association, the Association of Marketing Service Providers provides educational content, networking opportunities, and legislative advocacy.

11250 **Composite Can and Tube Institute**
50 S Pickett Street
Suite 110
Alexandria, VA 22304-7206

703-823-7234; Fax: 703-823-7237
ccti@cctiwdc.org
www.cctiwdc.org

Kristine Garland, Executive Vice President
Janine Marczak, Associate Manager, Events
Wayne Vance, Association Counsel

CCTI is an international nonprofit trade association representing the interests of manufacturers of composite paperboard cans, containers, canisters, tubes, cores, edgeboard and related or similar composite products and suppliers to those manufacturers of such items as paper, machinery, adhesives, labels and other services and materials.
Founded in 1934

11251 **Containerization & Intermodal Institute**
960 Holmdel Road
Bldg 2, Suite 201
Holmdel, NJ 07733

732-817-9131; Fax: 732-817-9133
connie@containerization.org
www.containerization.org
LinkedIn

Brendan McCahill, Sr., Chairman
Allen Clifford, Vice Chairman
Michael DiVirgilio, President
Steven Blust, Vice President
Sue Coffey, Treasurer

Provides educational opportunities through existing programs and initiatives, including educational outreach, scholarships, and award programs.
Founded in 1960

11252 **Contract Packaging Association**
One Parkview Plaza
Suite 800
Oakbrook Terrace, IL 60181

630-544-5053; Fax: 630-544-5055
info@contractpackaging.org
www.contractpackaging.org
Twitter, LinkedIn

Vicky Smitley, President
Tim Koers, Vice President
Mark O'Malley, Treasurer
Chris Nutley, Past-President
John Mazelin, Executive Director

A national, not-for-profit trade association that includes dynamic and growing companies offering contract packaging services.
155 Members
Founded in 1992

11253 **Corrugated Packaging Alliance**
500 Park Blvd.
Suite 985
Itasca, IL 60143

847-364-9600; Fax: 847-364-9739
inquiries@corrugated.org
www.corrugated.org
LinkedIn

Rachel K Kenyon, Vice President
Dennis Colley, Executive Director

Develops and coordinates industry-wide programs to address corrugated packaging issues. The Council's mission is to inform consumers, manufacturers, retailers and government officials of corrugated packaging's performance and environmental attributes.
Founded in 1994

11254 **EPS Industry Alliance**
1298 Cronson Blvd.
Suite 201
Crofton, MD 21114

410-451-8340
800-607-3772; Fax: 410-451-8343
info@epsindustry.org
www.epspackaging.org
Facebook, Twitter

EPS-IA is a union of 60 companies dedicated to the sustainability of the expanded polystyrene (EPS) industry and environmental protection.
Founded in 2012

11255 **Envelope Manufacturers Association**
700 S Washington St
Suite 260
Alexandria, VA 22314

703-739-2200; Fax: 703-739-2209
www.envelope.org

Maynard H. Benjamin, President & CEO

Association representing the interests of the envelope manufacturing industry.
Founded in 1933

11256 **Express Carriers Association**
9532 Liberia Avenue
Suite 752
Manassas, VA 20110

703-361-1058
866-322-7447; Fax: 703-361-5274
eca@expresscarriers.org
www.expresscarriers.org

Paul Steffes, President
Jim Luciani, 1st Vice President
Mike Coyle, 2nd Vice President
Jim King, Treasurer
Jim Bernecker, Secretary

Trade association representing regional carriers. Presents annual marketplace to bring together carriers and shippers

11257 **Fibre Box Association**
25 Northwest Point Blvd
Suite 510
Elk Grove Village, IL 60007

847-364-9600; Fax: 847-364-9639
fba@fibrebox.org
www.fibrebox.org
LinkedIn

John Davis, Chairman
Mike Waite, First Vice Chairman
Bill Hoel, Second Vice Chairman
Dennis Colley, President
Rachel Kenyon, Vice President1

Represents 90 percent of the US corrugated paper board, packaging, manufacturing industry.
141 Members
Founded in 1940

11258 **Flexible Intermediate Bulk Container Association**
PO Box 241894
Saint Paul, MN 55124-7019

952-412-8867; Fax: 661-339-0023
info@fibca.com
www.fibca.com
Facebook, Twitter, LinkedIn, Youtube, Googleplus, blogspot

Lewis Anderson, Executive Director

Works to develop minimum standards of testing and performance for FIBC. Acts as a forum through seminars and other programs and serves as an advocate for the industry.
50 Members
Founded in 1983

11259 **Flexible Packaging Association**
185 Admiral Cochrane Drive
Suite 105
Annapolis, MD 21401

410-694-0800; Fax: 410-694-0900
fpa@flexpack.org
www.flexpack.org

Marla Donahue, President

One of the leading trade associations for converters of flexible packaging and suppliers to the industry. Also provides a wealth of information to its members through focused services and benefits of membership.

11260 **Foodservice & Packaging Institute**
7700 Leesburg Pike
Suite 421
Falls Church, VA 22043

703-592-9889; Fax: 703-592-9864
fpi@fpi.org
www.fpi.org
Facebook, Twitter, LinkedIn

Lynn Dyer, President
Natha Freiburg, Vice President
Rob Kittredge, Chair
Michael Evans, 1st Vice Chair
Tracy Pearson, 2nd Vice Chair

Manufacturers, suppliers and distributors of one-time use products used for food service, as well as packaging products made from paper, plastic, aluminum and other materials.
37 Members
Founded in 1933

11261 **Gemini Shippers Group**
137 West 25th Street
3rd Floor
New York, NY 10001

212-947-3424; Fax: 212-629-0361
info@geminishippers.com
www.geminishippers.com

Sara L. Mayes, CEO and President
Kenneth O'Brien, Chief Operating Officer
Nicole Uchrin, Managing Director
Rich Moore, Sales Director
Arlene L. Blocker, Membership Director

Shippers association with global contracts for all commodities.
200 Members
Founded in 1916

11262 **Glass Packaging Institute**
1220 North Fillmore Street
Suite 400
Arlington, VA 22201

703-684-6359; Fax: 703-546-0588
info@gpi.org
www.gpi.org
Facebook, Twitter

Andres Lopez, Chairman
Lynn M. Bragg, President
John Riordan, Board Member
Sanjay Gandhi, Board Member
John Gallo, Board Member

Develops and evaluates testing procedures and equipment, conducts advertising campaigns for generic products.
Founded in 1945

11263 **Healthcare Compliance Packaging Council**
2711 Buford Road
#268
Bon Air, VA 23235-2423

804-338-5778; Fax: 888-812-4272
www.hcpconline.org
Facebook, LinkedIn

Walt Berghahn, Executive Director

Promotes the many benefits of unit dose blister and strip packaging, especially its ability to be designed in compliance, promoting formats that help people take their medications properly.
Founded in 1990

11264 **Institute of International Container Lessors**
1120 Connecticut Avenue
Suite 440
Washington, DC 20036-3946

202-223-9800; Fax: 202-223-9810
info@iicl.org
www.iicl.org

Philip Brewer, Chairman
Steven Blust, President & Secretary
Simon Vernon, 1st Vice President
Keith Lovetro, 2nd Vice President
George Elkas, Treasurer

Represents international container and chassis leasing industry in technical, governmental and legal matters. Publishes leading worldwide manuals on inspection and repair of containers and inspector and maintenance of chassis. Sponsors container and chassis inspection examination once a year in over 40 countries and chassis examination in North America.
Founded in 1971

11265 **Institute of Packaging Professionals**
One Parkview Plaza
Suite 800
Oakbrook Terrace, IL 60181

630-544-5050; Fax: 630-544-5055
info@iopp.org
www.iopp.org
Facebook, Twitter, LinkedIn, YouTube

Jane Chase, Chair
Dan Alexander, Vice Chair
Dana Alexander, Executive VP- Finance & Operations
Robert Meisner, Executive VP- Education
Suzanne Simmons, Executive VP- Membership

Dedicated to creating networking and educational opportunities that help packaging professionals succeed.

11266 **International Air Transport Association**
800 Place Victoria
PO Box 113
Montreal, CA H4Z 1M1

514-874-0202; Fax: 514-874-9632
www.iata.org/
Twitter, LinkedIn, YouTube

Tony Tyler, Director General & CEO

Seeks to improve understanding of the industry among decision makers and increase awareness of the benefits that aviation brings to national and global economies. It fights for the interests of airlines across the globe, challenging unreasonable rules and charges, holding regulators and governments to account, and strivign for sensible regulation.
240+ Members
Founded in 1945

11267 **International Molded Fiber Association**
355 Lexington Avenue
Floor 15
New York, NY 10017

212-297-2150; Fax: 262-241-3766
Alan@IMFA.org
www.imfa.org
Facebook, Twitter, LinkedIn

Cassandra Niesing, Asst. Director
Joseph Grygny, Chairman

Acts as an information center for the molded fiber industry with worldwide membership of users and manufacturers of molded fiber producs. Promotes use of natural and recycled fibers.
Founded in 1997

11268 **Keep America Beautiful**
1010 Washington Blvd
Stamford, CT 06901

203-659-3000; Fax: 203-659-3001
info@kab.org
www.kab.org
Facebook, Twitter, Youtube

Howard Ungerleider, Chairman
Jennifer M. Jehn, President and CEO
Steve Navedo, VP Development
Mike Rogers, Chief Development Officer
Becky Lyons, Chief Operating Officer

National, nonprofit, education organization whose corporate members include packagers, retailers, bottlers, and makers of chemical, steel, glass, paper and aluminum products.
Founded in 1953

11269 **Lake Carriers Association**
20325 Center Ridge Road
Suite 720
Rocky River, OH 44116

440-333-4444; Fax: 440-333-9993
info@lcaships.com
www.lcaships.com

James H I Weakley, President
Glen Nekvasil, Vice President
Harold W. Henderson, General Counsel
Katie Gumeny, Administrative Assistant
Katherine A. Gumeny, Secretary/Treasurer

Members are US-Flag Great Lakes vessel operators engaged in transporting iron ore, coal, grain, limestone, cement and petroleum products.
Founded in 1880

11270 **National Customs Brokers and Forwarders Association of America, Inc.**
1200 18th St NW
Suite 901
Washington, DC 20036

202-466-0222; Fax: 202-466-0226
www.ncbfaa.org

Darrell Sekin, Jr., Chairman
Geoffrey Powell, President
Amy Magnus, Vice President
Scott E. Larson, Treasurer
William S. App. Jr., Secretary

Learn about new business leads, stay on top of Customs Service and other agency regulations that will impact your operations and provide invaluable professional development resources for your employees.
600+ Members
Founded in 1897

11271 **National Institute of Packaging, Handling, and Logistics Engineers**
5903 Ridgeway Drive
Grand Prairie, TX 75052

817-466-7490
866-464-7490
admin@niphle.com
www.niphle.com
Facebook, Twitter, LinkedIn

Sean Kernis, President
Anna Boulware, Board Member
Michael Werneke, Board Member
Sher Paul Singh, Board Member
Brian Ramsey, Board Member

An assemblage of professionals whose interest in the complex and diverse practice of distribution and logistics is a common bond.
600 Members
Founded in 1956

11272 **Paperboard Packaging Council**
1350 Main Street
Suite 1508
Springfield, MA 01103-1670

413-686-9191; Fax: 413-747-7777
www.ppcnet.org
Facebook, Twitter, LinkedIn, Youtube

Kyle Eldred, Chair
Charles Johnson, Vice Chair
Marc Anderson, Director at large
Michael Ukropina, Director at large
Steven Levkoff, Treasurer

The leading industry association serving suppliers and converters of all forms of paperboard packaging, works to grow, promote, and protect the paperboard packaging industry while providing its members with resources and tools to compete effectively and successfully in the marketplace.
Founded in 1967

11273 **Petroleum Packaging Council**
ATD Management Inc.
1519 Via Tulipan
San Clemente, CA 92673

949-369-7102; Fax: 949-366-1057
www.ppcouncil.org
LinkedIn

John Whittenhall, President
Elizabeth Wagg, Vice President
Sam Merenda, Secretary/ Treasurer
Darren Booth, Assistant Treasurer
Carolyn Booms, Director

Provides technical leadership and education to the petroleum packaging industry.
400 Members
Founded in 1950

11274 **Pressure Sensitive Tape Council**
One Parkview Plaza
Suite 800
Oakbrook Terrace, IL 60181

630-544-5048; Fax: 630-544-5055
info@pstc.org
www.pstc.org
Twitter, LinkedIn, Flickr

Michael Merkx, President
Curt Rutsky, Vice President
Charlie McKenna, Treasurer
Brad Boelkins, Directors
Tom Boyle, Directors

Trade association for tape manufacturers and affiliate suppliers, dedicated to helping the industry produce quality pressure sensitive adhesive tape products in the global marketplace. PSTC provides education and training, works with ASTM and global trade organizations to harmonize test methods and monitors legislative and regulatory activities.
Founded in 1953

11275 **Recycled Paperboard Technical Association**
P.O. Box 5774
Elgin, IL 60121-5774

847-622-2544; Fax: 847-622-2546
rpta@rpta.org
www.rpta.org

David Briere, President
Mark Sklar, Vice President
Peter Traeger, Treasurer
Amy E. Schaffer, Ex-Officio
Tim Hagenbuch, Chair

An association of US, Canadian and overseas companies interested in cooperative research and development in the industry.
33 Members
Founded in 1953

11276 **Retail Packaging Association**
105 Eastern Ave.
Suite 104
Annapolis, MD 21403

410-940-6459; Fax: 410-263-1659
info@retailpackaging.org
www.retailpackaging.org
Facebook, Twitter, Pinterest, Instagram

Molly Alton Mullins, Executive Director

Serves its members and the entire retail packaging industry. Also organizes the largest trade show and conference of its kind in the US. A self-governed not-for-profit organization comprised of professionals involved in all facets of production and distribution of retail packaging products.
Founded in 1989

11277 **Reusable Industrial Packaging Association**
51 Monroe Street
Suite 812
Rockville, MD 20850

301-577-3786; Fax: 301-577-6476
prankin@ripaus.com
www.reusablepackaging.org
Facebook, Twitter

Ricky Buckner, Chair
Jerry Butler, Vice Chair
Paul W. Rankin, President
Dan Burek, Treasurer
Tim O'Bryan, Secretary
Founded in 1942

11278 **Technical Association of the Pulp & Paper Industry**
15 Technology Parkway South
Suite 115
Peachtree Corners, GA 30092

770-446-1400
800-322-8686; Fax: 770-446-6947
webmaster@tappi.org
www.tappi.org
Facebook, Twitter, LinkedIn

Chris Luettgen, Chair
Paul R. Durocher, Vice Chair
Larry N. Montague, President & CEO
Peter R. Augustine, Director
Medwick V. Byrd, Director

To engage the people and resources of our association in providing technically sound solutions to the workplace problems and opportunities that challenge our current and future members.
12000 Members
Founded in 1915

11279 **The Independent Packaging Association Converters**
113 S. West Street
3rd Floor
Alexandria, VA 22314

703-836-2422
877-836-2422; Fax: 703-836-2795
info@aiccbox.org
www.aiccbox.org
Facebook, Twitter, LinkedIn, YouTube

Mark Williams, Chairman
Tony Schleich, First Vice Chairman
Joseph M. Palmeri, Vice Chairman
Jeff Pallini, Associate Vice Chairman
John Forrey, Director at Large

Provides a forum for discussion of problems and offers educational programs and seminars.
1100 Members
Founded in 1974

11280 **Transportation Intermediaries Association**
1625 Prince St
Suite 200
Alexandria, VA 22314-2883

703-299-5700; Fax: 703-836-0123
info@tianet.org
www.tianet.org

Robert Voltmann, President
Jeff Tucker, Chair
Jason Beardall, Vice Chair
Michael Riccio, Treasurer
Barcy Vidt, Secretary

Education and policy organization for North American transportation intermediaries. The only national association representing the interests of all third party transportation service providers. Members include logistics management firms, property brokers, perishable commodities brokers, freight forwarders, intermodal marketers and ocean and air forwarders.
700 Members
Founded in 1977

11281 **Transportation Marketing Communications Association (TMCA)**
9382 Oak Avenue
Waconia, MN 55387
952-442-5638; Fax: 952-442-3941
www.tmcatoday.org

John Ferguson, President
Tom Nightingale, VP
Tracy Robinson, Treasurer
Edward Moritz, Secretary
Brian Everett, Executive Director

The only association serving transportation marketing, sales and communications pros in all modes and market segments of the North American transportation industry.
225 Members
Founded in 1924

Newsletters

11282 **Air Cargo Report**
Phillips Publishing
1201 Seven Locks Road
Potomac, MD 20854-2931

301-541-1400; Fax: 301-424-2098
info@accessintel.com
www.accessintel.com

Richard Koulbanis, Publisher
Donald Pazour, CEO/President

Reports on emerging trends and business strategies for airline cargo, integrator, freight forwarding and all-cargo carrier operations.
Circulation: 1430

11283 **CanTube Bulletin**
Composite Can and Tube Institute
50 S Pickett Street
Suite 110
Alexandria, VA 22304-7206

703-823-7234; Fax: 703-823-7237
ccti@cctiwdc.org
www.cctiwdc.org

Excellent source of information about issues affecting this industry, as well as updates on CCTI activities.
Frequency: Bi-Monthly
Circulation: 800+

11284 **E-Catalyst Industry Update**
Adhesive & Sealant Council

7101 Wisconsin Avenue
Suite 990
Bethesda, MD 20814

301-986-9700; Fax: 301-986-9795
data@ascouncil.org
www.ascouncil.org

William Allmond, President

Delivers the latest ASC news, industry information and end-user trends.
Frequency: Monthly

11285 **Mail Center Management Report**
Institute of Management and Administration
3 Bethesda Metro Center
Suite 250
Bethesda, MD 20814-5377

800-372-1033; Fax: 800-253-0332
www.ioma.com

Shows you how to improve mail center productivity, reduce costs, and get you the recognition you deserve through buying and leasing new equipment, negotiating rates with carriers, and much more. Shows proven techniques to improve relations with the USPS and other service vendors. You'll find tactics for improving your dealing with senior management, purchasing, marketing and logistics.

11286 **Packaging Strategies**
Packaging Strategies
600 Willowbrook Lane
Suite 610
West Chester, PA 19382

610-436-4220
800-524-7225; Fax: 610-436-6277
www.packstrat.com
Facebook, Twitter, LinkedIn

Joe Pryweller, Editor/Conference Director
Janet Martinelli, Conference/Study Support Manager
Randy Green, Publisher
Karen Vaillancourt, Sales Manager
Karen Close, Senior Events Manager

A subscription newsletter focusing on news and analysis of technology and business issues in the packaging industry. Also producer of 4 conferences per year: structural packagingsummit, food packaging technologies summit, global pouch firum, sustainable packaging forum and multi-client industry studies.
Cost: $497.00
8 Pages
ISSN: 8755-6189
Founded in 1983
Printed in 2 colors on matte stock

11287 **PostScripts**
Association of Marketing Service Providers
1800 Diagonal Road
Suite 320
Alexandria, VA 22314-2806

703-836-9200; Fax: 703-548-8204
kgarner@mfsanet.org
www.amsp.org

Joseph P. Truncale, President & CEO

Each issue of PostScripts highlights a theme relevant to mailing or fulfillment operations, such as production management or information technology.
Frequency: Monthly

11288 **Transportation Intermediaries Update**
Transportation Intermediaries Association
1625 Prince St
Suite 200
Alexandria, VA 22314-2883

703-299-5700; Fax: 703-836-0123
voltmann@tianet.org
www.tianet.org

Robert Voltmann, President

Education and policy organization for North American transportation intermediaries. TIA is the only national association representing the interests of all third party transportation service providers. The members of TIA include logistics management firms, property brokers, perishable commodities brokers, freight forwarders, intermodal marketers, ocean and air forwarders, and NVOCC's.
700 Pages
Frequency: Monthly

Magazines & Journals

11289 **Advanced Packaging**
PennWell Publishing Company
98 Spit Brook Rd
Suite L11
Nashua, NH 03062-5737

603-891-0123; Fax: 603-891-9294
lwilliam@pennwell.com
www.pennwell.com

Christine Shaw, VP
Gail Flower, Editor

Focuses on materials, assembly, design and reliability issues facing the global packaging community.
Cost: $88.00
Frequency: Monthly
Circulation: 22,000
Founded in 1910

11290 **Air Cargo Focus**
Cargo Network Services Corporation
703 Waterford Way
Suite 680
Miami, FL 33126-4677

786-413-1000; Fax: 786-413-1005
cns@cnsc.us
www.cnsc.net

Fernando Garcia, VP
Anthony P Calabrese, President

A forum for professionals involved in the sale , marketing, services and movement of air cargo.
Frequency: Quarterly
Circulation: 8000
Founded in 1986

11291 **Air Cargo News**
PO Box 98
Portage, MI 49081-98

718-479-0716; Fax: 718-740-0761
judy@aircargonews.com
www.aircargonews.com

Geoffrey Arend, Publisher

CAB regulations, and other news of interest to those in the air cargo industry.
Cost: $39.95
Frequency: Monthly
Circulation: 100,000
Founded in 1975

11292 **American Shipper**
Howard Publications
300 W Adams Street Suite 600
PO Box 4728
Jacksonville, FL 32201-4728

904-355-2601
800-874-6422; Fax: 904-791-8836
www.americanshipper.com

Hayes H Howard, Publisher
Gary G. Burrows, Managing Editor

Provides those involved in domestic and global supply chain management with news and information of a strategic nature, useful in the formation of logistics polices and partnerships.
Cost: $30.00
100 Pages
Frequency: Monthly
Circulation: 13487
ISSN: 1074-8350
Founded in 1951
Printed in 4 colors on glossy stock

11293 **Cargo Facts**
Air Cargo Managment Group
520 Pike St
Suite 1010
Seattle, WA 98101-4058

206-587-6537; Fax: 206-587-6540
www.cargofacts.com

Edwin Laird, Manager
David Harris, Editor
Jackie Edinger, Circulation Manager

Includes fiscal reports, freighter aircraft transactions, short segments, international perspectives, and industry updates.
Cost: $395.00
24 Pages
Frequency: Monthly
Circulation: 7500
ISSN: 0278-0801
Founded in 1980

11294 **Cosmetic Personal Care Packaging**
O&B Communications
11444 W Olympic Boulevard
Los Angeles, CA 90064-1303

310-445-4200; Fax: 310-445-4299
www.cpcpkg.com

Patricia Spinner, Publisher
John Bethune, Editorial Director
Jennifer Kwok, Managing Editor

Provides information on new packaging containers, materials, equipment and services that are involved with the cosmetic industry.
Cost: $60.00
Frequency: Monthly
Circulation: 12,500
Founded in 1996

11295 **Courier Times**
Courier Times
27-16 168th Street
Flushing, NY 11358-1130

718-291-1253; Fax: 718-359-1959
www.couriertimes.com

Bill Goodman, Editor
C Tsamis, Owner

New products vital to the industry, discusses insurance and technology updates, also offers customer service guidelines.
Cost: $39.00
Frequency: Monthly
Circulation: 1100

11296 **Electronic Packaging & Production**
Reed Business Information

360 Park Ave S
New York, NY 10010-1737

646-746-6400; Fax: 646-756-7583
corporatecommunications@reedbusiness.com
www.reedbusiness.com

John Poulin, CEO
Michael Sweeney, Editorial Director
James Reed, Owner

Edited for engineers and managers who are involved in packaging design, printed circuit board fabrication and assembly, and production testing of electronic circuits, systems, products and equipment.
Founded in 1960

11297 **Flexible Packaging**
Flexible Packaging Association
971 Corporate Blvd
Suite 403
Linthicum, MD 21090-2253

410-694-0800; Fax: 410-694-0900
fpa@flexpack.org
www.flexpack.org

Marla Donahue, President

Offering subscribers up-to-the-minute information on industry news and trends, material and substrate developments, innovations in equipment, and the latest in business management. The only magazine in the market that dedicates 100 percent of its editorial content and circulation to flexible packaging converters.
Frequency: Monthly

11298 **Food & Beverage Packaging**
155 Pfingsten Road
Suite 205
Deerfield, IL 60015

847-405-4000; Fax: 847-405-4100
www.foodandbeveragepackaging.com

Randy Green, Publisher

Identifies and analyzes the market trends and packaging solutions that matter to food and beverage processors.
Frequency: Monthly
Circulation: 75140
Founded in 1959

11299 **Harbour & Shipping**
Progress Publishing Company, Ltd
1489 Marine Drive
Suite 510
West Vancouver, BC V7 T1

604-922-6717; Fax: 604-922-1739

Allison Smith, Editor
Murray McLellan, Publisher/Marketing

Serves the deep sea and coastal shipping, and ship building, repair and supply industries of Canada and worldwide. Accepts advertising.
Cost: $60.00
Frequency: Monthly
Circulation: 2200
ISSN: 0017-7637
Printed in 4 colors on glossy stock

11300 **International Paper Board Industry**
Brunton Publications & NV Public
43 Main Street
Avon By The Sea, NJ 07717-1051

732-502-0500; Fax: 732-502-9606
jcurley@NVPublications.com
nvpublications.com

Mike Brunton, Publisher
Jim Curley, Editor
Tom Vilardi, President

Information on corrugated paper and converting industry, encompassing news and production worldwide.
Cost: $60.00
Frequency: Monthly
Circulation: 6500

11301 **Journal of HazMat Transportation**
Packaging Research International
404 Price St
West Chester, PA 19382-3531

610-436-8292
877-429-7447; Fax: 610-436-9422
www.hazmatship.com

Vincent A Vitollo, Owner

A professionally prepared technical reporting system, focused exlusively on explaining changes to the hazardous materials transportation regulations. Thoroughly covers and provides technical reviews of the US 49CFR, International Civil Aviation Organization Technical Instructions, the International Maritime Dangerous Goods Code, and the European Road and Rail Regulations.
Cost: $209.00
Circulation: 1000
Founded in 1990
Printed in 4 colors on matte stock

11302 **MAIL: The Journal of Communication Distribution**
1 Elmcoft Road
Stamford, CT 06926-700

203-356-5000
800-672-6937; Fax: 203-739-3488
www.pb.com

Meg Reiley, President
Ina Steiner, Publisher

Manages change and positions customers for both tactical and long-term success with innovative, cost-effective, end-to-end messaging solutions.

11303 **Modern Bulk Transporter**
Tunnell Publications
PO Box 66010
Houston, TX 77266

713-523-8124; Fax: 713-523-8384
www.bulktransporter.com/
Facebook, Twitter

Charles Wilson, Editor
Martine Ewing, Advertising Director
Mary Davis, Associate Editor

Serves the truck industry that transports petroleum and petroleum products. Accepts advertising.
Frequency: Monthly
Circulation: 15000

11304 **PARCEL**
RB Publishing
2901 International Lane
Madison, WI 53704-3102

608-778-8785
800-536-1992; Fax: 608-241-8666
www.parcelindustry.com
LinkedIn

Marll Thiede, CEO
Chad Griepentrog, President
Mike Beacom, Editor

Brings the insights needed to improve parcel operations and keep costs under control. PARCEL gives you access to experts who look at the entire process, from order entry to the shipping dock to customer delivery, to give you information you can use.
Circulation: 30000
Founded in 1988

11305 **Packaging Digest Magazine**
UBM Canon
1200 Jorie Blvd.
Suite 230
Oak Brook, IL 60523-2260

630-990-2371; Fax: 630-990-8894
packagingdigest@ubm.com
www.packagingdigest.com

John Kalkowski, Editorial Director
Lisa McTigue Pierce, Editor
Jenni Spinner, Senior Editor

Serves the manufacturing, wholesale and service industries.
Cost: $75.00
Frequency: Monthly
Founded in 1963

11306 **Packaging Technology & Engineering**
North American Publishing Company
1500 Spring Garden St
12th Floor
Philadelphia, PA 19130-4094

215-238-5300
800-777-8074; Fax: 215-238-5342
customerservice@napco.com
www.napco.com

Ned S Borowsky, CEO
Richard Soloway, CEO/President
Glen Reynolds, Circulation Manager
Nolle Skodzinski, Editor

Reports on environmental concerns, legislation and regulation, product design, material availability, and economic trends.
Cost: $69.00
Frequency: Monthly
Circulation: 20271
Founded in 1958

11307 **Packaging World**
Summit Publishing Company
330 N Wabash Ave
Suite 2401
Chicago, IL 60611-7618

312-222-1010; Fax: 312-222-1310
reynolds@packworld.com
www.packworld.com

Lloyd Ferguson, Owner
Joseph Angel, Vice President
Patrick Reynolds, VP/Editor
Timothy Hammack, Circulation Director
Jim George, Marketing & Design Editor

Serves the manufacturing, wholesaling, and service industries.
Frequency: Monthly
Circulation: 92547
ISSN: 1073-7367
Founded in 1994
Printed in 4 colors on matte stock

11308 **Paperboard Packaging**
2835 North Sheffield Avenue
Suite 226
Chicago, IL 60657

773-880-2234; Fax: 773-880-2244
www.packaging-online.com
Facebook, Twitter

Marisa Palmieri, Editor

Publication edited for management and other key personnel involved in the manufacturing and marketing segments of the paperboard packaging industry.
Cost: $39.00
Frequency: Monthly
ISSN: 0031-1227

11309 **Pharmaceutical & Medical Packaging News**
Canon Communications

11444 W Olympic Blvd
Suite 900
Los Angeles, CA 90064-1555

310-445-4200; Fax: 310-445-4299
www.devicelink.com

Charlie Mc Curdy, President
Daphne Allen, Managing Editor
Bob Michaels, Managing Editor
Nicole Welter, Account Executive

Information and news on events, new technology, industry trends, regulatory matters, and health care trade associations for professionals involved in the pharmaceutical and medical product packaging industry.
Cost: $150.00
Frequency: Monthly
Circulation: 20000
ISSN: 1081-5481
Founded in 1978

11310 **Refrigerated Transporter**
Penton
PO Box 66010
Houston, TX 77266

713-523-8124
800-880-0368; Fax: 713-523-8384
refrigeratedtransporter.com

Ray Anderson, Publisher

The information source for those involved in the transportation and distribution of refrigerated products ranging from food to pharmaceuticals, from film and cosmetics to chemicals. Provides practical information derived from the experience of businesses in the field as well as up-to-the-minute news on developments and equipment for the industry.
Frequency: Monthly
Circulation: 15023
Founded in 1905

11311 **TAPPI Journal**
Technical Association of the Pulp & Paper Industry
15 Technology Parkway South
Norcross, GA 30092

770-446-1400
800-322-8686; Fax: 770-446-6947
webmaster@tappi.org
www.tappi.org

Larry N. Montague, President & CEO

Serves domestic and international pulp, paper, paperboard, packaging and converting industries; manufacturers and suppliers of machinery, equipment, chemicals and other material.
Cost: $350.00
130 Pages
Frequency: Monthly
Circulation: 5300
ISSN: 0734-1415
Founded in 1949
Printed in 4 colors on glossy stock

11312 **Trucker's Connection**
Megan Cullingford
5960 Crooked Creek Road
Suite 15
Norcross, GA 30092

770-416-0927; Fax: 770-416-1734
www.truckersconnection.com

Megan Cullingford, General Manager
Dan Barnhill, Editor
Reid Ramsay, Production Manager

Published for the use of long haul, over-the-road truck drivers, owner operators, small trucking company fleet owners, safety and recruiting of personnel for trucking companies in the US and Canada.
Frequency: Monthly
Circulation: 165000
Founded in 1986
Printed in 4 colors on glossy stock

11313 **World Wide Shipping (WWS)**
World Wide Shipping Guide
16302 Byrnwyck Ln
Odessa, FL 33556-2807

813-920-4788; Fax: 813-920-8268
www.wwship.com

Lee Di Paci, Publisher
Barbara Edwards, Marketing Manager
Bob Susor, Marketing Manager

Dedicated to the interests of North American exporters, importers, distributors, freight forwarders, NVOCC's and customs brokers requiring freight tranportation services and equipment.
Cost: $32.00
32 Pages
Frequency: Fortnightly
Circulation: 9000
ISSN: 1060-7900
Founded in 1919
Printed in 4 colors on glossy stock

Trade Shows

11314 **AMSP Annual Conference**
Association of Marketing Service Providers
1800 Diagonal Road
Suite 320
Alexandria, VA 22314-2806

703-836-9200; Fax: 703-548-8204
kgarner@mfsanet.org
www.amsp.org

Joseph P. Truncale, President & CEO
Leo Raymond, VP, Postal & Member Relations

Opportunity for marketing professionals to network, collaborate, and learn.
Frequency: Annual

11315 **International Molded Fiber Packaging Seminar**
International Molded Fiber Association
1425 W Mequon Rd
Suite C
Mequon, WI 53092-3262

262-241-0522; Fax: 262-241-3766
info@imfa.org
www.imfa.org
Facebook, Twitter, LinkedIn

Cassandra Niesing, Asst. Director
Joseph Grygny, Chairman

Opportunity to network, learn, and grow in the molded fiber industry.
Founded in 1996

11316 **LabelExpo**
Tarsus Group
9501 W Devon Avenue
Rosemont, IL 60018-4811

847-292-3700; Fax: 847-318-1506
www.tarsus.com

Steve Krogulski, Manager

The largest event for the lable, web printing, product decoration, converting and packaging industry in the Americas.
13700 Attendees
Frequency: Annual/September

11317 **Outlook & Strategies Conference**
Paperboard Packaging Council
1350 Main Street
Suite 1508
Springfield, MA 01103-1670

413-686-9191; Fax: 413-747-7777
www.ppcnet.org

Ben Markens, President
Lou Kornet, Vice President/Chief of Staff

Industry leaders specializing in sustainability, the economy, and education will come together to impart their knowledge, experience, and business predictions.
325 Attendees
Frequency: Annual/March

11318 **PROPAK Asia**
Reed Exhibition Companies
383 Main Avenue
PO Box 6059
Norwalk, CT 06851

203-840-4800; Fax: 203-840-9628

One hundred and seventy four exhibitors for an audience of manufacturers, packaging design and development professionals. International food processing and packaging technology exhibition.
Frequency: Annual

11319 **Shipper/Carrier Marketplace**
Express Carriers Association
9532 Liberia Ave
Suite 752
Manassas, VA 20110-1719

703-361-1058
866-322-7447; Fax: 703-361-5274
www.expresscarriers.org

Stuart Hyden, President
Lance Adams, First VP
Fiona Morgan, Executive Director

Brings about 500 representatives from regional and national companies together to explore business relationships through face-to-face interviews
500 Attendees
Frequency: Annual

11320 **Transportation Intermediaries Annual Convention & Trade Show**
Transportation Intermediaries Association
1625 Prince Street
Suite 200
Alexandria, VA 22314

703-299-5700; Fax: 703-836-0123
voltmann@tianet.org
www.tianet.org
Facebook, Twitter, LinkedIn

Robert Voltmann, President/CEO

The only meeting for third-party logistics providers. A once a year opportunity to interact with representatives from throughout North America and abroad. Key decision makers with buying authority attend this meeting.
700 Attendees
Frequency: Annual/March
Founded in 1978

11321 **World Packaging Conference**
Reed Business Information
2000 Clearwater Drive
Oak Brook, IL 60523

630-740-0825; Fax: 630-288-8686
www.reedbusiness.com

Jay Singh, Conference Chair
Bruce Harte, Consultant

One thousand three hundred and fourteen booths.
500 Attendees
Frequency: Annual/June

Directories & Databases

11322 **ABS International Directory of Offices**
American Bureau of Shipping

16855 Northchase Dr
Houston, TX 77060-6006

281-673-2800; Fax: 281-877-5801
www.abs-group.com

Tony Nassif, CEO

Over 175 operations offices of the bureau worldwide are listed.
122 Pages
Frequency: Semiannual

11323 Air Freight Directory
Air Cargo
1819 Bay Ridge Avenue
Suite 1
Annapolis, MD 21403-2899

410-805-5578
800-747-6505; Fax: 410-268-3154

Debbi Mayes

Gives contact details for 35,000 global air cargo companies including 24,000 freight forwarders and 1700 airports. Track and trace shipments, locate airfreight personnel, or just follow the latest air cargo industry news.
Cost: $84.00
Frequency: Bi-Monthly

11324 American Drop-Shippers Directory
World Wide Trade Service
PO Box 283
Medina, WA 98039-0283

206-236-4795

Over 200 firms are listed that are willing to drop ship single item orders at wholesale prices for mail order and other direct marketers.
Cost: $15.00
36 Pages
Frequency: Biennial
Circulation: 5,000

11325 Commercial Carrier Journal: Buyers' Guide Issue
Reed Business Information
1 Chilton Way
Wayne, PA 19089-0002

646-746-6400; Fax: 646-746-7433
www.reedbusiness.com
Facebook, Twitter, LinkedIn

Gerald F Standley, Editor
Stuart Whayman, CFO

List of vehicles, components and accessories suppliers for the truck and bus fleet markets.
Cost: $10.00
Frequency: Annual/October
Circulation: 85,000

11326 Commercial Carrier Journal: Top 100 Issue
Reed Business Information
360 Park Avenue
New York, NY 10010

212-450-0067; Fax: 646-746-7433
www.ccjdigital.com

List of top 100 for-hire motor carriers, ranked by gross revenues; also the next 200 carriers in gross revenue.
Cost: $10.00
Frequency: Annual/August
Circulation: 85,000

11327 Directory of Contract Packagers and their Facilities
Institute of Packaging Professionals
Ste 123
1833 Centre Point Cir
Naperville, IL 60563-4848

630-544-5050
800-432-4085; Fax: 630-544-5055
info@iopp.org
www.iopp.org

Edwin Landon, Executive Director
Patrick Farrey, General Manager

More than 400 contract packagers in the US and abroad.
Frequency: Biennial

11328 Directory of Corrugated Plants
Fibre Box Association
25 Northwest Point Blvd
Suite 510
Elk Grove Village, IL 60007

847-364-9600; Fax: 847-364-9639
fba@fibrebox.org
www.fibrebox.org
LinkedIn

Over 1,600 manufacturing facilities in the North American corrugated and solid fibre industry. Distributed in microsoft excel spreadsheet.
Cost: $200.00

11329 Directory of Freight Forwarders and Custom House Brokers
International Wealth Success
PO Box 186
Merrick, NY 11566-0186

516-766-5850
800-323-0548; Fax: 516-766-5919
admin@iwsmoney.com
www.iwsmoney.com
Facebook, LinkedIn

Tyler G Hicks, President

Lists hundreds of these firms throughout the U.S. who help in the export/import business.
Cost: $20.00
106 Pages
Frequency: Annual
ISBN: 1-561503-46-0
Founded in 1980

11330 Directory of Packaging Consultants
Institute of Packaging Professionals
Ste 123
1833 Centre Point Cir
Naperville, IL 60563-4848

630-544-5050
800-432-4085; Fax: 630-544-5055
info@iopp.org
www.iopp.org
Facebook, Twitter, LinkedIn

Edwin Landon, Executive Director
Patrick Farrey, General Manager

Packaging consultants in the US.
Cost: $25.00
Frequency: Annual

11331 Directory of US Flexographic Packaging Sources
JPC Directories
PO Box 488
Plainview, NY 11803-0488

516-822-6861

Joel J Shulman, Editor

Offers information on narrow web and wide web printer/converters and suppliers to the printing industry.
125 Pages
Frequency: Annual
Circulation: 50,000

11332 Flexible Packaging Association Membership Directory
Flexible Packaging Association
971 Corporate Boulevard
Suite 403
Linthicum, MD 21090-4769

410-694-0800; Fax: 410-694-0900
fpa@flexpack.org

Over 200 member companies that manufacture flexible packaging and supplies used in this industry are profiled.
Frequency: Annual
Circulation: 20,000

11333 Food & Beverage Market Place
Grey House Publishing
4919 Route 22
PO Box 56
Amenia, NY 12501

518-789-8700
800-562-2139; Fax: 845-373-6390
books@greyhouse.com
www.greyhouse.com
Facebook, Twitter

Leslie Mackenzie, Publisher
Richard Gottlieb, Editor

This information packed three-volume set is the most powerful buying and marketing guide for the US food and beverage industry. Includes thousands of industry and transportation listings. Contains a significant chapter on food and beverage transportation.
Cost: $595.00
2000 Pages
Frequency: Annual
ISBN: 1-592373-61-5
Founded in 1981

11334 Food & Beverage Marketplace: Online Database
Grey House Publishing
4919 Route 22
PO Box 56
Amenia, NY 12501
518-789-8700
800-562-2139; Fax: 845-373-6390
gold@greyhouse.com
gold.greyhouse.com
Facebook, Twitter

Richard Gottlieb, President
Leslie Mackenzie, Publisher

This complete updated Food & Beverage Market Place: Online Database is the go-to source for the food and beverage industry. Anyone involved in the food and beverage industry needs this 'industry bible' and the important contacts to develop critical research data that can make for successful business growth.
Frequency: Annual
Founded in 1981

11335 Modern Bulk Transporter: Buyers Guide
Tunnell Publications
PO Box 66010
Houston, TX 77266

713-523-8124; Fax: 713-523-8384

Charles Wilson, Editor

Directory of suppliers of products or services for companies operating tank trucks.
Frequency: Annual/October
Circulation: 16,000

11336 NCBFAA Membership Directory
National Customs Brokers & Forwarders Association
1200 18th St NW
Suite 901
Washington, DC 20036-2572

202-466-0222; Fax: 202-466-0226
www.ncbfaa.org

About 600 customs brokers, international air cargo agents, and freight forwarders in the

United States.
Cost: $24.00
Frequency: Annual

11337 **National Motor Carrier Directory and Additional Products**
Transportation Technical Services
500 Lafayette Boulevard
Fredericksburg, VA 22401-6070

540-899-9872
888-665-9887; Fax: 540-899-1948
truckinfo@ttstrucks.com
www.ttstrucks.com/www.fleetseek.com

Ronald D Roth, Executive VP

Over 46,000 motor carriers with revenues of $100,000 or more.
Cost: $495.00
1781 Pages
Frequency: Annual/November
Founded in 1989

11338 **Official Container Directory**
Advanstar Communications
641 Lexington Ave
8th Floor
New York, NY 10022-4503

212-951-6600; Fax: 212-951-6793
info@advanstar.com
www.advanstar.com

Joseph Loggia, CEO

Directory of services and supplies to the industry.
200 Pages
Circulation: 5,000

11339 **Official Freight Shippers Guide**
Official Motor Freight Guides
1700 W Cortland Street
Chicago, IL 60622-1121

773-342-1000
800-621-4650; Fax: 773-489-0482

E Koch, Editor
Eric J Robison, Editor

Major air, rail, water and motor carriers published in three local editions covering Chicago, New York and St. Louis.
Cost: $55.00
516 Pages
Frequency: Annual

11340 **Official Motor Carrier Directory**
Official Motor Freight Guides
1700 W Cortland Street
Chicago, IL 60622-1121

773-342-1000
800-621-4650; Fax: 773-489-0482

Edward K Koch, Editor

Approximately 2,100 general and specialized motor carriers and air cargo carriers; federal and state agencies concerned with the trucking industry; tariff publishing bureaus, US and Canadian port authorities; state associations.
Cost: $59.50
Frequency: SemiAnnual
Circulation: 6,000

11341 **Official Motor Freight Guide**
C&C Publishing Company
1700 W Cortland Street
Chicago, IL 60622-1121

773-536-2050

This directory is published in over 21 regional editions that list air and water freight transportation, motor carriers and warehouse facilities for the metropolitan areas of Baltimore, Boston, Chicago, Cincinnati, Cleveland, Denver, Detroit, Evansville, Ft. Wayne, Indianapolis, Kansas City, Philadelphia, Pittsburgh, Quad Cities and Toledo.
Cost: $45.00
500 Pages
Frequency: Semiannual

11342 **PMMI Packaging Machinery Directory**
Packaging Machinery Manufacturers Institute (PMMI)
11911 Freedom Drive
Suite 600
Reston, VA 20190

571-612-3200; Fax: 703-243-8556
info@pmmi.org
www.pmmi.org

Charles D. Yuska, President & CEO
Corinne G. Mulligan, Executive Assistant
Caroline Abromavage, Operations Director
Heather Harvey, Membership Manager
Fred Hayes, Technical Services Director

Contains listings of packaging and processing companies that make up the membership of the Packaging Machinery Manufacturers Institute (PMMI).
800+ Members
Founded in 1933

11343 **Packaging Digest: Machinery Materials Guide Issue**
Delta Communications
Ste 300
20900 Swenson Dr
Waukesha, WI 53186-4050

262-429-9111; Fax: 262-546-8820
delta@deltacommunications.com

Barbara McDonough, Editor

List of more than 3,100 manufacturers of machinery and materials for the packaging industry, and about 260 contract packagers.
Frequency: Annual

11344 **Rauch Guide to the US Packaging Industry**
Impact Marketing Consultants
PO Box 1226
Manchester Center, VT 05255

802-362-2325
802-362-3693
www.impactmarket.com

Donald R Dykes, Editor
C Verbanic, Editor

Analyzes the US packaging industry, with data on industry economics, raw materials, major products, and unique profiles of 50% producers.
Cost: $495.00
Frequency: Triennial

11345 **Transportation Telephone Tickler**
Commonwealth Business Media
50 Millstone Rd
Building 400, Suite 200
East Windsor, NJ 08520-1418

609-371-7700
800-215-6084; Fax: 609-371-7879
www.cbizmedia.com

Alan Glass, CEO
Edith Chaudoin-Stahlberger, Editor

Provides vital contact information for 24,000 suppliers of 160 types of transportation services in the US, Canada, Caribbean and parts of Latin America.
Cost: $124.95
2425 Pages
Frequency: Annual
Founded in 1949

11346 **Who's Who & What's What in Packaging**
481 Carlisle Drive
Herndon, VA 20170-4830

703-471-8922

Offers information on members of the Institute of Packaging Professionals, including placement firms, colleges that offer packaging curricula, and related organizations.
Cost: $125.00
240 Pages
Frequency: Annual

Industry Web Sites

11347 **http://gold.greyhouse.com**
G.O.L.D Grey House OnLine Databases

Grey House Publishing's online database platform, GOLD, offers Quick Search, Keyword Search and Expert Search for most business sectors including freight, packaging and transportation markets. The GOLD platform makes finding the information you need quick and easy - whether you're a novice searcher or an experienced database user. All of Grey House's directory products are available for subscription on the GOLD platform.

11348 **plastics.americanchemistry.com**
Polystyrene Packaging Council

Links to other associations.

11349 **www.adhesives.org**
Adhesive and Sealant Council

Association for the packaging industry.

11350 **www.aiccbox.org**
Association of Independent Corrugated Converters

Provides a forum for discussion of problems and offers educational programs and seminars.

11351 **www.amsp.org**
Association of Marketing Service Providers

Formerly known as the Mailing & Fulfillment Service Association, the Association of Marketing Service Providers provides educational content, networking opportunities, and legislative advocacy.

11352 **www.corrugated.org**
Corrugated Packaging Council

Develops and coordinates industry-wide programs to address corrugated packaging issues. The Council's mission is to inform consumers, manufacturers, retailers and government officials of corrugated packaging's performance and environmental attributes.

11353 **www.fibca.com**
Flexible Intermediate Bulk Container Association

Facebook, Twitter

11354 **www.fibrebox.org**
Fibre Box Association

Represents 90 percent of the US corrugated paper board, packaging, manufacturing industry.

11355 **www.flexpack.org**
Flexible Packaging Association

Trade association of manufacturers, converters and suppliers of paper, metal foil and plastic or cellulose film.

11356 **www.fpi.org**
Foodservice & Packaging Institute

Sanitation and environmental information, plus programs and services.

11357 **www.ftd.com**
Florists' Transworld Delivery Association
Has an annual budget of approximately $140 million.

11358 **www.geminishippers.com**
Gemini Shippers Group
Shippers association with global contracts for all commodities.

11359 **www.graysonassociates.com**
Grayson Associates
Association for those interested in marketing analysis of the package goods industry.

11360 **www.greyhouse.com**
Grey House Publishing
Authoritative reference directories for most business sectors including freight, packaging, and transportation markets. Users can search the online databases with varied search criteria allowing for custom searches by product category, geographic area, sales volume, keyword, subject and more. Full Grey House catalog and online ordering also available.

11361 **www.homefair.com**
Offers comprehensive content and services for people moving to a new home or relocating to another community.

11362 **www.iicl.org**
Institute of International Container Lessors
Represents international container and chassis leasing industry in technical, governmental and legal matters. Publishes leading worldwide manuals on inspection and repair of containers and inspector and maintenance of chassis. Sponsors container and chassis inspection examination once a year in over 40 countries and chassis examination in North America.

11363 **www.lcaships.com**
Lake Carriers Association
Members are US- Flag Great Lakes vessel operators engaged in transporting iron ore, coal, grain, limestone, cement and petroleum products.

11364 **www.mfsanet.org/**
Mailing & Fulfillment Service Association
For over 80 years, this national trade association has been serving the mailing and fulfillment services industry by providing opportunities for learning and professional development of the managers of these companies.

11365 **www.niphle.com**
National Institute of Packaging, Handling and
Logistics

Originally the DC chapter of the Society of Packaging and Handling engineers, the Institute became independent in an effort to give more emphasis on the governmental responsibilities of its members.

11366 **www.nmaonline.org**
National Meat Association
Association for meat packers, processors and jobbers through out the USA.

11367 **www.packagingnetwork.com**
Packaging Network
Searchable database of food industry related items.

11368 **www.palletcentral.com**
National Wooden Pallet & Container Association
Membership roster, tech talk, publications and industry watch.

11369 **www.pmmi.org**
Packaging Machinery Manufacturers Institute (PMMI)
Facebook, Twitter, LinkedIn, YouTube, Instagram
Association representing manufacturers of packaging and packaging-related converting equipment.

11370 **www.polysort.com**
Polysort LLC
Links to related companies.

11371 **www.ppcnet.org**
Paperboard Packaging Council
Represents industry before legislative and regulatory bodies. Conducts technical seminars on sales, marketing, costs and management methods. Publishes a quarterly newsletter

11372 **www.ppcouncil.org**
Petroleum Packaging Council
Provides technical leadership and education to the petroleum packaging industry.

11373 **www.tianet.org**
Transportation Intermediaries Association
Education and policy organization for North American transportation intermediaries. TIA is the only national association representing the interests of all third party transportation service providers. The members of TIA include logistics management firms, property brokers, perishable commodities brokers, freight forwarders, intermodal marketers, ocean and air forwarders, and NVOCC's.

11374 **www.unitdose.org**
Healthcare Compliance Packaging Council
A not-for-profit trade association that was established in 1990 to promote the many benefits of unit dose blister and ship packaging - especially its ability to be designed in compliance-promoting formats that help people take their medications properly.

11375 **www.unitedfresh.org**
United Fresh Fruit & Vegetable Association
Equipment, supplies, cartons, packaging machinery, computers, sorting and sizing equipment, harvesting equipment, film wrap manufacturing and commodity organizations.

Associations

11376 **American Innerspring Manufacturers Association**
1918 N Parkway
Memphis, TN 38112

901-749-9030
800-882-5604
www.sleepproducts.org/ispa/industry-links

Members make and sell innerspring units and box springs to mattress manufacturers. Also conducts year round public relations program directed at consumers, encouraging purchase of innerspring mattresses.
Founded in 1966

11377 **American Society of Furniture Designers**
PO Box 5445
4136 Coachmans Court
High Point, NC 27262-5445

336-307-0999; Fax: 910-576-1573

Jason Phillips, President
John Conrad, Executive Director
Jena Hall, Editor-in-Chief
Rick Schroeder, Chairman
Tim O'Hare, Vice President

An international non-profit professional organization dedicated to advancing, improving, and supporting the profession of furniture design and its positive impact in the marketplace.
Founded in 1981

11378 **Association of Progressive Rental Organizations**
1504 Robin Hood Trail
Austin, TX 78703

800-204-2776; Fax: 512-794-0097
cferguson@rtohq.org
www.rtohq.org
Facebook, Twitter, Youtube, Flickr

Gary Ferriman, President
Gopal Reddy, 1st Vice President
Mark Connelly, 2nd Vice President
Jonathan Rose, Secretary
Ernie Lewallen, Treasurer

Members include television, appliance and furniture dealers who rent merchandise with an option to purchase.
2000 Members
Founded in 1980
Mailing list available for rent

11379 **Authentic Home Furnishings Association**
PO Box 520
Spofford, NH 03462

518-832-7939
800-487-8321; Fax: 518-824-5719
www.unfinishedfurniture.org

Fred Moriarty, Executive Director
Tim Case, President
Lara Lindner, Secretary
Steve Cavanaugh, Treasurer
Anthony Sabatino, Vice President

Our mission is to promote the common business interests of the unfinished furniture industry, encourage the most efficient and professional organization and administration of firms in the unfinished furniture industry; and to conduct meetings and educational programs, and to collect and publish information about the unfinished furniture industry.
600 Members
Founded in 1990

11380 **Business and Institutional Furniture Manufacturers Association**
678 Front Avenue NW
Suite 150
Grand Rapids, MI 49504-5368

616-285-3963; Fax: 616-285-3765
email@bifma.org
www.bifma.org
Twitter, LinkedIn

Tom Reardon, Executive Director
Melissa Hubbel, Finance & Administration
Sylvain Garneau, President
Don Van Winkle, Vice President
Franco Bianchi, Treasurer

BIFMA is a not-for-profit trade association of furniture manufacturers and suppliers, addressing issues of common concern.
245+ Members
Founded in 1973

11381 **California Furniture Manufacturers Association**
2973 Harbor Boulevard
Suite 295
Costa Mesa, CA 92626

714-550-9955
cfma.com
Facebook, LinkedIn

The CFMA is one of the oldest trade associations in California that serves the best interests of the furniture industry througout the state.
Founded in 1911

11382 **Futon Association International**
PO Box 593730
Orlando, FL 32859

800-327-3262

Members are retailers, manufacturers, distributors, associates, sales representatives of their country in the industry.
400 Members
Founded in 1984

11383 **Home Furnishings Association**
500 Guiseppe Court
Suite 6
Roseville, CA 95678

800-422-3778
JoinHFA@myHFA.org
myhfa.org
Facebook, Twitter, LinkedIn, Instagram

Sharron Bradley, CEO
Mary Frye, Executive VP
Dan McCann, Director of Marketing/Branding
Jef Spencer, Director of Operations
Jana Sutherland, Program Director

A professional association for businesses and individuals involved in the retail furniture industry.

11384 **Illuminating Engineering Society of North America**
120 Wall St
Floor 17
New York, NY 10005-4001

212-248-5000; Fax: 212-248-5017
ies@ies.org
www.ies.org
Facebook, Twitter, LinkedIn

Daniel Salinas, President
Paul Mercier, President-Elect
William Hanley, Executive Vice President
Nick Bleeker, Treasurer
Nicole DeGirolamo, Executive Assistant

To advance knowledge and disseminate information for the improvement of the lighted environment to the benefit of society. Publishes a monthly magazine.

11385 **International Furniture Rental Association**
5008 Pine Creek Drive
#6
Westerville, OH 43081-4848

614-755-3910
800-367-7368

A non-profit trade organization devoted exclusively to furniture rental and leasing.
Founded in 1967

11386 **International Furniture Transportation and Logistics Council**
PO Box 889
Gardner, MA 01440-0889

978-632-1913; Fax: 978-630-2917
jsears@iftlc.org
www.iftlc.org

Raynard F Bohman Jr, Managing Director

Members are furniture manufacturers, retailers, carriers, wholesalers and warehouses of allied products.
150 Members

11387 **International Home Furnishings Representatives Association**
PO Box 670
High Point, NC 27261

336-889-3920; Fax: 336-802-1959
ihfra@ihfra.org
www.ihfra.org

Tommy Leflein, President
Kathy Parks, Executive Director

Association for the professional development of home furnishings representatives and the improvement of the home furnishings industry as a whole.

11388 **International Home Furnishings Center**
210 E Commerce Ave
High Point, NC 27260

336-888-3700
336-801-6102; Fax: 336-882-1873
www.imchighpointmarket.com

Nonprofit trade association of wholesale distributors, importers and manufacturers of finished goods. Supports furniture retailers by continuous improvement of the industry through advocacy, research and the exchange of ideas. Membership is open to any legitimate furniture wholesaler, importer, manufacturer, agent or any other firm operating within the supply chain of finished goods.
150 Members
Founded in 1928

11389 **International Housewares Association**
6400 Shafer Ct
Suite 650
Rosemont, IL 60018

847-292-4200; Fax: 847-292-4211
pbrandl@housewares.org
www.housewares.org
Facebook, Twitter, LinkedIn, YouTube

Derek Miller, President
Dean Kurtis, VP, Finance
Mark Adkison, VP, Member & Buyer Relations
Leana Salamah, VP, Marketing
Adreinne Tiritilli, VP, Trade Show

A full-service trade association dedicated to promoting the sales and marketing of housewares.
Founded in 1938

11390 **International Sleep Products Association**
501 Wythe Street
Alexandria, VA 22314-1917

703-683-8371; Fax: 703-683-4503
info@sleepproducts.org
www.sleepproducts.org
Facebook, Twitter, LinkedIn, Googleplus,Pinterest,Youtube

Ryan Trainer, President

Maintains a strong organization to influence government actions, inform and educate the membership and act on industry issues to enhance the growth, profitability and stature of the sleep products industry. Provides members with information and services to manage their business more effectively and efficiently. Publishes a magazine devoted exclusively to the mattress industry, BEDtimes covers a broad range of issue and news important to the industry.
Cost: $65.00
650 Members
Frequency: Monthly
Circulation: 3,500
Founded in 1915

11391 **Juvenile Products Manufacturers Association**
15000 Commerce Parkway
Suite C
Mt. Laurel, NJ 08054

856-638-0420; Fax: 856-439-0525
jpma@jpma.org
www.jpma.org/
Facebook, Twitter, LinkedIn

Mark Messner, Chairman
Andy Newmark, Vice Chairman
Michael Dwyer-CAE, President
Rob Conley, Treasurer
Kelly Mariotti, Executive Director

The Juvenile Products Manufacturers Association exists to advance the interests, growth and well-being of the juvenile products industry through advocacy,public relations, information sharing and business devrlopment opportunities.
Founded in 1962

11392 **National Association of Display Industries**
4651 Sheridan Street
Suite 200
Hollywood, FL 33021

954-893-7300; Fax: 954-893-7500
www.nadi-global.com

Klein Merriman, Executive Director
Tracy Dillon, Director Communications

Sponsors seminars and annual contests. Conducts research programs and maintains placement services.
400 Members
Founded in 1937

11393 **National Cotton Batting Institute**
4322 Bloombury St
Southaven, MS 38672

901-218-2393; Fax: 662-449-0046

Weston Arnall, President
Greg Windsperger, VP
Fred Middleton, Executive Secretary-Treasurer

NCBI respresents U.S. companies that manufacture and sell batting for use in mattresses, futons, home furnishing, and upholstered products. It provides a range of services to assist its members in expanding markets, monitoring and contributing to legislative and regulatory decisions that affect the industry, and conducting consumer education and information programs.
27 Members
Founded in 1954

11394 **National Furniture Association**
Info@NationalFurnitureAssociation.com
www.nationalfurnitureassociation.com

The National Furniture Association is an organization supporting business to business initiatives, surrounding the Furniture Industry in the United States and emerging into other world countries.

11395 **National Unfinished Furniture Institute**
1850 Oak Street
Northfield, IL 60093-3042

847-784-1225; Fax: 847-446-3523

Ray Passis, Executive Director

Provides publicity and insurance for industry, offers educational seminars and bestows awards.
1.2M Members
Founded in 1979

11396 **National Waterbed Retailers Association**
2 Greentree Center
Suit 225
Marlton, NJ 08053-3102

312-236-6662
800-832-3553; Fax: 312-236-1140

Promotes industry through educational seminars, sells educational materials on waterbeds, health care and conducts surveys.
500 Members
Founded in 1972

11397 **North America Home Furnishings Association**
2050 N Stemmons Fwy
Suite 292
Dallas, TX 75207

800-422-3778; Fax: 916-784-7697
info@hfia.com
www.nahfa.org
Facebook, Twitter, LinkedIn

Richard Howard, Chairman
Marty Cramer, President
Jeff Child, President-Elect
Sharron Bradley, CEO
Steve Kidder, Vice President

Committed to strengthening the home furnishing industry trhough collective support, services, and leadership.
Founded in 1923

11398 **Paint & Decorating Retailers Association**
1401 Triad Center Dr
St Peters, MO 63376

636-326-2636; Fax: 636-326-1823
info@pdra.org
www.pdra.org
Facebook, Twitter, LinkedIn

Phil Merlo, President
Bahia Taylor, Executive Vice President
Craig Bond, Treasurer
Jeff Baggaley, Past-President
Robert Mueller, Director at Large

Provides members with the tools they need and prosper such as information, sales training, and business operations programs.
1500 Members
Founded in 1947

11399 **Quarters Furniture Manufacturers Association**
1211 Popes Head Drive
Fairfax, VA 22030

240-215-9700; Fax: 276-632-7894

Michael Gittinger, President
Chris Arndt, Vice President
Malcolm Wilson, Secretary
Allyn Richert, Treasurer
Tom Chapman, Board Member

Represents companies who produce furniture for military markets. Monitors federal procurement policy as it relates to prison industries.
20 Members
Founded in 1995

11400 **Society of Glass & Ceramic Decorated Products**
PO Box 2489
Zanesville, OH 43702

740-588-9882; Fax: 740-588-0245
info@sgcd.org
www.sgcd.org

Chad Yaw, President
Jan Weyrich, Vice President
Mike Gervais, Treasurer
David Stanton, Secretary
Myra Warne, Executive Director

Provides designers, decorators and marketers of glass, ceramic and related products with resources for maximizing profitability, technical applications and regulatory compliance.
525 Members

11401 **Summer and Casual Furniture Manufacturers Association**
1912 Eastchester Drive
Suite 100
High Point, NC 27265

336-884-5000; Fax: 336-884-5303
jlogan@ahfa.us
www.ahfa.us
Facebook, LinkedIn

Ken Burrows, Chairman
George Revington, Immediate Past Chairman
KEVIN O'CONNOR, 1st Vice President
RICHARD MAGNUSSEN, 2nd Vice President
ROGER BLAND, Board Member

Sponsors the International Casual Furniture and Accessories Market in Chicago, the Apollo Awards, recognizing excellence in casual furniture retailing and the Casual Furniture Design Excellence Awards.
500+ Members
Founded in 1959

11402 **The American Home Furnishings Alliance**
1912 Eastchester Drive
Suite 100
High Point, NC 27265

336-884-5000; Fax: 336-884-5303
pbowling@ahfa.us
www.ahfa.us
Facebook, LinkedIn

Ken Burrows, Chairman
George Revington, Immediate Past Chairman
KEVIN O'CONNOR, 1st Vice President
RICHARD MAGNUSSEN, 2nd Vice President
ROGER BLAND, Board Member

The world's largest and most influential trade organization serving the home furnishings industry. AHFA is dedicated to fostering the growth and global well being of its member companies.
450 Members
Founded in 1905

11403 **The Association of Woodworking & Furnishings Suppliers**
2400 E Katella Avenue
Suite 340
Anaheim, CA 92806

323-838-9440
800-946-2937; Fax: 323-838-9443

www.awfs.org
Facebook, Twitter, LinkedIn

Daniel Hershbeger, President
Rob Howell, Secretary/Treasurer

The largest national trade association in the US representing the interests of the broad array of companies that supply the home and commercial furnishings industry. Members include manufacturers and distributors of machinery, hardware, lumber, upholstery materials, bedding components, wood products and other supplies to furnishings and wood products manufacturers.
Founded in 1979

11404 **Upholstered Furniture Action Council**
PO Box 2436
High Point, NC 27261

336-885-5065; Fax: 336-885-5072
info@ufac.org
www.ufac.org

Joseph Ziolkowski, Executive Director

Conducts research and disseminates information about adoption of guidelines for cigarette-resistant furniture. Educates public about safe use of smoking materials.
Founded in 1972

11405 **World Floor Covering Association**
2211 E Howell Ave
Anaheim, CA 92806

714-978-6440
800-624-6880; Fax: 714-978-6066
wfca@wfca.org
www.wfca.org
Facebook, Twitter

Scott Humphrey, CEO
Terry Hearne, Director of Operations
Cammie Weitzel, Director of Finance/Administration
Donna Archambault, Membership Operations Manager

Shapes and defines public policy through agressive, national legislative advocacy on behalf of our members. Provides continuing professional educational programming through educational forums and the Regional Installation and Training Education (RITE) program.
45 Members
Founded in 1973

Newsletters

11406 **AWFS Suppliers' Edge**
Association of Woodworking & Furnishings Suppliers
2400 E Katella Avenue
Suite 340
Anaheim, CA 92806

323-838-9440
800-946-2937; Fax: 323-838-9443
www.awfs.org
Facebook, Twitter, LinkedIn

Daniel Hershbeger, President
Rob Howell, Secretary/Treasurer

Industry events, manufacturing news, AWFS Fair news, member news and more.
Frequency: Tri-Annually
Founded in 1979

11407 **At The Table**
American Home Furnishings Alliance
317 High Avenue
10th Floor
High Point, NC 27260

336-884-5000; Fax: 336-884-5303
pbowling@ahfa.us
www.ahfa.us
Facebook, LinkedIn

Andy Counts, CEO

News from legislative and regulatory forums where AHRA is at the table, serving as the voice of the home furnishings industry.
450 Members
Frequency: Quarterly
Founded in 1905

11408 **Focus on Benefits**
American Furniture Manufacturers Association
PO Box Hp7
High Point, NC 27261

336-884-5000; Fax: 336-884-5303
pbowling@ahfa.us
www.ahfa.us

Patricia Bowling, VP Communications

Adresses timely benefits subjects along with developing trends.
Frequency: Quarterly

11409 **Furniture Executive**
American Furniture Manufacturers Association
PO Box Hp7
High Point, NC 27261

336-884-5000; Fax: 336-884-5303
pbowling@ahfa.us
www.ahfa.us

Patricia Bowling, VP Communications

Includes news on all upcoming programs and events, a message from the AHFA President, news from Washington, updates on the AHFA public relations program, and updates on AHFA member benefits and programs.
Frequency: Monthly

11410 **Human Resources Close-Up**
American Home Furnishings Alliance
317 High Avenue
10th Floor
High Point, NC 27260

336-884-5000; Fax: 336-884-5303
pbowling@ahfa.us
www.ahfa.us
Facebook, LinkedIn

Andy Counts, CEO

Online newsletter, addresses pertinent legal subjects in the employment/labor relations arena, along with relevant court and National Labor Relations Board cases.
450 Members
Frequency: Monthly
Founded in 1905

11411 **National Association of Display Industries Newsletter**
4651 Sheridan Street
Suite 470
Hollywood, FL 33021

954-893-7300; Fax: 954-893-7500
www.nadi-global.com

Klein Merriman, Executive Director
Tracy Dillon, Director Communications

Accepts advertising.
Cost: $45.00
16 Pages
Circulation: 8000
Founded in 1956

11412 **Square Yard**
American Floorcovering Association
2211 E Howell Avenue
Anaheim, CA 92806-6009

714-572-8370; Fax: 714-780-0488

Edward Korczak, Publisher

Offers full coverage of interior design in association with floor coverings, carpets and rug manufacturers.
8 Pages
Frequency: Monthly

11413 **Suppliers on Demand**
American Home Furnishings Alliance
317 High Avenue
10th Floor
High Point, NC 27260

336-884-5000; Fax: 336-884-5303
pbowling@ahfa.us
www.ahfa.us
Facebook, LinkedIn

Andy Counts, CEO

Online newsletter designed to help manufacturer members find the product and service suppliers they need, when they need them.
450 Members
Frequency: Quarterly
Founded in 1905

Magazines & Journals

11414 **Architectural Lighting**
One Thomas Circle, NW
Suite 600
Washington, DC 20005

202-452-0800; Fax: 202-785-1974
Twitter

Ned Cramer, Editor-in-Chief
Elizabeth Donoff, Editor

Covers design specifications and application of electrical lighting and daylighting systems.
Frequency: Monthly
Circulation: 54,000

11415 **BEDtimes Magazine**
International Sleep Products Association
501 Wythe Street
Alexandria, VA 22314-1917

703-683-8371; Fax: 703-683-4503
info@sleepproducts.org
www.sleepproducts.org

Julie Palm, Editor
Kerri Bellias, Administrative Assistant
Dana Jackson, Administrative Assistant
Mary Best, Managing Editor

A magazine covering the bedding industry. Target audience as mattress suppliers and manufacturers.
Cost: $50.00
Frequency: Monthly
Circulation: 3000
ISSN: 0893-5556
Founded in 1915
Printed in 4 colors on glossy stock

11416 **Designer**
HDC Publications
429 Montague Ave
Caro, MI 48723-1921

989-673-4121
800-843-6394; Fax: 989-673-2031
info@hdc-caro.org
www.hdc-caro.org

Maryann Vandemark, Executive Director

A magazine offering information on interior design.
Frequency: Monthly

11417 **Draperies and Window Coverings**
840 US Highway One
Suite 330
North Palm Beach, FL 33408

561-627-3393
847-548-3900; Fax: 561-694-6578
www.dwcdesignet.com

Carolyn Silberman, Publisher
Howard Shingle, Editor
Sarah Christy, Associate Editor

Covers trends and specific industry topics.
Cost: $33.00
160 Pages
Frequency: Monthly
Circulation: 28,000
Founded in 1981

11418 **Eastern Floors Magazine**
Specialist Publications
22801 Ventura Boulevard
Suite 115
Woodland Hills, CA 91364-1230

818-224-8035
800-835-4398; Fax: 818-224-8042
www.icsmag.com
Facebook, Twitter

Howard Olansky, Editor
Phil Johnson, Group Publisher
Evan Kessler, Publisher
Amy Levin, Production Manager

Serving the floor covering and tile industry.
Cost: $140.00
Frequency: Monthly
Founded in 1990

11419 **Furniture Today**
Reed Business Information
PO Box 2754
High Point, NC 27261-2754

336-605-1000
800-395-2329; Fax: 336-605-1143
www.reedbusiness.com
Facebook, Twitter

Kevin Castellani, President
Ray Allegeeza, Editor-in-Chief
Helene Checinski, Circulation Manager
Kim Bashford, Production Manager
Delaney Rudd, Ower

Business and fashion newspaper of the furniture industry, edited for retail furniture executives in furniture stores, department stores, mass merchants, furniture specialty stores and catalog showrooms, as well as manufacturing executives at all levels. Focus is on the business and fashion news that these executives need at key decision times in their merchandising and marketing cycles.
Cost: $159.97
Frequency: Weekly
Circulation: 21212
Founded in 1976
Printed in on glossy stock

11420 **Home Accents Today**
Reed Business Information
360 Park Ave S
New York, NY 10010-1737

646-746-6400; Fax: 646-756-7583
www.homeaccentstoday.com
Facebook, Twitter

John Poulin, CEO
Marion Kelly, Publisher
Gerard Van de Aast, CEO
Becky Boswell Smith, Editor-in-Chief
James Reed, Owner

Enables home furnishing retailers to develop merchandising programs, define new style statements, make buying decisions, and create retail strategies. Editorially covers the broad fashion mix of home accent products.
Cost: $24.94
Frequency: Monthly
Circulation: 21300

11421 **Home Furnishing Retailer**
National Home Furnishings Association
3910 Tinsley Drive
Suite 101
Highpoint, NC 27265-3610

336-886-6100
800-888-9590; Fax: 336-801-6102
info@nhfa.org
www.nhfa.org
Facebook, Twitter, LinkedIn, YouTube

Provides the latest information specifically for industry retailers; current trends and strategies to keep business profitable.
Cost: $70.00
Frequency: Monthly
Circulation: 10000
ISSN: 1073-5585

11422 **Home Lighting & Accessories**
Doctorow Communications
1011 Clifton Ave
Suite 1
Clifton, NJ 07013-3518

973-779-1600; Fax: 973-779-3242
www.homelighting.com

Jeffrey Doctorow, President
Jon Doctorow, Circulation Director

Home Lighting & Accessories is a magazine of lamps, lighting fixtures, shades and decorative home accessories. Articles cover marketing and retailing aspects applied to portable lamps, lamps shades, residential lighting fixtures and decorative home accessories - customer relations, sales training, trends, lighting showroom laycut, design and operations. Plus industry and company news, new promotions, appointments, literature, patents
Cost: $15.00
Founded in 1953

11423 **ICS Cleaning Specialist**
Business News Publishing Company
22801 Ventura Blvd
Suite 115
Woodland Hills, CA 91364-1230

818-224-8035
800-835-4398; Fax: 818-224-8042
www.bnpmedia.com

Phil Johnson, Publisher
Evan Kessler, Publisher
Jeffrey Stouffer, Editor
Amy Levin, Production Manager

For carpet cleaning, restoration and floor care service providers.
68 Pages
Frequency: Monthly
Circulation: 24250
ISSN: 1522-4708
Founded in 1963
Printed in 4 colors on glossy stock

11424 **Metropolis**
Bellerophon Publications
61 W 23rd St
Floor 4
New York, NY 10010-4246

212-627-9977; Fax: 212-627-9988
www.metropolismag.com

Horace Havemeyer, Publisher
Susan Szenasy, Editor in Chief
Julie Taraska, Editor
Denise Csaky, Marketing Director

The only magazine that covers all facets of design: architecture, interiors, furniture, preservation, urban design, graphics and crafts.
Cost: $27.95
Circulation: 51000
Founded in 1981

11425 **NHFA Trade Show**
National Home Furnishings Association
3910 Tinsley Drive
Suite 101
Highpoint, NC 27265-3610

336-886-6100
800-888-9590; Fax: 336-801-6102
info@nhfa.org
www.nhfa.org

Steve DeHaan, Executive VP
Karin Mayfield, Senior Director for Membership
Frequency: Annual

11426 **Panel World**
Hatton-Brown Publishers
PO Box 2268
Montgomery, AL 36102-2268

334-834-1170
800-669-5613; Fax: 334-834-4525
mail@hattonbrown.com
www.hattonbrown.com/

D K Knight, Editor-in-chief
Rich Donnell, Editor
David Ramsey, President
Rhonda Thomas, Marketing

A magazine covering the interior design community.
Cost: $40.00
Frequency: Monthly
Circulation: 12000
Printed in 4 colors on matte stock

11427 **RTOHQ: The Magazine**
Association of Progressive Rental Merchandise
1540 Robinhood Trail
Austin, TX 78703-2624

512-794-0095
800-204-APRO; Fax: 512-794-0097
cferguson@rtohq.org
www.rtohq.org

Bill Keese, Executive Director
John C Cleek, President
Bill Kelly, Secretary

Emphasis on larger issues facing it players in the rent-to-own industry. Readers are rent-to-own dealers, owners, managers, employees, manufacturers and suppliers to the industry.
Frequency: Bi-Monthly
Circulation: 11000

Trade Shows

11428 **APRO Rent-To-Own Convention & Trade Show**
Association of Progressive Rental Organizations
1504 Robin Hood Trail
Austin, TX 78703

512-794-0095
800-204-APRO; Fax: 512-794-0097
www.rtohq.org

Shannon Strunkec, President
John C Cleek, First VP
Jeannie Hutchison, Program Coordinator
Bill Keese, Manager

Seminar, reception and tours, plus 280 exhibits of products and services of interest to rent to own dealers: stereos, televisions, furniture, fabric protection and more.
1400 Attendees
Frequency: Annual

11429 **Association of College Unions International Conference**
120 W. Seventh St.
Suite 200
Bloomington, IN 47404
812-245-2284; Fax: 812-245-6710
www.acui.org
Jake Dawes, Events & Operations Coordinator
Devon Bray, Marketing Coordinator
One hundred exhibits of graphic supplies, recreation equipment, computer hardware and software, furnishings, entertainment and speaker bureau information, food service equipment, and more related information and supplies.
1000 Attendees
Frequency: Annual

11430 **Canyon County Home & Garden Show**
Spectra Productions
837 E State Street
PO Box 333
Eagle, ID 83616
208-939-6426; Fax: 208-939-6437
david@spectraproductions.com
www.spectraproductions.com
David Beale, Show Manager
Features exhibitors displaying building materials, contractors, decorators, doors and windows, pools and spas, heating and cooling systems and much more.
150 Attendees
Frequency: April

11431 **Denver Home Show**
Industrial Expositions
PO Box 480084
Denver, CO 80248-0084
303-892-6800
800-457-2434; Fax: 303-892-6322
www.bigasalloutdoors.com
Formerly the Spring Home & Patio Show.
23000 Attendees
Frequency: Annual/March

11432 **Evergreen Home Show**
Westlake Promotions
6020 Seaview Avenue NW
Seattle, WA 98107
206-783-5957; Fax: 206-782-6250
www.westlakepromo.com
Bill Bradley, VP
See what's new and what you can do for your home. Fresh ideas and practical advice from our remodeling and construction specialists. See demonstrations on how to make dramatic improvements to your home.
7500 Attendees

11433 **Fall Home and Garden Expo**
Mid-America Expositions, Inc
7015 Spring Street
Omaha, NE 68106
402-346-8003
800-475-7469; Fax: 402-346-5412
info@showofficeonline.com
www.showofficeonline.com
Robert P Mancuso, CEO
Mike Mancuso, VP/Manager
Displays on everything for the home including kitchens, room additions, bathrooms, interior decorating, fireplaces, outdoor equipment, heating and air conditioning, remodeling contractors, security, siding, appliances, windows, doors, fencing, roofing, fitness equipment, spas and much more.
Frequency: Annual/October

11434 **Furniture Expo**
Glahe International
PO Box 2460
Germantown, MD 20875-2460
301-515-0012; Fax: 301-515-0016
Annual show and exhibits of furniture making.

11435 **Glass & Ceramic Decorators Annual Seminar & Exposition**
Society of Glass & Ceramic Decorators
47 N 4th Street
PO Box 2489
Zanesville, OH 43702
202-298-8660; Fax: 740-588-0245
www.sgcd.org
Myra Warne, Exhibit
The SGCD show attracts major suppliers to the decorating industry, including several firms from overseas. With a full seminar program and first step program that attracts attendees on their own merits.
525 Attendees

11436 **Great Northeast Home Show**
Osborne/Jenks Productions
936 Silas Deane Highway
Wethersfield, CT 06109-4273
860-563-2111
800-955-7469; Fax: 860-563-3472
Two hundred and fifty booths.
25M Attendees
Frequency: Annual/February

11437 **Home and Outdoor Living Expo**
Tower Show Productions
800 Roosevelt Road
Building A, Suite 109
Glen Ellyn, IL 60137
630-469-4611
800-946-4611; Fax: 630-469-4811
www.towershow.com
J Lake, VP Home Shows
The largest and longest running home improvement show.
15000 Attendees
Frequency: January
Founded in 1977

11438 **ICFF International Contemporary Furniture**
George Little Management
10 Bank Street
White Plains, NY 10606-1933
914-486-6070
800-272-7469; Fax: 914-948-6180
www.icff.com
Facebook, Twitter
Troy Hansen, Show Manager
Alex Cabat, Show Coordinator
George Little II, President
Tony Orlando, Operations Manager
More than 500 exhibitors will display contemporary furniture, seating, lighting, carpet and flooring, wall coverings, textiles, accessories, kitchen and bath, outdoor furniture, and materials for residential and commercial interiors. The combination of domestic and international exhibitors provides easy access to the best and hippest home and contract products.
12000 Attendees
Frequency: Annual/December

11439 **International Bedding Exposition**
International Sleep Products Association
501 Wythe Street
Alexandria, VA 22314-1917
703-683-8371; Fax: 703-683-4503
info@sleepproducts.org
www.sleepproducts.org
Susan Perry, Executive VP, Business Development
Dana Jackson, Administrative Assistant
Mary Best, Managing Editor
200 booths, net 120,000 square feet with 200 exhibitors participating.
4M Attendees
Frequency: Annual/March

11440 **International Home Furnishings Market**
International Home Furnishings Market Authority
101 S Main Street
High Point, NC 27262
336-691-1000; Fax: 336-889-6999
www.highpointmarket.org
Judy Mendenhall, President
Jan Wellmon, Executive Assistant
Shannon Kennedy, Director of Marketing
Large home furnishings trade show with a variety of new opportunities to make your visit easy, cost effective and productive. Ten million square seet of exhibition space with 2,500 manufacturers represented.
75000 Attendees
Frequency: Bi-Annual
Founded in 1921

11441 **International Housewares Show**
National Housewares Manufacturers Association
6400 Shafer Court
Suite 650
Rosemont, IL 60018
708-292-4200; Fax: 847-292-4211
www.housewares.org
Adrienne Tiritilli, VP, Trade Show
See first-hand consumer lifestyle and product trends for all areas of the home, both inside and out, under one roof.
60000 Attendees

11442 **International Woodworking Machinery and Furniture Supply Fair: USA**
Reed Exhibition Companies
1350 E Touhy Avenue
Des Plaines, IL 60018-3303
847-294-0300; Fax: 847-635-1571
Paul Pajor, National Marketing Manager
The largest woodworking machinery and furniture supply manufacturing exposition held in the Western Hemisphere. Exhibitors interface with North American furniture, cabinet, and woodworking manufacturers. One thousand booths.
37M Attendees
Frequency: Biennial/August

11443 **Juvenile Products Manufacturers Association Trade Show**
PO Box 955
Marlton, NJ 08053-0955
856-231-8500; Fax: 856-985-2878
William Macmillan, Show Manager
Home acessories and products for children's rooms.
2.5M Attendees
Frequency: Annual/October

11444 **Kitchen & Bath Industry Show**
National Kitchen & Bath Association

687 Willow Grove Street
Hackettstown, NJ 07840

908-520-0033
800-843-6522; Fax: 908-852-1695
www.kbis.com

Lee Hershberg, Sales Manager
Grayson Lutz, Operations Manager
Targeting dealers, designers, distributors, retailers, consumers, home centers and many other high-quality kitchen and bath professionals. Showcasing the latest products and cutting-edge design ideas of the kitchen and bath industry.
40000 Attendees
Frequency: Annual/April

11445 **Kitchen/Bath Industry Show & Multi-Housing World Conference**
VNU Expositions
1145 Sanctuary Parkway
Suite 355
Alpharetta, GA 30004

770-691-1540
800-933-8735; Fax: 770-777-8700

Lee Hershberg, Sales Manager
The latest products and technologies, industry and consumer trends, design and business tools and more to stay ahead of your competitors.
35000 Attendees

11446 **LightFair**
AMC
120 Wall Street
17th Floor
New York, NY 10005

212-843-8358; Fax: 212-248-5017
www.iesna.org

Pamela R Weess, Circulation Director
Nini Schwenk, Manager
A major lighting trade show in North America featuring architectural lighting products from all spectrons of the industry. Containing 600 booths and 400 exhibits.
17M Attendees
Frequency: June
Mailing list available for rent: 10M names at $100 per M
Printed in 4 colors on glossy stock

11447 **Mid-Atlantic Industrial Woodworking Expo Supply Show**
Trade Shows
PO Box 2000
Claremont, NC 28610-2000

828-459-9894; Fax: 828-459-1312

Keith Eidson, Show Manager
Annual show of 300 manufacturers of woodworking and furniture industry equipment, supplies and services.
4500 Attendees
Frequency: Annual/April

11448 **National City Home & Garden Show**
Expositions
PO Box 550
Edgewater Branch
Cleveland, OH 44107-0550

216-529-1300; Fax: 216-529-0311
showinfo@expoinc.com
www.expoinc.com

Featuring showcases on how to make your dream home a reality. Create the garden oasis, backyard retreat or a relaxing sanctuary.
35000 Attendees
Frequency: Annual/February

11449 **National Hardware Show**
383 Main Avenue
Norwalk, CT 06851

203-840-5622
888-425-9377; Fax: 203-840-4824
inquiry@hardware.reedexpo.com
www.nationalhardwareshow.com
Facebook, Twitter, LinkedIn, Instagram, YouTube

Juliana Sherwood, Sales Director
Richard Russo, Industry Vice President
Emily DeMarco, Marketing Director
The prime time and place for face to face sourcing, trading and learning for the US home improvement and DIY markets.
70000 Attendees
Frequency: Annual

11450 **Old House New House Home Show**
Kennedy Productions
1208 Lisle Place
Lisle, IL 60532-2262

630-515-1160; Fax: 630-515-1165
www.kennedyproductions.com

Laura McNamara, Event Producer
Over 300 home improvement exhibitors displaying cutting-edge home enhancements for kitchens, baths, home and garden including landscape, interior remodeling, pools, spas, floors, doors and more.
8000 Attendees
Frequency: Biannual
Founded in 1984

11451 **PDRA Paint & Decorating Show**
Paint & Decorating Retailers Association
403 Axminister Drive
Fenton, MO 63026

636-326-2636
800-737-0107; Fax: 636-326-1823
tina@pdra.org
www.pdra.org

Dan Simon, Executive Vice President
Retailers from the paint and decorating products industry to discuss a variety of business topics. Gain insight from retailers who face the same problems that you do everyday.
1000 Attendees
Frequency: Annual/May

11452 **Remodeling and Decorating Expo**
893 N Jan Mar Ct
Olathe, KS 66061-3693

913-768-8148; Fax: 785-780-4777

Tom Reno, VP
Mary Jo Doherty, Executive Director
Four hundred booths of the latest products and services related to remodeling and decorating. Also a presentation of How-To stage presentations on remodeling, decorating and home repair.
40M Attendees
Frequency: Annual/February

11453 **Southern Home & Garden Show**
Home Builders Association
702 E McBee Avenue
Greensville, SC 29601

864-229-7722; Fax: 864-232-3541

Exhibitors include professional landscapers, nurseryment, interior designers and home and garden experts.
40000 Attendees
Frequency: Biannual

11454 **Spring Home Show**
Osborne/Jenks Productions
936 Silas Deane Highway
Wethersfield, CT 06109

860-563-2111; Fax: 860-563-3472

Exhibitors include remodelers, homebuilders, custom cabinets, kitchens & baths, chimneys, wood stoves, sunrooms, awnings & decks, duct & vent maintenance, storage buildings, heating & cooling services, windows, doors & siding, water treatment systems, banks & mortgage companies, home theatre systems, security systems, financial planners, building supplies, insulation, energy management companies and so much more.
Frequency: Annual/March

11455 **Surfaces Conference**
World Floor Covering Association
2211 E Howell Avenue
Anaheim, CA 92806

714-978-6440
800-624-6880; Fax: 714-978-6066
wfca@wfca.org
www.wfca.org

Casey Voorhees, Executive Director
Tina Krulich, Administrative Assistant
The event for the floor covering industry with the latest trends to keep your business competitive, proven strategies to increase sales and profitability and all the critical industry information you need to make the right decisions.
40000 Attendees
Frequency: Annual/January

11456 **West Week**
Pacific Design Center
8687 Melrose Avenue
West Hollywood, CA 90069

310-652-6992; Fax: 310-652-9576

Show featuring the top interior designers and decorators.
Frequency: Annual/March

11457 **Woodworking and Furniture Expo**
Glahe International
PO Box 2460
Germantown, MD 20875-2460

301-515-0012; Fax: 301-515-0016

Annual show and exhibits of woodworking and furniture making.

Directories & Databases

11458 **AHFA's Industry Resource Guide**
American Home Furnishing Alliance
PO Box HP-7
High Point, NC 27261

336-884-5000; Fax: 336-884-5303
www.ahfa.us

Andy Counts, Executive VP
A who's who in the furniture industry, supplying information on over 500 furniture manufacturers and their suppliers.
80 Pages
Founded in 1966

11459 **Casual Living: Casual Outdoor Furniture and Accessory Directory Issue**
Reed Business Information
360 Park Ave S
New York, NY 10010-1737

646-746-6400; Fax: 646-756-7583
www.reedbusiness.com

John Poulin, CEO
Toni Agpar, Editor
List of manufacturers, manufacturers' trepresentatives, and suppliers of outdoor furni-

ture, wicker and rattan furniture, and backyard accessories such as barbecue grills, picnic accessories, outdoor lighting cushions, pads, patio umbrellas, vinyl refinishing, and maintenance, products.
Cost: $10.00
Frequency: Annual
Circulation: 13,000

11460 Complete Directory of Discount & Catalog Merchandisers
Sutton Family Communications & Publishing Company
920 State Route 54 East
Elmitch, KY 42343

270-276-9500

Theresa Sutton, Publisher
Lee Sutton, Editor

Print-out from database of wholesalers, manufacturers, distributors, importers and close-out houses. Database is updated daily to guarantee the most current and up-to-date sources available.
Cost: $125.00
100 Pages

11461 Complete Directory of Home Furnishings
Sutton Family Communications & Publishing Company
920 State Route 54 East
Elmitch, KY 42343

270-276-9500

Theresa Sutton, Publisher
Lee Sutton, Editor

Print-out from database of wholesalers, manufacturers, distributors, importers and close-out houses. Database is updated daily to guarantee the most current and up-to-date sources available.
Cost: $44.50
100 Pages

11462 Complete Directory of Kitchen Accessories
Sutton Family Communications & Publishing Company
920 State Route 54 East
Elmitch, KY 42343

270-276-9500

Theresa Sutton, Editor
Lee Sutton, General Manager

Print-out from database of wholesalers, manufacturers, distributors, importers and close-out houses. Database is updated daily to guarantee the most current and up-to-date sources available.
Cost: $49.50
100+ Pages

11463 Complete Directory of Lamps, Lamp Shades & Lamp Parts
Sutton Family Communications & Publishing Company
955 Sutton Lane
20 State Route 54 East
Elmitch, KY 42343

270-276-9500

Theresa Sutton, Editor
Lee Sutton, General Manager

Print-out from database of wholesalers, manufacturers, distributors, importers and close-out houses. Database is updated daily to guarantee the most current and up-to-date sources available.
Cost: $39.50
100+ Pages

11464 Complete Directory of Serving Ware
Sutton Family Communications & Publishing Company
920 State Route 54 East
Elmitch, KY 42343

270-276-9500

Theresa Sutton, Editor
Lee Sutton, General Manager

Print-out from database of wholesalers, manufacturers, distributors, importers and close-out houses. Database is updated daily to guarantee the most current and up-to-date sources available.
Cost: $39.50
100+ Pages

11465 Complete Directory of Showroom Fixtures and Equipment
Sutton Family Communications & Publishing Company
920 State Route 54 East
Elmitch, KY 42343

270-276-9500

Theresa Sutton, Publisher
Lee Sutton, Editor

Print-out from database of wholesalers, manufacturers, distributors, importers and close-out houses. Database is updated daily to guarantee the most current and up-to-date sources available.
Cost: $39.50
100 Pages

11466 Complete Directory of Small Furniture
Sutton Family Communications & Publishing Company
920 State Route 54 East
Elmitch, KY 42343

270-276-9500

Theresa Sutton, Publisher
Lee Sutton, Editor

Print-out from database of wholesalers, manufacturers, distributors, importers and close-out houses. Database is updated daily to guarantee the most current and up-to-date sources available.
Cost: $39.50
100 Pages

11467 Complete Directory of Upholstery Materials Supplies and Equipment
Sutton Family Communications & Publishing Company
920 State Route 54 East
Elmitch, KY 42343

270-276-9500

Theresa Sutton, Publisher
Lee Sutton, Editor

Print-out from database of wholesalers, manufacturers, distributors, importers and close-out houses. Database is updated daily to guarantee the most current and up-to-date sources available. Over 600 American wholesale direct supplies in 3-ring binder.
Cost: $67.50
100 Pages

11468 Furniture Retailer Resource Guide
Pace Communications
PO Box 13607
Suite 100
Greensboro, NC 27415-3607

336-378-6065; Fax: 336-275-2864
www.pacecommunications.com

Bonnie McElveen, CEO

Directory of services and supplies to the industry.
Cost: $20.00
Frequency: Annual;
Circulation: 16,000

11469 Home Furnishing Retailers
Chain Store Guide
3710 Corporex Park Dr.
Suite 310
Tampa, FL 33619-1389

813-627-6700
800-972-9292; Fax: 813-627-6888
webmaster@chainstoreguide.com
www.chainstoreguide.com

Mike Jarvis, Publisher
Shami Choon, Manager

This database features detailed information on over 2700 companies in the U.S. and Canada, with contact information for over 8600 key executives and buyers.
Cost: $575.00
Frequency: Annual

11470 IFRA Member Directory
International Furniture Rental Association
5008 Pine Creek Drive
#6
Westerville, OH 43081-4848

614-755-3910
800-367-7368
www.ifra.org

About 100 member furniture rental companies.

11471 Market Resource Guide
International Home Furnishings Center
PO Box 828
High Point, NC 27261-0828

336-888-3700; Fax: 336-882-1873
marketing@ihfc.com

Bruce Miller, CEO

Two-volume directory offers over 1,500 manufacturers and distributors in the furniture industry with exhibits at the International Home Furnishings Market.
Cost: $25.00
624 Pages
Frequency: Semiannual
Founded in 1974
Printed in 4 colors on glossy stock

11472 Specialized Furniture Carriers Directory
National Furniture Traffic Conference
PO Box 889
Gardner, MA 01440-0889

978-632-1913; Fax: 978-630-2917

Ray Bohman, Editor

Nearly 200 trucking firms specializing in transportation of new furniture, not including household moving firms.
Cost: $39.95

Industry Web Sites

11473 http://gold.greyhouse.com
G.O.L.D Grey House OnLine Databases

Grey House Publishing's online database platform, GOLD, offers Quick Search, Keyword Search and Expert Search for most business sectors including furnishing, fixure and decorating markets. The GOLD platform makes finding the information you need quick and easy - whether you're a novice searcher or an experienced database user. All of Grey House's directory products are available for subscription on the GOLD platform.

11474 **www.ahfa.us**
American Home Furnishings Alliance

The largest and most influential trade organization serving the home furnishings industry. Dedicated to fostering the growth and global well being of its member companies.

11475 **www.awfs.org**
Association of Woodworking & Furnishings Suppliers

Organization for furniture and accessories manufacturers and suppliers that are covered in this comprehensive journal.

11476 **www.bifma.org**
Business and Institutional Furniture Manufacturers

The voice of the office furniture industry, BIFMA members are manufacturers and suppliers of goods and services to the industry.

11477 **www.greyhouse.com**
Grey House Publishing

Authoritative reference directories for most business sectors including furnishings, fixtures and decorating marekts. Users can search the online databases with varied search criteria allowing for custom searches by product category, geographic area, sales volume, keyword, subject and more. Full Grey House catalog and online ordering also available.

11478 **www.hfia.com/**
Home Furnishings International Association

Product categories include residential casegoods, upholstery, gift and decorative accessories, lighting and area floor coverings and beddings.

11479 **www.nhfa.org**
National Home Furnishings Association

Trade association of furniture retailers which works to improve retailer's business opportunities and management practices.

11480 **www.ofdanet.org**
Office Furniture Dealers Association

Explores the effect of office environment on productivity and uses contract sales staff to anticipate changes in market.

11481 **www.rtohq.org/**
Association of Progressive Rental Organizations

Members include television, appliance and furniture dealers who rent merchandise with an option to purchase.

11482 **www.unfinishedfurniture.org**
Unfinished Furniture Association

Associations

11483 **AugmentedReality.Org**
40600 Ann Arbor Road E.
Suite 201
Plymouth, MI 48170

571-293-2013
www.augmentedreality.org
Facebook, Twitter, LinkedIn, YouTube, Flickr

Ori Inbar, Co-Founder & CEO
Tish Shute, Co-Founder & Chief Content Officer
Patrick O'Shaughnessy, Chief Technology Officer

Non-profit organization seeking to advance the field of augmented reality through connecting industry professionals through events and an online platform.

11484 **Canadian Game Studies Assocation**

Home Page: gamestudies.ca
Twitter

The CGSA is devoted to the interdisciplinary study of digital games, and supports the work of researchers, graduate students, artists, game designers, programmers, theorists, and others working in the industry.
Mailing list available for rent

11485 **Corporate Esports Association**

administrator@cea.gg
cea.gg
Twitter, YouTube

Brad Tenenholtz, Chief Executive Officer
Michael Pleasant, Co-Founder & Chair
Terence Southard, Co-Founder & Board Member

Facilitates online esport tournaments for corporate professionals on Discord, to enocurage team-building and donate the proceeds to charity.

11486 **Digital Games Research Association**

coordinator@digra.org
www.digra.org

William Huber, President
Hanna Wirman, Vice President
Allan Fowler, Secretary
Jussi Holopainen, Treasurer
Cody Mejeur, Diversity Officer

DiGRA is an international association of academics and professionals interested in research into digital games and related products. It features a Digital Library, Gamesnetwork mailing list, and the ToDiGRA journal.
Founded in 2003
Mailing list available for rent

11487 **Entertainment Consumers Association**

Home Page: www.theeca.com

Hal Halpin, Founder & President
Heather Ellertson, VP, Marketing
Jennifer Mercurio, VP & General Counsel
Brett Schenker, Advocacy Director
Mike Conley, Digital Marketing Coordinator

Non-profit representing the interests of consumers of digital entertainment in the US and Canada.

11488 **Entertainment Software Association**
601 Massachusetts Avenue NW
Suite 300
Washington, DC 20001

esa@theesa.com
www.theesa.com
Facebook, Twitter, LinkedIn

Stanley Pierre-Louis, President & CEO
Gina Vetere, SVP & General Counsel
Andrew Bowins, SVP, Comm. & Public Affairs
Ana Molina, CFO
Michael O'Leary, SVP, Government Affairs

The trade association of the video game industry.
Founded in 2000

11489 **Entertainment Software Association of Canada**
#408, 130 Spadina Avenue
Toronto, ON M5V 2L4

416-620-7171
theesa.ca
Facebook, Twitter, Instagram, YouTube

Jayson Hilchie, President & CEO
Corinne Crichlow, Director, Communications & PR
Paul Fogolin, Director, Policy & Gov. Affairs
Dylan Boyd, Digital Content Manager

The ESAC is devoted to video game developers, publishers, and distributors in Canada

11490 **Entertainment Software Rating Board**
New York, NY

marketing@esrb.org
www.esrb.org
Facebook, Twitter

Patricia E. Vance, President
David Kassack, SVP, Finance & Operations
Bill Garrity, SVP, Ratings
John Falzone, VP, ESRB Privacy Certified
Randy Walker, SVP, Marketing & Communications

Non-profit, self-regulatory body devoted to informing consumers (especially parents) about the video games they play. The ESRB established and maintains a ratings system for all video games, from E for Everyone to AO for Adults Only.
Founded in 1994

11491 **Esports Trade Association**
541 N. Fairbanks Court
Suite 2200
Chicago, IL 60611

708-680-7133
info@esportsta.org
esportsta.org
Facebook, Twitter, LinkedIn, YouTube, Instagram

Megan Van Petten, Founder & CEO

The ESTA serves the eSports community by promoting, protecting, and advancing its interests through professional development programs, networking opportunities, industry research, and tools and resources for members.
Founded in 2018

11492 **Fantasy Sports & Gaming Association**
1818 Parmenter Street
Suite 300
Middleton, WI 53562

608-310-7540
thefsga.org
Facebook, Twitter, LinkedIn

Christina McCoy, Executive Director
Michael Fiez, Marketing
Emily Petersen, Membership

The FSGA is a national organization representing fantasy sports and gaming companies, and serving those companies and players with research and data, networking opportunities, and collective action.

11493 **Gaming Standards Association**
51777 Brandin Court
Fremont, CA 94538

510-492-4060
www.gamingstandards.com
Facebook, Twitter, LinkedIn, YouTube

Peter DeRaedt, President
Michelle Olesiejuk, Executive Director
Mark Pace, Managing Director
Ethan Tower, Protocol Director
Oscar Salgado, Documentation Manager

International trade association that identifies, defines, develops, promotes, and implements standards in the gaming industry. It serves manufacturers, suppliers, operators, and regulators.

11494 **International Age Rating Coalition**

info@globalratings.com
www.globalratings.com

The IARC unites many of the video game rating authorities around the world and provides a streamlined age classification process for digital games and mobile apps. The Entertainment Software Rating Board is the point of contact in North America.

11495 **International Game Developers Association**
#402, 150 Eglinton Avenue E.
Toronto, ON M4P 1E8

info@igda.org
www.igda.org
Facebook, Twitter, LinkedIn, YouTube, Instagram

Renee Gittins, Executive Director
Tristin Hightower, Director, Operations

The IGDA is the largest non-profit membership organization serving individuals who create video games. They are dedicated to improving developers' careers and lives through: Community, Professional Development, and Advocacy.
Founded in 1994

11496 **Major League Gaming**

Home Page: www.mlg.com
Facebook, Twitter, YouTube, Instagram, Snapchat

Steve Bornstein, Chairman
Pete Vlastelica, President & CEO
Michael Sepso, Co-Founder & SVP, Media Networks
Sundance DiGiovanni, Co-Founder & VP, Brands & Content
Pavel Murnikov, VP, Technology

A professional eSports organization. MLG.tv, its free video streaming eSports showcase, attracts 27 million users per month.
Founded in 2002

11497 **Professional Esports Association**

pea@cloud9.gg
www.proesports.org
Facebook, Twitter, Instagram

PEA is a coalition of eSports teams aiming to advance the industry and grow the business of eSports.
Founded in 2016

11498 **United States eSports Federation**

Home Page: www.esportsfederation.org
Instagram

Vlad Marinescu, President
Robin Kent, General Secretary
Lance Mudd, Sport Director
Ryan Terao, VP, Education Commission
Robert Davidman, VP, Integrity Commission

USeF is the U.S. member organization of the International e-Sports Federation and official governing body of eSports in the U.S. Its goal is

to promote eSports and protect athletes by uniting all facets of the industry: stakeholders, athletes, event organizers, technology producers, innovators and inventors, IP holders, parents, sponsors, and fans.
Founded in 2016

11499 **VR/AR Association**
Palo Alto, CA 94303

nathan@thevrara.com
www.thevrara.com
Facebook, Twitter, LinkedIn, YouTube

Nathan Pettyjohn, Founder & President
Kris Kolo, Global Executive Director

International organization with a mission to foster collaboration between companies and individuals in the virtual reality and augmented reality industry. It aims to accelerate growth, encourage research and education, develop industry standards, connect members, and promote their services.
Founded in 2015

11500 **Video Game Bar Association**
#2000, 222 N. Sepulveda Boulevard
El Segundo, CA 90245

818-564-7898
jolin@vgba.org
vgba.org
Twitter, LinkedIn

Patrick Sweeney, Co-Founder & President
Joseph Olin, Executive Director
Ida Ebeid, Project Manager

An international association of lawyers who specialize in the video game industry.
Founded in 2011

11501 **World Esports Association**

info@wesa.gg
www.wesa.gg
Facebook, Twitter

Pietro Fringuelli, Executive Chair & Commissioner
Sebastian Weishaar, Board Member
Ulrich Schulze, Board Member
Ralf Reichert, Board Member
Erik Anderson, Board Member

WESA is an international body aiming to professionalize eSports by introducing elements common among traditional sports associations, including player representation, standardized regulations, & revenue shares for teams. It is a joint effort between eSports teams and eSports company ESL.

11502 **XR Association**
1299 Pennsylvania Avenue NW
Washington, DC 20004

membership@xra.org
xra.org
Facebook, Twitter, LinkedIn

Elizabeth Hyman, Chief Executive Officer
Joan O'Hara, Senior Director, Public Policy
Laura Chadwick, Senior Director, Industry Relations
Michael Williams, Chief Operating Officer
Bethany Reitsma, Executive Assistant

Trade association for technology manufacturers in the virtual, augmented, and mixed reality industries.
Founded in 2016

Newsletters

11503 **ECA Today**
Entertainment Consumers Association

Home Page: www.theeca.com

Hal Halpin, Founder & President
Heather Ellertson, VP, Marketing
Mike Conley, Digital Marketing Coordinator

Newsletter for members only.
Frequency: Nightly

Magazines & Journals

11504 **ARtillery Intelligence**
VR/AR Association
Palo Alto, CA 94303

nathan@thevrara.com
www.thevrara.com
Facebook, Twitter, LinkedIn, YouTube

Nathan Pettyjohn, Founder & President
Kris Kolo, Global Executive Director

Research and data package for VR/AR professionals.
Founded in 2015

11505 **Essential Facts About the Computer and Video Game Industry**
Entertainment Software Association
601 Massachusetts Avenue NW
Suite 300
Washington, DC 20001

esa@theesa.com
www.theesa.com

Stanley Pierre-Louis, President & CEO
Gina Vetere, SVP & General Counsel
Andrew Bowins, SVP, Comm. & Public Affairs
Ana Molina, CFO

Tracks statistics about the video game industry in the US.
Frequency: Annual
Founded in 2000

11506 **Loading...**
Canadian Game Studies Association

jennifer.jenson@ubc.ca
gamestudies.ca

Suzanne de Catell, Editor
Jennifer Jenson, Co-Editor

Official journal of the Canadian Game Studies Association with articls on research into digital games.

11507 **Transactions of the Digital Games Research Association**
Digital Games Research Association
jose.zagal@utah.edu
todigra.org

Jose P. Zagal, Editor-in-Chief
Harald Warmelink, Support Contact

ToDiGRA is an international, open access, refereed, multidisciplinary journal for research on and practice in all aspects of digital games. It is both printed and available online.
ISSN: 2328-9422

Trade Shows

11508 **Augmented World Expo**
AugmentedReality.org

Home Page: www.awexr.com
Facebook, Twitter, LinkedIn, YouTube

Ori Inbar, CEO

Showcase for technologies making the world more interactive: augmented reality; virtual reality; and wearable technology.
4000 Attendees

11509 **BlizzCon**
Blizzard Entertainment Inc.
16215 Alton Parkway
Irvine, CA 92618
Home Page: blizzcon.com
Facebook, Twitter, YouTube, Instagram

Convention held by Blizzard Entertainment to promote their franchises, such as Warcraft, StarCraft, Diablo, Hearthstone, Heroes of the Storm, and Overwatch.
40K Attendees
Founded in 2005

11510 **Canadian Game Studies Association Annual Conference**
Canadian Game Studies Assocation

Home Page: gamestudies.ca

Kym Stewart, Local Arrangement Coordinator

Held in tandem with the Congress of the Humanities and Social Sciences.

11511 **Comicpalooza**

Home Page: www.comicpalooza.com
Facebook, Twitter, YouTube, Instagram

Multi-genre convention on gaming, tabletop games, films, comics, literature, anime, cosplay, and more.
50K Attendees
Founded in 2008

11512 **DEXCON**
Double Exposure Inc.
Morristown, NJ

Home Page: www.dexposure.com

Gaming conference with a focus on board gaming, Larping, video gaming, and wargaming.
2200+ Attendees
Founded in 1992

11513 **Denver Pop Culture Con**
info@popcultureclassroom.org
denverpopculturecon.com
Facebook, Twitter, YouTube, Instagram

Multi-genre fan convention on comic books and web-comics, tabletop and video games, anime and manga, costplay, horros and sci-fi, movies, TV, and literature.
114K Attendees
Founded in 2012

11514 **ESTA Conference**
Esports Trade Association
541 N. Fairbanks Court
Suite 2200
Chicago, IL 60611

708-680-7133
info@esportsta.org
esportsta.org
Facebook, Twitter, LinkedIn, YouTube, Instagram

Megan Van Petten, Founder & CEO

Conference of the Esports Trade Association.
Founded in 2018

11515 **Electronic Entertainment Expo**
Entertainment Software Association
601 Massachusetts Avenue NW
Suite 300
Washington, DC 20001

Home Page: www.e3expo.com
Facebook, Twitter, YouTube, Instagram

Stanley Pierre-Louis, President & CEO
Andrew Bowins, SVP, Comm. & Public Affairs

Video game industry showcase featuring technology debuts and product launches.
50000 Attendees

11516 **FSGA Winter Conference**
Fantasy Sports & Gaming Association
1818 Parmenter Street
Suite 300
Middleton, WI 53562

608-310-7540
thefsga.org
Facebook, Twitter, LinkedIn

Christina McCoy, Executive Director
Michael Fiez, Marketing
Emily Petersen, Membership

January meeting of Fantasy Sports & Gaming Association members.

11517 **Game Developers Conference**
Informa Tech

415-947-6926
800-216-4916
gdcfeedback@ubm.com
gdconf.com
Facebook, Twitter, LinkedIn, YouTube, Instagram

The GDC provides education, inspiration, and networking opportunities to the video game development community, including programmers, artists, producers, game designers, audio professionals, and business leaders. The conference features discussions, awards ceremonies, community spaces for networking, and the GDC Expo.
Founded in 1988

11518 **Game On Expo**
Phoenix, AZ

Home Page: www.gameonexpo.com

Gaming convention with a focus on video and arcade games, board games, and tabletop games.
Frequency: Annual
Founded in 2015

11519 **GameSoundCon**
SoundCon, LLC
4735 134th Place SE
Bellevue, WA 98006

425-956-3725
brian@gamesoundcon.com
www.gamesoundcon.com
Twitter

Conference devoted to the art, technology, and business of video game audio.
350+ Attendees
Founded in 2009

11520 **GameStorm**
Red Lion Jantzen Beach
909 N. Hayden Island Drive
Portland, OR 97217

Home Page: gamestorm.org
Facebook, Twitter, Tumblr

Non-profit gaming convention with panel discussions, role-playing games, video games, and tabletop games.
Founded in 1998

11521 **GaymerX**
San Francisco, CA

info@gaymerx.org
gaymerx.org
Facebook, Twitter, YouTube, Discord

Non-profit convention dedicated to LGBTQ+ people and culture in the world of gaming, particularly regarding video games.
Founded in 2013

11522 **Genericon**
Rensselaer Polytechnic Institute
110 Eighth Street
Troy, NY 12180

518-276-6000
chair.genericon@gmail.com
genericon.org

Convention for anime, science fiction, and gaming, featuring viewing rooms, karaoke, cosplay, video gaming and competitions, role-playing games, board games, and lectures.

11523 **Independent Games Festival**
Informa Tech
303 Second Street
Suite 900, S. Tower
San Francisco, CA 94107

chairperson@igf.com
igf.com
Twitter

The IGF recognizes the best independent game developers, and encourages innovation in game development.
Founded in 1998

11524 **IndieCade**
Culver City, CA

central@indiecade.com
www.indiecade.com
Facebook, Twitter, YouTube, Instagram

Stephanie Barish, Chief Executive Officer
Sam Roberts, Festival Director
Celia Pearce, Festival Chair
Erin Shaver, Director, Operations
Shawn Pierre, Games Manager

The International Festival of Independent Games is dedicated to showcasing and supporting independent game development through a series of international events.
Founded in 2005

11525 **MAGFest**
Washington, DC

contact@magfest.org
www.magfest.org
Facebook, Twitter, YouTube, Instagram, Snapchat

Music and gaming festival to celebrate video games and video game music, running 24 hours a day for four days straight.
Founded in 2002

11526 **MidSouthCon**
Mid-South Science and Fictions Conventions, Inc.

info@midsouthcon.org
midsouthcon.org

Science-fiction-themed convention with programming that also includes comics, horror, costuming, and gaming.
2200 Attendees
Founded in 1982

11527 **Midwest Gaming Classic**
, WI

Home Page: www.midwestgamingclassic.com
Facebook, YouTube, Instagram

Trade show for all types of video game consoles, pinball machines, arcade video games, table-top games, computers, crane games, collectible card games, air hockey, and more.

11528 **Mobicon**
Renaissance Riverview Plaza Hotel
64 S. Water Street
Mobile, AL 36602

833-662-4266
president@mobilecomiccon.org
mobilecomiccon.org
Facebook, Twitter

Multi-genre convention on science fiction, fantasy, gaming, comics, anime, manga, horror, paranormal, and mass media.
1000+ Attendees
Founded in 1998

11529 **MomoCon**
Atlanta, GA

Home Page: www.momocon.com
Facebook, Twitter, YouTube, Instagram

A geek culture convention for fans of anime, gaming, comics, and animation.
39000 Attendees
Founded in 2005

11530 **Penny Arcade Expo**

pax_questions@paxsite.com
www.paxsite.com

Video game expos held in cities across the States, and also in Australia. Expos feature exhibit halls, freeplay, tournaments, concerts, panels, and more.
Founded in 2004

11531 **Phoenix Fan Fusion**
Phoenix Convention Center
100 N. 3rd Street
Phoenix, AZ 85004

604-635-4306
phoenixfanfusion.com
Facebook, Twitter, YouTube, Instagram

Multi-genre convention on pop culture fandom, including comic books, sci-fi/fantasy, film and TV, anime and manga, animation, toys, card games, and video games.
57K Attendees
Founded in 2002

11532 **PortConMaine**
492 Main Street
Westbrook, ME 04092

331-704-0927
info@portconmaine.com
portconmaine.com
Facebook, Twitter, Instagram

Julie York, Founder

Convention dedicated to anime and gaming.

11533 **QuakeCon**
ZeniMax Media Inc.
1370 Piccard Drive
Rockville, MD 20850

questions@quakecon.org
www.quakecon.org
Facebook, Twitter, Instagram

Gaming convention to celebrate and promote video game studios owned by ZeniMax Media, with a large LAN party and other events.
Frequency: Annual
Founded in 1996

11534 **RTX**
Rooster Teeth
Austin, TX

888-512-7469
rtxevent@roosterteeth.com

rtxevent.com
Facebook, Twitter, YouTube, Instagram

Clarissa Gonzalez, Senior Events Manager
Patrick Matthews, Events Specialist
George Panga, Marketing Coordinator

Convention held to celebrate gaming and internet culture, with a focus on animation and comedy as well. Other events are held in Sydney, Australia, and London, England.
62000 Attendees
Founded in 2011

11535 **TooManyGames**
Greater Philadelphia Expo Center
100 Station Avenue
Oaks, PA

info@toomanygames.com
toomanygames.com
Facebook, Twitter, YouTube, Instagram

Gaming convention with a new and used game marketplace, artists and creators, musicians, panels and demonstrations, LARPing, celebrities, an indie game showcase, and gaming arenas.
15K Members
Founded in 2004

11536 **TwitchCon**
Twitch Interactive, Inc.
San Francisco, CA

Home Page: www.twitchcon.com
Facebook, Twitter, Instagram

Convention for the video game streaming and on-demand platform Twitch, where fans can meet streamers and the online community in person, as well as play new games. The convention is hosted twice a year, once in North America and once in Europe.
50K Attendees
Frequency: Annual
Founded in 2015

11537 **VR/AR Global Summit**
VR/AR Association
Palo Alto, CA 94303
am@thevrara.com
www.thevrara.com
Facebook, Twitter, LinkedIn, YouTube

Nathan Pettyjohn, Founder & President
Kris Kolo, Global Executive Director
Anne-Marie Enns, Executive Producer

Summits bring together enterprise, hardware, software, and content providers for educational sessions and networking.
Founded in 2015

11538 **Virtual Reality Developers Conference**
Informa Tech
415-947-6926
800-216-4916
gdcfeedback@ubm.com
www.gdconf.com/vrdc
Facebook, Twitter, LinkedIn, YouTube, Instagram

The VRDC is a two-day summit for developers of Virtual Reality and Augmented Reality entertainment.

11539 **Yama-Con**
LeConte Center
2986 Teaster Lane
Pigeon Forge, TN 37863

support@www.yamacon.org
www.yamacon.org
Facebook, Instagram

Multi-genre convention on anime, comics, cosplay, and gaming.
2600 Attendees
Founded in 2012

Industry Web Sites

11540 **www.augmentedreality.org**
AugmentedReality.Org
Non-profit organization seeking to advance the field of augmented reality through connecting industry professionals through events and an online platform.

11541 **www.cea.gg**
Corporate Esports Association
Facilitates online esport tournaments for corporate professionals on Discord, to enocurage team-building and donate the proceeds to charity.

11542 **www.digra.org**
Digital Games Research Association
DiGRA is an international association of academics and professionals interested in research into digital games and related products. It features a Digital Library, Gamesnetwork mailing list, and the ToDiGRA journal.

11543 **www.esportsfederation.org**
United States eSports Federation
USeF is the U.S. member organization of the International e-Sports Federation and official governing body of eSports in the U.S. Its goal is to promote eSports and protect athletes by uniting all facets of the industry: stakeholders, athletes, event organizers, technology producers, innovators and inventors, IP holders, parents, sponsors, and fans.

11544 **www.esportsta.org**
Esports Trade Association
The ESTA serves the eSports community by promoting, protecting, and advancing its interests through professional development programs, networking opportunities, industry research, and tools and resources for members.

11545 **www.esrb.org**
Entertainment Software Rating Board
Non-profit, self-regulatory body devoted to informing consumers (especially parents) about the video games they play. The ESRB established and maintains a ratings system for all video games, from E for Everyone to AO for Adults Only.

11546 **www.gamestudies.ca**
Canadian Game Studies Assocation
The CGSA is devoted to the interdisciplinary study of digital games, and supports the work of researchers, graduate students, artists, game designers, programmers, theorists, and others working in the industry.
Mailing list available for rent

11547 **www.gamingstandards.com**
Gaming Standards Association
International trade association that identifies, defines, develops, promotes, and implements standards in the gaming industry. It serves manufacturers, suppliers, operators, and regulators.

11548 **www.globalratings.com**
International Age Rating Coalition
The IARC unites many of the video game rating authorities around the world and provides a streamlined age classification process for digital games and mobile apps. The Entertainment Software Rating Board is the point of contact in North America.

11549 **www.igda.org**
International Game Developers Association
The IGDA is the largest non-profit membership organization serving individuals who create video games. They are dedicated to improving developers' careers and lives through: Community, Professional Development, and Advocacy.

11550 **www.mlg.com**
Major League Gaming
A professional eSports organization. MLG.tv, its free video streaming eSports showcase, attracts 27 million users per month.

11551 **www.proesports.org**
Professional Esports Association
PEA is a coalition of eSports teams aiming to advance the industry and grow the business of eSports.

11552 **www.theeca.com**
Entertainment Consumers Association
Non-profit representing the interests of consumers of digital entertainment in the US and Canada.

11553 **www.theesa.ca**
Entertainment Software Association of Canada
The ESAC is devoted to video game developers, publishers, and distributors in Canada

11554 **www.theesa.com**
Entertainment Software Association
The trade association of the video game industry.

11555 **www.thefsga.org**
Fantasy Sports & Gaming Association
The FSGA is a national organization representing fantasy sports and gaming companies, and serving those companies and players with research and data, networking opportunities, and collective action.

11556 **www.thevrara.com**
VR/AR Association
International organization with a mission to foster collaboration between companies and individuals in the virtual reality and augmented reality industry. It aims to accelerate growth, encourage research and education, develop industry standards, connect members, and promote their services.

11557 **www.vgba.org**
Video Game Bar Association
An international association of lawyers who specialize in the video game industry.

11558 **www.wesa.gg**
World Esports Association
WESA is an international body aiming to professionalize eSports by introducing elements common among traditional sports associations, including player representation, standardized regulations, & revenue shares for teams. It is a joint effort between eSports teams and eSports company ESL.

11559 **www.xra.org**
XR Association
Trade association for technology manufacturers in the virtual, augmented, and mixed reality industries.

Associations

11560 **American Community Gardening Association**
3271 Main Street
College Park, GA 30337
877-ASK-ACGA
info@communitygarden.org
communitygarden.org
Facebook, Twitter
Charlie Monroe, President
Cathy Walker, Vice President
Cordalie Benoit, Treasurer
A bi-national nonprofit membership organization of professionals, volunteers and supporters of community greening in urban and rural communities.
Founded in 1982

11561 **American Herbal Products Association**
8630 Fenton St
Suite 918
Silver Spring, MD 20910
301-588-1171; Fax: 301-588-1174
www.ahpa.org
Graham Rigby, Chair
Steven Dentali, Vice Chair
Michael McGuffin, President
Steven Yeager, Secretary
Mitch Coven, Treasurer
A organization that only focuses on herbs and herbal products.
200 Members
Founded in 1982

11562 **American Horticultural Society**
7931 E Boulevard Dr
Alexandria, VA 22308
703-768-5700
800-777-7931; Fax: 703-768-8700
www.ahs.org
Facebook, Twitter, Flickr
Amy Bolton, Chair
Jane Diamantis, 1st Vice Chair
Mary Pat Matheson, 2nd Vice Chair
Nancy Hargroves, Secretary
J. Landon Reeve, Treasurer
Educates and inspires people of all ages to become successful and environmentally responsible gardeners by advancing the art and science of hoticulture. It is an education, nonprofit, 501 organization that recognizes and promotes best practices in American horticulture. AHS is known for its educational programs and the dissemination of horticultural information.
27M Members
Founded in 1922
Mailing list available for rent

11563 **American Horticultural Therapy Association**
610 Freedom Business Centre
#110
King of Prussia, PA 19406
610-992-0020
800-634-1603; Fax: 610-225-2364
www.ahta.org
Facebook, Twitter, LinkedIn, Youtube, Pinterest
MaryAnne McMillan, President
Leigh Anne Starling, Vice President
Todd Schappell, Treasurer
Patricia Cassidy, Secretary
Advancing the practice of horticulture as therapy to improve human well-being.
Founded in 1973

11564 **American Institute of Floral Designers**
720 Light Street
Baltimore, MD 21230
410-752-3318; Fax: 410-752-8295
www.aifd.org
Facebook, Twitter, LinkedIn, YouTube
Joyce Mason-Monheim, President
Anthony Vigliotta, President-Elect
Kim Oldis, Vice President
Frank Feysa, Secretary
Tom Simmons, Treasurer
Nonprofit association to support the floral design industry.
1300 Members
Founded in 1962

11565 **American Nursery & Landscape Association**
1200 G Street NW
Suite 800
Washington, DC 20005
202-789-2900; Fax: 202-789-1893
Facebook
Bob Terry, President
Dale Deppe, President Elect
Michael V. Geary, Executive Vice President
The American Nursery and Landscape Association serves firms who grow, sell or use plants. ANLA advocates the industry's interests before government and provides its members with unique business knowledge essential to long-term growth and profitability.
2000 Members
Founded in 1876

11566 **American Rose Society**
8877 Jefferson Paige Road
PO Box 30000
Shreveport, LA 71130
318-938-5402
800-637-6534; Fax: 318-938-5405
www.rose.org
Facebook, Twitter, Flickr,Pinterest,Youtube
Steve Jones, President
Jeff Wycoff, VP
Laura Seabaugh, Executive Director
Carol Spiers, Assistant to Executive Director
Peggy Spivey, Administrative Assistant
Striving to provide educational services to encourage the greater use of our national flower in private and public gardens throughout the country.
24000 Members
ISSN: 1078-5833
Founded in 1892

11567 **American Society for Horticultural Science**
1018 Duke Street
Alexandria, VA 22314
703-836-4606; Fax: 703-836-2024
webmaster@ashs.org
www.ashs.org
Facebook, Twitter, LinkedIn, Pinterest
Louise Ferguson, President
Michael W. Neff, Executive Director
Heather W. Hilko, Member Services & Subscriptions
Negar Mahdavian, Conferences
Sylvia DeMar, Publication Submissions
A cornerstone of research and education in horticulture and an agent for active promotion of horticultural science.
1200 Members
Founded in 1903

11568 **American Society of Consulting Arborists**
9707 Key West Avenue
Suite 100
Rockville, MD 20850-3222
301-947-0483; Fax: 301-990-9771
asca@mgmtsol.com
www.asca-consultants.org
Facebook, Twitter, LinkedIn, Pinterest
Richard Adkins, President
Th,rŠse Oetegen Clemens, Executive Director
Grace Jan, Senior VP, Meetings Management
Julie Hill, Marketing Director
Julianne Clark, Coordinator, Member Services
The industry's premier professional association focusing solely on arboricultural consulting. Consulting Arborists are authoritative experts on trees, consulting property owners, municipalitites, attorneys, insurance professionals and others on tree disease, placement, preservation and dispute resolution in addition to providing consulting and experto testimony in the legal, insurance and environmental arenas.
Founded in 1967

11569 **American Society of Irrigation Consultants**
404 E 4th Street
Royal Oak, MI 48067
508-763-8140
carolc@asic.org
www.asic.org
Carol Colein, Executive Director
Michael Krones, President
Stacy Gardner, Vice President
Janet Luehrs, Treasurer
Carly Kardon, Operations and Member Services
Promotes education skills on data exchange landscape irrigation. Members are irrigation consultants, suppliers, and manufacturers.

11570 **American Society of Landscape Architects**
636 Eye Street NW
Washington, DC 20001-3736
202-898-2444
888-999-2752; Fax: 202-898-1185
info@asla.org
www.asla.org
Facebook, Twitter, LinkedIn, Houzz, Instagram, Pinterest
Nancy Somerville, Exec. VP & CEO
Michael O'Brien, Managing Director & CFO
Residential and commercial real estate developers, federal and state agencies, city planning commissions and individual property owners are all among the thousands of people and organizations in America and Canada that will retain the services of a landscape architect this year.
15000 Members
Founded in 1899

11571 **Association for Garden Communicators**
355 Lexington Avenue
15th Floor
New York, NY 10017
212-297-2198; Fax: 212-297-2149
info@gardenwriters.org
gardenwriters.org
Facebook, Twitter, LinkedIn, Pinterest, Instagram
Becky Heath, President
Jo Ellen Meyers Sharp, Vice President
Maria Zampini, Treasurer
Ellen Zachos, Secretary
The Association for Garden Communicators provides leadership and opportunities for edu-

cation, recognition, career development and a forum for diverse interactions for professionals in the field of gardening communications.

11572 **Association of Specialty Cut Flower Growers**
17 1/2 W. College St.
MPO Box 268
Oberlin, OH 44074
440-774-2887; Fax: 440-774-2435
mail@ascfg.org
www.ascfg.org
Facebook
John Dole, Executive Advisor
Frank Arnosky, President
Mike Hutchison, Vice-President
Josie Crowson, Treasurer
Barb Lamborne, Secretary
Trade association that provides cultural and marketing information to specialty cut flower growers.
700 Members
Founded in 1988

11573 **Floral Trade Council**
101 N Main Street
Ovid, MI 48866
989-341-1322; Fax: 517-339-1393
Will Carlson, Executive Director
Association of US fresh cut flower growers.
70 Members
Founded in 1988

11574 **Garden Centers of America**
2873 Saber Dr.
Clearwater, FL 33759
800-721-0024
www.gardencentersofamerica.org
Jeff Morey, Executive Director
Cheryl Morey, Executive Vice President
National association focused on the needs of retail nurseries.

11575 **Garden Writers Association of America**
7809 FM 179
Shallowater, TX 79363
806-832-1870; Fax: 806-832-5244
webtech@gardenwriters.org
www.gwaa.org
Facebook, Twitter
Kirk Brown, President
Becky Health, Vice President
Jo Ellen Meyers Sharp, Treasurer
Maria Zampini, Secretary
Robert LaGasse, Executive Director
A organization with materials of interest to garden writers and news on members of the Association.
1800 Members

11576 **Illinois Landscape Contractors Association**
Illinois Landscape Contractors Association
2625 Butterfield Road
Suite 204W
Oak Brook, IL 60523
630-472-2851; Fax: 630-472-3150
information@ilca.net
www.ilca.net
Kevin Vancina, President
Michael Schmechtig, Secretary/Treasurer
Rusty Maulding, Vice President
Charlie Keppel, Immediate Past President
Scott Grams, Executive Director
ILCA's mission is to enhance the professionalism and capabilities of members by providing leadership, education and valued services while promoting environmental awareness within the landscape industry. Sponsor or Mid-Am Horticulture Trade Show.
Founded in 1959

11577 **International Society of Arboriculture**
1400 W Anthony Drive
PO Box 3129
Champaign, IL 61826
217-355-9411
888-472-8733; Fax: 217-355-9516
isa@isa-arbor.com
www.isa-arbor.com
Facebook, Twitter, LinkedIn, YouTube, RSS
Jim Skiera, Executive Director
Karin Phelps, Executive Assistant
Mark Bluhm, Director, Finance & Operations
Keely Roy, Director, Marketing
Sharon Lilly, Director, Educational Goods
A worldwide professional organization dedicated to fostering a greater appreciation for trees and to promoting research, technology, and the professional practice of arboriculture.

11578 **Los Angeles Community Garden Council**
4470 W Sunset Blvd
#381
Los Angeles, CA 90027
847-864-5781; Fax: 847-448-8805
www.lagardencouncil.org
Facebook
Glen Dake, President
Ada Berman, Treasurer
Eileen Zwiers, Secretary
David De La Torre, Contact
Francesca de la Rosa, Contact
Connect people with community garden space in their neighborhoods.

11579 **Mailorder Gardening Association**
PO Box 429
LaGrange, GA 30241
706-298-0022; Fax: 706-883-8215
www.directgardeningassociation.com
Facebook, Twitter, LinkedIn
Noel Valdes, President
Polly Welch, 1st VP
Ken Oakes, 2nd VP
Matt Bollinger, Secretary
Alisa Meggison, Treasurer
Mail-order suppliers of gardening and nursery stock and supplies.
210 Members
Founded in 1934

11580 **National Council of Commercial Plant Breeders**
1701 Duke Street
Suite 275
Alexandria, VA 22314
703-299-6633
ajorss@amseed.org
www.nccpb.org
Stephen Smith, President
Andrew LaVigne, Executive Vice President
Tom Koch, 1st Vice President
Marcelo Queijo, 2nd Vice President
Ann Jorss, Secretary/Treasurer
A non-profit organization to promote the achievement and interest of American plant breeders both in the United States and abroad.

11581 **National Garden Clubs**
4401 Magnolia Avenue
St. Louis, MO 63110
314-776-7574; Fax: 314-776-5108
headquarters@gardenclub.org
www.gardenclub.org
Facebook, Twitter, YouTube, Pinterest, Instagram
Michelle Smith, Executive Director
Emily Huck, Member Services Coordinator
Bill Trapp, Accountant
A not-for-profit organization that brings together nearly 165,000 members and 5,000 local garden clubs coast-to-coast. The organization comprises many of the nation's most respected botanic gardens and plant societies.
165K Members
Founded in 1891

11582 **National Gardening Association**
237 Commerce St.
Suite 101
Williston, VT 05495
802-863-5251; Fax: 802-864-6889
Facebook, Twitter, Pinterest, YouTube, Instagram
Dave Whitinger, Executive Director
Trish Whitinger, Chief Operating Officer
A nonprofit promoting garden-based education.
Founded in 1982

11583 **National Pest Management Association**
10460 North Street
Fairfax, VA 22030
703-352-6762
800-678-6722; Fax: 703-352-3031
www.npmapestworld.org
Facebook, Twitter, Flickr
Dominique Stumpf, Chief Executive Officer
Andy Architect, Chief Operating Officer
Chris Forberg, VP, Finance & Administration
Rachel Dittman, VP, Marketing & Communications
Kelly Harris, Director, Membership
Represents the interests of its members and the structural pest control industry.
7000 Members
3500 Attendees
Founded in 1933

11584 **Professional Grounds Management Society**
720 Light St
Baltimore, MD 21230-3850
410-223-2861
800-609-7467; Fax: 410-752-8295
www.pgms.org
Facebook, Twitter, LinkedIn, YouTube, RSS
John Burns, President
Marion Bolick, President-Elect
Gerald Landby, Vice President
Jeff McManus, Treasurer/Secretary
John Burns, Past President
Members are professionals involved in the care and maintenance of public and private sites.
1400 Members
Founded in 1911

11585 **Professional Landcare Network**
950 Herndon Parkway
Suite 450
Herndona, GA 20170
703-736-9666
800-395-2522; Fax: 703-736-9668
webmaster@landcarenetwork.org
www.landscapeprofessionals.org
Facebook, Twitter, LinkedIn, YouTube
Scott Jamieson, President
Brett Lemcke, President-Elect
Jason Becker, Directors at Large
Sabeena Hickman, CEO
Scott Lindley, VP Sales
PLANET emerged from the joining of the PLCAA and the ALCA in 2005. It is an educational, professional resource for landcare, exte-

rior maintenance and interiorscape professionals and the lawn and landscape industry.
1200 Members
Founded in 1979

11586 Roanoke Community Garden Association
P.O. Box 4326
Roanoke, VA 24015

540-929-1390
roanokecommunitygarden.org
Facebook, Instagram

Tina Badger, Interim Director

Founded in 2008 to build community through gardening. RCGA has a broad reach within the city of Roanoke that includes five community gardens, free educational programs, and a host of schoolyard garden projects. RCGA serves the community by providing means to grow fresh produce in neighborhoods that are known food deserts.
Founded in 2008

11587 Society of American Florists
1601 Duke St
Alexandria, VA 22314-3406

703-836-8700
800-336-4743; Fax: 703-836-8705
info@safnow.org
www.safnow.org
Facebook, Twitter, LinkedIn

Robert Williams, Chairman
Shirley Lyons, President
Martin Meskers, President-Elect
Dwight Larimer, Treasurer
Peter J Moran, EVP/CEO

Represents all segments of the U.S. floral industry.
12K Members
Founded in 1884

11588 Turf Grass Producers International
2 East Main Street
East Dundee, IL 60118

847-649-5555
800-405-8873; Fax: 847-649-5678
info@turfgrasssod.org
www.turfgrasssod.org
Facebook

Den Gardner, Editor
Lynn Grooms, Managing Editor
Veronica Iwanski, Membership & Marketing Manager
Jim Novak, Public Relations Manager
Geri Hannah, Accounting & Office Manager

An organization featuring business news and updates on legislation and agronomics concerning the turf industry.
1000 Members
Founded in 1967

11589 U.S. Lawn Mower Racing Association
PO Box 628
Northbrook, IL 60065

Home Page: letsmow.com
Facebook, Twitter, Instagram, YouTube

An association run for racing enthusiasts who love to tinker and compete.
Founded in 1992

Newsletters

11590 Bulletin
Garden Club of America
590 Madison Ave
Suite 19
New York, NY 10022-2544

212-872-1000; Fax: 212-872-1002
www.akingump.com

Daniel H Golden, Partner

GCA's oldest publication, articles include news from GCA member clubs around the country, with reports from national committees, zones, and GCA conferences and meetings.
Cost: $8.00
Frequency: Bi-Monthly

11591 Front Page News
Professional Landcare Network, Inc
950 Herndon Parkway
Suite 450
Herndon, VA 20170

703-736-9666
800-395-2522; Fax: 703-736-9668
www.landscapeprofessionals.org

Dan Foley, Publisher

E-newsletter with timely association and industry news and topics.
16 Pages
Frequency: Monthly

11592 Landscape Architect and Specifier News
George Schmok
14771 Plaza Dr
Suite M
Tustin, CA 92780-8012

714-979-5276; Fax: 714-979-3543
webmaster@landscapeonline.com
www.landscapeonline.com

George Schmok, Publisher
Jim Lipot, Circulation Manager
Leslie McGuire, Managing Editor

A photographically oriented professional journal featuring topics of concern and state of the art projects designed or influenced by registered landscape architects worldwide.
Frequency: Monthly
Circulation: 29162
Printed in 4 colors on glossy stock

11593 PLANET News Magazine
Professional Landcare Network, Inc
950 Herndon Parkway
Suite 450
Herndon, VA 20170

703-736-9666
800-395-2522; Fax: 703-736-9668
info@actionletter.com
www.landscapeprofessionals.org

News and information of the gardening and landscaping industries.
Frequency: Monthly

11594 Quill and Trowel
Garden Writers Association of America
10210 Leatherleaf Ct
Manassas, VA 20111-4245

703-257-1032; Fax: 703-257-0213
webmaster@gardenwriters.org
www.gwaa.org

Robert C La Gasse, Executive Director
Ann Marie Van Nest, Vice President
Seymour Jordan, Publisher

Material of interest to garden writers and news of members of the Association.
12 Pages
Frequency: Monthly
Circulation: 1800
Founded in 1848

11595 The Cut Flower Quarterly
Association of Specialty Cut Flower Growers
17 1/2 W. College St.
MPO Box 268
Oberlin, OH 44074

440-774-2887; Fax: 440-774-2435
www.ascfg.org

Newsletter
Cost: $175.00
Frequency: Quarterly
Circulation: 1200
ISSN: 1068-8013

Magazines & Journals

11596 American Nurseryman
American Nurseryman Publishing Company
223 W Jackson Blvd
Suite 500
Chicago, IL 60606-6911

312-427-7318
800-621-5727; Fax: 312-427-7346
Facebook, Twitter

Allen Seidel, President
Sally Benson, Editor

Focuses on topics relevant to professional growers, landscapers and retail garden center operators.
Cost: $48.00
100 Pages
Frequency: Fortnightly
Circulation: 16000
ISSN: 0003-0198
Founded in 1904
Printed in 4 colors on glossy stock

11597 American Rose Magazine
American Rose Society
PO Box 30000
Shreveport, LA 71130

318-221-5026
800-637-6534; Fax: 318-938-5405

Mike Kromer, Executive Director
Beth Smiley, Editor
Benny Ellerbe, Executive Director
Marny Fife, Marketing Director

Publication focusing on rose growing, culture and enjoyment. Accepts advertising.
Cost: $37.00
Frequency: Monthly
Circulation: 21000
ISSN: 1078-5833
Founded in 1894

11598 Casual Living
Reed Business Information
PO Box 2754
Suite 200
High Point, NC 27261-2754

336-605-1000
800-652-2948; Fax: 336-605-1143
www.reedbusiness.com

Kevin Castellani, President
Becky B Smith, Editor-in-Chief
Delaney Rudd, Owner
Stuart Whayman, CFO

Content includes industry lifestyle features, business analysis and product trend information.
Frequency: Monthly
Circulation: 10000
Founded in 1958

11599 Fine Gardening
Taunton Press

63 South Main St
PO Box 5506
Newtown, CT 06470-5506

203-706-6206
800-888-8286; Fax: 203-426-3434
fg@taunton.com
www.taunton.com

LeeAnne White, Editor
Cathy Austermann, Advertising Manager
Todd Meier, Publisher
John Lagan, National Account Manager

Landscaping and ornamental gardening are the magazine's primary editorial focus. Step-by-step in-depth information for the country. Articles written by gardening experts and enthusiasts.
Cost: $29.95
83 Pages
Circulation: 202163
Founded in 1988

11600 Florists' Review
WildFlower Media Inc.
3300 SW Van Buren
Topeka, KS 66611

785-266-0888
800-367-4708; Fax: 785-266-0333
mail@floristsreview.com
www.floristsreview.com
Facebook, Twitter

Travis Rigby, President / Publisher
David L Coake, Editorial Director
Brenda Wettengel, Circulation Coordinator
Lisa Strydom, Advertising Sales Director
Teresa Salts, Account Executive

For wholesalers and retailers and desingers of fresh and dried flowers.
Cost: $42.00
Frequency: Monthly
Circulation: 28000
Founded in 1897

11601 Flowers&
Richard Salvaggio
11444 W Olympic Boulevard
Los Angeles, CA 90064-1549

310-966-3518
800-321-2665; Fax: 310-966-3610
www.flowersandmagazine.com

Bruce Wright, Editor
Jill Fox, Circulation Manager
Richard Salvaggio, Publisher

Business information and tips for the retail florist.
Cost: $54.00
Frequency: Monthly
Circulation: 30,000
Founded in 1985
Printed in 4 colors on glossy stock

11602 Garden Center Magazine
GIE Media
801 Cherry St.
Suite 960 Unit 2
Fort Worth, TX 76102

817-882-4110
800-456-0707; Fax: 817-882-4121
Facebook

Yale Youngblood, Publisher
Sarah Martinez, Managing Editor

Garden Center magazine has made the business decision to be the voice to serve the total market with the content to serve common needs; the business of buying, merchandising and selling of trees, ornamentals, bedding plants and related garden materials and accessories to homeowner consumers.
Cost: $90.00
Frequency: Monthly
Circulation: 16249

11603 Garden Center Merchandising & Management
Branch-Smith Publishing
120 St. Louis Avenue
PO Box 1868
Fort Worth, TX 76101

817-882-4120
800-433-5612; Fax: 817-882-4121
www.gardencentermag.com

Carol Miller, Editor
Patricia Kuhl, Publisher
Tiffany O'Kelley, Media Manager
Mike Branch, President
Frequency: Monthly

11604 Green Industry PRO
Cygnus Publishing
1233 Janesville Avenue
Fort Atkinson, WI 53538-0803

920-000-1111
800-547-7377; Fax: 920-563-1699
Grant.Dunham@cygnuspub.com

Rick Monogue, Publisher
Gregg Wartgow, Associate Publisher
Lisa Danes, Associate Editor

A national trade publication providing the critical business information landscape contractors need for success. Readership includes the leaders of companies performing landscape management, installation, lawn care, irrigation and maintenance. Covers how to topics such as surviving and thriving through the pinch-points of growth, maximizing productivity, matching the right tools and equipment to the appliation at ahnd, and taking innovative approaches to the marketplace.
Frequency: Monthly
Circulation: 55000
Founded in 1937

11605 Greenhouse Management
GIE Media
4020 Kinross Lakes Pkwy
Richfield, OH 44286

800-456-0707

Richard Foster, Publisher
Todd Davis, Editorial Director
Kristy O'Hara, Editor
Kelli Rodda, Managing Editor

National magazine for commercial greenhouse growers. Accepts advertising.
Frequency: Monthly

11606 Grounds Maintenance
Penton Media
249 W. 17th Street
New York, NY 10011

212-204-4200
www.grounds-mag.com

Keeping readers informed on the latest techniques and products for gounds care. The most popular source of information for grounds maintenance professionals. Readership includes golf course superintendants, corporate/municipal groundskeepers and landscape professionals, providing them with content they trust and creating a deep source of reference and how-to information.
Frequency: Monthly
Circulation: 70000
Founded in 1966

11607 Hearth & Home
Village West Publishing
P.O. Box 1288
Laconia, NH 03247

603-528-4285
800-258-3772; Fax: 888-873-3610
wright@villagewest.com
www.hearthandhome.com
Facebook, LinkedIn

Richard Wright, Editor
Jackie Avignone, Advertising Director
Erica Paquette, Art Director

Information for retailers and others selling hearth products, patio furnishing, barbecues, spas, garden accessories, and other outdoor products.
Frequency: Monthly
Circulation: 17,000
Founded in 1980

11608 HortScience
American Society for Horticultural Science
1018 Duke Street
Alexandria, VA 22314-2851

703-836-4606; Fax: 703-836-2024
webmaster@ashs.org
www.ashs.org
Facebook

Michael W. Neff, Executive Director

Journal of interest to a broad array of horticultural scientists and others interested in horticulture. Goals are to provide information on significant research, education, extension findings and methods, and developments and trends that affect the profession.
Frequency: Monthly
ISSN: 0018-5345
Founded in 1903

11609 HortTechnology
American Society for Horticultural Science
1018 Duke Street
Alexandria, VA 22314-2851

703-836-4606; Fax: 703-836-2024
webmaster@ashs.org
www.ashs.org
Facebook

Michael W. Neff, Executive Director
Ruth Gaumond, Managing Editor
Sylvia DeMar, Publications Submissions
Heather Hilko, Publications Subscriptions
James Brannon, Publications Billing

Brings reliable, current, peer-reviewed technical information to help solve problems and deal with current challenges in production, education, and extension.
Frequency: Bi-Monthly
Founded in 1903

11610 Horticulture Magazine
F+W Media
10151 Carver Road
Suite 200
Cincinnati, OH 45242

513-531-2690; Fax: 513-891-7153
www.hortmag.com
Facebook, Twitter

Dedicated to celebrating the passion of avid gardeners, who take delight not just in gardens but in garden-making. Our informative, engaging writing and brilliant photography enables gardeners to create spaces that make them proud, beautify their hometowns and provide a gathering place for family and friends.
Frequency: Monthly

11611 Journal of Arboriculture
International Society of Arboriculture
1400 W Anthony Drive
PO Box 3129
Champaign, IL 61826

217-355-9411
888-472-8733; Fax: 217-355-9516
isa@isa-arbor.com
www.isa-arbor.com

Jim Skiera, Executive Director
Jerri Moorman, Executive Assistant

Refereed journal devoted to the dissemination of knowledge in the science and art of planting and caring for trees in the urban environment. Published by the International Society of Arboriculture, whose mission is to foster a greater appreciation for trees and to promote the research, technology, and practice of professional arboriculture.
Cost: $105.00
Frequency: Bi-Monthly
Circulation: 17000
ISSN: 0278-5226
Founded in 1924

11612 Journal of the American Society for Horticultural Science
American Society for Horticultural Science
113 S West St
Suite 200
Alexandria, VA 22314-2851
703-836-4606; Fax: 703-836-2024
journal@ashs.org
journal.ashspublications.org/
Neal D. De Vos, Editor in Chief
Michael W. Neff, Publisher
Ruth Gaumond, Managing Editor
Publishes papers on the results of original research on horticultural plants and their products or directly related research areas. Its prime function is to communicate mission-oriented, fundamental research to other researchers. The journal includes detailed reports of original research results on various aspects of horticultural science and directly related subjects.
Frequency: Bi-Monthly
ISSN: 0003-1062
Founded in 1903
Mailing list available for rent: 2500 names at $100 per M

11613 Landscape & Irrigation
Adams Business Media
111 W Jackson Blvd
7th Floor
Chicago, IL 60604-3589
312-846-4600; Fax: 312-977-1042
www.adamsbusinessmedia.com
John Kmitta, Editor
Steve Brackett, VP/Group Publisher
Joanne Juda, Circulation Manager
Targets decision-makers throughout the landscape industry, from residential contractors to commercial grounds managers, to public works professionals and irrigation and water management professionals. Information includes advice from industry professionals, coverage of specific projects, details on the latest products and innovations, and news from around the world.
Cost: $57.50
Frequency: 9x Yearly
ISSN: 0745-3795

11614 Landscape Illinois
Illinois Landscape Contractors Association
2625 Butterfield Road
Suite 204W
Oak Brook, IL 60523
630-472-2851; Fax: 630-472-3150
information@ilca.net
www.ilca.net
Scott Grams, Executive Director
An annual publication geared toward homeowners, business owners and consumers
36 Pages
Frequency: Monthly
Circulation: 40,000
Printed in 4 colors on glossy stock

11615 Landscape Management
Advanstar Communications
7500 Old Oak Blvd
Cleveland, OH 44130-3343
440-243-8100
800-225-4569; Fax: 440-891-2740
www.ubmamericas.com
Facebook, Twitter
Tony D Avino, General Manager
Kevin Stoltman, Publisher
Michael Harris, Sales Manager
Stephanie Ricca, Managing Editor
Ron Hall, Editor In Chief
Covers news, market trends, business and operations management, technical information on horticulture and agronomy for 51,000 professional landscape contractors, lawncare operators and inhouse grounds managers.
Cost: $46.00
Frequency: Monthly
Circulation: 60,000
Founded in 1965
Printed in 4 colors on glossy stock

11616 Lawn & Landscape
Gie Publishing
4012 Bridge Avenue
Cleveland, OH 44113
216-961-4130
800-456-0707; Fax: 216-961-0364
www.gie.net
Ron Lowy, Publisher
Dan Moreland, Executive Vice President
National trade magazine for the landscape professional. Accepts advertising.
120 Pages
Frequency: Monthly
Circulation: 73000
Founded in 1980

11617 Nursery Management
GIE Media
4020 Kinross Lakes Pkwy
Richfield, OH 44286
800-456-0707
Todd Davis, Publisher
Kelli Rodda, Editor
Nurserymen, landscapers and garden centers. Accepts advertising.
Cost: $24.00
136 Pages
Frequency: Monthly
Founded in 1910

11618 Nursery Retailer
Brentwood Publications
3023 Eastland Boulevard
Clearwater, FL 33761-4106
727-724-0200; Fax: 727-724-0021
Jeff Morey, President & Publisher
Cheryl Morey, Vice President & Publisher
News of retail growers.
Cost: $15.00
Frequency: Bi-Monthly
Founded in 1955

11619 Outdoor Power Equipment
10405 6th Ave. N
Suite 210
Minneapolis, MN 55441
763-383-4421
dvoll@epgmediallc.com
www.outdoorpowerequipment.com
Facebook
David Voll, Publisher
John Kmitta, Assoc. Publisher/Editor
Samantha VanKempen, Production Manager
Serves retailers and distributors who sell and service outdoor power equipment products, including retailers, lawn and garden supply retailers, farm supply retailers, hardware store retailers, home centers, and building supply retailers.

11620 Power Equipment Trade
Hatton-Brown Publishers
225 Hanrick Street
PO Box 2268
Montgomery, AL 36102-2268
334-834-1170
800-669-5613; Fax: 334-834-4525
www.powerequipmenttrade.com
Facebook, Twitter, Google+, YouTube
David H Ramsey, Co-Publisher
DK Knight, CEO
Rich Donnell, Editor
Leading publication in the power equipment community. Articles include profiles on successful power equipment retailers (dealers) and manufacturers and accounts pertaining to technology, market trends and timely issues.
Frequency: Bimonthly
Circulation: 21788
ISSN: 0163-0414
Founded in 1952

11621 Southern Nursery Digest
Betrock Information Systems
7770 Davie Road Ext
Hollywood, FL 33024-2516
954-810-0300; Fax: 954-438-2632
Irv Betrock, Editor
Sean Patrick, Manager
This comprehensive magazine covers the gardening and nursery business in the south.
Frequency: Monthly

11622 The American Gardener
Amerian Horticultural Society
7931 E Boulevard Dr
Alexandria, VA 22308-1300
703-768-5700
800-777-7931; Fax: 703-768-8700
www.ahs.org
Tom Underwood, Executive Director
Harry Rissetto, Chair
Mary Pat Matheson, 1st Vice Chair
Leslie Ariail, Secretary
J. Landon Reeve, Treasurer
Features inspiring color photographs and in-depth articles on new and native plants, influetial garden personalities, garden history, and earth friendly gardening techniques and products. Also regular departments on design, children's gardening, conservation issues, and reviews of the latest gardening books, as well as a calendar of gardening events nationwide.
27M Members
Founded in 1922

11623 The Cut Flower Quarterly
Association of Specialty Cut Flower Growers
17 1/2 W. College St.
MPO Box 268
Oberlin, OH 44074
440-774-2887; Fax: 440-774-2435
www.ascfg.org
Judy Laushman, Executive Director
Vicki Stamback, President
Leah Cook, Vice-President
Andrea Gagnon, Treasurer
Carolyn Tschetter, Secretary
The only regular publication dedicated to information about the production, postharvest care and marketing of cut flowers.
700 Members
Frequency: Quarterly
Founded in 1988

11624 The Landscape Contractor
Illinois Landscape Contractors Association

2625 Butterfield Road
Suite 204W
Oak Brook, IL 60523

630-472-2851; Fax: 630-472-3150
information@ilca.net
www.ilca.net

Scott Grams, Executive Director

Providing readers with news and developments in the industry with emphasis on regional concerns. Read by ILCA members and nonmembers who own, manage or supervise exterior and interior design/guild and maintenance firms, nurseries and garden centers, landscape architectural firms, as well as the staffs of parks and recreation districts and landscape industry professionals throughout the Midwest.
Cost: $75.00
Frequency: Monthly
Founded in 1959

11625 **The National Gardener**
The National Garden Clubs
4401 Magnolia Avenue
St. Louis, MO 63110

314-776-7574; Fax: 314-776-5108
headquarters@gardenclub.org
www.gardenclub.org

Patricia Binder, Editor
Michelle Smith, Executive Director

The quarterly publication of The National Garden Clubs.
Cost: $8.00
Frequency: Quarterly
Founded in 1891

11626 **Tomato Country**
Columbia Publishing
8405 Ahtanum Rd
Yakima, WA 98903-9432

509-248-2452
800-900-2452; Fax: 509-248-4056
www.tomatomagazine.com

Brent Clement, Editor/Publisher
Mike Stoker, Publisher

Includes information on tomato production and marketing, grower and shipper feature stories, tomato research, from herbicide and pesticide studies to new varieties, market reports, feedback from major tomato meetings and conventions, along with other key issues and points of interest for USA and Canada tomato growers.
Cost: $12.00

11627 **Turf News**
Turf Grass Producers International
2 East Main Street
East Dundee, IL 60118

847-649-5555
800-405-8873; Fax: 847-649-5678
info@turfgrasssod.org
www.turfgrasssod.org

Kirk T Hunter, Executive Director

The only magazine devoted exclusively to turfgrass sod production. focuses on the business of turfgrass by targeting farm owners and managers. A valuable tool for suppliers and manufacturers, featuring industry trends, product news, technical information, marketing, research, government issues, human resources, seed & planting stock, equipment/machinery, farm profiles, as well as vital industry and association news.
Frequency: Bi-Monthly
Circulation: 1600
Founded in 1977

11628 **Yard and Garden**
Cygnus Publishing
PO Box 803
Fort Atkinson, WI 53538-0803

920-000-1111
800-547-7377; Fax: 920-563-1699
noel.brown@cygnuspub.com

John French, CEO
Dan Newman, Director of Public Relations
Kathy Scott, Director of Public Relations
Paul Bonaiuto, CFO

A national trade publication providing the critical business information independent outdoor power equipment servicing dealers need for success. Readership includes the owners and managers of full-service outdoor power equipment dealerships serving both commercial and residential customers. Focuses on retail trends, management strategies, dealer best practices, supplier news, and the latest products and services to hit the lawn and garden marketplace.
Frequency: 8x Yearl
Circulation: 17504
Founded in 1977

Trade Shows

11629 **ASCA Annual Conference**
American Society of Consulting Arborists
9707 Key West Avenue
Suite 100
Rockville, MD 20850-3222

301-947-0483; Fax: 301-990-9771
asca@mgmtsol.com
www.asca-consultants.org

Richard Adkins, President
Th,rŠse Oetegen Clemens, Executive Director
Grace Jan, Senior VP, Meetings Management
Barbara Bienkowski, Exhibits & Sponsorship Manager

Recognized as a high quality, in-depth conference with cutting edge speakers. Combining the best forum for discussion of current and relevant arboricultural issues, as well as consulting practice management issues and key consulting topics such as the role of the expert witness, risk assessment and tree appraisal.
Founded in 1967

11630 **ASHS Annual Conference**
American Society for Horticultural Science
1018 Duke Street
Alexandria, VA 22314-2851

703-836-4606; Fax: 703-836-2024
webmaster@ashs.org
www.ashs.org
Facebook, Twitter, LinkedIn

Curt Louise, Ferguson
Michael W. Neff, Executive Director
Angie Lower, Conference Manager
Negar Mahdavian, Conference Manager

Attracts US and international horticulturists who attend to learn about research and new developments in horticulture.
Cost: $560.00
Frequency: Annual

11631 **American Nursery & Landscape Association Convention**
American Nursery & Landscape Association
1200 G Street NW
Suite 800
Washington, DC 20005

202-789-2900; Fax: 202-789-1893
Facebook

Robert S. Lyons, President
Robert Terry, President-Elect

Serves firms who grow, sell or use plants. ANLA advocates the industry's interests before government and provides its members with unique business knowledge essential to long-term growth and profitability.
Frequency: Annual/July

11632 **American Society of Irrigation Consultants National Conference**
404 E 4th Street
Royal Oak, MI 48067

508-763-8140
carolc@asic.org
www.asic.org

Carol Colein, Executive Director
Michael Krones, President
Stacy Gardner, Vice President
Janet Luehrs, Treasurer
Carly Kardon, Operations and Member Services

Addressing major industry issues and learn from each other and leading experts in irrigation, water management and related fields. Member participate in the conference to showcase the latest in irrigation solution technology and services.
Frequency: Annual/September
Founded in 1970

11633 **Annual Convention of the International Lilac Society**
9500 Sperry Road
Kirtland, OH 44094

440-946-4400; Fax: 216-256-1655

Exhibits on lilacs, including innovative cultivation and the use of lilacs in public and private landscaping.
Frequency: Annual
Founded in 1974

11634 **Annual Fort Worth Home & Garden Show**
International Exhibitions
1635 W Alabama
Houston, TX 77006

713-295-5366; Fax: 713-529-0936

The place to experience what's new in home, gardening, remodeling, home decor, and much more. Meet over 400 experts and experience thousands of products and services.
40000 Attendees

11635 **Annual Gulf Coast Home & Garden Expo**
Exposition Enterprises of Alabama
PO Box 430
Pinson, AL 35126

205-680-0234; Fax: 205-680-0615

Like a well tended garden, the show keeps growing and growing.
12000 Attendees

11636 **Central Environmental Nursery Trade Show (CENTS)**
Ohio Nursery & Landscape Association
72 Dorchester Square
Westerville, OH 43081-3350

614-991-1195
800-825-5062; Fax: 614-899-9489
info@onla.org
www.onla.org/cents
Facebook, LinkedIn

Jay Daley, President
Andy Harding, President-Elect
Kevin Thompson, Executive Director
Tracie Zody, Trade Show/Even Manager

Innovations and ideas in an expanded market.
Frequency: Annual/January

11637 Farwest
2780 SE Harrison Street
Suite 102
Milwaukie, OR 97222-7574
FAX 503-653-1528
Clayton Hannon, Executive Director
775 booths promoting the sale and exchange of nursery/landscape products and services.
13M Attendees
Frequency: August

11638 GIE+EXPO - Green Industry & Equipment Expo
Professional Lawncare Network, Inc
222 Pearl Street
Suite 300
New Albany, IN 47150
812-949-9200
800-558-8767; Fax: 812-949-9600
info@gie-expo.com
www.gie-expo.com
Anna Demoret, Trade Show Coordinator
Annual show of 400 manufacturers, suppliers and distributors of lawn care equipment, supplies and services, including fertilizers, weed control materials, insurance information and power equipment. Take advantage of the education sessions and presentations and demos, as well as six-hundred and fifty booths.
Frequency: Annual

11639 Green Industry Conference - GIC
Professional Lawncare Network, Inc (PLANET)
950 Herndon Parkway
Suite 450
Herndon, VA 20170
703-736-9666
800-395-2522; Fax: 703-736-9668
info@gie-expo.com
www.landscapeprofessionals.org
Keep current as a green industry professional. Stay tuned in to the new technology, products and services hitting the market every year. Hone your skills with applicable education that you can practice immediately. Green industry firms in all market segments including landscape management, lawn care, design, build and installation, irrigation and water management should attend.
Frequency: Annual

11640 Green Industry Great Escape
Professional Landcare Network
950 Herndon Parkway
Suite 450
Herndona, GA 20170
703-736-9666
800-395-2522; Fax: 703-736-9668
webmaster@landcarenetwork.org
www.landscapeprofessionals.org
Facebook, Twitter, LinkedIn, YouTube
Gerald J. Grossi, President
Norman Goldenberg, President-Elect
An annual destination meeting for upper-level management, owners, and key personnel.
1200 Members
Founded in 1979

11641 Green Profit's Retail Experience
Green Profit Magazine
335 N River Street
Batavia, IL 60510
630-208-9080
888-888-0013; Fax: 630-208-9350
info@ballpublishing.com
www.ballpublishing.com/conferences
Michelle Mazza, Show Manager
Educational event and tradeshow dedicated exclusively to garden center retailing. Covers topics from store layout and design to merchandising strategies and business management. 20 booths
300 Attendees
Frequency: Annual/September
Founded in 2006

11642 Interior Plantscape Symopsium
Professional Landcare Network
950 Herndon Parkway
Suite 450
Herndon, VA 20170
703-736-9666
800-395-2522; Fax: 703-736-9668
webmaster@landcarenetwork.org
www.plcaa.org/conference
Facebook, Twitter, LinkedIn, YouTube
Education will offer practical training for the front line with opportunities to earn CEUs toward Landscape Industry Certified Technician recertification as well as pesticide credits. Attendees will walk away with knowledge on how to run their businesses more effectively and keep customers happy. Technicians will learn cutting-edge techniques to make their jobs easier.
Frequency: Annual/April

11643 International Floriculture Expo
207-842-5508; Fax: 207-842-5509
www.floriexpo.com
Where buyers and suppliers from each stage of the floriculture production cycle come together to network, teach and learn from one another. With the live products, equipment, technology and education necessary for cultivating and retailing, find the ideas, new products, suppliers, trends and tools to flourish in the US market. Open to all buyers within the floriculture industry.
Frequency: Annual

11644 International Floriculture Trade Fair (IFTF)
Trade Show Bookings
PO Box 499
Fresh Meadows, NY 11365-0499
George Birne, Show Manager
The industry wide event serving all segments of the floriculture chain, from breeders, propagators, growers to the fresh flower trade.
40M Attendees
Frequency: Annual/November

11645 International Lawn Garden & Power Equipment Expo
Andry Montgomery and Associates
550 S 4th Avenue
#200
Louisville, KY 40202-2504
FAX 502-473-1999
Warren Sellers, Show Manager
The dream trade show for those interested in the concept of more power. The show is filled with outdoor lawn equipment that could do more faster, more quietly, more efficiently, and with the least amount of emissions.
25M Attendees
Frequency: Annual/July

11646 International Symposium on Orchids and Ornamental Plants
Home Page: www.orchidsociety.com
There are 75 booths and 50 exhibits that include bonsai trees, pots, tools and supplies, orchids, live plants and supplies for orchids and more.
Frequency: Annual/January

11647 Lawn & Garden Marketing & Distribution Summit Conference
2105 Laurel Bush Road
Suite 200
Bel Air, MD 21015
443-640-1080; Fax: 443-640-1031
www.lgmda.org
Steven T King, Executive VP
Marci L Hickey, Director Meetings/Member Services
Amy Chetelat, Financial Manager
Lawn and garden products. 120 booths.
500 Attendees
Frequency: Bi-Annual

11648 Lawn, Flower and Patio Show
Mid-America Expositions, Inc
7015 Spring Street
Omaha, NE 68106-3518
402-346-8003
800-475-7469; Fax: 402-346-5412
info@showofficeonline.com
www.showofficeonline.com
Robert P Mancuso, CEO
Mike Mancuso, VP/Manager
Annual show and exhibits of equipment, supplies and services for the lawn, flower and patio.
Frequency: Annual/February

11649 Mid Atlantic Nursery Trade Show
PO Box 11739
Baltimore, MD 21206-0339
410-882-5300
Carville Akehurst, Executive VP
Landscaping materials and horticultural tools. 750 booths, nursery stock, garden center and greenhouse supplies. 750 booths.
7.1M Attendees
Frequency: Annual/January

11650 Mid-Atlantic Nursery Trade Show
Mid Atlantic Nurserymen's Trade Shows
PO Box 818
Brooklandville, MD 21022
800-431-0066; Fax: 410-296-8288
Widely known as the masterpiece of trade shows.
11M Attendees
Founded in 1970

11651 Midwest Herb and Garden Show
PO Box 3434
Omaha, NE 68103-0434
Jane Booth, Show Manager
With vendors from throughout the midwest and nationally known speakers, this event is geared for everyone from the novice to master gardeners. Exhibitors display a variety of items including fresh herbs, herbs for culinary, medicinal, and decorative use, bulbs, seeds, books on birds, herbs and gardening, plans, herbal cookbooks, gardening magazines, bird feeders, houses and baths, antiques, china, spices, trellises, gourds, orchids, fudge, and much more.
15M Attendees
Frequency: Annual/February

11652 National City Home & Garden Show
Expositions

PO Box 550
Edgewater Branch
Cleveland, OH 44107-0550

216-529-1300; Fax: 216-529-0311
showinfo@expoinc.com
www.expoinc.com

Featuring showcases on how to make your dream home a reality. Create the garden oasis, backyard retreat or a relaxing sanctuary.
35000 Attendees
Frequency: Annual/February

11653 **National Lawn & Garden Trade Show**
Great American Exhibitions
112 Main Street
Norwalk, CT 06851

203-498-8735; Fax: 203-845-9183

Ronald Gratt, Manager

Sole mission has been to provide an affordable, efficient, alternative to traditional tradeshows which assures buyer/vendor introductions in pre-set scheduled appointments.
5000 Attendees
Frequency: Annual

11654 **National Lawn and Garden Show**
Controlled Marketing Conferences
PO Box 1771
Monument, CO 80132
719-488-0226
888-316-0226; Fax: 719-488-8168
www.nlgshow.com
Facebook, Twitter, LinkedIn

Bob Mikulas, President

This is the lawn and gardens premier headlines event and features both a pre-set scheduled appointment division and a traditional booth division.
300 Attendees
Frequency: June
Founded in 1995

11655 **National Pest Management Association Annual Eastern Conference**
10460 North Street
Fairfax, VA 22030

703-352-6762; Fax: 703-352-3031
www.npmapestworld.org
Facebook, Twitter

Dominique Stumpf, Chief Executive Officer
Alexis Wirtz, SVP, Meetings & Management Services
Megan Moloney, Director, Meetings & Exhibits
7000 Members
3500 Attendees
Frequency: January
Founded in 1933

11656 **Nursery/Landscape Expo**
Texas Nursery & Landscape Association
7730 S IH-35
Austin, TX 78745-6698

512-280-5182
800-880-0343; Fax: 512-280-3012
www.txnla.org

Ed Edmonson, Show Manager
Amy Prenger, President
Nancy Sollohub, Executive Assistant
Darlene Lanham, Communications Manager

Learn about industry trends, experience the breadth and depth of the green industry all under one roof, network, hear about industry best practices from peers and industry experts, and find the best deals from the best dealers in the southwest and beyond.
11M Attendees
Frequency: Annual/August

11657 **Old House New House Home Show**
Kennedy Productions
1208 Lisle Place
Lisle, IL 60532

630-515-1160; Fax: 630-515-1165
info@kennedyproductions.com
www.kennedyproductions.com
Facebook

Laura McNamara, Event Producer

Over 300 home improvement exhibitors displaying cutting-edge home enhancements for kitchens, baths, home and garden including landscape, interior remodeling, pools, spas, floors, doors and more.
8000 Attendees
Frequency: Bi-Annual
Founded in 1984

11658 **Perennial Production Conference**
335 N River Street
Batavia, IL 60510

630-208-9080
888-888-0013; Fax: 630-208-9350
perennialplantconference.org

Michelle Mazza, Show Manager

Perennial producers of all levels are urged to attend this unique event, which offers an educational and networking experience focused 100 percent on perennials. Learn everything about perennial production and retailing through workshops, seminars, tours, and a trade show.
600 Attendees
Frequency: Annual/September
Founded in 2003

11659 **Tropical Plant Industry Exhibition**
Florida Nursery Growers Landscape Association
1533 Park Center Drive
Orlando, FL 32835

407-295-7994
800-375-3642; Fax: 407-295-1619
info@fngla.org
www.fngla.org/tpie/
Facebook, Twitter, LinkedIn

Linda Adams, Show Manager
Sabrina Haines, Trade Show Coordinator

The trade event showcasing the latest trends in foliage, floral and tropicals. More than an exhibit area, it's 200,000 square feet of living and vibrant plants creating a virtual indoor garden of showstopping displays.
8,000 Attendees
Frequency: Annual/January

Directories & Databases

11660 **Complete Directory of Home Gardening Products**
Sutton Family Communications & Publishing Company
920 State Route 54 East
Elmitch, KY 42343

270-276-9500

Theresa Sutton, Editor
Lee Sutton, General Manager

Print-out from database of wholesalers, manufacturers, distributors, importers and close-out houses. Database is updated daily to guarantee the most current and up-to-date sources available.
Cost: $39.50
100+ Pages

11661 **Complete Directory of Horticulture**
Sutton Family Communications & Publishing Company
920 State Route 54 East
Elmitch, KY 42343

270-276-9500

Theresa Sutton, Editor
Lee Sutton, General Manager

Print-out from database of wholesalers, manufacturers, distributors, importers and close-out houses. Database is updated daily to guarantee the most current and up-to-date sources available.
Cost: $39.50
100+ Pages

11662 **DGA Membership Directory**
Mailorder Gardening Association
5836 Rockburn Woods Way
Elkridge, MD 21075-7302

410-540-9830; Fax: 410-540-9827

Camille Cimino, Executive Director

Member catalogers who sell gardening and nursery stock and supplies to consumers.
Cost: $2.00
Frequency: Annual

Industry Web Sites

11663 **KidsGardening.org**
National Gardening Association
237 Commerce St.
Suite 101
Williston, VT 05495

800-538-7476; Fax: 802-864-6889
www.kidsgardening.org

Jennifer Tedeschi, Executive Director
Sarah Pounders, Youth Education Specialist

Educational resources and garden grants for youth.

11664 **http://gold.greyhouse.com**
G.O.L.D Grey House OnLine Databases

Grey House Publishing's online database platform, GOLD, offers Quick Search, Keyword Search and Expert Search for most business sectors including garden and lawncare markets. The GOLD platform makes finding the information you need quick and easy - whether you're a novice searcher or an experienced database user. All of Grey House's directory products are available for subscription on the GOLD platform.

11665 **www.ahs.org**
American Horticultural Society

Individuals, institutions and businesses interested in a wide range of horticultural concerns.

11666 **www.ahta.org**
American Horticultural Therapy Association

Professional therapists, rehabilitation specialists and others using horticulture as a medium of rehabilitation.

11667 **www.aifd.org**
American Institute of Floral Designers

Non-profit association to support the floral design industry.

11668 **www.ascfg.org**
Association of Specialty Cut Flower Growers

Trade association that provides cultural and marketing information to specialty cut flower growers.

11669 **www.asla.org**
American Society of Landscape Architects
Landscape architects.

11670 **www.emda.net**
Farm Equipment Wholesalers Association

International trade association of wholesale/distributors of ag equipment and related products.

11671 **www.gardenwriters.org**
Garden Writers Association of America

A organization with materials of interest to garden writers and news on members of the Association.

11672 **www.greyhouse.com**
Grey House Publishing

Authoritative reference directories for most business sectors including garden and lawncare markets. Users can search the online databases with varied search criteria allowing for custom searches by product category, geographic area, sales volume, keyword, subject and more. Full Grey House catalog and online ordering also available.

11673 **www.landcarenetwork.org**
Professional Landcare Network

Lawn care companies, manufacturers/suppliers, ground managers and university personnel comprise membership of PLCAA. PLCAA is an educational, professional resource for the lawn and landscape industry.

11674 **www.mailordergardening.com**
Mailorder Gardening Association

Mail-order suppliers of gardening and nursery stock and supplies.

11675 **www.nahsa.org**
North American Horticultural Supply Association

Promotes full service distributors in the greenhouse and nursery hard good supply market.

11676 **www.pgms.org/**
Professional Grounds Management Society

Members are professionals involved in the care and maintenance of public and private sites.

11677 **www.safnow.org**
Society of American Florists

Represents all segments of the U.S. floral industry.

11678 **www.turfgrasssod.org**
Turf Grass Producers International

An organization featuring business news and updates on legislation and agronomics concerning the turf industry.

11679 **www.turfzone.com**
Turf Zone

Includes, commerical lawn care, consumer lawn care, irrigation equipment, fertilizer and other turf products.

Associations

11680 **American Craft Council**
1224 Marshall St. NW
Suite 200
Minneapolis, MN 55413

612-206-3100
800-836-3470; Fax: 612-355-2330
council@craftcouncil.org
www.craftcouncil.org
Facebook, Twitter, Flickr, YouTube, RSS

Chris Amundsen, Executive Director
Alanna Nissen, Office Coordinator
Greg Allen, Director, Finance & Administration
Claudia Cackler, Director, Development
Pamela Diamond, Director, Marketing & Communication

The American Craft Council is a national, non-profit educational organization to champion craft.
Founded in 1943

11681 **Gift & Home Trade Association**
2550 Sandy Plains Road
Suite 225, PO Box 214
Marietta, GA 30066

877-600-4872
info@giftandhome.org
www.giftandhome.org
Facebook, Twitter, LinkedIn

Todd Litzman, Chairman
Bob Ricciardi, President
Joe Harris, Vice President
Fred Schmidt, Treasurer
Allison Barrows, Secretary

The association was designed to help and encourage vendors, sales agencies, industry affiliates and retailers to work together, improving relationships and making business better by providing members with the opportunity to exchange ideas and network with industry leaders.
Founded in 2000

11682 **Gift Association of America**
115 Rolling Hills Road
Johnstown, PA 15905-5225

814-288-3893

Michael Russo, President

Gift association comprised of retailers and wholesalers in the gift industry.
Founded in 1592

11683 **Gift Basket Association**
8550 N. 91st Avenue
Suite 67
Peoria, AZ 85345

408-307-3411
giftbasketassociation.com
Facebook, Twitter

Debbie Quintana, Founder

Provides a central point of support to everyone in the gift basket industry, and works with gift basket companies throughout the globe to provide a variety of resources to help them grow themselves and their companies.
Founded in 2009

11684 **Greeting Card Association**
1444 I St. NW
Suite 700
Washington, DC 20005

202-216-9627; Fax: 202-216-9646
gca@greetingcard.org
www.greetingcard.org

Peter Doherty, Executive Director

Trade association representing American and international publishers - large and small - and production and distribution providers.
Founded in 1941

11685 **Museum Store Association**
2025 M Street NW
Suite 800
Washington, DC 20036

202-367-1106; Fax: 202-367-2104
info@museumstoreassociation.org
www.museumstoreassociation.org
Facebook, Twitter, LinkedIn, Pinterest

Steven Antolick, Executive Director
2500 Members
Founded in 1955

11686 **National Gift Organization**
332 Hurst Mill N
Bremen, GA 30110

505-798-0375
800-446-2533
www.naled.org

Ken Shirley, President

Trade association for the gift and collectibles industry. Offers once yearly expositions, a newsletter, software, low cost credit card processing, telephone service discounts and more to help you run your business profitably.
350 Members

11687 **National Specialty Gift Association**
PO Box 843
Norman, OK 73070

405-329-7847

Joni Damico, Executive Director

Specialty gift resource center for retailers, wholesale vendors and related professionals.
Cost: $29.95
400 Members
Founded in 1998

11688 **Organization of Associated Salespeople in the Southwest/OASIS**
859 University Dr.
Estes Park, CO 80517

602-952-2050; Fax: 602-445-6936
info@oasis.org
www.oasis.org
Facebook

Kristi Thomas, Media Relations
Melanie Beck, OASIS Gift Show Manager

A gift trade association which represents the manufacturing, sales and distribution side of the giftware industry. OASIS exhibitors offer trend setting general merchandise, world imports, home d,cor, jewelry, Native American art and crafts, western flair and southwestern gifts.
Founded in 1976

11689 **Retail Gift Card Association**
4248 Park Glen Road
Minneapolis, MN 55416

952-928-4688
info@theRGCA.org
www.thergca.org
Facebook, Twitter, LinkedIn

Jayne Stegemiller, Chair
Erin Wood, Vice Chair
Tim Anderson, Treasurer

The only trade association representing the closed-loop gift card industry, and is comprised of members committed to promoting and protecting the use of retail gift cards. RGCA members follow a code of principles that promotes best practice standards to help the industry grow, shaping it in ways that benefit both members and consumers.
85 Members
Founded in 2008

Magazines & Journals

11690 **American Craft Magazine**
American Craft Council
1224 Marshall St. NW
Suite 200
Minneapolis, MN 55413

612-206-3100
800-836-3470; Fax: 612-355-2330
council@craftcouncil.org
www.craftcouncil.org

Chris Amundsen, Executive Director
Alanna Nissen, Office Coordinator
Greg Allen, Director, Finance & Administration
Claudia Cackler, Director, Development
Pamela Diamond, Director, Marketing & Communication

Official magazine of the American Craft Council containing contemporary craft art and happenings of the Council.
Cost: $25.00
Frequency: 6x/Year
Founded in 1943

11691 **Gift Basket Review**
Festivities Publications
815 Haines Street
Jacksonville, FL 32206-6025

904-634-1902
800-729-6338; Fax: 904-633-8764
www.festivities-pub.com

Debra Paulk, Publisher
Kathy Horak, Managing Editor

Magazine devoted to issues relating to the gift basket and gift packing industries.
Cost: $29.94
Frequency: Monthly
Circulation: 15000
Founded in 1990

11692 **Gifts & Decorative Accessories**
Reed Business Information
360 Park Ave S
4th Floor
New York, NY 10010-1737

646-805-0234; Fax: 646-756-7583
corporatecommunications@reedbusiness.com
www.giftsanddec.com

Caroline Kennedy, Editor in Chief
Kathy Krassner, Editor at Large
Pamela Brill, Editor at Large

Serves retailers of stationery, greeting cards, collectibles, china, glass, lamps, and accessories.
Cost: $49.95
Frequency: Monthly
Circulation: 23737
ISSN: 0016-9889
Founded in 1946
Printed in 4 colors on glossy stock

11693 **Giftware News**
Talcott Communications Corporation
20 W Kinzie St
12th Floor
Chicago, IL 60654-5827

312-849-2220
800-229-1967; Fax: 312-849-2174
www.talcott.com
Twitter

Daniel Von Rabenau, Executive Director
Claire Weingarden, Associate Editor
John Saxtan, Editor in Chief

Edited for gift, stationery and department stores.
Cost: $39.00
Frequency: 18x Yearly
Circulation: 60000
Founded in 1982

11694 **Museum Store**
Museum Store Association
2025 M Street NW
Suite 800
Washington, DC 20036
202-367-1106; Fax: 202-367-2104
info@museumstoreassociation.org
www.museumstoreassociation.org
Facebook, Twitter, LinkedIn
Steven Antolick, Executive Director
Providing ideas, tips, insights and unique product sources for nonprofit retailers.
2500 Members
Founded in 1955

11695 **Souvenirs, Gifts & Novelties Magazine**
Kane Communications
7000 Terminal Square
Suite 210
Upper Darby, PA 19082-2330
610-734-2420; Fax: 610-734-2423
Scott Borowsky, President
Mary Anne Peacocti, Director Circulation
Caroline Burns, Managing Editor
Larry White, VP Marketing
Serves the general gift and trend marketplace with a core readership in the tourism and resorts gift and apparel stores.
Cost: $30.00
140 Pages
Frequency: 8x Yearly
Circulation: 43085
Founded in 1962
Printed in 4 colors on glossy stock

Trade Shows

11696 **ASD/AMD National Trade Show**
ASD/AMD Merchandise Group
2950 31st Street
Suite 100
Santa Monica, CA 90405
310-255-4633; Fax: 310-396-8476
The nation's largest, most comprehensive merchandise trade show. Featuring thousands of exhibitors, carrying products in more than 100 catebories, from jewelry and home decor to fashion accessories and general discount merchandise items.
10000 Attendees
Frequency: Annual/March

11697 **ASD/AMD's Gift Expo**
ASD/AMD Merchandise Group
2950 31st Street
Suite 100
Santa Monica, CA 90405
310-396-6006
800-421-4511; Fax: 310-399-2662
Julie Ichiba, Show Director
A general merchandise event which attracts over 50,000 buyers to Las Vegas. Tens of thousands of unique products in hundreds of popular consumer product categories are on display at this event.
55000 Attendees
Frequency: Bi-Annual

11698 **Accent on Design**
George Little Management
10 Bank Street
Suite 1200
White Plains, NY 10606-1954
914-486-6070
800-272-7469; Fax: 914-948-2867
www.nyigf.com
Elizabeth Murphy, Manager
George Little II, President
370 booths of the latest and most innovative gift lines such as decorative accessories and home furnishings.
50M Attendees
Frequency: Annual/August
Founded in 1999

11699 **American Craft Council Show**
American Craft Council
1224 Marshall St. NW
Suite 200
Minneapolis, MN 55413
612-206-3100
800-836-3470; Fax: 612-355-2330
council@craftcouncil.org
www.craftcouncil.org
Chris Amundsen, Executive Director
Alanna Nissen, Office Coordinator
Greg Allen, Director, Finance & Administration
Claudia Cackler, Director, Development
Pamela Diamond, Director, Marketing & Communication
The American Craft Council Show presents outstanding works by America's leading craftspeople for purchase by the public and to the trade
Founded in 1943

11700 **Annual Dickens Christmas Show and Festival**
Leisure Time Unlimited
2101 N. Oak Street
Myrtle Beach, SC 29577
843-448-9483
800-261-5991; Fax: 843-626-1513
dickensshow@sc.rr.com
www.dickenschristmasshow.com
Facebook, Twitter
Linda Cremer, Show Director
Victorian craft and gift show.
28000 Attendees
Frequency: Annual/November
Founded in 1981

11701 **Annual Spring New Products Show**
Pacific Expositions
1580 Makaola Street
Suite 1200
Honnolulu, HI 96814-3801
808-945-3594; Fax: 808-946-6399
Pat Shine, General Sales Manager
Kimalar K Carrol, Show Director/Coordinator
Over 200 New Products Booth Displays featuring for the entire family. All categories of consumer products and service are presented: roofing, siding, jewerly, cosmetics, cars, boats, home improvement products. Over 75 Food & Crafts displays, Sportscards & memorabilia displays.
18000 Attendees
Frequency: Annual/April
Founded in 1974

11702 **GHTA Annual Conference**
Gift & Home Trade Association
4380 Brockton Drive SE
Suite 1
Grand Rapids, MI 49512
877-600-4872
info@giftandhome.org
www.giftandhome.org
Marc Rice, Chairman of the Board
Julie Dix, President
John Keiser, Vice President
Todd Litzman, Treasurer
Denny King, Secretary
GHTA has partnered with the Gift Associates Interchange Network, Inc. (GAIN) to form a new credit reporting interchange. The interchange will give GHTA members access to retailer payment experiences, flash notices, predictive payment scoring, educational resources and more.
Frequency: Annual
Founded in 2000

11703 **General Gifts: A Division of the New York International Gift Fair**
George Little Management
10 Bank Street
White Plains, NY 10606-1954
914-486-6070
800-272-7469; Fax: 914-948-6180
www.nyigf.com
George Little II, President
Featuring stationary, collectibles, ceramic giftware, toys, pet items, party lines, trend merchandise, premiums, trim-a-tree, souvenirs and novelties, specialty foods, home office, floral & garden accessories, Judaica, and general items.
Frequency: Biennial

11704 **Grand Strand Gift and Resort Merchandise Show**
Fairchild Urban Expositions
5500 Interstate N Parkway
Suite 520
Atlanta, GA 30328
770-952-6444; Fax: 770-956-9644
Facebook
Bringing the nation's retailers an unrivaled selection of themed merchandise, resort apparel, gifts and souvenirs.
300 Attendees
Frequency: Annual/December

11705 **Gulf Coast Gift Show**
Fairchild Urban Expositions
5500 Interstate N Parkway
Suite 520
Atlanta, GA
770-952-6444; Fax: 770-956-9644
www.urban-expo.com
Facebook
Offering retailers from the Florida Panhandle and surrounding Gulf Coast areas to New Orleans an opportunigy to buy last minute holiday merchandise and get a jump on their spring/summer resort buying.
4000 Attendees
Frequency: Annual/October

11706 **Holiday Market**
Gilmore Enterprises
3514 Drawbridge Pkwy
Suite A
Greensboro, NC 27410-8584
336-282-5550; Fax: 336-282-0555
contact@gilmoreshows.com
www.gilmoreshows.com
Facebook
Tami Gilmore, Show Manager
Clyde Gilmore, Executive Director
Jan Donovon, Marketing Manager

There are two Holiday Market Shows, one in Greensboro, NC and the others in N. Cahrleston, SC. celebrate the season at Holiday Market. Children visit with santa and you will come away with ideas, recipes, samples, beauty makeovers and treats and holiday gifts.
35000 Attendees
Frequency: Annual/November
Founded in 1989

11707 Immediate Delivery Show: Fall
AMC Trade Shows/DMC Expositions
240 Peachtree Street NW
Suite 2200
Atlanta, GA 30303
404-220-3000; Fax: 404-220-3030
Mary Ellen Jackson, Show Manger
A trade show that allows you to move discontinued merchandise, overstocked inventory, samples and one of a kind items.
9000 Attendees
Frequency: Annual/November

11708 Indoor/Outdoor Home Show
True Value
PO Box 17
Bethel Park, PA 15102
412-276-6292; Fax: 412-851-6975
www.pitthomeshow.com
Plenty of exhibits and vendors, and the ultimate displays for the home office, garage, backyard and patio, dream windows, home flooring, and bathroom.
61000 Attendees
Frequency: Annual/January

11709 International Jewelry Fair/General Merchandise Show
Helen Brett Enterprises
5111 Academy Drive
Lisle, IL 60532
630-241-9865
800-541-8171; Fax: 630-241-9870
dharrington@helenbrett.com
www.gift2jewelry.com
Dave Harrington, Show Manager
Containing 1500 booths during the fall show and 800 booths during the spring show. Tradeshow open to wholesale buyers only (credentials required to attend).
44000 Attendees
Frequency: Bi-Annual

11710 Licensing International Expo
310-857-7544
888-644-2022
www.licensingexpo.com
Talia Loggia, Marketing Manager
Annual show of 220 exhibitors of logos, corporate trademarks, characters, designs and other advertising techniques that require licensing.
7000 Attendees
Frequency: Annual/July

11711 MSA Annual Retail Conference and Expo
Museum Store Association
2025 M Street NW
Suite 800
Washington, DC 20036
202-367-1106; Fax: 202-367-2104
info@museumstoreassociation.org
www.museumstoreassociation.org
Steven Antolick, Executive Director
Identify new sales leads, enhance your image and visibility in this niche market, reach your target audience, personally meet your customers, introduce a new product or service, generate sales, and network.
2500 Attendees
Founded in 1955

11712 Memphis Gift & Jewelry Show-Fall
Helen Brett Enterprises
5111 Academy Drive
Lisle, IL 60532
630-241-9865
800-541-8171; Fax: 630-241-9870
dharrington@helenbrett.com
www.gift2jewelry.com
Dave Harrington, Show Manager
Containing over 350 booths during the fall show and 350 booths during the spring show. Tradeshow open to wholesale buyers only (credentials required to attend).
9000 Attendees
Frequency: Annual/August

11713 Memphis Gift & Jewelry Show-Spring
Helen Brett Enterprises
5111 Academy Drive
Lisle, IL 60532
630-241-9865
800-541-8171; Fax: 630-241-9870
dharrington@helenbrett.com
www.gift2jewelry.com
Dave Harrington, Show Manager
Containing over 350 booths during the spring show and 350 booths during the fall show. Tradeshow open to wholesale buyers only (credentials required to attend).
9000 Attendees
Frequency: Annual/February

11714 Mid-South Jewelry & Accessories Fair -Spring
Helen Brett Enterprises
5111 Academy Drive
Lisle, IL 60532
630-241-9865
800-541-8171; Fax: 630-241-9870
dharrington@helenbrett.com
www.gift2jewelry.com
Dave Harrington, Show Manager
Containing over 300 booths during the spring show and 500 booths during the fall show. Tradeshow open to wholesale buyers only (credentials required to attend).
8500 Attendees
Frequency: Annual/May

11715 Mid-South Jewelry & Accessories Fair-Fall
Helen Brett Enterprises
5111 Academy Drive
Lisle, IL 60532
630-241-9865
800-541-8171; Fax: 630-241-9870
dharrington@helenbrett.com
www.gift2jewelry.com
Dave Harrington, Show Manager
Containing 500 booths during the fall show and over 300 booths during the spring show. Tradeshow open to wholesale buyers only (credentials required to attend).
16000 Attendees
Frequency: Annual/November

11716 Motivation Show
Hall-Erickson
98 E Naperville Road
Westmont, IL 60559
630-963-9185
800-752-6312; Fax: 630-434-1216
Nancy A Petitti, Show Director
Connecting engagement, loyalty, and financial results, learn from professional seminars on the latest trends, topics and best practices from some of America's leading organizations.
24000 Attendees
Frequency: Annual/September
Founded in 1929

11717 Museum Source
George Little Management
10 Bank Street
Suite 1200
White Plains, NY 10606-2867
914-486-6070
800-272-7469; Fax: 914-948-6180
Chelsea A Weinert, Divisional Manager
George Little II, President
Semi-annual show devoted to manufacturers, importers and publishers whose products are appropriate for museum gift shops, bookshores, specialty shops, zoos, aquariums and galleries. Items displayed include calendars, novelties, ethnic and craft items, historical interpretational products, art objects, children's educational items and posters.
Frequency: SemiAnnual

11718 Museum Source: West
George Little Management
10 Bank Street
Suite 1200
White Plains, NY 10606-1954
914-486-6070
800-272-7469; Fax: 914-948-6180
Elizabeth Murphy, Division Manager
George Little II, President
Semi-annual show devoted to manufacturers, importers and publishers whose products are appropriate for museum gift shops, bookshores, specialty shops, zoos, aquariums and galleries. Items displayed include calendars, novelties, ethnic and craft items, historical interpretational products, art objects, children's educational items and posters.
Frequency: SemiAnnual

11719 National Gift Basket Convention
Gift Basket Association
8550 N. 91st Avenue
Suite 67
Peoria, AZ 85345
408-307-3411
giftbasketassociation.com
Debbie Quintana, Founder, Gift Basket Association
A national convention for professionals involved in the gift basket industry.
Founded in 2009

11720 National Halloween Convention
Transworld Exhibits
1850 Oak Street
Northfield, IL 60093
847-784-6905
800-323-5462; Fax: 847-446-3523
www.nationalhalloweenconvention.com
This once a year event is where over 10,000 attendees will converge on Chicago from all across the US and over 50 foreign countries to see what over 700 manufacturers and distributors are showcasing as new and exciting for parties, shops and haunted houses. Free educational seminars and workshops.
Frequency: Annual/May

11721 National Stationery Show
Gerorge Little Management

10 Bank Street
Suite 1200
White Plains, NY 10606

741-421-3200
800-272-7469; Fax: 914-948-2918
www.nationalstationeryshow.com

Lori Robinson, Show Manager

The National Stationery Show is the premiere market for stationery resources in the Unite States. The National Stationery Show presents more than 1,400 exhibitors and product in five distinctive sections; Presents, Celebrate, Take Note, HomeWork, and Indulgences. The show draws 15,000 domestic and international retailers representing department, chain and specialty stores, museum shops, galler and craft retailers, boutiques, stationery, greeting card and gift shops, bookstores, bridal shops
15000 Attendees
Frequency: Annual/May

11722 **New Orleans Gift & Jewelry Show-Fall**
Helen Brett Enterprises
5111 Academy Drive
Lisle, IL 60532

630-241-9865
800-541-8171; Fax: 630-241-9870
dharrington@helenbrett.com
www.gift2jewelry.com
Facebook

Dave Harrington, Show Manager

Containing 850 booths during the fall show and 750 booths during the spring show. Tradeshow open to wholesale buyers only (credentials required to attend).
27000 Attendees
Frequency: Annual/August

11723 **New Orleans Gift & Jewelry Show-Spring**
Helen Brett Enterprises
5111 Academy Drive
Lisle, IL 60532

630-241-9865
800-541-8171; Fax: 630-241-9870
dharrington@helenbrett.com
www.gift2jewelry.com

Dave Harrington, Show Manager

Containing 750 booths during the spring show and 850 booths during the fall show. Tradeshow open to wholesale buyers only (credentials required to attend).
20000 Attendees
Frequency: Annual/January

11724 **New Yorks Newest: A Division of the New York International Gift Fair**
George Little Management
10 Bank Street
White Plains, NY 10606-1954

914-486-6070
800-272-7469; Fax: 914-948-6180
www.nyigf.com

George Little II, President

Showcasing 250 exhibitors new to the NYIGF spanning all categories and featuring fresh and innovative lines.
Frequency: SemiAnnual

11725 **OASIS Gift Show**
Organization of Assn Salespeople in the Southwest
859 University Dr.
Estes Park, CO 80517

602-952-2050; Fax: 602-952-2244
info@oasis.org
www.oasis.org

Melanie Beck, OASIS Gift Show Manager

Brings success, opportunity, and convenience to buyers and exhibitors. Each show features an expansive product selection on the main floor, the jury-chosen artisans' showcase, and the gifts 2 go cash and carry area. Exhibitors offer trend setting general merchandise, world imports, home decor, jewelry, native american arts and crafts, western flair and southwestern gifts. OASIS is dedicated to providing a wholesale gift marketplace.
6000+ Attendees
Frequency: Annual/January

11726 **Offinger's Handcrafted Martketplace**
Offinger Management Company
1100-H Brandywine Boulevard
Zanesville, OH 43701-7303

888-878-4438; Fax: 740-452-2552
gift@offinger.com

Providing safe, convenient and inexpensive trade shows with rich collections of handmades, limited-production creations, traditional crafts and gifts, home furnishings, furniture and home accents. Meet the country's top producers of folk art, rustic primitives, museum quality replicas, handmade country collectibles, as well as one-of-a-kind, contemporary works of art.
3300 Attendees
Frequency: Triannual

11727 **San Francisco International Gift Fair**
San Francisco, CA

Home Page: sfigf.com

Top name manufacturers, innovative newcomers, and cutting edge designs.
2500 Attendees

11728 **Smoky Mountain Gift Show: Fall**
Smoky Mountain Gift Show
PO Box 50
Gatlinburg, TN 37738

865-436-4418
800-441-7889; Fax: 865-436-2878
www.smokymountaingiftshow.com

Eva Havlicek, Owner

The most beloved, most popular trade shows for the souvenir, resort and gift industry. Brings the top-name product selection, buyer base, service levels, and spirit of fun and hospitality that defined the show at its prime.
3000 Attendees
Frequency: Annual/November
Founded in 1966

11729 **Smoky Mountain Gift Show: Spring**
Smoky Mountain Gift Show
PO Box 50
Gatlinburg, TN 37738

865-436-4418
800-441-7889; Fax: 865-436-2878
www.smokymountaingiftshow.com

Eva Havlicek, Owner

Geared to the gift and souvenier market. Wholesale trade show open only to buyers in the retail industry. Buyers must present credentials upon registration.
12000 Attendees
Frequency: Annual/March

11730 **Southern Christmas Show**
Southern Shows
PO Box 36859
Charlotte, NC 28236

704-566-1898; Fax: 703-376-6345

Check out the holiday trees, mantels and doors, stroll the Christmas Village, munch on tasty treats and sway with yuletide entertainment.
13200 Attendees

11731 **Southern Ideal Home Show: Fall**
Southern Shows
PO Box 36859
Charlotte, NC 28236

704-566-1898
800-849-0248; Fax: 704-676-6345
dzimmerman@southernshows.com
southernshows.com

David Zimmerman, Show Manager
Brenda Crofts, Assistant Show Manager

Gardens, designer rooms, seminars, exhibitors, and experts on remodeling, decorating, home improvement and landscaping
20000 Attendees
Frequency: Annual/September

11732 **Toy Fair**
Toy Industry Association
1115 Broadway
Suite 400
New York, NY 10010

212-675-1141; Fax: 212-645-3246
toyfairs@toy-tia.org

Thomas Conley, President
Diane Cardinale, Public Information Manager

Products include: games, toys, puzzles, dolls, science and hobby craft kits, books, bicycles and ride-ons, computer and video games and software, playground and sporting equipment, costumes and holiday decorations.
22000 Attendees
Frequency: Annual/February

11733 **Variety Merchandise Show**
Miller Freeman Publications
One Penn Plaza
PO Box 2549
New York, NY 10116

212-714-1300; Fax: 212-714-1313

An emphasis on customer service, community building forums and practical business education seminars.
20000 Attendees

11734 **Western States Toy and Hobby Show**
Western Toy and Hobby Representative Association
9397 Reserve Drive
Corona, CA 92883

951-771-1598; Fax: 909-277-1599
www.wthra.com

Phylis St. John, Manager

The biggest assortment of toys, games, hobbies and educational fun.
3000 Attendees
Frequency: March

Directories & Databases

11735 **AR100 Award Show Guide**
Black Book Marketing Group
10 Aston Place
6th Floor
New York, NY 10003

212-956-1425; Fax: 212-539-9801

H Huntington Stehli, President/Publisher

Lists of winners at the AR100 Award Show, which recognizes excellence in the field of annual reports; includes photographers, design firms, illustrators, printers and paper companies; includes listings and ads for winners of past shows.
Cost: $60.00
Frequency: Annual
Circulation: 10,000

11736 **Complete Directory of Giftware Items**
Sutton Family Communications & Publishing Company
920 State Route 54 East
Elmitch, KY 42343
270-276-9500
Theresa Sutton, Publisher
Lee Sutton, Editor
Print-out from database of wholesalers, manufacturers, distributors, importers and close-out houses. Database is updated daily to guarantee the most current and up-to-date sources available. Approximately 1,500 American direct wholesale sources in a three-ring binder.
Cost: $107.50
100 Pages

11737 **Complete Directory of Tabletop Items**
Sutton Family Communications & Publishing Company
920 State Route 54 East
Elmitch, KY 42343
270-276-9500
Theresa Sutton, Editor
Lee Sutton, General Manager
Print-out from database of wholesalers, manufacturers, distributors, importers and close-out houses. Database is updated daily to guarantee the most current and up-to-date sources available.
Cost: $54.50
100+ Pages

11738 **Gift Associates Interchange Database**
1100 Main Street
Buffalo, NY 14209
716-885-4444; Fax: 716-878-2866
J Warren Wright, Secretary
An online credit interchange database.
240 Pages
Founded in 1974

11739 **Gift Associates Interchange Network**
716-887-9508
800-746-9428
www.gaingroup.com
Donna Mosteller, Director, Member Group Services
Rosanne Battaglia, Member, Development Representative
GAIN is an online credit interchange database designed by and for credit managers in giftware, greeting card, silk floral, and related industries.
200 Members

11740 **Giftware Manufacturers Credit Interchange**
1100 Main Street
Buffalo, NY 14209-2356
716-885-4444; Fax: 716-878-2866
www.gaingroup.com
J Warren Wright, Executive Secretary
Manufacturers and importers of giftware and china.
60 Pages

Industry Web Sites

11741 **http://gold.greyhouse.com**
G.O.L.D Grey House OnLine Databases
Grey House Publishing's online database platform, GOLD, offers Quick Search, Keyword Search and Expert Search for most business sectors including home and corporate gift markets. The GOLD platform makes finding the information you need quick and easy - whether you're a novice searcher or an experienced database user. All of Grey House's directory products are available for subscription on the GOLD platform.

11742 **www.greyhouse.com**
Grey House Publishing
Authoritative reference directories for most business sectors including home and corporate gift markets. Users can search the online databases with varied search criteria allowing for custom searches by product category, geographic area, sales volume, keyword, subject and more. Full Grey House catalog and online ordering also available.

11743 **www.museumstoreassociation.org**
Museum Store Association
Providing member representatives with the professional opportunities and educational resources they need to operate effectively and ethically.

11744 **www.naled.org**
National Gift Organization
Trade association for the gift and collectibles industry. Offers once yearly expositions, a newsletter, software, low cost credit card processing, telephone service discounts and more to help you run your business profitably.
350 Pages

11745 **www.oasis.org**
Organization of Associated Salespeople Southwest
A gift trade association which represents the manufacturing, sales and distribution side of the giftware industry.

11746 **www.shop.com**
Altura International
CatalogCity.com is a powerful and flexible e-commerce technology. This site includes recognized brand names such as Blair, Bombay, Chef's Catalog, Fisher-Price, Gump's by Mail, Hammacher Schlemmer, Ross-Simmons, The Sharper Image, and many more.

Associations

11747 ASM International
9639 Kinsman Road
Materials Park, OH 44073-0002

440-338-5151
800-336-5152; Fax: 440-338-4634
memberservicecenter@asminternational.org
www.asminternational.org
Facebook, Twitter, LinkedIn

Zi-Kui Liu, President
Diana Essock, Vice President
Raymond V. Fryan, Treasurer
William T. Mahoney, Secretary & CEO

The society for materials engineers and scientists, a worldwide network dedicated to advancing industry, technology and applications of metals and materials. ASM provides information references, education, research and international events.
30K Members
Founded in 1913

11748 American Art Pottery Association
Home Page: aapa.info
Facebook, Pinterest

Mark Latta, President
Mark Mazzuki, Vice President

Association of dealers and collectors of American Art Pottery.
Founded in 1983

11749 American Ceramic Society
600 N. Cleveland Ave.
Suite 210
Westerville, OH 43082

240-646-7054
866-721-3322; Fax: 301-206-9789
customerservice@ceramics.org
www.ceramics.org
Facebook, Twitter, LinkedIn, RSS

Charles Spahr, Executive Director
10000 Members
Founded in 1898

11750 American Cut Glass Association
PO Box 482
Ramona, CA 92065

760-789-2715; Fax: 760-789-7112
acgakathy@aol.com
www.cutglass.org
Facebook, YouTube

Kathy Emmerson, Executive Secretary
Judy Northrop, President

A non-profit organization devoted to the study and research of American Brilliant Cut Glass.
1500 Members
Founded in 1978

11751 American Flint Glass Workers Union
1440 S Byrne Road
Toledo, OH 43614-2363

419-385-6687; Fax: 419-385-8839
ljs@primenet.com

Timothy Tuttle, President

Organized as the United Flint Glass Workers.
21.7M Members
Founded in 1878

11752 American Scientific Glassblowers Society
PO Box 453
Machias, NY 14101

716-353-8062; Fax: 716-353-4259
natl-office@asgs-glass.org
www.asgs-glass.org
Facebook

Skip Huckaby, President
Joe Gregar, President-Elect
Philip Legge, Secretary
Victor Mathews, Treasurer
Jerry Cloninger, Executive Secretary

A not for profit organization that is dedicated to sharing the knowedge,techniques, and skills of scientific glassblowing to its worldwide membership.
650 Members
Founded in 1952

11753 Art Glass Association
5610 Pleasant View Dr.
Nashport, OH 43830

740-450-6547
866-301-2421; Fax: 661-264-5277
www.artglassassociation.com

Steve Shupper, Chairman
Jennifer Urbaniak, Vice Chair
Bill Bird, Treasurer
Craig Bradley, Secretary
Vickie Gillespie, Membership

International, nonprofit organization whose purpose is to create awareness, knowledge and involvement for the growth and prosperity of the art glass industry. Programs include an annual conference, group health insurance, marchant listings on our website and more.
Founded in 1986

11754 Ceramic Tile Distributors Association
800 Roosevelt Rd
Building C, Suite 312
Glen Ellyn, IL 60137

630-545-9415; Fax: 630-790-3095
info@ctdahome.org
www.ctdahome.org

Ruby Llerena, President
Steve Vogel, VP
Robert DeAngelis, Treasurer
Bill Ives, Legal Counsel
Rick Church, Executive Director

An international association of distributors, manufacturers and allied professionals of ceramic tile and related products. Mission is to provide educational and networking opportunities for distributors of ceramic tile and their suppliers to further the consumption of ceramic tile.
500 Members
Founded in 1978

11755 Ceramic Tile Institute of America
12061 Jefferson Blvd.
Culver City, CA 90230-6219

310-574-7800; Fax: 310-821-4655
ctioa@earthlink.net
www.ctioa.org

Thomas Brady, Board Member
Michael J, Nisenbaum, Board Member
Thomas Domenici, Board Member
Lindell Lummer, Board Member
Bill Klaser, Board Member

Promoting excellence in tile installation and encouraging greater consumption of tile through education, public relations and liaison with all facets of the construction industry as well as the general public.
Founded in 1992

11756 China Clay Producers Association-CCPA
113 Arkwright Landing
Macon, GA 31210

478-757-1211; Fax: 478-757-1949
info@georgiamining.org
www.kaolin.com/

Lee Lemke, Executive VP

Organized to advance and encourage the development and production of kaolin-based products, and to work together with the people of Georgia in the communities where the mineral is mined and products manufactured.
Founded in 1978

11757 Glass Art Society
6512 23rd Ave. NW
Suite 329
Seattle, WA 98117

206-382-1305; Fax: 206-382-2630
info@glassart.org
www.glassart.org
Facebook, Twitter, LinkedIn, Pinterest

Cassandra Straubing, President
Kim Harty, Vice President
Natali Rodrigues, VP
Roger MacPherson, Treasurer
Kelly Conway, Director

International nonprofit organization encouraging excellence, advancing education, promoting appreciation and development of the glass arts, and supporting the worldwide community of artists who work with glass. Members are artists, students, educators, collectors, gallery and museum personnel, writers and critics.
3100 Members
Founded in 1971

11758 Glass Association of North America
800 SW Jackson St.
Suite 1500
Topeka, KS 66612-1200

785-271-0208; Fax: 785-271-0166
gana@glasswebsite.com
www.glasswebsite.com

William M Yanek, Executive VP
Ashley M Charest, Account Executive
Urmilla Sowell, Technical Director
Sara Neiswanger, Technical Coordinator
Erin Roberts, Director of Marketing

Offers education on blueprint reading, labor and glass estimating and analysis; manuals on glazing guidelines, sealant compatibility and labor hours and a quarterly newsletter. Serves distributors, installers and fabricators of glass for use in the construction automotive and industrial industries.
250 Members
Founded in 1994

11759 Insulating Glass Certification Council
PO Box 730
Sackets Harbor, NY 13685

315-646-2234; Fax: 315-646-2297
www.igcc.org

John Kent, Program Administrator
Alicia Deveau, Program Administrator
Jennifer Mackey, Meetings & Events Administration
Andrew Mostley, Auditor

IGCC sponsors and directs an independent, true third-party certification program. Periodic accelerated laboratory tests, per American Society for Testing and Materials specifications, and unannounced plant quality audits and inspections assure the quality and performance of sealed insulating glass products.
48 Members
Founded in 1977

11760 National Glass Association
1945 Old Gallows Rd
Suite 750
Vienna, VA 22182

703-442-4890
866-342-5642; Fax: 703-442-0630
nga@glass.org

www.glass.org
Facebook, Twitter, LinkedIn
Philip J. James, President & CEO
Nicole Harris, Vice President & Publisher
Denise M Sheehan, VP, Industry Events
James Gandorf, VP, Association Services
Pamela S Paroline, Director, Administration & Finance

The National Glass Association is the largest trade association representing the flat (architectural and automotive) glass industy. Member companies and locations reflect the entire vertical flat glass market. To support this ever changing industry, NGA produces products and services specifically for the industry.
4900 Members
Founded in 1948

11761 National Industrial Sand Association
2011 Pennsylvania Avenue, NW
Suite 301
Washington, DC 20006

202-457-0200; Fax: 202-457-0287
info@sand.org
www.sand.org

Mark Ellis, President
Darrell K. Smith, Ph.D, Executive Vice President
Chris Greissing, VP Government Affairs
Paige Huggins, Financial Assistant

Trade association representing major manufacturers of industrial sand in North America. Committed to the safe use of industrial sand products and to advancing research and maintaining a dialogue with industry, legislators, regulatory agencies and the scientific community in support of the safety of empoyees and customers.
Founded in 1936

11762 Porcelain Enamel Institute
PO Box 920220
Norcross, GA 30010

770-676-9366; Fax: 770-409-7280
penamel@aol.com
www.porcelainenamel.com
Twitter, LinkedIn, RSS

Cullen Hackler, Executive Director
Kevin Coursin, Chairman
Glenn Pfendt, President
Phil Flasher, Treasurer
Cullen Hackler, Executive VP and Secretary

Dedicated to advancing the common interests of porcelain enameling plants and suppliers of porcelain enameling materials and equipment.
85 Members
Founded in 1930

11763 Refractory Ceramic Fiber Coalition
1200 Seventeenth Street, NW
Room 07-54
Washington, DC 20036-3006

202-663-9188; Fax: 202-354-4982
www.htiwcoalition.org

An association of the leading US producers of refractory ceramic fibers(RCFs). The RCF Coalition develops and promotes proper work practices and standards for the RCF industry, conducts RCF health research and disseminates information on the proper handling and use of refractory ceramic fiber.
Founded in 1992

11764 Safety Glazing Certification Council
100 West Main Street
PO Box 730
Sackets Harbor, NY 13685

315-646-2234; Fax: 315-646-2297
staff@amscert.com
www.sgcc.org

Bill Nugent, President
Bernie Herron, Vice President
June Willcott, Secretary
Elaine S. Rodman, Treasurer

A nonprofit corporation that provides for the certification of safety glazing materials. Comprised of safety glazing manufacturers and other parties concerned with public safety.
105 Members
Founded in 1971

11765 Society of Glass and Ceramic Decorated Products (SGCDpro)
47 N 4th Street
PO Box 2489
Zanesville, OH 43702

740-588-9882; Fax: 740-588-0245
info@sgcd.org
www.sgcd.org

Ed Weiner, President

Membership gives decorators and marketers of glass, ceramic and related products the confidence that they are part of a network of professionals who have shared knowledge and resources for nearly 50 years. Helps industry professionals identify new and profitable technology, keeps members abreast of the latest regulatory mandates and works with government and industry to provide reasonable solutions to regulatory compliance.
525 Members

11766 Stained Glass Association of America
9313 East 63rd Street
Raytown, MO 64133

816-737-2090
800-438-9581; Fax: 816-737-2801
headquarters@sgaaonline.com
www.stainedglass.org
Facebook, Twitter

Membership consists of the finest architectural stained and decorative art glass artists and studios in the US and around the world. Actively works for the betterment of the craft of stained glass and architectural art glass through various programs that are designed to benefit the members of the SGAA and the clients whom we serve.
Founded in 1903

11767 Technical Ceramics Manufacturers Association
25 N Broadway
Tarrytown, NY 10591-3221

914-332-0040; Fax: 914-332-1541

A organization of manufacturers of custom and standard technical ceramic products for use in commercial, residential or industrial applications.

11768 The American Ceramic Society
600 N Cleveland Ave.
Suite 210
Westerville, OH 43082

240-646-7054
866-721-3322; Fax: 240-396-5637
customerservice@ceramics.org
www.ceramics.org
Facebook, Twitter, LinkedIn, Google+, YouTube

Charlie Spahr, Executive Director

The National Institute of Ceramic Engineers, the Ceramic Manufacturing Council and the Ceramic Education Council are affiliated groups. All are leading organizations dedicated to the advancement of ceramics.
10000 Members
Founded in 1898

11769 United States Advanced Ceramics Association
1020 19th St NW
Suite 375
Washington, DC 20036-6118

202-467-5459; Fax: 202-467-5469
usaca@strategicmi.com
www.advancedceramics.org

Todd E Steyer, Chairman
Steve Johnson, Vice Chair
Tom Foltz, Treasurer
Kent W Buesking, Secretary
Glen Mandigo, Executive Director

The premier association that champions the common business interests of the advanced ceramic producer and end user industries.
Founded in 1985

11770 Wedgwood Society of Boston
132 Middle Street
Braintree, MA 02184

wedgwoodboston@gmail.com
wedgwoodsociety.org

Jeremy Hagger, President, Corporate Secretary, Recording Secretary
Ronald F. Frazier, Treasurer & Newsletter Editor

Organization for those who appreciate the work of the potter Josiah Wedgwood and related decorative arts.
Founded in 1969

Newsletters

11771 American Ceramic Society Bulletin
The American Ceramic Society
600 N. Cleveland Ave.
Suite 210
Westerville, OH 43082

866-720-3322; Fax: 301-206-9789
customerservice@ceramics.org
www.ceramics.org

L David Pye, President
Scott Steen, Executive Director

The undisputed authority on news and new developments in the Ceramics and Glass industries, focuses on five end-use industries: transportation, electronics, defense, energy and construction.
Cost: $75.00
Frequency: 9x Yearly
Circulation: 10,000
ISSN: 0002-7812
Founded in 1898
Printed in 4 colors on glossy stock

11772 The Hobstar
American Cut Glass Association
PO Box 482
Ramona, CA 92065

760-789-2715; Fax: 760-789-7112
acgakathy@aol.com
www.cutglass.org

ACGA's highly educational journal.
Frequency: 10x Yearly
Founded in 1876
Printed in 2 colors on glossy stock

11773 WDweekly
National Glass Association
1945 Old Gallows Rd
Suite 750
Vienna, VA 22182

703-442-4890
866-342-5642; Fax: 703-442-0630
nga@glass.org

www.glass.org
Facebook, Twitter, LinkedIn

Philip J. James, President & CEO
Nicole Harris, Vice President & Publisher
John Swanson, Editor & Associate Publisher

E-newsletter for manufacturers, distributors and dealers. The most thorough, convenient source for the latest industry news and insights on market, design, technology and economic trends.
4900 Members
Frequency: Weekly
Circulation: 30000
Founded in 1948

Magazines & Journals

11774 **AGRR Magazine**
Key Communications
PO Box 569
Garrisonville, VA 22463

540-577-7174; Fax: 540-720-5687
info@agrrmag.com
www.agrrmag.com
Facebook, Twitter, LinkedIn

Debra Levy, Publisher
Megan Headley, President

Source of unbiased, accurate information about auto glass repair and replacement industry.
Cost: $49.95
Frequency: 6x Yearly
Circulation: 10000+
Founded in 1993

11775 **Advanced Materials & Processes**
ASM International
9639 Kinsman Road
Materials Park, OH 44073-0002

440-338-5151
800-336-5152; Fax: 440-338-4634
magazines@asminternational.org
www.asminternational.org

William T. Mahoney, Secretary & CEO
Joanne Miller, Editor
Vicki Burt, Managing Editor

AM&P is the monthly technical magazine from ASM International, designed to keep readers aware of leading-edge developments and trends in engineering materials - metals and alloys, engineering polymers, advanced ceramics, and composites - and the methods used to select, process, fabricate, test, and characterize them.
30K Members
Frequency: Monthly
Circulation: 23000
Founded in 1913

11776 **American Flint Magazine**
American Flint Glass Workers Union
1440 S Byrne Road
Toledo, OH 43614-2363

419-385-6687; Fax: 419-385-8839

Timothy Tuttle, President

Union news and information for the glass industry.
Frequency: Monthly

11777 **Ceramic Bulletin**
American Ceramic Society
600 N. Cleveland Avenue
Suite 210
Westerville, OH 43082

240-646-7054
866-721-3322; Fax: 240-396-5637
customerservice@ceramics.org
www.ceramics.org

L David Pye, President
Scott Steen, Executive Director

Written for ceramic and materials engineers and production management teams involved in industrial ceramics manufacturing. Topics covered include government relations, environmental issues, developing technology, industry statistics, cutting-edge manufacturing processes and technology.
Cost: $75.00
Frequency: Monthly
Circulation: 50000
ISSN: 0027-812
Founded in 1953
Printed in 4 colors on glossy stock

11778 **Ceramic Industry**
Business News Publishing Company
6075 B Glick Rd
Powell, OH 43065

281-550-5855; Fax: 248-244-6439
ci@halldata.com
www.ceramicindustry.com

Amy Vallance, Publisher
Susan Sutton, Editor in Chief/Integrated Media
Teresa Mcpherson, Managing Editor
Cory Emery, Art Director
Karen Telan, Production Manager

Serves manufacturers of advanced ceramics, glass, whitewares, refractories and other ceramic businesses. CI's offerings include practical, real-world solutions to manufacturing problems, information on the latest technological advancements, and up-to-date coverage of news, issues and trends.
Frequency: Monthly
Circulation: 10000
Founded in 1926

11779 **Ceramics Monthly**
American Ceramic Society
735 Ceramic Pl
Suite 100
Westerville, OH 43081-8728

614-895-4213; Fax: 614-891-8960
editorial@ceramicsmonthly.org
www.ceramicsmonthly.org

Sherman Hall, Editor
Rich Guerrein, Publisher
Jennifer Poellot, Assistant editor
Susan Enderle, Marketing Manager
Erin Pfeifer, Advertising Manager

An internationally distributed magazine covering ceramic arts and crafts. Includes lists of conferences, exhibitions, festivals, fairs, sales and workshops for crafts people.
Cost: $32.00
Frequency: Monthly
Circulation: 35000
ISSN: 0009-0328
Founded in 1953
Printed in on glossy stock

11780 **Fired Arts and Crafts**
Jones Publishing
N7450 Aanstad Road
PO Box 5000
Iola, WI 54945-5000

715-445-5000
800-331-0038; Fax: 715-445-4053
jonespub@jonespublishing.com
www.jonespublishing.com

Joe Jones, CEO/President
Mick Harbridge, Editor
Branden Hardy, Marketing

Features on projects and patterns, celebrity clips, new products, show listings, industry news and book reviews.
Cost: $32.95
Frequency: Monthly
Circulation: 15000

11781 **Fusion**
American Scientific Glassblowers Society
PO Box 778
Madison, NC 27025

336-427-2406; Fax: 336-427-2496
natl-office@asgs-glass.org
www.asgs-glass.org

Marylin Brown, Editor

Contains technical articles, references and abstracts from other publications, book reviews, new product information, local section reports and announcements, committee reports, and information about health and safety concerns. An excellent source for vendor information with ads of goods and services.
Cost: $40.00
Frequency: Quarterly
Circulation: 850
Founded in 1954

11782 **Glass Craftsman**
Arts & Media
10 Canal Street
Suite 300
Bristol, PA 19007

215-826-1799; Fax: 215-826-1788
www.artglassworld.com

Joe Porcelli, Publisher

Providing the best professionally produced, technical, aesthetic and practical information to its readers and a strong, committed audience of glass enthusiasts and professionals to its family of advertisers.
Cost: $25.00
Circulation: 12000
ISSN: 1079-199X

11783 **Glass Magazine**
National Glass Association
1945 Old Gallows Rd
Suite 750
Vienna, VA 22182

703-448-1319; Fax: 703-442-0630
www.glassmagazine.com

Nicole Harris, VP
Nancy Davis, Editor-in-Chief

Provides subscribers informative coverage of glass industry news, trends and analysis, product introductions, and best business practices, in addition to glass industry statistics and supplier resource guides.
Cost: $34.95
Frequency: 11x Yearly
Circulation: 27098
Founded in 1948

11784 **Journal of Materials Engineering and Performance**
ASM International
9639 Kinsman Road
Materials Park, OH 44073-0002

440-338-5151
800-336-5152; Fax: 440-338-4634
memberservicecenter@asminternational.org
www.asminternational.org

William T. Mahoney, Secretary & CEO
Rajiv Asthana, Editor

Peer-reviewed journal that publishes contributions on all aspects of materials selection, design, characterization, processing and performance testing. The journal is useful for solving day-to-day engineering challenges - especially those involving components for larger systems.
30K Members
Frequency: Bi-Monthly
Founded in 1913

11785 **Journal of Phase Equilibria & Diffusion**
ASM International

9639 Kinsman Road
Materials Park, OH 44073-0002

440-338-5151
800-336-5152; Fax: 440-338-4634
memberservicecenter@asminternational.org
www.asminternational.org

William T. Mahoney, Secretary & CEO
John Morral, Editor
Ursula R. Kattner, Editor
H. Okamoto, Editor

Peer-reviewed journal containing basic and applied research results, evaluated phase diagrams, a survey of current literature, and comments or other material pertinent to the previous three areas. The aim of the journal is to provide a broad spectrum of information concerning phase equilibria for the materials community.
30K Members
Frequency: Bi-Monthly
Founded in 1913

11786 Journal of the American Art Pottery Association
American Art Pottery Association

Home Page: aapa.info/current-issue
Facebook, Pinterest

Linda Carrigan, Managing Director
Frank Norman, Advertising Director
Mark Mazzuki, Creative Director

Association of dealers and collectors of American Art Pottery.

11787 Journal of the American Ceramic Society
American Ceramic Society
735 Ceramic Pl
Suite 100
Westerville, OH 43081

866-721-3322; Fax: 301-206-9789
customerservice@ceramics.org
www.ceramics.org

David J. Green, Associate Editor
David W. Johnson, Jr., Associate Editor
Lisa Klein, Associate Editor
John Halloran, Associate Editor

Contains records of original research that provide or lead to fundamental principles in the science of ceramics and ceramic-based composites. These papers include reports of the discovery of new phases, phase relationships, processing approaches and microstructures that relate to ceramic materials and processes.
Cost: $1190.00
Frequency: Monthly
ISSN: 0002-7820
Founded in 1905

11788 Pottery Making Illustrated
Ceramic Publications Company
735 Ceramic Pl
Suite 100
Westerville, OH 43081

866-721-3322; Fax: 301-206-9789
customerservice@ceramics.org
www.ceramics.org

Charlie Spahr, Publisher
Bill Jones, Editor
Mona Thiel, Advertising Manager
Steve Hecker, Marketing Manager
Erin Pfeifer, Editorial Assistant

Provides intermediate to advanced potters with practical techniques, tips and information for the studio in a well-illustrated format. With articles on throwing, handbuilding, sculpture, decorating and firing, PMI covers every aspect of the studio ceramic process. In addition, PMI provides up-to-date information on tools, supplies and materials for the ceramic studio.
Cost: $22.00
Frequency: Bi-Monthly
Circulation: 20000
Founded in 1905

11789 Stained Glass
Stained Glass Association of America
9313 East 63rd Street
Raytown, MO 64133

816-737-2090
800-438-9581; Fax: 816-737-2801
headquarters@sgaaonline.com
www.stainedglass.org
Facebook, Twitter

Features articles about historical and contemporary installations that will show you what others in the field are doing.
Frequency: Quarterly
Founded in 1903

11790 The Hobstar
American Cut Glass Association
PO Box 482
Ramona, CA 92065

760-789-2715; Fax: 760-789-7112
acgakathy@aol.com
www.cutglass.org
Facebook, YouTube

Kathy Emmerson, Executive Secretary
Karen Parker, President

ACGA's highly educational journal.
1500 Members
Frequency: 10x Yearly
Founded in 1978

11791 US Glass, Metal & Glazing
Key Communications
PO Box 569
Garrisonville, VA 22463

540-577-7174; Fax: 540-720-5687
www.usglassmag.com
Facebook, Twitter, LinkedIn

Penny Stacey, Advertising Coordinator
Ellen Giard Chilcoat, Editor
Debra Levy, President

Serves manufactures/fabricators, contract glaziers, distributors and wholesalers, retailors/dealers of glass/metal and/or glass/metal products and others allied to the field.
Frequency: Monthly
Circulation: 25572
ISSN: 0041-7661
Founded in 1965
Printed in 4 colors on glossy stock

11792 Window & Door
National Glass Association
1945 Old Gallows Rd
Suite 750
Vienna, VA 22182

703-442-4890
866-342-5642; Fax: 703-442-0630
nga@glass.org
www.glass.org
Facebook, Twitter, LinkedIn

Philip J. James, President & CEO
Nicole Harris, Vice President & Publisher
John Swanson, Editor & Associate Publisher

Serves the entire fenestration industry, including manufacturers, distributors, and dealers. Offers readers focused news coverage, insightful articles on market and design trends, regular columns on codes, legal issues, and marketing ideas, full coverage of new products, expert articles on operations and technology, and much more.
4900 Members
Frequency: 8x Yearly
Founded in 1948

Trade Shows

11793 AAPA Convention
American Art Pottery Association
Home Page: aapa.info/convention
Facebook, Pinterest

Marie Latta, Registration

Association of dealers and collectors of American Art Pottery.

11794 ACGA Annual Convention
PO Box 482
Ramona, CA 92065-0482

760-789-2715; Fax: 760-789-7112
acgakathy@aol.com
www.cutglass.org

Kathy Emmerson, Executive Secretary
Karen Parker, President

Opportunity to learn about cut glass.
Frequency: Annual/July

11795 AeroMat Conference and Exposition
ASM International
9639 Kinsman Road
Materials Park, OH 44073-0002

440-338-5151
800-336-5152; Fax: 440-338-4634
memberservicecenter@asminternational.org
www.asminternational.org

William T. Mahoney, Secretary & CEO
Lindy Good, Global Conference & Exhibit Planner

Focuses on innovative aerospace materials, fabrication and manufacturing methods that improve aerospace structures, performance and durability.
900 Members
Frequency: Annual/May
Founded in 1913

11796 American Ceramic Society Annual Meeting and Expo
600 N. Cleveland Ave.
Suite 210
Westerville, OH 43082

866-721-3322; Fax: 240-396-5637
customerservice@ceramics.org
www.ceramics.org

George Wicks, President
Richard Brow, President-Elect
Ted Day, Treasurer
Charlie Spahr, Executive Director

Three-hundred booths of ceramic materials, products manufacturing, testing, processing, research, components and software. Technical conference on ceramic materials research and development with over 1000 papers presented in more than 25 topical areas.
2,500 Attendees
Frequency: Annual/April

11797 American Scientific Glassblowers Exhibition
American Scientific Glassblowers Society
PO Box 453
Machias, NY 14101

716-353-8062; Fax: 716-353-4259
natl-office@asgs-glass.org
www.asgs-glass.org

Patrick DeFlorio, President
Frank Meints, President-Elect
Steven Moder, Secretary
Victor Mathews, Treasurer
Jerry Cloninger, Executive Secretary

Great opportunity to expand glassblowing knowledge through seminars, demonstrations, technical papers and posters.
650 Members
Frequency: Annual/June
Founded in 1952

11798 **BEC Conference**
Glass Association of North America
800 SW Jackson St.
Suite 1500
Topeka, KS 66612-1200

785-271-0208; Fax: 785-271-0166
www.glasswebsite.com

William M Yanek, Executive VP
Ashley M Charest, Account Executive
Urmilla Sowell, Technical Director

Features educational seminars for glazing contractors and executives in contracting companies.
Frequency: Annual/March

11799 **DECO**
Society of Glass & Ceramic Decorators
4340 E West Highway
Suite 200
Bethesda, MD 20814

301-986-9800; Fax: 301-951-3801
www.sgcd.org

Focusing on technical and regulatory issues affecting glass and ceramic decorators.

11800 **Dealers Show of the American Cut Glass Association**
American Cut Glass Association
PO Box 482
Ramona, CA 92065-0482

760-789-2715; Fax: 760-789-7112
acgakathy@aol.com
www.cutglass.org

Kathy Emmerson, Executive Secretary

Annual show and exhibits of American brilliant period cut glass and related articles.

11801 **Electronic Materials and Applications**
American Ceramic Society
600 N. Cleveland Ave.
Suite 210
Westerville, OH 43082

240-646-7054
866-721-3322; Fax: 301-206-9789
customerservice@ceramics.org
www.ceramics.org

Charles Spahr, Executive Director

Focuses on electronic materials for energy generation, conversion and storage applications.
10000 Members
Frequency: Annual/January
Founded in 1898

11802 **GANA Annual Conference**
Glass Association of North America
800 SW Jackson St.
Suite 1500
Topeka, KS 66612-1200

785-271-0208; Fax: 785-271-0166
www.glasswebsite.com

William M Yanek, Executive VP
Ashley M Charest, Account Executive
Urmilla Sowell, Technical Director

Seven Divisions of GANA have meetings planned at this event, along with the non-Division Committees including Fire-Rated Glazing, Glazing Industry Code Committee, Marketing, and Protective Glazing.
250 Members
Founded in 1994

11803 **Glass & Optical Materials Division Annual Meeting**
American Ceramic Society
600 N. Cleveland Ave.
Suite 210
Westerville, OH 43082

240-646-7054
866-721-3322; Fax: 301-206-9789
customerservice@ceramics.org
www.ceramics.org

Charles Spahr, Executive Director

Involving the physical properties and technological processes important to glasses, amorphous solids and optical materials.
10000 Members
Frequency: Annual/May
Founded in 1898

11804 **Glass Art Society Conference**
Glass Art Society
6512 23rd Ave. NW
Suite 329
Seattle, WA 98117

206-382-1305; Fax: 206-382-2630
info@glassart.org
www.glassart.org

Jeremy Lepisto, President
Jutta-Annette Page, Vice-President
Caroline Madden, Secretary
Lance Friedman, Treasurer

Annual conference and exhibits for those who make, collect, exhibit and appreciate objects made with glass.
2000 Attendees
Frequency: Annual/June

11805 **Glass Craft Exposition**
Las Vegas Management
2408 Chapman Drive
Las Vegas, NV 89104

702-734-0070
800-217-4527; Fax: 702-734-0636
www.glasscraftexpo.com

Shirley Harvey, Director

Learn new techniques and create new things.
3500 Attendees
Frequency: Annual/March

11806 **Glass Expo Midwest**
US Glass Magazine
PO Box 569
Garrisonville, VA 22463

540-720-5584; Fax: 540-720-5687
expos@glass.com
www.glassexpos.com/

Patrick Smith, Marketing Manager

Annual show and exhibits of flat, container, heavy insulated and tempered glass, architectural sealants and hardware, mirror products and windows and doors.
800 Attendees
Frequency: Annual/August

11807 **Glass TEXpo**
Key Communications, Inc.
PO Box 569
Garrisonville, VA 22463-0569

540-720-5584; Fax: 540-720-5687
expos@glass.com
www.glassexpos.com

Patrick Smith, Marketing Manager

Annual show and exhibits of flat, container, heavy insulated and tempered glass, architectural sealants and hardware, mirror products and windows and doors. Hosted in Dallas, TX.
700 Attendees
Frequency: Annual/October

11808 **Heat Treating Society Conference & Expo**
ASM International
9639 Kinsman Road
Materials Park, OH 44073-0002

440-338-5151
800-336-5152; Fax: 440-338-4634
memberservicecenter@asminternational.org
www.asminternational.org

William T. Mahoney, Secretary & CEO
Lindy Good, Global Conference & Exhibit Planner

Conference and expo for heat treating equipment and supplies as well as information of interest to metallurgists, maintenance supervisors and production engineering staff.
30K Members
Frequency: October
Founded in 1913

11809 **International Conference and Expo on Advanced Ceramics and Composites**
American Ceramic Society
600 N. Cleveland Ave.
Suite 210
Westerville, OH 43082

240-646-7054
866-721-3322; Fax: 301-206-9789
customerservice@ceramics.org
www.ceramics.org

George Wicks, President
Richard Brow, President-Elect
Ted Day, Treasurer
Charlie Spahr, Executive Director

Showcases cutting-edge research and product developments in advanced ceramics, armor ceramics, solid oxide fuel cells, ceramic coating, bioceramics and more.
Frequency: Annual/January

11810 **International Conference and Exposition on Advanced Ceramics & Composites**
American Ceramic Society
600 N. Cleveland Ave.
Suite 210
Westerville, OH 43082

240-646-7054
866-721-3322; Fax: 301-206-9789
customerservice@ceramics.org
www.ceramics.org

Charles Spahr, Executive Director

Showcases cutting-edge research and product developments in advanced ceramics, armor ceramics, solid oxide fuel cells, ceramic coatings, bioceramics and more.
10000 Members
Frequency: Annual/January
Founded in 1898

11811 **International Glass Show**
Dame Associates
100 Lincoln Street
Boston, MA 02135

617-783-4777
800-843-3263; Fax: 617-783-4787
www.dameassoc.com

Annual show of 115 manufacturers and suppliers of windows, doors, sun enclosures, windshields and mirrors, glass, machinery, hardware and insulating units, sealants, adhesives, mastic, security glazing and thermal barriers, aluminum, curtain wall computers and trucks.
2500 Attendees
Frequency: Annual/May

11812 **International Symposium for Testing & Failure Analysis**
ASM International

9639 Kinsman Road
Materials Park, OH 44073-0002

440-338-5151
800-336-5152; Fax: 440-338-4634
memberservicecenter@asminternational.org
www.asminternational.org

William T. Mahoney, Secretary & CEO
Lindy Good, Global Conference & Exhibit Planner

Annual event focusing on failure analysis and makers of tools such as microscopes, stress and measurement analytical tools, etchants and chemicals, ESD protective materials and other products used for this purpose.
30K Members
Frequency: Annual/Oct/Nov
Founded in 1913

11813 **International Thermal Spray Conference & Exposition**
ASM International
9639 Kinsman Road
Materials Park, OH 44073-0002

440-338-5151
800-336-5152; Fax: 440-338-4634
memberservicecenter@asminternational.org
www.asminternational.org

William T. Mahoney, Secretary & CEO
Lindy Good, Global Conference & Exhibit Planner

International annual conference for professional thermal spray technologists, researchers, manufacturers and suppliers.
30K Members
Frequency: Annual/May
Founded in 1913

11814 **International Window Film Conference and Expo**
Window Film Magazine
PO Box 569
Garrisonville, VA 22463-0569

540-720-5584; Fax: 540-720-5687
www.glassexpos.com

Patrick Smith, Marketing Manager

Numerous opportunities to network, socialize, and learn from others in the window film industry.
Frequency: Annual/March

11815 **MCARE: Materials Challenges in Alternative & Renewable Energy**
American Ceramic Society
600 N. Cleveland Ave.
Suite 210
Westerville, OH 43082

240-646-7054
866-721-3322; Fax: 301-206-9789
customerservice@ceramics.org
www.ceramics.org

Charles Spahr, Executive Director

Facilitates information sharing on the latest developments involving materials for alternative and renewable energy systems. Emphasis will be on materials challenges and innovations in areas of solar energy, wind power, hydro, geothermal, biomass, nuclear, hydrogen, electric grid, materials availability, nanocomposites/manomaterials, and battery and energy storage.
10000 Members
Frequency: Annual/February
Founded in 1898

11816 **Porcelain Enamel Institute Technical Forum & Suppliers Mart**
4004 Hillsboro Pike
Suite B224
Nashville, TN 37215-2722

615-385-5357; Fax: 615-385-5463
penamel@aol.com
www.porcelainenamel.com

Cullen Hackler, Executive VP
Patricia Melton, Executive Secretary

Members include suppliers and makers of porcelain enamel products and raw materials. Attendees of the PEI conference and workshops attend this show. There will be 20 booths.
250 Attendees
Frequency: Annual/May
Founded in 1989

11817 **Seattle Gift Show**
George Little Management
10 Bank Street
Suite 1200
White Plains, NY 10606

914-486-6070
800-272-7469; Fax: 914-948-2918
www.washingtongiftshow.com

Louise Seeber, Show Manager
Laura Scott, Exhibit Sales Manager
George Little II, President

See new products and proven bestsellers that cater to the eclectic tastes of the discerning Pacific Northwest consumer.
6000 Attendees
Frequency: Annual/January

Directories & Databases

11818 **Ceramic Abstracts**
American Ceramic Society
600 N. Cleveland Ave.
Suite 210
Westerville, OH 43081

240-646-7054
866-721-3322; Fax: 240-396-5637
customerservice@ceramics.org
www.ceramics.org

Charles Spahr, Executive Director

Abstracting/indexing publication covering ceramic materials-related literature. 15,000 entries published annually.
Frequency: Bi-Monthly
Circulation: 2,500

11819 **CeramicSOURCE**
American Ceramic Society
735 Ceramic Pl
Suite 100
Westerville, OH 43081-8728

614-904-4700; Fax: 614-794-5892
www.ceramicsource.org

Patricia Janeway, Editor
Marc Bailey, Director Global Marketing

Annual buyer's guide/directory of equipment and materials' suppliers to the industrial ceramic manufacturing market.
Cost: $25.00
Frequency: 1 issue
Circulation: 14,500
ISSN: 0002-7812
Founded in 1985
Printed in 4 colors on glossy stock

11820 **Complete Directory of Glassware & Glass Items**
Sutton Family Communications & Publishing Company
920 State Route 54 East
Elmitch, KY 42343

270-276-9500

Theresa Sutton, Publisher
Lee Sutton, Editor

Print-out from database of wholesalers, manufacturers, distributors, importers and close-out houses. Database is updated daily to guarantee the most current and up-to-date sources available. Over 800 American firms which sell direct to small retailers, in three-ring binder format.
Cost: $94.50
100 Pages

11821 **Complete Guide: US Advanced Ceramic Industry**
Business Communications Company
49 Walnut Park
Building 2
Wellesley, MA 02481-1713

866-285-7215; Fax: 781-489-7308
sales@bccresearch.com
www.bccresearch.com

David Nydam, President
Kevin R. Fitzgerald, Editorial Director
Andrew Hunt, Marketing Director

Approximately 450 companies and institutions involved in the advanced ceramic industry in the US.

11822 **Data Book and Buyers' Guide**
Ceramic Industry
2540 Billingsley Road
Business News Publishing Company
Columbus, OH 43235-1990

FAX 440-498-9121

List of over 1300 suppliers of equipment and materials for the advanced and traditional ceramics and heavy clay products.
Cost: $25.00
Frequency: Biennially

11823 **Glass Factory Directory of North America**
Glass News
Box 2267
Hempstead, NY 11551-2267

516-481-2188
www.glassfactorydir.com

Liz Scott, Editor

Over 600 glass manufacturers and plants in the US, Canada and Mexico.
Cost: $25.00
Frequency: Annually
Circulation: 1,500

11824 **Porcelain Enamel Institute Source List**
4004 Hillsboro Pike
Suite B224
Nashville, TN 37215-2722

615-385-5357; Fax: 615-385-5463
penamel@aol.com
www.porcelainenamel.com

Tom Sanford, Executive VP
Patricia Melton, Executive Secretary
Frequency: Annual/Fall
Founded in 1930

11825 **Society of Glass & Ceramic Decorating Products Directory**
Society of Glass & Ceramic Decorating Products

PO Box 2489
Zanesville, OH 43702

740-588-9882; Fax: 740-588-0245
info@sgcd.org
www.sgcd.org

Directory of more than 700 member manufacturers, suppliers, decorators and designers of glass and ceramics; international coverage indexed by product type and decorating technology.
Cost: $250.00
172 Pages
Frequency: Annual
Circulation: 800
Founded in 1964

11826 **US Glass, Metal & Glazing: Buyers Guide**
Key Communications
PO Box 569
Garrisonville, VA 22463-0569

540-577-7174; Fax: 540-720-5687
www.usglass.com

Debra A Levy, Publisher

About 3,000 suppliers of glass and glazing supplies for the glass, metal and glazing industry.
Cost: $20.00
Frequency: Annual
Circulation: 21,000

Industry Web Sites

11827 **Ceramic Arts Daily**
Ceramic Publications Company
600 N Cleveland Ave.
Suite 210
Westerville, OH 43082

614-794-5843; Fax: 614-794-5842
ceramicartsdaily.org

The online community of potters and ceramic artists provides a daily newsletter promoting related products and services as well as tools for learning.

11828 **http://gold.greyhouse.com**
G.O.L.D Grey House OnLine Databases

Grey House Publishing's online database platform, GOLD, offers Quick Search, Keyword Search and Expert Search for most business sectors including glass and ceramic markets. The GOLD platform makes finding the information you need quick and easy - whether you're a novice searcher or an experienced database user. All of Grey House's directory products are available for subscription on the GOLD platform.

11829 **www.advancedceramics.org**
United States Advanced Ceramics Association

Promotes the use of advanced ceramic materials in industrial applications.

11830 **www.asgs-glass.org**
American Scientific Glassblowers Society

Encourages the free exchange of knowledge and the broadening of scientific glassblowing skills to assist scientists, educators and the industry by designing and constructing glass components and scientific apparatus.

11831 **www.ceramics.org**
American Ceramic Society

The National Institute of Ceramic Engineers, the Ceramic Manufacturing Council and the Ceramic Education Council are affiliated groups.

11832 **www.ctdahome.org**
Ceramic Tile Distributors Association

CTDA is an international association of distributors, manufacturers, and allied professionals of ceramic tile and related products.

11833 **www.ctioa.org**
Ceramic Tile Institute of America

This organization has over 500 member manufacturers of ceramic tile in the western United States.

11834 **www.cutglass.org**
American Cut Glass Association

A non-profit organization devoted to the study and research of Americal Brilliant Cut Glass.

11835 **www.dameassoc.com**
Dame Associates

An organization with a biennial show w/250 manufacturers and suppliers of windows, doors, sun enclosures, windshields, mirrors, glass machinery, hardware, insulating units, sealants, adhesives, mastic, security glazing, thermal barriers, aluminum, curtain wall computers and trucks.

11836 **www.glass.org**
National Glass Association

An organization with an annual show of 325 manufacturers, suppliers and distributors of glass and glass-related products, supplies, equipment, tools and machinery, automotive glazing, equipment/machinery, curtain wall, store front systems, doors/hardware, windows, mirrors, shower/tub enclosures and tools.

11837 **www.glasswebsite.com**
Glass Association of North America

Offers educational on blueprint reading, labor, and glass estimating and analysis; manuals on glazing guidelines, sealant compatibility and labor hours; and a quarterly newsletter. Serves distributors, installers, fabricators of glass for use in the construction automotive and industrial industries.

11838 **www.greyhouse.com**
Grey House Publishing

Authoritative reference directories for most business sectors including glass and ceramic markets. Users can search the online databases with varied search criteria allowing for custom searches by product category, geographic area, sales volume, keyword, subject and more. Full Grey House catalog and online ordering also available.

11839 **www.igcc.org**
Insulating Glass Certification Council

Sponsors and directs a program of laboratory testing and unannounced plant inspection to ensure continuing product information.

11840 **www.igmaonline.org**
Insulating Glass Manufacturers Alliance

11841 **www.porcelainenamel.com**
Porcelain Enamel Institute

Members include suppliers and makers of porcelain enamel products and raw materials.

11842 **www.sgcc.org**
Safety Glazing Certification Council

Information center for this nonprofit corporation that provides for the certification of safety glazing materials.

Associations

11843 **Academy for State and Local Government**
444 N Capitol St NW
Washington, DC 20001-1512

202-434-4850; Fax: 202-434-4851

The policy center for the national organizations for the chief elected and appointed officials for state and local governments, functioning as their joint technical assistance, training and research organization. Its mission is to promote cooperation among federal, state and local governments.

11844 **American Association of State Highway and Transportation Officials**
444 N Capitol St NW
Suite 249
Washington, DC 20001-1539

202-624-5800; Fax: 202-624-5806
info@aashto.org
Facebook, Twitter

Mike Hancock, President
John Cox, Vice-President
Carlos Braceras, Secretary/ Treasurer
Bud Wright, Executive Director
Selim Amah, Accounts Payable Specialist

Membership is composed of highway and transportation departments in the 50 states, the District of Columbia, and Puerto Rico.
52 Members

11845 **American Conference of Governmental Industrial Hygienists (NCGIH)**
1330 Kemper Meadow Drive
Cincinnati, OH 45240

513-742-2020; Fax: 513-742-3355
mail@acgih.org
www.acgih.org
Facebook, Twitter, LinkedIn, Google+

J Torey Nalbone, Chair
John S. Morawetz, ScM, Treasurer
Jeff Washington, Deputy Executive Director
A Anthony Rizzuto, Executive Director
India Vargas, Administrative Assistant

A professional society of government and university employees engaged in a full program of industrial hygiene.
Founded in 1938

11846 **American Correctional Association**
206 N Washington St
Alexandria, VA 22314-2528

703-224-0000
800-222-5646; Fax: 703-224-0179
jeffw@aca.org
www.aca.org
Facebook, Twitter

Jeff Washington, Deputy Executive Director
James Gondles Jr, Executive Director
Debbi Seeger, Director of the Executive Office
Hok Gao, Director of Finance
Larry Strother, Director of Management

For individuals involved in the correctional field.
20000 Members
Founded in 1870

11847 **American Federation of Government Employees**
80 F St NW
Washington, DC 20001-1528

202-737-8700; Fax: 202-639-6490
comments@afge.org
www.afge.com
Facebook, Twitter, Youtube, Flickr, RSS

J David Cox Sr., President
Eugene Hudson, Secretary/Treasurer
Augusta Thomas, VP for Women's & Fair Practices

The largest federal employee union representing workers nationwide and overseas. Workers in virtually all functions of government at every federal agency depend upon AFGE for legal representation, legislative advocacy, technical expertise and informational services.
600K Members
Founded in 1932

11848 **American Federation of State, County & Municipal Employees**
1625 L Street NW
Washington, DC 20036-5687

202-429-1000; Fax: 202-429-1293
afsa@afsaadmin.org
www.afscme.org
Facebook, Twitter, YouTube, RSS

Lee Saunders, President
Laura Reyes, Secretary/ Treasurer

With members in hundreds of different occupations, AFSCME advocates for fairness in the workplace, excellence in public services and prosperity and opportunity for all working families.

11849 **American Foreign Service Association**
2101 E St Nw
Washington, DC 20037-2990

202-338-4045; Fax: 202-338-6820
member@afsa.org
www.afsa.org
Facebook, Twitter, Youtube, RSS

Hon. Barbara Stephenson, President
Hon. Charles A Ford, Treasurer
William Haugh, Secretary
Steve Morrison, FCS Vice President
Mark Petry, FAS Vice President

Missions are to enhance the effectiveness of the Foreign Service, to protect the professional interests of its members, to ensure the maintenance of high professional standards for both career diplomats and political appointeese, and to promote understanding of the critical role of the Foreign service in promoting America's national security and economic prosperity.
11M Members
Founded in 1924

11850 **American Judges Association**
300 Newport Ave
Williamsburg, VA 23185-4147

757-259-1841; Fax: 757-259-1520
aia@ncsc.dni.us
aja.ncsc.dni.us

Judge Brian MacKenzie, President
Judge John E Conery, President-Elect
Justice Russell Otter, Vice President
Judge Catherine Shaffer, Secretary
Jugde Kevin S Burke, Treasurer

The objective and purpose of the Association is: to promote and improve the effective administration of justice; to maintain the status and independance of the judiciary; to provide a forum for the continuing education of its members and the general public; and for the exchange of new ideas among all judges.
2500 Members
Founded in 1959

11851 **American League of Lobbyists**
300 North Washington Street
Suite 205
Alexandria, VA 22314

703-960-3011
888-712-1357
grprofessionals.org
Facebook, Twitter, LinkedIn

Monte Ward, President
James Hickey, 1st Vice President
Paul T Kelly, 2nd Vice President
Wright Andrews, Secretary
Paul Kangas, Treasurer

National association dedicated to serving government relations and public affairs professionals. Provides programs and conferences of interest to lobbyists.
600+ Members
Founded in 1979

11852 **American Logistics Association**
1101 Vermont Ave NW
Suite 1002
Washington, DC 20005-2710

202-466-7636; Fax: 202-296-4419
membership@ala-national.org
www.ala-national.org

Patrick B Nixon, President
Russ Moffett, VP, Member Relations
Maurice Branch, VP, Operations
Tracey Durand, Director, Meetings & Expositions
Joseph Campagna, Chair

Organization that represents the private industry to promote food sales to commissaries on military bases.
Cost: $828.00
400 Members
Frequency: Membership Dues Vary
Founded in 1972

11853 **American National Standards Institute**
1899 L Street NW
11th Floor
Washington, DC 20036

202-293-8020; Fax: 202-293-9287
info@ansi.org
www.ansi.org
Facebook, Twitter, LinkedIn, YouTube, Google+, Instagram

S. Joe Bhatia, President & CEO

To enhance the global competition of business and quality of life by promoting and facilitating voluntary consensus standards and conformity assessment systems, and safeguarding their integrity.
27000 Members
Founded in 1918

11854 **American Public Human Services Association**
1133 19th Street NW
Suite 400
Washington, DC 20036-3623

202-682-0100; Fax: 202-289-6555
www.aphsa.org
Facebook, Twitter, LinkedIn

Reggie Bicha, President
Uma Ahluwalia, Treasurer
Tracy Wareing, Secretary

APHSA pusues excellence in health and human services by supporting state and local agencies, informing policymakers, and working with partners to drive innovative, integrated and efficient solutions in policy and practice.
Founded in 1930

11855 **American Society for Public Administration**
1301 Pennsylvania Avenue NW
Suite 700
Washington, DC 20004

202-393-7878; Fax: 202-638-4952
info@aspanet.org
www.aspanet.org
Facebook, Twitter, LinkedIn

Maria Aristigueta, President
Susan T. Gooden, President Elect
William P. Shields Jr., Executive Director

Lisa Sidletsky, Chief of Program Operations
Janice Lachance, Vice President

Offers a wide range of services and membership options for individuals in public administration careers. Sponsors 127 local chapters and 16 sections on specific areas of governments, such as the Section of Natural Resources and Environmental Administration and the Section on Human Resource Administration.
15M Members
Founded in 1939

11856 American Society of Access Professionals
1444 I(Eye) St. NW
Suite 700
Washington, DC 20005-6542

202-712-9054; Fax: 202-216-9646
asap@bostrom.com
www.accesspro.org
Facebook, Twitter

Amy Bennett, President
Cindy Allard, Vice President
Amy McNulty, Treasurer
Ginger McCall, Secretary
Jonathan Cantor, Director

Members are government employees, lawyers, journalists and others concerned with access to government data under current personal privacy and public informaiton statues.
Founded in 1980

11857 Americans for Democratic Action
1629 K Street NW
Suite 300
Washington, DC 20006-1611

202-785-5980; Fax: 202-204-8637
info@adaction.org
www.adaction.org
Facebook, Twitter, Flickr, YouTube

Lynn Woolsey, President
David Card, Treasurer
Mary Von Euler, Secretary
Elijah Cummings, VP
James K. Galbraith, VP

Liberal lobbying group.

11858 Association for Federal Information Resources Management
400 North Washington St.
Suite 300
Alexandria, VA 22314

703-778-4646; Fax: 703-683-5480
info@affirm.org
www.affirm.org
Facebook, Twitter, LinkedIn, Flickr

Robert Foster, President
Richard Young, Vice President
Deirdre Murray, VP, Industry
Christopher Hamm, VP
James Maas, VP

A non-profit, volunteer, educational organization whose overall purpose is to improve the management of information, and related systems and resources, within the Federal government. Members include information resource management professionals from the Federal, academic, and industry sectors.
350 Members
Founded in 1979

11859 Association for Postal Commerce
1800 Diagonal Road
Suite 600
Alexandria, VA 22314

703-524-0096; Fax: 703-997-2414
info@postcom.org
www.postcom.org
Twitter, LinkedIn

Michael Plunkett, President & CEO
Ellena Talbott, Director, Operations & Membership
Beth McConnell, Postal Consultant
Matthew Field, General Counsel

National organization representing those who use, or who support, the use of mail as a medium for communication and commerce. Publishes a weekly newsletter covering postal policy and operational issues.
231 Members
Founded in 1947

11860 Association of Boards of Certification
2805 SW Snyder Blvd.
Suite 535
Ankeny, IA 50023

515-232-3623; Fax: 515-965-6827
abc@abccert.org
www.abccert.org

Ray Olson, President
Mike Gosselin, President-Elect
Michael Bolt, Vice President
Brian Thorburn, Immediate Past-President
Paul D. Bishop, CAE, Ex-Officio

The Association of Boards of Certification is dedicated to protecting public health and the environment by advancing the quality and integrity of environmental certification programs through innovative technical support services, effective information exchange, professional and cost-effective examination services, and other progressive services for certifying members.
Founded in 1972

11861 Association of Civilian Technicians (ACT)
12620 Lake Ridge Dr
Lake Ridge, VA 22192-2335

703-494-4845; Fax: 703-494-0961
actnational@actnat.com
www.actnat.com
Facebook

Terry Garnett, President
Raul Toro, Treasurer

Labor organization of civilian employees of Air Force, Army, National Guard and Reserves.
12M Members

11862 Association of Fish and Wildlife Agencies
1100 First Street, NE
Suite 825
Washington, DC 20002

202-838-3474; Fax: 202-350-9869
info@fishwildlife.org
www.fishwildlife.org
Facebook, Twitter, Blogger

Ron Regan, Executive Director
Carol Bambery, Association Counsel
Kathy Boydston, Wildlife & Energy Liasion
John Bloom, Accounting Manager
Arpita Choudhury, Science & Research Liasion

The organization that represents all of North America's fish and wildlife agencies that promotes sound management and conservation, and speaks with a unified voice on important fish and wildlife issues.
Founded in 1902

11863 Association of Food and Drug Officials
2550 Kingston Rd
Suite 311
York, PA 17402-3734

717-757-2888; Fax: 717-650-3650
afdo@afdo.org
www.afdo.org
Twitter

Joseph Korby, Executive Director
Krystal Reed, Association Manager
Pat Smith, Support Staff
Randy Young, IT Administrator
Patty Fitzgerald, Admin/Special Projects Assistant

Promotes the enforcement of laws and regulations at all levels of government. Fosters understanding and cooperation between industry and regulators. Develops model laws and regulations and seeks their adoption.
800 Members
Founded in 1986

11864 Association of Former Agents of the US Secret Service
6919 Vista Drive West
Des Moines, IA 50266

515-282-8192; Fax: 515-282-9117
www.oldstar.org

Founded to bring together former and current employees of the Secret Service for comradeship, friendship and support in time of need. Members include Special Agents, Technical Specialists and other support personnel who carried out the investigative and protective responsibilities of the United States Secret Service.
950 Members
Founded in 1971

11865 Association of Labor Relations Agencies
38 Wolcott Hill Road
Wethersfield, CT 06109

860-263-6860; Fax: 860-263-6875
www.alra.org

Pat Sims, President
Ginette Brazeau, President-Elect
Sylvie Guilbert, VP, Administration
Scot Beckenbaugh, VP, Finance
Jennifer Abruzzo, Board Member

An association of impartial government agencies in the US and Canada responsible for administering labor-management relations laws or services. Promotes cooperation among these agencies, high professional standards, public interest in labor relations, improved employer-employee relationships, peaceful resolution of employment and labor disputes, and the exchange of information regarding the administration and improvement of agency services.

11866 Cannabis Council of Canada
111 Albert St.
P.O. Box 81071
Ottawa, ON K1P 1B1

647-206-1231
allan.rewak@cann-can.ca
www.cannabis-council.ca
Facebook, Twitter

Allan Rewak, Executive Director

Promotes industry standards; Supports the development, growth, and integrity of the regulated cannabis industry; Serves as a resource on issues related to the safe an responsible use of cannabis for medical and non-medical purposes.

11867 Cannabis Cultural Association

contact@cannabisculturalassociation.org
www.cannacultural.org
Facebook, Twitter, LinkedIn, YouTube

Nelson Guerrero, Co-Founder & Executive Director
Jake Plowden, Co-Founder & Deputy Director

Works to end the stigma around cannabis use by educating people about the benefits of canabis. Emphasizes criminal justice reform, promotes access to medical cannabis, and advocates legalization for adult-use of cannabis.
Founded in 2016

11868 **Center for Neighborhood Enterprise**
1625 K. Street NW
Suite 1200
Washington, DC 20006
202-518-6500; Fax: 202-588-0314
info@cneonline.org
www.cneonline.org
Facebook, Twitter, YouTube, Flickr
Robert L Woodson Sr, President
Clifford Ehrlich, Chair
Founded to help the residents of low-income neighborhoods address the problems of their communities. Mission is to transform lives, schools, and troubled neighborhoods, from the inside out. Current programs are the Violence-Free Zone youth violence reduction program; Training and Technical Assistance for Community-Based Organizations; and Adult Financial Literacy.
Founded in 1981

11869 **Center for an Urban Future**
120 Wall St.
20th Floor
New York, NY 10005
212-479-3344
cuf@nycfuture.org
www.nycfuture.org
Facebook, Twitter
Jonathan Bowles, Executive Director
Eli Dvorkin, Editorial & Policy Director
Bora Lee, Assoc. Dir., Events & Operations
Judith Messina, Sr. Fellow, Small Businesses
An independent, nonpartisan policy organization that is a catalyst for smart and sustainable policies that reduce inequality, increase economic mobility, and grow the economy in New York City.
Founded in 1998

11870 **Center for the Study of the Presidency and Congress (CSPC)**
601 Thirteenth St, NW
Suite 1050N
Washington, DC 20005
202-872-9800; Fax: 202-872-9811
email@thepresidency.org
www.thepresidency.org
Facebook, Twitter, YouTube
David M Abshire, Vice Chair
Maxmillian Angerholzer III, President/CEO
Dan Mahaffee, Director, Policy & Board Relations
Jonathan Murphy, Director, External Affairs
Elizabeth Perch, COO & CFO
CSPC strives to: promote leadership in the Presidency and Congress to generate innovative solutions to current national challenges; preserve the historic memory of the Presidency by identifying lessons from successes and failures of such leadership; draw on a wide range of talent to offer ways to better organize an increasingly compartmentalized Federal Government; educate and inspire the next generation of America's leaders to incorporate civility, inclusiveness, and character into their lives.

11871 **Citizens Against Government Waste**
1301 Pennsylvania Ave
Suite 1075
Washington, DC 20004
202-467-5300; Fax: 202-467-4253
membership@cagw.org
www.cagw.org
Facebook, Twitter, Youtube
Thomas A Schatz, President
Ariane E Sweeney, VP, Membership & Development
Leslie K Paige, VP Policy & Communications
Robert J Tedeschi, Treasurer/CFO
William M. Christian, Director of Government Affairs
Public advocacy, non-partisan organization committed to eliminate government waste, fraud, abuse, mismanagement and inefficiency.
1MM+ Members
Founded in 1984
Mailing list available for rent

11872 **Citizens for Global Solutions**
420 7th St SE
Washington, DC 20003-2707
202-546-3950; Fax: 202-546-3749
info@globalsolutions.org
www.globalsolutions.org
Facebook, Twitter, YouTube
Marvin Perry, CEO
Jordan Bankhead, MS, Chairman
Scott Paul,, Vice-Chair
Shirley Lee Davis, Secretary
Evan Freund, Treasurer
Nonprofit, tax deductible membership organization of 50 chapters and groups throughout the United States. We work to educate policy-makers and the American public on issues of global governance, international law and grassroots activism.
11000 Members
Founded in 1978

11873 **Coalition for Government Procurement**
1990 M St NW
Suite 450
Washington, DC 20036-3466
202-331-0975; Fax: 202-822-9788
info@thecgp.org
www.thecgp.org
Facebook, Twitter, LinkedIn, Flickr, RSS
Roger Waldron, President
Carolyn Alston, EVP & General Counsel
Robert Rendely, CFO
Denise Meliski, Director, Business Development
Matt Cahill, VP, Membership & Marketing
Representing commercial contractors in the Federal market. Advocating for common sense policies that improve the acquisition environment for government, industry and ultimately the American taxpayer. Focusing outreach efforts on the General Services Administration, Department of Veterans Affairs, Office of Management and Budget, Department of Defense, and Capitol Hill.
350 Members
Founded in 1979

11874 **Commissioned Officers Association of the United States Public Health Service**
8201 Corporate Dr
Suite 200
Landover, MD 20785-2230
301-731-9080
866-366-9593; Fax: 301-731-9084
gfarrell@coausphs.org
www.coausphs.org
Facebook
Jim Currie, Executive Director
John McElligott, Deputy Executive Director
Teresa Hayden Foley, Chief Financial Officer
Judith Rensberger, Government Relations Director
Erica Robinson, Administrative Assistant
Protects the interests of the Commissioned Corps officers of the US Public Health Service, who are leaders in the realms of public and global health. Dedicated to improving and protecting the public health of the US by addressing unmet health needs and providing support.
7M Members

11875 **Community Leadership Association**
1240 S Lumpkin Street
Athens, GA 30602
706-542-0301; Fax: 706-542-7007
www.claweb.org
Gene A Honn, Executive Director
Organization dedicated to nurturing leadership in communities throughout the US and internationally. Members include hundreds of diverse community leadership organizations at local, state and national levels, thousands of individual graduates of these organizations and others interested in community leadership development.
2M Members
Founded in 1979

11876 **Conference of Minority Public Administrators**
PO Box 1552
Norfolk, VA 23510
301-333-5282; Fax: 202-638-4952
www.compaspanet.com
Facebook
Stanley Skinner, President
Linda A. Harmon, President-Elect
Pamela Alexxander, Treasurer
Tiffany L. Smith, Recording Secretary
Lynn Cherry-Miller, Corresponding Secretary
COMPA is one of America's leading national organizations committed to excellence in public service and public administration in city, county, state and federal government.
500 Members
Founded in 1977

11877 **Contract Services Association of America**
1000 Wilson Boulevard
Suite 1800
Arlington, VA 22209-3920
703-243-2020; Fax: 703-243-3601
Christopher Jahn, President
Represents the government services contracting industry. Membership ranges from small businesses and corporations servicing federal and state government in numerous capacities. CSA acts to foster the effective implementation of the government's policy of reliance on the private sector for support services.
650 Members
Founded in 1965

11878 **Council of Chief State School Officers**
One Massachusetts Ave. NW
Suite 700
Washington, DC 20001
202-336-7000; Fax: 202-408-8072
communications@ccsso.org
www.ccsso.org
Facebook, Twitter, LinkedIn, YouTube
Carissa Moffat Miller, Interim Executive Director
Melissa Johnston, Deputy Executive Director
Nationwide, nonprofit organization is a voice for elementary and secondary school heads of departments to government and the public.

11879 **Council of State Community Development Agencies**
1825 K St NW
Suite 515
Washington, DC 20006-1261

202-293-5820; Fax: 202-293-2820
www.coscda.org

Steve Charleston, President
Keith Heaton, VP
Alison George, Secretary
Leslie Leager, Treasurer
Dianne E Taylor, Executive DIrector

The premier national association advocating and enhancing the leadership role of states in community development through innovative policy development and implementation, customer-driven technical assistance, education, and collaborative efforts.
Founded in 1974

11880 **Council of State Governments**
2760 Research Park Drive
PO Box 11910
Lexington, KY 40578-1910

859-244-8000
800-800-1910; Fax: 859-244-8001
www.csg.org
Facebook, Twitter, YouTube, RSS

David Adkins, Executive Director & CEO
Brian Sandoval, President
Luis Fortuno, President-Elect
Sen. Carl Marcellino, Chair
Sen. Beau McCoy, Chair-Elect

Members include every elected and appointed state and territorial official in the US. A nonpartisan organization that brings state leaders together to share capitol ideas, providing them the chance to learn valuable lessons from each other. Also foster innovation in state government and shine a spotlight on examples of how ingenuity and leadership are transforming the way state government serves residents of the states and territories.
Founded in 1933

11881 **Council of State Housing Agencies**
Hall of States
444 N Capitol St NW
Suite 438
Washington, DC 20001-1505

202-624-7710; Fax: 202-624-5899
bthompson@ncsha.org
www.ncsha.org
Facebook, Twitter

Brian A Hudson, President
Thomas R Gleason, Vice President
Grant S Whitaker, Secretary/Treasurer
Barbara J. Thompson, Executive Director
Cary D Knox, Executive Office Admin

A nonprofit, nonpartisan organization created to represent members in Washingtong before Congress, the Administration, and the several federal agencies concerned with housing, including the Department of Housing and Urban Development, the Department of Agriculture, and the Treasury, and with other advocates for affordable housing.

11882 **Council on Licensure, Enforcement and Regulation**
108 Wind Haven Drive
Suite A
Nicholasville, KY 40356

859-269-1289; Fax: 859-231-1943
rbrown@clearhq.org
www.clearhq.org
Facebook, Twitter, LinkedIn

Adam Parfitt, Executive Director
Tami Martin, Office Manager
Roda Brown, Administrative Associate
Nicolle Harkness, Membership Coordinator
Jodie Markey, Senior Program Coordinator

Supports all those involved in occupational, professional licensing and regulation. Members include occupational and professional licensing boards and agencies and private interests in the 50 states, territories and Canada.
Founded in 1994
Mailing list available for rent

11883 **Digital Government Institute**
1934 Old Gallows Road
Suite 350
Vienna, VA 22182

703-752-6243; Fax: 703-752-6201
info@digitalgovernment.com
www.digitalgovernment.com
Facebook, Twitter, LinkedIn, Flickr

Specializes in the design and production of leading edge educational programs on emerging trends and technologies for government IT management professionals. A trusted source for education, networking and results.
Founded in 1998

11884 **Energy Bar Association**
2000 M Street, N.W.,
Suite 715
Washington, DC 20036-3429

202-223-5625; Fax: 202-833-5596
admin@eba-net.org
www.eba-net.org
Facebook

Richard Meyer, President
Emma Hand, President-Elect
Robert A. Weishaar, JR, Vice President
Caileen N. Gamache, Secretary
Noha Sidhom, Treasurer

An international, nonprofit association of attorneys and non-attorney professionals active in all areas of energy law. EBA's voluntary membership is comprised of government, corporate and private attorneys, as well as non-attorney professionals from across the globe, and includes law students interested in energy law.
2600 Members
Founded in 1946

11885 **Federal Bar Association**
1220 North Fillmore St.
Suite 444
Arlington, VA 22201

571-481-9100; Fax: 571-481-9090
fba@fedbar.org
www.fedbar.org
Facebook, Twitter, LinkedIn

Karen Silberman, Executive Director
Stacy King, Executive Deputy Director
Heather Gaskins, Director, Development
Monique Dennis, Membership Coordinator
Maria Conticelli, Sections and Divisions Manager

Members are attorneys in the Federal Government or who have interest in federal law.
16000 Members
Founded in 1920

11886 **Federal Criminal Investigators Association**
5868 Mapledale Plaza
Suite 104
Woodbridge, VA 22193

630-969-8537
800-403-3374
www.fedcia.org

Mission of FCIA is to ensure that Federal Law Enforcement Professionals have the tools and the support network to meet the challenges of future criminal investigations while becoming more community oriented.
1500 Members
Founded in 1953

11887 **Federal Facilities Council**
500 Fifth St. NW
Washington, DC 20001

202-334-3374; Fax: 202-334-3370
sites.nationalacademies.org/DEPS/FFC/
Facebook, Twitter

James Rispoli, Chair
Carmelo Melendez, Vice Chair

Operating under the auspices of the BICE, the FFC's mission is to identify and advance technologies, processes, and management practices that improve the performance of federal facilities over their entire life-cycle, from planning to disposal.
130 Members
Founded in 1953

11888 **Federal Managers Association**
1641 Prince St
Alexandria, VA 22314-2818

703-683-8700; Fax: 703-683-8707
info@fedmanagers.org
www.fedmanagers.org

Patricia A Niehaus, President
Dora L. Quinlan, VP
Christine C. Parker, Secretary
Katie L Smith, Treasurer
Todd V Wells, Executive Director

Advocates excellence in public service through effective management and professionalism, as well as the active representation of its members' interests and concerns.
15M Members
Founded in 1913

11889 **Federal Physicians Association**
12427 Hedges Run Drive
Suite 104
Lake Ridge, VA 22192

703-426-8400
877-333-7497; Fax: 703-426-8400
info@fedphy.org
www.fedphy.org

Brian J Ribiero, MD, President
Indira Jevaji, MD, VP
Michael Nesemann, MD, Treasurer
Michael Borecky, MD, Secretary

Represents and advocates for Physicians employed by the Federal Government.
400 Members
Founded in 1979

11890 **Federation of Tax Administrators**
444 N. Capitol Street NW.
Suite 348
Washington, DC 20001

202-624-5890
support@taxadmin.org
www.taxadmin.org

Gale Garriott, Executive Director
Verenda Smith, Deputy Director
Ronald Alt, Sr. Manager, Economic & Tax
Cindy Anders-Robb, Sr. Manager, Motor Fuel & Tobacco
Ryan Minnick, Manager, Special Projects

A nonprofit corporation designed to improve the quality of state tax administration by providing services to state tax authorities and administrators. These services include research and information exchange, training, and intergovernmental and interstate coordination.
53 Members
Founded in 1937

11891 **Fund for Constitutional Government**
122 Maryland Ave NE
Washington, DC 20002-5610

202-546-3799; Fax: 202-543-3156
info@fcgonline.org
www.fcgonline.org

Anne B. Zill, President
John Cavanagh, Chairperson
Conrad Martin, Executive Director
Kat Saunders, Secretary
Steven Aftergood, Board Member

Seeks to expose and correct illegal activities, corruption, and lack of accountability in the federal government.
Founded in 1974

11892 **Government Finance Officers Association**
203 N La Salle St
Suite 2700
Chicago, IL 60601-1210

312-977-9700; Fax: 312-977-4806
inquiry@gfoa.org
www.gfoa.org

Marion M. Gee, President
Chris Morrill, Executive Director
Mike Mucha, Deputy Executive Director
John Jurkash, Chief Financial Officer

The purpose of the Government Finance Officers Association is to enhance and promote the professional management of governments for the public benefit by identifying and developing financial policies and practices and promoting them through education, training and leadership.
17300 Members
Founded in 1906

11893 **Hispanic Elected Local Officials**
National League of Cities
1301 Pennsylvania Ave NW
Suite 550
Washington, DC 20004-1747

202-626-3169; Fax: 202-626-3103
Facebook, Twitter, LinkedIn, Youtube, RSS, Google+

Oscar Trevino, President
Joel Navarro, 1st Vice President
Lydia N. Martinez, 2nd Vice President
Clarence E Anthony, Executive Director

Serves as a forum for communication and exchange among Hispanic local government officials within the framework of the National League of Cities.
100+ Members
Founded in 1976

11894 **Housing Assistance Council**
1025 Vermont Ave NW
Suite 606
Washington, DC 20005-3516

202-842-8600; Fax: 202-347-3441
hac@ruralhome.org
www.ruralhome.org
Facebook, Twitter, LinkedIn

Moises Loza, Executive Director
Joe Belden, Senior Policy Analyst
Lilla Sutton, Executive Coordinator
Leslie Strauss, Senior Policy Analyst
Stephen Sugg, Government Relations

Expands the pool of decent housing available to the rural poor. Creates and sustains interest and action from all levels of government concerning rural housing for low-income people and helps rural housing organizations become more productive and professional.
30 Members
Founded in 1971

11895 **Industry Coalition on Technology Transfer**
1400 L St NW
Suite 800
Washington, DC 20005-3502

202-371-5994; Fax: 202-371-5950

Coalition of major high technology trade associations concerned with the US Government export controls. Monitors and addresses federal regulations on technology transfer.
4 Members
Founded in 1983

11896 **International Association of Correctional Training Personnel**
PO Box 81826
Lincoln, NE 68501

312-341-6340
www.iactp.org

Pete Norris, President
Tracy Reveal, President Elect
Mary O'Connor, Secretary
Terry Satterfield, Conference Coordinator
Joe Bouchard, Higher Education

Correctional officers and juvenile administrators.
9.5M Members
Founded in 1974

11897 **International Association of Fire Chiefs**
4025 Fair Ridge Drive
Suite 300
Fairfax, VA 22033-2868

703-273-0911; Fax: 703-273-9363
thicks@iafc.org
www.iafc.org
Facebook, Twitter

Mark Light, Executive Director & CEO
Karin Soyster Fitzgerald, Chief Operations Officer
Chief John Sinclair, President & Chairman
Chief Thomas Jenkins, First Vice President
Chief Gary Curmode, Second Vice President

Represents the leadership of firefighters and emergency responders worldwide; members are the world's leading experts in firefighting, emergency medical services, terrorism response, hazardous materials spills, natural disasters, search and rescue, and public safety policy.
12000 Members
Founded in 1873

11898 **International Association of Official Human Rights Agencies**
444 N Capitol Street NW
Suite 536
Washington, DC 20001

202-624-5410; Fax: 202-624-8185
iaohra@sso.org
www.iaohra.org

Jean Kelleher Niebauer, President
Alisa Warren, 2nd Vice President
Paula Haley, Secretary
Merrill Smith, Jr., Treasurer
Robin S. Toma, First Vice-President

Private non-profit corporation consisting of human rights agencies in the US and Canada. Provides opportunities and forums for the exchange of ideas and information among human rights advocates. Also provides training opportunities for members and other concerned groups and organizations.
200 Members
Founded in 1968

11899 **International City/County Management Association (ICMA)**
777 North Capitol St. NE
Suite 500
Washington, DC 20002-4201

202-289-4262
800-745-8780; Fax: 202-962-3500
icma.org
Facebook, Twitter, LinkedIn, YouTube, Pinterest, Flickr

Robert J. O'Neill, Executive Director

A worldwide organization for the advancement of professional local government.
Founded in 1914

11900 **International Code Council**
500 New Jersey Ave NW
6th Floor
Washington, DC 20001-2005

888-422-7233; Fax: 202-783-2348
webmaster@iccsafe.org
www.iccsafe.org
Facebook

Dominic Sims, Chief Executive Officer
John Belcik, COO & CFO
Joan O'Neil, Chief Knowledge Officer
Mark Johnson, Executive Vice President

A nonprofit membership association dedicated to preserving the public health, safety and welfare in the built environment through the promulgation of model codes suitable for adoption by governmental entities and assisting code enforcement officials, design professionals, builders, manufacturers and others involved in the design, construction and regulatory processes.
16M Members
Founded in 1915

11901 **International Downtown Association**
1025 Thomas Jefferson Street, NW
Suite 500W
Washington, DC 20007

202-393-6801; Fax: 202-393-6869
customerservice@ida-downtown.org
www.ida-downtown.org
Facebook, Twitter, LinkedIn

David Downey, President & CEO
Kevin Moran, Communications & IT Manager
Rebecca Bishophall, Manager, Membership Services
Tracie Clemmer, Development & Exhibits Director
Patricia Stephenson, Director, Finance & Administration

The International Downtown Association has member organizations worldwide in North America, Europe, Asia and Africa. Through a network of committed individuals, a rich body of knowledge and unique capacity to nurture community-building partnerships, IDA is a guiding force in creating healthy and dynamic centers that anchor the well being of towns, cities and regions of the world.
650+ Members
Founded in 1954

11902 **International Economic Development Council**
734 15th Street NW
Suite 900
Washington, DC 20005

202-223-7800; Fax: 202-223-4745
www.iedconline.org/
Facebook, Twitter, LinkedIn

Dyan Lingle Brasington, CEc, Chair
Jeff Finkle, CEcD, President/CEO
Katelyn Palomo, Executive Assistant
Swati Ghosh, Director, Research
Carrie Mulcaire, Director, Federal Grants

Nonprofit membership organization dedicated to helping economic developmers do their job more effectively and raising the profile of the profession. Members create more high-quality jobs, develop more vibrant communities, and generally improve the quality of life in their regions.
1.8M Members
Founded in 1967

11903 Interstate Council on Water Policy
505 North Ivy Street
Arlington, VA 22220-1707

703-243-7383; Fax: 301-984-5841
www.icwp.org
Facebook, Twitter

Dru Buntin, 2nd Vice-Chairman
Ryan Mueller, Executive Director
Andrew Dehoff, Secretary & Treasurer
Jerry Schulte, 1st Vice Chairman

The ICWP is the national organization of state and regional water resources management agencies. It provides a means for members to exchange information, ideas and experience to work with federal agencies which share water management responsibilities.
70 Members
Founded in 1959

11904 Interstate Oil and Gas Compact Commission
900 NE 23rd Street
Oklahoma City, OK 73105

405-525-3556
800-822-4015; Fax: 405-525-3592
communications@iogcc.ok.gov
www.iogcc.state.ok.us

Mike Smith, Executive Director
Gerry Baker, Associate Executive Director
Hannah Barton, Member Services Coordinator
Amy Childers, Federal Projects Manager
Carol Booth, CommunicationsÿManager

A multi-state government agency that champions the conservation and efficient recovery of domestic oil and natural gas resources.
700 Members
Founded in 1935

11905 Minority Cannabis Business Association

Home Page: www.minoritycannabis.org
Facebook, Twitter, Instagram

Shanita Penny, MBA, President

Advances the cannabis industry by increasing diversity. Mission is to create equal access and economic empowerment for cannabis businesses, their patients, an the communities most affected by the war on drugs.
Founded in 2015

11906 National Academy of Public Administration
1600 K Street, NW
Suite 400
Washington, DC 20006

202-347-3190; Fax: 202-223-0823
feedback@napawash.org
www.napawash.org
Facebook, Twitter, LinkedIn, Vimeo

David Wennergren, Chair
Norton N. Bonaparte, Jr., Vice Chair
Teresa Gerton, President & CEO
Jane Fountain, Secretary
David Mader, Treasurer

Through its trusted and experienced leaders, the Academy improves the quality, performance, and accountability of governments in the nation and the world.
500 Members
Founded in 1967

11907 National Affordable Housing Management Association
400 N Columbus Street
Suite 203
Alexandria, VA 22314

703-683-8630; Fax: 703-683-8634
www.nahma.org

Kris Cook, Executive Director
Larry Keys, Jr., Director, Government Affairs
Rajni Agarwal, Director, Finance
Brenda Moser, Director, Meetings & Membership
Scott McMillen, Coordinator, Government Affairs

The leading voice for affordable housing, advocating on behalf of multifamily property managers and owners whose mission is to provide quality affordable housing. Membership includes the industry's most distinguished multifamily managers, owners, and industry stakeholders.
3000 Members
Founded in 1990

11908 National Alliance of State and Territorial AIDS Directors
444 N Capitol St NW
Suite 339
Washington, DC 20001

202-434-8090; Fax: 202-434-8092
nastad@nastad.org
www.nastad.org
Facebook, Twitter, LinkedIn, Blogger, Youtube

Julie Scofield, Executive Director
Addis Tilahun, Senior Manager Finance & Accounting
Anna Carroll, Manager Global Program
Anne Redmond Sites, Manager Global Program
Brent Parker, Senior Director

NASTAD strengthens state and territory-based leadership, expertise, and advocacy and brings them to bear in reducing the incidence of HIV and viral hepatitis infections and on providing care and support to all who live with HIV/AIDS and viral hepatitis. NASTAD's vision is a world free of HIV/AIDS and viral hepatitis.
59 Members
Founded in 1992

11909 National Assembly of State Arts Agencies
1200 18th Street NW
Suite 1100
Washington, DC 20036

202-347-6352; Fax: 202-737-0526
nasaa@nasaa-arts.org
www.nasaa-arts.org
Facebook

Pam Breaux, Chief Executive Officer
Kelly J. Barsdate, Chief Program and Planning Officer
Laura S. Smith, CFRE, Chief Advancement Officer
Sharon Gee, Director of Meetings and Events

Unites, represents and serves the nation's state and jurisdictional arts agencies. Representing state arts agencies by empowering their work through knowledge, and advance the arts as an essential public benefit.
56 Members
Founded in 1968

11910 National Association for County Community and Economic Development
2025 M St NW
Suite 800
Washington, DC 20036-3309

202-367-1149; Fax: 202-367-2149
www.nacced.org

John Murphy, Executive Director
Tony Agliata, President
Jim Vazquez, Vice President
Chuck Robbins, Secretary/Treasurer
Bill J. Lake, Director

Purpose is to develop the technical capacity of county government practitioners to professionally administer federally-funded affordable housing, community development, and economic development programs that benefit their low- and moderate-income households.
120+ Members
Founded in 1989

11911 National Association for Search and Rescue
PO Box 232020
Centreville, VA 20120-2020

703-222-6277
877-893-0702; Fax: 703-222-6277
meganr@nasar.org
www.nasar.org

Monty Bell, President
Christopher Boyer, Executive Director
Ross Robinson, Chief Financial Officer
Ellen Wingerd, Customer Care Manager
Mike Vorachek, Secretary

A not-for-profit membership association dedicated to advancing professional, literary, and scientific knowledge in fields related to search and rescue.
3M Members

11912 National Association of Clean Air Agencies
444 N Capitol Street NW
Suite 307
Washington, DC 20001-1506

202-624-7864; Fax: 202-624-7863
4cleanair@4cleanair.org
www.4cleanair.org

Stu A Clark, Co-President
Merlyn Hough, Co-President
Bill Becker, Executive Director
Nancy Kruger, Deputy Director
Dave Klemp, Co-Vice President

Represents state and local air pollution control officers from over 150 major metropolitan areas and 53 states and territories.

11913 National Association of Conservation Districts (NACD)
509 Capitol Court, NE
Washington, DC 20002-4937

202-547-6223; Fax: 202-547-6450
www.nacdnet.org
Facebook, Twitter, LinkedIn, Vimeo, Google Plus, Flickr

Earl Garber, President
Lee McDaniel, First Vice President
Brent Van Dyke, Second Vice President
John Larson, Chief Executive Officer
Laura Wood Peterson, Director of Government Affairs

NACD develops national conservation policies, influences lawmakers and builds partnerships with other agencies and organizations. NACD also provides services to its districts to help them share ideas in order to better serve their local communities.
17000 Members
Founded in 1946

11914 **National Association of Counties**
25 Massachusetts Ave NW
Suite 500
Washington, DC 20001-1450

202-393-6226
888-407-6226; Fax: 202-393-2630
nacomeetings@naco.org
www.naco.org/
Facebook, Twitter, LinkedIn, YouTube

Linda Langston, President
Riki Hokama, 1st Vice President
Sallie Clark, 2nd Vice President
Matthew D. Chase, Executive Director
Karen McRunnel, Executive Assistant to the CEO
The National Association of Counties (NACo) is an organization that represents county governments in the United States. NACo advances issues with a unified voice before the federal government, improves the public's understanding of county government, and assists counties in finding and sharing innovative solutions through education and research. NACo's membership totals more than 2,000 counties, representing over 80 percent of the nation's population.
Founded in 1935

11915 **National Association of County Engineers**
25 Mass. Ave, NW
Suite 580
Washington, DC 20001-1454

202-393-5041; Fax: 202-393-2630
nace@naco.org
www.countyengineers.org

Brian C Roberts, Executive Director
Rebecca Page, Director of Marketing & Membership
Constantine Connie Radoulovitch, Office Manager
Duane J. Ratermann, President
Brian D. Stacy, President Elect
Members are county engineering professionals or road management authorities.
1900 Members
Founded in 1956

11916 **National Association of Development Organizations (NADO)**
400 N Capitol St NW
Suite 390
Washington, DC 20001-6505

202-624-7806; Fax: 202-624-8813
info@nado.org
www.nado.org
Facebook, Twitter, RSS

Terry Bobrowski, President
Vicki Glass, Director of Meetings and Membership
Susan Howard, Director of Government Relations
Brian Kelsey, Director of Economic Development
Carrie Kissel, Associate Director
The National Association of Development Organizations (NADO) serves as the national voice for regional development organizations. NADO helps its members achieve their goals by providing effective advocacy and lobbying services at the federal level, producing timely information and research, and offering opportunities for professional and organizational growth.

11917 **National Association of Government Archives & Records Administrators**
444 N. Capitol Street, NW
Suite 237
Washington, DC 20001-6505

202-508-3800; Fax: 202-508-3801
nagara@caphill.com
www.nagara.org
LinkedIn

Pari Swift, President
Patty Davis, Vice President
Jannette Goodall, Secretary
Galen R. Wilson, Treasurer
Steve Grandin, Membership Services & Publications
Professional association dedicated to the improvement of federal, state, and local government records and information management and the professional development of government records administrators and archivists. Members include county, municipal, and special district governments, state agencies, the National Archives and Records Administration; individual federal employees; the General Archives of Puerto Rico; and a number of provincial and institutional programs.
Founded in 1974

11918 **National Association of Housing and Redevelopment Officials**
630 Eye Street, NW
Washington, DC 20001-3736

202-289-3500
877-866-2476; Fax: 202-289-8181
nahro@nahro.org
www.nahro.org

Saul Ramirez, Executive Director
Donald J Cameron, Senior VP
Joseph E Gray Jr, VP
Elizabeth C Morris, VP Housing
Saul Ramirez, Manager
A professional membership association representing local housing authorities, community development agencies and individual professionals in the housing, community development and redevelopment fields.
700 Members
Founded in 1933

11919 **National Association of Local Housing Finance Agencies**
2025 M St NW
Suite 800
Washington, DC 20036-2422

202-367-1197; Fax: 202-367-2197
info@nalhfa.org
www.nalhfa.org

Ron Williams, President
W. D. Morris, Vice President
Vivian Benjamin, Treasurer
Tom Cummings, Secretary
The national association of professionals working to finance affordable housing in the broader community development context at the local level. Nonprofit association working as an advocate before Congress and federal agencies on legislative and regulatory issues affecting affordable housing and provides technical assistance and educational opportunities to its members and the public.
Founded in 1982

11920 **National Association of Neighborhoods**
1300 Pennsylvania Ave NW
Suite 700
Washington, DC 20004-3024

202-332-7766; Fax: 202-588-5881
info@nanworld.org
www.nanworld.org

Sam Thompson Jr., Board Member
Debra K. Powell, Board Member
Mission is to improve the quality of life in the nation's most important communities- its neighborhoods. Remains an organization of neighborhood coalitions, block clubs, community councils, and individuals, united by a love of neighborhoods and a strong determination to make them better.
2500+ Members
Founded in 1975

11921 **National Association of Postmasters of the United States**
8 Herbert St
Alexandria, VA 22305-2600

703-683-9027; Fax: 703-683-6820
www.napus.org

Robert J. Rapoza, President
Michael E. Quinn, Secretary/ Treasurer
Mission is to represent, promote, and protect postmasters. To foster a favorable image of public service and to assure users of the mail the best possible service. To be an advocate with the Congress of the United States. And to work closely with the United States Postal Service in the development of strategies for the enhancement of Postmasters and the Postal Service.
41M Members
Founded in 1898

11922 **National Association of Regional Councils**
777 North Caoitol Street NE
Suite 305
Washington, DC 20002

202-618-5696; Fax: 202-986-1038
lindsey@narc.org
www.narc.org
Twitter

Joanna Turner,, Executive Director
Lindsey Riley, Deputy of Communications
Leslie Wollack,, Deputy Executive Director
Mia Colson,, Grants Manager
State of regional repositories of instructional materials or services.
250 Members
Founded in 1965

11923 **National Association of Regulatory Utility Commissioners (NARUC)**
1101 Vermont Ave NW
Suite 200
Washington, DC 20005-3553

202-898-2200; Fax: 202-898-2213
admin@naruc.org
www.naruc.org

Lisa Polak Edgar, President
Travis Kavulla, 1st Vice President
Robert F Powellson, 2nd Vice President
Charles D. Gray, Executive Director
David E. Ziegner, Treasurer
Representing the State Public Service Commissioners who regulate essential utility services, including energy, telecommunications, and water. Members are responsible for assuring reliable utility service at fair, just, and reasonable rates. The Association is an invaluable resource for members and the regulatory community, providing a venue to set and influence public policy, share best practices, and foster innovative solutions to improve regulation.
Founded in 1889

11924 **National Association of State Development**
12884 Harbor Drive
Woodbridge, VA 22192

703-490-6777; Fax: 703-880-0509

Miles Friedman, President/CEO
Sally Pope, Director Finance
Pofen Salem, Project Manager
Established to provide a forum for directors of state economic development agencies to exchange information, compare programs, and es-

tablish an organizational base to approach the Federal Government on issues of mutual interest.
250 Members
Founded in 1946

11925 National Association of State Facilities
2760 Research Park Drive
PO Box 11910
Lexington, KY 40578-1910
859-244-8000
800-800-1910; Fax: 859-244-8001
membership@csg.org
www.csg.org
Facebook, Twitter, YouTube, RSS
Carl Marcellino, Chair
Gov. Brian Sandoval, President
Sen. Kelvin Atkinson, Vice Chair
Sen. Beau McCoy, Chair-Elect
David Adkins, Executive Director/CEO
Brings state leaders together to share capitol ideas, providing them the chance to learn valuable lessons from each other. Fosters innovation in state government and shining a spotlight on examples of how ingenuity and leaderhsip are transforming the way state government serves residents of the states and territories.
Founded in 1933

11926 National Association of Towns and Townships
1130 Connecticut Ave NW
Suite 300
Washington, DC 20036-3981
202-454-3950
866-830-0008; Fax: 202-331-1598
www.natat.org
Larry Merrill, President
Matthew DeTemple, Vice President
Jennifer Imo, Federal Director
Bill Hanka, Deputy Federal Director
Mark Limbaugh, Senior Advisor
Seeks flexible and alternative approaches to federal policies to ensure that small communities can meet federal requirements. Advocates for fair share funding, technical assistance, and other affirmative steps to address the inherent disadvantages that small governments face in our present intergovernmental system.
13M Members

11927 National Border Patrol Council
2445 Fifth Ave.
Suite 350
San Diego, CA 92101
520-219-5152
800-620-1613; Fax: 520-219-5154
www.nbpc1613.org
Facebook
James Harlan, President
Dan Mais, 1st Vice President
Terence Shigg, 2nd Vice President
Robert Lopez, 3rd Vice President
Victor Cantu, Treasurer
Exclusive representative for non-supervisory Border Patrol Agents and support personnel assigned to the San Diego Sector of the United States Border Parol.
69000 Members
Founded in 1965

11928 National Cannabis Industry Association
126 C Street NW
3rd Floor
Washington, DC 20001
888-683-5650
info@thecannabisindustry.org
www.thecannabisindustry.org
Facebook, Twitter, LinkedIn, Instagram
F. Aaron Smith, Executive Director
Shannon Hayden, Chief Operating Officer
Michael Correia, Director, Government Relations
Morgan Fox, Director, Media Relations
Brooke Gilbert, Director, Events & Education
Represents businesses and cannabis professionals in protecting legal cannabis businesses, defending state laws, and advancing federal policy reforms.
2000 Members
Founded in 2010

11929 National Community Development Association
522 21st St NW
#120
Washington, DC 20006-5012
202-293-7587; Fax: 202-887-5546
www.ncdaonline.org
LinkedIn
Cardell Cooper, Executive Director
Vicki Watson, Assistant Director
Karen Parker, Operations Manager
National nonprofit organization at the forefront in securing effective and responsive housing and community development programs for local governments. Provides timely, direct information and technical support to its members on federal housing and community development programs.
550+ Members

11930 National Conference of State Legislatures
National Conference of State Legislatures
7700 E 1st Pl
Denver, CO 80230-7143
303-364-7700; Fax: 303-364-7800
www.ncsl.org
Facebook, Twitter, LinkedIn, Youtube
Terie Norelli, President
Jean Cantrell, Vice President
Patsy Spaw, Secretary/Treasurer
A bipartisan organization that serves the legislators and staffs of the nation's 50 states, its commonwealths and territories.
Cost: $49.00
15000 Members
Circulation: 18000
ISSN: 0147-0644
Founded in 1975
Printed in 4 colors

11931 National Council of State EMS Training Coordinators
201 Park Washington Court
Falls Church, VA 22046
888-240-4696; Fax: 703-241-5603
Members are supervisors or coordinators of state EMS training programs, and limited to three from each state.

11932 National Council of State Housing Agencies
Hall of States
444 N Capitol St NW
Suite 438
Washington, DC 20001-1505
202-624-7710; Fax: 202-624-5899
bthompson@ncsha.org
www.ncsha.org
Facebook, Twitter
Thomas R. Gleason, President
Grant S. Whitaker, Vice President
Barbara J. Thompson, Executive Director
Maury L. Edwards, Director of Meetings
Kevin B. Burke, CPA, Director of Finance and Operations
NCSHA represents its members in Washington before Congress, the Administration, and the several federal agencies concerned with housing, including the Department of Housing and Urban Development, the Department of Agriculture, and the Treasury, and with other advocates for affordable housing.
350 Members
Founded in 1974

11933 National District Attorneys Association
99 Canal Center Plaza
Suite 330
Alexandria, VA 22314-1548
703-549-9222; Fax: 703-836-3195
www.ndaa.org
Facebook
Kay Chopard Cohen, Executive Director
Rick Hasey, CFO
Richard Hanes, Chief of Staff
Duane Kokesch, Director, Traffic Program
Allie Phillips, Deputy Director
Serves as a nationwide, interdisciplinary resource center for training, research, technical assistance, and publications reflecting the highest standards and cutting-edge practices of the prosecutorial profession.
7000 Members
Founded in 1950

11934 National Emergency Management Association
2760 Research Park Drive
Lexington, KY 40578
859-244-8000; Fax: 859-244-8239
nemaadmin@csg.org
www.nemaweb.org
Facebook
Bryan Koon, President
Wendy Smith-Reeve, Vice President
Trina R. Sheets, NEMA Executive Director
Beverly Bell, Senior Policy Analyst
Karen Cobuluis, Meeting & Marketing Coordinator
A nonpartisan, nonprofit association dedicated to enhancing public safety by improving the nation's ability to prepare for, respond to, and recover from all emergencies, disasters, and threats to our nation's security. Provides national leadership and expertise in comprehensive emergency management, serves as a vital emergency management information and assistance resource, and advances continuous improvement in emergency management.
263 Members
Founded in 1970

11935 National Forum for Black Public Administrators
777 N Capitol St NE
Suite 807
Washington, DC 20002-4291
202-408-9300; Fax: 202-408-8558
webmaster@nfbpa.org
www.nfbpa.org
Facebook, YouTube
Verdenia C. Baker, President
Bruce T. Moore, 1st Vice President
Regina V. K. Williams, Interim Executive Director
Malick Diagne, Fiscal Director
Yvette Harris, Membership Coordinator
Committed to strengthening the position of Blacks within the field of public administration; increasing the number of Blacks appointed to executive positions in public service organizations; and, to groom and prepare younger, aspiring administrators for senior public management posts in the years ahead.
2.8M Members
Founded in 1983

11936 National Governors' Association
Hall of States

444 N Capitol St
Suite 267
Washington, DC 20001-1512

202-624-5300; Fax: 202-624-5313
www.nga.org
Facebook, Twitter

Governor Mary Fallin, Chair
Governor John Hickenlooper, Vice Chair
Dan Crippen, Executive Director
Barry Anderson, Deputy Director
David Quam, Deputy Director, Policy

Coordinates the formulation of state policies by governors, and works to ensure consideration of these positions in the development of national policies and programs. The governors belong to seven standing committees: agriculture; community and economic development; justice and public protection; energy and environment; human resources; international trade; and foreign relations.
Founded in 1908

11937 National Hemp Association
80 M St. SE
Suite 130
Washington, DC 20003

202-706-3911
www.nationalhempassociation.org
Facebook, Twitter, Google+

Erica Stark, Executive Director
Anna Chanthavongseng, Assistant Executive Director

Supports the growth and development of all aspects of the industrial hemp industry through education, creating community, and working with government, scientific, and industry professionals.

11938 National Housing Law Project
703 Market Street
Suite 2000
San Francisco, CA 94103

415-546-7000; Fax: 415-546-7007
nhlp@nhlp.org
www.nhlp.org

Robert C. Pearman, Jr., Chairperson
John Relman, Vice Chair
Gideon Anders, Senior Staff Attorney
Catherine M. Bishop, Senior Staff Attorney
James R. Grow, Deputy Director

A nonprofit corporation that provides assistance on public and private housing and community development matters to Legal Services attorneys and housing specialists throughout the country. The project's goals are to produce, maintain and conserve low and moderate income housing and protect and expand the rights of lower income persons to decent and affordable housing.
Founded in 1968

11939 National Institute of Governmental Purchasing/NIGP
2411 Dulles Corner Park
Suite 350
Herndon, VA 20170-5223

703-736-8900
800-367-6447; Fax: 703-736-9639
grante@co.cape-may.nj.us
www.nigp.org
Facebook, Twitter, LinkedIn

Marcheta E. Gillespie, CPPO, CPPB,, President
Rick Grimm, CPPO, CPPB, Chief Executive Officer
Brent Maas, Executive Director, Business
Catherine Patin, Communications Manager
Carol Hodes, CAE, Executive Director

An international not-for-profit educational and technical organization of public purchasing agencies. NIGP develops, supports and promotes the public procurement profession through premier educational and research programs, professional support, and advocacy initiatives that benefit members and constituents.
2600+ Members
Founded in 1944

11940 National League of Cities
1301 Pennsylvania Ave NW
Suite 550
Washington, DC 20004-1747

202-626-3180
877-827-2385; Fax: 202-626-3043
info@nlc.org
www.nlc.org
Facebook, Twitter, LinkedIn, RSS, Youtube, Google Plus

Ralph Becker, President
Melodee Colbert Kean, 1st Vice President
Matt Zone, 2nd Vice President
Clarence Anthony, Executive Director
David DeLorenzo, Chief Digital Officer

Dedicated to helping city leaders build better communities. The NLC advocates for cities and towns, provides programs and services, provides opportunities for involvement and networking, keeps leaders informed, strengthens leadership skills, recognizes municipal achievements, partners with state leagues, and promotes cities and towns.
1700 Members
Founded in 1924

11941 National Public Employer Labor Relations Association
1012 South Coast Highway
Suite M
Oceanside, CA 92054

760-433-1686
877-673-5721; Fax: 760-433-1687
www.npelra.org
Facebook, Twitter, LinkedIn

Michael T. Kolb, Executive Director
Yvonne Gillengerten, Operations Manager
Janessa Stephens, Association Specialist
Allison Wittwer, Administrative Assistant
Stephanie Biggs, Administrative Assistant

Provides Professional Development, Networking, and Advocacy Services to Labor Relations & Human Resources professionals, so that public sector employers may deliver the most efficient and effective services to citizens & taxpayers.
2000+ Members
Founded in 1971

11942 National Rural Housing Coalition
1331 G St NW
10th FL
Washington, DC 20002

202-393-5229; Fax: 202-393-3034
www.nrhcweb.org
Facebook, Twitter

Karen Speakman, President
Marty Miller, 1st Vice President
Kathleen Tyler, 2nd Vice President
Hope Cupit, Secretary
Lee Beaulac, Treasurer

Works to focus policy makers on the needs of rural areas by direct advocacy and by coordinating a network of rural housing advocates around the nation. National Rural Housing Coalition is supported entirely by donations, contributions and subscriptions.
300 Members
Founded in 1969

11943 National Urban League
120 Wall St.
New York, NY 10005

212-558-5300; Fax: 212-344-5332
nul.iamempowered.com
Facebook, Twitter, LinkedIn, YouTube

Marc H. Morial, President & CEO
Michael F. Neidorff, Chair

Historic civil rights organization focused on improving quality of life in underserved urban communities.
Founded in 1911

11944 National Urban League Annual Conference
National Urban League
120 Wall St.
New York, NY 10005

212-558-5300; Fax: 212-344-5332
conference.iamempowered.com
Facebook, Twitter, Instagram, YouTube

Marc H. Morial, President & CEO
Michael F. Neidorff, Chair

Historic civil rights organization focused on improving quality of life in underserved urban communities.
Founded in 1911

11945 National WIC Association
2001 S Street NW
Suite 580
Washington, DC 20009-1165

202-232-5492; Fax: 202-387-5281
crichardson@nwica.org
www.nwica.org
Facebook, Twitter, Pinterest

Rita Arni, Chair
Douglas Greenaway, President & CEO
Cecilia Richardson, VP, Nutrition Programs & Admin
Emily Gilcher, Membership Engagement
Stephen Padre, Communications, Media and Marketing

The National WIC Association (NWA) is the non-profit education arm and advocacy voice of the Special Supplemental Nutrition Program for Women, Infants and Children (WIC), the over 7 million mothers and young children served by WIC and the 12,000 service provider Agencies who are the front lines of WIC's public health nutrition services for the nation's nutritionally at-risk mothers and young children.
1389 Members
Founded in 1979

11946 North American Gaming Regulators Association
1000 Westgate Drive
Suite 252
St Paul, MN 55114-8612

651-203-7244; Fax: 651-290-2266
www.nagra.org

Lisa M. Christiansen, President
Dave Jeseritz, Vice President
Tracy L. Bigelow, Treasurer
Craig Durbin, Secretary

A nonprofit professional association of gaming regulators throughout North America. The organization brings together agencies that regulate gaming activities and provides them a forum for the mutual exchange of regulatory information and techniques. Collecting and disseminating regulatory and enforcement information, procedures, and experiences from all jurisdictions provides on-going gaming education and training for all members.
120 Members
Founded in 1984

11947 **North American Securities Administrators Association, Inc.**
750 First Street NE
Suite 1140
Washington, DC 20002-8034
202-737-0900; Fax: 202-783-3571
www.nasaa.org
Facebook, RSS
Judith Shaw, President
Russ Iuculano, Executive Director
John H. Lynch, Deputy Executive Director
Joseph Brady, General Counsel
Michael Canning, Director of Policy
NASAA is the international organization representing securities administrators from all 50 states, the District of Columbia, Canada, Mexico and Puerto Rico, and is responsible for investor protection and education. NASAA recommends national policies in the securities industry and provides model legislation for state securities agencies to adopt affecting the regulation of broker/dealers and investment advisers. Consumers can contact NASAA to get phone numbers of state securities regulators.
66 Members
Founded in 1919

11948 **Patent and Trademark Office Society**
PO Box 2089
Arlington, VA 22202-0089
703-305-8340
www.ptos.org
Matthew Troutman, President
Brandon Rosati, Vice President
David Sosnowski, Secretary
Fred Guillermety, Administrator
Tsung-Yin Tsai, Treasurer
Internationally recognized for its activities in the patent and trademark fields. The Society has actively influenced the patent and trademark systems- promoting the systems' growth and well-being.
1800 Members
Founded in 1917
Mailing list available for rent

11949 **Procurement Round Table**
1464 Nieman Road
Shady Side, MD 20764
301-261-9918
www.procurementroundtable.org
Allan V. Burman, Chairman
Bill Gormley, Vice Chair
Kenneth J. Oscar, Treasurer
Chartered by former federal acquisition officials concerned about the economy, efficiency and effectiveness of the federal acquisition system. Its Directors and Officers are private citizens who serve pro bono with the objective of advising and assisting the government in making improvements in federal acquisition.
40 Members
Founded in 1984

11950 **Public Employees Roundtable**
PO Box 75248
Washington, DC 20013-5248
202-927-4926; Fax: 202-927-4920
Committed to helping future public servants reach their goals. Supporting young people planning careers in public service through the scholarship, fellowship and internship programs of its members.

11951 **Public Housing Authorities Directors Association**
511 Capitol Court NE
Washington, DC 20002-4947
202-546-5445; Fax: 202-546-2280
www.phada.org
Timothy Kaiser, Executive Director
Ted Van Dyke, Director of Government Affairs
Yaniv Goury, Director of Communications
Jim Armstrong, Policy Analyst
Kathleen Whalen, Policy Analyst
Represents and serves the needs of executive directors of housing authorities of all sizes, in all regions of the nation. In pursuing the Association's goal of improving assisted housing, the corporation works with Congress and federal agencies as well as with all interested groups to improve the nation's housing programs.
1.6M Members
Founded in 1979

11952 **Republican Communications Association**
Longworth House Office Building
1317 Longworth
PO Box 550
Washington, DC 20515-0001
Home Page: www.joinrca.org
Rachel Ledbetter, President
Rachel Stephens, Vice-President
Miranda Dabney, Treasurer
Sponsors professional development and networking programs. Conducts seminars, briefings, and tours.
165 Members
Founded in 1970

11953 **Society of Government Economists**
PO Box 77082
Washington, DC 20013
202-643-1743
sge@sge-econ.org
www.sge-econ.org
Robert Lerman, President
Julia Lane, Vice-President
Marvin Ward, Executive Director
Andrew Felton, Website Director
Brian Sloboda, Outreach Director and Event Planner
Supports the professional development of government economists, and those who are interested in public policy economics, by providing them with research, publications, and professional communication opportunities.
500 Members
Founded in 1970

11954 **State Government Affairs Council**
108 North Columbus Street
2nd Floor
Alexandria, VA 22314
571-312-3426
eloudy@sgac.org
www.sgac.org
Facebook, Twitter, LinkedIn
Donna Gehlhaart, President
Elizabeth A. Loudy, Executive Director
Jon Burton, Vice President
Crislyn Lumia, Director, Education & Training
Katherine Kilgore, Manager, Communications
The premier national association for multi-state government affairs professionals, providing opportunities for networking and professional development.
200 Members
Founded in 1975

11955 **State Higher Education Executive Officers Association**
3035 Center Green Drive
Suite 100
Boulder, CO 80301-2205
303-541-1600; Fax: 303-541-1639
sheeo@sheeo.org
www.sheeo.org
Twitter
Peter A. Blake, Chair
George Pernsteiner, President
Julie Carnahan, Senior Associate
Glady Kerns, Director of Administration
Eileen I. Klein, Treasurer
A nonprofit, nationwide association of the chief executive officers serving statewide coordinating boards and governing boards of postsecondary education.
56 Members
Founded in 1954

11956 **The Cannabis Alliance**
info@thecannabisalliance.us
www.thecannabisalliance.us
Facebook, Twitter
Lara Kaminsky, Executive Director
Julia Lee, Executive Assistant
Kim Ducot,, Membership Director
Advances the cannabis industry through education, advocacy, and setting the highest possible industry standards.
Founded in 2016

11957 **The National Association for State Community Services Programs**
111 K Street NE
Suite 300
Washington, DC 20002
202-624-5866; Fax: 202-624-8472
nascsp@nascsp.org
www.nascsp.org
Facebook, Twitter
Jenae Bjelland, Executive Director
Joan Harris, Director
Brad Penney, General Counsel
Gretchen Knowlton, Policy Director
Tabitha Beck, Research Director
The premier national association charged with advocating and enhancing the leadership role of states in preventing and reducing poverty.
100 Members
Founded in 1968

11958 **Trust for Public Land**
101 Montgomery Street
Suite 900
San Francisco, CA 94104
415-495-4014; Fax: 415-495-4103
info@tpl.org
www.tpl.org
Facebook, Twitter, Youtube
William Rogers, President & CEO
Brian Beitner, Chief Investment Officer
Sean Connolly, Chief Marketing Officer
Ernest Cook, Senior Vice President
Kathy DeCoster, Vice President
A nonprofit land acquisition and conservation organization, working with community groups, landowners, public land management agencies and rural groups to preserve open space lands and to pioneer methods of community ownership of land. Through its Investment Lands Program, the Trust for Public Land also acquires underutilized properties by gift or bargain sales.
Founded in 1972

11959 **U.S. Chamber of Commerce**
1615 H St Nw
Washington, DC 20062-2000

202-659-6000
800-638-6582; Fax: 202-463-5836
press@uschamber.com
www.uschamber.org
Facebook, Twitter

Thomas J Donohue, President & CEO
David C. Chavern, Executive Vice President
Myron Brilliant, Executive Vice President
Lily Fu Claffee, Senior Vice President
Shannon DiBari, Senior Vice President

The mission of the Chamber of Commerce is to advance human progress through an economic, political and social system based on individual freedom, incentive, initiative, opportunity, and responsibility. The Chamber of Commerce provides a voice of experience and influence in Washington, D.C., and around the globe, fighting for business and free enterprise before Congress, the White House, regulatory agencies, and the courts.

11960 **United States Conference of Mayors**
1620 Eye Street, NW
Washington, DC 20006-4033

202-293-7330; Fax: 202-293-2352
www.usmayors.org
Facebook, Twitter

Mayor Scott Smith, President
Mayor Kevin Johnson, Vice President
Mayor Stephanie Rawlings-Blake, 2nd Vice President
Tom Cochran, CEO and Executive Director

Primary roles are to promote development of policies, strengthen federal-city relationships, ensure federal policy meets urban needs, provide mayors with leadership and management tools, and create a forum in which mayors can share ideas and information.
30000 Members
Founded in 1987

11961 **United States Interagency Council on Homelessness**
Federal Center SW
409 Third St. SW Suite 310
Washington, DC 20024

202-708-4663; Fax: 202-708-1216
usich@usich.gov
www.ich.gov
Facebook, Twitter

Barbara Poppe, Executive Director

Mission is to coordinate the federal response to homelessness and to create a national partnership at every level of government and with the private sector to reduce and end homelessness in the nation while maximizing the effectiveness of the Federal Government in contributing to the end of homelessness.
Founded in 1987

11962 **Urban Land Institute**
1025 Thomas Jefferson St NW
Suite 500 West
Washington, DC 20007-5230

202-624-7000; Fax: 202-624-7140
ulifoundation@uli.org
www.uli.org
Facebook, Twitter, LinkedIn, YouTube, Flickr, Google Plus

Randall Rowe, Chairman
Patrick L. Phillips, Chief Executive Officer
Michael Terseck, CFO
Kathleen B. Carey, Chief Content Officer
Jason Ray, Chief Technology Officer

Founded to provide a land-use information resource for both the professionals and the public. ULI conducts seminars, workshops, semiannual meetings, research programs and publishes books on all aspects of land use and development issues. ULI offers an advisory service, and gives annual Awards for Excellence.
14M Members
Founded in 1936

11963 **Urban and Regional Information Systems Association**
701 Lee Street
Suite 680
Des Plaines, IL 60016-4508

847-824-6300; Fax: 847-824-6363
info@urisa.org
www.urisa.org
Facebook, Twitter, LinkedIn

Rebecca Somers, President
Wendy Nelson, Executive Director
Keri Brennan, GISP, Education Manager
Patricia Francis, Meeting Coordinator
Verlanda McBride, Registrar & Database Manager

Concerned with the effective use of information systems technology at the state, regional and local levels. Members informed of current developments in the information systems field. Its goal is to stimulate and encourage the advancement of an interdisciplinary professional approach to planning, designing and operating information systems.
3000 Members
Founded in 1963

11964 **Western Governor's Association**
1600 Broadway
Suite 1700
Denver, CO 80202

303-623-9378; Fax: 303-534-7309
www.westgov.org
Facebook, Twitter, LinkedIn, Google+, Pinterest

James Ogbury, Executive Director
Holly Propst, Deputy Executive Director

Association for policy development, information exchange and collective action by the Governors of 19 Western states and 3 US-flag Pacific islands.
Founded in 1984

Newsletters

11965 **ADA Today**
Americans for Democratic Action
1625 K St NW
Suite 102
Washington, DC 20006-1611

202-785-5980; Fax: 202-785-5969
info@adaction.org
www.adaction.org

David Card, Editor

The nation's oldest liberal lobbying group. This newsletter describes national and local chapter activities and updates federal legislative action.
Cost: $20.00
Frequency: Quarterly
Circulation: 65000
Mailing list available for rent: 65000 names
Printed in 2 colors on matte stock

11966 **ADAction News and Notes**
Americans for Democratic Action
1625 K St NW
Suite 210
Washington, DC 20006-1611

202-785-5980; Fax: 202-785-5969
info@adaction.org
www.adaction.org

Allen Kukovich, Executive Committee Chair
Jim McDermott, CEO
Don Kufler, Circulation Manager

Offers information on legislative issues and lobbying.
Cost: $20.00
Frequency: Weekly
Circulation: 3000
Founded in 1948
Mailing list available for rent: 3000 names
Printed in one color on matte stock

11967 **AJA Benchmark**
American Judges Association
300 Newport Ave
Williamsburg, VA 23185-4147

757-259-1841; Fax: 757-259-1520
aja.ncsc.dni.us

Judge Kevin S. Burke, President
Judge Toni Manning Higginbotham, President-Elect
Judge Elliott L. Zide, Vice President
Judge Brian MacKenzie, Secretary
Judge Harold V. Froehlich, Treasurer

Latest news from the American Judges Association.
2500 Members
Frequency: Quarterly
Founded in 1959

11968 **ASAP Newsletter**
American Society of Access Professionals
1444 I St Nw
Suite 700
Washington, DC 20005-6542

202-712-9054; Fax: 202-216-9646
asap@bostrom.com
www.accesspro.org

Claire Shanley, Executive Director

Provides information about upcoming and recent ASAP events, insights, and information about changes in the laws, and court decisions.
Frequency: Yearly

11969 **Advocate**
PHADA
511 Capitol Court NE
Washington, DC 20002-4947

202-546-5445; Fax: 202-546-2280
www.phada.org

Timothy Kaiser, Executive Director

Provides members with insights into HUD and Congressional actions, funding opportunities, job vacancies, and major developments in the public housing field.
1.6M Members
Frequency: Bi-Weekly
Founded in 1979

11970 **American Planning Association**
American Planning Association
1030 15th St.
Suite 750 W
Washington, DC 20005

202-872-0611; Fax: 202-872-0643
CustomerService@planning.org
www.planning.org/
Facebook, Twitter, LinkedIn

Joel Albizo, CEO
Ann Simms, CFO/EOO
Harriet Bogdanowicz, Chief Communications Officer
Mark Ferguson, Chief Information Officer
Liz Lang, Marketing Director

The American Planning Association(APA) brings together thousands of people- practicing planners, citizens, elected officials-committed to making great communities.
Cost: $645.00
40000 Members
Frequency: Monthly
Founded in 1917

11971 Assisted Housing Accounts & Audits Insider
Brownstone Publishers
149 5th Ave
16th Floor
New York, NY 10010-6832

212-473-8200
800-643-8095; Fax: 212-473-8786
info@vendomegrp.com
www.vendomegrp.com

David B Klein, Editor
John M Striker, Publisher

Explains how to comply with regulatory STET requirements for accounting and auditing for HUD-assisted housing. Includes accounting control policies, audit preparation checklists, model accounting book entries, forms, staff memos and model letters.
Cost: $195.00
Frequency: Monthly
Founded in 1980
Printed in 2 colors on matte stock

11972 Assisted Housing Management Insider
Brownstone Publishers
149 5th Ave
16th Floor
New York, NY 10010-6832

212-473-8200
800-643-8095; Fax: 212-473-8786
info@hcmarketplace.com
www.hcmarketplace.com

John Striker, Publisher

Explains HUD regulatory requirements for federally-assisted housing, and gives advice on how to stay in compliance. Includes sample copies of model leases, clauses, letters, eviction notices, authorization forms, checklists and signs.
Printed in 2 colors on matte stock

11973 BNA's Eastern Europe Reporter
Bureau of National Affairs
1801 S Bell St
Arlington, VA 22202-4501

703-341-3000
800-372-1033; Fax: 800-253-0332
customercare@bna.com
www.bnabooks.com

Paul N Wojcik, CEO
William A. Beltz

This is just one of many biweekly notification services covering legislative, regulatory and legal developments affecting business, trade and investment in Eastern Europe and the former Soviet Union.
Cost: $1750.00
Frequency: Bi-annually

11974 CQ Congressional Quarterly
Congressional Quarterly
1414 22nd Street NW
Washington, DC 20037-1003

202-887-8500

Offers information on House and Senate committee hearings scheduled for up to two months from publication date.
Cost: $1299.00

11975 CQ Schedules
Congressional Quarterly
77 K Street NE
Washington, DC 20002-4681

202-650-6500
800-432-2250
customerservice@cqrollcall.com
www.cq.com

Susan Benkelman, Executive Editor
Randy Wynn, Deputy Executive Editor
Anne Q Hoy, Managing Editor, Spec. Publications
Caitlin Hendel, Managing Editor, CQ Today
Melanie Starkey, Editor, Daily News

A daily guide to what's happening in Washington.

11976 CQ Today
Congressional Quarterly
77 K Street NE
Washington, DC 20002-4681

202-650-6500
800-432-2250
customerservice@cqrollcall.com
www.cq.com

Susan Benkelman, Executive Editor
Randy Wynn, Deputy Executive Editor
Anne Q Hoy, Managing Editor, Spec. Publications
Caitlin Hendel, Managing Editor, CQ Today
Melanie Starkey, Editor, Daily News

CQ Today, available in print and online, delivers unparalleled coverage and analysis from the floor, committee markups, hearings and more. Subscribers receive updates throughout the day as news breaks on Capitol Hill.

11977 Cannabis Council of Canada Newsletter
Cannabis Council of Canada
111 Albert St.
P.O. Box 81071
Ottawa, ON K1P 1B1

647-206-1231
www.cannabis-council.ca
Facebook, Twitter

Allan Rewak, Executive Director

Contains news, announcements, and updates about Canada's cannabis industry.

11978 Census and You
Census Bureau
4700 Silver Hill Rd
Washington, DC 20233-0001

301-763-3030; Fax: 301-457-3670
www.census.gov

Thomas E Zebelsky, Plant Manager

Highlights data products and program of the US Census Bureau. Shows which reports, CD-ROMs, tapes, etc. to choose and also highlights releases on the Internet.
Cost: $21.00
12 Pages
Frequency: Monthly
Circulation: 11000
Founded in 1790
Printed in 2 colors on matte stock

11979 Civil Rights: From the State Capitals
Wakeman Walworth
PO Box 7376
Alexandria, VA 22307-7376

703-768-9600; Fax: 703-768-9690
www.statecapitals.com/civilrights.html

Keyes Walworth, Publisher

Covers ethnic, race and gender discrimination; including hate crime legislation, racial profiling, the current battle over affirmative action plus gay rights, domestic partner issues, rights of the disabled, rights of minors, women in the workforce, Hispanic issues. Includes legislation, judicial and administrative decisions across the country, as well as federal actions that affect the states.
Cost: $245.00
4 Pages
Frequency: Weekly
Founded in 1962
Printed in one color on matte stock

11980 Clearinghouse
NAGARA
1450 Western Avenue
Suite 101
Albany, NY 12203

518-694-8472; Fax: 518-463-8656
nagara@caphill.com
www.nagara.org

Paul R. Bergeron, President
Daphne DeLeon, Vice President
Caryn Wojcik, Secretary
Nancy Fortna, Treasurer

Illustrated newsletter of NAGARA. Features lively articles, informative announcements, a wide variety of news, and a column by the Archivist of the United States. Provides a forum for archivists to share information and learn from each other. Electronic publication only.
Frequency: Quarterly

11981 Connections
National Public Employer Labor Relations Assoc
1012 South Coast Highway
Suite M
Oceanside, CA 92054

760-433-1686
877-673-5721; Fax: 760-433-1687
www.npelra.org

The outstanding monthly e-newsletter, your connection to national, regional and local developments. For members only
Frequency: Monthly
Circulation: 2000

11982 Cooperative Housing Bulletin
National Association of Housing Cooperatives
1444 I St Nw
Suite 700
Washington, DC 20005-6542

202-737-0797; Fax: 202-216-9646
info@nahc.coop
www.coophousing.org

Provides up-to-date information on issues of interest to the cooperative housing community. Accepts advertising.
Frequency: Monthly
Circulation: 2500
Printed in 2 colors on matte stock

11983 Divisions Digest
Federal Bar Association
1220 North Fillmore St.
Suite 444
Arlington, VA 22201

571-481-9100; Fax: 571-481-9090
fba@fedbar.org
www.fedbar.org
Facebook, Twitter, LinkedIn

Fern C. Bomchill, President
Robert J. DeSousa, President-Elect
Hon. Gustavo Gelpi, Jr., Treasurer

Serves the Corporate and Association Counsel, Federal Career Service, Senior Lawyers, and the Younger Lawyers Divisions of the FBA.
16000 Members
Frequency: Bi-Annually
Founded in 1920

11984 Downtown Idea Exchange
Alexander Communications Group

1916 Park Ave
8th Floor
New York, NY 10037-3733

212-281-6099
800-232-4317; Fax: 212-283-7269
info@downtowndevelopment.com
www.downtowndevelopment.com

Laurence Alexander, Owner
Nadine Harris, Marketing Manager

News of downtown revitalization for downtown leaders and officials in local and state government.
Cost: $167.00
8 Pages
Frequency: Monthly
ISSN: 0012-5822

11985 **Downtown Promotion Reporter**
Alexander Communications Group
1916 Park Ave
8th Floor
New York, NY 10037-3733

212-281-6099
800-232-4317; Fax: 212-283-7269
info@downtowndevelopment.com
www.downtowndevelopment.com

Romauld Alexander, Owner
Laurence Alexander, CEO
Sarah Benardos, Production Manager
Paul Felt, Editor

Proven promotion ideas and methods to bring shoppers to downtown stores.
Cost: $189.00
12 Pages
Frequency: Monthly
Circulation: 1000
ISSN: 0363-2830
Founded in 1954

11986 **EBA UPDATE**
Energy Bar Association
1990 M St NW
Suite 350
Washington, DC 20036-3429

202-223-5625; Fax: 202-833-5596
admin@eba-net.org
www.eba-net.org
Facebook

Derek A. Dyson, President
Susan A. Olenchuk, President-Elect
Jason F. Leif, Vice President
Emma F. Hand, Secretary
Hugh E. Hilliard, Treasurer

Providing members with the latest news regarding the energy industry.
2600 Members
Frequency: Quarterly
Founded in 1946

11987 **EENR Pursuits**
Federal Bar Association
1220 North Fillmore St.
Suite 444
Arlington, VA 22201

571-481-9100; Fax: 571-481-9090
fba@fedbar.org
www.fedbar.org
Facebook, Twitter, LinkedIn

Fern C. Bomchill, President
Robert J. DeSousa, President-Elect
Hon. Gustavo Gelpi, Jr., Treasurer

EENR Section newsletter.
16000 Members
Frequency: Bi-Annually
Founded in 1920

11988 **Economic Development Now**
International Economic Development Council
734 15th Street NW
Suite 900
Washington, DC 20005

202-223-7800; Fax: 202-223-4745

Jeff Finkle, President & CEO
Dennis G. Coleman, Chair
Jay C. Moon, Vice Chair
Paul Krutko, Secretary/ Treasurer

Member publication providing a survey of current economic development news, original reports examining best practices, and updates concerning federal funding and activity.
1.8M Members
Frequency: Bi-Monthly
Founded in 1967

11989 **Economic Development: From the State Capitals**
Wakeman Walworth
PO BOX 7376
Alexandria, VA 22307-7376

703-768-9600; Fax: 703-768-9690
www.statecapitals.com/

Keyes Walworth, Publisher

Covers environmental requirements, land use regulation, mass transportation, highway construction plans, utility rates, changes in labor laws, tax policies, enterprise zones, parkland development, taxes, licensing and fees. Includes vital urban development programs: growth control legislation, state construction programs involving airports, stadiums, and building codes.
Cost: $245.00
8 Pages
Frequency: Weekly
Founded in 1963
Printed in one color on Y stock

11990 **Employee Policy for the Public and Private Sector: From the State Capitals**
Wakeman Walworth
PO Box 7376
Alexandria, VA 22307-7376
703-768-9600; Fax: 703-549-1372
www.statecapitals.com/employeepolicy.html

Keyes Walworth, Publisher

Provides a nationwide perspective on employee health insurance programs, sexual harassment policies, unemployment and workers' compensation, retirement policies, family medical leave, new ergonomic rules, pay equity programs, collective bargaining, dismissal practices, minimum wages, drug testing, background checks, day care centers, domestic partner rules.
Cost: $245.00
4 Pages
Frequency: Weekly
Printed in one color on matte stock

11991 **EuroWatch**
WorldTrade Executive
PO Box 761
Concord, MA 01742
978-287-0301; Fax: 978-287-0302
www.wtexec.com

Alison French, Production Manager

Analyzes the most recent EU judicial and legislative developments. Covers EU trade issues, labor issues, single market and currency issues, EU and individual country business law, trademark issues.
Cost: $797.00

11992 **Federal Action Affecting the States: From the State Capitals**
Wakeman Walworth
PO Box 7376
Alexandria, VA 22307-7376
703-768-9600; Fax: 703-768-9690
www.statecapitals.com/fedaction.html

Keyes Walworth, Publisher

Gives a state perspective on Federal court rulings, overseer programs, changes in state jurisdiction, federal funds for state programs, highway, drug abuse control, disaster, environmental and other programs that involve both the states and the Feds.
Cost: $245.00
4 Pages
Frequency: Weekly
Founded in 1955
Printed in one color on matte stock

11993 **Federal Assistance Monitor**
CD Publications
8204 Fenton St
Silver Spring, MD 20910-4571

301-588-6380
800-666-6380; Fax: 301-588-6385
www.cdpublications.com

Michael Gerecht, President
Dave Kittross, Editor

Comprehensive review of federal funding announcements, private grants, rule changes and legislative actions affecting the community programs.
Cost: $419.00
Frequency: Monthly
Founded in 1961
Mailing list available for rent: 2,000 names at $160 per M

11994 **Federal Employees News Digest**
1850 Centennial Park Drive
Suite 520
Reston, VA 20191

703-648-9551
800-989-3363; Fax: 703-648-0265

Publishes weekly newsletter and self-help books for federal and postal employees on retirement and pay, as well as other benefit-related topics. Accepts advertising.
Cost: $49.00
4 Pages
Frequency: 5x Yearly
Founded in 1951

11995 **Federal Times**
6883 Commercial Dr
Springfield, VA 22159

800-368-5718
armylet@atpco.com
www.defensenews.com

Mark Winans, VP
Elaine Howard, President/CEO
Alex Neill, Managing Editor
Jim Tice, Senior Writer
David Smith, Marketing

Timely news and information on the rapid changes impacting today's federal managers, managing staff, the latest technology, and financial and career decisions.
Cost: $55.00
Frequency: Weekly
Circulation: 1MM

11996 **Friday Flash**
Coalition for Government Procurement

1990 M St Nw
Suite 450
Washington, DC 20036-3466

202-331-0975; Fax: 202-822-9788
info@thecgp.org
www.thecgp.org

A weekly newsletter published by the Coalition for Government Procurement.
38387 Pages
Frequency: Weekly
Circulation: 1200
Founded in 1979

11997 **From the State Capitals**
Wakeman Walworth
PO BOX 7376
Alexandria, VA 22307-7376

703-768-9600; Fax: 703-768-9690
thecapitolcollection.com

Keyes Walworth, Publisher

Keeps readers informed of national trends in domestic lawmaking. Issues dealing with taxes, the environment, economic development, drug abuse, abortion and education.
Founded in 1955

11998 **GovManagement Daily**
American Society for Public Administration
1301 Pennsylvania Avenue NW
Suite 700
Washington, DC 20004

202-393-7878; Fax: 202-638-4952
info@aspanet.org
www.aspanet.org
Facebook, Twitter, LinkedIn

Erik O. Bergrud, President
Stephen E. Condrey, Vice-President
Kuotsai Tom Liou, President-Elect

Presenting headlines and brief summaries of news and other information and analysis on public-sector management at all levels of government.
15M Members
Frequency: Daily
Founded in 1939

11999 **Government Employee Relations Report**
Bureau of National Affairs
1801 S Bell St
Arlington, VA 22202-4501

703-341-3000
800-372-1033; Fax: 800-253-0332
customercare@bna.com
www.bnabooks.com

Paul N Wojcik, CEO

A notification service that covers federal, state and municipal government employee relations.
Cost: $1479.00
Frequency: Weekly

12000 **Government PROcurement**
Penton Media
1300 E 9th St
Suite 316
Cleveland, OH 44114-1503

216-696-7000; Fax: 216-696-6662
www.govpro.com

Jane Cooper, Marketing
Kristin M Atwater, Managing Editor
Kay Ross Baker, Publisher

Specifically for the public sector purchasing professional.
58 Pages
Circulation: 20000
ISSN: 1078-0769
Founded in 1892
Printed in 4 colors on glossy stock

12001 **Government Waste Watch Newspaper**
Citizens Against Government Waste
1301 Pennsylvania Ave NW
Suite 1075
Washington, DC 20004-1707

202-467-5300; Fax: 202-467-4253
membership@cagw.org
www.cagw.org

Thomas A. Schatz, President
Robert J. Tedeschi, Treasurer & CFO

A quarterly newspaper published by Citizens Against Government Waste.
Cost: $25.00
Frequency: Quarterly
Circulation: 108000
Founded in 1984
Mailing list available for rent

12002 **HAC News**
Housing Assistance Council
1025 Vermont Ave NW
Suite 606
Washington, DC 20005-3516

202-842-8600; Fax: 202-347-3441
hac@ruralhome.org
www.ruralhome.org

Moises Loza, Executive Director
Janice Clark, Editor

Newsletter publishing issues of rural and low-income housing. Free.
ISSN: 1093-8036

12003 **HOTLINE**
National Journal
The Watergate
600 New Hampshire Ave., NW
Washington, DC 20037

202-739-8400
800-207-8001; Fax: 202-833-8069
www.nationaljournal.com

Julie Abramson, Associate Production Editor
Tim Alberta, Sr Editor, National Journal Hotline
Ronald Brownstein, Editorial Director

Online daily newsletter offers information on US national, state and local political campaigns and issues.
Frequency: Weekly
Founded in 1987

12004 **Health Officer News**
US Conference of Local Health Officers
1620 I Street NW
Washington, DC 20006-4005

202-887-6120; Fax: 202-293-2352

Alan Campbell, Publisher
Stephen Horn, Editor

The official publication of the US conference of local health officers. Accepts advertising.
Cost: $35.00
12 Pages
Frequency: BiWeekly

12005 **Housing Law Bulletin**
National Housing Law Project
703 Market Street
Suite 2000
San Francisco, CA 94103

415-546-7000; Fax: 415-546-7007
nhlp@nhlp.org
www.nhlp.org

Marcia Rosen, Executive Director
James Grow, Deputy Director
Susan Stern, Deputy Director, Administration

Updates in housing law information for use by legal services organizations.
Cost: $175.00
Frequency: Monthly
Circulation: 400

12006 **ICBA NewsWatch Today**
Independent Community Bankers of America
518 Lincoln Rd.
P.O. Box 267
Sauk Centre, MN 56378

320-526-6546
800-422-7285; Fax: 320-352-5766
newswatchtoday@icba.org
www.icba.org

Rebeca Romero Rainey, President/CEO
Terry J. Jorde, Sr. Executive Vice President

Free electronic news bulletin highlighting breaking industry news and information.
Frequency: Daily

12007 **In Hot Pursuit**
Federal Bar Association
1220 North Fillmore St.
Suite 444
Arlington, VA 22201

571-481-9100; Fax: 571-481-9090
fba@fedbar.org
www.fedbar.org
Facebook, Twitter, LinkedIn

Fern C. Bomchill, President
Robert J. DeSousa, President-Elect
Hon. Gustavo Gelpi, Jr., Treasurer

Criminal Law Section newsletter.
16000 Members
Frequency: Bi-Annually
Founded in 1920

12008 **Inside Energy**
Platts, McGraw Hill Companies
1221 Avenue of the Americas
New York, NY 10020-1001

212-512-2000; Fax: 212-512-3840
support@platts.com
www.mcgraw-hill.com

Glenn S Goldberg, President
Georgia Safos, Circulation Director

Covers the Department of Energy including energy, science/technology, and environmental management programs as well as energy programs at the Interior Department.
Cost: $1395.00
16 Pages
Frequency: Weekly
Founded in 1884

12009 **International Association of Emergency Managers**
201 Park Washington Court
Falls Church, VA 22046-4513

703-538-1795; Fax: 703-241-5603
info@iaem.com
www.iaem.com

Elizabeth B Armstrong, Executive Director
Sharon L Kelly, Member Director
Elizabeth B Armstrong, CEO
Karen Thompson, Editor
Dawn Shiley, Communication Manager

Representatives of city and county government departments responsible for emergency management and disaster preparedness.
Cost: $160.00
20 Pages
Frequency: Monthly
Circulation: 2700
Founded in 1952
Printed in 2 colors on matte stock

12010 **Lottery, Parimutuel & Casino Regulation: From the State Capitals**
Wakeman Walworth

PO BOX 7376
Alexandria, VA 22307-7376

703-768-9600; Fax: 703-768-9690
www.statecapitals.com/lotterypari.html

Keyes Walworth, Publisher

Covers regulation, or attempts to regulate every form of gambling from internet gambling to cockfighting. It covers state lottery prize structures, ticket marketing policies, distribution of revenues, new games and equipment; Indian gaming, gambling compacts with tribes and revenue sharing; regulation and taxation of casinos, pari-mutuel wagering operations plus horse racing, dog racing, jai alai, riverboat gambling, bingo and other forms of gaming.
Cost: $345.00
4 Pages
Frequency: Weekly
Founded in 1962
Printed in one color on matte stock

12011 Managing Today's Federal Employees
LRP Publications
PO Box 980
Horsham, PA 19044-0980

215-784-0912
800-341-7874; Fax: 215-784-9639
webmaster@lrp.com
www.lrp.com

Todd Lutz, CFO
Patrick Byrne, Editor
Chris Donohue, Legal Editor

Keeping supervisors informed of their personnel management responsibilities has always been one of the most difficult tasks facing federal agency personnel officers. This newsletter is a working resource as well as a comprehensive training tool. Gives sensible solutions to common management challenges and covers controversial issues such as sexual harassment, contracting out of federal jobs, alternative dispute resolutions and more.
Cost: $155.00
8 Pages
Frequency: Monthly
Founded in 1977
Printed in 2 colors on matte stock

12012 Mediaite
584 Broadway
Suite 510
New York, NY 10012

info@mediaite.com
www.mediaite.com

Dan Abrams, Founder
Jon Nicosia, Senior Editor & Video Director
Nando Di Fino, Senior Editor & TV Reporter
Tommy Christopher, Political Editor & WH Correspondent
Colby Hall, Editor at Large

Mediaite is the site for news, information and smart opinions about print, online and broadcast media, offering original and immediate assessments of the latest news as it breaks.

12013 Motor Vehicle Regulation: From the State Capitals
Wakeman Walworth
PO Box 7376
Alexandria, VA 22307-7376

703-768-9600; Fax: 703-768-9690
www.statecapitals.com/motorreg.html

Keyes Walworth, Publisher

Covers all fifty states regarding inspections, tags, fees and taxes, emissions standards, drunken driving laws, motorist licensing, insurance and education . We report on helmet , seat belt, and child restraint seat laws; regulation of all motor vehicles including autos, trucks, motorcycles, school buses, electric vehicles, watercraft. We also cover motor vehicle department administrative changes.
Cost: $245.00
4 Pages
Frequency: Weekly
Founded in 1962
Printed in one color on matte stock

12014 NACCED Alerts
Nat'l Assoc. for County & Economic Development
2025 M St NW
Suite 800
Washington, DC 20036-3309

202-367-1163; Fax: 202-367-2149
www.nacced.org

John Murphy, Executive Director
Brian Paulson, President
Jack Exler, Vice President
Tony Agliata, Secretary/Treasurer
Bill J. Lake, Director

Analyze federal legislation and regulations, highlight innovative county activities, report on current developments in the field, and provide updates on association activities.
120+ Members
Frequency: Bi-Weekly
Founded in 1989

12015 NADC News
National Association of Development Companies
6764 Old McLean Village Dr
Mc Lean, VA 22101-3906

703-748-2575; Fax: 703-748-2582
www.nadco.org

Chris Crawford, President

Provides long-term fixed asset financing to small businesses. Publishes newsletter.
Frequency: Monthly
Circulation: 244
Founded in 1981

12016 NAHMA News
National Affordable Housing Management Association
400 N Columbus Street
Suite 203
Alexandria, VA 22314

703-683-8630; Fax: 703-683-8634
www.nahma.org

Trade association for professional property managers of federally assisted housing. Publishes a newsletter.
Cost: $95.00
Frequency: Bimonthly
Circulation: 3000

12017 NASAA Insight
NA Securities Administrators Association
750 First Street NE
Suite 1140
Washington, DC 20002-8034

202-737-0900; Fax: 202-783-3571
www.nasaa.org
Facebook

Jack Herstein, President
Preston DuFauchard, President-Elect
Rick Hancox, Secretary
Fred J. Joseph, Treasurer

Designed to keep readers informed of recent NASAA activities.
Frequency: Quarterly
Founded in 1919

12018 NASCSP Newsletter
Nat'l Assoc. for State Community Service Programs
444 N Capitol St NW
Suite 846
Washington, DC 20001-1556

202-624-5866; Fax: 202-624-7745
nascsp@nascsp.org
www.nascsp.org
Facebook, Twitter

Steve Payne, President
William Brand, Vice President
Jennifer Sexson, Treasurer
Ditzah Wooden-Wade, Secretary

Updates the Community Action Network on pertinent legislation, best practices, CSBG and WAP program highlights, and the latest events.
100 Members
Founded in 1968

12019 NASFA News
Natl' Assoc. of State Facilities Administrators
2760 Research Park Drive
PO Box 11910
Lexington, KY 40578-1910

859-311-1877
800-800-1910; Fax: 859-244-8001
nasfa@nasfa.net
www.nasfa.net/

Marcia Stone, Executive Director

State administrators of facilities and property. A newsletter is published for members.
Cost: $1800.00
Frequency: Quarterly
Circulation: 2000
Founded in 1987

12020 NATAT's Reporter
National Association of Towns and Townships
444 N Capitol St Nw
Suite 397
Washington, DC 20001-1512

202-624-8195; Fax: 202-624-3554
natat@sso.org
www.natat.org

Kelly Aylward, Manager
Larry Merrill, Vice President
Matthew DeTemple, Secretary, Treasurer

Covers federal legislation and regulation that pertain to local governments, with emphasis on compact or small towns (under 50,000; many under 1,000); also includes case studies of exemplary, creative local government, programs and association news from the National Association of Towns & Townships.
Cost: $36.00
24 Pages
Frequency: BiWeekly
Circulation: 15,200
Mailing list available for rent: 11700 names at $85 per M
Printed in 2 colors on newsprint stock

12021 NCDA News
National Community Development Association
522 21st St NW
Suite 120
Washington, DC 20006-5012

202-293-7587; Fax: 202-887-5546
www.ncdaonline.org

Shandra Western, Editor

A national nonprofit membership organization representing local governments that implement community development programs. The members administer federally supported community development, housing and human services programs. NCDA provides counsel at the federal level on new program design and current program implementation and advocates on behalf of responsive community development.
13 Pages

12022 **Nation's Cities Weekly**
National League of Cities
1301 Pennsylvania Ave NwW
Suite 550
Washington, DC 20004-1747

202-626-3180; Fax: 202-626-3043
info@nlc.org
www.nlc.org

Donald J Borut, Executive Director

News for and about cities.
Cost: $96.00
Frequency: Weekly
Circulation: 30000
ISSN: 0164-5935

12023 **National Association of Conservation Districts**
NACD
509 Capitol Court, NE
Washington, DC 20002-4937

202-547-6223; Fax: 202-547-6450
www.nacdnet.org

John Larson, CEO

Highlights forestry issues of importance to districts and to showcase district-related forestry projects and success stories.
17000 Members
Frequency: Monthly
Founded in 1946

12024 **National Association of Regional Councils**
National Association of Regional Councils
1666 Connecticut Ave NW
Suite 305
Washington, DC 20002

202-986-1032; Fax: 202-986-1038
lindsey@narc.org
www.narc.org

Fred Abousleman, Executive Director
Lindsey Riley, Deputy of Communications
Frequency: Weekly
Circulation: 2000

12025 **Navy Times**
Gannett Government Media
6883 Commercial Drive
Springfield, VA 22159-500

703-750-7400
800-368-5718; Fax: 703-750-8622
tnaegele@atpco.com
www.navytimes.com

Elaine Howard, President
Judy McCoy, Associate Publisher
David Smith, VP Marketing/Business Dev
Dick Howlett, AVP Circulation Operations
Tobias Naegele, Executive Editor

The trusted, independent source for news and information of the Navy community. Breaking news, personal finance information, healthcare, recreational resources, exclusive videos and photos, Guard and Reserve information, and an expanded community area connecting service members, military families and veterans.
Cost: $143.00
Frequency: Weekly

12026 **Outlook: From the State Capitals**
Wakeman Walworth
PO Box 7376
Alexandria, VA 22307-7376

703-768-9600; Fax: 703-549-1372
www.statecapitals.com/theoutlook.html

Keyes Walworth, Publisher

Gives an excellent perspective of trend- setting topics in state lawmaking: internet taxes, school choice, economic development, abortion, environmental issues, gambling laws. Each week is devoted to a different subject. In addition, a special feature called In the Works Around The Nation provides current highlights from other State Capitals newsletters.
Cost: $245.00
4 Pages
Frequency: Weekly
Printed in one color on matte stock

12027 **PA TIMES**
American Society for Public Administration
1301 Pennsylvania Avenue NW
Suite 700
Washington, DC 20004

202-393-7878; Fax: 202-638-4952
info@aspanet.org
www.aspanet.org
Facebook, Twitter, LinkedIn

Erik O. Bergrud, President
Stephen E. Condrey, Vice-President
Kuotsai Tom Liou, President-Elect

ASPA's newspaper covering developments in the professional field of public administration. Article topics include successful local state and federal government programs, PA trends and new PA methods. Focuses on the issues that face public managers today. Also highlights best practices in the field and updates members on how ASPA plays a role in the support of the public sector.
15M Members
Frequency: Monthly
Founded in 1939

12028 **Politico**
Capitol News Company
1100 Wilson Blvd
Suite 610
Arlington, VA 22209

703-647-7999
newsrelease@politico.com
www.politico.com

Robert L Allbritton, Publisher
Frederick J Ryan Jr, President & CEO
Kim Kingsley, Chief Operating Officer
John F Harris, Editor-In-Chief
Jim VandeHei, Executive Editor

Provides insider-like access to Washington and the latest from the world of politics.

12029 **PostCom Bulletin**
Association for Postal Commerce
1800 Diagonal Road
Suite 600
Alexandria, VA 22314

703-524-0096; Fax: 703-997-2414
info@postcom.org
www.postcom.org

Michael Plunkett, President & CEO
Ellena Talbott, Director, Operations & Membership
Beth McConnell, Postal Consultant

A source of postal news and opinion.
Founded in 1947

12030 **Public Health: From the State Capitals**
Wakeman Walworth
PO Box 7376
Alexandria, VA 22307-7376

703-768-9600; Fax: 703-768-9690
www.statecapitals.com

Keyes Walworth, Publisher

Reports on a wide range of health care legislation such as AIDS disclosure and testing, drug programs, abortion rulings, cancer prevention including smoking restrictions in public places, mental health and disability programs, disease control, regulation of hospitals and nursing homes, clinics, food inspection policies, organ donor management and Medicare. It covers such current issues as mail order through pharmacies on the internet.
Cost: $245.00
4 Pages
Frequency: Weekly
Printed in one color on matte stock

12031 **Public Safety and Justice Policies: From the State Capitals**
Wakeman Walworth
PO Box 7376
Alexandria, VA 22307-7376

703-768-9600; Fax: 703-768-9690
www.statecapitals.com/publicsafety.html

Keyes Walworth, Publisher

Covers gun control on school grounds, buy-back programs, gunmaker lawsuits, law enforcement, arrest procedures, drug law enforcement and penalties; financing and administration of substance-abuse counseling, school violence , police administration, truth in sentencing , prison administration, prisoner drug testing and AIDS testing, new evidence such as DNA, inmate work programs, gender bias in the courtroom, family and juvenile justice, victim compensation laws, inmate living conditions
Cost: $245.00
4 Pages
Frequency: Weekly
Printed in one color on matte stock

12032 **Roads and Bridges**
Scranton Gillette Communications
3030 W Salt Creek Lane
Suite 201
Arlington Heights, IL 60005-5025

847-391-1000; Fax: 847-390-0408
www.scrantongillette.com/roadsandbridges

Bill Wildon, Editorial Director
Allen Zeyher, Managing Editor
Rick Schwer, Publisher

Provides engineers, contractors and government officials with the latest advancements in the road and bridge industry, timely news coverage and important information on products beneficial to the job site of office.
Cost: $40.00
92 Pages
Frequency: Monthly
Circulation: 70000
ISSN: 8750-9229
Founded in 1905

12033 **SideBAR**
Federal Bar Association
1220 North Fillmore St.
Suite 444
Arlington, VA 22201

571-481-9100; Fax: 571-481-9090
fba@fedbar.org
www.fedbar.org
Facebook, Twitter, LinkedIn

Fern C. Bomchill, President
Robert J. DeSousa, President-Elect
Hon. Gustavo Gelpi, Jr., Treasurer

Federal Litigation Section Newsletter
16000 Members
Frequency: Quarterly
Founded in 1920

12034 **Tax Administrators News**
Federation of Tax Administrators
444 N. Capitol Street NW.
Suite 348
Washington, DC 20001

202-624-5890
www.taxadmin.org

Gale Garriott, Executive Director
Verenda Smith, Deputy Director
Kevin Sullivan, President

Covers state and federal legislation, U.S. Supreme Court and state court cases, and developments relating to state tax administration.
Frequency: Monthly
Founded in 1937

12035 Taxes-Property: From State Capitals
Wakeman Walworth
PO Box 7376
Alexandria, VA 22307-7376

703-689-9600; Fax: 703-768-9690
www.statecapitals.com/taxprop.html

Keyes Walworth, Publisher

Covers new property tax legislation, initiatives, referenda, property assessment programs, tax exemptions, tax incentives, and tax collection methods. This newsletter emphasizes the use of property taxes for school financing including state aid formulas, alternative school financing methods, budget issues related to teacher pay and class sizes.
Cost: $345.00
4 Pages
Frequency: Weekly
Printed in one color on matte stock

12036 The Certifier
Association of Boards of Certification
2805 SW Snyder Blvd.
Suite 535
Ankeny, IA 50023

515-232-3623; Fax: 515-965-6827
abc@abccert.org
www.abccert.org

Paul Bishop, Executive Director
Bob Hoyt, Vice President
Cheryl Bergener, President
Kathy Cook, VP

The newsletter for environmental certification authorities, filled with news and updates on the latest in certification and focuses on state and provincial certification programs, certification issues, and association events.
Frequency: Monthly
Founded in 1972

12037 The Government Standard
American Federation of Government Employees
80 F St NW
Washington, DC 20001-1528

202-737-8700; Fax: 202-639-6490
comments@afge.org
www.afge.com

John Gage, President
J. David Cox, Secretary/Treasurer
Augusta Thomas, VP for Women's & Fair Practices

AFGE's official membership publication keeping members up to date on what their local government is up to.
Frequency: Quarterly
Founded in 1932

12038 The Resolver
Federal Bar Association
1220 North Fillmore St.
Suite 444
Arlington, VA 22201

571-481-9100; Fax: 571-481-9090
fba@fedbar.org
www.fedbar.org
Facebook, Twitter, LinkedIn

Fern C. Bomchill, President
Robert J. DeSousa, President-Elect
Hon. Gustavo Gelpi, Jr., Treasurer

Turning conflict into resolution, Alternative Dispute Resolution Section newsletter.
16000 Members
Frequency: Bi-Annually
Founded in 1920

12039 The Resource
National Association of Conservation Districts
509 Capitol Ct. NE
Washington, DC 20002-4937

202-547-6223; Fax: 202-547-6450
www.nacdnet.org

Krysta Harden, CEO
Bob Cordova, Second Vice President

NACD's print publication provides in depth coverage of the association's recent activities and features columns by the NACD CEO and President, in addition to guest and partnership columns.
Cost: $35.00
12 Pages
Frequency: Monthly
Circulation: 25000
Founded in 1937

12040 This Week in Washington
American Public Human Services Association
1133 19th Street NW
Suite 400
Washington, DC 20036-3623

202-682-0100; Fax: 202-289-6555
www.aphsa.org

Tracy Wareing, Executive Director

Gives readers concise updates on initiatives of the administration, legislative action in human service programs, the latest information on federal regulations, and state agency personnel changes- everything the human service administrator needs to know from the nation's capital.
Frequency: Weekly
Founded in 1930

12041 URISA Newsletter
Association for GIS Professionals
701 Lee St.
Suite 680
Des Plaines, IL 60016-4508

847-824-6300; Fax: 847-824-6363
info@urisa.org
www.urisa.org

Susan Johnson, President
Wendy Nelson, Executive Director

Effective use of information systems technology at the state, regional and local levels Newsletter is published.
Frequency: Monthly
Founded in 1963

12042 US Mayor
US Conference of Mayors
1620 I St Nw
Suite 40
Washington, DC 20006-4034

202-464-0790; Fax: 202-293-2352
www.usmayors.org

Don Plusquellic, President
Tom Cochan, Editor
Guy Smith, Managing Editor
Michael Guido, Chair Advisory Board
J Thomas Cochran, CEO

Federal government and congressional activities.
Cost: $35.00
16 Pages
Circulation: 6000
Founded in 1933

12043 United Nations Jobs Newsletter
Thomas F Burola & Associates
6477 Telephone Road
Suite 7R
Ventura, CA 93003-4459

805- 64- 725; Fax: 805-654-1708
Thomas F Burola, Publisher

Focus of this newsletter is employment conditions within the United Nations System and vacancy notices.
Cost: $145.00
Circulation: 3,500
Founded in 1994
Printed in 2 colors on matte stock

12044 United States Conference of Mayors News
United States Conference of Mayors
1620 Eye Street, NW
Washington, DC 20006-4005

202-293-7330; Fax: 202-293-2352
www.usmayors.org/uscm/

J Thomas Cochran, President
William Fay, CEO

City government officials. Newsletter is available for members.
Circulation: 30000
Founded in 1932

12045 Washington Report
Federal Managers Association
1641 Prince St
Alexandria, VA 22314-2818

703-683-8700; Fax: 703-683-8707
info@fedmanagers.org
www.fedmanagers.org

Todd Wells, Manager
Darryl A Perkinson, President

News bulletin detailing the latest developments on Capitol Hill and in the nation's capital.
15M Members
Frequency: Quarterly
Founded in 1913

12046 Washington Spectator
Public Concern Foundation
PO Box 20065
New York, NY 10011

212-741-2365
www.washingtonspectator.com/

Kevin Walter, Publisher
Ben A Franklin, Editor
Lisa Vandepaer, Associate Editor
Marvin Shanken, Owner
Ruth Shikes, Co-Founder

News, comment and analysis on current national and international affairs; politics, economics, environment and social issues.
Cost: $15.00
4 Pages
Circulation: 60,000
Founded in 1974
Mailing list available for rent: 60000 names at $75 per M
Printed in one color on matte stock

12047 Washington Trade Daily
Trade Reports International Group
PO Box 1802
Wheaton, MD 20915-1802

301-946-0817; Fax: 301-946-2631
trigtrig@aol.com
Twitter

Jim Berger, CEO
D Kanth, Editor

The only digital daily newsletters of its kind that covers the goings-on in the nation's Capital related to imports, exports and foreign investment. It reports daily to readers on the Executive Branch - including the US Trade Representative's office and the Commerce Department - as well as Congress. Readers can gain insight every morning on what are likely to be new laws and regulations governing international business tomorrow.
Cost: $650.00
16 Pages
Frequency: Daily

Founded in 1991
Printed in one color

12048 Worldwide Government Report
Worldwide Government Directories
7979 Old Georgetown Road
Suite 900
Bethesda, MD 20814-2429

301-258-2677
800-332-3535; Fax: 301-718-8494

Jonathan Hixon, Publisher

Each issue provides detailed reports of elections, government and military turnover. Events covered include ousted heads of state, reshuffled governments, changes in ruling majorities, analyses of recent elections, outlooks for upcoming elections, and senior military appointments.
Cost: $247.00
Frequency: Monthly

12049 eNotes
National Association of Conservation Districts
509 Capitol Ct. NE
Washington, DC 20002-4937

202-547-6223; Fax: 202-547-6450
www.nacdnet.org

Krysta Harden, CEO
Bob Cordova, Second Vice President

NACD's weekly news briefs.
Cost: $35.00
12 Pages
Frequency: Monthly
Circulation: 25000
Founded in 1937

Magazines & Journals

12050 AASHTO Daily Transportation Update
Amer. Assoc. of State Highway & Trans. Officials
444 N Capitol St NW
Suite 249
Washington, DC 20001-1539

202-624-5800; Fax: 202-624-5806
info@aashto.org
Facebook, Twitter

Kirk T. Steudle, President
Michael P. Lewis, Vice-President
Carlos Braceras, Secretary/ Treasurer
John Horsley, Executive Director

To help members and other transportation professionals stay informed about critical industry happenings and events.
52 Members
Frequency: Daily

12051 AASHTO Journal
Amer. Assoc. of State Highway & Trans. Officials
444 N Capitol St NW
Suite 249
Washington, DC 20001-1539

202-624-5800; Fax: 202-624-5806
info@aashto.org
Facebook, Twitter

Kirk T. Steudle, President
Michael P. Lewis, Vice-President
Carlos Braceras, Secretary/ Treasurer
John Horsley, Executive Director

Electronic journal to help members and other transportation professionals stay informed about critical industry happenings and events.
52 Members

12052 APWA Reporter
American Public Works Association
1200 Main Street
Suite 1400
Kansas City, MO 64105-2100

816-472-6100
800-848-APWA; Fax: 816-472-1610
kclark@apwa.net
www.apwa.net

Scott Grayson, Executive Director
R. Kevin Clark, Editor

Prime communication link uniting the community of public works professionals that make up APWA.
Cost: $100.00
Frequency: Monthly
Circulation: 25000
ISSN: 0092-4873
Mailing list available for rent

12053 Armed Forces Journal
6883 Commercial Dr
Springfield, VA 22159

800-368-5718
armylet@atpco.com
www.defensenews.com

Mark Winans, VP
Elaine Howard, President/CEO
Alex Neill, Managing Editor
Jim Tice, Senior Writer
David Smith, Marketing

The leading joint service monthly magazine for officers and leaders in the US military community. AFJ has been providing essential review and analysis on key defense issues for more than 140 years. Offers in-depth coverage of military technology, procurement, logistics, strategy, doctrine and tactics. Also covers special operations, US Coast Guard and US National Guard developments.
Cost: $55.00
Frequency: Monthly
Circulation: 1MM

12054 Army Magazine
2425 Wison Boulevard
Arlington, VA 22201-3326

703-841-4300
800-336-4570; Fax: 703-525-9039
membersupport@ausa.org
www.ausa.org

Gen. Gordon Sullivan, President
Mary Blake French, Editor
Millie Hurlbut, Director of Marketing
Founded in 1950

12055 Army Times
Army Times Publishing Company
6883 Commercial Dr
Springfield, VA 22151-4202

703-750-9000
800-368-5718; Fax: 703-750-8622
jmccoy@atpco.com
www.armytimes.com

Elaine Howard, CEO
Judy McCoy, Associate Publisher
Tobias Naegele, Executive Editor
David Smith, Marketing Manager

Magazine soldiers and their families rely on as trusted, independent sources for news and information on the most important issues affecting their careers and personal lives. A single source for breaking news; personal finance information; healthcare; recreational resources; exclusive videos and photos; Guard and Reserve information; and an expanded community area connecting service members, military families and veterans.
Cost: $52.00
Frequency: Weekly

12056 C41SR Journal
Defense News
6883 Commercial Dr
Springfield, VA 22159

800-368-5718
armylet@atpco.com
www.defensenews.com

Mark Winans, VP
Elaine Howard, President/CEO
Alex Neill, Managing Editor
Jim Tice, Senior Writer
David Smith, Marketing

Dedicated to the rapidly advancing, high-tech realm of military intelligence, surveillance and reconnaissance. It was the first major periodical to specifically serve this key area of military growth and development, and has a strong following in the world's network-centric warfare community.
Cost: $55.00
Frequency: Monthly
Circulation: 1MM

12057 CLEAR Exam Review
Council on Licensure, Enforcement & Regulation
108 Wind Haven Drive
Suite A
Nicholasville, KY 40356

859-269-1289; Fax: 859-231-1943
rbrown@clearhq.org
www.clearhq.org

Adam Parfitt, Executive Director

A bi-annual journal with useful discussions of current licensing examination issues and is geared toward a general audience. Free of charge for CLEAR members.
Cost: $30.00
Frequency: Bi-Annual
Founded in 1994

12058 CQ Weekly
Congressional Quarterly
77 K Street NE
Washington, DC 20002-4681

202-650-6500
800-432-2250
customerservice@cqrollcall.com
www.cq.com

Susan Benkelman, Executive Editor
Randy Wynn, Deputy Executive Editor
Anne Q Hoy, Managing Editor, Spec. Publications
Caitlin Hendel, Managing Editor, CQ Today
Melanie Starkey, Editor, Daily News

This award-winning publication provides a clear perspective on how legislation is shaped, who is shaping it and how the process could affect your interests.

12059 Capitol Ideas
National Association of State Facilities
2760 Research Park Drive
PO Box 11910
Lexington, KY 40578-1910

859-244-8000
800-800-1910; Fax: 859-244-8001
www.csg.org
Facebook, Twitter, YouTube

Gov. Brian Schweitzer, President
Gov. Luis Fortuno, President-Elect
Bob Godfrey, Chair
Jay Emler, Chair-Elect
Gary Stevens, Vice Chair

Includes member-driven content, including a targeted focus for each issue, news from each region and association news, focusing on what is going on in the states that might be of interest to other states.

12060 Code Official
International Code Council

4051 Flossmoor Rd
Country Club Hl, IL 60478-5771

708-799-2300
800-214-4321
202-783-2348; Fax: 708-799-4981
www.bocai.org

Paul K Myers, CEO
Margaret M Leddin, Managing Editor

Serves a wide-ranging readership of professionals who are interested in the development, maintenance and enforcement of progressive and reponsive building regulations.
Cost: $30.00
Frequency: Monthly
Circulation: 16000
Founded in 1994
Printed in on glossy stock

12061 **Congressional Digest**
Congressional Digest Corporation
4416 East-West Highway
Suite 400
Bethesda, DC 20814-3389

301-634-3113
800-638-8380; Fax: 301-634-3189
www.congressionaldigest.com

Griff Thomas, President
Page Robinson, Publisher
Kathy Thorne, Circulation Manager
Sarah Orrick, Editor

The only publication about Congress that concentrates each month on a single legislative issue in a unique Pro and Con format. It is an indispensable education tool for students of national and world affairs.
Cost: $62.00
36 Pages
ISSN: 0010-5899
Founded in 1921
Printed in 2 colors on glossy stock

12062 **Contract Management**
National Contract Management Association
8260 Greensboro Drive
Suite 200
McLean, VA 22102-3728

571-382-0082
800-344-8096; Fax: 703-448-0939
cm@ncmahq.org
www.ncmahq.org

Neal J Couture, Executive Director
Kathryn Mullan, Assistant Editor

It covers the myriad aspects of government and commercial contract management. News and features provide information on such topics as procurement policy, on-the-job techniques, regulations, case law, ethics, contract administration, electronic commerce, international and small business matters, education and career development.
Cost: $178.00
80 Pages
Frequency: Monthly
Circulation: 22000
Founded in 1959
Printed in 4 colors on glossy stock

12063 **Cooperative Housing Bulletin**
National Association of Housing Cooperatives
1444 I Street, NW
Suite 700
Washington, DC 20005-6542

202-737-0797; Fax: 202-216-9646
info@nahc.coop
www.coophousing.org

Member benefit conatining articles for co-op board members and professionals, up-to-date news on legislative issues that NAHC is monitoring, and practical information on issues facing housing cooperatives.
Frequency: Quarterly
Printed in 2 colors on matte stock

12064 **Correctional Health Today**
American Correctional Association
206 N Washington St
Suite 200
Alexandria, VA 22314-2528

703-224-0000
800-222-5646; Fax: 703-224-0179
jeffw@aca.org
www.aca.org

Jeff Washington, Deputy Executive Director
James Gondles Jr, Executive Director

An interdisciplinary, peer-reviewed, academic publication devoted to examining all areas of health care within corrections. Available in print and electronically.
20000 Members
Frequency: Monthly
Founded in 1870

12065 **Corrections Compendium**
American Correctional Association
206 N Washington St
Suite 200
Alexandria, VA 22314-2528

703-224-0000
800-222-5646; Fax: 703-224-0179
jeffw@aca.org
www.aca.org

Jeff Washington, Deputy Executive Director
James Gondles Jr, Executive Director

The peer-reviewed, research-based journal of the American Correctional Association. Presents research findings and trends and examines events in corrections and criminal justice.
20000 Members
Frequency: Quarterly
Founded in 1870

12066 **Corrections Today**
American Correctional Association
206 N Washington St
Suite 200
Alexandria, VA 22314-2528

703-224-0000; Fax: 703-224-0179
execoffice@aca.org
www.aca.org
Facebook, Twitter

James Gondles, Executive Director

The professional membership publication of the ACA. Its international readership includes individuals involved in every sector of the corrections and criminal justice fields.
Frequency: 6x Yearly

12067 **Court Review**
American Judges Association
300 Newport Ave
Williamsburg, VA 23185-4147

757-259-1841; Fax: 757-259-1520
aja.ncsc.dni.us

Judge Kevin S. Burke, President
Judge Toni Manning Higginbotham, President-Elect
Judge Elliott L. Zide, Vice President
Judge Brian MacKenzie, Secretary
Judge Harold V. Froehlich, Treasurer

Court technology, managing your staff, controlling your docket-a bench's eye view of information you won't find anywhere else.
2500 Members
Frequency: Quarterly
Founded in 1959

12068 **Defense News**
6883 Commercial Dr
Springfield, VA 22151-4202

703-750-9000
800-424-9335; Fax: 703-658-8412
armylet@atpco.com
www.defensenews.com

Mark Winans, VP
Elaine Howard, President/CEO
Alex Neill, Managing Editor
Jim Tice, Senior Writer
David Smith, Marketing

Provides the global defense community with the latest news and analysis on defense programs, policy, business and technology. With bureaus and reporters around the world, Defense News sets the standard for accuracy, credibility and timeliness in defense reporting. Circulates to top leaders and decisionmakers in North America and in Europe, Asia and the Middle East.
Cost: $55.00
Frequency: Weekly
Circulation: 1MM

12069 **Democratic Communique**
Union for Democratic Communications
777 Glades Rd
Boca Raton, FL 33431

Home Page:
www.democraticcommunications.net

Janet Wasko, Publisher

News of Democratic and grassroots communications projects, issues and publications.
Cost: $20.00
12 Pages
Frequency: BiWeekly

12070 **Economic Development Journal**
International Economic Development Council
734 15th Street NW
Suite 900
Washington, DC 20005

202-223-7800; Fax: 202-223-4745

Jeff Finkle, President & CEO
Dennis G. Coleman, Chair
Jay C. Moon, Vice Chair
Paul Krutko, Secretary/ Treasurer

Premier publication of IEDC's diverse and dynamic discipline, featuring in-depth accounts of important programs, projects, and trends from the US and around the world.
1.8M Members
Frequency: Quarterly
Founded in 1967

12071 **Energy Law Journal**
Energy Bar Association
1990 M St NW
Suite 350
Washington, DC 20036-3429

202-223-5625; Fax: 202-833-5596
admin@eba-net.org
www.eba-net.org
Facebook

Derek A. Dyson, President
Susan A. Olenchuk, President-Elect
Jason F. Leif, Vice President
Emma F. Hand, Secretary
Hugh E. Hilliard, Treasurer

Providing members with the latest news regarding the energy industry.
2600 Members
Frequency: Bi-Annually
Founded in 1946

12072 **Federal Criminal Investigator**
P.O. Box 23400
Washington, DC 20026

800-403-3374
630-969-8537; Fax: 800-528-3492
fcianat@aol.com
www.fedcia.org

Richard Zehme, President
William Paulin, Vice President
Rich Ahern, National Treasurer/Secretary

This comprehensive publication covers legislation and federal information for the police official and officer.
Frequency: Quarterly
Founded in 1956

12073 **Federal Manager**
Federal Managers Association
1641 Prince St
Alexandria, VA 22314-2818

703-683-8700; Fax: 703-683-8707
info@fedmanagers.org
www.fedmanagers.org

Todd Wells, Manager
Darryl A Perkinson, President

Magazine focusing on current management issues.
15M Members
Frequency: Quarterly
Founded in 1913

12074 **Foreign Service Journal**
American Foreign Service Association
2101 E St NW
Washington, DC 20037-2990

202-338-4045
800-704-2572; Fax: 202-338-6820
member@afsa.org
www.afsa.org

Susan R. Johnson, President
Andrew Winter, Treasurer

Each issue covers foreign affairs from an insider's perspective, providing thoughtful articles on international issues, the practice of diplomacy and the US Foreign Service.
Cost: $40.00
68 Pages
Frequency: Monthly
Circulation: 12500
ISSN: 0146-3543
Founded in 1924
Printed in on glossy stock

12075 **Government Executive**
National Journal
600 New Hampshire Ave NW
Suite 4
Washington, DC 20037-2403

202-739-8400; Fax: 202-833-8069
webmaster@govexec.com
www.govexec.com
Facebook, Twitter

John Fox Sullivan, President
Shane Harris, Editor

Serving senior executives and managers in the federal government's departments and agencies. Subscribers are high-ranking civilian and military officials who are responsible for defending the nation and carrying out the many laws that define the government's role in our economy and society. Covers the business of the federal government and its huge departments and agencies.
Cost: $48.00
72 Pages
Frequency: Monthly
Circulation: 75,000
Founded in 1970

12076 **Government Product News**
Penton Media
1300 E 9th St
Suite 316
Cleveland, OH 44114-1503

216-696-7000; Fax: 216-696-6662
www.penton.com

Jane Cooper, Marketing
Kristin M Atwater, Managing Editor
Vaughn Rockhold, Group Publisher
Kay Ross-Baker, Publisher
Sarah Arnold, Marketing Director

Serves officials in the executive, legislative, administrative, engineering, purchasing, financial and other operational departments, within government agencies.
40 Pages
Frequency: Monthly
Circulation: 85000
ISSN: 0017-2642
Founded in 1962
Printed in 4 colors on glossy stock

12077 **Government Recreation & Fitness**
Executive Business Media
825 Old Country Road
PO Box 1500
Westbury, NY 11590

516-334-3030; Fax: 516-334-3059
mail@ebmpubs.com
www.ebmpubs.com

Murry Greenwald, Publisher
Paul Ragnoz, Managing Editor

Government Recreation and Fitness reaches recreation and fitness professionals in every department and agency of the federal government, goes directly to the people who purchase your products, with deep market penetration, and covers both appropriated and nonappropriated fund budgets.
Cost: $35.00
42 Pages
Frequency: 10x Yearly
Circulation: 8521
ISSN: 1086-7899
Founded in 1996
Printed in 4 colors on glossy stock

12078 **Government Technology**
GT Publications
150 Almaden Blvd
Suite 600
San Jose, CA 95113-2016

408-275-9000; Fax: 408-275-0582
www.grantthornton.com
Facebook

Jeffrey S Pera, Managing Partner
Sherese Graves, Advertising Director
Dennis McKenna, Publisher
Micki Gerardi, Manager

Covering information technology's role in state and local governments. Through in-depth coverage of IT case studies, emerging technologies, and the implications of digital technology on the policies and management of public sector organizations, Government Technology chronicles the dynamics of governing in the information age. Readers include managers, elected officials, CIOs and technology staff at all levels of government.
56 Pages
Frequency: Monthly

12079 **ICBA Independent Banker**
Independent Community Bankers of America
1615 L Street NW.
Suite 900
Washington, DC 20036

202-659-8111
800-422-8439; Fax: 202-659-3604
info@icba.org
www.independentbanker.org

Rebeca Romero Rainey, President/CEO
Terry J. Jorde, Sr. Executive Vice President
Matt Kusilek, Advertising Contact
Chris Lorence, Member Engagement & Strategy

Covers the news topics and trends that are important to the nation's community bank senior executives. Keeping members informed about and connected with their national association and its activities; and providing them with timely, relevant information on developments to growth their business franchise within the rapidly evolving financial services industry.
Frequency: Monthly

12080 **International Debates**
Congressional Digest Corporation
4416 E West Hwy
Suite 400
Bethesda, MD 20814-4568

301-634-3113
800-637-9915; Fax: 301-634-3189
info@congressionaldigest.com
www.pro-and-con.org/

Griff Thomas, President
Page Robinson, Publisher

Independent journal featuring controversies before the United Nations and other international forums. Each issue covers an important and timely international issue and includes in-depth background information, key documents, and diverse global perspectives.
Frequency: 9x Yearly
Founded in 1921

12081 **Journal of Food Protection**
International Association for Food Protection
6200 Aurora Ave
Suite 200W
Des Moines, IA 50322-2864

515-276-3344
800-369-6337; Fax: 515-276-8655
info@foodprotection.org
www.foodprotection.org
Facebook, Twitter, LinkedIn

Timothy C. Jackson, President

Internationally recognized as the leading publication in the field of food microbiology, each issue contains scientific research and authoritative review articles reporting on a variety of topics in food science pertaining to food safety and quality.
Cost: $335.00
Frequency: Monthly
Circulation: 11000+
ISBN: 0-362028-X -
Founded in 1911
Mailing list available for rent: 3000+ names at $150 per M
Printed in 4 colors on glossy stock

12082 **Journal of Housing Economics**
630 Eye St NW
Washington, DC 20001-3736

202-289-3500
877-866-2476; Fax: 202-289-8181
www.journals.elsevier.com

Saul Ramirez, Executive Director
Donald J Cameron, CEO

Provides a focal point for the publication of economic research related to housing and encourages papers that bring to bear careful analytical technique on important housing-related questions. The journal covers the broad spectrum of topics and approaches that constitute housing economics, including analysis of important

public policy issues.
Cost: $33.00
Founded in 1933

12083 **Journal of Medical Regulation**
Federation of State Medical Boards
400 Fuller Wiser Rd
Suite 300
Euless, TX 76039-3856
817-868-4043; Fax: 817-868-4099
dcarlson@fsmb.org
www.fsmb.org
Rhonda Olsobrook, Manager
Peer-reviewed scholarly publication that helps raise awareness of important trends and challenging issues in the regulatory community.
Frequency: Monthly

12084 **Journal of Occupational and Environmental Hygiene (JOEH)**
ACGIH
1330 Kemper Meadow Drive
Cincinnati, OH 45240
513-742-2020; Fax: 513-742-3355
mail@acgih.org
www.acgih.org
Facebook, Twitter, LinkedIn
Stephen J. Reynolds, President
Mark Nicas, Editor-in-Chief
Focuses on publishing information that practicing professionals can apply in their day-to-day activities. A joint publication of AIHA and ACGIH.
Frequency: Monthly
Founded in 1938

12085 **Journal of the Association of Food and Drug Officials**
2550 Kingston Road
Suite 311
York, PA 17402
717-757-2888; Fax: 717-755-8089
afdo@afdo.org
www.afdo.org
News and the latest legislation for the Food and Drug Association.
Cost: $80.00
Frequency: Quarterly
Founded in 1896

12086 **Legislative Update**
1250 Eye St NW
Suite 902
Washington, DC 20005-3947
202-393-5225; Fax: 202-393-3034
www.nrhcweb.org
Robert A Rapoza, Publisher/Executive Director
Published by the National Rural Housing Coalition.
Cost: $250.00
Frequency: 25x Yearly
Circulation: 300
Founded in 1969

12087 **McGraw-Hill's Federal Technology Report**
McGraw Hill
1200 G St Nw
Suite 900
Washington, DC 20005-3821
202-383-2377
800-223-6180; Fax: 202-383-2438
www.aviationweek.com
Jennifer Michels, Manager
Georgia Safos, Circulation Director
Brings readers inside those areas of the federal government where federal technology policy and legislation is made; also identifies commercial opportunities at federal labs.
Cost: $1015.00
16 Pages
Frequency: Weekly

12088 **NCOA Journal**
Todays NCOA
10635 N 35th
San Antonio, TX 78233-6627
210-653-6161
800-662-2620; Fax: 210-637-3337
membsvc@ncoausa.org
Gene Overstreet, President/CEO
Cathy John, Advertising Manager
The official magazine for the Non Commissioned Officers Association.
Frequency: Quarterly
Circulation: 60000
Founded in 1960

12089 **NIST Tech Beat**
National Institute of Standards & Technology
Public & Business Affairs
100 Bureau Drive, Stop 1070
Gaithersburg, MD 20899-1070
800-877-8339; Fax: 301-926-1630
media@nist.gov
www.nist.gov
Facebook, Twitter, YouTube, Flickr
Michael Baum, Segments Editor
Ben Stein, Segments Editor
Michael E Newman, Segments Editor
Evelyn Brown, Segments Editor
Laura Ost, Segments Editor
A biweekly lay-language newsletter of recent research results and other news from the National Institute of Standards and Technology. NIST is the nation's physical sciences and engineering measurement laboratory. Archives available online.
Frequency: Biweekly

12090 **Nation's Cities Weekly**
National League of Cities
1301 Pennsylvania Ave NW
6th Floor, Suite 550
Washington, DC 20004-1747
202-626-3180; Fax: 202-626-3043
memberservices@nlc.org
www.nlc.org
Donald J Borut, Executive Director
Cyndy Hogan, Managing Editor
Delivers top stories about advocacy activities, successful and innovative city programs, new research and networking opportunities for local elected officials and city employees.
Cost: $96.00
12 Pages
Frequency: Weekly
Circulation: 27000
Founded in 1978

12091 **National Journal**
National Journal
600 New Hampshire Ave NW
Suite 4
Washington, DC 20037-2403
202-739-8400
800-207-8001; Fax: 202-833-8069
nationaljournal.com
Facebook, Twitter
John Fox Sullivan, President
Delivers highly engaged consumers with all of the information and insights that they need to know to conduct business successfully in Washington. Trusted professional resource for Members of Congress and their senior staffs, the Executive branch, federal agency executives, government affairs professionals, corporate and association leaders, and the political news media.
Cost: $1799.00
Founded in 1969

12092 **Navy News and Undersea Technology**
Pasha Publications
1616 N Fort Myer Drive
Suite 1000
Arlington, VA 22209-3107
703-528-1244
800-424-2908; Fax: 703-528-1253
Harry Baisden, Group Publisher
Thomas Jandl, Editor
Tod Sedgwick, Publisher
This report on the Navy, as well as the Marine Corps and naval developments overseas. Frequently cited by experts in the field as the source for breaking developments in submarine and anti-submarine warfare technology, this newsletter sets the standard for Navy reporting.
Cost: $545.00
Frequency: Weekly

12093 **Off the Shelf**
Coalition for Government Procurement
1990 M St NW
Suite 450
Washington, DC 20036-3466
202-331-0975; Fax: 202-822-9788
info@thecgp.org
www.thecgp.org
Larry Allen, Executive VP
Providing vital updates on rules, regulations, and GSA Schedule developments that may impact your business.
Frequency: Monthly
Founded in 1979

12094 **Parameters**
US Army War College
122 Forbes Ave
Suite C34
Carlisle, PA 17013-5220
717-245-3131; Fax: 717-245-3323
Robert J Ivany, Manager
Refereed journal of ideas and issues. Provides a forum for mature thought on the art and science of land warfare, joint and combined matters, national and international security affairs, military strategy, military leadership and management, military history, ethics, and other topics of significant and current interest to the US Army and the Department of Defense.
Cost: $26.00
Frequency: Quarterly
Circulation: 1300

12095 **Policy & Practice**
American Public Human Services Association
1133 19th Street NW
Suite 400
Washington, DC 20036-3623
202-682-0100; Fax: 202-289-6555
www.aphsa.org
Tracy Wareing, Executive Director
Presents a lively and comprehensive look at key human service issues. Its aim is to highlight the experiences of those who administer public assistance programs and services; to examine cutting-edge public human service research and demonstration projects; and to provide readers with a variety of resources to guide them in their challenging roles in the human service arena.
Frequency: Bi-Monthly
Founded in 1930

12096 **Presidential Studies Quarterly**
Center for the Study of the Presidency & Congress

1020 19th St NW
Suite 250
Washington, DC 20036-6120

202-872-9800; Fax: 202-872-9811
www.thepresidency.org
Facebook, Twitter, YouTube

George C Edwards III, Editor

Available in print and online, PSQ is widely viewed by scholars and professionals as an indispensable resource for understanding the Presidency. The only scholarly journal that focuses on the most powerful political figure in the world - the President of the United States. Offers articles, features, review essays, and book reviews covering Presidential decision making, the operations of the White House, and much more.
Frequency: Quarterly
Circulation: 6000
ISSN: 0360-4918

12097 Prosecutor
National District Attorneys Association
44 Canal Center Plaza
Suite 110
Alexandria, VA 22314-1548

703-549-9222; Fax: 703-836-3195
www.ndaa.org

Jean Hemphill, Publications Director/Editor

Fascinating articles, names in the news, upcoming conferences, capital perspective, profiles, course announcements, message from the President, message from the Executive Director, and much more.
Frequency: Quarterly
Circulation: 7000

12098 Public Administration Review (PAR)
American Society for Public Administration
1301 Pennsylvania Avenue NW
Suite 700
Washington, DC 20004

202-393-7878; Fax: 202-638-4952
info@aspanet.org
www.aspanet.org
Facebook, Twitter, LinkedIn

Erik O. Bergrud, President
Stephen E. Condrey, Vice-President
Kuotsai Tom Liou, President-Elect

The preeminent journal in the field of public administration research and theory.
15M Members
Frequency: Bi-Monthly
Founded in 1939

12099 Public Integrity
American Society for Public Administration
1301 Pennsylvania Avenue NW
Suite 700
Washington, DC 20004

202-393-7878; Fax: 202-638-4952
info@aspanet.org
www.aspanet.org
Facebook, Twitter, LinkedIn

Erik O. Bergrud, President
Stephen E. Condrey, Vice-President
Kuotsai Tom Liou, President-Elect

Furthering the understanding of ethics in government by publishing articles of interest to practitioners and scholars.
15M Members
Frequency: Monthly
Founded in 1939

12100 Public Risk
Public Risk Management Association
500 Montgomery St
Suite 750
Alexandria, VA 22314-1565

703-647-6244; Fax: 703-739-0200
info@primacentral.org
www.primacentral.org
Facebook, LinkedIn

Jim Hirt, Executive Director
Jon Ruzan, Manager
Kerry Langley, Manager

Provides risk managers in the public sector with timely, focused information in an easy-to-read format. Features articles from risk management practitioners as well as industry experts.
Frequency: 10x Yearly
Circulation: 8000+
Founded in 1978

12101 Pull Together
1306 Dahlgren Avenue SE
Washington Navy Yard, DC 20374-5055

202-678-4333; Fax: 202-889-3565
nhfwny@navyhistory.org
www.navyhistory.org

Captain Charles Creekman, Executive Director
Robert F Dunn, President
Cost: $25.00
Founded in 1926

12102 Rural Housing Reporter
1250 Eye St NW
Suite 902
Washington, DC 20005-3947

202-393-5225; Fax: 202-393-3034
www.nrhcweb.org

Robert A Rapoza, Publisher/Executive Director

Published by the National Rural Housing Coalition.
Cost: $250.00
Frequency: Monthly
Founded in 1969

12103 Rural Voices
Housing Assistance Council
1025 Vermont Ave NW
Suite 606
Washington, DC 20005-3516

202-842-8600; Fax: 202-347-3441
hac@ruralhome.org
www.ruralhome.org
Twitter, LinkedIn

Moises Loza, Executive Director

Written in non-technical language for a general audience.
Frequency: Quarterly
Founded in 1971

12104 Society of Cost Estimating and Analysis Journal
Society of Cost Estimating and Analysis
527 Maple Ave E
Suite 301
Vienna, VA 22180-4753

703-938-5090; Fax: 703-938-5091
www.sceaonline.net

Elmer Cleg, Executive Director
Joseph Dean, National VP

Subscribers are professionals engaged primarily in the field of government contract estimating and pricing.
Cost: $40.00
Frequency: Annual+
Circulation: 4500
ISSN: 0882-3871
Founded in 1984

12105 State Legislatures
National Conference of State Legislatures
7700 E 1st Pl
Denver, CO 80230-7143

303-364-7700; Fax: 303-364-7800
pubs-info@ncsl.org
www.ncsl.org
Twitter, LinkedIn

William Pound, Executive Director
Edward Smith, Managing Editor
LeAnn Hoff, Director, Revenue & Sales

The national magazine of state government and policy.
Cost: $49.00
15000 Members
Circulation: 18000
ISSN: 0147-0644
Founded in 1975
Printed in 4 colors

12106 Supreme Court Debates
Congressional Digest Corporation
4416 E West Hwy
Suite 400
Bethesda, MD 20814-4568

301-634-3113
800-637-9915; Fax: 301-634-3189
info@congressionaldigest.com
www.pro-and-con.org/

Griff Thomas, President
Page Robinson, Publisher

Independent journal featuring controversies before the US Supreme Court. Each issue covers a current prominent case, along with in-depth historical and legal background and excerpts from lawyers' arguments before the Court. Each issue also lists cases expected to be considered by the High Court during the current term.
Frequency: 9x Yearly
Founded in 1921

12107 The Federal Lawyer
Federal Bar Association
1220 North Fillmore St.
Suite 444
Arlington, VA 22201

571-481-9100; Fax: 571-481-9090
fba@fedbar.org
www.fedbar.org
Facebook, Twitter, LinkedIn

Fern C. Bomchill, President
Robert J. DeSousa, President-Elect
Hon. Gustavo Gelpi, Jr., Treasurer

The only magazine written and edited for lawyers who practice in federal courts or have an interest in federal law as well as judges who sit on the federal bench. Editorial content covers immigration, Indian, antitrust, labor and employment, bankruptcy, criminal, intellectual property, environmental, and other types of law that fall within federal jurisdiction.
Cost: $35.00
16000 Members
Frequency: Monthly
Founded in 1920

12108 The Forum
National Forum for Black Public Administrators
777 N Capitol St NE
Suite 807
Washington, DC 20002-4291

202-408-9300; Fax: 202-408-8558
webmaster@nfbpa.org
www.nfbpa.org
Facebook, YouTube

Aretha R. Ferrell-Benavides, President
Verdenia C. Baker, 1st Vice President
Bruce T. Moore, 2nd Vice President
Jelynne LeBlanc Burley, Secretary/Treasurer
John E. Saunders, III, Executive Director

Has been used as a means of polishing and honing the skills of capable and experienced administrators by providing practical advice on professional development and insight on social and economic concerns impacting the Black community. Strives to present timely, factual,

and comprehensive information on subjects of critical importance to its readers who share a common commitment to excellence in public service.
2.8M Members
Frequency: Quarterly
Founded in 1983

12109 **Training & Simulation Journal**
6883 Commercial Dr
Springfield, VA 22159

800-368-5718
armylet@atpco.com
www.defensenews.com

Mark Winans, VP
Elaine Howard, President/CEO
Alex Neill, Managing Editor
Jim Tice, Senior Writer
David Smith, Marketing

About trends in the global military training and simulation market, and a forum for market leaders to obtain and exchange information on emerging issues, new technologies, and new products.
Cost: $55.00
Frequency: Bi-Monthly
Circulation: 1MM

12110 **Translog**
200 Stovall Street
Hoffman Building Room 11N57
Alexandria, VA 22332-5000

703-428-3207; Fax: 703-428-3312

An authorized online publication for members of the Department of Defense, published under supervision of the SDDC Director of Command Affairs to provide timely, relevant information concerning SDDC people, missions, policies, operations, technical developments, trends, and ideas of and about SDDC and the US Army.

12111 **Urban Land**
Urban Land Institute
1025 Thomas Jefferson St NW
Suite 500 West
Washington, DC 20007-5230

202-624-7000; Fax: 202-624-7140
ulifoundation@uli.org
www.uli.org
Facebook, Twitter, LinkedIn, YouTube

Patrick Phillips, CEO
Richard Rosan, President
Michael Terseck, CFO

Focuses on the information needs of land use and development professionals worldwide, providing them with timely, objective, practical, and accessible articles on a wide variety of subjects related to their professional interests.
14M Members
Frequency: Monthly
Founded in 1936

12112 **Washington Law & Politics**
100 W Harrison St
Suite 340
Seattle, WA 98119-4196

206-282-9527; Fax: 206-282-9601
www.superlawyers.com

Keith Goben, Publisher
Beth Taylor, Editor
Paul Englund, Circulation Manager
Tina Justison, Production Manager

A magazine for those who care about, or have a stake in, the public policy debate that is the basis of our editorial. Readers consist of those in positions of power in media, government, politics, law and business. Attracts a curious blend of readers ranging from corporate CEOs to political junkies.
48 Pages
Frequency: 6x Yearly
Circulation: 18000
Founded in 1977
Printed in 4 colors on glossy stock

12113 **Washington Remote Sensing Letter**
Dr. Murray Felsher
1057B National Press Building
Washington, DC 20045-2001

202-393-3640

Dr. Murray Felsher, Publisher
Murray Felsher, Editor
Dr. Murray Felsher, Publisher
Dr. Murray Felsher, Marketing
Dr. Murray Felsher, Circulation Manager

The recognized leader in reporting and analysis of US and international news dealing with all phases and applications of satellite remote sensing of the earth and global analyses research, including imagery, photography, surveillance and monitoring the Earth from space.
Cost: $1100.00
4 Pages
ISSN: 0739-6538
Founded in 1980
Printed in 2 colors on matte stock

12114 **Western City Magazine**
League of California Cities
1400 K St
4th Floor
Sacramento, CA 95814-3971

916-658-8200
800-262-1801; Fax: 916-658-8289
info@westerncity.com
www.cacities.org
Facebook

Pam Blodgett, Ad Manager
Eva Spiegel, Managing Editor
Chris McKenzie, Executive Director

The magazine of the League of California Cities.
Cost: $39.00
Frequency: Monthly
Circulation: 10500
Founded in 1924
Printed in 4 colors on glossy stock

Trade Shows

12115 **ACAP National Training Conference**
American Society of Access Professionals
1444 I(Eye) St. NW
Suite 700
Washington, DC 20005-6542

202-712-9054; Fax: 202-216-9646
asap@bostrom.com
www.accesspro.org

Anne Weismann, President
Will Kammer, Vice President
Karen Finnegan, Treasurer
Carmen L. Mallon, Secretary

Created to bring educational opportunities beyond the Washington, D.C. area. Combines training topics with the thought-provoking and practical issues associated with FOIA and Privacy Act processing and requesting.
Frequency: Annual/March
Founded in 1980

12116 **ASPA Annual Conference**
American Society for Public Administration
1301 Pennsylvania Avenue NW
Suite 840
Washington, DC 20004

202-393-7878; Fax: 202-638-4952
info@aspanet.org
www.aspanet.org

Antoinette Samuel, Executive Director
Lyric Jonze, Administration Assistant

Offers cutting-edge educational programming at this year's conference. There are over 150 educational options to choose from - Panel Sessions, Best Practice Workshops, and Roundtable Discussions.
550 Attendees
Frequency: Annual/May

12117 **AURP International Conference**
Association of University Research Parks
6262 N. Swan Road
Suite 100
Tucson, AZ 85718-8936

520-529-2521; Fax: 520-529-2499
info@aurp.net
www.aurp.net
Facebook, Twitter

Eileen Walker, CEO
Victoria Palmer, Events Manager
Chelsea Simpson, Membership & Marketing Manager

Bringing together the world's leaders in high-tech economic development, this conference features professional development for university research park professionals.
Frequency: Annual/September

12118 **America's Town Meeting**
National Association of Towns and Townships
1130 Connecticut Ave NW
Suite 300
Washington, DC 20036-3981

202-454-3954
866-830-0008; Fax: 202-331-1598
www.natat.org

NATaT's national conference is the largest national conference for grassroots government leaders. Educational workshops and legislative workshops help officials be more effective representatives for the citizens they serve. The conference provides a time for attendees to lobby members of Congress on issues important to their towns.
13M Members
Frequency: Annual

12119 **American Association of Port Authorities Annual Convention**
1010 Duke Street
Alexandria, VA 22314-3589

703-684-5700; Fax: 703-684-6321
info@aapa-ports.org
www.aapa-ports.org

Kurt Nagle, President/CEO

AAPA's largest membership meeting of the year. It includes technical and policy committee meetings, business sessions and social networking opportunities for port professionals and others in the marine transportation industry.
700 Attendees
Frequency: Annual/September
Founded in 1912

12120 **American Political Science Association Annual Meeting**
1527 New Hampshire Avenue NW
Washington, DC 20036-1206

202-483-2512; Fax: 202-483-2657
apsa@apsanet.org
www.apsanet.org

G. Bingham Powell, Jr., President
Jane Mansbridge, President-Elect
Jonathan Benjamin-Alvarado, Treasurer
Lisa L. Martin, Secretary
Michael A. Brintnall, Executive Director

Workshop, luncheon and 150 plus exhibits of publications and software relating to political science.
6500 Attendees
Frequency: Annual
Founded in 1903

12121 **CLEAR Annual Educational Conference**
Council on Legislative Enforcement & Regulation
108 Wind Haven Drive
Suite A
Nicholasville, KY 40356

859-269-1289; Fax: 859-231-1943
rbrown@clearhq.org
www.clearhq.org
Facebook

Adam Parfitt, Executive Director
Jodie Markey, Senior Program Manager

Conference content focuses on compliance and discipline, credentialing and licensing, examination issues, and legislative and policy issues/reulatory administration.
Frequency: Annual/September
Founded in 1994

12122 **CSG National Conference & North American Summit**
Council of State Governments
2760 Research Park Drive
PO Box 11910
Lexington, KY 40578-1910

859-244-8000
800-800-1910; Fax: 859-244-8001
www.csg.org
Facebook, Twitter

Key officials that shape and make today's economic decisions.
1000+ Attendees
Frequency: Annual/October

12123 **Congress of Cities & Exposition**
National League of Cities
1301 Pennsylvania Avenue NW
Suite 550
Washington, DC 20004

202-626-3100
800-564-4220; Fax: 202-626-3043
www.nlc.org

Ted Ellis, President
Marie Lopez Rogers, 1st Vice President
Chris Coleman, 2nd Vice President
Don Borut, Executive Director

Provides educational content on the most pressing challenges facing city leaders. Conference attendees hear from prominent speakers and issue experts, participate in leadership training sessions, attend issue-specific workshops, visit best practices keynote speakers, issue workshops, mobile workshops, and leadership training sessions.
4200 Attendees
Frequency: Annual/December
Founded in 1924

12124 **EANGUS National Conference**
Exhibit Promotions Plus
11620 Vixens Path
Ellicott City, MD 21042

301-596-3028; Fax: 410-997-0764
www.eangus.org

Kevin Horowitz, Exhibit Mgmt.

General conference and exhibition for the Enlisted Association of the National Guard of the United States. All attendees are either National Guard members, retirees or their families.
2000+ Attendees
Frequency: Annual/August
Founded in 1971

12125 **Energy - Exhibit Promotions Plus**
US Dept. of Energy/US Dept. of Defense/GSA
11620 Vixens Path
Ellicott City, MD 21042

301-596-3028; Fax: 410-997-0764
www.epponline.com

Harve Horowitz, President
Kevin Horowitz, Senior Association Manager

Energy is an exclusive Federal Grant sponsored annual educational forum and exhibition.
1000+ Attendees
Frequency: Annual/August

12126 **FOSE**
Contingency Planning & Management Conference
3141 Fairview Park Drive
Suite 777
Falls Church, VA 22042

703-876-5100
800-638-8510
www.fose.com
Facebook, Twitter, LinkedIn

Sylvia Griffiths, Customer Supervisor

Vendors in different marketplaces & pavilions, providing the opportunity to source effective & actionable IT solutions, in-depth conferences, workshops, camps, keynote & theater education designed to help achieve sucess with government IT mandates & initiatives. Association meetings, CIO Summits and peer networking opportunities, bringing the government IT community together.
80M Attendees
Frequency: April

12127 **Government Finance Officers Association Annual Conference**
203 N LaSalle Street
Suite 2700
Chicago, IL 60601-1210

312-977-9700; Fax: 312-977-4806
inquiry@gfoa.org
www.gfoa.org

Chris Morrill, Executive Director
Barbara Mollo, Director Operations & Marketing
Mike Mucha, Director Research & Consulting
John Jurkash, CFO/Financial Administration
Emily S. Brock, Director Federal Liaison

The Government Finance Officers Association's Annual Conference provides training and networking opportunities for public sector finance professionals from across the United States and Canada. 250 booths with 200 exhibitors.
4000 Attendees
Frequency: June

12128 **HFA Institute**
National Council of State Housing Agencies
444 N Capitol St NW
Suite 438
Washington, DC 20001-1505

202-624-7710; Fax: 202-624-5899
bthompson@ncsha.org
www.ncsha.org
Facebook, Twitter

Gerald M. Hunter, President
Brian A. Hudson, Vice President
Thomas R. Gleason, Secretary/ Treasurer
Barbara J. Thompson, Executive Director

Premier training event providing an unprecedented chance to network with peers and receive top-notch education and invaluable advice from key federal officials, leading trainers and consultants, noted industry professionals, and experienced HFA practitioners.
350 Members
Frequency: Annual/December
Founded in 1974

12129 **Housing Credit Conference & Marketplace**
National Council of State Housing Agencies
444 N Capitol St NW
Suite 438
Washington, DC 20001-1505

202-624-7710; Fax: 202-624-5899
bthompson@ncsha.org
www.ncsha.org
Facebook, Twitter

Gerald M. Hunter, President
Brian A. Hudson, Vice President
Thomas R. Gleason, Secretary/ Treasurer
Barbara J. Thompson, Executive Director

The industry event of the year. Only NCSHA brings leaders and top development and compliance staff from the state Housing Credit allocating agencies together with government officials, developmers, lenders syndicators, investors, attorneys, accountants, property managers, compliance experts, owners, and nonprofits.
350 Members
Frequency: Annual/June
Founded in 1974

12130 **IAEM Annual Conference**
International Association of Emergency Managers
201 Park Washington Court
Falls Church, VA 22046

703-538-1795; Fax: 703-241-5603
info@iaem.com
www.iaem.com

Provides a forum for current trends and topics, information about the latest tools and technology in emergency management and homeland security, and advances IAEM-USA committee work. Sessions encourage stakeholders at all levels of government, the private sector, public health and related professions to exchange ideas on collaborating to protect lives and property from disaster.
1000 Attendees
Frequency: Annual/November

12131 **ICMA Annual Conference**
International City/County Management Association
777 N Capitol Street NE
Suite 500
Washington, DC 20002

202-624-4600
800-745-8780; Fax: 202-962-3500
amahoney@icma.org

Robert J. O'Neill, Executive Director
David Ellis, Conference Committee Co-Chair
Maria A. Hurtado, Conference Committee Co-Chair

The largest annual event in the world for local government managers and staff.
3814 Attendees
Frequency: Annual/September
Founded in 1914

12132 **ICMA Regional Summit**
International City/County Management Association
777 N Capitol Street NE
Suite 500
Washington, DC 20002-4239

202-289-4262
800-745-8780; Fax: 202-962-3500

customerservices@icma.org
Facebook, Twitter, LinkedIn, YouTube, Flickr

Barry Sacks, Show Manager
Robert J. O'Neill, Executive Director

A networking and professional development opportunity for members and state officers in the four regions.
3.5M Attendees
Frequency: Annual/September

12133 **Legislative Conference**
National Council of State Housing Agencies
444 N Capitol St NW
Suite 438
Washington, DC 20001-1505

202-624-7710; Fax: 202-624-5899
bthompson@ncsha.org
www.ncsha.org
Facebook, Twitter

Gerald M. Hunter, President
Brian A. Hudson, Vice President
Thomas R. Gleason, Secretary/ Treasurer
Barbara J. Thompson, Executive Director

Join HFA leaders and their board members and stakeholders in Washington to learn about NCSHA's legislative priorities and strategize the best way to communicate our message to Congress with one unified voice. Hear from key Congressional staff and industry leaders about the issues of the day.
350 Members
Frequency: Annual/March
Founded in 1974

12134 **MMA Annual Meeting and Trade Show**
Massachusetts Municipal Association
One Winthrop Square
Boston, MA 02110

617-426-7272; Fax: 617-695-1314
www.mma.org

The largest regular gathering of Massachusetts local government officials. Features educational workshops, nationally recognized speakers, awards programs, a large trade show, and an opportunity to network with municipal officials from across the state.
1000 Attendees
Frequency: Annual/January

12135 **Marine West Military Expo**
Nielsen Business Media, USA
1145 Sanctuary Parkway
Suite 355
Alpharetta

703-488-2762

Ron Bates, Event Organizer

This event is fully dedicated to the defense industry. The event will showcase the latest products and equipments used for marine and related industry at one place. The visitors will be the military professionals, equipment buyers, decision makers and the other people related to the field of defense.
Frequency: Annual/February

12136 **NACE Annual Conference**
National Association County Engineers
25 Mass. Avenue NW
Suite 580
Washington, DC 20001

202-393-5041; Fax: 202-393-2630
nace@naco.org
www.countyengineers.org

Mark A. Craft, President
Richie Beyer, President-Elect
Mark K. Servi, Secretary/ Treasurer

Attendees will have many opportunities to meet road and bridge professionals and their counterparts from other counties around the country, to exchange ideas and have some fun. The exhibit show offers a friendly environment for delegates to learn about the latest products and services.
450 Attendees
Frequency: Annual/April

12137 **NACo Annual Conference and Exposition**
National Association of Counties
25 Massachusetts Avenue, NW
Suite 500
Washington, DC 20001

202-393-6226
888-407-6226; Fax: 202-393-2630
nacomeetings@naco.org

Larry E. Naake, Executive Director

Provides an opportunity for all county leaders and staff to learn, network and guide the direction of the association. Provides county officials with a great opportunity to vote on NACo's policies related to federal legislation and regulation; elect officers; network with colleagues; learn about innovative county programs; find out about issues impacting counties across the country; and view products and services from participating companies and exhibitors.
Frequency: Annual/July

12138 **NACo's Annual Conference and Exposition**
National Association of Counties
440 1st Street NW
Washington, DC 20001-2028

202-393-6226; Fax: 202-393-2630
webmaster@naco.org
www.naco.org

Amanda Clark, Conference & Meetings Associate
Kim Struble, Conference & Meetings Director
Larry Naake, CEO

The place for elected and appointed county officials to network, attend educational sessions and meet with companies that sell products to counties. It includes a variety of activities designed to meet the needs of all delegates. In addition to strong educational sessions, the conference includes affiliate, steering and subcommittee meetings, state association meetings and social events.
4000 Attendees
Frequency: Annual

12139 **NAHRO National Conference**
Nat'l Assn of Housing & Redevelopment Officials
630 Eye Street NW
Washington, DC 20001-3736

202-289-3500
877-866-2476; Fax: 202-289-8181
nahro@nahro.org
www.nahro.org

A wide array of products and services needed by the housing and community development field.
3M Attendees
Frequency: Annual/October

12140 **NARC Conference and Exhibition**
National Association of Regional Councils
1666 Connecticut Ave NW
Suite 305
Washington, DC 20002

202-986-1032; Fax: 202-986-1038
www.narc.org

Fred Abousleman, Executive Director
Lindsey Riley, Deputy of Communications
500+ Attendees
Frequency: Annual/June

12141 **NASTAD Annual Conference**
Nat'l Alliance of State/Territoral AIDS Directors
444 N Capitol St NW
Suite 339
Washington, DC 20001

202-434-8090; Fax: 202-434-8092
nastad@nastad.org
www.nastad.org

Julie Scofield, Executive Director

Apprenticeship directors from around the nation come together to problem solve, share innovative ideas to the Registered Apprenticeship model as well as to bring the association up to date on each state's activities.
Frequency: Annual/May

12142 **NCBM Annual Convention**
National Conference of Black Mayors
191 Peachtree Street, NE
Suite 849
Atlanta, GA 30303

404-765-6444; Fax: 404-765-6430
www.ncbm.org

Vanessa R. Williams, Executive Director
Robert L. Bowser, President
Jamie Mayo, Treasurer
Johnny L. DuPree, Ph.D, Secretary
John White, Sergeant-at-Arms

Serving as a catalyst for bringing together mayors and municipal leaders, including several international delegations, state and federal officials, as well as leaders in the public and private sectors for the purpose of networking and obtaining information on the latest policies and strategies for enhancing municipal government.
542 Members
Founded in 1974

12143 **NCSHA Housing Credit Conference & Marketplace**
444 N Capitol Street NW
Suite 438
Washington, DC 20001-1512

202-624-7710; Fax: 202-624-5899
www.ncsha.org

Louise Moors, Membership Coordinator
William Pound, Executive Director

Brings leaders and top development and compliance staff from the state Housing Credit allocating agencies together with government officials, developers, lenders, syndicators, investors, attorneys, accountants, property managers, compliance experts, owners, and nonprofits. Heavy hitters of the industry and their partners will deliver the latest news on how to make the housing Credit work in these unprecedented times.
700 Attendees
Frequency: Annual/June

12144 **NCSL Fall Forum**
National Conference of State Legislatures
7700 East First Place
Denver, CO 80230

303-364-7700; Fax: 303-364-7800
www.ncsi.org

Peg Coniglio, Manager
Deana Blackwood, Circulation Director

Focuses on how best to advance the States' Agenda and tackle the difficult policy issues of our time, including budget gaps, health care coverage, education affordability, transportation funding, energy costs and many others.
6700 Attendees
Frequency: Annual/November

12145 **NCSL Legislative Summit**
National Conference of State Legislatures

444 North Capitol Street NW
Suite 515
Washington, DC 20001

202-624-5400; Fax: 202-737-1069
deana.blackwood@ncsl.org
www.ncsl.org

William T Pound, Executive Director
Leticia Van de Putte, President
Steven Rauschenberger, VP
Max Arinder, Staff Chair

Four days of 150 policy sessions on the most pressing issues facing state legislatures. Some of the topics include budget conditions, education reform, health care implementation and renewable energy.
13M+ Members
4800+ Attendees
Frequency: Annual/August
Founded in 1975

12146 **NCWM Annual Meeting**
National Conference on Weights and Measures
1135 M Street
Suite 110
Lincoln, NE 68508

402-434-4880; Fax: 402-434-4878
info@ncwm.net
www.ncwm.net

Don Onwiler, Executive Director

Technical presentations are a way to stay on the cutting edge of new developments in the weights and measures community. Complete the business of the conference through open hearings and voting on national standards.

12147 **NEMA Mid-Year Conference**
National Emergency Management Association
PO Box 11910
Lexington, KY 40578

859-244-8000; Fax: 859-244-8239
nemaadmin@csg.org
www.nemaweb.org

Jim Mullen, President
John Madden, Vice President
Charley English, Treasurer
Tom Sands, Secretary
Brenda Bergeron, Legal Counsel

Gives the opportunity to discuss important issues in the field of emergency management and homeland security. Also hear from respected leaders working on many of these issues. Opportunities to meet and network with peers are invaluable in these times of rapid change and economic challenges.
Frequency: Annual/March

12148 **NFBPA FORUM**
National Forum for Black Public Administrators
777 N Capitol Street NE
Suite 807
Washington, DC 20002-4239

202-289-5851
800-745-8780; Fax: 202-962-3500
webmaster@nfbpa.org
www.nfbpa.org

Aretha R. Ferrell-Benavides, President
Verdenia C. Baker, 1st Vice President
Bruce T. Moore, 2nd Vice President
Jelynn LeBlanc Burley, Secretary/ Treasurer

Waves of change, oceans of opportunity repositioning our communities for the future. Plenary sessions and luncheons, public policy forum, workshops, banquet and brunch, corporate exhibit, vendor showcase, artist's gallery and more.
1.4M Attendees
Frequency: Annual/April

12149 **NPELRA Annual Training Conference**
National Public Employer Labor Relations Assoc.
1620 I Street NW
4th Floor
Washington, DC 20006-4005

202-591-1190; Fax: 202-293-2352
www.npelra.org
Facebook, Twitter, LinkedIn

Sam Penrod, President
Michael S. Bates, Executive Vice President
Christa Ballowe, Vice President
Walt Pellegrini, Vice President
Joel Kuhl, Secretary/ Treasurer

Attend the best training available for public sector Labor Relations & Human Resources professionals with over 30 program sessions; in addition the conference provides credit hours for CLE and HRCI recertification. Interact with colleagues representing public sector labor relations professionals from across the country.
350 Attendees
Frequency: Annual

12150 **NPELRA Training Conference**
National Public Employer Labor Relations Assoc
1012 South Coast Highway
Suite M
Oceanside, CA 92054

760-433-1686
877-673-5721; Fax: 760-433-1687
www.npelra.org
Facebook, Twitter, LinkedIn

Michael T Kolb, Executive Director
Janessa Stephens, Association Specialist
Yvonne Gillengerten, Operation Manager
Stephanie Biggs, Administrative Assistant
Allison Wittwer, Administrative Assistant

Attend the best training available for public sector Labor Relations and Human Resources professionals with over 30 program sessions; in addition the conference provides credit hours for CLE and HRCI recertification. Interact wth colleagues representing public sector labor relations professionals from across the country.
Frequency: Annual

12151 **NSCL Legislative Summit**
National Conference of State Legislatures
7700 E 1st Pl
Denver, CO 80230-7143

303-364-7700; Fax: 303-364-7800
pubs-info@ncsl.org
www.ncsl.org
Twitter, LinkedIn

William Pound, Executive Director
Edward Smith, Managing Editor
LeAnn Hoff, Director, Revenue & Sales

A bipartisan organization that serves the legislators and staffs of the nation's 50 states, its commonwealths and territories.
15000 Members
5500 Attendees
Founded in 1975

12152 **National Association Regional Councils**
1666 Conneticut Ave NW
Suite 305
Washington, DC 20002

202-986-1032; Fax: 202-986-1038
www.narc.org

Shawn Sample, Show Manager

80 booths.
1.2M Attendees
Frequency: June
Founded in 1965

12153 **National Council of State Housing Agencies Conference**
444 N Capitol St NW
Suite 438
Washington, DC 20001-1505

202-624-7710; Fax: 202-624-5899
bthompson@ncsha.org
www.ncsha.org
Facebook, Twitter

Gerald M. Hunter, President
Brian A. Hudson, Vice President
Thomas R. Gleason, Secretary/ Treasurer
Barbara J. Thompson, Executive Director

The premier gathering of state HFAs and NCSHA affiliate members. It is the main networking event of the year for HFAs and the partners who work with them to increase housing opportunities through the financing, developemnt, and preservation of affordable housing.
350 Members
Frequency: Annual/October
Founded in 1974

12154 **National Electricity Forum**
NARUC
1101 Vermont Ave NW
Suite 200
Washington, DC 20005-3553

202-898-2200; Fax: 202-898-2213
admin@naruc.org
www.naruc.org

David A. Wright, Chairman & President
Philip B. Jones, 1st Vice President
Colette D. Honorable, 2nd Vice President
David E. Ziegner, Treasurer
Charles D. Gray, Executive Director

Addressing cutting-edge issues and discuss how collaboration can successfully modernize the nation's electricity infrastructure. The forum will feature national thought leaders from all sectors of the electric power industry, academia, policymakers, equipment manufacturers, consumers, and other affected parties.
Frequency: Annual/February
Founded in 1889

12155 **National Hemp Association Annual Meeting**
National Hemp Association
80 M St. SE
Suite 130
Washington, DC 20003

202-706-3911
www.nationalhempassociation.org
Facebook, Twitter, Google+

Erica Stark, Executive Director
Anna Chanthavongseng, Assistant Executive Director

A meeting to discuss all aspects of the industrial hemp industry including education, community, legislation, and scientific and industry news.
Frequency: Annual

12156 **National League of Postmasters Annual National Convention**
National League of Postmasters
5904 Richmond Highway
Suite 500
Alexandria, VA 22303-1864

703-329-4550; Fax: 703-329-0466
exhibit@epponline.com
www.epponline.com

Mark W. Strong, President

Extensive training and educational opportunities.
1400 Attendees
Frequency: Annual/August
Founded in 1903

12157 **National Postal Forum**
3998 Fair Ridge Drive
Suite 300
Fairfax, VA 22033

703-218-5015; Fax: 703-218-5020
info@npf.org
www.npf.org
Facebook, Twitter, LinkedIn, Flickr

Mary Guthrie, Director, Marketing & Exhibits
Laurie Woodhams, Exhibits Assistant

The premier educational event and tradeshow available to mail professionals today. Attend the National Postal Forum to get a complete education in the Business of Mail.
Frequency: Annual/April

12158 **Norfolk NATO Festival**
440 Bank Street
Norfolk, VA 23510

757-282-2800; Fax: 757-282-2787
www.azaleafestival.org

Kelly Harlan, General Manager

A salute to the NATO's Allied Command Atlantic forces in order to create new friendships, provide a basis for cultural exchange, recognize the military's role in maintaining peace in the world and pursue new lines of trade between Norfolk and the world.
5M Attendees
Frequency: Canada
Founded in 1953

12159 **PHADA Annual Convention and Exhibition**
Public Housing Authorities Directors Association
511 Capitol Court NE
Washington, DC 20002-4937

202-546-5445; Fax: 202-546-2280
www.phada.org

Timothy G. Kaiser, Executive Director
Stephanie White, Director of Meetings

Provides the latest information and tools housing authorities need to run their agencies in these changing times. Also, many exciting housing suppliers and vendors will be on-hand to showcase their services. There are many sessions to provide attendees with important information emanating from Congress and HUD headquarters.
800 Attendees
Frequency: Annual/May

12160 **Quarterly Cannabis Caucus**
National Cannabis Industry Association
126 C Street NW
3rd Floor
Washington, DC 20001

888-683-5650
info@thecannabisindustry.org
www.thecannabisindustry.org
Facebook, Twitter, LinkedIn, Instagram

F. Aaron Smith, Executive Director
Shannon Hayden, Chief Operating Officer
Michael Correia, Director, Government Relations
Morgan Fox, Director, Media Relations
Brooke Gilbert, Director, Events & Education

This business-to-business networking event series provides an opportunity to meet with the cannabis industry's leading executives and policymakers and advance the cannabis industry nationally. Hosted in the industry's eight most active regions in the first month of each quarter.
2000 Members
Frequency: Quarterly
Founded in 2010

12161 **SGAC Annual National Summit**
State Government Affairs Council
108 North Columbus Street
2nd Floor
Alexandria, VA 22314

571-312-3426
eloudy@sgac.org
www.sgac.org

Donna Gehlhaart, President
Elizabeth A. Loudy, Executive Director
Jon Burton, Vice President
Holly Johnson, Operations Associate
Katherine Kilgore, Manager, Communications

Professional development and networking opportunity for SGAC members.
200 Members
Frequency: Annual
Founded in 1975

12162 **The Cannabis Alliance General Meeting**
The Cannabis Alliance

info@thecannabisalliance.us
www.thecannabisalliance.us
Facebook, Twitter

Lara Kaminsky, Executive Director
Julia Lee, Executive Assistant
Kim Ducot,, Membership Director

An open meeting held every second Thursday of the month. Discuss legislative and regulatory news, committee information, industry updates and events.
Frequency: Monthly
Founded in 2016

12163 **The Cannabis Alliance Lobby Day**
The Cannabis Alliance

info@thecannabisalliance.us
www.thecannabisalliance.us
Facebook, Twitter

Lara Kaminsky, Executive Director
Julia Lee, Executive Assistant
Kim Ducot,, Membership Director

Spend the day at the Washington State Capitol meeting with state legislators to discuss the cannabis industry. Followed by a dinner reception with legislators and their aides to continue the conversation.
Frequency: Annual
Founded in 2016

12164 **Transforming Local Government Conference**
Mid-America Regional Council
6604 Harney Road, Suite L
PO Box 16645
Tampa, FL 33687-6645

813-622-8484; Fax: 813-664-0051
www.tlgconference.org
Facebook, Twitter, Flickr, YouTube

Mary Laird, Executive Assistant
David Warm, Executive Director

Through innovative case study sessions, conference attendees will take an in-depth look at the ingenuity and creativity of successful government programs. TLG attracts participation from local governments that are deliberately seeking new and innovative ways to connect people, information and ideas that support their efforts to be the best communities in which to live, work, and prosper.
800 Attendees
Frequency: Annual
Printed in one color on matte stock

12165 **UDT: Undersea Defense Technology Conference and Exhibition**
Reed Exhibition Companies
255 Washington Street
Newton, MA 02458-1637

617-584-4900; Fax: 617-630-2222
Facebook, Twitter, LinkedIn

Elizabeth Hitchcock, International Sales

The world's leading exhibition and conference for undersea defence and security. Gain access to the latest technologies, connect with existing suppliers and create new business relationships. Gives the invaluable opportunity to network across the global maritime community. Suppliers exhibiting; UUVs and components, acoustic technologies, maritime surveillance solutions, harbour and port security products, mine detection systems, and submarine hardware and electronics.
Frequency: Annual/May

12166 **UNA-USA Annual Meeting**
United Nations Association of the USA
1800 Massachusetts Avenue NW
Suite 400
Washington, DC 20036

202-887-9040; Fax: 202-887-9021
www.unausa.org

Patrick Madden, Executive Director

Brings together UNA-USA's constituencies for a variety of skills trainings, issue briefings, networking opportunities and capacity-building.
400 Attendees
Frequency: Annual/November

12167 **Western Legislative Conference**
1107 9th Street
Suite 730
Sacramento, CA 95814

916-553-4423; Fax: 916-446-5760
csgw@csg.org
www.csgwest.org

Rosie Berger, Chair
Kelvin Atkinson, Chair-Elect
Craig Johnson, Vice Chair

Brings together legislators from western states to learn from each other and collaborate on issues of regional concern such as water, public lands, energy and transportation. Also offers training and professional development opportunities for all legislators.
500 Attendees
Frequency: Annual/July
Founded in 1933

Directories & Databases

12168 **Almanac of American Politics**
National Journal
1730 M St NW
Suite 800
Washington, DC 20036-4551

202-828-0300; Fax: 202-457-5160

Marcia Coyle, Manager

The definitive guide to understanding the forces that shape American politics. Has been established as a Washington institution in its own right and an indespensable resource for anyone involved or interested in the American political scene.
Cost: $59.95
1500 Pages
Frequency: Biennial

12169 **Almanac of the Federal Judiciary**
Prentice Hall Law & Business
270 Sylvan Avenue
Englewood Cliffs, NJ 07632-2521

201-569-0006

Providing balanced, responsible judicial profiles of every federal judge and all the key bankruptcy

judges and magistrate judges- profiles that include reliable inside information based on interviews with lawyers who have argued cases before the federal judiciary.
Cost: $1715.00
2130 Pages
Frequency: Annual
ISBN: 9-780735-56-8

12170 **American Bench**
Forster-Long
3280 Ramos Cir
Sacramento, CA 95827-2513

916-362-3276
800-328-5091; Fax: 916-362-5643
www.forster-long.com

Jay Long, Vice President, Marketing

Over 19,000 judges who sit in local, state and federal courts are profiled. The definitive biographical reference to the American judiciary.
Cost: $595.00
Frequency: Daily
Founded in 1977

12171 **BRB Publications**
BRB Publications
PO Box 27869
Tempe, AZ 85285-7869

480-829-7475
800-929-3811; Fax: 800-929-4981
brb@brbpublications.com
www.brbpublications.com
Facebook, LinkedIn

Mike Sankey, President

Comprehensive listing of government agencies that have placed public records online, both free and fee based.
Founded in 1988

12172 **Billcast Archive**
George Mason University, Public Choice Center
4400 University Dr
Fairfax, VA 22030-4444

703-993-1120

Clayton Austin, Manager

This database contains information on public bills introduced in the US House of Representatives and Senate during the preceding session of Congress.

12173 **Book of the States**
Council of State Governments
2760 Research Park Drive
PO Box 11910
Lexington, KY 40578-1910

859-244-8000
800-800-1910; Fax: 859-244-8001
research@csg.org
www.csg.org

Jodi Rell, President
Carol Juett, Director of Development
Roger Werholtz, Secretary

A reference tool of choice and includes comparative information on everything from highway miles to state government employment and everything in between.
Cost: $99.00
Frequency: Annually
Founded in 1935

12174 **CSG State Directories**
Council of State Governments
2760 Research Park Drive
PO Box 11910
Lexington, KY 40578-1910

859-244-8000
800-800-1910; Fax: 859-244-8001
research@csg.org
www.csg.org

Jodi Rell, President
Carol Juett, Director of Development
Roger Werholtz, Secretary

Includes the names and contact information for key state government officials.
Frequency: Annually

12175 **Canadian Almanac & Directory**
Grey House Publishing Canada
555 Richmond Street West
Suite 301
Toronto, ON M5V 3B1

416-644-6479
866-433-4739; Fax: 416-644-1904
info@greyhouse.ca
www.greyhouse.ca
Facebook, Twitter, LinkedIn

Richard Gottlieb, President
Leslie Mackenzie, Publisher

A combination of textual material, charts, colour photographs and directory listings, the Canadian Almanac & Directory provides the most comprehensive picture of Canada, from physical attributes to economic and business summaries to leisure and recreation.
Cost: $360.00
1936 Pages
Frequency: Annual
ISBN: 1-592377-69-5

12176 **Canadian Parliamentary Guide**
Grey House Publishing Canada
555 Richmond Street West
Suite 301
Toronto, ON M5V 3B1

416-644-6479
866-433-4739; Fax: 416-644-1904
info@greyhouse.ca
www.greyhouse.ca
Facebook, Twitter, LinkedIn

Richard Gottlieb, President
Leslie Mackenzie, Publisher

Canadian Parliamentary Guide provides the most complete and comprehensive information on elected and appointed members in federal and provincial government.
Cost: $229.00
1152 Pages
Frequency: Annual
ISBN: 1-592377-65-7

12177 **Capital Source**
National Journal
600 New Hampshire Ave NW
Suite 4
Washington, DC 20037-2403

202-739-8400; Fax: 202-833-8069

John Fox Sullivan, President

Directory brimming with key information on the most important players and institutions Inside-the-Beltway, The Capital Source is the place for essential and current contact information all year round. A must-have resource for anyone in the business of politics, policy, government relations or the media.
Cost: $29.95
160 Pages
Frequency: Monthly

12178 **Carroll's County Directory**
Carroll Publishing
4701 Sangamore Rd
Suite S-155
Bethesda, MD 20816-2532

301-263-9800
800-336-4240; Fax: 301-263-9805
customersvc@carrollpub.com
www.carrollpub.com
Twitter, LinkedIn

Bill Wade, President/COO
Kathleen Undegraff, VP Marketing
Cost: $350.00
Founded in 1973

12179 **Carroll's Federal Directory**
Carroll Publishing
4701 Sangamore Rd
Suite 155S
Bethesda, MD 20816-2532

301-263-9800
800-336-4240; Fax: 301-263-9805
info@carrollpub.com
www.carrollpub.com

Tom Carroll, President

Offers complete coverage of the headquarter offices of the Executive, Legislative, and Judicial branches of government. Includes over 38,000 positions offering direct contact information for all Executive departments, independent agencies, Congressional Agencies and US Federal Courts.
Cost: $500.00
450 Pages
Frequency: Annual

12180 **Carroll's Federal Regional Directory**
Carroll Publishing
4701 Sangamore Rd
Suite 155S
Bethesda, MD 20816-2532

301-263-9800
800-336-4240; Fax: 301-263-9805
info@carrollpub.com
www.carrollpub.com

Tom Carroll, President

The one regional resource that has it all. Covering regional and field offices of Federal government departments, home-state offices for members of Congress, federal district courts and more. Reach over 32,000 government people located outside of Washington.
Cost: $170.00
370 Pages
Frequency: Bi-Annually

12181 **Carroll's Municipal Directory**
Carroll Publishing
4701 Sangamore Rd
Suite 155S
Bethesda, MD 20816-2532

301-263-9800
800-336-4240; Fax: 301-263-9805
info@carrollpub.com
www.carrollpub.com

Tom Carroll, President

The most comprehensive municipal directory available anywhere. It includes more than 60,000 appointed officials, career officials and local authorities across the US. Covering more cities than any other source, this has nearly 8,000 cities, towns and villages.
Cost: $170.00
550 Pages
Frequency: Bi-Annually

12182 **Carroll's State Directory**
Carroll Publishing
4701 Sangamore Rd
Suite 155S
Bethesda, MD 20816-2532

301-263-9800
800-336-4240; Fax: 301-263-9805
www.carrollpub.com
Twitter, LinkedIn

Bill Wade, President/COO
Kathleen Updegraff, VP Marketing

Provides complete contact information for over 68,000 key officials in all 50 states, plus the District of Columbia, Puerto Rico and the American Territories.
Cost: $210.00
530 Pages
Frequency: TriAnnual

12183 **Congress at Your Fingertips: Congressional Directory**
Capitol Advantage
1255 22nd St NW
Washington, DC 20037-1217
703-899-9636
800-659-8708; Fax: 703-289-4678
www.capitoladvantage.com
Dr. John Hansan, Production Manager
Comprehensive directory lists members of the US Senate and House of Representatives, complete with color photos and a fold-out map of Capitol Hill.
Cost: $13.95
Frequency: Annual

12184 **Congressional Staff Directory**
Leadership Directories, Inc.
1167 K Street NW
Suite 801
Washington, DC 20006
202-628-7757; Fax: 202-628-3430
www.leadershipdirectories.com
Gretchen Teichgraeber, CEO
William Cressey, Chairman
Locate key decision-makers and support staff that work behind the scenes on important legislative issues. Pinpoint key contacts on committees who work day-to-day on legislation that's most important.
Cost: $69.00
1200 Pages
Frequency: SemiAnnual

12185 **Daily Defense News Capsules**
United Communications Group
11300 Rockville Pike
Suite 1100
Rockville, MD 20852-3030
301-816-8950; Fax: 301-816-8945
Greg Beaudoin, Editor
This database offers the complete text of Periscope - Daily Defense News Capsules, that provide abstracts of international press coverage of military and defense news.

12186 **Defense Industry Charts**
Carroll Publishing
4701 Sangamore Rd
Suite 155S
Bethesda, MD 20816-2532
301-263-9800
800-336-4240; Fax: 301-263-9805
info@carrollpub.com
www.carrollpub.com
Tom Carroll, President
19000 key personnel in top US defense contractors, including major aerospace, electronic, military hardware, information technology and systems integration companies. Serves as a road map to the critical players in this important industry.
Cost: $2050.00
Frequency: Quarterly

12187 **Defense Programs**
Carroll Publishing
4701 Sangamore Rd
Suite 155S
Bethesda, MD 20816-2532
301-263-9800
800-336-4240; Fax: 301-263-9805
info@carrollpub.com
www.carrollpub.com
Tom Carroll, President
Detailed description of more than 2,000 military research, development, test and evaluation programs and projects.
Cost: $1060.00
Frequency: Quarterly

12188 **Defense and Foreign Affairs Handbook**
International Strategic Studies Association
PO Box 19289
Alexandria, VA 22320-0289
703-548-1070; Fax: 703-684-7476
dfa@strategicstudies.org
www.strategicstudies.org
Gregory Copley, Editor
Important global reference encyclopedia for most world leaders .Comprehensive chapters on 238 countries and territories worldwide, with each chapter giving full cabinet and leadership listings, history, recent developments, demographics, economic statistics, political and constitutional data, news media,defense overview, defense structure.
Cost: $297.00
2500 Pages
Frequency: Monthly
Circulation: 4,000
ISBN: 1-892998-06-8
Founded in 1976

12189 **Directory of Congressional Voting Scores and Interest Group Ratings**
1414 22nd Street NW
Washington, DC 20037-1003
202-887-8500
800-432-2250; Fax: 800-380-3810
www.cqpress.com
Complete compilation of CQ voting studies and interest group rating data for every legislator who has served in Congress since 1947. This resource is perfect for quick or in-depth research and provides the easiest, most accurate way to gauge the political orientation of members of Congress over time. This is the best source for understanding the political preferences of US senators and representatives, and what it means about their choices on future votes.
Cost: $450.00
1700 Pages
Frequency: Triennial

12190 **Encyclopedia of Governmental Advisory Organizations**
Gale/Cengage Learning
PO Box 6904
Florence, KY 41022-6904
800-354-9706; Fax: 800-487-8488
gale.galeord@cengage.com
www.gale.com
Patrick C Sommers, President
Contains entries which describe the activities and personnel of groups and committees that function to advise the President of the United States and various departments and bureaus of the federal government, as well as detailed information about historically significant committees.
Frequency: Annual

12191 **Federal Benefits for Veterans, Dependents and Survivors**
US Department of Veterans Affairs
810 Vermont Ave NW
Washington, DC 20420-0002
202-273-5400; Fax: 202-273-4880
John R Gingirch, CEO
Health care benefits, disability benefits, pensions, home loan, insurance, and much more.
Cost: $3.25
Frequency: Annual

12192 **Federal Buyers Guide**
Gold Crest
650 Ward Dr # A
Santa Barbara, CA 93111-2395
805-683-9000
800-922-3233; Fax: 805-683-7661
Roger Edgar, CEO
Gunnar Sundstrom, OPS Manager
Companies that serve or wish to serve as vendors to the federal government. Reading specialty lights, giftware, manufacturer, distributor, Mighty Bright brand.
170 Pages
Frequency: Quarterly
ISSN: 1043-7568
Founded in 1979

12193 **Federal Directory of Contract Administration Services Components**
Contract Mgmt. Command/Defense Logistics Agency
Caremon Station
Alexandria, VA 22304
703-781-9807
Lists the names and telephone numbers of those DCMA and other agency offices that offer contract administration services within designated geographic areas and at specified contractor plants.
110 Pages
Frequency: Annually

12194 **Federal Government Certification Programs**
US National Institute of Standards & Technology
Administration Building
Room 629
Gaithersburg, MD 20899-0001
301-975-2281; Fax: 301-963-2871
A directory available certification programs.
Cost: $18.95
229 Pages

12195 **Federal Staff Direcotry**
1414 22nd Street NW
Washington, DC 20037-1003
202-887-8500
800-432-2250; Fax: 800-380-3810
www.cqpress.com
Penny Perry, Editor
Pinpoint senior officials and top aides working directly with the President and Vice President using the most well-researched information available. Find all the information needed to locate high-ranking policy-makers, their deputies, bureau chiefs, and division heads. Connect with top-level officials at agencies ranging from the American Red Cross to the Environmental Protection Agency.
Cost: $450.00
1700 Pages
Frequency: Monthly

12196 **Federal Technology Source**
Government Executive- National Journal Group
600 New Hampshire Ave NW
Suite 4
Washington, DC 20037-2403
202-739-8500
800-356-4838; Fax: 202-739-8511

webmaster@govexec.com
www.govexec.com

Matt Dunie, President
Sue Fourney, Managing Editor

A directory of most important people and organizations in the federal technology community.
Cost: $9.95
168 Pages
Frequency: Annual
Circulation: 73,500
ISSN: 0017-2626
Printed in 4 colors on glossy stock

12197 **Foreign Consular Offices in the United States**
Bureau of Public Affairs/US Department of State
2201 C Street NW
Washington, DC 20520-0001

202-647-6141

A complete and official listing of the foreign consular offices in the US, and recognized consular officers. Compiled by the US Department of State, with the full cooperation of the foreign missions in Washington, it is offered as a convenience to organizations and persons who must deal with consular government agencies, state tax officials, international trade organizations, chamber of commerce, and judicial authorities.
Cost: $4.00
290 Pages
Frequency: Annual

12198 **Getting Started in Federal Contracting: A Guide Through the Federal Maze**
Panoptic Enterprises
PO Box 11220
Burke, VA 22009-1220

703-451-5953
800-594-4766; Fax: 703-451-5953
www.fedgovcontracts.com

Vivina Mcvay, President
Barry L McVay, Editor

Information is given on over 65 government procurement offices, Department of Labor offices, General Services Administration business services and Small Business Administration regional and branch offices.
Cost: $39.95
395 Pages
ISBN: 0-912481-24-2
Founded in 1984

12199 **Government Assistance Almanac: Guide to all Federal Financial Programs**
Omnigraphics
615 Griswold
Detroit, MI 48226

313-961-1340
800-234-1340; Fax: 313-961-1383
editorial@omnigraphics.com
www.omnigraphics.com

Robert Dumouchel, Editor

Provides updated information on all 1,613 federal domestic assistance programs available. These programs represent $1.675 trillion worth of federal assistance earmarked for distribution to consumers, children, parents, veterans, senior citizens, students, businesses, civic groups, state and local agencies, and others.
Cost: $240.00
1,000 Pages
Frequency: Annual
ISBN: 0-780807-00-6

12200 **Government Phone Book USA**
Omnigraphics
615 Griswold Street
Detroit, MI 48226

313-961-1340
800-234-1340; Fax: 313-961-1383
editorial@omnigraphics.com
www.omnigraphics.com

David Bianco, Marketing Director

Key federal, state and local government offices in the US are profiled. More than 270,000 listings with complete contact data.
Cost: $275.00
2,700 Pages
Frequency: Annual
ISBN: 0-780806-93-X
Founded in 1992

12201 **Government Research Directory**
Gale/Cengage Learning
PO Box 09187
Detroit, MI 48209-0187

248-699-4253
800-877-4253; Fax: 248-699-8049
gale.galeord@cengage.com
www.gale.com

Patrick C Sommers, President

In this vital resource you'll find research facilities and programs of the US and Canadian federal governments. Listings include e-mail addresses, information on patents available for licensing and expanded coverage of key personal contact.
ISBN: 1-414420-23-4

12202 **Governments Canada**
Grey House Publishing Canada
555 Richmond Street West
Suite 301
Toronto, ON M5V 3B1

416-644-6479
866-433-4739; Fax: 416-644-1904
info@greyhouse.ca
www.greyhouse.ca
Facebook, Twitter, LinkedIn

Richard Gottlieb, President
Leslie Mackenzie, Publisher

Governments Canada is the most complete and comprehensive tool for locating people and programs in Canada. It provides regularly updated listings on federal, provincial and territorial government departments, offices and agencies across Canada. Branch and regional offices are also included, along with all associated agencies, boards, commissions and crown corporations. Listings include contact names, full address, telephone and fax numbers, as well as e-mail addresses.
Cost: $299.00
600 Pages
Frequency: 2x/Year
ISBN: 1-592379-85-9

12203 **Grey House Safety & Security Directory**
Grey House Publishing
4919 Route 22
PO Box 56
Amenia, NY 12501

518-789-8700
800-562-2139; Fax: 845-373-6390
books@greyhouse.com
www.greyhouse.com
Facebook, Twitter

Leslie Mackenzie, Publisher
Richard Gottlieb, Editor

Comprehensive guide to the safety and security industry, including articles, checklists, OSHA regulations and product listings. Focuses on creating and maintaing a safe and secure enviroment, and dealing specifically with hazardous materials, noise and vibration, workplace preparation and maintenance, electrical and lighting safety, fire and rescue and more.
Cost: $165.00
1600 Pages
ISBN: 1-592373-75-5
Founded in 1981

12204 **Guide to Management Improvement Projects in Local Government**
ICMA Publications
777 N Capitol St NE
Suite 600
Washington, DC 20002-4240

202-216-9408
800-745-8780; Fax: 202-962-3500
www.icma.org

Joan Mc Callen, President

Projects conducted by municipal governments that have resulted in improvements in efficiency or cost reductions are listed.
Cost: $65.00
50 Pages
Frequency: Quarterly

12205 **Hudson's Washington News Media Contacts Directory**
Grey House Publishing
4919 Route 22
PO Box 56
Amenia, NY 12501

518-789-8700
800-562-2139; Fax: 845-373-6390
books@greyhouse.com
www.greyhouse.com
Facebook, Twitter

Leslie Mackenzie, Publisher
Richard Gottlieb, President

A comprehensive guide to the entire Washington, D.C. press corps, broken down into categories.
Cost: $289.00
350 Pages
ISBN: 1-592378-53-6
Printed in one color on matte stock

12206 **Hudson's Washington News Media Contacts - Online Database**
Grey House Publishing
4919 Route 22
PO Box 56
Amenia, NY 12501

518-789-8700
800-562-2139; Fax: 845-373-6390
gold@greyhouse.com
gold.greyhouse.com
Facebook, Twitter

Leslie Mackenzie, Publisher
Richard Gottlieb, President

With 100% verification of data, Hudson's is the most accurate, most up-to-date source for media contacts in our nation's capital. With the largest concentration of news media in the world, having access to Washington's news media will get your message heard by these key media outlets.

12207 **IAEM Directory**
International Association of Emergency Managers
111 Park Pl
Falls Church, VA 22046-4513

703-538-1795; Fax: 703-241-5603
info@iaem.com
www.iaem.com

Shan Coffin, Editor
Sharon L Kelly, Circulation Director
Cost: $100.00
Circulation: 8,000

12208 **Immediate Need Resource Directory**
Gold Crest

650 Ward Dr
Suite A
Santa Barbara, CA 93111-2395

805-683-9000
800-922-3233; Fax: 805-683-7661

Roger Edgar, CEO
Gunnar Sundstrom, OPS Manager

A directory catering to the immediate needs of Federal government purchasing agents. Reading and speciality lights, giftware, manufacturer, distributor, Mighty Bright brand.
Cost: $20.00
50 Pages
Frequency: Monthly
Founded in 1990

12209 **Judicial Yellow Book**
Leadership Directories
104 5th Ave
New York, NY 10011-6901

212-627-4140; Fax: 212-645-0931
judicial@leadershipdirectories.com
www.leadershipdirectories.com

David Hurvitz, CEO
James M Petrie, Associate Publisher

Contact information for over 3,250 federal and state judges in federal and state appellate courts, including staff and law clerks, and the law schools they attended.
Cost: $245.00
1,100 Pages
Frequency: SemiAnnual
ISSN: 1082-3298
Founded in 1995
Mailing list available for rent: 13,000 names at $125 per M

12210 **Kaleidoscope: Current World Data**
ABC-CLIO
PO Box 1911
Santa Barbara, CA 93102-1911

805-968-1911; Fax: 805-685-9685
CustomerService@abc-clio.com
www.abc-clio.com

Ron Boehm, CEO

This comprehensive database takes a look at all aspects of the American culture. Listings of information include statistics and factual information on the population, culture, economy, military forces, government, and political systems of countries around the world, the US States and Canadian provinces.
Frequency: Full-text

12211 **Leadership Directories**
104 5th Ave
New York, NY 10011-6901

212-627-4140; Fax: 212-645-0931
info@leadershipdirectories.com
www.leadershipdirectories.com

David Hurvitz, CEO
Barry Graubart, Executive VP/CMO

The mission of Leadership Directories is to compile, produce and offer subscribers, in all media and in easily usable form, the most current and accurate directories of leaders in the major categories of American activity, including government, business, the professions, and the nonprofits.
Founded in 1969

12212 **Leadership Library in Print**
Leadership Directories
104 5th Ave
New York, NY 10011-6901

212-627-4140; Fax: 212-645-0931
info@leadershipdirectories.com
www.leadershipdirectories.com

David Hurvitz, CEO

Complete set of all 14 leadership directories. Provides subscribers with complete contact information for the 400,000 individuals who constitute the institutional leadership of the US.
Cost: $2300.00
Frequency: Semiannually
Founded in 1996

12213 **Leadership Library on Internet and CD-ROM**
Leadership Directories
104 5th Ave
New York, NY 10011-6901

212-627-4140; Fax: 212-645-0931
info@leadershipdirectories.com
www.leadershipdirectories.com

David Hurvitz, CEO

Makes all 14 leadership directories available over the Internet and on CD-ROM in one integrated directory. They provide subscribers with complete contact information, in one database. Subscription includes Internet access and four CD-ROM editions quarterly.
Cost: $3065.00
Frequency: Updated Daily
ISSN: 1075-3869
Founded in 1999
Mailing list available for rent
Printed in A colors on B stock

12214 **Member Data Disk**
CQ Staff Directories
815 Slaters Lane
Alexandria, VA 22314-1219

800-252-1722; Fax: 703-739-0234

Bruce B Brownson, Editor

Covers all members of the US Congress and their key staff members in Washington, DC and principal district offices.
Cost: $395.00
Frequency: Quarterly

12215 **Military Biographical Profiles**
CTB/McGraw Hill
20 Ryan Ranch Rd
Monterey, CA 93940-5770

831-393-0700
800-538-9547; Fax: 831-393-6528
www.ctb.com

Ellen Haley, President
Sandor Nagy, Chief Operating Officer

Offers valuable information on US military officers and Department of Defense officials.
Frequency: Full-text

12216 **Municipal Year Book**
ICMA Publications
777 N Capitol St NE
Suite 600
Washington, DC 20002-4240

202-216-9408
800-745-8780; Fax: 202-962-3500
cpmmail@icma.org

Joan Mc Callen, President
Gary Huff, Founder

Directory of services and supplies to the industry.
Cost: $79.95
416 Pages
Frequency: Annual

12217 **Municipal Yellow Book**
Leadership Directories
104 5th Ave
New York, NY 10011-6901

212-627-4140; Fax: 212-645-0931
www.leadershipdirectories.com

David Hurvitz, CEO
James M Petrie, Associate Publisher

Contact information for over 33,000 elected and administrative officials of US cities, counties, and local authorities.
Cost: $245.00
1,200 Pages
Frequency: SemiAnnual
ISSN: 1054-4062
Founded in 1991
Mailing list available for rent: 30,000 names at $125 per M

12218 **National Directory of Corporate Public Affairs**
Columbia Books
PO Box 251
Annapolis Junction, MD 20701-0251

888-265-0600; Fax: 240-646-7020
info@columbiabooks.com
www.columbiabooks.com

J Valerie Steele, Senior Editor

Tracks the public/government affairs programs of about 1,900 major US corporations and lists the 14,00 people who run them, Also lists: Washington area offices, corporate PACs, federal and state lobbyists, outside contract lobbyists. Indexed by subject and geographic area. Includes membership directory of the Public Affairs Council.
Cost: $109.00
Frequency: Annual January

12219 **National Directory of Women Elected Officials**
National Women's Political Caucus
1630 Connecticut Avenue NW
Suite 201
Washington, DC 20009

202-785-1100; Fax: 202-785-3605
info@nwpc.org
www.nwpc.org

Directory of services and supplies to the industry.
230 Pages
Frequency: Biennial

12220 **National and Federal Employment Report**
Federal Reports
1010 Vermont Ave NW
Suite 408
Washington, DC 20005-4945

202-393-1552; Fax: 202-393-1553

Richard L Hermann, Owner

Over 600 current attorney and law-related job opportunities with the US government are listed.
Cost: $111.20
Frequency: Monthly

12221 **New York State Directory**
Grey House Publishing
4919 Route 22
PO Box 56
Amenia, NY 12501

518-789-8700
800-562-2139; Fax: 845-373-6390
books@greyhouse.com
www.greyhouse.com
Facebook, Twitter

Leslie Mackenzie, Publisher
Richard Gottlieb, Editor

A comprehensive and easy-to-use guide to accessing public officials and private sector organizations and individuals who influence public policy in the state of New York. Includes important information on all New York state legislators and congressional representatives, including biographies and key committee assignments.
Cost: $145.00
800 Pages
ISBN: 1-592373-58-5
Founded in 1981

12222 **New York State Directory - Online Database**
Grey House Publishing
4919 Route 22
PO Box 56
Amenia, NY 12501
518-789-8700
800-562-2139; Fax: 845-373-6390
gold@greyhouse.com
gold.greyhouse.com
Facebook, Twitter
Leslie Mackenzie, Publisher
Richard Gottlieb, Editor
A comprehensive and easy-to-use guide to accessing public officials and private sector organizations and individuals who influence public policy in the state of New York. Includes important information on all New York state legislators and congressional representatives, including biographies and key committee assignments. With a subscription to the online database, you'll have immediate access to this wealth of contact information.
Founded in 1981

12223 **Organization Charts**
Carroll Publishing
4701 Sangamore Rd
Suite 155S
Bethesda, MD 20816-2532
301-263-9800
800-336-4240; Fax: 301-263-9805
www.carrollpub.com
Tom Carroll, President
Provide a unique graphic visualization of the personnel relationships in Federal, Defense and Defense Industry organizations. Traditionally used to display report relationships between individuals, these charts are the #1 authoritative source for getting an up-to-date picture of the hierarchy within government, defense and defense contractors, including major aerospace, military hardware and IT companies.
Cost: $1160.00
185 Pages
Frequency: 8x Yearly

12224 **PRRN Directory (Public Record Retriever Network)**
BRB Publications, LLC
3200 W. Pleasant Run Road
Suite 420
Lancaser, TX 75146
800-929-3811; Fax: 800-929-4981
prrn@brbpublications.com
www.prrn.us
Facebook, LinkedIn
Kimberly Sparger, Director of Operations
Offers listings for professional on-site researchers possessing skills in searching court dockets, local recorded documents, and obtaining court information.
Cost: $9.95
400+ Members
240 Pages
Frequency: Annual

12225 **Politics in America**
Congressional Digest
4416 East West Highway
Suite 400
Bethesda, MD 20814-4568
301-634-3113
800-637-9915; Fax: 301-634-3189
www.pro-and-con.org
Offers information on United States senators and representatives.
Cost: $89.95
1700 Pages
Frequency: Biennial

12226 **Profiles of Worldwide Government Leaders**
Worldwide Government Directories
7979 Old Georgetown Road
Suite 900
Bethesda, MD 20814-2429
301-258-2677
800-332-3535; Fax: 301-718-8494
Jonathan Hixon, Publisher
Spanning 195 countries, includes comprehensive biographical snapshots of as many as 30 or more ministers from each country. The material is obtained from primary and secondary sources including embassies, government ministries, offices of the United States government and proprietary global network of correspondents.
Cost: $297.00
850+ Pages
Frequency: Annual

12227 **Public Human Services Directory**
American Public Human Services Association
1133 19th Street NW
Suite 400
Washington, DC 20036-3623
202-682-0100; Fax: 202-289-6555
www.aphsa.org
Tracy Wareing, Executive Director
State-by-state guide to people, programs and a must-have for all human service professionals.
Frequency: Annual
Founded in 1930

12228 **Public Risk Management Association Membership Directory**
500 Montgomery Street
Suite 750
Alexandria, VA 22314
703-528-7701; Fax: 703-739-0200
info@primacentral.org
www.primacentral.org
Jim Hirt, Executive Director
Jon Ruzan, Manager
Kerry Langley, Manager
Lists all members alphabetically; by state/country; by category; government; private; associate. Yellow pages give vender and service provider 50-wind thumbnail descriptions. Advertising sold.
Circulation: 2,000

12229 **US Congress Handbook**
8120 Woodmont Ave.
Suite 110
Bethesda, MD 20814
info@uscongresshandbook.com
www.uscongresshandbook.com
Facebook, Twitter
Washington's most trusted source for information on Congressional offices and their staff. The most comprehensive Congressional directory available.
Frequency: Annually
Founded in 1974

12230 **United States Government Manual**
Office of the Federal Register
National Archives Administration
Washington, DC 20408-0001
202-564-2480; Fax: 202-501-0599
The official handbook of the United States government; includes descriptions and lists of principal personnel of agencies and government bodies.
Cost: $30.00
935 Pages
Frequency: Annual

12231 **Washington Information Directory**
Congressional Quarterly
1414 22nd Street NW
Washington, DC 20037-1003
202-887-8500; Fax: 202-822-6583
Paul McClure, Editor
Will Gardner, Associate Editor
5,000 governmental agencies, congressional committees and non-governmental associations considered competent sources of specialized information.
Cost: $105.00
Frequency: Annual June

12232 **Washington: Comprehensive Directory of the Key Institutions and Leaders**
Columbia Books
1212 New York Avenue NW
Suite 330
Washington, DC 20005-3969
202-641-1662
888-265-0600; Fax: 202-898-0775
info@columbiabooks.com
www.columbiabooks.com
Buck Downs, Senior Editor
Over 5,000 federal and district government offices, businesses, associations, publications, radio and television stations, labor organizations, religious and cultural institutions, health care facilities and community organizations in the District of Columbia area.
Cost: $75.00
Frequency: Annual May

12233 **Worldwide Directory of Defense Attorneys**
Worldwide Government Directories
7979 Old Georgetown Road
Suite 900
Bethesda, MD 20814-2429
301-258-2677
800-332-3535; Fax: 301-718-8494
Jonathan Hixon, Publisher
One-of-a-kind resource covering military and civilian defense and national security agencies from the ministry of defense down to service branches in 195 countries worldwide.
Cost: $647.00
1,100 Pages
Frequency: Annual

12234 **Worldwide Government Directory**
Worldwide Government Directories
7979 Old Georgetown Road
Suite 900
Bethesda, MD 20814-2429
301-258-2677
800-332-3535; Fax: 301-718-8494
Jonathan Hixon, Publisher
Offers valuable information on every senior government official in the executive, legislative, and judicial branches as well as the diplomatic and defense communities of 195 countries worldwide. Plus senior officials in over 100 international organizations. Each entry includes name, address, title, telephone, telex, facsimile number, and more. Also included are current state agencies and corporations, official forms of address, international dialing codes and central bank information.
Cost: $347.00
1,400 Pages
Frequency: Annual

12235 **Worldwide Government Directory with International Organizations**
1414 22nd Street NW
Washington, DC 20037-1003

202-887-8500
800-432-2250; Fax: 800-380-3810
www.cqpress.com

Linda Dziobek, Editor

Coverage includes over 1800 pages of executive, legislative and political branches; heads of state, ministers, deputies, secretaries and spokespersons as well as state agencies, diplomats and senior level defense officials. Also covers the leadership of more than 100 international organizations.
Cost: $450.00
1700 Pages
Frequency: Annually

Industry Web Sites

12236 **http://gold.greyhouse.com**
G.O.L.D Grey House OnLine Databases

Grey House Publishing's online database platform, GOLD, offers Quick Search, Keyword Search and Expert Search for most business sectors including govenment markets. The GOLD platform makes finding the information you need quick and easy - whether you're a novice searcher or an experienced database user. All of Grey House's directory products are available for subscription on the GOLD platform.

12237 **www.aashto.org**
American Association of State Highway and Transportation

Membership is composed of highway and transportation departments in the 50 states, the District of Columbia, and Puerto Rico.

12238 **www.abccert.org**
Association of Boards of Certification

The Association of Boards of Certification is dedicated to protecting public health and the environment by advancing the quality and integrity of environmental certification programs through innovative technical support services, effective information exchange, professional and cost-effective examination services, and other progressive services for certifying members.

12239 **www.accesspro.org**
American Society of Access Professionals

Members are government employees, lawyers, journalists and others concerned with access to government data under current personal privacy and public information statutes.

12240 **www.actnat.com**
Association of Civilian Technicians

Union of civilian employees of the Army and National Guard and Air Reserve.

12241 **www.affirm.org**
Associ for Federal Information Resources Mngt

Seeks to improve the management of information systems and resources of the Federal Government.

12242 **www.afge.org**
American Federation of Government Employees

The largest federal employee union representing 700,000 workers nationwide and overseas.

12243 **www.aglf.org/**
Association for Governmental Leasing and Finance

Provides an exchange of information among tax-exempt issuers, investment banking firms and party lease brokers.

12244 **www.alexandriagroup.com**
National Association of Government Communicators

A merger of Federal Editors Association, the Government Information Organization, and the Armed Forces Writers League.

12245 **www.alldc.org**
American League of Lobbyists

National association dedicated to serving government relations and public affairs professionals. Provides programs and conferences of interest to lobbyists.

12246 **www.ansi.org**
American National Standards Institute

To enhance the global competition of business and quality of life by promoting and facilitating voluntary consensus standards and conformity assessment systems, and safeguarding their integrity.

12247 **www.aphf.org**
American Federation of Police & Concerned Citizens

Operates the American Police Academy as its educational arm. Maintains the American Police Hall of Fame & Museum in Miami, Florida.

12248 **www.aspanet.org**
American Society for Public Administration

Offers a wide range of services and membership options for individuals in public administration careers. Sponsors 127 local chapters and 16 sections on specific areas of governments, such as the Section of Natural Resources and Environmental Administration and the Section on Human Resource Administration.

12249 **www.brbpub.com**
BRB Publications

Public Records Directory and Records search.

12250 **www.brbpublications.com**
BRB Publications

Key resource providing publications, manuals, and databases on finding information from public record sources.

12251 **www.clearhq.org**
Council on Licensure, Enforcement and Regulation

Members include occupational and professional licensing boards and agencies and private interests in the 50 states, territories and Canada.

12252 **www.communityleadership.org**
Community Leadership Association

Founded by 40 community leadership organizations.

12253 **www.coscda.org**
Council for State Community Development Agencies

Employees of state community affairs agencies.

12254 **www.csa-dc.org**
Contract Services Association of America

Represents the government services contracting industry in Washington, DC. Members range from small businesses to large corporations servicing federal and state government in numerous capacities. CSA acts to foster effective implementation of the government's policy of reliance on the private sector for support services.

12255 **www.eba-net.org**
Energy Bar Association

Lawyers engaged in promoting proper administration of federal laws relating to the production, development and economic regulation of energy.

12256 **www.epic.org**
Fund for Constitutional Government

Seeks to expose and correct illegal activities, corruption, and lack of accountability in the federal government.

12257 **www.fbi.gov**
Federal Investigators Association

Formerly the United States Treasury Agents.

12258 **www.fedphy.org**
Federal Physicians Association

The purpose of the Federal Physicians Association is to improve the practice of medicine within the federal government; and to improve the working conditions and benefits of Federal Civil Service Physicians.

12259 **www.foodprotection.org**
International Association for Food Protection

The International Association for Food Protection founded in 1911, is a nonprofit educational association with a mission to provide food safety professionals worldwide with a forum to exchange information on protecting the food supply. The Association is comprised of a cross-section of over 3,000 members from 50 nations. Affiliate chapters are located in the United States, Canada and South Korea.

12260 **www.govexec.com**
National Journal

The website of Government Executive Magazine.

12261 **www.greyhouse.com**
Grey House Publishing

Authoritative reference directories for most business sectors including government markets. Users can search the online databases with varied search criteria allowing for custom searches by product category, geographic area, sales volume, keyword, subject and more. Full Grey House catalog and online ordering also available.

12262 **www.healthfinder.gov**
Association of Food and Drug Officials

Promotes the enforcement of laws and regulations at all levels of government. Fosters understanding and cooperation between industry and regulators. Develops model laws and regulations and seeks their adoption.

12263 **www.ida-downtown.org**
International Downtown Association

Represents organizations and individuals involved in downtown development. Members include city center redevelopment organizations and local officials, businesses, property owners, financiers, planners, university and foundation representatives, and legal and accounting professionals. Offers conferences, technical assistance, consulting services and extensive information services.

12264 **www.iedconline.org**
International Economic Development Council

Nonprofit membership organization serving economic developers by providing information to its members. Members include public economic development directors, chamber of commerce staff, utility executives and academicians, plus the many other professionals who help design and implement development programs.

12265 **www.ihs.com**
International Code Council

Nonprofit membership association with more than 16,000 members who span the building community, from code enforcement officials to materials manufacturers. Dedicated to preserving the public health, safety and welfare in the built environment through the effective use and enforcement of model codes.

12266 **www.imsasafety.org**
International Municipal Signal Association
International resource for information, education and certification for public safety.

12267 **www.iogcc.state.ok.us**
Interstate Oil and Gas Compact Commission
Represents the governors of 37 states that produce virtually all the domestic oil and natural gas in the United States.

12268 **www.leadershipdirectories.com**
Leadership Directories
Offers free online directory of Presidential Transition Team, free online roster of newly elected congressman and subscription information.

12269 **www.nacced.org**
National Association for County Community and Economic Development
Members are directors and staff members of county, community and economic development agencies.

12270 **www.naco.org**
Nat'l Assn of County Information Technology Admin

12271 **www.nagra.org**
North American Gaming Regulators Association
Members are government entities involved in local, state, federal and provincial regulation of gambling activities.

12272 **www.nahma.org**
National Affordable Housing Management Association
Trade association representing companies and individuals involved in the management of affordable multifamily housing.

12273 **www.nahro.org**
Ntl Assoc of Housing & Redevelopment Officials
A professional membership association representing local housing authorities, community development agencies, and individual professionals in the housing, community development, and redevelopment fields.

12274 **www.nalhfa.org**
National Assn. of Local Housing Finance Agencies
County and city agencies which finance affordable housing using tax-exempt annual tools such as the low income housing tax credit and private activity bonds.

12275 **www.napawash.org**
National Academy of Public Administration
An independent, non-profit organization chartered by Congress to improve governance at all levels- local, regional, state, national and international.

12276 **www.napus.org**
National Association of Postmasters of the US
Sponsors and supports the Political Education for Postmasters Political Action Committee.

12277 **www.narc.org**
National Association of Regional Councils
State of regional repositories of instructional materials or services.

12278 **www.nasaa-arts.org**
National Assembly of State Arts Agencies
NASAA's mission is to advance and promote a meaningful role for the arts in the lives of individuals, families and communities throughout the United States. We empower state art agencies through strategic assistance that fosters leadership, enhances planning and decision making, and increases resources. TTD 202-347-5948.

12279 **www.nasaa.org**
North American Securities Administrators Assoc
NASAA is the international organization representing 66 securities administrators from all 50 states, the District of Columbia, Canada, Mexico and Puerto Rico, and is responsible for investor protection and education. NASAA recommends national policies in the securities industry and provides model legislation for state securities agencies to adopt affecting the regulation of broker/dealers and investment advisers. Consumers can contact NASAA to get phone numbers of state securities regulators.

12280 **www.nasar.org**
National Association for Search and Rescue
Members belong to various emergency medical, fire or survival rescue services.

12281 **www.nasda.com**
National Association of State Development Agencies
Established to provide a forum for directors of state economic development agencies to exchange information, compare programs, and establish an organizational base to approach the Federal Government on issues of mutual interest.

12282 **www.nast.net**
Ntl Assoc of State Facilities Administrators
State administrators of facilities and property.

12283 **www.nastad.org**
Nat'l Alliance of State/Territorial AIDS Directors
NASTAD strengthens state and territory-based leadership, expertise, and advocacy and brings them to bear in reducing the incidence of HIV and viral hepatitis infections and on providing care and support to all who live with HIV/AIDS and viral hepatitis. NASTAD's vision is a world free of HIV/AIDS and viral hepatitis.

12284 **www.natat.org**
National Association of Towns and Townships
A nonprofit membership organization offering technical assistance, educational services and public policy support to local officials from more than 13,000 town and township governments across the country. The purpose is to strengthen the effectiveness of town and township governments and promote their interests in the public and private sectors.

12285 **www.nationalhempassociation.org**
A source for news and information on all aspects of the industrial hemp industry, including scientific, legislative, and industry news.

12286 **www.nbpc.net**
National Border Patrol Council
A labor union representing employees of the US border patrol.

12287 **www.ncne.com**
National Center for Neighborhood Enterprise
A research demonstration and development organization providing support and technical assistance to grassroots organizations who are working toward revitalization of urban communities. The Center accomplishes this goal by promoting, and explaining alternative approaches to community development; identifies successful transferable program principles, strategies and techniques; and encouraging policy recommendations to assist neighborhood revitalization.

12288 **www.ncsha.org**
National Council of State Housing Agencies
Represents the views of state housing finance agencies in 48 states. A high priority for the Council is promoting the views of state housing agencies on the issue of delivery of housing financing for low and moderate income people. Other priorities include increasing the stock of affordable rental units and generating innovative approaches to providing public housing acceptable to residents and communities.

12289 **www.ncsl.org**
National Conference of State Legislatures
A bipartisan organization dedicated to serving the lawmakers and staffs of the nations 50 states, its commonwealths and territories.

12290 **www.ndaa.org**
National District Attorneys Association
Voice of America's prosecutors and to support their efforts to protect the rights and safety of the people.

12291 **www.nedaonline.org**
National Community Development Association
A national nonprofit membership organization representing local governments that implement community development programs. The members administer federally supported community development, housing and human services programs. NCDA provides counsel at the federal level on new program design and current program implementation and advocates on behalf of responsive community development.

12292 **www.nemaweb.org**
National Emergency Management Association
Members include federal agencies, local emergency management representatives and interested individuals, associations and corporations.

12293 **www.nfbpa.org**
National Forum for Black Public Administrators
An association for public administrators.

12294 **www.nhlp.org**
National Housing Law Project
A nonprofit corporation that provides assistance on public and private housing and community development matters to Legal Services attorneys and housing specialists throughout the country. The project's goals are to produce, maintain and conserve low and moderate income housing and protect and expand the rights of lower income persons to decent and affordable housing.

12295 **www.nlc.org**
National League of Cities
Advocates on behalf of cities and regularly monitors all three branches of the federal government. Promotes the National Municipal Pol-

icy developed and adopted by member cities at the annual Congress of Cities.

12296 **www.npelra.org**
National Labor Relations Board of Professionals
Represents members in contract negotiations and grievance laws.

12297 **www.nrhcweb.org**
National Rural Housing Coalition
A national membership organization that advocates improved housing for low-income rural families and works to increase public awareness of rural housing problems. The Coalition works with a network of state coalitions and nonprofit organizations to promote federal housing policy that benefits both rural housing and community development programs.

12298 **www.phada.org**
Public Housing Authorities Directors Association
Represents and serves the needs of executive directors of housing authorities of all sizes, in all regions of the nation. In pursuing the Association's goal of improving assisted housing, the corporation works with Congress and federal agencies as well as with all interested groups to improve the nation's housing programs.

12299 **www.postcom.org**
Association for Postal Commerce
National organization representing those who use, or support the use, of mail as a medium for communication and commerce. Postcom publishes a weekly newsletter covering postal policy and operational issues.

12300 **www.ptos.org**
Patent and Trademark Office Society
Members are examiners in the US Patent & Trademark Office, registered patent attorneys and agents, agencies, judges and other patent professionals.

12301 **www.ruralhome.org**
Housing Assistance Council
Expands the pool of decent housing available to the rural poor. Creates and sustains interest and action from all levels of government concerning rural housing for low-income people and helps rural housing organizatins become more productive and professional.

12302 **www.sgac.org**
State Government Affairs Council
Seeks to improve the state legislative process through interaction with major state governmental conferences. Conducts educational programs on public policies to further understanding between private sector businesses and state legislations.

12303 **www.sge-econ.org**
Society of Government Economists
Membership benefits economists employed in the public sector or who are interested in the economic aspects of government policies.

12304 **www.sheeo.org**
State Higher Education Executive Officers
Members are the full-time chief executive officers serving statewide coordinating or governing boards of postsecondary education.

12305 **www.sso.org**
Intl Assoc of Official Human Rights Agencies
Members are state and local government human rights and human relations agencies.

12306 **www.statenews.org**
Council of State Governments
Research and service agency for state governments and state officials.

12307 **www.theiacp.org**
International Association of Chiefs of Police
Has an annual budget of approximately $7 million.

12308 **www.urisa.org**
Urban & Regional Information Systems Association
Concerned with the effective use of information systems technology at the state, regional and local levels. Members informed of current developments in the information systems field. Its goal is to stimulate and encourage the advancement of an interdisciplinary professional approach to planning, designing and operating information systems.

12309 **www.usmayors.org/uscm/**
United States Conference of Mayors
An organization of city government officials.

Associations

12311 **ACM SIGs**
Association for Computing Machinery
1601 Broadway
10th Floor
New York, NY 10019-7434
212-869-7440
800-342-6626; Fax: 212-944-1318
cappo@hq.acm.org
www.acm.org/special-interest-groups
Facebook, Twitter, LinkedIn, YouTube, Google Plus, RSS
Donna Cappo, Director
Diana Brantuas, Conference Program Coordinator
Ashley Cozzi, Assistant Director
Irene Frawley, SIG & Conference Operations
Adrienne Griscti, SIG Publications Manager
The Association for Computing Machinery's Special Interest Group that promotes the generation and dissemination of information on computer graphics and interactive techniques. Areas of focus include programming languages, graphics and interactive techniques, computer-human interaction, artificial intelligence, education and more.
8300+ Members
Founded in 1974

12312 **American Institute of Graphic Arts**
164 Fifth Avenue
New York, NY 10010-5989
212-807-1990; Fax: 212-807-1799
www.aiga.org
Facebook, Twitter, LinkedIn
Richard Grefe, Executive Director
Katie Baker, Director of chapter development
Jennifer Bender, Director of Communications
Elaine Bowen, Director of strategic partnerships
Kathleen Bundy, Program director
To further excellence in design as a broadly defined discipline, strategic tool for business and cultural force. A professional association committed to stimulating thinking about design through the exchange of ideas and information, the encouragement of critical analysis and research and the advancement of education and ethical practice.
18575 Members
Founded in 1922

12313 **Association of Graphic Communications**
330 7th Ave
9th Floor
New York, NY 10001-5010
212-279-2100; Fax: 212-279-5381
www.aiga.org
Serves as a provider of graphic arts education and training, a network for industry information and idea exchange, an advocate for legislative and regulatory/environmental issues, and a vehicle for industry promotion.
560 Members
Founded in 1865

12314 **Design Management Institute**
38 Chauncy St.
Suite 800
Boston, MA 02111
617-338-6380; Fax: 617-338-6570
dmistaff@dmi.org
www.dmi.org
Facebook, Twitter, LinkedIn, YouTube, Flickr
Carole Bilson, President
International nonprofit seeking to improve organizations through design management.
27K Members
Founded in 1975

12315 **Graphic Artists Guild**
32 Broadway
Suite 1114
New York, NY 10004-1612
212-791-3400; Fax: 212-791-0333
admin@graphicartistsguild.org
www.graphicartistsguild.org
Facebook, Twitter, LinkedIn, Google Plus
Haydn Adams, President
Chuck Schultz, Vice President
Lauren Rabinowitz, Treasurer
Lara Kisielewska, Secretary
Patricia McKiernan, Executive Director
Promotes and protects the economic interests of member artists and is committed to improving conditions for all ceators of graphic arts and raising standards for the enitre industry.
1400 Members
Founded in 1967

12316 **Graphic Arts Association**
1210 Northbrook Dr
Suite 200
Trevose, PA 19053-8406
215-396-2300; Fax: 215-396-9890
gaa@gaaonline.org
www.graphicartsassociation.org
Facebook, Twitter
Melissa Jones, President
Bill Scotese, Director of Credit and Collections
Stephen Stankavage, Environmental, Health
Rita Donlan, Bookkeeper/Office Manager
Patti Rose, Administrative Assistant
Mission is to be the leading resource for the printing and graphic communications industry in advocacy, education, and information to enhance the strength and profitability of its members.
400 Members
Founded in 1886

12317 **Guild of Natural Science Illustrators**
Guild of Natural Science Illustrators
P.O. Box 42410
Ben Franklin Station
Washington, DC 20015
301-309-1514; Fax: 301-309-1514
gnsihome@his.com
www.gnsi.org
Amelia Janes, President
Britt Griswold, Vice President
Gail Guth, Membership Secretary
Ikumi Kayama, Secretary
Marjorie Leggitt, Treasurer
A nonprofit organization of persons employed or genuinely interested in the field of natural science illustration. It maintains and encourages high standards of competence and professional ethics by increasing communication among its members. Provides opportunities for professional and scholarly development, and seeks to promote better understanding of the profession among the general public and potential clients requiring the services of natural science illustrators.
1.1M Members
Founded in 1968

12318 **Idealliance**
1800 Diagonal Road
Suite 320
Alexandria, VA 22314
703-837-1070; Fax: 703-837-1072
info@idealliance.org
www.idealliance.org
Dick Ryan, CEO
David Steinhardt, Managing Director
Jordan Gorski, Senior Vice President
Tara Bowmna, Director, Finance & Operations
Evelyn Helminen, Dir., Media, Marketing & Comm.
Idealliance, a global think tank, is a non-profit graphic communications industry organization with 12 strategically located offices around the world. Idealliance serves brands, content and media creators, manufacturers, service providers in print and packaging, fulfillment, mail delivery, marketing, material suppliers, and technology partners worldwide.
3000+ Members
Founded in 1966

12319 **National Association for Printing Leadership (NAPL)**
One Meadowlands Plaza
Suite 1511
East Rutherford, NJ 07073
201-634-9600
800-642-6275; Fax: 201-634-0324
webmaster@napl.org
www.napl.org
Facebook, Twitter, LinkedIn, YouTube, Google Plus, Pinteres
Nigel Worme, Chairman
Niels Winther, Vice Chairman
Joseph P. Truncale, Ph.D., CAE,, President & CEO
Mike Philie, Senior Vice President
Mark R. Hahn, Senior Vice President
A not-for-profit national trade association serving companies in the $100 billion+ graphic communications industry. NAPL offers a comprehensive slate of business and building solutions that provides company leaders with the strategies, insights, and guidance they can use to make informed business decisions, minimize risk, anticipate change, and profitably grow their business.
2000 Members
Founded in 1933

12320 **Pacific Printing & Imaging Association**
6825 SW Sandburg Street
Portland, OR 97223
877-762-7742; Fax: 503-221-5691
info@ppiassociation.org
www.ppiassociation.org
Facebook, Twitter, LinkedIn, YouTube
Jules Van Sant, Executive Director
Dedicated to promoting members and their industries while providing a variety of benefits and money saving programs to Visual & Graphic Communications Companies and individuals in six states. Purpose is to deliver what it takes to help members become more successful and profitable in their businesses.
200 Members
Founded in 1948

12321 **Printing Industries of America**
200 Deer Run Rd
Sewickley, PA 15143-2600
412-741-6860
800-910-4283; Fax: 412-741-2311
info@printing.org
www.printing.org
Facebook, Twitter, LinkedIn, Pinterest
Michael F. Makin, President & CEO
Mary Garnett, Executive Vice President
Nicholas Stratigos, CFO
Ronnie Davis Senior, Vice President & Chief Economist
Lisbeth Lyons, Vice President, Government Affairs
A graphic arts trade association representing our members in this industry. Printing Industries of America, along with its affiliates, deliv-

ers products and services that enhance the growth, efficiency and profitability of its members and the industry through advocacy, education, research and technical information
10000 Members
Founded in 1887

12322 **Society for Environmental Graphic Design**
1900 L Street NW
Suite 710
Washington, DC 20036
202-638-5555; Fax: 202-478-2286
segd@segd.org
www.segd.org
Facebook, Twitter, LinkedIn, RSS
Cybelle Jones, CEO
Jennette Foreman, Director, Events
Sarah Miorelli, Graphic Design Assistant
Nadia Adona, Member Services Associate/Webmaster
Members work in the planning, design, fabrication, and implementation of communications in the built environment. SEGD is the global community of people working at the intersection of communication design and the built environment.
1600+ Members
Founded in 1974

12323 **Society of Publication Designers**
27 Union Square West
Suite 207
New York, NY 10003
212-223-3332; Fax: 212-223-5880
mail@spd.org
www.spd.org
Facebook, Twitter, LinkedIn, Instagram, Spotify
Jeff Glendenning, President
David Matt, Vice President
Trevett McCandliss, Vice President
Keisha Dean, Executive Director
Chelsey Lamwatt, Communications Director
An organization dedicated to promoting and encouraging excellence in editorial design. Members include art directors, designers, photo editors, editors, and graphics professionals.
Founded in 1965

12324 **Technical Association of the Graphic Arts**
200 Deer Run Road
Sewickley, PA 15143
412-259-1706
800-910-4283; Fax: 412-741-2311
www.printing.org/taga
Facebook, Twitter, LinkedIn, Pinterest, Google Plus
Michael F. Makin, President & CEO
Mary Garnett, Executive Vice President
Nicholas Stratigos, CFO
Ronnie Davis Senior, Vice President & Chief Economist
Lisbeth Lyons, Vice President, Government Affairs
Provides a worldwide forum for sharing and disseminating theoretical,functional and practical information on current and emerging technologies for Graphic Arts print production and related processes
900+ Members
Founded in 1948

12325 **The One Club For Creativity**
450 W. 31st St.
6th Floor
New York, NY 10001
212-979-1900; Fax: 212-979-5006
info@oneclub.org
www.oneclub.org
Facebook, Twitter, LinkedIn, Instagram, YouTube
Kevin Swanepoel, Chief Executive Officer
Yash Egami, VP, Content & Marketing
Lucila Lopez Travez, Director of Events & Membership
Jovanne Jerome, Inclusion & Diversity Coordinator
Crystal Ray, Financial Controller
A non-profit organization that supports and celebrates the success of the global creative community. Stimulates the intersection of art and commerce, and creates spaces for artists to grow.

12326 **University & College Designers Association**
199 Enon Springs Rd. W
Suite 400
Smyma, TN 37167
615-459-4559; Fax: 615-459-5229
info@ucda.com
www.ucda.com
Facebook, Twitter, Instagram, Flickr
Tadson Bussey, Executive Director
Chris Klonowski, Assistant Director
Inspires designers working in academia by delivering relevant programming and benefits. Provides for the professional and personal growth of its members, advocates for designers' and educators' roles in their institutions, and elevates the importance of design.
1000 Members
Founded in 1970

Newsletters

12327 **Graphic News**
Printing Industry of Minnesota
2829 University Avenue SE
Suite 750
Minneappolis, MN 55414-3222
612-379-3360
800-448-756; Fax: 618-379-6030
davidr@pimn.org
www.pimn.org
David Radziej, President
Arlene Roth, Director Public Relations
John Connelly, Director of Membership
Carla Steuck, Director of Education Services
Patricia Barnum, CFO
For the printing and graphic arts industries.
16 Pages
Frequency: Bi-Monthly
Circulation: 12000
Founded in 1955

12328 **Graphics Update**
Printing Association of Florida
6095 NW 167 Street
Suite D-7
Miami, FL 33015
305-558-4855
800-331-0461; Fax: 305-823-8965
www.flprint.org
Facebook, Twitter, LinkedIn, Flickr, YouTube
Gene Strul, Editor
Michael H Streibig, Staff Executive
Ron Davis, Chief Economist
A monthly newsletter to the members of the Printing Association of Florida. Full color publication with attractive advertising purchases and a focused buying circulation.
Cost: $200.00
Frequency: Monthly

12329 **Guild News**
Graphic Artists Guild
32 Broadway
Suite 1114
New York, NY 10004-1612
212-791-3400; Fax: 212-791-0333
www.graphicartistsguild.org
Patricia McKiernan, Executive Director
Haydn Adams, President
Chuck Schultz, Vice President
Lauren Rabinowitz, Treasurer
Lara Kisielewska, Secretary
Designed to keep individuals abreast of what's going on with the Guild, the industry, and in the area.
Frequency: Bimonthly

12330 **Holography News**
Reconnaissance International Consulting
PO Box 40976
Denver, CO 80204
303-628-5568; Fax: 303-628-5594
www.reconnaissance-intl.com
Ian Lancaster, Director
Jon Senft, VP
Lewis Kontnik, Publisher
Leading global source of business intelligence on holography and authentication for document security, personal identification and brand protection. Unique knowledge and experience of these highly-specialized and rapidly-changing industries, this newsletter is offering invaluable insight into and authoritative information on markets, strategic management and technical issues through reports, newsleters, conferences, executive briefings and consultancy.
Cost: $774.00
Frequency: Monthly
Founded in 1987

12331 **Messages**
Society of Environmental Graphic Designers
1000 Vermont Ave Nw
Suite 400
Washington, DC 20005-4903
202-638-0891; Fax: 202-638-0891
segd@segd.org
www.segd.org
Facebook, Twitter, LinkedIn
Be the first to hear about new SEGD initiatives, events, and educational resources. Also learn about new contracts, new products, personnel changes, and other news from SEGD member companies. Messages is also the conduit for special SEGD publications and resources such as the ADA White Papers, the SEGD Green Paper, and other valuable educational materials.
Frequency: Monthly

12332 **Postal Beat**
Idealliance
1800 Diagonal Road
Suite 320
Alexandria, VA 22314
703-837-1070; Fax: 703-837-1072
info@idealliance.org
www.idealliance.org
Timothy Baechle, CEO
Jordan Gorski, Global Dir., Certification Programs
Distributed to Idealliance members in the mailing and fulfillment segments of the graphic communications industry. It is designed to keep members regularly informed on key mailing issues and to support mail professionals in meeting the ongoing challenges of mail distribution.
3000+ Members
Frequency: Monthly
Founded in 1966

Magazines & Journals

12333 **Animation Magazine**
Animation Magazine
30941 Agoura Rd
suite 102
Westlake Villag, CA 91361-4637

818-991-2884; Fax: 818-991-3773
info@animationmagazine.net
www.animationmagazine.net

Jean Thoren, President

Covers the animation industry trends, technology, new products, historical perspectives coverage of current animated programming and features, and general news.
Cost: $65.07
Frequency: Monthly
Founded in 1985
Printed in 4 colors on glossy stock

12334 **Before & After: How to Design Cool Stuff**
Pagelab
323 Lincoln Street
Roseville, CA 95678-2229

956-78 -229
800-266-5783; Fax: 916-784-3995
www.bamagazine.com
Facebook, Twitter, YouTube

John McWade, Publisher
Gaye McWade, Editor

Practical approach to graphic design. Dedicated to making graphic design understandable, useful and even fun for everyone.
Cost: $36.00
Circulation: 26000
Founded in 1990

12335 **Cadalyst**
Longitude Media

Home Page: www.cadalyst.com
Facebook, Twitter

Nancy Spurling Johnson, Editor-in-Chief
Cyrena Respini-Irwin, Senior Editor

The most complete source of essential information about computer-aided design and related software and hardware technologies for the fields of AEC, manufacturing, and GIS. Delivers timely, objective, and practical product reviews and updates, tips, tutorials, insight, and advice to help CAD managers and users make informed decisions about technology, get productive, and get the job done.
Cost: $39.95
100 Pages
Frequency: Monthly
Circulation: 90000
ISSN: 0360-3520
Founded in 1987
Printed in 4 colors

12336 **Communication Arts**
Coyne & Blanchard
110 Constitution Dr
Menlo Park, CA 94025-1107

650-326-6040; Fax: 650-326-1648
editorial@commarts.com
www.commarts.com

Patrick Coyne, Publisher
Ernie Schenck, Creative Director
Mike Krigel, Marketing Executive

Features profile individuals, studios and agencies with examples of their work. Includes reviews of software, books and products, as well as discussing the latest in digital and broadcast design.
Cost: $53.00
Frequency: 8 issues per ye
Circulation: 71927
ISSN: 0010-3519
Founded in 1959
Printed in 4 colors

12337 **Computer Graphics World**
COP Communications, Inc.
620 W. Elk Ave
Glendale, CA 91204

603-432-7568
karen@cgw.com
www.cgw.com

Karen Moltenbrey, Chief Editor
William R. Rittwage, Publisher, President & CEO
Kelly Ryan, Marketing Coordinator
Michael Viggiano, Art Director

Covers specific applications of computer graphics, written by users and vendors of equipment and services to the industry. The magazine of 3D computer graphics for engineering and animation professionals.
Cost: $55.00
Frequency: Monthly
Circulation: 40597
Founded in 1977
Printed in 4 colors on glossy stock

12338 **Critique**
Neumeier Design Team
120 Hawthorne Avenue
#102
Palo Alto, CA 94301-1000

650-326-4396; Fax: 650-323-3298
www.critiquemag.com

Marty Neumeier, Editor

Features include methods and products to increase the creativity and technological advance of graphic artwork.
Cost: $60.00
Frequency: Quarterly
Circulation: 10000

12339 **Desktop Publishers Journal**
Desktop Publishing Institute
462 Boston Street
Topsfield, MA 01983-1200

FAX 978-887-9245

Thomas Tetreault, Publisher
Barry Harrigan, Editor

Desktop publishing topics and issues and association information.
Frequency: Weekly
Circulation: 60000

12340 **Digital Imaging**
Cygnus Publishing
3 Huntington Quadrangle
Suite 301N
Melville, NY 11747

631-845-2700
800-308-6397; Fax: 631-845-2798

Laureen Delaney, Associate Publisher
Kathy Schneider, Group Publisher
Andrew Darlow, Editorial Director
Liz Vickers, Advertising Sales Manager
Paul Bonaiuto, CFO

For the imaging professional. Dedicated to bridging the digital imaging gap between graphics and photography while providing in-depth solutions.
Circulation: 30,000
Founded in 1966

12341 **Dynamic Graphics**
Dynamic Graphics
6000 N Forest Park Drive
Peoria, IL 61614-3592

309-888-8851
888-698-8542; Fax: 800-488-3492
www.dynamicgraphics.com

Alan Meckler, President, JupiterMedia
David Moffly, President/CEO
Marcy Slane, Managing Editor

Encourages users to take their electronic tools to the next level of productivity and creativity. Emphasizes practical and real-world solutions.
Cost: $36.00
72 Pages
Frequency: 6
Circulation: 66143
ISSN: 1094-2548
Founded in 1964
Printed in on glossy stock

12342 **GATFWORLD Magazine**
Graphic Arts Technical Foundation Association
200 Deer Run Road
Sewickley, PA 15143-2324

412-741-6860
800-910-4283; Fax: 412-741-2311
www.gain.net

George Ryan, Executive VP/COO
Michael Makin, President/CEO
Deanna Gentile, Editor

A bi-monthly magazine for GATF members and subscribers that reports on research and technical trends in the graphic arts (printing) industry, environmental and safety news, developments in graphic communications education and news of emerging products, programs and services.
Cost: $75.00
Circulation: 18000
Founded in 1924

12343 **Gasp Report**
GASP Engineering
234 Benjamin W Avenue
Swarthmore, PA 19081-1421

610-543-5194
800-256-4282; Fax: 610-328-1358

Steve Hannaford, Publisher

Covers new technology, financing, marketing and other business concerns of the printing, graphics and publishing industries. In-depth articles highlight strategies for industry professionals.
Cost: $195.00
Frequency: Monthly
Circulation: 400

12344 **Graphic Arts Monthly**
360 Park Avenue S
New York, NY 10010

212-636-6834
800-217-7874; Fax: 646-746-7422

Phil Saran, Publisher
Roger Ynostroza, Editorial Director

The magazine of the printing industry including commercial, in-plant and related operations, such as color separations, composition, binding and pre-press service bureaus.
Frequency: Monthly
Circulation: 75,000

12345 **Graphic Design: USA**
Kaye Publishing Corporation

641 Lexington Ave
Suite 1202
New York, NY 10022-4503

212-259-0400; Fax: 212-489-4736
gkaye@gdusa.com
www.gdusa.com

M Kaye, Owner
Maria Mohamed, Circualtion Manager
Gordon D. Kaye, Publisher

A publication for the graphic designer, offering information and news of the industry.
Cost: $60.00
120 Pages
Frequency: Monthly
ISSN: 0274-7499
Founded in 1965

12346 **Graphics Pro**
Graphic Products Association
4709 N El Capitan Avenue
Suite 103
Fresno, CA 93722

559-276-8494
800-276-8428; Fax: 559-276-8496
www.gpionline.org

Michael R Neer, Publisher
Steven V Neer, Associate Publisher
Damara Torres, Owner

A bi-monthly journal published by the Graphic Products Association.
Cost: $55.00
Circulation: 7500
Founded in 1994
Printed in on glossy stock

12347 **Graphis**
Graphis Press
307 5th Ave
10th Floor
New York, NY 10016-6517

212-532-9387
866-648-2915; Fax: 212-213-3229
info@graphis.com
www.graphis.com

Martin Pederson, Owner
Walter Herdeg, Editor

Graphis is an international journal of design and visual communication, covering graphic arts, design, photography, architecture and related topics. The targeted readership includes professionals in these disciplines as well as all creative visual communicators.
Cost: $90.00
Circulation: 22000
Founded in 1944

12348 **HOW Magazine**
F&W Publications
4700 E Galbraith Rd
Cincinnati, OH 45236-2726

513-531-2690; Fax: 513-531-1843
editorial@howdesign.com

David Nussbaum, CEO
Bryn Mooth, Editor
William R. Reed, President
Jim Ogle, Chief Financial Officer
Kate Rados, Marketing Director

Business and creative resource for graphic designers. Latest business, technological and creative information.
Cost: $49.00
194 Pages
Circulation: 39946
ISSN: 0886-0483
Founded in 1900
Printed in 4 colors on glossy stock

12349 **ID Magazine**
38 East 29th Street
Floor 3
New York, NY 10016

212-447-1400
800-258-929; Fax: 212-447-5231
www.id-mag.com

Kelly N Kofron, Executive Editor
Dave Richmond, Executive Editor

Leading critical magazine covering the art, business and culture of design.
Frequency: 8 per year

12350 **PC Graphics & Video**
Advanstar Communications
Ste 300
17770 Cartwright Rd
Irvine, CA 92614-5815

714-513-8400; Fax: 714-513-8481
info@advanstar.com
www.advanstar.com

Michael Forcillo, Publisher
Gene Smarte, Chief Executive Officer

Covers graphics and video for personal computers.
Cost: $5.00
Circulation: 10,699

12351 **Print Magazine**
RC Publications
38 E 29th Street
3rd Floor
New York, NY 10016

212-447-1400; Fax: 212-447-5231
info@printmag.com
www.printmag.com

Joyce Rutter Kay, Editor in Chief
Joel Toner, Publisher
Stephany Skirvin, Art Director
Steven Kent, CEO
William Reed, President

News and information for the graphic design industry.
Cost: $53.00
160 Pages
Circulation: 45000
ISSN: 0032-8510
Founded in 1940
Printed in 4 colors on glossy stock

12352 **Printer's Northwest Trader**
Eagle Newspapers
650 N 1st Street
PO Box 96
Woodburn, OR 97071-450

503-981-3441; Fax: 503-981-1253
www.eaglenewspapers.com

Rod Stollery, Publisher
Sandy Hubbard, Founder
Elmo Smith, Founder

Reviews new equipment and techniques and highlights industry leaders of note. Serves the northwestern portion of the United States.
Cost: $10.00
Frequency: Monthly
Circulation: 16000
Founded in 1933

12353 **Publication Design Annual #39**
Society of Publication Designers
17 East 47th Street
6th Floor
New York, NY 10017

212-223-3332; Fax: 212-223-5880
mail@spd.org

Bruce Ramsay, President
Amid Capeci, Treasurer
Gail Bichler, Treasurer
Nancy Stamatopoulos, Secretary

A compendium of the best designed magazine/trade and consumer newspapers. Annual reports of the year as judged by a panel. Also includes web and interactive design sites and annual reports.
Cost: $195.00
Frequency: Monthly
Circulation: 15000
ISBN: 1-564966-21-6
Founded in 1969
Printed in 4 colors on matte stock

12354 **Publish How-to Magazine**
MacWorld Communications
501 2nd St
Suite 310
San Francisco, CA 94107-1496

415-243-0505; Fax: 415-442-0766

Mike Kisseberth, CEO
Susan Gubemat, Editor

The definitive source on how to use personal computers to integrate text and graphics into printed communication.
Cost: $4.00
Circulation: 98,819

12355 **Sign & Digital Graphics**
National Business Media
PO Box 1416
Broomfield, CO 80038-1416

303-469-0424
800-669-0424; Fax: 303-465-3424
www.sdgmag.com

Mary Tohill, Publisher
Ken Mergentime, Executive Editor
Matt Dixon, Managing Editor
James Kochevar, Associate Publisher
Sara Siauw, Production Coordinator

The most widely read industry trade publication covering the business of visual communications and offering a broad range of in-depth reporting for sign industry and wide-format digital graphics professionals. This distinguished and unique magazine provides comprehensive professional coverage on all aspects of commercial signage, commercial graphics production, electric LED-based signage and letter systems, architectural signage, electronic digital displays, vehicle wraps, and much more.
Frequency: Monthly

12356 **Southern Graphics**
PTN Publishing Company
445 Broadhollow Road
Suite 21
Melville, NY 11747-3601

FAX 631-845-7109

Rob Schweiger, Publisher
KJ Moran, Editor

Edited for those in the graphic arts industry throughout the southeastern US and the Caribbean.
Cost: $5.00
Circulation: 21,000

12357 **TAGA Journal of Graphic Technology**
Technical Association of the Graphic Arts
200 Deer Run Road
Sewickley, PA 15143

412-259-1706; Fax: 412-741-2311
www.taga.org

Mark Bohan, Managing Director

A peer-reviewed journal designed to meet the needs of the global professional graphic applications industries and to bring together the multi-disciplinary community in further development of printing as a manufacturing process. Embraces the fundamental science and technology, application and technology transfer and the genergic problems and experience associated

with the management and implementation of graphic applications.
900+ Members
Frequency: Bi-Annually
Founded in 1948

12358 **Trade Show Times**
Fichera Communications
441 S State Road
Suite 14
Margate, FL 33063

954-971-4360
800-327-8999; Fax: 954-971-4362
www.tradeshowtimes.com

Orazio Fichera, Publisher
Rick Kelly, Contact

Hand distributed to attendees at major graphic arts trade shows. Accepts advertising.
32 Pages
Frequency: Monthly
Founded in 1974

12359 **Visual Communications Journal**
Graphic Arts Technical Foundation Association
200 Deer Run Road
Sewickley, PA 15143-2324

412-741-6860
800-910-4283; Fax: 412-741-2311
www.gain.net

George Ryan, Executive VP/COO
Michael Makin, President/CEO
Peter Oresick, VP Publishing

Educational guide and news for scholars and students studying the graphic arts industry.

12360 **segdDESIGN**
Society for Environmental Graphic Design
1000 Vermont Ave NW
Suite 400
Washington, DC 20005-4921

202-638-5555; Fax: 202-638-0891
pat@segd.org
www.segd.org

The magazine of choice for creative professionals working at the intersection of communication design and the built environment. A rich source of information on the key people, research, technologies, materials, and resources that influence communications in the built environment. International Journal of Environmental Graphic Design
Frequency: Quarterly

Trade Shows

12361 **3D Design & Animation Conference & Expo**
Miller Freeman Publications
525 Market Street
Suite 500
San Francisco, CA 94110

415-955-5533; Fax: 415-278-5341
www.mfi.com

For animators and digital content creators, exibits include equipment supplies and services for the 3D design and animation industry. Conferences, reception and publications. Space rental available.
Frequency: Annual

12362 **Grafix**
Conference Management Corporation
200 Connecticut Avenue
Norwalk, CT 06854-1940

800-342-3238; Fax: 203-831-8446

Annual show of 200 exhibitors of computer hardware and software for graphic design and computer publishing, paper supplies, typesetting equipment and services, stock photography, clip art service and related equipment, supplies and services.
4000 Attendees

12363 **Graph Expo**
Graphic Arts Show Company
1189 Preston White Drive
Reston, VA 20191-5435

703-264-7200; Fax: 703-620-9187
www.graphexpo.com

Where top executives come to learn, network and make informed intelligent purchasing decisions. Leading manufacturers and suppliers will be exhibiting at the show and many of them will be showcasing newly released products, technologies and services. The year's largest and most exciting display of live running equipment in the Americas.
40000 Attendees
Frequency: Annual/September

12364 **Graph Expo West**
Graphic Arts Show Company
1899 Preston White Drive
Reston, VA 20191

703-264-7200; Fax: 703-620-9187
info@gasc.org
www.gasc.org

Lilly Kinney, Conference Manager
Chris Theil, Administrative Assistant
Erin Omwake, Administrative Assistant
Deborah Vieder, Director of Communications

Two hundred booths for the graphics industry.
13M Attendees
Frequency: November
Founded in 1982

12365 **Graphics Trade Show Expo Southwest**
910 W Mockingbird Lane
Dallas, TX 75247-5182
Jim Weinstein, Show Manager
Six hundred and fifty booths.
13M Attendees
Frequency: June

12366 **Graphics of the Americas**
Printing Association of Florida
6275 Hazeltine National Drive
Orlando, FL 32822

407-240-8009; Fax: 407-240-8333
www.flprint.org

Holly Price, Booth Sales & Marketing
Michelle Torres, Attendee Info.

Largest annual international graphic commincations education and exhibit showplace. Over 450 exhibitors in 500,000 square feet.
22000 Attendees
Frequency: February

12367 **Gutenberg & Digital Outlook**
Graphic Arts Show Company
1189 Preston White Drive
Reston, VA 22091

703-264-7200; Fax: 703-620-9187
info@gasc.org
www.gasc.org

Chris Thiel, VP
Kelly Kilga, Administrative Assistant
Erin Omwake, Administrative Assistant
Deborah Vieder, Director of Communications

Largest graphic design, digital prepress, printing, publishing, and converting trade show in the Westen United States. Over 100 exhibitors with the widest selection of vendors.
8000 Attendees
Frequency: Annual,June

12368 **IMPA Annual Conference**
In-Plant Printing and Mailing Association
125 S. Jefferson
Suite B-4
Kearney, MO 64060

816-903-4762; Fax: 816-902-4766
www.ipma.org

John Sarantakos, Administrator
Larry Wright, Treasurer

Annual educational conference and vending show.

12369 **Printing Expo Conference Mid America**
Graphics Arts Show Company
1899 Preston White Drive
Reston, VA 20191

703-264-7200; Fax: 703-620-9187
info@gasc.org
www.gasc.org

Paul Kaplan, Show Manager
Erin Omwake, Administrative Assistant
Deborah Vieder, Director of Communications

Exhibits by manufacturers and dealers of the latest graphics equipment and services.
3000 Attendees
Frequency: June
Founded in 1982

12370 **Sunbelt Computer and Graphics**
Printing Industry Association of Georgia
5020 Highlands Parkway
Smyrna, GA 30082

770-433-3050
800-288-1894; Fax: 770-433-3062

Dianne McPherson, Trade Show Director
Denise Holland, VP Communications

Two hundred and fifty exhibitors of current printing technology.
18M Attendees

12371 **UCDA Design Conference**
University & College Designers Association
199 Enon Springs Rd. W
Suite 400
Smyma, TN 37167

615-459-4559; Fax: 615-459-5229
info@ucda.com
www.ucda.com
Facebook, Twitter, Instagram, Flickr

Tadson Bussey, Executive Director
Chris Klonowski, Assistant Director

A national conference for design students and professionals. Features keynotes, panels, workshops, a design show, and plenty of networking opportunities.
1000 Members
Frequency: Annual, Fall
Founded in 1970

12372 **UCDA Design Education Summit**
University & College Designers Association
199 Enon Springs Rd. W
Suite 400
Smyma, TN 37167

615-459-4559; Fax: 615-459-5229
info@ucda.com
www.ucda.com
Facebook, Twitter, Instagram, Flickr

Tadson Bussey, Executive Director
Chris Klonowski, Assistant Director

A national summit for design educators, chairs, and students that offers many opportunities for professional participation and development.

Features keynotes, panels, workshops, and paper and poster presentations.
1000 Members
Frequency: Annual, Spring
Founded in 1970

12373 **UCDA Design Summit**
University & College Designers Association
199 Enon Springs Rd. W
Suite 400
Smyma, TN 37167

615-459-4559; Fax: 615-459-5229
info@ucda.com
www.ucda.com
Facebook, Twitter, Instagram, Flickr

Tadson Bussey, Executive Director
Chris Klonowski, Assistant Director

Features experienced speakers and focused sessions on key topics in design, including technologies and resources that can help your daily work flow.
1000 Members
Frequency: Annual, Spring
Founded in 1970

Directories & Databases

12374 **365: AIGA Year In Design**
American Institute of Graphic Arts
164 Fifth Avenue
New York, NY 10010-5989

212-807-1990
www.aiga.org
Facebook, Twitter, LinkedIn

Doug Powell, President
Zia Khan, Secretary/ Treasurer
Richard Grefe, Executive Director

About 500 works of graphic designers that have been cited for outstanding design by the American Institute of Graphic Arts.
Cost: $45.00
Frequency: Annual

12375 **Graphic Artist's Guide to Marketing and Self-Promotion**
North Light Books
1557 Dana Avenue
Cincinnati, OH 45207-1005

FAX 513-531-4082

A list of publishers of resources about marketing for the graphic artist.
Cost: $19.95

12376 **Graphic Arts Blue Book**
AF Lewis & Company
360 Lexington Ave
Suite 21
New York, NY 10017-6529

212-682-8448; Fax: 212-682-2442
www.d-net.com/graphartsbb

Andrew Lewis, Owner
Timothy Lewis, Editor

Offers information on printing plants, bookbinders, imagesetters, platemakers, paper merchants, paper manufacturers, printing machinery manufacturers and dealers and others serving the graphic arts industry.
Cost: $85.00
Frequency: 8 Annual Editions
Circulation: 51500

12377 **Graphic Arts Monthly Sourcebook**
Reed Business Information
2000 Clearwater Dr
Oak Brook, IL 60523-8809

630-574-0825; Fax: 630-288-8781
www.reedbusiness.com

Jeff Greisch, President
Bill Esler, Editor-in_Chief
Roger Ynostroza, Editorial Director

About 1,400 manufacturers and distributors of graphic arts equipment, supplies and services, as well as over 700 graphic arts dealers.
Cost: $50.00
Frequency: Annual March
Circulation: 85,000

12378 **Publication Design Annual**
Society of Publication Designers
27 Union Square West
Suite 207
New York, NY 10003

212-223-3332; Fax: 212-223-5880
mail@spd.org
www.spd.org

Keisha Dean, Executive Director
Chelsey Lamwatt, Communications Director

Celebrates the journalists, editorial directors, photographers, and other talented individuals who brought the year with all its triumphs and disasters to light. Featuring work published in a wide range of mediums and created by journalistic, design, and publishing talent from around the world.
ISBN: 1-592531-81-4
Founded in 1965

12379 **RSVP: Directory of Illustration and Design**
RSVP
PO Box 050314
Brooklyn, NY 11205

718-857-9267
info@rsvpdirectory.com
www.rsvpdirectory.com

Kathleen Creighton, Co-Publisher/Co-Editor
Richard Lebenson, Co-Publisher/Co-Editor

Fully illustrated resource book for the graphic arts/media industry. Showcases work of illustrators and designers, nationwide.
Circulation: 18,000

Industry Web Sites

12380 **Creative Business**
38 Indian Rd.
Suite 200
Marshfield, MA 02050
617-451-0041
mail@creativebusiness.com
www.creativebusiness.com
Facebook, LinkedIn, YouTube

Cameron S. Foote, Editor

Business resources - forms, articles, books - for creative services organizations and freelancers.

12381 **http://gold.greyhouse.com**
G.O.L.D Grey House OnLine Databases

Grey House Publishing's online database platform, GOLD, offers Quick Search, Keyword Search and Expert Search for most business sectors including graphic design markets. The GOLD platform makes finding the information you need quick and easy - whether you're a novice searcher or an experienced database user. All of Grey House's directory products are available for subscription on the GOLD platform.

12382 **www.aiga.org**
American Institute of Graphic Arts

The purpose of the AIGA is to further excellence in a communication design as a broadly defined discipline, as a strategic tool for business and as a cultural force. The AIGA is the place design professionals turn first to exchange ideas and information, participate in critical analysis and research and advance education and ethical practice.

12383 **www.gaa1900.com**
Graphic Arts Association

Promotes the interests of graphic art professionals. Members consist of suppliers and distributors of graphic arts equipment.

12384 **www.gatf.org**
Graphic Arts Technical Foundation Association

To serve the graphic comunications community as the leading source for the technical information and services through research and education.

12385 **www.graphicartistsguild.org**
Graphic Artists Guild

Promotes and protects the economic interests of member artists and is committed to improving conditions for all ceators of graphic arts and raising standards for the enitre industry.

12386 **www.greyhouse.com**
Grey House Publishing

Authoritative reference directories for most business sectors including graphic design markets. Users can search the online databases with varied search criteria allowing for custom searches by product category, geographic area, sales volume, keyword, subject and more. Full Grey House catalog and online ordering also available.

12387 **www.idealliance.org**
Idealliance

Provides the opportunity for those who create, produce, manage, and deliver content to interface with those who develop the software tools to facilitate these functions.

12388 **www.myfonts.com**
MyFonts.com

Allows a user to find fonts with simple keywords. The user can test a font. The site also offers a MyFonts forum, where users can ask the experts

12389 **www.nagasa.org**
North American Graphic Arts Suppliers Association

The association for the channel that distributes printing and imaging technologies.

12390 **www.napl.org**
National Association for Printing Leadership

NAPL publishes industry specific books and periodicals for the graphic arts community. Topics cover management in the areas of sales, marketing, human resources, finance and operations technology.

12391 **www.ppi-assoc.org**
Pacific Printing & Imaging Association

To provide programs, offer services, and promote an environment, which assists members to see and adapt to the future, while continuing to improve and profit in the present.

12392 **www.recouncil.org**
Research and Engineering Council of the National
Association for Printing Leadership

A technical trade association established to identify graphic arts industry problems, coordinate graphic arts technical activities and develop industry associated technical/education programs, conference and seminars.

12393 **www.siggraph.org**
Special Interest Group on Computer Graphics

A forum for the promotion and distribution of current computer graphics research and technology.

12394 **www.taga.org**
Technical Association of the Graphic Arts

Organized to advance the science and technology of graphic arts. Disseminates graphic arts research internationally via annual technical conference and proceedings.

12395 **www.ucda.org**
University & College Designers Association

Inspires designers working in academia by delivering relevant programming and benefits. Provides resources for design professionals in all aspects of design.

Associations

12396 American Ladder Institute
330 N. Wabash
Suite 200
Chicago, IL 60611

312-321-6806; Fax: 312-673-6929
info@americanladderinstitute.org
www.americanladderinstitute.org
Facebook, Twitter, LinkedIn, YouTube

Pam O'Brien, Executive Director
Martin Jimenez, Operations Coordinator
Claire Sereiko, Marketing Senior Coordinator
Emily Palmeri, Marketing Association

Members include manufacturers of wood, metal and fiberglass ladders. Represents US companies engaged in the research, development, manufacture and safety ladders. Develops appropriate standards.

12397 Associated Locksmiths of America
3500 Easy St
Dallas, TX 75247

214-819-9733
800-532-2562; Fax: 214-819-9736
jim@aloa.org
www.aloa.org
Facebook, Twitter, LinkedIn

Mary May, Executive Director
Tom Foxwell, President
Clyde Roberson, Secretary

International professional organization of highly qualified security professionals engaged in consulting,sales,installation and maintenance of locks,keys,safes,premises security,access controls,alarms, and other secutriy relates endeavors.
10000 Members

12398 Builders Hardware Manufacturers Association
355 Lexington Avenue
15th Floor
New York, NY 10017

212-297-2122; Fax: 212-370-9047
www.buildershardware.com
LinkedIn

Patricia Yulkowski, President
John Cringole, 1st Vice President
Mark Bloom, 2nd Vice President
Tim Weller, 3rd Vice President

The trade association for North American manufacturers of commercial builders hardware. Nationally recognized for its leadership role in ensuring the quality and performance of builders hardware. Any organization that manufactures and sells builders hardware in the United States is eligible for Association membership.
Founded in 1925

12399 Door & Hardware Institute
2001 K Street NW
Washington, DC 20006

202-367-1134; Fax: 202-367-2134
www.dhi.org
Facebook, Twitter, LinkedIn

Sharon Newport, CAE, Chief Executive Officer
Laura Frye Weaver, VP, Education
Adam Berkshire, Communications/Marketing Manager

The Door & Hardware Institute (DHI) is the only professional association dedicated to the Architectural Openings Industry. DHI represents the North American openings marketplace as the advocate and primary resource for information, professional development and certification.

12400 Hand Tools Institute
25 North Broadway
Tarrytown, NY 10591-3221

914-332-0040; Fax: 914-332-1541
info@hti.org
www.hti.org

Trade association of North American manufacturers of non-powered hand tools and tool boxes. The objectives of the Institute are to promote and further the interests of its members relative to manufacturing, safety, standardization, international trade and government relations.
Founded in 1935

12401 International Door Association
1 Parkview Plaza
Suite 800
Oakbrook Terrace, IL 60181

202-591-2457
800-355-4432; Fax: 202-591-2445
info@doors.org
www.doors.org
Facebook, Twitter, LinkedIn, YouTube

Mike Fischer, Executive Director
Monica Saunders, Meetings/Exposition Manager
Lori Barker-Cummings, Managing Director
Melanie Goff, Member Service & Engagement Manager
Delia Murphy, Communications Program Director

Supports all those in the door and door operator industry, especially garage doors, installation hardware, roller shades and garage door openers. Publishes bimonthly magazine.
Founded in 1996

12402 Midwest Hardware Association
5000 Woodward Dr. Suite A
P.O. Box 8033
Stevens Point, WI 54481

800-888-1817; Fax: 715-341-4080
johnh@midwesthardware.com
www.midwesthardware.com

John Haka, Managing Director
Andrea Ramage, Meber Services Coordinator
Sam Schmidt, Communications Coordinator

Nonprofit supporting independent hardware, lumber and building supply retailers.
Founded in 1896

12403 National Lumber & Building Material Dealers Association (NLBMDA)
2025 M Street, NW
Suite 800
Washington, DC 20036-3309

202-367-1169; Fax: 202-367-2169
membersupport@dealer.org
www.dealer.org
Facebook, Twitter, LinkedIn

Jonathan M. Paine, CAE, President & CEO
Kevin McKenney, Director, Government Affairs
Alex McIntyre, Legislative & Regulatory Coord.
Allison Ward, Membership & Operations Associate
Corie Stretton, Event Manager

Promoting the industry and educating legislators and public policy personnel, assising legislative, regulatory, standard-setting and other government or private bodies in the development of laws, regulations and policies affecting lumber and building material dealers, its customers and suppliers.
6M Members
Founded in 1917

12404 North American Retail Hardware Association
136 N. Delaware St.
Suite 200
Indianapolis, IN 46204

317-275-9400
800-772-4424; Fax: 317-275-9403
nrha@nrha.org
www.nrha.org
Facebook, Twitter, YouTube

Serving the needs of independent hardware retailers in the United States and Canada. Purpose is to help independent home improvement retailers become better and more profitable merchants. Providing members with a wide array of educational and training programs, financial management resources and human resource tools that are all available online with unlimited access.
Founded in 1805

Newsletters

12405 Door & Hardware IndustryWatch
Door & Hardware Institute
2001 K Street NW
Washington, DC 20006

202-367-1134; Fax: 202-367-2134
www.dhi.org

Sharon Newport, CAE, Chief Executive Officer
Laura Frye Weaver, VP, Education
Adam Berkshire, Communications/Marketing

Electronic newsletter with the latest industry news and trends.
Frequency: Biweekly

Magazines & Journals

12406 Brushware
750-B NW Broad St.
Southern Pines, NC 28387

910-693-2644; Fax: 910-246-1681
www.brushwaremag.com

Norman J. Finegold, President
Karen Grinter, Publisher

Contains information of interest to manufacturers and suppliers of brushes, mops, rollers, brooms, pads, mitts, and the like. Topics include application techniques, news, product information, development, sales, and interviews.
Cost: $65.00
Frequency: Bimonthly
Circulation: 3000
Founded in 1898

12407 Door Security & Safety Magazine
Door & Hardware Institute
2001 K Street NW
Washington, DC 20006

202-367-1134; Fax: 202-367-2134
www.dhi.org

Sharon Newport, CAE, Chief Executive Officer
Laura Frye Weaver, VP, Education
Adam Berkshire, Communications/Marketing Manager

Offers information and articles from the industry's only publication dedicated solely to the architectural openings industry.
Frequency: Monthly

12408 Hardware Retailing
North American Retail Hardware Association
136 N. Delaware St.
Indianapolis, IN 46204

317-275-9400
800-772-4424; Fax: 317-275-9403

nrha@nrha.org
www.hardwareretailing.com

Bob Cutter, President & CEO
Dan Tratensek, Executive VP & Publisher
Lowell Huffman, National Sales Manager
Whitney Daulton, Director of Communications

The hardware and home improvement industry's leading trade publication. Covers hard hitting issues many retailers in the industry face. Content includes practical profitability advice and up-and-coming new products from the industry's leading manufacturers.
Cost: $50.00
Frequency: Monthly
Circulation: 36000
Founded in 1901

12409 **Hearth & Home**
Village West Publishing
P.O. Box 1288
Laconia, NH 03247

603-528-4285
800-258-3772; Fax: 888-873-3610
wright@villagewest.com
www.hearthandhome.com
Facebook, LinkedIn

Richard Wright, Editor
Jackie Avignone, Advertising Director
Erica Paquette, Art Director

Information for retailers and others selling hearth products, patio furnishing, barbecues, spas, garden accessories, and other outdoor products.
Frequency: Monthly
Founded in 1980

12410 **International Door & Operator Industry**
International Door Association
1 Parkview Plaza
Suite 800
Oakbrook Terrace, IL 60181

202-591-2457
800-355-4432; Fax: 202-591-2445
info@doors.org
www.doors.org

Greg Opt, Magazine Production, Sales, Ads
Tina Opt, Magazine Press Releases
LeAnne Munoz, Marketing Communications Manager

The first magazine published specifically for the door and access systems industry. Informing the industry about new products, new services, and the latest industry news. In addition, the publication features articles directed to help both door and access systems dealers and those who provide them products and services.
Circulation: 14000
Founded in 1996

12411 **Keynotes**
Associated Locksmiths of America
3500 Easy St.
Dallas, TX 75247

214-819-9733
800-532-2562; Fax: 214-819-9736
www.aloa.org

Betty Handerson, Editor
Mary May, Executive Director

Technical magazine for locksmiths.
Frequency: Monthly
Circulation: 8000
Founded in 1956

12412 **Outdoor Power Equipment**
10405 6th Ave. N
Suite 210
Minneapolis, MN 55441

763-383-4421
dvoll@epgmediallc.com
www.outdoorpowerequipment.com
Facebook

David Voll, Publisher
John Kmitta, Assoc. Publisher/Editor
Samantha VanKempen, Production Manager

Serves retailers and distributors who sell and service outdoor power equipment products, including retailers, lawn and garden supply retailers, farm supply retailers, hardware store retailers, home centers, and building supply retailers.

12413 **Power Equipment Trade**
Hatton-Brown Publishers
PO Box 2268
Montgomery, AL 36102-2268

334-834-1170
800-669-5613; Fax: 334-834-4525
www.powerequipmenttrade.com
Facebook, Twitter, Google+, YouTube

David Knight, Co-Owner/Editor-in-Chief
Dan Shell, Managing Editor
Rich Donnell, Editor
Dianne Sullivan, General Manager
Dave Ramsey, Co-Owner Advertising Sales Manager

Service-oriented and technical articles, product evaluations, industry news, dealer surveys and business management information.
Frequency: Bimonthly
Circulation: 21441
ISSN: 0163-0414
Founded in 1952
Printed in on glossy stock

Trade Shows

12414 **Ace Hardware Fall Convention and Exhibit**
Ace Hardware Corporation
2200 Kensington Court
Oak Brook, IL 60521

630-990-6900; Fax: 708-990-0278
myace@acehardware.com

Over 950 exhibitors with hardware related products for Ace Hardware dealers. Also features training classes and information on retail programs.
17000 Attendees
Frequency: Annual/October

12415 **Ace Hardware Spring Convention and Exhibit**
Ace Hardware Corporation
2200 Kensington Court
Oak Brook, IL 60521

630-990-6900; Fax: 708-990-0278
myace@acehardware.com

Over 900 exhibitors with hardware related products for Ace Hardware dealers. Also features training classes and information on retail programs.
8000 Attendees
Frequency: Annual

12416 **DHI conNextions**
Door & Hardware Institute
2001 K Street NW
Washington, DC 20006

202-367-1134; Fax: 202-367-2134
www.dhi.org

Sharon Newport, CAE, Chief Executive Officer
Laura Frye Weaver, VP, Education
Adam Berkshire, Communications/Marketing Manager

The Door & Hardware Institute (DHI) is the only professional association dedicated to the Architectural Openings Industry. DHI represents the North American openings marketplace as the advocate and primary resource for information, professional development and certification.
4200 Attendees
Frequency: Annual

12417 **National Hardware Show**
383 Main Avenue
Norwalk, CT 06851

203-840-5622
888-425-9377; Fax: 203-840-4824
inquiry@hardware.reedexpo.com
www.nationalhardwareshow.com
Facebook, Twitter, LinkedIn, Instagram, YouTube

Juliana Sherwood, Sales Director
Richard Russo, Industry Vice President
Emily DeMarco, Marketing Director

Held in conjunction with International Hardware Week, this is the industry's leading hardware/home improvement event, with products from over 2,000 manufacturers from around the world. Includes hardware and allied lines, plumbing, paint and home decorating, lawn and garden, building products and housewares. Also international pavilions.
70000 Attendees
Frequency: Annual
Founded in 1945

12418 **True Value Fall Reunion**
True Value Company
8600 West Bryn Mawr Ave.
Chicago, IL 60631

773-695-5000; Fax: 773-695-5172
www.truevaluecompany.com

A gathering of True Value co-op members, vendors, its retailers & associates to share details about big ideas and game changers and shape the future of the retail industry.
1500 Attendees
Frequency: Annual

12419 **True Value Spring Reunion**
True Value Company
8600 W Bryn Mawr Avenue
Chicago, IL 60631-3505

773-695-5000; Fax: 773-695-5172
www.truevaluecompany.com

A gathering of True Value co-op members, vendors, its retailers & associates to share details about big ideas and game changers and shape the future of the retail industry.
1500 Attendees
Frequency: Annual

Directories & Databases

12420 **Directory and Buyer's Guide of the Door & Hardware Institute**
Door & Hardware Institute
2001 K Street NW
Washington, DC 20006

202-367-1134; Fax: 202-367-2134
www.dhi.org

Sharon Newport, CAE, Chief Executive Officer
Laura Frye Weaver, VP, Education
Adam Berkshire, Communications/Marketing

More than 700 firms which supply doors, hinges, locks, cabinets and closet hardware, door motors, smoke clothing and detection devices.
Frequency: Annual

12421 **Door & Hardware Institute: Membership Directory**
Door & Hardware Institute

2001 K Street NW
Washington, DC 20006

202-367-1134; Fax: 202-367-2134
www.dhi.org

Sharon Newport, CAE, Chief Executive Officer
Laura Frye Weaver, VP, Education
Adam Berkshire, Communications/Marketing Manager

Includes names and addresses of more than 5,000 members, including 700 manufacturing firms. Excellent resource for networking and staying in touch with your colleagues. Advertising is available.
Frequency: Annually

12422 Home Center Operators & Hardware Chains
Chain Store Guide
3710 Corporex Park Dr.
Suite 310
Tampa, FL 33619-1389

813-627-6700
800-927-9292; Fax: 813-627-6888
webmaster@chainstoreguide.com
www.chainstoreguide.com

Mike Jarvis, Publisher
Arthur Rosenberg, Editor
Shami Choon, Manager

The facts on more than 4,600 company headquarters and subsidiaries operating almost 23,500 units in the vast Home Improvement Building Material Industry. Also included are 19 major buying/marketing groups and coops that contribute approximately $30 billion and serve 103,243 accounts.
Cost: $545.00
Frequency: Annual, Paperback

Industry Web Sites

12423 http://gold.greyhouse.com
G.O.L.D Grey House OnLine Databases

Grey House Publishing's online database platform, GOLD, offers Quick Search, Keyword Search and Expert Search for most business sectors including hardware markets. The GOLD platform makes finding the information you need quick and easy - whether you're a novice searcher or an experienced database user. All of Grey House's directory products are available for subscription on the GOLD platform.

12424 www.aloa.org
Associated Locksmiths of America

Facebook, Twitter, LinkedIn

Strives to educate and provide information to the locksmith industry. Maintains referral service and offers insurance and bonding programs. Holds technical training.

12425 www.americanladderinstitute.org
American Ladder Institute

Members include manufacturers of wood, metal and fiberglass ladders. Represents US companies engaged in the research, development, manufacture and safety ladders.

12426 www.greyhouse.com
Grey House Publishing

Authoritative reference directories for most business sectors including hardware markets. Users can search the online databases with varied search criteria allowing for custom searches by product category, geographic area, sales volume, keyword, subject and more. Full Grey House catalog and online ordering also available.

12427 www.hti.org
Hand Tools Institute

Provides safety education and concerned with product standards.

12428 www.nrha.org
North American Retail Hardware Association

An organization which features news and information for hardware retailers.

Associations

12429 **AAPA Center for Healthcare Leadership and Management**
2318 Mill Rd.
Suite 1300
Alexandria, VA 22314

571-319-4444
chlm@aapa.org
www.chlm.org
Facebook, Twitter, LinkedIn

Jennifer Broderick, Managing Director
Bianca Belcher, PA-C, MPH, Director
Rebecca Winkler, MA, Program Manager
Lawrence Herman, MPA, PA-C, Senior Advisor

Offers a wide range of professional development tools and resourcesto help physician assistants and nurse practitioners foster leadership and management skills in the healthcare setting.

12430 **ALS Association**
1275 K Street NW
Suite 250
Washington, DC 20005

202-407-8580; Fax: 202-464-8869
www.alsa.org
Facebook, Twitter, LinkedIn, YouTube

Calaneet Balas, President & CEO
Gregory L. Mitchell, Exec. VP, Finance & Administration
Brian Frederick, PhD, Exec. VP, Communications
Lucie Bruijn, PhD, MBA, Chief Scientist
Lance Slaughter, Exec. VP, Chapter Relations

National nonprofit organization fighting Lou Gehrig's Disease—leads the way in research, care services, public education, and public policy.
Founded in 1869

12431 **ARMA International**
11880 College Boulevard
Suite 450
Overland Park, KS 66210

913-444-9174
844-565-2120; Fax: 913-257-3855
headquarters@armaintl.org
www.arma.org
Facebook, Twitter, LinkedIn

Nate Hughes, Exec. Dir, Operations
Jennifer Millett, National Accounts Manager
Heather Skags, Sr. Manager Membership

ARMA International is a not-for-profit association and a source for authoritative education, the latest legislative updates, standards & best practices. The association was established in 1955. Its approximately 27,000 members include records managers, archivists, corporate librarians, imaging specialists, legal professionals, IT managers, consultants, and educators, all of whom work in a wide variety of industries.
27000 Members
Founded in 1955

12432 **ASET - The Neurodiagnostic Society**
402 East Bannister Road
Suite A
Kansas City, MO 64131-3019

816-931-1120; Fax: 816-931-1145
info@aset.org
www.aset.org
Facebook, Twitter

Arlen Reimritz, Executive Director
Maliha Khan, Marketing & Social Media Manager
Jennifer Montgomery, Government & Grassroots Advocacy
Kathy Wolff, Membership Manager
Faye McNall, MEd, R. EEG T., Director of Education

Professional association dedicated to the promotion and advocacy of best practices in the study of electrical activity in the brain and nervous system., with a focus on bettering the quality of patient care.
5600 Members
Founded in 1959

12433 **Academy of Dental Materials**
4425 Cass St.
Suite A
San Diego, CA 92109

858-272-1018; Fax: 858-272-7687
admin@academydentalmaterials.org
www.academydentalmaterials.org

Dr. Jeffrey W. Stansbury, President (2018-19)
Dr. Milena Cadenaro, Secretary (2018-20)
Dr. Carmen Pfeifer, Treasurer (2016-20)
Dr. Ricardo M. Carvalho, Membership Chair
Lynn Reeves, Executive Manager

Objectives of the Academy are; to provide a forum for the exchange of information on all aspects of dental materials, to enhance communication between industry, researchers and practicing dentists, to encourage dental materials research and its applications and to promote dental materials through its activities.
Founded in 1941

12434 **Academy of General Dentistry**
560 W. Lake Street
Sixth Floor
Chicago, IL 60611-6600

888-243-3368; Fax: 312-335-3432
membership@agd.org
www.agd.org
Facebook, Twitter, LinkedIn, Instagram, YouTube

Max G. Moses, JD, CPA, MBA, Executive Director
Dr. Neil Gajjar, DDS, MAGD, President

Mission is to serve the needs and represent the interest of general dentists, to promote the oral health of the public, and to foster continued proficiency of general dentists through quality continuing dental education in order to better serve the public.
37M Members
Founded in 1952

12435 **Academy of Nutrition and Dietetics**
120 South Riverside Plaza
Suite 2190
Chicago, IL 60606-6995

312-899-0040
800-877-1600
info@eatright.org
www.eatright.org
Facebook, Twitter, LinkedIn, Youtube

Patricia M. Babjak, MLIS, CEO

Striving to improve the nation's health and advance the profession of dietetics through research, education, and advocacy.
70M Members
Founded in 1917

12436 **Academy of Osseointegration**
85 W Algonquin Rd
Suite 550
Arlington Heights, IL 60005-4460

847-439-1919
800-656-7736; Fax: 847-427-9656
academy@osseo.org
www.osseo.org

Established to provide a focus for the rapidly advancing biotechnology involving the natural bond between bone and certain alloplastic reconstructive materials. Special focus on dental implants.
5200 Members
Founded in 1987

12437 **Acoustic Neuroma Association**
600 Peachtree Pkwy
Suite 108
Cumming, GA 30041-6899

770-205-8211
877-200-8211; Fax: 770-205-0239; Fax: 877-202-0239
info@anausa.org
www.anausa.org
Facebook, Twitter, YouTube, Instagram, Pinterest

Allison Feldman, CEO
Summer Duperon, Development Director
Melanie Hutchins, Manager, Volunteer Programs
Stephanie Rommer, Project Manager
Melissa Baumbick, Communications Specialist

A patient organization that provides education and support to thosediagnosed with an acoustic neuroma.
Founded in 1981

12438 **Adult Congenital Heart Association**
3300 Henry Ave.
Suite 112
Philadelphia, PA 19129

215-849-1260
888-921-ACHA; Fax: 215-849-1261
info@achaheart.org
www.achaheart.org
Facebook, Twitter, LinkedIn, Instagram

Mark Roeder, President & CEO
Beth Coimbra, CPA, Director, Finance & Administration
Jessica DiGiovanni, Development Manager
Jessica Freely, Director, Community Outreach
Terri Schaefer, Communication Manager

Information, resources, and support for adults with congenital heart disease.
Founded in 1998

12439 **Advanced Medical Technology Association**
701 Pennsylvania Ave, NW
Suite 800
Washington, DC 20004-2654

202-783-8700; Fax: 202-783-8750
info@advamed.org
www.advamed.org
Facebook, Twitter, LinkedIn, Youtube

Scott Whitaker, President & CEO
Jen Brearey, Chief Finance Officer
Greg Crist, Chief Advocacy Officer
Andrew Fish, Chief Strategy Officer, AdvaMed
Christopher L. White, Chief Operating Officer

Advocates for a legal, regulatory and economic environment that advances global health care by assuring worldwide patient access to the benefits of medical technology. Promoting policies that foster the highest ethical standards, rapid product approvals, appropriate reimbursement, and access to international markets.
1100 Members
Founded in 1980

12440 **Aerospace Medical Association**
320 S Henry St
Alexandria, VA 22314-3579

703-739-2240; Fax: 703-739-9652
inquiries@asma.org
www.asma.org
Facebook, Twitter, LinkedIn

Jeffrey C. Sventek, MS, CAsP, Executive Director
Gisselle Vargas, Operations Manager
Gloria Carter, Director, Member Services

Sheryl Kildall, Subscriptions Manager
Frederick Bonato, PhD, Journal Editor-in-Chief

Organized exclusively for charitable, educational, and scientific purposes. It is the largest, most-representative professional membership organization in the fields of aviation, space, and environmental medicine.
3200 Members
Founded in 1929
Mailing list available for rent

12441 **Alexander Graham Bell Association for the Deaf and Hard of Hearing**
3417 Volta Place, NW
Washington, DC 20007

202-337-5220
TTY: 202-337-5221; Fax: 202-337-8314
info@agbell.org
www.agbell.org
Facebook, Twitter, LinkedIn, YouTube, Instagram

Emilio Alonso-Mendoza, Chief Executive Officer
Lisa Chutjian, Chief Development Officer
Susan Boswell, Director of Communications
Robin Bailey, Programs Specialist
Judy Harrison, Director of Programs

A resource, support network and advocate for listening, learning, talking, and living independently with hearing loss.
Founded in 2005

12442 **Alzheimer's Association**
225 N. Michigan Ave.
Floor 17
Chicago, IL 60601-7633

312-335-8700
800-272-3900; Fax: 866-699-1246
advocate@alz.org
www.alz.org
Facebook, Twitter, YouTube

Michelle Helton, Vice President, Financial Operation
Christine Foh, Vice President, Legal
Beth Kallmyer, Vice President, Care & Support
Maria Carrillo, Chief Science Officer
Richard Hovland, Chief Operations Officer

Information on Alzheimer's disease and dementia symptoms, diagnosis, stages, treatment, care and support resources.

12443 **Ambulatory Surgery Center Association**
1012 Cameron Street
Alexandria, VA 22314-2427

703-836-8808; Fax: 703-549-0976
asc@ascassociation.org
www.ascassociation.org
Facebook, Twitter, LinkedIn

Bill Prentice, Chief Executive Officer

Membership and advocacy organization that provides member benefits and services, combats legislative, regulatory and other challenges at the federal and state level, assists state ASC association, enhances ASC representation at the state and federal level, and has established a political action committee.

12444 **America's Health Insurance Plans (AHIP)**
601 Pennsylvania Ave. NW
South Building, Suite 500ÿ
Washington, DC 20004

202-778-3200; Fax: 202-331-7487
info@ahip.org
www.ahip.org
Facebook, Twitter, LinkedIn, Pinterest

Matt Eyles, President & CEO
Dawn Banda, Chief Financial Officer
John Mathewson, Chief Operating Officer
Yvonne Chanatry, Sr. VP, Marketing
Kristine Grow, Sr. VP, Communications

The national trade association representing the health insurance industry. Members provide health and supplemental benefits to more than 200 million Americans through employer-sponsored coverage, the individual insurance market, and public programs such as Medicare and Medicaid. Advocates for public policies that expand access to affordable health care coverage to all Americans through a competitive marketplace that fosters choice, quality and innovation.

12445 **American Academy for Cerebral Palsy and Developmental Medicine**
555 East Wells
Suite 1100
Milwaukee, WI 53202-3800

414-918-3014; Fax: 414-276-2146
info@aacpdm.org
www.aacpdm.org
Facebook, Twitter

Tracy Burr, CAE, Executive Director
Erin Trimmer, Senior Meetings Manager
Heather Schrader, Manager, Membership & Admin.
Elizabeth Mueller, Meetings Coordinator
Kay Whalen, MBA, CAE, Managing Partner

Mission is to provide multidisciplinary scientific education for health professionals and promote excellence in research and services for the benefit of people with cerebral palsy and childhood-onset disabilities. A global leader in the multidisciplinary scientific education of health professionals and researchers.
1100 Members
Founded in 1947

12446 **American Academy of Allergy, Asthma and Immunology**
555 E Wells St
Suite 1100
Milwaukee, WI 53202-3823

414-272-6071
info@aaaai.org
www.aaaai.org
Facebook, Twitter

The largest professional medical specialty organization in the United States, representing allergists, asthma specialists, clinical immunologists, allied health professionals, and others with a special interest in the research and treatment of allergic disease.
6M Members
Founded in 1943

12447 **American Academy of Child and Adolescent Psychiatry**
3615 Wisconsin Ave NW
Washington, DC 20016-3007

202-966-7300; Fax: 202-464-0131
cme@aacap.org
www.aacap.org
Facebook, Twitter

Membership based organization, composed of child and adolescent psychiatrists and other interested physicians. Members actively research, evaluate, diagnose, and treat psychiatric disorders and pride themselves on giving direction to and responding quickly to new developments in addressing the health care needs of children and their families.
7500 Members
Founded in 1953

12448 **American Academy of Dermatology**
P.O. Box 1968
Des Plaines, IL 60017

847-240-1280
866-503-7546; Fax: 847-240-1859
president@aad.org
www.aad.org
Facebook, Twitter, Instagram

Elaine Weiss, CEO

The largest, most influential and most representative dermatology group in the United States. Represents virtually all practicing dermatologists in the US, as well as a growing number of international dermatologists.
13700 Members
Founded in 1938

12449 **American Academy of Family Physicians**
P.O. Box 11210
Shawnee Mission, KS 66207-1210

913-906-6000
800-274-2237; Fax: 913-906-6075
aafp@aafp.org
www.aafp.org
Facebook, Twitter

Douglas E. Henley, EVP & CEO
Todd C. Dicus, Dep. EVP & COO

The national association of family doctors.
Founded in 1947

12450 **American Academy of Fixed Prosthodontics**
Office of the Secretary
6661 Merwin Rd.
Columbus, OH 43235

614-761-1927; Fax: 614-292-0941
aafpsec@gmail.com
www.fixedprosthodontics.org
Facebook, Twitter

Dr. Steve Rosenstiel, Secretary

Mission is to foster excellence in the field of prosthodontics, implants and esthetic dentistry through mutual study, participation, and cooperation.
Founded in 1950

12451 **American Academy of Forensic Sciences**
410 N. 21st Street
Colorado Springs, CO 80904

719-636-1100; Fax: 719-636-1993
info@aafs.org
www.aafs.org
Facebook, RSS, YouTube

Anne Warren, Executive Director
Kimberly Wrasse, Exec. Assistant & Education Coord.
Sondra Doolittle, Meetings & Expositions Manager
Cheryl Hunter, Membership Coordinator
Nancy Jackson, Accreditation & Outreach Coord.

A professional society dedicated to the application of science to the law, the AAFS is committed to the promotion of education and the elevation of accuracy, precision, and specificity in the forensic sciences. Membership includes physicians, attorneys, dentists, toxicologists, anthropologists, document examiners, digital evidence experts, psychiatrists, engineers, physicists, chemists, criminalists, educators, and others from the US, Canada and 70 other countries worldwide.
6700 Members
Founded in 1948
Mailing list available for rent: 6500 names

12452 **American Academy of Home Care Medicine**
8735 W. Higgins Road
Suite 300
Chicago, IL 60631

847-375-4719; Fax: 847-375-6395
info@aahcm.org

www.aahcm.org
Facebook, Twitter, LinkedIn, YouTube

Brent T. Feorene, MBA, Executive Director
Val Good-Turney, Executive Administrator

Organization working towards the goal of improving healthcare services for those who receive homecare. Offers news, information, and resources to home care physicians, nurses, social workers, and other industry professionals.
Founded in 1988

12453 American Academy of Implant Dentistry
211 East Chicago Avenue
Suite 750
Chicago, IL 60611

312-335-1550
877-335-2243; Fax: 312-335-9090
info@aaid.com
www.aaid.com
Facebook, Twitter, LinkedIn, YouTube, Google Plus

Cheryl R. Parker, CAE, Executive Director
Christine DiGiovanni, Director, Education
Carolina Hernandez, CAE, Director, Membership & Credentials
William Rohe, Chief Financial Officer
Karina Devine, Social Media & Web Content Coord.

AAID offers a rigorous implant dentistry credentialing program which requires at least 300 hours of post-docroal or continuing education instruction in implant dentistry, passing a comprehensive exam, and presenting successful cases of different types of implants to a group of examiners. It is one of the most comprehensive credentialing programs in dentistry.
4000 Members
Founded in 1951

12454 American Academy of Medical Administrators
300 N. Wabash
Suite 2000
Chicago, IL 60611

312-321-6815
Facebook, Twitter, LinkedIn, Google+

Linda Larin, Chair

Organization whose mission is to advance excellence in healthcare leadership through the improvement of individual relationships, multi-disciplinary interaction, practical business tools and active engagement.
2000 Members
Founded in 1957

12455 American Academy of Neurology
201 Chicago Avenue
Minneapolis, MN 55415

612-928-6000
800-879-1960; Fax: 612-454-2746
memberservices@aan.com
www.aan.com
Facebook, Twitter, LinkedIn, YouTube, Instagram, Google+

Catherine M. Rydell, CAE, Executive Director & CEO
Bruce Levi, JD, General Counsel
Chris Becker, Chief Business Development Officer
Timothy Engel, CPA, Chief Financial Officer
Angela Babb, CAE, APR, Chief Communications Officer

An international professional association of neurologists and neuroscience professionals dedicated to promoting the highest quality patient-centered neurologic care. The AAN is strongly committed to its mission and focuses its efforts on ensuring the reality of the principles and standards set forth in AAN mission statement.
18000 Members
Founded in 1948

12456 American Academy of Ophthalmology
655 Beach Street
P.O. Box 7424
San Francisco, CA 94120-7424

415-561-8500; Fax: 415-561-8533
customer_service@aao.org
www.aao.org
Facebook, Twitter, LinkedIn, YouTube, RSS, Google+

David W. Parke II, MD, Chief Executive Officer
Jane Aguirre, VP, Membership & Alliances
Jill Boyett, CFO and VP, Organizational Services
Renaldo Juanso, VP, Communications & Marketing
Debra Rosencrance, CMP, CAE, VP, Meetings & Exhibits

Mission is to advance the lifelong learning and professional interests of opthalmologists to ensure that the public can obtain the best possible eye care.
80000 Members
Founded in 1979

12457 American Academy of Optometry
2909 Fairgreen Street
Orlando, FL 32803

321-319-4860
844-323-3937; Fax: 407-893-9890
aaoptom@aaoptom.org
www.aaopt.org
Facebook, Twitter, LinkedIn, Youtube, Instagram

Lois Schoenbrun, CAE, FAAO, Executive Director
Richard Jones, CPA, Deputy Exec. Dir., Finance & Admin.
Betty Taylor, Director, Meetings & Exhibits
Jenny Brown, Dir., Membership & Communications
Helen Viksnins, Sr. Director, Programs

A philanthropic organization that develops and provides financial support for optometric research and education in vision and eye health.
5000 Members
Founded in 1922

12458 American Academy of Oral and Maxillofacial Surgeons
9700 West Bryn Mawr Avenue
Rosemont, IL 60018-5701

847-678-6200
800-822-6637; Fax: 847-678-6286
inquiries@aaoms.org
www.aaoms.org
Facebook, Twitter, LinkedIn, YouTube, Vimeo, Instagram

Scott Farrell, MBA, CPA, Executive Director

The professional organization representing oral and maxillofacial surgeons in the US, supporting its members' ability to practice their specialty through education, research, and advocacy. Members comply with rigorous continuing education requirements and submit to periodic office examinations, ensuring the public that all office procedures and personnel meet stringent national standards.
11412 Members
Founded in 1946

12459 American Academy of Orofacial Pain
174 S. New York Ave
PO Box 478
Oceanville, NJ 08231

609-504-1311; Fax: 609-573-5064
aaopexec@aaop.org
www.aaop.org
Facebook, Twitter

Kenneth S. Cleveland, Executive Director

Dedicated to alleviating pain and suffering through the promotion of excellence in education, research and patient care in the field of orofacial pain and associated disorders.
Founded in 1975

12460 American Academy of Orthopaedic Surgeons
9400 West Higgins Rd.
Rosemont, IL 60018

847-823-7186; Fax: 847-823-8125
member@aaos.org
www.aaos.org
Facebook, Twitter, LinkedIn, YouTube, Instagram

Thomas E. Arend Jr., Esq., CAE, Chief Executive Officer
Laura Abrahams, Chief Human Resources Officer
Dino Damalas, MBA, Chief Operating Officer
Anna Salt Troise, MBA, Chief Education Strategist
Jennifer Wolff-Jones, CAE, Chief Membership Officer

Provider of medical education to orthopaedic surgeons.
Founded in 1933

12461 American Academy of Osteopathy
3500 DePauw Boulevard
Suite 1100
Indianapolis, IN 46268-1136

317-879-1881
800-875-6360; Fax: 317-879-0563
info@academyofosteopathy.org
www.academyofosteopathy.org
Facebook, Twitter, LinkedIn, YouTube

Sherri L. Quarles, Executive Director
Taylor Bridgeforth, Communications & Administration
Bev Searcy, Finance & Membership
Gennie Watts, Events
Amber Rausch, Education Coordinator

Mission is to teach, advocate, and research the science, art and philosophy of osteopathic medicine, emphasizing the integration of osteopathic principles, practices and manipulative treatment in patient care.
Founded in 1937

12462 American Academy of Otolaryngology-Head and Neck Surgery
1650 Diagonal Road
Alexandria, VA 22314-2857

703-836-4444
memberservices@entnet.org
www.entnet.org
Facebook, Twitter, LinkedIn, YouTube

The world's largest organization representing specialists who treat the ear, nose, throat, and related structures of the head and neck. Represents otolaryngologist- head and neck surgeons who diagnose and treat disorders of those areas.
12M Members
Founded in 1896

12463 American Academy of Pain Medicine
8735 W. Higgins Rd.
Suite 300
Chicago, IL 60631-2738

847-375-4731; Fax: 847-375-6477
info@painmed.org
www.painmed.org
Facebook, Twitter, LinkedIn

Phil Saigh, Executive Director

Has evolved as the primary organization for physicians practicing the specialty of Pain Medicine in the US. Purpose is to optimize the health of patients in pain and eliminate the major public health problem of pain by advancing the practice and the specialty of pain medicine.
Founded in 1983

12464 **American Academy of Pediatric Dentistry**
211 East Chicago Avenue
Suite 1600
Chicago, IL 60611-2637

312-337-2169; Fax: 312-337-6329
www.aapd.org
Facebook, Twitter, Instagram

John Rutkauskas, DDS, MBA, Chief Executive Officer
C. Scott Litch, Esq., CAE, Chief Operating Officer & Counsel
Margaret Bjerklie, Governance & Operations Manager
Mary Essling, RDH, MS, Dental Benefits Director
Erika Hoeft, Public Relations Director

Mission is to advocate policies, guidelines, and programs that promote optimal oral health and oral health care for infants and children through adolescence, including those with special health care needs. Serves and represents its membership in the areas of professional development and governmental and legislative activities. It is a liaison to other health care groups and the public.
8M Members
Founded in 1948

12465 **American Academy of Periodontology**
737 N. Michigan Avenue
Suite 800
Chicago, IL 60611-6660

312-787-5518; Fax: 312-787-3670
staff@abperio.org
www.perio.org
Facebook, Twitter, YouTube, Google Plus

Erin O'Donnell Dotzler, Executive Director

Purpose is to advance the periodontal and general health of the public and promote excellence in the practice of periodontics. Membership includes periodontists and general dentists from all 50 states as well as around the world.
8,400 Members
Founded in 1914

12466 **American Academy of Physical Medicine and Rehabilitation (AAPMR)**
9700 West Bryn Mawr Avenue
Suite 200
Rosemont, IL 60018-5701

847-737-6000
877-227-6799; Fax: 847-754-4368
info@aapmr.org
www.aapmr.org
Facebook, Twitter, YouTube, Instagram

Thomas E. Stautzenbach, MBA, CAE, Executive Director & CEO

Exclusively serving the needs of today's physical medicine and rehabilitation physician.
9000+ Members
Founded in 1938

12467 **American Academy of Physician Assistants**
2318 Mill Road
Suite 1300
Alexandria, VA 22314

703-836-2272; Fax: 703-684-1924
customercare@aapa.org
www.aapa.org
Facebook, Twitter, LinkedIn, Youtube, Huddle

Jennifer L. Dorn, Chief Executive Officer
Lisa Gables, CFO & Chief Development Officer
Catherine Gahres, VP, Membership Development & Svcs.
Carrie Munk, VP, Communications
Daniel Pace, VP, Education & Chief Strategy Off.

Advocates and educates on behalf of the profession and the patients PAs serve. AAPA works to ensure the professional growth, personal excellence and recognition of physician assistants. It also works to enhance their ability to improve the quality, accessibility and cost-effectiveness of patient-centered health care.
81M Members
Founded in 1968

12468 **American Academy of Professional Coders**
2233 S. Presidents Dr.
Suite F
Salt Lake City, UT 84120

801-236-2200
800-626-2633; Fax: 801-236-2258
info@aapc.com
www.aapc.com
Facebook, Twitter, LinkedIn

Jason VandenAkker, Chief Executive Officer

Founded to provide education and professional certification to physician-based medical coders and to elevate the standards of medical coding by providing student training, certification, ongoing education, networking, and job opportunities.
111M Members
Founded in 1988

12469 **American Alliance for Medical Cannabis**
44500 Tide Ave.
Arch Cape, OR 97102

503-436-1882
contact@letfreedomgrow.com
www.letfreedomgrow.com
Facebook, Twitter, LinkedIn
Arthur H. Livermore, National Director

Dedicated to bringing patients, caregivers, and volunteers the facts needed to make informed decisions about medical cannabis. Provides information on medical marijuana legislation, political activism, recipes, and growing guides.

12470 **American Art Therapy Association**
4875 Eisenhower Avenue
Suite 240
Alexandria, VA 22304

703-548-5860
888-290-0878; Fax: 703-783-8468
info@arttherapy.org
www.arttherapy.org
Facebook, Twitter, LinkedIn, RSS

Cynthia Woodruff, Executive Director
Christina Easterly, Coordinator, Events & Operations
Barbara Florence, Director, Events & Education
Clara Keane, Coordinator, Communication & Policy
Kat Michel, Manager. Membership

A U.S. national professional association of over 5,000 practicing art therapy professionals, including students, educators, and related practitioners in the field art therapy.

12471 **American Association for Cancer Research**
615 Chestnut St.
17th Fl.
Philadelphia, PA 19106-4404

215-440-9300
866-423-3965; Fax: 215-440-9313
aacr@aacr.org
www.aacr.org
Facebook, Twitter, LinkedIn, YouTube

Margaret Foti, Chief Executive Officer

The AACR is the oldest and largest cancer research organization in the world.
Founded in 1907

12472 **American Association for Clinical Chemistry**
900 Seventh Street, NW
Suite 400
Washington, DC 20001

202-857-0717
800-892-1400; Fax: 202-887-5093
executiveoffice@aacc.org
www.aacc.org
Facebook, Twitter, LinkedIn, YouTube

Janet B.ÿ Kreizman, Chief Executive Officer

An international scientific/ medical society of clinical laboratory professionals, physicians, research scientists and other individuals involved with clinical chemistry and related disciplines. Vision is to provide leadership in advancing the practice and profession of clinical laboratory science and its application to health care.
10M Members
Founded in 1948

12473 **American Association for Continuity of Care**
Fort Worth, TX

860-586-7525
info@continuityofcare.org
www.continuityofcare.org
Facebook, LinkedIn, RSS

Cindy Cowan, Communications/Admin

A national nonprofit multidisciplinary professional organization dedicated to providing leadership and supporting excellence in practice among those involved in continuity of care within the health care system through education and pationt focused advocacy.
Founded in 1982

12474 **American Association for Geriatric Psychiatry**
6728 Old McLean Village Drive
McLean, VA 22101

703-556-9222; Fax: 703-556-8729
main@aagponline.org
www.aagponline.org
Facebook, Twitter, LinkedIn

Christopher N. Wood, Executive Director
Victoria LaLiberte Cooper, Executive Assistant
Carrie Stankiewicz, Consultant

National association that has products, activities, and publications which focus exclusively on the challenges of geriatric psychiatry.
Founded in 1978

12475 **American Association for Hand Surgery**
500 Cummings Center
Suite 4400
Beverly, MA 01915

978-927-8330; Fax: 978-524-0498
www.handsurgery.org
Facebook, Twitter

Represents a diverse but cohesive mix of hand surgeons and hand therapists with a mission to work together to advance global hand care and education.

12476 **American Association for Laboratory Animal Science**
9190 Crestwyn Hills Drive
Memphis, TN 38125-8538
901-754-8620; Fax: 901-753-0046
info@aalas.org
www.aalas.org
Facebook, Twitter, LinkedIn, YouTube
Ann Turner, Executive Director
Jennifer C. Smith, DVM, Past President
An association of professionals that advances responsible laboratory animal care and use to benefit people and animals. Dedicated to the humane care and treatment of laboratory animals and the quality research that leads to scientific gains that benefit people and animals.
11M+ Members
Founded in 1950

12477 **American Association for Marriage and Family Therapy**
112 South Alfred St
Alexandria, VA 22314-3061
703-838-9808; Fax: 703-838-9805
central@aamft.org
www.aamft.org
Facebook, Twitter, LinkedIn, Youtube
Marvareneў Oliver, EdD, President
Christopher Habben, PhD, President-Elect
Michaelў Chafin, MEd, Past President
Thomas Smith, PhD, Secretary
Mike Fitzpatrick, MSW, Treasurer
The professional association for the field of marriage and family therapy. Representing the professional interests of marriage and family therapists throughout the US, Canada, and abroad. The Association facilitates research, theory development and education.
25M Members
Founded in 1942

12478 **American Association for Pediatric Ophthalmology and Strabismus**
655 Beach Street
San Francisco, CA 94109-1336
415-561-8505; Fax: 415-561-8531
aapos@aao.org
www.aapos.org
Facebook, Twitter, Google+
Jennifer ў Hull, Client Services Manager
Marjan Hazrati, Client Services Coordinator
Maria A.ў Schweers, CO, Scientific Program Coordinator
An academic association of pediatric ophthalmologists and strabismus surgeons.

12479 **American Association for Respiratory Care**
9425 N MacArthur Blvd
Suite 100
Irving, TX 75063-4706
972-243-2272; Fax: 972-484-2720
info@aarc.org
www.aarc.org
Facebook, Twitter, LinkedIn, YouTube
Tom Kallstrom, Executive Director/CEO
Tim Myers, Chief Business Officer
Shawna Strickland, Associate Executive Director
Doug Laher, Associate Executive Director
Anne Marie Hummel, Associate Executive Director
Leading the respiratory care profession in science, education and research. Its members are committed to providing exemplary respiratory care and improving lung health worldwide.
38M Members
Founded in 1947

12480 **American Association for Thoracic Surgery**
800 Cummings Center
Suite 350-V
Beverly, MA 01915
978-252-2200; Fax: 978-522-8469
admin@aats.org
www.aats.org
Facebook, Twitter, LinkedIn, YouTube
Cindy VerColen, CEO/Executive Director
Bill Maloney, AATS Consultant
Melissa Binette, Director, Meetings
Lisa McEvoy, Director, Marketing & Communication
Spencer McGrath, Director, Scientific Publications
The promotion and fostering of education and research in the field of cardiothoracic surgery, membership consists of the world's foremost cardiothoracic surgeons representing 35 countries. Surgeons must have a proven record of distinction within the cardiothoracic surgical field and have made meritorious contributions to the extant knowledge base about cardiothoracic disease and its surgical treatment to be considered for membership.
1231 Members
Founded in 1917

12481 **American Association for the Advancement of Science**
1200 New York Ave NW
Washington, DC 20005
202-326-6400
www.aaas.org
Facebook, Twitter, LinkedIn, YouTube, Instagram
Alan I. Leshner, Interim Chief Executive Officer
Andrew Black, Chief of Staff & External Affairs
Michael Savelli, Chief Operating Officer
Maureen Kearney, Chief Program Officer
Tiffany Lohwater, Chief Communications Officer
A nonprofit organization that has research news, issue papers, educational programs, etc.
Founded in 1848

12482 **American Association for the Study of Liver Disease**
1001 North Fairfax Street
Suite 400
Alexandria, VA 22314
703-299-9766; Fax: 703-299-9622
aasld@aasld.org
www.aasld.org
Facebook, Twitter, LinkedIn, Instagram, YouTube
Julie Deal, Executive Director
Organization of scientists and health care professionals committed to preventing and curing liver disease.
Founded in 1950

12483 **American Association of Bioanalysts**
906 Olive Street
Suite 1200
Saint Louis, MO 63101-1448
314-241-1445; Fax: 314-241-1449
aab@aab.org
www.aab.org
Facebook
Mark S Birenbaum PhD, Executive Director
Professional Association representing clinical laboratory directors, owners, managers and supervisors, medical technologistsm medical laboratory technicians,and physical office laboratory technicians. AAB provides a broad range of services, including representation before federal and state legislative and regulatory agencies, educational programs, and publications.
Founded in 1956

12484 **American Association of Blood Banks**
4550 Montgomery Ave.
Suite 700, North Tower
Bethesda, MD 20814
301-907-6977; Fax: 301-907-6895
aabb@aabb.org
www.aabb.org
Facebook, Twitter, LinkedIn, YouTube
Debra BenAvram, Chief Executive Officer
Advances the practice and standards of transfusion medicine and cellular therapies to optimize patient and donor care and safety. AABB vision is to be the pre-eminent knowledge-based organization focused on improving health through advancing the science and practice of transfusion medicine and cellular therapies.
Founded in 1947

12485 **American Association of Cardiovascular & Pulmonary Rehabilitation**
330 N. WabashўAvenue
Suite 2000
Chicago, IL 60611
312-321-5146; Fax: 312-673-6924
aacvpr@aacvpr.org
www.aacvpr.org
Facebook
Megan Cohen, CAE, Executive Director
Jessica Eustice, Director, Corporate Relations
Mollie Corbett, Operations Manager
Kirk Terry, Education Manager
Andrew Miller, Membership Senior Coordinator
Mission is to reduce morbidity, mortality, and disability from cardiovascular and pulmonary diseases through education, prevention, rehabilitation, research, and disease management.
Founded in 1985

12486 **American Association of Clinical Endocrinologists**
245 Riverside Avenue
Suite 200
Jacksonville, FL 32202-4933
904-353-7878; Fax: 904-353-8185
info@aace.com
www.aace.com
Facebook, Twitter, LinkedIn
Paul Markowski, Chief Executive Officer
Tom Conway, Chief Financial Officer
Michele Lentz, Chief Strategic Alliance Officer
Elizabeth A. Lepkowski, MATD, Chief Learning Officer
Robin Shelly, Chief Marketing Officer
Professional medical organization devoted to the enhancement of the practice of clinical endocrinology. Maintains high standards in a society of qualified medical, pediatric, reproductive and surgical endocrinologists to futher the practice through advocacy and education.
6200 Members
Founded in 1991

12487 **American Association of Colleges of Nursing**
655 K Street NW
Suite 750
Washington, DC 20001
202-463-6930; Fax: 202-785-8320
aercolino@aacnnursing.org

www.aacnnursing.org
Facebook, Twitter, LinkedIn, Instagram

Deborah Trautman, President & CEO
Alexis Ercolino, Executive Assistant
Robert Rosseter, Chief Communications Officer
Joan Stanley, Chief Academic Officer
Jennifer Ahearn, Chief Operating Officer

Education, research, federal advocacy, data collection, publications, and special programs for nursing education.
765 Members
Founded in 1969

12488 **American Association of Critical-Care Nurses**
101 Columbia
Aliso Viejo, CA 92656-4109

949-362-2000
800-809-2273; Fax: 949-362-2020
info@aacn.org
www.aacn.org
Facebook, Twitter, LinkedIn, Instagram, YouTube

Dana Woods, Chief Executive Officer

The largest specialty nursing organization in the world, representing the interests of nurses who are charged with the responsibility of caring for acutely and critically ill patients. The Association is dedicated to providing members with the knowledge and resources necessary to provide optimal care to critically ill patients.
Founded in 1969

12489 **American Association of Diabetes Educators**
200 W Madison Street
Suite 800
Chicago, IL 60606

800-338-3633
info@diabeteseducator.org
www.diabeteseducator.org
Facebook, Twitter, LinkedIn, Google+, Pinterest, Instagram

Charles Macfarlane, FACHE, CAE, Chief Executive Officer
Crystal Broj, Chief Tech. & Innovation Officer
Gina Tassio McClure, Chief Operating Officerÿ
Leslie Kolb, MBA, BSN, RN, Chief Science and Practice Officerÿ
Brad Neal, MBA, CAE, Chief Finance Officerÿ

A multidisciplinary association of healthcare professionals dedicated to integrating self-management as a key outcome in the care of people with diabetes and related chronic conditions.
10M Members
Founded in 1973

12490 **American Association of Healthcare Administrative Management**
11240 Waples Mill Road
Suite 200
Fairfax, VA 22030-6078

703-281-4043; Fax: 703-359-7562
info@aaham.org
www.aaham.org
Facebook, Twitter, LinkedIn, YouTube, Google+, Pinterest

Sharon R. Galler, CMP, Executive Director
Moayad Zahralddin, Operations & Membership Director
Matthew Hundley, Certification Director
Danielle Burns, Conference & Meetings Manager
Julia Tiffany, Certification Manager

The premier professional organization in healthcare administrative management. Actively represents the interests of healthcare administrative management professionals through a comprehensive program of legislative and regulatory monitoring and its participation in industry goups such as ANSI, DISA, and NUBC. AAHAM is a major force in shaping the future of health care administrative management.
Founded in 1968

12491 **American Association of Hip and Knee Surgeons**
9400 W. Higgins Rd.
Suite 230
Rosemont, IL 60018-4976

847-698-1200; Fax: 847-698-0704
www.aahks.org
Facebook, Twitter, LinkedIn

Michael J. Zarski, JD, Executive Director
Renalin J. Malvar-Ledda, Director of Operations
Eileen M. Lusk, Director of Membership
Sigita Wolfe, Director of Education & Research
Jeff Mitchell, Dir., Marketing & Corp. Relations

Specialty society for orthopedic surgeons who specialize in hip andknee replacements. Mission is to advance hip and knee patient care through education and advocacy.
4400 Members
Founded in 1991

12492 **American Association of Immunologists**
9650 Rockville Pike
Bethesda, MD 20814

301-634-7178; Fax: 301-634-7887
infoaai@aai.org
www.aai.org
Facebook

Michele Hogan, Executive Director
Bethany Coulter, Director of Communications
Maria Zavarello, Director of Finance
Jennifer Woods, Membership Manager
Gale Guerrieri, Meetings Manager

An association of professionally trained scientists from all over the world dedicated to advancing the knowledge of immunology and its related disciplines, fostering the interchange of ideas and information among investigators, and addressing the potential integration of immunologic principles into clinical practice.
Founded in 1913

12493 **American Association of Integrated Healthcare Delivery Systems**
4435 Waterfront Drive
Suite 101
Glen Allen, VA 23060

804-747-5823; Fax: 804-747-5316
www.aaihds.org
Facebook, Twitter, LinkedIn, Google+

A nonprofit organization dedicated to the educational advancement of provider-based managed care professionals involved in integrated healthcare delivery. Mission is to provide managed healthcare professionals in IPAs, PHOs, health systems, hospitals and other integrated delivery systems with the tools, education, skills and resources to be successful in the marketplace.
1000 Members
Founded in 1993

12494 **American Association of Managed Care Nurses**
4435 Waterfront Drive
Suite 101
Glen Allen, VA 23060-3393

804-747-9698; Fax: 804-747-5316
keads@aamcn.org
www.aamcn.org
Facebook, Twitter, LinkedIn, Google+

Jacquelyn Smith, President
Gloria J. Hayman, RN, CMCN, Board of Director
LaNita Knoke RN, BS, CMCN, Board of Director
Veronica Sheffield, CMCN, Board of Director
Joyce Thiem, RN, BSN, CCM, Board of Director

Nonprofit organization representing Registered Nurses, Nurse Practitioners and Licensed Practical Nurses. AAMCN seeks to offer those nurses the opportunity to become more successful, both in their workplace and their community, through interactive membership services, quality educational resources and unparalleled networking with other managed care nurses throughout the industry.
Founded in 1994

12495 **American Association of Medical Assistants**
20 N Wacker Dr
Suite 1575
Chicago, IL 60606-2963

312-899-1500
800-228-2262; Fax: 312-899-1259
www.aama-ntl.org
Facebook, YouTube, WordPress

Ann Naegele, President
Chris Hollander, Vice President
Charlene Couch, Secretary/ Treasurer

Mission is to provide the medical assistant professional with education, certification, credential acknowledgment, networking opportunities, scope-of-practice protection, and advocacy for quality patient-centered health care.
Founded in 1955

12496 **American Association of Naturopathic Physicians**
818 18th Street, NW
Suite 250
Washington, DC 20006

202-237-8150
866-538-2267; Fax: 202-237-8152
member.services@naturopathic.org
www.naturopathic.org
Facebook, Twitter, LinkedIn, Google+

Kasra Pournadeali, ND, President
Jaclyn Chasse, ND, President-Elect
Michelle Simon, ND, PhD, AANP Treasurer
Michael Cronin, ND, Board of Director
Laura Farr, Board of Director

Vision is to transform the healthcare system from a disease management system to a comprehensive health program incorporating the principles of naturopathic medicine.
1800 Members
Founded in 1985

12497 **American Association of Neurological Surgeons**
5550 Meadowbrook Drive
Rolling Meadows, IL 60008-3852

847-378-0500
888-566-2267; Fax: 847-378-0600
info@aans.org
www.aans.org
Facebook, Twitter, LinkedIn, Youtube, iTunesU

H. Hunt Batjer, President
Deborah L. Benzil, Vice President
Frederick A. Boop,ÿMD, FAANS, FACS, President-Elect
Alex B. Valadka, Treasurer
Christopher I. Shaffrey,ÿMD, FAANS, Secretary

The organization that speaks for all of neurosurgery. The AANS is dedicated to advancing the specialty of neurological surgery in order to promote the highest quality of patient care.
6500+ Members
Founded in 1931

12498 **American Association of Neuromuscular and Electrodiagnostic Medicine**
2621 Superior Drive NW
Rochester, MN 55901
507-288-0100; Fax: 507-288-1225
aanem@aanem.org
www.aanem.org
Facebook, Twitter, LinkedIn, YouTube
Vincent J. Tranchitella, MD, President
Vern C. Juel, MD, President Elect
Francis O. Walker, MD, Past President
Shirlyn A. Adkins, JDÿ, Executive Director
Anthony E.ÿ Chiodo, MD, Secretary-Treasurer
A nonprofit membership association dedicated to the advancement of neuromuscular, musculoskeletal medicine.
Founded in 1953

12499 **American Association of Neuromuscular and Electrodiagnostic Medicine**
2621 Superior Drive NW
Rochester, MN 55901-8350
507-288-0100; Fax: 507-288-1225
aanem@aanem.org
www.aanem.org
Facebook, Twitter, LinkedIn, Youtube
Vincent J. Tranchitella, MD, President
Vern C. Juel, MD, President Elect
Francis O. Walker, MD, Past President
Shirlyn A. Adkins, JDÿ, Executive Director
Anthony E.ÿ Chiodo, MD, Secretary-Treasurer
Dedicated to the advancement of neuromuscular, musculoskeletal, and electrodiagnostic medicine. Physician members- primarily neurologists and physiatrists- now are joined by allied health professionals and PhD Researchers working to improve the quality of medical care provided to patients with muscle and nerve disorders.
5200 Members
Founded in 1953

12500 **American Association of Neuroscience Nurses**
8735 W. Higgins Road
Suite 300
Chicago, IL 60631
847-375-4733
888-557-2266; Fax: 847-375-6430; Fax: 732-460-7313ÿ
info@aann.org
www.aann.org
Jan Hinkle, RN PhD CNRN, President
Cindy M.ÿ Sullivan, President Elect
Sandra J. Brettler, MSN RN CNRN, Secretary/Treasurer
Megan Keiser, RN DNP CNRN, Immediate Past President
Joan Kram, MBA RN FACHE, Executive Director
The leading authority in neuroscience nursing, inspires passion in nurses and creates the future for the specialty. AANN is committed to the advancement of neuroscience nursing as a specialty through the development and support of nurses to promote excellence in patient care.
3000 Members
Founded in 1968

12501 **American Association of Nurse Anesthetists**
222 South Prospect Avenue
Park Ridge, IL 60068-4001
847-692-7050
855-526-2262; Fax: 847-692-6968
info@aana.com
www.aana.com
Facebook, Twitter, LinkedIn, Youtube
Juan F. Quintana, President
Bruce A.ÿ Weiner, MS, CRNA, Vice President
Kathryn L.ÿ Jansky, CRNA, ARNP, Treasurer
Cheryl L.ÿ Nimmo, CRNA, DNP, President-Elect
Robertÿ Gauvin, CRNA, MS, Director, Region 1
The AANA promulgates education and practice standards and guidelines, and affords consultation to both private and governmental entities regarding nurse anesthetists and their practice.
Founded in 1931

12502 **American Association of Occupational Health Nurses**
7794 Grow Drive
Pensacola, FL 32514
850-474-6963
800-241-8014; Fax: 850-484-8762
AAOHN@aaohn.org
www.aaohn.org/
Facebook, Twitter, LinkedIn
Jeannie Tomlinson, MSN, RN, President
Ronda Weiss, MS, MPH, MBA, Secretary
Mary Gene Ryan, President-Elect
Phyllis Berryman, Director
David Allcott, Director
Dedicated to advancing and maximizing the health, safety and prductivity of domestic and global workforces by providing education, research, public policy and practice resources for occupational and environmental health nurses. Mission is to advance the profession of occupational and environmental health nursing.

12503 **American Association of Orthodontists**
401 North Lindbergh Boulevard
St. Louis, MO 63141-7816
314-993-1700
800-424-2841; Fax: 314-997-1745
info@aaortho.org
www.aaoinfo.org
Facebook, Twitter, LinkedIn
Jill Nowak, Director Of Finance & Admin
Linda Gladden, Director Of Comm. & Marketing
Sarah Dvorak, Meetings Coordinator
Sherry Nappier, Member Coordinator
Mike Nappier, Shipping And Receiving Coordinator
Official organization for board qualified and board certified orthodontists.
Founded in 1900

12504 **American Association of Physician Specialists Inc.**
5550 West Executive Drive
Suite 400
Tampa, FL 33609
813-433-2277; Fax: 813-830-6599
wcarbone@aapsus.org
www.aapsus.com
Martin E. Thornton, D.O., FAAEP, President
Surinder K. Kad, M.D., FAAIM, Secretary/Treasurer
Craig S. Smith, M.D., President-Elect
Mark DeSantis, D.O., Membership Officer
Kenneth A. Wallace, III, M.D., Vice President
AAPS was founded to fill a professional need among physicians practicing in medical specialities. Distinct from other medical societies, the AAPS accepts qualified physicians into membership who have either an allopathic (MD) or osteopathic (DO) degree.
Founded in 1950

12505 **American Association of Poison Control Centers**
515 King St.
Suite 510
Alexandria, VA 22314
703-894-1858
800-222-1222
info@aapcc.org
www.aapcc.org
Facebook, Twitter, RSS, WordPress
Jay L. Schauben, PharmD, President
William Banner, MD, PhD, President Elect
Marsha Ford, MD, FACMT, Past President
Stuart Heard, PharmD, FCSHP, Treasurer
Julie Weber, RPh, CSPIÿ, Secretary
National voluntary health organization that supports poison centersto prevent poisonings, provide education, conduct scientific research and treat individuals exposed to poisoning.

12506 **American Association of Public Health Physicians**
1605 Pebble Beach Blvd.
Green Cove Springs, FL 32043-8077
888-447-7281; Fax: 202-333-5016
membership@aaphp.org
www.aaphp.org
Katrina Rhodes, President
The AAPHP speaks on behalf of all public health physicians on major issues affecting public health.
Founded in 1954

12507 **American Association of Retired Persons**
601 E Street NW
Washington, DC 20049-0003
202-434-3525
888-687-2277; Fax: 202-434-7599
member@aarp.org
www.aarp.org
Facebook, Twitter, YouTube
Jo Ann Jenkins, CEO
Lawrence Flanagan, President, AARP Services
Scott Frisch, Chief Operating Officer
Nancy Smith, Corporate Secretary
Martha M. Boudreau, Chief Comm. & Marketing Officer
A nonprofit, nonpartisan membership organization for people age 50 and over. AARP is dedicated to enhancing quality of life for all.
21 Members
Founded in 1958

12508 **American Association of Sexuality Educators, Counselors & Therapists**
1444 I Street NW
Suite 700
Washington, DC 20005
202-449-1099; Fax: 202-216-9646
info@aasect.org
www.aasect.org
Konnie McCaffree, President
Debby Herbenick, President Elect
Douglas Braun-Harvey, LMFT, Treasurer
Chris F. Fariello, PhD, MA, Secretary
Michael Chan, Executive Director
A not-for-profit, interdisciplinary professional organization that is devoted to the promotion of sexual health by the development and advancement of the fields of sexual therapy, counseling and education.
Founded in 1967

12509 **American Association of Suicidology**
5221 Wisconsin Avenue, NW
Washington, DC 20015
202-237-2280
800-273-TALK; Fax: 202-237-2282

www.suicidology.org
Facebook, Twitter, YouTube

David Miller, PhD, President
Julie Cerel, PhDÿ, President Elect
Amy Boland, CPAÿ, Treasurer
Marnin J. Heisel, Secretary
Michelle Cornette, PhDÿ, Executive Director

A membership organization for those involved in suicide prevention and intervention, or touched by suicide.

12510 American Association on Intellectual and Developmental Disabilities
501 3rd Street, NW
Suite 200
Washington, DC 20001

202-387-1968; Fax: 202-387-2193
www.aaidd.org/
Facebook, Twitter, LinkedIn, YouTube

Susan B. Palmer, PhD, President
William Gaventa, MDiv, President Elect
Susan Havercamp, PhD, VP
Patti N. Martin, MEd, Secretary-Treasurer
Amy S. Hewitt, PhD, Immediate Past President

An American nonprofit professional organization concerned with intellectual disability and related developmental disabilities.
Founded in 1876

12511 American Autoimmune Related Diseases Association
22100 Gratiot Ave.
Eastpointe, MI 48021

586-776-3900; Fax: 586-776-3903
www.aarda.org
Facebook, Twitter, YouTube, RSS

Betty Diamond, M.D., Chairperson
Noel R. Rose, M.D., Ph.D., Chairman Emeritus
Edward K. Christian, Advisor
Stephanie P. Halesÿ, Advisor
Virginia T. Ladd, President and Executive Director

Includes patient information about autoimmunity and autoimmune related diseases.

12512 American Behcet's Disease Association
PO Box 80576
Rochester, MN 48308

631-656-0537
800-723-4238; Fax: 480-247-5377
info@behcets.com
www.behcets.com

Deb Kleber, President
Mary Burke, VP
Belinda Rivasÿ, Treasurer
Marcia Wiseÿ, Executive Secretary
Mirta Avila Santos, MD, Executive Dir. & Comm Coordinator

Provides information and support for patients with Behcet's Diseaseand for their family members and caretakers.

12513 American Brain Tumor Association
8550 W. Bryn Mawr Ave.
Suite 550
Chicago, IL 60631

773-577-8750
800-886-2282; Fax: 773-577-8738
info@abta.org
www.abta.org
Facebook, Twitter, YouTube

Jeff Fougerousse, Chair
Brian Olson, Vice Chair
Carla Varner, Treasurer
James Reilly, Secretary
Elizabeth M. Wilson, MNA, President and CEO

National nonprofit organization dedicated to providing support services and programs to brain tumor patients and their families, as well as the funding of brain tumor research.
Founded in 1973

12514 American Burn Association
311 S. Wacker Drive
Suite 4150
Chicago, IL 60606

312-642-9260; Fax: 312-642-9130
www.ameriburn.org
Facebook, Twitter

Edward E. Tredget, MD, MSc, President
Michael D. Peck, MD, ScD, FACS, President Elect
Linwood R. Haith, MD, FACS, First Vice President
Ernest J. Grant, RN, BSN, MSNÿ, Second Vice President
William L. Hickerson, MD, FACS, Treasurer

Involved in research in the methods of treating burn injuries and fostering prevention efforts.
3500+ Members

12515 American Cannabis Nurses Association
750 National Press Building
529 14th St. NW
Washington, DC 20045

720-881-6047
www.cannabisnurses.org
Facebook, Twitter

Carey Clark, President
Ed Glick, Founder

A national organization that expands the knowledge base of endo-cannabinoid therapeutics among nurses.
Founded in 2010

12516 American Chronic Pain Association
PO Box 850
Rocklin, CA 95677

800-533-3231; Fax: 916-632-3208
ACPA@theacpa.org
Facebook, Twitter, YouTube, Pinterest

Penney Cowan, Founderÿ& CEO
Mary Jane Bentÿ, Board of Director
Chris Duncan, Board of Director
Daniel Galia, Board of Director
Steve Feinberg, MD, Board of Director

Information is provided concerning services, conditions, and pain management issues.
Founded in 1980

12517 American College Health Association
1362 Mellon Road
Suite 180
Hanover, MD 21076

410-859-1500; Fax: 410-859-1510
contact@acha.org
www.acha.org
Facebook, Twitter, YouTube

Jake Baggott, MLS, 1SG, President
Jamie Davidson, PhD, President Elect
Stephanieÿ Hanenberg, RN, MSN, Vice President
Beverly Kloeppel, MD, MBA, Treasurer
Sarah Van Orman, MD, MMM, FA, Immediate Past President

The American College Health Association (ACHA) is the principal advocate and leadership organization for college and university health. The association provides advocacy, education, communications, products, and services, as well as promoting research and culturally competent practices to enhance its members' ability to advance the health of all students and the campus community.
2600 Members
Founded in 1920

12518 American College of Allergy, Asthma and Immunology
85 West Algonquin Road
Suite 550
Arlington Heights, IL 60005-4460

847-427-1200; Fax: 847-427-1294
mail@acaai.org
www.acaai.org
Facebook, Twitter, LinkedIn, YouTube, Pinterest

Michael B Foggs, MD, President
Bryan L Martin, MD*, Vice President
Bradley E Chipps, MD, FACAAI*, Treasurer
James L Sublett, MD, FACAAI*, President-Elect
Bob Q Lanier, MD, Executive Medical Director

Information and news service for patients, parents of patients, members, the news media, and purchasers of health care programs.
5200 Members
Founded in 1942

12519 American College of Cardiology
Heart House
2400 N Street NW
Washington, DC 20037-1153

202-375-6000
800-253-4636; Fax: 202-375-7000
resource@acc.org
www.acc.org
Facebook, Twitter, LinkedIn, YouTube

Robert A.ÿ Shor, MD, FACC, Chair
Matthewÿ Phillips, MD, FACC, Chair-Elect
Michael Mansour, MD, FACC, Immediate Past Chairÿ
Kim Allan Williams, President
Richard A.ÿ Chazal, MD, FACC, President-Elect

The mission is to advocate for quality cardiovascular care-through education, research promotion, development and application of standards and guidelines-and to influence health care policy.
39M Members
Founded in 1949

12520 American College of Cardiovascular Administrators (ACCA)
American Academy of Medical Administrators
701 Lee Street
Suite 600
Des Plaines, IL 60016-4516

847-759-8601; Fax: 312-673-6705
info@aameda.org
www.acc.org

Renee L. Mazeroll, President
Kathy A. Miller, President-Elect

Mission is to advance ACCA members and the field of cardiovascular management and promote excellence and integrity in cardiovascular leadership.

12521 American College of Emergency Physicians
1125 Executive Circle
Irving, TX 75038-2522

972-550-0911
800-798-1822; Fax: 972-580-2816
membership@acep.org
www.acep.org
Facebook

Rebecca B. Parker, MD, FACEP, Chair
Michael J. Gerardi, President
Paul D. Kivela, MD, FACEP, VP
Jay A. Kaplan, MD, FACEP, President-Elect
John J. Rogers, MD, FACEP, Secretary-Treasurer

Promoting the highest quality emergency care, ACEP is the leading advocate for emergency physicians and their patients.
28M Members
Founded in 1968

12522 **American College of Healthcare Executives**
One North Franklin Street
Suite 1700
Chicago, IL 60606-3529
312-424-2800; Fax: 312-424-0023
contact@ache.org
www.ache.org
Facebook, Twitter, LinkedIn, Youtube
Edward H. Lamb, Chairman
Charles D. Stokes, Chairman-Elect
Deborah J.ÿ Bowen, FACHE, President & CEO
Thomas C. Dolan, PhD, President & CEO
Richard J. Stull, Executive Vice President
An international professional society of healthcare executives who lead hospitals, healthcare systems and other healthcare organizations.
40M Members
Founded in 1933

12523 **American College of Healthcare Information Administrators (ACHIA)**
701 Lee Street
Suite 600
Des Plaines, IL 60016-4516
847-759-8601; Fax: 847-759-8602
info@aameda.org
www.aameda.org/Colleges/ACHIA/healthcareinformation.html
Charles D. Chapdelaine, President
Develops innovative concepts in the field of healthcare information and promotes the advancement of its members in knowledge, professional standing, and personal achievements through continuing education and research in healthcare information administration. ACHIA focuses on providing education, support and opportunity for information technology leaders in the healthcare industry.
300 Members
Founded in 1991

12524 **American College of Medical Practice**
104 Inverness Terrace East
Englewood, CO 80112-5306
303-799-1111
877-275-6462
support@mgma.org
www.mgma.com
Facebook, Twitter, LinkedIn, Google+
Stephen A. Dickens, JD, FACMPE, F, Board Chair
Debra J. Wiggs, FACMPE, Vice Chair
Susan L. Turney, MD, MS, FACP,, President and CEO
Ronald W. Holder, Jr., MHA, FACM, Finance/Audit Chair
Delivering networking, professional education and resources and political advocacy for medical practice management.
3000 Members
Founded in 1926

12525 **American College of Medical Quality**
5272 River Road
Suite 630
Bethesda, MD 20816
301-718-6516; Fax: 301-656-0989
www.acmq.org
Facebook, Twitter, LinkedIn
Prathibha Varkey, President
Mark Lyles, MD, MBA, FACMQ, President Elect
Donald E. Casey, Jr MD, MPH, Vice President
John Vigorita, Secretary
Henry C. L. Johnson, Jr., MD, MPH, Treasurer
The mission of the American College of Medical Quality is to provide leadership and education in healthcare quality management.
Founded in 1973

12526 **American College of Oncology Administrators**
701 Lee Street
Suite 600
Des Plaines, IL 60016-4516
847-759-8601; Fax: 847-759-8602
info@aameda.org
www.aameda.org/Colleges/ACOA/oncology.html
Margaret A. O'Grady, President
Bonnie J. Miller, President-Elect
Focuses on providing support and opportunity for oncology administrators and managers in all types of healthcare institutions.
300 Members
Founded in 1991

12527 **American College of Oral and Maxillofacial Surgeons**
2025 M Street NW
Suite 800
Washington, DC 20036
202-367-1182
800-522-6676; Fax: 202-367-2182
admin@acoms.org
www.acoms.org
Facebook, Twitter, LinkedIn, RSS
Pedro F. Franco, President
R. Bryan Bell, President-Elect
Steven C. Kemp, Executive Director
Jeffrey Bennett, Treasurer
Kevin L. Rieck, Secretary
The diplomates have joined together in the College for the purpose of enhancing the level of patient care. This enhancement of surgical care through the furthering of research and education in OMS surgergy is achieved by the College's sponsoring of educational programs, research activities, and fellowships as a service to not only the members of the College, but to the profession at large.
2M+ Members
Founded in 1975

12528 **American College of Osteopathic Family Physicians**
330 E. Algonquin Road
Suite 1
Arlington Heights, IL 60005-4665
800-323-0794; Fax: 847-228-9755
membership@acofp.org
www.acofp.org
Facebook, Twitter, LinkedIn, Youtube
Kevin D. de Regnier, DO, FACOFP, President
Peter L Schmelzer, CAE, Executive Director
Rodney M. Wiseman, DO, FACOFPÿ, Vice President
Duane G. Koehler, DO, FACOFP, Secretary/Treasurer
Annie DeVries, Sr. Administrative Assistant
Works to promote excellence in osteopathic family medicine through quality education, visionary leadership and responsible advocacy.
20M Members
Founded in 1950

12529 **American College of Osteopathic Surgeons**
123 North Henry Street
Alexandria, VA 22314-2903
703-684-0416
800-888-1312; Fax: 703-684-3280
info@facos.org
www.facos.org
Facebook, Twitter, LinkedIn, YouTube
Linda Ayers, MHCM, CAE, CEO
Don Kaveny, Director of Postdoctoral Trainingÿ
Sonjya Johnson, Director of Membership Recruitment
Brandon Roberts, Director of Finance
Allison Hamrick, Manager, Marketing & Communication
Committed to assuring excellence in osteopathic surgical care through education, advocacy, leadership, development and the fostering of professional and personal relationship.
2147 Members
Founded in 1927

12530 **American College of Physicians**
190 North Independence Mall West
Philadelphia, PA 19106-1572
215-351-2400
800-523-1546; Fax: 215-351-2759
archives@acponline.org
www.acponline.org
Facebook, Twitter, LinkedIn, RSS
Tanveer P.ÿ Mir, MD, MACP, Chair, Board of Regents
Wayne J. Riley, President
Steven E. Weinberger, EVP/CEO
Robert A Gluckman, MD, FACP, Treasurer
David A. Fleming, MD, MA, FACP, Immediate Past President
Mission is to enhance the quality and effectiveness of health care by fostering excellence and professionalism in the practice of medicine.
Founded in 1915

12531 **American College of Rheumatology**
2200 Lake Boulevard NE
Atlanta, GA 30319
404-633-3777; Fax: 404-633-1870
www.rheumatology.org/
Facebook, Twitter, LinkedIn, YouTube
E. William St.Clair, MD, President
Joan Von Feldt, MD, MSEd, President Elect
Mark Andrejeski, Executive Director
Steve Echard, CAE, IOM,, Foundation Executive Director
David I. Daikh, MD, PhD, Foundation Secretary
Mission is advancing rheumatology. The organization is for physicians, health professionals, and scientists that meets the mission through programs of education, research, advocacy and practice support.
Founded in 1934

12532 **American College of Sports Medicine**
401 West Michigan Street
Indianapolis, IN 46202-3233
317-637-9200; Fax: 317-634-7817
www.acsm.org
Facebook, Twitter, YouTube, Pinterest, Instagram
Lawrence E. Armstrong, President
NiCole Keith, Ph.D., FACSM, First Vice President
Walter Thompson, Ph.D., FACSM, First Vice President
Craig Harms, Ph.D., FACSM, Second Vice Presidentÿ
Kathryn Schmitz, Ph.D., FACSM, Second Vice Presidentÿ
From academicians to students and from personal trainers to physicians, the association of sports medicine, exercise science, and health and fitness professionals is dedicated to helping people worldwide live longer, healthier lives.
50,00 Members
Founded in 1954

12533 **American College of Surgeons**
633 N Saint Clair Street
Chicago, IL 60611-3211
312-202-5000
800-621-4111; Fax: 312-202-5001
postmaster@facs.org
www.facs.org
Facebook, Twitter, LinkedIn, Youtube

Ronald J. Weigel, MD, PhD, FACS, Chair, Board of Governors
Taylor Riall, MD, PhD, FACS, Vice-Chair, Board of Governors
Mika Sinanan, MD, PhD, FACS, Secretary, Board of Governors
David B. Hoyt, MD, FACS, Executive Director
Patti Anderson, Admin. & Mailing List Contact

Dedicated to improving the care of the surgical patient and to safeguarding standards of care in an optimal and ethical practice environment.
82K Members
Frequency: Contact Re: Mailing List
Founded in 1913
Mailing list available for rent

12534 **American Congress of Obstetricians and Gynecologists**
409 12th Street SW
PO Box 70620
Washington, DC 20024-2188

202-638-5577
800-673-8444
sales@acog.org
www.acog.org
Facebook, Twitter, Youtube, RSS

Mark S. DeFrancesco, MD, MBA, President
Dr. Hal C Lawrence IIIÿ, EVP, CEO
Richard C Bailey, CPA, MBA, CFO, VP - Finance
Thomas M. Gellhaus, MD, President Elect
Dr Sandra Ann Carson, MD, Vice President, Education

Serving as a strong advocate for quality health care for women, maintaining the highest standards of clinical practice and continuing education for its members, promoting patient education and stimulating patient understanding of and involvement in medical care, and increasing awareness among its members and the public of the changing issues facing women's health care.
45M Members
Founded in 1951

12535 **American Congress of Rehabilitation Medicine**
11654 Plaza America Drive
Suite 535
Reston, VA 20190-4700

703-435-5335; Fax: 866-692-1619
info@ACRM.org
www.acrm.org
Facebook, Twitter, LinkedIn, Google+

Sue Ann Sisto, PT, MA, PhD, President
Jon W Lindberg, MBA, CAE, Chief Executive Officer
Douglas Katz, MD, FACRM, FAAN, Vice President
Wayne A. Gordon, PhD ABPP-CN, Treasurer
Cindy Harrison-Felix, Secretary

An organization of rehabilitation professionals dedicated to serving people with disabling conditions by supporting research that; promotes health, independence, productivity, and quality of life, and meets the needs of rehabilitatio clinicians and people with disabilities.
Founded in 1923

12536 **American Council of Academic Plastic Surgeons**
500 Cummings Center
Suite 4550
Beverly, MA 01915

978-927-8330; Fax: 978-524-0498
www.acaplasticsurgeons.org/

W. John Kitzmiller, M.D., President
C. Scottÿ Hultman, M.D., President-Elect
Michael L. Bentz, M.D., VP Finance and Communication
Donald R.ÿ Mackay, MD, FACS, VP Academic Administration
Anthony Aÿ Smith, M.D., Vice President of Education

Goal is to provide leadership and support for educational programs for plastic surgery residents.

12537 **American Counseling Association (ACA)**
6101 Stevenson Ave
Suite 600
Alexandria, VA 22304-3302

703-823-9800
800-347-6647; Fax: 703-823-0252
membership@counseling.org
www.counseling.org
Facebook, Twitter, LinkedIn

Thelma Duffey, Ph.D., President
Catherine Roland, President-Elect
Elias Zambrano, Treasurer
Richard Yep, CEO
Robert L. Smith, Past President

Dedicated to the growth and development of the counseling profession and those who are served.
45M Members
Founded in 1952

12538 **American Dance Therapy Association**
10632 Little Patuxent Parkway
Suite 108
Columbia, MD 21044

410-997-4040; Fax: 410-997-4048
www.adta.org
Facebook, LinkedIn, YouTube, Pinterest

Jody Wager, MS, BC-DMT, President
Margaret Migliorati, R-DMT, VP
Meghan Dempsey, MS, BC-DMT, Treasurer
Gail Wood,ÿMA, BC-DMT, NCC, Secretary
Susan D. Imus, Board of Director

Establishes and maintains standards of professional education in the field of dance/movement therapy.
Founded in 1966

12539 **American Dental Association**
211 East Chicago Avenue
Chicago, IL 60611-2678

312-440-2500; Fax: 312-440-2800
affiliates@ada.org
www.ada.org
Facebook, Twitter, LinkedIn, YouTube

Dr. Maxine Feinberg, President
Dr. Carol Gomez Summerhays, President Elect
Dr. Kathleen T. T. O'Loughlin, Executive Director

The oldest and largest national dental society in the world. Becoming the leading source of oral health related information for dentists and their patients. The professional association of dentists that fosters the success of a diverse membership and advances the oral health of the public.
156M Members
Founded in 1859

12540 **American Dental Education Association**
655 K Street, NW
Suite 800
Washington, DC 20001ÿ

202-289-7201; Fax: 202-289-7204
membership@adea.org
www.adea.org
Facebook, Twitter, YouTube

Huw F. Thomas, Chair of the Board
Cecile A. Feldman, Chair-elect of the Board
Lily T Garcia, Immediate Past Chair of the Boardÿ
David M. Shafer, D.M.D.ÿ, Board Director for Hospitals
Richard W. Valachovic, President and CEO

The voice of dental education. Members include all US and Canadian dental schools and many allied and postdoctoral dental education programs, corporations, faculty, and students. Mission is to lead individuals and institutions of the dental education community to address contemporary issues influencing education, research, and the delivery of oral health care for the health of the public.
21,00 Members
Founded in 1983

12541 **American Dental Hygenists Association**
444 North Michigan Avenue
Suite 3400
Chicago, IL 60611-3980

312-440-8900; Fax: 312-440-8929
member.services@adha.net
www.adha.org
Facebook, Twitter, LinkedIn, YouTube, Instagram

Jill Rethman, RDH, BA, President
Betty Kabel, RDH, BS, President Elect
Tammy Filipiak, RDH, MS, VP
Donnellaÿ Miller, RDH, BS, MPS, Treasurer
Kelli Swanson Jaecks, Immediate Past President

Mission is to advance the art and science of dental hygiene, and to promote the highest standards of education and practice in the profession.
Founded in 1993

12542 **American Dental Society of Anesthesiology**
211 E Chicago Ave
Suite 780
Chicago, IL 60611-6983

312-664-8270
877-255-3742; Fax: 312-224-8624
adsahome@mac.com
www.adsahome.org
Facebook, Twitter, Vimeo, Instagram

Kenneth L. Reed, DMD, President
Edward C. Adlesic, DMD, Board of Director
Michael Rollert, DDSÿ, President-Elect
Morton B. Rosenberg, DMD, Treasurer
Daniel S. Sarasin, DDS, VP

Mission is to provide a forum for education, research, and recognition of achievement in order to promote safe and effective patient care for all dentists who have an interest in anesthesiology, sedation and the control of anxiety and pain.
5000 Members
Founded in 1953

12543 **American Diabetes Association**
C/o Center for Information
2451 Crystal Drive
Arlington, VA 22202

703-549-1500
800-342-2383; Fax: 703-549-6995
askada@diabetes.org

www.diabetes.org
Facebook, Twitter, Vimeo, Instagram, Pinterest

Robin Richardson, Chair
Margaret Powers, President, Health Care & Education
Desmond Schatz, President, Medicine & Science
Lorrie W. Liang, Secretary/Treasurer
Kevin L. Hagan, Chief Executive Officer

Leading the fight against the deadly consequences of diabetes and fight for those affected. Funding research to prevent, cure and manage diabetes. Delivering services to hundreds of communitites. Providing objective and credible information. Giving a voice to those denied their rights because of diabetes.
Founded in 1940

12544 American Gastroenterological Association
4930 Del Ray Avenue
Bethesda, MD 20814

301-654-2055; Fax: 301-654-5920
member@gastro.org
www.gastro.org
Facebook, Twitter, LinkedIn, YouTube

Michael Camilleri, MD, AGAF, President
Sheila E. Crowe, MD, AGAF, Vice President
Francis M. Giardiello, MD, AGAF, Secretary/Treasurer
Timothy C.ÿ Wang, MD, AGAF, President-Elect
Martin Brotman, MD, AGAF, Foundation Chair

Advancing the science and practice of gastroenterology.
16000 Members
Founded in 1897

12545 American Head and Neck Society
11300 W Olympic Boulevard
Suite 600
Los Angeles, CA 90064

310-437-0559; Fax: 310-437-0585
admin@ahns.info
Facebook, Twitter, YouTube

Dennis Kraus, MD, President
Jonathan Irish, MD, Vice President
Brian B Burkey, MD MEd, Secretary
Ehab Hanna, MD, Treasurer
Jeffery Myers, MD, President-Elect

The single largest organization in North American for the advancement of research and education in head and neck oncology.
Founded in 1998

12546 American Headache Society
19 Mantua Road
Mount Royal, NJ 08061

856-423-0043; Fax: 856-423-0082
achehq@talley.com
www.americanheadachesociety.org
Facebook, Twitter

Paul Winner, DO, Chair

Professional society of health care providers dedicated to the study and treatment of headache and face pain. Members collaborate in producing educational programs and materials, coordinating the support groups, and undertaking public awareness initiatives all aimed at improving care for headache sufferers.
1500 Members
Founded in 1990

12547 American Health Care Association
1201 L Street, N.W.
Washington, DC 20005-4046

202-842-4444; Fax: 202-842-3860
webmaster@ahca.org
www.ahcancal.org
Facebook, Twitter, YouTube, Flickr, Blogspot

Represents the long term care community to the nation at large- to government, business leaders, and the general public. Serves as a force for change, providing information, education, and administrative tools that enhance quality at every level.
12M Members
Founded in 1949

12548 American Health Information Management Association
233 N. Michigan Avenue
21st Floor
Chicago, IL 60601-5809

312-233-1100
800-335-5535; Fax: 312-233-1090
Facebook, Twitter, LinkedIn, RSS, YouTube

Cassi Birnbaum, President/Chair
Melissa M. Martin, President/Chair-elect
Laura Pait, RHIA, CDIP, CCS, Speaker of The HoD
Lynne Thomas Gordon, CEO
Susan W.ÿ Carey, RHIT, PMP, Treasurer

Professional organization for the field of effective management of health data and medical record needed to deliver quality healthcare to the public management.
71,00 Members
Founded in 1928

12549 American Health Information Management Association
233 N. Michigan Avenue
21st Floor
Chicago, IL 60601-5809

312-233-1100
800-335-5535; Fax: 312-233-1090
info@ahima.org
www.ahima.org
Facebook, Twitter, LinkedIn, RSS, YouTube

Wylecia Wiggs Harris, PhD, CAE, Chief Executive Officer
Amy Mosser, MBA, Chief Operating Officer
Leslie M. Stokes, MBA, Chief Product/Marketing/Sales Off.
Cheryl D. Martin, HIM Strategic Advisor

Mission is to be the professional community that improves healthcare by advocating best practices and standards for health information management and the trusted source for education, reasearch, and professional credentialing.
103K Members
Founded in 1928

12550 American Health Quality Association
7918 Jones Branch Drive
Suite 300
McLean, VA 22102

202-331-5790; Fax: 202-331-9334
info@ahqa.org
www.ahqa.org

Dawn FitzGerald, MS, MBA, President
Jane Brock, MD, MSPH, President Elect
Kathleen D.ÿ Merrill, Immediate Past President
Rick Potter, Treasurer
Colleenÿ Delaney Eubanks, CAE, Executive Director

Represents Quality Improvement Organizations and professionals working to improve the quality of health care in communities across America. QIOs share information about best practices with physicians, hospitals, nursing homes, home health agencies, and others. Working together with health care providers, QIOs identify opportunities and provide assistance for improvement.

12551 American Heart Association
7272 Greenville Ave
Dallas, TX 75231-4596

214-373-6300
800-242-8721; Fax: 214-570-5930
Review.personal.info@heart.org
www.americanheart.org
Facebook, Twitter, YouTube, Google Plus

Bernie Dennis, Chairman
Mariell Jessup, President
Nancy Brown, CEO
Sunder Joshi, Chief Administrative Officer
Suzie Upton, Chief Development Officer

A nonprofit organization funding research and providing information on the diagnosis, treatment, and prevention of heart diseases and stroke. Mission is to build healthier lives, free of cardiovascular diseases and stroke.
Founded in 1924

12552 American Horticultural Therapy Association (AHTA)
610 Freedom Business Center
Suite 110
King of Prussia, PA 19406

610-992-0020; Fax: 610-225-2364
www.ahta.org
Facebook, Twitter, LinkedIn, Pinterest, Youtube, RSS

MaryAnne McMillan, HTR, President
Leigh Anne Starling, MS, CRC, Vice President
Todd Schappell, OTR/L, Treasurer
Patricia Cassidy, HTR, Secretary
Gabriela Harvey, HTR, Immediate Past President

A champion of barrier-free, therapeutic gardens that enable everyone to work, learn, and relax in the garden. Horticultural therapists are skilled at creating garden spaces that accommodate people with a wide range of abilities.
Founded in 1973

12553 American Hospital Association
155 N. Wacker Dr.
Chicago, IL 60606

312-422-3000
800-424-4301; Fax: 312-422-4500
ddavidson@aha.org
www.aha.org
Facebook, Twitter, YouTube

Benjamin K Chu, M.D., Chairman
Richard J Pollack, President and CEO
John Evans, CFO, SVP
Alicia Mitchell, SVP, Communications
Richard Umbdenstock, Past President, CEO

Represents and serves all types of hospitals, health care networks, and their patients and communities. Provides education for health care leaders and is a source of information on health care issues and trends.
43,00 Members
Founded in 1898

12554 American Industrial Hygiene Association
3141 Fairview Park Drive
Suite 777
Falls Church, VA 22042

703-849-8888; Fax: 703-207-3561
infonet@aiha.org
www.aiha.org
Facebook, Twitter, LinkedIn, RSS, YouTube

Steven E. Lacey, PhD, CIH, CSP, President
Cynthia A. Ostrowski, CIH, Vice President
J. Lindsay Cook, CIH, CSP, Treasurer
Kathleen S. Murphy, CIH, Secretary
Deborah Imel Nelson, PhD, CIH, President-Elect

Organization of professionals in the science of occupational and environmental health and safety. Devoted to achieving and maintaining the highest professional standards for members. Promoting certification of industrial hygienists.
10000 Members
Founded in 1939

12555 **American Institute of Ultrasound in Medicine**
14750 Sweitzer Lane
Suite 100
Laurel, MD 20707-5906
301-498-4100
800-638-5352; Fax: 301-498-4450
cvalente@aium.org
www.aium.org
Facebook, Twitter, LinkedIn, YouTube, Instagram
Beryl R. Benacerraf, MD, President
Joseph R Wax, MD, First Vice President
Charlotte G. Henningsen, Second Vice President
Michael Blaivas, MD, Third Vice President
Brian D. Coley, MD, President-Electÿ
A multidisciplinary association dedicated to advancing the safe and effective use of ultrasound in medicine through professional and public education, research, development of guidelines, and accreditation.
85M Members
Founded in 1952

12556 **American Institute of Ultrasound in Medici ne**
14750 Sweitzer Lane
Suite 100
Laurel, MD 20707-5906
301-498-4100
800-638-5352; Fax: 301-498-4450
cvalente@aium.org
www.aium.org
Facebook, Twitter, LinkedIn, YouTube, Instagram
Beryl R. Benacerraf, MD, President
Joseph R Wax, MD, First Vice President
Charlotte G. Henningsen, Second Vice President
Michael Blaivas, MD, Third Vice President
Brian D. Coley, MD, President-Electÿ
A multidisciplinary association dedicated to advancing the safe and effective use of ultrasound in medicine through professional and public education, research, development of guidelines, and accreditation.
9.8M Members
Founded in 1952

12557 **American Lung Association**
1301 Pennsylvania Ave. NW
Suite 800
Washington, DC 20004
202-785-3355; Fax: 202-452-1805
info@lungusa.org
www.lung.org
Facebook, Twitter, YouTube, Google Plus, RSS
Albert A. Rizzo, Chair
Ross P. Lanzafame, Esq., Chair-Elect
Christine L. Bryant, Secretary/ Treasurer
Dedicated to the prevention, cure, and control of lung diseases such as asthma, emphysema, tuberculosis, and lung cancer. The Association offers community service, public health education, advocacy, and research.
Founded in 1904

12558 **American Massage Therapy Association**
500 Davis Street
Suite 900
Evanston, IL 60201
847-864-0123
877-905-0577; Fax: 847-864-5196
info@amtamassage.org
www.amtamassage.org/
Facebook, Twitter, LinkedIn, RSS, YouTube
Jeff Smoot, President
Nathan J. Nordstrom, President Elect
Nancy M. Porambo, Immediate Past President
Glyn Desmond, Board of Director
Maureen P.ÿ Hoock, Board of Director
Nonprofit, professional association serving massage therapists, massage students and massage schools.

12559 **American Medical Association**
330 N. Wabash Avenue
Chicago, IL 60611-5885
800-621-8335
robin_rusell@ama-assn.org
www.ama-assn.org
Facebook, Twitter, LinkedIn, Google+
James L. Madara, MD, CEO, EVP
Bernard L. Hengesbaugh, Chief Operating Officer
Denise M Hagerty, SVP, CFO
Robert W Davis, SVP, HR & Corporate Services
Kenneth J. Sharigian, SVP, Chief Strategy Officer
Mission is to promote the art and science of medicine and the betterment of public health. The American Medical Association helps doctors help patients by uniting physicians nationwide to work on the most important professional and public health issues.
Founded in 1847

12560 **American Medical Directors Association**
11000 Broken Land Parkway
Suite 400
Columbia, MD 21044
410-740-9743
800-876-2632; Fax: 410-740-4572
info@amda.com
www.amda.com
Facebook, Twitter, LinkedIn
Naushira Pandya, MD, FACP, CMD, President
Heidi K. White, Vice President
Daniel Haimowitz, Secretary
Arif Nazir, MD, FACP, CMD, Treasurer
Susan M. Levy, MD, CMD, AGSF, President-Elect
Professional association of medical directors, attending physicians, and others practicing in the long term care continuum, is dedicated to excellence in patient care and provides education, advocacy, information, and professional development to promote the delivery of quality long term care medicine.
Founded in 1978

12561 **American Medical Group Association**
One Prince Street
Alexandria, VA 22314-3318
703-838-0033; Fax: 703-548-1890
dfisher@amga.org
www.amga.org
Facebook, Twitter, LinkedIn, YouTube, Flickr
Don L. Wreden, M.D., Chair
Donald W Fisher, Ph.D., CAE, President and CEO
Donn E. Sorensen, Chair Elect
Barbara A. Walters, D.O., M.B.A., Treasurer
Clyde L. Morris, C.P.A., CFO
Represents medical groups and organized systems of care, including some of the nation's largest, most prestigious integrated healthcare delivery systems. Mission is to improve health care for patients by supporting multispecialty medical groups and other organized systems of care.
113M Members
Founded in 1950

12562 **American Medical Informatics Association**
4720 Montgomery Lane
Suite 500
Bethesda, MD 20814
301-657-1291; Fax: 301-657-1296
www.amia.org
Facebook, Twitter, LinkedIn, YouTube
Karen Greenwood, EVP, COO & Interim CEO
Krista Martin, VP, Marketing & Communications
Lee Ann Pirrello, VP, Membership
Jasmine Casteel, Director, Finance
Dasha Cohen, Director, Meetings
Aims to lead the way in transforming health care through trusted science, education, and the practice of informatics. Connecting a broad community of professionals and students interested in informatics, AMIA is the bridge for knowledge and collaboration across a continuum, from basic and applied research to the consumer and public health arenas.
3200 Members
Founded in 1990

12563 **American Medical Marijuana Association**
Home Page: www.ammainfo.com
Facebook
A leading organization for professionals, advocates, and those interested in the benefits, application, and proper use of medical marijuana (cannabis) in the treatment of health conditions.

12564 **American Medical Marijuana Physicians Asso ciation**
407-917-0887
medicalmarijuanaphysicians@gmail.com
www.ammpa.net
Facebook, Twitter, YouTube
Savara Hastings, Executive Director
Supports physicians and other healthcare professionals who use medical marijuana as a treatment for a legally indicated diagnosis.
Founded in 2016

12565 **American Medical Student Association**
45610 Woodland Road
Suite 300
Sterling, VA 20166
703-620-6600
800-767-2266; Fax: 703-620-6445
members@amsa.org
www.amsa.org
Facebook, Twitter, Inex, Youtube
Deborah Vozzella Hall, MD, National President
Kelly Thibert, President Elect
Joshua Weinstock, VP for Internal Affairs
Rinku Skaria, VP for Membership
Perry Tsai, VP for Program Development
The oldest and largest independent association of physicians-in-training in the United States. Committed to improving the lives of medical students.
40M Members
Founded in 1950

12566 **American Medical Technologists**
10700 West Higgins Road
Suite 150
Rosemont, IL 60018-3722
847-823-5169
800-275-1268; Fax: 847-823-0458
mail@americanmedtech.org
www.americanmedtech.org
Facebook, Twitter, LinkedIn, Youtube
Everett Bloodworth, President
Jeffrey Lavender, Vice President

Heather Herring, Secretary
Jeannette Hobson, Treasurer
Edna Anderson, Executive Councillor

Mission is to manage, promote, expand upon and continuously improve their certification programs for allied health professionals who work in a variety of disciplines and settings, to administer certification examinations in accordance with the highest standards of accreditation, and to provide continuing education, information, advocacy services and other benefits to members.
Founded in 1939

12567 **American Medical Women's Association**
1100 E. Woodfield Road
Suite 350
Schaumburg, IL 60173
847-517-2801; Fax: 847-517-7229
associatedirector@amwa-doc.org
www.amwa-doc.org
Facebook, Twitter, LinkedIn, Flickr

Connie Newman, MD, President
Eliza Lo Chin, MD, MPH, Executive Director
Sharon Batista, MD, Treasurer
Lynda Kabbash, MD, Secretary
Roberta Gebhard, DO, President-Elect

An organization of women physicians, medical students and other persons dedicated to serving as the unique voice for women's health and the advancement of women in medicine.
10000 Members
Founded in 1915

12568 **American Music Therapy Association (AMTA)**
8455 Colesville Road
Suite 1000
Silver Spring, MD 20910-3392
301-589-3300; Fax: 301-589-5175
info@musictherapy.org
www.musictherapy.org
Facebook, Twitter, YouTube

Andrea Farbman, Executive Director
Mary Ellen Wylei, AMTA President

AMTA's purpose is the progressive development of the therapeutic use of music in rehabilitation, special education, and community settings. AMTA is committed to the advancement of education, training, professional standards, credentials, and research in support of the music therapy profession.
3800 Members
Founded in 1998

12569 **American Nephrology Nurses Association**
East Holly Avenue
Box 56
Pitman, NJ 08071-0056
856-256-2320; Fax: 856-589-7463
anna@annanurse.org
www.annanurse.org
Facebook, Twitter, RSS

Cindy A. Richards, BSN RN CNN, President
Sheila J.ÿ Doss-McQuitty, President-Elect
Sharon M.ÿ Longton, Immediate Past President
Susan Cary, MN APRN NP CNN, Treasurer
Lynda K. Ball, MSN RN CNN, Secretary

Mission is to promote excellence by advancing nephrology nursing practice and positively influence outcomes for individuals with kidney disease.
Founded in 1969

12570 **American Nurses Association**
8515 Georgia Avenue
Suite 400
Silver Spring, MD 20910-3492
800-274-4ANA; Fax: 301-628-5001
anf@ana.org
www.nursingworld.org
Facebook, Twitter, LinkedIn, YouTube

Pamela F. Cipriano, PhD, RN, President
Cindy R. Balkstra, MS, RN, Vice President
Gingy Harshey-Meade, MSN, Treasurer
Patricia Travis, PhD, RN, CCRP, Secretary
Andrea C. Gregg, PhD, RN, Director at Large

Advances the nursing profession by fostering high standards of nursing practice, promoting the rights of nurses in the workplace, projecting a positive and realistic view of nursing, and by lobbying the Congress and regulatory agencies on health care issues affecting nurses and the public.

12571 **American Occupational Therapy Association**
4720 Montgomery Lane
Ste 200
Bethesda, MD 20814-3449
301-652-6611
800-729-2682; Fax: 301-652-7711
www.aota.org
Facebook, Twitter, LinkedIn, RSS

Florence Clark, President
Ginny Stoffel, Vice President
Paul A. Fontana, Secretary
Saburi Imara, Treasurer

Representing the interests and concerns of occupational therapy practitioners and students of occupational therapy and to improve the quality of occupational therapy services.
42M Members
Founded in 1917

12572 **American Optometric Association**
243 N Lindbergh Blvd
Flr. 1
St Louis, MO 63141-7881
314-991-4100
800-365-2219; Fax: 314-991-4101
Facebook, Twitter, LinkedIn, RSS, Youtube

Mitchell T. Munson, O.D, President
Steven A. Loomis, O.D., Vice President
Andrea P. Thau, O.D., Secretary/ Treasurer

National organization of optometrists, evaluates ophthalmic products and sponsors continuing education programs.
36M Members
Founded in 1898

12573 **American Optometric Student Association**
243 N Lindbergh Blvd
Suite 311
St Louis, MO 63141-7881
314-983-4231
rfoster@theaosa.org
www.theaosa.org/

Robert Foster, Executive Director
Alan Wegener, Vice President
Vicky Wong, Secretary
Elizabeth Turnage, Treasurer

Committed to promoting the optometric profession, enhancing the education and welfare of optometry students, as well as enhancing the vision and ocular health of the public.
6M Members

12574 **American Orthopaedic Foot & Ankle Society**
9400 West Higgins Road
Suite 220
Rosemont, IL 60018-4263
847-698-4654
800-235-4855; Fax: 847-823-8125
www.aofas.org
Facebook, Twitter, LinkedIn

Mark E. Easley, MD, President
Jeffrey E.ÿ Johnson, MD, President-Elect
ThomasÿH. Lee, MD, Vice President
J. Chris Coetzee, MD, Treasurer
Bruce J. Sangeorzan, MD, Immediate Past President

Mission is to promote quality, ethical and cost effective patient care through education, research and training of orthopaedic surgeons and other health care providers, create public awareness for the prevention and treatment of foot and ankle disorders, provide leadership, and serve as a resource for government, industry and the national and international health care community.
35000 Members
Founded in 1969

12575 **American Orthopaedic Foot and Ankle Society**
9400 West Higgins Road
Suite 220
Rosemont, IL 60018-4975
847-698-4654
800-235-4855; Fax: 847-692-3315
aofasinfo@aofas.org
www.aofas.org/
Facebook, Twitter, LinkedIn

Mark E. Easley, MD, President
Jeffrey E.ÿ Johnson, MD, President-Elect
ThomasÿH. Lee, MD, Vice President
J. Chris Coetzee, MD, Treasurer
Bruce J. Sangeorzan, MD, Immediate Past President

Specialty society for orthopedic surgeons with training and interest in the prevention and treatment of foot and ankle conditions.
Founded in 1969

12576 **American Orthopaedic Society for Sports Medicine**
9400 W. Higgins Road
Suite 300
Rosemont, IL 60018ÿ
847-292-4900
877-321-3500; Fax: 847-292-4905
www.sportsmed.org
Facebook, Twitter

Irvin E. Bomberger, Executive Director
Camille Petrick, Managing Director
Heather Hodge, Education Director
Kevin M. Boyer, MPHÿÿ, Director of Research
Lisa Weisenberger, Director of Communications

Promotes sports medicine education, research, communication, and fellowship and includes national and international orthopaedic sports medicine leaders.

12577 **American Orthopsychiatric Association**
C/o Clemson University, IFNL
225 S. Pleasantburg Dr.
Suite B-11
Greenville, SC 29607
864-250-4622; Fax: 864-250-4633
www.bhjustice.org

Andres J. Pumariega, President
Donald Wertlieb, President-Elect
Jan L. Culbertson, Secretary
William Reay, Treasurer
Robin Kimbrough-Melton, Executive Officer

Provides a common ground for collaborative study, research, and knowledge exchange among individuals from a variety of disciplines engaged in preventive, treatment, and advocacy approaches to mental health.
Founded in 1923

12578 **American Orthotic & Prosthetic Association**
330 John Carlyle Street
Suite 200
Alexandria, VA 22314
571-431-0876; Fax: 571-431-0899
info@aopanet.org
www.aopanet.org
Facebook, Twitter, LinkedIn, Youtube
Michael Oros, President
Chris Nolan, Vice President
Jim Weber, President Elect
Jeff Collins, Treasurer
Tom Fise, Executive Director
A national trade association committed to providing high quality, unprecedented business services and products to O&P professionals.
Founded in 1917

12579 **American Osteopathic Association**
142 E Ontario St
Chicago, IL 60611-2864
312-202-8000
800-621-1773; Fax: 312-202-8200
info@osteotech.org
www.osteopathic.org
Facebook, Twitter, LinkedIn, Youtube, Pinterest
John W. Becher, DO, President
Adrienne White-Faines, MPA, CEO
Geraldine O'Shea, DO, Second Vice President
Frank M. Tursi, DO, Third Vice President
Boyd R. Buser, DO, President-Electÿ
Promotes public health, encourages scientific research, and is the accrediting agency for all osteopathic medical schools and health care facilities.
52M Members
Founded in 1897

12580 **American Osteopathic College of Dermatology**
2902 North Baltimore Street
P.O. Box 7525
Kirksville, MI 63501
660-665-2184
800-449-2623; Fax: 660-627-2623
www.aocd.org
Facebook, Twitter, Tumblr
Marsha Wise, Executive Director
John Grogan, Resident Coordinator
Shelley Wood, Grants Coordinator
Alpesh Desai, President
Specialty college that promotes the practice of osteopathic dermatology.
Founded in 1958

12581 **American Pain Society**
8735 W. Higgins Road
Suite 300
Chicago, IL 60631
847-375-4715; Fax: 847-375-6479; Fax: 732-460-7318
info@americanpainsociety.org
www.americanpainsociety.org/
Facebook, Twitter, LinkedIn, Youtube
Roger Fillingim, PhD, President
Catherine H Underwood, MBA CAE, Executive Director
David A. Williams, PhD, Treasurer
Kathleen Sluka, PT PhD, Secretary
Gregory W Terman, MD PhD, President-Elect
The American Pain Society is a multidisciplinary community that brings together a diverse group of scientists, clinicians and other professionals to increase the knowledge of pain and transform public policy and clinical practice to reduce pain-related suffering.
Founded in 1977

12582 **American Pediatric Surgical Association**
One Parkview Plaza
Suite 800
Oakbrook Terrace, IL 60181
847-686-2237; Fax: 847-686-2253
www.eapsa.org/
Twitter
Mary Fallat, Presidentÿ
Diana Farmer, President-Elect
Michael D. Klein, Immediate Past Presidentÿ
Daniel Von Allmen, Treasurer
John H.T. Waldhausen, Secretary
Pediatric surgical care of patients and their families.

12583 **American Pharmacists Association (APhA)**
2215 Constitution Avenue NW
Suite 400
Washington, DC 20037-2985
202-628-4410
800-237-2742; Fax: 202-783-2351
www.pharmacist.com
Facebook, Twitter, LinkedIn, RSS, Youtube
Stacie Maass, SVP, Pharmacy Practice
Thomas E. Menighan, BSPharm, MBA, Chief Executive Officer
Jule Miller, SVP, Human Resources
Joseph J. Janela, Chief Financial Officer
Elizabeth K. Keyes, Chief Operating Officer
The American Pharmacists Association (APhA) is an organization whose members are recognized in society as essential in all patient care settings for optimal medication use that improves health, wellness, and quality of life. Through information, education, and advocacy, APhA empowers its members to improve medication use and advance patient care.
60000 Members
Founded in 1852

12584 **American Physical Therapy Association**
1111 North Fairfax Street
Alexandria, VA 22314-1488
703-683-6748
800-999-2782; Fax: 703-684-7343
memberservices@apta.org
www.apta.org
Facebook, Twitter, LinkedIn, Youtube
Sharon L.ÿ Dunn, PT, PhD, OCS, President
Lisa K. Saladin, Vice President
J. Michael Bowers, CEO
Rob Batarla, MBA, CPA, CAE, EVP, Financial and Business Affairs
Elmer Platz, PT, Treasurer
The principal membership organization representing and promoting the profession of physical therapy, is to furhter the profession's role in the prevention, diagnosis, and treatment of movement dysfunctions and the enhancement of the physical health and functional abilities of members of the public.
74000 Members

12585 **American Physiological Society**
9650 Rockville Pike
Bethesda, MD 20814-3991
301-634-7164; Fax: 301-634-7241
webmaster@the-aps.org
www.the-aps.org
Facebook, Twitter, LinkedIn, YouTube
Patricia Molina, M.D., Ph.D.ÿ, President
David M.ÿ PollockÿPh.D, Past President
Jane Reckelhoff, Ph.D., President Elect
Martin Frank, PhD, Executive Director
Robert Price, Director of Finance
A nonprofit devoted to fostering education scientific research and dissemination of information in the physiological sciences. A member of the Federation of American Societies for Experimental Biology (FASEB) a coalition of 18 independent societies that plays an active role in lobbying for the interests of biomedical scientists.
10,50 Members
Founded in 1887

12586 **American Podiatric Medical Association**
9312 Old Georgetown Road
Bethesda, MD 20814-1621
301-581-9200; Fax: 301-530-2752
www.apma.org
Facebook, Twitter, LinkedIn, YouTube
Matthew G. Garoufalis, DPM, President
Phillip E. Ward, DPM, Vice President
R. Daniel Davis, DPM, Treasurer
Glenn B. Gastwirth, DPM, Secretary
An association of podiatrists providing services and information on foot problems and foot health.
11000 Members
Founded in 1912

12587 **American Porphyria Foundation**
4900 Woodway
Suite 780
Houston, TX 77056-1837
713-266-9617
866-APF-3635; Fax: 713-840-9552
www.porphyriafoundation.com
James V. Young, Chairman, Board of Trustee
Desiree H. Lyon, Executive Director
Dr. William McCutchen, Board Member
Warren Hudson, Board Member
Andrew Turell, Board Member
Dedicated to improving the health and well-being of individuals andfamilies affected by Porphyria. Also advocates for public, private, and government agencies interested in funding research and educational programs.
Founded in 1982

12588 **American Psychiatric Association**
1000 Wilson Boulevard
Suite 1825
Arlington, VA 22209-3901
703-907-7300
888-357-7924; Fax: 703-907-1085
apa@psych.org
www.psychiatry.org
Facebook, Twitter, LinkedIn
Saul M. Levin, M.D., M.P.A., CEO, Medical Director
Maria A. Oquendo, President
Association for manufacturers, suppliers, distributors, publishers, state/federal agencies and psychiatric facilities.
Founded in 1844

12589 **American Psychological Association**
750 First St. NE
Washington, DC 20002-4242
202-336-5500
800-374-2721; Fax: 202-336-5518
www.apa.org
Facebook, Twitter, LinkedIn, YouTube, Google+, RSS
Barry S. Anton, PhD, President
Norman B. Anderson, PhD, Chief Executive Officer, EVP
Susan McDaniel, PhDÿ, President Elect
Nadine J. Kaslow, PhDÿ, Past President
Bonnie Markham, PhD, PsyDÿ, Treasurer
The largest scientific and professional organization representing psychology in the United States and the largest association of psychologists in the world, dedicated to advancing psychology as a

science and as a means of promoting health, education, and human welfare.
12250 Members
Founded in 1892

12590 **American Public Health Association**
800 I Street NW
Washington, DC 20001

202-777-2742; Fax: 202-777-2534
comments@apha.org
www.apha.org
Facebook, Twitter

Georges C. Benjamin, Executive Director

Influencing policies and setting priorities for over 125 years. Thoughout its history it has been in the forefront of numerous efforts to prevent disease and promote health.
Founded in 1872

12591 **American Public Human Services Association**
1133 19th Street, NW
Suite 400
Washington, DC 20036-3623

202-682-0100; Fax: 202-289-6555
www.aphsa.org
Facebook, Twitter, LinkedIn

Reggie Bicha, President
Tracy Wareing, Executive Director
Nicole Lobban, Human Resources Director
Raymond Washington III, Director of Finance
Anita Light, Senior Deputy Executive Director

Pursues excellence in health and human services by supporting state and local agencies, informing policymakers, and working wtih our partners to drive innovative, integrated and efficient solutions in policy and practice.
Founded in 1930

12592 **American Rhinologic Society**
PO Box 495
Warwick, NY 10990

845-988-1631; Fax: 845-986-1527
www.american-rhinologic.org/

Roy Casiano, MD, President
Joseph Jacobs, MD, Executive Vice President
Peter Hwang, MD, President-elect
John DelGaudio, MD, 1st Vice President
Richard Orlandi, MD, 2nd Vice President

Physician organization whose focus is upon the medical and surgicaltreatment of patients with diseases of the nose and paranasal sinuses.

12593 **American School Health Association**
7918 Jones Branch Drive
Suite 300
McLean, VA 22102

703-506-7675; Fax: 703-503-3266
info@ashaweb.org
www.ashaweb.org
Facebook, Twitter, LinkedIn, YouTube

Linda Morse, RN, MA, CHES, President
Ty Oehrtman, VP
Sharon Murray, MHSE, FASHA, Treasurer
Sharon Miller, Secretary
Sandy Klarenbeek, Chair of Advocacy

Concerned with all health factors that are necessary for students to be ready to learn, including optimum nutrition, physical fitness, emotional well-being, and a safe and clean environment.
2000 Members
Founded in 1927

12594 **American Sleep Apnea Association**
1717 Pennsylvania Avenue, NW
Suite 1025
Washington, DC 20006

888-293-3650; Fax: 888-293-3650
www.sleepapnea.org/
Facebook, Twitter, Google+, YouTube, Vimeo

Will Headapohl, Chair
Adam Amdurÿ, COO
Addison Closson, Treasurer
Nancy Rothstein, Secretary
Tracy R. Nasca, Executive Director

A nonprofit organization that promotes education, awareness and research into sleep apnea.
Founded in 1990

12595 **American Society for Aesthetic Plastic Surgery**
36 W 44th Street
New York, NY 10036

212-921-0500; Fax: 212-921-0011
media@surgery.org
www.surgery.org
Facebook, Twitter, LinkedIn

Jack Fisher, MD, President
James C. Grotting, MD, Vice President
Daniel C. Mills, II, MD, Treasurer
Clyde H. Ishii, MD, Secretary

Organization of plastic surgeons certified by the American Board of Plastic Surgery who specialize in cosmetic surgery of the face and body.

12596 **American Society for Cell Biology**
8120 Woodmont Avenue
Suite 750
Bethesda, MD 20814-2762

301-347-9300; Fax: 301-347-9310
ascbinfo@ascb.org
www.ascb.org
Facebook, Twitter, LinkedIn, Vimeo

Shirley M. Tilghman, President
Stefano Bertuzzi, PhD, Executive Director
Thea Clarke, Director of Comm. & Education
John Fleischman, Senior Science Writer
Christina Szalinski, Science Writer/Program Coordinator

A nonprofit membership organization of biologists studying the cell, the fundamental unit of life. Membership is open to all research scientists, students, educators, and technicians who have education or research experience in cell biology or an allied field.
10M Members
Founded in 1960

12597 **American Society for Dermatologic Surgery**
5550 Meadowbrook Drive
Suite 120
Rolling Meadows, IL 60008

847-956-0900; Fax: 847-956-0999
www.asds.net
Facebook, Twitter, LinkedIn, YouTube

Naomi Lawrence, MDÿ, President
Lisa M. Donofrio, MD, Vice President
Katherine J. Duerdoth, CAE, Executive Director
Thomas Rohrer, MD, President Elect
Mathew M. Avram, MD, JD, Treasurer

To promote optimal quality care for patients as well as support and develop investigative knowledge in the field of dermatologic surgery.
5,800 Members
Founded in 1973

12598 **American Society for Healthcare Risk Management**
155 N. Wacker Drive
Suite 400
Chicago, IL 60606-4425

312-422-3980; Fax: 312-422-4580
ashrm@aha.org
www.ashrm.org
Facebook, Twitter, LinkedIn, YouTube

Denise Shope, President
Hala Helm, President Elect
Faye Sheppard, Past-President
Matt B. Hornberger, MBA, CAE, Executive Director
Virginia Petrancosta, CAE, Director, Marketing & Comm.

National organization for the health care industry risk management equipment, supplies and services.
6000+ Members
Founded in 1980
Mailing list available for rentat $129 per M

12599 **American Society for Histocompatability and Immunogenetics**
1120 Route 73
Suite 200
Mt. Laurel, NJ 08054

856-638-0428; Fax: 856-439-0525
info@ashi-hla.org
www.ashi-hla.org
Facebook, Twitter, LinkedIn

Kathy Miranda, Executive Director
Mandi Cruz, Assistant Executive Director
Melissa Weeks, Accreditation Manager

Dedicated to advancing the science, education, and application of immunogenetics and transplant immunology.
Founded in 1974

12600 **American Society for Laser Medicine and Surgery, Inc.**
2100 Stewart Avenue
Suite 240
Wausau, WI 54401-1709

715-845-9283
877-258-6028; Fax: 715-848-2493
information@aslms.org
www.aslms.org
Facebook, Twitter, LinkedIn, Google+, YouTube, Pinterest

Dianne Dalsky, Executive Director
Corri Marschall, Conference Specialist
Paula Deffner, Accounting Specialist
Diane Dodds, Member and Customer Service
Andrea Alstad, Marketing & Communications Mgr.

Promotes excellence in patient care by advancing biomedical application of lasers and other related technologies worldwide.
Founded in 1980

12601 **American Society for Microbiology**
1752 N Street, N.W.
Washington, DC 20036-2904

202-737-3600; Fax: 202-942-9341
service@asmusa.org
www.asm.org
Facebook, Twitter, LinkedIn, Instagram, Youtube

Jeffery Miller, President
Joseph M. Campos, Secretary

The world's largest scientific society of individuals interested in the microbiological sciences.
39,00 Members

12602 **American Society for Nutrition**
9650 Rockville Pike
Bethesda, MD 20814

301-634-7050; Fax: 301-634-7894
www.nutrition.org
Facebook, LinkedIn, Youtube, RSS

Patrick J. Stover, PhD, President
Marian Neuhouser, PhD, RD, Vice-President
Simin Nikbin Meydani, Past President
Barbara Lyle, PhD, Treasurer
Susan Percival, PhD, Secretary

A non-profit organization dedicated to bringing together the world's top researchers, clinical nutritionists and industry to advance our knowledge and application of nutrition for the sake of humans and animals.
Founded in 1928

12603 **American Society for Pharmacology and Experimental Therapeutics**
9650 Rockville Pike
Bethesda, MD 20814-3995

301-634-7060; Fax: 301-634-7061
info@aspet.org
www.aspet.org
Facebook, Twitter, LinkedIn, Flickr

Judith A. Siuciak, Ph.D., Executive Director
Matthew Hilliker, Chief Financial Officer
Suzie Thompson, Director of Marketing
Richard Dodenhoff, Director of Journals
Cecilia Fox, Meetings and Admin. Coordinator

Members research efforts help develop new medicines and therapeutic agents to fight existing and emerging diseases.
5,000 Members
Founded in 1909

12604 **American Society for Surgery of the Hand**
822 W. Washington Boulevard
Suite 600
Chicago, IL 60607

312-880-1900; Fax: 847-384-1435
info@assh.org
www.assh.org
Facebook, Twitter, LinkedIn

Mark C. Anderson, FASAE, CAE, EVP, CEO
Pamela Schroeder, CAE, Deputy EVP
Angie Legaspi, CMP, VP, Professional Development
Bill Chandler, Director of Finance
Tara Spiess, Director of Publishing, Marketingÿ

The oldest medical specialty society in the United States devoted entirely to continuing medical education related to hand surgery.
3,500 Members
Founded in 1946

12605 **American Society for Therapeutic Radiology And Oncology**
8280 Willow Oaks Corporate Drive
Suite 500
Fairfax, VA 22031

703-502-1550
800-962-7876; Fax: 703-502-7852
meetings@astro.org
www.astro.org
Facebook, Twitter, LinkedIn, YouTube

Bruce D. Minsky,ÿ MD, FASTRO, Chairman
David C. Beyer,ÿ MD, FASTRO, President
Jeff M. Michalski, Secretary/Treasurer
Brian Kavanagh, President-elect
Bruce G. Haffty,ÿ MD, FASTRO, Immediate Past Chair

Provides members with the continuing medical education, health policy analysis, patient information resources and advocacy that they need to succeed in today's ever-changing health care delivery system.
10M Members
Founded in 1958

12606 **American Society of Addiction Medicine**
11400 Rockville Pike
Suite 200
Rockville, MD 20852

301-656-3920; Fax: 301-656-3815
email@asam.org
www.asam.org
Facebook, Twitter, LinkedIn, YouTube

Penny S. Mills, Executive Vice President
Carolyn C. Lanham, Chief Operating Officer

ASAM represents professionals in the addiction field. It promotes research and prevention, education for physicians and the public and improving access to, and quality of, treatment.
5000+ Members
Founded in 1954

12607 **American Society of Anesthesiologists**
1061 American Lane
Schaumburg, IL 60173-4973

847-825-5586; Fax: 847-825-1692
info@asahq.org
www.asahq.org
Facebook, Twitter, LinkedIn, YouTube

J.P. Abenstein, President
Daniel J.ÿ Cole, MD, President Elect
Jane C. K. Fitch, M.D., Immediate Past President
Jeffrey Plagenhoef, M.D.ÿ, First Vice President
James D.ÿ Grant, MD, Treasurer

An educational, research and scientific association of physicians organized to raise and maintain the standards of the medical practice of anesthesiology and improve the care of the patient.
39M Members
Founded in 1905
Mailing list available for rent

12608 **American Society of Angiology**
708 Glen Cove Ave
Glen Head, NY 11545

516-671-1975; Fax: 516-759-5524
anngailius@amsocang.org
www.amsocang.org/

David K Jackson, MD, President
Ann Gailius, Director, Membership

Striving to incorporate a variety of disciplines to encourage education and interaction in our common fields of endeavor.

12609 **American Society of Cataract & Refractive Surgery**
4000 Legato Rd
Suite 700
Fairfax, VA 22033-4055

703-591-2220
800-451-1339; Fax: 703-591-0614
ascrs@ascrs.org
www.ascrs.org
Facebook, Twitter, YouTube, Flickr

Robert J. Cionni, MD, President
Kerry D. Solomon, MD, Vice President/President Elect
Richard A. Lewis, MD, Immediate Past President
Bonnie An Henderson, MD, Treasurer
Thomas W. Samuelson, MD, Secretary

The mission of the American Society of Cataract and Refractive Surgery is to advance the art and science of ophthalmic surgety and the knowledge and skills of ophthalmic surgeons. It does so by providing clinical and practice management education and by working with patients, government, and the medical community to promote the delivery of quality eye care.
9,000 Members
Founded in 1974

12610 **American Society of Clinical Oncology**
2318 Mill Road
Suite 800
Alexandria, VA 22314

571-483-1300; Fax: 703-299-1044
abstracts@asco.org
www.asco.org
Facebook, Twitter, LinkedIn, Youtube

Julie M. Vose, MD, MBA, FASCO, President
Craig R. Nichols, MD, Treasurer
Daniel F. Hayes, MD, FASCO, President-Elect
Peter Paul Yu, Past-President
Richard L. Schilsky, Chief Medical Officer

Goal is to improve cancer care and prevention. Members include physicians and health-care professionals in all levels of the practice of oncology.
30M Members
Founded in 1964
Mailing list available for rent

12611 **American Society of Clinical Pathologists**
33 West Monroe Street
Suite 1600
Chicago, IL 60603

312-541-4999; Fax: 312-541-4998
www.ascp.org
Facebook, Twitter, LinkedIn, Youtube

William G. Finn, MD, FASCP, President
William E. Schreiber, MD, FASCP, Vice President
Melissa Perry Upton, MD, FASCP, Secretary
Gregory N. Sossaman, MD, FASCP, Treasurer
David N.B. Lewin, MD, FASCP, President Elect

Mission is to provide excellence in education, certification and advocacy on behalf of patients, pathologists and laboratory professionals across the globe.
100M+ Members

12612 **American Society of Colon and Rectal Surgeons**
85 West Algonquin Road
Suite 550
Arlington Heights, IL 60005

847-290-9184
800-791-0001; Fax: 847-290-9203
ascrs@fascrs.org
www.fascrs.org
Facebook, Twitter, LinkedIn

Charles Littlejohn, MD, President
Patricia L. Roberts, MD, President-Elect
Terry C. Hicks, MD, Past President
Guy R. Orangio, MD, Vice President
Neil H. Hyman, MD, Treasurer

The premier society for colon and rectal surgeons and other surgeons dedicated to advancing and promoting the science and practice of the treatment of patients with diseases and disorders affecting the colon, rectum and anus.
3,300 Members
Founded in 1899

12613 **American Society of Cytopathology**
100 West 10th Street
Suite 605
Wilmington, DE 19801-6604

302-543-6583; Fax: 302-543-6597
asc@cytopathology.org
www.cytopathology.org
Facebook, Twitter, LinkedIn, YouTube

Michael R. Henry, MD, President
Eva M. Wojcik, MD, MIAC, President Elect

Edmund S. Cibas, MD, Vice President
Daniel F. I. Kurtycz, MD, Treasurer
Elizabeth Jenkins, Executive Director

A professional organization dedicated to the science and study of cells. Membership includes physicians, cytotechnologists and scientists who practice the cytologic method of diagnostic pathology. Committed to education, research, and advocacy on behalf of its membership, with the ultimate goal of improving the standards and quality of patient care.
3,000 Members
Founded in 1951

12614 **American Society of ExtraCorporeal Technology**
2209 Dickens Road
Richmond, VA 23230-2005

804-565-6363; Fax: 804-282-0090
www.amsect.org
Facebook, Twitter, LinkedIn, YouTube

Jeffrey B. Riley MHPE CCT CCP, President
Kenny Shann CCP, President-Elect
Robert C. Groom MS CCP, Treasurer
Susan J. Englert RN CCP CPBMT, Secretary
Stewart Hinckley, Executive Director

Enhancing the quality of extracorporeal (involving heart and lung machines) technology rendered to the public by engaging in the programmatic activities that will further the knowledge, skills, abilities and general proficiency of practitioners.
2000 Members
Founded in 1964

12615 **American Society of Forensic Odontology**
4414 82nd Street
Suite 212
Lubbock, TX 79424

Home Page: www.asfo.org
Facebook, Twitter

Dr. Roger Metcalf, President
Dr. Bruce Schrader, Executive Director
Dr.ÿJacquelineÿ Reid, Secretary
Dr. Eric Wilson, Treasurer
Dr.ÿDavid Senn, President Elect

ASFO is one of the largest organizations representing all of those interested in forensic dentistry worldwide. Mission and goal to encourage and stimulate investigation and research in forensic odontology and related disciplines.
Founded in 1970

12616 **American Society of Health-System Pharmacists**
7272 Wisconsin Avenue
Bethesda, MD 20814-4861

301-657-3000
866-279-0681; Fax: 301-664-8877
custserv@ashp.org
connect.ashp.org
Facebook, Twitter, LinkedIn, YouTube, RSS

John A. Armitstead, President
Philip J. Schneider, Treasurer
Lisa M. Gersema, President-Elect
Paul W. Abramowitz, CEO
Christene M. Jolowsky, Immediate Past President

ASHP is a national professional association that represents pharmacists who practice in hospitals, health maintenance organizations, long-term care facilities, home care, and other compnents of health care systems.
30K Members
Founded in 1936

12617 **American Society of Hematology**
2021 L Street NW
Suite 900
Washington, DC 20036-3508

202-776-0544; Fax: 202-776-0545
ash@hematology.org
www.hematology.org
Facebook, Twitter, LinkedIn, Youtube

David A. Williams, MD, President
Charles S. Abrams, MD, President-Elect
Kenneth C. Anderson, MD, Vice President
Stephanie J. Lee, MD, MPH, Secretary
Susan B. Shurin, MD, Treasurer

Mission is to further the understanding, diagnosis, treatment, and prevention of disorders affecting the blood, bone marrow, and the immunologic, hemostatic and vascular systems, by promoting research, clinical care, education, training, and advocacy in hematology.
15,00 Members
Founded in 1958

12618 **American Society of Human Genetics, Inc.**
9650 Rockville Pike
Bethesda, MD 20814-3998

301-634-7300
866-HUM-GENE; Fax: 301-634-7079
society@ashg.org
www.ashg.org
Facebook, Twitter, LinkedIn, YouTube, RSS

Neil J. Risch, PhD, President
Cynthia C. Morton, PhD, Past President
Harry C. Dietz, MD, President-Elect
Geoffrey M. Duyk, MD PhDÿ, Treasurer
Brendan Lee, MD PhD, Secretary

The primary professional membership organization for human genetics worldwide. Members include researchers, academicians, clinicians, laboratory practice professionals, genetic counselors, nurses and others involved in or with special interest in human genetics.
8000 Members
Founded in 1948

12619 **American Society of Nephrology**
1510 H Street, NW
Suite 800
Washington, DC 20005

202-640-4660; Fax: 202-637-9793
email@asn-online.org
www.asn-online.org
Facebook, Twitter, LinkedIn, YouTube, Google+, Flickr, RSS

Jonathan Himmelfarb, MD, FASN, President
Sharon M. Moe, MD, FASN, Past President
Raymond C. Harris, MD, FASN, President-Elect
John R. Sedor, MD, FASN, Secretary-Treasurer
Tod Ibrahim, Executive Director

Leads the fight against kidney disease by educating health professionals, sharing new knowledge, advancing research, and advocating the highest quality care for patients.

12620 **American Society of Neuroradiology**
800 Enterprise Dr.
Suite 205
Oak Brook, IL 60523

630-574-0220; Fax: 630-574-0661
ltannehill@asnr.org
www.asnr.org
RSS

Laurie A. Loevner, MD, President
Howard A. Rowley, MD, President-Elect
Joshua A. Hirsch, MD, Treasurer
Tina Y. Poussaint, MD, Secretary
James B. Gantenberg, FACHE, Executive Director

Active members must devote approximately one half or more of their professional practice to nueroradiology. Publishes a monthly journal and holds an annual meeting.
3000 Members
Founded in 1962

12621 **American Society of Ophthalmic Administrators**
4000 Legato Road
Suite 700
Fairfax, VA 22033

703-788-5777
800-451-1339; Fax: 703-547-8827
asoa@asoa.org
www.asoa.org
Facebook, Twitter

John S. Bell, MBA, COE, CMPE, President
William T. Koch, COE, COA, CPC, Vice President
Daniel Chambers, MBA, COE, President-Elect
Sondra Soffman, COE, CPC, Immediate Past President
Laureen Rowland, CAE, Executive Director

The premier organization for the business side of the ophalmic practice.
Founded in 1986

12622 **American Society of Plastic Surgeons**
444 E Algonquin Road
Arlington Heights, IL 60005

847-228-9900
888-475-2784; Fax: 847-228-9131
webmaster@plasticsurgery.org
www.plasticsurgery.org
Facebook, Twitter, YouTube, Google+, Instagram, P

Scot Bradley Glasberg, MD, President
Michael D. Costelloe, JD, Executive Vice President
Keith M. Hume, Staff Vice President
Carol L. Lazier, Staff Vice President
Mark Espinosa, Staff Vice President

Promotes the specialty of plastic surgery and supports the highest quality patient care, professionalism and ethical standards through our role as patient and physician advocates.
Founded in 1931

12623 **American Speech-Language-Hearing Association**
2200 Research Boulevard
Rockville, MD 20850-3289

301-897-5700
800-638-8255; Fax: 301-296-8580
actioncenter@asha.org
www.asha.org
Facebook, Twitter, LinkedIn, YouTube, Instagram, Pinterest

Patricia A. Prelock, PhD, CCC-SLP, President
Donna Fisher Smiley, PhD, CCC-A, Vice President for Audiology
Howard Goldstein, PhD, CCC-SL, Vice President for Science
Carolyn W. Higdon, EdD, CCC-SLP, Vice President for Finance
Barbara J. Moore, EDD, CCC-SLP, Vice President for Planning

Represents the interests of medical specialists in speech, language, and hearing science and advocates for people with communication-related disorders.
Founded in 1925

12624 **American Stroke Association (ASA)**
7272 Greenville Ave
Dallas, TX 75231-5129

214-706-1556
888-478-7653; Fax: 214-570-5930
www.strokeassociation.org
Facebook, Twitter, YouTube, RSS

Lee Schwamm, Chairman

The American Stroke Association (ASA) is the division of the American Heart Association that's solely focused on reducing disability and death from stroke through research, education, fundraising and advocacy. The ASA offers a wide array of programs, products and services, from patient education materials to scientific statements.

12625 **American Tinnitus Association**
522 SW Fifth Avenue
Suite 825
Portland, OR 97204-2143
503-248-9985
800-634-8978; Fax: 503-248-0024
tinnitus@ata.org
www.ata.org/
Facebook, Twitter, YouTube

Melanie F. West, Chair
Scott C. Mitchell, J.D., C.P.A., Vice Chair
Gary P. Reul, Ed.D., Treasurer
David M. Sykes, Secretary
Paul F. Morris, CFRE, Development Director

The American Tinnitus Association (ATA) exists to cure tinnitus through the development of resources that advance tinnitus research. ATA board and staff work with researchers, tinnitus sufferers, donors, legislators and other concerned individuals to support vital tinnitus research.

Founded in 1971

12626 **American Urological Association**
1000 Corporate Boulevard
Linthicum, MD 21090-2260

410-689-3700
866-746-4282; Fax: 410-689-3800
aua@AUAnet.org
www.auanet.org
Facebook, Twitter, LinkedIn, YouTube

William F. Gee, MD, FACS, President
Richard K. Babayan, MD, President-Elect
William W. Bohnert, MD, FACS, Immediate Past President
Manoj Monga, MD, FACS, Secretary
Steven M. Schlossberg, MD, MBA, Treasurer

The premier professional association for the advancement or urologic patient care, and works to ensure that its members are current on the latest research and practices in urology.

12627 **Americans for Safe Access**
1624 U St. NW
Suite 200
Washington, DC 20009

202-857-4272; Fax: 202-618-6977
info@safeaccessnow.org
www.safeaccessnow.org
Facebook, Twitter, Google+, Instagram, YouTube

Steph Sherer, Executive Director
Debbie Churagi, Deputy Director
Geoffrey Marshall, Office & Membership Coordinator
Reenal Doshi, Director, Outreach & Communications
David Mongone Esq., Director, Government Affairs

Works to ensure safe and legal access to cannabis for therapeutic use and research.

Founded in 2002

12628 **Arthroscopy Association of North America**
9400 W. Higgins Road
Suite 200
Rosemont, IL 60018

847-292-2262; Fax: 847-292-2268
info@aana.org
www.aana.org

Jeffrey S. Abrams, MDÿÿ, President
John C. Richmond, MD, First Vice-President
Robert E. Hunter, MDÿÿÿÿÿÿ, Second Vice-President ÿ
Louis F. McIntyre, MD, Treasurerÿÿÿÿ
Larry D. Field, MD, Secretary

Goal is to promote, encourage, support and foster through continuing medical education functions, the development and dissemination of knowledge in the discipline of arthroscopic surgery.

12629 **Association for Gerontology in Higher Education**
1220 L Street NW
Suite 901
Washington, DC 20005-4018

202-289-9806; Fax: 202-289-9824
aghe@aghe.org
www.aghe.org
Facebook, Twitter, LinkedIn, YouTube, Google+

Donna L. Wagner, President
Christine A. Fruhauf, Treasurer
Lydia Manning, Secretary
Nina M. Silverstein, President-Elect
M Angela Baker, Director

A membership organization devoted primarily to gerontological education, the Association for Gerontology in Higher Education (AGHE) strives to develop and sponsor education and training initiatives and to involve students, educators, researchers, and officials from across the country in providing resources for older adults and for those who serve them.
Founded in 1974

12630 **Association for Healthcare Documentation Integrity**
4120 Dale Road
Suite J8-233
Modesto, CA 95356

209-527-9620
800-982-2182; Fax: 209-527-9633
ahdi@ahdionline.org
www.ahdionline.org
Facebook, Twitter, LinkedIn, Pinterest

Jay Vance, President
Sheila Guston, CHDS, AHDI-F, President-Elect
Sheryl Williams, CHDS, AHDI-F, Treasurer
Diane Warth, CHDS, RHIT, CPC, Secretary
Susan Dooley, Immediate Past President

AHDI works tirelessly to give thousands of medical transcriptionists a voice before legislative and regulatory agencies and to ensure MTs are recognized for their contributions to patient safety and risk management.
7000 Members
Founded in 1978

12631 **Association for Medical Imaging Management**
490B Boston Post Rd
Suite 200
Sudbury, MA 01776-3367

978-443-7591
800-334-2472; Fax: 978-443-8046
memberservices@ahraonline.org
www.ahraonline.org
Facebook, Twitter, LinkedIn, YouTube

Ernie Cerdena, CRA, FAHRA, President
Chris Tomlinson, CRA, FAHRA, Finance Director
Edward J Cronin, Jr., Chief Executive Officer
Kerri Hart-Morris, Associate Editor
Jason Newmark, CRA, FAHRA, President Elect

Professional association of radiology administrators from the US, Canada and several other countries. AHRA is a resource and catalyst for the development of professional leaders in imaging sciences and other health care disciplines.
5,000 Members
Founded in 1973

12632 **Association for Professionals in Infection Control and Epidemiology, Inc.**
1275 K St NW
Suite 1000
Washington, DC 20005-4006

202-789-1890; Fax: 202-789-1899
info@apic.org
www.apic.org
Facebook, Twitter, LinkedIn, Youtube

Mary Lou Manning, President
Marc Oliver Wright, MT, MS, Treasurer
Connie Steed, RN, MSN, CICÿ, Secretary
Susan A. Dolan, RN, MS, CICÿ, President-Elect
Katrina Crist, MBA, CEO

Mission is to improve health and patient safety by reducing risks of infection. APIC advances its mission through education, research, collaboration, practice guidance, public policy, and credentialing.
15,00 Members
Founded in 1972

12633 **Association for the Advancement of Medical Instrumentation**
4301 N. Fairfax Drive
Suite 301
Arlington, VA 22203-1633

703-525-4890; Fax: 703-276-0793
customerservice@aami.org
www.aami.org
Facebook, Twitter, LinkedIn, Youtube

Michael Scholla, PhD, Chair
Mary Logan, JD, CAE, President
Eamonn V. Hoxey, PhD BPharm, Treasurer/Secretary
C. Phillip Cogdill, Chair Elect
Ray Laxton, Immediate Past Chair

Mission is to increase the understanding and beneficial use of medical instrumentation through effective standards, educational programs, and publications.
Founded in 1967

12634 **Association of Air Medical Services**
909 N. Washington Street
Suite 410
Alexandria, VA 22314-3143

703-836-8732; Fax: 703-836-8920
information@aams.org
www.aams.org/
RSS

Cameron Curtis, President & CEO
Garet Turner, VP, Member Experience
Christopher Eastlee, VP, Public Affairs
Christina Childs, Director, Special Events
Diana ÿ Lundie, Tradeshow Manager

Voluntary, nonprofit organization, encourages and supports its members in maintaining a standard of performance reflecting safe operations and efficient, high quality patient care. Built on the idea that representation from a variety of medical transport services and businesses can be brought together to share information, collectively resolve problems and provide leadership in the medical transport community.
Founded in 1980

12635 **Association of American Physicians and Surgeons**
1601 N Tucson Boulevard
Suite 9
Tucson, AZ 85716-3450
800-635-1196; Fax: 520-325-4230
aaps@aapsonline.org
www.aapsonline.org
Facebook, Twitter
Tom Kendall, Sr., M.D., President, Executive Director
David Stumph
AAPS is a nonpartisan professional association of physicans in all types of practices and specialties across the country.
Founded in 1943

12636 **Association of Applied Psychophysiology and Biofeedback**
10200 West 44th Avenue
Suite 304
Wheat Ridge, CO 80033-2837
303-422-8436
800-477-8892; Fax: 303-422-8894
info@aapb.org
www.aapb.org
Facebook, Twitter
Richard Harvey, PhD, President
Thomas Collura, PhD, President-Elect
Stuart C. Donaldson, PhD, Past-President
Fred B. Shaffer, PhD, Treasurer
David Stumph, CAE, AAPB, Executive Director
Goals of the association are to promote a new understanding of biofeedback and advance the methods used in this practice. Mission is to advance the development, dissemination and utilization of knowledge about applied psychophysiology and biofeedback to improve health and the quality of life through research, education and practice.
Founded in 1969

12637 **Association of Cannabis Specialists**
62 Old Stage Rd.
Litchfield, NH 03052
800-645-0807
info@cannabis-specialist.org
www.cannabis-specialists.org
Twitter, LinkedIn
Jordan Tishler, MD, President
Danielle Feldman, Committee Coordinator
Rachel Schecter, Committee Coordinator
Ensures the highest standards in the practice of cannabis medicine, safeguards patient care with best practices, and collaborates with other stakeholders in the cannabis community.
Founded in 2017

12638 **Association of Family Medicine Administration**
11400 Tomahawk Creek Parkway
Leawood, KS 66211-2672
800-274-2237; Fax: 913-906-6084
www.afmaonline.org/
Star Andrews, C-TAGME, President
Eileen Morroni, C-TAGME, President-Elect
Debbie Blackburn, C-TAGME, Immediate Past President
Gina Silvey, C-TAGME, Co-Treasurer
Bobbi Kruse, AA, Edu. Comm.ÿ-ÿRAD Workshop, Chair
Promotes professionalism in family practice administration. Serves as a network for sharing information and fellowship among members. Provides technical assistance to members, functions as a liaison to related professional organizations.

12639 **Association of Family Medicine Residency Directors**
11400 Tomahawk Creek Parkway
Suite 670
Leawood, KS 66211-2672
913-906-6000
800-274-2237; Fax: 913-906-6105
www.afmrd.org
Michael Mazzone, MD, President
Todd D. Shaffer, MD, MBA,ÿ, Immediate Past President
Lisa Maxwell, MD, President Elect
Karen Mitchell, MD, Treasurer
Katy Kirk, MD, MPH, Resident Representative
Inspires and empowers family medicine residency program directors to achieve excellence in family medicine residency training.
410 Members
Founded in 1990

12640 **Association of Healthcare Internal Auditors**
One Parkview Plaza
Suite 800
Oakbrook Terrace, IL 60181
303-327-7546
888-275-2442; Fax: 720-881-6101
info@ahia.org
www.ahia.org
LinkedIn, YouTube
Mary Jane Schroeder, Chair
Cavell Alexander, Vice Chair
Todd Havens, Secretary/Treasurer
Michelle Cunningham, Executive Director
The Association of Internal Auditors (AHIA) is a network of experienced healthcare internal auditing professionals who come together to share tools, knowledge and insight on how to assess and evaluate risk within a complex and dynamic healthcare environment. AHIA is an advocate for the profession, continuing to elevate and champion the strategic importance of healthcare internal auditors with executive management and the Board.
Founded in 1981

12641 **Association of Otolaryngology Administrators**
2400 Ardmore Boulevard
Suite 302
Pittsburgh, PA 15221
412-243-5156; Fax: 412-243-5160
Facebook, LinkedIn
Jo Ann LoForti, President
Jeff Dudley, President-Elect
James Benson, Secretary-Treasurer
Robin L. Wagner, Executive Director
Seeks to promote the concept of professional management in otolaryngology, provide a forum for interaction and exchange of information between otolaryngological managers and present educational programs. Maintains data exchange service for members researching specific topics.
1000 Members
Founded in 1983

12642 **Association of Pediatric Hematology/ Oncology Nurses**
8735 W. Higgins Rd
Ste 300
Chicago, IL 60631
847-375-4724; Fax: 847-375-6478
info@aphon.org
www.aphon.org
Jami Gattuso, MSN RN CPON, President
Dave Bergeson, PhD CAE, Executive Director
Nicole Wallace, Senior Operations Manager
Jennifer Schap, Education Manager
Stephanie Sayen, Marketing Manager
Members are dedicated to promoting optimal nursing care for children, adolescents, and young adults with cancer and blood disorders, and their families. APHON provides the leadership and expertise to pediatric hematology/oncology nurses by defining and promoting the highest standards of practice and care to the pediatric, adolescent, and young adult communities.
3,000 Members
Founded in 1973

12643 **Association of Perioperative Registered Nurses**
2170 South Parker Rd
Suite 400
Denver, CO 80231-5711
303-755-6300
800-755-2676; Fax: 800-847-0045
custserv@aorn.org
www.aorn.org
Facebook, Twitter, LinkedIn, Slideshare, Pinterest, Youtube
Renae Battie, MN, RN, CNOR, President
Martha Stratton, President-Elect
Nathalie Walker, MBA, RN, CNOR, Secretary
Stephanie S.ÿ Davis, MSHA, RN, CNOR, Treasurer
Callie Craig, VP
A nonprofit membership association that represents the interests of perioperative nurses by providing nursing education, standards, and clinical practice resources.
41,00 Members
Founded in 1954

12644 **Case Management Society of America**
6301 Ranch Drive
Little Rock, AR 72223
501-225-2229; Fax: 501-221-9068
cmsa@cmsa.org
www.cmsa.org
Facebook, Twitter, LinkedIn
Kathy Fraser, President
Rebecca Perez, RN, BSN, CCM, Secretary
Catherine Campbell, RN, MSN, MBA, Treasurer
Cheri A Lattimer, RN, BSN, Executive Director
Mary McLaughlin-Davis, President-Elect
The leading memberhsip association providing professional collaboration across the health care continuum to advocate for patients' wellbeing and improved health outcomes.
Founded in 1990

12645 **Catholic Health Association**
4455 Woodson Road
St Louis, MO 63134-3797
314-427-2500; Fax: 314-427-0029
khewitt@chausa.org
www.chausa.org
Facebook, Twitter, LinkedIn, YouTube
Carol Keehan, DC, President
Adele Gianino, Director, Meetings & Travel
Ana Hilton, Government Relations Coordinator
Betsy Taylor, Associate Editor, Catholic Health
Betty Crosby, Executive Assistant
Led by dedicated women and men, both religious and lay, who combine advanced technology and innovative treatment with caring traditdion. As provider, employer, and advocate, Catholic health care is committed to improving the health status of communities and creating quality and compassionate health care that works for everyone, especially the vulnerable.
2000+ Members
ISSN: 0882-1577
Founded in 1915

12646 **Christopher & Dana Reeve Paralysis Resource Center**
636 Morris Turnpike
Suite 3A
Short Hills, NJ 07078-2608
973-467-8270
800-225-0292; Fax: 973-912-9433
www.christopherreeve.org
Facebook, Twitter, LinkedIn, YouTube, Google+, Pinterest, F
John M. Hughes, Chairman
John E. McConnell, Vice Chairman
Peter T. Wilderotter, President and CEO
Susan Howley, Executive Vice President, Research
Maggie Goldberg, Vice President, Policy and Programs
The Christopher & Dana Reeve Paralysis Resource Center (PRC) promotes the health and well-being of people living with paralysis and their families by providing comprehensive information resources and referral services.
Founded in 2001
Mailing list available for rent

12647 **Clinical Laboratory Management Association**
330 N. Wabash Avenue
Suite 2000
Chicago, IL 60611
312-321-5111; Fax: 610-995-9568
info@clma.org
www.clma.org
Facebook, Twitter, LinkedIn, YouTube
Patty Eschliman, President
Jane Mÿ Hermansen, President Elect
Rodney W Forsman, Treasurer
Paul L. Epner, Past-President
Deborah Wells, Board Member
Founded in 1976

12648 **Consumer Healthcare Products Association**
1625 Eye Street, NW
Suite 600
Washington, DC 20006-2105
202-429-9260; Fax: 202-223-6835
eassey@chpa-info.org
www.chpa.org
Twitter, YouTube, Pinterest
Scott Melville, President and CEO
Brian Green, Vice President, Finance, CFO
John F Gay, Vice President, Government Affairs
Barbara A Kochanowski, Ph.D, Vice President, Regulatory Affairs
Theodore L Peterson, Vice President, Corporate Dev
Promotes industry growth through consumer understanding, appreciation, and acceptance of responsible self-care in America's health care system by developing and sustaining a climate that provides consumers with convenient access to safe and effective nonprescription medicines and other self-care products marketed without undue restrictions.
Founded in 1881

12649 **Cremation Association of North America**
499 Northgate Parkway
Wheeling, IL 60090-2646
312-245-1077; Fax: 312-321-4098
info@cremationassociation.org
www.cremationassociation.org
Facebook, Twitter, LinkedIn, Youtube
Sheri Stahl, President
Michael Sheedy, First Vice President
Mitch Rose, Second Vice Presidentÿ
Timothy R. Borden, President-Elect (Treasurer)
Robert M Boetticher, Jr.ÿ, Past Presidentÿ
founded in 1913, the Cremation Association of North America is an international association of over 3,300 members comprised of funeral homes, cemeteries, crematories, consultants and suppliers. CANA members believe that cremation is prepareation for memorialization.

12650 **Dental Group Management Association**
North Point Dental Group
2525 E Arizona Biltmore Circle
Suite 127
Phoenix, AZ 85016
602-381-8980; Fax: 602-381-1093
www.dgma.org
Vincent Cardillo, President
Jill Nesbtt, Vice President
The DGMA is a national organization which recognizes the importance of professional management in group dental practices. The purpose of the Association is to advance dental group management and practice administration.
200 Members
Founded in 1951

12651 **Digital Phenom**
700 Princess Street
Suite 2M
Alexandria, VA 22314
202-393-0000
800-432-3247; Fax: 202-737-8406
staff@digitalphenom.com
Atilla Kocsis, President
Ismaila Togola, Sr. Developer - Content Management
James Patterson, Project Management
Siaka Togola, Junior Dev. -ÿContent Management
A non-profit educational foundation with a membership of companies engaged in the manufacture, preparation, compounding or processing of aspirin and aspirin products. AFA serves as a central source of information on the health benefits of aspirin and aspirin products, when used as directed.
Founded in 1995

12652 **Doctors for Cannabis Regulation**
601 Ewing St.
Suite C-10
Princeton, NJ 08540
202-930-0097; Fax: 202-754-9817
media@dfcr.org
www.dfcr.org
Facebook, Twitter
Brian Muraresku, JD, Legal Counsel
Antoinette O'Neil, Financial Controller
Suzanne Wills, CPA, Accountant
Represents physicians who oppose prohibition and believe that the misuse of cannabis is a health issue, not a criminal one. Promotes evidence-based strategies for legalization and effective regulation of cannabis in the U.S.

12653 **Emergency Nurses Association**
915 Lee Street
Des Plaines, IL 60016-6569
847-460-4100
800-900-9659; Fax: 847-698-9406
membership@ena.org
www.ena.org
Facebook, Twitter, Google Plus
JoAnn Lazarus, MSN, RN, CEN, President
Susan M. Hohenhaus, LPD,ÿRN, CE, Executive Director
Matthew F Powers, MS, BSN, RN, M, Secretary/Treasurer
Deena Brecher,ÿMSN, RN, APRN, President-Elect
Founded in 1968

12654 **Federation of American Health Systems**
750 9th Street, NW
Suite 600
Washington, DC 20001-4524
202-624-1500; Fax: 202-737-6462
info@fah.org
www.fah.org
Facebook, Twitter, LinkedIn, RSS
Chip Kahn, President and CEO
Keith Pitts, Vice Chairman
Matthew D. Klein, Treasurer
William F. Carpenter III, Secretary
Michael D. Bromberg, Vice Chair of the Board
Founded in 1966

12655 **Gerontological Society of America**
1220 L Street NW
Suite 901
Washington, DC 20005
202-842-1275; Fax: 202-842-1150
geron@geron.org
www.geron.org
Facebook, Twitter, LinkedIn, YouTube, Google+
Rita Effros, President
Nancy Morrow, President Elect
Rosemary Blieszner, Past President
Suzanne Kunkel, Treasurer
Tamara Baker, Secretary
800+ Members
Founded in 1945

12656 **Health Industry Distributors Association**
310 Montgomery Street
Alexandria, VA 22314
703-549-4432
rowan@hida.org
www.hida.org
Matthew Rowan, President and CEO
Elizabeth Hilla, SVP
Linda Rouse O'Neill, VP, Govt. Affairs
Balvinder Bains, VP, Finance & Operations
The trade association representing medical products distributors. Provides leadership in the healthcare distribution industry.
Founded in 1902

12657 **Health Industry Manufacturers Association**
1200 G Street NW
Washington, DC 20005-3814
FAX 202-783-8750
Established as the Wholesale Surgical Trade Association. Represents manufacturers of health care technology, including medical devices, diagnostic products, and health care information systems.

12658 **Healthcare Compliance Packaging Council**
2711 Buford Road
#268
Bon Air, VA 23235-2423
804-338-5778; Fax: 888-812-4272
pgmayberry@aol.com
www.hcpconline.org
Facebook, LinkedIn
Peter G Mayberry, Executive Director
Kathleen Hemming, Staff Consultant
Nonprofit trade association promoting the benefits of unit dose blister and strip packaging — especially its ability to be designed in compliance prompting formats that help people take their medications properly.
Founded in 1990

12659 **Healthcare Convention & Exhibitors Association**
1100 Johnson Ferry Rd.ÿ
Suite 300
Atlanta, GA 30342-1733
678-298-1183; Fax: 404-836-5595
hcea@kellencompany.com
www.hcea.org
Facebook, Twitter, LinkedIn
Christine Farmer, President
Kyle Wood, Vice President
Sue Huff, Secretary/Treasurer
Don Schmid, MBA, CME/H, President-Elect
Diane Benson, CTSM, Immediate Past President
Trade association of organizations involved in health care exhibiting or providing services to health care conventions, exhibitions and/or meetings.
600 Members
Founded in 1930

12660 **Healthcare Distribution Alliance**
901 North Glebe Road
Suite 1000
Arlington, VA 22203
703-787-0000; Fax: 703-812-5282
www.hda.org
Twitter, LinkedIn
Chester Davis, Jr., President/CEO
Ann W. Bittman, EVP/COO
Elizabeth A. Gallenagh, General Counsel/SVP, Supply Chain
A national association representing primary, full-service healthcare distributors. HDMA and its members are the vital link in the healthcare system, working daily to provide value, remove costs and develop innovative solutions.
Founded in 1876

12661 **Healthcare Financial Management Association**
3 Westbrook Corporate Center
Suite 600
Westchester, IL 60154-5723
708-531-9600
800-252-4362; Fax: 708-531-0032
jfifer@hfma.org
www.hfma.org
Facebook, Twitter, LinkedIn, YouTube
Joseph J Fifer, FHFMA, CPA, CEO & President
Joyce Zimowski, FHFMA, CPA, Executive Vice President & CFO
Susan Brenkus, Vice President, Human Resources
Richard L Gundling, FHFMA, CMA, Vice President, Healthcare
Brings perspective and clarity to the industry's complex issues for the purpose of preparing our members to succeed. Through our programs, publications and partnerships we enhance the capabilities that strengthen not only individual careers, but also the organizations from which our members come.
34000 Members
Founded in 1946

12662 **Healthcare Marketing & Communications Council**
1525 Valley Center Parkway
Bethlehem, PA 18017
610-868-8299; Fax: 610-868-8387
www.hmc-council.org
Janis Cohen, President/CEO
Gary J Gyss, Founder
Enhancing the professional development of its members by providing continuing education and career development opportunities. The council also works toward a better understanding of the role of marketing, education, and communications in health care.

12663 **Home Medical Equipment and Services Association of New England**
515 Kempton St
New Bedford, MA 02740-3852
508-993-0700; Fax: 508-993-0797
www.homesne.org
Karyn Estrella, Executive Director
Brian Simonds, President
Jim Greatorex, VP
Rebecca Godley, Secretary
Paula Finamore, Treasurer
Works together supporting the common goals and interests of the home medical equipment, respiratory, and rehab/assistive techology and home infusion therapy industry.
15 Members
Founded in 1988

12664 **Infectious Diseases Society of America**
1300 Wilson Blvd.
Suite 300
Arlington, VA 22209
703-299-0200; Fax: 703-299-0204
www.idsociety.org
Facebook, Twitter, LinkedIn
Paul G. Auwaerter, President
The IDSA represents health care professionals specializing in infectious diseases.

12665 **Infusion Nurses Society**
315 Norwood Park South
Norwood, MA 02062-4694
781-440-9408
800-694-0298; Fax: 781-440-9409
ins@ins1.org
www.ins1.org
Facebook, Twitter, LinkedIn, Youtube
Cheryl Dumont, PhD, RN, CRNI, President
Mary Alexander, MA, RN, Chief Executive Officerÿÿ
Christopher Hunt, Executive Vice Presidentÿ
Lisa Bruce, BSN, RN, CRNI, Secretary/Treasurer
Richelle Hamblin, MSN, RN, CRNI, President-Elect
The INS is committed to bringing innovative new resources and opportunities to a wide range of healthcare professionals who are involved with the specialty practice of infusion therapy.
6000 Members
Founded in 1973

12666 **International Anesthesia Research Society**
44 Montgomery Street
Suite 1605
San Francisco, CA 94104-4703
415-296-6900; Fax: 415-296-6901
info@iars.org
www.iars.org
Alex Evers, MD, Chair
Thomas A Cooper, Executive Director
Davy C H Cheng, MD, Treasurer
Makoto Ozaki, MD, PhD, Secretary
Laura J Kuhar, Education Director
Founded in 1922

12667 **International Association For Healthcare Security & Safety**
PO Box 5038
Glendale Heights, IL 60139
630-529-3913
888-353-0990; Fax: 630-529-4139
info@iahss.org
www.iahss.org
Facebook, Twitter, LinkedIn
David LaRose, CHPA, CPP, President
Dana Frentz,ÿCHPA, Vice-President/Treasurerÿ
Ben Scaglione, CHPA, CPP, Vice-President/Secretaryÿ
Jeff A. Young, CHPA, CPP, President-Electÿ
Colleen Kucera, Executive Director
The International Association for Healthcare Security and Safety, (IAHSS) is an organization dedicated to professionals involved in managing and directing security and safety programs in healthcare institutions. Its members have joined together to develop educational and credentialing programs and create a body of knowledge that meets the needs of today's fast paced and ever changing environment.
2000 Members
Founded in 1968

12668 **International Association for Cannabinoid Medicines**
Am Mildenweg 6
59602 Ruethen
Germany
+49-2952-9708571; Fax: +49-2952-902651
info@cannabis-med.org
www.cannabis-med.org
Twitter
Franjo Grotenhermen, Executive Director
Michael Krawitz, Patient Representative, USA
Alison Myrden, Patient Representative, Canada
Advances knowledge on cannabis, cannabinoids, the endocannabinoid ystem, and related topics, especially with regard to their therapeutic potential.
Founded in 2000

12669 **International Association for Worksite Health Promotion**
401 West Michigan Street
Indianapolis, IN 46202
317-637-9200
iawhp@acsm.org
www.acsm-iawhp.org/
Facebook, LinkedIn
George Pfeiffer, MSE, President
Stephen Cherniak, MS, MBA, Secretary/Treasurer
Charlie Estey, MS, President Elect
Wolf Kirsten, MSÿ, Past President
Kristine Holbrook, MEd, Board of Director
Mission is to advance the global community of worksite health promotion practitioners through high-quality information, services, educational activities, personal and professional development and networking opportunities.

12670 **International Association of Healthcare Central Service Material Management**
213 W Institute Place
Suite 307
Chicago, IL 60610-3195
312-440-0078
800-962-8274; Fax: 312-440-9474
mailbox@iahcsmm.com
www.iahcsmm.com
Sharon Greene-Golden, CRCST,, President
Susan Adams, Executive Director
Marilyn T Conde, CRCST, MAOM, FC, Secretary/Treasurer
Nick Baker, Certification Manager
Elizabeth Berrios, Member Services Coordinatorÿ
Membership consists of persons serving in a technical, supervisory or management capacity in hospital central service departments responsible for the sterilization management and distribution of supplies.
9000 Members
Founded in 1958
Mailing list available for rent: 13000 names

12671 **International Bone and Mineral Society**
330 N Wabash
Suite 1900
Chicago, IL 60611

312-321-5113; Fax: 312-673-6934
Twitter

John Eisman, President
Theresa Guise, Immediate Past President
Anna Teti, Vice Presidentÿ
Richard Eastell, Treasurer Secretary
David Schmahl, Executive Director
3600 Members
Founded in 1960

12672 **International Oxygen Manufacturers Association**
1025 Thomas Jefferson Street, NW
Suite 500 East
Washington, DC 20007

202-521-9300; Fax: 202-833-3636
www.iomaweb.org

The International Oxygen Manufacturers Association is the truly worldwide trade association of companies in the industrial and medical gas business
190 Members
Founded in 1943

12673 **International Sleep Products Association**
501 Wythe Street
Alexandria, VA 22314-1917

703-683-8371; Fax: 703-683-4503
info@sleepproducts.org
www.sleepproducts.org
Facebook, Twitter, LinkedIn, Youtube, Flickr, Google Plus,

Debi Sutton, VP, Marketing & Member Services

Maintains a strong organization to influence government actions, inform and educate the membership and act on industry issues to enhance the growth, profitability and stature of the sleep products industry. Provides members with information and services to manage their business more effectively and efficiently. Publishes a magazine devoted exclusively to the mattress industry, BEDtimes covers a broad range of issue and news important to the industry.
Cost: $65.00
650 Members
Frequency: Monthly
Circulation: 3,500
Founded in 1915

12674 **International Society for Quality-of-Life Studies**
2056 Pamplin
Virginia Tech
Blacksburg, VA 24061-0236

540-231-5110; Fax: 540-231-3076
sirgy@vt.edu
www.isqols.org
RSS

Rhonda Phillips, President
Mariano Rojas, President Elect
Denis Huschka, Executive Director/Treasurer
Peter Krause, VP-Programs
Don Rahtz, VP-Publications

Was founded to stimulate interdisciplincary research in quality-of-life studies and closer cooperation among scholars. Members are academic and government social/behavioral science researchers drawn from such fields as marketing, management, applied psychology, applies sociology, political science, economics, public administration, educational administration family/child development leisure/recreation studies and technology development.
Founded in 1995

12675 **International Virtual Reality Healthcare Association**
2021 L Street NW
Suite 100-242
Washington, DC 20037

202-684-6207
bob@ivrha.org
ivrha.org

Robert Fine, Executive Director
Tom Augeri, Membership Director

The organization advocates for and provides information on applications of virtual reality technology in a healthcare setting.

12676 **Interstate Postgraduate Medical Association**
PO Box 5474
Madison, WI 53705

608-231-9045
866-446-3424; Fax: 877-292-4489
cmehelp@ipmameded.org
www.ipmameded.org
Facebook

Carolyn C. Lopez, MD, Board Chair
Robert A.ÿ Lee, MD, Vice Chair
William E.ÿ Kobler, MD, Board Treasurer
Don Klitgaard, MD, Board of Trustee
Rodney A. Erickson, MD, Board of Trustee

Dedicated to sponsoring clinically relevant education for primary care clinicians.
Founded in 1916

12677 **Leading Age**
2519 Connecticut Avenue NW
Washington, DC 20008-1520

202-783-2242; Fax: 202-783-2255
info@leadingage.org
www.leadingage.org
Facebook, Twitter, LinkedIn, Google+, RSS

William L. Minnix, Jr., President & CEO
Katrinka Smith Sloan, COO & Sr. Vice President
Robyn I. Stone, Senior Vice President of Research
Cheryl Phillips, Senior Vice President
Majd Alwan, Senior Vice President of Technology

Focused on advocacy, leadership development, and applied research and promotion of effective services, home health, hospice, community services, senior housing, assisted living residences, continuing care communities, nursing homes, as well as technology solutions, to seniors, children, and others with special needs.
6M Members
Founded in 1961

12678 **Leukemia & Lymphoma Society**
3 International Dr
Suite 200
Rye Brook, NY 10573

914-949-5213; Fax: 914-949-6691
www.lls.org
Facebook, Twitter, LinkedIn, Instagram, Pinterest, YouTube

Louis J. DeGennaro, President & CEO
Rosemarie Loffredo, CFO
Ingo Gefeke, COO

Volunteer organization dedicated to funding blood cancer research and ensuring access to treatment.
Founded in 1949

12679 **Medical Group Management Association**
104 Inverness Terrace East
Englewood, CO 80112-5306

303-799-1111
877-275-6462; Fax: 303-643-9599
support@mgma.org
www.mgma.com
Facebook, Twitter, LinkedIn, Google+

William Jessee, CEO
Nicholas H Kupferle, Board Chair
Jyl D Bradley, Chair
Warren C White Jr, Chair
Nicholas H Kupferle III, Chair

The mission of the MGMA is to continually improve the performance of medical group practice professionals and the organizations they represent.
19000 Members
Founded in 1926

12680 **Medical Library Association**
65 East Wacker Place
Suite 1900
Chicago, IL 60601-7246

312-419-9094; Fax: 312-419-8950
info@mlahq.org
www.mlanet.org
Facebook, Twitter, LinkedIn, Youtube

Michelle Kraft, AHIP, President
Kevin Baliozian, Executive Director
Teresa L.ÿ Knott, AHIP, President-Elect
Linda Walton, AHIP, Immediate Past President
Chris Shaffer, AHIP, Treasurer

A nonprofit, educational organization that is a leading advocate for health sciences information professionals worldwide. Through it's programs and services, we provide lifelong educational opportunities, supports a knowledgebase of health information research and works with a global network of partners to promote the importance of quality information for improved health to the health care community and the public.
4500 Members
Founded in 1898
Mailing list available for rent

12681 **Medical Marketing Association**
10293 N Meridian Street
Suite 175
Indianapolis, IN 46290

317-816-1640; Fax: 317-816-1633
www.medicalmarketingassociation.org/
Facebook, Twitter, Google+, RSS

Michael L Boner, President
Steve Hamburger, Treasurer
Stewart Marsden, Secretary

Builds diagnostic industry leadership by providing market education, professional development and a forum for fellowship and the exchange of ideas.

12682 **National Association Medical Staff Services**
2025 M Street NW
Suite 800
Washington, DC 20036-2422

202-367-1196; Fax: 202-367-2196
info@namss.org
www.namss.org
Facebook, LinkedIn, YouTube, Flickr, RSS

Sharon Kimbrough, CPCS, CPMSM, President
Lynn Boyd, Executive Director
Tiffany Boykin, Operations Manager
Andrew Miller, Member Services Coordinator
Chris Murphy Peck, Education & Learning Services

NAMSS' vision is to advance a healthcare environment that maximizes the patient experience through the delivery of quality services.
4000 Members
Founded in 1978

12683 **National Association for Healthcare Recruitment**
18000 W. 105th St.
Suite 103
Olathe, KS 66061-7543
913-895-4627; Fax: 913-895-4652
www.nahcr.com
Facebook, Twitter, LinkedIn, Blogger, youtube
Jude Hill, President
Sheilaÿ O'Neal, Executive Director
Christie Ross, CAE, Education Director
Candice Miller, Administrative Assistant
Debbie Jennings, Meeting Planner
Individuals employed directly by hospitals and other health care organizations which are involved in the practice of professional health care recruitment. Promotes sound principles of professionals health care recruitment. Provides financial assistance to aid members in planning and implementing regional educational programs. Offers technical assistance and consultation services. Compiles statistics.
800 Members
Founded in 1975

12684 **National Association for Home Care and Hospice**
228 Seventh Street, SE
Washington, DC 20003-4306
202-547-7424; Fax: 202-547-3540
ads@nahc.org
www.nahc.org
Facebook, Twitter, Pinterest
Denise Schrader, Chairman
Lucy Andrews, Vice Chair
Val J. Halamandaris, President
Walter W. Borginis, Treasurer
Karen Marshall Thompson, Secretary

12685 **National Association for Medical Direction of Repiratory Care (NAMDRC)**
8618 Westwood Center Drive
Suite 210
Vienna, VA 22182-2222
703-752-4359; Fax: 703-752-4360
ExecOffice@namdrc.org
www.namdrc.org
Timothy A. Morris, MD, President
Phillip Porte, Executive Director
Vickie Parshall, Director Member Services
Charles W. Atwood, MD, President-Elect
Karen Lui, RN, Associate Executive Director
The National Association for Medical Direction of Respiratory Care, our mission is to improve access to quality care for patients with respiratory disease by removing regulatory and legislative barriers to appropriate treatment. It advises on coding issues and federal reimbursement policies; provides economic and regulatory updates; and offers unique educational opportunities.
700 Members
Founded in 1977

12686 **National Association of County & City Health Officials**
1100 17th Street NW
Seventh Floor
Washington, DC 20036-4619
202-783-5550; Fax: 202-783-1583
info@naccho.org
www.naccho.org
Facebook, Twitter
Paul Yeghiayan, President, NACCHO Foundation
Mark Jorritsma, COO
John Mericsko, Chief Financial Officer
LaMar Hasbrouck, Executive Director
William Barnes, Chief Program Officer
Administrators of freestanding and hospital-based long-term care facilities owned and operated by county governments or city-county consolidations; elected local officials. Promotes interests of county long-term care facilities; offers guidance in relevant legislative and regulatory areas. Provides technical assistance; conducts training workshops. Compiles statistics on public policy changes, such as changes in the Medicaid program, which affect long-term care facilities.
250 Members
Founded in 1977

12687 **National Association of School Nurses**
1100 Wayne Avenue
Suite 925
Silver Spring, MD 20910
240-821-1130
866-627-6767; Fax: 301-585-1791
nasn@nasn.org
www.nasn.org
Beth Mattey, MSN, RN, NCSN, President
Susan Zacharski, Vice President
Donna J. Mazyck, RN, MS, NCSN, Executive Director
Catherine Davis, BSN, RN, NCSN, Secretary/Treasurer
Nina Fekaris, President Elect
15500 Members
Founded in 1968

12688 **National Athletic Trainers Association**
1620 Valwood Parkway
Suite 115
Carrollton, TX 75006
214-637-6282
860-437-5700; Fax: 214-637-2206
webmaster@nata.org
www.nata.org
Scott Sailor, EdD, ATC, President
MaryBeth Horodyski, Vice President
Kathy Dieringer, Secretary/Treasurer
Dave Saddler, Executive Director
Rachael Oats, Associate Executive Director
35,00 Members
Founded in 1950

12689 **National Cancer Institute**
9609 Medical Center Drive
Bethesda, MD 20892-9760
800-422-6237
cancergovstaff@mail.nih.gov
www.cancer.gov
Facebook, Twitter, LinkedIn, Google+, YouTube, Instagram, R
Douglas R. Lowy, M.D., Acting Director
Lynn Austin, PhD, Deputy Director for Management
Jeffrey S. Abrams, MD, Acting Director, Clinical Research
Stephen J. Chanock, MD, Director
Peter Greenwald, MD, Associate Director, Prevention
Conducts and supports research, training, health information dissemination and other programs with respect to the cause, diagnosis, prevention and treatment of cancer, rehabilition from cancer and the continuing care of cancer patients.

12690 **National Council for Behavioral Health**
1701 K Street NW
Suite 400
Washington, DC 20005
202-684-7457; Fax: 202-386-9391
communications@thenationalcouncil.org
www.TheNationalCouncil.org
Facebook, Twitter, LinkedIn, YouTube, Pinterest, Google+
Susan Blue, Chair
Donald Miskowiec, Vice Chair
Jeff Richardson, Second Vice Chair
Linda Rosenberg, President & CEO
Jeannie Campbell, Executive Vice President and COO
Advocates for public policies in mental and behavioral health that ensure that people who are ill can access comprehensive healthcare services.
2,500 Members

12691 **National Council on the Aging**
251 18th Street South
Suite 500
Arlington, VA 22202
571-527-3900; Fax: 202-479-0735
info@ncoa.org
www.ncoa.org
Facebook, Twitter, LinkedIn, Youtube, RSS
Carol Zernial, Chair
James Firman, EdD, President and CEO
Richard Browdie, Immediate Past-Chair
Donna Whitt, SVP, CFO
Wendy Zecker, SVP, Public/Private Programs
Founded in 1950

12692 **National Environmental Health Association**
720 S Colorado Blvd
Suite 1000-N
Denver, CO 80246-1926
303-756-9090
866-956-2258; Fax: 303-691-9490
staff@neha.org
www.neha.org
Facebook, Twitter, LinkedIn
Bob Custard REHS, CP-FS, President
David Riggs, President Elect
Adam London MPA, RS, First VP
Vince Radke, 2nd VP
David T. Dyjack Dr.PH, CIH, Executive Director
NEHA offers a variety of programs that are all in keeping with the association's mission which is as relevant today as it was when the organization was founded. The mission of NEHA is to advance the environmental health and protection professional for the purpose of providing a healthful environment for all.
5000 Members
Founded in 1937

12693 **National Managed Health Care Congress**
71 2nd Avenue
3rd Floor
Waltham, MA 02154
888-882-2500; Fax: 941-365-0157
www.nmhcc.org

12694 **National Medical Association**
8403 Colesville Road
Suite 820
Silver Spring, MD 20910
202-347-1895
800-257-8290; Fax: 202-347-0722
cme@nmanet.org
www.nmanet.org
Facebook, Twitter, LinkedIn, YouTube
Garfield Clunie, M.D, Chair of the Board
Edith P. Mitchell, M.D., President
Lawrence Sanders, Immediate Past President
Richard Allen Williams, M.D., President-Elect
Traci C. Burgess, M.D., M.P.H., Secretary
The mission of the NMA is to advance the art and science of medicine for people of African

descent through education, advocacy, and health policy to promote health and wellness, eliminate health disparities, and sustain physician viability.
Founded in 1895

12695 National Renal Administrators Association
100 North 20th Street
Suite 400
Philadelphia, PA 19103-1462

215-320-4655; Fax: 215-564-2175
nraa@nraa.org
Facebook, Twitter, LinkedIn

Helen Currier, President
Karen Kelley, MHA, BSN, CNN, President-Elect
Anthony Messana, Secretary
Rob Bomstad,ÿRN, BSBA, MS, Treasurer
Deb Cote, Past-President

Administrative personnel involved with dialysis programs for patients suffering from kidney failure. Provides a vehicle for the development of educational and informational services for members. Maintains contact with health care facilities and government agencies. Operates placement serve; compiles statistics; conducts political action committee.
475 Members
Founded in 1977

12696 National Rural Health Association
4501 College Blvd
#225
Leawood, KS 66211-1921

816-756-3140; Fax: 816-756-3144
mail@NRHArural.org
www.ruralhealthweb.org
Facebook, Twitter, LinkedIn

Jodi Schmidt, President
Lisa Kilaweeÿ, President-Elect
Dave Pearson, Treasurer
Tommy Barnhart, Secretary
Raymond G. hristensen, MD, Past-President

A national membership organization, whose mission is to improve the health care of rural Americans and to provide leadership on rural issues through advocacy, communications, education and research.
20,00 Members

12697 National Society Of Certified Healthcare Business Consultants
12100 Sunset Hills Road
Suite 130
Reston, VA 20190-3233

703-234-4099; Fax: 703-435-4390
info@nschbc.org
www.nschbc.org
Facebook, Twitter, LinkedIn, Pineterst, Youtube

H. Christopherÿ Zaenger, CHBC, President
Michael J. Dejno, CHBC, CPA, President-Elect
Robert C. Scroggins, Secretary/Treasurer
Reed Tinsley, Immediate Past-President
Carol Wynne, Executive Director

Maintains code of ethics, rules of professional conducts, and certification program; administers exams and conduct certification course. Membership by successful completion of certification examination only.
350 Members
Founded in 1975

12698 National Society for Histotechnology
8850 Stanford Boulevard
Suite 2900
Columbia, MD 21045

443-535-4060; Fax: 443-535-4055
histo@nsh.org
www.nsh.org
Facebook, Twitter, LinkedIn

Elizabeth Sheppard, President
Sharon Kneebone, Executive Director
Jerry Santiago, Vice President
Diane Sterchi, Secretary
Monty Hyten, Treasurer

A non-profit organization, committed to the advancement of histotechnology, its practitioners and quality standards of practice through leadership, education and advocacy.
Founded in 1974

12699 National Strength and Conditioning Association
1885 Bob Johnson Drive
Colorado Spring, CO 80906-4000

719-632-6722
800-815-6826; Fax: 719-632-6367
nsca@nsca.com
www.nsca.com/Home/

G. Gregory Haff, President
Colin Wilborn, PhD, ATC, VP
Joel T. Cramer, PhD, CSCS, Treasurer
Lee Madden, Sr. Director of Admin. Services
Wayde Rivinius, Sr. Director of Technology

Develops and presents the most advanced information regarding strength training and conditioning practices, injury prevention, and research findings.
30000 Members
Founded in 1978

12700 Northwest Urological Society
914 164th St. SE
Suite 145
Mill Creek, WA 98012

866-800-3118; Fax: 800-808-4749
support@nwurologicalsociety.org
www.nwurologicalsociety.org/

William Ellis, MD, President
John Corman, MD, VP
Stan Myers, MD, VP
John Corman, MD, Secretary-Treasurer
Michael Conlin, MD, Immediate Past President

12701 OMA: Optical Industry Association
6055A Arlington Boulevard
Falls Church, VA 22044-2721

703-237-8433; Fax: 703-237-0643

Members are makers and importers of spectacle frames, and related products.
57 Members
Founded in 1916

12702 Obesity Medicine Association
101 University Boulevard
Suite 330
Denver, CO 80206

303-770-2526
877-266-6834; Fax: 303-779-4834
info@obesitymedicine.org
obesitymedicine.org
Facebook, Twitter, LinkedIn, Youtube, RSS

Ethan Lazarus, MD, FOMA, President
Claudia Randall, MBA, Executive Director
Christin Hammond, MBA, Director, Marketing

Formerly known as the American Society of Bariatric Physicians, the Obesity Medicine Association is the largest organization of physicians, nurse practitioners, physician assistants, and other healthcare providers dedicated to preventing, treating, and reversing the disease of obesity. Members of OMA believe treating obesity requires a scientific and individualized clinical approach comprised of nutrition, physical activity, behavior, and medication.
2900+ Members
Founded in 1950

12703 Optical Society of America
2010 Massachusetts Avenue NW
Washington, DC 20036

202-223-8130; Fax: 202-223-1096
info@osa.org
www.osa.org
Facebook, Twitter, LinkedIn, YouTube

Elizabeth A. Rogan, CEO
Elizabeth Nolan, Chief Publishing Officer
Sean Bagshaw, COO/CIO
Suzanne Ffolkes, Chief Communications Officer
Genaro Montanez, Chief Employee/Membership Officer

The Optical Society of America (OSA) was organized to increase and diffuse the knowledge of optics, pure and applied; to promote the common interests of investigators of optical problems, of designers and of users of optical apparatus of all kinds; and to encourage cooperation among them. The purposes of the Society are scientific, technical and educational.
20K Members
Founded in 1916

12704 Orthopedic Surgical Manufacturers Association
BioMet
7302 Texas Heights Ave
Kalamazoo, MI 49009

269-303-3831; Fax: 574-372-1790
secretary@osma.net
www.osma.net/

Sharon Starowicz, President
Lynnette Jackson, Vice President
Lori Burns, Secretary
Ed Chin, Treasurer
Susan Krasny, Past President

Members are manufacturers of orthopedic surgical items. Sponsors research, information and ethics programs.
25 Members
Founded in 1954

12705 Pacific Dermatological Association
575 Market Street
Suite 2125
San Francisco, CA 94105

415-927-5729
888-388-8815; Fax: 415-764-4915
www.pacificderm.org

Janellen Smith, MD, President
Tina Suneja, MD, President Elect
Keith Duffy, MD, Vice President
Hege Grande Sarpa, MD, Secretary-Treasurer
Catherine Ramsay, MD, Immediate Past President

Provides opportunitites for exchange of information and advancement of knowledge of dermatology among physicians within the membership area. Execlusively for education, scientific and charitable purposes.
Founded in 1948

12706 Pacific Northwest Radiological Society
2001 6th Aveÿ
Ste 2700
Seattle, WA 98121

206-956-3650
800-552-0612; Fax: 206-441-5863
lmk@wsma.org
www.pnwrs.org

Tess Chapman, MD, President
Greg Kicska, MD, First Vice President
Debra Alderman, Association Director
Jonathan Helwig, MD, Secretary/Treasurer
Shane Greek, MD, Immediate Past President

12707 **Professional Association of Health Care Office Management**
1576 Bella Cruz Drive
Suite 360
Lady Lake, FL 32159
847-375-4717
800-451-9311; Fax: 407-386-7006
info@pahcom.com
www.pahcom.com
Facebook, Twitter, LinkedIn, Youtube
Richard Blanchette, MS, Founder
Daniel Labelle, CISSP CEH, Chief Technology Officer
Karen Blanchette, MBA, Association Director
Darlene Born, CMM, HITCM-PP, Business Development
Aaron Miller, Web Developer
A national organization dedicated to promoting professionalism in physician office practice by providing professional development opportunities, continuing education in health care office management principles and practice, and certification for health care office managers.
Founded in 1988

12708 **Radiological Society of North America**
820 Jorie Blvd
Oak Brook, IL 60523-2251
630-571-2670
800-381-6660; Fax: 630-571-7837
www.rsna.org
Facebook, Twitter, LinkedIn, Flickr, Youtube
Richard L. Ehman, MD, Chairman
Ronald L. Arenson, MD, President
Richard L.ÿ Baron, MD, President-Elect/Secretary-Treasurer
William P. Dillon, MD, First Vice-President
William G. Bradley Jr, MD, PhD, Second Vice-President
The mission is to promote and develop the highest standards of radiology and related sciences through education and research. The society seeks to provide radiologists and allied health scientists with educational programs and materials of the highest quality and to constantly improve the content and value of these educational activities.
54,00 Members

12709 **Radiology Business Management Association**
10300 Eaton Place
Suite 460
Fairfax, VA 22030
703-621-3355
888-224-7262; Fax: 703-621-3356
info@rbma.org
www.rbma.org
Facebook, Twitter, LinkedIn
Suzanne Taylor, BS, FRMBA, President
Keith E. Chew, MHA, CMPEÿÿ, Immediate Past President
Jim Hamilton, President Elect
Thomas C. Dickerson, Treasurer, MidWestern Director
Michael R.ÿ Mabry, Executive Director
The only radiology-specific business organization in existence today. Dedicated to providing managers with information, resources, educatio and networking to run a successful radiology business.
2200 Members
Founded in 1968

12710 **Sisters Network: National Headquarters**
2922 Rosedale Street
Houston, TX 77004
713-781-0255
866-781-1808; Fax: 713-780-8998
infonet@sistersnetworkinc.org
www.sistersnetworkinc.org
Facebook, Twitter, Youtube
Karen Eubanks Jackson, Founder & CEO
Bettie Eubanks, Vice Chair
Dr John Green, Treasurer
Erie E. Calloway, Executive Director
Monica Jones, Administrative Assistant
Committed to increasing local and national attention to the devastating impact that breast cancer has in the African American community.
3000 Members
Founded in 1994

12711 **Society for Healthcare Strategy and Market Development**
155 North Wacker Drive
Chicago, IL 60606-3421
312-422-3888; Fax: 312-278-0883
shsmd@aha.org
www.shsmd.org/
Facebook, Twitter, LinkedIn
Christine Gallery, President
Lawrence Margolis, President Elect
Mark Parrington, Immediate Past Presidentÿ
Diane Weber, RN, Executive Director
Lisa Hinkle, Education Manager
The society of choice for thousands of healthcare marketing, public relations, strategic planning, communications and business development professionals.
4,000 Members
Founded in 1996

12712 **Society for Imaging Informatics In Medicine**
19440 Golf Vista Plaza
Suite 330
Leesburg, VA 20176-8264
703-723-0432; Fax: 703-723-0415
info@siim.org
www.siim.org
Facebook, Twitter, LinkedIn, Google+, YouTube, Instagram
David E. Brown, CIIP, Chair
William W Boonn, MD, Secretary
Rasu B. Shrestha, MD, MBA, Treasurer
Paul G. Nagy, PhD, FSIIM, CIIP, Chair-Elect
Anna Marie Mason, MS,CAE, Executive Director
Devoted to advance informatics and information technology in medical imaging through education and research. Provides an open environment for imaging information professionals to access expert and cutting edge resources in a collegial and practical atmosphere.
2200 Members
Founded in 1980

12713 **Society for Pediatric Research**
9303 New Trails Dr.
The Woodlands, TX 77381
346-980-9710
info@societyforpediatricresearch.org
www.societyforpediatricresearch.org
Facebook, Twitter, Instagram
Eileen G. Fenton, Executive Director
Belinda Thomas, PAS Education Program Director
Cynthia Bearer, Managing Editor, Pediatric Research
Antonio Moreno, Information Technology Director
Coordinates meetings, research and further education of health professionals. Features policies, publications and details of research programs.
Founded in 1929

12714 **Society of Cannabis Clinicians**
6842 21st Ave. NE
Seattle, WA 98115
Home Page: www.cannabisclinicians.org
Facebook, Twitter
Ellen Kuwana, Executive Director
An educational and scientific society of qualified physicians and other professionals dedicated to the promotion, protection, and support of cannabis for medical use.
Founded in 2004

12715 **Society of Critical Care Medicine**
500 Midway Drive
Mount Prospect, IL 60056-5811
847-827-6869; Fax: 847-827-6886
info@sccm.org
www.sccm.org
Facebook, Twitter, Google+
Carol Thompson, President
David Julian Martin, CAE, CEO, EVP
Brian Schramm, CAE, Director Business Affairs
James Flanigan, CAE, Director, Marketing
Pamela S. Dallstream, CMP, CMM, Director of Education
Professional organization devoted exclusively to the advancement of multidisciplinary, multiprofessional intensive care through excellence in patient care, education, research, and advocacy.
11000 Members
Founded in 1972

12716 **Society of Health and Physical Educators**
1900 Association Drive
Reston, VA 20191-1598
703-476-3400
800-213-7193; Fax: 703-476-9527
membership@shapeamerica.org
www.shapeamerica.org
Facebook, Twitter, Instagram
Stephanie A. Morris, Chief Executive Officer
Mission is to promote and support leadership, research, education, and best practices in the professions that support creative, healthy, and active lifestyles. AAHPERD envisions a society in which all individuals enjoy an optimal quality of life through appreciation of and participation in an active and creative, health-promoting lifestyle.
25M Members
Founded in 1885

12717 **Society of Medical-Dental Management**
125 Strafford Avenue
Suite 300
Wayne, PA 19087-3318
800-826-2264; Fax: 610-687-7702
patricia01@aol.com
www.smdmc.org
Joseph Cobo, President
Richard G Bock, Regional Director/Coordinator
Rex Stanley, Secretary/Treasurer
Professional medical and/or dental management consultants associated for educational and information sharing purposes. Objectives are to: advance the profession; share management techniques; improve individual skills; provide clients with competent and capable business management. Provides information on insur-

ance and income tax. Conducts surveys; compiles statistics.
60+ Members
Founded in 1968

12718 **Society of NeuroInterventional Surgery**
3975 Fair Ridge Drive
Suite 200 North
Fairfax, VA 22033

703-691-2272; Fax: 703-537-0650
info@snisonline.org
www.snisonline.org
Facebook, Twitter

Donald F. Frei, MD, President
Blaise W. Baxter, MD, Vice President
Charles J. Prestigiacomo, MD, President Elect
Richard P. Klucznik, MD, Treasurer
Adam S. Arthur, MD, Secretary

Formerly the American Society of Interventional and Therapeutic Neuroradiology, mission is to promote excellence in patient care, provide education, support research, influence health care policy, and foster the growth of the specialty.
3000 Members
Founded in 1992

12719 **Society of Nuclear Medicine & Molecular Imaging**
1850 Samuel Morse Dr
Reston, VA 20190-5316

703-708-9000; Fax: 703-708-9015
volunteer@snmmi.org
www.snm.org
Facebook, Twitter, LinkedIn, Youtube

Hossein Jadvar, MD,PhD,MPH,MBA, President
Sally W. Schwarz, MS, RPh, BCNP, President-Elect
Bennett S. Greenspan, Vice President-Elect
Michael L. Middleton, MD, FACNMÿ, Secretary/Treasurer
Peter Herscovitch, Immediate Past President

International scientific and professional organization that promotes the science, technology and practical applications of nuclear medicine.
18,00 Members
Founded in 1954

12720 **Society of Robotic Surgery**
c/c Veritas Meeting Solutions
1061 E. Main Street
Suite 300
East Dundee, IL 60118

847-752-5355
info@srobotics.org
www.srobotics.org
Facebook, Twitter

Farid Gharagozloo, MD, FACS, President
Vipul R. Patel, MD, FACS, Executive Director
Sue O'Sullivan, Administrative Director

Society providing education about robotic surgery, as well as studies, funding and development events for professionals in the field.
Founded in 2009

12721 **Southern Medical Association**
35 W. Lakeshore Drive
Suite 201
Birmingham, AL 35209-7254

205-945-8903
800-423-4992; Fax: 205-945-1840
CustomerService@sma.org
www.sma.org
Facebook, Twitter, Youtube

Mark S. Williams, President
Benjamin M. Carmichael, President-Elect
Ajoy Kumar, President-Electÿ
Stuart J. Goodman, Immediate Past President
William L. Hartsfield FLMI, Executive Director

Physician's choice for education and support to enhance practice and performance and career development.
88 Members
Founded in 1906

12722 **TLPA Annual Convention & Trade Show**
Taxicab, Limousine & Paratransit Association
3200 Tower Oaks Boulevard
Suite 220
Rockville, MD 20852

301-984-5700; Fax: 301-984-5703
info@tlpa.com
www.tlpa.org

James Campolongo, PA, President
Alfred LaGasse, MD, Chief Executive Officer
Carl Ward, KY, Treasurer
Robert McBride, CO, Vice President
Harold Morgan, MD, Secretary

Shares information vital to owners or taxicab, limousine, airport shuttle, paratransit and nonemergency medical transportation fleets. 100 supplier exhibits of the newest products available to the industry.
1000 Attendees
Frequency: Annual
Founded in 1917

12723 **The American Association of Tissue Banks**
8200 Greensboro Drive
Suite 320
McLean, VA ÿ22102

703-827-9582; Fax: 703-356-2198
www.aatb.org
Facebook, Twitter, LinkedIn

Daniel Schultz, MD, Chairman
Frank Wilton, President & Chief Executive Officer
Louis Barnes III, Chairman-Elect
Kevin Cmunt, Immediate Past Chairman
Diana Buck, Secretary/Treasurer

Transplant trade organization dedicated to ensuring that human tissues intended for transplantation are safe and free of infectious disease and available in quantities sufficient to meet national needs.
Founded in 1976

12724 **The American Board of Surgery**
1617 John F. Kennedy Blvd.
Suite 860
Philadelphia, PA 19103

215-568-4000; Fax: 215-563-5718
www.absurgery.org
Facebook, Twitter

Jo Buyske, Executive Director
Jessica Schreader, Chief Operating Officer

Independent, nonprofit organization promoting excellence in surgical practice.
Founded in 1937

12725 **The American Chiropractic Association**
1701 Clarendon Boulevard
Suite 200
Arlington, VA 22209

703-276-8800; Fax: 703-243-2593
memberinfo@acatoday.org
www.acatoday.org
Facebook, Twitter, LinkedIn, RSS, YouTube, Instagram

John Falardeau, SVP, Public Policy and Advocacy
Janet Ridgely, Deputy Executive Vice President
Kim Hodes, Senior Director, Finance
Felicity Clancy, SVP, Communications
Dean Millard, Vice President, Information Systems

Professional organization representing chiropractors.

12726 **The American Geriatrics Society**
40 Fulton St.
18th Fl.
New York, NY 10038

212-308-1414; Fax: 212-832-8646
info.amger@americangeriatrics.org
www.americangeriatrics.org
Facebook, Twitter, LinkedIn, Instagram

Nancy E. Lundebjerg, Chief Executive Officer
Steven Counsell, President

AGS is a nonprofit dedicated to improving the lives of the elderly.
6000 Members

Newsletters

12727 **AAB Bulletin**
American Association of Bioanalysts
906 Olive Street
Suite 1200
Saint Louis, MO 63101-1448

314-241-1445; Fax: 314-241-1449
aab@aab.org
www.aab.org

Mark S Biernbaum PhD, Executive Director

Newsletter that provides the latest information on meetings, conferences, legislative and regulatoryy issues and developments.
Frequency: Quarterly
Founded in 1956

12728 **AAMI News**
Assoc for the Advancement of Medical Instrumentat
4301 N. Fairfax Drive
Suite 301
Arlington, VA 22203-1633

703-525-4890; Fax: 703-276-0793
publications@aami.org
www.aami.org

Sean Loughlin, Publications Director
Robert King, Editor

Keeps individuals up-to-date with timely and relevant infustry news, breaking information about new standards activities and AAMI benefits, and guidance from experts in the field.
Cost: $160.00
Frequency: Monthly
Circulation: 6000

12729 **AAMI News Extra!**
Assoc for the Advancement of Medical Instrumentat
4301 N. Fairfax Drive
Suite 301
Arlington, VA 22203-1633

703-525-4890; Fax: 703-276-0793
publications@aami.org
www.aami.org

Sean Loughlin, Publications Director

Online newsletter that includes the top stories of the month; an up-to-date listing of career opportunities in the field; and updates on AAMI's standards, benefits, and services.
Frequency: Monthly

12730 **ACOG Clinical Review**
American College of Obstetricians/Gynecologists

409 12th Street SW
PO Box 96920
Washington, DC 20090-6920

202-638-5577; Fax: 202-484-5107
resources@acog.org
www.acog.org

Kathleen Harrison, Advertising
Frequency: 6 X

12731 **ACOS News**
American College of Osteopathic Surgeons
123 N Henry Street
Alexandria, VA 22314-2903

703-684-0416; Fax: 703-684-3280
info@facos.org
www.facos.org

Guy Beaumont, Executive Director
Judith T Mangum, Director Finance
Frequency: Monthly

12732 **ACOS Review**
American College of Osteopathic Surgeons
330 E Algonquin Rd
Suite 1
Arlington Hts, IL 60005-4665

847-228-6090
800-323-0794; Fax: 847-228-9755
www.acofp.org

Peter Schmelzer, Executive Director
Frequency: Monthly

12733 **ACS NewsScope**
American College of Surgeons
633 N Saint Clair Street
Chicago, IL 60611-3211

312-202-5000
800-621-4111; Fax: 312-202-5001
postmaster@facs.org
www.facs.org

David B. Hoyt, MD, FACS, Executive Director

Electronic newsletter with news about the College's activites, programs, and events.
Frequency: Weekly
Founded in 1913

12734 **AMGA's Advocacy ENewS**
American Medical Group Association
One Prince Street
Alexandria, VA 22314-3318

703-838-0033; Fax: 703-548-1890
www.amga.org

Don Fisher, CEO
Ryan O'Connor, VP, Membership/Marketing

Timely analysis on the latest issues that affect medical groups on the federal legislative and regulatory front.
375 Members

12735 **AMWA Connections**
American Medical Women's Association
1100 E. Woodfield Road
Suite 350
Schaumburg, IL 60173

847-517-2801; Fax: 847-517-7229
associatedirector@amwa-doc.org
www.amwa-doc.org

Connie Newman, MD, President
Eliza Lo Chin, MD, MPH, Executive Director
Sharon Batista, MD, Treasurer
Lynda Kabbash, MD, Secretary
Roberta Gebhard, DO, President-Elect

The electronic quarterly newsletter of the American Medical Women's Association, Connections, covers news and timely events of the association and informative topics regarding advocacy, practice management, and medical legal, women's health, and gender related issues.
Frequency: Quarterly
Founded in 1915

12736 **AOA News**
American Optometric Association
243 N Lindbergh Blvd
Suite 1
St Louis, MO 63141-7881

314-991-4100; Fax: 314-991-4101

Barry Barresi, Executive Director
Tom Cappucci, First Vice President
Michael Jones, CEO

Official newspaper of the American Optometric Association
Cost: $93.50
Circulation: 30000
ISSN: 0094-9620
Founded in 1896
Mailing list available for rent: 22,500 names at $70 per M
Printed in 4 colors on glossy stock

12737 **AOPA in Advance SmartBrief**
American Orthotic & Prosthetic Association
330 John Carlyle Street
Suite 200
Alexandria, VA 22314

571-431-0876; Fax: 571-431-0899
info@aopanet.org
www.aopanet.org
Facebook, Twitter, LinkedIn

Tom Fise, Executive Director
Michael Oros, President
Lauren Anderson, Manager, Communications
Don DeBolt, Chief Operating Officer

Provides updates and information to the O&P community.
Frequency: Twice-Weekly

12738 **ASA Monthly Activist Newsletter**
Americans for Safe Access
1624 U St. NW
Suite 200
Washington, DC 20009

202-857-4272; Fax: 202-618-6977
info@safeaccessnow.org
www.safeaccessnow.org
Facebook, Twitter, Google+, Instagram, YouTube

Steph Sherer, Executive Director
Debbie Churagi, Deputy Director
Geoffrey Marshall, Office & Membership Coordinator
Reenal Doshi, Director, Outreach & Communications
David Mongone Esq., Director, Government Affairs

A monthly newsletter bringing you the latest developments in the field of medical cannabis.
Founded in 2002

12739 **ASET News**
American Society of Electroneurodiagnostic Tech
402 East Bannister Road
Suite A
Kansas City, MO 64131-3019

816-931-1120; Fax: 816-931-1145
info@aset.org
www.aset.org

Arlen Reimnitz, Executive Director
Anne Bonner, Director, Publications

Newsletter detailing society updates, news briefings, and other information of interest to neurodiagnostic technologists.
Frequency: Quarterly

12740 **ASHI Quarterly**
American Society for Histocompatability
1120 Route 73
Suite 200
Mt. Laurel, NJ 08054

856-638-0428; Fax: 856-439-0525
info@ashi-hla.org
www.ashi-hla.org

Kathy Miranda, Executive Director
Sarah Black, Publication Manager

Latest updates and news on society activities as well as scholarly insights.
Frequency: Quarterly

12741 **Adult Day Services Letter**
Health Resources Publishing
1913 Atlantic Ave
Suite 200
Manasquan, NJ 08736-1067

732-292-1100; Fax: 732-292-1111
info@healthresourcesonline.com
www.hin.com/ehealthcare

Robert K Jenkins, Publisher
Brett Powell, Regional Director
Alice Burron, Director

A monthly newsletter that contains management information, reports on trends and new developments and information about other adult day care programs across the country.
Cost: $147.00
38574 Pages
Frequency: Monthly
ISSN: 0885-4572
Founded in 1985

12742 **AdvaMed SmartBrief**
Advanced Medical Technology Association
701 Pennsylvania Ave. NW
Suite 800
Washington, DC 20004-2654

202-783-8700; Fax: 202-783-8750
info@advamed.org

Scott Whitaker, President & CEO

12743 **American Academy of Forensic Sciences Academy Newsfeed**
American Academy of Forensic Sciences
410 N. 21st Street
Colorado Springs, CO 80904

719-636-1100; Fax: 719-636-1993
awarren@aafs.org
www.aafs.org

Anne Warren, Executive Director
Zeno J. Geradts, PhD., President
Jeri D. Ropero-Miller, PhD., President-Elect
Carl R. McClary, BA, Vice President
Susan M. Ballou, MS, Past President

An online newsletter for members that includes industry news, announcements, job postings, and more.
Frequency: Monthly
Founded in 1948

12744 **American Alliance for Medical Cannabis New sletters**
American Alliance for Medical Cannabis
44500 Tide Ave.
Arch Cape, OR 97102

503-436-1882
contact@letfreedomgrow.com
www.letfreedomgrow.com
Facebook, Twitter, LinkedIn

Arthur H. Livermore, National Director

An e-newsletter dedicated to bringing patients, caregivers, and volunteers the facts needed to make informed decisions about medical cannabis. Provides information on medical marijuana legislation, political activism, recipes, and growing guides.

12745 **BNA's Health Law Reporter**
Bureau of National Affairs
1801 S Bell St
Arlington, VA 22202-4501
703-341-3000
800-372-1033; Fax: 800-253-0332
customercare@bna.com
www.bnabooks.com
Paul N Wojcik, CEO
Of many newsletters from BNA, this contains information on health care policy, bankruptcy, antitrust, insurance and state developments, employment issues as well as a congressional and a regulatory calendar.
Cost: $1782.00
Frequency: Weekly

12746 **Biomedical Market Newsletter**
Biomedical Market
3237 Idaho Pl
Costa Mesa, CA 92626-2207
714-434-9500
800-875-8181; Fax: 714-434-9755
info@biomedical-market-news.com
www.biomedical-market-news.com
David G Anast, President
Steve Baker, Director of Marketing/Sales
Richard Guiss, Senior Editor
George Anast, CFO
New business development, FDA, regulatory, financial, and marketing NL on medical equipment, device, diagnostic test and instrument industries worldwide.
Cost: $199.00
Frequency: Monthly
ISSN: 1064-4180
Founded in 1991
Printed in 4 colors on matte stock

12747 **Bulletin on Long-Term Care Law**
Health Resources Publishing
1913 Atlantic Ave
Suite 200
Manasquan, NJ 08736-1067
732-292-1100; Fax: 732-292-1111
info@healthresourcesonline.com
www.hin.com/ehealthcare
Robert K Jenkins, Publisher
Lisa Mansfield, Regional Director
Brett Powell, Regional Director
Alice Burron, Director
A newsletter that covers compliance problems, Medicaid and Medicare overhauls, charges of abuse, fraud, negligence, needless litigation and other concerns of those involved in long-term health care.
Cost: $227.00
Frequency: Monthly
ISSN: 1093-6939
Founded in 1978

12748 **Communique**
213 W Institute Place
Suite 307
Chicago, IL 60610-3195
312-440-0078
800-962-8274; Fax: 312-440-9474
mailbox@iahcsmm.com
www.iahcsmm.com
Betty Hanna, Executive Director
Marilyn Corida, Secretary/Treasurer
Lisa Huber, President
Bi-monthly publication separates supervisors/directors from technicians.
Cost: $40.00
Frequency: 6/Annual
Circulation: 15M
ISBN: 1-605309-30-9
Mailing list available for rent: 13000 names

12749 **Dermatology World Weekly**
American Academy of Dermatology
P.O. Box 1968
Des Plaines, IL 60017
847-240-1280
866-503-7546; Fax: 847-240-1859
dweditor@aad.org
www.jaad.org
A brief, concise digest of the latest news, hand-picked by Dermatology World's editorial team with analysis of why it matters to dermatologists.
Frequency: Monthly

12750 **Diagnostic Testing & Technology Report**
Institute of Management and Administration
1 Washington Park
Suite 1300
Newark, NJ 07102
212-244-0360; Fax: 973-622-0595
www.ioma.com
Contains up-to-the minute information and unique perspectives on where diagnostic testing is headed, covering every innovation, new product, manufacturer, market and end-user applications.
Cost: $549.00
Frequency: Monthly

12751 **Directions: Looking Ahead in Healthcare**
Health Resources Publishing
1913 Atlantic Ave
Suite 200
Manasquan, NJ 08736-1067
732-292-1100
888-843-6242; Fax: 732-292-1111
info@healthresourcesonline.com
www.hin.com/ehealthcare
Robert K Jenkins, Publisher
Lisa Mansfield, Marketing Assistant
Carolin Pense, Publisher
Brett Powell, Regional Director
Alice Burron, Director
Provides management news on such topics as alerts, trends, forecasts, profitable innovations, facts and statistics.
Cost: $127.00
Frequency: Monthly
ISSN: 1093-6920
Founded in 1978

12752 **Dispatch & Division Newsletters**
Taxicab, Limousine & Paratransit Association
3200 Tower Oaks Blvd
Suite 220
Rockville, MD 20852
301-984-5700; Fax: 301-984-5703
info@tlpa.org
www.tlpa.org
Alfred LaGasse, CEO
Victor Dizengoff, President
Dispatch features articles on industry business issues, provides advice on running a transportation company, and comes with division specific bi-monthly newsletters.
Frequency: Bimonthly
Circulation: 6000

12753 **Elderly Health Services Letter**
Health Resources Publishing
1913 Atlantic Ave
Suite 200
Manasquan, NJ 08736-1067
732-292-1100
888-843-6242; Fax: 732-292-1111
info@themcic.com
www.hin.com/ehealthcare
Robert K Jenkins, Publisher
Lisa Mansfield, Regional Director
Brett Powell, Regional Director
Alice Burron, Director
A newsletter on projections and trends for health services provided for the elderly. Subjects include inpatient care, long-term care, outpatient, home care, primary care, ambulatory care, day care, health promotion, disease prevention, support groups, health education and residental care.
Cost: $227.00
Frequency: Monthly
ISSN: 0891-9275

12754 **Emergency Department Law**
Business Publishers
8737 Colesville Road
Suite 1100
Silver Spring, MD 20910-3928
301-876-6300
800-274-6737; Fax: 301-589-8493
custserv@bpinews.com
www.bpinews.com
Leonard A Eiserer, Publisher
James Lawlor, Editor
Devoted entirely to legal issues pertinent to emergency medicine, and covers monthly the latest case law, legal trends, risk management, tort reform and explains how they could impact your emergency care facility.
Cost: $357.00
Frequency: Monthly

12755 **Employee Assistance Program Management Letter**
Health Resources Publishing
1913 Atlantic Ave
Suite 200
Manasquan, NJ 08736-1067
732-292-1100
888-843-6242; Fax: 732-292-1111
info@themcic.com
Robert K Jenkins, Publisher
Lisa Mansfield, Regional Director
Brett Powell, Regional Director
Alice Burron, Director
A briefing published monthly on the range of influences surrounding your employee assistance program.
Cost: $237.00
Frequency: Monthly
ISSN: 0896-0941
Founded in 1978

12756 **Executive Report on Integrated Care & Capitation**
Managed Care Information Center
1913 Atlantic Ave
Suite 200
Manasquan, NJ 08736-1067
732-292-1100
888-843-6242; Fax: 732-292-1111
info@themcic.com
www.themcic.com
Robert K Jenkins, Publisher
Joseph Schmidt, Editor
A newsletter published twice a month to keep readers informed of the competitive market. Gives facts on strategic issues, mergers and acquisitions, market facts, economics, network alliances and plan affiliations.
Cost: $447.00
Frequency: Monthly
ISSN: 1085-3103

12757 **Executive Report on Managed Care**
Managed Care Information Center

1913 Atlantic Ave
Suite 200
Manasquan, NJ 08736-1067

732-292-1100
888-843-6242; Fax: 732-292-1111
info@themcic.com
www.themcic.com

Robert K Jenkins, Publisher

A monthly report that gives news of how major employers are implementing their managed care programs. The report also aids companies in preparing to evaluate and monitor different managed care proposals to determine cost effectiveness, quality and liability to the employer.
Cost: $437.00
ISSN: 0898-9753

12758 **Executive Report on Physician Organizations**
Managed Care Information Center
1913 Atlantic Ave
Suite 200
Manasquan, NJ 08736-1067

732-292-1100
888-843-6242; Fax: 732-292-1111
info@themcic.com
www.themcic.com

Robert K Jenkins, Publisher

The newsletter covers mergers, acquisitions, practice management agreements and strategic planes implemented in the physician marketplace. Also provides information about the ways that managed care and goverment regulations affect the physician marketplace.
Cost: $257.00
8-10 Pages
Frequency: 12 per year
ISSN: 1097-7309
Founded in 1998

12759 **Eye-Mail Monthly**
American Academy of Optometry
2909 Fairgreen St.
Orlando, FL 32803

321-319-4860
844-323-3937; Fax: 407-893-9890
aaoptom@aaoptom.org
www.aaopt.org

Lois Schoenbrun, Executive Director

The electronic newsletter of the American Academy of Optometry. Each issue features an article of interest, Annual Meeting and Academy information, links to useful websites and more.
Frequency: Monthly

12760 **G-2 Compliance Report**
Institute of Management and Administration
1 Washington Park
Suite 1300
Newark, NJ 07102

212-244-0360; Fax: 973-622-0595
www.ioma.com

Designed to guide hospital, lab, and pathology professionals in developing, implementing and revising compliance programs to meet federal standards.
Cost: $469.00

12761 **HCEA Edge**
Healthcare Convention & Exhibitors Association
5775 Peachtree Dnwdy Rd
Building G, Suite 500
Atlanta, GA 30342-1556

404-252-3663; Fax: 404-252-0774
hcea@kellencompany.com
www.hcea.org

Eric Allen, Executive Vice President
Nancy Hoppe, President

News and events of the trade association of over 600 organizations involved in healthcare exhibiting or providing services to healthcare conventions, exhibitions and/or meetings.
Frequency: Monthly, Members Only

12762 **HFMA's The Business of Caring**
Healthcare Financial Management Association
Two Westbrook Corporate Center
Suite 700
Westchester, IL 60154-5700

708-319-9600
800-252-4362; Fax: 708-531-0032
www.hfma.org/boc

Robert Fromberg, Editor-in-Chief
Maggie Van Dyke, Product Manager & Editor
Chris Burke, Advertising Manager
Kurt Belisle, Sponsorhip Manager

Helps nurse managers navigate the business side of health care to become successful hospital leaders. Topics discussed include: budgeting, workforce management, cost containment, and IT implementation. Available Free Online.
Frequency: Quarterly

12763 **HMFA Healthcare Cost Containment Newsletter**
Healthcare Finance Management Association
3 Westbrook Corporate Center
Suite 600
Westchester, IL 60154

708-531-9600; Fax: 708-531-0032
www.hfma.org/publications/healthcarecost

Issues illustrate how to implement strategic cost management that will reduce labor and supply expenses, enhance operational efficiency, satisfy your patients, and improve your competitive position.
Cost: $125.00
Frequency: Quarterly
Mailing list available for rent

12764 **HMFA Revenue Cycle Stragetist Newsletter**
Healthcare Finance Management Association
3 Westbrook Corporate Center
Suite 600
Westchester, IL 60154

708-531-9600; Fax: 708-531-0032
www.hfma.org/publications/

Improve your organization's bottom line while maintaining regulatory compliance.
Cost: $165.00
Frequency: Quarterly
Mailing list available for rent

12765 **Health Care Reimbursement Monitor**
Health Resources Publishing
1913 Atlantic Ave
Suite 200
Manasquan, NJ 08736-1067

732-292-1100
888-843-6242; Fax: 732-292-1111
info@themcic.com

Robert K Jenkins, Publisher
Lisa Mansfield, Regional Director
Brett Powell, Regional Director
Alice Burron, Director

A monthly newsletter that covers the latest details of actions taken or proposals in Washington concerning changes to the BBA; updates on Medicaid and Medicare budget and reimbursement issues; reimbursement news for hospital operations executives as well as top financial management. Reimbursement briefings cover hospitals, home health care, long-term care, hospice, ambulatory care and physician payment.
Cost: $257.00
Frequency: Monthly

12766 **Health Product Marketing**
PRS Group
6320 Fly Rd
Suite 102
East Syracuse, NY 13057-9792

315-431-0511; Fax: 315-431-0200
custserv@prsgroup.com
www.prsgroup.com

Mary Lou Walsh, President
Ben McTernan, Managing Editor
Patti Davis, Circulation Manager
Patty Redhead, Production Manager

Provides current information, analysis and ideas for strategic planning in the health industry.
ISSN: 1520-3271
Founded in 1979

12767 **Healthcare Market Reporter**
Managed Care Information Center
1913 Atlantic Ave
Suite 200
Manasquan, NJ 08736-1067

732-292-1100
888-843-6242; Fax: 732-292-1111
info@themcic.com
www.themcic.com

Robert K Jenkins, Publisher

Twice-a-month newsletter to help you abreast of the fiercely competitive market. Get the facts and details you'll need on strategies issues, market facts, mergers and acquisitions, economics, network alliances and plan affiliations.
Cost: $457.00
10 Pages
ISSN: 1073-6816

12768 **Healthcare Marketers Executive Briefing**
Health Resources Publishing
1913 Atlantic Ave
Suite 200
Manasquan, NJ 08736-1067

732-292-1100; Fax: 732-292-1111
info@healthresourcesonline.com

Robert K Jenkins, Publisher
Lisa Mansfield, Regional Director
Brett Powell, Regional Director
Alice Burron, Director

Helps managers stay informed of the latest innovations and changes in the health care field. Gives contact information for other community relations, publication practioners, administrators and marketing and advertising professionals.
Cost: $237.00
Frequency: Monthly
ISSN: 0894-9980

12769 **Healthcare PR & Marketing News**
Phillips Business Information
1201 Seven Locks Road
Potomac, MD 20854-2931

301-354-1400
888-707-5814; Fax: 301-309-3847
www.prandmarketing.com

Matthew Schwartz, Editor
Diane Schwartz, Publisher
Amy Urban, Marketing Manager

Issues faced by health care executives in PR firms and hospitals. Regular features include industry surveys, case studies and executive profiles.
Cost: $397.00
Founded in 1944

12770 **Healthcare e-Business Manager**
Managed Care Information Center
1913 Atlantic Ave
Suite 200
Manasquan, NJ 08736-1067

732-292-1100
888-843-5242; Fax: 732-292-1111
info@themcic.com
www.themcic.com

Robert K Jenkins, Publisher

Monthly executive briefing on the latest developments in the proliferation of electronic commerce among healthcare and managed care organization. Focuses on the internet marketplace, reports on trends in the industry and predictions of where the market seems to be heading.
Cost: $477.00
10 Pages
ISSN: 1526-6052

12771 **Hospice Letter**
Health Resources Publishing
1913 Atlantic Ave
Suite 200
Manasquan, NJ 08736-1067

732-292-1100
888-843-6242; Fax: 732-292-1111
info@themcic.com

Robert K Jenkins, Publisher
Lisa Mansfield, Regional Director
Brett Powell, Regional Director
Alice Burron, Director

Monthly newsletter reporting the latest development in the rapidly hospice concept of caring for the terminally ill. Ready by administrators and directors who follow Medicare reimbursement and hospice accreditation. How hospices are raising money and staging community events; new legislation and regulations and the latest on nursing care, volunteers and counseling programs. Delivery options: via mail or e-mail (indicate PDF or HTML format)
Cost: $227.00
10 Pages
Frequency: Monthly
ISSN: 0913-6816
Founded in 1978

12772 **IACM-Bulletin**
International Association for Cannabinoid Medicine
Am Mildenweg 6
59602 Ruethen
Germany

+49-2952-9708571; Fax: +49-2952-902651
info@cannabis-med.org
www.cannabis-med.org
Twitter

Franjo Grotenhermen, Executive Director
Michael Krawitz, Patient Representative, USA
Alison Myrden, Patient Representative, Canada

An e-newsletter containing news on all aspects of cannabis as medicine.
Frequency: Bi-Weekly
Founded in 2000

12773 **Integrated Healthcare News**
American Association of Integrated Healthcare
4435 Waterfront Drive
Suite 101
Glen Allen, VA 23060

804-747-5823; Fax: 804-747-5316
www.aaihds.org

Jerry Williams, Editorial
Mark Abernathy, Managing Director
Dalal Haldeman, PhD, MBA, Director, Marketing Operations

12774 **Journal of the American Association of Forensic Dentists**
1000 N Avenue
Waukegan, IL 60085

847-244-0292
info@andent.net
www.andent.net

Quarterly journal that brings forensic dental knowledge not only to dentists and their staff, but also to anthropologists, attorneys and law enforcement personnel.
3000 Pages
Founded in 1978

12775 **Legislative Alert**
Taxicab, Limousine & Paratransit Association
3200 Tower Oaks Blvd
Suite 220
Rockville, MD 20852

301-984-5700; Fax: 301-984-5703
info@tlpa.org
www.tlpa.org

Alfred LaGasse, CEO
William Rouse, President
Harold Morgan, Executive Vice President
Michelle A. Hariston, CMP, Manager of Meetings
Leah New, Manager of Communications

TLPA's members-only bulletin of early alerts to critical changes in the industry, announcing threats and opportunities on issues that are before Congress and federal agencies. Organizes operators to take action, and provides knowledge and awareness.
Circulation: 6000
Founded in 1917
Mailing list available for rent

12776 **Medical Group Management Update**
Medical Group Management Association
104 Inverness Ter E
Englewood, CO 80112-5313

303-799-1111; Fax: 303-643-9599
infocenter@mgma.com
www.mgma.com

William Jessee, CEO
Eileen Barker, senior Vice President
Anders Gilberg, senior Vice President
Natalie Jamieson, Administrative Assistant

Monthly association newspaper offering up-to-the-minute articles on current legislation, practical management, health care trends, association activities and other timely subjects.
Frequency: Monthly

12777 **National Intelligence Report**
Institute of Management and Administration
1 Washington Park
Suite 1300
Newark, NJ 07102-3130

212-244-0360; Fax: 973-622-0595
customercare@bna.com
www.ioma.com

Provides concise, independent coverage and analysis of fast-breaking lab, pathology, blood banking, imaging and diagnostic radiology news from the Nation's Capital.
Cost: $489.00
Frequency: Biweekly

12778 **Nephrology News and Issues**
Nephrology News and Issues
17797 N Perimeter Dr
Suite 109
Scottsdale, AZ 85255-5455

480-443-4635; Fax: 480-443-4528

Melissa Laudenschlager, Publisher
Mark Neumann, Editor
Marcia Coutts, Circulation Manager
Cost: $55.00
Frequency: Monthly
Circulation: 22000
Founded in 1986

12779 **Neurology Today**
American Academy of Neurology
201 Chicago Ave.
Minneapolis, MN 55415

612-928-6000
800-879-1960; Fax: 612-454-2746
memberservices@aan.com
journals.lww.com/neurotodayonline
Facebook, Twitter

Catherine M. Rydell, CAE, Executive Director & CEO
Joseph Safdieh, MD, FAAN, Editor-in-Chief
Kim Jansen, Executive Publisher

The official news source of the American Academy of Neurology reports on breaking news, issues, and trends in the practice and science of neurology, reaching over 20,000 professionals.
Frequency: Bimonthly

12780 **News Now**
American Physical Therapy Association
1111 N Fairfax St
Alexandria, VA 22314-1488

703-684-2782; Fax: 703-706-8536
memberservices@apta.org
www.apta.org
Facebook, Twitter, LinkedIn

Maryann DiGiacomo, Editor
John D. Barnes, Chief Executive Officer
Janet Bezner, VP, Education, Governance
Rob Batarla, VP, Finance & Business Development
Felicity Clancy, VP, Communications & Marketing

Reports timely legislative, health care, and Association news to APTA members and subscribers.
80000 Members
Frequency: Weekly
Mailing list available for rent

12781 **Nurses' Notes**
American Association of Managed Care Nurses
4435 Waterfront Dr
Suite 101
Glen Allen, VA 23060-3393

804-747-9698; Fax: 804-747-5316
keads@aamcn.org
www.aamcn.org

Bill Williams, President

A quarterly newsletter published by the American Association of Managed Care Nurses. Available to members only.
Circulation: 2000

12782 **Nursing News Update**
American Association of Managed Care Nurses
4435 Waterfront Dr
Suite 101
Glen Allen, VA 23060-3393

804-747-9698; Fax: 804-747-5316
keads@aamcn.org
www.aamcn.org

Bill Williams, President
Laura Givens, Executive Admin

A weekly electronic newsletter published by the American Association of Managed Care Nurses. Available to members only.
Circulation: 2000

12783 **Physician's News Digest**
Physician's New Digest

230 Windsor Ave
Suite 216
Narberth, PA 19072-2217

610-668-1040
800-220-6109; Fax: 610-668-9177
info@physiciansnews.com
www.physiciansnews.com

Jeffery Barg, CEO/President
Christopher Gaudagnino, Business Manager
Ben Birenbaum, Business Manager
Cost: $35.00
Frequency: Monthly
Circulation: 40000
ISSN: 1079-6312
Founded in 1987
Printed in 4 colors on newsprint stock

12784 **Public Health**
State Capitals Newsletters
PO Box 7376
Alexandria, VA 22307-7376

703-768-9600; Fax: 703-768-9690
thecapitolcollection.com
Cost: $245.00

Frequency: Weekly

12785 **Sisters Network/National Newsletter**
Sisters Network
2922 Rosedale St
Suite 4206
Houston, TX 77004-6188

713-781-0255
866-781-1808; Fax: 713-780-8998
infonet@sistersnetworkinc.org
www.sistersnetworkinc.org

Erie Calloway, Executive Director
Karen E. Jackson, CEO
Caleen Burtonalleen, Public Relations Manager
Cherlyn K Latham, Project Director
Kelly P. Hodges, National Program Director

Publication of the group committed to awareness of the impact that breast cancer has on the African American community, with the latest information, medical research and news about events taking place within the Sisters National Network of affiliate chapters.
Frequency: Monthly
Founded in 1994

12786 **Today's School Psychologist**
LRP Publications
747 Dresher Road
PO Box 980
Horsham, PA 19044-2247

215-784-0912
800-341-7874; Fax: 215-784-9639
webmaster@lrp.com
www.lrp.com

Caroline Miller, Editor

In-depth guide to a school psychologists job, offering proactive strategies and tips for handling day-to-day tasks and responsibilities, encouraging change and improving professional standing and performance.
Cost: $135.00
Frequency: Monthly

12787 **US Medicine Newsletter**
US Medicine
39 York Street
Suite 400
Lambertville, NJ 08530

609-397-5522; Fax: 609-397-4237
www.usmedicine.com

James F Breuning, Publisher
Brenda L. Mooney, Editorial Director
Stephen Spotswood, Correspondent
Beth Scholz, Account Manager
Anita Crandall, Production Manager

US Medicine is an organization that supports physicians and healthcare workers with medical and legal information. Publishes a newspaper. Founded in 1964.
9 Members
Founded in 1964

12788 **Walking Tomorrow**
Christopher Reeve Paralysis Foundation
500 Morris Ave
Springfield, NJ 07081-1027

973-467-5915
800-225-0292; Fax: 973-912-9433
www.christopherreeve.org/

Julie Kwon, Director of Marketing
Kathy Lewis, Controller
Ed Jobst, Controller

Newsletter of the Christopher Reeve Paralysis Foundation.
Frequency: Monthly
Founded in 1982

12789 **Wellness Program Management Advisor**
Health Resources Publishing
1913 Atlantic Ave
Suite 200
Manasquan, NJ 08736-1067

732-292-1100
888-843-6242; Fax: 732-292-1111
info@themcic.com

Robert K Jenkins, Publisher
Lisa Mansfield, Regional Director
Brett Powell, Regional Director
Alice Burron, Director

A newsletter that is designed to help professionals manage their organization's health promotion and wellness programs. Gives information about how other wellness programs are doing in such areas as strategies adopted, expenses and return on investments. Also included are in depth profiles of wellness programs around the country that list the problems that they encountered and the steps that they took to alter them.
Cost: $247.00
Frequency: Monthly
ISSN: 1085-7125

Magazines & Journals

12790 **24 X 7**
HealthTech Publishing Company
6100 Center Drive
Suite 1000
Los Angeles, CA 90045

310-642-4400; Fax: 310-641-4444
www.24x7mag.com

Tony Ramos, Publisher
Kelly Stephens, Editor
Jennifer Bezahler, Circulation Manager

News and business magazine for the healthcare service support and technology management industry.
Frequency: Monthly
Circulation: 15000
ISSN: 1091-1626
Founded in 1996
Printed in 4 colors on glossy stock

12791 **AABB News**
American Association of Blood Banks
4550 Montgomery Ave.
Suite 700, North Tower
Bethesda, MD 20814-2747

301-907-6977; Fax: 301-907-6895
aabb@aabb.org
www.aabb.org

Debra BenAvram, Chief Executive Officer

Monthly print magazine offering news and feature stories on critical issues affecting transfusion medicine, cellular therapies and patient blood management.
Frequency: Monthly

12792 **AAOS Now**
American Academy of Orthopaedic Surgeons
9400 West Higgins Rd.
Rosemont, IL 60018

847-823-7186; Fax: 847-823-8125
aaosnow@aaos.org
www.aaos.org

Thomas E. Arend Jr., Esq., CAE, Chief Executive Officer
Eeric Truumees, MD, Editor-in-Chief
Dennis Coyle, Publisher

Offers a unique blend of clinical news and information, advocacy updates, practice management advice, reports on research and quality, and the latest news from the American Association of Orthopaedic Surgeons (AAOS).
Frequency: Monthly

12793 **AAPS Newsmagazine**
American Association of Pharmaceutical Scientists
2107 Wilson Blvd
Suite 700
Arlington, VA 22201-3042

703-243-2800; Fax: 703-243-9054
aaps@aaps.org
www.aaps.org

John Lisack, Executive Director
Joy Metcalf, Managing Editor
Janelle Kihlstrom, Editorial Assistant
Ken Corch, Executive Assistant

Exclusive to AAPS members. Features expanded coverage of the industry, complete with expert information on marketplace trends, regulatory matters, and career opportunities.
Mailing list available for rent

12794 **AAPS PharmSciTech Journal**
American Association of Pharmaceutical Scientists
2107 Wilson Blvd
Suite 700
Arlington, VA 22201-3042

703-243-2800; Fax: 703-243-9054
aaps@aaps.org
www.aaps.org

John Lisack, Executive Director
Joy Metcalf, Managing Editor
James Greif, Communications Specialist
Ken Corch, Executive Assistant

An online-only journal published and owned by the American Association of Pharmaceutical Scientists. The journal's mission is to disseminate scientific and technical information on drug product design, development, evaluation and processing to the global pharmaceutical research community, taking full advantage of web-based publishing by presenting innovative text with 3-D graphics, interactive figures and databases, video and audio files.
ISSN: 1530-9932
Mailing list available for rent

12795 **AARP The Magazine**
American Association of Retired Persons
601 E St NW
Washington, DC 20049-0003

202-434-2277
888-687-2277
202-434-3525; Fax: 202-434-7599
member@aarp.org
www.aarp.org

Hop Backus, Executive Vice President
Steve Cone, Executive Vice President

Joann Jenkins, Foundation President
A. Barry Rand, Chief Executive Officer
Cindy Lewin, General Counsel

AARP is a nonprofit, nonpartisan organization with a membership that helps people age 50 and over have independence, choice and control in ways that are beneficial and affordable to them and society as a whole, ways that help people 50 and over improve their lives. Founded through support from staffed offices in all 50 states.
Frequency: Monthly
Founded in 1958
Mailing list available for rent

12796 **ACSM's Health & Fitness Journal**
Lippincott Williams & Wilkins
351 W Camden St
Baltimore, MD 21201-2436

410-949-8000
800-222-3790; Fax: 410-528-4414
www.lww.com

J Arnold Anthony, Operations
Michael Hargrett, Publisher
Edward Howley, Editor-in-Chief

The Journal strives to help health and fitness practitioners improve their knowledge and experience through reports and recommendations from experts, CEC offerings, opportunities to question the experts, listings of job openings and more.
Cost: $40.00
Frequency: Fortnightly
Circulation: 11144
ISSN: 1091-5397
Founded in 1997
Printed in 4 colors on matte stock

12797 **ADA Courier**
American Dietetic Association
120 South Riverside Plaza
Suite 2000
Chicago, IL 60606-6995

312-990-0040
800-877-1600; Fax: 312-899-4757
affiliate@eatright.org
www.eatright.org

Susan H Laramee, President
Ronald S Moen, CEO
Patricia M. Babjak, Executive VP
Jennifer Herendeen, Editorial Director
Jason Switt, Editor

Readers look to the Courier for current association activities, membership news, updates on continuing education opportunities, ADA policies and coverage of the Associations' lobbying efforts in Washington.
Cost: $315.00
10 Pages
Frequency: Monthly
Circulation: 80000
ISSN: 1050-7434
Founded in 1917
Printed in 4 colors on glossy stock

12798 **ADA News**
American Dental Association
211 E Chicago Ave
Chicago, IL 60611-2678

312-440-2897; Fax: 312-440-3538
www.ada.org

Judy Jakush, Editor
Jill Philbein, Circulation Manager
James Bramson, CEO
Cost: $64.00
Founded in 1859

12799 **AGD Impact**
Academy of General Dentistry
560 W. Lake St.
Sixth Floor
Chicago, IL 60611

888-243-3368; Fax: 312-335-3432
membership@agd.org
www.agd.org

Contains information of interst to dentists, including practice management, continuing education, dental products, and in-depth articles on new and innovate developments in general dentistry.
Frequency: Monthly
Founded in 1954

12800 **AHA News**
AHA
1 N Franklin St
Suite 700
Chicago, IL 60606-4425

312-895-2500
800-242-2626; Fax: 312-895-2501
storeservice@aha.org
www.aha.org

Anthony Burke, CEO
Cliff Lehman, Director Membership Services

Provides extensive coverage of regulatory, judicial and legislative developments while also providing news and information from the AHA.
Cost: $45.00
Frequency: Weekly
Circulation: 40000
Founded in 1917

12801 **AMA Alliance Today**
AMA
515 N State St
Chicago, IL 60654-9104

312-464-4470; Fax: 312-464-5020
amaa@ama-assn.org
www.ama-assn.org

Jo Posselt, Executive Director
Megan Pellegrini, General Counsel
Jon Ekdahl, General Counsel
Bernard Hengesbaugh, Chief Operating Officer
Jacqueline Drake, Secretary
Circulation: 30,000
Founded in 1922

12802 **Advance for Health Information Executives**
Advance Newsmagazines/Merion Publications
2900 Horizon Dr
King of Prussia, PA 19406-2651

610-265-8249
800-355-5627; Fax: 610-962-0639

Frank Irving, Editor
Maryann Kurkowski, Circulation Manager

Coverage of emerging e-health and computer-based patient record technologies.
Frequency: Monthly
Founded in 1997

12803 **Aesthetic Plastic Surgery**
6277 Sea Harbor Drive
Orlando Florida
Orlando, Fl 32887-7703

407-345-4000
800-364-2147; Fax: 407-363-9661
elspcs@elsevier.com
www.surgery.org/

Elizabeth Sadati, Executive Editor
Paul Bernstein, Scientific Forum Editor
Stanley A Klatsky, Managing Director
Cost: $196.00
Frequency: Monthly
Founded in 1996

12804 **Air Medical Journal**
Mosby
11830 Westline Industrial Drive
Saint Louis, MO 63146-3318

314-453-4307
800-325-4307; Fax: 314-872-9164
elspcs@elsevier.com

David Dries, Editor
Liz Bennett-Bailey, Publisher
Eric Ferguson, Issue Manager
Cost: $85.00
Frequency: bi-monthly
Founded in 1986

12805 **American Academy of Osteopathy Journal**
3500 DePauw Boulevard
Suite 1100
Indianapolis, IN 46268-1136

317-879-1881
800-875-6360; Fax: 317-879-0563
editoraaoj@gmail.com
www.academyofosteopathy.org

Sherri L. Quarles, Executive Director
Taylor Bridgeforth, Communications & Administration
Janice Upton Blumer, DO, FAAO, Editor-in-Chief
Lauren Good, Managing Editor

The official publication of the American Academy of Osteopathy. Contains scholarly articles and latest news.
Frequency: Quarterly

12806 **American Family Physician**
American Academy of Family Physicians
11400 Tomahawk Creek Pkwy.
Leawood, KS 66211-2672

913-906-6205; Fax: 913-906-6086
www.aafp.org/journals/afp.html
Facebook, Twitter, YouTube

Sumi M. Sexton, MD, Editor-in-Chief
Kenny Lin, MD, MPH, Deputy Editor

Peer-reviewed clinical journal of the American Academy of Family Physicians.
Cost: $240.00
Frequency: Monthly
ISSN: 0002-838X
Founded in 1947

12807 **American Health Line**
600 New Hampshire Avenue NW
Washington, DC 20037

202-295-5381
800-717-3245; Fax: 202-266-5700
www.americanhealthline.com

Joshua Perin, Editor-in-Chief
Josh Kotzman, Editors
Frequency: Weekly
Founded in 1992

12808 **American Imago: Studies In Psychoanalysis and Culture**
Johns Hopkins University Press
2715 N Charles St
Baltimore, MD 21218-4319

410-516-6900
800-548-1784; Fax: 410-516-6998
webmaster@jhupress.jhu.edu
www.press.jhu.edu/journals

William Brody, President
Kathleen Keane, Director
William M. Breichner, Publisher
Founded in 1878

12809 **American Journal of Clinical Medicine**
American Association of Physician Specialists, Inc

5550 West Executive Drive
Suite 400
Tampa, FL 33609

813-433-2277; Fax: 813-830-6599
wcarbone@aapsus.org
www.aapsus.com

Nadine Simone, Executive Administrative Assistant
Debi Colmorgen, Communications Coordinator
William Carbone, Chief Executive Officer
Anthony Durante, Director of Finance & Operations
Sandy Martin, Finance & Operations Coordinator

The official peer-reviewed journal of the AAPS, an organization dedicated to promoting the highest intellectual, moral, and ethical standards of its members.
1000 Attendees

12810 **American Journal of Cosmetic Surgery**
737 N Michigan Ave
Suite 2100
Chicago, IL 60611-5641

312-981-6760; Fax: 312-981-6787
info@cosmeticsurgery.org
www.cosmeticsurgery.org

Jeffrey Knezovich, Executive VP
Charlie Baase, Marketing Manager

12811 **American Journal of Geriatric Psychiatry**
American Association for Geriatric Psychiatry
6728 Old McLean Village Drive
McLean, VA 22101

703-556-9222; Fax: 703-556-8729
main@aagponline.org
www.ajgponline.org

Christopher N. Wood, Executive Director
Victoria LaLiberte Cooper, Executive Assistant
Charles F. Reynolds, III, MD, Editor-in-Chief

The authoritative source of information for the rapidly developing field of geriatric psychiatry. Contains peer-reviewed articles on the diagnosis and classification of psychiatric disorders of later life, epidemiological and biological correlates of mental health of older adults, and psychopharmacology and other somatic treatments.
Frequency: Annual
Founded in 1978

12812 **American Journal of Health Education (AJHE)**
Society of Health and Physical Educators
1900 Association Dr
Reston, VA 20191-1502

703-476-3400
800-213-7193; Fax: 703-476-9527
tlawson@shapeamerica.org
www.shapeamerica.org

Stephanie A. Morris, Chief Executive Officer
Thomas F. Lawson, Managing Editor

Covers today's health education and health promotion issues head on with timely, substantive, and thought provoking articles for professionals working in medical care facilities, professional preparation, colleges and universities, community and public health agencies, schools, and businesses.
25000 Members
Frequency: Bimonthly
Founded in 1885

12813 **American Journal of Human Genetics**
American Society of Human Genetics
9650 Rockville Pike
Bethesda, MD 20814-3998

301-634-7300
866-HUM-GENE; Fax: 301-634-7079
society@ashg.org
www.ashg.org
Facebook, Twitter, LinkedIn

Joann Boughman, PhD, Executive VP
Chuck Windle, Director of Finance/Administration
Karen Goodman, Executive Assistant
Pauline Minhinnett, Dir. of Meetings/Exhibit Management
Mary Shih, Membership Manager

ASHG is the primary professional membership organization for human genetics specialists worldwide.
8000 Members
Frequency: Monthly
Circulation: 7,199
ISSN: 0002-9297
Founded in 1948
Mailing list available for rent

12814 **American Journal of Hypertension**
148 Madison Ave
Fifth Floor
New York, NY 10016-6700

212-532-0537; Fax: 212-696-0711
journal@ash-us.org
www.ash-us.org

John H Laragh, Editor In Chief
Ellen Twyne, President
Cost: $246.00
Frequency: Monthly
Founded in 1985

12815 **American Journal of Managed Care**
American Medical Publishing
241 Forsgate Drive
Jamesburg, NJ 08831

732-656-1006; Fax: 732-656-0818
info@ajmc.com
www.ajmc.com

Jim King, Publisher
Lyn Beamesderfer, Editor

The American Journal of Managed Care is an independent, peer-reviewed forum for the publication of clinical research and opinion related to quality, value, and policy in health care delivery. The Journal delivers original research on patient outcomes, clinical effectiveness, cost effectiveness, quality management, and health policy to managed care decision makers.
Frequency: Monthly
Circulation: 53000
ISSN: 1088-0224
Founded in 1995

12816 **American Journal of Neuroradiology**
2210 Midwest Rd
Suite 207
Oak Brook, IL 60523-8205

630-574-1487
800-783-4903; Fax: 630-786-6251
www.ajnr.org

Karen Halm, Managing Editor
Victor M Haughton MD, VP

Relays news and schedules of events for members.
Cost: $235.00
Circulation: 7000
Founded in 1937

12817 **American Journal of Roetgenology**
American Roentgen Ray Society
1891 Preston White Dr
Reston, VA 20191-4326

703-729-3353
800-438-2777; Fax: 703-729-4839
info@arrs.org
www.arrs.org

Susan Brown, Executive Director
Connie Wolfe, Publications Assistant
Fran Schuweiler, Managing Editor
Charles Kahn, Vice President
Melissa Rosado, Secretary

A monthly journal published by the American Roentgen Ray Society.
Cost: $275.00
Frequency: Monthly
Circulation: 25,000
Founded in 1900
Mailing list available for rent: 10000 names at $160 per M

12818 **American Medical News**
American Medical Association
515 N State St
9th Floor
Chicago, IL 60654-9104

312-464-4429
800-621-8335; Fax: 312-464-4445
ben_mindell@ama-assn.org
www.ama-assn.org

Ben Mindell, Vice President
John Nelson, CEO/President
Kathryn Trombatore, Manager
Jon Ekdahl, General Counsel
Bernard Hengesbaugh, Chief Operating Officer

Intended to serve as an impartial forum for information affecting physicians and their practices. The views expressed in AMNews are not necessarily endorsed by the American Medical Association.
Cost: $95.00
Frequency: Weekly
Circulation: 230,000
Founded in 1847

12819 **American Nurse Today**
American Nurses Association
600 Maryland Avenue SW
Washington, DC 20024-2571

202-651-7000; Fax: 202-651-7003
www.NursingWorld.org

Pamela Cipriano PhD RN FAAN, Editor-in-Chief

Serves registered nurses in North America.
Frequency: 6 per year
Printed in 4 colors on glossy stock

12820 **Anesthesiology News**
545 W 45th St
8th Floor
New York, NY 10036-3409

212-957-5300; Fax: 212-957-7230
marsap@mcmahonmed.com
www.anesthesiologynews.com

Adam Marcus, Managing Editor
Raymond E. McMahon, CEO/Publisher
Marsha Radebaugh, Circulation Coordinator
Cost: $65.00
Frequency: Monthly
Circulation: 39720
Founded in 1975

12821 **Annals of Allergy, Asthma & Immunology**
85 W Algonquin Road
Suite 550
Arlington Heights, IL 60005-4460

847-427-1200; Fax: 847-427-1294
mail@acaai.org
www.acaai.org
Facebook, Twitter, LinkedIn, YouTube

Dana Wallace, MD, President
Stanley Fineman, MD, MBA, President-Elect

Information and news service for patients, parents of patients, members, the news media, and purchasers of health care programs.
5200 Members
Frequency: Monthly
Circulation: 5100
ISSN: 1081-1206
Founded in 1942

12822 **Annals of Emergency Medicine**
Elsevier Publishing
1125 Executive Circle
P.O. Box 619911
Irving, TX 75038-2522

972-550-0911
800-798-1822; Fax: 972-580-2816
customerservice@acep.org
www.acep.org

Nancy B Medina, CAE, Editorial Director
Tracy Napper, Managing Editor
Michael L Callaham, MD, Editor-in-Chief
Dean Wilkerson, Executive Director
Marco Coppola, Council Speaker

An international, peer-reviewed journal dedicated to improving the quality of care by publishing the highest quality science for emergency medicine and related medical specialties.
Frequency: Monthly
Circulation: 30000
ISSN: 0196-0644
Mailing list available for rent

12823 **Annals of Opthalmology**
Am. Society of Cont. Medicine, Surgery & Opth.
North Cisero Avenue
Suite 208
Chicago, IL 60712

847-677-9093
800-621-4002; Fax: 847-677-9094
iaos@aol.com

Mikhail Krasnov, Editor-in-Chief
Randall Bellows MD, CEO/President

Exclusive articles written and peer-reviewed by doctors.
Frequency: bi-monthly
Founded in 1884

12824 **Annals of Plastic Surgery**
530 Walnut St
Philadelphia, PA 19106-3603

215-521-8300; Fax: 215-521-8411
www.lww.com

Melissa Ricks, Manager
Cost: $375.00
Frequency: Monthly

12825 **Applied Clinical Trials**
Advanstar Communications
6200 Canoga Avenue
2nd Floor
Woodland Hills, CA 91367

818-593-5000; Fax: 818-593-5020
www.appliedclinicaltrialsonline.com
Facebook, Twitter, LinkedIn

Joseph Loggia, President
Chris DeMoulin, VP
Susannah George, Marketing Director

Practical information for clinical research professionals in industry and academia who develop, execute and manage clinical trials worldwide. Regular topics include regulatory affairs, protocol development, data management and harmonization updates.
Frequency: Monthly
Circulation: 16255
ISSN: 1064-8542
Founded in 1987
Mailing list available for rent

12826 **Archives of Physical Medicine and Rehabilitation**
American Congress of Rehabilitation Medicine
11654 Plaza America Drive
Suite 535
Reston, VA 20190

703-435-5335; Fax: 866-692-1619
www.acrm.org

Jon W. Lindberg, Executive Director
Dinara Suleymanova, Director of Operations
Judy Reuter, Publications & Web Development
Cindy Robinson, Marketing Coordinator
Margo Holen, Chief Meetings Officer

Available with membership to American Congress of Rehabilitation Medicine.
Frequency: Monthly
Circulation: 900
Founded in 1923

12827 **Art Therapy: Journal of the American Art T herapy Association**
American Art Therapy Association
4875 Eisenhower Avenue
Sute 240
Alexandria, VA 22304

703-548-5860
888-290-0878; Fax: 703-783-8468
info@arttherapy.org
www.arttherapy.org

Cynthia Woodruff, Executive Director
Christina Easterly, Coordinator, Events & Operations
Barbara Florence, Director, Events & Education
Clara Keane, Coordinator, Communication & Policy
Kat Michel, Manager, Membership

The leading scholarly research publication in art therapy with up-to-date professional knowledge of the field; a broad spectrum of ideas in therapy, practice, professional issues, and research; and peer-reviewed research, theory and practice papers, viewpoints, reviews of current literature, and best practices.

12828 **Arthritis Hotline**
2824 Swift Avenue
Dallas, TX 75204

972-286-6664; Fax: 214-363-2817

12829 **Arthroplasty Today**
American Association of Hip & Knee Surgeons
9400 W. Higgins Rd.
Suite 230
Rosemont, IL 60018-4976

847-698-1200; Fax: 847-698-0704
www.arthroplastytoday.org

Michael J. Zarski, JD, Executive Director
Brian J. McGrory, MD, Editor-in-Chief
Gregory J. Golladay, MD, Deputy Editor

A peer-reviewed journal that publishes original research and articles relating to joint replacement or the treatments of its complications in an open-access, online format. Sister publication of the Journal of Arthroplasty.

12830 **Arts & Health: An International Journal fo r Research, Policy and Practice**
American Art Therapy Association
4875 Eisenhower Avenue
Sute 240
Alexandria, VA 22304

703-548-5860
888-290-0878; Fax: 703-783-8468
info@arttherapy.org
www.arttherapy.org

Cynthia Woodruff, Executive Director
Christina Easterly, Coordinator, Events & Operations
Barbara Florence, Director, Events & Education
Clara Keane, Coordinator, Communication & Policy
Kat Michel, Manager, Membership

An international forum for the fast-emerging field of arts and health including ways in which the arts contribute to health, wellbeing, social inclusion, and healthcare practice.

12831 **Aviation Medicine and Human Performance**
Aerospace Medical Association
320 S Henry St
Alexandria, VA 22314-3579

703-739-2240; Fax: 703-739-9652
AMHPJournal@asma.org
www.asma.org

Frederick Bonato, PhD, Editor-in-Chief
Pamela C. Day, B.A., Managing Editor

A peer-reviewed journal that provides contact with physicians, life scientists, bioengineers and medical specialists working in both basic medical research and in its clinical applications.
Frequency: Monthly
Mailing list available for rent

12832 **BNA's Health Care Policy Report**
3 Bethesda Metro Center
Suite 250
Bethesda, MD 20814

202-452-4107
800-372-1033; Fax: 202-452-4084
edcontactslitigation@bna.com
www.bna.com

Josh Eastright, CEO
Frequency: Weekly
Founded in 1929

12833 **Behavioral Health Management**
MEDQUEST Communications
3800 Lakeside Ave E
Suite 201
Cleveland, OH 44114-3857

216-391-9100; Fax: 216-391-9200
www.behavioral.net

Mark Goodman, Manager
Monica E Oss, Editor-in-Chief

Largest publication reporting on the cutting edge trends and management practices in the behavioral health field.
Cost: $94.00
52 Pages
Circulation: 21615
ISSN: 1075-6701
Printed in 4 colors on glossy stock

12834 **Behavioral Neuroscience**
750 1st St NE
Washington, DC 20002-4242

202-336-5500
800-374-2721; Fax: 202-336-5549
journals@apa.org
www.apa.org/pubs/journals/bne/index.aspx

Rebecca Burwell, Editor
Cost: $235.00
Circulation: 200,000
Founded in 1988

12835 **Biomedical Instrumentation & Technology**
Assoc for the Advancement of Medical Instrumentat

4301 N. Fairfax Drive
Suite 301
Arlington, VA 22203-1633

703-525-4890; Fax: 703-276-0793
publications@aami.org
www.aami.org

Sean Loughlin, Managing Editor

Filled with practical guidance and regular features on troubleshooting, certification, career trends, management issues, sterilization, quality assurance, and more.
Cost: $182.00
Frequency: Bimonthly
Circulation: 6000
Mailing list available for rent

12836 **Biomedical Safety & Standards**
Aspen Publishers
280 Orchard Ridge Drive
Suite 200
Gaithersburg, MD 20878-1978

301-417-7591

Jack Bruggeman, Publisher

12837 **Birth-Issues in Perinatal Care**
350 Main Street
6th Floor
Malden, MA 02148-5023

781-388-8200
800-759-6102; Fax: 781-388-8210
www.blackwellpublishing.com

Diony Young, Editor
Gordon Tibbitts III, President
Robert Campbell, Publisher
Ginny Foley, Manager
Cost: $36.00
Frequency: Quarterly
Circulation: 1709
Founded in 1897

12838 **Body Positive**
19 Fulton Street
Suite 308 B
New York, NY 10038-2100

212-566-7333
800-566-6599; Fax: 212-566-4539
www.bodypos.org/

Raymond A Smith, Editor
Eric Rodriguez, Executive Director
Cost: $40.00
Frequency: Quarterly
Circulation: 10000
Founded in 1987

12839 **Brain & Life**
American Academy of Neurology
201 Chicago Ave.
Minneapolis, MN 55415

612-928-6000
800-879-1960; Fax: 612-454-2746
memberservices@aan.com
www.brainandlife.org
Facebook, Twitter, Instagram

Catherine M. Rydell, CAE, Executive Director & CEO
Orly Avitzur, MD, MBA, FAAN, Editor-in-Chief

The only magazine focused on the intersection of neurologic disease and brain health. Covers a range of topics including multiple sclerosis, Alzheimer's disease and dementia, epilepsy, concussion, Parkinson's disease and movement disorders, neuropathy, sleep disorders, migraines and much, much more.
Frequency: Bimonthly

12840 **Bulletin**
1650 Diagonal Road
Alexandria, VA 22314-3357

703-836-4444; Fax: 703-683-5100
membership@entnet.org
www.entnet.org
Facebook, Twitter

Marty Stewart, Sr Manager, Media/Public Relations
James L. Netterville, President
J. Gavin Setzen, Secretary/Treasurer
David R. Nielsen, Executive Vice President and CEO
Paul T. Fass, Director - Private Practice

Features articles written by member otolaryngologists and Academy staff, as well as regular segments on political advocacy, the grassroots member network, practice management, and the latest specialty news and information.
Frequency: Monthly
Circulation: 12,000
ISSN: 0731-8359
Mailing list available for rent

12841 **Business and Health**
Medical Economics Publishing
131 West First Street
Duluth, Mi 55802-2065

218-723-9200
888-346-0085; Fax: 218-723-9437
info@advanstar.com
www.advanstar.com

Tracey Walker, Senior Editor
Julie Miller, Managing Editor
Daniel Corcoran, Publisher
Joseph Loggia, Chief Executive Officer
Thomas Ehardt, Chief Administrator

Provides the business and industry fields with information on manufacturing, wholesale, retail and financial, insurance companies, law/accounting firms, hospitals, HMO/PPOs, labor unions, consulting firms, and Medicare/Medicade.
Cost: $64.00
Frequency: Monthly
Circulation: 39736
Founded in 1987
Printed in 4 colors on glossy stock

12842 **CA: A Cancer Journal for Clinicians**
1599 Clifton Road NE
Atlanta, GA 30329-4251

404-929-6902; Fax: 404-325-9341
caonline.amcancersoc.org

Harmon J Eyre, Editor
Vickie Thaw, Publisher
John R. Seffrin, CEO
Circulation: 90,000
Founded in 1913

12843 **CVS InStep with Healthy Living**
Drug Store News Consumer Health Publications
425 Park Ave
New York, NY 10022-3526

212-756-5220
845-426-7612; Fax: 212-756-5250
www.drugstorenews.com

Lebhar Friedman, Publisher
John Tanzola, National Sales Manager

Helps educate and inform over 25 millions 45+ shoppers that visit CVS every month. Topics include health, nutrition, fitness, lifestyle, travel, coupons and CVS programs and events.
Frequency: Quarterly
Circulation: 950000
Founded in 2002

12844 **Cancer Discovery**
American Association for Cancer Research
615 Chestnut St.
17th Fl.
Philadelphia, PA 19106-4404

215-440-9300
866-423-3965; Fax: 215-440-9313
cancerdiscovery@aacr.org
cancerdiscovery.aacrjournals.org

Margaret Foti, Chief Executive Officer
Lewis C. Cantley, Editor-in-Chief
Jos, Baselga, Editor-in-Chief

Publishes high-impact, peer-reviewed articles describing major advances in research and clinical trials.
Frequency: Monthly
Founded in 1907

12845 **Cancer Epidemiology, Biomarkers & Preventi on**
American Association for Cancer Research
615 Chestnut St.
17th Fl.
Philadelphia, PA 19106-4404

215-440-9300
866-423-3965; Fax: 215-440-9313
cebp@aacr.org
cebp.aacrjournals.org

Margaret Foti, Chief Executive Officer
Timothy R. Rebbeck, Editor-in-Chief

Publishes original peer-reviewed, population-based research on cancer etiology, prevention, surveillance, and survivorship.
Frequency: Monthly
Founded in 1907

12846 **Cancer Immunology Research**
American Association for Cancer Research
615 Chestnut St.
17th Fl.
Philadelphia, PA 19106-4404

215-440-9300
866-423-3965; Fax: 215-440-9313
cancerimmunolres@aacr.org
cancerimmunolres.aacrjournals.org

Margaret Foti, Chief Executive Officer
Robert D. Schreiber, Editor-in-Chief
Philip D. Greenberg, Editor-in-Chief

Publishes outstanding original articles reporting major advances in cancer immunology that span the discipline from basic investigations in host-tumor interactions to developmental therapeutics in model systems, early translational studies in patients, and late-stage clinical trials.
Frequency: Monthly
Founded in 1907

12847 **Cancer Prevention Research**
American Association for Cancer Research
615 Chestnut St.
17th Fl.
Philadelphia, PA 19106-4404

215-440-9300
866-423-3965; Fax: 215-440-9313
cancerprevres@aacr.org
cancerpreventionresearch.aacrjournals.org

Margaret Foti, Chief Executive Officer
Scott M. Lippman, Editor-in-Chief

Publishes important original studies, reviews, and perspectives within the major topic areas of biology of premalignancy, risk factors and risk assessment, early detection research, immunoprevention, and chemopreventive and other interventions, including the basic science behind them.
Frequency: Monthly
Founded in 1907

12848 **Cancer Research**
American Association for Cancer Research
615 Chestnut St.
17th Fl.
Philadelphia, PA 19106-4404

215-440-9300
866-423-3965; Fax: 215-440-9313

cancerres@aacr.org
cancerres.aacrjournals.org

Margaret Foti, Chief Executive Officer
Chi Van Dang, Editor-in-Chief

Publishes original studies, reviews, and opinion pieces offering significance and broad impact to a diverse audience. Primary subsections include genome and epigenome, metabolism and chemical biology, molecular cell biology, tumor biology and immunology, translational science, convergence an technologies, population and prevention science.
Frequency: Twice Monthly
Founded in 1907

12849 Cancer Today
American Association for Cancer Research
615 Chestnut St.
17th Fl.
Philadelphia, PA 19106-4404

215-440-9300
866-423-3965; Fax: 215-440-9313
info@cancertodaymag.org
www.cancertodaymag.org

Margaret Foti, Chief Executive Officer
William G. Nelson, MD, PhD, Editor-in-Chief

The authoritative resource for cancer patients, survivors and their family members and friends. Offers information and inspiration as you face the challenges of diagnosis, treatment, survivorship or caregiving.
Frequency: Quarterly
Founded in 1907

12850 Cannabinoids
International Association for Cannabinoid Medicine
Am Mildenweg 6
59602 Ruethen
Germany

+49-2952-9708571; Fax: +49-2952-902651
info@cannabis-med.org
www.cannabis-med.org
Facebook, Twitter, LinkedIn

Franjo Grotenhermen, Executive Director & Editor
Michael Krawitz, Patient Representative, USA
Alison Myrden, Patient Representative, Canada
Mark Ware, Editor

The official journal of the IACM is peer-reviewed and published online in several languages. A source of information on medical and scientific aspects of cannabis and cannabinoids.
ISSN: 2378-8763
Founded in 2000

12851 Cannabis and Cannabinoid Research
International Association for Cannabinoid Medicine
Am Mildenweg 6
59602 Ruethen
Germany
+49-2952-9708571; Fax: +49-2952-902651
info@cannabis-med.org
www.cannabis-med.org
Facebook, Twitter, LinkedIn

Franjo Grotenhermen, Executive Director
Michael Krawitz, Patient Representative, USA
Alison Myrden, Patient Representative, Canada
Daniele Piomelli, PhD, PharmD, Editor-in-Chief

A peer-reviewed journal dedicated to the scientific, medical, and psychosocial exploration of clinical cannabis, cannabinoids, and the endocannabinoid system. Affiliated with the IACM.
ISSN: 2378-8763
Founded in 2000

12852 Case Manager
Mosby
10801 Executive Center Drive
Suite 509
Little Rock, AR 72211

501-223-5165; Fax: 501-220-0519

Catherine Mullahy, Editor
Tom Strickland, Editor-in-Chief
Cheri Lattimer, Executive Director

Exclusively for the case management profession.
Cost: $52.00
80 Pages
Frequency: Bi-Monthly
Circulation: 20M
Founded in 1990
Printed in 4 colors on glossy stock

12853 Circulation Research
PO Box 1620
Suite 230
Hagerstown, MD 21741

301-223-2300
800-638-3030; Fax: 301-223-2400
educsales@lww.com
www.lww.com

Eduardo Marb n, Editor
Cost: $377.00
Founded in 1792

12854 CleanRooms Magazine
PennWell Publishing Company
98 Spit Brook Rd
Nashua, NH 03062-5737

603-891-0123; Fax: 603-891-9294
georgem@pennwell.com
www.pennwell.com

Christine Shaw, VP
John Haystead, Editor
James Enos, Publisher
Adam Japko, President
Heidi Barnes, Circulation Manager

Serves the contamination control and ultrapure materials and process industries. Written for readers in the microelectronics, pharmaceutical, biotech, health care, food processing and other user industries. Provides technology and business news and new product listings.
Circulation: 34019
Founded in 1910

12855 Clinical Advances in Periodontics
American Academy of Periodontology
737 N. Michigan Avenue
Suite 800
Chicago, IL 60611-6660

312-787-5518; Fax: 312-787-3670
staff@abperio.org
www.perio.org

Erin O'Donnell Dotzler, Executive Director

Dedicated to advancing clinical management of patients by translating scientific knowledge into practical therapy.

12856 Clinical Cancer Research
American Association for Cancer Research
615 Chestnut St.
17th Fl.
Philadelphia, PA 19106-4404

215-440-9300
866-423-3965; Fax: 215-440-9313
ccr@aacr.org
clincancerres.aacrjournals.org

Margaret Foti, Chief Executive Officer
Keith T. Flaherty, Editor-in-Chief

Publishes innovative clinical and translational cancer research studies that bridge the laboratory and the clinic.
Frequency: Twice Monthly
Founded in 1907

12857 Clinical Chemistry
American Association for Clinical Chemistry
900 Seventh St. NW
Suite 400
Washington, DC 20001

202-857-0717
800-892-1400; Fax: 202-887-5093
journals@aacc.org
www.aacc.org

Janet B. Kreizman, Chief Executive Officer
Nader Rifai, Editor-in-Chief

8,000 Members
Frequency: Monthly
Mailing list available for rent

12858 Clinical Lab Products
MWC Allied Healthcare Group
6100 Center Drive
Suite 1000
Los Angeles, CA 90045

310-642-4400; Fax: 310-641-4444
www.clpmag.com

Scott Anderson, Publisher
Carol Andrews, Editor
Sharon Marsee, Production Manager
Tony Ramos, President
Jennifer Bezahler, Circulation Director

CLP is the leading monthly product news magazine on key decision makers in the clinical diagnostic laboratory. New product annoucements and editorial features assist lab professionals in providing cost effective timely and accurate patient diagnostic information.
Cost: $125.00
Frequency: Monthly
Circulation: 45000
Founded in 1976
Printed in 4 colors on glossy stock

12859 Clinical Pulmonary Medicine
530 Walnut St
Philadelphia, PA 19106-3603

215-521-8300
800-638-6423; Fax: 215-521-8411
www.lww.com

Barry Morrill, Publisher
Michael S Niederman MD, Editor-in-Chief
Jay Lippincott, President

Provides a forum for the discussion of important new knowledge in the field of pulmonary medicine that is of interest and relevance to the practitioner.

12860 Comparative Medicine
American Association for Laboratory Animal Science
9190 Crestwyn Hills Drive
Memphis, TN 38125

901-754-8620; Fax: 901-753-0046
info@aalas.org
www.aalas.org

Ann Turner, Executive Director

Disseminates high-quality, peer-reviewed information that expands biomedical knowledge and promotes human and animal health through the study of laboratory animal disease, animal models of disease, and basic biologic mechanisms related to disease in people and animals.

12861 **Computers and Biomedical Research**
525 B Street
Suite 1900
San Diego, CA 92101-4401

619-231-6616
800-321-5068; Fax: 619-699-6422
www.elsevier.com

Gilbert Laporte, Editor
Bill Godfrey, Chief Information Officer
David Clark, Senior Vice President
Frequency: Monthly
Founded in 1974

12862 **Computers, Informatics, Nursing**
Lippincott Williams & Wilkins
10 A Beech Street
Suite 2
Portland, ME 04101

207-553-7750; Fax: 207-553-7751
www.nursingcenter.com

Leslie H. Nicoll, Editor
Lippin Cott, Publisher/President

Computer and informatics applications and product selection in nursing and education for nurse managers, patient care executives, nurses in direct patient care, nurse educators and researchers.
Cost: $63.00
Circulation: 4112
Founded in 1985

12863 **Contemporary Urology**
Medical Economics Publishing
5 Paragon Dr
Montvale, NJ 07645-1791

973-944-7777
888-581-8052; Fax: 973-944-7778

Curtis Allen, President
Culley C Carson MD, Editor-in-Chief
Matthew J Holland, Publisher
Don Berman, Director Business Development

Comtemporary Urology serves medical and osteopathic physicians specializing in urology.
Cost: $120.00
Frequency: Monthly
Circulation: 4276
ISSN: 1042-2250
Founded in 1992
Printed in 4 colors on glossy stock

12864 **Contingency Planning & Management**
Witter Publishing Corporation
20 Commerce Street
Flemington, NJ 08822

908-788-0343; Fax: 908-788-3782
www.witterpublishing.com

Bob Joudanin, Publisher
Paul Kirvan, Editor-in-Chief
Mike Viscel, Production Manager
Andrew Witter, President

Serves the fields of financial/banking, manufacturing industrial, transportation, utilities, telecommunications, health care, government, insurance and other allied fields.
Cost: $195.00
Frequency: Monthly
Founded in 1987

12865 **Continuing Care**
Stevens Publishing Corporation
5151 Belt Line Rd
10th Floor
Dallas, TX 75254-7507

972-687-6700; Fax: 972-687-6767
www.stevenspublishing.com

Craig S Stevens, President/CEO
Mike Valenti, Executive Vice President
Angela Neville, Editor

To provide case management and discharge planning professions with practical and professional information to ensure quality patient services at a cost-effective price.
Cost: $119.00
Founded in 1925

12866 **Continuum**
American Academy of Neurology
201 Chicago Ave.
Minneapolis, MN 55415

612-928-6000
800-879-1960; Fax: 612-454-2746
memberservices@aan.com
journals.lww.com/continuum
Facebook

Catherine M. Rydell, CAE, Executive Director & CEO
Steven L. Lewis, MD, FAAN, Editor-in-Chief

An in-depth clinically oriented review journal for the practicing neurologist, residents and fellows, advanced practice providers, and neurology professionals.
Frequency: Bimonthly

12867 **Coping with Allergies and Asthma**
Media America
P.O. Box 682268
Franklin, TN 37068-2268

615-790-2400
info@copingmag.com
www.copingmag.com
Facebook, Twitter

Paula Chadwell, Publisher
Laura Shipp, Editor

Information, tips and news for sufferers of allergies or asthma.
Founded in 1986

12868 **Coping with Cancer**
Media America
P.O. Box 682268
Franklin, TN 37068-2268

615-790-2400
info@copingmag.com
www.copingmag.com
Facebook, Twitter

Paula Chadwell, Executive
Laura Shipp, Editor

A magazine for people whose lives have been touched by cancer. Provides knowledge, hope and inspiration to its readers including cancer patients, cancer survivors, and their families, caregivers, healthcare teams and support group leaders.
Cost: $19.00
Founded in 1986

12869 **Cosmetic Surgery Times**
Advanstar Communications
7500 Old Oak Blvd
Cleveland, OH 44130-3343

440-243-8100
888-527-7008; Fax: 440-891-2740
info@advanstar.com
www.advanstar.com

Claudia Shayne-Ferguson, Group Publisher
Maureen Hrehocik, Editor-in-Chief
Michelle Tackla, Senior Editor
Ray Lender, General Manager
Carol Bessick, Manager

Provides cosmetic surgeons with the most current clinical news available. Covers latest surgical techniques, medicolegal issues, updates on new technologies, and suggestions for practice management.
Cost: $95.00
Frequency: 10x/yr
Circulation: 10,003
ISSN: 1094-6810
Founded in 1987

12870 **Cost Reengineering Report**
National Health Information
PO Box 15429
Atlanta, GA 30333-0429

404-607-9500
800-597-6300; Fax: 404-607-0095
www.nhionline.com

David Schwartz, President

Contains strategies for reengineering clinical and operational functions, and cutting costs while maintaining or improving quality.
Cost: $299.00
Frequency: Monthly

12871 **Counseling Today**
5999 Stevenson Ave
Alexandria, VA 22304-3302

703-823-9800
800-347-6647; Fax: 703-823-0252
membership@counseling.org
www.counseling.org
Facebook, Twitter
Marvin D. Kuehn, Executive Director
Tom Evenson, President

The mission of the American Counseling Association (ACA) is to enhance the quality of life in society by promoting the development of professional counselors, advancing the counseling profession, and using the profession and practice of counseling to promote respect for human dignity and diversity. ACA is a not-for-profit, professional and educational organization.
Frequency: Monthly
Circulation: 50000
Founded in 1952
Mailing list available for rent: 60M names

12872 **Critical Strategies: Psychotherapy in Managed Care**
Bill Cohen
10 Alice Street
Binghamton, NY 13904-1580

607-722-5857
800-342-9678; Fax: 607-722-6362
www.haworthpressinc.com

Frank DePiano, Editor
Sandra J Sickels, Marketing VP
William Cohen, Owner

Resource for innovative and effective approaches to clinical practice in relation to managed care.
Cost: $35.00
Frequency: 2 per year

12873 **Data Strategies & Benchmarks**
National Health Information
PO Box 15429
Atlanta, GA 30333-429

404-607-9500
800-597-6300; Fax: 404-607-0095
www.nhionline.net

David Schwartz, Publisher
Steve Larose, Editor
David Schwartz, CEO
Edgardo Rivera, Director

Provides insightful guidance and how-to advice to help them meet all the key challenges faced under managed care.
Cost: $339.00
Frequency: Monthly
Founded in 1994

12874 **Dental Economics**
PennWell Publishing Company
1421 S Sheridan Rd
Tulsa, OK 74112-6619

918-831-9421
800-331-4463; Fax: 918-831-9476

joeb@pennwell.com
www.pennwell.com

Robert Biolchini, President
Lyle Hoyt, Publisher
Cost: $105.76
Frequency: Monthly
Founded in 1910

12875 **Dental Lab Products**
MEDEC Dental Communications
2 Northfield Plaza
Suite 300
Northfield, IL 60093-1219

847-441-3700
800-225-4569; Fax: 847-441-3702

Bob Kehoe, Editorial Director
Gail Weisman, Editor
Fran Martin, Managing Editor
Richard Fischer, Publisher
Tom Delaney, National Sales Manager

Serves the dental profession and the dental industry, list rentals, classifieds and other services to complete your marketing plan.$35 subscription per year
35 Pages
Circulation: 19,000
ISSN: 0146-9738
Founded in 1967
Printed in 4 colors on glossy stock

12876 **Dental Materials**
Academy of Dental Materials
4425 Cass St.
Suite A
San Diego, CA 92109

858-272-1018; Fax: 858-272-7687
dentistry.dentmatj@manchester.ac.uk
www.demajournal.com

Dr. David C Watts PhD FADM, Editor-in-Chief
Nick Silikas, Editorial Advisor
Diana Knight, Editorial Assistant

Provides a forum for the exchange of information on dental materials, to enhance communication between industry, researchers and practicing dentists, and to promote dental materials through its activities.
Frequency: Monthly

12877 **Dental Practice**
MEDEC Dental Communications
2 Northfield Plaza
Suite 300
Northfield, IL 60093-1219

847-441-3700
800-225-4569; Fax: 440-826-2865

Richard Fischer, Publisher
Bob Kehoe, Editorial Director
Steven Diogo, Editor
Daniel McCann, Senior Editor
Tom Delaney, National Sales Manager

Serves the dental industry. Subscription
75 Pages
Circulation: 120,000
ISSN: 1078-1250
Printed in 4 colors on glossy stock

12878 **Dental Products Report**
MEDEC Dental Communications
2 Northfield Plaza
Suite 300
Northfield, IL 60093-1219

847-441-3700; Fax: 847-441-3702

Dolph Sharp, Publisher
Gail Weisman, Editor
Matthew LaFleur, Illustrator

Serves the dental profession and the dental industry. $120 subscription per year
141 Pages
Frequency: 12 per year
ISSN: 0011-8737
Founded in 1967
Printed in 4 colors on glossy stock

12879 **Dental Products Report Europe**
MEDEC Dental Communications
Two Northfield Plaza
Suite 300
Northfield, IL 60093-1219

847-441-3700; Fax: 847-441-3702

Richard Fisher, Publisher
Pam Johnson, Editor
Keith Easty, Circulation Director
Dennis Spaeth, Editor
Bob Kehoe, Editorial Director

Designed to inform dentists in Europe and selected Middle Eastern and North African countries and dental distributors and depot personnel worldwide of new developments and ongoing trends in the dental market.
Cost: $40.00
Circulation: 50000
Founded in 1987

12880 **Dentistry Today**
100 Passaic Ave
Fairfield, NJ 07004-3508

973-882-4700; Fax: 973-783-7112
admin@dentistrytoday.com
www.dentistrytoday.com/

Paul Radcliffe, Owner
Phillip Bonner, Editor
Susan Oettinger, Treasurer, Manager
Jan Nigro, Production Manager
Janice Yawdoszyn, Director

The nation's leading clinical news magazine for dentists
Cost: $65.00
122 Pages
Frequency: Monthly
Circulation: 150,000
ISSN: 8750-2186
Founded in 1981
Printed in 4 colors on glossy stock

12881 **Dermatology World**
American Academy of Dermatology
P.O. Box 1968
Des Plaines, IL 60017

847-240-1280
866-503-7546; Fax: 847-240-1859
dweditor@aad.org
www.jaad.org

As the official magazine of the Academy, Dermatology World is members' trusted inside source for balanced news about managing their practices, understanding legislative and regulatory issues, and incorporating clinical and research developments into patient care.
Frequency: Monthly

12882 **Devices and Diagnostics Letter**
300 N Washington Street
Suite 200
Falls Church, VA 22046-3431

703-538-7600
888-838-5578; Fax: 703-538-7676
customerservice@fdanews.com
www.fdanews.com

Robert Barton, Editorial Director
Matt Salt, Publisher
Maritza Lizama, Marketing Director
Cynthia Carter, President
Cost: $987.00
Frequency: Weekly
Circulation: 3300
Mailing list available for rent

12883 **Diabetes Care**
1701 N Beauregard St
Alexandria, VA 22311-1742

703-549-1500
800-342-2383; Fax: 703-739-0290
askada@diabetes.org
www.diabetes.org

Donna Lucas, Human Resources
Joseph Scheffer, Editor
Peter Banks, Publisher
Joe Herget, Marketing Manager
Cost: $314.00
Frequency: Monthly
Circulation: 13637
Founded in 1940

12884 **Diabetes Digest Family**
Drug Store News Consumer Health Publications
425 Park Ave
New York, NY 10022-3526

212-756-5220; Fax: 212-756-5250
www.drugstorenews.com

Lebhar Friedman, Publisher

Contains health news of importance to those with diabetes.
Frequency: Annual
Circulation: 6.8mm

12885 **Diabetes Educator**
American Association of Diabetes Educators
200 W Madison St.
Suite 800
Chicago, IL 60606

312-424-2426
800-338-3633; Fax: 312-424-2427
info@diabeteseducator.org
www.diabeteseducator.org

Charles Macfarlane, FACHE, CAE, Chief Executive Officer
James Fain, PhD, RN, BC-ADM, Editor-in-Chief

A peer-reviewed, bi-monthly journal publishes papers on aspects of patient education and professional education, and serves as a reference for the art and science of diabetes management.
Frequency: Bimonthly
Founded in 1973
Mailing list available for rent: 10000 names at $160 per M

12886 **Diabetes Interview**
6 School St
Suite 160
Fairfax, CA 94930-1655

415-258-2828
800-234-1218; Fax: 415-258-2822
www.diabeteshealth.com

Nadia Al-Samarrie, Publisher
Scott King, Editorial
Daniel Trecroci, Managing Editor
Dick Young, Production
Susan Art, Director
Cost: $12.00
Frequency: Monthly
Circulation: 120,000
Founded in 1989

12887 **Diagnostic Imaging**
Miller Freeman Publications
600 Harrison Street
San Francisco, CA 94107

415-947-6478; Fax: 415-947-6099
www.diagnosticimaging.com

John C. Hayes, Editor
Gary Marshall, President
Suzanne Johnston, Publisher
Kathy Mischak, Associate Publisher

The news magazine of imaging innovation and economics.
Cost: $113.00
90 Pages
Frequency: Monthly
Circulation: 31240
ISSN: 0194-2514
Founded in 1984
Printed in 4 colors on glossy stock

12888 **Diagnostic Imaging America Latina**
Miller Freeman Publications
600 Harrison Street
San Francisco, CA 94107

415-947-6478; Fax: 415-947-6099
www.diagnosticimaging.com

Suzanne Johnston, Editor/Publisher
John Hayes, Editorial
Buckley Dement, Circulation
Heidi Torpey, Marketing
Cost: $113.00
Frequency: Monthly
Founded in 1996

12889 **Diagnostic Imaging Asia Pacific**
Miller Freeman Publications
600 Harrison Street
San Francisco, CA 94107

415-947-6491; Fax: 415-947-6099
www.diagnosticimaging.com

Philip Ward, Editor
David E Lese, Publisher

A newsmagazine aimed at radiologists and allied medical professionals involved in the practice of diagnostic imaging, and provides timely articles on new diagnostic and technical developments in the field mixed with extensive coverage of important political, commercial and economic trends in the specialty.
Cost: $120.00
42 Pages
Frequency: Quarterly
Circulation: 10,000
Printed in 4 colors on glossy stock

12890 **Diagnostic Imaging Europe**
Miller Freeman Publications
600 Harrison Street
San Francisco, CA 94107

415-947-6478; Fax: 415-947-6099
www.diagnosticimaging.com

Philip Ward, Editor
Suzanne Johnston, Publisher
Jose Joaquin, Circulation
Kim Spinoso, National Sales Manager

A newsmagazine aimed at radiologists and allied medical professionals involved in the practice of diagnostic imaging. Provides a balanced mix of timely articles on new diagnostic and technical developments in the field mixed with extensive coverage of important political, commercial and economic trends in the specialty.
Cost: $125.00
58 Pages
Circulation: 10062
Founded in 1996
Printed in 4 colors on glossy stock

12891 **Dialysis and Transplantation**
Creative Age Publications
7628 Densmore Ave
Van Nuys, CA 91406-2042

818-782-7560
800-442-5667; Fax: 818-782-7450
www.creativeage.com

Deborah Carver, Publisher/CEO
Joseph G Herman, Executive Editor
Carlos Benskin, Circulation Manager
Gail Edwards, Accounting Manager
Diane Jones, Advertising Director

Serves the renal care community. Subscription: $17.50.
Cost: $35.00
Frequency: Monthly
Founded in 1975
Printed in 4 colors on glossy stock

12892 **Director**
National Funeral Director Association
13625 Bishops Dr
Brookfield, WI 53005-6607

262-789-1880
800-228-6332; Fax: 262-789-6977
nfda@nfda.org
www.nfda.org

Coverage concentrates on funeral service education and licensure, community service and public relations as well as public health concerns and legal, ethical and moral issues.
Cost: $45.00
84 Pages
Frequency: Monthly
Circulation: 13906
ISSN: 0199-3186
Founded in 1882
Printed in 4 colors on glossy stock

12893 **Diseases of the Colon & Rectum**
American Society of Colon & Rectal Surgeons
85 W Algonquin Road
Suite 550
Arlington Heights, IL 60005

847-290-9184
800-791-0001; Fax: 847-290-9203
ascrs@fascrs.org
www.fascrs.org
Facebook

Pat Oldenburg, Managing Editor
Rick Slawny, Executive Director
Stella Zedalis, Associate Executive Director
Julie Weldon, Assistant Director
John Nocera, Chief Financial Officer
2800 Members
Mailing list available for rent

12894 **Drug Store News**
Lebhar-Friedman
425 Park Ave
New York, NY 10022-3526

212-756-5088
800-216-7117; Fax: 212-838-9487
www.nrn.com

Heather Martin, Manager
Tony Lisanti, Editor/Associate Publisher
Terry Nicosia, Senior Production Manager
K Dement, Circulation Manager
Wayne Bennett, Advertising Manager

Publication consists of merchandising trends and pharmacy developments. Provides extensive coverage of every major segment of chain drug retailing and combination stores.
Frequency: Monthly
Circulation: 44372
Founded in 1925

12895 **Emergency Medicine**
7 Century Dr
Siute 302
Parsippany, NJ 07054-4609

973-206-3434; Fax: 973-206-9378
www.quadranthealth.com

Susan Alburtus, Manager
Michael Pepper, Publisher
Martin Dicarlantonio, Editor
Donna Sickles, Circulation Manager
Kathleen Corbett, Advertising Coordinator
Cost: $90.00
Frequency: Monthly
Circulation: 158000
Founded in 1967

12896 **Emerging Trends**
Trends Analysis Group
1 N Franklin
29th Floor
Chicago, IL 60606-3421

312-422-3990; Fax: 312-422-4569

Marcia Foley, Editor

Published as a community hospital trends which focuses on financial performance, personnel, utilization and facilities.
Cost: $135.00
Frequency: Quarterly
Circulation: 1,700

12897 **EndoNurse**
Virgo Publishing LLC
3300 N Central Ave
Suite 300
Phoenix, AZ 85012-2532

480-990-1101; Fax: 480-990-0819
jsiefert@vpico.com
www.vpico.com

Jenny Bolton, President
John Siefert, CEO
Jennifer Janos, Controller
Kelly Ridley, Executive VP, CFO, Copado

EndoNurse provides the practical information and updated protocol for those practicing in hospitals and freestanding facilities.
Mailing list available for rent: 13000+ names at $var per M

12898 **Endocrine**
505 NW 185th Avenue
Beaverton, OR 97006-3448

503-690-5350; Fax: 503-690-5245
www.bioscience.org

P Michael Conn, Editor-in-Chief
Peter O Kohler, President
Cost: $365.00
Founded in 1867

12899 **Endocrine Practice**
American Association of Clinical Endocrinologists
245 Riverside Avenue
Suite 200
Jacksonville, FL 32202

904-353-7878; Fax: 904-353-8185
info@aace.com
www.aace.com

Paul A. Markowski, Chief Executive Officer
Lori Clawges, Dir., Communications & Publications
Derek LeRoithm MD, PhD, FACE, Editor-in-Chief

To enhance the health care of patients with endocrine diseases through continuing education of practicing endocrinologists
Cost: $350.00
Frequency: Monthly
Circulation: 5000
Mailing list available for rent

12900 **Endocrine Reviews**
The Endocrine Society
8401 Connecticut Ave
Suite 900
Chevy Chase, MD 20815-5817

301-941-0200
888-363-6274; Fax: 301-941-0259
societyservices@endo-society.org
www.endo-society.org

Scott Hunt, Executive Director
Anthony R. Means, Secretary
John Marshall, Secretary
Cost: $252.00
Circulation: 5907
Founded in 1916

12901 **European Medical Device Manufacturer**
Canon Communications
11444 W Olympic Blvd
Los Angeles, CA 90064-1555
310-445-4200; Fax: 310-445-4299
www.cancom.com
Charlie Mc Curdy, President
Cost: $150.00
Circulation: 15,048
Founded in 1978

12902 **Exercise and Sport Sicence Reviews**
Lippincott Williams & Wilkins
530 Walnut St
Philadelphia, PA 19106-3604
215-521-8300; Fax: 215-521-8902
support@ovid.com
www.lww.com
Gordon Macomber, CEO
Lori A Tish, Editorial Assistant
Michael A. Hargrett, Associate Publisher
This Journal provides premier reviews of the most contemporary scientific, medical and research-based topics emerging in the field of sports medicine and exercise science, targeted to students, professors, clinicians, scientists and professionals for practical and research applications.
192 Pages
Frequency: Quarterly
ISSN: 0091-6331
Founded in 1998
Printed in 4 colors on matte stock

12903 **Extended Care Product News**
HMP Communications
83 General Warren Blvd
Suite 100
Malvern, PA 19355-1252
610-560-0500
800-237-7285; Fax: 610-560-0502
pnorris@hmpcommunications.com
www.hmpcommunications.com
Christine Franey, VP
Elizabeth Klumpp, Executive Editor
Peter Treaill, CEO/President
Bonnie Shannon, Manager
Michelle Koch, Circulation Manager
Serves purchasing professionals in acute, long term, and home care, offering product information, reimbursement updates, legislative news, industry trends, and a health care business focus.
24 Pages
Circulation: 100000
ISSN: 0895-2906
Founded in 1989
Printed in 4 colors on glossy stock

12904 **Family Medicine**
11400 Tomahawk Creek Parkway
Leawood, KS 66211
913-906-6000
800-274-2237; Fax: 913-906-6096
fmjournal@stfm.org
www.stfm.org
Traci Nolte, Publisher
John Saultz, President/Editor
Stacy Brungardt, Executive Director
Circulation: 6000
Founded in 1967

12905 **Family Therapy Magazine**
American Assoc for Marriage and Family Therapy
112 S Alfred Street
Alexandria, VA 22314-3061
703-838-9808; Fax: 703-838-9805
central@aamft.org
www.aamft.org
Facebook, Twitter, LinkedIn
Linda S. Metcalf, PhD, President
Michael L. Chafin, President-Elect
Michael Bowers, Executive Director
Robin Stillwell, MA, Secretary
Silvia M. Kaminsky, MsED,, Treasurer
AAMFT Association has been involved with the problems, needs and changing patterns of couples and family relationships. The assocation leads the way to increasing understanding, research and education in the field of marriage and family therapy, and ensuring that the public's needs are met by trained practitioners. The AAMFT provides individuals with the tools and resources they need to succeed as marriage and family therapists.
25000 Members
Frequency: Bi-Monthly
Circulation: 25,000
Founded in 1942

12906 **First Messenger**
American Association of Clinical Endocrinologists
245 Riverside Avenue
Suite 200
Jacksonville, FL 32202
904-353-7878; Fax: 904-353-8185
www.aace.com
Paul Markowski, Chief Executive Officer
Lori Clawges, Dir., Communications & Publications
Serves as a fast track communications tool for AACE members. AACE members utilize The First Messenger to remain in touch with the latest news that may impact their practices, including legislative and socioeconomic issues, cutting edge educational programs, practice management issues and new coding changes.
Frequency: Bi-Monthly
Circulation: 5000
Mailing list available for rent

12907 **Frontiers of Health Services Management**
American College of Healthcare Executives
One North Franklin Street
Suite 1700
Chicago, IL 60606-3529
312-424-2800; Fax: 312-424-0023
contact@ache.org
www.ache.org
Trudy Land, FACHE, Editorial
Frequency: Quarterly

12908 **General Dentistry**
Academy of General Dentistry
560 W. Lake St.
Sixth Floor
Chicago, IL 60611-2637
888-243-3368; Fax: 312-335-3432
membership@agd.org
www.agd.org
Max G. Moses, JD, CPA, MBA, Executive Director
A peer-reviewed journal featuring clinical articles on general dentistry. Topics include diagnostic case reports, solutions to common treatment dilemmas, evidence-based practices, and science and technology.
Frequency: Bimonthly
Circulation: 37,000
Founded in 1951

12909 **General Surgery News**
545 W 45th St
8th Floor
New York, NY 10036-3409
212-957-5300; Fax: 212-957-7230
cdahnke@mcmahonmed.com
www.mcmahonmed.com
Raymond E Mc Mahon, CEO
Van Velle, Director
James Prudden, Director
Megan Roloff, Managing Editor
Cost: $60.00
Frequency: Monthly
Circulation: 37,268
Founded in 1974

12910 **Grant Funding for Elderly Health Services**
Health Resources Publishing
1913 Atlantic Ave
Suite F4
Manasquan, NJ 08736-1067
732-292-1100
888-843-6242; Fax: 732-292-1111
info@healthresourcesonline.com
Robert K Jenkins, Publisher
Lisa Mansfield, Marketing Assistant
Robert Jenkins, Editor
Brett Powell, Regional Director
Alice Burron, Director
This report will give insight into which proposals will get funds for which organization. Lists the organizations that will recieve the most funds from grantmakers during this decade and beyond. Also studies different case histories of successful grant proposals.
Cost: $147.00
Frequency: Monthly
ISBN: 1-882364-46-5
Founded in 1969

12911 **Group Practice Data Management**
SourceMedia
550 W Van Buren
Suite 1100
Chicago, IL 60607-6680
312-913-1334; Fax: 312-913-1959
www.sourcemedia.com
Howard Anderson, Publisher/Editor
Melissa Sefic, Director of Sales
Analyses of trends, insights on technology and practice advice from automation pioneers for executive and physician administrators of medical groups in charge of making decisions about information technology investments. Profiles on practices, new software development updates, and ideas on plans for implementing information technology.
Frequency: Semiannual
Circulation: 15M

12912 **Hand**
American Association for Hand Surgery
500 Cummings Center
Suite 4400
Beverly, MA 01915
978-927-8330; Fax: 978-524-0498
www.handsurgery.org
Michael Neumeister, MD, FRCSC, Editor-in-Chief
An internationally peer-reviewed journal that publishes articles written by clinicians detailing current research and clinical work in the field of hand surgery.

12913 **Harvard Mental Health Letter**
Harvard Health Publcations

10 Shattuck Street
Boston, MA 02115

617-432-1485
877-649-9457; Fax: 617-432-1506
mental_health@hms.harvard.edu
www.health.harvard.edu/mental

Michael Craig Miller, Editor in Chief
Edward Coburn, Publishing Director
Cost: $59.00
Frequency: Monthly
Circulation: 50000
Founded in 1985

12914 **Harvard Public Health Review**
Harvard School of Public Health
665 Huntington Ave
Boston, MA 02115-6018

617-495-1000; Fax: 617-384-8989
fphelps@hsph.harvard.edu
www.hsph.harvard.edu/review

Martha Cassin, Manager
Barry R. Bloom, Dean of the School
Martha Cassin, Manager

Flagship magazine of the Harvard School of Public Health.
60 Pages
Frequency: Bi-annually
Circulation: 10000
Founded in 1922
Printed in 4 colors on glossy stock

12915 **Health Data Management**
SourceMedia
550 W Van Buren
Suite 1100
Chicago, IL 60607-6680

312-913-1334; Fax: 312-913-1959
www.healthdatamanagement.com/

Howard J Anderson, Publisher
Bill Siwicki, Editorial Director
Greg Gillespie, Managing Editor
Bill Briggs, Senior Editor
Jim Siebert, Sales/Marketing Manager

Reporting on important information technology issues in health care with emphasis on computerization trends that improve health care efficiency.
Frequency: Monthly
Circulation: 41116
Founded in 1994

12916 **Health Facilities Management**
American Hospital Publishing
1 N Franklin St
29th Floor
Chicago, IL 60606-3530

312-893-6800
800-821-2039; Fax: 312-422-4500
www.hfmmagazine.com

Mary Grayson, Publisher
Mike Hrickiewicz, Managing Editor
Gary A. Mecklenburg, Chairman
Neil J. Jesuele, Director

Reflects their highly specialized needs such as changes in codes and standards, industry news, new products and technical developments of suppliers.
Cost: $30.00
Frequency: Monthly
Circulation: 28160
Founded in 1998

12917 **Health Management Technology**
Nelson Publishing
2500 Tamiami Trl N
Nokomis, FL 34275-3476

941-966-9521; Fax: 941-966-2590
www.healthmgttech.com
Facebook, Twitter

A Verner Nelson, Owner
Robin Blair, Editor

Serves the health care industry including hospitals/multi-hospital systems, managed care organizations and others allied to the field.
Cost: $60.00
66 Pages
Frequency: Monthly
Circulation: 45751
ISSN: 0745-1075
Founded in 1965
Printed in 4 colors on glossy stock

12918 **Health Progress**
Catholic Health Association
4455 Woodson Rd
St Louis, MO 63134-3797

314-427-2500; Fax: 314-427-0029
rmueller@chausa.org
www.chausa.org

Rhonda Mueller, Senior Vice President of Operations
Monica Heaton, Editor
Martha Slover, Circulation Manager

Focuses on management concepts, ethical issues, legislative trends, and theological issues.
Cost: $50.00
Frequency: Monthly
Circulation: 12000
Founded in 1914

12919 **Healthcare Executive**
American College of Healthcare Executives
One North Franklin Street
Suite 1700
Chicago, IL 60606-3529

312-424-2800; Fax: 312-424-0023
contact@ache.org
www.ache.org
Facebook, Twitter, LinkedIn

Edward H. Lamb, Chairman
Charles D. Stokes, Chairman-Elect
Deborah J. Bowen, FACHE, President & CEO
Thomas C. Dolan. PhD, President & CEO
Richard J. Stull, Executive Vice President

Serves members of the American College of Health care executives, whose primary business/industries include hospitals, managed care organizations, long-term care facilities and others allied to the field.
Cost: $110.00
Frequency: Bi-Monthly
ISSN: 0883-5381
Mailing list available for rent
Printed in 4 colors on glossy stock

12920 **Healthcare Financial Management**
2 Westbrook Corporate Ctr
Westchester, IL 60154-5723

708-531-9614; Fax: 708-531-0032
www.hfma.org

Richard L Clarke, President

12921 **Healthcare Foodservice Magazine**
International Publishing Company of America
664 La Villa Dr
Miami Springs, FL 33166-6030

305-887-1700
800-525-2015; Fax: 305-885-1923
www.healthcarefoodservice.org

Alexander Morton, Owner
Melora Grattan, Assistant Editor

Devoted to foodservice topics for foodservice directors, foodservice managers, dieticians, foodservice supervisors, chefs, purchasing managers, purchasing agents, administrators and others.
Cost: $25.00
24 Pages
Frequency: Quarterly
Printed in 4 colors on glossy stock

12922 **Healthcare Informatics**
McGraw Hill
4530 W 77th St
Suite 350
Edina, MN 55435-5018

952-832-7887; Fax: 952-832-7908

Jim Dougherty, Publisher

12923 **Healthcare Purchasing News**
Nelson Publishing
7650 S Tamiami Trail N
Suite 10
Sarasota, FL 34275

941-927-9345; Fax: 941-927-9588
www.hpnonline.com

Rick Dana Barlow, Senior Editor
Jeannie Akridge, New Products Editor
Kristine Russell, Publisher
Julie Williamson, Features Editor
Susan Cantrell, Infection Control Editor

Serves the field of hospital materials management, purchasing, central services and administration.
Cost: $63.00
27 Pages
Frequency: Monthly
Circulation: 33000
ISSN: 0279-4799
Founded in 1965
Printed in 4 colors on glossy stock

12924 **Healthplan**
American Association of Health Plans
601 Pennsylvania Ave NW
Suite 500
Washington, DC 20004-2601

202-778-3200; Fax: 202-955-4394
ahip@ahip.org
www.ahip.org

Kevin New, Editor

A magazine of trends, insights and best practices.
Cost: $60.00
Circulation: 19000
Founded in 2004

12925 **Hepatology**
American Assn for the Study of Liver Disease
1001 North Fairfax Street
Suite 400
Alexandria, VA 22314

703-299-9766; Fax: 703-299-9622
hepatology@aasld.org
www.aasld.org

Julie Deal, Executive Director
David E. Cohen, MD, PhD, FAASLD, Editor-in-Chief

The official journal of AASLD. Contains the latest research findings, as well as other relevant scientific data.
Frequency: Bimonthly
Founded in 1950

12926 **Home Health Products**
Stevens Publishing Corporation
5151 Belt Line Rd
Dallas, TX 75254-7507

972-687-6700; Fax: 972-687-6767
www.stevenspublishing.com

Craig S Stevens, President
Mike Valenti, Executive Vice President
Randy Dye, Publisher
Sandra Bienkowski, Editor
Cost: $119.00
Circulation: 20000
Founded in 1925

12927 **Home Medical Equipment News**
United Publications

106 Lafayette Street
PO Box 998
Yarmouth, ME 04096

207-846-0600; Fax: 207-846-0657
www.hmenews.com

Rick Rector, Publisher
Brook Taliaferro, Editorial Director
Brenda Boothby, Circulation Director
James G. Taliaferro, President
Jim Sullivan, Editor

Serves home medical equipment providers.
Cost: $84.00
Frequency: Monthly
Circulation: 17100
Founded in 1995

12928 **HomeCare**
Penton Media Inc
249 W 17th St
New York, NY 10011-5390

212-204-4200; Fax: 212-206-3622
www.penton.com

Sharon Rowlands, CEO
Gail Walker, Editor
David Kieselstein, Chief Executive Officer
Kurt Nelson, Vice President, Human Resources
Andrew Schmolka, Senior Vice President

For business leaders in home medical equipment
Frequency: Monthly
Founded in 1989
Mailing list available for rent

12929 **Hospital Law Manual**
Publishers
111 Eighth Avenue
7th Floor
New York, NY 10011-1978

212-771-0600
800-234-1660; Fax: 212-771-0885
customer.service@aspenpubl.com
www.aspenlawschool.com

Robert Becker, CEO
Stacey Caywood, Publisher
Richard H Kravitz, VP

Hospital law.
Cost: $1325.00
Frequency: Quarterly
Founded in 1965

12930 **Hospital Outlook**
801 Pennsylvania Ave NW
Suite 245
Washington, DC 20004-2697

202-624-1500
202-624-1500; Fax: 202-737-6462
info@fah.org
www.fah.org

Charles Kahn, President
LaQuanda Washington, Editor Asst.
Richard P Coorsh, Publisher
Letitia Faison-Mahoney, Controller
Founded in 1966

12931 **Hypertension**
1516 Jefferson Highway
BH 514
New Orleans, LA 70121

504-842-3700; Fax: 504-842-3258

12932 **Immediate Care Business**
Virgo Publishing LLC
3300 N Central Ave
Suite 300
Phoenix, AZ 85012-2532

480-990-1101; Fax: 480-990-0819
jsiefert@vpico.com
www.vpico.com

Jenny Bolton, President
John Siefert, CEO
Jennifer Janos, Controller
Kelly Ridley, Executive VP, CFO, Copado

Immediate Care Business provides practical business solutions to professionals who own, operate or are planning to open an urgent care/immediate care facility.
Mailing list available for rent

12933 **Infection Control Today**
Virgo Publishing LLC
3300 N Central Ave
Suite 300
Phoenix, AZ 85012-2532

480-990-1101; Fax: 480-990-0819
jsiefert@vpico.com
www.vpico.com

Jenny Bolton, President
John Siefert, CEO
Jennifer Janos, Controller
Kelly Ridley, Executive VP, CFO, Copado

Infection Control Today provides science based articles for the general ward, operating room, sterile processing and environmental services departments of healthcare facilities as well as for the public health community.
Mailing list available for rent: 30000+ names at $var per M

12934 **Information Management**
ARMA International
11880 College Boulevard
Suite 450
Overland Park, KS 66215

913-444-9174
844-565-2120; Fax: 913-257-3855
headquarters@armaintl.org
magazine.arma.org
Facebook, Twitter, LinkedIn

Nick Inglis, Exec. Dir., Content & Programming
Jeff Whited, Sr. Content Writer
Ann Snyder, Manager, Content Development

Also known as ARMA Magazine, it is a major source of information on topics and issues central to the management of records and information worldwide. Each issue features articles written by experts in the management of records and information.
61 Pages
Frequency: 6/Year
Founded in 1955

12935 **International Journal of Trauma Nursing**
Mosby/Professional Opportunities
11830 Westline Industrial Drive
St Louis, MO 63146-3318

314-453-4338
800-237-9851; Fax: 314-872-9164
c.kilzer@elsevier.com

Judith Stoner Halpern, Editor
Sarah Papke Kalamazoo, EDITORIAL ASSISTANT
Carol Kilzer, Advertising Sales Service

Reaches today's trauma nurses, coordinators,and managers who direct the nursing aspects of patient care. The journal's multidisciplinary and collaborative approach to the unique needs of the trauma patient represents the vision and clinical expertise of each nursing specialty. These professionals influence the purchase of supplies and equipment for use in emergency and trauma departments.
Cost: $42.00
Frequency: Quarterly
Circulation: 1298
Founded in 1995

12936 **Internet Healthcare Strategies**
Dean Anderson
PO Box 50507
Santa Barbara, CA 93150

805-564-2177; Fax: 805-564-2146
www.corhealth.com

12937 **JAAPA**
American Academy of Physician Assistants
2318 Mill Road
Suite 1300
Alexandria, VA 22314

703-836-2272; Fax: 703-684-1924
membership@aapa.org
journals.lww.com/jaapa

Reamer L. Bushardt, PharmD, PA-C, Editor-in-Chief
Harrison Reed, MMSc, PA-C, Associate Editor

Official journal of the American Academy of Physican Assistants.
92 Pages
Frequency: Monthly
Circulation: 52500
ISSN: 0893-7400

12938 **Journal Of Oncology Management**
Alliance Communications Group
810 E 10th St
Lawrence, KS 66044-3018

785-843-1235
800-627-0932; Fax: 785-843-1274
www.acgpublishing.com

Gerald Lillian, CEO
Jorgene Hallett, Chief Financial Officer
Rob Chestnut, Chief Financial Officer
Barbara Buzzi, Manager

Bi-monthly, peer-reviewed journal. Includes original research, case studies and other features pertinent to improving performance of oncology administrators.
Cost: $87.00
32 Pages
Circulation: 10000
ISSN: 1061-9364
Founded in 1935
Printed in 4 colors on glossy stock

12939 **Journal Watch**
860 Winter Street
Waltham, MA 02154

781-893-3800
800-843-6356; Fax: 781-893-3914
jwatch@mms.org
www.jwatch.org

Allan S Brett, Editor In Chief
Alberta L Fitzpatrick, Publisher
Founded in 1987

12940 **Journal of AAPOS**
AAPOS
655 Beach Street
San Francisco, CA 94109-1336

415-561-8505; Fax: 415-561-8531
me@jaapos.org
www.jaapos.org

William V. Good, MD, Editor-in-Chief
Paul H. Phillips, MD, Sr. Associate Editor

The official publication of the American Association for Pediatric Ophthalmology and Strabismus. Presents expert information on children's eye diseases and on strabismus as it impacts all age groups.
Frequency: Bimonthly

12941 **Journal of Allergy and Clinical Immunology**
American Academy of Allergy, Asthma and Immunology
University of Iowa Hospitals & Clinics
Iowa City, IA 52242

319-467-7583; Fax: 319-356-7739
jaci@aaaai.org
www.aaaai.org

Zuhair K. Ballas, MD, Editor-in-Chief
Rachel L. Miller, MD, Deputy Editor
David P. Huston, MD, Deputy Editor

The official scientific journal of the American Academy of Allergy, Asthma and Immunology and the premiere journal in the field. Each issue features the very latest and best research in the allergy/immunology specialty.
6000+ Members
Frequency: Monthly
Founded in 1943

12942 **Journal of American Dietetic Association**
American Dietetic Association
120 South Riverside Plaza
Suite 2000
Chicago, IL 60606-6995

312-990-0040
800-877-1600; Fax: 312-899-4757
elspcs@elsevier.com
www.adajournal.org

Linda Van Horn, Editor-in-Chief
Jason T Switt, Editors:

The Journal of American Dietetic Association serves the dietetic field.
Cost: $220.00
Frequency: Monthly
Circulation: 65000
ISSN: 0002-8223
Founded in 1925
Printed in 4 colors on glossy stock

12943 **Journal of Applied Laboratory Medicine**
American Association for Clinical Chemistry
900 Seventh St. NW
Suite 400
Washington, DC 20001

202-857-0717
800-892-1400; Fax: 202-887-5093
journals@aacc.org
www.aacc.org

Janet B. Kreizman, Chief Executive Officer
Robert H. Christenson, Editor-in-Chief

An online, international, peer-reviewed publication that showcases applied research on clinically relevant laboratory topics as well as commentary on the practice of clinical chemistry and laboratory medicine.
8,000 Members
Frequency: Bimonthly
Mailing list available for rent

12944 **Journal of Arthroplasty**
American Association of Hip & Knee Surgeons
9400 W. Higgins Rd.
Suite 230
Rosemont, IL 60018-4976

847-698-1200; Fax: 847-698-0704
journalofarthroplasty@gmail.com
www.arthroplastyjournal.org

Michael J. Zarski, JD, Executive Director
John J. Callaghan, MD, Editor-in-Chief
Michael Mont, MD, Assistant Editor-in-Chief

A peer-reviewed journal that publishes original research and articles relating to joint replacement or the treatments of its complications.
Frequency: Monthly

12945 **Journal of Cardiopulmonary Rehabilitation and Prevention**
American Assn of Cardiovascular & Pulmonary Rehab
330 N. WabashýAvenue
Suite 2000
Chicago, IL 60611

312-321-5146; Fax: 312-673-6924
aacvpr@aacvpr.org
www.aacvpr.org
Facebook

Megan Cohen, CAE, Executive Director
Jessica Eustice, Director, Corporate Relations
Mollie Corbett, Operations Manager
Kirk Terry, Education Manager
Andrew Miller, Membership Senior Coordinator

The only professional journal for the entire cardiovascular and pulmonary rehabilitation team. Covers all aspects of cardiac, peripheral vascular, and pulmonary rehabilitation.
Founded in 1985

12946 **Journal of Cardiovascular Management**
Alliance Communications Group
810 E 10th St
Lawrence, KS 66044-3018

785-843-1235
800-627-0932; Fax: 785-843-1274
info@aameda.org
www.acgpublishing.com

Gerald Lillian, CEO
Jorgene Hallett, Publishing Manager
Renee S Schleicher, CEO/President
Rob Chestnut, Chief Financial Officer

Bi-monthly, peer-reviewed journal of articles pertinent to cardiovascular administration.
Cost: $87.00
32 Pages
Circulation: 12,500
ISSN: 1053-5330
Founded in 1957
Mailing list available for rent: 400 names at $350 per M
Printed in 4 colors on glossy stock

12947 **Journal of Clinical Epidemiology**
Elsevier Publishing
PO Box 28430
St Louis, MO 63146-0930

314-872-8370
800-545-2522; Fax: 314-432-1380
www.elsevier.com

Erik Engstrom, CEO
Bill Godfrey, Chief Information Officer
David Clark, Senior Vice President

12948 **Journal of Clinical Investigation**
11830 Westline Industrial Drive
St Louis, MO 63146

314-453-7010
800-460-3110; Fax: 314-453-7095
www.elsevier.com

A Knottnerus, Editor
P Tugwell, Editor
Laurence Zipson, Group Advertisement Manag
Karlyn Messinger, Communications Manager
Cost: $274.00
Frequency: Monthly
Founded in 1955

12949 **Journal of Craniofacial Surgery**
Lippencott Williams & Wilkins
16522 Hunters Green Pkwy
Hagerstown, MD 21740-2116

301-223-2300
800-638-3030; Fax: 301-223-2398
service@lww.com
www.nursingdrugguide.com

Mutaz B Habal MD, Editor
Jay Lippioctt, CEO

An international journal dedicated to the art and science essential to the practice of craniofacial surgery. Online version available.
Cost: $586.00
ISSN: 1049-2275
Founded in 1998

12950 **Journal of Dentistry for Children**
American Academy of Pediatric Dentistry
211 East Chicago Ave.
Suite 1600
Chicago, IL 60611-2637

312-337-2169
800-992-8044; Fax: 312-337-6329
www.aapd.org
Facebook, Twitter

John Rutkauskas, DDS, MBA, Chief Executive Officer
C. Scott Litch, Esq., CAE, Chief Operating Officer & Counsel
Margaret Bjerklie, Governance & Operations Manager
Erika Hoeft, Public Relations Director
Bob Gillmeister, Reprints & Copyright Permissions

An internationally renowned journal that promotes the practice, education and research specifically related to the specialty of pediatric dentistry.
Frequency: 3/Year

12951 **Journal of Digital Imaging**
Society for Imaging Informatics in Medicine
19440 Golf Vista Plaza
Suite 330
Leesburg, VA 20176-8264

703-723-0432; Fax: 703-723-0415
info@siimweb.org
www.siimweb.org

Janice Honeyman-Buck PhD, Editor-in-Chief

Goal is to enhance the exchange of knowledge encompassed by the general topic of Imaging Informatics in Medicine such as research and practice in clinical, engineering, information technologies and techniques in all medical imaging environments. JDI topics are of interest to researchers, developers, educators, physicians, and imaging informatics professionals.
Frequency: Bi-Monthly

12952 **Journal of Emergency Nursing**
Mosby/Professional Opportunities
PO Box 1510
Clearwater, FL 33757-1510

727-443-3047
800-237-9851; Fax: 727-445-9380

Presents original, peer-reviewed clinical articles as well as the annual ENA Scientific Assembly program.
Circulation: 27240

12953 **Journal of ExtraCorporeal Technology**
American Society of ExtraCorporeal Technology
2209 Dickens Road
Richmond, VA 23230-2005
804-565-6363; Fax: 804-282-0090
judyr@amsect.org
www.amsect.org

Stewart Hinckley, Executive Director
Donna Pendarvis, Associate Manager
Michael Troike, Government Relations Chairman
Kimberly Robertson, CPA, Controller

Greg Leasure, Membership Services
Cost: $225.00
2,000 Members
Frequency: Quarterly
Circulation: 2000
ISSN: 0022-1058
Founded in 1964

12954 **Journal of Forensic Psychology Practice**
Bill Cohen
10 Alice Street
Binghamton, NY 13904-1580
607-225-5857
607-722-5857; Fax: 607-771-0012
getinfo@haworthpress.com
www.haworthpressinc.com
Bill Cohen, President/Publisher
Jim Hom, Editor
Provides the forensic psychology practicioner and professional with timely information and regional research that examines the impact of new knowledge in the field as it relates to their practice.
Cost: $60.00
Frequency: Quarterly
Circulation: 700
Founded in 1978

12955 **Journal of Hand Surgery**
American Society for Surgery of the Hand
822 W. Washington Boulevard
Suite 600
Chicago, IL 60607
312-880-1900; Fax: 847-384-1435
info@assh.org
www.assh.org
Roy A Meals, Editor-in-Chief
Publishes original, peer-reviewed articles related to the diagnosis, treatment, and pathophysiology of diseases and conditions of the upper extremity; these include both clinical and basic science studies, along with case reports.
Frequency: Monthly
Mailing list available for rent

12956 **Journal of Healthcare Management**
American College of Healthcare Executives
One North Franklin Street
Suite 1700
Chicago, IL 60606-3529
312-424-2800; Fax: 312-424-0023
contact@ache.org
www.ache.org
Facebook, Twitter, LinkedIn
Deborah J. Bowen, FACHE, President & CEO
Thomas C. Dolan, PhD, President & CEO
Founded in 1933

12957 **Journal of Healthcare Quality**
National Association for Healthcare Quality
4700 W Lake Ave
Glenview, IL 60025-1468
847-375-4732
800-966-9392; Fax: 888-576-4349
info@nahq.org
www.nahq.org
Sheila Lee, Manager
John D Hartley, President
Professional forum that advances quality in a diverse and changing health care environment. Health care professionals worldwide depend upon the Journal for its creative solutions and scientific konwledge in the pursuit of quality.
Cost: $115.00
54 Pages
ISSN: 1062-2551
Founded in 1976
Printed in 4 colors on glossy stock

12958 **Journal of Magnetic Resonance**
525 B Street
Suite 1900
San Diego, CA 92101-4401
619-231-6616
800-321-5068; Fax: 619-699-6280
www.elsevier.com/
S.J. Opella, Editor
JJH Ackerman, Associate Editor
L Frydman, Associate Editor
W.S. Brey, Founding Editor
Founded in 1880

12959 **Journal of Managed Care Medicine**
American Assoc of Integrated Healthcare Delivery
4435 Waterfront Drive
Suite 101
Glen Allen, VA 23060
804-747-5823; Fax: 804-747-5316
phulcher@aaihds.org
www.aaihds.org
Bill Edwards, Managing Editor
Jeremy Williams, Communications Director
Mark Abernathy, Managing Director
David Tyler, Manager
Steven M. Abramson, Senior Manager

12960 **Journal of Marriage & Family Therapy**
American Assoc for Marriage and Family Therapy
112 S Alfred Street
Alexandria, VA 22314-3061
703-838-9808; Fax: 703-838-9805
central@aamft.org
www.aamft.org
Facebook, Twitter, LinkedIn
Linda S. Metcalf, PhD, President
Michael Chafin, President-Elect
Michael Bowers, Executive Director
Robin K. Stillwell, MA, Secretary
Silvia M. Kaminsky, MSEd, Treasurer
The AAMFT has been involved with the problems, needs and changing patterns of couples and family relationships. The association leads the way to increasing understanding, research and education in the field of marriage and family therapy, ensuring that the public's needs are met by trained practitioners.
25000 Members
Frequency: Quarterly
Circulation: 25,000
Founded in 1942

12961 **Journal of Midwifery & Women's Health**
American College of Nurse-Midwives
8403 Colesville Road,Suite 1550
Silver Spring, MD 20910
240-485-1815; Fax: 240-485-1817
jmwh@acnm.org
www.jmwh.org/
tekoa king, Editor
Tekoa King, President, Chief Executive Officer
Kalpana Raina, Managing Partner
Cost: $130.00
Circulation: 8000

12962 **Journal of Music Therapy**
8455 Colesville Rd
Suite 1000
Silver Spring, MD 20910-3392
301-589-3300; Fax: 301-589-5175
info@musictherapy.org
www.musictherapy.org
Facebook, Twitter
Andrea Farbman, Executive Director
Mary Ellen Wylei, AMTA President
Founded in 1998, AMTA's purpose is the progressive development of the therapeutic use of music in rehabilitation, special education, and community settings. AMTA is committed to the advancement of education, training, professional standards, credentials, and research in support of the music therapy profession.
3800 Members
Frequency: 4 Issues Per Year
Founded in 1998

12963 **Journal of Neurotherapy**
Taylor & Francis Group LLC
325 Chestnut Street
Suite 800
Philadelphia, PA 19106
215-625-8900
800-354-1420; Fax: 215-625-2940
haworthorders@taylorandfrancis.com
www.haworthpressinc.com
Timothy Tinius PhD, Editor
David Kaiser PhD, Editor
Provides an integrated multidisciplinary perspective on clinically relevant research, treatment and public policy for neurotherapy. The journal reviews important findings in clinical neurotherapy and electroencephalography for use in assessing baselines and outcomes of various procedures.
Frequency: Monthly

12964 **Journal of Nuclear Medicine**
Society of Nuclear Medicine
1850 Samuel Morse Dr
Reston, VA 20190-5316
703-708-9000; Fax: 703-708-9015
volunteer@snm.org
www.snm.org
Virginia Pappas, Executive Director
Vincent Pistilli, Chief Financial Officer
Matt Dickens, Director, Information Services
Judy Brazel, Director, Meeting Services
Joanna Spahr, Director, Marketing

12965 **Journal of Occupational and Environmental Hygiene (JOEH)**
American Industrial Hygiene Association
3141 Fairview Park Drive
Suite 777
Falls Church, VA 22042
703-849-8888; Fax: 703-207-3561
infonet@aiha.org
www.aiha.org
Facebook, Twitter, LinkedIn, RSS, YouTube
Stephen J. Reynolds, President
Mark Nicas, Editor-in-Chief
A joint publication of AIHA and ACGIH that is published to enhance the knowledge and practice of occupational and environmental hygiene and safety.
Frequency: Monthly
Founded in 1939

12966 **Journal of Oral Implantology**
American Academy of Implant Dentistry
211 E Chicago Avenue
Suie 750
Chicago, IL 60611
785-843-1234; Fax: 785-843-6153
orim@allenpress.com
www.joionline.org
Facebook, Twitter, LinkedIn
James Rutkowski, Editor-in-Chief
Sheldon Winkler, Senior Editor
Dedicated to providing valuable information to general dentists, oral surgeons, prosthodontists, periodontists, scientists, clinicians, laboratory owners and technicians, manufacturers, and edu-

cators
Cost: $140.00
Frequency: Bimonthly
Circulation: 4200
ISSN: 0160-6972

12967 Journal of Periodontology
American Academy of Periodontology
737 N. Michigan Avenue
Suite 800
Chicago, IL 60611-6660

312-787-5518; Fax: 312-787-3670
staff@abperio.org
www.perio.org

Erin O'Donnell Dotzler, Executive Director

Publishes original papers of the highest scientific quality to support practice, education, and research in the dental specialty of periodontics.

12968 Journal of Physical Education, Recreation & Dance (JOPERD)
Society of Health and Physical Educators
1900 Association Dr
Reston, VA 20191-1502

703-476-3400
800-213-7193; Fax: 703-476-9527
lstrecker@shapeamerica.org
www.shapeamerica.org

Stephanie A. Morris, Chief Executive Officer
Laura E. Strecker, Managing Editor

Provides a variety of information on health, physical education, recreation, and dance issues than any other publication in the field.
25000 Members
Frequency: 9/Year
Founded in 1885

12969 Journal of Prosthetics and Orthotics
351 W Camden St
Baltimore, MD 21201-7912

410-528-4000
800-638-6423; Fax: 410-528-4452
webmaster@lww.com
www.lww.com

Jeffrey A Nemeth, Editor
Cost: $91.00
Frequency: Quarterly
Founded in 1792

12970 Journal of Robotic Surgery
Society of Robotic Surgery
1061 E. Main Street
Suite 300
East Dundee, IL 60118

info@srobotics.org
link.springer.com/journal/11701

Vipul R. Patel, MD, Executive Director

Journal exploring minimally invasive surgical techniques and the role of robotics in surgery.
Cost: $99.00
Circulation: 40K+
ISSN: 1863-2483
Founded in 2009

12971 Journal of School Nursing (JOSN)
Sage Publications
2455 Teller Rd
Newbury Park, CA 91320-2234

805-499-9774
800-818-7243; Fax: 805-499-0871
info@sagepub.com
www.sagepub.com

Blaise R Simqu, CEO
Janice Denehy, Executive Editor

A forum for advancing the specialty of school nursing, promoting professional growth of school nurses, and improving the health of children in school. Published bi-monthly, this is the official journal of the National Association of School Nurses.
Cost: $164.00
Frequency: bi-Monthly
Mailing list available for rent

12972 Journal of Social Behavior & Personality
Drawer 37
Corte Madera, CA 94976

415-209-9838; Fax: 415-209-6719
www.sbp-journal.com

Rick Crandall, CEO/President
Rick Crandall, Editor
Cost: $70.00
Frequency: Quarterly
Founded in 1985

12973 Journal of Thoracic and Cardiovascular Surgery
American Association for Thoracic Surgery
800 Cummings Center
Suite 350-V
Beverly, MA 01915

978-252-2200; Fax: 978-522-8469
admin@aats.org
www.jtcvs.org
Facebook

Cindy VerColen, CEO/Executive Director
Richard D. Weisel, MD, Editor-in-Chief
Spencer McGrath, Director, Scientific Publications

Presents original, peer-reviewed articles on diseases of the heart, great vessels, lungs and thorax with emphasis on surgical interventions.
Cost: $354.00
Frequency: Monthly
Circulation: 6000
Founded in 1917
Mailing list available for rent

12974 Journal of Trauma & Dissociation
Taylor & Francis Group LLC
325 Chestnut Street
Suite 800
Philadelphia, PA 19106

215-625-8900
800-354-1420; Fax: 215-625-2940
haworthorders@taylorandfrancis.com
www.haworthpressinc.com

Jennifer J Freyd PhD, Editor

Dedicated to publishing peer reviewed scientific literature on psychological trauma, dissociation, and traumatic memory in children and adults. The journal addresses issues ranging from controlled management of traumatic memories and successful interventions to the ethical and philosophical issues entailed by trauma.
Frequency: Quarterly

12975 Journal of Ultrasound in Medicine
American Institute of Ultrasound in Medicine
14750 Sweitzer Ln
Suite 100
Laurel, MD 20707-5906

301-498-4392
800-638-5352; Fax: 301-498-4450
admin@aium.org
www.aium.org

Dr Beryl R Benacenraf, Editor-in-Chief
Bruce Totaro, Director of Publications
Thomas R. Nelson, Deputy Editor

Dedicated to the rapid, accurate publication of original articles dealing with all aspects of diagnostic ultrasound, particularly its direct application to patient care, but also relevant basic science, advances in instrumentation and biologic effects. Research papers, case reports, review articles, technical notes and letters to the editor are published.
Cost: $265.00
Frequency: Monthly
Circulation: 8200
ISSN: 0278-4297
Founded in 1952
Mailing list available for rent
Printed in 4 colors on glossy stock

12976 Journal of the American Academy of Child and Adolescent Psychiatry
American Academy of Child & Adolescent Psychiatry
3615 Wisconsin Ave NW
Washington, DC 20016-3007

202-966-7300; Fax: 202-464-0131
support@aacap.org
www.jaacap.org
Facebook, Twitter

Douglas K. Novins, MD, Editor-in-Chief
Robert R. Althoff, MD, PhD, Associate Editor

Advancing the science of pediatric mental health and promoting the care of youth and their families.
Founded in 1953
Mailing list available for rent

12977 Journal of the American Academy of Child & Adolescent Psychiatry
Lippincott Williams & Wilkins
351 W Camden St
Baltimore, MD 21201-2436

410-949-8000; Fax: 410-528-4414
www.lww.com
Facebook, Twitter

J Arnold Anthony, Operations
AndrSs Martin, MD/MPH, Editor-Elect
Rebecca Jensen, Managing Editor

The official journal of the American Academy of Child & adolescent Psychiatry, the journal is recognized as the major journal exclusivley on todays psychiatric research and treatment of the child and adolescent.
Frequency: Monthly
ISSN: 0890-8567

12978 Journal of the American Academy of Dermato logy
American Academy of Dermatology
P.O. Box 1968
Des Plaines, IL 60017

847-240-1280
866-503-7546; Fax: 847-240-1859
president@add.org
www.jaad.org

Detra N. Davis, Managing Editor
Jane M. Grant-Kels, MD, Deputy Editor
Dirk M. Elston, MD, Editor
Jason Winkler, Senior Publisher

Dedicated to the clinical and continuing education needs of the entire dermatologic community and is internationally known as the leading journal in the field.
Frequency: Annual
Founded in 1940

12979 Journal of the American Academy of Orthopa edic Surgeons
American Academy of Orthopaedic Surgeons
9400 West Higgins Rd.
Rosemont, IL 60018

847-823-7186; Fax: 847-823-8125
jaaos@aaos.org
www.aaos.org

Thomas E. Arend Jr., Esq., CAE, Chief Executive Officer
William N. Levine, MD, Editor-in-Chief
Jeffrey S. Fischgrund, MD, Editor, Research

Peer-reviewed articles that cover the expanse of orthopaedic medicine.
Frequency: Monthly
Founded in 1993

12980 **Journal of the American Assocation for Lab oratory Animal Science**
American Association for Laboratory Animal Science
9190 Crestwyn Hills Drive
Memphis, TN 38125

901-754-8620; Fax: 901-753-0046
info@aalas.org
www.aalas.org

Ann Turner, Executive Director

The official journal of the AALAS disseminates high-quality, peer-reviewed information on animal biology, technology, facility operations, management, and compliance as relevant to the AALAS membership.

12981 **Journal of the American College of Surgeons**
American College of Surgeons
633 N Saint Clair Street
Chicago, IL 60611-3211

312-202-5316
jacsedit@facs.org
www.journalacs.org
Facebook, Twitter, YouTube, RSS

David B. Hoyt, MD, FACS, Executive Director
Matthew R. Carmichael, Managing Editor
Alan Ross, Publisher

Official scientific journal of the College.
Frequency: Monthly
Founded in 1913

12982 **Journal of the American Dental Association**
American Dental Association
211 E Chicago Ave
Chicago, IL 60611-2678

312-440-2897; Fax: 312-440-2800
www.ada.org

Lawrence H Meskin, Editor
Daniel M Castagna, Editorial Board

Serves the dental profession and dental industry.
Cost: $95.00
Frequency: Monthly
Circulation: 135361
ISSN: 0002-8177
Founded in 1859
Printed in 4 colors on glossy stock

12983 **Journal of the American Health Information Management Association**
American Health Information Management Association
633 N St. Clair Street
Chicago, IL 60611-3211

312-202-5000
800-621-4111; Fax: 312-202-5001
postmaster@facs.org
www.facs.org/

Barry M. Manuel, Editor-in-chief
Paul F. Nora, Editor

Provides information in the field of health information and medical record management in all health care settings. Subscription: non-members $72,
Cost: $25.00
Frequency: Monthly
Founded in 1913
Printed in 4 colors on glossy stock

12984 **Journal of the American Medical Marijuana Association**
American Medical Marijuana Association

convention@ammainfo.com
www.ammainfo.com
Facebook

Contains scientific research, news, and current events that is of interest to professionals, advocates, and those interested in the benefits, application, and proper use of medical marijuana (cannabis) in the treatment of health conditions.
Frequency: Quarterly

12985 **Journal of the Medical Library Association**
Medical Library Association
65 E Wacker Drive
Suite 1900
Chicago, IL 60601-7246

312-419-9094; Fax: 312-419-8950
info@mlahq.org
www.mlanet.org

Elizabeth Lund, Director Publication
Carla J Funk, Executive Officer
Susan Talmage, Editorial Assistant
Scott Plutchak, Editor
Cost: $163.00
Frequency: Quarterly
Circulation: 5000
Founded in 1898
Mailing list available for rent

12986 **Journal of the National Medical Association**
4930 Del Ray Avenue
Bethesda, MD 20814

301-654-2055; Fax: 301-654-5920
member@gastro.org
www.gastro.org

Robert Greenberg, Executive Vp
Michael Stolar, Senior Vp

12987 **Journals of the American Osteopathic College of Dermatology**
American Osteopathic College of Dermatology
2902 North Baltimore Street
Kirksville, MO 63501

660-665-2184
800-449-2623; Fax: 660-627-2623
journalaocd@gmail.com
www.aocd.org

Karthik Krishnamurthy, Co-Editor-in-Chief
Derrick Adams, Co-Editor-in-Chief

Offers scholarly research and education for members.
Founded in 1958

12988 **Laboratory Animal Science Professional**
American Association for Laboratory Animal Science
9190 Crestwyn Hills Drive
Memphis, TN 38125

901-754-8620; Fax: 901-753-0046
info@aalas.org
www.aalas.org

Ann Turner, Executive Director

Contains reliable, practical information, including the latest developments and strategies in laboratory animal science, such as management, professional development, occupational health and safety, facility design, technologies, and much more.
Frequency: Quarterly

12989 **MS Connection**
Lippincott Williams & Wilkins
351 W Camden St
Baltimore, MD 21201-2436

410-949-8000
800-787-8981; Fax: 410-528-4414
www.lww.com

J Arnold Anthony, Operations
Michael Levin-Epstein, Managing Editor
Michele Swain, Marketing Manager

12990 **Managed Healthcare**
Advanstar Communications
7500 Old Oak Blvd
Cleveland, OH 44130-3343

440-243-8100; Fax: 440-891-2740
info@advanstar.com

Daniel J. Corcoran, Publisher
Michael T. McCue, Editor-In-Chief
Craig Roth, Group Publisher
Tracey L. Walker, Senior Editor
Julie Miller, Managing Editor

Valuable resource for managers charged with controlling health care costs and quality.
Cost: $64.00
Frequency: Monthly
Circulation: 40000
ISSN: 1060-1392
Founded in 1987

12991 **McKnight's Long-Term Care News**
McKnight Medical Communications
1 Northfield Plz
Suite 300
Northfield, IL 60093-1216

847-784-8706
800-558-1703; Fax: 847-784-9346
www.mcknightsonline.com

William Pecover, CEO
Lee Maniscalco, Executive VP
Jim Berklan, Editor
Jeff Hartford, Circulation Director

Serves the field of long term care including nursing homes, senior housing centers, assisted living facilities, hospitals with LTC units, continuing care retirement communities, nursing home chains and other allied organizations in the field.
35 Pages
Frequency: Weekly
Circulation: 46000
ISSN: 1048-3314
Printed in 4 colors on glossy stock

12992 **Medical Cannabis and Cannabinoids**
International Association for Cannabinoid Medicine
Am Mildenweg 6
59602 Ruethen
Germany

+49-2952-9708571; Fax: +49-2952-902651
info@cannabis-med.org
www.cannabis-med.org
Facebook, Twitter, LinkedIn

Franjo Grotenhermen, Executive Director
Michael Krawitz, Patient Representative, USA
Alison Myrden, Patient Representative, Canada
Prof. Rudolf Brenneisen, Editor-in-Chief

A peer-reviewed journal offering an international forum to present and discuss recent advances in the medical use of cannabis and cannabinoids. Affiliated with the IACM.
ISSN: 2378-8763
Founded in 2000

12993 **Medical Economics**
Advanstar Communications
5 Paragon Dr
Montvale, NJ 07645-1791

973-944-7777; Fax: 973-944-7778

Curtis Allen, President
Marianne Dekker Mattera, Editor-in-Chief

Mike Graziani, Publisher
Sean Keating, Managing Editor
Laura Wagner, VP Operations

Medical Economics guides physicians in the business of practicing by giving advice about malpractice, third-party reimbursement, managed care, tax strategies, legal information and counseling, fraud, abuse and anti-trust strategies. It helps them manage their practice more efficiently so they can be more effective in delivering patient care.
Cost: $109.00
Frequency: Monthly
Circulation: 154897
Founded in 1987

12994 **Medical Reference Services Quarterly**
Taylor & Francis Group LLC
325 Chestnut Street
Suite 800
Philadelphia, PA 19106

215-625-8900
215-625-8900; Fax: 215-625-2940
haworthorders@taylorandfrancis.com
www.haworthpress.com

M Sandra Wood, Editor

Covers topics of current interest and practical value in the areas of reference in medicine and related specialties, the biomedical sciences, nursing and allied health.
Cost: $60.00
Frequency: Quarterly
ISSN: 0276-3869
Founded in 1978

12995 **Medical Research Funding Bulletin**
PO Box 7507
New York, NY 10150-7507

212-371-3398; Fax: 801-761-4200

John Connolly, CEO
Carroll Gordon, Circulation Manager
Cost: $75.00
Frequency: Fortnightly
Circulation: 4500
Founded in 1972

12996 **Modern Healthcare**
Crain Communications
360 N Michigan Ave
Chicago, IL 60601-3800

312-649-5200; Fax: 312-649-7937
info@crain.com
www.crain.com

Keith Crain, CEO

Examines and reports on the issues that have a direct impact on the business decisions healthcare professionals make every day.
Frequency: Weekly
Circulation: 70180

12997 **Molecular Cancer Research**
American Association for Cancer Research
615 Chestnut St.
17th Fl.
Philadelphia, PA 19106-4404

215-440-9300
866-423-3965; Fax: 215-440-9313
mcr@aacr.org
mcr.aacrjournals.org

Margaret Foti, Chief Executive Officer
Karen E. Knudsen, Editor-in-Chief

Publishes articles describing novel basic cancer research discoveries of broad interest to the field.
Frequency: Monthly
Founded in 1907

12998 **Molecular Cancer Therapeutics**
American Association for Cancer Research
615 Chestnut St.
17th Fl.
Philadelphia, PA 19106-4404

215-440-9300
866-423-3965; Fax: 215-440-9313
mct@aacr.org
mct.aacrjournals.org

Margaret Foti, Chief Executive Officer
Napoleone Ferrara, Editor-in-Chief

Publishes the best science in the discovery and preclinical development of novel therapeutic agents for oncology, preclinical studies of approved therapeutics, mechanisms of drug action, mechanisms of drug resistance, biomarkers of drug response, novel models and technologies, and occasional drug toxicity mechanisms.
Frequency: Monthly
Founded in 1907

12999 **Molecular Endocrinology**
Molecular Society Journals
8401 Connecticut Avenue
Suite 900
Chevy Chase, MD 20815-4410

301-941-0200
888-363-6274; Fax: 301-941-0259
societyservices@endo-society.org
www.endo-society.org

John A Cidlowski, Editor-in-chief
Scott Hunt, Executive Director
Maggie Haworth, Managing Editor
Jessica Peterson, Marketing Manager
John Marshall, Secretary
Cost: $376.00
Frequency: Weekly
Circulation: 11000
Founded in 1916

13000 **NASN Newsletter**
National Association of School Nurses
163 US Route 1
PO Box 1300
Scarborough, ME 04074-9060

207-883-2117
877-627-6476; Fax: 207-883-2683
nasn@nasn.org
www.nasn.org

Devin Dinkel, Editor
Wanda Miller, Executive Director
Donna Mazyck, President
Gloria Durgin, Administrator/Sponsorship
Kenny Lull, Communications Manager
Cost: $2.00
Founded in 1968

13001 **Neurology**
American Academy of Neurology
201 Chicago Ave.
Minneapolis, MN 55415

612-928-6000
800-879-1960; Fax: 612-454-2746
memberservices@aan.com
n.neurology.org

Catherine M. Rydell, CAE, Executive Director & CEO
Robert A. Gross, MD, PhD, FAAN, Editor-in-Chief
Bradford B. Worrall, MD, MSc, FAAN, Deputy Editor

The official journal of the American Academy of Neurology and the leading clinical neurology journal worldwide. The journal's purpose is to advance the field by presenting new basic and clinical research with emphasis on knowledge that will influence the way neurology is practiced.
Frequency: Weekly

13002 **Neurology: Clinical Practice**
American Academy of Neurology
201 Chicago Ave.
Minneapolis, MN 55415

612-928-6000
800-879-1960; Fax: 612-454-2746
memberservices@aan.com
cp.neurology.org

Catherine M. Rydell, CAE, Executive Director & CEO
John R. Corboy, MD, FAAN, Editor

An official journal of the American Academy of Neurology that focuses on the day-to-day needs of practicing neurologists. Regular features include: approaches to the patient with various neurologic conditions; case-based articles on ethical issues; Five New Things updates on diseases and disorders; office-based issues and practice management tips; and health policy discussions.
Frequency: Bimonthly

13003 **Neurology: Genetics**
American Academy of Neurology
201 Chicago Ave.
Minneapolis, MN 55415

612-928-6000
800-879-1960; Fax: 612-454-2746
memberservices@aan.com
ng.neurology.org

Catherine M. Rydell, CAE, Executive Director & CEO
Stefan M. Pulst, MD, FAAN, Editor

An online open access journal publishing peer-reviewed reports in the field of neurogenetics. Publishes original articles in all areas of neurogenetics including rare and common genetic variations, genotype-phenotype correlations, outlier phenotypes as a result of mutations in known disease genes, and genetic variations with a putative link to diseases.
Frequency: Bimonthly

13004 **Neurology: Neuroimmunology & NeuroInflamma tion**
American Academy of Neurology
201 Chicago Ave.
Minneapolis, MN 55415

612-928-6000
800-879-1960; Fax: 612-454-2746
memberservices@aan.com
nn.neurology.org

Catherine M. Rydell, CAE, Executive Director & CEO
Josep O. Dalmau, MD, PhD, Editor

An official journal of the American Academy of Neurology that publishes rigorously peer-reviewed open access reports of original research and in-depth reviews of topics in neuroimmunology & neuroinflammation, affecting the full range of neurologic diseases.
Frequency: Bimonthly

13005 **New England Journal of Medicine**
Massachusetts Medical Society
10 Shattuck St
Boston, MA 02115-6094

617-734-9800; Fax: 617-739-9864
comments@nejm.org
www.nejm.org

Debra Weinstein, Chair
Jeffrey M Drazen, Editor-in-Chief
Gregory Curfman, Executive Editor

General medicine journal that publishes new medical research findings, review articles, and editorial opinion on a wide variety of topics of importance to biomedical science and clinical practice. Published with an emphasis on internal medicine and specialty areas including allergy/immunology, cardiology, endocrinology, gastroenterology, hematology, kidney disease, oncology, pulmonary disease, rheumatology,

HIV, and infectous diseases.
Cost: $149.00
Frequency: Weekly

13006 **Nursing**
Ambler Office of Lippincott Williams and Wilkins
323 Norristown Rd
Suite 200
Ambler, PA 19002-2758

215-646-8700
800-346-7844; Fax: 215-654-1328
www.lww.com

Mary Gill, Human Resources
Cheryl Mee, Publisher & Editor
Keith Sollweiler, Marketing
Cost: $34.00
Frequency: Monthly
Circulation: 300000
Founded in 1971

13007 **Nursing News**
48 W Street
Concord, NH 03301-3595

603-225-3783; Fax: 603-228-6672
www.nhnurses.org

Bob Desc, CEO
Susan Fetzer, President
Cost: $26.00
Frequency: Quarterly
Circulation: 18000
Founded in 1906

13008 **Nursing Outlook**
1111 Middle Drive
Indiana, IN 46202

317-274-1486; Fax: 317-278-1842
mbroome@iupui.edu

Marion Broome, Editor
Adam Herberg, President, Circulation Manager

13009 **Nutrition Business Journal**
4452 Park Boulevard
Suite 306
San Diego, CA 92116

619-295-7685; Fax: 619-295-5743
info@nutritionbusiness.com
www.nutritionbusiness.com

David Nussbaum, CEO
Preston Vice, CFO
Cost: $995.00
Frequency: Monthly
Founded in 1892

13010 **O&P Almanac**
American Orthotic & Prosthetic Association
330 John Carlyle Street
Suite 200
Alexandria, VA 22314

571-431-0876; Fax: 571-431-0899
info@aopanet.org
www.aopanet.org
Facebook, Twitter, LinkedIn

Tom Fise, Executive Director
Michael Oros, President
Josephine Rossi, Editor, O&P Almanac
Bob Heiman, Advertising Sales Director
84 Pages
Frequency: Monthly
Circulation: 13000
Founded in 1951
Mailing list available for rent
Printed in 4 colors on glossy stock

13011 **Occupational Health & Safety**
Stevens Publishing Corporation
5151 Belt Line Rd
10th Floor
Dallas, TX 75254-7507

972-687-6700; Fax: 972-687-6767
jlaws@stevenspublishing.com
www.stevenspublishing.com

Craig S Stevens, President
Jerry Laws, Executive Vice President
Mike Valenti, Executive Vice President
Craig Stevens, CEO
Margaret Perry, Circulation Director
Practical advice on workplace safety and compliance with laws and regulations. Feature articles and product information.
Frequency: Monthly
Circulation: 84000
Founded in 1925

13012 **Oncology Times**
333 7th Ave
19th Floor
New York, NY 10001-5015

646-674-6544
800-933-6525; Fax: 646-674-6500
ot@lww.com
www.lww.com

Serena Stockwell, Manager
Ken Senerth, Publisher
Frank Cox, Advertising Manager
Larry Klein, Director
Cost: $189.00
Circulation: 45000
Founded in 1972

13013 **Optometry and Vision Science**
American Academy of Optometry
2909 Fairgreen St.
Orlando, FL 32803

321-319-4860
844-323-3937; Fax: 407-893-9890
aaoptom@aaoptom.org
www.aaopt.org

Lois Schoenbrun, Executive Director
Michael D. Twa, OD, PhD, FAAO, Editor-in-Chief
The official journal of the American Academy of Optometry, and an authoritative source for current developments in optometry, visual optics, and eye & vision science.
Frequency: Monthly

13014 **Optometry: Journal of the American Optometric Association**
American Optometric Association
243 N Lindbergh Blvd
St Louis, MO 63141-7881

314-991-4100; Fax: 314-991-4101
journalsonlinesupport-usa@elsevier.com
www.optometryjaoa.com

Paul B. Freeman, OD, Editor-in-Chief
Most widely circulated scholarly optometry journal, provides a forum for research that advances the art and science of the practice of primary care optometry.
Cost: $95.00
68 Pages
Frequency: Monthly
Circulation: 34000
ISSN: 1529-1839
Founded in 1898
Printed in 4 colors on glossy stock

13015 **Ostomy Wound Management**
HMP Communications
83 General Warren Blvd
Suite 100
Malvern, PA 19355-1252

610-560-0500
800-237-7285; Fax: 610-560-0502
subscriptions@hmpcommunications.com
www.hmpcommunications.com
Facebook, Twitter, LinkedIn

Jeff Hennessy, CEO
Barbara Zeiger, Editor
Jeremy Bowden, Publisher
Bonnie Shannon, Circulation Manager
Information on the disciplines of ostomy care, wound care, incontinence care, and related skin and nutritional issues.
Cost: $39.95
Frequency: Monthly
Circulation: 230000
ISSN: 0889-5099
Founded in 1980
Printed in 4 colors on glossy stock

13016 **PM&R**
American Academy of Physical Medicine & Rehab.
9700 West Bryn Mawr Ave.
Suite 200
Rosemont, IL 60018-5701

847-737-6000
877-227-6799; Fax: 847-754-4368
info@aapmr.org
www.pmrjournal.org

Thomas E. Stautzenbach, MBA, CAE, Executive Director & CEO
Janna L. Friedly, MD, Editor-in-Chief
A peer-reviewed journal that delivers timely, clinical relevant, and evidence-based research and review information.
Frequency: Annual, November

13017 **PT in Motion**
American Physical Therapy Association
1111 N Fairfax St
Alexandria, VA 22314-1488

703-684-2782; Fax: 703-706-8536
memberservices@apta.org
www.apta.org
Facebook, Twitter, LinkedIn

Don Tepper, Editor
John D. Barnes, Chief Executive Officer
Janet Bezner, VP, Education, Governance
Rob Batarla, VP, Finance & Business Development
Felicity Clancy, VP, Communications & Marketing
Formerly PT Magazine, published to meet the needs and interests of APTA members and to promote physical therapy as a vital professional career, PT provides legislative, health care, human interest, and Association news and serves as a forum for discussion of professional issues and ideas in physical therapy practice.
80000 Members
Mailing list available for rent

13018 **Patient Care**
Medical Economics Publishing
5 Paragon Dr
Montvale, NJ 07645-1791

973-944-7777; Fax: 973-944-7778
www.patientcareonline.com

Curtis Allen, President
Stuart Williams, Publisher
Christine Shappell, Circulation Manager
Don Berman, Director Business Development
Patient care serves selected medical and osteopathic physicians.
Cost: $51.50
Frequency: Monthly
Founded in 1967
Printed in 4 colors

13019 **Pediatric Dentistry**
American Academy of Pediatric Dentistry

211 East Chicago Ave.
Suite 1600
Chicago, IL 60611-2637

312-337-2169
800-992-8044; Fax: 312-337-6329
www.aapd.org
Facebook, Twitter

John Rutkauskas, DDS, MBA, Chief Executive Officer
C. Scott Litch, Esq., CAE, Chief Operating Officer & Counsel
Margaret Bjerklie, Governance & Operations Manager
Erika Hoeft, Public Relations Director

The official publication of the American Academy of Pediatric Dentistry, the American Board of Pediatric Dentistry and the College of Diplomates of the American Board of Pediatric Dentistry. Promotes the practice, education and research specifically related to the specialty of pediatric dentistry. This peer-reviewed journal features scientific articles, case reports and abstracts of current pediatric dental research.
2500 Attendees
Frequency: Bimonthly
Founded in 1948

13020 Pediatric Research
Society for Pediatric Research
9303 New Trails Dr.
The Woodlands, TX 77381

346-980-9710
info@societyforpediatricresearch.org
www.nature.com/pr

Cynthia Bearer, Editor In Chief

The official publication of the American Pediatric Society, the European Society for Paediatric Research, and the Society for Pediatric Research.
Cost: $789.00
Frequency: Monthly
ISSN: 0031-3998

13021 Physicians & Computers
Moorhead Publications
810 S Waukegan Road
#200
Lake Forest, IL 60045-2672

847-615-8333; Fax: 847-615-8345

Tom Moorhead, Publisher

Provides physicians with information on computer advances helpful in the private practice of medicine. Practice management, current medical and non-medical software, computer diagnostics, etc.
Cost: $40.00
Frequency: Monthly
Circulation: 90M

13022 Pneumogram
1961 Main Street
#246
Sacremento, CA 95076

916-441-2222
888-730-2772; Fax: 916-442-4182
www.csrc.org/

Janyth Bolden, President
Abbie Rosenberg, Secretary
Sherry Blansfield, Secretary
Frequency: Quarterly
Founded in 1968

13023 Psychoanalytic Psychology
211 E 70th Street
Suite 17 H
New York, NY 10021

212-633-9162; Fax: 212-628-8453

Lori Sloan, Executive Director

13024 Psychology of Addictive Behaviors
University of South Florida
BEH 339
Department of Psychology
Tampa, FL 33620

813-974-4826
800-374-2721; Fax: 202-336-5568
www.apa.org
Facebook, Twitter

Stephen A. Maisto, Editor
Norman B. Anderson, Chief Executive Officer
L. Michael Honaker, Chief Operating Officer
Cynthia D. Belar, Executive Director
Tony Habash, Chief Information Officer
Mailing list available for rent

13025 Public Health Nursing
350 Main Street
6th Floor
Malden, MA 02148

781-388-8200; Fax: 781-388-8210
www.blackwellpublishing.com/

Sarah E Abrams, Editor
Judith C Hays, Editor
Otis Dean, Publisher
Alice Meadows, Senior Manager, Circulation
Paige Larkin, Sr. Marketing Manager
Cost: $149.00
Founded in 1922

13026 Quality Matters
385 Highland Colony Parkway
Suite 120
Ridgeland, MS 39157

601-957-1575
800-844-0500; Fax: 601-956-1713

13027 RDH
PennWell Publishing Company
1421 S Sheridan Rd
Tulsa, OK 74112-6619

918-831-9421; Fax: 918-831-9476
www.pennwell.com

Robert Biolchini, President
Mark Hartley, Editor

National magazine for dental hygiene professionals.
Cost: $48.00
60 Pages
Frequency: Monthly
Founded in 1910

13028 RN Magazine
Medical Economics Publishing
5 Paragon Dr
Montvale, NJ 07645-1791

973-944-7777
888-581-8052; Fax: 973-944-7778

Curtis Allen, President
Wendy Raupers, Associate Publisher
Joy Puzzo, Marketing/Circulation Manager
Don Berman, Director Business Development

Published to serve professional nurses in hospitals, physician's offices, extended care facilities, schools of nursing, occupational and community health agencies and other professional nurses.
Cost: $35.00
Frequency: Monthly
Circulation: 2500
ISSN: 0033-7021
Founded in 1937

13029 Radiology
820 Jorie Boulevard
Oak Brook, IL 60523-2251

630-571-2670
800-381-6660; Fax: 630-571-7837
reginfo@rsna.org
www.rsna.org

Anthony V. Proto, Editor
Michael Ulezlo, Senior Marketing Manager
Cost: $250.00
Frequency: Monthly
Circulation: 35000
Founded in 1915

13030 Radiology Management
American Healthcare Radiology Administrators
490B Boston Post Rd
Suite 200
Sudbury, MA 01776-3367

978-443-7591
800-334-2472; Fax: 978-443-8046
info@ahraonline.org
www.ahraonline.org
Facebook, Twitter, LinkedIn

Edward Cronin, Jr., CEO
Sarah Murray, Executive Assistant
Emily Ryan, Membership Coordinator
Debra Murphy, Publications Director

A peer reviewed journal with an editorial review board of AHRA members.
Cost: $65.00
64 Pages
Circulation: 4,000
ISSN: 0198-7097
Founded in 1978
Printed in 4 colors on glossy stock

13031 Remington Report
Remington Report
30100 Town Center Drive
Suite 421
Laguna Niguel, CA 92677

800-247-4781
800-247-4781; Fax: 949-715-1797
remrptedit@aol.com
www.remingtonreport.com

Lisa Remington, Publisher
Cost: $44.50
Founded in 1993

13032 Renal Business Today
Virgo Publishing LLC
3300 N Central Ave
Suite 300
Phoenix, AZ 85012-2532

480-990-1101; Fax: 480-990-0819
jsiefert@vpico.com
www.vpico.com

Jenny Bolton, President
John Siefert, CEO
Jennifer Janos, Controller
Kelly Ridley, Executive VP, CFO, Copado

Renal Business Today delivers editorials for practice management professionals. Editorials include the latest business and technology trends in renal care, expert advice, strategic business solutions written by industry leaders and human interest articles.
Mailing list available for rent

13033 Research Quarterly for Exercise and Sport
Society of Health and Physical Educators
1900 Association Dr
Reston, VA 20191-1598

703-476-3400
800-213-7193; Fax: 703-476-9527
tlawson@shapeamerica.org
www.shapeamerica.org

Stephanie A. Morris, Chief Executive Officer
Thomas F. Lawson, Managing Editor

RQES is a professional journal providing members with numerous articles and research on subjects that focus on the art and science of hu-

man movement studies.
Cost: $295.00
128 Pages
Frequency: Quarterly
Circulation: 6000
ISSN: 0270-1367
Mailing list available for rent
Printed in one color on glossy stock

13034 **Respiratory Care**
American Association for Respiratory Care
9425 N Macarthur Blvd
Suite 100
Irving, TX 75063-4725

972-514-7710; Fax: 972-484-2720
info@aarc.org
www.rcjournal.com

Tom Kallstrom, Executive Director/CEO
Richard D. Branson, MSc, RRT, Editor-in-Chief

Journal for the professional respiratory care therapist. Member publication of the American Association for Respiratory Care.
Cost: $89.95
Frequency: Monthly
Founded in 1947

13035 **Review of Optometry**
11 Campus Boulevard
Newton Square, PA 19073

610-492-1000; Fax: 610-492-1039
reviewofoptometry@jobson.com
www.revoptom.com

Amy Hellem, Editor-in-Chief
Jeffrey S Eisenberg, Director
Paul Karpecki, Director
Frequency: Monthly

13036 **Risk Management Handbook**
NACHA: The Electronic Payments Association
13450 Sunrise Valley Drive
Suite 100
Herndon, VA 20171

703-561-1100; Fax: 703-787-0996
info@nacha.org
www.nacha.org

Jane Larimer, CEO
Marcie Haitema, Chairperson

A comprehensive guide to ACH Risk Issues and Control Procedures. Explains the types of ACH payments risk, assesses the operational implications, and provides best practices for developing an effective risk management program.
Cost: $65.00
Frequency: Monthly
Founded in 1991

13037 **Rite Aid Be Healthy & Beatiful**
Drug Store News Consumer Health Publications
425 Park Ave
New York, NY 10022-3526

212-756-5220; Fax: 212-756-5250
www.drugstorenews.com

Lebhar Friedman, Publisher

Provides health and beauty tips to millions of women who visit Rite Aid stores.
Frequency: Quarterly
Circulation: 950,000
Founded in 2002

13038 **Scrip Magazine**
270 Madison Ave
New York, NY 10016-0601

212-262-8230; Fax: 212-262-8234
www.pjbpubs.com

Ken May, Executive Director
Alice Dunmore, Circulation Manager
Jenefer Trevena, Marketing Manager
Phillip Every, Worldwide Advertising Sales

An in-depth view of the issues and challenges facing all sectors of the pharmaceutical industry worldwide. Analytical features are written by pharmaceutical experts and opinion leaders as well as specialist journalists.
Cost: $ 1190.00

13039 **Sports Medicine Digest**
351 W Camden St
Baltimore, MD 21201-7912

410-528-4000
800-787-8981; Fax: 410-528-4452
www.lww.com

Daniel Schwartz, Publisher
Michael Levin-Epstein, Managing Editor
Cost: $125.00
12 Pages
Frequency: Monthly
ISSN: 0731-9770
Founded in 1978
Printed in one color on matte stock

13040 **Strategies: A Journal for Physical and Sport Educators**
Society of Health and Physical Educators
1900 Association Dr
Reston, VA 20191-1502

703-476-3400
800-213-7193; Fax: 703-476-9527
lstrecker@shapeamerica.org
www.shapeamerica.org

Stephanie A. Morris, Chief Executive Officer
Laura E. Strecker, Managing Editor

Delivers practical ideas, how-to information, and tips for sport and physical educators.
Frequency: Bimonthly

13041 **SurgiStrategies**
Virgo Publishing LLC
3300 N Central Ave
Suite 300
Phoenix, AZ 85012-2532

480-990-1101; Fax: 480-990-0819
jsiefert@vpico.com
www.vpico.com

Jenny Bolton, President
John Siefert, CEO
Jennifer Janos, Controller
Kelly Ridley, Executive VP, CFO, Copado

SurgiStrategies identifies and analyzes the high level trends impacting physician and corporation owned outpatient healthcare facilities with relevant, timely, ahead of the curve content.
Mailing list available for rent: 22000+ names at $var per M

13042 **Surgical Products**
Reed Business Information
100 Enterprise Drive
Suite 600
Rockaway, NJ 07866-912

973-920-7000; Fax: 630-288-8686
rritsma@reedbusiness.com
www.surgprodmag.com/

Noreen Costelloe, Group VP/Publisher
Richard Ritsma, Editor-in-Chief
James Reed, Owner
Sabrina Crow, Managing Director
Steve Koppelman, Circulation Manager

Surgical products provides surgeons, OR supervisors and OR materials managers working in hospitals and surgi-centers with new product technology and equipment.
Frequency: Monthly
Circulation: 71000
Founded in 1946

13043 **The Consultant Pharmacist**
American Society of Consultant Pharmacists
1321 Duke St
Alexandria, VA 22314-3563

703-739-1300
800-355-2727; Fax: 703-739-1321
info@ascp.com
www.ascp.com

Frank Grosso, RPh, Executive Director & CEO
Kelly Jennings, Chief Financial Officer
Marlene Bloom, Editor
Debbie Furman, Circulation

Official peer reviewed journal of the American Society of Consultant Pharmacists. Editorial deals with geriatric pharmacotherapy.
76 Pages
Frequency: Monthly
Circulation: 11000
Founded in 1969
Mailing list available for rent
Printed in 4 colors on glossy stock

13044 **The Neurodiagnostic Journal**
American Society of Electroneurodiagnostic Tech
402 East Bannister Road
Suite A
Kansas City, MO 64131-3019

816-931-1120; Fax: 816-931-1145
info@aset.org
www.aset.org

Arlen Reimritz, Executive Director
Anna M. Bonner, Managing Editor

Peer-reviewed journal that contains research articles, case studies, technical articles and book reviews.
Frequency: Quarterly
Circulation: 5000
ISSN: 2164-6821
Founded in 1961

13045 **Transfusion**
American Association of Blood Banks
4550 Montgomery Ave.
Suite 700, North Tower
Bethesda, MD 20814-2747

301-907-6977; Fax: 301-907-6895
aabb@aabb.org
www.aabb.org

Debra BenAvram, Chief Executive Officer

Scholarly, peer-reviewed monthly journal, publishing on the latest technological advances, clinical research, and controversial issues related to transfusion medicine, cellular and gene therapies, and tissue transplantation.
Frequency: Monthly

13046 **Transplantation**
351 W Camden St
Baltimore, MD 21201-7912

410-528-4000
800-222-3790; Fax: 410-528-4452
www.lww.com

Sherry Reed, Manager
Mark A Hardy, Editor
Jim Mulligan, Publisher
Taron Buttler, National Sales Manager
Jeff Hargrove, Manager
Cost: $657.00
Circulation: 2556

13047 **Transportation Leader**
Taxicab, Limousine & Paratransit Association
3200 Tower Oaks Blvd
Suite 220
Rockville, MD 20852

301-984-5700; Fax: 301-984-5703
info@tlpa.org
www.tlpa.org

Alfred LaGasse, CEO
William Rouse, President

Harold Morgan, Executive Vice President
Michelle A. Hariston, CMP, Manager of Meetings
Leah New, Manager of Communications

Leading resource for news and information on issues, trends, and people in the private, for-hire passenger transportation industry. Provides readers with an array of features, articles, and columns that include information on managing a transportation company, industry trends, driver's tips, an industry calendar of events, coverage of TLPA events, and advertisements from the industry's leading suppliers.
Cost: $4.00
48 Pages
Frequency: Quarterly
Circulation: 6000
Founded in 1917
Mailing list available for rent: 6,000 names at $100 per M
Printed in 4 colors on glossy stock

13048 Urologic Nursing
Society of Urologic Nurses and Associates
East Holly Avenue
PO Box 56
Pitman, NJ 08071

856-256-2300; Fax: 856-589-7463
uronsg@ajj.com
www.suna.org

Nancy Mueller, President
Robert McIlvaine, Circulation Manager
Mike Cunningham, Marketing
Jane Hokanson Hawks, Editor
Anthony Jannetti, Executive Director
Cost: $40.00
Circulation: 4500
Founded in 1981
Printed in 4 colors on glossy stock

13049 Virology
125 Park Avenue
23rd Floor
New York, NY 10017

212-309-5498
800-821-5068; Fax: 212-309-5480
d.weerd@elsevier.com
www.reed-elsevier.com/

A Pinczuk, Editor-in-Chief
Karlyn Messinger, Communications Manager
Cost: $139.00
Frequency: Monthly
Circulation: 280
Founded in 1993

13050 Volunteer
119 W 24th Street
9th Floor
New York, NY 10011-1913

212-870-4940; Fax: 212-367-1236

Esperanza Jorge-Garcia, Executive Director

13051 Walgreens Diabetes & You
Drug Store News Consumer Health Publications
425 Park Ave
New York, NY 10022-3526

212-756-5220; Fax: 212-756-5250
www.drugstorenews.com

Lebhar Friedman, Publisher
Edward H King, Director

Contains health news of importance to those with diabetes.

13052 World Disease Weekly
2900 Paces Ferry Road
Bldg D 2nd Floor
Atlanta, GA 30339

770-507-7777
800-726-4550; Fax: 770-435-6800
subscribe@newsrx.com
Cost: $2329.00

Frequency: Weekly
Founded in 1984

Trade Shows

13053 AAAAI Annual Conference and Exhibition
American Academy Allergy, Asthma, and Immunology
555 E Wells Street
Suite 100
Milwaukee, WI 53202-3823

414-272-6071
800-822-2762; Fax: 414-272-6070
info@aaaai.org
www.aaaai.org

Katie Ferguson, Sr. Meetings Manager

Exhibits, pharmaceuticals, medical supplies and books.
7000 Attendees
Frequency: Annual
Founded in 1943

13054 AAAAI Annual Meeting
American Academy of Allergy, Asthma and Immunology (AAAAI)
555 E. Wells Street, Suite 1100
Milwaukee, WI 53202-3823

414-272-6071; Fax: 414-272-6070
annualmeeting@aaaai.org
annualmeeting.aaaai.org

Annual gathering of immunology and allergy experts. Those attending the annual meeting include academicians, allied health professionals and clinicians.
6000+ Members
Frequency: Annual
Founded in 1943

13055 AAB Annual Meeting and Educational Conference
American Association of Bioanalysts
906 Olive Street
Suite 1200
Saint Louis, MO 63101-1448

314-241-1445; Fax: 314-241-1449
aab@aab.org
www.aab.org

Mark S Biernbaum PhD, Executive Director

Educational programs, abstract presentations, poster presentations and exhibits.
Frequency: Annual
Founded in 1956

13056 AACAP Annual Meeting
American Academy of Child & Adolescent Psychiatry
3615 Wisconsin Avenue NW
Washington, DC 20016-3007

202-966-7300; Fax: 202-464-0131
communications@aacap.org
www.aacap.org
Facebook, Twitter

Founded in 1953
Mailing list available for rent

13057 AAHP Institute & Display Forum
American Association of Health Plans
1129 20th Street NW
Washington, DC 20036

202-778-3200; Fax: 202-778-8506

13058 AAMFT Conference
American Assoc for Marriage and Family Therapy
112 S Alfred Street
Alexandria, VA 22314-3061

703-838-9808; Fax: 703-838-9805
central@aamft.org
www.aamft.org
Facebook, Twitter, LinkedIn

Linda S. Metcalf, PhD, President
Michael L. Chafin, President-Elect
Michael Bowers, Executive Director
Robin K. Stillwell, MA, Secretary
Silvia M. Kaminsky, MSEd, Treasurer

AAMFT represents the professional interests of more than 25,000 marriage and family therapists throughout the United States, Canada and abroad.
25000 Members
1500 Attendees
Frequency: Annual
Founded in 1942

13059 AAMI Conference & Expo
Assoc for the Advancement of Medical Instrumenta
4301 N. Fairfax Drive
Suite 301
Arlington, VA 22203-1633

703-525-4890; Fax: 703-276-0793
customerservice@aami.org
www.aami.org

Michael Miller, President
Ed Leonardo, Meetings/Expositions Director

Offers educational, networking, and personal-development opportunities that wil lenable you to expand your expertise, increasr your productivity, develop lasting relationships with peers, and ultimately advance your career.
Frequency: Annual

13060 AANEM Annual Meeting
American Assoc of Neuromuscular & Electro Medicine
2621 Superior Drive NW
Rochester, MN 55902-3018

507-288-0100; Fax: 507-288-1225
aanem@aanem.org
www.aanem.org

Shirlyn A Adkins, Executive Director
Patrick D Aldrich, Finance Director
Emily Spaulding, Executive Assistant
Loretta Bronson, Senior Director of Operations
Catherine French, Director of Health Policy

Forty exhibits of electromyographic and electrodiagnosis equipment and accessories. Seminar, workshop and breakfast.
1000 Attendees
Mailing list available for rent

13061 AAO-HNSF Annual Meeting & OTO Experience
American Academy of Otolaryngology-Head & Neck
1650 Diagonal Road
Alexandria, VA 22314

703-836-4444
www.entannualmeeting.org
Facebook, Twitter, LinkedIn, YouTube

Over 300 exhibits of otolaryngology, diseases of the ear, nose and throat, head and neck surgery equipment, supplies and services plus seminar.
9000+ Attendees
Frequency: Annual
Founded in 1896

13062 AAO-HNSF Leadership Forum & BOG Spring Mee ting
American Academy of Otolaryngology-Head & Neck
1650 Diagonal Road
Alexandria, VA 22314

703-836-4444
www.entnet.org
Facebook, Twitter, LinkedIn, YouTube

Includes leadership discussions, Board of Governors (BOG) meetings, informative speakers, advocacy updates, and mentoring/networking opportunities.
9000+ Attendees
Frequency: Annual
Founded in 1896

13063 AAOMS Scientific Meeting
American Assn. of Oral & Maxillofacial Surgeons
9700 W Bryn Mawr Avenue
Rosemont, IL 60018-5701

847-678-6200
800-822-6637; Fax: 847-678-6286
inquiries@aaoms.org
www.aaoms.org
Facebook, Twitter, LinkedIn

J. David Johnson, Treasurer
A. Thomas Indresano, Vice President

Educational session, reception, tours. Over 275 exhibits relating to the profession.
4000 Attendees
Frequency: Annual
Founded in 1918

13064 AAOS Annual Meeting
American Academy of Orthopaedic Surgeons
9400 West Higgins Rd.
Rosemont, IL 60018

847-823-7186; Fax: 847-823-8125
meeting@aaos.org
www.aaos.org

Thomas E. Arend Jr., Esq., CAE, Chief Executive Officer
Laura Abrahams, Chief Human Resources Officer
Dino Damalas, MBA, Chief Operating Officer
Anna Salt Troise, MBA, Chief Education Strategist
Jennifer Wolff-Jones, CAE, Chief Membership Officer

Three hundred and fifty-five exhibits of surgical equipment, supplies and services used by the orthopedic professional.
28000 Attendees
Frequency: Annual
Founded in 1933

13065 AAPA CHLM Executive Leadership Conference
2318 Mill Rd.
Suite 1300
Alexandria, VA 22314

571-319-4444
chlm@aapa.org
www.chlm.org
Facebook, Twitter, LinkedIn

Jennifer Broderick, Managing Director
Bianca Belcher, PA-C, MPH, Director
Rebecca Winkler, MA, Program Manager
Lawrence Herman, MPA, PA-C, Senior Advisor

A 3-day conference consisting of a unique blend of sessions and speakers that will challenge you to refine your healthcare leadership competencies, effectively measure your workforce, and stay ahead of the latest trends in healthcare.
230 Attendees
Frequency: Annual

13066 AAPA Leadership & Advocacy Summit
American Academy of Physician Assistants
2318 Mill Road
Suite 1300
Alexandria, VA 22314

703-836-2272; Fax: 703-684-1924
customercare@aapa.org
www.aapa.org
Facebook, Twitter, LinkedIn, Youtube, Huddle

Jennifer L. Dorn, Chief Executive Officer
Lisa Gables, CFO & Chief Development Officer
Catherine Gahres, VP, Membership Development & Svcs.
Carrie Munk, VP, Communications
Daniel Pace, VP, Education & Chief Strategy Off.

A full day dedicated to federal advocacy and afternoon visits with legislators on Capitol Hill, as well as sessions focused on critical issues facing the profession, best practices for constituent organization leaders, and advocacy skill-building.
81M Members
Frequency: Annual
Founded in 1968

13067 AAPC HEALTHCON
American Academy of Professional Coders
2233 S. Presidents Dr.
Suite F
Salt Lake City, UT 84120

801-236-2200
800-626-2633; Fax: 801-236-2258
conference@aapc.com
www.aapc.com

Jason VandenAkker, Chief Executive Officer
Provides the opportunity to attend educational sessions, espos, exhibits, and networking. Mingle with local chapters from all over the country. Get education on the most popular and needed subject matter taught by industry experts.
Frequency: Annual, Spring
Founded in 1988
Mailing list available for rent

13068 AAPS Annual Scientific Meeting
American Association of Physician Specialists, Inc
5550 West Executive Drive
Suite 400
Tampa, FL 33609-1035

813-433-2277; Fax: 813-830-6599
wcarbone@aapsus.org
www.aapsus.com

Esther Berg, Director of CME/Meetings/Membership
Keely Clarke, Membership/CME Coordinator
William Carbone, Chief Executive Officer

The American Association of Physician Specialists, Inc.(AAPS) annual meeting is used to educate medical professionals on relevant medical topics that include continuing medical education(CME) credits. The association also holdsbusiness meetings at this time.
1000 Attendees

13069 AARC International Respiratory Congress
American Association for Respiratory Care
9425 N MacArthur Boulevard
Suite 100
Irving, TX 75063-4706

972-243-2272; Fax: 972-484-2720
info@aarc.org
www.aarc.org

Tom Kallstrom, Executive Director/CEO
Tim Myers, Chief Business Officer
Annissa Buchanan, Meetings & Conventions Manager
Kathy Blackmon, Meetings & Conventions Coordinator
Pam Russell, Exhibits Coordinator

Largest respiratory care meeting in the world. Offers the latest information in all aspects of respiratory care. The congress offers you an opportunity to earn all the continuing education hours required for your state license annually.
7000 Attendees
Frequency: Annual, December
Founded in 1947
Mailing list available for rent

13070 AARC Summer Forum
American Association for Respiratory Care
9425 N MacArthur Boulevard
Suite 100
Irving, TX 75063-4706

972-243-2272; Fax: 972-484-2720
info@aarc.org
www.aarc.org

Tom Kallstrom, Executive Director/CEO
Tim Myers, Chief Business Officer
Annissa Buchanan, Meetings & Conventions Manager
Kathy Blackmon, Meetings & Conventions Coordinator
Pam Russell, Exhibits Coordinator

An opportunity for managers and educators in respiratory care meet to learn about new developments in the field, share ideas, network, and strategize for the future.
7000 Attendees
Frequency: Annual, July
Founded in 1947
Mailing list available for rent

13071 ACA Annual Conference & Expo
Journal of Counseling and Development
5999 Stevenson Ave
Alexandria, VA 22304-3302

703-823-9800; Fax: 703-823-0252
membership@counseling.org
www.counseling.org
Facebook, Twitter

Marvin D. Kuehn, Executive Director
Tom Evenson, President

The mission of the American Counseling Association (ACA) is to enhance the quality of life in society by promoting the development of professional counselors, advancing the counseling profession, and using the profession and practice of counseling to promote respect for human dignity and diversity. ACA is a not-for-profit, professional and educational organization. The annual expo features over 100 exhibitors.
4000 Attendees
Frequency: Annual
Founded in 1952
Mailing list available for rent

13072 ACOFP Convention & Scientific Seminar
American College of Osteopathic Family Physicians
330 E Algonquin Road
Arlington Heights, IL 60005

847-228-6090; Fax: 800-323-0794

2500 Attendees

13073 ACOMS Annual Scientific Conference and Exhibition
American College of Oral & Maxillofacial Surgeons
2025 M Street Nw
Suite 800
Washington, DC 20036

202-367-1182
800-522-6676; Fax: 202-367-2182
admin@acoms.org

www.acoms.org
Facebook, Twitter, LinkedIn

Pedro F. Franco, President
R. Bryan Bell, President-Elect
Steven C. Kemp, Executive Director
Jeffrey Bennett, Treasurer
Kevin L. Rieck, Secretary
Frequency: Annual

13074 AG Bell Convention
Alexander Graham Bell Association
3417 Volta Place, NW
Washington, DC 20007

202-337-5220
TTY: 202-337-5221; Fax: 202-337-8314
info@agbell.org
www.agbell.org
Facebook, Twitter, LinkedIn, YouTube, Instagram

Emilio Alonso-Mendoza, Chief Executive Officer
Lisa Chutjian, Chief Development Officer
Susan Boswell, Director of Communications
Robin Bailey, Programs Specialist
Judy Harrison, Director of Programs

An opportunity to learn, network, and connect with professionals, individuals, and parents of individuals who are deaf or hard of hearing.
Frequency: Annual
Founded in 2005

13075 AHIA Annual Conference
Association of Healthcare Internal Auditors
One Parkview Plaza
Suite 800
Oakbrook Terrace, IL 60181

303-327-7546
888-275-2442; Fax: 720-881-6101
info@ahia.org
www.ahia.org

Mary Jane Schroeder, Chair
Cavell Alexander, Vice Chair
Todd Havens, Secretary/Treasurer
Michelle Cunningham, Executive Director

Exhibits concerning cost containment and increased productivity in health care institutions through internal auditing.
Founded in 1981

13076 AHRA Annual Meeting and Exposition
Association for Medical Imaging Management
490B Boston Post Road
Suite 200
Sudbury, MA 01776

978-443-7591
800-334-2472; Fax: 978-443-8046
info@ahraonline.org
www.ahraonline.org
Facebook, Twitter, LinkedIn

Edward Cronin, Jr., CEO
Sarah Murray, Executive Assistant
Emily Ryan, Membership Coordinator
Debra Murphy, Publications Director

Educational event for Radiology Administration. Topics that are covered include human resources, finance, operations and communication.
3000 Attendees
Frequency: Annual

13077 AMGA's Annual Conference
American Medical Group Association
One Prince Street
Alexandria, VA 22314-3318

703-838-0033; Fax: 703-548-1890
www.amga.org
Facebook, Twitter, LinkedIn

Donald W Fisher PhD, CAE, President/CEO
Ryan O'Connor, VP Membership/Marketing
April Noland, Assistant to the President/CEO
Clyde L. Morris, C.P.A., CFO
Nanette Lewis, Administrative Asst/Office Manager

Brings together physician and nonphysician executives from the nation's leading health care organizations, medical groups and physician owned and operated IPAs. It offers both an interactive exhibit area and a relaxed environment for meeting one-on-one with management from the nation's leading health care organizations. National conference dedicated to leadership development in multispecialty medical groups.
375 Members
1100+ Attendees
Frequency: March, Arizona
Founded in 1949
Mailing list available for rent: 600 names

13078 AMIA Annual Symposium
American Medical Informatics Association
4720 Montgomery Lane
Suite 500
Bethesda, MD 20814

301-657-1291; Fax: 301-657-1296
www.amia.org

Douglas B. Fridsma, MD, PhD, President & CEO
Lauren Koleszar, Sr. Meetings/Exhibits Coordinator

Features an outstanding program of scientific papers, posters, tutorials and other educational events that provide information about cutting-edge work in medical informatics.
2000 Attendees
Frequency: Annual/November

13079 AMMA Convention & Expo
American Medical Marijuana Association
convention@ammainfo.com
www.ammainfo.com
Facebook

Offers an expo and educational courses for professionals, advocates, and those interested in the benefits, application, and proper use of medical marijuana (cannabis) in the treatment of health conditions.
Frequency: Annual

13080 AMMPA Annual Conference
American Medical Marijuana Physicians Association

407-917-0887
medicalmarijuanaphysicians@gmail.com
www.ammpa.net
Facebook, Twitter, YouTube

Savara Hastings, Executive Director

Features physician-led education lectures with CME credit, product presentations, panel discussions, and networking opportunities.
Frequency: Annual
Founded in 2016

13081 AORN Congress
Association of PeriOperative Registered Nurses
2170 S Parker Road
Suite 300
Denver, CO 80231-5711

303-755-6300
800-755-2676; Fax: 303-755-4511
sales@aorn.org
www.aorn.org

Garth Jordan, VP Marketing/Business
Lori Ropa, Manager

Surgical tradeshow featuring medical devices and supplies for the operating room and facilities recruiting for open OR nursing positions.
7000 Attendees
Frequency: Annual
Founded in 1954

13082 AORN World Conference of Perioperative Nurses
Association of PeriOperative Registered Nurses
2170 S Parker Road
Suite 300
Denver, CO 80231-5711

303-755-6300; Fax: 303-755-5411
sales@aorn.org
www.aorn.org

Christine Lindmark, Exhibits Director
Lori Ropa, Manager

Seminar and 82 equipment & supplies displays used in operating room suites, and pre-surgical areas.
2500 Attendees
Frequency: Biennial
Founded in 1978

13083 APHA Annual Meeting & Expo
American Public Health Association
800 I Street NW
Washington, DC 20001

202-777-2742; Fax: 202-777-2534
annualmeeting@apha.org
www.apha.org

Lynn Schoen, Exhibition Manager

Five-hundred seventy exhibits of medical interest, pharmaceuticals, publishers, educational, governmental, software, helth promotion products and more. Scientific Sessions available.
13000 Attendees

13084 APTA Annual Conference & Exposition
American Physical Therapy Association
1111 N Fairfax Street
Alexandria, VA 22314

703-684-2782; Fax: 703-706-3396
memberservices@apta.org
www.apta.org

R Scott Ward, President
John Barnes, CEO

The national event for physical therapy.
Frequency: June

13085 ARMA InfoCon
ARMA International
11880 College Boulevard
Suite 450
Overland Park, KS 66210

913-444-9174
844-565-2120; Fax: 913-257-3855
headquarters@armaintl.org
www.arma.org
Facebook, Twitter, LinkedIn

Nate Hughes, Exec. Dir., Operations
Jennifer Millett, National Accounts Manager
Karen Skaggs, Sales & Event Specialist

Conference, seminar, workshop, banquet, award ceremony and 175 exhibits of micrographics, optical disk, automated document storage and retrieval systems and more technology of interest to information professionals.
3500 Attendees
Frequency: Annual
Founded in 1956

13086 ARVO
FASEB/OSMC
9650 Rockville Pike
Bethesda, MD 20814

301-634-7100; Fax: 301-634-7014
info@faseb.org
www.faseb.org/meetings

Jacquelyn Roberts, Marketing Manager
David Craven, Executive Director

13087 **ASC Association Annual Conference**
Ambulatory Surgery Center Association
1012 Cameron Street
Alexandria, VA 22314-2427
703-836-8808; Fax: 703-549-0976
asc@ascassociation.org
www.ascassociation.org
Facebook, Twitter, LinkedIn
Bill Prentice, Chief Executive Officer
Features more than 50 educational sessions designed for ASC professionals, networking opportunities with more than 1000 colleagues, and hundreds of exhibitors.
71000 Attendees
Frequency: Annual, Spring
Founded in 1970

13088 **ASC Association Winter Seminar**
Ambulatory Surgery Center Association
1012 Cameron Street
Alexandria, VA 22314-2427
703-836-8808; Fax: 703-549-0976
asc@ascassociation.org
www.ascassociation.org
Facebook, Twitter, LinkedIn
Bill Prentice, Chief Executive Officer
Three days of educational seminars in three specialized tracks. Attendees can move freely between the tracks and attend any of the sesions offered.
71000 Attendees
Frequency: Annual, Spring
Founded in 1970

13089 **ASCRS Annual Meeting**
American Society of Colon & Rectal Surgeons
85 W Algonquin Road
Suite 550
Arlington Heights, IL 60005
847-290-9184
800-791-0001; Fax: 847-290-9203
ascrs@fascrs.org
www.fascrs.org
Facebook
James W J Felshman MD, President
John H Pemberton MD, VP
Alan G Thorson MD, Treasurer
Rick Slawny, Executive Director
Stella Zedalis, Associate Executive Director
2800 Members
Mailing list available for rent

13090 **ASCRS Symposium & ASOA Congress**
American Society of Cataract & Refractive Surgery
American Society of Opthalmic Administrators
4000 Legato Road, # 850
Fairfax, VA 22033-4003
703-912-2220
800-451-1339; Fax: 703-591-0614
ascrs@ascrs.org
www.ascrs.org
Jane Krause, Show Manager
Seminar and 700 exhibits of opthalmic related intruments of interest to opthalmologists, administrators, nurses and technicians.
7000 Attendees
Frequency: June
Founded in 1986

13091 **ASET Annual Conference**
American Society of Electroneurodiagnostic Tech
402 East Bannister Rd
Suite A
Kansas City, MO 64131-3019
816-931-1120; Fax: 816-931-1145
info@aset.org
www.aset.org
Facebook, Twitter
Arlen Reimnitz, Executive Director
Maliha Khan, Marketing & Social Media Manager
The premier education and exposition opportunity for the Neurodiagnostic technologists in the country. A must attend event for all neurodiagnostic professionals whether you are a technologist, laboratory manager, physician or representing a supplier.
500+ Attendees
Frequency: Annual

13092 **ASHCSP Annual Conference: American Society for Heathcare Central Servi**
American Hospital Association
One N Franklin
Chicago, IL 60601
312-422-2000; Fax: 312-422-4572
Conference and exhibition of health care administration supplies and services.

13093 **ASHHRA'S Annual Conference & Exposition**
American Society of Healthcare & Human Resources
155 North Wacker
Suite 400
Chicago, IL 60606
312-422-3720; Fax: 312-422-4577
www.ashhra.org
Facebook, Twitter, LinkedIn
Ricky Iovino, Exhibit Manager
ASHHRA's Annual Conference & Exposition is the opportunity to connect face-to-face with the top human resource executives and decision-makers in the healthcare field. The attendees come from hospital, hospital system, ambulatory care, long-term care and hospice organizations. Attendee job titles include: Chief Human Reosurce Officer; Vice President/Director of Human Resources; Director/Manager of Recruitment, Compensation, Benefits, Organizational Development or Employee Relations
500 Attendees
Frequency: September, Disneyland
Mailing list available for rent

13094 **ASHI Annual Meeting**
American Society for Histocompatability
1120 Route 73
Suite 200
Mt. Laurel, NJ 08054
856-638-0428; Fax: 856-439-0525
info@ashi-hla.org
www.ashi-hla.org
Kathy Miranda, Executive Director
Jessica Hayes, Meeting Manager
Exhibits from medical suppliers relating to tissue typing.
Frequency: Annual/October
Founded in 1974

13095 **ASHP Midyear Clinical Meeting**
American Society of Health-System Pharmacists
7272 Wisconsin Avenue
Bethesda, MD 20814-4836
301-657-3000
866-279-0681; Fax: 301-657-1641
www.ashp.org
Facebook, Twitter, LinkedIn
Kathryn R. Schultz, President
Paul W. Abramowitz, Chief Executive Officer
Philip J. Schneider, Treasurer
Gerald Meyer, Vice-Chairman
Containing 1,160 booths and 320 exhibits.
Mailing list available for rent

13096 **ASHRM Academy**
American Society for Healthcare Risk Management
155 N. Wacker Drive
Suite 400
Chicago, IL 60606-4425
312-422-3980; Fax: 312-422-4580
ashrm@aha.org
www.ashrm.org
Denise Shope, President
Hala Helm, President Elect
Faye Sheppard, Past-President
Matt B. Hornberger, MBA, CAE, Executive Director
Virginia Petrancosta, CAE, Director, Marketing & Communication
Four days of education, professional development, and networking for healthcare risk management professionals.
Frequency: Annual

13097 **ASNP Convention & Exhibition**
American Association of Naturopathic Physicians
4435 Wisconsin Avenue NW
Suite 403
Washington, DC 20016
202-237-8150
866-538-2267; Fax: 202-237-8152
member.services@naturopathic.org
www.naturopathic.org
Karen Howard, Executive Director
Michael Cronin, ND, President
Joe Pizzorno, ND, Treasurer
Shelly Nichols, Executive Administrator
Stephanie Geller, Membership Associate
900 Attendees
Frequency: Annual/August
Mailing list available for rent

13098 **ASPET Annual Meeting**
ASPET
9650 Rockville Pike
Bethesda, MD 20814
301-347-7060; Fax: 301-634-7061
info@aspet.org
www.aspet.org
Jean Lash, Exhibit Manager
Christine Carrico, Secretary, Treasurer
Paul Czoty, Secretary, Treasurer
The American Society for Pharmacology & Experimental Therapeutics annual meeting consisting of four-hundred exhibits of pharmacology and toxicology equipment, supplies and services.
13000 Attendees
Frequency: April

13099 **ASPRS/PSEF/ASMS Annual Scientific Meeting**
American Society of Plastic Surgeons
444 E Algonquin Road
Arlington Heights, IL 60005
847-228-9900
888-475-2784; Fax: 847-228-9131
webmaster@plasticsurgery.org
www.plasticsurgery.org
Bonnie Burkoth, Exhibit Manager
Close to four hundred exhibits of plastic surgery products, patient education and software to assist plastic surgeons, nurses and paramedical staff.
4000 Attendees
Frequency: October
Mailing list available for rentat $750 per M

13100 **ASSH Annual Meeting**
American Society for Surgery of the Hand

822 W. Washington Boulevard
Suite 600
Chicago, IL 60607

312-880-1900; Fax: 847-384-1435
info@assh.org
www.assh.org

Mark Anderson, CEO
Daniel Nagle, President
W P Andrew Lee, Secretary/VP
3500 Members
Frequency: September
Mailing list available for rent

13101 Academy of Dental Materials Conference
Academy of Dental Materials
4425 Cass St.
Suite A
San Diego, CA 92109

858-272-1018; Fax: 858-272-7687
adm@res-inc.com
www.academydentalmaterials.org

Lynn Reeves, Executive Manager
Nick Silikas, Abstract Coordinator
Dr. Arzu Tezvergil-Mutluay, Paffenbarger Award Chair
Dr. Mutlu Ozcan, Travel Award Chair
Dr. Will Palin, Marshalls Postdoctoral Award Chair

The annual meeting of the Academy of Dental Materials. Features speakers, awards, and educational sessions.
Frequency: Annual

13102 Academy of General Dentistry Annual Meeting
Academy of General Dentistry
560 W. Lake St.
Sixth Floor
Chicago, IL 60611

888-243-3368; Fax: 312-335-3432
membership@agd.org
www.agd.org

Educational session and over 225 dental manufacturers and supplier exhibits. Attended by dentists and the general public.
5000 Attendees
Frequency: Annual
Founded in 1954

13103 Academy of Osseointegration Annual Meeting
85 W Algonquin Rd
Suite 550
Arlington Heights, IL 60005-4460

847-439-1919
800-656-7736; Fax: 847-427-9656
registration@osseo.org
www.osseo.org

Kevin P. Smith, MA, MBA, Executive Director
Kelly Burns, Meeting Registration

Scientific sessions, workshops, and forums related to implant dentistry.
5200 Members
Founded in 1987

13104 Academy of Osseointegration Convention
Smith, Bucklin and Associates
401 N Michigan Avenue
Chicago, IL 60611-4267

312-644-6610; Fax: 312-245-1082
info@smithbucklin.com
www.smithbucklin.com

Henry S. Givray, President & CEO
C. Albert Koob, Executive Vice President
Carolyn Dolezal, Executive Vice President
Michael L. Payne, Executive Vice President
Cele Fogarty, Vice President - Event Services

Osseointegration medical exhibition.
Founded in 1949

13105 Adult Day Services Exposition
VNU Expositions
Dulles International Airport
PO Box 17413
Washington, DC 20041

703-318-0300
800-765-7616; Fax: 703-318-8833

Luellen Hoffman, Show Director

Adult/geriatric health care professionals gather to see exhibits of equipment, supplies, services and consulting for those who represent senior centers, adult day centers, nursing homes, hospitals and other health care markets.
300 Attendees
Frequency: Annual

13106 Aerospace Medical Association Annual Scien tific Meeting
Aerospace Medical Association
320 S Henry Street
Alexandria, VA 22314-3579

703-739-2240; Fax: 703-739-9652
www.asma.org

Jeffrey C. Sventek, MS, CAsP, Executive Director
Gisselle Vargas, Operations Manager
Gloria Carter, Director, Member Services

Provides a multi-faceted forum for all aerospace medical disciplines and concurrently provides continuing education credits for those attending the meeting.
3000 Attendees
Frequency: Annual
Mailing list available for rent

13107 Air Medical Transport Conference
Association of Air Medical Services
526 King Street
Sutie 415
Alexandria, VA 22314-3143

703-836-8732; Fax: 703-836-8920
information@aams.org
www.aams.org

Christina Childs, Director, Special Events

Annual exhibit of air medical transport equipment, supplies and services.
1500 Attendees
Frequency: November

13108 AmSECT International Conference
American Society of ExtraCorporeal Technology
2209 Dickens Road
Richmond, VA 23230-2005

804-565-6363; Fax: 804-282-0090
judyr@amsect.org
www.amsect.org

Stewart Hinckley, Executive Director
Donna Pendarvis, Associate Manager
Michael Troike, Government Relations Chairman
Kimberly Robertson, CPA, Controller
Greg Leasure, Membership Services
2000 Members
600 Attendees
Frequency: Annual
Founded in 1964
Mailing list available for rent

13109 Amer. Assoc. for Pediatric Ophthalmology & Strabismus Annual Meeting
AAPOS
655 Beach Street
San Francisco, CA 94109-1336

415-561-8505; Fax: 415-561-8531
aapos@aao.org
www.aapos.org

Jennifer ÿ Hull, Client Services Manager
Marjan Hazrati, Client Services Coordinator
Maria A.ÿ Schweers, CO, Scientific Program Coordinator

Poster presentations, educational sessions, and exhibitors in the field of pediatric ophthalmology and strabismus.
Frequency: Annual

13110 American Academy for Cerebral Palsy and Developmental Medicine Meeting
Amer. Academy for Cerebral Palsy/Dev. Medicine
555 E Wells St
Suite 1100
Milwaukee, WI 53202-3800

414-918-3014; Fax: 414-276-2146
info@aacpdm.org
www.aacpdm.org
Facebook, Twitter

Tracy Burr, CAE, Executive Director
Erin Trimmer, Senior Meetings Manager
Heather Schrader, Manager, Membership & Admin.
Elizabeth Mueller, Meetings Coordinator
Kay Whalen, MBA, CAE, Managing Partner

Provides dissemination of current and emerging information in the basic sciences, prevention, diagnosis, treatment and technical advances as applied to persons with cerebral palsy and developmental disabilities.
800 Attendees
Frequency: Annual
Founded in 1940

13111 American Academy of Dermatology Annual Meeting
American Academy of Dermatology
P.O. Box 1968
Des Plaines, IL 60017

847-240-1280
866-503-7546; Fax: 847-240-1859
president@add.org
www.aad.org

Seven hundred exhibits from 300 technical companies relating to skin care, professional and scientific organizations.
Frequency: Annual
Founded in 1940

13112 American Academy of Environmental Medicine Conference
American Academy of Environmental Medicine
7701 E Kellog
Suite 625
Wichita, KS 67207-1705

316-684-5500; Fax: 316-684-5709
centraloffice@aaem.com
www.aaem.com

D E Rodgers, Executive Director

Environmental medicine equipment, supplies and services of interest to physicans.
175 Attendees
Frequency: October
Mailing list available for rent

13113 American Academy of Family Physicians Family Medicine Experience
American Academy of Family Physicians

11400 Tomahawk Creek Parkway
Leawood, KS 66211-2680

913-906-6000
800-274-2237; Fax: 913-906-6075
www.aafp.org

Sondra Biggs CMP, Meetings/Convention Director

Gather with your family medicine peers to earn CME, experience dynamic and inspiring presentations, and find patient care solutions to implement when you return to practice.
20000 Attendees
Frequency: Annual

13114 **American Academy of Fixed Prosthodontics Scientific Session**
American Academy of Fixed Prosthodontics
6661 Merwin Road
Columbus, OH 43235

614-761-1927
800-860-5633; Fax: 614-292-0941
aafpsec@gmail.com
www.fixedprosthodontics.org
Facebook, Twitter

Stephen F. Rosenstiel, Secretary

World-renowned speakers present on topics of their expertise. Concepts and techniques presented enhance attendees' knowledge of various complex topics related to fixed prosthodontics.
800 Attendees
Frequency: Annual Feb.
Founded in 1951

13115 **American Academy of Forensic Sciences Annual Meeting**
American Academy of Forensic Sciences
410 N. 21st Street
Colorado Springs, CO 80904

719-636-1100; Fax: 719-636-1993
awarren@aafs.org
www.aafs.org

Anne Warren, Executive Director
Zeno J. Geradts, PhD., President
Jeri D. Ropero-Miller, PhD., President-Elect
Carl R. McClary, BA, Vice President
Susan M. Ballou, MS, Past President

Each February, the AAFS scientific meeting gathers together approximately 5,000 world-renowned professionals to present the most current information, research, and updates in their fields. More than 900 scientific papers, seminars, workshops, and other special sessions are presented. In addition, approximately 150 exhibitors showcase the cutting-edge technology and services of this ever-changing profession.
6700 Members
5000 Attendees
Frequency: Annual/February
Founded in 1948

13116 **American Academy of Home Care Medicine Annual Meeting**
8735 W. Higgins Road
Suite 300
Chicago, IL 60631

847-375-4719; Fax: 847-375-6395
info@aahcm.org
www.aahcm.org
Facebook, Twitter, LinkedIn, YouTube

Brent T. Feorene, MBA, Executive Director
Val Good-Turney, Executive Administrator

Focused on the issues and challenges that face the broad spectrum of healthcare professionals providing in-home primary care, you will learn from innovators in the field about the latest advancements in delivering and managing home care medicine.
Founded in 1988

13117 **American Academy of Implant Dentistry Annual Meeting**
American Academy of Implant Dentistry
211 E Chicago Avenue
Suite 750
Chicago, IL 60611

312-335-1550
877-335-2243; Fax: 312-335-9090
info@aaid.com
www.aaid.org
Facebook, Twitter, LinkedIn

Cheryl R. Parker, CAE, Executive Director
Christine DiGiovanni, Director, Education
Carolina Hernandez, CAE, Director, Membership & Credentials
William Rohe, Chief Financial Officer
Karina Devine, Social Media & Web Content Coord.
1500 Attendees
Frequency: Annual

13118 **American Academy of Neurology: Annual Meeting**
American Academy of Neurology
201 Chicago Ave.
Minneapolis, MN 55415

612-928-6000
800-879-1960; Fax: 612-454-2746
memberservices@aan.com
www.aan.com

Catherine M. Rydell, CAE, Executive Director & CEO
Bruce Levi, JD, General Counsel
Chris Becker, Chief Business Development Officer
Timothy Engal, CPA, Chief Financial Officer
Angela Babb, CAE, APR, Chief Communications Officer

Innovative programs and customizable, experiential, and inspirational learning opportunities for professional and personal knowledge and growth.
6500 Attendees
Frequency: Annual, May

13119 **American Academy of Ophthalmology Annual Meeting**
American Academy of Ophthalmology
655 Beach Street
P.O. Box 7424
San Francisco, CA 94120-7424

415-618-8500; Fax: 415-561-8533
meetings@aao.org
www.aao.org

David W. Parke II, MD, Chief Executive Officer
Debra Rosencrance, CMP, CAE, VP, Meetings & Exhibits
Elizabeth Washburn, Abstract Submission
Anna Zammataro, Exhibition
Abigail Greber, Promotional Opportunities

An opportunity to advance your education, present scientific papers, and visit with exhibitors in the ophthalmology field.
25000 Attendees
Frequency: Annual, Fall
Founded in 1896
Mailing list available for rent

13120 **American Academy of Optometry Annual Meeting**
American Academy of Optometry
2909 Fairgreen Street
Orlando, FL 32803

321-319-4860
844-323-3937; Fax: 407-893-9890
aaoptom@aaoptom.org
www.aaopt.org

Includes nearly 300 hours of lectures & workshops, symposia, and scientific lecture and poster presentations over 4 days. Also features an extensive exhibit hall, with over 200 booths displaying a variety of optometric products and services.
4000 Attendees
Frequency: Annual

13121 **American Academy of Oral and Maxillofacial Radiology Annual Session**
American Academy of Oral & Maxillofacial Radiology
PO Box 55722
Jackson, MS 39296

601-984-6060; Fax: 601-984-6086
www.aaomr.org

Dr. Sanjay Mallya, President
Dr. Debra Gander, President-Elect
Dr. Robert Cederberg, Executive Director
Professor Gail Williamson, Associate Executive Director

Over 20 exhibits relating to dental radiology, equipment, software and accessories.
120 Attendees
Frequency: November
Founded in 1949

13122 **American Academy of Orofacial Pain Annual Scientific Meeting**
American Academy of Orofacial Pain
174 S. New York Ave.
P.O. Box 478
Oceanville, NJ 08231

609-504-1331; Fax: 609-573-5064
aaopexec@aaop.org
www.aaop.org

Kenneth S. Cleveland, Executive Director

Exhibits, educational sessions, and networking opportunities relating to orofacial pain and temporomandibular disorders.
350 Attendees
Frequency: Annual

13123 **American Academy of Pain Medicine Annual Meeting**
American Academy of Pain Medicine
8735 W. Higgins Rd.
Suite 300
Chicago, IL 60631-2738

847-375-4731; Fax: 847-375-6477
info@painmed.org
www.painmed.org

Phil Saigh, Executive Director

Meeting and exhibits relating to pain medicine, particularly related socioeconomic and governmental issues.
Frequency: Annual

13124 **American Academy of Pediatric Dentistry Annual Meeting**
American Academy of Pediatric Dentistry
211 East Chicago Ave.
Suite 1600
Chicago, IL 60611-2637

312-337-2169
800-992-8044; Fax: 312-337-6329
annual.aapd.org
Facebook, Twitter

John Rutkauskas, DDS, MBA, Chief Executive Officer
C. Scott Litch, Esq., CAE, Chief Operating Officer & Counsel
Margaret Bjerklie, Governance & Operations Manager
Erika Hoeft, Public Relations Director

Features speakers, exhibitors, and networking opportunities.
2500 Attendees
Frequency: Annual, May
Founded in 1948

13125 **American Academy of Pediatrics Annual Meeting**
American Academy of Pediatrics
141 NW Point Boulevard
Elk Grove Village, IL 60009

847-434-4000; Fax: 847-434-8000
kidsdocs@aap.org
www.aap.org

E Stephen Edwards MD FAAP, President
Joe M Sanders Jr, MD FAAP, Executive Director
Joann Barbour, Manager

Three hundred and fifty exhibits relating to prescription and over the counter drugs, infant formulas medical equipment and publications. Reception, tours and meeting.
10000 Attendees
Frequency: Annual

13126 **American Academy of Periodontology Annual Meeting & Exhibition**
American Academy of Periodontology
737 N Michigan Avenue
Suite 800
Chicago, IL 60611

312-787-5518; Fax: 312-787-3670
meetings@perio.org
www.perio.org

Erin O'Donnell Dotzler, Executive Director
Lisa Parse, Registration & Housing
Marge Palonis, Exhibits
Linda Cooper, Logistics
Audra Rothermal, Speakers & Moderators

Two hundred and seventy-five exhibits of products and services relating to periodontics, including dental instruments, literature, X-ray equipment, furniture, software and more. Also features educational sessions and networking opportunities.
5800 Attendees
Frequency: Annual
Founded in 1914

13127 **American Academy of Physical Medicine and Rehabilitation Annual Assembly**
American Academy of Physical Medicine & Rehab.
9700 West Bryn Mawr Ave.
Suite 200
Rosemont, IL 60018-5701

847-737-6000
877-227-6799; Fax: 847-754-4368
info@aapmr.org
www.aapmr.org

Thomas E. Stautzenbach, MBA, CAE, Executive Director & CEO

Exhibitors, sponsors, plenary speakers, and networking opportunities.
3000 Attendees
Frequency: Annual, November
Founded in 1938

13128 **American Academy of Physician Assistants C onference**
American Academy of Physician Assistants
2318 Mill Road
Suite 1300
Alexandria, VA 22314

703-836-2272; Fax: 703-684-1924
customercare@aapa.org
www.aapa.org
Facebook, Twitter, LinkedIn, Youtube, Huddle

Jennifer L. Dorn, Chief Executive Officer
Lisa Gables, CFO & Chief Development Officer
Catherine Gahres, VP, Membership Development & Svcs.
Carrie Munk, VP, Communications
Daniel Pace, VP, Education & Chief Strategy Off.

Board of Directors meeting, CME sessions & workshops, career fair, exhibit hall, poster presentations, networking opportunities and much more.
Frequency: Annual

13129 **American Ambulance Association Annual Conference & Trade Show**
Executive Management Services
1255 23rd Street NWrd
Suite 200
Washington, DC 20037

202-213-3999
800-523-4447; Fax: 202-452-0005
www.the-aaa.org

David Saunders, Executive Director
Maria Bianchi, Executive Vice President
6100 Attendees
Frequency: Annual, October

13130 **American Art Therapy Association Conference**
American Art Therapy Association
4875 Eisenhower Avenue
Sute 240
Alexandria, VA 22304

703-548-5860
888-290-0878; Fax: 703-783-8468
info@arttherapy.org
www.arttherapy.org

Cynthia Woodruff, Executive Director
Christina Easterly, Coordinator, Events & Operations
Barbara Florence, Director, Events & Education
Clara Keane, Coordinator, Communication & Policy
Kat Michel, Manager, Membership

Advanced practice courses, papers, workshops, plenary sessions, panels, exhibitors, and a town hall with the AATA board of directors.
800 Attendees
Frequency: Annual
Founded in 1969

13131 **American Assn of Hip & Knee Surgeons Annua l Meeting**
American Association of Hip & Knee Surgeons
9400 W. Higgins Rd.
Suite 230
Rosemont, IL 60018-4976

847-698-1200; Fax: 847-698-0704
meeting@aahks.org
meeting.aahks.org

Michael J. Zarski, JD, Executive Director
Renalin J. Malver-Ledda, Director of Operations
Eileen M. Lusk, Director of Membership
Sigita Wolfe, Director of Education & Research
Jeff Mitchell, Dir., Marketing & Corp. Relations

Features exhibitors, educational sessions, speakers, poster presentations, and more related to the care of patients with arthritis and degenerative disease.
Frequency: Annual, November

13132 **American Assn of Hip & Knee Surgeons Sprin g Meeting**
American Association of Hip & Knee Surgeons
9400 W. Higgins Rd.
Suite 230
Rosemont, IL 60018-4976

847-698-1200; Fax: 847-698-0704
www.aahks.org

Michael J. Zarski, JD, Executive Director
Renalin J. Malver-Ledda, Director of Operations
Eileen M. Lusk, Director of Membership
Sigita Wolfe, Director of Education & Research
Jeff Mitchell, Dir., Marketing & Corp. Relations

Equips orthopaedic surgeons with the latest information and cutting-edge strategies to enhance overall surgeon competence related to the care of patients with arthritis and degenerative disease. Combines general and break-out sessions, emphasizing case-based learning in small group settings for most effective results.
Frequency: Annual, Spring

13133 **American Assocation for Cancer Research An nual Meeting**
American Association for Cancer Research
615 Chestnut St.
17th Fl.
Philadelphia, PA 19106-4404

215-440-9300
866-423-3965; Fax: 215-440-9313
aacr@aacr.org
www.aacr.org

Margaret Foti, Chief Executive Officer

Covers the latest discoveries across the spectrum of cancer research-from population science and prevention; to cancer biology, translational, and clinical studies; to survivorship and advocacy-and highlights the work of the best minds in research and medicine from institutions all over the world.
Frequency: Annual
Founded in 1907

13134 **American Association for Continuity of Care Annual Conference**
American Association for Continuity of Care
Fort Worth, TX

860-867-7525; Fax: 203-586-7550
info@continuityofcare.org
www.continuityofcare.org

Seminar, reception and 35 exhibits of suppliers of health care delivery resources, products and services.
Frequency: Annual
Founded in 1982

13135 **American Association for Geriatric Psychiatry Annual Meeting**
American Association for Geriatric Psychiatry
6728 Old McLean Village Drive
McLean, VA 22101

703-556-9222; Fax: 703-556-8729
main@aagponline.org
www.aagponline.org

Christopher N. Wood, Executive Director
Victoria LaLiberte Cooper, Executive Assistant
Carrie Stankiewicz, Consultant

The largest meeting of physicians and other health care professionals focused on late-life mental illness. Features workshops, speakers, and exhibitors.
Frequency: Annual
Founded in 1978

13136 **American Association for Hand Surgery Annu al Meeting**
American Association for Hand Surgery
500 Cummings Center
Suite 4400
Beverly, MA 01915

978-927-8330; Fax: 978-524-0498
www.handsurgery.org

Features instructional courses, panels, workshops, and exhibitors.
Frequency: Annual

13137 **American Association for Laboratory Animal Science National Meeting**
American Association for Laboratory Animal Science

9190 Crestwyn Hills Drive
Memphis, TN 38125

901-754-8620; Fax: 901-753-0046
info@aalas.org
www.aalas.org

Ann Turner, Executive Director

During the five days of the meeting, members and nonmembers come together to enjoy the workshops, lectures, poster sessions, and exhibits.
4,500 Attendees
Frequency: Annual, Fall

13138 **American Association for Medical Transcription Annual Meeting**
PO Box 576187
Modesto, CA 95357-6187

209-551-0883
800-982-2182; Fax: 209-551-9317

Daryl Ochs, Director Marketing
Terri White, Operations Manager

Exhibitors are medical transcription businesses, hardware, software, publishers and services.
750 Attendees
Frequency: Annual
Founded in 1978

13139 **American Association for Thoracic Surgery Annual Meeting**
American Association for Thoracic Surgery
800 Cummings Center
Suite 350-V
Beverly, MA 01915

978-252-2200; Fax: 978-522-8469
meetings@aats.org
www.aats.org

Cindy VerColen, CEO/Executive Director
Bill Maloney, AATS Consultant
Melissa Binette, Director, Meetings
Lisa McEvoy, Director, Marketing & Communication
Spencer McGrath, Director, Scientific Publications
4700 Attendees
Frequency: Annual
Founded in 1917
Mailing list available for rent

13140 **American Association for the Advancement of Science Annual Meeting**
American Assn for the Advancement of Science
1200 New York Ave NW
Washington, DC 20005

202-326-6400
www.aaas.org

Alan I. Leshner, Interim Chief Executive Officer
Founded in 1848

13141 **American Association for the Study of Headache Meeting**
19 Mantua Road
Mount Royal, NJ 08061

856-423-0043; Fax: 856-423-0082
ahshq@talley.com
www.americanheadachesociety.org

Paul Winner, President
David Dodick, Treasurer

Twenty-five exhibits of research equipment supplies, and services related to headache study.
650 Attendees
Frequency: Annual
Founded in 1958

13142 **American Association of Nurse Anesthetists Midyear Assembly**
222 S Prospect Avenue
Park Ridge, IL 60068-4001

847-927-7055; Fax: 847-692-6968
info@aana.org
www.aana.com

Wanda Wilson, President
Daniel Vigness, Vice President

Exhibits relating to nurse anesthetists.
350 Attendees

13143 **American Association of Blood Banks Annual Meeting**
American Association of Blood Banks
4550 Montgomery Ave.
Suite 700, North Tower
Bethesda, MD 20814-2749

301-907-6977; Fax: 301-907-6895
aabb@aabb.org
www.aabb.org

Debra BenAvram, Chief Executive Officer

The must-attend educational and networking meeting for health care professionals in the field of transfusion medicine and cellular therapy. Earn CME/CE credits, network with colleagues, learn about latest issues and technology in the profession.
7500 Attendees
Frequency: Annual, Fall
Founded in 1947
Mailing list available for rent

13144 **American Association of Cardiovascular & Pulmonary Rehab. Annual Meeting**
American Assoc of Cardiovascular & Pulmonary Rehab
330 N. Wabash Ave.
Suite 2000
Chicago, IL 60611

312-321-5146; Fax: 312-673-6924
aacvpr@aacvpr.org
www.aacvpr.org

Megan Cohen, CAE, Executive Director
Maria Loiotile, Event Services Senior Coordinator

Seminar and workshop, plus 70 exhibits of cardiovascular and pulmonary rehabilitation equipment, supplies and services.
1800 Attendees
Frequency: Annual
Founded in 1985

13145 **American Association of Diabetes Educators Annual Meeting & Educational Prog.**
American Association of Diabetes Educators
200 W Madison St.
Suite 800
Chicago, IL 60606

312-424-2426
800-338-3633; Fax: 312-424-2427
www.aademeeting.org

Charles Macfarlane, FACHE, CAE, Chief Executive Officer
Gregg Lapin, CMP, Director of Meetings
Ken Zielske, CAE, Director of Learning

Six hundred exhibits of dietary food and beverages, testing and screening tools, educational programs and publications. AADE Sessions on Demand available for those who can't make the conference.
Frequency: Annual, Summer
Mailing list available for rent: 10000 names at $160 per M

13146 **American Association of Homes and Services for the Aging Convention**
American Association of Homes and Services/Aging
901 E Street NW
Suite 500
Washington, DC 20004-2037

202-661-5700; Fax: 202-783-2255
mraynor@aahsa.org
www.leadingage.org

Daniel Smith, VP
Mary-Louise Raynor, Secretary
Bonnie Gauthier, Secretary
Douglas Struyk, Treasurer

One thousand eight hundred exhibitors of equipment, supplies and services for housing and long term care facilities for the aged, conference and tours.
4000 Attendees
Frequency: Annual
Founded in 1980

13147 **American Association of Immunologists Annual Meeting**
American Association of Immunologists
9650 Rockville Pike
Bethesda, MD 20814

301-634-7178; Fax: 301-634-7887
infoaai@aai.org
www.aai.org
Facebook

M Michele Hogan PhD, Executive Director
Gale Guerrieri, Meetings Manager

Exhibits related to immunological research, equipment and supplies.
7,600 Members
10000 Attendees
Frequency: May
Founded in 1913

13148 **American Association of Managed Care Nurses Annual Conference**
American Association of Managed Care Nurses
4435 Waterfront Drive
Suite 101
Glen Allen, VA 23060

804-747-9698; Fax: 804-747-5316
keads@aamcn.org
www.aamcn.org

Sloane Reed, VP Sales
Laura Givens, Executive Admin

The AAMCN Annual Conference is designed to provide registered nurses, licensed practical nurses, advanced practice, executive nurses and other healthcare professionals with current information they can use to influence their marketplace.

13149 **American Association of Medical Assistants National Convention**
American Association of Medical Assistants
20 N Wacker Drive
Suite 1575
Chicago, IL 60606-2963

312-899-1500
800-228-2262; Fax: 312-899-1259
info@aama-ntl.org
www.aama-ntl.org

David Balasa, Executive Director
Kathy Langley, Director Of Board Services

Main exhibits, data processing equipment, pharmaceuticals, publications, insurance services, text books, coding system reference guides, health care services and more.
500 Attendees
Frequency: Annual

13150 **American Association of Naturopathic Physicians Convention**
American Association of Naturopathic Physicians
4435 Wisconsin Avenue NW
Suite 403
Washington, DC 20016
202-237-8150; Fax: 202-237-8152
www.naturopathic.org
Karen Howard, Executive Director
Michael Cronin, ND, President
Joe Pizzorno, ND, Treasurer
Shelly Nichols, Executive Administrator
Stephanie Geller, Membership Associate
One hundred and twenty exhibits of Naturopathic medicine, supplies and services plus conference and banquet.
750 Attendees
Frequency: Annual
Founded in 1986
Mailing list available for rent

13151 **American Association of Neurological Surgeons Annual Meeting**
American Association of Neurologists
5550 Meadowbrook Drive
Rolling Meadows, IL 60008
847-378-0500
888-566-2267; Fax: 847-378-0600
info@aans.org
www.aans.org
John Robertson, President
Troy Tippett, Vice President
Griffith R. Harsh, Chairperson
Two hundred manufacturers and suppliers have 500 booths of equipment, publications and supplies.
2400 Attendees
Frequency: Annual
Mailing list available for rent

13152 **American Association of Neuroscience Nurses Convention**
224 N Des Plaines
#601
Chicago, IL 60661
312-258-1200
800-477-2266; Fax: 312-993-0362
info@aann.org
www.aann.org
Thomas O'Dowd, Manager Meetings
Sixty exhibits of nuerological and neurosurgical supplies, services and industry related recruiters.
900 Attendees
Frequency: Annual
Founded in 1968

13153 **American Association of Nurse Anesthetists Annual Meeting**
222 S Prospect Avenue
Park Ridge, IL 60068-4001
847-985-5400; Fax: 847-692-6968
meetings@aana.com
www.aana.com
Cindy Wood, Director Programs
325 exhibits of equipment, supplies, publications and recruiters. Seminar and workshop, as well as a banquet.
3500 Attendees

13154 **American Association of Nurse Anesthetists Assembly of School Faculty**
222 S Prospect Avenue
Park Ridge, IL 60068-4001
847-927-7055; Fax: 847-692-6968
info@aana.com
www.aana.com
Wanda Wilson, President
Daniel Vigness, Vice President
Nurse anesthetist related exhibits
250 Attendees
Frequency: Annual

13155 **American Association of Office Nurses Annual Meeting & Convention**
52 Park Avenue
Suite B4
Park Ridge, NJ 07656
201-391-2600
800-457-7504; Fax: 201-573-8543
www.aaacn.org
Michelle Aronowitz, Managing Director
Sherry Levy, Associate Managing Director
American Association of Office Nurses annual meeting and convention at the Eden Roc Hotel in Miami Beach, Florida.
150 Attendees
Frequency: Sept
Founded in 1988

13156 **American Association of Orthodontists Trade Show and Scientific Session**
401 N Lindbergh Boulevard
Saint Louis, MO 63141-7816
314-993-1700; Fax: 314-997-1745
info@aaortho.org
Chris Varanas, Manager
Five hundred and fifty exhibits of orthodontic equipment, publications, supplies and services.
9000 Attendees
Frequency: Annual

13157 **American Association of Suicidology Conference**
4201 Connecticut Avenue NW
Suite 408
Washington, DC 20008
202-237-2280; Fax: 202-237-2282
www.suicidology.org
Alan Berman PhD, Executive Director
Exhibits relating to the advancement of studies to prevent suicide and life threatening behavior.
Frequency: Annual
Founded in 1969

13158 **American Association of Tissue Banks Meeting**
1320 Old Chain Bridge Road
Suite 450
Mc Lean, VA 22101
703-827-9582; Fax: 703-356-2198
aatb@aatb.org
www.aatb.org
Robert Rigney, CEO
Scott Brubaker, Chief Policy Officer
Exhibits for the revival, preservation, storage, and distribution of tissues for transplantation.

13159 **American Association on Mental Retardation Annual Meeting**
444 N Capitol Street
Suite 846
Washington, DC 20001-1512
202-387-1968
800-424-3688; Fax: 202-387-2193
dcroser@aamr.org
www.aamr.org
Doreen Croser, Executive Director
Paul Aitken, Director Of Finance Administration
2000 Attendees
Founded in 1876

13160 **American Chiropractic Association Annual Convention and Exhibition**
1701 Clarendon Boulevard
Arlington, VA 22209
703-276-8800
800-986-4636; Fax: 703-243-2593
http://www.acatoday.org
Kevin Corcoran, VP
Fifty displays of chiropractic tables and products, mattress companies, nutritional supplements, computer software, services and supplies.
500 Attendees
Frequency: Annual
Founded in 1963

13161 **American Cleft Palate Craniofacial Association Annual Meeting**
American Cleft Palate-Craniofacial Association
1504 E. Franklin St.
Suite 102
Chapel Hill, NC 27514
919-933-9044; Fax: 919-933-9604
meetings@acpa-cpf.org
www.acpa-cpf.org
Kathy Bogie, Manager Meetings
Nancy Smythe, Administrative Assistant
Hillary Jones, Administrative Assistant
Scientific meeting.
600 Attendees
Frequency: April
Founded in 1943

13162 **American Clinical Neurophysiology Society Convention**
1 Regency Drive
PO Box 30
Bloomfield, CT 06002
860-447-9408; Fax: 860-286-0787
info@acns.org
www.acns.org
Mark Ross, President
Alan Legatt, First Vice President
Over 40 exhibits of electroencephalographic and neurophysiology equipment, seminar, workshop and conference.
400 Attendees
Frequency: Annual
Founded in 1946

13163 **American College Health Association Annual Meeting**
American College Health Association
1362 Mellon Road
Suite 180
Hanover, MD 21076
410-859-1500; Fax: 410-859-1510
contact@acha.org
www.acha.org
Facebook, Twitter
Jenny Haubenreiser, President
Pat Ketcham, President-Elect
Doyle Randall, Executive Director
The largest conference for college professionals. This year we honor the spirit of service and compassion that college health professionals have shown in their dedication to serving college students and their campus communities.
1800 Attendees
Frequency: Annual
Founded in 1922

13164 American College of Allergy, Asthma and Immunology Annual Meeting
85 W Algonquin Road
Suite 550
Arlington Heights, IL 60005-4460

847-427-1200; Fax: 847-427-1294
mail@acaai.org
www.acaai.org

Richard G Gowes MD, President
Sami L Bahna MD, President-Elect

2006 Annual Meeting will be held November 9-15 in Philadelpia, Pennsylvania
Frequency: November
Founded in 1942
Mailing list available for rent: 4500 names at $100 per M

13165 American College of Angiology Conference
295 Northern Boulevard
Suite 104
Great Neck, NY 11021-4701

516-466-4055; Fax: 516-466-4099
www.intlcollegeofangiology.org

Joan Shaffer, Executive Director

CME Seminars and 50 exhibits from commercial and scientific suppliers.
300 Attendees
Frequency: October
Founded in 1954

13166 American College of Cardiology Annual Scientific Session
American College of Cardiology
2400 N Street, NW
Washington, DC 20037-1699

202-375-6000
800-253-4636; Fax: 202-375-7000
resource@acc.org
www.acc.org

Christine McEntee, CEO
Julie Miller, Assistant Professor of Medicine

Seminar, workshop, dinner and 385 exhibits of products, supplies and services related to cardiovascular medicine.
30000 Attendees
Founded in 1949

13167 American College of Cardiovascular Administrator Leadership Conference
American Academy of Medical Administrators
701 Lee Street
Suite 600
Des Plaines, IL 60016

847-759-8601; Fax: 847-759-8602
www.acc.org

Holly Estal Ed M, Director Education
Gen Hedland, Manager of Exhibits
S. Patrick Alford, Chairman
Linda R. Larin, Treasurer
Tina R. Brinton, Vice Chairman

Featuring keynote and concurrent sessions on human relations, finance and business developments, CV program development technology plus exhibitors that include the latest technological and innovative systems and products in cardiovascular health care. There are 30-40 booths.
300 Attendees
Frequency: March
Mailing list available for rent: 3,000 names at $150 per M

13168 American College of Emergency Physicians Scientific Assembly
American College of Emergency Physicians
PO Box 619911
Dallas, TX 75261-9911

972-550-0911
800-798-1822; Fax: 972-580-2816
publicaffairs@acep.org
www.acep.org

Dana Bellantone, Manager Meetings

Five hundred and twenty-five exhibits of products and services related to emergency medicine.
4400 Attendees
Frequency: Annual
Founded in 1972

13169 American College of Medical Quality Annual Meeting
4334 Montgomerey Avenue
2nd Floor
Bethesda, MD 20814-4402

301-913-9149
800-924-2149; Fax: 301-656-0989
acmq@aol.com
www.acmq.org

Louis H. Diamond MB, ChB, President
Alan Krumholz, MD, Vice President

Seminar, reception and exhibits of computer hardware and software, publications, phamaceuticals and supplies. Medical professionals and others involved in quality assurance and utilization review and risk management attend.
150 Attendees
Founded in 1973
Mailing list available for rent

13170 American College of Nurse Practitioners
J Spargo & Associates
11208 Waples Mill Road
Suite 112
Fairfax, VA 22030

703-631-6200
800-564-4220; Fax: 703-654-6931
www.afcea.org
Facebook, Twitter, LinkedIn

June LaMountain, Exhibit Sales Account Manager
Kent Schneider, President and CEO
Pat Miorin, Chief Financial Officer
Al Grasso, Chairman

The premier educational offering for nurse practitioners. It offers the opportunity to earn a full scope of continuing education contact hours at sessions led by top clinical experts in many areas.
1200 Attendees
Frequency: October
Mailing list available for rent

13171 American College of Obstetricians and Gynecologists Clinical Meeting/Expo
American College of Obstetricians
409 12th Street SW
Washington, DC 20024

202-857-3288; Fax: 202-484-3933
http://www.acog.org

Professionally related exhibits.

13172 American College of Physicians Annual Convention
American College of Physicians
Independence Mall W
6th Street & Race
Philadelphia, PA 19106

215-351-2400
http://www.acponline.org

John Tooker, CEO

Five hundred exhibits of medical supplies and services, as well as a seminar.
8000 Attendees

13173 American College of Rheumatology Scientific Meeting
Slack
4930 Del Ray Avenue
Bethesda, MD 20814

301-654-2055; Fax: 301-654-5920
member@gastro.org
www.gastro.org

Robert Greenberg, Executive Vp
Michael Stolar, Senior Vp

Two hundred and ten exhibits of diagnostic testing kits, pharmaceuticals, equipment and supplies, of interest to professionals in Rheumatology.
4500 Attendees
Frequency: Annual
Founded in 1934

13174 American College of Surgeons Annual Clinical Congress
American College of Surgeons
633 N Saint Clair Street
Chicago, IL 60611
312-202-5000
800-621-4111; Fax: 312-202-5001
postmaster@facs.org
www.facs.org

David B. Hoyt, MD, FACS, Executive Director
Bob Hope, Convention & Meetings Director

Exhibits of medical and patient care products, equipment and supplies. Conference, seminar and workshop, as well as luncheon and tours.
Frequency: Annual
Founded in 1913

13175 American College of Surgeons Leadership and Advocacy Summit
American College of Surgeons
633 N Saint Clair Street
Chicago, IL 60611

312-202-5000
800-621-4111; Fax: 312-202-5001
postmaster@facs.org
www.facs.org

David B. Hoyt, MD, FACS, Executive Director
Bob Hope, Convention & Meetings Director

Topics on effective surgeon leadership, plus advocacy training.
Frequency: Annual
Founded in 1913

13176 American College of Surgeons Quality and Safety Conference
American College of Surgeons
633 N Saint Clair Street
Chicago, IL 60611

312-202-5000
800-621-4111; Fax: 312-202-5001
postmaster@facs.org
www.facs.org

David B. Hoyt, MD, FACS, Executive Director
Bob Hope, Convention & Meetings Director

Dedicated to surgical quality improvement initiatives.
Frequency: Annual
Founded in 1913

13177 American Congress of Rehabilitation Medicine Annual Meeting
6801 Lake Plaza Drive
Suite B- 205
Indianapolis, IN 46220

317-915-2250; Fax: 317-915-2245
crobinson@acrm.org
www.acrm.org

Richard D Morgan, Executive Director

Seminar, workshop and conference with 20 exhibits of rehabilitation supplies and equipment.
250 Attendees
Frequency: September/October
Founded in 1923
Mailing list available for rent: 750 names at $275 per M

13178 American Dental Association Annual Session & Technical Exhibition
211 E Chicago Avenue
Suite 200
Chicago, IL 60611-2678

312-440-2500; Fax: 312-440-2707
donovanj@ada.org
www.ada.org

James P Donovan, Exhibit Manager
Patricia A Johnson, Manager Program Development
Vicki Guinta, Director
James Bramson, CEO

The annual session scientific program consists of over 180 programs, including science of dentistry, practice of dentistry, dental technology and general insterest programs as well as participation workshops. The leading suppliers will showcase their products and services. Dental professionals can compare products, see demonstrations, and make decisions about applying the latest technology. Attendees visiting the Technical Exhibition can also look for the ADA Seal which has long been recognizd
30000 Attendees
Frequency: October

13179 American Dental Education Association Annual Session and Exposition
1400 K Street NW
Suite 1100
Washington, DC 20005

202-289-7201; Fax: 202-289-7204
www.adea.org

Rhonda Buford, Meetings Manager
Renee Latimer, Meeting Manager
Simone Smith, Meetings Manager
Novella Abrams, Senior Administrative Associate
Cassandra Allen, Program Associate

One hundred commercial and educational exhibits of supplies, video equipment, publications and more.
3000 Attendees
Frequency: Annual
Founded in 1983

13180 American Dental Hygienists Association Conference
444 N Michigan Avenue
Suite 3400
Chicago, IL 60611

312-440-8900; Fax: 312-440-8929
www.adha.org

Ann Battrell, Executive Director
Kathy Madryk, Marketing Manager
Katie Powell, Director, Members Service
Ann Lynch, Director, Governmental Affairs
Isaac Carpenter, Director, Finance and MIS

Educational session and 120 exhibits of dental products.
1500 Attendees
Frequency: Annual
Founded in 1993
Mailing list available for rent

13181 American Dental Society of Anesthesiology Scientific Meeting
211 E Chicago Avenue
Suite 948
Chicago, IL 60611

312-664-8270
800-722-7788; Fax: 312-642-9713

R Knight Charlton, Executive Director

Meeting and over 15 exhibits of anesthetics and monitoring equipment.
200 Attendees
Frequency: Annual
Founded in 1954

13182 American Diabetes Association Annual Scientific Sessions
American Diabetes Association
2451 Crystal Drive
Suite 900
Arlington, VA 22202

703-549-1500
800-342-2383; Fax: 703-549-6995
meetings@diabetes.org
www.diabetes.org
Facebook, Twitter, YouTube

Robin Richardson, Chair
Kevin L. Hagan, Chief Executive Officer

Three hundred and fifty exhibits of medical and dietary products and services, seminar and workshop.
Frequency: June
Founded in 1940

13183 American Health Care Association Annual Convention and Exhibition
1201 L Street NW
Washington, DC 20005

202-842-4444; Fax: 202-842-3860
webmaster@ahca.org
www.ahcancal.org
Facebook, Twitter, LinkedIn

Dave Kyllo, VP

Three hundred and fifty exhibits of supplies and information for the long term health care industry, banquet, luncheon and tours.
5000 Attendees
Frequency: Annual
Mailing list available for rent

13184 American Health Information Management Association Annual Convention
American Health Information Management Association
233 N. Michigan Avenue
21st Floor
Chicago, IL 60601-5809

312-233-1100
800-335-5535; Fax: 312-233-1090
info@ahima.org
www.ahima.org

Wylecia Wiggs Harris, PhD, CAE, Chief Executive Officer
Amy Mosser, MBA, Chief Operating Officer
Leslie M. Stokes, MBA, Chief Product/Marketing/Sales Off.
Cheryl D. Martin, HIM Strategic Advisor
Founded in 1928

13185 American Health Quality Association Annual Session
1140 Connecticut Avenue NW
Washington, DC 20036

202-331-5790
info@ahqa.org
www.ahqa.org

David Thomas MD, President
David Adler, Public Affairs Associate

Quality Improvement Organizations (QIOs) and professionals working to improve the quality of health care in communities across America gather for educational sessions and networking.
Frequency: March

13186 American Heart Association Scientific Sessions
American Heart Association
7272 Greenville Avenue
Dallas, TX 75231

214-736-6300; Fax: 214-373-3406
www.amhrt.org

M Cass Wheeler, CEO

Conference, seminar and tours, plus 325 exhibits relating to exercise, equipment, pharmceuticals and services related to cardiovascular health care.
29000 Attendees

13187 American Hospital Association Convention
155 N. Wacker Dr.
Chicago, IL 60606

312-422-3000
800-424-4301; Fax: 312-422-4500
ddavidson@aha.org
www.aha.org
Twitter, YouTube

Richard Umbdenstock, President & CEO
Richard Pollack, VP, Advocacy
Neil Jesuelo, SVP Business Development

Exhibits of equipment, supplies and services for the medical and hopsital industry.

13188 American Industrial Hygiene Conference & Exposition (AIHce)
American Industrial Hygiene Association
3141 Fairview Park Drive
Suite 777
Falls Church, VA 22042

703-849-8888; Fax: 703-207-3561
infonet@aiha.org
www.aiha.org
Facebook, Twitter, LinkedIn

Bethany Chirico, Director, Global Meeting & Expos
Alison Daniels, Manager , Exposition
Laura Cilano Garcia, Program Director

Attracts OEHS professionals that are industrial hygienists, EHS specialists, safety professionals, risk management professionals and other who are esponsible for safety, health and the environment at their organization.
Frequency: Annual
Founded in 1939

13189 American Lung Association/American Thoracic Society Int Conference
1740 Broadway
New York, NY 10019-4374

212-315-8700; Fax: 212-265-5642

John Kirkwood, CEO

Two hundred and fifty exhibits of pharmaceuticals, equipment and books.
8500 Attendees
Frequency: Annual
Founded in 1904

13190 American Medical Directors Association Annual Symposium
American Medical Directors Association
11000 Broken Land Parkway, Suite 400
Suite 760
Columbia, MD 21044

410-740-9743
800-876-2632; Fax: 410-740-4572

info@amda.com
www.amda.com

Megan Brey, Director Meetings
Lorraine Tarnove, Manager

Exhibits relating to geriatrics, pharmaceuticals and medical administration of long term care facilities. Long term health care physicians and professionals attend educational sessions, receptions and special events. Spouse/guest program offered.
1400 Attendees
Frequency: April
Founded in 1978

13191 **American Medical Student Association Convention**
American Medical Student Association
1902 Association Drive
Reston, VA 20191

703-620-6600
800-767-2266; Fax: 703-620-5873
amsa@amsa.org
www.amsa.org

One hundred exhibits relating to medical supplies and equipment, residency programs, physician recruitment and professional associations.
1500 Attendees

13192 **American Medical Technologists Convention**
American Medical Technologists
10700 West Higgins Road
Rosemont, IL 60018

847-823-5169
800-275-1268; Fax: 847-823-0458
dianepowell.amt@juno.com
www.amtc.com

Diane Powell, Show Manager

Forty eight exhibits of clinical laboratory books, supplies and equipment, seminar, workshop, banquet and tours.
600 Attendees
Frequency: Annual
Founded in 1991

13193 **American Medical Women's Association Annual Meeting**
American Medical Women's Association
1100 E. Woodfield Road
Suite 350
Schaumburg, IL 60173

847-517-2801; Fax: 847-517-7229
associatedirector@amwa-doc.org
www.amwa-doc.org

Connie Newman, MD, President
Roberta Gebhard, DO, President-Elect
Eliza Lo Chin, MD, MPH, Executive Director
Sharon Batista, MD, Treasurer
Lynda Kabbash, MD, Secretary

Seminar, banquet, tours and 60 exhibits of medical equipment, supplies and services.
1000 Attendees
Frequency: Annual
Founded in 1915

13194 **American Nephrology Nurses Association Symposium**
Society of Urologic Nurses and Associates
E Holly Avenue
Box 56
Pittman, NJ 08071

856-256-2350; Fax: 856-589-7463

Mike Cunningham, Manager

One hundred fifteen companies have exhibits of equipment, supplies, pharmaceuticals and services for nephrology.
2000 Attendees
Frequency: Annual
Founded in 1970

13195 **American Nurses Association Convention**
600 Maryland Avenue SW
Suite 100
Washington, DC 20024-2571

202-651-7000; Fax: 301-628-5001
exhibits@ana.org
www.nursingworld.org

Exhibits of nursing professional equipment, supplies and services.
Frequency: Annual

13196 **American Occupational Health Conference & Exhibits**
Slack
4930 Del Ray Avenue
Bethesda, MD 20814

301-654-2055; Fax: 301-654-5920
member@gastro.org
www.gastro.org
Facebook, Twitter, LinkedIn

Robert Greenberg, Executive Vp
Michael Stolar, Senior Vp
Derek Randolph, Director of Building Services
Arceli Bacsinila, Senior Director of Finance
Hillina Fetehawoke, Staff Accountant

Four hundred exhibits of pharmaceuticals, equipment, software and supplies for health professionals, offices and labs.
4500 Attendees
Mailing list available for rent

13197 **American Occupational Therapy Association Annual Conference**
American Occupation Therapy Association
4720 Montgomery Lane
PO Box 31220
Bethesda, MD 20824-1220

301-652-2682; Fax: 301-652-7711
www.aota.org

M Carolyn Baum, President
Lizette Rosales, Manager
7000 Attendees
Frequency: May
Founded in 1919

13198 **American Optometric Student Association Annual Meeting**
243 N Lindbergh Boulevard
Saint Louis, MO 63141

314-993-8575; Fax: 314-993-8919
www.iaccnorthamerica.org
Facebook, Twitter, LinkedIn

James Mahon, Director Marketing
Tom Cappucci, First Vice President

Optometry equipment, supplies and services.
Frequency: Annual

13199 **American Organization of Nurse Executives Meeting and Exposition**
American Hospital Association
1 N Franklin
Suite 27
Chicago, IL 60606

312-222-2000
312-422-4519
aone@aha.org
www.aha.org

Pamela Thompson, CEO
Cliff Lehman, Director Membership Services

One hundred fifty exhibits of patient care equipment and supplies, computer hardware and software, communications systems and information for the professional in health care.
Frequency: Annual

13200 **American Orthopsychiatric Association Annual Meeting**
330 7th Avenue
18th Floor
New York, NY 10001

212-564-5930; Fax: 212-564-6180

Rachel L MacAulay, Program Associate

Meeting and exhibits by social service agencies, publications, computer software companies and more.
1928 Members
700 Attendees
Frequency: Annual
Founded in 1923

13201 **American Orthotic & Prosthetic Association National Assembly**
American Orthotic & Prosthetic Association
330 John Carlyle Street
Suite 200
Alexandria, VA 22314

571-431-0876; Fax: 571-431-0899
info@aopanet.org
www.aopanet.org

Michael Oros, President
Tom Fise, Executive Director
Don DeBolt, Chief Operating Officer
Betty Leppin, Manager, Membership & Operations

AOPA's goal is to advocate for policies that improve patient care.
2200 Attendees
Frequency: Annual
Founded in 1917

13202 **American Osteopathic Association Meeting & Exhibits**
American Osteopathic Hospital Association
142 E Ontario Street
Chicago, IL 60611

312-587-3709; Fax: 312-202-8212

John Crosby, Executive Director

Over 25 exhibits of products and services relating to the osteopathic health care industry, including building and financing, marketing and operations.
500 Attendees
Founded in 1983

13203 **American Pain Society Scientific Meeting**
4700 W Lake Avenue
Glenview, IL 60025

847-375-4715; Fax: 877-734-8758
info@ampainsoc.org
www.ampainsoc.org

Judith A Paice, President
Catherine Underwood, Executive Director
Marilyn Rutkowski, Marketing Manager
Kathryn Checea, Director of Sales
Deborah Pinkston, Managing Editor

Designed for a diverse group of pain clinicians, scientists and other professionals, the Annual Scientific Meeting features a prominent faculty presenting basic, translational, and clinical research advancements. Seminar, banquet, luncheon, breakfast and 150 exhibits of pharmceutical and medical instruments, medical equipment, products, supplies, services, and alternative delivery systems.
Frequency: Annual
Founded in 1977

13204 **American Physical Therapy Association Annual Conference**
American Physical Therapy Association

1111 N Fairfax Street
Alexandria, VA 22314

703-684-2782
800-999-2782; Fax: 703-706-8575
webmaster@apta.org
www.apta.org

Kelly Glascoe, Director/Exposition
Frank Mallon, CEO

450 exhibits of physical therapy equipment, supplies and services.
4000 Attendees
Frequency: Annual

13205 **American Physical Therapy Association: Private Practice Session**
1111 N Fairfax Street
Alexandria, VA 22314

703-684-2782
800-999-2782; Fax: 703-706-8575
http://www.apta.org

Frank Mallon, CEO

Seminar, workshop, dinner and 120 exhibits of physical therapy and rehabilitation equipment, supplies and services.
1200 Attendees
Frequency: Annual
Founded in 1983

13206 **American Podiatric Medical Association Annual Meeting**
9312 Old Georgetown Road
Bethesda, MD 20814

301-581-9200; Fax: 301-530-2752
Facebook, Twitter, LinkedIn

Anne Martinez CMP, Meetings Administrator

One-hundred and fifty exhibits of medical and laser equipment, supplies and podiatric services.
1,500 Attendees
Frequency: August

13207 **American Psychiatric Association Annual Meeting**
American Psychiatric Association
1000 Wilson Boulevard
Suite 1825
Arlington, VA 22209-3901

703-907-7300
888-357-7924; Fax: 703-907-1085
apa@psych.org
www.psychiatry.org
Facebook, Twitter, LinkedIn

Saul M. Levin, M.D., M.P.A, CEO & Medical Director
Maria A. Oquendo, President

Conference, seminar, workshop and 850 exhibits of computer online service and software, media products, criminal justice, dianostic tools and much more.
18000 Attendees
Frequency: Annual
Founded in 1844

13208 **American Psychological Association Annual Convention**
American Psychological Association
750 1st Street NE
Washington, DC 20002-4242

202-336-5500
800-374-2721; Fax: 202-336-5568
www.apa.org

James H Bray PhD, President
Norman Anderson PhD, Executive VP/CEO
Paul L Craig PhD, Treasurer
12000 Attendees
Frequency: Annual, August

13209 **American Roentgen Ray Society Meeting**
American Roentgen Ray Society
44211 Slatestone Court
Leesburg, VA 20176

703-729-3353
800-438-2777; Fax: 703-729-4839
info@arrs.org
www.arrs.org

Maureen Robertson, Show Manager
Noel Montesa, Vice President
Charles Kahn, Vice President
Melissa Rosado, Secretary

Forty-one and a half hours of Category ICME credits available; Categorical course on Body CT; 30 commercial exhibits; 300 scientific exhibits; scientific paper presentations.
2,500 Attendees
Frequency: April-May

13210 **American School Health's Annual School Health Conference**
American School Health Association
4340 East West Highway
Suite 403
Bethesda, MD 20814

301-652-8072
800-445-2742; Fax: 301-652-8077
info@ashaweb.org
www.ashaweb.org
Facebook, Twitter, LinkedIn

Mary Bamer Ramsier, Meeting Planner
Thomas Reed, Manager
Stephen Conley, Executive Director
Julie Greenfield, Marketing and Conferences Director
Lori Lawrence, Membership/Database Manager

Join school health professionals who will come together to learn, share perspectives and resources, and network during the more than 120 educational sessions and workshops. General Sessions, multiple break-outs, and exhibits.
800 Attendees
Frequency: Annual
Founded in 1927
Mailing list available for rent: 650 names

13211 **American Society for Aesthetic Plastic Surgery Conference**
American Society for Aesthetic Plastic Surgery
36 W 44th Street
Suite 630
New York, NY 10036

212-921-0500; Fax: 212-921-0011
www.surgery.org

Educational sessions and displays of the latest prdoducts and developments.
2500 Attendees
Frequency: May

13212 **American Society for Artificial Internal Organs Meeting and Exhibits**
PO Box C
Boca Raton, FL 33429-8589

561-391-8589; Fax: 561-368-9153
www.asaio.com

Workshop, and over 30 exhibits of interest to physicians, nurses, engineers, perfusionists and technicians.
1000 Attendees
Frequency: Annual
Founded in 1954

13213 **American Society for Bone and Mineral Research Congress**
1200 19th Street NW
Suite 300
Washington, DC 20036

202-289-5900; Fax: 202-857-1880
www.asbmr.org

Joan Goldberg, Executive Director

Exhibits for the research of bone and mineral diseases.
Frequency: Annual
Founded in 1977

13214 **American Society for Cell Biology Annual Meeting**
9650 Rockville Pike
Bethesda, MD 20814

301-530-7153; Fax: 301-530-7139
enewman@ascb.org
www.ascb.org/ascb

Edward Newman, Director Marketing
Joan Goldberg, Manager
Jean Schwarzbauer, Secretary

Conference and 425 exhibits of interest to biomedical researchers, scientists, and related trade professionals.
8000 Attendees
Frequency: Annual
Founded in 1961

13215 **American Society for Dermatologic Surgery Annual Meeting**
American Society for Dermatologic Surgery
5550 Meadowbrook Drive
Suite 120
Rolling Meadows, IL 60008

847-956-0900; Fax: 847-956-0999
www.asds.net

Alastair Carruthers, President
Kimberly Butterwick, Board of Directors

Educational session, banquet and tours plus 80 exhibits of surgical instruments, dressings, closure materials and dermatologic pharmceuticals.
800 Attendees
Founded in 1973

13216 **American Society for Health Care Human Resources Administration Meeting**
American Hospital Association
1 N Franklin
Chicago, IL 60606

312-222-2000; Fax: 312-422-4519
www.aha.org

Human resources administration in health care exhibition.

13217 **American Society for Healthcare Management Convention**
Corcoran Expositions
100 W Monroe Street
Suite 1001
Chicago, IL 60603

312-541-0567; Fax: 312-541-0573

13218 **American Society for Laser Medicine and Surgery Conference**
2100 Stewart Avenue
Suite 240
Wausau, WI 54401-1709

715-845-9283; Fax: 715-848-2493
information@aslms.org
www.aslms.org

Richard O Gregory MD, Board Secretary
Dianne Dalsky, Executive Director

Seventy five exhibits of laser medicine and supplies of interest to physicians, physicists, nurses, veterinarians, dentists, podiatrists and technicians.
Frequency: Annual
Founded in 1980

13219 **American Society for Microbiology: General Meeting**
1325 Massachusetts Anvenue NW
Washington, DC 20005

202-942-9252; Fax: 202-942-9340

Professionally related exhibits.

13220 **American Society for Nutrition Annual Meeting**
9650 Rockville Pike
Bethesda, MD 20814-3998

301-634-7050; Fax: 301-634-7892
www.nutrition.org

Teresa A. Davis, President
John E Courtney PhD, Executive Officer
Gordon L. Jensen, VP
Cheryl Rock, Treasurer
Catherine Field, Secretary

Exhibits relating to clinical nutrition of interest to physicians and scientists.
Frequency: Annual
Mailing list available for rent

13221 **American Society for Surgery of the Hand Annual Meeting**
American Society for Surgery of the Hand
6300 N River Road
Suite 600
Rosemont, IL 60018

847-384-8300; Fax: 847-384-1435
info@assh.org
www.assh.org

Carissa Wehrman, Meetings/Exhibits Coordinator
Mark Anderson, Executive Director

Meeting plus exhibits of microsurgical instruments, finger splinting devices, surgical telescopes, trauma products, external fixation systems and more.
2,000 Attendees
Frequency: September

13222 **American Society for Therapeutic Radiology and Oncology Annual Meeting**
American Society for Therapeutic Radiology & Onc.
12500 Fairlakes Circle
Suite 375
Fairfax, VA 22033

703-502-1550
800-962-7876; Fax: 703-502-7852
meetings@astro.org
www.astro.org

Laura Mulay, ASTRO Meetings Manager

Eight-hundred exhibits of products, supplies and services for the treatment of cancer.
10000 Attendees
Frequency: October

13223 **American Society of Aesthetic Plastic Surgery Meeting**
11081 Winners Circle
Suite 200
Los Alamitos, CA 90720-2813

562-799-2356; Fax: 310-427-2234

Robert Stanton, Manager

Meeting and 100 exhibits of plastic surgery medical instruments and equipment.
Frequency: Annual

13224 **American Society of Anesthesiologists Annual Meeting**
American Society of Anesthesiologists
520 N Northwest Highway
Park Ridge, IL 60068-2573

847-825-5586; Fax: 847-825-1692
www.asahq.org

Ronald Bruns, Executive Director
18000 Attendees
Frequency: Annual, October

13225 **American Society of Clinical Oncology Annual Convention**
J Spargo & Associates
11208 Waples Mill Road
Suite 112
Fairfax, VA 22030

703-631-6200
800-564-4220; Fax: 703-299-1044
www.jspargo.com

John Spargo, President

Three hundred exhibits of medical equipment, supplies and services used in the practice of clinical oncology.
20000 Attendees
Frequency: Annual
Founded in 1964

13226 **American Society of Clinical Pathologists and College of American Pathologist**
American Society of Clinical Pathologists
2100 W Harrison Street
Chicago, IL 60612

312-738-1336; Fax: 312-738-1619

John Ball, Executive VP
4500 Attendees

13227 **American Society of Cytopathology Annual Scientific Meeting**
100 West 10th Street
Suite 605
Wilmington, DE 19801

302-543-6583; Fax: 302-543-6597
asc@cytopathology.org
www.cytopathology.org
Facebook, Twitter, LinkedIn

Christy Myers, Meetings Manager
Elizabeth Jenkins, Manager
Andrew Renshaw, President

Premier event in the field of cytopathology. The objectives of the Annual Meeting are to update cytologists on the current practice of cytopathology, foster research in early diagnosis and effective treatment of human disease and provide a forum for advocacy on behalf of cytologists and their patients.
850 Attendees
Frequency: November
Founded in 1951

13228 **American Society of Directors of Volunteer Services Leadership Training Conf**
1 N Franklin
Chicago, IL 60606

312-223-3937; Fax: 312-442-4575

Audrey Harris, Executive Director

Workshop, banquet, luncheon and 55 exhibits of health care administration equipment, supplies and services.
700 Attendees
Frequency: Annual
Founded in 1964

13229 **American Society of Extra-Corporeal Tech. International Conference**
503 Carlisle Drive
Suite 125
Herndon, VA 20170-4838

703-435-8556; Fax: 703-435-0056
www.amsect.org

Judy Luther, Deputy Executive Director

Seminar, workshop, conference and 75 exhibits relating to the practice of extra-corporeal technology (involving heart and lung machines).
Frequency: Annual

13230 **American Society of Hand Therapists Convention**
Smith, Bucklin and Associates
401 N Michigan Avenue
Chicago, IL 60611-4267

312-644-6610; Fax: 312-245-1082
info@smithbucklin.com
www.smithbucklin.com

Henry S. Givray, President & CEO
C. Albert Koob, Executive Vice President
Carolyn Dolezal, Executive Vice President
Michael L. Payne, Executive Vice President
Cele Fogarty, Vice President - Event Services

Workshop and 40 - 60 exhibits of books, and hand therapy equipment.
800 Attendees
Frequency: Annual
Founded in 1949

13231 **American Society of Health Care Marketing & Public Relations**
1 N Franklin Street
31st Floor
Chicago, IL 60606-3421

773-327-1064; Fax: 312-422-4579

Lauren Barnett, Executive Director

Sixty booths of communications, printing, computer equipment, public relations and fund raising consultants in the health care profession.
600 Attendees
Frequency: September

13232 **American Society of Hematology Annual Meeting & Exposition**
1200 19th Street NW
Suite 300
Washington, DC 24226

202-857-1118; Fax: 202-847-1164

Gail Sparks

Four hundred fifty exhibits of equipment and supplies of interest to hematologists and related professionals.
15000 Attendees
Founded in 1958

13233 **American Society of Human Genetics Annual Meeting**
American Society of Human Genetics
9650 Rockville Pike
Bethesda, MD 20814-3998

301-634-7300; Fax: 301-634-7079
society@ashg.org
www.ashg.org
Facebook, Twitter, LinkedIn

Joann Boughman, PhD, Executive VP
Chuck Windle, Director of Finance/Administration
Karen Goodman, Executive Assistant
Pauline Minhinnett, Dir. of Meetings/Exhibit Management
Mary Shih, Membership Manager

A meeting of researchers, clinicians, trainees and others who share the most recent research findings in human genetics. Includes invited speaker sessions and about 3000 contributed abstracts;

266 to platform and the remainder to poster presentations.
8000 Members
6,000 Attendees
Founded in 1948

13234 **American Society of Nephrology**
American Society of Nephrology
1200 19th Street NW
Suite 300
Washington, DC 20036

202-857-1190; Fax: 202-429-5112

13000 Attendees

13235 **American Society of PeriAnesthesia Nurses**
American Gastroenterological Association
4930 Del Ray Avenue
Bethesda, MD 20814

301-654-2055; Fax: 301-654-5920
member@gastro.org
www.gastro.org

13236 **American Society of Post Anesthesia Nurses Meeting**
Slack
4930 Del Ray Avenue
Bethesda, MD 20814

301-654-2055; Fax: 301-654-5920
member@gastro.org
www.gastro.org

Robert Greenberg, Executive Vp
Michael Stolar, Senior Vp

One hundred seventy exhibits of pharmaceuticals and recovery room supplies.
1700 Attendees
Frequency: Annual
Founded in 1981

13237 **American Society of Psychoprophylaxis in Obstetrics/Lamaze Conference**
Smith, Bucklin and Associates
1200 19th Street NW
Suite 300
Washington, DC 20036-2412

202-861-6416; Fax: 202-429-5112

Leigh McMillan, Senior Convention Director

One hundred exhibitors of educational materials for Lamaze method of prepared childbirth, obstetric equipment and supplies, infant products, breast pumps and more.
500 Attendees
Frequency: Annual
Founded in 1960

13238 **American Society of Transplant Physicians Scientific Meeting**
Slack
4930 Del Ray Avenue
Bethesda, MD 20814

301-654-2055; Fax: 301-654-5920
member@gastro.org
www.gastro.org

Robert Greenberg, Executive Vp
Michael Stolar, Senior Vp

Fifty exhibits of medical supplies and services of interest to physicans and others actively involved with transplantaion.
800 Attendees
Frequency: Annual
Founded in 1981

13239 **American Society of Transplant Surgeons Annual Meeting**
Wright Organization
716 Lee Street
Des Plaines, IL 60016-4515

847-245-5700; Fax: 708-824-0394

Sixty exhibitors of medical equipment, supplies and services relating to renal and cardiac transplants.
750 Attendees
Founded in 1974

13240 **American Society of Tropical Medicine and Hygiene Annual Scientific Meeting**
60 Revere Drive
Suite 500
Northbrook, IL 60062

847-480-9592; Fax: 847-480-9282
info@astmh.org
www.astmh.org

Madhuri Carson, Conference Administrator
Judy DeAcetis, Director
Karen Goraleski, Executive Director

Reception and over 20 exhibits related to tropical medicine and hygiene, including the areas of arboviology, entomology, medicine, nursing and parasitology.
1500 Attendees
Frequency: November
Founded in 1951

13241 **American Speech-Language-Hearing Association Annual Convention**
American Speech- Language Hearing Association
10801 Rockville Pike
Rockville, MD 20852

301-897-5700
800-498-2071; Fax: 301-296-8580
productsales@asha.org
www.asha.org

Mary Harding, Exhibition Manager
Arlene Pietranton, Associate Director
Amy Hasselkus, Associate Director

Four hundred exhibits of medical, educational and testing equipment, plus publications.
12000 Attendees

13242 **American Urological Association Convention**
1000 Corporate Boulevard
Linthicum, MD 21090

410-689-3700; Fax: 410-689-3800
convention@auanet.org
www.auanet.org/

Jane Conway, Advertising & Exhibit Sales
Sarah Hardy, Exhibitor Customer Service
Andrew Niles, Exhibit Operations
Michael T Sheppard, Executive Director
Paul F Schellhammer, Board of Directors President

At the American Urological Association (AUA)'s Annual Meeting there are more than 10,000 urologists and health care professionals in attendance and over 300 exhibitors showcasing their urological products or services-there is no better place to learn about the latest advances in urology.
10000 Attendees
Frequency: Annual

13243 **Annual Clinical Assembly of Osteopathic Specialists**
American College of Osteopathic Surgeons
123 N Henry Street
Alexandria, VA 22314

703-684-0416; Fax: 703-684-3280
info@facos.org
www.facos.org
Facebook, Twitter, LinkedIn

Guy Beaumont, Executive Director
Judith T Mangum, Director Finance
Jennifer B. Colwell, Director of Continuing Education
Sonjya Johnson, Director of Membership Recruitment
Brandon Roberts, Director of Finance
700 Members
Frequency: Annual
Mailing list available for rent

13244 **Annual Conference on Healthcare Marketing**
Alliance for Healthcare Strategy & Marketing
11 S LaSalle Street
Suite 2300
Chicago, IL 60603

312-704-9700; Fax: 312-704-9709
www.shsmd.org

Workshop and social events plus 50 exhibits of marketing communications, health care information lines, strategic planning and more.
600 Attendees
Frequency: Annual
Founded in 1984

13245 **Annual Contact Lens and Primary Care Seminar, MOA**
Michigan Optometric Association
530 W Ionia Street
Suite A
Lansing, MI 48933-1062

517-482-0616; Fax: 517-482-1611
www.themoa.org

William D Dansby CAE, Executive VP
Mark Margolies, Treasurer

Continuing education program and trade show for optometrists and optometric technicians/assistants.
1100 Attendees
Frequency: October, Annually
Founded in 1968

13246 **Annual Convention of American Institute of Ultrasound in Medicine**
American Institute of Ultrasound in Medicine
14750 Sweitzer Lane
Suite 100
Laurel, MD 20707

301-498-4392
800-638-5352; Fax: 301-498-4450
conv_edu@aium.org
www.aium.org

Jenny Clark, Director of Development
Brenda Kinney, Meeting Coordinator
Lisa Shendan, Sales Manager
Frequency: June

13247 **Annual Convention of the American College of Osteopathic Obstetricians**
American College Of Osteopathic Obstetricians
900 Auburn Road
Pontiac, MI 48342

248-332-6360
800-875-6360; Fax: 248-332-4607

Jaki Britton, Administrator

Workshop, reception and banquet as well as exhibits relating to women's health, medical equipment and supplies.
350 Attendees
Frequency: Annual
Founded in 1934

13248 **Annual Critical Care Update**
National Professional Education Institute

2525 Ossen Fort Road
PO Box 118
Glencoe, MO 63068-1107

636-735-5570
800-575-5575; Fax: 561-743-9596
JJMcDaid@aol.com
www.npeinursing.com

Judie McDaid, Exhibitor Relations Manager
Leslie Brock, Registration Manager

The Annual Critical Care Update and Nurse Managers Conference/EXPO provides a fully integrated program dedicated to the continuing education of critical care nurses, nurse managers and other healthcare professionals. Exhibitors showcase their latest healthcare products, pharmaceuticals, services, research and facilities. Knowledge gained in the informative, entertaining EXPO Hall, will influence these nurses' purchasing decisions throughout the year.
1500 Attendees
Frequency: Annual, April
Founded in 1973

13249 Annual Disease Management Congress: Innnovative Strategies

National Managed Health Care Congress
71 2nd Avenue
3rd Floor
Waltham, MA 02154

888-882-2500; Fax: 941-365-0157
www.nmhcc.org

Frances Pratt, Director/Marketing

One hundred exhibits of targeted disease management and services.
1700 Attendees
Frequency: Annual
Founded in 1996

13250 Annual Educational Conference and Exhibits

Society for Healthcare Strategy & Market Dev.
One N Franklin
Chicago, IL 60606

312-422-3840; Fax: 312-422-4579
stratsoc@aha.org

Frequency: September

13251 Annual Meeting & Clinical Lab Exposition

American Association for Clinical Chemistry
900 Seventh St. NW
Suite 400
Washington, DC 20001

202-857-0717
800-892-1400; Fax: 202-887-5093
education@aacc.org
www.aacc.org

Janet B. Kreizman, Chief Executive Officer

Six hundred exhibitors of clincal laboratory equipment, supplies and services for lab automation, information, robotics and OEM products. Seminar, worhshop and conference.
20000 Attendees
Frequency: Annual
Mailing list available for rent: 11000 names at $150 per M

13252 Annual Meeting & Homecare Expo

National Association for Home Care and Hospice
228 7th Street SE
Washington, DC 20003

202-547-7424; Fax: 202-547-3540
webmaster@nahc.org
www.nahc.org

Gathering of Home Care and Hospice professionals.
4000 Attendees
Frequency: October

13253 Annual Meeting of the American Association on Mental Retardation

American Association on Mental Retardation
444 N Capitol Street NW
Suite 846
Washington, DC 20001-1512

202-387-1968
800-424-3688; Fax: 202-387-2193
dcroser@aamr.org
www.aamr.org

Doreen Croser, Executive Director
Paul Aitken, Director Of Finance Administration
2000 Attendees
Frequency: Annual, May

13254 Annual Meeting of the Microscopy Society of America

Bostrom Corporation
230 E Ohio
Suite 400
Chicago, IL 60611-3265

312-644-1527
800-538-3672; Fax: 312-644-8557
www.msa.microscopy.com

Judy Janes, Manager

Microscopes and related supplies of interest to medical, biological, metalurgical, and polymer research scientists, technicians and physicists interested in instrument design and improvement.
Frequency: Annual, August

13255 Annual National Managed Health Care Congress

71 2nd Avenue
3rd Floor
Waltham, MA 02154

888-882-2500; Fax: 941-365-0157
www.nmhcc.org

Seminar, workshop, conference, and 600 exhibits of services and products dedicated to improving the quality of health care.
10000 Attendees
Frequency: Annual
Founded in 1989

13256 Annual PPO Forum

American Assn of Preferred Provider Organizations
222 South First Street
Suite 303
Louisville, KY 40202

502-403-1122; Fax: 502-403-1129
www.aappo.org

Melissa Cox, Event Coordinator
Michael Taddeo, Chairperson
Keith Vangeison, Vice-Chairman
Kenneth Hamm, Treasurer
William Ross, Secretary
Frequency: San Diego
Founded in 1983

13257 Annual Scientific & Clinical Congress

American Association of Clinical Endocrinologists
245 Riverside Avenue
Suite 200
Jacksonville, FL 32202

904-353-7878; Fax: 904-353-8185
www.aace.com

Paul Markowski, Chief Executive Officer
Tom Conway, Chief Financial Officer
Michele Lentz, Chief Strategic Alliance Officer
Elizabeth A. Lepkowski, MATD, Chief Learning Officer
Robin Shelly, Chief Marketing Officer

Clinical endocrinologists and endocrine surgeons gather for meeting and exhibits of equipment, supplies and services.
2000 Attendees
Frequency: Annual, April

13258 Annual Scientific Meeting of the Gerontological Society of America

Gerontological Society of America
1030 15th Street NW
Suite 250
Washington, DC 20005

202-842-1275; Fax: 202-842-1150
www.geron.org

Carol Schutz, Executive Director

13259 Applied Ergonomics Conference

Institute of Industrial Engineers
3597 Parkway Lane
Suite 200
Norcross, GA 30097

770-449-0461
800-494-0460; Fax: 770-263-8532
webmaster@iienet.org

Carol LeBlanc, Conference Manager

An exclusive event for ergonomists, engineers, and safety professionals. The conference focuses on how companies have successfully implemented programs that provide excellent return on their ergonomics investment.
800 Attendees
Frequency: March
Founded in 1998

13260 Arthroscopy Association of North America Annual Meeting

6300 N River Road
#104
Rosemont, IL 60018
847-292-2262; Fax: 847-292-2268
www.aana.org

Holly Albert, Meetings Manager
Edward Goss, Executive Director

Seminar, reception and 100 exhibits of video and arthroscopy equipment, braces, books and more.
1000 Attendees

13261 Assisted Living Expo

VNU Expositions
Dulles International Airport
PO Box 17413
Washington, DC 20041

703-318-0300
800-765-7616; Fax: 703-318-8833

Displays of assisted living information and equipment.

13262 Association for Applied Psychophysiology & Biofeedback Annual Meeting

Association for Applied Psychophysiology
10200 W 44th Avenue
Suite 304
Wheat Ridge, CO 80033

303-228-8436
800-477-8892; Fax: 303-422-8894

info@aapb.org
www.aapb.org

Tina Watkins, Meetings Manager
Francine Butler, Treasurer
Fred Schaffer, Treasurer

Exhibits of biofeedback equipment, supplies, and training programs, medical supplies and software, as well as annual meeting.
500 Attendees
Frequency: March
Founded in 1969

13263 **Association for Healthcare Philanthropy Annual Int'l Educational Conference**
Association for Healthcare Philanthropy
313 Park Avenue
Suite 400
Falls Church, VA 22046

703-532-6243; Fax: 703-532-7170
ahp@ahp.org
www.ahp.org

Conference and 120 exhibits with information about equipment and services for the fundraising and helatcare development community, including computer software, recognition gifts, direct mail companies, executive recriuters, special events and more.
900 Attendees
Frequency: September

13264 **Association for Professionals in Infection Control & Epidemiology**
Association for Professionals in Infection Control
1275 K Street NW
Suite 1000
Washington, DC 20005-4006

202-789-1890
800-650-9570; Fax: 202-789-1899
apicinfo@apic.org
www.apic.org

Christine J Nutty, President
Carolyn E Jackson, Secretary
Katrina Crist, CEO
Jacqueline Manson, Accounting
Sara Haywood, Education

Workshop, banquet, reception and 150 exhibits of infection control products, pharmaceuticals, disinfectants, soaps, dataprocessing software, housekeeping equipment and supplies.
2700 Attendees
Frequency: Annual
Founded in 1974

13265 **Association for Worksite Health Promotion Annual International Conference**
60 Revere Drive
Suite 500
Northbrook, IL 60062-1577

847-480-9574; Fax: 847-480-9282
www.awhp.org

Liz Freyn, Conference Manager

One hundred twenty two booths of information and supplies to promote and develop quality programs of health and fitness in business and industry. Seminar, workshop, conference, tours and luncheon.
950 Attendees
Founded in 1974

13266 **Association of Behavioral Healthcare Management Convention**
60 Revere Drive
Suite 500
Northbrook, IL 60062

847-480-9626; Fax: 847-480-9282

Exhibits related to the administation of services for the emotionally disturbed, mentally ill, mentally retarded, developmentally disabled, and those with substance abuse problems.
Frequency: Annual

13267 **Association of Pediatric Oncology Nurses Annual Conference**
Association of Pediatric Nurses
4700 W Lake Avenue
Glenview, IL 60025-1485

847-375-4724; Fax: 847-375-4777
www.apon.org

Pamela Asfahani, Product Manager
Elizabeth Sherman, senior marketing Manager

Exhibits on caring for children who have cancer.

13268 **Association of Rehabilitation Nurses Annual Educational Conference**
4700 W Lake Avenue
Glenview, IL 60025-1485

847-375-4710
800-229-7530; Fax: 847-375-4777

Conference, educational session, workshop and 225 exhibits of rehabilitational aids and supplies, medical equipment, hospitals and rehbilitation facilities and publications of interest to rehabilitation nurses.
2300 Attendees
Founded in 1974

13269 **Benefits Health Care New York Show**
Flagg Management
353 Lexington Avenue
New York, NY 10016

212-286-0333; Fax: 212-286-0086
flaggmgmnt@msn.com
www.flaggmgmt.com

Russell Flagg, President

Sponsored by Employee Benefit News, the conference will focus on the recent health care reform, as well as coping with the economic downturn. Human resources, personnel, administration and training marketplace. HRMS, systems and services 250 exhibits. $295.
Frequency: Annual
Mailing list available for rent

13270 **Building Bridges VII**
American Association of Health Plans
1129 20th Street NW
Washington, DC 20036

202-778-3200; Fax: 202-778-8506

13271 **CHPA Annual Executive Conference**
Consumer Health Care Products Association
900 19th St NW
Suite 700
Washington, DC 20006-2105

202-429-9260; Fax: 202-223-6835
www.chpa-info.org

Paul L. Sturman, Chair

Join top healthcare executives from across the nation and participate in high-level education sessions focused on the industry's rapidly shifting environment.

13272 **Center for School Mental Health Assistance National Convention**
Exhibit Promotions Plus
11620 Vixens Path
Ellicott City, MD 21042

301-596-3028; Fax: 410-997-0764

Harve C Horowitz, President

Supports school health, mental health professionals by offering ongoing consutation to address administrative, clinical and systems issues relevant to school health services.
Frequency: October

13273 **Clinical Laboratory Expo**
AACC; c/o Scherago International
11 Penn Plaza
Suite 1003
New York, NY 10001

212-643-1750; Fax: 212-643-1758

Tony Maiorino, Vice President
20000 Attendees
Frequency: July-August

13274 **Clinical Laboratory Management Association Annual Conference & Exhibition**
Clinical Laboratory Management Association
989 Old Eagle School Road
Suite 815
Wayne, PA 19087

610-995-9580; Fax: 610-995-9568
info@clma.org
www.clma.org

Dana Procsal, VP
Ruth Nelson, Director of Operations

CLMA-ASCP have combined forces to offer the largest, most comprehensive laboratory conference and exhibition ever, specifically designed for laboratory professionals at all levels.
4800 Attendees
Frequency: June

13275 **Clinical and Scientific Congress of the Int'l Anesthesia Research Society**
International Anesthesia Research Society
2 Summit Park Drive
Suite 140
Cleveland, OH 44131

216-642-1124; Fax: 216-642-1127
info@iars.org
www.iars.org

Donald S Prough, Chair
Hugo Van Aken, Chairman
1200 Attendees
Frequency: March

13276 **Congress on Invitro Biology**
Society for Invitro Biology
9315 Lango Drive W
Suite 255
Lango, MD 20774

301-324-5054
800-741-7476; Fax: 301-324-5057
sivb@sivb.org
www.sivb.org

Marietta Ellis, Managing Director
Richard Heller, Treasurer

Focus on issues pertinent to the Vertebrate, Invertebrate, and Cellular Toxicology Sections and will give participants a unique learning experience on animal cell culture and biotechnology.
1,000 Attendees
Frequency: June

13277 **Consumer Directed Health Care Conference**
Po Box 448, East Cary Street
Suite 102
Richmond, VA 23219

804-266-7422; Fax: 804-225-7458
www.galen.org

Carlotta Farmer, Director of Programming
Frequency: December, Washington

13278 **Digestive Disease Week Meeting & Exhibition**
American Gastroenterological Association

4930 Del Ray Avenue
Bethesda, MD 20814

301-654-2055; Fax: 301-652-3890
member@gastro.org
www.gastro.org

14000 Attendees
Frequency: March

13279 **Distribution Management Conference & Expo**
Healthcare Distribution Alliance
900 N Glebe Road
Suite 1000
Arlington, VA 22203

703-787-0000; Fax: 703-812-5282
www.hda.org

Chester Davis, Jr., President/CEO
Ann W. Bittman, EVP/COO
Elizabeth A. Gallenagh, General Counsel/SVP, Supply Chain

Provides the latest information on the most important topics affecting healthcare distribution.
Frequency: Annual

13280 **Drug Discovery Technology**
Hynes Convention Center
900 Boylston Street
Boston, MA 02115

617-954-2000
800-845-8800; Fax: 617-954-2125
info@mccahome.com

2000 Attendees
Frequency: August

13281 **Emergency Nurses Association Scientific Assembly & Exhibits**
Emergency Nurses Association
915 Lee Street
Des Plaines, IL 60016-6569

847-460-4100
800-900-9659; Fax: 847-460-4001
webmaster@ena.org
www.ena.org

David Westman, CEO
Anita Dorr, Co-Founder
Kathy Szumanski, Director
3500 Attendees
Frequency: Annual, September

13282 **Endocrine Society Annual Meeting**
Scherago International
11 Penn Plaza
Suite 1003
New York, NY 10001

212-643-1750; Fax: 212-643-1758

6500 Attendees

13283 **Experimental Biology**
FASEB/OSMC
9650 Rockville Pike
Bethesda, MD 20814

301-634-7100; Fax: 301-634-7014
info@faseb.org
www.faseb.org/meetings

Pauline Minhinnett, Meeting Manager
Jean Lash, Marketing Manager
Jacquelyn Roberts, Marketing Manager
David Craven, Executive Director
12M Attendees
Frequency: April

13284 **FASEB Conference Federation for American Societies for Experimental Biology**
FASEB/OSMC
9650 Rockville Pike
Bethesda, MD 20814

301-634-7100; Fax: 301-634-7014
info@faseb.org
www.faseb.org/meetings

Jean Lash, Exhibit Manager
Marcella Jackson, Marketing Manager
Jacquelyn Roberts, Marketing Manager
David Craven, Executive Director
900 Attendees
Frequency: March

13285 **Fall Symposium**
American College of Emergency Physicians
PO Box 619911
Dallas, TX 75261

972-550-0911; Fax: 972-580-2816

325 Attendees

13286 **Federation of Hospitals Public Policy Conference & Business Exposition**
Federation of American Health Systems
801 Pennsylvania Avenue NW
Suite 245
Washington, DC 20004-2604

202-624-1500; Fax: 202-737-6462
info@fah.org
www.fah.org

Bonnie Moneypenny, Senior VP Administrative Services
Letitia Faison-Mahoney, Controller

The conference brings together hospital executives and leading policymakers each Spring for important discussions. It also affords an important opportunity for suppliers to meet face-to-face with hospital managers and buyers.
Frequency: Annual, March
Founded in 1966

13287 **Fire-Rescue International**
International Association of Fire Chiefs
4025 Fair Ridge Drive
Suite 300
Fairfax, VA 22033

703-273-0911; Fax: 703-273-9363
lyonkers@iafc.org
www.iafc.org

Mark Light, Executive Director & CEO
Lisa Yonkers, Director, Conference & Education
Jason Nauman, Education & Learning Manager
Leanne Shroeder, Conference Manager

Conference and exposition of the fire service industry.
Frequency: Annual

13288 **Food & Nutrition Conference & Expo**
American Dietetic Association
120 South Riverside Plaza
Suite 2000
Chicago, IL 60606

312-899-0040
800-877-1600; Fax: 312-899-0008
gandruch@eatright.org
www.eatright.org
Facebook, Twitter

Greg Andruch, Exhibits Manager
Allison MacMunn, Public Relations Manager
Donna Wickstrom, Manager
Karen Didriksen, Purchasing Manager

More than 8,000 professionals come to the Food & Nutrition Conference & Expo for the latest technological and nutritional advancements. This is the premier selling opportunity in the fields of nutrition and food service management. The event continues to expand-attracting a wider audience of professionals, including hotel and restarurant managers, sports, health and nutrition professionals and executive chefs.
8000 Attendees
Frequency: September, Pennsylvania
Circulation: 65000

13289 **HCEA Annual Meeting**
Healthcare Convention & Exhibitors Association
1100 Johnson Ferry Rd NE
Suite 300
Atlanta, GA 30342-1733

404-252-3663; Fax: 404-252-0774
hcea@kellencompany.com
www.hcea.org

Eric Allen, Executive Vice President
Jackie Beaulieu, Associate Director
Michelle Hall, Staff Associate
Carol Wilson, Meetings Director
Frank Skinner, Executive Director

Cost varies; approximately 50 booths; 800 attendees.
200 Attendees
Frequency: Annual
Founded in 1930
Mailing list available for rent: 1400 names

13290 **HCEA Marketing Summit**
Healthcare Convention & Exhibitors Association
1100 Johnson Ferry Rd NE
Suite 300
Atlanta, GA 30342-1733

404-252-3663; Fax: 404-252-0774
hcea@kellencompany.com
www.hcea.org

Eric Allen, Executive Vice President
Jackie Beaulieu, Associate Director
Michelle Hall, Staff Associate
Carol Wilson, Meetings Director
Frank Skinner, Executive Director

Cost varies; no exhibits; 200-250 attendees.
200 Attendees
Frequency: Annual
Founded in 1930
Mailing list available for rent: 1400 names

13291 **HDA Business and Leadership Conference**
Healthcare Distribution Alliance
900 N Glebe Road
Suite 1000
Arlington, VA 22203

703-787-0000; Fax: 703-812-5282
www.hda.org

Chester Davis, Jr., President/CEO
Ann W. Bittman, EVP/COO
Elizabeth Gallenagh, General Counsel/SVP, Supply Chain

Provides a unique opportunity for senior-level retailer and supplier member executives to interact and discuss strategic issues.

13292 **HIDA Streamlining Healthcare Expo and Business Exchange**
Health Industry Distributors Association
310 Montgomery Street
Alexandria, VA 22314

703-549-4432
rowan@hida.org
www.hida.org

Matthew J. Rowan, President/CEO
Elizabeth Hilla, SVP
Linda Rouse O'Neil, VP, Govt. Affairs
Balvinder Bains, VP, Finance & Operations

Includes education sessions, training rotation, and the best-attended trade showin the industry.
Frequency: September

13293 **HMFA's ANI: The Healthcare Finance Conference**
Healthcare Finance Management Association
3 Westbrook Corporate Center
Suite 600
Westchester, IL 60154
708-531-9600; Fax: 708-531-0032
www.hfma.org/events/ani
Access to education programs, speaker sessions and hundreds of vendors, as well as networking and best practices sharing opportunities.
Mailing list available for rent

13294 **HMFA's Virtual Healthcare Finance Conference & Career Fair**
Healthcare Finance Management Association
3 Westbrook Corporate Center
Suite 600
Westchester, IL 60154
708-531-9600
800-252-4362; Fax: 708-531-0032
virtualhcfc@hfma.org
www.hfma.org
Facebook, Twitter, LinkedIn
Access live education programs and on-demand sessions from your office. Keynote speakers and presenters, and a virtual exhibit hall and career fair.
39000 Members
Founded in 1991
Mailing list available for rent

13295 **Healthcare Information and Management Systems Society**
HIMSS/Healthcare Information and Management
230 E Ohio
Suite 500
Chicago, IL 60611
312-664-4467; Fax: 312-664-6143

13296 **IACM Conference**
International Association for Cannabinoid Medicine
Am Mildenweg 6
59602 Ruethen
Germany
+49-2952-9708571; Fax: +49-2952-902651
info@cannabis-med.org
www.cannabis-med.org
Twitter
Franjo Grotenhermen, Executive Director
Michael Krawitz, Patient Representative, USA
Alison Myrden, Patient Representative, Canada
A conference on cannabinoids in medicine featuring programs, lectures, and poster presentations.
Frequency: Biennial
Founded in 2000

13297 **IAHCSMM Annual Conference**
213 W Institute Place
Suite 307
Chicago, IL 60610-3195
312-440-0078
800-962-8274; Fax: 312-440-9474
mailbox@iahcsmm.com
www.iahcsmm.com
Betty Hanna, Executive Director
Marilyn T. Conde, Secretary/Treasurer
Bruce T. Bird, President
David Jagrosse, Executive Board Member
David Narance, Executive Board Member
Internationational Association of Healthcare Central Service Material Management - 125 EXHIBITORSlication separates supervisors/directors from technicians.
600+ Attendees
Frequency: Annual

13298 **IAHSS Annual General Meeting**
International Association for Healthcare Security
PO Box 5038
Glendale Heights, IL 60139
888-353-0990
888-353-0990; Fax: 630-529-4139
info@iahss.org
www.iahss.org
Bryan Warren, President
Evelyn Meserve, Executive Director
Jim Stankevich, President-Elect
Lisa Pryse, VP/Treasurer
Bryan Warren, VP/Secretary
Non-profit organization of healthcare security and safety executives from around the world. The association works to improve and professionalize security and safety in healthcare facilities through the exchange of information and experiences among members.
1700 Members
Founded in 1968

13299 **INTERPHEX - The World's Forum for the Pharmaceutical Industry**
Reed Exhibition Companies
383 Main Avenue
Norwalk, CT 06851
203-840-4800; Fax: 203-840-4804
Chet Burchett, President
11000 Attendees

13300 **Infusion Nurses Society**
Infusion Nurses Society
315 Norwood Park South
Norwood, MA 02062
781-440-9408
800-694-0298; Fax: 781-440-9409
ins@ins1.org
www.ins1.org
Facebook, Twitter, LinkedIn
Britt Meyer, President
Mary Alexander, CEO
Chris Hunt, Executive VP
Michaelle Frost, Accounting Manager
Chelsea McCue, Accounting Coordinator
7000 Members
1000 Attendees
Frequency: Annual
Founded in 1973
Mailing list available for rentat $200 per M

13301 **Infusion Nurses Society Annual Meeting**
Infusion Nurses Society
315 Norwood Park South
Norwood, MA 02062
781-440-9408
800-694-0298; Fax: 781-440-9409
ins@ins1.org
www.ins1.org
Facebook, Twitter, LinkedIn
Cora Vizcarra, President
Mary Alexander, CEO
Chris Hunt, Executive VP
Michaelle Frost, Accounting Manager
Chelsea McCue, Accounting Coordinator
Mailing list available for rentat $200 per M

13302 **International Conference on Head and Neck Cancer**
American Head and Neck Society
1805 Ardmore Boulevard
Pittsburgh, PA 15221
412-243-5156; Fax: 412-243-5160
Robin Wagner, Show Manager
Sixty exhibits of equipment and supplies, conference, luncheon and reception.
2,500 Attendees
Frequency: August

13303 **International Congress on Ambulatory Surgery Conference**
Hynes Convention Center
900 Boylston Street
Boston, MA 02115
617-954-2000; Fax: 617-954-2125
info@mccahome.com
1500 Attendees
Frequency: May

13304 **International Society for Magnetic Resonance in Medicine**
International Society for Magnetic Resonance
2118 Milvia Street
Suite 201
Berkeley, CA 94704
510-841-1899; Fax: 510-841-2340
info@ismrm.org
www.ismrm.org
Frequency: May

13305 **International Vision Exposition & Conference**
Association Expositions & Services
383 Main Avenue
Norwalk, CT 06851
203-840-4820
800-811-7151; Fax: 203-840-4824
visionexpo.com
Eileen Baird
Ed Gallo, Sales Manager
Tracy Flacherty, Marketing Director
As the most comprehensive vision care show and conference in the US, International Vision Expo is where today's eye care professionals meet, learn and conduct business. International vision expo draws optical professionals from all career path including: Ophthalmologist, Optometrist, Opticians, Lab Personnel, Practice managers, Ophthalmic Medical Personnel, Retailers, Manufacturing Executives, Import Export buyers, Ophthalmic Assistants, Optical Interns and more.
15000 Attendees
Frequency: March/September

13306 **Listening and Spoken Language Symposium**
Alexander Graham Bell Association
3417 Volta Place, NW
Washington, DC 20007
202-337-5220
TTY: 202-337-5221; Fax: 202-337-8314
info@agbell.org
www.agbell.org
Facebook, Twitter, LinkedIn, YouTube, Instagram
Emilio Alonso-Mendoza, Chief Executive Officer
Lisa Chutjian, Chief Development Officer
Susan Boswell, Director of Communications
Robin Bailey, Programs Specialist
Judy Harrison, Director of Programs
An opportunity to learn, network, and connect with colleagues from all over the world. Learn about the latest research and innovative practices.
Frequency: Annual
Founded in 2005

13307 **Managed Care Institute & Display Forum**
American Association of Health Plans
601 Pennsylvania Avenue, NW
South Building, Suite 500
Washington, DC 20004
202-778-3200; Fax: 202-331-7487
ahip@ahip.org
www.aahp.org
Twitter
Michael Abbott, President
William Cameron, Chairman
Two hundred exhibits by suppliers to the managed health care industry, conference and reception.
2000 Attendees
Frequency: Annual
Founded in 1986

13308 **Managed Care Law Conference**
American Association of Health Plans
1129 20th Street NW
Washington, DC 20036
202-778-3200; Fax: 202-778-8506

13309 **Medical Design & Manufacturing Conference & Exhibition West**
Canon Communications
11444 W Olympic Boulevard
Los Angeles, CA 90064
310-445-4200; Fax: 310-996-9499
www.cancom.com
Diane O'Conner, Trade Show Director
Dan Cutrone, Show Marketing Manager
Devoted to the design, development, and manufacture of medical products. Visitors can preview the latest advances in medical-grade materials, assembly components, machinery, electronics, systems, software, services and more. Held at the Anaheim Convention Center in Anaheim, California.
8,500 Attendees
Frequency: January

13310 **Medical Design and Manufacturing Minneapolis Conference**
Canon Communications
11444 W Olympic Boulevard
Los Angeles, CA 90064
310-445-4200; Fax: 310-996-9499
www.mdm-minneapolis.com
Diane O'Connor, Trade Show Director
Dan Cutrone, Show Marketing Manager
Four hundred thirty three exhibitors in 52,500 square feet of the Minneapolis Convention Center. Medical supplies and information promotional opportunities in show directory, web site advertising, conference program, sponsorships and product previews.
3374 Attendees
Frequency: October
Founded in 1994

13311 **Medical Equipment Design & Technology Exhibition & Conference**
Canon Communications
11444 W Olympic Boulevard
Los Angeles, CA 90064-1549
310-445-4200; Fax: 310-445-4299
www.medtecshow.com
Diane O'Conner, Trade Show Director
Dan Cutrone, Show Marketing Manager
Devoted to the design, development and manufacture of medical products. Visitors can preview the latest advances in medical-grade materials, assembly components, electronics, machinery, software, systems, services and more. Held at the RAI International Exhibition and Congress Center in Amsterdam, Netherlands.
2231 Attendees
Frequency: October

13312 **Medical Group Management Association**
Medical Group Management Association
104 Inverness Terrace E
Englewood, CO 80112-5306
303-991-1111
800-275-6462; Fax: 877-329-6462
infocenter@mgma.com
www.mgma.com
William Jessee, President, Chief Executive Officer
Anders Gilberg, senior Vice President
Natalie Jamieson, Administrative Assistant
3800 Attendees
Frequency: Annual, October

13313 **Medical Meetings**
Penton Media Inc
249 W. 17th St., third floor
New York, NY 10011
847-763-9504
866-505-7173
shatch@meetingsnet.com
www.meetingsnet.com
Susan Hatch, Editor
Betsy Bair, Director, Content and Media
Melissa Fromento, Group Publisher
Regina McGee, Religious Conference Manager
Susan Hatch, Executive Editor
International guide for health care and meeting planners.
Cost: $57.00
106 Pages
Circulation: 12000
Founded in 1989
Printed in 4 colors on glossy stock

13314 **Medicare and Medicaid Conference**
American Association of Health Plans
1129 20th Street NW
Washington, DC 20036
202-778-3200; Fax: 202-778-8506

13315 **Medtrade West**
VNU Expositions
Dallas International Airport
PO Box 17413
Washington, DC 20041
703-318-0300; Fax: 703-318-8833

13316 **Medtrade/Comtrade**
VNU Communications
1130 Hightower Trail
Atlanta, GA 30350
770-569-1540; Fax: 703-318-8833

13317 **NCPA Rx Exposition**
NCPA
100 Daingerfield Road
Alexandria, VA 22314
703-683-8200
800-544-7447; Fax: 703-683-3619
www.ncpanet.org
Donnie Calhoun, President
B. Douglas Hoey, Chief Executive Officer
2000 Attendees
Frequency: Annual, October
Mailing list available for rent

13318 **National Athletic Trainers Association**
National Athletic Trainers
2952 Stemmons Freeway
#200
Dallas, TX 75247
214-637-6282; Fax: 214-637-2206
webmaster@nata.org
www.nata.org
Charles Kimmel, President
Charles Rozanski, VP
Mailing list available for rent

13319 **National Convention: Opticians Association of America**
Opticians Association of America
10341 Democracy Lane
Fairfax, VA 22030
703-916-8856; Fax: 703-691-8929

13320 **National Council on the Aging Annual Conference**
National Council on the Aging
1901 L Street Nw
4th Fl
Washington, DC 20036
202-479-1200; Fax: 202-479-0735
info@ncoa.org
www.ncoa.org
Facebook, Twitter
James Firman, President/CEO
Richard Browdie, Chair
Andrew Greene, Treasurer
Jay Greenberg, Senior Vice President
Donna Whitt, Senior Vice President
Mailing list available for rent

13321 **National Managed Healthcare Congress**
Po Box 3685
Boston, MA 02441-3685
888-670-8200; Fax: 941-365-2507
Frequency: March Atlanta

13322 **National Medical Association Annual Convention & Scientific Assembly**
National Medical Association
8403 Colesville Road
Suite 920
Silver Spring, MD 20910
703-631-6200
800-564-4220; Fax: 703-654-6931
www.nmanet.org
Facebook, Twitter
June LaMountain, Exhibit Sales Account Manager
Rahn K. Bailey, President
C. Freeman, Treasurer
Darryl R. Matthews, Executive Director
Promotes the collective interests of physicians and patients of African descent. NMA carries out this mission by serving the collective voice of physicians of African descent and a leading force for purity in medicine, elimination of health disparities and optimal health.
3000 Attendees
Frequency: August
Founded in 1895

13323 **National Safety Council Congress Expo**
National Safety Council
1121 Spring Lake Drive
Itasca, IL 60143
630-775-2213
800-621-7619; Fax: 630-285-0798
customerservice@nsc.org
www.congress.nsc.org
Nancy Gavin, Expo Manager
Bill Steinbach, Exhibit Sales
Janet Froetscher, CEO

Annual event for safety, health and the environment.
16000 Attendees
Frequency: September

13324 **National Society for Histotechnology Symposium/Convention**
National Society for Histotechnology
8850 Stanford Blvd
Suite 2900
Columbia, MD 21045
443-535-4060; Fax: 443-535-4055
histo@nsh.org
www.nsh.org
Aubrey M J Wanner, Meeting Manager
Carrie Diamond, Executive Director
Kerry Crabb, President
Kristin Ramseur, Administrative Assistant
Beth Wise, Administrative Assistant
National gathering for all chapters, advancing professional growth through educational sessions and the exchange of ideas.
1500 Attendees
Frequency: October
Founded in 1964

13325 **Neocon South**
Designfest/NeoCon South
200 World Trade Center Chicago
Chicago, IL 60654
312-527-7999; Fax: 312-527-7782
http://www.neocon.com
Chris Kennedy, President

13326 **Neocon West**
Designfest/Neocon South
200 World Trade Center
Chicago, IL 60654
312-527-7999; Fax: 312-527-7782
http://www.neocon.com
Chris Kennedy, President

13327 **Neocon's World Trade Fair**
Design/Neocon South
200 World Trade Center
Chicago, IL 60654
312-527-7999; Fax: 312-527-7782
Chris Kennedy, President

13328 **Northwest Urological Society**
Northwest Urological Society
914 164th Street Se
Suite B-12 #145
Mill Creek, WA 98012
866-800-3118; Fax: 800-808-4749
www.nwus.org
S Larry Goldenberg, President
Martin Gleave, VP
180 Attendees

13329 **Nurse Managers Update**
National Professional Education Institute
2525 Ossen Fort Road
PO Box 118
Glencoe, MO 63068-1107
636-735-5570
800-575-5575; Fax: 561-743-9596
JJMcDaid@aol.com
www.npeinursing.com
Judie McDaid, Exhibitor Relations Manager
Leslie Brock, Registration Manager
The Nurse Managers Update and Critical Care Conference/EXPO provides a fully integrated program dedicated to the continuing education of critical care nurses, nurse managers and other healthcare professionals. Exhibitors showcase their latest healthcare products, pharmaceuticals, services, research and facilities. Knowledge gained in the informative, entertaining EXPO Hall, will influence these nurses' purchasing decisions throughout the year.
1500 Attendees
Frequency: Annual, April
Founded in 1989

13330 **Obesity Medicine**
Obesity Medicine Association
101 University Boulevard
Suite 330
Denver, CO 80206
303-770-2526
877-266-6834; Fax: 303-779-4834
info@obesitymedicine.org
obesitymedicine.org
Ethan Lazarus, MD, FOMA, President
Claudia Randall, MBA, Executive Director
Christin Hammond, MBA, Director, Marketing
Spring conference of the Obesity Medicine Association.
Founded in 1950

13331 **Optometry's Meeting**
American Optometric Association
243 N Lindbergh Boulevard
Saint Louis, MO 63141
314-993-8575; Fax: 314-993-8919
www.iaccnorthamerica.org
Tom Bolman, Executive VP
Jerry White, Director of Education
Main exhibits: optometric equipment, supplies and services.
8000 Attendees
Frequency: June

13332 **Osteopathic Physicians & Surgeons Annual Convention**
Osteopathic Physicians & Surgeons of California
455 Capitol Mall
Suite 230
Sacramento, CA 95814
916-561-0724
Kathleen Creason, Executive Director

13333 **Overcoming Obesity**
Obesity Medicine Association
101 University Boulevard
Suite 330
Denver, CO 80206
303-770-2526
877-266-6834; Fax: 303-779-4834
info@obesitymedicine.org
obesitymedicine.org
Ethan Lazarus, MD, FOMA, President
Claudia Randall, MBA, Executive Director
Christin Hammond, MBA, Director, Marketing
Fall conference of the Obesity Medicine Association.
Founded in 1950

13334 **Pacific Dermatological Association**
Pacific Dermatological Association
575 Market Street
Suite 2125
San Francisco, CA 94105
415-927-5729
888-388-8815; Fax: 415-764-4915
www.pacificderm.org
Edgar F. Fincher, President
Catherine Ramsay, VP
Anita Gilliam, Secretary/Treasurer
Kent Lindeman, Executive Director
Ben Hsu, Executive Committee
Exclusively for education, scientific and charitable purposes. Provides opportunities for exchange of information and advancement of knowledge of dermatology among physicians within the membership area.
Frequency: August
Founded in 1948
Mailing list available for rent

13335 **Pacific Northwest Radiological Society**
Pacific Northwest Radiological Society
2033 6th Avenue
Suite 1100
Seattle, WA 98121
206-441-9762
800-552-0612; Fax: 206-441-5863
lmk@wsma.org
www.pnwrs.org
Gautham Reddy, President
Eric Stern, VP
Pauline Proulx, Association Executive
Jason Clement, Secretary/Treasurer

13336 **Pediatric Academic Societies Annual Meeting**
Society for Pediatric Research
9303 New Trails Dr.
Suite 350
The Woodlands, TX 77381
346-890-9717
info@pasmeeting.org
www.societyforpediatricresearch.org/events
Eileen G. Fenton, Executive Director
Belinda Thomas, PAS Education Program Director
Cynthia Bearer, Managing Editor, Pediatric Research
Antonio Moreno, Information Technology Director
An international gathering of researchers, academics, clinical care providers, and community practitioners to improve the health and well-being of children worldwide.
4500 Attendees
Frequency: Annual, Spring

13337 **Pediatric Perfusion**
American Society of ExtraCorporeal Technology
2209 Dickens Road
Richmond, VA 23230-2005
804-565-6310; Fax: 804-282-0090
judyr@amsect.org
www.amsect.org
Stewart Hinckley, Executive Director
Donna Pandarvis, Manager
Michael Troike, Government Relations Chairman
Kimberly Robertson, CPA, Controller
Greg Leasure, Membership Services
2000 Members
100 Attendees
Frequency: Bi-Annual
Founded in 1964
Mailing list available for rent

13338 **Perfusion Safety & Best Practices in Perfusion**
American Society of ExtraCorporeal Technology
2209 Dickens Road
Richmond, VA 23230-2005
804-532-2323; Fax: 804-282-0090
judyr@amsect.org
www.amsect.org
Stewart Hinckley, Executive Director
Donna Pandarvis, Manager
Michael Troike, Government Relations Chairman
Kimberly Robertson, CPA, Controller
Greg Leasure, Membership Services
2000 Members
150 Attendees

Frequency: Annual/October
Founded in 1964
Mailing list available for rent

13339 **Policy Conference**
American Association of Health Plans
1129 20th Street NW
Washington, DC 20036
202-778-3200; Fax: 202-778-8506

13340 **Postgraduate Assembly in Anesthesiology**
New York State Society of Anesthesiologists
85 5th Avenue
8th Floor
New York, NY 10003
212-867-7140; Fax: 212-867-7153
www.nyssa-pga.org
Kurt G Becker, Executive Director
David Wlody, Director
Annual conference for anesthesia professionals, held each December in New York City.
7000 Attendees
Frequency: December

13341 **Primary Care Update**
Interstate Postgraduate Medical Association
PO Box 5474
Madison, WI 53705
608-231-9045
866-446-3424; Fax: 877-292-4489
cmehelp@ipmameded.org
www.ipmameded.org
Designed to enhance your practice and improve the patient's health.
Frequency: November

13342 **Radiological Society of North America's Scientific Assembly**
Radiological Society of North America
2021 Spring Road
Suite 600
Oak Brook, IL 60521
630-571-5424
62000 Attendees

13343 **SCCM Educational & Scientific Symposium**
Society of Critical Care Medicine
8101 E Kaiser Blouevard
Anaheim, CA 92808
714-282-6000
2500 Attendees

13344 **SHAPE America National Convention & Expo**
Society of Health and Physical Educators
1900 Association Drive
Reston, VA 20191
703-476-3400
800-213-7193; Fax: 703-476-9527
membership@shapeamerica.org
convention.shapeamerica.org
Stephanie A. Morris, Chief Executive Officer
National convention and exposition that features many exhibits focusing on products, services and equipment within the fields of health, physical education, recreation and dance.
5000 Attendees
Frequency: Annual
Mailing list available for rent

13345 **SIIM Annual Meeting & Conference**
Society for Imaging Informatics in Medicine
19440 Golf Vista Plaza
Suite 330
Leesburg, VA 20176-8264
703-723-0432; Fax: 703-723-0415
www.siimweb.org
Facebook, Twitter, LinkedIn
Andrea Saris, Meetings Director
Provides a vibrant community and collegial forum for learning and networking with peers and thought leaders in the imaging informatics field. This is where physicians, health care IT decision-makers, PACS administrators, and vendors from around the world come together to explore the emerging field of informatics.
2000 Members
1800 Attendees
Frequency: June
Founded in 1980

13346 **Society for Disability Studies Annual Meeting**
Exhibit Promotions Plus
11630 Vixens Path
Ellicott City, MD 21042
301-596-3028; Fax: 410-997-0764
www.epponline.com
Harve C Horowitz, President
Frequency: June

13347 **Society for Neuroscience**
Herlitz Company
1890 Palmer Avenue
Suite 202 A
Larchmont, NY 10538
914-833-1979; Fax: 914-833-0920
Bruce Herlitz, President

13348 **Society of Nuclear Medicine Annual Meeting**
Society of Nuclear Medicine
1850 Samuel Morse Drive
Reston, VA 20190
703-708-9000; Fax: 703-708-9015
volunteer@snm.org
www.snm.org
Rebecca Maxey, Director
Vincent Pistilli, Chief Financial Officer
Matt Dickens, Director, Information Services
Judy Brazel, Director, Meeting Services
Joanna Spahr, Director, Marketing
7000 Attendees

13349 **Society of Thoracic Surgeons Annual Meeting**
Society of Thoracic Surgeons
633 N Saint Clair Street
Suite 2320
Chicago, IL 60611
312-202-5800; Fax: 312-202-5801
sts@sts.org
www.sts.org
Facebook, Twitter
Robert A Wynbrandt, Executive Director
Cheryl D. Wilson, Administrative Manager & Executive
Natalie Boden, Director of Marketing
Phillip A. Bongiorno, Director of Government Relations
Courtney Donovan, Director of Meetings
4200 Attendees
Mailing list available for rent

13350 **Society of Toxicology Annual Meeting**
Society of Toxicology
1821 Michael Faraday Drive
Suite 300
Reston, VA 20190
703-438-3115; Fax: 703-438-3113
sothq@toxicology.org
www.toxicology.org
Shawn Lamb, Executive Director
Clarissa Russell Wilson, Contact
Professional and scholarly organization meeting of scientists from academic institutions, government and industry representing the great variety of scientists who practice toxicology in the US and abroad.
5000 Attendees
Frequency: March

13351 **Southeastern Surgical Congress Annual Assembly**
South Med. Associates
PO Box 330
Pelham, AL 35124
205-991-3552; Fax: 205-991-6771

13352 **Southern Association for Primary Care**
Southern Medical Association
35 Lake Shore Drive
Birmingham, AL 35209
205-945-1840
800-423-4992; Fax: 205-945-1830
www.sma.org
Facebook, Twitter, LinkedIn
Michael C. Gosney, President
Ed Waldron, Administration
G. Richard Holt, Editor-in-Chief

13353 **Southern Medical Association Meeting**
Southern Medical Association
PO Box 190088
Birmingham, AL 35219
205-451-1840
800-423-4992; Fax: 205-945-1830
Ed Waldron, CEO
2500 Attendees

13354 **Symposium of the Protein Society**
FASEB
9650 Rockville Pike
Bethesda, MD 20814
301-634-7100; Fax: 301-530-7001
info@faseb.org
www.faseb.org
David Craven, Executive Director
Jacquelyn Roberts, Marketing Manager
Richard Dunn, Director

13355 **Symposium on New Advances in Blood Management**
American Society of ExtraCorporeal Technology
2209 Dickens Road
Richmond, VA 23230-2005
804-532-2323; Fax: 804-282-0090
www.amsect.org
Stewart Hinckley, Executive Director
Donna Pandarvis, Manager
Michael Troike, Government Relations Chairman
Kimberly Robertson, CPA, Controller
Greg Leasure, Membership Services
2000 Members
150 Attendees
Frequency: Annual/August
Founded in 1964
Mailing list available for rent

13356 TLPA Annual Convention & Trade Show
Taxicab, Limousine & Paratransit Association
3200 Tower Oaks Boulevard
Suite 220
Rockville, MD 20852
301-984-5700; Fax: 301-984-5703
info@tlpa.com
www.tlpa.org
Alfred LaGasse, CEO
William Rouse, President
Harold Morgan, Executive Vice President
Michelle A. Hariston, CMP, Manager of Meetings
Leah New, Manager of Communications
Shares information vital to owners or taxicab, limousine, airport shuttle, paratransit and nonemergency medical transportation fleets. 100 suppliers and exhibitors of the newest products available to the industry.
1000 Attendees
Frequency: Annual
Founded in 1917
Mailing list available for rent

13357 The MedTech Conference
Advanced Medical Technology Association
701 Pennsylvania Ave. NW
Suite 800
Washington, DC 20004-2654
202-783-8700; Fax: 202-783-8750
www.themedtechconference.com
Scott Whitaker, President & CEO
Features speakers, educational programming, networking, and business development opportunities for medtech companies.

13358 The Synergist
American Industrial Hygiene Association
3141 Fairview Park Drive
Suite 777
Falls Church, VA 22042
703-849-8888; Fax: 703-207-3561
infonet@aiha.org
www.aiha.org
Steven E. Lacey, PhD, CIH, CSP, President
Cynthia A. Ostrowski, CIH, Vice President
AIHA's official magazine, offering information and resources on health and safety for occupational environments.
Frequency: Monthly

13359 Today's Surgicenter Conference
Virgo Publishing LLC
3300 N Central Avenue
Suite 300
Phoenix, AZ 85012
480-675-8177; Fax: 602-567-6841
mikes@vpico.com
www.xchangemag.com
Facebook, Twitter, LinkedIn
Mike Saxby, Group Publisher
Craig Galbraith, Senior Online Managing Editor
Buffy Naylor, Managing Editor
Khali Henderson, Contributing Editor
Melissa Budwig, Online Advertising
Offers owners and operators of ambulatory surgery centers high-caliber instructive seminars by leading industry veterans, exhibits, and networking opportunities. Decision makers attend to learn more about construction and design, technology, equipment, legal and regulatory issues, marketing and finance and development. Approximately 50 booths.
200+ Attendees
Frequency: September
Founded in 2004
Mailing list available for rent: 15000+ names

13360 United States and Canadian Academy of Pathology
Herlitz Company
1890 Palmer Avenue
Suite 202A
Larchmont, NY 10538
914-833-1979; Fax: 914-833-0929
kris@herlitz.com
www.herlitz.com
Kris Herlitz, Show Manager
3000 Attendees
Frequency: March

13361 Vision New England
Hynes Convention Center
900 Boylston Street
Boston, MA 07115
617-954-2000; Fax: 617-954-2125
info@mccahome.com
24000 Attendees
Frequency: January

13362 World Congress on Pediatric & Intensive Care
Hynes Convention Center
900 Boylston Street
Boston, MA 02115
617-954-2000
800-845-8800; Fax: 617-954-2125
info@mccahome.com
2500 Attendees
Frequency: June

13363 Yankee Dental Congress
Hynes Convention Center
900 Boylston Street
Boston, MA 07115
617-954-2000; Fax: 617-954-2125
info@mccahome.com
2400 Attendees
Frequency: January

Directories & Databases

13364 ARMA International's Buyers Guide
ARMA International
11880 College Boulevard
Suite 450
Overland Park, KS 66215
913-444-9174
844-565-2120; Fax: 913-257-3855
headquarters@armaintl.org
armabuyersguide.org
Facebook, Twitter, LinkedIn
Nick Inglis, Exec. Dir., Content & Programming
Jeff Whited, Sr. Content Writer
Ann Snyder, Manager, Content Development
75-100 companies listed. Free.
Frequency: Annual

13365 Catalog of Professional Testing Resources
Psychological Assessment Resources
PO Box 998
Odessa, FL 33556
800-331-8378; Fax: 800-727-9329
www.parinc.com

13366 Comparative Guide to American Hospitals
Grey House Publishing
4919 Route 22
PO Box 56
Amenia, NY 12501
518-789-8700
800-562-2139; Fax: 845-373-6390
books@greyhouse.com
www.greyhouse.com
Facebook, Twitter
Leslie Mackenzie, Publisher
Richard Gottlieb, Editor
This new edition compares all of the nation's hospitals by 24 measures of quality in the treatment of heart attack, heart failure, pneumonia, and, new to this edition, surgical procedures and pregnancy care. Plus, this edition is now available in regional volumes, to make locating information about hospitals in your area quicker and easier than ever before.
Cost: $350.00
2000 Pages
ISBN: 1-532371-82-5
Founded in 1981

13367 Complete Directory for Pediatric Disorders
Grey House Publishing
4919 Route 22
PO Box 56
Amenia, NY 12501
518-789-8700
800-562-2139; Fax: 845-373-6390
books@greyhouse.com
www.greyhouse.com
Facebook, Twitter
Leslie Mackenzie, Publisher
Richard Gottlieb, Editor
Provides parents and caregivers with information about pediatric conditions, disorders, diseases and disabilities. Contains understandable descriptions of major bodily systems, descriptions of more than 200 disorders and a resource section.
Cost: $165.00
1200 Pages
ISBN: 1-592371-50-7
Founded in 1981

13368 Complete Directory for People with Disabilities
Grey House Publishing
4919 Route 22
PO Box 56
Amenia, NY 12501
518-789-8700
800-562-2139; Fax: 845-373-6390
books@greyhouse.com
www.greyhouse.com
Facebook, Twitter
Leslie Mackenzie, Publisher
Richard Gottlieb, Editor
Comprehensive resource for people with disabilities, detailing independent living centers, rehabilitation facilities, state and federal agencies, associations and support groups. This one-stop resource also provides immediate access to the latest products and services for people with disabilities, such as periodicals and books, assistive devices, employment and education programs and travel groups.
Cost: $165.00
1200 Pages
ISBN: 1-592373-67-4
Founded in 1981

13369 Complete Directory for People with Chronic Illness
Grey House Publishing

4919 Route 22
PO Box 56
Amenia, NY 12501

518-789-8700
800-562-2139; Fax: 845-373-6390
books@greyhouse.com
www.greyhouse.com
Facebook, Twitter

Leslie Mackenzie, Publisher
Richard Gottlieb, Editor

This directory provides a comprehensive overview of the support services and information resources available for people diagnosed with a chronic illness. It details the wide range of organizations, educational materials, books, newsletters, web sites, periodicals and databases that address 88 specific chronic illness.
Cost: $165.00
1200 Pages
ISBN: 1-952371-83-3
Founded in 1981

13370 **Complete Learning Disabilities Directory**
Grey House Publishing
4919 Route 22
PO Box 56
Amenia, NY 12501

518-789-8700
800-562-2139; Fax: 845-373-6390
books@greyhouse.com
www.greyhouse.com
Facebook, Twitter

Leslie Mackenzie, Publisher
Richard Gottlieb, Editor

The most comprehensive database of programs, services, curriculum materials, professional meetings and resources, camps, newsletters and support groups for teachers, students and families concerned with learning disabilities. Includes information about associations and organizations, schools, colleges and testing materials, government agencies, legal resources and more.
Cost: $145.00
800 Pages
ISBN: 1-592373-68-2
Founded in 1981

13371 **Complete Learning Disabilities Directory - Online Database**
Grey House Publishing
4919 Route 22
PO Box 56
Amenia, NY 12501-0056

518-789-8700
800-562-2139; Fax: 518-789-0556
gold@greyhouse.com
gold.greyhouse.com
Facebook, Twitter

Leslie Mackenzie, Publisher
Richard Gottlieb, President

The most comprehensive database of important learning disability resources, details associations and organizations, national and state programs, schools, colleges and learning centers, publishers, publications and periodicals, classroom resources, testing materials, exchange programs, and more. Locating learning disability resources has never been easier - it's only a click away.
Founded in 1981

13372 **Complete Mental Health Directory**
Grey House Publishing
4919 Route 22
PO Box 56
Amenia, NY 12501

518-789-8700
800-562-2139; Fax: 845-373-6390
books@greyhouse.com
www.greyhouse.com
Facebook, Twitter

Leslie Mackenzie, Publisher
Richard Gottlieb, Editor

Comprehensive information covering the field of behavioral health, with critical information for both the layman and mental health professional. Provides the layman with understandable descriptions of 25 mental health disorders, as well as detailed information on associations, media, support groups and mental health facilities. Offers the professional critical and comprehensive information on managed care organizations, information systems, government agencies and provider organizations.
Cost: $165.00
800 Pages
ISBN: 1-592372-85-6
Founded in 1981

13373 **Complete Mental Health Directory - Online Database**
Grey House Publishing
4919 Route 22
PO Box 56
Amenia, NY 12501-0056

518-789-8700
800-562-2139; Fax: 518-789-0556
gold@greyhouse.com
gold.greyhouse.com
Facebook, Twitter

Leslie Mackenzie, Publisher
Richard Gottlieb, President

This award-winning directory, now available in a quick-to-search, easy-to-use, online database provides the most comprehensive compilation of mental health resources available anywhere, with data for both layman and mental health professionals.
Founded in 1981

13374 **Detwiler's Directory of Health and Medical Resources**
Information Today
143 Old Marlton Pike
Medford, NJ 08055-8750

609-654-6266
800-300-9868; Fax: 609-654-4309
custserv@infotoday.com
www.infotoday.com

Thomas H Hogan, President
Roger R Bilboul, Chairman Of The Board
Joe Menendez, Marketing Manager
John Brokenshire, Chief Financial Officer
Michael V. Zarrello, Advertising Director

A comprehensive guide to over 2,000 health and medical corporations,associations, state and federal agencies, helathcare market research firms, foundations, institutes, and more.
Cost: $195.00
ISBN: 1-573871-55-9

13375 **Directory for Pediatric Disorders - Online Database**
Grey House Publishing
4919 Route 22
PO Box 56
Amenia, NY 12501-0056

518-789-8700
800-562-2139; Fax: 518-789-0556
gold@greyhouse.com
gold.greyhouse.com
Facebook, Twitter

Leslie Mackenzie, Publisher
Richard Gottlieb, President

The Complete Directory for Pediatric Disorders - Online Database is an important reference tool that provides parents and caregivers with information about common pediatric and adolescent conditions, disorders, diseases, and disabilities. This comprehensive, informative database is designed to meet the growing consumer demands for current, understandable medical information on pediatric disorders.
Founded in 1981

13376 **Directory for People with Chronic Illness - Online Database**
Grey House Publishing
4919 Route 22
PO Box 56
Amenia, NY 12501-0056

518-789-8700
800-562-2139; Fax: 518-789-0556
gold@greyhouse.com
gold.greyhouse.com
Facebook, Twitter

Leslie Mackenzie, Publisher
Richard Gottlieb, President

This important database is structured around the 80 most prevalent chronic illnesses and provides a comprehensive overview of the support services and information resources available for people diagnosed with a chronic illness. With a subscription to the Complete Directory for People with Chronic Illness - Online Database, your organization will have immediate access to a wealth of resources available for people diagnosed with a chronic illness, their families and support systems.
Founded in 1981

13377 **Directory for People with Disabilities - Online Database**
Grey House Publishing
4919 Route 22
PO Box 56
Amenia, NY 12501-0056

518-789-8700
800-562-2139; Fax: 518-789-0556
gold@greyhouse.com
gold.greyhouse.com
Facebook, Twitter

Leslie Mackenzie, Publisher
Richard Gottlieb, President

Comprehensive resource for people with disabilities, detailing independent living centers, rehabilitation facilities, state and federal agencies, associations and support groups. This one-stop resource also provides immediate access to the latest products and services for people with disabilities, such as periodicals and books, assistive devices, and more. With a subscription to the online databse, your organization will have immediate access to a wealth of resources available.
Founded in 1981

13378 **Directory of Health Care Group Purchasing Organizations**
Grey House Publishing
4919 Route 22
PO Box 56
Amenia, NY 12501

518-789-8700
800-562-2139; Fax: 845-373-6390
books@greyhouse.com
www.greyhouse.com
Facebook, Twitter

Leslie Mackenzie, Publisher
Richard Gottlieb, Editor

This comprehensive directory profiles over 800 Purchasing Organizations that negotiate more than 65% of all health care products purchased by hospitals and related facilities, and the institutions they represent.
Cost: $465.00
800 Pages
ISBN: 1-592372-87-2
Founded in 1981

13379 **Directory of Health Care Group Purchasing Organizations - Online Database**
Grey House Publishing
4919 Route 22
PO Box 56
Amenia, NY 12501-0056
518-789-8700
800-562-2139; Fax: 518-789-0556
gold@greyhouse.com
gold.greyhouse.com
Facebook, Twitter
Leslie Mackenzie, Publisher
Richard Gottlieb, President
This interactive online database offers immediate access to detailed information about over 800 GPOs, over 3,000 key contacts and 16,000 member hospitals and institutions they represent. These 800+ organizations represent billions of dollars in purchasing power for the medical and device supplies industry. This data is so critical for market research, sales plans and market development.
Founded in 1981

13380 **Directory of Hospital Personnel**
Grey House Publishing
4919 Route 22
PO Box 56
Amenia, NY 12501
518-789-8700
800-562-2139; Fax: 845-373-6390
books@greyhouse.com
www.greyhouse.com
Facebook, Twitter
Leslie Mackenzie, Publisher
Richard Gottlieb, Editor
A Who's Who of the hospital universe, The Directory of Hospital Personnel puts you in touch with over 100,000 key decision makers. This comprehensive directory contains listings of over 6,000 hospitals within the US, arranged alphabetically by city within state.
Cost: $325.00
2300 Pages
ISBN: 1-592372-86-4
Founded in 1981

13381 **Directory of Hospital Personnel - Online Database**
Grey House Publishing
4919 Route 22
PO Box 56
Amenia, NY 12501-0056
518-789-8700
800-562-2139; Fax: 518-789-0556
gold@greyhouse.com
gold.greyhouse.com
Facebook, Twitter
Richard Gottlieb, President
Leslie Mackenzie, Publisher
The DHP Online Database is the best resource you can have at your fingertips when researching or marketing a product or service to the hospital market. A 'Who's Who' of the hospital universe, this database puts you in touch with over 140,000 key decision-makers at 5,800 hospitals nationwide.
Founded in 1981

13382 **Employee Assistance Program Management Yearbook**
Health Resources Publishing
1913 Atlantic Ave
Suite 200
Manasquan, NJ 08736-1067
732-292-1100
888-843-6242; Fax: 732-292-1111
info@themcic.com
Robert K Jenkins, Publisher
Lisa Mansfield, Regional Director
Brett Powell, Regional Director
Alice Burron, Director
Explore major areas of involvement for EAPS. Investigate tools for effectively managing your EAP. Learn how screening tools for mental illness can help EAPS manage care. Learn how to help families deal with workplace changes. Learn how to identify potentially violent situations in the workplace and much more.
Cost: $149.00
ISBN: 1-882364-25-2

13383 **HCEA Directory of Healthcare Meetings and Conventions**
Healthcare Convention & Exhibitors Association
1100 Johnson Ferry Rd NE
Suite 300
Atlanta, GA 30342-1556
404-252-3663; Fax: 404-252-0774
hcea@kellencompany.com
www.hcea.org
Susan Huff, President
Carol Wilson, Meetings Director
Michelle Hall, Staff Associate
Jackie Beaulieu, Associate Director
Frank Skinner, Executive Director
Information on 6,000 health care meetings, available to members only.
500 Pages
Founded in 1930
Mailing list available for rent: 1400 names

13384 **HMO/PPO Directory**
Grey House Publishing
4919 Route 22
PO Box 56
Amenia, NY 12501
518-789-8700
800-562-2139; Fax: 845-373-6390
books@greyhouse.com
www.greyhouse.com
Facebook, Twitter
Leslie Mackenzie, Publisher
Richard Gottlieb, Editor
The HMO/PPO Directory is a comprehensive source that provides detailed information about Health Maintenance Organizations and Preferred Provider Organizations nationwide. Within the HMO/PPO Profiles, over 1,300 HMOs, PPOs and affiliated companies are listed, arranged alphabetically by state.
Cost: $325.00
600 Pages
ISBN: 1-592373-69-0
Founded in 1981

13385 **HMO/PPO Directory - Online Database**
Grey House Publishing
4919 Route 22
PO Box 56
Amenia, NY 12501-0056
518-789-8700
800-562-2139; Fax: 518-789-0556
gold@greyhouse.com
gold.greyhouse.com
Facebook, Twitter
Leslie Mackenzie, Publisher
Richard Gottlieb, President
The HMO/PPO Directory - Online Database is your in-depth searchable guide to health plans nationwide - their contact information, key executives, plan information and more. The online database is a necessary tool when researching or marketing a product or service to this important industry.
Founded in 1981

13386 **Health Funds Grants Resources Yearbook**
Health Resources Publishing
1913 Atlantic Ave
Suite 200
Manasquan, NJ 08736-1067
732-292-1100
888-843-6242; Fax: 732-292-1111
info@themcic.com
Robert K Jenkins, Publisher
Judy Granholm, Regional Director
Brett Powell, Regional Director
Alice Burron, Director
A resource book that gives dollar amounts, descriptions of previous grant recipients and programs that attract funding and details of future funding trends.
Cost: $165.00
ISBN: 1-882364-30-9

13387 **Managed Care Yearbook**
Health Resources Publishing
1913 Atlantic Ave
Suite 200
Manasquan, NJ 08736-1067
732-292-1100
888-843-6242; Fax: 732-292-1111
info@themcic.com
Robert K Jenkins, Publisher
Judy Granholm, Regional Director
Brett Powell, Regional Director
Alice Burron, Director
Resource book that includes critical facts, statistics cost, analysis, comparisions, enrollment and trends studies on managed care. Topics also include member retention, international markets and disease management.
Cost: $29.00
608 Pages
ISBN: 1-882364-26-0

13388 **Medical Abbreviations: 24,000**
Niel M Davis Associates
2049 Stout Dr
B-3
Warminster, PA 18974-3861
215-442-7430; Fax: 888-333-4915
med@neilmdavis.com
www.neilmdavis.com
Neil M Davis, Owner
This current edition paperback pocket book contains 16,000 medical related abbreviations and 24,000 of their possible meanings. It is current, comprehensive, and formatted so that it is easy to use. It also contains a cross-referenced listing of 3,300 generic and trade drug names.
Cost: $24.95
Frequency: Monthly
ISBN: 0-931431-09-3
Founded in 1981

13389 **Medical Device Register**
Grey House Publishing
4919 Route 22
PO Box 56
Amenia, NY 12501
518-789-8700
800-562-2139; Fax: 845-373-6390
books@greyhouse.com
www.greyhouse.com
Facebook, Twitter
Leslie Mackenzie, Publisher
Richard Gottlieb, Editor

The only one-stop resource of every medical supplier licensed to sell products in the US. This edition offers fast access to over 13,000 companies - and more than 65,000 products. This comprehensive resource saves you hours of time and trouble when searching for the equipment and supplies you want and the manufacturers who provide them.
Cost: $350.00
3000 Pages
ISBN: 1-592373-73-9
Founded in 1981

13390 **National Directory of Integrated Healthcare Delivery Systems**
Health Resources Publishing
1913 Atlantic Ave
Suite 200
Manasquan, NJ 08736-1067
732-292-1100
888-843-6242; Fax: 732-292-1111
info@themcic.com
Robert K Jenkins, Publisher
Lisa Mansfield, Regional Director
Brett Powell, Regional Director
Alice Burron, Director
Gives facts and stastics on more than 850 health care delivery systems and affiliations. Includes profiles of IHDSs by state and by alphabetical order. Also includes a directory of health care associations, a ranking of systems by revenues and an analysis of IHDSs growth projections.
Cost: $995.00
ISBN: 1-882364-31-7

13391 **National Directory of Managed Care Organzatons**
Health Resources Publishing
1913 Atlantic Ave
Suite 200
Manasquan, NJ 08736-1067
732-292-1100
888-843-6242; Fax: 732-292-1111
info@themcic.com
Robert K Jenkins, Publisher
Lisa Mansfield, Regional Director
Brett Powell, Regional Director
Alice Burron, Director
Published by Health Resources Publishing. Available in print ($325), database ($1695) or CD-Rom ($695).
Cost: $325.00
ISSN: 0898-9753

13392 **National Directory of Physician Organizations Database On Cd-Rom**
Health Resources Publishing
1913 Atlantic Ave
Suite 200
Manasquan, NJ 08736-1067
732-292-1100
888-843-6242; Fax: 732-292-1111
info@themcic.com
Robert K Jenkins, Publisher
Judy Granholm, Regional Director
Brett Powell, Regional Director
Alice Burron, Director
Detailed profiles on over 1,800 physician organizations. Listings include physician hospitals organizations (PHOs), independent practice associations, management services organizations and physician practice management companies. Key elements of the data profile include: executive officers; year founded; profits status, statue of incorporation; numbers of associates physician; market area; market analysis; affiliated/participating hospital; management service organizations used.
Cost: $995.00
ISBN: 1-882364-18-X

13393 **Older Americans Information Directory**
Grey House Publishing
4919 Route 22
PO Box 56
Amenia, NY 12501
518-789-8700
800-562-2139; Fax: 845-373-6390
books@greyhouse.com
www.greyhouse.com
Facebook, Twitter
Leslie Mackenzie, Publisher
Richard Gottlieb, Editor
Important resources for older americans, including national, regional, state and local organizations, government agencies, research centers, legal resources, discount travel information, continuing education programs, disability aids and assistive devices, health, print media and electronic media.
Cost: $165.00
1200 Pages
ISBN: 1-592373-57-7
Founded in 1981

13394 **Older Americans Information Directory - Online Database**
Grey House Publishing
4919 Route 22
PO Box 56
Amenia, NY 12501-0056
518-789-8700
800-562-2139; Fax: 518-789-0556
gold@greyhouse.com
gold.greyhouse.com
Facebook, Twitter
Leslie Mackenzie, Publisher
Richard Gottlieb, President
The Older Americans Information Directory is an easy to use source that offers up-to-date information on the prevalent social, health and financial issues facing older Americans in the 21st century, as well as recreational and educational opportunities to enrich their lives. With a subscription to the online database, you'll have immediate access to over 8,000 resources including national, regional, state and local organziations, government agencies, health facilities and more.
Founded in 1981

13395 **Wellness Program Management Yearbook**
Health Resources Publishing
1913 Atlantic Ave
Suite 200
Manasquan, NJ 08736-1067
732-292-1100
888-843-6242; Fax: 732-292-1111
info@themcic.com
Robert K Jenkins, Publisher
Lisa Mansfield, Regional Director
Brett Powell, Regional Director
Alice Burron, Director
This yearbook highlights such issues as obtaining senior management support, encouraging employment participation in programs, finding, funding and developing different programs. Also helps in planning initiatives by providing details of the components that will be important to include about the programs that will help you to meet your goals.
Cost: $155.00
ISBN: 1-882364-39-2

Industry Web Sites

13396 **http://gold.greyhouse.com**
G.O.L.D Grey House OnLine Databases
Grey House Publishing's online database platform, GOLD, offers Quick Search, Keyword Search and Expert Search for most business sectors including healthcare markets. The GOLD platform makes finding the information you need quick and easy - whether you're a novice searcher or an experienced database user. All of Grey House's directory products are available for subscription on the GOLD platform.

13397 **sors.memberclicks.net**
Society of Robotic Surgery
Facebook, Twitter
Society providing education about robotic surgery, as well as studies, funding and development events for professionals in the field.

13398 **www.aaaai.org**
American Academy of Allergy, Asthma And Immunology
The largest professional medical specialty organization in the United States, representing allergists, asthma specialists, clinical immunologists, allied health professionals, and others with the special interest in the research and treatment of allergic disease.

13399 **www.aaham.org**
American Association of Healthcare Administrative
Management
Business offices, credit and collection managers, and admitting officers for hospitals, clincis and other health care organizaitons. To educate members, exchange information and techniques, and keep members abreast of new regulations relating to their field. Seeks proper recognition for the financial aspect of hospital and clinic managememnt.

13400 **www.aahperd.org**
American Alliance for Hlth, Phys. Edu. Rec. Dance
Recreation & Dance

13401 **www.aaid.org**
American Academy of Implant Dentistry
Offers a rigorous implant dentistry credentialing program which requires at least 300 hours of post-docroal or continuing education instruction in implant dentistry, passing a comprehensive exam, and presenting successful cases of different types of implants to a group of examiners. It is one of the most comprehensive credentialing programs in dentistry.

13402 **www.aaihds.org**
American Association of Integrated Healthcare
Delivery Systems
Physicians, hospital executives and board members, health plan executives, and other key entities and professionals employed by all forms of IDDSs including PHOS, IPA POSOS, and MSOS. Seeks to provide advocacy for issues related to integrated health care through research, education, and communication. Conducts educational and research programs; maintains speakers' bureau and information clearinghouse.

13403 **www.aamft.org**
American Assoc for Marriage and Family Therapy
AAMFT represents the professional interests of more than 25,000 marriage and family therapists in the United States, Canada and abroad.

13404 **www.aami.org**
Assoc for the Advancement of Medical Instrumentati
The Association for the Advancement of Medical Instrumentation (AAMI), founded in 1967, is a unique alliance of over 6,000 members united by the coommon goal of increasing the understanding and use of medical instrumentation. AAMI is the primary source of consensus and timely information on medical instrumentation and technology for the industry, professionals, and the government for national and intemational standrards.

13405 **www.aaos.org**
American Academy for Cerebral Palsy and Developmental Medicine

13406 **www.aap.org**
American Academy of Pediatrics

13407 **www.academydentalmaterials.org**
Academy of Dental Materials
Formerly known as American Academy for Plastics Research in Dentistry.

13408 **www.ache.org**
American College of Healthcare Executives
International professional society of more than 30,000 healthcare executives. Credentialing and educational programs, Congress on Healthcare Management. ACHE's publishing division, Health Administration Press, is one of the largest publishers of books.

13409 **www.acpe.org**
American College of Physician Executives
Physicians whose primary professional responsibility is the management of health care organizations. Provides for continuing education and certification of the physician executive and the profession. Offers specialized career planning, counseling, recruitment and placement services, and research and information data on physican managers.

13410 **www.acrm.org**
American Congress of Rehabilitation Medicine

13411 **www.acsm.org**
American College of Sports Medicine
The ACSM promotes and integrates scientific research, education, and practical applications of sports medicine and exercise science to maintain and enhance physical performance, fitness, health, and quality of life.

13412 **www.afprd.org**
Association of Family Practice Residency Directors
Provides representation for residency directors at a national level and provides a political voice for them to approprite arenas. Promotes cooperation and communication between residency programs and different branches of the family practice specialty. Dedicated to improving of education of family physicians. Provides a network for mutual assistance among FP, residency directors.

13413 **www.aha.org**
American Hospital Association

13414 **www.ahia.org**
Association of Healthcare Internal Auditors
Promotes cost containment and increased productivity in health care institutions through internal auditing. Serves as a forum for the exchange of experience, ideas, and information among members; provides continuing professional education courses and informs members of developments in health care internal auditing. Offers employment clearinghouse services.

13415 **www.ahqa.org**
American Health Quality Association
Central news area for the group that represents quality inprovement organizations and professionals working to improve the quality of health care in communities across America.

13416 **www.ahraonline.org**
Association for Medical Imaging Management
For radiology administrators from the US, Canada, and several other countries.

13417 **www.ama-assn.org**
American Medical Association
A partnership of physicians and their professional associations dedicated to promoting the art and science of medicine and the betterment of the public health. To serve physicians and their patients by establishing and promoting ethical, educational, and clinical standards for the medical profession and by advocating for the highest principle of all - the integrity of the physician/patient relationship.

13418 **www.amga.org**
American Medical Group Association

13419 **www.apta.org**
American Physical Therapy Association
The principal membership organization representing and promoting the profession of physical therapy, is to furhter the profession's role in the prevention, diagnosis, and treatment of movement dysfunctions and the enhancement of the physical health and functional abilities of members of the public.

13420 **www.arrs.org**
American Roentgen Ray Society
102 years strong radiological association for all subspecialties.

13421 **www.ascrs.org**
American Society of Ophthalmic Administrators
A division of the American Society of Cataract and Retractive Surgery. Persons involved with the administration of an ophthalmic office or clinic. Facilitates the exchange of idease and information in order to improve management practices and working conditions. Offers placement services.

13422 **www.asma.org**
Aerospace Medical Association
Our mission is to apply and advance scientific knowledge to promote and enhance the health, safety and performance of those involved in aerospace and related activities.

13423 **www.asnr.org**
American Society of Neuroradiology

13424 **www.asrm.org**
American Society for Reproductive Medicine
Organization devoted to advancing knowledge and expertise in reproductive medicine and biology. Members of this voluntary nonprofit organization must demonstrate the high ethical principals of the medical profession, evince an interest in reproductive medicine and biotechnology, and adhere to the objectives of the Society.

13425 **www.assh.org**
American Society for Surgery of the Hand
The oldest medical specialty society in the United States devoted entirely to continuing medical education related to hand surgery.

13426 **www.awhp.org**
Association for Worksite Health Promotion
Exists to advance the profession of worksite health promotion and the career development of its practitioners and to improve the performance of the programs they administer. Represents a variety of disciplines and worksites, for decision-makers in the areas of health promotion/disease prevention and health-care cost management.

13427 **www.cdc.gov**
Centers for Disease Control and Prevention
The official website of CDC, the government's public health agency.

13428 **www.chpa-info.org**
Consumer Healthcare Products Association
Members are producers of nonprescription medicines and dietary supplements for self-care. Has an annual budget of approximately $10 million.

13429 **www.claims.org**
Alliance of Claims Assistance Professionals
Professionals dedicated to the effective management of health insurance claims. Our members are claims assistance professionals who work for patients.

13430 **www.cleftline.org**
American Cleft Palate Craniofacial Association
Organization of plastic surgeons, dentists, orthodontists, speech pathologists, geneticists, social workers and others.

13431 **www.cmsa.org**
Case Management Society of America
Exclusively for the case management profession.

13432 **www.crnusa.com**
Council for Responsible Nutrition
Government relations, scientific and regulatory affairs, publications.

13433 **www.docinfo.org**
A national data bank of disciplinary histories on US licensed physicians from the Federation of State Medical Boards; charges $9.95 per report

13434 **www.entnet.org**
American Academy of Otolarygngology-Head & Neck

13435 **www.foodallergy.org**
Food Allergy & Anaphylaxis Network
Facts, common questions, resources and news.

13436 **www.greyhouse.com**
Grey House Publishing
Authoritative reference directories for most business sectors including healthcare markets. Users can search the online databases with varied search criteria allowing for custom searches by product category, geographic area, sales volume, keyword, subject and more. Full Grey House catalog and online ordering also available.

13437 **www.hcea.org**
Healthcare Convention & Exhibitors Association
Trade association of over 650 organizations involved in health care exhibiting or providing services to health care conventions, exhibitions and/or meetings.

13438 **www.healthfinder.gov**
A comprehensive guide to resources for health information from the federal government and related agencies

13439 **www.hfma.org**
Healthcare Financial Management Association
Brings perspective and clarity to the industry's complex issues for the purpose of preparing our members to succeed. Through our programs, publications and partnerships, we enhance the capabilities that strengthen not only individuals careers, but also the organizations from which our members come.

13440 **www.hida.org**
Health Industry Distributors Association
HIDA keeps members current on healthcare reform, government affairs, industry trends and forecasts, provider news, and sales tips.

13441 **www.iahss.org**
International Association for Healthcare Security

Non-profit professional organization of healthcare security and safety executives from around the world.

13442 **www.ichbc.org**
Institute of Healthcare Business Consultants
Maintains code of ethics, rules of professional conducts, and certification program, administers examination and conducts certification course. Membership by successful completion of certification examination only.

13443 **www.jamesbeard.org**
James Beard Foundation
Not-for-profit organization dedicated to preserving the country's culinary heritage and fostering the appreciation and development of gastronomy by recognizing and promoting excellence in all aspects of the culinary arts.

13444 **www.letfreedomgrow.com**
American Alliance for Medical Cannabis
Dedicated to bringing patients, caregivers, and volunteers the facts needed to make informed decisions about medical cannabis. Provides information on medical marijuana legislation, political activism, recipes, and growing guides.

13445 **www.mgma.com**
American College of Medical Practice Executives
Professional credentialing organization. Works to encourage medical group practice administrators to improve and maintain their proficiency and to provide appropriate recognition; to establish a program with uniform standards of admission, advancement, certification and fellowship in order to achieve the highest possible standards in the profession of medical group practice administration; to participate in the development of educational and research programs.

13446 **www.mwsearch.com/**
Medical world search.

13447 **www.naher.com**
National Association for Healthcare Recruitment
Individuals employed directly by hospitals and other health care organizations which are involved in the practice of professional health care recruitment. Promotes sound principles of professionals health care recruitment. Provides financial assistance to aid members in planning and implementing regional educational programs. Offers technical assistance and consultation services. Compiles statistics.

13448 **www.namdrc.org**
National Association of Medical Directors for
Respiratory Care

Works to provide educational opportunities to fit the needs of medical directors of respiratory care and represents the interests of members to regulatory agencies to ensure that the needs of respiratory patients are not overlooked. Offers educational programs; maintains speakers' bureau.

13449 **www.namss.org**
National Association Medical Staff Service
Individuals involved in the management and administration of health care provider services. Seeks to enhance the knowledge and experience of medical staff services professionals and promote the certification of those involved in the profession.

13450 **www.nerf.org**
National Eye Research Center
Improving your vision through eyecare, education and research.

13451 **www.oncolink.com**
Founded by specialist at the University of Pennsylvania, provides information on wide range of childhood and adult cancers

13452 **www.pahcom.com**
Professional Association of Health Care Office
Management

Office managers of small group and solo medical practices. Operates certification program for health care office managers.

13453 **www.paralysis.org**
Christopher Reeve Paralysis Foundation
Our mission is to raise money to help fing spinal cord injury research.

13454 **www.quackwatch.com**
A nonprofit corporation whose purpose is to combat health - related frauds, myths, fads, and fallacies and investigate phony medical news

13455 **www.rbma.org**
Radiology Business Management Association
Business managers for private radiology groups; corporate members include: vendors of equipment, services, or supplies. Purposes are to improve business administration of radiologists' practices to better serve patients and the medical profession; and to provide opportunities for professional development and recognition. Offers extensive educational and networking opportunities and informal placement service. Maintains information services emphasizing those aspects unique to the business.

13456 **www.safeaccessnow.org**
Americans for Safe Access
Works to ensure safe and legal access to cannabis for therapeutic use and research. Home to newsletters, fact sheets, state legal manuals, reports, and booklets.

13457 **www.siim.org**
Society for Imaging Informatics in Medicine
Devoted to advance informatics and information technology in medical imaging through education and research. Provides an open environment for imaging information professionals to access expert and cutting edge resources in a collegial and practical atmosphere.

13458 **www.sleepproducts.org**
International Sleep Products Association
Maintains a strong organization to influence government actions, inform and educate the membership and act on industry issues to enhance the growth,profitability and stature of the sleep products industry. Provides members with information and services to manage their business more effectively and efficiently. Publishes a magazine devoted exclusively to the mattress industry, BEDtimes covers a broad range of issue and news important to the industry.

13459 **www.themcic.com**
Healthcare IS/IT Yearbook
The Health care IS/IT Market Yearbook is a unique and valuable sales and marketing reference tool for IT companies selling into the health and managed care industries. Great for sales and marketing research; developing reports or preparing presentations. Now, it's easy to identify what hospitals are contracting for, get information on hundreds of millions of dollars in healthcare. IT contract deals, discover what other companies are doing.

13460 **www.toxicology.org**
Society Of Toxicology
Members are scientists concerned with the effects of chemicals on man and the environment. Promotes the aquisition and utilization of knowledge in toxicology, aids in the protection of public health and facilitates disiplines. The society has a strong commitment to education in toxicology and to the recruitment of students and new members into the profession.

Associations

13461 **ASHRAE**
1791 Tullie Circle, N.E.
Atlanta, GA 30329-2398
404-636-8400
800-527-4723; Fax: 404-321-5478
ashrae@ashrae.org
www.ashrae.org
Facebook, Twitter
Jeff H. Littleton, Executive VP
Kim Mitchell ÿ, Chief Development Officer
Vanita Gupta, Director, Marketing
Joyce Abrams, Director, Member Services
Craig Wright, Director, Finance & Admin. Services
An international organization that fulfills its mission of advancing heating, ventilation, air conditioning and refrigeration to serve humanity and promote a sustainable world through research, standards writing, publishing and continuing education.
55000 Members
Founded in 1894
Mailing list available for rent

13462 **ASM International**
9639 Kinsman Road
Materials Park, OH 44073-0002
440-338-5151
800-336-5152; Fax: 440-338-4634
memberservicecenter@asminternational.org
www.asminternational.org
Facebook, Twitter, LinkedIn
Zi-Kui Liu, President
Diana Essock, Vice President
Raymond V. Fryan, Treasurer
William T. Mahoney, Secretary & CEO
The society for materials engineers and scientists, a worldwide network dedicated to advancing industry, technology and applications of metals and materials. ASM provides information references, education, research and international events.
30K Members
Founded in 1913

13463 **Air Conditioning Contractors of America**
2800 S Shirlington Road
Suite 300
Arlington, VA 22206
703-575-4477
membership@acca.org
www.acca.org
Facebook, Twitter, LinkedIn, YouTube
Barton James, President & CEO
Samuel Awotwi, Director of Finance
Christine Gibson, VP, Marketing & Partnerships
Sean Robertson, VP, Membership/Business Operations
Kimya Bailey, Director, Events & Benchmarking
ACCA is a non-profit association serving the HVACR community, working to promote professional contracting, energy efficiency, and healthy, comfortable indoor environments.
60000 Members
Founded in 1968

13464 **Air Diffusion Council**
1901 North Roselle Road
Suite 800
Schaumburg, IL 60195
847-706-6750; Fax: 847-706-6751
info@flexibleduct.org
www.flexibleduct.org
Jack Lagershausen, President
The purpose of the Air Diffusion Council is to promote and further the interests of the manufacturers of air distribution equipment, more specifically, flexible air ducts and related products, and the interests of the general public in the areas of safety, quality, efficiency and energy conservation. Also, to develop programs approved and supported by the membership that legally promote and further these interests.
40 Members
Founded in 1961

13465 **Air Movement and Control Association International, Inc.**
30 W University Dr.
Arlington Heights, IL 60004
847-394-0150; Fax: 847-253-0088
communications@amca.org
www.amca.org
Facebook, Twitter, LinkedIn
Tim O'Hare, Chairman
Doug Yamashita, President
Mark Stevens, Executive Director
AMCA represents manufacturers of air movement devices from 34 countries.
330 Members
Founded in 1917

13466 **Air-Conditioning, Heating, and Refrigeration Institute (AHRI)**
2111 Wilson Blvd.
Suite 500
Arlington, VA 22201
703-524-8800; Fax: 703-562-1942
www.ahrinet.org
Facebook, Twitter, YouTube, Instagram
Stephen Yurek, President & CEO
John Lanier, COO
Francis Dietz, VP, Public Affairs
James Walters, VP, International Affairs
Donna Morris, Director, Accounting
Institute members manufacture 90 percent of the residential and commercial HVAC equipment in North America.

13467 **American Boiler Manufacturers Association**
8221 Old Courthouse Road
Suite 380ÿ
Vienna, VA 22015
703-356-7172; Fax: 703-356-4543
info@abma.com
www.abma.com
Facebook, Twitter, LinkedIn
Scott Lynch, President & CEO
Shaunica Jayson, Membership & Marketing Manager
Bethany Jones, Administrative Coordinator
Hugh K. Webster, General Counsel
Marissa Torres, Director of Meetings
Manufacturers' trade association representing companies involved in utility, industrial and commercial steam generation. Includes associate memberships for companies who sell to or work with these companies and those who own boilers. Holds technical and production conferences and publishes technical guideline publications.
Founded in 1888

13468 **American Supply Association**
1200 Arlington Heights Road
Itasca, IL 60143
630-467-0000; Fax: 630-467-0001
info@asa.net
www.asa.net
Facebook, Twitter, LinkedIn
Mike Adelizzi, CEO
Aaron Scheiwe, CFO
ASA is a not-for-profit national organization serving wholesale distributors and their suppliers in the plumbing, heating, cooling and industrial and mechanical pipe, valves and fittings industries.
Founded in 1969

13469 **Association of Professional Energy**
3916 W Oak Street
Suite D
Burbank, CA 91505
818-972-2159; Fax: 818-972-2863
www.apem.org
John Sykes, Communications
Mark Martinez, Chair/Chapter Development
Bernell Loveridge, Chair/Treasurer
Lynne Eichner Kelley, Chair/Membership
Members include individuals responsible for energy production, consumption or management decisions.
1.5M Members
Founded in 1982

13470 **Cooling Technology Institute**
PO Box 681807
Houston, TX 77268
281-583-4087; Fax: 281-537-1721
vmanser@cti.org
www.cti.org
Jack Bland, President
Frank Michell, Vice-President
Steven Chaloupka, Treasurer
Thomas Toth, Secretary
Helene Troncin, Director
Seeks to improve technology, design and performance of water conservation apparatus. Provides inspection services and conducts research.
400 Members
Founded in 1950

13471 **Heating, Air Conditioning & Refrigeration Distributors International**
445 Hutchinson Avenue
Suite 550
Columbus, OH 43235
614-345-4328
888-253-2128; Fax: 614-345-9161
www.hardinet.org
Facebook, Twitter, LinkedIn, Flickr, Youtube, Instagram
Talbot H. Gee, CEO
Emily Saving, EVP
Palmer Schoening, VP, Gov't Affairs
Alex Ayers, Director, Gov't Affairs
Eileen Mantel, Manager, Networking & Conference
Nonprofit organization dedicated to advancing the science of wholesale distribution in the HVACR industry.
1200 Members
Founded in 1947

13472 **International Microwave Power Institute**
PO Box 1140
Mechanicsville, VA 23111-5007
804-559-6667; Fax: 804-559-4087
info@impi.org
www.impi.org
Facebook, Twitter, LinkedIn
Bob Schifmann, President
John Mastela, VP
Jerome Czajkowski, Secretary
John Gerling, Treasurer
Molly Poisant, Executive Director
To be the global organization that provides a forum for the exchange of information on all aspects of microwave and RF heating technologies.
Founded in 1966

13473 **Masonry Heater Association of North America**
2180 S Flying Q Lane
Tuscon, AZ 85731
520-883-0191; Fax: 480-371-1139
execdir@mha-net.org
www.mha-net.org
Richard Smith, Executive Director
Tim Seaton, VP
Rod Zander, Treasurer
Beverly Marois, Administrator
Promotes use of masonry heaters, increases public awareness and encourages reasonable governmental regulation.
115 Members
Founded in 1989

13474 **Mechanical Contractors Association of America**
1385 Piccard Drive
Rockville, MD 20850-4329
301-869-5800; Fax: 301-990-9690
www.mcaa.org
Represents heating, piping and air conditioning professionals.
1.4M Members

13475 **Mobile Air Conditioning Society Worldwide**
225 S. Broad Street
P.O. Box 88
Lansdale, PA 19446
215-631-7020; Fax: 215-631-7017
macsworldwide@macsw.org
www.macsw.org
Facebook, Twitter, LinkedIn, Youtube, WordPress
Elvis Hoffpauir, President/COO
Marion Posen, VP Marketing/Membership
Provides technical training, information and communication for the professionals in the automotive air-conditioning industry.
1700 Members
Founded in 1981

13476 **National Air Duct Cleaners Association**
1120 Route 73
Suite 200
Mt Laurel, NJ 08054
856-380-6810
855-GON-ADCA; Fax: 856-439-0525
info@nadca.com
www.nadca.com
Facebook, Twitter, LinkedIn, Youtube
Jodi Araujo, Chief Executive Officer
Kristy Cohen, Executive Director
Mike Dwyer, Chief Relationship Officer
Amanda Paolini, Membership & Certification Coord.
Sarah Black, Editor, DucTales
The trade association of the HVAC/Heating-Ventilation-Air Conditioning industry.
1000 Members
Founded in 1989

13477 **National Association of Plumbing, Heating and Cooling Contractors Association**
180 S Washington Street
Suite 100
Falls Church, VA 22046
703-237-8100
800-533-7694; Fax: 703-237-7442
naphcc@naphcc.org
www.phccweb.org
Facebook, Twitter, LinkedIn
Dawn Dalton, Administrative Coordinator
Katie Gilbert, Membership Coordinator
Merry Beth Hall, Director, Apprentice and Journeyman
Don Hawkins, Accounts Receivable Clerk
Patrice L Jackson, Coordinator, QSC Member Services
National organization designed for suppliers of equipment, supplies and services for the plumbing, heating and cooling industries.
3700 Members
Founded in 1883

13478 **National Association of Power Engineers**
One Springfield Street
Chicopee, MA 01013-2672
413-592-6273; Fax: 413-592-1998
nape@powerengineers.com
www.powerengineers.com
Facebook, Twitter, LinkedIn
Michael Morin, National President
Shawn Fitzpatrick, National Vice President
William Love, National Treasurer/Secretary
Members include power plant operators and maintenance personnel who supply the industry with process power and related building and plant services.

13479 **National Environmental Balancing Bureau**
8575 Grovemont Circle
Gaithersburg, MD 20877-4121
301-977-3698
866-497-4447; Fax: 301-977-9589
glenn@nebb.org
www.nebb.org
Tiffany Suite, Executive Vice President
Christina Spence, Office & Scheduling Coordinator
Sumayyah Milstein, Firm Certification Coordinator
NEBB is an international certification association for firms that deliver high performance building systems. Members perform testing, adjusting and balancing (TAB) of heating, ventilating and air-conditioning systems, commission and retro-commission building systems commissioning, execute sound and vibration testing, and test and certify lab fume hoods and electronic and bio clean rooms. NEBB holds the highest standards in certification.
Founded in 1971

13480 **Wholesalers Association of the Northeast**
1200 N. Arlington Heights Rd.
Suite 150
Itasca, IL 60143
630-467-0000; Fax: 508-923-1044
wane5@asa.net
www.wane5.org
Chris Murin, Executive Director
Presently comprised of the leading wholesale distributors of pluming, heating, cooling and industrial pipe supplies, located throughout the northeast states.
Founded in 1932

Newsletters

13481 **HVACR News**
Trade News International
4444 Riverside Drive
Suite 202
Burbank, CA 91505
818-848-6397; Fax: 818-848-1306
www.hvacrnews.com
Gary McCarty, Editor-in -Chief
Mark Deitch, Publisher
Jordan Tolila, Associate Publisher
Barb Kerr, Executive Assistant
A monthly national trade newspaper serving contractors, technicians, mechanical engineers, manufactures, manufacturer representatives, wholesalers, distributors, trade associations, government representatives, schools, students and other in the heating, ventilating, air conditioning, refrigerating, hydronics, sheet metals, solar, and allied trades.
Frequency: Monthly
Circulation: 50000
Founded in 1981
Printed in 4 colors on n stock

13482 **Heating/Combustion and Equipment News**
Business Communications Company
1 Penn Plz
Suite 42
New York, NY 10119-4200
212-273-7100
800-685-4488; Fax: 212-244-3721
www.firstalbany.com
Equipment, materials and supplies for the heating and air conditioning industry.
Cost: $12.00
Frequency: Monthly

13483 **Impact Compressor/Turbines News And Patents**
Impact Publishers
PO Box 3113
Ketchum, ID 83340-3113
208-726-2332; Fax: 208-726-2115
Mary Jo Helmeke, Publisher
Regular features include new product announcements, patent information and up-to-date industry news and information on current books, brochures, software, seminars and meetings.
Cost: $60.00
30 Pages
Frequency: Annual

13484 **Impact Pump News and Patents**
Impact Publishers
PO Box 3113
Ketchum, ID 83340-3113
208-720-4876; Fax: 208-726-2115
Mary Jo Helmeke, Publisher
Regular features include new product announcements, patent information and up-to-date industry news and information on current books, brochures software, seminars and meetings.
Cost: $100.00
25 Pages

13485 **Indoor Air Quality Update**
Cutter Information Corporation
37 Broadway
Suite 1
Arlington, MA 02474-5500
718-648-8700; Fax: 718-648-8707
www.cutter.com
Facebook, Twitter
Karen Coburn, President and CEO
Paul Bergeron, CFO and COO
Israel Gat, Director, Agile Practice
Anne Mullaney, VP, Prodct Development
Cuitlahuac Osorio, Director, Cutter Latin America
Practical control of indoor air problems.
Cost: $287.00
Frequency: Monthly

13486 **MACS Service Reports**
Mobile Air Conditioning Society Worldwide

225 S. Broad Street
P.O. Box 88
Lansdale, PA 19446
215-631-7020; Fax: 215-631-7017
macsworldwide@macsw.org
www.macsw.org
Elvis Hoffpauir, President/COO
Marion Posen, VP Marketing/Membership
Technical newsletter for mobile air conditioning industry.
Frequency: Monthly
Circulation: 13000
Founded in 1981

13487 Residential Heat Recovery Ventilators Directory
Cutter Information Corporation
37 Broadway
Suite 1
Arlington, MA 02474-5500
781-648-1950; Fax: 781-648-1950
www.cutter.com
Verna Allee, Senior Consultant
A comprehensive comparative guide and product directory to heat exchangers and ventilators.
Cost: $75.00

13488 Superinsulated House Design and Construction Workbook
Cutter Information Corporation
37 Broadway
Suite 1
Arlington, MA 02474-5500
781-648-1950; Fax: 781-648-1950
www.cutter.com
Verna Allee, Senior Consultant
Detailed, graphic information to design and build superior houses.
Cost: $85.00

Magazines & Journals

13489 AHRI Trends Magazine
Air Conditioning & Refrigeration Institute
2111 Wilson Boulevard
Suite 500
Arlington, VA 22201
703-524-8800; Fax: 703-528-3816
ahri@ahri.net
www.ahrinet.org
Facebook
Stephen Yurek, President & CEO
A resource for HVAC contractors and technicians.
300+ Members
Frequency: Monthly

13490 ASHRAE Journal
1791 Tullie Circle NE
Atlanta, GA 30329
404-636-8400
800-527-4723; Fax: 404-321-5478
ashrae@ashrae.org
www.ashrae.org
Facebook
Mark Owen, Director, Publications & Education
Sarah Foster, Editor
Explores topical technical issues, such as: indoor air quality, energy management, thermal storage, alternative refrigerants, fire and life safety and more.
Printed in 4 colors on matte stock

13491 Air Conditioning Today
PO Box 311776
New Braunfels, TX 78131
830-627-0605
877-669-4228; Fax: 830-627-0614
ac-today.com
Joe Eaton, Editor
Updates readers on the latest products, materials and technologies available.
Frequency: Monthly
Circulation: 19000
Founded in 1986

13492 Air Conditioning, Heating & Refrigeration News
Business News Publishing Company
1050 IL Route 83
Suite 200
Bensenville, IL 60106-1096
630-377-5909
www.bnpmedia.com
Katie Rotella, Manager
Timely information to contractors, wholesalers, distributors, manufacturers, owner/operators and consulting engineers. Features technical, marketing, design, engineering, installation, management, governmental and labor aspects of the heating and cooling industry. Regular columns highlight new products and literature, legal rulings, manufacturer announcements, industry events and the latest HVAC/r patents.
Cost: $49.00
Frequency: Weekly
Circulation: 32854
Founded in 1926
Mailing list available for rent: 35M names
Printed in 4 colors on glossy stock

13493 American Supply Association News
American Supply Association
1200 Arlington Heights Road
Itasca, IL 60143
630-467-0000; Fax: 630-467-0001
info@asa.net
www.asa.net
Mike Adelizzi, CEO
Aaron Scheiwe, CFO
Articles on plumbing, heating, cooling, and piping products.
50 Pages
Frequency: Monthly
Circulation: 2500
Founded in 1969
Mailing list available for rent: 4,000 names
Printed in 4 colors on matte stock

13494 Automotive Cooling Journal
National Automotive Radiator Service Association
3000 Villiage Run Rd
Suite 103, #221
Wexford, PA 15090-6315
412-847-5747
800-551-3232; Fax: 724-934-1036
info@narsa.org
www.narsa.org
Jim Holowka, National President
Chuck Braswell, National Chairman-Past President
Rick Fuller, National 1st VP
Maarten Taal, National 2nd VP
Angelo Miozza, National Treasurer
Auto cooling system service data. Free to members.
Cost: $30.00
60 Pages
Frequency: Monthly
Circulation: 10,000
Founded in 1954

13495 Boiler Systems Engineering Magazine
HPAC Engineering
1300 E 9th Street
Cleveland, OH 44144
216-696-7000; Fax: 216-696-3432
www.hpac.com
Facebook, Twitter
Mike Well, Editorial Director
Scott Arnold, Executive Editor
Ron Rajecki, Senior Editor
The official publication of the American Boiler Manufacturers Association, assists consulting engineers, in-house engineers, and building managers with the design, installation, operations, maintenance and commissioning of steam and hot water systems for institutional, commercial and industrial buildings.

13496 Contracting Business
Penton Media
249 W 17th St
New York, NY 10011
212-204-4200; Fax: 216-696-6662
information@penton.com
www.penton.com
Jane Cooper, Marketing
Michael S Weil, Editor-in-Chief
Gwen Hostnik, Marketing Manager
Directed to the residential, commercial and industrial mechanical systems contracting marketplace. HVAC mechanical systems and Design/Build/Maintain contractors, wholesalers and commercial/industrial in-house service organizations.
Cost: $75.00
120 Pages
Frequency: Monthly
Circulation: 49,001
Founded in 1944
Printed in 4 colors on glossy stock

13497 Contractor Magazine
Penton Media
1300 E 9th St
Cleveland, OH 44114-1503
216-696-7000; Fax: 216-696-6662
information@penton.com
www.contractormag.com
Facebook, Twitter
Jane Cooper, Marketing
Bob Mader, Managing Editor
David B. Nussbaum, CEO
For contractors who sell, install, service air conditioning, heating, piping, plumbing, air handling, heat transfer and fluid controls equipment. Accepts advertising.
70 Pages
Frequency: Monthly
Circulation: 50000
Founded in 1892

13498 District Energy
International District Enery Association (IDEA)
24 Lyman Streetad
Suite 230
Westborough, MA 01581
508-366-9339; Fax: 508-366-0019
idea@districtenergy.org
www.districtenergy.org
Peter Myers, Editor
Rob Thornton, President
Journal of district heating and cooling industry, congeneration, physical plants and energy efficiency. Accepts advertising.
Cost: $40.00
Frequency: Quarterly

13499 **Engineered Systems**
Business News Publishing Company
1050 IL Route 83
Suite 200
Bensenville, IL 60106-1096

630-377-5909
www.esmagazine.com

Katie Rotella, Manager
Peter E Moran, Publisher

Research conducted by us shows that end users, consulting engineers, and contractors work together closely on the specification and selection of engineered HVAC/r systems and components. We give this receptive audience solid editorial information about real-world solutions to the everyday situations faced in the industry.
72 Pages
Frequency: Monthly
Circulation: 57515
Founded in 1985
Mailing list available for rent: 57.5M names
Printed in 4 colors on glossy stock

13500 **Fuel Oil News**
Hunter Publishing Limited
3100 S King Dr
7th Floor
Chicago, IL 60616-3483

312-567-9981; Fax: 312-846-4632
www.fueloilnews.com

Luke Hunter, Partner
Joanne Juda, Circulation Director
Kate Kenny, Publisher
Chris Traczek, Editor-in-Chief
Patricia McCartney, Associate Editor

For home heating oil retailers.
Cost: $28.00
70 Pages
Frequency: Monthly
Circulation: 15200
Founded in 1935
Printed in 4 colors on glossy stock

13501 **HEI Standards**
Heat Exchange Institute
1300 Sumner Avenue
Cleveland, OH 44115

216-241-7333; Fax: 216-241-0105
www.heatexchange.org/standards.html

Outlines standards developed by the Heat Exchange Institute for the heat exchange industry.

13502 **HEI Tech Sheets**
Heat Exchange Institute
1300 Sumner Avenue
Cleveland, OH 44115

216-241-7333; Fax: 216-241-0105
www.heatexchange.org/tech_sheets.html

Information on heat exchange subjects, covering vacuum technology among other topics.

13503 **HVAC Insider**
Retailing Newspapers
PO Box 81489
Conveyors, GA 30013

770-787-0115; Fax: 770-787-1213

Jerry M Lawson, Publisher
Robert Scott, Chief Information Officer

Up to date information on technical tips, product reviews, commercial and industrial industry new, a job bulletin, new businesses and promotions, and a calendar of events. Retailing Newspapers issues a monthly publication for the Appliance and Electronics trade. Insiders Newspapers issues a quarterly national and 14 monthly regionals for the HVAC trade and a monthly regional publication for the plumbing trade.
Frequency: Monthly
Circulation: 118740
Founded in 1969
Printed in 4 colors on newsprint stock

13504 **HVAC/R Distribution Today**
HARDI
445 Hutchinson Avenue
Suite 550
Columbus, OH 43235
614-345-4328
888-253-2128; Fax: 614-345-9161
www.hardinet.org

Talbot H. Gee, CEO

Official publication of Heating, Air Conditioning and Refrigeration International. Uniting world class distribution.
Frequency: Quarterly
Founded in 1960

13505 **HVACR & Plumbing Distribution**
Penton Media
1300 E 9th St
Cleveland, OH 44114-1503

216-696-7000; Fax: 216-696-6662
information@penton.com
www.penton.com

Jane Cooper, Marketing
Perry Clark, Publisher

Exclusively for plumbing and heating equipment distributors.
Circulation: 10,000
Founded in 1890

13506 **Hearth & Home**
Village West Publishing
P.O. Box 1288
Laconia, NH 03246

603-528-4285
800-258-3772; Fax: 888-873-3610
wright@villagewest.com
www.hearthandhome.com
Facebook, LinkedIn

Richard Wright, Editor
Jackie Avignone, Advertising Director
Erica Paquette, Art Director

Information for retailers and others selling hearth products, patio furnishing, barbecues, spas, garden accessories, and other outdoor products.
Cost: $36.00
Frequency: Monthly
Circulation: 18000

13507 **Industrial Heating**
Business News Publishing Company
1910 Cochran Road
Manor Oak One, Suite 450
Pittsburgh, PA 15220

412-531-3370; Fax: 412-531-3375
www.industrialheating.com
Facebook, Twitter

Ed Kubel, Editor
Beth McClelland, Production Manager
Doug Glenn, Publisher
Kathy Pisano, Advertising Director
Patrick Connolly, Sales Representative

We have been applying the latest advances in thermal technology to practical use since 1931. With over 22,000 BPA audited circulation comprised of mostly thermal processing engineers, technical articles cover heat treatments, brazing, sintering, melting, process control, instrumentation, refractories, burners, heating elements, and other thermal processes typically in excess of 1000 degrees.
Cost: $55.00
70 Pages
Circulation: 22100
ISSN: 0019-8374
Founded in 1931
Printed in 4 colors on glossy stock

13508 **International Journal of Energy Management**
Association of Energy Engineers
3168 Mercer University Drive
Atlanta, GA 30341

770-447-5083
www.aeecenter.org
Facebook, Twitter, LinkedIn

Albert Thumann, Executive Director
Steven Parker, Editor

Exclusively written for engineers, energy managers, facility managers, utility professionals, VP's of operations, governmental energy managers and plant engineers involved in the design and application of energy management and facility improvement technologies.

13509 **MACS ACtion Magazine**
Mobile Air Conditioning Society Worldwide
225 S. Broad Street
P.O. Box 88
Lansdale, PA 19446

215-631-7020; Fax: 215-631-7017
macsworldwide@macsw.org
www.macsw.org

Elvis Hoffpauir, President/COO
Marion Posen, VP Marketing/Membership

A trade association news magazine for the Mobile Air Conditioning Society Worldwide.
Frequency: 8x Yearly
Circulation: 13000
Founded in 1981

13510 **PM Engineer**
Business News Publishing Company
1050 IL Route 83
Suite 200
Bensenville, IL 60106-1096

630-377-5909
www.pmengineer.com
Facebook, Twitter

Bob Miodonski, Group Publisher & Editor
Mike Miazga, Senior Editor
Julius Ballanco, Editorial Director
Suzette Rubio, Online Editor
John Siegenthaler, Hydronics Editor

Provides technical sheets, manufacturer product brochures, news features and analysis of useful industry information on the engineering and design of plumbing, piping, hydronics, cooling/heating, and fire protection/sprinkler systems. Free to trade engineers.
Cost: $64.00
80 Pages
Frequency: Monthly
Circulation: 25000
Founded in 1926
Printed in 4 colors on glossy stock

13511 **RSES Journal**
Refrigeration Service Engineers Society
1666 Rand Rd
Des Plaines, IL 60016-3552
847-297-6464
800-297-5660; Fax: 847-297-5038
general@rses.org
www.rses.org
Facebook, Twitter, LinkedIn

John Iwanski, Publishing Director
Lori A Kasallis, Editor

Providing quality technical content in digital and printed forms that can be applied on the job site.
Frequency: Monthly
Circulation: 15231

13512 **Reeves Journal**
23421 S Pointe Drive
Suite 280
Laguna Hills, CA 92654
949-830-0881; Fax: 949-859-7845
www.reevesjournal.com
Ellyn Fishman, Publisher
John Fultz, Editor
Tagg Henderson, CEO
An invaluable tool for Western plumbing contractors and industry professionals for more than 80 years.
Frequency: Monthly
Circulation: 13545
Founded in 1926

13513 **Refrigeration**
John W Yopp Publications
73 Sen Island Parkway Suite 21
PO Box 1147
Beaufort, SC 29901-1147
843-521-0239
800-849-9667; Fax: 843-521-1398
www.refrigeration-magazine.com
John W Yopp, Chairman
Joe Cronley, Publisher
Mary Yopp Cronley, Associate Publsiher
Cheryl Graffo, Editor
About the plants and processes used in ice manufacture, marketing and merchandising information, news of associations, meetings and new products available.
Cost: $20.00
Frequency: Monthly
Circulation: 3200
Founded in 1919
Printed in 4 colors on glossy stock

13514 **Snips**
Business News Publishing Company
2401 W. Big Beaver Road
Suite 700
Troy, MI 48084
248-362-3700; Fax: 248-362-0317
snips@halldata.com
www.snipsmag.com
Katie Rotella, Manager
Sally Fraser, Advertising Sales
Karen Koppins, Advertising Productions
Ann Kalb, Customer Service
Michael McConnel, Editorial Director
Magazine directed to the heating, air conditioning, sheet metal and ventilation industry. Accepts advertising.
Cost: $18.00
120 Pages
Frequency: Monthly
Circulation: 22000
Founded in 1926
Printed in 4 colors on glossy stock

13515 **Tab Journal**
Associated Air Balance Council
1518 K Street NW
Washington, DC 20005-1203
202-737-0202; Fax: 202-638-4833
www.aabchq.com/
Kenneth M Sufka, Publisher
Mike Young, President
Case studies, industry updates, as well as other news of importance to engineers.
Cost: $24.00
Frequency: Quarterly
Circulation: 12000
Founded in 1965

13516 **Todays A/C and Refrigeration News**
Todays Trade Publications
PO Box 521247
130 W Pine Ave
Longwood, FL 32750-1247
407-332-4959
866-320-2773; Fax: 407-332-5319
www.todays-ac.com
Thomas Fatchell, Editor
Covers industry legislation, building codes, licensing requirements and continuing educations. New product reviews and personnel changes are also included.
Frequency: Monthly
Circulation: 20000
Founded in 1988

Trade Shows

13517 **ABMA Annual Meeting**
American Boiler Manufacturers Association
8221 Old Courthouse Road
Suite 207
Vienna, VA 22182-3839
703-356-7172; Fax: 703-356-4543
www.abma.com
Scott Lynch, President/CEO
Shaunica Jayson, Membership & Marketing Manager
Marissa Torres, Director of Meetings
The association's premier membership networking events. In casual and relaxed settings, members have the opportunity to not only learn about developments and trends, both inside and outside their industry, that are likely to influence their business, members are also afforded the opportunity, through committee and product/market group meetings to focus on issues and concerns of specific relevance to their product and market segments.
Frequency: Bi-Annual
Founded in 1888

13518 **ABMA Manufacturers Conference**
American Boiler Manufacturers Association
8221 Old Courthouse Road
Suite 207
Vienna, VA 22182-3839
703-356-7172; Fax: 703-356-4543
www.abma.com
Scott Lynch, President/CEO
Bethany Jones, Administrative Coordinator
Marissa Torres, Director of Meetings
Gene Tompkins, Technical Team Lead
Hugh K. Webster, Association General Counsel
Designed to bring together manufacturing plant, office and others concerned with the design, fabrication, sales and distribution of ABMA'products and services to network, discuss trends and developments, and problem solve with others in the industry and with outside experts.
Frequency: Annual/October
Founded in 1888

13519 **AMCA Annual Meeting**
Air Movement and Control Assoc. Intl., Inc.
30 West University Dr.
Arlington Heights, IL 60004
847-394-0150
www.amca.org
Facebook, Twitter, LinkedIn
Dr. Geoff Sheard, Chairman
Patrick Cockrum, President
Mark Stevens, Executive Director

13520 **ASA CONNECT**
American Supply Association
1200 Arlington Heights Road
Itasca, IL 60143
630-467-0000; Fax: 630-467-0001
info@asa.net
www.asa.net
Mike Adelizzi, CEO
Aaron Scheiwe, CFO
Annual conference for wholesalers, distributors and manufacturers of plumbing and heating pipes, valves and fittings.
1800 Attendees
Frequency: Annual

13521 **Air Conditioning Contractors of America Annual Conference**
Air Conditioning Contractors of America
2800 S Shirlington Road
Suite 300
Arlington, VA 22206
703-575-4477
membership@acca.org
www.acca.org
Barton James, President & CEO
Samuel Awotwi, Director of Finance
Kimya Bailey, Director, Events & Benchmarking
Sean Robertson, VP, Membership/Business Operations
Annual meeting and exhibits of heating, air conditioning and refrigeration equipment, supplies and services. Over 140 exhibitors, plus seminar, workshop and banquet.
1000 Attendees

13522 **Air Conditioning Heating & Refrigeration Expo Mexico - AHR**
Industrial Shows of America
164 Lake Front Drive
Hunt Valley, MD 21030-2215
410-771-1445
800-638-6396; Fax: 410-771-1158
www.isoa.com
Bryan Mayes, President
Phillip McKay, Managing Director
300 exhibitors with air conditioning, heating and refrigerating equipment, supplies and information. Attended by professionals.
5000 Attendees
Frequency: Annual

13523 **Annual Campus Energy Conference**
International District Energy Association
24 Lyman Street
Suite 230
Westborough, MA 01581
508-366-9339; Fax: 508-366-0019
idea@districtenergy.org
www.districtenergy.org
Robert Thornton, President
Vincent Bedeli, Chair
Leonard Phillips, Director of Business Development
IDEA fosters the success of its members as leaders in providing reliable, economical, and environmentally sound district energy services.
600 Attendees
Frequency: Annual/June
Founded in 1909

13524 **Hearth Products Association**
1555 Wilson Boulevard
Suite 300
Arlington, VA 22209-2405
703-522-0086; Fax: 703-812-8875
Facebook, Twitter
Joan Letch Worth, Show Manager

900 booths of products related to the residential alternative fuel heating industry.
8M Attendees
Frequency: Annual/March

13525 Heating, Air Conditioning & Refrigeration Distributors International
445 Hutchinson Avenue
Suite 550
Columbus, OH 43235

614-345-4328
888-253-2128; Fax: 614-345-9161
www.hardinet.org

Talbot H. Gee, CEO

Annual show of 200 exhibitors of heating and air conditioning equipment, supplies and services.
1200 Attendees
Founded in 2003

13526 International Air Conditioning, Heating & Refrigerating Expo
International Exposition Company
15 Franklin Street
Westport, CT 06880

203-221-9232; Fax: 203-221-9260
info@ahrexpo.com
www.ahrexpo.com

Mark Stevens, Vice President
Jeff Stevens, Sales Vice President

Co-sponsored by American Society of Heating, Refrigeration and Air Conditioning Engineers and the Air Conditioning and Refrigeration Institute, this expo features exhibits that include equipment and services of industrial, commercial and residential heating, refrigeration, air conditioning and ventilation.
37292 Attendees
Frequency: Annual/January
Founded in 1930

13527 International Air Conditioning, Heating, & Refrigerating Expo
ASHRAE
1791 Tullie Circle NW
Atlanta, GA 30329

404-636-8400
800-527-4723; Fax: 404-321-5478
ashrae@ashrae.org
www.ashrae.org

Jeff H. Littleton, Executive VP

The largest HVAC&R event in America featuring over 1,600 exhibiting companies. Held every year in conjunction with the ASHRAE Winter Meeting.
30000 Attendees
Frequency: Annual/January
Founded in 1894

13528 International District Energy Association (IDEA) Show
1200 19th Street NW
Suite 300
Washington, DC 20036-2428

202-429-5131; Fax: 202-429-5113
www.districtenergy.org

John L Fiegel, Editor
Tammie Jackson, Advertising Manager

Show of the district heating and cooling industry, cogeneration, physical plants, energy efficiency.
40 booths.
450 Attendees
Frequency: Annual/June

13529 International Institute of Ammonia Refrigeration Annual Conference
1001 N Fairfax St
suite 503
Alexandria, VA 22314

703-312-4200; Fax: 202-857-1104
iiar_request@iiar.org

Adolfo Blasquez, Chair
Robert Port Jr, Vice Chair
Joe Mandato, Chair Elect
Marcos Braz, Treasurer
Bruce Badger, President

Show of the district heating and cooling industry, cogeneration, physical plants, energy efficiency.
40 booths.
750 Attendees
Frequency: Annual/March

13530 International Thermal Spray Conference & Exposition
ASM International
9639 Kinsman Road
Materials Park, OH 44073-0002

440-338-5151
800-336-5152; Fax: 440-338-4634
memberservicecenter@asminternational.org
www.asminternational.org

William T. Mahoney, Secretary & CEO
Lindy Good, Global Conference & Exhibit Planner

International annual conference for professional thermal spray technologists, researchers, manufacturers and suppliers.
30K Members
Frequency: Annual/May
Founded in 1913

13531 MACS Convention & Trade Show
Mobile Air Conditioning Society Worldwide
225 S. Broad Street
P.O. Box 88
Lansdale, PA 19446

215-631-7020; Fax: 215-631-7017
macsworldwide@macsw.org
www.macsw.org

Elvis Hoffpauir, President/COO
Marion Posen, VP Marketing/Membership
2000 Attendees
Frequency: Annual

13532 Midwest Contractors Expo
Kansas Assn of Plumbing, Heating & Cooling Contr
320 Laura Street
Wichita, KS 67211-1517

316-262-8860; Fax: 316-262-2782

Ray Katzenmeier, Owner

Annual show and exhibits of plumbing, heating and cooling equipment, supplies and services.

13533 National Plumbing, Heating, Cooling and Piping Products Exposition
Nat'l Assn of Plumbing-Heating-Cooling Contractors
180 S Washington Street
PO Box 6808
Falls Church, VA 22046

703-237-8100
800-533-7694; Fax: 703-237-7442
www.phccweb.org
Facebook, LinkedIn

Elicia Magruder, VP of Member Services
Cynthia A Sheridan, Foundation Chief Operating Officer
Charlotte R Perham, Senior Director of Communications

Annual show of 500 manufacturers and suppliers of equipment, supplies and services for the plumbing, heating and cooling industries.
15M Attendees
Frequency: Annual/October

13534 North American Thermal Analysis Society
Complete Conference
1540 River Park Drive
Suite 111
Sacramento, CA 95815-4608

916-922-7032; Fax: 916-922-7379

Marilyn Hauck, President

30 booths.
300 Attendees
Frequency: Annual/September

13535 Oil Heat Business and Industry Expo
20 Summer Street
#9137
Watertown, MA 02472-3468

FAX 781-924-1022

Bernard A Smith, Executive VP
Nancy Spinney, Expo Manager

This show provides a marketplace for prime purchasers of heating oil; oil heating, and air conditioning, as well as accessory equipment; fuel oil distribution equipment, trucks, transports, service and salesmen's vehicles; computers, office equipment; insurance programs and more.
8.5M Attendees
Frequency: Annual/June

13536 RSES Annual Conference and HVAC Technology Expo
Refrigeration Service Engineers Society
1666 Rand Road
Des Plaines, IL 60016-3552

847-297-6464
800-297-5660
general@rses.org
www.rses.org
Facebook, Twitter, LinkedIn

Mark Lowry, Executive Vice President
Josh Flaim, Operations Manager
Jean Birch, Conference & Seminar Manager

80 booths consisting primarily of products and services.

13537 Sheet Metal Air Conditioning Contractors National Association Show
4201 Lafayette Center Drive
Chantilly, VA 20151-1209

703-032-2980
http://www.smacna.org

Mary Lou Taylor, Convention Director
John Sroka, Executive VP

250 booths.
2.3M Attendees
Frequency: Annual/October

13538 Southwestern Ice Association Show
823 Congress Avenue
1300
Austin, TX 78701

512-479-0425; Fax: 512-495-9031

Andrea Barnard, Executive Director

30 booths.
200 Attendees
Frequency: Annual/February
Founded in 1891

Directories & Databases

13539 **Air Conditioning, Heating & Refrigeration News Directory Issue**
The Air-Conditioning, Heating & Refrigeration New
2401 W. Big Beaver Road
Suite 700
Troy, MI 48084

248-362-3700
www.achrnews.com

John Conrad, Publisher
Mike Murphy, Editor-in-Chief
Kyle Gargaro, Managing Editor
Greg Mazurkiewicz, Web Editor
Barbary Checket-Hanks, Service & Maintenance Editor

This issue offers a list of over 2,000 manufacturers, 5,000 wholesalers and factory outlets. Over 10,000 HVAC/R products, exporters and related trade organizations are also covered.
Cost: $35.00
618 Pages
Frequency: Annual
Circulation: 38,000
Printed in 4 colors on glossy stock

13540 **Annual Member Directory**
Air Conditioning & Heating Contractors of America
1712 New Hampshire Avenue NW
Washington, DC 20009-2502

202-483-9370; Fax: 202-234-4721

Rae Dorsey, Production Manager

A publication for the members of the Air Conditioning and Heating Contractors of America.
Circulation: 5,000

13541 **Directory of Certified Applied Air-Conditioning Products**
Air-Conditioning & Refrigeration Institute
4301 Fairfax Drive
Suite 425
Arlington, VA 22203-1634

703-248-8800

A list of 50 manufacturers of air conditioning and heating products.
Cost: $8.50
Frequency: Bi-Annual

13542 **Directory of Certified Unitary Air-Conditioners & Heat Pumps**
Air-Conditioning & Refrigeration Institute
4301 Fairfax Drive
Suite 425
Arlington, VA 22203-1634

703-248-8800

Air and coil heating and cooling units and air-to-air heat pumps manufacturers are profiled.
Cost: $13.00
Frequency: Bi-Annual

13543 **HPAC Engineering Information**
Penton Media
1300 E 9th St
Cleveland, OH 44114-1501

216-696-7000; Fax: 216-696-1752
information@penton.com
www.penton.com

Jane Cooper, Marketing
Cost: $30.00
300 Pages
Frequency: Annual
Circulation: 56,000
ISSN: 1527-4055
Printed in 4 colors on glossy stock

13544 **Industrial Heating Buyers Guide and Reference Handbook**
Business News Publishing
1050 IL Route 83
Suite 200
Bensenville, IL 60106-1096

630-377-5909
www.industrialheating.com
Facebook, Twitter, LinkedIn

Katie Rotella, Manager

Companies are profiled that have over 1,200 heating products, and heat treating, and other services in the worldwide industrial heating market.
Cost: $25.00
250 Pages
Circulation: 20,000

13545 **LP/Gas: Industry Buying Guide Issue**
Advanstar Communications
131 W 1st St
Duluth, MN 55802-2065

218-740-7200
800-346-0085; Fax: 218-723-9122
info@advanstar.com
www.advanstar.com

Kent Akervik, Manager

List of about 1,000 liquid propane gas equipment manufacturers and suppliers; list of about 700 distributors of gas appliances and equipment.
Cost: $50.00
Frequency: Annual
Circulation: 16,000
Printed in 4 colors on glossy stock

13546 **PM Directory & Reference Issue**
Business News Publishing
1050 IL Route 83
Suite 200
Bensenville, IL 60106-1096

630-377-5909
www.bnpmedia.com

Katie Rotella, Manager

Manufacturers, wholesalers, exporters, associations, products, consultants and manufacturers' representatives in the industries of plumbing, piping and hydronic heating.
Cost: $30.00
Frequency: Annual/December
Circulation: 42,000

13547 **Refrigeration: Ice Industry's Buyer's Guide Issue**
John W Yopp Publications
PO Box 1147
Beaufort, SC 29901-1147

843-521-0239
800-849-9677; Fax: 800-849-8418

Joe Cronley

Directory of services and supplies to the industry.
Cost: $3.00
Frequency: Annual
Circulation: 3,000

Industry Web Sites

13548 **http://gold.greyhouse.com**
G.O.L.D Grey House OnLine Databases

Grey House Publishing's online database platform, GOLD, offers Quick Search, Keyword Search and Expert Search for most business sectors including heating and air conditioning markets. The GOLD platform makes finding the information you need quick and easy - whether you're a novice searcher or an experienced database user. All of Grey House's directory products are available for subscription on the GOLD platform.

13549 **www.abma.com**
American Boiler Manufacturers Association

Manufacturers trade association representing companies involved in utility, industrial and commercial steam generation. Includes associate memberships for companies who sell to or work with these companies and those who own boilers. Holds technical and production conferences, and publishes technical guideline publications.

13550 **www.achrnews.com**
BNP Media

News, tips and a calendar of events for the heating & cooling industry.

13551 **www.aga.com**
American Gas Association

Events, publications, information, etc.

13552 **www.ari.org**
Air Conditioning & Refrigeration Institute

Trade association representing manufacturers of more than 90% of North American produced air-conditioning and commercial refrigeration equipment.

13553 **www.asa.net**
American Supply Association

ASA is a not-for-profit national organization serving wholesale distributors and their suppliers in the plumbing, heating, cooling and industrial and mechanical pipe, valves and fittings industries.

13554 **www.ashrae.org**
American Society of Heating, Refrigeration, AC

Research, activities, education and publications.

13555 **www.construction.com**

McGraw-Hill Construction (MHC), part of The McGraw-Hill Companies, connects people and projects across the design and construction industry, serving owners, architects, engineers, general contractors, subcontractors, building product manufacturers, suppliers, dealers, distributors and adjacent markets.

13556 **www.districtenergy.org**
International District Energy Association

Journal of district heating and cooling industry, congeneration, physical plants and energy efficiency. Accepts advertising.

13557 **www.gamanet.org**
Gas Appliance Manufacturers Association

Represents manufacturers of residential, commercial and industrial gas and oil fired appliances, associated controls and accessories, as well as equipment used in the production, transmission and distribution of fuel gases.

13558 **www.greyhouse.com**
Grey House Publishing

Authoritative reference directories for most business sectors including heating and air conditioning markets. Users can search the online databases with varied search criteria allowing for custom searches by product category, geographic area, sales volume, keyword, subject and more. Full Grey House catalog and online ordering also available.

13559 **www.impi.org**
International Microwave Power Institute

IMPI's members include scientists, researchers, lab technicians, product developers, marketing managers and a variety of other professionals in the microwave industry. The Institute serves the information needs of all specialists working with dielectric (microwave and RF) heating sytems, and was expanded in 1977 to meet the information needs relating to consumer microwave ovens and related products.

13560 www.macsw.org
Mobile Air Conditioning Society Worldwide

Information on technical training for professionals in the automotive air-conditioning industry.

13561 www.mha-net.org
Masonry Heater Association of North America

Promotes use of masonry heaters, increases public awareness and encourages reasonable governmental regulation.

13562 www.sweets.construction.com
McGraw Hill Construction

In depth product information that lets you find, compare, select, specify and make purchase decisions in the industrial product marketplace.

Associations

13563 **American Camping Association**
5000 State Road 67 North
Martinsville, IN 46151-7902

765-342-8456
800-428-2267; Fax: 765-342-2065
shallway@aca-camps.org
www.acacamps.org
Facebook, Twitter, LinkedIn, YouTube, Pinterest, Google+

Tisha Bolger, Chair
Rue Mapp, Vice Chair
Craig Whiting, Treasurer
Tom Holland, CEO
Steve Baskin, Board Member
6600+ Members
Founded in 1910
Mailing list available for rent

13564 **American Craft Council**
1224 Marshall Street NE.
Suite 200
Minneapolis, MN 55413

612-206-3100
800-836-3470; Fax: 612-355-2330
council@craftcouncil.org
www.craftcouncil.org
Facebook, Twitter, LinkedIn, YouTube, Pinterest, Google+, I

Stuart Kestenbaum, Board Chair
Gariel Ofiesh, Board Vice Chair
Libba Evans, Board Secretary
Kevin Buchi, Board Treasurer
Barbara Berlin, Board of Trustee Member

National nonprofit, educational organization dedicated to promotion, understanding and appreciation of contemporary American craft. Sponsors annual wholesale and retail shows, a magazine, a library and seminars.
Founded in 1943
Mailing list available for rent

13565 **American Home Sewing and Craft Association**
PO Box 369
Monroeville, PA 15146

412-372-5950; Fax: 212-714-1655
info@sewing.org
www.sewing.org

13566 **American Philatelic Society**
100 Match Factory Place
Bellefonte, PA 16823-1367

814-933-3803; Fax: 814-933-6128
apsinfo@stamps.org
www.stamps.org
Facebook, Twitter, LinkedIn, YouTube, Pinterest

Mick Zais, President
Scott English, Executive Director
Ken Martin, Chief Operating Officer
Judy Johnson, Membership Administration Manager
Mercer Bristow, Director, Expertizing

National organization for postage stamp collectors.
30000 Members
Founded in 1886

13567 **American Quilt Study Group**
American Quilt Study Group
1610 L Street
Lincoln, NE 68508-2509

402-477-1181; Fax: 402-477-1181
aqsg2@americanquiltstudygroup.org
www.americanquiltstudygroup.org

Lisa Erlandson, President
Lenna DeMarco, Vice President
Kathy Moore, Vice President
Judy J. Brott Buss, Ph.D., Executive Director
Anne E. Schuff, Member Services Coordinator

Establishes, sustains, and promotes the highest standards for quilt-related studies. We stimulate, nurture, and affirm engagement in quilt studies and provide opportunities for its dissemination.
1000 Members
Founded in 1980
Mailing list available for rent

13568 **American Specialty Toy Retailing Association**
432 N. Clark St.ÿ
Suite 305
Chicago, IL 60654

312-222-0984
800-591-0490; Fax: 312-222-0986
info@astratoy.org
www.astratoy.org
Facebook, Twitter

Dean May, Chair
Michael Levins, Past Chair
Ann Kienzle, Chair Electÿ
Tim Holliday, Treasurer
Erik Quam, Secretary

Providing a unified voice for the specialty toy industry, and opportunities to exchange information and ideas with counterparts. Membership benefits include workshops and seminars, vendor representative roundtables, membership directory and annual convention.
1000 Members
Founded in 1992

13569 **American Stamp Dealers Association**
PO Box 858
Suite 205
Morris Plains, NJ 07950

973-267-1644
800-369-8207; Fax: 800-369-8207
asda@americanstampdealer.com
www.asdaonline.com

Mark Reasoner, President
Stanley Piller, Vice President
Richard A. Friedberg, Secretary
James F. Bardo, Treasurer
Robert Prager, Director
800 Members
Founded in 1914

13570 **Archery Trade Association**
PO Box 70
101 N German St
New Ulm, MN 56073-0070

507-233-8130
866-266-2776; Fax: 507-233-8140
www.archerytrade.org
Facebook, Twitter

Jay McAninch, President/CEO
Kurt Weber, Director of Marketing
Patrick Durkin, Contributing Editor and Writer
Mitch King, Director of Government Relations
John Nelson, Director of Finance and Operations

Provides core funding and direction for two new foundations critical to the future of archery and bowhunting: Arrow Sport and the Bowhunting Preservation Alliance. In addition the ATA continues to direct the industry's annual archery and bowhunting trade show.
Founded in 1953
Mailing list available for rent

13571 **Association of Traditional Hooking Artists**
600 1/2 Maple Street
Endicott, NY 13760

jcahill29@aol.com
www.rughookersnetwork.com
Facebook

Joan Cahill, Membership Chairperson
Karen Balon, Guild Secretary
Mary Henck, President

Provides educational material about rug hooking, free patterns, supplies information, chapter/rug camp meetings and teacher information that is not available through any other source. Membership includes all 50 states, England, Japan and Australia.
Founded in 1996

13572 **Canadian Game Studies Assocation**

Home Page: gamestudies.ca
Twitter

The CGSA is devoted to the interdisciplinary study of digital games, and supports the work of researchers, graduate students, artists, game designers, programmers, theorists, and others working in the industry.
Mailing list available for rent

13573 **Corporate Esports Association**

administrator@cea.gg
cea.gg
Twitter, YouTube

Brad Tenenholtz, Chief Executive Officer
Michael Pleasant, Co-Founder & Chair
Terence Southard, Co-Founder & Board Member

Facilitates online esport tournaments for corporate professionals on Discord, to enocurage team-building and donate the proceeds to charity.

13574 **Digital Games Research Association**

coordinator@digra.org
www.digra.org

William Huber, President
Hanna Wirman, Vice President
Allan Fowler, Secretary
Jussi Holopainen, Treasurer
Cody Mejeur, Diversity Officer

DiGRA is an international association of academics and professionals interested in research into digital games and related products. It features a Digital Library, Gamesnetwork mailing list, and the ToDiGRA journal.
Founded in 2003
Mailing list available for rent

13575 **Embroidery Trade Association**
PO Box 793967
Dallas, TX 75379-3967

972-247-0415
888-628-2545; Fax: 972-755-2561
info@embroiderytrade.org
www.mesadist.com/trade_associations

John Swinburn, Executive Director
Dolores Cheek, Director of Membership
Keith Amen, VP

An organization with the objective to continually strengthen the commercial embriodery business.
1200 Members
Founded in 1990

13576 **Entertainment Consumers Association**

Home Page: www.theeca.com

Hal Halpin, Founder & President
Heather Ellertson, VP, Marketing
Jennifer Mercurio, VP & General Counsel

Brett Schenker, Advocacy Director
Mike Conley, Digital Marketing Coordinator

Non-profit representing the interests of consumers of digital entertainment in the US and Canada.

13577 Entertainment Software Association
601 Massachusetts Avenue NW
Suite 300
Washington, DC 20001

esa@theesa.com
www.theesa.com
Facebook, Twitter, LinkedIn

Stanley Pierre-Louis, President & CEO
Gina Vetere, SVP & General Counsel
Andrew Bowins, SVP, Comm. & Public Affairs
Ana Molina, CFO
Michael O'Leary, SVP, Government Affairs

The trade association of the video game industry.
Founded in 2000

13578 Entertainment Software Association of Canada
#408, 130 Spadina Avenue
Toronto, ON M5V 2L4

416-620-7171
theesa.ca
Facebook, Twitter, Instagram, YouTube

Jayson Hilchie, President & CEO
Corinne Crichlow, Director, Communications & PR
Paul Fogolin, Director, Policy & Gov. Affairs
Dylan Boyd, Digital Content Manager

The ESAC is devoted to video game developers, publishers, and distributors in Canada

13579 Entertainment Software Rating Board
New York, NY

marketing@esrb.org
www.esrb.org
Facebook, Twitter

Patricia E. Vance, President
David Kassack, SVP, Finance & Operations
Bill Garrity, SVP, Ratings
John Falzone, VP, ESRB Privacy Certified
Randy Walker, SVP, Marketing & Communications

Non-profit, self-regulatory body devoted to informing consumers (especially parents) about the video games they play. The ESRB established and maintains a ratings system for all video games, from E for Everyone to AO for Adults Only.
Founded in 1994

13580 Esports Trade Association
541 N. Fairbanks Court
Suite 2200
Chicago, IL 60611

708-680-7133
info@esportsta.org
esportsta.org
Facebook, Twitter, LinkedIn, YouTube, Instagram

Megan Van Petten, Founder & CEO

The ESTA serves the eSports community by promoting, protecting, and advancing its interests through professional development programs, networking opportunities, industry research, and tools and resources for members.
Founded in 2018

13581 Fantasy Sports & Gaming Association
1818 Parmenter Street
Suite 300
Middleton, WI 53562

608-310-7540
thefsga.org
Facebook, Twitter, LinkedIn

Christina McCoy, Executive Director
Michael Fiez, Marketing
Emily Petersen, Membership

The FSGA is a national organization representing fantasy sports and gaming companies, and serving those companies and players with research and data, networking opportunities, and collective action.

13582 Game Manufacturers Association
240 N. Fifth St.
Suite 340
Columbus, OH 43215

614-255-4500; Fax: 614-255-4499
president@gama.org
www.gama.org
Facebook

John ÿ Stacy, Executive Director
Chris Materni, Deputy Director
Melissa Jacobs, Education Manager
Paul McGraw, Events Manager
Kelly Mignogna, Communications Manager

A non-profit trade association dedicated to the advancement of the hobby game business.
Founded in 1977
Mailing list available for rent

13583 Handweavers Guild of America
1255 Buford Highway
Suite 209
Suwanee, GA 30024-8421

678-730-0010; Fax: 678-730-0836
hga@weavespindye.org
www.weavespindye.org
Facebook, Twitter, YouTube, Pinterest

Elizabeth Williamson, Executive Director
Ingrid Sciscoe, Membership/Development Coordinator
Kathi Grupp, Advertising & Marketing Manager
Whitney Young, Program Coordinator
Sally Orgren, Editor

An association that educations, supports, and inspires the fiber art community. Offers networking, education, and grants.
Founded in 1969

13584 Hobby Industry Association
319 E 54th Street
Elmwood Park, NJ 07407-2712

201-835-1200; Fax: 201-797-0657
info@craftandhobby.org
www.craftandhobby.org
Facebook, Twitter, LinkedIn, Pinterest, Youtube

David Murray, Chair
Mark Hill, Interim President, CEO
Chuck McGonigle, Vice Chair
Natalie Cohn, Vice President, Finance & Admin.
Maureen Walsh, Vice President, Marketing

Trade association in the craft and hobby market. The group produces an international trade show open to qualified professionals and is the industry's only market research show.
4000 Members
Founded in 1940
Mailing list available for rent

13585 Hobby Manufacturers Association
1410 East Erie Avenue
Philadelphia, PA 07405-0315

267-341-1604; Fax: 215-744-4699
heather.stoltzfus@hmahobby.org
www.hmahobby.org

Richard Janyszek, President
Bill Jeric, Vice President
Fred Hill, Treasurer
Abby Robey, Secretary
Mike MacDowell, Board of Director

The mission of the Hobby Manufacturers Association is to stimulate the growth of the model hobby industry.
292 Members
Founded in 2005

13586 International Council of Toy Industries
ICTI Secretariat, c/o Toy Industry Association
1375 Broadway, Suite 1001
New York, NY 10018

202-459-0355
icti@toyassociation.org
www.toy-icti.org

May Liang, President

Association of toy brands from 20 countries acting on issues of importance to the toy industry.
Founded in 1975

13587 International Game Developers Association
#402, 150 Eglinton Avenue E.
Toronto, ON M4P 1E8

info@igda.org
www.igda.org
Facebook, Twitter, LinkedIn, YouTube, Instagram

Renee Gittins, Executive Director
Tristin Hightower, Director, Operations

The IGDA is the largest non-profit membership organization serving individuals who create video games. They are dedicated to improving developers' careers and lives through: Community, Professional Development, and Advocacy.
Founded in 1994

13588 Major League Gaming
Home Page: www.mlg.com
Facebook, Twitter, YouTube, Instagram, Snapchat

Steve Bornstein, Chairman
Pete Vlastelica, President & CEO
Michael Sepso, Co-Founder & SVP, Media Networks
Sundance DiGiovanni, Co-Founder & VP, Brands & Content
Pavel Murnikov, VP, Technology

A professional eSports organization. MLG.tv, its free video streaming eSports showcase, attracts 27 million users per month.
Founded in 2002

13589 Museum Store Association
2025 M Street NW
Suite 800
Washington, DC 20036

202-367-1106; Fax: 202-367-2104
info@museumstoreassociation.org
www.museumstoreassociation.org
Facebook, Twitter, LinkedIn, Pinterest

Steven Antolick, Executive Director
2500 Members
Founded in 1955

13590 **National School Supply Equipment Association**
8380 Colesville Rd
Suite 250
Silver Spring, MD 20910-6225
301-495-0240
800-395-5550; Fax: 301-495-3330
www.nssea.org
Facebook, Twitter, LinkedIn, Youtube
Jim McGarry, President/CEO
Bill Duffy, Vice President - Operations
Adrienne Dayton, Vice President - Marketing
Joe Tucker, CEM, CMP, Director of Meetings & Experiences
Michael Nercesian, Exhibits Manager
Trade Association for the educational products industry.
1400+ Members
Founded in 1916

13591 **Professional Esports Association**
pea@cloud9.gg
www.proesports.org
Facebook, Twitter, Instagram
PEA is a coalition of eSports teams aiming to advance the industry and grow the business of eSports.
Founded in 2016

13592 **Toy Industry Association**
1115 Broadway
Suite 400
New York, NY 10010-3466
212-675-1141; Fax: 212-633-1429
info@toyassociation.org
www.toyassociation.org/
Facebook, Twitter, LinkedIn, Youtube
John Gessert, Chairman
David Hargreaves, Vice Chairman
Steve Pasierb, President and CEO
Bob Wann, Secretary-Treasurer
Shirley Price, Member of the Executive Committeeÿ
National organization with toy, game and holiday decoration manufacturers and their representatives, as well as toy designers, testing laboratories, licensors, sales representatives and trade magazines.
400+ Members
Founded in 1916

13593 **United States eSports Federation**
Home Page: www.esportsfederation.org
Instagram
Vlad Marinescu, President
Robin Kent, General Secretary
Lance Mudd, Sport Director
Ryan Terao, VP, Education Commission
Robert Davidman, VP, Integrity Commission
USeF is the U.S. member organization of the International e-Sports Federation and official governing body of eSports in the U.S. Its goal is to promote eSports and protect athletes by uniting all facets of the industry: stakeholders, athletes, event organizers, technology producers, innovators and inventors, IP holders, parents, sponsors, and fans.
Founded in 2016

13594 **Western Toy & Hobby Representatives Association**
PO Box 14874
Long Beach, CA 90853
833-869-3378; Fax: 909-697-2014
toyshow@wthra.com
toyfestwest.com
Carrie Scanlan, Show Manager
Bill St. John, President
Blake Goldenberg, Chairman
A nonprofit organization that produces and promotes ToyFest West.
75 Members
Founded in 1961

13595 **World Esports Association**
info@wesa.gg
www.wesa.gg
Facebook, Twitter
Pietro Fringuelli, Executive Chair & Commissioner
Sebastian Weishaar, Board Member
Ulrich Schulze, Board Member
Ralf Reichert, Board Member
Erik Anderson, Board Member
WESA is an international body aiming to professionalize eSports by introducing elements common among traditional sports associations, including player representation, standardized regulations, & revenue shares for teams. It is a joint effort between eSports teams and eSports company ESL.

Newsletters

13596 **American Stamp Dealers Association Newsletter**
American Stamp Dealers Association
3 School St
Suite 205
Glen Cove, NY 11542-2548
516-759-7000; Fax: 800-369-8207
www.asdaonline.com
Joseph Savarese, Executive VP
Elizabeth Pope, Secretary
Kim Kellermann, Secretary
Thomas Jacks, Treasurer
Association news.
Frequency: Monthly
Circulation: 810
Founded in 1914
Printed in on matte stock

13597 **Bill Nelson Newsletter**
Nelson Newsletter Publishing Corporation
PO Box 90890
Tucson, AZ 85752-0890
520-297-8240
800-368-8434; Fax: 520-629-0387
James Lee, President
Features news on the pin collecting hobby.
Cost: $20.00
8 Pages
Frequency: Monthly
Printed in one color on matte stock

13598 **ECA Today**
Entertainment Consumers Association
Home Page: www.theeca.com
Hal Halpin, Founder & President
Heather Ellertson, VP, Marketing
Mike Conley, Digital Marketing Coordinator
Newsletter for members only.
Frequency: Nightly

13599 **Guild of Natural Science Illustration**
Guild of Natural Science Illustrators
PO Box 652
Ben Franklin Station
Washington, DC 20044-652
301-309-1514; Fax: 301-309-1514
gnsihome@his.com
www.gnsi.org
Gretchen Kai Halpert, President
Erica Beade, Vice President
Non-profit organization for those interested in the field of natural science illustrations. Newsletter is published 10 times a year.
Cost: $75.00
Frequency: 10x Yearly
Circulation: 1000
Founded in 1968

13600 **This Time**
Homeworkers Organized for More Employment
PO Box 10
Orland, ME 04472
207-469-7961; Fax: 207-469-1023
info@homecoop.net
www.homecoop.net/
Lucy Toulin, President
J Ralph, Editor
F Eldridge, Volunteer Coordinator
Home community newsletter, part of the world Emmaus movement, offering information on craft store items and antiques. Member of rural coalition , Washington D.C..
Cost: $5.00
16 Pages
Frequency: Quarterly
Circulation: 300
Founded in 1970

Magazines & Journals

13601 **ABCs of Retailing**
Hobby Industry Association
319 E 54th St
Suite 348
Elmwood Park, NJ 07407-2712
201-794-1133; Fax: 201-797-0657
www.craftandhobby.org
Steve Berger, CEO
Guide to opening and maintaining a craft/hobby retail store.
20 Pages
Founded in 1940

13602 **American Craft Magazine**
72 Spring St
New York, NY 10012-4090
212-274-0630; Fax: 212-274-0650
council@craftcouncil.org
www.craftcouncil.org
Andrew Wagner, Manager
John Gourlay, Publisher
Lois Moran, Editor-in-Chief
Celebrates the excellence of contemporary craft, focusing on masterful achievements in the craft media — clay, fiber, metal, glass, wood and other materials — with the goal to create intellectual and visual interest for the reader on today's craft.
Cost: $40.00
Founded in 1943

13603 **American Philatelist**
American Philatelic Society
100 Match Factory Place
Bellefonte, PA 16823-1367
814-237-3803; Fax: 814-933-6128
apsinfo@stamps.org
www.stamps.org
Facebook, Twitter, LinkedIn, YouTube, Pinterest
Jay Bigalke, Editor
Jeff Stage, Editorial Associate
Doris Wilson, Editorial Associate
Helen Bruno, Advertising Manager
Scott English, Executive Director
Monthly magazine for stamp collectors, including articles, society news, and calendar of

events.
Cost: $80.00
30000 Members
100 Pages
Frequency: Monthly
Circulation: 37500
ISSN: 0003-0473
Founded in 1886

13604 **Antiques and Collecting Hobbies**
Lightner Publishing Corporation
1006 S Michigan Ave
Chicago, IL 60605-2216

312-939-4767; Fax: 312-939-0053

Antiques and collectible news articles.
Cost: $32.00
88 Pages
Frequency: Monthly
Circulation: 18,000
Founded in 1931

13605 **Bank Note Reporter**
F+W Media
38 E. 29th Street
New York, NY 10016

212-447-1400; Fax: 212-447-5231
contact_us@fwmedia.com
Facebook, Twitter, LinkedIn

Bill Bright, General Manager
Dave Harper, Editor
Buddy Redling, Manager
Chad Phelps, Chief Digital Officer
Stacie Berger, Communications Director

Recognized as the finest publication for paper money collectors available. Contains news on market values, 'Bank Note Clinic' (a collector Q&A), an up-to-date foreign exchange chart, 'Fun Notes' (interesting, odd & unusual notes), a price guide, a world currency section, historical features on paper money worldwide (emphasizing US issues), & hundreds of display & classified ads offering to buy, sell, & trade bank notes of all kinds. Contributors include some of the top experts in the field.
Cost: $21.98
84 Pages
Frequency: Monthly
Circulation: 8072
Founded in 1952
Mailing list available for rent

13606 **Blade**
F+W Media
38 E. 29th Street
New York, NY 10016

212-447-1400; Fax: 212-447-5231
contact_us@fwmedia.com
Facebook, Twitter, LinkedIn

David Nussbaum, CEO/Chairman
Steve Shackleford, Editor
Jim Ogle, Chief Financial Officer
Chad Phelps, Chief Digital Officer
Stacie Berger, Communications Director

Provides knifemakers, collectors, and knife enthusiasts with information concerning new knife-making techniques and processes, field tests, and the latest news and features on knives and their makers. Also includes a Q&A section, letters to the editor, features about individual knifemakers, an extensive listing of upcoming knife shows, and a reader feature entitled, 'The Knife I Carry.'
Cost: $25.98
140 Pages
Frequency: Monthly
Circulation: 38068
ISSN: 1064-5853
Founded in 1973
Mailing list available for rent

13607 **Cast On Magazine**
The Knitting Guild Association (TKGA)
1100-H Brandywine Blvd.
Zanesville, OH 43701-7303

740-452-4541
tkga@tkga.com
tkga.org
Facebook, Twitter, LinkedIn

Arenda Holladay, Editor & Executive Director

Educational journal for knitters.
10000 Members
Frequency: Quarterly
Circulation: 11,000
Mailing list available for rent

13608 **Coin Prices**
F+W Media
38 E. 29th Street
New York, NY 10016

212-447-1400; Fax: 212-447-5231
contact_us@fwmedia.com
Facebook, Twitter, LinkedIn

Bill Bright, General Manager
Bob Van Ryzin, Editor
Jim Ogle, Chief Financial Officer
Chad Phelps, Chief Digital Officer
Stacie Berger, Communications Director

Coin Prices is a complete guide to retail values for collectible US coins. A market update section (value guide) by market editor Joel Edler beings each issue. Rotating special sections provide values for Canadian and Mexican coins, Colonial coins, territorial coins, errors and varieties and selected issues of US paper money. Regular departments include a guide to grading US coins.
Cost: $18.98
96 Pages
Circulation: 56611
Founded in 1952
Mailing list available for rent

13609 **Coins**
F+W Media
38 E. 29th Street
New York, NY 10016

212-447-1400; Fax: 212-447-5231
contact_us@fwmedia.com
Facebook, Twitter, LinkedIn

Bill Bright, General Manager
Bob Van Ryzin, Editor
Jim Ogle, Chief Financial Officer
Chad Phelps, Chief Digital Officer
Stacie Berger, Communications Director

Covers market trends, buying tips, and historical perspectives on all aspects of numismatics. The news section, 'Bits and Pieces,' wraps up the latest happenings in numismatics. Regular columns and departments include 'Basics& Beyond,' 'Budget Buyer,' 'Coin Clinic' (Q&A), the editor's column, coin finds, a calendar of upcoming shows nationwide, 'Coin Values Guide' and 'Market Watch.'
Cost: $20.98
120 Pages
Frequency: Monthly
Circulation: 52660
Founded in 1955
Mailing list available for rent

13610 **Comics & Games Retailer**
F+W Media
38 E. 29th Street
New York, NY 10016

212-447-1400; Fax: 212-447-5231
contact_us@fwmedia.com
Facebook, Twitter, LinkedIn

Mark Williams, Publisher
John Miller, Editor
Norma Jean Fochs, Ad Manager

Provides information to retailers about marketing, industry news, and practical how-to tips on selling comics and games at the retail level. Regular columns include 'Suggested for Mature Retailers,' 'Small Store Strategy,' 'Trade Show Calendar,' 'Retailer News,' and 'Distributor News.' Special issue focus on the comic book industry, trade shows, trading cards, gaming, display racks, and other retail store supplies. 'Market Beat' gives a national overview of the comics market.
Cost: $29.95
72 Pages
Frequency: Monthly
Circulation: 5,201
Founded in 1971
Mailing list available for rent

13611 **Comics Buyer's Guide**
F+W Media
38 E. 29th Street
New York, NY 10016

212-447-1400; Fax: 212-447-5231
contact_us@fwmedia.com
Facebook, Twitter, LinkedIn

David Nussbaum, CEO/Chairman
Maggie Thompson, Editor
Jim Ogle, Chief Financial Officer
Chad Phelps, Chief Digital Officer
Stacie Berger, Communications Director

The longest-running magazine about comic books. Each 200+ page monthly issue features new comic reviews, nostalgic retroviews, interviews and the largest monthly price guide. Aslo included is the latest convention news, opinion pieces from celebrity columnists and expanded coverage of anime, manga and other comics-related auctions.
Cost: $38.95
244 Pages
Frequency: Monthly
Circulation: 30,000
ISSN: 1064-5853
Founded in 1952
Mailing list available for rent

13612 **Craftrends**
Primedia Enthusiast Group Publishing
741 Corporate Circle
Suite A
Golden, CO 80401

303-278-1010
800-881-6634; Fax: 303-277-0370
www.enthusiastnetwork.com

Bill Gardner, Editorial Director
Beth Hess, Managing Editor
Dave O'Neil, VP Group Publishing
Kelly P. Conlin, President/CEO

Includes new products, coverage of industry trade shows, merchandising and promotion ideas. Also has timely information to operate a craft business and stay on top of a rapidly changing retail environment.
Cost: $26.00
Frequency: Monthly
Circulation: 22000
Founded in 1989

13613 **Crafts Magazine**
Primedia Enthusiast Group Publishing
PO Box 420494
Palm Coast, FL 32142-9524

800-727-2387; Fax: 386-447-2321
papercrafts@palmcoastd.com
www.craftcouncil.org

Valerie Pingree, Editor-in-Chief
Mike Irish, Associate Publisher
Kelly P Conlin, CEO/President

Monthly craft consumer magazine reaching the crafting enthusiast.
Cost: $15.97
112 Pages
Circulation: 300272
ISSN: 0148-9127
Founded in 1989
Printed in 4 colors on glossy stock

13614 Crafts Report
Crafts Reports Publishing
100 Rogers Road
Wilmington, DE 19801

302-656-2209
800-777-7098; Fax: 302-656-4894
www.craftsreport.com

Lammot Copeland Jr, Publisher
Heather Skelly, Editor
Stewart Abowitz, Marketing Director
Deborah Copeland, Co-Publisher

Monthly business magazine for the crafts professional, providing information on marketing, growing your craft business, time management, studio safety, retail relationships, artist/retailer profiles, show listings and more.
Cost: $29.00
Frequency: Monthly
Circulation: 30000
ISSN: 0160-7650
Founded in 1975
Printed in 4 colors on glossy stock

13615 Creative Knitting
House of White Birches
306 E Parr Rd
Berne, IN 46711-1100

260-589-8741
800-829-5865; Fax: 260-589-8093
customer_service@drgbooks.com
www.whitebirches.com

David J McKee, CEO
John Boggs, Advertising Sales Director
Carl Musselman, Editor
David J McKee, Publishing Director
Greg Deily, Marketing Director

Serves the knitting industry.
Cost: $13.00
64 Pages
Frequency: Monthly
Founded in 1947

13616 Doll Artisan
Jones Publishing
N7 450 Aanstad Road
PO Box 5000
Iola, WI 54945-5000

715-445-5000; Fax: 715-445-4053
joejones@jonespublishing.com
www.dollsbeautiful.com

Edited to entertain, fascinate and educate the doll maker in reproduction of antique porcelain dolls. Encourages and promotes efforts to make porcelain doll making easier, safer and more accessible to a growing number of enthusiasts.
Cost: $5.95
Frequency: Bi-Monthly

13617 Doll World
Jones Publishing
N7 450 Aanstad Road
PO Box 5000
Iola, WI 54945-5000

715-445-5000
800-331-0038; Fax: 715-445-4053
jonespub@jonespublishing.com
www.jonespublishing.com

Joe Jones, President
Nayda Rondon, Editor
Trina Laube, Assistant Editor
Virginia Adams, Marketing
Brandan Hardie, Circulation Manager
Cost: $32.95
Frequency: Monthly

13618 Dollmaking
Jones Publishing
N7 450 Aanstad Road
PO Box 5000
Iola, WI 54945-5000

715-445-5000; Fax: 715-445-4053
jonespub@jonespublishing.com
www.Dollmaking/Artisan.com

Resource for makers of porcelain and sculpted modern dolls, is edited for the serious costume and doll maker.
Cost: $4.95
Frequency: Bi-Monthly

13619 Essential Facts About the Computer and Video Game Industry
Entertainment Software Association
601 Massachusetts Avenue NW
Suite 300
Washington, DC 20001

esa@theesa.com
www.theesa.com

Stanley Pierre-Louis, President & CEO
Gina Vetere, SVP & General Counsel
Andrew Bowins, SVP, Comm. & Public Affairs
Ana Molina, CFO

Tracks statistics about the video game industry in the US.
Frequency: Annual
Founded in 2000

13620 Essentials Magazine
National School Supply Equipment
8300 Colesville Rd
Suite 250
Silver Spring, MD 20910-6225

301-495-0240
800-395-5550; Fax: 301-495-3330
www.nssea.org
Facebook, Twitter, LinkedIn

Jim McGarry, President/CEO
Rashad Cheeks, Meetings Coordinator
Tamara Davis, Bookkeeper/Office Manager
Karen Prince, Director of Membership
Bill Duffy, Vice President - Operations

13621 Family Tree
B&W Publications
1507 Dana Avenue
Cincinnati, OH 45207-1056

513-943-9464; Fax: 513-531-1843

Ideas and advice for discovering, preserving and celebrating family history.

13622 Family Tree Magazine
F+W Media
38 E. 29th Street
New York, NY 10016

212-447-1400; Fax: 212-447-5231
contact_us@fwmedia.com
Facebook, Twitter, LinkedIn

David Nussbaum, CEO/Chairman
Allison Stacy, Editor
Kelly Klener, Marketing
Chad Phelps, Chief Digital Officer
Stacie Berger, Communications Director

America's most popular family history magazine. It covers all areas of potential interest to family history enthusiasts, reaching beyond strict genealogy research to include ethnic heritage, family reunions, memoirs, oral history, scrapbooking, historical travel and other ways that families connect with their pasts. Each issue features the latest tools, how-to tips and expert advice to guide readers through the journey of discovering, preserving and celebrating their roots.
Cost: $27.00
84 Pages
Circulation: 80050
Founded in 1952
Mailing list available for rent

13623 Fine Woodworking
Taunton Press
63 S Main Street
PO Box 5506
Newtown, CT 06470-5506

203-270-6206
800-926-8776; Fax: 203-426-3434
fw@taunton.com
www.taunton.com

David Grey, Publisher
Linda Abbett, Advertising Manager
Anatole Burkin, Editor
John Lagan, National Account Manager

Published since 1975, written by woodworkers for woodworkers regularly shows the finest work in wood being done today.
Cost: $34.95
120 Pages
Circulation: 295000
Founded in 1975
Mailing list available for rent: 185M names
Printed in 4 colors on glossy stock

13624 Gun Digest
F+W Media
38 E. 29th Street
New York, NY 10016

212-447-1400; Fax: 212-447-5231
contact_us@fwmedia.com
Facebook, Twitter, LinkedIn

David Nussbaum, CEO/Chairman
Steve Hudziak, Marketing
Jim Ogle, Chief Financial Officer
Chad Phelps, Chief Digital Officer
Stacie Berger, Communications Director

An all-advertising, nationwide marketplace for buyers and sellers of new, used and antique firearms. Display advertising from the nation's top dealers, manufacturers, distributors, and suppliers is found in each bi-weekly issue, along with thousands of classified word ads, organized alphabetically, from collectors all over the world. The nation's leading indexed firearms paper. Hundreds of gun show listings and knife show listings are included to help readers schedule their show attendance.
Cost: $37.98
136 Pages
Circulation: 81120
Founded in 1952
Mailing list available for rent

13625 HIA Craft/Hobby Consumer Study
Hobby Industry Association
319 E 54th St
Elmwood Park, NJ 07407-2712

201-794-1133; Fax: 201-797-0657
www.craftandhobby.org

Steve Berger, CEO

An extensive study of consumer behavior and buying habits relevant to the hobby/craft/creative industry. Executive summary is available on-line.
Cost: $400.00
Circulation: 5000
Founded in 2004

13626 Hobby Merchandiser
Hobby Publications
207 Commercial Court
PO Box 102
Morganville, NJ 07751-102

732-536-5160
800-969-7176; Fax: 732-536-5761
info@hobbymerchandiser.com
www.hobbymerchandiser.com/

Robert Gherman, Publisher
Jeff Troy, Editor
Patrick Sarver, Associate Publisher

Trade magazine for the model hobby industry, available to professionals only.
Cost: $20.00
96 Pages
Frequency: Monthly
Circulation: 7000
ISSN: 0744-1738
Founded in 1947
Mailing list available for rent: 8,300 names at $241 per M
Printed in 4 colors on glossy stock

13627 **Hobby Rocketry**
California Rocketry Publishing
PO Box 1242
Claremont, CA 91711-1242

760-389-2233; Fax: 661-824-0868
www.v-serv.com/crp

Jerry Irvine, Publisher

Covers consumer rocket products which are available in hobby, toy and retail outlets. Product reviews, manufacturers notes, consumer feedback and more. Back issues available.
Cost: $16.00
16 Pages
Frequency: Quarterly
Circulation: 8M
Founded in 1992
Printed in on newsprint stock

13628 **Horizons**
Hobby Industry Association
319 E 54th St
Elmwood Park, NJ 07407-2712

201-794-1133; Fax: 201-797-0657
www.craftandhobby.org

Steve Berger, CEO

Available only to members of the Hobby Association of America. This magazine offers information and updates on what is happening in the industry.
6 Pages
Frequency: Quarterly

13629 **Loading...**
Canadian Game Studies Assocation

jennifer.jenson@ubc.ca
gamestudies.ca

Suzanne de Catell, Editor
Jennifer Jenson, Co-Editor

Official journal of the Canadian Game Studies Assocation with articls on research into digital games.

13630 **Master Embroidery Manual**
Embroidery Trade Association
P.O. Box 794534
Suite 414
Dallas, TX 75379-4534

972-247-0415
888-628-2545; Fax: 972-755-2561
www.mesadist.com/trade_associations
Twitter, LinkedIn

John Swinburn, Executive Director
Dolores Cheek, Director Of Membership
Keith Amen, VP

Developed and published by ETA, this manual is an embroiderer's encyclopedia, especially for those new to the embroidery industry. Chapters include hooping & framing, backings & toppings, common goods and fabrics, and much more.
1200 Members
Founded in 1990

13631 **Model Retailer**
Kalmbach Publishing Company
21027 Crossroads Circle
PO Box 1612
Waukesha, WI 53187

262-796-8776
800-533-6644; Fax: 262-796-8776

Kevin Keefe, Publisher
Hal Miller, Editor
Rick Albers, Advertising Sales Manager
Jim Meinhardt, Circulation Manager

The business of hobbies, from financial and shop management issues to industry news and trends, as well as the latest in product releases. Provides hobby shop entreprenuers with the information, ideas and examples they need in order to be successful retailers.
Frequency: Monthly
Circulation: 6350
Founded in 1934

13632 **Needlework Retailer**
Yarn Tree Designs
117 Alexander Avenue
PO Box 2438
Ames, IA 50010-2438

515-232-3121
800-247-3952; Fax: 515-232-0789
info@needleworkretailer.com
www.needleworkretailer.com

Larry Johnson, VP
Megan Chriswisser, Editor

Highlights a variety of new products and designs in needlework. Includes infornation on upcoming needlework trade shows and association news.
Cost: $12.00
Circulation: 11000

13633 **Numismatic News**
F+W Media
38 E. 29th Street
New York, NY 10016

212-447-1400; Fax: 212-447-5231
contact_us@fwmedia.com
Facebook, Twitter, LinkedIn

Bill Bright, General Manager
Dave Harper, Editor
Jim Ogle, Chief Financial Officer
Chad Phelps, Chief Digital Officer
Stacie Berger, Communications Director

Provides timely reports on market happenings and news concerning collectible coins. 'Coin Clinic' is a very popular weekly Q&A column that gives readers a chance to learn all about numismatics. The 'Coin Market' section provides comprehensive pricing monthly. Each issue also includes columns with practical how-to advice and historical features by some of the top experts in the field including 'Making the Grade' and 'Facts about Fakes.' Sponsors the annual Mid-America Coin Convention.
Cost: $35.99
72 Pages
Frequency: Weekly
Circulation: 34392
Founded in 1952
Mailing list available for rent

13634 **Play Meter**
Skybird Publishing Company
PO Box 337
Metairie, LA 70004-0337

504-488-7003
888-473-2376; Fax: 504-488-7083
news@playmeter.com
www.playmeter.com
Facebook, Twitter, LinkedIn

Bonnie Theard, Editor
Carol P. Lally, Publisher
Carol Ann Lally, President
Bonnie Theard, Managing Editor
Courtney McDuff, Assistant Editor

Trade publication that provides members with information on the coin-operated entertainment industry, including upcoming trade shows, new products, ongoing trends and more.
Cost: $60.00
Frequency: Monthly
Circulation: 60000
Founded in 1974

13635 **Playthings**
Reed Business Information
360 Park Ave S
4th Floor
New York, NY 10010-1737

646-746-6400
800-309-3332; Fax: 646-756-7583
mlaporte@reedbusiness.com
www.reedbusiness.com
Twitter, LinkedIn

John Poulin, CEO
Larry Oliver, VP/Group Publisher
Micki LaPorte, Circulation Director
James Reed, Owner
Andrew Rak, Senior Vice President

Emphasizes a merchandising approach for improving sales and promotional techniques. Features include new product listings, market reports, licensing updates and general industry trends.
Cost: $33.95
80 Pages
Frequency: Monthly
Founded in 1903
Printed in 4 colors on glossy stock

13636 **SCRYE**
F+W Media
38 E. 29th Street
New York, NY 10016

212-447-1400; Fax: 212-447-5231
contact_us@fwmedia.com
Facebook, Twitter, LinkedIn

Mark Williams, Publisher
Joyce Greenholdt, Editor
Jim Ogle, Chief Financial Officer
Chad Phelps, Chief Digital Officer
Stacie Berger, Communications Director

The most respected price guide in the industry for collectible card games and collectible miniatures. SCRYE also provides collectors and players the latest news, checklists, player strategies, deck building tips and tricks for collectible card games. The latest collectible card games are reviewed in each issue in addition to related role-playing and board games.
Cost: $29.98
160 Pages
Frequency: Monthly
Circulation: 47000
Founded in 1994
Mailing list available for rent

13637 **Shuttle Spindle & Dyepot**
Handweavers Guild of America
1255 Buford Highway
Suite 209
Suwanee, GA 30024-8421

678-730-0010; Fax: 678-730-0836
hga@weavespindye.org
www.weavespindye.org

Sally Orgren, Editor
Elizabeth Williamson, Executive Director
Kathi Grupp, Advertising Manager

Contains articles about the fibre arts covering topics such as design, history, shows, educations, products, books, and news.
Frequency: Quarterly

13638 **Snapshot Memories**
PRIMEDIA Consumer Magazine & Internet Group

2 News Plaza
PO Box 1790
Peoria, IL 61656-1790

309-682-6626; Fax: 309-679-5057

Mike Irish, Associate Publisher
Miram Olson, Editor-in-Chief

Scrapbook page idea magazine.
Cost: $16.98
92 Pages
Frequency: Quarterly
Circulation: 90,000
Founded in 1998
Printed in 4 colors on glossy stock

13639 **Sports Collectors Digest**
F+W Media
38 E. 29th Street
New York, NY 10016

212-447-1400; Fax: 212-447-5231
contact_us@fwmedia.com
Facebook, Twitter, LinkedIn

Dean Listle, Publisher
TS O'Connell, Editor
Jim Ogle, Chief Financial Officer
Chad Phelps, Chief Digital Officer
Stacie Berger, Communications Director

The Bible of Hobby covers every aspect of modern sports collecting, including cards, memorabilia, equipment, lithographs, figurines, and autographed material. Online collecting, graded cards, memorabilia and auction news are covered each week in specially designed sections that complement columns from some of the most respected experts in the hobby and up-to-date card pricing checklisting data from expert analysts, along with display advertisements from all the major dealers in the country.
Cost: $49.95
96 Pages
Frequency: Weekly
Circulation: 23356
Founded in 1973
Mailing list available for rent

13640 **Stamp Collector**
F+W Media
38 E. 29th Street
New York, NY 10016

212-447-1400; Fax: 212-447-5231
contact_us@fwmedia.com
Facebook, Twitter, LinkedIn

Wayne Youngblood, Publisher
Jill Ruesch, Ad Manager
Jim Ogle, Chief Financial Officer
Chad Phelps, Chief Digital Officer
Stacie Berger, Communications Director

Covers a wide variety of US & foreign stamp news. Sepcial inserts cover topicals, errors, postal history, and many others. Regular columns and features include 'Decoding the Catalog,' 'Q&A,' 'Meet the Designer,' 'Postal History,' 'New Stamps of the World,' 'Stamp Values Today,' an auction guide and the most extensive stamp show calendar in the hobby. The first issue each month cotains Stamp Wholesaler - stamp dealer info that is used as a 'philatelic phone book' by the entire industry.
Cost: $32.98
60 Pages
Circulation: 13251
Founded in 1931
Mailing list available for rent

13641 **Tole World**
EGW.com
4075 Papazian Way
Suite 208
Fremont, CA 94538-4372

510-668-0268; Fax: 510-668-0280
www.toleworld.com

Chris Slaughter, VP
Rickie Wilson, Advertisement Manager

Serving crafters in the decorative painting field; each issue features 10 to 12 projects complete with full color photographs, step-by-step instructions and line art patterns. Project designs come from the nation's leading decorative artists, many of whom are also teachers in the field.
Cost: $35.94
84 Pages
Frequency: Quarterly
Circulation: 85956
Founded in 1977

13642 **Toy Book**
Adventure Publishing Group
1107 Broadway
Suite 1204
New York, NY 10010

212-575-4510; Fax: 212-575-4521
www.adventurepub.com

Owen Shorts, Owner
Nelson Lombardi, Editor
A Schwartz, Marketing
Anthony Guardiola, Production Manager

Keeps readers abreast of new products and marketing information related to the industry.
Cost: $48.00
Frequency: Monthly
Circulation: 18000
Founded in 1980

13643 **Toy Shop**
F+W Media
38 E. 29th Street
New York, NY 10016

212-447-1400; Fax: 212-447-5231
contact_us@fwmedia.com
Facebook, Twitter, LinkedIn

Mark Williams, Publisher
Tom Bartsch, Editor
David Nussbaum, CEO/Chairman
Chad Phelps, Chief Digital Officer
Stacie Berger, Communications Director

A complete marketplace for buyers and sellers of toys, action figures, Barbie, Hot Wheels, character toys, and more. Offers thousands of easy-to-read, categorized classified ads, display ads, and a complete editorial package covering baby-boomer toys, vintage collectibles, TV toys, action figures, and many helpful Q&A columns. Also contains up-to-date market trends as well as thorough auction updates and reports from toy shows nationwide.
Cost: $33.98
76 Pages
Circulation: 11577
Founded in 1988
Mailing list available for rent

13644 **Transactions of the Digital Games Research Association**
Digital Games Research Association

jose.zagal@utah.edu
todigra.org

Jose P. Zagal, Editor-in-Chief
Harald Warmelink, Support Contact

ToDiGRA is an international, open access, refereed, multidisciplinary journal for research on and practice in all aspects of digital games. It is both printed and available online.
ISSN: 2328-9422

13645 **Trapper & Predator**
F+W Media
38 E. 29th Street
New York, NY 10016

212-447-1400; Fax: 212-447-5231
contact_us@fwmedia.com
Facebook, Twitter, LinkedIn

Hugh McAloon, Publisher
Paul Wait, Editor
Jim Ogle, Chief Financial Officer
Chad Phelps, Chief Digital Officer
Stacie Berger, Communications Director

Contains news, in-depth features, and how-to tips on trapping, the art of predator calling, and animal damage control. Contributors include the top names in the business. Regular columns and departments include 'The Fure Shed,' 'Let's Swap Ideas,' 'Q&A,' and news from state trapping associations nationwide.
Cost: $18.95
80 Pages
Circulation: 38260
Founded in 1975
Mailing list available for rent

13646 **Tuff Stuff**
F+W Media
38 E. 29th Street
New York, NY 10016

212-447-1400; Fax: 212-447-5231
contact_us@fwmedia.com
Facebook, Twitter, LinkedIn

Dean Listle, Publisher
Rocky Landsverk, Editor
Jim Ogle, Chief Financial Officer
Chad Phelps, Chief Digital Officer
Stacie Berger, Communications Director

A guide to the sports card and collectibles hobby. Coverage of sports cards includes the latest prices on baseball, football, basketball, hockey, racing, and more. Each issue lists pricing information on Hall of Fame baseball and football memorabilia, autographed items, and commentary on the sports card industry. Columns and opinion pieces include a Q&A section, directories to professional teams, geographical and product directories, and hobby dealer listings for the US and Canada.
Cost: $29.95
Frequency: Monthly
Circulation: 175,682
Founded in 1983
Mailing list available for rent

13647 **Turkey & Turkey Hunting**
F+W Media
38 E. 29th Street
New York, NY 10016

212-447-1400; Fax: 212-447-5231
contact_us@fwmedia.com
Facebook, Twitter, LinkedIn

David Nussbaum, CEO/Chairman
James Schlender, Editor
Jim Ogle, Chief Financial Officer
Chad Phelps, Chief Digital Officer
Stacie Berger, Communications Director

Edited for serious, technical, year-round, gun and bow turkey hunters. Features emphasize success and enjoyment of the sport. Articles focus on hunting, scouting, turkey behavior and biology, hunting ethics, new equipment, methodologies, turkey management, and current research. Columns include 'Tree Call,' 'Mail Pouch,' 'Turkey Biology,' a Q&A column, 'Hunter's Library,' 'Turkey Gear,' and 'Last Call.'
Cost: $15.95
72 Pages
Circulation: 68962
Founded in 1975
Mailing list available for rent

13648 **Weekend Woodcrafts**
EGW.com

1041 Shary Circle
Concord, CA 94518-2407

925-671-9852; Fax: 925-671-0692
www.weekendwoodcrafts.com

Chris Slaughter, Circulation Director
Rickie Wilson, Advertising

Wide selection of easy-to-finish wood projects ranging from craft fair novelties and decorative home-accents to useful housewares and wooden toys.
Cost: $35.94
68 Pages
Frequency: Monthly
Founded in 1980

13649 Wood Strokes
EGW.com
1041 Shary Circle
Concord, CA 94518-2407

925-671-9852; Fax: 925-671-0692

Chris Slaughter, Circulation Manager

Wide selection of easy-to-finish decorative wood painting projects ranging from craft fair novelties and decorative home accents to useful housewares and wooden toys.
Cost: $5.99
76 Pages
Circulation: 110437

13650 World Coin News
F+W Media
38 E. 29th Street
New York, NY 10016

212-447-1400; Fax: 212-447-5231
contact_us@fwmedia.com
Facebook, Twitter, LinkedIn

Bill Bright, General Manager
Dave Harper, Editor
Jim Ogle, Chief Financial Officer
Chad Phelps, Chief Digital Officer
Stacie Berger, Communications Director

Recognized as the leading authority on world coins. It regularly reports on new issues, auctions and other coin news from around the world. Features by some of the top experts in the field provide in-depth historical information on coins and the countries that issue them. Regular features include World Coin Clinic (Q&A), World Coin Roundup (newly issued coins), Rule Britannia, Nautical Numismatics, Mexican Potpourri, and Coin Critters. Each issue provides a calendar of shows.
Cost: $30.99
84 Pages
Frequency: Monthly
Circulation: 8729
Founded in 1952
Mailing list available for rent

Trade Shows

13651 ACC Craft Show
American Craft Council
21 S Eltings Corner Road
Highland, NY 12528

845-883-6100
800-836-3670; Fax: 845-883-6130
shows@craftcouncil.org
www.craftcouncil.org

Craft fair.
Frequency: Annual

13652 APS AmeriStamp Expo
American Philatelic Society
100 Match Factory Place
Bellafonte, PA 16823-1367

814-933-3803; Fax: 814-933-6128
stampshow@stamps.org
www.stamps.org

Scott English, Executive Director
Megan Orient, Manager, Shows & Exhibitions
Kathleen Edwards, Shows & Exhibitions Assistant

Annual event for postage stamp collectors, featuring 75 dealers, 50 meetings and services, auction, 5,000 pages of exhibits and beginner actions.
Frequency: Annual/February-March
Founded in 1957

13653 APS Stampshow
American Philatelic Society
100 Match Factory Place
Bellefonte, PA 16823-1367

814-933-3803; Fax: 814-933-6128
stampshow@stamps.org
www.stamps.org

Scott English, Executive Director
Megan Orient, Manager, Shows & Exhibitions
Kathleen Edwards, Shows & Exhibitions Assistant

Annual show for postage stamp collectors. Includes 150 dealers buying and selling material, more than 100 seminars, and 10,000 pages of stamps in collection.
Frequency: Annual/August

13654 AQSG Conference and Annual Meeting
American Quilt Study Group
1610 L St
Lincoln, NE 68508-2509

402-477-1181; Fax: 402-477-1183
aqsg2@americanquiltstudygroup.org
www.americanquiltstudygroup.org
Twitter, LinkedIn

Lisa Erlandsonn, President
Lenna DeMarco, VP
Flavin Glover, VP
Judy J. Brott Buss, Ph.D., Executive Director
Anne E. Schuff, Member Services Coordinator

For members. Research presentations and quilt and textile study
200 Attendees
Frequency: Annual
Mailing list available for rent

13655 ASD/AMD Group
Fletcher
2950 31st Street
Suite 100
Santa Monica, CA 90405

310-255-4633; Fax: 310-396-8476

15000 Attendees

13656 American Camping Association Conference & Exhibits
5000 State Road 67 N
Martinsville, IN 46151-7902

765-342-8456
800-428-2267; Fax: 765-342-2065
bwilliems@aca-camps.org
http://www.acacamps.org

Peg Smith, CEO
Bill Willems, Director Business

One hundred fifty booths of arts and crafts, computer software, sporting goods, waterfront equipment and more plus a seminar and workshop.
1,200 Attendees
Frequency: Annual
Founded in 1943

13657 American Craft Council Fairs
ACC
21 S Elting Corners Road
Highland, NY 12528-2805

845-883-6100
800-836-3470; Fax: 612-355-2330
shows@craftcouncil.org
www.craftcouncil.org

Nine fairs nationwide each year. Each show incorporates crafts from the ceramics, wood, metal, mixed media, fiber, glass, jewelry, accessories and related industries. Most fairs include retail portion (public sales); some fairs also have wholesale (trade) component.

13658 American International Toy Fair
Toy Industry Association
1115 Broadway
Suite 400
New York, NY 10010

212-675-1141; Fax: 212-675-3246

Laura Green, VP Trade Shows/Meetings
Diane Cardinale, Public Information Manager

1,800-2,000 booths for producers of all types of toys and games, party and holiday items, models, hobby products, as well as collectibles, dolls, plush and miniatures. Attendees are retail buyers and trade professionals. Seminar and program.
20000 Attendees
Frequency: Annual
Founded in 1903

13659 American Needlepoint Guild Show
3410 Valley Creek Circle
Middleton, WI 53562-1990

608-831-3328; Fax: 608-831-0651
seminars@needlepoint.org
www.needlepoint.org

Estelle Kelley, Seminars Director

Two hundred exhibits of needlework pieces, banquet and luncheon.
830 Attendees
Frequency: Annual
Founded in 1972

13660 American Numismatic Association Trade Show
8181 N Cascade Avenue
Colorado Springs, CO 80903

719-632-2646
webmaster@money.org
www.money.org

Brenda Bishop, Show Manager
Nancy Green, Manager

Four hundred twenty five booths of coins, medals and paper money.
15M Attendees
Frequency: August

13661 American Quilt Study Group
American Quilt Study Group
1610 L St
Lincoln, NE 68508-2509

402-477-1181; Fax: 402-477-1181
aqsg2@americanquiltstudygroup.org
www.americanquiltstudygroup.org
Twitter, LinkedIn

Lisa Erlandsonn, President
Lenna DeMarco, Vice President
Kathy Moore, VP
Judy J. Brott Buss, Ph.D., Executive Director
Anne E. Schuff, Member Services Coordinator

Annual Seminar, Annual Journal member organization
Frequency: October, Kansas
Founded in 1980
Mailing list available for rent

13662 **American Stamp Dealers Association Stamp Shows**
3 School Street
Suite 201
Glen Cove, NY 11542-2548
516-759-7000; Fax: 800-369-8207
Joseph Savarese, Show Manager/Executive VP
Two hundred booths.
12.5M Attendees

13663 **Americover**
American First Day Cover Society
PO Box 1335
Maplewood, NJ 07040
973-762-2012; Fax: 973-762-7916
webmaster@afdcs.org
www.afdcs.org
Steve Ripley, Show Manager
US and international first day postal covers, USPS first day ceremonies at most shows, 50 stamp dealers, cover dealers, cachetmalchers philatelic suppliers.
1500 Attendees
Frequency: Annual

13664 **Annual Spring-Easter Arts & Crafts Show & Sale**
Finger Lakes Craftsmen Shows
1 Freshour Road
Shortsville, NY 14548
585-289-9439; Fax: 585-289-9440
Ronald L Johnson, President
Annual show of 150 exhibitirs of arts and crafts manufacturers. Exhibits include handcrafted arts and crafts, including photos and prints.
9000 Attendees
Frequency: March
Founded in 1999

13665 **Antique Arms Show**
P.O. Box 2917
Cathedral City, CA 92234
760- 20- 448; Fax: 760-202-4793
www.antiquearmsshow.com
Wallace Beinfield
Public show with 850 booths of antiques and collectibles.
4M Attendees
Frequency: January

13666 **Association of Crafts and Creative Industries Show: ACCI Show**
Offinger Management Company
1100-H Brandywine Boulevard
PO Box 3388
Zanesville, OH 43702
740-452-4541
888-360-2224; Fax: 740-452-2552
accishow@offinger.com
www.accicrafts.org
Facebook, Twitter, LinkedIn
Marrijane Jones, Executive Director
Erica McKenzie, ACCI Communications Manager
The ACCI Show is sponsored by the Association of Crafts and Creative Industries. Over 1,300 booths are represented, featuring general crafts, softcrafts, art materials and framing, scrapbooking materials and floral, home and garden items.
8000+ Attendees
Frequency: Annual

13667 **Canadian Game Studies Association Annual Conference**
Canadian Game Studies Assocation
Home Page: gamestudies.ca
Kym Stewart, Local Arrangement Coordinator
Held in tandem with the Congress of the Humanities and Social Sciences.

13668 **Christmas Gift & Hobby Show**
HSI Show Productions
PO Box 502797
Indianapolis, IN 46250
317-576-9933
800-215-1700; Fax: 317-576-9955
info@hsishows.com
www.hsishows.com
Donell Hebererwalton, Sales Director
Todd Jameson, Show Manager
45000 Attendees

13669 **Christmas Gift and Hobby Show**
HSI Show Productions
PO Box 502797
Indianapolis, IN 46250-7797
317-576-9933
800-215-1700; Fax: 317-576-9955
www.hsishows.com
Donell Hebererwalton, Sales Director
Todd Jameson, Show Manager
Annual show of 360 exhibitors of arts, crafts and giftware.
70M Attendees

13670 **Coin and Stamp Exposition: San Francisco**
Bick International
PO Box 854
Van Nuys, CA 91408
818-997-6496; Fax: 818-988-4337
iibick@sbcglobal.net
www.bickinternational.com
Israel I Bick, Managing Director
5000 Attendees
Frequency: June/September, Annually

13671 **Comicpalooza**
Home Page: www.comicpalooza.com
Facebook, Twitter, YouTube, Instagram
Multi-genre convention on gaming, tabletop games, films, comics, literature, anime, cosplay, and more.
50K Attendees
Founded in 2008

13672 **Convergence**
Handweavers Guild of America
1255 Buford Highway
Sutie 209
Suwanee, GA 30024-8421
678-730-0010; Fax: 678-730-0836
hga@weavespindye.org
www.weavespindye.org
Elizabeth Williamson, Executive Director
Ingrid Sciscoe, Membership Coordinator
Kathi Grupp, Advertising Manager
Linda Campbell, Exhibit & Editorial Assistant
Conference for everyone who loves and works in fiber.
3000 Attendees
Frequency: June, Biennial
Founded in 1969

13673 **DEXCON**
Double Exposure Inc.
Morristown, NJ
Home Page: www.dexposure.com
Gaming conference with a focus on board gaming, Larping, video gaming, and wargaming.
2200+ Attendees
Founded in 1992

13674 **Denver Pop Culture Con**
info@popcultureclassroom.org
denverpopculturecon.com
Facebook, Twitter, YouTube, Instagram
Multi-genre fan convention on comic books and web-comics, tabletop and video games, anime and manga, costplay, horros and sci-fi, movies, TV, and literature.
114K Attendees
Founded in 2012

13675 **Doll, Teddy Bear & Toy Show & Sale**
Jones Publishing
9572 Forest Hills Lodge & Route 173
Rockford, IL 54945-5000
715-445-5000
JoAnn Reynolds, Contact
Great assortment of toys featuring teddy bears of all kinds.

13676 **EDspaces**
National School Supply & Equipment Association
8380 Colesville Road
Suite 250
Silver Spring, MD 20910
800-395-5550; Fax: 301-495-3330
www.ed-spaces.com
Jim McGarry, President/CEO
Adrienne Dayton, VP, Communications & Education
Karen Prince, VP, Membership & Operations
Joe Tucker, VP, Meetings & Events
Scott Beyer, Director, Sales & Development
EDspaces is the country's premier event for manufacturers, distributors and service providers offering products to educational facilities.
3000 Attendees
Frequency: Annual/Oct-Nov

13677 **ESTA Conference**
Esports Trade Association
541 N. Fairbanks Court
Suite 2200
Chicago, IL 60611
708-680-7133
info@esportsta.org
esportsta.org
Facebook, Twitter, LinkedIn, YouTube, Instagram
Megan Van Petten, Founder & CEO
Conference of the Esports Trade Association.
Founded in 2018

13678 **Eastern States Doll, Toy, and Teddy Bear Show and Sale**
Maven Company
PO Box 937
Plandome, NY 11030
914-248-4646; Fax: 914-248-0800
www.mavencompany.com
N Chittenden, VP
Wide variety of dolls, toys and teddy bears. Largest show of its kind in the northeast.
5000 Attendees
Frequency: November/April
Founded in 1982

13679 **Electronic Entertainment Expo**
Entertainment Software Association
601 Massachusetts Avenue NW
Suite 300
Washington, DC 20001
Home Page: www.e3expo.com
Facebook, Twitter, YouTube, Instagram
Stanley Pierre-Louis, President & CEO
Andrew Bowins, SVP, Comm. & Public Affairs

Video game industry showcase featuring technology debuts and product launches.
50000 Attendees

13680 Evolution Championship Series
Home Page: evo.shoryuken.com
Facebook, Twitter

Annual open eSports tournament focused on fighting games.
Frequency: Annual
Founded in 1996

13681 FSGA Winter Conference
Fantasy Sports & Gaming Association
1818 Parmenter Street
Suite 300
Middleton, WI 53562

608-310-7540
thefsga.org
Facebook, Twitter, LinkedIn

Christina McCoy, Executive Director
Michael Fiez, Marketing
Emily Petersen, Membership

January meeting of Fantasy Sports & Gaming Association members.

13682 Game Developers Conference
Informa Tech

415-947-6926
800-216-4916
gdcfeedback@ubm.com
gdconf.com
Facebook, Twitter, LinkedIn, YouTube, Instagram

The GDC provides education, inspiration, and networking opportunities to the video game development community, including programmers, artists, producers, game designers, audio professionals, and business leaders. The conference features discussions, awards ceremonies, community spaces for networking, and the GDC Expo.
Founded in 1988

13683 Game On Expo
Phoenix, AZ

Home Page: www.gameonexpo.com

Gaming convention with a focus on video and arcade games, board games, and tabletop games.
Frequency: Annual
Founded in 2015

13684 GameSoundCon
SoundCon, LLC
4735 134th Place SE
Bellevue, WA 98006

425-956-3725
brian@gamesoundcon.com
www.gamesoundcon.com
Twitter

Conference devoted to the art, technology, and business of video game audio.
350+ Attendees
Founded in 2009

13685 GameStorm
Red Lion Jantzen Beach
909 N. Hayden Island Drive
Portland, OR 97217

Home Page: gamestorm.org
Facebook, Twitter, Tumblr

Non-profit gaming convention with panel discussions, role-playing games, video games, and tabletop games.
Founded in 1998

13686 Genericon
Rensselaer Polytechnic Institute
110 Eighth Street
Troy, NY 12180

518-276-6000
chair.genericon@gmail.com
genericon.org

Convention for anime, science fiction, and gaming, featuring viewing rooms, karaoke, cosplay, video gaming and competitions, role-playing games, board games, and lectures.

13687 HIA: Hobby Industries of America Trade Show
Hobby Industries of America
319 E 54th Street
PO Box 348
Elmwood Park, NJ 07407

201-794-1133; Fax: 201-798-0657
www.hobby.org

Steve Berger, Executive Director

International trade show open to qualified professionals and is the industry's only market research show.
10000 Attendees

13688 Halloween Costume and Party Show
TransWorld Exhibits
1850 Oak Street
Northfield, IL 60093

847-784-6905
800-323-5462; Fax: 847-446-3523
www.transworldexhibits.com

Don Olstinske, Manager
Stephanie Geitner, Operations Director

13689 Independent Games Festival
Informa Tech
303 Second Street
Suite 900, S. Tower
San Francisco, CA 94107

chairperson@igf.com
igf.com
Twitter

The IGF recognizes the best independent game developers, and encourages innovation in game development.
Founded in 1998

13690 IndieCade
Culver City, CA

central@indiecade.com
www.indiecade.com
Facebook, Twitter, YouTube, Instagram

Stephanie Barish, Chief Executive Officer
Sam Roberts, Festival Director
Celia Pearce, Festival Chair
Erin Shaver, Director, Operations
Shawn Pierre, Games Manager
The International Festival of Independent Games is dedicated to showcasing and supporting independent game development through a series of international events.
Founded in 2005

13691 International Coin + Stamp Collection Society
Bick International
PO Box 854
Van Nuys, CA 91408

818-997-6496; Fax: 818-988-4337
iibick@sbcglobal.net
www.bickinternational.com

Israel I Bick, Managing Director
5000 Attendees
Frequency: Annual/December/May, NV

13692 International Gift and Collectible Expo
F+W Media
38 E. 29th Streett
New York, NY 10016

212-447-1400; Fax: 212-447-5231
contact_us@fwmedia.com
Twitter, LinkedIn

Claude Chmiel, Show Producer
John Swinburn, Executive Director
17000 Attendees
Frequency: June

13693 International JPMA Show
Juvenile Products Manufacturers Association
15000 Commerce Parkway
Suite C
Mt Laurel, NJ 08054

856-439-0500; Fax: 856-439-0525
www.jpma.org

Linda Still, Director of Trade Show

Items of interest to retailers of children's apparel and toys.
3000 Attendees
Frequency: Annual

13694 International Miniature Collectibles Trade Show
10 Estes Street
Ipswich, MA 1938

978-356-6500
800-653-2726; Fax: 978-356-6565
www.miniatures.org/showlist
Facebook, Twitter, LinkedIn

Frequency: August

13695 Just Kidstuff & The Museum Source
George Little Management
10 Bank Street
Suite 1200
White Plains, NY 10606

914-486-6070
800-272-7469; Fax: 914-948-2918

George Little II, President
45000 Attendees

13696 Knitting Guild Association Conference
The Knitting Guild Association (TKGA)
1100-H Brandwine Blvd.
Zanesville, OH 43701-7303

740-452-4541; Fax: 740-452-2552
tkga@tkga.com
tkga.org
Facebook, Twitter, LinkedIn

Arenda Holladay, President & Executive Director

The TKGA conference is held twice each year and offers items such as fiber, stitching tools, patterns, books, finishing accessories and more.
10000 Members
Mailing list available for rent

13697 MAGFest
Washington, DC

contact@magfest.org
www.magfest.org
Facebook, Twitter, YouTube, Instagram, Snapchat

Music and gaming festival to celebrate video games and video game music, running 24 hours a day for four days straight.
Founded in 2002

13698 **MidSouthCon**
Mid-South Science and Fictions Conventions, Inc.
info@midsouthcon.org
midsouthcon.org
Science-fiction-themed convention with programming that also includes comics, horror, costuming, and gaming.
2200 Attendees
Founded in 1982

13699 **Midwest Gaming Classic**
, WI
Home Page: www.midwestgamingclassic.com
Facebook, YouTube, Instagram
Trade show for all types of video game consoles, pinball machines, arcade video games, table-top games, computers, crane games, collectible card games, air hockey, and more.

13700 **Mobicon**
Renaissance Riverview Plaza Hotel
64 S. Water Street
Mobile, AL 36602
833-662-4266
mobilecomiccon.org
Facebook, Twitter
Multi-genre convention on science fiction, fantasy, gaming, comics, anime, manga, horror, paranormal, and mass media.
1000+ Attendees
Founded in 1998

13701 **MomoCon**
Atlanta, GA
Home Page: www.momocon.com
Facebook, Twitter, YouTube, Instagram
A geek culture convention for fans of anime, gaming, comics, and animation.
39000 Attendees
Founded in 2005

13702 **National Dollhouse & Miniatures Trade Show & Convention**
Miniatures Association of America
10 Estes Street
Ipswich, MA 1938
978-356-6500
800-653-2726; Fax: 978-356-6565
miniatures.org/ShowList
Facebook, Twitter, LinkedIn
1400 Attendees

13703 **National Merchandise Show**
Miller Freeman Publications
One Penn Plaza
PO Box 2549
New York, NY 10119
212-714-1300; Fax: 212-714-1313
16000 Attendees

13704 **National NeedleArts Association Trade Show**
National Needlework Association
PO Box 3388
Zanesville, OH 43702-3388
740-452-4541
800-889-8662; Fax: 740-452-2552
tnna.info@offinger.com
www.tnna.org
Kelsey Kwasniak, Trade Show Senior Associate
Frequency: January

13705 **National Sewing Show: Home Sewing Association**
American Home Sewing and Craft Association
1350 Broadway
Suite 1601
New York, NY 10018
212-714-1633; Fax: 212-714-1655
info@sewing.org
www.sewing.org
Pat Kobishyn, Show Manager
Two hundred exhibits of fabric, notions, patterns, sewing and trimmings. Attended by professionals from major chain stores, independent retailers, wholesalers and manufacturers.
3000 Attendees
Frequency: Annual

13706 **Penny Arcade Expo**
pax_questions@paxsite.com
www.paxsite.com
Video game expos held in cities across the States, and also in Australia. Expos feature exhibit halls, freeplay, tournaments, concerts, panels, and more.
Founded in 2004

13707 **Phoenix Fan Fusion**
Phoenix Convention Center
100 N. 3rd Street
Phoenix, AZ 85004
604-635-4306
phoenixfanfusion.com
Facebook, Twitter, YouTube, Instagram
Multi-genre convention on pop culture fandom, including comic books, sci-fi/fantasy, film and TV, anime and manga, animation, toys, card games, and video games.
57K Attendees
Founded in 2002

13708 **PortConMaine**
492 Main Street
Westbrook, ME 04092
331-704-0927
info@portconmaine.com
portconmaine.com
Facebook, Twitter, Instagram
Julie York, Founder
Convention dedicated to anime and gaming.

13709 **QuakeCon**
ZeniMax Media Inc.
1370 Piccard Drive
Rockville, MD 20850
questions@quakecon.org
www.quakecon.org
Facebook, Twitter, Instagram
Gaming convention to celebrate and promote video game studios owned by ZeniMax Media, with a large LAN party and other events.
Frequency: Annual
Founded in 1996

13710 **RTX**
Rooster Teeth
Austin, TX
888-512-7469
rtxevent@roosterteeth.com
rtxevent.com
Facebook, Twitter, YouTube, Instagram
Clarissa Gonzalez, Senior Events Manager
Patrick Matthews, Events Specialist
George Panga, Marketing Coordinator
Convention held to celebrate gaming and internet culture, with a focus on animation and comedy as well. Other events are held in Sydney, Australia, and London, England.

13711 **SHOPA**
SHOPA
3131 Elbee Road
Dayton, OH 45439-1900
937-297-2250
800-854-7467; Fax: 937-297-2254
www.shopa.org
Steven Jacober, President
Doris Condron, Director of Communications
7500 Attendees
Frequency: November

13712 **Souvenirs Gifts & Novelties Trade Association**
Kane Communications
7000 Terminal Square
Suite 210
Upper Darby, PA 19082-2330
610-734-2420; Fax: 610-734-2423
Al Barry, Show Manager
Larry White, VP Marketing
Trade show serving amusements, museums, zoos, entertainment, bowling, and retailers. Seminars and networking party.
5000 Attendees
Frequency: July

13713 **Staff Development For Educators (SDE) National Conference**
National School Supply & Equipment Association
8380 Colesville Road
Suite 250
Silver Spring, MD 20910
800-395-5550; Fax: 301-495-3330
www.edmarket.org
Facebook, Twitter, LinkedIn
Jim McGarry, President/CEO
Adrienne Dayton, VP, Communications & Education
Karen Prince, VP, Membership & Operations
Joe Tucker, VP, Meetings & Events
Scott Beyer, Director, Sales & Development
Source new products, engage in industry discussion, hear perspectives on current issues, and network with existing and potential new suppliers, distributors and purchasing influencers.
Frequency: Annual/July

13714 **TooManyGames**
Greater Philadelphia Expo Center
100 Station Avenue
Oaks, PA
info@toomanygames.com
toomanygames.com
Facebook, Twitter, YouTube, Instagram
Gaming convention with a new and used game marketplace, artists and creators, musicians, panels and demonstrations, LARPing, celebrities, an indie game showcase, and gaming arenas.
15K Members
Founded in 2004

13715 **ToyFest West**
Western Toy & Hobby Representatives Association
PO Box 14874
Long Beach, CA 90853
833-869-3378; Fax: 909-697-2014
toyshow@wthra.com
toyfestwest.com
Carrie Scanlan, Show Manager
Bill St. John, President
Blake Goldenberg, Chairman
Toy trade show in the US.
75 Members
Frequency: Annual
Founded in 1961

13716 **TwitchCon**
Twitch Interactive, Inc.
San Francisco, CA

Home Page: www.twitchcon.com
Facebook, Twitter, Instagram

Convention for the video game streaming and on-demand platform Twitch, where fans can meet streamers and the online community in person, as well as play new games. The convention is hosted twice a year, once in North America and once in Europe.
50K Attendees
Frequency: Annual
Founded in 2015

13717 **Variety Merchandise Show**
Miller Freeman Publications
One Penn Plaza
PO Box 2549
New York, NY 10119

212-714-1300; Fax: 212-714-1313

20000 Attendees

13718 **Virtual Reality Developers Conference**
Informa Tech

415-947-6926
800-216-4916
gdcfeedback@ubm.com
www.gdconf.com/vrdc
Facebook, Twitter, LinkedIn, YouTube, Instagram

The VRDC is a two-day summit for developers of Virtual Reality and Augmented Reality entertainment.

13719 **Western States Toy and Hobby Show**
Western Toy and Hobby Representative Association
9397 Reserve Drive
Corona, CA 92883

951-771-1598; Fax: 909-277-1599
www.wthra.com

Phylis St. John, Contact

If it's for kids, it's here. Show is for trade members only, not open to the public.
3000 Attendees
Frequency: March

13720 **Yama-Con**
LeConte Center
2986 Teaster Lane
Pigeon Forge, TN 37863

Home Page: www.yamacon.org
Facebook, Instagram

Multi-genre convention on anime, comics, cosplay, and gaming.
2600 Attendees
Founded in 2012

13721 **iHobby Expo**
Hobby Manufacturers Association
PO Box 315
Butter, NJ 07405-0315

973-283-9088; Fax: 973-838-7124
pat.koziol@hmahobby.org
www.hmahobby.org
Twitter, LinkedIn

Patricia S. Koziol, Executive Director
Jodi Araujo, Expositions and Events Manager

Models, trains, rc, cars, boats, planes and more
Frequency: October

Directories & Databases

13722 **American International Toy Fair Official Directory of Showrooms & Exhibits**
Toy Industry Association
1115 Broadway
Suite 400
New York, NY 10010-3466

212-675-1142; Fax: 212-633-1429

Thomas Conley, President
Diane Cardinale, Public Information Manager

Over 1,500 toy, game and hobby decoration manufacturers and their representatives are profiled.
Cost: $50.00
400 Pages
Frequency: Annual
Circulation: 12,000

13723 **Complete Directory of Collectibles**
Sutton Family Communications & Publishing Company
920 State Route 54 East
Elmitch, KY 42343

270-276-9500

Theresa Sutton, Publisher
Lee Sutton, Editor

Print-out from database of wholesalers, manufacturers, distributors, importers and close-out houses. Database is updated daily to guarantee the most current and up-to-date sources available.
Cost: $67.50
100 Pages

13724 **Complete Directory of Crafts and Hobbies**
Sutton Family Communications & Publishing Company
920 State Route 54 East
Elmitch, KY 42343

270-276-9500

Theresa Sutton, Editor
Lee Sutton, General Manager

Print-out from database of wholesalers, manufacturers, distributors, importers and close-out houses. Database is updated daily to guarantee the most current and up-to-date sources available.
Cost: $54.50
100+ Pages

13725 **Complete Directory of Figurines**
Sutton Family Communications & Publishing Company
920 State Route 54 East
Elmitch, KY 42343

270-276-9500

Theresa Sutton, Publisher
Lee Sutton, Editor

Print-out from database of wholesalers, manufacturers, distributors, importers and close-out houses. Database is updated daily to guarantee the most current and up-to-date sources available.
Cost: $44.50
100 Pages

13726 **Complete Directory of Games**
Sutton Family Communications & Publishing Company
920 State Route 54 East
Elmitch, KY 42343

270-276-9500

Theresa Sutton, Publisher
Lee Sutton, Editor

Print-out from database of wholesalers, manufacturers, distributors, importers and close-out houses. Database is updated daily to guarantee the most current and up-to-date sources available.
Cost: $39.50
100 Pages

13727 **Complete Directory of Novelties**
Sutton Family Communications & Publishing Company
920 State Route 54 East
Elmitch, KY 42343

270-276-9500

Theresa Sutton, Publisher
Lee Sutton, Editor

Print-out from database of wholesalers, manufacturers, distributors, importers and close-out houses. Database is updated daily to guarantee the most current and up-to-date sources available.
Cost: $79.50
100 Pages

13728 **Complete Directory of Pewter Items**
Sutton Family Communications & Publishing Company
920 State Route 54 East
Elmitch, KY 42343

270-276-9500

Theresa Sutton, Publisher
Lee Sutton, Editor

Print-out from database of wholesalers, manufacturers, distributors, importers and close-out houses. Database is updated daily to guarantee the most current and up-to-date sources available.
Cost: $39.50
100 Pages

13729 **Complete Directory of Plush and Stuffed Toys and Dolls**
Sutton Family Communications & Publishing Company
920 State Route 54 East
Elmitch, KY 42343

270-276-9500

Theresa Sutton, Editor
Lee Sutton, General Manager

Print-out from database of wholesalers, manufacturers, distributors, importers and close-out houses. Database is updated daily to guarantee the most current and up-to-date sources available.
Cost: $39.50
100+ Pages

13730 **Complete Directory of Posters, Buttons and Novelties**
Sutton Family Communications & Publishing Company
920 State Route 54 East
Elmitch, KY 42343

270-276-9500

Theresa Sutton, Editor
Lee Sutton, General Manager

Print-out from database of wholesalers, manufacturers, distributors, importers and close-out houses. Database is updated daily to guarantee the most current and up-to-date sources available.
Cost: $39.50
100+ Pages

13731 **Complete Directory of Toys and Games**
Sutton Family Communications & Publishing Company

920 State Route 54 East
Elmitch, KY 42343

270-276-9500

Theresa Sutton, Editor
Lee Sutton, General Manager

Print-out from database of wholesalers, manufacturers, distributors, importers and close-out houses. Database is updated daily to guarantee the most current and up-to-date sources available.
Cost: $44.50
100+ Pages

13732 **Directory of Manufacturer Representatives Service Suppliers**
Hobby Industry Association
319 E 54th St
Elmwood Park, NJ 07407-2712

201-794-1133; Fax: 201-797-0657
www.craftandhobby.org

Steve Berger, CEO

Two hundred manufacturers representatives and 105 trade show booth demonstrators working in the hobby equipment industry.
Cost: $25.00
Frequency: Biennial

13733 **Game Manufacturers Association Membership Directory**
Game Manufacturers Association
240 N. Fifth St.
Suite 340
Columbus, OH 43215

614-255-4500; Fax: 614-255-4499
www.gama.org
Twitter, LinkedIn

John Stacy, Executive Director

Approximately 350 member manufacturers and distributors of adventure games.
Frequency: Annual
Founded in 1977
Mailing list available for rent

13734 **Games and Entertainment on CD-ROM**
Mecklermedia Corporation
20 Ketchum Street
Westport, CT 06880-5908

203-341-2806; Fax: 203-454-5840

Over 1,300 multimedia encyclopedias, children's educational software and interactive 'board games'.
Cost: $29.95

13735 **Hobby Industries of America Trade Show Program and Buyers Guide**
Hobby Industry Association
319 E 54th St
Elmwood Park, NJ 07407-2712

201-794-1133; Fax: 201-797-0657
www.craftandhobby.org

Steve Berger, CEO

Over 1000 manufacturers are listed that exhibit at the HIA trade show.
Cost: $25.00
170 Pages
Frequency: Annual
Founded in 1940

13736 **Hobby Merchandiser Annual Trade Directory**
Hobby Publications
207 Commercial Ct
Morganville, NJ 07751-1099

732-536-5160; Fax: 732-536-5761

David Gherman, President
Jeff Troy, Editor
Ellen Gherman, Circulation Director
Tracey Decesure, Production Manager

Offers valuable information on manufacturers, wholesalers, industry suppliers and publishers of books and periodicals in the hobby trade industry.
Cost: $35.00
140 Pages
Frequency: Annual
Circulation: 7,000
Founded in 1945
Mailing list available for rent: 8M names
Printed in 4 colors on glossy stock

13737 **Hobby RoundTable**
GE Information Services
401 N Washington Street
Rockville, MD 20850-1707

301-388-8284

Cathy Ge, Owner

This database offers a forum enabling participants to share information on hobby-related topics, the hobby industry and hobby-related software.
Frequency: Bulletin Board

13738 **Radio Control Hobby Membership Directory**
Radio Control Hobby Trade Association
31632 N Ellis Avenue
Unit 111
Volo, IL 60073

847-740-1111; Fax: 847-740-1111

Members and manufacturers of radio control products.
Founded in 1983

Industry Web Sites

13739 **http://gold.greyhouse.com**
G.O.L.D Grey House OnLine Databases

Grey House Publishing's online database platform, GOLD, offers Quick Search, Keyword Search and Expert Search for most business sectors including hobby and game markets. The GOLD platform makes finding the information you need quick and easy - whether you're a novice searcher or an experienced database user. All of Grey House's directory products are available for subscription on the GOLD platform.

13740 **www.asdaonline.com**
American Stamp Dealers Association

Holds annual International Philatelic Exhibition Interpex. Sponsors the annual International Dealers course. Postage stamp mega event twice a year (spring and fall).

13741 **www.craftdesigners.org**
Society of Craft Designers

The Society of Craft Designers (SCD), founded in 1975, is a professional organization for those who believe that quality craft design is the basis of a strong and viable craft industry. It is the only membership organization exclusively serving those who design for the consumer craft industry.

13742 **www.greyhouse.com**
Grey House Publishing

Authoritative reference directories for most business sectors including hobby and game markets. Users can search the online databases with varied search criteria allowing for custom searches by product category, geographic area, sales volume, keyword, subject and more. Full Grey House catalog and online ordering also available.

13743 **www.hubcityhobby.com**
5182 Old Highway 11
Suite 3
Hattiesburg, MS 39402

601-264-1040
www.hubcityhobby.com
Facebook, Twitter

Links to clubs, events, races and shows of interest to hobbyists.

13744 **www.mria.org**
Model Railroad Industry Association

Works to publicize the hobby and to keep members informed on the industry. Assists clubs and retailers in their shows.

13745 **www.nrhsa.org**
National Retail Hobby Stores Association

Association serving manufacturers and distributors of model hobby kits and hobby equipment.

13746 **www.nssea.org**
Naitonal School Supplu Equipment

Trade Association for the educational products industry.

13747 **www.stamps.org**
American Philatelic Society

National organization for stamp collectors, offering services including a lending library; insurance for philatelic materials; sales division, seminars and annual conventions open to the public.

13748 **www.tkga.com**
The Knitting Guild Association (TKGA)

Membership organization for knitters with focus on knitting education and enhancing knitter's skills

13749 **www.tnna.org**
National Needlework Association

For maufacturers, suppliers and distributers of needlework and related equipment, supplies and services.

13750 **www.toyassociation.org**
Toy Industry Association

National organization for U.S. producers and importers of toys, games and children's entertainment products. Represents more than 500 member companies including designers, safety consultants, testing laboratories, licensors, communication professionals and inventors.

Associations

13751 African American Association of Innkeepers International
919-907-1055
africanamericaninns@yahoo.com
www.africanamericaninns.com
Association dedicated to increasing awareness of African American-owned inns.

13752 American Hotel & Lodging Educational Institute
800 N. Magnolia Avenue
Suite 300
Orlando, FL 32803
407-999-8100
800-344-4381; Fax: 407-236-7848
info@ahlei.org
www.ahlei.org/
Facebook, Twitter, LinkedIn, Google Plus, Youtube, Instagra
Minaz Abji, Board Chairman
S. Kirk Kinsell, Vice Chairman
Paul Kirwin, Secretary/Treasurerÿ
Joori Jeon, Chief Executive Officer
Brenda Moons, CMHS, Senior Vice President, Sales
Fosters education, research programming, and information regarding operating techniques in the lodging industry.
11000 Members
Founded in 1953

13753 American Hotel and Lodging Association
1250 I Street NW
Suite 1100
Washington, DC 20005
202-289-3100; Fax: 202-289-3199
www.ahla.com
Facebook, Twitter, LinkedIn
Katherine Lugar, President & CEO
Organization focused on the needs of every aspect of the lodging industry.

13754 Asian American Hotel Owners Association
1100 Abernathy Road
Suite 1100
Atlanta, GA 30328-6707
404-816-5759; Fax: 404-816-6260
info@aahoa.com
www.aahoa.com
Facebook, Twitter, LinkedIn, YouTube, Instagram
Bharat (Bruce) Patel, CHO, Chairman
Bhavesh B. Patel, CHO, Vice Chairman
Chip Rogers, President & CEO
Hitesh Patel, CHO, Treasurer
Jagruti Panwala, CHO, Secretary
Supports Asian/American hotel and motel owners and operators.
16600 Members
Founded in 1989

13755 Associated Luxury Hotels International
1667 K Street, NW
Suite 610
Washington, DC 20006
202-887-7020; Fax: 202-887-0085
midatlantic@alhi.com
www.alhi.com
Facebook, Twitter, YouTube
Jim Schultenover, President
David Gabri, Chief Executive Officer
Chris Riccardi, Division VP
Mike Coutu, Executive VP & CFO
Ashly Balding, Division VP - East
Provided a National Sales Network to associations and corporations in America for the distinguished hotels and resorts now in 26 states, Canada, Mexico, and the Caribbean.
Founded in 1986

13756 Bed and Breakfast League
PO Box 9490
Washington, DC 20016-9490
202-363-7767; Fax: 202-363-8396
Millie Groobey, Director
A reservation service for bed and breakfasts in Washington, DC, that welcome selected travelers into their homes.
Founded in 1976

13757 Educational Institute of the American Hotel & Lodging Association
2113 N High St
Lansing, MI 48906-4221
517-372-8800
800-752-4567; Fax: 517-372-5141
info@ei-ahla.org
www.ahlei.org
Facebook, Twitter
George Glazer, VP
Anthony Farris, Chairman
Thomas J. Corcoran Jr., Vice Chair
Brenda Moons, Senior Vice President of Sales
K.V. Simon, Regional Vice President
A nonprofit educational foundation of the American Hotel & Lodging Association and the world's largest provider of hospitality education training resources, videos, books, workbooks, seminars, management courses, complete training systems and professional certification programs.
120 Members
Founded in 1953

13758 Green Hotels Association
PO Box 420212
Houston, TX 77242-0212
713-789-8889; Fax: 713-789-9786
green@greenhotels.com
www.greenhotels.com
Facebook, Twitter
Patricia Griffin, President
Association of hoteliers for environmentally-friendly properties.
Founded in 1993

13759 Hospitality Financial & Technology Professionals
11709 Boulder Lane
Suite 110
Austin, TX 78726-1832
512-249-5333
800-646-4387; Fax: 512-249-1533
membership@hftp.org
www.hftp.org
Facebook, Twitter, LinkedIn
Daniel N. Conti, Jr., CHAE, CAM, President
Arlene Ramirez, Vice President
Lyle Worthington, CHTP, Treasurer
Jerry M. Trieber, Immediate Past President
Connie Hong, Executive Services Administrator
Professional society for those in the financial segment of the hospitality industry.
4,700 Members
Founded in 1952
Mailing list available for rent

13760 Hotel Employees and Restaurant Employees
275 7th Avenue
16th Floor
New York, NY 10001-6708
212-265-7000
ccarrera@unitehere.org
www.unitehere.org
Facebook, Twitter, Google Plus
D. Taylor, General President
Nia Winston, General VP
Gwen ÿ Mills, Secretary-Treasurerÿ
Rich Maroko, Recording Secretary
Annemarie Strassel, Communications
Hosts a diverse membership, comprised largely of immigrants and including high percentages of African-American, Latino, and Asia-American workers. The majority of members are women.
850m Members
Founded in 1891

13761 International Council on Hotel, Restaurant and Institutional Education
2810 North Parham Road
Suite 230
Richmond, VA 23294
804-346-4800; Fax: 804-346-5009
webmaster@chrie.org
www.chrie.org
Facebook, Twitter, LinkedIn
Maureen Brookes, President
Martin O'Neillÿ, Immediate Past President
Margaret Steiskal, ViceÿPresident
Wanda Costen, Secretary
Stephanie Hein, Treasurer
A nonprofit professional association which provides programs and services to continually improve the quality of global education, research, service, and business operations in the hospitality and tourism industry.
Founded in 1946

13762 International Executive Housekeepers Association
1001 Eastwind Drive
Suite 301
Westerville, OH 43081-3361
614-895-7166
800-200-6342; Fax: 614-895-1248
excel@ieha.org
www.ieha.org
Facebook, Twitter, LinkedIn
Michael Patterson, President
Wayne Bledy, Director at Large
Wanda Joyce, Secretary/Treasurer
Lorrie Tripp, President-Elect
Sarah Larsen Miller, Convention Manager
An organization for persons working in the housekeeping area of the lodging industry.
3,500 Members
Founded in 1930

13763 International Facility Management Association
800 Gessner Rd
Suite 900
Houston, TX 77024-4257
713-623-4362; Fax: 713-623-6124
ifma@ifma.org
www.ifma.org
Facebook, Twitter, LinkedIn, Flickr, Youtube, RSS
Michael D. Feldman, FMP, CM, Chair
Tony Keane, CAE, President and CEO
Maureen Ehrenberg, FRICS, CRE, First Vice Chair
William M. O'Neill, CFM, Second Vice Chair
John Perry, Chief Operating Officer

Certifies facility managers, conducts research, provides educational programs, recognizes facility management degree and certificate programs and produces World Workplace, the world's largest facility management conference and exposition.
24,00 Members
Founded in 1980
Mailing list available for rent

13764 **NEWH: The Hospitality Industry Network**
PO Box 322
Shawano, WI 54166
715-526-5267
800-593-6394; Fax: 800-693-6394
newh.org
Facebook, Twitter, LinkedIn
Shelia Lohmiller, Executive Director
Jena Seibel, Deputy Director
The Network of Executive Women in Hospitality promotes the professional development of women in hospitality and related industries.
Founded in 1984

13765 **National Bed & Breakfast Association**
1011 W Fifth Street
Suite 300
Austin, TX 78703
512-322-2710; Fax: 512-320-0883
www.bedandbreakfast.com
Facebook, Twitter, Pinterest, Google Plus
John Banczac, Vice President
Denis Kashkin, Sr. Directory of Technology
Eric Goldreyer, Founder & President
An organization of services and supplies to the industry offering a list of the best in bed and breakfast accommodations in the USA, Canada and the Caribbean.
Founded in 1981
Mailing list available for rent

13766 **Preferred Hotels and Resorts Worldwide**
311 S Wacker Dr
Suite 1900
Chicago, IL 60606-6676
312-913-0400
866-990-9491; Fax: 312-913-5124
info@preferredhotels.com
www.preferredhotels.com
Facebook, Twitter, Pinterest, Instagram
John Ubberoth, CEO
Nora Gainer, Director Marketing
Independently owned luxury hotels and resorts. Each provides the highest standards of quality and extraordinary service.
120 Members
Founded in 1968

13767 **Professional Association of Innkeepers International**
295 Seven Farms Drive
Suite 236-C
Charleston, SC 29492
856-310-1102
800-468-7244; Fax: 856-895-0432
www.paii.org
Facebook, Twitter, Pinterest, Google+
Jay Karen, CEO
Isabel Abreu, Membership Sales Manager
Brook Patterson, Director of Vendor Services
Ingrid Thorson, Marketing & Communications Manager
Kris Ullmer, Executive Director
Serving bed and breakfast/country inn owners, aspiring innkeepers, inn sitters, vendors with educational and consultative services. International conference.
3000 Members
Founded in 1988

13768 **Select Registry**
295 Seven Farms Drive
Suite C-279
Charleston, SC 29492
269-789-0393
800-344-5244; Fax: 269-789-0970
maincontact@selectregistry.com
www.selectregistry.com/
Facebook, Twitter
Emily Cisewski, Content Manager
Carol Riggs, Director of Membership Services
Renee Flowers, Director of Marketing
Susan Galvin, Director of Membership Development
Susan Butler, Operations Manager
Represents the finest country inns, B&Bs, and unique small hotels from California to Nova-Scotia. The very best the travel industry has to offer.
400 Members
Founded in 1968
Mailing list available for rent

13769 **Small Luxury Hotels**
370 Lexington Avenue
Suite 1506
New York, NY 10017
212-953-2064
800-608-0273
reservation@slh.com
www.slh.com
Facebook, Twitter, LinkedIn, Pinterest, Instagram, Google+,
Members are independent owners and managers of deluxe hotels with fewer than 200 rooms.
233 Members
Founded in 1991

13770 **Small Luxury Hotels of the World**
370 Lexington Avenue
Suite 1506
New York, NY 10017
212-953-2064
800-608-0273; Fax: 212-953-0576
reservation@slh.com
www.slh.com
Facebook, Twitter, LinkedIn, Pinterest, Instagram, Google+,
Lanny Grossman, Marketing
Johnathan Slater, Chairman
Ed Donaldson, Manager
Collection of independently owned exclusive hotels in more than 50 countries. Selected for style and comfort, properties include spas, country houses, golf resorts, island retreats, city sanctuaries, game and wilderness lodges. Publishes directory.
300 Members
Founded in 1991

13771 **Textile Rental Services Association**
1800 Diagonal Road
Suite 200
Alexandria, VA 22314-2842
703-519-0029
877-770-9274; Fax: 703-519-0026
trsa@trsa.org
www.trsa.org
Facebook, Twitter, LinkedIn, RSS, YouTube
Roger Cocivera, President
George F. Ferencza, VP
Develops new programs and services to help textile rental operators meet today's challenges.
1400 Members
Founded in 1913

Newsletters

13772 **AHA Hotline Newsletter**
American Hospitality Association
603 S Pulaski
PO Box 3866
Little Rock, AR 72201
501-376-2323
800-472-5022; Fax: 501-376-6517
www.arhospitality.org
Facebook, Twitter, LinkedIn
Montine McNulty, Executive Director
Rita Walker, Executive Assistant
Amanda Glover, Education Coordinator
Holly Heer, Director of Membership
Kristen Smith, Director of Finance
For members, focuses on trends in the hospitality industry, upcoming events, training and education opportunities and more.
Frequency: Monthly

13773 **Cameron's Foodservice Marketing Reporter**
Cameron's Publications
5423 Sheridan Drive
PO Box 676
Williamsville, NY 14231
519-586-8785; Fax: 519-586-8816
www.cameronpub.com
Bob McClelland, CEO
Nina Cameron, Editor
Successful promotion and advertising case histories for the restaurant and hotel industry.

13774 **Epicurean Revue**
PO Box 35128
Sarasota, FL 34242-5128
FAX 941-349-4370
Jean-Noel Prade, Publisher
Georgia Brown, Editor
JN Prade, Circulation Manager
The publication for the jetsetters exclusive recommendations on top class hotels and restaurants. Total analysis of the various issues of the Michelin Guide and results of the wine auctions.
Cost: $79.00
8 Pages
Frequency: Monthly
Circulation: 5,000
Printed in one color on matte stock

13775 **Hospitality Law**
LRP Publications
PO Box 24668
West Palm Beach, FL 33416-4668
561-622-6520
800-341-7874; Fax: 561-622-0757
webmaster@lrp.com
www.lrp.com
Kenneth Kahn, President
Dave Light, Editor
Details and analyzes significant cases in the hospitality industry so you can learn from the mistakes that landed other properties in court. You receive summaries of the latest court cases - without legalese - involving hotels, inns, resorts and restaurants.
Cost: $229.00
12 Pages
Frequency: Monthly
Circulation: 1400

13776 **Hotel Technology Newsletter**
Chervenak, Keane and Company

307 E 44th Street
New York, NY 10017

212-986-8230; Fax: 212-983-5275
www.hospitalityleaderonline.com

J Christmas, Publisher
L Chervenak, Editor

Covers hotel information processing, telecommunications, security, fire safety, energy and audio-visual systems.
Cost: $180.00
Frequency: Annual

13777 **Hotel and Casino Law Letter**
William F Harrah College of Hotel Administration
4505 Maryland Parkway
Box 456013
Las Vegas, NV 89154-6013

702-895-3161; Fax: 702-895-4109
hotel.unlv.edu/

Annette Kannenberg, Business Manager
Stuart H Mann, Dean
Alice Baker, Administrative Assistant
Pat Merl, Management Assistant
Sherri Theriault, Director

Legislative news for executive level management of hotels and motels.

13778 **Hyatt Overseas**
Hyatt International Corporation
71 S Wacker Dr
Chicago, IL 60606-4637

312-701-7063; Fax: 312-750-8578

Thomas Pritzker, CEO

A summary of news, packages and events happening at Hyatt Hotels.
2 Pages

13779 **Inn Side Issues**
Hotel and Motel Brokers of America
10220 N Executive Boulevard
Suite 610
Kansas City, MO 64153

816-891-8776; Fax: 816-891-7071

Robert Kralicek, Editor

News of hotel owners and investors with articles about hospitality real estate.

Magazines & Journals

13780 **Bottomline**
Hospitality Financial & Technology Professionals
11709 Boulder Lane
Suite 110
Austin, TX 78726-1832

512-249-5333
800-646-4387; Fax: 512-249-1533
Sales@hftp.org
www.hftp.org

Jen Gonzales, Communications Manager
Theresa Pulley, Advertising Director

Official publication of the international association for individuals employed as controllers and financial officers in the hospitality industry. Articles include topics such as technology, personnel management, financial analysis, ethics and financial controls.
Cost: $200.00
Circulation: 4300
Founded in 1952
Printed in on glossy stock

13781 **Cameron's Worldwide Hospitality Marketing Reporter**
53256 Sheridan Drive
Williamsville, NY 14221-3503

416-636-5666; Fax: 416-636-5026

13782 **Cheers**
257 Park Avenue S
3rd Floor, Suite 303
New York, NY 10010

212-967-1551; Fax: 646-654-2099

John Eastman, Owner

Every issue is designed to help on-premise operators enhance the profitability of their beverage operations.

13783 **Club Management Magazine**
Finan Publishing Company
107 W Pacific
Saint Louis, MO 63119-3776

314-961-6644; Fax: 314-961-4809
www.cmaa.org

Thomas J Finan, IV, Managing Editor
Dee Kaplan, Publisher
Dianne Dierkes, Circulation Manager

The resource for successful club operations.
Cost: $26.95
150 Pages
Founded in 1921
Mailing list available for rent: 21,000 names
Printed in 4 colors on glossy stock

13784 **Consortium of Hospitality Research Information Services**
Quanta Press
1313 5th St SE
Suite 223A
Minneapolis, MN 55414-4513

612-379-3618

Nancy J Hall, Owner

Consists of academic and industry groups which together have produced a comprehensive index of hospitality literature in CD-ROM format. Over 47,000 bibliographic records with abstracts from over 50 journals serving the hospitality industry.

13785 **Cornell Hotel & Restaurant Administration Quarterly**
Elsevier Science Publishing Company
415 Horsham Road
Horsham, PA 19044

212-633-3730
888-437-4636; Fax: 212-633-3680
www.hotelschool.cornell.edu/

Glenn Withiam, Executive Editor
Dr. Michael Sturman, Editor
Thomas Cullen, Associate Professor

A journal devoted to the development and exchange of management ideas for the hospitality industry.
Cost: $113.00
Frequency: Quarterly
Circulation: 4500
Founded in 1960

13786 **Developments Magazine**
American Resort Development Association
1201 15th St NW
Suite 400
Washington, DC 20005-2842

202-371-6700; Fax: 202-289-8544
customerservice@arda.org
www.ardafoundation.org

Howard Nusbaum, President/CEO
Lou Ann Burney, Vice President of Marketing
Robert Craycraft, Vice President of Industry Relation
Rob Dunn, Vice President of Finance
Jason C. Gamel, Vice President of State Governments

13787 **Executive Housekeeping Today (EHT)**
International Executive Housekeepers Association
1001 Eastwind Dr
Suite 301
Westerville, OH 43081-3361

614-895-7166
800-200-6342; Fax: 614-895-1248
excel@ieha.org
www.ieha.org
Facebook, Twitter, LinkedIn

Beth Risinger, CEO
Laura DiGiulio, Advertising/Sales/Ed

Magazine for management personnel in the institutional housekeeping industry. Highlighting products, services, association news and industry trends.
Cost: $40.00
3500 Members
30 Pages
Frequency: Monthly
Circulation: 4130
ISSN: 0738-6583
Founded in 1930

13788 **Foodservice Equipment & Supplies Specialist**
Reed Business Information
2000 Clearwater Dr
Oak Brook, IL 60523-8809

630-574-0825; Fax: 630-288-8781
411_webmaster@reedbusiness.com
www.reedbusiness.com

Jeff Greisch, President
Maureen Slocum, Publisher
Paulette Cortopassi, Managing Editor
Victoria Jones, Production Manager
Andrew Rak, Senior Vice President

Magazine for professionals who specify, sell and distribute foodservice equipment, supplies and furnishings.
Frequency: Monthly
Circulation: 22719
Founded in 1948
Printed in 4 colors on glossy stock

13789 **Hospitality News**
PO Box 11960
Prescott, AZ 86304-1960

206-686-7378
800-685-1932; Fax: 206-463-0090
www.hospnews.com

Linda Sanders, Publisher
Miles Small, Editor-in-Chief

Serves restaurants, lodges, health care facilities, schools, clubs, casino's, caterers, and culinary and beverage marketplaces.
Circulation: 105000
ISSN: 1084-2551
Founded in 1988

13790 **Hospitality Product News**
Advanstar Communications
2501 Colorado Avenue
Suite 280
Santa Monica, CA 90404

310-857-7500
888-527-7008; Fax: 310-857-7510
info@advanstar.com
www.advanstar.com/

Doug Ferguson, Group Publisher
Helen Gardner, General Manager
Georgiann Decenzo, Director of Corporate mar
Joseph Loggia, CEO
Thomas Ehardt, Chief Administrator

Contains ADA compliance, maintenance and cleaning, fitness, leisure and entertainment, food and beverage, foodservice equipment and supplies, furnishings and fixtures, guest amenities, tabletop, technology, uniforms, and bedding and linens.
Cost: $35.00
Circulation: 30019
Founded in 1987

13791 **Hospitality Technology**
Edgell Communications
4 Middlebury Boulevard
Randolph, NJ 07869

973-252-0100; Fax: 973-252-9020
www.htmagazine.com

Lenore O'Meara, Associate Publisher
Reid Paul, Editor
Gerald Ryerson, President
Jan Miciak, Production Manager
Leah Segarra, Account Executive

Aimed at owners/operators, franchise and chain executives, and managers in operations, finance, sales/marketing and information systems. Emphasis on applications, new products, industry news and trade show highlights.
Circulation: 16000
Founded in 1984
Printed in 4 colors on glossy stock

13792 **Hotel & Motel Management**
Advanstar Communications
757 3rd Avenue
New York, NY 10017-2013

212-951-6600; Fax: 212-951-6793
info@advanstar.com
www.advanstar.com

Scott E Pierce, President
Mike Malley, Publisher
Jeff Higley, Editor-in-Chief
Mary M. Malloy, National Sales Manager

Publication reaching more than 57,000 management personnel in hotels, motels, motor inns and other related businesses.
Circulation: 53058
ISSN: 0018-6082
Founded in 1875

13793 **Hotels**
Reed Business Information
2000 Clearwater Dr
Oak Brook, IL 60523-8809

605-3 8-09; Fax: 630-288-8781
hotels_webmaster@reedbusiness.com
www.reedbusiness.com

Jeff Greisch, President
Andrew Rak, Senior Vice President
Jeff Weinstein, Editor

The magazine for the worldwide hotel industry
Cost: $125.90
Frequency: Monthly
Circulation: 62000
ISSN: 1047-2975
Printed in 4 colors on glossy stock

13794 **Infoline**
Hospitality Financial & Technology Professionals
11709 Boulder Lane
Suite 110
Austin, TX 78726-1832

512-249-5333
800-646-4387; Fax: 512-249-1533
eliza.selig@hftp.org
www.hftp.org

Eliza Selig, Editor
Lance Peterson, Director Marketing
Frank Wolfe, Executive ViP

Chapter and officer activities.
Frequency: Monthly
Circulation: 4000
Founded in 1952

13795 **Journal of Quality Assurance in Hospitality & Tourism**
Bill Cohen
10 Alice Street
Binghamton, NY 13904-1580

607-722-5857
800-342-9678; Fax: 607-722-6362
www.haworthpressinc.com

Timothy R Hinkin, Editor
Pyo Sungsoo, Editor
William Cohen, Owner

Serves as a medium to share and disseminate information coming from new research findings and superior practices in tourisim and hospitality; covers planning, development, management and marketing.
Cost: $50.00
Frequency: Quarterly
Founded in 1978

13796 **Journal of Teaching in Travel & Tourism**
Bill Cohen
10 Alice Street
Binghamton, NY 13904-1580

607-722-5857
800-342-9678; Fax: 607-722-6362
getinfo@haworthpress.com
www.haworthpressinc.com

Timothy R Hinkin, Editor
Pyo Sungsoo, Editor
Cathy HC Hsu, Editor
William Cohen, Owner

Serves as an international interdisiplinary forum and reference source for travel and tourisim education at professional schools and universities.
Founded in 1978

13797 **Lodging Hospitality**
Penton Media
1300 E 9th St
Cleveland, OH 44114-1503

216-696-7000; Fax: 216-696-6662
www.penton.com

Jane Cooper, Marketing
Edward Watkins, Editor
David Kieselstein, CEO
Preston L. Vice, Chief Financial Officer
Andrew Schmolka, Senior Vice President

Serving the US hotel, motel and resort industry. Published 16 times per year, LH provides owners and operators with the latest trends and information on the development, operations and marketing of lodging properties
Frequency: Monthly
Circulation: 50,976
ISSN: 0148-0766
Founded in 1892
Mailing list available for rent
Printed in 4 colors on glossy stock

13798 **Market Watch**
M Shanken Communications
387 Park Ave S
Floor 8
New York, NY 10016-8872

212-684-4224; Fax: 212-684-5424
www.cigaraficionado.com

Marvin Shanken, Publisher
Felicia Bedoya, President

Up-to-date information for individuals and businesses working in the beverage and alcohol industry.
Cost: $75.42
200 Pages
Circulation: 65000
Founded in 1981
Printed in 4 colors

13799 **Nation's Restaurant News**
Informa USA Inc.
101 Arthur Andersen Pkwy.
Sarasota, FL 34232-6323

508-616-6600
800-944-4676; Fax: 508-616-5522
jenna.telesca@knect365.com
www.nrn.com

Jenna Telesca, Editor-in-Chief
Kent Scholla, Director, Sales
Laura Viscusi, VP, Market Leader

Serves commercial and onsite food service and lodging establishments including restaurants, schools, universities, hospitals, nursing homes and other health and welfare facilities, hotels and motels with food service, government installations, clubs and other related firms.
Cost: $44.95
Circulation: 85,999
Founded in 1925
Mailing list available for rent: 100,000 names at $100 per M
Printed in 4 colors on matte stock

13800 **Restaurant Hospitality**
Penton Media
1300 E 9th St
Cleveland, OH 44114-1503

216-696-7000; Fax: 216-696-6662
information@penton.com
www.penton.com

Jane Cooper, Marketing
Jennifer Daugherty, Communications Manager
David Kieselstein, Chief Executive Officer
Kurt Nelson, Vice President, Human Resources
Andrew Schmolka, Senior Vice President

A national trade publication that covers the full-service restaurant industry. If offers cover story features, an extensive food section with recipes, a multi-page news section and a variety of one page profiles on rising stars, equipment, food safety, beverages, design and more.
130 Pages
Frequency: Monthly
Circulation: 117721
ISSN: 0147-9989
Founded in 1892
Mailing list available for rent
Printed in 4 colors on glossy stock

13801 **Restaurants & Institutions**
Reed Business Information
2000 Clearwater Dr
Oak Brook, IL 60523-8809

605-3 8-09; Fax: 630-288-8781
privacymanager@reedbusiness.com
www.reedbusiness.com

Patricia B Dailey, Editor-in-Chief
Scott Hume, Managing Editor
Jim Casella, CEO
Brion Palmer, Publisher
Andrew Rak, Senior Vice President

Commercial and noncommercial foodservice establishments including restaurant, hotels, motels, fast-food chains,coffee shops, food stores with foodservice
Cost: $477.00
Frequency: Monthly
Circulation: 154,110
Founded in 1937
Printed in 4 colors on glossy stock

13802 **Ski Area Management**
Beardsley Publishing Corporation

PO Box 644
Woodbury, CT 06798-644

203-263-0888; Fax: 203-266-0452
www.saminfo.com

Jennifer Rowan, Publisher
Rick Kahl, Editor
Donna Jacobs, Production Manager

Content includes technologies of skilifts, snowmaking and slope grooming, at year-round resort operations. Other features include product and supplier directories, resort architecture and design, new products, marketing, real estate and rental.
Cost: $42.00
Frequency: Monthly
Circulation: 3100
Printed in 4 colors on glossy stock

13803 **Textile Rental Magazine**
Textile Rental Services Association
1800 Diagonal Rd
Suite 200
Alexandria, VA 22314-2842

703-519-0029
877-770-9274; Fax: 703-519-0026
trsa@trsa.org
www.trsa.org
Facebook, Twitter, LinkedIn

Roger Cocivera, President/CEO
Jack Morgan, Editor

Packed with valuable tips and ideas.
Frequency: Monthly
Founded in 1912

13804 **The National Culinary Review**
American Culinary Federation
180 Center Place Way
St. Augustine, FL 32095

904-824-4468
800-624-9458; Fax: 904-940-0741
www.acfchefs.org

Heidi Cramb, Executive Director
Edward G Leonard, President
Brent T. Frei, Director of Marketing
Kay Orde, Editor
Michael Feierstein, Administrative Assistant

Flagship publication of the American Culinary Federation.
Frequency: 6x/yr
Circulation: 21000
Founded in 1932

Trade Shows

13805 **AAHOA Annual Convention and Trade Show**
Asian American Hotel Owners Association
1100 Abernathy Road
Suite 1100
Atlanta, GA 30328-6707

404-816-5759; Fax: 404-816-6260
info@aahoa.com
www.aahoa.com
Facebook, Twitter, LinkedIn, YouTube, Instagram

Chip Rogers, President & CEO
Bharat Patel, CHO, Chairman
Bhavesh B. Patel, CHO, Vice Chairman
Hitesh Patel, CHA, CHO, Treasurer
Jagruti Panwala, CHO, Secretary

Bringing together experts and professionals in the hotel and motel businesses to discuss and share industry tips, insights, and trends among Asian American owners.
16600 Members
Founded in 1989

13806 **American Hotel & Motel Association Annual Conference/Leadership Forum**
1201 New York Avenue NW
Suite 600
Washington, DC 20005-3931

202-289-3100; Fax: 202-289-3158
webmaster@ahla.com
www.ahlef.org

Gerald Petitt, Chairman
Joseph A. McInerney, President/Ceo
Pam Inman, Executive Vice President & COO
Joori Jeon, Executive Vice President & CFO
Marlene M. Colucci, Executive Vice President

189 exhibits of hotel supplies, equipment and information, conference and workshop.
1500 Attendees
Frequency: Annual
Founded in 1910

13807 **American Hotel & Motel Association Annual Convention**
1201 New York Avenue NW
Suite 600
Washington, DC 20005-3931

202-289-3100; Fax: 202-289-3199
webmaster@ahla.com
www.ahlef.org

Gerald Petitt, Chairman
Joseph A. McInerney, President/Coo
Pam Inman, Executive Vice President & COO
Joori Jeon, Executive Vice President & CFO
Marlene M. Colucci, Executive Vice President

125 booths consisting of telecommunication systems, supplies and equipment for the hotel and motel industry.
1.5M Attendees
Frequency: April

13808 **American Resort Development Association Convention**
1201 15th Street NW
Suite 400
Washington, DC 20005-2842

202-371-6700; Fax: 202-289-8544
customerservice@arda.org
www.arda.org

Howard C Nusbaum, President/CEO
Lou Ann Burney, Vice President of Marketing
Robert Craycraft, Vice President of Industry Relation
Rob Dunn, Vice President of Finance
Jason C. Gamel, Vice President of State Government

One hundred fifty booths.
3600 Attendees
Frequency: April

13809 **Annual Council on Hotel, Restaurant and Institutional Education Conference**
Int'l Council on Hotel & Restaurant Education
2810 North Parham Roaf
Suite 230
Richmond, VA 23294

804-346-4800; Fax: 804-346-5009
publications@chrie.org
www.chrie.org

Kathy McCarty, Executive VP/CEO
Bill Shoemaker, Treasurer
Joseph Bradley, Treasurer

Terrific opportunity to gain knowledge, exchange ideas, and enjoy the camaraderie and fellowship of colleagues in the hospitality industry
6MM Attendees
Frequency: July

13810 **Annual Hotel, Motel and Restaurant Supply Show of the Southeast**
Leisure Time Unlimited
708 Main Street
PO Box 332
Myrtle Beach, SC 29577

843-448-9483
800-261-5991; Fax: 843-626-1513
hmrss@sc.rr.com
www.hmrsss.com

Brooke P Baker, Show Director

Trade show for the hospitality industry.
23000 Attendees
Frequency: January
Founded in 1975

13811 **Fall Conference for Hospitality Supply Management**
Institute for Supply Management
Po Box 22160
Tempe, AZ 85285-2160

480-752-6276
800-888-6276; Fax: 480-752-7890
www.ism.ws
Facebook, Twitter, LinkedIn

Sidney Johnson, Chairman
Thomas W. Derry, Chief Executive Officer
Debbie Webber, Senior VP/Corporate Treasurer
Holly LaCroix Johnson, Senior VP/Corporate Secretary
Nora Neibergall, CPM, Senior VP
Frequency: Oct, Dallas, TX
Mailing list available for rent

13812 **Great Southwest Lodging & Restaurant Show**
Arizona Hotel and Lodging Association
1240 East Missouri Avenue
Phoenix, AZ 85014

602-604-0729
800-788-2462; Fax: 520-604-0769
www.southwestshow.com

Britt Kimball, Show Manager

Seminars, workshops and 450+ exhibits of food service and lodging equipment, marketing, decorations, berverage services (alcoholic and non), cleaning services and pest control, furnishings, lighting, insurance, transportation and more.
5000 Attendees
Frequency: Annual
Founded in 1970

13813 **IEHA's Association Convention/in Conjunction with ISSA Interclean**
International Executive Housekeepers Association
1001 Eastwind Drive
Suite 301
Westerville, OH 43081-3361

614-895-7166
800-200-6342; Fax: 614-895-1248
excel@ieha.org
www.ieha.org
Facebook, Twitter, LinkedIn

Beth Risinger, CEO

Educational seminars and exhibits by firms engaged in manufacturing, marketing and distribution of cleaning and maintenance suppliers. Containing 750 exhibits.
3500 Members
15M Attendees
Frequency: Oct 23-26 Orlando Florida

13814 **Innkeeping**
PAII
Box 97010
Santa Barbara, CA 93190

805-965-4525

JoAnn Bell, Publisher

Offers a forum for innkeepers, hotel and motel managers, owners and operators.
500 Attendees
Frequency: March/April

13815 **International Hotel/Motel & Restaurant Show**
George Little Management
10 Bank Street
Suite 1200
White Plains, NY 10606-1954
914-486-6070
800-272-7469; Fax: 914-948-6180
www.ihmrs.com
Christian Falkemberg, Show Manager
George Little II, President
Products and services for lodging and food service properties organized in 12 categories: Technology; Uniforms, Linens and Bedding; Tabletop; Guest amenities and services; Food and Beverage; Cleaning and Maintenance; Food Service Equipment and Supplies; Franchise, Finance and Management; Furnishings and Fixturtes; Fitness, Leisure and Entertainment; The Environment; Advertising and Promotion
45000 Attendees
Frequency: Early November

13816 **Marine Hotel Catering Duty Free Conference**
PO Box 1659
Sausalito, CA 94966
415-332-1903; Fax: 415-332-9457
mha@mhaweb.org
www.mhaweb.org
Caroline Prichard, Administrator
100 booths.
700 Attendees
Frequency: April

13817 **Pacific Hospitality Expo Convention Center**
1801 Kalakaua Avenue
Honolulu, HI 96815-2558
808-973-9790
Joanie Gribbin, Director
220 booths.
2.5M Attendees
Frequency: June

13818 **Rocky Mountain Hospitality Convention and Expo**
899 Logan Street
Suite 300
Denver, CO 80203-3155
303-792-9621
Bruce Whiticker, Convention Director
413 booths.
7M Attendees
Frequency: June

Directories & Databases

13819 **AHLA Allied Member Directory**
American Hotel & Lodging Association
1201 New York Ave NW
Suite 600
Washington, DC 20005-3931
202-289-3100; Fax: 202-289-3199
webmaster@ahla.com
www.ahla.com
Katherine Lugar, President & CEO
Lists over 1,000 companies that own, manage or franchise properties worldwide. Also lists, in 7 sections: companies by type, company/brand web site, company listings, geographical, company rankings, hotel brokers, and vendors.
Cost: $100.00
Frequency: Annual
Founded in 1931

13820 **All Suite Hotel Guide**
Ten Speed Press
PO Box 7123
Berkeley, CA 94707-0123
510-559-1600
800-841-2665; Fax: 510-559-1629
www.tenspeedpress.com
Phil Wood, President
Over 1,600 hotels are offered which have suites available consisting of two or more rooms for rent.
Cost: $14.95
336 Pages
Frequency: Annual
ISBN: 1-580080-91-

13821 **America's Wonderful Little Hotels & Inns**
St. Martin's Press
175 5th Ave
4th Floor
New York, NY 10010-7703
212-674-5151; Fax: 212-674-3179
John Sargent, CEO
A directory listing hotels and inns that are located throughout the United States and Canada in various volumes. Prices vary per region, per volume.
ISBN: 0-312081-30-8
Founded in 1952

13822 **Bed & Breakfast Home Directory: Homes Away from Home, West Coast**
Knighttime Publications
890 Calabasas Road
Watsonville, CA 95076-0418
Diane Knight, Author
Suzy Blackaby, Author
Kevin McElvain, Author
Over 250 bed and breakfast homes are listed that are located in the areas of California, Oregon, Washington and British Columbia, Canada.
Cost: $12.95
203 Pages
Frequency: Biennial
ISBN: 0-942902-03-3

13823 **Bed and Breakfast Guest Houses and Inns of America**
PO Box 38066
Germantown, TN 38183-0066
901-946-1902; Fax: 901-758-0816
Directory of services and supplies to the industry.
Cost: $45.00
350 Pages
Frequency: Annual
ISSN: 1056-8069

13824 **Cabin Guide to Wilderness Lodging**
Hammond Publishing
1500 E Tropicana Ave
Suite 110
Las Vegas, NV 89119-6515
702-878-2008
Jim Smith, Manager
Information is given on over 500 cabins in national and state forests, preserves and other wildlife areas.
Cost: $14.95
250 Pages
Frequency: Annual

13825 **Complete Guide to Bed & Breakfasts, Inns and Guesthouses in US & Canada**
Lanier Publishing International
963 Transport Way
Petaluma, CA 94954-8011
707-763-0271; Fax: 707-763-5762
lanier@travelguides.com
www.travelguides.com
Pamela Lanier, Owner
Directory of services and supplies to the industry.
Cost: $16.95
536 Pages
Frequency: Annual

13826 **Country Inns and Back Roads, North America**
HarperCollins
10 E 53rd St
Cellar 1 Floor
New York, NY 10022-5299
212-207-7000; Fax: 212-207-6964
feedback2@harpercollins.com
www.harpercollins.com
Brian Murray, CEO
Over 200 country inns in the United States and Canada are listed.
Cost: $13.00
450 Pages
Frequency: Annual

13827 **Hotel Development Guide**
Hospitality Media
17950 Preston Rd
Suite 710
Dallas, TX 75252-5637
972-934-2040; Fax: 972-934-2070
Info@hospitalitymgt.com
www.hospitalitymgt.com
Leo Spriggs, CEO
John Connor, Director of Operations
Bill Sullivan, Chief Financial Officer
Offers a list of suppliers of equipment, fixtures and services needed for new motels.
Cost: $100.00

13828 **Hotel and Travel Index**
Reed Travel Group
904 Haddonfield Rd
Subscription Department
Cherry Hill, NJ 08002-2745
856-665-4455
800-442-0900; Fax: 856-488-4867
Over 45,000 hotels worldwide are profiled in this travel directory.
Cost: $125.00
2000 Pages
Frequency: Quarterly
Circulation: 60,000

13829 **Inspected, Rated and Approved Bed and Breakfast Country Inns**
American Bed & Breakfast Association
10800 Midlothian Tpke
Suite 254
Richmond, VA 23235-4700
Home Page: www.abba.com
Beth Burgreen Stuhlman, Editor
Information on over 500 overnight accommodations in North American bed and breakfast locations are listed.
Cost: $17.95
350 Pages
ISBN: 0-934473-27-7
Founded in 1996

13830 **National Directory of Budget Motels**
Pilot Books

127 Sterling Avenue
#2102
Greenport, NY 11944-1439

631-477-0978
800-79 -ILOT; Fax: 631-477-0978

Guide to the best in economy-priced chain motel accommodations in the United States and Canada.
Cost: $12.95
346 Pages
Frequency: Annual

13831 National Trust Guide to Historic Bed & Breakfasts, Inns & Small Hotels
Preservation Press
1785 Massachusetts Ave NW
Washington, DC 20036-2117

202-588-6083; Fax: 202-588-6172

James Schwartz, Manager

Directory of services and supplies to the industry.
Cost: $13.95
416 Pages
Frequency: Biennial

13832 Official Bed and Breakfast Guide
National Bed & Breakfast Association
148 E Rocks Road
Norwalk, CT 06851

203-847-6196; Fax: 203-847-0469
www.nbba.com

Phyllis Featherston, President

A who's who directory of services and supplies to the industry offering a list of the best in bed and breakfast accommodations in USA, Canada and the Carribbean.
Cost: $17.95
560 Pages

13833 Official Hotel Guide
Reed Hotel Directories Network
500 Plaza Drive
Secaucus, NJ 07094-3619

201-902-1960; Fax: 201-319-1628

Wilma Goldenberg, Editor

3 volumes of 25,000 hotels, motels and resorts worldwide.
Cost: $385.00
Frequency: Annual
Circulation: 20,000

13834 Pelican's Select Guide to American Bed and Breakfast
Pelican Publishing Company
1000 Burmaster St
Gretna, LA 70053-2246

504-368-1175; Fax: 504-368-1195
sales@pelicanpub.com
www.pelicanpub.com

Milburn Calhoun, Publisher
Joseph Billingsley, Sales Manager

Independent guest houses, inns and bed and breakfast accommodations are profiled.
Cost: $14.95
216 Pages
ISBN: 1-589800-61-8
Printed in 2 colors on matte stock

13835 Preferred Hotels Directory
Preferred Hotels & Resorts Worldwide
311 S Wacker Dr
Suite 1900
Chicago, IL 60606-6676

312-913-0400
800-323-7500; Fax: 312-913-5124
www.preferredhotels.com

John Ubberoth, CEO
Casey Ueberroth, Managing Director
80 Pages
Frequency: Annual
Circulation: 25,000

13836 Recommended Country Inns
Globe Pequot Press
246 Goose Lane
PO Box 480
Guilford, CT 06437

203-458-4500
888-249-7586; Fax: 800-820-2329
www.globepequot.com

Elizabeth Squier
Elenor Berman

This series of directories offers information on country inns located in certain parts of the United States.
Cost: $18.95
416 Pages
Frequency: Biennial
ISBN: 0-762728-48-5

13837 Salem Press Online Platform
Grey House Publishing
4919 Route 22
PO Box 56
Amenia, NY 12501

800-221-1592; Fax: 201-968-0511
csr@salempress.com
online.salempress.com

The new Salem Press platform houses more than 500 titles including all of Salem's Health, Literature, History and Science titles in addition to select titles from the Grey House Publishing and H.W. Wilson product lines. Online access is free with each print purchase and includes an unlimited number of simultaneous users and remote access.

13838 Where to Stay USA
Prentice Hall Law & Business
1 Lake St
Upper Saddle Rv, NJ 07458-1828

201-236-7000; Fax: 201-236-3381

Information is given on over 1,200 places to stay and eat from $4 to $35 a night.
Cost: $16.00
350 Pages
Frequency: Biennial

Industry Web Sites

13839 http://gold.greyhouse.com
G.O.L.D Grey House OnLine Databases

Grey House Publishing's online database platform, GOLD, offers Quick Search, Keyword Search and Expert Search for most business sectors including hotel, motel and hospitality markets. The GOLD platform makes finding the information you need quick and easy - whether you're a novice searcher or an experienced database user. All of Grey House's directory products are available for subscription on the GOLD platform.

13840 www.abba.com
American Bed & Breakfast Association

National organization with information on over 500 overnight accomodations in North American bed and breakfast locations.

13841 www.biztravel.com
Biztravel.com

Internet travel service offering discounts on flights, hotels, car rentals, packages and cruises.

13842 www.chrie.org
Int'l Council on Hotel & Restaurant Education

To enhance professionalism at all levels of the hospitality and tourism industry through education and training.

13843 www.expedia.com
Expedia.com

Internet travel service offers access to airlines, hotels, car rentals, vacation packages, cruises and corporate travel.

13844 www.goworldnet.com/cgi-bin
Worldnet USA

A database of states with hotels, theaters and museums.

13845 www.greyhouse.com
Grey House Publishing

Authoritative reference directories for most business sectors including hotel, motel and hospitality markets. Users can search the online databases with varied search criteria allowing for custom searches by product category, geographic area, sales volume, keyword, subject and more. Full Grey House catalog and online ordering also available.

13846 www.hanyc.org
Hotel Association of New York City

One of the oldest professional trade associations in the nation.

13847 www.hotels.com
Hotels.com

Provides discount accommodations worldwide.

13848 www.hotwire.com
Hotwire.com

Internet travel service offering discounts on flights, hotels, car rentals, packages and cruises.

13849 www.ieha.org
International Executive Housekeepers Association

An organization for persons working in the housekeeping area of the lodging industry.

13850 www.innbook.com
Bed and Breakfast Inns & Small Luxury Hotels

Includes the finest inns, B&Bs, and getaway retreats in Canada and the Us, carefully chosen and inspected to maintain the highest standards.

13851 www.masslodging.com
Massachusetts Lodging Association

A trade association representing and promoting the lodging industryin Massachusetts.

13852 www.nmhotels.com
New Mexico Lodging Association

New Mexico's trade association representing the lodging industry.

13853 www.orbitz.com
Orbitz.com

Internet travel service offering discounts on flights, hotels, car rentals, packages and cruises.

13854 www.paii.org
Professional Association of Innkeepers

International

Serving bed and breakfast/country inn owners, aspiring innkeepers, inn sitters, vendors with educational and consultative services. International conference.

13855 **www.preferredhotels.com**
The Luxury Hotels of Preferred Hotels & Resorts
Worldwide

An exclusive group of independent luxury hotels in the United States.

13856 **www.travel.lycos.com**
Lycos.com
Internet travel service offering discounts on flights, hotels, car rentals, packages and cruises.

13857 **www.travel.yahoo.com**
Yahoo.com
Internet travel service providing access to flights, hotels, car rentals, vacation packages and cruises.

13858 **www.travelocity.com**
Sabre Holdings
Travel service offering consumers access to hundreds of airlines and thousands of hotels, as well as cruises, last-minute and vacation packages and best-in-class car rental companies.

13859 **www.travelweb.com**
Travelweb.com
Internet provider of hotel accommodations.

Associations

13860 **ASIS International**
1625 Prince St.
Alexandria, VA 22314-2882

703-519-6200; Fax: 703-519-6299
pr@asisonline.org
www.asisonline.org
Facebook, Twitter, LinkedIn, YouTube

Richard E. Chase, International President
Peter J. O'Neil, CEO

The largest organization for security professionals. ASIS is dedicated to increasing the effectiveness and productivity of security professionals by developing educational programs and materials that cover broad security interests, such as the ASIS Annual Seminar and Exhibits, as well as specific topics. ASIS also advocates the role and value of the security management profession to the media, governmental entities, and the public.
Founded in 1955

13861 **ASM International**
9639 Kinsman Road
Materials Park, OH 44073-0002

440-338-5151
800-336-5152; Fax: 440-338-4634
memberservicecenter@asminternational.org
www.asminternational.org
Facebook, Twitter, LinkedIn

Zi-Kui Liu, President
Diana Essock, Vice President
Raymond V. Fryan, Treasurer
William T. Mahoney, Secretary & CEO

The society for materials engineers and scientists, a worldwide network dedicated to advancing industry, technology and applications of metals and materials. ASM provides information references, education, research and international events.
30K Members
Founded in 1913

13862 **American Coatings Association**
1500 Rhode Island Ave., NW
Washington, DC 20005

202-462-6272; Fax: 202-462-8549
members@paint.org
www.coatingstech.org
Facebook, Twitter, LinkedIn, Reddit, Digg, MySpace, Stumble

J. Andrew Doyle, President & CEO
Thomas J. Graves, Vice President, General Counsel
Allen Irish, Counsel / Director
Alison Keane, Vice President, Government Affairs
Robin Eastman Caldwell, Senior Gov. Affairs Specialist

Provides technical education and professional development to its members and to the global industry through its multinational Constituent Societies and collectively as a Federation
Founded in 1922

13863 **American Composites Manufacturers Association**
3033 Wilson Blvd.
Suite 420
Arlington, VA 22201-4749

703-525-0511; Fax: 703-525-0743
info@acmanet.org
www.acmanet.org
Facebook, Twitter, LinkedIn, RSS

Jeff Craney, Chairman
Leon Garoufalis, Vice Chairman
Tom Dobbins, CAE, President
John Schweitzer, Vice President, Government Affairs
Heather Rhoderick, CMP, CAE, SVP, Events & Information

A trade association serving the composites industry.
1100 Members
Founded in 1979

13864 **American Electroplaters and Surface Finishers Society (AESF)**
1155 15th Street NW
Suite 500
Washington, DC 20005

202-457-8401; Fax: 202-530-0659
info@aesf.org
www.aesf.org
Facebook, Twitter, LinkedIn, Google+, RSS

John Flatley, Executive Director
Courtney Mariette, Bookstore/Education
Holly Wills, Membership
Carrie Hoffman, Deputy Executive Director
Cheryl Clark, Director of Events

AESF is an international society that advances the science of surface finishing to benefit industry and society through education, information and social involvement, as well as those who provide services, supplies and support to the industry.
5000 Members
Founded in 1909

13865 **Asphalt Recycling and Reclaiming Associates**
15 Harold Court
Suite 250
Bayshore, NY 11706

631-231-8400; Fax: 631-434-1116
sales@arra.com
www.arra.com

Mike Krissoff, Executive Director

Promotes the interest of owners and manufacturers of recycling equipment, engineers, suppliers and businesses involved in the asphalt recycling industry. Newsletter published quarterly.
200 Members
Founded in 1957
Mailing list available for rent

13866 **Associated Equipment Distributors**
650 E Algonquin Road
Suite 305
Schaumburg, IL 60173

630-574-0650
help@aednet.org
aednet.org
Facebook, Twitter, LinkedIn

Brian P. McGuire, President/CEO
Robert K. Henderson, EVP & Chief Operating Officer
Agnes Baczek, Director, Finance
Jon Cruthers, VP, Sales
Sara Smith, Editor-In-Chief & Marketing & Comm.

International trade association supporting companies specializing in eqipment used in construction, mining, forestry, power generation, agriculture and industrial applications.
1000 Members
Founded in 1919

13867 **Association for Manufacturing Excellence**
3701 Algonquin Rd.
Suite 225
Rolling Meadows, IL 60008-3150

224-232-5980; Fax: 224-232-5981
info@ame.org
www.ame.org
Facebook, Twitter, LinkedIn, YouTube

George Saiz, President & CEO

Organization promoting personal and enterprise improvement in the manufacturing industry.
4000 Members
Founded in 1985

13868 **Association of Equipment Manufacturers**
6737 West Washington Street
Suite 2400
Milwaukee, WI 53214-5647

414-272-0943; Fax: 414-272-1170
aem@aem.org
www.aem.org
Facebook, Twitter, LinkedIn, YouTube

Jeffrey R. Reed, Chair

The trade and business development resource for companies that offer equipment, products and services for the construction, agricultural, mining, forestry, and utility fields.
900+ Members

13869 **Association of Machinery and Equipment Appraisers**
315 South Patrick Street
Alexandria, VA 22314

703-836-7900
800-537-8629; Fax: 703-836-9303
amea@amea.org
www.amea.org
Facebook, LinkedIn, YouTube

Randall Koster, President
Jean Harris, Director
Terrance Jacobs, Director
Doris Toronyi, Director
Curt Roskelley, Director

Certifies and accredits qualified capital equipment appraisers in the appraisal industry, as well as offering opportunities for networking with other professionals.
300 Members
Founded in 1983
Mailing list available for rent

13870 **Athletic Equipment Managers Association**
207 E. Bodman
Bement, IL 13068-9643

217-678-1004; Fax: 217-678-1005
www.equipmentmanagers.org

Dan Siermine E.M., C., President
Mike Royster, Executive Director
Matthew Althoff E.M.,C., Associate Executive Director
Meli Resendiz E.M.,C, Vice Presidentў
Clifton Perry, Vice President

The purpose of the AEMA is to promote, advance, and improve the Equipment Managers Profession in all of its many phases
700 Members
Founded in 1974

13871 **Casting Industry Suppliers Association**
14175 West Indian School Road
Suite B4-504
Goodyear, AZ 85395

623-547-0920; Fax: 623-536-1486
www.cisa.org
RSS

Lew Fish, President
Roger A Hayes, Executive Director
Lew Fish, 2nd Vice President
Mike Bartol, 1st Vice President

Fosters better trade practices. Serves as industry representative before the government and public. Encourages member research into new processes and methods of foundry operation. Association

of suppliers to the worldwide metal casting industry.
70 Members
Founded in 1919
Mailing list available for rent

13872 Composite Can and Tube Institute
50 South Pickett Street
Suite 110
Alexandria, VA 22304-7206
703-823-7234; Fax: 703-823-7237
ccti@cctiwdc.org
www.cctiwdc.org
Kristine Garland, Executive Vice President
Wayne Vance, Association Councel
Janine Marczak, Associate Manager, Events
CCTI is an international nonprofit trade association representing the interests of manufacturers of composite paperboard cans, containers, canisters, tubes, cores, edgeboard and related or similar composite products and suppliers to those manufacturers of such items as paper, machinery, adhesives, labels and other services and materials.
Founded in 1933

13873 Conveyor Equipment Manufacturers Association (CEMA)
5672 Strand Ct.
Suite 2
Naples, FL 34110
239-514-3441; Fax: 239-514-3470
kim@cemanet.org
www.cemanet.org
Facebook, Twitter, LinkedIn, YouTube
Paul Ross, President
E.A. Thompson, Vice President
Robert Reinfried, Executive Vice President
Noel Bell, Director
Bob Callahan, Director
CEMA seeks to support manufacturers of conveyors and conveying systems. The association sponsors an annual Engineering Conference that allows members to meet and develop the industry standards that affect the conveyor industry.
Founded in 1933

13874 Equipment Dealers Association
165 North Meramec Avenue
Suite 430
St. Louis, MO 63105
636-349-5000; Fax: 636-349-5443
info@equipmentdealer.org
www.equipmentdealer.org
Facebook, Twitter, LinkedIn
Kim Rominger, President & CEO
Michael Williams, VP, Operations
Joseph Dykes, VP, Industry Relations
Doug Kreienkamp, Operations Coordinator
Alex Hoffman, Communications & Marketing Director
The association provides a variety of educational, financial, legislative and legal services to equipment dealers in the United States and Canada. Industries served by association members include agriculture, construction, industrial, forestry and outdoor power.
4500 Members
Founded in 1900

13875 Equipment Leasing and Finance Association
1625 Eye St. NW
Suite 850
Washington, DC 20006
202-238-3400; Fax: 202-238-3401
rpetta@elfaonline.org
www.elfaonline.org
Facebook, Twitter, LinkedIn, RSS, YouTube
Ralph Petta, President and CEO
Paul Stilp, Chief Financial & Operating Officer
Amy Vogt, VP, Communications
Julie Benson, VP, Membership Marketing
Andy Fishburn, VP, Federal Government Relations
Represents financial services companies and manufacturers involved in the dynamic equipment finance sector to the business community, government and media.
700+ Members
Founded in 1961
Mailing list available for rent

13876 Fluid Controls Institute
1300 Sumner Avenue
Cleveland, OH 44115-2851
216-241-7333; Fax: 216-241-0105
www.fluidcontrolsinstitute.org
Manufacturers of equipment for fluid (liquid or gas) control and conditioning. This institute is organized into product specific sections which address issues that are relevant to particular products and or/or technologies.
Founded in 1921

13877 Fluid Sealing Association
994 Old Eagle School Rd
Suite 1019
Wayne, PA 19087-1802
610-971-4850; Fax: 610-971-4859
info@fluidsealing.com
www.fluidsealing.com
Robert Ecker, Executive Director
Hope Silverman, Administrative Director
Influence and support the development of related standards and to provide education in the fluid sealing area.
57 Members
Founded in 1933
Mailing list available for rent

13878 Hoist Manufacturers Institute
8720 Red Oak Boulevard
Suite 201
Charlotte, NC 28217-3996
704-676-1190; Fax: 704-676-1199
cmiller@mhi.org
www.mhi.org
Facebook, Twitter, LinkedIn
E Larry Strayhorn, Last Retiring Executive Chairman
Dave Young, Executive Vice Chairman
John Paxton, President
Gregg E. Goodner, VP
Carol Miller, VP, Marketing
An affiliate of Material Handling Industry, also a trade association of maufacturers of overhead handling hoists. The products of member companies include hand chain hoists, ratchet lever hoists, trolleys, air chain and air rope hoists, and electric chain and electric wire rope hoists.
800 Members
Founded in 1945
Mailing list available for rent

13879 Independent Lubricant Manufacturers Association
400 N. Columbus Street
Suite 201
Alexandria, VA 22314-2264
703-684-5574; Fax: 703-836-8503
tmack@ilma.org
www.ilma.org
Facebook, Twitter
Holly Alfano, Chief Executive Officer
Brenda Gillinson, Sr. Director, Communications
Tim Mack, Sr. Director, Member Engagement
Amber Lopez, Sr. Manager, Marketing & Digital
Meg Thaxton, Manager, Meetings
Independent blenders and compounders of lubricants.
320 Members
Founded in 2004
Mailing list available for rent: 2000 names at $750 per M

13880 Industrial Diamond Association of America
PO Box 29460
Columbus, OH 43229
614-797-2265; Fax: 614-797-2264
tkane-ida@insight.rr.com
www.superabrasives.org
Mike Mustin, President
Terry M Kane, Executive Director
Troy Heuermann, Vice President
Keith Reckling, Secretary/Treasurer
Trade association for those in the superabrasives industry. Products and services provided and used in most manufacturing and constuction industries such as: stone processing, glass, construction, woodworking, electronics, medical, etc.
Founded in 1946

13881 Industrial Heating Equipment Association
5040 Old Taylor Mill Rd., PMB 13
Taylor Mill, KY 41015
859-356-1575; Fax: 859-356-0908
ihea@ihea.org
www.ihea.org
Facebook
Anne Goyer, Executive Vice President
Amanda Goyer, Marketing
Andy Goyer, Accounting & Government Relations
Kelly LeCount, Conference Manager & Speaker Coord.
Bruce Bryan, VP, Sales & Education
A voluntary national trade association representing the major segments of the industrial heat processing equipment industry. Provides services to member companies that will enhance member company capabilities to serve end users in the industrial heat processing industry and improve the member company's business performance as well.
Founded in 1929
Mailing list available for rent

13882 Industrial Supply Association
3435 Concord Road
Unit 21889
York, PA 17402
866-460-2360
info@isapartners.org
www.isapartners.org
Facebook, Twitter, LinkedIn, YouTube
Ed Gerber, President & CEO
The primary focus of the Inudstrial Supply Association is to improve the industrial supply channel through its mission-critical activities, including conventions, forums and the gathering and dissemination of critical information. The association supports distributors, manufacturers and representatives of MROP products/industrial equipment.
900+ Members
Founded in 2007

13883 Institute for Supply Management
2055 E. Centennial Circle
Tempe, AZ 85284-1802
480-752-6276
800-888-6276; Fax: 480-752-7890
custsvc@instituteforsupplymanagement.org
www.ism.ws

Facebook, Twitter, LinkedIn, Youtube, Google Plus

Thomas Derry, CEO
Nora Neibergall, CPSM CPO
Cindy Urbaytis, Managing Director
Mary Lue Peck, Managing Director

The mission of ISM is to enhance the value and performance of procurement and supply chain management practitioners and their organizations worldwide.
45000 Members
Founded in 1915
Mailing list available for rent

13884 **Institute of Industrial Engineers**
3577 Parkway Lane
Suite 200
Norcross, GA 30092

770-449-0460
800-494-0460; Fax: 770-441-3295
cs@iienet.org
Facebook, Twitter, LinkedIn, Google+, YouTube

Don Greene, P.E., C.A.E., Chief Executive Officerÿ
Donna Calvert, Chief Operating Officer
Hope Teaque, Dir. - Multimedia Advertising Sales
Nancy LaJoice, Director of Membership
Monica Elliott, Director of Communications

Supports all industrial engineers with training, education, publications, conferences, etc.
15000 Members
Founded in 1948
Mailing list available for rent

13885 **International Staple, Nail and Tool**
8735 W. Higgins Road
Suite 300
Chicago, IL 60631ÿ

847-375-6454; Fax: 847-375-6455
info@isanta.org
www.isanta.org

John Kurtz, Executive VP
David Rapp, Codes/Technical Services

An international organization of premier power fastening companies involved in the design, and manufacturing, and sales of power fastening tools and the fasteners they drive.
22 Members
Founded in 1966

13886 **Machinery Dealers National Association**
315 S Patrick Street
Alexandria, VA 22314

703-836-9300
800-872-7807; Fax: 703-836-9303
office@mdna.org
www.mdna.org
Facebook, Twitter, LinkedIn

Mark Robinson, Executive Vice President
Will Keys, Accounting Manager
Joyce Fitzgerald, Administration Director

Represents dealers of used industrial equipment, providing members with business standards and development opportunities.
400 Members
Founded in 1941

13887 **NIBA - The Belting Association**
1818 Parmenter Street
Suite 300
Middleton, WI 53562

608-310-7549; Fax: 608-492-0523
staff@niba.org
www.niba.org
Facebook, Twitter, LinkedIn

Michael Battaglia, Executive Director

NIBA is an association dedicated to promoting the interaction between value added distributors and manufacturers of conveyor belt and components. Its mission is to promote the common business interests of all distributor'fabricators and manufacturers of conveyor and flat power transmission belting and material that enhances and changes belt.
270 Members
Founded in 1927
Mailing list available for rent

13888 **National Corrugated Steel Pipe Association**
14070 Proton Road
Suite 100 LB9
Dallas, TX 75244

972-850-1907; Fax: 972-490-4219
info@ncspa.org
www.ncspa.org
Twitter, LinkedIn, Youtube, RSS

Mike Mihelick, President
Dan Kadrmas, First Vice President
Roger Loding, Treasurer
Wallace Johnson, Immediate Past President
Pat Loney, Secretary

Seeks to promote sound public policy relating to the use of corrugated steel drainage structures in private and public construction.
60 Members
Founded in 1956

13889 **National Spray Equipment Manufacturers**
PO Box 2147
Skokie, IL 60076

440-366-6808; Fax: 847-763-9538
ipp@halldata.com

Bruce Bryan, Advertising Director
Ted Klaiber, Sales Manager

Serves as a technical forum for safety and environmental matters pertaining to the spray finishing industry.
16 Members
Founded in 1922

13890 **New England Equipment Dealers Association**
PO Box 895
Concord, NH 03302-0895

603-225-5510; Fax: 603-225-5510

George M Becker, Managing Director

The New England Equipment Association serve equipment manufacturing companies who provide products and services to the food and beverage industry.

13891 **North American Sawing Association**
1300 Sumner Avenue
Cleveland, OH 44115-2851

216-241-7333; Fax: 216-241-0105

Charles M Stockinger, Secretary/Treasurer

The purpose of this association is to improve the band sawing and power tool accessoried industries.
8 Members
Founded in 1959

13892 **Power Transmission Distributors Association**
230 West Monroe Street
Suite 1410
Chicago, IL 60606-4703

312-516-2100; Fax: 312-516-2101
ptda@ptda.org
www.ptda.org
Twitter, LinkedIn

Jim Williams, President
Ann Arnott, Executive Vice President & CEO
Brenda Holt, Membership Director
Andrea Lebron, Operations Manager
Ginger Wheeler, Marketing & Communications Director

Association whose members are industrial power transmission/motion control distributor firms dealing in equipment such as bearings, belts, drives, motors, gears, couplings, clutches and brakes. The association offers member companies development programs and networking opportunities.
Founded in 1960

13893 **Society of Tribologists & Lubrication Engineers**
840 Busse Hwy
Park Ridge, IL 60068-2302

847-825-5536; Fax: 847-825-1456
information@stle.org
www.stle.org
Facebook, Twitter, LinkedIn, Youtube

Dr. Martin N. Webster, President
Dr. Aliÿ Erdemir, Vice President
Mr. Michaelÿ Anderson, Secretary
Greg Croce, Treasurer
Dr. Maureen E. Hunter, Past President

Purpose is to advance the science of tribology and the practice of lubrication engineering in order to foster innovation, improve the performance of equipment and products, conserve resources and protect the environment.
4000 Members
Founded in 1944
Mailing list available for rent

13894 **The National Council for Advanced Manufacturing (NACFAM)**
2025 M St. NW
Suite 800
Washington, DC 20036

202-367-1247
www.nacfam.org

Rusty Patterson, Chairman & CEO
Fred Wentzel, Executive Vice President

The non-partisan Council advocates for federal policies that will spur innovation in U.S. manufacturing and make it more competitive globally.

13895 **ToolBase Services**
NAHB Research Center
400 Prince George's Boulevard
Upper Marlboro, MD 20774

301-494-4000
800-898-2842

The housing industry's resource for technical information on building products, materials, new technologies, business management, and housing systems.
Mailing list available for rent

13896 **Unified Abrasive Manufacturers' Association**
30200 Detroit Road
Cleveland, OH 44145-1967

440-899-0010; Fax: 440-892-1404
contact@uama.org
www.uama.org

Jeff Wherry, Executive Director

The purpose is to undertake those activties that can be pursued more effectively by an association than individual companies in order to enable the industry to freely create and market safe, productive abrasive products throughout the world.
30 Members
Founded in 1999

13897 **WaterJet Technology Association-Industrial & Municipal Cleaning Association**
906 Olive Street
Suite 1200
Saint Louis, MO 63101

314-241-1445; Fax: 314-241-1449
wjta-imca@wjta.org
www.wjta.org
Facebook, Twitter, LinkedIn, Google+

Peter Wright, Association Manager
LeAnn Hampton, Association Manager
Pat DeBusk, Director
Luis Garcia, Director
Bill Krupowicz, Director

A professional association of high pressure waterjet and industrial technology and industrial cleaning. Members are contractors, end users, job shops, manufacturers, researchers, and academicians.
Founded in 1983

13898 **Web Sling & Tiedown Association**
9 Newport Drive
Suite 200
Forest Hill, MD 21050

443-640-1070; Fax: 443-640-1031
wstda@stringfellowgroup.net
www.wstda.com
LinkedIn

Jeff Iden, President
Greg Pilgrim, Vice-President
Jim Bailey, Secretary/Treasurer
Kathleen A.ÿ DeMarco, CAE, Executive Director
Amy Chetelat, CAE, Director of Finance

Manufacturers of web slings which are used as hoists in various industrial lifting operations.
79 Members
Founded in 1973

Newsletters

13899 **Asphalt Recycling and Reclaiming Association**
Asphalt Recycling and Reclaiming Association
3 Church Cir
PMB Box 250
Annapolis, MD 21401-1933

410-267-0023; Fax: 410-267-7546
www.arra.com

Mike Krissoff, Executive Director

Promotes the interest of owners and manufacturers of recycling equipment, engineers suppliers and businesses involved in the asphalt recycling industry.
Frequency: Quarterly
Circulation: 1200
Founded in 1976
Mailing list available for rent

13900 **Belt Line**
The Belting Association
1818 Parmenter Street
Suite 300
Middleton, WI 53562

608-310-7549; Fax: 608-492-0523
staff@niba.org
www.niba.org

Michael Battaglia, Executive Director

The official newsletter for members of The Belting Association.
Frequency: Quarterly

13901 **Can Tube Bulletin**
Composite Can & Tube Institute
50 S Pickett Street
Suite 110
Alexandria, VA 22304-7206

703-823-7234; Fax: 703-823-7237
www.cctiwdc.org

Kristine Garland, Executive VP
Wayne Vance, Association Counsel
Janine Marczak, Associate Manager, Events
Frequency: Bi-monthly
Circulation: 800+

13902 **ELFA QuickBrief**
Equipment Leasing And Finance Association
1625 Eye St. NW
Suite 850
Washington, DC 20006

202-238-3400; Fax: 202-238-3401
avogt@elfaonline.org
www.elfaonline.org

Amy Vogt, Managing Editor

A weekly newsletter for equipment finance professionals. Features compelling, industry-focused content.
Frequency: Weekly
Founded in 1961
Printed in 4 colors on glossy stock

13903 **Equipment Dealer News**
Equipment Dealers Association
165 North Meramec Avenue
Suite 430
St. Louis, MO 63105

636-349-5000; Fax: 636-349-5443
info@equipmentdealer.org
www.equipmentdealer.org
Facebook, Twitter

Kim Rominger, President & CEO
Michael Williams, VP, Operations
Joseph Dykes, VP, Industry Relations
Alex Hoffman, Communications & Marketing Director

Features news relevant to equipment manufacturers, as well as advocacy and government policy updates, management tips and more.
4500 Members
Founded in 1900

13904 **Fastener Industry News**
Business Information Services
5028 Dumont Place
Woodland Hills, CA 91364-2407

818-248-5023
800-929-5586; Fax: 818-249-1169
info@biscomputer.com
www.biscomputer.com

Richard Callahan, Publisher
John Wolz, Editor
Miro Macho, CEO/President

Publication written for executives and administrators in the fastener industry. Focuses on providing readers with business and financial news from within the industry. Includes personnel notices, management ideas and related materials.
Cost: $200.00
8 Pages
Frequency: Monthly
Founded in 1971
Mailing list available for rent
Printed in 2 colors on matte stock

13905 **Instrumentation and Automation News**
Chilton Company
201 King of Prussia Rd
Radnor, PA 19087-5147

610-964-4762
800-274-2207; Fax: 610-964-1888

Matt DeJulio, Publisher

The control technology/instrumentation market's only product news tabloid.

13906 **Jet News**
WaterJet Technology Association (WJTA)
906 Olive St.
Suite 1200
St. Louis, MO 63101

314-241-1445; Fax: 314-241-1449
www.wjta.org/wjta/Newsletters.asp

Bill McClister, President
Kerry Siggins, Vice President
George A. Savanick, Treasurer
Gary Noto, Secretary

Newsletter for members of the WaterJet Technology Association. The newsletter provides the latest information on applications, equipment, news from members, new developments, meetings, conferences, and technical issues.
Frequency: Bimonthly
Founded in 1983

13907 **Journal of the National Spray Equipment Manufacturers Association**
550 Randall Road
Elyria, OH 44035-2974

440-366-6808; Fax: 440-892-2018

Don R Scarbrough, Executive Secretary

Includes editorial on safety and environmental matters pertaining to the spray finishing industry. Regular monthly features.
16 Pages
Founded in 1922

13908 **Manufacturing Automation**
Vital Information Publications
754 Caravel Lane
Foster City, CA 94404-1712

650-345-7018
www.sensauto.com

Peter Adrian, Owner
Gary Kuba, Marketing Director

Provides market research data and vital information about key products, applications, and technologies for a wide range of industrial automation segments, such as CAD/CAM, supply chain management, e-Commerce solutions, enterprise resource planning, automation software, manufacturing technology, industrial controls, and manufacturing systems.

13909 **Sensor Business Digest**
Vital Information Publications
754 Caravel Lane
Foster City, CA 94404-1712

650-345-7018
www.sensauto.com

Peter Adrian, Owner
Gary Kuba, Marketing Director

A widely recognized as a major source of information about the sensors industry-provides unique information about vital sensor markets, products, and applications, sensor technology, as well as in-depth company profiles
Frequency: Monthly

13910 **Sensor Technology**
John Wiley & Sons
111 River St
Hoboken, NJ 07030-5774

201-748-6000
800-825-7550; Fax: 201-748-6088
info@wiley.com
www.wiley.com

William J Pesce, CEO

Written for companies and enterprises involved in a broad range of industrial disciplines. Publication follows advances in sensor technologies

and their applications, along with opportunities for their use in the industrial marketplace.
Cost: $565.00
10 Pages
Frequency: Daily
Founded in 1807
Mailing list available for rent: 25000 names at $180 per M
Printed in 2 colors on newsprint stock

13911 Spotlight
Power Transmission Distributors Association
230 West Monroe Street
Suite 1410
Chicago, IL 60606-4703

312-516-2100; Fax: 312-516-2101
ptda@ptda.org
www.ptda.org/resources/ptda-publications.aspx

Jim Williams, President
Ann Arnott, Executive Vice President & CEO
Brenda Holt, Membership Director
Andrea Lebron, Operations Manager
Ginger Wheeler, Marketing & Communications Director

Newsletter containing content on industry and PTDA association news and policy updates for companies dealing in industrial power transmission/motion control equipment.
Frequency: Bi-Monthly
Circulation: 3000+
Founded in 1960

13912 Transmissions
Power Transmission Distributors Association
230 West Monroe Street
Suite 1410
Chicago, IL 60606-4703

312-516-2100; Fax: 312-516-2101
ptda@ptda.org
www.ptda.org/resources/ptda-publications.aspx

Jim Williams, President
Ann Arnott, Executive Vice President & CEO
Brenda Holt, Membership Director
Andrea Lebron, Operations Manager
Ginger Wheeler, Marketing & Communications Director

Newsletter containing content on industry trends for companies dealing in industrial power transmission/motion control equipment.
Circulation: 4300+
Founded in 1960

Magazines & Journals

13913 Advanced Materials & Processes
ASM International
9639 Kinsman Road
Materials Park, OH 44073-0002

440-338-5151
800-336-5152; Fax: 440-338-4634
magazines@asminternational.org
www.asminternational.org

William T. Mahoney, Secretary & CEO
Joanne Miller, Editor
Vicki Burt, Managing Editor

AM&P is the monthly technical magazine from ASM International, designed to keep readers aware of leading-edge developments and trends in engineering materials - metals and alloys, engineering polymers, advanced ceramics, and composites - and the methods used to select, process, fabricate, test, and characterize them.
30K Members
Frequency: Monthly
Circulation: 23000
Founded in 1913

13914 American Industry
Publications for Industry
21 Russell Woods Road
Great Neck, NY 11021-4644

516-487-0990; Fax: 516-487-0809

Jack S Panes, Publisher

Created for those executives responsible for overall plant operations and maintenance. Editorial focus is on new products and related services.
Cost: $25.00
Circulation: 300000
Founded in 1946
Printed in 4 colors on newsprint stock

13915 American Tool, Die & Stamping News
Eagle Publications
42400 Grand River Ave
Suite 103
Novi, MI 48375-2572

248-347-3487
800-783-3491; Fax: 248-347-3492
www.ameritooldie.com

Applications, techniques, equipment and accessories of metal stamping, moldmaking, electric discharge machining; and new product information relating to the tool and die industry. Accepts advertising.
70 Pages
Frequency: Monthly
Circulation: 30000
ISSN: 0192-5709
Founded in 1971
Printed in 5 colors on glossy stock

13916 Asian Industrial Report
Keller International Publishing Corporation
150 Great Neck Rd
Great Neck, NY 11021-3309

516-829-9722; Fax: 516-829-9306

Gerald E Keller, President
Bryan DeLuca, Editorial Director
Terry Beirne, Publisher
Bob Herlihy, Sales manager

English language tabloid presenting new products, equipment and services.
36 Pages
Circulation: 37107
ISSN: 1076-8351
Founded in 1882
Printed in 4 colors on glossy stock

13917 Business & Industry
Business Magazines
1720 28th Street
Suite B
West Des Moines, IA 50266-1400

515-225-2545; Fax: 515-225-2318
www.locu.com

James V Snyder, Publisher
RJ Balch, Editor

Industrial news publication
Cost: $24.00
56 Pages
Frequency: Monthly
Circulation: 14M
ISSN: 0021-0463
Founded in 1946
Printed in 4 colors on glossy stock

13918 Cleaner
COLE Publishing
1720 Maple Lake Dam Road
PO Box 220
Three Lakes, WI 54562-0220

715-546-3346
800-257-7222; Fax: 715-546-3786
info@cleaner.com
www.cleaner.com
Facebook, Twitter

Jeff Bruss, President
Winnie May, Advertising Sales/Subscriptions
Ted Rulseh, Editor
Bob Kendall, Co-founder

The latest tools and equipment promoting safety and efficiency, employment and enviromental concerns, as well as industry profiles.
Cost: $15.50
Frequency: Monthly
Circulation: 22780
Founded in 1979

13919 Composites Manufacturers Magazine
American Composites Manufacturers Association
1010 N Glebe Rd
Suite 450
Arlington, VA 22201-5761

703-525-0511; Fax: 703-525-0743
info@acmanet.org
www.acmanet.org

Tom Dobbins, Chief Staff Executive
Patti Washburn, Deputy Chief Staff Executive
Frequency: Monthly

13920 Crane & Hoist Canada
Capamara Communications
815 1st Ave
#301
Seattle, WA 98104

250-474-3982
800-936-2266; Fax: 250-478-3979
www.naqua.com

Peter Chetteburgh, Editor-in-Chief
Jeremy Thain, Sales Manager
James Lewis, Production Department

Only magazine focused exclusively on Canada's crane and hoist sectors. Provides essential news and information that Canadian crane and hoist professionals need in order to operate successfully and profitably. Articles on company profiles, practical crane & rigging information, new product news, industry trends, policy & regulations, safety/training/certification, and risk management.
Cost: $27.95
Frequency: Bi-monthly
Circulation: 3,500
Founded in 1985

13921 Equipment Leasing & Finance
Equipment Leasing And Finance Association
1625 Eye St. NW
Suite 850
Washington, DC 20006

202-238-3400; Fax: 202-238-3401
avogt@elfaonline.org
www.elfaonline.org

Amy Vogt, Managing Editor

As the flagship publication of the Equipment Leasing and Finance Association, Equipment Leasing & Finance is the trusted leader, bringing readers unrivaled coverage of the people, trends and issues that have an impact on the $628 billion equipment finance industry. Information of funding sources, portfolio management, sales and marketing strategy, large ticket leasing, transportation leasing, the computer leasing market, remarketing equipment, and the role of the equipment manager.
Frequency: 6x/Year
Circulation: 10000
Founded in 1961
Printed in 4 colors on glossy stock

13922 Filtration News
Eagle Publishers

42400 Grand River Ave
Suite 103
Novi, MI 48375-2572

248-347-3487; Fax: 248-347-3492
info@filtnews.com

Arthur Brown, Editor
Antoinette DeWaal, Associate Publisher/VP
Ken Norberg, Editor-in-Chief

New products and events on the special aspects of filtraion ranging from new equipment applications to new trends in the filtraion industry.
Cost: $65.00
Frequency: Bi-Monthly
Founded in 1981

13923 **Finer Points Magazine**
Industrial Diamond Association of America
PO Box 29460
Columbus, OH 43229

614-797-2265; Fax: 614-797-2264
tkane-ida@insight.rr.com
www.superabrasives.org

Terry Kane, Publisher/Editor
Joe Tabling, President

Information for people who are involved in superabrasives or superabrasive products in some way.
Cost: $35.00
Frequency: Quarterly
Circulation: 7,500
Founded in 1946

13924 **Flow Control**
Grand View Media Group
200 Croft Street
Suite 1
Birmingham, AL 35242

888-431-2877; Fax: 205-408-3799
flowcontrol@grandviewmedia.com
www.flowcontrolnetwork.com
Facebook, Twitter, LinkedIn

John P Harris, Publisher
Matt Migliore, Editor
Matt Migliore, Executive Director of Content
Amy W. Richardson, Managing Editor
Mary Beth Timmerman, Marketing Manager

Technology information and new products for fluid handling engineers

13925 **Hauler**
Hauler Magazine
166 S Main Street
PO Box 508
New Hope, PA 18938

800-220-6029
800-220-6029; Fax: 215-862-3455
mag@thehauler.com
www.thehauler.com

Thomas N Smith, Publisher/Editor
Barbara Gibney, Circulation Manager
Leslie T Smith, Marketing Director

Dedicated to the refuse and solid waste industry. It is the acknowledged leader in the new and used refuse truck and equipment marketplace, and now lists hundreds of new and used trash trucks, trailers, containers, services, plus parts and accessories from the best suppliers in the industry.
Cost: $12.00
Frequency: Monthly
Circulation: 18630
Founded in 1978

13926 **High Performance Composites**
Ray Publishing
P.O.Box 992
Morrison, CO 80465-0992

303-467-1776; Fax: 303-467-1777
www.compositeworld.com

Approach is technical, offering cutting-edge design, engineering, prototyping, and manufacturing solutions for aerospace and other traditional and emerging structural applications for advanced composites.

13927 **I&CS-Instrumentation & Control Systems**
PennWell Publishing Company
1421 S Sheridan Rd
Tulsa, OK 74112-6619

918-831-9421
800-331-4463; Fax: 918-831-9476
headquarters@pennwell.com
www.pennwell.com

Robert Biolchini, President

Regular issue features include new systems analyses, new products listings, application ideas, and tutorial technology features.
Cost: $65.00
Frequency: Monthly
Circulation: 92,618
Founded in 1910

13928 **ICS Cleaning Specialist**
BNP Media
22801 Ventura Boulevard
#115
Woodland Hills, CA 91364

818-224-8035
800-835-4398; Fax: 818-224-8042
www.icsmag.com
Facebook, Twitter, LinkedIn

Phil Johnson, Group Publisher
Evan Kessler, Publisher
Jeffrey Stouffer, Editor

Dedicated to providing cleaning and restoration/remediation professionals with the most current and relevant information available to the industry.
Frequency: Annual+
Circulation: 25000
Mailing list available for rent

13929 **Industrial Distribution**
199 East Badger Road
Suite 201
Madison, WI 53713

781-734-8000; Fax: 781-734-8070
www.manufacturing.net/ind
Facebook, Twitter

Eric Wixom, Publisher
Jeff Reinke, Editorial Director
Joel Hans, Managing Editor
Mary Ann Gajewski, Production Manager

Provides current, comprehensive, issues-oriented editorial unique to the distribution industry including news, product updates, profitable product selection, management techniques, features on distribution-manufacturer relationships, legal issues and sales improvement.
Cost: $89.90
Frequency: Monthly
Circulation: 38000+
Mailing list available for rent

13930 **Industrial Equipment News**
Thomas Publishing Company
5 Penn Plaza
Manhattan, NY 10001

212-695-0500
800-733-1127; Fax: 212-290-7206
www.ien.com

Mark Maskin, Editorial Director
Deborah Maskin, Managing Editor
Ciro Buttacavoli, Publisher
Marie Urbanowicz, Marketing Director

Serves the industrial field including manufacturing, mining, utilities, construction, transportation, governmental establishments, and educational services.
Frequency: Monthly
Circulation: 205,000+
ISSN: 0019-8258
Founded in 1898

13931 **Industrial Laser Solutions**
PennWell Publishing Company
1421 S Sheridan Rd
Tulsa, OK 74112-6619

918-831-9421; Fax: 918-831-9476
www.pennwell.com

Robert Biolchini, President
Laureen Belleville, Associate Publisher/Senior Editor

Devoted exclusively to global coverage of industrial laser applications, technology, and the people and companies who participate in this, the largest commerical portion of the global laser market.
45 Pages
Frequency: Monthly
Circulation: 10000
ISSN: 1523-4266
Founded in 1910

13932 **Industrial Literature Review**
Thomas Publishing Company
5 Penn Plz
12th Floor
New York, NY 10001-1860

212-695-0500; Fax: 212-290-7362
www.thomaspublishing.com

Carl Holst-Knudsen, CEO

Created to provide the dissemination of manufacturer catalogs and literature and mailed to buyers and specifies at plants with more than twenty employees.
Founded in 1976

13933 **Industrial Maintenance & Plant Operation**
Advantage Business Media
199 E Badger Road
Suite 201
Madison, WI 53713

973-920-7787; Fax: 973-607-5599
www.impomag.com

Tom Lynch, Group Publisher
Eric Wixom, Associate Publisher
Anna Wells, Editor
Jeff Reinke, Editorial Director

provides timely, relevant coverage of manufacturing news, technology breakthrough, and in-plant advancements for plant managers and engineers looking to increase productivity, operate more efficiently and improve competitiveness.
Frequency: Monthly
Founded in 1940

13934 **Industrial Management**
Institute of Industrial Engineers
3577 Parkway Lane
Suite 200
Norcross, GA 30092

770-449-0460
800-494-0460; Fax: 770-441-3295
cs@iienet.org

Elaine Fuerst, Marketing Director
Don Greene, Chief Executive Officer
Donna Calvert, Chief Operating Officer
Heather Bradley, Director of Membership
Monica Elliott, Director of Communications

Directed to the full range of management issues including adapting and evaluating new technologies, improving productivity and quality, and motivating employees.
Cost: $35.00
Frequency: Monthly
Circulation: 8500
Founded in 1948
Mailing list available for rent

13935 Industrial Market Place
Wineberg Publications
7842 Lincoln Avenue
Skokie, IL 60077

847-676-1900
800-323-1818; Fax: 847-676-0063
info@industrialmktpl.com
www.industrialmktpl.com

Joel Wineberg, President
Jakie Bitensky, Editor

Has advertisements on machinery, industrial and plant equipment, services and industrial auctions in each issue.
Cost: $175.00
Frequency: Bi-Weekly
Circulation: 14,000
Founded in 1951
Mailing list available for rent: 120 names at $70 per M
Printed in 4 colors on glossy stock

13936 Industrial Purchasing Agent
Publications for Industry
21 Russell Woods Road
Great Neck, NY 11021-4644

516-487-0990; Fax: 516-487-0809
www.PublicationsforIndustry.com

Jack Panes, Publisher
Pearl Shaine, Editor

New products publication for industrial purchasing agent executives in largest plants in the United States. Contains new releases on products, brochures, materials handling, etc.
Cost: $25.00
Frequency: Monthly
Circulation: 27000
Founded in 1958
Printed in 4 colors on newsprint stock

13937 International Journal of Purchasing & Materials Management
National Association of Purchasing Management
2055 E Centennial Circle
PO Box 22160
Tempe, AZ 85285-2160

480-752-2277; Fax: 480-491-7885
www.capsresearch.com
Twitter

Phillip L Carter, CEO/President
Richard A. Boyle, Director of Corporate
Kristina Cahill, Research Specialist
Phillip L. Carter, Executive Director
Kim Dixon-Williams, Executive Programs Manager

Publishes articles dealing with concepts from business, economics, operations management, information systems, the behavioral sciences, and other disciplines which contribute to the advancement of knowledge in the various areas of purchasing, materials management, and related fields.
Cost: $59.00
Frequency: Quarterly
Circulation: 2800
Founded in 1986

13938 Journal of Coatings Technology
Federation of Societies for Coatings Technology
1500 Rhode Island Ave., NW
Suite 415
Washington, DC 20005

202-462-6272; Fax: 202-462-8549
www.coatingstech.org

J. Andrew Doyle, President & CEO
Thomas J. Graves, VP, General Counsel
Allen Irish, Counsel / Director, Industry Affair
Alison Keane, Vice President, Government Affairs
Robin Eastman Caldwell, Senior Government Affairs

Includes practical articles, Q&A features, and roundtable discussions with coatings professionals related to industry segments, manufacturing processes, business operations, environmental concerns, and other pertinent topics.
Frequency: 11x/Year

13939 Journal of Materials Engineering and Performance
ASM International
9639 Kinsman Road
Materials Park, OH 44073-0002

440-338-5151
800-336-5152; Fax: 440-338-4634
memberservicecenter@asminternational.org
www.asminternational.org

William T. Mahoney, Secretary & CEO
Rajiv Asthana, Editor

Peer-reviewed journal that publishes contributions on all aspects of materials selection, design, characterization, processing and performance testing. The journal is useful for solving day-to-day engineering challenges - especially those involving components for larger systems.
30K Members
Frequency: Bi-Monthly
Founded in 1913

13940 Journal of Phase Equilibria & Diffusion
ASM International
9639 Kinsman Road
Materials Park, OH 44073-0002

440-338-5151
800-336-5152; Fax: 440-338-4634
memberservicecenter@asminternational.org
www.asminternational.org

William T. Mahoney, Secretary & CEO
John Morral, Editor
Ursula R. Kattner, Editor
H. Okamoto, Editor

Peer-reviewed journal containing basic and applied research results, evaluated phase diagrams, a survey of current literature, and comments or other material pertinent to the previous three areas. The aim of the journal is to provide a broad spectrum of information concerning phase equilibria for the materials community.
30K Members
Frequency: Bi-Monthly
Founded in 1913

13941 Journal of Protective Coatings & Linings
Technology Publishing Company
2100 Wharton St
Suite 310
Pittsburgh, PA 15203-1951

412-431-8300
800-837-8303; Fax: 412-431-5428
webmaster@paintsquare.com
www.paintsquare.com
Facebook, Twitter

Harold Hower, Owner
Karen Kapsanis, Editor
Milissa Bogats, Production Director
Pam Simmons, Director of Marketing
Julie Birch, Marketing Manager

Focuses on good practice in the use of protective coatings for steel and concrete surfaces. Features articles on such topics as coatings selection for specific service environments, surface preparation, coating application, quality control, cost-effectiveness in maintenance programs, safety issues, and environmental regulations.
Cost: $80.00
Frequency: Monthly
Circulation: 15000
Mailing list available for rent

13942 Lift Equipment
Group III Communications
204 W Kansas Street
Suite 103
Independence, MO 64050

816-254-8735; Fax: 816-254-2128

Terry Ford, President
Michael Scheibach, Publisher
Tracy L Bennett, Editor/Associate Publisher

The buyer's source for equipment, technology and trends. Free to qualified subscribers.
Cost: $24.00
80 Pages
Frequency: 10 per year
Circulation: 18,000
ISSN: 1056-0149
Printed in 4 colors on glossy stock

13943 Lubes-N-Greases
LNG Publishing Company
6105 Arlington Blvd
Suite G
Falls Church, VA 22044-2708

703-536-0800; Fax: 703-536-0803
info@LNGpublishing.com
www.lngpublishing.com

Gloria Stienberg, Owner
Tim Sullivan, Managing Editor
Sheryl Unangst, Circulation Manager
Michele Persaud, Senior Editor
Richard Beercheck, Senior Editor

Features and informed opinions covering automotive and industrial lubricants, metalworking fluids, greases, base stocks, additives, packaging, biodegradable and synthetic products, companies, people, issues and trends affecting the industry.
Frequency: Monthly
Circulation: 16000
ISSN: 1080-9449
Founded in 1995
Printed in 4 colors

13944 Lubricating Engineering
Society of Tribologists & Lubrication Engineers
840 Busse Hwy
Park Ridge, IL 60068-2376

847-825-5536; Fax: 847-825-1456
information@stle.org
www.stle.org

Ed Salek, Executive Director
Karl Phipps, Associate Managing Editor
Tracy Nicholas, National Sales Manager

Technical papers and news articles with up to date developments in the lubrication industry.
Frequency: Monthly
Circulation: 6000

13945 MRO Today
Pfingsten Publishing
730 Madison Avenue
Fort Atkinson, WI 53538-606

920-563-5225
800-932-7732; Fax: 920-563-4269
www.mrotoday.com

Todd Rank, VP
Tom Hammel, Associate Publisher/Editorial Dir
John Mansavage, Circulation and Research
Jill Sheppard, Marketing Manager

Provides best practices for industrial maintanence, production, MRO purchasing, quality and safety personnel. MRO Today helps these pros do their jobs cheaper, better, faster and smarter.
Circulation: 120,000
ISSN: 1091-0638
Founded in 1996
Printed in on glossy stock

13946 **Maintenance Technology**
Applied Technology Publications
1300 S Grove Ave
Suite 105
Barrington, IL 60010-5246

847-382-8100; Fax: 847-304-8603
www.mt-online.com

Arthur Rice, President/CEO
Bill Kiesel, Vice President/Publisher
Jane Alexander, Editor-In-Chief
Rick Carter, Executive Editor
Randy Buttstadt, Director of Creative Services

Maintenance Technology magazine serves the business and technical information needs of managers and engineers responsible for assuring availability of plant equipment and systems. It provides readers with articles on advanced technologies, strategies, tools, and services for the life-cycle management of capital assets.
Frequency: Monthly
Circulation: 50,827
Mailing list available for rent: 35,263 names at $$15 per M

13947 **Measurements & Control**
100 Wallace Avenue
Suite 100
Sarasota, FL 34237

941-954-8405
800-883-8894; Fax: 941-366-5743

13948 **Modern Paint & Coatings**
Cygnus Publishing
445 Broad Hollow Road
Melville, NY 11747-3601

631-845-2700; Fax: 631-845-2723

Esther D'Amico, Editor
Paul Bonaiuto, CFO
Kathy Scott, Director of Public Relations

The latest technology and news including chemical innovations, new production equipment,new trends and coverage of regulatory affairs.
Cost: $45.00
Frequency: Monthly
Circulation: 14,000

13949 **New Equipment Digest**
Penton Media
1300 E 9th St
Cleveland, OH 44114-1503

216-696-7000; Fax: 216-696-6662
information@penton.com
www.penton.com

Jane Cooper, Marketing
Diane Madzelonka, Production Manager
David Kieselstein, Chief Executive Officer
Kurt Nelson, Vice President, Human Resources
Andrew Schmolka, Senior Vice President

Serves the general industrial field which includes manufacturing, processing, engineering services, construction, transportation, mining, public utilities, wholesale distributors, educational services, libraries, and governmental establishments.
Frequency: Monthly
Circulation: 206154
Founded in 1936
Mailing list available for rent

13950 **OEM Off-Highway**
1233 Janesville Avenue
PO Box 803
Fort Atkinson, WI 53538-803

920-563-6388
800-547-7377; Fax: 920-328-9029
Leslie.Shalabi@cygnuspub.com
www.oemoffhighway.com

Richard Reiff, Executive VP
Leslie Shalabi, Publisher/Editor
Paul Mackler, President/CEO
Barb Hesse, Circulation Manager

Offers information on off-road machinery and farm equipment.
Founded in 1965

13951 **Purchasing Magazine's Buying Strategy Forecast**
Reed Business Information
275 Washington St
Newton, MA 02458-1611

617-964-3030; Fax: 617-558-4327
kbecker@reedbusiness.com

Kathy Doyle, Publisher
Paul Teague, Chief Editor
Kathy Becker, Publisher's Assistant

Provides insight and forecasts of numerous industrial and commercial raw materials products.
Circulation: 95,095
Founded in 1960

13952 **Rental Product News**
Cygnus Business Media
3 Huntington Quadrangle
Suite 301N
Melville, NY 11747

631-845-2700
800-308-6397; Fax: 631-845-2741
info@cygnus.com

Dave Davel, VP Publishing
Kris Flitcroft, Group Publisher
Carrier Grall, Publisher
Paul Bonaiuto, Chief Financial Officer
John French, Chief Executive Officer

Provides professional rental operators with the latest insights on equipment asset management so they can make their businesses more productive and competitive. Also provides insight on how leaders in the equipment rental field are getting the best return from their assets through better equipment selection, application, maintenance and safety techniques.
Circulation: 20000
Founded in 1966

13953 **Robotics World**
Douglas Publications
2807 N Parham Road
Suite 200
Richmond, VA 23294

804-762-9600
800-791-8699
570-567-1982; Fax: 570-320-2079
www.douglaspublications.com

Jack Browne, Editor
Andrew Dwyer, Publisher

Covers key developments in the field of flexible automation and intelligent machines for an audience of management level automation professionals.
Frequency: Monthly
Circulation: 87000
Founded in 1985

13954 **The Cutting Edge**
International Association of Diecutting/Diemaking
651 W Terra Cotta Avenue
Suite 132
Crystal Lake, IL 60014

815-455-7519
800-828-4233; Fax: 815-455-7510
staff@iadd.org
www.iadd.org

Shaun Larson, President
Cindy Crouse, CEO
Jenny Holliday, Membership & Technical Services
Stella Quimby, Meetings & Marketing

Journal presenting technical articles on matters of interest to the diecutting industry and members of the International Association of Diecutting and Diemaking.
Founded in 1972

13955 **Twin Plant News**
5400 Suncrest
Suite D-5
El Paso, TX 79912

915-532-1567; Fax: 915-544-7556
www.twinplantnews.com

Michele Lee, President
Rosa Ma Nibbe, Executive Publisher
Mike Patten, Managing Editor

Focuses on the operations of major companies in the United States and the maquiladoras in Mexico. Includes articles about changes affecting the automotive, electronics, plastics and metal industries, as well as information about customs regulations on both sides of the border and other relevant topics.
Frequency: Monthly
Founded in 1985

13956 **World Industrial Reporter**
Keller International Publishing Corporation
150 Great Neck Rd
Great Neck, NY 11021-3309

516-829-9722; Fax: 516-829-9306
www.supplychainbrain.com

Bryan DeLuca, Editor
Terry Beirne, Publisher
Jerry Keller, President
Mary Chavez, Director of Sales

New equipment, machinery and techniques for the industry.
34 Pages
Circulation: 37,107
Founded in 1882

Trade Shows

13957 **ASIS Annual CSO Summit**
American Society of Industrial Security
1625 Prince St.
Alexandria, VA 22314-2882

703-519-6200; Fax: 703-519-6299
www.asisonline.org

Richard E. Chase, President
Peter J. O'Neil, CEO

Annual meeting of international security executives.
14M Attendees
Mailing list available for rent

13958 **AeroMat Conference and Exposition**
ASM International
9639 Kinsman Road
Materials Park, OH 44073-0002

440-338-5151
800-336-5152; Fax: 440-338-4634
memberservicecenter@asminternational.org
www.asminternational.org

William T. Mahoney, Secretary & CEO
Lindy Good, Global Conference & Exhibit Planner

Focuses on innovative aerospace materials, fabrication and manufacturing methods that improve aerospace structures, performance and durability.
900 Members
Frequency: Annual/May
Founded in 1913

13959 **Association of Machinery and Equipment Appraisers Forum**
315 South Patrick Street
Alexandria, VA 22314
703-836-7900
800-537-8629; Fax: 703-836-9303
amea@amea.org
www.amea.org
Randall Koster, President
Jean Harris, Director
Terrance Jacobs, Director
Doris Toronyi, Director
Curt Roskelley, Director
Forum for machinery and equipment appraisers.
300 Members
Founded in 1983
Mailing list available for rent

13960 **CCTI Annual Meeting**
Composite Can & Tube Institute
50 S Pickett Street
Suite 110
Alexandria, VA 22304-7206
703-823-7234; Fax: 703-823-7237
www.cctiwdc.org
Kristine Garland, Executive VP
Wayne Vance, Association Counsel
Janine Marczak, Associate Manager, Events
Frequency: May

13961 **Capital Industrial Show**
Industiral Shows of America
1794 The Alameda
San Jose, CA 95126-1729
408-947-0233; Fax: 408-286-8836
Annual show and exhibits of industrial equipment, supplies and services.
4000 Attendees

13962 **Dynamic Positioning Conference**
Marine Technology Society
1100 H St., Nw
Suite LL-100
Washington, DC 20005
202-717-8705; Fax: 202-347-4302
membership@mtsociety.org
www.mtsociety.org
Facebook, Twitter, LinkedIn
Kathleen Herndon, Executive Director
Recognized as the leading symposium covering developments and technology associated with Dynamic Positioning. Industry leaders discuss DP-related vessel design, and operations, and DP manufacturers and service companies exhibit their products and services to a highly targeted and focused audience.
2M Members
Founded in 1963

13963 **Equipment Leasing & Finance Association An nual Convention**
Equipment Leasing and Finance Association
1625 Eye St. NW
Suite 850
Washington, DC 20006
202-238-3400; Fax: 202-238-3401
hstaverman@elfaonline.org
www.elfaonline.org
Heather Staverman, Director, Meetings & Exhibits
Ralph Petta, President & CEO
Kelli J. Nienaber, Executive Director
1,200 Attendees
Frequency: October

13964 **FABFORM**
Industrial Shows of America
164 Lake Front Drive
Hunt Valley, MD 21030-2215
410-771-1445
800-638-6396; Fax: 410-771-1158
This is the most effective way to reach forming, fabricating and welding equipment buyers in the Northern California area.
3000 Attendees
Frequency: April

13965 **Federation of Societies for Coatings Technology**
Federation of Societies for Coatings Technology
492 Norristown Road
Blue Bell, PA 19422-2350
610-940-0777; Fax: 610-940-0292
www.coatingstech.com
Robert Ziegler, Publisher
Patricia D Ziegler, Semior Editor
Ray Dickie, Editor
Provides a major service to the coatings industry, serves as a link between users and supplies of raw materials, production equipment, coatings, adhesives, inks, sealants, testing equipment, containers and laboratory apparatus.International Coating Expo November, Georgia World Congress Center in Atlanta, Georgia.

13966 **Great Lakes Industrial Show**
North American Expositions Company
33 Rutherford Avenue
Boston, MA 02129
617-242-6092
800-225-1577; Fax: 617-242-1817
www.greatlakesindustrialcontrols.com
Denise Novack, Contact
With over 300 companies exhibiting, showcases the latest technology, products, services and solutions for your manufacturing needs.
14319 Attendees
Frequency: November
Founded in 1972

13967 **Heat Treating Society Conference & Expo**
ASM International
9639 Kinsman Road
Materials Park, OH 44073-0002
440-338-5151
800-336-5152; Fax: 440-338-4634
memberservicecenter@asminternational.org
www.asminternational.org
William T. Mahoney, Secretary & CEO
Lindy Good, Global Conference & Exhibit Planner
Conference and expo for heat treating equipment and supplies as well as information of interest to metallurgists, maintenance supervisors and production engineering staff.
30K Members
Frequency: October
Founded in 1913

13968 **IADD Annual Meeting**
International Association of Diecutting/Diemaking
651 W Terra Cotta Avenue
Suite 132
Crystal Lake, IL 60014
815-455-7519
800-828-4233; Fax: 815-455-7510
staff@iadd.org
www.iadd.org
Shaun Larson, President
Cindy Crouse, CEO
Jenny Holliday, Membership & Technical Services
Stella Quimby, Meetings & Marketing
A meeting for professionals of the diecutting and diemaking industries. Programs offered cover emerging technologies, professional development and networking.
Founded in 1972

13969 **ISA Convention**
Industrial Supply Association
3435 Concord Road
Unit 21889
York, PA 17402
866-460-2360
info@isapartners.org
www.isapartners.org
Facebook, Twitter, LinkedIn
Ed Gerber, President/CEO
Convention for distributors and manufacturers of industrial (MROP) supplies.
Founded in 2007

13970 **Industrial Marketing Expo**
Lobos Services
16016 Perkins Road
Baton Rouge, LA 70810
225-751-5626
Debbie Balough, Show Manager
250 booths.
6M Attendees
Frequency: April

13971 **Industrial Products Expo and Conference**
Key Productions
94 Murphy Road
Hartford, CT 06114-2121
860-247-8363
880-753-9776; Fax: 860-947-6900
www.keypro.com
Maura Lewis, Show Manager
This show features exhibits and/or services used in manufacturing, management and warehousing.
6M Attendees
Frequency: September

13972 **Industrial Show Pacific Coast**
Industrial Shows of America
164 Lake Front Drive
Hunt Valley, MD 21030-2215
410-771-1445
800-638-6396; Fax: 410-771-1158
James K Donahue, President
Four hundred booths.
11M Attendees
Frequency: November

13973 **International Fastener and Precision Formed Parts Manufacturing Expo**
Pemco
383 Main Avenue
Norwalk, CT 06851-1543
203-840-7700
800-323-5155; Fax: 630-260-0395
Biennial show and exhibits of cold headers and header tooling, tools and dies, forming machines, parts feeding and handling equipment and test equipment for the industrial fastener and precision formed parts manufacturing industry.

13974 **International Off-Highway and Power Plant Meeting and Exposition**
Society of Automotive Engineers

400 Commonwealth Drive
Warrendale, PA 15096-0001

724-776-4841; Fax: 724-776-4026
www.sae.org

Diane Rogne, Show Manager
Sam Barill, Treasurer
Andrew Brown, Treasurer

Annual show of 270 suppliers of parts, components, materials and systems utilized in farm and industrial machinery and off-road and recreational vehicles.
5000 Attendees
Circulation: 84,000

13975 **International Symposium for Testing & Failure Analysis**
ASM International
9639 Kinsman Road
Materials Park, OH 44073-0002

440-338-5151
800-336-5152; Fax: 440-338-4634
memberservicecenter@asminternational.org
www.asminternational.org

William T. Mahoney, Secretary & CEO
Lindy Good, Global Conference & Exhibit Planner

Annual event focusing on failure analysis and makers of tools such as microscopes, stress and measurement analytical tools, etchants and chemicals, ESD protective materials and other products used for this purpose.
30K Members
Frequency: Annual/Oct/Nov
Founded in 1913

13976 **Mid South Industrial, Material Handling and Distribution Expo**
Industrial Shows of America
164 Lake Front Drive
Hunt Valley, MD 21030-2215

410-771-1445
800-638-6396; Fax: 410-771-1158

James K Donahue, President

300 booths of industrial and business related products and services.
8M Attendees
Frequency: June

13977 **National Association of Industrial Technology Convention**
National Association of Industrial Technology
3300 Washtenaw Avenue
Suite 220
Ann Arbor, MI 48104-4294

734-677-0720; Fax: 734-677-2407
www.nait.org

Dr. Alvin Thadisill, Show Manager
Dave Monporan, Exhibit Manager
Rick Coscarelli, Executive Director

Annual convention of National Association of Industrial Technology, professional association of two and four year Industrial Technology program, faculty, standards and professionals in industry. Exhibitors desired in textbooks, training manuals, software and video; testing and training equipment, computer hardware and software, ISP's and distance learning hosts; CAD/CAM; Rapid Protyping; PC's. There are 25 booths. Next show is in Pittsburgh, Pennsylvania.
500 Attendees
Frequency: November

13978 **PTDA Industry Summit**
Power Transmission Distributors Association
230 West Monroe Street
Suite 1410
Chicago, IL 60606-4703

312-516-2100; Fax: 312-516-2101
ptda@ptda.org
www.ptda.org/events/industrysummit.aspx

Jim Williams, President
Ann Arnott, Executive Vice President & CEO
Brenda Holt, Membership Director
Andrea Lebron, Operations Manager
Ginger Wheeler, Marketing & Communications Director

Summit for companies dealing in industrial power transmission/motion control equipment.
Founded in 1960

13979 **Pacific Coast Industrial and Machine Tool Show**
ISOA
1794 The Alameda
San Jose, CA 95126-1729

408-947-0233
800-286-2882; Fax: 408-286-8836

Annual show of 260 exhibitors of industrial equipment, machine tools, business services, hand tools and related equipment, supplies and services.
12M Attendees
Frequency: November, Santa Clara

13980 **Rocky Mountain Industrial and Machine Tool Show**
Trade Shows West
360 S Fort Ln
Suite 2C
Layton, UT 84041-5708

801-485-0176; Fax: 801-485-0241
www.facetofacemarketing.net

A three day exhibit focusing on the needs of the industrial, manufacturing and plant maintenance industries.
8463 Attendees
Frequency: Annual/May

13981 **Salt Lake Machine Tool & Manufacturing Exposition**
Trade Shows West
2880 S Main Street
Suite 110
Salt Lake City, UT 84115

801-485-0176; Fax: 801-485-0241
jeffwfredericks@hotmail.com
www.facetofacemarketing.net

13982 **Tidewater Industrial & Manufacturing Technology Show**
Industrial Shows of America
164 Lake Front Drive
Hunt Valley, MD 21030-2215

410-771-1445
800-638-6396; Fax: 410-771-1158
www.isoa.com

Annual show of 250 suppliers and distributors of industrial and marine equipment, machine and hand tools, business services and related equipment, supplies and services.
Frequency: September, VA Beach

13983 **Tri-State Industrial & Machine Tools Show**
Industrial Shows of America
164 Lake Front Drive
Hunt Valley, MD 21030-2215

410-771-1445
800-638-6396; Fax: 410-771-1158

This show will bring together exhibitors and customers to preview products and discuss new technologies for the metalworking and manufacturing industries. The show will feature machine tools, metalworking equipment, services for manufacturing industrial products and supplies. Thousands of qualified decision-makers involved in management, engineering, purchasing and manufacturing will attend.
Frequency: April

13984 **USA/Mexico Industrial Expo**
Industrial Shows of America
164 Lake Front Drive
Hunt Valley, MD 21030-2215

410-771-1445
800-638-6396; Fax: 410-771-1158

This event draws attendees from avariety of manufacturing and assembly companies. Product categories include material handling, safety equipment, compressors, maintenance equipment, industrial water products, hydraulic/pneumatics, tools and many more. On average, attendees spend over $100,000 per year obn these products.
9000 Attendees
Frequency: June

13985 **WJTA Expo**
WaterJet Technology Association (WJTA)
906 Olive St.
Suite 1200
St. Louis, MO 63101

314-241-1445; Fax: 314-241-1449
www.wjta.org

Bill McClister, President
Kerry Siggins, Vice President
George A. Savanick, Treasurer
Gary Noto, Secretary

Expo for professionals working in the hydroblasting, vacuum truck, industrial cleaning and waterjet markets.
Founded in 1983

Directories & Databases

13986 **Capital Cities Regional Industrial Buying Guide**
Thomas Publishing Company
5 Penn Plaza
New York, NY 10001-1810

212-950-0500

A who's who directory of supplies to the industry.
Cost: $65.00
1200 Pages
Frequency: Annual

13987 **Directory of the Association of Machinery and Equipment Appraisers**
Association of Machinery and Equipment Appraisers
315 South Patrick Street
Alexandria, VA 22314

703-836-7900
800-537-8629; Fax: 703-836-9303
amea@amea.org
www.amea.org
Facebook, LinkedIn, YouTube

Randall Koster, President
Jean Harris, Director
Terrance Jacobs, Director
Doris Toronyi, Director
Curt Roskelley, Director

Database of nearly 300 member certified machinery appraisers, specializing in metalworking, plastics, construction, woodworking, textile, food processing and various other areas.
300 Members
Frequency: Annual

Founded in 1983
Mailing list available for rent

13988 **IADD Products and Services Directory**
International Association of Diecutting/Diemaking
651 W Terra Cotta Avenue
Suite 132
Crystal Lake, IL 60014
815-455-7519
800-828-4233; Fax: 815-455-7510
staff@iadd.org
www.iadd.org
Shaun Larson, President
Cindy Crouse, CEO
Jenny Holliday, Membership & Technical Services
Stella Quimby, Meetings & Marketing
A directory of products and services offered by members of the International Association of Diecutting and Diemaking.
Founded in 1972

13989 **IGWB Buyer's Guide**
BNP Media
PO Box 1080
Skokie, IL 60076-9785
847-763-9534; Fax: 847-763-9538
igwb@halldata.com
James Rutherford, Editor
Lynn Davidson, Marketing
Nikki Smith, Director
A comprehensive resource listing over 1000 gaming products and services suppliers.
Frequency: Annual

13990 **Industrial Machinery Digest**
Cygnus Interactive
262 Yeager Parkway
Suite C
Pelham am, AL 35124
866-833-5346; Fax: 866-826-5918
william.strickland@cygnusb2b.com
www.indmacdig.com
Facebook, Twitter, LinkedIn
William Strickland, Publisher
Adrienne Gallender, Associate Publisher
Lisa Hanschu, Sales Consultant
Amy Boelk, Art Director / Print Product
Susan Hopkins, Accounting
A leader among industrial trade publications distributed to machine shops, job shops, fabricating shops, gear manufacturers, industrial warehouses & distribution centers, large industrial facilities & manufacturing plants, material handling, retro & rebuilding machine maintenance, pipe & tube manufacturers and manchinery dealers and wholesalers.

13991 **SBC Industrial Purchasing Guide**
100 E Big Beaver Rd
Suite 700E
Troy, MI 48083-1248
248-524-4800
800-331-1385; Fax: 248-524-4849
www.smartpages.com
Susan Wright, Industrial Operations Manager
Nicole Howard-Combs, Director
Providers of industrial products and services; seperate regional editions cover Illinois, Wisconsin, Indiana, Michigan, and Ohio.

13992 **Sweets Directory**
Grey House Publishing/McGraw Hill Construction
1221 Avenue of the Americas
New York, NY 10020-1095
212-512-2000
800-442-2258; Fax: 212-512-3840
www.mcgraw-hill.com
Facebook, Twitter
Harold W McGraw III, CEO
The leading desktop reference and preliminary research guide, featuring more than 10,000 building product manufacturers and their products.
Cost: $145.00
950 Pages
Frequency: Annual
ISBN: 1-592378-50-1
Founded in 1906

13993 **ThomasNet**
Thomas Publishing Company, LLC
User Services Department
5 Penn Plaza
New York, NY 10001
212-695-0500
800-699-9822; Fax: 212-290-7362
contact@thomaspublishing.com
www.thomasnet.com
Facebook, Twitter, LinkedIn
Carl Holst-Knudsen, President
Robert Anderson, VP, Planning
Mitchell Peipert, VP, Finance
Ivy Molofsky, VP, Human Resources
A way to reach qualified businesses that list their company information on ThomasNet.com. Detailed profiles promote their products, services, capabilities and brands carried. The ThomasNet.com web site is the most up-to-date compilation of 650,000 North American manufacturers, distributors, and service companies in 67,000 industrial categories.
Founded in 1898
Mailing list available for rent

13994 **WJTA's Directory of Products, Systems and Services**
WaterJet Technology Association (WJTA)
906 Olive St.
Suite 1200
St. Louis, MO 63101
314-241-1445; Fax: 314-241-1449
www.wjta.org
Bill McClister, President
Kerry Siggins, Vice President
George A. Savanick, Treasurer
Gary Noto, Secretary
A directory listing products, systems and services offered by members of the WaterJet Technology Association.
Founded in 1983

13995 **World Industrial Reporter: Directory of Distributors Issue**
Keller International Publishing Corporation
150 Great Neck Rd
Great Neck, NY 11021-3309
516-829-9722; Fax: 516-829-9306
www.supplychainbrain.com
Jerry Keller, President
Mary Chavez, Director of Sales
A list of over 3,000 international advertisers and their distributors with product line related to the industrial supplies and equipment industry.
Cost: $45.00
Frequency: Annual

13996 **World Industrial Reporter: International Buyer's Guide Issue**
Keller International Publishing Corporation
150 Great Neck Rd
Great Neck, NY 11021-3309
516-829-9722; Fax: 516-829-9306
www.supplychainbrain.com
Jerry Keller, President
Mary Chavez, Director of Sales
Over 275 international advertisers are listed that offer industrial supplies and equipment for export.
Cost: $5.00
Frequency: Annual
Circulation: 40,000

Industry Web Sites

13997 **http://gold.greyhouse.com**
G.O.L.D Grey House OnLine Databases
Grey House Publishing's online database platform, GOLD, offers Quick Search, Keyword Search and Expert Search for most business sectors including industrial equipment markets. The GOLD platform makes finding the information you need quick and easy - whether you're a novice searcher or an experienced database user. All of Grey House's directory products are available for subscription on the GOLD platform.

13998 **www.amea.org**
Association of Machinery and Equipment Appraisers
Facebook, LinkedIn, YouTube
The premier international association of appraisers who specialize in machinery and equipment.

13999 **www.arra.org**
Asphalt Recycling and Reclaiming Association
Promotes the interest of owners and manufacturers of recycling equipment, engineers suppliers and businesses involved in the asphalt recycling industry.

14000 **www.atmae.org**
Assoc of Tech, Management, and Applied Engineering
Faculty, students and industry professionals dedicated to solving complex technological probelms and developing the competitive technologist and applied engineering workforce.

14001 **www.greyhouse.com**
Grey House Publishing
Authoritative reference directories for most business sectors including industrial equipment markets. Users can search the online databases with varied search criteria allowing for custom searches by product category, geographic area, sales volume, keyword, subject and more. Full Grey House catalog and online ordering also available.

14002 **www.iadd.org**
International Association of Diecutting/Diemaking
Facebook, Twitter, LinkedIn, YouTube
Association for diecutters, diemakers, and industry suppliers worldwide.

14003 **www.isapartners.org**
Industrial Supply Association
The primary focus of the Industrial Supply Association is to improve the industrial supply channel through its mission-critical activities, including conventions, forums and the gathering and dissemination of critical information. The association supports distributors, manufacturers and representatives of MROP products'industrial equipment.

14004 **www.mdna.org**
Machinery Dealers National Association
Facebook, Twitter, LinkedIn
Represents dealers of used industrial equipment, providing members with business standards and development opportunities.

14005 **www.mt-online.com**
Applied Technology Publications

MT-online.com is the premier source of capacity assurance and best practice solutions for manufacturing, process and service operations worldwide. Online home of Maintenance Technology magazie, the dynamic MT-online.com portal serves the critical technical, business and professional-development needs of engineers, managers and technicians from across all industrial, institutional and commercial sectors.

14006 **www.polysort.com**
Polysort.com

A portal for the plastics and rubber industry, providing news, information about plastics and rubber industry trade shows, company links, as well as plastics and rubber classified advertising

14007 **www.ptda.org**
Power Transmission Distributors Association

Twitter, LinkedIn

Association whose members are industrial power transmission/motion control distributor firms dealing in equipment such as bearings, belts, drives, motors, gears, couplings, clutches and brakes.

14008 **www.sweets.construction.com**
McGraw Hill Construction

In depth product information that lets you find, compare, select, specify and make purchase decisions in the industrial product marketplace.

14009 **www.thomasregister.com Thomas Register**
Thomas Register

Comprehensive online resource for defining companies and products manufactured in North America. Use it for placing orders, downloading computer-aided design drawings, and viewing thousands of online company catalogs and websites.

14010 **www.wjta.org**
WaterJet Technology Association (WJTA)

Facebook, Twitter, LinkedIn, Google+

A professional association of high pressure waterjet and industrial technology and industrial cleaning. Members are contractors, end users, job shops, manufacturers, researchers, and academicians.

Associations

14011 Alliance of Claims Assistance Professionals
9600 Escarpment
Suite 745-65
Austin, TX 78749

512-394-0008
888-394-5163
capinfo@claims.org
www.claims.org
Twitter

Rebecca Stephenson, Co-President
Katalin Goencz, Co-President

Professionals dedicated to the effective management of health insurance claims. Our members are claims assistance professionals who work for patients.
50 Members
Founded in 1991

14012 America's Health Insurance Plans
601 Pennsylvania Ave., NW
South Building, Suite 500
Washington, DC 20004-2601

202-778-3200; Fax: 202-331-7487
info@ahip.org
www.ahip.org
Facebook, Twitter, LinkedIn, Pinterest

Matt Eyles, President & CEO
Dawn Banda, Chief Financial Officer
John Mathewson, Chief Operating Officer

Mission is to be an effective advocate for a workable legislative and regulatory environment at the federal and state levels in which our members can advance their vision of a health care system that meets the needs of consumers, employers and public purchasers.
1300 Members
Founded in 2003
Mailing list available for rent

14013 American Academy of Actuaries
1850 M Street NW
Suite 300
Washington, DC 20036

202-223-8196; Fax: 202-872-1948
webmaster@actuary.org
www.actuary.org
Facebook, Twitter, LinkedIn, Youtube

Mary D. Miller, President
Tom Wildsmith, President-Elect
Tom Terry, Immediate Past President
Art Panighetti, Treasurer
John Moore, Secretary

AAA is a public policy organization for actuaries within the US. The Academy acts as the public information organization for the profession. Assisting public policy process through the presentation of clear actuarial analysis, the Academy regularly prepares testimony for Congress, provides information to federal elected officials, regulators and congressional staff, comments on proposed federal regulations, and works closely with state officials on issues related to insurance.
18,00 Members
Founded in 1965
Mailing list available for rent

14014 American Agents Alliance
1231 I Street
Suite 201
Sacramento, CA 95814

916-283-9473
866-497-9222; Fax: 916-283-9479
info@agentsalliance.com
www.agentsalliance.com
Facebook, Twitter, LinkedIn, Google Plus

Ken May, President
Brady Harrigan, Vice President
Charlie Garrison, Chief Financial Officer
Mike D'Arelli, Executive Director
Toni Damberger, Secretary

We're a national insurance association dedicated to serving the professional needs of independent insurance agents & brokers.
Founded in 1962

14015 American Association for Long Term Care Insurance
3835 E. Thousand Oaks Blvd.
Suite 336
Westlake Village, CA 91362

818-597-3227; Fax: 818-597-3206
info@aaltci.org
www.aaltci.org

Jesse Slome, Media Inquiries
Joseph Howard, Board of Advisor
Don Hansen, Board of Advisor
Tom Hebrank, Board of Advisor
Larry Thomas, Board of Advisor

National trade organization for the long term care insurance industry in the United States.
Founded in 1998

14016 American Association of Crop Insurers
1 Massachusetts Ave NW
Suite 800
Washington, DC 20001-1401

202-789-4100; Fax: 202-408-7763
www.cropinsurers.com

Michael Davenport, President

A organization that represents companies involved with the Federal crop insurance program.
25 Members
Founded in 1980

14017 American Association of Dental Consultants
10032 Wind Hill Drive
Greenville, IN 47124

812-923-2600
800-896-0707; Fax: 812-923-2900
www.aadc.org

Dr.ÿMichael D. Weisenfeld, President
Dr. Marc K. Zweig, President-Elect
Dr. Lawrence M Hoffman, Secretary-Treasurer
Dr. Kay D. Eckroth, PastÿPresident
Judith K. Salisbury, Executive Director

Members are dentists, insurance consultants, benefits programs administrators and other dental professionals.
350 Members
Founded in 1979

14018 American Association of Insurance Management Consultants
Eaglemark Consulting Group
PO Box 20
Lemoyne, PA 17043

717-763-7717; Fax: 717-763-7989
lesley.Perkins@aaimco.com
www.aaimco.com

Lee M Hoffman, President
Mary LaPorte, Membership Director
Lesley Perkins, Executive Director
Kevin Hromas, Membership Inquiries
Van Hedges, General Inquiries

THe premier association of consultants to the insurance industry: insurance companies, agents, brokers, and their consumers. Also dedicated to helping the insurance industry operate more efficiently and more profitably, thus enabling improved service to the buying public.
35 Members
Founded in 1979

14019 American Association of Insurance Services
701 Warrenville Roadÿ
Lisle, IL 60532

630-681-8347
800-564-AAIS; Fax: 630-681-8356
www.aaisonline.com
Facebook, LinkedIn

Edmund J. Kelly, President, CEO
Joan Zerkovich, SVP, Operations
Robin Westcott, VP, Govt. Affairs
John Kadous, CPCU, CPM, VP, Personal Lines
Bill Bickerton, VP, Data Analytics

A member-owned, nonprofit national insurance advisory organization that provides specialized services to property/casualty insurers.

14020 American Association of Retired Persons (AARP)
American Association of Retired Persons
601 E Street NW
Suite A1-200
Washington, DC 20049-0003

202-434-2277
888-687-2277
202-434-3525; Fax: 202-434-7599
member@aarp.org
www.aarp.org
Facebook, Twitter, RSS

Gail E. Aldrich, Board Chair
Josh Collett, VP, International Affairs
Jeffrey Gullo, Policy Analyst
Holly Schulz, Editorial Manager
Bradley Schurman, Senior Advisor

AARP is a nonprofit membership organization of persons 50 and older dedicated to addressing their needs and interests. Services include: informing members and the public on issues important to this age group; advocating on legislative, consumer and legal issues; promoting community service, and offering a wide range of special products and services to members. There are 39+ million members within the United States.
Founded in 1958
Mailing list available for rent

14021 American Association of State Compensation Insurance Funds
P.O. Box 20073
Towson, MD 21284

877-494-3237; Fax: 800-925-9420
dgarfield@wcf.com
www.aascif.org/
Facebook

Ray Pickup, President and CEO
Tom Phelan, Past President
Kristin Walls, Vice President
Gerard Adams, Vice President
Dennis Lloyd, Treasurer/Secretary

An association of workers' compensation insurance companies from 27different states, plus 11 workers' compensation boards in Canada.

14022 American Cargo War Risk Reinsurance
30 Broad Street
7th floor
New York, NY 10004

212-405-2835; Fax: 212-344-1664
www.ahtins.org

TD Montgomery, Chairman
RJ Decker, Vice Chairman
TA Haig Dick, Secretary/Director
Warren C Dietz, Treasurer

Reinsurance pool of member companies.
Founded in 1939

14023 American Council of Life Insurers
101 Constitution Avenue NW.
Suite 700
Washington, DC 20001-2133

202-624-2000
webadmin@acli.com
www.acli.com
Facebook, Twitter, LinkedIn

Daniel Houston, Chair
Susan K. Neely, President & CEO
David C. Turner, EVP & Corporate Secretary
Joyce Y. Meyer, EVP, Government Relations
Jill Kozeny, SVP, Comm. & Public Affairs

Trade association advocating federal, state, and international forums for public policy that supports the industry marketplace. ACLI members offer life insurance, annuities, retirement plans, long-term care, disability income insurance, and reinsurance.
290 Members
Founded in 1976

14024 American Fraternal Alliance
1301 West 22nd Street
Suite 700
Oak Brook, IL 60523-6022

630-522-6322; Fax: 630-522-6326
info@fraternalalliance.org
www.fraternalalliance.org
Facebook, Twitter

Harald Borrmann, Chair
Patrick Dees, Vice Chair
Joseph J. Annotti, President, CEO
Allison Koppel, Executive Vice President
Melanie Hinds, Director, Advocacy

The trade association of America's fraternal benefit societies.
69 Members
Founded in 1886

14025 American Institute of Marine Underwriters
14 Wall Street
Suite 820
New York, NY 10005-2145

212-233-0550; Fax: 212-227-5102
aimu@aimu.org
www.aimu.org

Frank Costa, Chairman of the Boardÿ
Drew Feldman, Vice Chairman
John A Miklus, President
Michael McKenna, Director of Finances
Eileen Monreale, Education/Training Specialist

Provides information of interest to marine underwriters and promotes their interests.

14026 American Insurance Association
555 12th Street NW
Suite 550
Washington, DC 20004

202-828-7100; Fax: 202-293-1219
info@aiadc.org
www.aiadc.org
Facebook, Twitter

John Degnan, President & CEO
J. Stephen Zielezienski, SVP & General Counsel
Joseph DiGiovanni, SVP, State Affairs

A property, casualty insurance trade organization representing more than 40,000 insurers that write more than $120 billion in premiums each year. AIA member companies offer all types of property-casualty insurance, including personal and commercial auto insurance, commercial property and liability coverage for small businesses, worker's compensation, medical malpractice coverage, and product liability insurance.
320 Members
Founded in 1866

14027 American Insurance Marketing & Sales Society
PO Box 35718
Richmond, VA 23235

804-674-6466
877-674-2742; Fax: 703-579-8896
info@aimssociety.org
www.aimssociety.org
Facebook, Twitter, LinkedIn, RSS

Craig Most, CPIA, CIC, President
Jim Mansfield, CPIA, Vice President
Donna Gray, Executive Director
Carlos Vargas, CPIA, Secretary
Bob Klinger, CPIA LUTCF, Treasurer

A sales training organization that is managed by agents for agents; makes an active effort to ensure that its sales training material is current and takes into consideration today's agency sales approaches.
Founded in 1968

14028 American Nuclear Insurers
95 Glastonbury Boulevard
Suite 300
Glastonbury, CT 06033-4453

860-682-1301; Fax: 860-659-0002
www.amnucins.com
Facebook, Twitter

George Turner, President/CEO
John Quatrocchi, Senior VP

A joint underwriting association, and and organization created by some of the largest stock insurance companies in the United States. The purpose is to pool the financial assets pledged by these member companies to provide significant amount of property and liability insurance we make available to nuclear power plants and related facilities throughout the world.
60 Members
Founded in 1957

14029 American Risk and Insurance Association ARIA
716 Providence Road
Malvern, PA 19355-3402

610-640-1997; Fax: 610-725-1007
aria@TheInstitutes.org
www.aria.org

Andreas Richter, President
Richard Phillips, Vice President
Paul Thistle, President-Elect
Patricia Born, Immediate Past President
Anthony Biacchi, Executive Director

ARIA is the premier academic organization devoted to the study and promotion of knowledge about risk management and insurance.
500 Members
Founded in 1932

14030 American Society of Appraisers
11107 Sunset Hills Road
Suite 310
Reston, VA 20190

703-478-2228
800-272-8258; Fax: 703-742-8471
asainfo@appraisers.org
www.appraisers.org
Facebook, Twitter, LinkedIn, YouTube

Johnnie White, Chief Executive Officer
Bonny Price, Chief Operations Officer
Joseph Noselli, Chief Financial Officer
Todd Paradis, Chief Marketing Officer
Sarah Sebastian, Director of Membership Development

Organization provides education and accreditation for appraisers.
Founded in 1939

14031 American Society of Pension Professionals and Actuaries
4245 N. Fairfax Drive
Suite 750
Arlington, VA 22203

703-516-9300; Fax: 703-516-9308
customercare@asppa.org
www.asppa.org
Facebook, LinkedIn, RSS, YouTube

Kyla M. Keck, CPC, QPA, QKA, President
Joseph A. Nichols, MSPA, President-Elect
Richard A. Hochman, APM, VP
David M. Lipkin, MSPA, Immediate Past President
Brian H. Graff, Esq., APMÿ, Executive Director

(ASPPA) ia a national organization for career retirement plan professionals. The membership consists of the many disciplines supporting retirement income management and benefits policy. Its members are part of the diversified, technical, and highly regulated benefits industry. ASPPA represents those who have made a career of retirement plan and pension policy work.
7,000 Members
Founded in 1966

14032 American Society of Safety Engineers
520 N. Northwest Hwy
Park Ridge, IL 60068

847-699-2929; Fax: 847-768-3434
customerservice@asse.org
www.asse.org
Facebook, Twitter, LinkedIn, Instagram, Blog

Michael Belcher, CSP, President
Thomas F. Cecich, CSP, CIH, President Elect
James D. Smith, CSP, M.S., Senior Vice President
Stephanie A. Helgerman, CSP, Vice President, Financeÿ
Fred J. Fortman, Jr., LL.M., Secretary & Executive Director

The oldest and largest professional safety organization. Its members manage, supervise and consult on safety, health, and environmental issues in industry, insurance, government and education.
30000 Members
Founded in 1911

14033 Appraisers Association of America
212 W. 35th Street
11th Floor South
New York, NY 10001

212-889-5404; Fax: 212-889-5503
referrals@appraisersassociation.org
www.appraisersassociation.org
Facebook, Twitter, LinkedIn

Linda Selvin, Executive Director
Teresa Caputo, Program Manager
Patrick McIntyre, Membership Manager
Yasemin Yeldener, Communications Coordinator
Jennifer Buonocore, CASP Coordinator

A national association of personal property appraisers who focus on fine and decorative arts. Appraiser Association appraisers work with private and corporate art collections as well as partner with collectors, attorneys, accountants, museums, educational institutions, trusts, brokers and insurance carriers to reflect the highest industry standards.
900+ Members
Founded in 1949

14034 Arbitration Forums
3820 Northdale Boulevard
Suite 200A
Tampa, FL 33624

813-915-2263
866-977-3434; Fax: 813-915-4153
status@arbfile.org
www.arbfile.org

Russ Smith, President & CEO
Jay Arcila, CFO/Secretary Treasurer
John Shedd, Director of Information Technology
Geoff Engert, Director of Mktg, Corp Compliance
Ken Butler, Director, Human Resource

Arbitration Forums is a not-for-profit provider of intercompany insurance dispute resolution services. More than 2,000 insurers and self-insurers participate in AF's programs. AF resolves over 250,000 disputes with a claim value approaching one billion dollars.
Founded in 1943

14035 Associated Risk Managers International
Two Pierce Place
20th Floor
Itasca, IL 60143-3141

630-285-4324; Fax: 630-285-3590
www.armiweb.com
Facebook, LinkedIn

Priscilla Hottle, Chairman
Greg Easley, Vice Chairman
Brenda Case, Immediate Past President
Richard Simmons, Treasurer
Mary Pursell, Secretary

Develops specialized insurance/risk management services for trade associations, professional groups and other industry organizations. Conducts seminars and sponsors competitions.
505 Members
Founded in 1969

14036 Association of Advanced Life Underwriters
11921 Freedom Drive
Suite 1100
Reston, VA 20190

703-641-9400
888-275-0092; Fax: 703-641-9885
stertzer@aalu.org
www.aalu.org

Mark B. Murphy, President
Richard A. DeVita, Vice President & Treasurer
David J Stertzer, Chief Executive officer
David F. Byers Jr., Secretary
Chris Foster, President - Elect

Offers services in complex fields of estate analysis, business, insurance, pension planning, employee benefit plans.
1.4M Members
Founded in 1957

14037 Association of Average Adjusters of the United States and Canada
126 Midwood Avenue
Farmingdale, NJ 11735

973-597-0824
averageadjusters@aol.com
www.averageadjustersusca.org/

Phil Gran, Chair
Richard P Carney, Executive Chairman
Eileen M Fellin

Marine insurance and general average adjusters, ship and cargo surveyors and admiralty lawyers. Has no paid staff. Membership principally in New York area.
700+ Members
Founded in 2011

14038 Association of Finance and Insurance Professionals
4104 Felps Drive
Suite H
Colleyville, TX 76034

817-428-2434; Fax: 817-428-2534
info@afip.com
www.afip.com
Facebook, Twitter, LinkedIn

David N Robertson, Executive Director
Tarrah Lett, Sr VP
Heather M Barnett, Communications Director

A nonprofit educational foundation that serves the needs of in-dealership finance and insurance personnel for the automobile, RV, commercial truck and equipment, motorcycle, and motorized sports industries while assisting the lenders, vendors, and independent general agents who support the F&I function.
Cost: $95.00
3500 Members
Frequency: $2,500 for Company's
Founded in 1989
Mailing list available for rent

14039 Association of Financial Guaranty Insurers
139 Lancaster Street
Albany, NY 12210-1903

518-449-4698; Fax: 212-391-6920
tcasey@mackinco.com
www.afgi.org

Bruce E.ÿ Stern, AFGI Chairman
Teresa M.ÿ Casey, Executive Director
Margaret Towers, Contact Person

A trade association of the insurers and reinsurers of municipal bonds and asset-backed securities.
10 Members
Founded in 1986

14040 Association of Home Office Underwriters
1155 15th Street, Nw
Suite 500
Washington, DC 20005

202-962-0167; Fax: 202-530-0659
memberservices@ahou.org
www.ahou.org
Facebook, Twitter, LinkedIn

Cheryl Johns, FALU, CLU, FLMI, President
Traci Davis, AALU, ACS, FLMI, Executive Vice President
Jean Pfundtner, RN, BSN, VP, Publications & Secretary
Tim Ranfranz, Vice President, Treasurer
Bob Cicchi, Vice President, Program Development

Founded when the Home Office Life Underwriters Association and Institute of Homes Office Underwriters joined forces to provide one unified underwriting voice. The mission is to advance the knowledge of sound underwriting of life and disability insurance risks, toward which end it holds meetings, publishes papers and discussions, and promotes educational programs.
Cost: $100.00
1,400 Members
Frequency: Membership Fee
Founded in 2002
Mailing list available for rent

14041 Association of Insurance Compliance Professionals
12100 Sunset Hills Road
Suite 130
Reston, VA 20190

703-437-4377; Fax: 703-435-4390
aicp@aicp.net
www.aicp.net

Sue Eckler-Kerns, President
Roger Osgood, AINS, BA, MBA, Vice President
Karen L. Pollitt, AIRC, CCP, Secretary
Jim Morgan, Treasurer
Elaine Douglas, Past President

Formerly the Society of State Filers. AICP represents individuals involved or interested in statutes, state filing methods, and/or regulatory requirements. Associate members are consultants, attorneys, association managers, education/service organizations and other interested individuals.
Cost: $175.00
1200 Members
Frequency: Membership Fee
Founded in 1985

14042 Association of Life Insurance Counsel
17 South High Street
Suite 200
Columbus, OH 43215

614-221-1900; Fax: 614-221-1989
www.alic.cc/

Raymond J. Manista, President
Carl Wilkerson, President-Elect
Jason Walters, Secretary-Treasurer

Association for life insurance counsel.
Founded in 1913

14043 Association of Professional Insurance Women
990 Cedar Bridge Avenue
suite B7 PMB210
Brick, NJ 08723-4157

973-941-6024; Fax: 732-920-1260
scb@thebeaumontgroup.com
www.apiw.org
LinkedIn

Cheryl Vollweiler, President
Susan Zdroik, CPCU, ARe, First Vice President
Bina Dagar, Senior Vice President
Lucy Mendieta, Treasurer
Kathryn Turck-Rose, Corporate Secretary

Provides women in the insurance insudtry with opportunities for professional development and assistance in advancing their careers. Our membership consists of professional insurance women, highly regarded, decision makers with primary insurers, reinsurers, insurance brokers, risk management, professional services firms and other industry related organizations.
135 Members
Founded in 1976

14044 Association of Professional Insurance Agen ts
400 North Washington Street
Alexandria, VA 22314

703-836-9340; Fax: 703-836-1279
web@pianet.org
www.pianet.com
Facebook, Twitter, LinkedIn, RSS

Richard A. Clements, President
Robert W Hansen, President-Elect
Gareth W Blackwell, Jr., Vice President/Treasurer
John G. Lee, Past President
Mike Becker, Executive Vice President & CEO

Represents professional independent insurance agents in all 50 states, Puerto Rico and the District of Columbia. Our members are local Main

Street Agents who serve their communities throughout America
Founded in 1931
Mailing list available for rent

14045 Automobile Insurance Plans Service Office
302 Central Ave
Johnston, RI 02919-4995

401-275-1000; Fax: 401-528-1350
www.aipso.com

David Kohlhammer, President

AIPSO's mission is to provide high quality services for the insurance residual market at the lowest possible cost.

14046 Aviation Insurance Association
7200 W. 75th Street
Overland Park, KS 66204

913-627-9632; Fax: 913-381-2515
mandie@aiaweb.org
www.aiaweb.org
Facebook, Blog

Jim Gardner, President
Amanda Loroff, Executive Director

A not-for-profit association dedicated to expanding the knowledge of and promoting the general welfare of the aviation insurance industry through numerous educational programs and events.
900 Members
Founded in 1976

14047 Blue Cross and Blue Shield Association
225 North Michigan Avenue
Chicago, IL 60601-6026

312-540-0460; Fax: 312-297-6609
bcbswebmaster@bcbsa.com
www.bcbs.com
Facebook, Twitter, RSS, YouTube

Scott P Serota, Presidentÿ& Chief Executive Officer
William A. Breskin, VP, Govt. Programs
Bhaskar Bulusu, VP, Enterprise Information
Kathy Didawick, VP, Congressional Relations
John T. Ericksen, VP, Federal Relations

Formerly Blue Cross Association and National Association of Blue Shield Plans. Members must be medical and/or hospital plans and operate according to established standards. Offers information, consulting, representation and operation services to members. Member plans represent over 68.1 million health care consumers.
55 Members
Founded in 1946
Mailing list available for rent

14048 Captive Insurance Companies Association
4248 Park Glen Road
Minneapolis, MN 55416

952-928-4655; Fax: 952-929-1318
info@cicaworld.com
www.cicaworld.com
Facebook, Twitter, LinkedIn

Scott Beckman, Board Chair
Michael Bemi, Board Vice Chair
Joel Chansky, Secretary/Treasurer
Dennis P. Harwick, President
Amy Sellheim, CICA Staff

An organization dedicated to networking, educating, and promoting the captive insurance industry. Its mission is to be the first and best source of unbiased information, knowledge, and leadership for captive insurance decision makers.
Founded in 1972

14049 Casualty Actuarial Society
4350 N. Fairfax Drive
Suite 250
Arlington, VA 22203-1620

703-276-3100; Fax: 703-276-3108
office@casact.org
www.casact.org
Facebook, Twitter, LinkedIn, RSS, YouTube, Flickr

Robert S. Miccolis, President
Stephen P. Lowe, President Elect
G. Chris Nyce, Vice President- Administration
Steven D. Armstrong, Vice President-Admissions
Jeff Courchene, Vice President- Internation

The purpose is to advance the body of knowledge of actuarial science applied to property, casualty and similar risk exposures, to establish and maintain standards of qualification for membership, to promote and maintain highstandards of conduct and competence for the members, and to increase the awareness of actuarial science.
6,300 Members
Founded in 1914
Mailing list available for rent

14050 Certified Claims Professional Accreditation Council
PO Box 550922
Jacksonville, FL 32255-0922

301-292-1988; Fax: 301-292-1787
www.ccpac.com

Dave Nordt, CCP, President
Judy R. Johnson, CCP, Vice President - Certifications
Deborah Baker, CCP, Vice President - Membership
Brenda Baker, CCP, Secretary
Jean Zimmerman, CCP, Treasurer

A nonprofit organization that seeks to raise the professional standards of individuals who specialize in the administration and negotiation of freight claims. Specifically it seeks to give recognition to those who have acquired the necessary degree of experience, education, and expertise in domestic and international freight claims to warrant acknowledgment of their professional stature.
Founded in 1981

14051 Chartered Property Casualty Underwriters
720 Providence Road
Suite 100
Malvern, PA 19355-3446

610-251-2733
800-932-2728; Fax: 610-725-5969
MemberResources@theinstitutes.org
www.cpcusociety.org
Facebook, Twitter, LinkedIn

Jane M. Wahl, President and Chairman
Kevin H Brown, Esq., CPCU, CAE, SVP, Executive Director
Brian P. Savko, CPCU, CLU, ChFC, President Elect
Stanley W. Plappert, Secretary/Treasurer
Cynthia A. Baroway, CPCU, M.Ed., Immediate Past President, Chairman

A community of credentialed property and casualty insurance professionals who promote excellence through ethical behavior and continuing education. Mission is to meet the career development needs of a diverse membership pf professionals who have earned the CPCU designation, so that they may serve others in a competent and ethical manner
22,00 Members
Founded in 1944

14052 Coalition Against Insurance Fraud
1012 14th St. NW
Suite 200
Washington, DC 20005

202-393-7330
info@insurancefraud.org
www.insurancefraud.org
Facebook, Twitter, YouTube

Dennis Jay, Executive Director

The Coalition fights insurance fraud on behalf of consumers, insurance companies and government.
Founded in 1993

14053 Conference of Consulting Actuaries
3880 Salem Lake Drive
Suite H
Long Grove, IL 60047-5292

847-719-6500; Fax: 847-719-6506
conference@ccactuaries.org
www.ccactuaries.org
Twitter, LinkedIn

Philip A. Merdinger, President
Donald E. Fuerst, President-Elect
Donald J. Segal, President-Elect
Edward M. Pudlowski, Treasurer
John H. Lowell, Secretary

The Conference advances the quality of consulting practice, supports the needs of consulting actuaries, and represents their interests.
1200+ Members
Founded in 1950

14054 Consumer Credit Industry Association
6300 Powers Ferry Road
Suite 600-286
Atlanta, GA 30339

678-858-4001
webmaster@cciaonline.com
www.cciaonline.com

Dick Williams, Chair
Jim Pangburn, President
Rebecca Smart, VP
Tom Keepers, EVP
Stephanie Neal, Director of Member Services

Preserves, promotes and enhances the availability, utility and integrity of insurance and related products and services delivered in connection with financial transactions.
140+ Members
Founded in 1951

14055 Council on Employee Benefits
1501 M Street, N.W
Suite 620
Washington, DC 20005

202-861-6025; Fax: 202-861-6027
info@ceb.org
www.ceb.org
LinkedIn

Donna A Sexton, President
Shane Canfield, Executive Director
Karen M Welch, Vice President
John R. Collins, Treasurer
Julie R Sheehy, Secretary

Composed of major corporations having a common interest in the management of employee benefits. Stimulates the development and improves the adminstration of sound, progressive employee benefit plan among its members. Also provides an excellent medium for the exchange of ideas, thought and information on the design, operation and financing of such plans.
Founded in 1946

14056 **Crop Insurance and Reinsurance Bureau**
440 First St NW
Suite 500
Washington, DC 20001

202-544-0067; Fax: 202-330-5255
mtorrey@cropinsurance.org
www.cropinsurance.org

Zane Vaughn, Chair
Mike Torrey, Executive Vice President
Tara Smith, Federal Affairs Vice President
Barbara Patterson, Director Of Government Relations
Perry Harlow, Manager Of Membership & Events

National trade association made up of insurance providers and related organization who provide a variety of insurance products for our Nation's Farmers.
Founded in 1964

14057 **Eastern Claims Conference**
PO Box 863902
Ridgewood, NY 11386

732-922-7037; Fax: 212-615-7345
easternclaimsconference@gmail.com
www.easternclaimsconference.com

Jenniferÿ Cobb, Conference Chair
Christine Prutting, Program
Melissa J Thomas, Marketing
Ann Healy, Ad Journal/Publications
Arlene Walsh, Ad Journal/Publications

Provides education and training to examiners, managers, and officers who review medical and disability claims. Holds seminars for life, health and disability clinics.
Founded in 1977

14058 **Employee Benefit Research Institute**
1100 13th St NW
Suite 878
Washington, DC 20005-4051

202-659-0670; Fax: 202-775-6312
www.ebri.org

Dallas L Salisburyÿ, President
Stephen Blakely, Communications Director
Martha Bobbino, Director, Library Resourcesÿ
Marcene Pugh, Director of Finance and Admin.
Jack VanDerhei, Director of Researchÿ

Mission is to contribute to, to encourage, and to enhance the development of sound employee benefit programs and sound public policy through objective research and education.
Founded in 1978
Mailing list available for rent

14059 **Federal Insurance Administration**
500 C Street SW
Washington, DC 20472-2110

202-646-3535; Fax: 202-646-4320

Bud Schaurte, Administrator

Administers the federal flood insurance and crime insurance programs.

14060 **Federation of Defense & Corporate Counsel**
11812 North 56th Street
Tampa, FL 33617-1528

813-983-0022; Fax: 813-988-5837
www.thefederation.org
Facebook, Twitter, LinkedIn

Victoria H. Roberts, Board Chair
Steven E. Farrar, President
J. Scott Kreamer, Secretary-Treasurer
H. Mills Gallivan, President-Elect
Walter Dukes, Senior Director

The Federation is an organization of recognized leaders in the legal community dedicated to representation of insurers and corporations.
1400+ Members
Founded in 1936

14061 **Financial & Insurance Conference Planners**
330 N. Wabash Avenue
Suite 2000
Chicago, IL 60611

312-245-1023; Fax: 312-321-5150
www.ficpnet.com
Facebook, Twitter, LinkedIn, YouTube, Flickr

Shelia R. Cleary, Chair
Caryn Taylor Lucia, Chair Elect and Treasurer
Marla Hannigan, CMP, Chair Elect and Treasurer
Sherri Lindenberg, CLU, Chair Elect and Treasurer
Kathy Roche, Chair Elect and Treasurer

An association of insurance and financial services industry meeting planners who exchange proven meeting management techniques and explore trends and new ideas that may enhance the value of conferences.
Founded in 1957

14062 **Financial Planning Association**
7535 E. Hampden Ave.
Suite 600
Denver, CO 80231

303-759-4900
800-322-4237; Fax: 303-759-0749
info@onefpa.org
www.fpanet.org
Facebook, Twitter, LinkedIn

Mary Tuttle, CEO
Maureen Peck, Executive Communications Manager
Lauren Schadle, Assoc Exec Dir, COO
Curt Niepoth, Assoc Exec Dir, CFO
Ian MacKenzie, Managing Dir Bus Dev, CMO

Members include accountants, financial planners, lawyers, bankers, stockbrokers, insurance professionals and others who provide financial advice and services to individuals.
15M Members
Founded in 2000
Mailing list available for rent

14063 **Fraternal Field Managers' Association**
Concordia Mutual Life
3020 Woodcreek Drive
Downers Grove, IL 60515

630-971-8000; Fax: 630-971-9332
www.ffma.co

William J. Murray, President
Jay Schenk, VP

FFMA is dedicated to the promotion of higher ethical standards and the professional development of the fraternal field force, fostering harmony, unity of purpose and the exchange of ideas among the member societies.
70 Members
Founded in 1935

14064 **GAMA International**
3112 Fairview Park Dr.
Falls Church, VA 22042

571-499-2300
800-345-2687
membership@gamaweb.com
www.gamaweb.com
Facebook, Twitter, LinkedIn

Bonnie Godsman, Chief Executive Officer
Debra Grommons, CEO, GAMA Foundation
Phillip Reid, Chief Operating Officer
Noreen Rich, Director, Marketing & Communication

The only association dedicated to promoting the professional development needs of managers in the insurance and financial services industry. Also the only volunteer organization that focuses on the agency building tasks and skills of successful career agenices and firms.
Cost: $300.00
7000 Members
Frequency: Membership Fee

14065 **General Agents and Managers Conference of NALU**
2901 Telestar Ct
Suite 140
Falls Church, VA 22042-1205

703-770-8184
800-345-2687; Fax: 571-499-4302
membership@gamaweb.com
www.gamaweb.com
Facebook, Twitter, LinkedIn

Bonnie Godsman, Chief Executive Officer
Debra Grommons, Chief of Staff / EVP
John Behn, Executive Vice President
Steven Mandurano, Sr. Director, Media & Marketing
Kathryn Kellam, CEO, GAMA Foundation

Seeks to improve quality of management and life insurance selling through educational programs, code of ethical practices, and research programs.
7.2M Members
Founded in 1951
Mailing list available for rent

14066 **Great American Insurance Group Tower**
301 E Fourth Street
Cincinnati, OH 45202

513-369-5000
800-545-4269; Fax: 212-885-1535
service@fcia.com
www.greatamericaninsurancegroup.com
Facebook, LinkedIn, YouTube

Lindley M Franklin, CEO

To provide credit insurance covering teh risk of non-payment on foreign and,in certain cases, domestic receivables.
Founded in 1961

14067 **Group Underwriters Association of America**
P.O. Box 735
Northbrook, IL 60065-0735

205-427-2638; Fax: 205-981-2901
info@guaa.com
www.guaa.com/

Steve Ginsburg, President
Joe Iannetti, Vice President
Matt Clark, Treasurer
Mariam Kaufman, Secretary
Shawn Dutremble, Past President

Comprised of industry professionals that promote the study, analysis, and discussion of all matters relating to the underwriting of group products.
225 Members

14068 **Health Insurance Association of America**
601 Pennsylvania Avenue, NW South Building
Suite 500
Washington, DC 20004

202-778-3200; Fax: 202-331-7487
ahip@ahip.org
www.ahip.org

A national political advocacy and trade association with about 1,300 member companies that sell health insurance coverage to Americans.

14069 Highway Loss Data Institute
1005 N. Glebe Road
Suite 800
Arlington, VA 22201-5759

703-247-1500; Fax: 703-247-1588
rrader@iihs.org
www.iihs.org
Twitter, YouTube, RSS

Adrian Lund, President
Russ Rader, Senior Vice President
Shelley M.ÿ Shelton, CAP, Senior Legal & Admin. Associate
Brenda O'Donnell, Vice President, Insurer Relations
Andrew Hauff, Communications Specialist

Provides the public with insurance industry data concerning human and economic loss resulting from crashes.
12 Members
Founded in 1959
Mailing list available for rent

14070 Home Office Life Underwriters Association
Minnesota Mutual Life
400 Robert Street N
Suite A
Saint Paul, MN 55101-2098

651-665-3500; Fax: 651-665-4488

Lynn Patterson, President
Jane Hall, Executive Vice President

Offers educational programs through the Academy Life Underwriting designed for professional home office underwriters.
560 Members
Founded in 1930

14071 I-Car
5125 Trillium Blvd
Hoffman Estates, IL 60192-3600

847-590-1198
800-422-7872; Fax: 800-590-1215
tom.mcgee@i-car.com
www.i-car.com
LinkedIn, Google+, YouTube

William Brower, Chair
John S. Van Alstyne, CEO & President
Rollie Benjaminÿ, Vice Chair
Dustin Wombleÿ, Secretaryÿ
Bob Keith, Treasurer

Formed by the collision industry, an international not-for-profit training organization. Develops and delivers technical training programs to professionals in all areas of the collision industry. Also provides a communication forum for anyone interested in proper collision repair.
100 Members
Founded in 1979

14072 Independent Automotive Damage Appraisers Association
PO Box 12291
Columbus, GA 31917-2291

800-369-IADA; Fax: 888-423-2669
admin@iada.org
www.iada.org

Mark Nathan, President
Bill Ambrosino, First Vice President
John Williams, Executive Vice President
Michael M. Sellman, Secretary/Treasurer
Mike Wilson, Regional Vice President

A nationwide network of appraiser specialists with the knowledge and experience to assess vehicle damage and to make unbiased repair decisions based on the manufacturer's specifications, accepted industry procedures, and safety concerns.
731 Members
Founded in 1947

14073 Independent Insurance Agents & Brokers of America
127 S Peyton Street
Alexandria, VA 22314-2803

703-683-4422
800-221-7917; Fax: 703-683-7556
info@iiaa.org
www.independentagent.com/
Facebook, Twitter, LinkedIn, Vimeo

Robert A Rusbuldt, CEO
Ronald Tubertini, Chairman

A national alliance of business owners and their employees who offer all types of insurance and financial services products. IIABA agents and brokers not only advise clients about insurance, they recommend loss-prevention ideas that can cut costs.
300M+ Members
Founded in 1896
Mailing list available for rent

14074 Information, Incorporated
2025 M Street NW
Washington, DC 20036

301-215-4688
800-497-5636; Fax: 301-215-4600
www.infoinc.com

Alain Carr, Manager

Organization offers evaluations of companies on their claims-paying ability. Association news services.
Founded in 1979
Mailing list available for rent

14075 Inland Marine Underwriters Association
14 Wall Street
8th Floor
New York, NY 10005

212-233-0550; Fax: 212-227-5102
lcolson@imua.org
www.imua.org
Facebook, Twitter, LinkedIn

Michelle Hoehn, Chair
Kevin O'Brien, President & CEO
William Rosa, Deputy Chair
Lloyd J. Stoik, Vice Chair
Lillian L. Colson, Vice President & Secretary

Serves as the collective voice of the U.S. inland marine insurance industry. Also provides its members with education, research and communications services that support the inland marine underwriting discipline.
Cost: $1750.00
400+ Members
Frequency: Membership Fee
Founded in 1930
Mailing list available for rent

14076 Institute of Home Office Underwriters
General American Life Insurance Company
1155 15th Street, Nw
Suite 500
Washington, DC 20005

202-962-0167; Fax: 202-530-0659
www.ahou.org
Facebook, Twitter, LinkedIn

Cheryl Johns, FALU, CLU, FLMI, President
Traci Davis, AALU, ACS, FLMI, Executive Vice President
Jean Pfundtner, RN, BSN, VP, Publications & Secretary
Tim Ranfranz, Vice President, Treasurer
Bob Cicchi, Vice President, Program Development

Goals are to increase underwriting knowledge of members through educational programs. Prepares program and examinations leading to Fellowship in Academy of Life Underwriting.
1,400 Members
Founded in 1937
Mailing list available for rent

14077 Insurance Accounting Systems Association
3511 Shannon Rd, Suite 160
PO Box 51340
Durham, NC 27707-6330

919-489-0991; Fax: 919-489-1994
info@iasa.org
www.iasa.org
Facebook, Twitter, LinkedIn, YouTube

Laurie Macklosky, President
Kerry Crockett, CEO
Chuck Gunkel, VP, Business Development
Parshy Phillips, Director, Marketing & Communication
Kelli Bohannon, Director, Membership

Membership includes insurance companies of all types, as well as companies that serve the insurance industry, regulators and also organizations more broadly representative of the financial services industry, including banks and investment brokerage firms.
1.7M Members
Founded in 1928
Mailing list available for rent

14078 Insurance Accounting and Systems Association
3511 Shannon Road, Suite 160
PO Box 51340
Durham, NC 27707

919-489-0991; Fax: 919-489-1994
info@iasa.org
www.iasa.org/
Facebook, Twitter, LinkedIn, YouTube

Laurie Macklosky, President
Kerry Crockett, CEO

A nonprofit education association that strives to enhance the knowledge of insurance professionals and participants from similar organizations closely allied with the insurance industry.

14079 Insurance Committee for Arson Control
3601 Vincennes Road
Indianapolis, IN 46268

317-575-5601; Fax: 317-879-8408
info@arsoncontrol.org
www.arsoncontrol.org
Facebook, Twitter, LinkedIn, Google+

Jerry Mulhearn, Chairman
Scott Sanderson, Vice Chairman
Rick Hammond, Executive Director
Don Hancock, Technical Director
Larry Baile, Event Director

Serves as a national resource, education and communications organization. ICAC works to increase public awareness of the arson problem, what can be done and how the industry is responding on both the national and local levels.
Founded in 1978
Mailing list available for rent

14080 Insurance Consumer Affairs Exchange
PO Box 746
Lake Zurich, IL 60047

847-991-8454
nbrebner@icae.com
www.icae.com

Kendra Franklin, President
Kristi Colbert, Secretary
Erica Hiemstra, Treasurer
Joan Holson, VP
Nancy Brebner, Executive Director

A not-for-profit organization that promotes professionalism and shapes the standards of behavior in relationships between insurance organizations, regulators and customers through proactive dialogue, research, communication and education.
110 Members
Founded in 1976

14081 Insurance Cost Containment Service
330 S Wells
Chicago, IL 60606-4701
312-427-2520; Fax: 312-368-8336
Robert Kissane, President
Assists insurance companies with property claims adjustment and arson and fraud claims investigation.

14082 Insurance Information Institute
110 William Street
New York, NY 10038-3908
212-346-5500
800-942-4242; Fax: 212-732-1916
members@iii.org
www.iii.org
Facebook, Twitter, LinkedIn, Google+, YouTube, Flickr
Andrea C. Basora, Executive Vice President
Jeanne M Salvatore, SVP, Public Affairs
Michael Barry, VP, Media Relations
Loretta Worters, Vice President, Communications
James P. Ballot, Director, Digital Communications
A factfinding communication and media organization for all lines of insurance except life and health insurance. Affiliated with Western Insurance Information Services offering consumer information services to 10 western states. Also offers a national insurance consumer helpline.
250 Members
Founded in 1959

14083 Insurance Loss Control Association
PO Box 346
Morton, IL 61550
309-696-2551; Fax: 317-879-8408
president@insurancelosscontrol.org
www.insurancelosscontrol.org
Ron Huber, CSP, ALCM, President
Robert J. Cruse, CSP, ARM, ALCM, First Vice President
Daniel Finn, ALCM, CFPS, AIM, Second Vice President
Mark Bates, CSP, Secretary
Stig T Ruxlow, CSP, Financial Secretary
Supports loss control professionals. Publishes quarterly newsletter.
Founded in 1931

14084 Insurance Marketing & Communications Association
4248 Park Glen Road
Minneapolis, MN 55416
952-928-4644; Fax: 952-929-1318
info@imcanet.com
www.imcanet.com
Facebook, Twitter, LinkedIn, Youtube
Valerie Foster, Chair
Christopher Nance, Executive Vice-Chair
Hank Pinkowski, Treasurer
Megan Flanagan, Executive Director
An international organization of insurance communications professionals who specialize in marketing, marketing communications, advertising, sales promotion, and public relations.
Cost: $350.00
120+ Members
Frequency: Annual Membership Fee
Founded in 1923
Mailing list available for rent

14085 Insurance Premium Finance Association
2890 Niagara Falls Boulevard
PO Box 726
Amherst, NY 14226
716-695-8757; Fax: 716-695-8758
Eric Bouskill, Contact
Firms licensed by New York State to finance property and casualty insurance premiums.
16 Members
Founded in 1961

14086 Insurance Research Council
718 Providence Road
Malvern, PA 19355-0725
610-644-2212; Fax: 610-640-5388
irc@theinstitutes.org
Facebook, Twitter, LinkedIn, Pinterest, Google+
Victoria McCarthy, Chairperson
Elizabeth A. Sprinkel, SVP
David Corum, Vice President
Victoria Kilgore, Director of Research
Patrick Schmid, PhD, Director of Research
Non profit division of the American Institute for Chartered Property Casualty Underwriters and the Insurance Institute of America. Addresses subjects relating to all lines of property-casualty insurance, including coverages of automobiles, homes, businesses, municipalities, and professionals.
Founded in 1977

14087 Insurance Value Added Network Services
1455 E Putnam Avenue
Old Greenwich, CT 06870-1307
203-698-1900
800-548-2675; Fax: 203-698-7299
ivans.info@ivans.com
www.ivans.com
Twitter, LinkedIn
Clare DeNicola, President/CEO
Jeffery K Dobish, Sr VP/CFO
Linda Welsh, CAO
Industry-sponsored organization offering value added data communications network linking agencies, companies and healthcare providers to the insurance industry.
Founded in 1983

14088 Insured Retirement Institute
1100 Vermont Avenue, NW
10th Floor
Washington, DC 20005
202-469-3000; Fax: 202-469-3030
www.irionline.org
Twitter, LinkedIn, YouTube, RSS
Nick Lane, Chairman
William Benjaminÿ, Vice Chairman
Catherine J Weatherford, President, CEO
Lee Covington, SVP, General Counsel
Danielle Holland, SVP, Communications, Marketing
An association for the retirement income industry.

14089 Intermediaries and Reinsurance Underwriters Association
3626 East Tremont Avenue
Suite 203
Throggs Neck, NY 10465
718-ÿ89- 022; Fax: 908-203-0213
mcs@irua.com
www.irua.com
Mike Sowa, President
Amy Barra, Executive Director
A not-for-profit corporation, organized for the purposes of reinsurance education and research and the dissemination of information relevant to the reinsurance industry.
60 Members
Founded in 1967

14090 International Association for Insurance Law: United States Chapter
Chase Communications
PO Box 3028
Malvern, PA 19355-0728
FAX 914-966-3264
Stephen C Acunto, VP
Members are attorneys, professors, regulators and others who are interested in international or comparative aspects of insurance law.
700 Members
Founded in 1963

14091 International Association of Accident Reconstruction Specialists
1036 Gretchen Lane
Grand Ledge, MI 48837-1873
517-622-3135
www.iaars.org
Fred Rice, President
Eino Butch Thompson, Vice President
Composed of members and associates from 38 states, as well as abroad. Membership comprised of law enforcement officers and civilian personnel.
152 Members
Founded in 1980

14092 International Association of Arson Investigators
2111 Baldwin Avenue
Suite 203
Crofton, MD 21114
410-451-3473
800-468-4224; Fax: 410-451-9049
iaai@firearson.com
www.firearson.com
Facebook, Twitter, LinkedIn, Youtube
Daniel Heenan, President
George Codding, First Vice President
Scott Bennett, Second Vice President
Peter Mansi, IAAI-CFI, MIAAI, Immediate Past President
Deborah Keeler, Executive Director
Dedicated to improving the professional development of fire and explosion investigators by being the global resource for fire investigation, technology and research.
7500 Members
Founded in 1949

14093 International Association of Defense Counsel
303 West Madison
Suite 925
Chicago, IL 60606-3300
312-368-1494; Fax: 312-368-1854
info@iadclaw.org
www.iadclaw.org
Facebook, Twitter, LinkedIn
Joseph E. O'Neil, President
John T. Lay, Jr., President Elect
Tripp Haston, Immediate Past President
Albert C. Hilber, Vice President of Insurance
Alfred R. Paliani, Vice President of Corporate
Formerly the International Association of Insurance Counsel. Members are defense attorneys and insurance and corporate counsels, by invitation only.
Cost: $650.00
2400 Members
Frequency: Membership Fee
Founded in 1920

14094 **International Association of Industrial Accident Boards and Commissions**
5610 Medical Circle
Suite 24
Madison, WI 53719
608-663-6355; Fax: 608-663-1546
webmaster@iaiabc.org
www.iaiabc.org
Facebook, Twitter, LinkedIn
R.D. Maynard, President
Dave Threedy, President Elect
Dwightÿ Lovan, Immediate Past President
Matt Carey, Secretary/Treasurer
Jennifer Wolf Horejsh, Executive Director
A not for profit trade association representing government agencies charged with the administration of workers' compensation systems throughout most of the United States and Canada, and other nations and territories.
300+ Members
Founded in 1914

14095 **International Association of Insurance Receivers**
610 Freedom Business Center
Suite 110
King of Prussia, PA 19406
610-992-0017; Fax: 610-992-0021
nancy@iair.org
www.iair.org
Bart Boles, President
Alan Gamse, Esq., First Vice President
Bruce Gilbert, Second Vice President
Donna Wilson, CIR-ML, Treasurer
James Kennedy, Esq., Corporate Secretary
Founded to provide an association to individuals involved with insurance receiverships in order to receive education, promote information exchange, and enhance the standards followed those who work in this position.
Founded in 1991

14096 **International Association of Insurance Pro fessionals Corporate Centre**
3525 Piedmont Road
Building Five, Suite 300
Atlanta, GA 30305ÿ
404-789-3153
800-766-6249; Fax: 404-240-0998
www.internationalinsuranceprofessionals.org
Facebook, Twitter, LinkedIn
Rebecca Clusserathÿÿ, Education
Beth Chitnis, CAE, Managementÿ
John C McColloch, Membership
Michael North, Accounting
Betsey Blimlineÿÿ, Marketing
Serves its members by providing professional education, an environment in which to build business alliances and the opportunity to make connections with people of differing career paths and levels of experience within the insurance industry.
2000 Members
Founded in 1940
Mailing list available for rent

14097 **International Association of Special Investigation Units (IASIU)**
N83 W13410 Leon Road
Menomonee Falls, WI 53051
414-375-2992; Fax: 414-359-1671
info@iasiu.org
www.iasiu.org
Facebook, LinkedIn
Wade Wickre, CIFI, FCLA, President
J. Michael Skiba, Vice President
Ellen Withers, Secretary
John D. Kloc, FCLS, Treasurer
Bill Elliott, Executive Director
An association of more than 870 insurance company SIU professionals representing 130 of the largest property and casualty companies in the country.
4000 Members
Founded in 1984

14098 **International Claim Association**
1155 15th Street NW
Suite 500
Washington, DC 20005
202-452-0143; Fax: 202-530-0659
cmurphy@claim.org
www.claim.org
Facebook
Emily E. Sudermann, Chairperson
David W. Grannan, CFE, President
Erin M. Worthington, President Elect
Rebecca L. Huerta, Secretary
Lester L. Bohnert, ALHC, FLMI, Treasurer
Provides a forum for information exchange and a program of education tailored to the needs of its member life and health insurance companies, reinsurers, managed care companies, TPAs, and Blue Cross and Blue Shield organizations worldwide
Founded in 1909
Mailing list available for rent

14099 **International Claim Association Newsletter**
International Claim Association
1155 15th Street NW
Suite 500
Washington, DC 20005
202-452-0143; Fax: 202-530-0659
cmurphy@claim.org
www.claim.org
Facebook
Emily E. Sudermann, Chairperson
David W. Grannan, CFE, President
Erin M. Worthington, President Elect
Rebecca L. Huerta, Secretary
Lester L. Bohnert, ALHC, FLMI, Treasurer
Frequency: Quarterly
Founded in 1909
Mailing list available for rent

14100 **International Cooperative and Mutual Insurance Federation**
8400 Westpark Drive
Second Floor
McLean, VA 22102-5116
703-245-8077; Fax: 703-610-0211
ww.icmif.org
Edward L Potter, CAE, Executive Director
Formerly the North American Association of the International Cooperative Insurance Federation.

14101 **International Foundation of Employee Benefit Plans**
18700 W. Bluemound Rd
P.O. Box 69
Brookfield, WI 53045
262-786-6700
888-334-3327; Fax: 262-786-8780
pr@ifebp.org
www.ifebp.org
Facebook, Twitter, LinkedIn, Youtube
Thomas T. Holsman, President and Chair of the Board
Michael Wilson, Chief Executive Officer
Thomas W. Stiedeÿ, Treasurer
Regina C Reardon, President-Elect
Kenneth R Boyd, Immediate Past President
The largest educational association serving the employees and compensation industry.
Cost: $295.00
35000 Members
Frequency: $575/Organization Fee
Founded in 1954

14102 **International Insurance Society**
101 Astor Place
Suite 202
New York, NY 10003
212-277-5171; Fax: 212-277-5172
ej@iisonline.org
www.iisonline.org
Facebook, Twitter, LinkedIn
Greig Woodring, Chairman
Michael Morrissey, President & Chief Executive Officer
Takeo Inokuchi, Vice Chairman
Chang Jae Shin, Vice Chairman
Yassir Albaharna, Board Member
Provides a world forum for leading insurance executives, academicians and others interested in insurance to share interests and ideas on timely global issues.
1000 Members
Founded in 1965

14103 **International Risk Management Institute**
12222 Merit Drive
Suite 1600
Dallas, TX 75251-3297
972-996-0800
800-827-5991; Fax: 972-371-5128
www.zeroriskhr.com
Facebook, Twitter, LinkedIn, Google+
Jack P Gibson, Chairman
Mike Poskey, President
Dr. Robert Kinsel Smith, Senior Adviser/Consultant
Heath Hilliard, National Sales Manager
Michelle Lima, Operations Manager
Provides important risk and insurance information to business, legal, risk management, and insurance professionals
Founded in 1978

14104 **International Society of Appraisers**
225 West Wacker Drive
Suite 650
Chicago, IL 60606ÿ
312-981-6778; Fax: 312-265-2908
isa@isa-appraisers.org
www.isa-appraisers.org/
Facebook, Twitter, LinkedIn, RSS
Christine Guernsey, ISA CAPP, President
Perri Guthrie, ISA CAPP, Vice President
Steven R. Roach, JD, ISA CAPP, Treasurer
Karen S. Rabe, ISA CAPP, Secretary
Hughene D. Acheson, ISA AM, Director
A nonprofit, professional personal property appraisal association representing appraisers in the United States and Canada.
Founded in 1979

14105 **International Tax and Investment Center**
1800 K St NW
Suite 718
Washington, DC 20006-2202
202-530-9799; Fax: 202-530-7987
Washington@iticnet.org
www.iticnet.org
Facebook, Twitter, RSS
Daniel A. Witt, President
Blake Marshall, Vice President
Irene Savitsky, Vice President
Brian Mandel, Program Manager
Diana McKelvey, Communications Manager

A trade association that advances the use of structured settlements as a means of using periodic payments to resolve personal injury claims, workers compensation, and other types of claims.
600+ Members
Founded in 1993

14106 **Intersure Ltd**
3 Hotel St
Warrenton, VA 20186-3221
540-349-0969; Fax: 540-349-0971
www.intersure.com
Vimeo
Millie Curtis, Executive Officer
Formerly the Association of International Insurance Agents. Founded to promote the principles of a free exchange of ideas and mutual cooperation based on the highest standards of intergrity, confidentiality and trust.
45 Members
Founded in 1965

14107 **LIMRA International**
300 Day Hill Road
Windsor, CT 6095
860-688-3358
800-235-4672; Fax: 860-298-9555
customer.service@limra.com
www.limra.com
Facebook, Twitter, LinkedIn, Google+, RSS, YouTube
Tim Stonehocker, Chair
Deanna Strable, Vice Chair
Robert A. Kerzner, CLU, ChFC, President
Alison Salka, Ph.D., SVP, Director - Research
Sean F. O'Donnell, Vice President, Member Relations
800 Members
Founded in 1916
Mailing list available for rent

14108 **LOMA: Life Office Management Association**
6190 Powers Ferry Road
Suite 600
Atlanta, GA 30339
770-951-1770
800-275-5662; Fax: 770-984-0441
askloma@loma.org
www.loma.org
Facebook, Twitter, LinkedIn, YouTube
Robert A Kerzner, CLU, ChFC, President and CEO
Jeffrey Hasty, FLMI, ACS, SVP, Corporate Secretary
Michele LaBouff, SVP, Human Resources
Kathy Milligan, FLMI, ACS, Senior Vice President, Education
Ian J Watts, SVP, Managing Director
Insurance worldwide association of insurance companies specializing in research and education.
1200+ Members
Founded in 1924
Mailing list available for rent

14109 **Life Insurance Marketing & Research Association (LIMRA)**
300 Day Hill Rd.
Windsor, CT 06095
860-688-3358; Fax: 860-285-7792
customer.service@limra.com
www.limra.com
Facebook, Twitter, LinkedIn, Google+, YouTube
Catherine Theroux, Director, Public Relations
We offer our clients insight in the form of cooperative research and value added marketing and distribution expertise. Insight that helps you identify trends, evaluate options and implement solutions. All of which leads to one clear outcome; the growth of your company.
800 Members
Founded in 1916
Mailing list available for rent

14110 **Life Insurance Settlement Association**
225 South Eola Drive
Orlando, FL 32801
407-894-3797
www.lisa.org/
Facebook, Twitter, LinkedIn, Google+, RSS, YouTube
Cynthia Poveda, Chairman
Michael Freedman, Vice Chairman
Phil Loy, Treasurer
James W. Maxson, Secretary
Alan Buerger, Board Member
Promotes the development, integrity, and reputation of the life settlement industry and promotes a competitive market for the people it serves.
85+ Members
Founded in 1994

14111 **Life Insurers Council**
2300 Windy Ridge Parkway
Suite 600
Atlanta, GA 30339
770-984-3724
800-275-5662; Fax: 770-984-3780
askloma@loma.org
www.loma.org/lic/
Robert A Kerzner, CLU, ChFC, President and CEO
Jeffrey Hasty, FLMI, ACS, Senior Vice President, Assessment
Michele LaBouff, Senior Vice President
Kathy Milligan, FLMI, ACS, A, Senior Vice President, Education
Ian J Watts, Senior Vice President
In 1997, the LIC merged with (LOMA) Life Office Management Association which added extensive benefits for all LIC members. Serving the basic insurance needs of the general public, including the underserved market, through various distribution methods.
62 Members
Founded in 1910
Mailing list available for rent

14112 **Lightning Protection Institute**
25475 Magnolia Drive
PO Box 99
Maryville, MO 64468
804-314-8955
800-488-6864; Fax: 660-582-0430
lpi@lightning.org
www.lightning.org
Facebook, Twitter
Harold VanSickle III, Executive Director
Kim Loehr, Communications Director
A not-for-profit organization whose members are dedicated to insuring that today's lightning protection systems are the best possible quality in design, materials and installation, so that precious live and property can be protected from the damaging and costly effects of one of nature's most exciting phenomenons, lightning.
100 Members
Founded in 1955

14113 **Loss Executives Association**
Industrial Risk Insurers
P.O. Box 37
Tenafly, NJ 07670
201-569-3346
info@lossexecutives.com
www.lossexecutives.com
Edward J. Ryan, President
Jean L. Broderick, Vice President
Paul Aviles, Treasurer
Raymond Mattia, Secretary
Harris E. Berenson, Esq., Board Member
A professional association of property loss executives providing education to the industry.

14114 **Mass Marketing Insurance Institute**
3007 Tilden Street, NW
Suite 7M-103
Washington, DC 20008
816-221-7575; Fax: 816-772-7765
gregc@robstan.com
www.mi2.org
Facebook, Twitter, LinkedIn, Google Plus, Youtube, Pinteres
Mark Smith, Director
Laurie Weber, Associate Director
Jim Barrett, First VP
Mary Walsh, VP Membership
Jennifer Branfort, Associate Director
The oldest not-for-profit membership organization that promotes the voluntary benefits industry by providing a forum for education, business development and fellowship.
300 Members
Frequency: Annual Meeting (Spring)
Founded in 1970

14115 **Massachusetts Association of Insurance Agents**
91 Cedar Street
Milford, MA 01757
508-634-2900
800-972-9312; Fax: 508-634-2929
info@massagent.com
www.massagent.com
Facebook, LinkedIn, Google+
Raymond Sirois, AAI, Chairman
G. L. Gaudette, III, CPCU, Chairman Elect
Glen E. Davis, CIC, CRM, LIA, Vice Chairman
Ely Kaplansky, Secretary-Treasurer
Raymond D.ÿ Gallant, National Director
Trade show for everyday use in the insurance agency office.
1800 Members
Frequency: November
Mailing list available for rent

14116 **Million Dollar Round Table**
325 West Touhy Ave
Park Ridge, IL 60068-4265
847-692-6378; Fax: 847-518-8921
info@mdrt.org
www.mdrt.org
Facebook, Twitter, LinkedIn, Pinterest
Brian Heckert, CLU, ChFC, President
Caroline Banks, FPFS, Immediate Past President
Mark Hanna, CLU, ChFC, First Vice President
James Douglas Pittman, Second VP
Ross Vanderwolf, CFP, Secretary
Provides its members with resources to improve their technical knowledge, sales and client service while maintaining a culture of high ethical standards. Mission is to be a valued, member-driven international network of leading insurance and investment financial services professionals/advisors who serve their clients by exemplary performance and the highest standards of ethics, knowledge, service and productivity.
35000 Members
Founded in 1927
Mailing list available for rent

14117 **Mortgage Bankers Association**
1919 M Street NW
5th Floor
Washington, DC 20036
202-557-2700
800-793-6222

www.mba.org
Facebook, Twitter

Robert Broeksmit, President & CEO
Marcia Davies, COO
Lisa Haynes, CFO/Chief of Diversity & Inclusion
Peter Grace, SVP, Strategy & Member Servies
Michael Briggs, SVP, HR & General Counsel

A national association representing the entire real estate finance industry. This association develops innovative business tools and provides education and training for industry professionals.

14118 Mortgage Insurance Companies of America
1425 K St Nw
Suite 210
Washington, DC 20005-3590

202-682-2683; Fax: 202-842-9252
www.privatemi.com

Suzanne Hutchinson, Executive VP

Representing the private mortgage insurance industry.
4 Members
Founded in 1973

14119 National African American Insurance Association
1718 M Street, NW
Box #1110
Washington, DC 20036

866-56 -AAIA; Fax: 513-563-9743
www.naaia.org
Facebook, Twitter, LinkedIn

Leslie L. Skinner-Leslieÿ, Chairman
Jerald L. Tillman,ÿLUTCF, Founder
Quincy Branch, Vice Chair
Cherie Coffey, Treasurer
Henry Pippins, Secretary

Helps create a network among minorities who are employed by insurance companies or self-employed in the insurance industry.
Founded in 1997

14120 National Alliance for Insurance Education & Research
3630 North Hills Drive
PO Box 27027
Austin, TX 78755-2027

512-457-7932
800-633-2165; Fax: 512-349-6194
alliance@scic.com
www.scic.com/
Facebook, Twitter, LinkedIn, Google Plus, RSS

William T Hold, Ph.D, CIC, CPCU, President and CEO
Skyla Badger, Assistant Vice President, Marketing
Theresa Bucek, CISR, Assistant Vice President
Paula Cook, CISR, SVP, Program Administration
Bettie Duff, SVP, Customer Care

National education providers offering programs for all insurance and risk management professionals in property, liability and life insurance, with a continuing education requirement upon designation.
75000 Members
Founded in 1969

14121 National Association of Professional Agents
8430 Enterprise Circle
Suite 200
Lakewood Ranch, FL 34202

800-593-7657; Fax: 800-411-4771
www.napa-benefits.org/
Facebook, Twitter, LinkedIn

Offers insurance agents direct access to insurance benefits and professional services.
Founded in 1989

14122 National Association of Bar-Related Title Insurers
1430 Lee Street
Des Plaines, IL 60018

847-298-8300; Fax: 847-298-8388
joanne@elliottlaw.com

Joanne P Elliott, Executive Vice President
Kathleen Waters, Secretary/Treasurer

Members are bar-related title insurance companies registered with the US Patent Office.
10 Members
Founded in 1965

14123 National Association of Casualty and Surety Agents
316 Pennsylvania Avenue SE
Suite 400
Washington, DC 20003-1172

202-543-7500; Fax: 202-293-1219

Lawrence Zippin, Executive Director

A trade organization of insurance agentswho represent and sell for stock insurers. Its purpose is to foster the growth of its members through cooperation with the insurers its members represent.

14124 National Association of Catastrophe Adjusters
P.O. Box 499
Alvord, TX 76225

817-498-3466; Fax: 817-498-0480
naca@nacatadj.org
www.nacatadj.org
Facebook, Twitter, LinkedIn

Chris Hatcher, President
Jon Joyceÿ, Vice President
Jimmy Clarkÿ, Secretary/Treasurer

Provides a professional organization focused on excellence in catastrophe insurance adjusting for members through education, shared resources, and technology.
347 Members
Founded in 1976

14125 National Association of Dental Plans
12700 Park Central Drive
Ste. 400
Dallas, TX 75251

972-458-6998; Fax: 972-458-2258
info@nadp.org
www.nadp.org
Facebook, Twitter, LinkedIn, Youtube

Chris Swanker, FSA, MAAA, Chair
Theresa McConeghey, Vice Chair
Dr Gene Sherman, Secretary
Kirk Andrews, Treasurer
Evelyn F. Ireland, CAEÿÿ, Executive Director

Non profit trade association representing the entire dental benefits industry; dental HMOs, dental PPOs, discount dental plans and dental indemnity products. Members include major commercial carriers, regional and single state companies, as well as companies organized as Delta and Blue Cross Blue Shield plans.
80 Members
Founded in 1989

14126 National Association of Disability Evaluating Professionals
13801 Village Mill Drive
Midlothian, VA 23113

804-378-7275
www.nadep.com

Virgil Robert May III, Executive Director

Members are lawyers, medical doctors and other professionals involved in the evaluation and rehabilitation of persons with disabilities resulting from work or personal injuries.
Cost: $150.00
1000 Members
Frequency: Membership Fee
Founded in 1984

14127 National Association of Fire Investigators , International
857 Tallevast Road
Sarasota, FL 34243

941-359-2800
877-506-6234; Fax: 941-351-5849
info@nafi.org
www.nafi.org
Facebook, Twitter, LinkedIn

Heather Perkins, Executive Director
Kathryn Smith, Vice Chairman

Primary purpose of this association is to increase the knowledge and improve the skills of persons engaged in the investigation and analysis of fires, explosions, or in the litigation that ensues from such investigations. The Association also originated and implemented the National Certification Board.
7000 Members
Founded in 1961

14128 National Association of Fraternal Insurance Counselors
211 Canal Road
Waterloo, WI 53594

920-478-4901
866-478-3880; Fax: 920-478-9586
office@nafic.org
www.nafic.org
Facebook

James Dietrich, FIC, AFA, President
Joy Collins, FICF, Vice President
Rick Kremel, CLU, LUTCF, Secretary/Treasurer
Robert Cooper, FICF, Immediate Past President
Anna Maenner, Executive Director

Promotes and educates the sales force in fraternal life insurance. Bestows quality service award and production awards annually.
3.1M Members
Founded in 1950

14129 National Association of Health Underwriters
1212 New York Avenue NW
Suite 1100
Washington, DC 20005

202-552-5060; Fax: 202-747-6820
info@nahu.org
www.nahu.org
Facebook, Twitter, LinkedIn, Youtube, RSS, B2B

Janet Trautwein, Executive Vice President & CEO
Jennifer B Murphy, CFO, COO
Illana Maze, Senior Vice President of Technology
Brooke Willson, Vice President of Leadership
Melanie Gibson, VP, Member & Corporate Relations

The mission is to improve its members' ability to meet the health, financial and retirement se-

curity needs of all Americans through education, advocacy and professional development.
18000 Members
Founded in 1930
Mailing list available for rent: 18000 names at $350 per M

14130 National Association of Independent Insurance Adjusters (NAIIA)
1880 Radcliff Ct.
Suite 117-C&B
Tracy, CA 95376
209-832-6962; Fax: 209-832-6964
admin@naiia.com
www.naiia.com
Matt Ouellette, President
Peter Crosa, President Elect
Susan Daniels, Secretary/Treasurer
James Hunt, Immediate Past President
Brenda Reisinger, Executive Director
Members are companies and individuals adjusting claims for insurance companies on a fee basis.
300 Members
Founded in 1937

14131 National Association of Independent Insura nce Adjusters (NAIIA)
1880 Radcliff Ct.
Suite 117-C & B
Tracy, CA 95376
209-832-6962; Fax: 209-832-6964
admin@naiia.com
www.naiia.com
Matt Ouellette, President
Peter Crosa, President Elect
Susan Daniels, Secretary/Treasurer
James Hunt, Immediate Past President
Brenda Reisinger, Executive Director
Membership consists of property-liability companies Supports the National Association of Independent Insurers Political Action Committee.

14132 National Association of Independent Life Brokerage Agencies
11325 Random Hills Road
Suite 110
Fairfax, VA 22030
703-383-3081; Fax: 703-383-6942
jnormandy@nailba.org
www.nailba.org
Facebook, Twitter, LinkedIn, RSS
David Long, Chairman
Jack Chiasson, CAE, Chief Executive Officer
George C. Van Dusen IV, Chair Elect
James Sorebo, Secretary/Treasurerÿ
Susan D. Haning, CEM, CMP, Director, Business Development
Influencing the independent life and health brokerage community.
300+ Members
Founded in 1981

14133 National Association of Insurance Commissioners
1100 Walnut Street
Suite 1500
Kansas City, MO 64106-2197
816-842-3600; Fax: 816-783-8175
news@naic.org
www.naic.org
Facebook, Twitter, LinkedIn, YouTube, RSS
Monica J. Lindeen, NAIC President, Commissioner
Sharon P. Clark, NAIC Vice President Commissioner
John M. Huff, NAIC President Elect Director
Sen. Ben Nelson, NAIC Chief Executive Officer
Ted Nickel, NAIC Secretary-Treasurer
Assists state insurance regulators, individually and collectively, in serving the public interest and achieving the following fundamental insurance regulatorygoals in a responsive, efficient and cost effective manner, consistent with the wishes of its members.
Founded in 1871
Mailing list available for rent

14134 National Association of Insurance and Financial Advisors
2901 Telestar Court
PO Box 12012
Falls Church, VA 22042-1205
877-866-2432
877-866-2432; Fax: 703-770-8201
membersupport@naifa.org
www.naifa.org
Facebook, Twitter, LinkedIn, Youtube
Cammie Scott, President
Kevin M. Mayeux, CAE, Chief Executive Officer
Tom Michel, President Elect
Brock Jolly, Treasurer
Lawrence Holzberg, Secretary
Mission is to advocate for a positive legislative and regulatory environment, enhance business and professional skills, and promote the ethical conduct of our members.
Founded in 1890

14135 National Association of Mutual Insurance Companies
3601 Vincennes Road
Indianapolis, IN 46268-0700
317-875-5250; Fax: 317-879-8408
www.namic.org
Facebook, Twitter, LinkedIn, YouTube, RSS
Charles Chamness, President/CEO
Neil Allredge, SVP, Corporate Affairs
Gregg Dykstra, COO, General Counsel
David Middleton, VP, Finance
Crista Hassett, VP, Event Operations
A full service nationaltrade association with more than 1,400 member companies that underwrite 43 percent of the property/casualty insurance premium in the United States.
1400 Members
Founded in 1985
Mailing list available for rent

14136 National Association of Professional Insur ance Agents
400 North Washington Street
Alexandria, VA 22314
703-836-9340; Fax: 703-836-1279
web@pianet.org
www.pianet.org/
Facebook, Twitter, LinkedIn, RSS
Mike Becker, Executive Vice President & CEO
Ted Besesparis, SVP, Comm./Public Relations
Patricia A. Borowski, CPIW, SVP, Government/Industry Affairs
Alexi Papandon, CAE, SVP, Products & Services
Jon Gentile, Director of Federal Affairs
Voluntary, membership based, trade association representing professional independent insurance agents throughout the United States.
Founded in 1931

14137 National Association of Public Insurance Adjusters
21165 Whitfield Place
Suite 105
Potomac Falls, VA 20165
703-433-9217; Fax: 703-433-0369
info@napia.com
www.napia.com
Scott deLuise, SPPAÿ, President
Diane Swerling, SPPA, First Vice President
Jeff Gould, CPA, Second Vice President
Damon Faunce, Third VP
Greg Raab, Fourth VP
Experts on property loss adjustment who are retained by policy holders to assist in preparing, filing and adjusting insurance claims. NAPIA members have joined together for the purpose of professional education, certification, and promotion of a code of professional conduct.
Founded in 1951
Mailing list available for rent

14138 National Association of State Comprehensive Health Insurance
580-512-1488
www.naschip.org/
Tanya Case, Chair
Vic Kensler, Chair-Elect/Vice President
Cecil Bykerk, Treasurerÿ
Vernita McMurtrey, Secretary
Michele Eberle, Board Member
Provides educational opportunities and information for state high risk health insurance pools that have been, or are yet to be, established by state governments to serve the medically uninsurable population.

14139 National Association of Surety Bond Producers
1140 19th Street
Suite 800
Washington, DC 20036-5104
202-686-3700; Fax: 202-686-3656
info@nasbp.org
www.nasbp.org
Facebook, Twitter, LinkedIn
Susan Hecker, President
Lynne Cook, First Vice President
Howard Cowan, Second VP
Robert Shaw, Third VP
Mark McCallum, CEO
International organization of professional surety bond producers and brokers.
500+ Members
Founded in 1942

14140 National Cargo Bureau
17 Battery Place
Suite 1232
New York, NY 10004-1110
212-785-8300; Fax: 212-785-8333
ncbnyc@natcargo.org
www.natcargo.org
Ian J. Lennard, President
Kristian Wiede, Corporate Secretary
Philip Anderson, Chief, Technical Department
Capt. Thomasÿ Sheridan, Deputy Chief Surveyor
Capt. Peter Ho, Deputy Chief Surveyor
The Bureau was created to render assistance to the United States Coast Guard in discharging its responsibilities under the 1948 International Convention for Safety of Life at Sea and for other purposes closely related thereto.
Founded in 1952

14141 National Conference of Insurance Legislators
385 Jordan Road
Troy, NY 12180
518-687-0178; Fax: 518-687-0401
info@ncoil.org
www.ncoil.org
Facebook, Twitter
Sen. Neil Breslin, President
Sen. Travis Holdman, IN, Vice President
Rep. Steve Riggs, Secretary
Sen. Jason Rapert, Treasurer
NCOIL is an organization of state legislators whose main area of public policy concern is in-

surance legislation and regulation. Many legislators active in NCOIL either chair or are members of the committees reponsible for insurance legislation in their respective state houses across the country.
Founded in 1969

14142 **National Conference of Insurance Legislato rs (NCOIL)**
1100 13th Street NW
Suite 1000
Washington, DC 20005

202-955-3500; Fax: 202-955-3599
www.ncqa.org
Facebook, Twitter, LinkedIn, YouTube, Google+, Pinterest

David Chin, MD, Chair
Margaret E. O'Kane, President
Michael S. Barr, MD, MBA, FACP, EVP, Quality Measurement
Tom Fluegel, Chief Operating Officer
Patricia Barrett, VP, Product Design and Support

Independent, non profit organization dedicated to improving healthcare quality.
Founded in 1990
Mailing list available for rent

14143 **National Council of Self-Insurers**
P.O. Box 98248
Des Moines, WA 98198

206-409-6995; Fax: 206-212-9488
dave.kaplan@natcouncil.com
www.natcouncil.com

Dave Kaplan, Executive Director
Robin R Obetz, VP

The Council believes that the workers' compensation system, properly administered by the states, is a vital part of the economic and social fabric of the United States. The Council aime to preserve it and protect it as the most effective means of resolving claims for industrial injuries and occupational diseases between employers and employees.
3500 Members
Founded in 1946

14144 **National Council on Compensation Insurance**
901 Pennisula Corporate Circle
Boca Raton, FL 33487-1362

561-893-1000; Fax: 561-893-1191
robert_pierson@ncci.com
www.ncci.com

Cheryl Budd, Chief Communications Officerÿ
Robert Pierson, Affiliate Services Executive
Jennie Dennison, Account Manager
Gregory Quinn, Media Relations Directorÿ
Judy Joffe, Community Relations Directorÿ

Manages the nation's largest database of workers' compensation insurance information. They analyze industry trends, prepares workers compensation insurance rate recommendations, determines the cost of propsed legislation, and provides a variety of services and tools to maintain a healthy workers compensation system.
Founded in 1922

14145 **National Independent Statistical Service**
3601 Vincennes Road
PO Box 68950
Indianapolis, IN 46268-0950

317-876-6200; Fax: 317-876-6210
questions@niss-stat.org
www.niss-stat.org

Theresa Szwast, President

A unique resource for the property/casualty insurance industry. Collect and report timely, quality insurance data, and perform other related functions, at a reasonable cost.
Founded in 1966

14146 **National Insurance Association**
1133 Desert Shale Avenue
Las Vegas, NV 89120

702-269-2445; Fax: 702-269-2446

Josephine King, Executive Director

Organization of about 14 insurance companies owned or controlled by African Americans.
14 Members
Founded in 1921

14147 **National Insurance Crime Bureau**
1111 E Touhy Ave
Suite 400
Des Plaines, IL 60018-5804

847-544-7000
800-447-6282; Fax: 847-544-7100
rjones@nicb.org
www.nicb.org
Facebook, Twitter, LinkedIn, Youtube

Joseph H Wehrle, Jr, President
James K Schweitzer, SVP, COO
Daniel G Abbott, SVP, Chief Information Officer
Robert Jachnicki, SVP, CFO
Andrew J Sosnowski, SVP, General Counsel

Not for profit organization that receives support from property/casualty insurance companies. Partners with insurers and law enforcement agencies to facilitate the identification, detection and prosecution of insurance criminals. Formed from the merging of the National Automobile Theft Bureau and the Insurance Crime Prevention Institute.
1000 Members
Founded in 1992

14148 **National Organization of Life and Health Insurance Guaranty Associations**
13873 Park Center Road
Suite 329
Herndon, VA 20171

703-481-5206; Fax: 703-481-5209
info@nolhga.com
www.nolhga.com/

Deborah J.ÿ Long, Esq., Chair
Lee Douglassÿ, Vice Chair
Deborah Bello, Treasurer
Margaret M . Parker, Secretary
Melody R. J.ÿ Jensen, Esq., Immediate Past Chair

A voluntary, U.S. association made up of the life and health insurance guaranty associations of all 50 states and the District of Columbia.
Founded in 1983

14149 **National Risk Retention Association**
16133 Ventura Blvd.
Suite 1055
Encino, CA 91436

818-995-3274
800-928-5809; Fax: 818-995-6496; Fax: 800-421-5981
joe@riskretention.org
www.nrra-usa.org

Dan Labrie, Chair
Michael J. Schroeder, Chair Elect/Vice Chair
Sanford Elsass, Immediate Past Chair
Jon Harkavy, Secretary
Nancy Gray, Treasurer

Promotes Risk Retention Act-authorized group insurance programs as a practical, economical, efficient and financially sound option for distributing the liability risks of member insuerds.
Founded in 1987

14150 **National Underwriter Company**
5081 Olympic Blvd
Erlanger, KY 41018-3164

859-692-2100
800-543-0874; Fax: 859-692-2295
www.nationalunderwriter.com

Charlie Smith, CEO

Organization with listings which include companies, brokers and agents in each area handling all lines of insurance.

14151 **National Viatical Association**
1030 15th Street NW
Washington, DC 20005

202-347-7361
800-741-9465; Fax: 202-393-0336

Charles C Reely, Executive Director

NVA is dedicated to financially assisting and effectively promotingthe needs of people coping with terminal illnesses in a compassionate, professional and ethical manner. The National Viatical Association is further dedicated to educating and informing the public on the viatical settlement processs.
60 Members
Founded in 1993

14152 **New England Professional Insurance Agents Association**
1 Ash Street
Hopkinton, MA 01748-1822

508-497-2590

Stella Di Camilo, Manager

Supports all those in professional agents in the insurance industry in the New England region. Hosts annual trade show.

14153 **Nonprofit Risk Management Center**
204 South King Street
Leesburg, VA 20175

202-785-3891; Fax: 703-443-1990
info@nonprofitrisk.org
www.nonprofitrisk.org
Twitter

Melanie Lockwood Herman, Executive Director
Whitney Thomey, Project Manager
Katharine Nesslage, Project Manager
Kay Nakamura, Director, Client Solutions

Provides assistance and resources for community serving organizations.
Founded in 1990
Mailing list available for rent

14154 **North American Pet Health Insurance Association**
200 - 692 Osborne Street
Winnipeg, MB R3L 2B9

877-962-7442
info@naphia.org
www.naphia.org
Facebook, Twitter, LinkedIn, YouTube

Dennis Rushovich, President and Past Treasurer
Laura Bennett, Past President
Steve Popovich, Treasurer
Tim Graff, Secretary
Randy Valpy, Board Member

Represents experienced and reputable pet health insurance companiesand pet health professionals.

14155 Physician Insurers Association of America
2275 Research Blvd
Suite 250
Rockville, MD 20850-6213
301-947-9000; Fax: 301-947-9090
membership@piaa.us
www.piaa.us
Twitter
Gloria H. Everett, Chair
Paul C. McNabb, II, MD, Vice Chair
Richard E. Anderson, MD, Secretary
Brian Atchinson, President & CEO
Eric Anderson, VP of Marketing & Communications
An organization of healthcare liability insurance entities which share the common values of its founders to advocate on behalf of physicians, dentists, and other healthcare providers in the areas of legislation, education, risk management and research.
1000 Members
Founded in 1977

14156 Professional Insurance Communicators of America
3601 Vincennes Road
Po Box 60700
Indianapolis, IN 46268-0700
317-875-5250; Fax: 317-879-8408
pica.informe.com
Twitter, LinkedIn
Janet EH Wright, Secretary/Treasurer
Members are editors of insurance company newsletters.
90 Members
Founded in 1955

14157 Professional Insurance Marketing Association
35 E. Wacker Dr.
Suite 850
Chicago, IL 60601-2106
817-569-7462; Fax: 312-644-8557
www.pima-assn.org
Twitter, LinkedIn
Michael Mercer, President
Mark Kelsey, President-Elect
Daniel O'Brien, CLU, Imm. Past President
William Suneson, Treasurer
Mona Buckley, CEO (ex-officio)
The leading national membership association of third-party administrators, insurance carriers and allied business partners involved in the direct marketing of insurance products. Also provides educational conferences, legislative updates, networking opportunities, publications and manuals to all those whose primary business is insurance marketing.
117 Members
Founded in 1974

14158 Professional Liability Underwriting Society
5353 Wayzata Blvd
Suite 600
Minneapolis, MN 55416-1335
952-746-2580
800-845-0778; Fax: 952-746-2599
info@plusweb.org
www.plusweb.org
Twitter, LinkedIn, RSS
James Skarzynski, President
Heather Fox, President-Elect
Peter Herron, Imm. Past President
Debbie Schaffel, RPLU, Secretary-Treasurer
Robbie Thompson, Executive Director
Enhances the professionalism of its members through education and other activities and to responsibly address issues related to professional liability.
7000 Members
Founded in 1986

14159 Property Casualty Insurers Association of America
8700 West Bryn Mawr Avenue
Suite 1200S
Chicago, IL 60631-3512
847-297-7800; Fax: 847-297-5064
pcinet@pciaa.net
www.pciaa.net
Facebook, Twitter, YouTube
David A. Sampson, President
Paul C. Blume, Senior Vice President
Nathaniel Wienecke, Senior Vice President
Randi Cigelnik, Senior Vice President
Joanne M. Orfanos, Senior Vice President
Established by the Merger of the Alliance of American Insurers and the National Association Association of Independent Insurers. Provides a responsible and effective voice on public policy questions affecting insurance products and services, fosters a competitive insurance marketplace for the benefit of insurers and consumers, and provides members with the highest quality products, information and services at a reasonable cost.
1000 Members
Founded in 2004

14160 Property Insurance Loss Register
700 New Brunswick Avenue
Rahway, NJ 07065-3819
732-388-0332; Fax: 732-388-0537
Lawrence Zippin, President
A voluntary nonprofit organization administered by the American Insurance Services Group; maintains a computerized registry of property loss claims which can be used by its subscribers to fight insurance fraud, and provides data for nonactuarial/statistical research.

14161 Property Loss Research Bureau (PLRB/LIRB)
3025 Highland Parkway
Suite 800
Downers Grove, IL 60515-1291
630-724-2200
888-711-7572; Fax: 630-724-2260
www.plrb.org
Facebook, Twitter, Instagram
Tom Mallin, President
Paul C Despensa, VP/General Counsel
PLRB/LIRB provides legal research, consulting and educational services in auto liablility and CGL lines, in addition to promoting education and new, beneficial developments within the property and casualty insurance industry. Members are stock and mutual insurance companies.
252 Members
Founded in 1990
Mailing list available for rent

14162 Public Agency Risk Managers Association
PO Box 6810
San Jose, CA 95150
888-907-2762; Fax: 888-412-5913
Info@parma.com
www.parma.com
Facebook, Twitter, LinkedIn, Vimeo, Instagram
Jim Thyden, President
Kim Hunt, Vice President
Susan Eldridge, Secretary Treasurer
Coni Hernandez, Alliance of Schools
Jeff J Rush, Senior Claims Administrator
A forum promoting, developing and advancing education and leadership in public agency risk management. PARMA is dedicated to facilitating the exchange of ideas and innovative solutions toward risk management in government.
600+ Members
Founded in 1974

14163 Registered Mail Insurance Association
100 William Street
New York, NY 10038-4512
212-612-4000
800-969-7462; Fax: 212-425-2539
Cheryl Martinez, Assistant VP
Insurance companies providing insurance for shipments of currency, securities and other valuables. LSTD Instrument Bonds are provided to facilitate the reproduction of lost documents.
3 Members
Founded in 1921

14164 Reinsurance Association of America
1445 New York Ave
7th Floor
Washington, DC 20005
202-638-3690; Fax: 202-638-0936
infobox@reinsurance.org
www.reinsurance.org
Facebook, Twitter, LinkedIn
Franklin W Nutter, President
Dennis C Burke, Vice President, State Relations
Marsha A Cohen, SVP, Director of Education
Tracey W Laws, SVP, General Counsel
Karalee C Morell, VP, Assistant General Counsel
Non profit association committed to an activist agenda that represents the interests of reinsurance professionals across the United States.
Founded in 1968

14165 Risk and Insurance Management Society
5 Bryant Park
13th Floor
New York, NY 10018-0713
212-286-9292; Fax: 212-986-9716
www.rims.org
Facebook, Twitter, LinkedIn
Mary Roth, Executive Director
Deborah Flam, Human Resoures Manager
Lynn Chambers, CFO
Stephanie Orange, Chief Marketing Officer
Valerie Cammiso, Membership/Chapter Services
Dedicated to advancing the practice of risk management, a professinal discipline that protects physical, financial and human resources.
3900 Members
Founded in 1950
Mailing list available for rent

14166 SNL Financial
212 7th Street NE
One SNL Plaza
Charlottesvle, VA 22902
434-977-1600; Fax: 434-977-4466
customerservice@snl.com
www.snl.com
Facebook, Twitter, LinkedIn, YouTube, Google+
Michael Chinn, President
Reid Nagle, CEO
Bjorn Turnquist, Director Product Management
This organization offers the most up-to-date information available in the insurance industry featuring the latest news releases, filings and important events. Provides current data on top-performing stocks, insider trades, ownership filings, company news and events and legislative issues.
Founded in 1987
Mailing list available for rent

14167 Securities Industry and Financial Markets Association (SIFMA)
1101 New York Avenue, NW
8th Floor
Washington, DC 20005-4279
202-962-7300; Fax: 202-962-7305
www.sifma.org
Facebook, Twitter, LinkedIn
Kenneth ÿ Benten, President & CEO
Joseph ÿ Seidel, Chief Operating Officer
David Krasner, Chief Financial & Admin. Officer
Salvatore Chiarelli, EVP, Conferences & Events
Cheryl Crispen, EVP, Communications & Marketings
SIFMA's mission is to champion policies and practices that benefit investors and issuers, expand and perfect global capital markets, and foster the development of new products and services. SIFMA provides an enhanced member network of access and forward-looking services, as well as premiere educational resources for the professionals within the industry and the investors whom they serve.
Mailing list available for rent

14168 Self Insurance Institute of America
PO Box 1237
Simpsonville, SC 29681
800-851-7789; Fax: 864-962-2483
administration@siia.org
www.siia.org
Facebook, Twitter
Donald K. Drelich, Chairman of the Board
Steven J. Link, Chairman Elect
Ronald K. Dewsnup, Treasurer/Corporate Secretary
Mike Ferguson, President, CEO
Erica Massey, EVP
Dedicated to protecting and promoting the self insurance and alternative risk transfer industry.
1500 Members
Founded in 1981

14169 Shipowners Claims Bureau
1 Battery Park Plaza
31st Floor
New York, NY 10004-1487
212-847-4500; Fax: 212-847-4599
info@american-club.com
www.american-club.com
J. Arnold Witte, Chairman
Markos K. Marinakis, Deputy Chairman
Arpad A. Kadi, Senior Vice President - Treasurer
Donald R. Moore, Senior Vice President
Members are claim managers and adjusters for shipping lines and protection and indemnity clubs.
31 Members
Founded in 1917
Mailing list available for rent

14170 Society of Actuaries
475 North Martingale Rd.
Suite 600
Schaumburg, IL 60173-2252
847-706-3500
888-697-3900; Fax: 847-706-3599
customerservice@soa.org
www.soa.org
Twitter, LinkedIn, YouTube
Roy Goldmanÿÿ, President
Greg Heidrich, Executive Director
Stacy Lin, Deputy Executive Director & CFO
Jennifer Gillespie, President-Elect
An educational, research and professional organization dedicated to serving the public and Society members. The vision is for actuaries to be recognized as the leading professionals in the modeling and management of finanacial risk and contingent events.
17000 Members
Founded in 1949

14171 Society of Certified Insurance Counselors
3630 North Hills Drive
Austin, TX 78731-3028
512-457-7932
800-633-2165; Fax: 512-349-6194
alliance@scic.com
www.scic.com
Facebook, Twitter, LinkedIn, Google+, RSS
William Hold, Ph.D, CIC, CPCU, President/CEO
Skyla Badger, Assistant Vice President, Marketing
Theresa Bucek, CISR, Assistant Vice President
Paula Cook, CISR, SVP, Program Administration
Bettie Duff, SVP, Customer Care
National education program in property, liability and life insurance, with a continuing education requirement upon designation.

14172 Society of Financial Examiners
12100 Sunset Hills Rd
Suite 130
Reston, VA 20190-3221
703-234-4140
800-787-7633; Fax: 888-436-8686
sofe@sofe.org
www.sofe.org
Facebook, LinkedIn
Joanne Campanelli, President
Cindy Dodson, Executive Director
Katie McRee, Assistant Executive Director
Rhenda Davis, Membership & Customer Care
The one organization where financial examiners of inusrance companies, banks, savings and loans, credit unions come together for training and to share exchange information on a formal and informal level.
1600 Members
Founded in 1973

14173 Society of Financial Service Professionals
3803 West Chester Pike
Suite 225
Newtown Square, PA 19073-3230
610-526-2500; Fax: 610-359-8115
info@societyoffsp.org
national.societyoffsp.org
Facebook, Twitter, LinkedIn, Flickr, RSS
David M. Maola, Chief Executive Officer
Michael J. McGlothlin, President
Brian D. Horn, Chief Operating/Information Officer
Donna M. Conrad, Chief Financial Officer
Members are dedicated to the highest standards of competence and service in insurance and financial services.
9000 Members
Founded in 1928
Mailing list available for rent

14174 Society of Insurance Research
631 Eastpoint Drive
Shelbyville, IN 46176-2291
317-398-3684; Fax: 317-642-0535
www.sirnet.org
Sharon Markovsky, President
Tom Forristell, CPA, Vice President - Controller
Karen Imbrogno, Vice President - Annual Conference
Michael Warner, VP Marketing
Carol Smith, Vice President - Membership
Provides a forum for the free exchange of ideas in all areas of insurance research. The Society includes representation from many different organizations such as insurance and non-insurance companies, government agencies, institutions of higher education, and trade associations.
350 Members
Founded in 1970
Mailing list available for rent

14175 Society of Insurance Trainers and Educators
1821 University Ave W
Ste S256
St. Paul, MN 55104
651-999-5354; Fax: 651-917-1835
ed@insurancetrainers.org
www.insurancetrainers.org
Facebook, Twitter, LinkedIn, Instagram
Deborah Davenport, CIC, ITP, President
Brad Gutcher, Immediate Past President
Elise Quadrozzi, CPCU, AIC,, VP Annual Conference
Treg Camper, VP Membership Services
Heather Hubbard, MSHRM, Vice President - Marketing
Professional organization of trainers and educators in insurance.
600 Members
Founded in 1953

14176 Society of Professional Benefit Administrators
2 Wisconsin Circle
Suite 670
Chevy Chase, MD 20815
301-718-7722; Fax: 301-718-9440
info@spbatpa.org
www.spbatpa.org
Twitter
Anne C Lennan, President
National Association of Third Party Administrators (TPAs) of employee benefit health and pension plans. SPBA represents TPAs who offer comprehensive services.
300 Members
Founded in 1975

14177 Society of Risk Management Consultants
621 North Sherman Avenue
Madison, WI 53704
800-765-SRMC; Fax: 212-572-6499
webmaster@srmcsociety.org
www.srmcsociety.org
Christopher Moss, President
Roy Ivins, President-Elect
Peter Murdough, Secretary
Lori Ussery, Treasurer
The mission is to advance these professions to benefit the consultants themselves, their clients and the public through research, education, the exchange of information, anf the promotion of professional and ethical guidlines.
150 Members
Founded in 1984

14178 Sun States Professional Insurance Agents Association
13416 N 32nd Street
Suite 106
Phoenix, AZ 85032-6000
602-482-3333
Maryls M Graser, Executive VP
Supports all those professional insurance agents who serve the southern region of the country. Hosts annual trade show.

14179 **Teachers Insurance and Annuity Association**
730 Third Avenue
New York, NY 10017
800-842-2252; Fax: 800-842-2252
www.tiaa-cref.org
Facebook, Twitter, LinkedIn, YouTube, Google+
Roger Ferguson, President, CEO
Gina Wilson, EVP, CFO
Connie Weaver, EVP, Chief Marketing Officer
Ron Pressman, EVP, Chief Operating Officer
Annabelle Bexiga, EVP, Chief Information Officer
Financial services organization that is a retirement provider for people who work in the academic, research, medical and cultural fields.

14180 **The American Society of Law, Medicine & Ethics**
765 Commonwealth Avenue
Suite 1634
Boston, MA 02215-1401
617-262-4990; Fax: 617-437-7596
info@aslme.org
www.aslme.org
Facebook, Twitter, LinkedIn
Ted Hutchinson, Executive Director
Margo Smith, Membership Department
Katie Kenney Johnson, Conference Director
Courtney McClellan, Assistant Editor
Arthur R. Derse, MD, JD, FACEP, Board of Director
Provides high-quality scholarship, debate, and critical thought to the community of professionals at the nexus of law, medicine, and ethics.
Founded in 1972
Mailing list available for rent

14181 **The Blue Cross and Blue Shield Association**
225 North Michigan Avenue
Chicago, IL 60601
bcbswebmaster@bcbsa.com
www.bcbs.com/
Facebook, Twitter, YouTube, RSS
Scott P. Serota, President, CEO
William A.ÿ Breskin, VP, Government Programs
Doug Porter, SVP, Operations, CIO
Maureen E. Sullivan, SVP, Strategic Services
Robert Kolodgy, SVP, Financial Services, CFO
Trade association for the independent, locally operated Blue Cross and Blue Shield plans in the USA.

14182 **The Council of Insurance Agents & Brokers**
701 Pennsylvania Avenue NW
Suite 750
Washington, DC 20004-2661
202-783-4400; Fax: 202-783-4410
ciab@ciab.com
www.ciab.com
Facebook, Twitter, LinkedIn
Bill D. Henry, Chairman
Ken A Crerar, President/CEO
Robert Cohen, Vice Chairman
David L. Eslick, Treasurer
Martin P.ÿ Hughes, Secretary
Formerly the National Association of Casualty and Surety agents. The council represents the nation's largest commercial property and casualty insurance agencies and brokerage firms. Council members annually place some 80% of the commercial property/casualty insurance premiums in the United States. Council members who operate both nationally and internationally, specialize in a wide range of insurance products and risk management services for business, industry, government and the public.
300 Members
Founded in 1913

14183 **The Griffith Insurance Education Foundation**
720 Providence Rd
Suite 100
Malvern, PA 19355
855-288-7743; Fax: 610-725-5967
info@griffithfoundation.org
www.griffithfoundation.org
Facebook, Twitter
Susan Krieger, Chair
James Jones, MBA, CPCU, ARM, Vice Chair
Dana Rudmose, CPA, Treasurer
Janice M. Abraham, Immediate Past Chairman
Kevin Brown, Esq., CAE, Executive Director
Nonprofit, nonadvocacy, educational organization that provides riskmanagement and insurance education for students and public policymakers.
Founded in 1960

14184 **The Institutes**
720 Providence Road
Suite 100
Malvern, PA 19355-3433
610-644-2101
800-644-2101
610-644-2100ÿ; Fax: 610-640-9576
cserv@cpcuiia.org
www.theinstitutes.org
Facebook, Twitter, LinkedIn
Peter L. Miller, CPCU, President
Anita Z. Bourke, CPCU, AINS, EVP
Kevin H. Brown, Esq., CPCU, CAE, SVP, General Counsel, Exe. Dir.
Jeffrey Scheidt, SVP
Elizabeth A. Sprinkel, CPCU, SVP
An independent, nonprofit organization offering educational programs and professional certification to people in all segments of the property and liability insurance business. More than 150,000 insurance practitioners around the world are involved in Institute programs.
Mailing list available for rent

14185 **The National Association for Fixed Annuities**
1155 F Street NW
Suite 1050
Washington, DC 20004
414-332-9306; Fax: 415-946-3532
bailey@nafa.com
www.nafa.com
Facebook, Twitter, LinkedIn
S. Christopher Johnson, NAFA Chair
Nathan Zuidema, NAFA Vice Chair
Dominicÿ Cursio, NAFA Treasurer
Brian D. Mann, Secretaryÿ
Chip Anderson, Executive Director
Trade association dedicated to promoting fixed annuities.

14186 **The National Association of Independent Insurance Adjusters**
1880 Radcliff Ct.
Tracy, CA 95376
209-832-6962; Fax: 209-832-6964
admin@naiia.com
www.naiia.com
Matt Ouellette, President
Peter Crosa, President Elect
Susan Daniels, Secretary/Treasurer
James Hunt, Immediate Past President
Brenda Reisinger, Executive Director
Trade group of property and casualty claims companies.

14187 **The National Association of Mutual Insurance Companies**
122 C Street N.W.ÿ
Suite 540
Washington, DC 20001
202-628-1558; Fax: 202-628-1601
www.namic.org
Facebook, Twitter, LinkedIn, RSS, YouTube
Randall K. Druvenga, Chair
Steven C. Sliver, Vice Chair
Robert Zak, Chair Elect
Charles Chamnessÿ, President, CEO
Gregg Dykstraÿ, COO & General Counsel
National trade association of mutual property and casualty insurance companies.

14188 **The Society of Chartered Property and Casualty Underwriters (CPCU)**
720 Providence Road
Malvern, PA 19355
800-932-2728; Fax: 610-725-5969
MemberResources@theinstitutes.org
www.cpcusociety.org/
Facebook, Twitter, LinkedIn
Jane M. Wahl, CPCU, CSSBB, President, Chair
Brian P. Savko, CPCU, CLU, ChFC, President-Elect
Stanley W. Plappert, JD, CPCU, Treasurer, Secretary
Cynthia A. Baroway, CPCU, M.Ed., Immediate Past President, Chairman
Kevin H. Brown, Esq., CPCU, CAE, SVP, Executive Director
A community of credentialed property and casualty insurance professionals.
22,00 Members

14189 **Think Believe Act**
220 West 42nd Street
10th Floor
New York, NY 10036
646-445-7000; Fax: 646-445-7001
Facebook, Twitter, LinkedIn, Instagram
Robert Geddes, CEO
TBA is a privately-held company that is now one of the world's leading producers and marketers of brand events and experiences for Fortune 1000 companies

14190 **Transportation & Logistics Council**
120 Main Street
Huntington, NY 11743
631-549-8988; Fax: 631-549-8962
tlc@transportlaw.com
www.tlcouncil.org
Reed Tepper, Chairman
Nadia Martin, CCP, President
Curtis Hart, VP
Phillip Lamb, Secretary/Treasurer
George CarlÿPezold, Executive Director
Formerly the Transportation Consumer Protection Council, a not for profit trade association dedicated to the education of shippers, carriers and others involved in the transportation of goods, the prevention of transit loss and damage, the promulgation of reasonable practices, laws and regulations, and the equitable resolution of disputes invloving frieght claims, freight charges and related maters.
250 Members
Founded in 1974

14191 **US Travel Insurance Association**
2080 Western Avenue
Guilderland, NY 12084
800-224-6164
president@ustia.org
www.ustia.org
Bruce Kirby, President
Mark Carney, Vice President
Linda Finkle, Treasurer
Mike Kelly, Past President
Henry Carpenter, Secretary
National association of insurance carriers, third-party administrators, insurance agencies and related businesses involved in the development, administration and marketing of travel insurance and travel assistance products.
Founded in 2004

14192 **Underwriters Laboratories**
333 Pfingsten Road
Northbrook, IL 60062-2096
847-272-8800
877-854-3577; Fax: 847-272-8129
CustomerExperienceCenter@ul.com
www.ul.com
Facebook, Twitter, LinkedIn, YouTube, Google+, Pinterest
Keith E Williams, President/CEO
Michael Saltzman, SVP & CFO
Christian Anschuetz, Senior VP and CIO
Adrian Groom, Senior Vice President
Terry Brady, SVP & Chief Legal Officer
An independent, not for profit product safety testing and certification organization. They have also tested products for public safety for more than a century.
Founded in 1894
Mailing list available for rent

14193 **Wholesale & Specialty Insurance Association**
4131 N. Mulberry Drive
Suite 200
Kansas City, MO 64116
816-741-3910
info@wsia.org
www.wsia.org
Twitter, LinkedIn
Brady Kelley, Executive Director
Julie Fritz, Director of Operations
Susan Henderson, Director of Marketing
Bryan Sanders, President
Davis Moore, Vice President
Formed in 2017 through the merger of the American Association of Managing General Agents (AAMGA) and the National Association of Professional Surplus Lines Offices (NAPSLO), the WSIA is a world-class member service organization representing the entirety of the wholesale, specialty and surplus lines industry.
Founded in 2017

14194 **Women In Insurance and Financial Services**
136 Everett Road
Albany, NY 12205
518-694-5506
866-264-9437; Fax: 518-935-9232
office@wifsnational.org
www.w-wifs.org
Facebook, Twitter, LinkedIn
Susan L. Combs, PPACA, President
Susan Glass, LUTC, President-Elect
Evelyn Gellar, LUTCF, Secretary
Lisa Pilgrim, Deputy Treasurer
Angelia Z. Shay, Immediate Past President
Vision is to provide a strong network of women helping each other develop the success that lies within each of us.
1.5M Members
Founded in 1987

14195 **Women in Insurance and Financial Services**
136 Everett Road
Albany, NY 12205
518-694-5506
866-264-9437; Fax: 518-935-9232
office@wifsnational.org
www.wifsnational.org
Facebook, Twitter, LinkedIn
Susan L. Combs, PPACA, President
Susan Glass, LUTC, President-Elect
Evelyn Gellar, LUTCF, Secretary
Lisa Pilgrim, Deputy Treasurer
Angelia Z. Shay, Immediate Past President
National organization devoted to the success of women in the insurance and financial services fields.

14196 **Workers Compensation Reinsurance Bureau**
2 Hudson Place
Hoboken, NJ 07030-5515
201-798-6312; Fax: 201-792-4441
Alfred O Weller, President
An association of insurance companies which pool their workers compensation excess losses as an alternative to purchasing reinsurance.
Founded in 1912

14197 **Workers Compensation Research Institute**
955 Massachusetts Ave.
Cambridge, MA 02139
617-661-9274; Fax: 617-661-9284
wcri@wcrinet.org
www.wcrinet.org
Dr. John W. Ruser, President & CEO
Ramona P. Tanabe, Executive VP & Counsel
WCRI conducts research into public policy issues surrounding workers' compensation systems.

Newsletters

14198 **ARIA Newsletter**
American Risk and Insurance Association
716 Providence Road
Malvern 19355-3402
610-640-1997; Fax: 610-725-1007
diana.lee@pciaa.net
www.aria.org
Frequency: 2x/Year

14199 **AWCP Newsletter**
Association of Workers' Compensation Professionals
PO Box 760
Rancho Cordova, CA 95741-0760
916-290-8017; Fax: 916-914-1706
info@awcp.org
www.awcp.org
Debra Real, President
Connie Conley, Executive Director
An educational newsletter with information about our constantly changing industry, how to contact our sponsors as well as announcing our upcoming events.
Frequency: Monthly

14200 **Actuarial Studies in Non-Life Insurance**
Astin Bulletin
B641 Locust Walk
Philadelphia, PA 19104-6218
215-898-2741
Jean Lemaire, Chairman
Promotes actuarial research and study and publishes the ASTIN Bulletin.
2.2M Pages
Founded in 1957

14201 **Advanced Underwriting Services**
Dearborn Financial Publishing
155 N Wacker Drive
Floor 1
Chicago, IL 60606-6819
312-836-4400; Fax: 312-836-1146
Georgia Mann, Publisher
Information on the law.
Cost: $395.00
Frequency: Monthly

14202 **Best's Agents Guide to Life Insurance Companies**
AM Best Company
Ambest Rd
Oldwick, NJ 08858
908-439-2200
800-544-2378; Fax: 908-439-3296
webmaster@ambest.com
www.ambest.com
Arthur Snyder, CEO
Offers information on over 1,400 life and health insurance companies nationwide.
Cost: $150.00
Frequency: Monthly
Founded in 1899

14203 **Compensation & Benefits for Law Offices**
Institute of Management and Administration
1 Washington Park
Suite 1300
Newark, NY 07102-3130
212-244-0360; Fax: 973-622-0595
customercare@bna.com
www.ioma.com
An indespensible reference for law firm recruitment, training, compensation, benefits, and HR managers who want and need to keep pace with what it takes to successfully, recruit, retain, train, reward, recognize, and compensatetop legal talent.
Cost: $449.00

14204 **Crittenden Insurance Markets Newsletter**
Crittenden Publishing
45 Leveroni Court
Suite 204
Novato, CA 94949-5721
415-475-1522
800-421-3483; Fax: 619-923-3518
ins@crittendenonline.com
www.crittendenonline.com
Twitter
Offers readers a behind-the-scenes look at everything going on in the commercial insurance market. Provides all the coverage necessary for agents to be successful in the board field of commercial insurance
Frequency: Weekly
Founded in 1972

14205 **Disability Eval and Rehab Review**
National Association of Disability Evaluating

13801 Village Mill Drive
Midlothian, VA 23113

804-378-7275
www.nadep.com

This periodical is peer reviewed and addresses issues which are impacting the field of medicine and rehabilitation and which specifically address impairment rating, disability determination, functional capacity evaluation, vocational evaluation and current trends in reimbursement and how the Americans with Disabilities Act of 1990 has changed the practice of medicine and rehabilitation.
Frequency: Quarterly

14206 HELP Newsletter
Insurance Loss Control Association
PO Box 346
Morton, IL 61550

309-696-2551; Fax: 317-879-8408
ccarson@namic.org
www.insurancelosscontrol.org

Brock Bell, President
Daniel Finn, VP
Stig Ruxlow, Financial Secretary

Association news and activities.
Frequency: Quarterly
Circulation: 325
Founded in 1931
Printed in 2 colors on matte stock

14207 Highlights
American Association of Retired Persons
601 E St Nw
Washington, DC 20049-0003

202-434-2277; Fax: 202-434-7599
PCMNationalOffice@aarp.org
www.aarp.org

A Barry Rand, CEO
Ethel Andrus, Founder

Offers information and updates on the association, tax information and legal statistics.
4 Pages
Frequency: BiWeekly

14208 IMCA Newsletter
Insurance Marketing & Communications Association
4248 Park Glen Road
Minneapolis, MN 55416

952-928-4644; Fax: 952-929-1318
info@imcanet.com
www.imcanet.com

Megan Flanagan, Executive Director

Available to members of the Insurance Marketing & Communications Association.
Mailing list available for rent

14209 IOMA's Report on Hourly Compensation
Institute of Management and Administration
1 Washington Park
Suite 1300
Newark, NJ 07102-3130

212-244-0360; Fax: 973-622-0595
customercare@bna.com
www.ioma.com

RHC is a sister publication for IOMA's Report on Salary Surveys and takes compensation and salary dates from major surveys produced by firms like Watson Wyatt Data Services, the Big Six Accounting firms and local HR groups to show benefits and compensation managers the going rate for hourly workers in a variety of positions.

14210 Insurance Daily
SNL Financial
One SNL Plaza
PO Box 2124
Charlottesville, VA 22902

434-977-1600; Fax: 434-293-0407
www.snl.com
Facebook, Twitter, LinkedIn

Akash Sinha, Editor
Tom Mason, Editor

The most comprehensive news source on the insurance sector. The news desk researches filings and investor presentations, conducts exclusive interviews with industry executives and analysts for the stories that impact the insurance market
Cost: $995.00
Frequency: Daily
Mailing list available for rent

14211 Insurance Finance & Investment
Institutional Investor
488 Madison Ave
New York, NY 10022-5701
212-303-3100
800-715-9195; Fax: 212-224-3491
iieditor@institutionalinvestor.com
www.institutionalinvestor.com

Erik Kolk, Publisher
Chris Brown, CEO/President
Stuard Wise, Senior Editor
Nick Ferris, Marketing Director

Provides reviews of investment performance, financing strategies, overviews of ratings, and highlights of new issues.
Cost: $1495.00
Frequency: Monthly
Founded in 1905

14212 Insurance Forum
Insurance Forum
PO Box 245
Ellettsville, IN 47429

812-876-6502; Fax: 812-876-6572
www.theinsuranceforum.com

Joseph M Belth, Editor
Ann I Belth, Business Manager
Jeffrey E Belth, Circulation Manager

Provides objective information and incisive analysis of important insurance topics.
Cost: $120.00
Frequency: Monthly
Founded in 1974

14213 Insurance Performance Graph
SNL Financial
PO Box 2124
Charlottesvle, VA 22902-2124

434-977-1600; Fax: 434-977-4466
isales@snl.com
www.snl.com

Mike Deane, Editor
Matt Mueller, Chief Operating Officer
Nick Cafferillo, Chief Operating Officer
Adam Hall, Managing Director

For publicly traded insurance companies and law, accounting and consulting firms. Compares the investment performance of an insurance company to a specific SNL index or to a selected peer group and the appropriate broad multi-industry index. Covers a 5-year period or the period beginning with the IPO date.
Cost: $399.00
Frequency: Monthly
Founded in 1987

14214 Insurance Regulation
Wakeman Walworth Inc
PO Box 7376
Alexandria, VA 22307-7376

703-768-9600; Fax: 703-768-9690
statecapitals.com

Keyes Walworth, Publisher

The best way to track day-to-day changes and innovations at the state level □ covers health insurance including HMOs, CHIP programs and the battle to increase health insurance benefits. It also covers life, automobile, homeowner, unemployment insurance, workers compensation and malpractice. It reports on tort reform, licensing, self-insurance, plus new approaches such as lifestyle considerations.
Cost: $245.00
Frequency: Weekly

14215 Insurance Weekly: Life & Health
SNL Financial
One SNL Plaza
PO Box 2124
Charlottesville, VA 22902-2124

434-977-1600; Fax: 434-977-4466
www.snl.com
Facebook, Twitter, LinkedIn

Akash Sinha, Editor
Tom Mason, Editor

Super-focused coverage of the dynamic life and health, managed care and insurance agency sectors
Cost: $396.00
Frequency: Weekly
ISSN: 1098-8149
Mailing list available for rent

14216 Insurance Weekly: Property & Casualty
SNL Financial
One SNL Plaza
PO Box 2124
Charlottesville, VA 22902-2124

434-977-1600; Fax: 434-977-4466
www.snl.com
Facebook, Twitter, LinkedIn

Akash Sinha, Editor
Tom Mason, Editor

Complete, current coverage of the property and casualty, title, financial and mortgage guaranty and insurance agency sectors
Cost: $396.00
Frequency: Weekly
ISSN: 1098-8130
Mailing list available for rent

14217 Journal for Insurance Compliance Professionals Newsletter
Association of Insurance Compliance Professionals
12100 Sunset Hills Road
Suite 130
Reston, VA 20190

703-234-4074; Fax: 703-435-4390
aicp@aicp.net
www.aicp.net

Doug Simino, President
Darrell Turner, Editor
Elaine Douglas, Vice President
Dawn Murphy, Secretary
Doug Geraci, Treasurer

Includes topical information for members, covering regulatory and industry issues, along with the latest techniques in filings nad news from each Association Region and Chapter
Frequency: Quarterly
Founded in 1998

14218 LIC Newsletter
Life Insurers Council
2300 Windy Ridge Pkwy SE
Suite 600
Atlanta, GA 30339-5665

770-951-1770
800-275-5662; Fax: 770-984-0441

askloma@loma.org
www.loma.org

Jeff Shaw, Executive Director
Rose Hoyt, Administrative Assistant

Includes news and analysis about issues of concern to executives and those involved in operations, plus information on upcoming events and company activities
Frequency: Monthly
Mailing list available for rent

14219 **Mealey's Catastrophic Loss**
LexisNexis Mealey's
555 W 5th Avenue
Los Angeles, CA 90013

213-627-1130
800-253-4182
mealeyinfo@lexisnexis.com
www.lexisnexis.com/mealeys
Facebook, Twitter, LinkedIn, RSS, Youtube

Tom Hagy, CEO
Maureen McGuire, Editorial Director
Gina Cappello, Editor
Mike Wash, Chief Executive Officer, Legal
Lisa Agona, Chief Marketing Officer

This report focuses on business interruption insurance claims in the aftermath of the Hurricane Katrina, September 11th, and other catastrophic loss tragedies. Additionally, the report will go beyond these claims and will offer important business interruption insurance coverage news related to computer viruses, computer failures, and natural disasters.
Cost: $1075.00
100 Pages
Frequency: Monthly
Founded in 2001
Mailing list available for rent

14220 **Mealey's Emerging Insurance Disputes**
LexisNexis Mealey's
555 W 5th Avenue
Los Angeles, CA 90013

213-627-1130
800-253-4182
mealeyinfo@lexisnexis.com
www.lexisnexis.com/mealeys
Facebook, Twitter, LinkedIn, RSS, Youtube

Tom Hagy, CEO
Maureen McGuire, Editorial Director
Gina Cappello, Editor
Mike Wash, Chief Executive Officer, Legal
Lisa Agona, Chief Marketing Officer

The report tracks new areas of coverage liability, novel policy applications, and conflicting policy language interpretations as they arise in insurance litigation. Some areas of coverage featured are: sexual harassment and discrimination, assault and battery, professional liability, patent and trademark infringement, construction defects, directors and officers claims, emotional distress, intentional acts, technology, and insurance business practices.
Cost: $ 1229.00
100 Pages
Frequency: Semi-Monthly
Founded in 1996
Mailing list available for rent

14221 **Mealey's Litigation Report: Asbestos**
LexisNexis Mealey's
555 W 5th Avenue
Los Angeles, CA 90013

213-627-1130
800-253-4182
mealeyinfo@lexisnexis.com
www.lexisnexis.com/mealeys
Facebook, Twitter, LinkedIn, RSS, Youtube

Tom Hagy, CEO
Maureen McGuire, Editorial Director
Bryan Redding, Editor
Mike Wash, Chief Executive Officer, Legal
Lisa Agona, Chief Marketing Officer

The report offers unsurpassed coverage of litigation arising from asbestos-related injury and death. Key issues include: massive class action settlements involving present and future claimants, state and federal verdicts, litigation experts, medical monitoring claims, suits against the tobacco industry, discovery battles, discovery rule decisions, insurance coverage rulings, and asbestos property decisions.
Cost: $1789.00
100 Pages
Frequency: Semi-Monthly
Founded in 1984
Mailing list available for rent

14222 **Mealey's Litigation Report: California Insurance**
LexisNexis Mealey's
555 W 5th Avenue
Los Angeles, CA 90013

213-627-1130
800-253-4182
mealeyinfo@lexisnexis.com
www.lexisnexis.com/mealeys
Facebook, Twitter, LinkedIn, RSS, Youtube

Tom Hagy, CEO
Maureen McGuire, Editorial Director
Jennifer Hans, Editor
Mike Wash, Chief Executive Officer, Legal
Lisa Agona, Chief Marketing Officer

The Report focuses on ever-changing California and federal Ninth Circuit insurance coverage disputes and developments. Topics include California developments in bad faith litigation, earthquake damage coverage, disability insurance, products liability coverage, environmental insurance coverage, mold coverage, asbestos coverage, aviation litigation coverage, entertainment law and more.
Cost: $949.00
100 Pages
Frequency: Monthly
Founded in 2001
Mailing list available for rent

14223 **Mealey's Litigation Report: Disability Insurance**
LexisNexis Mealey's
555 W 5th Avenue
Los Angeles, CA 90013

213-627-1130
800-253-4182
mealeyinfo@lexisnexis.com
www.lexisnexis.com/mealeys
Facebook, Twitter, LinkedIn, RSS, Youtube

Tom Hagy, CEO
Maureen McGuire, Editorial Director
Karen Miehle, Editor
Mike Wash, Chief Executive Officer, Legal
Lisa Agona, Chief Marketing Officer

This report tracks the burgeoning number of disputes involving complex disability coverage claims. Topics covered include: claims for chronic fatigue, chronic pain, stress, psychiatric disabilities, chemical dependency and risk of relapse, plus key issues like total disability, own occupation, bad faith, ERSA, class actions and much more.
Cost: $849.00
100 Pages
Frequency: Monthly
Founded in 2000
Mailing list available for rent

14224 **Mealey's Litigation Report: Insurance**
LexisNexis Mealey's
555 W 5th Avenue
Los Angeles, CA 90013

213-627-1130
800-253-4182
mealeyinfo@lexisnexis.com
www.lexisnexis.com/mealeys
Facebook, Twitter, LinkedIn, RSS, Youtube

Tom Hagy, CEO
Maureen McGuire, Editorial Director
Vivi Gorman, Editor
Shawn Rice, Co-Editor
Mike Wash, Chief Executive Officer, Legal

The report tracks declaratory judgment actions regarding coverage for litigation arising from long-tail claims, including environmental contamination and latent damage and injury allegedly caused by asbestos, tox chemicals and fumes, lead, breast implants, medical devices, construction defects, and more. Key issues: allocation, occurrence, policy exclusion, choice of law, discovery, duty to defend, notice, trigger of coverage and known loss.
Cost: $2115.00
100 Pages
Frequency: Weekly
Founded in 1984
Mailing list available for rent

14225 **NACA NEWS**
National Association of Catastrophe Adjusters
P.O. Box 499
Alvord, TX 76225

817-498-3466; Fax: 817-498-0480
naca@nacatadj.org
www.nacatadj.org
Facebook, Twitter, LinkedIn

Lori Ringo, Executive Administrator
Chris Hatcher, President
Jon Joyce, Vice President

Contains information of interest and benefit to the members of NACA and the president of the association provides his insights for the quarter.
Frequency: Quarterly
Circulation: 2500
Founded in 1976

14226 **NAPIA Newsletter**
National Association of Public Insurance Adjusters
21165 Whitfield Place
Suite 105
Potomac Falls, VA 20165

703-433-9217; Fax: 703-433-0369
info@napia.com
www.napia.com

David W Barrack, Executive Director
Ronald R. Reitz, President
Frequency: Quarterly
Circulation: 600
Mailing list available for rent

14227 **NCOILetter**
National Conference of Insurance Legislators
385 Jordan Road
Troy, NY 12180

518-687-0178; Fax: 518-687-0401
info@ncoil.org
www.ncoil.org

Susan F. Nolan, Executive Director
Candace Thorson, Deputy Executive Director
Simone Smith, Director, Operations/Administration
Mike Humphreys, Director,State-Federal Relations
Jordan Estey, Dir, Legislative Affairs/Education

NCOIL is an organization of state legislators whose main area of public policy concern is insurance legislation and regulation. Many legis-

lators active in NCOIL either chair or are members of the committees responsible for insurance legislation in their respective state houses across the country.
Frequency: Monthly
Circulation: 2500
Founded in 1969

14228 **NFPA Journal Update**
National Fire Protection Association
1 Batterymarch Park
Quincy, MA 02169-7471
617-770-3000
800-344-3555; Fax: 617-770-0700
www.nfpa.org
James M. Shannon, President/CEO
Peg O'Brien, Administrator - Public Affairs
Sharon Gamache, Executive Director
Bruce Mullen, CFO
Paul Crossman, VP, Marketing
Member newsletter that contains the latest articles, features, and special online exclusives from NFPA Journal , as well as quick access to the information and resources on NFPA's codes and standards-making process, research, training, safety information, and more.
75000 Members
Frequency: Monthly
Founded in 1896

14229 **PIA Connection**
Association of Professional Insurance Agents
400 N Washington Street
Alexandria, VA 22314-2312
703-836-9340; Fax: 703-836-1279
web@pianet.org
www.pianet.com
Facebook, Twitter, LinkedIn
Andrew C. Harris, President
John G. Lee, President-elect
Richard A. Clements, Vice President, Treasurer
Robert W. Hansen, Secretary/Assistant Treasurer
Contains current insurance industry news that is particularly relevant to independent insurance agents
Cost: $24.00
Frequency: 10x/Year
Mailing list available for rent

14230 **Report on Property/Casualty Rates & Ratings**
Institute of Management and Administration
1 Washington Park
Suite 1300
Newark, NJ 07102-3130
212-244-0360; Fax: 973-622-0595
customercare@bna.com
www.ioma.com
Helps agents and brokers get competitive premium rates for their clients.
Cost: $389.00
16 Pages
Frequency: Monthly
Founded in 1755

14231 **Risk Management Essentials**
Nonprofit Risk Management Center
15 N King Street
Suite 203
Leesburg, VA 20176
202-785-3891; Fax: 703-443-1990
info@nonprofitrisk.org
www.nonprofitrisk.org
Melanie Herman, Executive Director
Whitney Thomey, Project Manager
Katharine Nesslage, Project Manager
Kay Nakamura, Director of Client Solutions
Each issue covers a selection of issues, showcases the Center's training and workshops, and/or highlights new publications offering risk management advice from a nonprofit perspective
16 Pages
Frequency: 3 times a year
Mailing list available for rent

14232 **Riskwatch**
Public Risk Management Association
700 S. Washington St.
Suite 218
Alexandria, VA 22314-1565
703-528-7701; Fax: 703-739-0200
info@primacentral.org
www.primacentral.org
Facebook, Twitter, LinkedIn
Marshall Davies, Executive Director
Jennifer Ackerman, Deputy Executive Director
Bles Dones, Manager, Member Services
Jennifer W. Morris, Manager, Meetings and Conferences
Paulette Washington, Office Administrator
E-news service that delivers handpicked, high-quality news articles relating to the public risk management industry. Provides PRIMA members with valuable association-related news. Keeps you on top of the latest news and trends in the public sector risk management field.
Frequency: Weekly
Mailing list available for rent

14233 **SFFA Newsletter**
Surety & Fidelity Association of America
1101 Connecticut Avenue NW
Suite 800
Washington, DC 20036
202-463-0600; Fax: 202-463-0606
information@surety.org
www.surety.org
Facebook, Twitter
Lynn Schubert, President
Mailing list available for rent

14234 **Surety Association of America**
Surety Association of America
1101 Connecticut Ave Nw
Suite 800
Washington, DC 20036-4347
202-463-0600; Fax: 202-463-0606
information@surety.org
www.surety.org
Lynn Schubert, President

Magazines & Journals

14235 **AHIP Health IT Directory**
America's Health Insurance Plans
601 Pennsylvania Ave NW
South Building, Suite 500
Washington, DC 20004-2601
202-778-3200
877-291-2247; Fax: 202-331-7487
info@ahip.org
www.ahip.org
Twitter
Matt Eyles, President & CEO
Kristine Grow, Sr. VP, Communications
More than 3,400 key executives listed, types of products offered such as HMO, PPO, POS, etc., company contact information, national enrollment by type of products, and national and state level enrollment data by company. There is also a CD-ROM availablie for $1,495.00
Cost: $492.00
Mailing list available for rent

14236 **ASPPA Journal**
American Society of Pension Professionals & Act
4245 Fairfax Dr
Suite 750
Arlington, VA 22203-1648
703-516-0512; Fax: 703-516-9308
asppa@asppa.org
www.asppa.org
Thomas Finnegan, President
A technical publication providing critical insight into legislative and regulatory developments. Also features technical analysis of benefit plan matters as well as information regarding ASPPA's programs.
Frequency: Quarterly
Circulation: 7500

14237 **Actuarial Digest**
Actuarial Digest Publishing Company
PO Box 1127
Ponte Vedra, FL 32004-1127
904-273-1245
Gene Hubbard, Editor
Covers fields such as life, group, health, reinsurance, pension/employee benefits, government regulations and educational institutions.
Founded in 1982

14238 **Actuarial Studies in Non-Life Insurance**
Peeters
1600 Arch St
Philadelphia, PA 19103-2032
215-567-0097; Fax: 215-567-0107
webmaster@actuaries.org
www.actuaries.org
Lucy Peters, Owner
Andrew Cairns, Editor
David G Hartman, Chairman
Carla Melvin, Executive Assistant
Katy Martin, Project Manager
Promotes actuarial research and study and publishes the ASTIN Bulletin.
Cost: $65.00
500 Pages
Frequency: Quarterly
Circulation: 3000
Founded in 1957

14239 **Advisor Today**
Natl Assoc of Insurance and Financial Advisors
2901 Telestar Court
Falls Church, VA 22042
703-770-8100
877-866-2432
membersupport@naifa.org
www.advisortoday.com
Facebook, Twitter, LinkedIn
Ayo Mseka, Editor-In-Chief
Julie Britt, Senior Editor
Preeti Vasishtha, Editor
Tara Heuser, Publication and Circulation
Provides practical information, sales idas resources and business strategies to hel pinsurance and financial advisors succeed.
Founded in 1906
Mailing list available for rent

14240 **American Journal of Law & Medicine**
American Society of Law, Medicine and Ethics
765 Commonwealth Ave
Suite 1634
Boston, MA 02215-1401
617-262-4990; Fax: 617-437-7596
info@aslme.org
www.aslme.org
Facebook, Twitter, LinkedIn
Ted Hutchinson, Executive Director
Courtney McClellan, Assistant Editor
Katie Kenney Johnson, Conference Director

Margo Buege, Membership Department
Courtney McClellan, Assistant Editor

A law review fulfilling the need to improve communication between leagal and medical professionals. Contains professional articles and case notes on themes in health law and policy, and on the legal, ethical, and economic aspects of medical practice, research, and education-and health law court decisions and book reviews.
Cost: $150.00
Frequency: Quarterly
Mailing list available for rent

14241 **Annuity Shopper**
Annuity Shopper
28 Harrison Ave.
D209
Englishtown, NJ 07726

732-521-5110
877-206-8141; Fax: 732-521-5113
www.annuityshopper.com

Hersh Stern, Owner
Laura Stern, Editor

Helps consumers purchase the safest and most reliable lifetime income annuities for their retirement.
Frequency: Semi-annually
ISSN: 1071-4510
Founded in 1986
Mailing list available for rent

14242 **Beacon**
American Association of Dental Consultants
10032 Wind Hill Dr
Greenville, IN 47124-9673

812-923-2600
800-896-0707; Fax: 812-923-2900
www.aadc.org

Judith Salisburty, Executive Director
Dr Larry Hoffman, Secretary/Treasurer

Informs members about the latest issues affecting dentistry and dental benefits.
Frequency: Twice/Year
Circulation: 350

14243 **Benefits Magazine**
International Foundation of Employee Benefit Plans
18700 W Bluemound Road
Brookfield, WI 53045

262-786-6700
888-334-3327; Fax: 262-786-8670
pr@ifebp.org
www.ifebp.org
Facebook, Twitter, LinkedIn

Michael Wilson, CEO
Terry Davidson, VP, Business Development
Beth Harwood, VP, Educ Program/Content Management

Covers issues such as healthcare, retirement and related trends. Authors are experienced professionals in the field.
Cost: $175.00
35000 Members
Frequency: Monthly
Circulation: 28336
ISSN: 2157-6157
Founded in 1954

14244 **Benefits Quarterly**
Int'l Society of Certified Employee Benfit Special
18700 W Bluemound Road
PO Box 209
Brookfield, WI 53008-0209

262-786-8771; Fax: 262-786-8650
iscebs@iscebs.org
www.iscebs.org
Facebook, Twitter, LinkedIn

Daniel W Graham, CEBS, Executive Director
Sandra L. Becker, Director
Jennifer Mathe, Manager Member Services
Kathy Frank, Administrative Assistant
Julie Dickow, Department Assistant

Offers comprehensive coverage of the latest trends and innovations in benefits and compensation. Features articles on health care, retirement and total compensation, each issue includes a section focused on a topic of special interest.
Cost: $125.00
Frequency: Quarterly
Circulation: 15000
Founded in 1981
Mailing list available for rent

14245 **Best's Review**
AM Best Company
Ambest Rd
Oldwick, NJ 08858

908-439-2200
800-424-2378; Fax: 908-439-3296
www.ambest.com

Arthur Snyder, Chairman & President
Paul Tinnirello, CIO
Larry Mayewski, Chief Rating Officer

Best's Review, the insurance industry's premier news magazine, contains insightful, award-winning coverage of the worldwide insurance industry, giving you the information you need to make informed decisions about your business and career.
Cost: $60.00
Frequency: Monthly
ISSN: 1527-5914
Founded in 1900

14246 **BestWeek**
AM Best Company
Ambest Rd
Oldwick, NJ 08858

908-439-2200; Fax: 908-439-3296
bestweek@ambest.com
www.ambest.com

Arthur Snyder, Chairman and President
Paul Tinnirello, CIO
Larry Mayewski, Chief Rating Officer

BestWeek, the cornerstone of a Best's Insurance News & Analysis subscription, now provides even more ratings information and A.M. Best-generated analytical content in three region-focused editions.
Frequency: Weekly
ISSN: 1945-4139
Founded in 1953

14247 **Broker World**
Insurance Publications
9404 Reeds Road
PO Box 11310
Overland Park, KS 66207-1010

913-383-9191
800-762-3387; Fax: 913-383-1247
info@brokerworldmag.com
www.brokerworldmag.com

Rita S Reeves, Sales Manager
Sharon A Chace, Editor
Stephen P Howard, Publisher
Betsy Masters, Production Manager
Patty L Godfrey, Director of Circulation

The first and only national insurance magazine founded, focused and edited to specifically address the unique informational needs of independent like and health producers.
Frequency: Monthly
Circulation: 28600
Founded in 1980

14248 **Business Insurance**
Crain Communications
711 3rd Ave
New York, NY 10017-4014

212-210-0785; Fax: 212-210-0200
info@crain.com
www.businessinsurance.com

Norm Feldman, Manager
Charmain Benton, Assistant Managing Editor
Paul Bomberger, Managing Editor
Roberto Ceniceros, Senior Editor
Matt Dunning, Associate Editor

Reports on risk management, risk financing, employee benefits management and workers compensation. Our audience also includes insurance brokers, agents, consultants, insurers, reinsurers, and others concerned with corporate insurance, risk management, alternative risk financing, employee benefits, workers compensation and reinsurance.
Frequency: Weekly
Circulation: 44639
Mailing list available for rentat $89y per M

14249 **CICA International Conference**
Captive Insurance Companies Association
4248 Park Glen Road
Minneapolis, MN 55416

952-928-4655; Fax: 952-929-1318
info@cicaworld.com
www.cicaworld.com

Dennis Harwick, President

2012 International Conference is located in Scottsdale, AZ during March 11-13.
500 Attendees
Frequency: Annual

14250 **CPCU Journal**
Chartered Property Casualty Underwriters
720 Providence Rd
Malvern, PA 19355-3446

610-251-2733; Fax: 610-251-2761
www.cpcusociety.org

Steve McElhiney, President
Cynthia Barouex, Vice President

14251 **CPCU e-Journal**
Chartered Property Casualty Underwriter Society
720 Providence Road
Suite 100
Malvern, PA 19355

610-512-2728
800-932-2728; Fax: 610-725-5969
membercenter@cpcusociety.org
www.cpcusociety.org
Facebook, Twitter, LinkedIn

James R Marks, CEO
David C Marlett, Editor
Mark A. Robinson, President and Treasurer

Provides information on practical and timely issues of interest to financial services and property and casualty insurance professionals.
Frequency: Monthly

14252 **Contingencies**
American Academy of Actuaries
1850 M Street NW
Suite 300
Washington, DC 20036

202-223-8196; Fax: 202-872-1948
webmaster@actuary.org
www.actuary.org

Linda Mallon, Editor
Cindy Johns, Marketing/Publications Production

Magazine of the actuarial profession, available in print and digital editions; its circulation includes legislators, regulators, CEOs, and all

Academy members
Cost: $24.00
Frequency: Bi-Monthly
ISSN: 1048-9851
Founded in 1965
Printed in 4 colors on glossy stock

14253 **Contingency Planning & Management**
Witter Publishing Corporation
20 Commerce Street
Flemington, NJ 08822

908-788-0343; Fax: 908-788-3782
www.witterpublishing.com

Bob Joudanin, Publisher
Paul Kirvan, Editor-in-Chief
Mike Viscel, Production Manager
Courtney Witter, Circulation Manager
Andrew Witter, President

Serves the fields of financial/banking, manufacturing industrial, transportation, utilities, telecommunications, health care, government, insurance and other allied fields.
Cost: $275.00
Frequency: Monthly
Circulation: 62000
Founded in 1987

14254 **Crittenden Excess & Surplus Insider**
Crittenden Publishing
250 Bel Marin Keys Boulevard
PO Box 1150, #A
Novato, CA 94948-1150

415-382-2400; Fax: 415-382-2476
ins@crittendenonline.com
www.crittendenonline.com

Robert Fink, Publisher

Focuses on new products, trade literature, industry news, and personnel changes.
Cost: $411.00
Frequency: Weekly
Circulation: 20,000

14255 **EXAMINER Magazine**
Society of Financial Examiners
174 Grace Blvd
Altamonte Spgs, FL 32714-3210

407-682-4930
800-787-7633; Fax: 407-682-3175
www.sofe.org
Facebook, LinkedIn

Cindy Dodson, Executive Director
Joanne Campanelli, President

A quarterly magazine offering association news and information.
Cost: $65.00
Frequency: Quarterly
Circulation: 2500
Founded in 1973
Printed in 2 colors on glossy stock

14256 **GAMA International Journal**
GAMA International
3112 Fairview Park Dr.
Falls Church, VA 22042

571-499-4300
800-345-2687
membership@gamaweb.com
www.gamaweb.com
Facebook, Twitter, LinkedIn

Bonnie Godsman, Chief Excecutive Officer
Debra Grommons, CEO, GAMA Foundation
Jennifer McNally, Publisher
Jon Kia, Advertising Sales

Devoted to the professional development of leaders in the insurance and financial services industry.
Cost: $300.00
56 Pages
Frequency: Bimonthly
Circulation: 5000
ISSN: 1095-7367
Founded in 1951
Mailing list available for rent
Printed in 4 colors on glossy stock

14257 **Health Insurance Underwriters**
National Association of Health Underwriters
1212 New York Avenue NW
Suite 1100
Washington, DC 20005

202-552-5060; Fax: 202-747-6820
editor@nahu.org
www.nahu.org
Facebook, Twitter, LinkedIn

Martin Carr, Publisher/Editor

Covers technology, legislation and product news-everything that affects how health insurance professionals do business
Cost: $40.00
Frequency: Monthly
Circulation: 30,000
ISSN: 0017-9019
Founded in 1930
Mailing list available for rent: 19000 names at $350 per M
Printed in 4 colors on glossy stock

14258 **IAIABC Journal**
Int'l Assoc of Industrial Accident Boards/Commis.
5610 Medical Circle
Suite 24
Madison, WI 53719

608-663-6355; Fax: 608-663-1546
hlore@iaiabc.org
www.iaiabc.org

Robert Aurbach, Editor
Jennifer Wolf Horejsh, Executive Director
Faith Howe, Manager
Christina Klein, Events and Office Administrator
Heather Lore, Manager of Membership and Marketing

Advances the understanding and management of workers' compensation system administration through the availability of data, research, policy analysis, and thoughtful opinion.
Frequency: 2x/Year
Mailing list available for rent

14259 **Independent Agent Magazine**
Independent Insurance Agents & Brokers of America
127 S Peyton St
Alexandria, VA 22314-2803

703-683-4422
800-221-7917; Fax: 703-683-7556
info@iiaba.net
www.iiaba.net
Facebook, Twitter

Robert A Rusbuldt, CEO
Ronald Tubertini, Chairman

Regular issue features include agency management and automation, insurance products and markets, legislative issues, and analysis of industry trends.
Cost: $24.00
Frequency: Monthly
Circulation: 57,814
Mailing list available for rent

14260 **Inquiry**
Excellus Health Plan
1807 Glenview Rd
Suite 100
Glenview, IL 60025-2944

847-724-9280; Fax: 847-729-2199
INQEditor@sagepub.com
www.inquiryjournal.org

Howard J Berman, Publisher
Kevin P Kane, Editor-In-Chief
Alan Monheit, Editor
Ronny G. Frishman, Managing Editor

Seeks to contribute to the continued improvement of the nation's health care system by providing a thoughtful forum for the communication and discussion of relevant public policy issues, innovative concepts, and original research and demonstrations in the areas of health care organization, provision and financing
Cost: $1.00
Frequency: Quarterly
ISSN: 0046-9580

14261 **Insurance & Financial Meetings Managment**
Coastal Communications Corporation
2700 N Military Trail
Suite 120
Boca Raton, FL 33431

561-989-0600; Fax: 561-989-9509
www.themeetingmagazines.com

Harvey Grotsky, Publisher/Editor-In-Chief
Susan Wyckoff Fell, Managing Editor
Susan Gregg, Managing Editor

The executive source for planning meetings and incentives for the financial and insurance sectors. With regular features and special focus on site selection, destinations, industry-related studies and activities, motivational and incentive programs, program and event planning.
Frequency: Monthly
Circulation: 40,000
Founded in 1983

14262 **Insurance & Technology**
TechWeb
240 West 35th Street
New York, NY 10011

212-600-3000; Fax: 212-600-3060
www.insurancetech.com

Katherine Burger, Editorial Director
Anthony O'Donnell, Executive Editor
Nathan Golia, Associate Editor
Cara Latham, Online Managing Editor

Information on how technology can help life, health, property and casualty and multi-line insurance companies perform more productively, profitably, and competitively.
Frequency: Monthly
ISSN: 1054-0733
Mailing list available for rent

14263 **Insurance Advocate**
PO Box 14367
Cincinatti, OH 45250-0367

908-859-0893

Chris Luke, Publisher
Phil Gusman, Editor
Eric V Gilkey, Assistant Editor
Steve Acunto, Associate Publisher

Covers the people and issues affecting the insurance industry in New York, New Jersey, Connecticut and beyond. Also the source for new markets and coverages, financial trends, legislative isssues, M&A, insurance law and industry developments.
Cost: $59.00
Frequency: Weekly
Circulation: 7200
Founded in 1889
Printed in 4 colors on glossy stock

14264 **Insurance Conference Planner**
Penton Media Inc
249 W. 17th St., third floor
New York, NY 10011

847-763-9504
866-505-7173

shatch@meetingsnet.com
www.meetingsnet.com

Susan Hatch, Editor
Betsy Bair, Director, Content and Media
Melissa Fromento, Group Publisher
Regina McGee, Religious Conference Manager
Susan Hatch, Executive Editor

Meeting and incentive strategies for the financial services industry.
Cost: $57.00
148 Pages
Circulation: 9000
Founded in 1989
Printed in 4 colors on glossy stock

14265 **Insurance Insight**
Professional Independent Insurance Agents of IL
4360 Wabash Ave
Springfield, IL 62711-7009

217-793-6660
800-628-6436; Fax: 217-793-6744
info@IIAofIllinois.org
www.iiaofillinois.org

Sandy Cuffle, Manager
Dennis Garrett, VP Marketing/Membership
Mark Kuchar, CPA, CFO
Mike Tate, CAE, Chief Operating Officer
Peter Gulatto, Marketing Representative

Features articles that are relevant to the Illinois insurance industry, and includes topics such as industry news, technology, markets and coverages, financial planning, sales and marketing, state and federal issues, agency management, The Middleton Letter, and education.
Cost: $65.00
68 Pages
Frequency: Monthly
Circulation: 2500
Founded in 1993
Mailing list available for rent

14266 **Insurance Journal West**
3570 Camino Del Rio N
Suite 200
San Diego, CA 92108-1747

619-584-1100
800-897-9965; Fax: 619-584-5889
info@insurancejournal.com
www.insurancejournal.com
Facebook, Twitter, LinkedIn

Mark Wells, Publisher
Mitch Dunford, Chief Operating Officer
Katie Robley, Circulation Manager
Suzie Song, Marketing Manager
Andrea Ortega-Wells, Editor-In-Chief

Insurance Journal is written for the independent agent and broker. Insurance Journal West covers California and the western states, while Insurance Journal Texas/South Central covers Texas, Arkansas, Oklahoma & Louisiana. We cover legal issues, people, markets, regulations and legistation, the very things that affect our readers.
Cost: $58.00
Circulation: 40000
Founded in 1923
Printed in 4 colors on matte stock

14267 **Insurance Networking News**
SourceMedia
550 W. Van Buren St.
Suite 1110
Chicago, IL 60607

847-933-5183; Fax: 312-566-0656
www.insurancenetworking.com
Facebook, Twitter

Carrie Burns, Editor-In-Chief

A trusted source for information on how technology is being implemented to support insurers' strategic business objectives, providing insightful analysis of-and case studies on-how technology is being innovatively utilized to automate critical processes.
Frequency: Monthly
Founded in 1997
Mailing list available for rent

14268 **Journal of Healthcare Risk Management**
American Society for Healthcare Risk Management
155 N. Wacker Dr.
Suite 400
Chicago, IL 60606-4425

312-422-3980; Fax: 312-422-4580
ashrm@aha.org
www.ashrm.org

Denise Shope, President
Hala Helm, President Elect
Faye Sheppard, Past-President
Matt B. Hornberger, MBA, CAE, Executive Director
Virginia Petrancosta, CAE, Director, Marketing & Communication

Contains latest peer-reviewed research, trends, and developments in the health care risk management field. Topics include patient safety, emergency preparedness, insurance, legal issues, and leadership.
Cost: $80.00
Frequency: Quarterly
Circulation: 4500
Mailing list available for rent: 4400 names

14269 **Journal of Law, Medicine & Ethics**
American Society of Law, Medicine and Ethics
765 Commonwealth Ave
Suite 1634
Boston, MA 02215-1401

617-262-4990; Fax: 617-437-7596
info@aslme.org
www.aslme.org
Facebook, Twitter, LinkedIn

Ted Hutchinson, Executive Director
Ted Hutchinson, Publications Director
Katie Kenney Johnson, Conference Director
Margo Buege, Membership Department
Courtney McClellan, Assistant Editor

Provides articles on such timely topics as health care quality and access, managed care, pain relief, genetics, child/maternal health, reproductive health, informed consent, assisted dying, ethics committees, HIV/AIDS, and public health. Issues review significant policy developments, health law court decisions, and books.
Cost: $140.00
Frequency: Quarterly
Circulation: 4,500+
Mailing list available for rent

14270 **Journal of Reinsurance**
Intermediaries and Reinsurance Underwriters Assoc
971 Rte 202 North
Branchburg, NJ 08876

908-203-0211; Fax: 908-203-0213
info@irua.com
www.irua.com

Paul Walther, Editor

To encourage an exchange of ideas and to disseminiate educational information for the benefit and betterment of the Intermediaries & Reinsurance Underwriters Association membership and the reinsurance community.
Cost: $195.00
Frequency: Quarterly

14271 **Journal of Risk and Insurance**
Wiley-Blackwell Publishing
111 River Street
Hoboken, NJ 07030-5774

201-748-6000; Fax: 201-748-6088
info@wiley.com
www.wiley.com

Georges Dionne, Editor

The flagship journal for the American Risk and Insurance Association. The JRI is the most well recognized academic risk management and insurance journal in the world and is currently indexed by the American Economic Association's Economic Literature Index, the Finance Literature Index, RePEc, the Social Sciences Citation Index, ABI/Inform, Business and Company ASAP, Lexis-Nexis, Dow Jones Interactive, and others.
Frequency: Quarterly
ISSN: 0022-4367

14272 **LIMRA's MarketFacts Quarterly**
LIMRA
300 Day Hill Rd.
Windsor, CT 06095

860-688-3358; Fax: 860-285-7792
bragaglia@limra.com
www.limra.com

Wendy Weston, Contact

Features in-depth, timeless articles devoted to the critical issues of the day, including such topics as distribution, technology, marketing strategies, retirement, globalization, demographics, financial integration and products and services.
Cost: $500.00
Frequency: Quarterly
Circulation: 7500

14273 **Leader's Edge Magazine**
Council of Insurance Agents & Brokers
701 Pennsylvania Ave NW
Suite 750
Washington, DC 20004-2661

202-783-4400; Fax: 202-783-4410
webmaster@ciab.com
www.ciab.com

Ken A Crerar, President
Pat Wade, Director of Communications
Brianne Mallaghan, Director of Communications
Scott Sinder, General Counsel

Comprised of vital information and news for the industry of insurance agents and brokers.
Cost: $100.00
Frequency: Bi-Monthly

14274 **Liability & Insurance Week**
JR Publishing
PO Box 6654
McLean, VA 22106-6654

703-532-2235; Fax: 703-532-2236

John Reistrup, Publisher

Reports on political, legislative and regulatory actions affecting the insurance and legal industries.

14275 **Life & Health Advisor**
JonHope Communications
71 Emerson Road
PO Box 613
Walpole, MA 02081

508-668-8025
888-578-8025; Fax: 508-668-8056
www.lifehealth.com
Facebook, Twitter, LinkedIn

Sally O'Connell, Publisher/Ad Sales Manager
Peter Kelley, Editor

Access, exposure & market visibility for financial services, investment and retirement income planningo.
Frequency: Monthly
Founded in 1995
Mailing list available for rent

14276 **Life Insurance Selling**
Summit Buiness Media
5081 Olympic Blvd.
Suite 550
Erlanger, KY 41018
859-692-2100; Fax: 859-692-2000
www.lifeinsuranceselling.com
Facebook, Twitter, LinkedIn, RSS
Dave O'Neil, Group Publisher
John K Moore, Publisher
Brian Anderson, Editor
Tashawna Rodwell, Publisher
Bill Coffin, Group Editorial Director
The leading sales publication for life, health and financial planning professionals.

14277 **Life and Health Insurance Sales Magazines**
Rough Notes Company
11690 Technology Drive
Carmel, IN 46032-5600
317-582-1600
800-321-1909; Fax: 317-816-1000
rnc@roughnotes.com
www.roughnotes.com
Walter Gdowski, Owner
Nancy Doucette, Senior Editor
Elisabeth Boone, CPCU, Associate Editor
Dennis Pillsbury, Associate Editor
For life and health agents, general agents, managers and brokers with prospects to culivate and clients to serve. Accepts advertising.
48 Pages
Frequency: Monthly
Founded in 1878
Mailing list available for rent

14278 **Long-Term Care Insurance Sales Strategies**
Sales Creators
3835 E Thousand Oaks Boulevard
Suite 336
Westlake Village, CA 91362
818-597-3205
888-599-5997; Fax: 818-597-3206
jslome@ltcsales.com
www.ltcsales.com
Jesse Sloame, Publisher/President
Mindy Hartman, Ad Director
Content covers successful sales approaches, new and unexplored marekts, industry trends, and upcoming training seminars.
Cost: $24.00
Frequency: Quarterly
Circulation: 7500
Founded in 1998

14279 **Momentum**
Metropolitan Life Insurance Company
1 Madison Ave
New York, NY 10010-3603
212-867-2165; Fax: 212-685-8042
www.metlife.com
Robert H Benmosche, CEO
Magazine covering the Metropolitan Life Insurance Company.
Frequency: Monthly
Founded in 1970

14280 **NRRA News**
National Risk Retention Association
4248 Park Glen Road
Minneapolis, MN 55416-4758
952-284-4643
800-999-4505; Fax: 952-929-1318
www.captive.com
Judith Harrington, Editor
Cost: $195.00
Frequency: Quarterly
Circulation: 250,000

14281 **National Underwriter Life & Health Financial Services Edition**
33-41 Newark Street
2nd Floor
Hoboken, NJ 07030
201-526-1230; Fax: 201-526-1260
cms.nationalunderwriter.com
Stephen Piontek, Editor-In-Chief
Jim Connolly, Senior Editor
Uniquely positioned to provider producers, brokers, marketers and company executives with timely, insightful information. Each week, identifies, analyzes and comments on the latest trends and developments for their significance to the market-giving our readers the information they need to make critical business decisions.
Frequency: Weekly

14282 **National Underwriter: Life & Health Insurance Edition**
National Underwriter Company
5081 Olympic Blvd
Erlanger, KY 41018-3164
859-692-2100
800-543-0874; Fax: 859-692-2295
www.nationalunderwriter.com
Charlie Smith, CEO
Offers features on agent activities, stocks and marketing, brokers and financial planners, trade meetings, business trends and outside developments in the industry.
Cost: $75.00
Frequency: Weekly
Circulation: 48,5070

14283 **National Underwriter: Property & Casualty Risk & Benefits Management**
National Underwriter Company
5081 Olympic Blvd
Erlanger, KY 41018-3164
859-692-2100
800-543-0874; Fax: 859-692-2295
www.nationalunderwriter.com
Charlie Smith, CEO
Covers industry trends, risk management, state and federal legislation, and judicial affairs.
Cost: $149.00
Frequency: Weekly
Circulation: 485070
Founded in 1897

14284 **Proceedings**
Conference of Consulting Actuaries
3880 Salem Lake Drive
Suite H
Long Grove, IL 60047-5292
847-719-6500; Fax: 847-719-6506
conference@ccactuaries.org
www.ccactuaries.org
Rita K DeGraaf, Executive Director
Keith G Stewart, Director of Operations
Patricia D Johnson, Project Manager
Matthew D Noncek, Member Services Manager
The professional journal of the Conference of Consulting Actuaries. Promotes the interchange of information among actauries and the various actuarial organizations, and to keep its publics informed of the viewpoints and activities of the professional consulting actuary.
Cost: $95.00
500 Pages
Circulation: 1,200
Founded in 1950

14285 **Professional Agent**
Association of Professional Insurance Agents
400 N Washington Street
Alexandria, VA 22314-2312
703-836-9340; Fax: 703-836-1279
piainfo@pianet.org
www.pianet.com
Magazine for the insurance professional.
Cost: $24.00
65 Pages
Frequency: Monthly
Circulation: 35000
Founded in 1931

14286 **Property/Casualty Insurance**
National Association of Mutual Insurance Companies
3601 Vincennes Road
PO Box 68700
Indianapolis, IN 46268
317-875-5250; Fax: 317-879-8408
webmaster@namic.org
www.namic.org
Bart Anderson, Publisher
Laura Biddle-Bruckman, Managing Editor
Matt Keating, Editor
Kristen Eichhorn, Program Director
Highlights insurance industry news, personnel announcements, industry events, and new products in the field.
Cost: $20.00
Frequency: Monthly
Circulation: 2500
Founded in 1895

14287 **Public Risk**
Public Risk Management Association
700 S. Washington St.
Suite 218
Alexandria, VA 22314-1565
703-528-7701; Fax: 703-739-0200
info@primacentral.org
www.primacentral.org
Facebook, Twitter, LinkedIn
Marshall Davies, Executive Director
Jon Ruzan, Editor
Jennifer Ackerman, Deputy Executive Director
Bles Dones, Manager, Member Services
Paulette Washington, Office Administrator
Magazine exclusively targeting risk management practitioners in the public sector: state and local governments.
Cost: $130.00
Frequency: 1 Year 10 Issue
Circulation: 8250
ISSN: 0891-7183
Founded in 1978
Mailing list available for rent

14288 **Resource Magazine**
Life Office Management Association
2300 Windy Ridge Pkwy SE
Suite 600
Atlanta, GA 30339-5665
770-951-1770
800-275-5662; Fax: 770-984-0441
resource@loma.org
www.loma.org
Thomas P Donaldson, President/CEO
Jerry Woo, Director
Robert Lai, Managing Director
Covers every topic of interest to management of insurance and financial services companies.
Frequency: Monthly

14289 **Risk & Insurance**
LRP Publications
PO Box 980
Horsham, PA 19044-0980
215-784-0912
800-341-7874; Fax: 215-784-9639
custserv@lrp.com
www.lrp.com
Todd Lutz, CFO
Jack Roberts, Editor-in-Chief
Cyril Tuohy, Managing Editor
Provides business executives and insurance professionals with the insight, information and strategies they need to mitigate challenging business risks. Published monthly and semi-monthly in April when publish two special editions focusing on the Risk and Insurance Management Society's annual RIMS conference.
Frequency: Monthly
Circulation: 51541
Founded in 1977

14290 **Risk Management**
Risk Management Society Publishing
1065 Avenue of the Americas
13th Floor
New York, NY 10018-5637
212-286-9292; Fax: 212-986-9716
tdonovan@rims.org
www.rims.org
Facebook, Twitter, LinkedIn
Ted Donovan, Publisher
Bill Coffin, Editor-In-Chief
Morgan O'Rouke, Managing Editor
Jared Wade, Editor
Callie Nelson, Circulation Manager
The premier source of analysis, insight and news for corporate risk managers. RM strives to explore existing and emerging techniques and concepts that address the needs of those who are tasked with protecting the physical, financial, human and intellectual assets of their companies.
Cost: $64.00
Frequency: Monthly
Circulation: 17000
Founded in 1950
Mailing list available for rent

14291 **Risk Management and Insurance Review**
Wiley Publications
111 River Street
Hoboken, NJ 07030-5774
201-748-6000; Fax: 201-748-6088
info@wiley.com
www.wiley.com
Mary A Weiss, Editor
Publishes respected, accessible, and high-quality applied research, and well-reasoned opinion and discussion in the field of risk and insurance. The Review's Feature Articles section includes original research involving applications and applied techniques. The Perspectives section contains articles providing new insights on the research literature, business practice, and public policy.
Frequency: Bi-Annual
ISSN: 1098-1616

14292 **Risk Report**
International Risk Management Institute
12222 Merit Dr
Suite 1450
Dallas, TX 75251-3297
972-996-0800
800-827-5991; Fax: 972-371-5128
www.zeroriskhr.com
Facebook, Twitter, LinkedIn
Mike Poskey, Vice President
Jack P Gibson, President
Paul D Murray, VP Marketing/Sales
Robert Kinsel Smith, Senior Adviser/Consultant
Mike Wojcik, Information Technology Director
Helps risk and insurance professionals in both of these areas with analysis and interpretation of the latest innovations in insurance
Cost: $219.00
Frequency: Monthly
Founded in 1987

14293 **Rough Notes**
Rough Notes Company
PO Box 1990
Carmel, IN 46082-1990
317-582-1600
800-428-4384; Fax: 317-816-1000
rnc@roughnotes.com
www.roughnotes.com
Monthly sales and management magazine for property and casualty insurance agents.
Cost: $357.00
120 Pages
Frequency: Monthly
Founded in 1878
Printed in 4 colors on glossy stock

14294 **Round the Table Magazine**
Million Dollar Round Table
325 W Touhy Ave
Park Ridge, IL 60068-4265
847-692-6378; Fax: 847-518-8921
editor@mdrt.org
www.mdrt.org
Guy E Baker, President
Kathyrn F Keuneke, Associate Editor
John Prast, Executive VP
Scott Brennan, Secretary
Productivity ideas, reaching your clients, professional knowledge, motivational stories, all this to share with clients and to help you make the sale.
Cost: $14.00
Frequency: Bi-Monthly

14295 **Standard**
Standard Publishing Corporation
155 Federal St
13th Floor
Boston, MA 02110-1752
617-457-0600; Fax: 617-457-0608
e.ayers@spcpub.com
www.standardpub.com
John Cross, President/Publisher
Content focuses on all aspects involving legislative and regulatory developments at the state and federal levels, court decisions, trade association positions and more. Coverage includes news, feature articles and opinion pieces, with an emphasis on property/casualty insurance.
Cost: $80.00
Frequency: Weekly
Circulation: 5000
Founded in 1870

14296 **The Brief (Tort & Insurance Practice Section)**
American Bar Association
321 N Clark St
Chicago, IL 60654-7598
312-988-5000
800-285-2221; Fax: 312-988-6281
askaba@abanet.org
www.abanet.org
Facebook, Twitter
Jane Harper-Alport, Staff Editor
John Warren May, Editor
Janet Jackson, Director
Bill Pritchard, Assistant to the Director
The Brief explores all aspects of tort and insurance law, including the many facets of trial practice essential to the profession.
Cost: $50.00
400,0 Members
60 Pages
Frequency: Quarterly
Circulation: 30000
ISSN: 0273-0995
Founded in 1878
Printed in 4 colors

14297 **Today's Insurance Woman**
National Association of Insurance Women
1847 E 15th Street
PO Box 4410
Tulsa, OK 74159-0410
918-744-5195; Fax: 918-743-1968
Melissa Carlson, Editor
Focus is on business careers, legislation, leadership, management and social issues facing women in the industry.
Cost: $15.00
Frequency: Bi-Monthly
Circulation: 12,887

14298 **Underwriters' Report**
National Underwriters Company
5081 Olympic Boulevard
Erlanger, KY 41018
859-922-2100
800-543-0874; Fax: 800-874-1916
www.nationalunderwriter.com
Charlie Smith, CEO
Offering complete information on fire, casualty and life insurance every week.
Cost: $45.00
40 Pages
Frequency: Weekly
Circulation: 5000

14299 **Worker's Compensation Monitor**
LRP Publications
PO Box 24668
West Palm Beach, FL 33416-4668
561-622-6520; Fax: 561-622-0757
webmaster@lrp.com
www.lrp.com
Kenneth Kahn, President
Leslie Lake, Managing Editor
Josh Clifton, Editor
Information on worker's compensation laws.
Cost: $210.00
Frequency: Monthly
Founded in 1977

Trade Shows

14300 **AADC Annual Spring Workshop**
American Association of Dental Consultants
10032 Wind Hill Drive
Greenville, IN 47124
812-923-2600
800-896-0707; Fax: 812-923-2900
www.aadc.org
Dr George Koumaras, President
Dr Larry Hoffman, Secretary/Treasurer
Judith K. Salisbury, Executive Director
These meetings provide a forum to discuss topical subjects involving the Dental Benefit Industry and Clinical Dentistry as a whole. AADC presenters and lectures are recognized as leaders in the Dental Industry. 10 exhibitors.
300 Attendees
Frequency: Annual/May
Founded in 1979

14301 **AHIP Institute & Expo**
America's Health Insurance Plans

601 Pennsylvania Avenue NW
South Building, Suite 500
Washington, DC 20004

202-778-3200
877-291-2247; Fax: 202-331-7487
info@ahip.org
www.ahip.org

Matt Eyles, President & CEO
Kristine Grow, Sr. VP, Communications

This meeting continues to be the nation's leading health care conference where all segments of the health insurance industry convene to share perspectives on, and analysis of, the most recent developments in health care. Includes educational sessions, networking opportunities, and product exhibits.
300 Attendees
Frequency: Annual

14302 AHOU Annual Conference
Association of Home Office Underwriters
22300 Windy Ridge Parkway
Suite 600
Atlanta, GA 30339-8443

770-984-3715; Fax: 770-984-6418
ahou@loma.org
www.ahou.org

Jennifer Richards, Convention VP
Lee Janecek, Convention Assistant VP

Providing career development, underwriting solutions, the latest medical issues and valuable insight to keep you prepared.
Frequency: Annual/October
Founded in 2001

14303 AIA Annual Conference
Aviation Insurance Association
400 Admiral Blvd
Suite 200
Kansas City, MO 64106-1508

816-221-8488; Fax: 816-472-7765
www.aiaweb.org
Facebook

Jim Gardner, President

Provides a forum for the biggest names and best minds in the aviaiton insurance industry. Offers top-notch speakers, continuing education classes, time with vendors and opportunities to network and develop relationships that last a lifetime.
900 Members
Frequency: April/May
Founded in 1976

14304 AICP Annual Conference
Association of Insurance Compliance Professionals
12100 Sunset Hills Road
Suite 130
Reston, VA 20190

703-234-4074; Fax: 703-435-4390
aicp@aicp.net
www.aicp.net

Richard A Guggolz, Executive Director
Elaine Bailey, Conference Chair

Learning opportunities for a broad range of compliance professionals, sessions for beginners and seasoned professionals and networking opportunities with colleagues, peers and state regulators.
680 Attendees
Frequency: Annual/Sept-Oct

14305 ASPPA Annual Conference
American Society of Pension Professionals & Act
4245 N Fairfax Drive
Suite 750
Arlington, VA 22203

703-160-0512; Fax: 703-516-9308
asppa@asppa.org
www.asppa.org

Tom Finnegan, President

Attendees of this conference share quality time with representatives from every aspect of the retirement plan industry. Offers 20 hours of ASPPA continuing education credits and provides Joint Board for the Enrollemnt of Actuaries credit hours for enrolled actuaries.
1600 Attendees

14306 ASSE Annual Conference & Exposition
American Society of Safety Engineers
1800 E Oakton Street
Des Plaines, IL 60018

847-699-2929; Fax: 847-768-3434
customerservice@asse.org
www.asse.org
Facebook, Twitter, LinkedIn, Blogger, Pinterest, Tumblr

Fred Fortman, Executive Director
Jim Drzewiecki, Finance/Controller Director
Diane Hurns, Manager Public Relations Department
Richard A. Pollock, President
Stephanie A. Helgerman, Vice President, Finance

Featuring more than 200 sessions, an exposition with 300 exhibitors, special pre- and post-conference seminars, conference proceedings on CD, numerous networking events and more! Learn the latest strategies to expand your knowledge base and network with other safety, health and environmental professionals
3500 Attendees
Frequency: Annual/June
Mailing list available for rent

14307 Advanced Life Underwriting Association
1922 F Street NW
Washington, DC 20006-4302

202-331-6099; Fax: 202-331-2164

Karen G Keating, Director
22 booths.
1.1M Attendees
Frequency: February

14308 Alliance of Insurance Agents and Brokers Convention & Expo
1029 J. Street
Suite 120
Sacramento, CA 95814

916-283-9473
866-497-9222; Fax: 916-283-9479
info@agentsalliance.com
www.agentsalliance.com
Facebook, Twitter

Joe Jimenez, President
David Nelson, Executive Direcetor
Mike D'Arelli, Executive Vice President
Yolanda Olquin, Sales/Marketing Manager

The largest insurance industry trade show in the western U.S. Offers the perfect blend of business networking opportunities, education seminars, and fun and laughs with old and new friends.
Frequency: Annual
Founded in 1962

14309 American Fraternal Alliance Annual Meeting
American Fraternal Alliance
1301 W 22nd St
Suite 700
Oak Brook, IL 60523-6022

630-522-6322; Fax: 630-522-6326
info@fraternalalliance.org
www.fraternalalliance.org
Facebook, Twitter

Joseph Annotti, President & CEO
Linda McLaughlin, Admin Services Manager
Melanie Hinds, Director, Advocacy
Allison Koppel, Executive Vice President
Andrea Litewski, Executive Administrator

Keeps members abreast of industry trends, to promote the spirit of fraternalism and to resolve mutual concerns.
Frequency: September

14310 American Society for Healthcare Risk Management Annual Conference
American Society for Healthcare Risk Management
115 N. Wacker Dr.
Suite 400
Chicago, IL 60606-4425

312-422-3840; Fax: 312-422-4580
ashrm@aha.org

Denise Shope, President
Hala Helm, President Elect
Faye Sheppard, Past-President
Matt B. Hornberger, MBA CAE, Executive Director
Virginia Petrancosta, CAE, Director, Marketing & Communication

Annual convention and exhibits of health care industry risk management equipment, supplies and services.
Frequency: Annual/October

14311 American Society of CLU and CHFC Annual Conference
American Society of CLU and CHFC
270 S Bryn Mawr Avenue
Suite 2
Bryn Mawr, PA 19010-2195

215-726-3160; Fax: 610-527-1400

Annual conference and exhibits for insurance agents and financial services professionals who hold Chartered Life Underwriter or Chartered Financial Consultant designations.
Frequency: October, San Diego

14312 Annual Conference for Public Agencies
Public Risk Management Association
1815 Fort Myer Drive
Suite 1020
Arlington, VA 22209-1805

703-527-5546; Fax: 703-528-7966
info@primacentral.org
www.primacentral.org

James F Coyle, Executive Director
Tony D'Alba, Manager
Kerry Langley, Manager

Largest conference in North America for state and local government risk managers who purchase insurance, safety and training products, computer software, TPA and consultant services.
150 booths.
2000 Attendees
Frequency: June
Founded in 1979
Mailing list available for rent: 2000 names

14313 **Annual National Association of Insurance Women International**
1847 E 15th
PO Box 4410
Tulsa, OK 74159
918-744-5195
800-766-6249; Fax: 918-743-1968
www.naiw.org
Mark Adams, Executive Vice-President
Equipment, information and supplies for women in the insurance industry.
900 Attendees
Frequency: Annual

14314 **Appraisers Association of America National Conference**
Appraisers Association of America
212 W. 35th Street
11th Floor South
New York, NY 10001
212-889-5404; Fax: 212-889-5503
referrals@appraisersassociation.org
www.appraisersassociation.org
Linda Selvin, Executive Director
Yasemin Yeldener, Communications Coordinator
Exhibits of interest to appraisers, workshops, and presentations.
Founded in 1949

14315 **Association for Advanced Life Underwriting**
2901 Telester Court
Falls Church, VA 22042
703-641-9400
888-275-0092
Karen Keating, Communications Director
David Stertzer, Executive VP
Twenty two booths.
1M Attendees
Frequency: March

14316 **CEB Spring Conference**
Council on Employee Benefits
1311 King Street
Alexandria, VA 22314
703-549-6025; Fax: 703-549-6027
scanfiled@ceb.org
www.ceb.org
Shane Canfield, Executive Director
Robert B. Arthur, President
John R. Collins, Treasurer
Donna A. Sexton, Vice President
Charles A. Jordan, Secretary
For members only and affords a great opportunity to exchange ideas in an interactive workshop format.
Frequency: April

14317 **CIRB Annual Meeting**
Crop Insurance Research Bureau
201 Massachusetts Avenue, NE
Suite C5
Washington, DC 20002
202-544-0067; Fax: 202-330-5255
mtorrey@cropinsurance.org
www.cropinsurance.org
Mike Torrey, Executive VP/Federal Affairs Rep
Perry Harlow, Manager Of Membership & Events
W. Kurt Henke, Legal Counsel
The annual meeting brings together crop industry leaders to learn from expert speakers and newtwork with others in their industry.
Frequency: Annual/January-February

14318 **CPCU Annual Meeting & Seminar**
Chartered Property Casualty Underwriter Society
720 Providence Road
PO Box 3009
Malvern, PA 19355-0709
610-251-2728
800-932-2728; Fax: 610-251-2780
lrizzo@cpcusociety.org
www.cpcusociety.org
Liliana Rizzo, CMP, Meeting Services Director
Join your fellow society members, new designees and industry leaders for the best in education, networking and leadership the property and casualty insurance industry has to offer.
2600 Attendees
Frequency: Annual/October
Founded in 1944

14319 **CPCU Conferment Ceremony**
American Institute for CPCU
720 Providence Road
PO Box 3016
Malvern, PA 19355
610-251-2733
800-644-2101; Fax: 610-640-9576
cserv@cpcuiia.org
www.aicpcu.org
Karen Burger CPCU CPIW, Public Relations
Roch Parayre, Senior Partner
Annual graduation ceremony for people who have earned the Chartered Property Casualty Underwriter - CPCU - designation.
Frequency: October

14320 **Captive Insurance Companies Association Conference**
Captive Insurance Companies Association
4248 Park Glen Road
Minneapolis, MN 55416
952-928-4655; Fax: 952-928-1318
www.cicaworld.com
Annual conference and exhibits of captive insurance equipment, supplies and services.

14321 **Chartered Property Casualty Underwriters Society Fall Seminar**
Chartered Property Casualty Underwriter Society
720 Providence Road
Malvern, PA 19355-3402
610-512-2728
http://www.cpcusociety.org
Joseph Wisniewski, VP Finance
Jim Marks, Executive Director
Offers a forum for the exchange of ideas between insurance representatives.
3M Attendees
Frequency: October

14322 **Employee Benefits Annual Conference**
International Foundation of Employee Benefit Plans
18700 W Bluemound Road
Brookfield, WI 53045
262-786-6700
888-334-3327; Fax: 262-786-8780
pr@ifebp.org
www.ifebp.org
Facebook, Twitter, LinkedIn
Michael Wilson, CEO
Terry Davidson, VP, Business Development
Beth Harwood, VP, Educ Program/Content Management
This conference is designed to meet the specific needs of multiemployer and public sector plan trustees and administrators, attorneys, accountants, actuaries, investment managers and others who provide services or who are involved in the overall management and administration of benefit trust funds. The 2011 conference will be in New Orleans, LA.
35000 Members
4500 Attendees
Frequency: Annual/Nov 4-7

14323 **FICP Conference**
Financial & Insurance Conference Planners
330 N. Wabash Avenue
Suite 2000
Chicago, IL 60611
312-245-1023; Fax: 312-321-5150
www.ficpnet.com
James Schultze, CMP, Conference Manager
Laura Vanderbur, Conference Associate
Steve Bova, CAE, Executive Director
Mark Swets, Membership Manager
Ellie Hurley, Events Senior Manager
Exhibits, education and networking activities.
Frequency: Annual/November

14324 **Financial Service Forum**
Society of Financial Service Professionals
3803 West Chester Pike
Suite 225
Newtown Square, PA 19073-3230
610-526-2500
800-392-6900; Fax: 610-359-8115
info@societyoffsp.org
national.societyoffsp.org
Facebook, Twitter, LinkedIn
David M. Maola, Chief Executive Officer
Michael J. McGlothlin, President
Composed of motivational speakers, break-out educational session with continuing education for insurance, CFP, PACE, CLE, CPE, ICB, and EA. Exhibithall includes demo theaters.
3000+ Attendees
Frequency: October

14325 **General Agents and Managers Life Agency Management Program**
1922 F Street NW
Washington, DC 20006-4302
202-331-6099; Fax: 202-785-5612
Jo Anne Kohler, Show Manager
80 booths including publishers, computer software and hardware manufacturers and office management services.
2.7M Attendees
Frequency: March

14326 **Health Law Professors Conference**
American Society of Law, Medicine and Ethics
765 Commonwealth Avenue
16th Floor
Boston, MA 02215
617-262-4990; Fax: 617-437-7596
conferences@aslme.org
www.aslme.org
Facebook, Twitter, LinkedIn
Ted Hutchinson, Executive Director
Katie Kenney Johnson, Conference Director
Margo Buege, Membership Department
Courtney McClellan, Assistant Editor
Frequency: June
Mailing list available for rent

14327 **I-Car International Annual Meeting**
3701 W Algonquin Road
Suite 400
Rolling Meadows, IL 60008
925-961-0393
800-422-7872; Fax: 800-590-1215
webmaster@i-car.com
www.i-car.com
Pat Perren, Meetings Manager
Matt Forpanek, Customer Care Manager

A important event that brings together collision industry leaders from across the United States, Canada and New Zealand to address current trends and issues in the industry. Attendees will have the opportunity to learn about new products and technologies and share ideas with other industry leaders.
Frequency: Annual/July

14328 **IAAI Annual Conference and General Meeting**
International Association of Arson Investigators
12770 Boenker Road
Bridgeton, MO 63044

314-739-4224; Fax: 314-739-4219
orders@firearson.com
www.firearson.com

Marsha Sipes, Conference/Meeting Services
Dolores Nelson, Executive Director
Dave Allen, Executive Director

Provides the means to stay abreast of the latest techniques and theories in the investigation of the crime of arson.
Frequency: Annual/April

14329 **IADC Annual Meeting**
International Association of Defense Counsel
303 West Madison
Suite 925
Chicago, IL 60606

312-368-1494; Fax: 312-368-1854
info@iadclaw.org
www.iadclaw.org
Facebook, Twitter, LinkedIn

Mary Beth Kurzak, Executive Director
Mathew Hornberger, Director Membership/Administration
Liz Anderson, Administrative Assistant
Carmela Balice, Senior Manager, Member Services
Ashley Fitzgerald, Communications Coordinator

Offering interests CLE and excellent networking opportunities in family friendly environment.
Frequency: Annual/July

14330 **IAIABC Annual Convention**
Int'l Assoc of Industrail Accident Boards/Commissi
5610 Medical Circle
Suite 24
Madison, WI 53719

608-663-6355; Fax: 608-663-1546
hlore@iaiabc.org
www.iaiabc.org

Jennifer Wolf Horejsh, Executive Director
Faith Howe, EDI Manager
Christina Klein, Events/Education Coordinator
Christina Klein, Events and Office Administrator
Heather Lore, Manager of Membership and Marketing
Brings together regulators and administrators of workers' compensation agencies and private sector professionals to discuss the industry's most common and pressing problems.
Frequency: August
Mailing list available for rent

14331 **IAIR Roundtable and Meetings**
International Association of Insurance Receivers
174 Grace Boulevard
Altamonte Springs, FL 32714

407-682-4513; Fax: 407-682-3175
info@iair.org
www.iair.org

Daniel A Orth III, Meetings VP
Mary Cannon Veed, Vice President
Douglas Hartz, Vice President

Quarterly meetings that provides an opportunity to share information about important industry issues and topics in insurance and reinsurance as they relate specifically to insurance receiverships.
Frequency: June, Sept, December

14332 **IASA Annual Conference**
Insurance, Accounting & Systems Association
3511 Shannon Road
Suite 160
Durham, NC 27707

919-489-0991; Fax: 919-489-1994
info@iasa.org
www.iasa.org

Thom Hoffman, Exhibit Manager
R Iovino, Account Manager

Providing the most comprehensive education program and business show targeted for financial and technology professionals in the industry.
1800 Attendees
Frequency: June

14333 **ICAE's Annual Exchange**
Insurance Consumer Affairs Exchange
PO Box 746
Lake Zurich, IL 60047

847-997-8454
www.icae.com

Mike Hammond, President
Kendra Franklin, VP
Nancy Brebner, Executive Director
Chad Batterson, Executive Committee
Gail Cleary, Secretary

A not-for-profit organization that promotes professionalism and shapes the standards of behavior in relationships between insurance organizations, regulators and customers through proactive dialogue, research, communication and education.
110 Members
Frequency: Annual/October
Founded in 1976

14334 **IMCA Annual Conference**
Insurance Marketing & Communications Association
4248 Park Glen Road
Minneapolis, MN 55416

952-928-4644; Fax: 952-929-1318
info@imcanet.com
www.imcanet.com

Megan Flanagan, Executive Director

To promote education and development of its members.
Mailing list available for rent

14335 **IRU Spring Conference**
Intermediaries and Reinsurance Underwriters Assoc
971 Rte 202 North
Branchburg, NJ 08876

908-203-0211; Fax: 908-203-0213
info@irua.com
www.irua.com

Amy Barra, Executive Director
Frequency: Annual, March

14336 **Insurance and Financial Communications Association Annual Conference**
1037 N 3rd Ave
Tucson, AZ 85705

602-350-0717
info@ifcaonline.com
www.ifcaonline.com
Facebook, Twitter, LinkedIn, YouTube

Susan o'Neill, President
Ralph Chaump, VP
Kim Schultz, Secretary
Kim Schultz, Secretary

An international organization dedicated to the ongoing professional development of its members in life insurance and related financial services communications.
700 Members
Founded in 1933

14337 **International Claim Association Conference**
International Claim Association
1155 15th Street NW
Suite 500
Washington, DC 20005

202-452-0143; Fax: 202-530-0659
www.claim.org

Marlon Nettleton, President
Christopher Murphy, Executive Director
Lisa Phillips, Secretary
400 Attendees
Frequency: Annual
Founded in 1909
Mailing list available for rent

14338 **LAMP Annual Meeting**
GAMA International
3112 Fairview Park Dr.
Falls Church, VA 22042

571-499-4300
800-345-2687
membership@gamaweb.com
www.gamaweb.com

Bonnie Godsman, Chief Executive Officer
Debra Grommons, CEO, GAMA Foundation
Phillip Reid, Chief Operating Officer
Gail Mutnik, Director, Meetings
Noreen Rich, Director, Marketing & Communication
The event for field leaders in the insurance and financial services industry. Featuring top-notch main platform speaker presentations, more than 30 leading practices concurrent sessions, resource center with more than 50 exhibitors that will be offering valuable products and services and networking opportunities with your peers.
Frequency: Annual/March
ISSN: 1095-7367
Printed in 4 colors on glossy stock

14339 **LIC Annual Meeting**
Life Insurers Council
2300 Windy Ridge Parkway
Suite 600
Atlanta, GA 30339-8443

770-984-3724
800-275-5662; Fax: 770-984-3780
askloma@loma.org

Michael H Siris, Executive Director
Rose Hoyt, Administrative Assistant

Designed to educate members about critical issues for competing in today's regulatory, legislative and business climates.
Frequency: Annual/May
Mailing list available for rent

14340 **MDRT Annual Meeting**
Million Dollar Round Table

325 W Touhy Avenue
Park Ridge, IL 60068-4265

847-926-6378; Fax: 847-518-8921
meetings@mdrt.org
www.mdrt.org

Ray Kopcinski, Meeting Services Director
Jody Egel, Meeting Coordinator
Kathyrn H Pagura, Meeting Coordinator
John Prast, Executive Vice President
Scott Brennan, Secretary

Known throughout the industry as the premier meeting for financial professionals. Motivational stories, educational sessions, experienced colleagues, networking opportunities come together at these annual meetings.
Frequency: Annual/June

14341 **NACA Convention**
National Association of Catastrophe Adjusters
P.O. Box 499
Alvord, TX 76225

817-498-3466; Fax: 817-498-0480
naca@nacatadj.org
www.nacatadj.org
Facebook, Twitter, LinkedIn

Chris Hatcher, President
Jon Joyce, Vice President
Rebecca Wheeling, Communications Committee Chair

Annual convention and business meeting offering continuing education credits for some states; also a vendor show. Convention is held in Las Vegas, NV.
200 Attendees
Frequency: January
Founded in 1976

14342 **NADP Annual Conference**
National Association of Dental Plans
8111 LBJ Freeway
Suite 935
Dallas, TX 75251-1347

972-458-6998; Fax: 972-458-2258
info@nadp.org
www.nadp.org

Evelyn F Ireland, CAE, Executive Director
Tim Brown, Executive Assistant
Jeremy May, Executive Assistant

Get the greater industry insight, re-energized creativity and influential contacts.
Frequency: Annual/September

14343 **NAFIC Annual Convention**
National Association of Fraternal Insurance Counselors
211 Canal Road
Waterloo, WI 53594

920-478-4901
866-478-3880; Fax: 920-478-9586
office@nafic.org
www.nafic.org
Facebook

James Dietrich, President
Joy Collins, Vice President
Anna Maenner, Executive Director
Frequency: Annual

14344 **NAIFA Convention and Career Conference**
Ntl Association of Insurance & Financial Advisors
2901 Telestar Court
PO Box 12012
Falls Church, VA 22042-1205

703-770-8100
877-866-2432; Fax: 703-770-8201
membersupport@naifa.org
www.naifa.org

Cammie Scott, President
Brock Jolly, Treasurer
Lawrence Holzberg, Secretary
Kevin M. Mayeux, CEO

Features educational workshops from more than a dozen prominent speakers and the NAIFA Expo, one of the largest exhibits of financial services and products in the nation.
2000 Attendees
Frequency: Annual/September
Founded in 1890

14345 **NAIIA Annual Conference**
National Association of Independent Insurance Adj.
825 W State Street
Suite 117-C&B
Geneva, IL 60134

630-397-5012; Fax: 630-397-5013
www.naiia.com

David F Mehren, Executive Director
Brenda Reisenger, President
Mark Nixon, Secretary, Treasurer

Attendance is open to claims handling professionals.
Frequency: Annual

14346 **NAPIA Annual Meeting**
National Association of Public Insurance Adjusters
21165 Whitfield Place
Suite 105
Potomac Falls, VA 20165

703-433-9217; Fax: 703-433-0369
info@napia.com
www.napia.com

David W Barrack, Executive Director
Ronald R. Reitz, President

Education sessions, networking and social events and exhibits by industry suppliers.
Frequency: Annual/June
Mailing list available for rent

14347 **National Association of Independent Life Brokerage Agencies Conference**
National Assn of Independent Life Brokerage Agents
8201 Greensboro Drive
Suite 300
Mc Lean, VA 22102-3814

703-610-9011; Fax: 703-524-2303

Annual conference and exhibits of equipment, supplies and services for licensed independent life brokerage agencies that represent at least 3 insurance companies, but are not controlled or owned by an underwriting company.
Frequency: November, San Diego

14348 **National Association of Life Underwriters Conference**
1922 F Street NW
Washington, DC 20006-4394

202-331-6099; Fax: 202-331-2179

William V Regan III, Executive VP
Teresa Bonnema, Advertising Account

Sales professionals in life and health insurance and other financial services. 110 booths.
3.5M Attendees
Frequency: September

14349 **National Association of Mutual Insurance Companies Annual Convention & Expo**
National Association of Mutual Insurance Companies
3601 Vincennes Road
#68700
Indianapolis, IN 46268-1154

317-875-5250; Fax: 317-879-8408
bnastally@namic.org
www.namic.org

Charles Chamness, President
Barbara Nastally, Program Director
Kristen Eichhorn, Program Director
Gregg Dykstra, COO

Convention and exhibit show for property/casualty insurance executives. Four day event.
1700 Attendees
Frequency: Fall
Founded in 1895

14350 **New England Professional Insurance Agents Association Conference**
1 Ash Street
Hopkinton, MA 01748-1822

508-497-2590

Stella Di Camilo, Show Manager

100 booths of insurance-related products.
1.5M Attendees
Frequency: November

14351 **PIA Annual Convention and Trade Fair**
Professional Insurance Agents Association of
VA & DC
8751 Park Central Dr., Suite 140
Richmond, VA 23227

804-264-2582; Fax: 804-266-1075
pia@piavadc.com
www.piavadc.com
Facebook, Twitter

Dennis Yooom, Executive VP
Lori Lohr, Education Manager
Carol Throokmorton, Accounting Manager
Founded in 1936

14352 **PLRB/LIRB Claims Conference & Insurance Expo**
PLRB/LIRB-Property Loss Research Bureau
3025 Highland Parkway
Suite 800
Downers Grove, IL 60515-1291

630-242-2250
888-711-7572; Fax: 630-724-2260
pdispensa@lirb.org

Tom Mallin, President
Paul C Despensa, VP/General Counsel

Concept sessions that feature a thorough presentation of a topic by expert panelists. A forum of experts/panels that will discuss controversial topics in response to questions and comments from participants on a range of subjects outlined in the agenda for that forum. Participants form a small discussion group to reach consensus on hypothetical problems. Each table debates and defends its conclusions with other groups.
Frequency: April
Mailing list available for rent

14353 **PRIMA Annual Conference Trade Show**
700 S. Washington St.
Suite 218
Alexandria, VA 22314

703-528-7701; Fax: 703-739-0200
info@primacentral.org
www.primacentral.org
Facebook, Twitter, LinkedIn

Marshall Davies, Executive Director
Jon Ruzan, Editor
Jennifer Ackerman, Deputy Executive Director

Bles Dones, Manager, Member Services
Paulette Washington, Office Administrator

Containing 150 exhibits concerning insuring the public.
2,200 Attendees
Frequency: June
Founded in 1976
Mailing list available for rent

14354 Physician Insurers Association of America Annual Conference
Physician Insurers Association of America
2275 Research Boulevard
Rockville, MD 20850-3268

301-947-9000; Fax: 301-947-9090

Annual exhibits related to physician liability insurance.

14355 Professional Insurance Agents National Annual Conference & Exhibition
National Association of Prof. Insurance Agents
400 N Washington Street
Alexandria, VA 22314-2312

703-836-9340; Fax: 703-836-1279
http://www.pianet.com

Ted Besesparis, VP

Annual conference and exhibits of equipment, supplies and services for independent property and casualty agents.

14356 Public Agency Risk Managers Association Convention
Public Agency Risk Managers Association
PO Box 6810
San Jose, CA 95150-6810

Annual convention and exhibits of risk management equipment, supplies and services.

14357 Risk Insurance Management Society
1065 Avenue of Americas
13th Floor
New York, NY 10018

212-286-9292
chapterservices@RIMS.org
www.rims.org

Brian Stevenson, Show Manager
Mary Roth, Manager
Fran Jordan, Manager

500 booths of premier insurance companies and associated service companies.
5M Attendees

14358 Securities Industry and Financial Markets Association (SIFMA) Annual Meeting
1101 New York Avenue Nw
8th Floor
Washington, DC 20005

202-962-7300; Fax: 202-962-7305
www.sifma.org
Facebook, Twitter, LinkedIn

Kenneth Bentsen, President/CEO

The Securities Industry and Financial Markets Association/SIFMA Annual Meeting and Conference program addresses a variety of topics that may include competitiveness of the U.S. capital markets, global exchange consolidation, regulatory and legal initiatives, and trends in the fixed-income and capital markets.
Mailing list available for rent

14359 Society of Insurance Trainers and Educators Conference
2120 Market Street
Suite 108
San Francisco, CA 94114

415-621-2830; Fax: 415-621-0889
www.insurancetrainers.org

Lois A Markovich, Executive Director

Forty booths. A major conference for those involved with training and education in the insurance industry.
200 Attendees
Frequency: June-July
Founded in 1953

14360 Sun States Professional Insurance Agents Association
13416 N 32nd Street
Suite 106
Phoenix, AZ 85032-6000

602-482-3333
Facebook, Twitter, LinkedIn

Maryls M Graser, Executive VP

50 booths.
300 Attendees
Frequency: May

14361 Vermont Captive Insurance Association
Vermont Captive Insurance Association
180 Battery Street
Suite 200
Burlington, VT 05401-5212

802-658-8242; Fax: 802-658-9365
vcia@vcia.com
www.vcia.com

Richard Smith, President
Diane Leach, Education/Program Planning Director
Janice Valgoi, Membership/Development Director
Elizabeth Halpern, Communications Director
Peggy Companion, Director of Finance
Frequency: August
Founded in 1985

14362 WCRI Annual Issues & Research Conference
Workers Compensation Research Institute
955 Massachusetts Ave.
Cambridge, MA 02139

617-661-9274; Fax: 617-661-9284
wcri@wcrinet.org
www.wcrinet.org/conference.html

Vincent Armentano, Chair
Richard A. Victor, President & CEO

14363 WSIA Annual Marketplace
Wholesale & Specialty Insurance Association
4131 N. Mulberry Drive
Suite 200
Kansas City, MO 64116

816-741-3910
info@wsia.org
www.wsia.org

Brady Kelley, Executive Director
Julie Fritz, Director of Operations
Bryan Sanders, President

A conference that includes three days of business meetings and networking opportunities.
4500 Attendees
Frequency: Annual/September
Founded in 2017

14364 WSIA Automation Conference
Wholesale & Specialty Insurance Association
4131 N. Mulberry Drive
Suite 200
Kansas City, MO 64114

816-741-3910
info@wsia.org
www.wsia.org

Brady Kelley, Executive Director
Julie Fritz, Director of Operations
Susan Henderson, Directory Of Marketing
Bryan Sanders, President
Davis Moore, Vice President

A forum for educating, sharing and networking for any industry professional interested in ensuring their organization is able to manage technology disruptions and advancements.
Frequency: Annual

14365 WSIA Underwriting Summit
Wholesale & Specialty Insurance Association
4131 N. Mulberry Drive
Suite 200
Kansas City, MO 64116

816-741-3910
info@wsia.org
www.wsia.org

Brady Kelley, Executive Director
Julie Fritz, Director of Operations
Bryan Sanders, President

This conference will include networking for the underwriting and delegated authority segment of the WSIA membership and an opportunity for the leadership of all member firms to collaborate on strategic issues facing the marketplace.
1500 Attendees
Frequency: Annual/February
Founded in 2017

14366 Women Life Underwriters Confederation
1126 S 70th Street
Suite S-106
Milwaukee, WI 53214-3151

800-776-3008; Fax: 414-475-2585

Ann Wells, Managing Director

For women insurance agents, their managers and their companies. 20 booths.
100 Attendees
Frequency: September

Directories & Databases

14367 ADP Parts Exchange New
ADP Claims Services Group
2010 Crow Canyon Place
San Ramon, CA 94583

925-866-1100
www.adpclaims.com

Provides an electronic link from your ADP estimating system to comprehensive database of new replacement parts. Data on over three and a half million parts facilitates the writing of complete, cost-effective damage reports.

14368 Adjusters Reference Guide
Bar List Publishing Company
425 Huehl Road
Building 6B
Northbrook, IL 60062-2323

847-498-6133
800-726-1007; Fax: 847-498-6695
info@barlist.com
www.barlist.com

Bruce Rodgers, President
Leslie Rodgers, Production Manager

A professional service for anyone who handles insurance claims. It contains a complete set of

ISO Policy and Forms and is divided into two major categories; Personal Lines and Commercial Lines.
Frequency: Annual

14369 **Best's Directory of Recommended Insurance Attorneys and Adjusters**
AM Best Company
Ambest Rd
Oldwick, NJ 08858

908-439-2200; Fax: 908-439-3296
webmaster@ambest.com
www.ambest.com

Arthur Snyder, CEO

Includes over 5,300 insurance defense law firms and over 1,200 insurance adjusters companies recommended by the insurance industry. Includes a section on expert services providers, insurance company groups or fleets, legal and claims services, officials and a digest of insurance laws.
Cost: $1205.00
5100 Pages
Frequency: Annual
Circulation: 19,000
Founded in 1928

14370 **Best's Insurance News & Analysis**
AM Best Company
Ambest Rd
Oldwick, NJ 08858

908-439-2200
800-424-2378; Fax: 908-439-3296
www.ambest.com

Arthur Snyder, Chairman & President
Paul Tinnirello, CIO
Larry Mayewski, Chief Rating Officer

Best's Insurance News & Analysis makes it easy to take advantage of A.M. Best's extensive insurance news and industry research. A Best's Insurance News & Analysis subscription grants you access to a full range of news products as well as unique statistical studies and special reports - all of which are accessible from one convenient online location. Allows access to receive BestDay, BestWeek, Best's Review, and Best's Special Reports.

14371 **Best's Insurance Reports**
AM Best Company
Ambest Rd
Oldwick, NJ 08858

908-439-2200; Fax: 908-439-3296
webmaster@ambest.com
www.ambest.com

Arthur Snyder, CEO

Published in two editions - life-health insurance and property-casualty insurance, United States and Canada.
Cost: $570.00
Frequency: Annual

14372 **Best's Insurance Reports: International Edition**
AM Best Company
Ambest Rd
Oldwick, NJ 08858

908-439-2200; Fax: 908-439-3296
webmaster@ambest.com
www.ambest.com

Arthur Snyder, CEO

Offers information on over 800 insurance companies in Canada, Europe, Asia, Africa, Australia, and South America that offer life/health and property/casulaty insurance policies.
Cost: $495.00
1200 Pages
Frequency: Annual

14373 **Best's Key Rating Guide**
AM Best Company
Ambest Rd
Oldwick, NJ 08858

908-439-2200; Fax: 908-439-3296
webmaster@ambest.com
www.ambest.com

Arthur Snyder, CEO
Larry Mayewski, Editor

Financial and operating characteristics on over 2,600 major property/casualty insurance companies, over 1,750 major life and health insurance companies.
Cost: $95.00
Frequency: Annual August

14374 **Best's Market Guide**
AM Best Company
Ambest Rd
Oldwick, NJ 08858

908-439-2200; Fax: 908-439-3296
webmaster@ambest.com
www.ambest.com

Arthur Snyder, CEO

In each volume, separate volumes for corporate stocks, corporate bonds, and municipal bonds, a list of insurance company investment officers are offered.
Cost: $1425.00
Frequency: 3-Volume Set

14375 **Business Insurance Directory of Reinsurance Intermediaries**
Crain Communications
360 N Michigan Ave
Chicago, IL 60601-3800

312-649-5200
800-678-9595; Fax: 312-649-7937
www.crain.com

Keith Crain, CEO
Sandra L Budde, Editor

Lists nearly 100 reinsurance intermediaries in the United States and Bermuda.
Cost: $4.00
Frequency: Annual
Circulation: 53,000

14376 **Captive Insurance Company Directory**
Tillinghast/Towers Perrin Company
263 Tresser Boulevard
Stamford, CT 06901-3236

203-631-1900; Fax: 203-326-5498

Corinne Ramming, Editor

Lists over 3,000 captive insurance companies and their parent or sponsor companies; management companies and insurance subsidiary investment advisors.
Cost: $210.00
270 Pages
Frequency: Annual

14377 **Certified Claims Professional Accreditation Council**
PO Box 441110
Fort Washington, MD 20749-1110

301-292-1988; Fax: 301-292-1787
www.lattmag.com

Dale L Anderson, Editor

Offers a variety of information on members of the CCPAC and certified claims professionals.
76 Pages
Circulation: 350

14378 **Claim Service Guide**
Bar List Publishing Company
425 Huehl Road
Building 6B
Northbrook, IL 60062-2323

847-498-6133
800-726-1007; Fax: 847-498-6695
info@barlist.com
www.barlist.com

Bruce Rodgers, President
Edna MacMillan, Editor

National Directory of Independent Insurance Adjusters, Appraisers, Expert Consultants and Property Specialists. Distributed to every home and branch office insurance company claims manager.
Cost: $80.00
Frequency: Annual
Circulation: 13,000

14379 **Corporate Yellow Book**
Leadership Directories
104 5th Ave
New York, NY 10011-6901

212-627-4140; Fax: 212-645-0931
corporate@leadershipdirectories.com
www.leadershipdirectories.com
Facebook, Twitter

David Hurvitz, CEO

Contact information for over 48,000 executives at over 1,000 companies and more than 9,000 board members and their outside affiliations.
Cost: $360.00
1,400 Pages
Frequency: Quarterly
ISSN: 1058-2098
Founded in 1969

14380 **Custom Publishing & News Services**
Information
7707 Old Georgetown Rd
Suite 700
Bethesda, MD 20814

301-215-4688; Fax: 301-215-4600
www.infoinc.com

Alain Carr, Owner

Offers evaluations of companies on their claims-paying ability.

14381 **Directory of Corporate Buyers**
Crain Communications Inc
360 N Michigan Ave
Chicago, IL 60601-3800

312-649-5200; Fax: 312-649-7937
www.crain.com

Keith Crain, CEO

Provides complete contact information for more that 3,200 top level corporate executives from Fortune 500 companies involved in risk management and employee benefits.
Frequency: Annual

14382 **Directory of Employee Assistance Program Providers**
Crain Communications Inc
360 N Michigan Ave
Chicago, IL 60601-3800

312-649-5200; Fax: 312-649-7937
www.crain.com

Keith Crain, CEO

Lists organizations that provide a variety of EAP services to employers on a direct, stand alone basis.
Frequency: Annual
Circulation: 50,000

14383 **Directory of Property Loss Control Consultants**
Crain Communications

360 N Michigan Ave
Chicago, IL 60601-3800

312-649-5200; Fax: 312-649-7937
www.crain.com

Keith Crain, CEO

Lists companies that provide loss control services on a direct, unbundled basis. Consultants that provide loss control assistance only in conjunction with other services such as brokering insurance are not listed.
Frequency: Annual
Circulation: 53,000

14384 Directory of Specialty Markets Issue

Insurance Journal
9191 Towne Centre Drive
Suite 550
San Diego, CA 92122-1231

619-584-1100; Fax: 619-584-1200

Mark Wells, Editor

Lists about 200 insurance companies and surplus lines brokers offering specialty lines to insurance agents and brokers in California, Arizona, Alaska, Oregon, Hawaii and Washington.
Cost: $10.00
Frequency: SemiAnnual
Circulation: 10,400

14385 HMO/PPO Directory

Grey House Publishing
4919 Route 22
PO Box 56
Amenia, NY 12501

518-789-8700
800-562-2139; Fax: 845-373-6390
books@greyhouse.com
www.greyhouse.com
Facebook, Twitter

Leslie Mackenzie, Publisher
Richard Gottlieb, Editor

The HMO/PPO Directory is a comprehensive source that provides detailed information about Health Maintenance Organizations and Preferred Provider Organizations nationwide. Within the HMO/PPO Profiles, over 1,300 HMOs, PPOs and affiliated companies are listed, arranged alphabetically by state.
Cost: $325.00
600 Pages
ISBN: 1-592373-69-0
Founded in 1981

14386 HMO/PPO Directory - Online Database

Grey House Publishing
4919 Route 22
PO Box 56
Amenia, NY 12501-0056

518-789-8700
800-562-2139; Fax: 518-789-0556
gold@greyhouse.com
gold.greyhouse.com
Facebook, Twitter

Leslie Mackenzie, Publisher
Richard Gottlieb, President

The HMO/PPO Directory - Online Database is your in-depth searchable guide to health plans nationwide - their contact information, key executives, plan information and more. The online database is a necessary tool when researching or marketing a product or service to this important industry.
Founded in 1981

14387 III Data Base Search

Insurance Information Institute
110 William St
New York, NY 10038-3908

212-346-5500; Fax: 212-732-1916
www.iii.org

Gary Johnson, Manager
Cary Schneider, Executive Vice President

Provides citations and abstracts of insurance-related literature appearing in magazines, newspapers and trade publications and books.

14388 III Insurance Daily

Insurance Information Institute
110 William St
New York, NY 10038-3908

212-346-5500; Fax: 212-732-1916
www.iii.org

Gary Johnson, Manager
Cary Schneider, Executive Vice President

This insurance database provides summaries of news and articles relating to the property and casualty insurance industry.
Frequency: Full-text

14389 IRU Members +

Intermediaries and Reinsurance Underwriters Assoc
971 Rte 202 North
Branchburg, NJ 08876

908-203-0211; Fax: 908-203-0213
info@irua.com
www.irua.com

Jim Brost, President

List of all member companies and contacts; conference and attendee list provided to attendees only.
Founded in 1967

14390 Independent Insurance

Independent Insurance Agents of America
127 S Peyton St
Alexandria, VA 22314-2803

703-683-4422
800-221-7917; Fax: 703-683-7556
info@iiaba.net
www.independentagent.com
Facebook, Twitter

Robert A Rusbuldt, CEO
Alex Soto, President

This web site contains information for consumers on property and casualty insurance including homeowner, renter, landlord, and automobile insurance.
Frequency: Full-text
Founded in 1896
Mailing list available for rent

14391 Insurance Almanac

Underwriter Printing & Publishing Company
244 North Main St.
P.O. Box 622
New City, NY 10956

845-634-2720; Fax: 845-634-2989
jgcrothers@criterionpub.com

Over 3,000 insurance companies that write fire, casualty, accident, health and life insurance policies.
650 Pages
Frequency: Annual
Circulation: 10,000

14392 Insurance Bar Directory

Bar List Publishing Company
425 Huehl Road
Building 6B
Northbrook, IL 60062-2323

847-498-6133
800-726-1007; Fax: 847-498-6695
info@barlist.com
www.barlist.com

Bruce Rodgers, President
Edna MacMillin, Editor
Leslie Rodgers, Production Manager

National Directory of Insurance Defense Attorneys that is distributed to all insurance company home office and branch office company executives and claims personnel.
Cost: $80.00
Frequency: Annual
Circulation: 40,000

14393 Insurance Companies' Directory List of Mortgage Directors

Communication Network International
3918 Avenue T
Brooklyn, NY 11234-5028

718-396-6245

Listing of 210 mortgage offices of major insurance companies that make real estate mortgages and related investments.
Cost: $75.00
Founded in 1993

14394 Kelly Casualty Insurance Claims Directory

Francis B Kelley & Associates
123 Veteran Avenue
Los Angeles, CA 90024-1900

800-328-4144; Fax: 310-472-1290
www.fbka.com

Francis B Kelley, Editor

Lists only casualty insurance claims payment offices. Workers' Compensation and Auto Insurance can pay health care providers for their services. Directory covers Casualty Insurance Companies, Independent Claims Companies, Insurance Commissioners with their Web sites.
Cost: $150.00
280 Pages
Frequency: Annual

14395 LEXIS Insurance Law Library

Mead Data Central
9443 Springboro Pike
Dayton, OH 45401

888-223-6337; Fax: 518-487-3584
www.lexis-nexis.com

Andrew Prozes, CEO
Rebecca Schmitt, Chief Financial Officer

This full database contains the complete text of the insurance statutes for 50 states, the District of Columbia and Puerto Rico.
Frequency: Full-text

14396 LOMA's Information Center Database

Life Office Management Association
2300 Windy Ridge Pkwy SE
Suite 600
Atlanta, GA 30339-5665

770-951-1770
800-275-5662; Fax: 770-984-0441
infoctr@loma.org
www.loma.org

Thomas P Donaldson, President/CEO
Jerry Woo, Director
Robert Lai, Managing Director

A team of experienced researchers provide current data utilizing our comprehensive database. More than 10,000 documents are maintained and updated. A comprehensive list of Industry Research Links can also be found in this area.
Frequency: Available to Members

14397 Life Insurance Selling: Sources Issue

Commerce Publishing Company

330 N 4th Street
Suite 200
Saint Louis, MO 63102-2041

314-421-5445; Fax: 314-421-1070

Larry Albright, Editor

Lists life insurance companies, publishers of software used in the insurance field and financial planning corporations.
Cost: $7.00
Frequency: 45000

14398 Life Office Management Association Directory
5770 Powers Ferry Road NW
Atlanta, GA 30327-4350

770-953-6872; Fax: 770-984-0441

Philippa Griffith, Editor

Offers information on life insurance and financial service companies.
190 Pages
Frequency: Annual

14399 Morningstar
Morningstar
225 W Washington Street
Chicago, IL 60602

312-384-4000; Fax: 312-696-6001
productinfo@morningstar.com
www.morningstar.com

Joe Mansueto, Chairman & CEO
Chris Boruff, President, Software Division
Peng Chen, President, Global Investment Div.
Bevin Desmond, President, International Operations
Scott Cooley, Chief Financial Officer

Morningstar provides data on approximately 330,000 investment offerings, including stocks, mutual funds, and similar vehicles, along with real-time global market data on more than 5 million equities, indexes, futures, options, commodities, and precious metals, in addition to foreign exchange and Treasury markets. Morningstar also offers investment management services and has more than $167 billion in assets under advisement and management.

14400 NAIC Database
National Association of Insurance Commissioners
1100 Walnut Street
Suite 1500
Kansas City, MO 64106-2197

816-842-3600; Fax: 816-783-8175
www.naic.org

Sandy Praeger, President
Andrew Beal, CEO
Kevin M. McCarty, President
James J. Donelon, President-Elect
Monica J. Lindeen, Secretary-Treasurer
Mailing list available for rent

14401 National Association of Catastrophe Adjusters Membership Directory
National Association of Catastrophe Adjusters
P.O. Box 499
Alvord, TX 76225

817-498-3466; Fax: 817-498-0480
naca@nacatadj.org
www.nacatadj.org

Chris Hatcher, President
Jon Joyce, Vice President
Jimmy Clark, Secretary/Treasurer
Founded in 1976

14402 National Insurance Law Service/Insource Insurance
NILS Publishing Company
PO Box 2507
Chatsworth, CA 91313-2507

818-998-8830
800-423-5910; Fax: 818-718-8482

Jon Fish, Circulation Director
Karen G Beaudoin, VP Marketing
Jonathon K Fish, Production Manager

This insurance database contains the complete text of insurance codes, related laws, regulations, bulletins and selected attorney general opinions for all 50 states and the federal government. Available on CD-ROm and in looseleaf print. The CD-ROM service 'Insource Insurance' is accessible for licensed users on the NILS Publishing Website.
Cost: $520.00
Frequency: Monthly Updates
Circulation: 5,000

14403 National Underwriter Kirschner's Insurance Directories (Red Book)
National Underwriter Company
5081 Olympic Blvd
Erlanger, KY 41018-3164

859-692-2100; Fax: 859-692-2295
www.nationalunderwriter.com

Charlie Smith, CEO
Charlie Smith, Chief Executive Officer

This series of 24 directories are published by state or region. Listings include companies, brokers and agents and services for each state handling property and casualty.
Cost: $19.95
150+ Pages
Frequency: Semi-Annual/Annual
Printed in on matte stock

14404 Profiles: Health Insurance Edition
National Underwriter Company
5081 Olympic Blvd
Erlanger, KY 41018-3164

859-692-2100
800-543-0874; Fax: 859-692-2295
www.nationalunderwriter.com

Charlie Smith, CEO

Your reliable resource for up-to-date news and information in the life & health insurance/financial services industry.
Cost: $39.95
300 Pages
Frequency: Annual

14405 Profiles: Property and Casualty Insurance Edition
National Underwriter Company
505 Gest Street
Cincinnati, OH 45203-1716

513-723-0012

Edward A Lyon, Editor

Offers information on more than 1,500 property and liability insurance companies.
Cost: $39.95
852 Pages
Frequency: Annual

14406 Register of North American Insurance Companies
American Preeminent Registry
PO Box 622
Old Bridge, NJ 08857-0622

732-225-5533

Brian Axelrod, Publisher

Directory of services and supplies to the industry.
Cost: $125.00
450 Pages
Frequency: Annual

14407 Risk Retention Group Directory and Guide
Insurance Communications
PO Box 50147
Pasadena, CA 91115-0147

626-796-4972; Fax: 626-796-4972
http://www.rrr.com

Karen Cutts, Editor

Offers information on over 80 risk retention groups formed under the 1986 Risk Retention Act or the 1981 Product Liability Risk Retention Act through 1990.
Cost: $165.00
144 Pages
Frequency: Annual

14408 Salem Press Online Platform
Grey House Publishing
4919 Route 22
PO Box 56
Amenia, NY 12501

800-221-1592; Fax: 201-968-0511
csr@salempress.com
online.salempress.com

The new Salem Press platform houses more than 500 titles including all of Salem's Health, Literature, History and Science titles in addition to select titles from the Grey House Publishing and H.W. Wilson product lines. Online access is free with each print purchase and includes an unlimited number of simultaneous users and remote access.

14409 Shortcut 2: Insurance Markets Tracking Systems
National Underwriter Company
505 Gest Street
Cincinnati, OH 45203-1716

513-723-0012

Directory of services and supplies to the industry.
Cost: $300.00

14410 Society of Professional Benefit Administrators
Society of Professional Benefit Administrators
2 Wisconsin Circle
Suite 670
Chevy Chase, MD 20815

301-718-7722; Fax: 301-718-9440
info@spbatpa.org
www.spbatpa.org

Anne Lennan, President

For members only. Discusses and analyzes government compliance requirements of administration and plan design and industry and market trends
300 Members
350 Attendees
Frequency: 2x/Year
Founded in 1975

14411 Statistics of Fraternal Benefit Societies
1240 Iroquois Avenue
Suite 300
Naperville, IL 60563-8476

630-355-6633; Fax: 630-355-0042

Anthony Snyder, Communications Director

NFCA membership is currently made up of 82 fraternal benefit societies in the United States and Canada. Each of these societies pay annual membership dues to belong to the organization and it is their executives, employees and grassroots members who serve on the NFCA Board of Directors and various NFCA committees and sections.
Cost: $11.00

14412 **TPA Directory**
Society of Professional Benefit Administrators
2 Wisconsin Circle
Suite 670
Chevy Chase, MD 20815
301-718-7722; Fax: 301-718-9440
info@spbatpa.org
www.spbatpa.org
Frederick D Hunt Jr, President
Anne C Lennan, President-Elect
Detailed description of contact information and types of plans and services and size of each firm in an easy-to-cross-reference and compare format.
Cost: $495.00
Mailing list available for rent

14413 **WESTLAW Insurance Library**
West Publishing Company
610 Opperman Drive
Eagan, MN 55123-1340
651-687-7327
www.westgroup.com
This database offers information on US state laws relating to the insurance industry.
Frequency: Full-text

14414 **Weiss Ratings Consumer Box Set**
Grey House Publishing
4919 Route 22
PO Box 56
Amenia, NY 12501
518-789-8700
800-562-2139; Fax: 845-373-6390
books@greyhouse.com
www.greyhouse.com
Facebook, Twitter
Leslie Mackenzie, Publisher
Richard Gottlieb, Editor
Each guide in the Weiss Ratings Consumer Box Set is packed with accurate, unbiased information, including helpful, step-by-step Worksheets & Planners. The set consists of Consumer Guides to Variable Annuities, Elder Care Choices, Medicare Supplement Insurance, Medicare Prescription Drug Coverage, Homeowners Insurance, Automobile Insurance, Long-Term Care Insurance, and Term Life Insurance.
Cost: $249.00
600 Pages
Frequency: Quarterly
Founded in 1981

14415 **Weiss Ratings Guide to Health Insurers**
Grey House Publishing
4919 Route 22
PO Box 56
Amenia, NY 12501
518-789-8700
800-562-2139; Fax: 845-373-6390
books@greyhouse.com
www.greyhouse.com
Facebook, Twitter
Leslie Mackenzie, Publisher
Richard Gottlieb, Editor
Weiss Ratings Guide to Health Insurers is the first and only source to cover the financial stability of the nation's health care system, rating the financial safety of more than 6,000 health maintenance organizations (HMOs) and all of the Blue Cross Blue Shield plans - updated quarterly to ensure the most accurate, up-to-date informations.
Cost: $249.00
600 Pages
Frequency: Quarterly
Founded in 1981

14416 **Weiss Ratings Guide to Life & Annuity Insurers**
Grey House Publishing
4919 Route 22
PO Box 56
Amenia, NY 12501
518-789-8700
800-562-2139; Fax: 845-373-6390
books@greyhouse.com
www.greyhouse.com
Facebook, Twitter
Leslie Mackenzie, Publisher
Richard Gottlieb, Edtior
Each easy-to-use edition provides independent, unbiased ratings on the financial strength of 1,000 life and annuity insurers, including companies providing life insurance, annuities, guaranteed investment contracts (GICs) and other pension products.
Cost: $249.00
600 Pages
Frequency: Quarterly
Founded in 1981

14417 **Weiss Ratings Guide to Property & Casualty Insurers**
Grey House Publishing
4919 Route 22
PO Box 56
Amenia, NY 12501
518-789-8700
800-562-2139; Fax: 845-373-6390
books@greyhouse.com
www.greyhouse.com
Facebook, Twitter
Leslie Mackenzie, Publisher
Richard Gottlieb, Editor
Updated quarterly, this publication is the only resource that provides independent, unbiased ratings and analyses on the 2,400 insurers offering auto & homeowners, business, worker's compensation, product liability, medical malpractice and other professional liability insurance in the United States.
Cost: $249.00
600 Pages
Frequency: Quarterly
Founded in 1981

14418 **Yearbook of the Insurance Industry**
American Association of Managing General Agents
150 S Warner Rd
Suite 156
King of Prussia, PA 19406-2832
610-225-1999; Fax: 610-225-1996
www.aamga.org
Bernie Heinz, Executive Director
250 managing general agents of insurance companies and more than 500 branch offices; coverage includes Canada.
Frequency: Annual Spring

Industry Web Sites

14419 **http://gold.greyhouse.com**
G.O.L.D Grey House OnLine Databases
Grey House Publishing's online database platform, GOLD, offers Quick Search, Keyword Search and Expert Search for most business sectors including insurance markets. The GOLD platform makes finding the information you need quick and easy - whether you're a novice searcher or an experienced database user. All of Grey House's directory products are available for subscription on the GOLD platform.

14420 **www.aaimco.com**
American Association of Insurance Management Consultants
Supports the insurance management industry.

14421 **www.aaimedicine.org**
American Academy of Insurance Medicine
This organization offers information and legislative updates for people in the medical insurance field.

14422 **www.actuary.org**
American Academy of Actuaries
The AAA is a public policy organization for actuaries within the US The Academy acts as the public information organization for the profession. Assisting public policy process through the presentation of clear actuarial analysis, the Academy regularly prepares testimony for Congress, provides information to federal elected officials, regulators and congressional staff, comments on proposed federal regulations, and works closely with state officials on issues related to insurance.

14423 **www.ahou.org**
Association of Home Office Underwriters
Association offering educational and professional resources for insurance and financial services professionals working as home office underwriters.

14424 **www.aicpcu.org**
Insurance Institute of America
Sponsors programs for property and casualty insurance firms, conducts exams and award certificates. Maintains a library.

14425 **www.allianceai.org**
Alliance of American Insurers
Trade association of property and casualty insurers providing educational, legislative and safety services to its members.

14426 **www.apiw.org**
Association of Professional Insurance Women
Promotes cooperation and understanding among members. Maintains high professional standards and provides a network of professional contacts. Encourages women in industry.

14427 **www.arminet.com**
Associated Risk Managers International
Develops specialized insurance/risk management services for trade associations, professional groups and other industry organizations. Conducts seminars and sponsors competitions.

14428 **www.ashrm.org**
American Society for Healthcare Risk Management
Facebook, Twitter, LinkedIn, YouTube
National organization for the health care industry risk management equipment, supplies and services.

14429 **www.asppa.org**
American Society of Pension Professionals & Act
(ASPPA) ia a national organization for career retirement paln professionals. The membership consists of the many disciplines supporting retirement income management and benefits policy. Its members are part of the diversified, technical, and highly regulated benefits industry. ASPPA represents those who have made a career of retirement plan and pension policy work.

14430 **www.ccactuaries.org**
Conference of Consulting Actuaries

Full-time consulting actuaries.

14431 www.easternclaimsconference.com
Eastern Claims Conference
Provides education and training to examiners, managers, and officers who review medical and disability claims. Holds seminars for life, health and disability clinics.

14432 www.financialpro.org
Society of Financial Service Professionals
Members are dedicated to the highest standards of competence and service in insurance and financial services.

14433 www.financialratingsseries.com
Grey House Publishing
Financial Ratings Series Online combines the strength of Weiss Ratings and TheStreet Ratings to offer the library community with a single source for financial strength ratings and financial planning tools covering Banks, Insurers, Mutual Funds and Stocks. This powerful database will provide the accurate, independent information consumers need to make informed decisions about their financial planning.

14434 www.fraternalalliance.org
American Fraternal Alliance
The trade association of America's fraternal benefit societies.

14435 www.greyhouse.com
Grey House Publishing
Authoritative reference directories for most business sectors including insurance markets. Users can search the online databases with varied search criteria allowing for custom searches by product category, geographic area, sales volume, keyword, subject and more. Full Grey House catalog and online ordering also available.

14436 www.highwaysafety.org
Insurance Institute for Highway Safety
Traffic and motor vehicle safety organization supported by auto insurers.

14437 www.icae.com
Insurance Consumer Affairs Exchange
Promotes professionalism and shapes the standards of behavior in relationships between insurance organizations, regulators and customers through proactive dialogue, research, communication and education.

14438 www.irua.org
Intermediaries & Reinsurance Underwriters Assoc
A not-for-profit corporation, organized for the purposes of reinsurance education and research and the dissemination of information relevant to the reinsurance industry.

14439 www.ivans.com
Insurance Value Added Network Services
Industry-sponsored organization offering value added data communications network linking agencies, companies and providers of data to the insurance industry.

14440 www.nacatadj.org
National Association of Catastrophe Adjusters
Association of Catstrophe Insurance Adjusters and independent adjustment companies.

14441 www.nafi.org
National Association of Fire Investigators
Primary purpose of this association is to increase the knowledge and improve the skills of persons engaged in the investigation and analysis of fires, explosions, or in the litigation that ensues from such investigations. The Association also originated and implemented the National Certification Board.

14442 www.nahu.org
National Association of Health Underwriters
Sponsors advanced health insurance underwriting and research seminars. Testifies before federal and state committees on pending health insurance legislation. Presents numerous awards.

14443 www.naiw.org
National Association of Insurance Women
Professional membership association for employees in all facets of the insurance industry. The association exists to promote continuing education and networking for the professional advancement of its members, and offers education programs, meetings, publications, services and leadership opportunities for its members' benefits.

14444 www.ncci.com
National Council on Compensation Insurance
Develops and administers rating plans and systems for workers compensation insurance.

14445 www.ncoil.org
National Conference of Insurance Legislators
NCOIL is an organization of state legislators whose main area of public policy concern is insurance legislation and regulation. Many legislators active in NCOIL either chair or are members of the committees responsible for insurance legislation in their respective state houses across the country.

14446 www.nonprofitrisk.org
Nonprofit Risk Management Center
Publishes materials and delivers workshops and conferences on risk management, liability and insurance issues of special concern to nonprofit organizations.

14447 www.plrb.org
Property Loss Research Bureau
Provides access to legal and technical databases, legal research on property and inland marine coverage issues countrywide, claims education, and daily catastrophe information for a membership of 570 property/casualty insurance companies.

14448 www.sirnet.org
Society of Insurance Research
Members are individuals actively engaged in some form of insurance research.

14449 www.snl.com
SNL Securities
News articles on banks and thrifts, insurance and other financial services. Also features vital company information.

14450 www.snlnet.com
SNL Securities
This organization offers the most up-to-date information available in the insurance industry featuring the latest news releases, filings and important events. Provides current data on top-performing stocks, insider trades, ownership filings, company news and events and legislative issues.

14451 www.soa.org
Society of Actuaries
Nonprofit professional society of 17,000 members involved in the modeling and management of financial risk and contingent events. The mission of the SOA is to advance actuarial knowledge and to enhance the ability of actuaries to provide expert advice and relevant solutions for financial, business and societal problems involving uncertain future events.

14452 www.spbatpa.org
Society of Professional Benefit Administrators
National Association of Third Party Administrators (TPAs) of employee benefit health and pension plans. SPBA represents TPAs who offer comprehensive services.

14453 www.thefederation.org
Federation of Insurance and Corporate Counsel
For members of the bar who are actively engaged in the legal aspects of the insurance business, executives of insurance companies and associations and corporate counsel engaged in the defense of claims.

14454 www.thepiaa.org
Physician Insurers Association
Represents domestic and international medical malpractice insurance companies which are practioner-owned or controlled.

14455 www.transportlaw.com
Transportation Consumer Protection Council
Dedicated to the reduction of transit losses and the improvement of freight claim and freight charge payment procedures in domestic and international commerce.

Associations

14456 **American Floorcovering Alliance**
210 West Cuyler Street
Dalton, GA 30720
706-278-4101
800-288-4101; Fax: 706-278-5323
afa@americanfloor.org
www.americanfloor.org
Facebook, RSS
Wanda J. Ellis, Executive Director
Promotes the industry's products and services to the world, and educates the members and others through seminars, press releases, and trade shows.
Founded in 1979

14457 **American Lighting Association**
2050 N Stemmons Freeway
Ste 10046
Dallas, TX 75207
214-698-9898
800-605-4448
www.americanlightingassoc.com
Facebook, YouTube
Ray S. Angelo, Chair
Eric Jacobson, CAE, President/CEO
W. Lawrence Lauck, Vice President, Communications
Michael Weems, Vice President, Government Affairs
Beth Bentley, CMP, LA, Director of Confrences
A trade association uniting lighting; component manufacturers, showrooms/distributors, manufacturer representatives; industry related companies dedicated to providing quality residential illumination in the U.S., Canada and the Caribbean.
700 Members
Founded in 1945

14458 **American Society of Interior Designers**
1152 15th St. NW
Suite 910
Washington, DC 20005
202-546-3480; Fax: 202-546-3240
membership@asid.org
www.asid.org
Facebook, Twitter, LinkedIn, Instagram, YouTube, Pinterest
Randy W. Fiser, Hon. FASID, Chief Executive Officer
Susan L. Wiggins, CAE, Hon. IDC, Chief Operating Officer
Susan Chung, PhD, Dir., Research & Knowledge Mgmt.
Laurie Enceneat, Dir., Marketing & Communications
Kerri L. McGovern, MPP, CAE, Dir., Membership
The American Society of Interior Designers (ASID) is a community of people-designers, industry representatives, educators and students committed to interior design. Through education, knowledge sharing, advocacy, community building and outreach, the Society strives to advance the interior design profession and, in the process, to demonstrate and celebrate the power of design to positively change people's lives.
34500 Members
Founded in 1975

14459 **Association of University Interior Design**
1652 Cross Center Drive
Norman, OK 73019-5050
FAX 405-325-4164
www.auid.org
Debra Barresse, President
Sara Powell, First VP
Debi Miller, Second VP
Susan Carlyle, Secretary
Lisa Kring, Treasurer
Provides a network for individuals who work within institutions of higher education and to promote activities designed to benefit its members through education, research, and communication.
Founded in 1979

14460 **Association of the Wall and Ceiling Industry**
513 West Broad Street
Suite 210
Falls Church, VA 22046
703-538-1600; Fax: 703-534-8307
info@awci.org
www.awci.org
Facebook, Twitter, LinkedIn, YouTube
Michael Stark, Chief Executive Officer
Brenton Stone, Associate Publisher & Sr. Director
Karen Bilak, Dir., Convention & Conferences
Laura Porinchak, Communications Director
Chris Williams, Director, Membership
Represents acoustic systems, ceiling systems, drywall systems, exterior insulation and finishing systms, fireproofing, flooring systems, insulation, and stucco contractors, suppliers and manufacturers and those in allied trades.
2400 Members
Founded in 1918
Mailing list available for rent

14461 **Carpet Cushion Council**
5103 Brandywine Drive
Eagleville, PA 19043
484-687-5170; Fax: 610-885-5131
www.carpetcushion.org
Chris Bradley, President
Gary Lanser, Vice President
Bob Ambrose, Secretary
Mark Vitale, Treasurer
G. William Haines, Executive Director
Encourages distribution and use of seperate carpet cushions. Works with regulatory agencies at the national, state and local levels.
33 Members
Founded in 1976

14462 **Carpet and Rug Institute**
100 South Hamilton Street
P.O. Box 2048
Dalton, GA 30720
706-278-3176; Fax: 706-278-8835
www.carpet-rug.org
Facebook, Twitter, LinkedIn, YouTube, Google+
Jim Jolly, CEO
Georgina Sikorski, Executive Director
Werner Braun, President
CRI is a nonprofit trade association representing the manufacturers of more than 95 percent of all carpet made in the United States, as well as service providers and their suppliers.To help increase consumers' satisfaction with carpet and to show them how carpet creates a better environment, they coordinate with other segments of the industry, such as installers, distributors, and retailers.
115 Members
Founded in 1969

14463 **Certified Interior Decorators International, Inc.**
649 SE Central Pkwy.
Stuart, FL 34994
772-287-1855
800-624-0093; Fax: 772-287-0398
www.cidinternational.org
Facebook, Twitter, LinkedIn
Ron Renner, President
Worldwide certifying body and professional association for interior decorators.

14464 **Council for Interior Design Accreditation**
206 Grandville Avenue
Suite 350
Grand Rapids, MI 49503-4014
616-458-0400; Fax: 616-458-0460
info@accredit-id.org
www.accredit-id.org
Facebook
Pamela K. Evans, Ph.D., FIDEC, Chair
Jan Johnson, FIIDA, Industry Rep. Secretary-Treasurer
Holly Mattson, Executive Director
Laura Hozeska, Office Manager
Stacy I. Peck, Director of Public Relations
Leads the interior design profession to excellence by setting standards and accrediting academic programs.
135 Members
Founded in 1970

14465 **Custom Electronic Design & Installation Association**
7150 Winton Drive
Suite 300
Indianapolis, IN 46268
317-328-4336
800-669-5329; Fax: 317-735-4012
info@cedia.org
www.cedia.net
Facebook, Twitter, RSS
Larry Pexton, Chairman
Dennis Erskine, Chairman Elect
David Humphries, Treasurer
Richard Millson, Secretary
Vin Bruno, CEO
The Custom Electronic Design & Installation Association (CEDIA) is an international trade association of companies that specialize in planning and installing electronic systems for the home. CEDIA provides educational conferences, industry professional training, and certification focused on the installation and integration of residential electronic systems that consumers use to enhance their lifestyles.
3,500 Members
Mailing list available for rent

14466 **Designer Society of America**
866-721-7857
support@dsasociety.org
www.dsasociety.org
Natasha Lima Younts, CEO
The Society offers networking and showcasing opportunities for practicing designers.

14467 **Foundation for Design Integrity**
1950 N Main Street
Suite 139
Salinas, CA 93906
650-326-1867; Fax: 408-449-7040
www.ffdi.org
Justin Binnix, President
Eleanor McKay, Chairman
Susan E. Farley, Esquire
Promotes original design and to fight the unethical and illegal practice of manufacturing

knockoffs. Honors those who conceive, design, engineer and develop innovative new products for the Interior and Architectural Design Community and their clients.
150+ Members
Founded in 1994

14468 **Home Fashion Products Association**
355 Lexington Ave.
15th Fl.
New York, NY 10017
212-297-2122
www.homefashionproducts.com
Association for the promotion of manufacturers of bedding, window, floor and wall coverings, kitchen textiles and allied home fashion products.
Founded in 1996

14469 **Illuminating Engineering Society**
120 Wall St
17th Floor
New York, NY 10005-4001
212-248-5000; Fax: 212-248-5017
ies@ies.org
www.iesna.org
Daniel Salinas, President
Clayton Gordon, Marketing Manager
William Hanley, Executive Vice President
Calyton Gordon, Marketing Manager
Nick Bleeker, Treasurer
To advance knowledge and disseminate information for the improvement of the lighted environment to the benefit of society. Publishes a monthly magazine.
8500 Members
Founded in 1906

14470 **Institute of Inspection Cleaning and Restoration Certification**
4317 NE Thurston Way
Ste 200
Vancouver, WA 98662
360-693-5675
800-835-4624; Fax: 360-693-4858
info@iicrc.org
www.iicrc.org
Facebook, Twitter, LinkedIn, Google+
Patrick Winters, President & CEO
Hank Unck, 1st Vice President
Pete Duncanson, 2nd Vice President
Norm Maia, Treasurer
Kevin Pearson, Secretary
Sets standards of skill and ethics in fabric restoration industry. Works with regulatory bodies to develop proficiency standards and issues certification.
1.6M Members
Founded in 1972

14471 **Interior Design Educators Council**
One Parkview Plaza
Suite 800
Oakbrook Terrace, IL 60181
630-544-5057; Fax: 317-280-8527
info@idec.org
www.idec.org
Facebook, Twitter, LinkedIn, YouTube, Google+, Yahoo, Flick
Lori Barker-Cummings, Executive Director
Toni Wilkerson, Coordinator
Kirsten Lew, Associate Account Executive
Darrell McCook, Events Manager
Dedicated to the advancement of education and research in interior design. IDEC fosters exchange of information, improvement of educational standards, and development of the body of knowledge relative to the quality of life and human performance in the interior environment.
Founded in 1963

14472 **Interior Design Society**
164 S. Main St.
Suite 404
High Point, NC 27260
336-884-4437; Fax: 336-885-3291
info@interiordesignsociety.org
www.interiordesignsociety.org
Facebook, Twitter, LinkedIn, YouTube, Blogspot, Instagram,
Bruce Knott, President
Anna Mavrakis, Past President
Jan Cregier, Vice President
Kimberly Joi McDonald, Treasurer/Secretary
Snoa Garrigan, Executive Director
The largest design organization exclusively dedicated to serving the residential interior design industry. Promote retail interior design, emphasizing education and skills improvement.
2500 Members
Founded in 1973

14473 **International Federation of Interior Archi tects/Designers**
708 3rd Ave.
6th Floor
New York, NY 10017
212-884-6275; Fax: 212-884-6247
staff@ifiworld.org
www.ifiworld.org
Facebook, Twitter, LinkedIn
Shashi Caan, Chief Executive Officer
The only international federating body for Interior Architecture/Design organizations. Connects the international community to further the knowledge, impact, influence, and application of the design of interiors, promote global social responsibility, and raise the status of the profession worldwide.
Founded in 1963

14474 **International Feng Shui Guild**
705-B SE Melody Ln.
Suite 166
Lees Summit, MO 64063
816-246-1898
office@ifsguild.org
www.ifsguild.org
Laura Morris, Chair
Deb Dermyer-Lamb, Interim CEO
Professional organization for Feng Shui consultants of all perspectives.

14475 **International Furnishings and Design Association**
610 Freedom Business Center
Suite 110
King of Prussia, PA 19406
610-992-0011; Fax: 610-992-0021
info@ifda.com
www.ifda.com
Facebook, Twitter, LinkedIn
Diane Nicolson, FIFDA, President
Linda Kulla, FIFDA, Treasurer
Jennifer Jones, MPA, Executive Director
Diane Fairburn, Immediate Past President
Athena Charis, Immediate Past Treasurer
The only all-industry association whose members provide services and products to the furnishings and design industry. IFDA is the driving force, through its programs and services, to enhance the professionalism and strature of the industry worlwide.
1400 Members
Founded in 1947

14476 **International Interior Design Association**
111 E. Wacker Dr.
Suite 222
Chicago, IL 60601
312-467-1950
888-799-4432
+01-312-467-1950
iidahq@iida.org
www.iida.org
Facebook, Twitter, LinkedIn, Instagram
Cheryl Durst, Executive VP & CEO
Lisa Taylor, Director, Finance
Lauren Haras, Director, Marketing & Communication
Monae Redmond, Director, Member Services
Tracey Thomas, Director, Strategic Sales
Association that provides its members with sources, knowledge, and contacts necessary in the interior design field.

14477 **Museum Store Association**
2025 M Street NW
Suite 800
Washington, DC 20036
202-367-1106; Fax: 202-367-2104
info@museumstoreassociation.org
www.museumstoreassociation.org
Facebook, Twitter, LinkedIn, Pinterest
Steven Antolick, Executive Director
2500 Members
Founded in 1955

14478 **National Association of Decorative Fabric Distributors**
One Windsor Cove
Suite 305
Columbia, SC 29223
800-445-8629; Fax: 803-765-0860
info@nadfd.com
www.nadfd.com
Ted Sargetakis, President
Debbye Lustig, Vice President, Membership Chair
Frank Governal, 1st Vice Presiden
Dee Duncan, Director
Kathy Gowdy, Secreatry-Treasurer
Comprised of the leading fabric distributors who reach the reupholsterers, made to order drapery and home decorator markets, and more than fifty of their major suppliers, fabric mills, fabric finishers, manufacturers of upholstery and drapery supplies.
75 Members
Founded in 1968

14479 **National Council for Interior Design Qualification, Inc.**
1602 L Street, NW
Suite 200
Washington, DC 20036-5681
202-721-0220; Fax: 202-721-0221
inquiries@ncidqexam.org
www.ncidq.org
Facebook, Twitter, LinkedIn, Pinterest
Laurie McRae, President
David Hanson, President Elect
Victoria Horobin, Past President
Carol Williams-Nickelson, Executive Director
Lola Liao, Director of Finance & Admin.
Serves to identify to the public those interior designers who have met the minimum standards for professional practice by passing the NCIDQ examination in addition to protecting the public by identifying those individuals who are competent to practice interior design.
10000 Members
Founded in 1974

14480 National Guild of Professional Paperhangers, Inc.
136 S Keowee Street
Dayton, OH 45402
937-222-6477
800-254-6477; Fax: 937-222-5794
ngpp@ngpp.org
www.ngpp.org
Facebook, Twitter, LinkedIn
Kimberly Fantaci, Executive Director
Bob Banker, Secretary
Cyndi Green, President
Carl Bergaman, Treasurer
Vincent LaRusso, Vice President
Promotes products, upgrades skills of paperhangers and encourages good business ethics. Holds workshops and seminars.
650 Members
Founded in 1974

14481 National Home Furnishings Association
3910 Tinsley Drive
Suite 101
High Point, NC 27265-3610
336-886-6100
800-422-3778; Fax: 916-784-7697
info@nhfa.org
www.nhfa.org
Facebook, Twitter, LinkedIn, YouTube
Rick Howard, Chairman
Marty Cramer, President
Jeff Child, President Elect
Steve Kidder, Vice President
Jim Fee, Secretary/Treasurer
The nation's largest organization devoted specifically to the needs and interests of home furnishings retailers. Also to provide members with the information, education, products and services they need to remain successful.
2800 Members
Founded in 2013

14482 National Ice Cream Retailers Association
743 Spirit 40 Park Dr.
Suite 121
Chesterfield, MO 63005
636-778-1822
866-303-6960; Fax: 636-898-4326
info@nicra.org
www.nicra.org
Facebook
Steve Christensen, Executive Director
Members are in retail frozen dessert businesses. Some offer food services either full of limited and some operate convenience stores. The common denominator is that all members offer frozen desserts for take home or on site consumption.
350 Members
Founded in 1933

14483 North American Association of Floor Covering Distributors
330 N Wabash Avenue
Suite 2000
Chicago, IL 60611
312-321-6836
800-383-3091; Fax: 312-673-6962
info@nafcd.org
www.nafcd.org
LinkedIn, YouTube
Kevin Gammonley, Executive Director
Elaura Dunning, Operations Coordinator
Lauren Willett, Marketing Manager
Robb Shrader, Sales Coordinator
Lindsey Kallai, Conference Manager
The North American Association of Floor Covering Distributors (NAFCD) was organized to foster trade and commerce for those having a business, financial or professional interest as wholesale distributors or manufacturers of floor coverings and allied products.

14484 Paint and Decorating Retailers Association
1401 Triad Center Drive
St Peters, MO 63376
636-326-2636
800-737-0107; Fax: 636-229-4750
info@pdra.org
www.pdra.org
Facebook, Twitter, LinkedIn
Phil Merlo, President
Bahia Taylor, VP
Craig Bond, Treasurer
Jeff Baggaley, Past President
Dan Simon, Executive Vice President/Publisher
PDRA serves the independent dealer through education, membership benefits and trade shows. The Board of Director's initiative to bring top-quality, efficient education to all independent dealers has resulted in development of a new online seminar. The PDRA Coatings Specialist course eliminates the time and expense of traveling to a seminar site. This new course can be taken right in the store, during slow times or at the dealer's convenience.
1500 Members
Founded in 1947

14485 Painting Contractors Association
2316 Millpark Drive
Maryland Heights, MO 63043
314-514-7322
800-332-7322; Fax: 314-890-2068
bhoran@pdca.org
www.pcapainted.org
Facebook, Twitter, LinkedIn, YouTube
Nigel Costolloe, Executive Director
Chad Schirmerÿ, Creative Director
Marsha Bass, Operations Manager
Marcie Haselden, Member Experience Manager
Andrew Couch, Content Production Specialist
PDCA exists to lead the industry by providing quality products, programs, services, and opportunities essential to the success of our members.
5M Members
Founded in 1884
Mailing list available for rent

14486 Professional Picture Framers Association
2282 Springport Road
Suite F
Jackson, MI 49202
517-788-8100
800-762-9287; Fax: 517-788-8371
info@ppfa.com
www.ppfa.com
Facebook, Twitter, LinkedIn
John Pruitt, President
Elaine Truman, Administrative
Jeff Frazine, Trade Exhibit Sales
Nick Shaver, Membership
Sheila Pursglove, FMQ
An international trade association for the art and framing industry. Supporting a membership of custom picture framers, art galleries, manufacturers, and distibutors.
3000+ Members
Founded in 1971

14487 Retail Design Institute
126A West 14th St.
2nd Floor
Cincinnati, OH 45202
513-751-5815
www.retaildesigninstitute.org
Facebook, Twitter, LinkedIn, YouTube, Flickr
Ray Ehscheid, RDI, International President
Promotes the advancement and collaborative practice of creating selling environments. A community of the retail industry's creative professionals who share ideas, knowledge, and passion. Members include graphic designers, lighting designers, interior designs, store planners, visual merchandisers, resource designers, brand strategists, educators, trade partners, editors and publishers, and students.

14488 Society of Glass & Ceramic Decorated Products
PO Box 2489
Zanesville, OH 43702
740-588-9882; Fax: 740-588-0245
sgcd@sgcd.org
www.sgcd.org
Mark Kelly, President
Walter Lumley, VP
Nancy Klinefelter, Secretary/Treasurer
Provides decorating professionals with a competitive edge in business by providing opporotunities for networking to learn about new decorating technologies and techniques.
525 Members

14489 The One Club For Creativity
450 W. 31st St.
6th Floor
New York, NY 10001
212-979-1900; Fax: 212-979-5006
info@oneclub.org
www.oneclub.org
Facebook, Twitter, LinkedIn, Instagram, YouTube
Kevin Swanepoel, Chief Executive Officer
Yash Egami, VP, Content & Marketing
Lucila Lopez Travez, Director of Events & Membership
Jovanne Jerome, Inclusion & Diversity Coordinator
Crystal Ray, Financial Controller
A non-profit organization that supports and celebrates the success of the global creative community. Stimulates the intersection of art and commerce, and creates spaces for artists to grow.

14490 Window Coverings Association of America
P.O. Box 731
Wake Forest, NC 27588
919-263-9850
888-298-9222; Fax: 919-426-2047
www.wcaa.org
Facebook, LinkedIn, YouTube, Google+
Michele Williams, President
Julie A. Wood, VP
Sandra VanSickle, Treasurer
Ronica VanGelder, Secretary
Linda Principe, Past President
The only national non-profit trade association dedicated to the retail window covering industry and to the dealers, decorators, and workrooms that are our members.
1200 Members
Founded in 1987

Newsletters

14491 Architectural Lighting
1515 Broadway
34th Floor
New York, NY 10036-8901
212-360-0660
847-763-9050; Fax: 646-654-4484

archl@halldata.com
www.archlighting.com

Gary Gyss, Group Publisher
Emilie Worth Sommerhoff, Editor-in-Chief
Elizabeth Donoff, Managing Editor
Carolyn Cunningham, Brand Manager
Cliff Smith, Sales Manager

Showcases the application of lighting in architectural and interior design applications.
Circulation: 25,000
Founded in 1964

14492 Installer
National Guild of Professional Paperhangers
136 S Keowee Street
Dayton, OH 45402

937-222-6477
800-254-6477; Fax: 937-222-5794
ngpp@ngpp.org
www.ngpp.org

Elsie Kaptetna CP, President
Phil Curtis CP, First VP
Vincent Larusso CP, Second VP

Promotes products, upgrades skills of paperhangers and encourages good business ethics.
Frequency: Bimonthly
Circulation: 900

14493 Mirror News
Market Power
103 2nd Street N
Hopkins, MN 55343-9276

feedback@mirror.co.uk
www.mirror.co.uk

Wil Tiller, Publisher
Paul Hodd, Head of Digital

Offers interior design news and developments for professionals in the industry.
Cost: $16.00
24 Pages
Frequency: Monthly

14494 National Guild of Professional Paperhangers
136 S Keowee Street
Dayton, OH 45402

937-222-6477
800-254-6477; Fax: 937-222-5794
www.ngpp.org

Kim Fantaci, Executive VP
Joseph Parker, President

Accepts advertising.
16 Pages
Founded in 1974

14495 NewsFash
American Society of Interior Designers
608 Massachusetts Avenue NE
Washington, DC 20002-6006

202-546-3480; Fax: 202-546-3240
asid@asid.org

Julie Warren, Editor
Jennifer Lipner, Associate Editor
Rick McCosh, Director of Chapter Services
Thom Banks, COO
Rick Peluso, CFO

Bi-weekly newsletter published by the American Society of Interior Designers (ASID) that provides need-to-know design and Society news delivered biweekly. Through education, knowledge sharing, advocacy, community building and outreach, the Society strives to advance the interior design profession and, in the process, to demonstrate and celebrate the power of design to positively chang
Frequency: Bi-Weekly
Founded in 1975
Mailing list available for rent

Magazines & Journals

14496 ASID ICON
American Society of Interior Designers
608 Massachusetts Avenue NE
Washington, DC 20002-6006

202-546-3480; Fax: 202-546-3240
asid@asid.org

Julie Warren, Editor
Jennifer Lipner, Associate Editor
Rick McCosh, Director of Chapter Services
Thom Banks, COO
Rick Peluso, CFO

ASID ICON, the magazine of the American Society of Interior Designers/ASID, provides readers with success strategies bi-monthly. ASID is a community of people-designers, industry representatives, educators and students committed to interior design. Through education, knowledge sharing, advocacy, community building and outreach, the Society strives to advance the interior design profession and, in the process, to demonstrate and celebrate the power of design to positively change people's lives.
Frequency: Monthly
Circulation: 40,000
Founded in 1975
Mailing list available for rent

14497 Better Homes and Gardens
Meredith Corporation
1716 Locust St
Des Moines, IA 50309-3023

515-284-3000
800-678-8091; Fax: 515-284-3371
shareholderhelp@meredith.com
www.meredith.com

Stephen M Lacy, CEO
Daniel M. Lagani, V.P./Publisher
Karol DeWulf Nickell, Editor in Chief

Ideas and how-to information on both new and remodeled kitchen and bath.
Cost: $11.00
Frequency: Monthly
Circulation: 7.6 mill
Founded in 1902

14498 Country Home Product Guide
Meredith Corporation
1716 Locust St
Des Moines, IA 50309-3023

515-284-2015; Fax: 515-284-3684
shareholderhelp@meredith.com
www.meredith.com

David Kahn, Publisher

Offers information on residential projects focusing on innovative design work for homes with a country motif.
Frequency: Monthly

14499 Decor
Pfingsten Publishing
330 N 5th Street
Saint Louis, MO 63102-2036

314-421-5445
800-867-9285; Fax: 314-421-1070
www.decormagazine.com

Gary S Goldman, Publisher
Alice C Gibson, Editor

In the business of furnishing helpful information, education, and marketing services that will assist art and framing retailers, distributors, and wholesalers in the manufacture and sale of their products and services, and in the successful management of their business. Every article of Decor must give art and framing retailers helpful information that they can use to make their business stronger.
Cost: $20.00
Frequency: 13 per year
Circulation: 27,000

14500 Design Solutions Magazine
Architectural Woodwork Institute
46179 Westlake Drive
Suite 120
Potomac Falls, VA 20165-5874

571-323-3636; Fax: 571-323-3630
www.awinet.org

David Ritchey, Editor
Judith Durham, Executive VP
Matthew Lundahl, President
Randy Jensen, Vice President
Bruce Spitz, Treasurer

Covers new commercial construction, as well as renovation. Updates on doors, paneling, laminatem plywood, architectural hardware and finishes.
Cost: $25.00
Frequency: Quarterly
Circulation: 25000
Mailing list available for rent

14501 Designers West
Designers World Corporation
8914 Santa Monica Boulevard
Los Angeles, CA 90069-4902

213-748-8291; Fax: 213-748-0039

Carol Soucek King, Editor
Rafael Nadal, President

For interior designers, architects and other design professionals involved in residential, office and hospitality projects. Accepts advertising.
Cost: $30.00
120 Pages
Frequency: Monthly
Founded in 1953

14502 Designing with Tile and Stone
Tile & Stone
20 Beekman Pl
20th Floor
New York, NY 10022-8043

212-929-0500; Fax: 212-376-7723
www.ashlee.com

Michelle Tillou, Owner

Articles on design, selection, installation and maintenance.
Frequency: Quarterly
Circulation: 12000

14503 Donna Dewberry's One-Day Decorating
F+W Media
38 E. 29th Street
New York, NY 10016

212-447-1400; Fax: 212-447-5231
contact_us@fwmedia.com
Facebook, Twitter, LinkedIn

Colleen Cannon, Publisher
David Nussbaum, CEO
Jim Ogle, Chief Financial Officer
Chad Phelps, Chief Digital Officer
Stacie Berger, Communications Director

A how-to magazine for decorative painters, crafters, and do-it-yourself home decorators. Its goal is to inspire anyone interested in embellishing their home, and it features easy-to-complete, step-by-step project ideas using decorative painting, stamping, faux finishing, stenciling, and other crafting techniques.
Cost: $27.00
76 Pages
Frequency: Monthly
Circulation: 100000
Founded in 1945
Mailing list available for rent

14504 Eye on Design
American Society of Interior Designers
608 Massachusetts Avenue NE
Washington, DC 20002-6006

202-546-3480; Fax: 202-546-3240
asid@asid.org

Julie Warren, Editor
Jennifer Lipner, Associate Editor
Rick McCosh, Director of Chapter Services
Thom Banks, COO
Rick Peluso, CFO

Eye on Design, provided by the American Society of Interior Designers\ASID, focuses on industry news and developments and is delivered electronically on a weekly basis. Through education, knowledge sharing, advocacy, community building and outreach, the Society strives to advance the interior design profession and, in the process, to demonstrate and celebrate the power of design to positively change people's lives.
Founded in 1975
Mailing list available for rent

14505 Facilities Design & Management
1515 Broadway
34th Floor
New York, NY 10036-8901

212-840-0595
800-950-1314; Fax: 212-302-6273

Anne Fallucchi, Editor-in-Chief

Covers all aspects of the planning, design and management of facilities for corporate offices and related facilities, health care, government, hospitality and education.
Frequency: Monthly

14506 Flora-Line
Berry Hill Press
7336 Berry Hill Drive
Palos Verdes Estates, CA 90275-4404

310-377-7040

Dody Lyness, Editor

Targeted to the home-based business person engaged in dried floral design. Its format keeps readers abreast of the floral trends in herbal growing and the most modern techniques for drying and designing with flowering herbs. Accepts advertising.
Cost: $16.95
20 Pages
Frequency: Quarterly
Circulation: 1,000
Founded in 1981

14507 Furniture Style
400 Knightsbridge Parkway
Lincolnshire, IL 60069-3613

847-634-4339
800-621-2845; Fax: 847-634-4379
info@vancepublishing.com
www.vancepublishing.com

Michael R Reckling, Publisher
Judy Riggs, Director
Steve Chair, Marketing Manager
Douglas A. Riemer, Circulation Manager
William C Vance, Chairman
Cost: $49.95
Frequency: Monthly
Circulation: 25000
Founded in 1937

14508 HOW Design Ideas at Work
F&W Publications
4700 E Galbraith Rd
Cincinnati, OH 45236-2726

513-531-2690
800-333-1115; Fax: 513-531-1843
editorial@howdesign.com

David Nussbaum, CEO
Bryn Mooth, Chief Financial Officer
Jim Ogle, Chief Financial Officer
Kate Rados, Marketing Director
Stacie Berger, Communications Director

HOW reaches visual communicators, including art directors, graphic designers, type designers, typographers, illustrators, advertising and sales promotion managers, and other design-minded executives; also manufacturers and suppliers of graphic arts products and services.
Cost: $29.96
194 Pages
Frequency: Monthly
Circulation: 39946
ISSN: 0886-0483
Founded in 1990
Printed in 4 colors on glossy stock

14509 Home Furnishings Executive
305 W High Ave
Suite 400
High Point, NC 27260-4950

336-885-6981
800-888-9590; Fax: 336-885-4424

14510 Home Lighting & Accessories
Doctorow Communications
1011 Clifton Ave
Clifton, NJ 07013-3518

973-779-1600; Fax: 973-779-3242
www.homelighting.com

Jeffrey Doctorow, President
Cost: $15.00
Frequency: Monthly
Founded in 1953

14511 Homeworld Business
45 Research Way
Suite 106
East Setauket, NY 11733

631-246-9300; Fax: 631-246-9496
www.homeworldbusiness.com

Ian Gittlitz, Publisher/Editor-in-Chief
Peter Giannetti, Editor
Bill McLoughlin, Executive Editor
Peter Chamberlin, Circulation Manager
Hope Rosenzweig, Classified Advertising
Cost: $185.00

14512 House Beautiful
959 8th Ave
New York, NY 10019-3737

212-649-2098; Fax: 212-765-3528
www.housebeautiful.com

Kate Kelly Smith, Publisher
Victor F Ganzi, CEO
Bruce Paisner, VP
Michael A Hurley, Marketing Director
Cost: $19.97
Frequency: Monthly
Circulation: 854627
Founded in 1887

14513 Interior Design
Reed Business Information
360 Park Avenue South
17th floor
New York, NY 10010

212-772-8300; Fax: 630-288-8686
custserv@espcomp.com
www.reedbusiness.com
Facebook, Twitter, LinkedIn, RSS

Lawrence S Reed
Woody Goldfien, Owner
Jim Casella, CEO

Offers information on quality residential and contract design work. Recent issues include corporate offices, remodeling/restoration, kitchen and bath design, health care and hospitality.
Cost: $64.95
250 Pages
Frequency: Monthly
Circulation: 59,000
Founded in 1932
Printed in 4 colors on glossy stock

14514 Interiors and Sources
840 US Highway 1
Suite 330
North Pal Beach, FL 33408

561-627-3393; Fax: 561-694-6578
www.isdesignet.com

Robert Nieminen, Editor
Guy De Silva, Publisher
Charlotte Vann, Circulation Manager
Adam Moore, Managing Editor

Offers national commercial and residential design work articles. Emphasizes design solutions and focuses on challenges encountered by designers.
Cost: $27.00
Frequency: Monthly
Circulation: 28,000
Founded in 1990

14515 Kitchen & Bath Design News
Cygnus Publishing
PO Box 803
Fort Atkinson, WI 53538-0803

920-000-1111; Fax: 920-563-1699

John French, CEO
Eliot Sefrin, Director of Public Relations
Kathy Scott, Director of Public Relations
Paul Bonaiuto, CFO

Offers articles for kitchen and bath dealers, interior designers and architects.
Frequency: Monthly
Circulation: 50000
Founded in 1966

14516 Laminating Design & Technology
Cygnus Publishing
PO Box 803
Fort Atkinson, WI 53538-0803

920-000-1111; Fax: 920-563-1699

John French, CEO
Rich Reiff, Director of Public Relations
Kathy Scott, Director of Public Relations
Paul Bonaiuto, CFO

Global design and color trends, as well as surfacing solutions for furniture architecture and interior design. Focuses on surface design, performance and application.
Cost: $30.00
44 Pages
Frequency: Monthly
Circulation: 40006
Founded in 1937

14517 Lighting Dimensions
Primedia
PO Box 12901
Shawnee Mission, KS 66282-2901

913-341-1300; Fax: 913-514-6895

Eric Jacobson, Senior VP
David Barbour, Editorial Director
Cost: $34.97
Frequency: Monthly

14518 Metropolis
Bellerophon Publications
61 W 23rd St
23rd Street
New York, NY 10010-4246

212-627-9977
800-344-3046; Fax: 212-627-9988

info@metropolismag.com
www.metropolismag.com

Horace Havemeyer, Publisher
Susan S Szenasy, Editor-in-Chief
Denise Csaky, Marketing Director
Tamara Costa, Advertising Manager
Peter Sangiorgio, Circulation Controller

The only magazine that covers all facets of design: architecture, interiors, furniture, preservation, urban design, graphics and crafts.
Cost: $32.95
Circulation: 54000
Founded in 1980

14519 Michaels Create!
F+W Media
38 E. 29th Streett
New York, NY 10016

212-447-1400; Fax: 212-447-5231
contact_us@fwmedia.com

Debbie Knauer, Publisher
Jane Beard, Editor

Features contemporary designs reflecting the latest trends with clear instructions. The home decorating, fashion, and gift ideas will inspire experienced crafters as well as seasonal crafters to explore new possibilities. Step-by-step instructions, tips, and techniques will engage crafters of all ages - including kids - with the creative skills of crafting to be enjoyed as a year-round activity.
Cost: $21.97
116 Pages
Frequency: Monthly
Circulation: 24991
Founded in 1952

14520 Midwest Retailer
8528 Columbus Ave S
Bloomington, MN 55420-2460

952-854-7610; Fax: 952-854-6460

Joan Thomasberg, Owner
Cost: $10.00
38588 Pages
Circulation: 5000
Founded in 1972
Printed in 2 colors on newsprint stock

14521 NHFA Trade Show
National Home Furnishings Association
3910 Tinsley Drive
Suite 101
Highpoint, NC 27265-3610

336-886-6100
800-888-9590; Fax: 336-801-6102
info@nhfa.org
www.nhfa.org

Steve DeHaan, Executive VP
Karin Mayfield, Senior Director for Membership
Frequency: Annual

14522 National Floor Trends
Business News Publishing Company
22801 Ventura Blvd
Suite 113
Woodland Hills, CA 91364-1230

818-224-8035; Fax: 818-224-8042
privacy@BNPMedia.com
www.bnpmedia.com

Phil Johnson, Publisher
Rick Arvidson, Director

For interior designers.
Frequency: Monthly
Founded in 1952

14523 Paint & Decorating Retailer Magazine
Paint and Decorating Retailers Association
1401 Triad Center Dr
St. Peters, MO 63376-7353

636-326-2636
800-737-0107; Fax: 636-229-4750
info@pdra.org
www.pdra.org

Dan Simon, Executive VP/Publisher
Tina Sullivan, Dir Membership/Education/Tradeshows
Diane Capuano, Managing Editor
Renee Nolte, Director, Finance/Human Resources
Tony Sarantakis, Account Executive

Monthly trade magazine dedicated to the informational needs of paint and decorating store owners, managers and employees.
1500 Members
Frequency: Annual May
Circulation: 26,000+
Founded in 1947

14524 Panel World
Hatton-Brown Publishers
225 Hanrick Street
PO Box 2268
Montgomery, AL 36102

334-834-1170; Fax: 334-834-4525
rich@hattonbrown.com
www.hattonbrown.com

Rich Donnell, Editor
David Knight, Co-Owner
Rhonda Thomas, Circulation Director
Dianne Sullivan, Chief Operating Officer
Phil Grissett, Operations Manager
Cost: $30.00
Frequency: Monthly
Circulation: 12754
ISSN: 1048-826X
Founded in 1948
Printed in on glossy stock

14525 Perspective
International Interior Design Association
111 E. Wacker Dr.
Suite 222
Chicago, IL 60601

312-467-1950
888-799-4432; Fax: 312-467-0779
www.iida.org

International magazine of IIDA.
Cost: $30.00
Frequency: Semi-Annually
Circulation: 10000
Founded in 1994
Mailing list available for rent: 10000 names
Printed in on matte stock

14526 Picture Framing Magazine
Hobby Publications
225 Gordon's Corner Road
PO Box 420
Manalapan, NJ 07726

732-446-4900
800-969-7176; Fax: 732-446-5488
gcoughlin@hobbypub.com
www.pictureframingmagazine.com

Bruce Gherman, Executive Publisher
Anne Vazquez, Editor
Deborah Salmon, Circulation Director
Alan Pegler, Production Manager of Advertising

News and trends in the picture framing trade, marketing strategies, and economic developments.
Cost: $20.00
Frequency: Monthly
Circulation: 23000
ISSN: 1052-9977
Founded in 1995

14527 Progressive Architecture
Progressive Scale
382 S Beach Avenue
Old Greenwich, CT 06870-2223

203-792-2854; Fax: 203-748-2456

Valerie Kanter Sisca, Managing Editor

This magazine has been covering the fields of architecture and interiors for more than 60 years and publishes projects that illustrate both current trends and innovative design solutions.
Cost: $48.00
Frequency: Monthly
Circulation: 65,000

14528 Upholstery Journal
Industrial Fabrics Association International
1801 County Road B W
Roseville, MN 55113-4061

651-222-2508
800-225-4324; Fax: 651-631-9334
generalinfo@ifai.com
www.ifai.com

Steve Schiffman, President & CEO

Serves as the industry resource for after-market furniture, marine and automotive upholstery. Provides education for both the craft and business of upholstery.
Frequency: Bimonthly
Circulation: 5,000

14529 Wall Paper
Waldman Publishers
570 Fashion Ave
New York, NY 10018-1603

212-730-9590; Fax: 212-391-6610

Edited for wallcovering retailers and the wallcovering industry. Accepts advertising.
Cost: $25.00
40 Pages
Frequency: Monthly
Circulation: 18,000
Founded in 1980

14530 Wallcoverings, Windows and Interior Fashion
Cygnus Publishing
445 Broad Hollow Road
Melville, NY 11747-3669

631-845-2700; Fax: 631-845-2723

Paul Bonaiuto, CFO
Kathy Scott, Director of Public Relations

14531 Walls & Ceilings
Business News Publishing Company
2401 W. Big Beaver Rd
Suite 700
Troy, MI 48084

248-362-3700
www.bnpmedia.com
Facebook, Twitter, LinkedIn

Katie Rotella, Manager

Information regarding management, building methods, technology, government regulations, consumer trends, and product information for the contractor involved in exterior finishes, waterproofing, insulation, metal framing, drywall, fireproofing, partitions, stucco and plaster.
Cost: $49.00
140 Pages
Frequency: Monthly
Circulation: 32800
Founded in 1939
Printed in 4 colors

Trade Shows

14532 Accent on Design
George Little Management

10 Bank Street
Suite 1200
White Plains, NY 10606-1954

914-486-6070
800-272-7469; Fax: 914-948-2867
www.nyigf.com

George Little II, President
Elizabeth Murphy, Show Manager

370 booths of the latest and most innovative gift lines such as decorative accessories and home furnishings.
50M Attendees
Frequency: August
Founded in 1984

14533 **Aidex: Asian International Interior Design Exposition**
Reed Exhibition Companies
383 Main Avenue
PO Box 6059
Norwalk, CT 06851

203-840-4800; Fax: 203-840-9628

Audio visual systems, bathroom equipment, supplies and services, plus interior decorations. More than 22 exhibitors, for trade professionals.
Frequency: Annual

14534 **American Society of Interior Designers National Conference**
American Society of Interior Designers
1152 15th St. NW
Suite 910
Washington, DC 20005

202-546-3480; Fax: 202-546-3240
asid@asid.org
www.asid.org

Randy W. Fiser, Hon. FASID, Chief Executive Officer
Susan L. Wiggins, CAE, Hon. IDC, Chief Operating Officer

Workshop and annual conference with 100 manufacturers and suppliers. Exhibits include interior design merchandise, wall coverings, laminates, lighting fixtures, plumbing fixtures, carpets, furniture, office systems and fabrics.
3000 Attendees
Frequency: Annual
Founded in 1975
Mailing list available for rent

14535 **Annual IIDA Advocacy Symposium**
International Interior Design Association
111 E. Wacker Dr.
Suite 222
Chicago, IL 60601

312-467-1950
888-799-4432; Fax: 312-467-0779
advocacy@iida.org
www.iida.org

Cheryl Durst, Executive VP & CEO
Abby Wilson, Manager, Advocacy & Public Policy

Features a keynote speaker and a panel discussion on advocacy and legislation.
Cost: $30.00
Frequency: Annual
Founded in 1994
Mailing list available for rent: 10000 names

14536 **Dickens Christmas Show & Festival**
Leisure Time Unlimited
708 Main Street
Myrtle Beach, SC 29577

843-448-9483; Fax: 843-362-6153
www.dickenschristmasshow.com

Offers a unique blend of craft and gift exhibits presented in a 19th century setting
25000 Attendees
Frequency: Annual November

14537 **Evergreen Home Show**
Westlake Promotions
8740 Golden Gardens Dr. NW
Seattle, WA 98117

206-783-5957; Fax: 206-708-7406
www.westlakepromo.com
Facebook, Twitter

Bill Bradley, VP
Sam Scott, Marketing Director, Operations
Michael R. Scott, President

See what's new and what you can do for your home. Fresh ideas and practical advice from our remodeling and construction specialists. See demonstrations on how to make dramatic improvements to your home.
7500 Attendees

14538 **Fall Decor**
Paint & Decorating Retailers Association
403 Axminister Drive
Fenton, MO 63026

636-326-2636; Fax: 314-991-5039
info@pdra.org
www.pdra.org

Tina Sullivan, Show Coordinator
Kathy Witmeyer, Director of Trade Shows

Annual show of 350 manufacturers, suppliers and distributors of decorating and office products and related equipment, supplies and services.
4000 Attendees
Frequency: October

14539 **Galeria**
Decor Magazine
330 N 4th Street
Saint Louis, MO 63102

314-421-5445; Fax: 314-421-1070

12000 Attendees

14540 **Holiday Fair**
Textile Hall Corporation
25 Woodslake Road
Greenville, SC 29607

864-331-2277; Fax: 864-293-0619
http://www.holidayfairgreenville.com

25000 Attendees

14541 **Home Furnishings Summer Market**
1355 Market Street
San Francisco, CA 94103-1324

415-934-1380

Donald Preiser, Show Manager

600 booths.
30M Attendees

14542 **Home and Garden Show**
Reed Exhibition Companies
255 Washington Street
Newton, MA 02458-1637

617-584-4900; Fax: 617-630-2222

Elizabeth Hitchcock, International Sales

Home products and services.
75M Attendees
Frequency: March

14543 **IDS National Conference**
Interior Design Society
164 S Main Street
Suite 404
High Point, NC 27260

336-884-4437
888-884-4469; Fax: 336-885-3291
info@interiordesignsociety.org
www.interiordesignsociety.org
Facebook, Twitter, Youtube, Blogger

Domnick Minella, President
Snoa Garrigan, Executive Director
Dennis Novosel, Treasurer
Anna Mavrakis, VP

IDS is the largest design organization exclusively dedicated to serving the residential interior design industry. Promotes retail interior design, emphasizing education and skills improvement.
3000 Members
Founded in 1973

14544 **IFAI Annual Expo**
Industrial Fabrics Association International
1801 County Road BW
Roseville, MN 55113-4061

651-222-2508
800-225-4324; Fax: 651-631-9334
generalinfo@ifai.com
www.ifai.com
Facebook, Twitter, LinkedIn, Youtube

Aaron Monson, Education & Events Manager
Christian Weiland, Marketing & Communications Manager

Trade event in the American for the technical textiles and specialty fabrics industry.
Frequency: Annual/September

14545 **IFI Congress**
Int'l Federation of Interior Architects/Designers
708 3rd Ave.
6th Floor
New York, NY 10017

212-884-6275; Fax: 212-884-6247
staff@ifiworld.org
www.ifiworld.org
Facebook, Twitter, LinkedIn

Shashi Caan, Chief Executive Officer

Brings together professionals from around the globe. Features keynote speakers and an art exhibition.
Frequency: Biennial
Founded in 1963

14546 **International Home Furnishings Market**
International Home Furnishings Market Authority
POBox 5243
High Point, NC 27262

336-888-3794
800-874-6492; Fax: 336-889-6999
www.highpointmarket.org

Judy Mendenhall, President
G Bruce Miller, CEO
Tammy Covington, Director Operations
Jan Wellmon, Executive Assistant
Shannon Kennedy, Director of Marketing

Large home furnishings trade show with a variety of new opportunities to make your visit easy, cost effective and productive. Ten million square feet of exhibition space with 2,500 manufacturers represented.
80000 Attendees
Frequency: April & October
Founded in 1921

14547 **International Silk Flower Accessories Exhibition**
Dallas Market Center
2000 N Stemmons Freeway
Dallas, TX 75207

214-655-6100
800-325-6587; Fax: 214-655-6238

8000 Attendees

14548 **LightFair**
AMC

120 Wall Street
17th Floor
New York, NY 10005

212-843-8358; Fax: 212-248-5017
www.iesna.org

Pamela R Weess, Circulation Director
Nini Schwenk, Manager

A major lighting trade show in North America featuring architectural lighting products from all spectrons of the industry. Containing 600 booths and 400 exhibits.
17M Attendees
Frequency: June
Mailing list available for rent: 10M names at $100 per M
Printed in 4 colors on glossy stock

14549 **Living Product Expo**
International Living Future Institute
1501 East Madison St.
Suite 150
Seattle, WA 98122

206-223-2028
info@living-future.org
www.living-future.org
Facebook, Twitter, LinkedIn, Instagram

KC Gauldine, Chief Executive Officer
James Connelly, VP, Products & Strategic Growth
Kathleen Smith, VP, Living Building Challenge
Miranda Berger, VP, Development & Communications
Julie Tonroy, Events Director

Connect with industry leaders who are part of the movement to create beautiful, healthy and sustainable products. Features educational sessions, speakers, workshops, networking opportunities, and a trade show.
Frequency: Annual

14550 **NGPP National Convention & Trade Show**
National Guild of Professional Paperhangers
136 S Keowee Street
Dayton, OH 45402

937-222-6477
800-254-6477; Fax: 937-222-5794
www.ngpp.org

Elsie Kaptetna CP, President
Phil Curtis CP, First VP
Vincent Larusso CP, Second VP

Promotes products, upgrades skills of paperhangers and encourages good business ethics. Workshops and product launches with over 130 vendors.
Frequency: Annual

14551 **National Decorating Product Show**
Paint & Decorating Retailers Association
403 Axminister Drive
Fenton, MO 63026-2941

636-326-2636; Fax: 314-991-5039

James B Savens III, Executive Director

430 booths for home supplies, equipment and services.
10M Attendees
Frequency: November

14552 **National Decorating Products Association: Western Show**
1050 N Lindbergh Boulevard
Saint Louis, MO 63132-2912

314-432-6001; Fax: 314-991-5039

Ruth Williams, Convention Manager

230 booths of decorating products such as paint, furniture and more.
2.5M Attendees
Frequency: March

14553 **National Decorating Products Southern Show**
Paint & Decorating Retailers Association
403 Axminister Drive
Fenton, MO 63026-2941

636-326-2636; Fax: 314-991-5039

Ruth Williams, Convention Manager

850 display booths of floor coverings, paint, furniture and various interior decorating products.
4M Attendees
Frequency: February

14554 **Needlework Markets**
Needlework Markets
PO Box 533
Pine Mountain, GA 31822

706-663-0140; Fax: 706-663-0202
www.stitching.com

Emily Castleberry, Owner
Frequency: February

14555 **Old House New House Home Show**
Kennedy Productions
1208 Lisle Place
Lisle, IL 60532-2262

630-515-1160; Fax: 630-515-1165
info@kennedyproductions.com
www.kennedyproductions.com

Laura McNamara, Event Producer
Joanne Kennedy, President

Over 300 home improvement exhibitors displaying cutting-edge home enhancements for kitchens, baths, home and garden including landscape, interior remodeling, pools, spas, floors, doors and more.
8000 Attendees
Frequency: Feb/Sept
Founded in 1977

14556 **PDCA Painting & Decorating Expo**
Paint and Decorating Retailers Association
1401 Triad Center Dr
St. Peters, MO 63376-7353

636-326-2636
800-737-0107; Fax: 636-229-4750
info@pdra.org
www.pdra.org

Dan Simon, Executive VP/Publisher
Tina Sullivan, Dir Membership/Education/Tradeshows
Diane Capuano, Managing Editor
Renee Nolte, Director, Finance/Human Resources
Tony Sarantakis, Account Executive

Over thiry education sessions, multiple special networking events and the latest in products and services to support the trade.
2000 Members
Frequency: May
Founded in 1947

14557 **Paint Industries Show**
492 Norristown Road
Blue Bell, PA 19422-2355

610-940-0777; Fax: 215-840-0292

Robert F Ziegler, Show Manager

Exhibits of raw materials, production equipment, instrumentation and testing apparatus for the coatings, inks and adhesives manufacturing industries. 920 booths.
3.5M Attendees
Frequency: October

14558 **Painting and Decorating Contractors of America National Convention**
3913 Old Lee Highway
Suite 301
Fairfax, VA 22030-2433

703-359-0826; Fax: 703-359-2976

Mary S DePersig, Director Meetings

200 booths of painting, wallcoverings, coatings and sundries.
1.2M Attendees
Frequency: March

14559 **SCALE: The ASID National Student Summit**
American Society of Interior Designers
1152 15th St. NW
Suite 910
Washington, DC 20005

202-546-3480; Fax: 202-546-3240
asid@asid.org
www.asid.org

Randy W. Fiser, Hon. FASID, Chief Executive Officer
Susan L. Wiggins, CAE, Hon. IDC, Chief Operating Officer
Susan Chung, PhD, Dir., Research & Knowledge Mgmt.

Prepare students to take on their first professional roles, while educators will explore relevant topics and resources to augment their curricula.
Frequency: Annual

14560 **Surtex**
George Little Management
10 Bank Street
Suite 1200
White Plains, NY 10606-1954

914-486-6070
800-272-7469; Fax: 914-948-6180
www.SURTEX.com

Gina DeLuca, Show Coordinator
Rita Malek, Show Manager
George Little II, President

Annual show of 350 exhibitors featuring prints and patterns for all applications-decorative fabrics, linens, and domestics, apparel and contract textiles, wall and floor coverings, greeting cards, giftwrap and other paper products, tabletop, ceramics and packaging. Available for sale and/or license.
5000 Attendees
Frequency: May

14561 **TEXBO**
Reed Exhibition Companies
255 Washington Street
Newton, MA 02458-1637

617-584-4900; Fax: 617-630-2222

Elizabeth Hitchcock, International Sales

International trade fair for the interior design industry.
7M Attendees
Frequency: January

14562 **Tabletop Market**
George Little Management
577 Airport Boulevard
Burlingame, CA 94010-2020

650-548-1200
800-272-SHOW; Fax: 650-344-5270

Susan Corwin, VP

Annual show of 90 exhibitors featuring tableware, table linens, better housewares and decorative accessories.
1500 Attendees
Frequency: October

14563 West Coast Art and Frame
Art Trends/Picture Framing/Digital Fine Arts
PO Box 594
Lynbrook, NY 11563
516-596-3937; Fax: 516-596-3941
3500 Attendees

Directories & Databases

14564 Carpet & Rug Industry Buyers Guide Issue
Rodman Publishing
17 S Franklin Tpke
Ramsey, NJ 07446-2522
201-252-2552
More than 300 suppliers of machinery, equipment and colors and dyes used in the making of carpets and rugs.
Cost: $7.00
Frequency: Annual
Circulation: 5,500

14565 Carpet Cleaners Institute of the Northwest Membership Roster
Carpet Cleaners Institute of the Northwest
PMB #40 2421 South Union Avenue
Suite L-1
Tacoma, WA 98405
253-759-5762
877-692-2469; Fax: 253-761-9134
info@ccinw.org
www.ccinw.org
Lyle Neville, President
Matt O'Haleck, Treasurer
Jim Thomas, Secretary
Mike Elias, Director of Education
Over 330 member companies involved in the carpet cleaning industry in Washington, Oregon, and Montana, USA and Alberta and British Columbia, Canada.
Frequency: Annual

14566 Decor-Sources Issue
Commerce Publishing Company
330 N 4th Street
Suite 200
Saint Louis, MO 63102-2041
314-421-5445
Over 1,200 wholesale suppliers of pictures, frames, interior accessories and mirrors to art galleries and home accessories retailers are profiled.
Cost: $5.00
Frequency: Annual
Circulation: 35,000

14567 Decorating Registry
Paint and Decorating Retailers Association
1401 Triad Center Dr
St. Peters, MO 63376-7353
636-326-2636
800-737-0107; Fax: 636-229-4750
info@pdra.org
www.pdra.org
Dan Simon, Executive VP/Publisher
Tina Sullivan, Dir Membership/Education/Tradeshows
Diane Capuano, Managing Editor
Renee Nolte, Director, Finance/Human Resources
Tony Sarantakis, Account Executive
A searchable industry database listing paint and decorating companies, products, trademarks, distributors and manufacturer reps.
Cost: $15.00
1500 Members
200 Pages
Frequency: Annual, Magazine
Founded in 1947
Printed in on glossy stock

14568 Decorating Retailer's Decorating Registry
National Decorating Products Association
1050 N Lindbergh Boulevard
Saint Louis, MO 63132-2912
314-432-6001
800-737-0107; Fax: 314-991-5039
Ernest Stewart, Executive VP
Cindy Nusbaum, Directories Editor
Trademark and brand name directory covering paint, wallcovering, window covering, floor covering and related sundries.
Cost: $9.00
Frequency: Annual
Circulation: 30,000
Mailing list available for rent: 30,000+ names
Printed in 4 colors on glossy stock

14569 Decorating Retailer: Directory of the Wallcoverings Industry Issue
National Decorating Products Association
1050 N Lindbergh Boulevard
Saint Louis, MO 63132-2912
314-432-6001
800-737-0107; Fax: 314-991-5039
Ernest Stewart, Publisher
Cindy Nusbaum, Editor
Over 1,000 manufacturers and distributors of wallcoverings and related products are listed.
Cost: $25.00
Frequency: Annual
Circulation: 5,000
Printed in 4 colors

14570 DesignSource: Official Specifying and Buying Directory
PO Box 5059
Hoboken, NJ 07030-1501
201-963-9000
More than 10,000 companies that manufacture or supply products or services for interior designers.
Cost: $25.00
Frequency: Annual
Circulation: 40,000

14571 Directory of African American Design Firms
San Francisco Redevelopment Agency
770 Golden Gate Avenue
San Francisco, CA 94102
415-749-2400; Fax: 415-749-2526
Over 100 architectural, engineering, planning and landscape design firms.
Frequency: Annual December

14572 Draperies & Window Coverings: Directory and Buyer's Guide Issue
LC Clark Publishing Company
840 US Highway 1
Suite 330
North Palm Beac, FL 33408-3878
561-627-3393; Fax: 561-694-6578
John Clark, Owner
Sarah Christy, Associate Editor
Katie Sosnowchik, Senior Editor
Over 2,000 manufacturers and distributors of window coverings and other products used in the window coverings and interior fashions industry.
Cost: $15.00
Frequency: Annual

14573 ENR Directory of Design Firms
McGraw Hill
PO Box 182604
Columbus, OH 43272
877-833-5524; Fax: 614-759-3749
www.mcgraw-hill.com
Facebook, Twitter, LinkedIn, Blog, Youtube, Social
Paul Hermannsfeldt, Editor
Harold McGraw III, Chairman, President
Jack F. Callahan, Executive Vice President
John Berisford, Executive Vice President
Mary Jo Vittor, Executive Vice President
Profiles of 88 architects, architectural engineers, consultants and other design firms; limited to advertisers.
Cost: $95.00
Frequency: Biennial
Mailing list available for rent

14574 ENR: Top 500 Design Firms Issue
McGraw Hill
1221 Avenue of the Americas
Suite C3A
New York, NY 10020-1095
212-512-2000; Fax: 212-512-3840
www.mcgraw-hill.com
Harold W McGraw III, CEO
List of 500 leading architectural, engineering and specialty design firms selected on basis of annual billings.
Cost: $35.00
Frequency: Annual April
Circulation: 71,000

14575 Flooring: Buying and Resource Guide Issue
Leo Douglas
9609 Gayton Road
Suite 100
Richmond, VA 23233-4904
Lists various manufacturers, workrooms, manufacturers' representatives and distributors of floor, and other interior surfacing products and equipment.
Cost: $38.50
Frequency: Annual
Circulation: 24,000

14576 Home Lighting & Accessories Suppliers Directory
Doctorow Communications
1011 Clifton Ave
Clifton, NJ 07013-3518
973-779-1600; Fax: 973-779-3242
info@homelighting.com
www.homelighting.com
Jeffrey Doctorow, President
Linda Longo, Editor-in-Chief
Susan Grisham, Managing Editor
Dina Tamburro, Associate Publisher
A list of over 1,000 suppliers of lighting fixtures and other products for use in the retail lighting industry are provided.
Cost: $6.00
Frequency: Semi-Annual
Circulation: 9,690

14577 Interior Decorators Handbook
EW Williams Publications
370 Lexington Ave
Suite 1409
New York, NY 10017-6583
212-661-1516; Fax: 212-661-1713
Philippa Hochschild, Publisher
Phillip Russo, Publishing Director
Lynne Lancaster, Advertising Sales Director
Designers resource guide with over 600 product/service categories. 3,000 suppliers are listed with their headquarters, showrooms. Addresses,

phone numbers, fax numbers and e-mail.
Cost: $36.00
230 Pages
Frequency: Bi-annual
Circulation: 25,000
Founded in 1922
Printed in 4 colors on glossy stock

14578 LDB Interior Textiles Annual Buyers' Guide
EW Williams Publications
370 Lexington Ave
Room 1409
New York, NY 10017-6583

212-661-1516; Fax: 212-661-1713

Philippa Hochschild, Publisher

Over 2,000 manufacturers and importers of home accessories and interior design products are listed.
Cost: $40.00
Frequency: Monthly
Circulation: 14000
Founded in 1927

14579 Market Resource Guide
International Home Furnishings Center
PO Box 828
High Point, NC 27261-0828

336-888-3700; Fax: 336-882-1873
marketing@ihfc.com

Bruce Miller, CEO

Two-volume directory offers over 1,500 manufacturers and distributors in the furniture industry with exhibits at the International Home Furnishings Market.
Cost: $25.00
624 Pages
Frequency: Semiannual
Founded in 1974
Printed in 4 colors on glossy stock

14580 Painting and Wallcovering Contractor
Painting Contractors Association
2316 Millpark Drive
Suite 220
Maryland Heights, MO 63043

314-514-7322
800-332-7322; Fax: 314-514-9417
www.pcapainted.org
Facebook

Gina Koert, Chair

Offers a list of over 3,300 member contractors engaged in painting, decorating and special coatings applications.
Frequency: Annual
Circulation: 3,500
Mailing list available for rent

14581 Rauch Guide to the US Paint Industry
Grey House Publishing
4919 Route 22
PO Box 56
Amenia, NY 12501

518-789-8700
800-562-2139; Fax: 845-373-6390
books@greyhouse.com
www.greyhouse.com
Facebook, Twitter

Leslie Mackenzie, Publisher
Richard Gottlieb, Editor

Provides industry structure and current market information about this $16.6 billion industry. The report is divided into five major chapters with 100+ tables and 20 figures in its 500 pages. Unique to the Guide is a profile over 800 industry manufacturers, with sales estimates, products, mergers and acquisitions, divestitures and other information for the 400 largest companies.
Cost: $595.00
500 Pages
ISBN: 1-592371-27-2
Founded in 1981

14582 Specifiers' Guide and Directory of Contract Wallcoverings
Wall Publications
570 Fashion Ave
New York, NY 10018-1603

212-730-9590

Anne Gober, Owner

A who's who directory of services and supplies to the industry.
Cost: $15.95
Frequency: Annual
Circulation: 15,000

14583 Tile & Decorative Surfaces
18 E 41st Street
New York, NY 10017-6222

212-376-7722; Fax: 212-376-7723
www.ashlee.com/tile

Jordan M Wright, President/Publisher

The Tile industry including ceramic, natural stone, terrazzo, agglomerated, cement glasstiles and others allied to the field. Architects, designers, importers, retail floor covering dealers, distributors, installers and contractors. Also, firms involved with renovation and restoration of tile. Accepts advertising.
Cost: $25.00
Frequency: Monthly
Circulation: 24,000
ISSN: 0192-9550
Founded in 1950

14584 Wallcovering Pattern Guide and Source Directory
Home Fashion Information Network
557 S Duncan Avenue
Clearwater, FL 33756-6255

A list of wallcovering manufacturers and distributors are offered in this comprehensive directory aimed at the interior design community.
Cost: $78.00
Frequency: Semiannual
Circulation: 10,000

14585 Western Floors: Buyers Guide & Directory
Specialist Publications
17835 Ventura Boulevard
Suite 312
Encino, CA 91316-3634

818-709-1437

A list of firms which manufacture, import or distribute floor coverings.
Cost: $15.00
Frequency: Annual
Circulation: 17,000

14586 Who's Who in Floor Covering Distribution
National Association of Floor Covering Distributor
122 S. Michigan Avenue
Suite 1040
Chicago, IL 60603

312-461-9600; Fax: 312-461-0777
info@nafed.org
www.nafed.org

Jack Lidenschmidt, President
Danny Harris, Executive Director/CEO
Norbert Makowka, Vice President, Technical
Tamara Matthews, Communications Coordinator
Socorro Garcia, Office Manager

Offers information on over 400 member distributors and suppliers of floor coverings.
40 Pages
Frequency: Annual
Mailing list available for rent

Industry Web Sites

14587 http://gold.greyhouse.com
G.O.L.D Grey House OnLine Databases

Grey House Publishing's online database platform, GOLD, offers Quick Search, Keyword Search and Expert Search for most business sectors including interior design, decorating and lighting markets. The GOLD platform makes finding the information you need quick and easy - whether you're a novice searcher or an experienced database user. All of Grey House's directory products are available for subscription on the GOLD platform.

14588 www.carpet-rug.com
Carpet and Rug Institute

National association of carpet and rug manufacturers. Source for product information.

14589 www.greyhouse.com
Grey House Publishing

Authoritative reference directories for most business sectors including interior design, decorating and lighting markets. Users can search the online databases with varied search criteria allowing for custom searches by product category, geographic area, sales volume, keyword, subject and more. Full Grey House catalog and online ordering also available.

14590 www.homeshows.net
Home Show Management

Organizes three annual south Flordia home design and remodeling shows in Coconut Grove, Ft. Lauderdale and Miami Beach convention centers. Open to the trade and public.

14591 www.i-d-d.com
Interior Design Directory

Sources and links for the interior designer.

14592 www.iesna.org
Illuminating Engineering Society of North America

To advance knowledge and disseminate information for the improvement of the lighted environment to the benefit of society. Publishes a monthly magazine.

14593 www.iida.org
International Interior Design Association

Members are professionals from various facets of the interior design trade.

14594 www.interiordesignsociety.org
Interior Design Society

The largest design organization exclusively dedicated to serving the residential interior design industry. Promotes retail interior design, emphasizing education and skills improvement.

14595 www.nadfd.com
National Assn of Decorative Fabric Distributors

Promotes the textile and home furnishings manufacturers and distributors.

14596 www.nafcd.org
National Assn of Floor Covering Distributors

This organization offers information on over 500 member distributors and suppliers of floor coverings. Publications available to members.

14597 **www.ncidq.org**

National Council for Interior Design Qualification

Serves to identify to the public those interior designers who have met the minimum standards for professional practice by passing the NCIDQ examination.

14598 **www.ngpp.org**

National Guild of Professional Paperhangers

Promotes products, upgrades skills of paperhangers and encourages good business ethics. Holds workshops and seminars.

14599 **www.nhfa.org**

National Home Furnishings Association

A federation of local home furnishings representatives association.

14600 **www.pdra.org**

Paint and Decorating Retailers Association

This organization lists 1,500 manufacturers, manufacturers' representatives, distributors, and suppliers of decorating merchandise.

14601 **www.resources.com**

Resources

Organized into easy point and click directories under a highly interactive database.

Associations

14602 Academy of International Business
Eppley Center
645 N Shaw Ln., Rm. 7
East Lansing, MI 48824-1121

517-432-1452; Fax: 517-432-1009
aib@aib.msu.edu
aib.msu.edu
Facebook, Twitter, LinkedIn

Tomas Hult, Executive Director
Tunga Kiyak, Managing Director
Dan Rosplock, Communications Coordinator
Kathy Kiessling, Membership Coordinator

Global community of scholars focused on creating, advancing, and disseminating knowledge in international business research, education, policy, and practice with 18 chapters around the world.
3500 Members
Founded in 1959
Mailing list available for rent: 3000 names at $250 per M

14603 American Association of Exporters and Importers
1717 K Street, NW
Suite 1120
Washington, DC 20006

202-857-8009; Fax: 202-857-7843
hg@aaei.org
www.aaei.org
Facebook, Twitter, LinkedIn, Google+

Phyliss Wigginton, Chair
Karen Kelly, Vice Chair
Lori Goldberg, Vice Chair
Theresa Walker, Secretary/Treasurer
Marianne Rowden, President, CEO

Supports those involved in trade development with other countries and conducting business in the United States, as well as developments affecting trade originating from Treasury, Customs, US Courts, Commerce Department, International Trade Commission, Federal Maritime Commission and other regulatory agencies. Hosts annual trade show.
Founded in 1921

14604 American Foreign Service Association
2101 E Street NW
Washington, DC 20037

202-338-4045; Fax: 202-338-6820
www.afsa.org
Facebook, Twitter, YouTube, Flickr

Barbara Stephenson, President
Sharon Wayne, Vice President
Angie Bryan, State Vice President
Hon. Charles A. Ford, Treasurer
Ian Houston, Executive Director

Organization dedicated specifically to preserving and enhancing theintegrity of the U.S. Foreign Service.
31000 Members
Founded in 1924

14605 American League for Exports and Security Assistance
122 C St NW
Suite 740
Washington, DC 20001-2109

202-393-3903; Fax: 202-737-4727

David Lewis, President

Encourages and supports the sale of American defense products abroad in agreement with foreign policy, security and economic goals of the nation.
38 Members
Founded in 1976

14606 Assist International
90 John Street
Room 505
New York, NY 10038

212-244-2074; Fax: 831-439-9602
www.assist-intl.com

International trade promotion and consulting firm: mailing lists, seminars, conferences, international business expo.

14607 Association Of American Chambers of Commerce in Latin America
1615 H. Street, NW
Washington, DC 20062-2000

202-463-5485
info@aaccla.org
www.aaccla.org

Nicholas Galt, Chair
Thomas H. Kenna, Vice Chair
Aldo Defilippi, VP for Executive Management
Neil Herrington, Executive Vice President
Reuben Smith-Vaughan, Executive Director

Promotes trade and investment between the United States and the countries of the region through free trade, free markets, and free enterprise.
20000 Members

14608 CalChamber Council for International Trade
1215 K Street
Suite 1400
Sacramento, CA 95814

916-444-6670
800-649-4921; Fax: 916-325-1272
www.calchamber.com
Facebook, Twitter, LinkedIn

Allan Zaremberg, President/CEO
Ann Amioka, VP, Communications
Drew Savage, VP, Corporate Relations
Karen Olson, VP, Marketing
Denise Davis, Vice President, Media Relationsÿ

Formed by the merging of California Council for International Trade and California Chamber of Commerce International Trade Committee. The foundation is dedicated to preserving and strengthening the California business climate and private enterprise through accurate, impartial research and education on public policy issues of interest to the California business and public policy communities.
15000 Members
Founded in 1890
Mailing list available for rent

14609 Customs and International Trade Bar Association
Home Page: www.citba.org

Joseph W. Dorn, President
Lawrence M. Friedman, Vice President
Melvin S. Schwechter, Chair, Export Committee
Kathleen W. Cannon, Secretary
William Sjoberg, Treasurer

Members represent importers, exporters, and domestic producers in matters involving U.S. customs laws, antidumping and countervailing duty laws, safeguards, export licensing, and other federal laws and regulations that affect imported or exported merchandise or international commerce.
Founded in 1917

14610 FSC/DISC Tax Association
Council for International Tax Education
PO Box 1012
White Plains, NY 10602

914-328-5656
800-207-4432; Fax: 914-328-5757
www.citeusa.org

Robert Ross, Owner

The only organization operating on a national level devoted to educational interests of companies that have set up a foreign sales corporation.
300 Members
Founded in 1984
Mailing list available for rent

14611 Foreign Trade Association
437 S. Cataract Avenue
Suite #4B
San Dimas, CA 91773

888-223-6459; Fax: 310-220-4474
info@foreigntradeassociation.com
www.foreigntradeassociation.com
Facebook, Twitter, LinkedIn

Keith Sanchez, Chairman
Tom Gould, President
Adonna Martin, 1st VP
Cameron Roberts, 2nd VP
Glenn Patton, Treasurer

Business association of European and International commerce that promotes the values of free trade.

14612 Forum for International Trade Training
116 Lisgar Street
Suite 100
Ottawa, ON K2P 0C2

613-230-3553
800-561-3488; Fax: 613-230-6808
info@fitt.ca
www.fitt.ca
Facebook, Twitter, LinkedIn, Google+

Bill Walsh, Chair
Leslie Meingast, Vice Chair
Paloma Healey, Board Member
Scott Forbes, Board Member
Carl Burlock, Treasurer

Nonprofit organization that develops international business programs, sets competency standards, designs the certification and accreditation programs for the Certified International Trade Professional (CITP) designation, and generally ensures continuing professional development in the practice of international trade.
Founded in 1992

14613 Futures Industry Association
2001 Pennsylvania Avenue NW
Suite 600
Washington, DC 20006-1823

202-466-5460; Fax: 202-296-3184
info@fia.org
www.futuresindustry.org/
Facebook, Twitter, LinkedIn, Flickr

Gerald Corcoran, Chair
Walter L. Lukken, President & CEO
Mary Ann Burns, EVP & COO
M. Clarkÿ Hutchison, Treasurer
Emily Portney, Secretary

Trade association in the United States composed of futures commission merchants.
Founded in 1955

14614 Gemini Shippers Group National Fashion Accessories Assoc
137 West 25th Street
3rd Floor
New York, NY 10001

212-947-3424; Fax: 212-629-0361
info@geminishippers.com

www.geminishippers.com
Facebook, Twitter, LinkedIn, Google+

Sara L.ÿ Mayes, President
Kenneth O'Brien, Chief Operating Officer
Nicole Uchrin, Managing Director
Rich Moore, SalesÿDirector
Arlene L. Blocker, Membership Director

Offers membership to importers and exporters of various products.
200 Members
Founded in 1916

14615 **Hong Kong Association of New York**
115 East 54th Street
New York, NY 10022-4563

646-770-1676
contact@hkany.org
www.hkany.org
Facebook, LinkedIn, Instagram

Mary Wadsworth Darby, Chairman
Sylvia S. Ng, Vice Chairman
Amy Shang, Vice Chairman
Sebastien J.ÿ Granier, Treasurer
Raymond H. Wong, Secretary

Nonprofit organization that promotes global co-operation, communication exchange and synergy among the Hong Kong business associations worldwide.
1100 Members
Founded in 1987

14616 **Hong Kong Trade Development Council**
219 E 46th Street
New York, NY 10017

212-838-8688; Fax: 212-838-8941
new.york.office@hktdc.org
www.hktdc.com
Facebook, Twitter, LinkedIn, Google+, YouTube, RSS, Weibo

Anna Fan, Director, New York

Promotes trade between the United States and Hong Kong.
Founded in 1966
Mailing list available for rent

14617 **International Chamber of Commerce (ICC)**
33-43 Ave. du President Wilson
Paris, Fr 75116

33- 0 -1 49; Fax: 3- 0- 1 4
icc@iccwbo.org
www.iccwbo.org
Facebook, Twitter, LinkedIn, Google+, YouTube

Harold McGraw III, Chairman
Sunil Bharti Mittalÿ, Vice Chairman
Frederico Fleury Curadoÿ, Vice Chairman
Dennis M. Nally, Vice Chairman
Gerard Worms, Honorary Chairman
Founded in 1919
Mailing list available for rent

14618 **International Reciprocal Trade Association**
524 Middle Street
Portsmouth, VA 23704

FAX 757-257-4014
www.irta.com
Facebook, LinkedIn, Google+, YouTube

Annette Riggs, President
Scott Whitmer, Vice President
Ron Whitney, Executive Director
Chong Kee Tan, Secretary
Mary Ellen Rosinski, Treasurer

A nonprofit organization committed to promoting just and equitable standards of practice and operation within the Modern Trade and Barter and otherAlternative Capital Systems Industry.
Founded in 1979

14619 **International Trade Administration**
U.S. Department of Commerce
1401 Constitution Ave NW
Washington, DC 20230

800-USA-TRAD
trade.gov
Facebook, Twitter, LinkedIn, Blog

Tim Rosado, CFO & CAO
Arthur Paiva, Chief Information Officer
Stefan M. Selig, Under Secretary
Kenneth E. Hyatt, Deputy Under Secretary
Arun Venkataraman, Policy Director

An agency in the United States Department of Commerce that promotesUnited States exports of nonagricultural U.S. services and goods.

14620 **International Trade and Finance Association**
PO Box 2145
Kingsville, TX 78363

itfaconf@ymail.com
www.itfaconference.org

Khosrow Fatemi, President
Janina Witkowska, VP of Membership
Alfred Eckes, EVP
Scheherazade Rehman, President Elect
Pompeo Della Posta, Board Member

A multidisciplinary association for academics and professionals interested in studying international trade and finance and in promoting a general awareness of these fields and related global economic issues.
Founded in 1988

14621 **International Trademark Association**
655 Third Avenue
10th Floor
New York, NY 10017

212-642-1700; Fax: 212-768-7796
memberservices@inta.org
www.inta.org
Facebook, Twitter, LinkedIn

J. Scott Evans, President
Joseph Ferrettiÿ, Vice President
Ronald Van Tuijlÿ, President Elect
Tish Berard, VP
Etienne Sanz de Acedo, CEO

A global association of trademark owners and professionals dedicated to supporting trademarks and related intellectual property in order to protectconsumers and to promote fair and effective commerce.
6400 Members
Founded in 1878

14622 **International Warehouse Logistics Association**
2800 S River Road
Suite 260
Des Plaines, IL 60018

847-813-4699; Fax: 847-813-0115
mail@iwla.com
www.iwla.com
Facebook, Twitter, LinkedIn, YouTube

Steve W. Dehaan, President & CEO
Jay D. Strother, Vice President
Jennifer Rezny, Membership Director
Hank Vaughan, Education & Meetings Director
Robert Budo, Finance & Accounting Manager

The unified voice of the global logistics outsourcing industry, representing third party warehousing, transportation and logistics service providers. Our member companies provide the most timely and cost-effective global logistics solutions for their customers and are committed to protecting the free flow of products across international borders.
500 Members
Founded in 1997

14623 **Italian Trade Agency**
33 East 67th Street
New York, NY 10065-5949

212-980-1500; Fax: 212-758-1050
newyork@ice.it
www.italtrade.com

Maurizio Forte, Trade Commissioner & Executive Dir.
Gemma Di Gangi, Executive Secretary
Gioia Gatti, Food and Wine section
Marc Littell, Graphic Design
Alessandro Greco, Fashion and Start Up

Trade promotion section of the Italian Consulate.

14624 **Latin American Studies Association**
University of Pittsburgh
416 Bellefield Hall
University of Pittsburgh
Pittsburgh, PA 15260

412-648-7929; Fax: 412-624-7145
lasa@pitt.edu
lasa.international.pitt.edu/
Facebook, Twitter, LinkedIn

Gilbertÿ Joseph, President
Joanne Rappaport, Vice President-President Elect
Timothy J. Power, Treasurer
Debra Castillo, Past President
Milagros Pereyra-Rojas, Executive Director

To foster intellectual discussion, research, and teaching on Latin America, the Caribbean, and its people throughout the Americas, promote the interests of its diverse membership, and encourage civic engagement through network building and public debate.
5000+ Members
Mailing list available for rent

14625 **MIQ Logistics, LLC**
11501 Outlook St
Suite 500
Overland Park, KS 66211

913-696-7100
877-232-1845; Fax: 913-696-7501
contact_us@miq.com
www.miq.com
Facebook, Twitter, LinkedIn, Google+, RSS

John E. Carr, President/CEO
Dan Bentzinger, Chief Information Officer
Brenda Stasiulis, Chief Financial Officer
Paul Fitzpatrick, General Counsel
Clint Dvorak, Mng. Dir., Global North America

Plans and coordinates the movement of goods throughout the world.
Founded in 2002

14626 **NEXCO, Inc.**
Grand Central Station
PO Box 3949
New York, NY 10163

877-291-4901; Fax: 646-349-9628
director@nexco.org
www.nexco.org
Facebook, Twitter, LinkedIn, YouTube

Barney Lehrer, President
David Reiff, Secretary
Susan T.ÿ Gilligan, B.O.D.
Henry Lapidos, Director
Neil Lenok, B.O.D.

Members are import and export trading and import and export management companies, international trade service vendors and other international trade companies.
300 Members
Founded in 1963

14627 **National Association of College Stores**
528 E Lorain St.
Oberlin, OH 44074
800-622-7498; Fax: 440-775-4769
service@nacscorp.com
www.nacs.org
Bob Walton, CEO
Provides educational and support services and products to college stores. Promotes business methods and ethics. Conducts manager certification, educational services and research.
3.9M Members
Founded in 1963

14628 **National Council on International Trade Development**
1901 Pennsylvania Ave. NW
Suite 804
Washington, DC 20006
202-872-9280; Fax: 202-293-0495
www.ncitd.org
Mary Fromyer, Executive Director
David Joy, Senior Counsel
Cathleen Ryan, Asst. Dir. Of Enforcement
kevin J. Wolf, Asst. Secretary of Commerce
Gerard Horner, Head of Economic Analysis Program
Non-profit membership organization dedicated to providing direct expertise on a wide range of international trade topics. Our mission is to identify impediments to all aspects of international commerce and to provide solutions to faciliting the global process.
Founded in 1967

14629 **National Foreign Trade Council**
1625 K Street, NW
Suite 200
Washington, DC 20006
202-887-0278; Fax: 202-452-8160
nftcinformation@nftc.org
www.nftc.org
Facebook, Twitter
William A. Reinsch, President & CEO
J. Daniel O'Flaherty, Vice President
Marshall Lane, Sr Director of Operations
Andrew Watrous, Program Manager
Catherine Schultz, VP, Tax Policy
Business organization advocating a rules-based world economy.
300 Members
Founded in 1914

14630 **PromaxBDA**
5700 Wilshire Blvd
Suite 275
Los Angeles, CA 90036
310-788-7600; Fax: 310-788-7616
steve.kazanjian@promaxbda.org
www.promaxbda.org
Facebook, Twitter, LinkedIn, RSS
Steve Kazanjian, President/CEO
Randy Smith, SVP & CFO
Stacy La Cotera, General Manager and Vice President
Lucian Cojescu, CIO
Stephen Earley, VP, Strategic Partnerships
International association of promotion and marketing, professionals in electronic media. Promotes the effectiveness of promotion and marketing within the industry and the academic community.
2400 Members
Founded in 1952

14631 **Russian Trade Development Association**
Palms & Company
6421 Lake Washington Boulevard North East
Penthouse Suite 408
Kirkland, WA 98033-6876
425-828-6774; Fax: 425-821-9101
Palms@PeterPalms.com
www.peterpalms.com
Variety of industrial trade shows by SIC code occuring in the Russian Federation throughout the year. Export services from USA to purchasing agent services in Russia for buyers worldwide.
25000 Members
Founded in 1934

14632 **Small Business Exporters Association**
800-345-6728
info@sbea.org
www.sbea.org
Jody Milanese, Government Affairs
Patrick Post, Membership
Molly Day, Media/ Press Inquires
Association for small and mid-sized exporters and serves as the international trade arm of the National Small Business Association (NSBA), the nation's first small-business advocacy organization with more than 65,000 members across the country.
65000 Members

14633 **The Association of Women in International Trade**
4070 52nd Street NW
Washington, DC 20016
202-293-2948
info@wiit.org
www.wiit.org
Twitter, LinkedIn
Stefanie Holland, President
Rowan M. Dougherty, VP of Programming
Jennifer Shore, VP of Communications
Dana Watts, VP of Professional Development
Peggy A. Clarke, Secretary
Provides educational and networking opportunities to professional women involved in international trade and business.
Founded in 1987

14634 **The Federation of International Trade Associations**
172 Fifth Avenue
#118
Brooklyn, NY 11217
888-491-8833
www.fita.org
Kimberly Park, President & CEO
Provides resources, benefits and services to the international trade community.
45000 Members
Founded in 1984

14635 **The Women in International Trade Charitable Trust**
Home Page: www.wiittrust.org
Nicole Bivens Collinson, Chair
Amy Breeman-Rhodes, Treasurer
Emily Ruger-Beline, Advisory Committee
Amanda DeBusk, Advisory Committee
Cami Mazard, Advisory Committee
Funds charitable, scientific, and educational activities in international trade.
Founded in 2001

14636 **US China Business Council**
1818 N Street, NW
Suite 200
Washington, DC 20036
202-429-0340; Fax: 202-775-2476
info@uschina.org
www.uschina.org
Facebook, Twitter, LinkedIn, Google+
Mark Fields, Chair
Robert A. Iger, Vice Chair
Paul D. Conway, Vice Chair
Indra K. Nooyi, Vice Chair
John Frisbie, President
Membership association for US companies doing business with the People's Republic of China. Provides representation, practical assistance, and up-to-date information to members.
240 Members
Founded in 1973
Mailing list available for rent

14637 **US Council for International Business**
1212 Avenue of the Americas
New York, NY 10036
212-354-4480; Fax: 212-575-0327
info@uscib.org
www.uscib.org
Facebook, Twitter, LinkedIn, RSS, Flickr, YouTube
Harold McGraw III, Chair
Dennis Nally, Vice Chair
Thomas M. T. Niles, Vice Chair
Donald Monks, Treasurer
Peter M. Robinson, President, CEO
Addresses a broad range of policy issues with the objective of promoting an open system of world trade, finance and investment in which business can flourish and contribute to economic growth, human welfareand protection of the environment.
300 Members
Founded in 1945

14638 **US International Trade Association**
1401 Constitution Ave Nw
U.S. Department of Commerce
Washington, DC 20230
202-482-2867
800-USA-TRAD; Fax: 202-482-2867
www.trade.gov
Facebook, Twitter, LinkedIn, Blog, YouTube
Tim Rosado, CFO & CAO
Arthur Paiva, Chief Information Officer
Stefan M. Selig, Under Secretary
Kenneth E. Hyatt, Deputy Under Secretary
Arun Venkataraman, Policy Director
Association for those interested in export opportunities for United States businesses.

14639 **US Russia Business Council**
1110 Vermont Avenue, NW
Suite 350
Washington, DC 20005
202-739-9180; Fax: 202-659-5920
info@usrbc.org
www.usrbc.org
LinkedIn
Klaus Kleinfield, Chairman of the Board
Daniel A. Russell, President, CEO
Randi Levinas, EVP, Chief Operating Officer
Jeff Barnett, Senior Director of Policy
Marc Luet, Board Member
A Washington-based trade association that provides significant business developme, dispute resolution, government relations, and market intelligence services to its American and Russian member companies.

14640 **United States Council for International Business**
1212 Avenue of the Americas
New York, NY 10036
212-354-4480; Fax: 212-575-0327
info@uscib.org

www.uscib.org
RSS, Flickr, YouTube

Harold McGraw III, Chair
Dennis Nally, Vice Chair
Thomas M. T. Niles, Vice Chair
Donald Monks, Treasurer
Peter M. Robinson, President, CEO

Promotes open markets, competitiveness and innovation, sustainable development and corporate responsibility, supported by international engagement and regulatory coherence.
300 Members
Founded in 1945

14641 **WESTCONN International Trade Association**

Home Page: www.westconn.org
Facebook, Twitter, LinkedIn

George Woods, President
Edward Carey, Vice President
Sam Fischel, Treasurer
Mark Bishop, Co-Secretary
Susan Leavitt, Co-Secretary

Promotes industrial and academic awareness of the importance of international trade to our national economy.
Founded in 1972

14642 **Women's International Shipping & Trading Association**

Home Page: www.wista.net
Facebook, Twitter

Karin Orsel, President
Rachel Lawton, Treasurer
Despina Panayiotou Theodosiou, Secretary
Katerina Stathopoulou, Board Member
Sanjam Gupta, Board Member

An international organization for women in management positions involved in the maritime transportation business and related trades worldwide.
2,100 Members
Founded in 1997

Newsletters

14643 **AAMA News**

Asian American Manufacturers Association
3300 Zanker Road
Maildrop Sj2f8
San Jose, CA 95134

408-955-4505; Fax: 408-955-4516

Robert M Lee, Executive Director
Cost: $30.00
Frequency: Monthly
Circulation: 1000

14644 **AIB Newsletter**

Academy of International Business
Michigan State University
7 Eppley Center
East Lansing, MI 48824-1121

517-432-1452; Fax: 517-432-1009
aib@aib.msu.edu
aib.msu.edu

G Tomas M Hult, Executive Director
Tunga Kiyak, Managing Director
Irem Kiyak, Treasurer

Provides feature reports and news articles. Information on upcoming events such as conference announcements, calls for papers, and publishing opportunities are also featured.
Frequency: Quarterly
ISSN: 1520-6262

14645 **Asahi Shimbun Satellite Edition**

Japan Access
757 3rd Avenue
Front 3
New York, NY 10017-2013

212-869-7018; Fax: 212-317-3025

Mo Matsuchita, Publisher
Cost: $3.00
Circulation: 12,000

14646 **Asian Economic News**

Kyodo News International
50 Rockefeller Plz
Room 803
New York, NY 10020-1605

212-603-6600; Fax: 212-397-3721
kni@kyodonews.com
www.kyodonews.com

Economic business news of Asian countries and regions.

14647 **Buisness IP Services in Brazil**

Probe Research
3 Wing Drive
Suite 240
Cedar Knolls, NJ 07927-1000

973-285-1500; Fax: 973-285-1519
www.proberesearch.com

Provides an overview of the business IP services market in Brazil; one of the most active IP markets in South America. Breakdown of Brazil companies. IT investment in B2B and networking applications. We discuss cable and ADSL broadband services and the e-government project. Profile of over 15 service providers.

14648 **Business Russia**

Economist Intelligence Unit
111 W 57th Street
New York, NY 10019-2211

212-586-1115
800-938-4685; Fax: 212-586-1181
www.eiu.com

Hyunkyu Lee, Owner

Monthly newsletter providing financial and market information as well as current business statistics, economic forecasts and political risk analysis for Russia.
Cost: $865.00
12 Pages
Frequency: Monthly
ISSN: 1357-0293

14649 **Business Africa**

Economist Intelligence Unit
111 W 57th Street
New York, NY 10019-2211

212-861-1115
800-938-4685; Fax: 212-586-1181
www.eiu.com

Daniel Franklin, Editorial Director
Richard Epstein, Director
Ingersoll Rand, Managing Director
Jane Morley, Senior Editor

Fortnightly newsletter identifying key business issues across Africa; forecasting future developments and trends and analysing their implications on Africa's business environment.
Cost: $1095.00
12 Pages
ISSN: 0968-4468
Founded in 1946

14650 **Business Asia**

Economist Intelligence Unit
111 W 57th Street
New York, NY 10019-2211

212-861-1115
800-938-4685; Fax: 212-586-1181
www.eiu.com

Daniel Franklin, Editorial Director
David Butter, Editor
Euan Rellie, Executive Director

Fortnightly newsletter focusing on operating issues and analyzing current political, business and economic developments across Asia.
Cost: $1055.00
12 Pages
Frequency: Fortnightly
ISSN: 0572-7545
Founded in 1946

14651 **Business China**

Economist Intelligence Unit
111 W 57th Street
New York, NY 10019-2211

212-586-1115
800-938-4685; Fax: 212-586-1181
www.eiu.com

Daniel Franklin, Editorial Director
Richard Epstein, Advertising Manager

Fortnightly newsletter alerting business executives to the political economic and legal changes that will affect corporate interests. Provides corporate case studies. Analysis financial issues in, and affecting, China. Offers practical, detailed advice.
Cost: $895.00
12 Pages
Frequency: 50 issues per y
ISSN: 1016-9766
Founded in 1946

14652 **Business Eastern Europe**

Economist Intelligence Unit
111 W 57th Street
New York, NY 10019-2211

212-861-1115
800-938-4685; Fax: 212-586-1181
www.eiu.com

Daniel Franklin, Editorial Director
Richard Epstein, Advertising Manager

Fortnightly newsletter providing information for business planning on the latest political and economic developments in Eastern Europe on a country-by-country basis.
Cost: $1395.00
12 Pages
Frequency: Weekly
ISSN: 1351-8763
Founded in 1946

14653 **Business Europe**

Economist Intelligence Unit
111 W 57th Street
New York, NY 10019-2211

212-861-1115
800-938-4685; Fax: 212-586-1181
www.eiu.com/

Lou Hencken, CEO/President
Paul Lewis, Editor
Nina Andrikian, Marketing

Fortnightly newsletter providing hard facts about changes in the EU's business environment; identifying opportunities for growth and analysing the impact of current issues on business in Europe.
Cost: $1435.00
12 Pages
Frequency: 44 issues per y
ISSN: 1351-8755
Founded in 1946

14654 **Business India Intelligence**

Economist Intelligence Unit

111 W 57th Street
New York, NY 10019-2211

212-586-1115
800-938-4685; Fax: 212-586-1181
www.eiu.com

Helen Alexander, CEO
Lou Kelly, Marketing Manager
Louis Ceil, VP

Monthly newsletter tracking the issues and trends in India's business environment; providing information on infrastructure and industries, tariffs, taxes and economic policy and consumer markets.
Cost: $660.00
16 Pages
Frequency: Monthly
ISSN: 1352-8335
Founded in 1946

14655 **Business Latin America**
Economist Intelligence Unit
111 W 57th Street
New York, NY 10019-2211
212-861-1115
800-938-4685; Fax: 212-586-1181
www.eiu.com

Daniel Franklin, Editorial Director
Richard Epstein, Director, Business Development

Weekly newsletter covering vital issues affecting business in Latin America, identifying the opportunities, and forecasting the risks to help executives make competetive corporate decisions.
Cost: $1370.00
12 Pages
Founded in 1946

14656 **Caribbean Update**
52 Maple Avenue
Maplewood, NJ 07040-2626

973-762-1565; Fax: 973-762-9585
mexcarib@cs.com

Kal Wagenheim, Editor/Publisher

Monthly newsletter focusing on trade and investment opportunities in the Caribbean and Central America.
Cost: $267.00
24 Pages
Frequency: Monthly
Founded in 1985
Mailing list available for rent: 2500 names
Printed in one color on newsprint stock

14657 **Country Finance**
Economist Intelligence Unit
111 W 57th Street
New York, NY 10019-2211

212-861-1115
800-938-4685; Fax: 212-586-1181
www.eiu.com

Daniel Franklin, Editorial Director
Richard Epstein, Director, Business Development

Covering 47 countries, this service is a comprehensive overview of global financial issues and conditions. Provides case studies and resources to help companies find and manage finances in countries around the globe. A weekly alert service highlights changes as they happen.
Cost: $445.00
Frequency: 41 issues per y
Founded in 1946

14658 **Country Forecasts**
Economist Intelligence Unit
111 W 57th Street
New York, NY 10019-2211

212-861-1115
800-938-4685; Fax: 212-586-1181
www.eiu.com

Daniel Franklin, Editorial Director

Five-year forecasts of political, economic and business trends in 60 countries. Each quarterly updated forecast focuses on the key factors affecting a country's political and economic outlook and its business environment over the next five years.
Cost: $845.00
36 Pages
Frequency: Quarterly

14659 **Country Monitor**
Economist Intelligence Unit
111 W 57th Street
New York, NY 10019-2211

212-861-1115
800-938-4685; Fax: 212-586-1181
www.eiu.com

Daniel Franklin, Editorial Director
Richard Epstein, Director, Business Development

Weekly newsletter analysing the latest global economic and political events; providing risk assessment in emerging markets and facts on global trends and markets.
Cost: $895.00
12 Pages
Frequency: Weekly
Founded in 1946

14660 **Country Reports**
Economist Intelligence Unit
111 W 57th Street
New York, NY 10019-2211

212-861-1115
800-938-4685; Fax: 212-586-0248
www.eiu.com

Daniel Franklin, Editorial Director
Emily Morris, Senior Editor

Quarterly updates on the situation in over 180 countries. Each report includes and analysis of a country's current political and economic climate as well as 12-18 month economic projection.
Cost: $425.00
Founded in 1946

14661 **Country Risk Service**
Economist Intelligence Unit
111 W 57th Street
New York, NY 10019-2211

212-861-1115
800-938-4685; Fax: 212-586-1181
www.eiu.com

Daniel Franklin, Editorial Director

Information to assist financial risk management in emerging countries. Country Risk Service is an exclusive two-year forecasting service, assessing the solvency of 100 indebted countries. Each report includes projections of GDP, the budget deficit, trade and current account balances, financing requirements and debt-service ratio.
Cost: $760.00
60 Pages
Frequency: Quarterly
Founded in 1946

14662 **East Asian Business Intelligence**
International Executive Reports
717 D St Nw
Suite 300
Washington, DC 20004-2815

202-737-6366; Fax: 202-628-6618
execrep@aol.com

William Hearn, Publisher

Twice-a-month newsletter containing business leads and market studies on Far East business.
Cost: $345.00
8 Pages
Frequency: 22 per year
Circulation: 300
ISSN: 0888-058X
Founded in 1986
Printed in on matte stock

14663 **East/West Executive Guide**
WorldTrade Executive
PO Box 761
Concord, MA 01742

978-287-0301; Fax: 978-287-0302
www.wtexec.com

Alison French, Production Manager

Provides detailed information on how to do business in Russia, the CIS, and East/Central Europe. Focuses on key mechanical issues such as accounting and tax matters, local sourcing, the due diligence process, labor, finance, permits, environmental issues etc.
Cost: $656.00
Frequency: Monthly

14664 **European Community**
US Council for International Business
1212 Ave of the Americas
Suite 1800
New York, NY 10036-1689

212-354-4480; Fax: 212-575-0327
www.uscib.org

Peter Robinson, President

Newssheet on developments in the European community affecting business on council activities.
Circulation: 2,800

14665 **Export Update**
Trade Communications
733 15th Street NW
Suite 1100
Washington, DC 20005-2112

202-737-1060; Fax: 202-783-5966

Stephen Pfeiderer, Publisher

Includes significant buying trends, specific sales leads, in-depth country market profiles, latest figures on trade activity, schedules for trade affairs and missions and insight on the affects of international news.

14666 **Hong Kong Trade Development Council Newsletter**
Hong Kong Trade Development Council
219 E 46th Street
New York, NY 10017

212-838-8688; Fax: 212-838-8941
new.york.office@hktdc.org
www.hktdc.com
Facebook, Twitter, LinkedIn, Google+, YouTube, RSS, Weibo

Anna Fan, Director, New York

Promotes trade between the United States and Hong Kong.
Frequency: Weekly
Founded in 1966

14667 **Indonesia Letter**
Asia Letter Group
12508 Whitley Street
Whittier, CA 90601-2729

FAX 852-526-2950

14668 **International Finance & Treasury**
WorldTrade Executive

PO Box 761
Concord, MA 01742

978-287-0301; Fax: 978-287-0302
www.wtexec.com

Alison French, CEO

Focus on techniques used by leading firms to manage worldwide financial resources. Topics covered include: tax, accounting and regulatory changes, currency and interest rate risk, cash management techniques, risk management strategies, regional treasury alerts.
Cost: $1245.00
Frequency: Weekly

14669 International Observer
PO Box 5997
Washington, DC 20016-1597

202-244-7050; Fax: 202-244-5410

J Wagner, Publisher

Informs on world developments in political, diplomatic, government, security, and economic origins.
Cost: $240.00
10 Pages
Frequency: Monthly
Printed in one color

14670 International Securitization & Structured Finance
WorldTrade Executive
PO Box 761
Concord, MA 01742

978-287-0301; Fax: 978-287-0302
www.wtexec.com

Jill McKenna, Production Manager
George Veoger, Editor
Pierre Brown, Publisher
Alleesa Aughas, Marketing Manager

A twice monthly report devoted exclusively to asset-backed securities in international markets. Covers all aspects of international asset-backed securitization, including innovative product trends, issuer considerations, regulatory matters, and tax and accounting considerations. Examines what is working in emerging markets and spotlights unique US transactions.
Cost: $1296.00
Frequency: Bi-monthly
Founded in 1996

14671 International Trade Alert
American Association of Importers and Exporters
1200 G Street NW
Suite 800
Washington, DC 20005

212-944-2230; Fax: 202-661-2185
www.aaei.org

Mathew Mermigousis, Production Manager
Stuart Iserber, Director of Events
Michelle Measel, Director of Events

Reports on current trade developments and advance notices of changes in rules for conducting business in the United States, as well as developments affecting trade originating from Treasury, Customs, US Courts, Commerce Department, International Trade Commission, Federal Maritime Commission and other regulatory agencies.
10 Pages
Frequency: Monthly
Circulation: 2,200

14672 International Trade Reporter Current Reports
Bureau of National Affairs
1801 S Bell St
Arlington, VA 22202-4501

703-341-3000
800-372-1033; Fax: 800-253-0332
customercare@bna.com
www.bnabooks.com
Facebook, Twitter, LinkedIn

Paul N Wojcik, Chairman
Gregory C. McCaffery, President and CEO
John Camp, Vice President
Lisa A. Fitzpatrick, Vice President
Audrey Hipkins, Vice President

A comprehensive source that reports and analyzes legislative and regulatory developments as well as private sector activities affecting international trade (both export and import).
Cost: $1744.00
Frequency: Weekly
Founded in 1929

14673 International Trade Reporter Decisions
Bureau of National Affairs
1801 S Bell St
Arlington, VA 22202-4501

703-341-3000
800-372-1033; Fax: 800-253-0332
customercare@bna.com
www.bnabooks.com
Facebook, Twitter, LinkedIn

Paul N Wojcik, Chairman
Gregory C. McCaffery, President and CEO
John Camp, Vice President
Lisa A. Fitzpatrick, Vice President
Audrey Hipkins, Vice President

Only available source of digested, classified and indexed judicial and administrative decisions dealing with legal issues arising from US trade law (mostly import cases).
Cost: $2265.00
ISSN: 0748-0709

14674 International Trade Reporter Import Reference Manual
Bureau of National Affairs
1801 S Bell St
Arlington, VA 22202-4501

703-341-3000
800-372-1033; Fax: 800-253-0332
customercare@bna.com
www.bnabooks.com
Facebook, Twitter, LinkedIn

Paul N Wojcik, Chairman
Gregory C. McCaffery, President and CEO
John Camp, Vice President
Lisa A. Fitzpatrick, Vice President
Audrey Hipkins, Vice President

A complete guide to the entire import process with analysis and full text of statutes, regulations, and executive orders on subjects such as customhouse brokers, dumping, countervailing duties, escape clauses, and presidential retaliation.
Cost: $1781.00

14675 Investing, Licensing & Trading
Economist Intelligence Unit
111 W 57th Street
New York, NY 10019-2211

212-586-1115
800-938-4685; Fax: 212-586-1181
www.eiu.com

Updated twice a year, ILT outlines business requirements for operating successfully in the world's major markets. This reference service, shows how the laws work in practice, with case studies of how leading multinationals obtain government approvals, set up local companies, calculate corporate and personal taxes and overcome restrictions and other legal hurdles in 60 countries and the European Union.
Cost: $345.00

14676 Managing Imports and Exports
Institute of Management and Administration
1 Washington Park
Suite 1300
Newark, NJ 07102-3130

212-244-0360; Fax: 973-622-0595
customercare@bna.com
www.ioma.com

The source of information on customs policies and procedures, BIS rules and regulations, and how to best enhance the compliance programs.
Cost: $437.00

14677 Market Europe
PRS Group
6320 Fly Rd
Suite 102
East Syracuse, NY 13057-9792

315-431-0511; Fax: 315-431-0200
custserv@prsgroup.com
www.prsgroup.com

Mary Lou Walsh, President
Doris Walsh, Chairman

Demographic and lifestyle information about consumers in Europe to help businesses do a better job marketing to those consumers.
Cost: $397.00
Frequency: Monthly
Circulation: 325
Founded in 1985
Printed in one color on matte stock

14678 Mexican Forecast
WorldTrade Executive
2250 Main St
Suite 100
Concord, MA 01742-3838

978-287-0301; Fax: 978-287-0302

Gary Brown, President
Jay Stanley, Sales Manager

Provides up-to-date information and forecasts on Mexican business. Includes coverage of foreign trade, currency, major industry sectors, market trends and investment climates.
Cost: $535.00

14679 Middle East Business Intelligence
International Executive Reports
717 D St Nw
Suite 300
Washington, DC 20004-2815

202-737-6366; Fax: 202-628-6618
execrep@aol.com

William Hearn, Publisher

Twice-a-month newsletter containing business leads and market studies on Middle East business.
Cost: $345.00
8 Pages
Circulation: 400
ISSN: 0731-5305
Printed in one color on matte stock

14680 Middle East Trade Letter
PO Box 472986
Charlotte, NC 28247-2986

704-536-9847; Fax: 704-543-6161

Leslie B Cohen, Publisher

Business in the Middle East.
Cost: $139.00
4 Pages
Frequency: Quarterly
Circulation: 500
Printed in one color on newsprint stock

14681 Nielsen's International Investment Letter
Nielsen & Nielsen

1901 South Bay Rd Ne
Olympia, WA 98506-3532

360-352-7485; Fax: 360-352-7485
www.nelsonfurnitureworks.com

Paul Nelson, President

Tracks domestic and international stock markets and economics, precious metals and other commodities, USA and foreign bonds, interest rates, foreign currencies and real estate; offers clients specific buy and sell recommendations on domestic and international investments for both traders and investors.
Cost: $360.00
10 Pages
Frequency: Monthly
Printed in on matte stock

14682 **North American Free Trade & Investment**
WorldTrade Executive
PO Box 761
Concord, MA 01742

978-287-0301; Fax: 978-287-0302
www.wtexec.com

Alison French, Production Manager
Gary Brown, CEO/President
Gary Brown, Editor
Dana Pierce, Marketing Manager
Dana Pierce, Circulation Manager

Covers NAFTA trade and investment developments. Key topics include rules of origin, tariff phaseouts, intellectual property protection, compliance and planning options, and business opportunities.
Cost: $734.00
Frequency: Annual+
Circulation: 100
Founded in 1992

14683 **Practical Latin American Tax Strategies**
WorldTrade Executive
PO Box 761
Concord, MA 01742

978-287-0301; Fax: 978-287-0302
www.wtexec.com

Alison French, Production Manager

A monthly report on how leading companies are reacting to changes and developments in Latin American tax practice. Includes commentary from senior practitioners at major law and accounting firms and case studies from major corporations.
Cost: $645.00
Frequency: Monthly

14684 **Practical US/International Tax Strategies**
WorldTrade Executive
PO Box 761
Concord, MA 01742-761

978-287-0301; Fax: 978-287-0302
www.wtexec.com

Dana Pierce, Production Manager
Gary Brown, CEO/Publisher
David Cooper, Editor
John Nartel, Marketing Manager
Jay Stanley, Sales Manager

Analyzes how leading companies are reacting to changes in US-international tax practice. Leading experts provide practical guidance covering every area of international transactions.
Cost: $614.00
Frequency: Fortnightly
Circulation: 200
Founded in 1992

14685 **Russian Far East Update**
Russian Far East Update
PO Box 22126
Seattle, WA 98122-0126

206-447-2668; Fax: 206-628-0979

Trade and economic information plus news analysis of Russia's far east.
Cost: $20.00
Circulation: 1,300

14686 **Vietnam Business Info Track**
Vietnam Access
PO Box 1210
Port Hueneme, CA 93044-1210

FAX 805-985-0839

Kahn Le, Editor

Comprehensive coverage of Vietnam market. Focuses on trade, investment and sector reports. Gives you an immediate advantage in evaluating the potential of doing business in Vietnam and operating in a timely and cost effective matter.

14687 **Vietnam Market Watch**
Vietnam Market Resources
375 Lexington Avenue
New York, NY 10017

212-499-2000; Fax: 203-256-9790
mail@inc.com
www.inc.com/

Khoung Ho, Publisher
Aaron Goldstein, Chief Operating Officer
Caroline Basquez, Owner

For companies and professionals doing business in Vietnam.
Cost: $295.00
Frequency: Monthly
Circulation: 500
Founded in 2004

14688 **Weekly International Market Alert**
International Business Communications
114 E 32nd Street
#602
New York, NY 10016

212-686-1460

Johnathan Block, Publisher

International trade news.
Frequency: Monthly

14689 **World Trade**
Taipan Press
4199 Campus Drive
Suite 230
Irvine, CA 92612-4684

949-410-0980; Fax: 949-725-0306

Will Swaim, Publisher

Articles aim to help companies expand international opportunities. Accepts advertising.
Cost: $24.00
96 Pages
Frequency: Monthly

Magazines & Journals

14690 **AIB Insights**
Academy of International Business
Michigan State University
7 Eppley Center
East Lansing, MI 48824-1121

517-432-1452; Fax: 517-432-1009
aib@aib.msu.edu
aib.msu.edu

Ilan Alon, Editor

Provides an outlet for short, interesting, topical, current, and thought provoking articles. Articles can discuss theoretical, empirical, practical or pedagogical issues affecting the international business community.
Frequency: Quarterly
ISSN: 1938-9590

14691 **Aaonline**
Africa-America Institute
420 Lexington Ave
Suite 1706
New York, NY 10170-0007

212-949-5666; Fax: 212-682-6174
aainy@aaionline.org
www.aaionline.org

Amber Jones, Executive Assistant
Mora McLean, Vice President
Joy Phumaphi, Vice President
Frequency: Quarterly
Circulation: 3000
Founded in 1953

14692 **American Business in China**
Caravel
23545 Crenshaw Blvd
Suite 101E
Torrance, CA 90505-5201

310-325-0100; Fax: 310-325-2583
info@china4us.com
www.china4us.com

Directory of US firms operating in China and Hong Kong; Hong Kong: a special administrative region; exporting to China - best US exporting prospects; China's major cities for foreign investments; marketing, advertising and exhibiting in China.
Cost: $99.00
288 Pages
Circulation: 10,000
ISBN: 0-964432-29-3
Founded in 1993
Mailing list available for rent: 2,000 names at $95 per M

14693 **Asian Finance**
Asian Finance Publications
14 Davis Drive
Armonk, NY 10504-3005

Focuses on international banking and finance.
Circulation: 13147

14694 **Asian Industrial Report**
Keller International Publishing Corporation
150 Great Neck Rd
Great Neck, NY 11021-3309

516-829-9722; Fax: 516-829-9306

Robert Herihly, Publisher
Brian Deluca, Editor
Jerry Keller, President

New machinery and equipment.
Cost: $85.00
36 Pages
Frequency: Monthly
Circulation: 20000
Founded in 1882
Printed in 4 colors on matte stock

14695 **Business America: the Magazine of International Trade**
US Department of Commerce
200 Constitution Ave NW
Washington, DC 20210-0001

202-693-5000; Fax: 202-219-8822
www.dol.gov
Facebook, Twitter, LinkedIn, Pinterest, Blogger, Tumblr

Hilda L Solis, CEO

Designed to help American exporters penetrate overseas markets by providing them with timely information on opportunities for trade and

methods of doing business in foreign countries.
Cost: $2.00
Circulation: 13,000
Mailing list available for rent

14696 **Cross Border**
Economist Intelligence Unit
111 W 57th Street
New York, NY 10019-2211
212-586-1115; Fax: 212-586-1181
Debrah Langley, Publisher
Focuses on multinational management issues faced by managers of international businesses.
Circulation: 55,000

14697 **East Asian Executive Report**
International Executive Reports
717 D St NW
Suite 300
Washington, DC 20004-2815
202-737-6366; Fax: 202-628-6618
execrep@aol.com
William Hearn, Publisher
Monthly magazine covering the legal and practical requirements of doing business in Far Eastern countries.
Cost: $455.00
28 Pages
Frequency: Monthly
Circulation: 600
ISSN: 0272-1589
Founded in 1979
Printed in on matte stock

14698 **Economist**
PO Box 58524
Boulder, CO 80322-8524
303-945-1917
800-456-6086; Fax: 303-604-7455
ukpressoffice@economist.com
www.economist.com
Helen Alexander, CEO
Kate Cooke, Group Communications Manager
David Hanger, Publisher
James Wilson, Founder
The Economist is a news and business publication written for top business decision-makers and opinion leaders who need a wide range of information and views on world events. It explores the close links between domestic and international issues, business, finance, current affairs, science and technology.
160 Pages
Frequency: Weekly
Circulation: 1009759
ISSN: 0013-0613
Founded in 1843
Printed in 4 colors on glossy stock

14699 **Export**
Adams/Hunter Publishing
2101 S Arlington Heights Road
Suite 150
Arlington Heights, IL 60005-4142
FAX 847-427-2006
David Thayer, Publisher
Covers all aspects of international trade for distributors of consumer durables in 183 countries.

14700 **Foreign Affairs**
Foreign Affairs
58 E 68th St
New York, NY 10065-5953
212-434-9522
800-829-5539; Fax: 212-861-2759
order@wshein.com
www.foreignaffairs.org
David Kellogg, Publisher
Gideon Rose, Editor
Michael Pasuit, Marketing Coordinator
Eugnia Chang, Circulation Director
Reviews on events, news, people, and foreign relations.
Cost: $44.00
Founded in 1921

14701 **Global Trade**
North American Publishing Company
1500 Spring Garden St
Suite 1200
Philadelphia, PA 19130-4094
215-238-5300; Fax: 215-238-5342
www.napco.com
Ned S Borowsky, President and CEO
Bennett Zucker, Publisher
Assists international cargo decision makers in planning, financing and documenting goods and commodities in international trade. Accepts advertising.
Cost: $45.00
Frequency: Monthly
Founded in 1958

14702 **IGT Magazine**
World Trade Winds
610 Old Campbell Rd
Suite 108
Richardson, TX 75080-3379
972-994-9816
877-861-1188; Fax: 972-699-1189
Offers information for exporters to find international buyers.
ISSN: 0259-9880
Founded in 1975

14703 **Journal of International Business Studies**
Academy of International Business
Michigan State University
7 Eppley Center
East Lansing, MI 48824-1121
517-432-1452; Fax: 517-432-1009
managing-editor@jibs.net
www.aib.msu.edu
Lorraine Eden, Editor
The leading peer-reviewed, scholarly journal that publishes research across the entire range of topics encompassing the domain of international business studies.
Frequency: 9x/Year
ISSN: 0047-2506

14704 **LASA Forum**
Latin American Studies Association
946 William Pitt Union
University of Pittsburgh
Pittsburgh, PA 15260
412-648-7929; Fax: 412-624-7145
lasa@pitt.edu
lasa.international.pitt.edu/
Hane Horowitz, Exhibit Management Head
Arturo Arias, Associate Editor
Sonia E Alvarez, President/Editor
Charles R Hale, VP
Milagros Pereyra-Rojas, Managing Editor
Published by the Latin American Studies Association.
Cost: $30.00
Frequency: Quarterly
Founded in 1969
Mailing list available for rent

14705 **Latin Trade Magazine**
Freedom Latin America
1001 Brickell Bay Drive
Suite 2700
Miami, FL 33131
305-749-0880; Fax: 786-513-2407
info@latintrade.com
www.latintrade.com
Facebook, Twitter, LinkedIn, RSS
Rosemary Winters, Chief Executive Officer
Maria Lourdes Gallo, Executive Director & Publisher
Santiago Gutierrez, Executive Editor
Elida Bustos, Managing Editor
Manny Melo, Art & Production Director
Comprehensive news coverage and analysis of business issues in Latin America and the Caribbean. Available in English or Spanish
Cost: $64.00
Frequency: Monthly
Circulation: 92,319
Founded in 1993

14706 **Middle East Executive Reports**
International Executive Reports
717 D St NW
Suite 300
Washington, DC 20004-2815
202-737-6366; Fax: 202-628-6618
execrep@aol.com
William Hearn, Publisher
Monthly magazine covering the legal and practical requirements of doing business in the Middle East.
Cost: $455.00
28 Pages
Frequency: Monthly
Circulation: 1,000
ISSN: 0271-0498
Founded in 1978
Printed in 2 colors on matte stock

14707 **Showcase USA**
Bobit Publishing Company
23210 Crenshaw Blvd
Torrance, CA 90505-3181
310-539-1969; Fax: 310-539-4329
www.bobit.com
John Bebout, Owner
International marketing vehicle for American manufacturing.
Cost: $12.00
165 Pages
Founded in 1979

14708 **Trade and Culture Magazine**
Key Communications
PO Box 569
Garrisonville, VA 22463-0569
540-657-7174
800-544-5684; Fax: 540-720-5687
www.key-com.com
Debra Levy, Owner
Kim White, Managing Editor
Penny Stacey, Advertising Coordinator
Published to help executives make their companies competitive worldwide, featuring 22 trade zone presentations in each issue covering every country. Trade and Culture blends cultural insight with practical how-to business information.
Cost: $39.95
96 Pages
Frequency: Quarterly
Circulation: 45000
Founded in 1993

14709 **US Council for International Business**
1212 Avenue of the Americas
Suite 1805
New York, NY 10036-1689
212-354-4480; Fax: 212-575-0327
info@uscib.org
www.uscib.org
Peter Robinson, President
Davis Hodge, Marketing & Advertising

Monthly newsletter that supports those involved in the developments in the European community affecting business on council activities.
Frequency: Monthly
Founded in 1945

14710 **US-China Business Council**
US China Business Council
1818 N St NW
Suite 200
Washington, DC 20036-2470

202-429-0340; Fax: 202-775-2476
info@uschina.org
www.uschina.org

John Frisbie, President
Erin Ennis, VP
Ryan Ong, Director/Business Advisory Services

Covers all aspects of doing business with China and Hong Kong.
Cost: $100.00
240+ Members
Circulation: 6000
ISSN: 0163-7169
Founded in 1973
Printed in on glossy stock

14711 **Vietnam Business Journal**
VIAM Communications Group
535 W 114th Street
New York, NY 10027

212-854-2271; Fax: 212-854-9099

Kenneth Felderbaum, Publisher

Research and experience based articles and graphics produces by journalists.

14712 **World Trade**
Freedom Magazine
2401 W. Big Beaver Rd
Suite 700
Troy, MI 48084

248-362-3700
www.bnpmedia.com
Facebook, Twitter, LinkedIn

Steve Beyer, Director

Articles are aimed at helping companies to expand their international opportunities.
Frequency: Monthly
Circulation: 70590
Founded in 1987

Trade Shows

14713 **AIB Annual Meeting**
Academy of International Business
645 N. Shaw Ln
Rm 7
East Lansing, MI 48824-1121

517-432-1452; Fax: 517-432-1009
aib@aib.msu.edu
www.aib.msu.edu

G Tomas M Hult, Executive Director
Tunga Kiyak, Managing Director
Irem Kiyak, Treasurer
Robert Grosse, President
Elizabeth Rose, Vice President Administration

Features a combination of plenaries, panels, and papers.
Frequency: June-July

14714 **American-Turkish Council Annual Meeting**
Ideea
6233 Nelway Drive
McLean, VA 22101

703-760-0762; Fax: 703-760-0764
qwhiteree@ideea.com
www.ideea.com

Quentin C Whiteeree, President

High level military and government officials and businessmen from Turkey and the United States. Seminar and over 25 exhibits of trade, defense, banking, investments and tourism.
1000 Attendees
Frequency: Annual
Founded in 1983

14715 **Annual Convention and Trade Show**
American Association of Exporters and Importers
1050 17th Street NW
Suite 810
Washington, DC 20036

202-857-8009; Fax: 202-857-7843
hq@aaei.org
www.aaei.org
Facebook, Twitter

Kathy Corrigan, Director Meetings/Events
Marianne Rowden, President and CEO
Terri A Lankford, Director Membership & Marketing
David A Potts, Manager Office Administration
Megan Montgomery, Director of Government Affairs

Reports on current trade developments and advance notices of changes in rules for conducting business in the United States, as well as developments affecting trade originating from Treasury, Customs, US Courts, Commerce Department, International Trade Commission, Federal Maritime Commission and other regulatory agencies. 50 exhibitors with 50 booths.
550 Attendees
Frequency: May
Founded in 1921

14716 **International Business Expo**
Assist International
90 John Street
Room 505
New York, NY 10038

212-442-2074; Fax: 212-725-3312

Peter Robinson, Director

This expo has 170 exhibitors with 170 booths.
1800 Attendees
Frequency: April
Founded in 1999

14717 **Showcase USA Trade Show**
Bobit Publishing Company
3520 Challenger Street
Torrance, CA 90503

310-533-2400; Fax: 310-533-2500
webmaster@bobit.com
www.bobit.com

Mike Spivak, Editor
Ty Bobit, CEO

International marketing vehicle for American manufacturing.
165 Attendees
Founded in 1979

14718 **USRBC Annual Meeting**
US Russia Business Council
1701 Pennsylvania Avenue NW
Suite 520
Washington, DC 20006

202-739-9180; Fax: 202-659-5920
lawson@usrbc.org
www.usrbc.org

Eugene K Lawson, President

Highlights the opportunities and risks that are emerging in the Russian market as it enters a new stage of development.

Directories & Databases

14719 **A Basic Guide to Exporting**
World Trade Press
1450 Grant Avenue
Suite 204
Novato, CA 94945

415-549-9934
800-833-8586; Fax: 415-898-1080
www.worldtradepress.com

Alexandra Woznick

Includes significant new information on export regulations, customs benefit, and tax incentives. There are also hundreds of new sources of assistance available with updated addresses and telephone numbers.
188 Pages
ISBN: 1-885073-83-6
Founded in 1999

14720 **AIMCAL SourceBook**
Association of International Metallizers/Coaters
201 Springs Street
Fort Mill, SC 29715

803-948-9470; Fax: 803-948-9471
aimcal@aimcal.org
www.aimcal.org/sourcebook.html

Craig Sheppard, Executive Director
Tracey Messina, Operations Manager
Melissa Crandall, Administrative Assistant
Kevin Lifsey, Web & IT Manager

An index from the Association of International Metallizers, Coaters and Laminators listing member services, products and equipment. Some topics include management techniques, roll to roll markets and technology development.

14721 **American Business in China**
Caravel
23545 Crenshaw Blvd
Sutie 101E
Torrance, CA 90505-5201

310-325-0100; Fax: 310-325-2583
info@china4us.com
www.china4us.com

Davisson Chang, Owner
Sheryl Chang, Production Manager
Betty Yao, Marketing Manager

Directory of US firms operating in China and Hong Kong; Hong Kong as a special administrative region; exporting to China - best US exporting prospects; China's major cities for foreign investments; marketing, advertising and exhibiting in China. Also contains 1,000+ US contacts and 1,800+ China & Hong Kong contacts
Cost: $99.00
288 Pages
Frequency: Annual
ISBN: 0-964432-29-3
Founded in 1995
Mailing list available for rent: 2,000 names at $95 per M

14722 **Arthur Andersen North American Business Sourcebook**
Triumph Books

601 S La Salle St
Suite 500
Chicago, IL 60605-1725

312-939-3330; Fax: 312-663-3557
www.triumphbooks.com

Mitch Rogatz, President/Publisher
Tom Bast, Editorial Director
Blythe Hurley, Managing Editor
Kelley Thornton, Associate Editor

Government and trade agencies and trade-related databases in the United States, Canada and Mexico are profiled.
Cost: $150.00
Founded in 1994

14723 AtoZ World Business
World Trade Press
800 Lindberg Lane
Suite 190
Petaluma, CA 94952

707-778-1124
800-833-8586; Fax: 707-778-1329
egh@worldtradepress.com
www.worldtradepress.com

Edward Hinkelman, Publisher

The world's most comprehensive country-by-country resource for success in international business and trade. Consists of 100 Country Business Guides and 76 World Trade Resources. Offers entrepreneurs, business professionals and researchers access to vetted international business and trade intelligence, compiled into a single, reliable source.
Founded in 1993

14724 Brazil Tax, Law, & Business Briefing
WorldTrade Executive
2250 Main St
Suite 100
Concord, MA 01742-3838

978-287-0301; Fax: 978-287-0302

Gary Brown, Owner
Jay Stanley, Sales Manager

Coverage includes economic analysis and risk assessment, new transfer pricing rules, foreign direct investment, labor regulation, environment, privatization, accessing the Mercosur market, litigation, arbitration, and debt collection in Brazil, antitrust concerns for foreign acquisition, securitizing infrastructure projects, foreign investor access to the telecommunications market, and choices in creating Brazilian subsidiaries.
Cost: $297.00
340 Pages
ISBN: 1-893323-57-9

14725 CSI Market Statistics
Commodity Systems
200 W Palmetto Park Rd
Suite 200
Boca Raton, FL 33432-3788

561-392-1556
800-274-4727; Fax: 561-392-7761
info@csidata.com
www.csidata.com

Bob Pelletier, President

Offers information on daily, weekly and monthly time series of price and trading data for commodity markets worldwide, cash, futures options, index options, US stocks and mutual funds and government instruments.

14726 Chinese Business in America
Caravel
23545 Crenshaw Blvd
Suite 101E
Torrance, CA 90505-5201

310-325-0100; Fax: 310-325-2583
info@china4us.com
www.china4us.com

Davisson Chang, Owner
Sheryl Chang, CEO

Directory of ethnic Chinese importers and exporters in the US; marketing, sourcing and establishing a business in the US; US business laws and immigration regulations; money saving tips and business bargains.
Cost: $88.00
288 Pages
Frequency: Annual
Circulation: 5,000
ISBN: 0-964432-26-9
Founded in 1997

14727 DACA Directory
Distributors & Consolidators of America
2240 Bernays Dr.
York, PA 17404

888-519-9195
daca@comcast.net
www.dacacarriers.com

Firms and individuals active in the shipping, warehousing, receiving, distribution or consolidation of freight shipments.

14728 DRI Europe
DRI/McGraw-Hill
24 Hartwell Ave
Lexington, MA 02421-3103

781-860-6060; Fax: 781-860-6002
support@construction.com
www.construction.com

Walt Arvin, President

Subjects covered in this database include macroeconomic, microeconomic, and financial indicators for the European countries.

14729 DRI Middle East and African Forecast
DRI/McGraw-Hill
24 Hartwell Ave
Lexington, MA 02421-3103

781-860-6060; Fax: 781-860-6002
support@construction.com
www.construction.com

Walt Arvin, President

This large database offers more than 500 annual historical and forecast time series for 10 Middle Eastern and African economies.

14730 DRI/TBS World Sea Trade Forecast
DRI/McGraw-Hill
24 Hartwell Ave
Lexington, MA 02421-3103

781-860-6060; Fax: 781-860-6002
support@construction.com
www.construction.com

Walt Arvin, President

This comprehensive database covers cargo movements over major water trade routes worldwide.

14731 DRI/TBS World Trade Forecast
DRI/McGraw-Hill
24 Hartwell Ave
Lexington, MA 02421-3103

781-860-6060; Fax: 781-860-6002
support@construction.com
www.construction.com

Walt Arvin, President

Offers over 82,000 annual historical and forecast time series on import and export volumes, and prices in current US dollars.

14732 Dictionary of International Trade
World Trade Press
1450 Grant Avenue
Suite 190
Petaluma, CA 94952

707-778-1124
800-833-8586; Fax: 707-778-1329
egh@worldtradepress.com
www.worldtradepress.com

Edward G Hinkelman

The most respected and largest-selling dictionary of trade in the world. It is in use in more than 100 countries by importers, exporters, bankers, shippers, logistics professionals, attorneys, economists, and government officials.
Cost: $55.00
688 Pages
ISBN: 1-885073-72-0
Founded in 2004

14733 Directory of US Exporters
Journal of Commerce
33 Washington Street
Floor 13
Newark, NJ 07102

973-848-7000
amiddlebrook@cbizmedia.com
www.cbizmedia.com

Amy Middlebrook, Group Publisher

Provides logistics professionals with active confirmed leads for over 60,000 US companies involved in world trade.
Cost: $450.00
Frequency: Annual

14734 Directory of US Importers
Journal of Commerce
33 Washington Street
13 Floor
Newark, NJ 07102

973-848-7000
www.cbizmedia.com

Amy Middlebrook, Group Publisher

Provides logistics professionals with active confirmed leads for over 60,000 US companies involved in world trade.
Cost: $450.00

14735 Export Yellow Pages
US West Marketing Resources Group
1101 30th Street NW
Suite 200
Washington, DC 20007-3769

202-934-4584
800-228-2582; Fax: 202-944-4680

David Lee, President

Approximately 16,000 US suppliers distributed worldwide through US commerce department channels.

14736 Foreign Exchange Forecast Data Base
Global Insight
800 Baldwin Tower
Eddystone, PA 19022
610-490-4000; Fax: 610-490-2770
info@wefa.com
www.wefa.com

Ben G Hackett, International Trade/Transportation

This large database covers over 130 monthly and 60 quarterly time series of historical and forecast data for foreign exchange rates.

14737 Foreign Representatives in the US Yellow Book
Leadership Directories

104 5th Ave
New York, NY 10011-6901

212-627-4140; Fax: 212-645-0931
info@leadershipdirectories.com
www.leadershipdirectories.com
Facebook, Twitter

David Hurvitz, CEO
James M Petrie, Associate Publisher

Contact information for foreign representatives of over 187 nations at embassies, consulates, and intergovernmental organizations in the US, US executives of over 1,100 foreign corporations, over 275 foreign financial institutions with offices in the US, and over 300 international media outlets with bureaus in the US.
Cost: $245.00
850+ Pages
Frequency: SemiAnnual
ISSN: 1089-5833
Founded in 1969
Mailing list available for rent: 12,000 names at $125 per M

14738 **GIN International Database**
Global Information Network
146 W 29th St
Suite 7E
New York, NY 10001-5303

212-244-3123
www.g-i-n.net/home

Lisa Vives, Owner

This large database offers all sorts of information on developing countries, ranging from economics and finance to health and social trends.
Frequency: Full-text

14739 **GLOBAL Vantage**
Standard & Poor's Corporation
55 Water St
New York, NY 10041-0003

212-438-1000
800-525-8640; Fax: 212-438-0299

Deven Sharma, President

This database provides corporate financial data covering more than 2,500 US companies and over 1,500 companies in 23 other countries.

14740 **Global Report**
Citicorp
800 3rd Ave
New York, NY 10022-7669

212-688-1308
www.citibank.com

One of the most comprehensive databases in the world offering information on foreign exchange, country reports, money markets, bonds, companies, industries and news.
Frequency: Full-text

14741 **Importers Manual USA**
World Trade Press
800 Lindberg Lane
Suite 190
Petaluma, CA 94952

707-778-1124
800-833-8586; Fax: 707-777-1329
egh@worldtradepress.com
www.worldtradepress.com

Edward Hinkelman, Publisher
James Nolan, Editor
Karla Shippey, Editor

Lists of trade fairs, embassies, chambers of commerce, banks, and other sources of information on various aspects of international trade.
Cost: $145.00
960 Pages
Frequency: 2-3 per year
Circulation: 3,000
ISBN: 1-885073-93-3
Founded in 1993

14742 **International Directory of Importers**
1741 Kekamek NW
Poulsbo, WA 98730

360-779-1511
800-818-0140; Fax: 360-697-4696
www.export-leads.com

Esther Camacho, Circulation

Publishes reference guides for worldwide importers, wholesalers, agents, and distributors.
Cost: $250.00
5000 Pages
Frequency: Annual
Founded in 1978

14743 **Japan Economic Daily**
Kyodo News International
747 3rd Ave
Suite 1803
New York, NY 10017-2803

212-935-4440; Fax: 212-508-5441
kni@kyodonews.com
www.kyodonews.com

This full coverage database contains news on Japanese business, industry, economics and finance developments.
Frequency: Full-text

14744 **LEXIS International Trade Library**
Mead Data Central
9443 Springboro Pike
Dayton, OH 45401

888-223-6337; Fax: 518-487-3584
www.lexis-nexis.com

Andrew Prozes, CEO
Rebecca Schmitt, Chief Financial Officer

This database contains information on international trade regulation decisions handed down from the Supreme Court and other legislative bodies.
Frequency: Full-text

14745 **Local Chambers of Commerce Which Maintain Foreign Trade Services**
US Chamber of Commerce-International Division
1615 H St NW
Washington, DC 20062-0002

202-659-6000; Fax: 202-463-5836
www.uschamber.org

Thomas J Donohue, CEO
Jean Hunt, Administrative Assistant
Cost: $15.00

14746 **Mexico Tax, Law,& Business Briefing**
WorldTrade Executive
2250 Main St
Suite 100
Concord, MA 01742-3838

978-287-0301; Fax: 978-287-0302

Gary Brown, Owner
Jay Stanley, Sales Manager

A single volume special report that provides guidance on tax and legal issues investors should consider when evaluating a possible company aquisition, starting a business or entering into a joint venture or strategic alliance in Mexico. Also featuring important guidance prepared by major accounting and law firms.
Cost: $297.00
291 Pages
ISBN: 1-893323-67-6

14747 **North American Export Pages**
US West Marketing Resources Group
1101 30th Street NW
Suite 200
Washington, DC 20007-3769

202-934-4584
800-288-2582; Fax: 202-944-4680

David Lee, President

Approximately 50,000 suppliers from the United States, Canada, and Mexico wishing to export products worldwide.
Cost: $39.95

14748 **Official Export Guide**
North American Publishing Company
1500 Spring Garden St
Suite 1200
Philadelphia, PA 19130-4094

215-238-5300; Fax: 215-238-5342
www.napco.com

Ned S Borowsky, President and CEO

Offers information on customs officials, port authorities, embassies and consulates, chambers of commerce and other organizations involved in international trade.
Cost: $399.00
1800 Pages
Frequency: Annual
Founded in 1958

14749 **Political Handbook of the World**
McGraw Hill
PO Box 182604
Columbus, OH 43272

614-866-5769; Fax: 614-759-3759
www.mcgraw-hill.com

Arthur S Banks, Editor
Thomas C Muller, Editor

Annual reference book containing separate sections on every country in the world and more than 100 intergovernment organizations. Each edition completely updates political developments over the past year while retaining the extensive background information necessary for researchers to place current events in a comprehensive historical perspective.
1400 Pages
Founded in 1979

14750 **Practical Guide: Doing Business in Ukraine**
WorldTrade Executive
PO Box 761
Concord, MA 01742-0761

978-287-0301; Fax: 978-287-0302
www.wtexec.com

Alison French, Production Manager

Topics covered include: common business structures, registration procedures, real property transactions, tax and foreign investment legislation, currency reforms and regulations, privatization programs, intellectual property.
Cost: $145.00

14751 **Protecting Intellectual Property in Latin America**
WorldTrade Executive
PO Box 761
Concord, MA 01742-0761
978-287-0301; Fax: 978-287-0302
www.wtexec.com

Alison French, Production Manager

A complete guide to the protection of intellectual property in Latin America, including in-depth coverage of copyright law, patents and trademarks, software, pharmaceuticals, etc. Also deals with issues of enforcement and prosecution.
Cost: $235.00

14752 **Russian Far East: A Business Reference Guide**
Russian Far East Advisory Group
PO Box 22126
Seattle, WA 98122-0126

206-447-2668; Fax: 206-628-0979

Elisa Miller, Editor
Alexander Karp, Editor

Sourcebook for business people, travelers, and researchers focusing on trends and economic developments in the Russian Far East. Includes reviews of each of the ten administrative regions and 27 maps
Cost: $79.00
270 Pages
ISBN: 0-964128-63-2

14753 **Selling Successfully in Mexico**
WorldTrade Executive
PO Box 761
Concord, MA 01742-0761

978-287-0301; Fax: 978-287-0302
www.wtexec.com

Alison French, Production Manager

A detailed guide to market research, advertising, direct marketing, and trade show exhibition in Mexico, written by marketing professionals and supplemented by extensive data and key contracts.
Cost: $129.00

14754 **Showcase USA: American Export-Buyers Guide and Membership**
Bobit Publishing Company
3623 Artesia Boulevard
Redondo Beach, CA 90278

FAX 310-376-9043

List of member companies and organizations of Sell Overseas America.

14755 **Trade Opportunity**
US International Trade Association
1401 Constitution Ave NW
Washington, DC 20230-0001

202-482-2867
800-872-8723; Fax: 202-482-2867

David L Aaron, Manager
Renee Macklin, Chief Information Officer

Leads to export opportunities for United States businesses.

14756 **Trade Shows Worldwide**
Gale/Cengage Learning
PO Box 09187
Detroit, MI 48209-0187

248-699-4253
800-877-4253; Fax: 248-699-8049
gale.galeord@cengage.com
www.gale.com
Facebook, Twitter, Google+, Youtube

Patrick C Sommers, President

Each edition of this resource includes listings for more than 10,000 trade shows; approximately 6,000 trade show sponsoring organizations and more than 5,900 facilities, services and information sources on trade shows and exhibitions held in the United States and around the globe.
Frequency: Annual
ISBN: 1-414435-24-X

14757 **US Custom House Guide**
U.S. Custom House Guide

609-371-7825
888-215-6084; Fax: 609-371-7885

Monica McCarthy, Associate Editor
Amy Middlebrook, Vice President, Directories
Dennis Ferrere, Advertising Sales Rep

List of ports having customs facilities, customs officials, port authorities, chambers of commerce, embassies and consulates, foreign trade zones and other organizations; related trade services.
Cost: $399.00
Frequency: Annual January

14758 **World Trade Almanac**
World Trade Press
1450 Grant Avenue
Suite 204
Novato, CA 94945

415-454-9934
415-898-1124
www.worldtradepress.com

Gayle Madison
Peter Jones

Industry Web Sites

14759 **http://gold.greyhouse.com**
G.O.L.D Grey House OnLine Databases

Grey House Publishing's online database platform, GOLD, offers Quick Search, Keyword Search and Expert Search for most business sectors including international trade markets. The GOLD platform makes finding the information you need quick and easy - whether you're a novice searcher or an experienced database user. All of Grey House's directory products are available for subscription on the GOLD platform.

14760 **www.aib.msu.edu/**
Academy of International Business

Members are executives and teachers in the international business field.

14761 **www.fancyfoodshows.com**
National Association for the Specialty Food Trade

Members are manufacturers, importers, distributors and retailers of specialty gourmet and fancy foods. Has an annual budget of approximately $15 million. Publications available to members.

14762 **www.geminishippers.com**
Gemini Shippers Group

Shippers association with global contracts for all commodities.

14763 **www.greyhouse.com**
Grey House Publishing

Authoritative reference directories for most business sectors including international trade markets. Users can search the online databases with varied search criteria allowing for custom searches by product category, geographic area, sales volume, keyword, subject and more. Full Grey House catalog and online ordering also available.

14764 **www.hktdc.com**
Hong Kong Trade Development Council

Promotes trade between United States and Hong Kong.

14765 **www.iwla.com**
International Warehouse Logistics Association

The unified voice of the global logistics outsourcing industry, representing third party warehousing, transportation and logistics service providers. Our member companies provide the most timely and cost-effective global logistics solutions for their customers and are committed to protecting the free flow of products across international borders.

14766 **www.ncitd.org**
National Council on Int'l Trade Development

For exporters and importers and other professionals serving the international commerce industry.

14767 **www.uschina.org**
US China Business Council

Membership association for US companies doing business with the People's Republic of China. Provides representation, practical assistance, and up-to-date information to members.

14768 **www.vita.com**
VMEbus International Trade Association (VITA)

Association for manufacturers of microcomputer boards, hardware, software, military products, controllers, bus interfaces and other accessories compatible with VMEbus architecture.

International Trade Resources

14769 **Albania to the United Nations**
320 E 79th Street
New York, NY 10075

212-249-2059; Fax: 212-535-2917
albania.un@albania-un.org
www.albania-un.org
Facebook, Twitter, LinkedIn, RSS Feed, Google+

Ferit Hoxha, Ambassador
Petrik Jorgji, Minister Counselor
Olisa Cifligu, Second Secretary
Ermal Frasheri, Adviser, legal Issues
Admira Jorgji, Counselor

14770 **Antigua and Barbuda Department of Tourism and Trade**
25 S.E. 2nd Avenue
Suite 300
Miami, FL 33131

305-381-6762; Fax: 305-381-7908
www.antigua-barbuda.org

Byron Spencer, Manager

14771 **Austrian Trade Commission**
120 West 45th Street
9th Floor
New York, NY 10036

212-421-5250; Fax: 212-421-5251
newyork@advantageaustria.org
www.advantageaustria.org/us
Facebook, Twitter, RSS Feed

Peter Athanasiadis, Manager
Sabine Miller, Project Manager
Walter HAfle, Director

14772 **Azerbaijan - Permanent Mission to the United Nations**
866 United Nations Plaza, Ste 560
48 str. & 1 Avenue
New York, NY 10017

212-371-2559; Fax: 212-371-2784
www.un.int/azerbaijan/

Eldar Kouliev, Manager

14773 **Bahamas Consulate General**
231 E 46th Street
New York, NY 10017

212-421-6420; Fax: 212-688-5926
consulate@bahamasny.com

Hon Eldred E Bethel, Contact
Forrester J. Carroll, JP, Consul General
Sandra N. McLaughlin, Vice Consul

Clemmy Eneas-varence, Sr. Information Clerk
Carolyn Young-Miller, Administrative Asst.

14774 **Bulgarian General Consulate**
121 E 62nd Street
New York, NY 10021

212-935-4646; Fax: 212-319-5955
consulate.newyork@mfa.bg
www.consulbulgaria-ny.org

14775 **Business Council for the United Nations**
801 2nd Avenue
Ste 900
New York, NY 10017

212-697-3315; Fax: 212-682-9185
unahq@unausa.org
www.unfoundation.org
Facebook, Twitter, YouTube, RSS Feed

Allison B MacEachron, Executive Director
Kathy Calvin, President & CEO
Richard S. Parnell, COO
Walter Cortes, CFO
Aaron Sherinian, VP, Communications

14776 **Chile Trade Commission**
866 United Nations Plaza
Suite 603
New York, NY 10017

212-207-3266; Fax: 212-207-3649

Alejandro Cerda, Trade Commissioner

14777 **Consulate General of Bahrain**
866 2nd Avenue
14th Floor
New York, NY 10017

212-223-6200; Fax: 212-319-0687

Jassim Buallay, Manager

14778 **Consulate General of Belgium in New York**
1065 Avenue of Americas
22nd Floor
New York, NY 10018

212-586-5110
212-586-7472; Fax: 212-582-9657
NewYork@diplobel.fed.be
www.diplomatie.be/newyork/

Piet Morisse, Manager
Marc Calcoen, Consul General
Leon Cortens, Deputy Consul General

14779 **Consulate General of Brazil**
220 E. 42nd St.
26th Floor
New York, NY 10017

917-777-7777; Fax: 212-827-0225
cg.novayork@itamaraty.gov.br
http://novayork.utamaraty.gov.br/en-us/

Julio Cesar Gomes Dos Sant, Manager

14780 **Consulate General of Costa Rica**
14 Penn Plaza, #1202
225 West 34th Street
New York, NY 10122

212-509-3066
212-509-3066; Fax: 212-509-3068; Fax: 212-509-3068
www.costaricaembassy.com

Otto Barcas, Manager

14781 **Consulate General of Germany**
871 United Nations Plaza
New York, NY 10017

212-610-9700; Fax: 212-940-0402

Bernhard Von Der Planit, Manager

14782 **Consulate General of Haiti**
815 2nd Ave.
6th Floor
New York, NY 10017

212-697-9767; Fax: 212-681-6991
www.haitianconsulate-nyc.org

Marie Therese, Manager
Charles A. Forbin, Consul General

14783 **Consulate General of Honduras**
255 West 36th Street
First Level
New York, NY 10018

212-714-9451; Fax: 212-714-9453
www.hondurasemb.org
Facebook, Twitter

14784 **Consulate General of India**
3 E 64th Street
New York, NY 10065

212-774-0600; Fax: 212-861-3788
www.indiacgny.org

Ambassador Prabhu Dayal, Consul General
Mr. P.K. Bajaj, Consul (Head of Chancery)
Shambhu Amitabh, Vice Consul (Passport & Consular)
Ajay Purswani, Consul (Visa)
Dhirendra Singh, Counsel

14785 **Consulate General of Indonesia**
5 E 68th Street
New York, NY 10021

212-879-0600

14786 **Consulate General of Israel in New York**
800 Second Avenue
New York, NY 10017

212-499-5000
info@newyork.mfa.gov.il
embassies.gov.il/new-york
Facebook, Twitter, YouTube, flickr

Ido Aharoni, Consul General
Founded in 1948

14787 **Consulate General of Kenya**
866 UN Plaza
Suite 4016
New York, NY 10017

212-421-4741; Fax: 212-486-1985
kenyahighcommission.ca

Rolando Visconti, Manager

14788 **Consulate General of Lebanon in New York**
9 E 76th Street
New York, NY 10021

212-744-7905; Fax: 212-794-1510
lebconsny@aol.com
www.lebconsny.org

Hassan Saad, Manager

14789 **Consulate General of Lithuania**
420 5th Avenue
3rd Floor
New York, NY 10018

212-354-7840; Fax: 212-354-7911
kons.niujorkas@urm.lt
ny.mfa.lt

Rimantas Morkvenas, Manager
Valdemaras Sarapinas, Consul General

14790 **Consulate General of Malta**
249 E 35th Street
New York, NY 10016

212-725-2345; Fax: 212-779-7097

14791 **Consulate General of Morocco**
10 East 40th Street
New York, NY 10016

212-758-2625; Fax: 646-395-8077
info@moroccanconsulate.com
www.moroccanconsulate.com

Ramon Xilotl, Manager
Mohammed Benabdeljalil, Consul general
Sidi Mohammed El Bakkari, Deputy Consul

14792 **Consulate General of Nigeria**
828 2nd Avenue
New York, NY 10017

212-808-0301; Fax: 212-687-1476
cgny@nigeriahouse.com
www.nigeriahouse.com

14793 **Consulate General of Paraguay**
801 2nd . Ave.
Suite 600
New York, NY 10017

212-682-9441
212-682-9442; Fax: 212-682-9443
info@consulparny.com

Juan Baiardi, Manager

14794 **Consulate General of Peru**
241 East 49th St.
New York, NY 10017

646-735-3828; Fax: 646-735-3866
consulado@conperny.org
www.consuladoperu.com

Fortunato Ricar Quesada Seminario, Consul General

14795 **Consulate General of Qatar**
2555 M St NW
Washington, DC 20037-1305

202-274-1600; Fax: 202-237-9880

Mohammad Al-Madadi, Consul

14796 **Consulate General of Saudi Arabia**
866 United Nations Plaza
Suite 480
New York, NY 10017

212-752-2740

Abdulrahman Gdaia, Execellency

14797 **Consulate General of Slovenia**
120 East 56th Street
Suite 320
New York, NY 10022

212-370-3006; Fax: 212-421-1532
nky@gov.si

Reimo Pettai, Manager

14798 **Consulate General of South Africa**
333 E 38th Street
9th Floor
New York, NY 10016

212-213-4880; Fax: 212-213-0102
consulate.ny@foreign.gov.za
www.southafrica-newyork.net

Fikile Magubane, Consul-General
Thami Sono, Consul
Leon Naidoo, Consul
George Monyemangene, Consul General

14799 Consulate General of St. Lucia
2005 Massachusetts Ave., NW
Washington, DC 20036-1030

202-558-2216
800-345-6541
202-364-6795; Fax: 202-318-0771
info@visahq.com
saint-lucia.visahq.com

Julian Hunte, Manager

14800 Consulate General of Switzerland
633 3rd Avenue
30th Floor
New York, NY 10017-6706

212-599-5700; Fax: 212-599-4266
www.eda.admin.ch

Raymond Loretan, Excellency

14801 Consulate General of Trinidad & Tobago
125 Maidan Lane
4th Floor
New York, NY 10038

212-682-7272; Fax: 212-232-0368
www.ttcgnewyork.com
Facebook, Twitter, YouTube, RSS Feed

Hon Harold Robertson, Contact
Rudrawatee Nan Ramgoolam, Consul General

14802 Consulate General of Ukraine
240 E 49th Street
New York, NY 10017

212-371-5690; Fax: 212-371-5547
gc_usn@mfa.gov.ua
ny.mfa.gov.ua

Serhii Pohoreltsev, Consul General

14803 Consulate General of Uruguay
420 Madison Street
6th Floor
New York, NY 10017

212-753-8581
212-753-8192; Fax: 212-753-1603
consulado@consuladouruguaynewyork.com
www.consuladouruguaynewyork.com

Basil Bryan, Manager
Carlos Orlando, Consul General

14804 Consulate General of Venezuela
7 East 51st Street
New York, NY 10022

212-826-1660; Fax: 212-644-7471
ven.newyork@gmail.com
nuevayork.consulado.gob.ve

Carol Delgado Arria, Consul General
Ayerim Flores Rivas, Consul General of the Second

14805 Consulate General of the Dominican Republic
1715 22nd Street, NW
Washington, DC 20008

202-332-6280
202-332-7670; Fax: 202-265-8057
www.domrep.org
Facebook, Blogspot

Jose Luis Dominguez, Minister Counselor
Felipe Herrera, Cunselor
Morela Baez, Commercial Affairs
Alejandra Hernandez, Minister Counselor
Ligia Reid Bonetti, Minister Counselor

14806 Consulate General of the Netherlands
666 Third Avenue
19th floor
New York, NY 10017

877-388-2443; Fax: 212-333-3603
nyc@minbuza.nl
Facebook, Twitter, YouTube, RSS Feed

Wanda Fleck, Manager

14807 Consulate General of the Principality of Monaco
565 5th Avenue
23rd Floor
New York, NY 10017

212-286-0500; Fax: 212-286-1574
info@monaco-consulate.com
www.monaco-consulate.com
Facebook, Twitter

Maguy Maccario-Doyle, Consul General, Minister Couseller

14808 Consulate General of the Republic of Belarus
708 3rd Avenue
20th Floor
New York, NY 10017

212-682-5392; Fax: 212-682-5491
RSS Feed

Sergei Kolos, Manager

14809 Consulate General of the Russian Federation
2343 Massachusettes Ave, NW
Washington, DC 20008-2803

202-588-5899; Fax: 202-588-8937
www.croatiaemb.org

14810 Consulate of Guyana
370 7th Avenue
New York, NY 10017

212-947-5110; Fax: 212-573-6225
www.guyana.org
Facebook, Twitter, Gmail, StumbleUpon,Pinterest,G

Samuel Insanally, Ambassador, Permanent Rep
Edwin Carrington, Secretary
Mohammed A. O. Ishmael, Managing Director
Amral Khan, Administrator & Editor

14811 Consulate of the Republic of Uzbekistan in New York City
801 Second Ave
20th Floor
New York, NY 10017

212-754-7403; Fax: 212-838-9812
info@uzbekconsulny.org
www.uzbekconsulny.org

14812 Croatia Consulate, United States
369 Lexington Avenue
11th Floor
New York, NY 10017

212-599-3066; Fax: 212-599-3106
us.mvep.hr/en

Abdul Seraj, Manager

14813 Ecuadorian Consulate
2535 15th Street NW
Washington, DC 20009

202-234-7200
866-ECU-DOR; Fax: 202-667-3482
consuladodc@ecuador.org

Pablo Yanez, Consul General

14814 Egyptian Consulate Economic & Commercial Office
3521 International Ct. NW
Washingotn, DC 20008

202-895-5400; Fax: 202-244-5131
embassy@egyptembassy.net
www.egyptembassy.net
Facebook

Ayden Nour, Executive Director
Mohamed M. Tawfik, Ambassador

14815 Embassy of Australia
1601 Massachusetts Avenue NW
Washington, DC 20036

202-797-3000; Fax: 202-797-3168
www.usa.embassy.gov.au
Facebook, Twitter

Kim Beazley, Ambassador

14816 Embassy of Benin
2124 Kalorama Road NW
Washington, DC 20008

202-232-6656; Fax: 202-232-2611
info@beninembassy.us
www.beninembassy.us

Boni T. Yayi, President
Cyrille S. Oguin, Ambassador

14817 Embassy of Bosnia and Herzegovina
2109 East Street NW
Washington, DC 20037

202-337-1500; Fax: 202-337-1502
info@bhembassy.org
www.bhembassy.org
Facebook

Haris Hrle, Ambassador
Milenko Misic, Minister Counselor
Sanja Juric, First Secretary
Denita Lelo, 1st Consular Officer
10 Members

14818 Embassy of Cambodia
4530 16th Street NW
Washington, DC 20011

202-726-7742
202-726-7824; Fax: 202-726-8381
www.embassyofcambodia.org
Facebook

Hem Heng, Ambassador
Mouth Keo Thida, Commercial Counselor
Koeut navuth, Defense Attache
Neang Chanthou, Finance Attache

14819 Embassy of Estonia
2131 Massachusetts Avenue NW
Washington, DC 20008

202-588-0101; Fax: 202-588-0108
www.estemb.org
Facebook, Twitter, Flickr

Marina Kaljurand, Ambassador

14820 Embassy of Ethiopia
3506 International Drive NW
Washington, DC 20008

202-364-1200; Fax: 202-587-0195
ethiopia@ethiopianembassy.org
www.ethiopianembassy.org

Girma Birru, Ambassador
Tsegab Kebebew, Minister Counselor
Kidist Yakob, Counselor (Politcal Affairs)
Wahide Belay, Minister Counselor
Yohannes Getahun, Minster Counselor

14821 Embassy of Finland
3301 Massachusetts Avenue NW
Washington, DC 20008

202-298-5800; Fax: 202-298-6030
sanomat.was@formin.fi

www.finland.org
Facebook, Twitter

Ritva Koukku-Ronde, Ambassador

14822 **Embassy of Georgia**
2209 Massachusettes Avenue, NW
Washington, DC 20008

202-387-2390; Fax: 202-387-0864
embgeo.usa@mfa.gov.ge
www.embassy.mfa.gov.ge

Temur Yakobashvili, Ambassador
David Rakviashvili, Envoy
Mikheil Darchiashvili, Minister
Thea Kentchadze, Sr. Counselor
Mariam Lebanidze, Counselor

14823 **Embassy of Grenada**
1701 New Hampshire Ave, NW
Washington, DC 20009-2501

202-265-2561; Fax: 292-265-2468
gdaembassydc@gmail.com
www.grenadaembassyusa.org
Facebook, Twitter, Google+

E. Angus Friday, Ambassador
Patricia D.M. Clarke, Counsellor
Dianne C. Perrotte, Adminstrative Asst
Lucia Amedee, Receptionist/ Clerical Asst.

14824 **Embassy of Jamaica (JAMPRO)**
1520 New Hampshire Ave, NW
Washington, DC 20036

202-452-0660; Fax: 202-452-0036
firstsec@jamaicaembassy.org
www.embassyofjamaica.org

Audrey P. Marks, Ambassador

14825 **Embassy of Jordan**
3504 International Drive NW
Washington, DC 20008

202-966-2664; Fax: 202-966-3110
www.jordanembassyus.org
Facebook, Twitter, YouTube, RSS Feed, Pinterest,

Alia Hatoung Bouran, Ambassador
Amjad Hatem Al-Mbideen, Consul
Fawaz Bilbesi, Deputy Chief of Mission
Aishabint Al hussein, Military Attache
Qais Biltaji, Fist Secretary

14826 **Embassy of Mali**
2130 R Street NW
Washington, DC 20008

202-332-2249; Fax: 202-332-6603
info@maliembassy.us
www.maliembassy.us

Al Maamoun Baba Lamine Kehta, Ambassador
Muhamed Ouzouna Maiga, 1st Counselor
Ahmadou Barazi Maiga, 2nd Counselor
Colonel Bourama Sangare, Defence Attache
Mahama Dicko, Financial Attache

14827 **Embassy of Mongolia**
2833 M Street NW
Washington, DC 20007

202-333-7117; Fax: 202-298-9227
www.mongolianembassy.us

Khasbazaryn Bekhbat, Ambassador

14828 **Embassy of Panama**
2862 McGill Terrace NW
Washington, DC 20008

202-483-1407
202-483-1407; Fax: 202-483-8413
info@embassyofpanama.org
www.embassyofpanama.org
Facebook

Mario E. Jaramillo, Ambassador

14829 **Embassy of Tanzania**
1232 22nd St, NW
Washington, DC 20037

202-884-1080
202-939-6125, 202-; Fax: 202-797-7408
ubalozi@tanzaniaembassy-us.org
www.tanzaniaembassy-us.org
Facebook, Twitter

Liberata Mulamula, Ambassador
Lily Munanka, Minister/ Head of Chancery
Paul Mwafongo, Minister, Economic Affairs
B.G. Emmanuel Maganga, Defense Attache
Edward Masanja, Finacial Attache

14830 **Embassy of Tunisia**
1515 Massachusetts Avenue NW
Washington, DC 20005

202-862-1850; Fax: 202-862-1858
www.tunconsusa.org/

Gordon Gray, Ambassador

14831 **Embassy of Uganda**
5911 16th Street NW
Washington, DC 20011

202-726-7100; Fax: 202-726-1727
info@ugandaembassyus.org
www.ugandaemb.org

Oliver Wonekha, Ambassador
Alfred Nnam, Deputy Chief of Commission
Dickson Ogwang, Minister Counselor
Patrick Muganda Guma, Counselor
Sam Bhoi Omara, 1st Secretary

14832 **Embassy of Vietnam**
1233 20th Street NW
Suite 400
Washington, DC 20036

202-861-0737; Fax: 202-861-0917
www.vietnamembassy-usa.org

Nguyen Quoc Cuong, Ambassador

14833 **Embassy of Zimbabwe**
1608 New Hampshire Avenue NW
Washington, DC 20009

202-332-7100; Fax: 202-483-9326
www.zimbabwe-embassy.us

Dr. Machivenyik Mapuranga, Ambassador
Richard T. Chibuwe, Minister Counselor & Deputy Chief
Whatmore Goora, Counselor (Political)
R. Matsika, Counselor
Lt. Col. George Chinoingira, Defence Attache

14834 **Embassy of the Lao People's Democratic Republic**
2222 S Street NW
Washington, DC 20008

202-332-6416
202-667-0076; Fax: 202-332-4923
embasslao@gmail.com
www.laoembassy.com

H.E. Seng Soukhathivong, Ambassador
Thongmoon Phongphailath, 1st Secretary
Somxai Kittanouvong, 2nd Secretary (Consular)
Kerlor Yangko, 3rd Secretary (Economy And Culture)
Sounthone Duangxaty, Attache (Economic & Culture)

14835 **Embassy of the People's Republic of China**
3505 International Place NW
Washington, DC 20008

202-495-2266; Fax: 202-495-2138
chinaembpress_us@mfa.gov.cn
www.china-embassy.org

Cui Tiankai, Ambassador
Lu Kang, Minister

14836 **Embassy of the Republic of Angola**
2100-2108 16th Street, NW
Washington, DC 20009

202-785-1156; Fax: 202-822-9049
angola@angola.org
www.angola.org

Alberto do Carmo Bento Ribeiro, Ambassador
Sofia Pegado da Silva, Minster Counselor
Manuel Fransisco Lourenco, 1st Secretary
Ismael Filipe, 2nd secretary- Political Affairs
Gil Cardoso, Financial Attache

14837 **Embassy of the Republic of Botswana and GlobeScope, Inc.**
1531-1533 New Hampshire Avenue NW
Washington, DC 20036

202-244-4990
www.botswanaembassy.org

H.E. Dr.Tebelel Mazile Seretse, Ambassador
Ms. Sophie Heide Mautle, Deputy Head of Mission
Innocent Matengu, Counselor (Politcal Affairs)
Dineo Mpuchane, 1st Secretary (Administration)
Mighty Mohurutshe, Administrative Attache
Founded in 1965

14838 **Embassy of the Republic of Fiji**
2000 M Street,NW
Suite 710
Washington, DC 20036

202-466-8320; Fax: 202-466-8325
info@fijiembassydc.com
www.fijiembassydc.com

Winston Thompson, Ambassador
Akuila Vuira, 1st Secretary
Teresita R. Sauler-Cooke, Executive Asst.
Lathanzuala Phillips, Chauffer

14839 **Embassy of the Republic of Latvia**
2306 Massachusettes Ave, NW
Washington, DC 20008

202-328-2840; Fax: 202-328-2860
embassy.usa@mfa.gov.lv
www.mfa.gov.lv/en/usa
Facebook, Twitter, Flickr

Andris Teikmanis, Ambassador
Juris Pekalis, Deputy Chief of Mission

14840 **Embassy of the Republic of Yemen**
2319 Wyoming Ave, NW
Washington, DC 20008

202-965-4760; Fax: 202-337-2017
ambassador@yemenembassy.org
www.yemenembassy.org

Abdulwahab Abdulla Al-Hajjri, Ambassador
Nadia Fhashem, Asst to the Ambassador

14841 **Embassy of the Republic of the Marshall Islands**
2433 Massachusetts Avenue NW
Washington, DC 20008

202-234-5414; Fax: 202-232-3236
info@rmiembassyus.org
www.rmiembassyus.org

Charles R. Paul, Ambassador
Dixie Lomae, 1st Secretary
Donna Dizon, Office Manager

14842 **Export-Import Bank of the United States**

800-565-3946
www.exim.gov
Twitter, LinkedIn, YouTube

Fred P. Hochberg, Chairman & President

An agency of the Executive Branch of the U.S. Government, EXIM is the official export credit agency of the United States.

14843 Export.gov

Home Page: www.export.gov

Export.gov is managed by the U.S. Department of Commerce's International Trade Administration. It connects businesses with U.S. Government resources that will assist them in their international sales efforts.

14844 Fair Trading Commission

Good Hope, Green Hill
St. Michael, Ba BB12003

246-424-0260; Fax: 246-424-0300
info@ftc.gov.bb
www.ftc.gov.bb

Peggy Griffith, CEO
Sir Neville Nicholls, Chairman
Andrew Downes, Deputy chairman
Monique Taitt, Commissioner
Kendrid Sargeant, Commissioner

14845 French Trade Commission

200 N Colombus Dr.
Chicago, IL 60601

312-565-8000; Fax: 312-856-1032
www.firmafrance.com
Facebook, Twitter, LinkedIn, RSS Feed, Google +

14846 Gambia Mission to the United Nations

800 2nd Avenue
Suite 400 F
New York, NY 10017

212-949-6640; Fax: 212-856-9820

Tamsir Jallow, Ambassador

14847 General Consulate of Luxembourg

17 Beekman Place
New York, NY 10022

212-888-6664; Fax: 212-888-6116
newyork.cg@mae.etat.lu
www.newyork-cg.mae.lu/

Jean-Claude Knebelar, Consul General
Saba Amroun-Forbes, Consular Officer

14848 Gibraltar Information Bureau

1156 15th Street NW
Suite 1100
Washington, DC 20005

202-452-1108; Fax: 202-452-1109

Perry Stieglitz, Executive Director

14849 Greek Trade Commission

150 E 58th Street
17th Floor
New York, NY 10155

212-751-2404; Fax: 212-593-2278

Yannis Papadimitriou, Manager

14850 Hungarian Trade Commission

425 Bloor Street, East
Suite 501
Toronto-Ontario M4W 3R4

416-923-3596; Fax: 416-923-2097

Gyula Cseko, Trade Commissioner

14851 Icelandic Consulate General

800 3rd Avenue
36th Floor
New York, NY 10022

646-282-9360; Fax: 646-282-9369
icecon.ny@mfa.is
www.iceland.is/us/nyc

Hlynur Gudjonsson, Consul & Trade Commissioner

14852 International Chamber of Commerce (ICC)

1212 Avenue of the Americas
New York, NY 10036-1689

212-703-5065; Fax: 212-575-0327
www.iccwbo.org
Facebook, Twitter, LinkedIn, Google+, YouTube

Sunil Bharti Mittal, Vice-Chairman
Harold McGraw III, Chairman
Gerard Worms, Honorary Chairman
Jean-Guy Carrier, Secretary General
Founded in 1919
Mailing list available for rent

14853 Irish Trade Board

345 Park Avenue
17th Floor
New York, NY 10154

212-180-0800

Jean McCluskey, Marketing Executive

14854 Japanese External Trade Organization

1221 Avenue of the Americas
McGraw Hill Building, 42nd Floor
New York, NY 10020

212-997-0400; Fax: 212-997-0464
jetrony@jetro.go.jp
www.jetro.org
Facebook, Twitter

Hiroyuki Ishige, Chairman
Masaki Fujihara, Dir., Business Development
Daiki Nakajima, ICT/ Environment

14855 Kazakhstan Mission to the United Nations

305 East 47th Street
3rd Floor
New York, NY 10017

212-230-1900; Fax: 212-230-1172
kazakhstan@un.int
www.kazakhstanun.org

Byrganym Aitimova, Ambassador
Akan Rakhmetulin, Deputy Permanent Rep
Israil Tilegen, Minister Counsellor
Ruslan Bultrikov, Counsellor
Col. Alexander Kabentayev, Counsellor Military Adviser

14856 Korea Trade Promotion Center (KOTRA)

460 Park Avenue
14th Floor
New York, NY 10022

212-826-0900; Fax: 212-888-4930
kotrany@hotmail.com
www.kotrana.org

Sungpil Um, Presiden/North America
Il Hoon Ko, Deputy Director

14857 Kyrgyzstan Mission to the United Nations

866 United Nations Plaza
Room 477
New York, NY 10017

212-486-4214; Fax: 212-486-5259

Talaibek Kydyrov, Ambassador
Nuran Niyazaliev, Counsellor/DPR
Nurbek Kasymov, 1st secretary
Asel Davydova, Chief Administrative Specialist
Salamat Supataev, Administrative Officer

14858 Malaysia Mission to the United Nations

313 E 43rd Street
3rd Floor
New York, NY 10017

212-986-6310; Fax: 212-490-8576
www.kln.gov.my
RSS Feed

Hussein Haniff, Ambassador

14859 Mexico Trade Commission

757 3rd Ave
Suite 2400
New York, NY 10017-2042

212-826-2978; Fax: 212-826-2979
www.mexconnect.com
Facebook, Twitter

14860 Moldova Mission to the United Nations

35 East 29th Street
New York, NY 10016

212-447-1867; Fax: 212-447-4067
unmoldova@aol.com

Vlad Lupan, Ambassador
Larisa Miculet, Counsellor, Deputy Permanent Rep
Carolina Podoroghin, 3rd Secretary
Tatiana Dudnicenco, CFO,Head of Chancery
Litvac Sergiu, Administrator

14861 New Zealand Trade Development Board

222 East 41st Street
New York, NY 10017-6739

212-497-0200

14862 Norwegian Trade Council

2720 34th Street NW
Washington, DC 20008

202-333-6000; Fax: 202-469-3990
emb.washington@mfa.no
www.norway.org
Facebook, Twitter, Flickr, Instagram

Kare A. Aas, Ambassador
Berit Enge, Minister Counselor
Beate Anderson Varrecchia, Officer for Administrative
Harald W. Storen, Counselor
Olav Heian-Engdal, 1st Secretary

14863 Pakistan Trade Commission

12 E 65th Street
4th Floor
New York, NY 10021

212-879-5800

Abbas Zaidi, Manager

14864 Permanent Mission of Armenia to the United Nations

119 E 36th Street
New York, NY 10016

212-686-9079; Fax: 212-686-3934
www.un.mfa.am/
RSS

Andrezej Towpik, Manager
Garen Nazarian, Permanent Representative to the UN
Tigran Samvelian, Counsell, Deputy Permanent Rep
Nikolay Sahakov, 1st Secretary
Sahak Sargsyan, 2nd Secretary

14865 **Permanent Mission of Bangladesh to the United Nations**
820 East 2nd Avenue, Diplomat Centre
4th Floor
New York, NY 10017

212-867-3434; Fax: 212-972-4038

Sheikh Hasina, Prime Minister

14866 **Permanent Mission of Belize to the United Nations**
675 Third Avenue
Suite 1911
New York, NY 10017

212-986-1240; Fax: 212-593-0932
www.belizemission.com
Facebook, Twitter

Mohamed Latheef, Manager
Paulette Erlington, Counselor
Han Dean Barrow, Prime Minister
Lois M. Young, Ambassador
Janine felson, Deputy Permanent Representative

14867 **Permanent Mission of Ghana to the United Nations**
19 E 47th Street
New York, NY 10017

212-832-1300; Fax: 212-751-6743
ghanaperm@aol.com
www.un.int/ghana

Ken Kanda, Ambassador
William A. Awinador-Kanyirige, Minister
Henry Tachie-Menson, Minister-Counsellor
N.A. Abayena, Counsellor
A. Ayebi Arthur, 1st Secretary

14868 **Permanent Mission of Myanmar (Formerly Burma)**
10 E 77th Street
New York, NY 10075

212-744-1271; Fax: 212-744-1290
www.myanmarmissionny.org

Janis Priedkalns, Manager
U Han Thu, Deputy Permanent Representative
U Aung Kyaw Zan, Minister Counsellor
U kyaw Tin, Permanent representative
U Ko Ko Shein, Minister Counselor

14869 **Permanent Mission of Saint Vincent & the Grenadines**
800 2nd Avenue
Suite 400-G
New York, NY 10017

212-599-0950; Fax: 212-599-1020
Facebook, Twitter, YouTube

Camillo M. Gonsalves, Ambassador
Nedra Miguel, Minister Counsellor
Mozart Carr, Attache
Maglyn Carrington, Secretary/ Accountant
N. Pepper Alexander, Security Officer/ Aide de Camp

14870 **Permanent Mission of Slovakia to the United Nations**
801 2nd Ave.
New York, NY 10017

212-286-8880
un.newyork@mzv.sk
www.mzv.sk/unnewyork

Founded in 1993

14871 **Permanent Mission of Tajikistan to the United Nations**
216 East 49th St.
4th Floor
New York, NY 10017

212-207-3315; Fax: 212-207-3855
www.un.int/

Khamrokhon Zaripov, President
Sirodjidin Aslov, Ambassador

14872 **Permanent Mission of the Czech Republic to the United Nations**
1109-1111 Madison Avenue
New York, NY 10028

646-981-4000; Fax: 646-981-4099
un.newyork@embassy.mzv.cz
www.mzv.cz/un.newyork
RSS

Edita Hrda, Ambassador
David Cervenka, Minister Counsellor
Peter Urbanek, Counsellor
Ladislav Steinhubel, 1st Secretary
Petra Benesova, 3rd Secretary

14873 **Permanent Mission of the Kingdom of Bhutan to the United Nations**
343 East 43rd Street
New York, NY 10017

212-682-2268; Fax: 212-661-0551

Lhatu Wangchuk, Ambassador

14874 **Permanent Mission of the Republic of Sudan to the United Nations**
305 East 47th Street
3 Dag Hammarskjold Plaza, 4th Floor
New York, NY 10017

212-573-6033; Fax: 212-573-6160
sudan@sudanmission.org

Jenine Selson, Manager

14875 **Permanent Mission of the Solomon Islands to the United Nations**
800 2nd Avenue
Suite 400
New York, NY 10017-4709

212-599-6192; Fax: 212-661-8925

B Jagne, Manager

14876 **Philippines Commercial Office**
556 5th Avenue
New York, NY 10036

212-764-1330

14877 **Poland Trade Commission**
675 3rd Avenue
19th Floor
New York, NY 10017

212-351-1713

Phyllis Poland, Owner

14878 **Portuguese Trade Commission**
590 5th Avenue
3rd Floor
New York, NY 10036

212-354-4627; Fax: 212-575-4737

Soto Moura, Manager

14879 **Romanian Consulate General**
11766 Wilshire Blvd
Suite 560
Los Angeles, CA 90025

310-444-0043; Fax: 310-445-0043
http://www.romanian.com
RSS

Corina Suteu, Manager
Eugen Chivu, Consul General

14880 **Singapore Trade Commission**
55 E 59th Street
Suite 21-B
New York, NY 10022

212-421-2200

Kc Yeoh, Executive Director

14881 **Swedish Trade Council**
150 N Michigan Avenue
Chicago, IL 60601

312-781-6222

Stefam Bergstrom, Manager

14882 **Syrian Arab Republic Embassy**
2215 Wyoming Avenue NW
Washington, DC 20008

202-232-6316; Fax: 202-265-4585
www.syrianembassy.us/

14883 **Taiwan Trade Center**
1 Penn Plaza
Suite 2025
New York, NY 10119

212-904-1677; Fax: 212-904-1678
newyork@taitra.org.tw
http://newyork.taiwantrade.com.tw/

Kevin K. H. Wei, Director

14884 **Thailand Trade Center-Consulate General of Thailand**
401 N Michigan Avenue
Suite 544
Chicago, IL 60611

312-467-0044; Fax: 312-467-1690

14885 **Trade Commission of Denmark**
3565 Piedimont Rd
NE #1-400
Atlanta, GA 30305

404-588-1588; Fax: 404-835-0799
atlhkt@um.dk
/www.dtcatlanta.um.dk

Henrik Bronner, Manager

14886 **Trade Commission of Spain**
500 N Michigan Avenue
Suite 1500
Chicago, IL 60611

312-644-1154

14887 **Turkish Trade Commission**
821 United Nations Plaza
4th Floor
New York, NY 10017

212-687-1530

14888 Turkmenistan Mission to the United Nations
866 United Nations Plaza
Suite 424
New York, NY 10017

212-486-8908; Fax: 212-486-2521

Aksoltan Ataeva, Manager

14889 UK Trade & Investment
1 Victoria St.
London, UK SW1H OET

212-745-0495
www.ukti.gov.uk
Twitter, LinkedIn, Youtube, Flickr, Open to Expor

Nick Baird, CEO
Sandra Rogers, Managing Dir., Marketing
Jon Harding, COO
Charu Gorasia, Dir., Finance & IT
Michael W. Boyd, MD, Strategic Investments

14890 United Nations Mission to El Salvador
46 Park Avenue
New York, NY 10016

212-679-1616; Fax: 212-725-3467

Antonio Montiero, Manager
Mauricio Fiunes, President

Associations

14891 American Gem Society Laboratories
8917 W Sahara Ave
Las Vegas, NV 89117-5826

702-233-6120; Fax: 702-233-6125
support@agslab.com
www.agslab.com
Facebook, Twitter, RSS, Youtube, Tumblr, Blogger,

Frank Delahan, CEO
Donna Jolly, Marketing Executive

Seeks to build consumer confidence in the retail jeweler by promoting ethical business standards and professional excellence.
4.4M Members
Founded in 1996

14892 American Gem Trade Association
3030 LBJ Freeway
Ste 840
Dallas, TX 75342-643

214-742-4367
800-972-1162; Fax: 214-742-7334
info@agta.org
www.agta.org
Facebook, Twitter, YouTube

Ruben Bindra, Board President
Jeffrey Bilgore, Board VP
Gerry Manning, Board VP
Douglas K. Hucker, CEO
Joan Allen, Chief Financial Officer

Trade association for the colored gemstone industry in North America. Operates a gemological testing laboratory in New York.
750+ Members
Founded in 1981
Mailing list available for rent

14893 American Jewelry Design Council
P.O. Box 1149
Hermitage, PA 16148

724-979-4992
800-376-3609
www.ajdc.org
Facebook, RSS

Barbara Heinrich, President
Alishan Halebian, VP
Jane Bohan, Secretary
Mark Schneider, Treasurer
Pascal Lacroix, Board Member

The American Jewelry Design Council is a non-profit educational corporation that recognizes and promotes the understanding of original jewelry designs as art.
Founded in 1988

14894 American Watch Association
1201 Pennsylvania Avenue NW
PO Box 464
Washington, DC 20044

434-963-7773; Fax: 434-963-7776
egcollado@earthlink.net
www.americanwatchassociation.com

David Periman, Chairman
Timothy Michno, First Vice President
Mark Goldberg, Second Vice President
Michael Kaplan, Treasurer
Steven Kaiser, Secretary

Trade association for communication among professionals and legislative advocacy.
45 Members
Founded in 1933

14895 American Watchmakers-Clockmakers Institute
701 Enterprise Drive
Harrison, OH 45030-1696

513-367-9800
866-367-2924; Fax: 513-367-1414
awci@awci.com
www.awci.com
Facebook, RSS, Instagram

Fred White, President
Drew Zimmerman, VP
Manuel Yazijian, Treasurer
Chris Carey, Secretary
Paul Wadsworth, Immediate Past President

Examines and certifies master watchmakers and clockmakers. Maintains a placement service. Conducts home study courses.
2500 Members
Founded in 1892
Mailing list available for rent

14896 Appraisers Association of America
212 W. 35th Street
11th Floor South
New York, NY 10001

212-889-5404; Fax: 212-889-5503
referrals@appraisersassociation.org
www.appraisersassociation.org
Facebook, Twitter, LinkedIn

Linda Selvin, Executive Director
Teresa Caputo, Program Manager
Patrick McIntyre, Membership Manager
Yasemin Yeldener, Communications Coordinator
Jennifer Buonocore, CASP Coordinator

A national association of personal property appraisers who focus on fine and decorative arts. Appraiser Association appraisers work with private and corporate art collections as well as partner with collectors, attorneys, accountants, museums, educational institutions, trusts, brokers and insurance carriers to reflect the highest industry standards.
900+ Members
Founded in 1949

14897 Brotherhood of Traveling Jewelers
Leys, Christie & Company
342 Madison Avenue
Suite #1530
New York, NY 10013

212-869-9162

Represents traveling jewelers.
300 Members

14898 Cultured Pearl Information Center
331 E 53rd Street
New York, NY 10022-4923

212-688-5580; Fax: 212-688-5857
www.pearlinfo.com

Devin MacNow, Executive Director

Conference information and buying guide for pearls.

14899 Diamond Council of America
3212 West End Ave
Suite 400
Nashville, TN 37203

615-385-5301
877-283-5669; Fax: 615-385-4955
www.diamondcouncil.org
Facebook

Peter Engel, Chairman
Terry Chandler, President/CEO

Provides courses in diamontology and gemology to retail jewelers and their employees who are DCA members. Sixty-six retailers representing 1,800 locations.
70 Members
Founded in 1944

14900 Diamond Dealers Club
580 Fifth Avenue
Floor 10
New York, NY 10036

212-790-3600; Fax: 212-869-5164
mhochbaum@nyddc.com
www.nyddc.com
Facebook, Twitter, LinkedIn

Reuven Kaufman, President
Israel Ashkenazy, VP
Abraham Einhorn, Treasurer
Elliot Krischer, Secretary
William Lerner, General Counsel

Seeks to foster the interest of the diamond industry, promote equitable trade principles and eliminate abuses and unfair trading practices.
Founded in 1931

14901 Diamond Manufacturers and Importers Association of America
580 Fifth Avenue
Suite 2000
New York, NY 10036

212-944-2066
800-223-2244; Fax: 212-202-7525
www.dmia.net

Ronald VanderLinden, President
Stuart Samuels, Secretary
Parag Shah, Treasurer
Eli Haas, VP
Steve Eisen, Director, Board Member

Represents and promotes manufacturers and importers of diamonds and rare gems.
150 Members
Founded in 1931

14902 Diamond Peacock Club Kebadjian Brothers
Kebadjian Brothers
333 Washington Street
Suite 638
Boston, MA 02108-5111

617-523-5565; Fax: 617-523-7193
info@kebadjian.com
www.kebadjian.com

Claude Kebadjian, Founder And Designer
Seta Kebadjian, Designing
Michael Kebadjian, Jewelry Design
Founded in 1957

14903 Diamond Promotion Service
466 Lexington Avenue
New York, NY 10017-9998

800-370-6789; Fax: 877-276-1224
www.diamondpromotions.com
Facebook, Twitter

Resource for the tools and strategies to sell more diamonds. Buy marketing materials, train your staff, find the suppliers of advertised jewelry and more.

14904 Estate Jewelry Association of America
209 Post Street
Suite 718
San Francisco, CA 94108-5209

415-834-0718
800-584-5522; Fax: 212-840-1644
jaa@aol.com

14905 Fashion Jewelry Association of America
3 Davol Sq
Unit 135
Providence, RI 02903-4710

401-273-1515

Nick Macris, President
150 Members
Founded in 1985

14906 Gem & Lapidary Dealers Association
120 Derwood Circle
Rockville, MD 20850

301-294-1640; Fax: 301-294-0034
info@glda.com
www.glda.com
Facebook, Twitter, Google+, Pinterest

Arnold Duke, President
Brandy Swanson, Customer Service
Jennifer Guillot, Exhibit Sales/Services
Monique Anderson, PR/ Marketing & New Media
Don Wyatt, PR/ Marketing & New Media

G.L.D.A. is a firmly established, successful wholesale gem & jewelry show promotion company. For the past 30 years, our Tucson show has enjoyed a booming success growth rate. Our show has included 400 exhibit booths which is the maximum that this facility would accomodate.

14907 Gold Prospectors Association of America
43445 Business Park Drive
Suite #113
Temecula, CA 92590

951-699-4749
800-551-9707; Fax: 951-699-4062
info@goldprospectors.org
www.goldprospectors.org
Facebook, Twitter, LinkedIn, YouTube

Thomas Massie, CEO

GPAA is the largest recreational gold prospecting club. Owner of The Outdoor Channel, a cable TV channel featuring real outdoors for real people.
35M Members
Founded in 1985
Mailing list available for rent

14908 Independent Jewelers Organization
136 Old Post Road
Southport, CT 06890-1302

203-846-4215
800-624-9252; Fax: 203-254-7429
www.ijo.com
Facebook, Twitter, LinkedIn

Penny Palmer, Member Services Director

Jewelry buying group and service organization for retail jewelers.
850 Members
Founded in 1972

14909 Indian Arts & Crafts Association
4010 Carlisle NE
Suite C
Albuquerque, NM 87107

505-265-9149; Fax: 505-265-8251
www.iaca.com
Facebook, Twitter

Jacque Foutz, President
Joseph P. Zeller, President
Kathi Ouellet, Treasurer
Georgia Fischel, Secretary
Beth Hale, Membership Director

Nonprofit trade association whose mission is to promote, protect and preserve Indian arts.
700 Members
Founded in 1974
Mailing list available for rent

14910 Industrial Diamond Association of America
PO Box 29460
Columbus, OH 43229

614-797-2265; Fax: 614-797-2264
tkane-ida@insight.rr.com
www.superabrasives.org

Terry M. Kane, Executive Director
Mike Mustin, President
Keith Reckling, Secretary/Treasurer
Troy Heuermann, Vice President
Edward E. Galen, Executive Director

Association of industrial diamond, cvd diamond and polycrystalling supplies, toolmakers. Products and services provided and used in most manufacturing and constuction industries such as: stone processing, glass construction, electronics, medical, woodworking, etc.
190 Members
Founded in 1946

14911 International Colored Gemstone Association
30 West 47th Street
Suite 201
New York, NY 10036

212-352-8814; Fax: 212-352-9054
claudiu@gemstone.org
www.gemstone.org
RSS Feed

Benjamin Hackmanÿ, President
Damien Cody, VP
Santpal Sinchawla, Vice-President
Marcelo Ribeiro Fernandes, Treasurer
Ehud Harel, Secretary

Nonprofit association representing the international gemstone industry. Works to increase the understanding, appreciation and sales of colored gemstones worldwide.
Founded in 1984

14912 International Fine Jewelers Guild
257 Adams Lane
Hewlett, NY 11557

516-295-2516; Fax: 516-374-5060
www.iwjg.com

Bertram Kalisher, Chairman
Olivia Cornell, President
Berge Abajian, Jewelry Industry Advisory Board
Kari Allen, Jewelry Industry Advisory Board
Zoltan David, Jewelry Industry Advisory Board

14913 International Precious Metals Institute
5101 North 12th Avenue
Suite C
Pensacola, FL 32504

850-476-1156; Fax: 850-476-1548
mail@ipmi.org
www.ipmi.org
Facebook, LinkedIn, YouTube

Robert Bullen Smith, Chairman
Jon Potts, Vice Chairman
Sascha Biehl, Treasurer
Bodo Albrecht, Secretary
Chris Jones, Immediate Past Chairman

International association of producers, refiners, fabricators, scientists, users, financial institutions, merchants, private and public sector groups and the general precious metals community created to provide a forum for the exchange of information and technology.
Founded in 1976

14914 International Society of Appraisers
225 West Wacker Drive
Suite 650
Chicago, IL 60606

312-981-6778; Fax: 312-265-2908
isa@isa-appraisers.org
www.isa-appraisers.org
Facebook, Twitter, LinkedIn

Christine Guernsey, ISA CAPP, President
Perri Guthrie, ISA CAPP, Vice President
Steven R. Roach, JD, ISA CAPP, Treasurer
Karen S. Rabe, ISA CAPP, Secretary
Hughene D. Acheson, ISA AM, Director

Nonprofit professional association of personal property appraisers. ISA provides education and organizational support to its members, to serve the public by producing highly qualified and ethical appraisers who are recognized authorities in personal property appraising.
1400+ Members
Founded in 1979
Mailing list available for rent

14915 Jewelers Board of Trade
95 Jefferson Boulevard
Warwick, RI 02888

401-467-0055; Fax: 401-467-6070
jbtinfo@jewelersboard.com
www.jewelersboard.com
Twitter

Dione Kenyen, President

Trade Association: credit and collection for the jewelry industry.
3300 Members
Founded in 1884

14916 Jewelers Vigilance Committee
801 2nd Avenue
Suite 303
New York, NY 10017

212-997-2002; Fax: 212-997-9148
clg@jvclegal.org
www.jvclegal.org
Facebook, LinkedIn

Berylÿ Raff, Chairman
Steven P. Kaiser, 1st Vice President
Scott Berg, 2nd Vice President
Mark Goldberg, Treasurer
Cecilia L. Gardner, President, CEO, General Counsel

The sole legal compliance association in the jewelry industry. Educates the trade to understand complex rules governing the manufacture, sale and marketing of fine jewelry.
1300 Members
Founded in 1917

14917 Jewelers of America
120 Broadway
Suite 2820
New York, NY 10271

646-658-0246
800-223-0673; Fax: 646-658-0256
www.jewelers.org
Facebook, Twitter, LinkedIn, Pinterest, Instagram

David J Bonaparte, President & CEO
Matthew Tratner, Dir., Membership & Sales
Molly Fallon, Dir., Marketing & Communications

Center of knowledge for the jeweler and an advocate for professionalism and high social, ethical and environmental standards in the jewelry trade. Our mission is to assist all members in improving their business skills and profitability. JA will provide acess to meaningful educational programs and services, leadership in public and industry

affairs, and encourage members with common interests to act in the industry's best interest.
Founded in 1906
Mailing list available for rent

14918 **Jewelry Industry Distributors Association**
703 Old Route 422 West
Butler, PA 16001

jidainfo@gmail.com
www.jidainfo.com

Bill Esslinger, President
Chris Gaber, Vice President
Richard Livesay, Treasurer

Sets standards of service and facilitates the exchange of information of all types among members in order to improve business, maximize opportunities, and minimize risks.
Founded in 1946

14919 **Jewelry Information Center**
120 Broadway
Suite 2820
New York, NY 10271

646-658-0246
800-223-0673; Fax: 646-658-0256
info@jewelers.org
www.jic.org
Facebook, Twitter, RSS

Matthews Runzi, President and CEO
Robert Headley, Vice President & COO
Carlon Alexandr, Administrative Assistant
Carey Miller, Membership Manager

Identifies deceptive trade practices and misleading advertising. Provides advice on marketing and assists in prosecution of violations. The media side of the Jewelers Vigilance Committee.
1000 Members
Founded in 1946
Mailing list available for rent

14920 **Jewelry Manufacturers Guild**
PO Box 46099
Los Angeles, CA 90046

909-769-1820
800-359-0340; Fax: 909-769-1920

Paula Glick Hill, Operations Manager

Promotes and improves conditions in the fine jewelry manufacturing industry.
400 Members

14921 **Leading Jewelers Guild**
PO Box 64609
Los Angeles, CA 90064

310-820-3386; Fax: 310-820-3530
www.love-story.com
Facebook, Twitter, Google+, Pinterest

James West, President
Mailing list available for rent

14922 **Manufacturing Jewelers & Suppliers of America**
8 Hayward St.
Attleboro, MA 2703

508-316-2132
800-444-6572; Fax: 508-316-1429
info@mjsa.org
www.mjsa.org
Facebook, Twitter, LinkedIn, Pinterest

Ann Arnold, Chair
Darrell Warren, Vice Chair
Steven A. Cipolla, Vice Chair
David W. Cochran, President, CEO
James K. McCarty, Chief Operating Officer & CFO

National trade association for the manufacturing jewelers and silversmiths. Sponsors trade shows, expositions and social events.
1.8M Members
Founded in 1903

14923 **Manufacturing Jewelers and Silversmiths**
8 Hayward St.
Attleboro, MA 2703

508-316-2132
800-444-6572; Fax: 508-316-1429
info@mjsa.org
www.mjsa.org
Facebook, Twitter, LinkedIn

Ann Arnold, Chair
Darrell Warren, Vice Chair
Steven A. Cipolla, Vice Chair
David W. Cochran, President, CEO
James K. McCarty, Chief Operating Officer & CFO

The trade association for all segments of the American jewelry manufacturing and supply industry.
Founded in 1903

14924 **National Association of Jewelry Appraisers**
P.O. Box 18
Rego Park, NY 11374-0018

718-896-1536; Fax: 718-997-9057
office@NAJAAppraisers.com
www.najaappraisers.com
Facebook

Gail Brett Levine, Executive Director

Purpose is to maintain professional standards and education in the field of jewelry appraising and provide members benefits at lower cost than can be attained individually.
830 Members
Founded in 1981

14925 **Platinum Guild International USA**
620 Newport Center Dr
Suite 800
Newport Beach, CA 92660-6420

212-404-1600
800-207-PLAT; Fax: 949-760-8780
www.preciousplatinum.com
Facebook, Twitter, Google+, Pinterest

Laurie A Hudson, President

Organization promoting platinum jewelry. Maintains a website where the press and the public can find helpful information.
Founded in 1975

14926 **Plumb Club**
157 Engle Street
Englewood, NJ 07631

201-816-8881; Fax: 201-816-8882
www.plumbclub.com

Jonathan Goodman Cohen, President
Michael Lerche, VP
Michael Langhammer, Treasurer
Roger Forman, Secretary
Jeffrey Cohen, Director

Exclusive social organization within the jewelry industry holding black tie events for members and their clients and exhibitor shows.

14927 **Schneider National**
3101 S Packerland Drive
Po Box 2545
Green Bay, WI 54306-2545

920-592-2000
800-558-6767
www.schneider.com
RSS

Don Schneider, Chairman
Christopher Lofgren PhD, President & CEO

A leading provider of transportation and logistics services with a comprehensive reach across North America and a growing presence in Europe and Asia.
Founded in 1935

14928 **Silver Institute**
1400 I Street, NW
Suite #550
Washington, DC 20005

202-835-0185; Fax: 202-835-0155
info@silverinstitute.org
www.silverinstitute.org

Fernando Alanis, President
Michael DiRienzo, Executive Director and Secretary
Mitchell Krebs, Vice President
Thomas Angelos, Treasurer
Mark Spurbeck, Assistant Treasurer

International association of miners, refiners, fabricators and wholesalers of silver and silver products.
Founded in 1971

14929 **Silver Users Association**
3930 Walnut Street
Suite 210
Fairfax, VA 22030

703-930-7790
800-245-6999; Fax: 703-359-7562
pmiller@mwcapitol.com
www.silverusersassociation.org

Bill LeRoy, President
Mike Huber, VP
Jack Gannon, Immediate Past President
Bill Hamelin, Treasurer
John King, Secretary

Represents manufacturers and distributors of products in which silver is an essential element, such as photographic materials, medical and dental supplies, batteries and electronic and electrical equipment, silverware, mirrors, commemorative art and jewelry.
27 Members
Founded in 1947

14930 **Society of American Silversmiths**
P.O.Box 786
West Warwick, RI 02893

401-461-6840; Fax: 401-828-0162
sas@silversmithing.com
www.silversmithing.com

Jeffrey Herman, Founder/Executive Director

Organization devoted to the preservation and promotion of the silversmithing art and craft.
240 Members
Founded in 1989
Mailing list available for rent

14931 **Society of North American Goldsmiths**
PO Box 1355
Eugene, OR 97440

541-345-5689; Fax: 541-345-1123
info@snagmetalsmith.org
www.snagmetalsmith.org
Facebook, Twitter, LinkedIn, Pinterest, Flickr, RSS, YouTub

Renee Zettle-Sterling, President
Anne Havel, Treasurer
Gwynne Rukenbrod, Executive Dir.
Tara Jecklin, Operations Manager
John Garbett, Advertising & Production Director

Promotes a favorable and enriching environment in which contemporary metalsmiths practice their art. One aspect of this process is educating the public about the quality and rich diversity within the field of metalsmithing. Exhibitions, public forums, lectures, and published documents are our primary methods of reaching out to the public. SNAG sponsors workshops, seminars, audio-visual services and an annual conference.
Founded in 1968

14932 **The Fashion Jewelry & Accessories Trade Association**
25 Sea Grass Way
North Kingstown, RI 02852
401-667-0520; Fax: 401-267-9096
bcleaveland@fjata.org
www.fjata.org
Twitter
Brent Cleaveland, Executive Director
The voice of jewelry and accessories manufacturers, suppliers and retailers to regulatory agencies.
225 Members

14933 **Women's Jewelry Association**
80 Washington Street
Suite 205
Poughkeepsie, NY 12601
845-473-7323; Fax: 646-355-0219
info@womensjewelryassociation.com
www.womensjewelryassociation.com
Andrea Hansen, President
Brandee Dallow, President Elect
Tryna Kochanek, Immediate Past President
Kristie Nicolosi, Treasurer
Bernadette Mack, Executive Director
To empower women to achieve their highest goals in the international jewelry, watch and related businesses.
Founded in 1983

14934 **World Gold Council**
685 Third Avenue
27th Floor
New York, NY 10017
212-317-3800; Fax: 212-688-0410
info@gold.org
www.gold.org
Facebook, Twitter, LinkedIn, YouTube Flickr, RSS Feed, Goog
Aram Shishmanian, CEO
Brenda Bates, Managing Director, Corporate Comm.
Natalie Dempster, Managing Director, Central Banks
Roland Wang, Managing Director, China
William Rhind, Managing Director, Investment
Organization formed and funded by the world's leading gold mining companies with the aim of stimulating and maximizing the demand for, and holding of gold by consumers, investors, industry and the official sector.
23 Members
Founded in 1987

Newsletters

14935 **Benchmark**
Manufacturing Jewelers & Suppliers of America
57 John L Dietsch Sq
Attleboro Falls, MA 02763-1027
401-274-3840
800-444-6572; Fax: 401-274-0265
info@mjsa.org
www.mjsa.org
James McCarthy, COO
Bruce Coltin, Operations Manager
Kristin Kopaz, Operations Manager
Corrie Berry, Sales Manager
Offers details of association activities and industry events for members.
4 Pages
Frequency: Bi-Monthly

14936 **Costume Jewelry Review**
Retail Reporting Bureau
302 5th Ave
11th Floor
New York, NY 10001-3604
212-279-7000
Offers news and information on the costume jewelry industry, suppliers and manufacturers.
Cost: $108.00
Frequency: Monthly

14937 **Diamond Insight**
Tryon Mercantile
790 Madison Avenue
New York, NY 10021-6124
212-288-9011; Fax: 212-772-1286
www.newsletteraccess.com
Guido Giovannini-Torelli, Editor
Penetrates the multifaceted world of diamonds, giving intelligence on the world's important stones, future price indicators, key individuals behind the trends, jewelry auctions and DeBeers/CSO Activities.
Cost: $325.00
12 Pages
Frequency: Monthly
Circulation: 250
Printed in one color on glossy stock

14938 **Diamond Registry Bulletin**
Diamond Registry
580 5th Avenue
New York, NY 10036-4701
212-575-0444
800-223-7955; Fax: 212-575-0722
info@diamondregistry.com
www.diamondregistry.com
Facebook
Joseph Schlussel, Founder
Nissan Perla, President & CEO
Monthly newsletter offering the latest trends, prices and forecasts concerning diamonds, diamond jewelry and diamond mining.
Frequency: Monthly
ISSN: 0199-9753
Founded in 1961

14939 **Jewelers' Security Alliance Newsletter**
Jewelers' Security Alliance
6 E 45th St
Suite 1305
New York, NY 10017-2469
212-687-0328
800-537-0067; Fax: 212-808-9168
jsa2@jewelerssecurity.org
www.jewelerssecurity.org
John J Kennedy, President
Robert W. Frank, Vice President
Helen M. Buck, Manager of Membership Services
Principal activity is providing education and information to jewelers so they can guard against loss through crimes, including burglary, robbery and theft.
Cost: $375.00
Frequency: Annual+
Founded in 1883

14940 **Jewelers' Security Bulletin**
Jewelers' Security Alliance
6 E 45th St
Suite 1305
New York, NY 10017-2469
212-687-0328
800-537-0067; Fax: 212-808-9168
jsa2@jewelerssecurity.org
www.jewelerssecurity.org
John J Kennedy, President
Robert W. Frank, Vice President
Helen M. Buck, Manager of Membership Services
Principal activity is providing education and information to jewelers so they can guard against loss through crimes, including burglary, robbery and theft.
19500 Members
Founded in 1883
Mailing list available for rent

14941 **Jewelry Newsletter International**
Newsletters International
7710 T Cherry Park Drive
#421
Houston, TX 77095
888-972-4662
www.jewellerybusiness.com
Len Fox, Editor
Informs manufacturers, wholesalers, suppliers, and retailers of jewelry how to stimulate sales, increase profits, and cut costs.
Cost: $250.00
4-8 Pages
Frequency: Monthly
Founded in 1975
Printed in on matte stock

14942 **Precious Metals News**
International Precious Metals Institute
5101 N 12th Avenue
Suite C
Pensacola, FL 32504
850-476-1156; Fax: 850-476-1548
mail@ipmi.org
www.ipmi.org
Robert Ianniello, President
Frequency: Quarterly
Circulation: 1000

14943 **Spectra**
American Gem Society
8917 W Sahara Ave
Las Vegas, NV 89117-5826
702-233-6120; Fax: 702-233-6125
support@agslab.com
www.agslab.com
Frank Delahan, CEO
Society news covering all aspects of the jewelry world.
12 Pages
Frequency: Quarterly
Founded in 1934

Magazines & Journals

14944 **AJM Magazine: The Authority on Jewelry Manufacturing**
Manufacturing Jewelers & Suppliers of America
57 John L Dietsch Sq
Attleboro Falls, MA 02763-1027
401-274-3840
800-444-6572; Fax: 401-274-0265
info@mjsa.org
www.mjsa.org
James McCarthy, COO
Corrie Silvia Berry, Director of Sales & Business
David W. Cochran, President & CEO
Kristin Kopaz, Operations Manager
Dawn Britland, Assistant Controller
This is the only magazine dedicated solely to jewelry manufacturers. It delivers the three T's of jewelry manufacturing: trends, technology and techniques.
Cost: $47.00
Frequency: Monthly
Founded in 1903
Printed in 4 colors on glossy stock

14945 **Accent Magazine**
Larkin Group

485 Fashion Ave
Suite 1400
New York, NY 10018-6804

212-594-1439; Fax: 212-594-8556

AJ Larkin, Publisher

Provides trend analysis and market forecasts for buyers and designers, for accessories, clothing, and footwear. Also covers convention and tradeshow news, and new product launches.
Cost: $24.00
Frequency: Monthly
Circulation: 13,000

14946 **Adornment: Newsletter of Jewelry and Related Arts**
1333A N Avenue
New Rochelle, NY 10804

914-636-3784
ekarlin@usa.net

Elyse Karlin, Publisher/Editor/CEO
Cost: $60.00
Frequency: Quarterly
Circulation: 800
Founded in 1999

14947 **Chronos**
Golden Bell Press
2403 Champa St
Denver, CO 80205-2621

303-296-1600; Fax: 303-295-2159
print@goldenbellpress.com
www.goldenbellpress.com

Editorial material looks at timepieces of the past, present and future, bringing you the latest, the best and the most intriguing creation from the leading international watch and clock makers. The history of timepiece manufacturers and their significant milestones are also reported as well as armchair tours of the world's most prestigious horological museums.
Cost: $2250.00
Frequency: Quarterly
Circulation: 20000
Founded in 1933

14948 **Colored Stone**
PRIMEDIA
60 Chestnut Avenue
Suite 201
Devon, PA 19333-1312

610-964-6300
610-232-5700; Fax: 610-293-1717
www.colored-stone.com

Joseph Breck, Publisher
Morgan Beard, Editor-in-Chief

Contains news and information on the gem and gemstone jewelry industry.
Cost: $29.95
64 Pages
Circulation: 10000
Founded in 1986

14949 **Couture International Jeweler**
Miller Freeman Publications
770 Broadway
5th Floor
New York, NY 10003-9595

212-780-0400; Fax: 847-763-9037
ijmag@halldata.com
www.couturejeweler.com

Debra De Roo Ballard, Publisher
Lynda Roguso, Operations Director
Karen Stewart, Operations Director

Publication features information on hot trends in fine jewelry and fashion.
Cost: $60.00
Circulation: 20000
Founded in 1964

14950 **GZ (European Jeweler)**
JCK International Publishing Group
360 Park Ave S
New York, NY 10010-1710

646-746-6400; Fax: 646-746-7131
www.jckgroup.com

Ted Smith, CEO
Donna Borrelli, Associate Publisher
Hedda Schupak, Editor-in-Chief
Tracey Peden, Marketing Manager
Nancy Walsh, Senior Vice President
Cost: $49.95
Frequency: Monthly
Founded in 1874

14951 **High-Volume Jeweler**
Reed Business Information
201 King of Prussia Road
Radnor, PA 19087-5114

610-889-9577; Fax: 630-288-8686
www.reedbusiness.com

Shawn Mery, Publisher
Lisa Reed, CFO
Stuart Whayman, CFO

Provides original market research and in-depth analysis of current news and industry trends affecting this segment of the jewelry and watch market. Features operational strategies and new technological developments that can make and save money for retailers and vendors.
Cost: $60.00
Frequency: Bi-Monthly
Circulation: 5,000

14952 **Horological Times**
American Watchmakers-Clockmakers Institute
701 Enterprise Drive
Harrison, OH 45030-1696

513-367-9800
866-367-2924; Fax: 513-367-1414
www.awci.com
Facebook, RSS

James Lubic, Executive Director
Tom Pack, Operations Director
Jennifer Bilodeau, Assistant Editor
Elizabeth Janszen, Membership Coordinator

Contains articles dealing with the techniques of servicing and repairing watches and clockes; the uses of shop tool and equipment; the functional characteristics of mechanical, electronic, and antique timepieces.
Frequency: Monthly
Founded in 1892
Mailing list available for rent

14953 **International Wristwatch Magazine USA**
International Publishing Corporation
979 Summer Street
PO Box 110204
Stamford, CT 06905

203-259-8100; Fax: 203-295-0847
www.iwmagazine.com

Gary George, Editor-in-Chief
Patricia Russo, General Manager

Editorial content provides a consumer-oriented focus on new, vintage, and collectable watches.
Cost: $7.95
150 Pages
Frequency: Bi-Monthly
Circulation: 30,000
ISBN: 0-744706-22-2
Founded in 1989
Printed in 4 colors on glossy stock

14954 **JCK Magazine**
JCK International Publishing Group
1018 W Ninth Avenue
King of Prussia, PA 19406-1

610-205-1100
800-305-7759; Fax: 610-205-1139
www.jckgroup.com

Nancy Walsh, Senior VP
Fran Pennella, Marketing Director
Mark Smelzer, Publisher
Hedda Schupak, Editor-in-chief
Jay Jackson, Chief Operating Officer

Serves retailers, manufacturers, and vendors of fine jewerly and selected upscale gift categories, providing valuable market and design trend information and how-to information about gemology, financial management, employee relations, marketing, advertising, and visual merchandising, e-commerce, and other topics.
Cost: $49.95
Frequency: Monthly
Founded in 1869

14955 **JQ Limited Edition**
JQ Publishing
585 5th Street W
Sonoma, CA 95476-6831

707-938-1082; Fax: 707-935-6585
www.retailmerchandising.net

Audrey Bromstad, Publisher
Cynthia Unninayar, Editor
Deborah Rittenberg, Marketing Manager

Issues contain articles presented with illustrations on precious colored gems and diamonds, creative jewelry designs, designers, and luxury watches.
Frequency: Monthly
Circulation: 300000
Founded in 1985

14956 **Jewelers' Circular: Keystone**
Reed Business Information
360 Park Ave S
New York, NY 10010-1737

646-746-6400; Fax: 646-756-7583
hschupak@reedbusiness.com
www.reedbusiness.com
Twitter, LinkedIn

John Poulin, CEO
Hedda Schupak, Editor
Victoria Jones, Production Manager
James Reed, Owner
Andrew Rak, Senior Vice President

Discusses news of interest mainly to the jewelry shop owner and manager. Covers such topics as; product notices, manufacturer news and tips on operating a successful business.
Cost: $49.95
Frequency: Monthly
Circulation: 25000
Founded in 1874
Printed in on glossy stock

14957 **Jewelry Appraiser**
National Association of Jewelry Appraisers
P. O. Box 18
Rego Park, NY 11374-0018

718-896-1536; Fax: 718-997-9057
office@najaappraisers.com
www.najaappraisers.com

Gail Brett Levine, Executive Director

An important source for all jewelry appraisers.
Frequency: Quarterly
Founded in 1981

14958 **Lapidary Journal**
300 Chesterfield Parkway
Suite 100
Malvern, PA 19355-937

610-232-5700
800-676-4336; Fax: 610-232-5754
www.lapidaryjournal.com

Merle White, Editor
Karen Nuckols, Sales Director
Joe Breck, Publisher

This publication focuses fundamentally on the all aspects of the jewelry industry.
Cost: $29.95
Frequency: Monthly
Circulation: 45000
Founded in 1947

14959 **Link**
National Cuff Link Society
PO Box 5970
Vernon Hills, IL 60061-5970

847-816-0035; Fax: 847-816-0035
www.cufflink.com

Gena Klompus, President
Founded in 1990

14960 **Lustre**
Cygnus Publishing
19 W 44th St
Suite 1405
New York, NY 10036-6101

212-921-1091; Fax: 212-921-5539
lorraine.depasque@cygnuspub.com

Tim Murphy, Publisher
Roy Kim, Sales Director
Lorraine DePasque, Editor In Chief
Barb Hesse, Circulation Manager
Paul Mackler, President/CEO
Circulation: 4000
Founded in 1966

14961 **Modern Jeweler**
3 Huntington Quadrangle
Suite 301N
Melville, NY 11747-3602

631-845-2700
800-255-5113; Fax: 631-845-7109
tim.murphy@cygnuspub.com

Matthew Kramer, Managing Editor
Timothy Murphy, Publisher
Cheryl Kremkow, Editor in Chief
Barb Hesse, Circulation Manager
Jeff Prine, Executive Editor

A trade publication serving retail jewelers, wholesalers and manufacturers of jewelry, watches and related items. Accepts advertising.
Cost: $66.00
90 Pages
Frequency: Monthly
Circulation: 30000

14962 **Monroe Originals**
Karen Monroe
14014 Moorpark Street
Apartment 122
Sherman Oaks, CA 91423-3492

FAX 818-783-5009

Handmade wholesale jewelry designs magazine.
Cost: $2.00
50 Pages
Frequency: Monthly

14963 **Ornament Magazine**
PO Box 2349
San Marcos, CA 92079-9806

760-599-0222
800-888-8950; Fax: 760-599-0228
ornament@sbcglobal.net
ornamentmagazine.com

Robert Liu, Co-Editor
Carolin Denish, Co-Editor

Offers information on contemporary, ethnic, ancient jewelry and costumes.
Cost: $26.00
Frequency: Quarterly
Circulation: 38,000
Founded in 1976

14964 **Professional Jeweler**
Bond Communications
1500 Walnut Street
Suite 1200
Philadelphia, PA 19102-3523

215-670-0727
888-557-0727; Fax: 215-545-9629
askus@professionaljeweler.com
www.professionaljeweler.com

Lee Lawrence, Publisher/President
Peggy Jo Donahue, Editor-in-Chief
Peter James, Manager
Carole Masciantonio, Marketing Coordinator
Lisa Pastore, Advertising Manager

Editorial content provides these professionals with the information they need to meet business objectives and ensure success. Regular departments offer the latest news, trends, technical and practical information on all aspects of the jewelry industry.
Cost: $49.95
105 Pages
Frequency: Monthly
Circulation: 24000
ISSN: 1097-5314
Founded in 1998
Printed in 4 colors on glossy stock

14965 **Southern Jewelry News**
Mullen Publications
9629 Old Nations Ford Rd
Charlotte, NC 28273-5719

704-527-5111
800-738-5111; Fax: 704-527-5114
www.mullenpublications.com

Chip Smith, Publisher
Bill Newnam, Production Manager
Robert Cutshaw, Production Manager
Elesa Dillon, Sales Manager

Dedicated to the southern jewelry industry and contains industry news, local and regional events, personnel announcements, and pricing information.
Frequency: Monthly
Circulation: 13,431
Founded in 1945

14966 **Watch and Clock Review**
Golden Bell Press
2403 Champa St
Denver, CO 80205-2621

303-296-1600; Fax: 303-295-2159
print@goldenbellpress.com
www.goldenbellpress.com

Offers news and information on fashion accessories and jewelry.
Cost: $19.50
48 Pages
ISSN: 1082-2453
Founded in 1935

Trade Shows

14967 **ASD/AMD Las Vegas Variety Merchandise Show**
ASD/AMD Merchandise Group
Las Vegas Convention Center
3150 Paradise Road
Las Vegas, NV 89109

702-892-0711; Fax: 702-892-2933
www.lvcva.com

Features tens of thousands of unique products in hundres of popular categories.
10000 Attendees
Frequency: March

14968 **Accent on Design**
George Little Management
10 Bank Street
Suite 1200
White Plains, NY 10606-1954

914-486-6070
800-272-7469; Fax: 914-948-2867
www.nyigf.com

Elizabeth Murphy, Show Manager
George Little II, President

Three hundred and seventy booths of the latest and most innovative gift lines such as decorative accessories and home furnishings.
50M Attendees
Frequency: August
Founded in 1984

14969 **American Gem Society Conclave**
8881 W Sahara Avenue
Las Vegas, NV 89117

702-255-6500; Fax: 702-255-7420
www.ags.org

Glory Wade, Show Manager

One hundred and sixty booths. Conference and exhibitors.
1M Attendees
Frequency: April

14970 **American Gem Trade Association Expo**
3030 LBJ Freeway
Suite 840
Dallas, TX 75234

214-742-4367
800-972-1162; Fax: 214-742-7334
info@agta.org
www.agta.org

Elizabeth Ross, Marketing Manager
Rick Krementz, President

Two booths featuring exhibits of loose colored gemstones and diamonds.
10.3M Attendees
Frequency: February

14971 **Annual Spring New Products Show**
Pacific Expositions
1600 Kapiolani Boulevard
Suite 1660
Honnolulu, HI 96814

808-945-3594; Fax: 808-946-6399

48000 Attendees
Frequency: Annual

14972 **Appraisers Association of America National Conference**
Appraisers Association of America
212 W. 35th Street
11th Floor South
New York, NY 10001

212-889-5404; Fax: 212-889-5503
referrals@appraisersassociation.org
www.appraisersassociation.org

Linda Selvin, Executive Director
Yasemin Yeldener, Communications Coordinator

Exhibits of interest to appraisers, workshops, and presentations.
Founded in 1949

14973 **Bead and Button Show**
Kalmbach Publishing Company
21027 Crossroads Circle
PO Box 1612
Waukesha, WI 53187-1612

262-796-8776
800-553-6644
262-796-8776; Fax: 262-796-1615
www.beadandbuttonshow.com
Facebook, Pinterest

3500 Attendees

14974 **Best Bead Show**
Crystal Myths
PO Box 3243
Albuquerque, NM 87190

505-883-9295; Fax: 505-889-9553

14975 **Business to Business Gem Trade Show**
Gem & Lapidary Wholesalers
Holiday Inn Palo Verde/Holidome
Tucson, AZ

601-879-8832; Fax: 601-879-3282
info@glwshows.com
www.glwshows.com

Frequency: February

14976 **Catalog in Motion**
Bell Group
Tucson E Hilton
Tucson, AZ

505-839-3249; Fax: 505-839-3248
www.riogrande.com

Frequency: February

14977 **Fashion Accessories Expo**
Business Journals
50 Day Street
Norwalk, CT 06854

203-853-6015; Fax: 203-852-8175
www.busjour.com

Britton Jones, President
Lizette Chin, Show Director Market
14000 Attendees

14978 **Fashion Accessories Expo Accessories to Go**
Business Journals
50 Day Street
Norwalk, CT 06854

203-853-6015; Fax: 203-852-8175
www.busjour.com

Britton Jones, President
Lorrie Frost, Accessories Publisher
14000 Attendees

14979 **GJX Gem and Jewelry Show**
198 S Granada Avenue
Tucson, AZ

520-824-4200; Fax: 520-882-4203

Allan Norville, President
Frequency: February

14980 **GLDA Gem and Jewelry Show**
Gem & Lapidary Dealers Association
PO Box 2391
Tucson, AZ 85702

520-792-9431; Fax: 520-882-2836
info@glda.com
www.glda.com

Paul Page, Director Marketing

Qualified buyers receive free admission. Buyers are jewelry retailers, manufacturers, wholesalers, gem dealers.
16000 Attendees
Frequency: February

14981 **Gem & Jewelry Show**
International Gem & Jewelry Show
120 Derwood Circle
Rockville, MD 20850-1264

301-294-1640; Fax: 301-294-0034

Herb Duke, Owner

Annual show and exhibits of jewelry and gemstones and related equipment, supplies and services.
Frequency: October, Denver

14982 **Gem, Jewelry & Mineral Show**
Trade Shows International
PO Box 8862
Tucson, AZ 85738

520-791-2210; Fax: 520-825-9115

14983 **IJO Trade Show & Seminars**
Independent Jewelers Organization
25 Seir Hill Rd
Norwalk, CT 06850-1322

203-846-4215
800-624-9252; Fax: 203-846-8571
www.ijo.com

Penny Palmer, Member Services Director

For members only
3500 Attendees
Frequency: Semi-Annual

14984 **IPMI Conference**
International Precious Metals Institute
5101 N 12th Avenue
Suite C
Pensacola, FL 32504

850-476-1156; Fax: 850-476-1548
mail@ipmi.org
www.ipmi.org

Robert Ianniello, President
Frequency: Annual

14985 **International Gem & Jewelry Show**
120 Derwood Circle
Rockville, MD 20850

301-294-1640; Fax: 301-294-0034
www.intergem.net

Herb Duke, Owner

Jewelry, gemstones and related equipment, supplies and services.

14986 **International Gift Show: The Jewelry & Accessories Expo**
Business Journals
50 Day Street
Norwalk, CT 06854

203-853-6015; Fax: 203-852-8175

14000 Attendees

14987 **International Jewelry Fair/General Merchandise Show-Spring**
Helen Brett Enterprises
5111 Academy Drive
Lisle, IL 60532-2171

630-241-9865
800-541-8171; Fax: 630-241-9870
dharrington@helenbrett.com
www.gift2jewelry.com
Facebook

Dave Harrington, Show Manager

Containing 800 booths during the spring show and 1500 booths during the fall show. Tradeshow open to wholesale buyers only (credentials required to attend).
24000 Attendees
Frequency: May
Founded in 1946
Mailing list available for rent

14988 **International Watch and Jewelry Show**
Burley and Olg Bullock
5901-Z Westheimer Road
Houston, TX 77057

713-783-8188
800-554-4992; Fax: 281-589-8987
info@iwjg.com
www.iwjg.com

JJ Gilbreath
Christina LeDoux
Frequency: June-Nov./January-March

14989 **JCK Orlando International Jewelry Show**
Reed Exhibition Companies
383 Manin Avenue
Norwalk, CT 06850

203-404-4800; Fax: 203-840-5830
www.jckgroup.com

Jay Jackson, Chief Operating Officer
Matthew Stuller, Founder
John Bachman, Secretary

Conference and exhibition.
2000 Attendees
Frequency: February

14990 **Jewelers International Showcase (JIS)**
6421 Congress Avenue
Suite 105
Boca Raton, FL 33487-2858

561-998-0205; Fax: 561-998-0209
www.jisshow.com

Michael G Breslow CEM, President
Jordan Tuchband, Sales Director
Vito J. Miceli, Sales Manager
Cindy Corrente, Financial Coordinator
Michele Carter, Show Director

Worldwide manufacturers and wholesalers of jewelry exhibit to trade buyers from Florida, Caribbean, Central and South America, plus other USA states. Exhibits of 1000 suppliers of fine jewelry, fashion jewelry and related products and services. The leading and largest independent Jewelery Trade-Only Show in the Western Hemisphere.
12000 Attendees
Frequency: October, January, April
Founded in 1979

14991 **Merchandise Mart Gift/Jewelry/ Resort Show**
Denver Merchandise Mart
451 E 58th Avenue #470
Suite 4270
Denver, CO 80216

303-292-6278
800-289-6278; Fax: 303-298-8473
www.denvermart.com

Bridget Oakes, Gift Show Exhibit Manager

A wholesale market for retail store buyers for resorts, theme parksand national parks, specialty gift stores and interior designers. Semi - Annual Show.
7000 Attendees
Frequency: February/August

14992 **Mid-South Jewelry & Accessories Fair -Spring**
Helen Brett Enterprises
5111 Academy Drive
Lisle, IL 60532-2171

630-241-9865
800-541-8171; Fax: 630-241-9870
dharrington@helenbrett.com
www.gift2jewelry.com
Facebook

Dave Harrington, Show Manager

Containing over 300 booths during the spring show and 500 booths during the fall show. Tradeshow open to wholesale buyers only (credentials required to attend).
8500 Attendees
Frequency: May
Founded in 1946
Mailing list available for rent

14993 **Mid-South Jewelry & Accessories Fair-Fall**
Helen Brett Enterprises
5111 Academy Drive
Lisle, IL 60532-2171

630-241-9865
800-541-8171; Fax: 630-241-9870
dharrington@helenbrett.com
www.gift2jewelry.com
Facebook

Dave Harrington, Show Manager

Containing 500 booths during the fall show and over 300 booths during the spring show. Tradeshow open to wholesale buyers only (credentials required to attend).
16000 Attendees
Frequency: November
Founded in 1946
Mailing list available for rent

14994 **Midwest Jewelry Expo**
Wisconsin Jewelry Assocation
1 East Main Street
Suite 305
Madison, WI 53703

608-257-3541; Fax: 608-257-8755

Mary Kaja, Executive Director

The next jewelry trade show exposition is scheduled for March 24th to March 25th in 2007.
3000 Attendees
Frequency: March

14995 **NAJA Summer Education Conference**
National Association of Jewelry Appraisers
P. O. Box 18
Rego Park, NY 11374-0018

718-896-1536; Fax: 718-997-9057
office@najaappraisers.com
www.najaappraisers.com

Gail Brett Levine, Executive Director

An opportunity for professional gem and jewelry appraiders to increase their skills, learn new information, and network.
Frequency: Annual, August
Founded in 1981

14996 **NAJA Winter Education Conference**
National Association of Jewelry Appraisers
P. O. Box 18
Rego Park, NY 11374-0018

718-896-1536; Fax: 718-997-9057
office@najaappraisers.com
www.najaappraisers.com

Gail Brett Levine, Executive Director

An opportunity for professional gem and jewelry appraiders to increase their skills, learn new information, and network.
Frequency: Annual, February
Founded in 1981

14997 **National Accessory Maintenance Exposition**
240 Peachtree Street NW
Suite 2200
Atlanta, GA 30303-1327

404-203-3000; Fax: 404-607-8682

Jeff Portman, CEO
Charles Sydney, Manager

Offers a forum for the exchange of ideas between manufacturers and suppliers of fashion accessories.
10M Attendees
Frequency: January

14998 **Pacific Jewelry Show**
California Jewelers Association
911 Wilshire Boulevard
Suite 1740
Los Angeles, CA 90017-3446

213-235-5722; Fax: 213-623-5742

Richard Trujillo, Owner
Alberta E Hultman, Manager

Annual show of 250 exhibitors of jewelry and related items.
3000 Attendees
Frequency: August
Founded in 1999

14999 **Stylemax**
Merchandise Mart Properties Inc
222 Merchandise Mart Plaza
Suite 470
Chicago, IL 60654

312-527-4141
800-677-6278
sglick@mmart.com
www.mmart.com
Facebook

Susan Glick, VP

A women's apparel and accessory trade show with over 4,000 exhibitors.
5000 Attendees
Founded in 1920
Mailing list available for rent

15000 **The Whole Bead Show**
PO Box 1100
Nevade City, CA 95959

530-652-2725
800-292-2577; Fax: 530-265-2776
www.wholebead.com
Facebook

Ava Motherwell, Owner

An international bread trade show that occurs thirteen times per year. Contemporary pieces made from glass, stone, metal, pearl, amber and porcelain. Offering antique beads, handmade, findings, buttons, charms and beaded jewelry. Access merchants, bead makers and importers who are direct suppliers of many professional and novice jewelry makers.
N/A Attendees
Frequency: Jan/Feb/Mar/Apr
Founded in 1993
Mailing list available for rent

15001 **Trade Show for Jewelry Making**
Manufacturing Jewelers & Suppliers of America
57 John L Dietsch Sq
Attleboro Falls, MA 02763-1027

401-274-3840
800-444-6572; Fax: 401-274-0265
info@mjsa.org
www.mjsa.org

James McCarthy, COO
Corrie Silvia Berry, Director of Sales & Business
David W. Cochran, President & CEO
Kristin Kopaz, Operations Manager
Dawn Britland, Assistant Controller

New regional trade show designed to service jewelry makers and manufacturers of all sizes throughout New England and surrounding areas. Providing a full range of products that industry professionals need to make their jewelry and operate their business.
1000 Attendees
Frequency: September
Founded in 1903

15002 **Transworld's Jewelry, Fashion & Accessories Show**
Transworld Exhibits
1850 Oak Street
Northfield, IL 60093

847-446-8434
800-323-5462; Fax: 847-446-3523

Don Olstinske, Show Manager
Yianna Manokas, Creative Director
Donna Connolly, Customer Service Rep
Ron Carlson, Logistics Manager

Hundreds of the country's finest exhibitors. Thousands of the best buyers nationwide. The perfect venue for the latest jewelry collections, the most current fashion ideas and new accessories.
25000 Attendees
Frequency: July/October/December

15003 **Tucson Gem and Mineral Show (tm)**
Tucson Gem and Mineral Society
PO Box 42588
Tucson, AZ 85733

520-322-5773; Fax: 520-322-6031
tgms@tgms.org
www.tgms.org

Sponsored by the Tucson Gem and Mineral Society. Retail show open to the public at the Tucson Convention Center every February for four days. Over 200 dealers, over 100 exhibitors, children's activities.
25000 Attendees
Frequency: February
Founded in 1946

Directories & Databases

15004 **AJM Technology Sourcebook**
Manufacturing Jewelers & Suppliers of America
57 John L Dietsch Sq
Attleboro Falls, MA 02763-1027

401-274-3840
800-444-6572; Fax: 401-274-0265
info@mjsa.org
www.mjsa.org

James McCarthy, COO
Corrie Silvia Berry, Director of Sales & Business
David W. Cochran, President & CEO
Kristin Kopaz, Operations Manager
Dawn Britland, Assistant Controller

This publication provides listings and specs on machinery, equipment, raw materials, and software specifically geared to jewelry manufacturing.
Cost: $4.50
Frequency: Annual
Circulation: 5,000
Founded in 1903
Printed in 4 colors on glossy stock

15005 **Accent Source Book**
Larkin Group
100 Wells Avenue
Newton, MA 02459-3210

617-326-6525
800-869-7469; Fax: 617-964-2752

Lauren Parker, Editor
Michael Corkin, Owner

Information on over 1,500 manufacturers of jewelry, watches and accessories is available in this comprehensive directory aimed at the gemology and related industries.
Cost: $25.00
200 Pages
Frequency: Annual
Circulation: 15,000
ISSN: 0192-7507

15006 **Accessories Resource Directory**
Business Journals
50 Day Street
Norwalk, CT 06854-3100

203-853-6015; Fax: 203-852-8175

Britton Jones, President

Over 1,500 manufacturers, importers and sales representatives that produce accessories are profiled.
Frequency: Annual
Circulation: 10,000

15007 **Complete Directory of Cubic Zirconia Jewelry**
Sutton Family Communications & Publishing Company
920 State Route 54 East
Elmitch, KY 42343

270-276-9500

Theresa Sutton, Editor
Lee Sutton, General Manager

Print-out from database of wholesalers, manufacturers, distributors, importers and close-out houses. Database is updated daily to guarantee the most current and up-to-date sources available.
Cost: $39.50
100+ Pages

15008 **Complete Directory of Earrings & Necklaces**
Sutton Family Communications & Publishing Company
920 State Route 54 East
Elmitch, KY 42343

270-276-9500

Theresa Sutton, Editor
Lee Sutton, General Manager

Print-out from database of wholesalers, manufacturers, distributors, importers and close-out houses. Database is updated daily to guarantee the most current and up-to-date sources available.
Cost: $37.00
100+ Pages

15009 **Complete Directory of Jewelry Close-Outs**
Sutton Family Communications & Publishing Company
920 State Route 54 East
Elmitch, KY 42343

270-276-9500

Theresa Sutton, Editor
Lee Sutton, General Manager

Print-out from database of wholesalers, manufacturers, distributors, importers and close-out houses. Database is updated daily to guarantee the most current and up-to-date sources available.
Cost: $34.50
100+ Pages

15010 **Complete Directory of Jewelry: General**
Sutton Family Communications & Publishing Company
920 State Route 54 East
Elmitch, KY 42343

270-276-9500

Theresa Sutton, Editor
Lee Sutton, General Manager

Print-out from database of wholesalers, manufacturers, distributors, importers and close-out houses. Database is updated daily to guarantee the most current and up-to-date sources available.
Cost: $54.50
100+ Pages

15011 **Complete Directory of Low-Price Jewelry & Souvenirs**
Sutton Family Communications & Publishing Company
920 State Route 54 East
Elmitch, KY 42343

270-276-9500

Theresa Sutton, Editor
Lee Sutton, General Manager

Print-out from database of wholesalers, manufacturers, distributors, importers and close-out houses. Database is updated daily to guarantee the most current and up-to-date sources available.
Cost: $39.50
100+ Pages

15012 **Complete Directory of Watches and Watch Bands**
Sutton Family Communications & Publishing Company
920 State Route 54 East
Elmitch, KY 42343
270-276-9500

Theresa Sutton, Editor
Lee Sutton, General Manager

Print-out from database of wholesalers, manufacturers, distributors, importers and close-out houses. Database is updated daily to guarantee the most current and up-to-date sources available.
Cost: $39.50
100+ Pages

15013 **Diamond Report**
Rapaport Diamond Corporation
15 W 47th Street
Suite 600
New York, NY 10036-3305

212-540-0575; Fax: 212-840-0243
rap@diamonds.net
www.diamond.net

Amber Michelle, Editor
Eillene Furrel, Advertising Manager

This large directory database offers background information and current prices for more than 100,000 stores.
Cost: $185.00
Frequency: Annual

15014 **International Society of Appraisers**
International Society of Appraisers
Ste 400
230 E Ohio St
Chicago, IL 60611-3646

206-241-0359; Fax: 312-265-2908
isa@isa-appraisers.org
www.isa-appraisers.org

Nan B Shelton, President
Connie Davenport, Vice President
Charles Pharr, Treasurer
Philip Hawkins, Secretary

Be Certain of its Value - A Consumer's Guide To Hiring a Competent Personal Property Appraiser is available complimentary to the public. Alphabetical list of appraisers with specialty areas plus indexes: area of expertise, zip code, state and city, company, and related services.
Cost: $15.00
305 Pages
Frequency: Annual
Circulation: 1500
Founded in 1979
Printed in 2 colors

15015 **Jewelers Board of Trade: Confidential Reference Book**
Jewelers Board of Trade
95 Jefferson Blvd
Warwick, RI 02888-1046

401-467-0055; Fax: 401-467-1199
jbtinfo@jewelersboard.com
www.jewelersboard.com

Dione Kenyen, President

Importers, distributors and retailers, close to 45,000, are profiled that are directly related to the jewelry industry.
Frequency: Semiannual
Circulation: 3,400

15016 **Jewelers' Circular/Keystone: Brand Name and Trademark Guide**
Chilton Company
1 Chilton Way
Wayne, PA 19089-0002

610-964-4243
800-866-0206; Fax: 610-964-4481

L Roberts, Editor

Over 5,000 manufacturers of jewelry store products.
Cost: $49.95

15017 **Jewelers' Circular/Keystone: Jewelers' Directory Issue**
Chilton Company
PO Box 2045
Radnor, PA 19089

610-964-4000; Fax: 610-964-4512

Kathleen Ellis, Editor

About 10,000 manufacturers, importers and wholesale jewelers providing merchandise and supplies to the jewelry retailing industry and related trade organizations.
Cost: $32.00
Frequency: Monthyly
Circulation: 30,000

15018 **Lapidary Journal: Annual Buyers' Directory Issue**
Lapidary Journal
60 Chestnut Avenue
Suite 201
Devon, PA 19333-1312

610-325-5700
800-676-GEMS; Fax: 610-293-1717

Michele Erazo, Marketing Executive

List of 4,000 suppliers and retailers of gem-cutting and jewelry making and mineral collecting equipment, beads, fossils, minerals and gems, gem and mineral clubs, bead societies, museums, schools and shops.
Cost: $6.50
Frequency: Annual May
Circulation: 67,000

15019 **MJSA Buyers' Guide**
Manufacturing Jewelers & Suppliers of America
57 John L Dietsch Sq
Attleboro Falls, MA 02763-1027

401-274-3840
800-444-6572; Fax: 401-274-0265
info@mjsa.org
www.mjsa.org

James McCarthy, Coo
Bruce Coltin, Operations Manager
Kristin Kopaz, Operations Manager
Corrie Berry, Sales Manager

Contains finished jewelry as well as equipment, supplies, and components necessary for jewelry manufacturing.
Cost: $45.00
Frequency: BiAnnual
Circulation: 5,000

15020 **National Jeweler: Industry Yellow Pages**
Miller Freeman Publications
28 East 28th Street
12th Floor
New York, NY 10016
212-378-0400; Fax: 212-378-0470
sedorusa@optonline.net
www.governmentvideo.com
RSS
Gary Rhodes, International Sales Manager
Approximately 5,000 companies providing products and services in the jewelry and watch industries.
Cost: $10.00
Frequency: Annual December
Circulation: 36,000

Industry Web Sites

15021 **Gemological Institute of America**
The Robert Mouawad Campus
5345 Armada Dr.
Carlsbad, CA 92008
760-603-4000
800-421-7250; Fax: 760-603-4080
www.gia.edu
Facebook, Twitter, LinkedIn, Google+, YouTube
John A. Green, Chair
Susan M. Jacques, President & CEO
The jewellery industry's source for knowledge, standards and education since 1931.
Founded in 1931

15022 **http://gold.greyhouse.com**
G.O.L.D Grey House OnLine Databases
Grey House Publishing's online database platform, GOLD, offers Quick Search, Keyword Search and Expert Search for most business sectors including jewelry and watch markets. The GOLD platform makes finding the information you need quick and easy - whether you're a novice searcher or an experienced database user. All of Grey House's directory products are available for subscription on the GOLD platform.

15023 **www.agta.org**
American Gem Trade Association
A trade association for the colored gemstone industry in North Africa. Operates gemological testing in New York.

15024 **www.cufflink.com**
National Cuff Link Society
For cuff link wearers and collectors.

15025 **www.greyhouse.com**
Grey House Publishing
Authoritative reference directories for most business sectors including jewelry and watch markets. Users can search the online databases with varied search criteria allowing for custom searches by product category, geographic area, sales volume, keyword, subject and more. Full Grey House catalog and online ordering also available.

15026 **www.iaca.com**
Indian Arts & Crafts Association
Not for profit trade association. Our mission is to promote, protect and preserve Indian arts.

15027 **www.ipmi.org**
International Precious Metals Institute
International association of producers, refiners, fabricators, scientists, users, financial institutions, merchants, private and public sector groups and the general precious metals community created to provide a forum for the exchange of information and technology.

15028 **www.isa-appraisers.org**
International Society of Appraisers
A not-for-profit professional association of personal property appraisers. ISA provides education and organizational support to its members, to serve the public by producing highley qualified and ethical appraisers who are recognized authorities in personal property appraising.

15029 **www.jewelers.org**
Jewelers of America

15030 **www.jewelersboard.com**
Trade association providing credit reporting, collections and marketing services to the US and overseas jewelry industries. Our members are wholesalers, manufacturers and service providers to the jewelry industry.

15031 **www.jewelerssecurity.org**
Jewelers' Security Alliance
Principal activity is providing education and information to jewelers so they can guard against loss through crimes, including burglary, robbery and theft.

15032 **www.jewelryinfo.org**
Jewelery Information Center
Identifies deceptive trade practices and misleading advertising. Provides advice on marketing and assists in prosecution of violations. The media side of the Jewelers Vigilance Committee.

15033 **www.jvclegal.org**
Jewelers Vigilance Committee
Identifies deceptive trade practices and misleading advertising. Provides advice on marketing and assists in prosecution of violations.

15034 **www.love-story.com**
Leading Jewelers Guild

15035 **www.silverinstitute.org**
Silver Institute

15036 **www.silversmithing.com**
Society of American Silversmiths

15037 **www.silverusersassociation.org**
Silver Users Association
Represents manufacturers and distributors of products in which silver is an essential element, such as photographic materials, medical and dental supplies, batteries and electronic and electrical equipment, silverware, mirrors, commemorative art and jewelry.

15038 **www.superabrasives.org**
Industrial Diamond Association of America

15039 **www.womensjewelry.org**
Women's Jewelry Association
For jewelry industry professionals.

Associations

15040 **Accrediting Council on Education in Journalism and Mass Communications**
1435 Jayhawk Blvd
Lawrence, KS 66045-7575

785-864-3973; Fax: 785-864-5225
www2.ku.edu/~acejmc/

Christopher Callahan, Chair
Marie Hardin, Vice Chair
David Boardman, President
Doug Anderson, Vice President
Cindy Reinardy, Assistant to the Executive Dir.

ACEJMC members are journalism and media departments, education associations and professional organizations.
113 Members
Founded in 1945

15041 **American Agricultural Editors' Association**
120 Main Street W
PO Box 156
New Prague, MN 56071

952-758-6502; Fax: 952-758-5813
www.ageditors.com
Facebook, Twitter, LinkedIn

Elaine Shein, President
Kurt Lawton, Immediate Past President
Mike Wilson, President Elect
Den Gardner, Executive Director
Doug Rich, Board Member

National professional development member association for agricultural communicators.
Founded in 1921

15042 **American Association of Sunday & Feature Editors**
1921 Gallows Road
Suite 600
Vienna, VA 22182-3900

703-902-1639; Fax: 703-620-4557
contact@aasfe.org
www.aasfe.org

Chris Beringer, President
Gina Seay, VP
Denise Joyce, VP
Kim Marcum, Secretary-Treasurer

An organization of editors from the United States and Canada dedicated to the quality of features in newspapers and the craft of feature writing.

15043 **American Copy Editors Society**
155 E. Algonquin Road
Arlington Heights, IL 60005-4617

info@copydesk.org
www.copydesk.org
Facebook, Twitter, LinkedIn, RSS

Teresa Schmedding, President
David Sullivan, Vice President
Sara Ziegler, Treasurer
Brady Jones, Secretary
Christine Steele, Director of Membership

A professional nonprofit association for copy editors at U.S. newspapers, magazines, websites, and corporations.
Founded in 1997

15044 **American Copy Editors Society (ACES)**
7 Avenida Vista Grande
Suite B7 #467
Santa Fe, NM 87508
info@copydesk.org
www.copydesk.org
Facebook, Twitter, LinkedIn, RSS

Teresa Schmedding, President
Lisa McLendon, Vice President Conferences
Sara Ziegler, Treasurer
Rudy Bahr, Executive Director
David F. Sullivan, Secretary

ACES is a professional organization working toward the advancement of editors. Their aim is to provide opportunities through training, discussion and advocacy that promote the editing profession.
Founded in 1997

15045 **American Medical Writers' Association**
30 W Gude Dr
Suite 525
Rockville, MD 20850-4347

240-238-0940; Fax: 301-294-9006
amwa@amwa.org
www.amwa.org
Facebook, Twitter, LinkedIn

Susan Krug, CAE, Executive Director
Ann Silveira, Membership Manager & Database Coor
Shari Rager, CAE, Deputy Director
Julia Shedlin, Membership Program Assistant
Josie Zeman, Education Program Assistant

Concerned with the advancement and improvement of medical communications.
5000+ Members
Founded in 1940
Mailing list available for rent

15046 **American Newspaper Representatives**
2075 W Big Beaver Rd
Suite 310
Troy, MI 48084-3439

248-643-9910
800-550-7557; Fax: 248-643-9914
accountsales@gotoanr.com
gotoanr.com

Hilary Howe, President
Robert Sontag, Executive VP/COO
John Jepsen, Controller
Melanie Cox, Regional Sales Manager

Supports those newspaper representatives and distributors in the United States. Hosts annual trade show.
Founded in 1943

15047 **American Press Institute**
4401 Wilson Boulevard
Suite 900
Arlington, VA 22203

571-366-1200
hello@pressinstitute.org
www.americanpressinstitute.org/
Facebook, Twitter, YouTube, RSS

Robert J. Weil, Chair
Michael G. Abernathy, Vice Chair
Tom Rosenstiel, Executive Director
Jeff Sonderman, Deputy Director
Jane Elizabeth, Senior Research Project Manager

Conducts research, training, convenes thought leaders and creates tools to help chart a path ahead for journalism in the 21st century.
Founded in 1946

15048 **American Press Institute (API)**
4401 Wilson Blvd.
Ste 900
Arlington, VA 22203

571-366-1200; Fax: 571-366-1195
hello@pressinstitute.org
www.americanpressinstitute.org
Facebook, Twitter, RSS, YouTube

Robert J. Weil, Chair
Michael G. Abernathy, Vice Chair
Tom Rosenstiel, Executive Director
Jeff Sonderman, Deputy Director
Jane Elizabeth, Senior Research Project Manager

API is the trusted source for career leadership development for the newsmedia industry in North America and around the world. They help companies innovate and leaders realize their full potential.
Founded in 1946

15049 **American Society of Business Press Editors**
214 North Hale Street
Wheaton, IL 60187

630-510-4588; Fax: 630-510-4501
info@asbpe.org
www.asbpe.org
Facebook, Twitter, LinkedIn, RSS

Jessica Zemler, President
Dominick Yanchunas, Vice President
Janet Svazas, Executive Director
Steve Ross, Treasurer
Robin Sherman, Associate Dir. & Newsletter Editor

ASBPE is the professional association for full-time and freelance editors and writers employed in the business, trade, and specialty press. It is widely known for its annual Awards of Excellence competition, which recognizes the best editorial, design, and online achievement.
Founded in 1964
Mailing list available for rent

15050 **American Society of Business Publication Editors**
214 North Hale St.
Wheaton, IL 60187

630-510-4588; Fax: 630-510-4501
info@asbpe.org
www.asbpe.org
Facebook, Twitter, LinkedIn, YouTube

Jessica Zemler, President
Dominick Yanchunas, Vice President
Janet Svazas, Executive Director
Steve Ross, Treasurer

Professional association for full-time and freelance editors and writers employed in the business, trade, and specialty press.
Founded in 1964

15051 **American Society of Journalists and Authors**
355 Lexington Avenue
15th Floor
New York, NY 10017-6603

212-997-0947; Fax: 212-937-2315
webeditor@asja.org
www.asja.org
Facebook, Twitter, LinkedIn, Google+, Instagram

Randy Dotinga, President
Sherry Beck Paprocki, Vice President
Alexandra Cantor Owens, Executive Director
Meredith Taylor, General Manager
Neil O'Hara, Treasurer

For freelance nonfiction writers whose bylines appear in periodicals and in books.
1000+ Members
Founded in 1948

15052 American Society of Magazine Editors
757 Third Avenue
11th Floor
New York, NY 10017
212-872-3700
mpa@magazine.org
www.magazine.org/
Facebook, Twitter, LinkedIn, YouTube, Google+
Mary G. Berner, President, CEO
Nancy Telliho, Interim CEO
Sid Holt, Chief Executive
Eric John, SVP, Digital Strategy & Initiatives
Rita Cohen, SVP/ Legislative & Reg Policy
An industry trade group for editors of magazines published in the United States.
Founded in 1919

15053 American Society of Media Photographers (ASMP)
150 North 2nd Street
Philadelphia, PA 19106
215-451-2767; Fax: 215-451-0880
info@asmp.org
asmp.org
Facebook, Twitter, LinkedIn
Tom Kennedy, Executive Director
Victor Perlman, General Counsel
Elena Goertz, General Manager
Chris Chandler, Bookkeeper
Ellen Khlystova, IT Specialist
ASMP is the premier trade association for the world's most respectd photograhers. ASMP is the leader in promoting photographers' rights, providing education in better business practices, producing business publications for photographers, and helping to connect purchasers with professional photographers.
7000 Members
Founded in 1944

15054 American Society of News Editors (ASNE)
209 Reynolds Journalism Institute
Mission School of Journalism
Columbia, MO 65211
573-884-2405; Fax: 573-884-3824
asne@asne.org
www.asne.org
Facebook, Twitter, Storify
Pam Fine, President
Mizell Stewart III, Vice President
Teri Hayt, Executive Director
Arnie Robbins, Senior Adviser
Cindy L. Roe, Finance Director
ASNE is a membership organization for editors, producers or directors in charge of journalistic organizations or departments, deans or faculty at university journalism schools, and leaders and faculty of media-related foundations and training organizations.
Founded in 1922

15055 Asian American Journalists Association (AAJA)
5 Third Street
Suite 1108
San Francisco, CA 94103
415-346-2051; Fax: 415-346-6343
national@aaja.org
www.aaja.org
Facebook, Twitter, LinkedIn
Paul Cheung, President
Kathy Chow, Executive Director
Glenn E. K. Sugihara, Accounting Consultant
Karen A. Sugihara, Accounting Consultantŷ
Derric Jones, Event Manager Consultant
AAJA provides support among Asian American and Pacific Islander journalists. It provides encouragement, information, advice and scholarship assistance to Asian American and Pacific Islander students who aspire to professional journalism careers.
Founded in 1981

15056 Associated Press
1825 K Street NW
Suite 800
Washington, DC 20006-1202
212-621-1500; Fax: 202-736-1107
info@ap.org
www.ap.org
Facebook, Twitter, LinkedIn, Google+, Youtube
Mary Junck, Chairman
Gary Pruitt, President and CEO
Jessica Bruce, SVP, Director of Human Resources
Ken Dale, Senior Vice President and CFO
Ellen Hale, SVP, Director of Corporate Comm.
Seeks to advance journalism through radio and television, and cooperates with the AP to promote accurate and impartial news.
5.9m Members
Founded in 1846

15057 Associated Press Media Editors
450 West 33rd Street
New York, NY 10001
212-621-7007
sjacobsen@ap.org
www.apme.com
Facebook, Twitter, Blog
Bill Church, President
Jim Simon, Vice President
Angie Muhs, Secretary
Dennis Anderson, Treasurer
Members are managing editors or executives of Associated Press News Executives.
Founded in 1930

15058 Associated Press Sports Editors
9000 N. Broadway
Oklahoma City, OK 73114
405-475-3164; Fax: 405-475-3315
apsportseditors.com
Facebook, Twitter, RSS
Mike Sherman, Chairman
Mary Byrne Byrne, President
Tommy Deas, First Vice President
John Bednarowski, Third VP
Jack Berninger, Executive Director
A national organization that strives to improve professional standards of sports departments.

15059 Association for Education in Journalism and Mass Communication
234 Outlet Pointe Boulevard
Suite A
Columbia, SC 29210-5667
803-798-0271; Fax: 803-772-3509
www.aejmc.org
Facebook, Twitter, LinkedIn, YouTube, Pinterest, Instagram
Tim P. Vos, President
Jennifer McGill, Executive Director
Belinda Pearson, Association Business Manager
Felicia G. Brown, Assistant Executive Director
Lillian Coleman, Newsletter Editor/Project Manager
AEJMC promotes the highest possible standards for education in journalism and mass communication, encouraging the widest possible range of communication research and the implementation of a multi-cultural society in the classroom and curriculum, defending and maintaining the freedom of expression in day-to-day living.
Founded in 1912

15060 Association for Women in Communications
1717 E Republic Road
Suite A
Springfield, MO 65804
417-886-8606; Fax: 417-886-3685
chair@womcom.org
www.womcom.org
Facebook, Twitter, LinkedIn, Google+, YouTube
Anita K. Parran, Chair
Kandice Mollitiam, Data Protection Officer
Professional organization that champions the advancement of women across all communications disciplines by recognizing excellence, promoting leadership and positioning its members at the forefront of the evolving communications era. Hosts a bi-annual conference.
1000 Members
Founded in 1909
Mailing list available for rent: 1000+ names at $n/a per M

15061 Association for Women in Sports Media
7742 Spalding Dr.
#377
Norcross, GA 30092
Home Page: www.awsmonline.org
Facebook, Twitter, LinkedIn, Instagram
Lydia Craver, Chair of the Board
Jennifer Overman, President
Rachel Whittaker, VP, Administration
Jill Ann Bouffard, VP, Convention
Allison Creekmore, VP, Digital
Nonprofit organization founded as a support network and advocacy group for women who work in sports writing, editing, broadcast and production, andpublic and media relations.

15062 Association of Alternative Newsmedia
116 Cass Street
Traverse City, MI 49684
703-470-2996; Fax: 866-619-9755
web@aan.org
www.altweeklies.com
Facebook, Twitter, RSS, Google+
Molly Willmott, Association Manager
Britt Ervin, Admin. & Marketing Associate
Susan Torregrossa, Events Manager
Christy Bryan, Events Manager
Amy Howarth, Accounting Manager
Trade association of alternative weekly newspapers in North America.
Founded in 1978

15063 Association of American Editorial Cartoonists
PO Box 460673
Fort Lauderdale, FL 33346
717-703-3003; Fax: 717-703-3008
www.editorialcartoonists.com
Twitter
Jack Ohman, President
Jen Sorensen Sorensen, Vice President
R.C. Harvey, Secretary-Treasurer

15064 Association of Food Journalists
Home Page: www.afjonline.com
Facebook
Debbie Moose, President
Bob Batz, Jr., Vice President
Jennifer Palcher-Silliman, Executive Director

Nancy Stohs, Secretary
Patricia West-Barker, Treasurer
Founded in 1974

15065 Association of Health Care Journalists
Missouri School of Journalism
10 Neff Hall
Columbia, MO 65211

573-884-5606; Fax: 573-884-5609
www.healthjournalism.org
Facebook, Twitter

Karl Stark, President
Ivan Oransky, M.D., Vice President
Len Bruzzeseў, Executive Director
Jeff Porter, Special Projects Director
Pia Christensen, Managing Editor/Online Services
1,400 Members
Founded in 1997

15066 Association of Magazine Media
757 Third Avenue
11th Floor
New York, NY 10017

212-872-3700; Fax: 212-906-0128
mpa@magazine.org
www.magazine.org
Facebook, Twitter, LinkedIn, Youtube, Pinterst

Mr. Stephen M. Lacy, Chairman
Ms. Nancy Telliho, Interim President and CEO
Sid Holt, Chief Executive
Nina Fortuna, Director, ASME
Julie Ryu, Marketing and Events Coordinator

ASME is the principal organization for magazine journalists in the United States. ASME works to defend the First Amendment, protect editorial independence and support the development of journalism.
700 Members
Founded in 1919

15067 Association of Opinion Journalists
2301 Vanderbilt Place
VU Station B 351669
Nashville, TN 37233-1699

opinionjournalists@gmail.com
www.opinionjournalists.org/
Facebook, Twitter

David D. Haynes, President
Jennifer Hemmingsen, Secretary
Dan Morain, Treasurer
Founded in 1947

15068 Baptist Communicators Association
1519 Menlo Drive
Kennesaw, GA 30152

770-425-3728
www.baptistcommunicators.org
Facebook, RSS

Brian Hobbs, Program Chair
Eric Yarbrough, Awards Chairman
Ian Richardson, President
Neisha Fuson Roberts, Membership Vice President
Brooke Zimny, Communications Vice President

PR and journalism profesionals.
300 Members
Founded in 1953

15069 Center for Investigative Reporting
1400 65th St.
Suite 200
Emeryville, CA 94608

510-809-3160; Fax: 510-849-6141
www.revealnews.org
Facebook, Twitter, Tumblr, RSS

Phil Bronstein, Executive Chair
Joaquin Alvarado, CEO
Laurel Leichter, Human Resources Consultant
Robert J. Rosenthal, Executive Director
Christa Scharfenberg, Head of Studio
Founded in 1977

15070 Center for Media Literacy
22837 Pacific Coast Highway
#472
Malibu, CA 90265

310-804-3985
cml@medialit.com
www.medialit.org
YouTube

Tessa Jolls, President & CEO
Founded in 1977

15071 Collegiate Press Association
330 21st Avenue S
Minneapolis, MN 55455-0480

612-625-3500; Fax: 612-626-0720

Tom Rolnicki, Manager

Supports all those involved in the development and betterment of collegiate press. Hosts annual trade show.

15072 Committee of Concerned Journalists
Administrative Offices
Suite 300
Columbia, MO 65211

573-884-9121; Fax: 573-884-3824
rji@rjionline.org
www.rjionline.org
Facebook, Twitter, LinkedIn, Google+, YouTube

Randy Picht, Executive Director
Roger Gafke, Director of Program Development
Edward McCain, Digital Curator of Journalism
Brian Steffens, Director, Communications
Esther Thorson, Director, Research
Founded in 2004

15073 Committee to Protect Journalists
330 7th Avenue
11th Floor
New York, NY 10001

212-465-1004; Fax: 212-465-9568
info@cpj.org
www.cpj.org/
Facebook, Twitter, YouTube, Tumblr, RSS

Joel Simon, Executive Director
Robert Mahoney, Deputy Director
John Weis, Development & Outreach Director
Sue Marcoux, Director, Finance & Admin.
Kavita Menon, Senior Program Officer
Founded in 1981

15074 Dart Center for Journalism & Trauma
Columbia University
Graduate School of Journalism, 2950
New York, NY 10027

212-854-8056
bruce.shapiro@dartcenter.org
www.dartcenter.org
Facebook, Twitter

Bruce Shapiro, Executive Director
Kate Black, Associate Director
Kelly Boyce, Administrative Coordinator
Ariel Ritchin, Website Editor

15075 Education Writers Association
3516 Connecticut Avenue NW
Washington, DC 20008

202-452-9830; Fax: 202-452-9837
www.ewa.org
Facebook, Twitter, LinkedIn, Google+

Scott Elliott, President
Greg Toppo, Vice President (Journalists)
Christine Tebben, Vice President (Community Members)
Caroline W. Hendrie, Executive Director
George Dieter, Chief Operating Officer

The Education Writers Association is the national professional organization of education reporters and intent of improving education reporting to the public.

15076 First Amendment Center
555 Pennsylvania Ave. N.W.
Washington, DC 20001

202-292-6288; Fax: 202-292-6295
kcatone@newseum.org
www.firstamendmentcenter.org
Facebook, Twitter, RSS

Ken Paulson, President and CEO
Gene Policinski, SVP and Executive Director
John Seigenthaler, Founder
Karen Catone, Director
Ashlie Hampton, Event Coordinator

15077 Football Writers Association of America
18652 Vista del Sol
Dallas, TX 75287

972-713-6198
webmaster@sportswriters.net
www.sportswriters.net
Twitter

Kirk Bohls, President
Steve Richardson, Executive Director
Lee Barfknecht, 1st VP
Mark Anderson, Second VP
1,000 Members
Founded in 1941

15078 Garden Writers Association of America
7809 FM 179
Shallowater, TX 79363

806-832-1870; Fax: 806-832-5244
webtech@gardenwriters.org
www.gardenwriters.org/
Facebook, Twitter, LinkedIn, Pinterest, Google+

Kirk Brown, President
Becky Heath, Vice President
Jo Ellen Meyers Sharp, Treasurer
Robert LaGasse, Executive Director
Debra Prinzing, Past President

15079 Gay and Lesbian Press Association
PO Box 8185
Universal City, CA 91618-8185

FAX 818-902-9576

Supports those gay and lesbian professionals in the field of journalism. Publishes quarterly newsletter.

15080 Hollywood Foreign Press Association
646 N Robertson Blvd
West Hollywood, CA 90069

310-657-1731; Fax: 310-939-9034
info@hfpa.org
www.hfpa.org
Facebook, Twitter, Youtube, RSS

Lorenzo Soria, President
Meher Tatna, VP
Serge Rakhlin, Executive Secretary
Jorge Camara, Treasurer
Meher Tatna, Treasurer

Foreign correspondents covering Hollywood and the entertainment industry.
Mailing list available for rent

15081 Inland Press Association
701 Lee Street
Suite 925
Des Plaines, IL 60016
847-795-0380; Fax: 847-795-0385
inland@inlandpress.org
www.inlandpress.org/
Facebook, Twitter, LinkedIn
Tom Slaughter, Executive Director
Patty Slusher, Director, Membership & Programming
Tim Mather, Financial Studies Manager
Mark Fitzgerald, Publications Editor
Maria Choronzuk, Graphic Designer
Founded in 1885

15082 Inter American Press Association
Jules Dubois Building
1801 Sw 3rd Ave
Miami, FL 33129
305-634-2465; Fax: 305-635-2272
info@sipiapa.org
www.sipiapa.org
Facebook, Twitter, Blogger, Youtube
Ricardo Trotti, Executive Director
Martha Estrada, Assistant Executive Director
Melba Jimenez, Assistant Press Freedom Committee
Carlos Fernandez, Financial counselor
Ana Maria Perez, Accounting
Supports all those involved in the media and journalism industry. Hosts annual trade show.
Founded in 1926

15083 International Center for Journalists
2000 M St. NW
Suite 250
Washington, DC 20036
202-737-3700; Fax: 202-737-0530
www.icfj.org
Facebook, Twitter, LinkedIn, YouTube, Instagram, Google+
Michael Golden, Chairman
James F. Hoge, Jr., Vice Chair
Pamela Howard, Vice Chair
Matthew Winkler, Vice Chair
Joyce Barnathan, President

15084 International Communication Association
1500 21st St Nw
Washington, DC 20036
202-955-1444; Fax: 202-955-1448
icahdq@icahdq.org
www.icahdq.org
Facebook, Twitter, LinkedIn, Google+, Tumblr, Reddit
Laura Sawyer, Executive Director
Tom Mankowski, Director, Publishing Operations
Julie Arnold, Sr. Manager, Governance
Jennifer Le, Sr. Manager, Conference Services
Kristine Rosa, Manager, Member Services/Marketing
Supports all students and professionals in the international communications industry. Publishes bi-monthly newsletter.
3400 Members
Founded in 1950
Mailing list available for rent

15085 International Food, Wine and Travel Writers Association
39252 Winchester Rd.
Ste 107 #418
Murrieta, CA 92563
877-439-8929
951-970-8326; Fax: 909-396-0014
admin@ifwtwa.org
www.ifwtwa.org
Facebook, Twitter, LinkedIn, RSS, Youtube, Instagram
Linda Kissam, President, Officer, Chair Marketing
Allen Cox, VP, Officer, Chair Excellence Award
Elizabeth Willoughby, Secretary
Michelle M. Winner, Director
Andrew M. Harris, Director, Culinary Advisor
Staff and/or freelance writers in the food, wine and travel field. Also includes other media professionals and industry associate members in 28 countries worldwide.
300 Members
Founded in 1956

15086 International Food, Wine and Travel Writer
39252 Winchester Rd
Ste 107 #418
Murrieta, CA 92563
877-439-8929
951-970-8326; Fax: 877-439-8929
admin@ifwtwa.org
www.ifwtwa.org/
Facebook, Twitter, LinkedIn, YouTube, RSS, Instagram
Linda Kissam, President, Officer, Chair Marketing
Allen Cox, VP, Officer, Chair Excellence Award
Elizabeth Willoughby, Secretary
Michelle M. Winner, Director
Andrew M. Harris, Director, Culinary Advisor

15087 International News Media Association
PO Box 740186
Dallas, TX 75374
214-373-9111
972-991-3151; Fax: 214-373-9112
www.inma.org
Facebook, Twitter, LinkedIn, RSS
Ross McPherson, Executive Chairman
Mark Challinor, President
Yasmin Namini, Senior VP, Chief Consumer Officer
Earl J. Wilkinson, Executive Director/CEO
Brie Logsdon, Social Media Editor
Individuals in marketing, circulation, research and public relations of newspapers.
1100 Members
Founded in 1930
Mailing list available for rent

15088 Investigative Reporters and Editors
141 Neff Annex
Missouri School of Journalism
Columbia, MO 65211
573-882-2042; Fax: 573-882-5431
info@ire.org
www.ire.org
Sarah Cohen, Board President
Matt Goldberg, Vice President
Andrew Donohue, Treasurer
Mark Horvit, Executive Director
Jaimi Dowdell, Senior Training Directorÿ
For individuals involved in investigative journalism.
Founded in 1975

15089 Journalism Center on Children and Families
Knight Hall, Room 1100
College Park, MD 20742
301-405-8808
info@journalismcenter.org
www.journalismcenter.org
Facebook, Twitter, LinkedIn
Julie Drizin, Director
Aysha Khan, Editorial Intern
Zoe King, Editorial Intern
Fatimah Waseem, Editorial Intern
Founded in 1993

15090 Magazine Publishers of America
757 Third Avenue
11th Floor
New York, NY 10017
212-872-3700
mpa@magazine.org
www.magazine.org
Facebook, Twitter, LinkedIn, YouTube, Google+
Mr. Stephen M. Lacy, Chairman
Ms. Nancy Telliho, Interim President and CEO
Sid Holt, Chief Executive
Eric John, SVP
Rita Cohen, SVP / Legislative & Reg Policy
Founded in 1919

15091 Media Financial Management Association
550 W. Frontage Road
Ste. 3600
Northfield, IL 60093
847-716-7000; Fax: 847-716-7004
info@mediafinance.org
www.infe.org
Ralph Bender, Chairman
Mary M. Collins, President & CEO
Jamie L. Grande, Director of Operations
Arcelia Pimentel, Director of Sales
Caitlin Hahne, Membership Coordinator
Focuses on newspaper financial management, with members representing most North American newpaper companies, as well as many offshore. INFE's activities include publishing, conferences, workshops, industry surveys and studies, and offers members networking opportunities.
1200 Members
Founded in 1961

15092 National Academy of Television Journalists
PO Box 289
Salisbury, MD 21803
410-251-2511; Fax: 410-543-0658
www.angelfire.com/md/NATJ/
Dr Catherine North, Executive Director
Dr Cathy Roche, Director
Works with newly graduated journalist school students to assist them as they enter in the world of television news. Honors those in the industry for excellence in their field of endeavour.
Founded in 1985

15093 National Association of Black Journalists
1100 Knight Hall
Suite 3100
College Park, MD 20742
301-405-0248; Fax: 301-314-1714
www.nabj.org
Facebook, Twitter
Sarah Glover, President
Dorothy Tucker, Vice President/Broadcast
Marlon A. Walker, Vice President/Print
Ben,t Wilson, Vice President/Digital
Sherlon Christie, Secretary
An organization of journalists, students and media-related professionals that provides quality programs and services and advocates on behalf of black journalists worldwide.
Founded in 1975

15094 **National Association of Broadcast Employees & Technicians**
501 3rd St Nw
Washington, DC 20001
202-434-1254; Fax: 202-434-1426
guild@cwa-union.org
www.nabetcwa.org
Facebook, Youtube, RSS, Flickr
Charles G. Braico, Sector President
Lou Marinaro, Sector Vice President
William Murray, Staff Representative
Eric Seggi, Staff Representative
Jodi Fabrizio-Clontz, Assistant to the President
Organization covering the newspaper industry, its employment practices, press freedom and labor movement.
Founded in 1934

15095 **National Association of Hispanic Journalists**
1050 Connecticut Avenue NW
10th Floor
Washington, DC 20036
202-662-7145; Fax: 202-662-7144
nahj@nahj.org
www.nahj.org
Facebook, Twitter, LinkedIn, YouTube
Mekahlo Medina, President
Rebecca Aguilar, VP, Online
Barbara Rodriguez, VP Print
Francisco Cortes, Financial Officer
Sid Garcia, Secretary
NAHJ is dedicated to the recognition and professional advancement of Hispanics in the news industry. NAHJ created a national voice and unified vision for all Hispanic journalists.
2300 Members
Founded in 1984

15096 **National Association of Hispanic Journalis ts**
1050 Connecticut Avenue NW
10th Floor
Washington, DC 20036
202-662-7145
NAHJ@nahj.org
www.nahj.org
Facebook, Twitter, LinkedIn, YouTube
Mekahlo Medina, President
Rebecca Aguilar, VP, Online
Barbara Rodriguez, VP, Print
Francisco Cortes, Financial Officer
Sid Garcia, Secretary
Founded in 1984

15097 **National Association of Science Writers**
P.O. Box 7905
Berkeley, CA 94707
510-647-9500
www.nasw.org
Facebook, Twitter, LinkedIn, Google+
Robin Marantz Henig, President
Laura Helmuth, Vice President
Jill Adams, Treasurer
Deborah Franklin, Secretary
Tinsley Davis, Executive Director
Founded in 1934

15098 **National Book Critics Circle**
160 Varick Street
11th Floor
New York, NY 10013
info@bookcritics.org
www.bookcritics.org
Twitter
Tom Beer, President
Jane Ciabattari, VP, Online
Rigoberto Gonzalez, VP/Awards
Michael Miller, VP/Treasurer
Karen Long, VP/Secretary
Founded in 1974

15099 **National Federation of Press Women**
200 Little Falls Street
Ste.405
Falls Church, VA 22046
703-237-9804
800-780-2715; Fax: 703-237-9808
www.nfpw.org
Facebook, Twitter, LinkedIn, RSS, Flickr, Youtube
Teri Ehresman, President
Marsha Hoffman, 1st VP
Marianne Wolf, 2nd VP (Membership Adviser)
Gay Porter DeNileon, Secretary
Ellen Crawford, Treasurer (Financial Advisor)
Members are writers, editors and other communication professionals for newspapers, magazines, wire services, agencies and freelance.
2000 Members
Founded in 1937
Mailing list available for rent: 1700 names at $40 per M

15100 **National Journalism Center**
Young America's Foundation
11480 Commerce Park Dr.
Suite 600
Reston, VA 20191
800-872-1776; Fax: 703-318-9122
njc@yaf.org
Elizabeth Donatelli, Director
Kelleigh Huber, Program Officer
Journalism training with a conservative edge.
Founded in 1977

15101 **National Lesbian & Gay Journalists Association**
2120 L St, NWÿ
Suite 850
Washington, DC 20037ÿ
202-588-9888
info@nlgja.org
www.nlgja.org/
Facebook, Twitter, LinkedIn
Jen Christensen, President
Sarah Blazucki, Vice President of Print & Online
Ken Miguel, Vice President of Broadcast
Sharif Durhams, Treasurer
Rick Stuckey, Secretary
Founded in 1990

15102 **National Lesbian and Gay Journalists Association (NLGJA)**
2120 L Street NW
Suite 850
Washington, DC 20037
202-588-9888
info@nlgja.org
www.nlgja.org
Facebook, Twitter
Jen Christensen, President
Sarah Blazucki, Vice President of Print & Online
Ken Miguel, Vice President of Broadcast
Sharif Durhams, Treasurer
Rick Stuckey, Secretary
NLGJA is an organization of journalists, media professionals, educators and students working within the news industry to foster fair and accurate coverage of LGBT issues. NLGJA opposes all forms of workplace bias and provides professional development to its members.
220 Members
Founded in 1990
Mailing list available for rent

15103 **National Newspaper Association**
900 Community Drive
Springfield, IL 62703
217-241-1400; Fax: 217-241-1301
membership@nna.org
www.nnaweb.org
Facebook, Twitter, RSS Feeds
Matthew Paxton, President
Susan Rowell, Vice President
Tonda Rush, Director, Public Policy
Dennis DeRossett, Chief Operating Officer
Lynne Lance, Director, Membership Services
To protect, promote and enhance America's community newspapers.
2100 Members
Founded in 1885

15104 **National Press Club**
529 14th St NW
13th Floor
Washington, DC 20045
202-662-7500; Fax: 202-662-7512
press.org/
Facebook, Twitter, Google+, RSS
angela Greiling Keane, President
Myron Belkind, Vice President
Joel Whitaker, Secretary
John Hughes, Treasurer
Marc Wojno, Membership Secretary
A private organization composed of professional journalists who are directly related to the media. Persons must qualify to be admitted.
4.6M Members
Founded in 1921

15105 **National Press Foundation**
1211 Connecticut Ave NW
Suite 310
Washington, DC 20036
202-663-7280; Fax: 202-662-1232
www.nationalpress.org
Facebook, Twitter, Flickr, Youtube, Google+, Scri
Sandy Johnson, President/COO
Amun Nadeem, Program Manager
Linda Topping Streitfeld, Director of Training and Content
Jenny Ash-Maher, Director of Operations
Reyna Abigale Levine, Digital Media Manager
Supports all those involved with national press and the media. Publishes bi-weekly newsletter.
Founded in 1976

15106 **National Scholastic Press Association**
2221 University Ave SE
Suite 121
Minneapolis, MN 55414
612-625-8335; Fax: 612-605-0072
info@studentpress.org
www.studentpress.org
Facebook, Twitter, Flickr, RSS
Diana mitsu Klos, Executive Director
Paul Schwarzkopf, Dir. Of Communications & Technology
Lindasy Grome, Dir. Of Community Engagement
Albert R. Tims, President
Christopher J. Ison, Treasurer
Supports all those involved in yearbook printing and photographic services, college journalism departments and video yearbook production services. Hosts annual trade show.
Founded in 1921
Mailing list available for rent

15107 Native American Journalists Association (NAJA)
OU Gaylord College
395 W. Lindsey St.
Norman, OK 73019-4201

405-325-1649; Fax: 405-325-6945
www.naja.com/
Facebook, Twitter, RSS

Jason Begay, President
Bryan Pollard, Vice President
Tristan Ahtone, Treasurer
Shannon Shaw-Duty, Secretary

NAJA serves and empowers Native journalists through programs and actions designed to enrich journalism and promote Native cultures. NAJA educates and unifies its membership through journalism programs that promote diversity and defends challenges to free press.
Founded in 1983

15108 New England Newspaper and Press Association
370 Common Street, Barletta Hall
3rd Floor, Suite 319
Dedham, MA 02026

781-320-8050; Fax: 781-320-8055
www.nenpa.org
Facebook, Twitter

Peter Haggerty, President
Mark S. Murphy, VP
Linda Conway, Executive Director
Megan Sherman, PR and Events Manager
Robin LaPolla, Business Manager

This organization offers a publication about the newspaper industry specifically focusing on New England newspapers and the issues that affect them, which goes to every newspaper in New England.
460 Members
Founded in 1950

15109 New Jersey Press Association
810 Bear Tavern Rd
Suite 307
West Trenton, NJ 08628-1022

609-406-0600; Fax: 609-406-0300
www.njpa.org

Stanley M. Ellis, Chairman
Thomas M. Donovan, President
Brett Ainsworth, 1st Vice President
Michael Lawson, 2nd Vice President
George H. White, Executive Director/ Secretary

Supports all those involved in the development and betterment of collegiate press. Hosts annual trade show.
49 Members
Founded in 1857

15110 News Media Alliance
4401 N. Fairfax Drive
Suite 300
Arlington, VA 22203

571-366-1000
info@newsmediaalliance.org
www.newsmediaalliance.org
Facebook, Twitter, LinkedIn, YouTube

David Chavern, President & CEO
Robert Walden, Chief Financial Officer
Rebecca Frank, VP, Research & Insights
Danielle Coffey, SVP & General Counsel
Paul Boyle, SVP, Public Policy

Formerly known as the Newspaper Association of America, the News Media Alliance represents large daily papers, non-daily/small-market publications, as well as digital and multiplatform products across North America.
2000 Members
Founded in 1992

15111 Overseas Press Club of America
40 West 45th Street
New York, NY 10036

212-626-9220; Fax: 212-626-9210
info@opcofamerica.org
opcofamerica.org
Facebook, Twitter, LinkedIn, Instagram, YouTube, Google+

Deidre Depke, President
Deborah Amos, First Vice President
Patricia Kranz, Executive Director
Boots R. Duque, Office Manager
Chad Bouchard, Web Manager & Social Media Editor

Association of journalists working in the area of international news. The club aims to maintain high news reporting standards, advocate for press freedom and encourage networking between press members.
450 Members
Founded in 1939

15112 Pulic Radio News Directors Incorporated
PO Box 838
Sturgis, SD 57785

605-490-3033; Fax: 605-490-3085
www.prndi.org
Facebook, Twitter, RSS

George Bodarky, President
Rachel Osier Lindley, Treasurer
Teresa Collier, Large Station Rep
Catherine Welch, Medium Station Rep
Christine Paige Diers, Business Manager

A non-profit professional association that exists to improve local news and information programming by serving public radio journalists.
Founded in 1985

15113 Society for Features Journalism

Home Page: www.featuresjournalism.org
Facebook, Twitter, RSS

Lisa Glowinski, President
Kathy Lu, First Vice-President
Jim Haag, Second Vice-President
Margaret Myers, Secretary-Treasurer
Andrew Nynka, Executive Director
Founded in 1947

15114 Society for News Design
424 E. Central Blvd.
Suite 406
Orlando, FL 32801

407-420-7748; Fax: 407-420-7697
snd@snd.org
www.snd.org
Facebook, Twitter, LinkedIn, RSS, Pinterest

Lee Steele, President
Sara Quinn, Vice President
Douglas Okasaki, Secretary/Treasurer
Stephen Komives, Executive Director
Jonathon Berlin, Immediate Past President

An international professional organization that encourage high standards of journalism through design. An international forum and resource for all those interested in news design, SND works to recognize excellence and strengthen visual journalism as a profession.
1500 Members
Founded in 1979
Mailing list available for rent

15115 Society of American Business Editors and Writers
ASU, Walter Cronkite School of Journalism & Mas
555 North Central Ave, Suite 302
Phoenix, AZ 85004-1248

602-496-7862; Fax: 602-496-7041
sabew@sabew.org
www.sabew.org
Facebook, Twitter, RSS

Joanna Ossinger, President
Cory Schouten, VP
Kathleen Graham, Executive Director
Spring Eselgroth, Web/ Membership Director
Liisa Straub, Fiscal Manager

Members are financial and economic news writers and editors for print and broadcast outlets.
3200 Members
Founded in 1964

15116 Society of American Travel Writers
One Parkview Plaza
Suite 800
Oakbrook Terrace, IL 60181

414-359-1625; Fax: 414-359-1671
info@satw.org
www.satw.org
Facebook, Twitter, LinkedIn

Paul Lasley, President
Barbara Orr, Vice President, Membership
Marla Schrager, Executive Director
John Kingzette, Membership Coordinator
Cindy Lemek, Executive Director

Photographers and 35 associate member representatives of airlines, hotels, resorts, tourist agencies and public relations firms.
Founded in 1955

15117 Society of Professional Journalists
3909 N Meridian Street
Indianapolis, IN 46208

317-927-8000; Fax: 317-920-4789
webmaster@spj.org
www.spj.org
Facebook, Twitter, LinkedIn, RSS, Pinterest, Flickr, Storif

Paul Fletcher, President
Rebecca Baker, Secretary/Treasurer
Joe Skeel, Executive Director
Chris Vachon, Associate Executive Director
Linda Hall, Director of Membership

Broad-based journalism organization, dedicated to encouraging the free practice of journalism and stimulating high standards of ethical behavior.
7500 Members
Founded in 1909
Mailing list available for rent

15118 The American Society of Journalists and Authors
355 Lexington Avenue
15th Floor
New York, NY 10017-6603

212-997-0947
www.asja.org/
Facebook, Twitter, LinkedIn, Instagram, Google+

Randy Dotinga, President
Sherry Beck Paprocki, Vice President
Neil O'Hara, Treasurer
Alexandra Cantor Owens, Executive Director
Meredith Taylor, General Manager
Founded in 1948

15119 The Fund for Investigative Journalism
529 14th Street NW
13th Floor
Washington, DC 20045

202-662-7564
fundfij@gmail.com
www.fij.org/
Facebook, Twitter, RSS

Ricardo Sandoval Palos, President
Marcia Bullard, Vice President
Clarence Page, Treasurer
Founded in 1969

15120 The Gridiron Club
Prestigious organization of Washington, D.C. journalists. Membership is by invitation only. The Club is best known for its annual dinner featuring skits and speeches by politicians of both parties.
65 Members
Founded in 1885

15121 The Poynter Institute for Media Studies
801 Third Street South
St. Petersburg, FL 33701
727-821-9494
www.poynter.org
Facebook, Twitter, LinkedIn, YouTube, Instagram
Neil Brown, President
Kelly McBride, Vice President
Non-profit journalism school begun by Nelson Poynter, owner of the St. Petersburg Times (now the Tampa Bay Times).
Founded in 1975

15122 The Society of Environmental Journalists
PO Box 2492
Jenkintown, PA 19046
215-884-8174; Fax: 215-884-8175
sej@sej.org
www.sej.org
Facebook, Twitter, RSS
Jeff Burnside, President
Beth Parke, Executive Director
Jennifer Bogo, First Vice Pres. & Programs Chair
Kate Sheppard, SVP/Membership Chair
Gloria Gonzalez, Treasurer & Finance Chair
Mission is to strengthen the quality. reach and viability of journalism across all media to advance public understanding of environmental issues.
Founded in 1990
Mailing list available for rent

15123 UNITY Journalists for Diversity, Inc.
Eugene S. Pulliam National Journalism Center
3909 N Meridian St
Indianapolis, IN 46208
414-335-1478
Facebook, Twitter, LinkedIn, Google+, Tumblr, Reddit
Neal Justin, President
Alliance of Asian American Journalists Association, National Lesbian and Gay Journalists Association and the Native American Journalists Association. Advocates fair and accurate coverage of diversity issues.
Founded in 1994

Newsletters

15124 AEJMC News
AEJMC
234 Outlet Pointe Boulevard
Suite A
Columbia, SC 29210-5667
803-798-0271; Fax: 803-772-3509
www.aejmc.org
Jennifer McGill, Executive Director
Lillian Coleman, Newsletter Editor/Project Manager
Newsletter of the Association for Education in Journalism and Mass Communication.
Frequency: Monthly
Circulation: 3425
Founded in 1912

15125 AGENDA
National Federation of Press Women
PO Box 34798
Alexandria, VA 22334-0798
800-780-2715; Fax: 703-812-4555
www.nfpw.org
Facebook, Twitter, LinkedIn, RSS, Flickr, Youtube
Lori Potter, President
A quarterly newletter published by the National Federation of Press Women.
Cost: $51.50
4 Pages
Frequency: Quarterly
Circulation: 2000
Founded in 1937
Mailing list available for rent: 1700 names at $40 per M

15126 APME Update
Associated Media Press Editors
450 West 33rd Street
New York, NY 10001
212-621-7007
sjacobsen@ap.org
www.apme.com
Facebook, Twitter
Bill Church, President
Jim Simon, Vice President
Kathleen Carroll, AP SVP & Executive Editor
Brian Carovillano, AP Managing Editor
Mark Baldwin, Program Chair
APME is an association of U.S. and Canadian editors, broadcasters and educators whose entitites are members of The Associated Press.
Founded in 1933

15127 ASBPE News
American Society of Business Publication Editors
214 North Hale Street
Wheaton, IL 60187
630-510-4588; Fax: 630-510-4501
info@asbpe.org
www.asbpe.org
Facebook, Twitter, LinkedIn, RSS
Amy Florence Fischbach, President
Erin Erickson, Vice President
Tina Grady Barbaccia, Secretary/Treasurer
Janet Svazas, Executive Director
Robin Sherman, Associate Dir. & Newsletter Editor
ASBPE is the professional association for full-time and freelance editors and writers employed in the business, trade, and specialty press. It is widely known for its annual Awards of Excellence competition, which recognizes the best editorial, design, and online achievement.
Founded in 1964
Mailing list available for rent

15128 ASJA Newsletter
American Society of Journalists and Authors
1501 Broadway
Suite 403
New York, NY 10036-5505
212-997-0947; Fax: 212-937-2315
staff@asja.org
www.asja.org
Facebook, Twitter, LinkedIn, Goggle+
Alexandra Cantor Owens, Executive Director
Minda Zetlin, President
Barbara DeMarco- Barrett, Newsletter Editor
Dave Mosso, Art Director
Confidential news for journalists and authors, available only to members of the Society.
Frequency: Monthly
Founded in 1948
Mailing list available for rent

15129 ASMP Bulletin
American Society of Media Photographers
150 North 2nd Street
Philadelphia, PA 19106
215-451-2767
info@asmp.org
www.asmp.org
Facebook, Twitter, LinkedIn, Pinterest, Blogger, Tumblr
Peter Dyson, Director of Communications
Victor Perlman, General Counsel
Eugene Mopsik, Executive Director
Elena Goertz, General Manager
Khaisha Allford, Member Services Coordinator
ASMP is the premier trade association for the world's most respectd photograhers. The ASMP Bulletin is a newsletter benefit for members.
Founded in 1944
Mailing list available for rent

15130 Bulldog Reporter
James Sinkinson/InfoCom Group
124 Linden Street
Suite L
Oakland, CA 94607
510-596-9300
800-959-1059
www.bulldogreporter.com
Facebook, Twitter, RSS, Pinterest, Google+
James Sinkson, President
Jacques Guatreaux, Vice President
Journalist contact updates and intelligence on how to successfully place stories with the most influential business media and journalists in the US.
Cost: $449.00
Frequency: 24 issues per y
Founded in 1980
Mailing list available for rent

15131 Clio Among the Media
Association for Education in Journalism
234 Outlet Pointe Blvd
Suite A
Columbia, SC 29210-5667
803-798-0271; Fax: 803-772-3509
aejmc@aejmc.org
www.asjmc.org
Georgia NeSmith, Assistant Editor
Jennifer McGill, Executive Director
This newsletter is aimed directly at scholars and educators of Journalism and Mass Communications.
Cost: $107.50
24 Pages
Frequency: Quarterly
Circulation: 450
Founded in 1966

15132 Communicator
American Institute of Parliamentarians
550m Ritchie Highway #271
Severna Park, MD 21146
888-664-0428; Fax: 410-544-4640
aip@aipparl.org
www.aipparl.org
Rob James, Vice President
Alison Wallis, President
Mary Remson, Treasurer
Jim Jones, CPP-T, Accrediting Director
Jeanette Williams, CP-T, Education Director
Quarterly newsletter listing AIP's board of directors, committees, parliamentary activities, chapter news and activities.
Founded in 1958

15133 GP Reporter
Star Reporter Publishing Company
PO Box 60193
Staten Island, NY 10306-0193
718-981-5700; Fax: 718-981-5713
RA Lindberg, Publisher

Covers journalism for educational purposes.
Cost: $9.00
20 Pages

15134 **Guild Reporter**
Newspaper Guild: CWA
501 3rd St Nw
6th Floor
Washington, DC 20001-2760

202-434-1254; Fax: 202-434-1426
guild@cwa-union.org
www.nabetcwa.org
Facebook, Youtube, RSS, Flickr

John Clark, President
Carol D Rothman, Secretary/Treasurer
Andy Zipser, Guild Reporter
Charles G. Braico, Sector Vice President

Covers the newspaper industry, its employment practices, press freedom and labor movement.
Cost: $20.00
6 Pages
Frequency: Monthly
Founded in 1933

15135 **ICA Newsletter**
International Communications Association
1500 21st St Nw
Washington, DC 20036-1000

202-955-1444; Fax: 202-530-9851
icahdq@icahdq.org
www.icahdq.org
Facebook, Twitter, LinkedIn, Google+

Michael L. Haley, Executive Director
Sam Luna, Member Services Director
John Paul Gutierrez, Communication Director
Jennifer Le, Executive Assistant
Michael J. West, Publications Manager

Trade association publication for scholars in the field of communication.
Cost: $20.00
Frequency: 10 times a year
Founded in 1950
Mailing list available for rent
Printed in on matte stock

15136 **Journalist and Financial Reporting**
TJFR Publishing Company
82 Wall Street
Suite 1105
New York, NY 10005-3600
212-422-2456; Fax: 212-663-3260

Dean Rotbart, Publisher

Financial and business news.
Cost: $549.00
12 Pages
Frequency: BiWeekly

15137 **Media Reporter**
Gay and Lesbian Press Association
PO Box 8185
Universal City, CA 91618-8185

FAX 818-902-9576

RJ Curry, Publisher

Accepts advertising.
Cost: $40.00
16 Pages
Frequency: Quarterly

15138 **N2 Newspaper Next:**
American Press Institute
4401 Wilson Boulevard
Suite 900
Arlington, VA 22203

703-620-3611; Fax: 703-620-5814
www.americanpressinstitute.org
Facebook, Twitter, LinkedIn

Thomas A. Silvestri, Chairman
Peter Bhatia, Editor
Caroline H. Little, President and CEO
Margaret G. Vassilikos, Finance & Operations
Mary Peskin, Training Programs

N2 Newspaper Next: is the forward-thinking project undertaken by API - to identify and test new business models for newspaper companies. It has grown to include not just research, but two reports of the project's findings as well as cuountless seminars, worksops, tailored programs offerings and special events.
Founded in 1946
Mailing list available for rent

15139 **National Press Foundation Update**
National Press Foundation
1211 Connecticut Ave Nw
Suite 310
Washington, DC 20036-2709

202-663-7280; Fax: 202-662-1232
www.nationalpress.org
Facebook, Twitter, RSS, Youtube, Google+, Scribd,

Bob Meyers, President/COO
Gerald Seib, Vice Chairman
Linda Topping Streitfeld, Director of Programs
Maha Masud, Programs Manager
Kerry Buker, Director of Operations

News.
4 Pages
Frequency: BiWeekly
Founded in 1993

15140 **New England Press Association Bulletin**
New England Press Association
360 Huntington Avenue
428CP
Boston, MA 02115-5005

617-254-4880; Fax: 617-373-5615
www.nepa.org

Brenda Need, Publisher
Linda Conway, Marketing Director
Thomas Guenette, Circulation Manager
Brenda Need, Editor

A monthly publication about the newspaper industry specifically focusing on New England newspapers and the issues that affect them.
Cost: $15.00
Frequency: Monthly
Circulation: 1500
Founded in 1950
Printed in 4 colors on newsprint stock

15141 **OPC Bulletin**
Overseas Press Club of America
40 West 45th Street
New York, NY 10036

212-626-9220; Fax: 212-626-9210
info@opcofamerica.org
opcofamerica.org/opc-bulletin

Deidre Depke, President
Patricia Kranz, Executive Director
Boots R. Duque, Office Manager
Chad Bouchard, Web Manager & Social Media Editor

Features foreign correspondence news as well as news on the operations of the Overseas Press Club of America.
450 Members
Frequency: Monthly
Founded in 1939

15142 **Platform News You Can Use**
Newspaper Association of America
4401 N. Fairfax Drive
Suite 300
Arlington, VA 22203

571-366-1000
info@newsmediaalliance.org
www.newsmediaalliance.org

David Chavern, President & CEO
Michael Maloon, VP, Innovation & Communications
Rebecca Frank, VP, Research & Insights
Lindsey Loving, Manager, Communications
Jennifer Peters, Reporter, Trends & Insights

Members-only e-newsletter with developments on large tech platforms and their relationships with the news industry and journalism.
Frequency: Monthly

15143 **Publisher's Auxiliary**
National Newspaper Association
900 Community Drive
Springfield, IL 62703

217-241-1400; Fax: 217-241-1301
www.nnaweb.org
Facebook, Twitter

Matthew Paxton, President
Tonda Rush, Director, Public Policy
Stan Schwartz, Managing Editor

The only national publication serving America's community newspapers. First published in 1865, Publishers' Auxiliary is also the oldest newspaper serving the newspaper industry.
Founded in 1865

15144 **dailyXchange**
Newspaper Association of America
4401 N. Fairfax Drive
Suite 300
Arlington, VA 22203

571-366-1000
info@newsmediaalliance.org
www.newsmediaalliance.org

David Chavern, President & CEO
Michael Maloon, VP, Innovation & Communications
Rebecca Frank, VP, Research & Insights
Lindsey Loving, Manager, Communications
Jennifer Peters, Reporter, Trends & Insights

Members-only e-newsletter with relevant Alliance and industry news from the past day.
Frequency: Daily

15145 **newsXchange**
Newspaper Association of America
4401 N. Fairfax Drive
Suite 300
Arlington, VA 22203

571-366-1000
info@newsmediaalliance.org
www.newsmediaalliance.org

David Chavern, President & CEO
Michael Maloon, VP, Innovation & Communications
Rebecca Frank, VP, Research & Insights
Lindsey Loving, Manager, Communications
Jennifer Peters, Reporter, Trends & Insights

News brief from the News Media Alliance with news media industry news, as well as information on digital, advertising, trends, and Alliance products and services.
Frequency: Weekly (Wed.)

Magazines & Journals

15146 **APME News Magazine**
Associated Press Media Editors
450 W 33rd St
New York, NY 10001-2647

212-621-1849; Fax: 212-833-7574
info@ap.org
www.apme.com

Bill Church, President
Kathleen Carroll, AP SVP & Executive Editor
Brian Carovillano, AP Managing Editor
Frequency: Quarterly
Circulation: 7000
Founded in 1848

15147 Alternative Press Review
P.O. Box 444
Columbia, MD 21045

Home Page: www.alternativepressreview.org

Jason McQuinn, Editor

Covers alternative press including humor, opinion and art.
Cost: $16.00
Frequency: Quarterly
Circulation: 7000

15148 American Editor
American Society of Newspaper Editors
11690B Sunrise Valley Drive
Reston, VA 20191-1409

703-453-1122; Fax: 703-453-1133
www.asne.org

Arnie Robbins, Executive Director
Kathy Bates, Development Director
Cindy L. Roe, Finance Director
Diana Mitsu Klos, Senior Project Director
Megan Schumacher, Sr. Information Specialist

A magazine published by the American Society of Newspaper Editors.
30 Pages
Frequency: Daily
Founded in 1922

15149 American Journalism Review
University of Maryland
1117 Journalism Building
College Park, MD 20742-1

301-405-8803
800-827-0771; Fax: 301-405-8323
www.ajr.org

Tom Kunkel, President
Rem Rieder, Editor
Reese Cleghorn, Publisher
Kathy Darragh, Circulation Manager
Kevin Klose, Senior Vice President

Monthly magazine for media professionals.
Cost: $24.00
Circulation: 25000
Founded in 1972

15150 American Prospect
5 Broad Street
Boston, MA 02109

617-570-8030; Fax: 617-570-8028
editors@prospect.org
www.prospect.org

Robin Hutson, Publisher
Tim Lysler, Associate Publisher
Robert Kuttner, President

Progressive liberal publication
Cost: $19.95
Frequency: Monthly
Circulation: 55000
Founded in 1990
Printed in 4 colors on matte stock

15151 Brilliant Ideas for Publishers
Creative Brilliance Associates
Mathey Road
PO Box 32
Clam Lake, WI 94517

715-749-2186
800-975-5474; Fax: 715-749-2180

Naomi Shapiro, Editor

Edited and published for the newspaper industry.

15152 Catholic Journalist
3555 Veterans Memorial Highway
Unit O
Ronkonkoma, NY 11779

631-471-4730; Fax: 631-471-4804
www.catholicpress.org

Penny Wiegert, President
Tim Walker, Executive Director
Cost: $12.00
Frequency: Quarterly

15153 Columbia Journalism Review
Columbia University
2960 Broadway
New York, NY 10027-6900

212-854-1754
888-425-7782; Fax: 212-749-0397
subscriptions@cjr.org
www.columbia.edu

Robert Kasdin, Executive VP
Evan Cornog, Publisher
Michael Hoyt, Executive Editor

Evaluates all of the media as well as establishes standards for the profession.
Cost: $19.95
72 Pages

15154 ESD Technology
Kelvin Publishing
22700 Wood Street
Saint Clair Shores, MI 48080-1762

586-777-0440; Fax: 586-774-3892

John Kelvin, Editor
Kevin Campbell, VP Marketing

Technical articles highlighting new applications and research.
Founded in 1936

15155 Ideas
International Newspaper Marketing Association
10300 N Central Expressway
Suite 467
Dallas, TX 75231

214-373-9111; Fax: 214-373-9112
www.inma.org
Facebook, Twitter, LinkedIn, RSS

Earl Wilkinson, Executive Director
Marise Trevino, Editor
Earl Wilkinson, CEO/President
Dawn McMullan, Editor
Ravi Dhariwal, President

Marketing and promotion ideas for newspaper executives.
32 Pages
Frequency: Monthly
Circulation: 1200
Founded in 1930
Mailing list available for rent

15156 International Communications Association
1500 21st St NW
Washington, DC 20036-1000

202-955-1444; Fax: 202-955-1448
icahdq@icahdq.org
www.icahdq.org
Facebook, Twitter, LinkedIn, Google+

Michael L. Haley, Executive Director
Sam Luna, Member Services Director
John Paul Gutierrez, Communication Director
Jennifer Le, Executive Assistant
Michael J. West, Publications Manager

Bi-monthly newsletter that supports all students and professionals in the international communications industry.
Mailing list available for rent
Printed in on matte stock

15157 Journal of Advertising Education
AEJMC
234 Outlet Pointe Boulevard
Suite A
Columbia, SC 29210-5667

803-798-0271; Fax: 803-772-3509
www.aejmc.org

Jay Newell, Editor

Peer-reviewed academic journal devoted to research and commentary on instruction, curriculum, and leadership in advertising education. Official journal of the Advertising Division of the Association for Education in Journalism and Mass Communication, and available to members of the American Academy of Advertising.

15158 Journalism & Mass Communication Quarterly (JMCQ)
AEJMC
234 Outlet Pointe Boulevard
Suite A
Columbia, SC 29210-5667

803-798-0271; Fax: 803-772-3509
www.aejmc.org

Jennifer McGill, Executive Director
Louisa Ha, Editor

Published by the Association for Education in Journalism and Mass Communication, the JMC Quarterly focuses on research in journalism and mass communication. Each issue features reports of original investigation, presenting the latest developments in theory and methodology of communication, international communication, journalism history, and social and legal problems. Also contains book reviews. Refereed. Four times per year. (est. 1924)
Circulation: 4800
Mailing list available for rent

15159 Latinos in the US: A Resource Guide for Journalists
National Association of Hispanic Journalists
529 14th St Nw # 1240
Washington, DC 20045-2520

202-789-1157; Fax: 202-347-3444
rnutting@marketwatch.com
www.marketwatch.com

Rex Nutting, Manager
Joseph Torres, Communications Director
Rex Nutting, Manager

Purposes are to increase educational and career opportunities in journalism for Hispanic Americans.
Cost: $8.50
Mailing list available for rentat $500 per M

15160 Magazine Media Factbook (ASME)
American Society of Magazine Editors
810 Seventh Avenue
24th Floor
New York, NY 10019

212-872-3700; Fax: 212-906-0128
info@magazine.org
www.magazine.org
Facebook, Twitter, LinkedIn, Youtube, Pinterst

Mary Berner, President & CEO
Nina Fortuna, Program Coordinator
Larry Hackett, President
Peggy Northrop, Vice President
Lucy Danziger, Secretary

A comprehensive guide of magazine media facts for advertisers, advertising agencies, media planners and consumer magazine marketers.
700 Members
Founded in 1963

15161 Newspapers & Technology
Conley Magazines

1623 Blake Street
Suite 250
Denver, CO 80202

303-575-9595; Fax: 303-575-9555
www.newsandtech.com/

Mary Van Meter, Publisher
Chuck Moozakis, Editor-in-Chief
Tara McMeekin, Editor
Hays Goodman, Associate Editor/Webmaster
Jessica Shade, Creative Services Assistant

Newspapers & Technology is a monthly trade publication for newspaper publishers and department managers involved in applying and integrating technology. Written by industry experts, News & Tech provides regular coverage of the following departments: prepress, press, postpress and new media.
Circulation: 16,874
Mailing list available for rent

15162 **OPC Dateline Magazine**
Overseas Press Club of America
40 West 45th Street
New York, NY 10036

212-626-9220; Fax: 212-626-9210
info@opcofamerica.org
opcofamerica.org

Deidre Depke, President
Deborah Amos, First Vice President
Patricia Kranz, Executive Director
Chad Bouchard, Web Manager & Social Media Editor

Magazine from the Overseas Press Club of America featuring international news coverage.
450 Members
Frequency: Annual
Founded in 1939

15163 **Parliamentary Journal**
American Institute of Parliamentarians
550m Ritchie Highway #271
Severna Park, MD 21146

888-664-0428; Fax: 410-544-4640
aip@aipparl.org
www.aipparl.org

Rob James, Vice President
Alison Wallis, President
Mary Remson, Treasurer
Jim Jones, CPP-T, Accrediting Director
Jeanette Williams, CP-T, Education Director

Wide range of subjects for AIP members
Founded in 1958

15164 **Ways With Words**
American Society of News Editors
11690B Sunrise Valley Drive
Reston, VA 20191-1409

703-453-1122
asne@asne.org
www.asne.org
Facebook, Twitter, Storify

Cindy L. Roe, Finance Director
Arnie Robbins, Executive Director
Diana Mitsu Klos, Senior Project Director
Megan Schumacher, Sr. Information Specialist
Kevin Goldberg, Legal Counsel

Ways With Words is the result of unusual, perhaps unique, collaboration among a diverse group of people who care about newspapers and reading. It may well be a model for joint research and development by journalism scholars and practitioners into the future of newspaper journalism.
Cost: $1.00
Founded in 1922

Trade Shows

15165 **AEJMC Annual Conference**
AEJMC
234 Outlet Pointe Boulevard
Suite A
Columbia, SC 29210-5667

803-798-0271; Fax: 803-772-3509
www.aejmc.org

Jennifer McGill, Executive Director
Amanda Caldwell, Confernece/Meetings Manager

Annual conference of the Association for Education in Journalism and Mass Communication.
2000 Attendees
Frequency: August
Founded in 1912

15166 **APME/ASNE/APPM Annual Conference**
Associated Press Media Editors
450 West 33rd Street
New York, NY 10001

212-621-7007
sjacobsen@ap.org
www.apme.com
Facebook, Twitter

Bill Church, President
Jim Simon, Vice President
Angie Muhs, Secretary
Mark Baldwin, Program Chair

APME is an association of U.S. and Canadian editors, broadcasters and educators whose entitites are members of The Associated Press.
Frequency: Annual
Founded in 1933

15167 **AWC National Conference**
Association for Women in Communications
1717 E Republic Road
Suite A
Springfield, MO 65804

417-886-8606; Fax: 417-886-3685
chair@womcom.org
www.womcom.org
Facebook, Twitter, LinkedIn, Youtube

Anita K. Parran, Chair
Allison Buehner, Vice Chair
Peggy Fleming, Secretary
Patricia Meads, Treasurer

For members designed to enhance professional and personal development.
Frequency: Bi-Annual

15168 **American Society of Journalists and Authors Conference**
1501 Broadway
Suite 403
New York, NY 10036-5501

212-997-0947; Fax: 212-937-2315
www.asja.org
Facebook, Twitter, LinkedIn, Goggle+

Alexandra Cantor Owens, Executive Director
Minda Zetlin, President
Barbara DeMarco- Barrett, Newsletter Editor
Dave Mosso, Art Director
Bruce Miler, Web Master

A forum for the exchange of ideas between journalists.
700 Attendees
Frequency: May
Mailing list available for rent

15169 **American Society of News Editors (ASNE) Convention**
11690B Sunrise Valley Drive
2660 Woodley Road, NW
Reston, VA 20191-1409

703-453-1122
800-656-4622
registrar@naa.org
www.asne.org
Facebook, Twitter

Cindy L. Roe, Finance Director
Arnie Robbins, Executive Director
Diana Mitsu Klos, Senior Project Director
Megan Schumacher, Sr. Information Specialist
Kevin Goldberg, Legal Counsel

ASNE's annual convention is the largest annual gathering of newsroom leaders from daily newspapers and other news organizations. Editors and leaders in the field of journalism education will gather to refresh their spirits and create a roadmap to transform their newsrooms and shape the future of professional journalism.
Frequency: April
Founded in 1922

15170 **Annual Multimedia Convention & Career Expo (NAHJ)**
National Association of Hispanic Journalists
Disney's Coronado Spings Resort
1000 W Buena Vista Drive
Lake Buena Vista, FL 32830

866-257-5990
www.nahjconvention.org
Facebook, Twitter, LinkedIn, YouTube

Michele Salcedo, President
Manuel De La Rosa, Vice President/Broadcast
Russell Contreras, VP Print/Financial Officer

NAHJ is dedicated to the recognition and professional advancement of Hispanics in the news industry. NAHJ created a national voice and unified vision for all Hispanic journalists.
2300 Members
Frequency: August
Founded in 1984

15171 **Collegiate Press Association Trade Show**
330 21st Avenue S
Minneapolis, MN 55455-0480

612-625-3500; Fax: 612-626-0720

Tom Rolnicki, Show Manager

20 booths including learning sessions and press conferences.
1.2M Attendees
Frequency: November

15172 **Edward R. Murrow Forum on Issues in Journalism**
Tufts University
95 Talbot Ave.
Medford, MA 02155

617-627-2155; Fax: 617-627-3449
fms@tufts.edu
ase.tufts.edu/cms/murrow.html

Annual interdisciplinary panel reflecting on contemporary issues in journalism.
Frequency: Annual
Founded in 2006

15173 **International American Press Association Trade Show**
2911 NW 39th Street
Miami, FL 33142-5148

305-634-2465

Julio Munoz, Executive Director

12 booths.
500 Attendees
Frequency: September
Mailing list available for rent

15174 **International Newspaper Marketing Association Central**
World-Herald Square
Omaha, NE 68102
402-734-7632; Fax: 402-444-1370
Terry Ausenbaugh
20 booths.
100 Attendees
Frequency: October

15175 **Magazine Media Factbook (ASME)**
American Society of Magazine Editors
810 Seventh Avenue
24th Floor
New York, NY 10019
212-872-3700; Fax: 212-906-0128
www.magazine.org
Facebook, Twitter, LinkedIn, Pinterest, Youtube
Sid Holt, Chief Executive
Nina Fortuna, Program Coordinator
Larry Hackett, President
Peggy Northrop, Vice President
Lucy Danziger, Secretary
A comprehensive guide of magazine media facts for advertisers, advertising agencies, media planners and consumer magazine marketers.
700 Members
Founded in 1963

15176 **National Conference of the American Copy Editors Society**
Sheraton New Orleans Hotel
500 Canal Street
Nw Orleans, LA 70130
504-525-2500
866-716-8106; Fax: 504-595-5552
www.sheratonneworleans.com
Facebook, Twitter, LinkedIn
Teresa Schmedding, President
Lisa McLendon, Vice President Conferences
Sara Hendricks, Vice President Membership
Rudy Bahr, Executive Director
Gerri Berendzen, Content Editor
ACES is a professional organization working toward the advancement of editors. Their aim is to provide opportunities through training, discussion and advocacy that promote the editing profession.
Frequency: April
Founded in 1997

15177 **National Convention & Annual LGBT Media Summit**
National Lesbian and Gay Journalists Association
2120 L Street NW
Suite 850
Washington, DC 20037
202-588-9888
info@nlgja.org
www.nlgja.org
Facebook, Twitter
Bach Polakowski, National Office Administrator
Matthew Rose, Membership Coordinator
Michael Tune, Executive Director
David Steinberg, President
Jen Christensen, Vice President/Broadcast
NLGJA is an organization of journalists, media professionals, educators and students working within the news industry to foster fair and accurate coverage of LGBT issues. NLGJA opposes all forms of workplace bias and provides professional development to its members.
220 Members
Founded in 1990
Mailing list available for rent

15178 **National Editorial Conference**
American Society of Business Publication Editors
The Gleacher Center
450 N. Cityfront Plaza Drive
Chicago, IL 60611
312-464-8787; Fax: 312-464-8683
info@gleachercenter.com
www.gleachercenter.com
Facebook, Twitter, LinkedIn
Amy Florence Fischbach, President
Erin Erickson, Vice President
Tina Grady Barbaccia, Secretary/Treasurer
Janet Svazas, Executive Director
Robin Sherman, Associate Dir. & Newsletter Editor
The National Editorial Conference focuses on the skills and ideas you need to weather the down economy and thrive in the new B2B publishing landscape.
Frequency: August

15179 **National Magazine Awards**
American Society of Magazine Editors
810 Seventh Avenue
24th Floor
New York, NY 10019
212-872-3700; Fax: 212-906-0128
www.magazine.org
Facebook, Twitter, LinkedIn, Pinterest, Youtube
Sid Holt, Chief Executive
Nina Fortuna, Program Coordinator
Larry Hackett, President
Peggy Northrop, Vice President
Lucy Danziger, Secretary
The National Magazine Awards honor magazines, published in print and on digital platforms, that consistently demonstrate superior execution of editirial objectives, innovative techniques, noteworthy journalistic enterprise and imaginative art direction.
Founded in 1966

15180 **National Scholastic Press Association Conference**
National Scholastic Press Association
330 21st Avenue S
Suite 620
Minneapolis, MN 55455-0479
612-625-8335; Fax: 612-626-0720
Tom Rolnicki, Executive Director
Annual conference and exhibits of information on yearbook printing and photographic services, college journalism departments and video yearbook production services.
1800 Attendees

15181 **Newspaper Association of America/ Circulation Managers International**
1921 Gallows Road
Suite 600
Vienna, VA 22182-3995
703-902-1600; Fax: 703-902-1600
James Abbott, VP
Newspaper management forum.
1M Attendees

15182 **SABEW Annual Conference**
Society of American Business Editors & Writers
ASU, Walter Cronkite School of Journalism
555 North Central Ave, Suite 302
Phoenix, AZ 85004-1248
602-496-7862; Fax: 602-496-7041
sabew@sabew.org
www.sabew.org
Facebook, Twitter, LinkedIn, RSS
Warren Watson, Executive Director
Lacey Clements, Marketing Director
Mark Scarp, Membership Director
Spring Eselgroth, Web/ Membership Coordinator
Defines and inspires excellence in business journalism.
Frequency: April

15183 **West Coast Practicum**
American Institute of Parliamentarians
550m Ritchie Highway #271
Severna Park, MD 21146
888-664-0428; Fax: 410-544-4640
aip@aipparl.org
www.aipparl.org
Rob James, Vice President
Alison Wallis, President
Mary Remson, Treasurer
Jim Jones, CPP-T, Accrediting Director
Jeanette Williams, CP-T, Education Director
Topics being covered are convention committees, boards and problems related to boards, reference committees and the parliamentarian's role in consulting with boards.
Founded in 1958

15184 **adXchange**
News Media Alliance
4401 N. Fairfax Drive
Suite 300
Vienna, VA 22203
571-366-1000
info@newsmediaalliance.org
www.newsmediaalliance.org
David Chavern, President & CEO
Rachel Fox, Event Planner & Executive Assistant
Hosted by the News Media Alliance to bring members of the news industry together with advertisers.
Frequency: Annual

Directories & Databases

15185 **1,000 Worldwide Newspapers**
Albertsen's
PO Box 339
Nevada City, CA 95959-0339
Over 500 English-language newspapers overseas and in the United States are listed.
Cost: $10.00
54 Pages
Frequency: Annual

15186 **American Society of Journalists and Authors Directory**
ASJA
1501 Broadway
Suite 403
New York, NY 10036-5505
212-997-0947; Fax: 212-937-2315
www.asja.org
Facebook, Twitter, LinkedIn, Goggle+
Alexandra Cantor Owens, Executive Director
Minda Zetlin, President
Barbara DeMarco- Barrett, Newsletter Editor
Dave Mosso, Art Director
Lists over 800 member freelance nonfiction writers.
Cost: $75.00
90 Pages
Mailing list available for rent

15187 American Society of News Editors (ASNE) Database
11690B Sunrise Valley Drive
Reston, VA 20191-1409
703-453-1122
asne@asne.org
www.asne.org
Facebook, Twitter, Storify

Cindy L. Roe, Finance Director
Arnie Robbins, Executive Director
Diana Mitsu Klos, Senior Project Director
Megan Schumacher, Sr. Information Specialist
Kevin Goldberg, Legal Counsel

Free access to ASNE's extensive online archive of reports and journalism studies, the gold standard in newsroom-related research.
Founded in 1922

15188 Asian American Journalists Accountants Directory
1182 Market St
Suite 320
San Francisco, CA 94102-4919
415-346-2051; Fax: 415-346-6343
www.aaja.org

Ellen Endo, Executive Director
Luke Stangel, Co-Founder
Christine Choy, Director
Marcus Brauchli, Executive Editor

Student development, job referrals, fellowship and internship reports.
700 Pages
Founded in 1981

15189 Bacon's Newspaper & Magazine Directories
Cision U.S., Inc.
322 South Michigan Avenue
Suite 900
Chicago, IL 60604
312-263-0070
866-639-5087
info.us@cision.com
us.cision.com

Joe Bernardo, President & CEO
Heidi Sullivan, VP & Publisher
Valerie Lopez, Research Director
Jessica White, Research Director
Rachel Farrell, Research Manager

Two volume set listing all daily and community newspapers, magazines and newsletters, news service and syndicates, syndicated columnists, complete editorial staff listings of each publication provided, covers U.S., Canada, Mexico, and Carribean.
Cost: $350.00
4,700 Pages
Frequency: Annual
ISSN: 1088-9639
Founded in 1951
Printed in one color on matte stock

15190 Bacon's Radio/TV/Cable Directory
Cision U.S., Inc.
332 South Michigan Avenue
Suite 900
Chicago, IL 60604
312-263-0070
866-639-5087
info.us@cision.com

Joe Bernardo, President & CEO
Heidi Sullivan, VP & Publisher
Valerie Lopez, Research Director
Jessica White, Research Director
Rachel Farrell, Research Manager

Includes comprehensive coverage for contact and programming information for more than 3,500 televsion networks, cable networks, television syndicators, television stations, and cable systems in the United States and Canada.
Cost: $350.00
Frequency: Annual
ISSN: 1088-9639
Printed in one color on matte stock

15191 Burrelle's Media Directory
BurrellesLuce
75 E Northfield Rd
Livingston, NJ 07039-4532
973-992-6600
800-631-1160; Fax: 973-992-7675
www.burrellesluce.com
Facebook, Twitter, LinkedIn, RSS

Robert C Waggoner, CEO
Johna Burke, Senior Vice President, Marketing

Approximately 60,000 media listings in North America. Listings cover newspapers, magazines (trades and consumer), broadcast, and internet outlets.
Cost: $795.00
Frequency: Annual

15192 Directory of Selected News Sources Issue
American Journalism Review
8701 Adelphi Road
Suite 310
Adelphi, MD 20783-1716
800-827-0771; Fax: 301-405-8323

Rem Reider, Editor

List of about 400 companies, organizations and associations that provide information to newspapers and freelance reporters.
Cost: $2.95
Frequency: Annual
Circulation: 28,295

15193 FYI Directory of News Sources and Information
JSC Group
PO Box 868
Severna Park, MD 21146-0868
410-647-1013; Fax: 410-647-9557

Julia Stocks Corneal, Editor

About 400 associations, corporations, individuals and sources for background story gathering for journalists.
Cost: $19.95
Frequency: Annual
Circulation: 20,000

15194 Find A Photographer Database
American Society of Media Photographers
150 North 2nd Street
Philadelphia, PA 19106
215-451-2767
info@asmp.org
www.asmp.org
Facebook, Twitter, LinkedIn, Pinterest, Blogger, Tumblr

Peter Dyson, Director of Communications
Victor Perlman, General Counsel
Eugene Mopsik, Executive Director
Elena Goertz, General Manager
Khaisha Allford, Member Services Coordinator

Find a Photographer is a search engine to help ASMP members connect with the most respected photographers in the industry.
Founded in 1944
Mailing list available for rent

15195 Journalism Forum
CompuServe Information Service
5000 Arlington Centre Blvd
Columbus, OH 43220-5439
614-326-1002
800-848-8199

This database provides information on all aspects of professional journalism.
Frequency: Full-text

15196 National Directory of Community Newspapers
American Newspaper Representatives
1000 Shelard Parkway
Suite 360
Minneapolis, MN 55426-4933
612-545-1116
800-752-6237; Fax: 612-545-1116

Hilary Howe, President

A directory of community and weekly newspapers in the United States offering rates, circulation, etc.
Cost: $85.00
550 Pages
Frequency: Annual
Circulation: 2,000

15197 News Media Yellow Book
Leadership Directories
104 5th Ave
New York, NY 10011-6901
212-627-4140; Fax: 212-645-0931
www.leadershipdirectories.com
Facebook, Twitter

David Hurvitz, CEO
James M Petrie, Associate Publisher

Contact information for over 39,000 journalists at over 2,500 new services, networks, newspapers, television, radio stations, as well as independent journalists and syndicated columnists.
Cost: $325.00
1,200 Pages
Frequency: Quarterly
ISSN: 1071-8931
Founded in 1969
Mailing list available for rent: 32,000 names at $125 per M

15198 Newswire ASAP
Information Access Company
362 Lakeside Drive
Foster City, CA 94404-1171
650-378-5200
800-227-8431

Provides citations and the complete text of more than 1 million news releases and wire stories from the international news wire agencies. Subjects covered include banking, commodities, companies, currency and economics.
Frequency: Full-text
Founded in 1983

15199 Salem Press Online Platform
Grey House Publishing
4919 Route 22
PO Box 56
Amenia, NY 12501
800-221-1592; Fax: 201-968-0511
csr@salempress.com
online.salempress.com

The new Salem Press platform houses more than 500 titles including all of Salem's Health, Literature, History and Science titles in addition to select titles from the Grey House Publishing and H.W. Wilson product lines. Online access is free with each print purchase and includes an unlimited number of simultaneous users and remote access.

Industry Web Sites

15200 **http://gold.greyhouse.com**
G.O.L.D Grey House OnLine Databases
Grey House Publishing's online database platform, GOLD, offers Quick Search, Keyword Search and Expert Search for most business sectors including communication, broadcast and journalism markets. The GOLD platform makes finding the information you need quick and easy - whether you're a novice searcher or an experienced database user. All of Grey House's directory products are available for subscription on the GOLD platform.

15201 **opcofamerica.org**
Overseas Press Club of America
Facebook, Twitter, LinkedIn, Instagram, YouTube, Google+
Association of journalists working in the area of international news.

15202 **www.aarwba.org**
American Auto Racing Writers and Broadcasters
Association
Members are professional journalists who regularly cover auto racing and other related sports events.

15203 **www.apme.com**
Associated Press Managing Editors
Members are executives of Associated Press News Executives.

15204 **www.asja.org**
American Society of Journalists and Authors
For freelance nonfiction writers whose bylines appear in periodicals and in books.

15205 **www.asne.org**
American Society of Newspaper Editors
Directing editors who determine editorial and news policy on daily newspapers and news gathering operations of daily newspapers.

15206 **www.cjr.org/resources**
Columbia Journalism Review
Contains resource guides and other journalism-related lists.

15207 **www.drudgereport.com**
Links to international news sources and columnists.

15208 **www.greyhouse.com**
Grey House Publishing
Authoritative reference directories for most business sectors including communication, broadcast and journalism markets. Users can search the online databases with varied search criteria allowing for custom searches by product category, geographic area, sales volume, keyword, subject and more. Full Grey House catalog and online ordering also available.

15209 **www.house.gov**
Association of House Democratic Press Assistants
Promotes education and professional standards of members through speakers, series, seminars and papers. Offers placement services.

15210 **www.inma.org**
International Newspaper Marketing Association
Individuals in marketing, circulation, research and public relations of newspapers.

15211 **www.ire.org**
Investigative Reporters and Editors
For individuals involved in investigative journalism.

15212 **www.kausfiles.com**
Site for journalists and media specialists.

15213 **www.nepa.org**
New England Press Association
This organizatiom offers a publication about the newspaper industry specifically focusing on New England newspapers and the issues that affect them, which goes to every newspaper in New England.

15214 **www.newsmediaalliance.org**
News Media Alliance
Formerly known as the Newspaper Association of America, the News Media Alliance represents large daily papers, non-daily/small-market publications, as well as digital and multiplatform products across North America.

15215 **www.nnaweb.org**
National Newspaper Association
To protect, promote and enhance America's community newspapers.

15216 **www.poynter.org**
Poynter Institute is dedicated to teaching and inspiring journalists and media leaders. Promotes excellence and integrity in the practice of craft and in the practical leadership of successful businesses.

15217 **www.press.org**
National Press Club
A private organization composed of professional journalists who are directly related to the media. Persons must qualify to be admitted.

Associations

15218 **Academy of Criminal Justice Sciences**
PO Box 960
Suite A
Greenbelt, MD 20768-0960

301-446-6300
800-757-2257; Fax: 301-446-2819
info@acjs.org
www.acjs.org

Lorenzo M. Boyd, President
Nicole Leeper Piquero, First Vice-President
Faith Lutze, Second Vice-President
Mary K. Stohr, Executive Director
Heather L. Pfeifer, Secretary

An international association established to foster professional and scholarly activities in the field of criminal justice.
2800 Members
Founded in 1963

15219 **Air Force Security Forces Association**
818 Willow Creek Cir
San Marcos, TX 78666

512-396-5444
888-250-9876; Fax: 512-396-7328
afsfaonline.com

Scott Castillo, President
Jim Saulnier, Vice President
John Probst, Executive Director
Jerry Bullock, Executive Director Emeritus
Lucille Bullock, Executive Treasurer-Secretary

The mission is to bring together all those currently serving in the US Air Force as Security Forces members, past Air Police and Security Police members, as well as future Security forces members.
Founded in 1947

15220 **Airborne Law Enforcement Association**
50 Carroll Creek Way
Suite 260
Frederick, MD 21701

301-631-2406; Fax: 301-631-2466
webmaster@alea.org
www.alea.org
Facebook, Twitter, LinkedIn

Steve Roussell, Chair:Executive Committee
Daniel B. Schwarzbach, Executive Director/CEO
Benay Osborne, CEM, CMP, Operations Manager
Don Ruby, Training Program Manager
Bryan Smith, Safety Program Manager

Supports and encourages the use of aircraft in public safety and provides networking systems, educational seminars and product expositions.
3500 Members
Founded in 1968

15221 **American Academy of Forensic Sciences**
410 N. 21st Street
Colorado Springs, CO 80904

719-636-1100; Fax: 719-636-1993
awarren@aafs.org
www.aafs.org
Facebook, YouTube, RSS

Zeno J. Greadts, PhD., President
Carl R. McClary, BA, Vice President
Jeri D. Ropero-Miller, PhD., President-Elect
Anne Warren, Executive Director
Susan M. Ballou, MS, Past President

A professional society dedicated to the application of science to the law, the AAFS is committed to the promotion of education and the elevation of accuracy, precision, and specificity in the forensic sciences. Membership includes physicians, attorneys, dentists, toxicologists, anthropologists, document examiners, digital evidence experts, psychiatrists, engineers, physicists, chemists, criminalists, educators, and others from the US, Canada and 70 other countries worldwide.
6700 Members
Founded in 1948
Mailing list available for rent: 6500 names

15222 **American Association of Motor Vehicle Administrators**
4401 Wilson Boulevard
Suite 700
Arlington, VA 22203

703-522-4200; Fax: 703-522-1553
info@aamva.org
www.aamva.org
Facebook, Twitter, YouTube, Flickr

Neil D Schuster, President & CEO
Sandy Bloomfield, Executive Asst.
Philip Quinlan, VP, Business Solutions
Marc Saitta, Vice President & CFO
Kathy King, Director, Program Business Services

A nonprofit association that supports both state and provincial official members throughout North America who oversee the administration and enforcement of motor vehicle laws. Services include development and research in motor vehicle administration, law enforcement and highway safety as well as being an information clearinghouse.
Founded in 1933
Mailing list available for rent

15223 **American Association of Police Polygraphists**
3223 Lake Ave
Unit 15c-168
Wilmette, IL 60091-1069

847-635-3980
888-743-5479; Fax: 937-488-1046
NOM@policepolygraph.org
www.policepolygraph.org
Facebook

Karen Clark, Chairperson
James Wardwell, President
Tracey Hilton, Vice President
Robert C. Heard, Secretary
Gordon W. Moore, Treasurer

Promote and maintain the highest standards of ethics, integrity, honor and conduct in the polygraph profession; provide an opportunity and forum for the exchange of information regarding polygraph experiences, studies and research; cooperate with other national, regional and state polygraph associations and other professional organizations in matters of mutual interest and benefit to the profession.
900 Members
Founded in 1977

15224 **American Association of Police Officers**
1109 W 6th St
Suite 205
Austin, TX 78703

800-961-9773; Fax: 800-227-1042
policeusa@gmail.com
www.policeusa.com
Facebook

Phil LeConte, Executive Officer
David Dierks, Financial Officer
Suzanne D'Ambrose, Law Enforement Instructor
Dennis Haley, Veteran Homicide Investigator
Curt Schwake, General Counsel & Advisor

Dedicated to bringing the wisdom of America's law enforcement veterans to the next generation of police officers and citizens. AAPO has provided a national stage for veteran law enforcement officers to share their wisdom and experience. Guided by an advisory council of law enforcement veterans and distinguished citizens, AAPO is committed to tapping into this often overlooked resource - veteran law enforcers both active duty and retired - and putting this unique knowledge to a useful purpose.

15225 **American Association of State Troopersÿ**
1949 Raymond Diehl Road
Tallahassee, FL 32308

800-765-5456
850-765-5456; Fax: 850-385-8697
joan@statetroopers.org
www.statetroopers.orgÿ
Facebook

Keith Barbier, President
Jeffrey Lane, First Vice President
Lee Burch, Second Vice President
Noel Houze Jr., Secretary
Kenneth Musick, Treasurer
Founded in 1989

15226 **American Correctional Association**
206 N Washington St
Alexandria, VA 22314

703-224-0000
800-222-5646; Fax: 703-224-0179
jeffw@aca.org
www.aca.org
Facebook, Twitter, LinkedIn, YouTube

Mary L Livers, President
Michael Wade, Vice President
Gary C Mohr, Treasurer
James A Gondles, Jr., Secretary

For individuals involved in the correctional field.
20000 Members
Founded in 1870
Mailing list available for rent

15227 **American Criminal Justice Association**
PO Box 601047
Sacramento, CA 95860-1047

916-484-6553; Fax: 916-488-2227
acjalae@aol.com
www.acjalae.org

Preston Koelling, President
Steve Atchley, VP
Jeanne Church-Elson, Region 1 President
Karen Campbell, Executive Secretary
David Redford, Region 2 President

Objectives are to improve criminal justice through educational activities, foster professionalism in law enforcement personnel and agencies, promote professional, academic and public awareness of criminal justice issues and promote high standards of ethical conduct, professional training and higher education within the criminal justice field.
7200 Members
Founded in 1937

15228 **American Jail Association**
1135 Professional Ct
Hagerstown, MD 21740-5853

301-790-3930; Fax: 301-790-2941
rickn@aja.org
www.aja.org
Facebook, Twitter, LinkedIn, YouTube, Instagram

Robert J. Kasabian, Executive Director
Steve Custer, Director of Communications
Patty Vermillion, Program Manager
Lauren Pirri, Marketing and Sales Coordinator
Nico Gentile, Dir. Of Business Development

Dedicated to supporting those who work in and operate our nations's jails. AJA is the only national association that focuses exclusively on is-

sues specific to the operations of local correctional facilities.
5000 Members
Founded in 1981

15229 **American Police Hall of Fame and Museum**
6350 Horizon Drive
Titusville, FL 32780

321-264-0911; Fax: 321-264-0033
policeinfo@aphf.org
www.aphf.org
Facebook

Donna Shepherd, CEO
Barry Shepherd, Executive Director
Debra Chitwood, CFO
Jamie Maynard, Dir. Of Communications
Brent Shepherd, Director of Operations

Offers benefits and various types of awards to members, magazine, line of duty benefits, film and training library as well as support services, scholarships and financial assistance for police family survivors.
Founded in 1960

15230 **American Police Hall of Fame and Museum**
6350 Horizon Drive
Titusville, FL 32780

321-264-0911; Fax: 321-264-0033
policeinfo@aphf.org
www.aphf.org
Facebook

Donna Shepherd, CEO
Barry Shepherd, Executive Director
Debra Chitwood, Chief Financial Officer
Brent Shepherd, Director of Operations
Jamie Maynard, Director of Communications

The nation's first national police museum dedicated to law enforcement officers who have died in the line of duty.
104M Members
Founded in 1960

15231 **American Polygraph Association**
PO Box 8037
Chattanooga, TN 37414-0037

423-892-3992
800-272-8037; Fax: 423-894-5435
manager@polygraph.org
www.polygraph.org
Facebook, Twitter

Steve Duncan, President

Representing experienced polygraph examiners in private business; law enforcement and government. Professional APA polygraph examiners administer hundreds of thousands of polygraph exams each year worldwide. The APA establishes standards of ethical practices, techniques, instrumentation and research, as well as provides advanced training and continuing education programs.
2700+ Members
Founded in 1966

15232 **American Probation and Parole Association**
1776 Avenue of the States
Lexington, KY 40511-8482

859-244-8203; Fax: 859-244-8001
appa@csg.org
www.appa-net.org
Facebook, Twitter, LinkedIn

Veronica Cunningham, Executive Director
Diane Kincaid, Dep. Dir./Information Specialist

An international association composed of members from the United States, Canada and other countries actively involved with probation, parole and community based corrections, in both adult and juvenile sectors.
30K Members
Founded in 1975

15233 **American Psychiatric Association**
1000 Wilson Blvd
Suite 1825
Arlington, VA 22209-3901

703-907-7300
888-35 -7792; Fax: 703-907-1085
apa@psych.org
www.psychiatry.org
Facebook, Twitter, LinkedIn

Saul M. Levin, M.D., M.P.A, CEO & Medical Director
Maria A. Oquendo, President

U.S. and international member physicians work together to ensure humane care and effective treatment for all persons with mental disorder, including mental retardation and substance-related disorders. It is the voice and conscience of modern psychiatry. Its vision is a society that has available, accessible quality psychiatric diagnosis and treatment.

15234 **American Society of Crime Laboratory Directors**
65 Glen Road
Suite 123
Garner, NC 27529

919-773-2044
asclddirector@gmail.com
www.ascld.org
Facebook, Twitter, LinkedIn, RSS

Matthew Gamette, President
Jean Stover, Executive Director
Timothy Scanlan, Training & Education Chair
Rite Dyas, Treasurer
Linda Jackson, Secretary

A nonprofit professional society, composed of crime laboratory directors and forensic science managers, that aims to foster professional interests, to assist in laboratory management principles and technqiues, to maintain communication among crime laboratory directors, to disseminate and acquire forensic based information, and to promote high standards of practice within the field.
660 Members
Founded in 1974
Mailing list available for rent: 660 names at $800 per M

15235 **American Society of Criminology**
1314 Kinnear Rd
Suite 212
Columbus, OH 43212-1156

614-292-9207; Fax: 614-292-6767
asc@asc41.com
www.asc41.com
Twitter, LinkedIn

Bonnie Fisher, Treasurer
Joanne Belknap, President-Elect
Christopher Uggen, Executive Secretary
Robert Agnew, President
Becky Block, VP

Objectives are to encourage the exchange, in a multidisciplinary setting, of those engaged in research, teaching, and practice so as to foster criminological scholarship, and to serve as a forum for the dissemination of criminological knowledge.
Founded in 1941

15236 **American Speaker Association**
32 East Riverhead Drive
Houstan, TX 77042-2501

713-914-9444
800-636-2722
www.nsaspeaker.org
Facebook, LinkedIn

Mary Lue Peck, President & CEO
Rhette Baughman, Chief Revenue Officer
Nikki Harris, Director, Member Success
Jessi Leonardo, Director, Operations
Matt Longdon, Manager, Marketing & Communications

Assists in proceedings involving legislation and arbitration.
37 Members
Founded in 1979
Mailing list available for rent

15237 **American Traffic Safety Services Association**
15 Riverside Parkway
Suite 100
Fredericksburg, VA 22406-1022

540-368-1701
800-272-8772; Fax: 540-368-1717
foundation@atssa.com
www.atssa.com
Facebook, Twitter, LinkedIn, Pinterest, Google+, YouTube

Sue Reiss, President
Kathleen Holst, Vice President
Chad England, Traffic Director
john Tobin, Director, Manufacturers & Suppliers
Juan Arvizu, At-Large Director

Promotes uniform use of lights, signs, pavement markings and barricades. Distributes technical information and sponsors training courses for worksite traffic supervisors.
1600 Members
Founded in 1969

15238 **Americans for Effective Law Enforcement**
P.O. Box 75401
Chicago, IL 60675-5401

847-685-0700; Fax: 847-685-9700
info@aele.org
www.aele.org
RSS

Daniel B. Hales, President
Wayne W. Schmidt, Esq., Executive Director
Bernard J. Farber, Editor/ Research Counsel
Helen Finkel, Staff Vice President
Missy Taki, Supervisor/Manager

Incorporated as a not for profit educational organization for the purpose of establishing an organized voice for the law-abiding citizens regarding this country's crime problem, and to lend support to professional law enforcement.
Founded in 1966

15239 **Association of Firearm and Tool Mark Examiners**
525 Carter Hill Rd.
Montgomery, AL 36106

334-242-2938; Fax: 334-240-3284
kathy.richert@adfs.alabama.gov
www.afte.org

Brandon Giroux, President
Travis Spinder, 1st Vice President
Justine Kreso, Secretary
Alison Quereau, Membership Secretary
Melissa Oberg, Treasurer

15240 **Association of Paroling Authorities Inernational**
Sam Houston State University
Huntsville, TX 77341-2296

877-318-2724; Fax: 936-294-1671
www.apaintl.org

Cyndi Mausser, President
Tena Pate, Vice President
Keith Hardison, Chief Administrative Officer

David Blumberg, Treasurer
Dan Fetsco, Secretary
511 Members
Founded in 1970

15241 **Association of Public-Safety Communication s Officials International (APCO)**
351 N Williamson Boulevard
Daytona Beach, FL 32114-1112

386-322-2500
888-272-6911; Fax: 386-322-2501
apco@apcointl.org
www.apcointl.org/
Facebook, Twitter, LinkedIn

Brent Lee, President
Cheryl J. Greathouse, RPL, 1st Vice President
Martha K. Carter, ENP, 2nd Vice President
Doreen Geary, Accounting
Sarah Hill, Awards

International, nonprofit organization fostering the development and progress of the art of public safety communications by means of research, planning, training and education. Promotes cooperation between towns, cities, counties, states and federal, public safety agencies in the area of communications.
15000 Members
Founded in 1935

15242 **Border Patrol Supervisors' Association**
3755 Avocado
Blvd #404
La Mesa, CA 91941

Home Page: www.bpsups.org

Richard Haynes, President
Richard Marzec, Vice President
Linwood Knowles, Secretary
Logan Snider, Treasurer
Mike Diaz, Sergeant at Arms
500 Members
Founded in 1990

15243 **Commission on Accreditation for Law Enforcement Agencies, Inc.**
13575 Heathcote Boulevard
Suite 320
Gainesville, VA 20155

703-352-4225
800-368-3757; Fax: 703-890-3126
calea@calea.org
www.calea.org
RSS, Pinterest, Google+, Myspa

W. Craig Hartley, Jr., Executive Director
Travis Parrish, Dir, Client Services and Relations
Antonio T. Beatty, Administrative Services Manager
Margaret Giglio, Program Specialist
Wendi Jones, Contract Specialist

Established as an independent accrediting authority by the four major law enforcement membership associations: International Association of Chiefs of Police; National Organization of Black Law Enforcement Executives; National Sheriffs' Association; and Police Executive Research Forum.
21 Members
Founded in 1979

15244 **Concerns of Police Survivors**
846 Old South 5
PO Box 3199
Camdenton, MO 65020

573-346-4911; Fax: 573-346-1414
cops@nationalcops.org
www.concernsofpolicesurvivors.org
Facebook, Twitter, YouTube

Emilio Miyares, President
Dianne Bernhard, Executive Director
Sarah Slone, Director of Public Relations
Shelley Jones, Director of Operations
Lynn Kuse, Financial Manager

Providing resources and services that help rebuild the shattered lives of surviving families and co-workers affected by line-of-duty death.
51000 Members
Founded in 1984
Mailing list available for rent: 55000 names

15245 **Congressional Fire Services Institute**
900 2nd St NE
Suite 303
Washington, DC 20002-3557

202-371-1277; Fax: 202-682-3473
update@cfsi.org
www.cfsi.org
Facebook

William Jenaway, President
Jim Estepp, Vice President
Bill Webb, Executive Director
Sean Carroll, Director of Government Affairs
Brian Goldfeder, Special Events Manager

Designed to educate members of Congress about the needs and challenges of our nation's fire and emergency services so that the federal government provides the types of training and funding needed by our first responders.
Founded in 1989

15246 **Cops Who Careÿ**
PO Box 20688
Wickenburg, AZ 85358

860-500-8926
www.copswhocare.org

Founded in 1982

15247 **Criminal Justice Center**
Sam Houston State University
PO Box 2296
Huntsville, TX 77341

936-294-1635; Fax: 281-294-1653
icc_www@shsu.edu

Vincent Webb, Director/Dean
Kristi Kreier, Business Office Director

Established to provide an educational program for students seeking careers in law enforcement, cours and corrections and for the development of a continuing education program for professionals working in the field.

15248 **D.A.R.E. America**
PO Box 512090
Los Angeles, CA 90051-0090

310-215-0575
800-223-DARE; Fax: 310-215-0180
www.dare.com

Louis Miller, Chair
David M. Horn, Vice Chair
Francisco X Pegueros, President and CEO
Thomas Hazelton, President of Development
Anita Bryan, Deputy Director of Education

A police officer led series of classroom lessons that teaches children from kindergarten through 12th grad how to resist peer pressure and live productive drug and violence free lives.
Mailing list available for rent

15249 **Dogs Against Drugs/Dogs Against Crime National Law Enforcement K9 Assn.**
3320 Main St.
Suite G
Anderson, IN 46013

765-642-9447
888-323-3227; Fax: 765-642-4899
daddac.tripod.com
Facebook

Darron Sparks, President/National Director

Dedicated to the betterment of law enforcement K9 operations and to educating the youth on the dangers of drug abuse. DAD/DAC provides grants to officers for purchasing highly trained special purpose dogs and related training equipment and supplies and to provide training for the officer and/or dog. Working/training seminars are offered for K9 officers on numerous topics related to police service dogs.

15250 **Evidence Photographers International Council**
229 Peachtree St. NE
Ste #2200
Atlanta, GA 30303

570-253-5450
866-868-3742; Fax: 404-614-6404
www.evidencephotographers.com
Facebook

Robert F Jennings, Executive Director

Nonprofit scientific/educational organization with a primary purpose of advancement of forensic photography/videography in civil evidence and law enforcement.
Founded in 1968

15251 **FBI National Academy Associates**
422 Garrisonville Road
Suite 103
Stafford, VA 22554

540-628-0834; Fax: 703-632-1993
www.fbinaa.org

Barry Thomas, Association President
Steve Tidwell, Executive Director
Korri Roper, CFO/COO
Denise MacLane, Financial Accountant
Ashley Sutton, Communications Manager

A non-profit international organization of senior law enforcement professionals dedicated to providing the communities and profession with the highest degree of law enforcement expertise, training, education and information.
17000 Members
Founded in 1935

15252 **Federal Criminal Investigators Association**
5868 Mapledale Plaza
Suite 104
Woodbridge, VA 22193

800-403-3374
www.fedcia.orgÿ

Founded in 1991

15253 **Federal Law Enforcement Officers Association**
7945 MacArthur Blvd
Suite 201
Cabin John, MD 20818

202-870-5503
866-553-5362
fleoa@fleoa.org
www.fleoa.orgÿ
Facebook, Twitter, Reddit, Pinterest

Jon Adler, National President
Nate Catura, Executive Vice President
Chris Schoppmeyer, Vice President - Agency Affairs
Frank Terreri, Vice President- Legislative Affairs
John Ramsey, Vice President - Membership Benefit
Founded in 1977

15254 **Fire Equipment Manufacturers' Association**
1300 Sumner Avenue
Cleveland, OH 44115

216-241-7333
www.femalifesafety.org

Facebook, LinkedIn, YouTube, Wikipedia, Slideshare

Bill Vegso, President

Trade association representing manufacturers of fire protection equipment. Products made by member companies include portable fire extinguishers, fire hose/interior equipment and pre-engineered fire suppression systems.
Founded in 1930

15255 Fire Suppression Systems Association
3601 East Joppa Road
Baltimore, MD 21234

410-931-8100; Fax: 410-931-8111
fssa@clemonsmgmt.com
www.fssa.net
Facebook, Twitter, LinkedIn, Reddit, Pinterest, Blooger

Tim Carman, President
Ray Aldridge, Vice President
Helen Lowery, Secretary/Treasurer
Tim Carman, Secretary/Treasurer
Eric Burkland, VP

An organization of manufacturers, suppliers, and design-installers, dedicated to providing a higher level of fire protection. Members are specialists in protecting high value special hazardareas from fire.
Founded in 1982

15256 Fire and Emergency Manufacturers and Services Association
P.O. Box 147
Lynnfield, MA 01940-0147

781-334-2771; Fax: 781-334-2771
info@femsa.org
www.femsa.org
Twitter, LinkedIn

William Van Lent, President
James Long, Vice President

The leading trade association for the fire and emergency services industry whose members provide products and services to millions of fire and EMS professionals throughout the world. Works to strengthen its membership, planning for future development and directing programs that build industry opportunities.
160 Members
Founded in 1966

15257 Flight Safety Foundation
801 N. Fairfax Street
Suite 400
Alexandria, VA 22314-1774

703-739-6700; Fax: 703-739-6708
www.flightsafety.org
Facebook, Twitter, LinkedIn

Hassan Shahidi, President & CEO
Frank Jackman, VP, Communications
Louise Martin, VP, Membership
Kenneth P. Quinn, General Counsel & Secretary
Jerry Lederer, Founder

Independent, nonprofit, international organization engaged in research, auditing, education, advocacy and publishing to improve aviation safety.
Founded in 1947

15258 Fraternal Order of Police
701 Marriott Dr
Nashville, TN 37214-5043

615-399-0900; Fax: 615-399-0400
webmaster@grandlodgefop.org
www.fop.net

Chuck Canterbury, National President
Ed Brannigan, National VP
Les Neri, National Second Vice President
Tom Penoza, National Treasurer
Patrick Yoes, National Secretary

This is the world's largest organization of sworn law enforcement officers, with more than 324,000 members in more than 2,100 lodges. It is the voice of those who dedicate their lives to protecting and serving our communities, and is committed to improving the working conditions of law enforcement officers and the safety of those served through education, legislation, information, community involvement,and employeee representation.
324M Members
Founded in 1915
Mailing list available for rent

15259 Hispanic National Law Enforcement Association
PO Box 766
Cheltenham, MD 20623

240-244-9189
www.hnlea.com

Mike Rodriguez, President
Luis Rodriguez, Executive Director
Miguel I. Core, Vice President
Jose Perez, Treasurer
Adriane Clayton, Secretary

Non-profit organization of professionals involved in the administration of justice and dedicated to the advancement of Hispanic(Latino) and minority interests within the law enforcement profession.
Founded in 1988

15260 Institute of Investigative Technology
AccuQuest
6950 Phillips Hwy, #46
Jacksonville, FL 32216-6087

904-296-0212; Fax: 904-296-7385

John Ramming, Director

Provides training for law enforcement and corporate clients. Programs can be designed from one-day to multiple week training courses.

15261 Institute of Police Technology and Management
University of North Florida
12000 Alumni Dr
Jacksonville, FL 32224-2678

904-620-4786; Fax: 904-620-2453
info@iptm.org
www.iptm.org
Facebook

Teresa R. Dioquino, Management Section Coordinator
Cameron Pucci, Diector
Tony Becker, Administration
Kenin Al Roop, Marketing
Harry Walters, Traffic Enforcement

Mission of the Institute is to provide the law enforcement community with the highest quality of training at competitive prices. By providing this service, IPTM continues to support law enforcement's efforts in building and maintaining safer communitites.
Founded in 1980

15262 Insurance Institute for Highway Safety
1005 N Glebe Rd
Suite 800
Arlington, VA 22201

703-247-1500; Fax: 703-247-1588
rrader@iihs.org
www.iihs.org
Twitter, RSS, YouTube

Adrian Loud, President
Russ Rader, Senior Vice President
Shelley Shelton, Executive Assistant, Legal Affairs
Brenda O'Donnell, Vice President, Insurer Relations
Chamelle Matthew, Communications Associate

Independent, nonprofit, scientific and educational organization dedicated to reducing the losses (deaths, injuries, and property damage) from crashes on the nation's highways.
Founded in 1959
Mailing list available for rent

15263 International Association for Identification
2131 Hollywood Blvd.,
Suite 403
Hollywood, FL 33020

954-589-0628; Fax: 954-589-0657
www.theiai.org
Facebook

Bridget Lewis, President
Harold Ruslander, 1st Vice President
Ray Jorz, 2nd Vice President
Lisa Hudson, 3rd Vice President
Glen Calhoun, Chief Operations Officer
Founded in 1915

15264 International Association for Property Evidence, Inc.
903 N San Fernando Boulevard
Suite 4
Burbank, CA 91504-4327

818-846-2926
800-449-4273; Fax: 818-846-4543
Mail@IAPE.org
www.iape.org
Facebook

Joseph T. Latta, Executive Director/Lead Instructor
William Kiley, Board Member, Instructor
Steve Campbell, Secretary, Instructor
Suzanne Cox, Tresurer
Robin Lynn Trench, Founder

Established to further the education, training and professional growth of Law Enforcement Property and Evidence Personnel.
Founded in 1993

15265 International Association of Arson Investigators
2111 Baldwin Avenue
Suite 203
Crofton, MD 21114

410-451-3473
800-468-4224; Fax: 410-451-9049
www.firearson.com
Facebook, Twitter, LinkedIn, YouTube

Daniel Heenan, President
George Codding, 1st Vice President
Scott Bennett, 2nd Vice President
Deborah Keeler, Executive Director
Debra Miller, Accounting & Finanace Manager

Dedicated to improving the professional development of fire and explosion investigators by being the global resource for fire investigation, technology and research.
7500 Members
Founded in 1949

15266 International Association of Auto Theft Investigators
PO Box 223
Clinton, NY 13323-0223

315-853-1913; Fax: 315-883-1310
jvabounader@iaati.org
www.iaati.org

Todd M. Blair, President
Robert C. Hasbrouck, Treasurer
John V Abounader, Executive Director
Heidi M. Jordan, 1st VP
Todd M. Blair, 3rd VP

Provides members who are auto theft investigators with resources to develop and maintain professional standards within the industry.
3604 Members
Founded in 1952

15267 International Association of Bloodstain Pattern Analysts

Home Page: www.iabpa.org

Pat Laturnus, President
Donald Schuessler, VP
Norman Reeves, Secretary/ Treasurer
Jeff Scozzafava, Sergeant at Arms
Stuart H James, Historian

15268 International Association of Bomb Technicians and Investigators

1120 International parkway
Fredricksburg, VA 22406

540-752-4533; Fax: 540-752-2796
admin@iabti.org
www.iabti.org
Facebook, Twitter, LinkedIn

Ralph Way, Executive Director

An independent professional association formed for countering the criminal use of explosives. This is sought through the exchange of training, expertise and information among personnel employed in the fields of law enforcement, fire and emergency services, the military, forensic science and other related fields.
4000 Members
Founded in 1973

15269 International Association of Campus Law Enforcement Administrators

342 N Main Street
West Hartford, CT 06117-2507

860-586-7517; Fax: 860-586-7550
info@iaclea.org
www.iaclea.org
Facebook

William F. Taylor, President
Christopher Blake, CAE, Executive Director
Kendra Pheasant, CAE, Associate Director
Susan Koczka, Corporate Relations
Eva Storrs, Membership Services

Advances public safety for educational institutions by providing educational resources, advocacy and professional development.
Founded in 1958
Mailing list available for rent

15270 International Association of Directors of Law Enforcement Standards/Training

1330 N. Manship Pl.
Meridian, ID 83642

208-288-5491; Fax: 517-857-3826
www.iadlest.org

David Harvey, President
Brian Grisham, First Vice-President
Dan Zivkovich, Second Vice-President
Michael N. Becar, Executive Director
Mark Damitio, Secretary

An international organization of training managers and executives dedicated to the improvement of public safety personnel. The Association serves as the national forum of Peace Officer Standards and Training (POST) agencies, boards and commissions as well as statewide training academies throughout the United States.
Mailing list available for rent

15271 International Association of Law Enforcement Firearms Instructors

25 Country Club Road
Suite 707
Gilford, NH 03249

603-524-8787; Fax: 603-524-8856
info@ialefi.com
www.ialefi.com

R Steven Johnson, President
Robert D Bossey, Executive Director/Treasurer
Michial Dunlap, Secretary
John T. Meyer, 1st VP
Emanuel Kapelson, 2nd VP

An independent, non-profit association whose mission is to update and modernize the instruction and teaching techniques used to train the majority of law enforcement officers.
Founded in 1981

15272 International Association of Undercover Officers

142 Banks Drive
Brunswick, GA 31523

800-876-5943; Fax: 800-876-5912
charlie@undercover.org
www.undercover.org

Brian Sallee, President
Brian Sallee, President
Steve Cook, First Vice-President
David Redemann, Second Vice-President
Frank Swirko, Treasurer

Established for the purpose of promoting safety and professionalism among undercover officers. The association continues to foster mutual cooperation, discussion and interests among its members. It provides vast international network of intelligence gathering means for today's undercover officer and sponsors high quality training programs for undercover officers.

15273 International Association of Women

1352 NE 47th Avenue
Portland, OR 97213

301-464-1402; Fax: 301-464-1402
carolpaterick@gmail.com
www.iawp.org
Twitter

Margaret Shorter, President
Deborah Friedl, First Vice President
Andrea Humphrys, Executive Director
Michelle Lish, Foundation Treasurer
Julia Jaeger, Recording Secretary
Founded in 1915

15274 International Association of Women Police

1352 NE 47th Avenue
Portland, OR 97213

301-464-1402; Fax: 301-464-1402
carolpaterick@gmail.com
www.iawp.org
Twitter

Margaret Shorter, President
Deborah Friedl, First Vice President
Andrea Humphrys, Executive Director
Michele Lish, Foundation Treasurer
Julia Jaeger, Recording Secretary

To strengthen, unite, and raise the profile of women in criminal justice internationally.
24000 Members
Founded in 1915

15275 International Board of Certification for Safety Managers

173 Tucker Road
Suite 202
Helena, AL 35080

205-664-8412; Fax: 205-663-9541
info@ibfcsm.org
www.ibfcsm.org
Facebook

James Tweedy, Executive Director

A professional credentialing organization that promotes the application of managerial techniques to eliminate or control unsafe and unhealthy conditions, behavior and other factors detrimental to people and property. Offers credentials in safety, product safety, healthcare safety, patient safety, and healthcare emergency management.
2500 Members
Founded in 1976

15276 International Crime Scene Investigator's Association

15774 S. LaGrange Road
Orland Park, IL 60462

708-460-8082
www.icsia.org

Hayden B Baldwin, Executive Director
Christopher Anderson, Caribbean Director
Paul Echols, Board of Directors
Chad Pitfield, Board of Directors
Steven W Hulsey, Board of Directors

15277 International Critical Incident Stress Foundation

3290 Pine Orchard Ln
Suite 106
Ellicott City, MD 21042

410-750-9600; Fax: 410-750-9601
info@icisf.org
www.icisf.org
Facebook, Twitter

Dave Evans, CPA, Chairman
Lisa Joubert, Finance Director
Richard Barton, CEO
C. Kenneth Bohn, Director of Operations
Jeannie Gow, General Information Requests

A foundation dedicated to the prevention and mitigation of disabling stress through the provision of; Education, training and support services for all Emergency Services professions, continuing education and training in Emergency Mental Health Services for Psychologists, Psychiatrists, Social Workers and Licensed Professional Counselors and Consultation in the establishment of Crisis and Disaster Response Programs for varied organizations and communities worldwide.

15278 International Footprint Association

PO Box 1652
Walnut, CA 91788

323-981-1488
877-432-3668; Fax: 323-265-4657
www.footprinter.org

Robert H. Hubbell, Grand President
Doug Partlow, First Grand Vice President
Michael Leary, Second Grand Vice President
Maura Mattson, Grand Secretary/Treasurer
Michael Leary, Assistant Grand Secretary/Treasurer

A non-profit association that promotes and encourages fellowship, respect, cooperation, and helpfulness between all arms of law enforcement and all others who are sympathetic with and understanding toward law enforcement and all of its agencies.
4000 Members
Founded in 1929

15279 International Law Enforcement Educators & Trainers Association

4742 79 Street
Kenosha, WI 53142

262-767-1406; Fax: 262-767-1813
info@ILEETA.org

www.ileeta.org
Facebook

Harvey Hedden, Executive Director
Brian Wills, Deputy Executive Dir.
Alexis Artwohl, Advisory Board Member
Massad Ayoob, Advisory Board Member
Steve Ashley, Advisory Board Member

An organization by, for and about instructors and training for the criminal justice professions. Committed to the reduction of law enforcement risk through the enhancement of training for criminal justice practitioners.
Founded in 2003

15280 International Narcotic Enforcement Officers Association
112 State Street
Suite 1200
Albany, NY 12207-2079

518-463-6232
www.ineoa.org

John J Bellizer Jr, Executive Director
Michael Harris, President

Basic purpose is to promote and foster mutual interest in the problems of narcotic control; provide a medium for the exchange of ideas, conduct seminars, conferences and study groups and issue publications.

15281 International Police Associationÿÿ
PO Box 516
Greystone Station
Yonkers, NY 10703-0516

855-241-9998
www.ipa-usa.org
Facebook, Twitter

Kevin Gordon, President
Calvin Chow, 1st VP
Cory Freadling, 2nd VP
Joe Johnson, 3rd VP
Viola Powrie, Treasurer
Founded in 1950

15282 International Union of Police Associations
1549 Ringling Blvd
6th Fl.
Sarasota, FL 34236

800-247-4872; Fax: 941-487-2570
iupa@iupa.org
iupa.org
Facebook, LinkedIn, YouTube

Samuel A. Cabral, President
Hugh J. Cameron, Secretary-Treasurer

The voice of the law enforcement community within the organized labor movement.
Founded in 1954

15283 Law Enforcement & Emergency Services Video Association
84 Briar Creek Road
Whitesboro, TX 76273

469-285-9435; Fax: 469-533-3659
www.leva.org
Facebook, Twitter, LinkedIn

Alan Salmon, Chairman of the Board
Tracy Peloquin, Vice Chairman
Juan Ruano, President
Scott Olar, Executive Vice President
Scott Sullivan, Forensic Training, Program Manager

Committed to improving the quality of video training and promoting the use of state-of-the-art, effective equipment in the law enforcement and emergency services community.
Mailing list available for rent

15284 Law Enforcement Alliance of America
12427 Hedges Run Drive
Suite 113
Lake Ridge, VA 22192-1715

202-706-9218; Fax: 703-556-6485
membership@leaa.org
www.leaa.org

Jim Fotis, Executive Director
Kevin Watson, Communications Director

Nation's largest nonprofit, non-partisan coalition of law enforcement professionals. Crime victims, and concerned citizens united for justice; with a major focus on public education, LEAA is dedicated to providing hard facts and real world insights into the world of law enforcement and the battle against violent crime. Fighting at every level of government for legislation that reduces violent crime while preserving the rights of honest citizens, particularly the right of self-defense.
Founded in 1992

15285 Law Enforcement Bloodhound Association
PO Box 190442
Anchorage, AL 99519-0442

907-602-3542
leba@gci.net
www.npba.com

Gerry Nichols, President

LEBA is a professional nonprofit organization dedicated to the promotion of bloodhounds in law enforcement. Also provides beginning, continuing and advanced education to law enforcement professionals and thier bloodhound partners.
Founded in 1998
Mailing list available for rent

15286 Law Enforcement Executive Development Association, Inc.
5 Great Valley Pkwy.
Suite 125
Malvern, PA 19355

484-321-7821
877-772-7712; Fax: 610-644-3193
info@fbileeda.org
www.fbileeda.org
Facebook, Twitter, LinkedIn

Chief David Boggs, President
Paul Shastany, First Vice President
Thomas Alber, Second Vice President
Chief John Horsman, Third Vice President
Charles Robb, Executive Director

Purpose of the association is to advance the Science and Art of Police Management and Administration; to develop and disseminate improved administrative and technical practices; promote the exchange of information and training for executives of law enforcement.

15287 Law Enforcement Legal Defense Fundÿ
1428 Duke Street
Alexandria, VA 703-807-18

info@leldf.org
www.policedefense.orgÿ
Facebook, Twitter, LinkedIn, YouTube

Alfred S Regnery, Chairman
John J Burke, Vice Chairman
Ron Hosko, President
Edwin Meese, Director
Daniel J DeSimone, Secretary-Treasurer
Founded in 1995

15288 Law Enforcement Standards Office
100 Bureau Drive
MS 8102
Gaithersburg, MD 20899-8102

301-975-6478; Fax: 301-948-0978
inquiries@nist.gov
www.nist.gov

Patrick D. Gallagher, Director
Michael D. Herman, Executive Officer
Kevin Kimball, Chief of Staff
Henry N. Wixon, Chief Counsel
Mary Saunders, Associate Director

OLES's mission is to serve as the principal agent for standards development for the criminal justice and public safety communities. Helping criminal justice and public safety agencies acquire, on a cost-effective basis, the high quality resources they need to do their jobs.
Founded in 1901

15289 Major Cities Chiefs Police Association
P.O. Box 8717
Salt Lake City, UT 84047

stephens@majorcitieschiefs.com
www.majorcitieschiefs.com

J. Thomas Manger, President
Art Acevedo, 1st Vice President
George Turner, 2nd Vice President
Darrel W. Stephens, Executive Director

An organization bringing together Chiefs and Sheriffs from the largest cities of the United States, Canada, and the United Kingdom, with the intent of creating a forum for shared ideas and insights across international borders.
Founded in 1949

15290 Metropolitan Alliance of Police
215 Remington Blvd.
Suite C
Bolingbrook, IL 60440

630-759-4925; Fax: 630-759-1902
mapunion@msn.com
www.mapunion.org

Joseph Andalina, President
Keith George, Vice President
Richard Tracy, Secretary
Joseph R. Mazzone, Chief Counsel
Richard J. Reimer, Co-Counsel

15291 Narcotic Enforcement Officers Association
29 N Plains Hwy
Suite 10
Wallingford, CT 06492

203-269-8940; Fax: 203-284-9103
www.neoa.org

Michael R Rinaldi, President
Gabriel Lupo, VP
Richard Stook, Treasurer
Duane Tompkins, Secretary

A non-profit educational organization of more than a thousand law enforcement personnel and others in the criminal justicce system, includin state and local police, D.E.A., F.B.I. and customs.

15292 National Asian Peace Officers' Association
1776 I Street, NW,
Suite 900
Washington, DC 20006

646-632-5384; Fax: 202-756-1301
www.napoablue.org

James Ng, President
Taerance Oh, 1st Vice President
Thomas Masters, 3rd Vice President
Rolland Ogawa, Secretary
Siamone Bangphraxay, Treasurer

15293 National Association School Resource Officers
2020 Valleydale Road
Suite 207A
Hoover, AL 35244
205-739-6060
888-316-2776; Fax: 205-536-9255
www.nasro.org
Facebook, Twitter, RSS, Youtube
Joe Carter, President
Don Bridges, 1st Vice President
Bill West, 2nd Vice President
Jon Carrier, Secretary
Jennifer Thornton, Marketing Manager
A not-for-profit organization for school based law enforcement officers, school administrators, and school security/safety professionals working as partners to protect students, school faculty and staff and the schools they attend.

15294 National Association of Attorneys General
2030 M Street NW
8th Floor
Washington, DC 20036
202-326-6000; Fax: 202-331-1427
feedback@naag.org
www.naag.org
Facebook, Twitter
Jim McPherson, Executive Director
Theresia Heller, Chief Financial Officer
Janet Fernandes, Accounting Manager
Al Lama, Chief of Staff
Marjorie Tharp, Director of Communications
Founded to help Attorneys General fulfill the responsibilities of their office and to assist in the delivery of high quality legal services to the states and territorial jurisdictions.
Founded in 1907
Mailing list available for rent

15295 National Association of Chiefs of Police
6350 Horizon Drive
Titusville, FL 32780-8002
321-264-0911; Fax: 321-264-0033
policeinfo@aphf.org
www.aphf.org
Jamie Maynard, Director of Communications
Barry Shepherd, Executive Director
Debra Chitwood, Chief Financial Officer
Brent Shepherd, Director of Operations
The mission is to encourage through the leadership of persons who hold a command law enforcement or security position within the United States and her territories and possessions, educational activities and services to upgrade law enforcement and security on a professional level.
Founded in 1967
Mailing list available for rent

15296 National Association of Drug Court Professionals
1029 N. Royal St
Suite 201
Alexandria, VA 22314
703-575-9400; Fax: 703-706-0577
www.nadcp.org
Facebook, Twitter, YouTube, Instagram
West Huddleston, CEO
Meghan Wheeler, Project Director
Seeks to reduce substance abuse, crime and recidivism by promoting and advocating for the establishment and funding of Drug Courts and providing for collection and dissemination of information, technical assistance, and mutual support to association members.
Founded in 1997
Mailing list available for rent

15297 National Association of Field Training Officers
7942 W. Bell Rd.
Suite C5 #463
Glendale, AZ 85308
812-483-6588
info@nafto.org
www.nafto.org
Facebook, Twitter, RSS
Lt. Bob Smith, President
Officer Jeff Crippen, First VP
Sgt. Daniel Greene, Second VP
Sgt. Jeff Chapman, Executive Director
An educational and professional association concerned with apprenticeship and advance ongoing training for law enforcement, communications, and corrections personnel. Educators, administrators and other criminal justice practitioners are also encouraged to participate.

15298 National Association of Fleet Administrators
125 Village Boulevard
Suite 200,Princeton Forrestal Villa
Princeton, NJ 08540
609-720-0882; Fax: 609-452-8004
info@nafa.org
www.nafa.org
Facebook, Twitter, LinkedIn, Youtube, RSS
Charles A Gibbens, President
Gayle Pratt, Senior VP
Serving the needs of those managing fleets of automobiles, light duty trucks and/or vans for US and Canadian organizations. Offers statistical research, publications, including NAFA's Fleet Executive monthly magazine, regional meetings, government representation, conferences, trade shows and seminars.
2600+ Members
Mailing list available for rent

15299 National Association of Police Organizations
317 S Patrick St
Alexandria, VA 22314-3501
703-549-0775; Fax: 703-684-0515
info@napo.org
www.napo.org
Facebook, Twitter
Mick McHale, President
John Flynn, Vice President
William J. Johnson, Executive Director
Craig Lally, Executive Secretary
Sean Smoot, Treasurer
A coalition of police unions and associations from across the United States that serves to advance the interests of America's law enforcement officers through legislative and legal advocacy, political action and education.
241k Members
Founded in 1978
Mailing list available for rent

15300 National Black Police Association
3100 Main Street
#256
Dallas, TX 75226
855-879-6272; Fax: 202-986-0410
nationaloffice@blackpolice.org
www.blackpolice.org
Malik Aziz, Chairperson
Rochelle Bilal, Vice Chairperson
Carlos Bratcher, Sergeant at Arms
Sherri V. Lockett, Secretary
Donna Ross, Fiscal Officer
Law enforcement association to improve the relationship between Police Departments as institutions and the minority.
35000 Members
Founded in 1972

15301 National Burglar & Fire Alarm Association
2300 Valley View Lane
Suite 230
Irving, TX 75062-1733
214-260-5970
888-447-1689; Fax: 214-260-5979
www.alarm.org
Facebook, Twitter, Youtube
Merlin Guilbeau, Executive Director
Georgia Calaway, Communications/PR Director
Representing, promoting and enhancing the growth and professional development of the electronic life safety, security, and integrated systems industry. In cooperation with a federation of state associations, NBFAA provides government advocacy and delivers timely information, professional development tools, products and services that members use to grow and prosper their businesses.
Founded in 1948

15302 National Constables Association (NCA)
16 Stonybrook Drive
Levittown, PA 19055-2217
215-943-3110
800-292-1775; Fax: 215-943-0979
www.angelfire.com/la/nationalconstable
Hal Lefcourt APR, Executive Director
John Sindt, President
Leo Bullock, Secretary
Helping to preserve and clearly define the significant role of the constable in the delivery of justice system in the United States; to train, educate and upgrade the quality of performance of the constable; to serve as a clearing house for all positive actions to give a continued rebirth to the dignity, respect, status and duties and responsibilities of the position of constable as the heritage of the law enforcement community.
Founded in 1973

15303 National Correctional Industries Association
800 North Charles Street
Suite 550B
Baltimore, MD 21201
410-230-3972; Fax: 410-230-3981
memberservices@nationalcia.org
www.nationalcia.org
Facebook
Gina Honeycutt, Executive Director
Wil Heslop, Director of Operations
Karl Wiley, Accounting Manager
Rebekah Zinno, Sales and Marketing Manager
Farrah Marriott, Systems Coordinator
An affiliate body of the American Correctional Association, the Jail Industries Association and The Workman Fund. The mission is to promote excellence and credibility in correctional industries through professional development and innovative business solutions.
Founded in 1941
Mailing list available for rent

15304 National Crime Prevention Council
1201 Connecticut Avenue, NW
Suite 200
Washington, DC 20036
202-466-6272; Fax: 202-296-1356
webmaster@ncpc.org
www.ncpc.org
David A. Dean, Chairman
Robert F. Diegelman, Vice Chairman
Ann M. Harnkins, President/CEO
John P. Box, Treasurer
Jean Adnopoz, Secretary
Aids people in keeping themselves, their families, and their communities safe from crime.

NCPC produces tools that communities can use to learn crime prevention strategies, engage community members, and coordinate with local agencies.
136 Members
Founded in 1982
Mailing list available for rent

15305 National Crime and Punishment Learning Center
300 S 25th Ave
Hattiesburg, MS 39401-7301
228-447-0285; Fax: 228-896-8696
ncplc@crimeandpunishment.net
www.crimeandpunishment.net
William H Sanford, President/Founder
Provide free information on the most common crimes and their punishments in each state. The center is unique in its dedicated endeavor to accomplish this task by providing information to bridge the gap between the legal justice system and the American people.

15306 National Criminal Justice Association
720 7th St Nw
3rd Floor
Washington, DC 20001-3902
202-628-8550; Fax: 202-448-1723
info@ncja.org
www.ncja.org
Facebook, Twitter, LinkedIn, RSS
Jeanne Smith, President
Karhlton Moore, Vice President
Cabell Cropper, Executive Director
David Fredenburgh, Director of Program Services
Bethany Broida, Director of Communications
A national voice in shaping and implementing criminal justice policy since its founding. As the representative of state, tribal and local criminal and juvenile justice practitioners, the NCJA works to promote a balanced approach to communities' complex public safety and criminal and juvenile justice system problems.
Founded in 1971

15307 National Criminal Justice Reference Service
PO Box 6000
Rockville, MD 20849-6000
301-519-5500
800-851-3420
202-836-6998; Fax: 301-240-5830
www.ncjrs.gov
Facebook, Twitter, LinkedIn, RSS, Youtube, Google+, Vimeo,
Dolores Kozloski, Executive Director
A federally funded resource offering justice and substance abuse information to support research, policy, and program development worldwide.
Founded in 1972
Mailing list available for rent

15308 National District Attorneys Association
99 Canal Center Plz
Suite 330
Alexandria, VA 22314-1548
703-549-9222; Fax: 703-836-3195
berryb@co.yamhill.or.us
www.ndaa.org
Facebook, Twitter
William Fitzpatrick, President
Kay Chopard Cohen, Executive Director
Rick Hanes, Chief of Staff
Development resource for prosecutors at all levels of government. APRI has become a vital resource and national clearinghouse for information on the prosecutorial function. The Institute is committed to providing interdisciplinary responses to the complex problems of criminal justice. It is also committed to supporting the highest professional standards among officials entrusted with the crucial responsibility for public safety.
Founded in 1950

15309 National Drug Court Institute
1029 N. Royal St
Suite 201
Alexandria, VA 22314
703-575-9400; Fax: 703-575-9402
webmaster@nadcp.org
www.ndci.org
Facebook, Twitter, RSS, Youtube
Lars Levy, President
Milly Merrigan, President-Elect
Promote education, research and scholarship for drug court and other court-based intervention programs.

15310 National Drug Enforcement Officers Association
Drug Enforcement Administration
Office of Training/TRDS
FBI Academy, PO Box 1475
Quantico, VA 22134-1475
202-298-9653
paul.stevens@state.mn.us
www.ndeoa.org
Paul Stevens, President
Steve Peterson, First VP
NDEOA's purpose and objective is to promote the cooperation, education and exchange of information among all Law Enforcement Agencies involved in the enforcement of controlled substance laws.
Founded in 1970

15311 National Emergency Number Association
1700 Diagonal Road
Suite 500
Alexandria, VA 22314
202-466-4911; Fax: 202-618-6370
rhixson@nena.org
www.nena.orgÿ
Facebook, Twitter, YouTube
Christy Williams, President
Renee Hardwick, ENP, 1st Vice President
Rob McMullen, ENP, 2nd Vice President
Brian Fontes, Chief Executive Officer
Trey Forgety, Director of Government Affairs

15312 National Fire Protection Association
1 Batterymarch Park
Quincy, MA 02169-7471
617-770-3000
800-344-3555; Fax: 617-770-0700
www.nfpa.org
Facebook, Twitter, LinkedIn, Youtube, RSS, Google+, Flickr
Ernest J. Grant, RN, MSN, PhD, Chair
Randolph W. Tucker, First Vice Chair
Jim Pauley, President and CEO
Amy R. Acton, Secretary
Thomas A. Lawson, Treasurer
Mission is to reduce the worldwide burden of fire and other hazards on the quality of life by providing and advocating scientifically based concensus codes and standards, research, training, and education. Also serves as the world's leading advocate of fire prevention and is an authoritive source on public safety.
70000 Members
Founded in 1896

15313 National Gang Crime Research Center
Research Center
PO Box 990
Peotone, IL 60468-0090
708-258-9111; Fax: 708-258-9546
gangcrime@aol.com
www.ngcrc.com
George W Knox, Director
Research on gangs and gang members, disseminate information through publications and reports, and provide training and consulting services.
Founded in 1990

15314 National Institute of Justice
US Department Of Justice
810 7th Street NW
Washington, DC 20531
202-664-4000
800-851-3420; Fax: 202-307-6394
askncjrs@ncjrs.org
www.ojp.usdoj.gov
Facebook, Twitter, RSS, YouTube
Leigh Benda, Chief Financial Officer
Karol Virginia Mason, Assistant Attorney General
Phillip Merkle, Director
Mary Lou Leary, Principal Deputy Assistant Attorney
James H. Burch, II, Deputy Assistant Attorney General
Research, development and evaluation agency of the US department of Justice. Supports all those in the justice industry with education and training, publications and trade shows.
Mailing list available for rent

15315 National Insurance Crime Bureau
1111 E Touhy Ave
Suite 400
Des Plaines, IL 60018-5804
847-544-7002
800-447-6282; Fax: 708-544-7100
rjones@nicb.org
www.nicb.org
Facebook, Twitter, LinkedIn, Youtube
Joseph H. Wehrle, President/CEO
James K. Schweitzer, Senior Vice President
Daniel G. Abbott, Senior Vice President
Robert Jachnicki, Senior Vice President
Andrew J. Sosnowski, Senior Vice President
A not for profit organization that recieves support from approximately 1,000 property/casualty insurance companies. NICB partners with insurers and law enforcement agencies to facilitate the identification, detection and prosecution of insurance criminals.
1000 Members
Founded in 1992

15316 National Latino Peace Officers Association
PO Box 23116
23116
Santa Ana, CA 92711
nlpoamgr@gmail.com
www.nlpoa.com
Facebook
Andrew P Peralta, National President
Alfredo Dean, Vice President
Maria B. Thomas, Secretary
Cindy Rodriguez, Treasurer
Vicente Calderon, Founder
Founded in 1972

15317 National Native American Law Enforcement Association
PO Box 171
Washington, DC 20040

202-207-3065; Fax: 866-506-7631
www.nnalea.org

Joseph Wicks, President
Mark Murtha, Vice President
Gary Edwards, CEO
Dave Nichols, CFO
Daryll Davis, Senior Director

NNALEA is a nonprofit organization that promotes and fosters mutual cooperation between American Indian Law Enforcement Officers/Agents/Personnel, their agencies, tribes, private industry and public.
Founded in 1993

15318 National Organization for Victim Assistance
510 King St
Suite 424
Alexandria, VA 22314-3132

703-535-6682
800-879-6682; Fax: 703-535-5500
www.trynova.org
Facebook, Twitter, RSS

Will Marling, Executive Director
Claire Ponder Selib, Director of Education
James Gierke, Director of Victim Services
Deborah Baroch, Director of Finance and Operations
Barbara Kendall, Director of Training

A private, non-profit organization of victim and witness assistance programs and practitioners, criminal justice agencies and professionals, mental health professionals, researchers, former victims and survivors, and others committed to the recognition and implementation of victim rights and services.

15319 National Organization of Black Law Enforcement Executives
4609 Pinecrest Office Park Dr
Alexandria, VA 22312-1442

703-658-1529; Fax: 703-658-9479
jakers@noblenatl.org
www.noblenatl.org
Facebook, Twitter, LinkedIn, Tumblr, Stumbleupon, Pinterest

Gregory Thomas, National President
Perry Tarrant, National First Vice President
Clarence Cox, National Second Vice President
Hubert Bell, Treasurer
Thomas Nelson, National Recording Secretary

Ensure equity in the administration of justice in the provision of public service to all communities, and to serve as the conscience of law enforcement by being committed to justice by action.
Founded in 1976

15320 National Police Athletic/Activities League , Inc.
1662 N. US Highway 1
Suite C
Jupiter, FL 33469

561-745-5535; Fax: 561-745-3147
mdillhyon@nationalpal.org
www.nationalpal.org
Facebook, Twitter

Christopher Hill, President
Barbara Bonilla, 1st Vice President
Ronald Allen, 2nd Vice President
Donna Miller, 3rd Vice President
Frank Williams, Secretary

Exists to prevent juvenile crime and violence by providing civic, athletic, recreational, and educational opportunities and resources to PAL Chapters.
Founded in 1940

15321 National Police Bloodhound Association

president@npba.com
www.npba.com
Facebook

Doug Lowry, President
Roger G. Titus, Vice President
Kevin Osuch, Secretary
Coby Webb, Treasurer
Roger G. Titus, Training
Founded in 1966

15322 National Police Institute
Central Missouri State University
200 Ming Street
Warrensburg, MO

660-543-4090; Fax: 660-543-4709
www.theipti.org

Dr Mike Wiggins, Director

An internationally recognized police training center. Provides advanced police training in a number of areas as well as housing the Regional Police Academy.

15323 National Public Safety Information Bureau
PO Box 365
Stevens Point, WI 54481

715-345-2772
800-647-7579; Fax: 715-345-7288
info@safetysource.com
www.safetyresource.com

Steve Cywinski, President/Publisher
Ronald Tippel, VP Information Services
Laura Gross, VP Data Procurement
Celia Piesik, Data Procurement Specialist
Christina Scott, Data Procurement Specialist

Working hand in hand with law enforcement, fire and emergency departments to develop the most accurate database in the public safety industry with over 70,000 contacts. The result is; the most current and comprehensive reference tools available.
Founded in 1964

15324 National Public Safety Telecommunications Council
8191 Southpark Lane
Unit 205
Littleton, CO 80120-4641

407-836-9668
866-907-4755; Fax: 303-649-1844
support@npstc.org
www.npstc.org
Facebook, Twitter, LinkedIn, YouTube, Blogger

Don Root, Committee Vice Chair
Stu Overby, Committee Vice Chair
Marilyn Ward, Ecexutive Director
Charles Bryson, Outreach News Editor
Mark Grubb, Participant Development Coordinator

NPSTC is a federation of associations representing public safety telecommunications. They follow up on the recommendations of the Public Safety Wireless Advisory Committee.
Founded in 1997
Mailing list available for rent

15325 National Reserve Law Officers Association
PO Box 6505
San Antonio, TX 78209

210-805-8917; Fax: 210-653-9655

Capt. Chuck Mantkus, Director of Training

Provides members with training information and services plus the best, most extensive, and lowest cost in-line-of-duty accidental insurance coverage available.

15326 National Safety Council
1121 Spring Lake Dr
Itasca, IL 60143-3201

630-285-1121
800-621-7615; Fax: 630-285-1434
www.nsc.org
RSS

John P. Surma, Chairman
Deborah Hersman, President & CEO
Patrick Phelan, Chief Financial Officer
Shay Gallagher, Vice President, General Manager
Michael Pollock, VP, Relationship Management

Provides information sharing opportunities, continuing education and professional fellowship to people with environmental health and safety responsibilities in higher education.
936 Members
Founded in 1912
Mailing list available for rent

15327 National Sheriffs' Association
1450 Duke St
Alexandria, VA 22314-3490

703-836-7827
800-424-7827; Fax: 703-683-5349
jthompson@sheriffs.org
www.sheriffs.org
Facebook, Twitter, LinkedIn, Googe+

Aaron D. Kennard, Executive Director
John Thompson, Chief of Staff and Deputy Executive
Fred G. Wilson, Director of Operations
Ed Hutchison, Director of Traffic Safety & Triad
Greg J. MacDonald, Director of Homeland Security

Devoted to helping sheriffs and other law enforcers to execute their duties most effectively and professionally.
21M Members
Founded in 1940
Mailing list available for rent: 3M names

15328 National Tactical Officers Association
PO Box 797
Doylestown, PA 18901

215-230-7552
800-279-9127; Fax: 215-230-7552
membership@ntoa.org
www.ntoa.org
Facebook, Twitter

Deputy Chief Bo Chabali, Board Chairman
Mark Lomax, Executive Director
Rob Cartner, Director of Training
Corey Luby, Marketing Director
Marsha Martello, Membership Coordinator

Enhance the performance and professional status of law enforcement personnel by providing a credible and proven training resource, as well as a forum for the development of tactics and information exchange. The Association's ultimate goal is to improve public safety and domestic security through training, education, and tactical excellence.
32000 Members
Founded in 1983

15329 National Technical Investigators Association (NATIS)
1069 West Broad Street
Box 757
Falls Church, VA 22046

703-237-9338
800-966-2842

770-485-1820; Fax: 703-832-2600
admin@natia.org

Michael Woods, President

The purpose of NATIA is to further knowledge, develop skills and promote fellowship between those law enforcement and intelligence professionals who support their agencies' and departments' technical surveillance, tactical operations, and forensic activities.

15330 **National United Law Enforcement Officers**
256 E McLemore Avenue
Memphis, TN 38106-2833

901-774-1118; Fax: 901-774-1139

Clyde Venson, Executive Director
Samantha Macklin, Secretary

Protects the needs and interests of persons in the law enforcement industry.
5000 Members
Founded in 1969

15331 **National White Collar Crime Center**
10900 Nuckols Rd
Suite 325
Glen Allen, VA 23060-9288

804-967-6200
Facebook, Twitter, Youtube

Don Brackman, Director
Ken Brooks, Deputy Director

Through a combination of training and critical support services, law enforcement agencies are given the skills and resources they need to tackle emerging economic and cyber crime problems.
Mailing list available for rent

15332 **Naval Criminal Investigative Services**
27130 Telegraph Road
Suite 2000
Quantico, VA 22134

202-433-8800; Fax: 724-794-3293
www.ncis.navy.mil

Andrew L. Traver, Director
John Beattie, Senior Intelligence Officer
Mark D. Ridley, Deputy Director
Rod Baldwin, Executive Assistant Director
Charlton Howard, Chief Intelligence Officer

Primary law enforcement and counterintelligence arm of the United States Department of the Navy. It works closely with other local, state, federal and foreign agencies to counter and investigate the most serious crimes.

15333 **Organized Crime Task Force**
The Capitol
Albany, NY 12224-0341

518-474-7330; Fax: 914-422-8795
www.ag.ny.gov

John Amodeo, Assistant Attorney General
Colleen Glavin, Public Integrity Officer

A forum that brings government, law enforcement and a range of agencies together to set priorities for tackling organized crime.
Founded in 1970

15334 **Park Law Enforcement Association**

Home Page: www.myparkranger.org

Tom Wakolbinger, President
William Westerfield, Vice President
Dale Steele, Secretary
Capt. Carl Nielsen, Executive Director
Steve Newsom, Treasurer
Founded in 1979

15335 **Police & Firemen's Insurance Association**
101 E 116th St
Carmel, IN 46032-5629

317-581-1913
800-221-7342; Fax: 317-571-5946
www.pfia.net

Mark Kemp, President
Jeanie Williams, Operations VP

Mission of the association is to create and operate a Supreme Lodge and Subordinate Branches for the purpose of inculcating principles of friendship and brotherhood among police officers and fire fighters. Providing financial assistance to its members through disability certificates and pay final expenses for members with legal reserve life insurance policies.

15336 **Police Executive Research Forum**
1120 Connecticut Ave NW
Suite 930
Washington, DC 20036-3951

202-466-7820; Fax: 202-466-7826
www.policeforum.org

Chief J. Scott Thomson, President
Chief Tom Manger, VP
Chief Robert White, Secretary
Chief Roberto Villase□or, Treasurer
Shannon Branly, Deputy Chief of Staff

A national membership organization of progressive police executives from the largest city, county and state law enforcement agencies. Dedicated to improving policing and advancing professionalism through research and involvement in public policy debate.
100 Members
Founded in 1976
Mailing list available for rent

15337 **Police Foundation**
1201 Connecticut Ave NW
Suite 200
Washington, DC 20036-2636

202-833-1460; Fax: 202-659-9149
info@policefoundation.org
www.policefoundation.org
Facebook, Twitter, RSS, Google+, YouTube

Weldon J. Rougeau, Chairman
Chief Jim Bueermann, President
Karen L. Amendola, PhD, Chief Behavioral Scientist
Tari Lewis, CPA, Chief Financial Officer
Blake Norton, VP/COO

A national, nonpartisan, nonprofit organization dedicated to supporting innovation and improvement in policing through its research and evaluation, technical assistance, training, technology, professional services, and communication programs.
Founded in 1970
Mailing list available for rent

15338 **Public Safety Diving Association**

904-743-3025

David Scoggins, President
Mark Reese, Director
Founded in 1972

15339 **Public Services Health and Safety Association**
4950 Yonge Street
Suite 902
Toronto, ON M2N 6K1

416-250-2131
877-250-7444; Fax: 416-250-7484
elearning@pshsa.ca
www.pshsa.ca

Michael Papadakis, Chair
Thomas Hayes, Vice Chair
Ron Kelusky, CEO
Joanne Clark, Director, Marketing and Comm.
Susan Sun, Director, Finance & Administration
Founded in 2009

15340 **Reserve Police Officers Association**
89 Rockland Ave
Yonkers, NY 10705

800-326-9416
800-326-9416; Fax: 212-555-1234

Brooke Webster, President

Dedicated to the support of law enforcement with an emphasis on the role of the reserve and auxiliary law enforcement officer.
Founded in 1996

15341 **Texas Department of Public Safety Officer's Association**
5821 Airport Boulevard
Austin, TX 78752

512-451-0571
800-933-7762; Fax: 512-451-0709
www.dpsoa.com
Facebook, Twitter, RSS, Google+, Tumblr

Sgt. Gary Chandler, President
Lt. Jimmy Jackson, VP
John M. Pike, Executive Director
Trooper Clay Taylor, Secretary/Treasurer
Patti Benson, Membership Services

Offers and executes programs that benefit Texas Troppers and the communitites around them. Also publishes DPSOA a quarterly magazine.
2650 Members
Founded in 1974

15342 **The Association of Certified Fraud Specialists**
4600 Northgate Blvd.
Suite 105
Sacramento, CA 95834

916-419-6319; Fax: 916-419-6318
headquarters@acfsnet.org
www.acfsnet.org
Facebook, LinkedIn

Bill Cramer, President
Mark Menz, National Vice President
Charles Raborn, Executive Director
Jeremy Krater, Information Technology Specialist
Brittany Cyrus, Graphic Designer
Founded in 1993

15343 **The Commission on Accreditation forÿLaw Enforcement Agencies**
13575 Heathcote Boulevard
Suite 320
Gainesville, VI 20155

703-352-4225; Fax: 703-890-3126
jgregory@calea.org
www.calea.org
Facebook, Twitter, LinkedIn, Reddit, Google+, Tumblr

J. Grayson Robinson, President
Craig Webre, Vice-President
W. Craig Hartley, Jr., Executive Director
Richard Myers, Secretary
Gary Margolis, Treasurer

15344 **The Federal Law Enforcement Associationÿ**
7945 MacArthur Blvd
Suite 201
Cabin John, MD 20818

202-870-5503
866-553-5362
fleoa@fleoa.org
www.fleoa.org
Facebook, Twitter, Reddit, Google+, Tumblr

Jon Adler, National President
Nate Catura, Executive Vice President
Chris Schoppmeyer, Vice President - Agency

Affairs
Frank Terreri, Vice President- Legislative Affairs
Enid Febus, National Secretary
Founded in 1977

15345 **The International Association of Chiefs of Police**
44 Canal Center Plaza
Suite 200
Alexandria, VA 22314
703-836-6767
www.theiacp.org
Facebook, Twitter, LinkedIn, YouTube
Richard Beary, President
Vincent Talucci, Executive Director/CEO
Gwen Boniface, Deputy Executive Director
John Firman, Director of Strategic Partnerships
Jacqueline Gooding, Director of Human Resources
Founded in 1893

15346 **The Monitoring Association**
8150 Leesburg Pike
Suite 700
Vienna, VA 22182
703-242-4670; Fax: 703-242-4675
communications@tma.us
www.csaaintl.org
Facebook, Twitter, LinkedIn, RSS
Celia Trigo Besore, Executive Director
Represents companies offering security (alarm) monitoring systems through a central station. It also represents companies that provide services and products to the industry.
300+ Members
Founded in 1950

15347 **TheÿAssociationÿofÿPublic-Safety Communications Officials**
351 N. Williamson Blvd
Daytona Beach, FL 32114-1112
386-322-2500; Fax: 386-322-2501
apco@apcointl.org
www.apcointl.org
Facebook, Twitter
Brent Lee, President
Cheryl J. Greathouse, RPL, First Vice President
Martha K. Carter, ENP, Second Vice President
Gigi Smith, Immediate Past President
Derek Poarch, Executive Director
Founded in 1982

15348 **Transportation Research Board National Research Council**
500 Fifth Stret NW
Washington, DC 20001
202-334-2934; Fax: 202-334-2003
www.trb.org
Facebook, Twitter, LinkedIn, RSS, Blogger, Pinterest, Tumbl
Neil Pedersen, Executive Director
Rosa Allen, Administrative Coordinator
Stephen J. Andrle, Deputy Director
Javy Awan, Director, Publications
Terri M. Baker, Senior Program Assistant
A division of the National Research Council, which serves as an independent advisor to the federal government and others on scientific and technical questions of national importance.

15349 **Transportation Technology Center**
55500 DOT Rd.
Pueblo, CO 81001-0130
719-584-0750; Fax: 719-584-0711
ttci_marketing@ttci.aar.com
www.aar.com
Facebook, Twitter, Youtube
Roy Allen, Manager
Michele Johnson, Administrative Assistant
Mark Nordling, Assistant Director Business
Ron Lang, Manager Business Development
Michele Johnson, Executive Assistant
A wholly owned subsidiary of the Association of American Railroads. TTCI is a world-class transportation research and testing organization, providing emerging technology solutions for the railway industry throughout North America and the world.

15350 **U.S. First Responders Association**
Panama City, FL
520-907-2153
Corporate@usfra.org
www.usfra.org
Facebook, Twitter, LinkedIn, RSS
Traycee Biancamano, CEO & President
Janet Liebsch, Executive Vice President
Capt. D. Lewis, Vice President
Bobby Biancamano, Secretary/Treasurer
A professional and social network of first responders including firefighters, EMS, rescue, police, military, and civilian support teams.

15351 **United States Conference of Mayors**
1620 Eye St NW
Washington, DC 20006
202-293-7330; Fax: 202-293-2352
www.usmayors.org
Facebook, Twitter
Mayor Stephanie Rawlings-Blake, President
Mick Cornett, VP
Mitchell J. Landrieu, Second Vice President
Tom Cochran, CEO and Executive Director
An organization of city government officials whose primary roles are to promote the development of effective national urban/suburban policy; strengthen federal-city relationships; ensure that federal policy meets urban needs; provide mayors with leadership and management tools; and create a forum in which mayors can share ideas and information.
Founded in 1932

15352 **United States Deputy Sheriff's Association**
2909 S Spruce
Wichita, KS 67216
316-263-2583
info@usdeputy.org
www.usdeputy.org
Facebook, Twitter, YouTube
David Hinners, Executive Director/National Trainer
Mike Willis, Law Enf. Prog. Coord.
Laura Rainwater, Comms. and Publ. Rels. Dir.
Organization dedicated to the support and training of underfunded law enforcement agencies.
Founded in 1995

15353 **United States Police Canine Association**
PO Box 80
Springboro, OH 45066
937-751-6469
800-531-1614
uspcadir@aol.com
www.uspcak9.com
Facebook
Russ Hess, Executive Director
Kevin Johnson, President
Melinda Roupp, Secretary
James Matarese, Treasurer
Nonprofit organization striving for the establishment of minimum standards for Police K-9 dogs through proper methods of training. Police K-9 dogs, properly trained and handled, give Law Enforcement officers one of the finest non-lethal aids in the prevention and detection of crime.
Founded in 1971

Newsletters

15354 **American Academy of Forensic Sciences Academy Newsfeed**
American Academy of Forensic Sciences
410 N. 21st Street
Colorado Springs, CO 80904
719-636-1100; Fax: 719-636-1993
awarren@aafs.org
www.aafs.org
Anne Warren, Executive Director
Zeno J. Geradts, PhD., President
Jeri D. Ropero-Miller, PhD., President-Elect
Carl R. McClary, BA, Vice President
Susan M. Ballou, MS, Past President
An online newsletter for members that includes industry news, announcements, job postings, and more.
Frequency: Monthly
Founded in 1948

15355 **CGAA Signals**
Central Station Alarm Association
8150 Leesburg Pike
Suite 700
Vienna, VA 22182-2721
703-242-4670; Fax: 703-242-4675
communications@csaaul.org
www.csaaul.org
Facebook, Twitter, LinkedIn
Stephen P Doyle, Executive VP/CEO
Celia Besore, VP Marketing & Programs
Robert R. Bean, President
Jay Hauhn, First Vice President
Peter Lowitt, Secretary
300+ Members
Frequency: Quarterly
Circulation: 1200
Founded in 1950
Mailing list available for rent

15356 **Correctional Education Bulletin**
LRP Publications
747 Dresher Road Suite 500
PO Box 980
Horsham, PA 19044
215-784-0912
800-341-7874; Fax: 215-784-9639
webmaster@lrp.com
www.lrp.com
Kim Yablonski, Editor
Combines and analyzes corrections education issues and management topics. You'll learn how educators are coping with shrinking budgets and the growing number of youths being sentenced as adults. Expert analysis of current legal issues and the latest regulatory updates given.
Cost: $125.00
Frequency: Monthly
Founded in 1977

15357 **Corrections Professional**
LRP Publications
PO Box 980
Horsham, PA 19044
215-840-0912
800-341-7874; Fax: 215-784-9639
webmaster@lrp.com
www.lrp.com
Debi Pelletier, Editor
Kenneth Kahn, President
Tracks innovative strategies, proven techniques and legal developments impacting correction facilities across the country. Gives profiles of other professionals and their institutions, giving an opportunity to learn from their experiences and avoid costly mistakes. Contains Q-A section that

addresses difficult situations.
Cost: $210.00
Frequency: 104 issues per
Founded in 1977

15358 Criminal Justice Newsletter
Pace Publications
443 Park Ave S
New York, NY 10016-7322

212-685-5450; Fax: 212-679-4701

Sid Goldstein, Publisher
Craig Fischer, Editor
Peter Kiers, Executive Director

Independent publication providing system-wide perspective of law enforcement.
Cost: $219.00
Frequency: BiWeekly

15359 Emergency Preparedness News
Business Publishers
2222 Sedwick Dr
Suite 101
Durham, NC 27713

800-223-8720; Fax: 800-508-2592
custserv@bpinews.com
www.bpinews.com

Dedicated solely to disaster management: from securing pre-disaster mitigation and counter terrorism funds, to staying prepared for hurricanes, terrorist threats, fires, floods and other natural disasters.
Cost: $327.00

15360 FEMSA News
Fire & Emergency Manufacturers & Services Assn.
P.O. Box 147
Lynnfield, MA 01940-0147

781-334-2771; Fax: 781-334-2771
info@femsa.org
www.femsa.org

William Van Lent, President
James Long, Vice President

Member newsletter.
Frequency: 2x/Year

15361 FLEOA Newsletter
Federal Law Enforcement Officers Association
PO Box 326
Lewisberry, PA 17339-2900

717-938-2300; Fax: 717-932-2262
fleoa@fleoa.org
www.fleoa.org
Facebook, Twitter

Jon Adler, National President
Nate Catura, National Executive VP

Federal newsletter offering information, legislative updates and news for law enforcement officers nationwide.
12 Pages
Circulation: 2400
Founded in 1976

15362 HOPE Magazine
Concerns of Police Survivors
846 Old South 5
PO Box 3199
Camdenton, MO 65020

573-346-4911; Fax: 573-346-1414
cops@nationalcops.org
www.concernsofpolicesurvivors.org

Dianne Bernhard, Executive Director
Shelley Jones, Director Of Operations

Providing resources and services that help rebuild the shattered lives of surviving families and co-workers affected by line-of-duty death.
Frequency: 3x/year

15363 Journal of the American Association of Forensic Dentists
1000 N Avenue
Waukegan, IL 60085

847-223-5077
www.andent.net
RSS

Quarterly journal that brings forensic dental knowledge not only to dentists and their staff, but also to anthropologists, attorneys and law enforcement personnel.
Cost: $8.00
Frequency: Quarterly
Founded in 1978

15364 Keepers' Voice
International Association of Correctional Officers
PO Box 53
Chicago, IL 60690

312-996-5401; Fax: 312-413-0458

Jim Clark, Publisher
Jess Maghan, Editor

Of special interest to correctional officers because it focuses on current developments in the field, including practical, day-to-day training topics, current legislation, resources, conference notices and job openings.

15365 Law Enforcement Legal Publications
421 Ridgewood Avenue
Suite 100
Glen Ellyn, IL 60137-4900

630-858-6092; Fax: 630-858-6392
lelp@xnet.com
www.lelp.com

James Manak, Publisher/President

Publication for law enforcement, legal professional civil liability, personnel law, labor law, criminal law and law libraries.
ISSN: 1070-9967
Founded in 1970
Printed in 3 colors on newsprint stock

15366 Law Enforcement Legal Review
Law Enforcement Legal Publications
421 Ridgewood Avenue
Suite 100
Glen Ellyn, IL 60137-4900

630-858-6392; Fax: 630-858-6392
lelp@xnet.com
www.lelp.com/

James Manak, Publisher
Glen Manak, VP Marketing

Case reporter for law enforcement, legal profession and law libraries, covering criminal law, civil liability and personnel law.
Cost: $98.00
16 Pages
Frequency: Bi-monthly
Circulation: 500
ISSN: 1070-9967
Founded in 1975

15367 Legal Employment Weekly Law Bulletin Publishing Company
415 N State Street
Chicago, IL 60610-4674

312-644-7800; Fax: 312-644-1215
editor@lbpc.com
www.lawbulletin.com

Bernard Judge, Publisher
Stephen Brown, Managing Editor
Lanning Macfarland, Chairman

Legal employment opportunities.
Frequency: Weekly
Founded in 1854
Printed in 2 colors on newsprint stock

15368 National Constables Association Newsletter
National Constables Association
PO Box 1172
Haverhill, MA 01831-1572

978-373-5234
800-272-1775; Fax: 978-373-1191
mike@constables.com
www.constables.com

Hal Lefcourt, Executive Director
John Sindt, President

A newsletter published for the members of National Constables Association.
4 Pages
Frequency: Quarterly
Printed in one color on glossy stock

15369 Police Executive Research Forum
1120 Connecticut Avenue NW
Suite 930
Washington, DC 20036

202-466-7820; Fax: 202-466-7826
www.policeforum.org

Chuck Wexler, Executive Director
Chief John Timoney, VP
Daniel Woods, Research Associate
Jessica Toliver, Deputy Director
Raquel Rodriguez, Accounting Manager

Members are chief executives of city, county and state police agencies. Membership dues are general $300.00, subscribing $125.00.
Cost: $35.00
Frequency: Monthly
Circulation: 1000
Founded in 1977
Mailing list available for rent

15370 Signal
American Traffic Safety Services Association
15 Riverside Parkway
Suite 100
Fredericksburg, VA 22406-1022

540-368-1701
800-272-8772; Fax: 540-368-1717
www.atssa.com

James Baron, Communications Director
Douglas Danko, Chairman

Covers legislative updates, industry news and meeting information, as well as other items of interest to the roadway safety industry as is a full-color publication.
Frequency: Quarterly
Mailing list available for rent

15371 Women Police
International Association of Women Police
PO Box 690418
Tulsa, OK 74169

918-234-6445
jvanland@aol.com
www.iawp.org/

Mona Moore, Publisher
Kim Covert, Treasurer

Accepts advertising.
Cost: $25.00
50 Pages
Frequency: Quarterly

Magazines & Journals

15372 Air Beat Magazine
Airborne Law Enforcement Association

50 Carroll Creek Way
Suite 260
Frederick, MD 21701-4786

301-631-2406; Fax: 301-631-2466
www.alea.org

Steven Ingley, Executive Director
Kevin R. Caffery, VP
Nicole Gentile, Operations Manager
Keith Johnson, Safety Program Director
Carrie Cosens, Membership Manager

Dedicated to Airborne Law Enforcement. The subscription also includes the annual Buyer's Guide and special Convention issue with membership.
Cost: $40.00
3500 Members
Frequency: Bi-Monthly
Circulation: 6500
Founded in 1968

15373 **Campus Safety Journal**
Bricepac
12228 Venice Boulevard
PO Box 66515
Los Angeles, CA 90066

310-390-5277; Fax: 310-390-4777

John Van Horn, Publisher
Tom Nelson, Managing Editor
Wendy Rackley, Production Manager

Provides a vehicle for communicating campus safety and security issues to all interested parties at the middle, secondary, college and university levels.
40 Pages
Frequency: Monthly
Circulation: 20100
Founded in 1992
Printed in 4 colors on glossy stock

15374 **Contingency Planning & Recovery Journal**
Management Advisory Services & Publications
PO Box 81151
Wellesley Hills, MA 02481-0001

781-235-2895; Fax: 781-235-5446
www.masp.com/

An independent, subscription supported to all issues of contingency planning, disaster recovery and business continuity. Includes tutorial extensive literature review on the fields of business continuity.
Cost: $75.00
Frequency: Quarterly
Founded in 1972
Printed in on glossy stock

15375 **Corrections Today**
4380 Forbes Boulevard
Lanham, MD 20706

301-918-1800
800-222-5646; Fax: 301-918-1900
customerservice@corrections.com
www.corrections.com/aca

Susan Clayton, Editor
Gwendolyn C Chunn, President
Harry Wilhelm, Marketing Manager
Alice Heiserman, Publications and Research Manager

Published by the American Correctional Association.
Cost: $25.00
200 Pages
Circulation: 20000
Founded in 1870
Mailing list available for rent

15376 **Credit Card Crime, Law Enforcement Kit**
9770 S Military Trail
Suite 380
Boynton Beach, FL 33436-4011

561-737-8700; Fax: 561-737-5800

Larry Schwartz, Editor

Ways to catch and punish the thieves, including corporate support of police, reverse sting operations, paying informants. Case histories, specific recommendations.
Cost: $59.95
ISBN: 0-914801-05-8
Founded in 1982

15377 **Crime & Delinquency**
Sage Publications
2455 Teller Rd
Newbury Park, CA 91320-2234

805-499-9774
800-818-7243; Fax: 805-499-0871
info@sagepub.com
www.sagepub.com

Blaise R Simqu, CEO
Janice Denehy, Executive Editor

Offers information to probation and parole executives as well as criminologists and lawyers.
Cost: $105.00
Frequency: Quarterly
Circulation: 3250
Founded in 1965
Mailing list available for rent

15378 **Fluid Power Journal**
Fluid Power Safety Institute
2170 South 3140 West
West Valley City, UT 84119

801-908-5456; Fax: 801-908-5734
art@fluidpowerjournal.com
fluidpowerjournal.com
Facebook, Twitter, LinkedIn

Paul Prass, Co-Founder
Lisa Prass, Co-Founder
Robert McKinney, Associate Publisher
Gerald Irving, Editor
Dan Helgerson, Technical Editor

Resource for fluid power professionals. The journal contains reports and news on the fluid power industry, including information about hydraulic, pneumatic, vacuum and motion control products.

15379 **Journal of Forensic Sciences**
Wiley Subscription Services, Inc.
American Academy of Forensic Sciences
410 N. 21st Street
Colorado Springs, CO 80904

719-636-1100; Fax: 719-636-1993
www.aafs.org

Brenda K. Peat, Managing Editor
Anne Warren, Executive Director
Zeno J. Geradts, Phd., President
Carl R. McClary, BA, Vice President
Jeri D. Ropero-Miller, PhD., President-Elect

The official publication of the American Academy of Forensic Sciences (AAFS). It is devoted to the publication of original investigations, observations, scholarly inquiries, and reviews in the various branches of the forensic sciences.
Frequency: Bi-Monthly
ISSN: 0022-1198
Founded in 1948

15380 **Justice Quarterly**
Academy of Criminal Justice Sciences
7339 Hanover Parkway
Suite A
Greenbelt, MD 20770

301-446-6300
800-757-2257; Fax: 401-446-2819
info@acjs.org
www.acjs.org

Dr. Cassia Spohn, Editor

The official ACJS journal offering articles of professional insight and industry news on crime and criminal justice.
Frequency: 6 times a year
ISSN: 0741-8825

15381 **Law Enforcement Legal Review**
Law Enforcement Legal Publications
421 Ridgewood Avenue
Suite 100
Glen Ellyn, IL 60137-4900

630-858-6392; Fax: 630-858-6392
lelp@xnet.com
home.xnet.com/~lelp

James Manak, President
Glen P Manak, VP Marketing

Civil liability, driminal law and personnel law case reporter for law enforcement, legal professional and law libraries.
Cost: $98.00
Circulation: 1000
ISSN: 1070-9967
Founded in 1970
Printed in on n stock

15382 **Law Enforcement Product News**
100 Garfield Street
2nd Floor
Denver, CO 80206

303-322-6400
800-291-3911; Fax: 303-322-0627
www.law-enforcement.com

Michael George, Publisher
Jeannine Heinecke, Editor
Paul Mackler, CEO
Chuck Cummings, Sales Manager
Circulation: 57000
Founded in 1966

15383 **Law Enforcement Technology**
Cygnus Publishing
PO Box 803
Fort Atkinson, WI 53538-0803

920-000-1111; Fax: 920-563-1699
Patrick.Bernardo@cygnuspub.com

John French, CEO
Scott Cravens, Circulation Director
Gordon Gavin, VP
Ronnie Garrett, Editor
Kathy Scott, Director of Public Relations

Covers the innovative products and technology available to the law enforcement manager. Accepts advertising.
64 Pages
Frequency: Monthly
Circulation: 30,000
Founded in 1966

15384 **Law and Order**
Hendon
130 Waukegan Rd
Deerfield, IL 60015-4912

847-444-3300
800-843-9764; Fax: 847-444-3333
info@hendonpub.com
hendonpub.com

Henry Kingwill, Owner
Bruce Cameron, Editor
Pete Kingwill, National Director
Yesenia Salcedo, Managing Editor
Tim Davis, Graphic Designer

Tailored to the law enforcement officer, the magazine updates professionals on trends, covers new methods and incorporates articles with spe-

cial focuses.
Cost: $24.00
100 Pages
Frequency: Monthly
Circulation: 32304
Founded in 1953

15385 **National Fire Protection Association Newsletter**
1 Batterymarch Park
Quincy, MA 02169-7471
617-770-3000
800-344-3555; Fax: 617-770-0700
www.nfpa.org
James M. Shannon, President/CEO
Peg O'Brien, Administrator - Public Affairs
Lorraine VP - Communications, Executive Director
Bruce Mullen, CFO
Paul Crossman, VP, Marketing
Written for various fire safety professionals and covers major topics in fire protection and suppression. The Journal carries investigation reports written by NFPA specialists, special NFPA statistical studies on large-loss fires, multiple deaths, fire fighter deaths and injuries, and others annually. Articles on fire protection advances, public education and information of interest to NFPA members.
Cost: $135.00
70000 Members
Circulation: 85000
Founded in 1896

15386 **Peace Officer**
Dale Corporation
22150 W 9 Mile Road
Southfield, MI 48034
248-204-2244; Fax: 248-204-2240
Dale Jabolonski, President
Covers areas of interest to law enforcement personnel.
Cost: $12.00
40 Pages
Founded in 1958

15387 **Perspectives Journal**
American Probation and Parole Association
PO Box 11910
Lexington, KY 40578-1910
859-244-8203; Fax: 859-244-8001
appa@csg.org
www.appa-net.org
Facebook, Twitter, LinkedIn
Carl Wicklund, Executive Director
Barbara Broderick, President
Diane Kincaid, Deputy Director
Carrie Abner, Research Associate
John Higgins, Graphic Designer
Mailing list includes mailing addresses only, no email
Frequency: Quarterly
Circulation: 2200
Mailing list available for rent: 2200 names

15388 **Police**
Bobit Publishing Company
3520 Challenger St
Torrance, CA 90503-1640
310-533-2400; Fax: 310-533-2500
webmaster@bobit.com
www.bobit.com
Edward J Bobit, CEO
The law officer's magazine. Accepts advertising.
Cost: $35.00
104 Pages
Frequency: Monthly
Circulation: 50000
Founded in 1961

15389 **Police Chief**
International Association of Chiefs of Police
515 N Washington St
Alexandria, VA 22314-2340
703-836-6767
800-843-4227; Fax: 703-836-4543
www.theiacp.org
Facebook, Twitter, RSS, Youtube
Dan Rosenblatt, Executive Director
Mark L. Whitman, Chair Commissioner
A monthly magazine published by the International Association of Chiefs of Police.
Cost: $25.00
80 Pages
Frequency: Monthly
Circulation: 21300
Founded in 1893
Mailing list available for rent

15390 **Police Times**
American Federation of Police & Concerned Citizens
6350 Horizon Drive
Titusville, FL 32780
321-264-0911; Fax: 321-573-9819
policeinfo@aphf.org
www.aphf.org
Facebook
Barry Shepard, Executive Director
Deputy Dennis Wise, National President
Debra Chitwood, CEO
Brent Shephard, Director of Operations
Quarterly publication focusing on law enforcement, security and police survivors.
Circulation: 31,000
Founded in 1978

15391 **Public Safety Communications/APCO Bulletin**
Assn of Public Safety Communication Officials
351 N Williamson Boulevard
Daytona Beach, FL 32114-1112
386-322-2500
888-272-6911; Fax: 386-322-2501
apco@apcointl.org
https://www.apcointl.org/about-apco/current-annual-report/past-re
Toni Edwards, Editor
George S Rice Jr, President
Susan Stowell, Member Services Director
Garry Mendez, Marketing/Communications Director
Robert Gurss Esq., Legal/Government Affairs Director
The world's oldest and largest professional organization dedicated to the enhancement of public safety communications and to serving its more than 15,000 members, the people who use public safety communications systems and services.
Cost: $12.00
Frequency: Monthly
Circulation: 13000
ISSN: 1526-1646
Founded in 1935

15392 **Public Safety Product News**
Cygnus Publishing
PO Box 803
Fort Atkinson, WI 53538-0803
920-000-1111
800-547-7377; Fax: 920-563-1699
Patrick.Bernardo@cygnusB2B.com
John French, CEO
Sharon Haberkorn, Development Manager
Ronnie Garrett, Editor-in-Chief
Kathy Scott, Director of Public Relations
Paul Bonaiuto, CFO
Frequency: Monthly

15393 **Sheriff**
National Sherriff's Association
1450 Duke St
Alexandria, VA 22314-3490
703-836-7827
800-424-7827; Fax: 703-836-6541
nsamail@sheriffs.org
www.sheriffs.org
Suzanne Kitts, Editor
Aaron Kennard, President
Thomas N Faust, Executive Director
Published for the law enforcement official.
Cost: $25.00
Circulation: 20,000
Founded in 1948

15394 **Tactical Edge**
National Tactical Officers Association
PO Box 797
Doylestown, PA 18901
215-230-7616
800-279-9127; Fax: 215-230-7552
membership@ntoa.org
www.ntoa.org
Facebook, Twitter, LinkedIn, Google+, Blogger, Bloggy, Pint
Phil Hansen, Board Chairman
Jim Torkar, Treasurer
Bob Chabali, Secretary
Mark Lomax, Executive Director
Rob Cartner, Director of Training
Cost: $40.00
Frequency: Quarterly
Circulation: 12000
Mailing list available for rent

15395 **Today's Policeman**
Towerhigh Productions
PO Box 875108
Los Angeles, CA 90087-208
Donald Mack, President
General philosophy of the police services.
Cost: $9.00
40 Pages
Founded in 1961

Trade Shows

15396 **APCO Annual Conference & Expo**
351 N Williamson Boulevard
Daytona Beach, FL 32114-1112
386-322-2500
888-272-6911; Fax: 386-322-2501
apco@apcointl.org
www.apcointl.org/
Barbara Myers, Director Conference Services
Casey Epton Roush, Conference/Meeting Services Manager
Brigid Blaschak, Tradeshow Manager
Patricia Giannini, Senior Meeting Coordinator
Garry Mendez, Marketing/Communications Director
APCO's Annual Conference and Exposition brings together more than 300 vendors to provide hands-on demonstrations of new technologies you might use in your agency or call centers. The Conference also offers sessions on personal and professional development and a variety of technical skills. Banquet, breakfast and exhibitors of radio, computer, and supporting equipment companies.
6000 Attendees
Frequency: Annual
Founded in 1935

15397 **Academy of Criminal Justice Sciences Annual Meeting**
Academy of Criminal Justice Sciences

7339 Hanover Parkway
Suite A
Greenbelt, MD 20770
301-446-6300
800-757-2257; Fax: 401-446-2819
info@acjs.org
www.acjs.org
Lorenzo M. Boyd, President
Nicole Leeper Piquero, First-Vice President
Faith Lutze, Second Vice-President
L. Edward Day, Treasurer
Criminal justice educators, researchers, practicioners, students and the general public visit 45 exhibits and seminars.
2000 Attendees
Frequency: Annual
Founded in 1963

15398 **Airborne Law Enforcement Annual Conference & Expo**
Airborne Law Enforcement Association
50 Carroll Creek Way
Suite 260
Frederick, MD 21701-4786
301-631-2406; Fax: 301-631-2466
www.alea.org
Steven Ingley, Executive Director
Kevin R. Caffery, VP
Nicole Gentile, Operations Manager
Keith Johnson, Safety Program Director
Carrie Cosens, Membership Manager
Containing 157 booths.
1100 Attendees
Frequency: July
Founded in 1968

15399 **American Academy of Forensic Sciences Annual Meeting**
American Academy of Forensic Sciences
410 N. 21st Street
Colorado Springs, CO 80904
719-636-1100; Fax: 719-636-1993
awarren@aafs.org
www.aafs.org
Zeno J. Geradts, PhD., President
Anne Warren, Executive Director
Jeri D. Ropero-Miller, PhD., President-Elect
Carl R. McClary, BA, Vice President
Susan M. Ballou, MS, Past President
Each February, the AAFS scientific meeting gathers together approximately 5,000 world-renowned professionals to present the most current information, research, and updates in their fields. More than 900 scientific papers, seminars, workshops, and other special sessions are presented. In addition, approximately 150 exhibitors showcase the cutting-edge technology and services of this ever-changing profession.
6700 Members
5000 Attendees
Frequency: Annual/February
Founded in 1948

15400 **American Correctional Association Congress**
206 N Washington St
Suite 200
Alexandria, VA 22314
703-224-0000
800-222-5646; Fax: 703-224-0179
pres@aca.org
www.aca.org
Daron Hall, President
James Gondles Jr, Executive Director
Jeff Washington, Deputy Executive Director
Five hundred booths featuring association whose membership is concerned with correctional services.
3900 Attendees
Mailing list available for rent

15401 **American Correctional Association Winter Conference**
206 N Washington St
Suite 200
Alexandria, VA 22314
703-224-0000
800-222-5646; Fax: 703-224-0179
pres@aca.org
www.aca.org
James Gondles Jr, Executive Director
Daron Hall, President
Jeff Washington, Deputy Executive Director
Three hundred and fifty booths.
3M Attendees
Frequency: January
Founded in 1935
Mailing list available for rent

15402 **American Criminal Justice Association National Conference**
American Criminal Justice Association
PO Box 601047
Sacramento, CA 95860-1047
916-484-6553; Fax: 916-488-2227
acjalae@aol.com
www.acjalae.org
Joe Davenport, President
Karen Campbell, Executive Secretary
Abby Schofield, Region 1 President
Preston Koelling, Vice-President
Business meetings, awards, competitions, job fairs, physical agility competitions, safety meetings and crime scene competitions
7200 Members
Founded in 1937

15403 **American Jail Association Training Conference & Jail Expo**
1135 Professional Court
Hagerstown, MD 21740
301-790-3930; Fax: 301-790-2941
dorothyd@aja.org
www.aja.org
Facebook
Dorothy Drass, Marketing Director
Holly Nicarry, Assistant Marketing Director
Robert J. Kasabian, Executive Director
Patty Vermillion, Training Coordinator
Leslie Brozna, Marketing and Sales Coordinator
Brings together more than 2,200 participants from around the world and over 275 companies who provide products and services to jails.
2200 Attendees
Frequency: May
Founded in 1981

15404 **American Society of Criminology Show**
1314 Kinnear Road
Columbus, OH 43212
614-292-9207; Fax: 614-292-6767
webmaster@asc41.com
www.asc41.com
Bonnie Fisher, Treasurer
Twenty-five tables.
1.5M Attendees
Frequency: October

15405 **Convention & Traffic Expo**
American Traffic Safety Services Association
15 Riverside Parkway
Suite 100
Fredericksburg, VA 22406-1022
540-368-1701
800-272-8772; Fax: 540-368-1717
www.atssa.com
Douglas Danko, Chairman
The premier meeting place for roadway professionals around the world. The program and exhibits are dedicated to issues and products related to all aspects of temporary traffic control and roadway safety.
Frequency: Annual/February
Mailing list available for rent

15406 **FBINAA Conference**
FBI National Academy Associates
422 Garrisonville Road
Suite 103
Stafford, VA 22554
540-628-0834; Fax: 703-632-1993
info@fbinaa.org
www.fbinaa.org
Timothy D Overton, National President
Steve Tidwell, Executive Director
Rhonda Stites, Administrative Assistant
Becky Storm, Business Manager
Nell Cochran, Financial Manager
Frequency: July
Mailing list available for rent

15407 **FEMSA Annual Conference**
Fire & Emergency Manufacturers & Services Assn.
P.O. Box 147
Lynnfield, MA 01940-0147
781-334-2771; Fax: 781-334-2771
info@femsa.org
www.femsa.org
William Van Lent, President
James Long, Vice President
Works to strengthen its membership, planning for future development, and directing programs that build industry opportunities. Conference open to members only.
160 Members
100+ Attendees
Frequency: Fall
Founded in 1966

15408 **GovSec: The Govenment Security Conference & Expo**
1105 Media
9201 Oakdale Avenue
Suite 101
Chatsworth, CA 91311
818-734-5200; Fax: 818-734-1522
info@1105media.com
www.1105media.com
Jules Gagne, Exhibits & Sponsorships
Deborah Lovell, Conference Program
Brad Wills, Press & Media
Neal Vitale, President & Chief Executive Officer
Richard Vitale, Senior Vice President & CFO
GovSec is the premier government security conference & expo that has joined forces with the Contingency Planning & Management Network (Centric Security) and U.S. Law Enforcement Conferences, to strengthen its focus on critical infrastructure protection, cybercrime and cyberterrorism, counterterrorism and homeland security. Washington Convention Center, Washington, DC.
Frequency: Annual/April
Founded in 2001

15409 **Int'l Assn of Campus Law Enforcement Administrators Annual Conference**
International Assn of Campus Law Enforcement Admin
342 North Main Street
West Hartford, CT 06117-2507
860-586-7522; Fax: 860-586-7550
info@iaclea.org
www.iaclea.org
Pamela Hayes, Exhibitor Contact
Peter Berry, Executive Director

Offers members an opportunity to attend informative programs to learn more about current issues and developments in campus public safety, network with peers, visit exhibitor booths, and enjoy special events.
Frequency: Annual

15410 **International Association of Chiefs of Police Annual Conference**
International Association of Chiefs of Police
515 N Washington Street
Alexandria, VA 22314-2357

703-836-6767
800-843-4227; Fax: 703-836-4543
www.theiacp.org
Facebook, Twitter, RSS, Youtube

Lia Muwwakkil, Exhibits & Conferences
Colleen Phalen, Exhibits & Sponsorships
Dan Rosenblatt, Executive Director

Enables professionals to examine the state of the police industry through highly rated seminars, forums, and technical workshops. Only open to IACP members and their guests.
Frequency: Annual,September
Mailing list available for rent

15411 **Major Cities Chiefs Conference**
Major Cities Chiefs Police Association
P.O. Box 8717
Salt Lake City, UT 84047

stephens@majorcitieschiefs.com
www.majorcitieschiefs.com

J. Thomas Manger, President
Art Acevedo, 1st Vice President
George Turner, 2nd Vice President
Darrell W. Stephens, Executive Director

Association meetings held three times a year - winter, summer, and fall.
Founded in 1949

15412 **National Conference on Law Enforcement Wellness and Trauma**
Concerns of Police Survivors
846 Old South 5
PO Box 3199
Camdenton, MO 65020

573-346-4911; Fax: 573-346-1414
cops@nationalcops.org
www.concernsofpolicesurvivors.org

Dianne Bernhard, Executive Director
Shelley Jones, Director of Operations

This conference offers a focus on officer wellness and the need to pro-actively address the cumulative stresses that can occur over an officer's career. Attendees include active and retired law enforcement officers nationwide.
Cost: $300.00
Frequency: Annual/November

15413 **National Education & Training Conference**
National Black Police Association
3100 Main Street
#256
Dallas, TX 75226

855-879-6272; Fax: 202-986-0410
www.blackpolice.org

Ronald Hampton, Executive Director
Malik Aziz, Chairperson
Walter L Holloway, Vice Chairperson
Sherri Lockett, Secretary
Donna Ross, Fiscal Officer
400 Attendees
Frequency: Annual

15414 **National Forensic League**
125 Watson Street
PO Box 38
Ripon, WI 54971

920-748-6206; Fax: 920-748-9478

Diane Rasmussen, Associate Secretary
J Scott, Executive Director

Ten booths.
2.8M Attendees
Frequency: June

15415 **National Police Survivors' Conference**
Concerns of Police Survivors
846 Old South 5
PO Box 3199
Camdenton, MO 65020

573-346-4911; Fax: 573-346-1414
cops@nationalcops.org
www.concernsofpolicesurvivors.org

Dianne Bernhard, Executive Director
Shelley Jones, Director of Operations

During the activities that comprise National Police Week, C.O.P.S. hosts the annual National Police SurvivorsB Conference. Law enforcement survivors, co-workers, and agencies from across the nation gather to meet others who understand how they feel, attend seminar sessions specifically designed for their needs, and hear presentations delivering inspirational messages on hope and survival.
Frequency: Annual/May

15416 **National Sheriff's Association**
1450 Duke Street
Alexandria, VA 22314-3490

703-836-7827
800-424-7827
kbright@sheriffs.org
www.sheriffs.org

Kimberly Bright, Director, Marketing & Exhibits
Thomas Faust, Executive Director

More than 500 exhibits.
3M Attendees
Frequency: June

15417 **Tactical Operations Conference**
National Tactical Officers Association
PO Box 797
Doylestown, PA 18901

215-230-7616
800-279-9127; Fax: 215-230-7552
membership@ntoa.org
www.ntoa.org
Facebook, Twitter, LinkedIn, Google+, Blogger, Bloggy, Pint

Mark Lomax, Executive Director
Laura Gerhart, Conference Coordinator
Rob Cartner, Director of Training
Mary Heins, Editor
Michelle Griffin, Assistant Editor
1000 Attendees
Frequency: September
Mailing list available for rent

Directories & Databases

15418 **Directory of Law Enforcement and Criminal**
Law Enforcement Standards Office
US National Institute of Standards
100 Bureau Drive M/S 8102
Gaithersburg, MD 20899-8102

301-975-2757; Fax: 301-948-0978

Marilyn Leach, Editor
Ruth Joel, Editor

More than 200 local, national and international organizations involved in the fields of law enforcement, corrections, forensic science and criminal justice in the US.

15419 **FEMA Educational Articles**
Fire Equipment Manufacturers' Association
1300 Sumner Avenue
Cleveland, OH 44115

216-241-7333
www.femalifesafety.org/articles.html

Bill Vegso, President

Articles from the Fire Equipment Manufacturers' Association covering information on fire equipment, safety procedures and laws.
Founded in 1930

15420 **Fire Chief: Equipment and Apparatus Directory Issue**
Primedia
1300 E 9th St
Cleveland, OH 44114-1503

216-696-7000; Fax: 216-696-6662
www.penton.com

Eric Jacobson, Senior VP
Jane Cooper, Marketing
David Kieselstein, Chief Executive Officer
Kurt Nelson, Vice President, Human Resources
Andrew Schmolka, Senior Vice President

List of approximately 1,000 suppliers of fire protection equipment, including ladder trucks, protective clothing, alarms, alternators and others.
Cost: $10.00
Frequency: Monthly
Circulation: 52901
Mailing list available for rent

15421 **Grey House Homeland Security Directory**
Grey House Publishing
4919 Route 22
PO Box 56
Amenia, NY 12501

518-789-8700
800-562-2139; Fax: 845-373-6390
books@greyhouse.com
www.greyhouse.com
Facebook, Twitter

Leslie Mackenzie, Publisher
Richard Gottlieb, Editor

Features the latest contact information for government and private organizations involved with Homeland Security along with the latest product information. The directory provides detailed profiles of nearly 1,500 Federal & State Organizations & Agencies and over 3,000 Officials and Key Executives involved with Homeland Security.
Cost: $195.00
800 Pages
ISBN: 1-592370-75-6
Founded in 1981

15422 **Grey House Homeland Security Directory - Online Database**
Grey House Publishing
4919 Route 22
PO Box 56
Amenia, NY 12501-0056

518-789-8700
800-562-2139; Fax: 518-789-0556
gold@greyhouse.com
gold.greyhouse.com
Facebook, Twitter

Leslie Mackenzie, Publisher
Richard Gottlieb, President

This comprehensive database presents a wide range of information that is scattered and hard to

find elsewhere, providing subscribers with access to the most comprehensive, up-to-date and detailed information on the nation's homeland security contacts and services. This online database contains over 1,100 profiles of Federal and State agencies and companies along with the names of 11,000 key contacts.
Founded in 1981

15423 **Grey House Safety & Security Directory**
Grey House Publishing
4919 Route 22
PO Box 56
Amenia, NY 12501
518-789-8700
800-562-2139; Fax: 845-373-6390
books@greyhouse.com
www.greyhouse.com
Facebook, Twitter
Leslie Mackenzie, Publisher
Richard Gottlieb, Editor
Comprehensive resource guide to the safety and security industry, including articles, checklists, OSHA regulations and product listings. Focuses on creating and maintaing a safe and secure enviroment, and dealing specifically with hazardous materials, noise and vibration, workplace preparation and maintenance, electrical and lighting safety, fire and rescue and more.
Cost: $165.00
1600 Pages
ISBN: 1-592373-75-5
Founded in 1981

15424 **Law Enforcement Technology Directory**
Hendon
130 Waukegan Rd
Deerfield, IL 60015-4912
847-444-3300
800-843-9764; Fax: 847-444-3333
info@hendonpub.com
www.lawandordermag.com
Henry Kingwill, Owner
Directory of manufacturers and suppliers of one type of law enforcement equipment such as computers, weapons, training, surveillance, forensics and radio and communications equipment.
Cost: $60.00
Frequency: Annual December

15425 **Law and Order Magazine: Police Management Buyer's Guide Issue**
Hendon
130 Waukegan Rd
2nd Floor
Deerfield, IL 60015-4912
847-444-3300
800-843-9764; Fax: 847-444-3333
esanow@hendonpub.com
www.hendonpub.com
Henry Kingwill, Owner
Jennifer Gavigan, Managing Editor
Yesenia Salcedo, Managing Editor
Tim Davis, Graphic Designer
Marilou Go, Office Manager
Monthly publication for police managers, covering all aspects of law enforcement including a list of manufacturers, dealers and distributors of products and services for police departments.
Cost: $15.00
Frequency: Annual February

15426 **National Directory of Law Enforcement Administrators Correctional Inst**
National Public Safety Information Bureau
PO Box 365
Stevens Point, WI 54481
715-345-2772
800-647-7579; Fax: 715-345-7288
info@safetysource.com
www.safetysource.com
Steve Cywinski, Publisher
John Diser, Account Manager
Christina Scott, Business Development Manager
Listing of police departments, sheriffs, criminal prosecutors, state law enforcement, criminal investigation agencies, federal law enforcement and homeland security.
Cost: $129.00
924 Pages
Frequency: Annual, paperback
Circulation: 9,000
ISBN: 1-880245-22-1
ISSN: 1066-5595
Founded in 1964

15427 **National Employment Listing Service Bulletin**
Criminal Justice Center
Sam Houston State University
1803 Avenue I
Huntsville, TX 77341
936-295-6371
Kay Billingsley, Editor
Job openings in police departments, sheriff's departments, courts and other law enforcement and security agencies.

15428 **Police: Buyer's Guide Issue**
Bobit Publishing Company
23210 Crenshaw Blvd
Torrance, CA 90505-3181
310-539-1969; Fax: 310-539-4329
police@bobit.com
John Bebout, Owner
List of suppliers of police products and services.
Cost: $10.00
Frequency: Annual August

15429 **Transportation Security Directory & Handbook**
Grey House Publishing
4919 Route 22
PO Box 56
Amenia, NY 12501
518-789-8700
800-562-2139; Fax: 845-373-6390
books@greyhouse.com
www.greyhouse.com
Facebook, Twitter
Leslie Mackenzie, Publisher
Richard Gottlieb, Editor
Provides information on everything from Regulatory Authorities to Security Enforcement, this top-flight directory brings together the relevant information necessary for creating and maintaining a security plan for a wide range of transportation facilities.
Cost: $195.00
800 Pages
ISBN: 1-592370-75-6
Founded in 1981

15430 **Who's Who in Jail Management Jail Directory**
American Jail Association
1135 Professional Ct
Hagerstown, MD 21740-5853
301-790-3930; Fax: 301-790-2941
www.aja.org
Gwyn Smith-Ingley, Executive Director
Kelton Chapman, Manager
Sheryl Ebersole, Business Manager
Connie Lacy, Director
Offers the most current information available on local jails in the US. Also offers an up-to-date listing of all the jails in the US that is available for rent electronically and a valuable resource for sheriffs, jail administrators and vendors.
Cost: $85.00

Industry Web Sites

15431 **http://gold.greyhouse.com**
G.O.L.D Grey House OnLine Databases
Grey House Publishing's online database platform, GOLD, offers Quick Search, Keyword Search and Expert Search for most business sectors including law enforcement and public safety markets. The GOLD platform makes finding the information you need quick and easy - whether you're a novice searcher or an experienced database user. All of Grey House's directory products are available for subscription on the GOLD platform.

15432 **www.aamva.org**
American Assn. of Motor Vehicle Administrators
Nonprofit organization represents state and provincial officials in the US and Canada who administer and enforce motor vehicle laws. Strives to develop model programs in motor vehicle administration, police traffic services and highway safety.

15433 **www.aca.org**
American Correctional Association
This organization offers information on the correctional field.

15434 **www.alea.org**
Airborne Law Enforcement Association
Members are law enforcement officers who use both fixed and rotary wing air craft, in law enforcement, and equipment suppliers.

15435 **www.apco911.org**
Association of Public-Safety Communications Officials International
The world's oldest and largest professional organization dedicated to the enhancement of public safety communications and to serving its more than 15,000 members, the people who use public safety communications systems and services.

15436 **www.aphf.org**
American Police Hall of Fame
Offers benefits, and various types of awards to members, magazine, line of duty death benefits, film and training library as well as support services, scholarships and financial assistance for police family survivors.

15437 **www.atssa.org**
American Traffic Safety Services Association
Promotes uniform use of lights, signs, pavement markings and barricades. Distributes technical information and sponsors training courses for worksite traffic supervisors.

15438 **www.blr.com**
Business & Legal Reports
Provides essential tools for safety and environmental compliance and training needs

15439 **www.corrections.com/**
Corrections Professionals
Information about events, careers, news, legal happenings and newsletters.

15440 **www.dpsoa.com**
Texas Department of Public Safety Officer's Association

15441 **www.fema.gov**
Federal Emergency Management Agency.

15442 **www.femsa.org**
Fire & Emergency Manufacturers & Services Assn.
The leading trade association for the fire and emergency services industry whose members provide products and services to millions of fire and EMS professionals throughout the world.

15443 **www.fluidpowersafety.com**
Fluid Power Safety Institute
An organization whose mission is to educate people about workplace safety within the fluid power industry.

15444 **www.footprinter.org**
International Footprint Association

15445 **www.fssa.net**
Fire Suppression Systems Association
Designers, suppliers and installers of special hazard fire suppression equipment, gases and detectors.

15446 **www.greyhouse.com**
Grey House Publishing
Authoritative reference directories for most business sectors including law enforcement and public safety markets. Users can search the online databases with varied search criteria allowing for custom searches by product category, geographic area, sales volume, keyword, subject and more. Full Grey House catalog and online ordering also available.

15447 **www.highwaysafety.org**
Insurance Institute for Highway Safety
Traffic and motor vehicle safety organization supported by auto insurers.

15448 **www.iaati.org**
International Association of Auto Theft Investigators

Provides members who are auto theft investigators with resources to develop and maintain professional standards within the industry.

15449 **www.iawp.org**
International Association of Women Police
To strengthen, unite and raise the profile of women in criminal justice internationally.

15450 **www.ncpc.org**
National Crime Prevention Council

15451 **www.neoa.org**
Narcotic Enforcement Officers Association
A non-profit educational organization of more than a thousand law enforcement personnel and others in the criminal justicce system, includin state and local police, D.E.A., F.B.I. and customs.

15452 **www.ntoa.org**
National Tactical Officers Association
Enhance the performance and professional status of law enforcement personnel by providing a credible and proven training resource as well as a forum for the development of tactics and information exchange.

15453 **www.policeforum.org**
Police Executive Research Forum
For chief executives of city, county and state police agencies.

15454 **www.polygraph.org**
American Polygraph Association
A merger of Academy of Scientific Interrogation, American Academy of Polygraph Examiners and National Board of Polygraph examiners.

15455 **www.psa.com**
Production Services Associates,Inc.
Dealers and dealer banks who underwrite and trade federal, state and local government securities and mortgage-backed securities.

15456 **www.sheriffs.org**
National Sherriff's Association
Devoted to helping sheriffs and other law enforcers to execute their duties most effectively and professionally.

15457 **www.theiacp.org**
International Association of Chiefs of Police
Organization that focuses on topics of interest to professional law enforcers.

15458 **www.toxicology.org**
Society of Toxicology
Members are scientists concerned with the effects of chemicals on man and the environment. Promotes the aquisition and utilization of knowledge in toxicology, aids in the protection of public health and facilitates disiplines. The society has a strong commitment to education in toxicology and to the recruitment of students and new members into the profession.

Associations

15459 **American Leather Chemists Association**
1314 50th Street
Suite 103
Lubbock, TX 79412

806-744-1798; Fax: 806-744-1785
alca@leatherchemists.org
www.leatherchemists.org

Mike Bley, President
Joseph Hoefler, Vice President
Steven Lange, JALCA Editor
Carol Adcock, Executive Secretary

Group of leather chemists who are interested in the development of methods that could be utilized to standardize both the supply and application of the tanning agents utilized by the industry.
500 Members
Founded in 1903
Mailing list available for rent

15460 **American Saddle Makers Association**
12155 Donovan Lane
Black Forest, CO 80908

729-494-2848
info@saddlemakers.org
www.saddlemakers.org

Cheryl Rifkin, President
Bob Brenner, Executive Director
Steve Bowen, Director of Membership

Representing manufacturers of Western and English saddles in the US.

15461 **International Federation Leather Guild**
2264 Logan Drive
New Palestine, IN 46163

317-691-0321
eddjanlucas@sbcglobal.net
www.ifolg.org

David Smith, Executive Director
Alex Madson, Assistant Director
Carol Higgins, Secretary
Monica Nibbes, Treasurer
Roger Bligan, Web Master

Supports all leather craftsmen via education, training, publications and trade shows.

15462 **Leather Apparel Association**
19 W 21st Street
Suite 403
New York, NY 10010

212-727-1210; Fax: 212-727-1218

Morris Goldfarb, President
Richard Harrow, Executive Director

Represents the nation's leading leather retailers, manufacturers, cleaners and other businesses in promoting leather apparel in the US.
Founded in 1990

15463 **Leather Industries of America**
3050 K St NW
Suite 400
Washington, DC 20007-5100

202-342-8497; Fax: 202-342-8583
info@leatherusa.com
www.leatherusa.com

John Wittenborn, President
John M. Pike, Executive Director

A trade association representing the leather industry: tanners; chemical suppliers; hide, skin and leather suppliers; and product manufacturers. Provides environmental, technical, educational, statistical, and marketing services.
Founded in 1917

15464 **Leathercraft Guild**
9108 Garvey Ave
Rosemead, CA 91770

Home Page: www.theleathercraftguild.com
Facebook, Twitter, Myspace

Preserves and promotes the art of leather carving and stamping. Seeks to improve skills of members, raise standards of crafts and promote the product.
200 Members
Founded in 1949

15465 **National Shoe Retailers Association**
7386 N La Cholla Blvd.
Tucson, AZ 85741

520-209-1710
800-673-8446; Fax: 410-381-1167
info@nsra.org
www.nsra.org
Facebook, Twitter, Pinterest

Chuck Schuyler, President

Membership association for independent shoe ratailers. Provides busisness services such as credit-card processing and shipping at special low members only prices. Also provides educational and training programs, consulting and other services.
1400 Members
Founded in 1912

15466 **Pedorthic Footwear Association**
1610 East Forsyth Street
Suite D
Americus, GA 31709

229-389-3440
703-995-4456; Fax: 888-563-0945
info@pedorthics.org
www.pedorthics.org
Facebook, Twitter, LinkedIn, Google+, Blogger, Bloggy, Pint

Rob Sobel, C. Ped., President
Dean Mason, Vice President
Matt Almeida, Secretary
Christopher J. Costantini, C. Ped., Treasurer
Rebecca Fazzari, Meeting and Convention Manager

Membership organization for individuals and companies involved in the design, manufacture, modification and fit of therapeutic footwear. Provides educational programs, publications, legislative monitoring, marketing materials, professional liason and business operations services.
Cost: $55.00
2000 Members
Founded in 1958

15467 **Proleptic, Inc.**
PO Box 17817
Asheville, NC 28816

828-505-8474; Fax: 828-505-8476
www.proleptic.net
Facebook

Daniel S Preston, PhD, Director

A Comprehensive Source for Sewing Machines, Leather working Equipment, Supplies, Tools, Horse Healthcare and Finished Products Repair Shops Retailers, Crafters, Collectors.
320 Members
Founded in 1984

15468 **Sponge and Chamois Institute**
10024 Office Center Ave
Suite 203
Saint Louis, MO 63128

314-842-2230; Fax: 314-842-3999
scwaters@swbell.net

Members are suppliers and dealers of natural sponges and chamois leather.

15469 **Travel Goods Association**
259 Nassau Street
#119
Princeton, NJ 08542

877-842-1938; Fax: 877-842-1938
tga@travel-goods.org
www.travel-goods.org
Facebook, Twitter, LinkedIn, YouTube

Michele Marini Pittenger, President/CEO
Rob Holmes, Vice President/ CFO
Kim Wong, Creative Director
Kate Ryan, Media Relations
Nate Herman, Director, Government Relations

Trade association that represents manufacturers of luggage, business and computer cases,handbags and accessories. Formerly the Luggage and Leather Goods Association.
294 Members
Founded in 1938
Mailing list available for rent

15470 **Western-English Trade Association**
451 East 58th Avenue
Suite 4323
Denver, CO 80216-8468

303-295-2001; Fax: 303-295-6108

Glenda Chipps, Executive Director

Members are manufacturers and retailers of western and english style riding equipment and clothes.
158 Members
Founded in 1963

Newsletters

15471 **Leather Conservation News**
Minnesota Historical Society
345 Kellogg Blvd W
St Paul, MN 55102-1906

651-259-3000; Fax: 651-296-1004
webmaster@mnhs.org
www.mnhs.org

Nina Archabal, Executive Director
Jackie Swanson, Secretary
Sue Leas, Executive Assistant

Research and advancements in the specialty of leather conservation and preservation; articles on materials science research and treatments; news of conferences and workshops.
Cost: $15.00
24 Pages
Frequency: 2 per year
Circulation: 250
ISSN: 0898-0128
Printed in on matte stock

15472 **Leather Facts**
US Hide, Skin & Leather Association
1700 N Moore Street
Suite 1600
Arlington, VA 22209

703-841-2400; Fax: 703-527-0938

John Reddington, President

Association news covering the leather and hide industry.

15473 **Leather International**

Home Page: www.leathermag.com

Carl Friedmann, Editor

In-depth coverage of every aspect of the international leather industry.

Magazines & Journals

15474 **Journal of the American Leather Chemists Association (JALCA)**
American Leather Chemists Association
1314 50th Street
Suite 103
Lubbock, TX 79412

806-744-1798; Fax: 806-744-1785
alca@leatherchemists.org
www.leatherchemists.org

Carol Adcock, Executive Secretary
Robert F. White, Editor
Steven Gilberg, President
Steve Lange, Vice President
Cost: $175.00
Frequency: Monthly
Circulation: 500
Founded in 1903
Mailing list available for rent

15475 **Leather Crafters & Saddlers Journal**
222 Blackburn St
Rhinelander, WI 54501

715-362-5393
888-289-6409; Fax: 715-362-5391
journal@newnorth.net
www.leathercraftersjournal.com
Facebook

Dot Reis, Editor

Publication for leather workers. Sponsors several trade shows throughout the year which attract vendors of leather, tools, equipment and supplies.
Cost: $32.00
Frequency: Bi-Monthly
Circulation: 6000
ISSN: 1082-4480

15476 **Travel Goods Showcase**
Travel Goods Association
259 Nassau Street
#119
Princeton, NJ 08542

877-842-1938; Fax: 877-842-1938
tga@travel-goods.org
www.travel-goods.org
Facebook, Twitter, LinkedIn, YouTube

Michele Marini Pittenger, President/CEO

The largest trade magazine devoted to travel products whose 21,000 readers include retailers, consumer press and trade media.
Founded in 1975

Trade Shows

15477 **ALCA Annual Meeting**
American Leather Chemists Association
1314 50th Street
Suite 103
Lubbock, TX 79412

806-744-1798; Fax: 806-744-1785
www.leatherchemists.org

Carol Adcock, Executive Secretary
Robert F. White, Editor
Steven Gilberg, President
Steve Lange, Vice President
100 Attendees
Mailing list available for rent

15478 **International Federation Leather Guild Trade Show**
748 NW Wood Street
Burleson, TX 76028-2619

817-478-2335

Ernie Wayman, Executive Director

Open exhibition of leather craftsmen.
400 Attendees

15479 **Leather Allied Trade Show**
2214 S Brentwood Boulevard
Saint Louis, MO 63144-1804

314-961-2829

Virginia Breen, Secretary

Exhibition of leathers and components.
2.1M Attendees
Frequency: February

15480 **PFA Annual Symposium & Exhibition**
Pedorthic Footwear Association
1610 E Forsyth St.
Suite D
Americus, GA 31709

229-389-3440; Fax: 888-563-0945
pedorthicsusa@gmail.com
www.pedorthics.org
Facebook, Twitter, LinkedIn

Robert Sobel, President

One hundred fifty booths plus educational sessions regarding the design, manufacture or modification and fit of shoes and foot orthoses to alleviate foot problems caused by disease, congenital condition, overuse or injury.
1000 Attendees
Frequency: November

15481 **The Travel Goods Show**
Travel Goods Association
259 Nassau Street
#119
Princeton, NJ 08542

877-842-1938; Fax: 877-842-1938
tga@travel-goods.org
www.thetravelgoodsshow.org

Michele Marini Pittenger, President/CEO
Cathy Trecartin, VP, Trade Show

To learn about the latest and greatest travel industry innovations and trends.

Directories & Databases

15482 **Complete Directory of Leather Goods & Luggage**
Sutton Family Communications & Publishing Company
920 State Route 54 East
Elmitch, KY 42343

270-276-9500

Theresa Sutton, Publisher
Lee Sutton, Editor

Print-out from database of wholesalers, manufacturers, distributors, importers and close-out houses. Database is updated daily to guarantee the most current and up-to-date sources available.
Cost: $39.50
100 Pages

15483 **LIA Member Directory & Buyer's Guide**
Leather Industries of America
3050 K St. NW
Suite 400
Washington, DC 20007

202-342-8497; Fax: 202-342-8583
info@leatherusa.com
www.leatherusa.com

John Wittenborn, President
30 Pages
Frequency: Annual/March
Founded in 1917

15484 **Leather Manufacturer Directory**
Shoe Trades Publishing Company
323 Cornelia
Suite 274
Plattsburg, NY 12901

514-457-8787
800-973-7463; Fax: 514-457-5832
www.shoetrades.com

George McLeish, Group Publisher
Inta Huns, Managing Editor

Classified directory of major leather finishers, tanneries and hide processors in the United States and Canada, and their suppliers.
Cost: $61.00
413 Pages
Frequency: Annual
Circulation: 1,200

15485 **U.S. Leather Industry Statistics**
Leather Industries of America
3050 K St. NW
Suite 400
Washington, DC 20007

202-342-8497; Fax: 202-342-8583
info@leatherusa.com
www.leatherusa.com

John Wittenborn, President

Statistical record of the U.S. leather industry for over 85 years.
Cost: $18.00
10 Pages
Frequency: Annual
Founded in 1917

Industry Web Sites

15486 **http://gold.greyhouse.com**
G.O.L.D Grey House OnLine Databases

Grey House Publishing's online database platform, GOLD, offers Quick Search, Keyword Search and Expert Search for most business sectors including leather markets. The GOLD platform makes finding the information you need quick and easy - whether you're a novice searcher or an experienced database user. All of Grey House's directory products are available for subscription on the GOLD platform.

15487 **www.greyhouse.com**
Grey House Publishing

Authoritative reference directories for most business sectors including leather markets. Users can search the online databases with varied search criteria allowing for custom searches by product category, geographic area, sales volume, keyword, subject and more. Full Grey House catalog and online ordering also available.

15488 **www.hidenet.com**
Hidenet

Furnishes detailed information on the daily hide market worldwide.

15489 **www.leatherusa.com**
Leather Industries of America

Works to promote the leather industry through collection of statistics, chemical and technical research and public relations.

15490 **www.ssia.info**
Shoe Service Institute of America

Shop to shop chat room, links and listings of manufacturers and wholesalers plus shoe care tips.

15491 **www.travel-goods.org**
Travel Goods Association

Trade association that represents manufacturers of luggage, business and computer cases, handbags and accessories. Formerly the Luggage and Leather Goods Association.

Associations

15492 **ABA Young Lawyers Division**
American Bar Association
321 N Clark St
Chicago, IL 60654-7598

312-988-5000
800-285-2221; Fax: 312-988-5280
yld@staff.abanet.org
www.abanet.org/yld/home.html
Facebook, Twitter, LinkedIn, Youtube

Patricia Lee Refo, President
Barbara Howard, Chair, House of Delegates
Jack L. Rives, Executive Director
Pauline Weaver, Secretary
Kevin L. Shepherd, Treasurer

The Division is committed to assuring it is best able to represent the newest members of the profession, ensuring that it reflects the society it serves, and providing young lawyers wth the tools and opportunities for professional and personal success.
194K Members
Founded in 1878

15493 **AILA's Immigration Lawyer Search**
ils@aila.org
www.ailalawyer.com

15494 **Academy of Family Mediators**
PO Box 51090
Eugene, OR 97405

541-345-1629
admin@mediate.com
www.mediate.com
Facebook, Twitter, LinkedIn, Google+

Jim Melamed, CEO
Carol Knapp, CTO
Josh Remis, COO
John Blair, Business Advisor & Board Member
Byron Knapp, Systems Administrator

Produce conflict management specialists who can advance conflict resolution and engagement, as well as a functional approach to conflict within our communities and society.
2M Members
Founded in 1981
Mailing list available for rent

15495 **Adjutants General Association of the United States**
One Massachusetts Ave, N.W.
Washington, DC 20001

504-278-8357; Fax: 302-326-7196
agausinfo@gmail.com
www.agaus.org

MG Matthew T. Quinn, President
MG Timothy P. Williams, VP Army
MG Michael A. Loh, VP Air
MG Francis J. Evon, Jr., Treasurer
MG Christopher Callahan, Secretary

Composed of the commander of the National Guard in each state and territory.
54 Members

15496 **Alliance for Justice**
11 Dupont Cir NW
2nd Floor
Washington, DC 20036-1206

202-822-6070; Fax: 202-822-6068
alliance@afj.org
www.afj.org
Facebook, Twitter, Youtube, Google Plus

Paulette Meyer, Chair
Nan Aron, President
Norman Rosenberg, Vice-Chair
Holly Tippett, Director of Foundation Relations
Myesha Braden, Director, Justice Initiatives

Nonprofit association of public interest advocacy organization. Offers workshops, advocacy projects, legal guides, techinical assistance and public education. Publishes a directory of public interest law centers.
Founded in 1979
Mailing list available for rent

15497 **American Academy of Psychiatry and the Law**
One Regency Drive
PO Box 30
Bloomfield, CT 06002-2310

860-242-5450
800-331-1389; Fax: 860-286-0787
office@aapl.org
www.aapl.org

Liza Gold, MD, President
Hal Wortzel, MD, Vice President
Britta Ostermeyer, MD, Vice President
Karen Rosenbaum, MD, Secretary
Stuart Anfang, MD, Treasurer

Members are psychiatrists who have a professional interest in psychiatry and the law.
2000 Members
Founded in 1969

15498 **American Alliance of Paralegals**
4023 Kennett Pike
Suite 146
Wilmington, DE 19807-2018

info@aapipara.org
www.aapipara.org
Facebook, Twitter, LinkedIn

John C. Goudie, AACP, President
Dawn Carey, Vice President
Diana J. Gruber, AACP, Treasurer
Keelie J. Fike, AACP, Secretary
Stephanie Rubio, AACP, Director of Education
2000 Members
Founded in 2003

15499 **American Arbitration Association**
1633 Broadway
Floor 10
New York, NY 10019-6707

212-716-5800; Fax: 877-304-8457
websitemail@adr.org
www.adr.org

William K Slate II, CEO
Debi Miller-Moore, VP

Available to resolve a wide range of disputes through mediation, arbitration, elections and other out-of-court settlement procedures.
Founded in 1996

15500 **American Association for Justice**
777 6th Street, NW
Suite 200
Washington, DC 20001

202-965-3500
800-424-2725
membership@justice.org
www.justice.org
Facebook, Twitter, LinkedIn

Tobi Millrood, President
Tad Thomas, Vice President
Sean Dominick, Secretary
Lori Andrus, Treasurer
Navan Ward, President-Elect
56000 Members
Founded in 1946
Mailing list available for rent

15501 **American Association for Paralegal Education**
222 S. Westmonte Drive
Suite 101
Altamonte Springs, FL 32714

407-774-7880; Fax: 407-774-6440
info@aafpe.org
www.aafpe.org
Facebook, Twitter, LinkedIn

Toni Marsh, President
Tonya Wade, Executive Director
Gregory L. Richard, J.D., Director, Baccalaureate Programs
Lisa Hutton, Secretary
Marie Harrigan, Treasurer

National organization serving paralegal education and institutions which offer paralegal education programs.
Founded in 1981

15502 **American Association of Attorney-Certified Public Accountants**
P.O. Box 706
Warrendale, PA 15095

703-352-8064
888-288-9272; Fax: 703-352-8073
info@attorney-cpa.com
www.attorney-cpa.com
Facebook, Twitter, LinkedIn

Howard O. Bernstein, President
Michele B. Friend, Vice President
Deron R. Harrington, Treasurer
Marc L. Schwartz, Secretary
Daniel S. Rosefelt, Assistant Secretary/Treasurer

The AAA-CPA is the only association in the nation whose members are comprised of professionals dually qualified as both attorneys and certified public accountants. Their mission is to provide members with quality education, opportunities to interface with other Attorney-CPAs, and resources to support and develop their professional practices.
Founded in 1964

15503 **American Association of Law Libraries**
105 W Adams Street
Suite 3300
Chicago, IL 60603-6225

312-939-4764; Fax: 312-431-1097
aallhq@aall.org
www.aallnet.org
Facebook, Twitter, LinkedIn, RSS

Kate Hagan, Executive Director
Emily Feltren, Director of Government Relations
Paula Davidson, Director of Finance and Admin
Cara Schillinger, Director
Ashley St. John, Director Marketing/Communications

Promotes and enhances the value of law libraries to the legal and public communities, fosters the profession of law librarianship and provides leadership in the field of legal information.
3956 Members
Founded in 1906

15504 **American Bail Coalition**
P.O. Box: 352
Franklinville, NJ 08322

877-735-2240
ambailcoalition.com
Facebook, Twitter, LinkedIn, Youtube

William B Carmichael, President
Thomas Ritchey, Treasurer
Jeffrey J. Clayton, Executive Director

Dedicated to the long term growth and continuation of the surety bail bond industry.
Founded in 1992

15505 **American Bar Association**
321 N Clark St
Chicago, IL 60654-7598

312-988-5000
800-285-2221; Fax: 312-988-5280
service@americanbar.org
americanbar.org
Facebook, Twitter, LinkedIn

Barbara Howard, Chair
Patricia Lee Refo, President
Jack L. Rives, Executive Director
Kevin L. Shepherd, Treasurer
Pauline Weaver, Secretary

The American Bar Association is the largest coluntary professional association in the world, with over 400,000 members. The ABA provides law school accreditation, continuing legal education, information about the law, programs to assist lawyerd and judges in their work, and initiatives to improve the legal system for the public.
400K Members
Founded in 1878
Mailing list available for rent

15506 **American Bar Foundation**
750 N Lake Shore Dr
Chicago, IL 60611-4403

312-988-6500; Fax: 312-988-6579
www.americanbarfoundation.org

E. Thomas Sullivan, President
Jimmy K. Goodman, Vice President & Secretary
Walter L. Sutton, Treasurer
Francine Blazowski, Executive Assistant
Ann Pikus, Grants and Program Officer

Memberships are elected and limited to one third of one percent of the lawyers in the United States.
Founded in 1952
Mailing list available for rent

15507 **American Civil Liberties Union**
125 Broad St
18th Floor
New York, NY 10004-2427

212-549-2500; Fax: 212-549-2646
membership@aclu.org
www.aclu.org
Facebook, Twitter, RSS, Youtube

Susan N. Herman, President
Anthony D Romero, Executive Director
David Cole, Legal Director
Terence Dougherty, Chief Development Officer
Dorothy M. Ehrlich, Deputy Executive Director

Protection of civil liberties and constitutional rights through litigation, public education and legislative lobbying.
Founded in 1920
Mailing list available for rent

15508 **American College of Legal Medicine**
9700 West Bryn Mawr Avenue
Suite 210
Rosemont, IL 60018

847-447-1713; Fax: 847-447-1150
info@aclm.org
www.aclm.org
Facebook, Twitter

Laurie Krueger, Executive Director
Daniel L. Orr, President
C. William Hinnant, President-Elect
Veling Tsai, Secretary
David Donnersberger, Treasurer

Organization related to the field of health law, legal medicine or medical jurisprudence.
1400 Members
Founded in 1960

15509 **American Health Lawyers Association**
1099 14th Street NW
Suite 925
Washington, DC 20005

202-833-1100; Fax: 202-833-1105
americanhealthlaw.org
Facebook, Twitter, LinkedIn

Maureen Dubois, Senior Director Of HR
David S. Cade, Executive Vice President
Emily Morris, Senior Manager
Felicia Dillard, Chief Financial Officer
Stefan R. Bradham, Sr. Director, Marketing

Health Lawyers offers numerous services for their members and most are freely available to nonmembers as well.
Mailing list available for rent

15510 **American Immigration Lawyers Association**
1331 G St NW
Suite 300
Washington, DC 20005-3142

202-507-7600; Fax: 202-783-7853
info@aila.org
www.aila.org
Facebook, Twitter, LinkedIn, Youtube

Jennifer Minear, President
Jeremy L. McKinney, First Vice President
Farshad Owji, Second Vice President
Kelli Stump, Treasurer
Jeff Joseph, Secretary

Attorneys practicing in the field of immigration and naturalization law.
15K Members
Founded in 1946
Mailing list available for rent

15511 **American Inns of Court**
225 Reinekers Lane
Suite 770
Alexandria, VA 22314

703-684-3590; Fax: 703-684-3607
info@innsofcourt.org
home.innsofcourt.org
Facebook, Twitter, LinkedIn, Pinterest, Tumblr, Blogger, St

Hon. Kent A. Jordan, President
Hon. Barbara Lynn, Vice President
Malinda E. Dunn, Executive Director
Cindy Dennis, Awards & Scholarships Coordinator
Andrew Young, Director of Knowledge Resources

AIC is designed to improve skills, professionalism and ethics of the bench and bar. The American Inns of Court is an amalgam of judges, lawyers, and in some cases, law professors and law students.
Mailing list available for rent

15512 **American Institute of Parliamentarians**
1100 E Woodfield Rd.
Suite 350
Schaumburg, IL 60173

888-664-0428; Fax: 847-517-7229
aip@aipparl.org
www.aipparl.org

Al Gage, CPP, PRP, PAP, President
Robert M. President, DDS, Vice President
C.J. Cavin, CP, PRP, Treasurer
Atul Kapur, CPP, PRP, MD, Secretary
Joe Theobald, CP-T, PRP, Education Director

Promotes the use of effective, democratic and parliamentary practices by teaching of parliamentary procedures; training and certification of parliamentarians; promoting the use of parliamentarians; and maintaining a representative, democratic organization.
1.4M Members
Founded in 1958

15513 **American Intellectual Property Law Association**
1400 Crystal Drive
Suite 600
Arlington, VA 22202

703-415-0780; Fax: 703-415-0786
aipla@aipla.org
www.aipla.org
Facebook, Twitter, LinkedIn, Pinterest, Tumblr, Blogger, St

Joseph R. Re, President
Vincent Garlock, Executive Director
Meghan Donohoe, Chief Operating Officer
Cathleen Clime, Director of Meetings & Events
Randy Sagara, Information Technology Manager

Lawyers whose specialty is trademark, patent or copyright laws.
Founded in 1897
Mailing list available for rent

15514 **American Judicature Society**
P.O. Box 656
Honolulu, HI 96809

808-386-6987; Fax: 808-523-0842
americanjudicaturesociety.org
Facebook, Twitter, Youtube

Martha Hill Jamison, President
Rebecca Lee Wiggs, Vice President
Jon Comstock, Vice President
James Alfini, Interim Executive Director
Cynthia Gray, Director, Center Judicial Ethics

Lawyers, judges and educators interested in the effective administration of justice.
5000 Members
Founded in 1913

15515 **American Law & Economics Association**
PO Box 208245
New Haven, CT 06520-8245

203-432-7801; Fax: 203-432-7225
ALEA@yale.edu
www.amlecon.org

Aaron Edlin, President
W. Bentley Macleod, Vice President
Kathryn Zeiler, Secretary-Treasurer

Dedicated to the advancement of economic understanding of law and related areas of public policy and regulation.
Founded in 1991

15516 **American Law Institute**
4025 Chestnut St
Suite 5
Philadelphia, PA 19104-3099

215-243-1600
800-253-6397; Fax: 215-243-1636
ali@ali.org
www.ali.org
Facebook, Twitter, LinkedIn, Vimeo

David F. Levi, President
Lee H. Rosenthal, 1st Vice President
Teresa Wilton Harmon, 2nd Vice President
Wallace B. Jefferson, Chief Financial Officer
Richard L. Revesz, Director

A private, nonprofit organization that seeks to promote the clarification and simplification of the law through legal research and reform activities.
Founded in 1923
Mailing list available for rent

15517 **American Law Institute Continuing Legal Education Group (ALI CLE)**
4025 Chestnut St
Suite 5
Philadelphia, PA 19104
215-243-1600
800-253-6397; Fax: 215-243-1664
www.ali-cle.org
Julie Scribner, CFO and Director
Nancy Cline, Customer Service/MCLE Director
Diane Schnitzer, Director of Human Resources
Frank Paul Tomasello, Director
Provides continuing legal education courses, books, and periodicals for practicing attorneys and others in the legal profession. This organization is a collaborative effort of the ALI and the ABA.
Founded in 2012

15518 **American Lawyers Auxiliary**
321 North Clark Street
Chicago, IL 60610-4714
312-988-6387; Fax: 312-988-5494
Facebook, RSS
Sue Patterson, President
Anne Santorelli, First Vice President
Marilyn McDowell, Second Vice Presidentў
Connie Meigs, Secretary
Sharon Chappelear, Treasurer
Acts as a clearinghouse for state and local groups throughout the country and suggests educational programs pertaining to the law. Encourages members to volunteer their services.
75M Members
Founded in 1958

15519 **American Lawyers Newspapers Group**
1730 M Street NW
Washington, DC 20036-4513
202-457-0686
Supports all those involved in the reporting of legal issues. Publishes a weekly newsletter.
Founded in 1977

15520 **American Prepaid Legal Services Institute**
321 N Clark Street
Chicago, IL 60654
312-988-5751; Fax: 312-932-6436
glsaonline.org
Facebook, Twitter, LinkedIn
Nicolle Schippers, President
Stephen Ginsberg, Treasurer
Jean Clauson, Secretary
Professional trade organization representing the legal services plan industry. The members include lawyers, sponsor representatives, administrators and marketers of legal service plans. These people have invested their time, money and organizational resources to build legal service plans into the premier mechanism for supplying affordable legal services.
Founded in 1975

15521 **American Society for Legal History**
185 West Broadway
PO Box R
New York, NY 10013
574-631-6984; Fax: 574-631-3595
walter.f.pratt.1@nd.edu
www.aslh.net
Michael Grossberg, President
Sally Hadden, Secretary
Craig Evan Klafter, Treasurer
Rebecca J. Scott, President-Elect
Exhibits relating to legal history and its uses in formulating legal policy, decisions and actions; unearthing historical items; and preserving legal and legislative records.
1200 Members
Founded in 1956
Mailing list available for rent

15522 **American Society of Comparative Law**
University of Baltimore
1420 N. Charles Street
Baltimore, MD 21201
410-837-4689; Fax: 410-837-4560
lschnitzer@ubalt.edu
David J. Gerber, President
Vivian Curran, Vice President
Franklin Gervurtz, Secretary
Mortimer Sellers, Treasurer
Helge Dedek, Editor
An organization of institutional and individual members devoted to study, research, and write on foreign and comparative law as well as private international law.
60 Members
Founded in 1951
Mailing list available for rent

15523 **American Society of International Law**
2223 Massachusetts Ave Nw
Washington, DC 20008-2864
202-939-6001; Fax: 202-797-7133
services@asil.org
www.asil.org
Facebook, Twitter, LinkedIn, Youtube
Catherine Amirfar, President
Patrick Lipton Robinson, Honorary President
Mark Agrast, Executive Director
James Nafziger, Secretary
Nancy L. Perkins, Treasurer
Supports all those involved with overseas litigation. Publishes monthly newsletter.
4000 Members
Founded in 1906
Mailing list available for rent

15524 **American Society of Notaries**
PO Box 5707
Tallahassee, FL 32314-5707
850-671-5164; Fax: 850-671-5165
www.asnnotary.org
Kathleen Butler, Executive Director
Carly Hayes, Member Services Director
Helps to organize, improve and uphold high standards for notaries public.
21K Members
Founded in 1965

15525 **American Society of Trial Consultants**
6 Lawrence Square
Springfield, IL 62704
217-321-0337; Fax: 217-525-1271
ASTCOffice@astcweb.org
www.astcweb.org
Leslie Ellis, President
Amy Cheatham, Executive Director
Sean Hanko, Treasurer & Board Member
Suann Ingle, MS, Secretary & Board Member
Members come from diverse professional fields: communication, psychology, theatre, marketing, linguistics, political science and law.
500+ Members
Founded in 1982
Mailing list available for rent

15526 **American Society of Trial Consultants Foun dation**
10951 West Pico Blvd.
Suite 203
Los Angeles, CA 90064
424-832-3641
info@astcfoundation.org
www.astcfoundation.org
Daniel Wolfe, J.D., Ph.D., Board of Director
Karen Ohnemus Lisko, Ph.D., Board of Director
Mark Modlin, M.S., N.C.C., Board of Director
Ken Broda-Bahm, Ph.D., Board of Director
Ted Donner, Esq., Board of Director
Founded in 2004

15527 **Association of American Law Schools**
1614 20th Street, Northwest
Washington, DC 20009-1001
202-296-8851; Fax: 202-296-8869
aals@aals.org
www.aals.org
Facebook, Twitter, LinkedIn, YouTube, RSS
Darby Dickerson, President
Judith Areen, Executive Director/CEO
Jeff Allum, Director, Research & Analytics
James Greif, Communications Coordinator
Marisa Guevaa-Michalski, Chief Strategy Officer
An association of law schools that serves as the law teachers' learned society.
Founded in 1900
Mailing list available for rent

15528 **Association of Corporate Counsel**
1001 G Street NW
Suite 300W
Washington, DC 20001
202-293-4103; Fax: 202-293-4701
acc.chair@acc.com
www.acc.com
Facebook, Twitter, LinkedIn, RSS
Jo Anne Schwendinger, Chair
Mike Madden, Vice-Chair
Adrian Goss, Treasurer
Tracy Preston, Secretary
David Bamlango, Director
Lawyers who practice law in a corporation or other private sector entity and do not hold themselves out to the public to practice law.
15000 Members
Founded in 1982
Mailing list available for rent

15529 **Association of Family and Conciliation**
6525 Grand Teton Plaza
Madison, WI 53719
608-664-3750; Fax: 608-664-3751
afcc@afccnet.org
www.afccnet.org
Facebook, Twitter, LinkedIn, RSS
Hon. Peter Boshier, President
Annette T. Burns, JD, Vice President
Peter Salem, MA, Executive Director
Leslye Hunter, MA, LMFT, Associate Director
Carly Wieman, BA, Program Director
AFCC is an interdisciplinary, international association of professionals dedicated to improving the lives of children and families through the resolution of family conflict.
3700 Members
Founded in 1963

15530 **Association of Insolvency Advisors and Restructuring Advisors**
221 W. Stewart Avenue
Suite 207
Medford, OR 97501

541-858-1665; Fax: 541-858-9187
aira@aira.org
www.aira.org

Jim Lukenda, Executive Director
Terry Jones, Director, CIRA & CDBV Programs
Michael Stull, Director, Information Technology
Michele Michael, Director, Member Services

AIRA is a nonprofit professional association serving the bankruptcy, restructuring and turnaround practice area. AIRA's membership consists of accountants, financial advisors, investment bankers, attorneys, workout consultants, trustees, and others in the field of business turnaround, restructuring and bankruptcy. AIRA members are among the most trusted and sought-after professionals in matters dealing with limited capital resources and deteriorating operating performance.
2000+ Members
Founded in 1982

15531 **Association of Legal Administrators**
8700 W. Bryn Mawr Ave.
Suite 110S
Chicago, IL 60631-3512

847-267-1252; Fax: 847-267-1329
publications@alanet.org
www.alanet.org
Facebook, Twitter, LinkedIn

Paul Farnsworth, President
Oliver Yandle, JD, CAEÿ, Executive Director
Renee Tibbettsÿ, Director of Administration
Gwen Biasi, CAEÿ, Director of Marketing
Michelle Goldberg, Sr. Director Marketing

Professional support for management of private law firms and other legal organizations worldwide.
10000 Members
Founded in 1971

15532 **Association of Professional Responsibility Lawyers (APRL)**
20 South Clark Street
Suite 1050
Chicago, IL 60603

312-782-4396; Fax: 312-782-4725
admin@aprl.net
aprl.net

Arthur J Lachman, President
Charles Lundberg, President-Elect
Lynda C Shely, Secretary
Donald Campbell, Treasurer

An organization of lawyers who concentrate on professional responsibilities issues.
300 Members
Founded in 1990

15533 **Association of Prosecuting Attorneys**
11 DuPont Circle NW
Suite 240
Washington, DC 20036

202-861-2480; Fax: 202-816-8597
info@apainc.org
www.apainc.org
Facebook, Twitter

David LaBahn, President & CEO
Steven Naugle, Treasurer & CFO

Advocacy body and global forum focused on proactive and innovative prosecutorial practices.

15534 **Biz Law Association**
PO Box 247
Springdale, UT 84767-0247

FAX 435-635-9817

Suppports all those involved in business law, especially business owners and managers. Publishes newsletter.

15535 **Business & Legal Reports**
100 Winners Circle
Suite 300
Brentwood, TN 37027

860-510-0100
800-727-5257; Fax: 860-510-7225
service@blr.com
www.blr.com
Facebook, Twitter, LinkedIn

Robert L Brady, JD, Founder
Dan Oswald, Chief Executive Officer
Elizabeth Petersen, Vice President of Healthcare
Lawton Miller, Chief Financial Officer
Brad Forrister, VP, Training and Legal

Provides essential tools for safety and environmental compliance and training needs.
32 Members
Mailing list available for rent

15536 **Center for Professional Responsibility**
American Bar Association
321 North Clark Street
Chicago, IL 60654

312-988-5000
800-285-2221; Fax: 312-988-5491
cpr@staff.abanet.org
www.americanbar.org
Facebook, Twitter, LinkedIn

James R. Silkenat, President
Jack L. Rives, Executive Director
Robert M. Carlson, Chair, House of Delegates
Lucian T. Pera, Treasurer
Cara Lee T. Neville, Secretary

Since 1978, the Center has provided national leadership and vision in developing and interpreting standards and scholarly resources in legal ethics, professional regulation, professionalism and client protection mechanisms.
Founded in 1878
Mailing list available for rent

15537 **Center on Children and the Law**
American Bar Association Young Lawyers Division
1050 Connecticut Ave. N.W.
Suite 400
Washington, DC 20036

202-662-1000
800-285-2221; Fax: 202-662-1755
ctrchildlaw@abanet.org
www.americanbar.org
Facebook, Twitter, LinkedIn

James R. Silkenat, President
Jack L. Rives, Executive Director
Robert M. Carlson, Chair, House of Delegates
Lucian T. Pera, Treasurer
Cara Lee T. Neville, Secretary

This is a program of the Young Lawyers Division that aims to improve children's lives through advances in law, justice, knowledge, practice and public policy. Areas of expertise include child abuse and neglect, child welfare and protective services system enhancement, foster care, family preservation, termination of parental rights, parental substance abuse, adolescent health, and domestic violence.
15 Members
Founded in 1878

15538 **Commercial Law League of America**
3005 Tollview Drive
Rolling Meadows, IL 60008

312-240-1400; Fax: 312-240-1408
info@clla.org
www.clla.org
Facebook, Twitter, LinkedIn, YouTube

Phil Lattanzio, Executive Vice President
Dawn Federico, Associate Director
Linda Herbst, Marketing & Communications
Lillian Novak, Member Services

Supports those involved in bankruptcy, collections, debt and insolvency legislation, and connects experienced attorneys with gredit grantors, lending instutitions and other commercial credit, bankruptcy, and general finance industry members.
Founded in 1895

15539 **Commission on Mental & Physical Disability Law**
American Bar Association
1050 Connecticut Ave. N.W.
Suite 400
Washington, DC 20036

202-662-1000
800-285-2221; Fax: 202-442-3439
cdr@americanbar.org
www.americanbar.org
Facebook, Twitter, LinkedIn

Mark D. Agrast, Esq., Chair
Amy L. Allbright, Director
M. Tovah Miller, Program Specialist
Michael J. Stratton, Administrative Coordinator
Brandon M. Moore-Rhodes, Technology Associate

The Commission's mission is 'to promote the ABA's commitment to justice and the rule of law for persons with mental, physical, and sensory disabilities and to promote their full and equal participation in the legal profession.' The Commission consists of 15 members appointed by the ABA President-elect on an annual basis. It meets bi-annually at its headquarters in Washington, D.C., to map out future plans and to direct the current activities.
15 Members
Founded in 1973
Mailing list available for rent

15540 **Copyright Society of The USA**
1 East 53rd Street
8th Floor
New York, NY 10022

Home Page: www.csusa.org
Facebook, Twitter, LinkedIn

Eric J. Schwartz, President
Nancy E. Wolff, Vice President
Michael Donaldson, Treasurer
Judith Finell, Secretary
Kaitland Kubat, Director of Operations
Founded in 1953

15541 **Council of State Governments**
2760 Research Park Drive
PO Box 11910
Lexington, KY 40578-1910

859-244-8000
800-800-1910; Fax: 859-244-8001
press@csg.org
www.csg.org
Facebook, Twitter, LinkedIn, YouTube, RSS

Sen. Carl Marcellino, Chair
Brian Sandoval, President
David Adkins, Executive Director/CEO
Carl Marcellino, Vice Chair
Mark Norris, Chair-Elect
Founded in 1933
Mailing list available for rent

15542 **Council on Legal Education Opportunity**
1101 Mercantile Lane
Suite 294
Largo, MD 20774

240-582-8600
866-886-4343; Fax: 240-582-8605
cleo@cleoinc.org
www.cleoscholars.org
Facebook, Twitter

Cassandra Sneed Ogden, Executive Director
Bernetta J Hayes, Admissions Administrator
Leigh R. Allen II, Mentoring & Development Director
Lynda Cevallos, Pre-Law Coordinator
Julie D Long, Project Research Assistant

Provides law school preparation assistance for minority and disadvantaged students. Program is six-week summer institute paid for by the program. Scholarship of approximately $16,000 for the three years of law study is granted to selected and certified students, after completion of the summer program.

15543 **Council on Licensure, Enforcement and Regulation**
108 Wind Haven Drive
Suite A
Nicholasville, KY 40356

859-269-1289; Fax: 859-231-1943
rbrown@clearhq.org
www.clearhq.org
Facebook, Twitter, LinkedIn

Tami Martin, Office Manager
Adam Parfitt, Executive Director
Rosa Brown, Administrative Associate
Nicolle Harkness, Membership Coordinator
Jodie Markey, Senior Program Coordinator

Supports all those involved in occupational, professional licensing and regulation.
Founded in 1994
Mailing list available for rent

15544 **DRI-The Voice Of The Defense Bar**
55 W. Monroe Street
Suite 2000
Chicago, IL 60603

312-951-1101; Fax: 312-795-0749
dri@dri.org
www.dri.org
Facebook, Twitter, LinkedIn, Youtube

Laura E. Proctor, President
John F. Kuppens, First Vice President
Toyja E. Kelley, Second Vice President
Kathleen M. Guilfoyle, Secretary-Treasurer
John Parker Sweeney, President-Elect

Service organization to improve the administration of justice and defense lawyers' skills.
Founded in 1960

15545 **Education Law Association**
2121 Euclid Avenue
LL 212
Cleveland, OH 44115-2214

216-523-7377; Fax: 216-687-5284
ela@educationlaw.org
www.educationlaw.org
Facebook, Twitter, LinkedIn

Patrick D. Pauken, J.D., Ph.D., President
Lynn Rossi Scott, J.D, Vice President
Cate K. Smith, J.D., M.P.A, Executive Director
Pat Petrusky, Member Services Coordinator
Pamela Hardy, Publications Specialist

Brings together educational and legal scholars and practitioners to inform and advance educational policy and practice through knowledge of the law. Together, our professional community anticipates trends in educational law and supports scholarly research through the highest value print and electronic publications, conferences, seminars and professional forums.
1400 Members
Founded in 1954

15546 **Environmental Law Alliance Worldwide**
1412 Pearl St.
Eugene, OR 97401

541-687-8454; Fax: 541-687-0535
elawus@elaw.org
www.elaw.org

Bern Johnson, Executive Director
Lori Maddox, Associate Director

Attorneys, scientists and others advocating for a healthy planet.

15547 **Equal Justice Works**
1730 M Street NW
Suite 1010
Washington, DC 20036-4511

202-466-3686; Fax: 202-429-9766
mail@equaljusticeworks.org
www.equaljusticeworks.org
Facebook, Twitter, LinkedIn, Youtube, Flickr

Kim Koopersmith, Chair
David Stern, Executive Director
Jeanne Van Vlandren, Chief Operating Officer
Tammy Sun, Senior Manager, Fellowships
Anne Bloom, Director of Public Programs

Founded by law students dedicated to surmounting barriers to equal justice that affect millions of low income individuals and families. Equal Justice organizes, trains and supports public service minded law students, and in creating summer and postgraduate public interest jobs.
Founded in 1986
Mailing list available for rent

15548 **Federal Bar Association**
1220 North Fillmore St.
Suite 444
Arlington, VA 22201ÿ

571-481-9100; Fax: 571-481-9090
fba@fedbar.org
www.fedbar.org
Facebook, Twitter, LinkedIn

Matthew B. Moreland, President
Mark K. Vincent, President Elect
Michael J. Newmanÿ, Treasurer
Karen Silberman, Executive Director
Heather Gaskins, Director of Development
Founded in 1920

15549 **Federal Circuit Bar Association**
1620 Eye St NW
Suite 801
Washington, DC 20006-4035

202-466-3923; Fax: 202-833-1061
ehaugFCBA@FLHlaw.com
www.fedcirbar.org

Edgar H. Haug, Esquire, President
James E. Brookshire, Executive Director
Marcia Foster, Office Operations
Jeremy Atkinson, IT/Administration
Darren Davis, Membership Coordinator

FCBA is a national organization of attorneys who practice before the United States Court of Appeals for the Federal Circuit.
Mailing list available for rent

15550 **Federal Communications Bar Association**
1020 19th St NW
Suite 325
Washington, DC 20036-6101

202-293-4000; Fax: 202-293-4317
fcba@fcba.org
www.fcba.org

Christopher J. Wright, President
Julie M. Kearney, Secretary
Natalie G. Roisman, Assistant Secretary
Erin L. Dozier, Treasurer
Lee G. Petro, Assistant Treasurer

A nonprofit organization of attorneys and other professionals involved in the development, interpretation, implementation and practice of communications law and policy.
3000 Members
Founded in 1936
Mailing list available for rent

15551 **Federal Mediation & Conciliation Service**
2100 K St NW
Washington, DC 20427

202-606-8100; Fax: 202-606-4251
jpinto@fmcs.gov
www.fmcs.gov

John Pinto, Manager of Field Operations

15552 **Federation of Defense & Corporate Counsel**
11812 N 56th St
Tampa, FL 33617-1528

813-983-0022; Fax: 813-988-5837
www.thefederation.org
Facebook, Twitter, LinkedIn

Victoria H. Roberts, Board Chair
Smith Moore Leatherwood, President
Martha J. Streeper, FDCC Executive Director
Michael W. Streeper, FDCC Financial Director
Susan J. Coone, Executive Administration

The objective and purposes of this Federation are to establish and maintain an organization consisting of members of the bar who are actively engaged in the legal aspects of the insurance business, executives of insurance companies an associations and corporate counsel engaged in the defense of claims; to assist in establishing standards for providing competent, efficient and economical legal services; to encourage and provide for legal education of the members of this Federation.
Founded in 1960

15553 **First Amendment Lawyers Association**
1875 K Street NW
4th Floor
Washington, DC 20006

202-540-9817; Fax: 202-289-7499
therberghs@firstamendmentlawyers.org
www.firstamendmentlawyers.org

Todd Herberghs, Director, Operations

FALA is a not-for-profit, nation-wide association devoted to the protection of Free Expression under the First Amendment, who represent businesses and individuals engaged in constitutionally protected activities. Members practice throughout the U.S., Canada, and elsewhere in defense of the First Amendment and free speech and advocate against all forms of governmental censorship.
180 Members
Founded in 1965

15554 **Hispanic National Bar Association**
1020 19th Street NW
Suite 505
Washington, DC 20036
202-223-4777; Fax: 202-223-2324
info@hnba.com
www.hnba.com
Facebook, Twitter, RSS
Robert Maldonado, President
Alba Cruz-Hacker, HNBA COO & Executive Director
Anjanette Cabrera, VP of Membership
Jaime Areizaga-Soto, VP of Regions & Affiliates
Raquel Matas, VP of External Affairs
Supports all Latino attorneys and legal professionals with publications and educational conferences.
25000 Members
Founded in 1972
Mailing list available for rent

15555 **Institute of Management & Administration**
3 Bethesda Metro Center
Suite 250
Bethesda, MD 20814-5377
703-341-3500
800-372-1033; Fax: 800-253-0332
customercare@bna.com
www.ioma.com
Facebook, Twitter, LinkedIn, YouTube
Gregory C. McCaffery, CEO & President
Sue Martin, Chief Operating Officer
Jean Lockhart, Chief of Staff
Michael Newborn, VP/Chief Security Officer
Rich Thompson, Chief Technology Officer
An independent source of exclusive business management information for experienced senior and middle management professionals.

15556 **Inter-American Bar Association**
1889 F Street, NW
3rd. Floor, Suite 355
Washington, DC 20006
202-466-5944; Fax: 202-466-5946
iaba@iaba.org
www.iaba.org
Facebook, Twitter, LinkedIn, YouTube
Alejandro Lapad£, President
Alejandro Solano, Vice President
Tina di Battista, Secretary
The main purposes of this association are to establish and maintain relations among organizations of lawyers, national and local, in the Americas; to provide a forum for the exchange of views; to advance the science of jurisprudence particularly in the study of comparative law; to promote uniformity of the law; to disseminate knowledge of the laws; to promote the Rule of Law and the administration of justice; to preserve and defend human rights and liberties.
3M Members
Founded in 1940

15557 **International Association of Defense Counsel**
303 West Madison
Suite 925
Chicago, IL 60606-3401
312-368-1494; Fax: 312-368-1854
info@iadclaw.org
www.iadclaw.org
Facebook, Twitter, LinkedIn
Joseph E. O'Neil, President
Mary Beth Kurzak, Executive Director
Amy O'Maley, Esq., Director, Professional Development
Carmela Balice, Senior Manager, Member Services
Ashley Fitzgerald, Manager, Communications
Offers continuing legal education and conducts research projects.
Cost: $650.00
2.5M Members
Founded in 1920

15558 **International Bar Association**
1667 K Street, NW
Suite 1230
Washington, DC 20006
202-827-3250; Fax: 202-733-5657
iba@int-bar.org
www.ibanet.org
Facebook, Twitter, LinkedIn, YouTube
David W Rivkin, President
Martin Solc, Vice President
Horacio Bernardes-Neto, Secretary-General
Mark Ellis, Executive Director
Ele Dexter, Executive Assistant
Founded in 1947

15559 **International BarÿAssociation**
1667 K Street, NW
Suite 1230
Washington, DC 20006
202-827-3250; Fax: 202-733-5657
www.ibanet.org
Facebook, Twitter, LinkedIn, YouTube
David W Rivkin, President
Martin Solc, Vice President
Horacio Bernardes-Neto, Secretary-General
Mark Ellis, Executive Director
Ele Dexter, Executive Assistant
Founded in 1947

15560 **International Paralegal Management Association**
980 N. Michigan Ave
Suite 1400
Chicago, IL 60611
312-214-4991; Fax: 888-662-9155
www.theipma.org
Facebook, Twitter, LinkedIn
Victoria L.ÿ Snook, President
Gary L. Melhuish, Vice President - Membership
Lynda S. McNie, Secretary-Treasurer
Jennifer Karns, Vice President - Trends & Positions
Larry C. Smith, CAE, Executive Director
Founded in 1984

15561 **International Probate Research Association**
c/o Josh Butler & Company
PO Box 27
Cuyahoga Falls, OH 44222-0027
330-506-6400
inforequest@joshbutler.com
www.lostheir.com/ipa.htm
Josh Butler, President
IPRA members are probate research companies.
Founded in 1989

15562 **International Society of Barristers**
210 Science Drive
802 Legal Research Building
Durham, NC 27708-0360
919-613-7085; Fax: 734-764-8309
isob.com
John W Reed, Administrative Secretary
Members are trial lawyers interested in encouraging advocacy under the adversary system and preserving trial by jury.
750 Members
Founded in 1965

15563 **Investigative Professionals, Inc.**
PO Box 35
Hardyville, KY 42746
928-451-1598; Fax: 877-657-6691
www.investigativeprofessionals.com
Facebook, Twitter, Google+, Blogger
Larry Troxel
NALI was formed with its primary focus to conduct investigations related to litigation. Membership in NALI is open to all professional legal investigators who are actively engaged in negligence investigations for the plaintiff and/or criminal defense, and who are emplyoed by investigative firms, law firms or public defender agencies.
Founded in 1996
Mailing list available for rent

15564 **Japanese American Society for Legal Studies**
University of WA Law School-1100 NE Cam.
Seattle, WA 98105
206-233-9292; Fax: 206-685-4469
John Haley, Editor
Association for those interested in Japanese law and legal issues.

15565 **Law and Society Association**
383 South University Street
Suite 205
Salt Lake City, UT 84112
801-581-3219; Fax: 888-292-5515
lsa@lawandsociety.org
www.lawandsociety.org
Facebook, Twitter, LinkedIn
Valerie Hans, President
Susan Olson, Executive Director
Kris Monty, Administrative and Events Manager
Megan Crowley, Communication Specialist
Susan Olson, Executive Director
Founded in 1964

15566 **Legal Education and Admissions to the Bar Association**
321 N Clark Street
21st Floor
Chicago, IL 60611-4403
312-988-5000
800-285-2221; Fax: 312-988-5681
www.abanet.org/legaled/resources
Facebook, Twitter
Barry Currier, Managing Director
William E. Adams, Deputy Managing Director
Camille deJorna, Associate Consultant
Carl A. Brambrink, Director of Operations
Beverly Holmes, Program Associate
Association for state bar admission administrators in the United States and its territories.
10000 Members
Founded in 1878
Mailing list available for rent

15567 **Legal Marketing Association**
330 North Wabash Ave.
Suite 2000
Chicago, IL 60611
312-321-6898; Fax: 312-673-6894
membersupport@legalmarketing.org
www.legalmarketing.orgÿ
Facebook, Twitter, LinkedIn, YouTube
Timothy B. Corcoran, President
Susan Lane, Director of Operations
Lisa Rottler, Membership Services Coordinator
Adrianne Stokes, Membership Services Associate
Betsi Roach, Executive Directorÿ
Founded in 1985

15568 Maritime Law Association of the United States
400 Poydras Street
27th Floor Texaco Center
New Orleans, LA 70130-324

504-680-8433; Fax: 904-421-8437
www.mlaus.org

Robert B. Parrish, President
Robert G. Clyne, First VP
Harold K. Watson, Second VP
William Robert Connor III, Treasurer
David J. Farrell, Secretary

To advance reforms in the Maritime Law of the United States, to facilitate justice in its administration to promote uniformity in its enactment and interpretation, to furnish a forum for the discussion and consideration of problems affecting the Maritime Law and its administration to participate as a constituent member of the Comite Maritime International and as an affiliated organization of the American Bar Association.
Founded in 1899
Mailing list available for rent

15569 Mid-America Association of Law Libraries
jeri_hopkins@ca8.uscourts.gov
www.aallnet.org/chapter/maall/

Cynthia Bassett, President
Jennifer Prilliman, Vice President/ President Elect
Erika Cohn, Secretary
Jenny Watson, Treasurer

Association for suppliers of law library equipment, supplies and services.
Founded in 1973

15570 NALS/The Association For Legal Professionals
8159 East 41st Street
#210
Tulsa, OK 74145

918-582-5188; Fax: 918-582-5907
www.nals.org
Facebook, Twitter, LinkedIn, RSS, Youtube, Google+, Flickr

Carl H. Morrison, PP-SC, AACP, President
Tammy Hailey, CAE, Executive Director
April Collins, Meetings & Communications Manager
Saundra Bates, Membership Services Manager
Melissa Wells, Certification/Education

Supports all those involved with the technology of the legal profession and the education and training of the legal administrative staff. Publishes quarterly magazine. NALS is dedicated to enhancing the competencies and contributions of members in the legal field.
Founded in 1929
Mailing list available for rent

15571 National Academy of Elder Law Attorneys
1577 Spring Hill Road
Suite 220
Vienna, VA 22182-2223

703-942-5711; Fax: 703-563-9504
naela@naela.org
www.naela.org

Shirley Berger Whitenack, President
Hyman G. Darling, CELA, CAP, Vice President
Peter G. Wacht, CAE, Executive Director
Ann Watkins, Operations Manager
Courtney White, Marketing Coordinator

Non-profit association for attorneys specializing in Elder Law and Special Needs Law.
4200 Members
Founded in 1987

15572 National American Indian Court Clerks Association
National Association of Tribal Court Personnel
920 Spring Creek Circle
Green Bay, WI 54311
Robert Miller, President

Devoted to upgrading the integrity capabilities and management of tribal courts through training, testing and certification of court clerks and court administrators.
257 Members

15573 National American Indian Court Judges
1942 Broadway
Suite 215
Boulder, CO 80303

303-449-4112; Fax: 303-449-4038
info@naicja.org
www.naicja.org
Facebook, Youtube

Hon. Jill E. Tompkins, President
Richard Blake, First VP
Kevin Briscoe, Second VP
Winona Tanner, Treasurer
Catherine Bryan, Associate Director

National voluntary association of tribal court judges. Primarily devoted to the support of the American Indian and Alaska Native justice systems through education, information sharing and advocacy.
256 Members
Founded in 1969
Mailing list available for rent

15574 National Association for Community Mediation
PO Box 3376
STE 252
Cumming, GA 30028

602-633-4213; Fax: 202-545-8873
jordway@nafcm.org
www.nafcm.org
Facebook, Twitter, LinkedIn, Youtube, Blogger, Google+

Joanne Galindo, Senior Director
Victoria Tobin, Executive Director
D.G. Mawn, Associate Executive Director
LaDessa Croucher, Secretary
Laura Jeffords, Treasurer

Supports the maintenance and growth of community-based mediation program and processes: presents a compelling voice in appropriate policy-making, legislative, professional, and other arenas; and encourages the development and sharing of resources for these efforts.
779 Members
Founded in 1994
Mailing list available for rent

15575 National Association for Court Management
300 Newport Avenue
Williamsburg, VA 23185-4147

757-259-1841
800-616-6165; Fax: 757-259-1520
nacm@ncsc.org
www.nacmnet.org
Facebook, Twitter, LinkedIn

David W. Slayton, President
Stephanie Hess, Vice President
Scott C. Griffith, Secretary/Treasurer

Members are clerks of court, court administration and others serving in a court management capacity.
1700 Members
Founded in 1985
Mailing list available for rent

15576 National Association for Legal Career Professionals
1220 19th Street NW
Suite 401
Washington, DC 20036-2405

202-835-1001; Fax: 202-835-1112
info@nalp.org
www.nalp.org
Facebook, Twitter, LinkedIn, YouTube

Jean A. Durling, President
Beth Moeller, Vice-President for Member Services
Christina Fox, Vice-President for Finance
James G. Leipold, Executive Director
Frederick E. Thrasher, Deputy Director

Deals with issues such as career planning, recruiting and ethics.
Founded in 1971

15577 National Association of Attorneys General
2030 M Street Nw
8th Floor
Washington, DC 20036

202-326-6000; Fax: 202-331-1427
feedback@naag.org
www.naag.org
Facebook, Twitter

Jim McPherson, NAAG Executive Director
Chris Toth, NAAG Deputy Executive Director
Al Lama, NAAG Chief of Staff
Jeffrey Hunter, NAAG Executive Assistant
Marjorie Tharp, NAAG Communications Director

Fosters interstate cooperation on legal and law enforcement issues, conducts policy research and analysis, provides advocacy.
56 Members
Founded in 1907
Mailing list available for rent: 56 names

15578 National Association of Black Criminal
1801 Fayetteville Street 106
Whiting Criminal Justice Building
Durham, NC 27707

919-683-1801
866-846-2225; Fax: 919-683-1903
office@nabcj.org
www.nabcj.org
Facebook, Twitter, RSS

Carlyle I. Holder, President
Terri Mcgee, Vice President
Vernise Robinson, Secretary
Charles Lockett, Treasurer
Andre Turner, Assistant Treasurer
Founded in 1974

15579 National Association of Blacks in Criminal Justice
1801 Fayetteville St.
106 Whiting Criminal Justice Bldg.
Durham, NC 27707

919-683-1801
866-846-2225; Fax: 919-683-1903
office@nabcj.org
www.nabcj.org
Facebook, Twitter, RSS

Carlyle Holder, President
Terrie McGee, Vice President
Vernise Robinson, Secretary
Charles Lockett, Treasurer

Supports all black persons who are involved in the criminal justice system. Hosts annual trade show.
Founded in 1974

15580 National Association of College and University Attorneys
One Dupont Circle
Suite 620
Washington, DC 20036-1134

202-833-8390; Fax: 202-296-8379
nacua@nacua.org
www.nacua.org

Kathleen Curry, CEO
Jeanna L. Grimes, Manager of Membership and Marketing
John R. Bishop, Director of Information Services
Meredith L. McMillan, Meetings and Events Planner
Paul L. Parsons, Deputy CEO

Educates attorneys and administrative executives about campus legal issues.
Mailing list available for rent

15581 National Association of Consumer Advocates
1215 17th Street NW
5th Floor
Washington, DC 20036

202-452-1989; Fax: 202-452-0099
info@consumeradvocates.org
www.consumeradvocates.org
Facebook, Twitter

David Philips, Co-Chair
Michael J. Quirk, Co-Chair
Brian Bromberg, Treasurer
Ronald Wilcox, Secretary
Ira Rheingold, Executive Director

The National Association of Consumer Advocates (NACA) is a nonprofit association of more than 1,500 attorneys and consumer advocates committed to representing consumers' interests. NACA's members and their clients are actively engaged in promoting a fair and open marketplace that forcefully protects the rights of consumers, particularly those of modest means.
1500 Members
Founded in 1994

15582 National Association of Counsel for Children
13123 E. 16th Avenue
B390
Aurora, CO 80045

303-864-5320
Advocate@NACCchildlaw.org
www.naccchildlaw.org
Facebook, LinkedIn, Blog

Gerard Glynn, MS, JD / LLM, President
H.D. Kirkpatrick, Vice President
Kendall Marlowe, Executive Director
Daniel Trujillo, Certification Director
Sara Whalen, Membership Director
Founded in 1977

15583 National Association of County Civil Attorneys
1100 17th St NW
Second Floor
Washington, DC 20036-4619

202-783-5550; Fax: 202-783-1583
info@naccho.org
www.naccho.org
Facebook, Twitter, LinkedIn, RSS, Blogger, Pinterest, Tumbl

Paul Yeghiayan, President
Mark Jorritsma, Chief Operating Officer
John Mericsko, Chief Financial Officer
LaMar Hasbrouck, Executive Director
Laura Hanen, Chief, Government & Public Affairs

An affiliate of the National Association of Counties.
240 Members
Founded in 1994
Mailing list available for rent

15584 National Association of Criminal Defense Lawyers
1660 L Street NW
12th Floor
Washington, DC 20036

202-872-8600; Fax: 202-872-4000
jstepan@nacdl.org
www.nacdl.org
Facebook, Twitter, LinkedIn, YouTube

Nina Ginsberg, President
Chris Adams, President-Elect
Martin Sabelli, First Vice President
Andrew Birrell, Treasurer
Norman L. Reimer, Executive Director

America's preeminent voluntary bar association supporting the Criminal Defense profession.
8500 Members
Founded in 1958

15585 National Association of Legal Assistants
7666 E. 61st Street
Suite 315
Tulsa, OK 74133

918-587-6828; Fax: 918-582-6772
nalanet@nala.org
www.nala.orgÿ

Kelly A. LaGrave, ACP, President
Cassandra Oliver, ACP, First Vice President
Jill Francisco, ACP, Second Vice President
Debra L. Overstreet, ACP, Treasurer
Marge Dover, CAE, Executive Director

15586 National Association of Legal Investigator s
235 N. Pine Street
Lansing, MI 48933

517-702-9835
866-520-NALI; Fax: 517-372-1501
info@nalionline.org
www.nalionline.org
Facebook, LinkedIn
David W. Luther, CLI, National Director
Don C. Johnson, CLI, CII, Assistant National Director
Neeta McClintock, National Secretary
Julian Vail, LLC, Association Management
John Hoda, CLI, Regional Director, Northeast Region
Founded in 1967

15587 National Association of Legal Vendors
Juris
5106 Maryland Way
Brentwood, TN 37027-7501

615-377-3740

Mel Goldenburg, Chairman

Trade association of organizations who sell products to the legal community.
100 Members

15588 National Association of Parliamentarians (NAP)
213 South Main Street
Independence, MO 64050-3808

816-833-3892
888-627-2929; Fax: 816-833-3893
hq@nap2.org
www.parliamentarians.org
Facebook, Twitter, RSS

Mary Randolph, President
James Jones, VP
Cyndy Launchbaugh, Executive Director
Courtney Emery, Membership Marketing & Comm.
Stefanie Luttrell, Administrative Coordinator

An association for those interested in parliamentary law and procedure, NAP's primary objectives are teaching, promoting, and disseminating the philosophy and principles underlying the rules of deliberative assemblies.
3500 Members
Founded in 1930

15589 National Association of Women Lawyers
321 North Clark Street
Chicago, IL 60654

312-988-6186; Fax: 312-932-6450
nawl@nawl.org
www.nawl.org

Marsha L. Anastasia, President
Angela Beranek Brandt, Vice President
Jennifer A. Waters, Executive Director
Caitlin Kepple, Marketing and Development Director
Karen M. Richardson, Program Director

Promotes the advancement and welfare of women in the legal profession. NAWL is a professional association of attorneys, judges and law students serving the educational, legal and practical interests of the organized bar and women generally. Founded in 1899, long before most local and national bar associations admitted women.
800 Members
Founded in 1899

15590 National Bar Association
1225 11th St Nw
Washington, DC 20001-4217

202-842-3900; Fax: 202-289-6170
headquarters@nationalbar.org
www.nationalbar.org
Facebook, Twitter, LinkedIn, YouTube

Benjamin Crump, President
Keith Andrew Perry, Executive Director
Chris Tinker, CFO
Heidi Franklin, Director
Nanjiba Hlemi, Director of Membership and Programs
Represents the interests of minority attorneys, offers education and research programs.
18000 Members
Founded in 1925
Mailing list available for rent

15591 National Cannabis Bar Association
244 California St.
Suite 507
San Francisco, CA 94111

415-723-6222
info@canbar.org
www.canbar.org
Facebook, Twitter, LinkedIn
Christopher J. Davis, Executive Director

Connects cannabis industry lawyers for the purpose of continuing education and providing excellent, ethical, and advanced legal assistance to the growing cannabis industry.
Founded in 2015

15592 National Center for State Courts
300 Newport Ave
Williamsburg, VA 23185-4147

757-259-1819
800-616-6164; Fax: 757-220-0449
mmcqueen@ncsc.org
www.ncsc.org
Facebook, Twitter, LinkedIn, Google+, Flickr, Vimeo, Pinter

David Gilbertson, Chair
Patricia W. Griffin, Vice-Chair
Mary McQueen, President

Thomas Clarke, VP, Research and Technology
Daniel Hall, Vice President of Court Consulting
Provides a forum for the state courts.
Founded in 1971
Mailing list available for rent

15593 National College of District Attorneys
99 Canal Center Plaza
Suite 330
Alexandria, VA 22314
703-549-9222; Fax: 703-836-3195
www.ndaa.org
Facebook, Yahoo
William Fitzpatrick, President
Rick Hasey, Chief Financial Officer
Rick Hanes, Chief of Staff
Kay Chopard Cohen, Executive Director
Ann Ratnayake, Staff Attorney
Provides continuing legal education and training for prosecuting attorneys and their investigators and office administrators through programs specifically tailored to meet their needs. Programs include resident courses held each summer at the University of Houston Law Center, short courses conducted in locations throughout the country, and courses presented cooperatively with state associations and local offices.
Founded in 1950
Mailing list available for rent

15594 National Conference of Bar Examiners
302 South Bedford Street
Madison, WI 53703-3622
608-280-8550; Fax: 608-280-8552
contact@ncbex.org
www.ncbex.org
Erica Moeser, President
A non-profit organization offering tests and services to state boards of bar examiners.
Founded in 1931

15595 National Conference of Bar Foundations
ABA Division For Bar Services
321 North Clark Street
Suite 2000
Chicago, IL 60654
312-988-5344; Fax: 312-988-5492
info@ncbf.org
www.ncbf.org
Leonard Pataki, President
Leslie Barineau, Secretary
Alison Belfrage, Treasurer
Lorrie Albert, Secretary
Serves bar foundations in the United States and Canada; conducts biannual conferences; maintains information clearinghouses.
Founded in 1977
Mailing list available for rent

15596 National Conference of Bar Presidents
321 North Clark Street
Suite 2000
Chicago, IL 60654-7598
312-988-5344; Fax: 312-988-5492
www.ncbp.org
Facebook, Twitter
Lanneau W. Lambert Jr., President
Christine H. Hickey, Treasurer
Jennifer L. Parent, Secretary
Provides a forum for the exchange of ideas and seeks to stimulate work in bar associations.
1M Members
Founded in 1950

15597 National Conference of Commissioners on US Law
211 E Ontario St
Suite 1300
Chicago, IL 60611-3242
312-283-5200; Fax: 312-915-0187
www.uniformlaws.org
John A. Sebert, Executive Director
J. Elizabeth Cotton-Murphy, Chief Administrative Officer
Robert Stein, Secretary
Carl Lisman, Treasurer
Elizabeth Cotton, Manager
Designed to foster interstate cooperation in legal issues.
Founded in 1892
Mailing list available for rent

15598 National Conference of Women's Bar Associations
PO Box 82366
Portland, OR 97282
503-775-4396
info@ncwba.org
www.ncwba.org
Facebook, Twitter, LinkedIn
Katherine L. Brown, President
Barbara L. Harris Chiang, Vice President - Membership
Robin Bresky, VP, Fundraising & Strategic Part.
Monica Parham, Vice-President-Finance
Celia J. Collins, Secretary
To promote and assist the growth of local and statewide women's bar associations and ideas among women's bar associations and women's bar sections of local and statewide bar associations; to serve as a vehicle for the exchange and dissemination of information and ideas among women's bar associations and women's bar sections of local and statewide bar associations.

15599 National Conference of Womens' Bar Associations
PO Box 82366
Portland, OR 97282
503-775-4396; Fax: 503-657-3932
info@ncwba.org
www.ncwba.org
Facebook, Twitter, LinkedIn
Katherine L. Brown, President
Barbara L. Harris Chiang, Vice President - Membership
Robin Bresky, VP, Fundraising & Strategic Part.
Monica Parham, Vice-President-Finance
Celia J. Collins, Secretary
Supports women who are involved in the legal community and provides a forum for the exchange of ideas, thus stimulating work in bar associations.
30000 Members
Founded in 1981
Mailing list available for rent

15600 National Court Reporters Association
12030 Sunrise Valley Drive
Suite 400
Reston, VA 20191
703-556-6272
800-272-6272; Fax: 703-391-0629
msic@ncra.org
www.ncraonline.org
Facebook, Twitter, LinkedIn, Youtube, RSS
Stephen A. Zinone, RPR, President
Christine J. Willette, Vice President
Doreen Sutton, RPR, Secretary-Treasurer
Stephen A. Zinone, RPR, Secretary/Treasurer
Toni O'Neill, FAPR, RPR, Director
18000 Members
Founded in 1899

15601 National District Attorneys Association
99 Canal Center Plaza
Suite 330
Alexandria, VA 22314-1548
703-549-9222; Fax: 703-836-3195
www.ndaa.org
Facebook, Yahoo
William Fitzpatrick, President
Rick Hasey, Chief Financial Officer
Mary McQueen, President
Thomas Clarke, VP, Research and Technology
Daniel Hall, Vice President of Court Consulting
Supports district attorneys nationwide with education, publications, and regular conferences.
7000 Members
Founded in 1950

15602 National Federation of Paralegal Associations, Inc.
23607 Highway 99
Suite 2-C
Edmonds, WA 98026
425-967-0045; Fax: 425-771-9588
info@paralegals.org
www.paralegals.org
Facebook, LinkedIn
Lisa Vessels, RP, CP, FRP, President
Allen F. Mihecoby, CLAS, RP, VP/Director of Profession Dev
Lynne-Marie Reveliotis, VP/Director of Positions and Issues
Yvonne DeAntoneo, VP/Director of Membership
Nita Serrano, RP, VP/Director of Paralegal Cert.
Nonprofit, professional organization comprising state and local paralegal associations throughout the United States and Canada. NFPA affirms the paralegal profession as an independent, self-directed profession which supports increased quality, efficiency and accessibility in the delivery of legal services. NFPA promotes the growth, development and recognition of the profession as a integral partner in the delivery of legal services.
15000 Members
Founded in 1974

15603 National Forensic Center
17 Temple Terrace
Lawrenceville, NJ 08648
609-883-0550
800-526-5177
jon@midi.com
expertindex.com
Association for those interested in the application of scientific knowledge in litigation.

15604 National Institute for Trial Advocacy
1685 38th Street
Suite 200
Boulder, CO 80301-2735
800-225-6482; Fax: 720-890-7069
www.nita.org
Karen Lockwood, Executive Director
Michelle Rogness, Director of Programs
Katie Grosso, Program Specialist, Public Programs
Jennifer Schneider, Director of Publications
Daniel McHugh, Director of Sales & Marketing
60 Members
Founded in 1971

15605 National Law Foundation
P. O. Box 218
Montchanin, DE 19710
302-656-4757; Fax: 302-764-8697
www.nlfcle.com

15606 **National Lawyers Association**
PO Box 327
Suite 400
Lee's Summit, MO 64063
844-917-1787
www.nla.org
Facebook, Twitter, LinkedIn, Pinterest, Google+
Joshua McCaig, President
Paul Brodersen, Vice President
Lenny A. Best, CEO
Jeremiah Morgan, Board Member
Cynthia Dunbar, Board Member
Founded in 1993

15607 **National Lawyers Guild**
132 Nassau St
Suite 922
New York, NY 10038
212-679-5100; Fax: 212-679-2811
www.nlg.org
Facebook, Twitter, Instagram, Vimeo
Pooja Gehi, Executive Director
Traci Yoder, Director, Education & Research
Tasha Moro, Director, Communications
Lisa Drapkin, Director, Membership
King Downing, Director, Mass Defense
Dedicated to seeking economic justice, social equality and the right to political dissent.
5000 Members
Founded in 1937
Mailing list available for rent

15608 **National Legal Aid and Defender Associatio n**
1901 Pennsylvania Avenue NW
Suite 500
Washington, DC 20006
202-452-0620; Fax: 202-872-1031
www.nlada100years.org
John Mauldin, Chairperson
Rosita Stanley, Vice-Chairperson
Alex Gulotta, Vice-Chairperson
Jo-Ann Wallace, President & CEO
Helen Katz, Chief Development Officer
Private, nonprofit association that dedicates all its resources to ensuring the availability of high quality legal assistance for the poor.
3500 Members
Founded in 1911
Mailing list available for rent

15609 **National Notary Association**
9350 De Soto Avenue
Chatsworth, CA 91311-4926
818-739-4000
800-876-6827; Fax: 818-700-1942
hotline@nationalnotary.org
www.nationalnotary.org
Facebook, Twitter, LinkedIn, Google+
Milton G Valera, Chairman
Thomas A. Heymann, President And CEO
Deborah M Thaw, Executive VP
Rob Clarke, Chief Financial Officer
Dave Stephenson, Vice President, CIO/CTO
Supports all those involved in identity fraud and electronic notarization. Publishes newlsetter.
200M Members
Founded in 1957

15610 **National Organizations of Bar Counsel**
275 N. York Street
Ste 401
Elmhurst, IL 60126
630-617-5153
BloomL@dcobc.org
www.nobc.org
Facebook, Twitter
Paul J. Burgoyne, President
Kathleen M. Uston, Treasurer
Melinda Bentley, Secretary
NOBC is a non-proft of legal professionals whose members enforce ethics rules that regulate the professional conduct of lawyers who practice in the U.S., Canada and Australia. Via the website, locate your local member office for information.
Founded in 1965

15611 **National Paralegal Association**
23607 Highway 99
Suite 2-C
Edmonds, WA 98026
425-967-0045; Fax: 425-771-9588
info@paralegals.org
www.paralegals.org
Facebook, LinkedIn
Lisa Vessels, RP, CP, FRP, President
Allen F. Mihecoby, CLAS, RP, VP/Director of Profession Dev.
Lynne Marie Reveliotis, VP & Director of Positions
Yvonne DeAntoneo, VP, Director of Membership
Nita Serrano, RP, VP, Dir. of Paralegal Certification
Founded in 1974

15612 **Native American Rights Fund**
1506 Broadway St
Boulder, CO 80302-6296
303-447-8760; Fax: 303-443-7776
webmaster@narf.org
www.narf.org
Facebook
Moses K. N. Haia III, Chairman
Mark Macarro, Board Vice-Chairman
John E. Echohawk, Executive Director
Michael Kennedy, Chief Financial Officer
Eric Anderson, Legal Administrative Assistant
National legal defense fund. Provides legal services and technical assistance to Indian tribes, organizations and individuals in the areas of preservation of tribal existence, protection of tribal natural resources, promotion of human rights, accountability of governments and development of Indian law.
35000 Members
Founded in 1971
Mailing list available for rent

15613 **People Against Racist Terror**
PO Box 70447
Oakland, CA 94612
510-893-4648; Fax: 818-848-2680
info@prisonactivist.org
www.prisonactivist.org
Michael Novick, Publisher
Association for those interested in anti-racist activism, research and education covering neo-nazi and other racist violence, efforts at conflict resolution and social justic reforms.

15614 **Practising Law Institute**
1177 Avenue of the Americas
2nd Floor
New York, NY 10036
212-824-5700
800-260-4754; Fax: 212-581-4670
cfbook@loc.gov
www.pli.edu
Facebook, Twitter, LinkedIn, YouTtube, Pinterest
John Y Cole, Director
Anne Boni, Program Specialist
Nonprofit continuing legal education organization chartered by the Regents of the University of the State of New York. Dedicated to providing the legal community and allied professionals with the most up-to-date, revelant information and techniques which are critical to the development of a professional, competitive edge.
Founded in 1977
Mailing list available for rent

15615 **RAND Institute for Civil Justice**
1776 Main Street
Santa Monica, CA 90407-3208
310-393-0411; Fax: 310-393-4898
webmaster@monroecc.edu
www.rand.org/icj
Facebook, Twitter, LinkedIn, Instagram, YouTube
John L. Bartolotta, Chair
Grace S. Tillinghast, Vice Chair
Anne M. Kress, Ph.D., President
Andrea C. Wade, Ph.D., Provost/VP, Academic Services
Lloyd A. Holmes, Ph.D., Vice President, Student Services
Nonprofit research organization within the RAND Corporation dedicated to interdisciplinary, empirical research to facilitate change in the civil justice system.
1.1M Members
Founded in 1961

15616 **Rocky Mountain Mineral Law Foundation**
9191 Sheridan Blvd
Suite 203
Westminster, CO 80031-3011
303-321-8100; Fax: 303-321-7657
www.rmmlf.org
Facebook, Twitter, Flickr, Tumblr, Youtube
Stephen Schwartz, President
Ralph Sevush, Executive Director, Business
Gary Garrisonÿ, Executive Director
Joey Stocks, Director of Publications
Deborah Murad, Director of Business Affairs
6M+ Members
Founded in 1920
Mailing list available for rent

15617 **The Center for HIV Law & Policy**
65 Broadway
Suite 832
New York, NY 10006
212-430-6733; Fax: 212-430-6734
www.hivlawandpolicy.org
Facebook, Twitter, LinkedIn, Instagram
Catherine Hanssens, Executive Director
Mayo Schreiber Jr., Deputy Director
Center works to reduce impact of HIV on vulnerable communities.

15618 **The Sports Lawyers Association**
12100 Sunset Hills Road
Suite 130
Reston, VA 20190
703-437-4377; Fax: 703-435-4390
ewa@ewa.org
www.sportslaw.org
Scott Elliott, President
Caroline W. Hendrie, Executive Director
George Dieter, Chief Operating Officer
Tracee Eason, Administrative Coordinator
Kenneth Terrell, Project Director
800 Members
Founded in 1947

15619 **Trial Lawyers Marketing**
1 Boston Place
Suite 1260
Boston, MA 02108-4471
617-720-5356; Fax: 617-742-5417
James Sokolve, President
Provides education and marketing information to personal injury attorneys.
300 Members
Founded in 1986

Newsletters

15620 **AAACPA Newsletter**
American Association of Attorney-CPAs
P.O. Box 706
Warrendale, PA 15095
703-352-8064
888-288-9272; Fax: 703-352-8073
info@attorney-cpa.com
www.attorney-cpa.com
Robert Driegert, President
Domenick Lioce, President Elect
Joseph Cordell, Treasurer
John Pramberg, Secretary
To promote the study and understanding of law and accounting and those related professions.
Frequency: Quarterly
Founded in 1964

15621 **ABA Child Law Practice**
ABA Center on Children and the Law
740 15th Street, NW
Washington, DC 20005
202-662-1000
800-285-2221; Fax: 202-662-1755
www.abanet.org
Facebook, Twitter
Laurel Bellows, President
Jack L. Rives, Executive Director
Robert M. Carlson, Chairman
Lucian T. Pera, Treasurer
Cara Lee T. Neville, Secretary
An online periodical for lawyers who advocate for children and youth, judges handling child protection-related cases, and other professionals who want to keep abreast of cutting edge legal issues affecting children. Includes litigation strategies, analyses of new laws, policies and research, and how they apply to practice, expert interviews, advice from judges, and more.
Cost: $50.00
Frequency: Online
Founded in 1878
Mailing list available for rent

15622 **ABA Washington Letter**
American Bar Association Government Affairs Office
321 N Clark St
Chicago, IL 60654-7598
312-988-5000
800-285-2221; Fax: 202-662-1762
www.abanet.org/poladv/home.html
Facebook, Twitter
Thomas M. Susman, Director, GAO
Denise A. Cardman, Deputy Director
Jared D. Hess, Legislative Coordinator
Laurel Bellows, President
Jack L. Rives, Executive Director
A monthly publication produced by the GAO to report and analyze congressional and executive branch action on legislation issues of interest to the ABA and the legal profession, highlighting ABA involvment in the federal legislative process.
Cost: $30.00
Frequency: Monthly
Founded in 1957
Mailing list available for rent

15623 **ACC Docket**
American Corporate Counsel Association
1025 Connecticut Ave Nw
Suite 200
Washington, DC 20036-5425
202-293- 410; Fax: 202-293-4701
acc.chair@acc.com
www.acc.com
Tiffani Alexander, Managing Editor
Ken Lawrence, Director Publishing
Fred Krebs, President/CEO
Moustafa W. Abdel-Kader, Marketing Manager
David Barre, Director Communications
Frequency: Monthly
Mailing list available for rent

15624 **ALA News**
Association of Legal Administrators
75 Tri-State International
Suite 222
Lincolnshire, IL 60069-4435
847-267-1252; Fax: 847-267-1329
publications@alanet.org
www.alanet.org
Larry Smith, Executive Director
Debbie Thomas, Director, Accounting & Finance
Renee Mahovsky, Director, Administration/Operations
Bob Abramson, Director, Marketing & Communication
Jan Waugh, Director, Member Services
Member magazine focusing on association news and career improvements for administrators in the association.
Cost: $36.00
40 Pages
Circulation: 9000
Founded in 1971
Mailing list available for rent
Printed in 4 colors on glossy stock

15625 **ATLA Advocate**
Association of Trial Lawyers of America
1050 31st Street NW
Washington, DC 20007
202-965-3500
800-424-2725
www.justice.org
Kathleen Flynn Peterson, President
Linda Lipsen, Chief Executive Officer
Charles Jeffress, Chief Operating Officer
Kathi Berge, Chief Financial Officer
Anjali Jesseramsing, Executive Vice President
Keeps association members abreast of association news. Not available by subscription. No advertising or announcements.
Cost: $5.00
Frequency: Monthly
Mailing list available for rent
Printed in 2 colors

15626 **Administrative & Regulatory Law News**
American Bar Association-Administrative/Regulatory
740 15th St NW
11th Floor
Washington, DC 20005-1022
202-662-1000
800-285-2221; Fax: 202-662-1592
www.abanet.org
Facebook, Twitter
Laurel Bellows, President
Jack L. Rives, Executive Director
Robert M. Carlson, Chairman
Lucian T. Pera, Treasurer
Cara Lee T. Neville, Secretary
Newsletter for Section members providing information about recent developments affecting clients and practices with features such as Supreme Court News, News From the Circuits, and more.
16 Pages
Frequency: Quarterly
Circulation: 6000
Founded in 1878
Mailing list available for rent

15627 **Admiralty Law Newsletter**
American Bar Association - TIPS Admiralty/Maritime
321 N Clark St
Chicago, IL 60654-7598
312-988-5000
800-285-2221; Fax: 312-988-5280
askaba@abanet.org
www.abanet.org
Facebook, Twitter
Laurel Bellows, President
Jack L. Rives, Executive Director
Robert M. Carlson, Chairman
Lucian T. Pera, Treasurer
Cara Lee T. Neville, Secretary
Focuses on summaries of recent case law development, CLE programs in maritime law area, and information and articles on programs and projects.
Frequency: Quarterly
Founded in 1878
Mailing list available for rent

15628 **Allen's Trademark Digest**
Congressional Digest Corporation
152413 29th Street NW
Washington, DC 20007-2756
202-333-7332
800-637-9915; Fax: 202-625-6670
ededitor@aol.com
Griff Thomas, President
Page Robinson, Publisher
Brooke Beyer, Editor
Monthly digest of citable and uncitable tradmark decisions issues by the US Patent and Trademark Office.
Cost: $695.00
Frequency: 12 per year
ISSN: 8990-191X
Founded in 1989

15629 **American Association of Visually Impaired Attorneys**
American Blind Lawyers Association
c/o American Council of the Blind
1703 N. Beauregard St., Suite 420
Alexandria, VA 22311
202-467-5081
800-424-8666; Fax: 703-465-5085
info@acb.org
www.acb.org
Eric Bridges, Executive Director
12000 Members
Frequency: Audio
Circulation: 150
Founded in 1961

15630 **American Corporate Counsel Association Newsletter**
Americna Corporate Counsel Association
1025 Connecticut Ave NW
Suite 200
Washington, DC 20036-5425
202-293-8439; Fax: 202-331-7454
http://www.acc.com
Deneen Stambone, Editor

Association news.
16 Pages
Frequency: Bi-Monthly
Circulation: 9,700
Printed in 2 colors on matte stock

15631 American Foreign Law Association Newsletter
Forman Law School
140 W 62nd Street
New York, NY 10023
212-636-6844; Fax: 212-636-6899
James Maxelner, Publisher
Reports on programs sponsored by the Association of American Foreign Law.
Cost: $20.00
4 Pages
Frequency: Monthly

15632 American Lawyers Newspapers Group
American Lawyers Newspapers
1730 M St Nw
Suite 802
Washington, DC 20036-4550
202-296-1995; Fax: 202-457-0718
Ted Goldman, Manager
Supports all those involved in the reporting of legal issues.
Founded in 1977

15633 American Notary
American Society of Notaries
PO Box 5707
Tallahassee, FL 32314
850-671-5164
800-522-3392; Fax: 850-671-5165
www.notaries.org
Lisa K Fisher, Publisher
Joanna Lilly, Executive Director
Kathleen Butler, Executive Director
Legislation news.
Cost: $21.00
20 Pages
Frequency: Quarterly
Circulation: 21000
Printed in 4 colors on glossy stock

15634 American Society of International Law Newsletter
American Society of International Law
2223 Massachusetts Ave Nw
Washington, DC 20008-2864
202-939-6000; Fax: 202-797-7133
http://www.asil.org
Charlotte Ku, Executive Director
Association news and updates on overseas litigation.
6 Pages
Frequency: Monthly

15635 Antitrust and Trade Regulation Report
Bureau of National Affairs
1801 S Bell St
Arlington, VA 22202-4501
703-341-3000
800-372-1033; Fax: 800-253-0332
customercare@bna.com
www.bnabooks.com
Facebook, Twitter, LinkedIn
Paul N Wojcik, Chairman
Gregory C. McCaffery, President and CEO
John Camp, Vice President and Chief Technology
Lisa A. Fitzpatrick, Vice President
Audrey Hipkins, Vice President
Weekly comprehensive coverage of significant competition and deceptive trade practice law developments on the federal, state and international levels.
Cost: $1894.00
Frequency: Weekly

15636 Attorneys Marketing Report
James Publishing
3505 Cadillac Avenue
Suite H
Costa Mesa, CA 92626
714-755-5450
800-440-4780; Fax: 714-751-2709
customer-service@jamespublishing.com
www.jamespublishing.com
Jim Pawell, Founder/President
Linda Standke, Editor
The latest practice development tips and news for law firms from Yellow Pages advertising to referral management.
Founded in 1981
Mailing list available for rent

15637 BNA's Bankruptcy Law Reporter
Bureau of National Affairs
1801 S Bell St
Arlington, VA 22202-4501
703-341-3000
800-372-1033; Fax: 800-253-0332
customercare@bna.com
www.bnabooks.com
Facebook, Twitter, LinkedIn
Paul N Wojcik, Chairman
Gregory C. McCaffery, President and CEO
John Camp, Vice President and Chief Technology
Lisa A. Fitzpatrick, Vice President
Audrey Hipkins, Vice President
Weekly notification service covering various areas of bankruptcy law.
Cost: $1331.00
Frequency: Weekly

15638 BNA's Corporate Counsel Weekly Corporate Practice Series
Bureau of National Affairs
1801 S Bell St
Arlington, VA 22202-4501
703-341-3000
800-372-1033; Fax: 800-253-0332
customercare@bna.com
www.bnabooks.com
Facebook, Twitter, LinkedIn
Paul N Wojcik, Chairman
Gregory C. McCaffery, President and CEO
John Camp, Vice President and Chief Technology
Lisa A. Fitzpatrick, Vice President
Audrey Hipkins, Vice President
A weekly roundup of the latest developments in law that affect business, including coverage of the courts, federal regulatory agencies, the executive branch, states and professional associations.
Cost: $722.00
8 Pages
Frequency: Weekly
Printed in one color on matte stock

15639 BNA's Medicare Report
Bureau of National Affairs
1801 S Bell St
Arlington, VA 22202-4501
703-341-3000
800-372-1033; Fax: 800-253-0332
customercare@bna.com
www.bnabooks.com
Facebook, Twitter, LinkedIn
Paul N Wojcik, Chairman
Gregory C. McCaffery, President and CEO
John Camp, Vice President and Chief Technology
Lisa A. Fitzpatrick, Vice President
Audrey Hipkins, Vice President
Biweekly notification service covering legislative, regulatory and legal developments affecting or pertaining to the Medicare program; also provides information about relevant developments in the Medicaid program that could have implications for Medicare.
Cost: $1108.00
Frequency: Weekly

15640 Bankruptcy Court Decisions
LRP Publications
PO Box 980
Horsham, PA 19044-0980
215-784-0912
800-341-7874; Fax: 215-784-9639
webmaster@lrp.com
www.lrp.com
Todd Lutz, CFO
Kenneth Khan, CEO
Full-text loose leaf bankruptcy reporting service with an expanded and informative newsletter.
Cost: $900.00
Founded in 1977
Mailing list available for rent
Printed in one color on matte stock

15641 Bankruptcy Law Letter
Thomson West Publishing
610 Opperman Dr
Eagan, MN 55123-1340
651-687-7000
800-344-5008; Fax: 651-687-5581
www.west.thomson.com
Facebook, Twitter, LinkedIn, Blogger, Pinterest, Tumblr, St
Charles B Cater, Executive VP
Laurie Zenner, VP
Highly specialized coverage of case developments in the bankruptcy field. No outside submissions accepted.
Cost: $621.00
Frequency: Monthly
Circulation: 3000

15642 Biotechnology Law Report
Mary Ann Liebert
2 Madison Ave
Larchmont, NY 10538-1947
914-834-4348
800-6 5-3 23; Fax: 914-834-3688
info@liebertpub.com
www.liebertpub.com/
Mary Ann Liebert, President
Gerry J Elman, Editor
Harry Matisco, Marketing
Legislative news for the world of biotechnology and science.
Cost: $1858.00
96 Pages
ISSN: 0730-031X
Founded in 1980

15643 Business Crime: Criminal Liability of the Business Community
Matthew Bender and Company
11 Penn Plz
Suite 5101
New York, NY 10001-2006
212-000-1111; Fax: 212-244-3188
Eric Blood, Data Processing
The most complete guide to the many criminal questions that can arise in modern business practice.

15644 Business Information Alert
Alert Publications

401 W Fullerton Parkway
Suite 1403E
Chicago, IL 60614-2801

773-525-7594
866-492-5266; Fax: 773-525-7015
www.alertpubs.com

Donna T Heroy, Publisher/Editor
Nina Wendt, Director Marketing

Newsletter for business and law librarians to help them make purchasing decisions for their companies. Includes product reviews and columns on industry news. Discounted price of $99 for non-profit organizations.
Cost: $167.00
12 Pages
ISSN: 1042-0746
Founded in 1981

15645 **CLE Guidebook**
Law Bulletin Publishing Company
415 N State St
Suite 1
Chicago, IL 60654-8116

312-644-7800; Fax: 312-644-4255
www.lawbulletin.com

Lanning Macfarland Jr, President
Bernard M Judge, Publisher
Michael Loquercio, Sales Manager

Lists hundreds of CLE courses by date, subject and provider.
Cost: $219.00
34 Pages
Printed in 4 colors on matte stock

15646 **Chapter 11 Update**
Federal Managers Association
1641 Prince St
Alexandria, VA 22314-2818

703-683-8700; Fax: 703-683-8707
info@fedmanagers.org
www.fedmanagers.org

Todd Wells, Executive Director
George J. Smith, National VP
Patricia J. Niehaus, National President
Richard J. Oppedisano, National Secretary
Katie L. Smith, National Treasurer

Management issues and concerns.
Frequency: Monthly
Mailing list available for rent

15647 **Civil RICO Report**
LRP Publications
PO Box 24668
West Palm Beach, FL 33416-4668

561-622-6520
800-341-7874; Fax: 561-622-0757
webmaster@lrp.com
www.lrp.com

Kenneth Kahn, President
Robert K Latzko, Editor

Weekly report and analysis of litigation under the civil provisions of the Racketeer Influenced and Corrupt Organizations Act as well as legislative developments and state little RICO laws.
Cost: $812.00
Printed in 2 colors on matte stock

15648 **Client Counseling Update**
American Bar Association
321 N Clark St
Chicago, IL 60654-7598

312-988-5000
800-285-2221; Fax: 312-988-5280
askaba@abanet.org
www.abanet.org
Facebook, Twitter

Laurel Bellows, President
Jack L. Rives, Executive Director
Robert M. Carlson, Chairman
Richard J. Oppe Pera, Treasurer
Cara Lee T. Neville, Secretary

e-Newsletter contains summaries of publications and news articles concerning client counseling.
Founded in 1878
Mailing list available for rent

15649 **Collective Bargaining Negotiations and Contracts**
Bureau of National Affairs
1801 S Bell St
Arlington, VA 22202-4501

703-341-3000
800-372-1033; Fax: 800-253-0332
customercare@bna.com
www.bnabooks.com
Facebook, Twitter, LinkedIn

Paul N Wojcik, Chairman
Gregory C. McCaffery, President and CEO
John Camp, Vice President and Chief Technology
Lisa A. Fitzpatrick, Vice President
Audrey Hipkins, Vice President

A biweekly notificaiton and reference service containing information designed to help unions and management prepare, negotiate and administer contracts.
Cost: $1541.00
Frequency: Monthly
Founded in 1929

15650 **Commercial Laws of the World**
Foreign Tax Law
PO Box 2189
Ormond Beach, FL 32175-2189

386-341-7405
www.foreignlaw.com

Contains company laws, commercial codes, and related law for over 100 countries.
Cost: $100.00

15651 **Communications Lawyer**
American Bar Association Forum - Communication Law
321 N Clark St
Chicago, IL 60654-7598

312-988-5000
800-285-2221; Fax: 312-988-5280
askaba@abanet.org
www.abanet.org
Facebook, Twitter

Laurel Bellows, President
Jack L. Rives, Executive Director
Robert M. Carlson, Chairman
Lucian T. Pera, Treasurer
Cara Lee T. Neville, Secretary

Newsletter reviews significant activities and developments in communications law and reports on Forum activities.
Cost: $45.00
30 Pages
Frequency: Quarterly
ISSN: 0737-7622
Founded in 1878
Mailing list available for rent

15652 **Computer & Internet LAWCAST**
Vox Juris
PO Box 389
Pennington, NJ 08534

609-737-6543
800-LAW-CAST; Fax: 609-737-3860
www.lawcast.com

Jason Meyer, Publisher

Groundbreaking law arising from life and commerce in the digital age...in licensing, torts, intellectual property securities, contracts, privacy, joint ventures, antitrust, content regulation and more. If your clients use email or the internet, have their own websites, produce hardware or software or provide on-line service, listen up here. 60 minute audio and outline twice monthly
Cost: $25.00

15653 **Computer Industry Litigation Reporter**
Andrews Publications
175 Strafford Avenue
Building 4 Suite 140
Wayne, PA 19087

610-225-0510
800-345-1101; Fax: 610-225-0501

Donna Higgins, Editor
Mary Ellen Fox, Publisher
Jodine Mayberry, Executive Editor

Covers litigation involving copyright, patent, trade secrets, employment, securities, trademark, contracts and other issues related to the computer industry.
Cost: $1226.00
Founded in 1983

15654 **Construction Claims Monthly**
Business Publishers
2222 Sedwick Dr
Suite 101
Durham, NC 27713

800-223-8720; Fax: 800-508-2592
custserv@bpinews.com
www.bpinews.com

Contains summaries of important decisions from the federal and state courts, boards of contract appeals, and the Office of Comptroller General on such topics as change orders, design problems, inspection, delay, home office overhead, claims administration, termination, waivers, differing site conditions, subcontractors and insurance.
Cost: $244.00
8 Pages
Frequency: Monthly
Founded in 1962

15655 **Construction Litigation Reporter**
McGraw Hill
1221 Avenue of the Americas
New York, NY 10020-1095

212-512-2000
800-352-3566; Fax: 212-512-3840
www.mcgraw-hill.com

Harold W McGraw III, CEO

Summaries of judicial and agency decisions.
Cost: $300.00
24 Pages
Frequency: Monthly

15656 **Consumer Financial Services Law Report**
LRP Publications
PO Box 980
Horsham, PA 19044-0980

215-784-0912
800-341-7874; Fax: 215-784-9639
webmaster@lrp.com
www.lrp.com

Todd Lutz, CFO
Kenneth Kahn, President

Keeps you up-to-date with the latest changes and developments in the area of consumer financial services litigation. Provides timely coverage of legal developments involving fair lending, debt collection, state UDAP laws and fraud, automobile lending and leasing, damage theories and class actions, and more.
Cost: $220.00
Founded in 1977

15657 **Consumer Product Litigation Reporter**
Andrews Publications

175 Strafford Avenue
Building 4, Suite 140
Wayne, PA 19087-3331
610-225-0510
800-345-1101; Fax: 610-225-0501

Robert Maroldo, Publisher
Eileen Gonyeau, Editor

Covers areas such as strict liability, assumption of risk, insurance coverage, adequacy of warning merchantability, punitive damages, component liability, forseeability and more.
Cost: $46.00

15658 Controlling Law Firm Costs
Institute of Management and Administration
1 Washington Park
Suite 1300
Newark, NJ 07102-3130

212-244-0360; Fax: 973-622-0595
customercare@bna.com
www.ioma.com

Laurel Bellows, President

Shows law office administrators how to reduce overhead, improve the firm's profitability and efficiency, get more value for the firm's budget dollar, and improve their own professional standing. Includes strategies to control the costs of support staff, insurance, leases, taxes, computers and more.
Cost: $300.00
Frequency: Annual+

15659 Corporate Counsel LAWCAST
Vox Juris
PO Box 389
Pennington, NJ 08534

609-737-6543
800-LAW-CAST; Fax: 609-737-3860
www.lawcast.com

Jason Meyer, Publisher

Everything for the in-house counsel in one lively and substantive program. In-house ethics and privileges, the law of the workplace, intellectual property, corporate governance, contracts, regulations, and more...close-ups on how top counsel meet the demands of the in-house practice. 75 minute audio and online, 15 times per year
Cost: $25.00

15660 Corporate Legal Times
Corporate Legal Times
656 West Randolph Street
Suite 500 East
Chicago, IL 60611

312-654-3500; Fax: 312-654-3525
www.cltmag.com

Nat Slavin, Publisher
Larry Lannon, CEO

Written for general counsel and other in house corporate attourneys to provide information relevant to strategic planning and day-to-day operation of legal departments including in-house counsel's relationships with outside law firms.
Cost: $10.00
Frequency: Monthly
Circulation: 40000
Founded in 1991

15661 Corporate Practice Series
Bureau of National Affairs
1801 S Bell St
Arlington, VA 22202-4501

703-341-3000
800-372-1033; Fax: 800-253-0332
customercare@bna.com
www.bnabooks.com
Facebook, Twitter, LinkedIn

Paul N Wojcik, Chairman
Gregory C. McCaffery, President and CEO
John Camp, Vice President and Chief Technology
Lisa A. Fitzpatrick, Vice President
Audrey Hipkins, Vice President

A corporate law reference service organized into a series of portfolios written by legal experts, with a weekly newsletter. Each portfolio covers a different legal subject with detailed analyses, working papers and a bibliography.
Cost: $2426.00
ISSN: 0162-5691

15662 Criminal Law Reporter
Bureau of National Affairs
1801 S Bell St
Arlington, VA 22202-4501

703-341-3000
800-372-1033; Fax: 800-253-0332
customercare@bna.com
www.bnabooks.com
Facebook, Twitter, LinkedIn

Paul N Wojcik, Chairman
Gregory C. McCaffery, President and CEO
John Camp, Vice President and Chief Technology
Lisa A. Fitzpatrick, Vice President
Audrey Hipkins, VP

A weekly notification service providing coverage of court decisions, federal legislative activities and administrative developments in the field of criminal law. Fulltext of the cases highlighted in each issue are available free on CrL's web site. Subscribers can also recieve free email notification of Supreme Court decisions.
Cost: $1108.00
Frequency: Weekly
Founded in 1929

15663 DataLaw Report
Clark Boardman Company
155 Pflingsten Road
Deerfield, IL 60015

847-374-0400; Fax: 847-948-7099

Amelia Boss, Editor

Analyzes the changing global legal environment for electronic information.

15664 Death Care Business Advisor
LRP Publications
747 Dresher Road
PO Box 980
Horsham, PA 19044-980

215-784-0912
800-341-7874; Fax: 215-784-9639
webmaster@lrp.com
www.lrp.com

Jay Kravetz, Editor
Dionne Ellis, Managing Editor

The only twice a month newsletter that offers you in-depth business coverage of memorialization and remembrance issues. You'll recieve news and tips on the latest trends and developments in funeral service, cemetery management and cremation and learn innovative strategies to capture the expanding preneed market and more.
Cost: $215.00
Founded in 1977

15665 Digest of Environmental Law
Strafford Publications
PO Box 13729
Atlanta, GA 30324-0729

404-881-1141
800-926-7926; Fax: 404-881-0074
customerservice@straffordpub.com
www.straffordpub.com

Richard Ossoff, Presdient
Jennifer Vaughan, Managing Editor

Monthly digest of nationally significant litigation related to the full range of environmental issues, includes annual index.
Cost: $547.00
Frequency: Monthly
ISSN: 1073-9521
Founded in 1984

15666 Disability Compliance for Higher Education
LRP Publications
747 Dresher Road
PO Box 980
Horsham, PA 19044-980
215-784-0912
800-341-7874; Fax: 561-622-2423
webmaster@lrp.com
www.lrp.com

Marsha Jaquays, Editor
Nancy Grover, Managing Editor

Helps colleges determine if they are complying with the Americans with Disabilities Act (ADA) and section 504 of the Rehabilitation Act. Readers find out how to fulfill legal obligations under the law and save their college from costly litigation.
Cost: $198.00
Frequency: Monthly
Founded in 1977

15667 ELA Notes
Education Law Association
300 College Park Ave
Dayton, OH 45469-0001

937-229-3589; Fax: 937-229-3845
ela@educationlaw.org
www.educationlaw.org

Mandy Schrenk, Executive Director
Jody Thornburg, Publications Editor
Cate K Smith, Executive Director
Judy Pleiman, Member Services Coordinator
Jody Thornburg, Publications Manager

ELA is a nonprofit, nonadvocacy, member-based organization found in 1954 to provide an unbiased forum for the dissemination of information about current issues in education law. Membership is open to all individuals and organizations with a special interest in education law. ELA's mission is to bring together educational and legal scholars and practioners to inform and advance educational policy and practice through knowledge of the law.
Cost: $125.00
Frequency: Quarterly
Circulation: 1300
ISSN: 0047-8997
Founded in 1954
Printed in 2 colors on matte stock

15668 Employee Benefits Cases
Bureau of National Affairs
1801 S Bell St
Arlington, VA 22202-4501
703-341-3000
800-372-1033; Fax: 800-253-0332
customercare@bna.com
www.bnabooks.com
Facebook, Twitter, LinkedIn

Paul N Wojcik, Chairman
Gregory C. McCaffery, President and CEO
John Camp, Vice President and Chief Technology
Lisa A. Fitzpatrick, Vice President
Audrey Hipkins, VP

A weekly decisional service that reports the full text of federal and state court opinions and selected decisions of arbitrators and the NLRB on employee benefits issues.
Cost: $1582.00
54 Pages
Frequency: Weekly
Circulation: 6000+
ISSN: 0273-236X

Founded in 1929
Printed in on matte stock

15669 **Employment Law Report Strategist**
Data Research
PO Box 490
Rosemount, MN 55068-0490

952-452-8694
800-365-4900; Fax: 952-452-8694

Covers the latest court cases and late-breaking legislation along with the most recent law review articles affecting employment.
Cost: $120.00
Frequency: Monthly
ISSN: 1058-1308

15670 **Entertainment Law and Finance**
345 Park Avenue S
New York, NY 10010-1707

212-779-6611
800-888-8300; Fax: 212-696-1848

Stan Soocher, Editor
Stuart M Wise, Production Manager
Kerry Kyle, Circulation Director

Laws and news in the entertainment field.
Cost: $195.00
8 Pages
Frequency: Monthly
ISSN: 0883-2455
Printed in 2 colors

15671 **Entertainment and Sports Lawyer**
American Bar Association
Forum-Entertainment/Sport
321 N Clark St
Chicago, IL 60654-7598

312-988-5000
800-285-2221; Fax: 312-988-5280
askaba@abanet.org
www.abanet.org
Facebook, Twitter

Laurel Bellows, President
Vered Yakovee, Editor
Jack L. Rives, Executive Director
Robert M. Carlson, Chairman
Lucian T. Pera, Treasurer

Newsletter on recent developments in the sports and entertainment industries, public policy and scholarly viewpoints.
Cost: $60.00
40 Pages
Frequency: Quarterly
ISSN: 0732-1880
Founded in 1878
Mailing list available for rent

15672 **Estate Planner's Alert**
Thomson Reuters
2395 Midway Rd
Suite 4
Carrollton, TX 75006

646-822-2000
800-231-1860; Fax: 646-822-2800
trta.lei-support@thomsonreuters.com
www.ria.thomsonreuters.com

Laurel Bellows, President
Thomas H Glocer, CEO & Director
Robert D Daleo, Chief Financial Officer
Kelli Crane, Senior Vice President & CIO

Offers complete coverage of estate planning and law.
Cost: $195.00
Frequency: Monthly
Founded in 1935

15673 **Exercise Standards and Malpractice Reporter**
PRC Publishing
3976 Fulton Dr Nw
Canton, OH 44718-3043

330-492-6063
800-336-0083; Fax: 330-492-6176

Molly Romig, VP
Dr. Doyice Cotton, Publisher
Mary Cotton, Publisher

Designed to cover topics of interest and concern to the exercise professionals.
Cost: $39.95
16 Pages
Circulation: 750
ISSN: 0891-0278
Founded in 1997
Printed in 2 colors on matte stock

15674 **FCBA Newsletter**
Federal Communications Bar Association
1020 19th St Nw
Suite 325
Washington, DC 20036-6113

202-293-4000; Fax: 202-293-4317
fcba@fcba.org
www.fcba.org

Stanley Zenor, Executive Director
Kerry Loughney, Director of Membership Services
Diane J Cornell, Treasurer
Wendy Jo Parish, Administrative Assistant
Beth Phillips, Bookkeeper

A non-profit organization of attorneys and other professionals involved in the development, interpretation, implementation and practice of communications law and policy.
Frequency: Monthly
Founded in 1936
Mailing list available for rent

15675 **Family Law Reporter**
Bureau of National Affairs
1801 S Bell St
Arlington, VA 22202-4501

703-341-3000
800-372-1033; Fax: 800-253-0332
customercare@bna.com
www.bnabooks.com
Facebook, Twitter, LinkedIn

Paul N Wojcik, Chairman
Gregory C. McCaffery, President and CEO
John Camp, Vice President and Chief Technology
Lisa A. Fitzpatrick, Vice President
Audrey Hipkins, VP

A weekly notification and reference service dealing with all significant state and federal developments in the field of family law.
Cost: $974.00
Frequency: Weekly
Founded in 1929

15676 **Federal Contract Disputes**
Business Publishers
2222 Sedwick Dr
Suite 101
Durham, NC 27713

800-223-8720; Fax: 800-508-2592
custserv@bpinews.com
www.bpinews.com

A monthly newsletter designed to help you avoid disputes, and successfully resolve those you can't avoid. Each issue brings you concise synopses of a dozen major decisions, from the courts, the Comptroller General, and the boards of contract appeals.
Cost: $285.00
Frequency: Monthly

15677 **Federal Contracts Report**
Bureau of National Affairs
1801 S Bell St
Arlington, VA 22202-4501

703-341-3000
800-372-1033; Fax: 800-253-0332
customercare@bna.com
www.bnabooks.com
Facebook, Twitter, LinkedIn

Paul N Wojcik, Chairman
Gregory C. McCaffery, President and CEO
John Camp, Vice President and Chief Technology
Lisa A. Fitzpatrick, Vice President
Audrey Hipkins, VP

A weekly reporting service providing comprehensive coverage of the latest significant developments affecting federal contracts and grants.
Cost: $1887.00
Frequency: Weekly
Founded in 1929

15678 **Federal Discovery News**
LRP Publications
747 Dresher Road
PO Box 980
Horsham, PA 19044-980

215-784-0912
800-341-7874; Fax: 215-784-9639
webmaster@lrp.com
www.lrp.com

John Massaro, Editor
Dionne Ellis, Managing Editor

Each issue covers the whole realm of pretrial case management and discovery, especially the impact of the new civil procedure rules on discovery in federal cases. Provides a timely review of how district developments pertain to your practice.
Cost: $275.00
Frequency: Monthly
Founded in 1977

15679 **Federal EEO Advisor**
LRP Publications
747 Dresher Road
PO Box 980
Horsham, PA 19044-980

215-784-0912
800-341-7874; Fax: 215-784-9639
webmaster@lrp.com
www.lrp.com

Allison Uehling, Editor
Clarrisa Spasyk, Staff Writer

One-of-a-kind publication provides readers with essential tips, strategies and news about the constanly changing EEO profession. Each issue includes insightful coverage on topics such as: details on major developments and trends in federal EEO; tips on how to accomplish specific objectives within the EEO program; synopses of decisions by the EEOC and related courts, etc.
Cost: $220.00
Frequency: Monthly
Founded in 1977

15680 **Federal Human Resources Week**
LRP Publications
747 Dresher Road Suite 500
PO Box 980
Horsham, PA 19044

215-840-0912
800-341-7874; Fax: 215-784-9639
custserve@lrp.com
www.feds.com

Daniel J Gephart, Editorial Director
Julie Davidson, Managing Editor
Kathleen Filipczyk, Staff Writer

Federal Human Resources Week helps you stay on top of changes affecting you and your workplace. This revolutionary resource enables you to experience each major development as it oc-

curs.
Cost: $365.00
12 Pages
Frequency: Weekly
Founded in 1977
Printed in 2 colors on matte stock

15681 **Financial Management Newsletter**
Association of Legal Administrators
75 Tri-State International
Suite 222
Lincolnshire, IL 60069-4435

847-267-1252; Fax: 847-267-1329
publications@alanet.org
www.alanet.org

Larry Smith, Executive Director
Debbie Thomas, Director, Accounting & Finance
Renee Mahovsky, Director, Administration/Operations
Bob Abramson, Director, Marketing & Communication
Jan Waugh, Director, Member Services
8 Pages
Frequency: Monthly
Founded in 1971

15682 **Forum**
Federal Bar Association
1220 North Fillmore St.
Ste. 444
Arlington, VA 22201

571-481-9100; Fax: 571-481-9090
fba@fedbar.org
www.fedbar.org
Facebook, Twitter, LinkedIn

Karen Silberman, Executive Director
Lori Beth Gorman, Executive Assistant
Stacy King, Deputy Executive Director
April Davis, Staff Accountant
Patty Richardson, Receptionist

A forum for the exchange of ideas, news, updates, and cases for lawyers.
Cost: $35.00
8 Pages
Frequency: Monthly
Founded in 1920
Mailing list available for rent

15683 **HRFocus**
Institute of Management and Administration
1 Wasington Park
Suite 1300
Newark, NJ 07102-3130

212-244-0360; Fax: 973-622-0595
customercare@bna.com
www.ioma.com

Provides HR managers with timely information on a variety of topics, including talent management, HR legal and compliance issues, performance reviews, and workplace policies and standards.
Cost: $429.00
16 Pages
Frequency: Monthly
Printed in 4 colors

15684 **Hastings Communications & Entertainment Law Journal**
Hastings College of Law
200 McAllister St
2nd Floor, Room 213
San Francisco, CA 94102-4978

415-565-4600; Fax: 415-565-4854
www.uchastings.edu

Nell Jessup Newton, Manager
Karen Gibbs, Editor

Specializing in a host of legal issues generally grouped under the rubric of communications and entertainment law. Focuses on, but is not limited to, telecommunications, broadcasting, cable and other non-broadcast video, and the print media.
Cost: $7.00
Frequency: Monthly
Circulation: 1300
Founded in 1878

15685 **Health Law Week**
Strafford Publications
PO Box 13729
Atlanta, GA 30324-0729

404-881-1141
800-926-7926; Fax: 404-881-0074
customerservice@straffordpub.com
www.straffordpub.com

Richard Ossoff, President

Case digest of judicial decision affecting all aspects of health care operations. Topics covered include AIPS abortion antitrust, drugs, ERISA, expert testimony, informed consent, amd much more.
Cost: $1397.00
Frequency: Weekly
ISSN: 1063-4061
Founded in 1984
Mailing list available for rent: 25M names

15686 **Hospital Litigation Reporter**
Strafford Publications
PO Box 13729
Atlanta, GA 30324-0729

404-881-1141
800-926-7926; Fax: 404-881-0074
customerservice@straffordpub.com
www.straffordpub.com

Richard Ossoff, President
Jennifer Vaughan, Editor

Monthly digest of judicial decisions that concern or affect the hospital environment. Cases are screened and selected to provide concise, comprehensive coverage of issues important to hospital attorneys and administrators.
Cost: $397.00
18 Pages
Frequency: Monthly
ISSN: 1048-5201
Founded in 1984
Mailing list available for rent: 11M names
Printed in one color

15687 **Human Resources Report**
Bureau of National Affairs
1801 S Bell St
Arlington, VA 22202-4501

703-341-3000
800-372-1033; Fax: 800-253-0332
customercare@bna.com
www.bnabooks.com
Facebook, Twitter, LinkedIn

Paul N Wojcik, Chairman
Gregory C. McCaffery, President and CEO
John Camp, Vice President and Chief Technology
Lisa A. Fitzpatrick, Vice President
Audrey Hipkins, VP

Covers current developments in every area of human resources; includes in-depth analysis of important events, developments or trends affecting human resource professionals.
Cost: $1140.00
28 Pages
Frequency: Weekly
ISSN: 1095-6239
Founded in 1929
Printed in one color on matte stock

15688 **I-CBC Newsletter**
Institute of Certified Business Counselors
18831 Willamette Dr
West Linn, OR 97068-1711

503-751-1856
877-422-2674; Fax: 503-292-8237
www.theicbc.org

Roger Murphy, Director, Newsletter

For counselors, brokers and attorneys qualified to act as advisors for persons with business problems. Regular editorial features.
Frequency: 6/Year
Mailing list available for rent

15689 **IOMA's Report on Controlling Law Firm Costs**
Institute of Management and Administration
1 Washington Park
Suite 1300
Newark, NJ 07102-3130

212-244-0360; Fax: 973-622-0595
customercare@bna.com
www.ioma.com

Information to control costs of law firms management.
Cost: $175.00
12 Pages
Frequency: Monthly

15690 **IRR News Report**
ABA Section - Individual Rights & Responsibilities
740 15th Stree, NW
10th Floor
Washington, DC 20005

202-662-1000
800-285-2221; Fax: 202-662-1031
askaba@abanet.org
www.abanet.org
Facebook, Twitter

Laurel Bellows, President
Jack L. Rives, Executive Director
Robert M. Carlson, Chairman
Lucian T. Pera, Treasurer
Cara Lee T. Neville, Secretary

A quarterly newsletter including updates on Section events, news about members, a review of recent legislative events and decision by the Supreme Court.
Circulation: 6000
Founded in 1878
Mailing list available for rent

15691 **Individual Employment Rights**
Bureau of National Affairs
1801 S Bell St
Arlington, VA 22202-4501

703-341-3000
800-372-1033; Fax: 800-253-0332
customercare@bna.com
www.bnabooks.com
Facebook, Twitter, LinkedIn

Paul N Wojcik, Chairman
Gregory C. McCaffery, President and CEO
John Camp, Vice President and Chief Technology
Lisa A. Fitzpatrick, Vice President
Audrey Hipkins, VP

Case reference and notification on individual employment rights issues including employment at will, privacy, polygraph testing, and other employee rights issues outside the traditional labor-management relations context.
Cost: $1227.00
Frequency: Monthly
ISSN: 0148-7981
Founded in 1929

15692 **Intellectual Property LAWCAST**
Vox Juris

PO Box 389
Pennington, NJ 08534-389

609-737-6543; Fax: 609-737-3860
www.lawcast.com

Jason Meyer, Publisher

US legal news in patents, trademarks, copyrights, trade secrets, unfair trade, etc. including comprehensive coverage of PTO policies and a regular Listening Post on legal issues in the digital age. The buzz for thousands of IP lawyers, nationwide. 60 minute audio and online, twice monthly.
Cost: $488.00

15693 **Intellectual Property Law Review**
Clark Boardman Company
375 Hudson St
Room 201
New York, NY 10014-3658

585-546-5530
800-323-1336

David Doughty, Publisher

Compilation of the best law review articles.
Frequency: Monthly
Founded in 1916

15694 **Intellectual Property Litigation Reporter**
Andrews Publications
175 Strafford Avenue
Building 4 Suite 140
Wayne, PA 19087-3331

610-225-0510
800-345-1101; Fax: 610-225-0501

Robert Maroldo, Publisher
Jodine Mayberry, Editor

Covers litigation and regulation of intellectual property issues including patents, copyrights, and tradeworks.
Cost: $83.00

15695 **Intellectual Property Today**
Omega Communications
29 E Maryland Street
Indianapolis, IN 46204-7258

317-264-4010; Fax: 317-264-4020
planet@iptoday.com
www.omegac.com

Douglas Dean, Editor
Steve Barnes, Vice President
Laura Moore, Vice President

Emphasizes developments in leading edge technology, including multimedia, genetic engineering and computer software, and how they effect disciplines of law.
Cost: $96.00
Frequency: Monthly
Circulation: 20000
Founded in 1971

15696 **Inter-American Bar Association Newsletter**
Inter-American Bar Association
1211 Connecticut Ave Nw
Suite 202
Washington, DC 20036-2712

202-466-5944; Fax: 202-466-5946
iaba@iaba.org
www.iaba.org
Facebook

Marianne Cordier, Secretary General
Rafael Veloz, President
Cost: $60.00
Frequency: Quarterly

15697 **International Law News**
American Bar Association Internat'l Law & Practice
321 N Clark St
Chicago, IL 60654-7598

312-988-5000
800-285-2221; Fax: 312-988-5280
askaba@abanet.org
www.abanet.org
Facebook, Twitter

Angela Gwizdala, Managing Editor
Laurel Bellows, President
Jack L. Rives, Executive Director
Robert M. Carlson, Chairman
Lucian T. Pera, Treasurer

Provides information concerning current, important developments pertaining to international law and practice, Section news, and other information of professional interest.
28 Pages
Frequency: Quarterly
Circulation: 15000
ISSN: 0047-0813
Founded in 1878
Mailing list available for rent

15698 **Internet Lawyer**
GoAhead Productions
123 7th Avenue
#137
Brooklyn, NY 11215-1301

718-399-6136; Fax: 718-499-6039
www.internetlawyer.com

Tatia L Gordon-Troy, Editor-in-Chief
Christopher Eddings, Publisher

Gives legal advice and examines how to use the Net for research, marketing and communications purposes. Includes book reviews as well as information on current law office technology.
Cost: $149.00
Frequency: Monthly

15699 **Judicial Division Record**
American Bar Association Judicial Division
321 N Clark St
Chicago, IL 60654-7598

312-988-5000
800-285-2221; Fax: 312-988-6281
askaba@abanet.org
www.abanet.org
Facebook, Twitter

Laurel Bellows, President
Jack L. Rives, Executive Director
Robert M. Carlson, Chairman
Lucian T. Pera, Treasurer
Cara Lee T. Neville, Secretary

The Record is the only newsletter published by the Division, providing news about Division activites, products, publications and programs. It contains sections for each Division Conference, and an insert.
Cost: $25.00
Frequency: Free Online
Founded in 1878
Mailing list available for rent

15700 **Labor Arbitration and Dispute Settlements**
Bureau of National Affairs
1801 S Bell St
Arlington, VA 22202-4501

703-341-3000
800-372-1033; Fax: 800-253-0332
customercare@bna.com
www.bnabooks.com
Facebook, Twitter, LinkedIn

Paul N Wojcik, Chairman
Gregory C. McCaffery, President and CEO
John Camp, Vice President and Chief Technology
Lisa A. Fitzpatrick, Vice President
Audrey Hipkins, VP

Contains the full-text of arbitration cases, and digests of court decisions involving arbitration.
Cost: $1686.00
Frequency: Weekly
ISSN: 1043-5662
Founded in 1929

15701 **Labor Arbitration in Government**
LRP Publications
PO Box 980
Horsham, PA 19044-0980

215-784-0912
800-341-7874; Fax: 215-784-9639
webmaster@lrp.com
www.lrp.com

Todd Lutz, CFO
Dionne Ellis, Marketing

Selected awards involving city, state, and federal employers (other than those employed by schools) are covered by this reporting service. Some of the issues arbitrated include: absenteeism, smoking policies, layoffs, and substance abuse.
Cost: $120.00
Frequency: Monthly
Founded in 1977
Printed in 2 colors on glossy stock

15702 **Labor Lawyer**
American Bar Association - Labor & Employment Law
321 N Clark St
Chicago, IL 60654-7598

312-988-5000
800-285-2221; Fax: 312-988-5814
laboremplaw@abanet.org
www.abanet.org
Facebook, Twitter

Laurel Bellows, President
Jack L. Rives, Executive Director
Robert M. Carlson, Chairman
Lucian T. Pera, Treasurer
Cara Lee T. Neville, Secretary

Substantive articles on developments in labor and employment law.
Frequency: Quarterly
Circulation: 2300
Founded in 1878
Mailing list available for rent

15703 **Labor Relations Reporter**
Bureau of National Affairs
1801 S Bell St
Arlington, VA 22202-4501

703-341-3000
800-372-1033; Fax: 800-253-0332
customercare@bna.com
www.bnabooks.com
Facebook, Twitter, LinkedIn

Paul N Wojcik, Chairman
Gregory C. McCaffery, President and CEO
John Camp, Vice President and Chief Technology
Lisa A. Fitzpatrick, Vice President
Audrey Hipkins, VP

A multi-part notification and reference service covering labor-management relations, wages and hours, labor arbitration, fair employment practices, individual employment rights and more.
Cost: $6175.00
Frequency: Weekly
ISSN: 0148-7981
Founded in 1929

15704 **Labor Relations Week**
Bureau of National Affairs
1801 S Bell St
Arlington, VA 22202-4501

703-341-3000
800-372-1033; Fax: 800-253-0332

customercare@bna.com
www.bnabooks.com
Facebook, Twitter, LinkedIn

Paul N Wojcik, Chairman
Gregory C. McCaffery, President and CEO
John Camp, Vice President and Chief Technology
Lisa A. Fitzpatrick, Vice President
Audrey Hipkins, VP

A weekly reporting service that provides a comprehensive overview of developments influencing labor relations in the private sector.
Cost: $1472.00
Frequency: Weekly
ISSN: 0891-4141
Founded in 1929

15705 **Labor and Employment Law**
American Bar Association - Labor & Employment Law
321 N Clark St
Chicago, IL 60654-7598

312-988-5000
800-285-2221; Fax: 312-988-6281
askaba@abanet.org
www.abanet.org
Facebook, Twitter

Laurel Bellows, President
Jack L. Rives, Executive Director
Robert M. Carlson, Chairman
Lucian T. Pera, Treasurer
Cara Lee T. Neville, Secretary

Offers news items of interest to members and information on the latest developments in the labor field.
Cost: $5.00
16 Pages
Frequency: Quarterly
Circulation: 22000
ISSN: 0193-5739
Founded in 1878
Mailing list available for rent

15706 **Labor and Employment Law News**
American Bar Association - Labor & Emplyment Law
321 N Clark St
Chicago, IL 60654-7598

312-988-5000
800-285-2221; Fax: 312-988-5280
service@abanet.org
www.abanet.org
Facebook, Twitter

Laurel Bellows, President
Jack L. Rives, Executive Director
Robert M. Carlson, Chairman
Lucian T. Pera, Treasurer
Cara Lee T. Neville, Secretary

Legal issues and trends of interest to lawyers who represent employees, unions, and management.
Cost: $5.00
16 Pages
Frequency: Monthly
Circulation: 22000
ISSN: 0193-5739
Founded in 1878
Mailing list available for rent
Printed in 4 colors

15707 **Labor-Management Relations**
Bureau of National Affairs
1801 S Bell St
Arlington, VA 22202-4501

703-341-3000
800-372-1033; Fax: 800-253-0332
customercare@bna.com
www.bnabooks.com
Facebook, Twitter, LinkedIn

Paul N Wojcik, Chairman
Gregory C. McCaffery, President and CEO
John Camp, Vice President and Chief Technology
Lisa A. Fitzpatrick, Vice President
Audrey Hipkins, VP

Contains a table of cases, digest-summaries of all published NLRB decisions and full-text of opinions of the US Supreme Court, US Courts of Appeals and other courts, in one bound volume, issued several times a year.
Cost: $ 1776.00
Frequency: Monthly
ISSN: 1043-5506
Founded in 1929

15708 **Labor-Management Relations Analysis/News and Background Information**
Bureau of National Affairs
1801 S Bell St
Arlington, VA 22202-4501

703-341-3000
800-372-1033; Fax: 800-253-0332
customercare@bna.com
www.bnabooks.com
Facebook, Twitter, LinkedIn

Paul N Wojcik, Chairman
Gregory C. McCaffery, President and CEO
John Camp, Vice President and Chief Technology
Lisa A. Fitzpatrick, Vice President
Audrey Hipkins, VP

This weekly section of the Labor Relations Reporter summarizes developments and rulings in the field of labor law, covers major non-decisional developments and recent significant arbitration awards, and provides in-depth analysis and evaluation of the week's labor news.
Cost: $507.00
Frequency: Weekly
Founded in 1929

15709 **Land Use Law Report**
Business Publishers
8737 Colesville Road
10th Floor
Silver Spring, MD 20910-3928

301-876-6300
800-274-6737; Fax: 301-589-8493
custserv@bpinews.com
www.bpinews.com/

Leonard Eiserer, Publisher
James Esq, Editor

Zoning and land use decisions at all levels of government; impact on business community and environment.
Cost: $397.00
Founded in 1963

15710 **Latin America Law and Business Report**
WorldTrade Executive
2250 Main St
Suite 100
Concord, MA 01742-3838

978-287-0301; Fax: 978-287-0302

Gary Brown, President
Jay Stanley, Sales Manager

Provides practical, current information on how to do business in Latin America. Covers areas such as capital markets, accounting matters, labor issues, privatization, project finance techniques, joint venture regulation, local sourcing, export/import, taxation, intellectual property, environment.
Cost: $893.00
Frequency: Monthly

15711 **Law Bulletin**
Andrews Publications
175 Strafford Avenue
Building 4, Suite 140
Wayne, PA 19087-3331

610-225-0510
800-345-1101; Fax: 610-225-0501

Donna Higgins, Editor
Rose MacDonald, Production Manager

Newsletter covering the legal issues raided by the Millenium. Bug along with insightful commentary from attorneys and other experts.
Cost: $25.00
Frequency: Monthly
Founded in 1872

15712 **Law Firm Profit Report**
James Publishing
3505 Cadillac Avenue
Suite H
Costa Mesa, CA 92626

714-755-5450
800-440-4780; Fax: 714-751-2709
customer-service@jamespublishing.com
www.jamespublishing.com

Jim Pawell, Founder/President
Lorraine Thinnes, Editor

How to manage a small to medium-sized law firm profitably, with tips on cost-cutting, managing automation, personnel and more.
Founded in 1981
Mailing list available for rent

15713 **Law Office Management & Administration Report**
Institute of Management and Administration
1 Washington Park
Suite 1300
Newark, NJ 07102-3130

212-244-0360; Fax: 973-622-0595
customercare@bna.com
www.ioma.com

Covers the daily management concerns relevant for law firm administrators, office managers, and others.
Cost: $489.00
Frequency: Monthly
Founded in 1983

15714 **Law Practice Today**
American Bar Association
321 N Clark St
Chicago, IL 60654-7598

312-988-5000
800-285-2221; Fax: 312-988-5280
askaba@abanet.org
www.abanet.org
Facebook, Twitter

Laurel Bellows, President
Jack L. Rives, Executive Director
Robert M. Carlson, Chairman
Lucian T. Pera, Treasurer
Cara Lee T. Neville, Secretary

An e-newsletter focusing on how lawyers can improve their personal productivity in the hands-on practice of law.
Frequency: Monthly
Founded in 1878
Mailing list available for rent

15715 **Law and Society Association Newsletter**
Denver College of Law
1900 Olive Street
Denver, CO 80220-1857

303-871-6306
www.lawandsociety.org

Joyce Sterling, Publisher

Legal updates and information on the Society.
Frequency: Monthly

15716 **LawPractice.news**
American Bar Association - Law Practice Management
321 N Clark St
Chicago, IL 60654-7598

312-988-5000
800-285-2221; Fax: 312-988-5280
askaba@abanet.org
www.abanet.org/lpm/home.shtml
Facebook, Twitter, Youtube

Laurel Bellows, President
Jack L. Rives, Executive Director
Robert M. Carlson, Chairman
Lucian T. Pera, Treasurer
Cara Lee T. Neville, Secretary

A monthly e-newsletter for Law Practice Management Section members, keeping them abreast of Section events, publications, promotions and member news.
Frequency: Monthly
Founded in 1974
Mailing list available for rent

15717 **Lawyer's PC**
West Group
1428 Dewey Ave
Rochester, NY 14613-1128

585-254-9585
800-327-2665; Fax: 585-258-3707
west.support@thomson.com
www.west.thomson.com

Computer and electronics information aimed at the legal profession.
Cost: $299.00
16 Pages
Circulation: 4000
Founded in 1872
Printed in one color

15718 **Lawyering Tools and Techniques**
American Bar Association
321 N Clark St
Chicago, IL 60654-7598

312-988-5000
800-285-2221; Fax: 312-988-5280
askaba@abanet.org
www.abanet.org
Facebook, Twitter

Laurel Bellows, President
Jack L. Rives, Executive Director
Robert M. Carlson, Chairman
Lucian T. Pera, Treasurer
Cara Lee T. Neville, Secretary

Focuses on specific tools lawyers can use to improve the productivity of their work including electronic communications, laptops, desk publishing and resources.
Cost: $50.00
Frequency: Quarterly
Founded in 1878
Mailing list available for rent

15719 **Lawyers Tax Alert**
Research Institute of America
90 5th Avenue
2nd Floor
New York, NY 10011-7696

212-367-6300

Peter Grean, Manager

Tax laws and news.
Frequency: Monthly

15720 **Lawyers' Letter**
American Bar Association
321 N Clark St
Chicago, IL 60654-7598

312-988-5000
800-285-2221; Fax: 312-988-5280
askaba@abanet.org
www.abanet.org
Facebook, Twitter

Laurel Bellows, President
Jack L. Rives, Executive Director
Robert M. Carlson, Chairman
Lucian T. Pera, Treasurer
Cara Lee T. Neville, Secretary

Newsletter informing lawyers of new developments in court improvement and reports on Conference activities.
Founded in 1878
Mailing list available for rent

15721 **Legal Advisory**
WPI Communications
55 Morris Ave
Suite 300
Springfield, NJ 07081-1422

973-467-8700
800-323-4995; Fax: 973-467-0368
info@wpicomm.com
www.wpicomm.com

Steve Klinghoffer, President
Marilyn Lang, Chairman

Offers updates, news and the latest legislation for lawyers.
Frequency: Monthly
Founded in 1952

15722 **Legal Assistant Today Magazine**
James Publishing
3505 Cadillac Avenue
Suite H
Costa Mesa, CA 92626

714-755-5450
800-440-4780; Fax: 714-751-2709
customer-service@jamespublishing.com
www.jamespublishing.com

Jim Pawell, Founder/President
Rod Hughes, Managing Editor

Written exclusively for paralegals and legal assistants. Each issue includes coverage if industry news and trends, how-to articles as well as colorful and informative pieces on unique areas and persons in the profession and sound advice for becoming more efficient in the workplace., buy wisely and use their investments to maximize productivity and profitability.
Cost: $47.98
56 Pages
Circulation: 13000
ISSN: 1055-128X
Founded in 1981

15723 **Legal Review**
Native American Rights Fund
1506 Broadway St
Boulder, CO 80302-6296

303-447-8760; Fax: 303-443-7776
webmaster@narf.org
www.narf.org
Facebook

John E Echohawk, Executive Director
Carly Hare, Director Development
Rose Cuny, Office Manager
Katrina Mora, Office Services Assistant
Mireille Martinez, Development Projects Manager

A bi-annual case update published by the Native American Rights Fund.
Frequency: Bi-annually
Circulation: 30000
ISSN: 0739-862x
Mailing list available for rent
Printed in 4 colors on matte stock

15724 **Litigation LAWCAST**
Vox Juris
PO Box 389
Pennington, NJ 08534

609-737-6543
800-529-2278; Fax: 609-737-3860
www.lawcast.com

Jason Meyer, Editor & Publisher
Linda Delp, General Manager

Analysis of legal departments and advanced strategic ideas for the most demanding litigators - whatever the subject of your litigation. Stay up to date on substance and tactics in evidence, discovery, advocacy, damages, client management and selection, settlement, ADR, and ethics, plus coverage of groudbreaking decisions affecting personal injury, commercial, and employment law. 60 min./monthly
Cost: $399.00
Frequency: Monthly
Founded in 1994

15725 **Litigation News**
American Bar Association Section of Litigation
321 N Clark St
Chicago, IL 60654-7598

312-988-5000
800-285-2221; Fax: 312-988-5280
askaba@abanet.org
www.abanet.org
Facebook, Twitter

Laurel Bellows, President
Jack L. Rives, Executive Director
Robert M. Carlson, Chairman
Lucian T. Pera, Treasurer
Cara Lee T. Neville, Secretary

Present articles on the latest developments in law, litigation trends, and topics of interest to litigators.
Frequency: Quarterly
Circulation: 60000
Founded in 1878
Mailing list available for rent

15726 **Marketing for Lawyers**
Leader Publications
345 Park Avenue S
New York, NY 10010-1707

212-799-9200; Fax: 212-696-1848

Sam Adler, Editor
Kerry Kyle, Circulation Director

Helps lawyers expand their practice through marketing.
Cost: $17.50

15727 **Mealey's Asbestos Bankruptcy Report**
LexisNexis Mealey's
555 W 5th Avenue
Los Angeles, CA 90013

213-627-1130
800-253-4182
mealeyinfo@lexisnexis.com
www.lexisnexis.com/mealeys
Facebook, Twitter, LinkedIn, RSS, Youtube

Tom Hagy, CEO
Maureen McGuire, Editorial Director
Lisa Schaeffer, Editor
Mike Wash, Chief Executive Officer, Legal
Lisa Agona, Chief Marketing Officer

The report provides in-depth news and analysis of asbestos bankruptcy law and the progress of bankrupt asbestos companies through the ever-evolving Chapter 11 process. Topics include: insurance issues, impacts on settlements, how asbestos bankruptcies are affecting the landscape of the litigation and which companies may be forced to file for Chapter 11 protection in the future.
Cost: $475.00
100 Pages
Frequency: Quarterly

Founded in 2000
Mailing list available for rent

15728 Mealey's California Section 17200 Report
LexisNexis Mealey's
555 5th Avenue
Los Angeles, CA 90013
213-627-1130
800-253-4182
mealeyinfo@lexisnexis.com
www.lexisnexis.com/mealeys
Facebook, Twitter, LinkedIn, RSS, Youtube
Tom Hagy, CEO
Maureen McGuire, Editorial Director
Bryan Redding, Editor
Mike Wash, Chief Executive Officer, Legal
Lisa Agona, Chief Marketing Officer

Monitors litigation and provides legislative updates on California's Unfair Competition Law. This monthly report will offer readers hard-to-find filings and briefs, new complaints, breaking news, concise case summaries, and trial updates. All major cases involving Section 17200 of the state's Business and Professions Code will be reported, including those dealings with insurance, employment, consumer law, the Internet, telecommunications, securities, fraud, product liability and many more.
Cost: $959.00
100 Pages
Frequency: Monthly
Founded in 2002
Mailing list available for rent

15729 Mealey's Catastrophic Loss
LexisNexis Mealey's
555 W 5th Avenue
Los Angeles, CA 90013
213-627-1130
800-253-4182
mealeyinfo@lexisnexis.com
www.lexisnexis.com/mealeys
Facebook, Twitter, LinkedIn, RSS, Youtube
Tom Hagy, CEO
Maureen McGuire, Editorial Director
Gina Cappello, Editor
Mike Wash, Chief Executive Officer, Legal
Lisa Agona, Chief Marketing Officer

This report focuses on business interruption insurance claims in the aftermath of the Hurricane Katrina, September 11th, and other catastrophic loss tragedies. Additionally, the report will go beyond these claims and will offer important business interruption insurance coverage news related to computer viruses, computer failures, and natural disasters.
Cost: $1075.00
100 Pages
Frequency: Monthly
Founded in 2001
Mailing list available for rent

15730 Mealey's Daubert Report
LexisNexis Mealey's
555 W 5th Avenue
Los Angeles, CA 90013
213-627-1130
800-253-4182
mealeyinfo@lexisnexis.com
www.lexisnexis.com/mealeys
Facebook, Twitter, LinkedIn, RSS, Youtube
Tom Hagy, CEO
Maureen McGuire, Editorial Director
Kristin Casler, Editor
Mike Wash, Chief Executive Officer, Legal
Lisa Agona, Chief Marketing Officer

This newsletter covers the interpretation, adoption and/or rejection of the Supreme Court's landmark expert admissibility ruling, Daubert v. Merrell Dow Pharmaceutical Inc. As the nation's jurisdictions grapple with so called junk science testimony, this monthly newsletter offers subscribers the latest key rulings in this contentious components of civil and criminal litigation.
Cost: $735.00
100 Pages
Frequency: Monthly
Founded in 1997
Mailing list available for rent

15731 Mealey's Emerging Drugs & Devices
LexisNexis Mealey's
555 W 5th Avenue
Los Angeles, CA 90013
213-627-1130
800-253-4182
mealeyinfo@lexisnexis.com
www.lexisnexis.com/mealeys
Facebook, Twitter, LinkedIn, RSS, Youtube
Tom Hagy, CEO
Maureen McGuire, Editorial Director
Tom Moylan, Editor
Mike Wash, Chief Executive Officer, Legal
Lisa Agona, Chief Marketing Officer

The report covers cases involving a variety of prescription drug vaccines, implants and devices. Duract, Parlodel, Accutane, fen-phen, Rezulin, Propulsid, dietary supplements and blood products are among the topics tracked. Medical devices covered include heart catheters, breast implants, heart valves, intraocular lenses, jaw implants, joint replacements, latex gloves, pacemakers, pedicle screws, penile implants, and surgical lasers.
Cost: $1249.00
100 Pages
Frequency: Semi-Monthly
Founded in 1996
Mailing list available for rent

15732 Mealey's Emerging Insurance Disputes
LexisNexis Mealey's
555 W 5th Avenue
Los Angeles, CA 90013
213-627-1130
800-253-4182; Fax: 610-768-0880
mealeyinfo@lexisnexis.com
www.lexisnexis.com/mealeys
Facebook, Twitter, LinkedIn, RSS, Youtube
Tom Hagy, CEO
Maureen McGuire, Editorial Director
Gina Cappello, Editor
Mike Wash, Chief Executive Officer, Legal
Lisa Agona, Chief Marketing Officer

The report tracks new areas of coverage liability, novel policy applications, and conflicting policy language interpretations as they arise in insurance litigation. Some areas of coverage featured are: sexual harassment and discrimination, assault and battery, professional liability, patent and trademark infringement, construction defects, directors and officers claims, emotional distress, intentional acts, technology, and insurance business practices.
Cost: $ 1229.00
100 Pages
Frequency: Semi-Monthly
Founded in 1996
Mailing list available for rent

15733 Mealey's Emerging Securities Litigation
LexisNexis Mealey's
555 W 5th Avenue
Los Angeles, CA 90013
213-627-1130
800-253-4182; Fax: 610-768-0880
mealeyinfo@lexisnexis.com
www.lexisnexis.com/mealeys
Facebook, Twitter, LinkedIn, RSS, Youtube
Tom Hagy, CEO
Maureen McGuire, Editorial Director
Mike Lello, Editor
Mike Wash, Chief Executive Officer, Legal
Lisa Agona, Chief Marketing Officer

The report covers fiduciary duties to shareholders, 401k and pension implications, class actions, damage calculations, causation questions. Daubert issues, debt bondholder implications, bankruptcy issues and accountant liability in the securities law context.
Cost: $875.00
100 Pages
Frequency: Monthly
Founded in 2002
Mailing list available for rent

15734 Mealey's Emerging Toxic Torts
LexisNexis Mealey's
555 W 5th Avenue
Los Angeles, CA 90013
213-627-1130
800-253-4182; Fax: 610-768-0880
mealeyinfo@lexisnexis.com
www.lexisnexis.com/mealeys
Facebook, Twitter, LinkedIn, RSS, Youtube
Tom Hagy, CEO
Maureen McGuire, Editorial Director
Bill Lowe, Editor
Mike Wash, Chief Executive Officer, Legal
Lisa Agona, Chief Marketing Officer

The report focuses on the hottest areas of toxic tort litigation including: chemical sensitivity; indoor air quality; groundwater, soil and air contamination; radiation; workplace exposure; pesticides; solvents; latex gloves; EMF's; MTBE; endocrine disruptors, and more. The report provides in-depth coverage of medical monitoring; fear of cancer/disease; stigma damages; expert admissibility; federal preemption; class actions; punitive damages and market share theory.
Cost: $1539.00
100 Pages
Frequency: Semi-Monthly
Founded in 1992
Mailing list available for rent

15735 Mealey's International Arbitration Quarterly Law Review
LexisNexis Mealey's
555 W 5th Avenue
Los Angeles, CA 90013
213-627-1130
800-253-4182; Fax: 610-768-0880
mealeyinfo@lexisnexis.com
www.lexisnexis.com/mealeys
Facebook, Twitter, LinkedIn, RSS, Youtube
Tom Hagy, CEO
Maureen McGuire, Editorial Director
Edie Scott, Editor
Mike Wash, Chief Executive Officer, Legal
Lisa Agona, Chief Marketing Officer

The report provides thought-provoking commentary articles authored by arbitrators, scholars and attorneys with first-hand knowledge of the complex field of commercial dispute resolution. Each issue contains analytical discussions and practical insights on current case law, new treaties and statues, arbitration principles, dispute resolution techniques, and more from our prestigious international authors.
Cost: $475.00
100 Pages
Frequency: Quarterly
Founded in 2000
Mailing list available for rent

15736 Mealey's International Arbritation Report
LexisNexis Mealey's

555 W 5th Avenue
Los Angeles, CA 90013

213-627-1130
800-253-4182; Fax: 610-768-0880
mealeyinfo@lexisnexis.com
www.lexisnexis.com/mealeys
Facebook, Twitter, LinkedIn, RSS, Youtube

Tom Hagy, CEO
Maureen McGuire, Editorial Director
Edie Scott, Editor
Mike Wash, Chief Executive Officer, Legal
Lisa Agona, Chief Marketing Officer

The report examines arbitration and related litigation in courts world-wide. Covers enforcement, jurisdictional disputes, forum selection, use of experts by arbitral parties, enforcement, judicial supervision, the Iran-US Claims Tribunal, the United Nations Compensation Commission, and events of interest at arbitration institutions around the globe.
Cost: $2049.00
100 Pages
Frequency: Monthly
Founded in 1986
Mailing list available for rent

15737 **Mealey's International Asbestos Liability Report**
LexisNexis Mealey's
555 W 5th Avenue
Los Angeles, CA 90013

213-627-1130
800-253-4182; Fax: 610-768-0880
mealeyinfo@lexisnexis.com
www.lexisnexis.com/mealeys
Facebook, Twitter, LinkedIn, RSS, Youtube

Tom Hagy, CEO
Maureen McGuire, Editorial Director
Lisa Schaeffer, Editor
Mike Wash, Chief Executive Officer, Legal
Lisa Agona, Chief Marketing Officer

The report covers the latest litigation, regulatory, and medical news related to worldwide asbestos exposure - including the emerging issue of subsidiary liability and the question of US jurisdiction - with in-depth case summaries and news of medical findings, full-text court documents, and exclusive expert commentary articles.
Cost: $959.00
100 Pages
Frequency: Monthly
Founded in 2003
Mailing list available for rent

15738 **Mealey's Litigation Report: Insurance Fraud**
LexisNexis Mealey's
555 W 5th Avenue
Los Angeles, CA 90013

213-627-1130
800-253-4182; Fax: 610-768-0880
mealeyinfo@lexisnexis.com
www.lexisnexis.com/mealeys
Facebook, Twitter, LinkedIn, RSS, Youtube

Tom Hagy, CEO
Maureen McGuire, Editorial Director
Teresa Kent Zink, Editor
Mike Wash, Chief Executive Officer, Legal
Lisa Agona, Chief Marketing Officer

The report reviews civil and criminal cases arising from efforts by policyholders and third parties to defraud insurance carriers. Topics include false and fraudulent claims, arson, reverse bad faith, restitution, RICO, incontestability clauses, material misrepresentation, rescission, qui tam actions and fraud rings. Readers receive reports on schemes involving property & casualty, health care, automobile, life, homeowners, and workers' compensation fraud.
Cost: $839.00
100 Pages
Frequency: Monthly
Founded in 1994
Mailing list available for rent

15739 **Mealey's Litigation Report: Asbestos**
LexisNexis Mealey's
555 W 5th Avenue
Los Angeles, CA 90013

213-627-1130
800-253-4182; Fax: 610-768-0880
mealeyinfo@lexisnexis.com
www.lexisnexis.com/mealeys
Facebook, Twitter, LinkedIn, RSS, Youtube

Tom Hagy, CEO
Maureen McGuire, Editorial Director
Bryan Redding, Editor
Mike Wash, Chief Executive Officer, Legal
Lisa Agona, Chief Marketing Officer

The report offers unsurpassed coverage of litigation arising from asbestos-related injury and death. Key issues include: massive class action settlements involving present and future claimants, state and federal verdicts, litigation experts, medical monitoring claims, suits against the tobacco industry, discovery battles, discovery rule decisions, insurance coverage rulings, and asbestos property decisions.
Cost: $1789.00
100 Pages
Frequency: Semi-Monthly
Founded in 1984
Mailing list available for rent

15740 **Mealey's Litigation Report: Baycol**
LexisNexis Mealey's
555 W 5th Avenue
Los Angeles, CA 90013

213-627-1130
800-253-4182; Fax: 610-768-0880
mealeyinfo@lexisnexis.com
www.lexisnexis.com/mealeys
Facebook, Twitter, LinkedIn, RSS, Youtube

Tom Hagy, CEO
Maureen McGuire, Editorial Director
Dylan McGuire, Editor
Mike Wash, Chief Executive Officer, Legal
Lisa Agona, Chief Marketing Officer

This report tracks the litigation surrounding Baycol and other statin-based anti-cholesterol drug cases. Since the voluntary withdrawl of Bayer's Baycol and Lipobay brand cerivastatin anti-cholesterol drugs, numerous complaints have been filed. The report will cover hard-to-find filings, new complaints, class actions, MDL developments, trial updates and more.
Cost: $950.00
100 Pages
Frequency: Monthly
Founded in 2002
Mailing list available for rent

15741 **Mealey's Litigation Report: California Insurance**
LexisNexis Mealey's
1016 W Ninth Avenue
1st Floor
King of Prussia, PA 19406-1221

215-564-1788
800-448-1515; Fax: 610-768-0880
mealeyinfo@lexisnexis.com
www.lexisnexis.com/mealeys
Facebook, Twitter, LinkedIn, Itunes, Youtube

Kumsal Bayazit, Global Senior Vice President
Haywood Talcove, Chief Executive Officer, Government
Ian McDougall, Executive Vice President
Mike Walsh, CEO
Alex Watson, Executive Vice President

The Report focuses on ever-changing California and federal Ninth Circuit insurance coverage disputes and developments. Topics include California developments in bad faith litigation, earthquake damage coverage, disability insurance, products liability coverage, environmental insurance coverage, mold coverage, asbestos coverage, aviation litigation coverage, entertainment law and more.
Cost: $949.00
100 Pages
Frequency: Monthly
Founded in 2001

15742 **Mealey's Litigation Report: Class Actions**
LexisNexis Mealey's
1016 W Ninth Avenue
1st Floor
King of Prussia, PA 19406-1221

215-564-1788
800-448-1515; Fax: 610-768-0880
mealeyinfo@lexisnexis.com
www.lexisnexis.com/mealeys
Facebook, Twitter, LinkedIn, Itunes, Youtube

Kumsal Bayazit, Global Senior Vice President
Haywood Talcove, Chief Executive Officer, Government
Ian McDougall, Executive Vice President
Mike Walsh, CEO
Alex Watson, Executive Vice President

This report will provide in-depth coverage of class action litigation involving mass torts and beyond - including consumer law, employment law, securities litigation and e-commerce disputes. Get the latest on: hard-to-find filings, notice plans, fairness hearings, class certification rulings, settlements, trial news and verdicts, attorney fee news, appeals, breaking news stories, new complaints, Supreme Court battles, and much more.
Cost: $1195.00
100 Pages
Frequency: Semi-Monthly
Founded in 1997

15743 **Mealey's Litigation Report: Construction Defects**
LexisNexis Mealey's
1016 W Ninth Avenue
1st Floor
King of Prussia, PA 19406-1221

215-564-1788
800-448-1515; Fax: 610-768-0880
mealeyinfo@lexisnexis.com
www.lexisnexis.com/mealeys
Facebook, Twitter, LinkedIn, Itunes, Youtube

Kumsal Bayazit, Global Senior Vice President
Haywood Talcove, Chief Executive Officer, Government
Ian McDougall, Executive Vice President
Mike Walsh, CEO
Alex Watson, Executive Vice President

The Report tracks the growing area of construction defect litigation, including cases involving water intrusion, building settlement, concrete corrosion, mold and other defects. Topics covered include: recovery of damages, warranty issues, contractor liability, sub-contractor liability, developer liability, architect liability and related insurance cover actions.
Cost: $979.00
100 Pages
Frequency: Monthly
Founded in 2000

15744 **Mealey's Litigation Report: Copyright**
LexisNexis Mealey's
1016 W Ninth Avenue
1st Floor
King of Prussia, PA 19406-1221

215-564-1788
800-448-1515; Fax: 610-768-0880
mealeyinfo@lexisnexis.com

www.lexisnexis.com/mealeys
Facebook, Twitter, LinkedIn, Itunes, Youtube

Kumsal Bayazit, Global Senior Vice President
Haywood Talcove, Chief Executive Officer, Government
Ian McDougall, Executive Vice President
Mike Walsh, CEO
Alex Watson, Executive Vice President

The report offers timely and practical analysis on the hot issues in the field. Also features in-depth reporting of copyright law, including court decisions, new suits, settlements, and trials, plus full-text court documents.
Cost: $849.00
100 Pages
Frequency: Monthly
Founded in 2002

15745 **Mealey's Litigation Report: Cyber Tech & E -Commerce**
LexisNexis Mealey's
1016 W Ninth Avenue
1st Floor
King of Prussia, PA 19406-1221

215-564-1788
800-448-1515; Fax: 610-768-0880
mealeyinfo@lexisnexis.com
www.lexisnexis.com/mealeys
Facebook, Twitter, LinkedIn, Itunes, Youtube

Kumsal Bayazit, Global Senior Vice President
Haywood Talcove, Chief Executive Officer, Government
Ian McDougall, Executive Vice President
Mike Walsh, CEO
Alex Watson, Executive Vice President

The Report covers disputes arising from e-commerce. The report tracks emerging legal issues, including: Internet security, data destruction and/or alteration, defamation on the Web, software errors, hardware failure, electronic theft, e-mail trespass, online privacy, government action, shareholder lawsuits, Internet jurisdiction issues, file sharing (copyright) disputes and much more.
Cost: $999.00
100 Pages
Frequency: Monthly
Founded in 1999

15746 **Mealey's Litigation Report: Disability Insurance**
LexisNexis Mealey's
1016 W Ninth Avenue
1st Floor
King of Prussia, PA 19406-1221

215-564-1788
800-448-1515; Fax: 610-768-0880
mealeyinfo@lexisnexis.com
www.lexisnexis.com/mealeys
Facebook, Twitter, LinkedIn, Itunes, Youtube

Kumsal Bayazit, Global Senior Vice President
Haywood Talcove, Chief Executive Officer, Government
Ian McDougall, Executive Vice President
Mike Walsh, CEO
Alex Watson, Executive Vice President

This report tracks the burgeoning number of disputes involving complex disability coverage claims. Topics covered include: claims for chronic fatigue, chronic pain, stress, psychiatric disabilities, chemical dependency and risk of relapse, plus key issues like total disability, own occupation, bad faith, ERSA, class actions and much more.
Cost: $849.00
100 Pages
Frequency: Monthly
Founded in 2000

15747 **Mealey's Litigation Report: Discovery**
LexisNexis Mealey's
1016 W Ninth Avenue
1st Floor
King of Prussia, PA 19406-1221
215-564-1788
800-448-1515; Fax: 610-768-0880
mealeyinfo@lexisnexis.com
www.lexisnexis.com/mealeys
Facebook, Twitter, LinkedIn, Itunes, Youtube

Kumsal Bayazit, Global Senior Vice President
Haywood Talcove, Chief Executive Officer, Government
Ian McDougall, Executive Vice President
Mike Walsh, CEO
Alex Watson, Executive Vice President

This report covers all of the discovery litigation essentials, including how different districts and judges interpret federal discovery rules, procedural changes, the work product, attorney-client and common interest privileges, and discovery abuse.
Cost: $785.00
100 Pages
Frequency: Monthly
Founded in 2003

15748 **Mealey's Litigation Report: ERISA**
LexisNexis Mealey's
1016 W Ninth Avenue
1st Floor
King of Prussia, PA 19406-1221

215-564-1788
800-448-1515; Fax: 610-768-0880
mealeyinfo@lexisnexis.com
www.lexisnexis.com/mealeys
Facebook, Twitter, LinkedIn, Itunes, Youtube

Kumsal Bayazit, Global Senior Vice President
Haywood Talcove, Chief Executive Officer, Government
Ian McDougall, Executive Vice President
Mike Walsh, CEO
Alex Watson, Executive Vice President

The report focuses on the hottest areas of ERISA litigation, including preemption, health plan actions, exhaustion of administrative remedies, contingent worker litigation, class actions 401k plans, attorney's fees, breach of fiduciary duty, what courts consider to be equitable relief, downsizing and benefit cutbacks, blackout periods and bad faith claims against disability insurers.
Cost: $875.00
100 Pages
Frequency: Monthly
Founded in 2002

15749 **Mealey's Litigation Report: Ephedra/PPA**
LexisNexis Mealey's
1016 W Ninth Avenue
1st Floor
King of Prussia, PA 19406-1221

215-564-1788
800-448-1515; Fax: 610-768-0880
mealeyinfo@lexisnexis.com
www.lexisnexis.com/mealeys
Facebook, Twitter, LinkedIn, Itunes, Youtube

Kumsal Bayazit, Global Senior Vice President
Haywood Talcove, Chief Executive Officer, Government
Ian McDougall, Executive Vice President
Mike Walsh, CEO
Alex Watson, Executive Vice President

The report tracks every facet of the growing area of litigation resulting from injuries and deaths associated with over-the-counter decongestant and appetite suppressant, phenylpropanolamine (PPA), and the chemically similar weight-loss herb, ephedra. The report offers true litigation reporting of new complaints, answers, discovery motions, appeals, trials, verdicts, settlements, plus covers the latest regulatory news.
Cost: $995.00
100 Pages
Frequency: Monthly
Founded in 2001

15750 **Mealey's Litigation Report: Fen-Phen/Redux**
LexisNexis Mealey's
1016 W Ninth Avenue
1st Floor
King of Prussia, PA 19406-1221

215-564-1788
800-448-1515; Fax: 610-768-0880
mealeyinfo@lexisnexis.com
www.lexisnexis.com/mealeys
Facebook, Twitter, LinkedIn, Itunes, Youtube

Kumsal Bayazit, Global Senior Vice President
Haywood Talcove, Chief Executive Officer, Government
Ian McDougall, Executive Vice President
Mike Walsh, CEO
Alex Watson, Executive Vice President

The report provides detailed coverage of the litigation surrounding fen-phen, Redux and other diet drugs. The report covers new filings, class actions, MDL proceedings, trials, settlements, rulings, medical studies, FDA activity and more.
Cost: $995.00
100 Pages
Frequency: Monthly
Founded in 1997

15751 **Mealey's Litigation Report: Insurance**
LexisNexis Mealey's
1016 W Ninth Avenue
1st Floor
King of Prussia, PA 19406-1221

215-564-1788
800-448-1515; Fax: 610-768-0880
mealeyinfo@lexisnexis.com
www.lexisnexis.com/mealeys
Facebook, Twitter, LinkedIn, Itunes, Youtube

Kumsal Bayazit, Global Senior Vice President
Haywood Talcove, Chief Executive Officer, Government
Ian McDougall, Executive Vice President
Mike Walsh, CEO
Alex Watson, Executive Vice President

The report tracks declaratory judgment actions regarding coverage for litigation arising from long-tail claims, including environmental contamination and latent damage and injury allegedly caused by asbestos, tox chemicals and fumes, lead, breast implants, medical devices, construction defects, and more. Key issues: allocation, occurrence, policy exclusion, choice of law, discovery, duty to defend, notice, trigger of coverage and known loss.
Cost: $2115.00
100 Pages
Frequency: Weekly
Founded in 1984

15752 **Mealey's Litigation Report: Insurance Bad Faith**
LexisNexis Mealey's
1016 W Ninth Avenue
1st Floor
King of Prussia, PA 19406-1221

215-564-1788
800-448-1515; Fax: 610-768-0880
mealeyinfo@lexisnexis.com
www.lexisnexis.com/mealeys
Facebook, LinkedIn, Itunes, Youtube

Kumsal Bayazit, Global Senior Vice President
Haywood Talcove, Chief Executive Officer, Government
Ian McDougall, Executive Vice President
Mike Walsh, CEO
Alex Watson, Executive Vice President

The report details insurance coverage disputes arising from alleged breaches of the implied covenant of good faith and fair dealing. The topics covered involve third-party and first-party actions, statutory suits, punitive damage claims, coverage denials and delays, the definition of bad faith, relevant legislation, verdicts, and discovery disputes.
Cost: $1325.00
100 Pages
Frequency: Semi-Monthly
Founded in 1987

15753 **Medical Liability Advisory Service**
Business Publishers
8737 Colesville Road
10th Floor
Silver Spring, MD 20910-3928

301-876-6300
800-274-6737; Fax: 301-589-8493
custserv@bpinews.com
www.bpinews.com

Eric Easton, Publisher
Bonita Becker, Editor

Gives you practical information on just what triggers a lawsuit. Information you can pass on to your staff to claim-proof your procedures.
Founded in 1963

15754 **Medical Malpractice Reports**
Matthew Bender and Company
11 Penn Plz
Suite 5101
New York, NY 10001-2006

212-000-1111; Fax: 212-244-3188

Eric Blood, Data Processing

All the facts, background information and expert analysis you need to keep on top of new legislation, new theories of liability, the impact of new medical technology and more.

15755 **Mental and Physical Disability Law Reporter: On-Line**
American Bar Association
740 15th Street NW
Washington, DC 20005-1019

202-662-1000; Fax: 202-442-3439
Facebook, Twitter, LinkedIn

Stephen N. Zack, President
Katherine H. O'Neil, Commission Chair
John W. Parry, Commission Director
Jack L. Rives, Executive Director
Alice Richmond, Treasurer

A new online searchable database allows subscribers to research disability law cases and legislation by case name, federal or state legislation, subject area, jurisdiction, and year (beginning 2003). There are 22 subject areas that cover three main areas: civil mental disability law; criminal mental disability law; and disability discrimination law. The database, which is updated every two months, contains over 12,000 summaries of key cases and legislation.
Cost: $299.00
15 Members
Frequency: 6 X/Year
ISSN: 0883-7902
Founded in 1973

15756 **Mergers & Acquisitions Litigation Reporter**
Thomson Reuters
610 Opperman Dr
St Paul, MN 55123-1340

651-687-7000
800-344-5008; Fax: 651-687-5581
www.store.westlaw.com/default.aspx

Charles B Cater, Executive VP
Laurie Zenner, VP

Provides summaries and fulltext documents in key litigation concerning mergers and acquisitions. Offers general buyout and acquisition coverage as well as cases related to leveraged buyouts.
Cost: $1234.20
Frequency: Monthly
Mailing list available for rent

15757 **Money Laundering Alert**
Alert Global Media
80 SW 8th Street
Suite 2300
Miami, FL 33130-3031

305-530-0500
800-232-3652; Fax: 305-530-9434
customerservice@moneylaundering.com
www.moneylaundering.com

Charles Intriago, President

Covers legal issues, including new laws, regulations and cases related to money laundering and the bank secrecy act in the US and worldwide. Provides practical guidance and analysis and serves as a training tool. Also full text on the internet.
Cost: $945.00
15 Pages
Frequency: Monthly
ISSN: 1046-3070
Founded in 1989

15758 **Municipal Litigation Reporter**
Strafford Publications
PO Box 13729
Atlanta, GA 30324-0729

404-881-1141
800-926-7926; Fax: 404-881-0074
customerservice@straffordpub.com
www.straffordpub.com

Richard Ossoff, President
Jennifer Vaughan, Managing Editor

Monthly digest of key court decisions on litigation involving local governments. Cases are screened and selected to provide concise, comprehensive coverage of issues important to municipal attorneys and others involved with the local government.
Cost: $497.00
16 Pages
ISSN: 0278-1301
Founded in 1984
Mailing list available for rent: 7.4M names
Printed in one color

15759 **NAELA News**
National Academy of Elder Law Attorneys
1577 Spring Hill Road
Suite 220
Vienna, VA 22182-2223

703-942-5711; Fax: 703-563-9504
naela@naela.org
www.naela.org

Peter G Wacht, CAE, Executive Director
Nancy Sween, Director Publications
Kirsten Brown Simpson, Director, Membership & Marketing
Ann Watkins, Operations Manager
Roger Naoroji, Meetings & Education Coordinator

Communicates the activities, goals, and mission of its publisher, the National Academy of Elder Law Attorneys and seeks out and publishes information and diverse views related to Elder Law and Special Needs.
Frequency: 6x Year

15760 **NCWBA Newsletter**
National Conference of Women's Bar Associations
PO Box 82366
Portland, OR 97282

info@ncwba.org
www.ncwba.org

Jeanne Cezanne Collins, President
Pamela Berman, President-Elect
Diane Rynerson, Executive Director

To promote and assist the growth of local and statewide women's bar associations and ideas among women's bar associations and women's bar sections of local and statewide bar associations; to serve as a vehicle for the exchange and dissemination of information and ideas among women's bar associations and women's bar sections of local and statewide bar associations.
Frequency: Monthly

15761 **National Association of Consumer Advocates Newsletter**
National Association of Consumer Advocates
1215 17th Street NW
5th Floor
Washington, DC 20036

202-452-1989; Fax: 202-452-0099
info@consumeradvocates.org
www.consumeradvocates.org

David Philips, Co-Chair
Michael J. Quirk, Co-Chair
Ira Rheingold, Executive Director

A newsletter for NACA members that oncludes the latest updates on consumer finance and consumer protection legislative and regulatory issues.
Founded in 1994

15762 **National Bankruptcy Reporter**
Andrews Communications
175 Stafford, Building 4
Suite 140
Wayne, PA 19087

610-225-0510
800-345-1101; Fax: 610-225-0501

Robert Maroldo, Publisher

Commercial bankruptcy news.
Frequency: Monthly

15763 **National Bar Bulletin**
National Bar Association
1225 11th St Nw
Washington, DC 20001-4217

202-842-3900; Fax: 202-289-6170
www.nationalbar.org

John Crump, Executive Director
Kim M Keenan, Manager
Teka Miller, Manager

Association news and activities, legislative updates and information for lawyers.
Cost: $20.00
8 Pages
Frequency: Monthly
Founded in 1925

15764 **National Financing Law Digest**
Strafford Publications
PO Box 13729
Atlanta, GA 30324-0729

404-881-1141
800-926-7926; Fax: 404-881-0074
customerservice@straffordpub.com
www.straffordpub.com

Richard Ossoff, President
Jennifer Vaughan, Managing Editor

Monthly digest of nationally significant litigation concerning secured and unsecured financing transactions, including bonds, bankruptcy

collection, and lender liability.
Cost: $597.00
Frequency: Monthly
ISSN: 1073-953X
Founded in 1984

15765 National Notary
National Notary Association
9350 DeSoto Avenue
PO Box 2402
Chatsworth, CA 91311-2402

818-394-4000
800-876-6827; Fax: 800-833-1211
publications@nationalnotary.org
www.nationalnotary.org

Deborah Thaw, Executive VP
Armando Aguirre, Editor
Milton G. Valera, Chairman
Thomas A. Heymann, President /CEO
Deborah M. Thaw, Executive Vice President

Contents range from indentity fraud and electronic notarization, to legislation and practicing tips. Also includes human interest stories involving notaries.
Circulation: 250,000
ISSN: 0894-7872
Founded in 1957
Printed in 4 colors on glossy stock

15766 National Paralegal Reporter
National Federation of Paralegal Associations
2815 Eastlake Ave E
Suite 160
Seattle, WA 98102-3278

206-285-1851; Fax: 206-284-3481
info@akpreparedness.com
www.akproductions.com

Founded in 1981

15767 National Property Law Digests
Strafford Publications
PO Box 13729
Atlanta, GA 30324-0729

404-881-1141
800-926-7926; Fax: 404-881-0074
customerservice@straffordpub.com
www.straffordpub.com

Richard Ossoff, Presdient

Case digests of national significant court decisions affecting the acquisition, development, management, transfer and financing of real property.
Cost: $697.00
Frequency: Monthly
ISSN: 0363-8340
Founded in 1984
Mailing list available for rent: 25M names

15768 National Report on Work & Family
Business Publishers
2222 Sedwick Dr
Suite 101
Durham, NC 27713

800-223-8720; Fax: 800-508-2592
custserv@bpinews.com
www.bpinews.com

Independent, authoritative resource covering the latest federal and state legislative, legal and regulatory developments concerning work/family issues. Includes case studies of organizations that have implemented family-friendly policies.
Cost: $497.00
Frequency: 25 per year

15769 National Security Law Report
American Bar Association-Law & National Security
740 15th St Nw
Suite 8
Washington, DC 20005-1022

202-662-1000; Fax: 202-662-1032
orders@abanet.org
www.americanbar.org/aba.html
Facebook, Twitter

Laurel G. Bellows, President

The Report includes reports of committee conferences, pertinent law and national security updates, recent cases, book reviews, pending legislation, and other writing relevant to the field.
Frequency: Monthly
Circulation: 4000
Founded in 1991

15770 Newswire
Commercial Law League of America
3005 Tollview Drive
Rolling Meadows, IL 60008

312-240-1400; Fax: 312-240-1408
info@clla.org
www.clla.org

Phil Lattanzio, Executive Vice President
Dawn Federico, Associate Director

Provides news and information on bankruptcy, collections, debt and insolvency information, as well as recent events essential information and community news.
Founded in 1895

15771 Nolo News: Legal Self-Help Newspaper
Nolo Press
950 Parker St
Berkeley, CA 94710-2576

510-704-2248; Fax: 510-859-0027
www.nolo.com

Maggie Wang, Manager
Mary Randolph, Editor

Self-help legal newspaper.
Cost: $39.99
Frequency: Weekly
Circulation: 120000
Founded in 1971

15772 On the Line: Union Labor Reports Guide
Bureau of National Affairs
1801 S Bell St
Arlington, VA 22202-4501

703-341-3000
800-372-1033; Fax: 800-253-0332
customercare@bna.com
www.bnabooks.com
Facebook, Twitter, LinkedIn

Paul N Wojcik, CEO

Reports on shopfloor issues affecting union stewards. Includes summaries of arbitration awards and court cases. $4.00 per year each subscription.
Cost: $4.00
ISSN: 1526-2863
Founded in 1929

15773 Parascope
American Bar Association
321 N Clark St
Chicago, IL 60654-7598

312-988-5000
800-285-2221; Fax: 312-988-6281
askaba@abanet.org
www.americanbar.org/aba.html
Facebook, Twitter

Tommy H Wells Jr, President
Laurel G. Bellows, President

Newsletter for nation's appellate staff attorneys. Contains book reviews and articles on matters concerning appellate courts.
Cost: $19.00
Frequency: Quarterly

15774 Partner's Report for Law Firm Owners
Institute of Management and Administration
3 Bethesda Metro Center
Suite 250
Bethesda, MD 20814-5377

703-341-3500
800-372-1033; Fax: 800-253-0332
www.ioma.com

Keeps partners up to date on salary guidelines and benefits, aw well as provide the reader with tips on increasing profit margins and exercising leadership skills.
Frequency: Monthly
Founded in 1984

15775 Patent/Trade/Copyright Newsletter
American Bar Association
321 N Clark St
Chicago, IL 60654-7598

312-988-5000
800-285-2221; Fax: 312-988-6281
www.americanbar.org/aba.html
Facebook, Twitter

Tommy H Wells Jr, President
Laurel G. Bellows, President

Activities of the Section, recent developments in intellectual property law and calendar of events.
Frequency: Quarterly
Founded in 1878

15776 People and Programs
American Bar Association
321 N Clark St
Chicago, IL 60654-7598

312-988-5000
800-285-2221; Fax: 312-988-6281
askaba@abanet.org
www.americanbar.org/aba.html
Facebook, Twitter

Tommy H Wells Jr, President
Laurel G. Bellows, President

A newsletter for donors and volunteers for the ABA fund for Justice and Education, which supports over 150 public service and law-related education programs.
Founded in 1878

15777 People-to-People Newsletter
Association of Legal Administrators
75 Tri-State International
Suite 222
Lincolnshire, IL 60069-4435

847-267-1252; Fax: 847-267-1329
publications@alanet.org
www.alanet.org

Larry Smith, Executive Director
Debbie Thomas, Director, Accounting & Finance
Renee Mahovsky, Director, Administration/Operations
Bob Abramson, Director, Marketing & Communication
Jan Waugh, Director, Member Services

Offers the newest information and legislative updates for legal administrators.
Frequency: Monthly
Founded in 1971

15778 Personal Injury Verdict Reviews
LRP Publications
PO Box 980
Horsham, PA 19044-0980

215-784-0912
800-341-7874; Fax: 215-784-9639

webmaster@lrp.com
www.lrp.com

Todd Lutz, CFO
David Light, Managing Editor
Brooke Doran, Research Associate

Each twice-monthly issue contains a statistically based feature article backed by nationwide personal injury case summaries. Each case summary includes description of the incident, names and locations of counsel and expert witnesses, verdict or settlement amount, amount of medical expense and wage loss and date and docket number.
Cost: $375.00
Founded in 1977

15779 **Personnel Legal Alert**
Alexander Hamilton Institute
70 Hilltop Rd
Suite 2200
Ramsey, NJ 07446-2816

201-825-3377
800-879-2441; Fax: 201-825-8696
editorial@ahipubs.com
www.ahipubs.com

Schuyler T Jenks, President

Deals with legal aspects of personnel.
Cost: $97.00
4 Pages
Frequency: Fortnightly
Circulation: 4000
Founded in 1989
Mailing list available for rent: 7,000 names at $125 per M
Printed in 2 colors on matte stock

15780 **Personnel Manager's Legal Letter**
Institute of Management and Administration
3 Bethesda Metro Center
Suite 250
Bethesda, MD 20814-5377

703-341-3500
800-372-1033; Fax: 800-253-0332
www.ioma.com

PMLL regularly covers title VII, the Americans with Disabilities Act, ERISA, the Family and Medical Leave Act, and human resources legal issues around hiring, teminations, compensation and much more.

15781 **Practical Law Books Reviews**
Library Managemental Services
5914 Highland Hills Drive
Austin, TX 78731-4057

512-320-0320

Judith Helburn, Publisher

Reference book separated by field specification.

15782 **Premises Liability Report**
Strafford Publications
PO Box 13729
Atlanta, GA 30324-0729

404-881-1141
800-926-7926; Fax: 404-881-0074
customerservice@straffordpub.com
www.straffordpub.com

Richard Ossoff, President
Jennifer Vaughan, Managing Editor

Digest of legal developments offering liability of property owners and managers. Warning system for potential lawsuits for injuries resulting from conditions on or near premises.
Cost: $287.00
Frequency: Monthly
ISSN: 1055-730X
Founded in 1984

15783 **Preview of US Supreme Court Cases**
American Bar Association
321 N Clark St
Chicago, IL 60654-7598

312-988-5000
800-285-2221; Fax: 312-988-6281
askaba@abanet.org
www.americanbar.org/aba.html
Facebook, Twitter

Tommy H Wells Jr, President
Laurel G. Bellows, President

Previews cases coming before the US Supreme Court.
Cost: $130.00
Frequency: Annual

15784 **Private Security Case Law Reporter**
Strattford Publishers
590 Dutch Valley Road NE
Atlanta, GA 30324-729

404-881-1141
800-926-7926; Fax: 404-881-0074
customerservice@straffordpub.com
www.straffordpub.com

Richard Ossoff, Publisher
Albert J Pucciarelli, VP

Monthly digest decisions on litigation involving private security operations; includes insights and trend analysis by nations leading security expert.
Cost: $347.00
Frequency: Monthly
Founded in 1984

15785 **Probate and Property**
American Bar Association
321 N Clark St
Chicago, IL 60654-7598

312-988-5000
800-285-2221; Fax: 312-988-6281
askaba@abanet.org
www.americanbar.org/aba.html
Facebook, Twitter

Tommy H Wells Jr, President
Laurel G. Bellows, President

Aimed at lawyers who devote a large part of their practice to real estate law and laws dealing with wills, trusts and estates.
Cost: $60.00
Founded in 1978

15786 **Public Contract Newsletter**
American Bar Association
321 N Clark St
Chicago, IL 60654-7598

312-988-5000
800-285-2221; Fax: 312-988-6281
askaba@abanet.org
www.americanbar.org/aba.html
Facebook, Twitter

Tommy H Wells Jr, President
Laurel G. Bellows, President

Contains informative articles on a wide range of timely topics including current developments in federal and grant law, recent developments in state and local public contract law, upcoming educational programs and legislative developments.
Cost: $60.00
Frequency: Quarterly

15787 **Purchasing Law Report**
Institute of Management and Administration
3 Bethesda Metro Center
Suite 250
Bethesda, MD 20814-5377

703-341-3500
800-372-1033; Fax: 800-253-0332
www.ioma.com

Purchasing Law Report is the most practical, least expensive and quickest way to understand and apply new purchasing laws and regulations in your day-to-day operations without wasting time sorting through hundreds of legal documents.

15788 **Report on Disability Programs**
Business Publishers
8737 Colesville Road
Suite 1100
Silver Spring, MD 20910-3928

301-876-6300
800-274-6737; Fax: 301-589-8493
custserv@bpinews.com
www.bpinews.com

Leonard A Eiserer, Publisher

Follows legislation, regulations, legal actions and funding in areas import to all persons with disabilities including health care, employment, civil rights, housing, and transportation.
Cost: $227.00
8 Pages
Frequency: Monthly
Founded in 1963
Printed in on matte stock

15789 **School Law Reporter**
Education Law Association
300 College Park Ave
Dayton, OH 45469-0001

937-229-3589; Fax: 937-229-3845
ela@educationlaw.org
www.educationlaw.org
Facebook, Twitter, LinkedIn

W Brad Colwell, President
Mandy Schrank, Executive Director
Cate K. Smith, Executive Director
Judy Pleiman, Member Services Coordinator
Jody Thornburg, Publications Manager

Member association for those with an iunterest in school law issues, such as attorneys, law professors, education professors, school administrators, and teachers.
Frequency: Monthly
ISSN: 1059-4094
Founded in 1954

15790 **Search and Seizure Law Report**
Clark Boardman Company
375 Hudson St
Room 201
New York, NY 10014-3658

585-546-5530
800-323-1336

Robert Bouchard, Publisher
Elizabeth Brooks, Editor

Provides detailed, current coverage of the law, procedure, trends, and developments evolving in search and seizure law.
Cost: $175.00
8 Pages
Frequency: Monthly
Circulation: 2,000
Printed in 2 colors on matte stock

15791 **Section of Taxation Newsletter**
American Bar Association
321 N Clark St
Chicago, IL 60654-7598

312-988-5000
800-285-2221; Fax: 312-988-6281
askaba@abanet.org
www.americanbar.org/aba.html
Facebook, Twitter

Tommy H Wells Jr, President
Laurel G. Bellows, President

Update on current tax developments, committee projects, meeting information and order forms.
Cost: $15.00
Frequency: Quarterly

15792 **Security Law**
Strafford Publications

PO Box 13729
Atlanta, GA 30324-0729

404-881-1141
800-926-7926; Fax: 404-881-0074
customerservice@straffordpub.com
www.straffordpub.com

Richard Ossoff, President

Monthly updates on security law without all the legal jargon.
Cost: $297.00
Frequency: Monthly
ISSN: 0889-0625
Founded in 1984
Mailing list available for rent: 31.6M names
Printed in one color

15793 Sexual Harassment Litigation Reporter
Andrews Publications
175 Strafford Avenue
Building 4 Suite 140
Wayne, PA 19087-3317

610-225-0510
800-345-1101; Fax: 610-225-0501

Robert Maroldo, Publisher
Linda Coady, Editor
Cost: $49.00
Frequency: Monthly

15794 Small Firm Profit Report: Attorney Edition
Professional Newsletters
Atlanta, GA 30366-1143

770-819-4151
Robert Palmer, Publisher

Practice management and marketing help for small law firms and solo practitioners.

15795 Software Law Bulletin
Andrews Publications
1735 Market Street
Suite 1600
Wayne, PA 19087

610-225-0510
800-345-1101; Fax: 610-225-0501

Donna Higgins, Editor

As pantenting becomes the predominant method of protecting software, and as cases involving technological copy protection measures wind through the court system, Andrews' Software Law Bulletin provides coverage of decisions and opinions in the key cases. Detailed articles put individual developments into the big picture of the changing law landscape.
Cost: $588.00
Frequency: Monthly
Founded in 1972

15796 Special Court News
American Bar Association
321 N Clark St
Chicago, IL 60654-7598

312-988-5000
800-285-2221; Fax: 312-988-6281
askaba@abanet.org
www.abanet.org

Tommy H Wells Jr, President

Newsletter apprises members of the current activities and plans of the Conference. Also provides active, continual contact with members and solicits more active participation.
Cost: $11.00
Frequency: Quarterly

15797 Special Education Law Monthly
LRP Publications
747 Dresher Road Suite 500
PO Box 980
Horsham, PA 19044-980

215-784-0912
800-341-7874; Fax: 215-784-9639
webmaster@lrp.com
www.lrp.com

Jessyca Harrington, Editor
Dionne Ellis, Managing Editor

Covers court decisions and administrative rulings affecting the education of students with disabilities. Each issue begins with a brief overview of the case summaries covered allowing you to quickly focus on the decisions and hearings that affect you most.
Cost: $140.00
Frequency: Monthly
Founded in 1977

15798 Sports & Entertainment Litigation Reporter
Andrews Publications
175 Strafford Avenue
Building 4 Suite 140
Wayne, PA 19087-3317

610-225-0510
800-345-1101; Fax: 610-225-0501

Robert Maroldo, Publisher
Robert Sullivan, Editor

Covers the latest news in the fast-changing world of entertainment litigation.
Cost: $775.00
Frequency: Monthly
Founded in 1960

15799 Sports Medicine Standards and Malpractice Reporter
PRC Publishing
3976 Fulton Dr Nw
Canton, OH 44718-3043

330-492-6063
800-336-0083; Fax: 330-492-6176

Molly Romig, VP

Designed to keep sports medicine professionals informed about current trends in their challenging professions. Accepts advertising.
Cost: $29.95
16 Pages
Frequency: Quarterly
Circulation: 500
ISSN: 0141-696X
Founded in 1984
Printed in 2 colors on matte stock

15800 Sports, Parks and Recreation Law Reporter
PRC Publishing
3976 Fulton Dr Nw
Canton, OH 44718-3043

330-492-6063
800-336-0083; Fax: 330-492-6176

Molly Romig, VP

For those professionals in the sports, parks and recreational law. Accepts advertising.
Cost: $39.95
16 Pages
Frequency: Quarterly
Circulation: 500
ISSN: 0893-8210
Founded in 1997
Printed in 2 colors on matte stock

15801 State Legislative Report
American Bar Association
1800 M Street NW
#450S
Washington, DC 20036-5802

202-662-1000; Fax: 202-331-2220

Patrick Sheehan, Publisher
Diane Gibson, Editor

A summary of key legislative developments of interest to attorneys.
Cost: $50.00
4 Pages
Circulation: 800

15802 State and Local Law News
American Bar Association
321 N Clark St
Chicago, IL 60654-7598

312-988-5000
800-285-2221; Fax: 312-988-6281
askaba@abanet.org
www.americanbar.org/aba.html
Facebook, Twitter

Tommy H Wells Jr, President
Laurel G. Bellows, President
Richard W. Bright, Staff Editor

Informs members regarding Section activities and important issues of law.
Cost: $40.00
Frequency: Quarterly
Circulation: 6000
Founded in 1878

15803 Summary and Reports
American Bar Association
321 N Clark St
Chicago, IL 60654-7598

312-988-5000
800-285-2221; Fax: 312-988-6281
askaba@abanet.org
www.americanbar.org/aba.html
Facebook, Twitter

Tommy H Wells Jr, President
Laurel G. Bellows, President

Contains recommendations and informational reports to the ABA House of Delegates.

15804 Summary of Labor Arbitration Awards
LRP Publications
PO Box 980
Horsham, PA 19044-0980

215-784-0912
800-341-7874; Fax: 215-784-9639
webmaster@lrp.com
www.lrp.com

Todd Lutz, CFO
Ken Kahn, CEO
Dana Eynon, Marketing Director
Claude Werder, VP
Marcy Witt, Marketing Director

Since 1959, the summary has been providing digests of private-sector labor arbitration decisions, covering the latest topics in collective bargaining with non-governmental employers.
Cost: $120.00
16 Pages
Frequency: Monthly
Founded in 1977
Printed in 2 colors on glossy stock

15805 Syllabus
American Bar Association
321 N Clark St
Chicago, IL 60654-7598

312-988-5000
800-285-2221; Fax: 312-988-6281
askaba@abanet.org
www.americanbar.org/aba.html
Facebook, Twitter

Tommy H Wells Jr, President
Laurel G. Bellows, President

Newspaper describing and commenting on developments in legal education.
Cost: $15.00
Frequency: Quarterly
Founded in 1978

15806 **Tax Laws of the World**
Foreign Tax Law
PO Box 2189
Ormond Beach, FL 32175-2189

386-253-5785; Fax: 386-257-3003
www.foreignlaw.com

Income, corporate and related tax laws for over 100 countries. Many full text translations.
Cost: $100.00

15807 **Testifying Expert**
LRP Publications
747 Dresher Road
PO Box 980
Horsham, PA 19044-2247

215-784-0912
800-341-7874; Fax: 215-784-9639
webmaster@lrp.com
www.lrp.com

Patrick Byrne, Editor
Gary Bagin, Circulation Manager

A newsletter designed to help experts develop a reputation or improve their present standing as an expert. Each monthly issue contains relevant decisions affecting the expert, book reviews and seminar listings.
Cost: $140.00
Frequency: Monthly
Founded in 1977

15808 **The ALI Reporter**
American Law Institute-American Bar Association
Continuing Professional Education
4025 Chestnut Street, Suite 5
Philadelphia, PA 19104

215-243-1600; Fax: 215-243-1664
ali@ali.org
www.ali-aba.org
Facebook, Twitter, LinkedIn

Julene Franki, Executive Director
Lawrence F. Meehan, Deputy Executive Director
Judith Cole, Executive Assistant
Bennett Boskey, Treasurer

This newsletter reports on the activities of the ALI and is primarily for its members.
Frequency: Quarterly
Founded in 1947

15809 **The Air and Space Lawyer**
American Bar Association Forum on Air & Space Law
321 N Clark St
Chicago, IL 60654-7598

312-988-5000
800-285-2221; Fax: 312-988-6281
askaba@abanet.org
www.americanbar.org/aba.html
Facebook, Twitter

Kenneth P. Quinn, Editor-in-Chief
John Palmer, Staff Editor
Laurel G. Bellows, President

Newsletter of significant developments in the field of air and space law as well as reports of Forum Committee activities.
Cost: $40.00
24 Pages
Frequency: Quarterly
Circulation: 2000
ISSN: 0747-7449
Printed in 4 colors

15810 **The Construction Lawyer**
American Bar Association
321 N Clark St
Chicago, IL 60654-7598

312-988-5000
800-285-2221; Fax: 312-988-5280
askaba@abanet.org
www.americanbar.org/aba.html
Facebook, Twitter

Thomas J. Campbell, Staff Editor
John W. Ralls, Editor-in-Chief
Laurel G. Bellows, President

Newsletter containing articles on recent developments in the construction industry as well as announcements pertaining to the Forum Committee or to other organizations in the field.
Cost: $50.00
48 Pages
Frequency: Quarterly

15811 **The Health Lawyer**
American Bar Association Section on Health Law
321 N Clark St
Chicago, IL 60654-7598

312-988-5000
800-285-2221; Fax: 312-988-5280
askabanet@abanet.org
www.americanbar.org/aba.html
Facebook, Twitter

Laurel G. Bellows, President

Provides informative articles that focus on a wide range of areas in the health law field and offers incisice analysis of key issues.
Cost: $60.00
Frequency: Bi-monthly

15812 **The National Notary**
Po Box 2402
Chatsworth, CA 91313-2402

818-739-4000
800-876-6827; Fax: 818-700-1942
hotline@nationalnotary.org
www.nationalnotary.org
Facebook, Twitter, LinkedIn

Milton G Valera, President
Deborah M Thaw, Executive VP
Marc Reiser, CEO
Jane Eagle, Executive VP & CFO
Ron Johnson, VP Systems & Operations

The National Notary addresses pertinent cutting-edge notarial issues in depth, and also features helpful how-to articles on every phase of operating as a professional Notary Public in the venue of American law and commerce.
200M Members
Frequency: Bi-Monthly
Circulation: 200,000
Founded in 1957

15813 **The Procurement Lawyer**
American Bar Association - Public Contract Law
321 N Clark St
Chicago, IL 60654-7598

312-988-5000
800-285-2221; Fax: 312-988-5280
pubcontract@abanet.org
www.americanbar.org/aba.html
Facebook, Twitter

John A. Burkholder, Editor-in-Chief
Laurel G. Bellows, President

Newsletter providing news on federal, state and local government procurement professionals.
Frequency: Quarterly

15814 **The SciTech Lawyer**
American Bar Association Science & Technology Law
321 N Clark St
Chicago, IL 60654-7598

312-988-5533
800-285-2221
sciencetech@abanet.org
www.americanbar.org/aba.html
Facebook, Twitter

Shawn T Kaminski, Section Director
Julie Fleming, Co-Editor-in-Chief
Eleanor Kellett, Co-Editor-in-Chief
Laurel G. Bellows, President

Quarterly practice specific magazine featuring cutting edge news.

15815 **Tobacco Products Litigation Reporter**
TPLR
PO Box 1162
Back Bay Annex
Boston, MA 02117-1162

617-373-2026; Fax: 617-373-3672
www.tplr.com

Lissy Friedman, Publisher
Richard Daynard, Editor

Tobacco industry news.
Cost: $995.00
Founded in 1975

15816 **Transnational Bulletin**
Lewis, D'Amato, Brisbois & Bisgaard
221 N Figueroa St
Suite 1200
Los Angeles, CA 90012-2663

213-250-1800; Fax: 213-250-7900

Legal information for the international business community written by lawyers of the firm.

15817 **Trial Judges News**
American Bar Association
321 N Clark St
Chicago, IL 60654-7598

312-988-5000
800-285-2221; Fax: 312-988-6281
askaba@abanet.org
www.americanbar.org/aba.html
Facebook, Twitter

Tommy H Wells Jr, President
Laurel G. Bellows, President

This newsletter informs membership of the National Conference of State Trial Judges of the activities and programs of that conference.
Frequency: Quarterly
Founded in 1978

15818 **Turning the Tide**
People Against Racist Terror
PO Box 1990
Burbank, CA 91507-1990

FAX 818-848-2680

Michael Novick, Publisher

Bimonthly newsletter of anti-racist activism, research and education covering neo-nazi and other racist violence, efforts at conflict resolution and social justic reforms.
Cost: $10.00
24 Pages
Frequency: BiWeekly
Circulation: 7,500
Printed in 2 colors on newsprint stock

15819 **Urban Lawyer**
American Bar Association
321 N Clark St
Chicago, IL 60654-7598

312-988-5000
800-285-2221; Fax: 312-988-6281
askaba@abanet.org

www.americanbar.org/aba.html
Facebook, Twitter

Tommy H Wells Jr, President
Laurel G. Bellows, President

Articles on various areas of urban, state and local government law.
Cost: $49.95
Frequency: Quarterly
Circulation: 6000
Founded in 1879

15820 **Utility Section Newsletter**
American Bar Association
321 N Clark St
Chicago, IL 60654-7598

312-988-5000
800-285-2221; Fax: 312-988-6281
www.americanbar.org/aba.html
Facebook, Twitter

Tommy H Wells Jr, President
Laurel G. Bellows, President

Articles pertaining to the field of public utility law.
Frequency: Quarterly
Founded in 1878

15821 **Washington Employment Law Letter**
M Lee Smith Publishers
PO Box 5094
Brentwood, TN 37219-2407

615-737-7517
800-274-6774; Fax: 615-256-6601
www.mleesmith.com

M Lee Smith, Publisher
Michael Reynvaan, Editor

Reviews of employment laws.
Cost: $157.55
8 Pages
Frequency: Monthly
Circulation: 54,000
Founded in 1975
Mailing list available for rent
Printed in 2 colors on matte stock

15822 **Washington Summary**
American Bar Association
740 15th St Nw
Suite 8
Washington, DC 20005-1022

202-662-1000; Fax: 202-662-1032
cmpdi@abanet.org
www.americanbar.org/aba.html
Facebook, Twitter

Stephanie A Marella, Editor
Laurel G. Bellows, President

Tracks legislation and federal regulations of interest to lawyers by abstracting the Congressional Record and Federal Register.
Cost: $55.00
Frequency: Daily
Founded in 1878

15823 **White-Collar Crime Reporter**
Andrews Publications
175 Strafford Avenue
Building 4, Suite 140
Wayne, PA 19087-3317

610-225-0510
800-345-1101; Fax: 610-225-0501

Robert Maroldo, Publisher
Edith McFail, Editor

Major articles guest written by practitioners in the area of white collar crame and covering such topics as sentencing guidelines, corporate liability, banking and securities fraud and government contract fraud.
Cost: $66.00
Frequency: Monthly
Founded in 1872

15824 **Word Progress**
American Bar Association
321 N Clark St
Chicago, IL 60654-7598

312-988-5000
800-285-2221; Fax: 312-988-6281
askaba@abanet.org
www.americanbar.org/aba.html
Facebook, Twitter

Tommy H Wells Jr, President
Laurel G. Bellows, President

Newsletter of the Word Processing User Group, includes updates on more effective word processing in the law office.
Cost: $50.00
Frequency: Quarterly

15825 **World Jurist**
World Jurist Assn of the World Peace Through Law
1000 Connecticut Avenue NW
Suite 202
Washington, DC 20036

202-466-5428; Fax: 202-452-8540
http://www.worldjurist.net

Sona Pancholy, Editor
M Henneberry, Executive VP

Research for international development as a basis for future world peace.
Cost: $80.00
Frequency: Fortnightly
Circulation: 6000
Founded in 1963
Printed in on glossy stock

15826 **Your School and the Law**
LRP Publications
747 Dresher Road Suite 500
PO Box 980
Horsham, PA 19044-2247

215-840-0912
800-341-7874; Fax: 215-784-9639
webmaster@lrp.com
www.lrp.com

Stephen Bekiiacqwa, Editor

A monthly newsletter providing practical information on current judicial decisions affecting schools.
Cost: $190.00
Founded in 1977
Mailing list available for rent
Printed in one color on matte stock

Magazines & Journals

15827 **AALL Spectrum**
American Association of Law Libraries
105 W Adams Street
Suite 3300
Chicago, IL 60603

312-939-4764; Fax: 312-431-1097
support@aall.org
www.aallnet.org
Facebook, Twitter

Mark Estes, Editorial Director
Hillary Baker, Marketing and Communications
Kate Hagan, Executive Director
Kim Rundle,, Executive Assistant
Emily Feltren, Director of Government Relations

Publishes substantive, well-written articles on topics of real interest to law librarians, as well as news about the American Association of Law Libraries, including its chapters, committees and Special Interest Sections
Cost: $ 75.00

15828 **ABA Journal**
American Bar Association
321 N Clark St
6th Floor
Chicago, IL 60654-7598

312-988-5000
800-285-2221; Fax: 312-988-6281
abajournal@abanet.org
www.abanet.org

Tommy H Wells Jr, President
Robert Brouwer, Associate Publisher
Elizabeth Sullivan, Marketing Manager

Its editorial materials include news of interest to members of the legal profession. Editorial highlights include reviews of general interest and legal books, a US Supreme Court Digest section, a section listing significant rulings of other courts and news from government agencies.
Cost: $75.00
Frequency: Monthly
Circulation: 389420
Founded in 1878

15829 **AIRA Journal**
Association of Insolvency & Restructuring Advisors
221 W. Stewart Avenue
Suite 207
Medford, OR 97501

541-858-1665; Fax: 541-858-9187
aira@aira.org
www.aira.org

Jim Lukenda, Executive Director
Valda Newton, Managing Editor

A quarterly publication of the Association of Insolvency & Restructuring Advisors that publishes professional papers, articles and commentary by members as well as other professionals in the turnaround, bankruptcy, restructuring and related fields, such as banking, tax, law and government.
Frequency: Quarterly
Founded in 1982

15830 **APA Magazine**
American Polygraph Association
PO Box 8037
Chattanooga, TN 37414-0037

423-892-3992
800-272-8037; Fax: 423-894-5435
manager@apapolygraph.org
www.polygraph.org

Lisa Jacocks, Contact
Cost: $125.00
Frequency: Bi-Monthly
Founded in 1966

15831 **Administrative Law Review**
American University Washington College of Law
4801 Massachusetts Ave Nw
Suite 622
Washington, DC 20016-8180

202-274-4433; Fax: 202-274-4130
alr-editor-in-chief@wcl.american.edu
www.wcl.american.edu/journal/alr/
Facebook, LinkedIn

Stacey L.Z. Edwards, Editor-In-Chief
Keeley McCarty, Executive Editor
Brittany Ericksen, Managing Editor
Sharon Wolfe, Journal Coordinator

Scholarly legal journal on developments in the field of administrative law and regulatory practice.
Cost: $40.00
Frequency: Quarterly
Founded in 1949

15832 Advance Sheet
150 Lincoln Street
Boston, MA 02111
617-695-3660; Fax: 617-695-3656

15833 AmLaw Tech
American Lawyer Media
345 Park Avenue S
New York, NY 10010
212-799-9434
800-888-8300; Fax: 212-972-6258
www.americanlawyermedia.com
William L Pollak, President
Aric Press, Editorial Director
Kevin Vermeulen, Senior Vice President of Legal
Frequency: Annual+
Circulation: 16,500
Founded in 1997

15834 American Bankruptcy Law Journal
American Bankruptcy Institute
66 Canal Center Plaza
Suite 600
Alexandria, VA 22314-1546
703-739-0800; Fax: 703-739-1060
info@abiworld.org
www.abiworld.org
Sameul Gerdano, Executive Director
Amy Quackenboss, Deputy Executive Dir./Gen. Counsel
Benefit to ABI members. Written by experts in the insolvency community, the Journal addresses timely issues involving consumer bankruptcy, the intersection of state laws and the Bankrupcy Code, valuation, turnaround management concerns, recent legislative developments, the US trustee system and more. Available in print or online.
Frequency: Monthly
Founded in 1982

15835 American Lawyer
American Lawyer Corporation
Lbby L5
120 Broadway
New York, NY 10271-0096
917-562-2000
800-603-6571; Fax: 212-696-1845
www.americanlawyermedia.com
Barbara Eskin, Circulation Director
Issues affecting lawyers and the legal profession, with an emphasis on the business aspect of law firms.
Cost: $349.00
102 Pages
Frequency: Monthly

15836 American Lawyers Quarterly
American Lawyers Company
853 Westpoint Pkwy
Suite 710
Cleveland, OH 44145-1546
440-871-8700
800-843-4000; Fax: 440-871-9997
alq@alqlist.com
www.alqlist.com
Thomas W Hamilton, Executive VP
Frequency: Quarterly
Founded in 1899

15837 American University Business Law Review
American University Washington College of Law
4801 Massachusetts Ave Nw
Suite 615-A
Washington, DC 20016-8180
202-274-4433; Fax: 202-274-4130
www.wcl.american.edu/blr/
Averell Sutton, Editor-In-Chief
Cameron Chong, Executive Editor
Sara Hill, Managing Editor
Sharon Wolfe, Journal Coordinator
Scholarly legal journal publishing articles providing cutting-edge legal analysis for the business law community, scholarly articles, case law analysis, and coverage of developing trends in a variety of areas to include financial regulation, international trade, antitrust, communications, healthcare and energy.
Cost: $40.00
Frequency: Quarterly
Founded in 2011

15838 American University International Law Review
American University Washington College of Law
4801 Massachusetts Ave Nw
Suite 610
Washington, DC 20016-8180
202-274-4433; Fax: 202-274-4130
www.auilr.org
LinkedIn
Lauren R Dudley, Editor-In-Chief
Daniel F Martini, Executive Editor
Michelle Mora Rueda, Managing Editor
Sharon Wolfe, Journal Coordinator
Scholarly legal journal publishing articles, critical essays, comments, and casenotes on a wide variety of international law topics, including public and private international law, the law of international organizations, international trade law, international arbitration, and international human rights. AUILR also publishes pieces on topics of foreign and comparative law that are of particular interest to the international legal community.
Cost: $40.00
Frequency: Quarterly
Founded in 1986

15839 American University Journal of Gender, Social Policy & the Law
American University Washington College of Law
4801 Massachusetts Ave Nw
Suite 632
Washington, DC 20016-8180
202-274-4433; Fax: 202-274-4130
www.wcl.american.edu/journal/genderlaw/
Facebook
Rafael Roberti, Editor-In-Chief
J. Peter Bodri, Executive Editor
Claire Griggs, Managing Editor
Sharon Wolfe, Journal Coordinator
Scholarly legal journal that publishes articles addressing social and political equality under the law.
Cost: $40.00
Frequency: Quarterly
Founded in 1992

15840 American University Law Review
American University Washington College of Law
4801 Massachusetts Ave Nw
Suite 616
Washington, DC 20016-8180
202-274-4433; Fax: 202-274-4130
alr-editor-in-chief@wcl.american.edu
www.wcl.american.edu/journal/alr/
Facebook, Twitter, LinkedIn
Brian R Westley, Editor-In-Chief
Mary M Gardner, Executive Editor
Christopher J Walsh, Managing Editor
Sharon Wolfe, Journal Coordinator
Scholarly legal journal, which publishes articles from professors, judges, practicing lawyers, and renowned legal thinkers. It is the only journal in the nation to publish an annual issue dedicated to decisions of the Court of Appeals for the Federal Circuit regarding patent law, international trade, government contracts, and trademark law.
Cost: $40.00
Frequency: Quarterly
Founded in 1952

15841 Animal Law Report
American Bar Association
321 N Clark St
Chicago, IL 60654-7598
312-988-5000
800-285-2221; Fax: 312-988-6281
askaba@abanet.org
www.americanbar.org/aba.html
Facebook, Twitter
Tommy H Wells Jr, President
Laurel G. Bellows, President
Summarizes recent legislation, case decisions and literature.
Cost: $10.00
Frequency: SemiAnnual

15842 AntiShyster
AntiShyster
PO Box 540786
Dallas, TX 75354-786
FAX 972-386-8604
Alfred Adask, Editor
Critical examination of the American legal system.
Circulation: 10000

15843 Antitrust Law Journal
American Bar Association
321 N Clark St
Chicago, IL 60654-7598
312-988-5000
800-285-2221; Fax: 312-988-6281
askaba@abanet.org
www.americanbar.org/aba.html
Facebook, Twitter
Tommy H Wells Jr, President
Laurel G. Bellows, President
MaryAnn Dadisman, Staff Editor
Covers proceedings of Section meetings, Section reports and positions on legislation, as well as content of National Institutes on antitrust law.
Cost: $120.00
Circulation: 10,000
Founded in 1878

15844 Arbitration Journal
American Arbitration Association
1633 Broadway
Suite 2c1
New York, NY 10019-6707
212-716-5800
800-778-7879; Fax: 212-716-5905
www.adr.org
William K Slate II, CEO
Christine Newhall, Senior Vice President
Harry Kaminsky, Vice President
Cost: $30.00
Frequency: Quarterly
Founded in 1926

15845 Association of Legal Administrators
Association of Legal Administrators

75 Tri-State International
Suite 222
Lincolnshire, IL 60069-4435

847-267-1252; Fax: 847-267-1329
publications@alanet.org
www.alanet.org

Larry Smith, Executive Director
Debbie Thomas, Director, Accounting & Finance
Renee Mahovsky, Director, Administration/Operations
Bob Abramson, Director, Marketing & Communication
Jan Waugh, Director, Member Services

Professional support for management of private law firms and other legal organizations worldwide.
Cost: $10.00
9500 Members
Founded in 1971
Printed in 4 colors on glossy stock

15846 **BNA's Patent, Trademark and Copyright Journal**
Bureau of National Affairs
1801 S Bell St
Arlington, VA 22202-4501

703-341-3000
800-372-1033; Fax: 800-253-0332
www.bnabooks.com
Facebook, Twitter, LinkedIn

Paul N Wojcik, CEO

Provides an in-depth review of significant current developments in the intellectual property field. Covers congressional activity, court decisions, relevant conferences, professional associations, international developments, plus actions of the Patent and Trademark Office and the Copyright Office.
Cost: $1968.00
Frequency: Weekly

15847 **Barrister**
American Bar Association
321 N Clark St
Chicago, IL 60654-7598

312-988-5000
800-285-2221; Fax: 312-988-6281
www.americanbar.org/aba.html
Facebook, Twitter

Tommy H Wells Jr, President
Laurel G. Bellows, President

Magazine containing general articles about the profession, the law and society in general.
Cost: $19.95
Frequency: 5 per year

15848 **Broadcasting and the Law**
One SE 3rd Avenue
#1450
Miami, FL 33131-1714

305-530-1322; Fax: 305-539-0013
broadlaw@aol.com

Matthew L Leibowitz

Addresses legal issues within the broadcasting industry.
Frequency: Monthly
Circulation: 400

15849 **Business Law Today**
American Bar Association Section on Business Law
321 N Clark St
Chicago, IL 60654

312-988-5000
800-285-2221; Fax: 312-988-5280
askaba@abanet.org
www.americanbar.org/aba.html
Facebook, Twitter

John Palmer, Staff Editor
Arthur F. Ferguson, Editor
Laurel G. Bellows, President

The Business Law Section's magazine edited for busy professionals: no footnotes and lots of the latest in business law.
64 Pages
Frequency: Bimonthly
Circulation: 55000
ISSN: 1059-9436
Printed in 4 colors

15850 **Business Lawyer**
American Bar Association
321 N Clark St
Chicago, IL 60654-7598

312-988-5000
800-285-2221; Fax: 312-988-6281
askaba@abanet.org
www.americanbar.org/aba.html

Tommy H Wells Jr, President

Journal of business and financial law, with articles on current legal topics and substantive section programs.
Cost: $20.00
Frequency: Quarterly
Circulation: 60000
Founded in 1915

15851 **Business Lawyer's Computer News**
American Bar Association
321 N Clark St
Chicago, IL 60654-7598

312-988-5000
800-285-2221; Fax: 312-988-6281
askaba@abanet.org
www.americanbar.org/aba.html
Tommy H Wells Jr, President
Information on new developments in technology for the business lawyer and news on how business lawyers are applying technology in their practices.
Cost: $50.00
Frequency: Quarterly

15852 **CLEAR Exam Review**
Council on Licensure, Enforcement & Regulation
108 Wind Haven Drive
Suite A
Nicholasville, KY 40356

859-269-1289; Fax: 859-231-1943
rbrown@clearhq.org
www.clearhq.org

Adam Parfitt, Executive Director

A bi-annual journal with useful discussions of current licensing examination issues and is geared toward a general audience. Free for CLEAR members.
Cost: $30.00
Frequency: Bi-Annual
Founded in 1994

15853 **Champion Magazine**
National Association of Criminal Defense Lawyers
1660 L Street NW
12th Floor
Washington, DC 20036

202-872-8600; Fax: 202-872-4000
memberservices@nacdl.org
www.nacdl.org

Quintin Chatman, Senior Editor
Offers timely, informative articles written for and by criminal defense lawyers, featuring the latest developments in search and seizure laws, DUI/DWI, grandy jury proceedings, habeas, the exclusionary rule, death penalty, RICO, federal sentencing guidelines, forfeiture, white-collar crime, and more.
Cost: $70.00
Frequency: 10x/Year
Circulation: 13000

15854 **Chinese Law and Government**
ME Sharpe
80 Business Park Dr
Suite 202
Armonk, NY 10504-1715

914-273-1800
800-541-6563; Fax: 914-273-2106
www.mesharpe.com

Myron E Sharpe, President
James Tong, Executive Editor
George Lobell, Executive Editor

Translations of significant works and policy documents, primarily from the Peoples Republic of China.
Cost: $144.00
Frequency: 1 Year 6 Issues

15855 **Clearinghouse Reference Guide**
American Bar Association
1800 M Street NW
Washington, DC 20036-5802

202-662-1000; Fax: 202-331-2220

Patrick Sheehan, Editor
Diane Gibson, Publications Coordinator

A summary of key state legislative developments of interest to attorneys.
Frequency: Annual
Circulation: 800

15856 **Columbia Law School Magazine**
Columbia Law School
435 West 116 Street
Box A-2
New York, NY 10027

212-854-2640; Fax: 212-854-7801
webmaster@law.columbia.edu
http://web.law.columbia.edu
Facebook, Twitter, LinkedIn

Matthew Malady, Editor
Joy Wang, Managing Editor

Features contributions that promotes ongoing discussion of social change and related issues.
Frequency: Biennial
Founded in 1754

15857 **Commercial Law Journal**
Commercial Law League of America
3005 Tollview Drive
Rolling Meadows, IL 60008

312-240-1400; Fax: 312-240-1408
info@clla.org
www.clla.org

Phil Lattanzio, Executive Vice President
Dawn Federico, Associate Director

Law review journal covering such issues as credit, debt, insolvency, banking and the Uniform Commercial Code.
Frequency: Quarterly
Circulation: 6000
Founded in 1895

15858 **Commercial Law World Magazine**
Commercial Law League of America
3005 Tollview Drive
Rolling Meadows, IL 60008

312-240-1400; Fax: 312-240-1408
info@clla.org
www.clla.org

Phil Lattanzio, Executive Vice President
Dawn Federico, Associate Director
Wanda Borges, Editor-in-Chief

Reports, discusses the changing and developing commercial collections sector utilizing an editorial board of leading industry insights.
Founded in 1895

15859 **Communications and the Law**
Fred B Rotham Company
10368 W Cenntenial Road
Littleton, CO 80127-4205
800-828-7971; Fax: 716-883-8100
Theodore Kupfeman, Publisher
Features articles and book reviews on communications law, new technologies and law.
Cost: $25.00
Circulation: 585

15860 **Complete Lawyer**
American Bar Association
321 N Clark St
Chicago, IL 60654-7598
312-988-5000
800-285-2221; Fax: 312-988-6281
askaba@abanet.org
www.americanbar.org/aba.html
Tommy H Wells Jr, President
Magazine provides practical articles directed to general practitioners, on substantive areas of law, news of council and committee activities.
Cost: $23.00
Frequency: Quarterly
Circulation: 16743

15861 **Computer Industry Litigation Reporter**
Andrews Publications
175 Strafford Avenue
Building 4, Suite 140
Wayne, PA 19087-3331
610-225-0510
800-345-1101; Fax: 610-225-0501
Robert Maroldo, Publisher
Legal issues as they relate to hardware, software electronic databaes and the computer industry in general.
Cost: $875.00

15862 **Computer Law Strategist**
Leader Publications
345 Park Avenue S
New York, NY 10010-1707
212-799-9200; Fax: 212-696-1848
Stuart Wise, Publisher
For lawyers operating in the area of computer law and intellectual property.
Frequency: Monthly

15863 **Corporate Control Alert**
The Deal, LLC.
14 Wall Street
New York, NY 10005
212-313-9200
888-667-3325; Fax: 212-481-8128
customerservice@thedeal.com
www.thedeal.com
Twitter
Mickey Hernandez, Advertising Sales
Elena Freed, Marketing
Frequency: Monthly
Founded in 1999

15864 **Corporate Counsel**
American Lawyer Media
345 Park Avenue S
New York, NY 10010
212-779-9434
800-234-4256; Fax: 212-696-1845
www.americanlawyermedia.com

15865 **Court Review**
American Judges Association
300 Newport Ave
Williamsburg, VA 23185-4147
757-259-1841; Fax: 757-259-1520
aja@ncsc.dni.us
aja.ncsc.dni.us
James McKay, President
Highlights court decicions and precedents through articles written by US jurists and legal scholars.
Cost: $35.00
Frequency: Quarterly
Circulation: 2000
ISSN: 0011-0647
Founded in 1959

15866 **Criminal Justice**
American Bar Association
321 N Clark St
Chicago, IL 60654-7598
312-988-5000
800-285-2221; Fax: 312-988-6281
askaba@abanet.org
www.americanbar.org/aba.html
Tommy H Wells Jr, President
Magazine providing practical treatment of aspects of the criminal law and reporting on legislative, policy-making and educational activities of the ABA Criminal Justice Section.
Cost: $38.00
Frequency: Quarterly
Circulation: 9000
Founded in 1915

15867 **Cyber Esq.**
Daily Journal Corporation
PO Box 54026
Los Angeles, CA 90054-0026
213-229-5300; Fax: 213-229-5481
www.dailyjournal.com
Gerald L Salzman, CEO
Cyber Esq. is a guide for lawyers who use technology and whose practices are affected by the impact on the latest hardware and software and analysis of cutting-edge legal issues.
52 Pages
Frequency: Quarterly
Printed in 4 colors on n stock

15868 **Daily Journal**
Daily Journal Corporation
PO Box 54026
Los Angeles, CA 90054-0026
213-229-5300; Fax: 213-229-5481
www.dailyjournal.com
Gerald L Salzman, CEO
Ray Chagolla, Circulation Manager
The Daily Journal Corporation provides lawyers with concise, comprehensive and intelligent coverage of legal news throughout the city, state, and nation. Through our family of publications we are able to serve the nation's largest legal markets.
Cost: $628.00
28 Pages
Frequency: Daily
Circulation: 11000
ISSN: 1059-2636
Founded in 1888
Printed in on n stock

15869 **Decisions & Developments**
PO Box 98
Bolton, MA 01740-0098
781-890-5678; Fax: 781-890-1150

15870 **Dispute Resolution**
American Bar Association Sec. Dispute Resolution
321 N Clark St
Chicago, IL 60654-7598
312-988-5000
800-285-2221; Fax: 312-988-5280
askaba@abanet.org
www.americanbar.org/aba.html
Thomas J. Campbell, Staff Editor
Chip Stewart, Editor
A clearinghouse of information on programs related to the study of existing methods for prompt and effective resolution of disputes.
Cost: $45.00
32 Pages
Frequency: Quarterly
Founded in 1978

15871 **Dispute Resolution Journal**
206 Hulston Hall
University of Missouri
Columbia, MO 65211
573-823-3645; Fax: 212-716-5906
umclawcdr@missouri.edu
www.law.missouri.edu
Jonathan R Bunch, Editor-in-Chief
Cassandra A Rogers, Managing Editor
Leonard Riskin, Manager
Cost: $21.00
Founded in 1984

15872 **Docket**
150 Lincoln Street
Boston, MA 02111
617-695-3660; Fax: 617-695-3656

15873 **Duke Law Journal**
Duke University School of Law
210 Science Drive
Box 90362
Durham, NC 27708
919-613-7006; Fax: 919-681-8460
dlj@law.duke.edu
www.law.duke.edu
Facebook, Twitter, LinkedIn, Youtube
Sarah Boyce, Editor-in-Chief
Julia Wood, Managing Editor
Jennifer Brady, Executive Editor
Philip Alito, Research Editor
The journal's purpose is to publish legal writing of superior quality, to publish a collection of outstanding scholarship from established legal writers, up and coming authors, and student editors.
Frequency: 8x/year
Founded in 1951

15874 **EEOC Compliance Manual**
Bureau of National Affairs
1801 S Bell St
Arlington, VA 22202-4501
703-341-3000
800-372-1033; Fax: 800-253-0332
customercare@bna.com
www.bnabooks.com
Facebook, Twitter, LinkedIn
Paul N Wojcik, CEO
A two-binder monthly service containing the complete text of the EEOC Compliance Manual, as issued by the EEOC, with monthly notification to related developments.
Cost: $410.00

15875 **Education Law Association**
Education Law Association

300 College Park Ave
Dayton, OH 45469-0001

937-229-3589; Fax: 216-687-5284
ela@educationlaw.org
www.educationlaw.org
Facebook, Twitter, LinkedIn

Mandy Schrenk, Executive Director
Cate K. Smith, Executive Director
Judy Pleiman, Member Services Coordinator
Jody Thornburg, Publications Manager

Brings together educational and legal scholars and practitioners to inform and advance educational policy and practice through knowledge of the law. Together, our professional community anticipates trends in educational law and supports scholarly research through the highest value print and electronic publications, conferences, seminars and professional forums.
Cost: $125.00
1400 Pages
Frequency: Monthly
Circulation: 1200
Founded in 1954

15876 **Energy Law Journal**
Federal Energy Bar Association
1990 M St Nw
Suite 350
Washington, DC 20036-3429

202-223-5625; Fax: 202-833-5596
admin@eba-net.org
www.eba-net.org

Lorna Wilson, Administrator
Clinton A. Vince, Secretary, Treasurer
Michelle Grant, Secretary, Treasurer
Peter Trombley, Vice President

Lawyers and consultants engaged in energy and public utility law.
Cost: $35.00
Frequency: Monthly
Circulation: 2600
ISSN: 0270-9163
Founded in 1946
Printed in 2 colors on matte stock

15877 **Environmental Forum**
Environmental Law Institute
2000 L St Nw
Suite 620
Washington, DC 20036-4919

202-939-3800
800-433-5120; Fax: 202-939-3868
law@eli.org
www.eli.org

John Cruden, President
Stephen R. Dujack, Editor
Linda Ellis, Manager Customer Service
Carolyn Fischer, Editorial Associate

Uses diverse points of view to stimulate the exchange of ideas and foster solutions for pressing environmental issues.
Cost: $115.00
60 Pages
Circulation: 2100
Founded in 1985
Printed in 4 colors on matte stock

15878 **Environmental Law Journal**
State Bar of Texas
1515 S Capitol of Texas Highway
Suite 415
Austin, TX 78746-6544

512-322-5800; Fax: 512-478-7750

Jimmy Alan Hall, Editor-in-Chief
Charles Jordan, Chairman

Provides members with current legal activities, recent developments and information pertaining to environmental and natural resource law, as well as section activities and other events pertaining to this area of the law.
Cost: $ 10.00
68 Pages
Frequency: Monthly
Founded in 1969

15879 **Experience**
American Bar Association
321 N Clark St
Chicago, IL 60654-7598

312-988-5000
800-285-2221; Fax: 312-988-6281
askaba@abanet.org
www.americanbar.org/aba.html

Tommy H Wells Jr, President

News magazine for one of the fastest-growing sections in the ABA. Articles cover elderlaw, Council relationships, aspects of retirement including housing and health, and other topics of interest to lawyers pre- and post retirement.
Cost: $45.00
Frequency: Quarterly
Founded in 1878

15880 **Expert and the Law**
National Forensic Center
17 Temple Terrace
Lawrenceville, NJ 08648-3254

800-562-5177
info@nfstc.org
www.nfstc.org/

Betty Lipscher, Publisher
David Epstein, Chief Operations Officer
Mike Berry, Program Manager

Appilcation of scientific, medical and technical knowledge to litigation.

15881 **Fair Employment Practices/Labor Relations Reporter**
Bureau of National Affairs
1801 S Bell St
Arlington, VA 22202-4501

703-341-3000
800-372-1033; Fax: 800-253-0332
customercare@bna.com
www.bnabooks.com
Facebook, Twitter, LinkedIn

Paul N Wojcik, CEO

A guide to the regulation of fair employment practices, including federal laws, orders and regulations; policy guides and ground rules; and state and local fair employment practice laws.
Cost: $1576.00
Frequency: Weekly
Founded in 1929

15882 **Family Advocate**
American Bar Association
321 N Clark St
Chicago, IL 60654-7598

312-988-5000
800-285-2221; Fax: 312-988-6281
www.americanbar.org/aba.html
Facebook, Twitter

Tommy H Wells Jr, President
Laurel G. Bellows, President
Amelia Stone, Marketer
Adrienne Cook, Development Editor

A practical journal in magazine format, containing information on divorce, mental health, juveniles, custody, support and problems of the aging as well as current trends, recent court decisions and new legislation.
Cost: $39.50
Frequency: Quarterly
Circulation: 11000
Founded in 1984

15883 **Family Law Quarterly**
American Bar Association
321 N Clark St
Chicago, IL 60654-7598
312-988-5000
800-285-2221; Fax: 312-988-6281
askaba@abanet.org
www.americanbar.org/aba.html
Facebook, Twitter

Tommy H Wells Jr, President
Laurel G. Bellows, President

A scholarly journal, including regular coverage of judicial decisions, legislation, taxation, summaries of state and local bar association projects and book reviews.
Cost: $79.95
Frequency: Quarterly
Circulation: 11000
Founded in 1998

15884 **Federal Communications Law Journal**
University of California-Los Angeles
Box 951476
Los Angeles, CA 90095-1476

310-825-7768; Fax: 310-206-6489
webmaster@law.ucla.edu
www.law.ucla.edu

John Alden, Editor in Chief
David Matheson, Advertising Director

Articles on legal issues relating to the communications industry.
Cost: $10.00
Circulation: 2500

15885 **Federal Lawyer**
Federal Bar Association
1220 North Fillmore St.
Ste. 444
Arlington, VA 22201

571-481-9100; Fax: 571-481-9090
fba@fedbar.org
www.fedbar.org
Facebook, Twitter, LinkedIn

Jack D. Lockridge, Executive Director
Lori Beth Gorman, Executive Assistant
Lisa Sidletsky, Director Membership
Robert J. DeSousa, President
Hon. Gustavo Gelpi, Jr., President-Elect

Chronicles the news of the association and its members as well as providing practical coverage of issues affecting federal attorneys.
Cost: $35.00
Circulation: 15200
Founded in 1931

15886 **Fidelity and Surety News**
American Bar Association
321 N Clark St
Chicago, IL 60654-7598

312-988-5000
800-285-2221; Fax: 312-988-6281
askaba@abanet.org
www.americanbar.org/aba.html
Facebook, Twitter

Tommy H Wells Jr, President
Laurel G. Bellows, President

Summarizes selected recent cases on fidelity and surety law for professionals and lawyers.
Cost: $165.00
Frequency: Quarterly
Circulation: 1000
Founded in 1878

15887 **Firestation Lawyer**
Quinlan Publishing Company

23 Drydock Avenue
Boston, MA 02215-2336

617-542-0048; Fax: 617-345-9646
www.quinlan.com

E Michael Quinlan, Publisher
Hoss Homaier, President, Chief Executive Officer

Case summaries of recent lawsuits involving fire departments. Discusses residency requirements of firefighters, worker's compensation, pensions, discrimination, and fire department rules and regulations.
Frequency: Monthly
Founded in 1950

15888 Franchise Law Journal
American Bar Association
321 N Clark St
Chicago, IL 60654-7598

312-988-5000
800-285-2221; Fax: 312-988-6281
www.americanbar.org/aba.html
Facebook, Twitter

Tommy H Wells Jr, President
Laurel G. Bellows, President
Robert A Stein, Executive Director

Journal in newsletter format primarily on current legal trends in franchising; also reports on activities of the Forum.
Cost: $50.00
Frequency: Quarterly

15889 Health Law Litigation Reporter
Andrews Publications
175 Strafford Avenue
Building 4, Suite 140
Wayne, PA 19087-3331

610-225-0510
800-345-1101; Fax: 610-225-0501
www.andrewspub.com/

John E Backe, Publisher

Focus on cases involving ERSA, experimental insurance coverage, patient dumping, Medicare and Medicaid, medical devices, and federal and state legislation.
Frequency: Monthly
Circulation: 4100

15890 Hospital Law Manual
Publishers
200 Orchard Ridge Drive
Gaithersburg, MD 20878-1978

301-417-7500
800-234-1660; Fax: 301-698-7931
customer.service@aspenpubl.com
www.aspenlawschool.com

Patricia Younger, Director

Hospital law.
Cost: $1325.00
Frequency: Quarterly
Founded in 1959

15891 Human Rights
American Bar Association
321 N Clark St
Chicago, IL 60654-7598

312-988-5000
800-285-2221; Fax: 312-988-6281
askaba@abanet.org
www.americanbar.org/aba.html
Facebook, Twitter

Tommy H Wells Jr, President
Laurel G. Bellows, President

Magazine containing news articles, features and commentary with relevance to human rights and individual rights and responsibilities.
Cost: $17.00
Frequency: Quarterly
Circulation: 6000
Founded in 1878

15892 IP Worldwide
American Lawyer Media
345 Park Avenue S
New York, NY 10010

212-779-9434; Fax: 212-592-4900
www.americanlawyermedia.com

Steve Pressman, Editor
William L Pollak, CEO/President
Kevin Vermeulen, Publisher
Frequency: Quarterly
Circulation: 8000
Founded in 1997

15893 Institute of Management & Administration Newsletter
Institute of Management and Administration
3 Bethesda Metro Center
Suite 250
Bethesda, MD 20814-5377

703-341-3500
800-372-1033; Fax: 800-253-0332
www.ioma.com

Monthly newsletter that supports law office administrators by offering training on how to reduce overhead, improve the firm's profitability and efficiency, get more value for the firm's budget dollar, and improve their own professional standing.
Frequency: Monthly

15894 International Commercial Litigation
Euromoney Publications
173 W 81st Street
New York, NY 10024-7227

212-874-4265; Fax: 212-501-8926

International litigation and dispute resolution news and developments in commercial law.

15895 International Lawyer
American Bar Association
321 N Clark St
Chicago, IL 60654-7598

312-988-5000
800-285-2221; Fax: 312-988-6281
askaba@abanet.org
www.americanbar.org/aba.html
Facebook, Twitter

Tommy H Wells Jr, President
Laurel G. Bellows, President

Practical issues facing lawyers engaged in an international practice.
Cost: $7.00
Circulation: 11000

15896 Journal of Court Reporting
National Court Reporters
8224 Old Courthouse Rd
Vienna, VA 22182-3808

703-556-6272
800-272-6272; Fax: 703-556-6291
www.ncraonline.org
Facebook, Twitter

Melanie Humphrey-Sonntag, President
Mark Golden, Executive Director & CEO
Tami Smith, VP
Bruce Matthews, Secretary/Treasurer

Covers information and views on matters related to the court recording and captioning professions.
20000 Members
Circulation: 34000
Founded in 1905

15897 Journal of Internet Law
Apen Publishers
111 Eighth Avenue
7th Floor
New York, NY 10011

212-771-0600
800-638-8437; Fax: 212-771-0885
www.aspenlawschool.com

Mark F Radcliffe, Editor-in-Chief
Stacey Caywood, VP/Publisher
Mark Radcliffe, Editor
Gerry Centrowitz, VP Marketing And Communication
Robert Becker, CEO

Discusses strategies utilized by top intellectual property, computer law and information technology industry experts.
Cost: $380.00
Frequency: Monthly

15898 Journal of Legal Medicine
American College of Legal Medicine
9700 West Brun Mawr Avenue
Suite 210
Rosemont, IL 60018

847-447-1713; Fax: 847-447-1150
info@aclm.org
www.aclm.org
Facebook, Twitter

Laurie Krueger, Executive Director
Frequency: Quarterly
Founded in 1960

15899 Judges' Journal
American Bar Association
321 N Clark St
Chicago, IL 60654-7598

312-988-5000
800-285-2221; Fax: 312-988-6281
askaba@abanet.org
www.americanbar.org/aba.html
Facebook, Twitter

Tommy H Wells Jr, President
Laurel G. Bellows, President

Created to help judges and lawyers improve the administration of justice.
Cost: $23.00
Frequency: Quarterly
Founded in 1878

15900 Judicature
American Judicature Society
The Opperman Center at Drake University
2700 University Avenue
Des Moines, LA 50311

515-271-2281
800-626-4089; Fax: 515-279-3090
www.ajs.org

Seth S. Andersen, Executive Director
Krista Maeder, Assistant to the Executive Director
Laury Lieurance, Accountant/Membership Coordinator
Danielle Mitchell, Program Manager
David Richert, Editor

A forum for fact and opinion relating to all aspects of the administration of justice and its improvement.
Cost: $60.00
Frequency: Bi-Monthly
ISSN: 0022-5800

15901 Jurimetrics: Journal of Law, Science and Technology
American Bar Association
321 N Clark St
Chicago, IL 60654-7598

312-988-5000
800-285-2221; Fax: 312-988-6281
askaba@abanet.org

www.americanbar.org/aba.html
Facebook, Twitter

Tommy H Wells Jr, President
Laurel G. Bellows, President

Covers a wide range of topics on legal issues in science and technology.
Cost: $29.00
Frequency: Quarterly

15902 **Juvenile and Child Welfare Law Reporter**
American Bar Association
321 N Clark St
Chicago, IL 60654-7598

312-988-5000
800-285-2221; Fax: 312-988-6281
askaba@abanet.org
www.americanbar.org/aba.html
Facebook, Twitter

Tommy H Wells Jr, President
Laurel G. Bellows, President

Contains abstracts of case law on juvenile delinquency, abuse and neglect, adoption, termination of parental rights and other topics on child welfare.
Cost: $145.00
Frequency: Monthly

15903 **Law**
National Association of Legal Professionals
314 E 3rd Street
Suite 210
Tulsa, OK 74120-2409

918-582-5188; Fax: 918-582-5907
www.nals.org

Jay Moore, Editor
Tammy Hailey, Publisher
Jay Moore, Communications Manager
Tammy Hailey, Executive Director
Cindy Rosser, Executive Assistant

Published content focuses on new products, technology and items of interest to the administrative staff within the legal profession.
Cost: $40.00
Frequency: Quarterly
Circulation: 7000
Founded in 1929

15904 **Law Office Computing Magazine Services Section**
James Publishing
PO Box 25202
Santa Ana, CA 92799-5202

714-755-5450
800-440-4780; Fax: 714-751-2709
customer-service@jamespublishing.com
www.jamespublishing.com

Jim Pawell, Founder/President
Tina Dhamija, Assistant Editor
Adrianne Choi, Production Manager

Focuses on law office automation. Issues contain independent reviews of legal software with side-by-side comparisons of the top programs, plus how-to articles and expert columns. Targeted editorial attracts legal technology buyers and helps them plan effectively for their purchases, buy wisely and use their investments to maximize productivity and profitability.
Cost: $49.00
96 Pages
Founded in 1981

15905 **Law Practice Management**
American Bar Association
321 N Clark St
Chicago, IL 60654-7598

312-988-5000
800-285-2221; Fax: 312-988-6281
askaba@abanet.org
www.americanbar.org/aba.html
Facebook, Twitter

Tommy H Wells Jr, President
Laurel G. Bellows, President
Jody Thornburg, Publications Editor

The pre-eminent magazine on all phases of law office management. Includes feature articles, book reviews, reports on technical innovations and announcements of forthcoming events.
Cost: $40.00
Founded in 1878

15906 **Law Reporter**
The American Association for Justice
777 6th Street, NW
Washington, DC 20001

202-965-3500
800-424-2725
membership@justice.org
www.justice.org/

Peter C Quinn, Editor-in-Chief
Linda Lipsen, Chief Executive Officer
Charles Jeffress, Chief Operating Officer
Kathi Berge, Chief Financial Officer
Anjali Jesseramsing, Executive Vice President

Covers civil law, including automobile ,civil rights, insurance, commercial, employment and family law, medical negligence, premises liability and products liability, and workplace safety.
Cost: $135.00
40 Pages
Circulation: 53000
ISSN: 1052-4649
Founded in 1947
Printed in 2 colors

15907 **Law Technology News**
American Lawyer Media
345 Park Avenue S
New York, NY 10010

212-779-9434; Fax: 212-592-4900
www.americanlawyermedia.com

Kevin Vermuellen, Publisher
Monica Bay, Editor
William L Pollak, President/CEO

Covers the use of technology in the law profession.
Cost: $99.00
Frequency: Monthly
Circulation: 40000
Founded in 1997

15908 **Law and Social Inquiry: Journal of the American Bar Foundation**
American Bar Association
321 N Clark St
Chicago, IL 60654-7598

312-988-5000
800-285-2221; Fax: 312-988-6281
askaba@abanet.org
www.americanbar.org/aba.html
Facebook, Twitter

Tommy H Wells Jr, President
Laurel G. Bellows, President

An academic and legal journal containing a wide range of research reports relating to the law, the profession and legal institutions.
Frequency: Weekly
Circulation: 4,00,000
Founded in 1878

15909 **Law in Japan**
Japanese American Society for Legal Studies
University of WA Law School-1100 NE Cam.
Seattle, WA 98105

206-233-9292; Fax: 206-685-4469

John Haley, Editor

Academic journal with translation, original articles, comments and case notes on Japanese law and legal issues.
Cost: $13.00
Circulation: 1,400

15910 **Lawyers Weekly USA**
Lawyers Weekly Publications
10 Milk Street
Suite 1000
Boston, MA 02111-1203

617-451-7300
366-294-8963; Fax: 617-451-1466
www.lawyersweeklyusa.com
Facebook, Twitter, LinkedIn

Scott Murdock, Circulatlon Manager
Susan Bocamazo, Editor
Reni Germer, Managing Editor

Features profiles, practice tips, technology, marketing, management and other topics related to law practice.
Cost: $249.00
Frequency: Monthly
Circulation: 2500
Founded in 1972

15911 **Lawyers' Professional Liability Update**
American Bar Association
321 N Clark St
Chicago, IL 60654-7598

312-988-5000
800-285-2221; Fax: 312-988-6281
askaba@abanet.org
www.americanbar.org/aba.html
Facebook, Twitter

Tommy H Wells Jr, President
Laurel G. Bellows, President

Current reports and articles on legal malpractice insurance marketplace and other aspects of legal malpractice.
Cost: $45.00
Circulation: 23,000

15912 **Leadership and Management Directions**
American Bar Association
321 N Clark St
Chicago, IL 60654-7598

312-988-5000
800-285-2221; Fax: 312-988-6281
askaba@abanet.org
www.americanbar.org/aba.html
Facebook, Twitter

Tommy H Wells Jr, President
Laurel G. Bellows, President

Focuses on trends, principles, and practices in law office management including financial matters, marketing, human resources, facilities and technology.
Cost: $50.00
Frequency: Quarterly

15913 **Legal Management: Journal of the Association of Legal Administrators**
Association of Legal Administrators
75 Tri-State International
Suite 222
Lincolnshire, IL 60069-4435

847-267-1252; Fax: 847-267-1329
publications@alanet.org
www.alanet.org

Larry Smith, Executive Director
Debbie Thomas, Director, Accounting & Finance
Renee Mahovsky, Director, Administration/Operations
Bob Abramson, Director, Marketing & Communication
Jan Waugh, Director, Member Services

Covers personnel management, finance, strategic planning, the legal industry, business soft-

ware, technology. leadership, interpersonal communication, time and stress management, and disaster planning.
Circulation: 25000
Founded in 1971

15914 Legal Tech
Leader Publications
345 Park Avenue S
New York, NY 10010-1707

212-799-9200
800-888-8300; Fax: 212-696-1848

Stuart Wise, Publisher
Frequency: Monthly

15915 Legal Times
American Lawyers Newspapers Group
1730 M St Nw
Suite 802
Washington, DC 20036-4550

202-296-1995; Fax: 202-457-0718
www.legaltimes.com

Peter Scheer, Editor
Ann Pelham, Publisher
Eva Rodriguev, Editor-in-Chief
Gwen Jones, Circulation Manager
Rose Mahoney, Sales Manager

Covers law, lobbying and politics.
Cost: $349.00
36 Pages
Frequency: Weekly
Circulation: 6200
Founded in 1977

15916 Lender Liability Litigation Reporter
Andrews Communications
175 Stafford Building 4
Suite 140
Wayne, PA 19087

610-225-0510
800-328-4880; Fax: 610-225-0501

Robert Maroldo, Publisher

Journal of record, of litigation proceedings involving lender liability issues.
Cost: $650.00
Frequency: Monthly

15917 License
1 Park Avenue
2nd Floor
New York, NY 10016

212-951-6600
888-527-7008; Fax: 212-951-6714
info@advanstar.com
www.licensemag.com

Joyceann Cooney, Editor-in-Chief
Lorri Freifeld, Managing Editor
Steven Ekstract, Publisher
Sharon Weisman, Sales Manager

Patents, trademarks and copyrights
Frequency: Monthly
Circulation: 25000
Founded in 1987

15918 Litigation
American Bar Association
321 N Clark St
Chicago, IL 60654-7598

312-988-5000
800-285-2221; Fax: 312-988-6281
askaba@abanet.org
www.americanbar.org/aba.html
Facebook, Twitter

Tommy H Wells Jr, President
Laurel G. Bellows, President

A journal for trial lawyers and judges, each issue of which focuses on a particular topic involving trial practice.
Cost: $39.50
Frequency: Quarterly

15919 M and A Lawyer
Glasser LegalWorks
150 Clove Road
Little Falls, NJ 07424-2138

973-890-0008; Fax: 973-890-0042
www.legalwks.com

Steven E Bochner, Editor
Stephen W Seemer, President

News affecting all types of mergers and acquisitions transactions, including securities law, state law, international, taxation, accounting and practice areas like intellectual property, employee benefits/compensation, antitrust and environmental.
Cost: $317.00
Circulation: 500
Founded in 1995

15920 Mental & Physical Disability Law
American Bar Association
740 15th St Nw
Suite 8
Washington, DC 20005-1022

202-662-1000; Fax: 202-662-1032
cmpdi@abanet.org
www.americanbar.org/aba.html
Facebook, Twitter

William Neukom, President
Laurel G. Bellows, President
John Parry, Executive Director

A bi-monthly journal published by the Commission on Mental and Physical Disability Law, containing timely summaries of reported legal developments in 22 disability subject areas - over 1600 summaries annually.
Founded in 1878

15921 Mental & Physical Disability Law Reporter
American Bar Association
740 15th Street NW
Washington, DC 20005-1019

202-662-1570; Fax: 202-442-3439
cmpdl@abanet.org
www.abanet.org/disability
Facebook, Twitter, LinkedIn

Stephen N. Zack, President
Katherine H. O'Neil, Commission Chair
John W. Parry, Commission Director
Jack L. Rives, Executive Director
Alice Richmond, Treasurer

Published since 1976, the Reporter is the only periodical that comprehensively covers civil and criminal mental disability law and disability discrimination law. Organized by 22 subject areas, the Reporter allows you to target your research and save time. A perfect complement to your online legal research databases.
Cost: $325.00
15 Members
Frequency: 6 X/Year
Circulation: 300+
ISSN: 0883-7902
Founded in 1973

15922 Mental Health Law Reporter
Business Publishers
2222 Sedwick Drive
Durham, NC 27713

800-223-8720; Fax: 800-508-2592
custserv@bpinews.com
www.bpinews.com

Sarah Terry, Managing Editor

Court decisions affecting mental health professionals.
Cost: $277.00
Frequency: Monthly
Founded in 1963

15923 Midwest Alternative Dispute Resolution Guide
Law Bulletin Publishing Company
415 N State St
Suite 1
Chicago, IL 60654-8116

312-644-7800; Fax: 312-644-4255
www.lawbulletin.com

Lanning Macfarland Jr, President

Profiles of midwest attorneys.
Cost: $219.00
156 Pages
Frequency: Monthly
Founded in 1854

15924 Midwest Legal Staffing Guide
Law Bulletin Publishing Company
415 N State St
Suite 1
Chicago, IL 60654-8116

312-644-7800; Fax: 312-644-4255
editor@lbpc.com
www.lawbulletin.com

Lanning Macfarland Jr, President
Bernard Judge, Editor
Stephen E Brown, Publisher

Monthly magazine about law, people and opportunity.
Frequency: Daily
Founded in 1854
Printed in 4 colors

15925 Midwest Legal Technology Guide
Law Bulletin Publishing Company
415 N State St
Suite 1
Chicago, IL 60654-8116

312-644-7800; Fax: 312-644-4255
www.lawbulletin.com

Lanning Macfarland Jr, President

Supplement to the Chicago Daily Law Bulletin and Chicago Lawyer. Eliminates the confusion arising from the many new technological service and product providers.
60 Pages

15926 NAELA Journal
National Academy of Elder Law Attorneys
1577 Spring Hill Road
Suite 220
Vienna, VA 22182-2223

703-942-5711; Fax: 703-563-9504
naela@naela.org
www.naela.org

Peter G Wacht, CAE, Executive Director
Nancy Sween, Director, Comm. & Publications
Kirsten Brown Simpson, Director, Membership & Marketing
Ann Watkins, Operations Manager
Roger Naoroji, Meetings & Education Coordinator

Peer-reviewed, scholarly publication of substantive articles on Elder and Special Needs Law topics.
Frequency: 2x Year

15927 National Bar Association Magazine
National Bar Association
1225 11th St Nw
Washington, DC 20001-4217

202-842-3900; Fax: 202-289-6170
headquarters@nationalbar.org
www.nationalbar.org
Facebook, Twitter, LinkedIn

John Crump, Executive Director

Founded in 1925, the National Bar Association (NBA) is the nation's oldest and largest associa-

tion of African American lawyers and judges.
Cost: $32.00
Circulation: 25,000
Founded in 1925

15928 **National Jurist**
PO Box 939039
Sandy, CA 92193
858-503-7786; Fax: 858-503-7588
www.nationaljurist.com
Jack Crittenden, Editor-in-Chief
Keith Carter, Managing Editor
Rebecca Luczycki, Editor
Mike Wright, National Accounts Manager
Information, advice, news and entertainment for law and pre-law students to help them succeed in law school.
Cost: $30.00
Circulation: 100000
Founded in 1996

15929 **National Notary**
National Notary Association
9350 Desoto Avenue
Post Office Box 2402
Chatsworth, CA 91313-2402
818-739-4000
800-876-6827; Fax: 800-833-1211
www.nationalnotary.org
Deborah M. Thaw, Executive Vice President
Milton Valera, President
Mark Valera, Managing Director
Thomas Hayden, Director of Marketing
Focuses on the importance of notaries as public servants and updates readers on related news.
Founded in 1957

15930 **National Paralegal Reporter**
National Federation of Paralegal Association
PO Box 2018
Edmonds, WA 98020
425-967-0045; Fax: 425-771-9588
info@paralegals.org
www.paralegals.org
Features in-depth articles on timely topics such as paralegal roles and choosing vendors; how-toarticles providing readers with practical information that can be directly applied to their careers; and provides legal updated providing information that affects the paralegal profession such as case law, legislation, and technology education.
Cost: $30.00
Frequency: Bi-Monthly
Circulation: 10,000

15931 **Natural Resources and Environment**
American Bar Association
740 15th St Nw
Suite 8
Washington, DC 20005-1022
202-662-1000
800-285-2221; Fax: 202-662-1032
service@abanet.org
www.abanet.org
Practical magazine on the latest developments in the field of natural resources law.
Cost: $60.00
Frequency: Quarterly
Circulation: 12000

15932 **Negotiation Journal**
Plenum Publishing Corporation
513 Pound Hall
Cambridge, MA 02138
617-495-1684; Fax: 617-495-7818
www.pon.harvard.edu
Michael Wheeler, Editor
Nancy Waters, Managing Editor
Investigates theoretical and practical developments in the conflict resolution field.
Cost: $79.00
Frequency: Quarterly
Founded in 1998

15933 **Older Americans Report**
Business Publishers
8737 Colesville Road
Suite 1100
Silver Spring, MD 20910-3928
301-876-6300
800-274-6737; Fax: 301-589-8493
custserv@bpinews.com
www.bpinews.com
Leonard A Eiserer, Publisher
Beth Early, Operations Director
Mark Sherman, Editor
Covers every issue and program that affects your decision-making: Older Americans Act, long term care, Social Security & SSI, nutrition, nursing home regulation, housing, retirement/pension issues, all block grants for the aged, and more.
Cost: $427.00
Frequency: Weekly
Founded in 1963

15934 **Payroll Administration Guide**
Bureau of National Affairs
1801 S Bell St
Arlington, VA 22202-4501
703-341-3000
800-372-1033; Fax: 800-253-0332
customercare@bna.com
www.bnabooks.com
Facebook, Twitter, LinkedIn
Paul N Wojcik, CEO
A notification and reference service for payroll professionals. Covers federal and state employment tax, wage-hour and wage-payment laws.
Cost: $896.00
Frequency: Bi-Weekly
Founded in 1929

15935 **Preview of United States Supreme Court Cases**
American Bar Association
321 N Clark St
Chicago, IL 60654-7598
312-988-5000
800-285-2221; Fax: 312-988-6281
askaba@abanet.org
www.americanbar.org/aba.html
Facebook, Twitter
Tommy H Wells Jr, President
Laurel G. Bellows, President
Advance analysis by legal experts of the issues, facts and significance of each case being argued before the Supreme Court, plus special summer issue with all court decisions.
Cost: $340.00
Frequency: 10-12 issues

15936 **Probate Lawyer**
3415 S Sepulveda Boulevard
Suite 460
Los Angeles, CA 90034-6014
310-478-4454
Offers legislative news for probate courts.
Frequency: Annual

15937 **Professional Lawyer**
American Bar Association
321 N Clark St
Chicago, IL 60654-7598
312-988-5000
800-285-2221; Fax: 312-988-6281
askaba@abanet.org
www.americanbar.org/aba.html
Facebook, Twitter
Tommy H Wells Jr, President
Laurel G. Bellows, President
A magazine providing a forum for exchange of views and ideas on professionalism issues for bar leaders, lawyers, law school education and others interested in professionalism.
Cost: $40.00
Founded in 1878

15938 **Prosecutor**
National District Attorneys Association
44 Canal Center Plz
Suite 110
Alexandria, VA 22314-1548
703-549-4253; Fax: 703-836-3195
www.ndaa.org
Thomas Charron, Executive Director
Paul F Walsh Jr, Manager
Bill Gibbs, Manager
Covers a variety of criminal justice topics including child abuse, telemarketing fraud, violence against women, vehicular crime, DNA, juvenile justice and community prosecution.
48 Pages
Circulation: 7000
ISSN: 0027-6383
Founded in 1977
Mailing list available for rent: 6,500 names
Printed in 4 colors on glossy stock

15939 **Public Contract Law Journal**
American Bar Association
321 N Clark St
Chicago, IL 60654-7598
312-988-5000
800-285-2221; Fax: 312-988-6281
askaba@abanet.org
www.americanbar.org/aba.html
Facebook, Twitter
Tommy H Wells Jr, President
Laurel G. Bellows, President
Contains articles on all phases of federal, state and local procurement and grant law by leading authoritiies.
Cost: $60.00
Frequency: Annual+

15940 **Real Property, Property and Trust Journal**
American Bar Association
740 15th St Nw
Suite 8
Washington, DC 20005-1022
202-662-1000; Fax: 202-662-1032
www.americanbar.org/aba.html
Facebook, Twitter
William Neukom, President
Laurel G. Bellows, President
Jennifer Collins, Advertising Sales Coordinator
Scholarly articles in the fields of estate planning, trust law and real property law.
Cost: $60.00
Frequency: Quarterly

15941 **Review of Banking and Financial Services**
Standard & Poor's Corporation
55 Water St
New York, NY 10041-0003
212-438-1000; Fax: 212-438-0299
clientsupport@standardandpoors.com
www.standardandpoors.com
Deven Sharma, President
Hendrik Kranenburg, Executive VP
Focuses on laws and regulations affecting the banking and related industries.
Founded in 1941

15942 **Review of Securities & Commodities Regulation**
Standard & Poor's Corporation
55 Water St
44th Floor
New York, NY 10041-0003

212-438-1000; Fax: 212-438-0299

Deven Sharma, President

Information on the laws and regulations affecting the securities and future industries.
Cost: $8.55
Frequency: 22 per year
Printed in on newsprint stock

15943 **Right of Way**
International Right of Way
19750 S Vermont Ave
Suite 220
Torrance, CA 90502-1144

310-538-0233; Fax: 310-538-1471
info@irwaonline.org
www.irwa.net

Mark Rieck, Executive VP
Barbara Billitzer, Publisher
Cost: $425.00
Founded in 1985

15944 **Specialization Update**
American Bar Association
321 N Clark St
Chicago, IL 60654-7598

312-988-5000
800-285-2221; Fax: 312-988-6281
askaba@abanet.org
www.abanet.org

Tommy H Wells Jr, President

A compilation of current news briefs and articles of interest on lawyer specialization and related topics.
Circulation: 4,00,000
Founded in 1878

15945 **Student Lawyer**
American Bar Association
321 N Clark St
Chicago, IL 60654-7598

312-988-5000
800-285-2221; Fax: 312-988-6281
askaba@abanet.org
www.americanbar.org/aba.html
Facebook, Twitter

Tommy H Wells Jr, President
Laurel G. Bellows, President

Magazine for law students featuring articles on legal, political, social issues, law school and the profession.
Cost: $20.00
Frequency: Monthly
ISSN: 0039-274X
Founded in 1972
Printed in 4 colors on glossy stock

15946 **Tax Lawyer**
American Bar Association
321 N Clark St
Chicago, IL 60654-7598

312-988-5000
800-285-2221; Fax: 312-988-6281
askaba@abanet.org
www.americanbar.org/aba.html
Facebook, Twitter

Tommy H Wells Jr, President
Laurel G. Bellows, President

Journal of scholarly articles written by highly respected attorneys in the field and a thought-provoking student notes and comments section.
Cost: $53.00
Frequency: Quarterly

15947 **Technology and Practice Guide**
ABA Publishing
321 N Clark St
Chicago, IL 60654-7598

312-988-5000
800-285-2221; Fax: 312-988-6281
askaba@abanet.org
www.americanbar.org/aba.html
Facebook, Twitter

Tommy H Wells Jr, President
Laurel G. Bellows, President

Helps law professionals of general practice in making decisions about legal information management and technology.
Cost: $18.00
Frequency: SemiAnnual
Circulation: 13,477

15948 **The Bar Examiner Magazine**
National Conference of Bar Examiners
302 South Bedford Street
Madison, WI 53703

608-280-8550; Fax: 608-280-8552
contact@ncbex.org
www.ncbex.org

Erica Moeser, President

Published by the NCBE as a servuce to courts, academia, bar admissions administrators, members of bar examining boards and character committees, and others with special interest in the bar admissions process. Views and opinions in the articles are not to be taken as official expressions of the NCBE's policy unless so stated.
Frequency: 4/Year
Founded in 1931

15949 **The Paralegal Educator**
American Association for Paralegal Education
222 S Westmonte Drive
Suite 101
Altamonte Springs, FL 32714

407-774-7880; Fax: 407-774-6440
info@aafpe.org
www.aafpe.org

Ronald Goldfarb, President

A journal offering news, information, and scholarly articles pertaining to paralegal education.
Frequency: Annual

15950 **The Rules of the Game**
Alliance for Justice
11 Dupont Cir Nw
Suite 200
Washington, DC 20036-1206

202-822-6070; Fax: 202-822-6068
alliance@afj.org
www.afj.org

Nan Aron, President
Mailing list available for rent

15951 **Tort and Insurance Law Journal**
American Bar Association
740 15th St Nw
Suite 8
Washington, DC 20005-1022

202-662-1000; Fax: 202-662-1032
cmpdi@abanet.org
www.americanbar.org/aba.html
Facebook, Twitter

William Neukom, President
Laurel G. Bellows, President
Rick Paszkiet, Development Editor
Jennifer Collins, Advertising Sales Coordinator

Scholarly journal on current or emerging issues of national scope in the fields of tort and insurance law.
Cost: $23.00
Frequency: Quarterly

15952 **Trial**
The American Association for Justice
777 6th Street, NW
Washington, DC 20001

202-965-3500
800-424-2725
membership@justice.org
www.justice.org/

Kathleen Flynn Peterson, President
Linda Lipsen, Chief Executive Officer
Charles Jeffress, Chief Operating Officer
Kathi Berge, Chief Financial Officer
Anjali Jesseramsing, Executive Vice President

In depth articles by experts on socio-legal issues. Evaluates legal practices, points of law, civil law and recent developments in law.
Cost: $79.00
Frequency: Monthly
Circulation: 60000
Founded in 1946

15953 **Utilities Law Review**
John Wiley & Sons
111 River St
Hoboken, NJ 07030-5790

201-748-6000
800-825-7550; Fax: 201-748-6088
info@wiley.com
www.wiley.com

William J Pesce, CEO

Edited by a team of specialist UK and European lawyers, it is the leading journal in this fast-changing field. Providing detailed coverage of electricity, gas, telecommunications, transport, water and broadcasting.
Founded in 1807

15954 **Verdicts & Settlement**
Daily Journal Corporation
PO Box 54026
Los Angeles, CA 90054-0026

213-229-5300; Fax: 213-229-5481
www.dailyjournal.com

Gerald L Salzman, CEO
Malisha Anderson, Editor
Ray Chagolla, Marketing Head
Ama Sanchev, Circulation Manager
Frequency: Weekly
Circulation: 11000
Founded in 1888

15955 **Women Lawyers Journal**
National Association of Women Lawyers
American Bar Center 15.2
321 N Clark Street
Chicago, IL 60610-4403

312-988-6186; Fax: 312-988-5491
nawl@nawl.org
www.abanet.org/nawl/journal/wlj.html

Janice Sperow, Editor
Peggy Golden, Managing Editor
Stephanie Scharf, President

Published since 1911 as a forum for the exchange of ideas and information of interest to women lawyers. Unsolicited articles and press releases about non members will not be published.
Cost: $45.00
Circulation: 1200
ISSN: 0043-7468
Founded in 1899

15956 **Young Lawyers Division Newsletter**
Young Lawyers
104 Marietta St Nw
Suite 100
Atlanta, GA 30303-2743

404-527-8700
800-334-6865; Fax: 404-527-8717

webmaster@gabar.org
www.gabar.org

Cliff Brashier, Executive Director
Bryan Scott, Director
Natalie Kelly, Director
Frequency: Quarterly
Circulation: 21000
Founded in 1978

Trade Shows

15957 **ABA Annual Meeting**
American Bar Association
740 15th Street NW
9th Floor
Washington, DC 20005

202-662-1570; Fax: 202-442-3439
cmpdl@abanet.org
www.americanbar.org/aba.html
Facebook, Twitter

Carolyn B Lamm, President
Alex J Hurder, Commission Chair
Laurel G. Bellows, President

The meeting includes a CLE event on incompetency and Miranda rights, and also a reception for lawyers with disabilities.

15958 **AFCC Annual Conference**
Association of Family and Conciliation Courts
6525 Grand Teton Plaza
Madison, WI 53719

608-664-3750; Fax: 608-664-3751
afcc@afccnet.org
www.afccnet.org

Peter Salem, Executive Director

Over 20 exhibits relating to family judicial issues, including child custody and marriage, family, and divorce counseling. Attended by judges, couselors, attorneys, court personnel, mediators, teachers and researchers.
Frequency: June

15959 **AIRA Annual Bankruptcy & Restructuring Conference**
Association of Insolvency & Restructuring Advisors
221 Stewart Avenue
Suite 207
Medford, OR 97501

541-858-1665; Fax: 541-858-9187
aira@airacira.org
www.airacira.org

Grant Newton, Executive Director

Exhibits for professionals involved in insolvency and restructuring.
Frequency: Annual/June
Founded in 1984

15960 **AIRA Bankruptcy & Restructuring Conference**
Association of Insolvency & Restructuring Advisors
221 W. Stewart Avenue
Suite 207
Medford, OR 97501

541-858-1665; Fax: 541-858-9187
aira@aira.org
www.aira.org

Jim Lukenda, Executive Director
Cheryl Campbell, Conference Director

A conference for AIRA members to connect and network with colleages, as well as learn from experts in the field.
Frequency: Annual
Founded in 1982

15961 **ALA Annual Educational Conference and Exposition**
Association of Legal Administrators
75 Tri-State International
Suite 222
Lincolnshire, IL 60069-4435

847-267-1252; Fax: 847-267-1329
publications@alanet.org
www.alanet.org

Larry Smith, Exhibits Manager
Debbie Thomas, Director, Accounting & Finance
Renee Mahovsky, Director, Administration/Operations
Bob Abramson, Director, Marketing & Communication
Jan Waugh, Director, Member Services

Seminar, luncheon, tours and 200 exhibitors of information about computer hardware and software, facilities management, publications, printers, suppliers, litigation support, travel consultants and more.
2000 Attendees
Frequency: May

15962 **Academy of Criminal Justice Sciences**
Northern Kentucky University
402 Nunn Hall
Highland Heights, KY 41099

859-572-5100
800-757-ACJS; Fax: 859-572-6665

Patricia Delancey, Executive Director

Exhibits of publications pertaining to criminal justice and related areas. 45 booths.
1.8M Attendees
Frequency: March

15963 **Academy of Legal Studies in Business Annual Meeting**
School of Business-Forsyth
Western Carolina University
Cullowhee, NC 28723
Daniel Hebron, Executive Secretary

15 booths.
300 Attendees
Frequency: August

15964 **Adjutants General Association of the United States Annual Meeting**
1 Massachusetts Avenue NW
Washington, DC 20001-1401

302-326-7008; Fax: 302-326-7196
www.agaus.org

Government legislation.
300 Attendees
Frequency: Spring

15965 **American Association for Paralegal Education Conference**
American Association for Paralegal Education
222 S Westmonte Drive
Suite 101
Altamonte Springs, FL 32714

407-774-7880; Fax: 407-774-6440
info@aafpe.org
www.aafpe.org

Dave Wenhold, Executive Director
Cristina Griffin, Exhibits & Meetings Manager

Annual conference of 20 exhibitors of computer hardware and software, paralegal publications and educational materials and related supplies.
Founded in 1981

15966 **American Association of Attorney-Certified Public Accountants Annual Meeting**
American Association of Attorney-CPAs
P.O. Box 706
Warrendale, PA 15095

703-352-8064
888-288-9272; Fax: 703-352-8073
info@attorney-cpa.com
www.attorney-cpa.com

Howard O. Bernstein, President
Kimmy Headland, Director, Membership & Chapters
Jennifer Welding, Meetings Manager

Exhibits for persons licensed both as attorneys and CPAs for learning and networking purposes.
Frequency: Annual/July
Founded in 1964
Mailing list available for rent

15967 **American Association of Law Libraries Meeting & Conference**
American Association of Law Libraries
105 W Adams Street
Suite 3300
Chicago, IL 60603

312-939-4764; Fax: 312-431-1097
support@aall.org
www.aallnet.org
Facebook, Twitter

Paul Graller, Exhibits Manager
Susan Fox, Executive Director
Kate Hagan, Executive Director
Kim Rundle,, Executive Assistant
Emily Feltren,, Director of Government Relations

Annual show of 200 booths and 175 exhibitors of library equipment, supplies and services, including computer hardware and software/publishers of legal materials/information.
2000 Attendees
Frequency: July

15968 **American Bar Association Annual Meeting/ ABA Expo**
American Bar Association
321 N Clark Street
Chicago, IL 60610

312-988-5000
800-285-2221
askaba@abanet.org
www.americanbar.org/aba.html
Facebook, Twitter

William Neukom, President
Laurel G. Bellows, President

Annual meeting and 200 exhibits of legal technology, law books, computers, data processing equipment and other products and services related to the legal profession.
15000 Attendees
Frequency: August
Founded in 1887

15969 **American College of Legal Medicine Annual Meeting**
American College of Legal Medicine
9700 West Bryn Mawr Avenue
Suite 210
Rosemont, IL 60018

847-447-1713; Fax: 847-447-1150
info@aclm.org
www.aclm.org
Facebook, Twitter

Laurie Krueger, Executive Director
Daniel L. Orr, President

Annual conference and exhibits related to the field of legal medicine or health care related issues.

15970 **American Corporate Counsel Association Conference**
1025 Connecticut Avenue NW
Suite 200
Washington, DC 20036-5425

202-318-8327; Fax: 202-331-7454
http://www.acc.com

Frederick J Krebs, Executive Director

Corporate law.
600 Attendees
Frequency: November

15971 **American Immigration Lawyers Association Trade Show**
American Immigration Lawyers Association
1331 G Street NW
Suite 300
Washington, DC 20005-3142

202-507-7600; Fax: 202-783-7853
executive@aila.org
www.aila.org

Charles H Kuck, President
Bernard P Wolfadorf, President-Elect
David W Leopold, First VP
Gregory Chen, Director of Advocacy
Susan D. Quarles, Deputy Executive Director

628 booths.
600 Attendees
Frequency: June

15972 **American Society for Legal History Annual Meeting**
American Society for Legal History
Notre Dame Law School
PO Box R
Notre Dame, IN 46556-0780

574-631-6627; Fax: 574-631-3595
www.aslh.net

Walter F Pratt Jr, Secretary/Treasurer

Annual meeting of scholarly presses. Exhibits relating to legal history and its uses in formulating legal policy, decisions and actions; unearthing historical items; and preserving legal and legislative records.
1200 Attendees
Frequency: Annual
Founded in 1956

15973 **American Society of International Law Conference**
2223 Massachusetts Avenue NW
Washington, DC 20008-2847

202-939-6005; Fax: 202-797-7133
http://www.asil.org

Rosemarie Rauzino-Heller, Show Manager
Charlotte Ku, Executive Director

30 tables.
1M Attendees

15974 **Annual Education Conference & Resource Center Exhibition**
National Association for Law Placement
1666 Connecticut Avenue NW
Suite 1110
Washington, DC 20009

202-835-1001; Fax: 202-835-1112
info@nalp.org
www.nalp.org

Fred Thrasher, Deputy Director
Mark Weber, Senior Vice President
Pamela Malone, Senior Vice President

Annual conference and exhibits relating to recruitment and placement of lawyers.
800 Attendees
Frequency: Annual

15975 **Association of American Law Schools Annual Meeting**
Association of American Law Schools
1201 Connecticut Avenue NW
Suite 800
Washington, DC 20036-2605

202-296-8851; Fax: 202-296-8869
aals@aals.org
www.aals.org

Mary E Cullen, Director Meetings
Carl Monk, Executive Director

Annual meeting of 51 book publishers, suppliers and distributors, computer software suppliers.
4100 Attendees
Founded in 1896

15976 **Association of Trial Lawyers Annual Summer Meeting**
The American Association for Justice
777 6th Street, NW
Washington, DC 20001

202-965-3500
800-424-2725
membership@justice.org
www.justice.org/

Kathleen Flynn Peterson, President
Linda Lipsen, Chief Executive Officer
Charles Jeffress, Chief Operating Officer
Kathi Berge, Chief Financial Officer
Anjali Jesseramsing, Executive Vice President

45 booths.
3M Attendees
Frequency: July/August

15977 **Association of Trial Lawyers Mid Winter Meeting**
The American Association for Justice
777 6th Street, NW
Washington, DC 20001

202-965-3500
800-424-2725
membership@justice.org
www.justice.org/

Kathleen Flynn Peterson, President
Linda Lipsen, Chief Executive Officer
Charles Jeffress, Chief Operating Officer
Kathi Berge, Chief Financial Officer
Anjali Jesseramsing, Executive Vice President

55 booths.
1.5M Attendees
Frequency: January/Febuary

15978 **Association of Trial Lawyers of America Convention/Exposition**
The American Association for Justice
777 6th Street, NW
Washington, DC 20001

202-965-3500
800-424-2725
membership@justice.org
www.justice.org/

Kathleen Flynn Peterson, President
Linda Lipsen, Chief Executive Officer
Charles Jeffress, Chief Operating Officer
Kathi Berge, Chief Financial Officer
Anjali Jesseramsing, Executive Vice President

Semi-annual convention and exhibits of 130 manufacturers, suppliers and distributors of legal products/service, including computer animation videos, computer software/hardware, demonstrative evidence products, expert witness services and marketing firms, as well as high end consumer gifts.
3000 Attendees
Frequency: July
Founded in 1946

15979 **CLLA National Conference**
Commercial Law League of America
3005 Tollview Drive
Rolling Meadows, IL 60008

312-240-1400; Fax: 312-240-1408
info@clla.org
www.clla.org

Phil Lattanzio, Executive Vice President
Dawn Federico, Associate Director
Linda Herbst, Marketing & Communications
Lillian Novak, Member Services

A networking opportunity for professionals who are involved in bankruptcy, collections, debt and insolvency legislation.
Frequency: Annual
Founded in 1895

15980 **DRI- Annual Conference**
DRI-The Voice of the Defense Bar
55 W. Monroe Street
Suite 2000
Chicago, IL 60603

312-951-1101; Fax: 312-795-0749
dri@dri.org
www.dri.org
Facebook, Twitter, LinkedIn

Mary Massaron Ross, President
J. Michael Weston, President-Elect
John Parker Sweeney, First Vice President
Laura E. Proctor, Second Vice President
John E. Cuttino, Secretary/Treasurer

DRI is an international organization of attorneys defending the interests of business and individuals in civil litigation. DRI provides numerous educational and informational resources to DRI members and offers many opportunities for liaison among defense trial lawyers.

15981 **Education Law Association Annual Conference**
Education Law Association
300 College Park Avenue
Dayton, OH 45469

937-229-3589; Fax: 216-687-5284
ela@educationlaw.org
www.educationlaw.org
Facebook, Twitter, LinkedIn

Mandy Schrank, Executive Director
Cate K. Smith, Executive Director
Judy Pleiman, Member Services Coordinator
Jody Thornburg, Publications Manager

Annual conference with over 100 presenters giving presentations on current education law issues. Ten to twelve exhibitors of education law resources.
350 Attendees
Frequency: November

15982 **Federal Bar Association Convention**
Federal Bar Association
1220 North Fillmore St.
Ste. 444
Arlington, VA 22201

571-481-9100; Fax: 571-481-9090
fba@fedbar.org
www.fedbar.org
Facebook, Twitter, LinkedIn

Jack D. Lockridge, Executive Director
Lori Beth Gorman, Executive Assistant
Robert J. DeSousa, President
Hon. Gustavo Gelpi, Jr., President-Elect

Annual convention and exhibits of legal publications, computer software and insurance information.
300 Attendees

15983 **Federal Taxation Institute**
11 W 42nd Street
New York, NY 10036-8002

212-921-2300

Lorrie Ann England, Show Manager

11 booths.
1M Attendees
Frequency: November

15984 **Institute of Federal Taxation**
USC Law Center
University Park
Suite 124
Los Angeles, CA 90089-0001

FAX 213-740-9442

Karen Sprague, Director

10 booths.
1M Attendees
Frequency: January

15985 **Law and Society Association Annual Meeting**
University of Massachusetts
Hampshire House
Amherst, MA 01003

413-545-0111; Fax: 413-545-1640
www.lawandsociety.org

Ronald Pipkin, Executive Officer
Lissa Ganter, Administrative Coord

The annual meeting brings together 800-1000 scholars from the US and around the world to present research in the field of socio-legal studies. This includes the place of law in relation to other social institutions, legal decision making, legal systems, and operations, and a variety of research methods and modes of analysis. 50 booths including publishers exhibit, mainly academic, in the fiels of legal studies, and social science.
Frequency: May

15986 **Legal Administrators Association**
Association of Legal Administrators
75 Tri-State International
Suite 222
Lincolnshire, IL 60069-4435

847-267-1252; Fax: 847-267-1329
publications@alanet.org
www.alanet.org

Larry Smith, Executive Director
Debbie Thomas, Director, Accounting & Finance
Renee Mahovsky, Director, Administration/Operations
Bob Abramson, Director, Marketing & Communication
Jan Waugh, Director, Member Services

350 booths of products and services related to the legal industry.
2M Attendees
Frequency: April
Founded in 1971

15987 **Mid-America Association of Law Libraries Convention**
Mid-America Association of Law Libraries
105 W Adams Street
Suite 3300
Chicago, IL 60603

312-939-4764; Fax: 312-431-1097
www.aallnet.org/chapter/maall/
Facebook, Twitter

Annual show and exhibits of law library equipment, supplies and services.
Frequency: October, Omaha
Founded in 1973
Mailing list available for rent

15988 **NACA Fair Credit Reporting Act Conference**
National Association of Consumer Advocates
1215 17th Street NW
5th Floor
Washington, DC 20036

202-452-1989; Fax: 202-452-0099
info@consumeradvocates.org
www.consumeradvocates.org

David Philips, Co-Chair
Michael J. Quirk, Co-Chair
Ira Rheingold, Executive Director

Provides innovative, in-depth content to help private, public interest, and legal service attorneys address the unique needs of their clients.
Founded in 1994

15989 **NACB Symposiums**
National Association of Cannabis Businesses
1918 E. Lafayette Place
Milwaukee, WI 53202

720-926-6881
info@nacb.com
www.nacb.com
Facebook, Twitter, LinkedIn

Gina Kranwinkel, Chief Executive Officer
Mark Gorman, Executive VP & COO
Tom Nolasco, Dir., Legal & Strategic Initiatives
Meggan Hau, Operations Manager
Mary Clifton, Cannabis Research Advisor

A series of day-long symposiums on the most pressing legal and business issues facing the cannabis industry. Features presentations by premier law, accounting, and advisory firms.

15990 **NFPA Convention**
National Federation of Paralegal Associations
23607 Highway 99
Suite 2-C
Edmonds, WA 98026

425-967-0045; Fax: 425-771-9588
info@paralegals.org
www.paralegals.org
Facebook, LinkedIn

Dana Murphy-Love, Managing Director
Celeste Allen, Assistant Director
Rodney Dunham, Assistant Director

The premier annual event for legal professionals to gather for education seminars, dynamic speakers, knowledge sharing, networking, and of course product-shopping.
350 Attendees
Frequency: Annual

15991 **National Association of Black Criminal Justice**
1900 N Loop W
Suite 255
Houston, TX 77018-8116

713-681-3700; Fax: 713-956-8664

Keith Branch Esq, Chairman
Howard Thompson, Owner

60 booths.
700 Attendees
Frequency: July

15992 **National Association of Parliamentarians (NAP) Conference**
National Association of Parliamentarians
213 South Main Street
Independence, MO 64050-3850

816-833-3892
888-627-2929; Fax: 816-833-3893
hq@nap2.org
www.parliamentarians.org

Ronald R Stinson, President
Naurice S Henderson, VP
Sandra K Olson, Secretary

The NAP sponsors a conference and exhibit relating to parliamentary law and procedure on a biennial basis. In addition, the Association also holds a national event once each year, providing the opportunities for members, prospective members, and guests to learn more about effective meetings, how to help others learn the fundamentals of parliamentary procedure, and how to be an effective parliamentarian.

15993 **National Bar Association Annual Convention**
National Bar Association
1225 11th Street NW
Washington, DC 20001-4217

202-842-3900; Fax: 202-289-6170
www.nationalbar.org
Facebook, Twitter, LinkedIn

Maurice Foster, Director Special Projects
Reese Marshall, Coordinator Special Projects
John Crump, Executive Director

Annual convention and exhibits of computers and legal software, office products, accounting services, financial planners, temporary employment agencies, legal publications, travel agencies, luggage and leather goods, fine arts and jewelry. Containing 50 booths.
2500 Attendees
Frequency: July-August
Founded in 1925

15994 **National Court Reporters Association Annual Convention & Expo**
National Court Reporters Association
8224 Old Courthouse Road
Vienna, VA 22182-3808

703-556-6272
800-272-6272; Fax: 703-556-6291
msic@ncra.org
www.ncra.org
Facebook, Twitter, LinkedIn, Youtube

James M. Cudahy, Executive Director & CEO
18000 Members
1200 Attendees
Founded in 1899

15995 **National Federation Paralegal Associations**
PO Box 33108
Kansas City, MO 64114

816-421-5989; Fax: 816-941-2725
info@paralegals.org
www.paralegals.org

Tena Nichols, Assistant Managing Director

Thirty-five booths.
300 Attendees
Frequency: April

15996 **National Forensic Center Trade Show**
National Forensic Center
17 Temple Ter
Lawrenceville, NJ 08648-3254

609-883-0550
800-526-5177; Fax: 609-883-7622
expertindex.com

Betty Lipschner, Director

Coverage of the application of scientific, medical and technical knowledge to litigation.
200 Attendees
Printed in one color on matte stock

15997 **National Judges Association**
P.O. Box 325
Glendale, OR 97442

FAX 541-832-2674
njaoffice@yahoo.com
www.nationaljudgesassociation.org

Whitney Sullivan, Executive Director
Charlene Hewitt, Secretary
Ralph Zeller, Vice President

10 booths.
150 Attendees
Frequency: May

15998 National Notary Association Annual National Conference
Po Box 2402
Chatsworth, CA 91313-2402
818-739-4000
800-876-6827; Fax: 818-700-1942
hotline@nationalnotary.org
www.nationalnotary.org
Facebook, Twitter, LinkedIn
Milton G Valera, President
Deborah M Thaw, Executive VP
Marc Reiser, CEO
Jane Eagle, Executive VP & CFO
Ron Johnson, VP Systems & Operations
200M Members
500+ Attendees
Frequency: Bi-Monthly
Circulation: 200,000
Founded in 1957

15999 VALCON
ABI/AIRA
221 W. Stewart Avenue
Suite 207
Medford, OR 97501
541-858-1665; Fax: 541-858-9187
aira@aira.org
www.aira.org
Jim Lukenda, Executive Director
Cheryl Campbell, Conference Director
A joint conference by the American Bankruptcy Association and the Association of Insolvency & Restructuring Advisors where professionals can connect with leadinge experts and dealmakers in the distressed-debt, restructuring and valuation industry.
Frequency: Annual
Founded in 1982

Directories & Databases

16000 ABA Journal Directory of Legal Software and Hardware
American Bar Association
321 N Clark St
Chicago, IL 60654-7598
312-988-5000
800-285-2221; Fax: 312-988-6281
askaba@abanet.org
www.americanbar.org/aba.html
Facebook, Twitter
Tommy H Wells Jr, President
Laurel G. Bellows, President
Directory of supplies to the industry.
Cost: $7.00
Frequency: Annual
Circulation: 400,000

16001 Agricultural Law Update
American Agricultural Law Association
University of Arkansas Law Programs Building
Fayetteville, AR 72701
479-575-4671; Fax: 479-575-5830
Susan Williams, Admininstrative Assistant
Linda McGormic, Editor
Monthly update of legal issues concerning the agricultural industry(members only)
Frequency: Biennial
Circulation: 1,500

16002 American Association of Attorney-Certified Public Accountants Directory
American Association of Attorney-CPAs
P.O. Box 706
Warrendale, PA 15095
703-352-8064
888-288-9272; Fax: 703-352-8073
info@attorney-cpa.com
www.attorney-cpa.com
Howard O. Bernstein, President
Kimmy Headland, Director, Membership & Chapters
Offers names, addresses and biographical data on members licensed as both attorneys and CPAs for a one-time rental.
Founded in 1964

16003 American Bar Association Legal Education Database
American Bar Association
321 N Clark St
Chicago, IL 60654-7598
312-988-5000
800-285-2221; Fax: 312-988-6281
askaba@abanet.org
www.americanbar.org/aba.html
Facebook, Twitter
Tommy H Wells Jr, President
Laurel G. Bellows, President
Contains the complete text of the Third Tenative Draft of Law School Library Accreditation Standards.
Frequency: Full-text

16004 American College of Legal Medicine Member Directory
American College of Legal Medicine
9700 West Bryn Mawr
Suite 210
Rosemont, IL 60018
847-447-1713; Fax: 847-447-1150
www.aclm.org
Facebook, Twitter
Laurie Krueger, Executive Director
Daniel L. Orr, President
Lists members alphabetically, specialty or area(s) of expertise, and geographic location.
Circulation: 1,425
Founded in 1960

16005 American Law Reports Library
Lawyers Co-operative Publishing Company
50 Broad Street E
Rochester, NY 14694-0001
585-719-9760
A database, updated periodically, that contains the complete text of analyses of state and federal case law.
Frequency: Full-text

16006 BNA Criminal Practice Manual
Pike & Fischer
8505 Fenton St
Suite 1400
Silver Spring, MD 20910-4499
301-562-1530
800-255-8131; Fax: 301-562-1521
www.pf.com
Meg Hargreaves, President
David Heyman, Director Marketing
Karen James-Cody, Director of Communications
Kirk Swanson, Managing Editor

16007 BNA's Directory of State and Federal Courts, Judges and Clerks
BNA Books
1231 25th Street NW
Washington, DC 20037-1164
732-346-0089
800-960-1220; Fax: 732-346-1624
books@bna.com
www.bnabooks.com
Margaret Hullinger, Executive Editor
Lois Smith, Marketing Manager
Janie Meidhof, Media Specialist
Complete contact information including e-mail addresses on the nation's judges and clerks, as well as comprehensive details on the structure of federal, state, and territorial courts. Includes 2,201 state courts, 214 federal courts, 14,432 judges, and 5,303 clerks, list of nominations for federal judgeships, federal appellate court jurisdiction map and list, state court structure charts, reports of judicial decisions, directory of electronic public-access services, and personal name index.
714 Pages
Frequency: Annual
Circulation: 1,300
ISBN: 1-570184-11-9
ISSN: 1078-5582
Founded in 1986

16008 Best Lawyers in America
Woodward/White
129 1st Ave Sw
Aiken, SC 29801-4862
803-648-0300; Fax: 803-641-4794
info@bestlawyers.com
www.bestlawyers.com
Steven Naifeh, President
Over 11,000 attorneys who are selected as the best in their specialities by a survey of over 150,000 lawyers are profiled.
Cost: $110.00
1000 Pages
Frequency: Biennial

16009 Business Litigation Database
Trans Union Credit Information Company
20 Constance Ct
Hauppauge, NY 11788-4200
631-582-2690; Fax: 516-582-2767
Over 8 million court records on companies from New York and New Jersey are included in this database.
Frequency: Directory

16010 CEMC/ENR Directory of Law Firms
Construction Education Management Corporation
8133 Leesburg Pike
Suite 700
Vienna, VA 22182-2706
703-734-2399; Fax: 703-734-2908
Over 70 construction-oriented law firms located nationwide and overseas are listed.
Cost: $75.00
Frequency: Annual

16011 Common Market Law Review
Kluwer Law and Taxation Publishers
101 Philip Drive
Assinippi Park
Norwell, MA 02061
781-871-6600
866-269-9527; Fax: 781-681-9045
Serves as a medium for the dissemination of legal thinking on community law matters, meeting the need of both the academic and the practitioner.

16012 Comprehensive Guide to Bar Admission Requirements
Legal Education and Admissions to the Bar

321 N Clark Street
21st Floor
Chicago, IL 60610

312-988-6738; Fax: 312-988-5681
www.americanbar.org/aba.html
Facebook, Twitter
Laurel G. Bellows, President

Offers a list of state bar admission administrators in the United States and its territories.
Cost: $5.00
Frequency: Annual

16013 Corporate Counsel's Law Library
LexisNexis Matthew Bender
1275 Broadway
Menands, NY 12204-2694

518-487-3385
888-223-1940; Fax: 518-487-3083
info.in@lexisnexis.com
www.lexisnexis.com

George Bearese, VP
Rebecca Schmitt, Chief Financial Officer

This database contains court decisions covering statutory and common law concepts related to the formation, maintenance and dissolution of corporations.
Cost: $2484.00

16014 Criminal Justice Information Exchange Directory
US National Criminal Justice Reference Service
P.O. Box 60769
Harrisburg, PA 17106-0769

717-232-7554; Fax: 717-232-2162

Carroll Penyak, Director
Lori Dabbondanza, Executive Secretary
Lucas Martsolf, Manager

Over 100 criminal justice-related organizations are listed.
95 Pages
Frequency: Annual

16015 Criminal Justice Periodical Index
University Microfilms International
125 Chapman Hall
1219 University of Oregon
Eugine, OR 97403-1219

541-346-5129; Fax: 541-346-2804

Mary Ann Gilbert, Editor

Offers information on more than 180,000 citations to articles in 145 magazines, journals, newsletters and law reporting periodicals on the administration of justice and law enforcement.
Cost: $315.00
Frequency: TriAnnual

16016 Current Index to Legal Periodicals
Marian Gould Gallagher Law Library-Univ. of Wash.
William H Gates Hall
Box 353025
Seattle, WA 98195-3025

206-543-4089; Fax: 206-685-2165

Susan M Sorensen, Editor
Muriel Quick, Information Specialist

List of publishers of titles indexed in the database.
Cost: $192.00
Frequency: 52 issues
Founded in 1948
Printed in on matte stock

16017 Deskbook Encyclopedia of Employment Law
Data Research
PO Box 490
Rosemount, MN 55068-0490

952-452-8694
800-365-4900; Fax: 952-452-8694

An up-to-date compilation of summarized federal and state appellate court decisions which affect employment. The full legal citation is supplied for each case. A brief introductory note on the American judicial system is provided along with updated appendices of recent US Supreme Court cases and recently published law review articles. Also included are portions of the US Constitution which are most frequently cited in employment cases.
Cost: $85.75
500 Pages
Frequency: Annual
ISBN: 0-939675-55-2
Founded in 1996

16018 Deskbook Encyclopedia of Public Employment Law
Data Research
PO Box 490
Rosemount, MN 55068-0490

952-452-8694
800-365-4900; Fax: 952-452-8694

An up-to-datre compilation of summarized federal and state appellate court decisions which affect public employment. The full legal citation is cupplied for each case. A brief introductory note on the American judicial system is provided along with updated appendices of recent US Supreme Court cases and recently published law review articles.
Cost: $987.54
531 Pages
Frequency: Annual
ISBN: 0-939675-56-0
Founded in 1996

16019 Directory of Bar Associations
American Bar Association
321 N Clark St
Chicago, IL 60654-7598

312-988-5000
800-285-2221; Fax: 312-988-6281
askaba@abanet.org
www.americanbar.org/aba.html
Facebook, Twitter

Tommy H Wells Jr, President
Laurel G. Bellows, President

Offers information on more than 57 state bar associations, local bar associations and other local associations represented in the American Bar Association House of Delegates.
Cost: $95.00
40 Pages
Frequency: Annual

16020 Directory of Certified Business Counselors
Institute of Certified Business Counselors
18831 Willamette Dr
West Linn, OR 97068-1711

503-751-1856
877-422-2674; Fax: 503-292-8237

David Finsterwald, President

120 member counselors, brokers and attorneys qualified to act as advisors for persons with business problems.

16021 Directory of Courthouses, Abstract and Title Companies of the USA
Harbors International
7020 S Yale Avenue
Suite 206
Tulsa, OK 74136-5744

918-496-3232; Fax: 918-496-8905

A who's who directory of counties, parishes and boroughs with a section on abstract and title companies.
Cost: $95.00
368 Pages
ISSN: 0896-7830

16022 Directory of Law-Related CD-ROMs
Infosource Publishing
140 Norma Road
Teaneck, NJ 07666-4234

201-836-7072

Arlene Eis, Editor

A who's who directory of supplies to the industry.
Cost: $64.00
200 Pages
Frequency: Annual

16023 Directory of Lawyer Disciplinary Agencies & Lawyers' Funds/Client Protection
Center for Professional Responsibility
321 North Clark Street
Chicago, IL 60610

312-988-5000; Fax: 312-988-6281
www.americanbar.org/aba.html
Facebook, Twitter

Laurel G. Bellows, President
35 Pages
Frequency: Annual

16024 Directory of Lawyer Referral Services
American Bar Association
321 N Clark St
Chicago, IL 60654-7598

312-988-5000
800-285-2221; Fax: 312-988-6281
askaba@abanet.org
www.americanbar.org/aba.html
Facebook, Twitter

Tommy H Wells Jr, President
Laurel G. Bellows, President

Names of services, sponsoring organizations, phones and names of the directors are listed for over 330 services.
Cost: $10.00
40 Pages
Frequency: Annual

16025 Directory of Legal Aid & Defender Offices in the United States & Territories
National Legal Aid and Defender Association
1140 Connecticut Ave NW
Suite 900
Washington, DC 20036-4019

202-452-0620; Fax: 202-872-1031
www.nlada100years.org

Jo Ann Wallace, President & CEO
Julie Clark, Secretary
Alex Gulotta, Treasurer
Cost: $70.00

16026 Directory of Opportunities in International Law
John Bassett Moore Society of International Law
School of Law: University of VA
Charlottesville, VA 22901

Offers hundreds of possible employers in international law.
Cost: $10.00
204 Pages

16027 **Directory of Private Bar Involvement Programs**
American Bar Association
321 N Clark St
Chicago, IL 60654-7598
312-988-5000
800-285-2221; Fax: 312-988-6281
askaba@abanet.org
www.americanbar.org/aba.html
Facebook, Twitter
Tommy H Wells Jr, President
Laurel G. Bellows, President
A list of over 900 programs that provide free or low-cost legal services.
Cost: $7.50
210 Pages
Frequency: Annual

16028 **Directory of Public Interest Law Centers**
Alliance for Justice
11 Dupont Cir NW
2nd Floor
Washington, DC 20036-1206
202-822-6070; Fax: 202-822-6068
alliance@afj.org
www.afj.org
Nan Aron, President
Nonprofit association of public interest advocacy organization. Offers workshops, advocacy projects, legal guides, techinical assistance and public education. Lists addresses, branch offices and directors of 200 public interest law centers around the country. Indexed by state and subject area.
Cost: $10.00
48 Pages
Founded in 1996
Mailing list available for rent

16029 **Directory of State Court Clerks & County Courthouses**
WANT Publishing Company
420 Lexington Ave
Room 300
New York, NY 10170-0002
212-687-3774; Fax: 212-687-3779
rwant@msn.com
www.wantpublishing.com
Robert S Want, President
Allows easy access to vital information including court decisions, real estate records, UCC and tax liens, and other important documents maintained by State appellate and trial courts and county courthouses nationwide.
Cost: $ 75.00
380 Pages
Frequency: Annual
ISBN: 0-970122-91-8

16030 **FCBA Directory**
Federal Communications Bar Association
1020 19th St NW
Suite 325
Washington, DC 20036-6113
202-293-4000; Fax: 202-293-4317
fcba@fcba.org
www.fcba.org
Stanley Zenor, Executive Director
Kerry Loughney, Director Of Membership Services
Wendy Jo Parish, Administrative Assistant
A nonprofit organization of attorneys and other professionals involved in the development, interpretation, implementation and practice of communications law and policy.
Founded in 1936

16031 **Federal Careers for Attorneys**
Federal Reports
1010 Vermont Ave NW
Suite 408
Washington, DC 20005-4945
202-393-1552
Richard L Hermann, Owner
United States government general counsel and other legal offices throughout the federal system.
Cost: $23.95
150 Pages

16032 **Federal Law-Related Careers Directory**
Federal Reports
1010 Vermont Ave NW
Suite 408
Washington, DC 20005-4945
202-393-1552
800-296-9611; Fax: 202-393-1553
Richard L Hermann, Owner
Richard L Hermann, Editor
Listings of over 1,000 federal government recruiting offices.
Cost: $16.95

16033 **General Bar Law Directory**
General Bar
25000 Center Ridge Rd
Suite 3
Cleveland, OH 44145-4108
440-835-2000
800-533-2500; Fax: 440-835-3636
service@generalbar.com
www.generalbar.com
Charles Sonnhalter, Owner
700 Pages
Circulation: 10000
Founded in 1941

16034 **Insider's Guide to Law Firms**
Mobius Press
PO Box 3339
Boulder, CO 80307
303-188-8205
800-529-5627; Fax: 303-499-5389
Directory of services and supplies to the industry.
Cost: $28.95
740 Pages
Frequency: Annual

16035 **Judicial Yellow Book**
Leadership Directories
104 5th Ave
New York, NY 10011-6901
212-627-4140; Fax: 212-645-0931
judicial@leadershipdirectories.com
www.leadershipdirectories.com
David Hurvitz, CEO
James M Petrie, Associate Publisher
Contact information for over 3,250 federal and state judges in federal and state appellate courts, including staff and law clerks, and the law schools they attended.
Cost: $245.00
1,100 Pages
Frequency: SemiAnnual
ISSN: 1082-3298
Founded in 1995
Mailing list available for rent: 13,000 names at $125 per M

16036 **Latin American Labor Law Handbook**
WorldTrade Executive
PO Box 761
Concord, MA 01742-0761
978-287-0301; Fax: 978-287-0302
www.wtexec.com
Alison French, Production Manager
Designed to give firms doing business in Latin America some basic knowledge of labor and employment law in the region. Covers countries where US and foreign investment is particularly high: Argentina, Brazil, Venezuela, Colombia, Costa Rica and Chili - providing an overview of the complex network of laws, regulations, and customs affecting social security, wages, employment security, and labor organizing.
Cost: $185.00

16037 **Law Books and Serials in Print**
R R Bowker LLC
630 Central Ave
New Providence, NJ 07974-1506
908-286-0288
888-269-5372; Fax: 908-464-3553
www.bowker.com
R R Bowker
L Yuster-Freeman, Editor
Focusing on core legal and related titles, Law Books & Serials in Print includes descriptive annotations that provide expert guidance on selecting the right sources for every research need.
ISBN: 0-835249-42-3
Mailing list available for rent

16038 **Law Books in Print**
Glanville Publishers
75 Main St
Dobbs Ferry, NY 10522-1673
914-693-1320
Publishers of law books in English are listed.
Cost: $750.00
Frequency: Base Edition

16039 **Law Firms Yellow Book**
Leadership Directories
104 5th Ave
New York, NY 10011-6901
212-627-4140; Fax: 212-645-0931
lawfirms@leadershipdirectories.com
www.leadershipdirectories.com
David Hurvitz, CEO
James M Petrie, Associate Publisher
Contact information for over 24,000 attorneys and administrators who make the business decisions and manage the practice areas in over 800 of the nation's leading law firms.
Cost: $245.00
1,100 Pages
Frequency: SemiAnnual
ISSN: 1054-4054
Founded in 1991
Mailing list available for rent: 19,000 names at $125 per M

16040 **Law Office Computing Directory**
James Publishing
Po Box 25202
Suite E
Santa Ana, CA 92799-5202
714-755-5450; Fax: 714-751-2709
www.jamespublishing.com
Jim Pawell, Owner
Approximately 25 computer products and services designed for use by the legal profession.
Cost: $49.95
Frequency: Bi-Monthly
Circulation: 9,000

16041 **Law Office Economics & Management: Directory of Law Office Software**
Clark Boardman Callaghan

155 Pfingsten Road
Deerfield, IL 60015
847-374-0400
800-323-1336; Fax: 847-948-9340
Paul S Hoffman, Editor
List of about 100 suppliers of data processing equipment and software.
Cost: $15.00
Frequency: Annual June

16042 **Law and Legal Information Directory**
Gale/Cengage Learning
27500 Drake Road
Farmington Hills, MI 48331-3535
248-699-4253
800-877-4253; Fax: 877-363-4253
gale.galeord@cengage.com
www.gale.cengage.com
Facebook, Twitter, Youtube
Patrick C Sommers, President
Jacqueline O'Brien, Editor
Provides descriptions and contact information for more than 21,000 institutions, services and facilities in the law and legal information industry.
Frequency: Annual
ISBN: 1-414421-26-5

16043 **Lawyers Referral Directory**
PO Box 40335
Cleveland, OH 44140-0335
440-899-8660
800-LAW-LIST; Fax: 440-899-1005
www.lawlistil.com
Ted M McManamon, Editor
Richard T Ostovitz, Production Manager
Bonded reference guide to lawyers specializing in commercial law, creditors' rights and collection litigation. Free to users registering referrals sent.
700 Pages
Frequency: Annual

16044 **Lawyers' List**
Commercial Publishing Company
PO Box 2430
Easton, MD 21601-2430
410-820-4494
800-824-9911; Fax: 410-820-4474
DA Schwartz, President
A listing of law offices engaged in general, corporation and trial practice or patent, trademark and copyright practice.
1700 Pages
Frequency: Annual

16045 **Legal Information Alert**
Alert Publications
401 W Fullerton Parkway
Apartment 1403E
Chicago, IL 60614-2805
773-525-7594
Donna Tuke-Heroy, President
Publishers of books, databases, CD-ROM products and loose-leaf services for the legal profession are listed.
Cost: $149.00

16046 **Legal Looseleafs in Print**
Infosource Publishing
140 Norma Road
Teaneck, NJ 07666-4234
201-836-7072
aeis@carroll.com
www.infosourcespub.com
Over 230 publishers offering 3,600 looseleaf legal information services.
Cost: $106.00
400 Pages
Frequency: Annual March
Founded in 1981

16047 **Legal Newsletters in Print**
Infosource Publishing
140 Norma Road
Teaneck, NJ 07666-4234
201-836-7072
Arlene Eis, Editor
Directory of services and supplies to the industry.
Cost: $90.00
400 Pages
Frequency: Annual

16048 **Legal Researcher's Desk Reference**
Infosource Publishing
140 Norma Road
Teaneck, NJ 07666-4234
201-836-7072
Arlene Eis, Editor
Information is provided on federal and state government officials and departments are listed, as well as publishers and law book dealers and much more.
Cost: $58.00
416 Pages
Frequency: Biennial

16049 **Legal Resource Directory**
McFarland & Company Publishers
PO Box 611
Jefferson, NC 28640-0611
336-246-4460; Fax: 336-246-5018
info@mcfarlandpub.com
www.mcfarlandpub.com
Facebook, Twitter, LinkedIn
Information is given on national, state and local organizations providing free or inexpensive legal advice to low-income families.
Cost: $30.95
148 Pages
Mailing list available for rent

16050 **Legal Resources Index**
Information Access Company
362 Lakeside Drive
Foster City, CA 94404-1171
650-378-5200
800-227-8431
This database contains more than 500,000 citations, with selected abstracts, to articles published in more than 800 key law journals, bar association publications and legal newspapers.

16051 **Martindale-Hubbell Law Directory**
Martindale-Hubbell/Reed Reference Publishing
121 Chanlon Rd
New Providence, NJ 07974-1544
908-464-6800
800-526-4902; Fax: 908-771-8704
info@martindale.com
www.martindale.com
Ralph Colistri, President
Directory of services and supplies to the industry.
Cost: $690.00
50000 Pages
Frequency: 26 Volumes

16052 **NACB Signals**
National Association of Cannabis Businesses
1918 E. Lafayette Place
Milwaukee, WI 53202
720-926-6881
info@nacb.com
www.nacb.com
Facebook, Twitter, LinkedIn
Gina Kranwinkel, Chief Executive Officer
Mark Gorman, Executive VP & COO
Tom Nolasco, Dir., Legal & Strategic Initiatives
Meggan Hau, Operations Manager
Mary Clifton, Cannabis Research Advisor
A cannabis, marijuana, and hemp legislation tracking tool available only to members of the NACB.

16053 **NALP Directory of Legal Employers**
National Association for Law Placement
1025 Connecticut Ave NW
Suite 1110
Washington, DC 20036-5413
202-835-1001; Fax: 202-835-1112
info@nalp.org
www.nalp.org
M Liepold, Executive Director
Fred Thrasher, Senior Vice President
Pamela Malone, Senior Vice President
Information on more than 1,700 employers nationwide and is an invaluable tool for job searchers, career counselors, and legal recruiters alike. Published both on-line and in print, this directory includes indexes by location and by practice area keyword.
Cost: $75.00
Frequency: Annual
Founded in 1971
Mailing list available for rent: CBC names

16054 **NLADA Directory of Legal Aid and Defender Offices in the US & Territories**
National Legal Aid and Defender Association
1140 Connecticut Ave NW
Suite 900
Washington, DC 20036-4019
202-452-0620; Fax: 202-872-1031
www.nlada100years.org
Jo Ann Wallace, President & CEO
Julie Clark, Secretary
Alex Gulotta, Treasurer
About 3,600 civil legal aid and indigent defense organizations in the US.
Cost: $70.00
Frequency: Biennial

16055 **NSA Directory**
National Sheriff's Association
1450 Duke St
Alexandria, VA 22314-3490
703-836-7827
Suzanne B Litts, Editor
David Strigel, Advertising Manager
Sheriffs of the US address phone and fax.
Cost: $50.00
94 Pages
Frequency: Annual

16056 **National Directory of Corrections Construction**
National Institute of Justice

PO Box 6000
Rockville, MD 20849-6000

301-251-5500

Offers valuable information on over 150 correctional institutions constructed since 1985.
Cost: $32.00
354 Pages

16057 **National Directory of Courts of Law**
Information Resources
1110 N Glebe Road
Suite 550
Arlington, VA 22201-5762
703-525-4750

Directory of services and supplies to the industry.
Cost: $95.00
888 Pages
Frequency: Biennial

16058 **National Employment Listing Service Bulletin**
Criminal Justice Center
Sam Houston State University
Huntsville, TX 77341

936-295-6371; Fax: 281-294-1653

Kay Billingsley, Editor

Job openings in police departments, sheriff's departments, courts and other law enforcement and security agencies.

16059 **National Hispanic American Attorney Directory**
Hispanic National Bar Association
100 Seaview Drive
Secaucus, NJ 07094-1800

201-348-4900; Fax: 201-348-6609

Carlos G Ortiz

National directory listing Hispanic American Attorneys.
Cost: $65.00
Circulation: 4,000

16060 **National Law Journal: Directory of Current Law & Law-Related Books**
New York Law Publishing Company
345 Park Avenue S
8th Floor
New York, NY 10010-1700

212-799-9434; Fax: 212-696-1875
www.ljextra.com

Ben Gerson, Editor
Bill Pollak, General Counsel
Michael Holston, General Counsel
David Hechler, Executive Editor
Paula Martersteck, Managing Editor

Lists over 70 publishers of law and law-related books.
Cost: $124.00
Frequency: Annual January

16061 **National List**
PO Box 2486
Bismark, ND 58502-2486

701-237-7202
800-227-1675; Fax: 701-223-5634
info@nationallist.com
www.nationallist.com

Randy Nicola, VP
Gerry Cowgill, President
Kacey Rask, Account Executive
Leslie Herr, Director of Operations

A list of lawyers and law firms handling collections and general practice in the United States, Canada, and most foreign countries.
550 Pages
Frequency: Annual

16062 **National Trial and Deposition Directory**
321 W Franklin Street
Boise, ID 83702

208-344-3191; Fax: 208-345-8800
Cost: $39.95

490 Pages
Circulation: 2,000

16063 **National and Federal Legal Employment Report**
Federal Reports
1010 Vermont Ave NW
Suite 408
Washington, DC 20005-4945

202-393-1552
800-296-9611; Fax: 202-393-1553

Richard L Hermann, Owner
Richard L Hermann, Editor

Listings of approximately 600 current attorney and law-related job opportunities with the US government and other public and private employers in Washington DC, nationwide and abroad.
Cost: $35.80
Frequency: Monthly

16064 **Nelson's Law Office Directory**
Nelson Company
53 West Jackson Blvd.
Chicago, IL 60604

877-464-6656
www.nelson.com

Richard Nelson, Owner
Michael Andrews, Chief Financial Officer

A directory of the top rated law firms in the United States. Rated on legal ability, integrity and diligence by the leading lawyers in each state.
Cost: $23.00
210 Pages
Frequency: Annual
Founded in 1968

16065 **Now Hiring: Government Jobs for Lawyers**
American Bar Association
321 N Clark St
Chicago, IL 60654-7598
312-988-5000
800-285-2221; Fax: 312-988-6281
askaba@abanet.org
www.americanbar.org/aba.html
Facebook, Twitter

Tommy H Wells Jr, President
Laurel G. Bellows, President

Federal, quasi- and independent government agency jobs for lawyers.
Cost: $17.95
170 Pages

16066 **Parole and Probation Compact Administrator Association Mailing List**
Council of State Governments
2760 Research Park Drive
PO Box 11910
Lexington, KY 40578-1910

859-244-8000
800-800-1910; Fax: 859-244-8001
www.csg.org

Jodi Rell, President

16067 **Preview of United States Supreme Court Cases**
American Bar Association
321 N Clark St
Chicago, IL 60654-7598

312-988-5000
800-285-2221; Fax: 312-988-6281
askaba@abanet.org
www.americanbar.org/aba.html
Facebook, Twitter

Tommy H Wells Jr, President
Laurel G. Bellows, President

This database contains full-text reviews of cases orally argued before the US Supreme Court.
Frequency: Full-text

16068 **Representative Offices in the Russian Federation**
WorldTrade Executive
PO Box 761
Concord, MA 01742-0761

978-287-0301; Fax: 978-287-0302
www.wtexec.com

Alison French, Production Manager

Combines detailed information on the legal structure within which representative offices must operate, including tax and other requirements, with a user-friendly guide to the accreditation and registration process.
Cost: $135.00

16069 **Russell Law List**
Commercial Publishing Company
PO Box 2430
Easton, MD 21601-2430

410-820-4494
800-824-9911; Fax: 410-820-4474

DA Schwartz, President

A listing of law offices in general practice worldwide.
147 Pages
Frequency: Annual

16070 **Russia Business & Legal Briefing**
WorldTrade Executive
PO Box 761
Concord, MA 01742-0761

978-287-0301; Fax: 978-287-0302
www.wtexec.com

Alison French, Production Manager

Topics include: economic analysis; hard currency regulations; investment legislation in St. Petersburg; enforcing foreign judgements in Russia; new laws on limited liability companies and bankruptcy; new commercial arbitration court in St. Petersburg; changes in tax legislation; managing the Russian tax burden.
Cost: $265.00

16071 **Sourcebook of Local Court and County Records Retrievers**
BRP Publications
200 E Eager Street
Baltimore, MD 21202-3704

202-312-6060
800-822-6338; Fax: - - 047

Offers information on firms that specialize in finding court and county records, including civil, criminal, probate and bankruptcy files.
Cost: $45.00
432 Pages

16072 **Summer Legal Employment Guide**
Federal Reports
1010 Vermont Ave NW
Suite 408
Washington, DC 20005-4945

202-393-1552

Richard L Hermann, Owner

Directory of services and supplies to the industry.
Cost: $170.00
36 Pages
Frequency: Annual

16073 **US Supreme Court Employment Cases**
Data Research
PO Box 490
Rosemount, MN 55068-0490
952-452-8694
800-365-4900; Fax: 952-452-8694

A compilation of summarized US Supreme Court decisions which affect employment. The full legal citation is supplied for each case.
Cost: $64.70
288 Pages
Frequency: Annual
ISBN: 0-939675-51-0
Founded in 1995

16074 **United States Probation and Pretrial Services Officers Directory**
Probation Div./Admin. Office of US Courts
1 Columbus Circle NE
Suite 4-300
Washington, DC 20544-0001
FAX 202-273-1603

Federal probation offices and pretrial services offices.
Frequency: Annual

16075 **WESTLAW International Law Library**
West Publishing Company
610 Opperman Drive
Eagan, MN 55123-1340
651-687-7327
www.westgroup.com

Database containing the complete information of international and US federal court decisions.
Frequency: Full-text

16076 **WESTLAW Legal Services Library**
West Publishing Company
610 Opperman Drive
Eagan, MN 55123-1340
651-687-7327
www.westgroup.com

This database offers the complete text of US federal and state court decisions, statutes and regulations.

16077 **WESTLAW Litigation Library**
West Publishing Company
610 Opperman Drive
Eagan, MN 55123-1340
651-687-7327
www.westgroup.com

Offers information on law reviews, bar association journals and law-related texts.
Frequency: Full-text

16078 **Want's Federal-State Court Directory**
WANT Publishing Company
420 Lexington Ave
Room 300
New York, NY 10170-0002
212-687-3774; Fax: 212-687-3779
rwant@msn.com
www.wantpublishing.com
Robert S Want, President

The nation's number one court reference source, offering comprehensive information on the nation's federal, state and county courts.
Cost: $35.00
235 Pages
Frequency: Softcover

Industry Web Sites

16079 **http://gold.greyhouse.com**
G.O.L.D Grey House OnLine Databases

Grey House Publishing's online database platform, GOLD, offers Quick Search, Keyword Search and Expert Search for most business sectors including legal markets. The GOLD platform makes finding the information you need quick and easy - whether you're a novice searcher or an experienced database user. All of Grey House's directory products are available for subscription on the GOLD platform.

16080 **www.aallnet.org**
American Association of Law Libraries

Membership consists of national law library professionals.

16081 **www.abanet.org**
American Bar Association

The largest organization serving lawyers and all professionals involved in the law enforcement and legal industries. Conducts research and educational activities, encourages professional improvement and provides public service.

16082 **www.aclm.org**
American College of Legal Medicine

Organization related to the field of health law, legal medicine or medical jurisprudence.

16083 **www.aclu.org**
American Civil Liberties Union

Protection of civil liberties and constitutional rights through litigation, public education and legislative lobbying.

16084 **www.afccnet.org**
Association of Family and Conciliation

AFCC is an interdisciplinary, international association of professionals dedicated to improving the lives of children and families through the resolution of family conflict.

16085 **www.afj.org**
Alliance for Justice

Nonprofit association of public interest advocacy organization. Offers workshops, advocacy projects, legal guides, techinical assistance and public education. Publishes a directory of public interest law centers.

16086 **www.ali-aba.org**
American Law Institute - American Bar Association

Provides continuing legal education courses, books, and periodicals for practicing attorneys and others in the legal profession.

16087 **www.atlanet.org**
Association of Trial Lawyers of America

16088 **www.attorney-cpa.com**
American Association of Attorney-CPAs

Seeks to safeguard the professional and legal rights of CPA attorneys.

16089 **www.blr.com**
Business & Legal Reports

Provides essential tools for safety and environmental compliance and training needs

16090 **www.educationlaw.org**
Education Law Association

Association for manufacturers or suppliers of law education equipment, supplies and services.

16091 **www.fcba.org**
Federal Communications Bar Association

A non-profit organization of attorneys and other professionals involved in the development, interpretation, implementation and practice of communications law and policy.

16092 **www.findlaw.com**

Online Legal Resources. Legal, Professionals, Students, Business, Legal News, etc.

16093 **www.greyhouse.com**
Grey House Publishing

Authoritative reference directories for most business sectors including legal markets. Users can search the online databases with varied search criteria allowing for custom searches by product category, geographic area, sales volume, keyword, subject and more. Full Grey House catalog and online ordering also available.

16094 **www.lexis-nexis.com**
Mead Data Central

Contains the Lexis-Nexis Source Locator, a powerful new tool for retrieving targeted information about the more 31,000 Lexi-Nexis sources.

16095 **www.nacdl.org**
National Association of Criminal Defense Lawyers

America's preeminent voluntary bar association supporting the Criminal Defense profession.

16096 **www.naela.org**
National Academy of Elder Law Attorneys

Members are private attorneys, law professors and Title III interest in the provision of legal service to the elderly.

16097 **www.narf.org**
Native American Rights Fund

Provides legal services to Indian tribes, organizations and individuals in the areas of preservation of tribal existence, protection of tribal natural resources, promotion of human rights , accoutability of governments, development of Indian law.

16098 **www.ncraonline.org**
National Court Reporters Association

16099 **www.ncwba.org**
National Conference of Women's Bar Associations

To promote and assist the growth of local and statewide women's bar associations and ideas among women's bar associations and women's bar sections of local and statewide bar associations; to serve as a vehicle for the exchange and dissemination of information and ideas among women's bar associations and women's bar sections of local and statewide bar associations.

16100 **www.paralegals.org**
National Federation of Paralegal Association

For state and local paralegal associations throughout the United States and Canada.

16101 **www.parliamentarians.org**
National Association of Parliamentarians

An association for those interested in parliamentary law and procedure, NAP's primary objectives are teaching, promoting, and disseminating the philosophy and principles underlying the rules of deliberative assemblies.

16102 **www.rand.org/icj**
Institute for Civil Justice

Nonprofit research organization within the RAND Corporation dedicated to interdisciplinary empirical research to facilitate change in the civil justice system.

16103 www.rmmlf.org
Rocky Mountain Mineral Law Foundation

16104 www.romingerlegal.com
Is a Search Engine dedicated to Legal Links, Legal Research Page, Case Law and Professional Directories for Law, etc.

16105 www.searchcrawl.com/legal/justice.html
Searchcrawl
List of legal resources.

16106 www.worldjurist.org
World Jurist Association of the World Peace Through Law

Association for those interested in future world peace.

Associations

16107 **Africana Librarians Council**
African Studies Association
54 Joyce Kilmer Avenue
Piscataway, NJ 08854-8045

732-932-8173; Fax: 732-445-1366
kramer@tiac.net
www.africanstudies.org/

Eileen Kramer, President

Members consist of librarians, archivists or documentalists working with materials from and about Africa or scholars interested in the preseravtionof or access to Africana.
500 Members
Founded in 1983

16108 **American Association of Law Libraries**
105 W Adams Street
Suite 3300
Chicago, IL 60603

312-939-4764; Fax: 312-431-1097
admin@ifwtwa.org
www.aallnet.org
Facebook, Twitter, LinkedIn, Youtube, RSS, Instagram

Linda Kissam, President
Allen Cox, Vice President
Elizabeth Willoughby, Treasurer
Susan J Montgomery, Treasurer, Board Member
Marc d'Entremont, Director

Promotes and enhances the value of law libraries to the legal and public communities, fosters the profession of law librarianship and provides leadership in the field of legal information.
300 Members
Founded in 1956

16109 **American Association of School Librarians**
American Library Association
50 E Huron Street
Chicago, IL 60611

312-944-6780
800-545-2433; Fax: 312-280-5276
ala@ala.org
www.ala.org/aasl/
Facebook, Twitter, LinkedIn, Flickr, Pinterest, Google+, In

Sylvia Knight Norton, Executive Director
Jennifer Habley, Manager, Web Communications
Stephanie Book, Manager, Communications
Allison Cline, Deputy Executive Director
Meg Featheringham, Manager/Editor

Works to ensure that all members of the school library media field collaborate to provide leadership in the total education program, participate as active partners in the teaching and learning process, connect learners with ideas and information and prepare students for life long learning, informed decision making, a love of reading and the use of information technologies.
60000 Members

16110 **American Indian Library Association**
American Library Association
50 E Huron Street
Chicago, IL 60611

312-944-6780
800-545-2433; Fax: 312-664-7459
ala@ala.org
www.ala.org

Sari Feldman, President
Keith Michael Fiels, Executive Director
Sara Harris, Manager

Association for Native Americans and Native Alaskans libraries and librarians.
10000 Members
Founded in 1949

16111 **American Library Association**
American Library Association
50 E Huron St
Chicago, IL 60611-2788

312-944-6780
800-545-2433
ala@ala.org
www.ala.org

Sari Feldman, President
Keith Michael Fiels, Executive Director

To provide leadership for the development, promotion, and improvement of library and information services and the profession of librarianship in order to enhance learning and ensure access to information for all.
65000 Members
Founded in 1876

16112 **American Society of Indexing**
American Society for Indexing
1628 E. Southern Avenue
Suite 9-223
Tempe, AZ 85282

480-245-6750; Fax: 303-422-8894
nahj@nahj.org
www.asindexing.org
Facebook, Twitter, YouTube, RSS

Mekahlo Medina, President
Ivette Davila-Richards, Vice President/Broadcast
Rebecca Aguilar, Vice President, Online
Barbara Rodriguez, Vice President, Print
Francisco Cortes, Financial Officer

A national association with international membership and interests. A nonprofit charitable organization for indexers, librarians, abstractors, editors, publishers, database producers, and organizations concerned with indexing, seeking cooperation and membership of all persons, groups or institutions interested in indexing. Founded in 1968 to promote excellence in indexing and increase awareness of the value of well-written indexes.
2300 Members
Founded in 1984

16113 **American Theological Library Association**
The American Theological Library Association
300 S Wacker Dr
Suite 2100
Chicago, IL 60606-6701

312-454-5100
888-665-2852; Fax: 312-454-5505
www.atla.com
Facebook, Twitter, LinkedIn, Youtube, RSS, Flickr

Teri Ehresman, President
Marsha Hoffman, 1st Vice President
Marianne Wolf-Astrauskas, 2nd Vice President
Ellen Crawford, Treasurer (Financial Adviser)
Gay Porter DeNileon, Secretary

Provides indexing services in these formats: online database, CD-ROM versions, magnetic tape for OPAC tapeload and print publications. ATLA Religion indexes in print include Religious Index One: Periodicals, Religion Index Two: Multi-Author Works, Index to Book Reviews, Research in Ministry an Index to D. Min. Project Reports and Theses.
2000 Members
Founded in 1937

16114 **Americans For Libraries Council**
Americans For Libraries Council
347 Congress Street
Boston, MA 02210

855-533-9335
800-542-1918; Fax: 646-336-6318
natlwritersassn@hotmail.com
www.lff.org

Sandy Whelchel, Executive Director

Americans for Libraries Council (ALC) is a national non-profit organization that advocates for libraries at the national level and develops and promotes programs aimed at realizing the potential of libraries in the 21st century.
2000 Members
Founded in 1937

16115 **Art Libraries Society of North America**
Art Libraries Society of North America
7044 South 13th Street
Box 11
Oak Creek, WI 53154

403-247-3001
800-817-0621; Fax: 414-768-8001
info@owaa.org
www.arlisna.org
Facebook, Twitter, LinkedIn, RSS Feeds

Lisa Ballard, President
Brett Prettyman, 1st Vice President
Phil Bloom, 2nd Vice President
Tom Sadler, Executive Director
Jessica Seitz, Membership & Conference Services

Membership organization for art libraries in the US and Canada.
2.4M Members
Founded in 1927

16116 **Asian/Pacific American Librarians**
Asian/Pacific American Librarians
PO Box 677593
Orlando, FL 32867

415-422-5379
www.apalaweb.org

Alan Di Benedetto, President
Stan Cohen, Vice President / Online Director
Liz Kassler, Treasurer
Chris McDonough, Membership Director
George Kamper, Communications Director

Librarians and information specialists of Asian Pacific descent and those interested in APA librarianship.
Founded in 1984

16117 **Association for Information Science and Technology**
8555 16th Street
Suite 850
Silver Spring, MD 20910

301-495-0900; Fax: 301-495-0810
asist@asist.org
www.asist.org
Facebook, Twitter, LinkedIn

Lydia Middleton, Executive Director
Terrence Curtiss, Director of Membership
Cathy L. Nash, Director of Meetings & Events

Professional development organization for the information science and technology industry.

16118 **Association for Library & Information Science Education**
Association for Library & Information
2150 N 107th St
Suite 205
Seattle, WA 98133

206-209-5267; Fax: 206-367-8777
sabew@sabew.org

www.alise.org
Facebook, Twitter, LinkedIn, RSS

Joanna Ossinger, President
Cory Schouten, VP
Kathleen Graham, Executive Director
Crystal Beasley, Membership
Renee McGivern, Director of conference sponsorship

Provides a forum for library educators to share ideas, discuss issues and seek solutions to common problems.
3200 Members
Founded in 1964

16119 **Association for Library Collections & Technical Services**
American Library Association
50 E Huron Street
Chicago, IL 60611

312-944-6780
800-545-2433; Fax: 312-280-5033
ala@ala.org
www.ala.org/alcts

Norm Medeiros, President
Keri Cascio, Executive Director
Keri A Cascio, Director at Large
Norm Medeiros, Director at Large
Timothy T Strawn, Director at Large

Division of the American Library Association.
5M Members
Founded in 1957

16120 **Association for Library Service to Children**
American Library Association
50 E Huron Street
Chicago, IL 60611

312-944-6780
800-545-2433; Fax: 312-944-7671
ala@ala.org
www.ala.org/alsc/

Andrew Medlar, President
Betsy Orsburn, Vice-President/President-Elect
Jenna Nemec-Loise, ALSC Division Councilor
Diane Foote, Fiscal Officer
Kristen Sutherland, Program Officer

A network of more than 4,000 children's and youth librarians, children's literature experts, publishers, education and library school faculty members, and other adults committed to improving and ensuring the future of the nation through exemplary library service to children, their families, and others who work with children.
3500 Members

16121 **Association for Population/Family Planning**
Family Health International Library
PO Box 13950
Research Triangle Park, NC 27709

919-447-7040; Fax: 215-898-2124
info@satw.org
www.aplici.org
Facebook, Twitter, LinkedIn

Paul Lasley, President
Barbara Orr, Vice President, Membership
Marla Schrager, Executive Director
John Kingzette, Membership Coordinator
Peggy Bendel, Secretary

Global network of communication, information and resource professionals dedicated to providing assistance and support to members and to other population and reproductive health colleagues, especially in developing nations.
Founded in 1955

16122 **Association for Recorded Sound Collections**
Association for Recorded Sound Collections
1299 University of Oregon
Eugene, OR 97403-1299

440-564-9340
www.arsc-audio.org
Facebook, Twitter, LinkedIn, Google+

Scott Tilley, President
Kit Adams, VP
JP Osterman, Secretary
Peggy Insula, Treasurer
Bill Allen, Communications & Publicity

Persons in broadcasting and recording industries, librarians, sound archivists, curators, private collectors and reviewers.
Cost: $40.00
Frequency: 2 Per Year
Circulation: 1000
Founded in 1982
Mailing list available for rent

16123 **Association of Christian Libraries**
PO Box 4
Cedarville, OH 45314

937-766-2255; Fax: 937-766-5499
www.acl.org
Facebook, Twitter, Youtube,RSS

Howard A. Rodman, President
David A. Goodman, Vice President
Aaron Mendelsohn, Secretary-Treasurer

Membership is composed of over 500 evangelical Christian librarians representing primarily evangelical institutions of higher education.
9500 Members
Founded in 1912

16124 **Association of College and Research Libraries**
American Library Association
50 E Huron Street
Chicago, IL 60611

312-944-6780
800-545-2433; Fax: 312-280-2520
acrl@ala.org
www.ala.org/acrl/

Ann Campion Riley, President
Irene M. H. Herold, ACRL Vice-President
Margot Sutton Conahan, Manager of Professional Development
David Connolly, Classified Advertising Coordinator
Kathryn Deiss, Content Strategist
13M Members
ISSN: 0099-0086
Founded in 1940

16125 **Association of Independent Information Professionals (AAIP)**
Association of Independent Information
8550 United Plaza Boulevard
Suite 1001
Baton Rouge, LA 70809

225-408-4400; Fax: 225-922-4611
www.aiip.org

Lori Packwood, Director

Provides a forum for information professionals to meet and exchange views.
Founded in 2000

16126 **Association of Jewish Libraries**
Association of Jewish Libraries
PO Box 1118
Teaneck, NJ 07666

201-371-3255
info@ablusa.org
www.jewishlibraries.org
Facebook, Twitter, RSS

Warren Scheidt, President
John D Bodnovich, Executive Director
Susan Day Duffy, Director of Trade Relations
Jessica Anders, Manager, Comm. & Public Relations
Warren Scheidt, Vice President

Promotes the advancement of the interests of Jewish libraries and publications of Jewish biographical interest.
15000 Members
Founded in 1933

16127 **Association of Mental Health Librarians**
Cedarcrest Regional Hospital, Medical Libary
One Beach Street
Suite 100
San Francisco, CA 94133

415-955-2157; Fax: 845-398-5551
society@asev.org
www.mhlib.org/
Facebook, Twitter, LinkedIn, Picasa

Mark Greenspan, President
Dan Howard, Executive Director
Nichola Hall, First Vice President
James Harbertson, Second Vice President
Tom Collins, Secretary/Treasurer

Provides a forum for the introduction of new audiovisual and printed materials in the field of mental health.
2400+ Members
Founded in 1950

16128 **Association of Moving Image Archivists**
1313 North Vine Street
Hollywood, CA 90028

323-463-1500; Fax: 323-463-1506
asbc@scisoc.org
www.amianet.org
Facebook, Twitter, LinkedIn, Pinterest

Jeffery L Cornell, President
Christina Schoenberger, Vice President
Amy Hope, Executive Officer
Barbara Mock, Vice President of Finance
Kelly A Tretter, Secretary

A non-profit professional association established to advance the field of moving image archiving by fostering cooperation among individuals and organization concerned with the acquistion, description, preservation, exhibition and use of moving image materials.
750 Members
Founded in 1934

16129 **Association of Research Libraries**
Association of Research Libraries
21 Dupont Circle NW
Suite 800
Washington, DC 20036

202-296-2296; Fax: 202-872-0884
info@beerinstitute.org
www.arl.org
Facebook, Twitter, YouTtube

Joe McClain, President
Mary Jane Saunders, VP & General Counsel

Nonprofit organization striving to shape and influence forces affecting the future of research libraries in the process of scholarly communication.
100 Members
Founded in 1986

16130 **Beta Phi Mu**
University of South Florida
PO Box 42139
Philadelphia, PA 19101

267-361-5018; Fax: - - 8
info@brewersassociation.org
www.beta-phi-mu.org
Facebook, Twitter, Youtube

Charlie Papazian, President
Bob Pease, Chief Operating Officer

Paul Gatza, Director
Erin Glass, Membership Coordinator
Katie Marisic, Federal Affairs Manager

Beta Phi Mu is an organization that recognizes and encourages scholastic achievement among library and information studies students.
1900 Members
Founded in 1978

16131 **Black Caucus of ALA**
Gladys Smiley Bell
PO Box 5837
Lib. Med. Serv., Rm 161, Kent State
Chicago, IL 60680

330-672-3045; Fax: 330-672-3964
www.bcala.org
Facebook, Twitter

Peter H Cressy, President

Association that supports black librarians. Holds annual meeting in conjunction with the American Library Association conference.
32 Members
Founded in 1973

16132 **Catholic Library Association**
Catholic Library Association
8550 United Plaza Blvd
Ste 1001
Baton Rouge, LA 70809

225-408-4417
855-739-1776; Fax: 312-739-1778
www.cathla.org
Facebook, Twitter, YouTube, flickr, RSS

Anthony Perrone, International President
William T. McDonough, Executive Vice President, UFCW
Patrick J. O'Neill, International Secretary-Treasurer
Stuart Appelbaum, Executive Vice President
Paul Meinema, Executive Vice President

International membership organization, providing its members professional development through educational and networking experiences, publications, scholarships and other services.
14M Members
Founded in 1979

16133 **Center for Children's Books**
Center for Children's Books
501 E Daniel Street
Champaign, IL 61820

217-244-9331; Fax: 217-333-5603
ccb.lis.illinois.edu
Facebook, Twitter, Youtube

Mark Alston, President
Steven Haynes, VP
Ray Ault, Secretary
Allison Babock, Treasurer
Dee Roberson, Executive Director

A crossroads for critical inquiry, professional training and educational outreach related to literature for youth from birth through adolescence. In partnership with The Bulletin of the Center for Children's Books, it aims to inspire and inform adults who connect young people with resources in person, in print, and online.
Founded in 1976

16134 **Center for Childrens Books**
Center for Children's Books
501 E Daniel Street
Champaign, IL 61820

217-244-9331; Fax: 217-333-5603
newyork@ice.it
ccb.lis.illinois.edu

Michelle Jones, Editor
Robert Luongo, Executive Director

16135 **Chief Officers of State Library Agencies**
Chief Officers of State Library Agencies
201 E Main Street
Suite 1405
Lexington, KY 40507

859-514-9151; Fax: 859-514-9166
iwfi@aol.com
www.cosla.org

Lucio Caputo, President
Vincent Giampaoco, VP

Association for directors of state libraries.
Founded in 1983

16136 **Chinese-American Librarians Association**
UCI Libraries
PO Box 19557
Irvine, CA 92623-9557

949-824-6836; Fax: 949-857-1988
www.cala-web.org
Facebook, Twitter, Youtube

Stephen Larson, Chairman
James M. Sgueo, President & CEO
Jerome J. Janicki, Sr. VP of Operations, COO
Patricia Kelly, Sr. VP of Administration, CFO
Steven L. Schmidt, SVP, Public Policy/Communications
175 Members
Founded in 1938

16137 **Church and Synagogue Library Association**
10157 SW Barbur Boulevard
Suite 102C
Portland, OR 97219

503-244-6919
800-542-2752; Fax: 503-977-3734
info@nbwa.org
www.cslainfo.org
Facebook, Twitter, Youtube, Flickr

Craig A. Purser, NBWA President & CEO
Kimberly McKinnish, CPA, Chief Financial Officer
Rebecca Spicer, SVP Comm. and Public Affairs
Paul Pisano, SVP Industry Affairs & Gen. Counsel
Patti Rouzie, VP, Membership and Meetings

Provides educational guidance in the establishment and maintenance of congregational libraries
Founded in 1938

16138 **Coalition for Networked Information**
21 Dupont Circle
Suite 800
Washington, DC 20036-1109

202-296-5098; Fax: 202-872-0884
www.cni.org

Robert P Koch, President / Chief Executive Officer
Nancy Light, Vice President, Communications
Steve Gross, Vice President, State Relations
Allison Jordan, VP, Environmental Affairs
Steve Hayes, VP, Finance and Administration

The Coalition for Networked Information is an organization dedicated to supporting the transformative promise of networked information technology for the advancement of scholarly communication and the enrichment of intellectual productivity.
80 Members
Founded in 1934

16139 **Council on Library and Information Resources**
Council on Library and Information Resources
1707 L Street NW, Suite 650
Washington, DC 20036-2124

202-939-4750; Fax: 202-600-9628
info@wssa.com
www.clir.org
Facebook, Twitter, LinkedIn, RSS

V. James Andretta, Jr., Chairman of the Board
Louis Healey, President
Howard Jacobs, Vice President
Heather Randolph, Director of Operations
Alison Leavitt, Managing Director

The mission of the Council on Library and Information Resources is to expand access to information, however recorded and preserved, as a public good.
460 Members
Founded in 1976

16140 **Council on Library/Media Technicians**
PO Box 256
Oxon Hill, MD 20748

202-231-3836; Fax: 202-231-3838
Info@wswa.org
http://colt.ucr.edu/
Facebook, Twitter, YouTube, RSS, Google+

Brien Fox, Chairman
Doug Epstein, Vice Chairman
Craig Wolf, President and CEO
Jim Rowland, VP, Government Affairs
Dawson Hobbs, Vice President, State Affairs

Supports library and media techicians by offering publications, training, networking and annual conference in conjunction with the American Library Association conference.
450 Members
Founded in 1943

16141 **Ethnic Employees of the Library of Congress**
6100 Eastview Street
Bethesda, MD 20817-6004
George E Perry, President

Promotes and strengthens brotherhood among ethnic employees and ethnic members of society.
Founded in 1973

16142 **Federal Library and Information Network**
Library of Congress
101 Independence Ave SE
Washington, DC 20540-4935

202-707-4800; Fax: 202-707-4818
help@apawood.org
www.loc.gov/flicc
Facebook, Twitter

Tom Temple, Chairman
Don Grimm, Vice Chairman
Edward Elias, President
Marilyn Thompson, Director of Marketing and Comm.
Tom Kositzky, Director, Field Services Rep.

Representatives of departments and agencies of the federal government.
160 Members
Founded in 1933
Mailing list available for rent

16143 **Federal and Armed Forces Libraries Roundtable**
American Library Association
50 E Huron Street
Chicago, IL 60611

312-944-6780
800-545-2433
ala@ala.org
www.ala.org

Amanda J. Wilson, President
Stephen V. Pomes, Vice President
Theresa Taylor, Armed Forces Director

Bianna E. Ine-Ryan, Armed Forces Director
Anne Harrison, Federal Director

Association for libraries and information services.

16144 Friends of Libraries (FOLUSA)
Association of Library Trustees, Advocates, Friend
50 E Huron Street
Chicago, IL 60611

312-944-6780
800-545-2433; Fax: 215-545-3821
jkalonick@ala.org
www.ala.org

Ed McBride, President
Sally Gardner Reed, Executive Director
Beth Nawalinski, Deputy Executive Director
Jillian Kalonick, Marketing/PR Specialist
Bette M Kozlowski, Treasurer

Encourages the development of excellent library service to all residents of the US. Aids in forming local and state, friends branches in academic and special libraries.
1.8M Members
Founded in 1979

16145 Herbert Hoover Presidential Library Association
302 Park Side Drive
PO Box 696
West Branch, IA 52358

319-643-5327
800-828-0475; Fax: 319-643-2391
afa@fiberboard.org
www.hooverassociation.org
Twitter

Rina P. McGuire, President
Jim Pieczynski, VP
Louis E. Wagner, Executive Director
William C. Ives, Legal Counsel
Blair Ruzicka, Secretary/Treasurer
7 Members
Founded in 1990

16146 Insurance Library Association of Boston
Insurance Library
156 State St
Boston, MA 02109-2584

617-227-2087; Fax: 617-723-8524
info@afandpa.org
www.insurancelibrary.org
Facebook, Twitter, LinkedIn, Youtube

Mark R. Gardner, Chairman
Mark W. Kowlzan, President and CEO
Linda Massman, Second Vice Chairman
Samuel Kerns, VP, Administration and CFO
Chuck Fuqua, Executive Director, Strategic Comm.

Founded in 1887, the Insurance Library Association of Boston is a resource for and provider of literature, information services, and quality professional education for the insurance industry and related interests. The Association offers a wide variety of research services and materials. The collection includes contemporary and historical versions of books, pamphlets, articles and reference materials in all areas of the insurance industry.
550 Members
Founded in 1993
Mailing list available for rent

16147 Interagency Council on Information
American Nurses Association Library
8515 Georgia Avenue
Suite 400
Silver Spring, MD 20910-3492

301-628-5143; Fax: 301-628-5008
info@forestfoundation.org
www.icirn.org
Facebook, Twitter

Kenneth Stewart, Chairman
Connie Best, Vice-Chair
Nathan Truitt, Vice President of Development
Scott Smiley, Vice President, Finance
Kathy McGlauflin, SVP, Project Learning Tree

To esablish an effective use of information resources available to the nursing community, and to advance the profession through the promotion and use of its literature.
120 Members

16148 International Association of Aquatic & Marine Science Libraries
The International Association of Aquatic and Marin
2030 S Marine Science Drive
Newport, OR 97365

772-460-9977
brian.voss@noaa.gov
www.iamslic.org
Facebook, Twitter, YouTube

Ann Nichols, Chair
Scott Steen, President & CEO
Matthew Boyer, Vice President, Individual Giving
Peter Hutchins, VP/COO
Greg Meyer, VP, Corporate Partnerships

Encourages members to exchange scientific and technical information and explore issues of mutual concern. Conducts workshops about on line databases.
Founded in 1990

16149 International Association of School Librarianship
65 E. Wacker Place
Suite 1900
Chicago, IL 60601-7246

814-474-1115; Fax: 312-419-8950
www.iasl-online.org/

Michael Snow, Executive Director
An Di H Nguyen, Manager of International Programs
Stefani Brown, International Program Coordinator

IASL provides an international forum for those people interested in promoting effective school library media programs as viable instruments in the educational process.

16150 Library Binding Institute
4440 PGA Blvd.
Ste. 600
Palm Beach Gardens, FL 33410

561-745-6821; Fax: 561-472-8401
www.lbibinders.org

Don DeVisser P.E., Executive VP
Skeet Rominger, Director Quality Services
Mike Schoen, Controller
Robert A Horlacher, Senior District Manager, Eastern
John Zachariou, Senior District Manager, Western

Members are firms binding books for libraries and their suppliers.
Founded in 1952

16151 Library Leadership and Management Association
American Library Association
50 E Huron Street
Chicago, IL 60611

312-944-6780
800-545-2433; Fax: 312-280-5033
lama@ala.org
www.ala.org/llama/

Jeff Steely, President
Kerry Ward, Executive Director
Fred Reuland, Program Officer
Jim Rettig, Treasurer

Works to improve and develop all aspects and levels of administration in all types of libraries.
5M Members
Founded in 1957

16152 Library and Information Technology Association
American Library Association
50 E Huron Street
Chicago, IL 60611

312-944-6780
800-545-2433
lita@ala.org
www.ala.org/lita/

Thomas P. Dowling, President
Jenny Levine, Executive Director
Mark A. Beatty, Staff Liaison
Melissa Prentice, Program Planning and Marketing
Valerie A Edmonds, Program Coordinator

16153 Major Orchestra Librarians' Association
MOLA
1530 Locust Street
PMB 154
Philadelphia, PA 19102

alsc@alsc.org
www.mola-inc.org

Thomas D Searles, President, Chief Lumber Inspector

International organization whose objectives include: to improve communication among orchestra librarians; present a unified voice in publisher relations; and assist librarians in providing better service to their orchestras.
Founded in 1924

16154 Medical Library Association
65 E Wacker Place
Suite 1900
Chicago, IL 60601-7246

312-419-9094; Fax: 312-419-8950
info@sportsbuilders.org
www.mlanet.org
Facebook, LinkedIn, Blog

Dan Wright, CFB, Chairman
Pete Smith, CTB, Tennis Division President
Troy Rudolph, Track Division President
Joe Covington, Jr, Indoor Division President
Jim Catella, CFB, CTB, Fields Division President

A nonprofit, educational organization that is a leading advocate for health sciences information professionals worldwide. Through it's programs and services, we provide lifelong educational opportunities, supports a knowledgebase of health information research and works with a global network of partners to promote the importance of quality information for improved health to the health care community and the public.
50 Members
Founded in 1965

16155 Mid-America Association of Law Libraries
MidAmerican Energy Holdings Company
Po Box 657
Des Moines, IA 50306-0657

515-242-4300
800-358-6265; Fax: 515-242-4261
jackson@purdue.edu
www.midamerican.com

Brian Brookshire, Executive Director
Laura Brookshire, Comm. and Membership Manager
Beverly Heidbreder, Accountant

Association for suppliers of law library equipment, supplies and services.
8 Members
Founded in 1912

16156 **Middle East Librarians' Association**
Middle East Librarians Association
Main Library
Santa Barbara, CA 93106

805-637-7749
www.mela.us
Facebook, Twitter, LinkedIn, RSS

Kris J. Ormseth, Office Managing Partner

Interested in aspects of librarianship that support the study or dissemination of information about the Middle East. Publishes a bulletin (semi-annually) that is distributed to members and subscriber institutions in North America, Europe, the Middle East, Asia and Africa.
5 Members
Founded in 1907

16157 **Mountain Plains Library Association**
14293 W. Center Drive
'
Lakewood, CO 80228

303-985-7795; Fax: 605-677-5488
email@awpa.com
www.mpla.us

Colin McCown, Executive Vice President

Purpose is to promote the development of librarians and libraries by providing significant educational and networking opportunities. The association meets annually in joint conferences with member stats on a rotational basis, and its governed by an elected board of representatives from each member state and a number of selections and roundtables representing interests and types of libraries. In addition to its board and officers, MPLA activities are carried out by a number of committees.
900 Members
Founded in 1904

16158 **Music Library Association**
1600 Aspen Commons
Suite 100
Middleton, WI 53562

608-836-5825; Fax: 608-831-8200
tom@appalachianwood.org
www.musiclibraryassoc.org

Tom Inman, President
Dinah Farrington, Administrative Assistant

Promotes growth and establishment in the use of music libraries, musical instruments and musical literature.
154 Members
Founded in 1926

16159 **National Association of Media & Technology Centers**
PO Box 9844
Cedar Rapids, IA 52409-9844

319-654-0608; Fax: 319-654-0609
info@awinet.org
www.namtc.org
Facebook, Twitter, LinkedIn, YouTube, Flickr

Philip Duvic, Executive Vice President
Greg Heuer, Chief Learning Officer
Cassey Gibson, Chief Member Services Officer
Beth Holcomb, Meeting and Event Planner
Katie Allen, Project Manager

The National Association of Media & Technology Centers is an organization committed to promoting leadership among its membership through networking, advocacy, and support activities that will enhance the equitable access to media, technology, and information services to educational committees. Current membership is over 20 million students.
4000 Members
Founded in 1954

16160 **National Church Library Association**
National Church Library Association
275 3rd St S
Suite 101A
Stillwater, MN 55082-5094

651-430-0770
Mail@WorldMillworkAlliance.com
Twitter, LinkedIn

Joe Bayer, President
Dave Ondrasek, First Vice President
Timothy Lyons, Second Vice President
Rosalie Leone, Chief Executive Officer
Brian Welsh, Membership & Marketing Director

Non-profit support organization that endeavours to further the gospel through church libraries. New resources and support programs are always under development to serve the ever changing needs of the church librarian. Membership is open to individuals, churches or libraries of any denomination or size.
1200 Members
Founded in 1935

16161 **National Information Standards Organization**
3600 Clipper Mill Road
Suite 302
Baltimore, MD 21211

301-654-2512; Fax: 410-685-5278
www.niso.org
Facebook, Twitter, LinkedIn

Wade Gregory, President
Archie Thompson, VP
Angelo Gangone, Executive Vice President
Amy Bartz, Fair Sales Director
Nancy Fister, Education & Conference Director

A non-profit association accredited by the American National Standards Institute, identifies, develops, maintains, and publishes technical standards to manage information in our changing and ever-more digital environment.
425 Members
Founded in 1979

16162 **National Library Service for the Blind**
Library of Congress
1291 Taylor Street, NW
Washington, DC 20542

202-707-5100
800-424-8567; Fax: 202-707-0712
info@capital-lumber.com
www.loc.gov/nls
Facebook, Twitter, LinkedIn, Pinterest

Dan Merrill, Division Manager
Bill Bieker, Sales Manager
ISSN: 0363-3805
Founded in 1948
Mailing list available for rent

16163 **National Media Market**
National Media Market
PO Box 87410
Tucson, AZ 85754-7410

520-743-7735; Fax: 800-952-0442
info@capital-lumber.com
www.nmm.net
Facebook, Twitter, LinkedIn, Pinterest

Matt Yates, Branch Manager
Darren Henderson, Operations Manager
Bill Butner, Sales Manager
Cindy DeLand, Office Manager
Phillip Floyd, Account Manager

Presents an exceptional opportunity for media professionals who purchase for public libraries, universities, media/technology centers and educational broadcasting to screen the newst and best quality motion medis from fifty-five prominent producers and distributors.
Founded in 1999

16164 **New England Library Association**
New England Library Association
55 North Main Street, Unit 49
Belchertown, MA 01007

413-813-5254; Fax: 978-282-1304
info@cedarbureau.com
www.nelib.org
Facebook, Twitter

Kent Gibson, Chairman
Ed Watkins, Vice-chairman
Terry Kost, Secretary-Treasurer
Lynne Christensen, MBA, CAE, Director of Operations
Barbara Enns, Accountant

Promotes excellence in library services to the people of New England and advances the leadership role of it's members. Holds an annual conference.
350 Members
Founded in 1915

16165 **Public Library Association**
Public Library Association
50 E Huron Street
Chicago, IL 60611-5295

312-280-5752
800-545-2433; Fax: 312-280-5029
pla@ala.org
www.ala.org/pla
Facebook

Vailey Oehlke, President
Barb Macikas, Executive Director
Julianna Kloeppel, Program Director
Melissa Faubel Johnson, CMP, Meeting & Special Events Planner
Mary Hirsh, Project Manager

Exists to provide a diverse program of communications and programming for its members and others interested in the advancment of public libaries.
Founded in 1944

16166 **Reference and User Services Association**
American Library Association
50 E Huron St
Chicago, IL 60611-2729

312-280-4395
800-545-2433; Fax: 312-944-8085
rusa@ala.org

Susan Hornung, Executive Director
Andrea Hill, Manager, Web Services
Leighann Wood, Membership Assistant
Marianne Braverman, Marketing & Programs Manager

Reference and User Services Association is responsible for stimulating and supporting excellence in the delivery of general library services and materials to adults, and the provision of reference and information services, collection development, and resource sharing for all ages, in every type of library.
5000 Members
Founded in 1876

16167 **Society of American Archivists**
17 North State Street
Suite 1425
Chicago, IL 60602

312-606-0722
866-722-7858; Fax: 312-606-0728
admin@decorativesurfaces.org
www2.archivists.org/

Jackson Morrill, President
Donald Bisson, VP, Gov. and Industry Affairs
Jeannie Ervin, VP, Membership and Administration

Gary Heroux, Vice President, Product Acceptance
Allyson O'Sullivan, Director of Marketing

Association for those interested in archival theory and practice in North America.
232 Members
Founded in 1960

16168 **Southeastern Library Association**
P.O. Box 950
Rex, GA 30273

678-466-4334; Fax: 678-466-4349
www.selaonline.org/

James Mathers, President
Larry R Frye, Executive Director

For over 60 years, the Association has been a unifying force strong enough to influence legislation and to attract foundation and federal funds for regional library projects. The accomplishments of the Association include 2 regional library surveys; the adoption of school library standards; the establishment of state library agencies and the position of state school library supervisor; the founding of library schools; the sponsoring of a variety of informative workshops.
15 Members
Founded in 1933

16169 **Special Libraries Association**
331 S Patrick St
Alexandria, VA 22314-3501

703-647-4900; Fax: 703-647-4901
license@landmobile.com
www.sla.org
Facebook, Twitter

Kevin Mc Carthy, President

International association of information professionals who work in special libraries serving business, research, government and institutions that produce specialized information.
600 Members
Founded in 1947

16170 **State University of New York Librarians Association**
Office of Library & Information Services
SUNY Plaza
Albany, NY 12246

518-443-5577; Fax: 518-443-5358
info@forestlandowners.com
www.sunyla.org
Facebook, Twitter

Joe Hopkins, President
Scott P. Jones, Chief Executive Officer
Susan Johnson Klco, Director of Administration
Kent Sole, Director of Development
Katelin Baker, Marketing Coordinator

Statewide professional librarian organization.
10500 Members
Founded in 1941

16171 **Substance Abuse Librarians and Information**
Substance Abuse Librarians & Information Specialis
PO Box 9513
Berkeley, CA 94709-0513

510-865-6225; Fax: 510-865-2467
info@forestprod.org
www.salis.org
Facebook, Twitter, LinkedIn

Maureen Puettman, President
David DeVallance, Vice President
Stefan A. Bergmann, Executive Vice President

Provides professional development and exchange of information and concerns about access to and dissemination of information on substance abuse.
Founded in 1947

16172 **Theatre Library Association**
40 Lincoln Center Plaza
New York, NY 10023

friendsofthetrees@yahoo.com
www.tla-online.org

Michael Pilarski, Founder and Director

Supports librarians and archivists affiliated with theatre, dance, performance studies, popluar entertainment, motion picture and broadcasting collections. Promotes professional best practices in acquistion, organization, access and preservation of performing arts resources in libraries, archives, museums, private collections, and the digital environment.
Founded in 1978

16173 **United for Libraries**
600 Eagleview Boulevard
Suite 300
Exton, PA 19341

312-280-2161
800-545-2433; Fax: 484-698-7868
united@ala.org
www.ala.org/united

Beth Nawalinski, Executive Director
Jillian Wentworth, Manager of Marketing & Membership

United for Libraries: The Association of Library Trustees, Advocates, Friends and Foundations, is a division of the American Library Association with group members representing hundreds of thousands of library supporters. United for Libraries supports those who govern, promote, advocate, and fundraise for libraries, and brings together library trustees, advocates, friends, and foundations into a partnership that creates a powerful force for libraries in the 21st century.
4000 Members
Founded in 1979

16174 **Urban Libraries Council**
1333 H Street, NW
Suite 1000 West
Washington, DC 20005

202-750-8650; Fax: 312-676-0950
jackhillman@woodtank.com
www.urbanlibraries.org

Jack Hillman, Company Contact

Works to strengthen public libraries as an essential part of urban life. Serves as a forum for research widely recognized and used by public and prrivate sector leaders.
Founded in 1854

Newsletters

16175 **AASL Presidential Hotline**
American Library Association
50 E Huron St
Chicago, IL 60611-2788

312-280-2518
800-545-2433
kfiels@ala.org
www.ala.org

Keith Michael Fiels, Executive Director

School library media association news.
Frequency: Monthly
Founded in 1951

16176 **Corporate Library Update**
Reed Business Information
30 Technology Parkway South
Suite 100
Norcross, GA 30092

646-746-6400
800-424-3996; Fax: 646-756-7583
webmaster@reedbusiness.com
www.reedbusiness.com

John Poulin, CEO
Lynn Blumenstein, Senior Editor
Susan DiMattia, Editor
Cost: $69.95
Frequency: Fortnightly
Circulation: 2500

16177 **Libraries Alive**
National Church Library Association
275 3rd St S
Suite 101A
Stillwater, MN 55082-5094

651-430-0770
Facebook

Sue Benish, Executive Director
Chuck Mann, President Board of Directors

Features informative articles, reviews of books and other media, a sharing of ideas, Internet resources, chapter news, news of authors and upcoming regional and national workshops.
Frequency: Quarterly

16178 **Library Hotline**
Library Journal/School Library Journal
360 Park Ave S
New York, NY 10010-1710

646-746-6819
800-446-6551; Fax: 646-746-6734
www.libraryjournal.com

Ron Shank, Publisher
Justin Torres, Production Manager
Lynn Blumenstein, Senior Editor
Carol Batt, COO
Patty Braden, Director
Cost: $115.00
Frequency: Weekly
Founded in 1876

16179 **MLA News**
Medical Library Association
65 E Wacker Place
Suite 1900
Chicago, IL 60601-7298

312-419-9094; Fax: 312-419-8950
info@mlahq.org
www.mlanet.org

Lynanne Fielen, Director Publications
Carla Funk, Editor
Lynanne Fielen, Circulation Manager
Elizabeth Rodriguez, Graphic Designer

Covers MLA programs and services as well as the medical librarian profession in general.
Cost: $58.00
Frequency: Monthly
Founded in 1898
Mailing list available for rent

16180 **Marcato**
MOLA/Editor
1530 Locust Street
PMB 154
Philadelphia, PA 19102

202-416-8131; Fax: 202-416-8132
sfriedman@kennedy-center.org
www.mola-inc.org

Shelley Friedman, Editor
Gordon Rowley, Treasurer
Elena Lence Talley, President

Newsletter of Major Orchestra Librarians' Association.
Cost: $20.00
Frequency: Quarterly

16181 **Marketing Treasures**
Chris Olson & Associates

857 Twin Harbor Drive
Arnold, MD 21012-1027

410-647-6708; Fax: 410-647-0415
www.chrisolson.com

Christine Olson, Publisher

Provinding creative ideas, helpful hints and insights on how libraries can promote thier services
6 Pages
Frequency: Monthly
Circulation: 1000
Founded in 1987
Printed in 2 colors on matte stock

16182 Report on Literacy Programs
Business Publishers
8737 Colesville Road
Suite 1100
Silver Spring, MD 20910-3928

301-876-6300
800-274-6737; Fax: 301-589-8493
custserv@bpinews.com
www.bpinews.com

Dave Speights, Editor
Leonard A Eiserer, Publisher
Beth Early, Operations Director

Covers all aspects of literacy including legislation, funding, training programs, important conferences, job skills and much more.
Cost: $317.00
Founded in 1963

16183 Research Library Issues
Association of Research Libraries
21 Dupont Circle NW
Suite 800
Washington, DC 20036

202-296-2296; Fax: 202-872-0884
www.arl.org
Facebook, Twitter, LinkedIn, Flickr, YouTube

Charles B Lowry, Executive Director
Prudence S. Adler, Associate Executive Director
Sue Baughman, Deputy Executive Director
Julia Blixrud, Assistant Executive Director
Mary Jane Brooks, Assistant Executive Director

Member representatives
Frequency: Bi-Monthly
ISSN: 1947-4911

16184 State University of New York Librarians Association
Office of Library & Information Services
SUNY Plaza
Albany, NY 12246

518-443-5577; Fax: 518-443-5358
drewwe@morrisville.edu
www.sunyla.org
Facebook, Twitter

Wilfred Drew, President
John Schumacher, Electronic Resources Coordinator

Provides news, notes and information from SUNY campus libraries.
Frequency: 2-3/Year

16185 Technicalities
Westport Publishing
802 Broadway Street
Kansas City, MO 64105

816-842-0641

Brian Alley, Editor

A professional journal presenting discussion, opinions, and reviews on library-management topics. Typical issues include articles ranging from computer applications, on-line public access catalogs, library budgets, collection building, book reviews, automation, software, library marketplace trends, and the Library of Congress. Articles are indexed in Library Literature and LISA: Library Information Science Abstracts and are available on microfilm from UMI.
Cost: $ 47.00
16 Pages
Frequency: Monthly
Circulation: 700
Mailing list available for rent
Printed in one color on matte stock

16186 Urban Libraries Council Exchange Letter
1603 Orrington Avenue
Suite 1080
Evanston, IL 60201

847-866-9999; Fax: 847-866-9989
info@urbanlibraries.org
www.urbanlibraries.org/

Eleanor Rodger, President/CEO
Linda Crismond, Editor

Newsletter for public libraries in cities with over 100,000 people. Free to members, also available without membership.
Cost: $50.00
150 Pages
Circulation: 6000
Founded in 1971

Magazines & Journals

16187 AALL Spectrum
American Association of Law Libraries
105 W Adams Street
Suite 3300
Chicago, IL 60603

312-939-4764; Fax: 312-431-1097
support@aall.org
www.aallnet.org
Facebook, Twitter

Mark Estes, Editorial Director
Hillary Baker, Marketing and Communications
Kate Hagan, Executive Director
Kim Rundle,, Executive Assistant
Emily Feltren,, Director of Government Relations

Publishes substantive, well-written articles on topics of real interest to law librarians, as well as news about the American Association of Law Libraries, including its chapters, committees and Special Interest Sections
Cost: $ 75.00

16188 Advanced Technology/Libraries
GK Hall & Company
1239 Broadway
Suite 1601
New York, NY 10001-4327

212-685-0602; Fax: 212-654-4751
sales@gkimport.com
www.gkimport.com

Dina Groudan, President
Audrey Ismal, Owner

Concise, practical information on the advances in development, implementation and use of library automation. Articles cover new products, new services, legislation and grant information.
Cost: $95.00
Frequency: Monthly

16189 American Archivist
Society of American Archivists
527 S Wells Street
5th Floor
Chicago, IL 60607-3922

312-922-0140; Fax: 312-347-1452
www.archivists.org

Susan Fox, Executive Director
Philip B Eppard, Editor
Teresa Brinati, Director of Publications

Offers information and essays on archival theory and practice in North America.
Cost: $85.00
Circulation: 4800+
Founded in 1936

16190 American Libraries
American Library Association
50 E Huron St
Chicago, IL 60611-2788

312-280-2518
800-545-2433
customerservice@ala.org
www.ala.org

Claire Knowles, Manager
Carla D Hayden, President

Library development news.
Cost: $60.00
Frequency: Monthly
Founded in 1876

16191 Book Report: Magazine for Secondary School Librarians
Linworth Publishing
480 East Wilson Bridge Road
Suite L
Worthington, OH 43085

614-436-7107
800-786-5017; Fax: 614-436-9490
linworth@linworthpublishing.com
www.linworth.com

Marlene Woo-Lun, Publisher
Amy Robinson, Marketing Manager

In-depth articles, helpful hints, and reviews on books, software, videos, and CD-Roms for secondary school librarians.
Cost: $49.00
105 Pages
Circulation: 15000
Founded in 1981
Printed in 4 colors on glossy stock

16192 Booklist
American Library Association
50 E Huron St
Chicago, IL 60611-2788

312-280-2518
800-545-2433
customerservice@ala.org
www.ala.org

Claire Knowles, Manager

To provide a guide to current library materials in many formats appropriate for use in public libraries and school library media centers.
Cost: $89.95
Circulation: 25000
Founded in 1876

16193 Bulletin of Bibliography
Greenwood Publishing Group
88 Post Road W
P O Box 5007
Westport, CT 06881-5007

203-226-3571
800-225-5800; Fax: 203-226-6009
www.greenwood.com

Bernard McTigue, Editor-in-Chief
Gerry Katz, Executive Editor
Naomi Caldwell Wood, Author

Offers bibliographies in humanities and social sciences.
Cost: $125.00
100 Pages
Frequency: Quarterly
Circulation: 1000
ISSN: 0190-745X
Printed in 2 colors on matte stock

16194 Bulletin of the Center for Children's Books
501 E Daniel Street
MC-493
Champaign, IL 61820

217-244-0324; Fax: 217-244-3302

Deborah Stevenson, Editor
Marlow Welshon, Dean

Reviews of children's books for librarians, teachers, booksellers and parents.
Cost: $50.00
34 Pages
Frequency: Monthly
Circulation: 6500
Founded in 1893

16195 CD-ROM Librarian
Mecklermedia Corporation
11 Ferry Lane W
Westport, CT 06880-5808

FAX 203-454-5840

Alan Meckler, Editor

A periodical intended for the library professional.
Cost: $80.00
Frequency: Monthly
Founded in 1986

16196 Catholic Library World
Catholic Library Association
205 W Monroe St, Ste 314
Pittsfield, MA 01201-5178

413-443-2252; Fax: 413-442-2252
cla@cathla.org
www.cathla.org
Facebook

Nancy K Schmidtmann, President
Malachy R McCarthy, VP
Jean R Bostley SSJ, Executive Director

Articles and news of interest to the library profession. Extensive section of book and media reviews
Frequency: Quarterly
ISSN: 0008-820X

16197 Choice
Association of College and Research Libraries
575 Main Street
Suite 300
Middletown, CT 06457

800-545-2433
acrl@ala.org
www.ala.org/acrl/choice

Lori Goetsch, President
Irving Rockwood, Publisher
Francine Graf, Editorial Director
Lisa Gross, Information/Production Manager
Rita Balasco, Choice Reviews

Publishes reviews of books, internet sites, and microcomputer software suitable for college and university libraries.
Cost: $280.00
Frequency: Monthly
Circulation: 5000
Founded in 1938

16198 Congregational Libraries Today
Church and Synagogue Library Association
10157 SW Barbur Boulevard
Suite 102C
Portland, OR 97219-4055

503-244-6919
800-542-2752; Fax: 503-977-3734
www.cslainfo.org
Facebook, Twitter

Sue Poss, Publications Editor
Marcia Trauernicht, President

Contains news about CSLA and its chapters, feature stories about congregational libraries and librarians, promotion ideas, information on using computers and the internet in the library, and reviews of books, videos, CDs, and audiotapes for adults and children.
Cost: $40.00
800 Members
28 Pages
Frequency: Quarterly
Founded in 1967

16199 Information Retrieval & Library Automation
Lomond Publications
PO Box 88
Mount Airy, MD 21771-0088

202-362-1361; Fax: 202-362-6156

Thomas Hattery, Publisher

New technology, products and equipment that improve information systems and library services, for science, social, social science, law, medicine, academic institutions and the public.
Cost: $75.00
Frequency: Monthly

16200 Journal of the Medical Library Association
Medical Library Association
65 E Wacker Drive
Suite 1900
Chicago, IL 60601-7298

312-419-9094
800-462-6420; Fax: 312-419-8950
www.mlanet.org

Lynanne Feilen, Director Publication
Carla J Funk, Executive Director
Susan C Talmage, Editorial Assistant
Bleu caldwell, Production Assistant
Barbara Redmond, Advertising Coordinator
Cost: $163.00
Frequency: Quarterly
Mailing list available for rent

16201 Knowledge Quest
American Library Association
50 E Huron St
Chicago, IL 60611-2788

312-280-2518
800-545-2433
kfiels@ala.org
www.ala.org

Keith Michael Fiels, Executive Director
Andria Parker, Marketing
Vickie William, Circulation Manager

Articles on teaching, learning process, ideas and information to prepare students for life long learning.
Cost: $40.00
Circulation: 5000
ISSN: 1094-9046
Founded in 1879
Printed in 4 colors on matte stock

16202 Library Bookseller
PO Box 9544
Berkeley, CA 94709-544
Scott Saifer, Publisher
Gail Russin, Editor

A journal focusing on suppliers to libraries.
Cost: $100.00
36 Pages

16203 Library Journal
Media Source
160 Varick Street
11th Floor
New York, NY 10013

646-380-0700; Fax: 646-380-0756
ljinfo@mediasourceinc.com
www.libraryjournal.com

Ron Shank, Publisher
Francine Fialkoff, Editor-in-Chief
Brian Kenney, Editorial Director
Bette-Lee Fox, Managing Editor
Rebecca Miller, Executive Editor

Provides groundbreaking features and analytical news reports covering technology, management, policy and other professional concerns to public, academic and institutional libraries. Evaluates 8000 reviews annually of books, ebooks, audiobooks, videos/DVDs, databases, systems and websites.
Cost: $141.00
Circulation: 17936
Founded in 1876
Printed in 4 colors on glossy stock

16204 Library Resources & Technical Services
American Library Association
50 E Huron St
Chicago, IL 60611-2788

312-280-2518
800-545-2433
kfiels@ala.org
www.ala.org

Keith Michael Fiels, Executive Director
Steven L Hofman, Circulation Manager
Andrea Parker Parker, Marketing Head

Offers articles to technical service librarians on acquisitions, cataloging and classification.
Cost: $30.00
Frequency: Bi-annually
Circulation: 60000
Founded in 1951

16205 Library Software Review
Sage Publications
Vanderbilt University
419 21st Avenue S
Nashville, TN 37240-0001

615-343-6094; Fax: 615-343-8834
info@sagepub.com
www.sagepub.com

Marshall Breeding, Editor

Provides the library professional with information necessary to make intelligent software evaluation, procurement, integration and installation decisions. Issues review software and software books and periodicals.
Cost: $52.00
Frequency: Quarterly
Circulation: 1M

16206 Library Talk: Magazine for Elementary School Librarians
Linworth Publishing
480 E Wilson Bridge Road
Suite L
Worthington, OH 43085-2372

614-436-7107
800-786-5017; Fax: 614-436-9490
linworth@linworthpublishing.com
www.linworth.com

Marlene Woo-Lun, Publisher
Amy Robinson, Marketing Manager
Carol Simpson, Consulting Editor

In-depth articles, helpful hints, and reviews on books, software, and CD-ROMS for elementary school library media and technology specialist.
Cost: $49.00
68 Pages
Circulation: 10000

Founded in 1988
Printed in 4 colors on glossy stock

16207 **Library Trends**
University of Illinois Press
1325 S Oak St
Champaign, IL 61820-6975

217-333-0950
866-244-0626; Fax: 217-244-8082
journals@uillinois.edu
www.press.uillinois.edu

Willis Regier, Director
Ann Lowry, Journals Manager
Cheryl Jestis, Manager
Pat Hoefling, Marketing and Sales Director

A journal which offers a medium for current thought and information in the library field.
Cost: $75.00
Frequency: Quarterly
Circulation: 2600
ISBN: 0-252725-23-9
Founded in 1918

16208 **Medical Reference Services Quarterly**
Taylor & Francis
325 Chestnut Street
Suite 800
Philadelphia, PA 19106

800-354-1420; Fax: 215-625-2940
www.tandf.co.uk

M Sandra Wood, Editor

An essential working tool for medical and health sciences librarians. Covers topics of current interest and practical value in the areas of reference in medicine and related specialities, the biomedical sciences, nursing and allied health.
Cost: $110.00
Frequency: Quarterly
ISSN: 0276-3869
Founded in 1975

16209 **Reference and User Services Quarterly (RUSQ)**
American Library Association
50 E Huron St
Chicago, IL 60611-2788

312-280-2518
800-545-2433; Fax: 312-664-7459
customerservice@ala.org
www.ala.org

Keith Michael Fiels, Executive Director
Andrea Parker, Marketing Specialist
Steven L Hofmann, Manager, Communications
Connie Van Fleet, Editor in Chief

News of interest to reference and adult services librarians.
Cost: $60.00
Frequency: Quarterly
Circulation: 6,246
Founded in 1951

16210 **School Library Journal**
Media Source
160 Varick Street
11th Floor
New York, NY 10013

646-380-0700; Fax: 646-380-0756
sljinfo@mediasourceinc.com

Ron Shank, Publisher
Francine Fialkoff, Editor-in-Chief
Brian Kenney, Editorial Director
Bette-Lee Fox, Managing Editor
Rebecca Miller, Executive Editor

Provides groundbreaking features and analytical news reports covering technology, management, policy and other concerns to school libraries. Evaluates 8000 reviews annually of books, ebooks, audiobooks, videos/DVDs, databases, systems and websites.
Frequency: Monthly
Circulation: 100000
Founded in 1954
Printed in 4 colors on glossy stock

16211 **School Library Media Research**
American Library Association
50 E Huron St
Chicago, IL 60611-2788

312-280-2518
800-545-2433
kfiels@ala.org
www.ala.org

Keith Michael Fiels, Executive Director

Available online only. Current developments in the media and library field. Evaluates the most currently available print and nonprint materials for library media centers.

16212 **Science and Technology Libraries**
Taylor & Francis
325 Chestnut Street
Suite 800
Philadelphia, PA 19106

800-354-1420; Fax: 215-625-2940
www.tandf.co.uk

Tony Stankus, Editor-in-Chief

A peer-reviewed, scholarly journal covering all ascpects of the profession as librarians serving science, engineering, clinical investigation, and agriculture.
Cost: $110.00
Frequency: Quarterly
ISSN: 0194-262X
Founded in 1978

16213 **Today's Librarian**
Virgo Publishing LLC
3300 N Central Ave
Suite 300
Phoenix, AZ 85012-2532

480-990-1101; Fax: 480-990-0819
mikes@vpico.com
www.vpico.com

Jenny Bolton, President
John Siefert, CEO
Kelly Ridley, Executive VP, CFO
Heather Wood, VP, Human Resources
Jon Benninger, VP, Health & Nutrition Network

Of interest to librarians and media professionals.

16214 **Video Librarian**
Video Librarian
3435 NE Nine Boulder Drive
Poulsbo, WA 98370

360-626-1259; Fax: 360-626-1260
vidlib@videolibrarian.com
www.videolibrarian.com

Randy Pitman, Publisher
Anne Williams, Graphic Designer
Carol Kaufman, Graphic Designer

Offers video reviews and news for public, school, academic and special libraries.
Cost: $64.00
56 Pages
Circulation: 2000
ISSN: 0887-6851
Founded in 1986
Printed in 4 colors on glossy stock

Trade Shows

16215 **ACL Conference**
Association of Christian Librarians
PO Box 4
Cedarville, OH 45314

937-766-2255; Fax: 937-766-5499
info@acl.org
www.acl.org
Facebook, Twitter, Delicious

Jo Ann Rhodes, President
Alice Ruleman, VP
Janelle Mazelin, Executive Director
Sheila O. Carlblom, Treasurer
Carrie Beth Lowe, Secretary

The purpose of the conference is to provide professional information, promote Christian philosophy and ethic of librarianship, provide an opportunity for exchange of ideas and promote service to the academic community worldwide
550 Members
Founded in 1954

16216 **ALA National Conference on Asian Pacific American Librarians**
American Library Association
50 E Huron Street
Chicago, IL 60611

800-545-2433
customerservice@ala.org
www.ala.org

16217 **American Association of School Librarians National Conference & Exhibition**
50 E Huron Street
Chicago, IL 60611-5295

312-280-4386
800-545-2433; Fax: 312-664-7459
customerservice@ala.org
www.ala.org/aasl

Judy King, Director Program Development
Lissa Salvatierra, Meeting Planner

Biennial continuing education conference and 300-500 exhibits of equipment, supplies and services for school library media centers, including print and nonprint materials and other equipment.
3500 Attendees
Frequency: October
Founded in 1876

16218 **American Indian Library Association Conference**
American Indian Library Assn Univ. of Pittsburgh
207 Hillman Library
Pittsburgh, PA 15260

412-621-4470; Fax: 412-648-1245
http://www.ailanet.org

Lisa A Mitten

Annual conference and exhibits relating to the development, maintenance and cultural information services on reservations and in communities of Native Americans and Native Alaskans.
Founded in 1979

16219 **American Library Association Annual Conference**
American Library Association
50 E Huron Street
Chicago, IL 60611

800-545-2433
customerservice@ala.org
www.ala.org

Loriene Roy, President
Keith Michael Fiels, Executive Director

Annual meeting and exhibits of books, periodicals, reference works, audio visual equipment, films, data processing services, computer hardware and software, library equipment and supplies.

16220 **American Library Association Midwinter Meeting**
American Library Association

50 E Huron Street
Chicago, IL 60611

800-545-2433
customerservice@ala.org
www.ala.org

Loriene Roy, President
Keith Michael Fiels, Executive Director

Annual meeting and 418 exhibits of books, periodicals, reference works, audio visual equipment, films, data processing services, computer hardware and software, library equipment and supplies.

16221 **Art Libraries Society of North America Annual Conference**
Art Libraries Society of North America
4101 Lake Boone Trail
Suite 201
Raleigh, NC 27607-7506

919-518-1919
800-892-7547; Fax: 919-787-4916
arlisna@mercury.interpath.com

Annual conference and show of publishers, book dealers, library suppliers and visual resources suppliers.
500 Attendees
Founded in 1977

16222 **Association for Library & Information Science Education Annual Conference**
11250 Roger Bacon Drive
Suite 8
Reston, VA 20190-5202

703-360-0500; Fax: 703-435-4390
www.alise.org/index.shtml

John Budd, President
Deborah York, Executive Director
Frequency: January

16223 **Association for Population/Family Planning Libraries & Information Centers**
Assn for Population Family Planning Libraries
Surgical Contraception-79 Madison
New York, NY 10016

212-780-2687; Fax: 212-779-9439

William Record

Annual conference and exhibits for effective documentation, information systems and services in the field of population/family planning.

16224 **Association of College and Research Libraries**
American Library Association
50 E Huron Street
Chicago, IL 60611-5295

312-280-2511
800-545-2433; Fax: 312-280-2520
customerservice@ala.org
www.ala.org/acrl

Mary Ellen Davis, Executive Director

Two hundred exhibitors with computers and web products, audiovisual products, furniture and library equipment.
3000 Attendees
Frequency: Biennial
ISSN: 0099-0086
Founded in 1978
Mailing list available for rent

16225 **CSLA Conference**
Church and Synagogue Library Association
10157 SW Barbur Boulevard
Suite 102C
Portland, OR 97219-4055

503-244-6919
800-542-2752; Fax: 503-977-3734
csla@worldaccessnet.com
www.cslainfo.org
Facebook, Twitter

Judith Janzen, Administrator
Marcia Trauernicht, President
Frequency: Annual/July

16226 **Culture Keepers: Making Global Connections**
Black Caucus of the American Library Association
Newark Public Library
5 Washington Street
Newark, NJ 07101
973-961-2540; Fax: 973-522-4827

Dr. Alex Boyd

Biennial show and exhibits of books, journals and library products.

16227 **Federal and Armed Forces Libraries Roundtable Conference**
American Library Association
50 E Huron St
Chicago, IL 60611-2729

312-944-6780
800-545-2433; Fax: 312-944-8085
ala@ala.org
www.ala.org/faflrt/front

Emily Sheketoff, Executive Director

Annual conference and exhibits of equipment, supplies and services for libraries and information services.

16228 **International Association of Aquatic & Marine Science Libraries Conference**
Harbor Branch Oceanographic Institution
5600 US 1 N
Fort Pierce, FL 34946

800-333-4264; Fax: 772-465-2446

Annual conference and exhibits of equipment, supplies and services for marine-related libraries and information centers.
Frequency: October, Charleston

16229 **Mid-Atlantic Regional Library Federation**
South Maryland Regional Library
37 606 New Market Road
Charlotte Hall, MD 20622

301-884-0436

Katharine Hurrey, President

Offers exhibits by vendors who provide services and products useful to libraries and information brokers.
1M Attendees
Frequency: March

16230 **Mountain Plains Library Association Annual Conference**
Mountain Plains Library Association
University of SD-I D Weeks Library
Vermillion, SD 57069

FAX 605-677-5488

Annual conference and exhibits of publications and library equipment, supplies and services.
600 Attendees

16231 **New England Library Association Annual Conference**
New England Library Association
14 Main Street
Gloucester, MA 03031

978-820-0787; Fax: 978-282-1304
www.nelib.org

Mary Ann Rupert, Technology Manager
Barry Blaisdell, Manager

Annual show of publishers, distributors and suppliers of books, media, supplies, furniture, equipment, hardware, software and services used by libraries. Containing 160 booths and 130 exhibits.
1,000 Attendees
Frequency: October

16232 **Public Library Association National Conference**
Public Library Association
50 E Huron Street
Chicago, IL 60611-5295

312-280-5752
800-545-2433; Fax: 312-280-5029
pla@ala.org

Barb Macikas, Show Manager

Biennial show of 200 exhibitors of books and other equipment, supplies and services for libraries.
3500 Attendees
Frequency: March

16233 **Southeastern Library Association**
Combined Book Exhibit
P.O. Box 950
Rex, GA 30273

678-466-4334; Fax: 678-466-4349
http://selaonline.org/

This biennial conference, offers attendees from over 12 states. The convention offers exhibits, meetings and an open reception in the exhibit hall. The three biggest states, Georgia, North Carolina and South Carolina spend twice as much of expenditures on CD-ROM and 8% more on books than the national average, which makes this the perfect exhibition for sellers.
2.1M+ Attendees
Frequency: Fall

16234 **Special Libraries Association**
331 South Patrick St
Alexandria, VA 22314-3501

703-647-4900; Fax: 703-647-4901
janice@sla.org
www.sla.org

James Mears, Conference Manager
Janice Lschance, CEO

An international professional association of people working in special libraries serving institutions and organizations that use or produce specialized information.
6M Attendees
Frequency: June

Directories & Databases

16235 **Address List, Regional and Subregional Libraries for the Handicapped**
Library of Congress
101 Independence Avenue SE
Washington, DC 20540

202-707-4800
888-657-7323; Fax: 202-707-0712
nls@loc.gov
www.loc.gov/nls
Facebook, Twitter, LinkedIn

Kurt Cykle, Director
25 Pages
Frequency: Semi-Annual

ISSN: 0363-3805
Mailing list available for rent

16236 **American Library Association Handbook**
American Library Association
50 E Huron St
Chicago, IL 60611-2788
312-280-2518
800-545-2433
customerservice@ala.org
www.ala.org
Claire Knowles, Manager
Offers 56 regional groups comprised of libraries, trustees, librarians and others interested in the responsibilities of libraries in the educational and cultural needs of society.

16237 **American Library Directory**
Information Today
143 Old Marlton Pike
Medford, NJ 08055-8750
609-654-6266
800-300-9868; Fax: 609-654-4309
custserv@infotoday.com
www.infotoday.com
Thomas H Hogan, President
Roger R Bilboul, Chariman Of The Board
Detailed profiles for more than 35,000 public, academic, special, and government libraries and library related organizations in the US and Canada. These include addresses, phone and fax numbers, e-mail addresses, network participation, expenditures, holdings and special collections, key personnel, special services and more than 40 categories of library information in all. A two volume set.
Cost: $299.00
4000 Pages
ISBN: 1-573872-04-0
Mailing list available for rent

16238 **Association of Jewish Libraries Membership List**
Ramaz Upper School Library
60 E 78th St
New York, NY 10075-1838
212-517-2103
Ira Miller, Principal
Cost: $100.00
100 Pages
Frequency: Annual

16239 **BookQuest**
ABACIS
135 Village Queen Drive
Owings Mills, MD 21117-4470
FAX 410-581-0398
This database offers descriptions of book dealers' offerings and books being sought by libraries, dealers and collectors.
Frequency: Full-text

16240 **Chief Officers of State Library Agencies Directory**
Chief Officers of State Library Agencies
201 E Main St
Suite 1405
Lexington, KY 40507-2004
859-514-9151; Fax: 859-514-9166
www.cosla.org
Tracy Tucker, Executive Director
Directors, staff and consultants of state libraries.
Cost: $25.00
Frequency: Annual April

16241 **Computers in Libraries: Buyer's Guide & Consultants Directory Issue**
Mecklermedia Corporation
11 Ferry Lane W
Westport, CT 06880-5808
This comprehensive directory offers a list of suppliers of computer products and services for use in libraries.
Cost: $30.00
Frequency: Annual

16242 **DataLinx**
Faxon Company
1001 W Pines Road
Oregon, IL 61061-9507
815-732-9001
800-732-9001; Fax: 815-732-2132
www.faxon.com
This online system was established to provide technical support to libraries for serials acquisition and control.

16243 **Directory of Special Libraries and Information Centers**
Gale Research
27500 Drake Road
Farmington Hills, MI 48331-3535
248-699-4253
800-877-4253; Fax: 877-363-4253
gale.galeord@cengage.com
www.gale.cengage.com
Facebook, Twitter, Youtube
Patrick C Sommers, President
Provides detailed contact and descriptive information on subject-specific resource collections maintained by various government agencies, businesses, publishers, educational and non-profit organizations, and associations around the world.
3600 Pages
Frequency: Annual
ISBN: 1-414433-49-2

16244 **Directory of US Government: Depository Libraries**
Joint Committee on Printing, US Congress
1309 Longworth
Washington, DC 20515
202-225-8281; Fax: 202-225-9957
Directory of federal depository libraries, regional and select throughout the United States. Includes list of GPO bookstores.
91pp Pages
Frequency: Annual

16245 **EBSCONET**
EBSCO Publishing
Po Box 682
Ipswich, MA 01938-0682
978-356-1372
800-653-2726; Fax: 978-356-6565
http://www.ebsco.com
Timothy S Collins, President
This database provides technical support to libraries, information centers and purchasing departments for serials acquisitions and control.

16246 **Employment Sources in the Library and Information Professions**
National Center for Information Media & Technology
University of Hertfordshire, College Lane
Chicago, IL 60611
773-846-7300
customerservice@ala.org
www.ala.org
Directory of services to the industry.
140 Pages
Frequency: Annual

16247 **Gale Directory of Databases**
Gale/Cengage Learning
27500 Drake Road
Farmington Hills, MI 48331-3535
248-699-4253
800-877-4253; Fax: 877-363-4253
gale.galeord@cengage.com
www.gale.cengage.com
Facebook, Twitter, Youtube
Patrick C Sommers, President
Bob Romanick, Editor
Profiles thousands of databases available worldwide in a variety of formats. Entries include producer name and contact information, description, cost and more.
ISBN: 1-414420-79-X

16248 **Interlibrary Loan Policies Directory**
Neal-Schuman Publishers
100 William St
New York, NY 10038-5017
212-925-8650
800-584-2414; Fax: 212-219-8916
www.neal-schuman.com
Patricia Schuman, Owner
A brand new edition of the standard source of current information about the policies of over 1,425 academic, public and other libraries that offer books through interlibrary loans in the United States, Canada and Puerto Rico. Updated to include all the members of the Association of Research Libraries, Internet addresses, Ariel addresses and libraries that loan periodicals, government documents, microfilms, software, newspapers, media and foreign countries.
Cost: $119.95
800 Pages

16249 **Librarian's Yellow Pages**
Garance
7823 Stratford Road
Bethesda, MD 20814
240-354-1281
www.lyponline.com
A database offering information on products and services intended for use by libraries and information centers in the United States.

16250 **Library Fax/Ariel Directory**
CBR Consulting Services
PO Box 22421
Kansas City, MO 64113-0421
Over 10,500 libraries with telefacsimile services in the United States and Canada and worldwide.
Cost: $49.50
475 Pages
Frequency: Annual

16251 **Library Literature & Information Science**
HW Wilson Company
950 Dr Martin L King Jr Blvd
Bronx, NY 10452-4297
718-588-8405; Fax: 718-590-1617
www.hwwilson.com
Harold Regan, CEO
Kathleen McEvoy, Director of Public Relations
Comprehensive listings are offered in this database on more than 25,000 citations to articles and reviews of books, periodicals and audiovisual materials in the library and information science areas.

16252 **Library Periodicals: An Annual Guide for Subscribers, Authors and Publicists**
Periodical Guides Publishing

1633 Pearl Street
Alameda, CA 94501-3065

510-865-7439

Over 150 journals and newsletters in the United States and Canada of national or international scope devoted to library science.
Cost: $18.00
55 Pages
Frequency: Annual

16253 **One Hundred and One Software Packages to Use in Your Library**
American Library Association
50 E Huron St
Chicago, IL 60611-2788

312-280-2518
800-545-2433
customerservice@ala.org
www.ala.org

Claire Knowles, Manager

Directory of services and supplies to the industry.

16254 **Salem Press Online Platform**
Grey House Publishing
4919 Route 22
PO Box 56
Amenia, NY 12501

800-221-1592; Fax: 201-968-0511
csr@salempress.com
online.salempress.com

The new Salem Press platform houses more than 500 titles including all of Salem's Health, Literature, History and Science titles in addition to select titles from the Grey House Publishing and H.W. Wilson product lines. Online access is free with each print purchase and includes an unlimited number of simultaneous users and remote access.

16255 **Subject Directory of Special Libraries & Information Centers**
Gale/Cengage Learning
27500 Drake Road
Farmington Hills, MI 48331-3535

248-699-4253
800-877-4253; Fax: 877-363-4253
gale.galeord@cengage.com
www.gale.cengage.com
Facebook, Twitter, Youtube

Patrick C Sommers, President

Presents entries culled from the Directory of Special Libraries and Information Centers in three volumes arranged by subject matter. This rearrangement is especially important for all users who frame their searches in a subject context. In addition to expanded international coverage, users will also find fax numbers, E-mail addresses, Web and Internet addresses and increased reporting of online services
Frequency: Annual/Set
ISBN: 1-414434-59-6

16256 **Univ. of Missouri School of Journalism: Freedom of Information Center**
University of Missouri
133 Neff Annex
Columbia, MO 65210-0012

573-882-7539; Fax: 573-884-6204
www.missouri.edu/~foiwww

Charles N Davis, Executive Director
Kathleen M Edwards, Center Manager

Reference and research library serving the public and media regarding access to government information. The center has a collection of over a million articles and documents concerning access to information at state, federal and local levels and offers a wide variety of online documents through its webpage.

16257 **Who's Who in Special Libraries**
Special Libraries Association
1700 18th St Nw
Washington, DC 20009-2508

202-234-4700; Fax: 202-265-9317

Directory of services and supplies to the industry.
Cost: $50.00
364 Pages
Frequency: Annual

Industry Web Sites

16258 **http://gold.greyhouse.com**
G.O.L.D Grey House OnLine Databases

Grey House Publishing's online database platform, GOLD, offers Quick Search, Keyword Search and Expert Search for most business sectors including library markets. The GOLD platform makes finding the information you need quick and easy - whether you're a novice searcher or an experienced database user. All of Grey House's directory products are available for subscription on the GOLD platform.

16259 **www.aallnet.org**
American Association of Law Libraries

16260 **www.acl.org**
Association of Christian Librarians

Membership is composed of over 500 evangelical Christian librarians representing primarily evangelical institutions of higher education.

16261 **www.aiip.org**
Association Independent Information Professionals

16262 **www.akla.org**
Alaska Library Association

16263 **www.ala.org**
American Library Association

Association for librarians, libraries, trustees, students and academics, encompassing all aspects of librarianship.

16264 **www.ala.org./alcts**
Assn for Library Collections & Technical Services

A division of the American Library Association.

16265 **www.ala.org/aasl**
American Association of School Librarians

Works to ensure that all members of the school library media field collaborate to: provide leadership in the total eduction program; participate as active partners in the teaching/learning process; connect learners with ideas and information; and prepare students for life-long learning. The American Association of School Librarians is a division of the American Library Association.

16266 **www.ala.org/acrl**
Association of College and Research Libraries

A division of the American Library Association. Represents academic and research librarians.

16267 **www.ala.org/alsc**
Association for Library Service to Children

A division of the American Library Association. For persons interested in the improvement and extension of library services to children.

16268 **www.ala.org/yalsa**
The Young Adult Library Services Association

Responsible for the evaluation and selection of books and nonbook materials and the interpretation and use of materials for teenagers and young adults. The Young Adult Library Services Association is a division of the American Library Association.

16269 **www.alise.org/index.shtml**
Association for Library & Information Science
Education

16270 **www.allanet.org**
Alabama Library Association

16271 **www.amianet.org**
Association of Moving Image Archivists

16272 **www.arl.org**
Association of Research Libraries

Non profit organization striving to shape and influence forces affecting the future of research libraries in the process of scholarly communication.

16273 **www.arlib.org**
Arkansas Library Association

Includes constitution and bylaws, conference information, publication, membership, and links to the Arkansas State Library.

16274 **www.arlisna.org**
Art Libraries Society of North America

Membership organization for art libraries in the US and Canada.

16275 **www.arma.org**
Assoc. for Information Management Professionals

16276 **www.arsc-audio.org**
Association for Recorded Sound Collections

Persons in broadcasting and recording industries, librarians, sound archivists, curators, private collectors and reviewers.

16277 **www.asindexing.org**
American Society of Indexers

A national association with international membership and interests. A nonprofit charitable organization for indexers, librarians, abstractors, editors, publishers, database producers, and organizations concerned with indexing, seeking cooperation and membership of all persons, groups or institutions interested in indexing. Founded in 1968 to promote excellence in indexing and increase awareness of the value of well-written indexes.

16278 **www.azla.org**
Arizona Library Association

16279 **www.bcala.org**
Black Caucus of the American Library Association

Meets annually in conjunction with the American Library Association in August.

16280 **www.cal-webs.org/aboutus.html**
Colorado Association Of Libraries

16281 **www.cala-web.org**
Chinese-American Librarians Association

16282 **www.cla-net.org**
California Library Association

16283 **www.clir.org**
Council on Library & Information Resources

16284 **www.cni.org**
Coalition for Networked Information

16285 **www.csla.org**
Church and Synagogue Library Association
Provides educational guidance in the establishment and maintenance of congregational libraries

16286 **www.ctlibraryassociation.org**
Connecticut Library Association
Professional organization of librarians, library staff, friends, and trustees working together: to improve library service to Connecticut, to advance the interests of librarians, library staff, and librarianship, and to increase public awareness of libraries and library services.

16287 **www.flalib.org**
Florida Library Association

16288 **www.glma-inc.org/**
Georgia Media Library Association

16289 **www.greyhouse.com**
Grey House Publishing
Authoritative reference directories for most business sectors including library markets. Users can search the online databases with varied search criteria allowing for custom searches by product category, geographic area, sales volume, keyword, subject and more. Full Grey House catalog and online ordering also available.

16290 **www.hlaweb.org**
Hawaii Library Association

16291 **www.idaholibraries.org**
Idaho Library Association

16292 **www.ifla.org**
International Federation of Library Associations

16293 **www.ila.org**
Illinois Library Association

16294 **www.ilfonline.org**
Indiana Library Federation

16295 **www.iowalibraryassociation.org**
Iowa Library Association

16296 **www.kylibasn.org**
Kentucky Library Association

16297 **www.lff.org**
Americans for Libraries Council

16298 **www.lita.org**
Library and Information Technology Association
Concerned with information dissemination in the areas of library information technology and automation. The Library and Information Technology Association is a division of the American Library Association.

16299 **www.llaonline.org**
Louisiana Library Association

16300 **www.mainelibraries.org**
Maine Library Association

16301 **www.masslib.org**
Massachusetts Library Association

16302 **www.mdlib.org**
Maryland Library Association

16303 **www.misslib.org**
Mississippi Library Association

16304 **www.mla.lib.mi.us**
Michigan Library Association

16305 **www.mlanet.org**
Medical Library Association
MLA is dedicated to the dissemination of quality health sciences information for use in education, research, and patient care.

16306 **www.mnlibraryassociation.org**
Minnesota Library Association

16307 **www.molib.org**
Missouri Library Association

16308 **www.mtlib.org**
Montana Library Association
The mission of the Montana Library Association is to develop, promote, and improve library and information services and the profession of librarianship in order to enhance learning and ensure accesss to information to all.

16309 **www.musiclibraryassoc.org**
Music Library Association
Promotes growth and establishment in the use of music libraries, musical instruments and musical literature.

16310 **www.namtc.org**
National Association of Media & Technology Centers

16311 **www.nativeculture.com/lisamitten/aila.html**
American Indian Library Association
Association for Native Americans and Native Alaskans libraries and librarians.

16312 **www.nclaonline.org**
North Carolina Library Association

16313 **www.nelib.org**
New England Library Association

16314 **www.nevadalibraries.org**
Nevada Library Association

16315 **www.niso.org**
National Information Standards Organization

16316 **www.njla.org**
New Jersey Library Association

16317 **www.nmla.org**
New Mexico Library Association

16318 **www.nmm.net**
National Media Market

16319 **www.nol.org/home/nla**
Nebraska Library Association

16320 **www.nyla.org**
New York Library Association

16321 **www.oelma.org**
Ohio Educational Library Media Association

16322 **www.oema.net**
Oregon Educational Media Association

16323 **www.oklibs.org**
Oklahoma Library Association

16324 **www.olaweb.org**
Oregon Library Association

16325 **www.olc.org**
Ohio Library Council

16326 **www.palibraries.org**
Pennsylvania Library Association

16327 **www.pla.org**
Public Library Association
Plans programs on current public library issues and concerns, develops publications for public librarians and disseminates statistics on public libraries. The Public Library Association is a division of the American Library Association.

16328 **www.pnla.org**
Pacific Northwest Library Association

16329 **www.rig.org**
Research Libraries Group

16330 **www.rusa.org**
Reference & User Services Association

16331 **www.salis.org**
Substance Abuse Librarians & Info. Specialists
Provides professional development and exchange of information and concerns about access to and dissemination of information on substance abuse.

16332 **www.scla.org**
South Carolina Library Association

16333 **www.sla.org**
Special Libraries Association
International association of information professionals who work in special libraries serving business, research, government and institutions that produce specialized information.

16334 **www.state.nh.us/nhla**
New Hampshire Library Association

16335 **www.tnla.org/**
Tennessee Library Association

16336 **www.txla.org**
Texas Library Association

16337 **www.uic.edu/depts/lib/projects/resources**
Asian/Pacific American Librarians Association
Librarians and information specialists of Asian Pacific descent working in the United States.

16338 **www.ula.org**
Utah Library Assocation

16339 **www.urbanlibraries.org**
Urban Libraries Council
Works to strengthen public libraries as an essential part of urban life. Serves as a forum for research widely recognized and used by public and private sector leaders.

16340 **www.uri.edu/library/rila/rila.html**
Rhode Island Library Association

16341 **www.vermontlibraries.org**
Vermont Library Association

16342 **www.vla.org**
Virginia Library Association

16343 **www.wla.org**
Washington Library Association

16344 **www.wvla.org**
West Virginia Library Association

16345 **www.wyla.org**
Wyoming Library Association

Associations

16346 **American Agricultural Editors' Association**
American Agricultural Editors' Association
120 Main Street W
PO Box 156
New Prague, MN 56071
952-758-6502; Fax: 952-758-5813
ljovanovich@hardwood.org
www.ageditors.com
Facebook, Twitter, Youtube, Pinterest
Susan M Regan, Executive VP
National professional development member association for agricultural communicators.
55 Members

16347 **American Independent Writers**
1001 Connecticut Ave Nw
Suite 701
Washington, DC 20036-5547
202-775-5150; Fax: 202-775-5810
hpva@hpva.org
www.amerindywriters.org/
Kip Howlett, HPVA President
Eva Mentel, Office Manager
Ketti Tyree, Membership and Conventions Manager
Matthew Windt, Marketing Manager
An association that seeks to create an open and inclusive community of authors, journalists and other writers.
73 Members
Founded in 1921

16348 **American Medical Writers' Association**
American Medical Writers' Association
30 W Gude Dr
Suite 525
Rockville, MD 20850-4347
240-238-0940; Fax: 301-294-9006
paraman@vt.edu
www.amwa.org
Philip Araman, President
Concerned with the advancement and improvement of medical communications.

16349 **American Society of Journalists and Authors**
American Society of Journalists and Authors
355 Lexington Avenue
15th Floor
New York, NY 10017-6603
212-997-0947; Fax: 212-937-2315
www.asja.org
Facebook, Twitter
Jack Goldman, President & CEO
David E. Woodbury, Jr., Director - Finance & Operations
Debbie Scerbo, Office Manager
Ryan Carroll, Director - Government Affairs
John Crouch, Director - Public Affairs
Association for journalists and authors.
2600 Members
Founded in 1980

16350 **American Translators Association**
225 Reinekers Lane
Suite 590
Alexandria, VA 22314
703-683-6100; Fax: 703-683-6122
ata@atanet.org
www.atanet.org
Facebook, Twitter, LinkedIn
Corinne McKay, President
Walter W. Bacak, Executive Director
Karen Tkaczyk, Secretary
John Milan, Treasurer
ATA membership is open to anyone with an interest in translation and interpreting as a profession or as a scholarly pursuit.
10500 Members
Founded in 1959

16351 **Association of American Collegiate Literary Societies**
Philomathean Society
College Hall
Box G
Philadelphia, PA 19104
Andrew Smith, Governor
Works with literary societies in the United States to promote the creation of new societies, existing societies and reviving old societies.
400 Members
Founded in 1978

16352 **Association of Authors' Representatives, Inc.**
302A West 12th St
Suite 122
New York, NY 10014
administrator@aaronline.org
aaronline.org
Gail Hochman, President
Professional organization whose members represent book authors and playwrights.
400+ Members

16353 **Association of Professional Writing**
Professional Writers Association
P.O. Box 7474
Daytona Beach, FL 32116
386-265-4279
info@iwpawood.org
www.prowriters.org
Facebook, Twitter, LinkedIn
Craig Forester, President
Bronson Newburger, Vice President
JoAnn Gillebaard Keller, Treasurer
Cindy L Squires, Esq., Executive Director
Joseph L. O'Donnell, Manager
Organization founded to establish standards for writing consultants. Other goals are to draw new members into the writing consulting field. Also offers a referral system for companies looking for writing consultants.
220 Members
Founded in 1956

16354 **Association of Writers & Writing Programs**
University of Maryland
5245 Greenbelt Rd., Box 246
College Park, MD 20740
301-226-9710; Fax: 301-226-9797
www.awpwriter.org
Facebook, Twitter, Pinterest
David W. Fenza, Executive Director
Support, resources and advocacy for writers and creative writing programs, conferences and centers.
Founded in 1967

16355 **Before Columbus Foundation**
The Raymond House
655 13th Street
Suite 302
Oakland, CA 94612
510-268-9775
www.beforecolumbusfoundation.com
Facebook, Twitter
Honorable Carro Breaux, President
Ronnie C Harris, Executive Director
Kerry Landry, Chief Financial Officer
Cliff Palmer, LaMATS Executive Director
Nikki Samrow, Events Coordinator
Participants are individuals interested in promoting contemporary American multicultural literature.
Founded in 1926

16356 **Boating Writers International**
108 Ninth Street
Wilmette, IL 60091
847-736-4142
info@bwi.org
www.bwi.org
Facebook, LinkedIn
Charlie Levine, President
Chris Woodward, First Vice President
Brady Kay, Second Vice President
Zuzana Prochazka, Executive Director
A nonprofit professional organization consisting of writers, broadcasters, editors, photgraphers, public relations specialists and other media professionals in communications serving the boating industry.
Founded in 1970

16357 **Center for the Book**
Library of Congress
101 Independence Avenue SE
Washington, DC 20540
202-707-5000; Fax: 202-707-0269
www.loc.gov/loc/cfbook
Steven Smith, President/Director
Elliott Smith, VP
Richard J Arde, Secretary/Treasurer
This organization strives to stimulate consumer interest in books and reading.
Founded in 1876
Mailing list available for rent

16358 **Children's Literature Association**
1301 W 22nd St.
Suite 202
Oak Brook, IL 60523
630-571-4520; Fax: 708-876-5598
info@childlitassn.org
www.childlitassn.org
Facebook, Twitter
Teya Rosenberg, President
ChLA is a nonprofit dedicated to promoting the study of children's literature.

16359 **Council of Biology Editors**
1000 East Henrietta Road
Rochester, NY 14623
585-292-2000
info@msrlumber.org
www.monroecc.edu
Dan Uskoski, President
Stacy Tiefenbach, Secretary/Treasurer
Sean Shields, Business Manager
Represents those members in life sciences who write for journals, medical science publications, and textbooks.
Founded in 1987

16360 **Council on National Literatures**
Council on National Literatures
68-02 Metropolitan Avenue
Middle Village, NY 11379
718-821-3916
mfma@maplefloor.org
www.annehenrypaolucci.homestead.com
Facebook, Twitter, Pinterest
Daniel F. Heney, Executive Director
Heather Currier, Marketing Communications Director
Daniel J. Krupa, Technical Director
Madhuri Carson, Conference Manager
Amber Montgomery, Order Processing Specialist

Provides a forum for scholars concerned with comparative study of literature.
175 Members
Founded in 1897

16361 **Dramatists Guild of America**
1501 Broadway
Suite 701
New York, NY 10036-5505
212-398-9366; Fax: 212-944-0420
www.dramatistsguild.com/
Facebook, Twitter, Pinterest, Houzz, YouTube
Kevin Anundson, MCR, CKBR, Chairman
Judy Mozen, CR, GCP, President
Tom Miller, Treasurer
Elsie Iturralde, CAE, Chief Operations Officer
Fred Ulreich, Chief Executive Officer
Protects the rights of its international membership of playwrights, composers and lyricists. Supports fair royalty, maintenance of subsidiary rights, artistic control and ownership of copyright.
Founded in 1983

16362 **Education Writers Association**
Education Writers Association
3516 Connecticut Avenue NW
Suite 201
Washington, DC 20008
202-452-9830; Fax: 202-452-9837
info@nfba.org
www.ewa.org
Facebook, RSS
Ken Gieseke, Chair
Todd Carlson, Secretary-Treasurer
Mike Dunipace, Director
Dan Nyberg, Director
Terry Burrow, Director
The Education Writers Association is the national professional organization of education reporters and intent of improving education reporting to the public.
Founded in 1969

16363 **Freelance Editorial Association**
PO Box 380835
Cambridge, MA 02238-0835
617-643-8626
membership@nhla.com
Facebook, Twitter, LinkedIn, RSS
Pem Jenkins, President
Brent Stief, 1st Vice President
Mark Barford, Chief Executive Officer
Kristina Bran, Digital Media Manager
Trisha Clariana, Office Manager
Offers editorial services that include editing, writing, proofreading, graphic design, desktop publishing, and project managemant.
1600 Members
Founded in 1898
Mailing list available for rent

16364 **International Food, Wine and Travel Writers Association**
39252 Winchester Rd
Ste 107 #418
Murrieta, CA 92563
877-439-8929
909-860-6914
951-970-8326; Fax: 877-439-8929
www.ifwtwa.org
Facebook, Twitter, LinkedIn
JD Saunders, Chair
Jonathan M. Paine, President/CEO
Laura DeMaria, Membership Services Manager
Ben Gann, VP, Legislative & Political Affairs
Frank Moore, Regulatory Counsel
Staff and/or freelance writers in the food, wine and travel field. Also includes other media professionals and industry associate members in 28 countries worldwide.
6000 Members
Founded in 1916

16365 **Mystery Writers of America**
1140 Broadway
Suite 1507
New York, NY 10001
212-888-8171; Fax: 212-888-8107
mysterywriters.org
Facebook, Twitter, YouTube, Instagram
Jeffery Deaver, President
Donna Andrews, Executive Vice President
Margery Flax, Administrative Director
Professional writers of crime and mystery stories and novels. Unpublished writers are affiliate members. MWA annually gives the Edgar Awards for excellence in the mystery genre.
3000 Members
Founded in 1985

16366 **National Association of Hispanic Journalists**
1050 Connecticut Avenue NW
Washington, DC 20036
202-662-7145; Fax: 202-662-7144
membersupport@wdma.com
www.nahj.org
Facebook, Twitter, LinkedIn, RSS Feeds
Al Babiuk, Chairman
Michael O'Brien, CAE, President & CEO
John McFee, Vice President, Certification
Jeff Lowinski, Vice President, Technical Services
Jeffrey Inks, VP, Code & Regulatory Affairs
NAHJ is dedicated to the recognition and professional advancement of Hispanics in the news industry. NAHJ created a national voice and unified vision for all Hispanic journalists.
140 Members
Founded in 1926

16367 **National Federation of Press Women**
National Federation of Press Women
200 Little Falls Street
Suite 405
Falls Church, VA 22046
703-237-9804
800-780-2715; Fax: 703-237-9808
www.nfpw.org
Facebook, Twitter, LinkedIn, YouTube
Brent J. McClendon, CAE, President/CEO
Isabel Sullivan, VP, Operations and Events
Brad Gething, PhD, Technical and PDS Manager
John A. McLeod III, Director
Annette Ferri, Comm. & Education Director
Members are writers, editors and other communication professionals for newspapers, magazines, wire services, agencies and freelance.
700+ Members
Founded in 1947
Mailing list available for rent: 1700 names at $40 per M

16368 **National Writers Association**
10940 S Parker Rd
Suite 508
Parker, CO 80134-7440
303-841-0246; Fax: 303-841-2607
sales@kiln-direct.com
www.nationalwriters.com
Exists to enhance the future of writers by fostering continuing education through award winning scholarships and providing no or low cost workshops and seminars. A non-profit organization, we provide education and an ethical resource for writers at all levels of experience.
650 Members
Founded in 1951

16369 **Newspaper Features Council**
22 Byfield Lane
Greenwich, CT 06830
203-661-3386; Fax: 203-661-7337
A forum for editors, writers, columnists, cartoonists and syndicates to exchange views and improve the content of newspapers.
130 Members
Founded in 1955

16370 **Outdoor Writers Association of America**
615 Oak St
Suite 201
Missoula, MT 59801-1896
406-728-7434
800-692-2477; Fax: 406-728-7445
info@nawla.org
www.owaa.org
Facebook, Twitter, LinkedIn
Scott Elston, Chairman
Jim McGinnis, First Vice Chairman
Bill Adams, Second Vice Chairman
Marc Saracco, Executive Director
Ben Barclay, Manager
Nonprofit, international organization representing over 2,000 professional outdoor communicators who report on diverse interests in the outdoors.
600+ Members
Founded in 1893

16371 **Self-Employed Writers and Artists Network**
PO Box 175
Towaco, NJ 07082
nela@northernlogger.com
www.njcreatives.org
Joseph E. Phaneuf, Executive Director
Eric A Johnson, Executive Editor
Mona Lincoln, Coordinator of Training and Safety
Debbie Haehl, Advertising Manager
Nancy E. Petrie, Circulation Manager
For more then 2 decades, companies and agencies alike have relied on the NJ Creatives Network organization as a cost-efficient, reliable source for freelance talent-from writers and artists to designers and photographers, plus film and video producers, and more.
2000 Members
Founded in 1952

16372 **Society of American Business Editors and Writers**
ASU, Walter Cronkite School of Journalism
555 North Central Ave, Suite 416
Phoenix, AZ 85004-1248
602-496-7862; Fax: 602-496-7041
www.sabew.org
Tom Partin, President
Members are financial and economic news writers and editors for print and broadcast outlets.
70 Members
Founded in 1987

16373 **Society of American Travel Writers**
One Parkview Plaza
Suite 800
Oakbrook Terrace, IL 60181
414-359-1625; Fax: 414-359-1671
info@nlassn.org
www.satw.org
Facebook
William Wood, Chairman of the Board
Cody Nuernberg, President
Abbie Diekmann, Membership & Financial Assistant

Jodie Fleck, Director of Conventions & Tours
Melanie Hultman, Communications Coordinator

Photographers and 35 associate member representatives of airlines, hotels, resorts, tourist agencies and public relations firms.
1.5M Members
Founded in 1890

16374 **Space Coast Writers Guild**
PO Box 262
Melbourne, FL 32902

Home Page: www.scwg.org

Nonprofit, tax-exempt organization of writers of all genres.
Cost: $35.00
Frequency: Annual
Founded in 1978

16375 **The Editorial Freelancers Association**
266 W 37th Street
20th Floor
New York, NY 10018

212-920-4816
866-929-5425
office@the-efa.org
www.the-efa.org
Facebook, Twitter, LinkedIn

Christina M. Frey, Co-Executive
William P. Keenan Jr., Co-Executive
Susannah Driver-Barstow, General Manager
Akiko Yamagata, Chapter Development
Jennifer Lawler, Education

The national professional association for freelance editorial service providers and those who hire them. Members include those skilled in various areas: editors, writers, indexers, proofreaders, researchers, translators, formatters and designers, and more.
2675+ Members
Founded in 1970

16376 **Writers Alliance**
12 Skylark Lane
Stony Brook, NY 11790-3121

516-751-7080

Writers' organization.

16377 **Writers Guild of America: West**
Writers Guild of America
7000 W 3rd St
Los Angeles, CA 90048-4329

323-951-4000
800-548-4532; Fax: 323-782-4800
www.wga.org
Facebook, Twitter

Rikki Wellman, Executive Director
Craig Olson, President
Ron Simon, Treasurer

An independent labor union representing writers in motion pictures, television and radio in the west.
550 Members
Founded in 1909

16378 **Writers Research Group LLC**
Po Box 891568
Oklahoma City, OK 73189-1568

405-682-2589; Fax: 405-685-3390
info@lumber-exporters.org
Facebook, Twitter, LinkedIn, Google+

David Stallcop, President
Chip Setzer, Vice-President
Mark Rodakowski, Secretary
Chris Knowles, Treasurer

Writers Research Group is a professional writing and research firm. Our knowledgeable employees gather, examine, edit, and compile data to your company's specifications. Our services include research, writing, directory listing updates and new entries, indexing, copyediting, proofreading, data entry, document markup and permissions negotiations.
Founded in 1923

Newsletters

16379 **AGENDA**
National Federation of Press Women
PO Box 34798
Alexandria, VA 22334-0798

800-780-2715; Fax: 703-237-9808
www.nfpw.org
Facebook, Twitter, LinkedIn, Youtube

A quarterly newletter published by the National Federation of Press Women.
Cost: $51.50
4 Pages
Frequency: Quarterly
Circulation: 2000
Founded in 1937
Mailing list available for rent: 1700 names at $40 per M

16380 **ASJA Newsletter**
American Society of Journalists and Authors
1501 Broadway
Suite 302
New York, NY 10036-5505

212-997-0947; Fax: 212-937-2315
staff@asja.org
www.asja.org
Facebook, Twitter, LinkedIn

Alexandra Owens, Executive Director
Lisa Collier Coloradool, President
Barbara Barrett, Newsletter Editor

Confidential news for journalists and authors, available only to members of the Society.
Frequency: Monthly
Founded in 1948

16381 **American Writer**
American Independent Writers
1001 Connecticut Ave Nw
Suite 701
Washington, DC 20036-5547

202-775-5150; Fax: 202-775-5810
www.amerindywriters.org/

Donald Graul, Executive Director

News and information for freelance writers.
Cost: $160.00
8 Pages
Frequency: Monthly
Founded in 1975

16382 **BWI Newsletters**
108 Ninth Street
Wilmette, IL 60091

847-736-4142
info@bwi.org
www.bwi.org

Charlie Levine, President
Zuzana Prochazka, Executive Director

Newsletter containing content of interest to recreational boating and fishing activities and the media professionals involved in covering boating industry news.
Founded in 1970

16383 **Copy Editor**
McMurry
1010 E Missouri Ave
Phoenix, AZ 85014-2602

602-395-5850
888-626-8779; Fax: 602-395-5853
www.mcmurry.com

Chris McMurry, CEO
Barbara Wallraff, Editor

Helps editors stay up-to-date with the changing language. Articles discuss new words, changes in usage and reference books. Each issue contains interviews with copy editors.
Cost: $69.00
8 Pages
Circulation: 2000
Founded in 1990
Printed in one color

16384 **Editorial Eye**
Editorial Experts
66 Canal Center Plz
Suite 200
Alexandria, VA 22314-5507

703-683-0683
800-683-8380; Fax: 703-683-4915
www.eeicom.com

Jim De Graffenreid, President
Candee Wilson, Director
Robin Cormier, VP Publications
Linda B Jorgensen, Editor
Keith C. Ivey, Technical Editor

Professional standards and practices for editors, writers and publication managers.
Cost: $139.00
12 Pages
Frequency: Monthly
Circulation: 3,000
Founded in 1972

16385 **Freelance Writer's Report**
CNW Publishing
PO Box A
North Stratford, NH 03590

603-922-8338
800-351-9278; Fax: 603-922-8339
info@writers-editors.com
www.writers-editors.com

Dana K Cassell, Executive Director

News and marketing information for freelance writers.
Cost: $39.00
Frequency: Monthly
Circulation: 1200

16386 **IDEAS Unlimited for Editors**
Omniprint
9700 Philadelphia Ct
Lanham, MD 20706-4405

301-731-7000
800-774-6809; Fax: 301-731-7001
www.omniprint.net

Ken Kaufman, President
Stephen Brownan, VP

Editorial ideas and graphics for editors of in-house, corporate newsletters. Provides 16 pages of fresh, ready-to-use items and ideas editors can use to fill out their publications.
Cost: $5.00
16 Pages
Frequency: Monthly
Circulation: 6310
Founded in 1973
Printed in one color on matte stock

16387 **KEYSTROKES**
Writers Alliance
12 Skylark Lane
Stony Brook, NY 11790-3121

516-751-7080

Kiel Stuart, Publisher
Howard Austerlitz, Editor
Charles Spataro, Circulation Manager

A writers newsletter containing marketing, how-to and computer information.
Cost: $10.00
16 Pages
Frequency: TriAnnual
Circulation: 250

Mailing list available for rent: 250 names
Printed in one color on matte stock

16388 **Linington Lineup**
1223 Glen Ter
Glassboro, NJ 08028-1315

856-589-1571

Rinehart S Potts, Editor

Editing, publishing, police procedural.
Cost: $12.00
16 Pages
Frequency: Bi-Monthly
Circulation: 400
Founded in 1984
Printed in one color on matte stock

16389 **NWA Newsletter**
National Writers Association
10940 S Parker Rd
Suite 508
Parker, CO 80134-7440

303-841-0246; Fax: 303-841-2607
natlwritersassn@hotmail.com
www.nationalwriters.com

Sandy Whelchel, Executive Director

A monthly e-mail newsletter that includes information on upcoming contests and conferences, announcements and job opportunities
2000 Members
Frequency: Monthly
Founded in 1938

16390 **Speechwriter's Newsletter**
Ragan Communications
316 N Michigan Ave
Suite 400
Chicago, IL 60601-3773

312-960-4100
800-493-4867; Fax: 312-960-4106
cservice@ragan.com
www.ragan.com

Jim Ylisela, Publisher
David Murray, Editor
Rebecca Anderson, Managing Editor

Offers speechwriting tips, examples and criticism.
Cost: $307.00
4 Pages
Frequency: Monthly
Founded in 1980

16391 **Story Bag: National Storytelling Newsletter**
5361 Javier St
San Diego, CA 92117-3215

858-569-9399; Fax: 858-569-0205
storybag@juno.com

Professional storytellers, whether freelance or working for a school or library, will find this newsletter stuffed full of tips on techniques, suggestions for handling the business, reviews of storytelling books and tapes, listings of events nationwide, bibliographies of suggested materials, and discussion of issues such as censorship. Note: Above phone is used on e-mail, if busy try again.
Cost: $15.00
8 Pages
Frequency: Bi-Monthly
Circulation: 300
Printed in one color on matte stock

16392 **Strategic Employee Publications**
Lawrence Ragan Communications
316 N Michigan Ave
Suite 400
Chicago, IL 60601-3773

312-960-4100
800-878-5331; Fax: 312-960-4106
cservice@ragan.com
www.ragan.com

Jim Ylisela, Publisher
David Murray, Editor
Diane Tillman, Marketing Manager

Designed to help organizational editors produce their company publications.
Cost: $139.00
8 Pages
Frequency: Monthly
Circulation: 2500
Founded in 1970
Printed in 2 colors on matte stock

16393 **Writers Connection**
Writers Connection
1826 Crossover Roade
PMB 108
Fayetteville, AR 72703

Home Page: www.thewritersconnection.com

Provides how-to information for writers, plus listings of markets, contests and events. Accepts advertising.
Cost: $45.00
16 Pages
Frequency: Monthly

Magazines & Journals

16394 **ATA Chronicle**
American Translators Association
225 Reinekers Lane
Suite 590
Alexandria, VA 22314

703-683-6100; Fax: 703-683-6122
ata@atanet.org
www.atanet.org
Facebook, Twitter, LinkedIn

Corinne McKay, President
Walter W. Bacak, Executive Director
Karen Tkaczyk, Secretary
John Milan, Treasurer

Contains feature articles, announcements, reviews, and association news.
Cost: $65.00
Frequency: Monthly
Circulation: 11,100

16395 **Latinos in the US: A Resource Guide for Journalists**
National Association of Hispanic Journalists
529 14th St Nw # 1240
Washington, DC 20045-2520

202-789-1157; Fax: 202-347-3444
rnutting@marketwatch.com
www.marketwatch.com

Rex Nutting, Manager
Joseph Torres, Communications Director
Rex Nutting, Manager

Purposes are to increase educational and career opportunities in journalism for Hispanic Americans.
Cost: $8.50
Mailing list available for rentat $500 per M

16396 **Modernism/Modernity**
2715 N Charles Street
Baltimore, MD 21218-4319

410-516-6900
800-548-1784; Fax: 410-516-6968

Jeffrey T Schnapp, Editor
Becky Brasington Clark, Marketing Director
Tom Lovett, Circulation Manager
Ken Sabol, Production Manager

Focuses systematically on the methodological, archival, and theoretical exigencies particular to modernist studies. It encourages and interdisciplinary approach linking music, architecture, the visual arts, literature, and social and intellectual history.
Cost: $40.00
Frequency: Quarterly
Founded in 1994

Trade Shows

16397 **ATA Annual Conference**
American Translators Association
225 Reinekers Lane
Suite 590
Alexandria, VA 22314

703-683-6100; Fax: 703-683-6122
ata@atanet.org
www.atanet.org
Facebook, Twitter

Corinne McKay, President
Walter W. Bacak, Executive Director
Karen Tkaczyk, Secretary
John Milan, Treasurer
Frequency: Annual/October

16398 **AWP Conference & Bookfair**
Association of Writers & Writing Programs
George Mason University
4400 University Dr., MSN 1E3
Fairfax, VA 22030

703-993-4301; Fax: 703-993-4302
registration@awpwriter.org
www.awpwriter.org/awp_conference/overview
Facebook, Twitter, Pinterest

The largest literary conference in North America.
12K+ Attendees
Frequency: Annual

16399 **Agricultural Publications Summit**
American Agricultural Editors' Association
120 Main Street W
PO Box 156
New Prague, MN 56071

952-758-6502; Fax: 952-758-5813
www.ageditors.com

Den Gardner, Executive Director
Holly Martin, President
Kenna Rathai, Associate Executive Director
Frequency: July

16400 **American Society of Journalists and Authors Conference**
American Society of Journalists and Authors
1501 Broadway
Suite 302
New York, NY 10036-5501

212-997-0947; Fax: 212-937-2315
www.asja.org
Facebook, Twitter, LinkedIn

Alexandra Owens, Executive Director
Salley Shannon, President
Barbara DeMarco- Barrett, Newsletter Editor
Stephen Morril, Web Editor
Bruce Miler, Web Master

A forum for the exchange of ideas between journalists.
700 Attendees
Frequency: May

16401 **Annual Multimedia Convention & Career Expo (NAHJ)**
National Association of Hispanic Journalists

Disney's Coronado Spings Resort
1000 W Buena Vista Drive
Lake Buena Vista, FL 32830

866-257-5990
www.nahjconvention.org
Facebook, Twitter, LinkedIn, YouTube

Michele Salcedo, President
Manuel De La Rosa, Vice President/Broadcast
Russell Contreras, VP Print/Financial Officer

NAHJ is dedicated to the recognition and professional advancement of Hispanics in the news industry. NAHJ created a national voice and unified vision for all Hispanic journalists.
2300 Members
Frequency: August
Founded in 1984

16402 **ChLA Conference**
1301 W 22nd St.
Suite 202
Oak Brook, IL 60523

630-571-4520; Fax: 708-876-5598
www.childlitassn.org/annual-conference

Roberta Seelinger Trites, Chair, Conf. Planning Committee
Jackie Stallcup, Committee Member
Annette Wannamaker, Committee Member
Eric Tribunella, Committee Member
Jennifer Miskec, Committee Member

Academic conference focused on the scholarly study of children's and adolescent literature.
Frequency: Annual/June
Founded in 1973

16403 **EFA National Conference**
The Editorial Freelancers Association
266 W 37th Street
20th Floor
New York, NY 10018

212-920-4816
866-929-5425
office@the-efa.org
www.the-efa.org

Christina M. Frey, Co-Executive
William P. Keenan Jr., Co-Executive
Susannah Driver-Barstow, General Manager
Jennifer Lawler, Education
Akiko Yamagata, Chapter Development

EFA's bi-annual event brings together editorial freelances to explore and discuss current trends and issues.
2675+ Members
Frequency: Bi-Annual
Founded in 1970

16404 **SABEW Annual Conference**
Society of American Business Editors & Writers
ASU, Walter Cronkite School of Journalism
555 North Central Ave, Suite 416
Phoenix, AZ 85004-1248

602-496-7862; Fax: 602-496-7041
sabew@sabew.org
www.sabew.org
Facebook, Twitter, LinkedIn

Carrie Paden, Executive Director
Rex Seline, VP
Jon Lansner, Secretary/Treasurer
Brant Houston, Executive Director
Frequency: April

Directories & Databases

16405 **AWP Official Guide to Writing Programs**
Association of Writers & Writing Programs
Mail Stop 1E3
Fairfax, VA 22030

703-993-4301; Fax: 703-993-4302
awp@awpwriter.org

Supriya Bhatngar, Director of Publications

About 300 colleges and universities offering workshops and degree programs in creative writing; approximately 100 writers' conferences, colonies and centers; coverage includes Canada and the United Kingdom.
Cost: $24.95
400 Pages
Frequency: Biennial

16406 **American Directory of Writer's Guidelines**
Dustbooks
PO Box 100
Paradise, CA 95967-0100

530-877-6110
800-477-6110; Fax: 530-877-0222
directories@dustbooks.com
www.dustbooks.com

Brigitte M Phillips, Editor
Susan D Klassen, Editor
Doris Hall, Editor

These guidelines help writers target their submissions to the exact needs of the individual publisher. A compilation of information for freelancers from more than 1,500 magazine editors and book publishers.
Cost: $29.95
752 Pages
ISBN: 1-884956-40-8

16407 **American Library Directory**
Information Today
143 Old Marlton Pike
Medford, NJ 08055-8750

609-654-6266
800-300-9868; Fax: 609-654-4309
custserv@infotoday.com
www.infotoday.com

Thomas H Hogan, President
Roger R Bilboul, Chariman Of The Board

Detailed profiles for more than 35,000 public, academic, special, and government libraries and library related organizations in the US and Canada. These include addresses, phone and fax numbers, e-mail addresses, network participation, expenditures, holdings and special collections, key personnel, special services and more than 40 categories of library information in all. A two volume set.
Cost: $299.00
4000 Pages
ISBN: 1-573872-04-0
Mailing list available for rent

16408 **American Society of Journalists and Authors Directory**
American Society of Journalists and Authors
1501 Broadway
Suite 302
New York, NY 10036-5505

212-997-0947; Fax: 212-937-2315
www.asja.org
Facebook, Twitter, LinkedIn

Alexandra Owens, Executive Director

Lists over 800 member freelance nonfiction writers.
Cost: $75.00
90 Pages

16409 **Applied Science & Technology Index**
HW Wilson Company
950 Dr Martin L King Jr Blvd
Bronx, NY 10452-4297

718-588-8405
800-367-6770; Fax: 718-590-1617
www.hwwilson.com

Harold Regan, CEO
Kathleen McEvoy, Director of Public Relations

Fast, convenient access to the cover-to-cover content of leading trade and industrial publications, journals issued by professional and technical societies, specialized subject periodicals, as well as buyers' guides, directories, and conference proceedings.
Frequency: Monthly on WlisonDisc

16410 **Association of Professional Writing Consultants Membership Directory**
Northwestern University
2315 Sheridan Rd
Evanston, IL 60201-2920

847-491-5500

Henry Bienen, President
Cost: $75.00
Frequency: Annual

16411 **Authors and Artists for Young Adults**
Gale/Cengage Learning
27500 Drake Road
Farmington Hills, MI 48331-3535

248-699-4253
800-877-4253; Fax: 877-363-4253
gale.galeord@cengage.com
www.gale.cengage.com
Facebook, Twitter, Youtube

Patrick C Sommers, President

A a source where teens can discover fascinating and entertaining facts about the writers, artists, film directors, graphic novelists and other creative personalities that most interest them.
ISBN: 0-787677-96-5

16412 **Children's Writer's and Illustrator's Market**
Writer's Market
1507 Dana Avenue
Cincinnati, OH 45207-1005

513-396-6160
800-289-0963; Fax: 513-531-4082

Offers valuable information about book and magazine publishers that publish works by authors and illustrators for young audiences.
Cost: $22.99
256 Pages
Frequency: Annual

16413 **Complete Guide to Self-Publishing**
Writer's Market
1507 Dana Avenue
Cincinnati, OH 45207-1005

513-396-6160
800-289-0963; Fax: 513-531-4082

Offers, in appendixes, a list of contacts and companies that help see to publication of a book at the author's expense.
Cost: $18.95

16414 **Contemporary Authors**
Gale/Cengage Learning
27500 Drake Road
Farmington Hills, MI 48331-3535

248-699-4253
800-877-4253; Fax: 877-363-4253
gale.galeord@cengage.com
www.gale.cengage.com
Facebook, Twitter, Youtube

Patrick C Sommers, President

Find biographical information on more than 130,000 modern novelists, poets, playwrights,

nonfiction writers, journalists and scriptwriters. Sketches typically include personal information, contact information, career history, writings, biographical and critical sources, authors' comments and informative essays about their lives and work.
ISBN: 0-810319-11-X

16415 **Directory of Literary Magazines**
Council of Literary Magazines and Presses
154 Christopher St
Suite 3C
New York, NY 10014-2840

212-741-9110; Fax: 212-741-9112
info@clmp.org
www.clmp.org

Contains names, addresses and phone numbers of nearly 600 magazines in the US and abroad that publish poetry, fiction, essays, literary reviews and more.
Cost: $17.00
Frequency: Annual

16416 **Directory of Poetry Publishers**
Dustbooks
PO Box 100
Paradise, CA 95967-0100

530-877-6110
800-477-6110; Fax: 530-877-0222
directories@dustbooks.com
www.dustbooks.com

Len Fulton, Editor

Over 2,100 magazines, small and commercial presses and university presses that accept poetry for publication.
Cost: $25.95
300 Pages
Frequency: Annual
Circulation: 2,000
ISBN: 0-916685-47-0

16417 **Directory of Small Magazines Press Magazine Editors & Publishers**
Dustbooks
PO Box 100
Paradise, CA 95967-0100

530-877-6110
800-477-6110; Fax: 530-877-0222
directories@dustbooks.com
www.dustbooks.com

Len Fulton, Editor

This directory contains more than 7,500 listings of editors and publishers in alphabetical order, along with their associated publishing companies, their addresses, phones, e-mail addresses and Web pages. Includes self publishers.
Cost: $25.95
460 Pages
Frequency: Annual
Circulation: 1,000
ISBN: 0-913218-28-6
Founded in 1967
Mailing list available for rent

16418 **EFA Membership Directory**
The Editorial Freelancers Association
71 West 23rd Street
4th Floor
New York, NY 10010

212-929-5400
866-929-5425; Fax: 212-929-5439
office@the-efa.org
www.the-efa.org
Facebook, Twitter, LinkedIn

Christina M. Frey, Co-Executive
William P. Keenan Jr., Co-Executive
Susannah Driver-Barstow, General Manager
Jennifer Maybin, Education

Offers clients free access to members of The Editorial Freelancers Association.
2500 Members
Founded in 1970

16419 **Editor & Publisher International Year Book**
Editor & Publisher Company
17782 Cowan
Suite C
Irvine, CA 92614

929-660-6150
888-732-7323; Fax: 949-660-6172
circulation@editorandpublisher.com
www.editorandpublisher.com

Duncan McIntosh, President/Publisher
Jeff Fleming, Editor-In-Chief
Kristina Ackermann, Managing Editor
Ralph Bayless, Sales Manager

It's the encyclopedia of the newspaper industry with listings for all dailies worldwide and all community and special interest U.S. and Canadian weeklies. Tabbed sections make it easy to find information from U.S. & Canadian dailies to foreign newspapers. Tables profile newspaper ad trends, circulation size by population groups, rankings by circulation size and more.
Cost: $125.00
600 Pages
Frequency: Annual
Founded in 1884

16420 **Editor & Publisher: Directory of Syndicated Services Issue**
Editor & Publisher Company
11 W 19th Street
10th Floor
New York, NY 10011-4209

212-929-1259

Michael Parker, President

A directory of several hundred syndicates serving newspapers in the United States and abroad with news, features and comic strips.
Cost: $7.00
Frequency: Annual

16421 **Guide to Literary Agents**
Writer's Market
1507 Dana Avenue
Cincinnati, OH 45207-1005

513-396-6160
800-289-0963; Fax: 513-531-4082
www.writersmarket.com

Agents and representatives for professional writers.
Cost: $18.95
240 Pages
Frequency: Annual

16422 **Guide to Writers Conferences & Workshops**
Shaw Guides
PO Box 231295
New York, NY 10023

212-799-6464; Fax: 212-724-9287
www.shawguides.com

Conferences, workshops, and seminars for amateur and professional writers.
Cost: $19.95
272 Pages

16423 **Key Guide to Electronic Resources: Language and Literature**
Information Today
143 Old Marlton Pike
Medford, NJ 08055-8750

609-654-6266
800-300-9868; Fax: 609-654-4309
custserv@infotoday.com
www.infotoday.com

Thomas H Hogan, President
Roger R Bilboul, Chairman Of The Board

Part of the ongoing topic related series of reference guides is an evaluative directory of electronic reference sources in the fields of language and literature.
Cost: $39.50
120 Pages
ISBN: 1-573870-20-x
Mailing list available for rent

16424 **Literary Agents of North America**
Author Aid/Research Associates International
340 E 52nd St
New York, NY 10022-6728

212-758-4213

Arthur Ormont, Editor

More than 1,00 US and Canadian literary agencies.
Cost: $33.00

16425 **Literary Forum**
CompuServe Information Service
5000 Arlington Centre Blvd
Columbus, OH 43220-5439

614-326-1002
800-848-8199

This database covers literature, including books and poetry, writing, stage and screen, journalism and comic books.
Frequency: Bulletin Board

16426 **Market Guide for Young Writers: Where and How to Sell What You Write**
Writer's Market
1507 Dana Avenue
Cincinnati, OH 45207-1005

513-396-6160
800-289-0963; Fax: 513-531-4082
www.writersmarket.com

A list of over 150 magazines and writers contests are profiles that all accept work from young writers for publishing purposes.
Cost: $16.95

16427 **Mystery Writer's Market Place and Sourcebook**
Writer's Market
1507 Dana Avenue
Cincinnati, OH 45207-1005

513-396-6160
800-289-0963; Fax: 513-531-4082
www.writersmarket.com

Offers various profiles of about 50 publishers of mystery and crime books.
Cost: $17.95

16428 **Novel & Short Story Writer's Market**
Writer's Market
1507 Dana Avenue
Cincinnati, OH 45207-1005

513-396-6160
800-289-0963; Fax: 513-531-4082
www.writersmarket.com

More than 2,000 literary magazines, publishers, agents and writer's organizations are profiled.
Cost: $19.95
Frequency: Annual

16429 **Poet's Market**
Writer's Market

1507 Dana Avenue
Cincinnati, OH 45207-1005

513-396-6160
800-289-0963; Fax: 513-531-4082
www.writersmarket.com

Over 1,500 publishers, periodicals and other markets that accept poetry for publication are profiled.
Cost: $22.99
528 Pages
Frequency: Annual
ISSN: 0883-5470

16430 **Professional Freelance Writers Directory**
National Writers Club
314 Peoria
Suite 290
Aurora, CO 80014

303-841-0246

Over 200 professional members selected from the total membership on the basis of significant articles books or movies published.
Cost: $12.50
75 Pages
Frequency: Annual

16431 **Salem Press Online Platform**
Grey House Publishing
4919 Route 22
PO Box 56
Amenia, NY 12501

800-221-1592; Fax: 201-968-0511
csr@salempress.com
online.salempress.com

The new Salem Press platform houses more than 500 titles including all of Salem's Health, Literature, History and Science titles in addition to select titles from the Grey House Publishing and H.W. Wilson product lines. Online access is free with each print purchase and includes an unlimited number of simultaneous users and remote access.

16432 **Science Fiction and Fantasy Writers of America Membership Directory**
PO Box 877
Chestertown, MD 21620

exedir@sfwa.org
www.sfwa.org

Mary Kowal, Vice-President
Robert Howe, Secretary
Amy Casil, Treasurer

Directory of services and supplies to the industry.
Cost: $60.00
40 Pages
Frequency: Annual

16433 **Self-Employed Writers and Artists Network Directory**
Po Box 175
Towacos, NJ 07653-0440

Facebook, Twitter

Phil Cantor, President
Wayne Rousck, VP Marketing

Over 140 freelance writers and graphic designers, as well as illustrators, photographers and more in northern New Jersey and Metropolitan New York City are profiled.
20 Pages
Frequency: Annual

16434 **Self-Publishing Manual: How to Write, Print and Sell Your Own Book**
Para Publishing
PO Box 8206
Santa Barbara, CA 93118-8206

805-968-7277
800-727-2782; Fax: 805-968-1379
www.parapublishing.com
Dan Poynter, Publisher

A list of wholesalers, reviewers and exporters, etc, are profiled.
Cost: $19.95
900 Pages
Frequency: Biennial
ISBN: 1-568600-73-9
Founded in 1979
Printed in one color on matte stock

16435 **Space Coast Writers Guild: Organization, Activities and Membership**
PO Box 262
Melbourne, FL 32902

Home Page: www.scwg.org
Facebook, Twitter, LinkedIn

Judy Mammay, President
Bill Allen, VP
Donna Chesher, President
Andy Vazquez, Vice-President
Carol Didier, Secretary

A who's who directory of professional writing services and training to the media industry.
25 Pages
Frequency: Annual

16436 **Who's Who in Writers, Editors and Poets: US and Canada**
December Press
Apt 406
2800 N Roadrunner Pkwy
Las Cruces, NM 88011-0859

847-940-4122

Curt Johnson, President

Directory of writers and editors.
Cost: $99.00
700 Pages
Frequency: Biennial

16437 **Writer's Digest: Writers Conference Issue**
F&W Publications
1507 Dana Avenue
Cincinnati, OH 45207-1005

513-531-2222; Fax: 513-531-1843

Directory of services and supplies to the industry.
Cost: $2.95
Frequency: Annual
Circulation: 225,000

16438 **Writer's Guide to Book Editors, Publishers and Literary Agents**
Prima Publishing
3000 Lava Ridge Ct
Roseville, CA 95661-2802

916-787-7000
800-632-8676; Fax: 916-787-7004
www.primagames.com

Julie Asbury, Publisher

Offers information on more than 200 publishing houses and their editors.
Cost: $19.95
370 Pages
Frequency: Annual

16439 **Writer's Handbook**
Kalmbach Publishing Company
21027 Crossroads Circle
PO Box 1612
Waukesha, WI 53186-1612

262-796-8776
800-533-6644; Fax: 262-796-1615
www.writermag.com

A list of more than 3,000 markets for the sale of manuscripts, ads and awards.
Cost: $29.95
Frequency: Annual

16440 **Writer's Market: Where and How to Sell What You Write**
Writer's Market
1507 Dana Avenue
Cincinnati, OH 45207-1056

513-396-6160; Fax: 513-531-4082

Directory of services and supplies to the industry.
Cost: $29.95
1000 Pages
Frequency: Annual
ISSN: 0084-2729

16441 **Writer's Northwest Handbook**
Media Weavers, Blue Heron Publishing
4140 S.E. 37
#10
Portland, OR 97202

Home Page: www.mediaweavers.net

Over 3,000 markets for writers, including newspapers, magazines and book publishers in Northwestern United States and British Columbia, Canada.
Cost: $18.95
232 Pages
Frequency: Biennial

16442 **Writers Conferences**
Poets & Writers
150 Broadway
New York, NY 10038-4381

212-566-2424; Fax: 212-587-9673
mpettus@pettuswilliams.com
www.pettuswilliams.com

Marvin K Pettus
Cost: $7.50
50 Pages
Frequency: Annual

16443 **Writers Directory**
St. James Press/Gale
27500 Drake Road
Farmington Hills, MI 48331-3535

248-699-4253
800-877-4253; Fax: 877-363-4253
gale.galeord@cengage.com
www.gale.cengage.com
Facebook, Twitter, Youtube

Patrick C Sommers, President

This comprehensive resource features uptodate bibliographical, biographical and contact information for approximately 20,000 living authors worldwide who have at least one English publication.
ISBN: 1-558626-20-4

16444 **Writers Guild Directory**
Writers Guild of America, West
8455 Beverly Blvd
Los Angeles, CA 90048-3445

323-651-2600; Fax: 323-782-4802

Bob Waters, Owner

Directory of services and supplies to the industry.
Cost: $17.50
450 Pages
Frequency: Annual

Industry Web Sites

16445 **http://gold.greyhouse.com**
G.O.L.D Grey House OnLine Databases
Grey House Publishing's online database platform, GOLD, offers Quick Search, Keyword Search and Expert Search for most business sectors including literary markets. The GOLD platform makes finding the information you need quick and easy - whether you're a novice searcher or an experienced database user. All of Grey House's directory products are available for subscription on the GOLD platform.

16446 **www.asja.org**
American Society of Journalists and Authors
Association for journalists and authors.

16447 **www.dramaguild.com**
Dramatists Guild
Protects the rights of its international membership of playwrights, composers and lyricists. Supports fair royalty, maintenance of subsidiary rights, artistic control and ownership of copyright.

16448 **www.greyhouse.com**
Grey House Publishing
Authoritative reference directories for most business sectors including literary markets. Users can search the online databases with varied search criteria allowing for custom searches by product category, geographic area, sales volume, keyword, subject and more. Full Grey House catalog and online ordering also available.

16449 **www.ifwtwa.org**
International Food, Wine and Travel Writers Association

Staff and/or freelance writers in the food, wine and travel field. Also includes other media professionals and industry associate members in 28 countries worldwide.

16450 **www.loc.gov/loc/cfbook/**
Library of Congress
This organization strives to stimulate the consumer interest in books and reading.

16451 **www.mysterywriters.org**
Mystery Writers of America
Professional writers of crime and mystery stories and novels. Unpublished writers are affiliate members. MWA annually gives the Edagar Awards for excellence in the mystery geare.

16452 **www.nationalwriters.com**
Membership organization for writers.

16453 **www.nfpw.org**
National Federation of Press Women
Members are writers, editors and other communication professionals for newspapers, magazines, wire services, agencies and freelance.

16454 **www.owaa.org**
Outdoor Writers Association of America
A nonprofit, international organization representing over 2,000 professional outdoor communicators who report on diverse interests in the outdoors.

16455 **www.the-efa.org**
The Editorial Freelancers Association
Facebook, Twitter, LinkedIn
The national professional association for freelance editorial service providers and those who hire them.

16456 **www.wga.org**
Writers Guild of America, West
An independent labor union representing writers in motion pictures, television and radio in the west.

Associations

16457 **American Fiberboard Association**
2118 Plum Grove Rd.
#283
Rolling Meadows, IL 60008
847-934-8394
richard@westernforestry.org
www.fiberboard.org
Richard Zabel, Executive Director
The national trade organization of manufacturers of cellulose fiberboard products used for residential and commercial construction.
125 Members
Founded in 1909

16458 **American Forest & Paper Association**
AF&PA
1101 K Street, NW
Suite 700
Washington, DC 20005
202-463-2700
800-878-8878; Fax: 202-463-2785
www.afandpa.org
Facebook, Twitter, Youtube, Pinterest
Peter Lang, General Manager
Edward Burke, Eastern Field Representative
Represents member companies and related trade associations which grow, harvest and process wood and wood fiber, manufacture pulp, paper and paperboard products from both virgin and recovered fiber and produce solid wood products.
Founded in 1954

16459 **American Forest Foundation**
2000 M Street, NW
Suite 550
Washington, DC 20036
202-765-3660; Fax: 202-827-7924
info@wwpa.org
www.forestfoundation.org
Michael O'Halloran, President
Tom Hanneman, VP/Director
Robert Bernhardt Jr, Director Information Services
Kevin CK Cheung, Director Technical Services
Kevin Binam, Director Economic Services
Committed to creating a future where North American forests are sustained by the public that understand and values the social, economic, and environmental benefits they provide to our communities, our nation, and the world.
135 Members
Founded in 1964
Mailing list available for rent

16460 **American Forest Resource Council**
5100 SW Macadam
Suite 350
Portland, OR 97239
503-222-9505; Fax: 503-222-3255
info@amforest.org
amforest.org
Facebook, Twitter, LinkedIn, Instagram, YouTube
Travis Joseph, President
Manufacturers and forest products companies working for responsible forestry.

16461 **American Forests**
1220 L Street NW
Suite 750
Washington, DC 20005
202-737-1944
membersupport@wdma.com
www.americanforests.org
Facebook, Twitter, LinkedIn, RSS
Michael O'Brien, CAE, President & CEO
Jeff Lowinski, Vice President, Technical Services
Jeffrey Inks, Vice President, Code & Regulatory
John McFee, VP, Certification Programs
Jonathan Paine, VP, Membership & Operations
Restoring watersheds to help provide clean drinking water and replanting forests destroyed by human action and by natural disasters.
Founded in 1927
Mailing list available for rent

16462 **American Hardwood Export Council**
American Hardwood Export Council
1825 Michael Faraday Dr
Reston, VA 20190
703-435-2900; Fax: 703-435-2537
wcma@wcma.com
www.ahec.org
Paul Dow, President
Sid Anderson, III, Vice President
Keith Malmstadt, Treasurer
AHEC provides the global hardwood industry with promotional assistance, technical information and sources of supply for American hardwoods from its international offices.
Founded in 1929

16463 **American Institute of Timber Construction**
American Institute of Timber Construction
7012 S Revere Parkway
Suite 140
Centennial, CO 80112
503-639-0651; Fax: 503-684-8928
info@wmma.org
www.aitc-glulam.org
Facebook, Twitter, LinkedIn
Jamison J. Scott, President
Chris Hacker, Vice President
Fred Stringfellow, Executive Director
Diane Schafer, Director of Meetings
Amy Chetelat, Director of Finance
The national trade association of the structural glued laminated (glulam) timber industry.
Founded in 1899

16464 **American Lumber Standard Committee**
American Lumber Standard Committee
PO Box 210
Germantown, MD 20875-0210
301-972-1700; Fax: 301-540-8004
www.alsc.org
Facebook
Kellie Schroeder, CMP, CAE, CEO / Exec. VP
Clark Malak, Legal Counsel
Sadie Dickinson, Member Services
Scott Biesecker, Finance
Ric Morrison, Technical Advisor
Comprised of manufacturers, distributors, users, and consumers of lumber, serves as the standing committee for the American Softwood Lumber Standard

16465 **American Sports Builders Association**
American Sports Builders Association
9 Newport Drive
Suite 200
Forest Hill, MD 21050
410-730-9595
888-501-2722; Fax: 410-730-8833
info@wmia.org
www.sportsbuilders.org
Facebook, Twitter
Scott Mueller, President
Dave Rakauskas, Vice President
Jim Besonen, Secretary/Treasurer
Liza Wentworth, Program Administrator
Dave Rakauskas, Secretary/Treasurer
Wood flooring manufacturers and distributors.
Founded in 1977

16466 **American Walnut Manufacturers Association**
American Walnut Manufacturers Association
505 East State Street
Jefferson City, MO 65101
573-635-7877; Fax: 573-636-2591
memberservices@asminternational.org
www.walnutassociation.org
Facebook, Twitter, LinkedIn
Dr. Sunniva R. Collins, FASM, President
Jon D. Tirpak, P.E., FASM, Vice President
Craig D. Clauser, P.E., Treasurer
Terry F. Mosier, Managing Director
Virginia Shirk, Foundation Executive Assistant
A national trade group representing manufacturers of walnut lumber, veneer, gunstock and dimensions.
35000 Members
Founded in 1913

16467 **American Wood Chip Export Association**
Stoel Rives
101 South Capitol Boulevard
Suite 1900
Boise, ID 83702
208-389-9000; Fax: 208-389-9040
www.stoel.com
Facebook, Wordpress
Chris Felix, President
Holly Hampton, Vice President
John Schultz, Executive Vice President
Ashley Davis, Administrative Assistant
Tina Schwart, Business & Finance Manager
Researches and compiles data on the wood chip export association.
Founded in 1981

16468 **American Wood Council**
222 Catoctin Circle SE
Suite 201
Leesburg, VA 20175
202-463-2766; Fax: 703-771-4079
www.awc.org
Twitter, LinkedIn, YouTube
Robert Glowinski, President & CEO
The wood products division of the American Forest & Paper Association promotes the use and manufacture of structural wood products.

16469 **American Wood Protection Association**
100 Chase Park S
Suite 116
Birmingham, AL 35244-1851
205-733-4077; Fax: 205-733-4075
webmaster@agma.org
www.awpa.com
Facebook, Twitter
Dean Burrows, Chairman
Joe T Franklin Jr, President
Amir Aboutaleb, Vice President, Technical Division
Jan Alfieri, Director, Education
Mary Ellen Doran, Web Communications Manager
A non-profit organization which is responsible for promulgating voluntary wood preservation standards.
400 Members
Founded in 1916

16470 **Appalachian Hardwood Manufacturers**
Appalachian Hardwood Manufacturers
PO Box 427
Suite 202
High Point, NC 27272
336-885-8315; Fax: 336-886-8865
info@amba.org
www.appalachianwood.org/
Todd Finley, President
Troy Nix, Executive Director
Kym Conis, Managing Director
Promotes the use of Appalachian hardwoods. Provides education and research programs.
400 Members
Founded in 1973

16471 **Architectural Woodwork Institute**
Architectural Woodwork Institute
46179 Westlake Drive
Suite 120
Potomac Falls, VA 20165-5874
571-323-3636; Fax: 571-323-3630
CustomerCare@asme.org
www.awinet.org
Facebook, Twitter, LinkedIn
Julio Guerrero, President
David Soukup, Managing Director, Governance
James W. Coaker, Secretary/Treasurer
John Delli Venneri, Assistant Secretary
William Garofalo, Assistant Treasurer
Members consist of architectural woodworkers, suppliers, design professionals and students from around the world
12000 Members
Founded in 1880

16472 **Association of Equipment Manufacturers**
6737 West Washington Street
Suite 2400
Milwaukee, WI 53214-5647
414-272-0943; Fax: 414-272-1170
aem@aem.org
www.aem.org
Facebook, Twitter, LinkedIn, YouTube
Jeffrey R. Reed, Chair
Association representing manufacturers of equipment for architectural, construction, forestry, materials handling and liability purposes.
900+ Members

16473 **Association of Woodworking & Furnishings Suppliers**
Association of Woodworking & Furnishings
2400 E Katella Avenue
Suite 340
Anaheim, CA 92806
323-838-9440
800-946-2937; Fax: 323-838-9443
www.awfs.org
Facebook, Twitter, Google+, YouTube
Daniel Hershbeger, President
Rob Howell, Secretary/Treasurer
Trade association for suppliers to the woodworking and furnishings industry. Services include three trade shows: Woodworking; Machinery and Supply Fair; Home and Commercial Furnishings.
500 Members

16474 **Capital Lumber Company: Boise**
Capital Lumber Company
5110 North 40th Street
Ste 242
Phoenix, AZ 85018
602-381-0709; Fax: 602-955-6191
info@AFE.org
www.capital-lumber.com
Facebook, Twitter, LinkedIn
Dennis M. Hydrick, CPMM, President & Chairman
Wayne P. Saya, CPE, CPMM, Executive Director
Fred King, Vice Chair of Finance
Virginia N Gibson, Vice Chair of Membership
Wayne P. Saya Sr., CPE, Executive Director
Serves Idaho with a 10,000 square foot warehouse on a five acre site.
Founded in 1915

16475 **Capital Lumber Company: Tacoma**
Capital Lumber Company
230 East F. Street
Ste 242
Tacoma, WA 98421
602-381-0709
877-479-5077; Fax: 602-955-6191
www.capital-lumber.com
Twitter, LinkedIn
Serves Western Washington, Alaska and Western Oregon through a seven acre asphalt covered yard and a 100,000 square foot fully enclosed warehouse.
Founded in 1991

16476 **Cedar Shake and Shingle Bureau**
Cedar Shake & Shingle Bureau
PO Box 1178
Sumas, WA 98295-1178
604-820-7700; Fax: 604-820-0266
amt@amtonline.org
www.cedarbureau.org
Facebook, Twitter, LinkedIn, Youtube
Douglas K Woods, President
Barbara Enns, Lead Accountant
Kathy Milne, Member Services Coordinator
Christine Inglis, Administrative Coordinator
Nonprofit trade association representing manufacturer's, distributors, approved installers and service suppliers of Certilabel™ cedar shakes and shingles.
400 Members
Founded in 1925

16477 **Composite Panel Association**
19465 Deerfield Avenue
Suite 306
Leesburg, VA 20176
703-724-1128; Fax: 703-724-1588
acmhelp@acm.org
www.compositepanel.org
Facebook, Twitter, LinkedIn, Google+, YouTube
Alexander L Wolf, President
Vicki Hanson, Vice President
Erik R Altman, Secretary/Treasurer
Vicki Hanson, Vice President
Erik AR. Altman, Secretary/ Treasurer
Represents Northern American Particle Board and Manufacturers' sister association, Composite Wood Council. Represents manufacturers and suppliers of Composite Wood Council.
Founded in 1947

16478 **Fine Hardwood Veneer Association**
American Walnut Manufacturers Association
260 S 1st Street
Suite 2
Zionsville, IN 46077
317-873-8780; Fax: 317-873-8788
amea@amea.org
www.hpva.org
LinkedIn, YouTube
Jack Mendenhall, CEA, President
Randy Koster, CEA, 1st Vice President
Don Bentley, Second VP
Dave Troutman, Treasurer
Represents the decorative veneer industry. Members are face veneer manufacturers, dealers, veneer custom cutters, rotary face and crossband manufacturers, hardwood industry suppliers, veneer salesman and veneer face plants.
284 Members
Founded in 1983

16479 **Forest Industries Telecommunications**
1565 Oak St
Eugene, OR 97401-4008
541-485-8441; Fax: 541-485-7556
avemexecsec@avem.org
www.landmobile.com
Organized to assist the forest industry in radio matters before the FCC.
49 Members
Founded in 1969

16480 **Forest Landowners Association**
900 Circle 75 Pkwy SE
Suite 205
Atlanta, GA 30339-3075
404-325-2954
800-325-2954; Fax: 404-325-2955
inquiries@clinicalrobotics.com
www.forestlandowners.com
Gyu-Seog Choi, President
Mark Dylewski, Vice President
Rajan Sudan, Vice President
Chung Ngai Tang, Secretary
Joseph Colella, Treasurer
Proactive, progressive, grassroots organization of timberland owners - large and small - who operate more than 47 million acres of timberland in 17 southern and eastern states.
Mailing list available for rent

16481 **Forest Products Society**
15 Technology Parkway South
Ste. 115
Peachtree Corners, GA 30092
855-475-0291; Fax: 608-231-2152
www.forestprod.org
John Addington, Manager
An international non-profit technical association founded to provide an information network for all segments of the forest products industry.
Founded in 1915

16482 **Forest Products Trucking Council**
1025 Vermont Avenue NW
Suite 1020
Washington, DC 20005-3516
202-149-9250
Douglas Domenech, Secretary
An affiliate of the American Pulpwood Association.
50 Members

16483 **Friends of the Trees**
PO Box 165
Hot Springs, MT 59845
406-741-5809
info@csda.org
www.friendsofthetrees.net
Facebook, LinkedIn, YouTube, Instagram
Kevin Baron, President
Jack Sondergard, Vice President
Pat O'Brien, Executive Director
Mike Orzechowski, Secretary/ Treasurer
500 Members
Founded in 1971
Mailing list available for rent

16484 **Great Lakes Timber Professionals Association**
3243 Golf Course Road
PO Box 1278
Rhinelander, WI 54501-1278
715-282-5828; Fax: 715-282-4941
aimcal@aimcal.org
www.timberpa.com
Facebook, Twitter, LinkedIn, YouTube, Instagram
Craig Sheppard, Executive Director
Tracey Ingram, Operations Manager
Melissa Crandall, Administrative Assistant
Ashley Wood, Event Planner
Colin Rupp, Web Designer
A nonprofit organization that is committed to leading the Forest Products industry in sustainable forest management through advocacy, professionalism, service to members, education and training.
Founded in 1984

16485 **Hall-Woolford Tank Co., Inc.**
5500 N Water St
PO Box 2755
Philadelphia, PA 19120
215-329-9022; Fax: 215-329-1177
kim@cemanet.org
www.woodtank.com
Facebook, Twitter, LinkedIn
Jerry Heathman, President
Garry Abraham, Vice President
Paul Ross, Secretary
Robert Reinfried, Executive Vice President of CEMA
E.A. Thompson, Treasurer
To promote the use and to guide the proper construction methods for wooden tanks as per NWTI S-82.
96 Members
Founded in 1933

16486 **Hardwood Manufacturers Association**
Hardwood Manufacturers Association
665 Rodi Road
Suite 305
Pittsburgh, PA 15235
412-244-0440; Fax: 412-244-9090
info@farmequip.org
www.hardwoodinfo.com
Twitter
Vernon Schmidt, Executive Vice President
Elaina Jackson, Membership Services
Tricia Kidd, Accounting and Meeting Services
Kristi Ruggles, Publications and Communications
Hannah Hamontree, Communications Director
Over 100 companies with over 150 locations in the US.
340 Members

16487 **Hardwood Plywood and Veneer Association**
1825 Michael Faraday Dr
Reston, VA 20190-5350
703-435-2900; Fax: 703-435-2537
www.hpva.org
LinkedIn, Youtube
Provides public relations, advertising, marketing, and technical services to manufacturers and distributors of hardwood plywood, veneers and engineered hardwood flooring and suppliers who sell to these industries.
24 Members
Founded in 1925

16488 **Hardwood Utilization Consortium**
USDA Forest Service
Southern Research Station
Blacksburg, VA 24061-0503
540-231-5341; Fax: 540-231-8868
info@fluidpowersafety.com
Rory S. McLaren, Founder & Director
The role is to improve hardwood resource viability through better utilization, technology, markets, cooperative extension and education in the eastern United States.

16489 **Hearth, Patio & Barbecue Association**
1901 N Moore St
Suite 600
Arlington, VA 22209-1708
703-522-0086; Fax: 703-522-0548
Askus@ifps.org
www.hpba.org
Marti Wendel, CFPE, CFPS, CF, President & Chairperson
Donna Pollander, ACA, Executive Director
Jeff Morrow, Business Development Manager
Adele Kayser, Website/Communications Manager
Sue Dyson, Client Data Manager
2600 Members
Founded in 1960

16490 **Intermountain Forest Association**
2218 Jackson Blvd
#10
Rapid City, SD 57702
605-341-0875; Fax: 605-341-8651
info@fpsa.org
www.intforest.org
Facebook, Twitter, LinkedIn, Google+
Gil Williams, Chairman
David Seckman, President & CEO
Robyn Roche, CFO
Andy Drennan, Senior VP, International Market
Adam Finney, VP of Membership and Communications
Seeks to provide a unified voice for the industry. Promotes a sustained timber yield. Monitors federal legislation.
350+ Members
Founded in 2005

16491 **International Wood Products Association**
4214 King St
Alexandria, VA 22302-1555
703-820-6696; Fax: 703-820-8550
www.iwpawood.org
John H Addington, Secretary-Treasurer
Craig H Addington, Account Executive
International trade association for the North American imported wood products industry, representing companies and trade organizations engaged in the import of hardwoods and softwoods from sustainably managed forests in more than 30 nations across the globe.
19 Members
Founded in 1933

16492 **Laminating Materials Association**
Louisiana Municipal Association
700 North 10th street
Baton Rouge, LA 70802
225-344-5001
800-234-8274; Fax: 225-344-3057
info@isapartners.org
www.lma.org
John Duffy, Director
Ed Gerber, Director
Nonprofit trade group representing all decorative overlays and edgebanding in North America. These products are applied to a composite wood substrate and used in the production of furniture, store fixtures, kitchen cabinets and more.
650 Members
Founded in 1988

16493 **Lumbermen's Credit Association**
20 N Wacker Dr
Suite 1800
Chicago, IL 60606-2905
312-553-0943; Fax: 312-553-2149
staff@iadd.org
Facebook, Twitter, LinkedIn
Jeremy T. Guest, President
Mauro Tomelleri, VP, International Activities
Ian Young, Vice President, Media & Content
Jennifer Thoroe, Vice President, Membership
Eric B. Anderson, Vice President, Sales & Marketing
Assist credit managers and salesmen by providing listings and credit ratings of companies which deal in lumber and wood products. Also publishes a directory.

16494 **MSR Lumber Producers Council**
MSR Lumber Producers Council
6300 Enterprise Lane
Madison, WI 53719
888-848-5339; Fax: 888-212-5110
websteward@iamaw.org
www.msrlumber.org
Facebook, Twitter, RSS, Ucubed
R Thomas Buffenbarger, CEO
Robert Martinez, Jr., General VP
Robert Roach, Jr., General Secretary-Treasurer
Diane Babineaux, Executive Assistant
Represents the interest of Machine Stress Rated Lumber Producers in the manufacturing, marketing, promotion, utilization and technical aspects of machine stress rated lumber.
Founded in 1888

16495 **Maple Flooring Manufacturers Association**
Maple Flooring Manufacturers Association
One Parkview Plaza
Suite 800
Oakbrook Terrace, IL 60181
847-480-9138
888-480-9138; Fax: 847-686-2251
www.maplefloor.org
International non-profit trade organization representing manufacturers of northern hard maple solid strip flooring along with flooring contractors, distributors and providers of instalation-related products and services. Maintains technical standards for product quality, grading, shipping and packaging, and quality central.
Founded in 1954

16496 **Mid America Lumbermens Association**
638 W 39th St
Kansas City, MO 64111
816-561-5323
800-747-6529; Fax: 816-561-1249
mail@themla.com
www.themla.com
Facebook, Twitter, LinkedIn
Olivia Holcombe, Executive Vice President
Lisa Stock, Event & Marketing Manager
Bridget Staker, Accountant & Taxes
Mike Griffith, Communications Director
Serves independent lumber and building material retailers in Arkansas, Kansas, Missouri, and Oklahoma.

16497 **National Association of the Remodeling Industry**
P.O. Box 4250
Des Plaines, IL 60016
847-298-9200
800-611-6274; Fax: 847-298-9225
office@mdna.org
www.nari.org
Facebook, Twitter, LinkedIn, Youtube
David Pekel, CEO
Elsie Iturralde, Chief Operaions Officer
Tracy Wright, Sr. Director, Membership & Chapters
Rob King, Director, Marketing
Kelsey Kazmierczak, Manager, Events & Communities
Purpose is to establish and maintain a firm commitment to developing and sustaining programs that expand and unite the remodeling industry; to ensure the industry's growth and security; to encourage ethical conduct, sound business practices and professionalism in the remodeling industry; and to present NARI as the recognized authority in the remodeling industry.
383 Members
Founded in 1941

16498 **National Food Flooring Association**
111 Chesterfield Industrial Boulevard
Suite B
Chesterfield, MO 63005
636-519-9663
800-422-4556
636-519-9663; Fax: 636-519-9664
www.nofma.org
Facebook, Twitter, LinkedIn, Youtube, RSS
Carlos M. Cardoso, Chairman
John M. Stropki, Vice Chairman
Stephen V. Gold, President
Cameron L. Mackey, Vice President, Sales and Marketing
Daniel J. Meckstroth, Vice President and Chief Economist
It's warmer with wood. Genuine hardwoods, plus one-of-a-kind beauty. You never get tired of solid hardware floors - provides the perfect setting.
500+ Members
Founded in 1933

16499 **National Frame Builders Association**
8735 W Higgins Road
Suite 300
Chicago, IL 60631
785-843-2444
800-557-6957; Fax: 847-375-6495
www.nfba.org
Facebook, Twitter, LinkedIn, Youtube, Blooger, RSS
Dave Young, Executive Chairman
John Paxton, President
Gregg E. Goodner, Vice President
Cathy Moose, Executive Assistant
Victoria Wheeler, Director Member Services
Building contractors, suppliers, design and code professionals and academic personnel specializing in the post frame construction industry.
22 Members
Founded in 1945

16500 **National Hardwood Lumber Association**
National Hardwood Lumber Association
PO Box 34518
Memphis, TN 38184
901-377-1818
800-933-0318
bob@mpta.org
www.nhla.com
Youtube
Robert Reinfried, Executive VP
Founded to establish a uniform system of grading rules for the measurement and inspection of hardwood lumber
23 Members
Founded in 1933

16501 **National Lumber & Building Material Dealers Association (NLBMDA)**
2025 M St NW
Suite 800
Washington, DC 20036-3309
202-367-1169
800-634-8645; Fax: 202-367-2169
membersupport@dealer.org
www.dealer.org
Facebook, Twitter, LinkedIn, Google+
Jonathan M. Paine, CAE, President & CEO
Kevin McKenney, Director, Government Affairs
Alex McIntyre, Legislative & Regulatory Coord.
Allison Ward, Membership & Operations Associate
Corie Stretton, Event Manager
Promoting the industry and educating legislators and public policy personnel, assising legislative, regulatory, standard-setting and other government or private bodies in the development of laws, regulations and policies affecting lumber and building material dealers, its customers and suppliers.
Founded in 1955

16502 **National Wood Flooring Association**
111 Chesterfield Industrial
Suite B
Chesterfield, MO 63005-1219
636-519-9663
800-422-4556; Fax: 636-519-9664
info@ntma.org
www.nwfa.org
Twitter, LinkedIn
Rob Akers, CEO
Rich Basalla, Membership Officer
Tiffany Bryson, Sales/Sponsorship Manager
John Capka, Chief Financial Officer
A not-for-profit trade association serving the wood flooring industry
2800 Members
Founded in 1943

16503 **National Wood Window and Door Association**
330 N. Wabash Avenue
Suite 2000
Chicago, IL 60611-4267
312-321-6802; Fax: 847-299-1286
naeda@naeda.com
www.wdma.com
Facebook, Twitter, LinkedIn
Blaine Bingham, Chairman
Richard Lawhun, President/CEO
Joseph Dykes, VP Industry Relations
Michael Williams, VP Operations
Doug Kreienkamp, Coordinator Operations
Members are makers of standard building products such as doors, windows and frames.
5000 Members
Founded in 1900

16504 **National Wooden Pallet & Container Association**
1421 Prince Street
Suite 340
Alexandria, VA 22314-2805
703-519-6104; Fax: 703-519-4720
info@opeesa.com
www.palletcentral.com
Twitter, LinkedIn
Jeff Plotka, President and Director
Nancy Cueroni, Executive Director
David Dollard, Director
Robert Smith, Director
Mark DeShetler, Director
An advocacy organization communicating regularly with key lawmakers and regulators, collaborating with a broad network of business groups and wood product organizations.

16505 **New England Kiln Drying Association**
SUNY
200A Progress Drive Ext,
Burgaw, NC 28425
910-259-9794; Fax: 910-259-1625
pmmiwebhelp@pmmi.org
www.kiln-direct.com
Facebook, Twitter, LinkedIn, Youtube
Charles D. Yuska, President and CEO
Tom Egan, Vice President, Industry Services
Maria Ferrante, VP, Education & Workforce Dev.
Patti Fee, Vice President Meetings And Events
Jim Pittas, Senior Vice President
Disseminates information on the dying of wood to the wood-using industry.
Founded in 1933

16506 **North American Wholesale Lumber Association**
330 N. Wabash Avenue
Suite 2000
Chicago, IL 60611
312-321-5133
800-527-8258; Fax: 312-673-6838
info@patmi.org
www.nawla.org
Scott Parker, Executive Director
Mark Swets, Senior Manager
Elizabeth Conner, Senior Coordinator
Supports the wholesale lumber industry. Publishes monthly NAWLA Bulletin that includes industry and association news, and produces the NAWLA Traders Market, an annual trade show bringing together over 1500 manufacturers and wholesale lumber traders at the premier event in the forest products industry. NAWLA also produces a variety of educational programs designed to enhance professionalism in the lumber industry.
600+ Members
Founded in 1951

16507 **Northeastern Loggers Association**
3311 State Route 28
PO Box 69
Old Forge, NY 13420-0069
315-369-3078
800-318-7561; Fax: 315-369-3736
www.northernlogger.com
Susan Young, Manager
Works to improve the industry in the Northeast and educate the public about policies and products of the industry.
Founded in 1968

16508 **Northern Woods Logging Association**
PO Box 270
Jackman, ME 04945-0270
Provides members with a workers compensation protection program. Conducts on-site inspections and offers a first aid course and safety training program.
213 Members
Founded in 1974

16509 **Northwest Forestry Association**
1500 SW 1st Ave
Suite 700
Portland, OR 97201-5837

503-222-9505; Fax: 503-222-3255
ptrahq@ptra.org
www.nwtrees.org

Doug Landgraf, President
Bill Taylor, First Vice President
Curt Benson, CPMR, Second Vice President
Susan Crolla, Executive Director
Walt Brooks, Treasurer

Promotes forestry throughout the region to assure a permanent industry and stable economy. Works to keep informed on current changes affecting forest products.
Founded in 1972

16510 **Northwestern Lumber Association**
701 Decatur Avenue N
Golden Valley, MN 55427

763-544-6822
888-544-6822; Fax: 763-595-4060
info@nlassn.org
www.nlassn.org
Facebook, Twitter, LinkedIn

Cody Nuernberg, President
Connie Johnson, Director, Professional Development
Jodie Fleck, CMP, Director, Conventions & Tours
Melanie Hultman, Office Manager
Tim Dressen, CONNECTION Editor

Connects member LBM retailers with people, programs, and resources to improve business. Serves Iowa, Minnesota, Nebraska, North Dakota, South Dakota, Upper Michigan, and Wisconsin.
Founded in 1890
Mailing list available for rent

16511 **OSBGuide**
Structural Board Association
25 Valleywood Drive
Unit 27
Markham, L3R 5L9, ON

905-475-1100; Fax: 905-475-1101
ria@robotics.org
osbguide.tecotested.com
Facebook, Twitter, LinkedIn, YouTube, Google+

Jeff Burnstein, Executive Director

Members are manufacturers of structural panels.
Founded in 1974

16512 **Pacific Logging Congress**
Pacific Logging Congress
PO Box 1281
Maple Valley, WA 98038

425-413-2808; Fax: 425-413-1359
rbrothers@wade-partners.com
www.pacificloggingcongress.com

Matt Thompson, President
Sean Ryan, Vice-President
Bill Wade, Executive Director
Toni Nastali, Treasurer
Randy Brothers, Manager

Logging firms.
140 Members
Founded in 1981

16513 **Pacific Lumber Exporters Association**
720 NE Flanders
Suite 207
Portland, OR 97232

503-701-6510; Fax: 503-467-5273
advertising@sme.org
www.lumber-exporters.org
Facebook, Twitter, LinkedIn, Youtube, RSS

Wayne F. Frost, CMfgE, President/Interim CEO
Jeffrey M. Krause, Chief Executive Officer
Dean L. Bartles, PhD, FSME, Secretary/Treasurer
Debbie Holton, Managing Director
Jeannine Kunz, Managing Director

Provide forum to discuss trade issues and problems; promote member companies through governmental and other trade association channels.
7000 Members
Founded in 1932

16514 **Pacific Lumber Inspection Bureau**
Pacific Lumber Inspection Bureau
909 S. 336th St.
Ste 203
Federal Way, WA 98003

253-835-3344; Fax: 253-835-3371
srs@wjweiser.com
www.plib.org
Facebook

Accredited for grading and grade stamping of softwood lumber. Issues certificates on domestic and export lumber shipments.

16515 **Pennsylvania Forest Products Association**
301 Chestnut Street
Suite 102
Harrisburg, PA 17101

717-901-0420
800-232-4562; Fax: 717-901-0360
pmmiwebhelp@pmmi.org
www.paforestproducts.org
Facebook, Twitter

Charles D. Yuska, President and CEO
Tom Egan, Vice President, Industry Services
Maria Ferrante, VP, Education & Workforce Dev.
Patti Fee, Vice President Meetings And Events
Jim Pittas, Senior Vice President

Created to provide members with a unified voice on state legislative and regulatory issues.
650 Members
Founded in 1933

16516 **Railway Tie Association**
Railway Tie Association
115 Commerce Dr
Suite C
Fayetteville, GA 30214-7335

770-460-5553; Fax: 770-460-5573
info@fpda.org
www.rta.org

Tim Gillig, President & Chairman
Patricia A. Lilly, Executive Director
Beth Hiltabidle, Marketing Specialist
Joseph M. Thompson, General Manager
Donald Smith, Accounting Manager

Members include crosstie producers, sawmill owners, chemical manufacturers, wood preservation companies, railroad maintenance engineers, purchasing officials and others.
180 Members
Founded in 1974

16517 **Redwood Inspection Service**
818 Grayson Road
Suite 201
Pleasant Hill, CA 94523

925-935-1499
888-225-7339; Fax: 925-935-1496
contact@uama.org
www.calredwood.org

Authorized by Department of Commerce to develop and supervise redwood lumber grading.
Founded in 1999

16518 **Society of American Foresters**
5400 Grosvenor Lane
Bethesda, MD 20814-2198

301-897-8720
866-897-8720; Fax: 301-897-3690
wsandler@vma.org
www.safnet.org

Terry Baker, Chief Executive Officer
Susi Metz, Director, Finance & Administration
Danielle Watson, Director, Policy & Public Affairs
Angela Colonna, Manager, Marketing & Communications
Steven Glover, Director, Membership

Provides access to information and networking opportunities to prepare members for the challenges and the changes that face natural resource professionals.
100 Members
Founded in 1938

16519 **Society of Wood Science & Technology**
PO Box 6155
Monona, WI 53716-6155

608-577-1342; Fax: 608-467-8979
information@vi-institute.org
www.swst.org
Facebook, Twitter, LinkedIn

Dave Corelli, President
Tom Spettel, Executive Vice President
Robin Ginner, Executive Director
Ellie Murphy, Finance Associate
Ronald L. Eshleman, Ph.D., Technical Director

Promotes policies and procedures which assure the wise use of wood and wood-based products; assures high standards for professional performance of wood scientists and technologists; fosters educational programs at all levels of wood science and technology and further the quality of such programs; represents the profession in public policy development.
3000 Members
Founded in 1972

16520 **Southeastern Lumber Manufacturers Association, Inc.**
Southeastern Lumber Manufacturers
200 Greencastle Road
Tyrone, GA 30290

770-631-6701; Fax: 770-631-6720
www.slma.org
Facebook, Twitter, LinkedIn, RSS, Google+

Victor J Rubino, President
Sandra R. Geller, Executive Vice President
William C. Cubberley, Vice President of Publishing
Anita C. Shapiro, Vice President of Programs
Donald F. Berbary, Chief Sales & Marketing Officer

Represents membership in local, regional, and national problems that affect southeastern lumber industry. Conducts marketing and promotional activity.
Founded in 1933

16521 **Southern Cypress Manufacturers Association**
Southern Cypress Manufacturers Association
400 Penn Center Boulevard
Suite 530
Pittsburgh, PA 15235

877-607-7262
zakaras@rand.org
www.cypressinfo.org
Facebook, Twitter

Michael D Rich, President/CEO
Richard Fallon, SVP and Chief Financial Officer

Andrew R Hoehn, SVP, Research and Analysis
Allison Elder, Vice President, Human Resources
Naveena Ponnusamy, Executive Director, Development

Administrative support provided by the Hardwood Manufacturers Association.
Founded in 1948
Mailing list available for rent

16522 Southern Forest Products Association
6660 Riverside Drive
Suite 212
Metairie, LA 70003

504-443-4464; Fax: 504-443-6612
mail@sfpa.org
www.sfpa.org
Facebook, Twitter, LinkedIn

Tami Kessler, Executive Director
Eric Gee, Deputy Director
Julia Milrod, Communications Manager
Rachel Elton, Accountant
Linda Patch, Program Coordinator

The Association and its members are committed to quality, and believe that Southern Pine forest products provide a smart, environmentally friendly way to meet the world's needs for a wide range of building and industrial products.
Founded in 1915

16523 Southern Pine Inspection Bureau
Southern Pine Inspection Bureau
Po Box 10915
Pensacola, FL 32524-0915

850-434-2611; Fax: 850-434-1290
www.spib.org

Anne Lytle, President

Develops grading standards for Southern pine lumber and provides an inspection service and grade marking systems.
Founded in 1984
Mailing list available for rent

16524 Southern Pressure Treaters' Association
PO Box 1784
Starkville, MS 39760

601-405-1116; Fax: 662-205-8589
www.spta.org
Facebook, Twitter, LinkedIn

Kevin Ragon, Executive Director

Southern Pressure Treaters' Association is composed of producers of industrial treated wood products, suppliers of AWPA approved industrial preservatives and preservative components, distributors, engineers, manufacturers, academia, inspection agencies and producers of untreated wood products.
Founded in 1954

16525 Structural Building Components Association
6300 Enterprise Lane
Madison, WI 53719

608-274-4849; Fax: 608-274-3329
www.sbcindustry.com

Kirk Grundahl, PE, Executive Director

Provide the services our membership needs to continue expanding the market share of all structural building components by promoting the common interests of those engaged in manufacturing trusses, wall panels and related structural components to ensure growth, continuity and increased professionalism.
Founded in 1983

16526 Temperate Forest Foundation
528 Hennepin Avenue
Suite 703
Minneapolis, MN 55403

612-333-0430; Fax: 612-333-0432
sla@sportslaw.org
www.forestinfo.org
Facebook, Twitter, LinkedIn

Matthew J. Mitten, President
Richard A. Guggolz, Executive Director
Ash Narayan, Treasurer
Vered Yakovee, Secretary
William M. Drohan, CAE, Deputy Executive Director

A tax-exempt, non-profit, public charity. Provides leadership by articulating the current realties, and a positive inspiring vision of the future. Helps people move toward the positive vision of living sustainably.

16527 Timber Products Manufacturers Association (TPM)
951 E 3rd Avenue
Spokane, WA 99202-2287

509-535-4646; Fax: 509-534-6106
secretariat@africanstudies.org
www.timberassociation.com
Facebook, Twitter, LinkedIn, Flickr

Toyin Samatar, President
Dorothy Hodgson, Vice President
Suzanne Moyer Baazet, Executive Director
Kathryn Salucka, Program Manager
Kathryn Salucka, Executive Assistant

Association of companies in the Timber and Wood products industry of the pacific northwest. TPM provides human resource and safety consulting, Training and employee benefits.
Founded in 1957

16528 Treated Wood Council
1101 K Street NW
Suite 700
Washington, DC 20005

202-641-5427; Fax: 202-463-2059
jeff_miller@treated-wood.org
www.treated-wood.org

Jeff Miller, Executive Director

To serve all segments of the treated wood industry in the field of government affairs.
450+ Members
Founded in 2003

16529 Tree Care Industry Association
Tree Care Industry Association
136 Harvey Road
Suite 101
Londonderry, NH 03053
603-314-5380
800-733-2622; Fax: 603-314-5386
aallhq@aall.org
www.tcia.org/
Facebook, Twitter, LinkedIn, Flickr

Kate Hagan, Executive Director
Kim Rundle, Executive Assistant
Emily Feltren, Director Government Relations
Julia O'Donnell, Director Membership Marketing
Ashley St. John, Director Marketing/Communications

Supports all those involved with trees and tree care by offering education and training, community events, and publications.
5000+ Members
Founded in 1906
Mailing list available for rent

16530 Truss Plate Institute
218 North Lee Street
Suite 312
Alexandria, VA 22314-2800

703-683-1010; Fax: 866-501-4012
www.tpinst.org
Facebook, Twitter, LinkedIn

Dr. Sandra G. Hirsh, President
Richard Hill, Executive Director
Jan Hatzakos, Director of Finance & Admin
Vanessa Foss, Director of Meetings and Membership
Sandra Holder, Receptionist, Office Assistant

The Truss Plate Institute's mission is '...to maintain the truss industry on a sound engineering basis..'. To accomplish its mission, TPI establishes methods of design and construction for trusses in accordance with the American National Standards Institute's accredited consensus procedures for coordination and development of American National Standards in addition to providing a Quality Assurance Inspection program and by contributing its expertise in other technical areas.
4000 Members
Founded in 1937

16531 West Coast Lumber Inspection Bureau
PO Box 23145
Portland, OR 97281-3145

503-639-0651; Fax: 503-684-8928
info@asindexing.org
www.wclib.org

Fred Leise, President
Diana Witt, Vice President and President-Elect
Gwen Henson, Executive Director
Janet Perlman, Treasurer
Judi Gibbs, Secretary

Supervises manufacturing practices, grade stamping, and inspecting.
1M Members
Founded in 1957

16532 Western Building Material Association
Western Building Material Association
909 Lakeridge Dr. SW
PO Box 1699
Olympia, WA 98502

360-943-3054
888-551-9262; Fax: 360-943-1219
sales@atla.com
www.wbma.org
Facebook

Casey Voorhees, Executive Director
Stephanie Masters, Office Manager

Regional trade association derving building material dealers throughout the states of Alaska, Idaho, Montana, Oregon and Washington and a federated association of the National Lumber and Building Material Dealers Association.
800 Members
Founded in 1991

16533 Western Forestry and Conservation Association
4033 SW Canyon Rd
Portland, OR 97221

503-226-4562
888-722-9416; Fax: 503-226-2515
info@lff.org
www.westernforestry.org

Richard Zabel, Executive Director

Offers high-quality continuing education workshops and seminars for professional foresters throughout Oregon, Washington, Idaho,

Montana, Northern California and British Columbia.
Founded in 1909
Mailing list available for rent

16534 Western Red Cedar Lumber Association
Western Red Cedar Lumber Association
1501-700 West Pender Street
Pender Place 1, Business Building
Vancouver, BC V6C 1G8

604-891-1262
800-266-1910; Fax: 604-687-4930
ww.realcedar.com
Facebook, Twitter, LinkedIn

Kristen Regina, President
Heather Gendron, Vice-President/President Elect
Jamie Lausch Vander Broek, Secretary
Mark Pompelia, Treasurer
Carol Graney, Editorial Director

Mission is to produce quality Western Red Cedar lumber products and support them with technical education and promotion.
Founded in 1972

16535 Western Wood Preservers Institute
12503 SE Mill Plain Blvd.
Suite 205
Vancouver, WA 98684

360-693-9958
wwpinstitute.org
Facebook, Twitter, LinkedIn

Dallin Brooks, Executive Director
Butch Bernhard, Sr. Program Manager
Ryan Pessah, Director of Government Relations
Becky Brock, Administrative Officer Manager

Western Wood Preservers Institute (WWPI) represents the interests of the preserved wood products industry throughout western North America. Its membership consists of companies that either manufacture products, are directly affiliated or provide a service to the preserved wood industry.
Founded in 1947

16536 Western Wood Products Association
1500 SW First Ave.
Suite 870
Portland, OR 97201

503-224-3930; Fax: 503-224-3935
webmaster@apalaweb.org
wwpa.org
Facebook, Twitter, LinkedIn, Flickr

Buenaventura Ven Basco, Executive Director

Represents lumber manufacturers in 12 Western states and Alaska. Provides lumber quality control, technical support, and business information to supporting mills.
310 Members
Founded in 1980

16537 Window & Door Manufacturers Association
Window & Door Manufacturers Association
330 N. Wabash Avenue
Suite 2000
Chicago, IL 60611-4267

312-321-6802
800-223-2301; Fax: 847-299-1286
office@alise.org
www.wdma.com
Facebook, Twitter, LinkedIn

John Budd, President
Connie Van Fleet, VP/President-Elect
Deborah York, Executive Director
Jeremy Uthank, Information Management

A trade association representing approximately 145 U.S. and Canadian manufacturers and suppliers of windows and doors for the domestic and export markiets.
Founded in 1915

16538 Wood Component Manufacturers Association
Wood Component Manufacturers Association
PO Box 662 Lindstrom
Ste 350
Minneapolis, MN 55045

651-332-6332; Fax: 651-400-3502
info@aplici.org
www.woodcomponents.org
Twitter

Allison Burns, President
Debbie Dickson, Vice President
Liz Nugent, Recording Secretary
Joann Donatiello, Acting Treasurer

Represents manufacturers of wood component products for furniture, cabinetry, building products, and decorative wood products.
Founded in 1968

16539 Wood Machinery Manufacturers of America
9 Newport Drive
Suite 200
Forest Hill, MD 21050

443-640-1052; Fax: 443-640-1031
info@wmma.org
www.wmma.org
Facebook, Twitter, LinkedIn

Chris Hacker, President
Stephen Carter, Vice President
Fred Stringfellow, Chief Executive Officer
Kristin Grove, Member Services Coordinator
Diane Schafer, Meetings Director

Organization dedicated to supporting and advocating for manufacturers of machinery and tooling used for processing wood.
Founded in 1899

16540 Wood Machining Institute
Wood Machining Institute
420 N Civic Dr.
Suite 406
Walnut Creek, CA 94596

925-943-5240; Fax: 925-943-5240
szymani@woodmachining.com
www.woodmachining.com

Ryszard Szymani, Ph.D., Editor/Publisher
Ryszard Szymani, Ph.D., Dir. & Machine Safety Consultant

Information on the latest technological advances in the field of wood machining, including sawing, planning and sanding operations as well as the production of veneers and chips.
Cost: $72.00
Frequency: Fortnightly
Circulation: 600
Founded in 1984

16541 Wood Moulding and Millwork Producers Association
MMPA
507 1st St
Woodland, CA 95695-4025

530-661-9591
800-550-7889; Fax: 530-661-9586
info@acl.org
www.wmmpa.com
Facebook, Twitter

Frank Quinn, President
Janelle Mazelin, Executive Director
Rodney Birch, Vice President
Sheila O Carlblom, Treasurer
Denise Nelson, Secretary

Promote quality products produced by its members, to develop sources of supply, to promote optimum use of raw materials to standardize products, and to increase the domestic and foreign usage of moulding and millwork products.
574 Members
Founded in 1956

16542 Wood Products Manufacturers Association
PO Box 761
Westminster, MA 01473-0761

978-874-5445; Fax: 978-874-9946
woodprod@wpma.org
www.wpma.org
Facebook, LinkedIn

Philip Bibeau, Executive Director

Information and services to support businesses in the industry.
Founded in 1929

16543 WoodWorks - Wood Products Council
1101 K Street NW
Suite 700
Washington, DC 20005

info@woodworks.org
www.woodworks.org

Jennifer Cover, PE, President & CEO

WoodWorks aims to facilitate project teams to design, engineer and construct successful commercial and multi-family wood buildings in the U.S. The council offers free project support, a nationwide education program, and publishes industry resources.

16544 Woodworking Machinery Industry Association
225 Reinekers Lane
Suite 410
Alexandria, VA 22314

571-279-8340; Fax: 571-279-8343
info@wmia.org
www.wmia.org
Facebook, Twitter, LinkedIn, YouTube

Larry Hoffer, President
Jeff Linder, Program Manager
Heather Jolley, Program Administrator
Rick Braun, Director
Andreas Muehlbauer, Director

Represents importers and distributors of woodworking machinery and ancillary equipment, as well as being a link between suppliers and manufacturers. The organization supports its members through industry awards, safety publications, scholarships and networking platforms.
Founded in 1977

16545 World Millwork Alliance
10047 Robert Trent Jones Parkway
New Port Richey, FL 34655-4649

727-372-3665; Fax: 727-372-2879
mail@worldmillworkalliance.com
www.worldmillworkalliance.com

Rosalie Leon, President/CEO
Tim Hicks, Chair
Carl McKenzie, 1st Vice Chair
Jeff Williams, Treasurer

Provides leadership, certification, education, promotion, networking and advocacy to, and for, the millwork distribution industry.
Founded in 1963

Newsletters

16546 AFRC News
American Forest Resource Council

5100 SW Macadam
Suite 350
Portland, OR 97239

503-222-9505; Fax: 503-222-3255
info@amforest.org
www.amforest.org

Tom Partin, President

Newsletter of the American Forest Resource Council.
Frequency: Monthly

16547 **American Wood Protection Association Newsletter**
American Wood Protection Association
100 Chase Park South
Suite 116
Birmingham, AL 35244-1851

205-733-4077; Fax: 205-733-4075
www.awpa.com

John Hall, Publisher

Reports on governmental issues and environmental news.
Cost: $7.50
12 Pages
Frequency: Monthly
Founded in 1921

16548 **Classified Exchange**
Miller Publishing Corporation
PO Box 34908
Memphis, TN 38184-0908

901-372-8280
800-844-1280; Fax: 901-373-6180
editor@millerwoodtradepub.com
www.millerpublishing.com

Paul J Miller, President
Sue Putnam, Editor

Pages and pages of bargains, several pages on raw material and service sources for everything from lumber to curved plywood, from dry kilns to sawmill equipment and boilers. Special liquidations and auctions offering everything from soup to nuts.
Cost: $65.00
Frequency: Monthly

16549 **Connected**
Association of Millwork Distributors
10047 Robert Trent Jones Pkwy
Trinity, FL 34655-4649

727-372-3665
800-786-7274; Fax: 727-372-2879
marketing@amdweb.com
www.amdweb.com

Rosalie Leone, CEO

Keeps you abreast of the latest breaking news within the millwork industry regarding economics & finance; the current housing industry; legislative updates; codes, standards and the AMD Certification Program information, Education special offers as well as comprehensive Millwork News.
Frequency: Weekly

16550 **Forestbytes**
American Forests
734 15th Street NW
Suite 800
Washington, DC 20005

202-737-1944
www.americanforests.org
Facebook, Twitter

Lynda Webster, Chair
Scott Steen, CEO

Features environmental stories and breakthroughs that impact our forests and trees and news and updates on American Forests projects and programs.
Frequency: Monthly
Founded in 1990

16551 **Forestry Source**
Society of American Foresters
5400 Grosvenor Ln
Bethesda, MD 20814-2198

301-897-8720; Fax: 301-897-3690
www.safnet.org
Facebook, Twitter, LinkedIn

Morgan Fincham, Director, Publications
Steve Wilent, Editor

Offers the latest information on national forestry trends, the latest developments in forestry at the federal, state, and local levels, the newest advances in forestry-related research and technology, and up-to-date information about SAF programs and activities.
Cost: $33.00
Frequency: Monthly
Founded in 1900
Printed in 4 colors

16552 **Import/Export Wood Purchasing News**
Miller Publishing Corporation
PO Box 34908
Memphis, TN 38184-0908

901-372-8280
800-844-1280; Fax: 901-373-6180
editor@millerwoodtradepub.com
www.millerpublishing.com

Paul J Miller, President
Sue Putnam, Editor

Read features about overseas buyers, U.S. factories buying imported forest products and North American exporters. Also carries forest products business trends on the domestic and international markets.
Cost: $75.00
Frequency: Bi-Monthly

16553 **MLA LINE**
Mid America Lumbermens Association
638 W 39th St
Kansas City, MO 64111

816-561-5323
800-747-6529; Fax: 816-561-1249
mail@themla.com
www.themla.com

Olivia Holcombe, Executive Vice President

Lumber Industry News Express is the e-newsletter of the MLA.
Frequency: Monthly

16554 **MSR Council Matters**
MSR Lumber Producers Council
6300 Enterprise Lane
Madison, WI 53719

888-848-5339; Fax: 888-212-5110
info@msrlumber.org
www.msrlumber.org

Steve Hardy, President

Provides updates on issues affecting members and customers
Frequency: Monthly
Founded in 1987

16555 **National Frame Builders Association Newsletter**
National Frame Builders Association
4700 W. Lake Avenue
Glenview, IL 60025

785-843-2444
800-557-6957; Fax: 847-375-6495
info@nfba.org
www.nfba.org

John Fullerton, VP
Tom Knight, President

Published by the National Frame Builders Association.

16556 **National Wooden Pallet & Container Association: Newsletter**
National Wooden Pallet & Container Association
1421 Prince Street
Suite 340
Alexandria, VA 22314-3501

703-519-6104; Fax: 703-519-4720
palletcomm@aol.com

Bruce N Scholnick, President
Pamela Wilson, Publisher
Kathy Conroy, Marketing Director
Sam McAdow, Interim President
Susan Cheney, Membership Coordinator

Newsletter published by The National Wooden Pallet and Container Association.
Cost: $2995.00

16557 **SFPA E-Newsletter**
Southern Forest Products Association
6660 Riverside Drive
Suite 212
Metairie, LA 70003

504-443-4464; Fax: 504-443-6612
mail@sfpa.org
www.sfpa.org

Tami Kessler, Executive Director
Eric Gee, Deputy Director
Julia Milrod, Communications Manager
Rachel Elton, Accountant
Linda Patch, Program Coordinator

The Association and its members are committed to quality, and believe that Southern Pine forest products provide a smart, environmentally friendly way to meet the world's needs for a wide range of building and industrial products.
Frequency: Bi-Weekly

16558 **Scene...in a Flash**
Northwestern Lumber Association
701 Decatur Avenue N
Golden Valley, MN 55427

763-544-6822
888-544-6822; Fax: 763-595-4060
info@nlassn.org
www.nlassn.org

Tim Dressen, Editor

Latest information on association activities and industry news.
Frequency: Monthly
Circulation: 1900
Mailing list available for rent

16559 **Softwood Forest Products Buyer**
Miller Publishing Corporation
PO Box 34908
Memphis, TN 38184-0908

901-372-8280
800-844-1280; Fax: 901-373-6180
editor@millerwoodtradepub.com
www.millerpublishing.com

Paul J Miller, President
Sue Putnam, Editor

Provides you with interesting feature articles on purchasing, inventory control, marketing, production, utilization and distribution of Softwood forest products such as lumber, plywood, moulding, etc.
Cost: $65.00
Frequency: Bi-Monthly

16560 **TPM Bulletin**
Timber Products Manufacturers Association

951 E 3rd Avenue
Spokane, WA 99202-2287

509-535-4646; Fax: 509-534-6106
tpm@tpmrs.com

Dick Molenda, Interim President
Shelley Jeffers, Publications Coordinator

Provides insightful overviews of key employment issues that can impact every business.
Frequency: Monthly
Circulation: 250

16561 TPM Newsletter
Timber Products Manufacturers (TPM) Association
951 E 3rd Avenue
Spokane, WA 99202-2287

509-535-4646; Fax: 509-534-6106
tpm@tpmrs.com

Dick MoLenda, Interim President
Jeff Bosma, Chairman

Official newsletter of Timber Products Manufacturers (TPM) Association.
Cost: $195.00
250 Members
Frequency: Monthly
Circulation: 700
Founded in 1916

16562 The Cutting Edge
Wood Machinery Manufacturers of America
9 Newport Drive
Suite 200
Forest Hill, MD 21050

443-640-1052; Fax: 443-640-1031
info@wmma.org
www.wmma.org

Chris Hacker, President
Stephen Carter, Vice President
Kristin Grove, Member Services Coordinator
Jennifer Miller, Associate Director

Newsletter featuring articles on woodworking equipment and the wood processing industry, as well as public policy updates that would affect business for members of the Wood Machinery Manufacturers of America organization.
Frequency: Monthly
Founded in 1899

16563 Timberline
Bear Creek Lumber
Po Box 669
Winthrop, WA 98862

800-597-7191; Fax: 509-997-2040
customerservice@bearcreeklumber.com
www.bearcreeklumber.com
Twitter, LinkedIn

Features articles about the timber industry, the construction industry, how-to information, and it also lets folks know what's new at Bear Creek Lumber.
Cost: $15.00
6000 Pages

16564 TreeWorker
Tree Care Industry Association
136 Harvey Road
Suite 101
Londonderry, NH 03053

603-314-5380
800-733-2622; Fax: 603-314-5386
tcia@tcia.org
www.tcia.org
Facebook, Twitter, LinkedIn, Youtube

Mark Garvin, Interim CEO/President
Peter Gerstenberger, Sr Adv Safety/Standards/Compliance
Frequency: Monthly
Founded in 1938

16565 Two-By-Four
Mountain States Lumber & Building Material Dealers
9034 E Easter Pl
#103
Centennial, CO 80112-2104

303-793-0859
800-365-0919; Fax: 303-290-9137
www.mslbmda.org

Geri Adams, Executive Director

16566 WMA Newsletter
World Millwork Alliance
10047 Robert Trent Jones Parkway
New Port Richey, FL 34655-4649

727-372-3665; Fax: 727-372-2879
mail@worldmillworkalliance.com
www.worldmillworkalliance.com

Rosalie Leone, President/CEO
Tim Hicks, Chair
Carl McKenzie, 1st Vice Chair
Jeff Williams, Treasurer

Updates for wholesale millwork distribution companies.
Frequency: Monthly
Circulation: 1500
Founded in 1963
Printed in 2 colors on glossy stock

16567 WMIA News
Woodworking Machinery Industry Association
225 Reinekers Lane
Suite 410
Alexandria, VA 22314

571-279-8340; Fax: 571-279-8343
info@wmia.org
www.wmia.org/wmia-newsletter

Larry Hoffer, President
Jeff Linder, Program Manager
Heather Jolley, Program Administrator
Rick Braun, Director

Newsletter from the Woodworking Machinery Industry Association providing updates on events and members.
Founded in 1977

16568 Wood Design Focus
Forest Products Society
2801 Marshall Court
Madison, WI 53705-2295

608-231-1361; Fax: 608-231-2152
info@forestprod.org
www.forestprod.org
Facebook, Twitter

Paul Merrick, President
Patrice Tardif, President-Elect
Timothy M. Young, Vice President
Stefan Bergmann, Executive Vice President

Online publication providing a communications link between design professionals, educators, researchers, building code officials, and manufacturers of engineered wood products through the publication of technical articles related to contemporary engineered wood construction.
Cost: $125.00
Frequency: Quarterly
Founded in 1947

Magazines & Journals

16569 AMD Millwork Magazine
Association of Millwork Distributors
10047 Robert Trent Jones Pkwy
Trinity, FL 34655-4649

727-372-3665
800-786-7274; Fax: 727-372-2879
marketing@amdweb.com
www.amdweb.com

Rosalie Leone, CEO

Digital news journal distributed to AMD members and industry professionals with an interest in the millwork industry. An inside look at the heartbeat of AMD and offers industry insights found nowhere else.
Frequency: Monthly

16570 American Forests
American Forests
734 15th Street NW
Suite 800
Washington, DC 20005

202-737-1944; Fax: 202-955-4588
www.americanforests.org
Facebook, Twitter

Deborah Gangloff, Executive Director
Lydia Scalettar, Art Director

Updates on forest management and environmental policy, as well as news on the programs and policies of the American Forests organization.
Cost: $25.00
Frequency: Quarterly
Circulation: 25000
Founded in 1875

16571 American Forests Magazine
American Forests
734 15th Street NW
Suite 800
Washington, DC 20005

202-737-1944
www.americanforests.org
Facebook, Twitter

Lynda Webster, Chair
Scott Steen, CEO

Topics covered include urban forestry methods and visiting champion trees, fighting invasive species and learning about the many incredible creatures that make their homes in forests.
Frequency: Bi-Annually
Founded in 1990

16572 Building Products CONNECTION
Northwestern Lumber Association
701 Decatur Avenue N
Golden Valley, MN 55427

763-544-6822
888-544-6822; Fax: 763-595-4060
info@nlassn.org
www.nlassn.org

Tim Dressen, Editor

Dedicated to providing information on issues important to the success of the lumber and building material industry in the upper Midwest.
Cost: $300.00
Frequency: Bi-Monthly
Circulation: 1900
Mailing list available for rent

16573 Crossties
Railway Tie Association
115 Commerce Dr
Suite C
Fayetteville, GA 30214-7335

770-460-5553; Fax: 770-460-5573
ties@rta.org
www.rta.org

Talty O'Connor, President/CEO

Highlights new products, industry news, and personnel changes.
Cost: $35.00
Circulation: 3000
Founded in 1983

16574 **Crow's Weekly Market Report**
CC Crow Publications
3635 N Farragut St
Portland, OR 97217-5954
503-241-7382; Fax: 503-646-9971
info@chadcrowe.com
www.chadcrowe.com
Facebook, Twitter, LinkedIn
Chad Crowe, President
Sam Sherrill, Editor
Tracks the wood and lumber industry, providing customers with accurate and timely pricing and analysis.
Cost: $285.00
Frequency: Weekly
Circulation: 2000
Founded in 1921
Mailing list available for rent

16575 **Custom Woodworking Business**
Vance Publishing
400 Knightsbridge Parkway
Lincolnshire, IL 60069
847-342-2600
800-343-2016; Fax: 847-634-4374
industrialinfo@vancepublishing.com
Facebook, Twitter, Youtube
William C Vance, CEO
Helen Kuhl, Editor
Harry Urban, VP Publishing
Bill Esler, Associate Publisher/Editor-in-Chief
Rich Christianson, Associate Publisher/Editor-at-Large
Founded in 1937

16576 **Design Solutions Magazine**
Architectural Woodwork Institute
46179 Westlake Drive
Suite 120
Potomac Falls, VA 20165
571-323-3636; Fax: 571-323-3630
info@awinet.org
www.awinet.org
Judy Durham, Executive VP
Philip Duvic, Marketing Director
Kirsten Ingham, President
Featuring beautiful woodwork projects manufactured by members of the Architectural Woodwork Institute (AWI). Many other related publications, including woodworking quality standards used by woodwork manufacturers and design professionals.
Cost: $25.00
Frequency: Quarterly
Circulation: 27000

16577 **Evergreen Magazine**
Evergreen Foundations
PO Box 1290
Bigfork, MT 59911
406-837-0966; Fax: 406-258-0815
editor@evergreenmagazine.com
www.evergreenmagazine.com
Facebook
James D Petersen, Publisher
Focuses on issues and events impacting forestry, forest communities, and the forest product industry. Includes profiles of industry leaders and advocates.
Frequency: Bi-Monthly
Circulation: 100000

16578 **Fine Woodworking**
Taunton Press
63 South Main Street
PO Box 5506
Newtown, CT 06470-2355
203-426-8171
800-477-8727; Fax: 203-426-3434
fwads@taunton.com
www.taunton.com
James Chiavelli, Publisher
Richard West, Advertising Manager
Published since 1975, written by woodworkers for woodworkers regularly shows the finest work in wood being done today.
Cost: $34.95
120 Pages
Frequency: 7 Issues (1yr)
Circulation: 250000
Founded in 1980
Printed in 4 colors on glossy stock

16579 **Forest Industries**
Miller Freeman Publications
600 Harrison Street
6th Fl
San Francisco, CA 94107
415-947-6000; Fax: 415-947-6055
www.mfi.com
Directed to foresters, loggers and manufacturers.
Cost: $55.00
90 Pages
Frequency: Monthly

16580 **Forest Landowner Magazine**
Forest Landowners Association
900 Circle 75 Pkwy Se
Suite 205
Atlanta, GA 30339-3075
404-325-2954
800-325-2954; Fax: 404-325-2955
info@forestlandowners.com
www.forestlandowners.com
Scott P Jones, Executive VP
Joy Moore, Circulation Director
Provides members with applied, practical and current forestry information written by the most experienced and successful forestry professionals.
Cost: $50.00
Circulation: 9000
Founded in 1941

16581 **Forest Products Journal**
Forest Products Society
2801 Marshall Ct
Madison, WI 53705-2295
608-231-1361; Fax: 608-231-2152
info@forestprod.org
www.forestprod.org
Facebook, Twitter, LinkedIn
Carol Lewis, VP
Covers the latest research and technology from every branch of the forest products industry.
Cost: $155.00
Founded in 1945

16582 **Forests and People**
Louisiana Forestry Association
PO Drawer 5067
Alexandria, LA 71307
318-443-2558; Fax: 318-443-1713
www.laforestry.com
Facebook, Twitter
Janet Tompkins, Editor
Mike Merritt, President
Buck Vandersteen, Executive Director
Karla Johnson, Admin. Assistant/Annual Meeting
Debbie Dodd, Membership/Tree Farm Magazine
Cost: $250.00
36 Pages
Frequency: Quarterly
Circulation: 5800
ISSN: 0015-7589
Founded in 1947
Printed in 4 colors on glossy stock

16583 **Frame Building News**
National Frame Builders Association
4700 W. Lake Avenue
Glenview, IL 60025
785-843-2444
800-557-6957; Fax: 847-375-6495
info@nfba.org
www.nfba.org
Facebook
John Fullerton, VP
Tom Knight, President
The official publication of National Frame Builders Association.

16584 **Great Lakes TPA Magazine**
Great Lakes Timber Professionals Association
3243 Golf Course Road
PO Box 1278
Rhinelander, WI 54501-1278
715-282-5828; Fax: 715-282-4941
info@timberpa.com
www.timberpa.com
Henry Schienebeck, Executive Director & Editor
The magazine provides education and information on the practice and promotion of sustainable forestry and seeks to instill a sense of pride and professionalism among manufacturers, operators, transporters, landowners, and foresters.
Cost: $24.00
Frequency: Monthly
Circulation: 2500

16585 **Hardwood Floors**
National Wood Flooring Association
111 Chesterfield Industrial
Chesterfield, MO 63005-1219
636-519-9663
800-422-4556; Fax: 636-519-9664
info@nwfa.org
www.nwfa.org
Ed Korczak, Executive Director
An essential educational tool, with articles on everything from sanding and finishing techniques to industry trends and tips on running a profitable business.
Frequency: 6x/Year
Circulation: 25000

16586 **International Journal of Forest Engineering**
Forest Products Society
2801 Marshall Court
Madison, WI 53705-2295
608-231-1361; Fax: 608-231-2152
info@forestprod.org
www.forestprod.org
Facebook, Twitter
Paul Merrick, President
Patrice Tardif, President-Elect
Timothy M. Young, Vice President
Stefan Bergmann, Executive Vice President
Committed to serving the international forest engineering community as the voice of new ideas and developments in forest engineering. Reporting on existing practices and innovations in forest engineering by scientists and professionals from around the world which promote environmentally sound forestry practices and contribute to sustainable forest management.
Frequency: Semiannually
Founded in 1947

16587 **International Wood: The Guide to Applications, Sources & Trends**
International Wood Products Association

4214 King St
Alexandria, VA 22302-1555

703-820-6696; Fax: 703-820-8550
info@iwpawood.org
www.iwpawood.org

Brent McClendon, Executive VP/CAE
Annette Ferri, Member Services
Brigid Shea, Government Affairs
Annette Ferri, Director, Finance & Administration
Ashley A. Amidon, Manager, Government

Formerly Imported Wood, International Wood continues to lead with innovative new designs and new product applications.
Frequency: Annual
Circulation: 25000

16588 **Journal of Forestry**
Society of American Foresters
5400 Grosvenor Ln
Bethesda, MD 20814-2198

301-897-8720; Fax: 301-897-3690
www.safnet.org

Morgan Fincham, Director, Publications

To advance the profession of forestry by keeping professionals informed about significant developments and ideas in the many facets of forestry: economics, education and communication, entomology and pathology, fire, forest ecology, geospatial technologies, history, international forestry, measurments, policy, recreation, silviculture, social sciences, soils anf hydrology, urban and community forestry, utilization and engineering, and wildlife management.
Cost: $85.00
Frequency: 8 Times
ISSN: 0022-1201
Founded in 1902
Printed in 4 colors on glossy stock

16589 **Loggers' World**
Loggers World Publications
4206 Jackson Hwy
Chehalis, WA 98532-8425

360-262-3376
800-462-8283; Fax: 360-262-3337
logworld@aol.com
www.loggersworld.com

Mike Crouse, Publisher
Kevin Core, Advertising Manager
Finley Hays, Editor
Darin Burt, Writer

Accepts advertising.
Cost: $12.00
56 Pages
Frequency: Monthly
Circulation: 16,000
Founded in 1966

16590 **Logging & Sawmilling Journal**
Logging & Sawmilling Journal
Po Box 86670
Vancouver, BC V7L-4L2

604-990-9970; Fax: 604-990-9971
stanhope@forestnet.com
www.forestnet.com
Facebook

Rob Stanhope, Publisher
Lil Fawcus, Production Manager
Mailing list available for rent

16591 **Lumber Cooperator**
Northeastern Retail Lumber Association
585 N Greenbush Rd
Rensselaer, NY 12144-9615

518-286-1010
800-292-6752; Fax: 518-286-1755
rferris@nrla.org
www.nrla.org

Rita Ferris, President

Includes the latest industry, legislative and regulatory news, as well as issues and trends that most influence the lumber and building materials business. Readers gain insight into the newest methods, management techniques, new product ideas, family owned business concerns and key industry issues.
Cost: $40.00
100 Pages
Circulation: 5000
Founded in 1894

16592 **Lumberman's Equipment Digest**
Lumbermen Online
PO Box 1146
Columbia, TN 38401

931-381-1638
800-477-7606; Fax: 931-388-3564
publisher@lumbermenonline.com
www.lumbermenonline.com

Brady Carr, Publisher
Tammy Coffman, Advertising Manager
Shana Hibdon, Internet Technical Support
Gina High, Graphics Department
Cost: $38.00
Frequency: Monthly
Circulation: 35,000

16593 **Millwork Magazine**
Association of Millwork Distributors
10047 Robert Trent Jones Pkwy
New Port Richey, FL 34655-4649

727-372-3665
800-786-7274; Fax: 727-372-2879
www.amdweb.com
Twitter, LinkedIn

Rosalie Leone, CEO/ Secretary
Dan Barber, President
John Crowder, 1st VP
Mark Hefley, Associate VP
George Kessel, Treasurer

Articles of interest to AMD members.
1200 Members
Frequency: Monthly
Founded in 1935

16594 **Modern Woodworking**
Modern Woodworking
90 West Afton Ave. #117
Yardley, PA 19067

267-519-1705
800-633-5953; Fax: 205-391-2081
www.farmhausmodern.com

Brooke Wisdom, Executive Editor
W.W. Chip Wisdom, VP/Group Publisher
Mailing list available for rent

16595 **National Hardwood Magazine**
Miller Publishing Company
PO Box 34908
Memphis, TN 38184-0908

901-372-8280
800-844-1280; Fax: 901-373-6180
editor@millerwoodtradepub.com
www.millerpublishing.com

Paul J Miller, President
Wayne Miller, VP
Sue Putnam, Editor

A monthly journal serving the hardwood industry including sawmillls, distillation, lumber yards, wholesalers and buyers and woodworkers.
Cost: $45.00
85 Pages
Frequency: Monthly
Circulation: 5000
Founded in 1927
Printed in 4 colors on glossy stock

16596 **Northern Journal of Applied Forestry**
Society of American Foresters
5400 Grosvenor Ln
Bethesda, MD 20814-2198

301-897-8720
866-897-8720; Fax: 301-897-3690
www.safnet.org
Facebook, Twitter, LinkedIn

Morgan Fincham, Director, Publications

Each regional journal of applies forestry focuses on research, practice, and techniques targeted to foresters and allied professionals in specific regions of the United States and Canada. This journal covers northeastern, midwestern, and boreal forests in the United States and Canada.
Cost: $75.00
Frequency: 4 Times
ISSN: 0742-6348

16597 **Pallet Enterprise**
Industrial Reporting
10244 Timber Ridge Dr
Ashland, VA 23005-8135

804-550-0323
800-805-0263; Fax: 804-550-2181
ed@ireporting.com
www.palletenterprise.com

Edward C Brindley Jr, Publisher
Chris Edwards, Production Manager
Chaille Brindley, Assistant Publisher
Scott Brindley, Marketing Director
Laura Seal, Circulation Manager

Written for those who manufacture, repair, sell or use wooden pallets and containers. Regular features include a market column, new products section and industry events.
Cost: $60.00
104 Pages
Frequency: Monthly
Circulation: 15000
Founded in 1981
Printed in 4 colors on glossy stock

16598 **PalletCentral**
National Wooden Pallet & Container Association
1421 Prince Street
Suite 340
Alexandria, VA 22314-2805

703-519-6104; Fax: 703-519-4720

John T. Swenby, Chair
James Ruder, Chair-Elect
James Schwab, Secretary/ Treasurer
Bruce N. Scholnick, President

The technical journal for the solid wood packaging industry published by the NWPCA. First with essential news and innovations affecting wood packaging companies, going beyond reporting to provide useful analysis and strategies for coping with industry changes.
700+ Members
Frequency: Montly
Circulation: 6000
Founded in 1947

16599 **Panel World**
Hatton-Brown Publishers
225 Hanrick Street(36104)
PO Box 2268
Montgomery, AL 36102-3317

334-834-1170
800-669-5613; Fax: 334-834-4525
mail@hattonbrown.com
www.hattonbrown.com

Rich Donnell, Editor
Rhonda Thomas, Circulation Manager
Dan Shell, Managing Editor
Jennifer McCary, Associate Editor
Tonya Cooner, Associate Editor

For people who deal with production, sales, marketing, distribution, fabrication and utilization of veneer, plywood and other panel prod-

ucts.
Cost: $40.00
Circulation: 12850
Founded in 1948
Printed in 4 colors on matte stock

16600 Popular Woodworking
F And W Publications
10151 Carver Road, Suite # 200
Blue Ash, OH 45242
513-531-2690; Fax: 513-531-1843
publicity@fwmedia.com
David Nussbaum, CEO
Don Schroder, Ad Manager
Everything woodworkers need to develop their skills; in-depth tool reviews and tests, shop tips, finishing secrets, projects and more.
Cost: $28.00
104 Pages
Frequency: Monthly
Circulation: 240151
Founded in 1981

16601 Rural Builder
F And W Publications
10151 Carver Road, Suite # 200
Blue Ash, OH 45242
513-531-2690; Fax: 715-445-4087
Steve Shanesy, Publisher
Don Schroder, Advertising Manager

16602 Southern Loggin' Times
Hatton-Brown Publishers
PO Box 2268
Montgomery, AL 36102-2268
334-834-1170
800-669-5613; Fax: 334-834-4525
mail@hattonbrown.com
www.hattonbrown.com
David H Ramsey, President
Rich Donnell, Editor
Monitors the south's forest products industry.
Cost: $65.00
Frequency: Monthly
Circulation: 13,408
ISSN: 0744-2106
Founded in 1948
Printed in 4 colors on glossy stock

16603 Southern Lumberman
Hatton-Brown Publishers
PO Box 2268
Montgomery, AL 36102-2268
334-834-1170
800-669-5613; Fax: 334-834-4525
mail@hattonbrown.com
www.hattonbrown.com
David H Ramsey, President
Rich Donnell, Editor
Industry news for sawmill operators and dimension manufacturers.
Cost: $21.00
60 Pages
Frequency: Monthly
Circulation: 13500

16604 Southern Pine Inspection Bureau Magazine
Southern Pine Inspection Bureau
PO Box 10915
Pensacola, FL 32524-0915
850-434-2611; Fax: 850-433-5594
spib@spib.org
www.spib.org
James Loy, President
Tom Jones, Executive Director
Founded in 1940
Mailing list available for rent

16605 Timber Harvesting
Hatton-Brown Publishers
225 Hanrick Street (36104)
PO Box 2268
Montgomery, AL 36102-3317
334-834-1170
800-669-5613; Fax: 334-834-4525
mail@hattonbrown.com
www.hattonbrown.com
Dave Ramsey, Co-Publisher
D K Knight, Co-Publisher
Rich Donnell, Editor
News and methods reported that are of particular interest to loggers.
Cost: $40.00
Frequency: Monthly
Circulation: 20130
ISSN: 0160-6433
Founded in 1953
Printed in 4 colors on matte stock

16606 Timber Processing
Hatton-Brown Publishers
225 Hanrick Street
PO Box 2268
Montgomery, AL 36102
334-834-1170
800-669-5613; Fax: 334-834-4525
rich@hattonbrown.com
www.hattonbrown.com
David H Ramsey, Co-Publisher
Rich Donnell, Editor-in-Chief
Dan Shell, Managing Editor
Timber Processing serves sawmill/chipmill operations; consultants in mill and processing operations; machinery manufacturers, dealers and distributors, others allied to the field.
Cost: $40.00
44 Pages
Circulation: 20780
ISSN: 0885-906X
Founded in 1948
Printed in 4 colors on glossy stock

16607 Timber West Journal
Logging & Sawmilling Journal
Po Box 86670
Vancouver, BC V7L-4L2
604-990-9970
866-221-1017; Fax: 604-990-9971
timberwest@forestnet.com
www.forestnet.com/timberwest
Facebook
Sheila Ringdahl, Publisher
Diane Mettler, Managing Editor
Packed with valuable and useful stories on successful mechanized harvesting and wood processing techniques and equipment, special editorial features, plus timely information on legislation, industry news, annual events, and people and products pertinent to America's largest forestry market.
Cost: $20.00
48 Pages
Circulation: 10500
ISSN: 0192-0642
Founded in 1975
Mailing list available for rent
Printed in 4 colors

16608 Timberline
Industrial Reporting
10244 Timber Ridge Dr
Ashland, VA 23005-8135
804-550-0323; Fax: 804-550-2181
editor@ireporting.com
www.palletenterprise.com
Edward C Brindley Jr, Publisher
Tim Cox, Editor
Laura Seal, Circulation
Highlights sawmill, logging, and pallet interests including environmental issues, new machinery and technologies that impact the industry.
52 Pages
Frequency: Monthly
Circulation: 30000
Founded in 1994
Mailing list available for rent: 28,000 names at $250 per M
Printed in 4 colors on newsprint stock

16609 Tree Care Industry
Tree Care Industry Association
136 Harvey Road
Suite 101
Londonderry, NH 03053
603-314-5380
800-733-2622; Fax: 603-314-5386
tcia@tcia.org
www.tcia.org
Facebook, Twitter, LinkedIn, Youtube
Mark Garvin, Interim CEO/President
Peter Gerstenberger, Sr Adv Safety/Compliance/Standards
Informative articles on tree care issues, leading advertisers, and industry almanac, and cutting edge product news combine to make TCI Magazine a must-read for tree workers, tree care company owners, and anyone who wants a fresh, insightful look at the industry
Founded in 1938

16610 Tree Farmer Magazine, the Guide to Sustaining America's Family Forests
American Forest Foundation
1111 19th St NW
Suite 780
Washington, DC 20036
202-463-2462; Fax: 202-463-2461
info@forestfoundation.org
www.forestfoundation.org
Facebook, Twitter, YouTube
Tom Martin, President & CEO
Brigitte Johnson APR, Director Communications, Editor
The official magazine of ATFS, this periodical provides practical, how-to and hands-on information and techniques, and services to help private fore landowners to become better stewards, save money and time, and add to the enjoyment of their land.

16611 Wood Digest
Cygnus Publishing
1233 Janesville Avenue
Fort Atkinson, WI 53538-0803
920-000-1111
800-547-7377; Fax: 920-563-1699
info@cygnus.com
www.cygnus.com
John French, CEO
John Anfderhaar, Associate Publisher
Paul Bowers, President
Jay Schneider, Publisher
Trade magazine, Accepts advertising.
64 Pages
Frequency: Monthly
Circulation: 51000
Founded in 1965

16612 Wood Finisher
7616 Banning Way
Inver Grove Heights, MN 55077-5819
Mitchell Kohansek, Editor
Wood finishing information.
Cost: $10.00
20 Pages
Frequency: Monthly
Founded in 1981

16613 **Wood and Fiber Science**
Society of Wood Science & Technology
PO Box 6155
Monona, WI 53716-6155

608-577-1342; Fax: 608-467-8979
vicki@swst.org
www.swst.org
Facebook

Victoria Herian, Executive Director
James Funck, President Elect

Publishes papers with both professional and technical content. Original papers of professional concer, or based on research dealing with the science, processing, and manufacture of wood and composite products of wood or wood fiber origin are considered for publication. All papers are peer-reviewed and must be unpublished research not offered for publication elsewhere.
Cost: $250.00
Frequency: Quarterly
Circulation: 950
ISSN: 0735-6161
Founded in 1958

16614 **Wood and Wood Products**
Vance Publishing
400 Knightsbridge Pkwy
Lincolnshire, IL 60069

847-634-2600; Fax: 847-634-4379
info@vancepublishing.com
www.vancepublishing.com

William C Vance, Chairman
Peggy Walker, Wood & Wood Products

Leading woodworking industry publication for solid wood and panel technology.
140 Pages
Frequency: Monthly
Circulation: 48000
ISSN: 0043-7662
Founded in 1937

16615 **World Wood Review**
Widman Publishing
601 West Broadway
Suite 400
Vancouver, BC V5Z 4C2

604-675-6923; Fax: 604-675-6924
tlhaugen@widman.com
www.widman.com

Janice Widman, Chair
Jason Roth, Director / Editor
Tamara Haugen, Director / Editor
Dick Brown, Associate Editor
Brian Haugen, Associate Editor

The premier newsletter serving the global wood products industry, with news of trends and developments in the solid wood and panel manufacturing sector.
Cost: $55.00
50 Pages
Frequency: Monthly

Trade Shows

16616 **AMD Annual Convention & Tradeshow**
Association of Millwork Distributors
10047 Robert Trent Jones Pkwy
Trinity, FL 34655-4649

727-372-3665
800-786-7274; Fax: 727-372-2879
marketing@amdweb.com
www.amdweb.com

Rosalie Leone, CEO

16617 **ATIC Annual Meeting**
7012 S Revere Parkway
Suite 140
Centennial, CO 80112

303-379-2955
www.aitc-glulam.org
Facebook

R Michael Caldwell PE, Executive VP
Frequency: Annual
Founded in 1952

16618 **American Forestry Association**
PO Box 2000
Washington, DC 20013-2000
202-955-4500

Billl Tikkala, Show Manager
Deborah Gangloff, Executive Director

30 booths of tree planting and care equipment.
1M Attendees
Frequency: November

16619 **Appalachian Hardwood Expo**
Mercer County Technical Education Center
105 Old Bluefield Road
Princeton, WV 24740-8901

304-425-4583

Linda Cox
100 tables.
2M Attendees
Frequency: June

16620 **Architectural Woodwork Institute Annual Convention**
46179 Westlake Drive
Suite 120
Potomac Falls, VA 20165

571-323-3636; Fax: 571-323-3630
info@awinet.org
www.awinet.org

Kimberly Haynes, Director Meetings & Conventions

Seminar, workshop and woodwork products such as casework, fixtures and panelings, equipment and supplies.

16621 **Forest Expo**
Prince George Regional Forest Exhibition Society
850 River Road
Prince George, BC V2L-5S8

250-563-8833; Fax: 250-563-3697
www.cnre.ca

Trudy Swaan, General Manager

Provides a showcase to display the latest in new technology, equipment, supplies and services, as well as educate the forest sector and the general public about the importance of our forests.

16622 **Forest Products Machinery & Equipment Expo**
Southern Forest Products Association
6660 Riverside Drive
Suite 212
Metairie, LA 70003

504-443-4464; Fax: 504-443-6612
mail@sfpa.org
www.sfpa.org

Tami Kessler, Executive Director
Eric Gee, Deputy Director
Rachel Elton, Accountant
Linda Patch, Program Coordinator
Julia Milrod, Communications Manager

An exhibition that provides the forest products industry with a venue to discuss trends, discover new technologies and manufacturing. Includes 200+ exhibitors.
Frequency: Biennial/June

16623 **Frame Building Expo**
National Frame Builders Association
4700 W. Lake Avenue
Glenview, IL 60025

785-843-2444
800-557-6957; Fax: 847-375-6495
info@nfba.org
www.nfba.org
Facebook

John Fullerton, VP
Tom Knight, President
Containing 200 booths.
2000+ Attendees
Frequency: February

16624 **Greenbuild International Conference and Expo**
Engineered Wood Association
7011 S 19th Street
Tacoma, WA 98466-5333

253-565-6600; Fax: 253-565-7265
tanya.rosendahl@apawood.org
www.apawood.org
Facebook, Twitter

Tanya Rosendahl, Tradeshow Coordinator

16625 **HPVA Sping Conference**
Hardwood Plywood & Veneer
1825 Michael Faraday Dr
Reston, VA 20190-5350

703-435-2900; Fax: 703-435-2537
hpva@hpva.org
www.hpva.org

Clifford Howlett, President
Kip Howlett, HPVA President
Eva Mentel, Office Manager
Frequency: May

16626 **HPVA Winter Conference**
Hardwood Plywood & Veneer
1825 Michael Faraday Dr
Reston, VA 20190-5350

703-435-2900; Fax: 703-435-2537
hpva@hpva.org
www.hpva.org

Clifford Howlett, President
Kip Howlett, HPVA President
Eva Mentel, Office Manager
Frequency: November

16627 **Hardwood Manufacturers Association**
400 Penn Center Boulevard
Suite 530
Pittsburgh, PA 15235-5605

412-244-0440; Fax: 412-244-9090

Susan Regan, Executive VP

Offers 20 booths of sawmill and logging machinery and services.
300 Attendees
Frequency: March

16628 **IWPA Annual Convention**
International Wood Products Association
4214 King St
Alexandria, VA 22302-1555

703-820-6696; Fax: 703-820-8550
info@iwpawood.org
www.iwpawood.org

Brent McClendon, Executive VP/CAE
Annette Ferri, Member Services
Brigid Shea, Government Affairs
Annette Ferri, Director, Finance & Administration
Ashley A. Amidon, Manager, Government

The largest gethering solely dedicated to the North American imported wood products industry.
Frequency: April

16629 **International Woodworking Machinery and Furniture Supply Fair: USA**
Reed Exhibition Companies
1350 E Touhy Avenue
Des Plaines, IL 60018-3303
847-294-0300; Fax: 847-635-1571
Paul Pajor, National Marketing Manager
The largest woodworking machinery and furniture supply manufacturing exposition held in the Western Hemisphere. Exhibitors interface with North American furniture, cabinet, and woodworking manufacturers. One thousand booths.
37M Attendees
Frequency: August/Biennial

16630 **Iowa Lumber Convention**
Northwestern Lumber Association
701 Decatur Ave. N
Golden Valley, MN 55427
763-544-6822
888-544-6822; Fax: 763-595-4060
info@nlassn.org
www.nlassn.org
Jodie Fleck, Director, Conventions & Tours
Hosts educational seminars and trade show.

16631 **Lake States Logging Congress & Equipment Expo**
Great Lakes Timber Professionals Association
3243 Golf Course Road
PO Box 1278
Rhinelander, WI 54501-1278
715-282-5828; Fax: 715-282-4941
info@timberpa.com
www.timberpa.com
Henry Schienebeck, Executive Director & Editor
Held in either Michigan or Wisconsin, the Logging Congress is a 3-day expo that takes place during the Fall season throughout the Lake States region of the United States.
3500 Attendees
Founded in 1945

16632 **Live Woods Show**
Pacific Logging Congress
PO Box 1281
Maple Valley, WA 98038
425-413-2808; Fax: 425-413-1359
www.pacificloggingcongress.com
Rikki Wellman, Executive Director
Craig Olson, President
Ron Simon, Treasurer
3000+ Attendees
Frequency: September

16633 **Logging Congress Pacific**
2300 SW 6th Avenue
Suite 200
Portland, OR 97201-4915
FAX 503-612-0344
Al Wilson, Executive Director
50 booths.
800 Attendees
Frequency: September

16634 **Lumbermen's Merchandising Conferences**
137 W Wayne Avenue
Wayne, PA 19087-4018
610-293-7000; Fax: 215-293-7098
Jack Reznor, Show Manager
Anthony Decarlo, President
325 booths.
1.6M Attendees
Frequency: March

16635 **MFMA Annual Conference**
Maple Flooring Manufacturers Association
111 Deer Lake Road
Suite 100
Deerfield, IL 60015
847-480-9138
888-480-9138; Fax: 847-480-9282
www.maplefloor.org
Madhuri Carson, Conference Manager
Containing 50 booths.
300 Attendees
Frequency: Annual/March

16636 **NHLA Annual Convention & Exhibit Showcase North American Hardwood Lumber Indu**
National Hardwood Lumber Association
6830 Raleigh Lagrange Road
Memphis, TN 38184
901-377-1818
www.nhla.com
Lisa Browne, Convention Director
The premier networking opportunity for the Hardwood Industry. Provides attendees time for direct, personal contact with industry leaders and exhibitors, giving them from the opportunity to ask meaningful questions, view and compare products and services and strengthen business relationships.
Frequency: Annual

16637 **NWFA Wood Flooring Convention and Expo**
National Wood Flooring Association
111 Chesterfield Industrial Boulevard
Chesterfield, MO 63005
636-519-9663
800-422-4556; Fax: 636-519-9664
www.nwfa.org
Michael Martin, CEO
The Wood Flooring Expo has become the international gathering place for wood flooring professionals: Manufacturers, Distributors, Dealer/Contractors, Inspectors, Installers, Import/Exporters, Architects & Designers of wood flooring.
2000 Attendees
Frequency: April

16638 **Northeastern Forest Products Equipment Expo**
Northeastern Loggers Association
3311 State Route 28 PO Box 69
Old Forge, NY 13420-0069
315-369-3078; Fax: 315-369-3736
nela@northernlogger.com
http://nefpexpo.net
Joseph Phaneuf, Show Manager
Annual expo on forest products equipment, suppliers, and services. Always listed as one of the top 100 shows in the U.S. with 200+ exhibitors and indoor/outdoor demonstrations.
6000 Attendees
Frequency: Annual/May

16639 **Northeastern Retail Lumber Association**
Northeastern Retail Lumber Association
585 N Greenbush Road
Rensselaer, NY 12144
518-286-1010
800-292-6752; Fax: 518-286-1755
rferris@nrla.org
www.nrla.org
Deborah Talar, Executive Assistant
Rita Ferris, President
500 booths or more of builiding materials and education relating to the lumber and building industry.
8M Attendees
Frequency: January

16640 **Northwestern Building Products Expo NORTH**
Northwestern Lumber Association
701 Decatur Avenue N
Golden Valley, MN 55427
763-544-6822
888-544-6822; Fax: 763-595-4060
info@nlassn.org
www.nlassn.org
Jodie Fleck, CMP, Director, Conventions & Tours
Building material retailers and their contractors attend this trade show and conference for continuing education and cammeraderie.
1200 Attendees
Frequency: Annual/January
Mailing list available for rent

16641 **Northwestern Building Products Expo SOUTH**
Northwestern Lumber Association
701 Decatur Avenue N
Golden Valley, MN 55427
763-544-6822
888-544-6822; Fax: 763-595-4060
info@nlassn.org
www.nlassn.org
Jodie Fleck, CMP, Director, Conventions & Tours
Building material retailers and their contractors attend this tradeshow and conference for continuing education and cammeraderie.
Frequency: Annual/March

16642 **Redwood Region Logging Conference California**
Redwood Region Logging Conference
5601 South Broadway Street
Eureka, CA 95503
707-443-4091; Fax: 707-443-0926
www.rrlc.net/
Charles Benbow, Show Manager
100 booths of timber and forestry related products and services.
3M Attendees
Frequency: March

16643 **Retail Lumbermen's Association Northeast**
339 E Avenue
Rochester, NY 14604-2627
John Brill, Show Manager
681 booths of lumber and related services.
10M Attendees
Frequency: January

16644 **Sawmill Logging Equipment Expo East Coast**
220 E Williamsburg Road
PO Box 160
Sandston, VA 23150-0160
804-737-5625; Fax: 804-737-9437
info@exporichmond.com
www.exporichmond.com
Mike Washko, Expo Manager
Logging and forestry production and distribution.
12M Attendees
Frequency: May

16645 **Southeastern Lumber Manufacturers Association**
Southeastern Lumber Manufacturers

200 Greencastle Road
Tyrone, GA 30290

770-631-6701; Fax: 770-631-6720
www.slma.org/

Steve Roundtree, President
Bryan Smalley, President
Will Telligman, Government Affairs Manager
Beverly Knight, Accounting Manager

50 booths.
350 Attendees
Frequency: July

16646 **Southern Forest Products Mid-Year Meeting**
Southern Forest Products Association
6660 Riverside Drive
Suite 212
Metairie, LA 70003

504-443-4464; Fax: 504-443-6612
mail@sfpa.org
www.sfpa.org

Tami Kessler, Executive Director
3000 Attendees

16647 **Southern Forestry Conference**
Forest Landowners Association
900 Circle 75 Pkwy Se
Suite 205
Atlanta, GA 30339-3075

404-325-2954
800-325-2954; Fax: 404-325-2955
info@forestlandowners.com
www.forestlandowners.com

Lisa Newsome, Manager
Stacie Lewis, Managing Editor
Frequency: May
Founded in 1941

16648 **Spring Meeting & Legislative Conference**
National Lumber & Building Material Dealers Assn.
2025 M St NW
Suite 800
Washington, DC 20036-3309

202-367-1169
800-634-8645; Fax: 202-367-2169
membersupport@dealer.org
www.dealer.org
Facebook, Twitter, LinkedIn

Jonathan M. Paine, CAE, President & CEO
Ben Gann, VP, Legislative & Political Affairs
Frank Moore, Regulatory Counsel
Kiersten Kochanowski, Membership & Operations
Corie Stretton, Event Manager

An opportunity to meet with members of Congress and share legislative priorities and concerns. Network with fellow industry partners, members of Congress and staff on Capitol Hill.
6000 Members
Frequency: Annual, Spring
Founded in 1917

16649 **TCI Expo**
Tree Care Industry Association
136 Harvey Road
Suite 101
Londonderry, NH 03053

603-314-5380
800-733-2622; Fax: 603-314-5386
www.tcia.org
Facebook, Twitter, LinkedIn, Youtube

Mark Garvin, Interim CEO/President
Peter Gerstenberger, Sr Adv Safety/Compliance/Standards
3500 Attendees
Frequency: Annual
Founded in 1938

16650 **Wisconsin Lumber Dealers Leadership Confer ence**
Northwestern Lumber Association
701 Decatur Avenue N
Golden Valley, MN 55427

763-544-6822
888-544-6822; Fax: 763-595-4060
info@nlassn.org
www.nlassn.org

Jodie Fleck, CMP, Director, Conventions & Tours

A one-day conference that brings together retail lumberyard owners, managers, and sales teams to network and learn from each other and featured speakers.
Frequency: Annual/February

16651 **Woodworking Industry Conference**
Wood Machinery Manufacturers of America
9 Newport Drive
Suite 200
Forest Hill, MD 21050

443-640-1052; Fax: 443-640-1031
info@wmma.org
woodworkingindustryconference.com

Chris Hacker, President
Stephen Carter, Vice President
Kristin Grove, Member Services Coordinator
Diane Schafer, Meetings Director

The conference will focus on business development, networking and practical knowledge for those working in the woodworking machinery industry.
Frequency: Annual/May
Founded in 1899

16652 **Woodworking Industry Conference 2018**
Woodworking Machinery Industry Association
225 Reinekers Lane
Suite 410
Alexandria, VA 22314

571-279-8340; Fax: 571-279-8343
info@wmia.org
www.wmia.org/events/event/wic-2018-save-the-date

Larry Hoffer, President
Jeff Linder, Program Manager
Heather Jolley, Program Administrator
Rick Braun, Director

Conference for the woodworking machinery industry, offering business development programs, networking, and education.
Founded in 1977

16653 **World of Wood Annual Convention**
International Wood Products Association
4214 King Street W
Alexandria, VA 22302-1507

703-820-6696; Fax: 703-820-8550
info@iwpawood.org
www.iwpawood.org

Brent J McClendon, Executive VP/CAE
Annette Ferri, Member Services
Brigid Shea, Government Affairs
Annette Ferri, Director, Finance & Administration
Ashley A. Amidon, Manager, Government

A gethering for imported wood products industry importers, distributers, manufacturers, offshore suppliers and service providers.
220 Attendees
Frequency: Annual/Spring

Directories & Databases

16654 **Cedar Shake and Shingle Bureau Membership Directory/Buyer's Guide**
Cedar Shake & Shingle Bureau
PO Box 1178
Sumas, WA 98295-1178

604-820-7700; Fax: 604-820-0266
info@cedarbureau.com
www.cedarbureau.org

Lynne Christensen, Director of Operations
Barb Enns, Accountant
Dave Mooney, Cedar Quality Auditor
Sharron Beauregard, Accounting Assistant
Suzie Quigley, Customer Service Representative

About 102 member manufacturing mills in the Pacific Northwest and British Columbia, Canada; approximately 163 affiliated roofing applicators, builders, architects, remodelers and suppliers of related products and services.
Cost: $17.00
Frequency: SemiAnnual
Circulation: 450

16655 **Dimension & Wood Components Buyer's Guide**
Miller Publishing Corporation
Po Box 34908
Memphis, TN 38184-0908

901-372-8280
800-844-1280; Fax: 901-373-6180
editor@millerwoodtradepub.com
www.millerpublishing.com

Paul J Miller, President
Sue Putnam, Editor

Instant access to manufacturers of furniture parts, mouldings, cabinet doors, stair parts, flooring, turnings, paneling, door parts, window parts, edge glued panels, etc. Gives the information on who to contact, firm name and address, phone number, fax number, number of employees, products manufactured, species of wood used, machining capabilities and marketing areas served.
Cost: $350.00

16656 **Forest Products Export Directory**
Miller Publishing Corporation
Po Box 34908
Memphis, TN 38184-0908

901-372-8280
800-844-1280; Fax: 901-373-6180
editor@millerwoodtradepub.com
www.millerpublishing.com

Paul J Miller, President
Sue Putnam, Editor

The only directory published listing all the major exporters of North American forest products. Edited to help the oversease buyer find reliable suppliers for the wide variety of Softwood and Hardwood forest products available in North America.
Cost: $175.00

16657 **Forest Products Research Society Membership Directory**
2801 Marshall Ct
Madison, WI 53705-2295

608-231-1361; Fax: 608-231-2152
info@forestprod.org
www.forestprod.org

Carol Lewis, VP
Stefan A. Bergmann, Executive Vice President

Joe Gravunder, Publications Manager
Cost: $125.00
1900 Pages
Frequency: 10 Per Year
Circulation: 3500
Founded in 1947

16658 **Gebbie Press: All-In-One Media Directory**
Gebbie Press
Po Box 1000
New Paltz, NY 12561
845-255-7560; Fax: 888-345-2790
www.gebbieinc.com
Facebook, Twitter, LinkedIn
Mark Gebbie, Associate Editor
Founded in 1955

16659 **Green Book's Hardwood Marketing Directory**
Miller Publishing Corporation
Po Box 34908
Memphis, TN 38184-0908
901-372-8280
800-844-1280; Fax: 901-373-6180
editor@millerwoodtradepub.com
www.millerpublishing.com
Paul J Miller, President
Sue Putnam, Editor
A sales booster that lists over 7,900 woodworking plants' Hardwood lumber and other Hardwood forest products purchasing needs. Gives up-to-date, documented facts on species, grades, thicknesses and quantities purchased by each plant annually in the U.S. and Canada.
Cost: $1200.00

16660 **Green Book's Softwood Marketing Directory**
Miller Publishing Corporation
Po Box 34908
Memphis, TN 38184-0908
901-372-8280
800-844-1280; Fax: 901-373-6180
editor@millerwoodtradepub.com
www.millerpublishing.com
Paul J Miller, President
Sue Putnam, Editor
Instant access to over 5,000 woodworking and industrial plants' Softwood lumber purchasing needs with complete, up-to-date, documented facts on species, grades, thicknesses, and quantities of Softwood lumber and other Softwood forest products bought regularly.
Cost: $900.00

16661 **Hardwood Manufacturers Association: Membership Directory**
Hardwood Manufacturers Association
665 Rodi Road
Suite 305
Pittsburgh, PA 15235
412-244-0440
800-373-9663; Fax: 412-244-9090
www.hardwoodinfo.com
Susan Regan, Executive VP
Over 100 companies with over 160 locations in the US.
Frequency: Annual December

16662 **Hardwood Purchasing Handbook**
Miller Publishing Corporation
Po Box 34908
Memphis, TN 38184-0908
901-372-8280
800-844-1280; Fax: 907-373-6180
editor@millerwoodtradepub.com
www.millerpublishing.com
Paul J Miller, President
Sue Putnam, Editor
An easy-to-use digest size directory that has all the major Hardwood suppliers in the U.S.A. and Canada of Hardwood lumber, plywood, veneers, etc. Up-to-date sections describe Hardwood sawmills, wholesalers, distribution yards, etc. Complete mailing addresses, phone numbers, fax numbers, email addresses, names of sales agents, main Hardwood species handled, specialty items listed and information on production facilities and shipping methods are given.
Cost: $175.00

16663 **Imported Wood Purchasing Guide**
Miller Publishing Corporation
Po Box 34908
Memphis, TN 38184-0908
901-372-8280
800-844-1280; Fax: 901-373-6180
editor@millerwoodtradepub.com
www.millerpublishing.com
Paul J Miller, President
Sue Putnam, Editor
A wide variety of imported suppliers of lumber, mouldings, veneers, wall paneling, furniture components, flooring, plywood, hardboard, doorskins, millwork, etc.
Cost: $175.00

16664 **Imported Wood: Guide To Applications, Sources and Trends**
International Wood Products Association
4214 King St
Alexandria, VA 22302-1555
703-820-6696; Fax: 703-820-8550
info@iwpawood.org
www.iwpawood.org
Facebook, Twitter, LinkedIn
Brent McClendon, Executive VP/CAE
Annette Ferri, Member Services
Brigid Shea, Government Affairs
An annual magazine featuring imported woods in applications, sustainable Forest Management issues and listing of IWPA members.
84 Pages
Frequency: Annual
Circulation: 15,000

16665 **International Green Front Report**
Friends of the Trees
PO Box 1064
Tonasket, WA 98855-1064
FAX 509-485-2705
michael@friendsofthetrees.net
Michael Pilarski, Editor
Organizations and periodicals concerned with sustainable forestry and agriculture and related fields.
Cost: $7.00
Frequency: Irregular

16666 **LBM Industry Buyer's Guide**
National Lumber & Building Material Dealers Assn.
2025 M St NW
Suite 800
Washington, DC 20036-3309
202-367-1169
800-634-8645; Fax: 202-367-2169
membersupport@dealer.org
www.dealer.org
Facebook, Twitter, LinkedIn
Jonathan M. Paine, CAE, President & CEO
Ben Gann, VP, Legislative & Political Affairs
Frank Moore, Regulatory Counsel
Kiersten Kochanowski, Membership & Operations
Corie Stretton, Event Manager
A platform for dealers and consumers to search for products and services provided by NLBMDA's preferred vendors to the LBM industry.
6000 Members
Founded in 1917

16667 **Lumbermen's Red Book**
Lumbermens Credit Association
20 N Wacker Drive
Suite 1800
Chicago, IL 60606-2905
312-553-0943; Fax: 312-533-1842
PD McLaughlin, Editor
Approximately 39,000 manufacturers and distributors of lumber and wood products in the US and Canada.
Cost: $1780.00
Frequency: SemiAnnual

16668 **MLA Buyer's Guide & Dealer Directory**
Mid America Lumbermens Association
638 W 39th St
Kansas City, MO 64111
816-561-5323
800-747-6529; Fax: 816-561-1249
mail@themla.com
www.themla.com
Olivia Holcombe, Executive Vice President

16669 **Manufacturers & Services Council Directory**
National Lumber & Building Material Dealers Assn.
2025 M St NW
Suite 800
Washington, DC 20036-3309
202-367-1169
800-634-8645; Fax: 202-367-2169
membersupport@dealer.org
www.dealer.org
Facebook, Twitter, LinkedIn
Jonathan M. Paine, CAE, President & CEO
Ben Gann, VP, Legislative & Political Affairs
Frank Moore, Regulatory Counsel
Kiersten Kochanowski, Membership & Operations
Corie Stretton, Event Manager
A directory of NLBMDA preferred providers.
6000 Members
Founded in 1917

16670 **North American Forest Products Export Directory**
International Wood Trade Publications
1235 Sycamore View Road
Memphis, TN 38134-7646
901-752-1246; Fax: 901-373-6180
Producers, exporters, agents, etc. of lumber, plywood, etc. in the US and Canada.
Cost: $150.00
Frequency: Annual August
Circulation: 10,000

16671 **Northeastern Retail Lumber Association Buyer's Guide**
Northeastern Retail Lumber Association
585 N Greenbush Rd
Rensselaer, NY 12144-9615
518-286-1010
800-292-6752; Fax: 518-286-1755
rferris@nrla.org
www.nrla.org
Rita Ferris, President
Offers information on over 2,000 retail dealers in lumber and forest products located in the North-

eastern states of the US.
Cost: $125.00
225 Pages
Frequency: Annual
ISSN: 0024-7294

16672 **Random Lengths Big Book: Buyers' & Sellers' Directory of the Forest**
Random Lengths Publications
PO Box 867
Eugene, OR 97440-0867

541-869-9925
888-686-9925; Fax: 800-874-7979
rlmail@rlpi.com
www.randomlengths.com

Dave Evans, Editor
Terri Richards, Editor

About 7,500 companies, consultants and associations involved in the softwood forest product industry in the US and Canada, including sawmills, treating plants, manufacturers of panels and specialty products, wholesalers and secondary manufacturers.
Cost: $188.00
Frequency: Annual February
Circulation: 2,200

16673 **Rauch Guide to the US and Canadian Pulp & Paper Industry**
Grey House Publishing
4919 Route 22
PO Box 56
Amenia, NY 12501

518-789-8700
800-562-2139; Fax: 845-373-6390
books@greyhouse.com
www.greyhouse.com
Facebook, Twitter

Leslie Mackenzie, Publisher
Richard Gottlieb, Editor

Provides current market information and trends; industry economics and government regulations; company share data for each of the leading product categories; technology and raw material information; industry sources of further data; and unique profiles of 500+ pulp and paper manufacturers, a section which includes all known companies with pulp and paper sales at or over $15 million annually.
Cost: $595.00
400 Pages
ISBN: 1-592371-31-0
Founded in 1981

16674 **Timber Harvesting: Logger's Resource Guide**
Hatton-Brown Publishers
Po Box 2268
Montgomery, AL 36102-2268

334-834-1170
800-669-5613; Fax: 334-834-4525
mail@hattonbrown.com
www.hattonbrown.com

David H Ramsey, President
Rich Donnell, Editor
Cost: $20.00
88 Pages
Frequency: Annually, January
Circulation: 20,179
ISSN: 0160-6433
Printed in on glossy stock

16675 **WMIA Member Directory**
Woodworking Machinery Industry Association
225 Reinekers Lane
Suite 410
Alexandria, VA 22314

571-279-8340; Fax: 571-279-8343
info@wmia.org
www.wmia.org/membership-2/wmia-member-directory

Larry Hoffer, President
Jeff Linder, Program Manager
Heather Jolley, Program Administrator
Rick Braun, Director

Directory of companies that are part of the membership of Woodworking Machinery Industry Association.
Founded in 1977

16676 **WMMA Company Directory**
Wood Machinery Manufacturers of America
9 Newport Drive
Suite 200
Forest Hill, MD 21050

443-640-1052; Fax: 443-640-1031
info@wmma.org
www.wmma.org

Chris Hacker, President
Stephen Carter, Vice President
Fred Stringfellow, Chief Executive Officer
Kristin Grove, Member Services Coordinator

Directory of member companies of the Wood Machinery Manufacturers of America (WMMA) as well as the wood processing equipment they sell.
Founded in 1899

16677 **Where to Buy Hardwood Plywood, Veneer & Engineered Hardwood Flooring**
Hardwood Plywood and Veneer Association
1825 Michael Faraday Drive
Reston, VA 20190-5350

703-435-2900; Fax: 703-435-2537
hpva@hpva.org
www.hpva.org

Kip Howlett, President
Eva Mentel, Office Manager
Ketti Tyree, Membership & Conventions Manager

The definitive annual guide to the species and products sold by HPVA members.
120 Pages
Frequency: Annual
Founded in 1921

16678 **Wood & Wood Products: Laminating Users Guide Issue**
Louisiana Municipal Association
700 North 10th street
Baton Rouge, LA 70802

225-344-5001
800-234-8274; Fax: 225-344-3057
www.lma.org

George Carter, Editor

List of approximately 100 manufacturers and importers of decorative overlays, wood substrates, adhesives, laminating equipment and laminated products.
Frequency: Annual June

16679 **Wood Components Buyer's Guide**
Wood Component Manufacturers Association
741 Butlers Gate NE
Suite 100
Marietta, GA 30068-4207

770-565-6660; Fax: 770-565-6663
wcma@woodcomponents.org
www.woodcomponents.org

Steven V Lawser, Executive Director

Over 150 member manufacturers of wood components.
Cost: $5.00
Frequency: Annual Summer

16680 **Wood Technology: Buyers' Guide Issue**
Miller Freeman Publications
600 Harrison Street
Suite 400
San Francisco, CA 94107-1391

800-227-4675; Fax: 415-905-2630
www.woodtechmag.com

David A Pease, Editorial Director

Companies supplying machinery, tools and other equipment to manufacturers of wood products worldwide.
Frequency: Annual

16681 **Wood and Wood Products: Red Book Issue**
Vance Publishing
400 Knightsbridge Parkway
Lincolnshire, IL 60069

847-634-2600; Fax: 847-634-4379
www.vancepublishing.com

William C Vance, Chairman
Peggy Walker, President

Annual directory that is the editorial and advertising leader for the woodworking industry. Listings and specifications of more than 3,000 industry suppliers.
Cost: $40.00
Frequency: Annual
Circulation: 50,000

Industry Web Sites

16682 **http://gold.greyhouse.com**
G.O.L.D Grey House OnLine Databases

Grey House Publishing's online database platform, GOLD, offers Quick Search, Keyword Search and Expert Search for most business sectors including lumber and wood markets. The GOLD platform makes finding the information you need quick and easy - whether you're a novice searcher or an experienced database user. All of Grey House's directory products are available for subscription on the GOLD platform.

16683 **www.afandpa.org**
American Forest and Paper Association

Represents member companies and related trade associations which grow, harvest and process wood and wood fiber, manufacture pulp, paper and paperboard products from both virgin and recovered fiber and produce solid wood products.

16684 **www.afma4u.org**
American Furniture Manufacturers Association

Provides a uniform voice in the furniture industry.

16685 **www.aitc-glulam.org**
American Institute of Timber Construction

The national trade association of the structural glued laminiated (glulam) timber industry.

16686 **www.alsc.org**
American Lumber Standard Committee

16687 **www.amdweb.com**
Association of Millwork Distributors

Provides leadership, certification, education, promotion, networking and advocacy to, and for, the millwork distribution industry.

16688 **www.apawood.org**
Engineered Wood Association

A nonprofit trade association that represents US and Canadian manufacturers of structural engineered wood products, including plywood, oriented strand board (OSB), glued-laminated timber (glulam), wood i-joists and structural composite lumber.

16689 **www.bearcreeklumber.com**
Bear Creek Lumber
Publishes a newsletter called the Timberline.

16690 **www.big-creek.com**
Big Creek
Produces a newspaper

16691 **www.calredwood.org**
California Redwood Association
Authorized by Department of Commerce to develop and supervise redwood lumber grading.

16692 **www.capital-lumber.com**
Capital Lumber Company
Dedicated to being the leading distributor of materials in the Western United States.

16693 **www.construction.com**
McGraw-Hill Construction
McGraw-Hill Construction (MHC), part of The McGraw-Hill Companies, connects people and projects across the design and construction industry, serving owners, architects, engineers, general contractors, subcontractors, building product manufacturers, suppliers, dealers, distributors and adjacent markets.

16694 **www.fiberboard.org**
American Fiberboard Association
The national trade organization of manufacturers of cellulosic fiberboard products used for residential and commercial construction.

16695 **www.forestinfo.org**
Temperate Forest Foundation
Source for information which is understandable, unbiased, fast, accurate, and available in a wide variety of formats.

16696 **www.forestnet.com**
Logging & Sawmilling Journal
A journal that provides information on logginf and sawmilling.

16697 **www.forestprod.org**
Forest Products Society
Focus is on the development and research of information for the wood industry.

16698 **www.gebbieinc.com**
Gebbie Press
A directory with all information that is needed for the lumber industry.

16699 **www.greyhouse.com**
Grey House Publishing
Authoritative reference directories for most business sectors including lumber and wood markets. Users can search the online databases with varied search criteria allowing for custom searches by product category, geographic area, sales volume, keyword, subject and more. Full Grey House catalog and online ordering also available.

16700 **www.hardboard.org**
American Hardboard Association
Represents major United States producers of hardwood.

16701 **www.hlma.org**
Pennsylvania Forest Products Association
Represents the state's entire forest products industry, including foresters, loggers, sawmills, and value-added processors.

16702 **www.iwpawood.org**
International Wood Products Association
International trade association representing companies handling imported wood products of all types.

16703 **www.lma.org**
Laminating Materials Association
Nonprofit trade group representing manufacturers and importers of decorative overlays, wood substrates, adhesives, laminating equipment and laminated products.

16704 **www.loggertraining.com**
A reference site for loggers in their pursuit of training programs where they work and live. Maintained by Northeastern Loggers' Association.

16705 **www.lumber.org**
North American Wholesale Lumber Association
NAWLA Bulletin is published monthly and includes industry and association news. The Association also produces the NAWLA Traders Market, an annual trade show bringing together over 2000 manufacturer and wholesale lumber traders at the premier event in the forest products industry. NAWLA also produces a variety of educational programs designed to enhance professionalism in the lumber industry.

16706 **www.maplefloor.org**
Maple Flooring Manufacturers Association
For manufacturers of northern hard maple solid strip flooring along with flooring contractors, distributors and providers of instalation-related products and services. Maintains technical standards for product quality, grading, shipping and packaging, and quality central.

16707 **www.millerpublishing.com**
Miller Publishing Corporation
Publishes many newspapers, magazines, and directories.

16708 **www.mslbmda.org**
Mountain States Lumber & Building Materials Dealer

16709 **www.nari.org**
National Association of the Remodeling Industry
Establishes and maintains a firm commitment to developing and sustaining programs that expand and unite the remodeling industry.

16710 **www.nfba.org**
National Frame Building Association
Nonprofit trade association supporting contractors, suppliers, manufacturers, material dealers, code and design professionals and engineers specializing in the post frame construction industry.

16711 **www.nlassn.org**
Northwestern Lumber Association
Connects member LBM retailers with people, programs, and resources to improve business. Serves Iowa, Minnesota, Nebraska, North Dakota, South Dakota, Upper Michigan, and Wisconsin.

16712 **www.nofma.org**
National Oak Flooring Manufacturers Association
Formulates and administers industry standards on hardwood floorings, inspection service, and semiannual Hardwood Flooring installation school.

16713 **www.nsdja.com**
National Sash and Door Jobbers Association
For wholesale millwork distribution companies.

16714 **www.nwfa.org**
National Wood Flooring Association
A not-for-profit trade association serving the wood flooring industry

16715 **www.pacificloggingcongress.org**
Pacific Logging Congress
Fulfills the need to provide sound technical education about the forest industry.

16716 **www.sfpa.org**
Southern Forest Products Association
The Association and its members are committed to quality, and believe that Southern Pine forest products provide a smart, environmentally friendly way to meet the world's needs for a wide range of building and industrial products.

16717 **www.spib.org**
Southern Pine Inspection Bureau
Develops grading standards for Southern pine lumber and provides an inspection service and grade marking systems.

16718 **www.sweets.construction.com**
McGraw Hill Construction
In depth product information that lets you find, compare, select, specify and make purchase decisions in the industrial product marketplace.

16719 **www.swst.org**
Society of Wood Science & Technology
Promotes policies and procedures which assure the wise use of wood and wood-based products; assures high standards for professional performance of wood scientists and technologists; foster educational programs at all levels of wood science and technology and further the quality of such programs; represents the profession in public policy development.

16720 **www.timberassociation.com**
Timber Products Manufacturers Association
Association of companies in the Timber and Wood products industry. The association provides human resource and safety consulting, training and employee benefits.

16721 **www.toc.org**
TOC Management Services
Serves membership in the fields of labor, industrial, and employee relations. Provides counsel in wage and contract negotiations. Provides training and safety programs.

16722 **www.wdma.org**
Window & Door Manufacturers Association
Trade association representing approximately 145 U.S. and Canadian manufacturers and suppliers of windows and doors for the domestic and export market.

16723 **www.westernforestry.org**
Western Forestry and Conservation Association
Offers high-quality continuing education workshops and seminars for professional foresters throughout Oregon, Washington, Idaho, Montana, Northern California and British Columbia.

16724 **www.wmia.org**
Woodworking Machinery Industry Association
Facebook, Twitter, LinkedIn
Represents importers and distributors of woodworking machinery. The organization supports its members through industry awards, safety publications, scholarships and networking platforms.

16725 **www.wmma.org**
Wood Machinery Manufacturers of America

Facebook, Twitter, LinkedIn

Organization dedicated to supporting and advocating for manufacturers of machinery and tooling used for processing wood.

16726 **www.woodcomponents.org**
Wood Component Manufacturers Association

Represents manufacturers of wood component products for urniture, cabinetry, building products, and decorative wood products.

16727 **www.woodfloors.org**
National Wood Flooring Association

For distributors, manufacturers, retailers, and contractors.

16728 **www.woodtank.com**
National Wood Tank Institute

To promote the use and to guide the proper construction methods for wooden tanks as per NWTI S-82.

16729 **www.wrcla.org**
Western Red Cedar Lumber Association

Association of 26 quality producers of Western Red Cedar lumber products in Washington, Oregon, Canada.

16730 **www.wwpa.org**
Western Wood Products Association

Represents lumber manufacturers in 12 Western states and Alaska. Provides lumber quality control, technical support, and business information to supporting mills.

Associations

16731 **ASM International**
9639 Kinsman Road
Materials Park, OH 44073-0002

440-338-5151
800-336-5152; Fax: 440-338-4634
memberservicecenter@asminternational.org
www.asminternational.org
Facebook, Twitter, LinkedIn

Zi-Kui Liu, President
Diana Essock, Vice President
Raymond V. Fryan, Treasurer
William T. Mahoney, Secretary & CEO

The society for materials engineers and scientists, a worldwide network dedicated to advancing industry, technology and applications of metals and materials. ASM provides information references, education, research and international events.
30K Members
Founded in 1913

16732 **American Amusement Machine Association**
450 E Higgins Rd
Suite 201
Elk Grove Village, IL 60007

847-290-9088
866-372-5190; Fax: 847-290-9121
info@coin-op.org
coin-op.org
Facebook, Twitter, Instagram

Peter Gustafson, Exec. VP
Ashley Ritschdorff, Marketing Coordinator
Tina Schwartz, Business and Finance Manager

Non-profit trade association representing the manufacturers, distributors and part suppliers to the coin-operated and out-of-home amusement industry.
Founded in 1981

16733 **American Gear Manufacturers Association**
1001 N. Fairfax Street
Suite 500
Alexandria, VA 22314-1587

703-684-0211; Fax: 703-684-0242
webmaster@agma.org
www.agma.org
Facebook, Twitter

Matthew Croson, President
Amir Aboutaleb, VP, Technical Division
Cindy Bennett, Executive Director, AGMA Foundation
Jenny Blackford, VP, Marketing
Rebecca Brinkley, Communications Director

Association dedicated to providing technical standards, education, and business information on mechanical power transmission components, including gears and geared speed changers.
495+ Members
Founded in 1916

16734 **American Mold Builders Association**
American Mold Builders Association
7321 Shadeland Station Way
Suite 285
Indianapolis, IN 46256

317-436-3102; Fax: 317-913-2445
info@amba.org
www.amba.org
Facebook, Twitter, LinkedIn, Flickr, YouTube, Google Plus

Justin McPhee, President
Toby Bral, Vice President
Alan Rothenbuecher, Secretary

Promotes the development of businesses engaged in the manufacturing of molds and related tools.
296 Members
Founded in 1973

16735 **American Society of Mechanical Engineers**
Two Park Avenue
New York, NY 10016-5990

973-882-1170
800-843-2763
CustomerCare@asme.org
www.asme.org
Facebook, Twitter, LinkedIn, Instagram

Bryan A. Erler, President
Thomas Costabile, Executive Director & CEO
William Garofalo, Chief Financial Officer
Allian Pratt, Managing Director, Board Operations

ASME aims to promote and enhance the technical competency and professional well-being of the members, and through quality programs and activities in mechanical engineering, better enable its practitioners to contribute to the well being of human kind.
100K+ Members
Founded in 1880

16736 **American Textile Machinery Association**
201 Park Washington Court
Falls Church, VA 22046

703-538-1789
info@atmanet.org
www.atmanet.org

Will Motchar, Chairman
Clay D. Tyeryar, President & Assistant Treasurer
Harry W. Buzzerd, Jr., Management Counsel
Susan A. Denston, EVP & Secretary

The association's mission is to advance the common interests of its members, improve business conditions within the US textile machinery industry from a global perspective, and market the industry and members' machinery, parts and services.
Founded in 1933

16737 **Associated Equipment Distributors**
650 E Algonquin Road
Suite 305
Schaumburg, IL 60173

630-574-0650
help@aednet.org
aednet.org
Facebook, Twitter, LinkedIn

Brian P. McGuire, President/CEO
Robert K. Henderson, EVP & Chief Operating Officer
Agnes Baczek, Director, Finance
Jon Cruthers, VP, Sales
Sara Smith, Editor-In-Chief & Marketing & Comm.

International trade association supporting companies specializing in eqipment used in construction, mining, forestry, power generation, agriculture and industrial applications.
1000 Members
Founded in 1919

16738 **Association for Advancing Automation**
900 Victors Way
Suite 140
Ann Arbor, MI 48108

734-994-6088; Fax: 734-994-3338
info@a3automate.org
www.a3automate.org
Facebook, Twitter, LinkedIn, YouTube

Jeff Burnstein, President
Dana Whalls, Vice President
Bob Doyle, Vice President, RIA & A3 Mexico
Robert Huschka, Director, Education Strategies
James Hamilton, Director, Sales

A3 is the umbrella association for the Robotic Industries Association, representing automation manufacturers, component suppliers, system integrators, end users, research groups, and consulting firms internationally.
1000 Members

16739 **Association for Computing Machinery**
1601 Broadway
10th Floor
New York, NY 10019-7434

212-869-7440
800-342-6626; Fax: 212-944-1318
acmhelp@acm.org
www.acm.org
Facebook, Twitter, LinkedIn, YouTube, Google+, Instagram

Vicki Hanson, Chief Executive Officer
Pat Ryan, Chief Operating Officer
John Stanik, Managing Editor
Darren Ramdin, Director, Finance
Cynthia Ryan, Associate Director, Membership

Organization serving a membership of computing educators, researchers, and professionals. The association offers relevant career development, professional networking, and education opportunities.
80000 Members
Founded in 1947

16740 **Association for Facilities Engineering**
1000 Potomac Street NW
Suite 500
Washington, DC 20007

202-791-9080; Fax: 571-766-2142
grodriguez@afe.org
www.afe.org
Facebook, Twitter, LinkedIn, Instagram

Gabriella Rodriguez, Senior Manager, Membership
Joshua Watkins, Manager, Professional Development

Provides education, certification, technical information and other relevant information for plant and facility engineering operations and maintenance professionals worldwide.

16741 **Association for Machine Translation in the Americas**

Home Page: amtaweb.org

Steve Richardson, President
Ray Flournoy, Vice President
Elaine O'Curran, Secretary
Jean Doyan, Treasurer
Priscilla Rasmussen, Business Manager

The North American branch of the International Association for Machine Translation (IAMT).
Founded in 1991

16742 **Association of Equipment Manufacturers**
6737 West Washington Street
Suite 2400
Milwaukee, WI 53214-5647

414-272-0943; Fax: 414-272-1170
aem@aem.org
www.aem.org
Facebook, Twitter, LinkedIn, YouTube

Jeffrey R. Reed, Chair

Membership association dedicated to supporting equipment manufacturers and their businesses,

with emphasis on the agriculture and construction industries.
900+ Members

16743 **Association of International Metallizers, Coaters and Laminators**
201 Springs Street
Fort Mill, SC 29715

803-948-9470; Fax: 803-948-9471
aimcal@aimcal.org
web.aimcal.org
Facebook, Twitter, LinkedIn, YouTube

Danis J. Roy, President
David Bryant, Vice President
Craig Sheppard, Executive Director
Tracey Messina, Operations Manager
Danielle Fletcher, Event Manager

Global nonprofit trade association supporting metallizers, coaters and laminators as well as suppliers of the industry. The association offers conferences, training, publications and other services for its members.
Founded in 1970

16744 **Association of Machinery and Equipment Appraisers**
315 South Patrick Street
Alexandria, VA 22314

703-836-7900
800-537-8629; Fax: 703-836-9303
amea@amea.org
www.amea.org
Facebook, LinkedIn, YouTube

Randall Koster, President
Jean Harris, Director
Terrance Jacobs, Director
Doris Toronyi, Director
Curt Roskelley, Director

Nonprofit professional association providing accreditation to certified equipment appraisers. The association also offers its members industry news, educational opportunities, networking opportunities and other membership benefits.
300 Members
Founded in 1983
Mailing list available for rent

16745 **Association of Vacuum Equipment Manufacturers (AVEM)**
201 Park Washington Court
Falls Church, VA 22046-4527

703-538-3543; Fax: 703-241-5603
aveminfo@avem.org
www.avem.org

Dawn M. Shiley, Executive Director
Clay Tyeryar, Assistant Treasurer
Kim Fay, Data Analyst
Harry Buzzerd, Management Counsel

Nonprofit U.S. association dedicated to supporting companies in the vacuum equipment manufacturing industry. AVEM promotes member interests and provides services to enhance the membership value and understanding of the global market.
202 Members
Founded in 1969

16746 **Automotive Parts Manufacturers' Association**
10 Four Seasons Place
Suite 801
Toronto, ON M9B 6H7

416-620-4220; Fax: 416-620-9730
apma.ca
Twitter, LinkedIn

Flavio Volpe, President
Roy Verstraete, Chairman

Canadian association representing suppliers of parts, equipment, tools, supplies, and services for the automotive industry. The association offers its members supports such as publications, industry events and news.
Founded in 1952

16747 **Clinical Robotic Surgery Association**
Two Prudential Plaza
180 North Stetson
Suite 3500
Chicago, IL 60601

312-268-5754
inquiries@clinicalrobotics.com
www.clinicalrobotics.com
Facebook, LinkedIn, YouTube, Instagram

Philip Clark, Executive Managing Director
Riccardo Terrosi, Technical Director
Danielle Jacobson, Membership Coordinator

Organization of surgeons practicing in Upper GI, HPB, Thoracic, Colorectal, Vascular, Transplant, ENT and other medical areas. The association's mission is to offer clinical, educational and innovative services related to use of robotics in medical procedures.
Founded in 2009

16748 **Compressed Air and Gas Institute**
1300 Sumner Avenue
Cleveland, OH 44115

216-241-7333; Fax: 216-241-0105
www.cagi.org
Facebook, LinkedIn

Rick Stasyshan, Technical Consultant

An organization representing manufacturers of compressed air system equipment, including air compressors, blowers, pneumatic tools and air and gas equipment.
Founded in 1967

16749 **Concrete Sawing and Drilling Association**
100 2nd Avenue South
Suite 402N
St. Petersburg, FL 33701

727-577-5004; Fax: 727-577-5012
info@csda.org
www.csda.org
Facebook, Twitter, LinkedIn, Flickr, YouTube

Patrick O'Brien, Executive Director
Erin O'Brien, Assistant to Executive Director
Russell Hitchen, Training Coordinator & Editor
Jacqueline Takach, Member Service Coordinator

An industrial trade association supporting professional specialty sawing and drilling contractors.
500 Members
Founded in 1972

16750 **Contractors Pump Bureau**
Association of Equipment Manufacturers
6737 West Washington Street
Suite 2400
Milwaukee, WI 53214-5647

414-272-0943; Fax: 414-272-1170
aem@aem.org
www.aem.org
Facebook, Twitter, LinkedIn, YouTube

Jeffrey R. Reed, Chair

A product group of the Association of Equipment Manufacturers. The Contractors Pump Bureau (CPB) supports contractor pump users, manufacturers and parts and component suppliers. The Bureau also publishes industry consensus standards for equipment.
Founded in 1938

16751 **Conveyor Equipment Manufacturers Association (CEMA)**
5672 Strand Ct.
Suite 2
Naples, FL 34110

239-514-3441; Fax: 239-514-3470
kim@cemanet.org
www.cemanet.org
Facebook, Twitter, LinkedIn, YouTube

Paul Ross, President
E.A. Thompson, Vice President
Robert Reinfried, Executive Vice President
Noel Bell, Director
Bob Callahan, Director

CEMA seeks to support manufacturers of conveyors and conveying systems. The association sponsors an annual Engineering Conference that allows members to meet and develop the industry standards that affect the conveyor industry.
Founded in 1933

16752 **Equipment Dealers Association**
165 North Meramec Avenue
Suite 430
St. Louis, MO 63105

636-349-5000; Fax: 636-349-5443
info@equipmentdealer.org
www.equipmentdealer.org
Facebook, Twitter, LinkedIn

Kim Rominger, President & CEO
Michael Williams, VP, Operations
Joseph Dykes, VP, Industry Relations
Doug Kreienkamp, Operations Coordinator
Alex Hoffman, Communications & Marketing Director

Nonprofit trade organization supporting equipment dealers of agriculture, construction, industrial, forestry, outdoor power, lawn and garden and turf industries.
4500 Members
Founded in 1900

16753 **Eta Kappa Nu**
445 Hoes Lane
Piscataway, NJ 08854

732-465-5846
800-406-2590
info@hkn.org
hkn.ieee.org

Edward Rezek, President

Eta Kappa Nu (HKN) is the electrical and computer engineering honor society of the Institute of Electrical and Electronics Engineers (IEEE).
Founded in 1904

16754 **Farm Equipment Manufacturers Association**
1000 Executive Parkway Drive
Suite 100
St. Louis, MO 63141-6369

314-878-2304
info@farmequip.org
www.farmequip.org
Facebook, Twitter, LinkedIn

Matt Westendorf, President
Vernon Schmidt, Executive Vice President
Tricia Kidd, Accounting & Meeting Services
Kristi Ruggles, Communications Director
Sarah Stevener, Meetings & Membership

An information gathering and distributing organization for farm equipment manufacturers and suppliers.
730+ Members
Founded in 1950

16755 Fire Equipment Manufacturers' Association
1300 Sumner Avenue
Cleveland, OH 44115

216-241-7333
www.femalifesafety.org
Facebook, LinkedIn, YouTube, Wikipedia, Slideshare

Bill Vegso, President

Trade association representing manufacturers of fire protection equipment. Products made by member companies include portable fire extinguishers, fire hose/interior equipment and pre-engineered fire suppression systems.
Founded in 1930

16756 Fluid Power Safety Institute
2170 South 3140 West
West Valley City, UT 84119

801-908-5456; Fax: 801-908-5734
info@fluidpowersafety.com
www.fluidpowersafety.com

Rory S. McLaren, Founder & Director

The purpose of the Fluid Power Safety Institute is to educate companies about occupational safety within the fluid power industry. A variety of resources are offered online on safety products and procedures.

16757 Fluid Power Society
1930 East Marlton Pike
Suite A2
Cherry Hill, NJ 08003

856-489-8983
800-308-6005; Fax: 856-424-9248
askus@ifps.org
www.ifps.org

Dean Houdeshell, President
Donna Pollander, Executive Director
Jeana Hoffman, Assistant Director
Patrick J. Maluso, Business Development Manager
Adele Kayser, Communications Manager

Nonprofit organization for fluid power and motion control professionals. Its mission is to provide members with certification and educational opportunities for professional development.
4500 Members
Founded in 1960

16758 Food Processing Suppliers Association (FPSA)
1451 Dolley Madison Boulevard
Suite 101
McLean, VA 22101-3850

703-761-2600; Fax: 703-761-4334
info@fpsa.org
www.fpsa.org
Facebook, Twitter, LinkedIn, Google+

David Seckman, President & CEO
Robyn Roche, Chief Financial Officer
Dolores Alonso, VP, Membership & Business Dev
Andy Drennan, International Market Development
Grace A. Cular Yee, Vice President, Sales

Trade association for food and beverage processing suppliers and those working in the packaging industry. The association offers advocacy, business solutions and trade shows. The five main industry areas covered are bakery, beverage, dairy, prepared foods and meat.
400+ Members
Founded in 1983

16759 Global Association for Vision Information
900 Victors Way
Suite 140
Ann Arbor, MI 48108

734-994-6088
www.visiononline.org
Facebook, Twitter, LinkedIn, YouTube

Jeff Burnstein, President
Alex Shikany, VP, Membership & Business
James Hamilton, Director, Sales
Robert Huschka, Director, Education Strategies
Bob McCurrach, Director, Standards Development

The AIA is dedicated to vision and imaging technologies, with members including manufacturers of vision components and systems, system integrators, distributors, OEMs, end users, consulting firms, academic institutions, and research groups.
380+ Members
Founded in 1984

16760 Heat Exchange Institute
1300 Sumner Avenue
Cleveland, OH 44115

216-241-7333; Fax: 216-241-0105
www.heatexchange.org
LinkedIn

A nonprofit trade association whose mission is the technical advancement and promotion of utility and industrial-scale heat exchange and vacuum apparatus. Governed by technical committees, the association aims to develop standards for the heat exchange industry.
4500 Members
Founded in 1933

16761 IEEE Circuits and Systems Society
Institute Of Electrical and Electronics Engineers
445 Hoes Lane
Piscataway, NJ 08854

Home Page: www.ieee-cas.org
Facebook, Twitter, LinkedIn

Amara Amara, President
Yoshifumi Nishio, VP, Membership
Myung Hoon Sunwoo, VP, Conferences
Guoxing Wang, VP, Financial Activities
Mohammad Sawan, VP, Publications

CASS fosters interdisciplinary and cross-disciplinary cooperation with regards to using circuits and systems to address humanity's greatest challenges.

16762 IEEE Computational Intelligence Society
445 Hoes Lane
Piscataway, NJ 08855

732-465-5892; Fax: 732-465-6435
cis-info@ieee.org
cis.ieee.org
Facebook, Twitter, LinkedIn

Bernadette Bouchon-Meunier, President
Pablo Estevez, VP, Finances
Marley Vellasco, VP, Conferences
James Keller, VP, Publications
Carlos Coello Coello, VP, Member Activities

The CIS seeks to advance computational intelligence in science and engineering.

16763 IEEE Control Systems Society
445 Hoes Lane
Piscataway, NJ 08854-1331

Home Page: ieeecss.org
Facebook, Twitter, LinkedIn

Anuradha Annaswamy, President
Jorge Cortes, Director, Operations

Subsidiary of the Institute of Electrical and Electronics Engineers dedicated to control system technology.

16764 IEEE Industrial Electronics Society
Institute Of Electrical and Electronics Engineers
445 Hoes Lane
Piscataway, NJ 08854

804-827-3999
president@ieee-ies.org
www.ieee-ies.org
Facebook, Twitter, LinkedIn, YouTube

Terry Martin, President
Thilo Sauter, VP, Publications
Juan Rodriguez-Andina, VP, Conference Activities
Kiyoshi Ohishi, VP, Workshops & Activities
Yousef Ibrahim, VP, Membership Activities

Conducts, through its members, range of technical activities dedicated to applying electronics and electrical sciences in an industrial setting, including current developments in intelligent and computer control systems, robotics, factory communications and automation, flexible manufacturing, data acquisition and signal processing, vision systems, and power electronics.

16765 IEEE Industry Applications Society
Institute Of Electrical and Electronics Engineers
445 Hoes Lane
Piscataway, NJ 08854

732-562-2663
p.mccarren@ieee.org
ias.ieee.org
Facebook, Twitter, LinkedIn

Patrick McCarren, Executive Director
Lynda Bernstein, IAS Program Specialist

Seeks to link theory and practice by advancing science and technology in the electrical and electronic systems.

16766 IEEE Robotics and Automation Society
445 Hoes Lane
Piscataway, NJ

732-562-3906
ras@ieee.org
www.ieee-ras.org
Facebook, Twitter, LinkedIn, YouTube

Kathy Colabaugh, Society Operations Manager
Amy Reeder, Society Program Specialist
Alexis Simoes, Society Program Coordinator

A scientific, literary and educational society of the Institute of Electrical and Electronics Engineers, seeking to facilitate scientific and technological knowledge exchange in robotics and automation.

16767 IEEE Society on Social Implications of Technology
Institute of Electrical and Electronics Engineers
445 Hoes Lane
Piscataway, NJ 08854

r.dent@ieee.org
technologyandsociety.org
Facebook, Twitter, LinkedIn

Robert Dent, President
Lew Terman, Secretary
Howard Wolfman, Treasurer

The SSIT focuses on the following areas: Sustainable Development & Humanitarian Technology; Ethics, Human Values and Technology; Technology Benefits for All; Future Societal Impact of Technology Advances; and Protecting the Planet & Sustainable Technology

16768 IEEE Systems, Man, and Cybernetics Society
Institute of Electrical and Electronics Engineers
445 Hoes Lane
Piscataway, NJ 08854

Home Page: www.ieeesmc.org
Facebook, Twitter, LinkedIn, Instagram

Imre Rudas, President
Sam Kwong, VP, Cybernetics
Andreas Nuernberger, VP, Conferences & Meetings
Adrian Stoica, VP, Systems Science & Engineering
Vladimir Marik, VP, Organization & Planning

Promotes all aspects of systems science and engineering, human-machine systems, and cybernetics, through conferences, publications, and other activities.

16769 IEEE Technology & Engineering Management Society
Institute of Electrical and Electronics Engineers
445 Hoes Lane
Piscataway, NJ 08854

Home Page: www.ieee-tems.org
Facebook, Twitter, LinkedIn

Andy Chen, President
Richard Evans, VP, Technical Activities
Sudeendra Koushik, VP, Conferences

Formerly the Engineering Management Society and the Technology Management Council, TEMS seeks to provide members with essential management and leadership knowledge and skills.
Founded in 1951

16770 Industrial Supply Association
3435 Concord Road
Unit 21889
York, PA 17402

866-460-2360
info@isapartners.org
www.isapartners.org
Facebook, Twitter, LinkedIn, YouTube

Ed Gerber, President & CEO

The primary focus of the Industrial Supply Association is to improve the industrial supply channel through its mission-critical activities, including conventions, forums and the gathering and dissemination of critical information. The association supports distributors, manufacturers and representatives of MROP products/industrial equipment.
900+ Members
Founded in 2007

16771 Institute of Electrical and Electronics Engineers
3 Park Ave.
17th Fl.
New York, NY 10016-5997

212-419-7900; Fax: 212-752-4929
www.ieee.org
Facebook, Twitter, LinkedIn, YouTube, Instagram

Toshio Fukuda, President & CEO
Stephen Welby, Executive Director & COO

Supports all those involved in the field of electrical engineering, and works to nurture technological innovation and excellence for the benefit of humanity.
422K Members
Founded in 1963

16772 International Association of Diecutting and Diemaking
651 West Terra Cotta Avenue
Suite 132
Crystal Lake, IL 60014

815-455-7519
800-828-4233; Fax: 815-455-7510
staff@iadd.org
www.iadd.org
Facebook, Twitter, LinkedIn, YouTube

Shaun Larson, President
Cindy Crouse, CEO
Jenny Holliday, Membership & Technical Services
Stella Quimby, Meetings & Marketing
Guadalupe Trejo, Social Media & Administrative

A notprofit international trade association serving diecutters, diemakers, and industry suppliers worldwide. The association provides conferences, educational and training programs, networking opportunities, a monthly magazine, technical articles and a variety of other resources.
Founded in 1972

16773 International Association of Machinists and Aerospace Workers
9000 Machinists Place
Upper Marlboro, MD 20772

301-967-4500; Fax: 301-967-4588
www.goiam.org
Facebook, Twitter, LinkedIn, YouTube, Instagram, Pinterest

Robert Martinez, Jr., President
Dora Cervantes, General Secretary, Treasurer
Sito Pantoja, VP, Transportation
Rickey Wallace, Vice President
Stan Pickthall, Vice President

Labor union whose mission is to improve job security, wages and benefits for machinists and aerospace workers.
700K+ Members
Founded in 1888

16774 International Association of Professional Mechanical Engineers
55 Public Square
Suite 612
Cleveland, OH 44113

216-453-0500
iapme.org

Organization of licensed mechanical engineers (PEs) and engineer interns (EIs). The association offers its members education, licensure advocacy, leadership training and networking in order to strengthen their practices.
Founded in 1951

16775 Machine Intelligence Research Institute
Berkeley, CA

contact@intelligence.org
intelligence.org
Facebook, Twitter, RSS

Nate Soares, Executive Director
Malo Bourgon, Chief Operating Officer

Uses foundational mathematics to ensure artificial intelligence systems have a positive impact.

16776 Machinery Dealers National Association
315 S Patrick Street
Alexandria, VA 22314

703-836-9300
800-872-7807; Fax: 703-836-9303
office@mdna.org
www.mdna.org
Facebook, Twitter, LinkedIn

Mark Robinson, Executive Vice President
Will Keys, Accounting Manager
Joyce Fitzgerald, Administration Director

Represents dealers of used industrial equipment, providing members with business standards and development opportunities.
400 Members
Founded in 1941

16777 Manufacturers Alliance for Productivity and Innovation
1600 Wilson Boulevard
Suite 1100
Arlington, VA 22209-2594

703-841-9000
info@mapi.net
www.mapi.net
Facebook, Twitter, LinkedIn, YouTube

Stephen Gold, President & CEO
Kris Bledowski, Council Director & Senior Economist
Dave Augliera, VP, Sales & Member Services
Jenn Callaway, VP, Research
Rae Ann Johnson, SVP, Admin & General Councel

A policy research organization whose members are companies drawn from the producers and users of capital goods and allied products. The association operates 22 councils covering the areas of finance, HR, or operations in businesses.
Founded in 1933

16778 Material Handling Institute
8720 Red Oak Boulevard
Suite 201
Charlotte, NC 28217-3996

704-676-1190; Fax: 704-676-1199
gbaer@mhi.org
www.mhi.org
Facebook, Twitter, LinkedIn, YouTube

George Prest, CEO
Brian Reaves, Executive Vice President
Donna Varner, Sr. Executive Administrator
Laurie Walker, Sr. Membership Coordinator
Greg Baer, Sales Director

Association for the material handling industry, offering industry groups, education, events and programming to support companies and professionals. Members include material handling and logistics equipment companies, software manufacturers, consultants and logistics providers.
800 Members
Founded in 1945

16779 Measurement, Control & Automation Association
200 City Hall Avenue
Suite D
Poquoson, VA 23662

757-258-3100
automationassociation.com
Facebook, Twitter, LinkedIn, YouTube

Teresa Sebring, President
Andrea Ambrose, Director, Member Relations
Elizabeth Horton, Programs Manager
Kim Malina, Marketing Communications Manager
Rebecca Moore, Administrative Manager

The MCAA is the national trade association for manufacturers and distributors of instrumentation, systems, and software products for industrial process control and factory automation.
Founded in 1944

16780 Mechanical Power Transmission Association
5672 Strand Ct.
Suite 2
Naples, FL 34110
239-514-3441; Fax: 239-514-3470
bob@mpta.org
mpta.org

Bob Hamilton, President
Don Sullivan, Vice President
Robert A. Reinfried, Executive Director
Karen Lampart, Meeting Coordinator

Organization serving those working in the power transmission field, including promoting the manufacturing and sale of mechanical power transmission equipment.
Founded in 1961

16781 Motion Control & Motor Association
900 Victors Way
Suite 140
Ann Arbor, MI 48108
734-994-6088
info@motioncontrolonline.org
www.motioncontrolonline.org
Facebook, Twitter, LinkedIn, YouTube

Matt French, Chair
Gunnar Block, Vice Chair
Paul Horvat, Vice Chair

The MCMA seeks to advance motion control and related automation technologies, and to help members and the industry grow.
Founded in 2006

16782 National Fluid Power Association
6737 W. Washington Street
Suite 2350
Milwaukee, WI 53214
414-778-3344; Fax: 414-778-3361
nfpa@nfpa.com
www.nfpa.com
Facebook, LinkedIn, Flickr, Pinterest

Eric Lanke, President & CEO
Pete Alles, VP, Member Services & Marketing
Leslie Miller, Membership Manager
Stephanie Scaccianoce, Association Program Manager
Amy Zignego, Executive Admin Coordinator

Association made up of a membership of companies that have designed, manufactured and nationally marketed fluid power components.
Founded in 1953

16783 National Tooling and Machining Association
1357 Rockside Road
Cleveland, OH 44134
440-799-8991
800-248-6862; Fax: 216-264-2840
info@ntma.org
www.ntma.org
Facebook, Twitter, LinkedIn, YouTube

Dave Tilstone, President
Candy Davis, Executive Assistant
Michel Conklin, NRL Program Manager
Matt Gilmore, Membership & Business Development
Doug DeRose, Chief Financial Officer

Membership association serving the precision custom manufacturing industry through business development support, education, events and advocacy.
1400 Members
Founded in 1943

16784 Outdoor Power Equipment and Engine Service Association
37 Pratt St.
Essex, CT 06426-1159
860-767-1770; Fax: 860-767-7932
info@opeesa.com
www.opeesa.com
Twitter, LinkedIn

Alex Wyatt, President
Lorri Sklar, Vice President, Annual Meeting
Nancy Cueroni, Executive Director
Arin Monroe, Secretary/Treasurer

Association made up of distributors and manufacturers of outdoor power equipment and air-cooled gas and diesel engines.
100+ Members

16785 Packaging Machinery Manufacturers Institute
11911 Freedom Drive
Suite 600
Reston, VA 20190
571-612-3200; Fax: 703-243-8556
info@pmmi.org
www.pmmi.org
Facebook, Twitter, LinkedIn, YouTube, Instagram

Charles D. Yuska, President & CEO
Corinne G. Mulligan, Executive Assistant
Caroline Abromavage, Operations Director
Jeremy Adams, Marketing & Communications
Heather Harvey, Membership Manager

Trade association for manufacturers of packaging and packaging-related converting equipment, components and materials.
800+ Members
Founded in 1933

16786 Powder Actuated Tool Manufacturers Institute
320 North 5th Street
St. Charles, MO 63301
636-578-5510; Fax: 314-884-4414
info@patmi.org
www.patmi.org

Represents manufacturers of construction tools used to fasten construction materials together, such as wood to concrete, steel to concrete, metal to concrete and steel to steel.
Founded in 1952

16787 Power Tool Institute
1300 Sumner Avenue
Cleveland, OH 44115-2851
216-241-7333; Fax: 216-241-0105
pti@powertoolinstitute.com
www.powertoolinstitute.com
YouTube

Organization with a mission to educate people about power tools and set standards of safety and quality control in the industry.
Founded in 1968

16788 Power Transmission Distributors Association
230 West Monroe Street
Suite 1410
Chicago, IL 60606-4703
312-516-2100; Fax: 312-516-2101
ptda@ptda.org
www.ptda.org
Twitter, LinkedIn

Jim Williams, President
Ann Arnott, Executive Vice President & CEO
Brenda Holt, Membership Director
Andrea Lebron, Operations Manager
Ginger Wheeler, Marketing & Communications Director

Association whose members are industrial power transmission/motion control distributor firms dealing in equipment such as bearings, belts, drives, motors, gears, couplings, clutches and brakes. The association offers member companies development programs and networking opportunities.
Founded in 1960

16789 Power-Motion Technology Representatives Association
5353 Wayzata Boulevard
Suite 350
Minneapolis, MN 55416
888-817-7872; Fax: 952-252-8096
ptrahq@ptra.org
ptra.org
Facebook, LinkedIn

Curt Benson, CPMR, President
Susan Crolla, Executive Director
Adam Cooler, Treasurer

The association is made up of independent manufacturers' representatives and those invested in promoting sales representatives within the power transmission and motion control industries. Supports will include education, networking opportunities and industry events.
Founded in 1972

16790 Precision Machined Products Association
6880 West Snowville Road
Suite 200
Brecksville, OH 44141
440-526-0300; Fax: 440-526-5803
info@pmpa.org
www.pmpa.org
Facebook, Twitter, LinkedIn, YouTube, Flickr

Bernard Nagle, Executive Director
Mari Kirchenbauer, Executive Assistant
Miles K. Free, Industry Research & Technology Dir
Renee A. Merker, Communications & Event Planner
Andrea J. Jeric, Accounting Assistant

International trade association supporting the precision machined products industry through educational opporunities for members, knowledge resources and professional development events.
Founded in 1933
Mailing list available for rent

16791 Robotic Industries Association
900 Victors Way
Suite 140
Ann Arbor, MI 48108
734-994-6088; Fax: 734-994-3338
info@robotics.org
www.robotics.org
Facebook, Twitter, LinkedIn, YouTube

Jeff Burnstein, President
Dana Whalls, Vice President, A3
Clarissa Carvalho, Marketing Specialist
James Hamilton, Sales Director
Bob Doyle, Vice President

Trade group serving the robotics industry. Members include robot manufacturers, users, system integrators, component suppliers, research groups, and consulting firms. The Robotic Industries Association offers educational resources, events and news for its members.
Founded in 1974
Mailing list available for rent

16792 Service Specialists Association
1221 Candlewick Drive NW
Poplar Grove, IL 61065

224-990-1005
service.specialists@outlook.com
www.truckservice.org

Jim Parsons, President
Craig Fry, Executive Director
Toni Nastali, Treasurer
Billy Burkholder, Director
Mark Broem, Director

Association whose members are persons, firms or corporations that operate a full line heavy duty repair service shop related to trucking.

16793 Society of Manufacturing Engineers
1000 Town Center
Suite 1910
Southfield, MI 48075

313-425-3000
service@sme.org
www.sme.org
Facebook, Twitter, LinkedIn, YouTube, Google+, Instagram

Sandra L. Bouckley, Executive Director & CEO
Craig Connop, Chief Financial Officer
Steve Prahalis, Chief Operating Officer
Erica Ciupak, Information Technology
Debbie Clark, Governance

The organization serves its members and others in the international manufacturing community by identifying, evaluating and explaining the adoption and integration of emerging information technologies to create business value.
65K Members
Founded in 1932

16794 Society of Robotic Surgery
c/c Veritas Meeting Solutions
1061 E. Main Street
Suite 300
East Dundee, IL 60118

847-752-5355
info@srobotics.org
www.srobotics.org
Facebook, Twitter

Farid Gharagozloo, MD, FACS, President
Vipul R. Patel, MD, FACS, Executive Director
Sue O'Sullivan, Administrative Director

Society providing education about robotic surgery, as well as studies, funding and development events for professionals in the field.
Founded in 2009

16795 The Association for Manufacturing Technology
7901 Jones Branch Drive
Suite 900
McLean, VA 22102-4206

703-893-2900
800-524-0475; Fax: 703-893-1151
amt@amtonline.org
www.amtonline.org
Facebook, Twitter, LinkedIn, YouTube

Douglas K. Woods, President
Rebecca Stahl, Chief Financial Officer
Kimberly L. Brown, Member Services Director
Peter R. Eelman, VP, Exhibitions & Business Dev.
Andrea Kuchinski, Dir, Marketing & Communications

Represents and supports the U.S.-based manufacturing technology industry, including distributors, producers and service providers. The association offers essential programs and services that help its members gain global recognition.

16796 The Conveyor & Sortation Systems Industry Group
MHI
8720 Red Oak Boulevard
Suite 201
Charlotte, NC 28217

704-676-1190
askidmore@mhi.org
www.mhi.org/conv

Todd Hunter, Chair
Sebastian Titze, Vice Chair
Ashley Skidmore, Manager

Association of providers of conveyors and sortation systems working together to promote their industry.

16797 The FPDA Motion & Control Network
180 Admiral Cochrane Drive
Suite 370
Annapolis, MD 21401

410-940-6347
info@fpda.org
www.fpda.org
Facebook, Twitter, LinkedIn

Kevin Kampe, President
Amy Luckado, Executive Director
Donald Smith, Chief Financial Officer
Dominique Abney, Director, Marketing/Sales
Courtney Truelove, Manager, Membership/Programs

Organization with the mission of supporting business performance for those working in the fluid power industry.
300+ Members
Founded in 1974

16798 Unified Abrasives Manufacturers' Association
30200 Detroit Road
Cleveland, OH 44145-1967

440-899-0010; Fax: 440-892-1404
uama.org

Allen Donahue, President
Brian Goers, Vice President
Jeff Wherry, Managing Director
Fred Rodgers, Director
Christian Pfeifer, Director

The mission of the association is to support the manufacturing and marketing of abrasive products by providing members with knowledge, networking opportunities, industry standards and more.
Founded in 1999

16799 Valve Manufacturers Association of America (VMA)
1050 17th Street NW
Suite 280
Washington, DC 20036-5521

202-331-8105; Fax: 202-296-0378
spartyke@vma.org
www.vma.org

William S. Sandler, President
Marc Pasternak, Vice President
Malena Malone-Blevins, Meetings Manager
Judy Tibbs, Education Director
Abby Brown, Education & Training Coordinator

Trade association representing manufacturers of valves, actuators and controls. The association offers supports in the form of meetings, publications, education and networking.
100 Members
Founded in 1938

16800 Vibration Institute
2625 Butterfield Road
Suite 128N
Oak Brook, IL 60523-3415

630-654-2254; Fax: 630-654-2271
information@vi-institute.org
www.vi-institute.org
Facebook, Twitter, LinkedIn

Dave Corelli, President
Michael Long, Executive Director
Ronald L. Eshleman, Technical Director
Peggy Dellaria, Membership Associate
Sean McDonald, Marketing & Communications Manager

An organization dedicated to the exchange of practical vibration information on machines and structures. The Institute offers various educational and training programs for this purpose.
Founded in 1972

16801 Wood Machinery Manufacturers of America
9 Newport Drive
Suite 200
Forest Hill, MD 21050

443-640-1052; Fax: 443-640-1031
info@wmma.org
www.wmma.org
Facebook, Twitter, LinkedIn

Chris Hacker, President
Stephen Carter, Vice President
Fred Stringfellow, Chief Executive Officer
Kristin Grove, Member Services Coordinator
Diane Schafer, Meetings Director

Organization dedicated to supporting and advocating for manufacturers of machinery and tooling used for processing wood.
Founded in 1899

16802 Woodworking Machinery Industry Association
225 Reinekers Lane
Suite 410
Alexandria, VA 22314

571-279-8340; Fax: 571-279-8343
info@wmia.org
www.wmia.org
Facebook, Twitter, LinkedIn, YouTube

Larry Hoffer, President
Jeff Linder, Program Manager
Heather Jolley, Program Administrator
Rick Braun, Director
Andreas Muehlbauer, Director

Represents importers and distributors of woodworking machinery and ancillary equipment, as well as being a link between suppliers and manufacturers. The organization supports its members through industry awards, safety publications, scholarships and networking platforms.
Founded in 1977

Newsletters

16803 APMA Newsletter
Automotive Parts Manufacturers' Association
10 Four Seasons Place
Suite 801
Toronto, ON M9B 6H7

416-620-4220; Fax: 416-620-9730
apma.ca/apma-newsletter

Flavio Volpe, President
Jonathon Azzopardi, Director
Mike Bilton, Director
Lisa T. Boulton, Director
Fred di Tosto, Director

Newsletter featuring news items on activities and events of the Automotive Parts Manufacturers' Association.
Founded in 1952

16804 **Bot Brief**
Robotic Industries Association
900 Victors Way
Suite 140
Ann Arbor, MI 48108
734-994-6088; Fax: 734-994-3338
info@robotics.org
www.robotics.org
Jeff Burnstein, President
Dana Whalls, Vice President, A3
Clarissa Carvalho, Marketing Specialist
Bob Doyle, Vice President
Weekly newsletter from the Robotic Industries Association with the latest industry news.
Frequency: Weekly
Founded in 1974

16805 **CEMA Bulletin**
Conveyor Equipment Manufacturers Association
5672 Strand Ct.
Suite 2
Naples, FL 34110
239-514-3441; Fax: 239-514-3470
kim@cemanet.org
www.cemanet.org
Paul Ross, President
E.A. Thompson, Vice President
Robert Reinfried, Executive Vice President
Noel Bell, Director
Newsletter by the Conveyor Equipment Manufacturers Association containing conveyor industry news as well as statistics and articles.
Founded in 1933

16806 **Caster and Wheel Handbook**
Youngs
55 E Cherry Ln
Souderton, PA 18964-1550
215-723-4400
800-523-5454; Fax: 800-544-3239
custrep@youngscatalog.com
www.youngscatalog.com
Paul O Young Jr, President
Technical news and information.
Frequency: Monthly
Founded in 1945

16807 **Computer Aided Design Report**
CAD/CAM Publishing
711 Van Nuys Street
San Diego, CA 92109-1053
858-488-0533; Fax: 858-488-0361
www.cadcampub.com/
Randall Newton, Editor
Uses of computers by engineers in the manufacturing trades.
Cost: $344.00
Frequency: Monthly
ISSN: 0276-749X
Founded in 1977

16808 **Computer Integrated Manufacture and Engineering**
Lionheart Publishing
2555 Cumberland Pkwy Se
Suite 299
Atlanta, GA 30339-3921
770-432-2551; Fax: 770-432-6969
Explores cutting edge developments in manufacturing systems operation management.
Circulation: 24,000

16809 **FPDA InMotion Newsletter**
The FPDA Motion & Control Network
180 Admiral Cochrane Drive
Suite 370
Annapolis, MD 21401
410-940-6347
info@fpda.org
www.fpda.org
Kevin Kampe, President
Amy Luckado, Executive Director
Dominique Abney, Director, Marketing/Sales
Donald Smith, Chief Financial Officer
Courtney Truelove, Manager, Membership/Programs
Newsletter for members of The FPDA Motion & Control Network, covering subjects of interest to the fluid power industry.
300+ Members
Frequency: Monthly
Founded in 1974

16810 **High-Tech Materials Alert**
John Wiley & Sons
111 River St
Hoboken, NJ 07030-5790
201-748-6000
800-825-7550; Fax: 201-748-6088
info@wiley.com
www.wiley.com
William J Pesce, CEO
Details significant developments in high-performance materials ranging from alloys and metallic whiskers to ceramic and graphite fibers, their fabrication and industrial applications.
Cost: $1152.00
Frequency: Monthly
Founded in 1807

16811 **Industrial Health & Hazards Update**
InfoTeam
PO Box 15640
Plantation, FL 33318-5640
954-473-9560; Fax: 954-473-0544
Merton Allen, Editor
Covers occupational safety, health, hazards, and disease, mitigatioin and control of hazardous situations; waste recycling and treaqtment; environmental pollution and control; product safety and liability; fires and explosions; plant and computer security,; air pollution; surface and ground water; wastewater; soil gases; combustion and incineration; earth warming; ozone layer depletion; electromagnetic radiation; toxic materials; and many other related topics.
Frequency: Monthlyth

16812 **Innovators Digest**
InfoTeam
PO Box 15640
Plantation, FL 33318-5640
954-473-9560; Fax: 954-473-0544
Merton Allen, Editor
A multidisciplinary publication covering developments in science, engineering, products, markets, business development, manufacturing and other technological developments having industrial or commercial significance.
Frequency: Bi-Weekly

16813 **Intelligent Manufacturing**
Lionheart Publishing
506 Roswell St Se
Suite 220
Marietta, GA 30060-4101
770-422-3139; Fax: 770-432-6969
lpi@lionhrtpub.com
www.lionhrtpub.com
John Llewellyn, Publisher
David Blanchard, Advertising Sales Manager
Marvin Diamond, Advertising Sales Manager
Provides expert solutions to manufacturing professionals covering production problems, developments in manufacturing systems.
Cost: $20.00
Frequency: Weekly
Circulation: 1598
Founded in 1987

16814 **MAPI Research Data**
Manufacturers Alliance for Productivity/Innovation
1600 Wilson Boulevard
Suite 1100
Arlington, VA 22209-2594
703-841-9000
info@mapi.net
www.mapi.net
Stephen Gold, President & CEO
Kris Bledowski, Council Director & Senior Economist
Rae Ann Johnson, SVP, Admin & General Councel
Jenn Callaway, VP, Research
Collection of research, forecasts, and analyses relevant to the manufacturing sector and covering energy, taxes, labor, trade, innovation, and regulations. The material is published by the Manufacturers Alliance for Productivity and Innovation.
Founded in 1933

16815 **Machinery Outlook**
Manfredi & Associates
20934 W Lakeview Pkwy
Mundelein, IL 60060-9502
847-949-9080; Fax: 847-949-9910
info@manfredi.com
www.machineryoutlook.com
Frank Manfredi, President
A newsletter about and for the construction and mining machinery industry.
Cost: $550.00
14 Pages
Frequency: Monthly
Founded in 1984
Printed in one color on matte stock

16816 **Manufacturing Technology**
National Technical Information Service
5285 Port Royal Rd
Springfield, VA 22161-0001
703-605-6000; Fax: 703-605-6900
info@ntis.gov
www.ntis.gov
Linda Davis, VP
Patrik Ekstrom, Business Development Manager
Reuel Avila, Managing Director
Covers CAD/CAM, robotics, robots, productivity, manufacturing, planning, processing and control, plant design and computer software.

16817 **Motion Control Market Report**
Motion Control & Motor Association
900 Victors Way
Suite 140
Ann Arbor, MI 48108
734-994-6088
info@motioncontrolonline.org
www.motioncontrolonline.org
Matt French, Chair
Gunnar Block, Vice Chair
Paul Horvat, Vice Chair
Quarterly release for members.
Founded in 2006

16818 **NTMA Record**
Tooling

9300 Livingston Road
Fort Washington, MD 20744-4905

301-248-5071
800-248-6862; Fax: 301-248-7104
www.ntma.org

Rob Akers, Operations Director/ Publisher
Richard Wills, CEO
Thomas Garcia, Manager, Marketing

Covers activities of 4,000 member companies of tool, die and precision machining industries.
Cost: $39.00
16 Pages
Frequency: Monthly
Circulation: 2000
Founded in 1943

16819 **OPEESA eNewsletter**
Outdoor Power Equipment and Engine Service Assoc
37 Pratt Street
Suite 2
Essex, CT 06426-1159

860-767-1770; Fax: 860-767-7932
info@opeesa.com
www.opeesa.com

Alex Wyatt, President
Lorri Sklar, Vice President, Annual Meeting
Nancy Cueroni, Executive Director
Arin Monroe, Secretary/Treasurer

Online newsletter for members of the Outdoor Power Equipment and Engine Service Association, covering topics relevant to outdoor power equipment.
100+ Members
Frequency: Monthly

16820 **PMPA Speaking of Precision**
Precision Machined Products Association
6880 West Snowville Road
Suite 200
Brecksville, OH 44141

440-526-0300; Fax: 440-526-5803
info@pmpa.org
pmpaspeakingofprecision.com

Bernard Nagle, Executive Director
Mari Kirchenbauer, Executive Assistant
Miles K. Free, Industry Research & Technology Dir
Renee A. Merker, Communications & Event Planner

Blog providing information and news about the precision machined products industry.
Frequency: Daily
Founded in 1933

16821 **Spotlight**
Power Transmission Distributors Association
230 West Monroe Street
Suite 1410
Chicago, IL 60606-4703

312-516-2100; Fax: 312-516-2101
ptda@ptda.org
www.ptda.org/resources/ptda-publications.aspx

Jim Williams, President
Ann Arnott, Executive Vice President & CEO
Brenda Holt, Membership Director
Andrea Lebron, Operations Manager
Ginger Wheeler, Marketing & Communications Director

Newsletter containing content on industry and PTDA association news and policy updates for companies dealing in industrial power transmission/motion control equipment.
Frequency: Bi-Monthly
Circulation: 3000+
Founded in 1960

16822 **The AMEA Appraiser newsletter**
Association of Machinery and Equipment Appraisers
315 South Patrick Street
Alexandria, VA 22314

703-836-7900
800-537-8629; Fax: 703-836-9303
amea@amea.org
www.amea.org
Facebook, LinkedIn, YouTube
Randall Koster, President
Jean Harris, Director
Terrance Jacobs, Director
Doris Toronyi, Director
Curt Roskelley, Director

The AMEA Appraiser is a newsletter published by the AMEA organization, containing articles on the subject of appraising, machinery and equipment.
300 Members
8 Pages
Frequency: Quarterly
Circulation: 6800
Founded in 1983
Mailing list available for rent: 282 names at $100 per M
Printed in 2 colors on matte stock

16823 **The Cutting Edge**
Wood Machinery Manufacturers of America
9 Newport Drive
Suite 200
Forest Hill, MD 21050

443-640-1052; Fax: 443-640-1031
info@wmma.org
www.wmma.org

Chris Hacker, President
Stephen Carter, Vice President
Kristin Grove, Member Services Coordinator
Jennifer Miller, Associate Director

Newsletter featuring articles on woodworking equipment and the wood processing industry, as well as public policy updates that would affect business for members of the Wood Machinery Manufacturers of America organization.
Frequency: Monthly
Founded in 1899

16824 **Transmissions**
Power Transmission Distributors Association
230 West Monroe Street
Suite 1410
Chicago, IL 60606-4703

312-516-2100; Fax: 312-516-2101
ptda@ptda.org
www.ptda.org/resources/ptda-publications.aspx

Jim Williams, President
Ann Arnott, Executive Vice President & CEO
Brenda Holt, Membership Director
Andrea Lebron, Operations Manager
Ginger Wheeler, Marketing & Communications Director

Newsletter containing content on industry trends for companies dealing in industrial power transmission/motion control equipment.
Circulation: 4300+
Founded in 1960

16825 **WMIA News**
Woodworking Machinery Industry Association
225 Reinekers Lane
Suite 410
Alexandria, VA 22314

571-279-8340; Fax: 571-279-8343
info@wmia.org
www.wmia.org/wmia-newsletter

Larry Hoffer, President
Jeff Linder, Program Manager
Heather Jolley, Program Administrator
Rick Braun, Director

Newsletter from the Woodworking Machinery Industry Association providing updates on events and members.
Founded in 1977

Magazines & Journals

16826 **Advanced Materials & Processes**
ASM International
9639 Kinsman Road
Materials Park, OH 44073-0002

440-338-5151
800-336-5152; Fax: 440-338-4634
magazines@asminternational.org
www.asminternational.org

William T. Mahoney, Secretary & CEO
Joanne Miller, Editor
Vicki Burt, Managing Editor

AM&P is the monthly technical magazine from ASM International, designed to keep readers aware of leading-edge developments and trends in engineering materials - metals and alloys, engineering polymers, advanced ceramics, and composites - and the methods used to select, process, fabricate, test, and characterize them.
30K Members
Frequency: Monthly
Circulation: 23000
Founded in 1913

16827 **American Tool, Die & Stamping News**
Eagle Publications
42400 Grand River Ave
Suite 103
Novi, MI 48375-2572

248-347-3487
800-783-3491; Fax: 248-347-3492
www.ameritooldie.com

Arthur Brown, President
Joan Oakley, CEO

Applications, techniques, equipment and accessories of metal stamping, moldmaking, electric discharge machining; and new product information relating to the tool and die industry. Accepts advertising.
70 Pages
Circulation: 36000
ISSN: 0192-5709
Founded in 1971
Printed in 4 colors on glossy stock

16828 **Circuits and Systems Magazine**
IEEE Circuits and Systems Society
445 Hoes Lane
Piscataway, NJ 08854

chaiwahwu@ieee.org
www.ieee-cas.org

Chai Wah Wu, Editor-in-Chief
Alyssa B. Apsel, Deputy Editor-in-Chief
Mohammad Sawan, VP, Publications

Feature articles with noteworthy results, surveys, and tutorials.

16829 **Compressed Air Magazine**
Ingersoll Rand Company
200 Chestnut Ridge Road
Woodcliff, NJ 07677

201-573-0123; Fax: 201-573-3172
www.irco.com

Michele Zayle, Circulation Director
Thomas McAloon, Editor

A magazine of applied technology and industrial management for middle and upper level managers in diversified industries.
Cost: $15.00
44 Pages
Frequency: 8 per year

Circulation: 125,000
Printed in 4 colors on matte stock

16830 **Compressed Air and Gas Handbook**
Compressed Air and Gas Institute
1300 Sumner Avenue
Cleveland, OH 44115

216-241-7333; Fax: 216-241-0105
www.cagi.org

Rick Stasyshan, Technical Consultant

Reference source containing information about compressed air and the management of compressors and pneumatic equipment.

16831 **Contact**
Furnas Electric Company
1000 McKee Street
Batavia, IL 60510-1682

630-879-6000; Fax: 630-879-0867

Steve Wilcox, Editor

Application of electric motor controls to electrically operated machinery and equipment.
Circulation: 4,000

16832 **Cutting Edge**
Int'l Assoc of Diecutting and Diemaking
651 W Terra Cotta Ave
Suite 132
Crystal Lake, IL 60014

815-455-7519
800-828-4233; Fax: 815-455-7510
ccrouse@iadd.org
www.iadd.org

Cindy Crouse, CEO
Jill May, Chapter Relations Coordinator

A technical journal and trade magazine written and edited specifically for diecutters, diemakers and industry suppliers who are faced with the need to stay ahead of technologies in an industry that is changing at breakneck speed.
Frequency: Monthly

16833 **Diesel Progress: North American Edition**
Diesel & Gas Turbine Publications
20855 Watertown Rd
Suite 220
Waukesha, WI 53186-1873

262-754-4100; Fax: 262-754-4175
www.dieselspec.com

Michael Osenga, President
S Bollwahn, Circulation Manager

Geared towards readers interested in state-of-the-art systems technology. Features include new product listings, systems design, research and product testing as well as systems maintenance and rebuilding.
Frequency: Monthly
Circulation: 26011

16834 **EE-Evaluation Engineering**
Nelson Publishing Inc
2500 Tamiami Trl N
Nokomis, FL 34275-3476

941-966-9521; Fax: 941-966-2590
www.healthmgttech.com
Facebook

A Verner Nelson, President

Leading source of information for the electronics testing and evaluation market.
Founded in 1962

16835 **Elevator World**
Elevator World
PO Box 6507
Mobile, AL 36660-0507

251-479-4514
800-730-5093; Fax: 251-479-7043

T Bruce Mackinnon, CEO
Robert S Caporale, Senior VP/Editor
Patricia Cartee, VP/Commercial Operations

International journal for those involved in short-range vertical transportation, including manufacturers, contractors, maintainers, consultants and inspectors.
Cost: $75.00
170 Pages
Frequency: Monthly
Circulation: 7,000
Founded in 1953
Printed in 4 colors on glossy stock

16836 **Equip-Mart**
Story Communications
116 N Camp Street
Seguin, TX 78155

830-303-3328
800-864-1155; Fax: 830-372-3011
www.equip-mart.com

Tammy Reilly, Publisher

Largest industrial equipment magazine in North America. Received by manufacturig executives who purchase or sell industrial equipment, tools, supplies and accessories.
Frequency: Monthly
Circulation: 108,000

16837 **Facilities Engineering Journal**
Association for Facilities Engineering
1000 Potomac Street NW
Suite 500
Washington, DC 20007

202-791-9080; Fax: 571-766-2142
grodriguez@afe.org
www.afe.org

Gabriella Rodriguez, Senior Manager, Membership
Joshua Watkins, Manager, Professional Development

Provides practical, in-depth information on the key issues faced by facilities engineers on the job every day.
Frequency: Quarterly

16838 **Gear Technology**
Randall Publishing Company
PO Box 1426
Elk Grove Village, IL 60009

847-437-6604; Fax: 847-437-6618
www.geartechnology.com

Michael Goldstein, Publisher
William R Stott, Managing Editor
Dan Pels, Business Development Mana
Carol Tratar, Circulation Coordinator
Richard Goldstein, Vice President

Gear Technology offers technical articles from the top names in the industry; feature articles dealing with management and technology; top-notch tradeshow coverage; industry and products news.
Circulation: 13025
Founded in 1934
Printed in 4 colors on glossy stock

16839 **High Performance Composites**
Ray Publishing
P.O.Box 992
Morrison, CO 80465-0992

303-467-1776; Fax: 303-467-1777
www.compositeworld.com

Approach is technical, offering cutting-edge design, engineering, prototyping, and manufacturing solutions for aerospace and other traditional and emerging structural applications for advanced composites.

16840 **Home Medical Equipment News**
United Publications
106 Lafayette Street
PO Box 998
Yarmouth, ME 04096

207-846-0600; Fax: 207-846-0657
www.hmenews.com

James G Taliaferro, CEO/President
Brenda Boothby, Circulation Director
Joline V Gilman, Production Director
Jim Sullivan, Editor
Rick Rector, Publisher

Serves home medical equipment providers.
Frequency: Monthly
Circulation: 17100
Founded in 1995

16841 **Home Shop Machinist**
Village Press
2779 Aero Park Drive
PO Box 968
Traverse City, MI 49685-968

231-946-3712
800-327-7377; Fax: 231-946-3289
info@villagepress.com
www.villagepress.com

Robert Goff, Publisher
Neil Knopf, Editor
Joe D. Rice, Editor in Chief
Angela Sagi, Advertising Director

Articles on precision machining and metal working and how-to projects geared towards the amateur machinist and small commercial machine shops.
Cost: $25.00
Circulation: 28000

16842 **IEEE Computational Intelligence Magazine**
IEEE Computational Intelligence Society
445 Hoes Lane
Piscataway, NJ 08855

732-465-5892; Fax: 732-465-6435
cis-info@ieee.org
cis.ieee.org

Bernadette Bouchon-Meunier, President
Hessein Abbass, VP, Technical Activities
James Keller, VP, Publications

CIM features peer-reviewed articles with noteworthy discoveries, insights, and tutorial surveys.

16843 **IEEE Control Systems Magazine**
IEEE Control Systems Society (CSS)
445 Hoes Lane
Piscataway, NJ 08854-1331

732-562-3937
m.david@ieee.org
www.ieee.org

Jonathan How, Editor-in-Chief
Rodolphe Sepulchre, Deputy Editor-in-Chief

Focuses on applications of technical knowledge and concentrates on industrial implementations, design tools, technology review, control education and applied research. Geared towards readers with many different responsibilities including applied research, device design, product development and design including software and semiconductor components.
Cost: $210.00
Founded in 1973
Mailing list available for rent

16844 **IEEE Industrial Electronics Magazine**
Institute Of Electrical and Electronics Engineers

445 Hoes Lane
Piscataway, NJ 08854

804-827-3999
eic-iem@ieee-ies.org
www.ieee-ies.org

Peter Palesnky, Editor-in-Chief

IEM features peer-reviewed articles presenting new trends and practices in industrial electronics research & development.

16845 IEEE Transactions on Engineering Management
IEEE Technology & Engineering Management Society
445 Hoes Lane
Piscataway, NJ 08854

tugrul.u.daim@pdx.edu
www.ieee-tems.org

Tugrul U. Daim, Editor-in-Chief
Alison Larkin, Peer Review Support Services
Mark Werwath, VP, Publications

Journal of the Technology and Engineering Management Society of IEEE, with peer-reviewed research on engineering, technology, and innovation management.
Frequency: Quarterly
Founded in 1954

16846 IEEE Transactions on Industry Applications
Institute Of Electrical and Electronics Engineers
445 Hoes Lane
Piscataway, NJ 08854

732-562-2663
t.nondahl@ieee.org
www.ieee.org

Thomas A. Nondahl, Editor-in-Chief

The development and applications of electrical systems, apparatus, devices and controls to the processes and equipment of industry and commerce.
Circulation: 5100
Founded in 1980

16847 InTech
ISA Services
67 Alexander Drive
PO Box 12277
Research Triangle Park, NC 27709

919-549-8411; Fax: 919-990-9434
info@isa.org
www.isa.org

Greg Hale, Editor
Richard Simpson, Publisher

Covers the most recent developments in the instrumention, measurement and control market.
Frequency: Monthly
Circulation: 75000
Founded in 1945

16848 Industrial Machine Trader
Heartland Industrial Group
1003 Central Avenue
PO Box 1415
Fort Dodge, IA 50501

515-955-1600
800-203-9960; Fax: 515-955-3753
www.industrialmachinetrader.com

Tony Smith, Publisher
Gele Mckinney, President
Angi Hesterman, Circulation Manager

Industrial machinery equipment, suppliers and manufacturers.
Cost: $67.85
8 Pages
Frequency: Weekly
Circulation: 234000
Founded in 1970

16849 Industrial Market Place
Wineberg Publications
7842 Lincoln Avenue
Skokie, IL 60077

847-676-1900
800-323-1818; Fax: 847-676-0063
info@industrialmktpl.com
www.industrialmktpl.com

Joel Wineberg, President
Jackie Bitensky, Editor

Has advertisements on machinery, industrial and plant equipment, services and industrial acution in each issue.
Cost: $175.00
Frequency: Every 2 weeks
Circulation: 14,000
Founded in 1951
Mailing list available for rent: 120 names at $70 per M
Printed in 4 colors on glossy stock

16850 Journal of Materials Engineering and Performance
ASM International
9639 Kinsman Road
Materials Park, OH 44073-0002

440-338-5151
800-336-5152; Fax: 440-338-4634
memberservicecenter@asminternational.org
www.asminternational.org

William T. Mahoney, Secretary & CEO
Rajiv Asthana, Editor

Peer-reviewed journal that publishes contributions on all aspects of materials selection, design, characterization, processing and performance testing. The journal is useful for solving day-to-day engineering challenges - especially those involving components for larger systems.
30K Members
Frequency: Bi-Monthly
Founded in 1913

16851 Journal of Robotic Surgery
Society of Robotic Surgery
1061 E. Main Street
Suite 300
East Dundee, IL 60118

info@srobotics.org
link.springer.com/journal/11701

Vipul R. Patel, MD, Executive Director

Journal exploring minimally invasive surgical techniques and the role of robotics in surgery.
Cost: $99.00
Circulation: 40K+
ISSN: 1863-2483
Founded in 2009

16852 Lead, Reach and Connect
Automotive Parts Manufacturers' Association
10 Four Seasons Place
Suite 801
Toronto, ON M9B 6H7

416-620-4220; Fax: 416-620-9730
accounting@matrixgroupinc.net
apma.ca/lead-reach-and-connect

Flavio Volpe, President
Jonathon Azzopardi, Director
Shoshana Weinberg, Customer Service Liaison
Alexandra Walld, Editor

The official magazine of the Automotive Parts Manufacturers' Association, providing the Canadian automotive industry with current information on business. Some subjects covered include automotive intelligence, industry events and industry standards.
Founded in 1952

16853 Locator Services
Locator Online
315 S Patrick St
Suite 3
Alexandria, VA 22314-3532

703-836-9700
800-537-1446; Fax: 703-836-7665
sales@locatoronline.com
www.locatoronline.com

Terry Pitman, Publisher

Used metalworking equipment.
Cost: $38.00
Frequency: Monthly
Circulation: 225000
Founded in 1969

16854 MPTA Publications
Mechanical Power Transmission Association
5672 Strand Ct.
Suite 2
Naples, FL 34110

239-514-3441; Fax: 239-514-3470
bob@mpta.org
mpta.org

Bob Hamilton, President
Don Sullivan, Vice President
Robert A. Reinfried, Executive Director
Karen Lampart, Meeting Coordinator

Publications by the Mechanical Power Transmission Association (MPTA) featuring industry standards on the subjects of pulleys, sheaves, chain and elastomeric couplings.
Founded in 1961

16855 Machine Shop Guide
Worldwide Communications
401 Worthington Avenue
Harrison, NJ 07029-2039

973-977-7555; Fax: 253-872-7603
www.wctower.com

Robert L Hatschek, Executive Editor
Frederick Mason, Editor

Information on manufacturing technology, new applications for manufacturing technology and new products. Focus is metal cutting machines and tooling.
Frequency: 10 per year
Circulation: 102,893
Founded in 1996
Printed in 4 colors on glossy stock

16856 Machinery Trader
Sandhills Publishing
PO Box 82545
Lincoln, NE 68501-2545

402-479-2181
800-247-4898; Fax: 402-479-2195
feedback@sandhills.com
www.sandhills.com

Tom Peed, CEO
Marva Wasser, Editor-in-Chief

Covering heavy equipment.
Cost: $59.00
160 Pages
Frequency: Weekly
Circulation: 20000
Founded in 1978

16857 Managing Automation
Thomas Publishing Company
5 Penn Plz
Suite 10
New York, NY 10001-1860

212-695-0500; Fax: 212-290-7362
www.thomaspublishing.com

Carl Holst-Knudsen, CEO
Robert Malone, Editor
Heather L Mikisch, Publisher
Kim Vennard, Marketing Manager

Serves the needs of those managers and engineers responsible for the planning and imple-

mentation of factory automation at both the plant and enterprise levels.
Frequency: Monthly
Circulation: 100246
Founded in 1898

16858 **Manufacturing Engineering**
Society of Manufacturing Engineers
1 SME Drive
Dearborn, MI 48128

313-425-3000
800-733-4763; Fax: 313-425-3400
service@sme.org
advancedmanufacturing.org

Jeffrey M. Krause, CEO
Alan Rooks, Editor-in-Chief
James A. Lorincz, Senior Editor
Patrick Waurzyniak, Senior Editor

Serves U.S. engineers and other manufacturing professionals by covering topics such as cybersecurity, automation, milling, robotics and more.
65K Members
Frequency: Monthly
Founded in 1932

16859 **Mechanical Engineering Magazine**
American Society of Mechanical Engineers
Two Park Avenue
New York, NY 10016-5990

973-882-1170
800-843-2763
falcionij@asme.org
www.asme.org/network/media/mechanical-engineering-magazine

John G. Falconi, Editor-in-Chief & Publisher
Chitra Sethi, Managing Editor

Flagship publication of the American Society of Mechanical Engineering.
Frequency: Monthly
Founded in 1880

16860 **Metallurgical and Materials Transactions**
ASM International
9639 Kinsman Rd
Materials Park, OH 44073-0002

440-338-5151
800-336-5152; Fax: 440-338-4634
memberservicecenter@asminternational.org
www.asminternational.org

William T. Mahoney, Secretary & CEO
Tresa M. Pollock, Principal Editor

Covers information on physical metallurgy and materials science with emphasis on processing, structure, and properties. Joint publication between ASM International and The Minerals, Metals and Materials Society.
Cost: $5658.00

16861 **Modern Machine Shop**
Gardner Publications
6915 Valley Ln
Cincinnati, OH 45244-3153

513-527-8800
800-950-8020; Fax: 513-527-8801
mmsmkt@gardnerweb.com
www.gardnerweb.com

Rick Kline Sr, CEO
Mark D Albert, Manager
John Campos, Manager
Brian Wertheimer, Account Manager
Eddie Kania, Sales Manager

Reaches metalworking plants of all sizes - from small job shops to giant aerospace and automotive plants. It is edited for those involved in metalworking operations, particularly those performed on machine tools.
Cost: $4.00
Frequency: Monthly
Circulation: 107000
Founded in 1928
Mailing list available for rent: 106M names
Printed in 4 colors on glossy stock

16862 **Motion Control**
ISA Services
PO Box 12277
Durham, NC 27709-2277

919-549-8411; Fax: 919-990-9434
info@isa.org
www.isa.org

Sam Batman, Editor
Richard Simpson, Publisher
Robert Renner, Executive Director

Information for those who design and maintain motion control systems.
Cost: $54.00
56 Pages
Circulation: 41000
ISSN: 1058-4644
Founded in 1945
Printed in 4 colors on glossy stock

16863 **Motion System Distributor**
Penton Media
1166 Avenue of the Americas/10th Fl
New York, NY 10036

212-204-4200; Fax: 216-696-6662
www.penton.com

Jane Cooper, Marketing
Chris Meyer, Director, Corporate Communications

Provides selling and technical information to individuals and distributors specializing in power transmission, motion control and fluid products.

16864 **OEM Worldwide**
Cygnus Publishing
PO Box 803
Fort Atkinson, WI 53538-0803

920-000-1111; Fax: 920-563-1699
tjheinlein@cableinet.co.uk

John French, CEO
Leslie Shalabi, Publisher
James S Rank, VP
Sue Cullen, Advertising Manager
Brett Apold, Corporate Production Director

Designed to be a resource of operational and general productivity information for original equipment manufacturers in Europe, competing in the global marketplace.
Cost: $6.00
Frequency: Monthly
Circulation: 16800
Founded in 1984

16865 **Outdoor Power Equipment**
10405 6th. Ave. N
Suite 210
Minneapolis, MN 55441

763-383-4421
dvoll@epgmediallc.com
www.outdoorpowerequipment.com

David Voll, Publisher
John Kmitta, Assoc. Publisher/Editor
Samantha VanKempen, Production Manager

Serves retailers and distributors who sell and service outdoor power equipment products, including retailers, lawn and garden supply retailers, farm supply retailers, hardware store retailers, home centers, and building supply retailers.
150 Pages
Founded in 1980

16866 **Plant Engineering**
Reed Business Information
30 Technology Parkway South
Suite 100
Norcross, GA 30092

646-746-6400
800-424-3996; Fax: 646-756-7583
webmaster@reedbusiness.com
www.reedbusiness.com

John Poulin, CEO
Richard L Dunn, Editor
Gerard Van de Aast, Director
Carel de Bos, Chief Information Officer

The magazine for plant engineering professionals responsible for the maintenance, repair and operations of plant facilities, equipment and systems.
Cost: $3.00
Circulation: 116700

16867 **Processing Magazine**
Grand View Media Group
200 Croft Street
Suite 1
Birmingham, AL 35242

888-431-2877; Fax: 205-408-3797
webmaster@grandviewmedia.com
www.gvmg.com/

Leading source for up-to-date product and equipment solutions.

16868 **Production Machining**
Gardner Publications
6915 Valley Ln
Cincinnati, OH 45244-3153

513-527-8800
800-950-8020; Fax: 513-527-8801
www.gardnerweb.com

Rick Kline Sr, CEO
Leo Rakowski, Senior Editor
John Jordan, Assistant Editor
Lori Beckman, Managing Editor
John Campos, Manager
Frequency: Monthly
Circulation: 200000
Founded in 1928

16869 **Pumps & Systems**
Randall Publishing Company
1900 28th Ave S
Suite 110
Homewood, AL 35209-2627

205-212-9402; Fax: 205-212-9452
www.pump-zone.com

Walter Evans, President
George Lake, Associate Publisher
Scott Kidwell, Advertising Sales:
Tom Cory, Circulation
Robert Windle, CEO
Frequency: Monthly
Founded in 2002

16870 **RIA Tech Papers**
Robotic Industries Association
900 Victors Way
Suite 140
Ann Arbor, MI 48108

734-994-6088; Fax: 734-994-3338
info@robotics.org
www.robotics.org/Tech-Papers

Jeff Burnstein, President
Dana Whalls, Vice President, A3
Clarissa Carvalho, Marketing Specialist
Bob Doyle, Vice President

Technical papers on various subjects relating to the robotics industry, including manufacturing challenges, software and safety concerns.
Frequency: Monthly
Founded in 1974

16871 **Robotics and Autonomous Systems**
Elsevier Science

230 Park Avenue
Suite 800
New York, NY 10169

212-309-8100
www.elsevier.com

K. Berns, Editor-in-Chief
M. Gini, Editor-in-Chief
J. Ota, Editor-in-Chief

Journal with articles on developments in the field of robotics, with an emphasis on autonomous systems.
Cost: $3008.00
ISSN: 0921-8890

16872 **SMC Magazine**
IEEE Systems, Man, and Cybernetics Society
445 Hoes Lane
Piscataway, NJ 08854

smcmagazine_eic@outlook.com
www.ieeesmc.org

Saeid Nahavandi, Editor-in-Chief
Enrique Herrera Viedma, VP, Publications

Articles relevant to the research areas of the IEEE Systems, Man, and Cybernetics Society, with information on the Society's activities, and educational material as well.

16873 **Science Robotics**
American Assn for the Advancement of Science
1200 New York Avenue NW
Washington, DC 20005-3941

202-326-6490; Fax: 202-789-4669
sciroboteditors@aaas.org
robotics.sciencemag.org

Alan I. Leshner, Interim Executive Publisher
Jeremy Berg PhD, Editor-in-Chief
Monica M. Bradford, Executive Editor

Publishes original, peer-reviewed, science- or engineering-based research articles that advance the field of robotics. The journal also features editor-commissioned reviews.
Frequency: Monthly

16874 **Sensors Magazine**
Advanstar Communications
7500 Old Oak Blvd
Cleveland, OH 44130-3343

440-243-8100; Fax: 440-891-2740
info@advanstar.com

Barbara G Goode, Editor-in-Chief
Donna Pellerin George, Associate Editor
Joseph Loggia, CEO
Georgiann Decenzo, Director of Corporate marketing
Francis Heid, Vice President of Publishing

Primary source among design and production engineers of information on sensor technologies and products, and topic integral to sensor-based systems and applications. Provides practical and in-depth yet accessible information on sensor operation, design, application, and implementation within systems. Covers the effective use of state-of-the-art resources and tools that enable readers to get the maximum benefit from their use of sensors.
Frequency: Monthly
Circulation: 75000
Founded in 1984

16875 **Technology and Society**
IEEE Society on Social Implications of Technology
445 Hoes Lane
Piscataway, NJ 08854

j.pitt@imperial.ac.uk
technologyandsociety.org
Facebook, Twitter, LinkedIn

Jeremy Pitt, Editor_in-Chief
Terri A. Bookman, Managing Editor

Flagship magazine of the IEEE Society on Social Implications of Technology, with peer-reviewed articles on the impact of technology on the world.

16876 **The American Mold Builder Magazine**
American Mold Builders Association
7321 Shadeland Station Way
Suite 285
Indianapolis, IN 46256

317-436-3102; Fax: 317-913-2445
info@amba.org
www.amba.org

Justin McPhee, President
Toby Bral, Vice President
Alan Rothenbuecher, Secretary

Publication containing information on the mold manufacturing industry, including industry trends, global and technical issues, goverment relations, sales and marketing, human resources and more.
296 Members
Frequency: Quarterly
Circulation: 5000
Founded in 1973
Printed in 4 colors

16877 **The Bridge**
IEEE-Eta Kappa Nu
445 Hoes Lane
Piscataway, NJ 08854

732-465-5846
800-406-2590
info@hkn.org
hkn.ieee.org/news-and-announcements/the-bridge

Sahra Sedigh Sarvestani, Editor-in-Chief
Stephen Williams, Editor-in-Chief

The award-winning digital magazine of the IEEE-HKN.
Frequency: 3x/year

16878 **Valve Magazine**
Valve Manufacturers Association of America
1050 17th Street NW
Suite 280
Washington, DC 20036-5521

202-331-8105; Fax: 202-296-0378
gparente@vma.org
www.valvemagazine.com

William S. Sandler, President & Publisher
Judy Tibbs, Editor-in-Chief
Genilee Parente, Managing Editor
Chris Guy, Assistant Editor
Sue Partyke, Advertising Director

Magazine promoting US and Canadian manufactured industrial valves and actuators.
100 Members
Frequency: Quarterly
Circulation: 26000
Founded in 1938

16879 **Vibrations Magazine**
Vibration Institute
2625 Butterfield Road
Suite 128N
Oak Brook, IL 60523-3415

630-654-2254; Fax: 630-654-2271
information@vi-institute.org
www.vi-institute.org

Dave Corelli, President
Michael Long, Executive Director
Ronald L. Eshleman, Technical Director
Peggy Dellaria, Membership Associate
Sean McDonald, Marketing & Communications Manager

Provides current information about activities of the Vibration Institute and news about vibration technology. Each issue contains practical, technical articles and case histories.
Frequency: Quarterly
Founded in 1972

16880 **World Industrial Reporter**
Keller International Publishing Corporation
150 Great Neck Rd
Suite 400
Great Neck, NY 11021-3309

516-829-9722; Fax: 516-829-9306
www.supplychainbrain.com

Bryan DeLuca, Editor
Terry Beirne, Publisher
Jerry Keller, President
Mary Chavez, Director of Sales

New equipment, machinery and techniques for the industry.
34 Pages
Frequency: Monthly
Circulation: 37107
Founded in 1882

Trade Shows

16881 **A3 Business Forum**
Association for Advancing Automation
900 Victors Way
Suite 140
Ann Arbor, MI 48108

734-994-6088; Fax: 734-994-3338
info@a3automate.org
www.a3automate.org

Jeff Burnstein, President
Maria Kurple, Event Marketing Manager
Mandy Pawczuk, Administrator, Event Services

Conference for professionals working in robotics, vision & imaging, motion control, and motors industries.
550+ Attendees
Frequency: Annual/January

16882 **AMTA Conference**
Association for Machine Translation in Americas
Home Page: www.conference.amtaweb.org

Steve Richardson, President

Conference held by the Association for Machine Translation in the Americas, bringing together researchers, developers, and users of Machine Translation technology to network and share ideas.
135 Attendees
Frequency: Biennial/March

16883 **APMA Annual Conference & Exhibition**
Automotive Parts Manufacturers' Association
10 Four Seasons Place
Suite 801
Toronto, ON M9B 6H7

416-620-4220; Fax: 416-620-9730
apma.ca

Flavio Volpe, President
Jonathon Azzopardi, Director
Mike Bilton, Director
Lisa T. Boulton, Director
Fred di Tosto, Director

Event for automotive equipment suppliers, focusing on key issues facing the industry.
Founded in 1952

16884 **ASME Annual Meeting**
American Society of Mechanical Engineers
Two Park Avenue
New York, NY 10016-5990

973-882-1170
800-843-2763
williamsk@asme.org
www.asme.org

Kim Williams, Meetings Manager

Forum for information exchange and professional growth for engineering professionals.

16885 **American Mold Builders Association Conference 2018**
American Mold Builders Association
7321 Shadeland Station Way
Suite 285
Indianapolis, IN 46256

317-436-3102; Fax: 317-913-2445
info@amba.org
www.amba.org
Facebook, Twitter, LinkedIn

Justin McPhee, President
Toby Bral, Vice President
Alan Rothenbuecher, Secretary

Conference for mold builders to learn about increasing profitability in their business as well as to connect with others in the field.
Cost: $795.00
296 Members
Frequency: Annual/February
Founded in 1973

16886 **Automate**
Motion Control & Motor Association
900 Victors Way
Suite 140
Ann Arbor, MI 48108

734-994-6088
info@motioncontrolonline.org
www.motioncontrolonline.org

Matt French, Chair
Gunnar Block, Vice Chair
Paul Horvat, Vice Chair

Trade show and conference on automation technologies.
20K Attendees

16887 **CRSA Worldwide Congress**
Clinical Robotic Surgery Association
Two Prudential Plaza
180 North Stetson, Suite 3500
Chicago, IL 60601

312-268-5754
inquiries@clinicalrobotics.com
www.clinicalrobotics.com

Philip Clark, Executive Managing Director

The annual meeting for surgeons using robotic systems in General Surgery to discuss methods, share ideas and network.
Frequency: Annual/September

16888 **FPDA Networking Summit**
The FPDA Motion & Control Network
180 Admiral Cochrane Drive
Suite 370
Annapolis, MD 21401

410-940-6347
info@fpda.org
www.fpda.org

Kevin Kampe, President
Amy Luckado, Executive Director
Dominique Abney, Director, Marketing/Sales
Donald Smith, Chief Financial Officer
Courtney Truelove, Manager, Membership/Program

Conference for distribution professionals from the fluid power industry.
300+ Members
Founded in 1974

16889 **FloorTek Expo**
American Floorcovering Alliance
210 West Cuyler St
Dalton, GA 30720-8209

706-278-4101
800-288-4101; Fax: 706-278-5323
afa@americanfloor.org
www.floor-tek.com

Wanda J Ellis, Executive Director

The only internationla flooring manufacturing tradeshow dedicated to the production and materials of the industry
3000+ Attendees
Frequency: Bi-Annual

16890 **IADD/FSEA Odyssey**
Int'l Assoc of Diecutting and Diemaking
651 W Terra Cotta Ave
Suite 132
Crystal Lake, IL 60014

815-455-7519
800-828-4233; Fax: 815-455-7510
cccrouse@iadd.org
www.iadd.org

Cindy Crouse, CEO
Jill May, Chapter Relations Coordinator

The premiere education and technology expo uniquely focused on diemaking, converting, foil stamping, embossing and bindery.
Frequency: Annual/May

16891 **IEEE SoutheastCon**
IEEE Meeting & Conference Management (MCM)
445 Hoes Lane
Piscataway, NJ 08854

732-562-3878
800-678-4333; Fax: 732-971-1203
conference-services@ieee.org
www.ieee.org
Facebook, LinkedIn, Instagram

A student conference, technical conference, and business meeting.
800 Attendees
Frequency: Annual

16892 **IMTS 2020 International Manufacturing Technology Show**
Association for Manufacturing Technology
7901 Jones Branch Drive
Suite 900
McLean, VA 22102-3316

703-827-5215
800-828-7469
info@imts.com
www.imts.com

Douglas K. Woods, President
Peter R. Eelman, VP, Exhibitions & Business Dev
Michelle Reynolds Edmonson, Sr Director, Exhibitions Operations
Jessica Aybar, Sr Manager, Exhibition Operations
Mark Kennedy, Exhibitions Sales Director

Industrial trade show featuring over 2,400 exhibiting companies in the business of manufacturing technology.

16893 **International Conference on Automation Science and Engineering**
IEEE Robotics and Automation Society
445 Hoes Lane
Piscataway, NJ

732-562-3906
ras@ieee.org
www.ieee-ras.org

Kathy Colabaugh, Society Operations Manager
Amy Reeder, Society Program Specialist
Alexis Simoes, Society Program Coordinator

CASE is the flagship conference of the IEEE Robotics and Automation Society.

16894 **International Conference on Electronics, Circuits, and Systems**
IEEE Circuits and Systems Society
445 Hoes Lane
Piscataway, NJ 08854

manager@ieee-cas.org
www.ieee-cas.org

Brittian Parkinson, Operations Manager
Myung Hoon Sunwoo, VP, Conferences
Frequency: Annual

16895 **International Conference on Intelligent Robots and Systems**
Robotics and Automation Society
445 Hoes Lane
Piscataway, NJ

732-562-3906
ras@ieee.org
www.ieee-ras.org

Kathy Colabaugh, Society Operations Manager
Amy Reeder, Society Program Specialist
Alexis Simoes, Society Program Coordinator

16896 **International Conference on Robotics and Automation**
Robotics and Automation Society
445 Hoes Lane
Piscataway, NJ

732-562-3906
ras@ieee.org
www.ieee-ras.org

Kathy Colabaugh, Society Operations Manager
Amy Reeder, Society Program Specialist
Alexis Simoes, Society Program Coordinator

16897 **International Conference on Shape Memory and Superelastic Technologies**
ASM International
9639 Kinsman Road
Materials Park, OH 44073-0002

440-338-5151
800-336-5152; Fax: 440-338-4634
memberservicecenter@asminternational.org
www.asminternational.org/web/smst

William T. Mahoney, Secretary & CEO
Lindy Good, Global Conference & Exhibit Planner

A forum for the discussion of SMA design in Irish Biotechnology.
30K Members
Frequency: May
Founded in 1913

16898 **International Integrated Manufacturing**
Reed Exhibition Companies
255 Washington Street
Newton, MA 02458-1637

617-584-4900; Fax: 617-630-2222

Elizabeth Hitchcock, International Sales

Expo and conference dedicated to the products and technology needed by engineering operations and management to automate and integrate manufacturing.
Frequency: March

16899 **International Manufacturing Technology Show**
7901 Westpark Drive
Mc Lean, VA 22102-4206
703-893-2900; Fax: 703-893-1151
www.amtonline.org
John Byrd, President
Peter Eelman, VP Exhibitions
Manufacturing equipment trade show.
85M Attendees
Frequency: Biennial
Founded in 1927

16900 **International Symposium on Circuits and Systems**
IEEE Circuits and Systems Society
445 Hoes Lane
Piscataway, NJ 08854
manager@ieee-cas.org
www.ieee-cas.org
Brittian Parkinson, Operations Manager
Myung Hoon Sunwoo, VP, Conferences
Frequency: Annual

16901 **International Woodworking Machinery and Furniture Supply Fair: USA**
Reed Exhibition Companies
1350 E Touhy Avenue
Des Plaines, IL 60018-3303
847-294-0300; Fax: 847-635-1571
Paul Pajor, National Marketing Manager
The largest woodworking machinery and furniture supply manufacturing exposition held in the Western Hemisphere. Exhibitors interface with North American furniture, cabinet, and woodworking manufacturers. One thousand booths.
37M Attendees
Frequency: August/Biennial

16902 **Job Shop Show: Midwest**
Edward Publishing LLC
16 Waterbury Road
Prospect, CT 06712-1215
203-758-6658; Fax: 203-758-4476
www.jobshoptechnology.com
Jennifer Bryda, Production Manager
Christoper Davis, Manager
Gerald Schmidt, President
A source for forming, fabricating, shaping, and assemblies. The show is designed to attract the highest caliber engineers and buyers from product manufacturers. There will be 170 exhibitors and booths.
1500 Attendees

16903 **MCAA Industry Forum**
Measurement, Control & Automation Association
200 City Hall Avenue
Suite D
Poquoson, VA 23662
757-258-3100
automationassociation.com
Teresa Sebring, President
Andrea Ambrose, Director, Member Relations
Elizabeth Horton, Programs Manager
Kim Malina, Marketing Communications Manager
Rebecca Moore, Administrative Manager
Education and networking event for manufacturers and distributors of instrumentation, systems, and software products for industrial process control and factory automation.
Founded in 1944

16904 **MCMA TechCon**
Motion Control & Motor Association
900 Victors Way
Suite 140
Ann Arbor, MI 48108
734-994-6088
info@motioncontrolonline.org
www.motioncontrolonline.org
Matt French, Chair
Gunnar Block, Vice Chair
Paul Horvat, Vice Chair
The Motion Control & Motor Association Technical Conference provides attendees with recent updates on motion control and automation.

16905 **MDNA Convention**
Machinery Dealers National Association
315 S Patrick Street
Alexandria, VA 22314
703-836-9300
800-872-7807; Fax: 703-836-9303
office@mdna.org
www.mdna.org
Mark Robinson, Executive Vice President
Will Keys, Accounting Manager
Joyce Fitzgerald, Administration Director
Convention for dealers of used industrial equipment.
400 Members
Frequency: Annual/May
Founded in 1941

16906 **Management Update Conference**
Precision Machined Products Association
6880 West Snowville Road
Suite 200
Brecksville, OH 44141
440-526-0300; Fax: 440-526-5803
rmerker@pmpa.org
www.pmpa.org
Bernard Nagle, Executive Director
Mari Kirchenbauer, Executive Assistant
Miles K. Free, Industry Research & Technology Dir
Renee A. Merker, Communications & Event Planner
Conference will provide updates on industry news for owners and managers of metalworking companies. It will also provide networking opportunities and information sessions for members of the Precision Machined Products Association.
Frequency: March
Founded in 1933

16907 **Motion + Power Expo**
American Gear Manufacturers Association
1001 N. Fairfax Street
Suite 500
Alexandria, VA 22314-1587
703-684-0211; Fax: 703-684-0242
gearexpo@agma.org
motionpowerexpo.com
Matthew Croson, President
Deneen Pratt, Exhibitor Customer Service
Jenny Blackford, VP, Marketing
Jenny Bogue, Attendee Customer Service
Provides networking opportunities for gear buyers, users, manufacturers, and engineers.
4.5M Attendees
Frequency: October
Founded in 1916

16908 **OPEESA Annual Meeting**
Outdoor Power Equipment and Engine Service Assoc
37 Pratt Street
Suite 2
Essex, CT 06426-1159
860-767-1770; Fax: 860-767-7932
info@opeesa.com
www.opeesa.com
Alex Wyatt, President
Lorri Sklar, Vice President, Annual Meeting
Nancy Cueroni, Executive Director
Arin Monroe, Secretary/Treasurer
Meeting for members of the Outdoor Power Equipment and Engine Service Association.
100+ Members
Frequency: Annual/February

16909 **PTDA Industry Summit**
Power Transmission Distributors Association
230 West Monroe Street
Suite 1410
Chicago, IL 60606-4703
312-516-2100; Fax: 312-516-2101
ptda@ptda.org
www.ptda.org/events/industrysummit.aspx
Jim Williams, President
Ann Arnott, Executive Vice President & CEO
Brenda Holt, Membership Director
Andrea Lebron, Operations Manager
Ginger Wheeler, Marketing & Communications Director
Summit for companies dealing in industrial power transmission/motion control equipment.
Founded in 1960

16910 **PTRA Annual Conference**
Power-Motion Technology Representatives Assoc.
5353 Wayzata Boulevard
Suite 350
Minneapolis, MN 55416
888-817-7872; Fax: 952-252-8096
ptrahq@ptra.org
ptra.org
Curt Benson, CPMR, President
Susan Crolla, Executive Director
Adam Cooler, Treasurer
Conference for independent manufacturers' representatives and those invested in promoting sales representatives within the power transmission and motion control industries.
Frequency: Annual/May
Founded in 1972

16911 **Powder and Bulk Solids Conference and Exhibition**
Reed Exhibition Companies
255 Washington Street
Newton, MA 02458-1637
617-584-4900; Fax: 617-630-2222
Elizabeth Hitchcock, International Sales
Equipment and technology for processing and handling of powder and bulk solids.
8.4M Attendees
Frequency: May

16912 **SOUTH-TEC**
Society of Manufacturing Engineers
1 SME Drive
Dearborn, MI 48128
313-425-3000
800-733-4763; Fax: 313-425-3400
service@sme.org
www.southteconline.com
Jeffrey M. Krause, CEO
Cynthia Bond, Exhibitor Services
Patti Miller, Marketing
Ashley Areeda, Media
Cathy Kowalewicz, Event Management

Exhibition of technologies and services applicable to manufacturing suppliers, distributors and equipment builders.
65K Members
Frequency: October
Founded in 1932

16913 **Service Specialists Association Annual Convention**
Service Specialists Association
1221 Candlewick Drive NW
Poplar Grove, IL 61065

224-990-1005
service.specialists@outlook.com
www.truckservice.org

Jim Parsons, President
Craig Fry, Executive Director
Toni Nastali, Treasurer
Billy Burkholder, Director

Forum providing technical and business information related to vehicle repair shop operation and safety.
Frequency: Annual

16914 **Society of Robotic Surgery Annual Meeting**
Society of Robotic Surgery
1061 E. Main Street
Suite 300
East Dundee, IL 60118

847-752-5355
info@srobotics.org
www.srobotics.org

Vipul R. Patel, MD, Executive Director

Conference exploring issues related to robotic surgery, including protocols, furture developments, artificial intelligence, training and curriculum and more.
Frequency: Annual/June
Founded in 2009

16915 **The MFG Meeting 2020**
Association for Manufacturing Technology
7901 Jones Branch Drive
Suite 900
McLean, VA 22102-3316
703-893-2900
800-524-0475; Fax: 703-893-1151
amt@amtonline.org
www.amtonline.org

Douglas K. Woods, President
Peter R. Eelman, VP, Exhibitions & Business Dev
Michelle Reynolds Edmonson, Sr Director, Exhibitions Operations
Amber L. Thomas, VP, Marketing & Communications
Andrea Kuchinski, Dir, Marketing & Communications

Conference for manufacturing technology industry professionals, organized to cover subjects of business, market forcasts, workforce development, and more.

16916 **The MPTA Annual Meeting**
Mechanical Power Transmission Association
5672 Strand Ct.
Suite 2
Naples, FL 34110

239-514-3441; Fax: 239-514-3470
bob@mpta.org
mpta.org/events

Bob Hamilton, President
Don Sullivan, Vice President
Robert A. Reinfried, Executive Director
Karen Lampart, Meeting Coordinator

Annual meeting for members of the Mechanical Power Transmission Association.
Frequency: Annual
Founded in 1961

16917 **The NFPA Annual Conference**
National Fluid Power Association
6737 W. Washington Street
Suite 2350
Milwaukee, WI 53214

414-778-3369; Fax: 414-778-3361
nfpahub.com/events/conferences/nfpa-annual-conference

Eric Lanke, President & CEO
Leslie Miller, Membership Manager
Stephanie Scaccianoce, Association Program Manager

Conference held by the National Fluid Power Association (NFPA) for professionals working in the fluid power supply chain and industry.
Frequency: Annual/February

16918 **The Vision Show**
Global Association for Vision Information
900 Victors Way
Suite 140
Ann Arbor, MI 48108

734-994-6088
www.visiononline.org
Facebook, Twitter

Jeff Burnstein, President
Maria Kurple, Event Marketing Manager
Mandy Pawczuk, Administrator, Event Services

North America's largest display of machine vision and imaging systems.
Frequency: June

16919 **Valve Industry Leadership Forum**
Valve Manufacturers Association of America
1050 17th Street NW
Suite 280
Washington, DC 20036-5521

202-331-8105; Fax: 202-296-0378
mmaloneblevins@vma.org
www.vma.org

William S. Sandler, President
Marc Pasternak, Vice President
Malena Malone-Blevins, Meetings Manager
Judy Tibbs, Education Director

Forum for the leaders of companies serving the valve industry.
100 Members
Founded in 1938

16920 **Vibration Institute Annual Training Conference**
Vibration Institute
2625 Butterfield Road
Suite 128N
Oak Brook, IL 60523-3415

630-654-2254; Fax: 630-654-2271
information@vi-institute.org
www.vi-institute.org

Dave Corelli, President
Michael Long, Executive Director
Peggy Dellaria, Membership Associate
Sue Fonck, Certification & Training Associate

Conference providing specific training in practical vibration technology.
Frequency: Annual
Founded in 1972

16921 **Woodworking Industry Conference**
Wood Machinery Manufacturers of America
9 Newport Drive
Suite 200
Forest Hill, MD 21050

443-640-1052; Fax: 443-640-1031
info@wmma.org
woodworkingindustryconference.com

Chris Hacker, President
Stephen Carter, Vice President
Kristin Grove, Member Services Coordinator
Diane Schafer, Meetings Director

The conference will focus on business development, networking and practical knowledge for those working in the woodworking machinery industry.
Frequency: Annual/May
Founded in 1899

16922 **Woodworking Industry Conference 2018**
Woodworking Machinery Industry Association
225 Reinekers Lane
Suite 410
Alexandria, VA 22314

571-279-8340; Fax: 571-279-8343
info@wmia.org
www.wmia.org/events/event/wic-2018-save-the-date

Larry Hoffer, President
Jeff Linder, Program Manager
Heather Jolley, Program Administrator
Rick Braun, Director

Conference for the woodworking machinery industry, offering business development programs, networking, and education.
Founded in 1977

Directories & Databases

16923 **ASM Handbooks Online**
ASM International
9639 Kinsman Road
Materials Park, OH 44073-0002

440-338-5151
800-336-5152; Fax: 440-338-4634
sales@asminternational.org
www.asminternational.org

William T. Mahoney, Secretary & CEO
Madrid Tramble, eDocument Production Manager

Contains information on ferrous and non-ferrous metals and materials technology presented through articles, illustrations, tables, graphs and practical examples.
30K Members
25000 Pages
Founded in 1913

16924 **American Machinist Buyers' Guide**
Penton Media
1166 Avenue of the Americas/10th Fl
New York, NY 10036

212-204-4200; Fax: 216-696-6662
information@penton.com
www.penton.com

Jane Cooper, Marketing
Pat Smith, Managing Editor
Chris Meyer, Director, Corporate Communications

Guide to over manufacturers of products and services used by metalworking industries.
Cost: $6.00
Frequency: Annual
Circulation: 80,000
Printed in 4 colors on glossy stock

16925 **American Mold Builders Association**
PO Box 404
Medinah, IL 60157-0404

630-980-7667; Fax: 630-980-9714
info@amba.org
www.amba.org

Jeanette Bradley, Editor
Kym Conis, Managing Director

Directory of services and supplies to the industry.
Cost: $25.00
50 Pages
Frequency: Annual

16926 **American Textile Machinery Association Official Directory**
201 Park Washington Ct
Falls Church, VA 22046-4527

703-538-1789; Fax: 703-241-5603
info@atmanet.org
www.atmanet.org

Harry W Buzzerd, Owner
Clay D Tyeryar, President/Assistant Treasurer
Susan Denston, Executive VP/Secretary
Judith O Buzzerd, Meetings Manager

The Directory of the American Textile Machinery Association/ATMA offers information on over 100 member textile machinery and accessory manufacturers. ATMA is a professional trade association devoted to the advancement of manufacturers of textile machinery, parts, and accessories in the textile industry.
100 Pages

16927 **Canadian Automotive Sourcing Guide**
Automotive Parts Manufacturers' Association
10 Four Seasons Place
Suite 801
Toronto, ON M9B 6H7

416-620-4220; Fax: 416-620-9730
canadianautomotivesourcingguide.com

Flavio Volpe, President
Jonathon Azzopardi, Director
Mike Bilton, Director
Lisa T. Boulton, Director
Fred di Tosto, Director

Directory of products and information for auto parts manufacturers and other industry professionals.
Founded in 1952

16928 **EDA Buyers Guide**
Equipment Dealers Association
165 North Meramec Avenue
Suite 430
St. Louis, MO 63105

636-349-5000; Fax: 636-349-5443
info@equipmentdealer.org
www.equipmentdealer.org
Facebook, Twitter

Kim Rominger, President & CEO
Michael Williams, VP, Operations
Joseph Dykes, VP, Industry Relations
Alex Hoffman, Communications & Marketing Director

Directory of products and services for equipment dealers of the agriculture, outdoor power and industrial equipment industries.
4500 Members
Frequency: Annually
Founded in 1900

16929 **Equip-Mart**
116 N Camp Street
Seguin, TX 78155

830-303-3328
800-864-1155; Fax: 830-372-3011
www.equip-mart.com

Directory of available used metalworking equipment.
Frequency: Weekly

16930 **FEMA Educational Articles**
Fire Equipment Manufacturers' Association
1300 Sumner Avenue
Cleveland, OH 44115

216-241-7333
www.femalifesafety.org/articles.html

Bill Vegso, President

Articles from the Fire Equipment Manufacturers' Association covering information on fire equipment, safety procedures and laws.
Founded in 1930

16931 **ISA Directory**
Instrumentation, Systems,and Automation Society
PO Box 12277
Durham, NC 27709-2277

919-549-8411; Fax: 919-990-9434
info@isa.org
www.isa.org

Premier guide to instrumentation, systems and automation
Printed in 4 colors

16932 **Industrial Machine Trader**
Heartland Industrial Group
1003 Central Avenue
PO Box 1415
Fort Dodge, IA 50501

515-955-1600
800-247-2000; Fax: 515-955-3753
www.industrialgroup.com
Facebook, Twitter, LinkedIn

Virginia Rodriguez, Publisher

Printed directory of available used metalworking equipment.
150+ Members
Frequency: Weekly
Founded in 1966

16933 **Locator Services**
315 S Patrick St
Alexandria, VA 22314-3532

703-836-9700
800-537-1446; Fax: 703-836-7665
sales@locatoronline.com
www.locatoronline.com

Terry Pitman, Publisher

Printed directory of available used metalworking equipment.
Frequency: Monthly
Circulation: 225,000

16934 **MPTA Member Products**
Mechanical Power Transmission Association
5672 Strand Ct.
Suite 2
Naples, FL 34110

239-514-3441; Fax: 239-514-3470
bob@mpta.org
mpta.org/member-products

Bob Hamilton, President
Don Sullivan, Vice President
Robert A. Reinfried, Executive Director
Karen Lampart, Meeting Coordinator

Directory of products sold by members of the Mechanical Power Transmission Association. Product groups include belt drive and pully equipment, chain and sprocket, and coupling equipment.
Founded in 1961

16935 **MTBuyers Guide**
Association for Manufacturing Technology
7901 Jones Branch Drive
Suite 900
McLean, VA 22102-3316

703-893-2900
800-524-0475; Fax: 703-893-1151
amt@amtonline.org
www.amtonline.org

Douglas K. Woods, President
Rebecca Stahl, Chief Financial Officer

Lists machine tools and related products built by members of the Association for Manufacturing Technology. Products include automated systems and cells, controls and software, forming equipment, material handling equipment, cleaning tools and more.

16936 **Machine Design Product Locator**
Penton Media
1166 Avenue of the Americas/10th Fl
New York, NY 10036

212-204-4200; Fax: 216-696-6662
information@penton.com
www.penton.com

Jane Cooper, Marketing
Chris Meyer, Director, Corporate Communications

Directory of services and supplies to the industry.
Cost: $35.00
325 Pages
Frequency: Annual
Circulation: 180,000
Printed in 4 colors on glossy stock

16937 **Metalworking Machinery Mailer**
Tade Publishing Group
29501 Greenfield Road
Suite 120
Southfield, MI 48076

248-552-8583
800-966-8233; Fax: 248-552-0466

Tom Lynch, Editor

Printed directory of available used metalworking equipment.
Frequency: Monthly

16938 **Motion Control Technical Reference and Buyers Guide**
ISA Services
PO Box 12277
Durham, NC 27709-2277

919-549-8411; Fax: 919-990-9434
info@isa.org
www.isa.org

The most comprehensive reference source for motion control market
Founded in 2000
Printed in 4 colors

16939 **Multimedia Monograph Series**
SIGDA Multimedia

Home Page: atrak.usc.edu/~sigda-mm/

Massoud Pedram, Program Director

Set of electronic media publications focusing on key talks/presentations given at various ACM sponsored conferences over the last few years.

16940 **NCFP Technical Papers**
National Fluid Power Association

6737 W. Washington Street
Suite 2350
Milwaukee, WI 53214

414-778-3347; Fax: 414-778-3361
www.nfpa.com/fluidpower/technicalpaperslocator.aspx

Eric Lanke, President & CEO
Pete Alles, VP, Member Services & Marketing
Leslie Miller, Membership Manager
Carrie Tatman Schwartz, Tech School Education Manager

A database of technical papers from the National Fluid Power Association (NCFP) conferences, written by technical and engineering professionals working in the fluid power industry.
Founded in 1953

16941 **NFPA Member and Product Directory**
National Fluid Power Association
6737 W. Washington Street
Suite 2350
Milwaukee, WI 53214

414-778-3344; Fax: 414-778-3361
nfpa@nfpa.com
www.nfpa.com

Eric Lanke, President & CEO
Pete Alles, VP, Member Services & Marketing
Leslie Miller, Membership Manager
Stephanie Scaccianoce, Association Program Manager

Directory listing companies and products of members of the National Fluid Power Association.
Founded in 1953

16942 **NTMA Manufacturing Suppliers Guide**
National Tooling and Machining Association
1357 Rockside Road
Cleveland, OH 44134

440-799-8991
800-248-6862; Fax: 216-264-2840
info@ntma.org
www.ntma.org
Facebook, Twitter, LinkedIn, YouTube

Dave Tilstone, President
Candy Davis, Executive Assistant
Michel Conklin, NRL Program Manager
Matt Gilmore, Membership & Business Development

Resource for members of the National Tooling and Machining Association and others in the industry. The guide helps locate industry-specific products and services.
1400 Members
Founded in 1943

16943 **OPEESA Membership Listing**
Outdoor Power Equipment and Engine Service Assoc
37 Pratt Street
Suite 2
Essex, CT 06426-1159

860-767-1770; Fax: 860-767-7932
info@opeesa.com
www.opeesa.com

Alex Wyatt, President
Lorri Sklar, Vice President, Annual Meeting
Nancy Cueroni, Executive Director
Arin Monroe, Secretary/Treasurer

Directory of members belonging to the Outdoor Power Equipment and Engine Service Association. Members include distributors and manufacturers of outdoor power equipment.
100+ Members

16944 **Orion Blue Book: Tools**
Orion Research Corporation
14555 N Scottsdale Rd
Suite 330
Scottsdale, AZ 85254-3487

480-951-1114
800-844-0759; Fax: 480-951-1117
www.bluebook.com

Roger Rohrs, Owner

List of manufacturers of tools.
Frequency: Annual

16945 **PMPA Buyer's Guide**
Precision Machined Products Association
6880 West Snowville Road
Suite 200
Brecksville, OH 44141

440-526-0300; Fax: 440-526-5803
info@pmpa.org
www.pmpa.org

Bernard Nagle, Executive Director
Mari Kirchenbauer, Executive Assistant
Miles K. Free, Industry Research & Technology Dir
Renee A. Merker, Communications & Event Planner

Contains a list of member companies associated with the Precision Machined Products Association. Members include all those who manufacture custom designed precision machined products or supply materials needed for the industry.
Founded in 1933

16946 **PMPA Knowledge Base**
Precision Machined Products Association
6880 West Snowville Road
Suite 200
Brecksville, OH 44141

440-526-0300; Fax: 440-526-5803
info@pmpa.org
www.pmpa.org

Bernard Nagle, Executive Director
Mari Kirchenbauer, Executive Assistant
Miles K. Free, Industry Research & Technology Dir
Andrea J. Jeric, Accounting Assistant

Contains information on topics related to precision machined products. Material covers human resources, environmental topics, industry trends, engineering, quality assurance and various other areas of relevance.
Founded in 1933

16947 **SSA Member List**
Service Specialists Association
1221 Candlewick Drive NW
Poplar Grove, IL 61065

224-990-1005
service.specialists@outlook.com
www.truckservice.org/members.html

Jim Parsons, President
Craig Fry, Executive Director
Toni Nastali, Treasurer
Billy Burkholder, Director

Contains a list of companies that are members of the Service Specialists Association. These include repair shop members, suppliers and associates.

16948 **Surplus Record Machinery & Equipment Directory**
Thomas Scanlan
20 N. Wacker Drive
Chicago, IL 60606-3004

312-372-9077; Fax: 312-372-6537
surplus@surplusrecord.com
surplusrecord.com

Thomas Scanlan, Publisher

Listing over 70,000 items of used/surplus machine tools, machinery, electrical apparatus, and capital equipment by more than 1200 suppliers worldwide.
Cost: $33.00
736 Pages
Frequency: Monthly
Circulation: 150000
ISSN: 0039-615X
Founded in 1924
Mailing list available for rent: 155000 names at $85 per M

16949 **ThomasNet**
Thomas Publishing Company, LLC
User Services Department
5 Penn Plaza
New York, NY 10001

212-695-0500
800-699-9822; Fax: 212-290-7362
contact@thomaspublishing.com
www.thomasnet.com
Facebook, Twitter, LinkedIn

Carl Holst-Knudsen, President
Robert Anderson, VP, Planning
Mitchell Peipert, VP, Finance
Ivy Molofsky, VP, Human Resources

A way to reach qualified businesses that list their company information on ThomasNet.com. Detailed profiles promote their products, services, capabilities and brands carried. The ThomasNet.com web site is the most up-to-date compilation of 650,000 North American manufacturers, distributors, and service companies in 67,000 industrial categories.
Founded in 1898

16950 **Used Machinery Buyer's Guide**
Machinery Dealers National Association
315 S Patrick Street
Alexandria, VA 22314

703-836-9300
800-872-7807; Fax: 703-836-9303
office@mdna.org
www.mdna.org

Mark Robinson, Executive Vice President
Will Keys, Accounting Manager
Joyce Fitzgerald, Administration Director

Lists over 400 dealers in used capital equipment.
Frequency: Annual, September

16951 **VMA's Product Finder for Valves, Actuators & Controls**
Valve Manufacturers Association of America
1050 17th Street NW
Suite 280
Washington, DC 20036-5521

202-331-8105; Fax: 202-296-0378
spartyke@vma.org
www.vma.org

William S. Sandler, President
Marc Pasternak, Vice President
Sue Partyke, Advertising Director
Chris Guy, Assistant Editor, News & Products

Lists U.S. and Canadian valves, actuators and controls produced by the member companies of the Valve Manufacturers Association of America.
100 Members
Founded in 1938

16952 **WMIA Member Directory**
Woodworking Machinery Industry Association
225 Reinekers Lane
Suite 410
Alexandria, VA 22314

571-279-8340; Fax: 571-279-8343
info@wmia.org

www.wmia.org/membership-2/wmia-member-directory

Larry Hoffer, President
Jeff Linder, Program Manager
Heather Jolley, Program Administrator
Rick Braun, Director

Directory of companies that are part of the membership of Woodworking Machinery Industry Association.
Founded in 1977

16953 **WMMA Company Directory**
Wood Machinery Manufacturers of America
9 Newport Drive
Suite 200
Forest Hill, MD 21050

443-640-1052; Fax: 443-640-1031
info@wmma.org
www.wmma.org

Chris Hacker, President
Stephen Carter, Vice President
Fred Stringfellow, Chief Executive Officer
Kristin Grove, Member Services Coordinator

Directory of member companies of the Wood Machinery Manufacturers of America (WMMA) as well as the wood processing equipment they sell.
Founded in 1899

Industry Web Sites

16954 **apma.ca**
Automotive Parts Manufacturers' Association

Facebook, Twitter, LinkedIn, Google+

Canadian association representing suppliers of parts, equipment, tools, supplies, and services for the automotive industry.

16955 **http://gold.greyhouse.com**
G.O.L.D Grey House OnLine Databases

Grey House Publishing's online database platform, GOLD, offers Quick Search, Keyword Search and Expert Search for most business sectors including machinery markets. The GOLD platform makes finding the information you need quick and easy - whether you're a novice searcher or an experienced database user. All of Grey House's directory products are available for subscription on the GOLD platform.

16956 **mpta.org**
Mechanical Power Transmission Association

Organization serving those working in the power transmission field.

16957 **ptra.org**
Power-Motion Technology Representatives Assoc.

Association for independent manufacturers' representatives and those invested in promoting sales representatives within the power transmission and motion control industries.

16958 **sors.memberclicks.net**
Society of Robotic Surgery

Facebook, Twitter

Society providing education about robotic surgery, as well as studies, funding and development events for professionals in the field.

16959 **www.agma.org**
American Gear Manufacturers Association

Manufacturers of gears and geared speed changers.

16960 **www.amba.org**
American Mold Builders Association

Promotes the development of businesses engaged in the manufacturing of molds.

16961 **www.amea.org**
Association of Machinery and Equipment Appraisers

Facebook, LinkedIn, YouTube

Organization made up of appraisers of the metalworking industry.

16962 **www.americanfloor.org**
American Floorcovering Alliance

Promotes the industry's products and services to the world, and educates the members and others through seminars, press releases, and trade shows.

16963 **www.avem.org**
Association of Vacuum Equipment Manufacturers

Nonprofit U.S. association dedicated to supporting vacuum equipment manufacturers.

16964 **www.cemanet.org**
Conveyor Equipment Manufacturers Association

Facebook, Twitter, LinkedIn, YouTube

Membership association and resource for conveyor safety dimensional and application standards.

16965 **www.equipmentdealer.org**
Equipment Dealers Association

Association promoting the general welfare of equipment dealers in the United States and Canada.

16966 **www.greyhouse.com**
Grey House Publishing

Authoritative reference directories for most business sectors including machinery markets. Users can search the online databases with varied search criteria allowing for custom searches by product category, geographic area, sales volume, keyword, subject and more. Full Grey House catalog and online ordering also available.

16967 **www.iadd.org**
Int'l Association of Diecutting and Diemaking

A not-for-profit international trade association serving diecutters, diemakers, and industry suppliers worldwide. IADD provides conferences, educational and training programs, networking opportunities, a monthly magazine, technical articles, regional chapter meetings, publications and training manuals, recommended specifications, videos and surveys.

16968 **www.mapi.net**
Manufacturers Alliance/MAPI

A policy research organization whose members are companies drawn from the producers and users of capital goods and allied products. Includes leading companies in heavy industry, automotive, electronics, precision instruments, telecommunications, computers, office systems, aerospace, oil/gas, chemicals and similar high technology industries.

16969 **www.mdna.org**
Machinery Dealers National Association

Facebook, Twitter, LinkedIn

Represents dealers of used industrial equipment, providing members with business standards and development opportunities.

16970 **www.nfpa.com**
National Fluid Power Association

Association serving companies and manufacturers within the fluid power industry.

16971 **www.ntma.org**
National Tooling and Machining Association

Association supporting professionals of the precision custom manufacturing industry.

16972 **www.pmmi.org**
Packaging Machinery Manufacturers Institute (PMMI)

Facebook, Twitter, LinkedIn, YouTube, Instagram

Association representing manufacturers of packaging and packaging-related converting equipment.

16973 **www.pmpa.org**
Precision Machined Products Association

Facebook, Twitter, LinkedIn, YouTube, Flickr

International trade association made up of member companies that are producers of high precision component products. The association provides educational and business development resources for members, emphasizing quality assurance and emerging technologies.

16974 **www.polysort.com**
Polysort.com

Includes materials, machinery and equipment, processors and industry services.

16975 **www.ptda.org**
Power Transmission Distributors Association

Twitter, LinkedIn

Association whose members are industrial power transmission/motion control distributor firms dealing in equipment such as bearings, belts, drives, motors, gears, couplings, clutches and brakes.

16976 **www.robotics.org**
Robotic Industries Association

Trade group serving the robotics industry through educational resources, events and news. Members include robot manufacturers, users, system integrators, component suppliers and more.

16977 **www.truckservice.org**
Service Specialists Association

Association whose members are persons, firms or corporations that operate a full line heavy duty repair service shop related to trucking.

16978 **www.vi-institute.org**
Vibration Institute

Facebook, Twitter, LinkedIn

An organization dedicated to the exchange of practical vibration information on machines and structures.

16979 **www.vma.org**
Valve Manufacturers Association of America

Trade association representing manufacturers of valves, actuators and controls.

16980 **www.wmia.org**
Woodworking Machinery Industry Association

Facebook, Twitter, LinkedIn

Represents importers and distributors of woodworking machinery. The organization supports its members through industry awards, safety publications, scholarships and networking platforms.

16981 **www.wmma.org**
Wood Machinery Manufacturers of America

Facebook, Twitter, LinkedIn

Organization dedicated to supporting and advocating for manufacturers of machinery and tooling used for processing wood.

Associations

16982 **AMR Management Services**
201 East Main Street
Suite 1405
Lexington, KY 40507

859-514-9150; Fax: 859-514-9207
info@amrms.com
www.amrms.com
Facebook, Twitter, LinkedIn

Nick Ruffin, President & Chief Operating Officer
Melanie Bowzer, Executive Director
Margaret Cloyd, Member Services Coordinator
Glen Ellwood, Conferences & Events Manager
Eric Sweden, Program Director

Organization dedicated to enhancing members' skills in management by offering consultative services that address strategic planning, training and leadership to help strengthen organizations.
Founded in 1997

16983 **ARMA International**
11880 College Boulevard
Suite 450
Overland Park, KS 66210

913-444-9174
844-565-2120; Fax: 913-257-3855
headquarters@armaintl.org
www.arma.org
Facebook, Twitter, LinkedIn

Nate Hughes, Exec. Dir, Operations
Jennifer Millett, National Account Manager
Heather Lehman, Sr. Manager, Membership

ARMA International is a not-for-profit association and a source for authoritative education, the latest legislative updates, standards & best practices. The association was established in 1955. Its approximately 27,000 members include records managers, archivists, corporate librarians, imaging specialists, legal professionals, IT managers, consultants, and educators, all of whom work in a wide variety of industries.
27000 Members
Founded in 1955

16984 **Academy of Human Resource Development**
1000 Westgate Drive
Suite 252
St. Paul, MN 55114

651-290-7466; Fax: 651-290-2266
office@ahrd.org
www.ahrd.orgÿ
Facebook, Twitter, LinkedIn, RSS

Ron Jacobs, President
Kathie Pugaczewski, CAE, CMP, Executive Director
Jeanne Demartino, Member Service Specialist
Jazzy McCroskey, Communications Specialist
Carissa Wolf, Meeting Planner
Founded in 1993

16985 **Adizes Institute Worldwide**
1212 Mark Avenue
Carpinteria, CA 93013

805-566-0742; Fax: 805-456-1959
info@adizes.com
adizes.com
Facebook, Twitter, LinkedIn, Google+

Dr. Ichak Kalderon Adizes, Founder & CEO
Pavel Golenchenko, Managing Director
Shoham Adizes, Vice President Operations
Sunil Dovedy, Professional Director
Paula Gray Lemons, Chief Executive Officer

Promotes Adizes management consulting to help support management within various organizations. Adizes facilitates discussion of ideas and conducts lectures and seminars on leadership, conflict resolution, customer service and other related areas.
Founded in 1971

16986 **American Academy of Medical Administrators**
300 N. Wabash
Suite 2000
Chicago, IL 60611

312-321-6815
Facebook, Twitter, LinkedIn, Google+

Linda Larin, Chair

Organization whose mission is to advance excellence in healthcare leadership through the improvement of individual relationships, multi-disciplinary interaction, practical business tools and active engagement.
2000 Members
Founded in 1957

16987 **American Business Women's Association**
9820 Metcalf Ave
Suite 110
Overland Park, KS 66212

800-228-0007; Fax: 913-660-0101
webmail@abwa.org
www.abwa.orgÿ
Facebook, Twitter, YouTube

Nancy Griffin, National President
Meg Bell, National ViceÿPresident
Lisa Montross, National Secretary - Treasurer
Gina Berry, Vice President, District I
Frances Nicholson, Vice President, District II

16988 **American Management Association**
1601 Broadway
New York, NY 10019

212-586-8100; Fax: 518-891-0368
customerservice@amanet.org
www.amanet.org
Facebook, Twitter, LinkedIn, YouTube

Manny Avramidis, President & CEO
Barbara Zung, SVP, Chief Human Resources Officer
Richard J. Barton, SVP, Chief Information Officer
Michel Wright, SVP, Chief of Sales & Marketing
Nissa Harvey, Vice President, Finance

Membership-based management development organization. The American Management Association provides practical action-oriented learning programs to people at all levels, in all industries, from companies and agencies of all sizes. Members can learn new skills and behaviors, gain more confidence and advance their careers through a wide range of seminars, conferences and executive forums, as well as publications, research, print and online self-study courses.
25000 Members
Founded in 1923

16989 **American Productivity and Quality Center**
123 N Post Oak Lane
3rd Floor
Houston, TX 77024

800-776-9676
713-681-4020; Fax: 713-681-8578
communications@apqc.org
www.apqc.org
Facebook, Twitter, LinkedIn, YouTube, RSS, Instagram

Jack Grayson, Founder
Dr. Carla O'Dell, Chairman & CEO
Lisa Higgins, Chief Operating Officer
Perry D Wiggins, Chief Financial Officer
Cathy Hill, Sales & Membership

Organization assisting other organizations by providing ways to improve benchmarking, best practices, process and knowledge management. The mission of the center is to help businesses, unions, academic and government agencies to improve productivity and quality.
500+ Members
Founded in 1977

16990 **American Society for Quality**
600 N Plankinton Avenue
Milwaukee, WI 53203

414-272-8575
800-248-1946; Fax: 414-272-1734
help@asq.org
asq.org
Facebook, Twitter, LinkedIn

Elmer Corbin, Chair
Bill Troy, CEO
Brian Savoie, Chief Financial Officer
Andrew Baines, Managing Director, Global
Ann Jordan, General Counsel

The association's mission is to facilitate continuous improvement and customer satisfaction in manufacturing by sharing ideas, tools, standards and expertise on quality management.
80K Members
Founded in 1946

16991 **American Society of Association Executives**
1575 I Street NW
Washington, DC 20005

202-626-2723
888-950-2723; Fax: 202-371-8315
ASAEservice@asaecenter.org
www.asaecenter.org
Facebook, Twitter, LinkedIn, YouTube, Instagram

John Graham, President & CEO
Francine Alestock, Executive Coordinator
Shaniece Brown, Member Relations Coordinator
Laura Gaske, Marketing Manager
Sabrina Kidwai, Senior Manager, Public Relations

Association providing advocacy and future-oriented research for member organizations in support of the association and nonprofit profession.
39K Members
Founded in 1920

16992 **Association For Strategic Planning**
Association for Strategic Planning
191 Clarksville Road
Princeton, NJ 08550

877-816-2080; Fax: 609-799-7032
www.strategyplus.org
Facebook, Twitter, LinkedIn, Youtube, Picasa

Neelima Firth, President
Lee Crumbaugh, Vice President
Tom Carter, Treasurer
Kimme Carlos, Executive Director

Dedicated to advancing thought and practice in strategy development and deployment for business, non-profit and government organizations. Provides opportunities to explore cutting-edge strategic planning principles and practices that enhance organizational success and advance members' and organizations' knowledge, capability, capacity for innovations and professionalism.
Founded in 1999

16993 **Association for Services Management International (AFSM)**
Association for Services Management

17065 Camino San Bernardo
Suite 200
San Diego, CA 92127

858-674-5491
800-333-9786; Fax: 239-275-0794
Facebook, Twitter, YouTube, Google+, Blog

J.B. Wood, President and CEO
Thomas Lah, Executive Director

A global organization dedicated to furthering the knowledge, understanding, and career development of executives, managers and professionals in the high-technology service industry.
5000 Members
Founded in 1975

16994 **Association for Systems Management**
Association for Systems Management
24587 Bagley Road
Cleveland, OH 44138

216-671-1919; Fax: 440-234-2930

Paula Winrod, Public Communication

Offers seminars and conferences in all phases of business systems and management.
5M Members
Founded in 1947

16995 **Association of Chamber of Commerce Executives**
1330 Braddock Place
Suite 300
Alexandria, VA 22314

703-998-0072; Fax: 888-577-9883
webmaster@acce.org
secure.acce.org
Facebook, Twitter, LinkedIn, YouTube, Instagram

Sheree Anne Kelly, President & CEO
Alysia Bell, VP, Education Business Coalitions
Stacey Breslin, VP, Benefits Services
Beth Bronder, VP, Development & Partnerships
Crystal Moore, VP, Professional Development

Serves chamber of commerce professionals, chambers of commerce, and other organizations like convention and visitors bureaus and economic development organizations.
1300+ Members
Founded in 1914

16996 **Association of Executive and Administrative Professionals**
900 South Washington Street
Suite G-13
Falls Church, VA 22046-4009

703-237-8616; Fax: 703-533-1153
headquarters@theaeap.com
www.theaeap.com
LinkedIn

Ruth Ludeman, Director

Has helped thousands of administrative and secretarial professionals grow in their chosen careers, and supported their efforts at becoming the best that they can be. Strives to provide its members with a pathway for setting and achieving accomplishments of all types and at all levels. Publishes a newsletter 11 times per year.
3000 Members
Founded in 1975

16997 **Association of Higher Education Facilities Officers (APPA)**
1643 Prince St
Alexandria, VA 22314-2818

703-684-1446; Fax: 703-549-2772
webmaster@appa.org
www.appa.org
Facebook, Twitter, LinkedIn, Youtube

Peter Strazdas, President
E. Landerÿ Medlin, Executive Vice President
John F Bernhardsÿ, Associate Vice President
Norm Young, VP, Information and Research
Paul Wuebold, VP, Professional Affairs

APPA is an association dedicated to leadership in educational facilities management and the ongoing evolution of its professionals into influential leaders in education.
5500 Members
Founded in 1914

16998 **Association of Investment Management Sales Executives**
Association of Investment Management
12100 Sunset Hills Road
Suite 130
Reston, VA 20190

703-234-4098; Fax: 703-435-4390
www.aimse.org/

P. MacKenzie Hurd, CFA, President
Christopher D. Rae, Vice President
Kathy Hoskins, Executive Director
Katie Earley, Deputy Executive Director
Glenn Beales, Director of Finance

The AIMSE mission is to provide an educational forum for those employed in the investment management sales and marketing services profession worldwide. AIMSE fosters high ethical and professional standards among members regarding representation of investment products and services, with an educational emphasis on improving skills, enabling members to adapt to the changing needs of the marketplace.
1400 Members
Founded in 1977

16999 **Association of Management**
Association of Management
920 Battlefield Boulevard
Suite 100
Chesapeake, VA 23322

757-482-2273; Fax: 757-482-0325
aomgt@aom-iaom.org
www.aom-iaom.org

Dr. Karin Klenke, Chairperson, Co-Founder and CEO
Dr. Willem Arthur Hamel, Co-Founder/President
T J Mills, VP Comptroller

Formerly the Association of Human Resources Management and Organizational Behavior (HRMOB).
3.5M Members
Founded in 1979

17000 **Association of Management Consulting Firms**
Association of Management Consulting Firms
370 Lexington Avenue
Suite 2209
New York, NY 10017

212-262-3055; Fax: 212-262-3054
info@amcf.org
www.amcf.org
Facebook, Twitter, LinkedIn, YouTube, RSS

Steve Goodrich, Chairman of the Board
Sally Caputo, President & Chief Operating Officer
Ayaka Sparks, Marketing & Events Coord.
Dina Bystryak, Marketing & Events Coordinator
MaryAnn Dogo, Admin Support & Project Coordinator

Seeks to unite management consulting firms in order to develop and improve professional standards and practice in the field. Offers information and referral services on management consultants.
65 Members
Founded in 1929

17001 **Automotive Trade Association Executives**
Automotive Trade Association Executives
8400 Westpark Dr
Mc Lean, VA 22102-5116

703-821-7072; Fax: 703-556-8581
sjewett@nada.org
www.asna-atae.com

Stacey Castle, ATAE Chairman
Joe Rohatynski, Senior Editor

Promotes interests of executives of state and local auto dealers associations.
106 Members
Founded in 2003

17002 **Awards and Recognition Association**
Awards and Recognition Association
8735 W. Higgins Road
Suite 300
Chicago, IL 60631

847-375-4800
800-344-2148; Fax: 847-375-6480
info@ara.org
Facebook, Twitter, Instagram

Mike May, President
Louise Ristau, CAE, Executive Director
Brian Fitzgerald, Senior Sales Manager
Tom Calvin, Sales Manager
Chris Schroll, Sales Manager

Membership organization of 4,000 companies dedicated to increasing the professionalism of recognition specialists and advancing the awards and engraving industry.
Founded in 1993

17003 **Best Employers Association**
Best Employers Association
17701 Mitchell North
Irvine, CA 92614-6028

866-706-2225
800-237-8543; Fax: 949-553-0883
info@bestlife.com
www.beassoc.org/
Facebook, Twitter, LinkedIn

Steve Course, President
Jennifer Bolton, Sales Account Manager
Ramon Duran, Sales Account Manager
Cristina Rios, Sales Account Manager
Dorothy Sehramm, Salews Account Manager

Providing group medical, dental, long-term disability, vision and life insurance to employers.
Founded in 1970

17004 **Business Management Daily**
National Institute of Business Management
PO Box 9070
McLean, VA 22102-0070

703-058-8000
800-543-2055; Fax: 703-905-8040
Customer@BusinessManagementDaily.com
www.businessmanagementdaily.com
Facebook, Twitter, LinkedIn, Google+

Steve Sturm, President

Career guidance for managers and executives.
Founded in 1937

17005 **Center for Breakthrough Thinking**
Center for Breakthrough Thinking
PO Box 18012
Los Angeles, CA 90018

213-740-6415; Fax: 213-740-1120
Twitter

Dr Gerald Nadler, President
George Hathaway, Executive Vice President
Dr. William Chandon, Vice President
Mr. Steven S. Benson, Vice President - Development

Organized to promote and institutionalize the teaching and application of Breakthrough Think-

ing in universities, corporations and governments for solving problems, leveraging opportunities, and achieving change.
15 Members
Founded in 1988

17006 Center for Creative Leadership
Center for Creative Leadership
One Leadership Place
PO Box 26300
Greensboro, NC 27410-6300
336-545-2810; Fax: 336-282-3284
info@ccl.org
www.ccl.org/Leadership/
Facebook, Twitter, LinkedIn, Youtube, Google Plus, Pinteres
Odd Ingar Skaug, Chairman
John Alexander, President
An international, nonprofit educational institution devoted to behavioral science research, executive development and leadership education.
Founded in 1970
Mailing list available for rent

17007 Center for Management Effectiveness
Center for Management Effectiveness
P. O. Box 1202
Pacific Palisades, CA 90272
310-459-6052; Fax: 310-459-9307
info@cmeinc.org
www.cmeinc.org
Facebook, Twitter, LinkedIn, RSS
Jerry Feist, President
Ron Smith, General Manager
Rob Wood, Publications Director
Sam Erdman, Manager Information Systems
Christie Randolph, Management Consultants
Conducts management training programs and publishes self-scoring inventories, trainer guides and workbooks on stress management, resolution of conflict, risk taking, decision making and building managerial skills.
Founded in 1981

17008 Center for Management Systems
Center for Management Systems
PO Box 159
Akron, IA 51001-0159
FAX 712-568-3427
Provides specialized education to improve management skills.
70M Members
Founded in 1978

17009 Center for Third World Organizing
Center For Third World Organizing
900 Alice Street
Suite 300
Oakland, CA 94607
510-433-0908; Fax: 510-433-0908
www.ctwo.org
Faron Mclurkin, Executive Director
Karey Leung, Research Director
Karissa Lewis, Senior Field Organizerÿ
Avery Bizzell, Organiser
A national organization of books, periodicals and audiovisuals on transnational corporations and labor issues.
Founded in 1980

17010 Christian Management Association
Christian Management Association
1825 Hamilton Drive
San Jose, CA 95125
408-703-6568; Fax: 408-703-6568
www.christianmanagementassociation.org
Facebook, Twitter, RSS
Frank Lofaro, CEO
Dick Bahruth, Senior Consultant
Sandy Huston, Member Services Manager
Joe Voorhies, Director Business Development
Charles S Blake, Director Finance
Designed to assist those involved in the management of Christian organizations.
3500+ Members
Founded in 1976

17011 Club Managers Association of America
1733 King St
Alexandria, VA 22314-2720
703-739-9500; Fax: 703-739-0124
cmaa@cmaa.org
www.cmaa.org
Facebook, Twitter, LinkedIn, Flickr
Tony D'Errico, CCM, CCE, President
Jill Philmon, CCM, CCE, Vice President
Jeff Morgan, FASAE, CAE, Chief Executive Officerÿ
Seth Gregg, Chief Operating Officerÿ
Margaret Meleney, Chief Financial Officer
Advances the professional of club management by fulfilling the educational and related needs of its members.
7000 Members
Founded in 1927

17012 Construction Financial Management Association
100 Village Boulevard
Suite 200
Princeton, NJ 08540-5783
609-452-8000
888-421-9996; Fax: 609-452-0474
info@cfma.org
www.cfma.org
Facebook, Twitter, LinkedIn, YouTube
Stuart Binstock, President & CEO
Brian Summers, VP, Operations
Catherine Wasner, VP, Member Services
Samantha Lake, VP, Marketing
Stacey Scholl, Director, Finance
CFMA is the only organization dedicated to bringing together construction financial professionals and those partners serving their unique needs. CFMA has 98 chapters located throughout the US and Canada.
8600 Members
Founded in 1981

17013 Data Processing Sciences Corporation
Data Processing Sciences Corporation
11370 Reed Hartman Hwy
Cincinnati, OH 45241
513-489-4200; Fax: 513-791-2371
www.dpsciences.com
Facebook, Twitter, LinkedIn, Youtube, Google+
Kurt Loock, President
Scott Nesbitt, CEO
Stephen Vandegriff, EVP
Tim Shelton, CFO
DPS delivers solutions that simplify and manage technology for our clients so they can aggressively pursue their strategic business goals.

17014 Decision Sciences Institute
Decision Sciences Institute
C.T. Bauer College of Business
334 Melcher Hall, Suite 325
Houston, TX 77204-6021
713-743-4815; Fax: 713-743-8984
info@decisionsciences.org
www.decisionsciences.org
Facebook, Twitter, LinkedIn
Morgan Swink, Publisher
Janelle Heineke, VP - Finance (Treasurer)
Gyula Vastag, VP - Global Activities
Kaushik Sengupta, VP - Marketing
Hope Baker, VP - Member Services
Scientific quantitative, behavioral and computational approaches to decision making.

17015 Distribution Business Management Association
2938 Columbia Ave
Suite 1102
Lancaster, PA 17603
717-295-0033; Fax: 717-299-2154
athorn@dbm-assoc.com
www.dcenter.com

17016 Diversified Business Communications
Diversified Business Communications
121 Free Street
Portland, ME 04101
207-842-5500; Fax: 207-842-5503
custserv@divcom.com
www.divbusiness.com
Theodore Wirth, President & Chief Executive Officer
Paul Clancy, Executive Vice President
Janice Rogers, Vice President, Human Resources
Vicki Hennin, Vice President, Strategic Marketing
Oakley R. Dyer, VP/Business Development
Has over 30 years of experience as trade magazine publishers and exhibition organizers. Provides exposition management services for associations and organizations seeking to expand domestically and overseas, as well as direct mail, internet, telemarketing campaigns and market research.
Founded in 1949

17017 Employer Associations of America
262-696-3473
Vicki.Vought@mranet.org
www.eaahub.orgÿ
Mary Lynn Fayoumi, Chair
Vicki Vought, Executive Director
Clayton Kamida, Secretary - Treasurer
Cassie Schauer, Web Tech Specialist
Pam Estergard, Financial Services

17018 Employers Group
Employers Group
1150 S Olive St
Suite 2300
Los Angeles, CA 90015-2211
213-748-0421
800-748-8484; Fax: 213-742-0301
serviceone@employersgroup.com
www.employersgroup.com
Facebook, Twitter, LinkedIn
Mark Wilbur, CEO
Aims to provide human resources management, management counseling and educational programs. Offers unemployment insurance services, and workers compensation programs.
3.9M Members

17019 Employers of America
Employers of America
310 Meadow Lane
Mason City, IA 50401
641-424-3187
800-728-3187; Fax: 641-424-3187
www.employersgroup.com
Jim Collison, President
Provides information and guidance to employers, managers, and supervisors to empower employees and make great things happen.
1600 Members
Founded in 1976

17020 Financial Management Association International
University of South Florida
4202 E. Fowler Avenue
BSN 3403
Tampa, FL 33620-5500

813-974-2084; Fax: 813-974-3318
fma@coba.usf.edu
www.fma.org
Facebook, Twitter, LinkedIn, YouTube

Michelle Lui, Executive Director
Dawn Appleby, Program Assistant
Linda Grimm, Manager, Admin. & Membership
Kieara Nunez, Manager, Marketing & Communications
Shannon Tompkins, Director, Student Programs

Serving the global finance community by: Promoting the development of high-quality research that extends the frontier of financial knowledge; Promoting the understanding of basic and applied research and of sound financial practices; Enhancing the quality and relevance of education in finance; Providing opportunities for professional interaction between and among academics, practitioners, and students.
Founded in 1970

17021 Floodplain Management Association
P.O. Box 712080
Santee, CA 92072

760-936-3676
admin@floodplain.org
www.floodplain.orgў
Facebook, Twitter, LinkedIn, Google+

Thomas Plummer, Chair
Mark Seits, Vice Chair
Andrew Treleaseў, Treasurer
George Booth, Secretary
John Moynier, Director

17022 Fulfillment Management Association
Fulfillment Management Association
225 West 34th Street
Suite 946
New York, NY 10122

818-487-2090; Fax: 818-487-4501
info@the-mcma.org
the-mcma.org
Facebook, Twitter, LinkedIn

Rochelle Boorstein, President
Suzanne Nicholas, Vice President
Raymond Dryden, Treasurer
Melissa Borduin, Executive Secretary
Jodi Sentementes, Recording Secretary

Educates, updates and maintains high standards of service in operations management and customer service. Sponsors four seminars per year. Members are direct mail fullfillment, marketing and circulation executives.
425 Members
Founded in 1945

17023 Independent Professional Representatives Organization (IPRO)
Independent Professional Representatives
34157 West 9 Mile Road
Farmington Hills, MI 48335

248-474-0522
800-420-4268; Fax: 248-514-4418
www.avreps.org
Facebook, LinkedIn

Dave Humphries, President
Frank Culotta, Vice President
Mark Adams, Secretary
Mike Pecar, Treasurer

The mission of IPRO is to provide new avenues of networking; provide new and emerging resources for sound business management; enhance valuable dialogue and commmunication with business partners; and to continue to develop resources and benefits for individual members beyond the resources of individual firms.

17024 Industrial Asset Management Council
Industrial Asset Management Council
6625 The Corners Parkway
Suite 200
Peachtree Corners, GA 30092

770-325-3461; Fax: 770-263-8825
info@iamc.org
www.iamc.org
Facebook, Twitter, LinkedIn, Pinterest, Tumblr, Blogger, St

Samantha L. Turner, Chair
Mr. Russell A. Burton, Vice Chair
J. Tate Godfrey, Executive Director
Rya Hazelwood, Director of Marketing & Conference
Joel Parker, Director of Research & Education

World's leading associates of industrial asset management and corporate real estate executives, their supplies and service providers and economic developers.
135 Members
Founded in 1963

17025 Information Resources Management Association
701 E Chocolate Avenue
Suite 200
Hershey, PA 17033-1240

717-533-8845; Fax: 717-533-8661
member@irma-international.org
www.irma-international.org

Mehdi Khosrowpour, Executive Director
Sherif Kamel, VP, Information Management

An international professional organization dedicated to advancing the concepts and practices of information resources management in modern organizations. The primary objective of IRMA is to assist organizations and professionals in enhancing the overall knowledge and understanding of effective information resources management in the early 21st century and beyond.
Mailing list available for rent

17026 Institute for Supply Management Association
2055 E Centennial Circle
PO Box 22160
Tempe, AZ 85284-1802

480-752-6276
800-888-6276; Fax: 480-752-7890
custsvc@instituteforsupplymanagement.org
www.ism.ws
Facebook, Twitter, LinkedIn, Youtube, google Plus

Thomas K. Linton, Chair
Bill Michels, CPSM, C.P.M., Senior Vice President
Nora Neibergall, CPSM, C.P., Senior Vice President
Thomas W. Derry, Chief Executive Officer, ISM
Janis Kellerman, Senior Vice President/Corporate

The mission of ISM is lead supply management.
43000 Members
Founded in 1915

17027 Institute of Business Appraisers
Institute of Business Appraisers
5217 South State Street
Suite 400
Salt Lake City, UT 84107

954-482-1812
800-299-4130; Fax: 866-353-5406
www.go-iba.org

Mark Walker, Board of Governor's Chair

The oldest professional society devoted solely to the appraisal of closely-held businesses.
3,000 Members
Founded in 1978

17028 Institute of Certified Business Counselors
Institute of Certified Business Counselors
222 N. LaSalle Street
Suiteў300
Chicago, IL 60601

312-856-9590
877-844-2535; Fax: 503-292-8237
info@amaaonline.org
www.amaaonline.com
Facebook, Twitter, LinkedIn, Google+

Michael Nail, Founder & Managing Director
Diane Niederman, Vice President of Alliances
MaryўLou Nall, Operations Manager
Nancy Reyes, Member Services Administrator
Nilla Cooper, Director of Accounting

Premier association of skilled, experienced practitioners focused on the needs of businesses in ownership transition.
120 Members
Founded in 1998

17029 Institute of Management & Administration
Institute of Management & Administration
3 Bethesda Metro Center
Suite 250
Bethesda, MD 20814-5377

703-341-3500
800-372-1033; Fax: 800-253-0332
customercare@bna.com
www.bna.com
Facebook, Twitter, LinkedIn, YouTube

Josh Eastright, CEO
Mike McCarty, Chief Financial Officer
Christina Correira, Chief Human Resources Officer
Cesca Antonelli, Editor-In-Chief

An independent source of exclusive business management information for experienced senior and middle management professionals.

17030 Institute of Management Accountants
10 Paragon Dr
Suite 1
Montvale, NJ 07645-1760

201-573-9000
800-638-4427; Fax: 201-474-1600
ima@imanet.org
www.imanet.org
Facebook, Twitter, LinkedIn, YouTube

Dana C. Riess, Chair
Jeffrey C. Thomson, President and CEO

To provide a dynamic forum for management accounting and finance professionals to develop and advance their careers through certification, research and practice development, education, networking, and the advocacy of the highest ethical and professional practices.
90K Members
Founded in 1919

17031 Institute of Management Consultants - USA
Institute of Management Consultants - USA
2025 M St NW
Suite 800
Washington, DC 20036-2422

202-367-1261
800-221-2557; Fax: 202-367-2134
norm@ecksteinconsult.com
www.imcusa.org
Facebook, Twitter, LinkedIn, RSS

Loraine Huchler CMC, P.E, Chair and CEO
Cynthia E. Currence CMC, Director

Lee Czarapata CMC, Director
Don Matheson, Treasurer
Manola Robinson CMC, Director

IMC is the leading association representing management consultants in the United States, organized to establish consulting as a self-regulating profession, meriting public confidence and respect. Toward the achievement of this goal IMC awards the international appelation CMC for certified management consultants.

17032 **Institute of Management and Administration**
Institute of Management and Administration
3 Bethesda Metro Center
Suite 250
Bethesda, MD 20814-5377

703-341-3500
800-372-1033; Fax: 800-253-0332
customercare@bna.com
www.bna.com
Facebook, Twitter, LinkedIn, YouTube

Josh Eastright, CEO
Mike McCarty, Chief Financial Officer
Christina Correira, Chief Human Resources Officer
Cesca Antonelli, Editor-In-Chief

An independent source of exclusive business management information for experienced senior and middle management professionals.

17033 **Int'l. Association of Healthcare Central Services Material Management**
Int'l. Association of Healthcare
55 West Wacker Drive
Suite 501
Chicago, IL 60601

312-440-0078
800-962-8274; Fax: 312-440-9474
mailbox@iahcsmm.com
Facebook, Twitter, LinkedIn

David Jagrosse, CRCST, President
Susan Adams, Executive Director
Nick Baker, Certification Manager
Josephine Colacci, Advocacy
Elizabeth Berrios, Office Manager

Membership consists of persons serving in a technical, supervisory or management capacity in hospital central service departments responsible for the sterilization management and distribution of supplies.
9000 Members
Founded in 1958

17034 **International Association for Conflict Management**
1 Liberty Street
New York, NY 5006

872-302-7567
brandon@iafcm.org
iafcm.org
Facebook, Twitter

Taya Cohen, President
Brandon Charpied, Executive Director

An association for scholars and practitioners to share theories, research, and experience towards forming an understanding of conflict management in various settings.
Founded in 1970

17035 **International Association for Worksite Health Promotion**
Association for Worksite Health Promotion
401 W. Michigan St.
Indianapolis, IN 46202

317-637-9200; Fax: 847-480-9282
iawhp@acsm.org
ww.acsm-iawhp.org
Facebook, LinkedIn

George Pfeiffer, MSE, President
Charlie Estey, President-Elect
Stephen Cherniak, MS, MBA, Secretary/Treasurer
Wolf Kirsten, MSÿ, Past President

Exists to advance the profession of worksite health promotion and the career development of its practitioners and to improve the performance of the programs they administer. Represents a variety of disciplines and worksites, for decision makers in the areas of health promotion/disease prevention and health care cost management.
3000 Members

17036 **International Association of Administrative Professionals**
10502 N. Ambassador Dr.
Suite 100
Kansas City, MO ÿ64153

816-891-6600; Fax: 816-891-9118
www.iaap-hq.orgÿ
Facebook, Twitter, LinkedIn, Pinterest, RSS, YouTube

Wendy Melby, CAP-OM, Chair
Kristiÿ Rotvold, CAP-OM, Chair-Elect
Jay Donohue,CAE, CMP, President & CEO
Melissa Mahoney, CAE, Senior Director, Operations
Melissa Sutphin, Executive Admin
Founded in 1942

17037 **International Council for Small Business**
2201 G Street NW
Funger Hall Suite 315
Washington, DC 20052

202-944-0704; Fax: 202-994-4930
info@icsb.org
www.icsb.org
Facebook, Twitter, Google+, RSS

Luca Iandoli, President
Dr. Robert S. Lai, President-Elect
Geralyn Franklin, VP/Finance/Control
Ayman El-Tarabishy, Executive Director
Michael Battaglia, Operations Manager

Founded in 1955, the International Council for Small Business (ICSB) was the first international membership organization to promote the growth and development of small businesses worldwide. The organization brings together educators, researchers, policy-makers and practitioners from around the world to share knowledge and expertise in their respective fields.
4000+ Members
Founded in 1955

17038 **International Council of Management Consulting Institutes**
International Council of Management
3860 BB NIJKERK Gld
P.O. Box 1058
Netherland

31 -0 3- 247; Fax: 31 -0 3- 246
info@icmci.org
www.icmci.org

Camera Gaylen, Executive Director
Michael Shays, Manager
John Roethle, Advisory Council

The global association of management consultants. The members of ICMCI are national institutes from around the world that certify professional management consultants. The ICMCI maintains an international code of professional conduct, an international uniform body of knowledge, and strict standards for certification and reciprocity between nations. It promotes professional development and networking between consultants and the highest standards of performance for clients.
39 Members
Founded in 1987

17039 **International Facility Management Association**
International Facility Management
800 Gessner Rd.
Ste. 900
Houston, TX 77024-4257

713-623-4362; Fax: 713-623-6124
ifma@ifma.org
www.ifma.org
Facebook, Twitter, LinkedIn, Youtube, Flickr, RSS

Michael D. Feldman, FMP, CM, Chair
Tony Keane, CAE, President and CEO
Maureen Ehrenberg, FRICS, First Vice President
William M. O'Neill, CFM, Second Vice President
Cheryl White, Director, Corporate Programs

Certifies facility, managers, conducts research, provides educational programs, recognizes facility management degree and certificate programs and produces World Workplace, the world's largest facility management conference and exposition.
Founded in 1980

17040 **International Leadership Association**
1110 Bonifant Street
Suite 510
Silver Spring, MD 20910-3358

202-470-4818; Fax: 202-470-2724
ila@ila-net.org
www.ila-net.org
Facebook, Twitter, LinkedIn, Google+, YouTube, Flickr

Cynthia Cherrey, President & CEO
Shelly Wilsey, Chief Operating Officer
Bridget Chisholm, Director of Conferences
Anita Marsh, Membership Manager
Jean Portianko, I.T. and Office Manager
Founded in 1999

17041 **International Personal Management and Association for Human Resources**
Int'l Public Management Assoc for Human Resources
1617 Duke St
Alexandria, VA 22314-3406

703-549-7100; Fax: 703-684-0948
ipma@ipma-hr.org
ipma-hr.org
Facebook, Twitter, LinkedIn

Neil Reichenberg, Executive Director
Sima Hassassian, Deputy Executive Director
Jenny Chang, Director of Communications
Jacob Jackovich, Assessment Services Coordinator
Andrey Pankov, Assessment Research Manager

Human resource professionals, representing the interests of over 6,000 individual and 1,300 agency members, at the federal, state and local levels of government. Promotes excellence in human resource management through the ongoing development of professional and ethical standards, and through its publishing and educational training programs.
6M Members
Founded in 1906

17042 International Project Management Association
1 Penn Plaza
Suite 6201
New York, NY 10119

diego.arimany@ipma-usa.org
www.ipma-usa.org
Facebook, Twitter, LinkedIn

Joel Carboni, President
Meghan Crumble, Vice President
Bill Duncan, Director of Certification
Diego Arimany, Director of Marketing
Nanci Love, Director of Education

Nonprofit professional society dedicated to supporting project management personnel through standards, leadership and certification.
200K Members
Founded in 1965
Mailing list available for rent: 520 names

17043 International Public Management Association
1617 Duke Street
Alexandria, VA 22314

703-549-7100; Fax: 703-684-0948
nreichenberg@ipma-hr.org
ipma-hr.orgÿ
Facebook, Twitter, LinkedIn

Neil Reichenberg, Executive Director
Sima Hassassian, Deputy Executive Director
Gabrielle Voorhees, Controller
Jenny Chang, Director of Communications
Linda Sun, Director of China Programs
Founded in 1906

17044 Life Office Management Association
Life Office Management Association
6190 Powers Ferry Road
Suite 600
Atlanta, GA 30339-5665

770-951-1770
800-968-1738; Fax: 770-984-0441
askloma@loma.org
www.loma.org
Facebook, Twitter, LinkedIn, Youtube

Robert A Kerzner, CLU, ChFC, President and CEO
Jeffrey Hasty, FLMI, ACS, SVP/Corporate Secretary
Michele LaBouff, SVP, Human Resources
Kathy Milligan, FLMI, ACS, A, SVP, Education and Training
Ian J Watts, SVP/Managing Director, Intl. Ops

Insurance worldwide association of insurance companies specializing in research and education.
1250 Members
Founded in 1924

17045 Marketing Management Association

Home Page: www.mmaglobal.orgÿ
Facebook, Twitter, LinkedIn, Google+, YouTube

Brain Vander Schee, President
Roscoe Hightower, Immediate Past President
Pam Kennett-Hensel, President Elect
Susan Geringer, VP, Marketing
Alex Miliovic
Founded in 1977

17046 Medical Group Management Association
Medical Group Management Association
104 Inverness Terrace East
Englewood, CO 80112-5306

303-799-1111
877-275-6462; Fax: 303-643-9599
support@mgma.org
www.mgma.com
Facebook, Twitter, LinkedIn, Youtube

Ronald S German, MBA, FACMPE, Chair of the Board
Kevin Spencer, Chief Operating Officer
Stephen A. Dickens, JD, FACMPE, F, Secretary/Treasurer

The oldest and largest professional membership association dedicated to medical practice management. Serves their members by offering timely and relevant networking and educational opportunities that keep the members up-to-date on the practice management field.
18M Members
Founded in 1926

17047 National Association Executive Club
1300 L Street NW
Suite 1050
Washington, DC 20005-4107

202-043-3001; Fax: 202-783-4410

Steven Fier, Secretary
Angela West, Manager

Provides networking services and facilities.
500 Members
Founded in 1953

17048 National Association for the Self-Employed
P.O. Box 241
Annapolis Junction, MD 20701-0241

800-649-6273
800-649-6273
www.nase.org
Facebook, Twitter, LinkedIn, Youtube

Keith R. Hall, President/CEO
John K. Hearrell, VP, Membership & Affiliate Programs
Thom Childers, Software Developer/Database Admin
Rosie Farris, Accounts Payable
Cameron T. Brown, Systems Administrator

Goal is to promote small business growth through education and discounts earned through NASE negotiating power.
225M Members
Founded in 1981
Mailing list available for rent

17049 National Association of Corporate Directors
2001 Pennsylvania Ave, NW
Suite 500
Washington, DC 20006

202-775-0509; Fax: 202-775-4857
Join@NACDonline.org
www.nacdonline.org
Facebook, Twitter, LinkedIn, Youtube, RSS

Kenneth Daly, President/CEO
Katherine Davis, COO
Peter Gleason, Managing Director, CFO
Henry Stoever, Chief Marketing Officer
Judy Warner, Editor in Chief

A national non-profit membership organization dedicated exclusively to serving the corporate governance needs of corporate boards and individual board members.
15500 Members
Founded in 1977

17050 National Association of Service Managers
PO Box 250796
Milwaukee, WI 53225

414-466-6060; Fax: 414-466-0840
www.nasm.com
Facebook

Ken Cook, Treasurer

Service manager association for professional development
100 Members
Founded in 1955

17051 National Business Owners Association
480 Broadway
PO Box 3373
Saratoga Springs, NY 12866

202-839-9000
866-639-1669; Fax: 866-224-0609
www.naboe.org

Ed Bolen, President

A non-profit organization representing small business owners' interests and offers several money-saving services, valuable benefits and assistance.
4.5M Members
Founded in 1986

17052 National Businesswomens Leadership Association
P.O. Box 419107
Kansas City, MI 64141-6107

913-432-7755
800-258-7246; Fax: 913-432-0824
cstserv@natsem.com
www.nationalseminarstraining.com/AboutNBLA.cfm
Facebook, Twitter, LinkedIn, Google+

Linda Truitt, President

Offers seminars and workshops on business related issues.
Founded in 1986

17053 National Career Development Association
305 N. Beech Circle
Broken Arrow, OK 74012

918-663-7060
866-367-6232; Fax: 918-663-7058
webeditor@ncda.org
www.ncda.org
Facebook, Twitter, LinkedIn, Pinterest

Cynthia Marco Scanlon, President
Mark Danaher, Past President
David M. Relie, President Elect
Deneen Pennington, Executive Director
Mary Ann Powell, CDF & Conference Director
Founded in 1913

17054 National Committee for Quality Assurance
1100 13th Street NW
Suite 1000
Washington, DC 20005

202-955-3500; Fax: 202-955-3599
www.ncqa.org
Facebook, Twitter, LinkedIn, Youtube, Google+, Pinterest

David Chin, MD, Chair
Margaret E. O'Kane, President
Tom Fluegel, Chief Operating Officer
Scott Hartranft, Chief Financial Officer
Rick Moore, Chief Information Officer

Independent, non profit organization dedicated to improving healthcare quality.
Founded in 1990
Mailing list available for rent

17055 National Conference of Personal Managers
964 2nd Avenue
New York, NY 10022-6304

212-421-2670
866-91N-COPM; Fax: 212-838-5105
www.ncopm.com/

Clinton Ford Billups Jr, National President
Jack Rollins, National First Vice President

Stanley Evans, National Second Vice President
Peggy Becker, National Secretary
Daniel Abrahamson, Eastern Executive Director

A personal manager is engaged in the occupation of advising and counseling talent and personalities in the enternainment industry. personal managers have the expertis to find and develop new talent and create opportunities for those artists which they represent.

17056 National Contract Management Association
21740 Beaumeade Circle
Suite 125
Ashburn, VA 20147

571-382-0082
800-344-8096; Fax: 703-448-0939
memberservices@ncmahq.org
www.ncmahq.org
Facebook, Twitter, LinkedIn, Youtube,Instagram

Russell J. Blaine, CPCM, Fellow, President
Michael Fischetti, J.D., CPCM,, Executive Director
John G. Horan, J.D., General Counsel
Penny L. White, J.D., Fellow, Director and Chair
Kim Rupert, CPCM, CFCM, Fe, Director and Chair, Finance

Formed in 1959 to foster the professional growth and educational advancement of its members.
19000 Members
Founded in 1959

17057 National Employee Services and Recreation Association
Employee Services Management Association
568 Spring Road
Suite D
Elmhurst, IL 60126-3896

630-559-0020
esmahq@esmassn.org

Pud Belek, President

Manufacturers and distributors offering products and services for employee discount programs and employee store merchandise to members.

17058 National Management Association
2210 Arbor Blvd
Moraine, OH 45439-1580

937-294-0421; Fax: 937-294-2374
nma@nma1.org
www.nma1.org
Facebook, Twitter, LinkedIn, YouTube

William T Mahaffey, Chairman
Wendell M Pichon, Vice Chairman
Steve Bailey, CM, President
Sue Kappeler, CM, Vice President
Robin Furlong, Manager

Seeks to develop and recognize management as a profession and to promote the free enterprise system.
22000 Members
Founded in 1925

17059 National Property Management Association
3525 Piedmont Road
Building 5, Suite 300
Atlanta, GA 30305

404-477-5811; Fax: 404-240-0998
hq@npma.org
www.npma.orgÿ
Facebook, LinkedIn, YouTube

Marcia Whitson CPPM CF, National Presidentÿ
Cinda Brockman CPPM CF, Executive Vice Presidentÿ
Cheri Cross CPPM CF, Immediate Past Presidentÿ
Ivonne Bachar CPPM CF, VP, Administration
Rosanne Green CPPM CF, VP, Certification
Founded in 1970

17060 National Small Business United
1156 15th St NW
Suite 1100
Washington, DC 20005-1755

202-293-8830
800-345-6728; Fax: 202-872-8543
info@nsba.biz
www.nsba.biz/
Facebook, Twitter, LinkedIn, Google+, Stumbleupon

Tim Reynolds, Chair
C. Cookie Driscoll, First Vice Chair
Todd McCracken, President and CEO
Cynthia Kay, Vice Chair for Advocacy
Marc Amato, Vice Chair for Membership

Merged with Small Business United in 1986 and sponsors and supports the NSBU Political Action Committee.

17061 National Training Systems Association
2111 Wilson Boulevard
Suite 400
Arlington, VA 22201-3061

703-247-9471; Fax: 703-243-1659
jrobb@ndia.org
www.trainingsystems.org
Facebook, Twitter, LinkedIn

De Voorhees, GD IT, Chairman
Pete Swan, VT MAK, Vice Chairman
James Robb, President
Debbie Dyson, Director/Exhibits
Patrick Rowe, Director of Membership Services

Represents companies in the simulation and training and training support industry. Provides forums, market surveys, and business development information and other services to members.
944 Members
Founded in 1988

17062 North America Human ResourceÿManagement Association
Facebook, Twitter, LinkedIn

Henry Jackson, President
Lic. Jorge Jauregui, HRMP, Immediate Past Presidentÿ
Cheryl Newcombeÿÿÿÿ, Secretary/Treasurer
Founded in 1997

17063 Operations Management Society
5400 Bosque Boulevard
Waco, TX 76710-4414

254-752-6315; Fax: 254-776-3767
www.poms.orgÿ

Sushil Gupta, Ph.D, Executive Director
Dr. Metin €akanyildirim, Associate Executive Director

Members are senior management and deans of business schools in the field of operations management.
Founded in 1989

17064 Organization Development Institute
11234 Walnut Ridge Road
Chesterland, OH 44026-1240

440-729-7419; Fax: 440-729-9319
donwcole@aol.com
Facebook, Twitter, LinkedIn

Dr. Donald W Cole RODC, President
Jim Gustafson, Editor Journal

Promotes the understanding of organization development and offers three categories of membership: professional consultant, regular and student. Offers the International Registry of O.D. Professionals and O.D. Handbook which lists names, addresses and E-mail addresses, publishes a monthly newsletter plus a quarterly journal of 100-150 pages. There are two conferences held every year, one in the USA and one International.
500 Members
Founded in 1991

17065 Product Development and Management Association
330 N. Wabash Avenue
Suite 2000
Chicago, IL 60611

312-321-5145
800-232-5241; Fax: 312-673-6885
pdma@pdma.org
www.pdma.org
Facebook, Twitter, LinkedIn

Charlie Noble, Chair
Charlie Noble, VP Academic Affairs
Peter Bradford, NPDP, VP of Certification
Peter Flentov, VP Chapters
Brad White, VP Conferences & Events

Provides essential information to help foster new product development, giving an overview of the total product innovation process and presenting the latest advancements in product innovation. Also assists managers in innovating and producing products more effectively and efficiently.
3200 Members
Founded in 1976

17066 Production and Operations Management Society
Home Page: www.poms.orgÿ

Sushil Gupta, Ph.D, Executive Director
Dr. Metin €akanyildirim, Associate Executive Director
Founded in 1989

17067 Professional Convention Management Association
35 East Wacker Drive
Suite 500
Chicago, IL 60601

312-423-7262
877-827-7262; Fax: 312-423-7222
communications@pcma.org
www.pcma.org
Facebook, Twitter, LinkedIn, YouTube,Google+

Ray Kopcinski, CMP, Chairman of Board
Deborah Sexton, President and CEO
Jason Paganessi, Vice President, Business Innovation
Sherrif Karamat, CAE, BAS, MBA, Chief Operating Officer
Michelle Russell, Editor in Chief

PCMA delivers superior and innovative education, to promote the value of professional convention management.
6100 Members
Founded in 1957

17068 Professional Managers Association
PO Box 77235
Washington, DC 20013

202-803-9597; Fax: 202-803-9044
info@promanager.org
www.promanager.org

Michael Leszcz, National President
Jeff Eppler, National Vice President
Jackie Jones, National Secretary
Tom Burger, Executive Director
Carlos Zepeda, National Treasurer

National membership association representing the interests of professional managers, management officials and non-bargaining unit employees in the federal government. Promote

leadership and management excellence within the federal services.
10000 Members
Founded in 1981

17069 Project Management Institute (PMI)
14 Campus Boulevard
Newtown Square, PA 19073-3299

610-356-4600; Fax: 610-356-4647
customercare@pmi.org
www.pmi.org
Facebook, Twitter, LinkedIn, YouTube,Google+

Sunil Prashara, President & CEO
Joe Cahill, COO
Cindy W. Anderson, VP, Brand Management
Dave Garrett, VP, Corporate Development
Christine Millaway, VP, Finance

Fosters recognition of the need for project management professionalism. Offers professional certification and bestows awards.
105M Members
Founded in 1969
Mailing list available for rent

17070 Public Risk Management Association
700 S. Washington St.
Suite 218
Alexandria, VA 22314

703-528-7701; Fax: 703-739-0200
info@primacentral.org
www.primacentral.org
Facebook, Twitter, LinkedIn

Jennifer Ackerman, Chief Executive Officer
Shaunda Ragland, Director, Education & Training
Monique Gilliam, Director, Meetings & Conferences
Melvin Bodmer, Director, Admin. & Member Services
Taquan Gilbert, Education Coordinator

17071 Small Business Assistance Center
90 Daniel Drive
Avondale, PA 19311

610-444-1720; Fax: 610-444-1724
inquire@sbacnetwork.org
www.sbacnetwork.org

Provides information and assistance to small businesses. To train and consult entrepreneurs through information services, seminars and professional consultations.
Founded in 1988

17072 Small Business Association of America
Washington, DC

Provider of insured benefits, discount benefit plans and services to small businesses and self-employed people.
Founded in 1964

17073 Society for Advancement of Management
6300 Ocean Drive - OCNR 383
Unit - 5808
Corpus Christi, TX 78412-5807

361-825-3045
888-827-6077; Fax: 361-825-5609
www.samnational.org
Facebook, LinkedIn

Moustafa H Abdelsamad, President/CEO
R. Clifton Poole, Secretary
Kent Byus, Treasurer

SAM members come from a variety of disciplines - productions, finance, marketing, accounting and more who all share a common bond of interest in becoming stronger managers. SAM abounds with opportunities for professional development.
3000 Members
Founded in 1912

17074 Society for Human Resource Management
SHRM/Society for Human Resource Management
1800 Duke St
Alexandria, VA 22314-3496

703-535-6000
800-283-7476
703-548-3440; Fax: 703-535-6490
www.shrm.org
Facebook, Twitter, LinkedIn, YouTube, RSS, Google+

Bette J. Francis, SPHR, Chair
Henry G. Jackson, CPA, President and CEO
J. Robert Carr, J.D., SPHR, SVP, Membership, Marketing
Deb Cohen, Ph.D., SPHR, SVP, Knowledge Development
Brian K. Dickson, SVP, Professional Development

World's largest association devoted to human resource management. Serves the needs of the human resource management professional by providing the most essential and comprehensive set of resources available.
18500 Members
Founded in 1948
Mailing list available for rent

17075 Stage Managers' Association
PO Box 275
Times Square Station
New York, NY 10108-0275

Home Page: www.stagemanagers.org
Facebook, Twitter, LinkedIn
Elynmarie Kazle, Chair
Mandy L. Berry, 1st Vice Chair
Hope Rose Kelly, 2nd Vice Chair
Eileen Arnold, Treasurer
Melissa A.ÿ Nathan, Secretary
Founded in 1981

17076 Strategic Management Association
19102 South Blackhawk Parkway
Unit 25
Mokena, IL 60448-4066

815-806-4908

Chris Glatz, Executive Director/Administration

The international society for strategic management and planning. Presents awards, conducts seminars and foundation research.
6.5M Members
Founded in 1985

17077 Strategic Management Society
Rice Building, 815 W Van Buren Street
Suite 215
Chicago, IL 60607

312-492-6224; Fax: 312-492-6223
sms@strategicmanagement.net
www.strategicmanagement.net
Facebook, Twitter, LinkedIn, YouTube

Robert Hoskisson, President
Marjorie Lyles, President Elect
Jay Barney, Past President
Steven Floyd, Treasurer
Nikolaus Pelka, Executive Director
Founded in 1981

17078 Support Services Alliance
Po Box 130
Schoharie, NY 12157-0130

518-295-7966
800-322-3920; Fax: 518-295-8556
membershipservices@ssamembers.com
www.ssainfo.com

Steven Cole, President

Multi-state membership organization that provides cost-savings services and legislative representation for small businesses and the self-employed. Also offers services to the memberships of more than 100 affiliated state, regional and national associations.
50 Members
Founded in 1977

17079 The Association of State Floodplain Managers
575 D'Onofrio Drive
Suite 200
Madison, WI 53719

608-828-3000; Fax: 608-828-6319
www.floods.orgÿ
Facebook, Twitter, LinkedIn

Bill Nechamen, Chair
Ceil Strauss, Vice Chair
Karen McHugh, Treasurer
Leslie Durham, Secretary
Chad Berginnis, Executive Director
Founded in 1977

17080 The Employers Association
3020 W. Arrowood Road
Charlotte, NC 28273

704-522-8011; Fax: 704-522-8105
info@employersassoc.com
www.employersassoc.com
Facebook, Twitter, LinkedIn, RSS

Paul DeVine, Chairman
Paul DeVine, Vice Chairman
Kenny Colbert, President, CEO
Tom L. Barnhardt, Past Chairman
Cathy Graham, SPHR, Director, Benefit Services

17081 The Sales Management Association
support@salesmanagement.org
www.salesmanagement.org
Facebook, Twitter, LinkedIn, RSS

Robert J. Kelly, Chairman
Laura Hall, Managing Director

17082 TheÿAmerican SocietyÿofÿAdministrativeÿ Professionals
121 Free Street
Portland, ME 4101

888-960-ASAP; Fax: 207-842-5603
membership@asaporg.com
www.asaporg.com
Facebook, Twitter, LinkedIn, Pinterest

Founded in 2005

17083 TheÿAssociationÿfor Financial Professionals
4520 East West Highway
Suite 750
Bethesda, MD 20814ÿ

301-907-2862; Fax: 301-907-2864
www.afponline.org
Twitter, LinkedIn, YouTube, RSS

Terry Crawford, Chair
Michael High, Vice Chair
Gaileon Thompson, Vice Chair

17084 Turnaround Management Association Headquarters
150 S Wacker Drive
Suite 900
Chicago, IL 60606

312-578-6900; Fax: 312-578-8336
info@turnaround.org

www.turnaround.org
Facebook, Twitter, LinkedIn

Ronald R Sussman, Chairperson
Thomas M Kim, President
Gregory J. Fine, CAE, Chief Executive Officer
Jim Gavin, Chief Financial Officer
Jennifer Bethke, Chief Learning & Certification

The only international nonprofit association dedicated to corporate renewal and turnaround management. TMA's 9,000 members in 46 regional chapters comprise a professional community of turnaround practitioners, attorneys, accountants, investors, lenders, venture capitalists, appraiser, liquidators, executive recruiters and consultants. Three international conferences each year offer networking and educational sessions on the latest trends and best practices in the restructuring field.
9000 Members
Founded in 1988

17085 U.S. Workplace Wellness Alliance
1615 H Street NW
Washington, DC 20062-2000

Home Page: www.uswwa.org

17086 WACRA: World Association for Case Method Research & Application
23 Mackintosh Avenue
Needham, MA 02492-1218

781-444-8982; Fax: 781-444-1548
wacra@rcn.com
www.wacra.org

Dr Hans E Klein, President/Executive Director
Dr. Joelle Piffault, Director, Development & Membership
Dr. Pavel Zufan, Director, Business & Economics
Dr. Juan Cortes, Director, Public Relations
Dr. Al Rosenbloom, Director, Communications

Advancing the use of the case method and other interactive methodologies in teaching, training and planning.
2200 Members
Founded in 1984

17087 Wiley
John Wiley & Sons
111 River Street
Hoboken, NJ 07030-5774

201-748-6000
800-825-7550; Fax: 201-748-6088
info@wiley.com
www.wiley.com

Matthew S. Kissiner, Chairman of the Board
Mark Allin, President and CEO
Vincent Marzano, Vice President & Treasurer
Ellis E. Cousens, Executive Vice President
John Kritzmacher, Executive Vice President

Provides information to help executives manage their companies effectively.

17088 Women in Management
Women in Management
PO Box 6690
Elgin, IL 60121-6690

877-946-6285; Fax: 847-683-3751
nationalwim@aol.com
www.wimonline.org

Dana Vierck, President
Ann Louis, Secretary
Tracey Carlstedt, Treasurer
Jane Gregory, Membership
Chris Awe, Administrator

Aims to promote self-growth in management. Sponsors speakers and discussion groups.
1.7M Members
Founded in 1976

17089 Young Presidents Organization
600 East Las Colinas Boulevard
Suite 1000
Irving, TX 75039ÿ

972-587-1500
800-773-7976; Fax: 972-587-1611
askypo@ypo.org
www.ypo.orgÿ
Facebook, Twitter, LinkedIn, YouTube, Google+, Instagram

Scott Mordell, Chief Executive Officer
Sean Magennis, Chief Operating Officer
Cynthia Abbott, Chief Marketing Officer
Terry Wilson, Chief Financial Officer
Dwight Moore, Chief Information Officer
Founded in 1950

17090 Young Presidents' Organization
Young Presidents' Organization
600 East Las Colinas Boulevard
Suite 1000
Irving, TX 75039

972-587-1500
800-773-7976; Fax: 972-587-1611
askypo@ypo.org
www.ypo.org
Facebook, Twitter, LinkedIn, Youtube, Google+, Instagram

Fulton Collins, Chairman
Scott Mordell, Chief Executive Officer

Members are corporate presidents under the age of fifty whose companies employ at least fifty employees.
8000 Members
Founded in 1950

Newsletters

17091 AMA e-Newsletters
American Management Association
1601 Broadway
New York, NY 10019

212-586-8100; Fax: 518-891-0368
customerservice@amanet.org
www.amanet.org

Manny Avramidis, President & CEO
Barbara Zung, SVP, Chief Human Resources Officer
Richard J. Barton, SVP, Chief Information Officer
Michel Wright, SVP, Chief of Sales & Marketing
Nissa Harvey, Vice President, Finance

Newsletters offering content related to business issues for management development organizations.
25000 Members
Founded in 1923

17092 AMR Association Management Tips Blog
AMR Management Services
201 East Main Street
Suite 1405
Lexington, KY 40507

859-514-9150; Fax: 859-514-9207
info@amrms.com
www.amrms.com

Nick Ruffin, President & Chief Operating Officer
Melanie Bowzer, Executive Director
Margaret Cloyd, Member Services Coordinator
Glen Ellwood, Conferences & Events Manager
Eric Sweden, Program Director

A blog containing various management-related tips for organization leaders covering strategic planning, event management, retirement and more.
Founded in 1997

17093 Adizes Around The World
Adizes Institute Worldwide
1212 Mark Avenue
Carpinteria, CA 93013

805-566-0742; Fax: 805-456-1959
info@adizes.com
www.adizes.com/news

Dr. Ichak Kalderon Adizes, Founder & CEO
Pavel Golenchenko, Managing Director
Shoham Adizes, Vice President Operations
Sunil Dovedy, Professional Director
Paula Gray Lemons, Chief Executive Officer

Newsletter covering news and events from the Adizes Institute.
Founded in 1971

17094 Best Practices Report
Management Roundtable
92 Crescent St
Waltham, MA 02453-4315

781-891-8080
800-338-2223; Fax: 781-398-1889
www.pharmcentric.com

A monthly newsletter on the best practices in product development. How to develop and deliver great products at the lowest cost in the shortest time.

17095 Better Supervision
Economics Press
12 Daniel Road
Fairfield, NJ 07004-2565

973-227-1224; Fax: 973-227-9742

Robert Guder, Publisher

Techniques for managing people successfully.
Cost: $1.00
Circulation: 43,000

17096 Better Work Supervisor
Clement Communications
Concord Industrial Park
Concordville, PA 19331

610-459-4200; Fax: 610-459-0936

Offers important information, articles and news to upper level management.
Cost: $48.50

17097 Blue Ribbon Service
Economics Press
12 Daniel Road
Fairfield, NJ 07004-2565

973-227-1224; Fax: 973-227-9742

Robert Guder, Publisher

Shows employees the importance of giving good customer service and methods of providing that service.
Circulation: 27,760

17098 Bridging the Gap
Section for Women in Public Administration
1301 Pennsylvania Avenue NW
Suite 700
Washington, DC 20004

202-393-7878; Fax: 202-638-4952
info@aspanet.org
www.aspanet.org
Facebook, Twitter, LinkedIn

Circulation: 400
Founded in 1939
Mailing list available for rent: 400 names

17099 Bulletin to Management
Bureau of National Affairs
1801 S Bell St
Arlington, VA 22202-4501

703-341-3000
800-372-1033; Fax: 800-253-0332

customercare@bna.com
www.bnabooks.com
Facebook, Twitter, LinkedIn

Paul N Wojcik, CEO

Features summaries of current developments in human resource/personnel management and labor relations. Discusses real life job situations and provides policy guides on how companies have successfully handled employee related problems. Recurring features include statistics.
Cost: $317.00
Frequency: Weekly
Founded in 1929

17100 **Business Journal**
Business Journals of North Carolina
120 W Morehead St
Suite 420
Charlotte, NC 28202-1874

704-973-1200
800-948-5323; Fax: 704-973-1201
www.citybiznetwork.com

George Conley, President
Robert Morris, Editor
David Harris, Managing Editor
72 Pages
Frequency: Weekly
ISSN: 0887-5588
Printed in 4 colors on newsprint stock

17101 **Business Courier**
101 W 7th St
Cincinnati, OH 45202-2306

513-621-6665
800-767-3263; Fax: 513-621-2462
www.bizjournals.com/cincinnati/

Douglas Bolton, Publisher
Rob Daumeyer, Editor
Cost: $83.00
Frequency: Weekly
Circulation: 11000
Founded in 1947

17102 **Case Strategies**
Cutter Information Corporation
37 Broadway
Suite 1
Arlington, MA 02474-5500

781-648-1950
800-888-8939; Fax: 781-648-1950
service@cutter.com
www.cutter.com/

Paul Harman, Editor
Kim Leonard, Customer Service Director
Karen Coburn, CEO/President
Hillel Glazer, Senior Consultant
Ron Blitstein, Director

Objective, timely information to help you successfully integrate CASE into your organization.
Cost: $387.00
16 Pages
Frequency: Monthly
Founded in 1986

17103 **Cash Flow Enhancement Report**
Institute of Management and Administration
3 Bethesda Metro Center
Suite 250
Bethesda, MD 20814-5377

703-341-3500
800-372-1033; Fax: 800-253-0332
www.ioma.com

Focuses on business strategies for increasing liquidity.
Cost: $245.00
16 Pages
Frequency: Monthly

17104 **Center for Creative Leadership Newsletter**
Center for Creative Leadership
Attn: Client Services
PO Box 26300
Greensboro, NC 27438-6300

336-887-7210; Fax: 336-282-3284
info@ccl.org
www.ccl.org

Walter Ulmer Jr, Publisher
John Alexander, President, Chief Executive Officer

A newsletter featuring issues and observations on the behavioral science research and development field.
Frequency: Monthly
Circulation: 35000
Founded in 1970

17105 **Chief Executive Officers Newsletter**
Center for Entreprenuel Management
47 West Street
Suite 5C
New York, NY 10014-4606

212-633-0060; Fax: 212-633-0063
mail@ceoclubs.org
www.ceoclubs.org

Joseph Mancuso, President
Christopher Jones, Office Manager

Unique management insights and sources for presidents of growing businesses.
Cost: $71.00
Frequency: Monthly
Circulation: 40000
Founded in 1978

17106 **Communications Insights**
Comquest
112 Schubert Drive
Downingtown, PA 19335-3382

610-269-2100; Fax: 610-269-2275

Mark Schubert, Publisher

Tips and techniques for sucessful communication.

17107 **Communique**
213 W Institute Place
Suite 307
Chicago, IL 60610-3195

312-440-0078
800-962-8274; Fax: 312-440-9474
www.iahcsmm.com

Betty Hanna, Executive Director
Marilyn Corida, Secretary/Treasurer
Lisa Huber, President
Bruce T. Bird, President

Bi-monthly publication separates supervisors/directors from technicians.
Cost: $40.00
Frequency: 6/Annual
Circulation: 15M
ISBN: 1-605309-30-9

17108 **Contractor's Business Management Report**
Institute of Management and Administration
3 Bethesda Metro Center
Suite 250
Bethesda, MD 20814-5377

703-341-3500
800-372-1033; Fax: 800-253-0332
www.ioma.com

Delivers practical, relevant, and insightful business management guidance to contractors, subcontractors and their consultants.
Cost: $424.00

17109 **Corporate EFT Report**
Phillips Publishing
95 Old Shoals Road
Arden, NC 28704

301-340-2100
866-599-9491
feedback@healthydirections.com
www.healthydirections.com
Facebook, Twitter

Newsletter on business, EFT operations for corporate cash managers.

17110 **Corporate Examiner**
Interfaith Center on Corporate Response
475 Riverside Dr
Suite 1842
New York, NY 10115-0034

212-870-2295; Fax: 212-870-2023
info@interfaithcommunity.org
www.interfaithcommunity.org

Laura Morrison, Program Coordinator
Diane Bratcher, Editor

Analyzes corporate social responsibility issues and trends, reports corporate action news, reviews publications and media and presents the ideas and opinions of leaders of the corporate social responsibility movement.
Cost: $ 35.00
8 Pages
Circulation: 1500
Founded in 1981
Printed in one color on matte stock

17111 **Cost Controller**
Siefer Consultants
PO Box 1384
Storm Lake, IA 50588-1384
712-732-7340; Fax: 712-732-7906

Dan Siefer, Publisher

Cost cutting techniques and ideas for business and industry.
Cost: $149.00
8 Pages
Frequency: Monthly

17112 **Customer Communicator**
Alexander Communications Group
1916 Park Ave
Suite 501
New York, NY 10037-3733

212-281-6099
800-232-4317; Fax: 212-283-7269
info@customerservicegroup.com
www.customerservicegroup.com

Romauld Alexander, President
Adam Reif, Marketing Manager

Provides customer service representatives with the skills, techniques and motivation they need to be more productive.
Cost: $200.00
Frequency: Monthly
ISSN: 0145-8450
Founded in 1990

17113 **Customer Service Manager's Letter**
Bureau of Business Practice
76 Ninth Avenue
7th Floor
New York, NY 10011

212-771-0600; Fax: 212-771-0885
www.aspenlawschool.com
Facebook, Twitter, LinkedIn

Mark Dorman, CEO
Gustavo Dobles, VP Operations

Specially designed to show managers how to reduce their costs, their customer base, and maximize their employee capability.
Cost: $179.00
8 Pages
Frequency: 2 per year
Circulation: 5200

17114 **Daily Report for Executives**
Bureau of National Affairs
1801 S Bell St
Arlington, VA 22202-4501
703-341-3000
800-372-1033; Fax: 800-253-0332
customercare@bna.com
www.bnabooks.com
Facebook, Twitter, LinkedIn
Paul N Wojcik, CEO
A daily notification service covering legislative, regulatory, legal, tax and economic developments which affect both national and international businesses.
Cost: $9399.00
Frequency: Daily
ISSN: 0148-8155
Founded in 1929

17115 **Deal**
The Deal, LLC.
14 Wall Street
New York, NY 10005
212-313-9200
888-667-3325
customerservice@thedeal.com
www.thedeal.com
Twitter
Mickey Hernandez, Advertising Sales
Elena Freed, Marketing
Dedicated solely to reporting and analyzing all the aspects of the booming, high stakes world of the deeal economy. Areas of coverage include mergers and acquisitions, IPO's, private equity, venture capital and bankruptcies. Published in newsletter and on website.
Cost: $249.00
26 Pages
Founded in 1999

17116 **Delphi Insight Series**
Delphi Group
Ten Post Office Square
Suite 580
Boston, MA 02109-4603
617-247-1511
800-335-7440; Fax: 617-247-4957
www.delphigroup.com
Thomas Koulopoulos, President
Hadley Reynolds, Director Research
Mary Ann Kozlowski, Director Public Relations
Timely and insightful analysis and review of the markets, developments, and business cases for knowledge management, corporate portals and e-business solutions. Incorporates original Delphi research findings. Written for all management titles. Includes weekly email news update on relevant issues and access to DelphiWeb, an extensive online resource of product and market information.
Cost: $20000.00
Frequency: Daily

17117 **Directorship**
Directorship Search Group
8 Sound Shore Drive
Suite 250
Greenwich, CT 06830-7276
203-618-7000; Fax: 203-618-7007
www.directorship.com
Russell Reynolds Jr, CEO/President
Barrett Stephens, VP
J.P. Donlon, Editor-in-Chief
Articles and news of interest to CEOs and directors of public companies, on every aspect of corporate governance.
Cost: $395.00
12 Pages
ISSN: 0193-4279
Founded in 1975
Printed in 4 colors on glossy stock

17118 **EAP Link**
International Education Services and Publishing
1537 Franklin Street
#201-203
San Francisco, CA 94109-4571
415-239-4171
800-551-3005
Kendall Van Blarcom, Publisher
International news for human resource professionals.
Cost: $197.00
8 Pages
Frequency: Monthly

17119 **Employee Assistance Program Management Letter**
Health Resources Publishing
1913 Atlantic Ave
Suite 200
Manasquan, NJ 08736-1067
732-292-1100
888-843-6242; Fax: 732-292-1111
info@healthresourcesonline.com
Robert K Jenkins, Publisher
Lisa Mansfield, Regional Director
Brett Powell, Regional Director
Alice Burron, Director
A monthly briefing on guidelines to help companies make decisions on managing their EAP programs. Contains information on what EAP's across the country are doing; help on policy issues dealing with and monitoring costs; framing coverages and limitations; and case histories.
Cost: $227.00
Frequency: Monthly
ISSN: 0896-0941
Founded in 1978

17120 **Enrollment Management Report**
LRP Publications
747 Dresher Road Suite 500
PO Box 980
Horsham, PA 19044-980
215-840-0912
800-341-7874; Fax: 215-784-9639
webmaster@lrp.com
www.lrp.com
Jay Margolis, Editor
Provides solutions and strategies for recruitment, admissions, retention and financial aid for higher-education institutions. Shows readers how to face the challenge of working across departmental lines to improve retention rates and how to respond to the upcoming surge in non-traditional students who apply.
Cost: $198.00
Frequency: Monthly
Founded in 1977

17121 **Executive Administrator**
Seifer Consultants
P.O.Box 1384
Storm Lake, IA 50588-1384
712-732-7340; Fax: 712-732-7906
John Siefer, Publisher
Management, job opportunities and news.
Cost: $70.00
Frequency: Monthly

17122 **Executive Advantage**
Briefings Publishing Group
1101 King St
Suite 110
Alexandria, VA 22314-2944
703-548-3800
800-888-2084; Fax: 703-684-2136
www.briefings.com
Tina Ragland, Editorial Assistant
Lois Willingham, Marketing Manager
Deirdre Hackett, Executive Editor
William Dugan, Group Publisher
Michelle Cox, Publisher
A publication designed to help you learn the key interpersonal secrets to business success through proper etiquette and protocol.
Cost: $147.00
8 Pages
Frequency: Monthly
Founded in 1981
Mailing list available for rent: 6000 names at $125 per M
Printed in 2 colors on matte stock

17123 **Executive Edge**
28 W 23rd Street
10th Floor
New York, NY 10010
212-367-4100; Fax: 212-367-4137
Rich Karlgaard, Publisher
David Hallerman, Editor
Covers quality customer service and marketing techniques.

17124 **Executive Issues**
Wharton School
255 S 38th St
Philadelphia, PA 19104-3706
215-386-8300; Fax: 215-573-6138
www.wharton.upenn.edu
Jason Fisher, President
Discusses current business issues, business continuing information.
Circulation: 40000

17125 **Executive Recruiter News**
Kennedy Information
1 Phoenix Mill Lane
Floor 3
Peterborough, NH 03458
603-924-1006
800-531-0007
www.kennedyinfo.com
Joseph McCool, Editor
William Allen, Managing Director
The authoritative voice of the recruiting industry, covering news, analysis, practice, advice, proprietary data and opinion.
Cost: $229.00
8 Pages
Frequency: Monthly
ISSN: 0271-0781
Founded in 1980
Printed in 2 colors on matte stock

17126 **Executive Report on Managed Care**
Health Resources Publishing
1913 Atlantic Ave
Suite 200
Manasquan, NJ 08736-1067
732-292-1100
888-843-6242; Fax: 732-292-1111
info@themcic.com
Robert K Jenkins, Publisher
Lisa Mansfield, Regional Director
Brett Powell, Regional Director
Alice Burron, Director
Bi-monthly report giving news of how major employers are implementing managed care programs. Helps companies prepare to evaluate and monitor various managed care proposals in

terms of their cost effectiveness, quality and liability to the employer.
Cost: $497.00
Frequency: Weekly
ISSN: 0898-9753
Founded in 1978

17127 **Executive Report on Physician Organizations**
Health Resources Publishing
1913 Atlantic Ave
Suite 200
Manasquan, NJ 08736-1067

732-292-1100
800-516-4343; Fax: 732-292-1111
info@themcic.com

Robert K Jenkins, Publisher
Lisa Mansfield, Marketing Assistant
Caroline Pense, Editor
Brett Powell, Regional Director
Alice Burron, Director

A bi-monthly newsletter published by Health Resources Publishing.
Cost: $197.00
Frequency: Monthly
Circulation: 5000
ISSN: 0898-9753
Founded in 1978

17128 **Executive Solutions**
Dartnell Corporation
4660 N Ravenswood Avenue
Chicago, IL 60640-4510

773-907-9500
800-727-1227; Fax: 561-622-2423
customerservice@dartnellcorp.com
www.dartnellcorp.com

Clark Fertridge, Publisher
John Aspley, Founder

Modern management techniques for executive training.

17129 **Executive Wealth Advisory**
National Institute of Business Management
Po Box 906
Williamsport, PA 17703-9933

703-058-8000
800-433-0622; Fax: 570-567-0166
customer@nibm.net
www.nibm.net

10 Pages
Frequency: Monthly
ISSN: 1049-4855

17130 **Federal Personnel Guide**
LRP Publications
360 Hiatt Drive
Palm Beach Gardens, FL 33418

561-622-6520
800-341-7874; Fax: 561-622-0757
webmaster@lrp.com
www.lrp.com

Kenneth Kahn, President

Annual almanac for US civilian federal personnel and training officers and individual federal and postal employees. An up-to-the-minute summary of rules and regulations affecting federal employees, including employment, pay and benefits.
Cost: $12.95
Circulation: 55000
ISBN: 1-881097-12-9
ISSN: 0163-7665
Founded in 1978

17131 **Financial Management Association International (FMA)**
University of South Florida
4202 E Fowler Ave
Tampa, FL 33620-9951

813-974-2011; Fax: 813-974-5530
www.usf.edu

Judy L Genshaft, President
William Christie, Financial Management Editor
Keith M Howe, Journal of Applied Finance Editor
James Schallheim, FMA Survey Synthesis Series Editor
John Finnerty, Editor FMA Online

Financial books, textbooks, databases, newspapers, research services, software and related products and services.
Frequency: Quarterly
Founded in 1970
Mailing list available for rent

17132 **Global Environmental Change Report**
Cutter Information Corporation
111 Eighth Avenue 7th Floor
New York, NY 10011-5552

212-771-0600; Fax: 212-771-0885
www.aspenlawschool.com

Wolters Kluwer, CEO
Richard Richard, Executive VP

An exclusive international service reporting on policy trends, industry actions and global environmental change.
Cost: $565.00
8 Pages
Frequency: Monthly

17133 **HIPAA Bulletin for Management**
Health Resources Publishing
1913 Atlantic Ave
Suite 200
Manasquan, NJ 08736-1067

732-292-1100
888-843-6242; Fax: 732-292-1111

Robert K Jenkins, Publisher
Lisa Mansfield, Regional Director
Brett Powell, Regional Director
Alice Burron, Director

A monthly newsletter published by Health Resources Publishing.
Cost: $147.00
Frequency: Monthly
ISSN: 0898-9753
Founded in 1978

17134 **HMFA Healthcare Cost Containment Newsletter**
Healthcare Finance Management Association
3 Westbrook Corporate Center
Suite 600
Westchester, IL 60154

708-531-9600; Fax: 708-531-0032
www.hfma.org/publications/healthcarecost

Issues illustrate how to implement strategic cost management that will reduce labor and supply expenses, enhance operational efficiency, satisfy your patients, and improve your competitive position.
Cost: $125.00
Frequency: Quarterly

17135 **HMFA Revenue Cycle Stragetist Newsletter**
Healthcare Finance Management Association
3 Westbrook Corporate Center
Suite 600
Westchester, IL 60154

708-531-9600; Fax: 708-531-0032
www.hfma.org/publications/

Improve your organization's bottom line while maintaining regulatory compliance.
Cost: $165.00
Frequency: Quarterly

17136 **HR Briefings**
Bureau of Business Practice
111 8th Avenue
New York, NY 10011

212-771-0733
800-243-1660; Fax: 800-901-9075
www.aspenlawschool.com/

Alicia Pierce, President

Designed to help HR professionals become more effective on the job. It offers hands-on advice from other personnel managers who have experienced the kinds of problems facing readers.
Cost: $259.00
8 Pages
Frequency: Monthly
Founded in 1925

17137 **HR News**
Int'l Public Management Assoc for Human Resources
1617 Duke St
Alexandria, VA 22314-3406

703-549-7100; Fax: 703-684-0948
ipma-hr.org

Neil Reichenberg, Executive Director
Sima Hassassian, COO
Tina Chiappetta, Sr Director Gov't Affairs/Comm
Frequency: Monthly
Circulation: 8000

17138 **HR Weekly**
SHRM/Society for Human Resource Management
1800 Duke St
Alexandria, VA 22314-3494

703-535-6000
866-898-4724; Fax: 703-535-6474
www.shrm.org
Facebook, Twitter, LinkedIn, Youtube

Susan R Meisinger, CEO

Weekly e-newsletter highlighting critical HR/Human Resourace issues.

17139 **HR on Campus**
LRP Publications
747 Dresher Road
PO Box 980
Horsham, PA 19044-980

215-784-0912
800-341-7874; Fax: 215-784-9639
webmaster@lrp.com
www.lrp.com

Jay Margolis, Editor/publisher

Gives you the tools you need to solve your institution's human resource challenges. Provides pratical tips for handling real-life, day-to-day problems, along with the latest news and significant developments in higher education.
Cost: $165.00
Frequency: Monthly
Founded in 1977

17140 **HRmadeEasy**
Employers of America

310 Meadow Lane
Mason City, IA 50401

641-424-3187
800-728-3187; Fax: 641-424-3187
www.employerhelp.org

Jim Collison, President

A weekly e-newsletter published by Employers of America.
Cost: $149.00
Frequency: Weekly
Circulation: 600
Founded in 1976

17141 **Hiring the Best**
Briefings Publishing Group
1101 King St
Suite 110
Alexandria, VA 22314-2944

703-548-3800
800-888-2084; Fax: 703-684-2136
www.briefings.com

Deirdre Hackett, Editor
William G Dugan, Publisher
Tina Ragland, Editorial Assistant
Lois Willingham, Marketing Manager

A publication designed to help executives recruit, screen, and retain the best employees.
Cost: $697.00
8 Pages
Frequency: Monthly
Circulation: 1300
Founded in 1981
Mailing list available for rent: 6000 names at $125 per M
Printed in 2 colors on matte stock

17142 **Human Resource Department Management Report**
Institute of Management and Administration
3 Bethesda Metro Center
Suite 250
Bethesda, MD 20814-5377

703-341-3500
800-372-1033; Fax: 800-253-0332
www.ioma.com

Shows HR department heads how to boost staff motivation and productivity, improve department automation, and cut costs while improving service.
Cost: $299.00
Frequency: Monthly

17143 **Human Resources Management Reporter**
Thomson Reuters
2395 Midway Rd
Carrollton, TX 75006

646-822-2000
800-431-9025; Fax: 888-216-1929
trta.lei-support@thomsonreuters.com
www.ria.thomsonreuters.com

Elaine Yadlon, Plant Manager
Thomas H Glocer, CEO & Director
Robert D Daleo, Chief Financial Officer
Kelli Crane, Senior Vice President & CIO

For personnel practitioners.
Founded in 1935

17144 **ICSB Bulletin Updates**
International Council for Small Business
2201 G Street NW
Suite 315
Washington, DC 20052

202-944-0704; Fax: 202-994-4930
icsb@gwu.edu
www.icsb.org
Facebook, Twitter

Luca Iandoli, President
Dr. Robert S. Lai, President-Elect
Geralyn Franklin, VP/Finance/Control
Ayman El Tarabishy, Executive Director
Michael Bataglia, Operations Manager

Provides monthly updates on ICSB events, news, and relevant information.
4000+ Members
Frequency: Monthly
Founded in 1955
Printed in 2 colors on glossy stock

17145 **IOMA's Pay for Performance Report**
Institute of Management and Administration
3 Bethesda Metro Center
Suite 250
Bethesda, MD 20814-5377

703-341-3500
800-372-1033; Fax: 800-253-0332
www.ioma.com

Helps human resource and compensation executives improve their company's productivity through the use of variable pay and bonus programs for all types of employees.

17146 **IOMA's Report on Managing Flexible Benefit Plans**
Institute of Management and Administration
3 Bethesda Metro Center
Suite 250
Bethesda, MD 20814-5377

703-341-3500
800-372-1033; Fax: 800-253-0332
www.ioma.com

Information to manage a firm's flex plan.
Cost: $245.00
16 Pages
Frequency: Monthly

17147 **IPMA-USA Newsletter**
International Project Management Association
1 Penn Plaza
Suite 6201
New York, NY 10119

diego.arimany@ipma-usa.org
www.ipma-usa.org/news-media

Joel Carboni, President
Meghan Crumble, Vice President
Nanci Love, Director of Education
Neil Goldman, Secretary/Treasurer
Bill Duncan, Director of Certification

Newsletter on the subjects of company development and performance improvement, including updates and news from the International Project Management Association.
Frequency: Monthly
Founded in 1965

17148 **IT Services Business Report**
Staffing Industry Analysts
881 Fremont Ave
Suite A3
Los Altos, CA 94024-5637

650-948-9303
800-950-9496; Fax: 650-232-2360

Ron Mester, President/CEO
Peter Yessne, Chairman/Publisher

Business news and industry trends analysis for professionals.
Cost: $297.00
Frequency: Monthly
Founded in 1989

17149 **Information Advisor**
Information Advisory Services
143 Old Marlton Pike
Medford, NJ 08055-8750

609-654-6266; Fax: 609-654-4309
www.informationadvisor.com

Robert Berkman, Editor

Compares and evaluates business information services - print, online and CD-ROM. Covers international data, information quality, and new noteworthy products.
Frequency: Monthly
Circulation: 700

17150 **International Management Council**
608 S 114th Street
Omaha, NE 68154-3153

402-330-6310
800-688-9622; Fax: 402-330-7424
www.cmc-global.org

Jodeen Sterba, National Administrator

Information on developing leadership and management skills through a network of shared experiences and education.
Printed in 2 colors on matte stock

17151 **International Quality**
Underwriters Laboratories
2600 N.W. Lake Rd.
Camas, WA 98607-8542

847-412-0136
877-854-3577; Fax: 360-817-6278
www.ul.com

Keith E Williams, CEO
John Drengenberg, Manager Consumer Affairs

Free standards and other quality management topics.
Frequency: Monthly
Circulation: 18000
Founded in 1894

17152 **Inventory Reduction Report**
Institute of Management and Administration
3 Bethesda Metro Center
Suite 250
Bethesda, MD 20814-5377

703-341-3500
800-372-1033; Fax: 800-253-0332
www.ioma.com

Focuses on reducing inventory costs, JIT methods and improving profitability.
Cost: $245.00
16 Pages
Frequency: Monthly

17153 **Issues and Observations**
Center for Creative Leadership & Jossay-Bass
350 Sansome Street
San Francisco, CA 94104-1304

415-334-4700
888-378-2537; Fax: 800-605-2665
info@ccl.org
www.ccl.org

John Alexander, President
Patricia Ohlott, President, Chief Executive Officer

Contains articles about leadership and management.
Cost: $99.00
Frequency: Quarterly
Circulation: 3000
ISSN: 1093-6092
Founded in 1970

17154 **Job Safety and Health**
Bureau of National Affairs
1801 S Bell St
Arlington, VA 22202-4501

703-341-3000
800-372-1033; Fax: 800-253-0332
www.bnabooks.com
Facebook, Twitter, LinkedIn

Paul N Wojcik, CEO

A biweekly review of workplace health and safety regulations, policies, practices and

trends.
Cost: $898.00
ISSN: 0149-7510
Founded in 1929

17155 **Jots and Jolts**
Economics Press
12 Daniel Road
Fairfield, NJ 07004-2565
973-227-1224; Fax: 973-227-9742
John Beckley, Publisher
Monthly planner for supervisors; includes information management theory.
Cost: $1.00
Circulation: 32000

17156 **Kennedy's Career Strategist**
Career Strategies
1150 Wilmette Avenue
Wilmette, IL 60091-2603
847-251-1661
800-728-1709; Fax: 847-251-5191
mmkcareer@aol.com
Marilyn Moat Kennedy, Editor
Linda Mitchell, Production Manager
Cost: $65.00
Frequency: Monthly
ISSN: 0891-2572
Founded in 1986

17157 **Laboratory Industry Report**
Institute of Management and Administration
3 Bethesda Metro Center
Suite 250
Bethesda, MD 20814-5377
703-341-3500
800-372-1033; Fax: 800-253-0332
www.ioma.com
An insider's view of the lab industry's most important business and financial trends.
Cost: $449.00

17158 **Law Office Management & Administration Report**
Institute of Management and Administration
3 Bethesda Metro Center
Suite 250
Bethesda, MD 20814-5377
703-341-3500
800-372-1033; Fax: 800-253-0332
www.ioma.com
Covers the daily management concerns relevant for law firm administrators, office managers, and others.
Cost: $489.00
Frequency: Monthly
Founded in 1983

17159 **Leadership Strategies**
Briefings Publishing Group
1101 King St
Suite 110
Alexandria, VA 22314-2944
703-548-3800
800-888-2084; Fax: 703-684-2136
www.briefings.com
Deirdre Hackett, Editor
Jacqueline Stonis, Production Manager
William G. Duggan, Group Publisher
Lois Willingham, Marketing Manager
A publication designed to sharpen your management and leadership abilities, improve your productivity, and accelerate your professional success.
Cost: $199.00
8 Pages
Frequency: Monthly
Circulation: 8500
Founded in 1981
Mailing list available for rent: 7000 names at $125 per M
Printed in 2 colors on matte stock

17160 **Management Policies and Personnel Law**
Business Research Publications
1533 H Street NW
Suite 200W
Washington, DC 20005-1005
202-364-6473
800-822-6338; Fax: 202-466-3509
Susan Sonnesyn-Brooks, Editor
Leading newsletter designed to give managers an inside view into the best run companies.
Frequency: BiWeekly

17161 **Manager's Legal Bulletin**
Alexander Hamilton Institute
70 Hilltop Rd
Suite 220
Ramsey, NJ 07446-2816
201-825-3377
800-879-2441; Fax: 201-825-8696
custsvc@ahipubs.com
www.ahipubs.com
Schuyler T Jenks, President
Shows managers how to handle problems in the workplace without provoking lawsuits for illegal discrimination in hiring, firing, promotions, sexual harassment or discipline decisions.
Cost: $66.00
4 Pages
Frequency: Fortnightly
Circulation: 20000
Founded in 1909
Mailing list available for rent: 8M names at $125 per M
Printed in 2 colors on matte stock

17162 **Managing Benefits Plans**
Institute of Management and Administration
3 Bethesda Metro Center
Suite 250
Bethesda, MD 20814-5377
703-341-3500
800-372-1033; Fax: 800-253-0332
www.ioma.com
The result of combining two newsletters into one, stronger report. Managers who oversee the enrollment, communications, and administration of employee benefits are the best subscribers to MBP.
Cost: $399.00
Founded in 1982

17163 **Managing Customer Service**
Institute of Management and Administration
3 Bethesda Metro Center
Suite 250
Bethesda, MD 20814-5377
703-341-3500
800-372-1033; Fax: 800-253-0332
www.ioma.com
Boost the productivity, efficiency and visibility of your department, and keep it on the cutting edge.

17164 **Managing Logistics**
Institute of Management and Administration
3 Bethesda Metro Center
Suite 250
Bethesda, MD 20814-5377
703-341-3500
800-372-1033; Fax: 800-253-0332
www.ioma.com
Covers new technologies and strategies, how to negotiate with outsourced service providers.

17165 **Managing Training & Development**
Institute of Management and Administration
3 Bethesda Metro Center
Suite 250
Bethesda, MD 20814-5377
703-341-3500
800-372-1033; Fax: 800-253-0332
www.ioma.com
Covers all aspects of measuring, learning, development, getting employees trained for their jobs, and justifying the cost of training to upper management.

17166 **Medical Group Management Update**
Medical Group Management Association
104 Inverness Ter E
Englewood, CO 80112-5313
303-799-1111; Fax: 303-643-9599
infocenter@mgma.com
www.mgma.com
William Jessee, CEO
Eileen Barker, senior Vice President
Anders Gilberg, senior Vice President
Natalie Jamieson, Administrative Assistant
Monthly association newspaper offering up-to-the-minute articles on current legislation, practical management, health care trends, association activities and other timely subjects.
Frequency: Monthly

17167 **Object-Oriented Strategies**
Cutter Information Corporation
37 Broadway
Suite 1
Arlington, MA 02474-5500
781-648-1950
800-888-8939; Fax: 781-648-1950
service@cutter.com
www.cutter.com
Paul Harman, Editor
Kim Leonard, Customer Service Director
Karen Coburn, CEO
Hillel Glazer, Senior Consultant
Ron Blitstein, Director
Designed for managers and developers of object-oriented systems.
Cost: $495.00
16 Pages
Frequency: Monthly
Founded in 1986

17168 **Orlando Business Journal**
Business Journals
Ste 700
255 S Orange Ave
Orlando, FL 32801-5007
407-649-8470
888-649-6254; Fax: 407-420-1625
orlando@bizjournals.com
www.bizjournals.com/orlando
Ann Sonntag, Publisher
Ken Cogburn, Editor
Cindy Barth, Managing Editor
Sue Ross, Ad Director
Alan Byrd, Director of Marketing/Circulation
Cost: $79.00
64 Pages
Frequency: Weekly
ISSN: 8750-8686
Founded in 1995
Printed in 4 colors on newsprint stock

17169 **PMI Today**
Project Management Institute
14 Campus Boulevard
Newtown Square, PA 19073-3299
610-356-4600; Fax: 610-356-4647
customercare@pmi.org
www.pmi.org
Sunil Prashara, President & CEO

A monthly newsletter published by the Project Management Institute.
6 Pages
Frequency: Monthly
Circulation: 150000
Founded in 1969
Mailing list available for rent

17170 **PSMJ Principal Strategies**
PSMJ Resources
10 Midland Avenue
Newton, MA 02458-1000
617-965-0055
800-537-7765; Fax: 617-965-5152
info@psmj.com
www.psmj.com
Frank Stasiowski, Production Manager
Offers management tactics and techniques for the design industry.
Cost: $195.00
8 Pages
Frequency: Monthly
Founded in 1974
Mailing list available for rentat $125 per M
Printed in 2 colors on matte stock

17171 **PSMJ Project Delivery**
PSMJ Resources
10 Midland Avenue
Newton, MA 02458-1000
617-965-0055
800-537-7765; Fax: 617-965-5152
www.psmj.com
Frank Stasiowski, Production Manager
Offers project management tactics and techniques to the design industry.
Cost: $196.00
8 Pages
Frequency: Monthly
Mailing list available for rentat $125 per M
Printed in 2 colors on matte stock

17172 **Payroll Manager's Letter**
Bureau of Business Practice
111 8th Avenue
7th Floor
New York, NY 10011
212-771-0600
800-638-8437
rfecustomer@aspenpubl.com
www.aspenlawschool.com
Marc Jennings, VP
Gerry Centrowitz, VP, Marketing and Commu
Contains concise, plain-English explanations of the latest federal payroll developments which helps companies comply with rapidly changing employment tax and minimum wage/overtime laws.
Cost: $235.00
8 Pages
Circulation: 7000
Founded in 1920
Printed in one color on glossy stock

17173 **Personal Report for the Administrative Professional**
National Institute of Business Management
1750 Old Meadow Rd
Suite 302
Mc Lean, VA 22102-4304
703-905-8000
800-543-2049; Fax: 703-905-8042
customer@nibm.net
www.nibm.net
Steve Sturm, President
Phil Ash, Marketing Director
Cost: $54.00
10 Pages
Frequency: Monthly
ISSN: 1049-4855
Founded in 1937

17174 **Preventing Business Fraud**
Institute of Management and Administration
3 Bethesda Metro Center
Suite 250
Bethesda, MD 20814-5377
703-341-3500
800-372-1033; Fax: 800-253-0332
www.ioma.com
Stop corporate fraud before it happens. Get guidance on how to avoid supplier collusion and kickbacks, false invoicing, health insurance and workers' compensation fraud, payroll, petty cash and T and E overstatements, theft of equipment and materials and more.

17175 **Professional Advisor**
Int'l Society of Speakers, Authors & Consultants
PO Box 6432
Kingwood, TX 77325-6432
281-441-3558; Fax: 281-441-3538
Bernard Zick, Publisher
Includes information of the consulting industry.
Cost: $120.00
10 Pages
Frequency: Monthly

17176 **Profit Line**
Ernst and Young
9920 Pacific Heights Blvd
Suite 200
San Diego, CA 92121
858-452-6800
800-200-7763; Fax: 858-452-6998
Gary Martino, Chief Financial Officer
Business information newsletter for entrepreneurs.

17177 **Quality Assurance Bulletin**
Bureau of Business Practice
76 Ninth Avenue
7th Floor
New York, NY 10011
212-771-0600; Fax: 212-771-0885
www.aspenlawschool.com
Facebook, Twitter, LinkedIn
Mark Dorman, CEO
Gustavo Dobles, VP Operations
Helps quality professionals improve the company's question-answer function.
Cost: $118.80
8 Pages
Frequency: 2 per year

17178 **Real Estate & Leasing Report**
Business Journals
120 W Morehead St
Suite 420
Charlotte, NC 28202-1874
704-973-1200; Fax: 704-973-1201
www.citybiznetwork.com
George Conley, President
Joanne Skoog, Editor
Cost: $70.00
70 Pages
Frequency: Weekly
ISSN: 0887-5588
Printed in 4 colors on newsprint stock

17179 **Report on Salary Surveys**
Institute of Management and Administration
3 Bethesda Metro Center
Suite 250
Bethesda, MD 20814-5377
703-341-3500
800-372-1033; Fax: 800-253-0332
www.ioma.com
Analyzes data from major salary surveys released during the year by the biggest compensation survey companies, WorldatWork, SHRM, state HR societies, and the Big Four accounting firms, to give readers an overview of those expensive, hard-to-manage services.
Cost: $429.00
Founded in 1993

17180 **Rodenhauser Report**
Consulting Information Services
191 Washington Street
Keene, NH 03431
603-355-1560
www.consultinginfo.com
Tom Rodenhauser, President
Rodenhauser Report is a monthly electronic briefing that forecasts consulting trends for senior management advisors and business executives.
Frequency: Monthly
Founded in 1998

17181 **Servicing Management**
LDJ Corporation
100 Willenbrock Road
Oxford, CT 06478
203-755-0158
800-325-6745; Fax: 203-755-3480
www.servicingmgmt.com
Paul Zackin, Publisher
Michael Bates, Editor
June Han, Circulation Manager
Jeanette Laliberte, Subscriptions
Delivers news and how-to advice to executives and personnel in the servicing of mortgage loans nationwide.
Cost: $48.00
Frequency: Monthly
Circulation: 18000
Founded in 1969

17182 **Signal Newsletter**
International Association for Conflict Management
1 Liberty Street
New York, NY 5006
872-302-7567
brandon@iafcm.org
iafcm.org
William Bottom, President-Elect Nominee
Zoe Barsness, President-Elect Nominee
Brandon Charpied, Executive Director
Cheryl Rivers, Editor
Newsletter covering activities of the International Association for Conflict Management.
Founded in 1970

17183 **Small-Biz Growth**
Support Services Alliance
PO Box 130
Schoharie, NY 12157-0130
518-295-7966
800-322-3920; Fax: 518-295-8556
info@ssamembers.com
www.smallbizgrowth.com
Steven Cole, President
Keeps SSA members and their employees up-to-date on developments affecting small-business communties.
Cost: $25.00
Frequency: Monthly
Circulation: 17,000
Founded in 1977

17184 **Small-Business Strategies**
Page Group
PO Box 116
Dundee, IL 60118-0116
847-695-7887
Phillip Grisolia, Publisher

Contains practical ideas for use in successfully starting and profitably managing small businesses. Accepts advertising.
Cost: $95.00
4 Pages
Frequency: BiWeekly

17185 **Sound Thinking**
Jay Mitchell Associates
PO Box 1285
Fairfield, IA 52556-0022

641-472-4087; Fax: 641-472-2071

Jay Mitchell, Publisher

Notes and comments on the radio industry and related fields, specializing in an outside-in view.
Cost: $65.00
2 Pages
Frequency: Monthly

17186 **Source**
Rachel PR Services
1650 S Pacific Coast Highway
Suite 200C
Redondo Beach, CA 90277-5625
Janis Brett-Elspas, Editor
Jamie Steiner, Advertising/Sales

Annual reference guide for job hunters in advertising, public relations, marketing and journalism offering more than 2,000 resources for finding jobs at all levels in all 50 states. Listings includes job banks, job hotlines, executive recruiters, books/directories, trade publications, industry associations and more.
Cost: $39.00
40 Pages
Frequency: Annual
Circulation: 30,000
Printed in on matte stock

17187 **Southeastern Association Executive**
Special Edition Publishing
999 Douglas Ave
Suite 3317
Altamonte Spgs, FL 32714-2063

407-862-7737; Fax: 407-862-8102
www.specedpub.com

A Sciuto, Publisher
Nichole Wunduke, Editor
Betty Harper, Director of Sales & Marke

Monthly news magazine serving associations meetings and hospitality executives in the southeast .
25 Pages
Frequency: Monthly
Circulation: 5200
Founded in 1973
Printed in 4 colors on glossy stock

17188 **Staffing Industry Report**
Staffing Industry Analysts
881 Fremont Ave
Suite A3
Los Altos, CA 94024-5637

650-948-9303
800-950-9496; Fax: 650-232-2360
memberservices@staffingindustry.com
www.staffingindustry.com

Ron Mester, Managing Director
Tim Murphy, Editor
Joyce Routson, Managing Editor
Greg Palmer, CEO
Jason Ezratty, Managing Partner

A twice monthly newsletter for temporary help, staff leasing and employment service companies. Industry information, company news, training and automation resource reviews, financial coverage, labor demand and supply analysis, key interviews. Association news, public company stock tables. SI Report sponsors an annual Staffing Industry Executive Forum in April. Emphasis is on business news. Includes advertising supplement.
Cost: $385.00
Circulation: 3000
Founded in 1989
Mailing list available for rent: 3500 names
Printed in 2 colors on matte stock

17189 **Success in Recruiting and Retaining**
National Institute of Business Management
1750 Old Meadow Rd
Suite 302
Mc Lean, VA 22102-4304

703-905-8000
800-543-2049; Fax: 703-905-8042
customer@nibm.net

Steve Sturm, President
10 Pages
Frequency: Monthly
ISSN: 1049-4855

17190 **Successful Self-Management**
Stahlka Associates
60 Westchester Road
Williamsville, NY 14221-5021

716-347-7070; Fax: 716-626-4188
wendystahlka@verizon.net
www.stahlkamarketing.com

Clayton A Stahlka, Production Manager
Wendy Stahlka, President

Mastering changes in yourself and your environment to be the best you can be with what you have.
Cost: $24.00
5 Pages
Frequency: Quarterly
Circulation: 1800
Founded in 1975
Printed in one color on matte stock

17191 **Supplier Selection and Management Report**
Institute of Management and Administration
3 Bethesda Metro Center
Suite 250
Bethesda, MD 20814-5377

703-341-3500
800-372-1033; Fax: 800-253-0332
www.ioma.com

Focuses on supplier selection, partnering and management issues.
Cost: $289.00
16 Pages
Frequency: Monthly
Circulation: 180,000
Founded in 1980

17192 **Travel Manager's Executive Briefing**
Health Resources Publishing
1913 Atlantic Ave
Suite 200
Manasquan, NJ 08736-1067

732-292-1100
888-843-6242; Fax: 732-292-1111
info@themcic.com

Robert K Jenkins, Publisher
Judith Granholm, Regional Director
Brett Powell, Regional Director
Alice Burron, Director

A digest published twice a month that covers developments in the field of travel and expense cost control. Topics include discounts in air fare, car rentals, hotel bills, travel alternatives, phone savings, planning for meetings trends in government legislation affecting business travel costs, and case histories of companies that have successfully cut costs. Ideal for travel managers of corporations, small businesses and nonprofit organizations.
Cost: $447.00
ISSN: 0272-569X
Founded in 1978

17193 **WACRA NEWSletter**
World Assoc for Case Method Research & Application
23 Mackintosh Avenue
Needham, MA 02492-1218

781-444-8982; Fax: 781-444-1548
wacra@rcn.com
www.wacra.org

Dr. Hans E Klein, President/Executive Director
Dr. Al Rosenbloom, Director, Communications
Frequency: Semiannual

17194 **Wage-Hour Compliance Report**
Institute of Management and Administration
3 Bethesda Metro Center
Suite 250
Bethesda, MD 20814-5377

703-341-3500
800-372-1033; Fax: 800-253-0332
www.ioma.com

Covers white-collar exemptions, how to pay employees for rest and overtime periods, legal holidays, how to handle vacation, severance and negotiated termination pay rules, and give managers a concise rundown of new federal and state withholding and minimum wage changes, new rules, rates and requirements.

17195 **What's Ahead in Personnel**
Remy Publishing Company
1439 W Summerdale Ave
Suite 440
Chicago, IL 60640-2115

773-769-6760
800-542-6670; Fax: 773-464-0166
www.passportnewsletter.com

Contains information on current HR trends, legal issues and company practices.
Frequency: SemiMonthly

17196 **What's Working In Consulting**
Kennedy Information
1 Pheonix Mill Lane
Floor 3
Fitzwilliam, NH 03447

603-924-1006
800-531-0007
www.kennedyinfo.com

Alan Weiss, Editor

Provides practical guidance on improving consulting skills and managing a consulting practice.
Cost: $197.00
Frequency: Monthly
ISSN: 1535-3036

17197 **Women in Business**
Business Journal of Portland
851 Sw 6th Ave
Suite 500
Portland, OR 97204-1342

503-274-8733
800-486-3289; Fax: 503-219-3450
www.bizjournals.com/portland

Craig Wessel, Publisher
Dan McMillan, Managing Editor
Rob Smith, Editor
George Vaughan, Advertising Director

Special supplement of The Business Journal that celebrates the achievements of women making a difference in the business world and community
Cost: $89.00
36 Pages
ISSN: 0742-6550
Printed in 4 colors on newsprint stock

17198 Work and Family Life
230 W 55th Street
Apartment 6B
New York, NY 10019-5212

212-557-3555; Fax: 212-557-6555
www.workandfamily.com

Ellen Galinsky, Executive Editor
Susan Ginsberg, Editor/Publisher
Anne Perryman, Editor
Susan Seitel, President

Provides information and practical solutions to a wide range of family, job and health issues. Purpose is to help readers find pleasure and satisfaction in their many roles at work, at home, and in their communities.
Cost: $ 295.00
Frequency: Monthly
Circulation: 50000
Founded in 1984
Printed in 4 colors on matte stock

17199 Working Smart
National Institute of Business Management
1750 Old Meadow Rd
Suite 302
Mc Lean, VA 22102-4304

703-905-8000
800-543-2055; Fax: 703-905-8042
customer@nibm.net
www.nibm.net

Steve Sturm, President
Morey Stettner, Editor
Phil Ash, Marketing Director

Ready, relevant and reliable advice for managers on workplace issues.
Cost: $48.00
10 Pages
Frequency: Monthly
ISSN: 1049-4855
Founded in 1937
Printed in 2 colors on matte stock

Magazines & Journals

17200 AFSM: Professional Journal
Assoication for Services Management International
11031 Via Frontera
Suite A
San Diego, CA 92127

239-275-7887
800-333-9786; Fax: 239-275-0794

Jb Wood, President/CEO
John Schoenewald, Executive Director

A journal aimed at management issues.
64 Pages
Frequency: Monthly
Founded in 1975

17201 AMA Quarterly
American Management Association
1601 Broadway
New York, NY 10019
212-586-8100; Fax: 518-891-0368
customerservice@amanet.org
www.amanet.org

Manny Avramidis, President & CEO
Barbara Zung, SVP, Chief Human Resources Officer
Richard J. Barton, SVP, Chief Information Officer
Michel Wright, SVP, Chief of Sales & Marketing
Nissa Harvey, Vice President, Finance

Quarterly management journal for American Management Association's executive and individual members, covering subjects such as 'How the Best Companies Stay Relevant in a Fast-Changing World'.
25000 Members
Frequency: Quarterly
Founded in 1923

17202 APICS: The Performance Advantage
APICS Association for Operations Management
8430 West Bryn Mawr Avenue
Suite 1000
Chicago, IL 60631

773-867-1777
800-444-2742; Fax: 773-639-3000
www.apics.org
Facebook, Twitter, LinkedIn, Youtube

Doug Kelly, Editor
Jennifer Procter, Managing Editor
Beth Rennie, Senior Editor

Provides comprehensive articles on enterprise resources planning, supply chain management, e-business, materials management and production and inventory management.
Cost: $65.00
64 Pages
Frequency: 10/Year
Circulation: 66,000
ISSN: 1056-0017
Mailing list available for rent: 40,000 names at $100 per M
Printed in 4 colors on glossy stock

17203 American Cemetery
Kates-Boylston Publications
11300 Rockville Pike
Suite 1100
Rockville, MD 20852

800-500-4585
800-500-4585; Fax: 301-287-2150
www.kates-boylston.com

Adrian F Boylston, Publisher
Thomas Lorge, Executive Director
Thomas Parmalee, Executive Director
Amy Fidalgo, Production Manager

Features articles on cemetery administration, maintenance, sales and public relations. Also includes coverage of conventions, new cemeteries and new building ideas.
Cost: $39.95
Frequency: Monthly
Circulation: 5800

17204 Association Management Magazine
American Society of Association Executives
1575 I St Nw
Suite 11
Washington, DC 20005-1103

202-626-2700
888-950-2723; Fax: 202-371-8315
publicpolicy@asaenet.org
www.asaenet.org/

Karl Ely, Publisher
Keith C Skillman, Editor

Serves the field of trade business professional and philanthropic associations.
Cost: $30.00
Frequency: Monthly
Circulation: 22507
Founded in 1920

17205 Benchmarking: A Practitioner's Guide for Becoming & Staying the Best
Quality & Productivity Management Association
300 N Martingale Road
Suite 230
Schaumburg, IL 60173-2407

FAX 847-619-3383

William Ginnodo, Publisher
Lesley Williams, Publications Manager

Promotes benchmarking as a technique for comparing processes, products or services with the world's best encouraging ways to do things faster, better, and less cost.

17206 Bits and Pieces
Economics Press
12 Daniel Road
Fairfield, NJ 07004-2565

973-227-1224; Fax: 973-227-9742

Arthur Lenehan, Publisher

Management and common sense plus anecdotes and quotes.
Cost: $1.00
Circulation: 266,000

17207 Bloomberg Businessweek
Bloomberg
731 Lexington Avenue
New York, NY 10022

212-318-2000
800-955-4003; Fax: 212-617-5999
www.bloomberg.com

Daniel L. Doctoroff, President/CEO
Peter T. Grauer, Chairman
Beth Mazzeo, Head of Global Data Products Div.
Thomas F. Secunda, Head of Global Financial Products
Matthew Winkler, Editor-in-Chief

Offers a global perspective to help senior executives profit from faster, smarter, and more informed decisions. Bloomberg Businessweek reaches more C-level executives than any other business magazine.
Cost: $4.95
Frequency: Weekly
Founded in 1981

17208 Building Operating Management
Trade Press Publishing Corporation
2100 W Florist Avenue
Milwaukee, WI 53209-3799

414-228-7701; Fax: 414-228-1134
info@tradepress.com
www.tradepress.com

Edward Sullivan, Editor
Bobbie Reid, Production Director
Scott Cunningham, Associate Publisher
Eric Muench, Director of Circulation
Robert J Wisniewski, President/CEO

Serves the field of facilities management, encompassing commercial building: office buildings, real estate/property management firms, developers, financial institutions, insurance companies, apartment complexes, civic/convention centers, including members of the Building Owners and Managers Association
Frequency: Monthly
Circulation: 70000
Founded in 1943

17209 Business Facilities
Group C Communications
PO Box 2060
Red Bank, NJ 07701-0901

732-842-7433
800-524-0337; Fax: 732-758-6634
webmaster@groupc.com
www.groupc.com

Edgar T Coene, President
Ted Coene, Publisher
Karim Khan, Editor
Beth Sicignano, Marketing Manager
Connie Donatantonio, Circulation Manager

Magazine covering the fields of corporation expansion, economic development and real estate.
Cost: $30.00
Frequency: Monthly
Circulation: 30309
Founded in 1969

17210 **Business First**
Business News
455 S 4th St
Suite 278
Louisville, KY 40202-2551

502-583-1731; Fax: 502-587-1703
www.bizjournals.com

Tom Monahan, President
Carol Brando Timmons, Editor
Judith Berzof, Associate Editor
Rebecca Ray, Assistant Editor
Cost: $83.00
Frequency: Monthly

17211 **C2M Consulting to Management**
Journal of Management Consulting
858 Longview Road
Burlingame, CA 94010-6974

650-342-1954; Fax: 650-344-5005
www.challenge2media.com

E Michael Shays, Publisher
Marsha Lewin, Chairman Editorial

The journal, which is read in over 60 countries, presents methods and processes for management consultants helping them to enlarge and perfect their skills and service to clients.
Cost: $80.00
Frequency: Quarterly
Circulation: 5000
ISSN: 0158-7778
Founded in 1981

17212 **CFMA Building Profits**
Construction Financial Management Association
100 Village Boulevard
Suite 200
Princeton, NJ 08540-5783

609-452-8000
888-421-9996; Fax: 609-452-0474
info@cfma.org
www.cfma.org
Facebook, Twitter, LinkedIn, YouTube

Stuart Binstock, President & CEO
Brian Summers, VP, Operations

Information for financial managers and CPAs concerned with financial management.
Frequency: Bi-Monthly
Circulation: 8,600
Founded in 1981

17213 **CFO: the Magazine for Chief Financial Officers**
CFO Publishing Corporation
253 Summer St
Suite 3
Boston, MA 02210-1114

617-345-9700; Fax: 617-951-4090
www.cfo.com

Frank Quigley, President

Features insurance, cash management, taxes, benefits, accounting, buyers guide.
Circulation: 365,409

17214 **COM-SAC, Computer Security, Audit & Control**
Management Advisory Services & Publications
PO Box 81151
Wellesley Hills, MA 02481-0001

781-235-2895; Fax: 781-235-5446
Info@masp.com
www.masp.com

Presents tutorials and articles of current interest in computer security and audit, presents a comprehensive digest of all key articles and books published on the fields of computer security and control.
Cost: $98.00
Frequency: Quarterly
Founded in 1973

17215 **Central Penn Business Journal**
Journal Publications
101 N 2nd Street
2nd Floor
Harrisburg, PA 17101-1600

717-236-4300; Fax: 717-909-6803
webmaster@journalpub.com
www.centralpennbusiness.com

David A Schankweiler, Publisher
Gary Nalbandian, CEO/President
Jason Klinger, Editor

Provides comprehensive news for the business community.
Cost: $64.95
56 Pages
Frequency: Weekly
Circulation: 10,500
ISSN: 1058-3599
Founded in 1985

17216 **Chain Leader**
Raymond Herrmann
2000 Clearwater Drive
Oak Brook, IL 60523

630-288-8242; Fax: 630-288-8215
www.chainleader.com

Mary Boltz Chapman, Editor-in-Chief
Maya Norris, Managing Editor
Ray Herrmann, Publisher

Targets senior management of chain restaurant companies.
Frequency: Monthly
Circulation: 17323
Founded in 1960

17217 **Chamber Executive Magazine**
Association of Chamber of Commerce Executives
1330 Braddock Place
Suite 300
Alexandria, VA 22314

703-998-0072; Fax: 888-577-9883
wburns@acce.org
secure.acce.org

Will Burns, VP, Communications & Networks

Magazine offering relavant information for chambers and the businesses they serve, including best practices, community issues and trends.
Cost: $32.00
Frequency: Quarterly
Founded in 1914

17218 **Chief Executive**
Chief Executive Group
110 Summit Avenue
Montvale, NJ 07645

201-930-5959; Fax: 201-930-5956
contact@chiefexecutive.net
www.chiefexecutive.net

Carol Evans, Publisher
Robin Uhl, Circulation Manager
William J. Holstein, Editor-in-Chief
Edward M. Kopko, CEO/Chairman
Chris Chalk, Vice President of Sales

A journal of strategy and analysis by and for chief executives.
75 Pages
Frequency: Monthly
Circulation: 42000
Founded in 1976

17219 **Club Management Magazine**
Finan Publishing Company
107 W Pacific
Saint Louis, MO 63119

314-961-6644; Fax: 314-961-4809
www.cmaa.org

Thomas J Finan, Publisher/Editor
Dee Kaplan, Publisher
Dianne Dierkes, Circulation Manager

The resource for successful club operations.
Cost: $26.95
Frequency: 3 Issues a year
Founded in 1927
Mailing list available for rent: 21,000 names
Printed in 4 colors on glossy stock

17220 **Commitment Plus**
Quality & Productivity Management Association
300 N Martingale Road
Suite 230
Schaumburg, IL 60173-2407

FAX 847-619-3383

William Ginnodo, Editor/Author

This monthly newsletter is for managers who want to improve quality, productivity and service through people. It contains brief case studies, written primarily by QPMA staff, showing how operating managers, or their people, went about implementing improvements in their organizations' operating managers, and regularly reinforce the improvement message. This newsletter is free to members.
Cost: $95.00
4 Pages
Frequency: Monthly

17221 **Competitive Intelligence Review**
John Wiley & Sons
111 River St
Hoboken, NJ 07030-5790

201-748-6000
800-825-7550; Fax: 201-748-6088
info@wiley.com
www.wiley.com

William J Pesce, CEO

Collection and analysis of business information.
Cost: $68.95
Frequency: Quarterly
Circulation: 3250
Founded in 1807

17222 **Consulting Magazine**
Kennedy Information
One Phoenix Mill Lane
Floor 3
Peterborough, NH 03458

603-924-1006
800-531-0007
www.kennedyinfo.com

Jack Sweeney, Editor-in-Chief
Mina Landrisina, Managing Director

The only magazine written exclusively for management consultants, consulting is dedicated to fostering performance excellence and career success. Consulting serves the information needs of those responsible for shaping the business strategies of their clients.
Cost: $99.00
Frequency: Monthly
ISSN: 1525-4321
Founded in 1970

17223 **Contingency Planning & Management**
Witter Publishing Corporation
20 Commerce Street
Flemington, NJ 08822

908-788-0343; Fax: 908-788-3782
www.witterpublishing.com

Bob Joudanin, Publisher
Paul Kirvan, Editor

Courtney Witter, Print Circulation/Subscriptions
Andrew Witter, President

Serves the fields of financial/banking, manufacturing industrial, transportation, utilities, telecommunications, health care, government, insurance and other allied fields.
Cost: $195.00
Frequency: Monthly
Founded in 1987

17224 **Contingency Planning & Recovery Journal**
Management Advisory Services & Publications
PO Box 81151
Wellesley Hills, MA 02481-0001

781-235-2895; Fax: 781-235-5446
Info@masp.com
www.masp.com

The only independent quarterly that is membership and subscriber supported. It presents current state of affairs in emergency preparedness, contingency planning and business resumption planning and business continuity.
Cost: $ 75.00
16 Pages
Frequency: Quarterly
Founded in 1972
Printed in 2 colors

17225 **Corporate Meetings & Incentives**
Penton Media Inc
10 Fawcett Street
Suite 500
Cambridge, MA 02138

847-763-9504
866-505-7173
shatch@meetingsnet.com
www.meetingsnet.com
Facebook, Twitter, LinkedIn

Susan Hatch, Editor

Serves those involved in organizing business meetings, conventions, corporate travel agencies, and related fields.
Cost: $87.00
Frequency: Monthly
Circulation: 32200
Founded in 1980
Printed in 4 colors

17226 **Corporate Security**
Strafford Publications
PO Box 13729
Atlanta, GA 30324-0729

404-881-1141
800-926-7926; Fax: 404-881-0074
customerservice@straffordpub.com
www.straffordpub.com

Richard Ossoff, Publisher
Joan McKenna, Editor
Marianne Mueller, Marketing

Intelligence briefing on the latest security developments, best practices, the most important trends and new technolgies.
Cost: $330.00
23 Pages
ISSN: 0889-0625
Founded in 1984

17227 **Cost Engineering Journal**
AACE International
1265 Suncrest Towne Centre Drive
Morgantown, WV 26505-1876

304-296-8444
800-858-2678; Fax: 304-291-5728
info@aacei.org
www.aacei.org

Marvin Gelhausen, Managing Editor
Noah Kinderknecht, Editor

International hournal of cost estimation, cost/schedule control, and project management read by cost professionals around the world to get the most up-to-date information about the profession.
Frequency: Monthly
Founded in 1956

17228 **Crain's New York Business**
Crain Communications
711 3rd Ave
New York, NY 10017-4014

212-210-0100; Fax: 212-210-0200
www.crainsnewyork.com
Facebook, Twitter, LinkedIn

Norm Feldman, President

Dedicated to exclusive coverage of business in New York City, Crain's keeps tabs on the people, the companies, the products, the politics and much more.
Frequency: Weekly
Circulation: 61000
Mailing list available for rent

17229 **Customer Interaction Solutions**
Technology Marketing Corporation
800 Connecticut Ave
1st Floor East
Norwalk, CT 06854-1936

203-852-6800
800-243-6002; Fax: 203-866-3326
tmc@tmcnet.com
www.tmcnet.com
Twitter

Rich Tehrani, CEO

Dedicated to teleservices and e-services outsourcing, marketing and customer relationship management issues.
Frequency: Monthly
Founded in 1972

17230 **Decision Sciences Journal**
Decision Sciences Institute
35 Broad Street
Atlanta, GA 30303

404-651-4000; Fax: 404-413-7714
dsi@gsu.edu
www.decisionsciences.org

Gary L Ragatz, President
Julie Kendall, Treasurer
Carol J. Latta, Executive Director
Terrell G. Williams, Marketing Director
Vicki Smith-Daniels, Editor

Scientific quantitative, behavioral and computational approaches to decision making.
Cost: $100.00
Frequency: Quarterly
Circulation: 5000
Founded in 1968

17231 **Destination KC**
Show-Me Publishing
306 E 12th Street
Suite 1014
Kansas City, MO 64106

816-358-8700; Fax: 814-474-1111

Joe Sweeney, Editor-in-Chief

Kansas City's business relocation and information guide.
Cost: $36.00
984 Pages
Frequency: Monthly
ISSN: 1046-9958
Printed in 4 colors on glossy stock

17232 **Direct**
Primedia
1166 Avenue of the Americas/10th Fl
New York, NY 10036

212-204-4200; Fax: 913-514-6895
www.penton.com

Eric Jacobson, Senior VP
Charles Vietri, Managing Editor
Cheryll Richter, Marketing Manager
Andria Gennlauderslager, Circulation Manager
Chris Meyer, Director, Corporate Communications

Serves the marketing and media industries.
Circulation: 46500
ISSN: 1046-4174
Printed in 4 colors

17233 **Director**
NFDA Publications
13625 Bishops Dr
Brookfield, WI 53005-6607

262-789-1880
800-228-6332; Fax: 262-789-6977
www.nfda.org

Christine Pepper, CEO
Chris Raymond, Editor
Benjamin Lund, Assistant Editor
Fay Spano, Director of Public Relations

The Director is specifically designed to inform and educate the funeral service professional in today's world.
Cost: $45.00
114 Pages
Frequency: Monthly
Circulation: 14,761
ISSN: 0199-3186
Founded in 1882
Printed in 4 colors on glossy stock

17234 **Discovery**
Cooper Group
381 Park Ave S
Suite 801
New York, NY 10016-8822

212-696-2512; Fax: 212-696-2517
www.cooperdirect.com

Harold Cooper, CEO

Focusing on critical management issues that drive growth, profitability and shareholder value.
Cost: $10.00
Circulation: 1500
Founded in 1984

17235 **Economist**
PO Box 58524
Boulder, CO 80322-8524

303-945-1917
800-456-6086; Fax: 303-604-7455
ukpressoffice@economist.com
www.economist.com

Helen Alexander, CEO
Kate Cooke, Group Communications Manager
David Hanger, Publisher
James Wilson, Founder

The Economist is a news and business publication written for top business decision-makers and opinion leaders who need a wide range of information and views on world events. It explores the close links between domestic and international issues, business, finance, current affairs, science and technology.
160 Pages
Frequency: Weekly
Circulation: 1009759
ISSN: 0013-0613
Founded in 1843
Printed in 4 colors on glossy stock

17236 **Executive Update**
Greater Washington Society of Assn Executives

1300 Pennsylvania Avenue NW
Washington, DC 20004

202-048-8014; Fax: 202-326-0995
www.gwsae.org

Liz Whittenmore, Publisher
Scott Briscoe, Editor
Theresa Magner, Director Advertising
Jam Armstrong, Circulation Manager
Susane Sarsati, CEO/President

Association news aimed at the executive level.
120 Pages
Frequency: Monthly
Circulation: 13300
Founded in 1980

17237 **Expansion Management**
Penton Media
1166 Avenue of the Americas/10th Fl
New York, NY 10036

212-204-4200; Fax: 216-696-6662
information@penton.com
www.penton.com

Jane Cooper, Marketing
Bill King, Chief Editor
Jodi Svenson, Production Manager
Chris Meyer, Director, Corporate Communications
Mary Abood, Vice President

Employs charts, graphs and art to lead readers through well organized sections, such as regional reviews, state reports, industry news, case studies and international reports. Addresses the key issues that attract executives in companies that need facts on resource management.
Frequency: Monthly
Circulation: 45015
Founded in 1986

17238 **Facilities Manager**
APPA
1643 Prince St
Alexandria, VA 22314-2818

703-684-1446; Fax: 703-549-2772
lander@appa.org
www.appa.org

Steve Glazner, Editor
Anita Dosik, Managing Editor
Cost: $120.00
Frequency: Bimonthly
Circulation: 5,500
ISSN: 0882-7249

17239 **Financial Management**
Financial Management Association International
University of South Florida
4202 E. Fowler Avenue, BSN 3403
Tampa, FL 33620-5500

813-974-2084; Fax: 813-974-3318
fma@coba.usf.edu
www.fma.org

Utpal Bhattacharya, Executive Editor

Financial Management serves the profession by publishing significant new scholarly research in finance that is of the highest quality. The principal criteria for publishability are originality, rigor, timeliness, practical relevance and clarity.
Frequency: Quarterly

17240 **Financial Manager**
Broadcast Cable Credit Association
550 W. Frontage Road
Suite 3600
Northfield, IL 60093-1243

847-881-8757; Fax: 847-784-8059
info@bccacredit.com
www.bccacredit.com

Mary Collins, President & CEO
Jamie Smith, Director, Operations
Arcelia Pimentel, Sales/Membership

A bi-monthly magazine published by the Broadcast Cable Credit Association.
Frequency: Bi-Monthly

17241 **Forbes Magazine**
Forbes Media LLC.
60 5th Ave
New York, NY 10011-8868

212-620-2200; Fax: 212-620-1857
readers@forbes.com
www.forbes.com

Malcolm S Forbes Jr, CEO
Bruce Rogers, VP Marketing
Paul Maidment, Executive Editor
Michael Smith Maidment, VP, GM Operations

A magazine giving detailed information about business and finance.
Frequency: Monthly

17242 **Fortune Magazine**
Time Inc./Time Warner
1271 Avenue of the Americas
16th Floor
New York, NY 10020-1393

212-522-1212
800-274-6800; Fax: 212-522-0602
www.timeinc.com
Facebook, Twitter

Laura Lang, CEO
Howard M. Averill, CFO
Leslie Picard, President
Stephanie George, Chief Marketing Officer
John Huey, Editor-in-Chief

FORTUNE is a global leader in business journalism. The magazine has a great history of providing analysis and news critical to business people.
Cost: $5.00
Frequency: Annual/18
Circulation: 1M
Founded in 1930

17243 **Global IT Consulting Report**
Kennedy Information
1 Kennedy Place
Route 12 S
Fitzwilliam, NH 03447

212-973-3855

Martin Zook, Editor

The business of information technology consulting, featuring news, analysis, benchmasking data and our exclusive Intelligence Briefing.
Cost: $895.00
16 Pages
Frequency: Monthly

17244 **Golf Course Management**
Golf Course Superintendents Association of America
1421 Research Park Dr
Lawrence, KS 66049-3859

785-841-2240
800-472-7878; Fax: 785-832-4488
hrmail@gcsaa.org
www.gcsaa.org

Mark Woodward, CEO
Lacy Stattelman, Marketing Specialist
Carla Sturgeon, Sales Coordinator
Shelly Howard, Publications Coordinator

Golf Course Superintendent, economical, research and commercial interests concerned with golf course management and improvement. Provides information, education and representation for golf course managment profession.
Cost: $ 48.00
Frequency: Monthly
Circulation: 40000
ISSN: 0192-3048
Founded in 1926

17245 **HR Magazine**
SHRM/Society for Human Resource Management
1800 Duke St
Alexandria, VA 22314-3494

703-535-6000
866-898-4724; Fax: 703-535-6474
www.shrm.org
Facebook, Twitter, LinkedIn, Youtube

Susan R Meisinger, CEO
Leon Rubis, Editor

The world's leading HR resource, offering perspective and in-depth information to leading HR professionals for over 50 years.
Cost: $70.00
Frequency: Monthly
Circulation: 197000
ISSN: 1047-3149
Founded in 1956

17246 **IJCRA**
World Assoc for Case Method Research & Application
23 Mackintosh Avenue
Needham, MA 02492-1218

781-444-8982; Fax: 781-444-1548
wacra@rcn.com
www.wacra.org

Dr. Hans E Klein, President/Executive Director
Dr. Al Rosenbloom, Director, Communications

Provides members and case writers and case teachers from around the world the opportunity to share their work with colleagues, to learn from colleagues and to create an international network for ccase writing, case teaching and interactive teaching applications. Published online in English and Spanish.
Frequency: Quarterly
ISSN: 1554-7752

17247 **Information Management**
ARMA International
11880 College Boulevard
Suite 450
Overland Park, KS 66215

913-444-9174
844-565-2120; Fax: 913-257-3855
headquarters@armaintl.org
magazine.arma.org
Facebook, Twitter, LinkedIn

Nick Inglis, Exec. Dir., Content & Programming
Jeff Whited, Sr. Content Writer
Ann Snyder, Manager, Content Development

Also known as ARMA Magazine, it is a major source of information on topics and issues central to the management of records and information worldwide. Each issue features articles written by experts in the management of records and information.
61 Pages
Frequency: 6/Year
Founded in 1955

17248 **Information Resources Management Journal**
Information Resources Management Association
701 E Chocolate Avenue
Suite 200
Hershey, PA 17033-1240

717-533-8845; Fax: 717-533-8861
members@irma-international.org
www.irma-international.org

Mehdi Khosrowpour, Executive Director
Sherif Kamel, VP, Information Management

An applied research, refereed, international journal providing coverage of challenges, opportunities, problems, trends, and solutions encountered by both scholars and practitioners in the field of

information technology management.
Cost: $95.00
Frequency: Quarterly
ISSN: 1040-1628

17249 **Institute of Management & Administration Newsletter**
Institute of Management and Administration
3 Bethesda Metro Center
Suite 250
Bethesda, MD 20814-5377

703-341-3500
800-372-1033; Fax: 800-253-0332
www.ioma.com

Monthly newsletter that offers information for all those involved in international sales, looking for new distribution channels and how to reduce exports costs and risks.
Circulation: 180,000

17250 **International Cemetery & Funeral Management**
International Cemetery & Funeral Association
1895 Preston White Drive
Suite 220
Reston, VA 20191-5434

703-391-8400
800-645-7700; Fax: 703-391-8416
www.icfa.org

Susan Loving, Managing Editor
Larry Stuart Jr, General Manager

Serves as the primary communication vehicle for ICFA news, membership activities, legislation, marketing and management, including the financial aspects of cemetery and funeral home operation.
Cost: $25.00
64 Pages
Circulation: 6200
ISSN: 0270-5281
Founded in 1887
Printed in 4 colors on glossy stock

17251 **Journal of Applied Corporate Finance**
Financial Management Association International
University of South Florida
4202 E. Fowler Avenue BSN 3403
Tampa, FL 33620-5500

813-974-2084; Fax: 813-974-3318
fma@coba.usf.edu
www.fma.org

Matt Staton, Managing Editor

The Journal of Applied Corporate Finance's goal is to be the leading bridging journal between practitioners and academics. The mission is to publish well-crafted papers of interest to practitioners and of use to academics in stimulating research and in their teaching function.
Frequency: 2 Times/Year

17252 **Journal of Corporate Renewal**
Turnaround Management Association
150 S Wacker Drive
Suite 900
Chicago, IL 60606

312-578-6900; Fax: 312-578-8336
info@turnaround.org
www.turnaround.org
Facebook, Twitter, LinkedIn

Lisa Poulin, President
Patrick Lagrange, Chairman
Linda Delgadillo, Executive Director

The only international nonprofit association dedicated to corporate renewal and turnaround management. TMA's 9,000 members in 46 regional chapters comprise a professional community of turnaround practitioners, attorneys, accountants, investors, lenders, venture capitalists, appraiser, liquidators, executive recruiters and consultants. Three international conferences each year offer networking and educational sessions on the latest trends and best practices in the restructuring field.
Frequency: 9/Year
Circulation: 9000+

17253 **Journal of Information Technology Management**
Association of Management
920 Battlefield Boulevard
Suite 100
Chesapeake, VA 23322

757-482-2273; Fax: 757-482-0325
aomgt@aom-iaom.org
www.aom-iaom.org

Dr Al Bento, Editor-in-Chief

A forum for the communication of solutions found by practitioners and academicians to the mulitfaceted problems associated with managing information and information technology as a corporate resource.
Frequency: Quarterly

17254 **Journal of Management Systems**
Association of Management
920 Battlefield Boulevard
Suite 100
Chesapeake, VA 23322

757-482-2273; Fax: 757-482-0325
aomgt@aom-iaom.org
www.aom-iaom.org

Dr John Saee, Editor-in-Chief

Promotes the integreation and cross-fertilization of the behavioral/organizational and information sciences and to encourage, sharpen and expand the dialogue between academicians and practitioners from an interdisiplinary perspective

17255 **Journal of Quality Technology**
American Society for Quality
600 N Plankinton Avenue
Milwaukee, WI 53203

414-272-8575
800-248-1946; Fax: 414-272-1734
help@asq.org
asq.org/pub/jqt/index.html

Elmer Corbin, Chair
Bill Troy, CEO
Brian Savoie, Chief Financial Officer
Andrew Baines, Managing Director, Global
Ann Jordan, General Counsel

Published by the American Society for Quality, the Journal of Quality Technology is a quarterly, peer-reviewed journal that focuses on the subject of quality control and the related areas of reliability and similar disciplines.
80K Members
Frequency: Quarterly
Founded in 1946

17256 **MSI**
Reed Business Information
30 Technology Parkway South
Suite 100
Norcross, GA 30092

630-574-0825
800-424-3996; Fax: 630-288-8781
webmaster@reedbusiness.com
www.reedbusiness.com

Jeff Greisch, President
Kevin Parker, Editorial Director
Jim Casella, CEO
Nancy Bartels, Senior Editor
Eric Roth, Circulation Manager
Frequency: Monthly
Founded in 1977

17257 **Maintenance Technology**
Applied Technology Publications
1300 S Grove Ave
Suite 105
Barrington, IL 60010-5246

847-382-8100; Fax: 847-304-8603
www.mt-online.com

Arthur Rice, President/CEO
Bill Kiesel, Vice President/Publisher
Jane Alexander, Editor-In-Chief
Rick Carter, Executive Editor
Randy Buttstadt, Director of Creative Services

Maintenance Technology magazine serves the business and technical information needs of managers and engineers responsible for assuring availability of plant equipment and systems. It provides readers with articles on advanced technologies, strategies, tools, and services for the life-cycle management of capital assets.
Frequency: Monthly
Circulation: 50,827
Mailing list available for rent: 35,263 names at $$15 per M

17258 **Manage**
National Management Association
2210 Arbor Blvd
Suite A
Moraine, OH 45439-1580

937-294-0421; Fax: 937-294-2374
nma@nma1.org
www.nma1.org

Douglas Shaw, Publisher
Richard Hergert, Owner
Steve Bailey, CEO
Mike McCulley, Chief Operations Officer

Association news for executives.
32 Pages
Frequency: Quarterly
Founded in 1925

17259 **Management Consultants International**
Kennedy Information
37 Beach Rd
Singapore 199597

65 -100-0688; Fax: 656-234-0688
corporate@cacmci.com
www.cacmci.com

News and business intelligence on management consulting worldwide. Monthly issues feature country by country surveys of local consulting firms.
Cost: $1122.00
16 Pages
Frequency: Monthly
ISSN: 0956-3253

17260 **Medical Group Management Journal**
Medical Group Management Association
104 Inverness Ter E
Englewood, CO 80112-5313

303-799-1111; Fax: 303-643-9599
infocenter@mgma.com
www.mgma.com

William Jessee, CEO
Eileen Barker, senior Vice President
Anders Gilberg, senior Vice President
Natalie Jamieson, Administrative Assistant

Encompasses pertinent problems, questions and issues relating to group practice management.
Frequency: Bi-Monthly

17261 **Negotiation and Conflict Management Research**
International Association for Conflict Management

1 Liberty Street
New York, NY 5006

872-302-7567
cs-journals@wiley.com
iafcm.org

William Bottom, President-Elect Nominee
Zoe Barsness, President-Elect Nominee
Brandon Charpied, Executive Director
Michael A. Gross, Editor
Mallory Wallace, Editorial Assistant

Articles on theory and research related to negotiation and conflict management of all kinds, including interpersonal, intergroup, organizational, and cross-cultural conflicts.
ISSN: 1750-4716
Founded in 1970

17262 **New Mobility**
PO Box 220
415 Horsham Road
Horsham, PA 19044

215-675-9133
888-850-0344; Fax: 215-675-9376
info@newmobility.com
www.newmobility.com
Facebook, Twitter, MySpace

Tim Gilmer, Editor
Jean Dobbs, Editorial Director, VP
Kim Brennan, Circulation/List Manager
Amy Blackmore, VP of Sales
Jeff Leonard, SVP of Marketing + Communication

New Mobility encourages the integration of active-lifestyle wheelchair users into mainstream society, while simultaneously reflecting the vibrant world of disability-related arts, media, advocacy and philosophy. Our stories foster a sense of community.
Cost: $27.95
Frequency: Monthly

17263 **Operations & Fulfillment**
Primedia
11 River Bend Drive South
PO Box 4242
Stamford, CT 06907-242

203-589-9900
800-775-3777; Fax: 203-358-5823
www.multichannelmerchant.com

Sherry Chiger, Editorial Director
Melisa Dowling, Executive Editor
Len Roberto, Circulation Manager
Kate Dimarco, Creative Director of Production
Barry Litwin, VP Sales/Marketing

Provides executives information they can't get anywhere else and reach executives and managers with purchasing authority in all areas of operations management. Information on direct to customer fulfillment..
Cost: $85.00
Circulation: 40000
Founded in 1984

17264 **Organization Development Journal**
Organization Development Institute
11234 Walnut Ridge Road
Chesterland, OH 44026-1240

440-729-7419; Fax: 440-729-9319
www.odinstitute.org/

Dr. Donald W Cole, Publisher
Dr. Donald W Cole, CEO/President
Jenny Maes, Editor

A journal published quarterly for human resource people, managers and organization development people. The most frequently cited OD/OB publication in the world.
Cost: $80.00
100 Pages
Frequency: Quarterly
Circulation: 700
ISSN: 0889-6402

Founded in 1968
Mailing list available for rent: 9M names
Printed in one color on newsprint stock

17265 **PM Network**
Project Management Institute
14 Campus Boulevard
Newtown Square, PA 19073-3299

610-356-4600; Fax: 610-356-4647
customercare@pmi.org
www.pmi.org

Sunil Prashara, President & CEO

A monthly magazine published by the Project Management Institute.
75 Pages
Frequency: Monthly
Mailing list available for rent

17266 **Print Solutions Magazine**
Document Management Industries Association
433 E Monroe Avenue
Alexandria, VA 22301-1693

703-836-6232
800-336-4641; Fax: 703-549-4966
www.printsolutionsmag.com/

Peter L Colaianni, Editor-in-Chief
Darin Painter, Managing Editor
Preeti Vasishtha, Assistant Editor
Andrew Brown, Assistant Editor

Source for marketing, management and product information.
Frequency: Monthly
Circulation: 42000
ISSN: 0532-1700
Founded in 1962
Printed in 4 colors on glossy stock

17267 **Professional Journal**
AFSM International
11031 Via Frontera
Suite A
San Diego, CA 92127-1709

858-673-3055
800-333-9786; Fax: 239-275-0794

John Schoenewald, Executive Director
Jb Wood, President/Ceo

A magazine for executives, managers and professionals in the high-technology services industry.
Cost: $90.00
114 Pages
Circulation: 7000
ISSN: 1049-2135
Founded in 1975
Printed in 4 colors on glossy stock

17268 **Project Management Journal**
Project Management Institute
14 Campus Boulevard
Newtown Square, PA 19073-3299

610-356-4600; Fax: 610-356-4647
customercare@pmi.org
www.pmi.org

Sunil Prashara, President & CEO
Dan Goldfischer, Editor-In-Chief

A quarterly journal published by the Project Management Institute.
65 Pages
Frequency: Quarterly
Mailing list available for rent

17269 **Purchasing**
Reed Business Information
6 Alfred Circle
Bedford, MA 00173

972-980-8810; Fax: 630-288-8686
www.designnews.com
Facebook, Twitter, LinkedIn

Kathy Doyle, Publisher
Lockie Montgomery, Production Manager
Anne Millen Porter, Business Manager
Paul Teague, Chief Editor.

About the purchasing professional in American industry.
Founded in 1920

17270 **Quality Engineering**
American Society for Quality
600 N Plankinton Avenue
Milwaukee, WI 53203

414-272-8575
800-248-1946; Fax: 414-272-1734
help@asq.org
asq.org/pub/qe/index.html

Elmer Corbin, Chair
Bill Troy, CEO
Brian Savoie, Chief Financial Officer
Andrew Baines, Managing Director, Global
Ann Jordan, General Counsel

Co-published by Taylor and Francis, this journal is for professional practitioners and researchers in quality engineering improvement and solutions. Subjects include quality assurance management, physical technology, statistical tools and more.
80K Members
Frequency: Quarterly
Founded in 1946

17271 **Quality Management Journal**
American Society for Quality
600 N Plankinton Avenue
Milwaukee, WI 53203

414-272-8575
800-248-1946; Fax: 414-272-1734
help@asq.org
asq.org/pub/qmj/index.html

Elmer Corbin, Chair
Bill Troy, CEO
Brian Savoie, Chief Financial Officer
Andrew Baines, Managing Director, Global
Ann Jordan, General Counsel

Quarterly, peer-reviewed journal focusing on research on the subject of quality management practice. The journal provides a discussion forum for both practitioners and academics.
80K Members
Frequency: Quarterly
Founded in 1946

17272 **Quality Progress**
American Society for Quality
600 N Plankinton Avenue
Milwaukee, WI 53203

414-272-8575
800-248-1946; Fax: 414-272-1734
help@asq.org
asq.org/qualityprogress

Elmer Corbin, Chair
Bill Troy, CEO
Brian Savoie, Chief Financial Officer
Andrew Baines, Managing Director, Global
Ann Jordan, General Counsel

Peer-reviewed journal exploring the subject of quality control, discussing the usage and implementation of quality principles. Topics include customer satisfaction, trends and developments.
80K Members
Founded in 1946

17273 **Recruiting Trends**
Kennedy Information
One Phoenix Mill Lane
Floor 3
Peterborough, NH 03458

603-924-1006
800-531-0007
www.kennedyinfo.com

Joseph McCool, Editor
Mina Landrisina, Managing Director

Provides strategies and tactics for creating and maintaining a competitive workforce.
Cost: $99.00
8 Pages
Frequency: Monthly
ISSN: 0034-1827
Founded in 1970

17274 **Retail Merchandiser**
MacFadden Publishing
233 Park Ave S
6th Floor
New York, NY 10003-1606

212-979-4800; Fax: 212-979-7342
www.retail-merchandiser.com

Jeff Friedman, Publisher
Greg Masters, Managing Editor
Toni Riggio, Sales Coordinator
Anita M Wise, Production Manager

Serves those in management positions of mass retail and discount companies.
Cost: $99.00
Frequency: Monthly
Circulation: 34,188
Founded in 1961

17275 **Risk Management**
Risk & Insurance Management Society
655 3rd Avenue
2nd Floor
New York, NY 10017

212-286-9292; Fax: 212-286-9716
chapterservices@RIMS.org
www.rims.org

Ted Donovan, Publisher
Bill Coffin, Editor-in-Chief
Jared Wade, Associate Editor
Callie Nelson, Circulation Manager
Todd Lockwood, Advertising Sales Manager
Cost: $64.00
Frequency: Monthly
Circulation: 15000
Founded in 1950

17276 **SAM Advanced Management Journal**
Society for Advancement of Management
Corpus Christi - College of Business
6300 Ocean Drive - Unit 5807
Corpus Christi, TX 78412-5807

361-825-6045; Fax: 361-825-2725
www.samnational.org

Moustafa H. Abdelsamad, President/CEO
R. Clifton Poole, Secretary
S.G. Fletcher, Treasurer
Everette Anderson, VP, Sales & Marketing
Anthony Buono, Director

A quarterly, refereed publication especially designed for general managers.
Cost: $64.00
3000 Members
Frequency: Quarterly
Founded in 1912

17277 **SAM Management In Practice**
Society for Advancement of Management
Corpus Christi - College of Business
6300 Ocean Drive, Unit 5807
Corpus Christi, TX 78412-5807

361-825-6045; Fax: 361-825-2725
www.samnational.org

Moustafa H. Abdelsamad, President/CEO
R. Clifton Poole, Secretary
S.G. Fletcher, Treasurer
Everette Anderson, VP, Sales & Marketing
Anthony Buono, Director

A quarterly, refereed publication especially designed for general managers.
3000 Members
Frequency: Quarterly
Founded in 1912

17278 **Shelby Report**
Shelby Publishing Company
517 Green St Nw
Gainesville, GA 30501-3300

770-534-8380; Fax: 770-535-0110
www.shelbypublishing.com

Ron Johnston, President
Chuck Gilmer, Editor

Serving the grocery industry in Arizona, Arkansas, Colorado, Kansas, Louisana, Missouri, New Mexico, Oklahoma, and Texas,
Cost: $36.00
Frequency: Monthly
Circulation: 25201
Founded in 1966

17279 **Si Review**
Staffing Industry Analysts
881 Fremont Ave
Suite A3
Los Altos, CA 94024-5637

650-948-9303
800-950-9496; Fax: 650-232-2360

Ron Mester, President
Theresa Daly, Production Manager

Tools and techniques for staffing industry professionals. How-to's and survey articles for branch management, upper management, owners, and sales/service personnel in employment service companies. Display advertising included.
Cost: $99.00
Frequency: 22 issues per y
Founded in 1989
Printed in 4 colors on glossy stock

17280 **Software Quality Professional**
American Society for Quality
600 N Plankinton Avenue
Milwaukee, WI 53203

414-272-8575
800-248-1946; Fax: 414-272-1734
help@asq.org
asq.org/pub/sqp/index.html

Elmer Corbin, Chair
Bill Troy, CEO
Brian Savoie, Chief Financial Officer
Andrew Baines, Managing Director, Global
Ann Jordan, General Counsel

Quarterly, peer-reviewed journal for software development professionals that focuses on the subject of quality practice principles in the implementation of software and the development of software systems.
80K Members
Frequency: Quarterly
Founded in 1946

17281 **South Florida Business Journal**
American City Business Journals
120 W Morehead St
Suite 400
Charlotte, NC 28202-1874

704-973-1000
800-486-3289; Fax: 704-973-1001
www.bizjournals.com

Whitney R Shaw, CEO
Megan Foley, Marketing Director
David Harris, Managing Editor

Covers all aspects of business in South Florida.
Cost: $99.00
Frequency: Weekly
ISSN: 1528-0527

17282 **Staffing Management**
SHRM/Society for Human Resource Management
1800 Duke St
Alexandria, VA 22314-3494

703-535-6000
866-898-4724; Fax: 703-535-6474
www.shrm.org
Facebook, Twitter, LinkedIn, Youtube

Susan R Meisinger, CEO
Leon Rubis, Editor

Formerly known as Employment Management Today, this magazine provides information on the latest techniques and trends in recruiting and retaining your most important commodity: your employees.
Cost: $35.00
56 Pages
Frequency: Quarterly
Circulation: 10000
Founded in 1995

17283 **Supermarket News - Retail/Financial**
Fairchild Publications
7 W 34th St
New York, NY 10001-8100

212-630-3880
800-204-4515; Fax: 212-630-3868
custserv@espcomp.com
www.supermarketnews.com

Dan Bagan, Publishing Director
David Orgel, Editor-in-Chief
Christina Veiders, Managing Editor
Joy Kulick, Marketing
Cost: $45.00
Frequency: Weekly
ISSN: 0039-5803
Founded in 1892

17284 **Supervision Magazine**
National Research Bureau
320 Valley St
Burlington, IA 52601-5513

319-752-5415; Fax: 319-752-3421
mail@national-research-bureau.com
www.national-research-bureau.com

Diane M Darnall, President
Teresa Levinson, Editor

Dedicated to providing the most timely and relevant information to today's supervisors and managers.
Frequency: Monthly
Circulation: 1200
Founded in 1930

17285 **Supply Chain Management Review**
Reed Business Information
225 Wyman St
Suite 3
Waltham, MA 02451-1216

781-734-8000; Fax: 781-734-8076
www.reedbusiness.com

Mark Finklestein, President
Frank Quinn, Chief Editor
Susan Lacefield, Associate Editor
Mary Ann Gajewski, Production Manager
Stuart Whayman, CFO

Contains in-depth feature articles on various aspects of Supply Chain Management. SCM is the science of integrating the flow of goods and information from initial souring and purchasing, order processing and fulfillment, production planning and scheduling, inventory management, transportation, distribution and customer service. Each issue delivers in-depth feature articles from the thought leaders in the supply chain community.
Cost: $199.00
Circulation: 12000

17286 **Supply Chain Technology News**
Penton Media

1166 Avenue of the Americas/10th Fl
New York, NY 10036

212-204-4200; Fax: 216-696-6662
information@penton.com
www.penton.com

Jane Cooper, Marketing
Chris Meyer, Director, Corporate Communications

Focuses on the practical application of technology accross a broad range of supply chain functions.

17287 **Tapping the Network Journal**
Quality & Productivity Management Association
300 N Martingale Road
Suite 230
Schaumburg, IL 60173-2407

708-619-2909; Fax: 847-619-3383

William Ginnodo, Editor/Author

This quarterly publication is, By and For Organizational Change Agents. Most articles are written by QPMA members. Its purpose is to share - in a straightforward, factual and practical manner - what has been learned within the authors' organization during the course of a particular change effort. It is provided free to members, and made available to non-member subscribers.

17288 **Training**
50 S 9th Street
Minneapolis, MN 55402

612-333-0471; Fax: 612-333-6526
www.vnu.com

Rob van den Bergh, CEO
Rob Ruijter, CFO
AC Nielsen, Marketing
Founded in 1960

17289 **Warehousing Management**
Reed Business Information
30 Technology Parkway South
Suite 100
Norcross, GA 30092

646-746-6400
800-424-3996; Fax: 646-756-7583
webmaster@reedbusiness.com
www.reedbusiness.com

John Poulin, CEO
John R Johnson, Editor-in-Chief
James Reed, Owner
Jane Burgess, Marketing Director

Warehousing Management targets warehousing and distribution center operations managers with analysis, news, trends, equipment and events.
Circulation: 47185
Founded in 1977

17290 **Workgroup Computing Report**
Patricia Seybold Group
Po Box 783
Needham Heights, MA 02492

617-742-5200
800-826-2424; Fax: 617-742-1028
www.psgroup.com
Twitter

Patricia Seybold, Founder/CEO

Provides information on implementing workflow, document management, groupware, and business process reengineering.
Cost: $440.00
Frequency: Monthly
Mailing list available for rent

17291 **World**
Economist
111 W 57th Street
The Economist Building
New York, NY 10019

212-541-5730; Fax: 212-541-9378

Dudley Fishburn, Editor
David Hanger, Publisher
124 Pages
ISBN: 0-862181-66-6
Printed in 4 colors on glossy stock

17292 **Young Presidents' Organization - Magazine**
Young Presidents' Organization
451 Decker Drive
Suite 200
Irving, TX 75062-3954

972-504-4600; Fax: 972-650-4777
www.ypo.org

Thomas Stauffer, Executive Director
Les Ward, Manager
Frequency: BiAnnual
Circulation: 8000
Printed in on glossy stock

Trade Shows

17293 **AACE Annual Meeting**
AACE International
1265 Suncrest Towne Centre Drive
Morgantown, WV 26505-1876

304-296-8444
800-858-2678; Fax: 304-291-5728
info@aacei.org
www.aacei.org
Facebook, LinkedIn

Andrew S Dowd Jr, Executive Director
Jennie Amos, Marketing/Meetings Manager
Frequency: June

17294 **ACCE Annual Convention**
Association of Chamber of Commerce Executives
1330 Braddock Place
Suite 300
Alexandria, VA 22314

703-998-0072; Fax: 888-577-9883
communications@acce.org
secure.acce.org

Sheree Anne Kelly, President & CEO
Crystal Moore, VP, Professional Development

Convention for chamber of commerce professionals.
Frequency: Annual/July
Founded in 1914

17295 **AHRA Annual Meeting & Exposition**
Association for Medical Imaging Management
490B Boston Post Road
Suite 200
Sudbury, MA 01776

978-443-7591
800-334-2472; Fax: 978-443-8046
info@ahraonline.org
www.ahraonline.org
Facebook, Twitter, LinkedIn

Edward Cronin, Jr., CEO
Sarah Murray, Executive Assistant
Emily Ryan, Membership Coordinator
Debra Murphy, Publications Director

A resource and catalyst for the development of professional leadership in imaging sciences. A driving force toward improving the healthcare environment. Containing 171 booths and 171 exhibits.
5000 Members
Mailing list available for rent: 4000 names at $250 per M

17296 **APQC's Annual Process Conference**
American Productivity and Quality Center
123 N Post Oak Lane
3rd Floor
Houston, TX 77024

800-776-9676
713-681-4020; Fax: 713-681-8578
confregistration@apqc.org
www.apqc.org

Jack Grayson, Founder
Dr. Carla O'Dell, Chairman & CEO
Nancy Troxel, Conference Contact
Perry D Wiggins, Chief Financial Officer
Cathy Hill, Sales & Membership

Conference dedicated to exploring best practices for businesses to improve performance.
500+ Members
Frequency: Annual
Founded in 1977

17297 **APQC's Knowledge Management Conference**
American Productivity and Quality Center
123 N Post Oak Lane
3rd Floor
Houston, TX 77024

800-776-9676
713-681-4020; Fax: 713-681-8578
confregistration@apqc.org
www.apqc.org

Jack Grayson, Founder
Dr. Carla O'Dell, Chairman & CEO
Nancy Troxel, Conference Contact
Perry D Wiggins, Chief Financial Officer
Cathy Hill, Sales & Membership

Conference dedicated to exploring knowledge management in businesses.
500+ Members
Frequency: Annual
Founded in 1977

17298 **ARMA InfoCon**
ARMA International
11880 College Boulevard
Suite 450
Overland Park, KS 66210

913-444-9174
844-565-2120; Fax: 913-257-3855
headquarters@armaintl.org
www.arma.org
Facebook, Twitter, LinkedIn

Nate Hughes, Exec. Dir., Operations
Jennifer Millett, National Accounts Manager
Karen Skaggs, Sales & Event Specialist

Conference, seminar, workshop, banquet, award ceremony and 175 exhibits of micrographics, optical disk, automated document storage and retrieval systems and more technology of interest to information professionals.
3500 Attendees
Frequency: Annual
Founded in 1956

17299 **ASAE Annual Meeting & Exposition**
American Society of Association Executives
1575 I Street NW
Washington, DC 20005

202-626-2723; Fax: 202-371-8315
lholzman@asaecenter.org
annual.asaecenter.org

John Graham, President & CEO
Susan Robertson, Executive Vice President
Ashley Anewalt, Marketing Manager
Sabrina Kidwai, Senior Manager, Public Relations
Melody Jordan-Carr, Senior Director, Member Relations

Exposition for association professionals and industry partners to share resources, information and solutions.
39K Members
Frequency: Annual/August
Founded in 1920

17300 **Administrative Assistants Executive Secretaries Seminar**
PA Douglas & Associates
644 Strander Boulevard
#411
Seattle, WA 98188

206-244-6441; Fax: 780-444-8002
www.padouglas.com

Dr. Paul A Douglas MBA, PhD, CMC, Leader

To provide seminars, workshops and educational materials to individuals from the United States, Canada, and Europe. Includes an intensive three-day workshop for exploring and developing intellectual, organizational and interpersonal abilities.
Founded in 1975

17301 **Association for Services Management**
11031 Via Frontera
Suite A
San Diego, CA 92127

239-275-7887
800-333-9786; Fax: 239-275-0794

John Schoenwald, Executive Director
Jb Wood, President/Ceo

Management convention and exposition.
Frequency: Fall

17302 **Association for Strategic Planning Annual Conference**
Association for Strategic Planning
12021 Wilshire Boulevard
Suite 286
Los Angeles, CA 90025-1200

877-816-2080; Fax: 323-954-0507
www.strategyplus.org
Facebook, Twitter, LinkedIn

Dr Stanley G Rosen, President
Janice Laureen, Executive Director

Nation's premier forum for professional discussion and exchange of information and experiences among strategic planning practitioners.
Frequency: February

17303 **Association for Worksite Health Promotion Annual International Conference**
60 Revere Drive
Suite 500
Northbrook, IL 60062-1577

847-480-9574; Fax: 847-480-9282
www.awhp.org

Liz Freyn, Conference Manager

122 booths of information and supplies to promote and develop quality programs of health and fitness in business and industry. Seminar, workshop, conference, tours and luncheon.
950 Attendees
Founded in 1974

17304 **Association of Management Meeting**
Association of Management
920 Battlefield Boulevard
Suite 100
Chesapeake, VA 23322

757-482-2273; Fax: 757-482-0325
aomgt@aom-iaom.org
www.aom-iaom.org

Dr Karin Klenke, Co-Founder/President
Dr WM A Hamel, CEO
T J Mills, VP Comptroller
800 Attendees
Frequency: Annual

17305 **CFMA Annual Conference & Exhibition**
Construction Financial Management Association
100 Village Boulevard
Suite 200
Princeton, NJ 08540

609-452-8000; Fax: 609-452-0474
info@cfma.org
www.cfma.org

Stuart Binstock, President & CEO
Brian Summers, VP, Operations

A resource for construction financial professionals.
Frequency: Annual/May

17306 **Chief's Edge**
International Association of Fire Chiefs
4025 Fair Ridge Drive
Fairfax, VA 22033-2868

703-273-0911; Fax: 703-273-9363
education@iafc.org
www.iafc.org
Facebook, Twitter

Mark Light, Executive Director & CEO
Lisa Yonkers, Director, Conferences & Education
Jason Nauman, Education & Learning Manager
Leanne Shroeder, Conference Manager

Fire service experts take participants through an intensive program that teaches lessons not taught in any school. Executive leadership program is designed for newly appointed fire chiefs and those preparing to become fire chiefs.
12000 Members
Founded in 1873

17307 **Circulation Managers Association International**
11600 Sunrise Valley Drive
Reston, VA 20191-1412

703-506-1661

Joseph Forsee, Show Manager

100 booths exhibiting products such as news racks, rubber products and software.
225 Attendees
Frequency: June

17308 **Coaching and Teambuilding Skills for Managers and Supervisors**
SkillPath Seminars
6900 Squibb Road
PO Box 2768
Mission, KS 66201-2768

913-623-3900
800-873-7545; Fax: 913-362-4241
webmaster@skillpath.com
www.skillpath.com

One-day workshop to sharpen your leadership skills and boost your team's productivity. Various locations and dates.

17309 **Conf-IRM**
Association for Information Systems
Member Service Center
PO Box 2712
Atlanta, GA 30301-2712

404-413-7445
membership@aisnet.org
aisnet.org

Lise Fitzpatrick, Chief Operating Officer
Robina Wahid, Conference Director

Provides forums for researchers and practitioners to share leading-edge knowledge in the global resource information management area.

17310 **Construction Specifications Institute Annual Show & Convention**
110 South Union Street
Suite 100
Alexandria, VA 22314

703-684-0300
800-689-2900; Fax: 703-684-8436
csi@csinet.org
www.csinet.org
Facebook, Twitter, LinkedIn, Youtube,Slideshare,Flickr

Eugene A Valentine, President
W Richard Cooper, VP

Education sessions that focus on industry topics such as; Business and Professional Development, Design & Pre-Construction Activities, Facility Management, Formats & Documents, Legal, Public Facilities & Communities, Safety & Security, Specialty Construction, and Specifications.
6,000 Attendees
Frequency: Annual
Founded in 1954

17311 **EMA Annual Conference & Exposition**
SHRM/Society for Human Resource Management
1800 Duke Street
Alexandria, VA 22314

703-535-6000
866-898-4724; Fax: 703-535-6474
www.shrm.org/
Facebook, Twitter, LinkedIn, Youtube

Johnny C Taylor Jr, Chairman
Susan Meisinger, President/CEO
Robert O Gonzales, Secretary
Robb E Van Cleave, Treasurer

Conference devoted to employment management issues.
700 Attendees
Frequency: March/April

17312 **FMA Annual Meeting**
Financial Management Association International
University of South Florida
4202 E. Fowler Avenue BSN 3403
Tampa, FL 33620-9951

813-974-2084; Fax: 813-974-3318
fma@coba.usf.edu
www.fma.org

Michelle Lui, Executive Director
Dawn Appleby, Program Assistant
Karen Wright, Special Events Coordinator

The Financial Management Association International (FMA) is the global leader in developing and disseminating knowledge about financial decision making. FMA's members include adademicians and practitioners worldwide.
Founded in 1970

17313 **Fundamentals of Personnel Law for Managers and Supervisors**
Human Resources Council

6900 Squibb Road
PO Box 804441
Kansas City -4441

800-601-4636

Rose Miller, Trainer

One-day seminar covering the legal issues affecting everyday management of employees. Various locations and dates.

17314 **Hartford Conference on Leadership Development & Teambuilding**
SkillPath Seminars
6900 Squibb Road
PO Box 2768
Mission, KS 66201-2768

913-623-3900
800-873-7545; Fax: 913-362-4241
enroll@skillpath.net

Conference teaches practical leadership skills thorough real-life examples, pratical methods and techniques. Suitable for managers, supervisors, team leaders and team members.

17315 **IAMC Conference**
International Association for Conflict Management
1 Liberty Street
New York, NY 5006
872-302-7567
brandon@iafcm.org
iafcm.org/index.php/2017-conference-philadelphia-pa

William Bottom, President-Elect Nominee
Zoe Barsness, President-Elect Nominee
Brandon Charpied, Executive Director

Conference on the topic of conflict management, welcoming scholarly papers covering conflict in religion, government, media, race and communities.
Frequency: Annual
Founded in 1970

17316 **ICSB Annual World Conference**
International Council for Small Business
2201 G Street NW
Suite 315
Washington, DC 20052

202-944-0704; Fax: 202-994-4930
icsb@gwu.edu
www.icsb.org
Facebook, Twitter

Luca Iandoli, President
Dr. Robert S. Lai, President-Elect
Geralyn Franklin, VP/Finance/Control
Ayman El Tarabishy, Executive Director
Michael Battaglia, Operations Manager

Annual business conference attended by entrepreneurs, policy makers, business service providers and researchers.
4000+ Members
Founded in 1955

17317 **Int'l. Association of Healthcare Central Svc. Material Management**
IAHCSMM Annual Conference
213 W Institute Place
Suite 307
Chicago, IL 60610-3195

312-440-0078
800-962-8274; Fax: 312-440-9474
www.iahcsmm.com

Betty Hanna, Executive Director
Marilyn Corida, Secretary/Treasurer
Lisa Huber, President
Bruce T. Bird, President

125 EXHIBITORSlication separates supervisors/directors from technicians.
600+ Attendees
Frequency: Annual

17318 **International Public Management Associatio n for Human Resources Trade Show**
Int'l Public Management Assoc for Human Resources
1617 Duke St
Alexandria, VA 22314-3406

703-549-7100; Fax: 703-684-0948
ipma-hr.org

Neil Reichenberg, Executive Director
Sima Hassassian, COO
Tina Chiappetta, Sr Director Gov't Affairs/Comm
500 Attendees

17319 **International WACRA Conference**
World Assoc for Case Method Research & Application
23 Mackintosh Avenue
Needham, MA 02492-1218

781-444-8982; Fax: 781-444-1548
wacra@rcn.org
www.wacra.org

Dr Hans E Klein, President/Executive Director
Dr Joelle Piffault, Director, Development/Membership
Dr Pavel Zufan, Director, Business/Economics
Dr. Juan Cortes, Director, Public Relations
Dr. Al Rosenbloom, Director, Communications

Conference on Case Method Research & Application
Frequency: Annual, Summer

17320 **Labor-Management Alliance (LMA)**
International Association of Fire Chiefs
4025 Fair Ridge Drive
Suite 300
Fairfax, VA 22033-2868

703-273-0911; Fax: 703-273-9363
jwoulfe@iafc.org
www.iafc.org

Mark Light, Executive Director & CEO
Karin Soyster Fitzgerald, Chief Operations Officer
Lisa Yonkers, Director, Conferences & Education
Jason Nauman, Education & Learning Manager
John Woulfe, Assistant Director, Hazmat

Provides exceptional networking opportunities and dynamic education to foster and enhance cooperative and collaborative labor-management relationships.
Frequency: Annual

17321 **Lean and Six Sigma Conference**
American Society for Quality
600 N Plankinton Avenue
Milwaukee, WI 53203

414-272-8575
800-248-1946; Fax: 414-272-1734
help@asq.org
asq.org/conferences/six-sigma

Elmer Corbin, Chair
Bill Troy, CEO
Brian Savoie, Chief Financial Officer
Andrew Baines, Managing Director, Global
Ann Jordan, General Counsel

Networking event for practitioners in the Lean Six Sigma community. Industries addressed will include operations, manufacturing, transactional, healthcare, financial, service and government.
80K Members
Frequency: Annual/February
Founded in 1946

17322 **New York Social Media Marketing Conference**
SkillPath Seminars
6900 Sqibb Road
PO Box 2768
Mission, KS 66201-2768

913-623-3900
800-873-7545; Fax: 913-362-4241
webmaster@skillpath.com
www.skillpath.com

Steve Nichols, Customer Care Representative
Robb Garr, President

This state-of-the-art conference walks through everything needed to start using social media to drive real business results, even for someone who doesn't know the difference between a tweet and a like button. There's no reason to miss out any longer on the proven, bottom-line benefits of marketing with social media.
Frequency: Semi-Annual, April

17323 **Project Management for IT Professionals**
CompuMaster
6900 Squibb Road
PO Box 2973
Mission, KS 66201-1373

913-362-3900
800-867-4340; Fax: 913-432-4930
compumaster@mcimail.com
www.compumaster.net

Casey Smith, Customer Service

A two-day workshop that will help you meet complex project deadlines and budgets. Held in various locations in November and December. Customization at your location available for groups of twenty or more.

17324 **Society for Advancement of Management, Inc. (SAM)**
Society for Advancement of Management
Corpus Christi - College of Business
6300 Ocean Drive, Unit 5808
Corpus Christi, TX 78412-5808

361-825-3045
888-827-6077; Fax: 361-825-5609
sam@samnational.org
www.samnational.org

Moustafa H. Abdelsamad, President/CEO
Ken E. Byus, Treasurer
Everette Anderson, VP, Sales & Marketing

Featuring speakers, sponsors, presentations, workshops and discussions.
2500 Members
Founded in 1912

17325 **Turnaround Management Association Annual Fall Conference**
Turnaround Management Association
150 S Wacker Drive
Suite 900
Chicago, IL 60606

312-578-6900; Fax: 312-578-8336
info@turnaround.org
www.turnaround.org
Facebook, Twitter, LinkedIn

Lisa Poulin, President
Patrick Lagrange, Chairman
Linda Delgadillo, Executive Director

The only international nonprofit association dedicated to corporate renewal and turnaround management. TMA's 9,000 members in 46 regional chapters comprise a professional community of turnaround practitioners, attorneys, accountants, investors, lenders, venture capitalists, appraiser, liquidators, executive recruiters and consultants. Three international conferences each year offer networking and educational sessions on the latest trends and best practices in the restructuring field.
600 Attendees
Frequency: Annual/Fall

17326 Turnaround Management Association Spring Conference
Turnaround Management Association
150 S Wacker Drive
Suite 900
Chicago, IL 60606
312-578-6900; Fax: 312-578-8336
info@turnaround.org
www.turnaround.org
Facebook, Twitter, LinkedIn
Lisa Poulin, President
Patrick Lagrange, Chairman
Linda Delgadillo, Executive Director
The only international nonprofit association dedicated to corporate renewal and turnaround management. TMA's 9,000 members in 46 regional chapters comprise a professional community of turnaround practitioners, attorneys, accountants, investors, lenders, venture capitalists, appraiser, liquidators, executive recruiters and consultants. Three international conferences each year offer networking and educational sessions on the latest trends and best practices in the restructuring field.
600 Attendees
Frequency: Annual/Spring

17327 VCOS Symposium in the West
International Association of Fire Chiefs
4025 Fair Ridge Drive
Suite 300
Fairfax, VA 22033-2868
703-273-0911; Fax: 703-273-9363
www.iafc.org
Mark Light, Executive Director & CEO
Lisa Yonkers, Director, Conferences & Education
Shannon Gilliland, Assistant Director, Conferences
Sara Stehle, Conference Specialist
Addresses the unique needs of volunteer and combination departmentsincluding transitioning from a volunteer to a combination department, recruitment and retention, leadership and management, staffing and more.
Frequency: Annual

17328 Valve Industry Leadership Forum
Valve Manufacturers Association of America
1050 17th Street NW
Suite 280
Washington, DC 20036-5521
202-331-8105; Fax: 202-296-0378
mmaloneblevins@vma.org
www.vma.org
William S. Sandler, President
Marc Pasternak, Vice President
Malena Malone-Blevins, Meetings Manager
Judy Tibbs, Education Director
Forum for the leaders of companies serving the valve industry.
100 Members
Founded in 1938

17329 Volunteer & Combination Officers Section Symposium in the Sun
International Association of Fire Chiefs
4025 Fair Ridge Drive
Suite 300
Fairfax, VA 22033-2868
703-273-0911; Fax: 703-273-9363
sstehle@iafc.org
www.iafc.org
Mark Light, Executive Director & CEO
Lisa Yonkers, Director, Conferences & Education
Sara Stehle, Conference Specialist
Shannon Gilliland, Assistant Director, Conferences
Addresses the unique needs of volunteer and combination departments including transitioning from a volunteer to a combination department, recruitment and retention, leadership and management, staffing and more.
Frequency: Annual

17330 WACRA Creative Teaching Conference
World Assn. for Case Method Research & Application
23 Mackintosh Ave.
Needham, MA 02492-1218
781-444-8982; Fax: 781-444-1548
www.wacra.org
Dr. Hans E Klein, President/Executive Director
Winter conference on Creative Teaching. A cooperation of WACRA and ACT (Academy for Creative Teaching).
Frequency: Annual, Winter
Founded in 1998

17331 World Conference on Quality and Improvement
American Society for Quality
600 N Plankinton Avenue
Milwaukee, WI 53203
414-272-8575
800-248-1946; Fax: 414-272-1734
help@asq.org
asq.org/conferences/wcqi
Elmer Corbin, Chair
Bill Troy, CEO
Brian Savoie, Chief Financial Officer
Andrew Baines, Managing Director, Global
Ann Jordan, General Counsel
Conference on quality and improvement exploring quality tools, techniques and methodologies.
80K Members
Frequency: Annual
Founded in 1946

Directories & Databases

17332 ABI/INFORM
UMI/Data Courier
620 S 3rd Street
Suite 400
Louisville, KY 40202-2475
800-626-2823; Fax: 502-589-5572
This database contains more than 675,000 citations, appearing in over 900 international periodicals covering business and management related areas.

17333 ACCE Business Directory
Association of Chamber of Commerce Executives
1330 Braddock Place
Suite 300
Alexandria, VA 22314
703-998-0072; Fax: 888-577-9883
bwills@acce.org
secure.acce.org
Sheree Anne Kelly, President & CEO
Ben Wills, Communications & Marketing Director
Sarah Melby, Information & Research Director
Jen Pack, Resource Coordinator
Tamara Philbin, COO & Membership Management
Directory of businesses connected with the Association of Chamber of Commerce Executives, including marketing professionals, management consultants and community development services.
Founded in 1914

17334 APQC's Knowledge Base
American Productivity and Quality Center
123 N Post Oak Lane
3rd Floor
Houston, TX 77024
800-776-9676
713-681-4020; Fax: 713-681-8578
communications@apqc.org
www.apqc.org
Jack Grayson, Founder
Dr. Carla O'Dell, Chairman & CEO
Lisa Higgins, Chief Operating Officer
Perry D Wiggins, Chief Financial Officer
Cathy Hill, Sales & Membership
Collection of best practices and business drivers, benchmarks, metrics and case studies.
500+ Members
Founded in 1977

17335 ARMA International's Buyers Guide
ARMA International
11880 College Boulevard
Suite 450
Overland Park, KS 66215
913-444-9174
844-565-2120; Fax: 913-257-3855
headquarters@armaintl.org
armabuyersguide.org
Facebook, Twitter, LinkedIn
Nick Inglis, Exec. Dir., Content & Programming
Jeff Whited, Sr. Content Writer
Ann Snyder, Manager, Content Development
75-100 companies listed. Free.
Frequency: Annual

17336 Analysis of Workers' Compensation Laws
Chamber of Commerce of the United States
1615 H St Nw
Washington, DC 20062-0002
202-659-6000; Fax: 202-463-5836
www.uschamber.org
Thomas J Donohue, CEO
Jean Hunt, Administrative Assistant
Offers a list of workers' compensation administrators.
Cost: $25.00
Frequency: Annual

17337 Association of Management Consulting Firms
AMCF
380 Lexington Avenue
Suite 1700
New York, NY 10168
212-551-7887; Fax: 212-551-7934
info@amcf.org
www.amcf.org
Elizabeth A Kovacs, President/CEO
Kathleen Fish, Director Programs
Samantha Colon, Executive Administrator
About 50 management consulting firms that are members of ACME.
Cost: $50.00
Frequency: Biennial
Founded in 1929

17338 Business Information Desk Reference: Where to Find Answers to Questions
Palgrave Macmillan
175 5th Ave
New York, NY 10010-7728
212-982-3900; Fax: 212-307-5035
www.ibtauris.com
Bruce McKenzie, President
Stuart Weir, Production Director

Paul Davighi, Marketing Director
Liz Stuckey, Secretary

Over 1,000 print material, online databases and federal agencies covering over 24 business areas are listed.

17339 Business Information Resources - Online Database
Grey House Publishing
4919 Route 22
PO Box 56
Amenia, NY 12501
518-789-8700
800-562-2139; Fax: 518-789-0556
gold@greyhouse.com
gold.greyhouse.com
Facebook, Twitter

Leslie Mackenzie, Publisher
Richard Gottlieb, Editor

This one-stop, business building database provides immediate access to the resources you need for success in the industry of your choice. This is the kind of must have information that, before now, could take hours to find. With a subscription to the Directory of Business Information Resources - Online Database, you'll have immediate access to over 17,000 associations, magazines, journals, newsletters, trade shows, directories, databases, and web sites for 100 industry groups.
Founded in 1981

17340 Business Library
Dow Jones & Company
4300 North Route 1
South Brunswick, NJ 08852
609-520-4000

Covers all types of topics and subjects that are of interest to US business markets.
Frequency: Full-text

17341 Business Opportunities Handbook
Enterprise Magazines
1020 N Broadway
Suite 111
Milwaukee, WI 53202-3157
414-272-9977; Fax: 414-272-9973
www.franchisehandbook.com

Betsy Green, Owner

Over 2,500 listings of franchises, dealers and distributors that offer business opportunities to individuals.
Cost: $5.99
150 Pages
Frequency: Quarterly

17342 Career Guide: Dun's Employment Opportunities Directory
Dun & Bradstreet Information Service
3 Sylvan Way
Parsippany, NJ 07054-3822
973-605-6000; Fax: 973-605-9630

Offers information on more than 5,000 companies, leading employers of the United States, that provide career opportunities in sales, marketing and management.
Cost: $385.00
2700 Pages
Frequency: Annual

17343 Company Intelligence
Information Access Company
362 Lakeside Drive
Foster City, CA 94404-1171
650-378-5200
800-227-8431

Offers company news and financial information with an emphasis placed on hard-to-find privately held companies in the United States and worldwide.

17344 Corporate Technology Database
One Source Information Services
300 Baker Ave
Concord, MA 01742-2131
978-318-4300
800-554-5501; Fax: 978-318-4690
sales@onesource.com
www.onesource.com

Philip J Garlick, President
John Brewer, Vice Chairman
Brad Haigis, VP/Products
Beth Jacaruso, VP/Content

Offers profiles of over 45,000 public and private US corporations and operating units of large corporations that develop or manufacture some 100,000 high-technology products.
Frequency: Directory

17345 Corporate Yellow Book
Leadership Directories
104 5th Ave
New York, NY 10011-6901
212-627-4140; Fax: 212-645-0931
corporate@leadershipdirectories.com
www.leadershipdirectories.com

David Hurvitz, CEO

Contact information for over 48,000 executives at over 1,000 companies and more than 9,000 board members and their outside affiliations.
Cost: $360.00
1,400 Pages
Frequency: Quarterly
ISSN: 1058-2098
Founded in 1986

17346 Directory of Business Information Resources
Grey House Publishing
4919 Route 22
PO Box 56
Amenia, NY 12501
518-789-8700
800-562-2139; Fax: 845-373-6390
books@greyhouse.com
www.greyhouse.com
Facebook, Twitter

Leslie Mackenzie, Publisher
Richard Gottlieb, Editor

The source for contacts in over 98 business areas, from advertising and agriculture to utilities and wholesalers. This carefully researched volume details, for each business industry, the associations representing each industry, the newsletters that keep members current, the magazines and journals that are important to the trade, the top conventions and industry web sites that provide important marketing information. Includes contact names with phone, fax, website and e-mail information.
Cost: $195.00
2300 Pages
Frequency: Annual
ISBN: 1-592371-93-0
Founded in 1981

17347 Directory of Executive Recruiters
Kennedy Information
One Phoenix Mill Lane
Floor 3
Peterboro, NH 03458
603-924-1006
800-531-0007
www.kennedyinfo.com

Lists over 8,900 offices of 5,678 executive search firms in the US, Canada and Mexico. Includes key data and contact info on each firm. Directory is indexed by recruiter specialities, function, industry, key principals, and geography. Corporate edition is specially designed for corporate buyers of search services and search providers.
Cost: $179.95
1180 Pages
Frequency: Annual
ISBN: 1-885922-81-7
ISSN: 0090-6484

17348 Directory of Management Consultants
Kennedy Information
1 Phoenix Mill Lane
Floor 3
Peterborough, NH 03458
603-924-1006
800-531-0007
www.kennedyinfo.com

The premier directory of management consulting firms, published since 1979. The 10th edition profiles more than 2,400 firms in North America. Indexed by services, industries, geography, and key contacts.
Cost: $295.00
850 Pages
Frequency: Biennial
ISBN: 1-885922-69-8
ISSN: 0743-6890
Founded in 1919
Mailing list available for rent: 7600 names at $200 per M

17349 Directory of Outplacement & Career Management Firms
Kennedy Information
One Phoenix Mill Lane
Floor 3
Peterborough, NH 03458
603-924-1006
800-531-0007
www.kennedyinfo.com

Profiles 365 firms in 1,351 offices worldwide and identifies 1,875 key principals. Includes key data on revenues, staff sizes, fees & expense policies, and contact information. Indexed by industry specialty, geography and individual outplacement professional.
Cost: $129.00
606 Pages
ISBN: 1-885922-65-5

17350 Directory of US Labor Organizations
BNA Books
3 Bethesda Metro Center
Suite 250
Bethesda, MA 02814-5377
703-341-3500
800-372-1033; Fax: 800-253-0332
customercare@bna.com
www.bna.com

Josh Eastright, CEO

Over 200 national unions and professional and state employees associations engaged in labor representation are profiled.
Cost: $55.00
110 Pages
Frequency: Annual

17351 Diversity in Corporate America
Hunt-Scanlon Corporation
700 Fairfield Avenue
Stamford, CT 06902
203-352-2920; Fax: 203-352-2930

James A Mueller, Founder
Scott Scanlon, CEO
Smooch S Reynolds, President
A David Brown, Managing Director
John D Delpino, Director - Executive Staffing

2,200 listings of executives responsible for managing corporate diversity in the US.
Cost: $179.00
Frequency: Biennial

17352 **Employee Service Management: NESRA Buyers Directory**
National Employee Services & Recreation Assn
568 Spring Road
Suite D
Elmhurst, IL 60126
630-559-0020; Fax: 630-559-0025
esmahq@esmassn.org
Renee Mula, Editor
Includes a list of over 200 member manufacturers and distributors offering products and services for employee discount programs and employee store merchandise to members.
Frequency: Annual

17353 **Employment, Hours and Earnings**
US Department Of Commerce
200 Constitution Ave Nw
Washington, DC 20210-0001
202-693-5000; Fax: 202-219-8822
webmaster@dol.gov
www.dol.gov
Hilda L Solis, CEO
Sonya Carrion, Director
This database aimed at employees and management cover US employment, hours and earnings.

17354 **Fortune Magazine**
Time Inc./Time Warner
1271 Avenue of the Americas
16th Floor
New York, NY 10020-1393
212-522-1212
800-274-6800; Fax: 212-522-0602
www.timeinc.com
Facebook, Twitter
Laura Lang, CEO
Howard M. Averill, CFO
Leslie Picard, President
Stephanie George, Chief Marketing Officer
John Huey, Editor-in-Chief
FORTUNE is a global leader in business journalism. The magazine has a great history of providing analysis and news critical to business people.
Founded in 1922

17355 **Fortune: Deals of the Year Issue**
Time Inc./Time Warner
1271 Avenue of the Americas
16th Floor
New York, NY 10020-1393
212-522-1212
800-274-6800; Fax: 212-522-0602
www.timeinc.com
Laura Lang, CEO
Howard M. Averill, CFO
Leslie Picard, President
Stephanie George, Chief Marketing Officer
John Huey, Editor-in-Chief
Offers information on 50 of the largest United States corporate financial transactions, including mergers, acquisitions and leveraged buyouts.
Cost: $5.00
Frequency: Annual
Founded in 1922

17356 **Gale Group Management Contents**
Gale/Cengage Learning
2250 Perimeter Park Drive
Suite 300
Morrisville, NC 27560
919-804-6400
800-334-2564; Fax: 919-804-6410
www.infotrac.galegroup.com
Facebook, Twitter, LinkedIn, Youtube
Patrick C Sommers, President
A specialized database that provides current information on business practices and management techniques from key management journals. The database provides theoretical background and practical how to approaches to key management disciplines.
Frequency: Weekly

17357 **International Directory of Executive Recruiters**
Kennedy Information
One Phoenix Mill Lane
Floor 3
Peterborough, NH 03458
603-924-1006
800-531-0007
www.kennedyinfo.com
A comprehensive source of worldwide executive recruiting firms and consultancies. List full contact information for search firms in 60 countries. Indexed by management function, industry, firm, and search firm principals.
Cost: $149.00
800 Pages
ISBN: 1-885922-53-1

17358 **International Registry of OD Professional**
Organization Development Institute
11234 Walnut Ridge Road
Chesterland, OH 44026-1240
440-729-7419
donwcole@aol.com
Dr. Donald W Cole RODC, President
A who's who directory of services and supplies to the industry. Includes: The OD Code of Ethics; a Statement on the Knowledge and Skill Necessary for Competence in O.D.; a listing of not just names and addresses, but the credential of all those registered with us; a list of all the OD organizations in the world and all the OD/OB academic programs in the world.
Cost: $25.00
300 Pages
Frequency: Annual

17359 **Labor Arbitration Information System**
LRP Publications
747 Dresher Road, Suite 500
PO Box 980
Horsham, PA 19044-0980
215-840-0912; Fax: 215-784-9639
webmaster@lrp.com
www.lrp.com
Sandy Johnson, Director/Manager
Comprehensive indexing system for arbitration awards available. The easy-to-use, one-stop indexing system covers all the major arbitration reporting services including AAA, BNA, and CCH.
Cost: $515.00
Frequency: Monthly
Founded in 1977

17360 **Meeting the Needs of Employees with Disabilities**
Resources for Rehabilitation
22 Bonad Road
Winchester, MA 01890
781-368-9094; Fax: 781-368-9096
www.rfr.org
Offers various descriptions of organizations and products that assist those involved in the employment of people with disabilities.
Cost: $42.95
Frequency: Biennial

17361 **SHRM Membership Directory Online**
SHRM/Society for Human Resource Management
1800 Duke St
Alexandria, VA 22314-3494
703-535-6000
866-898-4724; Fax: 703-535-6474
www.shrm.org
Facebook, Twitter, LinkedIn, Youtube
Susan R Meisinger, CEO
Robert O Gonzales, Secretary
Robb E Van Cleave, Treasurer
An exclusive benefit for SHRM members, the SHRM Membership Directory Online is a searchable database catagorized by by name, title, company, company size, job function or location.

17362 **Salem Press Online Platform**
Grey House Publishing
4919 Route 22
PO Box 56
Amenia, NY 12501
800-221-1592; Fax: 201-968-0511
csr@salempress.com
online.salempress.com
The new Salem Press platform houses more than 500 titles including all of Salem's Health, Literature, History and Science titles in addition to select titles from the Grey House Publishing and H.W. Wilson product lines. Online access is free with each print purchase and includes an unlimited number of simultaneous users and remote access.

17363 **Small Business Sourcebook**
Gale/Cengage Learning
27500 Drake Road
Farmington Hills, MI 48331-3535
248-699-4253
800-877-4253; Fax: 877-363-4253
gale.galeord@cengage.com
www.gale.cengage.com
Facebook, Twitter, Youtube
Patrick C Sommers, President
In this two volume annotated guide you'll discover more than 340 specific small business profiles and 99 general small business topics, small business programs and assistance programs in the US, its territories and Canadian provinces and US federal government agencies and offices specializing is small business issues, programs and assistance.
Frequency: Annual/2 Volumes
ISBN: 1-414421-75-3

17364 **Small Business or Entrepreneurial Related Newsletter**
Prosperity & Profits Unlimited
PO Box 416
Denver, CO 80201-0416
303-573-5564
A Doyle, Editor
A mini directory of listings for small businesses.
Cost: $19.95
8 Pages
Frequency: Every 2 Years
Circulation: 2,500
Founded in 1990
Printed in one color on matte stock

17365 **Staffing Industry Sourcebook**
Staffing Industry Analysts
881 Fremont Ave
Suite A3
Los Altos, CA 94024-5637
650-948-9303
800-950-9496; Fax: 650-232-2360
Ron Mester, Manager
Jeff Reeder, Mgr Editor/SI Review
Sona Sharma, Mgr Editor/IT Serv Business Report

Linda Hubbard, Director of Marketing
Leslie Austin, Customer/Membership

Source Book, Facts and Figures for Market Research on the staffing industry.
Cost: $285.00
451 Pages
Frequency: BiAnnual
ISBN: 1-883814-10-3

17366 **Transnational Corporations and Labor: A Directory of Resources**
Third World Resources
1218 E 21st Street
Oakland, CA 94606

510-533-7583; Fax: 510-533-0923

Danielle Mahones, Executive Director

This directory is a source for books, periodicals and audiovisuals on transnational corporations and labor issues.
Cost: $14.95
160 Pages

Industry Web Sites

17367 **http://gold.greyhouse.com**
G.O.L.D Grey House OnLine Databases

Grey House Publishing's online database platform, GOLD, offers Quick Search, Keyword Search and Expert Search for most business sectors including management markets. The GOLD platform makes finding the information you need quick and easy - whether you're a novice searcher or an experienced database user. All of Grey House's directory products are available for subscription on the GOLD platform.

17368 **iafcm.org**
International Association for Conflict Management

Facebook, Twitter

An association for scholars and practitioners to share theories, research, and experience related to conflict management.

17369 **www.afsmi.de**
Association for Services Management International

A global organization dedicated to furthering the knowledge, understanding, and career development of executives, managers and professionals in the high-technology service industry.

17370 **www.amanet.org**
American Management Association

Facebook, Twitter, LinkedIn, YouTube

Association offering a full range of business education and management development programs for individuals and organizations. Members can learn superior business skills and best management practices through a variety of seminars, conferences and special events.

17371 **www.amcf.org**
AMCF

Seeks to unite management consulting firms in order to develop and improve professional standards and practice in the field. Offers information and referral services on management consultants.

17372 **www.aom-iaom.org**
Association of Management

Formerly the Association of Human Resources Management and Organizational Behavior.

17373 **www.apics.org**
APICS Association for Operations Management

The primary purpose of this specific industry group is to educate food and beverage manufacturers on effective marketing strategies, market trends and material management.

17374 **www.apqc.org**
American Productivity and Quality Center

Facebook, Twitter, LinkedIn, YouTube, RSS, Instagram

Organization assisting other organizations by providing ways to improve benchmarking, best practices, process and knowledge management within businesses.

17375 **www.aspanet.org**
American Society for Public Administration

The nation's most respected society representing all forums in the public service arena. Advocate for greater effectiveness in government agents of goodwill and professionalism addressing key public service issues by promoting change at both the local and international levels, we can enhance the quality of lives worldwide.

17376 **www.asq.org**
American Society for Quality

Facebook, Twitter, LinkedIn

Associaion with the mission to promote quality principles concepts and technologies through information, contacts and development opportunities for management professionals in various industries.

17377 **www.awhp.org**
Association for Worksite Health Promotion

Exists to advance the profession of worksite health promotion and the career development of its practitioners and to improve the performance of the programs they administer. Represents a variety of disciplines and worksites, for decision-makers in the areas of health promotion/disease prevention and health-care cost management.

17378 **www.besthealthplans.com**
Best Employers Association

Market and administer medical and dental insurance for large and small groups. Specializes in group insurance and employee benefits.

17379 **www.cmaa.org**
Club Managers Association of America

Professional association for managers of membership clubs. Members manage country, city, athletic, faculty, yacht, town and military clubs. Objectives to promote and advance friendly relations among persons connected with the management of clubs and other associations of similar character.

17380 **www.cmaonline.org**
The Christian Management Association

Designed to assist those involved in the management of Christian organizations.

17381 **www.cmeinc.org**
Center for Management Effectiveness

Conducts management training programs and publishes self-scoring inventories, trainer guides and workbooks on stress management, resolution of conflict, risk taking, decision making and building managerial skills.

17382 **www.expedia.com**
Expedia.com

Internet travel service offers access to airlines, hotels, car rentals, vacation packages, cruises and corporate travel.

17383 **www.fma.org**
Financial Management Association International

Strives to facilitate exchanges of ideas among persons in financial management.

17384 **www.greyhouse.com**
Grey House Publishing

Authoritative reference directories for most business sectors including management markets. Users can search the online databases with varied search criteria allowing for custom searches by product category, geographic area, sales volume, keyword, subject and more. Full Grey House catalog and online ordering also available.

17385 **www.iamc.org**
Industrial Asset Management Council

Members are companies engaged in the management of two or more organizations on a professional client basis.

17386 **www.icmci.org**
ICMCI Intn'l Council of Mgnt Consulting Institutes

For national institutes from around the world that certify professional management consultants; promotes professional development and networking between consultants and the highest standards of performance for clients.

17387 **www.icsb.org**
International Council for Small Business

Management development, resources, and metworking for small business professionals.

17388 **www.imcusa.org/**
IMC-USA Institute of Management Consultants-USA

For management consultants in the United States, organized to establish consulting as a self-regulating profession, meriting public confidence and respect. Toward the achievement of this goal IMC awards the international appelation CMC for certified management consultants.

17389 **www.ioma.com**
Institute of Management & Administration

Organization helps to provides information and guidance to management teams for various businesses.

17390 **www.ipma-hr.org**
International/Public Management Assn For Human Res

Human resource professionals, representing the interests of over 6,000 individual and 1,300 agency members, at the federal, state and local levels of government. Promotes excellence in human resource management through the ongoing development of professional and ethical standards, and through its publishing and educational training programs.

17391 **www.members.aol.com/odinst**
Organization Development Institute

Promotes the understanding of organization development and offers three categories of membership: professional consultant, regular and student.

17392 **www.mgma.com**
Medical Group Management Association

The oldest and largest professional membership association dedicated to medical practice management. Serves their members by offering timely and relevant networking and educational opportunities that keep the members up-to-date on the practice management field.

17393 **www.mt-online.com**
Applied Technology Publications

MT-online.com is the premier source of capacity assurance and best practice solutions for manufacturing, process and service operations worldwide. Online home of Maintenance Technology magazie, the dynamic MT-online.com portal serves the critical technical, business and professional-development needs of engineers, managers and technicians from across all industrial, institutional and commercial sectors.

17394 **www.nacdonline.org**
National Association of Corporate Directors
Fosters research, surveys, seminars and director for corporate. Maintains placement service.

17395 **www.nsha.biz**
National Small Business United
Volunteer-led association. Primary mission is to advocate state and federal policies that are beneficial to small business, the state and the nation and to promote the growth of free enterprise.

17396 **www.pmi.org**
Project Management Institute
Fosters recognition of the need for project management professionalism. Offers professional certification and bestows awards.

17397 **www.promanager.org**
Professional Managers Association
A national membership association representing the interests of professional managers, management officials and non-bargaining unit employees in the federal government.

17398 **www.rbma.org**
Radiology Business Management Association
Promotes management education and study of practice economics, legislative issues and consumer trends.

17399 **www.samnational.org**
Society for Advancement of Management
SAM members come from a variety of disciplines - productions, finance, marketing, accounting and more who share a common bond of interest in becoming stronger managers.

17400 **www.shrm.org**
Society for Human Resource Management

17401 **www.wacra.org**
World Assn for Case Method Research & Application
Members are professional and academicians with an interest in the use of the case method in teaching, training and planning. Interactive, innovative teaching and learning methods.

17402 **www.ypo.org**
Young Presidents' Organization
Members are corporate presidents under the age of fifty whose companies employ at least fifty employees.

Associations

17403 **APICS: Association for Operations Management**
8430 West Bryn Mawr Avenue
Suite 1000
Chicago, IL 60631

773-867-1777
800-444-2742; Fax: 773-639-3000
www.apics.org
Facebook, Twitter, LinkedIn, Youtube

Robert D Boyle, Chair of the Board
Abe Eshkenazi, CSCP, CPA,, Chief Executive Officer
Sharon Rice, Executive Director
Dean Martinez, Executive Vice President
Jennifer K Daniels, Vice President, Marketing

Provides lifelong learning for lifetime success. APICS certification programs, training tools and networking opportunities increase workplace performance. The society supports 20,000 manufacturing and service industry companies worldwide.
Cost: $110.00
60000 Members
Frequency: Membership/Professional
Founded in 1957

17404 **ASM International**
9639 Kinsman Road
Materials Park, OH 44073-0002

440-338-5151
800-336-5152; Fax: 440-338-4634
memberservicecenter@asminternational.org
www.asminternational.org
Facebook, Twitter, LinkedIn

Zi-Kui Liu, President
Diana Essock, Vice President
Raymond V. Fryan, Treasurer
William T. Mahoney, Secretary & CEO

The society for materials engineers and scientists, a worldwide network dedicated to advancing industry, technology and applications of metals and materials. ASM provides information references, education, research and international events.
30K Members
Founded in 1913

17405 **Adhesive & Sealant Council**
7101 Wisconsin Ave
Suite 990
Bethesda, MD 20814-4805

301-986-9700; Fax: 301-986-9795
data@ascouncil.org
www.ascouncil.org
Twitter, LinkedIn

William Allmond, President
Steve Duran, Managing Dir., Membership
Malinda Armstrong, Sr. Dir., Meetings & Expositions
Valeryia Mikharava, Director, Finance & Admin.
Connie Howe, Sr. Director, Technical Services

A North American trade association dedicated to representing the adhesive and sealant industry. ASC is bound by the collective efforts of its members, and strives to improve the industry operating government and strengthen its member companies.
Founded in 1958

17406 **American Bearing Manufacturers Association**
330 North Wabash
Suite 2000
Chicago, IL 60611

202-367-1155; Fax: 202-367-2155
info@americanbearings.org
www.americanbearings.org
Facebook, Twitter

Chris Coughlin, Chair
Ben Succop, Vice Chair
Mark Thorsby, President & Secretary
Amanda Santoro, Director, Membership & Operations
Ashley Stenger, Director, Operations

Promotes bearing standardization. Sponsors Bearing Technical Committee.
Founded in 1917

17407 **American Brush Manufacturers Association**
736 Main Ave, Suite 7
Durango, CO 81301

720-392-2262; Fax: 866-837-8450
info@abma.org
www.abma.org
Facebook, Twitter, LinkedIn

David Park, Executive Director

Trade association representing North American manufacturers of brooms, brushes, mops and rollers.
175 Members
Founded in 1917

17408 **American Gear Manufacturers Association**
1001 N. Fairfax Street
Suite 500
Alexandria, VA 22314-1587

703-684-0211; Fax: 703-684-0242
webmaster@agma.org
www.agma.org
Facebook, Twitter

Matthew Croson, President
Amir Aboutaleb, VP, Technical Division
Cindy Bennett, Executive Director, AGMA Foundation
Jenny Blackford, VP, Marketing
Rebecca Brinkley, Communications Director

Association dedicated to providing technical standards, education, and business information on mechanical power transmission components, including gears and geared speed changers.
495+ Members
Founded in 1916

17409 **American Society for Quality**
600 N Plankinton Avenue
Milwaukee, WI 53203

414-272-8575
800-248-1946; Fax: 414-272-1734
help@asq.org
asq.org
Facebook, Twitter, LinkedIn

Elmer Corbin, Chair
Bill Troy, CEO
Brian Savoie, Chief Financial Officer
Andrew Baines, Managing Director, Global
Ann Jordan, General Counsel

The association's mission is to facilitate continuous improvement and customer satisfaction in manufacturing by sharing ideas, tools, standards and expertise on quality management.
80K Members
Founded in 1946

17410 **American Textile Machinery Association**
201 Park Washington Ct
Falls Church, VA 22046-4527

703-538-1789; Fax: 703-241-5603
info@atmanet.org
www.atmanet.org

Will Motchar, Chairman
Clay D Tyeryar, President/Assistant Treasurer
Harry W. Buzzerd, Jr., ATMA Management Counsel
Susan A. Denston, ATMA Executive Vice President
Carlos F. J. Moore, ATMA International Trade

The American Textile Machinery Association/ATMA's purpose is to advance the common interests of its members, improve business conditions within the US textile machinery industry from a global perspective and market the industry and members' machinery, parts and services.
Founded in 1933

17411 **Association for Rubber Products Manufacturers**
7321 Shadeland Station Way
Suite 285
Indianapolis, IN 46256

317-863-4072; Fax: 317-913-2445
www.arpminc.com

Dave Jentzsch, Director
Chris Wagner, Director
Tim Jarvis, Director
Charlie Braun, Director
Joe Walker, Director

Association dedicated to helping industry executives improve their businesses in rubber products manufacturing through waste reduction, benchmarking, networking, product standards, and educational opportunities provided to its members.
Founded in 2010

17412 **Association of Equipment Manufacturers**
6737 West Washington Street
Suite 2400
Milwaukee, WI 53214-5647

414-272-0943; Fax: 414-272-1170
aem@aem.org
www.aem.org
Facebook, Twitter, LinkedIn, YouTube

Jeffrey R. Reed, Chair

Composed of manufacturers of equipment used in mining and industrial processing. The association promotes and furthers the interests of members in safety, production, engineering, government relations and other industry matters.
900+ Members

17413 **Battery Council International**
330 North Wabash Avenue
Suite 2000
Chicago, IL 60611

312-245-1074; Fax: 312-527-6640
info@batterycouncil.org
www.batterycouncil.org
Facebook, LinkedIn

Mark O. Thornsby, CAE, Executive Vice President

A not-for-profit trade association formed to promote the interests of an international lead-acid battery industry.
265 Members
Founded in 1924

17414 **Contract Packaging Association**
One Parkview Plaza
Suite 800
Oakbrook Terrace, IL 60181

630-544-5053; Fax: 630-544-5055
info@contractpackaging.org
www.contractpackaging.org
Twitter, LinkedIn

Vicky Smitley, President
Chris Nutley, Past President
Tim Koers, Vice President
John Mazelin, Executive Director
Mark O' Malley, Treasurer

Formed for contract packaging firms and those businesses related to them. Promotes the growth and welfare of member firms.
155 Members
Founded in 1992

17415 **Conveyor Equipment Manufacturers Association (CEMA)**
5672 Strand Ct.
Suite 2
Naples, FL 34110

239-514-3441; Fax: 239-514-3470
kim@cemanet.org
www.cemanet.org
Facebook, Twitter, LinkedIn, YouTube

Paul Ross, President
E.A. Thompson, Vice President
Robert Reinfried, Executive Vice President
Noel Bell, Director
Bob Callahan, Director

CEMA seeks to support manufacturers of conveyors and conveying systems. The association sponsors an annual Engineering Conference that allows members to meet and develop the industry standards that affect the conveyor industry.
Founded in 1933

17416 **Flexible Packaging Association**
185 Admiral Cochrane Drive
Suite 105
Annapolis, MD 21401

410-694-0800; Fax: 410-694-0900
fpa@flexpack.org
www.flexpack.org

Marla Donahue, President

One of the leading trade associations for converters of flexible packaging and suppliers to the industry. Also provides a wealth of information to its members through focused services and benefits of membership.

17417 **Grocery Manufacturers Association**
1350 Eye St NW
Suite 300
Washington, DC 20005-3377

202-639-5900; Fax: 202-639-5932
info@gmaonline.org
Facebook, Twitter, RSS

Pamela G Bailey, President
Jim Flannery, Senior Executive Vice President
Dr. Leon Bruner, DVM, Ph.D., Senior Vice President
Louis Finkel, Executive Vice President
Sean Darragh, Executive Vice President, Global

Manufacturers of food and nonfood products sold through the grocery trade. US sales are more than $500 billion, GMA members employ more than 2.5 million workers in the nation.
135 Members
Founded in 1908

17418 **International Packaged Ice Association**
238 East Davis Blvd
Suite 213
Tampa, FL 33606

813-258-1690
jane@packagedice.com
www.packagedice.com
Facebook, YouTube

Bob Morse, Chairman
Bo Russell, Vice Chairman/Treasurer
John Smibert, Secretary/Assistant Treasurer
Mike Ringstaff, Associate Member

Manufacturers and distributors of ice and their suppliers.
150 Members
Founded in 1917

17419 **Manufacturers' Agents National Association**
6321 W. Dempster Street
Suite 110
Morton Grove, IL 60053

949-859-4040
877-626-2776; Fax: 949-855-2973
MANA@MANAonline.org
www.manaonline.org
Facebook, Twitter, LinkedIn, YouTube, Google+

ken McGregor, Chairman
Charles Cohon, CPMR, President and CEO
Jerry Leth, Vice President and General Manager
Lisa Ball, Member Services Coordinator
Doug Bower, Director of Strategic Alliances

Association for independent agents and firms representing manufacturers and other businesses in specified territories on a commission basis, including consultants and associate member firms interested in the manufacturer/agency method of marketing.
Founded in 1947

17420 **Material Handling Institute**
8720 Red Oak Boulevard
Suite 201
Charlotte, NC 28217-3996

704-676-1190; Fax: 704-676-1199
gbaer@mhi.org
www.mhi.org
Facebook, Twitter, LinkedIn, YouTube

George Prest, CEO
Brian Reaves, Executive Vice President
Donna Varner, Sr. Executive Administrator
Laurie Walker, Sr. Membership Coordinator
Greg Baer, Sales Director

Association for the material handling industry, offering industry groups, education, events and programming to support companies and professionals. Members include material handling and logistics equipment companies, software manufacturers, consultants and logistics providers.
800 Members
Founded in 1945

17421 **National Association of Display Industries**
4651 Sheridan Street
Suite 470
Hollywood, FL 33021

954-893-7300; Fax: 954-893-7500
www.nadi-global.com

Klein Merriman, Executive Director
Tracy Dillon, Director Communications

A leading association for the visual merchandising profession. As visual merchandising has evolved over the years into playing an integral role in retail, NADI has always taken the lead in information and educating members. The association's already significant support for the visual design profession has grown with NADI's exclusive sponsorship of GlobalShop's Visual Merchandising Show and StoreXpo.
350 Members
Founded in 1942

17422 **National Association of Manufacturers**
733 10th Street NW
Suite 700
Washington, DC 20001

202-637-3000
800-814-8468; Fax: 202-637-3182
manufacturing@nam.org
www.nam.org
Facebook, Twitter, LinkedIn, Youtube, RSS, Flickr

Gregg M. Lundgren, Chairman
John F. Lundgren, Vice Chairman
Jay Timmons, President
Linda E. Kelly, Senior Vice President, Legal
Richard I. Klein, Senior Vice President

Enhances the competitiveness of manufacturers and improves American living standards by shaping a legislative and regulatory environment conductive to US economic growth and to increase understanding among policy makers, the media and the general public about the importance of manufacturing to America's economic strength.
14000 Members
Founded in 1895

17423 **National Automatic Merchandising Association**
20 N Wacker Dr.
Suite 3500
Chicago, IL 60606

312-346-0370
800-331-8816; Fax: 312-704-4140
www.namanow.org
Facebook, Twitter, x, YouTube, Instagram

Carla Balakgie, President & CEO

Association serving the convenience services industry.
1250+ Members
Founded in 1936

17424 **North American Punch Manufacturers Association**
21 Turquoise Avenue
Naples, FL 34114

239-775-7245; Fax: 239-775-7245
www.exactapunch.com/associations.htm

Robert E May, Executive Secretary

Principal program of NAPMA is the standardization of all punches, dies and retainers manufactured by the various member companies.
23 Members
Founded in 1963

17425 **Power Transmission Distributors Association**
230 West Monroe Street
Suite 1410
Chicago, IL 60606-4703

312-516-2100; Fax: 312-516-2101
ptda@ptda.org
www.ptda.org
Twitter, LinkedIn

Jim Williams, President
Ann Arnott, Executive Vice President & CEO
Brenda Holt, Membership Director
Andrea Lebron, Operations Manager
Ginger Wheeler, Marketing & Communications Director

Association whose members are industrial power transmission/motion control distributor firms dealing in equipment such as bearings, belts, drives, motors, gears, couplings, clutches and brakes. The association offers member companies development programs and networking opportunities.
Founded in 1960

17426 **Pressure Vessel Manufacturers Association**
800 Roosevelt Rd.
Building C,Suite 312
Glen Ellyn, IL 60137

630-942-6590; Fax: 630-790-3095
info@pvma.org
www.pvma.org/

Rick Fryda, President
Bill Kahl, Vice President
Brooke Cornard, Secretary/Treasurer
GregÿMc Rae, Director
Michael Pischke, Immediate Past President

Members are manufacturers of ASME code pressure vessels and suppliers, components and services to pressure vessel manfacturers.
31 Members
Founded in 1975

17427 **Production and Operations Management Society**
Dept. of Management-Univ. of Baltimore
1420 N Charles Street
Baltimore, MD 21201-5720

410-837-4727; Fax: 410-837-5675
www.poms.org/

Sushil Gupta, PhD, Executive Director
Chelliah Sriskandarajah, Ph.D., Associate Executive Director
Metin €akanyildirim, Associate Professor of Operations

Members are professionals and academics with an interest in production and operations management.
1200 Members
Founded in 1989

17428 **Refractories Institute**
1300 Sumner Avenue
Cleveland, OH 44115

216-241-7333; Fax: 216-241-0105
www.refractoriesinstitute.org

Robert Crolius, President

National trade association for refractory manufacturers, suppliers of equipment and raw materials and installers of refractory products.
80 Members
Founded in 1951

17429 **Remanufacturing Industries Council**
RICI
4401 Fair Lakes Ct
Suite 210
Fairfax, VA 22033-3848

FAX 703-968-2878
www.rici.org
Facebook, LinkedIn, Google+

Larry Rice, CEO

A coalition of associations and companies in the remanufacturing industry.
Founded in 1997

17430 **Remanufacturing Institute**
Po Box 48
Lewisburg, PA 17837

570-523-0992; Fax: 705-555-5555

Ron Giuntini, Executive Director

A coalition of associations and companies in the entire manufacturing industry. There are over 73,000 companies in this industry. Our goal is to unite them into a powerful organization.
11 Members
Founded in 1997

17431 **The Association for Manufacturing Technology**
7901 Jones Branch Drive
Suite 900
McLean, VA 22102-4206

703-893-2900
800-524-0475; Fax: 703-893-1151
amt@amtonline.org
www.amtonline.org
Facebook, Twitter, LinkedIn, YouTube

Douglas K. Woods, President
Rebecca Stahl, Chief Financial Officer
Kimberly L. Brown, Member Services Director
Peter R. Eelman, VP, Exhibitions & Business Dev
Amber L. Thomas, VP, Marketing & Communications

Represents and supports the U.S.-based manufacturing technology industry, including distributors, producers and service providers. The association offers essential programs and services that help its members gain global recognition.

17432 **The Benchmarking Network**
4606 Fm 1960 Rd W
Suite #250
Houston, TX 77069-4617

281-440-5044; Fax: 281-440-6677
Facebook, Twitter

AMBC is a focused group of manufacturing process improvement professionals that looks to identify the best practices surrounding manufacturing issues for the overall operations of the members.

17433 **Ultrasonic Industry Association**
PO Box 2307
Dayton, OH 45401-2301

937-586-3725; Fax: 937-586-3699
uia@ultrasonics.org
www.ultrasonics.org

Mark Hodnett, President
Mark Schafer, VP
Ron Stault, Treasurer
Janet Devine, Secretary

Improving processes, techniques and materials through the application of ultasonic technology.
70 Members
Founded in 1956

17434 **Unified Abrasives Manufacturers' Association**
30200 Detroit Road
Cleveland, OH 44145-1967

440-899-0010; Fax: 440-892-1404
uama.org

Allen Donahue, President
Brian Goers, Vice President
Jeff Wherry, Managing Director
Fred Rodgers, Director
Christian Pfeifer, Director

The mission of the association is to support the manufacturing and marketing of abrasive products by providing members with knowledge, networking opportunities, industry standards and more.
Founded in 1999

17435 **United Association of Manufacturers Representatives**
P.O. Box 4216
Dana Point, CA 92669

949-481-5214; Fax: 417-779-1576
info@uamr.com
www.uamr.com/

Karen Kittrell Mazzola, Executive Director

Benefits manufacturers and independent sales representatives and is a national marketing association.
3,000 Members
Founded in 1965

17436 **Valve Manufacturers Association of America (VMA)**
1050 17th Street NW
Suite 280
Washington, DC 20036-5521

202-331-8105; Fax: 202-296-0378
spartyke@vma.org
www.vma.org

William S. Sandler, President
Marc Pasternak, Vice President
Malena Malone-Blevins, Meetings Manager
Judy Tibbs, Education Director
Abby Brown, Education & Training Coordinator

Trade association representing manufacturers of valves, actuators and controls. The association offers supports in the form of meetings, publications, education and networking.
100 Members
Founded in 1938

17437 **Waste Equipment Technology Association**
4301 Connecticut Ave Nw
Suite 300
Washington, DC 20008-2304

202-244-4700
800-424-2869; Fax: 202-966-4824
www.wasterecycling.org
Facebook, Twitter, LinkedIn, Youtube

Mike Savage, Chairman
Sharon H. Kneiss, President and CEO
Philip Hagan, Director, Safety
Sheila R. Alkire, Director, Education
Catherine Maimon, Manager, Meetings

Manufacturers of waste handling, collection and processing equipment.
Founded in 1972

Newsletters

17438 **Advanced Manufacturing Now**
Society of Manufacturing Engineers
1 SME Drive
Dearborn, MI 48128

313-425-3000
800-733-4763; Fax: 313-425-3400
service@sme.org
advancedmanufacturing.org

Jeffrey M. Krause, CEO
Alan Rooks, Editor-in-Chief
James A. Lorincz, Senior Editor
Patrick Waurzyniak, Senior Editor

News on manufacturing and new technologies.
Frequency: Weekly

17439 **Infocus Newsletter**
319 SW Washington Street
Suite 710
Portland, OR 97204-2618

503-227-3393; Fax: 503-274-7667

Lea Anne A Fuchs, President
Andy Palatka, Executive Director
Tonya Macalino, Adversiting and Sales

Infocus is a newsletter focused on industry topics and products.
Cost: $75.00
Circulation: 1,100
Founded in 1960
Mailing list available for rent: 1M names at $200 per M

17440 **Innovators Digest**
InfoTeam
PO Box 15640
Plantation, FL 33318-5640

954-473-9560; Fax: 954-473-0544

Merton Allen, Editor

A multidisciplinary publication covering developments in science, engineering, products, markets, business development, manufacturing and other technological developments having industrial or commercial significance.
Frequency: Bi-Annual

17441 **Intelligent Manufacturing**
Lionheart Publishing

2555 Cumberland Pkwy Se
Suite 299
Atlanta, GA 30339-3921

770-432-2551; Fax: 770-432-6969
llewellyn@lionhrtpub.com

John Llewellyn, Publisher
David Blanchard, Editor

Provides expert solutions to manufacturing professionals covering production problems, developments in manufacturing systems.
Cost: $20.00
Circulation: 1,598

17442 MHI Newswire
Material Handling Institute
8720 Red Oak Boulevard
Suite 201
Charlotte, NC 28217-3996

704-676-1190; Fax: 704-676-1199
shani@naylor.com
www.mhisolutionsmag.com

George Prest, CEO
Brian Reaves, Executive Vice President
Carol Miller, VP, Marketing & Communications
Shani Calvo, Editor

eNewsletter published by the Material Handling Institute (MHI), covering legislative news affecting the material handling industry.
800 Members
Frequency: Weekly
Founded in 1945

17443 Manufacturing Technology
National Technical Information Service
5285 Port Royal Rd
Springfield, VA 22161-0001

703-605-6000; Fax: 703-605-6900
info@ntis.gov
www.ntis.gov

Linda Davis, VP
Patrik Ekstr"m, Business Development Manager
Reuel Avila, Managing Director

Covers CAD/CAM, robotics, robots, productivity, manufacturing, planning, processing and control, plant design and computer software.

17444 Noise Regulation Report
Business Publishers
2222 Sedwick Drive
Durham, NC 27713

800-223-8720; Fax: 800-508-2592
custserv@bpinews.com
www.bpinews.com

Exclusive coverage of airport, highway, occupational and open space noise, noise control and mitigation issues.
Cost: $511.00
10 Pages
Frequency: 12 per year
Printed in on matte stock

17445 RPA News
Retail Packaging Association
105 Eastern Ave.
Suite 104
Annapolis, MD 21403

410-940-6459; Fax: 410-263-1659
info@retailpackaging.org
www.retailpackaging.org
Facebook, Twitter, Pinterest, Instagram

Frequency: bi-monthly
Founded in 1989

17446 Service Management
National Association of Service Management
PO Box 250796
Milwaukee, WI 53225

414-466-6060; Fax: 414-466-0840
www.nasm.com

Don Buelow, Publisher
Caryn Anderson, Editor
Ken Cook, Treasurer

Offers information on manufacturing and service companies.
40 Pages
Frequency: Quarterly
Circulation: 300

17447 Spotlight
Power Transmission Distributors Association
230 West Monroe Street
Suite 1410
Chicago, IL 60606-4703

312-516-2100; Fax: 312-516-2101
ptda@ptda.org
www.ptda.org/resources/ptda-publications.aspx

Jim Williams, President
Ann Arnott, Executive Vice President & CEO
Brenda Holt, Membership Director
Andrea Lebron, Operations Manager
Ginger Wheeler, Marketing & Communications Director

Newsletter containing content on industry and PTDA association news and policy updates for companies dealing in industrial power transmission/motion control equipment.
Frequency: Bi-Monthly
Circulation: 3000+
Founded in 1960

17448 Transmissions
Power Transmission Distributors Association
230 West Monroe Street
Suite 1410
Chicago, IL 60606-4703

312-516-2100; Fax: 312-516-2101
ptda@ptda.org
www.ptda.org/resources/ptda-publications.aspx

Jim Williams, President
Ann Arnott, Executive Vice President & CEO
Brenda Holt, Membership Director
Andrea Lebron, Operations Manager
Ginger Wheeler, Marketing & Communications Director

Newsletter containing content on industry trends for companies dealing in industrial power transmission/motion control equipment.
Circulation: 4300+
Founded in 1960

Magazines & Journals

17449 APICS: The Performance Advantage
APICS Association for Operations Management
5301 Shawnee Road
Alexandria, VA 22312-2317

703-548-8851; Fax: 703-354-8106
webmaster@apics.org
www.apics.org

Doug Kelly, Editor
Jennifer Procter, Managing Editor
Jeffery Raynes, CEO

Provides comprehensive articles on enterprise resources planning, supply chain management, e-business, materials management and production and inventory management.
Cost: $65.00
64 Pages
Circulation: 66000
ISSN: 1056-0017
Mailing list available for rent: 40,000 names at $100 per M
Printed in 4 colors on glossy stock

17450 Adhesives & Sealants
Business News Publishing Company
PO Box 400
Flossmoor, IL 60422

708-922-0761; Fax: 708-922-0762
mcphersont@bnpmedia.com
www.adhesivesmag.com

Susan Love, Publisher
Teresa Mc Pherson, Editor
Kari Rowe, Circulation Manager
Violeta Ivezaj, Senior Marketing Manager
Cost: $33.00
Frequency: Monthly
Circulation: 15000
Founded in 1926

17451 Adhesives Age
2 Grand Central Tower
140 East 45th Street,40th Floor
New York, NY 10017

212-884-9528; Fax: 212-884-9514
ltattum@chemweek.com
www.chemweek.com

Lyn Tattum, Group Vice President/Publisher
Joe Minnella, Global Sales Director

Adhesives Age provides readers with vital information: global industry coverage of the development, manufacture, and application of adhesives, sealants, and related products.
Cost: $75.00
62 Pages
Frequency: Weekly
Circulation: 22994
ISSN: 0001-821X
Founded in 1958
Mailing list available for rent
Printed in 4 colors on glossy stock

17452 Advanced Materials & Processes
ASM International
9639 Kinsman Road
Materials Park, OH 44073-0002

440-338-5151
800-336-5152; Fax: 440-338-4634
magazines@asminternational.org
www.asminternational.org

William T. Mahoney, Secretary & CEO
Joanne Miller, Editor
Vicki Burt, Managing Editor

AM&P is the monthly technical magazine from ASM International, designed to keep readers aware of leading-edge developments and trends in engineering materials - metals and alloys, engineering polymers, advanced ceramics, and composites - and the methods used to select, process, fabricate, test, and characterize them.
30K Members
Frequency: Monthly
Circulation: 23000
Founded in 1913

17453 American Fastener Journal
Tom Massar
6759 Oakfair Ave
Columbus, OH 43235

614-766-9669
800-528-1164; Fax: 614-766-9115
tom@fastenerjournal.com
www.fastenerjournal.com

Tom Massar, President/Publisher

This journal for the fastener industry covers technical articles, inspections, quality assurance, materials applications, specifications and standards, as well as manufacturer, distributors and supplier profiles. Publishes annual buyers

guide - The American Fastener Source Guide
Cost: $45.00
Circulation: 13000
Founded in 1981
Printed in 4 colors on glossy stock

17454 **American Funeral Director**
Kates-Boylston Publications
11300 Rockville Pike
Suite 1100
Rockville, MD 20852

800-500-4585
800-500-4585; Fax: 732-730-2515
www.kates-boylston.com

Adrian F Boylston, Publisher
Thomas Parmalee, Executive Director
Amy Fidalgo, Production Manager

Articles on funeral home construction, finance, mortuary law, shipment of human remains by air transportation, sales and display methods, advertising and public relations, new equipment and other association activiies. Also includes personnel news about funeral directors and related supply firms.
Cost: $49.95
Frequency: Monthly
Circulation: 12168
Founded in 1918

17455 **CNC West**
Arnold Publications
14340 Bolsa Chica Avenue E
PO Box 100
Westminster, CA 92684-100

714-899-0733; Fax: 714-899-0738
larnold@cnc-west.com
www.cnc-west.com

Shawn Arnold, Publisher
Chuck Bush, Editor
Shawn Arnold, CEO/President
Shawn Arnold, Circulation Manager
Shawn Arnold, Marketing Manager

News and trends on western jobshops and manufacturers
Cost: $32.50
Circulation: 22000
Founded in 1981
Printed in 4 colors on glossy stock

17456 **Card Manufacturing**
International Card Manufacturing Association
PO Box 727
Princeton Junction, NJ 08550-727

609-799-4900; Fax: 609-799-7032
info@icma.com
www.icma.com

Lynn McCullough, Association Manager
Jeffrey E Barnhart, Communications Manager
Kaitlin Friedmann, Communications Manager
Al Vrancart, Founder

Advertiser supported trade magazine featuring industry news and features on all aspects of the plastic card production worldwide, and the news of the ICMA.
Cost: $75.00
Circulation: 3000

17457 **Coatings World**
Rodman Publishing
70 Hilltop Rd
Suite 3000
Ramsey, NJ 07446-1150

201-825-2552; Fax: 201-825-0553
info@rodpub.com
www.nutraceuticalsworld.com
Facebook, Twitter, LinkedIn

Rodman Zilenziger Jr, President
Matt Montgomery, VP

Coatings World is directed at industry personnel concerned with developing and manufacturing paints, coatings, adhesives and sealants. Feature articles and industry news are directed at chemists, formulators and all levels of management that must keep abreast of technical products and market developments.
Cost: $50.00
136 Pages
Frequency: Monthly
Circulation: 17315
ISSN: 1527-1129
Mailing list available for rent
Printed in 4 colors on glossy stock

17458 **Composites Fabrication**
Composites Fabricators Association
1010 N Glebe Rd
Suite 450
Arlington, VA 22201-4749

703-525-0714; Fax: 703-525-0743
info@acmanet.org
www.acmanet.org/

Elly Shariat, Marketing Manager
Andy Rusnak, Editor
Roxanne Fraver, Marketing & Circulation
Sabeena Hickman, Deputy Director
Jessica Howard, Production Manager

Presents information on new technology, trends and techniques for manufacturers in the fiberglass and composites industry.
Cost: $41.00
114 Pages
Circulation: 8000
ISSN: 1084-841X
Printed in 4 colors on glossy stock

17459 **Consumer Goods Technology**
Edgell Communications
4 Middlebury Boulevard
Randolph, NJ 07869

973-252-0100; Fax: 973-252-9020
www.consumergoods.com

Andrew Gaffney, Group Publisher
Steve Rosenstock, Publisher
Tim Clark, Editor-in-Chief
Alliston Ackerman, Assistant Editor
Pat Wisser, Production Manager

Provides case histories, technology overviews, new products and industry news to assist corporations and management in the consumer goods industry.
Frequency: Monthly
Circulation: 25000
Founded in 1984

17460 **Contingency Planning & Management**
Witter Publishing Corporation
20 Commerce Street
Flemington, NJ 08822

908-788-0343; Fax: 908-788-3782
www.witterpublishing.com

Bob Joudanin, Publisher
Paul Kirvan, Editor In Chief
Courtney Writter, Circulation Manager
Andrew Witter, President

Serves the fields of financial/banking, manufacturing industrial, transportation, utilities, telecommunications, health care, government, insurance and other allied fields.
Frequency: Monthly
Founded in 1987

17461 **Contract Management**
National Contract Management Association
1912 Woodford Road
Vienna, VA 22182-3728

703-489-9231
800-344-8096; Fax: 703-448-0939
memberservices@ncmahq.org
www.ncmahq.org

Amy Miedema, Editor-in-Chief
Neal Couture, Executive Director

It covers the myriad aspects of government and commercial contract management. News and features provide information on such topics as procurement policy, on-the-job techniques, regulations, case law, ethics, contract administration, electronic commerce, international and small business matters, education and career development.
Cost: $75.00
80 Pages
Frequency: Monthly
Circulation: 22000
Founded in 1959
Printed in 4 colors on glossy stock

17462 **Control Design**
Putman Media
555 W Pierce Rd
Suite 301
Itasca, IL 60143-2626

630-467-1300; Fax: 630-467-0197
lgoldberg@putman.net
www.putman.net

John Cappelletti, President
Mike Bacidore, Editor-in-Chief/Publisher
Anetta Gauthier, Production Manager
Lori Goldberg, Operations Manager

Markets to the manufacturing facilities under the government's standard industry classification (SIC) code 35, which manufacture a broad range of products from turbines, conveyors and machine tools to food processing, printing presses and computers.
Cost: $96.00
Circulation: 50,046
ISSN: 1094-3366
Founded in 1938
Printed in 4 colors

17463 **Design News**
Reed Business Information
30 Technology Parkway South
Suite 100
Norcross, GA 30092

646-746-6400
800-424-3996; Fax: 646-756-7583
webmaster@reedbusiness.com
www.reedbusiness.com

John Poulin, CEO
Karen Auguston Field, Editor-in-Chief
James Reed, Owner

Informs professionals in the technology industry of all the latest in new product introductions in fields such as bearings, fastening/joining and new technology.
Circulation: 170000

17464 **Distributor's Link**
4297 Corporate Sq
Naples, FL 34104-4754

239-643-2713
800-356-1639; Fax: 239-643-5220
leojcoar@linkmagazine.com
www.linkmagazine.com/

Maryann Marzocchi, President
Tracey Lumia, Director of Sales and Marketing

Information aimed at the fastener distributors nationwide.
Cost: $45.00
Frequency: Quarterly
Circulation: 50000
Founded in 1975

17465 **Edplay**
Fahy-Williams Publishing

PO Box 1080
Geneva, NY 14456-8080

315-789-0458
800-344-0559; Fax: 315-789-4263
www.edplay.com

Kevin Fahy, Publisher
Tina Manzer, Editorial Director
Mark Stash, Art Director
Alyssa Lafaro, Associate Editor

Serves toy manufacturers and dealers. Offers product reviews, industry profiles, and reader surveys.
Circulation: 13000
Founded in 1984

17466 **Fastener Technology International**
Initial Publications
PO Box 5451
Akron, OH 44334-0451

330-864-2122; Fax: 330-864-5298
mcnulty@fastenertech.com
www.fastenertech.com

Job Lippincott, Publisher
Michael J. McNulty, Vice President and Editor

Contains articles on company profiles, new equipment, literature, products, fastener topics and patents.
Cost: $40.00
Circulation: 13,000
Founded in 1981
Printed in 4 colors on glossy stock

17467 **Fastening**
Mike McGuire
293 Hopewell Drive
Powell, OH 43065-9350

614-848-3232
800-848-0304; Fax: 614-848-5045
www.fastenerjournal.com

Mike McGuire, Publisher

In-depth and up-to-date information about fastening products, design/applications, people, companies, fastening industry events and specifications.
Cost: $30.00
Frequency: Quarterly
Circulation: 28,000
Founded in 1995
Printed in 4 colors on glossy stock

17468 **ITE Solutions**
Institute of Industrial Engineers
25 Technology Pkwy S
Suite 150
Norcross, GA 30092-2946

770-449-0461; Fax: 770-263-8532
webmaster@iienet.org

17469 **InTech**
Instrumentation, Systems,and Automation Society
67 Alexander Drive
Research Triangle Park, NC 27709

919-549-8411; Fax: 919-990-9434
info@isa.org
www.isa.org

Richard Simpson, Publisher
Greg Hale, Editor
Rob Renner, Executive Officer
Chip Lee, Publication Director

Regular issue features include new product developments, new processes, research updates and general industry news.
Cost: $75.00
Frequency: Monthly
Circulation: 67000
Founded in 1945

17470 **Industrial Equipment News**
Thomas Publishing Company
5 Penn Plz
Suite 10
New York, NY 10001-1860

212-695-0500
800-733-1127; Fax: 212-290-7362
www.thomaspublishing.com

Carl Holst-Knudsen, CEO
Joseph Rosta, Editor-in-Chief
Marie Urbanowicz, Marketing Manager

Serves the industrial field including manufacturing, mining, utilities, construction, transportation,governmental establishments, and educational services.
Frequency: Monthly
ISSN: 0019-8258
Founded in 1898

17471 **Industrial Maintenance & Plant Operation**
Reed Business Information
199 East Badger Road
Suite 201
Madison, WI 53713

973-920-7787; Fax: 973-920-7531
hpendrak@reedbusiness.com
www.impomag.com

Scott Sward, Publisher
Rick Carter, Editor-in-Chief
R Reed, Owner
Kyle Orr, Circulation Manager
Hank Pendrak, Marketing Director
Circulation: 100000
Founded in 1975

17472 **Industrial Market Place**
Wineberg Publications
7842 Lincoln Avenue
Skokie, IL 60077

847-676-1900
800-323-1818; Fax: 847-676-0063
www.industrialmktpl.com

Joel Wineberg, President
Jackie Bitensky, Editor

Has advertisements on machinery, industrial and plant equipment and services and industrial auctions in each issue.
Cost: $175.00
Circulation: 14000
Founded in 1951
Mailing list available for rent: 120 names at $70 per M
Printed in 4 colors on glossy stock

17473 **Job Shop Technology**
Edward Publishing
16 Waterbury Road
Prospect, CT 06712-1215

203-758-4474
800-317-0474; Fax: 203-758-3427
www.jobshoptechnology.com

Mark W Shortt, Editor
Cindy Wilkinson, Circulation Director

Published to aid product manufacturers who outsource parts and manufacturing services. Specializes in manufacturing processes for the metals, plastics, rubber, and electronics industries, including virtually any outsourced manufacturing service.
Frequency: Quarterly
Circulation: 100,000
Founded in 1986
Mailing list available for rent: 90875 names at $125 per M
Printed in 4 colors on glossy stock

17474 **Journal of Coatings Technology**
Federation of Societies for Coatings Technology
527 Plymouth Rd
Suite 415
Plymouth Meetin, PA 19462-1641

610-940-0777; Fax: 610-940-0292
www.coatingstech.org

Robert F Ziegler, Publisher
Patricia D Ziegler, Administrative Assistant
Shelby Ferguson, Administrative Assistant
Chris Hobson, Communications Manager
Lance Edwards, Director

For the industrial and service organizations in paint and manufacturing plants, raw materials suppliers for coatings, printing inks and sealants.
Cost: $120.00
Frequency: Monthly

17475 **Journal of Materials Engineering and Performance**
ASM International
9639 Kinsman Road
Materials Park, OH 44073-0002

440-338-5151
800-336-5152; Fax: 440-338-4634
memberservicecenter@asminternational.org
www.asminternational.org

William T. Mahoney, Secretary & CEO
Rajiv Asthana, Editor

Peer-reviewed journal that publishes contributions on all aspects of materials selection, design, characterization, processing and performance testing. The journal is useful for solving day-to-day engineering challenges - especially those involving components for larger systems.
30K Members
Frequency: Bi-Monthly
Founded in 1913

17476 **Journal of Phase Equilibria & Diffusion**
ASM International
9639 Kinsman Road
Materials Park, OH 44073-0002

440-338-5151
800-336-5152; Fax: 440-338-4634
memberservicecenter@asminternational.org
www.asminternational.org

William T. Mahoney, Secretary & CEO
John Morral, Editor
Ursula R. Kattner, Editor
H. Okamoto, Editor

Peer-reviewed journal containing basic and applied research results, evaluated phase diagrams, a survey of current literature, and comments or other material pertinent to the previous three areas. The aim of the journal is to provide a broad spectrum of information concerning phase equilibria for the materials community.
30K Members
Frequency: Bi-Monthly
Founded in 1913

17477 **Journal of Process Control**
Butterworth Heinemann
313 Washington Street
Newton, MA 02458-1626

617-928-5460; Fax: 781-933-6333

JD Perkins, Editor
T McAvoy, Regional Editor

Covers the application of control theory, operations research, computer science and engineering principles to the solution of process control problems.

17478 **Journal of Quality Technology**
American Society for Quality

600 N Plankinton Avenue
Milwaukee, WI 53203

414-272-8575
800-248-1946; Fax: 414-272-1734
help@asq.org
asq.org/pub/jqt/index.html

Elmer Corbin, Chair
Bill Troy, CEO
Brian Savoie, Chief Financial Officer
Andrew Baines, Managing Director, Global
Ann Jordan, General Counsel

Published by the American Society for Quality, the Journal of Quality Technology is a quarterly, peer-reviewed journal that focuses on the subject of quality control and the related areas of reliability and similar disciplines.
80K Members
Frequency: Quarterly
Founded in 1946

17479 **MHI Solutions**
Material Handling Institute
8720 Red Oak Boulevard
Suite 201
Charlotte, NC 28217-3996

704-676-1190; Fax: 704-676-1199
shani@naylor.com
www.mhisolutionsmag.com

George Prest, CEO
Brian Reaves, Executive Vice President
Carol Miller, VP, Marketing & Communications
Shani Calvo, Editor

Journal published by the Material Handling Institute (MHI), containing articles about technology, trends and developments in the material handling and logistics industry.
800 Members
Frequency: Quarterly
Founded in 1945

17480 **Maintenance Technology**
Applied Technology Publications
1300 S Grove Ave
Suite 105
Barrington, IL 60010-5246

847-382-8100; Fax: 847-304-8603
www.mt-online.com

Arthur Rice, President/CEO
Bill Kiesel, Vice President/Publisher
Jane Alexander, Editor-In-Chief
Rick Carter, Executive Editor
Randy Buttstadt, Director of Creative Services

Maintenance Technology magazine serves the business and technical information needs of managers and engineers responsible for assuring availability of plant equipment and systems. It provides readers with articles on advanced technologies, strategies, tools, and services for the life-cycle management of capital assets.
Frequency: Monthly
Circulation: 50,827
Mailing list available for rent: 35,263 names at $$15 per M

17481 **Managing Automation**
Thomas Publishing Company
5 Penn Plz
Suite 10
New York, NY 10001-1860

212-695-0500
800-733-1127; Fax: 212-290-7362
contact@thomaspublishing.com
www.thomaspublishing.com

Carl Holst-Knudsen, CEO
Greg MacSweeney, Managing Editor
Kim Vennard, Senior Marketing Manager
Shawn Jacobs, Director of Sales

Serves the needs of those managers and engineers responsible for the planning and implementation of factory automation at both the plant and enterprise levels.
Cost: $60.00
Frequency: Monthly
Circulation: 100246
Founded in 1898

17482 **Manufacturers Mart**
Philip G Cannon Jr
PO Box 310
Georgetown, MA 01833-0410

978-352-3320
800-835-0017; Fax: 401-348-0797
info@manufacturersmart.com
www.manufacturersmart.com

Phillip Cannon, Publisher
Linda Smith, Editor

Information and news on manufacturing companies with a regional focus in New England. New product articles, coverage of advances in technology, compliance issues, case studies, announcements and calendar events. Online version includes searchable index of products and services.
32 Pages
Frequency: Monthly
Circulation: 30000
Founded in 1978
Printed in 4 colors on newsprint stock

17483 **Manufacturing News**
Publishers & Producers
PO Box 36
Annandale, VA 22003

703-750-2664; Fax: 703-750-0064
www.manufacturingnews.com

Richard McCormack, Publisher/Editor

Gives in-depth analysis of critical manufacturing trends, insightful interviews with top players in industry and government and up-to-the-minute business news about issues that directly affect your ability to compete and prosper and takes a look at software and hardware, sucessful manufacturers, and profound technological changes.
Cost: $495.00
12 Pages
Frequency: Fortnightly
Circulation: 30,000
ISSN: 1078-2397
Founded in 1994
Printed in on matte stock

17484 **Manufacturing Systems**
2000 Clearwater Drive
Oak Brook, IL 60523-8809

630-288-8000; Fax: 630-320-7373
www.manufacturing.net

Michelle Palmer, Publisher
Mary Ann Brockway, Circulation Manager
David Greenfield, Editor

Information management for increased manufacturing productivity.
Cost: $6.00
Frequency: Monthly
Circulation: 114682

17485 **Marketeer**
1602 E Glen Avenue
Peoria, IL 61614-5451
VB Cook, Editor

New products for manufacturing.
Cost: $15.00
16 Pages
Frequency: Monthly
Founded in 1952

17486 **Marking Industry Magazine**
Marking Devices Publishing Company
136 W Vallette St
Suite 6
Elmhurst, IL 60126-4377

630-832-5200; Fax: 630-832-5206
www.markingdevices.com

David Hachmeister, President

New products, processes and services, MDAI and other association news, shows and seminars, sales and management methods.
Cost: $54.00
Frequency: Monthly
Circulation: 1300
Founded in 1907

17487 **Material Handling Equipment Distributors Association**
201 US Highway 45
Vernon Hills, IL 60061

847-680-3500; Fax: 847-362-6989
connect@mheda.org
www.mheda.org

Liz Richards, CEO
Jamie Aiwohi, Financial Manager
Kathy Cotter, Membership Manager
Susan Freibrun, Education/Meeting Manager
Cindy Thoren, Project Manager

The Material Handling Equipment Distributors Association is the only national association dedicated solely to improving the proficiency of the independent material handling equipment distributor.
Frequency: Quarterly
Circulation: 4000
Founded in 1954

17488 **Material Handling Network**
Network Publishing
252 E Washington Street
East Peoria, IL 61611-338

309-699-4431
800-447-6901; Fax: 309-698-0801
www.mhnetwork.com

Andra Stephens, Editor
Bob Behrens, General Manager
Andra Stephens, Advertising/Sales
Mindi Mitzelfelt, Graphic Designer

Monthly journal written for material handling distributors/dealers and people who sell racks, bins, conveyors, dock equipment, lift trucks, batteries, and pallet jacks - both power and non-power.
Cost: $65.00
156 Pages
Frequency: Monthly
Circulation: 12058
Founded in 1981
Printed in 4 colors on n stock

17489 **Material Handling Product News**
Reed Business Information
225 Wyman St
Suite 3
Waltham, MA 02451-1216

781-734-8000; Fax: 781-734-8076
www.reedbusiness.com

Mark Finklestein, President
Joseph Pagnotta, Editor-in-Chief
Joanna Schumann, Marketing Manager
Michael Holowchuck, Circulation Manager
Steve McCoy, Associate Publisher

Literature reviews, new product listings and new systems and services are featured regularly.
Frequency: Monthly
Founded in 1977

17490 **Materials at High Temperatures**
Butterworth Heinemann

313 Washington Street
Newton, MA 02458-1626

617-928-5460; Fax: 781-933-6333

T Suzuki, Co-Editor
TB Gibbons, Co-Editor

Serves the needs of those developing and using materials for high temperature applications in the power, chemical, engine, processing and furnace industries.

17491 **Mid-America Commerce & Industry**
Mid-America Commerce & Industry
2432 Sw Pepperwood Rd
Topeka, KS 66614-5293

785-272-5280; Fax: 785-272-3729
www.maci-mag.com/

David Lippe, President

Regional industrial magazine covering manufacturing in Missouri, Kansas, Nebraska, Oklahoma, Arizona and Iowa
Cost: $18.00
Frequency: Monthly

17492 **Midrange ERP**
MFG Publishing
9 W Street
Beverly, MA 01915-2225

978-927-1419; Fax: 978-921-1255

Deborah A Turbide, Publisher

Planning and scheduling issues, polices and procedures, as well as system improvements.
Circulation: 40000
Founded in 1996

17493 **Modern Applications News**
Nelson Publishing
2500 Tamiami Trl N
Nokomis, FL 34275-3476

941-966-9521; Fax: 941-966-2590
www.healthmgttech.com
Facebook

A Verner Nelson, President
John Mullaly, Editor
Bob Olree, Publisher
Joan Southerland, Marketing
Wyanne Harwell, Circulation Manager

Information includes coverage of abrasives and grinding, automated handling and robotics, CAD/CAM, coatings and finishings, coolants, lubricants and filters, cutting tools, heat treating, ID marking, lasers, machining centers, and shop control software.
Cost: $127.00
Frequency: Monthly
Circulation: 80340
Founded in 1962

17494 **NC Shop Owner**
Penton Media
1166 Avenue of the Americas/10th Fl
New York, NY 10036

212-204-4200; Fax: 216-696-6662
information@penton.com
www.penton.com

Jane Cooper, Marketing
Chris Meyer, Director, Corporate Communications

News of industry events, new product information, updates on manufacturing technology and a special technology focus section.
Frequency: Semiannual
Circulation: 120,000

17495 **National Association of Relay Manufacturers**
2500 Wilson Boulevard
Arlington, VA 22201

703-907-8025; Fax: 703-875-8908
www.ecaus.org/narm

Electronical relay and associated switching devices. Engrs. Relay HB - 5th Edition - $60.00 plus $7.00 postage and handling; IRC Proceeding 2002 - $60.00 plus $7.00 postage and handling
Cost: $60.00
Circulation: 1000
Founded in 1947

17496 **New Equipment Digest**
Penton Media
1166 Avenue of the Americas/10th Fl
New York, NY 10036

212-204-4200; Fax: 216-696-6662
information@penton.com
www.penton.com

Chris Meyer, Director, Corporate Communications
Robert F King, Editor
Sarah Hughes, Production Manager
Bobbie Macy, Circulation Manager
David B. Nussbaum, CEO

Serves the general industrial field which include manufacturing, processing, engineering services, construction, transportation, mining, public utilities, wholesale distributors, educational services, libraries, and governmental establishments.
Frequency: Monthly
Circulation: 206154
Founded in 1892

17497 **Off-Highway Engineering**
SAE
400 Commonwealth Dr
Warrendale, PA 15086-7511

724-776-4841
877-606-7323; Fax: 724-776-5760
sohe@sae.org

Richard O Schaum, President

Off-Highway Engineering serves the international off highway design and manufacturing field which consists of producers of construction, lawn and garden, agricultural equipment, and industrial vehicles. Also served are makers of engines and parts and components and others allied to the field.
Cost: $70.00
66 Pages
Circulation: 16308
ISSN: 1074-6919
Founded in 1905
Printed in 4 colors on glossy stock

17498 **Planning Guidebook**
Reed Business Information
6 Alfred Circle
Bedford, MA 00173

972-980-8810; Fax: 617-558-4700
corporatecommunications@reedbusiness.com
www.designnews.com

William Shordon, Editor
Jim Casella, CEO

Offers information and news on manufacturing companies.
Frequency: Monthly
Founded in 1946

17499 **Plant**
Rogers Media Publishing
777 Bay Street
Toronto, Ontario M5W1A

416-596-5729; Fax: 416-596-5552
www.plant.ca

Joe Terrett, Editor
Kathy Smith, Production Manager
Jessica Jubb, Manager

PLANT serves manufacturing and processing industries in Canada.
Cost: $125.00
Frequency: 18 per year
ISSN: 0845-4213
Founded in 1941

17500 **Plant Services**
Putman Media
555 W Pierce Rd
Suite 301
Itasca, IL 60143-2626

630-467-1300; Fax: 630-467-0197
mbrenner@putman.net
www.putman.net

John Cappelletti, CEO
Mike Bacidore, Editor-in-Chief
Mike Brenner, Group Publisher
Keith Larson, VP Content

For maintenance and engineering managers responsible for keeping manufacturing plants running efficiently.
Cost: $96.00
Circulation: 80100
Founded in 1938
Mailing list available for rent: 10,000 names
Printed in 4 colors on glossy stock

17501 **Plating and Surface Finishing**
1155 Fifteenth Street, NW
Suite 500
Washington, DC 20005

202-457-8401; Fax: 407-281-6446
www.aesf.org

Jon Bednerik CAE, Publisher
Tom Urban, Advertising Manager
Donn Berry, Editor
Dan Denston, Executive Director
John Flatley, Senior Advisor and NASF Liaison

AESF is an international society that advances the science of surface finishing to benefit industry and society through education information and social involvement, as well as those who provide services, supplies and support to the industry.
Cost: $125.00
Frequency: Monthly
Circulation: 4000
Founded in 1909

17502 **Powder Coating**
OSC Publishing
1300 E 66th Street
Minneapolis, MN 55423-2642

612-866-2242; Fax: 612-866-1939

Richard R Cress, Publisher
Richard Link, Manager

Our information focuses on the application, pre-treatment, materials, materials handling, and curing processes. Also features case histories.
Frequency: 9 per year
Circulation: 23587

17503 **Precision Manufacturing**
Minnesota Precision Manufacturing Association

3131 Fernbrook Ln N
Suite 111
Minneapolis, MN 55447-5336

763-473-4090; Fax: 763-473-2804
www.mpma.com

Dennis A Olson, President
Garry Bultnick, Sales Manager
LuAnn Bartley, Executive Director

Publication for job shop owners, managers and engineers and industrial suppliers, distributors, OEM buyers and purchasing agents, manufacturing representatives and technical colleges.
Circulation: 7900
Founded in 1958
Printed in on glossy stock

17504 Process Cooling & Equipment
Business News Publishing Company
1050 IL Route 83
Suite 200
Bensenville, IL 60106-1096

630-377-5909; Fax: 630-694-4002
www.process-cooling.com

Katie Rotella, President
Linda Becker, Editor
Sean Meaney, Sales Manager

Focuses on temperatures down through cryogenic levels in industrial processes and in equipment cooling.

17505 Process Heating
Business News Publishing Company
155 Pfingsten Road
Suite 205
Deerfield, IL 60015

847-405-4000; Fax: 248-502-1001
PHeditors@bnpmedia.com
www.process-heating.com
Facebook, Twitter

Anne Armel, Publisher
Linda Becker, Associate Publisher/Editor
Beth McClelland, Production Manager
Sean Meaney, Sales Manager
Caroline Eychenne, European Sales Representative

Magazine covers heat processing at temperatures up to 1000 degrees F at end user and OEM plants in 9 industries. Follow us at twitter.com/ProcessHeating, www.facebook.com/ProcessHeating
Circulation: 25000
Founded in 1994

17506 Products Finishing
Gardner Publications
6915 Valley Ln
Cincinnati, OH 45244-3153

513-527-8800
800-950-8020; Fax: 513-527-8801
narnold@gardnerweb.com
www.gardnerweb.com

Rick Kline Sr, CEO
Matthew J Little, Editor
Nancy Eigel-Miller, Marketing Director
Nancy Arnold, Circulation Manager
John Campos, Manager

Covers production, management, engineering, design, etc. in plants where metal and plastic products are eletroplated, anodized, painted, buffed, cleaned or otherwise finished.
Cost: $89.00
Frequency: Monthly
Circulation: 42000
Founded in 1928
Printed in 4 colors on glossy stock

17507 Progressive Distributor
Pfingsten Publishing
730 Madison Avenue
Fort Atkinson, WI 53538

920-563-5225
800-932-7732; Fax: 920-563-4269
www.progressivedistributor.com

Rich Vurva, Editor
Pat OBrien, Executive Director
Mitch Bouchard, Secretary, Treasurer

Sales and marketing magazines for top manager, salespeople and marketing executives in industrial and construction distribution firms.
Circulation: 24337
Founded in 1996
Printed in 4 colors on glossy stock

17508 Quality
Business News Publishing
1050 IL Route 83
Suite 200
Bensenville, IL 60106-1096

630-377-5909; Fax: 630-227-0204
www.qualitymag.com

Katie Rotella, President
Thomas A Williams, Publisher
Christopher Sheehy, Manager

Quality is a monthly business publication serving the quality assurance and process improvement needs of more than 80,000 North American manufacturing professionals.
Cost: $75.00
74 Pages
Frequency: Monthly
Circulation: 64000
ISSN: 0360-9936
Founded in 1962
Printed in 4 colors on glossy stock

17509 Quality Engineering
American Society for Quality
600 N Plankinton Avenue
Milwaukee, WI 53203

414-272-8575
800-248-1946; Fax: 414-272-1734
help@asq.org
asq.org/pub/qe/index.html

Elmer Corbin, Chair
Bill Troy, CEO
Brian Savoie, Chief Financial Officer
Andrew Baines, Managing Director, Global
Ann Jordan, General Counsel

Co-published by Taylor and Francis, this journal is for professional practitioners and researchers in quality engineering improvement and solutions. Subjects include quality assurance management, physical technology, statistical tools and more.
80K Members
Frequency: Quarterly
Founded in 1946

17510 Quality Management Journal
American Society for Quality
600 N Plankinton Avenue
Milwaukee, WI 53203

414-272-8575
800-248-1946; Fax: 414-272-1734
help@asq.org
asq.org/pub/qmj/index.html

Elmer Corbin, Chair
Bill Troy, CEO
Brian Savoie, Chief Financial Officer
Andrew Baines, Managing Director, Global
Ann Jordan, General Counsel

Quarterly, peer-reviewed journal focusing on research on the subject of quality management practice. The journal provides a discussion forum for both practitioners and academics.
80K Members
Frequency: Quarterly
Founded in 1946

17511 Quality Observer: ICSS Journal
Quality University Press
3970 Chain Bridge Road
PO Box 1111
Fairfax, VA 22030-3316

703-691-9496

Johnson A Edosomwan, Editor

Case studies, interviews, international and national news and regular colums covering service in manufacturing, high-tech, government agencies and non-profit organizations.
Cost: $139.00
50 Pages
Frequency: 4 per year
Circulation: 15,000
ISSN: 1057-9583
Printed in 4 colors on glossy stock

17512 Quality Progress
American Society for Quality
600 N Plankinton Avenue
Milwaukee, WI 53203

414-272-8575
800-248-1946; Fax: 414-272-1734
help@asq.org
asq.org/qualityprogress

Elmer Corbin, Chair
Bill Troy, CEO
Brian Savoie, Chief Financial Officer
Andrew Baines, Managing Director, Global
Ann Jordan, General Counsel

Peer-reviewed journal exploring the subject of quality control, discussing the usage and implementation of quality principles. Topics include customer satisfaction, trends and developments.
80K Members
Founded in 1946

17513 Scan Tech News
Reed Business Information
30 Technology Parkway South
Suite 100
Norcross, GA 30092

630-574-0825
800-424-3996; Fax: 630-288-8781
webmaster@reedbusiness.com
www.reedbusiness.com

Jeff Greisch, President

Updates in trends in ADC technology and standards, the latest news from leading industry events, and product developments that streamline the flow of essential information in industrial settings.
Frequency: Monthly
Circulation: 82M

17514 Smart Manufacturing Magazine
Society of Manufacturing Engineers
1 SME Drive
Dearborn, MI 48128

313-425-3000
800-733-4763; Fax: 313-425-3400
editorial@sme.org
advancedmanufacturing.org

Jeffrey M. Krause, CEO
Alan Rooks, Editor-in-Chief
James A. Lorincz, Senior Editor
Patrick Waurzyniak, Senior Editor

Covers advanced manufacturing technologies and tools and how they work with and are strengthened by integrated information technology.
65K Members
Frequency: Quarterly
Founded in 1932

17515 Software Quality Professional
American Society for Quality

600 N Plankinton Avenue
Milwaukee, WI 53203

414-272-8575
800-248-1946; Fax: 414-272-1734
help@asq.org
asq.org/pub/sqp/index.html

Elmer Corbin, Chair
Bill Troy, CEO
Brian Savoie, Chief Financial Officer
Andrew Baines, Managing Director, Global
Ann Jordan, General Counsel

Quarterly, peer-reviewed journal for software development professionals that focuses on the subject of quality practice principles in the implementation of software and the development of software systems.
80K Members
Frequency: Quarterly
Founded in 1946

17516 **Solid State Technology**
PennWell Publishing Company
1421 S. Sheridan Road
Tulsa, OK 74112

918-835-3161
800-331-4463; Fax: 603-891-9294
www.pennwell.com

Christine Shaw, VP
David Barach, Publisher

Serves firms involved in the manufacturing and testing of semi-conductor materials, equipment, device/circuits manufacturing and OEM manufacturing with in-house IC manufacturing facilities.
Cost: $213.00
Frequency: Monthly
ISSN: 0038-111X
Founded in 1958
Mailing list available for rent

17517 **Solid Surface**
Cygnus Publishing
PO Box 803
Fort Atkinson, WI 53538-0803

920-000-1111
800-547-7377; Fax: 920-563-1699
paul.bowers@cygnuspub.com

John French, CEO
Russ Lee, Editor
Paul Bowers, Group VP
Charlie Lillis, Content Licensing
Kathy Scott, Director of Public Relations

Solid surfaces link between fabricator, distributor, supplier, and manufacturer. It is dedicated to providing reliable and timely information, including updates on the latest fabrication trends and techniques, with a fresh perspective and a sense of humor.
Cost: $25.00
Circulation: 4,500
Founded in 1966

17518 **Springs Manufacturer Institute**
Spring Manufacturers Institute
2001 Midwest Rd
Suite 106
Oak Brook, IL 60523-1378

630-495-8588; Fax: 630-495-8595
info@smihq.org
www.smihq.org

Lynne Carr, President
Rita Schauer, Editor
Kim Kostecki, Member Services Coordinator
Pashun McNulty, Financial Admin Coordinator
Russ Bryer, Secretary, Treasurer

Provides how-to and technical articles on inspection methods, design, finishes, manufacturing proccesses, materials and equipment, also contains financial and management articles on the interests of precision mechanical spring manufacturers.
130 Pages
Frequency: Quarterly
Circulation: 12,000
Printed in 4 colors on glossy stock

17519 **Supply Chain e-Business**
Keller International Publishing Corporation
150 Great Neck Rd
Suite 400
Great Neck, NY 11021-3309

516-829-9722; Fax: 516-829-9306
www.supplychainbrain.com

Thomas A Foster, Editor-in-Chief
Russell W Goodman, Managing Editor
Jerry Keller, President
Mary Chavez, Director of Sales

Offers a thorough analysis of on-line solutions designed to help corporations achieve greater supply-chain visiblity and real-time connections with suppliers and customers
Frequency: Bi-Monthly
Circulation: 45M
ISSN: 1525-4887
Printed in 4 colors on glossy stock

17520 **Target**
Association for Manufacturing Excellence
380 W Palatine Road
Wheeling, IL 60090-5831

847-520-3282; Fax: 847-520-0163
info@ame.org
www.ame.org

Robert W Hall, Editor-in-Chief
Dick Barton, Director of Advertising

Contains coverage on educational events, opinion columns, a networking section and more, reflecting manufacturing competitiveness, and improvement concepts and activities for the members of the Association for Manufacturing Excellence and interested academia.
Cost: $125.00
Frequency: Quarterly
Circulation: 5000
Founded in 1985

17521 **US Industries Today**
Postitive Publications
225 Madison Avenue
Morristown, NJ 07960

973-292-2600; Fax: 973-292-2696
www.usitoday.com

Peter Mercer, Editor
Sabastian Fraser, CEO/President

Provides information on the latest developments across the whole range of the US manufacturing industry, covering stock market analysis, US business leaders, business profiles and industry sector reports, as well as new products and services.
Cost: $15.00
Circulation: 65000
Founded in 1998

17522 **Valve Magazine**
Valve Manufacturers Association of America
1050 17th Street NW
Suite 280
Washington, DC 20036-5521

202-331-8105; Fax: 202-296-0378
gparente@vma.org
www.valvemagazine.com

William S. Sandler, President & Publisher
Judy Tibbs, Editor-in-Chief
Genilee Parente, Managing Editor
Chris Guy, Assistant Editor
Sue Partyke, Advertising Director

Magazine promoting US and Canadian manufactured industrial valves and actuators.
100 Members
Frequency: Quarterly
Circulation: 26000
Founded in 1938

Trade Shows

17523 **AES/EPA Conference/Exhibit: Environmental Control for Surface Finishing**
American Electroplaters and Surface Finishers Soc.
1155 Fifteenth Street, NW
Suite 500
Washington, DC 20005

202-457-8401; Fax: 407-281-6446
exhibit@aesf.org
www.aesf.org

Kathy Shumacher, Show Manager
Dan Denston, Executive Director
John Flatley, Senior Advisor and NASF Liaison

One-hundred exhibitors of waste treatment, pollution control, surface finishing equipment and surfaces.
600 Attendees
Frequency: June

17524 **AESF SUR/FIN Annual Technical Conference and Exhibit of Surface Finishers**
American Electroplaters and Surface Finishers Soc.
1155 Fifteenth Street, NW
Suite 500
Washington, DC 20005

202-457-8401; Fax: 407-281-6446
exhibit@aesf.org
www.aesf.org

Dan Denston, Executive Director
John Flatley, Senior Advisor and NASF Liaison

More than 300 suppliers to the industry will attend.
Frequency: June

17525 **AESF Week - Society's Annual Winter Meeting**
American Electroplaters and Surface Finishers Soc.
1155 Fifteenth Street, NW
Suite 500
Washington, DC 20005

202-457-8401; Fax: 407-281-6446
www.aesf.org

Dan Denston, Executive Director
John Flatley, Senior Advisor and NASF Liaison
Frequency: June

17526 **AME Annual Conference**
Association for Manufacturing Excellence
380 W Palatine Road
Suite 7
Wheeling, IL 60090-5863
847-520-3282; Fax: 847-520-0163
info@ame.org
www.ame.org

Vivian Bartt, Manager
Dick Barton, Director of Advertising
Frequency: November
Founded in 1985

17527 **Adhesive and Sealant Council Fall Convention**
Adhesive & Sealant Council

7101 Wisconsin Avenue
Suite 990
Bethesda, MD 20814

301-986-9700; Fax: 301-986-9795
data@ascouncil.org
www.ascouncil.org

Malinda Armstrong, Director, Meetings & Expositions
Frequency: October

17528 **AeroMat Conference and Exposition**
ASM International
9639 Kinsman Road
Materials Park, OH 44073-0002

440-338-5151
800-336-5152; Fax: 440-338-4634
memberservicecenter@asminternational.org
www.asminternational.org

William T. Mahoney, Secretary & CEO
Lindy Good, Global Conference & Exhibit Planner

Focuses on innovative aerospace materials, fabrication and manufacturing methods that improve aerospace structures, performance and durability.
900 Members
Frequency: Annual/May
Founded in 1913

17529 **Annual Elevator Convention and Exposition**
356 Morgan Avenue
PO Box 6507
Mobile, AL 36660

251-479-4514
800-730-5093; Fax: 251-479-7043

Ricia S Hendrick, President/Publisher
Robert Caporale, Senior VP and Editor
Frequency: Annual

17530 **Annual Meeting & Leadership Conference**
Private Label Manufacturers Association (PLMA)
630 Third Avenue
New York, NY 10017

212-972-3131; Fax: 212-983-1382
info@plma.com
www.plma.com

Brian Sharoff, President
Myra Rosen, VP
Tom Prendergast, Director, Research Services

Members look at key issues for the years ahead.
3200+ Members
Frequency: Annual
Founded in 1979

17531 **Association of Loudspeaker Mfg. & Acoustics (ALMA) Symposium**
ALMA International
55 Littleton Road
13B
Ayer, MA 01432

978-772-6977
management@almainternational.org
www.almainternational.org

Spiro Iraclianos, President, VP

Unlike other audio-related events, ALMA Symposia focuses exclusively on products, services and technical and business topics relevant to the loudspeaker industry. Invited speakers present technical papers to keep attendees abreast of the latest developments and expert panelists discuss the latest topics. Training programs are also offered. Exhibit hall features more than 30 industry professionals.
100 Members
Frequency: Annual
Founded in 1962

17532 **Atlantic Design Engineering**
Canon Communications
11444 W Olympic Boulevard
Suite 900
Los Angeles, CA 90064-1549

310-445-4200; Fax: 310-445-4299
www.cancom.com/

Shannon Cleghorn, Customer & Media Coordinator
Erwin Laner, Promotional Manager

The Atlantic Design Engineering show serves the East Coast's design, process and manufacturing marketplace. Product classifications include Coatings & Finishes, composites, Computer Aided Design/Computer Aided Manufacturing, Electrical/Electronic, Electro Optical Components & Equipment, Engineered Safety Products, Engineering Management & Tools, Fasteners, Fluid Media, Fluid Power & Control and more. Held at the Jacob K. Javits Convention Center in New York, New York.
1319 Attendees
Frequency: June

17533 **BCI Annual Convention & Power Mart Expo**
Battery Council International
330 North Wabash Avenue
Suite 2000
Chicago, IL 60611

312-245-1074; Fax: 312-527-6640
info@batterycouncil.org
www.batterycouncil.org
Facebook, LinkedIn

Offers members the opportunity to exchange ideas and views with industry members from around the world in a working meeting atmosphere.
Frequency: Annual/Spring

17534 **CleanRooms East**
PennWell Conferences and Exhibitions
1421 S. Sheridan Road
Tulsa, OK 74112

918-835-3161
800-331-4463; Fax: 603-891-9200
andrear@pennwell.com
www.pennwell.com

Andrea Rollins, Show Manager
Lisa Gowern, Registration Manager
Meg Villeure, Conference Manager

CleanRooms shows, the international forums exclusively serving the contamination control industry, couples exhibits with 100% technology-driver conference programs.
3000 Attendees
Frequency: March
Mailing list available for rent

17535 **Close the Loop Technical Symposium**
2001 Midwest Road
Suite 106
Oak Brook, IL 60523-1335

630-495-8588; Fax: 630-495-8595
www.smihq.org

Russ Bryer, Secretary, Treasurer
Jim Kobrinetz, Technical Director
Christy Johnson, Manager

Symposium will highlight the latest technolgy and best practice solutions to difficult technical problems that are regularly experienced by the spring designer, spring user and manufacturing personel.

17536 **Contract Packaging Association Annual Meeting**
Contract Manufacturing & Packaging
1601 Bond Street
Suite 101
Naperville, IL 60563

630-544-5053; Fax: 630-544-5055
info@contractpackaging.org
www.contractpackaging.com

John Mazelin, President
John Riley, VP
Frequency: April

17537 **Dollar Store Expo**
Retail Dollar Store Association
11540 S Eastern Avenue
Suite 100
Henderson, NV 89052

702-893-9090
800-859-9247; Fax: 702-893-9227
www.asdonline.com/info/dollar-store

Kristina Mullen, Show Manager
Wendy Witherspoon, Manager

Four-hundred and fifty booths for products that retail for a dollar or less. Wholesalers, distributors, manufacturers, importers and representatives for surplus, jewelry, hair and beauty, automotive, food items, household goods, gifts, toys, party supplies, seasonal and closeouts.
2,500 Attendees
Frequency: June
Founded in 2002

17538 **EASTEC Exposition**
Society of Manufacturing Engineers
1 SME Drive
Dearborn, MI 48128

313-425-3000
800-733-4763; Fax: 313-425-3400
service@sme.org
www.easteconline.com/about/about-eastec

Jeffrey M. Krause, CEO
Nancy Totten, Conference Management
Kim Farrugia, CEM, Event Management
Chris Moody, Event Operations
Patti Miller, EASTEC Marketing

Exposition with over 500 exhibitors presenting information on technologies and manufacturing.
65K Members
Frequency: Annual/May
Founded in 1932

17539 **Heat Treating Society Conference & Expo**
ASM International
9639 Kinsman Road
Materials Park, OH 44073-0002

440-338-5151
800-336-5152; Fax: 440-338-4634
memberservicecenter@asminternational.org
www.asminternational.org

William T. Mahoney, Secretary & CEO
Lindy Good, Global Conference & Exhibit Planner

Conference and expo for heat treating equipment and supplies as well as information of interest to metallurgists, maintenance supervisors and production engineering staff.
30K Members
Frequency: October
Founded in 1913

17540 **Int'l Conference on Powder Injection Molding of Metals & Ceramics**
Innovative Material Solutions
605 Severn Drive
State College, PA 16803

814-867-1140; Fax: 814-867-2813

Frequency: March

17541 **International Integrated Manufacturing Technology Trade Exhibition**
Reed Exhibition Companies
383 Main Avenue
Norwalk, CT 06851
203-840-4800; Fax: 203-840-4801
inquiry@reedexpo.com
www.reedexpo.com/app/homepage
Elizabeth Hitchcock, International Sales
Expo and conference dedicated to the products and technology needed by engineering operations and management to automate and integrate manufacturing.
Frequency: June

17542 **International Manufacturing Technology Show**
7901 Westpark Drive
Mc Lean, VA 22102-4206
703-893-2900
800-828-7469; Fax: 703-827-5250
peelman@AMTonline.org
www.amtonline.org
Peter Eelman, VP Exhibitions
Michelle Edmonson, Exhibitions Operations Manager
Manufacturing equipment trade show.
85M Attendees
Frequency: Biennial
Founded in 1927

17543 **International Symposium for Testing & Failure Analysis**
ASM International
9639 Kinsman Road
Materials Park, OH 44073-0002
440-338-5151
800-336-5152; Fax: 440-338-4634
memberservicecenter@asminternational.org
www.asminternational.org
William T. Mahoney, Secretary & CEO
Lindy Good, Global Conference & Exhibit Planner
Annual event focusing on failure analysis and makers of tools such as microscopes, stress and measurement analytical tools, etchants and chemicals, ESD protective materials and other products used for this purpose.
30K Members
Frequency: Annual/Oct/Nov
Founded in 1913

17544 **International Thermal Spray Conference & Exposition**
ASM International
9639 Kinsman Road
Materials Park, OH 44073-0002
440-338-5151
800-336-5152; Fax: 440-338-4634
memberservicecenter@asminternational.org
www.asminternational.org
William T. Mahoney, Secretary & CEO
Lindy Good, Global Conference & Exhibit Planner
International annual conference for professional thermal spray technologists, researchers, manufacturers and suppliers.
30K Members
Frequency: Annual/May
Founded in 1913

17545 **Lean Management and Solutions Conference**
Institute of Industrial Engineers
3577 Parkway Lane
Suite 200
Norcross, GA 30092
770-449-0460
800-494-0460; Fax: 770-441-3295
cs@iienet.org
Elaine Fuerst, Marketing Director
The place to find the leaders in lean management and all the tools that you need for success.
300 Attendees
Frequency: September

17546 **Lean and Six Sigma Conference**
American Society for Quality
600 N Plankinton Avenue
Milwaukee, WI 53203
414-272-8575
800-248-1946; Fax: 414-272-1734
help@asq.org
asq.org/conferences/six-sigma
Elmer Corbin, Chair
Bill Troy, CEO
Brian Savoie, Chief Financial Officer
Andrew Baines, Managing Director, Global
Ann Jordan, General Counsel
Networking event for practitioners in the Lean Six Sigma community. Industries addressed will include operations, manufacturing, transactional, healthcare, financial, service and government.
80K Members
Frequency: Annual/February
Founded in 1946

17547 **METALfab**
532 Forest Parkway
Suite A
Forest Park, GA 30297-6137
404-363-4009; Fax: 404-366-1852
nommainfo@nomma.org
www.nomma.org
Martha Pennington, Show Manager
Todd Daniel, Editor
Barbara Cook, Executive Director
Martha Pennington, Meetings Manager
Trade show sponsored by National Ornamental and Miscellaneous Metals Association.
1000 Attendees
Frequency: March

17548 **MHI Spring Meeting**
Material Handling Institute
8720 Red Oak Boulevard
Suite 201
Charlotte, NC 28217-3996
704-676-1190; Fax: 704-676-1199
abose@mhi.org
www.eiseverywhere.com/ehome/295537
George Prest, CEO
Brian Reaves, Executive Vice President
Anupam Berry Bose, Solution & Product Groups Manager
Devon Birch, Membership Director
Kay Clark, Meetings & Events Director
A meeting for members of the Material Handling Institute, offering product and solutions group activities and networking opportunities with others in the industry.
800 Members
Founded in 1945

17549 **Medical Design & Manufacturing Exhibition East/West**
Canon Communications
11444 W Olympic Boulevard
Los Angeles, CA 15494
310-445-4200; Fax: 310-996-9499
www.cancom.com
Shannon Cleghorn, Customer & Media Coordinator
Erwin Laner, Promotional Manager
Design, development, and manufacture of medical products, from high-volume, single-use disposables to next-generation diagnostic instruments and advanced imaging systems. Preview the latest advances in medical-grade materials, assembly components, electronics, machinery, software, systems, services, and more.
Frequency: May

17550 **Medical Equipment Design & Technology Conference**
Canon Communications
11444 W Olympic Boulevard
Los Angeles, CA 90064-1549
310-445-4200; Fax: 310-996-9499
www.cancom.com
Shannon Cleghorn, Customer & Media Coordinator
Erwin Laner, Promotional Manager
Design, development, and manufacture of medical products, from high-volume, single-use disposables to next-generation diagnostic instruments and advanced imaging systems. Preview the latest advances in medical-grade materials, assembly components, electronics, machinery, software, systems, services and more.
Frequency: September

17551 **Midwest Job Shop Show**
Edward Publishing
16 Waterbury Road
Prospect, CT 06712-1215
203-758-4474; Fax: 203-758-4476
www.jobshoptechnology.com
Jennifer Bryda, Production Manager
Christoper Davis, Manager
Gerald Schmidt, President
A source for forming, fabricating, shaping, and assemblies. The show is designed to attract the highest caliber engineers and buyers from product manufacturers. There will be 170 exhibitors and booths.
1500 Attendees

17552 **Motion + Power Expo**
American Gear Manufacturers Association
1001 N. Fairfax Street
Suite 500
Alexandria, VA 22314-1587
703-684-0211; Fax: 703-684-0242
gearexpo@agma.org
motionpowerexpo.com
Matthew Croson, President
Deneen Pratt, Exhibitor Customer Service
Jenny Blackford, VP, Marketing
Jenny Bogue, Attendee Customer Service
Provides networking opportunities for gear buyers, users, manufacturers, and engineers.
4.5M Attendees
Frequency: October
Founded in 1916

17553 **National Manufacturing Week**
Reed Exhibition Companies
383 Main Street
Norwalk, CT 06851
203-840-4800; Fax: 203-840-4801
inquiry@reedexpo.com
www.reedexpo.com/app/homepage
Elizabeth Hitchcock, International Sales

The pre-eminent American forum for the display of industrial technology.
1.5M Attendees
Frequency: March

17554 **National Plant Engineering and Facilities Management Show and Conference**
Reed Exhibition Companies
383 Main Avenue
Norwalk, CT 06851
203-840-4800; Fax: 203-840-4801
inquiry@reedexpo.com
www.reedexpo.com/app/homepage
Frequency: June

17555 **PTDA Industry Summit**
Power Transmission Distributors Association
230 West Monroe Street
Suite 1410
Chicago, IL 60606-4703
312-516-2100; Fax: 312-516-2101
ptda@ptda.org
www.ptda.org/events/industrysummit.aspx
Jim Williams, President
Ann Arnott, Executive Vice President & CEO
Brenda Holt, Membership Director
Andrea Lebron, Operations Manager
Ginger Wheeler, Marketing & Communications Director
Summit for companies dealing in industrial power transmission/motion control equipment.
Founded in 1960

17556 **Pacific Design Engineering**
Canon Communications
11444 W Olympic Boulevard
Los Angeles, CA 90064
310-445-4200; Fax: 310-996-9499
www.cancom.com
Shannon Cleghorn, Customer & Media Coordinator
Erwin Laner, Promotional Manager
Serves the West Coast's dynamic design, process, and manufacturing marketplace. Product classifications include: Coatings and Finishes, Composites, Computer Aided Design/Computer Aided Manufacturing, Electrical/Electronic, Electrc Optical Compnents and Equipment, Engineered Safety Products, Engineering Management and Tools, Fasteners, Fluid Media, Fluid Power and Control.
Frequency: January

17557 **RPA Conference & Showcase**
Retail Packaging Association
105 Eastern Ave.
Suite 104
Annapolis, MD 21403
410-940-6459; Fax: 410-263-1659
info@retailpackaging.org
www.retailpackaging.org
Molly Alton Mullins, Executive Director
600 Attendees
Frequency: Annual

17558 **Roll-to-Roll Conference**
Association of International Metallizers/Coaters
201 Springs Street
Fort Mill, SC 29715
262-697-0525; Fax: 262-697-0525
aimcal@aimcal.org
www.aimcal.org/2018-r2r-usa.html
Craig Sheppard, Executive Director
Conference exploring the subject of roll to roll processing, and the converting industry.
400+ Attendees
Frequency: Annual

17559 **SOUTH-TEC**
Society of Manufacturing Engineers
1 SME Drive
Dearborn, MI 48128
313-425-3000
800-733-4763; Fax: 313-425-3400
service@sme.org
www.southteconline.com
Jeffrey M. Krause, CEO
Cynthia Bond, Exhibitor Services
Patti Miller, Marketing
Ashley Areeda, Media
Cathy Kowalewicz, Event Management
Exhibition of technologies and services applicable to manufacturing suppliers, distributors and equipment builders.
65K Members
Frequency: October
Founded in 1932

17560 **Simulation Solutions Conference**
Institute of Industrial Engineers
3577 Parkway Lane
Suite 200
Norcross, GA 30092
770-449-0460
800-494-0460; Fax: 770-441-3295
cs@iienet.org
Elaine Fuerst, Marketing Director
Simulation techniques. Tools and software used in a wide range of industries and applications.
250 Attendees

17561 **Southern Job Shop Show**
Edward Publishing
16 Waterbury Road
Prospect, CT 06712-1215
203-758-4474; Fax: 860-768-4475
www.jobshoptechnology.com
Mark W Shortt, Editor
Gerald Schmidt, President
Christopher Davis, Manager
The show is designed to attract the highest caliber engineers and buyers from your major DEM product manufacturers.
1500 Attendees
Frequency: March

17562 **Spring World Expo**
PO Box 1144
Highland Park, IL 60035
847-433-1335; Fax: 847-433-3769
info@casmi-springworld.org
www.springworld.org
Gerald H Reese, Executive Director
Tracy Hodge, Director
4500 Attendees
Frequency: October

17563 **The Smart Manufacturing Experience**
The Association for Manufacturing Technology
7901 Jones Branch Drive
Suite 900
McLean, VA 22102-3316
313-425-3000
800-733-4763
smartmfgexp@sme.org
www.smartmanufacturingexperience.com
Kim Farrugia, Event Management
Kris Cogliandro, Event Project Coordinator
Cynthia Bond, Exhibitor Services
Jackie Solack, Event Operations
Patti Miller, Marketing Manager
Exhibition for those working in the manufacturing technologies industry. Event covers topics such as automation and robotics, precision machining, digital manufacturing and more.

17564 **World Adhesive & Sealant Conference**
Adhesive & Sealant Council
7101 Wisconsin Avenue
Suite 990
Bethesda, MD 20814
301-986-9700; Fax: 301-986-9795
data@ascouncil.org
www.ascouncil.org
Twitter, LinkedIn, RSS
William Allmond, President
International event gathering together industry stakeholders from across the world for three days of keynote addresses, technical courses, and networking opportunities.
Frequency: Every Four Years/April

17565 **World Conference on Quality and Improvement**
American Society for Quality
600 N Plankinton Avenue
Milwaukee, WI 53203
414-272-8575
800-248-1946; Fax: 414-272-1734
help@asq.org
asq.org/conferences/wcqi
Elmer Corbin, Chair
Bill Troy, CEO
Brian Savoie, Chief Financial Officer
Andrew Baines, Managing Director, Global
Ann Jordan, General Counsel
Conference on quality and improvement exploring quality tools, techniques and methodologies.
80K Members
Frequency: Annual
Founded in 1946

Directories & Databases

17566 **AMT Member Product Directory**
The Association for Manufacturing Technology
7901 Jones Branch Drive
Suite 900
McLean, VA 22102-4206
703-893-2900
800-524-0475; Fax: 703-893-1151
amt@amtonline.org
www.amtonline.org
Douglas K. Woods, President
Rebecca Stahl, Chief Financial Officer
Kimberly L. Brown, Member Services Director
Peter R. Eelman, VP, Exhibitions & Business Dev
Amber L. Thomas, Director, Marketing & Communication
Directory listing equipment or services offered by companies serving the manufacturing industry. Categories include business services, cutting and forming tools, cleaning tools, software and more.

17567 **ARPM Member Roster**
Association for Rubber Products Manufacturers
7321 Shadeland Station Way
Suite 285
Indianapolis, IN 46256
317-863-4072; Fax: 317-913-2445
www.arpminc.com
Dave Jentzsch, Director
Chris Wagner, Director
Tim Jarvis, Director
Charlie Braun, Director
Joe Walker, Director
List of members of the Association for Rubber Products Manufacturers.
Founded in 2010

17568 **Agricultural & Industrial Manufacturers Membership Directory**
Agricultural & Industrial Manufacturers Rep Assn
7500 Flying Cloud Drive
Suite 900
Eden Prairie, MN 55344
952-253-6230
866-759-2467; Fax: 952-835-4774
www.aimrareps.org
Michael J Kowalczyk, President
Ronald R Reed, VP
Cost: $25.00
Frequency: Annual October

17569 **Directory of Manufacturing Research Centers**
Manufacturing Technology Information
10 W 35th Street
Chicago, IL 60616-3717
312-431-1442
800-421-0586; Fax: 312-567-4736
info@iitri.org
www.iitri.org
Paula Marggraf, Editor
Cost: $75.00
Frequency: Irregular

17570 **Directory of Waste Equipment Manufacturers and Distributors**
WASTEC Equipment Technology Association
4301 Connecticut Ave NW
Suite 300
Washington, DC 20008-2304
202-966-4701; Fax: 202-966-4818
www.wastec.org
Christine Hutcherson, Director Member Services
Bruce Parker, President
Gary T Satterfield, Executive VP
Sandra Price, Director Member Services
About 250 member manufacturers of waste handling, collection and processing equipment.
Cost: $5.00
Frequency: Annual

17571 **Encyclopedia of American Industries**
Grey House Publishing
4919 Route 22
PO Box 56
Amenia, NY 12501
518-789-8700
800-562-2139; Fax: 845-373-6390
books@greyhouse.com
www.greyhouse.com
Facebook, Twitter
Leslie Mackenzie, Publisher
Richard Gottlieb, Editor
A two volume set, Volume I provides separate coverage of nearly 500 manufacturing industries, while Volume II presents nearly 600 essays covering the vast array of services and other non-manufacturing industries in the United States. Combined, these two volumes provide individual essays on every industry recognized by the U.S. Standard Industrial Classification (SIC) system.
Cost: $650.00
3000 Pages
ISBN: 1-592372-44-9
Founded in 1981

17572 **Food & Beverage Marketplace Directory**
Grey House Publishing
4919 Route 22
PO Box 56
Amenia, NY 12501-0056
518-789-8700
800-562-2139; Fax: 518-789-0556
books@greyhouse.com
www.greyhouse.com
Facebook, Twitter
Richard Gottlieb, President
Leslie Mackenzie, Publisher
A three-volume set that is the most comprehensive resource in the food and beverage industry. Available in print, a subscription-based online database, as well as a mailing list and database formats.
Cost: $595.00
2000 Pages
Frequency: Annual
Founded in 1981

17573 **Manufacturers Representatives of America: Yearbook and Directory of Members**
Manufacturers Representatives of America
PO Box 150229
Arlington, TX 76015-6229
817-465-5511; Fax: 817-561-7275
WR Bess, Executive Director
Several hundred independent manufacturers' representatives in paper, plastic, packaging and sanitary supplies.
Cost: $250.00
Frequency: Annual Fall
Circulation: 1,200

17574 **Manufacturing & Distribution USA**
Gale/Cengage Learning
27500 Drake Road
Farmington Hills, MI 48331-3535
248-699-4253
800-877-4253; Fax: 877-363-4253
gale.galeord@cengage.com
www.gale.cengage.com
Facebook, Twitter, Youtube
Patrick C Sommers, President
This new edition also features enhanced coverage of input-output data by industrial sector when available as well as classifications of leading public and private corporations in each industry.
ISBN: 1-414408-67-6

17575 **Rauch Guide to the US Rubber Industry**
Grey House Publishing
4919 Route 22
PO Box 56
Amenia, NY 12501
518-789-8700
800-562-2139; Fax: 845-373-6390
books@greyhouse.com
www.greyhouse.com
Facebook, Twitter
Leslie Mackenzie, Publisher
Richard Gottlieb, Editor
Provides current market information and trends; industry economics and government regulations; company share data for each of the leading product categories; technology and raw material information; industry sources of further data; and unique profiles of 847 rubber manufacturers, a section which includes all known companies with rubber sales at or over $1 million annually.
Cost: $595.00
500 Pages
ISBN: 1-592371-30-2
Founded in 1981

17576 **Salem Press Online Platform**
Grey House Publishing
4919 Route 22
PO Box 56
Amenia, NY 12501
800-221-1592; Fax: 201-968-0511
csr@salempress.com
online.salempress.com
The new Salem Press platform houses more than 500 titles including all of Salem's Health, Literature, History and Science titles in addition to select titles from the Grey House Publishing and H.W. Wilson product lines. Online access is free with each print purchase and includes an unlimited number of simultaneous users and remote access.

17577 **Small Business Inovation Research**
1000 Independence Avenue SW
Washington, DC 20585-1207
202-571-1300
www.sbir.gov
Lawrence Small, CEO
Frequency: Annual

17578 **Sound and Vibration: Buyer's Guide Issue**
Acoustical Publications
PO Box 40416
27101 E. Oviatt Road
Bay Village, OH 44140-0416
440-835-0101; Fax: 440-835-9303
sv@mindspring.com
www.sandv.com
Jack Mowry, Editor and Publisher
Scott J Lothes, Assistant Editor/Webmaster
This directory offers a list of manufacturers of products for noise and vibration control.
Frequency: Monthly
Circulation: 19,000
ISBN: 0-038181-09-9
Mailing list available for rent: 21M names
Printed in 4 colors on glossy stock

17579 **ThomasNet**
Thomas Publishing Company, LLC
User Services Department
5 Penn Plaza
New York, NY 10001
212-695-0500
800-699-9822; Fax: 212-290-7362
contact@thomaspublishing.com
www.thomasnet.com
Facebook, Twitter, LinkedIn
Carl Holst-Knudsen, President
Robert Anderson, VP, Planning
Mitchell Peipert, VP, Finance
Ivy Molofsky, VP, Human Resources
A way to reach qualified businesses that list their company information on ThomasNet.com. Detailed profiles promote their products, services, capabilities and brands carried. The ThomasNet.com web site is the most up-to-date compilation of 650,000 North American manufacturers, distributors, and service companies in 67,000 industrial categories.
Founded in 1898

17580 **VMA's Product Finder for Valves, Actuators & Controls**
Valve Manufacturers Association of America
1050 17th Street NW
Suite 280
Washington, DC 20036-5521
202-331-8105; Fax: 202-296-0378
spartyke@vma.org
www.vma.org
William S. Sandler, President
Marc Pasternak, Vice President
Sue Partyke, Advertising Director
Chris Guy, Assistant Editor, News & Products

Lists U.S. and Canadian valves, actuators and controls produced by the member companies of the Valve Manufacturers Association of America.
100 Members
Founded in 1938

17581 **Who Audits America**
Data Financial Press
PO Box 668
Menlo Park, CA 94026-0668
650-321-4553; Fax: 650-321-4427
A who's who directory of services and supplies.
Cost: $133.00
600 Pages
Frequency: SemiAnnual

Industry Web Sites

17582 **http://gold.greyhouse.com**
G.O.L.D Grey House OnLine Databases
Grey House Publishing's online database platform, GOLD, offers Quick Search, Keyword Search and Expert Search for most business sectors including a wide variety of manufacturing markets. The GOLD platform makes finding the information you need quick and easy - whether you're a novice searcher or an experienced database user. All of Grey House's directory products are available for subscription on the GOLD platform.

17583 **www.abrasiveengineering.com**
Abrasive Grain Association
Members manufacture natural and artificial grains used in grinding wheels, coated abrasives etc.

17584 **www.aesf.org**
American Electroplaters and Surface Finishers Soc.
AESF is an international society that advances the science of surface finishing to benefit industry and society through education information and social involvement, as well as those who provide services, supplies and support to the industry.

17585 **www.agma.org**
American Gear Manufacturers Association
Manufacturers of gears and geared speed changers.

17586 **www.amtonline.org**
The Association for Manufacturing Technology
Facebook, Twitter, LinkedIn, YouTube
Association representing and supporting the U.S.-based manufacturing technology industry, including distributors, producers and service providers.

17587 **www.ararental.org**
American Rental Association
For rental business owners and equipment suppliers.

17588 **www.arcat.com**
National Association of Relay Manufacturers
NARM is a trade association for the electro-mechanical relay and associated switching devices industry. An affiliate of Electronic Industries Alliance.

17589 **www.arpminc.com**
Association for Rubber Products Manufacturers
Association dedicated to helping industry executives improve their businesses in rubber products manufacturing.

17590 **www.asphaltinstitute.org**
Asphalt Institute
Conducts education, research, and engineering services related to asphalt products; conducts seminars and sells publications and videos on asphalt technology.

17591 **www.asq.org**
American Society for Quality
Facebook, Twitter, LinkedIn
Associaion with the mission to promote quality principles concepts and technologies through information, contacts and development opportunities for management professionals in various industries.

17592 **www.awci.com/**
American Watchmakers-Clockmakers Institute
Examines and certifies master watchmakers and clockmakers. Maintains a placement service. Conducts home study courses.

17593 **www.awci.org**
Association of the Wall and Ceiling Industries
Offers information on contractors, manufacturers, suppliers and organizations affiliated with the interior design, building and contracting community. Strives to provide services and undertake activities that enhance the members ability to operate a successful business.

17594 **www.bia.org**
Brick Industry Association
Supports the industry by rendering technical assistance to architects and designers, by providing marketing assistance to the industry, by monitoring and positively influencing governmental actions, by working to assure the long term availability of bricklayers and by providing other member services as appropriate.

17595 **www.cancentral.com**
Can Manufacturers Institute
Industry, environmental and consumer information.

17596 **www.carpetcushion.org**
Carpet Cushion Council
Encourages distribution and use of seperate carpet cushions. Works with regulatory agencies at the national, state and local levels.

17597 **www.cottonseed.com**
National Cottonseed Products Association
Services include the administration of trading rules and standards, a research program, information service center and product promotion of cotton seed food and feed products.

17598 **www.cti.org**
Cooling Technology
Seeks to improve technology, design and performance of water conservation apparatus. Provides inspection services and conducts research.

17599 **www.divbusiness.com**
Diversified Business Communications
Provides management services for associations and organizations seeking to expand domestically and overseas, as well as direct mail, internet, telemarketing campaigns and market research.

17600 **www.fluidcontrolsinstitute.org**
Fluid Controls Institute
Manufacturers of devices for fluid control, such as temperature and pressure regulators, strainers, gauges, control valves, solenoid valves, steam traps, etc.

17601 **www.fluidsealing.com**
Fluid Sealing Association
An international association of manufacturers of mechanical packings, sealing devices, gaskets, rubber expansion joints and allied products.

17602 **www.greyhouse.com**
Grey House Publishing
Authoritative reference directories for most business sectors including a wide variedy of manufacturing markets. Users can search the online databases with varied search criteria allowing for custom searches by product category, geographic area, sales volume, keyword, subject and more. Full Grey House catalog and online ordering also available.

17603 **www.housewares.org**
National Housewares Manufacturers Association
Links to other associations.

17604 **www.iccsafe.org/**
International Code Council
Nonprofit membership association with more than 16,000 members who span the building community, from code enforcement officials to materials manufacturers. Dedicated to preserving the public health, safety and welfare in the built environment through the effective use and enforcement of model codes.

17605 **www.icea.net**
Insulated Cable Engineers Association
Professional organization dedicated to developing cable standards for the electric power, control and telecommunications industries. Ensures safe, economical and efficient cable systems utilizing proven state-of-the-art materials and concepts. ICEA documents are of interest to cable manufacturers, architects and engineers, utility and manufacturing plant personnel, telecommunication engineers, consultants and OEMs.

17606 **www.ifai.com**
Industrial Fabrics Association International
Provides many products, services and programs to industry members.

17607 **www.ilma.org**
Independent Lubricant Manufacturers Association
Independent blenders and compounders of lubricants.

17608 **www.iopp.org**
Institute of Packaging Professionals
Association for packing professionals.

17609 **www.ipc.org**
IPC-Association Connecting Electronics Industries
Works to develop standards in circuit board assembly equipment. Brings together all players in the electronic interconnection industry, including designers, board manufacturers, assembly companies, suppliers and original equipment manufacturers. Offers workshops, conferences, meetings and online communications.

17610 **www.isri.org**
Institute of Scrap Recycling Industries
Members include processors, brokers and consumers of scrap metal, rubber, paper, textiles, plastics and glass.

17611 www.marinecanvas.com
Marine Fabricators Association
Firms and individuals engaged in the design, construction, and installation of marine fabric products. Provides certification and product standards.

17612 www.mechanical.com
Mechanical.Com
Manufacturing industry database.

17613 www.mfgworld.com/index.html
Manufacturing World Online
Manufacturing news, software, industry reports and links.

17614 www.mhi.org
Material Handling Institute
Facebook, Twitter, LinkedIn, YouTube
Association for the material handling industry, offering industry groups, education, events and programming to support companies and professionals.

17615 www.mhia.org/psc/PSC_Products_Racks.cfm
Rack Manufacturers Institute
Makers of steel industrial storage racks.

17616 www.mt-online.com
Applied Technology Publications
MT-online.com is the premier source of capacity assurance and best practice solutions for manufacturing, process and service operations worldwide. Online home of Maintenance Technology magazie, the dynamic MT-online.com portal serves the critical technical, business and professional-development needs of engineers, managers and technicians from across all industrial, institutional and commercial sectors.

17617 www.naima.org
North American Insulation Manufacturers Assn

17618 www.nam.org
National Association of Manufacturers
Represents industry's views on national and international problems to government.

17619 www.naumd.com
North American Assoc. of Uniform Manufacturers
Promotes interests of manufacturers and distributors of uniforms and career wear.

17620 www.ncspa.org
National Corrugated Steel Pipe Association
NCSPA seeks to promote sound public policy relating to the use of corrugated steel drainage structures in private and public construction.

17621 www.nei.org
Nuclear Energy Institute
Members are of utilities, manufacturers of electrical generating equipment, researchers, architects, engineers, labor unions, and others interested in the generation of electricity by nuclear power.

17622 www.nomma.org
National Ornamental and Miscellaneous Metals
Association

Publishes the Ornamental and Miscellaneous Metals Fabricator magazine. Holds annual convention and trade show (METALfab). Membership dues: $275 fabricators, $250 local supplier, $325 regional supplier, $425 nationwide supplier.

17623 www.nwpca.org
National Wooden Pallet & Container Association
Represents manufacturers, recyclers and distributors of pallets, containers and reels.

17624 www.p3-ny.org/
Women in Production
Promotes the interests of women in the production profession.

17625 www.patmi.org
Powder Actuated Tool Manufacturers Institute
Represents manufacturers of construction tools used to fasten construction materials together.

17626 www.powertoolinstitute.com
Power Tool Institute
Organization with a mission to educate people about power tools and set standards of safety and quality control in the industry.

17627 www.ptda.org
Power Transmission Distributors Association
Twitter, LinkedIn
Association whose members are industrial power transmission/motion control distributor firms dealing in equipment such as bearings, belts, drives, motors, gears, couplings, clutches and brakes.

17628 www.reman.org
Remanufacturing Institute International
A coalition of associations and companies in the entire manufacturing industry. There are over 73,000 companies in this industry. Our goal is to unite them into a powerful organization.

17629 www.smma.org
SMMA: Small Motors & Motion Association
Manufacturing trade association. Members include electric motor and motion control companies, as well as suppliers, users, and associated businesses such as consultants, universities and distributors.

17630 www.steeltubeinstitute.org
Steel Tube Institute of North America
Members produce steel tubes and pipes from carbon, stainless or alloy steel for applications ranging from large structural tubing to small redrawn tubing.

17631 www.sunglassassociation.com
Sunglass Association of America
A nonprofit trade association of manufacturers and import-wholesale sunglasses, sunglass parts, components, materials, and reading glasses.

17632 www.thomasnet.com/index.html
Thomas Register of American Manufacturers
Industrial buying guide of US and Canadian manufacturers.

17633 www.tileusa.com
Tile Council of America
Manufacturers and suppliers of ceramic wall and floor tiles.

17634 www.tpatube.org
Tube & Pipe Association International
TPA is an educational technology association serving the metal tube and pipe producing and fabricating industries.

17635 www.ttmanet.org
Truck Trailer Manufacturers Association
News of interest to trailer manufacturers and suppliers.

17636 www.vending.org
National Automatic Merchandising Association
For makers and operators of automatic vending equipment.

17637 www.westernroofing.net/
Roof Tile Institute
Manufacturers of clay and concrete roof tiles. Emphasis is on technical issues and codes that involve tile. Has annual budget of approximately $300,000 a year. Publications available to members.

Associations

17638 **Academy of Marketing Science**
c/o Louisiana Tech University
P.O. Box 3072
Ruston, LA 71272

ams@latech.edu
www.ams-web.org
Facebook, Twitter, LinkedIn

Julie Moulard, President
Herold W. Berkman, EVP & Director
Brad D. Carlson, VP, Programs
Janna M. Parker, VP, Development
Nina Krey, Secretary/Treasurer

Fosters education professional standards in marketing science. Sponsers the AMS Foundation which provides grants for the advancement of teaching and research.
1500 Members
Founded in 1971

17639 **Advertising Educational Foundation**
10 Grand Central, 155 E. 44th Street
3rd Floor
New York, NY 10017

212-986-8060; Fax: 212-986-8061
gm@aef.com
www.aef.com
Facebook, Twitter, LinkedIn, YouTube, Instagram

Gord McLean, President & CEO
Elliot Lum, SVP, Talent Strategy & Program Dev.
Marcia Soling, VP & Content Manager
Sharon Hudson, VP & Program Manager
Sara Parrish, VP & Program Manager

The AEF is supported by ad agencies, advertisers and media companies. The foundation acts as a bridge between the advertising, marketing and academic communities, fostering a better understanding of of marketing and advertising in society. As of 2015, the AEF is the educational foundation of the Association of National Advertisers.
48 Members
Founded in 1983

17640 **Advertising Research Foundation**
432 Park Avenue S.
6th Floor
New York, NY 10016

212-751-5656; Fax: 212-689-1859
www.thearf.org
Facebook, Twitter, LinkedIn, YouTube

Scott McDonald, President & CEO
Paul Donato, Chief Research Officer
Tom Higgins, COO & CFO
Rachael Feigenbaum, SVP & Events Program Producer
Michael Heitner, EVP, Member Needs & Value

The Advertising Research Foundation (ARF) conducts research, experiments, and market tests to better guide marketers in the use of evolving technology. Research areas include ad effectiveness & ROI, analytics & data science, audience & media measurement, and creative & branded content.
400 Members
Founded in 1936

17641 **Advertising Specialty Institute**
4800 Street Road
Trevose, PA 19053

800-546-1350
ideas@asicentral.com
www.asicentral.com
Facebook, Twitter, LinkedIn, YouTube, Instagram, Pinterest

Norman Unger Cohn, Chair
Timothy Andrews, President & CEO
Steve Bright, EVP & General Counsel
Nancy Carmona, SVP, Business Strategy & Analysis
Andy Cohen, SVP, Editorial

The Advertising Specialty Institute (ASI) is a membership organization for the promotional product industry, offering media, technology, marketing, and educational services to members.
26000 Members
Founded in 1950

17642 **American Association of Advertising Agencies**
1065 Avenue of the Americas
16th Floor
New York, NY 10018

212-682-2500
www.aaaa.org
Facebook, Twitter, LinkedIn, YouTube, Instagram

Marla Kaplowitz, President & CEO
Adam Cotumaccio, COO
Alison Pepper, EVP, Government Relations
Mollie Rosen, EVP, Member Engagement & Dev.
Donna Tobin, EVP, Strategic Services

Dedicated to helping brands create, distribute, and measure effective and insightful advertising and marketing through the use of new technology and techniques.
600+ Members
Founded in 1917

17643 **American Association of Family & Consumer Sciences**
400 N. Columbus Street
Suite 202
Alexandria, VA 22314-2264

703-706-4600
800-424-8080; Fax: 703-706-4663
staff@aafcs.org
www.aafcs.org
Facebook, Twitter, LinkedIn, Flickr, Pintrest, Instagram

Carolyn Jackson, CEO
Nancy Bock, Sr. Director, Communications
Katy Kleemann, Sr. Director, Finance & Operations
Lori Myers, Sr. Director, Credentialing
Debbie Johnson, Director, Education

An association dedicated to Family & Consumer Sciences professionals. AAFCS strives to improve the quality and standards of individual and family life by providing educational programs, influencing public policy, and through communication.
10000 Members
Founded in 1909

17644 **American Marketing Association**
130 E. Randolph Street
22nd Floor
Chicago, IL 60601

800-262-1150
customersupport@ama.org
www.ama.org
Facebook, Twitter, LinkedIn

Russ Klein, Chief Executive Officer
Julie Schnidman, VP, Alliances
Adara Bowen, VP, Growth
Molly Soat, VP, Professional Development
Jeremy Van Ek, Chief Operations Officer

The AMA is a professional association for individuals and organizations leading the practice, teaching and development of marketing knowledge worldwide. Their principle role is to serve as a forum to connect like-minded individuals and foster knowledge sharing, provide resources, tools and training and support marketing practice and thought leadership around the globe.
40000 Members
Founded in 1953

17645 **Asian American Advertising Federation**
6230 Wilshire Boulevard
Suite 1216
Los Angeles, CA 90048

ghomfranzen@3af.org
www.3af.org
Facebook, Twitter, YouTube, Instagram

Jay Kim, President
Iris Yim, Vice President
Sandra Lee, Treasurer
Genny Hom-Franzen, Executive Director

3AF consists of Asian American advertising agency principals, media, advertisers and strategic partners that seek to grow the Asian American advertising and marketing industry, raise public awareness of the Asian community, and increase professionalism within the industry.

17646 **Association for Innovative Marketing**
34 Summit Avenue
Sharon, MA 02067-2149

781-784-8283
Facebook, Twitter, Google+

Facilitates sharing of innovative ideas; bestows awards, maintains library and speaker bureau.
Founded in 1989

17647 **Association for Postal Commerce**
1800 Diagonal Road
Suite 600
Alexandria, VA 22314

703-524-0096; Fax: 703-997-2414
info@postcom.org
www.postcom.org
Twitter, LinkedIn

Michael Plunkett, President & CEO
Ellena Talbott, Director, Operations & Membership
Beth McConnell, Postal Consultant
Matthew Field, General Counsel

National organization representing those who use, or who support, the use of mail as a medium for communication and commerce. Publishes a weekly newsletter covering postal policy and operational issues.
231 Members
Founded in 1947

17648 **Association of Canadian Advertisers**
21 St. Clair Avenue E.
Suite 1201
Toronto, ON M4T 1L9

416-964-3805
800-565-0109; Fax: 416-964-0771
communications@acaweb.ca
www.acaweb.ca
Twitter, LinkedIn

Ron Lund, President & CEO
Judy Davey, VP, Media Policy & Marketing
Davina Wong, Director, Membership
Jessica Yared, Manager, Digital Marketing

The Association of Canadian Advertisers (ACA) is a national, not-for-profit association exclusively dedicated to serving the interests of companies that market and advertise their products and services in Canada. Membership in the ACA is restricted to client marketers only, making it the premier Canadian marketing association. It cuts across all products and service sectors, and speaks on behalf of over 200 companies.
Founded in 1914

17649 **Association of Chamber of Commerce Executives**
1330 Braddock Place
Suite 300
Alexandria, VA 22314

703-998-0072; Fax: 888-577-9883
webmaster@acce.org

www.acce.org
Facebook, Twitter, LinkedIn, YouTube, Instagram

Sheree Anne Kelly, President & CEO
Alysia Bell, VP, Education Business Coalitions
Stacey Breslin, VP, Benefits Services
Beth Bronder, VP, Development & Partnerships
Crystal Moore, VP, Professional Development

Serves chamber of commerce professionals, chambers of commerce, and other organizations like convention and visitors bureaus and economic development organizations.
1300+ Members
Founded in 1914

17650 Association of Marketing Service Providers
1800 Diagonal Road
Suite 320
Alexandria, VA 22314-2806

703-836-9200; Fax: 703-548-8204
kgarner@mfsanet.org
www.amsp.org

Joseph P. Truncale, President & CEO
Ken Garner, Chief Operating Officer
Dean D'Ambrosi, Chief Financial Officer
Andrew D. Paparozzi, SVP & Chief Economist
Leo Raymond, VP, Postal & Member Relations

Formerly known as the Mailing & Fulfillment Service Association, the Association of Marketing Service Providers provides educational content, networking opportunities, and legislative advocacy.

17651 Association of Marketing and Communication Professionals
127 Pittsburgh Street
Dallas, TX 75207

214-377-3524
info@amcpros.com
amcpros.com
Facebook, Twitter, LinkedIn, RSS

AMCP oversees several international marketing and communication competitions, honoring excellence in concept, writing and design of marketing and communication programs and print, visual and audio materials. These are: MarCom Awards, AVA Digital Awards, Hermes Awards, Communitas Awards, and dotComm Awards.
Founded in 1995

17652 Association of National Advertisers
Association of National Advertisers
10 Grand Central, 155 E. 44th Street
New York, NY 10017

212-697-5950; Fax: 212-687-7310
info@ana.net
www.ana.net
Facebook, Twitter, LinkedIn, Instagram

Bob Liodice, Chief Executive Officer
Christine Manna, President & COO
Brian Davidson, EVP, Membership
Mark Liebert, SVP, Marketing Training & Dev.
Kathleen Hunter, EVP, Marketing Knowledge Center

The Association of National Advertisers (ANA) is the advertising industry's oldest trade association. Currently, the ANA leads the marketing community by providing its members insights, collaboration, and advocacy. ANA's membership includes 20,000 brands that collectively spend over $400 billion in marketing communications and advertising. ANA acquired the Brand Activation Association in 2014.
1000 Members
Founded in 1910

17653 Association of Sales & Marketing Companies
5225 Wisconsin Avenue NW
Suite 316
Washington, DC 20015-2055

202-293-1414; Fax: 202-293-1702
info@asmconline.net
www.asmconline.net

Gary Chartrand, Chair
Rick Abraham, President
Barry C. Maloney, Secretary-Treasurer & CFO

Association represents the interests of sales and marketing agencies and their clients in the food, beverage and consumer goods industries.
250 Members
Founded in 1995

17654 Biomedical Marketing Association
10293 N Meridian Street
Suite 175
Indianapolis, IN 46290

317-816-1640
800-278-7886; Fax: 317-816-1633
www.bmaonline.org

Michael L Boner, President

Builds diagnostic industry leadership by providing market education, professional development and a forum for fellowship and the exchange of ideas.

17655 Business Marketing Association
708 Third Avenue
Suite 123
New York, NY 10017

212-697-5950; Fax: 212-687-7310
info@marketing.org
www.marketing.org
Facebook, Twitter, LinkedIn

Katherine Button Bell, Chairman
Stephen Liguori, Vice Chair
George Stenitzer, VP, Thought Leadership
Chris Schermer, VP, Marketing
Bob Felsenthal, VP, Membership

The Business Marketing Association/BMA, a preeminent service organization for professionals, provides expertise in business-to-business marketing and communications. The BMA offers an information-packed Website, online skills-building, marketing certification programs, and industry surveys and papers. In addition, members have the opportunity to interact with peers at seminars, chapter training programs and the BMA Annual Conference.
Founded in 1922

17656 Business Marketing Association: Atlanta
2801 Buford Highway
Druid Chase Suite 375
Atlanta, GA 30329

404-641-9417
800-664-4262; Fax: 312-822-0054
Facebook, Twitter, LinkedIn, Youtube

Martine Hunter, President
Rory Carlton, Treasurer
Eduardo Esparza, Co-Chair of Marketing
Mark Potter, Membership Chairperson
Nancy Bistritz, Public Relations

The Atlanta chapter of the BMA includes marketing executives from a variety of industries and backgrounds including research, advertising, promotions, events, Web development, printing and more. The BMA offers an information-packed Website, online skills-building, marketing certification programs, and industry surveys and papers. In addition, members have the opportunity to interact with peers at seminars, participate in chapter training programs and the BMA Annual Conference.
Founded in 1922

17657 Business Marketing Association: Boston
246 Hampshire Street
Cambridge, MA 02130

617-418-4000
800-664-4262; Fax: 312-822-0054
www.thebmaboston.com/

Michael Lewis, President
Will Robinson, VP Public Relations
Matthew Mamet, VP Internet Marketing
Larry Perreault, VP Finance
Chris Perkett, VP Programming

BMA Boston helps members improve their ability to manage business-to-business marketing and communications for greater productivity and profitability by providing unique access to information, ideas, and the experience of peers. The BMA offers an information-packed Website, online skills-building, marketing certification programs, and industry surveys and papers. In addition, members have the opportunity to interact with peers at seminars, chapter training programs and the BMA Annual Conference.

17658 Business Marketing Association: Houston
PO Box 710350
Houston, TX 77271-0350

713-723-1325; Fax: 713-723-1326
www.bmahouston.org
Facebook, Twitter, LinkedIn, Youtube

Diana Salerno, President
Linda Ives, Executive Director
Megan Coffing, Vice President
Bob Wallace, Treasurer

Dedicated to serving the needs of business to business Associations worldwide.
Founded in 1922

17659 Business Marketing Association: Hudson Valley
304 Wall Street
Kingston, NY 12401

845-340-4708
800-664-4262
alviankamaly@gmail.com
www.hvdma.org

Bud Clarke, President
Joan Giewat, First Vice President
June Bisel, Second Vice President
Rebecca D Jones, Treasurer
John Bassler, Secretary

Offers ways for its members to expand their business expertise and grow professionally.

17660 Business Marketing Association: Indy
8650 Commerce Park Place
Indianapolis, IN 46268

800-664-4262; Fax: 317-285-2068

John Faust, President
Christine Johnston, Secretary
Judy Knafel, Treasurer

To promote the quality and effectiveness of Indiana-developed business-to-business marketing communications through the continuous learning of its members.

17661 Cable & Telecommunications Association for Marketing
120 Waterfront Street
Suite 200
National Harbor, MD 20745

301-485-8900
info@ctam.com

www.ctam.com
Twitter, LinkedIn

Vicki Lins, President & CEO
Angie Britt, SVP, Advanced Products
Zell Murphy, SVP, Finance & Administration
Mark Snow, SVP & GM, Consumer Marketing
Ken Leonardo, VP, Marketing

Provides marketing knowledge and industry scale to help its membersmanage the future and drive business results. Also provides consumer research, industry resources, a job bank, conferences and awards.

17662 Center for Marketing and Opinion Research

441 Wolf Ledges Parkway
Suite 103
Akron, OH 44311

330-564-4211
888-878-5875
info@cmoresearch.com
cmoresearch.com
Facebook, Twitter, LinkedIn

Michelle Henry, Principal
Amanda Barna, Principal
Anthony Matonis, Senior Dir., Research & Analytics
Sarah Brown, Research Manager
Laura Long, Accounts Manager

A non-profit organization which works on behalf of the survery research industry to improve respondent cooperation in research, and to promote positive legislation and prevent restrictive legislation which could impact the survey research industry.
150+ Members
Founded in 1992

17663 Color Marketing Group

1908 Mount Vernon Avenue
3rd Floor
Alexandria, VA 22301

703-329-8500; Fax: 703-535-3190
sgriffis@colormarketing.org
www.colormarketing.org
Facebook, Twitter, LinkedIn, Pinterest, Instagram

Judith van Vliet, President
Paula Lord, VP, Marketing
Sandy Sampson, VP, Communications & PR
Peggy van Allen, VP, Color Forecasting
Sharon Griffis, Executive Director

A nonprofit international association of color designers involved in the use of color as it applies to the profitable marketing of goods and services.
1300 Members
Founded in 1962

17664 Communications Marketing Association

204 S. Shaffer Drive
New Freedom, PA 17349

717-439-7391
cmaexecdirector@gmail.com
www.cma-cmc.org
Facebook, Twitter, LinkedIn, YouTube

Alex Hinerfeld, President
Carl Peek, Vice President
Rob Menees, Secretary
Cliff Peck, Treasurer
Sharon Boyle, Executive Director

Organization of manufacturers, manufacturer's representatives and distributors in the wireless communications industry.

17665 Communications Roundtable

1250 24th Street NW
Suite 250
Washington, DC 20037

202-755-5180; Fax: 202-466-0544

Michael Reichgut, Chairman
Shawn Dolley, CEO

Association of more than 20 public relations, marketing, graphics, advertising, training and other communications organizations with more than 12,000 professional members. The goals include furthering professionalism, cooperation between member organizations, career and employment support, and employer assistance.

17666 Construction Marketing Association

1220 Iroquois Avenue
Suite 210
Naperville, IL 60563

630-868-5061
www.constructionmarketingassociation.org
Facebook, Twitter, LinkedIn, YouTube

Rick Dean, Board Member
Paul Deffenbaugh, Board Member
Kevin Enke, Board Member
Denice Shuty, Board Member

Donates and provides pro-bono marketing services to nonprofit and needy relating to construction.
Founded in 2009

17667 Construction Marketing Research Council C/O CMPA

4625 South Wendler Drive
Suite 111
Tempe, AZ 85282

602-431-1441; Fax: 602-431-0637
www.nrc-cnrc.gc.ca/eng/rd/construction/index.html

Craig Schulz, President
Don Johnson, Director at Large
Jim McMahon, Treasurer

Members are professionals in the construction products industry with responsiblities for their firms' corporate strategic planning and the conduct of marketing research activities. Membership is restricted to the highest level marketing research or planning professional within a company.
25 Members
Founded in 1992

17668 Culture Marketing Council

8280 Willow Oaks Corporate Drive
Suite 600
Fairfax, VA 22031

703-745-5531; Fax: 703-610-0227
info@culturemarketingcouncil.org
culturemarketingcouncil.org
Facebook, Twitter, LinkedIn, YouTube

Gonzalo Del Fa, Chair
Isabella Sanchez, Treasurer
Horacio Gavilan, Executive Director

Formerly known as the Association of Hispanic Advertising Agencies and AHAA: The Voice of Hispanic Marketing, the Culture Marketing Council represents the Hispanic marketing, communications and media industry.
45000 Members
Founded in 1996

17669 Data-Driven Marketing

Direct Marketing Association
1120 Avenue of the Americas
New York, NY 10036-6700

212-768-7277; Fax: 212-302-6714
www.thedma.org
Facebook, Twitter, LinkedIn

Gunther Schmachar, Chairman
Eva Reda, Vice Chairman
JoAnne Monfradi Dunn, CEO & President, Direct Marketing
Bruce Bieger, Senior Managing Director
Cathy Butler, SVP, Group Account Director

17670 Destinations International

2025 M Street NW
Suite 500
Washington, DC 20036

202-296-7888; Fax: 202-296-7889
info@destinationsinternational.org
destinationsinternational.org
Facebook, Twitter, LinkedIn, YouTube

Don Welsh, President & CEO
Melissa Cherry, COO
Jack Johnson, Chief Advocacy Officer
Nina Winston, EVP, Global Development & Alliances
Caitlyn Blizzard, VP, Communications

Serves destination marketing and management professionals.
650+ Members
Founded in 1914

17671 Digital Analytics Association

401 Edgewater Place
Suite 600
Wakefield, WA 1880

781-876-8933; Fax: 781-224-1239
info@digitalanalyticsassociation.org
www.digitalanalyticsassociation.org
Facebook, Twitter, LinkedIn

Marilee Yorchak, Executive Director
Adrienne Segundo, Education Manager
Matt Dirks, Director, Sponsorships
Catherine Hackney, Community Manager
Brooke Weldon, Membership Manager

Formerly known as the Web Analytics Association, it is a global organization of practitioners, corporations, vendors, marketing and public relations agencies, consultants, academics, and more involved in the growing digital analytics industry.
Founded in 2004

17672 Direct Marketing Association

1120 Avenue of the Americas
New York, NY 10036-6700

212-768-7277; Fax: 212-302-6714
customerservice@the-dma.org
www.thedma.org
Facebook, Twitter, LinkedIn

Gunther Schmachar, Chairman
Eva Reda, Vice Chairman
JoAnne Monfradi Dunn, CEO & President, Direct Marketing
Thomas J. Benton, Chief Operating Officer
Jerry Cerasale, J.D., Senior Vice President

The leading global trade association of businesses and nonprofit organizations using and supporting multichannel direct marketing tools and techniques. DMA advocates standards for responsible marketing, promotes relevance as the key to reaching consumers with desirable offers, and provides cutting edge research, education and networking opportunities to improve results throughout the end to end direct marketing process.
3100 Members
Founded in 1917

17673 **Distributive Education Clubs of America**
1908 Association Drive
Reston, VA 20191
703-860-5000
info@deca.org
www.deca.org
Facebook, Twitter, LinkedIn, Youtube, Pinterest, Instagram
Frank Peterson, Acting Executive Director
Christopher Young, Chief Program Officer
Cindy Allen, Director, Sponsorships
Diane Pruner, Grants Program Director
Michael Mount, Director, Data Management
DECA seeks to enhance the co-curricular education of students with interest in marketing, management, and entrprenuership. It helps students to develop skills and competence for marketing careers, to build self-esteem, to experience leadership and to practice community service.
215K Members
Founded in 1946

17674 **Diving Equipment & Marketing Association**
858-616-6408
800-862-3483; Fax: 858-616-6495
info@dema.org
www.dema.org
Facebook, Twitter, LinkedIn, YouTube, RSS, Instagram
Tom Ingram, President & CEO
Nicole Russel, VP, Operations
Colleen Vasquez, VP, Finance
Rachelle Reimers, Communications Manager
Alicia Vasquez, Member Services Assistant
Trade association for the international scuba diving industry.
1400 Members

17675 **EMarketing Association**
251 W. 30th Street
6th Floor
New York, NY 10001
212-678-2520
admin@emarketingassociation.com
www.emarketingassociation.com
Twitter, LinkedIn, YouTube
International association of eMarketing professionals committed to enriching the marketing community and its members through recognition, research, advocacy, education, and service.
Founded in 1997

17676 **Entertainment Resource & Marketing Association**
73450 Country Club Drive
Suite 46
Palm Desert, CA 92260
424-231-7322
mail@erma.org
www.erma.org
Michael Schrager, President
ERMA is an organization for entertainment marketing professionals.

17677 **Financial Communications Society**
368 Ninth Avenue
9th Floor
New York, NY 10001
908-858-0427
admin@thefcs.org
thefcs.org
Tim Hart, Chair
Tom Jago, Vice Chair
Katherine Divney, Secretary
Kevin Windorf, CEO
The FCS is devoted to improving professional standards in financial marketing communications, with a membership comprised of managers in advertising, marketing, PR, IR, corporate communications, and social and digital media.
Founded in 1967

17678 **Foodservice Sales & Marketing Association**
5225 Wisonsin Avenue NW
Suite 316
Washington, DC 20015-2055
202-596-8112; Fax: 202-293-1702
info@fsmaonline.com
www.fsmaonline.com
Twitter, LinkedIn, Youtube
Jerry Campbell, Chair & President
Barry Maloney, General Counsel, CFO & Exec. Dir.
John Krattenmaker, Operations Manager
Arlene Murphy, Director, Member Development
Specializes in selling food and related products to foodservice companies.
150 Members
Founded in 2003
Mailing list available for rent

17679 **Global Retail Marketing Association**
Home Page: www.thegrma.com
Twitter, LinkedIn
Brian Beitler, Co-Chair
Tim Rea, Co-Chair
Provides members with networking platforms and other resources to aid in organizational growth, including an annual leadership forum, regional marketing events, an online community, research, reports, and case studies, newsletters, and partners.

17680 **Healthcare Public Relations & Marketing Association**
5406 Hazeltine Ave.
Sherman Oaks, CA 91401
714-647-2430
info@hprma.org
Facebook, Twitter, LinkedIn
Pamela Westcott, President
Ava Alexander, Sponsorships
Jennifer Heinley, Secretary
Kathleen Curan, Communications
Lisa Killen, Membership

17681 **Hospitality Sales & Marketing Association International**
7918 Jones Branch Drive
Suite 300
McLean, VA 22102
703-506-3280; Fax: 703-506-3266
info@hsmai.org
www.hsmai.org
Facebook, Twitter, LinkedIn, Flicker
Robert A. Gilbert, President & CEO
Fran Brasseux, EVP
Jason Smith, VP, Marketing & Communications
Juli Jones, Vice President
Chris Durso, VP, Content Development
Global organization of sales, marketing, and revenue management professionals involved in the hospitality industry.
5000 Members
Founded in 1927

17682 **Incentive Marketing Association**
4248 Park Glen Road
Minneapolis, MN 55416
952-928-4649
info@incentivemarketing.org
www.incentivemarketing.org
Twitter, LinkedIn
Karen Wesloh, Executive Director
Ione Terrio, Marketing & PR Director
Angie Newgren, Communications Manager
Audrey Daley, Membership Coordinator
Members are professional premium/incentive marketing executives.
500+ Members
Founded in 1998

17683 **Incentive Performance Center**
5008 Castle Rock Way
Naples, FL 34112
914-591-7600; Fax: 239-775-7537
info@incentivecentral.org
www.incentivecentral.org
Howard C Henry, Executive Director/CAE
Your portal to new ways of achieving business goals by capturing the power of your best customers and employees.
150 Members
Founded in 1984

17684 **Insurance Marketing & Communications Association**
4248 Park Glen Road
Minneapolis, MN 55416
952-928-4644; Fax: 952-929-1318
info@imcanet.com
www.imcanet.com
Facebook, Twitter, LinkedIn, Youtube
Valerie Foster, Chair
Christopher Nance, Executive Vice-Chair
Hank Pinkowski, Treasurer
Megan Flanagan, Executive Director
An international organization of insurance communications professionals who specialize in marketing, marketing communications, advertising, sales promotion, and public relations.
Cost: $350.00
120+ Members
Frequency: Annual Membership Fee
Founded in 1923
Mailing list available for rent

17685 **Interactive Advertising Bureau**
116 E. 27th Street
6th Floor
New York, NY 10016
212-380-4700
learning@iab.com
www.iab.com
Facebook, Twitter, LinkedIn, YouTube, Instagram
David Cohen, Board President & CEO
Dennis Buchheim, President
Randall Rothenberg, Executive Chair
Dave Grimaldi, EVP, Public Policy
Sheryl Goldstein, SVP, Member Engagement & Dev.
The Interactive Advertising Bureau (IAB) is comprised of leading media and technology companies that are responsible for selling the majority of online advertising in the United States. On behalf of its members, the IAB is dedicated to the growth of the interactive advertising marketplace, of interactive's share of total marketing spend, and of its members' share of total marketing spend. The IAB educates marketers, agencies, and media companies about the value of interactive advertising.
650+ Members
Founded in 1996

17686 **Intermarket Advertising Network**
401 Mendocino Avenue
Santa Rosa, CA 95401
info@theengineisred.com
www.intermarketnetwork.com
Alicia Wadas, President
Tom Flynn, Vice President
Dan Borgmeyer, Membership Chair

The Intermarket Agency Network (IAN) is a forum for leaders of noncompetitive marketing agencies to openly exchange knowledge in a collaborative setting. A nationwide association of carefully selected agencies, its members meet twice annually to freely discuss important issues like new business, financials, HR, creativity, growth and much more. No topic is off limits.
13 Members
Founded in 1967

17687 **International Advertising Association**
114 E. 25th Street
Suite 915
New York, NY 10009
646-722-2612; Fax: 646-722-2501
iaa@iaaglobal.org
www.iaaglobal.org
Facebook, Twitter, LinkedIn
Joel Nettey, Chair & World President
Sasan Saeidi, Senior Vice President
Suresh Mathai, VP, Area Director, USA
Fredrik Borestrom, VP, Corporate Members
Dagmara Szulce, Managing Director, IAA Global
International network comprising thousands of members working in all areas of marketing communications.
Founded in 1938

17688 **International Communications Agency Network**
P.O. Box 3417
Nederland, CO 80466
720-215-6674
info@icomagencies.com
www.icomagencies.com
Facebook, Twitter, LinkedIn, Instagram
Emma Keenan, Executive Director
Nancy Giges, Media Relations Manager
Diane Venturino, International Meeting Planner
Alice Freeman, Finance Manager
Jennifer Henderson, Online Manager
ICOM is one of the world's largest networks of independent advertising and marketing communications agencies. Their mission is: To provide effective integrated communications resources to clients internationally; To provide a free exchange of ideas, information & support for members.
80+ Members
Founded in 1950

17689 **Internet Marketing Association**
200 Spectrum Center Drive
Irvine, CA 92618
949-443-9300
info@imanetwork.org
imanetwork.org
Facebook, Twitter, LinkedIn, YouTube
Sinan Kanatsiz, Chair & Founder
Sean Conrad, CEO
Lei Lani Fera, Head Of Creative
Hall Roosevelt, General Manager
Marcus Volpe, Executive Director
Seeks to provide members with the chance to learn, network, and establish Internet Marketing best practices. Members are in fields such as sales, marketing, business ownership, programming, and creative development.
Founded in 2001

17690 **Legal Marketing Association**
330 North Wabash Avenue
Suite 2000
Chicago, IL 60611-4267
312-321-6898; Fax: 312-673-6894
membersupport@legalmarketing.org
www.legalmarketing.org
Facebook, Twitter, LinkedIn, Youtube
Betsi Roach, Executive Director
Susan Lane, Director of Operations
Adrianne Watson, Membership Services
Lizzie Duvall, Membership Services
Justine Gershak, Membership Services
LMA is a nonprofit organization dedicated to serving the needs and maintaining the professional standards of the men and women involved in marketing within the legal profession.
2700 Members
Founded in 1985

17691 **Life Insurance Direct Marketing Association**
3227 S. Cherokee Lane
Suite 1320
Woodstock, GA 30188
770-516-0207
866-890-5323
info@lidma.org
lidma.org
Robert Bland, President
Nicole Buckenmeyer, Vice President
Jeff McCauley, Secretary-Treasurer
Brian Barnes, Membership Vice Chair
A nonprofit organization dedicated specifically to supporting businesses and professionals active in direct sales of term life insurance products to consumers.

17692 **Manufacturers Agents National Association**
6321 W Dempster Street
Suite 110
Morton Grove, IL 60053
949-859-4040
877-626-2776; Fax: 949-855-2973
mana@manaonline.org
www.manaonline.org
John Davis, Chairman
Charles Cohon, CPMR, President & CEO
Jerry Leth, Vice President and General Manager
Susan Srouse, Secretary/Treasurer
A national organization for manufacturers' agents and manufacturers who contract for the services of these representatives.
3000 Members
Founded in 1947

17693 **Marketing Agencies Association Worldwide**
60 Peachcroft Drive
Bernardsville, NJ 07924
908-428-4300; Fax: 908-766-1277
www.maaw.org
Aldo Cundari, President
Aldo Cundari, 1st Vice President
Dan Mortimer, VP On-line Services
John Williams, Executive Director
Rick Shaver, Treasurer
The Marketing Agencies Assocation Worldwide (MAA) is the only global organization dedicated solely to the CEOs, Presidents,Managing Directors and Principals of top marketing services agencies.
75 Members
Founded in 1963

17694 **Marketing Education Association**
PO Box 27473
Tempe, AZ 85285-7473
602-750-6735
www.nationalmea.org
Fosters the development and expansion of education for and about marketing as a descrete, clearly defined profession. Members are high school and postsecondary marketing educations as well as university-level teacher educations and collegiate marketing teacher education students.
Founded in 1982

17695 **Marketing Research Association**
1156 15th Street NW
Suite 302
Washington, DC 20005
202-800-2545; Fax: 888-512-1050
membership@marketingresearch.org
www.marketingresearch.org
Facebook, Twitter, LinkedIn, Google+
David Almy, CEO
The Marketing Research Association's Blue Book Research Services Directory is the research industry number one reference source.
Founded in 1957

17696 **Marketing Science Institute**
Marketing Science Institute
1000 Massachusetts Avenue
Cambridge, MA 02138-5396
617-491-2060; Fax: 617-491-2065
msi@msi.org
www.msi.org
Facebook, Twitter, LinkedIn
Katherine N.ÿ Lemon, Executive Director
Marni Zea Clippinger, Chief Operating Officer
Earl Taylor, Chief Marketing Officer
Liza Hostetler-Ingalls, Administrative Assistant
Susan Keane, Editorial Director
MSI publishes research done on a variety of marketing topics, including: E - Commerce, Metrics, Branding, New Products and Innovations, Communications and more. Individual papers and subscriptions are available. We accept proposals and papers for grant consideration.
65 Members
Founded in 1961

17697 **Mass Marketing Insurance Institute**
3007 Tilden Street, NW
Suite 7M-103
Washington, DC 20008
816-221-7575; Fax: 816-772-7765
Jeffrey.M.Collins@MedStar.net
www.mi2.org
Twitter, Youtube, Pinterest, RSS, Googl
Greg Carlile, Executive Director
Laurie Weber, Associate Director
Provides a forum for professionals engaged in marketing, sales and administration of employee benefits such as worksite marketing, payroll deduction and other mass marketed services.

17698 **Materials Marketing Associates**
136 South Keowee Street
Dayton, OH 45402
937-222-1024; Fax: 937-222-5794
email@mma4u.com
www.mma4u.com
Kimberley Fantaci, President
Members are chemical distributors representing manufacturers marketing chemical raw material specialties to makers of coatings, inks, pharmaceuticals, adhesives, cosmetics, plastics, soaps, detergents, etc.
19 Members
Founded in 1963

17699 **Midwest Direct Marketing Association**
P.O. Box 75
Andover, MN 55304
763-607-2943; Fax: 763-753-2240
office@mdma.org
www.mdma.org
Ben DuBois, Communications Director
Jolee Molitor, Programs Director

Vicki Erickson, Secretary/Treasurer
Jolee Moiltor, Past President

Dedicated to the advancement of professional and ethical practice of direct response marketing by members throughout the Upper Midwest.
600 Members
Founded in 1960

17700 Mobile Marketing Association
41 E. 11th Street
11th floor
New York, NY 10003

646-257-4515
mma@mmaglobal.com
www.mmaglobal.com
Facebook, Twitter, LinkedIn

Greg Stuart, CEO
Sheryl Daija, Chief Strategy Officer
Vassilis Bakopoulos, SVP, Industry Research
Andy Goldman, VP, Finance

A global nonprofit trade association comprised of more than 800 member companies that strive to accelerate the transformation and innovation of marketing through mobile technology, including emerging technologies such as 5G and artificial intelligence, driving business growth with closer and stronger consumerengagement.
800 Members

17701 Mobile Marketing Research Association
1006 Morgans Landing Drive
Atlanta, GA 30350

404-308-7173
www.mmra-global.org
Facebook, Twitter, LinkedIn, YouTube

Rick West, President
Mark Michelson, Executive Director

A global trade association dedicated to the promotion and development of professional standards and ethics for conducting marketing research on mobile devices.
Founded in 2011

17702 Multi-Level Marketing International Association
119 Stanford Court
Irvine, CA 92612

949-854-0484
info@mlmia.com
www.mlmia.com
Facebook, Twitter

Doris Wood, Chair
Carrol Leclerc, President, Canada
Tony Cannuli, COO

A nonprofit professional trade organization representing all sectors of the networking marketing industry on a worldwide basis.
Founded in 1985

17703 Multicultural Marketing Resources
New York, NY

212-242-3351
lisa@multicultural.com
www.multicultural.com
Facebook, Twitter, LinkedIn

Lisa Skriloff, President
Dominika Peszko, Marketing

A place where corporate executives can find diverse resources, experts and information on how to market to multicultural (ethnic and niche) consumer markets.
Founded in 1994
Mailing list available for rent: 10,000 names at $850 per M

17704 National Association of Display Industries
4651 Sheridan Street
Suite 470
Hollywood, FL 33021

954-893-7300; Fax: 954-893-7500
www.nadi-global.com

Klein Merriman, Executive Director
Tracy Dillon, Director Communications

A leading association for the visual merchandising profession. As visual merchandising has evolved over the years into playing an integral role in retail, NADI has always taken the lead in informing and educating members. The association's already significant support of the visual design profession has grown with NADI's exclusive sponsorship of GlobalShop's Visual Merchandising Show and StoreXpo.
Founded in 1942

17705 National Energy Marketers Association
3333 K Street, NW
Suite 110
Washington, DC 20007

202-333-3288; Fax: 202-333-3266
www.energymarketers.com

Dan Verbanac, Chair, Executive Committee
Chris Hendrix, 1st Vice Chair, Executive Committee
Pierre Koshakji, 2nd Vice Chair, Executive Committee
Craig Goodman, President
Harry Warren, Chair Emeriti

17706 North American Farmers' Direct Marketing Association
6161 N. Hillside Avenue
Indianapolis, IN 46220

855-623-3621
suzi@farmersinspired.com
nafdma.com

Suzi Spahr, Executive Director
Lisa Dean, Membership & Communications Manager
Jeff Winston, Education & Operations Manager

A membership association that advances the prosperity of its members and the farm direct marketing industry through networking, participation, education, and innovation.

17707 Performance Marketing Association
364 East Main St.
Suite 444
Middletown, DE 19709

805-233-7987
thepma.org
Facebook, Twitter, LinkedIn, RSS, Google+

Brian Littleton, President
Tony Pantano, Treasurer
Tricia Meyer, Secretary
Todd Crawford, Board Member
Rachel Honoway, Board Member
20000 Members
Founded in 2008

17708 Petroleum Marketers Association of America
1901 North Fort Myer Drive
Suite 500
Arlington, VA 22209

703-351-8000; Fax: 703-351-9160
info@pmaa.org
www.pmaa.org
Facebook, Twitter

Grady Gaubert, Chairman
Mike Bailey, Vice Chair
Mark Whitehead, 2nd Vice Chair
Benny Hodges, Brands Division Director
Greg Benson, West Region Chair
Founded in 1909

17709 Photo Marketing Association International
7918 Jones Branch Drive
Suite 300
McLean, VA 22102

703-665-4416
800-762-9287; Fax: 703-506-3266
www.theimagingalliance.com
Facebook, Twitter, LinkedIn

Allen Showalter, President
Robert L. Hanson, Vice President
Jim Esp, Executive Director/Secretary
Bill Eklund, Treasurer
18000 Members
Founded in 1924

17710 Power Marketing Association
Home Page: www.powermarketers.com

Ralph E. Beaty III, Membership/Communications Manager
Carol Ofiesh, Member Services Manager
Phil Ofiesh, Data Services Manager
Scott Spiewak, Publisher

17711 Private Label Manufacturers Association
630 Third Avenue
New York, NY 10017-6770

212-972-3131; Fax: 212-983-1382
info@plma.com
www.plma.com

Trade Association promoting the Private Label Industry.
3200+ Members
Founded in 1979

17712 Produce Marketing Association
1500 Casho Mill Road
Newark, DE 19711

302-738-7100; Fax: 302-731-2409
www.pma.com
Facebook, Twitter, Pinterest, Flickr

Cathy Burns, CEO
Doug Bohr, Executive Officer
Yvonne Bull, Chief Financial Officer
Lauren Scott, Chief Marketing Officer
Max Teplitski, Chief Science Officer

17713 Producers Livestock Marketing Association
PO Box 540477
North Salt Lake, UT 84054-0477

801-936-2424
800-791-BEEF
homeoffice@producerslivestock.com
www.producerslivestock.com

Rick O'Brien, General Manager
Brad Jones, Branch Manager
Bob Elliot, Assistant Branch Manager
Vivian Reed, Office Manager
Founded in 1935

17714 Professional Insurance Marketing Association
35 E. Wacker Dr
Suite 850
Chicago, IL 60601-2106

817-569-PIMA; Fax: 312-644-8557
www.pima-assn.org
Twitter, LinkedIn

Daniel O'Brien, CLU, President
Mona F. Buckley, MPA, Chief Executive Officer
William Suneson, Secretary

Mark Kelsey, Treasurer
Dave Armstrong, Director
120 Members

17715 **Promotion Industry Council**
1805 N Mill Street
Naperville, IL 60563-1275

630-369-7781; Fax: 630-369-3773

Manufacturers, distributors and users of promotion premiums. Increases understanding of incentives and the premium promotion process.
100 Members
Founded in 1940

17716 **Re:Gender**
11 Hanover Square
24th Floor
New York, NY 10005-2819

212-785-7335; Fax: 212-785-7350
Facebook, Twitter, RSS

Lucie Lapovsky, Chair
Aine Duggan, President
Andrea Greenblatt, Vice President of Operations
Debbie Kellogg, Vice President for External Rel
Gail Cooper, Vice President for Programs

A network of 120 leading research, policy and advocacy centers committed to improving the lives of women and girls. Provides the latest news, information and strategies needed to ensure fully informed debates, effective policies and inclusive practices.
3,000 Members
Founded in 1981

17717 **Restaurant Marketing & Delivery Association**
3636 Menaul Blvd.
Ste. 323
Albuquerque, NM 87110

membership@rmda.info
www.rmda.info
Facebook, Twitter, LinkedIn

Paul Birrell, President
David Farmer, Vice President
Wes Garrison, Treasurer
Anu Mehra, Convention
Luke Katuin, Technology
Founded in 1990

17718 **Sales and Marketing Executives International**
PO Box 1390
Sumas, WA 98295-1390

312-893-0751; Fax: 312-893-0751
admin@smei.org
www.smei.org
Facebook, Twitter, LinkedIn, Youtube, RSS,Blog

Clinton J. Schroeder MBA, CME, CS, Chairman
Willis Turner CAE CME CSE, President & Chief Executive Officer
Hans-Benno Mastboom, Senior Vice Chair
Antonio Rios-Ramirez, Senior Vice Chair
Nathalie Roemer CME, Secretary Treasurer

Members are most commonly professionals in the fields of sales and marketing management, market research management, sales training, distribution management and other senior executives in small and medium businesses.
10000 Members
Frequency: Annual Meeting (Fall)
Founded in 1935

17719 **Search Engine Marketing Professional Organization**
401 Edgewater Pl.
Suite 600
Wakefield, MA 1880

718-876-8866
info@sempo.org
www.sempo.org
Facebook, Twitter, LinkedIn, Blogpot, YouTube, Google+,Pint

Mike Grehan, Chair
Mike Gullaksen, President
Simon Heseltine, VP of Education
Marc Engelsman, VP of Research
Krista LaRiviere, VP of Local Group
Founded in 2002

17720 **She Runs It**
1460 Broadway
New York, NY 10036

212-221-7969
info@sherunsit.org
sherunsit.org
Facebook, Twitter, LinkedIn, Instagram

Lynn Branigan, President & CEO
Rebekah Walter, Director, Business Development
Megan Heady, Director, Programming
Cheri Carpenter, Communications Lead

Formerly known as the League of Advertising Women and Advertising Women of New York, the organization was founded as the first women's association in the communications industry. Members now include women in marketing, media, and tech.
1700 Members
Founded in 1912

17721 **Society for Marketing Professional Services**
123 North Pitt Street
Suite 400
Alexandria, VA 22314

703-549-6117
800-292-7677; Fax: 703-549-2498
info@smps.org
www.smps.org
Facebook, Twitter, LinkedIn, Youtube,Pinterest

Ronald D. Worth, CAE, FSMPS, CPS, CEO
Lisa Bowman, Senior Vice President
Mark DellaPietra, Vice President of Education
Tina Myers, CAE, Senior Vice President
Michele Santiago, Director of Marketing

Serving marketing and business development professionals employed by architectural, engineering and construction firms, SMPS provides education and networking opportunities tailored to build your bottom line.
5600 Members
Founded in 1973
Mailing list available for rent: 6000 names at $200 per M

17722 **Society of Digital Agencies**
280 Interstate North Cir. SE
Suite 300
Atlanta, GA 30339

info@sodaspeaks.com
www.sodaspeaks.com
Facebook, Twitter, LinkedIn, Pinterest, Behance

Lakia Newman, Communications Manager

An international association of respected digital marketing agencies and production companies. Provides infrastructure, processes, and products to enable knowledge sharing around best practices and business success.
100 Members
Founded in 2007

17723 **Society of Independent Gasoline Marketers**
3930 Pender Drive
Suite 340
Fairfax, VA 22030

703-709-7000; Fax: 703-709-7007
sigma@sigma.org
www.sigma.org

Tom Gresham, President
Kenneth A. Doyle, CAE, Executive Vice President
Mary Alice Kutyn, Director Meetings
Dennis Cuevas, Director of Education
Mary Alice Kutyn, Director of Meetings

Members are independent gasoline marketers.
270 Members
Founded in 1958

17724 **Specialty Equipment Market Association**
1575 S. Valley Vista Drive
Diamond Bar, CA 91765-0910

909-610-2030; Fax: 909-860-0184
sema@sema.org
www.sema.org
Facebook, Twitter, Google+

Dough Evans, Chairman
Christopher J. Kersting, President and CEO
George Afremow, Vice President
Steve McDonald, Vice President of Government Affair
John Kilroy, Vice President/General Manager, PRI

Represents the automotive aftermarket industry with government agencies and trade and consumer groups.
5200 Members
Founded in 1963

17725 **Sport Marketing Association**
1972 Clark Ave.
Alliance, OH 44601

330-829-8207
smaoffice@mountunion.edu
www.sportmarketingassociation.com
Facebook, Twitter, LinkedIn

Jim Kadlecek, President
Khalid Ballouli, VP of Academic Affairs
Elizabeth Gregg, VP of Student Affairs
Steven McKelvey, VP of Industry Relations
Beth Grupsmith, Social Media Consultant
Founded in 2002

17726 **Strategic Account Management Association**
10 N. Dearborn St.
2nd Floor
Chicago, IL 60602

312-251-3131; Fax: 312-251-3132
napolitano@strategicaccounts.org
www.strategicaccounts.org
Facebook, Twitter, LinkedIn, Pinterest, Google+

Bernard Quancard, President/CEO
Katherine Gotsick, Chief Operations Officer
Frankie Cusimano, Senior Manager, Membership
Matt Fegley, Chief Business Development Officer
Richard Rottsolk, Senior Manager, Corporate Resource

The Strategic Account Management Association is a non-profit organization devoted to developing and promoting the concept of customer-supplier partnering. SAMA is dedicated to the professional and personal development of the executives charged with managing national, global, and strategic account relationships, and to elevating the status of the profession as a whole. SAMA provides literature, training and research into

best practices in large, complex, global customer account management.
2000 Members
Founded in 1964

17727 **Thomson Reuters**
Thomson Reuters
2395 Midway Rd
Carrollton, TX 75006

646-223-4000
888-885-0206; Fax: 888-216-1929
trta.lei-support@thomsonreuters.com
www.tax.thomsonreuters.com

David K R Thomson, Chairman
Thomas H Glocer, CEO & Director
Robert D Daleo, Chief Financial Officer
Kelli Crane, Senior Vice President & CIO

A national organization that focuses on marketing and sales intelligence for top level marketing executives.

17728 **Trade Show Exhibitors Association**
2214 NW 5th St.
Suite 1005
Bend, OR 97701

541-317-8768; Fax: 541-317-8749
tsea@tsea.org
Facebook

Amanda Helgemoe, President
Michael Mulry, Vice President
Glenda Brundgardt, Treasurer
Chris Griffin, Secretary

Members are companies using exhibits for marketing, advertising or public relations.
1800 Members
Founded in 1966

17729 **Transportation Marketing & Sales Association**
9382 Oak Avenue
Waconia, MN 55387

952-466-6270
www.tmsatoday.org/
Facebook, Twitter, LinkedIn, YouTube

David Hoppens, Chairman
Dino Moler, President
Beth Carroll, VP-Administration & Finance
Candi Cybator, VP- Content & Strategy
Andy Williams, VP- Membership & Outreach
Founded in 1924

17730 **Video Advertising Bureau**
830 3rd Avenue
2nd Floor
New York, NY 10022

212-508-1200
info@thevab.com
thevab.com
Twitter, LinkedIn

Sean Cunningham, President & CEO
Danielle Delauro, EVP
Jason Wiese, SVP & Director, Strategic Insights
Marianne Vita, SVP & Director, Integrated Strategy
Lauren Liff, VP, Public Relations & Comms.

VAB is a research and marketing organization for the video industry, providing insights and custom analysis, while embracing emerging technologies.

17731 **Word of Mouth Marketing Association**
200 East Randolph Street
Suite 5100
Chicago, IL 60601

312-577-7610; Fax: 312-275-7687
membership@womma.org
www.womma.org
Facebook, Twitter, LinkedIn, YouTube, Google+

Suzanne Fanning, President
Chris Spallino, Director of Marketing
Jennifer Connelly, Events Manager
Chelsea Hickey, Marketing Manager & Editor

The Word of Mouth Association is dedicated to word of mouth and social media marketing. It is the leader in ethical word of mouth marketing practices through eduation including the WOMMA summit, professional marketing opportunities and knowledge sharing.
Founded in 2004

Newsletters

17732 **AMS Quarterly**
Academy of Marketing Science
c/o Louisiana Tech University
P.O. Box 3072
Ruston, LA 71272

ams@latech.edu
www.ams-web.org

Obinna O. Obilo, Editor
Nina Krey, Editor

Newsletter of the Academy of Marketing Science.
Frequency: Quarterly

17733 **Advanced Selling Power**
Thompson Group
6850 Austin Center Blvd
Suite 100
Austin, TX 78731-3201

512-418-8869; Fax: 512-418-1209
carol@thompson-group.com
www.thompson-group.com

Terry E Thompson, Publisher
Valerie A Canaday, Editor
Carol Thompson, President

Provides sales tactics, strategies and ideas to sales professinals and entrepreneurs. Each issue helps salespeople learn how to put together presentations, develop openings that keep customers interested, use testimonials correctly and more.
Cost: $10.00
Circulation: 1000
Founded in 1993

17734 **Airline Financial News**
Phillips Business Information
1201 Seven Locks Road
Suite 300
Potomac, MD 20854-2931

301-541-1400; Fax: 301-309-3847

Grier Graham, Editor

Newsletter that provides the most timely financial reports and market analysis for the entire airline industry.
Cost: $695.00
Frequency: Weekly

17735 **Antin Marketing Letter**
Alan Antin/Antin Marketing Group
19888 Sw Monte Vista Dr
Suite 205
Beaverton, OR 97007-5412

503-356-0504; Fax: 913-663-5552

Brad Antin, President
Alan Antin, Director of Marketing
William Hammond, Director of Marketing

How-to info on marketing for professionals and entrepreneurs (service businessess, retailers, wholesalers, professional practice).
Cost: $197.00
Frequency: Monthly

17736 **Application Servers and Media Servers**
Probe Research
3 Wing Drive
Suite 240
Cedar Knolls, NJ 07927-1000

973-285-1500; Fax: 973-285-1519
www.proberesearch.com

This bulletin describes the market for both applications and media servers; examines key issues and provides a profile of selected players in various product categories.

17737 **Art of Self Promotion**
Ilise Benun/Creative Marketing and Management
PO Box 23
Hoboken, NJ 07030

201-653-0783
800-737-0783; Fax: 201-222-2494
ilise@marketing-mentor.com

Lisa Cyr, Author
Ilise Benun, Marketing Manager

Nuts'n bolts for manageable marketing for small business owners and self employed professionals.
Cost: $100.80
8 Pages
Frequency: Quarterly
Founded in 1995

17738 **Auctioneer**
National Auctioneers Association
8880 Ballentine
Overland Park, KS 66214

913-541-8084; Fax: 913-894-5281
hcombest@auctioneers.org
auctioneers.org

Robert Shively, CEO
Wendy Dellinger, Advertising Manager
Steve Baska, Publications Editor
Ryan Putnam, Assistant Editor

Keeps members of the National Auctioneers Association informed of trends and legal issues related to auctioneering. Chronicles activities of the Association and its membership.
Frequency: Monthly
Circulation: 7000
Founded in 1948

17739 **Automated and Self-Provisioning Servers**
Probe Research
3 Wing Drive
Suite 240
Cedar Knolls, NJ 07927-1000

973-285-1500; Fax: 973-285-1519
www.proberesearch.com

A look at service provider implementation of automated and self - provisioning software systems. An explanation of the causes of delay and QoS degradation in IP networks.

17740 **BDA**
BDA News
900 W Sunset Boulevard
Suite 900
Los Angeles, CA 90069

310-712-0040; Fax: 310-712-0039
www.bda.tv

Jill Masters, VP Member Services
Jim Chabin, President

Newsletter, awards annual, magazine and directory published by BDA for designers in the motion graphics industry.
Cost: $5.00
Frequency: Monthly
Circulation: 2000
Printed in 4 colors on glossy stock

17741 **Bandwidth Management: Driving Profitablity to the Botton Line**
Probe Research
3 Wing Drive
Suite 240
Cedar Knolls, NJ 07927-1000
973-285-1500; Fax: 973-285-1519
www.proberesearch.com
Provides an analysis of the type of issues that require Bandwidth Management solutions. Makes a comparison of the types of technical solutions implemented in different parts of the network and the major benefits of each solution. Also analyzes the trends seen in IP traffic and inter - relationship with bandwidth management.

17742 **Bulletproof Marketing for Small Businesses**
Kay Borden/Franklin-Sarrett Publishers
3761 Vinyard Trce Ne
Marietta, GA 30062-5227
770-578-9410; Fax: 770-977-5495
Kay Borden, President
Publicity for small businesses, particularly producing news releases that get printed.
Cost: $15.00
Frequency: SemiAnnual
Founded in 1994

17743 **Business Owner**
Mailing & Fulfillment Service Association
1421 Prince Street
Suite 410
Alexandria, VA 22314-2806
703-836-9200; Fax: 703-548-8204
www.mfsanet.org
Facebook, Twitter, LinkedIn
David L Perkins Jr, Editor
Leo Raymond, Vice President
Developed specifically to communicate with owners and CEOs on issues unique to them. You'll receive a wealth of knowledge on growing your business, tax issues, insurance, estate planning, management, finance and much more.
Frequency: Bi-Monthly

17744 **Business-2-Business Marketer**
Business Marketing Association
Ste 123
1833 Centre Point Cir
Naperville, IL 60563-4848
630-544-5054; Fax: 630-544-5055
info@marketing.org
www.marketing.org
Facebook, Twitter, LinkedIn
Jeffrey Hayzlett, Chairman
Gary Slack, Vice Chairman
Bob Goranson CBC, Treasurer
Editorial covers all apsects of integrated marketing disciplines, including: sales management, trade show marketing, datbase and direct mail marketing, presentations, telemarketing, public relations, advertising and electronic marketing.
Cost: $150.00
16 Pages
Circulation: 4300
ISSN: 1073-4538
Founded in 1922
Printed in 4 colors on glossy stock

17745 **Cable & Wireless**
Probe Research
3 Wing Drive
Suite 240
Cedar Knolls, NJ 07927-1000
973-285-1500; Fax: 973-285-1519
www.proberesearch.com
A look at cable & wireless IP infrastructure, how the company is operating it, and how it is managing services on its network.

17746 **Cable Headed Equipment Markets Upstarts**
Probe Research
3 Wing Drive
Suite 240
Cedar Knolls, NJ 07927-1000
973-285-1500; Fax: 973-285-1519
www.proberesearch.com
This bulletin analyses the CMTS market and the role the equipment plays in the plans of the major cable operators to move towards the goal of full service operators. A market forecast is included and the major players profiled.

17747 **Cambridge Reports Trends and Forecasts**
Cambridge Reports
955 Massachusetts Ave
Suite 8
Cambridge, MA 02139-3178
617-661-0110; Fax: 617-661-3575
Gene Pokorny, Publisher
Key changes in consumer and public opinions.

17748 **Career News Update**
American Marketing Association
311 S Wacker Dr
Suite 5800
Chicago, IL 60606-6629
312-542-9000
800-262-1150; Fax: 312-542-9001
www.marketingpower.com
Facebook, Twitter, LinkedIn, Youtube
Dennis Dunlap, CEO
You'll receive the latest career and hiring advice as well as useful job resources and employment listings.
Frequency: Monthly
Mailing list available for rent

17749 **Collegiate Trends**
Strategic Marketing
550 N Maple Ave
Suite 102
Ridgewood, NJ 07450-1611
201-612-8100; Fax: 201-612-1444
weil@studentmonitor.com
www.studentmonitor.com
Marketing and media trends for marketers targeting college students.
Cost: $95.00
Frequency: Quarterly
Founded in 1987

17750 **Colloquy**
Frequency Marketing
PO Box 610
Milford, OH 45150-0610
513-248-2882; Fax: 513-248-2672
info_de@epsilon.com
www.epsilon.com
Bryan Kennedy, President/CEO
Jill Z. McBride, Chief Operating Officer
Catherine Lang, Chief Operating Officer
Paul Dundon, Chief Financial Officer
Jeanette Fitzgerald, General Counsel
Frequency Marketing, is the publisher of the COLLOQUY newsletter and COLLOQUY.com Web site, which are dedicated tot he discrimination of information about analysis of frequency marketing strategies and programs worldwide. COLLOQUY also provides educational and research services on a global basis to the loyalty marketing industry, and offers substantial news, research libraries and program archives to qualified subscribers at COLLOQUY.com.
Frequency: Quarterly
Circulation: 16,000+
Founded in 1990

17751 **Color Alerts**
1908 Mount Vernon Avenue
3rd Floor
Alexandria, VA 22301
703-329-8500; Fax: 703-535-3190
sgriffis@colormarketing.org
www.colormarketing.org
Judith van Vliet, President
Paula Lord, VP, Marketing
Sandy Sampson, VP, Communications & PR
Peggy van Allen, VP, Color Forecasting
Sharon Griffis, Executive Director
News and relevant information for color designers involved in the use of color as it applies to the profitable marketing of goods and services.
Founded in 1962

17752 **Competitive Advantage**
Competitive Advantage
PO Box 10828
Portland, OR 97296-0828
503-274-2953; Fax: 503-274-4349
Jim Moran, Publisher
Tonya Shrives, Promotional Director
Provides sales, marketing and management tools to make careers and companies more prosperous.
Circulation: 10,000

17753 **Conference Board Management Briefing - Marketing**
Conference Board
845 3rd Ave
Suite 2
New York, NY 10022-6600
212-759-0900; Fax: 212-980-7014
june.shelp@conference-board.org
www.conference-board.org
Jonathan Spector, CEO
Trends and practices in marketing.
Frequency: Monthly

17754 **Creative Selling**
Bentley-Hall
120 E Washington St
Suite 913
Syracuse, NY 13202-4003
315-701-0308; Fax: 315-471-2138
Contains training material for sales managers and sales training managers.
Cost: $7.00
Circulation: 6,500

17755 **Current Global Carrier Market Environment, Global Carrier**
Probe Research
3 Wing Drive
Suite 240
Cedar Knolls, NJ 07927-1000
973-285-1500; Fax: 973-285-1519
www.proberesearch.com
Addresses a sweeping review of current strategic, business, economic, financial, network technology, network operations and service portfolio topics now at work in global and international carriage. Also includes a discussion of the potential risk assessment value of existing and future bandwidth trading and arbitrage exchanges.

17756 **Current Thinking on Network Evolution and Its Laws**
Probe Research
3 Wing Drive
Suite 240
Cedar Knolls, NJ 07927-1000
973-285-1500; Fax: 973-285-1519
www.proberesearch.com
This issue focuses on three laws of network evolution used by new entrants and by vendors. These three laws seem to be justified when the stock market rewarded new entrants with enormous valuations simply based on technology and expensive business plans. Now that the stock market no longer rewards such ventures, an analysis of these three laws is warranted and what impact thay have had on the carrier business.

17757 **Customers First**
Dartnell Corporation
4660 N Ravenswood Avenue
Chicago, IL 60640-4510
773-907-9500; Fax: 773-561-3801
Clark Fetridge, Publisher
Jim Nawrocki, Editor
A practical periodical that provides employees with an organized plan of action for building and improving customer relations.
Cost: $62.00

17758 **DECA Insight**
Distributive Education Clubs of America
1908 Association Drive
Reston, VA 20191
703-860-5000
info@deca.org
www.deca.org
Frank Peterson, Acting Executive Director
News and teaching tools for high school division chapter advisors.
Frequency: 4x Year
Founded in 1946

17759 **Daily News E-Mail (3D)**
Direct Marketing Association
1120 Avenue of the Americas
New York, NY 10036-6700
212-768-7277; Fax: 212-302-6714
customerservice@the-dma.org
www.the-dma.org
Lawrence M Kimmel, CEO
Delivers the essential news, research, hot trends, and technological developments from the nations leading newspapers, trade publications, and the government all in an easy-to-read, time-saving format.

17760 **Dance Travel News**
Multicultural Marketing Resources
New York, NY
212-242-3351
lisa@multicultural.com
www.multicultural.com
Lisa Skriloff, President
Dominika Peszko, Marketing
A place where corporate executives can find diverse resources, experts and information on how to market to multicultural (ethnic and niche) consumer markets.
Founded in 1994

17761 **Dartnell Sales and Marketing Executive Report**
Dartnell Corporation
4660 N Ravenswood Avenue
Chicago, IL 60640-4510
773-907-9500
800-341-7874; Fax: 773-907-0645
infochicago@insightpd.com
www.insightpd.com
Craig Scherer, Senior Partner
Anthony Annibale, General Manager
Cost: $168.00
Frequency: Monthly
Founded in 1917

17762 **Data Service: ISDN, Private Lines, Frame Relay and ATM**
Probe Research
3 Wing Drive
Suite 240
Cedar Knolls, NJ 07927-1000
973-285-1500; Fax: 973-285-1519
www.proberesearch.com
We survey and highlight four major data transport technologies detailing the technology's strengths, weakness, specific applications, and basic carrier strategies.

17763 **Defining the M-Commerce Value Chain**
Probe Research
3 Wing Drive
Suite 240
Cedar Knolls, NJ 07927-1000
973-285-1500; Fax: 973-285-1519
www.proberesearch.com
Defines and unifies all participants in a mobile commerce transaction using the sentence Selecting, ordering and paying for items using a mobile device in a secure fashion. Examines the m-commerce business models selected carriers, ASPs and other vendors.

17764 **Delaney Report**
PRIMEDIA Intertec-Marketing & Professional Service
149 5th Avenue
#725
New York, NY 10010-6801
212-979-7881; Fax: 212-979-0691
tdrinfo@aol.com
http://www.delaneyreport.com
Thomas Delaney, Editor
Provides information on personnel changes, trade literature and indsutry events for advertising, media, media, and public relations executives. Reports on global news and developments.
Cost: $74.00

17765 **Digital Subscriber Line Access Multiplexer Upstarts**
Probe Research
3 Wing Drive
Suite 240
Cedar Knolls, NJ 07927-1000
973-285-1500; Fax: 973-285-1519
www.proberesearch.com
This bulletin examines the major DSALM vendors and forecast the market for DSLAM ports and equipment revenue until 2006.

17766 **Downtown Promotion Reporter**
Alexander Communications Group
1916 Park Ave
Suite 501
New York, NY 10037-3733
212-281-6099
800-232-4317; Fax: 212-283-7269
info@downtowndevelopment.com
www.downtowndevelopment.com
Romauld Alexander, President
Nadine Harris, Marketing Manager
Tested ideas for promotion, public relations, marketing, increasing business, participation, downtown image building, sales, and events.
Cost: $189.00
Frequency: Monthly
Founded in 1954

17767 **Drop Shippng News**
Consolidated Marketing Services
PO Box 7838
New York, NY 10150
212-688-8797; Fax: 212-688-8797
www.cmsassociates.com
Nicholas T Scheel, Editor/Publisher
Covers all facets of Drop Shipping; source directory for 300,000 consumer products. Book 'Drop Shipping' marketing methods.
Cost: $25.00
Frequency: Monthly
Founded in 1977

17768 **Dynamic Selling**
Economics Press
12 Daniel Road
Fairfield, NJ 07004-2565
973-227-1224; Fax: 973-227-9742
Covers sales issues and ways to improve sales.

17769 **Effective Telephone Techniques**
Dartnell Corporation
4660 N Ravenswood Avenue
Chicago, IL 60640-4510
773-907-9500; Fax: 773-561-3801
Clark Fetridge, Publisher
Kim Anderson, Editor
Training bulletin helps your team build profitable customer relations with every call.
Cost: $62.00

17770 **Empoyment Points**
Mailing & Fulfillment Service Association
1421 Prince Street
Suite 410
Alexandria, VA 22314-2806
703-836-9200; Fax: 703-548-8204
www.mfsanet.org
Facebook, Twitter, LinkedIn
Leo Raymond, Vice President
The content is written for business owners and operators who want to stay informed about current employment issues. The editorial is targeted on human resource issues and employment practices in the mailing and fulfillment services industry.
Frequency: 4x/Year
Circulation: 2000

17771 **Fiberoptics Market Intelligence**
KMI Corporation
98 Spit Brook Rd
Suite 400
Nashua, NH 03062-5737
603-243-8100; Fax: 603-891-9172
Richard Mack, VP/General Manager
David Janoff, President
Kurt A Ruderman, Analyst/Editor
Markets, technologies, strategic planning, issues, standards and competition in the fiber optics industry.
Cost: $595.00
Frequency: Fortnightly
Founded in 1974

17772 **Frohlinger's Marketing Report**
Marketing Strategist Communications
7 Coppel Drive
Tenafly, NJ 07670-2903
201-569-6088; Fax: 201-568-8538
Joseph Frohlinger, Editor/Publisher

Global marketing, advertising and media NL with emphasis on strategic and trend articles.
Cost: $200.00
Frequency: Bi-Monthly
Founded in 1988

17773 **Growth Strategies**
Growth Strategies
2118 Wilshire Blvd
#826
Santa Monica, CA 90403-5704

310-721-6322; Fax: 310-828-0427

Roger Selbert, President

A newsletter published twice a monthly since 1981 has been presciently reporting on economic, social, political, technological, demographic, lifestyle, consumer, business, management, workforce and marketing trends.
Cost: $146.00
Frequency: Monthly
Founded in 1981
Printed in 2 colors on glossy stock

17774 **Guerrilla Marketing International**
Cascade Seaview Corporation
PO Box 1336
Mill Valley, CA 94942-1336

415-383-5426; Fax: 415-381-8361

William Shear, Publisher

Marketing insights, trends and tips for small business.
Cost: $59.00
8 Pages
Frequency: Bi-Monthly
Founded in 1989
Printed in one color on glossy stock

17775 **Home Business Idea Possibility Newsletter**
Prosperity & Profits Unlimited
PO Box 416
Denver, CO 80201-0416

303-573-5564

A Doyle, Editor

Possibilities for home businesses.
Cost: $7.50
4 Pages
Frequency: Annual
Circulation: 1,000
Founded in 1996
Printed in one color on matte stock

17776 **How Long Can Traffic Grow?**
Probe Research
3 Wing Drive
Suite 240
Cedar Knolls, NJ 07927-1000

973-285-1500; Fax: 973-285-1519
www.proberesearch.com

Carrier lack of agreement on standard metrics for traffic measurement allows for any interpretation of data, misleads investors and vendors. Optical networking's future depends on a more rational approach to traffic statistics. An assessment of the three drivers for optical networking are discussed.

17777 **IMCA Newsletter**
Insurance Marketing & Communications Association
4248 Park Glen Road
Minneapolis, MN 55416

952-928-4644; Fax: 952-929-1318
info@imcanet.com
www.imcanet.com

Megan Flanagan, Executive Director

Available to members of the Insurance Marketing & Communications Association.
Mailing list available for rent

17778 **INFO Marketing Report**
Towers Club Press
9170 NW 11th Avenue
Vancouver, WA 98665

360-574-3084

Jerry Buchanan, Editor

Focuses on marketing of HOW TO information in all its many forms: print, audio, video, public speaking, etc.
Cost: $69.95
Frequency: Monthly
Founded in 1974

17779 **Imaging Market Forum**
Technology Marketing Corporation
800 Connecticut Ave
1st Floor East
Norwalk, CT 06854-1936

203-852-6800
800-243-6002; Fax: 203-866-3326
tmc@tmcnet.com
www.tmcnet.com
Twitter

Rich Tehrani, CEO

Case studies and opinions.

17780 **Incentive Marketing Association - Fast Take Newsletter**
Incentive Marketing Association
4248 Park Glen Road
Minneapolis, MN 55416

952-928-4649
info@incentivemarketing.org
www.incentivemarketing.org

Provides members with news and updates on association activities

17781 **Incentive Source**
Association of Incentive Marketing
4248 Park Glen Road
Minneapolis, MN 55416

952-928-4649
info@incentivemarketing.org
www.incentivemarketing.org

Karen Wesloh, Executive Director
Angie Newgren, Communications Manager

Membership directory of the Association of Incentive Marketing.
Cost: $50.00
Frequency: Annual

17782 **Infomercial Marketing Report**
Steven Dworman and Associates
11533 Thurston Circle
Los Angeles, CA 90049-2426

310-472-6360

Steve Dworman, Editor/Publisher

Insider information on the infomercial industry.
Cost: $395.00
Frequency: Monthly

17783 **Information Advisor**
Information Today
143 Old Marlton Pike
Medford, NJ 08055-8750

609-654-6266
800-300-9868; Fax: 609-654-4309
custserv@infotoday.com
www.infotoday.com

Thomas H Hogan, President
Roger R Bilboul, Chairman Of The Board

Provides comprehensive evlauation of research tools, timely and specific information you will use, new sources valuable to researchers and head to head analysis of the most popular information services.
Cost: $165.00
Frequency: Monthly
Mailing list available for rent

17784 **International Marketing Service Newsletter**
IDG Communications
375 Cochituate Road
#9171
Framingham, MA 01701-4653
Frank Cutitta, Publisher

This newsletter concentrates on the overseas advertising and marketing industry.

17785 **International Product Alert**
Marketing Intelligence Service
482 N Main St
Canandaigua, NY 14424-1049

585-374-6326
800-836-5710; Fax: 585-374-5217

Tom Vierhile, Editor

Reports product introductions from Europe, Asia and throughout the world.
Cost: $795.00
Frequency: Fortnightly
Founded in 1983

17786 **JonesReport**
PO Box 50038
Indianapolis, IN 46250-7830

317-576-9889
800-878-9024; Fax: 317-576-0441
www.jonesreport.com

William Willburn, Publisher/President
William Willburn, Editor
Lue Dyar, Circulation Manager

Monthly newsletter for shopping center marketing professionals. Free Resource Guide in September. Salary Survey results in December. Christmas planner issues in April. STEALable marketing ideas in every issue. Sample copies are available.
Cost: $145.00
16 Pages
Frequency: Monthly
Circulation: 1000
Founded in 1980
Mailing list available for rent: 6M names at $110 per M
Printed in 2 colors on matte stock

17787 **Levin's Public Relations Report**
Levin Public Relations & Marketing
2 East Ave
Suite 201
Larchmont, NY 10538-2419

914-834-2570; Fax: 914-834-5919
www.saralevin.com

Sara B Levin, President
Sylvia Moss, Editor

Strategies, tactics for the CEO, VP Sales and Marketing seeking new marketing/public relations effectiveness.
Cost: $29.00
Frequency: Quarterly
Founded in 1978

17788 **Licensing Journal**
PO Box 1169
Stamford, CT 06904-1169

203-358-0848

Charles Grimes, Publisher

A publication directed to leaders in the Intellectual Property, Technology and Entertainment Communities. Accepts advertising.
Cost: $150.00
23 Pages
Frequency: Annual
Circulation: 1,000

17789 **Licensing Letter**
EPM Communications
19 W. 21st St., #303
New York, NY 10010
212-941-0099
888-852-9467; Fax: 212-941-1622
www.epmcom.com
Ira Mayer, President
Michele Khan, Marketing
Contains features on licensed properties, market trends and survey analysis.
Cost: $467.00
Frequency: 22x Year
Founded in 1977

17790 **Long Haul Market**
Probe Research
3 Wing Drive
Suite 240
Cedar Knolls, NJ 07927-1000
973-285-1500; Fax: 973-285-1519
www.proberesearch.com
In this report, we take a look into the long haul market space and discuss some of the reasons - supply, demand and the resulting prices - that have reversed these service providers fortunes so dramatically over the past year or so. We also discuss long haul product lines, new networking technology and provide a table comparing market participants for convenient reference.

17791 **M-Commerce Security**
Probe Research
3 Wing Drive
Suite 240
Cedar Knolls, NJ 07927-1000
973-285-1500; Fax: 973-285-1519
www.proberesearch.com
In this bulletin, we examine the issue of security in the m-commerce transaction and the technologies that are appering to address it. We also create international m-commerce forecasts by region.

17792 **Mainly Marketing**
Schoonmaker Associates
30150 Telegraph Road
Suite 155
Bringham Farms, MI 48025
248-594-7800; Fax: 866-211-5711
WK Schoonmaker, Publisher
Marketing high technology products.

17793 **Make It Happen**
Action Marketing
3747 NE Sandy Boulevard
Portland, OR 97232-1840
503-287-8321; Fax: 503-282-2980
CE Colwell, Publisher
Marketing news for starting a business and marketing products.

17794 **Market: Africa/Mid-East**
PRS Group
6320 Fly Rd
Suite 102
East Syracuse, NY 13057-9792
315-431-0511; Fax: 315-431-0200
custserv@prsgroup.com
www.prsgroup.com
Mary Lou Walsh, President
Patti Davis, Chairman
Ben McTernan, Managing Editor
Patty Redhead, Production Manager
Demographic and lifestyle information about consumers in Africa and the Middle East.
Cost: $397.00
Frequency: Monthly
Founded in 1979

17795 **Market: Asia Pacific**
PRS Group
6320 Fly Rd
Suite 102
East Syracuse, NY 13057-9792
315-431-0511; Fax: 315-431-0200
custserv@prsgroup.com
www.prsgroup.com
Mary Lou Walsh, President
Patti Davis, Chairman
Ben McTernan, Managing Editor
Patty Redhead, Production Manager
Population and lifestyle trend information about consumers in the Asia-Pacific region.
Cost: $397.00
Frequency: Monthly
Circulation: 225
Founded in 1979
Printed in 2 colors on matte stock

17796 **Market: Latin America**
PRS Group
6320 Fly Rd
Suite 102
East Syracuse, NY 13057-9792
315-431-0511; Fax: 315-431-0200
custserv@prsgroup.com
www.prsgroup.com
Mary Lou Walsh, President
Patti Davis, Chairman
Ben McTernan, Managing Editor
Patty Redhead, Production Manager
Population and lifestyle trend information about consumers in the Latin America region.
Frequency: Monthly
Founded in 1979

17797 **Marketing Academics Newsletter**
American Marketing Association
311 S Wacker Dr
Suite 5800
Chicago, IL 60606-6629
312-542-9000
800-262-1150; Fax: 312-542-9001
www.marketingpower.com
Facebook, Twitter, LinkedIn, Youtube
Dennis Dunlap, CEO
This newsletter provides news and information that affect and inform this important constituency. It reviews Academic Council activities, profiles Academic SIGS and highlights upcoming events.
Mailing list available for rent

17798 **Marketing Communications Report**
14629 SW 104 Street
#272
Miami, FL 33186-4929
305-595-0063; Fax: 305-595-0380
Pete Silver, Editor
Highlights prevalent thoughts on successful marketing strategies and reviews new products.
Frequency: Monthly

17799 **Marketing Dynamics**
Recognition Technologies Users Association
10 High Street
Suite 630
Boston, MA 02110-1605
FAX 617-426-8911
Franklin Cooper, Publisher
Focuses on strategic marketing and planning in technology and industrial areas including technology commercialization. Also features articles on government programs and how to participate in them. International market and business development also are featured.
Cost: $120.00
Frequency: Bi-Monthly
Circulation: 5,000
Printed in 2 colors on glossy stock

17800 **Marketing Insights**
WPI Communications
55 Morris Ave
Suite 300
Springfield, NJ 07081-1422
973-467-8700
800-323-4995; Fax: 973-467-0368
info@wpicomm.com
www.wpicomm.com
Steve Klinghoffer, President
Marilyn Lang, Chairman
Founded in 1952

17801 **Marketing Library Services**
Information Today
143 Old Marlton Pike
Medford, NJ 08055-8750
609-654-6266
800-300-9868; Fax: 609-654-4309
custserv@infotoday.com
www.infotoday.com
Thomas H Hogan, President
Roger R Bilboul, Chairman Of The Board
Provides information professional in all types of libraries with specfic ideas for marketing their services.
Cost: $79.95
Frequency: Bi Monthly
ISSN: 0896-3908
Mailing list available for rent

17802 **Marketing Matters Newsletter**
American Marketing Association
311 S Wacker Dr
Suite 5800
Chicago, IL 60606-6629
312-542-9000
800-262-1150; Fax: 312-542-9001
www.marketingpower.com
Facebook, Twitter, LinkedIn, Youtube
Dennis Dunlap, CEO
This e-newsletter updates readers on the latest happenings in the marketing profession through news briefs, indepth features and interviews
Frequency: 2x/Monthly
Mailing list available for rent

17803 **Marketing Power Newsletter**
American Marketing Association
311 S Wacker Dr
Suite 5800
Chicago, IL 60606-6629
312-542-9000
800-262-1150; Fax: 312-542-9001
www.marketingpower.com
Facebook, Twitter, LinkedIn, Youtube
Dennis Dunlap, CEO
This update of the latest news, research and trends in the marketing industry and allied fields.
Frequency: Weekly
Mailing list available for rent

17804 **Marketing Pulse**
Unlimited Positive Communications
11 N Chestnut Street
New Paltz, NY 12561-1706
845-565-0615; Fax: 845-255-2231
Bill Harvey, Editor/Publisher
Focus on all aspects of new electronic media, advertising, entertainment, and marketing.
Cost: $300.00
Frequency: Monthly
Founded in 1979

17805 **Marketing Report**
Progressive Business Publications
PO Box 3019
Malvern, PA 19355-0719
610-695-0201
800-220-5000; Fax: 610-647-8098
customer_service@pbp.com
www.pbp.com
Ed Satell, CEO
Christine Wheeler, Marketing Manager
Cost: $264.00
8 Pages
Founded in 1989

17806 **Marketing Researchers Newsletter**
American Marketing Association
311 S Wacker Dr
Suite 5800
Chicago, IL 60606-6629
312-542-9000
800-262-1150; Fax: 312-542-9001
www.marketingpower.com
Facebook, Twitter, LinkedIn, Youtube
Dennis Dunlap, CEO
This e-newsletter provides members with content designed to educate and inform researchers or any member interested in marketing research topics.
Mailing list available for rent

17807 **Marketing Science Institute Newsletter**
Marketing Science Institute
1000 Massachusetts Ave
Suite 1
Cambridge, MA 02138-5379
617-491-2060; Fax: 617-491-2065
msi@msi.org
www.msi.org
Russ Winer, Executive Director
Leana McAlister, CEO
Focuses on people and events of MSI.
Circulation: 8000
Founded in 1968

17808 **Marketing Technology**
Zhivago Marketing Partners
381 Seaside Dr
Jamestown, RI 02835-2376
401-423-2400; Fax: 401-423-2700
kristin@zhivago.com
www.zhivago.com
Kristin Zhivago, President
Philip Zhivago, CEO
Thomas Baker, Owner
Solutions to internal political problems encountered by high-tech marketers, critiques marketing campaigns, and discuss what's working.
Cost: $269.00
Frequency: Monthly
Founded in 1970

17809 **Marketing Thought Leaders Newsletter**
American Marketing Association
311 S Wacker Dr
Suite 5800
Chicago, IL 60606-6629
312-542-9000
800-262-1150; Fax: 312-542-9001
www.marketingpower.com
Facebook, Twitter, LinkedIn, Youtube
Dennis Dunlap, CEO
These articles focus on the issues and concepts that shape marketing today and tomorrow.
Frequency: Monthly
Mailing list available for rent

17810 **Marketing to Emerging Minorities**
EPM Communications
19 W. 21st St., #303
New York, NY 10010
212-941-0099
888-852-9467; Fax: 212-941-1622
www.epmcom.com
Ira Mayer, President
Michele Khan, Marketing
Melanie Shreffler, Editor
Research, trends and lifestyle coverage of minority markets.
Cost: $377.00
Frequency: Monthly

17811 **Marketscan International**
Miller Freeman Publications
2655 Seely Avenue
San Jose, CA 95134
408-943-1234; Fax: 408-943-0513
Paul W Kelash, Editor/Publisher
PC and Networking news in Europe, Asia, and Latin America.
Cost: $395.00
Frequency: Monthly
Founded in 1987

17812 **Master Salesmanship**
Clement Communications
10 LaCrue Avenue
PO Box 36
Concordville, PA 19331
610-459-4200
888-358-5858; Fax: 610-459-4582
customerservice@clement.com
www.clement.com
Andrew B Clancy, Managing Editor
George Clement, President
Newsletter for professional salespeople.
Cost: $156.00
Founded in 1919

17813 **Meditation Software Market**
Probe Research
3 Wing Drive
Suite 240
Cedar Knolls, NJ 07927-1000
973-285-1500; Fax: 973-285-1519
www.proberesearch.com
Examines the mediation market, the major and niche players, functionality of the solutions, and service provider deployments.

17814 **Multicultural Travel News**
Multicultural Marketing Resources
New York, NY
212-242-3351
lisa@multicultural.com
www.multicultural.com
Lisa Skriloff, President
Dominika Peszko, Marketing
Newsletter that covers travel news of interest to ethnic and niche travelers and those who market to them.
Founded in 1994

17815 **Multimedia Strategist**
Leader Publications
345 Park Avenue S
New York, NY 10010-1707
212-779-9200
800-888-8300; Fax: 212-696-1848
www.alm.com
Stuart M Wise, Editor
Kerry Kyle, Circulation Director
William L Pollak, CEO/President
Aric Press, Editorial Director
Kevin Vermeulen, Vice President, Group Publisher
Cost: $175.00
Frequency: Monthly
ISSN: 1080-3904
Founded in 1997

17816 **New Account Selling**
Dartnell Corporation
4660 N Ravenswood Avenue
Chicago, IL 60640-4510
773-907-9500; Fax: 773-561-3801
Clark Fetridge, Publisher
Terry Breen, Editor
Timely and effective techniques for building sales and improving profits. Instructive series ideal for training new sales people and for increasing the productivity of your sales veterans.
Cost: $62.00

17817 **New Age Marketing Opportunities Newsletter**
New Editions International
PO Box 2578
Sedona, AZ 86339-2578
928-282-9574
800-777-4751; Fax: 928-282-9730
www.newagemarket.com
Sophia Tarila PhD, Production Manager
Focuses on issues dealing with good marketing buys, resources and pertinent marketing programs dealing in the historic, visionary marketplace.
Cost: $24.00
4 Pages
Frequency: Bi-Monthly
Circulation: 450
Mailing list available for rent
Printed in one color on matte stock

17818 **Next Genaration IAD for SOHO Markets**
Probe Research
3 Wing Drive
Suite 240
Cedar Knolls, NJ 07927-1000
973-285-1500; Fax: 973-285-1519
www.proberesearch.com
Examines the market for VoDSL - comapatible Integrated Access Devices (IAD) targeted toward SOHO customers. Identifies key issues associated with development, analyzes competitive dynamics and market requirements and reviews selected vendor products.

17819 **On The Move**
Transportation Marketing Communications Assoc
9382 Oak Avenue
Waconia, MN 55387
952-442-5638; Fax: 952-442-3941
www.tmcatoday.org
John Ferguson, President
Tom Nightingale, VP
Tracy Robinson, Treasurer
Edward Moritz, Secretary
Brian Everett, Executive Director
Provides regular feature articles on ways to effectively create more impact in transportation marketing, sales and communications strategies.

17820 **Online Marketing Letter**
Cyberware Media
1005 Terminal Way
Suite 110
Reno, NV 89502
808-874-0089
www.cyberware.com
Jonathan Mizel, Editor/Publisher

Reviews the marketing of products and services over commercial online services of the internet.
Cost: $195.00
Frequency: Quarterly
Founded in 1993

17821 **Online Marketplace**
Jupiter Communications Company
627 Broadway
2nd Floor
New York, NY 10012-2612
212-533-8885; Fax: 212-780-6075
Adam Schoenfeld, Editor
Gene DeRose, Publisher
Interactive transaction.
Cost: $545.00
Frequency: Monthly

17822 **Organized Executive**
Briefings Publishing Group
1101 King St
Suite 110
Alexandria, VA 22314-2944
703-548-3800
800-722-9221; Fax: 703-684-2136
www.briefings.com
Stephanie Winston, Editor-in-Chief
Lois Willingham, Production Manager
A publication designed to help busy people more effectively master their activities and time by applying advanced organizational strategies developed by Stephanie Winston.
Cost: $97.00
8 Pages
Frequency: Monthly
Circulation: 30000
Founded in 1981
Mailing list available for rent: 6000 names at $125 per M
Printed in 2 colors on matte stock

17823 **Overcoming Objections**
Dartnell Corporation
4660 N Ravenswood Avenue
Chicago, IL 60640-4510
773-907-9500; Fax: 773-561-3801
Clark Fetridge, Publisher
Christen Heide, Editor
Designed to give sales team practical responses to every objection they're likely to face and imparts proven techniques for turning every type of sales objection into a sales opportunity.
Cost: $62.00

17824 **Perspectives**
1375 King Avenue
PO 12279
Columbus, OH 43212-2220
614-486-6708
800-448-0398; Fax: 614-486-1819
www.mark-ed.org
J Gleason, President
Mary Carlisi, Production Manager
Information on education and marketing. Provides professional support and materials. Primary clients are schools, colleges and educational institutions.
Cost: $25.00
Circulation: 7500
Founded in 1971
Printed in 4 colors on matte stock

17825 **Photo Marketing**
Photo Marketing Association International
3000 Picture Pl
Jackson, MI 49201-8853
517-788-8100; Fax: 517-788-8371
www.theimagingalliance.com
Ted Fox, CEO
Terri Cameron, Publisher
Cost: $30.00
Frequency: Monthly
Founded in 1980

17826 **PostCom Bulletin**
Association for Postal Commerce
1800 Diagonal Road
Suite 600
Alexandria, VA 22314
703-524-0096; Fax: 703-997-2414
info@postcom.org
www.postcom.org
Michael Plunkett, President & CEO
Ellena Talbott, Director, Operations & Membership
Beth McConnell, Postal Consultant
A source of postal news and opinion.
Founded in 1947

17827 **PostScripts**
Association of Marketing Service Providers
1800 Diagonal Road
Suite 320
Alexandria, VA 22314-2806
703-836-9200; Fax: 703-548-8204
kgarner@mfsanet.org
www.amsp.org
Joseph P. Truncale, President & CEO
Each issue of PostScripts highlights a theme relevant to mailing or fulfillment operations, such as production management or information technology.
Frequency: Monthly

17828 **Postal Points**
Mailing & Fulfillment Service Association
1421 Prince Street
Suite 410
Alexandria, VA 22314-2806
703-836-9200; Fax: 703-548-8204
www.mfsanet.org
Facebook, Twitter, LinkedIn
Leo Raymond, Editor
Leo Raymond, Vice President
Deals exclusively with current and pending postal and delivery issues. Here you will find the facts and analysis of developing postal issues.
Frequency: 18x/Year

17829 **Pricing Advisor**
Pricing Advisor
3535 Roswell Rd
Suite 59
Marietta, GA 30062-8828
770-509-9933; Fax: 770-509-1963
info@pricingsociety.com
www.pricingsociety.com
Eric Mitchell, President
Michelle Darko, Editor
Sobem Nwoko, COO
Pricing strategy and tactics for marketing and corporate executives.
Cost: $400.00
8 Pages
Frequency: Monthly

17830 **Product Alert**
Marketing Intelligence Service
482 N Main St
Canandaigua, NY 14424-1049
585-374-6326
800-836-5710; Fax: 585-374-5217
Christine Dengler, Marketing Manager
Tom Vierhile, CEO
Diane Beach, Editor
A twice-monthly briefing on new packaged goods introduced in North America. Featuring product pictures and descriptions with indexing provided in two convenient formats. Also available in a twice monthly, international version.
Cost: $795.00

17831 **Promos & Premiums**
New World Media
PO Box 95
Newton Centre, MA 02156
781-483-8967; Fax: 617-367-9151
Jennifer Sawyer English, Editor/Publisher
Barbara Kalunian, Publisher
Informs consumers, collectors, dealers, and marketing executives about the best special offers available nationwide.
Cost: $19.95
Frequency: Monthly
Founded in 1994

17832 **Research Alert**
EPM Communications
19 W. 21st St., #303
New York, NY 10010
212-941-0099
888-852-9467; Fax: 212-941-1622
www.epmcom.com
Ira Mayer, President
Michele Khan, Marketing
Melanie Shreffler, Editor
Analyzes research on consumer behavior and attitudes.
Cost: $389.00
Frequency: 24x Year

17833 **Revisiting R&D**
Probe Research
3 Wing Drive
Suite 240
Cedar Knolls, NJ 07927-1000
973-285-1500; Fax: 973-285-1519
www.proberesearch.com
With the collapse of the bull market and the apparent collapse of viable wireline competition, the ILECs must focus on the role of wireless as a major competitor. The new Bush administration appears to be pro-ILEC and this will translate into a series of reglatory initiatives that may in total favor the ILECs R&D agendas have to shift to support innovative solutions in the access domain and in mobile.

17834 **Roper's Public Pulse**
Roper Starch Worldwide
29 W 35th Street
5th Floor
New York, NY 10001-2299
212-240-5300; Fax: 212-564-0465
www.roper.com
Diane Crispell, Editor
Content includes the latest research on demographic trends, new insights from opinion research experts as to what Americans think, concise, brand-focused data, current consumer attitudes toward dozens of American themes, as well as news updates on special markets and brands.
Cost: $299.00
Frequency: Monthly
Circulation: 2000

17835 **SBC**
Probe Research
3 Wing Drive
Suite 240
Cedar Knolls, NJ 07927-1000
973-285-1500; Fax: 973-285-1519
www.proberesearch.com
Discussion and analysis of ILEC/vendor market dynamics; case study of SBC's metro optical architecture; technology evolution; new services offered; incorporation of passive optical networking and metro DWDM rollouts; strategy going forward.

17836 **Sales Bullet**
Economics Press
12 Daniel Road
Fairfield, NJ 07004-2565
973-227-1224; Fax: 973-227-9742
Robert Guder, Editor
Diane Cody, Promotional Director
Covers the fundamental and subtleties of professional selling with methods, principles and ideas all salespoeple will find useful.
Circulation: 9,000

17837 **Sales Manager's Bulletin**
Bureau of Business Practice
76 Ninth Avenue
7th Floor
New York, NY 10011
212-771-0600; Fax: 212-771-0885
www.aspenlawschool.com
Robert Becker, CEO
Gustavo Dobles, VP Operations
For front-line sales management. Focus on sales hiring, training, managing, motivation, results. Reports what people in sales management field are doing to produce measurable sales profits.
Cost: $9.00
Circulation: 4,290

17838 **Sales Productivity Review**
Penoyer Communications
PO Box 2509
Santa Clara, CA 95055-2509
408-248-5458
800-248-5458; Fax: 408-296-6917
info@penoyer.com
www.penoyer.com
Flyn Penoyer, President
Edited for sales management with an editorial focus that will assist in improving sales productivity and effectiveness.
Cost: $5.00
Frequency: 6 issues per ye

17839 **Sales Promotion Monitor**
Commerce Communications
418 N 3rd Street
Suite 303
Milwaukee, WI 55410-2444
414-225-9085; Fax: 414-225-9095
tom@com-broker.com
www.com-broker.com
K Sederberg, Publisher
Tom Millitzer, Contact
News and information concerning all aspects of sales promotion.

17840 **Sales Rep's Advisor**
Alexander Communications Group
1916 Park Ave
Suite 501
New York, NY 10037-3733
212-281-6099
800-232-4317; Fax: 212-283-7269
info@repsadvisor.com
www.repsadvisor.com
Romauld Alexander, President
Bill Keenan, Editor
Adam Reis, Marketing
For independent manufacturers sales representatives. Filled with concise advice and ideas for reducing costs and increasing profits.
Cost: $199.00
Frequency: Monthly
ISSN: 0278-5048
Founded in 1954

17841 **Sarah Stambler's E-Tactics Letter**
E-Tactics
370 Central Park W
#210
New York, NY 10025-6517
212-222-1713; Fax: 212-678-6357
info@e-tactics.com
www.e-tactics.com
Sarah Stambler, President
Shlomo Bar-Ayal, Circulation Manager
Publication devoted to the creative use of electronic alternative media in the design and implementation of customer driven marketing, research and publication strategies.
Circulation: 5000
ISSN: 1070-809X
Founded in 1984

17842 **School Marketing Newsletter**
School Market Research Institute
1721 Saybrook Road
PO Box 10
Haddam, CT 06438
860-345-8183
800-838-3444; Fax: 860-345-3985
Bob Stimolo, Publisher
Lynn Stimolo, Account Executive
Sally Chittenden, Account Executive
How to articles, trends, original research, interviews with experts on school marketing Pre-K - 12th.
Cost: $119.00
12 Pages
Frequency: Monthly
Circulation: 500
ISSN: 0882-701X
Founded in 1980
Printed in one color on matte stock

17843 **Selling Advantage**
Progressive Business Publications
PO Box 3019
Malvern, PA 19355-0719
610-695-0201
800-220-5000; Fax: 610-647-8098
webmaster@pbp.com
www.pbp.com
Ed Satell, CEO
Phillip Ahr, Editor
Business-to-business sales advice to assist sales staff and sales managers.
Cost: $94.56
Circulation: 60,000
Founded in 1989

17844 **Selling To Kids**
Phillips Publishing
PO Box 611130
Potomac, MD 20859-2931
301-208-6787; Fax: 301-340-1451
Angela Duff, Associate Publisher
Editorial offers news and practical advice on strategies in successful marketing. Includes information on market research, buying trends, and media opportunities and features news on conferences as well as a look at new products and services.
Cost: $495.00
Frequency: BiWeekly

17845 **Selling to Seniors**
CD Publications
8204 Fenton St
Silver Spring, MD 20910-4571
301-588-6380
800-666-6380; Fax: 301-588-6385
www.cdpublications.com
Michael Gerecht, President
Jean Van Ryzin, Editor
Published as a subscriber driven newsletter targeting marketers and advertisers of products and services for the mature market.
Cost: $294.00
Frequency: Monthly
Founded in 1961
Mailing list available for rent: 2,000 names at $160 per M

17846 **Service Level Agreements**
Probe Research
3 Wing Drive
Suite 240
Cedar Knolls, NJ 07927-1000
973-285-1500; Fax: 973-285-1519
www.proberesearch.com
Details service level agreements that are being offered by several major service providers, and examines many of the popular software solutions taht are being used in their networks. Also a briefly discusses XML, and its potential uses.

17847 **Siedlecki on Marketing**
Richard Siedlecki Business & Marketing
4767 Lake Forrest Drive NE
Atlanta, GA 30342-2539
770-436-8271; Fax: 403-303-9939
Richard Siedlecki, Editor
Tips, techniques, and insights on marketing.
Cost: $49.00
6 Pages
Frequency: BiWeekly
Circulation: 500
Printed in one color on matte stock

17848 **SmartBrief**
Culture Marketing Council
8280 Willow Oaks Corporate Drive
Suite 600
Fairfax, VA 22031
703-745-5531; Fax: 703-610-0227
info@culturemarketingcouncil.org
culturemarketingcouncil.org
Horacio Gavilan, Executive Director
E-mail newsletter of the Culture Marketing Council (formerly the Association of Hispanic Advertising Agencies).

17849 **Strategic Health Care Marketing**
Health Care Communications
11 Heritage Lane
PO Box 594
Rye, NY 10580-594
914-967-6741; Fax: 914-967-3054
healthcomm@aol.com
www.strategichealthcare.com
Michele von Dambrowski, Editor/Publisher
Michele von Dambrowski, CEO
Business development and marketing startegies for health care executives.
Cost: $279.00
12 Pages
Frequency: Monthly
Circulation: 1200
Founded in 1984
Printed in 2 colors on matte stock

17850 **Subscribe**
PO Box 194
Bryn Mawr, PA 19010-0194
Lynn Kerrigan, Editor
Gail Jennings, Administration
A newsletter offering marketing ideas to help gain new subscribers and retain old ones.
Cost: $49.00
Frequency: Quarterly

17851 **Successful Closing Techniques**
Dartnell Corporation
4660 N Ravenswood Avenue
Chicago, IL 60640-4510
773-907-9500; Fax: 773-561-3801
Clark Fetridge, Publisher
Terry Breen, Editor
Fail-safe techniques for acquiring bigger sales and more frequent closings.
Cost: $62.00

17852 **Target Market News**
Target Market News
228 S Wabash Ave
Suite 210
Chicago, IL 60604-2383
312-408-1881; Fax: 312-408-1867
TargetMarketNews@aol.com
www.targetmarketnews.com
Facebook, Twitter
Ken Smikle, President
Hallie Mummert, Editor
News and developments in the areas of black consumer marketing and black-oriented media.
Cost: $40.00
12 Pages
Frequency: Monthly
Founded in 1988

17853 **Trends Journal**
Trends Research Institute
P.O.Box 3476
Kingston, NY 12402-3476
845-876-6700; Fax: 845-758-5252
www.trendsresearch.com
Gerald Celente, Editor
Emily Arter, Manager
Offers the inside track on trends affecting your business, your profession, your life. Forecasts on over 300 trend categories - consumer, social, economic, political, media, health, family, education, and other domestic and international trends.
Cost: $185.00
Frequency: Quarterly
Founded in 1980
Printed in 2 colors on glossy stock

17854 **Upline**
MLM Publishing
106 W South Street
Charlottesvle, VA 22902-5039
FAX 434-979-1602
John Milton Fogg, Editor
Randolph Byrd, Publisher
Distribution training for network (multilevel) marketers.
Founded in 1990

17855 **Video Marketing Newsletter**
Outback Group Productions
PO Box 872
Harrison, AR 72602-0872
FAX 870-741-4727
Dan Reynolds, Editor/Publisher
Information, business opportunities, marketing tips, product reviews. For people interested in producing and marketing their own videos.
Cost: $185.00
Frequency: Monhtly
Founded in 1989

17856 **What's Working in Sales Management**
Progressive Business Publications
PO Box 3019
Malvern, PA 19355-0719
610-695-0201
800-220-5000; Fax: 610-647-8098
webmaster@pbp.com
www.pbp.com
Ed Satell, CEO
Richard Kern, Editor
Sales management news and issues.
Cost: $264.00
Founded in 1989

17857 **Youth Markets Alert**
EPM Communications
19 W. 21st St., #303
New York, NY 10010
212-941-0099
888-852-9467; Fax: 212-941-1622
www.epmcom.com
Ira Mayer, President
Michele Khan, Marketing
Larissa Faw, Editor
Research reports on trends in youth response to marketing techniques and buying.
Cost: $447.00
Frequency: 24x Year

Magazines & Journals

17858 **ADCLIP**
National Research Bureau
320 Valley St
Burlington, IA 52601-5513
319-752-5415; Fax: 319-752-3421
mail@national-research-bureau.com
www.national-research-bureau.com
Diane M Darnall, President
Nancy Heinzel, Circulation Manager
Individualized adclipping service providing market intelligence information on various retail operations. Includes full size, pages, market strategies, advertising promotion ideas, new store openings and more.

17859 **ANA Magazine**
Association of National Advertisers
10 Grand Central, 155 E. 44th Street
New York, NY 10017
212-697-5950; Fax: 212-687-7310
info@ana.net
www.ana.net
Bob Liodice, Chief Executive Officer
Duke Fanelli, EVP & CMO
The latest news and insights from the Association of National Advertisers.

17860 **Ad Age**
Crain Communications
684 Third Ave
New York, NY 10017
212-210-0100
adage.com
Facebook, Twitter, LinkedIn
Josh Golden, Publisher
Heidi Waldusky, Assoc. Publisher & General Manager
Editorial insights, exclusive analysis and proprietary data take readers beyond the day's news, helping our audience understand ongoing and emerging trends.
Frequency: Weekly
Circulation: 56650
Founded in 1930

17861 **Adage Global**
Crain Communications
711 3rd Ave
New York, NY 10017-4014
212-210-0785; Fax: 212-210-0200
info@crain.com
www.crain.com
Norm Feldman, President
Scott Donaton, Editor
David Klein, Publisher
Philip Scarano, Circulation Director
Vanessa Reed, Marketing Director
Dedicated to being the world's essential advertising, marketing and media publication, with editors around the world, Adage covers topics of significance form Times Square to Taiwan.
Cost: $69.95
Frequency: Weekly
Circulation: 57,800
Founded in 1943
Printed in 4 colors

17862 **Advantages**
Advertising Specialty Institute
4800 Street Road
Trevose, PA 19053
800-546-1350
ideas@asicentral.com
www.asicentral.com
Timothy Andrews, President & CEO
Dave Vagnoni, Editor
Written especially for the promotional products sales professional, with tips and sales tactics.
Frequency: 15x/Year

17863 **Advertising and Marketing Law in Canada**
Association of Canadian Advertisers
21 St. Clair Avenue E.
Suite 1201
Toronto, ON M4T 1L9
416-964-3805
800-565-0109; Fax: 416-964-0771
communications@acaweb.ca
www.acaweb.ca
Ron Lund, President & CEO
Judy Davey, VP, Media Policy & Marketing
Davina Wong, Director, Membership
Jessica Yared, Manager, Digital Marketing
Current information on advertising and marketing law in Canada, including the latest on social media advertising practices and changes to online behavioural advertising.
Founded in 1914

17864 **Adweek**
Prometheus Global Media
770 Broadway
New York, NY 10003-9595
212-493-4100; Fax: 646-654-5368
www.prometheusgm.com
Facebook, Twitter, RSS
Richard D. Beckman, CEO
James A. Finkelstein, Chairman
Madeline Krakowsky, Vice President Circulation
Tracy Brator, Executive Director Creative Service
Adweek is the source for advertising and agency news, information and opinion. Covering the industry from an agency perspective Adweek focuses on the image makersand those who create the strategy and the ads as well as those who buy the media and handle client rela-

tions.
Cost: $149.00
Frequency: Weekly
Circulation: 36032
Founded in 1978

17865 **Agency Sales Magazine**
Manufacturers Agents National Association
6321 W Dempster Street
Suite 110
Morton Grove, IL 60053

949-859-4040
877-626-2776; Fax: 949-855-2973
mana@manaonline.org
www.manaonline.org

Charles Cohon, CPMR, President & CEO

Chronicling the changes which continue to take place nationwide that affect businesses. Explores the latest tax developments, sales tips, market data, management aids, legal bulletins and more.
96 Pages
Frequency: Monthly
Circulation: 50000
Printed in on glossy stock

17866 **Agri Marketing Magazine**
Henderson Communications LLC
1422 Elbridge Payne Rd
Suite 250
Chesterfield, MO 63017-8544

636-728-1428; Fax: 636-777-4178
info@agrimarketing.com
www.agrimarketing.com

Lynn Henderson, President

Covers the unique interests of corporate agribusiness executives, their marketing communications agencies, the agricultural media, ag trade associations and other ag related professionals.
Circulation: 8000
Founded in 1962

17867 **AgriSelling Principles and Practices**
Henderson Communications LLC
1422 Elbridge Payne Rd
Suite 250
Chesterfield, MO 63017-8544

636-728-1428; Fax: 636-777-4178
info@agrimarketing.com
www.agrimarketing.com

Lynn Henderson, President
Marilyn Holschuh, Editor

This 448-page book is utilized by many major agribusiness corporations and academic institutions for training its sales and marketing staff and or students.

17868 **B-to-B Marketer**
Association of National Advertisers
10 Grand Central, 155 E. 44th Street
New York, NY 10017

212-697-5950; Fax: 212-687-7310
info@ana.net
www.ana.net

Bob Liodice, Chief Executive Officer
Duke Fanelli, EVP & CMO

Best practices, case studies and expert advice from the Association of National Advertisers.

17869 **Brand Marketing**
Fairchild Publications
7 W 34th St
New York, NY 10001-8100

212-988-2882; Fax: 212-630-3868
info@brandmarketingltd.com
www.brandmarketingltd.com

Richard Faul, Publisher
Mary Berner, President

Covers how manufactureres launch and build brands, and how they leverage brand equity in new ways using new techniques. These ways include partnerships with retailers via trade marketing and information technology and a variety of cost-reduction strategies such as everyday low pricing and efficient consumer response.
Cost: $90.00
Frequency: Monthly
Circulation: 18,543

17870 **Brandweek**
Prometheus Global Media
770 Broadway
New York, NY 10003-9595

212-493-4100; Fax: 646-654-5368
www.prometheusgm.com

Richard D. Beckman, CEO
James A. Finkelstein, Chairman
Madeline Krakowsky, Vice President Circulation
Tracy Brater, Executive Director Creative Service

Focuses on marketing strategy and services, brand identity, sponsorships, licensing, media usage and distribution and promotions.
Frequency: Weekly
Circulation: 25784
Founded in 1991

17871 **Broker News**
Broker Publishing
PO Box 20287
Fountain Hills, AZ 85269-0287

480-816-1400
800-475-3565; Fax: 480-836-7767
www.brokernews-online.com

Joanne Genualdi, Account Executive

Serving insurance producers and financial planners across the country.
Cost: $12.00
32+ Pages
Frequency: Bi-Monthly
Founded in 1990

17872 **BtoB Magazine**
Ad Age Group/ Division of Crain Communications
711 3rd Ave
New York, NY 10017-4014

212-210-0785; Fax: 212-210-0200
info@crain.com
www.crain.com

Norm Feldman, President

Dedicated to integrated business to business marketing. Every page is packed with substance news, reports, technologies, benchmarks, best practices served up by the most knowledgeable journalists.
Frequency: Monthly
Circulation: 45000

17873 **Business Journal**
120 W Morehead Street
Suite 200
Charlotte, NC 28202

704-472-2340
800-948-5323; Fax: 704-973-1102
www.bizjournals.com/charlotte

Robert Morris, Editor
Megan Foley, Marketing Manager
Jeannie Falknor, Publisher

Provides marketing solutions and caring service.
Cost: $82.00
Frequency: Monthly

17874 **CRM Magazine**
Information Today
143 Old Marlton Pike
Medford, NJ 08055-8750

609-654-6266
800-300-9868; Fax: 609-654-4309
custserv@infotoday.com
www.infotoday.com

Thomas H Hogan, President
Roger R Bilboul, Chairman Of The Board

Offers vital information that will help you benefit from the experience of others in the industry.
Cost: $23.95
Mailing list available for rent: 4M names
Printed in 4 colors on glossy stock

17875 **Catalog Success**
North American Publishing Company
1500 Spring Garden St
Suite 1200
Philadelphia, PA 19130-4094

215-238-5300; Fax: 215-238-5342
phatch@napco.com
www.catalogsuccess.com

Ned S Borowsky, CEO
Matt Griffin, Associate Editor
Peggy Hatch, VP Group Publishing

Putting marketing management to the test.
Frequency: Monthly
Circulation: 20000
ISSN: 1524-2307
Founded in 1999
Printed in 4 colors

17876 **Chamber Executive Magazine**
Association of Chamber of Commerce Executives
1330 Braddock Place
Suite 300
Alexandria, VA 22314

703-998-0072; Fax: 888-577-9883
wburns@acce.org
secure.acce.org

Will Burns, VP, Communications & Networks

Magazine offering relavant information for chambers and the businesses they serve, including best practices, community issues and trends.
Cost: $32.00
Frequency: Quarterly
Founded in 1914

17877 **Circulation Management**
Primedia
1166 Avenue of the Americas/10th Fl
New York, NY 10036

212-204-4200; Fax: 913-514-6895
www.penton.com

Eric Jacobson, Senior VP
Ron Wall, Chief Officer
Chris Meyer, Director, Corporate Communications

Serves consumer/special interest and business/trade/association publications.
Frequency: Monthly
ISSN: 0888-8191
Founded in 1986
Printed in 4 colors

17878 **Connect**
Media-Mark
114 Sansome St
Suite 1224
San Francisco, CA 94104-3803

415-743-6220; Fax: 415-421-6225
connect@media-mark.com
www.media-mark.com

Art Garcia, Publisher

Features report on news-making agencies and corporate departments making news, as well as the people managing them, and rate/review PR services and products. Regular sections also report on international PR/marketing andmedia, women in marketing, investor relations, internet marketing, senior-level moves and promotions, account changes, trends, case studies and industry chatter.

17879 **Consumer Goods Technology**
Edgell Communications
4 Middlebury Boulevard
Randolph, NJ 07869

973-252-0100; Fax: 973-252-9020
cs@e-circ.net

Gabriele A. Edgell, Chairman & CEO
Joe Skorupa, Editor-in-Chief
Andrew Gaffney, Group Publisher
Gerald Ryerson, President

Consumer Goods Technology serves manufacturers of accessories, shoes, apparel, appliances, consumer electronics, office products, automotive aftermarket products, seasonal merchandise, transporters of consumer products, consultants and others allied to the field.
Frequency: Monthly
Circulation: 25035
Founded in 1984
Printed in 4 colors on glossy stock

17880 **Counselor**
Advertising Specialty Institute
4800 Street Road
Trevose, PA 19053

800-546-1350
ideas@asicentral.com
www.asicentral.com

Timothy Andrews, President & CEO
Andy Cohen, VP, Editorial & Marketing Services

Counselor covers marketing trends and new products, and is aimed at distributor principals.
Frequency: Monthly

17881 **Currents**
Council for Advancement & Support of Education
1307 New York Ave Nw
Suite 1000
Washington, DC 20005-4726

202-393-1301; Fax: 202-387-4973
memberservicecenter@case.org
www.case.org

John Lippincott, President
Deborah Bongiorno, Editor in chief
Tracy Baird, Marketing
Anne Eigeman, Editor

Offers articles on integrated marketing, technology and other industry related information.
Cost: $115.00
Frequency: Monthly
ISSN: 0748-478X
Founded in 1975

17882 **Customer Interaction Solutions**
Technology Marketing Corporation
800 Connecticut Ave
1st Floor East
Norwalk, CT 06854-1936

203-852-6800
800-243-6002; Fax: 203-866-3326
tmc@tmcnet.com
www.tmcnet.com
Twitter

Rich Tehrani, CEO
Tracey Schelmetic, Editorial Director

Dedicated to teleservices ans e-services outsoucing, marketing and customer relationship management issues.
Frequency: Monthly
Circulation: 13400

17883 **CyberDealer**
Meister Publishing Company
37733 Euclid Ave
Willoughby, OH 44094-5992

440-942-2000
800-572-7740; Fax: 440-975-3447
www.meisternet.com

Gary Fitzgerald, President

Helps agricultural dealerships better manage their operations.
Frequency: 6 per year

17884 **DECA Direct**
Distributive Education Clubs of America
1908 Association Drive
Reston, VA 20191

703-860-5000
info@deca.org
www.deca.org

Frank Peterson, Acting Executive Director

News, updates, and best practices.
Founded in 1946

17885 **DECA Guide**
Distributive Education Clubs of America
1908 Association Drive
Reston, VA 20191

703-860-5000
info@deca.org
www.deca.org

Frank Peterson, Acting Executive Director

Resource for all of DECA's programs, produced for high school and college divisions.
Frequency: Annually
Founded in 1946

17886 **Daily Record**
11 E Saratoga St
Baltimore, MD 21202-2199

410-752-3849; Fax: 410-752-2894
editor@mddailyrecord.com
www.mddailyrecord.com

Chris Eddings, Publisher
Mark Chashir, Editor
Susan Hoettner, Marketing
Kris Charddo, Circulation Manager
Cost: $190.00
Frequency: Daily
Circulation: 9000
Founded in 1888

17887 **Dealerscope Merchandising**
North American Publishing Company
1500 Spring Garden St
Suite 1200
Philadelphia, PA 19130-4094

215-238-5300
800-818-8174; Fax: 215-238-5342
www.napco.com

Ned S Borowsky, CEO
Eric Schwartz, President
Grant Clauser, Editorial Director
David Dritsas, Editor-in-Chief
Sean Downey, Managing Editor

Offers news on the marketing of appliances and consumer electronics on a national and regional basis.
Frequency: Monthly
Circulation: 20000
Founded in 1958

17888 **Direct**
Primedia
3585 Engineering Drive
Suite 100
Norcross, GA 30092

678-421-3000
800-216-1423; Fax: 212-206-3622
www.primedia.com

Jack Condon, Chief Operating Officer
Ray Schultz, Editorial Director
Charles Vietri, Managing Editor
Elizabeth O'Connor, Publisher

Magazine of direct marketing management.
Cost: $85.00
Circulation: 46,527
Founded in 1989

17889 **Do-It-Yourself Retailing**
5822 W 74th St
Indianapolis, IN 46278-1756

317-297-1190; Fax: 317-328-4354
www.nrha.org

John Hammond, Executive Director

17890 **Exhibitor Magazine**
206 S Broadway
Suite 745
Rochester, MN 55903-0368

507-289-6556
888-235-6155; Fax: 507-289-5253
www.exhibitoronline.com
Facebook, Twitter, LinkedIn

Lee Knight, President
John Pavek, VP of Publishing

Mission is to provide trade show marketing professionals with the tools and education to produce high-performance programs with measurable results.
Cost: $78.00
Frequency: Monthly
ISSN: 0739-6821

17891 **Family & Consumer Sciences Research Journal**
American Association of Family & Consumer Sciences
400 N. Columbus St
Suite 202
Alexandria, VA 22314-2264

703-706-4600
800-424-8080; Fax: 703-706-4663
staff@aafcs.org
www.aafcs.org

Sharon A. DeVaney, Editor

New research on all aspects of family & consumer sciences, including consumerism, human development, and family studies to housing, technology, nutrition, and textiles. Published in partnership with Wiley-Blackwell.
Cost: $45.00
Frequency: Quarterly

17892 **Forward**
Association of National Advertisers
10 Grand Central, 155 E. 44th Street
New York, NY 10017

212-697-5950; Fax: 212-687-7310
info@ana.net
www.ana.net

Bob Liodice, Chief Executive Officer
Duke Fanelli, EVP & CMO

Thought leadership newsletter from the Association of National Advertisers.

17893 **Greenville Magazine**
303 Haywood Rd
Greenville, SC 29607-3426

864-271-1105; Fax: 864-271-1165
www.greenvillemagazine.com

Paul Gesimondo, President

Features content summary, web-only extras, advertiser links, and access to reader service forms and various contests and programs.
Frequency: Monthly
Circulation: 10,002

17894 **Journal of Advertising Research**
Advertising Research Foundation

432 Park Avenue S.
6th Floor
New York, NY 10016

212-751-5656; Fax: 212-689-1859
www.thearf.org

Scott McDonald, President & CEO
Paul Donato, Chief Research Officer

The mission of the Journal of Advertising Research is to act as the research and development vehicle for professionals in all areas of marketing including media, research, advertising and communications
Frequency: Quarterly

17895 **Journal of Family & Consumer Sciences**
American Association of Family & Consumer Sciences
400 N. Columbus St
Suite 202
Alexandria, VA 22314-2264

703-706-4600
800-424-8080; Fax: 703-706-4663
staff@aafcs.org
www.aafcs.org

Scott S. Hall, PhD, CFLE, Editor

Contains scholarly peer-reviewed articles, practical information geared toward family and consumer sciences professionals, and news and information about AAFCS.

17896 **Journal of International Marketing**
American Marketing Association
130 E. Randolph Street
22nd Floor
Chicago, IL 60601

800-262-1150
customersupport@ama.org
www.ama.org/ama-academic-journals

Kelly Hewett, Editor-in-Chief

Presents scholarly and managerially relevant articles on international marketing.
Frequency: Quarterly
ISSN: 1069-031X

17897 **Journal of Marketing**
American Marketing Association
130 E. Randolph Street
22nd Floor
Chicago, IL 60601

800-262-1150
customersupport@ama.org
www.ama.org/ama-academic-journals

Christine Moorman, Editor-in-Chief

Scholarly journal of the marketing discipline.
Frequency: Bimonthly
ISSN: 0022-2429
Founded in 1936

17898 **Journal of Marketing Research**
American Marketing Association
130 E. Randolph Street
22nd Floor
Chicago, IL 60601

800-262-1150
customersupport@ama.org
www.ama.org/ama-academic-journals

Rajdeep Grewal, Editor-in-Chief

Covers a wide range of marketing research concepts, methods and applications.
Frequency: Bimonthly
ISSN: 0022-2437
Mailing list available for rent

17899 **Journal of Nonprofit & Public Sector Marketing**
Taylor & Francis
325 Chestnut Street
Suite 800
Philadelphia, PA 19106

800-354-1420; Fax: 215-625-2940
www.tandf.co.uk

Gillian Sullivan Mort, Editor

A peer reviewed journal devoted to the study of the adaption of traditional marketing principles for use by nonprofit organizations and government agencies.
Cost: $186.00
Frequency: Quarterly
Circulation: 500
ISSN: 1049-5142
Founded in 1976

17900 **Journal of Public Policy & Marketing**
American Marketing Association
130 E. Randolph Street
22nd Floor
Chicago, IL 60601

800-262-1150
customersupport@ama.org
www.ama.org/ama-academic-journals

Scot Burton, Co-Editor
Pam Ellen, Co-Editor
Josh Weiner, Co-Editor

Each issue features a wide ranging forum for the research, findings and discussion of marketing subjects related to business and government.
Frequency: Semiannual
ISSN: 0743-9156

17901 **Journal of the Academy of Marketing Science**
Academy of Marketing Science
c/o Louisiana Tech University
P.O. Box 3072
Ruston, LA 71272

ams@latech.edu
www.ams-web.org

John Hulland, Editor

Promotes research and the dissemination of research results through the study and improvement of marketing as an economic, ethical and social force.
Frequency: Quarterly
Circulation: 1100
Founded in 1972

17902 **License Magazine**
Advanstar Communications
641 Lexington Ave
Suite 8
New York, NY 10022-4503

212-951-6600; Fax: 212-951-6793
sekstract@advanstar.com
www.licensemag.com

Joseph Loggia, CEO
Tony Lisanti, Editor

Detailed coverage and research on the $177+ billion licensed consumer product business including: retail and merchandising trends; promotional partnerships; available and recently granted property licenses; research reports; and case studies on licensed consumer product categories based on publishing and art, entertainment, brands, sports, fashion, home decor, and interactive media properties
Cost: $59.00
Frequency: Monthly
Circulation: 25000
Founded in 1998
Printed in 4 colors

17903 **Magnet Marketing & Sales**
Graham Communications
40 Oval Rd
Suite 2
Quincy, MA 02170-3813

617-328-0069
800-659-0069; Fax: 617-471-1504
www.grahamcomm.com

John R Graham, President
Cynthia Cantrell, Editor
John Graham, CEO
Jonathan Bloom, Marketing manager

A marketing and sales newsletter.
Cost: $18.95
9 Pages
Frequency: Quarterly
Printed in 2 colors on matte stock

17904 **Marketing**
Mane/Marketing
13901 NE 175th Street
#M
Woodinville, WA 98072-8548

425-487-9111; Fax: 425-487-3158
coff@marketings.com

Larry Coffman, Publisher

Features important area events, industry projects, awards and executives of note. Highlights the latest information on marketing trends and pattern analysis. Free subscription.
Frequency: Monthly
Circulation: 11M

17905 **Marketing Health Services**
American Marketing Association
311 S Wacker Dr
Suite 5800
Chicago, IL 60606-6629

312-542-9000
800-262-1150; Fax: 312-542-9001
www.marketingpower.com
Facebook, Twitter, LinkedIn, Youtube

Dennis Dunlap, CEO

Specifically aimed at senior level healthcare marketers and managers, offers targeted information, practical strategies and thought provoking commentary to help achieve your goals and shape your vision
Frequency: Quarterly
Mailing list available for rent

17906 **Marketing Management**
American Marketing Association
311 S Wacker Dr
Suite 5800
Chicago, IL 60606-6629

312-542-9000
800-262-1150; Fax: 312-542-9001
www.marketingpower.com
Facebook, Twitter, LinkedIn, Youtube

Dennis Dunlap, CEO

Focuses on strategic marketing issues that marketing managers face every day.
Frequency: 6x/Year
Mailing list available for rent

17907 **Marketing Recreation Classes**
Learning Resources Network
1554 Hayes Drive
Manhattan, KS 66502-5068

785-539-5376; Fax: 888-234-8633
draves@lern.org
www.lern.org/

William Draves, Editor

This magazine offers information on marketing and advertising trends.
8 Pages
Frequency: Monthly
Founded in 1980

17908 **Marketing Research**
American Marketing Association

311 S Wacker Dr
Suite 5800
Chicago, IL 60606-6629

312-542-9000
800-262-1150; Fax: 312-542-9001
www.marketingpower.com
Facebook, Twitter, LinkedIn, Youtube

Dennis Dunlap, CEO

Researchers and managers count on this resource to help stay on top of current methodologies and issues, management concerns and the latest books and software.
Frequency: Quarterly
Mailing list available for rent

17909 Marketing Science: INFORMS
INFORMS
7240 Parkway Dr
Suite 310
Hanover, MD 21076-1344

410-850-0300
800-446-3676; Fax: 410-757-3515
informs@informs.org
www.informs.org

Mark Doherty, Executive Director
Barry List, Director Marketing
Patricia Shaffer, Director Publications
Richard C Larson, President

Marketing journal offering marketing and advertising articles. Provides help for marketing decision makers and deeper understanding of marketing phenomena.
Cost: $172.00
Frequency: Quarterly
Circulation: 1800
ISSN: 0732-2399
Founded in 1982

17910 Marketing to Women
EPM Communications
19 W. 21st St., #303
New York, NY 10010

212-941-0099
888-852-9467; Fax: 212-941-1622
www.epmcom.com

Ira Mayer, President
Larissa Faw, Editor

Topics covers attitudes and buying behaviors of the female consumer, market segment demographics, gender gap and health issues, media preferences and the role of technology.
Cost: $35.00
Frequency: Monthly

17911 Marketrac
Marketrac San Diego
4 First American Way
Santa Ana, CA 92707

714-250-6400
800-345-7334

Gerald Schultz, Editor
Jim Lucich, Promotional Manager

Marketing communications: people, places, events, trends, new products, technology, public relations, advertising, broadcast, TV, radio, video production, promotions, market research, direct mail, trademark, copyright law, accounting, employee management printing, graphics, color separations, novelty promotions.
Cost: $15.00
32 Pages
Frequency: Monthly

17912 NAPRA ReView
109 N Beach Road
PO Box 9
Eastsound, WA 98245-9

360-376-2001
800-367-1907; Fax: 360-376-2704
marilyn@marilynmcguire.com
www.napra.com

Erin Johnson, Advertising Sales
Marilyn McGuire, Editor
Marilyn McGuire, CEO/President
Frequency: 10 issues ayear
Circulation: 180000
Founded in 1986

17913 POINT
Direct Marketing Association
1120 Avenue of the Americas
New York, NY 10036-6713

212-768-7277; Fax: 212-302-6714
www.the-dma.org
Facebook, Twitter, LinkedIn

John A. Greco Jr, President & CEO

DMA's digital magazine.

17914 POP Design
In-Store Marketing Institute
8550 W. Bryn Mawr
#200
Chicago, IL 60631

773-992-4450; Fax: 773-992-4455
info@instoremarketer.org
www.p2pi.org/

Peter Hoyt, President

Serves the news and product information needs of producers and designers of instore displays, signs and fixtures. Each issue features the latest trends and technologies vital to building and designing successful instore merchandising.
Frequency: Monthly
Circulation: 18000
Printed in 4 colors on glossy stock

17915 PSMJ Marketing Tactics
PSMJ Resources
10 Midland Avenue
Newton, MA 02458-1000

617-965-0055
800-537-7765; Fax: 617-965-5152
www.psmj.com

Frank Stasiowski, Production Manager

Provides marketing tactics and techniques for the design industry.
Cost: $267.00
8 Pages
Frequency: Monthly
Founded in 1975
Mailing list available for rentat $125 per M
Printed in 2 colors on matte stock

17916 Personal Selling Power
1140 International Parkway
PO Box 5467
Fredericksburg, VA 22406-467

540-752-7000
800-752-7355; Fax: 540-752-7001
feedback@sellingpower.com
www.sellingpower.com

John Nuzzi, VP / Associate Publisher
Laura Gschwandtner, CEO

Sales education/motivation magazine designed to train, educate, motivate salespeople.
Cost: $33.00
140 Pages
Frequency: 10 times a year
ISSN: 1093-2216
Printed in 4 colors on glossy stock

17917 Point of Purchase Magazine
1115 Northmeadow Parkway
Roswell, GA 30076

847-647-7987
800-241-9034; Fax: 847-647-9566
popmag@halldata.com

Murray Kasmenn, Publisher
Julie Andrews, Sales Manager
Larry Shore, Sales Manager
Ted Eshleman, Account Executive
Alison Medina, Executive Editor

Addresses the industry perspective of the brand marketer and the retailer and focuses on retail trends, case studies, statistics and profitability.
Cost: $60.00
Frequency: 9 per year
Circulation: 18,506

17918 Politically Direct
Direct Marketing Association
1120 Avenue of the Americas
New York, NY 10036-6700

212-768-7277; Fax: 212-302-6714
customerservice@the-dma.org
www.the-dma.org

Lawrence M Kimmel, CEO

Published both in print and digital versions, this newsletter on DMA advocacy efforts keeps DMA members informed and involved in the politics and policies that impact them today and ahead of the curve on developments that will affect them tomorrow.

17919 PromaxBDA
PROMAX
1522 Cloverfield Blvd.
Suite E
Santa Monica, CA 90404

310-788-7600; Fax: 310-788-7616
www.promaxbda.org

Jonathan Black-Verk, President & CEO
Jill Lindeman, General Manager

Magazine, newsletter and directory published by PROMAX for members only, promotion and marketing professionals in electronic media.
Frequency: Annual
Circulation: 2500
Founded in 1952
Printed in 4 colors on glossy stock

17920 Quirk's Marketing Research Review
Quirk Enterprises
4662 Slater Rd
Eagan, MN 55122-2362

651-379-6200; Fax: 651-379-6205
info@quirks.com
www.quirks.com
Facebook, Twitter, LinkedIn

Steve Quirk, President
Joe Rydholm, Editor
Evan Tweed, Vice President Sales
Alice Davies, Manager

Emphasizes marketing research case histories and techniques used by researchers in a variety of industries, from consumer products to advertising, includes directories of research services and new products and features personnel announcements.
Cost: $70.00
30000 Members
Circulation: 16013
Founded in 1986
Mailing list available for rent: 17000 names
Printed in 4 colors on glossy stock

17921 Recharger Magazine
Recharger Magazine

1050 E Flamingo Rd
Suite N237
Las Vegas, NV 89119-7427

702-438-5557
877-902-9759; Fax: 702-873-9671
info@rechargermag.com
www.rechargermag.com

Tom Enerson, Publisher
Amy Turner, Manager
Becky Fenton, Manager
Amy Weiss, Director
Nancy Calabrese, Sales Manager

Information including articles that cover business and marketing, technical updates, association and industry news, and company profiles. Related features focus on the importance of recycling, government legislation, and product comparisons.
Cost: $45.00
Frequency: Monthly
Circulation: 8000
Founded in 1997

17922 **Response TV**
Advanstar Communications
Ste 300
17770 Cartwright Rd
Irvine, CA 92614-5815

714-513-8400
800-527-7008; Fax: 714-513-8412
george@directresponsetv.com
www.directresponsetv.com

John Yarring, Publisher
Thomas Haire, Editor
Joe Logia, CEO/President
Jodi Dressig, Circulation manager
Gina Cohen, Manager

Addresses industry concerns regarding regulatory issues, production, fulfillment and aftermarketing. Designed for direct marketers, product owners and related agencies.
Cost: $39.00
Frequency: Monthly
Circulation: 21345
Founded in 1993

17923 **Sales Executive**
Sales Marketing Executives of Greater New York
13 E 37th Street
#8
New York, NY 10016-2821

212-685-3613; Fax: 212-725-3752

Edward Glanegan, Publisher
Patricia Israel, Editor

For sales executives in New York.
Circulation: 2,500

17924 **Sales Upbeat**
Economics Press
12 Daniel Road
Fairfield, NJ 07004-2565

973-227-1224; Fax: 973-227-9742

John Beckley, Publisher
Robert Guder, Editor

Sales methods and techniques, quotes and anecdotes about selling.
Cost: $2.00
Circulation: 52,000

17925 **Salesmanship**
LRP Publications/Dartnell Corporation
PO Box 980
Horsham, PA 19044-0980

215-784-0912
800-341-7874; Fax: 215-784-9639
webmaster@lrp.com
www.lrp.com

Todd Lutz, CFO

Enhances training program with engaging and instructive reminders and shape-up tips that pay off in greater gains from sales force.
Cost: $62.00

17926 **Say Yes Marketing Script Presentations**
Frieda Carrol Communications
PO Box 416
Denver, CO 80201-0416

303-575-5676

This reference contains marketing presentations for various kinds of businesses.
Cost: $52.95

17927 **Security Distributing & Marketing**
Reed Business Information
1050 IL Route 83
Suite 200
Bensonville, IL 60106

630-616-0200; Fax: 630-227-0214
www.sdmmag.com

Bill Zalud, Editorial Director
Susan Whitehurst, Production Manager
Lyn Sopala, Production Manager

Security Distributing and Marketing serves security installing dealers, security installing dealers with central station equipment, central station services, access control system specialists and systems integrators.
Cost: $82.00
104 Pages
Frequency: 19 per year
Circulation: 28,298
ISSN: 0049-0016
Founded in 1971
Printed in 4 colors on glossy stock

17928 **Selling Magazine**
Selling Magazine
477 Madison Avenue
New York, NY 10022-5802

212-751-0485; Fax: 212-224-3592

Marjorie Weiss, Publisher

Selling is targeted to business-to-business salespeople.
Cost: $5.00
Circulation: 155162

17929 **Senior Marketwatch**
Campbell Associates
185 Martling Ave
Tarrytown, NY 10591-4703

914-332-1177; Fax: 914-332-1177

Arnold Thiesfeldt, Publisher

Features research based on tastes, trends, and resources of the senior market, as a means for advertisers and marketers to target and focus their products.
Cost: $242.00
12 Pages
Frequency: Monthly
Founded in 1997

17930 **Southern California Marketing Media**
Southern California Marketing Media
5 Via Caseta
Rancho Santa Margarita, CA 92688-4947

949-713-3188; Fax: 714-713-3188

Gary Klayman, Publisher

Written to report on marketing strategies, techniques and new products for the Southern California area, includes various company, client and media updates, new trends, and guides to developing individualized marketing programs.

17931 **Subscription Marketing**
Blue Dolphin Communications
526 Boston Post Road
Wayland, MA 01778-1833

978-358-5795; Fax: 508-358-5795
subs@bluedolphin.com
www.bluedolphin.com

Donald L Nicholas, Publisher

Offers trade strategies for maximizing product profitability. Provides perspective on success and failure stories.
Cost: $195.00
Frequency: Monthly

17932 **Supermarket News**
Fairchild Publications
750 3rd Ave
New York, NY 10017-2703

212-630-4000
800-204-4515; Fax: 212-630-3563
www.supermarketnews.com

Mary G Berner, CEO
David Merrefield, Editorial Director
Cost: $44.50
40 Pages
Frequency: Weekly
Circulation: 36346
ISSN: 0039-5803
Founded in 1892

17933 **Supplier Global Resource**
Advertising Specialty Institute
4800 Street Road
Trevose, PA 19053

800-546-1350
ideas@asicentral.com
www.asicentral.com

Timothy Andrews, President & CEO
Michele Bell, Editorial Director

News on international commerce and forecasts for the promotional products industry.
Frequency: 6x/Year

17934 **TODAY - The Journal of Work Process Improvement**
Recognition Technologies Users Association
185 Devonshire Street
Suite 770
Boston, MA 02110-1407

617-426-1167; Fax: 617-521-8675
www.tawpi.org

Dan Bolita, Editor
Frank Moran, CEO/President
Jason Glass, VP Sales
Cost: $27.69
Circulation: 5000
ISSN: 1073-2233
Founded in 1997
Printed in 2 colors on glossy stock

17935 **Target Marketing**
North American Publishing Company
1500 Spring Garden St
Suite 1200
Philadelphia, PA 19130-4094

215-238-5300; Fax: 215-238-5342
www.targetmarketingmag.com
Facebook, Twitter, LinkedIn

Ned S Borowsky, CEO
Lisa Yorgey, Managing Editor
Drew James, Sales Manager

Covers telemarketing, list rental, testing and management, circulation, catalogue and online/web marketing, and direct response advertising.
Cost: $65.00
Frequency: Monthly
Circulation: 42,000
Mailing list available for rent

17936 **Telemarketing & Call Center Solutions**
Technology Marketing Corporation
800 Connecticut Ave
1st Floor East
Norwalk, CT 06854-1924

203-852-6800
800-243-6002; Fax: 203-866-3326
tmc@tmcnet.com
www.tmcnet.com
Twitter

Nadji Tehrani, President
Linda Driscoll, Editor

First and only authoritative guide to effective and profitable marketing through business telecommunications. Provides information on technology and services releases, new techniques and management strategies.
Cost: $7.00
Frequency: 24 times
Circulation: 31419
Founded in 1972

17937 **Velocity**
Strategic Account Management Association
33 N La Salle Street
Suite 3700
Chicago, IL 60602

312-251-3131; Fax: 312-251-3132
www.strategicaccounts.org

Greg Bartlett, Editor

Contains exclusive, in-depth articles on topics such as negotiation, customer management, internal alignment and effective team communications.
Cost: $65.00
52 Pages
Frequency: Quarterly
Circulation: 2000
Founded in 1964
Printed in 4 colors

17938 **Wearables**
Advertising Specialty Institute
4800 Street Road
Trevose, PA 19053

800-546-1350
ideas@asicentral.com
www.asicentral.com

Timothy Andrews, President & CEO
C.J. Mittica, Editor

Serves the apparel and accessories segment of the advertising specialty industry.
Frequency: 10x/Year

17939 **Wireless for the Corporate User**
Probe Research
3 Wing Drive
Suite 240
Cedar Knolls, NJ 07927-1000

973-285-1500; Fax: 973-285-1519

Jack Killion, Publisher

Edited for the corporate user/decision maker to keep abreast of the growth product and service offerings, the expanding uses and the technological, political and standardization issues of the wireless arena.
Circulation: 43000

17940 **World Trade**
BNP Media
2401 W. Big Beaver Rd, Suite 700
Troy, MI 48084

248-362-3700
www.bnpmedia.com
Facebook, Twitter, LinkedIn

Katie Rotella, President
Cost: $37.00
58 Pages
Frequency: Monthly

Trade Shows

17941 **3AF Asian Marketing Summit**
Asian American Advertising Federation
6230 Wilshire Boulevard
Suite 1216
Los Angeles, CA 90048

ghomfranzen@3af.org
www.3af.org
Facebook, Twitter, YouTube, Instagram

Genny Hom-Franzen, Executive Director

Two-day event aimed at Asian members of the marketing profession.
Frequency: Annual

17942 **4A's Data Summit**
American Association of Advertising Agencies
1065 Avenue of the Americas
16th Floor
New York, NY 10018

212-682-2500
www.aaaa.org

Marla Kaplowitz, President & CEO
Mollie Rosen, EVP, Member Engagement & Dev.

One-day event exploring how data will impact the advertising industry.

17943 **4A's Talent@2030**
American Association of Advertising Agencies
1065 Avenue of the Americas
16th Floor
New York, NY 10018

212-682-2500; Fax: 212-682-8391
www.aaaa.org
Twitter, Instagram, YouTube

Marla Kaplowitz, President & CEO
Mollie Rosen, EVP, Member Engagement & Dev.

Event explores how technology, social media and data are impacting people and culture.

17944 **AAFCS Annual Conference & Exposition**
American Association of Family & Consumer Sciences
400 N. Columbus Street
Suite 202
Alexandria, VA 22314-2264

703-706-4600
800-424-8080; Fax: 703-706-4663
annualconf@aafcs.org
www.aafcs.org

Carolyn Jackson, CEO
Sara Tantillo, Assoc. Director, Events & Outreach

Informative speakers, cutting-edge workshops, and a panel discussion.
Frequency: Annual/June

17945 **ACCE Annual Convention**
Association of Chamber of Commerce Executives
1330 Braddock Place
Suite 300
Alexandria, VA 22314

703-998-0072; Fax: 888-577-9883
communications@acce.org
secure.acce.org

Sheree Anne Kelly, President & CEO
Crystal Moore, VP, Professional Development

Convention for chamber of commerce professionals.
Frequency: Annual/July
Founded in 1914

17946 **AMA Annual Conference**
American Marketing Association
130 E. Randolph Street
22nd Floor
Chicago, IL 60601

800-262-1150
customersupport@ama.org
www.ama.org
Facebook, Twitter, LinkedIn

Russ Klein, Chief Executive Officer
Jeremy Van Ek, Chief Operating Officer

Premier educational and networking event of the American Marketing Association.

17947 **AMSP Annual Conference**
Association of Marketing Service Providers
1800 Diagonal Road
Suite 320
Alexandria, VA 22314-2806

703-836-9200; Fax: 703-548-8204
kgarner@mfsanet.org
www.amsp.org

Joseph P. Truncale, President & CEO
Leo Raymond, VP, Postal & Member Relations

Opportunity for marketing professionals to network, collaborate, and learn.
Frequency: Annual

17948 **ANA Advertising Financial Management Conference**
Association of National Advertisers
10 Grand Central, 155 E. 44th Street
New York, NY 10017

212-697-5950; Fax: 212-687-7310
info@ana.net
www.ana.net

Bob Liodice, Chief Executive Officer
Kristen McDonough, SVP, Conferences

Brings together top marketing finance and procurement professionals from the client side with agency CFOs and other key industry stakeholders interested in efficiencies, cost savings, return on investment, and delivering greater value to organizations.

17949 **ANA Advertising Law & Public Policy Conference**
Association of National Advertisers
10 Grand Central, 155 E. 44th Street
New York, NY 10017

212-697-5950; Fax: 212-687-7310
info@ana.net
www.ana.net

Bob Liodice, Chief Executive Officer
Kristen McDonough, SVP, Conferences

Keeping up with the digital revolution is becoming a nearly impossible task. This conference enters the battlefield by putting together a stellar faculty, including leading regulators, top practitioners, and serious critics, capped off by a session that puts it all together led by a leading law professor.

17950 **ANA Brand Activation Marketing Conference**
Association of National Advertisers

10 Grand Central, 155 E. 44th Street
New York, NY 10017

212-697-5950; Fax: 212-687-7310
info@ana.net
www.ana.net

Bob Liodice, Chief Executive Officer
Kristen McDonough, SVP, Conferences

Coordinated brand activation strategies from top marketers.

17951 ANA Chicago Nonprofit Conference
Association of National Advertisers
10 Grand Central, 155 E. 44th Street
New York, NY 10017

212-697-5950; Fax: 212-687-7310
info@ana.net
www.ana.net

Bob Liodice, Chief Executive Officer
Kristen McDonough, SVP, Conferences

Marketing, fundraising, and collaborative ideas to help nonprofits expand their donor base.

17952 ANA DC Nonprofit Conference
Association of National Advertisers
10 Grand Central, 155 E. 44th Street
New York, NY 10017

212-697-5950; Fax: 212-687-7310
info@ana.net
www.ana.net

Bob Liodice, Chief Executive Officer
Kristen McDonough, SVP, Conferences

Marketing, fundraising, and collaborative ideas to help nonprofits expand their donor base.

17953 ANA Data & Measurement Conference
Association of National Advertisers
10 Grand Central, 155 E. 44th Street
New York, NY 10017

212-697-5950; Fax: 212-687-7310
info@ana.net
www.ana.net

Bob Liodice, Chief Executive Officer
Kristen McDonough, SVP, Conferences

17954 ANA Digital & Social Media Conference
Association of National Advertisers
10 Grand Central, 155 E. 44th Street
New York, NY 10017
212-697-5950; Fax: 212-687-7310
info@ana.net
www.ana.net

Bob Liodice, Chief Executive Officer
Kristen McDonough, SVP, Conferences

Discussing how to use social media and digital technology to impact consumer decisions and how to effectively partner with other companies to maximize social media reach and more.

17955 ANA Email Evolution Conference
Association of National Advertisers
10 Grand Central, 155 E. 44th Street
New York, NY 10017

212-697-5950; Fax: 212-687-7310
info@ana.net
www.ana.net

Bob Liodice, Chief Executive Officer
Kristen McDonough, SVP, Conferences

A look at regulatory changes, privacy concerns, and technical advances in email marketing.

17956 ANA In-House Agency Conference
Association of National Advertisers
10 Grand Central, 155 E. 44th Street
New York, NY 10017

212-697-5950; Fax: 212-687-7310
info@ana.net
www.ana.net

Bob Liodice, Chief Executive Officer
Kristen McDonough, SVP, Conferences

Conference devoted to all aspects of in-house agencies, including digital asset management, culture and talent, the evolution of in-house agencies, starting a new agency, and more.

17957 ANA Influencer Marketing Conference
Association of National Advertisers
10 Grand Central, 155 E. 44th Street
New York, NY 10017

212-697-5950; Fax: 212-687-7310
info@ana.net
www.ana.net

Bob Liodice, Chief Executive Officer
Kristen McDonough, SVP, Conferences

17958 ANA Masters of B2B Marketing
Association of National Advertisers
10 Grand Central, 155 E. 44th Street
New York, NY 10017
212-697-5950; Fax: 212-687-7310
info@ana.net
www.ana.net

Bo Liodice, Chief Executive Officer
Kristen McDonough, SVP, Conferences

Insights into successful B2B approaches.

17959 ANA Masters of Data & Technology
Association of National Advertisers
10 Grand Central, 155 E. 44th Street
New York, NY 10017

212-697-5950; Fax: 212-687-7310
info@ana.net
www.ana.net

Bob Liodice, Chief Executive Officer
Kristen McDonough, SVP, Conferences

Discussions on the ever-changing marketing technology ecosystem.

17960 ANA Masters of Marketing Conference
Association of National Advertisers
10 Grand Central, 155 E. 44th Street
New York, NY 10017

212-697-5950; Fax: 212-687-7310
info@ana.net
www.ana.net

Bob Liodice, Chief Executive Officer
Kristen McDonough, SVP, Conferences

The conference offers an opportunity to learn from and engage with the leaders of the industry as they build brands, leverage the expanding array of media, make marketing more accountable and improve the quality of their marketing organizations.
2500 Attendees

17961 ANA Media Conference
Association of National Advertisers
10 Grand Central, 155 E. 44th Street
New York, NY 10017

212-697-5950; Fax: 212-687-7310
info@ana.net
www.ana.net

Bob Liodice, Chief Executive Officer
Kristen McDonough, SVP, Conferences

Actionable insights into today's important issues.

17962 ANA Multicultural Marketing & Diversity Conference
Association of National Advertisers
10 Grand Central, 155 E. 44th Street
New York, NY 10017

212-697-5950; Fax: 212-687-7310
info@ana.net
www.ana.net

Bob Liodice, Chief Executive Officer
Kristen McDonough, SVP, Conferences

17963 ANA Nonprofit Federation Leadership Summit
Association of National Advertisers
10 Grand Central, 155 E. 44th Street
New York, NY 10017
212-697-5950; Fax: 212-687-7310
info@ana.net
www.ana.net

Bob Liodice, Chief Executive Officer
Kristen McDonough, SVP, Conferences

17964 ANA/BAA Marketing Law Conference
Association of National Advertisers
10 Grand Central, 155 E. 44th Street
New York, NY 10017

212-697-5950; Fax: 212-687-7310
info@ana.net
www.ana.net

Bob Liodice, Chief Executive Officer
Kristen McDonough, SVP, Conferences

17965 Annual Conference and Mailing Fulfillment Expo
Mailing & Fulfillment Service Association
1421 Prince Street
Suite 410
Alexandria, VA 22314-2806

703-836-9200; Fax: 703-548-8204
www.mfsanet.org
Facebook, Twitter, LinkedIn

Ken Garner, President
Jennifer Root, Director
Bill Stevenson, Director Marketing
Leo Raymond, Vice President

Quality educational sessions, industry specific exhibit hall, networking and more.
Frequency: Annual

17966 Annual Conference for Catalog & Multichannel Merchants (ACCM)
Direct Marketing Association
1120 Avenue of Americas
New York, NY 10036

212-768-7277; Fax: 212-302-6714
www.the-dma.org
Facebook, Twitter, LinkedIn

Julie Hogan, SVP Conference & Events
10M Attendees

17967 Annual Conference on Healthcare Marketing
Alliance for Healthcare Strategy & Marketing
11 S LaSalle Street
Suite 2300
Chicago, IL 60603

312-704-9700; Fax: 312-704-9709

Workshop and social events plus 50 exhibits of marketing communications, health care information lines, stategic planning and more.
600 Attendees
Frequency: Annual
Founded in 1984

17968 AudiencexScience
Advertising Research Foundation

432 Park Avenue S.
6th Floor
New York, NY 10016

212-751-5656; Fax: 212-689-1859
www.thearf.org

Scott McDonald, President & CEO
Rachael Feigenbaum, SVP & Events Program Producer

Conference devoted to audience measurement and growth.
400 Members
Founded in 1936

17969 **Business Intelligence Conference**
The Conference Board
845 Third Avenue
New York, NY 10022

212-339-0345; Fax: 212-836-9740
www.conference-board.org/intelligence.htm

Shows how you can utilize business intelligence in your own organization to enhance performace and drive results.
Frequency: June, Chicago

17970 **CMC Annual Summit**
Association of Hispanic Advertising Agencies
8280 Willow Oaks Corporate Drive
Suite 600
Fairfax, VA 22031

703-745-5531; Fax: 703-610-0227
info@culturemarketingcouncil.org
culturemarketingcouncil.org

Horacio Gavilan, Executive Director

Examines the myriad of changes facing Hispanic agencies in and beyond including shifts in approaches to communications planning, demographics and client needs.

17971 **Communications Marketing Association Conference**
Communications Marketing Association
204 S. Shaffer Drive
New Freedom, PA 17349

717-439-7391
cmaexecdirector@gmail.com
www.cma-cmc.org

Alex Hinerfeld, President
Carl Peek, Vice President
Rob Menees, Secretary
Cliff Peck, Treasurer
Sharon Boyle, Executive Director

Training, education, and networking conference for manufacturers, manufacturer's representatives and distributors in the wireless communications industry.

17972 **DAA OneConference**
Digital Analytics Association
401 Edgewater Place
Suite 600
Wakefield, WA 1880

781-876-8933; Fax: 781-224-1239
info@digitalanalyticsassociation.org
www.digitalanalyticsassociation.org

Marilee Yorchak, Executive Director
Adrienne Segundo, Education Manager
Lesley Coussis, Symposia Manager

Conference of the Digital Analytics Association, which is a global organization of practitioners, corporations, vendors, marketing and public relations agencies, consultants, academics, and more involved in the growing digital analytics industry.
Founded in 2004

17973 **DEMA Show**

858-616-6408
800-862-3483; Fax: 858-616-6495
info@dema.org
www.dema.org

Tom Ingram, President & CEO
Nicole Russel, VP, Operations

Annual trade show produced by the Diving Equipment & Marketing Association, for companies doing business in the scuba diving, ocean water sports and adventure/dive travel industries.
10M Attendees
Frequency: Annual

17974 **DMA Annual Conference & Exhibition**
Direct Marketing Association
1120 Avenue of Americas
New York, NY 10036-6700

212-768-7277; Fax: 212-302-6714
dmaconferences@the-dma.org
www.the-dma.org

Lawrence M Kimmel, CEO
Julie A Hogan, SVP Conferences/Events

Brings together thousands of practitioners and experts from the entire marketing continuum to discuss solutions and best practices to achieve optimal channel mix and integration that lead to measurable results and increase real-time customer engagement.
12000 Attendees
Frequency: October

17975 **DMB: Direct Marketing to Business Conference**
Target Conference Corporation
11 Riverbend Drive S
Stamford, CT 06907-0949

203-358-9900; Fax: 203-358-5815

Ed Berkowitz

National conference for business to business direct marketers. 75 table tops
1000+ Attendees
Frequency: March
Mailing list available for rent

17976 **Destinations International Annual Convention**
Destinations International
2025 M St NW
Suite 500
Washington, DC 20036-3349

202-296-7888; Fax: 202-296-7889
info@destinationsinternational.org
destinationsinternational.org

Don Welsh, President & CEO
Barbra Gustis, EVP, Meetings & Event Design
1500 Attendees
Founded in 1914

17977 **Direct Marketing Conference National Conference**
DMB Miami
Fontainebleau Hilton Resort and Towers
Miami, FL 33152

203-358-3751
800-927-5007
www.directmac.org

Information on improving R.O.I. and stay ahead of the competition, create customer centric business, synthesize traditional marketing strategies with the internet.

17978 **Electronic Retailing Association Annual Convention**
Electronic Retailing Association
7918 Jones Branch Dr
Suite 300
McLean, VA 22102

703-841-1751
800-987-6462; Fax: 703-506-3266
Facebook, Twitter, LinkedIn, YouTube

Mary Katherine Bilowus, Director, Events

17979 **Email Evolution Conference**
Direct Marketing Association
1120 Avenue of Americas
New York, NY 10036-6700

212-768-7277; Fax: 212-302-6714
dmaconferences@the-dma.org
www.the-dma.org

Julie A Hogan, SVP Conference/Events
Lawrence M Kimmel, CEO

Focuses on the ever-changing and evolving world of email marketing, providing you with the best ways to capitalize on the high ROI this low-cost communication tool can provide both on its own, and integrated with social, search, mobile, video and other email enhancers.
10M Attendees
Frequency: Annual/February

17980 **Exhibitor Conference**
Exhibitor Magazine Group
206 S Broadway
Suite 745
Rochester, MN 55904-6565

507-289-6556
888-235-6155; Fax: 507-289-5253
www.exhibitoronline.com
Facebook, Twitter, LinkedIn

Carol Fojtik, Managing Director/Sr Vice President

Conference program combined with exhibit hall featuring latest products and resources shaping the future of exhibiting and corporate event programs. Anyone responsible for planning, managing or implementing trade show or corporate event marketing functions should attend. Conference is held annually in Las Vegas, NV.
5M Attendees
Frequency: March, Las Vegas
Founded in 1989

17981 **FCS Race for Kids**
Financial Communications Society
368 Ninth Avenue
9th Floor
New York, NY 10001

908-858-0427
admin@thefcs.org
thefcs.org

Tim Hart, Chair
Tom Jago, Vice Chair
Katherine Divney, Secretary
Kevin Windorf, CEO

Charity event and marketing summit held by the Financial Communications Society.
Founded in 1967

17982 **GRMA Growth & Innovation Forum**
Home Page: www.thegrma.com

Brian Beitler, Co-Chair
Tim Rea, Co-Chair

Event for C-level executives with education, resource exchanges, and networking.

17983 **High Performance Linux on Wall Street**
Flagg Management
353 Lexington Avenue
New York, NY 10016

212-286-0333; Fax: 212-286-0086
www.flaggmgmt.com

Russell Flagg, President

Featuring Linux and HPC futures discussions, virtualization, cloud computing and service-driven datacenters, open source meets low latency, VLDB architectures, cost reduction with Linux, and more.
1000 Attendees
Frequency: Annual
Founded in 2001

17984 **IAA World Congress**
International Advertising Association
114 E. 25th Street
Suite 915
New York, NY 10009

646-722-2612; Fax: 646-722-2501
iaa@iaaglobal.org
www.iaaglobal.org

Dagmara Szulce, Managing Director, IASA Global

Bi-annual event attracts more than a thousand marketing communications professionals from all over the world.
1200 Attendees
Frequency: Bi-annual

17985 **IAB ALM**
Interactive Advertising Bureau
116 E. 27th Street
6th Floor
New York, NY 10016

212-380-4700
learning@iab.com
www.iab.com
Facebook, Twitter, LinkedIn, YouTube, Instagram

David Cohen, Board President & CEO
Dennis Buchheim, President
Randall Rothenberg, Executive Chair
Dave Grimaldi, EVP, Public Policy
Sheryl Goldstein, SVP, Member Engagement & Dev.

AdTech conference hosted by the Interactive Advertising Bureau, dedicated to exploring the devices, systems, networks, regulations, and applications shaping marketing and media.
Cost: $2695.00
Frequency: Registration Fee
Founded in 1996

17986 **ICOM World Meeting**
International Communications Agency Network
P.O. Box 3417
Nederland, CO 80466

720-215-6674
info@icomagencies.com
www.icomagencies.com

Emma Keenan, Executive Director
Diane Venturino, International Meeting Planner

Networking opportunity with new business opportunities and information on industry developments.
Frequency: Annual

17987 **IMCA Annual Conference**
Insurance Marketing & Communications Association
4248 Park Glen Road
Minneapolis, MN 55416

952-928-4644; Fax: 952-929-1318
info@imcanet.com
www.imcanet.com

Megan Flanagan, Executive Director

To promote education and development of its members.
Mailing list available for rent

17988 **Incentive Marketing Association Annual Summit**
Incentive Marketing Association
4248 Park Glen Road
Minneapolis, MN 55416

952-928-4649
info@incentivemarketing.org
www.incentivemarketing.org

Karen Wesloh, Executive Director

Gathering of experts and professionals in the incentive marketing industry to share ideas and discuss business growth.
Frequency: Annual

17989 **LIDMA Conference and Business Showcase**
Life Insurance Direct Marketing Association
3227 S. Cherokee Lane
Suite 1320
Woodstock, GA 30188

770-516-0207
866-890-5323
info@lidma.org
lidma.org

Robert Bland, President
Nicole Buckenmeyer, Vice President
Jeff McCauley, Secretary-Treasurer
Brian Barnes, Membership Vice Chair

Annual conference of the Life Insurance Direct Marketing Association.

17990 **MBA Research Conclave**
MBAResearch and Curriculum Center
1375 King Avenue
PO Box 12279
Columbus, OH 43212

614-486-6708
800-448-0398; Fax: 614-486-1819
www.mbaresearch.org

Marsha Dyer, Customer Service Manager
Kimberly Holstlaw, Executive Adminstrator
James Gleason, President/CEO

Containing 20 booths and 15 exhibits.
500 Attendees
Frequency: June
Founded in 1971

17991 **MDMA's Annual Direct Marketing Conference & Expo**
Midwest Direct Marketing Association
P.O. Box 75
Andover, MN 55304

763-607-2943; Fax: 763-753-2240
office@mdma.org
www.mdma.org

Joan Forde, President
Cindy McCleary, Director

Containing 55 booths and 50 companies exhibiting.
Frequency: April
Mailing list available for rent: 1.1M+ names

17992 **MFSA Midwinter Executive Conference**
Mailing & Fulfillment Service Association
1421 Prince Street
Suite 410
Alexandria, VA 22314-2806

703-836-9200; Fax: 703-548-8204
www.mfsanet.org
Facebook, Twitter, LinkedIn

Ken Garner, President
Jennifer Root, Director
Bill Stevenson, Director Marketing
Leo Raymond, Vice President

Will address financial operations and business valuation, marketing your own company, the changing world of postal regulations, technology in fulfillment, building a sales team, being strong in digital printing and the landscape of employment law.

17993 **MLMIA Convention and Expo**
Multi-Level Marketing International Association
119 Stanford Court
Irvine, CA 92612

949-854-0484
info@mlmia.com
www.mlmia.com

Doris Wood, Chair
Tony Cannuli, COO

Seeks to strengthen and improve the Direct Sales/Network Marketing/Multi-Level Marketing industry in the United States and abroad. Members are companies which market their products and services directly to consumers through independent distributors, suppliers to the industry and distributors who interface with consumers.
Founded in 1985

17994 **Mailer Strategies Conference**
Mailing & Fulfillment Service Association
1421 Prince Street
Suite 410
Alexandria, VA 22314-2806

703-836-9200; Fax: 703-548-8204
www.mfsanet.org
Facebook, Twitter, LinkedIn

Ken Garner, President
Jennifer Root, Director
Bill Stevenson, Director Marketing
Leo Raymond, Vice President

This conference will focus solely on postal issues that are important to your operations.

17995 **Marketing Federation's Annual Conference on Strategic Marketing**
Marketing Federation
109 58th Avenue
Saint Petersburg, FL 33706-2203

727-363-7805; Fax: 727-367-6545

Greg Stemm

Offers attendees information on how to boost attendance at their seminars, conferences and expositions.

17996 **NCDM Conference**
Direct Marketing Association
1120 Avenue of Americas
New York, NY 10036-6700

212-768-7277; Fax: 212-302-6714
dmaconferences@the-dma.org
www.the-dma.org

Julie A Hogan, SVP Conference/Events
Lawrence M Kimmel, CEO

Presents industry experts and hard-hitting case studies from a variety of verticals, such as financial services, retail, automotive, publishing, non-profit and many more, who will share the latest strategies and methodologies in gathering, analyzing, leveraging and protecting your most valuable business asset - customer data.
10M Attendees
Frequency: Annual/December

17997 **NCDM Conferences National Center for Database Marketing**
Primedia Business Exhibitions
11 River Bend S
PO Box 4254
Stamford, CT 06907

203-358-9900; Fax: 203-358-5815

Ed Berkowitz, Director Sales

A conference offering a highly qualified audience of database marketing decision-makers from all over the country, including a high concentration of marketers from the Midwest and

West coast. Containing 210 booths and 100 exhibits.
2500 Attendees
Frequency: July/December

17998 **National Conference on Operations & Fulfillment (NCOF)**
Direct Marketing Association
1120 Avenue of Americas
New York, NY 1003-6700

212-768-7277; Fax: 312-302-6714
dmaconferences@the-dma.org
www.the-dma.org

Julie A Hogan, SVP Conference/Events
Lawrence M Kimmel, CEO

Focus on innovative solutions for warehouse, distribution, operations, and ecommerce needs in the ever-changing world of operations and fulfillment.
10M Attendees
Frequency: Annual/April

17999 **National Hispanic Market Trade Show and Media Expo (Se Habla Espanol)**
Hispanic Business
5385 Hollister Avenue, Ste. 204
Santa Barbara, CA 93111

805-964-4554
800-806-4268; Fax: 805-964-5539
www.expomediainc.com/en/home
Facebook, Twitter, LinkedIn

John Pasini, Cfo/Coo

Annual show of 100 exhibitors of market/research, media, advertising, public relations, information services and recruitment.
1500 Attendees
Mailing list available for rent

18000 **National Mail Order Merchandise Show**
Expo Accessories
47 Main Avenue
Clifton, NJ 07014-1917

973-661-9681

Martin Deeks, Show Manager

300 booths.
5M Attendees
Frequency: January

18001 **New York Nonprofit Conference**
Direct Marketing Association
1120 Avenue of Americas
New York, NY 10036-6700

212-768-7277; Fax: 212-302-6714
dmaconferences@the-dma.org
www.the-dma.org

Julie A Hogan, SVP Conference/Events
Lawrence M Kimmel, CEO

Discover which acknowledgement programs work best-and why, increase the revenue with membership options-as well as traditional fundraising appeals, learn how the Internet and e-mail campaigns can improve fundraising, lower costs and increase advocacy.
10M Attendees

18002 **PROMO Live**
Prism Business Media
PROMO Live
11 River Bend South
Stamford, CT 06907

508-743-0105
800-927-5007; Fax: 508-759-4552

Kim Stolfi, Conference/Show Coordinator
Florence Torres, Conference Program Manager
Frequency: Oct Chicago

18003 **Photo Marketing Association International**
3000 Picture Place
Jackson, MI 49201

517-788-8100; Fax: 517-788-8371
www.theimagingalliance.com

Ted Fox, Executive Director
Mary Anne LaMarre, Operations Officer

Containing 3,230 booths and 645 exhibits. Promoting the growth of the photography industry through coorperation.
24M Attendees
Frequency: February

18004 **Promo Expo**
Promo Expo Sales
The Navy Pier
Chicago, IL 60606

800-927-5007; Fax: 203-358-3751
prg.ca/promoexpo

The largest conference and exhibition dedicated to the promotion marketing industry, and the one event where you can meet with over four thousand promotion marketing decision makers.
Frequency: October

18005 **Publishers Multinational Direct Conference**
1501 3rd Avenue
New York, NY 10028-2101

212-734-7040; Fax: 212-986-3757

Alfred Goodloe, President

Offers publishers information and seminars on how to build sales and profits in foreign markets.
Frequency: March

18006 **Re:Think The ARF Annual Convention & Expo**
Advertising Research Foundation
432 Park Avenue S.
6th Floor
New York, NY 10016

212-751-5656; Fax: 212-689-1859
www.thearf.org

Scott McDonald, President & CEO
Rachael Feigenbaum, SVP & Events Program Producer

Re:Think is a research forum where the ad industry gathers to dispense, explore and challenge the latest knowledge driving the advertising and marketing industry. Showcases innovative market research services and products, high-level networking, free education, and leading-edge industry resources.
400 Members
Founded in 1936

18007 **Securities Industry and Financial Markets Association (SIFMA) Annual Meeting**
1101 New York Avenue NW
8th Floor
Washington, DC 20005

202-962-7300; Fax: 202-962-7305
www.sifma.org
Facebook, Twitter, LinkedIn

Kenneth Bentsen, President/CEO

The Securities Industry and Financial Markets Association/SIFMA Annual Meeting and Conference program addresses a variety of topics that may include competitiveness of the U.S. capital markets, global exchange consolidation, regulatory and legal initiatives, and trends in the fixed-income and capital markets.
Mailing list available for rent

18008 **SourceMedia Conferences & Events**
SourceMedia
One State Street Plaza
27th floor
New York, NY 10004

212-803-6093
800-803-3424; Fax: 212-803-8515
www.sourcemedia.com/
Facebook, Twitter, LinkedIn

James M Malkin, Chairman & CEO
William Johnson, CFO
Steve Andreazza, VP, Sales & Customer Service
Celie Baussan, SVP, Operations
Anne O'Brien, EVP Marketing & Strategic Planning

SourceMedia Conferences & Events attract over 20,000 attendees worldwide. The content embraces a variety of formats, including: conferences, executive roundtables, expositions, Web seminars, custom events and pod casts. With over 70 events annually, participants are provided with premier content as well as access to the industry's top solution providers. Markets served include: accounting; banking; capital markets; financial services; information technology; insurance; and real estate.
Mailing list available for rent

18009 **TMCA Annual Conference & Marketing Expo**
Transportation Marketing Communications Assoc
9382 Oak Avenue
Waconia, MN 55387

952-442-5638; Fax: 952-442-3941
www.tmcatoday.org

John Ferguson, President
Tom Nightingale, VP
Tracy Robinson, Treasurer
Edward Moritz, Secretary
Brian Everett, Executive Director
200 Attendees
Frequency: Annual

18010 **Top2Top Nexgen**
5225 Wisonsin Avenue NW
Suite 316
Washington, DC 20015-2055

202-596-8112; Fax: 202-293-1702
info@fsmaonline.com
www.fsmaonline.com

Jerry Campbell, Chair & President
Annual conference of the Foodservice Sales & Marketing Association.
Founded in 2003

18011 **impactSHOW**
Internet Marketing Association
200 Spectrum Center Drive
Irvine, CA 92618

949-443-9300
info@imanetwork.org
imanetwork.org
Facebook, Twitter, LinkedIn, YouTube

Sinan Kanatsiz, Chair & Founder
Sean Conrad, CEO
Lei Lani Fera, Head Of Creative
Hall Roosevelt, General Manager
Marcus Volpe, Executive Director

Conference of the Internet Marketing Association.
Founded in 2001

Directories & Databases

18012 **Adweek Directory**
Prometheus Global Media

770 Broadway
New York, NY 10003-9595

212-493-4100; Fax: 646-654-5368
www.prometheusgm.com

Richard D. Beckmand, CEO
James A. Finkelstein, Chairman
Madeline Krakowsky, Vice President Circulation
Tracy Brater, Executive Director Creative Service

Adweek Directories Online is where you will find searchable databases with comprehensive information on ad Agencies, brand marketers and multicultural media.
Frequency: Annual
Circulation: 800
Founded in 1981

18013 **Affluent Markets Alert**
EPM Communications
488 E 18th Street
Brooklyn, NY 11226-6702

FAX 718-469-7124

Offers complete coverage on affluent market trends containing complete contact and price information on books, monographs, journals and newspapers.
Frequency: Full-text

18014 **AmericanProfile**
Donnelley Marketing Information Services
25 Tremont Ave
#10250
Stamford, CT 06906-2330

203-325-9801
800-866-2255; Fax: 203-553-7276
www.donnellyestates.com

Richard Donnelly, Owner

A database retrieval and reporting system that contains 1980 and 1990 census data, current year updates and 5-year projections of selected demographic characteristics and proprietary statistics.

18015 **Annual Directory of Marketing Information Companies**
American Demographics
PO Box 4949
Stamford, CT 06907-0949

203-358-9900

Offers a list of firms offering demographic and research services, data retrieval and analysis, market evaluation and forecasting.
Frequency: Annual
Circulation: 5,000

18016 **Annual Mail Order Sales Directory & Mail Order 750 Report**
Marketing Logistics
1460 Cloverdale Avenue
Highland Park, IL 60035-2817

847-831-1575

Arnold L Fishman, President

This comprehensive directory offers a list of mail order businesses reporting at least 5 million dollars in annual sales. The 750 report gives mail order companies, businesses and mail order catalogs, 250 listings of each.
Cost: $1095.00
Frequency: Annual

18017 **Boomer Report**
FIND/SVP
625 Avenue of the Americas
New York, NY 10011-2020

212-807-2656
800-346-3787; Fax: 212-645-7681

Andrew P Garvin, President

With over 77 million baby boomers, this report carefully tracks news stories, market surveys, and interviews the experts to help you spot opportunities and position your products.
Cost: $195.00
8 Pages
Frequency: Monthly

18018 **Bradford's Directory of Marketing Research Agencies & Consultants**
Bradford's Directory of Marketing Research Agency
9991 Caitlin Center
Manassas, VA 20110-4282

703-614-4000

Thomas Bradford, Owner

Over 2,500 companies that are involved in management or market research are listed.
Cost: $90.00
400 Pages
Frequency: Biennial
Circulation: 5,000

18019 **Business Marketing Association Membership Directory & Yellow Pages**
Business Marketing Association
Ste 123
1833 Centre Point Cir
Naperville, IL 60563-4848

630-544-5054; Fax: 630-544-5055
info@marketing.org
www.marketing.org
Facebook, Twitter, LinkedIn

Jeffrey Hayzlett, Chairman
Gary Slack, Vice Chairman
Bob Goranson, Treasurer

Offers information on over 4,500 member business communications professionals in the field of advertising, marketing communications and marketing. Additional benefits of membership include opportunites for networking, professional development seminars, and access to marketing research and studies.
Frequency: Annual

18020 **CMC Hispanic Market Guide**
Association of Hispanic Advertising Agencies
8400 Westpark Drive
2nd Floor
McLean, VA 22102

703-610-9014; Fax: 703-610-0227
info@culturemarketingcouncil.org
culturemarketingcouncil.org

Horacio Gavilan, President

Digital guide with advertising, media and marketing companies that specialize in the Hispanic market.

18021 **Catalog Connection**
Holy B Pasiuk
210 E 5th Street
Greenville, NC 06437-0527

252-758-8612
www.catalogconnection.net

Over 400 companies that supply catalogs of their merchandise to consumers and businesses are profiled in this directory.
55 Pages
Frequency: Biennial

18022 **Catalog Handbook**
Enterprise Magazines
1020 N Broadway
Suite 111
Milwaukee, WI 53202-3157

414-272-9977; Fax: 414-272-9973
www.franchisehandbook.com

Offers information on companies that offer product catalogs.
Cost: $6.99
106 Pages
Frequency: Quarterly
Circulation: 30,000
Founded in 1989

18023 **Complete Directory of Mail Order Catalog Products**
Sutton Family Communications & Publishing Company
920 State Route 54 East
Elmitch, KY 42343

270-276-9500

Theresa Sutton, Editor
Lee Sutton, General Manager

Print-out from database of wholesalers, manufacturers, distributors, importers and close-out houses. Database is updated daily to guarantee the most current and up-to-date sources available.
Cost: $157.50
100+ Pages

18024 **Direct Marketing Marketplace**
National Register Publishing
430 Mountain Ave.
Suite 400
New Providence, NJ 07974

800-473-7020; Fax: 908-673-1189
nrpeditorial@marquiswhoswho.com

Provides contact information for direct marketers, service firms and suppliers.

18025 **Directory Marketplace**
Todd Publications
PO Box 635
Nyack, NY 10960-0635

845-358-6213; Fax: 845-358-1059
toddpub@aol.com

Barry Klein, Editor

Directories and Reference Books for business, education, and libraries; news of new directories.
Cost: $25.00
Frequency: Bi-Monthly
Founded in 1987

18026 **Directory of Franchising Organizations**
Pilot Books
127 Sterling Avenue
PO Box 2102
Greenport, NY 11944

631-477-0978
800-797-4568; Fax: 631-477-0978

Over 1,300 current franchise opportunities in 45 categories.
Cost: $12.95
Frequency: Annual
Circulation: 0
ISBN: 0-875762-15-8

18027 **Directory of Mail Order Catalogs**
Grey House Publishing
4919 Route 22
PO Box 56
Amenia, NY 12501

518-789-8700
800-562-2139; Fax: 845-373-6390
books@greyhouse.com

www.greyhouse.com
Facebook, Twitter

Leslie Mackenzie, Publisher
Richard Gottlieb, Editor

The premier source of information on the mail order catalog industry. Covers over 13,000 consumer and business catalog companies with 44 different product chapters from Animals to Toys and Games.
Cost: $395.00
1600 Pages
Frequency: Annual
ISBN: 1-592373-96-8
Founded in 1981

18028 **Directory of Mail Order Catalogs - Online Database**
Grey House Publishing
4919 Route 22
PO Box 56
Amenia, NY 12501

518-789-8700
800-562-2139; Fax: 845-373-6390
gold@greyhouse.com
gold.greyhouse.com
Facebook, Twitter

Leslie Mackenzie, Publisher
Richard Gottlieb, Editor

Reach over 10,000 consumer catalog companies in one easy-to-use source with The Directory of Mail Order Catalogs - Online Database. Filled with business-building detail, each company profile gives you the information you need to access that organization quickly and easily. Listings provide key contacts, sales volume, employee size, printing information, circulation, list data, product descriptions and much more.
Frequency: Annual
Founded in 1981

18029 **Entertainment Marketing Letter**
EPM Communications
19 W. 21st St., #303
New York, NY 10010

212-941-0099
888-852-9467; Fax: 212-941-1622
www.epmcom.com

Ira Mayer, Owner
Terence Keegan, Editor

Database covering marketing techniques used in the entertainment industry.
Cost: $449.00
Frequency: 24 Issues/Year

18030 **Food & Beverage Market Place**
Grey House Publishing
4919 Route 22
PO Box 56
Amenia, NY 12501

518-789-8700
800-562-2139; Fax: 845-373-6390
books@greyhouse.com
www.greyhouse.com
Facebook, Twitter

Leslie Mackenzie, Publisher
Richard Gottlieb, Editor

This information packed three-volume set is the most powerful buying and marketing guide for the US food and beverage industry. Includes thousands of industry freight and transportation listings.
Cost: $595.00
2000 Pages
Frequency: Annual
ISBN: 1-592373-61-5
Founded in 1981

18031 **Food & Beverage Marketplace: Online Database**
Grey House Publishing
4919 Route 22
PO Box 56
Amenia, NY 12501

518-789-8700
800-562-2139; Fax: 518-789-0556
gold@greyhouse.com
gold.greyhouse.com
Facebook, Twitter

Richard Gottlieb, President
Leslie Mackenzie, Publisher

This complete updated Food & Beverage Market Place: Online Database is the go-to source for the food and beverage industry. Anyone involved in the food and beverage industry needs this 'industry bible' and the important contacts to develop critical research data that can make for successful business growth.
Frequency: Annual
Founded in 1981

18032 **GreenBook: Worldwide of Market Research Companies and Services**
NY American Marketing Association
116 East 27th Street
6th Floor
New York, NY 10016-1799

212-687-3280; Fax: 212-202-7920
info@greenbook.org
www.greenbook.org
Twitter, LinkedIn

Lucas Pospichal, Managing Director

Comprehensive listings of over 1,500 market research firms in the US and Canada. Listings in over 300 service categories and market industries. The most reliable reference resource for buyers of marketing research services.
Cost: $350.00
880 Pages
Frequency: Yearly
Circulation: 4,500
Founded in 1962

18033 **Infomercial Marketing Sourcebook**
Prometheus Global Media
770 Broadway
New York, NY 10003-9595

212-493-4100; Fax: 646-654-5368
www.prometheusgm.com

Richard D. Beckman, CEO
James A. Finkelstein, Chairman
Madeline Krakowsky, Vice President Circulation
Tracy Brater, Executive Director Creative Service

A complete resource guide for everyone involved in the infomercial industry.

18034 **International Directory of Marketing Research Companies & Services**
New York Chapter/American Marketing Association
310 Madison Avenue
New York, NY 10017-6009

212-986-1418

Offers more than 1,500 marketing research consultants and suppliers of marketing research data.
Cost: $105.00
600 Pages
Frequency: Annual
Circulation: 6,000

18035 **International Network Marketing Reference Book & Resource Directory**
MLM Group Publications
12 Rose Center
Norwood, MA 02062-2603

Offers valuable information on over 800 companies in the multi-level marketing industry.
Cost: $15.75
85 Pages

18036 **Leadership Library on Internet and CD-ROM**
Leadership Directories
104 5th Ave
New York, NY 10011-6901

212-627-4140; Fax: 212-645-0931
info@leadershipdirectories.com
www.leadershipdirectories.com

David Hurvitz, CEO

Makes all 14 leadership directories available over the Internet and on CD-ROM in one integrated directory. They provide subscribers with complete contact information in one database. Subscription includes Internet access and four CD-ROM editions quarterly.
Cost: $3065.00
Frequency: Updated Daily
ISSN: 1075-3869
Founded in 1999
Mailing list available for rent
Printed in A colors on B stock

18037 **MDMA Membership and Resource Directory**
Midwest Direct Marketing Association
P.O. Box 75
Andover, MN 55304

763-607-2943; Fax: 763-753-2240

Ed Harrington, Manager
Cindy McCleary, Director
400 Pages
Frequency: April
Mailing list available for rent: 1.1M+ names

18038 **Mail Order Business Directory**
B Klein Publishers
PO Box 8503
Coral Springs, FL 33075-8503
Bernard Klein, Editor

A listing of over 12,000 corporations in the US and 500 international firms doing business by mail order and catalogs.
Cost: $95.00
400 Pages
Frequency: Annual

18039 **Mail Order Product Guide**
Todd Publications
PO Box 635
Nyack, NY 10960-0635

845-358-6213
800-747-1086

A listing of over 1,500 manufacturers and importers to the mail order industry worldwide.
Cost: $50.00
250 Pages
Frequency: Triennial
Circulation: 5,000

18040 **Market Scope**
Trade Dimensions
45 Danbury Rd
Wilton, CT 06897-4445

203-563-3000; Fax: 203-563-3131
www.tradedimensions.com

Lynda Gutierrez, Managing Editor

The definitive source of market share and category sales data for supermarkets. The book configures the information in Trade Dimensions' database to determine market share by Nielsen, DMA, MSA and IRI definitions - over 300 markets in all. Market Scope also provides extensive category sales data as reported by Nielsen and IRI.
Cost: $325.00
Frequency: Annual

18041 **Marketing Guidebook**
Trade Dimensions

45 Danbury Rd
Wilton, CT 06897-4445

203-563-3000; Fax: 860-563-3131
www.tradedimensions.com

Lynda Gutierrez, Managing Editor
Jane Sheulin, Editor

The 'blue book' sales and marketing professionals have depended on for 30 years. The directory details the supermarket industry from distribution standpoint, comprising over 800 profiles, organized into 52 market areas. Includes all grocery chains and wholesalers that do a minimum of $30 million in sales. Also includes food brokers, non-food distributors, and small wholesalers in each market.
Cost: $340.00
Frequency: Annual

18042 Marketing Made Easier: Directory of Mailing List Companies
Todd Publications
PO Box 635
Nyack, NY 10960-0635

845-358-6213
800-747-1056; Fax: 845-358-3203
toddpubQ@aol.com
toddpublications.com

Barry Klein, Editor

Over 1,100 companies that sell mailing lists and the type of lits they handle.
Cost: $55.00
100 Pages
Frequency: Biennial
Circulation: 5,000
ISBN: 0-915344-83-1
Founded in 1972
Mailing list available for rent: 1,000 names at $100 per M
Printed in 2 colors

18043 Marketing Tools Directory
American Demographics
PO Box 4949
Stamford, CT 06907-0949

203-358-9900
800-832-1486; Fax: 607-273-3196

List of firms offering demographic and research services, data retrieval, and analysis, market evaluation and forecasting media services.
Frequency: Annual

18044 Marketing on a Shoestring: Low-Cost Tips for Marketing Products & Services
John Wiley & Sons
111 River St
Hoboken, NJ 07030-5790

201-748-6000
800-825-7550; Fax: 201-748-6088
info@wiley.com
www.wiley.com

William J Pesce, CEO

Business and professional associations that can assist individuals or companies in improving their marketing are profiled.
Cost: $14.95
236 Pages

18045 National Directory of Addresses and Telephone Numbers
Omnigraphics
2500 Penobscot Building
Detroit, MI 48226

313-961-1340

This new edition provides the most current names and addresses for businesses and services throughout the United States, arranged alphabetically and by business type.
Cost: $60.00
1,500 Pages
Frequency: Hardcover
ISBN: 0-780800-20-6

18046 National Trade and Professional Associations of the United States
Columbia Books
1212 New York Avenue NW
Suite 330
Washington, DC 20005-3987
202-641-1662
888-265-0600; Fax: 202-898-0775
info@columbiabooks.com
www.columbiabooks.com

Buck Downs, Senior Editor

Lists 7,600 national trade associations, professional societies and labor unions. Five convenient indexes enable you to look up associations by subject, budget, geographic area, acronym and executive director. Other features include: contract information, serial publications, upcoming convention schedule, membership/staff size, budget figures, and background information.
Cost: $99.00
Frequency: Annual Feburary

18047 New Marketing Opportunities
New Editions International
PO Box 2578
Sedona, AZ 86339-2578

928-282-9574
800-777-4751; Fax: 928-282-9730
www.newagemarket.com

Sophia Tarila, Author
Pat Bush, CEO

7,000 New Age and Metaphysical publishers, events, retailers, distributors, services, publications, reviewers, catalogers, media connections, internet connections, associations and other resources.
Cost: $139.95
Frequency: Annual
ISBN: 0-944773-18-4
Mailing list available for rent

18048 Procter & Gamble Marketing Alumni Directory
Ward Howell International
300 S Wacker Drive
Suite 2940
Chicago, IL 60606-6703

Membership directory listings.
120 Pages
Frequency: Annual

18049 Quirk's Marketing Research Review
Quirk Enterprises
PO Box 23536
Minneapolis, MN 55423-0536

952-854-5101; Fax: 612-854-8191
evan@quirks.com
www.quirks.com

Thomas Quirk, Publisher
Evan Tweed, Associate Publisher
Joseph Rydholm, Editor
Alice Davies, Manager

Publishing case histories and discussions of techniques which can be used by purchasers of research products and services. Also directories of research services. Accepts advertising.
Cost: $60.00
64 Pages
Frequency: 11 per year
Circulation: 15,500
Mailing list available for rent: 15.5M names
Printed in 4 colors on glossy stock

18050 Shop-at-Home Directory
Belcaro Group
7100 E Belvue
Suite 305
Greenwood Village, CO 80111
Marc Braunstein, President

This valuable informational source offers information on over 400 companies that offer direct mail order sales.
Cost: $3.00
60 Pages
Frequency: SemiAnnual

18051 Source Book of Multicultural Experts
Multicultural Marketing Resources
New York, NY
212-242-3351
lisa@multicultural.com
www.multicultural.com
Facebook, Twitter, LinkedIn

Lisa Skriloff, President
Dominika Peszko, Marketing

An annual directory that includes companies with expertise in marketing to different cultural and lifestyle markets. Resources include how to reach ethnic consumers, and contacts and leads for possible business alliances.
Cost: $19.99
Frequency: Annually
Circulation: 4000
Founded in 1994
Mailing list available for rent: 10,000 names

18052 Sports Market Place Directory
Grey House Publishing
4919 Route 22
PO Box 56
Amenia, NY 12501

518-789-8700
800-562-2139; Fax: 518-789-0556
books@greyhouse.com
greyhouse.com
Facebook, Twitter

Leslie Mackenzie, Publisher
Richard Gottlieb, Editor

For over 20 years, this comprehensive, up-to-date directory has offered direct access to the Who, What, When & Where of the Sports Industry. With this directory on your desk, you have a comprehensive tool providing current key information about the people, organizations and events involving the explosive sports industry at your fingertips.
Cost: $225.00
1800 Pages
Frequency: Annual
ISBN: 1-592373-48-8
Founded in 1981

18053 State and Regional Associations of the United States
Columbia Books
1212 New York Avenue NW
Suite 330
Washington, DC 20005-3987

202-641-1662
888-265-0600; Fax: 202-898-0775
info@columbiabooks.com
www.columbiabooks.com

Buck Downs, Senior Editor

Lists 7,200 of the largest and most significant state and regional trade and professional organizations in the US Look up associations by subject, budget, state, acronym, or chief executive. Also lists contract information, serial publications, upcoming convention schedule, membership/staff size, budget figures, and background information.
Cost: $79.00
Frequency: Annual March

18054 **Who's Who: MASA Buyer's Guide to Blue Ribbon Mailing Services**
Mailing & Fulfillment Service Association
1421 Prince Street
Suite 410
Alexandria, VA 22314-2806

703-836-9200; Fax: 703-548-8204
www.mfsanet.org
Facebook, Twitter, LinkedIn

Ken Garner, President
Bill Stevenson, Director Marketing
Leo Raymond, Vice President

Offers a detailed listing of suppliers of equipment, products and services to the direct mail industry, most containing a description of the specific products they provide.
Frequency: Annual

Industry Web Sites

18055 **http://gold.greyhouse.com**
G.O.L.D Grey House OnLine Databases

Grey House Publishing's online database platform, GOLD, offers Quick Search, Keyword Search and Expert Search for most business sectors including advertising and marketing markets. The GOLD platform makes finding the information you need quick and easy - whether you're a novice searcher or an experienced database user. All of Grey House's directory products are available for subscription on the GOLD platform.

18056 **www.adweek.com**
Adweek

Leading decision makers in the advertising and marketing field go to Adweek.Com everyday for breaking news, insight, buzz, opinion, analysis, research and classifieds. The resources of all six regional editions of Adweek, as well as the national edition of Brandweek are combined with the knowledge of our online editors and the multimedia/interactive capabilities of the web to deliver vital information quickly and effectively to our target audience.

18057 **www.ama.org**
American Marketing Association

Represents marketers and keeps members informed of trends in advertising. Fosters research, sponsors seminars and provides educational placement service.

18058 **www.amsp.org**
Association of Marketing Service Providers

Formerly known as the Mailing & Fulfillment Service Association, the Association of Marketing Service Providers provides educational content, networking opportunities, and legislative advocacy.

18059 **www.assist-intl.com**
Assist International

International trade promotion and consulting firm: mailing lists, seminars, conferences, international business expo.

18060 **www.bmahouston.org**
Business Marketing Association: Houston

Dedicated to serving the needs of business to business Associations worldwide.

18061 **www.fmi.org**
Food Marketing Institute

Events, publications, industry and consumer information and media.

18062 **www.greyhouse.com**
Grey House Publishing

Authoritative reference directories for most business sectors including advertising and marketing markets. Users can search the online databases with varied search criteria allowing for custom searches by product category, geographic area, sales volume, keyword, subject and more. Full Grey House catalog and online ordering also available.

18063 **www.imanetwork.org**
Internet Marketing Association

Seeks to provide members with the chance to learn, network, and establish Internet Marketing best practices. Members are in fields such as sales, marketing, business ownership, programming, and creative development.

18064 **www.inma.org**
International Newspaper Marketing Association

Individuals in marketing, circulation, research and public relations of newspapers.

18065 **www.manaonline.org**
Manufacturers Agents National Association

A national organization for manufacturer's agents and manufacturers who contract for the services of these representatives.

18066 **www.mark-ed.org**
Marketing Education Center

Committed to education for and about marketing. Provides professional support and training materials. Primary clients are schools, colleges, and educational institutions.

18067 **www.marketing.org**
Business Marketing Association

Pre-eminent service organization for professional's in this vital industry.

18068 **www.marketingpower.com**
American Marketing Association

A professional association for individuals and organizations involved in the practice, teaching and study of marketing worldwide.

18069 **www.mlmia.com**
Multi-Level Marketing International Association

Seeks to strengthen and improve the multi-level marketing industry in the United States and abroad.

18070 **www.msi.org**
Marketing Science Institute

Seeks to improve marketing practice and education, conducts research.

18071 **www.nacda.com**
National Assn of Collegiate Marketing Admin.

Members are public relations and marketing professionals in college and university athletic departments. Promotes standards and provides professional support.

18072 **www.pdma.org**
Product Development and Management Association

International association serving those with a professional interest in improving the management of product innovation.

18073 **www.pma.com**
Produce Marketing Association

Products and services, issues and information, conventions and expos.

18074 **www.postcom.org**
Association for Postal Commerce

National organization representing those who use, or support the use, of mail as a medium for communication and commerce. Postcom publishes a weekly newsletter covering postal policy and operational issues.

18075 **www.printing.org**
Graphic Arts Marketing Information Service

A section of Printing Industries of American that provides market research and statistics to its members. Research is member selected and directed.

18076 **www.retailing.com**
Electronic Retailing Association

Members include infomercial producers, marketers, product developers, broadcasters and other industries serving the infomercial market.

18077 **www.sigma.org**
Society of Independent Gasoline Marketers

Members are independent gasoline marketers.

18078 **www.smps.org**
Society for Marketing Professional Services

Promotes new business development of architectural, engineering, planning, design and construction management firms.

18079 **www.strategicaccounts.org**
Strategic Account Management Association

Dedicated to the professional and personal development of the executives charged with managing national, global, and strategic account relationships, and to elevating the status of the profession as a whole.

18080 **www.the-dma.org**
Direct Marketing Association

Leading global trade association of business and nonprofit organizations using and supporting direct marketing tools and techniques.

18081 **www.thefcs.org**
Financial Communications Society

The FCS is devoted to improving professional standards in financial marketing communications, with a membership comprised of managers in advertising, marketing, PR, IR, corporate communications, and social and digital media.

International Trade Resources

18082 **Antigua and Barbuda Department of Tourism and Trade**
25 S.E. 2nd Avenue
Suite 300
Miami, FL 33131

305-381-6762; Fax: 305-381-7908
www.antigua-barbuda.org

Byron Spencer, Manager

18083 **Austrian Trade Commission**
120 West 45th Street
9th Floor
New York, NY 10036

212-421-5250; Fax: 212-421-5251
newyork@advantageaustria.org
www.advantageaustria.org/us

Peter Athanasiadis, Manager
Sabine Miller, Project Manager
Walter HAfle, Director

18084 **Belize Mission to the United Nations**
675 Third Avenue
Suite 1911
New York, NY 10017

212-986-1240; Fax: 212-593-0932

Janine Coye-Felson, Minister-Counsellor
Dina S. Shoman, Counsellor/Director of Trade
Alfonso Gahona, First Secretary

18085 **Botswana Embassy**
1531-1533 New Hampshire Avenue NW
Washington, DC 20036

202-244-4990
www.botswanaembassy.org

H.E. Ms. Tebelelo Seretse, Ambassador
Ms. Sophie Heide Mautle, Deputy Head of Mission

18086 **British Trade and Investment Office**
845 3rd Avenue
9th Floor
New York, NY 10022

212-745-0495
www.ukti.gov.uk
Twitter, LinkedIn, YouTube, flickr

Nick Baird, Chief Executive Officer
Jon Harding, Chief Operating Officer
Crispin Simon, Managing Director, Trade
Michael Boyd, Managing Director
Sandra Rogers, Managing Director, Marketing

18087 **Bulgarian General Consulate**
121 E 62nd Street
New York, NY 10021

212-935-4646; Fax: 212-319-5955
consulate.newyork@mfa.bg
www.consulbulgaria-ny.org

18088 **Business Council for the United Nations**
801 2nd Avenue
2nd Floor
New York, NY 10017

212-907-1300; Fax: 212-682-9185
unahq@unausa.org
www.unausa.org/bcun
Facebook, Twitter, YouTube, flickr

Allison B MacEachron, Executive Director

18089 **Chile Trade Commission**
866 United Nations Plaza
Suite 603
New York, NY 10017

212-207-3266; Fax: 212-207-3649

Alejandro Cerda, Trade Commissioner

18090 **Colombia Government Trade Bureau**
1701 Pennsylvania Avenue, N W
Suite 560
Washington, DC 20006

202-887-9000; Fax: 202-223-0526
Fadul@coltrade.org

18091 **Consulate General of Bahrain**
866 2nd Avenue
14th Floor
New York, NY 10017

212-223-6200; Fax: 212-319-0687

Jassim Buallay, Manager

18092 **Consulate General of Belgium**
1065 Avenue of Americas
22nd Floor
New York, NY 10018

212-586-5110
212-586-7472; Fax: 212-582-9657
NewYork@diplobel.fed.be
www.diplomatie.be/newyork/

Piet Morisse, Manager

18093 **Consulate General of Bolivia**
211 E 43rd Street
Suite 702
New York, NY 10017

212-599-6767; Fax: 212-687-0532

Jorge Heredia Cavero, Manager

18094 **Consulate General of Brazil**
1185 Avenue of the Americas
21st Floor
New York, NY 10036-2601

917-777-7777; Fax: 212-827-0225
cg.novayork@itamaraty.gov.br
http://novayork.itamaraty.gov.br/en-us/

Julio Cesar Gomes Dos Sant, Manager

18095 **Consulate General of Costa Rica**
14 Penn Plaza, #1202
225 West 34th Street
New York, NY 10122

212-509-3066
212-509-3066; Fax: 212-509-3068; Fax: 212-509-3068

Otto Barcas, Manager

18096 **Consulate General of Germany**
871 United Nations Plaza
New York, NY 10017
212-610-9700; Fax: 212-940-0402

Bernhard Von Der Planit, Manager

18097 **Consulate General of Haiti**
815 2nd Avenue
6th Floor
New York, NY 10017

212-697-9767; Fax: 212-681-6991
www.haitianconsulate-nyc.org
Facebook, Twitter

Marie Therese, Manager

18098 **Consulate General of Honduras**
255 West 36th Street
First Level
New York, NY 10018

212-714-9451; Fax: 212-714-9453
www.hondurasemb.org
Facebook, Twitter

18099 **Consulate General of India**
3 E 64th Street
New York, NY 10065

212-774-0600; Fax: 212-861-3788
www.indiacgny.org
Facebook, Twitter, Youtube

Dnyaneshwar M Mulay, Consul General
Mr. P.K. Bajaj, Consul (Head of Chancery)

18100 **Consulate General of Indonesia**
5 E 68th Street
New York, NY 10021

212-879-0600

18101 **Consulate General of Israel**
800 Second Avenue
New York, NY 10017

212-499-5000
info@newyork.mfa.gov.il
embassies.gov.il/new-york
Facebook, Twitter, YouTube, flickr

Ido Aharoni, Consul General

18102 **Consulate General of Kenya**
866 UN Plaza
Suite 4016
New York, NY 10017

212-421-4741; Fax: 212-486-1985

Rolando Visconti, Manager

18103 **Consulate General of Lebanon**
9 E 76th Street
New York, NY 10021

212-744-7905; Fax: 212-794-1510
lebconsny@aol.com
www.lebconsny.org/

Hassan Saad, Manager

18104 **Consulate General of Lithuania**
420 5th Avenue
3rd Floor
New York, NY 10018

212-354-7840

Rimantas Morkvenas, Manager

18105 **Consulate General of Malta**
249 E 35th Street
New York, NY 10016

212-425-2345

18106 **Consulate General of Morocco**
10 East 40th Street
New York, NY 10016

212-758-2625; Fax: 646-395-8077
www.moroccanconsulate.com/

Ramon Xilotl, Manager

18107 **Consulate General of Nicaragua**
820, 2nd Avenue, 8th floor.,
Suite 802
New York, NY 10017

212-983-1981; Fax: 212-989-5528
consuladodenicaragua.com

Jose Flores, Manager
Nohelia Urcuyo, Consul

18108 **Consulate General of Nigeria**
828 2nd Avenue
New York, NY 10017

212-808-0301; Fax: 212-687-1476
cgnny@nigeriahouse.com
www.nigeriahouse.com/
Facebook

18109 **Consulate General of Paraguay**
801 2nd Avenue
Suite 600
New York, NY 10017

212-682-9441; Fax: 212-682-9443
info@consulparny.com

Juan Baiardi, Manager

18110 **Consulate General of Peru**
215 Lexington Avenue
21st Floor
New York, NY 10016

212-481-7410
www.consuladoperu.com/

18111 **Consulate General of Qatar**
809 United Nations Plaza
4th Floor
New York, NY 10017

212-486-9335

18112 **Consulate General of Russia**
2790 Green St
San Francisco, CA 94123

415-928- 687; Fax: 415-929-0306

18113 **Consulate General of Saudi Arabia**
866 Second Avenue
5th Floor
New York, NY 10017

212-752-2740
www.saudiembassy.net

Abdulrahman Gdaia, Excellency

18114 **Consulate General of Slovenia**
600 3rd Avenue
24th Floor
New York, NY 10016

212-370-3007; Fax: 212-370-3581
www.culturalprofiles.net/slovenia

Reimo Pettai, Manager
Sayed Jahangir, Director of Publications

18115 **Consulate General of South Africa**
333 E 38th Street
9th Floor
New York, NY 10016

212-213-4880; Fax: 212-213-0102
consulate.ny@foreign.gov.za
www.southafrica-newyork.net/consulate/
Facebook

George Monyemangene, Consul General

18116 **Consulate General of St. Lucia**
800 2nd Avenue
9th Floor
New York, NY 10017

212-499-5000

Julian Hunte, Manager

18117 **Consulate General of Switzerland**
633 3rd Avenue
30th Floor
New York, NY 10017

212-599-5700

Raymond Loretan, Excellency

18118 **Consulate General of Trinidad & Tobago**
125 Maiden Lane
Unit 4A, 4th Floor
New York, NY 10038

212-682-7272; Fax: 212-232-0368
www.ttcgnewyork.com/
Facebook, Twitter, You Tube

Hon Harold Robertson, Contact

18119 **Consulate General of Ukraine**
240 E 49th Street
New York, NY 10017

212-371-6965; Fax: 212-371-5547
gc_usn@mfa.gov.ua

18120 **Consulate General of Uruguay**
420 Madison Avenue
6th Floor
New York, NY 10017

212-753-8191; Fax: 212-753-1603
www.consuladouruguaynewyork.com/english-1/

Basil Bryan, Manager

18121 **Consulate General of Venezuela**
7 E 51st Street
New York, NY 10022

212-826-1660

18122 **Consulate General of the Commonwealth of the Bahamas**
231 E 46th Street
2nd Floor
New York, NY 10017

212-717-5643

Hon Eldred E Bethel, Contact

18123 **Consulate General of the Dominican Republic**
1715 22nd Street NW
Washington, DC 20008

202-332-6280; Fax: 202-265-8057

18124 **Consulate General of the Netherlands**
666 Third Avenue
19th Floor
New York, NY 10017

877-388-2443; Fax: 212-246-9769
nyc@minbuza.nl
http://ny.the-netherlands.org/
Facebook, Twitter

Wanda Fleck, Manager

18125 **Consulate General of the Principality of Monaco**
565 5th Avenue
New York, NY 10017

212-286-0500

Magguy Maccario-Doyle, Manager

18126 **Consulate General of the Republic of Croatia**
369 Lexington Avenue
11th Floor
New York, NY 10017

212-972-2277

Abdul Seraj, Manager

18127 **Consulate General of the Republic of Belarus**
708 3rd Avenue
21st Floor
New York, NY 10017

212-682-5392

Sergei Kolos, Manager

18128 **Consulate of Guyana**
866 United Nations Plaza
New York, NY 10017

212-527-3215

Brentnold Evans, Manager

18129 **Consulate of the Republic of Uzbekistan**
866 United Nations Plaza
Suite 327-A
New York, NY 10017-7671

212-754-6178

18130 **Cyprus Embassy Trade Center**
13 E 40th Street
New York, NY 10016

212-213-9100; Fax: 212-213-2918
ctcny@cyprustradeny.org
www.cyprustradeny.org/

Aristos Constantine, Trade Commissioner

The commission's primary role is to further and expand the economic interests of the Republic of Cyprus through promoting, facilitating and attracting foreign investment and fostering the expansion of exports of Cyprus' goods and services, in addition to monitoring related market and policy issues.

18131 **Department of Trade- Government of Antigua & Barbuda**
610 5th Avenue
Suite 311
New York, NY 10020

212-541-4117

18132 **Ecuadorian Consulate**
2535 15th Street NW
Washington, DC 20009

202-234-7200; Fax: 202-667-3482
consuladodc@ecuador.org

Pablo Yanez, Consulate

18133 **Egyptian Consulate Economic & Commercial Office**
3521 International Ct. NW
Washingotn, DC 20008

202-895-5400; Fax: 202-244-4319
embassy@egyptembassy.net
www.egyptembassy.net
Facebook

Ayden Nour, Executive Director

18134 **Embassy of Australia**
1601 Massachusetts Avenue NW
Washington, DC 20036

202-797-3000; Fax: 202-797-3168
www.usa.embassy.gov.au
Facebook, Twitter

Kim Beazley, Ambassador

18135 **Embassy of Benin**
2124 Kalorama Road NW
Washington, DC 20008

202-232-6656; Fax: 202-265-1996
info@beninembassy.us
www.beninembassy.us

Cyrille Segbe Oguin, President

18136 **Embassy of Cambodia**
4530 16th Street NW
Washington, DC 20011

202-726-7742
202-726-7824; Fax: 202-726-8381
www.embassyofcambodia.org
Facebook

Hem Heng, Ambassador

18137 **Embassy of Ethiopia Trade Affairs**
3506 International Drive NW
Washington, DC 20008

202-364-1200; Fax: 202-587-0195
ethiopia@ethiopianembassy.org
www.ethiopianembassy.org

Girma Birru, Ambassador

18138 **Embassy of Finland**
3301 Massachusetts Avenue NW
Washington, DC 20008

202-298-5800; Fax: 202-298-6030
sanomat.was@formin.fi
www.finland.org
Facebook, Twitter

Ritva Koukku-Ronde, Ambassador
Kristiina Vuorenp„„, Assistant to the Ambassador
Tarja Thatcher, Social Secretary

18139 **Embassy of Georgia**
2209 Massachusettes Avenue, NW
Washington, DC 20008

202-387-2390; Fax: 202-387-0864
www.embassy.mfa.gov.ge

Temur Yakobashvili, Ambassador

18140 **Embassy of Grenada**
1701 New Hampshire Ave, NW
Washington, DC 20009-2501

202-265-2561; Fax: 292-265-2468
embassy@grenadaembassyusa.org
www.grenadaembassyusa.org
Facebook, Twitter, Google Plus

E. Angus Friday, Ambassador
Patricia D Clarke, Counsellor
Dianne C Perrotteÿ, Administrative Assistant
Lucia Amedee, Receptionist/Office Assistant

18141 **Embassy of Jamaica (JAMPRO)**
1520 New Hampshire Ave, NW
Washington, DC 20036

202-452-0660; Fax: 202-452-0036
firstsec@jamaicaembassy.org
www.embassyofjamaica.org

Dr Stephen Vasciannie, Ambassador

18142 **Embassy of Mali**
2130 R Street NW
Washington, DC 20008

202-332-2249; Fax: 202-332-6603
info@maliembassy.us
www.maliembassy.us

Al Maamoun Baba Lamine Keita, Ambassador
Muhamed Ouzouna Maiga, The First Counselor
Ahmadou Barazi Maiga, The Second Counselor
Salif Sanogo, The Third Counselor-Communication
Colonel Bourama Sangare, Defence Attache

18143 **Embassy of Mongolia**
2833 M Street NW
Washington, DC 20007

202-333-7117; Fax: 202-298-9227
www.mongolianembassy.us
Facebook, Twitter, Youtube

H.E. Altangerel Bulgaa, Ambassador
Gansukh Damdin, Minister Counsellor, Deputy Chief
Munkhjargal Byamba, Counsellor
Colonel Boldbat Khasbazar, Defense Attache
Gantulga Chadraabal, Political Affairs/ Counsellor

18144 **Embassy of Panama**
2862 McGill Terrace NW
Washington, DC 20008

202-483-1407
202-483-8416; Fax: 202-483-8413
info@embassyofpanama.org
www.embassyofpanama.org
Facebook

Mario E. Jaramillo, Ambassador

18145 **Embassy of Tanzania**
1232 22nd St, NW
Washington, DC 20037

202-884-1080
202-939-6125; Fax: 202-797-7408
ubalozi@tanzaniaembassy-us.org
www.tanzaniaembassy-us.org

H.E. Liberataÿ Mulamula, Ambassador
Lily Munankaÿ, Minister
Paul Mwafongoÿ, Minister Plenipotentiary, Economics
B. G.ÿEmmanuel Maganga, Defense Attach,
Edward Masanja, Financial Attache

18146 **Embassy of Tunisia**
1515 Massachusetts Avenue NW
Washington, DC 20005

202-862-1850; Fax: 202-862-1858
www.tunconsusa.org/

Gordon Gray, Ambassador

18147 **Embassy of Uganda**
5911 16th Street NW
Washington, DC 20011

202-726-7100; Fax: 202-726-1727
owonekha@ugandaembassyus.org
www.ugandaemb.org
Facebook, Twitter

Oliver Wonekha, Ambassador
Alfred Nnam, Deputy Chief of Mission (DCM)
Dickson Ogwang, Minister Counselor
Patrick Muganda Guma, Counselor
Sam Bhoi Omara, First Secretary

18148 **Embassy of Vietnam**
1233 20th Street NW
Suite 400
Washington, DC 20036

202-861-0737; Fax: 202-861-0917
info@vietnamembassy.us
www.vietnamembassy-usa.org

Nguyen Quoc Cuong, Ambassador

18149 **Embassy of Zimbabwe**
1608 New Hampshire Avenue
Washington, DC 20009

202-332-7100; Fax: 202-483-9326
www.zimbabwe-embassy.us

Machivenyika Mapuranga, Ambassador
Richard T Chibuwe, Minister Counselor and Deputy Chief
R Matsika, Counselor
Whatmore Goora, Counselor (Political)
Col. George Chinoingira, Defence Attache

18150 **Embassy of the Hashemite Kingdom of Jordan**
3504 International Drive NW
Washington, DC 20008

202-966-2664; Fax: 202-966-3110
www.jordanembassyus.org
Facebook, Twitter, Youtube, Pintrest

Alia Hatoug Bouran, Ambassador

18151 **Embassy of the Lao People's Democratic Republic**
2222 S Street NW
Washington, DC 20008

202-332-6416
202-667-0076; Fax: 202-332-4923
embasslao@gmail.com
www.laoembassy.com

Seng Soukhathivong, Ambassador

18152 **Embassy of the People's Republic of China**
3505 International Place NW
Washington, DC 20008

202-495-2266; Fax: 202-495-2138
chinaembpress_us@mfa.gov.cn
www.china-embassy.org

Zhang Yesui, Ambassador

18153 **Embassy of the Republic of Angola**
2100-2108 16th Street, NW
Washington, DC 20009

202-785-1156; Fax: 202-822-9049
angola@angola.org
www.angola.org

Alberto do Carmo Bento Ribeiro, Ambassador
Sofia Pegado da Silva, Minister Counselor
Manuel Francisco Louren‡o, First Secretary - Head of Consular
Ineclito Lima, First Secretary - Consular Section
ÿMercedes Quintino, First Secretary - Consular Section

18154 **Embassy of the Republic of Fiji**
2000 M Street,NW
Suite 710
Washington, DC 20036

202-466-8320; Fax: 202-466-8325
info@fijiembassydc.com
www.fijiembassydc.com

Winston Thompson, Ambassador

18155 **Embassy of the Republic of Latvia**
2306 Massachusettes Ave, NW
Washington, DC 20008

202-328-2840; Fax: 202-328-2860
embassy.usa@mfa.gov.lv
www.mfa.gov.lv/en/usa
Facebook, Twitter, Flickr

Andris Teikmanis, Ambassador
Juris Pekalis, Deputy Chief of Mission

18156 **Embassy of the Republic of Liberia**
5201 16th Street N. W.
Washington, DC 20011

202-723-0437; Fax: 202-723-0436
www.liberianembassyus.org/

Charles Minor, President

18157 **Embassy of the Republic of Yemen**
2319 Wyoming Ave, NW
Washington, DC 20008

202-965-4760; Fax: 202-337-2017
ambassador@yemenembassy.org
www.yemenembassy.org

Abdulwahab Abdulla Al-Hajjri, Ambassador
Nadia Hashem, Assistant to the Ambassador

18158 **Embassy of the Republic of the Marshall Islands**
2433 Massachusetts Avenue NW
Washington, DC 20008

202-234-5414; Fax: 202-232-3236
www.rmiembassyus.org

Charles R. Paul, Ambassador

18159 **Estonian Embassy in Washington**
2131 Massachusetts Avenue NW
Washington, DC 20008

202-588-0101; Fax: 202-588-0108
Embassy.Washington@mfa.ee
www.estemb.org

Marina Kaljurand, Ambassador
Tanel Sepp, Deputy Chief of Mission
Indrek Kannik, Counselor (Security Policy)
Oleg Dmitrijev, First Secretary (Political Affairs)
Marju Korts, Third Secretary (Economic Affairs)

18160 **Fair Trading Commission**
800 2nd Avenue
2nd Floor
New York, NY 10017

246-424-260; Fax: 246-424-0300
info@ftc.gov.bb
www.ftc.gov.bb

Peggy Griffith, CEO
Founded in 1955

18161 **French Trade Commission**
1 E Wacker Drive
Suite 3730
Chicago, IL 60601

312-661-1880; Fax: 310-843-1700
www.ubifrance.com
Facebook, Twitter, LinkedIn

18162 **Gambia Mission to the United Nations**
800 2nd Avenue
Suite 400 F
New York, NY 10017

212-949-6640; Fax: 212-856-9820
www.un.int/gambia

Tamsir Jallow, Ambassador

18163 **General Consulate of Luxembourg**
17 Beekman Place
New York, NY 10022

212-888-6664; Fax: 212-888-6116
newyork.cg@mae.etat.lu
http://newyork-cg.mae.lu/en/The-Consulate-General

Jean-Claude Knebeler, Consul General
Saba Amroun-Febres, Consular Officer

18164 **Gibraltar Information Bureau**
1156 15th Street NW
Suite 1100
Washington, DC 20005

202-452-1108; Fax: 202-452-1109

Perry Stieglitz, Executive Director

18165 **Greek Trade Commission**
150 E 58th Street
17th Floor
New York, NY 10155

212-751-2404; Fax: 212-593-2278

Yannis Papadimitriou, Manager

18166 **Guatemala Trade Office**
57 Park Avenue
New York, NY 10017

212-689-1014; Fax: 212-689-6414
guatrade@aol.com

Roberto Rosenberg, Manager

18167 **Hong Kong Trade Development Council**
219 E 46th Street
New York, NY 10017-2951

212-838-8688; Fax: 212-838-8941
new.york.office@hktdc.org
www.hktdc.com
Facebook, Twitter, LinkedIn, Google+, YouTube, RSS, Weibo

Anna Fan, Director, New York

Promotes trade between the United States and Hong Kong.
Founded in 1966
Mailing list available for rent

18168 **Hungarian Trade Commission**
425 Bloor Street, East
Suite 501
Toronto-Ontario M4W 3R4

416-923-3596; Fax: 416-923-2097

Gyula Cseko, Trade Commissioner

18169 **Icelandic Consulate General**
800 3rd Avenue
36th Floor
New York, NY 10022

212-593-2700
646-282-9360; Fax: 646-282-9369
icecon.ny@mfa.is
www.iceland.is/us/nyc
Facebook

Hlynur Gudjonsson, Consul & Trade Commissioner
Berg_¢ra Laxdal, Cultural Representative
Founded in 1939

18170 **International Chamber of Commerce (ICC)**
1212 Avenue of the Americas
New York, NY 10036-1689

212-703-5065; Fax: 212-575-0327
www.iccwbo.org
Facebook, Twitter, LinkedIn, Youtube

Gerard Worms, Chairman
Harold McGraw III, Vice-Chairman
Founded in 1919

18171 **Irish Trade Board**
345 Park Avenue
17th Floor
New York, NY 10154

212-180-0800

Jean McCluskey, Marketing Executive

18172 **Italian Trade Commission**
33 East 67th Street
New York, NY 10065-5949

212-980-1500; Fax: 212-758-1050
newyork@ice.it
www.italtrade.com/countries/americas/usa/newyork.htm

Michelle Jones, Editor
Robert Luongo, Executive Director

Developments in the Italian wine industry and market, as well as reviews of imported wines from Italy.

18173 **Japanese External Trade Organization**
1221 Avenue of the Americas
42nd Floor
New York, NY 10020

212-997-0400; Fax: 212-997-0464
jetrony@jetro.go.jp
www.jetro.org
Facebook, Twitter

Masaki Fujiharaÿ, Director, Business Developmentÿ
Daiki Nakajimaÿ, ICT/Environmentÿ

18174 **Kazakhstan Mission to the United Nations**
305 East 47th Street
3rd Floor
New York, NY 10017

212-230-1900; Fax: 212-230-1172
kazakhstan@un.int
www.kazakhstanun.org

Byrganym Aitimova, Ambassador
Akan Rakhmetulin, DeputyPermanent Representative
Israil Tilegen, Minister Counsellor
Ruslan Bultrikov, Counsellor
Tluezan Seksenbay, Counsellor

Historic contributions in the field of nuclearÿdisarmamentand non-proliferation by voluntarily eliminating its nuclear arsenal, acceding to the NPT as a non-nuclear state and shutting down the former Semipalatinsk nuclear testing ground, thus ensuring global and regional stability
Founded in 1992

18175 **Korea Trade Promotion Center (KOTRA)**
460 Park Avenue
14th Floor
New York, NY 10022

212-826-0900; Fax: 212-888-4930
kotrany@hotmail.com

Sungpil Umo, President
Il Hoon Ko, Deputy Director

18176 **Kyrgyzstan Mission to the United Nations**
866 United Nations Plaza
Suite 477
New York, NY 10017

212-486-4214; Fax: 212-486-5259

Talaibek Kydyrov, Ambassador
Nuran Niyazaliev, Counsellor
Nurbek Kasymov, First Secretary
Diana Sarygulova, Third Secretary
Asel Davydova, Chief Administrative Specialist

Landlocked republic in the eastern part of Central Asia which is bordered in the north by Kazakhstan, in the east by China, in the south by China and Tajikistan, and in the west by Uzbekistan. Bishkek is the capital and largest city.
Founded in 1993

18177 **Malaysia Trade Commission**
313 E 43rd Street
3rd Floor
New York, NY 10017

212-986-6310; Fax: 212-490-8576
www.kln.gov.my

Hussein Haniff, Ambassador

18178 **Mexico Trade Commission**
757 3rd Avenue
Suite 2400
New York, NY 10017-2042

212-826-2978

18179 **Moldova Mission to the United Nations**
35 East 29th Street
New York, NY 10016

212-447-1867; Fax: 212-447-4067
unmoldova@aol.com

Vlad Lupan, Ambassador
Larisa Miculet, Counsellor
Carolina Podoroghin, Third Secretary

Tatianana Dudnicenco, Chief Financial Officer
Litvac Sergiu, Administrator
Founded in 1992

18180 New Zealand Trade Development Board
222 East 41st Street
New York, NY 10017-6739

212-497-0200

18181 Norwegian Trade Council
2720 34th Street NW
Washington, DC 20008

202-333-6000; Fax: 202-469-3990
emb.washington@mfa.no
www.norway.org
Twitter, LinkedIn, Flickr, Instagram, Tumblr

Kare R.Aas, Ambassador
Lajla Jakhelin, Minister
Elin Kylvag, Personal Assistant
Berit Enge, Minister Counsellor

Innovation Norway promotes nationwide industrial development profitable to both the business economy and Norways national economy, and helps release the potential of different districts and regions by contributing towards innovation, internationalisation and promotion. Innovation Norway also promotes tourism to Norway

18182 Pakistan Trade Commission
12 E 65th Street
4th Floor
New York, NY 10021

212-879-5800

Abbas Zaidi, Manager

18183 Permanent Mission of Bangladesh to the United Nations
820 East Diplomat Center, 2nd Avenue
4th Floor
New York, NY 10017

212-867-3434; Fax: 212-972-4038

A.K.Abdul Momen, Ambassador
Mustafizur Rahman, Permanent Representative
Andalib Elias, Counsellor
Samia Anjum, Counsellor

Peaceful settlement of disputes, promotion of human rights, protection of environment, sustainable development and so on.
Founded in 1990

18184 Permanent Mission of Ghana to the United Nations
19 E 47th Street
New York, NY 10017

212-832-1300; Fax: 212-751-6743
ghanaperm@aol.com
www.un.int/ghana

Ken Kanda, Ambassador
William Kanyirige, Minister
Henry T.Menson, Minister-Counsellor
J.R Adogla, Minister-Counsellor
N.A Abayena, Counsellor
Founded in 1957

18185 Permanent Mission of Myanmar (Formerly Burma)
10 E 77th Street
New York, NY 10075

212-744-1271; Fax: 212-744-1290
www.myanmarmissionny.org

H.E.U. Kyaw Tin, Ambassador
A.Kyaw Zan, Minister counsellor
Ko Ko Shien, Minister Counsellor

18186 Permanent Mission of Saint Vincent & the Grenadines to the United Nations
800 2nd Avenue
Suite 400-G
New York, NY 10017

212-599-0950; Fax: 212-599-1020
www.svg-un.org
Facebook, Twitter, YouTube

Camillo M. Gonsalves, Ambassador
Nedra Miguel, Minister Counsellor
Mozart Carr, Attache
Maglyn Carrington, Secretary/Accountant

Primary channel for communications between the Vincentian Government and the United Nations in New York City.
Founded in 1998

18187 Permanent Mission of the Czech Republic to the United Nations
1109-1111 Madison Avenue
New York, NY 10028

646-981-4001; Fax: 646-981-4099
un.newyork@embassy.mzv.cz
www.mzv.cz/un.newyork
Facebook, Twitter, LinkedIn

Edita Hrda, Amabassador
David Cervanka, Deputy Permanent Representative
Founded in 1945

18188 Permanent Mission of the Kingdom of Bhutan to the United Nations
343 East 43rd Street
New York, NY 10017

212-682-2268; Fax: 212-661-0551

Lhtu Wangchuk, Ambassador

18189 Permanent Mission of the Republic of Sudan to the United Nations
655 3rd Avenue
Suite 500-10
New York, NY 10017

212-593-0999

Jenine Selson, Manager

18190 Permanent Mission of the Republic of Armenia to the United Nations
119 E 36th Street
New York, NY 10016

212-752-3370

Andrezej Towpik, Manager

18191 Permanent Mission of the Solomon Islands to the United Nations
800 2nd Avenue
Suite 400
New York, NY 10017

212-599-6192; Fax: 212-661-8925

Collin Beck, Ambassador
Hellen Beck, Counsellor
Vanessa M.Kenilorea, Third Secretary
B Jagne, Manager

18192 Philippines Commercial Office
556 5th Avenue
New York, NY 10036

212-764-1330

18193 Poland Trade Commission
675 3rd Avenue
19th Floor
New York, NY 10017

212-351-1713

Phyllis Poland, Owner

18194 Portuguese Trade Commission
590 5th Avenue
3rd Floor
New York, NY 10036

212-354-4403; Fax: 212-575-4737
chamber@portugal-us.com

18195 Romanian Consulate General
11766 Wilshire Blvd
Suite 560
Los Angeles, CA 90025

310-444-0043; Fax: 310-445-0043
http://www.romanian.com

Corina Suteu, Manager

The Romanian projects are on hold, as inhouse resources were diverted to more lucrative projects hosted at NetSide. If you have an interst to develop something in Romanian, please let me know and perhaps we can work something out.

18196 Singapore Trade Commission
55 E 59th Street
Suite 21-B
New York, NY 10022

212-421-2869; Fax: 212-421-2206
newyork@contactsingapore.org

Kc Yeoh, Executive Director

18197 Slovak Republic Mission to the United Nations
866 United Nations Plaza
Suite 493
New York, NY 10017

212-980-1558

18198 Swedish Trade Council
150 N Michigan Avenue
Chicago, IL 60601

312-781-6222
Facebook, Twitter

Stefam Bergstrom, Manager

18199 Syrian Arab Republic Embassy
2215 Wyoming Avenue NW
Washington, DC 20008

202-232-6313; Fax: 202-265-4585

18200 Taiwan Trade Center
5201 Great America Parkway
Suite 306
Santa Clara, CA 95054-112

408-988-5018; Fax: 408- 98-5029
office@taiwantradesf.org
http://sf.taiwantrade.com.tw/

Founded in 1970

18201 Tajikistan Mission to the United Nations
136 E 67th Street
New York, NY 10021

212-744-2196; Fax: 212-472-7645

Khamrokhon Zaripov, President
Abduvokhid Karimov, Minister

18202 Thailand Trade Center- Consulate General of Thailand
401 N Michigan Avenue
Suite 544
Chicago, IL 60611

312-467-0044; Fax: 312-467-1690

18203 **Trade Commission of Denmark**
285 Peachtree Road NE
Suite 920
Atlanta, GA 30303
404-588-1588; Fax: 678-904-9714
atlhkt@um.dk
Taksoe Jensen, Ambassador
Henrik Bronner, Manager

18204 **Trade Commission of Spain**
500 N Michigan Avenue
Suite 1500
Chicago, IL 60611
312-644-1154
www.spaintechnology.com

18205 **Turkish Trade Commission**
821 United Nations Plaza
4th Floor
New York, NY 10017
212-687-1530

18206 **Turkmenistan Mission to the United Nations**
866 United Nations Plaza
Suite 424
New York, NY 10017
212-486-8908; Fax: 212-486-2521
turkmenistan@un.int
Aksoltan Ataeva, Manager

18207 **United Nations Mission to El Salvador**
46 Park Avenue
New York, NY 10016
212-679-1616; Fax: 212-725-3467
Antonio Montiero, Manager

Associations

18208 **AMT: Association for Manufacturing Technology**
7901 Westpark Dr
Mc Lean, VA 22102-4206

703-893-2900
800-524-0475; Fax: 703-893-1151
AMT@amtonline.org
www.amtonline.org
Facebook, Twitter, LinkedIn, Youtube

Bob Simpson, President
Douglas K. Woods, First Vice Chairman
John Byrd, President

ÿThe Association For Manufacturing Technology represents and promotes U.S.-based manufacturing technology and its members-those who design, build, sell, and service the continuously evolving technology that lies at the heart of manufacturing
370 Members
Founded in 1902

18209 **APMI International Advancement of Powder Metallurgy**
105 College Road E
Princeton, NJ 08540-6992

609-452-7700; Fax: 609-987-8523
info@mpif.orgÿ
www.mpif.org

Dean Howard, President
Michael E Lutheran, Director
C James Trombino CAE, Director

A non-profit professional society which promotes the advancement of powder metallurgy (PM) and particulate materials as a science. Its purpose is to disseminate and exchange information about PM and particulate materials through publications, conferences, and other activities of the society.
Founded in 1959

18210 **ASM International**
9639 Kinsman Road
Materials Park, OH 44073-0002

440-338-5151
800-336-5152; Fax: 440-338-4634
memberservicecenter@asminternational.org
www.asminternational.org
Facebook, Twitter, LinkedIn

Zi-Kui Liu, President
Diana Essock, Vice President
Raymond V. Fryan, Treasurer
William T. Mahoney, Secretary & CEO

The society for materials engineers and scientists, a worldwide network dedicated to advancing industry, technology and applications of metals and materials. ASM provides information references, education, research and international events.
30K Members
Founded in 1913

18211 **Aluminum Anodizers Council (AAC)**
1000 North Rand Road
Suite 214
Wauconda, IL 60084

847-526-2010; Fax: 847-526-3993
mail@anodizing.org
www.anodizing.org
LinkedIn

Represents the interests of aluminum anodizers worldwide and is the principal trade organization for the andozing industry in North America. It promotes the interests of its members through technical exchange, ongoing education, statistical data, market promotion and industry representation.
85 Members
Founded in 1988

18212 **Aluminum Association**
Aluminum Association
1400 Crystal Drive
Suite 430
Arlington, VA 22209-2444

703-358-2960; Fax: 703-358-2961
info@aluminum.org
www.aluminum.org
Facebook, Twitter, LinkedIn

J Stephen Larkin, President
Joe Quinn, VP, Public Affairs
Heidi Biggs Brock, President
Ryan Olsen, Vice President, Business Informatio

Members are manufacturers of aluminum mill products and producers of aluminum.
70 Members

18213 **Aluminum Extruders Council**
1000 North Rand Road
Suite 214
Wauconda, IL 60084

847-526-2010; Fax: 847-526-3993
mail@aec.org
www.aec.org
Facebook, Twitter, LinkedIn, Blog

Matt McMahon, Chairman
Scott Kelley, Vice Chairman
Jeff Henderson, President
Nancy Molenda, Communications Manager

An international association dedicated to helping manufacturers, engineers, architects and others to discover why aluminum extrusoin is the preferred material process for better products
Founded in 1950

18214 **American Association of Professional Farriers**
1313 Washington Street
Unit 5
Shelbyville, KY 40065

Home Page: www.professionalfarriers.comÿ

Dave Farley APF CF, President
Steve Prescott APF CJF, Vice President
Roy Bloom APF CJF, Treasurer
Jeff Ridley APF CJF TE, Immediate Past President
Bryan Quinsey, Executive Director
Founded in 2011

18215 **American Ceramic Society**
600 N. Cleveland Ave.
Suite 210
Westerville, OH 43082

240-646-7054
866-721-3322; Fax: 240-396-5637
customerservice@ceramics.org
www.ceramics.org
Facebook, Twitter, LinkedIn, RSS, Google+, YouTube

18216 **American Electroplaters and Surface Finishers Society (AESF)**
1155 15th Street NW
Suite 500
Washington, DC 20005

202-457-8401; Fax: 202-530-0659
info@aesf.org
www.aesf.org
Facebook, Twitter, LinkedIn, RSS, Google+, YouTube

John Flatley, Executive Director
Courtney Mariette, Bookstore/Education
Holly Wills, Membership
Dan Denston, Executive Director
John Flatley, Senior Advisor and NASF Liaison

AESF is an international society that advances the science of surface finishing to benefit industry and society through education, information and social involvement, as well as those who provide services, supplies and support to the industry.
5000 Members
Founded in 1911

18217 **American Farriers Association**
4059 Iron Works Pkwy
Suite 1
Lexington, KY 40511-8488

859-233-7411; Fax: 859-231-7862
info@americanfarriers.org
www.americanfarriers.org

Craig Trnka, President
Bob S.Earle, VP
Bryan Quinsey, Executive Director
Rachel Heighton, Office Manager
Founded in 1971

18218 **American Foundry Society**
1695 N Penny Ln
Schaumburg, IL 60173-4555
847-824-0181
800-537-4237; Fax: 847-824-7848
library@afsinc.org
www.afsinc.org
Facebook, Twitter, LinkedIn

Jerry Call, Executive VP
Ian Kay, VP
David Peterson, Membership Director

Trade association representing the interests of foundry workers across the nation. Offers publications, seminars and networking to promote business in the trade.
10000 Members
Founded in 1896

18219 **American Galvanizers Association**
6881 S Holly Circle
Suite 108
Centennial, CO 80112

720-554-0900; Fax: 720-554-0909
aga@galvanizeit.org
www.galvanizeit.org
Facebook, Twitter, LinkedIn, Google+, YouTube

Philip G. Rahrig, Executive Director
Thomas Langill, PhD, Technical Director
Melissa Lindsley, Marketing Director

The American Galvanizers Association (AGA) is a non-profit trade association dedicated to serving the needs of after-fabrication galvanizers, fabricators, specifiers, architects, engineers, and contractors. The AGA provides technical support on today's innovative applications and state-of-the-art technological developments in hot-dip galvanizing for corrosion control. The AGA also provides a number of services to galvanizers and zinc producers in the industry.
Founded in 1933

18220 **American Galvinizers Association**
6881 South Holly Circle,
Suite 108
Centennial, CO 80112

720-554-0900; Fax: 720-554-0909
aga@galvanizeit.org
www.galvanizeit.orgÿ
Facebook, Twitter, LinkedIn, Google+, YouTube

Tommy Rose, President
John Gregor, First Vice President
Tim Pendley, Second Vice President
Philip G. Rahrig, Executive Director
Dr. Tom Langill, Technical Director
Founded in 1933

18221 American Institute of Mining, Metallurgical & Petroleum Engineers
8307 Shaffer Parkway
Po Box 270728
Littleton, CO 80127-0013

303-948-4255; Fax: 303-948-4260
aime@aimehq.org
www.aimeny.org

Rick Rolater, Executive Director
James R Jorden, President

Organized and operated exclusively to advance, record and disseminate significant knowledge of engineering and the arts and sciences involved in the production and use of minerals, metals, energy sources and materials for the benefits of humankind, both directly as AIME and through memeber societies.

18222 American Institute of Steel Construction
One East Wacker Drive
Suite 700
Chicago, IL 60601-1802

312-670-2400; Fax: 312-670-5403
solutions@aisc.org
www.aisc.org
RSS

Charles Carter, President
Scott Meinick, SVP
Carly Hurd, VP, Operational Engagement
Larry Kruth, CP, Engineering & Research
Brian Raff, VP, Market Development

18223 American Iron & Steel Institute
25 Massachusetts Ave., NW, Suite 800
Washington, DC 20001

202-452-7100; Fax: 202-496-9702
webmaster@steel.org
www.recycle-steel.org
Facebook, Twitter, Youtube,Google+,Blog

Chip Foley, VP
David Bell, VP/CEO

Works with market development communications programs in automotive, construction and container markets.

18224 American Society for Metals
9639 Kinsman Road
Materials Park, OH 44073-0002

440-338-5151
800-336-5152
memberservicecenter@asminternational.org
www.asminternational.org
Facebook, Twitter, LinkedIn

Founded in 1913

18225 American Welding Society
8669 Doral Boulevard, Suite 130
Doral, FL 33166

305-443-9353
800-443-9353; Fax: 305-443-7559
www.aws.org
Facebook, Twitter, Instagram

Ray Shook, Manager
Andy Cullison, Publisher
Amy Nathan, Public Relations Manager

Involved in writing industry standards.
48000 Members
Founded in 1919

18226 American Wire Cloth Institute
25 North Broadway
Tarrytown, NY 10591

914-332-0040; Fax: 914-332-1541
info@hti.org
www.hti.org

Richard C Byrne, Executive Director

Formerly the Industrial Wire Cloth Institute (1978)
Founded in 1933

18227 American Wire Producers Association
PO Box 151387
Alexandria, VA 22315

703-299-4434; Fax: 703-299-4434
info@awpa.org
www.awpa.org

Founded in 1981

18228 Artist-Blacksmiths Association of North America
259 Muddy Fork Road
Jonesborough, TN 37659

423-913-1022; Fax: 423-913-1023
abana@abana.org
www.abana.org
Facebook, Twitter

Eddie Rainey, President
Tina Chisena, First VP
John Fee, Second Vice President
Herb Upham, Secretary

For the professional and amateur blacksmith.
4500 Members
Founded in 1973
Mailing list available for rent

18229 Association for Iron & Steel Technology (AIST)
186 Thorn Hill Rd
Warrendale, PA 15086-7528

724-814-3000; Fax: 724-814-3001
memberservices@aist.org
www.aist.org
Facebook, Twitter, LinkedIn, YouTube

Ronald E Ashburn, Executive Director
Lori Wharrey, Board Administrator
Chris McKelvey, Assistant Board Administrator
Stacy Vermecky, Membership Services Manager
Penny English, Member Administrator

The Association for Iron & Steel Technology (AIST) is an international technical association representing iron and steel producers, their allied suppliers and related academia. The association is dedicated to advancing the technical development, production, processing and application of iron and steel.
12300 Members
Founded in 2004

18230 Association of Battery Recyclers
PO Box 290286
Tampa, FL 33687

813-626-6151; Fax: 813-622-8387
joycemorales@aol.com
batteryrecyclers.com

Joyce Morales, Secretary/Treasurer

Investigates means and methods to achieve compliance with OSHA and EPA regulations impacting the secondary lead smelting industry.
Founded in 1976

18231 Association of Industrial Metallizers, Coaters and Laminators (AIMCAL)
201 Springs Street
Fort Mill, SC 29715

803-948-9470; Fax: 803-948-9471
aimcal@aimcal.org
www.aimcal.org
Facebook, Twitter

Dan Bemi, President
Danis Roy, VP
Craig Sheppard, Executive Director
Tracey Ingram, Senior Administrator
David Bryant, Treasurer

Nonprofit trade organization for makes of coated, laminated and metalized papers.
Founded in 1970
Mailing list available for rent

18232 Association of Steel Distributors
401 N Michigan Avenue
Chicago, IL 60611

312-673-5793; Fax: 312-527-6705
www.steeldistributors.org
Facebook, Twitter, LinkedIn, Instagram

Ron Pietrzak, Executive Director
Brain Robbins, President
Andy Gross, Executive Vice President
Mike Sawyer, Vice President
Bill Vitucci, Treasurer

ASD is a nonprofit organization, providing the steel distribution industry a forum for ideas exchange and market information.
Founded in 1943

18233 Association of Women in the Metal Industries
19 Mantua Road
Mt Royal, NJ 08061

856-423-3201; Fax: 856-423-3420
awmi@talley.com
www.awmi.org
Facebook, Twitter, LinkedIn

Haley Brust, Executive Director
Donna Peters, President
Carol Chizmar, Vice President
Lauren Lebakken, Secretary
Lauren Kerekes, Treasurer

An international, professional organization dedicated to promoting and supporting the advancement of women in the metal industries.
Founded in 1981

18234 Cast Iron Soil Pipe Institute
2401 Fieldcrest Dr.
Mundelein, IL 60660

224-864-2910
www.cispi.org

Founded in 1949

18235 Cast Metals Institute
1695 N Penny Ln
Schaumburg, IL 60173-4555

847-824-0181
800-537-4237; Fax: 847-824-7848
library@afsinc.org
www.afsinc.org
Facebook, Twitter, LinkedIn

Mark Nagel, Executive VP
Sandy Salisbury-Linton, Vice Chairman

Supports all those involved in the cast metal industry. Hosts annual trade show.
Founded in 1956

18236 Closure & Container Manufacturers Association
14070 Proton Rd.
Suite 100, LB 9
Dallas, TX 75244-3601

972-333-9107; Fax: 972-490-4219
office@bevtech.org
www.bevtech.org/
Facebook, Twitter, LinkedIn

Brain Stegmann, President
Cloeann Durham, 1st Vice President
Sieg Muller, 2nd Vice President
Ron Puvak, Immediate Past President
Larry Hobbs, Executive Director

Conducts public relations for member companies and establishes industry standards.
38 Members
Founded in 1984

18237 Copper Development Association
7918 Jones Branch Dr.
Suite 300
McLean, VA 22102

212-251-7200
questions@copper.org
www.copper.org
Facebook, Twitter, LinkedIn, Google+

Thomas S. Passek, President
Andrew G. Kireta, Vice President, Market Development
Luis Lozano, Technical Consultant

CDA is committed to promoting the proper use of copper materials in sustainable, efficient applications for business, industry and the home.
52 Members
Founded in 1963

18238 Copper and Brass Servicenter Association
6734 W 121st Street
Overland Park, KS 66209

913-396-0697
cbsahq@copper-brass.org
www.copper-brass.org
Facebook, Twitter, LinkedIn, YouTube, Flickr

Susan Avery, Executive Director
Liz Novak, Senior Director

Distributors (service centers) of fabricated copper and copper alloy products (sheet, plate, coil, rod, bar tube, etc) and their brass mill suppliers.
78 Members
Founded in 1951

18239 Ductile Iron Pipe Research Association
P.O. Box 19206
Suite O
Golden, CO 80402

205-402-8700; Fax: 205-402-8730
info@dipra.org
www.dipra.org
Facebook, Twitter, YouTube

Jon R. Runge, CAE, President
Richard W Bonds, Technical Director
L. Gregg Horn, VP, Technical Services
Josh Blount, Staff Engineer/Project Manager

Established as the Cast Iron Pipe Publicity Bureau.
7 Members
Founded in 1915

18240 Ductile Iron Society
15400 Pearl Rd
Suite 234
Strongsville, OH 44136-6017

440-665-3686; Fax: 440-878-0070
jwood@ductile.org
www.ductile.org

Robert O.Rourke, President
MIke Galvin, VP
Pete Guidi, Treasurer
James N.Wood, Executive and Technical Director
Patricio Gil, Past President

A technical society servicing the ductile iron industry. To advance the technology, art, science of ductile iron production and to disseminate all such information to the members.
102 Members
Founded in 1958

18241 Edison Welding Institute
1250 Arthur E Adams Dr
Columbus, OH 43221-3585

614-688-5000; Fax: 614-688-5001
info@ewi.org
www.ewi.org
Facebook, Twitter

Henry Cialone, President
Dr Karl Graff, Executive Director
Richard Rogovin, Chair

Companies and organizations with an interest in new developments in welding equipment and technology.

18242 Electrical Manufacturing & Coil Winding Association
PO Box 278
Imperial Beach, CA 91933-0278

619-435-3629; Fax: 619-435-3639
cthurman@earthlink.net
www.emcwa.org

Richard Duke, President
Charles Thurman, Executive Director
Don Stankiewicz, Vice President

A non-profit voluntary organization dedicated to the furtherance of the conception, research, design, manufacturing, marketing and use of electrical products. The Association provides an array of educational opportunities that enhance the development, knowledge, and use of electrical technology and products. Providing an annual forum to display products, ideas and innovations is a key element in this educational process.
400 Members
Founded in 1973
Mailing list available for rent

18243 Fabricators & Manufacturers Association International
833 Featherstone Road
Rockford, IL 61107

815-399-8700
888-394-4362
info@fmanet.org
www.fmanet.org
Facebook, Twitter, LinkedIn, YouTube, Google+

Ed Youdell, President & CEO

Organization seeking to improve the metal forming and fabricating industry.
2300 Members
Founded in 1970

18244 Fabricators and Manufacturers Association
Fabricators and Manufacturers Association
833 Featherstone Road
Rockford, IL 61107-6302

815-399-8700; Fax: 815-484-7700
info@fmanet.org
www.fmanet.org
Facebook, Twitter, LinkedIn

Gerald M Shankel, President/CEO
Jim Warren, Director/Membership + Education
Vicki Webb, Director/Information Technology
Mark Hoper, Director/Expositions
Michael Long, Director/Education
1500 Members
Founded in 1971

18245 Forging Industry Association
1111 Superior Ave.
Suite 615
Cleveland, OH 44114

216-781-6260; Fax: 216-781-0102
info@forging.org
www.forging.org
Facebook, Twitter, LinkedIn

Roy W. Hardy, President
Joe Boni, CFO
Don Farley, Director of Marketing
Theresa Ferry, Executive Assistant
Pat Kasik, Executive Assistant

18246 Global Platinum & Gold
5380 S 154th St
Gilbert, AZ 85298-6138

480-946-1242; Fax: 480-946-1242

A natural resources mining company engaged in the processing and commercial extraction of precious metals from complex ores.

18247 Gold Prospectors Association of America
43445 Business Park Drive
Suite #113
Temecula, CA ÿ92590
951-699-4749
800-551-9707; Fax: 951-699-4062
info@goldprospectors.org
www.goldprospectors.org
Facebook, Twitter, LinkedIn, YouTube

Thomas Massie, CEO

GPAA is the largest recreational gold prospecting club. Owner of The Outdoor Channel, a cable TV channel featuring real outdoors for real people.
35M Members
Founded in 1985

18248 Industrial Diamond Association of America
P.O. Box 29460ÿ
Columbus, OH 43229

614-797-2265
614-425-0712; Fax: 614-797-2264
tkane-ida@insight.rr.com
www.superabrasives.org

Terry M. Kane, Executive Director

18249 Industrial Metal Containers Section of the Material Handling Institute
8720 Red Oak Boulevard
Suite 201
Charlotte, NC 28217-3996

704-676-1190; Fax: 704-676-1199
gbaer@mhia.org
www.mhi.org
Facebook, Twitter, LinkedIn, YouTube

Dave Young, Chairman
John Patrox, President
Gregg E.ÿ Goodner, Vice President
Steve Buccella, VP, Corporate Sales/BD
Bryan Carey, President and CEO

Promotes the market and develops a code of ethics. Serves as liaison among members and other groups.
9 Members
Founded in 1972

18250 Industrial Perforators Association
6737 W. Washington St
Milwaukee, WI 53214

414-389-8618; Fax: 414-276-7704
www.iperf.org
Facebook, Twitter

Delores Morris, Executive Secretary

Members are companies making perforated metal products.

18251 Innovative Material Solutions
225 Canterbury Drive
State College, PA 16803

814-867-1140; Fax: 814-867-2813

Supports all those involved in research in the materials industry. Hosts annual trade show.

18252 Institute of Scrap Recycling Industries
1615 L St NW
Suite 600
Washington, DC 20036-5664
202-662-8500; Fax: 202-626-0900
dennywhite@scrap.org
www.isri.org
Facebook, Twitter, LinkedIn, YouTube
Robin K.Wiener, President
Sandy Bishop, VP Finance/Administration
Rachel Bookman, Admin Assistant
Thomas Crane, Director of Membership
ISRI provides education, advocacy, and compliance training while promoting public awareness of the role recycling plays in the U.S. economy, global trade, the environment and sustainable development.

18253 International Chromium Development Association
43 rue de la Chauss,e d'Antinÿ
Paris 75009
014-076-0689; Fax: 014-076-0687
info@icdacr.com
www.icdacr.com
Samancor Chrome, Chairperson
Founded in 1984

18254 International Copper Association
260 Madison Ave
16th Floor
New York, NY 10016-2403
212-251-7240; Fax: 212-251-7245
info@copperalliance.org
www.copperalliance.org
Facebook, Twitter, LinkedIn, Google+
Francis J Kane, President
Promoting the use of copper by communicating the unique attributes that make this sustainable element an essential contributor to the formation of life, to advances in science and technology, and to a higher standard of living worldwide.
Founded in 1989

18255 International Council on Mining and Metals
35/38 Portman Square
London W1H 6LR
207-467-5070; Fax: 207-467-5071
info@icmm.com
www.icmm.com
Twitter, LinkedIn, YouTube, RSS
Tom Butler, CEO
Aidan Davy, Deputy President
John Atherton, Director, Materials Stewardship
Ross Hamilton, Director, Environment and Climate C
Brigid Janssen, Director, Communications
Founded in 2001

18256 International Hard Anondizing
P.O. Box 5
Moorestown, NJ 08054
856-234-0330; Fax: 856-727-9504
staff@ihanodizing.com
www.ihanodizing.com
Facebook
Denise Downing, Executive Director
Formed by companies in the hard anodizing business to provide a forum for the exchange of technical information and to act as a clearing house for information about the industry.
Founded in 1989

18257 International Lead Management Center
2525 Meridian Parkway
Suite 100
Durham, NC 27713
919-287-1872; Fax: 919-361-1957
www.ilmc.orgÿ

18258 International Lead Zinc Research Organization
1822 NC Highway 54 East
Suite 120
Durham, NC 27713-5243
919-361-4647; Fax: 919-361-1957
www.ilzro.org
Stephen Wilkinson, President
Judith Hendrickson, Corporate Secretary
Members are miners, smelters and refiners of lead and zinc. Supports research and development of new uses for the metals and refinement existing uses. Has an annual budget of approximately $5.3 million.
77 Members
Founded in 1958

18259 International Magnesium Association
1000 N Rand Rd
Suite 214
Wauconda, IL 60084-1180
847-526-2010; Fax: 847-526-3993
info@intlmag.org
www.intlmag.org
LinkedIn
Greg Patzer, Executive VP
Eileen Hoblit, Administrative Coordinator
Ken White, Chairman
Jan Guy, President
Dr. Karl Kainer, Immediate Past President
IMA is to promote the use of the metal magnesium in material selection and encourage innovative applications of the versatile metal.
125 Members
Founded in 1943

18260 International Platinum GroupÿMetals Association
Schiess-Staett-Strasse 30
Munich, Germany 80339
49-89-5199-6770; Fax: 49-89-5199-6719
info@ipa-news.com
www.ipa-news.com
Steve Phiri, President
Gabriele Randlshofer, Managing Director
Tania Bossi, Communications Manager
Julian K"hle, Government AffairsÿManager
Founded in 1987

18261 International Precious Metals Institute
5101 N 12th Avenue
Suite C
Pensacola, FL 32504
850-476-1156; Fax: 850-476-1548
mail@ipmi.org
www.ipmi.org
Facebook, LinkedIn, YouTube
Robert Ianniello, President
International association of producers, refiners, fabricators, scientists, users, financial institutions, merchants, private and public sector groups and the general precious metals community created to provide a forum for the exchange of information and technology.
Founded in 1987

18262 International Thermal Spray Association
Post Office Box 1638
Painesville, OH 44077
440-357-5400; Fax: 440-357-5430
itsa@thermalspray.org
www.thermalspray.org
Facebook, LinkedIn
Kathy M Dusa, Administrative Assistant
Bill Moiser, Chairman
Jim Rayan, Vice Chairman
David Wright, Executive Officer
Strengthens the level of awareness in general industry and government on the increasing capabilities and advantages of thermal spray technology for surface engineering through business opportunities, technical support and a social network. Contributes to growth and education in the thermal spray industry.
70 Members
Founded in 1948

18263 International Titanium Association
11674 Huron Street
Suite 100
Northglenn, CO 80234
303-404-2221; Fax: 303-404-9111
ita@titanium.org
www.titanium.org
titanium2011.pathable.com
Brett S.Paddock, President & CEO
Donn S.Hickton, VP
Hunter R.Dalton, Treasurer
Susan M.Abkowitz, Director
Jennifer Simpson, Executive Director
International Titanium Association is an international membership based trade association dedicated to the titanium metal industry. Established in 1984, ITA strives to connect the public interested in using titanium with specialists from across the globe who offer sales and technical assistance.
120 Members
Founded in 1984

18264 Lead Industries Association
13 Main Street
Sparta, NJ 07871
973-726-5323; Fax: 973-726-4484
www.leadinfo.com
Jeffrey T Miller, Executive Director
Nonprofit trade association representing the lead industries in the US and abroad. It collects and distributes information about the users of lead products in industry, vehicles, radioactive waste disposal and noise barriers. Its services are availble, generally free of charge, to anyone interested in the uses of lead and lead products.

18265 Machinery Dealers National Association
315 S Patrick Street
Alexandria, VA 22314
703-836-9300
800-872-7807; Fax: 703-836-9303
office@mdna.org
www.mdna.org
Facebook, Twitter, LinkedIn
Mark Robinson, Executive Vice President
Will Keys, Accounting Manager
Joyce Fitzgerald, Administration Director
Represents dealers of used industrial equipment, providing members with business standards and development opportunities.
400 Members
Founded in 1941

18266 Magnet Distributors and Fabricators Association
8 S Michigan Avenue
Suite 1000
Chicago, IL 60603

312-541-2667; Fax: 312-580-0165

August L Sisco, Executive Secretary

Distributors and magnetic materials and fabricators of magnetic components, plus suppliers to the distributor/fabricators.
31 Members
Founded in 1991

18267 Metal Building Contractors and Erectors Association
PO Box 499
Shawnee Mission, KS 66201

913-432-3800
800-866-6722; Fax: 913-432-3803
www.mbcea.org

Angela M Cruse, Executive Director
Tim Seyler, President

To support the professional advancement of metal building contractors, erectors, and the industry.
235 Members
Founded in 1968

18268 Metal Building Manufacturers Association
1300 Sumner Avenue
Cleveland, OH 44115-2851

216-241-7333; Fax: 216-241-0105
www.mbma.com
Twitter, LinkedIn, Google+

Tony Bouquot, General Manager
Vincent Sagan, Senior Staff Engineer
W Lee Shoemaker, Director of Research & Engineering

Promotes the design and construction of metal building systems in the low-rise, non-residential building marketplace.
Founded in 1956

18269 Metal Construction Association
8735 W. Higgins Rd.
Suite 300
Chicago, IL 60631

847-375-4718; Fax: 847-375-6488
mca@metalconstruction.org
www.metalconstruction.org
Facebook, LinkedIn

Jeff Henry, Executive Director
Peggy Doherty, Director, Operations
Jeff Irwin, Program Director
Bob Zabcik, Technical Dirctor
Andy Williams, Director, Codes & Standards

Dedicated to promoting the use of metal in construction. Initiative include market development, educational programs, issue and product awareness compaigns and publication of technical guidelines and specifications manuals. Also monitors and confronts challenges affecting the industry such as code restructions.
100 Members
Founded in 1983

18270 Metal Findings Manufacturers
30-R Houghton Street
Providence, RI 02904

401-861-4667; Fax: 401-861-0429

John Augustyn, Executive Officer

Makers of metal parts and fittings used in the assembly of jewelry.
Founded in 1930

18271 Metal Injection Molding Associationÿ
105 College Road East
Princeton, NJ 8540

609-452-7700
609-987-8523; Fax: 609-987-8523
info@mpif.org
www.mimaweb.org

18272 Metal Powder Industries Federation
105 College Rd E
Princeton, NJ 08540-6692

609-452-7700; Fax: 609-987-8523
info@mpif.org
www.mpif.org

Michael Latheran, President, CEO
Jilliane Regan, VP
Jim Adams, Manager
James R.Dale, VP

As its name states, it is aÿfederation of trade associations-six in all-that are concerned with some aspect of powder metallurgy, metal powders, or particulate materials.
210 Members
Founded in 1944

18273 Metal Service Center Institute
4201 Euclid Ave
Suite 550
Rolling Meadows, IL 60008-2025

847-485-3000; Fax: 847-485-3001
info@msci.org
www.msci.org
Facebook, Twitter, LinkedIn

Bob Weidner, President
Jonathan Kalkwarf, VP Finance/Administration
Rose Manfredini, VP Member Information Services
Chris Marti, VP Technology
375 Members
Founded in 1907

18274 Metals Service Center Institute
4201 Euclid Ave
Rolling Meadows, IL 60008

847-485-3000; Fax: 847-485-3001
info@msci.org
www.msci.org
Facebook, Twitter, LinkedIn

Bob Weidner, President/ Chief Executive Officer
Ann D'Orazio, Vice President, Marketing-Growth
Ashley DeVecht, Director of Communications
Rose Manfredini, Vice President, Membership
Chris Marti, Vice President, Research
400+ Members

18275 Mineral Information Institute
12999 E. Adam Aircraft Circle
Englewood, CO 80112-4167

303-948-4200; Fax: 800-763-3132
MEC@smenet.org
www.MineralsEducationCoalition.org
Facebook, Twitter, YouTube

Sharon Schonhaut, Director
Rebecca Smith, Curriculum Coordinator
Rachel Grimes, Outreach Coordinator
Carol Kiser, Purchases dept

Nonprofit organization dedicated to educating youth about the science of minerals and other natural resources and about their importance in our everyday lives.

18276 Minerals, Metals & Materials Society
184 Thorn Hill Road
Warrendale, PA 15086-7514

724-769-9000
800-759-4867; Fax: 724-776-3770
webmaster@tms.org
www.tms.org
Facebook, LinkedIn, YouTube

James Robinson, Executive Director
Nellie Luther, Professional Affairs Coordinator
Gail Miller, Executive Assistant
Nancy Lesko, Executive & Board Administrator
Steve Reubi, Controller

Supports all those devoted to exploring the many aspects of materials science and engineering. Publishes monthly magazine.
Founded in 1993

18277 Mining and Metallurgical Society of America
PO Box 810
Boulder, CO 80306-0810

303-444-6032; Fax: 415-897-1380
contactmmsa@mmsa.net
www.mmsa.net
Facebook, Twitter, LinkedIn

Betty L. Gibbs, Executive Director
Matt Bender, President
Barney Guarnera, VP
Paul C. Jones, Treasurer
Michael Blois, Secretary

Concerned with the conservation of the nation's mineral resources and the best interest of the mining and metallurgical industries.
350 Members
Founded in 1908

18278 National Association for Surface Finishing
1155 15th Street NW
Suite 500
Washington, DC 20005

202-457-8404; Fax: 202-530-0659
www.nasf.org
Facebook, Twitter

Erik Welys, President
Paul Brancato, VP
Brain Harrick, Secretary/Treasurer
Jery Wahlin, Executive

The National Association for Surface Finishing is a trade association whose mission is to promote the advancement of the surface finishing industry worldwide.

18279 National Association of Aluminum Developers
4201 Euclid Ave
Suite 550
Rolling Meadows, IL 60008-2025

847-485-3000; Fax: 847-485-3001
info@msci.org
www.msci.org
Facebook, Twitter, LinkedIn

Bob Weidner, President
Jonathan Kalkwarf, VP Finance/Administration
Rose Manfredini, VP Member Information Services
Chris Marti, VP Technology
Ann Zastrow, VP

NAAD is the trade association of North American service centers and principal suppliers engaged in marketing aluminum products.
400 Members
Founded in 1914

18280 National Blacksmiths and Welders
PO Box 123
Arnold, NE 69120

308-848-2913
www.arcat.com
Facebook, Twitter, Google+

Dave Christen, President
Jim Lindquist, First Director
Gerry Westhoff, Second VP
James Holman, Executive Director

Blacksmiths, welders and manufacturing machine shops. Organize and offer assistance to state organizations for the advancement of their members with education and guiding measures for the present and future prospects of the trade.
175 Members
Founded in 1895

18281 National Coil Coating Association
1300 Sumner Ave
Cleveland, OH 44115-2851

216-241-3333; Fax: 216-781-0621
www.coilcoating.org
Facebook, Twitter

NCCA is an established trade organization dedicated to the growth of coil coated products. A unified organization that provides resources and leadership in order to ensure that coil coated materials are the product of choice.
Founded in 1962

18282 National Institute for Metal Working Skills
10565 Fairfax Boulevard
Suite 203
Fairfax, VA 22030

703-352-4971; Fax: 703-352-4991
www.nims-skills.org

James Wall, Executive Director
David Morgan, Director of Business Development
Catherine Ross, Accrediation Incharge

A nonprofit organization formed by metalworking trade associations, national labor organizations, a council of state governors, companies and educators to support the development of a skilled workforce for the metalworking industry.
Founded in 1995
Mailing list available for rent

18283 National Ornamental & Miscellaneous Metals Association
P.O. Box 492167
Ste. 127 #311
Lawrenceville, GA 30049

888-516-8585; Fax: 888-279-7994
nommainfo@nomma.org
www.nomma.org
Facebook, Twitter, LinkedIn, YouTube, Vimeo, Flickr

Allyn Moseley, President
Cathy Vequist, VP/Treasurer
Keith Majka, President-Elect
Mark Koenke, Immediate Past President
Todd Daniel, Executive Director

Supports all those involved in the ornamental and miscellaneous metal industry. Publishes bi-monthly magazine.
1000 Members
Founded in 1958

18284 National Ornamental and Miscellaneous Metals
P.O. Box 492167
Ste. 127 #311
Lawrenceville, GA 30049

888-516-8585; Fax: 888-279-7994
nommainfo@nomma.org
www.nomma.org
Facebook, Twitter, LinkedIn, YouTube

Todd Daniel, Executive Director
Liz Harris, Member Care & Operations Manager
Martha Pennington, Meetings & Exposition Manager
Allyn Moseley, President
Cathy Vequist, VP/Treasurer
Founded in 1958

18285 National Tooling and Machining Association
1357 Rockside Road
Cleveland, OH 44134

440-799-8991
800-248-6862; Fax: 216-264-2840
info@ntma.org
www.ntma.org
Facebook, Twitter, LinkedIn, YouTube

Dave Tilstone, President
Candy Davis, Executive Assistant
Michel Conklin, NRL Program Manager
Matt Gilmore, Membership & Business Development
Doug DeRose, Chief Financial Officer

Trade organization representing the precision custom manufacturing industry throughout the US. Members are supported through business development programs, education, events and advocacy.
1400 Members
Founded in 1943

18286 National Welding Supply Association
Fernley & Fernley
1900 Arch St
Philadelphia, PA 19103-1404

215-564-3484; Fax: 215-564-2175
www.nwsa.com
Facebook, Twitter

William R. Surman, President
William Mehlenbeck, Vice President
R.J Kuhn, Treasurer
Bryan Beck, Immediate Past President
Jay Armstrong, Director
1200 Members
Founded in 1945

18287 Non-Ferrous Founders' Society
1480 Renaissance Drive
Suite 310
Park Ridge, IL 60068

847-299-0950; Fax: 847-299-3598
nffstaff@nffs.org
www.nffs.org
Facebook, Twitter

James L Mallory, Executive Director
Jerrod A Weaver, Director Of Education and Training
Ryan J Moore, Member Services Manager

Manufacturers of bronze, brass and aluminum castings.
185 Members
Founded in 1943

18288 North American Die Casting Association
3250 Arlington Heights Rd
Suite 101
Arlington Heights, IL 60004

847-279-0001; Fax: 847-279-0002
nadca@diecasting.org
www.diecasting.org
Facebook, Twitter, LinkedIn, YouTube, Instagram

Neal Shapiro, Affairs Committee Chairman

Supports all those involved in the die casting industry. Publishes bi-monthly magazine.
Founded in 1957

18289 Precision Metalforming Association
6363 Oak Tree Blvd
Cleveland, OH 44131-2500

216-901-9667; Fax: 216-901-9190
pma@pma.org
www.pma.org
Facebook, Twitter, LinkedIn, YouTube

Nels Leutwiler, Chairman
Dennis J Keat, First Vice Chairman
Bernie Rosselli Jr, Second Vice Chairman/Treasurer
William Gaskin, President

Members include producers of metal stampings, spinnings, washers and precision sheet metal fabrications as well as suppliers of equipment, materials and services.
1300 Members
Founded in 1913

18290 Resistance Welder Manufacturers
8669 NW 36 Street
Suite 130
Miami, FL 33166

305-443-9353; Fax: 305-442-7451
www.aws.org/rwma/
Facebook, LinkedIn

Mark Gramelspacher, Chairman
Ed Langhenry, Vice Chairman
Tom Snow, Vice Chairman

Strives to create widespread awareness and use of the various resistance welding processes and equipment, improve relations between individual manufacturers, foster higher ethical standards throughout the industry, develop industry standards to assist users of resistance welding equipment.
82 Members
Founded in 1935

18291 Sheet Metal Workers International Association
1750 New York Avenue, NW
6th Floor
Washington, DC 20006
Home Page: www.smwia.org

18292 Sheet Metal and Air Conditioning Contractors' National Association
4201 Lafayette Center Dr
Chantilly, VA 20151-1219

703-803-2980; Fax: 703-803-3732
www.smacna.org
Facebook, Twitter, LinkedIn, YouTube

Vincent Sandusky, CEO

An international trade association representing 4,500 contibuting contractor firms in the sheet metal and air conditioning industry. Develops technical standards and manuals addressing all facets of the sheet metal and air conditioning industry.
1944 Members
Founded in 1943

18293 Silver Institute
1400 I Street, NW
Suite 550
Washington, DC 20005

202-835-0185; Fax: 202-835-0155
info@silverinstitute.org
www.silverinstitute.org

Fernando Alanis, President
Mitchell Krebs, VP
Thomas Angelos, Treasurer
Michael Dirienzo, Executive Director and Secretary
Mark Spurbeck, Assistant Treasurer

International association of miners, refiners, fabricators and wholesalers of silver and silver products.
Founded in 1971

18294 Silver Users Association
3930 walnut Street
Suite 210
Fairfax, VA 22030

703-934-0219
800-245-6999; Fax: 703-359-7562

sas@silversmithing.com
www.silverusersassociation.org

Mike Merolla, President
John Gannon, VP

Represents the interests of corporations that make, sell and distribute products and services in which silver is an essential part. SUA membership includes representatives from the photographic, electronic, silverware and jewelry industries; producers of semi-fabricated and industrial products; and, mirror manufacturers.
30 Members
Founded in 1947

18295 **Society of American Silversmiths**
PO Box 786
West Warwick, RI 02893

401-461-6840; Fax: 401-461-0162
sas@silversmithing.com
www.silversmithing.com

Jeffrey Herman, Founder/Executive Director

Founded to preserve the art and history of handcrafted holloware and flatware plus provide support, networking and greater access to the market for its artisan members. Artisans are silversmiths both practicing and retired who now or used to smith as a livelihood. Educates the public as to the aesthetic and investment value of this art form and demystifies silversmithing techniques through its literature and national exhibits.
240 Members
Founded in 1989

18296 **Society of Manufacturing Engineers**
1000 Town Center
Suite 1910
Southfield, MI 48075

313-425-3000
service@sme.org
www.sme.org
Facebook, Twitter, LinkedIn, YouTube, Google+, Instagram

Sandra L. Bouckley, Executive Director & CEO
Craig Connop, Chief Financial Officer
Steve Prahalis, Chief Operating Officer
Erica Ciupak, Information Technology
Debbie Clark, Governance

The organization serves its members and others in the international manufacturing community by identifying, evaluating and explaining the adoption and integration of emerging information technologies to create business value.
65K Members
Founded in 1932

18297 **Society of North American Goldsmiths**
PO Box 1355
Eugene, OR 97440

541-345-5689; Fax: 541-345-1123
www.snagmetalsmith.org
Facebook, Twitter, LinkedIn

Nicole Jaquard, President
Peggy Eng, Conferences
Becky Mcdonah, Secretary
Anne Havel, Treasurer
Renee Zettle-Sterling, Past President

Promotes a favorable and enriching environment in which contemporary metalsmiths practice their art. One aspect of this process is educating the public about the quality and rich diversity within the field of metalsmithing. Exhibitions, public forums, lectures, and published documents are our primary methods of reaching out to the public. SNAG sponsors workshops, seminars, audio-visual services and an annual conference.
Founded in 1969

18298 **Specialty Steel Industry of North America**
3050 K Street, N.W.
Washington, DC 20007

202-342-8630
800-982-0355; Fax: 202-342-8451
www.ssina.comÿ

18299 **Steel Deck Institute**
PO Box 25
Fox River Grove, IL 60021-0025

847-458-4647; Fax: 412-487-3326
www.sdi.org

Steven A Roehrig, Managing Director

Trade association providing uniform industry standards for the engineering, design, manufacture and field usage of steel decks.
29 Members
Founded in 1939

18300 **Steel Door Institute**
30200 Detroit Rd
Cleveland, OH 44145-1967

440-899-0010; Fax: 440-892-1404
info@steeldoor.org
www.steeldoor.org

Jeff Wherry, Executive Director

Producers of all metal frames and doors for commercial, industrial and residential construction.

18301 **Steel Founders Society of America**
780 McArdle Dr
Unit G
Crystal Lake, IL 60014-8155

815-455-8240; Fax: 815-455-8241
monroe@sfsa.org
www.sfsa.org
Facebook

Raymond Monroe, Executive VP
Rick Boyd, Vice President of Technology
Kelly DiGiacomo, CPA, Director of Finance
Rob Blair, Manager of Information Services
David Poweleit, Director of Engineering

A technically oriented trade association serving the steel casting industry.
Founded in 1902

18302 **Steel Manufacturers Association**
1150 Connecticut Ave NW
Suite 715
Washington, DC 20036-4131

202-296-1515; Fax: 202-296-2506
www.steelnet.org

Philip K. Bell, President
Eric J. Stuart, VP, Energy & Environment
Adam B. Parr, VP, Policy & Communications
Annie Stefanec, Member Services Coordinator

The majority of SMA members are minimills companies engaged in electric air furnace/continuous caster steel productions as well as hot and cold rolling of steel mill products. A growing number of integrated steel producers are also members.

18303 **Steel Plate Fabricators Association**
944 Donata Ct
Lake Zurich, IL 60047-5025

847-438-8265; Fax: 847-438-8766
info@steeltank.com
www.steeltank.com
Facebook, LinkedIn, Youtube

Anne Kiefer, Director Of Administration
Wayne B. Geyer, President
J Michael Braden, VP
Jerry Stetzler, Treasurer

Protection of the environment and preservation of air and water quality are key concerns for the owners and operators of tanks, pressure vessels, specialty fabrications and piping systems.
Founded in 1916

18304 **Steel Service Center Institute**
701 West Mason Street
Springfield, OH 44128

217-528-4035
800-252-2516; Fax: 847-485-3001
www.ssoci.org
Facebook

Thomas Conley, President
S Harbke, Director
570 Members
Founded in 1909

18305 **Steel Shipping Container Institute**
120 Hatton Drive
Severna Park, MD 21146-4400

410-544-0385; Fax: 503-581-2221
snauman@industrialpackaging.org
whysteeldrums.org
Facebook, Twitter, LinkedIn, YouTube, Google+

Kyle R. Stavig, Chairman
Leonard H. Berenfield, Vice Chairman
John McQuaid, Senior Advisor

18306 **Steel Tank Institute**
944 Donata Ct
Lake Zurich, IL 60047-5025

847-438-8265; Fax: 847-438-8766
info@steeltank.com
www.steeltank.com
Facebook, LinkedIn, Youtube

Anne Kiefer, Director Of Administration
Wayne B. Geyer, President
J Michael Braden, VP
Jerry Stetzler, Treasurer

Protection of the environment and preservation of air and water quality are key concerns for the owners and operators of tanks, pressure vessels, specialty fabrications and piping systems.
Founded in 1916

18307 **Steel Tube Institute of North America**
2516 Waukegan Road, Suite 172
Glenview, IL 60025

847-461-1701; Fax: 847-660-7981
sti@apk.net
steeltubeinstitute.org
Facebook, LinkedIn

Timothy F Andrassy, Executive Director
Peggy Sams, Executive Assistant
Mary Gregel, Administrative Assistant
Dave Seeger, President

Members produce steel tubes and pipes from carbon, stainless or alloy steel, for applications ranging from large structural tubing to small redrawn tubing.
87 Members
Founded in 1930

18308 **The Aluminum Association**
1400 Crystal Drive
Suite 430
Arlington, VA 22202

703-358-2960
info@aluminum.org
www.aluminum.org
Facebook, Twitter, LinkedIn

Layle Smith, Chairman
Garney B. Scott, III, Vice Chairman
Michelle O'Neill, Second Vice Chair
Heidi Brock, President
Karen Bowden, Vice President, Administration

18309 **The American Institute of Mining, Metallur gical and Petroleum Engineers**
12999 East Adam Aircraft Circle
Englewood, CO 80112-5991

303-325-5185; Fax: 888-702-0049
aime@aimehq.org
www.aimehq.org
Facebook, LinkedIn, YouTube, RSS

Roland Moreau, President
Hani Henein, President-Elect
George Luxbacher, President-Elect Designate
John Speer, Past President
Michele Lawrie-Munro, Executive Director

Supporting member societies by exercising fiscal responsibility, distributing funds, facilitating interaction with the larger scientific and engineering community, and honoring the legacy and traditions of AIME.
130M Members
Founded in 1871

18310 **The Association for Manufacturing Technology**
7901 Jones Branch Drive
Suite 900
McLean, VA 22102-4206

703-893-2900
800-524-0475; Fax: 703-893-1151
amt@amtonline.org
www.amtonline.org
Facebook, Twitter, LinkedIn, YouTube

Douglas K. Woods, President
Rebecca Stahl, Chief Financial Officer
Kimberly L. Brown, Member Services Director
Peter R. Eelman, VP, Exhibitions & Business Dev.
Andrea Kuchinski, Dir, Marketing & Communications

Represents and supports the U.S.-based manufacturing technology industry, including distributors, producers and service providers. The association offers essential programs and services that help its members gain global recognition.

18311 **The Fabricators & Manufacturers**
833 Featherstone Road
Rockford, IL 61107

815-399-8700
888-394-4362
www.fmanet.org
Facebook, Twitter, LinkedIn, YouTube, Google+

Edwin Stanley, Chair
Al Zelt, First Vice Chairman
Vivek Kumar Gupta, Second Vice Chairman
Lyle Menke, Secretary/ Treasurer
Carlos Borjas, Immediate Past Chair
Founded in 1970

18312 **The Minerals, Metals, and Materials Society**
184 Thorn Hill Road
Warrendale, PA 15086-7514

800-759-4867; Fax: 724-776-3770
webmaster@tms.org
www.tms.org
Facebook, LinkedIn, YouTube

Hani Heneinÿ, President
Elizabeth A. Holm, Past President
Patrice E. A. Turchi, Vice President
James Robinson, Secretary/ Executive Director
Robert W. Hyers, Financial Planning Officer

18313 **The Silver Users Association**
3930 walnut Street
Suite 210
Fairfax, VA 22030

703-934-0219
800-245-6999; Fax: 703-359-7562
sas@silversmithing.com
www.silverusersassociation.orgÿ

Bill LeRoy, President
Mike Huber, Vice President
Jack Gannon, Immediate Past President
Bill Hamelin, Treasurer
John King, Secretary
Founded in 1947

18314 **Tube and Pipe Association International**
833 Featherstone Road
Rockford, IL 61107

815-399-8700
888-394-4362; Fax: 815-484-7700
www.fmanet.org
Facebook, Twitter, LinkedIn, YouTube, Google+

Gerald Shankel, President
Mike Hedges, VP Finance/CFO

TPA is an educational technology association serving the metal tube and pipe producing and fabricating industries. It is an affiliate association of the Fabricators and Manufacturers Association International.
Founded in 1970

18315 **US Magnetic Materials Association**
1120 East 23rd St.
Indianapolis, IN 46206

717-898-2294
www.usmagneticmaterials.com

Ed Richardson, Chairman/ President/ Treasurer
Peter Dent, Vice President
Daniel McGroarty, Vice President
Rob Strahs, Secretary/ Vice President
Kerry LaPierre, Board Member

18316 **US Pipe and Foundry Company**
Two Chase Corporate Drive
Suite 200
Birmingham, AL 35244

866-347-7473; Fax: 205-254-7494
info@uspipe.com
www.uspipe.com
Facebook, Twitter, LinkedIn, YouTube, Google+

Paul Ciolino, Chief Executive Officer
Bob Waggoner, SVP, Marketing and Sales
Norb Gross, VP, Supply Chain & Logistics
Brad Overstreet, Chief Financial Officer
Vinod Upadhyay, VP, Information Technology

Supports all those involved with the foundry industry. Publishes semi-monthly newsletter.
Founded in 1899

18317 **Unified Abrasives Manufacturers' Association**
30200 Detroit Road
Cleveland, OH 44145-1967

440-899-0010; Fax: 440-892-1404
uama.org

Allen Donahue, President
Brian Goers, Vice President
Jeff Wherry, Managing Director
Fred Rodgers, Director
Christian Pfeifer, Director

The mission of the association is to support the manufacturing and marketing of abrasive products by providing members with knowledge, networking opportunities, industry standards and more.
Founded in 1999

18318 **United States Cutting Tool Institute**
1300 Sumner Ave
Cleveland, OH 44115-2851

216-241-7333; Fax: 216-241-0105
www.uscti.com

Charles M Stockinger, Secretary-Treasurer
Thomas Hagg, President
Steve Stokey, Senior Vice President
Philip Kurtz, Vice President

The premier trade association for all manufacturers of any type of cutting tools designed and sold to the metalworking, woodworking, and other industrial and consumer markets.
60 Members
Founded in 1988

18319 **Welding Research Council**
PO Box 201547
Shaker Heights, OH 44122

216-658-3847; Fax: 216-658-3854
mprager@forengineers.org
www.forengineers.org

Coordinates welding research.
Founded in 1935

18320 **Welding Research Council, Inc.**
PO Box 201547
Shaker Heights, OH 44122

216-658-3847; Fax: 216-658-3854
mpc@forengineers.org
www.forengineers.org

Martin Prager, PhD, Executive Director

An outgrowth of the ASTM-ASME Joint Committee on the effect of temperature on the properties of metals which was founded in 1925 to meet the apparent need for information on the subject in the construction of central power stations.
600 Members
Founded in 1966

18321 **Wire Association International**
71 Bradley Rd.
Suite 9
Madison, CT 06443

203-453-2777; Fax: 203-453-8384
www.wirenet.org
Facebook, Twitter, LinkedIn, YouTube

Steven J Fetteroll, Executive Director
Marc Murray, Director, Education & Member Svcs.
Janice Swindells, Director, Marketing & Communication
Bob Xeller, Director, Sales
Chuck Szymaszek, Director, Technology

Technical association serving the global wire and cable industry by providing educational materials, sponsoring trade shows and international technical conferences.
2000 Members
Founded in 1930

18322 **Wiring Harness Manufacturers Association**
15490 101st Ave. N.
Suite 100
Maple Grove, MN 55369

763-235-6467; Fax: 763-235-6461
whma@whma.org
www.whma.org

Andrew Larsen, Executive Director
Rick Bromn, Chairman
Donnie Hill, Vice Chairman/Secretary
Randy Olson, Treasurer
Lyle Fahning, Immediate Past Chair

To provide the cooperative forum through which members companies can solve both their

specific problems and also help resolve industry problems.
4 Pages
Frequency: Quarterly
Circulation: 5,000

Newsletters

18323 **Abrasive Users News Fax**
Meadowlark Technical Services
144 Moore Rd
Butler, PA 16001-1312

724-282-6210; Fax: 724-234-2376
aes@abrasiveengineering.com
www.abrasivesmall.com

Ted Giese, Executive Director

Newsletter from the Abrasive Engineering Society.
Cost: $50.00
Circulation: 500
Founded in 1957

18324 **American Iron and Steel Institute News**
American Iron and Steel Institute
25 Massachusetts Ave., NW, Suite 800
Suite 705
Washington, DC 20001

202-452-7100; Fax: 202-496-9702
steelnews@steel.org
www.recycle-steel.org
Facebook, Twitter, Youtube

Chip Foley, VP
Dave James, Marketing

Publication of the nonprofit trade organization representing approximately 65 percent of steel companies in the US, Canada and Mexico.
Circulation: 6000
Founded in 1855

18325 **American Metal Market**
Michael G Botta
825 7th Avenue
New York, NY 10019-6014

212-887-8510; Fax: 212-887-8522
custserv@amm.com
www.amm.com

Gloria T LaRue, Editor
Catalino Abrei, Owner

A daily newspaper of the metals industry covering news and pricing information for corporate, purchasing and manufacturing management.
Frequency: Daily
Circulation: 10,500

18326 **Cables Industry Analyst**
CRU International
6305 Ivy Ln
Suite 422
Greenbelt, MD 20770-6339

301-441-8997; Fax: 301-441-4726
sales@crugroup.com
www.crugroup.com

Florence Kauffman, VP

Written for managers and executives in the wire industry around the globe. Spotlights effective management techniques and superior administrative skills in the industry, profiles industry leaders, notes personnel movements and features general industry news.
Cost: $965.00
12 Pages
Frequency: Monthly
ISSN: 1368-4191

18327 **Futuretech**
John Wiley & Sons
111 River St
Hoboken, NJ 07030-5790

201-748-6000
800-825-7550; Fax: 201-748-6088
www.wiley.com

William J Pesce, CEO

Edited for product development and technology transfer engineers. Intelligence service that deals with new technologies with demonstrated commercial appeal still in the early stages of development in leading corporate, academic and university labs. Contains analysis and exploitation information.
Cost: $1500.00
24 Pages
Frequency: Monthly

18328 **IMA Weekly Updates**
1000 N Rand Rd
Suite 214
Wauconda, IL 60084-1180

847-526-2010; Fax: 847-526-3993
info@intlmag.org
www.intlmag.org

Greg Patzer, Executive Vice-President
Heidi Diederich, Administrative Coordinator

Develops international use and acceptance of magnesium metal and its alloys in all product forms. Members are organizations or individuals engaged in the production, manufacture or marketing of metallic magnesium or those supplying materials, equipment or consulting.
Cost: $90.00
Frequency: Weekly
Circulation: 5000
Founded in 1943
Printed in 2 colors on glossy stock

18329 **IMPI Conference**
International Precious Metals Institute
5101 N 12th Avenue
Suite C
Pensacola, FL 32504

850-476-1156; Fax: 850-476-1548
mail@ipmi.org
www.ipmi.org

Robert Ianniello, President

annual conference holds technical sessions, evening social receptions and a golf tournament. Also some product demonstrations.
400 Attendees
Frequency: Annual

18330 **MBCEA Newsletter**
Metal Building Contractors & Erectors Association
PO Box 499
Shawnee Mission, KS 66201

913-432-3800; Fax: 913-432-3803
www.mbcea.org

Angela M Cruse, Executive Director
Tim Seyler, President

Official newsletter of the Metal Building Contractors and Erectors Association (MBCEA), a trade association, formed in 1968 to provide programs and services, as well as to support the interests of metal building contractors and erectors.

18331 **Precious Metals News**
International Precious Metals Institute
5101 N 12th Avenue
Suite C
Pensacola, FL 32504

850-476-1156; Fax: 850-476-1548
mail@ipmi.org
www.ipmi.org

Robert Ianniello, President
Cost: $30.00
Frequency: Quarterly
Circulation: 1000
Founded in 1976

18332 **R&D Focus**
International Lead Zinc Research Organization
2525 Meridian Parkway
PO Box 12036
Research Triangle Park, NC 27709-2036

919-361-4647; Fax: 919-361-1957
www.ilzro.org

Rob Putnam, Publisher
Doug Zabor, President

Reports on current research and development products in the metal industry.
Frequency: Quarterly
Circulation: 100
Founded in 1958

18333 **Steel Industry Weekly Review**
2 Uxbridge Road
Scarsdale, NY 10583-2725
Karl Keffer, Publisher

Offers industry news for steel workers.
Cost: $75.00
Frequency: Monthly

18334 **Titanium**
International Titanium Association
2655 W Midway Blvd
Suite 300
Broomfield, CO 80020-7187
303-404-2221
299-942-5371; Fax: 303-404-9111
jsimpson@titanium.org
www.titanium.org

Frequency: Quarterly
Circulation: 5000
Founded in 1960

18335 **US Piper**
US Pipe and Foundry Company
PO Box 10406
James Canada
Birmingham, AL 35202-406

205-547-7254; Fax: 205-254-7494
www.uspipe.com

George Bogs, Publisher
Ray Torok, President
Walter Knollenberg, VP

Articles deal with advantages of using new products.
16 Pages
Circulation: 9000
Founded in 1899

18336 **WRC Bulletin**
Welding Research Council
3 Park Avenue
27th Floor
New York, NY 10016-5902

212-591-7956; Fax: 212-591-7183
bulletinsales@forengineers.org
www.forengineers.org/wrc

CR Felmley Jr, Publisher

Offers information and updates for the welding community.
Cost: $300.00
Frequency: Monthly
Circulation: 900

Magazines & Journals

18337 **AISE Steel Technology**
Association of Iron & Steel Engineers
186 Thorn Hill Road
Warrendale, PA 15086
724-776-6040; Fax: 724-776-1880
info@aist.org
www.aise.org
Ronald Ashburn, Managing Director
Marge Baker, Editor
Gerry Kane, Sales Manager
Karen Hadley, Managing Editor
Janet McConnell, Production Editor
Information relating to the design and construction of equipment, machinery and plants for the production and processing of iron and steel.
Cost: $115.00
Frequency: Monthly
Circulation: 8000
Founded in 2004

18338 **APMI International**
105 College Road E
Princeton, NJ 08540-6622
609-452-7700; Fax: 609-987-8523
apmi@mpif.org
www.mpif.org
Christopher Adam, President
David L Schaefer, Director
Jim Adams, Manager
Monthly newsletter for all those involved the metal powder producing and consuming industries. Regular editorial features.
Founded in 1965

18339 **Abrasives**
PO Box 11
Byron Center, MI 49315
616-530-3220; Fax: 616-530-6466
www.abrasivesmagazine.com
Rose Trevino, Publisher/Editor
Covers research and development in the abrasives field including information about grinding and finishing applications.
Cost: $27.00
Frequency: Annual+
Circulation: 35000

18340 **Advanced Materials & Processes**
ASM International
9639 Kinsman Road
Materials Park, OH 44073-0002
440-338-5151
800-336-5152; Fax: 440-338-4634
magazines@asminternational.org
www.asminternational.org
William T. Mahoney, Secretary & CEO
Joanne Miller, Editor
Vicki Burt, Managing Editor
AM&P is the monthly technical magazine from ASM International, designed to keep readers aware of leading-edge developments and trends in engineering materials - metals and alloys, engineering polymers, advanced ceramics, and composites - and the methods used to select, process, fabricate, test, and characterize them.
30K Members
Frequency: Monthly
Circulation: 23000
Founded in 1913

18341 **Aluminum Recycling & Processing for Energy Conservation and Sustainability**
Aluminum Association
1525 Wilson Blvd
Suite 600
Arlington, VA 22209-2444
703-358-2960; Fax: 703-358-2961
www.aluminum.org
John Green, Editor
Heidi Biggs Brock, President
Nicholas Adams, Vice President, Business
Frequency: Yearly

18342 **American Machinist**
Penton Media
1166 Avenue of the Americas/10th Fl
New York, NY 10036
212-204-4200; Fax: 216-696-6662
www.penton.com
Jane Cooper, Marketing
Patricia L Smith, Executive Editor
Charles Bates, Senior Editor
Jim Benes, Associate Editor
Chris Meyer, Director, Corporate Communications
Magazine of the manufacturing business. Plays an integral role in educating and informing our readers of the significant developments of manufacturing technology. The intent of every issue is to describe new metalworking technologies that help the readership speed production, cut costs, and stay competitive in the global market.
Frequency: Monthly
Circulation: 80000
Founded in 1892
Printed in 4 colors

18343 **American Metal Market**
Reed Business Information
225 Park Avenue South
New York, NY 10003
646-274-6257; Fax: 630-288-8686
www.amm.com
Twitter, LinkedIn
Lawrence S Reed, President
Gloria LaRue, Editor-in-Chief
Catalino Abrei, Owner
Thoroughly covers the metals industry, from production to distribution to recycling. American Metal Market is comprehensive, timely, reliable and invaluable daily newspaper for today's metal industry professionals.
Cost: $725.00
16 Pages
Frequency: Daily
Circulation: 10000
Printed in on glossy stock

18344 **American Tool, Die & Stamping News**
Eagle Publications
42400 Grand River Ave
Suite 103
Novi, MI 48375-2572
248-347-3487
800-783-3491; Fax: 248-347-3492
Arthur Brown, President
Joan Oakley, CEO
Applications, techniques, equipment and accessories of metal stamping, moldmaking, electric discharge machining; and new product information relating to the tool and die industry. Accepts advertising.
70 Pages
Circulation: 36000
ISSN: 0192-5709
Founded in 1971
Printed in 5 colors on glossy stock

18345 **Anvil Magazine**
PO Box 1810
Georgetown, CA 95634-1810
530-333-2142
800-942-6845; Fax: 530-333-2906
www.anvilmag.com
Rob Edwards, Publisher
Timothy Sebastian, Editor-in-Chief
Jody Edwards, Advertising Manager
World-wide coverage of the blacksmithing and farrier trades.
Cost: $29.50
Frequency: Monthly
Circulation: 5000
Founded in 1980

18346 **Anvil's Ring**
Artist-Blacksmith's Association of North America
259 Muddy Fork Road
Jonesborough, TN 37659
423-913-1022; Fax: 423-913-1023
areditor@abana.org
www.abana.org
Facebook, Twitter
Dan Nauman, Editor
Covers such topics as architectural iron, decorative design, primitive artifacts, advice, and Association news. Also discusses supply sources, formal blacksmithing instruction and employment opportunities.
60 Pages
Frequency: Quarterly

18347 **Association of Iron and Steel Engineers Steel Technology**
Three Gateway Center
Suite 1900
Pittsburgh, PA 15222-1004
412-281-6323; Fax: 412-281-6216
rashburn@aist.org
www.aise.org
Ronald E Ashburn, Executive Director
Frank E Farmer, Graphic Designer
Chris Brown, Graphic Designer
Stacy Varmecky, General Manager
AISE Steel Technology is the monthly technical journal of AISE. Highly authorative, it contains exclusive technical information relating to all phases of iron and steelmaking and finishing.
50+ Pages
Frequency: Monthly
Printed in 4 colors

18348 **Automatic Machining Magazine**
Screw Machine Publishing Company
1066 Gravel Rd
Suite 201
Webster, NY 14580-1769
585-787-0820
800-610-6950; Fax: 585-787-0868
Wayne Wood, President
General industry news for professionals in the metal turning and cold forming fields.
Cost: $45.00
142 Pages
Frequency: Monthly
Circulation: 13000
Founded in 1941
Printed in 4 colors on glossy stock

18349 **Casting World**
Continental Communications
104 Florence Ln
Fairfield, CT 06824-2215
203-255-7752; Fax: 203-377-7230
Wilburt W Troland, President

In-depth news on all aspects of ferrous and non-ferrous casting.
Cost: $99.00
Frequency: Quarterly
Circulation: 35000

18350 Coil World
CJL Publishing
8 High Point
Cedar Grove, NJ 07009
973-571-7155; Fax: 973-571-7102
philcola@optonline.net
www.coilworld.com
Philip E Colaiacovo, Editor-in-Chief/Publisher
Carl Hoffman, Circulation Manager
Shawn A Savage, Creative Director
A L Colaiacovo, Production/Advertising Svcs Manager
Offers articles on coil coating operations, fabricators, service centers, OEMs which use prepainted metals, new products, upcoming events, industry news, personnel announcements and committee updates.
Frequency: Quarterly
Circulation: 10000

18351 Cutting Technology
Penton Media
1166 Avenue of the Americas/10th Fl
New York, NY 10036
212-204-4200; Fax: 216-696-6662
information@penton.com
www.penton.com
Jane Cooper, Marketing
Patricia Smith, Executive Editor
Gil Apelis, Manager
Chris Meyer, Director, Corporate Communications
Covers the full gamut of information essential to the success and productivity of those involved in metalcutting manufacturing.
Cost: $35.00
Circulation: 40000
Founded in 1892
Printed in 4 colors

18352 Cutting Tool Engineering
CTE Publications
40 Skokie Blvd
Suite 450
Northbrook, IL 60062-1698
847-498-9100
866-207-1450; Fax: 847-559-4444
www.ctemag.com
John Wm Roberts, CEO
Alan Richter, CEO
Alan Rooks, Director
Cutting Tool Engineering serves manufacturing plants in the metal working industries.
Cost: $65.00
72 Pages
Frequency: Monthly
Circulation: 34871
ISSN: 0011-4189
Founded in 1955
Printed in 4 colors on glossy stock

18353 Die Casting Engineer Magazine
North American Die Casting Association
241 Holbrook Drive
Wheeling, IL 60090
847-279-0001; Fax: 847-279-0002
nadca@diecasting.org
www.diecasting.org
Facebook, Twitter, LinkedIn, youtube, Flickr
Donna Peterson, Editor
Norwin A Merens, Managing Director
Provides members with the latest industry information, technology innovation and state-of-the-art developments. Each issue presents readers with up to date die casting news topics, opinion features of interest, and an editorial theme.
Cost: $150.00
1000 Pages
Frequency: Bi-Monthly
Founded in 1989

18354 Die Casting Management
C-K Publishing
PO Box 247
Wonder Lake, IL 60097-0247
815-728-0912; Fax: 815-728-0912
Rob Crofts, Publisher
The main content focuses on profitable management, and includes articles on finance, marketing, technology, engineering, industry developments, and government legislation.
Frequency: Bi-Monthly
Circulation: 4500

18355 Ductile Iron News
Ductile Iron Society
15400 Pearl Rd
Suite 234
Strongsville, OH 44136-6017
440-665-3686; Fax: 440-878-0070
jwood@ductile.org
www.ductile.org
Scott Gledhill, President
Patricio Gill, VP
Pete Guidi, Treasurer
The main material focuses on the technical data and applications, production statistics, and profiles of foundries.
Frequency: 3-4x/Year

18356 Engineering and Mining Journal
Mining Media
8751 E Hampden Ave
Suite C1
Denver, CO 80231-4930
303-751-5370; Fax: 303-283-0641
info@mining-media.com
www.e-mj.com
Peter Johnson, President
Steve Fiscor, Editor-in-Chief
Russ Carter, Managing Editor
Gina Tverdak, Assistant Editor
Serves the field of mining including exploration, development, milling, smelting, refining of metals and nonmetallics.
Cost: $79.00
Frequency: Monthly
Circulation: 10523
Founded in 1866
Printed in 4 colors on glossy stock

18357 Equip-Mart
116 N Camp Street
Seguin, TX 78155
830-303-3328
800-864-1155; Fax: 830-372-3011
www.equip-mart.com
James Story, President
Tammy Reilly, Publisher
Kim Wiemann, Circulation Manager
Used metalworking equipment.
Cost: $50.00
Frequency: Monthly
Circulation: 36000
Founded in 1994

18358 Fabricator
Fabricators and Manufacturers Association
833 Featherstone Road
Rockford, IL 61107
815-227-8281
866-879-9144; Fax: 815-484-7700
www.thefabricator.com
Dan Davis, Executive Editor
North America's leading magazine for the metal forming and fabricating industry that delivers the news, technical articles, and case histories that enable fabricators to do their jobs more efficiently.
Cost: $75.00
Frequency: Monthly
Circulation: 55000
Founded in 1970
Printed in 4 colors on glossy stock

18359 Forging
Penton Media
1166 Avenue of the Americas/10th Fl
New York, NY 10036
212-204-4200; Fax: 216-696-6662
www.penton.com
Jane Cooper, Marketing
Robert Brooks, Editor
Melody Berendt, Circulation
Chris Meyer, Director, Corporate Communications
Dedicated to providing industrial part forgers with current market, product, process and equipment news and trend analysis.
Cost: $31.50
62 Pages
Circulation: 5000
ISSN: 1054-1756
Founded in 1990
Printed in 4 colors on glossy stock

18360 Foundry Management & Technology
Penton Media
1166 Avenue of the Americas/10th Fl
New York, NY 10036
212-204-4200; Fax: 216-696-6662
jwright@penton.com
www.penton.com
Jane Cooper, Marketing
Dave Shanks, Publisher
Melody Berendt, Circulation Manager
Chris Meyer, Director, Corporate Communications
Received by management, production, engineering, research and technical professionals in the foundry industry.
Cost: $54.00
70 Pages
Frequency: Monthly
ISSN: 0360-8999
Printed in 4 colors on glossy stock

18361 Gases & Welding Distributor
Penton Media
1166 Avenue of the Americas/10th Fl
New York, NY 10036
212-204-4200; Fax: 216-696-6662
infomation@penton.com
www.penton.com
Jane Cooper, Marketing
Patricia L Smith, Executive Editor
Charles Bates, Senior Editor
Jim Benes, Associate Editor
Melody Berendt, Circulation Manager
Marketing, management and technology magazine that aids distributors of welding supplies, industrial/medical/specialty gases, and safety products to sell more effectively to diverse markets.
Cost: $55.00
74 Pages
Frequency: six issues ayea
ISSN: 1079-3909
Printed in 4 colors

18362 Heat Treating Progress
ASM International

9639 Kinsman Road
Materials Park, OH 44072-9603

440-338-5151
800-336-5152; Fax: 440-338-4634
MemberServiceCenter@asminternational.org
www.asminternational.org/news/magazines/htp-archive

Magazine no longer in print, but with an online archive available with editions from 2001-2009.
Founded in 1913

18363 **Industrial Paint & Powder Magazine**
Reed Business Information
30 Technology Parkway South
Suite 100
Norcross, GA 30092

630-574-0825
800-424-3996; Fax: 630-288-8781
webmaster@reedbusiness.com
www.reedbusiness.com

Jeff Greisch, President

Coatings on manufacturing.
Cost: $55.00
Frequency: Monthly
Circulation: 38000
Founded in 1924

18364 **Industrial Product Bulletin**
Gordon Publications
301 Gibraltar Drive
#650
Morris Plains, NJ 07950-3400

973-292-5100; Fax: 973-539-3476

Todd Baker, Publisher
Anita LaFond, Editor

Publication for executives and professionals in the process and metalworking industries.
Cost: $7.00
Circulation: 200,050

18365 **Inspection Trends**
American Welding Society
550 Nw 42nd Ave
Miami, FL 33126-5699

305-443-9353
800-443-9353; Fax: 305-443-7559
info@aws.org
www.aws.org

Ray Shook, President
Jeff Hufsey, Deputy Executive Director
Ray Shook, Executive Director
Kristin Campbell, Assistant Editor
Robert Pali, Treasurer

Our information assists inspection personnel through information and reports on new technology and equipment, tips on inspection techniques and interpretation, as well as by giving examples of practical methodology.
Cost: $50.00
Frequency: Quarterly
Circulation: 18000
Founded in 1989

18366 **International Journal of Powder Metallurgy**
APMI International
105 College Road E
Princeton, NJ 08540-6992

609-452-7700; Fax: 609-987-8523
apmi@mpif.org
www.mpif.org/apmi

Dr Alan Lawley, Editor-in-Chief
Peter K Johnson, Contributing Editor

Embraces a wide range of materials and processes including classical press and sinter PM and advanced particulate materials.
Cost: $230.00
Frequency: Bi-Monthly
ISSN: 0888-7462

18367 **Iron & Steel Technology**
Association for Iron & Steel Technolgy (AIST)
186 Thorn Hill Rd
Warrendale, PA 15086-7528

724-814-3000; Fax: 724-814-3001
memberservices@aist.org
www.aist.org
Facebook, Twitter, LinkedIn

Karen D Hickey, Managing Editor
Amanda Blyth, Technical Editor
Janet McConnell, Production Editor

The official monthly publication of AIST, this is the premier technical journal for metallurgical, engineering, operating and maintenance personnel in the global iron and steel industry.
Cost: $20.00
Frequency: Monthly
Circulation: 9600

18368 **Journal of Materials Engineering and Performance**
ASM International
9639 Kinsman Road
Materials Park, OH 44073-0002

440-338-5151
800-336-5152; Fax: 440-338-4634
memberservicecenter@asminternational.org
www.asminternational.org

William T. Mahoney, Secretary & CEO
Rajiv Asthana, Editor

Peer-reviewed journal that publishes contributions on all aspects of materials selection, design, characterization, processing and performance testing. The journal is useful for solving day-to-day engineering challenges - especially those involving components for larger systems.
30K Members
Frequency: Bi-Monthly
Founded in 1913

18369 **Journal of Minerals, Metals & Materials Society**
Minerals, Metals & Minerals Society
184 Thorn Hill Road
Warrendale, PA 15086-7511

724-776-9000; Fax: 724-776-3770
webmaster@tms.org
www.tms.org

Alexander R Scott, Executive Director
Robert Makowski, Communications Director

To promote the global science and engineering profession's concerned with minerals, metals and materials. Founded in 1871. Publishes a monthly magazine.
Cost: $20.00
Frequency: Monthly
Circulation: 10000
Founded in 1880

18370 **Journal of Phase Equilibria & Diffusion**
ASM International
9639 Kinsman Road
Materials Park, OH 44073-0002

440-338-5151
800-336-5152; Fax: 440-338-4634
memberservicecenter@asminternational.org
www.asminternational.org

William T. Mahoney, Secretary & CEO
John Morral, Editor
Ursula R. Kattner, Editor
H. Okamoto, Editor

Peer-reviewed journal containing basic and applied research results, evaluated phase diagrams, a survey of current literature, and comments or other material pertinent to the previous three areas. The aim of the journal is to provide a broad spectrum of information concerning phase equilibria for the materials community.
30K Members
Frequency: Bi-Monthly
Founded in 1913

18371 **Light Metal Age**
Fellom Publishing Company
170 S Spruce Ave
Suite 120
S San Francisco, CA 94080-4557

650-588-8832; Fax: 650-588-0901
lma@lightmetalage.com
www.lightmetalage.com

Ann Marie Fellom, Publisher

Technical trade magazine covering the aluminum industry, from primary to secondary production, including semi-fabrications processes such as extrusion and rolling, and applications.
Cost: $45.00
Frequency: Monthly
Circulation: 5000
ISSN: 0024-3345
Founded in 1944
Printed in 4 colors on glossy stock

18372 **Locator Services**
Locator Online
315 S Patrick St
Suite 3
Alexandria, VA 22314-3532

703-836-9700
800-537-1446; Fax: 703-836-7665
www.locatoronline.com

Terry Pitman, Publisher

Used metalworking equipment.
Frequency: Monthly
Circulation: 225000
Founded in 1969

18373 **Machine Shop Guide**
Worldwide Communications
401 Worthington Avenue
Harrison, NJ 07029-2039

973-497-7555; Fax: 973-497-7556

Robert L Hatschek, Executive Editor

Information on manufacturing technology, new applications for manufacturing technology and new products.
Circulation: 102893

18374 **Manufacturers Showcase**
Heartland Communications Group
1003 Central Avenue
Po Box 1052
Fort Dodge, IA 50501

515-955-1600
800-203-9960; Fax: 515-955-3753
www.industrialmachinetrader.com

Natalie Fevold, Operations Manager
Sandy Simonson, Sales Manager

A magazine for new metalworking machinery, tooling and supplies.
Frequency: Monthly

18375 **Metal Architecture**
Modern Trade Communications
7450 Skokie Blvd
Suite 200
Skokie, IL 60077-3374

847-674-2200; Fax: 847-674-3676
www.moderntrade.com

John Lawrence, President
Mark Wiebusch, Marketing & Operations
Shawn Zuver, Editorial & Production

Low-rise construction involving architects, engineers and specifiers.
Frequency: Monthly
Circulation: 29513

18376 **Metal Center News**
Reed Business Information
30 Technology Parkway South
Suite 100
Norcross, GA 30092

630-574-0825
800-424-3996; Fax: 630-288-8781
webmaster@reedbusiness.com
www.reedbusiness.com

Jeff Greisch, President

Reports on verious phases of metal center operations.

18377 **Metal Finishing**
Elsevier Science
655 Avenue of the Americas
New York, NY 10010-5107

212-633-3800; Fax: 212-633-3850
PressOffice@elsevier.com
www.elsevier.com

Young Suk Chi, President
Patti Ann Frost, Managing Editor
Susan Canalizo, Director, Manager
Greg Valero, Manager

Finishes and finishing of metal products.
Cost: $87.00
Frequency: Monthly
Circulation: 19824
Founded in 1903

18378 **Metal Mecanica**
Gardner Publications
901 poncedeleon blvd
sute 601
Coral Gables, FL 33134-3029

513-527-8977
800-950-8020; Fax: 305-448-9942
www.metalmecanica.com

David Ash, President
Eduardo Tovar, Editor
Holgar Hilkinger, Circulation Manager
Alfredo Domador, Publisher
Circulation: 12157
Founded in 1905

18379 **MetalForming**
Precision Metalforming Association
6363 Oak Tree Blvd
Cleveland, OH 44131-2500

216-901-9667; Fax: 216-901-9190
pma@pma.org
www.metalformingmagazine.com

Brad Kuvin, Editor
Kathy DeLollis, Publisher
William Gaskin, President
Daniel Ellashek, VP
Lou Kren, Senior Editor

Edited for decision makers in the precision metal forming industry.
Cost: $59.95
100 Pages
Frequency: Monthly
Circulation: 60000
Founded in 1967
Printed in 4 colors on matte stock

18380 **Metallurgical and Materials Transactions**
ASM International
9639 Kinsman Rd
Materials Park, OH 44073-0002

440-338-5151
800-336-5152; Fax: 440-338-4634
memberservicecenter@asminternational.org
www.asminternational.org

William T. Mahoney, Secretary & CEO
Tresa M. Pollock, Principal Editor

Covers information on physical metallurgy and materials science with emphasis on processing, structure, and properties. Joint publication between ASM International and The Minerals, Metals and Materials Society.
Cost: $5658.00

18381 **Metalsmith**
Society of North American Goldsmiths
5009 Londonderry Drive
Tampa, FL 33647-1336

813-977-5326; Fax: 813-977-8462
editor@snagmetalsmith.org
www.snagmetalsmith.org

Suzanne Ramljak, Editor
Dana Singer, Executive Director
Ken Bova, President
Jean Savarese, Advertising Director
Ellen Laing, Program Manager

Information which explores new work in the jewelry, holloware, blacksmithing, and sculpture fields. Profiles of master metalsmiths are included.
Cost: $65.00
Circulation: 13,500
Founded in 1969

18382 **Metalworking Digest**
Reed Business Information
30 Technology Parkway South
Suite 100
Norcross, GA 30092

973-920-7000
800-424-3996; Fax: 973-920-7531
webmaster@reedbusiness.com
www.reedbusiness.com

Rich Stevancsecz, Editor
Joe May, Publisher
Cloin Ungaro, CEO/President
Steve Koppelman, Circulation Manager
R Reed, Owner
Frequency: Monthly
Circulation: 115000
Founded in 1969

18383 **Metalworking Distributor**
Penton Media
1166 Avenue of the Americas/10th Fl
New York, NY 10036

212-204-4200; Fax: 216-696-6662
information@penton.com
www.penton.com

Jane Cooper, Marketing
Thomas Grasson, Editor
Susan Cubranich, Production Manager
Chris Meyer, Director, Corporate Communications

Publication exclusively devoted to distributors and wholesales in the metalworking industry to help improve marketing, management, and technology knowledge as well as provide information on new markets.
Frequency: Quarterly
Circulation: 5,000
Printed in 4 colors

18384 **Modern Applications News**
Nelson Publishing
2500 Tamiami Trl N
Nokomis, FL 34275-3476

941-966-9521; Fax: 941-966-2590
www.healthmgttech.com
Facebook

A Verner Nelson, President

Information includes coverage of abrasives and grinding, automated handling and robotics, CAD/CAM, coatings and finishings, coolants, lubricants and filters, cutting tools, heat treating, ID marking, lasers, machining centers, and shop control software.
Frequency: Monthly
Circulation: 84000
Founded in 1967

18385 **Modern Casting**
American Foundrymen's Society
1695 N Penny Ln
Schaumburg, IL 60173-4555

847-824-0181
800-537-4237; Fax: 847-824-7848
circ@afsinc.org
www.afsinc.org

Jerry Call, Executive VP
Sandy Salisbury-Linton, Vice Chairman
Kyle Bauer, Editor
Barbara Jackowski, Circulation Manager
Alfred Spada, Editor-In-Chief

Designed to promote the technological advances in the industry.
Cost: $50.00
Frequency: Monthly
Circulation: 19000
Founded in 1896

18386 **Modern Machine Shop**
Gardner Publications
6915 Valley Ln
Cincinnati, OH 45244-3153

513-527-8800
800-950-8020; Fax: 513-527-8801
www.gardnerweb.com

Rick Kline Sr, CEO
Mark D Albert, Editor-in-Chief
Dianne Hight, Circulation Manager
John Campos, Manager
Brian Wertheimer, Account Manager

Reaches metalworking plants of all sizes - from small job shops to giant aerospace and automotive plants. It is edited for those involved in metalworking operations, particularly those performed on machine tools.
Cost: $89.00
Frequency: Monthly
Circulation: 107000
Founded in 1928
Mailing list available for rent: 106M names
Printed in 4 colors on glossy stock

18387 **Occupational Hazards**
Penton Media
1166 Avenue of the Americas/10th Fl
New York, NY 10036

212-204-4200; Fax: 216-696-6662
information@penton.com
www.penton.com

Jane Cooper, Marketing
Bob Marinez, Publisher
David B Nussbaum, CEO
Jennifer Daugherty, Communications Manager
Chris Meyer, Director, Corporate Communications

Analysis of qualified recipients who have indicated that they recommend, select and/or buy the safety equipment, fire protection and other occupational health products.
65 Pages
Frequency: Monthly
Circulation: 65777
ISSN: 0029-7909
Founded in 1892
Printed in 4 colors on glossy stock

18388 **Ornamental and Miscellaneous Metals Fabricator**
National Ornamental & Miscellaneous Metals Assn
532 Forest Parkway
Suite A
Forest Park, GA 30297-6137

404-363-4009; Fax: 404-366-1852
nommainfo@nomma.org
www.nomma.org

Curt Witter, CEO/President
Todd Daniel, Editor

Magazine published by National Ornamental and Miscellaneous Metals Association.
Cost: $30.00
Circulation: 10000
Founded in 1958

18389 **Platt's Metals Week**
McGraw Hill
3333 Walnut Street
Boulder, CO 80301

720-548-5000
800-752-8878; Fax: 720-548-5701
metals@platts.com
www.mcgraw-hill.com

Jackie Roche, Editor-in-Chief
Terry McGraw, CEO
Harry Sachinsis, President
Jackie Roche, Publisher

Extensive price listings in four currencies.
Frequency: Weekly

18390 **Powder Coating**
OSC Publishing
1300 E 66th Street
Minneapolis, MN 55423-2642

612-866-2242; Fax: 612-866-1939

Richard R Cress, Publisher
Richard Link, Manager

Our information focuses on the application, pre-treatment, materials, materials handling, and curing processes. Also features case histories.
Cost: $95.00
Frequency: Monthly
Circulation: 23587

18391 **Practical Welding Today**
Fabricators and Manufacturers Association
833 Featherstone Road
Rockford, IL 61107-6302

815-399-8700; Fax: 815-484-7700
info@fmanet.org
www.fmanet.org

Gerald M Shankel, President/CEO
Michael Hedges, VP Finance/CFO
Scott Stevens, Publisher
Kim Clothier, Director of Circulation
Jim Gorzek, Marketing

Practical Welding Today is the only hands on, down-to-earth magazine with information that welders can use in the shop or out in the field. Published six times per year with more than 40,000 subcribers, it covers topics such as systems and equipment, safety, consumables, cutting and welding prep, welding inspection and more. In addition, Practical Welding Today has a regular lineup of application articles, welder profiles, product highlights and valuable buyers' guides.
Circulation: 40000
Printed in 4 colors on glossy stock

18392 **Products Finishing**
Gardner Publications
6915 Valley Ln
Cincinnati, OH 45244-3153

513-527-8800; Fax: 513-527-8801
www.gardnerweb.com

Rick Kline Sr, CEO
Beverly Graves, Manager
John Campos, Manager
Brian Wertheimer, Account Manager
Eddie Kania, Sales Manager

Covers production, management, engineering, design, etc. in plants where metal and plastic products are eletroplated, anodized, painted, buffed, cleaned or otherwise finished.
Cost: $89.00
Frequency: Monthly
Circulation: 45552
Founded in 1928
Printed in 4 colors on glossy stock

18393 **Projects in Metal**
Village Press
2779 Aero Park Drive
PO Box 629
Traverse City, MI 49686-9101

231-463-3712; Fax: 231-946-3289
villagepre@aol.com
www.members.aol.com/vpshop/pim/htm

Robert Goff, Publisher

In each issue you will find plans for valuable tools and accessories, and challenging hobby projects. Every project is complete in one issue.
Frequency: Bi-Monthly
Circulation: 15000

18394 **Recycling Today**
GIE Media
4012 Bridge Avenue
Cleveland, OH 44113-3320

216-961-4130
800-456-0707; Fax: 216-961-0364
btaylor@gie.net
www.recyclingtoday.com

Jim Keefe, Group Publisher
Brian Taylor, Editor
Richard Foster, CEO
Helen Duerr, Director of Production
Megan Ries, Advertising Coordinatior

Published for the secondary commodity processing/recycling market.
Cost: $30.00
Frequency: Monthly
Founded in 1980

18395 **SCRAP**
Institute of Scrap Recycling Industries
1615 L Street NW
Suite 600
Washington, DC 20036-5664

202-662-8500; Fax: 202-626-0900
kentkiser@scrap.org
www.scrap.org

Kent Kiser, Publisher
Marian Weiss, Production Manager
Rachel H Pollack, Editor-In-Chief
Valerie Hillyer, Circulation/Advertising Associate

A bi-monthly magazine that covers all aspects of the international scrap recycling industry, including market trends, business management, personnel issues, equipment and technology, regulations and legislation, and more.
Cost: $36.00
16 Pages
Frequency: 6 per year
Circulation: 7400
ISSN: 1092-8618
Founded in 1928

18396 **Secondary Marketing Executive Magazine**
Zackin Publications
100 Willenbrock Road
Oxford, CT 06478

203-262-4670
800-325-6745; Fax: 203-262-4680
www.secondarymarketingexec.com
Facebook, Twitter

Michael Bates, Publisher
Patrick Barnard, Editor
Vanessa Williams, Business Development

Delivers news, analysis and how-to advice to people involved in the buying and selling of mortgage loans and servicing rights nationwide.
Frequency: Monthly
Founded in 1986

18397 **Shop Owner**
Penton Media
1166 Avenue of the Americas/10th Fl
New York, NY 10036

212-204-4200; Fax: 216-696-6662
information@penton.com
www.penton.com

Jane Cooper, Marketing
Thomas J Grasson, Editorial Director
Charles Bates, Senior Editor
Melody Berendt, Circulation Manager
Janet Marioneaux, Administrative Assistant

Digest-sized publication covering information essential to the success of the small to medium manufacturing shop.
Frequency: Quarterly
Circulation: 120000
Founded in 1998
Printed in 4 colors

18398 **Stamping Journal**
Fabricators and Manufacturers Association
833 Featherstone Road
Rockford, IL 61107-6302

815-399-8700; Fax: 815-484-7700
info@fmanet.org
www.fmanet.org

Gerald Shankel, President/CEO
Michael Hedges, CFO
Scot Stevens, Publisher
Jim Gorzek, Sales Manager
Kim Clothier, Circulation Manager

Stamping Journal, the only North American magazine devoted exclusively to metal stamping, has been delivering the industry's latest techniques, news and ideas to subscribers worldwide for 13 years. Published six times per year, with more than 35,000 subscribers, Stamping Journal focuses on metal stamping technology including, tool and die, material handling, coil processing, stamping presses, press feeding, quick die change and more.
Cost: $65.00
Frequency: Monthly
Circulation: 35000
Founded in 1970
Printed in 4 colors on glossy stock

18399 **Tooling & Production**
NP Communications, LLC
2500 Tamiami Trail N
Nokomis, FL 34275

941-966-9521; Fax: 941-966-2590
vnelson@nelsonpub.com
www.toolingandproduction.com

Vern Nelson, Publisher/Editorial Director
Bob West, Managing Editor/Associate Publisher

Provides information to metalworking professionals working in large, high-throughput plants. Original editorial delivers technology, products, and processes applying to aerospace, automotive, medical equipment, mold, tool & die manufacturing, and much more.
100 Pages
Frequency: Monthly
Circulation: 70000
ISSN: 0040-9243
Founded in 1934
Printed in 4 colors on glossy stock

18400 **Tube & Pipe Journal**
Fabricators and Manufacturers Association
833 Featherstone Road
Rockford, IL 61107-6302

815-998-8700; Fax: 815-484-7701
info@fmanet.org
www.fmanet.org

Gerald Shankel, President/CEO
Michael Hedges, CFO

The Tube and Pipe Journal is North America's only magazine devoted exclusively to metal tube and pipe manufacturing. Published 8 times

per year and with more than 30,000 subscribers, TPJ covers topics such as tube producing, bending and forming, cutting and sawing, welding, tooling, coil and material handling, and more. TPJ also provides expanded coverage of hydroforming technology in the Hydroforming Journal, a separate supplement published four time per year alongside TPJ.
Cost: $200.00
Circulation: 30000
Founded in 1970
Printed in 4 colors on glossy stock

18401 **US Glass, Metal & Glazing**
Key Communications
PO Box 569
Garrisonville, VA 22463

540-577-7174; Fax: 540-720-5687
info@glass.com
www.glass.com

Debra Levy, Publisher
Ellen Giard Chilcoat, Editor
Penny Stacey, Advertising Coordinator

Serves manufactures/fabricators, contract glaziers, distributors and wholesalers, retailors/dealers of glass/metal and or glass/metal products and other allied to the field.
Frequency: Monthly
Circulation: 15000
ISSN: 0041-7661
Founded in 1995
Printed in 4 colors on glossy stock

18402 **Welding Design & Fabrication**
Penton Media
1166 Avenue of the Americas/10th Fl
New York, NY 10036

212-204-4200; Fax: 216-696-6662
information@penton.com
www.penton.com

Jane Cooper, Marketing
Dean Peters, Editor
David Nussbaum, CEO
Chris Meyer, Director, Corporate Communications

Reaches designers, engineers, managers, superviisors, and buyers in plants and field sites in the US and Canada who conduct welding and fabricating operations. Reports on processes and equipment, materials, safety, testing and inspection in the manufacturing of fabricated metal products, structural projects and equipment maintenance.
Frequency: Monthly
Circulation: 40000
Founded in 1892
Printed in 4 colors

18403 **Welding Innovation**
James F Lincoln Arc Welding Foundation
22801 Saint Clair Ave
Cleveland, OH 44117-2524

216-481-4300; Fax: 216-383-8220
www.jflf.org/

Roy Morrow, President
Richard D Seif, Chairman
Vicki Wilson, Administrative Assistant
Dave Manning, Executive Director

Informative articles related to welding steel structures such as bridges and buildings, as well as notices of related conferences.
Circulation: 40000
Founded in 1936

18404 **Welding Journal**
American Welding Society
550 Nw 42nd Ave
Miami, FL 33126-5699

305-443-9353
800-443-9353; Fax: 305-443-7559
info@aws.org
www.aws.org

Ray Shook, President
Jefferey Weber, Publisher
Cecilia Barbier, Senior Coordinator Market
Robert Pali, Treasurer

Our feature articles include new product listings, book reviews and the application of new operating procedures.
Frequency: Monthly
Circulation: 46000
Founded in 1919

18405 **Wire Rope News & Sling Technology**
Wire Rope News
PO Box 871
Clark, NJ 07066-871

908-486-3221; Fax: 732-396-4215
vsent@aol.com
www.wireropenews.com

Edward J Bluvias, Publisher
Conrad Miller, Editor

Wire Rope News & Sling Technology is edited for manufacturers and distributors of wire rope, chain, cordage, related hardware, and sling fabricators. Content includes technical articles, news, and reports describing the manufacture and use of wire rope in marine, construction, mining, aircraft and offshore drilling operations. Cordage, slings, chain and fittings are also covered. Editorial content contains articles about fabricating companies, new products and people in the news.
Cost: $20.00
Circulation: 4400
ISSN: 0740-1809
Founded in 1979
Printed in 4 colors on glossy stock

Trade Shows

18406 **AFS/CMI Advanced Foundry Operations Conference**
American Foundrymen's Society
1695 N Penny Ln
Schaumburg, IL 60173-4555

847-824-0181
800-537-4237; Fax: 847-824-7848
www.afsinc.org

Frequency: March

18407 **AISTech Conference & Exposition**
Association for Iron & Steel Technology
186 Thorn Hill Rd
Warrendale, PA 15086-7528

724-814-3000; Fax: 724-814-3001
memberservices@aist.org
www.aist.org
Facebook, Twitter, LinkedIn

Ronald E Ashburn, Executive Director
William A Albaugh, Technology Programs Manager
Joann Cantrell, Publications Manager/Editor
Mark Didiano, Finance & Administration Manager
Stacy Varmecky, Membership Communications Manager

Featuring technologies from across the globe, allowing steel producers to compete in today's global market. Submit technical papers for presentation at the event. 300 exhibitors. Registration starts at $425.
4500 Attendees
Frequency: Annual/Spring

18408 **AeroMat Conference and Exposition**
ASM International
9639 Kinsman Road
Materials Park, OH 44073-0002

440-338-5151
800-336-5152; Fax: 440-338-4634
memberservicecenter@asminternational.org
www.asminternational.org

William T. Mahoney, Secretary & CEO
Lindy Good, Global Conference & Exhibit Planner

Focuses on innovative aerospace materials, fabrication and manufacturing methods that improve aerospace structures, performance and durability.
900 Members
Frequency: Annual/May
Founded in 1913

18409 **American Foundrymen's Society Castings Congress and Cast Expo**
505 State St
Des Plaines, IL 60016-2267

847-824-0181; Fax: 847-824-7845

Kristy Glass, Show Manager

300 booths including technical papers and panel sessions for the metal casting industry.
12000 Attendees
Frequency: Annual

18410 **American Society Engineers: Design International**
Systems and Design Group
3 Park Avenue
Floor 27
New York, NY 10016-5902

212-903-4160

Fred Goldfarb, Program Manager
Virgil Carter, CEO

150 booths.
2.5M Attendees
Frequency: August

18411 **American Welding Show**
American Welding Society
8669 Doral Boulevard, Suite 130
Doral, FL 33166

305-443-9353
800-443-9353; Fax: 305-443-7559
www.aws.org

Ray Shook, Executive Director
Jefferey Weber, Publisher
Amy Nathan, Public Relations Manager

350 booths of welding and allied industries held in conjunction with metal form.
Frequency: Annual

18412 **American Zinc Association**
1112 16th Street NW
Suite 240
Washington, DC 20036-4818

202-478-8200; Fax: 202-835-0155
www.zinc.org

George Vary, Executive Director
David Adkins, Secretary
Frequency: February

18413 **Annual International Titanium Conference**
International Titanium Association
1871 Folsom Street
Suite 200
Boulder, CO 80302-5714

303-443-7515; Fax: 303-443-4406
www.titanium.org

Amy Fitzgerald, Manager
800 Attendees
Frequency: October
Founded in 1984

18414 Artist-Blacksmiths Association of North America Conference
Artist Blacksmith's Association of North America
259 Muddy Fork Road
Jonesborough, TN 37659

423-913-1022; Fax: 423-913-1023
abana@abana.org
www.abana.org
Facebook, Twitter

Eddie Rainey, President

Meeting and exhibitions, workshops, demonstrations and artistic metalwork for the professional and amateur blacksmith.

18415 Association of Industrial Metallizers, Coaters and Laminators Conference
201 Springs Street
Fort Mill, SC 29708

803-802-7820; Fax: 803-802-7821
aimcal@aimcal.org
www.aimcal.org

Craig Sheppard, Executive Director
Erin Davis, Communications Manager

Displays relating to coaters and laminators, metallizers and producers of metallized film and or paper on continuous rolls, suppliers of plastic films, papers and adhesives.
Frequency: Annual
Founded in 1970

18416 CBSA Annual Convention
Copper and Brass Servicenter Association
6734 W 121st Steet
Overland Park, KS 66209

913-396-0697
cbsahq@copper-brass.org
www.copper-brass.org

Susan Avery, Executive Director
Liz Novak, Senior Director

Distributors (service centers) of fabricated copper and copper alloy products (sheet, plate, coil, rod, bar tube, etc) and their brass mill suppliers.
78 Members
Founded in 1951

18417 Cast Expo
Cast Metals Institute
1695 N Penny Ln
Schaumburg, IL 60173-4555

847-824-0181
800-537-4237; Fax: 847-824-7848
www.castmetals.com
Facebook, Twitter, LinkedIn

CastExpo attracts thousands of decision-making metalcasters from around the world, all of whom are looking for the latest advancements in equipment, technology and services to use in their own facilities.
Frequency: May

18418 Electrical Manufacturing & Coil Winding Expo
PO Box 278
Imperial Beach, CA 91933-0278

619-435-3629; Fax: 619-435-3639
cthurman@earthlink.net
www.emcwa.org

Richard Duke, President
Charles Thurman, Executive Director
Don Stankiewicz, Vice President

An annual technical conference and exhibition related to the manufacture of electrical products. Exhibitors include suppliers of materials and process equipment used in manufacturing electric motors, trnasformers, and other electrical devices. 150 exhibitors, free admission.
2000 Attendees

18419 FABTECH International
Fabricators and Manufacturers Association
833 Featherstone Road
Rockford, IL 61107-6302

815-399-8700; Fax: 815-399-7279
www.fmametalfab.org

Mark Hoper, Director

Metal forming, fabricating, finishing and welding event that gives all the tools neded to improve productivity, increase profits and find new ways to survive in today's competitive business environment.
25000 Attendees
Frequency: Annual/November

18420 Furnaces North America
Metal Treating Institute
504 Osceola Ave
Jacksonville Beach, FL 32250

904-249-0448; Fax: 904-249-0459
www.heattreat.net

Tom Morrison, Show Manager

North America's Premier Heat Treat Only Event, Furnaces North America 2012, will be held October 1-3, 2012 in Nashville, TN.
340 Members
1200 Attendees
Frequency: September
Founded in 1933

18421 Heat Treating Society Conference & Expo
ASM International
9639 Kinsman Road
Materials Park, OH 44073-0002

440-338-5151
800-336-5152; Fax: 440-338-4634
memberservicecenter@asminternational.org
www.asminternational.org

William T. Mahoney, Secretary & CEO
Lindy Good, Global Conference & Exhibit Planner

Conference and expo for heat treating equipment and supplies as well as information of interest to metallurgists, maintenance supervisors and production engineering staff.
30K Members
Frequency: October
Founded in 1913

18422 International Anodizing Conference & Exposition
Aluminum Anodizers Council (AAC)
1000 North Rand Road
Suite 214
Wauconda, IL 60084

847-526-2010; Fax: 847-526-3993
mail@anodizing.org
www.anodizing.org

Terry D Snell, Chairman
Todd Hamilton, Vice Chairman
Gregory T Rajsky CAE, President
120 Attendees
Frequency: Annual

18423 International Symposium for Testing & Failure Analysis
ASM International
9639 Kinsman Road
Materials Park, OH 44073-0002

440-338-5151
800-336-5152; Fax: 440-338-4634
memberservicecenter@asminternational.org
www.asminternational.org

William T. Mahoney, Secretary & CEO
Lindy Good, Global Conference & Exhibit Planner

Annual event focusing on failure analysis and makers of tools such as microscopes, stress and measurement analytical tools, etchants and chemicals, ESD protective materials and other products used for this purpose.
30K Members
Frequency: Annual/Oct/Nov
Founded in 1913

18424 International Thermal Spray Conference & Exposition
ASM International
9639 Kinsman Road
Materials Park, OH 44073-0002

440-338-5151
800-336-5152; Fax: 440-338-4634
memberservicecenter@asminternational.org
www.asminternational.org

William T. Mahoney, Secretary & CEO
Lindy Good, Global Conference & Exhibit Planner

International annual conference for professional thermal spray technologists, researchers, manufacturers and suppliers.
30K Members
Frequency: Annual/May
Founded in 1913

18425 Iron & Steel Exposition
Association of Iron & Steel Engineers
3 Gateway Center
Suite 1900
Pittsburgh, PA 15222-1000

412-281-6323; Fax: 412-281-4657
www.aise.org

Ronald E Ashiurn, Managing Director
Chris Brown, Graphic Designer
Stacy Varmecky, General Manager

Includes technical sessions and exhibits of equipment, supplies and services for the metals producing industry.
25M Attendees

18426 MBCEA Annual Conference
Metal Building Contractors & Erectors Association
PO Box 499
Shawnee Mission, KS 66201

913-432-3800; Fax: 913-432-3803
www.mbcea.org

Angela M Cruse, Executive Director
Tim Seyler, President

Annual conference with the mission to support the professional advancement of metal building contractors, erectors and our industry.
Frequency: February

18427 METALFORM
Precision Metalforming Association
6363 Oak Tree Boulevard
Independence, OH 44131

216-901-8800; Fax: 216-901-9190
rjudson@pma.org

Amy Primiano, Director Expositions
William Gaskin, President

A regional networking and educational event that brings buyers and sellers from metal stamping and fabricating markets together in a dynamic and interactive environment.
5,000 Attendees
Frequency: March

18428 Metalworking Machine Tool Expo
Marketing International Corporation
200 N Glebe Road
Suite 900
Arlington, VA 22203-3728

703-527-8000; Fax: 703-527-8006

Annual show of 100 machine tools suppliers.
8000 Attendees

18429 **NFFS Summit Conference**
Non-Ferrous Founders' Society
1480 Renaissance Drive
Suite 310
Park Ridge, IL 60068

847-299-0950; Fax: 847-299-3598
staff@nffs.org
www.nffs.org

Frequency: February

18430 **National Ornamental and Miscellaneous Metals Association**
532 Forest Parkway
Suite A
Forest Park, GA 30297-6137

404-363-4009; Fax: 888-279-7994
nommainfo@nomma.org
www.nomma.org

Barbara Cook, Executive Director
Todd Daniel, Editor
Cyndi Smith, Office Manager
Martha Pennington, Meetings/Exposition Manager

This annual convention and trade show — METALfab — is for all those involved in the ornamental and metallury industries.
900 Attendees
Founded in 1958

18431 **PowderMet**
APMI International
105 College Road E
Princeton, NJ 08540-6992

609-452-7700; Fax: 609-987-8523
info@mpif.org
www.mpif.org

Nicholas T Mares, President
Michael E Lutheran, Director
C James Trombino CAE, Director

An annual international conference serving the powder metallurgy industry with a standalone exhibit featuring industry service providers and equipment suppliers.
1000 Attendees
Frequency: Annual

18432 **SMACNA Annual Convention**
Sheet Metal and Air Conditioning Contractor's Natl
4201 Lafayette Center Drive
Chantilly, VA 20151-1219

703-803-2980; Fax: 703-803-3732
info@smacna.org
www.smacna.org

Vincent R Sandusky, CEO

Sheet metal and air conditioning contractors explore the newest ideas, technologies, and trends in the construction industry.
Frequency: October

18433 **TMS Annual Meeting Exhibition**
Minerals, Metals & Materials Society
184 Thorn Hill Road
Warrendale, PA 15086

724-776-9000; Fax: 724-776-3770
webmaster@tms.org
www.tms.org

Cindy Wilson, Show Manager
Alexander Scott, Executive Director

International metals and materials exhibition. Production, processing, engineering and research. Held in Charlotte, North Carolina.
3,500 Attendees
Frequency: March

Directories & Databases

18434 **Aluminum Association Aluminum Standards & Data**
Aluminum Association
900 19th Street NW
Washington, DC 20006-2105
202-862-5100

Contains the nominal composition and composition limits, typical mechanical and physical properties and tensile properties limits for US wrought aluminum alloys. Updated periodically.

18435 **Aluminum Extruders Council Buyer's Guide**
1000 North Rand Road
Suite 214
Wauconda, IL 60084

847-526-2010; Fax: 847-526-3993
mail@aec.org
www.aec.org
LinkedIn

Matt McMahon, Chairman
Scott Kelley, Vice Chairman
Jeff Henderson, President
Nancy Molenda, Communications Manager

Offers listings of aluminum extruders.
Frequency: Annual
Founded in 1950

18436 **DRI Steel Forecast**
DRI/McGraw-Hill
24 Hartwell Ave
Lexington, MA 02421-3103

781-860-6060; Fax: 781-860-6002
support@construction.com
www.construction.com

Walt Arvin, President

This comprehensive database offers over 500 quarterly and annual forecasts on production, shipment, and consumption of raw steel and steel products in the United States.

18437 **Directory Iron and Steel Plants**
Association for Iron & Steel Technology
186 Thorn Hill Rd
Warrendale, PA 15086-7528

724-814-3000; Fax: 724-814-3001
memberservices@aist.org
www.aist.org
Facebook, Twitter, LinkedIn

Ronald E Ashburn, Executive Director
William A Albaugh, Technology Programs Manager
Joann Cantrell, Publications Manager/Editor
Mark Didiano, Finance & Administration Manager
Stacy Varmecky, Membership Communications Manager

The Directory lists more than 2,000 companies and 17,500 individuals. Featuring data on essentially ever steel producer in the USA, Canada and Mexico, including names and titles of executive, enginnering, maintenance and operating personnel. Also includes an alpha listing of all major equipment, product and service providers to the international iron and steel industry, and a listing of associations affiliated with the industry, with complete geo-indexing. Softbound book with CD.
Cost: $95.00
Frequency: M-$95/NM-$135
ISBN: 1-935117-00-1

18438 **Dun's Industrial Guide: Metalworking Directory**
Dun & Bradstreet Information Service
3 Sylvan Way
Parsippany, NJ 07054-3822

973-605-6000
800-526-0651; Fax: 973-605-9630

Over 78,000 original equipment manufacturers, metal distributors, and machine tools/metalworking machinery distributors.
Cost: $775.00
Frequency: Annual

18439 **EDM Today Yearbook**
EDM Publications
230 W Parkway
Suite 3-1
Pompton Plains, NJ 07444-1065

973-831-1334; Fax: 973-831-1195

Jack Sebzda, Editor
Frequency: Annual

18440 **Economic Handbook of the Machine Tool Industry**
AMT - The Association for Manufacturing Technology
7901 Jones Branch Drive
Suite 900
McLean, VA 22102-4206

703-893-2900
800-524-0475; Fax: 703-893-1151
amt@amtonline.org
www.amtonline.org

Douglas K. Woods, President
Matthew Lutz, Business Solutions Manager
Rebecca Stahl, Chief Financial Officer
Amber L. Thomas, VP, Marketing & Communications

Contains statistics for the US machine tool industry, including exports and imports.
Cost: $295.00
Printed in one color on matte stock

18441 **Equip-Mart**
116 N Camp Street
Seguin, TX 78155
830-303-3328
800-864-1155; Fax: 830-372-3011
www.equip-mart.com

Directory of available used metalworking equipment.
Frequency: Weekly

18442 **Foundry Management & Technology: Where to Buy Directory Issue**
Penton Publishing Company
1166 Avenue of the Americas/10th Fl
New York, NY 10036

212-204-4200; Fax: 216-696-1752
information@penton.com
www.penton.com

Dean Peters, Editor
Chris Meyer, Director, Corporate Communications

Listing of about 1,700 manufacturers of foundry products.
Cost: $15.00
Frequency: Annual, September
Circulation: 22,000

18443 **Fundamentals of Steel Product Physical Metallurgy**
Association for Iron & Steel Technology (AIST)
186 Thorn Hill Road
Warrendale, PA 15086-7528

724-814-3000; Fax: 724-814-3001
memberservices@aist.org

Bruno C De Cooman, Author
John G Speer, Author

This directory is an introduction to steel products for industry professionals. With its readily acces-

sible style, the book allows the reader to easily grasp important scientific topics that play an essential role in current steel research, product development and applications. ISBN: 978-1-935117-16-2
Cost: $110.00
Frequency: Annual

18444 Industrial Laser Review: Buyers' Guide of Companies & Products
PennWell Publishing Company
10 Tara Boulevard
5th Floor
Nashua, NH 03062-2800
603-891-0123; Fax: 603-891-0574
www.industrial-lasers.com/index.html
David Belforte, Editor
Frequency: Annual July

18445 Industrial Machine Trader
Heartland Industrial Group
1003 Central Avenue
PO Box 1415
Fort Dodge, IA 50501
515-955-1600
800-247-2000; Fax: 515-955-3753
www.industrialgroup.com
Facebook, Twitter, LinkedIn
Virginia Rodriguez, Publisher
Printed directory of available used metalworking equipment.
150+ Members
Frequency: Weekly
Founded in 1966

18446 International Lead and Zinc
WEFA Group
800 Baldwin Tower Boulevard
Eddystone, PA 19022-1368
610-490-4000; Fax: 610-490-2770
info@wefa.com
www.wefa.com
This database contains quarterly and annual time series on lead and zinc.

18447 International Powder Metallurgy Directory
Metal Powder Industries Federation
105 College Rd East
Princeton, NJ 08540-6692
609-452-7700; Fax: 609-987-8523
info@mpif.org
www.mpif.org
Michael Lutheran, President
Jim Adams, Director, Technical Services
C. James Trombino, Executive Director, CEO
Jillaine K. Regan, VP, Finance & Administration
Jessica Tamasi, Advertising & Exhibit Manager
Leading reference source for powder metallurgy parts producers and industry suppliers worldwide.
Cost: $30.00
210 Members
504 Pages
Frequency: Annual, Paperback
Founded in 1944

18448 Iron and Manganese Ore Databook
Metal Bulletin
220 5th Avenue
New York, NY 10001-7708
212-136-6202
800-MET-L 25; Fax: 212-213-6273
John Bailey, Editor
Iron and manganese ore producers and traders worldwide.
Cost: $179.00
Frequency: Quadrennial

18449 Iron and Steel Works of the World
Metal Bulletin
220 5th Avenue
19th Floor
New York, NY 10001-7781
212-213-6202; Fax: 202-213-1870
www.metalbulletin.com
Henry Cooke, Editor
Lists over 1,500 major iron and steel plants worldwide.
Cost: $439.00
730 Pages

18450 Locator Services
315 S Patrick St
Alexandria, VA 22314-3532
703-836-9700
800-537-1446; Fax: 703-836-7665
sales@locatoronline.com
www.locatoronline.com
Terry Pitman, Publisher
Printed directory of available used metalworking equipment.
Frequency: Monthly
Circulation: 225,000

18451 MDNA Machine Tool Reference Guide
Machinery Dealers National Association
315 S Patrick Street
Alexandria, VA 22314
703-836-9300
800-872-7807; Fax: 703-836-9303
office@mdna.org
www.mdna.org/resource-guides
Mark Robinson, Executive Vice President
Will Keys, Accounting Manager
Joyce Fitzgerald, Administration Director
Lists contact information of U.S. machine tool builders as well as non-U.S. builders.
Cost: $29.95

18452 Metal Bulletin's Prices and Data Book
Metal Bulletin
220 5th Avenue
19th Floor
New York, NY 10001-7781
212-213-6202; Fax: 212-213-1870
help@metalbulletin.com
www.metalbulletin.com
Richard ODonoghue, Manager
Ania Tumm, Marketing Manager
Julius Pike, Account Manager
A list of national and international associations and trading organizations concerned with iron, steel and nonferrous ores and metals.
Cost: $165.00
Frequency: Annual

18453 Metal Casting Industry Directory
Penton Media
1166 Avenue of the Americas/10th Fl
New York, NY 10036
212-204-4200; Fax: 216-696-6662
information@penton.com
www.penton.com
Jane Cooper, Marketing
Chris Meyer, Director, Corporate Communications
Directory of services and supplies to the industry.
Cost: $425.00
300 Pages

18454 Metal Center News: Metal Distribution Issue
Hitchcock Publishing Company
191 S Gary Avenue
Carol Stream, IL 60188-2095
630-690-5600
Joseph Marino, Editor
Offers a list of producers and industrial metals and metal products, manufacturers of metal processing and handling equipment.
Cost: $25.00
Frequency: Annual
Circulation: 14,000

18455 Metal Finishing Guidebook Directory
Metal Finishing/Elsevier Science
360 Park Ave S
New York, NY 10010-1736
212-633-3980; Fax: 212-633-3913
metalfinishing@elsevier.com
www.elsevier.com
Ys Chi, President
Patti Ann Frost, Managing Editor
Matthew Smaldon, Circulation Manager
Bill Godfrey, Chief Information Officer
Cost: $87.00
Founded in 1962

18456 Metal Finishing: Guidebook Directory
Metal Finishing/Elsevier Science
650 Avenue of Americas
New York, NY 10011
212-633-5100; Fax: 212-633-5140
www.metalfinishing.com
Eugene Nadel, Publisher
Don Walsh, Director of operations
Enthone Taps, Communications Manager
Jonathan Timms, Director of Marketing
Frequency: Annual January

18457 Metal Statistics
American Metal Market
350 Hudson Street
4th Floor
New York, NY 10014-4504
212-666-2420
800-662-4445; Fax: 212-519-7522
custserv@amm.com
www.amm.com
Gloria Larme, Editor-in-Chief
The statistical guide to North American metals. Hardcover $265.00, Softcover $185.00.
404 Pages
Frequency: Annual
ISBN: 0-910094-01-2
Founded in 1908

18458 Metal Statistics: Ferrous Edition
American Metal Market
350 Hudson Street
4th Floor
New York, NY 10014-4504
212-662-2420
800-662-4445; Fax: 818-487-4550
custserv@amm.com
www.amm.com
Machael Botta, Publisher
Gloria LaRue, Editor-in-Chief
Statistics for North American metals, also Canadian and Mexican statistucs, International tables and graphs, International trade labor contractsand recycling and scrap alternatives.
Cost: $265.00
Frequency: Annual
ISBN: 0-910094-00-4

18459 Metals Datafile
Materials Information

ASM International
Materials Park, OH 44073

440-930-4888; Fax: 440-338-4634

This database contains designation and specification numbers for ferrous and non-ferrous metals and alloys.
Frequency: Full-text

18460 Metalworking Machinery Mailer
Tade Publishing Group
29501 Greenfield Road
Suite 120
Southfield, MI 48076

248-552-8583
800-966-8233; Fax: 248-552-0466

Tom Lynch, Editor

Printed directory of available used metalworking equipment.
Frequency: Monthly

18461 Mineral and Energy Information
Mineral Information Institute
505 Violet St
Golden, CO 80401-6714

303-277-9190; Fax: 303-277-9198
www.mii.org

Profiles of associations, government agencies and special interest groups in North America that are sources of publications and products on mineral related subjects.
Cost: $15.00

18462 Modern Machine Shop: CNC & Software Guide Software Issue
Gardner Publications
6915 Valley Ln
Cincinnati, OH 45244-3153

513-527-8800; Fax: 513-527-8801
www.gardnerweb.com

Rick Kline Sr, CEO
Richard Kline, Manager
John Campos, Manager
Brian Wertheimer, Account Manager
Eddie Kania, Sales Manager
Frequency: Annual April

18463 Parts Cleaning: Master Source Buyer's Guide
Witter Publishing Corporation
84 Park Avenue
Suite 32
Flemington, NJ 08822-1172

908-788-0343; Fax: 908-788-3782
www.partscleaningweb.com

Andrew Witter, Owner
Frequency: Annual July

18464 Pipe and Tube Mills of the World with Global Technical Data
Preston Publishing Company
715 S Sheridan Rd
Tulsa, OK 74112-3139

918-834-2356; Fax: 918-299-4795
www.prestonpipe.com

Richard Preston, Owner
LaSondra L O'Farrell, President

We also have a monthly trade journal The Preston Pipe and Tube Report.
Cost: $245.00
842 Pages
Frequency: BiAnnual
Founded in 1995
Printed in one color on matte stock

18465 Powder Metallurgy Suppliers Directory
Metal Powder Industries Federation
105 College Rd East
Princeton, NJ 08540-6692

609-452-7700; Fax: 609-987-8523
info@mpif.org
www.mpif.org

Michael Lutheran, President
Jim Adams, Director, Technical Services
C. James Trombino, Executive Director, CEO
Jillaine K. Regan, VP, Finance & Administration
Jessica Tamasi, Advertising & Exhibit Manager

Over 50 producers and suppliers of metal powder who belong to the Metal Powder Producers Association or Refractory Metals Association.
210 Members
Frequency: Paperback
Founded in 1944

18466 Precision Cleaning: Master Source Buyer's Guide
Witter Publishing Corporation
84 Park Avenue
Suite 32
Flemington, NJ 08822-1172

908-788-0343; Fax: 908-788-3782

Andrew Witter, Owner
Frequency: Annual

18467 Purchasing Magazine
Reed Business Information
275 Washington St
Newton, MA 02458-1611

617-964-3030; Fax: 617-558-4327
www.designnews.com

About 1,800 metal producers, distributors, die casters, foundries, forgers, coil coaters and powder metals.
Cost: $15.00
Frequency: Annual

18468 Silver Refiners of the World and their Identifying Ingot Marks
Silver Institute
1112 16th St Nw
Suite 240
Washington, DC 20036-4818

202-347-8200
www.silverinstitute.org

Over 80 refiners in over 18 countries are profiled.
Cost: $33.00
85 Pages

18469 Welding Design & Fabrication
Penton Media
1166 Avenue of the Americas/10th Fl
New York, NY 10036

212-204-4200; Fax: 216-696-6662
information@penton.com
www.penton.com

Jane Cooper, Marketing
Chris Meyer, Director, Corporate Communications

For owner operators and managers of professional welding shops.
Frequency: Annual, December

18470 Who's Who in Powder Metallurgy Membership Directory
Metal Powder Industries Federation
105 College Rd East
Princeton, NJ 08540-6692

609-452-7700; Fax: 609-987-8523
info@mpif.org
www.mpif.org

Michael Lutheran, President
Jim Adams, Director, Technical Services
C. James Trombino, Executive Director, CEO
Jillaine K. Regan, VP, Finance & Administration
Jessica Tamasi, Advertising & Exhibit Manager

An annual listing of the members of the APMI International and the Metal Powder Industries Federation.
Cost: $105.00
210 Members
88 Pages
Frequency: Annual
ISSN: 0361-6304
Founded in 1944

Industry Web Sites

18471 http://gold.greyhouse.com
G.O.L.D Grey House OnLine Databases

Grey House Publishing's online database platform, GOLD, offers Quick Search, Keyword Search and Expert Search for most business sectors including metals and metalworking markets. The GOLD platform makes finding the information you need quick and easy - whether you're a novice searcher or an experienced database user. All of Grey House's directory products are available for subscription on the GOLD platform.

18472 www.ace.org
Aluminum Extruders Council

An international trade association representing aluminum extruders.

18473 www.aimcal.org
Association of Industrial Metallizers, Coaters
and Laminators

Packaging equipment.

18474 www.aisc.org
American Institute of Steel Construction

Nonprofit trade association and technical institute established to serve the structural steel industry in the US. Our purpose is to promote the use of structural steel through research activities, market development, education, codes and specifacations, technical assistance, quality certifacation and standardization.

18475 www.aise.org
Association of Iron & Steel Engineers

Production and processing of iron and steel.

18476 www.amea.org
Association of Machinery and Equipment Appraisers

Facebook, LinkedIn, YouTube

Organization made up of appraisers of the metalworking industry.

18477 www.amtonline.org
The Association for Manufacturing Technology

Facebook, Twitter, LinkedIn, YouTube

Membership organization supporting professionals in the manufacturing technology industry.

18478 www.asminternational.org

ASM International provides information and networking for metals and materials professionals through its website.

18479 www.aws.org
American Welding Society

18480 www.coilcoating.org
National Coil Coaters Association

18481 www.construction.com
McGraw-Hill Construction

McGraw-Hill Construction (MHC), part of The McGraw-Hill Companies, connects people and projects across the design and construction industry, serving owners, architects, engineers, general contractors, subcontractors, building product manufacturers, suppliers, dealers, distributors and adjacent markets.

18482 www.copper-brass.org
Copper and Brass Servicenter Association
Distributors (service centers) of fabricated copper and copper alloy products (sheet, plate, coil, rod, bar tube, etc) and their brass mill suppliers.

18483 www.copper.org
Copper Development Association
CDA is committed to promoting the proper use of copper materials in sustainable, efficient applications for business, industry and the home.

18484 www.ductile.org
Ductile Iron Society
A technical society servicing the ductile iron industry. To advance the technology, art, science of ductile iron production and to disseminate all such information to the members.

18485 www.emcw.org
Electrical Manufacturing & Coil Winding Assn
Promotes welfare of the motor and coil industry. Offers courses and workshops.

18486 www.fmanet.org
Fabricators and Manufacturers Association
FMA is an educational association serving the metal forming and fabricating industry. Technology areas include sheet metal fabrucating, stamping, roll forming, coil processing, punching, and plate structural fabricating.

18487 www.forengineers.org/wrc
Welding Research Council
Coordinates welding research.

18488 www.greyhouse.com
Grey House Publishing
Authoritative reference directories for most business sectors, incluidng metal and metalworking markets. Users can search the online databases with varied search criteria allowing for custom searches by product category, geographic area, sales volume, keyword, subject and more. Full Grey House catalog and online ordering also available.

18489 www.ilzro.org
International Lead Zinc Research Organization
For miners, smelters and refiners of lead and zinc. Supports research and developement of new uses for the metals and refinement existing uses.

18490 www.intlmag.org
International Magnesium Association
Develops international use and acceptance of magnesium metal and its alloys in all product forms. Members are organizations or individuals engaged in the production, manufacture or marketing of metallic magnesium or those supplying materials, equipment or consulting.

18491 www.ipmi.org
International Precious Metals Institute
Miners, refiners, producers and users of precious metals, as well as research scientists and mercantilists.

18492 www.mbcea.org
Metal Building Contractors & Erectors Association
To support the professional advancement of metal building contractors, erectors, and the industry.

18493 www.mdna.org
Machinery Dealers National Association
Facebook, Twitter, LinkedIn
Represents dealers of used industrial equipment, providing members with business standards and development opportunities.

18494 www.metalforming.com
Precision Metalforming Association
For producers of metal stampings, spinnings, washers and precision sheet metal fabrications as well as suppliers of equipment, materials and services.

18495 www.mmsa.net
Mining and Metallurgical Society of America
A professional organization dedicated to increasing public awareness and understanding about mining and why mined materials are essential to modern society and human well being.

18496 www.mpif.org
Metal Powder Industries Federation
Promotes the science and industry of powder metallurgy through technical meetings, seminars, conferences, and publications.

18497 www.naad.org
National Association of Aluminum Distributors
NAAD is the trade association of North American service centers and principal suppliers engaged in marketing aluminum products.

18498 www.nffs.org
Non-Ferrous Founder's Society
Manufacturers of bronze, brass and aluminum castings.

18499 www.nwsa.com
Fernley & Fernley

18500 www.powdercoating.org
Powder Coating Institute

18501 www.sdi.org
Steel Deck Institute
Trade association providing uniform industry standards for the engineering, design, manufacture and field usage of steel decks.

18502 www.silversmithing.com
Society of American Silversmiths
Founded to preserve the art and history of handcrafted holloware and flatware plus provide support, networking and greater access to the market forsilversmiths. Educates the public as to the aesthetic and investment value of this art form.

18503 www.smacna.org
Sheet Metal and Air Conditioning Contactor's Natl
An international trade association representing 4,500 contibuting contractor firms in the sheet metal and air conditioning industry. Develops technical standards and manuals addressing all facets of the sheet metal and air conditioning industry.

18504 www.spfa.org
Steel Plate Fabricators Association

18505 www.ssci.org
Steel Service Center Institute

18506 www.steel.org
American Iron and Steel Institute
Works to protect interests of manufacturers in the steel industry.

18507 www.steeldistributors.org/asd
Association of Steel Distributors
Bestows Steel Distributor of The Year Award and the Presidents Award of Merit.

18508 www.steelnews.com
Association for Iron and Steel Technology (AIST)
SteelNews.com is a publication created by the Association for Iron and Steel Technology (AIST) for the steel community. The site features daily updates of the latest global headlines.

18509 www.steeltubeinstitute.org
Steel Tube Institute of North America
Members produce steel tubes and pipes from carbon, stainless or alloy steel, for applications ranging from large structural tubing to small redrawn tubing.

18510 www.sweets.construction.com
McGraw Hill Construction
In depth product information that lets you find, compare, select, specify and make purchase decisions in the industrial product marketplace.

18511 www.thermalspray.org
International Thermal Spray Association
Strengthens the level of awareness in general industry and government on the increasing capabilities and advantages of thermal spray technology for surface engineering through business opportunities, technical support and a social network. Contributes to growth and education in the thermal spray industry.

18512 www.titanium.org
International Titanium Association
Contact ITA for mailing list price.

18513 www.wirenet.org
Wire Association International
Technical association serving the global wire and cable industry by providing educational materials, sponsoring trade shows and international technical conferences.

18514 www.zinc.org
American Zinc Association
Provides information on the zinc industry and hosts international conference on zinc.

Associations

18515 ASM International
9639 Kinsman Road
Materials Park, OH 44073-0002

440-338-5151
800-336-5152; Fax: 440-338-4634
memberservicecenter@asminternational.org
www.asminternational.org
Facebook, Twitter, LinkedIn

Zi-Kui Liu, President
Diana Essock, Vice President
Raymond V. Fryan, Treasurer
William T. Mahoney, Secretary & CEO

The society for materials engineers and scientists, a worldwide network dedicated to advancing industry, technology and applications of metals and materials. ASM provides information references, education, research and international events.
30K Members
Founded in 1913

18516 Alabama Surface Mining Commission
PO Box 2390
Jasper, AL 35502

205-221-4130; Fax: 205-221-5077
asmc@asmc.alabama.gov
www.surface-mining.state.al.us

Dr. Randall C. Johnson, Director
Ann Miles, Executive Secretary
Carla D.Lightsey, Chief Divison of SMCR
Milton McCarthy, Legal Division

Doing its part to balance civilization's demands for natural resources and environmental conservation in the state of Alabama.
Founded in 1972

18517 Alaska Miners Association
121 W. Fireweed
Suite 120
Anchorage, AK 99503-4575

907-563-9229; Fax: 907-563-9225
ama@alaskaminers.org
www.alaskaminers.org
Facebook, Twitter, LinkedIn, Google+

Jason Brune, President
Lorna Shaw, First Vice President
Mike Satre, SecondÿVice President
Kim Aasand, Treasurer
James Fueg, Past President

Works to promote the mining industry in Alaska. It advocates the development and use of Alaska's mineral resources to provide an economic base for the State. AMA monitors the activities of State and Federal Government, Congress and the Legislature that affect mineral development.

18518 American Association for Crystal Growth
6986 S. Wadsworth Court
Litteton, CO 80128

303-539-6907; Fax: 303-482-2775
AACG@comcast.net
www.crystalgrowth.org

Mariya Zhuravleva, President
Joan Redwing, VP
Luis Zepeda-Ruiz, Treasurer
Merry Koschan, Secretary

AACG is a nonprofit technical membership organization where the primary function is a organic conference in the fall of crystal growth and characterization. A newsletter is published 3 times per year and distributed to members.
600 Members
Founded in 1966

18519 American Coal Ash Association
38800 Country Club Drive
Farmington Hills, MI 48331

720-870-7897; Fax: 720-870-7889
info@acaa-usa.org
www.acaa-usa.org

Thomas H. Adams, Executive Director
Alyssa Barto, Member Liaison
John Ward, Communications Coordinator

A non-profit trade association devoted to recycling the materials created from burning coal.
Founded in 1968

18520 American Exploration and Mining Association
10 N Post St
Suite 305
Spokane, WA 99201-0722

509-624-1158; Fax: 509-623-1241
info@miningamerica.org
www.miningamerica.org

Mari-Ann Green, President
Ron Parratt, 1st Vice President
Steve Alfers, 2nd Vice President
Shelia Bush, Secretary
Laura Skaer, Executive Director

Provides liaison between mining, industry and government. Offers short course on current technology.
2000 Members
Founded in 1890

18521 American Geosciences Institute
4220 King St
Alexandria, VA 22302-1502

703-379-2480; Fax: 703-379-7563
www.agiweb.org
Facebook, Twitter

P.Patrick Leahy, Executive Director
Dr. Wayne D. Pennington, President
Dr. Sharon Mosher, President Elect
Ann Benow, Outreach and Development Director
Walter R.Sisson, Finance and administrator Director

A nonprofit federation of 45 geoscientific and professional associations that represents more than 120,000 geologists, geophysicists, and other earth scientists.
45 Members
Founded in 1948

18522 American Institute of Mining, Metallurgical & Petroleum Engineers
12999 East Adam Aircraft Circle
Eglewood, CO 80112-5991

303-325-5185; Fax: 888-702-0049
aime@aimehq.org
www.aimehq.org
Facebook, LinkedIn, YouTube, RSS

Brajendra Fattahi, President
Garry W. Warren, President-Elect
Nikhil C. Trivedi, President-Elect Designate
Dale E. Heinz, Past President
Drew Meyer, Trustee

Supporting member societies by exercising fiscal responsibility, distributing funds, facilitating interaction with the larger scientific and engineering community, enhancing collaboration among the member societies, and honoring the legacy and traditions of AIME.
130M Members
Founded in 1871

18523 American Institute of Professional Geologists
1333 W 120th Avenue
Suite 211
Westminster, CO 80234

303-412-6205; Fax: 303-253-9220
aipg@aipg.org
aipg.org
Facebook, LinkedIn

Aaron W Johnson, Executive Director
Wendy J Davidson, Assistant Director

Founded to certify the credentials of practicing geologists and to advocate on behalf of the profession.
5000 Members
Founded in 1963

18524 Arizona Mining Association
916 W Adams St
Suite B-134
Phoenix, AZ 85007

602-266-4416; Fax: 602-230-8413
www.azmining.org

Sydney Hay, President
June Castelhano, Administrative Assistant

Recognizes the importance of educating Arizona's citizens about the critical role the mining industry plays not only in our state and nation, but also in the world.
Founded in 1965

18525 Arizona State Mine Inspectors
1700 West Washington
4th Floor
Phoenix, AZ 85007-4655

602-542-5971; Fax: 602-542-5335
www.asmi.az.gov

John Stanford, Sr.Deputy Mine Inspector
Tim Evans, Assistant State Mine Inspector
Jack Speer, Deputy Mine Inspector Reclamation
Wiiliam Schifferns, Deputy Mine Inspector

Priority mission is to enforce state mining laws which protect mine employees, residents, and the Arizona environment. Focused on providing the best customer service to Arizona residents and mining enterprises.
330 Members
Founded in 1912

18526 Association for Mineral Exploration British Columbia
889 W Pender Street
Suite 800
Vancouver, BC V6C-3B2

604-689-5271; Fax: 604-681-2363
info@amebc.ca
www.amebc.ca
Facebook, Twitter

Gavin C Dirom, President/CEO
Rick Conte, Vice President
David McLelland, Chair
Diane Nicolson, Vice Chair
Sam Adkins, Director

AME BC is the predominant voice of mineral exploration and development in British Columbia.
5400 Members
Founded in 1912

18527 Association of Bituminous Contractors
1250 Eye St NW
Suite 620
Washington, DC 20005-5976

202-296-5745; Fax: 202-331-8049

William H Howe, President

Members are general and independent contractors constructing coal mines and coal mine facili-

ties and also bargains with the United Mine Workers.
150 Members
Frequency: Annual/March

18528 Association of Equipment Manufacturers
6737 West Washington Street
Suite 2400
Milwaukee, WI 53214-5647

414-272-0943; Fax: 414-212-1170
aem@aem.org
www.aem.org
Facebook, Twitter, LinkedIn, YouTube

Jeffrey R. Reed, Chair

Represents manufacturers of equipment, including machinery used in architectural, construction, forestry, mining and utility industries.
900+ Members

18529 Bureau of Land Management
1849 C Street NW
Room 5665
Washington, DC 20240

202-208-3801; Fax: 202-208-5242
www.blm.gov
Facebook, Twitter, LinkedIn, YouTube

Ted Bingham, President
Robert C Bruce, VP

18530 California Mining Association
1029 J Street
Suite 420
Sacramento, CA 95814

916-554-1000; Fax: 916-554-1042
spridmore@calcima.org
www.calcima.org

Adam Harper, Association Manager
Stephanie Pridmore, Association Administrator
Gary W. Hambly, President/CEO

Represents the breadth and depth of California's mining industry including producers of precious metals (such as gold and silver), industrial minerals (including borates, limestone, rare earth elements, clays, gypsum and tungsten) and rock, sand and gravel.

18531 Canadian Institute of Mining, Metallurgy and Petroleum
3500 de Maisonneuve Blvd. W.
Suite 1250
Westmount, QC H3Z-3C1

514-939-2710; Fax: 514-939-2714
cim@cim.org
www.cim.org
Facebook, Twitter, LinkedIn, YouTube

Russell E Hallbauer, CIM President
Jean Vavrek, CIM Executive Director
Danielle Langlois, Director
Benoit Sawyer, Controller
Jasen Coady, Web Developer

The leading technical society of professionals in the Canadian minerals, metals, materials and energy industries.
12000 Members
Founded in 1898

18532 China Clay Producers Association CCPA
113 Arkwright Landing
Macon, GA 31210

478-757-1211; Fax: 478-757-1949
info@georgiamining.org
www.kaolin.com/

Lee Lemke, Executive VP

The mission of the China Clay Producers Association is to promote the common business interest of producers of china clay and the development of coordinated policies, which assure the industry will continue to provide jobs and contribute to the Georgia economy. In addition, objectives also include informing members of proposed legislation, regulatory actions and other matters affecting the kaolin industry, and to maintain the industry's strong community commitment.
Founded in 1978

18533 Colorado Mining Association
216 16th St
Suite 1250
Denver, CO 80202-5161

303-575-9199; Fax: 303-575-9194
colomine@coloradomining.org
www.coloradomining.org
Facebook, Twitter

Stuart Sanderson, President
Fred J. Menzer, Chairman
William Zisch, Chairman-Elect
Stephen A. Onorofskie, Treasurer

Composed of both small and large enterprises engaged in the exploration for, production and refining of, metals, coal, oil shale, and industrial minerals; firms that manufacture and distribute mining and mineral processing equipment and supplies; and other institutions providing services and supplies to the mineral industry.
Founded in 1876

18534 Copper Development Association
7918 Jones Branch Dr.
Suite 300
McLean, VA 22102

212-251-7200
www.copper.org
Facebook, Twitter, LinkedIn, Google+

Thomas S. Passek, President
Andrew G. Kireta, Vice President, Market Development
Luis Lozano, Technical Consultant

CDA is committed to promoting the proper use of copper materials in sustainable, efficient applications for business, industry and the home.
52 Members
Founded in 1963

18535 Desert Research Institute
2215 Raggio Pkwy
Reno, NV 89512-1095

775-673-7300; Fax: 775-673-7421
www.dri.edu
Facebook, Twitter

Stephen G Wells, President
Ellen Oppenheim, SVP, Finance & Admin/COO
Dr. Alan Gertler, VP, Research/Chief Science Officer
Chris Fritsen, VP, Academic and Faculty Affairs
Chris Ipsen, Assistant VP IT/CIO

A nonprofit statewide division of the university and community college system of Nevada, DRI pursues a full-time program of basic and applied environmental research on a local, national, and international scale. DRI employees nearly 400 full and part-time staff scientists, technicians, and support personnel.
Founded in 1959

18536 Environmental Information Association
6935 Wisconsin Avenue
Suite 306
Chevy Chase, MD 20815-6112

301-961-4999
888-343-4342; Fax: 301-961-3094
info@eia-usa.org
www.eia-usa.org

Brent Kynoch, Managing Director
Kim Goodman, Membership and marketing Manager
Kelly Rut, Development Manager
Nehmesah Israel, Admin Assistant
Chris Gates, Treasurer

Providing the environmental industry with the information needed to remain knowledgeable, responsible, and competitive in the environmental health and safety industry.

18537 Excavation Engineering Associates
1352 SW 175th Street
Seattle, WA 98166

206-248-7388; Fax: 206-244-7994
www.crimsonengineering.com
Facebook, Twitter, LinkedIn, Google+

Estelle Friant, Secretary
James E.Friant, President

Underground excavation.

18538 Federal Mine Safety and Health Review Commission
1331 Pennsylvania Avenue, NW, Suite 520N
Suite 520N
Washington, DC 20004-1710

202-434-9900; Fax: 202-434-9906
fmshrc@fmshrc.gov
www.fmshrc.gov

Richard Baker, Executive Director

Independent adjudicative agency that provides administrative trial and apellate review of legal disputes arising under the Federal Mine Safety and Health Amendments Act of 1977 (mine act).

18539 Geological Society of America
PO Box 9140
Boulder, CO 80301-9140

303-357-1000
800-472-1988; Fax: 303-357-1070
gsa@geosociety.org
www.geosociety.org
Facebook, Twitter, LinkedIn, YouTube

Jonathan G. Price, President
Claudia I. Mora, Vice President
Bruce R. Clark, Treasurer
Vicki McConnell, Executive Director/Secretary
Nancy L. Wright, Technical Program Manager

Provides access to elements that are essential to the professional growth of earth scientists at all levels of expertise and from all sectors, academic, government, business, and industry. Membership unites thousands of earth scientists from every corner of the globe in a common purpose to study the mysteries of our planet and share scientific findings.
16000 Members
Founded in 1888

18540 Gold Prospectors Association of America
43445 Business Park Drive
Suite #113
Temecula, CA 92590

951-699-4749
800-551-9707; Fax: 951-699-4062
info@goldprospectors.org
www.goldprospectors.org
Facebook, Twitter, LinkedIn, YouTube

Thomas Massie, CEO

GPAA is the largest recreational gold prospecting club. Owner of The Outdoor Channel, a cable TV channel featuring real outdoors for real people.
35M Members
Founded in 1968

18541 Idaho Mining Association
802 W Bannock St
Suite 301
Boise, ID 83702-5840

208-342-0031; Fax: 208-345-4210
ima@mineidaho.com
www.mineidaho.com/
Twitter

Randy Vranes, President
Corey Millard, 1st Vice President
Dennis Facer, 2nd Vice President
Jack Lyman, Executive Vice President

Founded to further the interests of Idaho's mining industry and minerals production. Mission is to act as the unified voice for its members to ensure the long-term health and well being of Idaho's mining industry.

Founded in 1903

18542 International Lead Association
2 Bravingtons Walk
London N1 9AF

44 (0)20 7833 8090; Fax: 44 (0)20 7833 1611
enq@ila-lead.org
www.ila-lead.org
Twitter, LinkedIn

Nonprofit trade association representing the lead industries in the US and abroad. It collects and distributes information about the users of lead products in industry, vehicles, radioactive waste disposal and noise barriers. Its services are availble, generally free of charge, to anyone interested in the uses of lead and lead products.

18543 Lignite Energy Council
1016 E. Owens Avenue
PO Box 2277
Bismarck, ND 58502-2277

701-258-7117
800-932-7117; Fax: 701-258-2755
lec@lignite.com
www.lignite.com
Facebook, Twitter, LinkedIn, YouTube

Jason Bohrer, President/CEO
Alan Hodnik, Chairman
Robert McLennan, Chairman-Elect
Mike Jones, Ph. D., VP, Research and Development
Steve Van Dyke, VP, Communications

Regional Trade Association - promotes policies and activities that maintain a viable lignite industry and enhance development of our regions' lignite resources.

355 Members
Founded in 1974

18544 Mine Safety Institue of America
319 Paintersville Road
Hunker, PA 15139

724-925-5150
sikora.lisa@dol.gov

Frank Linkous, President
Ronnie Biggerstaff, 1st VP
Joseph Sbaffoni, 2nd VP
William Gerringer, 3rd VP
Gerald E. Davis, Secretary/Treasurer

The objectives of the Mine Safety Institute of America is to provide successful educational programs, safer and healthier working conditions, more productivity in the mining industry, and support of good legislature pertaining to mining.

Founded in 1908

18545 Mine Safety and Health Administration
1100 Wilson Blvd
21st Floor
Arlington, VA 22209-3939

202-693-9400
800-746-1553; Fax: 202-693-9401
www.msha.gov

David G Dye, Executive Director

Administers the Federal Mine Safety and Health Act of 1977 (Mine Act) and enforces compliance with mandatory safety and health standards as a means to eliminate fatal accidents; to reduce the frequency and severity of nonfatal accidents, to minimize health hazards and to promote mineral processing operations in the US, regardless of size, employees, commodity mined or method of extraction.

18546 Mineral Economics and Management Society
Colorado School Of Mines
Golden, CO 49931

303-273-3150; Fax: 906-487-2944

Patricia Dillon, President

A society for mineral, energy, and natural resource professionals who apply economics, finance and policy analysis to the issues facing the minerals and materials industries. These issues include supply and demand of mineral commodities, international trade in mineral and energy raw materials, environmental issues, natural resource, mineral and energy conservation, and related government policies.

200 Members
Founded in 1991

18547 Mineral Information Institute
12999 E. Adam Aircraft Circle
Englewood, CO 80112

303-948-4236; Fax: 303-948-4265
www.mineralseducationcoalition.org/
Facebook, Twitter, LinkedIn, YouTube

Jaqueline S. Dorr, Manager

Nonprofit organization dedicated to educating youth about the science of minerals and other natural resources and about their importance in our everyday lives.

18548 Minerals, Metals & Materials Society
184 Thorn Hill Road
Warrendale, PA 15086-7514

800-759-4867
800-759-4867; Fax: 724-776-3770
webmaster@tms.org
www.tms.org
Facebook, LinkedIn

James Robinson, Executive Director
Adrianne Carolla, Deputy Executive Director
Peter DeLuca, Accountant

Dedicated to the development and dissemination of the scientific and engineering knowledge bases for materials-centered technologies.

18549 Mining Foundation of the Southwest
PO Box 42317
Tucson, AZ 85733

520-577-7519; Fax: 520-577-7073
admin@miningfoundationsw.org
www.miningfoundationsw.org

Thomas Aldrich, President
Amanda W. Brick, Executive Manager

Advances the science of mining and related industries by educating members and the public. Annual American Mining Hall of Fame First Saturday in December. A newsletter is published.

92 Members
Founded in 1982

18550 Mining and Metallurgical Society of America
PO Box 810
PO Box 810
Boulder, CO 80306-0810

303-444-6032; Fax: 415-897-1380
contactmmsa@mmsa.net
www.mmsa.net
Facebook, Twitter, LinkedIn

Alan K Burton, Business Manager
Mark leVier, President
Robert Schafer, VP
Kenneth Brunk, Treasurer

Concerned with the conservation of the nation's mineral resources and the best interest of the mining and metallurgical industries.

350 Members
Founded in 1908

18551 National Association of State Land Reclamationists
Coal Research Center/Southern Illinois University
47 School Street
Suite 301
Philippi, WV 26416

304-940-0271; Fax: 618-453-7346
aharrington@crc.siu.edu
naslr.org

Sam Faith, President
Janet Yates, Vice President
Derek Giebell, Secretary/Treasurer
Jennifer Keese, Chairman

The National Association of State and Land Reclamationists advocates the use of research, innovative technology and professional discourse to foster the restoration of lands and waters affected by mining related activities.

140 Members
Founded in 1972

18552 National Lime Association
200 N Glebe Rd
Suite 800
Arlington, VA 22203-3728

703-243-5463; Fax: 703-243-5489
www.lime.org

William C.Herz, Executive Director
Arline Seeger, General Counsel
Hunter Prillaman, Director Of Government Affairs
Robert Hirsch, Director of Environment
Lori D.Oney, Admin Director

Trade association for US and Canadian manufacturers of high calcium quicklime, dolomitic quicklime and hydrated lime, collectively referred to as lime. NLA represents the interests of its members in Washington, provides input on standards and specifications for lime, and funds and manages research on current and new uses for lime.

63 Members
Founded in 1902

18553 National Mining Association
101 Constitution Ave Nw
Suite 500 East
Washington, DC 20001-2133

202-463-2600; Fax: 202-463-2666
webmaster@nma.org
www.nma.org
YouTube

Harry M. Conger, Chairman
Kevin Cruntchfield, Vice Chairman
Rich Nolan, Senior VP
Hal Quinn, President & CEO
Bruce Watzman, SVP, Regulatory Affairs

The voice of U.S. mining in Washington.

325 Members
Founded in 1995

18554 **National Ocean Industries Association**
1120 G St NW
Suite 900
Washington, DC 20005-3801

202-347-6900; Fax: 202-347-8650
jwilliams@noia.org
www.noia.org
Facebook, Twitter, LinkedIn, YouTube

Randall Luthi, President
Franki Stuntz, Sr.VP
Anna Chapman, VP, Conferences & Special Events
Nicoltte Nye, VP, Comm. &ÿIndustry Affairs
Jeff Vorberger, VP, Policy & Government Affairs

National organization engaged in offshore construction, drilling and petroleum production, geophysical exploration, ship building and repair, deep-sea mining and related activities in the development and use of marine resources.
300 Members
Founded in 1972

18555 **National Ready Mixed Concrete Association**
900 Spring St
Silver Spring, MD 20910-4015

240-485-1139; Fax: 301-585-4219
info@nrmca.org
www.nrmca.org
Facebook, Twitter, LinkedIn, YouTube

Michael Phillips, President
Nicole Maher, Chief Operating Officer
Joe Roche, Chief Financial Officer
Alex Land, Director, Memberhsip Engagement
Frank Cavaliere, Director, Special Programs & Coord.

The mission of the National Ready Mixed Concrete Association is to provide exceptional value for our members by responsibly representing and serving the entire ready mixed concrete industry through leadership, promotion, education, and partnering to ensure ready mixed concrete is the building material of choice.
1200 Members
Founded in 1930

18556 **National Stone, Sand & Gravel Association**
1605 King St
Alexandria, VA 22314-2726

703-525-8788
800-342-1415; Fax: 703-525-7782
jwilson@nssga.org
www.nssga.org
Facebook, Twitter, LinkedIn, YouTube

Michael Johnson, President & CEO
Jason Epstein, Director, Membership
Jennifer Dugas, VP, Meetings & Events
Chuck Fuqua, VP, Communications
Cesar ÿ Silva Orrego, VP, Finance & Administration

Represents the stone, sand and gravel — or aggregate — industries. Our members account for 90 percent of the crushed stone and 70 percent of the sand and gravel produced annually in the US.
25 Members
Founded in 1916

18557 **Nevada Mining Association**
201 W. Liberty Street
Suite 300
Reno, NV 89501

775-829-2121; Fax: 775-852-2631
www.nevadamining.org
Facebook, Twitter, YouTube

Tim Crowley, President
Dylan Shaver, Public Affairs
Lauren Arends, Office Manager
Joseph Riney, Information System Administrator

Represents all aspects of the mining industry. Provides representation for the broad mining industry in public outreach activities such as public relations, media relations, and community relations.

18558 **North American Insulation Manufacturers Association**
11 Canal Center Plaza
Suite 103
Alexandria, VA 22314

703-684-0084; Fax: 703-684-0427
www.naima.org

Curt Rich, President & CEO
Stacy Fitzgerald-Redd, Dir., Marketing & Communications

An authoritative resource on energy-efficiency, sustainable performance, and the application and safety of fiber glass, rock wool, and slag wool insulation products. The voice of the insulation industry for architects and builders, design, process and maintenance engineers, contractors, code groups and standards organizations, government agencies, public interest, energy and environmental groups, and homeowners.

18559 **Perlite Institute**
2207 Forest Hills Drive
Suite A
Harrisburg, PA 17112

717-238-9723; Fax: 717-238-9985
info@perlite.org
www.perlite.org
Facebook, Twitter

Denise Calabrese, Executive Director
Michelle Keyser, Communications Director
Lori Zelesko, Events Director
Jennifer Swartz, Finance Administrator

An international association which establishes product standards and specifications, and which encourages the development of new product uses through research.
183 Members
Founded in 1949

18560 **Rocky Mountain Association of Geologists**
910 16th Stÿ
Suite 1214
Denver, CO 80202-2997

303-573-8621; Fax: 303-476-2241
staff@rmag.org
www.rmag.org

Larry Rasmussen, President
Stephen Sturm, First VP
Catherine Campbell, Second VP
Barbara Kuzmic, Executive Director
2000 Members
Founded in 1922

18561 **Silver Institute**
1400 I Street, NW
Suite 550
Washington, DC 20005

202-835-0185; Fax: 202-835-0155
info@silverinstitute.org
www.silverinstitute.org

Robert Quartermain, President
Michael Dirienzo, Executive Director

International association of miners, refiners, fabricators and wholesalers of silver and silver products.

18562 **Silver Users Association**
3930 walnut Street
Suite 210
Fairfax, VA 22030

703-930-7790
800-245-6999; Fax: 703-359-7562
sas@silversmithing.com
www.silverusersassociation.org

Bill Le Roy, President
Mike Huber, VP
John King, Secretary
Bill Hamelin, Treasurer
29 Members
Founded in 1947

18563 **Silver Valley Mining Association**
604 Bank St.
Wallace, ID 83873

208-556-1621

Dedicated to promoting the Silver Valley of northern Idaho and its mining industry. Informs the public of the history and merits of the region, serving various beneficiary needs of the mining industry, and serving those who work in the industry and the investing public.

18564 **Society for Mining, Metallurgy & Exploration**
12999 E. Adam Aircraft Circle
Englewood, CO 80112

303-948-4200
800-763-3132; Fax: 303-973-3845
sme@smenet.org
www.smenet.org
Facebook, Twitter, LinkedIn, YouTube, Google+

John N. Murphy, President
Drew A. Meyer, President-Elect

Advances the worldwide mining and minerals community through information exchange and professional development.
13000 Members
Founded in 1957

18565 **Society of Economic Geologists**
7811 Shaffer Pkwy
Littleton, CO 80127-3732

720-981-7874; Fax: 720-981-7874
seg@segweb.org
www.segweb.org
Facebook, Twitter, LinkedIn, YouTube

Fran‡ois Robert, President
Robert P. Foster, President-Elect
A. Jamesÿ Macdonald, Vice President for Regional Affairs
Regina M. Baumgartner, VP, Student Affairs
Brian G Hoal, Executive Director

International organization of individual members with interests in the field of economic geology. Membership includes representatives from the industry, academia and government institutions. Annual meetings, publications, field conferences and short courses ensure active communication of economic geology related concepts with the membership and the economic geology profession at large.
3400 Members
Founded in 1920

18566 **Society of Exploration Geophysicists**
8801 South Yale
Suite 500
Tulsa, OK 74137-3575

918-497-5500; Fax: 918-497-5557
web@seg.org
www.seg.org
Facebook, Twitter, LinkedIn, YouTube, Google+

Dr. Bob A. Hardage, President
Dr. David James Monk, President-Elect
Dr. Wafik Bulind Beydoun, Vice-President
Nancy Jo House, Secretary/ Treasurer
Dr. Tamas Nemeth, Editor

The Society of Exploration Geophysicists/SEG is a not-for-profit organization that promotes the science of geophysics and the education of

applied geophysicists. SEG fosters the expert and ethical practice of geophysics in the exploration and development of natural resources, in characterizing the near surface, and in mitigating earth hazards.
Founded in 1930

18567 **Society of Mineral Analysts**
PO Box 50085
Sparks, NV 89435-0085

562-467-8980
Facebook, Twitter, LinkedIn

Patrick Brown, Director

The Society of Mineral Analysts is a non-profit organization, whose members are assayers, chemists, laboratory managers, geologists, suppliers and vendors both in and serving the mineral analysis industry.
250 Members
Founded in 1986

18568 **Sorptive Minerals Institute**
1155 15th St NW
Suite 500
Washington, DC 20005-2725

202-289-2760; Fax: 202-530-0659
www.sorptive.org

Lee Coogan, Executive Director

The Sorptive Minerals Institute represents the absorbent clay industry and is a not-for-profit industry trade association that would serve as the marketing, promotion and research arm of the absorbent clay indsutry with the goal of enhancing long-range growth and profitability.
Founded in 1970

18569 **Sulphur Institute**
1020 19th Street NW, Suite 520
Washington, DC 20036

202-331-9660; Fax: 202-293-2940
sulphur@sulphurinstitute.org
www.sulphurinstitute.org

Robert J Morris, President
Thomas W.Dunn, Director
Joshua C.Maak, Communications Manager
Donald S.Messik, VP,Communications

The Sulphur Institute (TSI) is an international, non-profit organization established in 1960. The Institute is the global advocate for sulphur, representing all stakeholders engaged in producing, consuming, trading, handling or adding value to sulphur. We seek to provide a common voice for all stakeholders to promote the uninterrupted, efficient and safe handling and transportation of all sulphur products while protecting the best interests of the environment
Founded in 1960

18570 **US Geological Survey**
950 National Ctr
Reston, VA 20192-0001

703-648-4302; Fax: 703-648-6373
dc_va@usgs.gov
www.usgs.gov

Founded in 1879

18571 **United Mine Workers of America International Union**
18354 Quantico Gateway Drive
Suite 200
Triangle, VA 22172

703-291-2400; Fax: 703-208-7227
www.umwa.org

Cecil E Roberts, President
Daniel J Kane, Secretary/Treasurer

The United Mine Workers of America International Union is an organization with a diverse membership that includes coal miners, clean coal technicians, health care workers, truck drivers, manufacturing workers and public employees throughout the United States and Canada. The Union works to fight for safe workplaces, good wages and benefits, and fair representation.
120M Members
Founded in 1890

18572 **Utah Mining Association**
136 S Main St
Suite 709
Salt Lake City, UT 84101-1683

801-364-1874; Fax: 801-364-2640
mining@utahmining.org
www.utahmining.org
Facebook, Twitter

Mark Karll, Chairman
Greg Gergory, Vice Chairman
Mark Compton, President
Mike Brown, 1st Vice President
Chadd Baker, 2nd Vice President

Provides its members with full-time professional industry representation before the State Legislature; various government regulatory agencies on the federal, state and local levels; other associations, and business and industry groups. Helps to promote and protect the mining industry.
Founded in 1915

18573 **Women in Mining National Organization**
PO Box 260246
Lakewood, CO 80226-0246

303-298-1535
866-537-9697
wim@womeninmining.org

Betty Mahaffey, President
Christine Ballard, Vice President
Stephen Tibbals, Treasurer
Hannah McNally, Secretary

Women in Mining/WIM was founded in 1972 in Denver, Colorado, by several women whose intent was to facilitate education about the mining industry for themselves and for those not acquainted with the role the industry plays in their lives. In addition to providing valuable educations benefits, the WIM organization offers members an opportunity to become acquainted and work with others involved in the mining industry and thereby acquire new personal and professional contacts.
600 Members

18574 **World Gold Council**
510 Madison Ave
9th Floor
New York, NY 10022

212-317-3800; Fax: 212-688-0410
www.gold.org
Facebook, Twitter, Google+

Organization formed and funded by the world's leading gold mining companies with the aim of stimulating and maximizing the demand for, and holding of gold by consumers, investors, industry and the official sector.
Founded in 1987

Newsletters

18575 **AME BC News**
Assoc for Mineral Exploration British Columbia
889 W Pender Street
Suite 800
Vancouver, BC V6C-3B2

604-689-5271; Fax: 604-681-2363
info@amebc.ca
www.amebc.ca

Gavin C Dirom, President/CEO

A member e-newsletter that captures essential mineral exploration and mining news, announces important upcoming events, gives an inside look at what is happening within AME BC, announces new and renewed members and more.
5400 Members
Frequency: Bi-Weekly
Founded in 1912

18576 **ASH at Work**
American Coal Ash Association
38800 Country Club Drive
Farmington Hill, MI 48331

720-870-7897; Fax: 720-870-7889
info@acaa-usa.org
www.acaa-usa.org

Thomas H. Adams, Executive Director
Alyssa Barto, Member Liaison
John Ward, Communications Coordinator

Published twice a year, it is the only magazine covering all facets of the coal combustion products industry.
160 Members
Frequency: 2x/Year
Founded in 1968
Printed in 4 colors on glossy stock

18577 **Alaska Geology Survey News**
Alaska Division of Geological Survey
3354 College Rd
Fairbanks, AK 99709-3707

907-451-5000; Fax: 907-451-5050
www.dggs.dnr.state.ak.us

Robert Swenson, Executive Director
Trudy Wassel, Business Manager
John Parrott, Manager

Alaska miners and earth scientists.
4 Pages
Frequency: Monthly
Printed in on glossy stock

18578 **Bulletin**
Northwest Mining Association
10 N Post St
Suite 220
Spokane, WA 99201-0722

509-624-1158; Fax: 509-623-1241
www.nwma.org

Laura Skaer, Executive Director
Mike Heywood, Marketing Director

Published every six weeks. 12-16 page newsletter covering issues relevant to the hardrock mining industry.
Circulation: 1500
Founded in 1895

18579 **Coal Week International**
McGraw Hill
PO Box 182604
Columbus, CO 43272

877-833-5524
800-752-8878; Fax: 614-759-3749
www.mcgraw-hill.com

John Slater, Publisher

Offers information and news to and of the mining industry in North America.
Cost: $467.00
Frequency: Monthly
Founded in 1884

18580 **Coaldat Productivity Report**
Pasha Publications
1600 Wilson Boulevard
Suite 600
Arlington, VA 22209-2510

703-528-1244
800-424-2908; Fax: 703-528-1253

Harry Baisden, Group Publisher
Michael Hopps, Editor
Kathy Thorne, Circulatin Manager

Shows quarterly and year-to-date total coal production in tons, productivity in tons per miner per

day, average number of employees for each mine, mining methods used, controlling company, mine location, district number, union affiliation and whether the mine is surface or underground. Both a controlling company and a state/country format are available.
Cost: $545.00
60 Pages
Frequency: Quarterly

18581 **Concentrates Newsletter**
PO Box 42317
Tucson, AZ 85733
520-577-7519; Fax: 520-577-7073
admin@miningfoundationsw.org
www.miningfoundationsw.org
Thomas Aldrich, President
Amanda W. Brick, Office Manager
Querterly newsletter providing members with news and updates regarding the Foundation
90 Pages
Frequency: Quarterly
Founded in 1973

18582 **Control**
Putman Media Company
555 W Pierce Rd
Suite 301,Pierce Road
Itasca, IL 60143-2626
630-467-1300; Fax: 630-467-0197
jcappelletti@putman.net
www.putman.net
John Cappelletti, President
Walter Boies, Circulation Manager
Designed for instrumentation and control systems professionals.
Frequency: Fortnightly
Circulation: 35000
Founded in 1945

18583 **Legal Quarterly Digest of Mine Safety and Health Decisions**
Legal Publication Services
888 Pittsford Mendon Center Road
Pittsford, NY 14534
585-582-3211; Fax: 585-582-2879
MineSafety@aol.com
www.minesafety.com
Ellen Smith, Owner/publisher
Melanie Aclander, Editor
Covers legal decisions on health and safety law in the mining industry.
Cost: $525.00
100 Pages
Frequency: Annual+
Founded in 1991

18584 **Machinery Outlook**
Manfredi & Associates
20934 W Lakeview Pkwy
Mundelein, IL 60060-9502
847-949-9080; Fax: 847-949-9910
frank@manfredi.com
www.machineryoutlook.com
Frank Manfredi, President
A newsletter about and for the construction and mining machinery industry.
Cost: $365.00
14 Pages
Frequency: Monthly
Founded in 1984
Printed in one color on matte stock

18585 **Mine Regulation Reporter**
Pasha Publications
1600 Wilson Boulevard
Suite 600
Arlington, VA 22209-2509
703-528-1244
800-424-2908; Fax: 703-528-1253
Harry Baisden, Group Publisher
Michael Hopps, Editor
Kathy Thorne, Circulation Manager
The only biweekly newsletter and document service in the US for mine safety and environmental managers and attorneys. It covers mine safety, health and environmental regulations, legislation and court decisions that affect mine operations.
Cost: $785.00
Frequency: BiWeekly

18586 **Mining and Metallurgical Society of America Newsletter**
476 Wilson Avenue
Novato, CA 94947-4236
415-897-1380; Fax: 415-899-0262
contactmmsa@mmsa.net
www.mmsa.net
Alan K Burton, Executive Director
Society news and information for professionals in the mining industry.
6 Pages
Founded in 1908

18587 **The Outcrop**
Rocky Mountain Association of Geologists
910 16th St
Suite 1214
Denver, CO 80202-2997
303-573-8621; Fax: 303-476-2241
staff@rmag.org
www.rmag.org
Facebook, Twitter, LinkedIn
Larry Rasmussen, President
Barbara Kuzmic, Executive Director
Will Duggins, Managing Editor
Cheryl Fountain, Associate Editor
RMAG newsletter detailing member activities, organization events, and topics of interest.
2000 Members
Founded in 1922

18588 **Utah Mining Association Newsletter**
Utah Mining Association
136 South Main Street
Suite 709
Salt Lake City, UT 84101-1683
801-364-1874; Fax: 801-364-2640
mining@utahmining.org
www.utahmining.org
Todd Bingham, President
Bryan Nielson, Chairman
Marilyn Tuttle, Office Manager
Provides updates on the mining industry.

18589 **e-DIGEST & Washington Watch Newsletter**
National Stone, Sand & Gravel Association
1605 King St
Alexandria, VA 22314-2726
703-525-8788
800-342-1415; Fax: 703-525-7782
jwilson@nssga.org
www.nssga.org
Jennifer Joy Wilson, President & CEO
Gus Edwards, Executive Vice President
Janice B. Springs, Executive Assistant
Member benefit of the NSSGA. Available online only.
25 Members
Frequency: Weekly
Founded in 1916

Magazines & Journals

18590 **Alaska Miner**
Alaska Miners Association
3305 Arctic Blvd
Suite 105
Anchorage, AK 99503-4575
907-563-9229; Fax: 907-563-9225
ama@alaskaminers.org
www.alaskaminers.org
Steven Borell, Executive Director
News and developments regarding Alaskan mining efforts.

18591 **Alaska Miners Association Journal**
Alaska Miners Association
3305 Arctic Boulevard
Suite 105
Anchorage, AK 99503-4575
907-563-9229; Fax: 907-563-9225
ama@alaskaminers.org
www.alaskaminers.org
Steven Borell, Executive Director

18592 **CIM Magazine**
Canadian Inst of Mining, Metallurgy & Petroleum
3400 de Maisonneuve Boulevard W
Suite 855
Montreal, QC H3Z-3B8
514-939-2710; Fax: 514-939-2714
www.cim.org
Dawn Nelley, Publications
Provides important information on mine developments, new technologies, safety, HR, products and services, and business issues.
Frequency: 8x's a Year
Circulation: 11,289

18593 **Canadian Mining Journal**
Northern Miner
320-255 Duncan Mill Rd.
Toronto, ON M3B 3K9
416-510-6789
888-502-3456; Fax: 416-510-5138
northernminer2@northernminer.com
www.northernminer.com
John Cumming, Editor-In-Chief
Anthony Vaccaro, Group Publisher
Joe Crofts, Advertising Sales Manager
Provides readers with news on Canadian mining and exploration, technologies, operations, corporate dvelopments, and industry events.
Cost: $51.95

18594 **Coal**
MacLean Hunter
29 N Wacker Drive
Floor 9
Chicago, IL 60606-3298
312-726-2802; Fax: 312-726-4103
Art Sanda, Editor
Elisabeth O'Grady, Executive Director
Articles cover maintenance and production of coal mines.
Cost: $62.50
Frequency: Monthly
Circulation: 22,000
Founded in 1964

18595 **Coal Age**
Primedia

29 N Wacker Avenue
10th Floor
Chicago, IL 60606

312-726-2802; Fax: 312-726-2574
www.coalage.com

Peter Johnson, Publisher
Stever P Fiscor, Editor-in-Chief
Ben Fromenthal, Production Manager

Geared primarily toward professionals in the coal mining and processing industries. Coal Age focuses on news, with in-depth features on coal mining operations and changing technologies.
Cost: $49.00
54 Pages
Frequency: Monthly
Circulation: 17900
ISSN: 1040-7820
Founded in 1911
Printed in 4 colors on glossy stock

18596 Coal Journal
PO Box 3068
Pikeville, KY 41502-3068

606-432-0206; Fax: 606-432-2162

Terry L May, Publisher

Information concentrating on government regulations, emerging technologies and trade literature, and analyzes governmental actions and their impact on the coal industry.
Frequency: Quarterly
Circulation: 10000

18597 Coal People
Al Skinner Enterprises
PO Box 6247
Charleston, WV 25362-247

304-342-4129
800-235-5188; Fax: 304-343-3124
cpm@newwave.net
www.coalpeople.com

Al Skinner, Editor
Christina Karaum, Managing Editor
Beth Terranova, Sales Manager
Angela McNealy, Circulation Manager

Features special news and product sections for the coal industry. Home interest, historical pices, coal industry personalities.
Cost: $25.00
60 Pages
Frequency: 10 times ayear
Circulation: 11500
Founded in 1976
Printed in 4 colors on glossy stock

18598 Diamonds in Canada
Northern Miner
320-255 Duncan Mill Rd.
Toronto, ON M3B 3K9

416-510-6789
888-502-3456; Fax: 416-510-5138
northernminer2@northernminer.com
www.northernminer.com

John Cumming, Editor-In-Chief
Anthony Vaccaro, Group Publisher
Joe Crofts, Advertising Sales Manager

Provides readers with information on the Canadian diamond industry, including round-ups of diamand exploration projects and engineering innovations.
Frequency: Bi-Annual

18599 EARTH Magazine
American Geosciences Institute
4220 King St
Alexandria, VA 22302-1502

703-379-2480; Fax: 703-379-7563
www.earthmagazine.org
Facebook, Twitter

Patrick Leahy, Executive Director
Dr. Wayne D. Pennington, President
Dr. Sharon Mosher, President Elect
Michael D. Lawless, Treasurer
Dr. Berry H. Tew, Jr., Secretary

The science behind the headlines.
Frequency: Monthly
Founded in 1948

18600 Engineering & Mining Journal
Primedia Publishing
330 N Wabash Avenue
Suite 2300
Chicago, IL 60611

312-595-1080; Fax: 312-595-0295
info@mining-media.com
www.e-mj.com

Peter Johnson, Publisher
Steve Fiscor, Editor

Serves the field of mining including exploration, development, milling, smelting, refining of metals and nonmetallics
108 Pages
Frequency: Monthly
Circulation: 20589
ISSN: 0095-8948
Founded in 1866
Printed in 4 colors on glossy stock

18601 Environmental & Engineering Geoscience
Geological Society of America
PO Box 9140
Boulder, CO 80301-9140

303-357-1019
800-472-1988; Fax: 303-357-1070
gsa@geosociety.org
www.geosociety.org
Facebook, Twitter, LinkedIn, YouTube

John W. Geissman, President
George H. Davis, Vice President
Jonathan G. Price, Treasurer
John W. Hess, Executive Director/ Secretary

Contains new theory, applications, and case histories illustrating the dynamics of the fast-growing environmental and applied disciplines.
16000 Members
Frequency: Quarterly
Founded in 1888

18602 GSA Today
Geological Society of America
PO Box 9140
Boulder, CO 80301-9140

303-357-1019
800-472-1988; Fax: 303-357-1070
gsa@geosociety.org
www.geosociety.org
Facebook, Twitter, LinkedIn, YouTube

John W. Geissman, President
George H. Davis, Vice President
Jonathan G. Price, Treasurer
John W. Hess, Executive Director/ Secretary

Lead science articles are refereed and should present the results of exciting new research or summarize and synthesize important problems or issues.
16000 Members
Frequency: Monthly
Founded in 1888

18603 Geology
Geological Society of America
PO Box 9140
Boulder, CO 80301-9140

303-357-1019
800-472-1988; Fax: 303-357-1070
gsa@geosociety.org
www.geosociety.org
Facebook, Twitter, LinkedIn, YouTube

John W. Geissman, President
George H. Davis, Vice President
Jonathan G. Price, Treasurer
John W. Hess, Executive Director/ Secretary

Articles cover all earth-science disciplines and include new investigations and provocative topics. Professional geologists and university-level students in the earth sciences use this widely read journal to keep up with scientific research trends.
16000 Members
Frequency: Monthly
Founded in 1888

18604 Geophysics
Society of Exploration Geophysicists
8801 South Yale
Suite 500
Tulsa, OK 74137-3575

918-497-5500; Fax: 918-497-5557
web@seg.org
www.seg.org
Facebook, Twitter, LinkedIn

Dr. Bob A. Hardage, President
Dr. David James Monk, President-Elect
Dr. Wafik Bulind Beydoun, Vice-President
Nancy Jo House, Secretary/ Treasurer
Dr. Tamas Nemeth, Editor

Encompasses all aspects of research, exploration, and education in applied geophysics.
Founded in 1930

18605 Geosphere
Geological Society of America
PO Box 9140
Boulder, CO 80301-9140

303-357-1019
800-472-1988; Fax: 303-357-1070
gsa@geosociety.org
www.geosociety.org
Facebook, Twitter, LinkedIn, YouTube

John W. Geissman, President
George H. Davis, Vice President
Jonathan G. Price, Treasurer
John W. Hess, Executive Director/ Secretary

Electronic journal, peer-reviewed covering all geoscience disciplines in a medium that accommodates animations, sound, and movie files.
16000 Members
Frequency: Bimonthly
Founded in 1888

18606 Geotimes
American Geological Institute
4220 King St
Alexandria, VA 22302-1502

703-379-2480; Fax: 703-379-7563
www.agiweb.org/
Facebook, Twitter

Dr. Wayne D. Pennington, President
Dr. Sharon Mosher, President Elect
Michael D. Lawless, Treasurer
Dr. Berry H. Tew, Jr., Secretary

Nonprofit federation of 40 geoscientific and professional associations that represents more than 100,000 geologists, geophysicsts, and other earth scientists. AGI provides information services to geoscientists, serves as a voice of shared interests in our profession, plays a major role in strengthening geoscience education, and strives to increase public awareness of the vital role the geosciences play in society's use of resources and interaction with the environment.
Cost: $42.95
250M Members
40 Pages
Frequency: Monthly
Circulation: 100000
Founded in 1948

18607 Hydrogeology Journal
Geological Society of America

PO Box 9140
Boulder, CO 80301-9140

303-357-1019
800-472-1988; Fax: 303-357-1070
gsa@geosociety.org
www.geosociety.org
Facebook, Twitter, LinkedIn, YouTube

John W. Geissman, President
George H. Davis, Vice President
Jonathan G. Price, Treasurer
John W. Hess, Executive Director/ Secretary

Features peer-reviewed papers on theoretical and applied hydrogeology. Describes worldwide progress in the science integrating subsurface hydrology and geology with supporting disciplines.
16000 Members
Frequency: Bi-Monthly
Founded in 1888

18608 JOM: The Member Journal of TMS
Minerals, Metals & Minerals Society
184 Thorn Hill Road
Warrendale, PA 15086-7514

724-776-9000
800-759-4867
724-776-9000; Fax: 724-776-3770
tmsgeneral@tms.org
www.tms.org
Facebook, LinkedIn

Garry W. Warren, President
Wolfgang A. Schneider, Vice President
Warren Hunt, Jr., Secretary/ Executive Director
Adrian C. Deneys, Director/ Chair

A technical journal devoted to exploring the many aspects of materials science and engineering. Reports scholarly work that explores the state-of-the-art processing, fabrication, design, and application of metals, ceramics, plastics, composites, and other materials.
Cost: $131.00
Frequency: Monthly
Circulation: 10000
Founded in 1948

18609 Journal of Electronic Materials
Minerals, Metals & Materials Society
184 Thorn Hill Road
Warrendale, PA 15086-7514

800-759-4867; Fax: 724-776-3770
webmaster@tms.org
www.tms.org
Facebook, LinkedIn

Reports on the science and technology of electronic materials while examining new applications for semiconductors, magnetic alloys, insulators, and optical and display materials.
Frequency: Monthly

18610 Lithosphere
Geological Society of America
PO Box 9140
Boulder, CO 80301-9140

303-357-1019
800-472-1988; Fax: 303-357-1070
gsa@geosociety.org
www.geosociety.org
Facebook, Twitter, LinkedIn, YouTube

John W. Geissman, President
George H. Davis, Vice President
Jonathan G. Price, Treasurer
John W. Hess, Executive Director/ Secretary

Peer-reviewed journal focusing on processes that affect the crust, upper mantle, landscapes, and/or sedimentary systems at all spatial and temporal scales.
16000 Members
Frequency: Bimonthly
Founded in 1888

18611 Metallurgical and Materials Transactions
ASM International
9639 Kinsman Rd
Materials Park, OH 44073-0002

440-338-5151
800-336-5152; Fax: 440-338-4634
memberservicecenter@asminternational.org
www.asminternational.org

William T. Mahoney, Secretary & CEO
Tresa M. Pollock, Principal Editor

Covers information on physical metallurgy and materials science with emphasis on processing, structure, and properties. Joint publication between ASM International and The Minerals, Metals and Materials Society.
Cost: $5658.00

18612 Mine Safety and Health News
Legal Publication Services
888 Pittsford Mendon Center Road
Pittsford, NY 14534

585-582-3211; Fax: 585-582-2879
MineSafety@aol.com
www.minesafety.com

Ellen Smith, Owner
Melanie Aclander, Editor
Cost: $525.00
Founded in 1991

18613 Mine and Quarry Trader
Primedia
7355 N Woodland Drive
PO Box 603
Indianapolis, IN 46206

317-991-1350
800-827-7468; Fax: 317-299-1356
www.mineandquarry.com

John Owen, Production Manager
Colleen Leath, Circulation Director
Kyle Agert, Publisher
Laura Larahaag, Marketing
Ellen Rolett, Manager

Equipment and services geared to the mining, aggregate and heavy construction industries.
Cost: $21.00
76 Pages
Frequency: Monthly
Circulation: 34406
Founded in 1976
Printed in 4 colors on matte stock

18614 Miners News
Miners News
9792 W Glen Ellyn Street
PO Box 4965
Boise, ID 83711

800-624-7212; Fax: 208-658-4901
minersnews@msn.com
www.minersnews.com

Gary White, Publisher
Shirley White, Public Relations

Information on mining history and provides insight into new technology and products used in mining.
Cost: $25.00
Circulation: 6512
ISSN: 0890-6157
Founded in 1985

18615 Mines Magazine
Colorado School of Mines Alumni Association
1600 Arapahoe Street
PO Box 1410
Golden, CO 80402

303-733-3143; Fax: 303-273-3583
www.minesmagazine.com
Facebook, Twitter, LinkedIn

Nick Sutcliffe, Editor
Anita Pariseau, CEO/President
Amie Chitwood, Manager
Heidi Boersma, Administrative Assistant

Mines magazine is a critical communication serving the Colorado School of Mines community. Its mission is to keep readers informed about the school, to further the goals of the school and the alumni association, and to foster connectedness.
Cost: $35.00
Frequency: Quarterly
Circulation: 20000
Founded in 1910
Printed in 4 colors on glossy stock

18616 Mining Record
Mining Record Company
PO Box 1630
Castle Rock, CO 80104-6130

303-888-8871
800-441-4708; Fax: 303-663-7823
customerservice@miningrecord.com
www.miningrecord.com

Don E Howell, Editor
Dale Howell, Marketing

Has been in continuous publication for 115 years and is recognized as the industry's leading newspaper. Focuses on timely and credible news reporting on exploration, discovery, development, production, joint ventures, acquisitions, operating results, legislation, government reports and metals prices. Its readership is concentrated in the mining industry proper; mining companies and all individuals engaged in large or small mine production.
Cost: $45.00
16 Pages
Frequency: Monthly
Circulation: 5100
ISSN: 0026-5241
Founded in 1889
Printed in on newsprint stock

18617 New Equipment Digest
Penton Media
1300 E 9th St
Suite 316
Cleveland, OH 44114-1503

216-696-7000; Fax: 216-696-6662
information@penton.com

Jane Cooper, Marketing
Jennifer Daugherty, Communications Manager
John DiPaola, Group Publisher
Robert F King, Editor
Bobbie Macy, Circulation Manager

Serves the general industrial field which includes manufacturing, processing, engineering services, construction, transportation, mining, public utilities, wholesale distributors, educational services, libraries, and governmental establishments.
Cost: $65.00
Frequency: Monthly
Circulation: 206000
Founded in 1892

18618 North American Mining
Mining Media
1005 Terminal Way
#140
Reno, NV 89502-2179

775-323-1553; Fax: 775-323-1553

Dorothy Y Kosich, Editor

Information broken into departments which include environment, finance, government, management, new product news, profiles, safety issues and development technology updates.
Frequency: Bi-Monthly
Circulation: 7000

18619 **Pay Dirt**
Copper Queen Publishing Company
Copper Queen Plaza
PO Drawer 48
Bisbee, AZ 85603-48
520-432-2244; Fax: 520-432-2247
Gary Dillard, Editor
Caryl Larkins, CEO
Frank Barco, Publisher
Gruce Rubin, Marketing
Keeps readers informed on current mining developments, changes in policies and decisions by state and federal agencies affecting mining. Accepts advertising.
Cost: $30.00
34 Pages
Frequency: Monthly
Circulation: 2200
ISSN: 0886-0920
Founded in 1938

18620 **Pit & Quarry Magazine**
The Aggregates Authority
1360 E. Ninth St.
Suite 1070
Cleveland, OH 44114
216-706-3700
800-669-1668; Fax: 216-706-3711
scarr@questex.com
www.pitandquarry.com
Sean Carr, Publisher
Exclusively for nonmetallic minerals producers.

18621 **Professional Geologist**
American Institute of Professional Geologists
1200 N Washington St
Suite 285
Thornton, CO 80241-3134
303-412-6205; Fax: 303-253-9220
aipg@aipg.org
www.aipg.org
William J Siok, Executive Director
Wendy Davidson, Assistant Director
Frequency: Bi-Monthly

18622 **Reclamation Matters**
American Society of Mining and Reclamation
1800 South Oak Street
Suite 100
Champaign, IL 61820-6974
859-335-6529
asmr@insightbb.com
www.asmr.us
Facebook
Robert Darmody, Executive Secretary
Pete Stahl, President
Kimery Vories, President Elect
Richard Barnhisel, Editor-in-Chief
Dissemination of technical information relating to the reclamation of lands disturbed by mineral extraction. Members yearly issue is paid out of proceeding.
Cost: $10.00
Frequency: Twice A Year
Founded in 1973

18623 **Silver Valley Mining Journal**
414 Sixth Street
Wallace, ID 83873
208-556-1621
silverminers@usamedia.tv
Provides information about silver mining.

18624 **Skillings Mining Review**
WestmorelandFlint
11 E Superior St
Suite 514
Duluth, MN 55802-3015
218-727-1552; Fax: 218-733-0463
www.westmorelandflint.com
John Hyduke, President
Ivan Hohnstadt, General Manager
Holly Olson, Circulation Manager
Skillings Mining Review covers breaking news about mining companies and their suppliers, dynamics of the global marketplace, technical aspects of mining and processing, people in the industry and their contributions to it. Also production and shipping reports, and the latest news from coal and power industries.
Cost: $69.00
28 Pages
Frequency: Monthly
Circulation: 1500
ISSN: 0037-6329
Founded in 1912
Printed in 4 colors on glossy stock

18625 **The Leading Edge**
Society of Exploration Geophysicists
8801 South Yale
Suite 500
Tulsa, OK 74137-3575
918-497-5500; Fax: 918-497-5557
web@seg.org
www.seg.org
Facebook, Twitter, LinkedIn
Dr. Bob A. Hardage, President
Dr. David James Monk, President-Elect
Dr. Wafik Bulind Beydoun, Vice-President
Nancy Jo House, Secretary/ Treasurer
Dr. Tamas Nemeth, Editor
Gateway publication introducing new geophysical theory, instrumentation, and established practices to scientists in a wide range of geoscience disciplines. Most material is presented in a semitechnical manner that minimizes mathematical theory and emphasizes practical applications.
Frequency: Monthly
Founded in 1930

18626 **The Mountain Geologist**
Rocky Mountain Association of Geologists
910 16th St
Suite 1214
Denver, CO 80202-2997
303-573-8621; Fax: 303-476-2241
staff@rmag.org
www.rmag.org
Larry Rasmussen, President
Barbara Kuzmic, Executive Director
RMAG's quarterly publication offering peer-reviewed articles from experts spanning a range of geologist sub-disciplines.
2000 Members
Frequency: Quarterly
Founded in 1922

18627 **The Northern Miner Newspaper**
Northern Miner
320-225 Duncan Mill Rd.
Toronto, ON M3B 3K9
416-510-6789
888-502-3456; Fax: 416-510-5138
northernminer2@northernminer.com
www.northernminer.com
Facebook, Twitter, LinkedIn, Google+, YouTube
John Cumming, Editor-In-Chief
Anthony Vaccaro, Group Publisher
Joe Crofts, Advertising Sales Manager
News and information for the mining industry.
Cost: $114.00
Frequency: Bi-Weekly
Founded in 1915
Printed in 4 colors on glossy stock

18628 **United Mine Workers Journal**
United Mine Workers of America
900 15th Street NW
Washington, DC 20005-2585
202-842-7200; Fax: 202-842-7227
sales@wmwa.net
www.wmwa.net
Doug Gibson, Editor
Information sent to members of the United Mine Workers of America, retirees, other labor unions, politicians and opinion makers in the United States and abroad. Reports on issues inside and outside the UMWA that are of interest to its members. Also contains features on politics, the arts, media and the culture of US workers.
Frequency: Monthly
Circulation: 200000

18629 **Valley Gazette**
Hometown Publications
1000 Bridgeport Ave
Suite 3-2
Shelton, CT 06484-4676
203-926-2080; Fax: 203-926-2091
Gina Burkhart, CEO
Susane Hunter, Editor
Sharon Sakal, Circulation Manager
John Schneider, Marketing Manager
Frequency: Weekly
Circulation: 12322

18630 **World Dredging, Mining & Construction**
Placer Corporation
PO Box 17479
Irvine, CA 92623-7479
949-474-1120; Fax: 949-863-9261
info@worlddredging.com
www.worlddredging.com
MJ Richardson, Publisher
Steve Richardson, Editor
Robert Lindaur, Circulation Manager
International and national news for the dredging.
Cost: $40.00
100 Pages
Frequency: Monthly
Circulation: 3400
ISSN: 1045-0343
Founded in 1965
Printed in 4 colors on glossy stock

18631 **World Mining Equipment**
13544 Eads Road
Prairieville, LA 70769
225-673-9400; Fax: 225-677-8277
info@mining-media.com
www.mining-media.com
Steve Fiscor, Editor in chief
Richard Johnson, Managing Editor
Russ Carter, Managing Editor
Victor Matteucci, National Sales Manager
Cost: $29.95
Frequency: Monthly
Circulation: 10,523
Founded in 1866

Trade Shows

18632 **ACAA Annual Meeting**
American Coal Ash Association
38800 Country Club Drive
Farmington Hills, MI 48331

720-870-7897; Fax: 720-870-7889
info@acaa-usa.org
www.acaa-usa.org

Thomas H. Adams, Executive Director
Alyssa Barto, Member Liaison
John Ward, Communications Coordinator

A non-profit trade association devoted to recycling the materials created from burning coal.
150 Attendees

18633 **ASMA Annual Meeting**
American Society of Mining and Reclamation
1800 South Oak Street
Suite 100
Champaign, IL 61820

217-333-9489; Fax: 859-335-6529
asmr@insightbb.com
www.asmr.us
Facebook

Robert Darmody, Executive Secretary
Pete Stahl, President
Kimery Vories, President Elect

Approximately 30 exhibitors.
300 Attendees
Frequency: Annual

18634 **Alaska Miners Association Convention**
Alaska Miners Association
3305 Arctic Boulevard
Suite 105
Anchorage, AK 99503-4575

907-563-9229; Fax: 907-563-9225
ama@alaskaminers.org
www.alaskaminers.org

Steven Borell, Executive Director

Forty booths supporting businesses of the mining industry and state and federal agencies involved with regulating the industry.
500 Attendees
Frequency: Annual/March

18635 **American Federation Mineralogical Society Rocky Mountain**
816 Whipporwhill Sourt
Bartlesville, OK 74006

918-827-6405

T Alf, President

One hundred tables of gems, minerals and fossils for wholesale and retail dealers.
4M Attendees
Frequency: September

18636 **American Gem & Mineral Suppliers Association**
PO Box 741
Patton, CA 92369-0741

760-241-3191

Renata Williams, Executive Chairman

Ten booths.
100 Attendees
Frequency: February

18637 **Arminera**
Marketing International
200 N Glebe Road
Suite 900
Arlington, VA 22203

703-527-8000; Fax: 703-527-8006

Seminar, banquet and 400 exhibits of supplies, equipment and services for the mining industry.
8500 Attendees
Frequency: Biennial

18638 **Ash at Work Transportation Research Board**
American Coal Ash Association
38800 Country Club Drive
Farmington Hills, MI 48331

720-870-7897; Fax: 720-870-7889
info@acaa-usa.org
www.acaa-usa.org

Thomas H. Adams, Executive Director
Alyssa Barto, Member Liaison
John Ward, Communications Coordinator

The only magazine covering all facets of the coal combustion products industry. Read by ACAA members and others interested in the use and management of coal combustion products.
160 Members
Frequency: 2x/Year
Founded in 1968
Printed in 4 colors on glossy stock

18639 **EIA National Conference & Exposition**
Environmental Information Association
6935 Wisconsin Avenue
Suite 306
Chevy Chase, MD 20815-6112

301-961-4999
888-343-4342; Fax: 301-961-3094
info@eia-usa.org
www.eia-usa.org

Dana Hudson, President
Mike Schrum, President Elect
Kevin Cannan, Vice President
Joy Finch, Secretary
Chris Gates, Treasurer

Providing the environmental industry with the information needed to remain knowledgeable, responsible, and competitive in the environmental health and safety industry.
Frequency: Annual/March

18640 **MIACON Construction, Mining & Waste Management Show**
Finocchiaro Enterprises
2921 Coral Way
Miami, FL 33145-3053

305-441-2865; Fax: 305-529-9217
www.miacon.com

Michael Finocchiaro, President
Jose Garcia, VP
Justine Finocchiaro, Chief Operations

Annual show of 650 manufacturers, suppliers, distributors and exporters of equipment, machinery, supplies and services for the construction, mining and waste managment industries. There will be 600 booths.
10M Attendees
Frequency: December
Founded in 1994

18641 **MINExpo International**
National Mining Association
101 Constitution Avenue NW
Suite 500 East
Washington, DC 20001-2133

202-463-2600; Fax: 202-463-2666
www.minexpo.com

Harold P. Quinn, Jr., President & CEO

MINExpo is the mining industry's premier showcase for companies specializing in every facet of mining: open pit, underground, processing and preparation, mine site development, exploration and surveying, smelting and refining, and reclamation.
30000 Attendees
Frequency: Annual/September

18642 **Mineral Exploration Roundup**
Assoc for Mineral Exploration British Columbia
889 W Pender Street
Suite 800
Vancouver, BC V6C 3B2

604-689-5271; Fax: 604-681-2363
info@amebc.ca
www.amebc.ca
Facebook, Twitter

Simone Hill, Acting Dir., Member Relations
Morgen Andoff, Acting Manager, Special Events
Roxanne Finnie, Manager, Member Relations

AME BC is the predominant voice of mineral exploration and development in British Columbia. AME BC represents members including geoscientists, prospectors, engineers, students, exploration and mining companies and suppliers who are engaged in mineral exploration and develoment in BC and throughout the world. AME BC annually hosts international guests from around the world during the annual Mineral Exploration Roundup conference that takes place every January.
5000 Members
Frequency: Annual/January
Founded in 1912

18643 **National Western Mining Conference & Exhibition**
Colorado Mining Association
216 16th Street
Suite 1250
Denver, CO 80202-5161

303-575-9199; Fax: 303-575-9194
colomine@coloradomining.org
www.coloradomining.org

Stuart Sanderson, President

Annual show of 90 exhibitors of equipment and support services for the mining industry.
1000 Attendees

18644 **Northwest Mining Association Annual Meeting and Exposition**
Northwest Mining Association
10 N Post Street
Suite 220
Spokane, WA 99201

509-624-1158; Fax: 509-623-1241
www.nwma.com

Pat Nelsen, Operations Director

Annual mining convention in the US. Containing 335 booths, 280 exhibits and more than 20 technical sessions. The second largest annual mining convention in the USA. Founded in 1895.
2.5M Attendees
Frequency: December

18645 **Randol Gold Forum**
Randol International Limited
18301 W Colfax Avenue
#T1B
Golden, CO 80401-4834

303-526-7618; Fax: 303-271-0334
http://www.randol.com

Hans Von Michaelis, President
Patti Hamilton, Sales Coordinator

Mining companies exposition.
350 Attendees
Frequency: September

18646 Rapid Excavation Tunneling Conference Expo
PO Box 625002
Littleton, CO 80162-5002
303-973-9550
DD Daley, Meeting Manager
75 booths.
1M Attendees
Frequency: June

18647 SME Annual Meeting
Society of Mining, Metallurgy, and Exploration
12999 E. Adam Aircraft Circle
Englewood, CO 80112
303-948-4200
800-763-3132; Fax: 303-973-3845
sme@smenet.org
www.smenet.org
Facebook, Twitter, LinkedIn
John N. Murphy, President
Drew A. Meyer, President-Elect
David L. Kanagy, Executive Director
Mine to Market: Now It's Global.
4M Attendees
Frequency: Annual/February

18648 UMA Annual Convention
Utah Mining Association
136 S Main St
Suite 709
Salt Lake City, UT 84101-1683
801-364-1874; Fax: 801-364-2640
mining@utahmining.org
www.utahmining.org
Todd Bingham, President
Terry Maio, Chairman
Marilyn Tuttle, Admininistrator
Frequency: August

Directories & Databases

18649 Coal Data
National Coal Association
100 Independence Ave, SW
Washington, DC 20585
202-586-8800
Offers important data on the 50 largest coal mines in the country.
Cost: $50.00

18650 Coal Mine Directory
Primedia
29 N Wacker Drive
10th Floor
Chicago, IL 60606-3203
312-726-2802
800-621-9907; Fax: 312-726-2574
Art Sanda, Editor
Patricia L Yos, Editor
Over 2,000 coal mines are profiled that are based in the United States and Canada.
Cost: $149.00
Frequency: Annual January
Circulation: 700

18651 DRI Coal Forecast
DRI/McGraw-Hill
24 Hartwell Ave
Lexington, MA 02421-3103
781-860-6060; Fax: 781-860-6002
support@construction.com
www.construction.com
Walt Arvin, President
Offers valuable information on the mining of coal by supply region and producing state; total coal by demand region; cost and demand by the consumer sector.

18652 Engineering and Mining Journal: Buying Directory Issue
Primedia
29 N Wacker Drive
10th Floor
Chicago, IL 60606
312-726-2802
800-621-9907; Fax: 312-726-2574
Robert Wyllie, Editor
List of manufacturers and suppliers of mining equipment.
Cost: $35.00
Frequency: Annual November
Circulation: 23,000

18653 Expanded Shale, Clay and Slate Institute Roster of Members
Expanded Shale, Clay and Slate Institute
35 East Wacker Dr.
Suite 850
Chicago, IL 60601
801-272-7070; Fax: 312-644-8557
info@escsi.org
www.escsi.org
John Riese, President
About 15 producers by the rotary kiln method of lightweight aggregates of expanded shales, clays, and slates; international coverage.

18654 Geophysical Directory
Geophysical Directory
PO Box 130508
Houston, TX 77219-0508
713-291-1922
800-929-2462; Fax: 713-529-3646
www.iagc.org
Claudia LaCalli, Editor
Stewart Schafer, Owner
About 4,500 companies that provide geophysical equipment, supplies or services and mining and petroleum companies that use geophysical techniques.
Cost: $135.00
400 Pages
Frequency: Annual March
Circulation: 2,000
Founded in 1946
Mailing list available for rent: 2500 names
Printed in 4 colors on glossy stock

18655 Iron and Manganese Ore Databook
Metal Bulletin
220 5th Avenue
#Enus-19T
New York, NY 10001-7708
212-136-6202
800-MET-L 25; Fax: 212-213-6273
John Bailey, Editor
Iron and manganese ore producers and traders worldwide.
Cost: $179.00
Frequency: Quadrennial

18656 Keystone Coal Industry Manual
Primedia
29 N Wacker Drive
10th Floor
Chicago, IL 60611
312-726-2802
800-621-9907; Fax: 312-726-2574
Art Sanda, Editor
Patricia L Yos, Editor
Coal companies and mines, coke plants, coal preparation plants, domestic and export coal sales companies.
Cost: $260.00
Frequency: Annual January
Circulation: 1,400

18657 Landmen's Directory and Guidebook
American Association of Professional Landmen
4100 Fossil Creek Boulevard
Fort Worth, TX 76137-2723
817-847-7700; Fax: 817-847-7704
aapl@landman.org
www.landman.org
Le'ann Callihan, Editor/Publications Department
About 7,500 member specialists in assembling or disposing of land or rights required for oil, gas, coal andmineral exploration and exploitation in the US and Canada.
Cost: $100.00
Frequency: Annual November
Circulation: 7,500
ISSN: 0272-8370

18658 Minerals Yearbook
US Geological Survey
1730 E Parham Rd
Richmond, VA 23228-2202
804-261-2600; Fax: 804-261-2659
dc_va@usgs.gov
www.usgs.gov
Charles G Groats, Director
The Minerals Yearbook discusses the performance of the worldwide minerals and materials industry and provides background information to assist in interpreting that performance. Contents of the individual Minerals Yearbook volumes are, Volume I, Metals and Minerals, Volume II, Area Reports:Domestic, and Volume III, Area Reports: International.
200+ Pages
Frequency: Annual
Founded in 1935

18659 Mining Directory
Metal Bulletin
220 5th Avenue
10th Floor
New York, NY 10001-7708
212-213-6202
800-MET-L 25; Fax: 212-213-6273
Don Nelson, Editor
Offers valuable information on mines, mining equipment manufacturers, suppliers of equipment and services to the industry and industry consultants.
Cost: $158.00

18660 Mining Engineering: SME Membership Directory
Society of Mining, Metallurgy & Exploration
12999 E. Adam Aircraft Circle
Englewood, CO 80112
303-948-4200
800-763-3132; Fax: 303-973-3845
sme@smenet.org
www.smenet.org
Facebook, Twitter, LinkedIn
John N. Murphy, President
Drew A. Meyer, President-Elect
A list of over 18,000 persons engaged in the location, exploration,treatment and marketing of all classes of minerals except petroleum.
Cost: $150.00
Frequency: Annual
Circulation: 20,000
ISSN: 0026-5187

18661 **National Ocean Industries Association: Directory of Membership**
National Ocean Industries Association
1120 G St NW
Suite 900
Washington, DC 20005-3801
202-347-6900; Fax: 202-347-8650
www.noia.org
Tom Fry, President
Over 300 firms engaged in offshore construction, drilling and petroleum production, geophysical exploration, ship building and repair, deep-sea mining and related activities in the development and use of marine resources.
Frequency: Annual

18662 **Pit & Quarry: Reference Manual & Buyers' Guide Issue**
Advanstar Communications
2501 Colorado Avenue
Suite 280
Santa Monica, CA 90404-4503
310-857-7500; Fax: 310-857-7510
info@advanstar.com
www.advanstar.com
List of approximately 1,000 manufacturers and other suppliers of equipment, products and services to the nonmetallic mining and quarrying industry.
Cost: $25.00
Frequency: Annual
Circulation: 25,000

18663 **Randol Buyer's Guide**
Randol International Limited
18301 W Colfax Avenue
#T-2
Golden, CO 80401-4834
303-526-7618
800-726-3652; Fax: 303-278-9229
http://www.randol.com
Hans Von Michaelis, Editor
Approximately 10,000 companies that offer equipment and services used in the mining industry.
Cost: $35.00
Frequency: Annual
Circulation: 10,000

18664 **Randol Mining Directory**
Randol International Limited
18301 W Colfax Avenue
#T1B
Golden, CO 80401-4834
303-526-7618; Fax: 303-271-0334
http://www.randol.com
Hans Von Michaelis, President
Patti Hamilton, Sales Coordinator
The most comprehensive source of information on all mines in the USA. Used for systematic marketing to mines and exploration companies, statistical research and more, offering 10,000 industry contacts.

18665 **Rock Products: Buyer's Guide Issue**
Primedia
29 N Wacker Drive
10th Floor
Chicago, IL 60606
312-726-2802; Fax: 312-726-2574
Rick Marley, Editor
Scot Bieda, Publisher
David Pistello, Classified
List of about 1,500 providers worldwide of equipment and services for the nonmetallic mineral mining and processing industry.
Cost: $100.00
Frequency: Annual November
Circulation: 23,000

18666 **Silver Refiners of the World and their Identifying Ingot Marks**
Silver Institute
1112 16th St NW
Suite 240
Washington, DC 20036-4818
202-347-8200
www.silverinstitute.org
Over 80 refiners in over 18 countries are profiled.
Cost: $33.00
85 Pages

18667 **Western Mining Directory**
Howell Publishing Company
1758 Blake St
Denver, CO 80202-1226
303-296-8000
800-441-4748; Fax: 303-296-1123
Dave Howell, Owner
Directory of mining companies and mines nationwide.
Cost: $49.00
Circulation: 5,000
Founded in 1968

18668 **World Aluminum: A Metal Bulletin Databook**
Metal Bulletin
220 5th Avenue
19th Floor
New York, NY 10001-7781
212-213-6202; Fax: 212-213-1870
help@metalbulletin.com
www.metalbulletin.com
Richard ODonoghue, Manager
Ania Tumm, Marketing Manager
Julius Pike, Account Manager
Offers information on producers and traders of aluminum and aluminum alloys.
Cost: $247.00
540 Pages
ISSN: 0951-2233

18669 **World Mining Equipment**
Metal Bulletin
220 5th Avenue
New York, NY 10001
212-213-6202; Fax: 212-213-6619
www.wme.com
Mike Woof, Editor
Manufacturers of mining equipment.
Cost: $246.00
66 Pages
Circulation: 13M
ISSN: 0746-729X
Printed in 4 colors on glossy stock

Industry Web Sites

18670 **http://gold.greyhouse.com**
G.O.L.D Grey House OnLine Databases
Grey House Publishing's online database platform, GOLD, offers Quick Search, Keyword Search and Expert Search for most business sectors including mining markets. The GOLD platform makes finding the information you need quick and easy - whether you're a novice searcher or an experienced database user. All of Grey House's directory products are available for subscription on the GOLD platform.

18671 **www.acaa-usa.org**
American Coal Ash Association
A non-profit trade association devoted to recycling the materials created from burning coal.

18672 **www.aem.org**
Vibrating Screen Manufacturers Association

18673 **www.agiweb.org**
American Geological Institute
Provides information services to geoscientists, serves as a voice of shared interests in our profession.

18674 **www.aimeny.org**
American Institute of Mining & Petroleum Engineers
Organization was founded to further the arts and sciences employed to recover the earth's minerals and convert them to useful products.

18675 **www.aipg.org**
American Institute of Professional Geologists
Founded to certify the credentials of practicing geologists and to advocate on behalf of the profession.

18676 **www.alaskaminers.org**
Alaska Miners Association
Encourage and support responsible mineral production in Alaska.

18677 **www.amebc.ca**
Assn for Mineral Exploration British Columbia
Supports and promotes the mineral exploration community and related services by disseminating information to the public and governments, thereby assisting in the creation of wealth and jobs through sustainable mineral developement.

18678 **www.asmi.state.az.us**
State Mine Inspector

18679 **www.asmr.us**
American Society of Mining and Reclamation

18680 **www.azcu.org**
Arizona Mining Association
Provides information about mining, specifically copper mining and the impact it has on our lives.

18681 **www.cim.org**
Canadian Inst of Mining, Metallurgy & Petroleum
Strives to be the association of choice for professionals in the minerals industries.

18682 **www.coloradomining.org**
Colorado Mining Association
Serves as a spokesman for the mining industry in Colorado.

18683 **www.copper.org**
Copper Development Association
CDA is committed to promoting the proper use of copper materials in sustainable, efficient applications for business, industry and the home.

18684 **www.crc.siu.edu/nasir.htm**
National Association of State Land Reclamationists

18685 **www.crystalgrowth.org**
American Association for Crystal Growth
For those interested in organic crystal growth.

18686 **www.dri.edu**
Desert Research Institute
Information on basic and applied environmental research on a local, national, and international scale. For scientists, technicians, and support personnel.

18687 **www.geosociety.org**
Geological Society of America

18688 **www.gold.org**
World Gold Council

18689 **www.goldprospecters.org**
Gold Prospectors Association

18690 **www.greyhouse.com**
Grey House Publishing
Authoritative reference directories for most business sectors, including mining markets. Users can search the online databases with varied search criteria allowing for custom searches by product category, geographic area, sales volume, keyword, subject and more. Full Grey House catalog and online ordering also available.

18691 **www.idahomining.org**
Idaho Mining Association
Founded to further the interests of Idaho's mining industry and minerals production.

18692 **www.kaolin.com**
China Clay Producers Association

18693 **www.leadinfo.com**
Lead Industries Association

18694 **www.lignite.com**
Lignite Energy Council
Promotes policies and directs activities that maintain a viable lignite industry and enhance the development of our regions lignite resources.

18695 **www.lime.org**
National Lime Association
Trade association for US and Canadian manufacturers of high calcium quicklime, dolomitic quicklime and hydrated lime, collectively referred to as lime.

18696 **www.miningfoundationsw.org**
Mining Foundation of the Southwest

18697 **www.miningusa.com**
Mining Associations-National
A list of associations throughout the United States.

18698 **www.mmsa.net**
Mining and Metallurgical Society of America
A professional organization dedicated to increasing public awareness and understanding about mining and why mined materials are essential to modern society and human well being.

18699 **www.msha.gov**
Mine Safety and Health Administration

18700 **www.naima.org**
Mineral Insulation Manufacturers Association
Trade association of North American manufacturwers of fiberglass, rock wool, and slag wool insulation products.

18701 **www.nevadamining.org**
Nevada Mining Association
Represents all aspects of the mining industry in the state of Nevada.

18702 **www.nma.org**
National Mining Association
The only national trade organization represents the interests of mining before Congress, the Administration, federal agencies, the judiciary and the media.

18703 **www.noia.org**
National Ocean Industries Association
National organization engaged in offshore construction, drilling and petroleum production, geophysical exploration, ship building and repair.

18704 **www.northernminer.com**
Northern Miner
Facebook, Twitter, LinkedIn, Google+, YouTube
Articles and press releases relevant to the mining industry.

18705 **www.nssga.org**
National Stone, Sand & Gravel Association

18706 **www.nwma.org**
Northwest Mining Association
Provides liaison between mining industry and government. Offers short course on current technology.

18707 **www.perlite.org**
Perlite Institute

18708 **www.pitandquarry.com**
The Aggregates Authority-Pit and Quarry
A magazine exclusively for nonmetallic minerals producers.

18709 **www.rheology.org**
Society of Rheology

18710 **www.rmag.org**
Rocky Mountain Association of Geologists

18711 **www.seg.org**
Society of Exploration Geophysicists

18712 **www.segweb.org**
Society of Economic Geologists
The society of economic geologists is an international organization of individual members with interest in the field of economic geology.

18713 **www.silverinstitute.org**
Silver Institute

18714 **www.smenet.org**
Society for Mining, Metallurgy & Exploration
Advances the worldwide mining and minerals community through information exchange and professional development.

18715 **www.sorptive.org**
Sorptive Minerals Institute

18716 **www.sulphurinstitute.org**
Sulphur Institute

18717 **www.surface-mining.state.al.us**
Alabama Surface Mining Commission
Balance civilization's demands for natural resources and environmental conservation in the state of Alabama.

18718 **www.tmra.com**
Texas Mining & Reclamation Association

18719 **www.tms.org**
Minerals, Metals & Materials Society
Dedicated to the development and dissemination of the scientific and engineering knowledge bases for materials-centered technologies.

18720 **www.umwa.org**
United Mine Workers of America

18721 **www.usgs.gov**
US Geological Survey

18722 **www.utahmining.org**
Utah Mining Association
Helps to promote and protect the mining industry. Provides its members with full-time professional industry representation before the State Legislature; various government regularoty agencies on the federal, state and local levels, other associations, and business and industry groups.

18723 **www.womeninmining.org**
Women in Mining

Associations

18724 Academy of Motion Picture Arts and Sciences
8949 Wilshire Blvd
Beverly Hills, CA 90211-1972

310-247-3000; Fax: 310-271-3395
www.oscars.org
Facebook, Twitter, LinkedIn, Youtube

The Academy was founded to advance the arts and sciences of motion pictures; foster cooperation among creative leaders for cultural, educational and technological progress; recognize outstanding achievments; cooperate on technical research and improvement of methods and equipment; provide a common forum and meeting ground for various branches and crafts; represent the viewpoint of actual creators of the motion picture. Hosts annual Academy Awards.
6000 Members
Founded in 1927

18725 Academy of Science Fiction Fantasy and Horror Films
334 W 54th St
Los Angeles, CA 90037-3806

323-752-5811; Fax: 323-752-5811
saturn.awards@ca.rr.com
www.saturnawards.org
Facebook, Twitter

Robert Holguin, President & CEO
David Brilbrey, Executive Administrator
Michael Laster, Director, Operations
Jeff Rector, Official Spokesperson
Kurt Reichenbach, Art Designer

Culminated from the Count Dracula Society, the Academy hosts the annual Science Fiction Film Awards, called the Saturn Awards.
Founded in 1972

18726 American Cinema Editors
100 Universal City Plaza
Verna Fields Building 2282 Room 190
Universal City, CA 91608

818-777-2900; Fax: 818-733-5023
www.americancinemaeditors.org
Facebook, Twitter

Alan Heim, President
Stephen Rivkin, VP
Lillian Bennson, Secretary
Ed Abroms, Treasurer
Jan Ambler, A.C.E

A non-profit corporation committed to the encouragement of mutually-beneficial dialogue with other members of the motion picture industry and to educating the general public. Holds the annual ACE Eddie Awards honoring the nominees for the Film Editing Award given by the Academy of Motion Pictures Arts and Sciences.
Founded in 1950

18727 American Film Institute
2021 North Western Ave.
Los Angeles, CA 90027-1657

323-856-7600; Fax: 323-467-4578
information@afi.com
www.afi.com
Facebook, Twitter, YouTube, Tumblr, Instagram

Bob Gazzale, President & CEO

The AFI is a nonprofit educational and cultural organization dedicated to preserving and honoring America's film heritage and educating its next generation of filmmakers.

18728 American Society of Cinematographers
1782 N Orange Drive
PO Box 2230
Hollywood, CA 90028

323-969-4333
800-448-0145; Fax: 323-882-6391
office@theasc.com
www.theasc.com
Facebook, Twitter, YouTube ,Instagram, Vimeo

Daryn Okadaan, President
Michael Negrin, Secretary
Victor J Kemper, Treasurer
Rachael K. Bosley, Managing Director

The ASC is not a labor union or guild, but is an educational, cultural and professional organization. Membership is possible by invitation and is extended only to directors of photography with distinguished credits in the industry. Publishes 'American Cinematographer' magazine.
Founded in 1919

18729 Art Directors Guild
11969 Ventura Blvd
Suite 200
Studio City, CA 91604-2619

818-762-9995; Fax: 818-762-9997
lydia@artdirectors.org
www.adg.org
Facebook, Twitter, Instagram, Vimeo

Scott Roth, Executive Director
Lisa Frazza, Secretary
Michael Baugh, Treasurer
Sasha Aronson, Executive Assistant to Scott Roth
Alexandra Schaaf, Manager Membership Department

The creative talents that concieve and manage the background and settings for most films and television projects are members of the Art Directors Guild, Local 800. They and most other crafts of the entertainment industry are members of the International Alliance of Theatrical Stage Employees, Moving Picture Technicians, Artists and Allied Crafts of the United States, its Territories and Canada.
935 Members
Founded in 1937

18730 Assistant Directors Training Program
15301 Ventura Blvd.
Bldg E #1075
Sherman Oaks, CA 91403

818-386-2545; Fax: 818-386-2876
www.trainingplan.org

Tom Joyner, Chair

Provides motion picture and television industry training as directed by the Alliance of Motion Picture and Television Producers and the Directors Guild of America.
Founded in 1965

18731 Association of Cinema and Video Laboratories
Bev Wood C/O Deluxe Laboratories
1377 North Serrano Avenue
Hollywood, CA 90027

323-462-6171; Fax: 206-682-6649
www.intersociety.org

Bev Wood, President
Chip Wilkenson, First VP
John Carlson, Second VP
Kevin Dillon, Treasurer
Bob Olson, Secretary

Provides opportunities for discussion and exchange of ideas in connection with administrative, technical and managerial problems in the motion picture and video industry. The Association is concerned with improvements in technical practices and procedures, public and industry relations, product specifications to vendors, the impact of current and impending governmental regulations, and any and all other areas of interest to the laboratory industry.
80 Members
Founded in 1953

18732 Association of Talent Agents
9255 Sunset Blvd
Suite 930
Los Angeles, CA 90069-3317

310-274-0628; Fax: 310-274-5063
www.agentassociation.com

Sandy Bresler, President
Sheldon Sroloff, VP
Jim Gosnell, Secretary/Treasurer
Karen Stuart, Executive Director
Shellie Jetton, Administrative Director

A non-profit trade association representing talent agencies in the industry. ATA is the voice of unified talent and literary agencies. ATA agencies represent the vast majority of working artists, including actors, directors, writers, and other artists in film, stage, television, radio, commercial, literary work, and other entertainment enterprises.
Founded in 1937

18733 Casting Society of America
1149 N. Gower Street
Suite 110
Los Angeles, CA 90038

323-785-1011; Fax: 323-463-4753
info@castingsociety.com
www.castingsociety.com

Richard Hicks, President
Matthew Lessall, Vice President
Sharon Bialy, Secretary
Mark Simon, Treasurer

CSA is the largest professional association of Casting Directors in the world. They work in all areas of entertainment in film, television and theatre. CSA continually seeks to expand their standing in the industry by providing information and opportunities that support is members.
500+ Members
Founded in 1982

18734 Children in Film
11271 Ventura Blvd.
Studio City, CA 91604

818-432-7400
800-902-9001
contact@childreninfilm.com
www.childreninfilm.com

Toni Casala, President
Trisha Noble, Director, Permit Services
Heather Broeker, Director, Marketing

To provide tools and information needed to successfully employ a child in the entertainment industry while also lending a healthy, positive view into the world of child actors.
Founded in 2000

18735 Directors Guild of America
7920 W Sunset Blvd
Los Angeles, CA 90046-3347

310-289-2000
800-421-4173; Fax: 310-289-2029
LDavis@dga.org
www.dga.org

Jay Roth, President
Steven Soderbergh, National VP
Gilbert Cates, Secretary/Treasurer

The DGA represents Film and Television Directors, Unit Production Managers, First Assistant Directors, Second Assistant Directors, Technical Coordinators and Tape Associate Directors, Stage Managers and Production Assistants.

18736 Film Society of Lincoln Center
70 Lincoln Center Plz
New York, NY 10023-6595

212-875-5601; Fax: 212-875-5636
webmaster@filmlinc.com
www.filmlinc.com
Facebook, Twitter, YouTube

Serge Joseph, Manager
Daniel H Stern, President
Wendy Keys, Secreatry
James Bouras, Treasurer
Lesli Klainberg, Executive Director

Celebrates American and international cinema, recognizes and supports new filmmakers, and enhances awareness, accessibility and understanding of the art among a broad and diverse film going audience. The Film Society is best known for two international festivals - the New York Film Festival and the New Directors/New Films festival.
Founded in 1969

18737 Greek Americans in the Arts and Entertainment
3916 Sepulveda Blvd
Suite 107
Culver City, CA 90230

323-651-3507; Fax: 310-933-0250
info@americanhellenic.org
www.americanhellenic.org
Facebook, Twitter, LinkedIn

Dr. Menas Kafatos, Chairman
Eleftheria Polychronis, Vice President
Aris Anagnos, Vice President of Political Action
Dr. Tasos Chassiakos, VP, Culture & Education, Secretary
Alexander Mizan, Treasurer

Follows the legacy of Greek-Americans in the arts and entertainment field.

18738 Historians Film Committee
711 E. Boldt Way
Box 80
Appleton, WI 54911

920-832-6649; Fax: 202-544-8307
center@filmandhistory.org
www.filmandhistory.org

Peter C Rollins, Editor-in-Chief

The Committee exists to further the use of film sources in teaching and research, to disseminate information about film and film use to historians and other social scientists, to work for an effective system of film preservation so that scholars may have ready access to film archives, and to organize periodic conferences dealing with film.
Founded in 1970

18739 Hollywood Arts Council
PO Box 931056
Hollywood, CA 90093

323-462-2355; Fax: 323-465-9240
www.hollywoodartscouncil.org
Facebook, LinkedIn, YouTube

David Warren, Chairman
Matthew Leum, Vice Chair
Patti Negri, Secretary
Steven P. Tronson, Treasurer
Joni Labaqui, Director

Promotes, nurtures and supports the arts in Hollywood. Has served the community through advocacy, coalition building, free public arts events and after school programs.
400 Members
Founded in 1978

18740 Independent Film & Television Alliance
10850 Wilshire Blvd
9th Floor
Los Angeles, CA 90024-4628

310-446-1000; Fax: 310-446-1600
www.ifta-online.org
Facebook, LinkedIn, YouTube

Michael Ryan, Chairman
Nicolas Chartier, Vice Chairperson
Kirk D' Amico, General Vice Chairperson
Charlotte Mickie, Vice Chairperson, Non-Californian
Lise Romanoff, Vice Chairperson/Secretary

A non-profit association whose mission is to provide the independent film and television industry with high-quality marketplace-oriented services and worldwide representation. The Alliance actively lobbies the United States and Eurpoean governments and the international organizations on measures that impact production and distribution.
Founded in 1980

18741 International Animated Film Society
2114 W Burbank Blvd
Burbank, CA 91506-1232

818-842-8330; Fax: 613-232-6315
info@asifa-hollywood.org
www.animationarchive.org

Amtran Manoogian, President

A California nonprofit organization established to promote and encourage the art and craft of animation. They support and encourage animation education, supports the preservation and critical evaluation of animation history, recognize achievement of excellence in the art and field of animation, strive to increase the public awareness of animation, act as a liaison to encourage the free exchange of ideas within the animation community, as well as a variety of other goals.
350 Members
Founded in 1974

18742 International Cinematographers Guild
7755 W Sunset Boulevard
Hollywood, CA 90046

323-876-0160; Fax: 323-876-6383
www.cameraguild.com
Facebook, Twitter

Steven Poster, President
Lewis Rothenberg, National VP
Alan M. Gitlin, Secretary/Treasurer
Bruce C Doering, Executive Director

The International Cinematographers Guild welcomes camera professionals from across the United States and around the world.

18743 International Documentary Association
3470 Wilshire Boulevard
Suite 980
Los Angeles, CA 90010

213-232-1660; Fax: 213-232-1669
michael@documentary.org
www.documentary.org
Facebook, Twitter, LinkedIn, Youtube

Simon Kilmurry, Executive Director
Dana Merwin, Program Officer
Niki Bhardwaj, Events Coordinator
Jina Chung, Director, Development
Veronica Monteyro, Membership Manager

A nonprofit membership organization dedicated to supporting the efforts of nonfiction film and video makers throughout the United States and the world; promoting the documentary form; and expanding opportunities for the production, distribution, and exhibition of documentary.
2631 Members
Founded in 1982

18744 International Stunt Association
11331 Ventura Boulevard
Suite 100
Studio City, CA 91604

818-760-2072; Fax: 818-501-5656
www.isastunts.com
Facebook, Twitter

Leading the industry in exciting action while holding safety above all else, ISA is a fraternal organization whose membership is by invitation only. It is comprised of the top stuntment, stunt coordinators and second unit directors that Hollywood has to offer and a safety record that is second to none.
Founded in 1980

18745 Motion Picture Association of America
15301 Ventura Boulevard
Building E
Sherman Oaks, CA 91403

818-995-6600; Fax: 818-285-4403
www.mpaa.org

Christopher J Dodd, President/CEO

Serves as the voice and advocate of the American motion picture, home video and television industries. The association advocates for strong protection of the creative works produced and distributed by the industry, fights copyright theft around the world, and provides leadership in meeting new and emerging industry challenges.
7 Members
Founded in 1922

18746 Motion Picture Editors Guild
7715 Sunset Boulevard
Suite 200
Hollywood, CA 90046

323-876-4770
800-705-8700; Fax: 323-876-0861
www.editorsguild.com
Facebook

Alan Heim, President
Gregg Rudloff, VP
Louis Bertini, Second Vice Presdient
Diane Adler, Secretary
Rachel B Igel, Treasurer

A national labor organization representing freelance and staff post-production professionals. MPED negotiates new collective bargaining agreements and enfoces existing agreements with employers involved in post-production. They provide assistance for securing better conditions, including but not limted to financial, medical, safety and artistic concerns.
6000 Members
Founded in 1937

18747 Motion Picture Pilots Association
7435 Valjean Avenue
Van Nuys, CA 91406

818-947-5454
www.moviepilots.com

Cliff Fleming, Board Director
Dirk Vahle, Board Director
Rick Shuster, Board Director
Neil Looy, Board Director
Kevin LaRosa, Board Director

The MPPA promotes aviation safety and the interest of aviators working in the motion picture, television and entertainment industries; establishes, conducts and maintains such activities which promote higher aviation standards and better business methods as may assist in the advancement of aviation in the Entertainment Aviation Profession; cooperates with those

government agencies, industry organizations, entities or association whose objective is the betterment or advancement of the industry.
Founded in 1997

18748 **Motion Picture Sound Editors**
10061 Riverside Dr.
PMB Box 751
Toluca Lake, CA 91602-2550

818-506-7731; Fax: 818-506-7732
mpse.org
Facebook, Twitter, LinkedIn, YouTube

Frank Morrone, President
Mark Lanza, Vice President

Organization for the improvement of the professional status of sound editors.

18749 **National Association of Theatre Owners**
1705 N St. NW
Washington, DC 20036

202-962-0054
nato@natodc.com
natoonline.org

John Fithian, President & CEO

Exhibition trade organization that helps its members influence federal policy-making on issues of concern.

18750 **Producers Guild of America**
8530 Wilshire Blvd
Suite 450
Beverly Hills, CA 90211-3115

310-358-9020; Fax: 310-358-9520
info@producersguild.org
www.producersguild.org

Marshall Herskovitz, President
Vance Van Paten, Executive Director
Grant Stoner, Director Membership
Courtney Cowan, Treasurer
Gale Ann Hurd, Secretary

The PGA represents, protects and promotes the interests of all members of the producing team by providing employment opportunities and health and welfare benefits for all members of the producing team; combating deceptive or uneraned credits within the producing team; and representing the interests of the entire producing team. The producing team consists of all those whose interdependency and support of each other are necessary for the creation of motion pictures and television programs.
500 Members
Founded in 1950

18751 **Society for Cinema & Media Studies**
640 Parrington Oval
Wallace Old Science Hall Room 300
Norman, OK 73019

405-325-8075; Fax: 405-325-7135
www.cmstudies.org
Facebook, Twitter

Steven Cohan, President
Victoria E.ÿ Johnson, Secretary
Amanda Klein, Treasurer
Jane Dye, Administrative Coordinator
Pamela Wojcik, President-Elect

A professional organization of college and university educators, filmmakers, historians, critics, scholars, and others devoted to the study of the moving image. The gaols of SCMS are to promote all areas of media studies within universities and two- and four-year colleges; to encourage and reward excellence in scholarship and writing; to facilitate and improve the teaching of media studies as disciplines and to advance multi-cultural awareness and interaction.
1M Members
Founded in 1959

18752 **Society of Camera Operators**
PO Box 2006
Toluca Lake, CA 91610

818-382-7070; Fax: 323-856-9155
www.soc.org
Facebook, Twitter

Kristin Petrovich Kennedy, Business Consultant
John Bosson, Member Services & Ops. Coordinator
Jeff Victor, Sales
Kate McCallum, Camera Operator Magazine Editor
Stephanie Cameron, Camera Operator Magazine Designer

Non-profit organization which advances the art and creative contribution of the operating cameraman in the Motion Picture and Television Industries.
Founded in 1979
Mailing list available for rent

18753 **Society of Motion Picture & Television Engineers**
3 Barker Ave
5th Floor
White Plains, NY 10601-1509

914-761-1100; Fax: 914-761-3115
www.smpte.org
Facebook, Twitter, LinkedIn, Youtube

Barbara Lange, Executive Director
Sally-Ann D'Amato, Director, Events
Roberta Gorman, Director, Membership
Frank Kunkle, Director, Marketing
Joyce Cataldo, Director, Business Development

The SMPTE is the leading technical society for the motion imaging industry. It was founded to advance theory and development in the motion imaging field. Today, it publishes ANSI-approved Standards, Recommended Practices, and Engineering Guidelines. SMPTE holds conferences and local Section meetings to bring people and ides together, allowing for useful interaction and information exchange.
100 Members
Founded in 1916

18754 **Stuntmen's Association of Motion Pictures**
5200 Lankershim Blvd.
Suite 190
North Hollywood, CA 91601

818-766-4334; Fax: 818-766-5943
hq@stuntmen.com
www.stuntmen.com

Chris Doyle, Manager
Alex Daniels, First VP
John Moio, Second VP
Oliver Keller, Secretary
Hugh Aodh O'Brien, Treasurer

Seeks to improve working conditions for stuntmen. Encourages members to uphold high professional standards.
135 Members
Founded in 1961

18755 **Stuntwomen's Association of Motion Pictures**
3760 Cahuenga Blvd
Suite 104
Studio City, CA 91604-2411

818-588-8888
888-817-9267; Fax: 818-762-0907
INFO@STUNTWOMEN.COM
www.stuntwomen.com
Facebook

Jane Austin, President

A professional association for stuntwomen and stunt coordinators which seeks to uphold professional standards and improve working conditions.
Founded in 1967

18756 **Sundance Institute**
1825 Three Kings Drive
PO Box 684429
Park City, UT 84060

435-658-3456; Fax: 435-658-3457
Institute@sundance.org
www.sundance.org
Twitter, LinkedIn, Instagram

Robert Redford, President
Keri Putnam, Executive Director
Geoffrey Gilmore, Director Sundance Film Festival
Brooke McAffee, Director Finance
Ellen Oh, Associate Director Marketing

Non-profit organization dedicated to the discovery and development of independent artists and audiences. The Institute seeks to discover, support, and inspire independent film and theatre artists from the United States and around the world, and to introduce audiences to their new work. The Institutes programs include the annual Sundance Film Festival, held in Park City, Utah each January.
Founded in 1981

18757 **United Stuntwomen's Association**
26893 Bouquet Canyon Rd.
Suite C, Box 218
Saugus, CA 91350

818-508-4651
usastunts@usastunts.com
www.usastunts.com

Bonnie Happy, President
Debbie Evans, Vice President

Trade association of professional stuntwomen, co-ordinators and second unit directors.
Founded in 1984

18758 **University Film and Video Association**
UFVA Membership Office C/O Cheryl Jestis
University of Illinois Press
1325 South Oak Street
Champaign, IL 61820-6903

217-244-0626
866-244-0626; Fax: 217-244-9910
ufvahome@gmail.com
www.ufva.org
Facebook, Twitter, LinkedIn, Instagram, YouTube

Francisco Menendez, President
Jennifer Machiorlatti, Executive VP
Brett Levner, Secretary
Tom Sanny, Treasurer
Cheryl Jestis, Membership Coordinator

Supports those interested in the fields of film and video production, history, criticism, and aesthetics. Provides training, education, and a quarterly magazine.
Cost: $75.00
Founded in 1947

18759 **Women in Film**
6100 Wilshire Blvd
Suite 710
Los Angeles, CA 90048-5107

323-935-2211; Fax: 323-935-2212
info@wif.org
www.wif.org
Facebook, Twitter, YouTube

Tichi Wilkerson-Kassel, Founder
Cathy Schulman, President
Glen Alpert, VP Membership
Nicole Katz, CFO
Gayle Nachlis, Executive Director

WIFs purpose is to empower, promote, nurture, and mentor women in the industry through a network of valuable contacts, events, and programs.
10000 Members
Founded in 1974

Newsletters

18760 **American Academy of Arts & Sciences Bulletin**
American Academy of Arts & Sciences
136 Irving Street
Cambridge, MA 02138

617-576-5000; Fax: 617-576-5050
vsp@amacad.org
www.amacad.org

Leslie Berkowitz, President
Mark Robinson, Director, Operations
Paul Karoff, Director, Communications

Features the following departments: Academy News; Around the Country; Noteworthy; and Remembrance.
Frequency: 2x/year

18761 **Festival Rag**
541 Main Street
Union, WV 24983

FAX 888-813-5457
markus@kemek.com

Markus Varjo, Publisher
Cil Ripley, Editor-In-Chief
Dave Roberts, Managing Editor
Carl Merrick, Content & Development

Dedicated to true independent filmmaking and filmmakers, and broadcast to thousands of media-industry subscribers. Provides information on film festivals worldwide, including interviews with filmmakers and programmers.

18762 **Film Advisory Board Monthly**
Film Advisory Board
263 W Olive Avenue
#377
Burbank, CA 91502

323-461-6541; Fax: 323-469-8541
www.filmadvisoryboard.org
Facebook, Twitter, LinkedIn

Janet Stokes, President

Information and news on the entertainment industry.
Frequency: Monthly
Founded in 1975
Printed in one color on glossy stock

18763 **Hollywood Arts Council**
PO Box 931056
Hollywood, CA 90093

323-462-2355; Fax: 323-465-9240
www.hollywoodartscouncil.org

Promotes, nurtures and supports the arts field in Hollywood. Newsletter is included with membership.
Founded in 1978
Printed in 4 colors on glossy stock

18764 **Preview Family Movie & TV Review**
Movie Morality Ministries
6302 Riverside Dr
Irving, TX 75039

972-409-9960
800-807-8071; Fax: 785-255-4316
preview@fni.com
www.merchantcircle.com

Dave Haverty, President
Greg Shull, Editor
Susan Haverty, Desktop Publisher/Office Manager

Reviews current films and TV series from a Christian and family values perspective.
Cost: $34.00
Frequency: Monthly
ISSN: 0892-6468
Printed in 2 colors on matte stock

Magazines & Journals

18765 **Advanstar**
Advanstar Communications
641 Lexington Ave
Suite 8
New York, NY 10022-4503

212-951-6600; Fax: 212-951-6793
info@advanstar.com
www.advanstar.com

Joseph Loggia, CEO

News and features emphasize innovation in equipment technology and creative technique for editing, graphics, and special effects. Covers all budget levels from desktop post to feature films.
130 Pages
Frequency: Monthly
Circulation: 31464
Founded in 1986

18766 **American Cinematographer**
American Society of Cinematographers
1782 North Orange Drive
PO Box 2230
Hollywood, CA 90078-2230

323-969-4333
800-448-0145; Fax: 323-876-4973
office@theasc.com
www.theasc.com

Covers feature films, television, commercials, music videos, digital video, new equipment, DVD and book releases and much more. An exploration and a reflection of today's cinematography. A publication of the American Society of Cinematographers.
Cost: $29.95
Frequency: Monthly
Circulation: 42000
Founded in 1919
Mailing list available for rent

18767 **Animation Magazine**
Animation Magazine
26500 W.Agoura Rd
Suite 102
Calabasas, CA 91302

818-883-2884; Fax: 818-883-3773
info@animationmagazine.net
www.animationmagazine.net

Jean Thoren, President

Promotes the art and business of animation and gives recognition to those animators and technicians who make the world of animation what it is today.
Cost: $50.00
Frequency: Monthly
Circulation: 30000
ISSN: 1041-617X
Founded in 1986
Printed in 4 colors on glossy stock

18768 **Celebrity Service**
8833 W Sunset Boulevard
Suite 401
Los Angeles, CA 90069-2171

213-883-3671; Fax: 310-652-9244

Robert Dean, Manager/Director

A listing of celebrities names and addresses. Publisher of the Celebrity Bulletin informing the entertainment and news industry of which celebrities are traveling to Hollywood and New York
Frequency: Bi-Monthly

18769 **Cineaste**
Cineaste Magazine
243 5th Ave
Suite 706
New York, NY 10016

212-366-5720; Fax: 212-366-5724
cineaste@cineaste.com
www.cineaste.com

Gary Crowdus, Editor-in-Chief
Cynthia Lucia, Editor
Richard Porton, Editor
Dan Georgakas, Consulting Editor
Vicki Robinson, Production Assistant

An internationally recognized independent film magazine. Features contributions from many of America's most articulate and outspoken writers, critics and scholars. Focussing on both the art and politics of the cinema.
Cost: $ 20.00
Frequency: Quarterly
Circulation: 11000
ISSN: 0009-7004
Founded in 1967
Mailing list available for rent

18770 **Cinefantastique**
CFQ Media
PO Box 34425
Los Angeles, CA 90034-0425

310-204-0825; Fax: 310-204-5882
www.cfq.com

Frederick Clarke, Editor

Provides coverage of genre entertainment. Each issue features in-depth coverage of sci-fi, fantasy and horror films, TV, DVDs, games, toys, books, comics and more.
Cost: $34.95
Frequency: Monthly
Circulation: 40,000

18771 **Cinefex**
79 Daily Drive
#309
Camarillo, CA 93010

805-383-0800; Fax: 805-383-0803
advertising@cinefex.com
www.cinefex.com

A quarterly magazine devoted to motion picture special effects.
Cost: $32.00
180 Pages
Frequency: Quarterly
Circulation: 30000
ISSN: 0198-1056
Founded in 1980
Printed in 4 colors

18772 **Cinema Journal**
University of Texas Press
2100 Comal
PO Box 7819
Austin, TX 78713-7819

512-471-7233
800-252-3206; Fax: 512-232-7178
utpress@uts.cc.utexas.edu
www.utexas.edu/utpress

Sponsored by the Society for Cinema and Media Studies. The journal presents recent scholarship by SCMS members. It publishes essays on a wide variety of subjects from diverse methodological perspectives. A 'Professional Notes' section informs Society of Cinema and Media Studies readers about upcoming events, research opportunities, and the latest published research. Cinema Journal is a member of the CELJ, the

Conference of Editors of Learned Journals.
Cost: $42.00
144 Pages
Frequency: Quarterly
Circulation: 2800
ISSN: 0009-7101
Founded in 1950
Printed in on matte stock

18773 **Daily Variety/Gotham**
360 Park Avenue South
New York, NY 10010-3659

646-746-7001; Fax: 646-746-6977
vtccustserv@cdsfulfillment.com
www.variety.com

Peter Bart, Editor-in-Chief
Timothy M Gray, Editor
Ted Johnson, Managing Editor
Kathy Lyford, Managing Editor
Phil Gallo, Associate Editor

Focus is on Broadway theater, network television headquarters, regional music business, and local film production. Explores the role of New York City in relation to the national and global entertainment industries.
Cost: $259.00
Frequency: Daily
Founded in 1905

18774 **Daily Variety/LA**
5900 Wilshire Boulevard
Suite 3100
Los Angeles, CA 90036-3659

323-617-9100; Fax: 323-857-0494
vtccustserv@cdsfulfillment.com
www.variety.com

Peter Bart, Editor-in-Chief
Timothy M Gray, Editor
Ted Johnson, Managing Editor
Kathy Lyford, Managing Editor
Phil Gallo, Associate Editor

Focus is on Hollywood, network television headquarters, regional music business, and local film production. Explores the role of Hollywood in relation to the national and global entertainment industries.
Cost: $259.00
Frequency: Daily
Founded in 1905

18775 **Documentary Magazine**
International Documentary Association
3470 Wilshire Boulevard
Suite 980
Los Angeles, CA 90010

212-232-1660; Fax: 213-232-1669
tom@documentary.org
www.documentary.org
Facebook, Twitter, LinkedIn, Instagram

Thomas White, Editor
Maria Elena Hewett, Account Executive
Simon Kilmurry, Executive Director

Devoted exclusively to nonfiction media.
Cost: $55.00
2631 Members
Frequency: Quarterly
Founded in 1982
Mailing list available for rent: 25000 names
Printed in 4 colors on glossy stock

18776 **Film & History**
Historians Film Committee
Lawrence University,Memorial Hall B5
711 E Boldt Way
Appleton, WI 54911

920-832-6649
www.h-net.org/~filmhis

Peter C Rollins, Director
Deborah Carmichael, Editor-in-Chief
Cynthia Miller, Associate Editor-in-Chief

An Interdisciplinary Journal of Film and Television Studies concerned with the impact of motion pictures on our society. Film and History focuses on how feature films and documentary films both represent and interpret history. Types of articles include: Analysis of individual films and/or television programs from a historical perspective, survey of documents related to the production of films, or analysis of history as explored through film.
Cost: $50.00
Frequency: Bi-annually
Circulation: 1000
ISSN: 0360-3695
Founded in 1970

18777 **Film & Video Magazine**
110 William Street
11th Floor
New York, NY 10038

212-621-4900; Fax: 212-621-4635
www.studiodaily.com/filmandvideo

Bryant Frazer, Editor-in-Chief
Pete Putman, Senior Editor
Alison Johns, Editor-in-Chief
Scott Gentry, Group Publisher
Jarrett Cory, Classified Sales

Covers new ideas in creating entertainment by focusing on technique in the production and finishing of features, TV programming, music videos and commercials. No longer publishes print copies, magazine is 100% digital
Frequency: Monthly
Founded in 1983
Printed in 4 colors

18778 **Film Journal International**
VNU Business Media
770 Broadway,7th Floor
New York, NY 10003-9595

212-493-4097; Fax: 646-654-7694
www.filmjournal.com

Penny Vane, President
Sid Holt, Editorial Director
Robert Sunshine, Publisher/Editor
Robin Klamfoth, Advertising Director
Kevin Lally, Executive Editor

A trade publication covering the motion picture industry, including theatrical exhibition, production, distribution, and allied activities. Articles report on US and international news, with features on current production, industry trends, theatre design, equipment, concessions, sound, digital cinema, screen advertising, and other industry-related news. Each issue also includes the Buying and Booking Guide, with comprehensive feature film reviews.
Cost: $65.00
Frequency: Monthly
Founded in 1934
Mailing list available for rent

18779 **Film Threat**
Film Threat International Headquarters
5042 Wilshire Boulevard
PMB 1500
Los Angeles, CA 90036

FAX 310-274-7985
www.filmthreat.com
Facebook, Twitter

Mark Bell, Editor-in-Chief
Eric Campos, Senior Contributing Editor
Chris Gore, Founder/Publishjer

The print edition of Film Threat retired in 1997, but the legend has lived on as an internet journalism mainstay. FilmThreat.com delivers film reviews, film festival coverage, exclusive filmmaker interviews and original video content.
Cost: $10.50
Frequency: Bi-Monthly
Circulation: 100,000
Founded in 1985

18780 **Hollywood Life**
Movieline Magazine
10537 Santa Monica Blvd
Suite 250
Los Angeles, CA 90025-4952

310-234-9501; Fax: 310-234-0332
hollywoodlife@pcspublink.com
www.hollywoodlive.net

Anne Volokh, President

Formerly called Movieline, an entertainment lifestyle featuring interviews with stars, directors and producers; as well as information on celebrity shopping, up and coming talent, soundtracks, electronics and fashion associated with hollywood style and trends.
Cost: $13.75
Frequency: Monthly
Founded in 1989
Printed in 4 colors on glossy stock

18781 **Hollywood Reporter**
Prometheus Global Media
770 Broadway
New York, NY 10003-9595

212-493-4100; Fax: 646-654-5368
www.prometheusgm.com
Facebook, Twitter, YouTube

Richard D. Beckman, CEO
James A. Finkelstein, Chairman
Madeline Krakowsky, Vice President Circulation
Tracy Brater, Executive Director Crative Service

Gives fresh ideas for film and TV. Covers the full spectrum of craft and commerce in the entertainment industry.
Cost: $199.00
Frequency: Weekly
Circulation: 34770

18782 **International Cinematographers Guild Magazine**
7755 W Sunset Blvd
Suite 300
Los Angeles, CA 90046-3911

323-876-0160; Fax: 323-876-6383
info@icgmagazine.com
www.cameraguild.com

Steven Poster, President
John McCarthy, Marketing

Serves as the journal of 'how to' for film and digital techniques. It incorporates a wide range of editorial for specific job categories in relation to cinematography for Film/Hi-Def/Digital production and defines the tools and technology necessary for advancement in this field. The magazine is written for members of the International Cinematographers Guild, including cinematographers, camera operators, camera assistants, still photographers, publicists, film loaders, and others in the field.
Cost: $48.00
Frequency: Monthly
Founded in 1929

18783 **Journal of Film and Video**
University Film and Video Association
University of Illinois Press
1325 S Oak Street
Champaign, IL 61820

217-244-0626
866-244-0626; Fax: 217-244-9910
journals@uiuc.edu
www.ufva.org

Stephen Tropiano, Editor
Cheryl Jestis, Membership

Focuses on scholarship in the fields of film and video production, history, criticism, and aesthetics. Topics include film and related media, education in these fields, and the function of

film and video in society.
Cost: $40.00
Frequency: Quarterly
Circulation: 1200

18784 Journal of Popular Film and Television
Heldref Publications
1319 18th St Nw
Suite 2
Washington, DC 20036-1802

202-296-6267
800-365-9753; Fax: 202-296-5149
subscribe@heldref.org
www.heldref.org

James Denton, Executive Director
Gary Edgerton, Co-Executive Editor

Articles discuss networks, genres, series and audiences, as well as celebrity stars, directors and studios. Regular features include essays on the social and cultural background of films and television programs, filmographies, bibliographies, and commisioned book and video reviews.
Cost: $51.00
Frequency: Quarterly
ISSN: 0195-6051
Founded in 1956

18785 Keyframe Magazine
DMG Publishing
2756 N Green Valley Pkwy
Suite 261
Henderson, NV 89014-2120

702-990-8656; Fax: 702-992-0471
www.dmgpublishing.com

Dariush Derakhshani, Editor-in-Chief
Cheri Madison, Managing Editor
Charles Edgin, Editorial Director
Alice Edgin, Executive Editor

In response to reader requests, Keyframe is adding to its LightWave and Photoshop tutorials and content additional bonus pages covering other tools used by digital artists. As Keyframe evolves into this larger, better magazine, its new title with be HDRI 3D.
Cost: $54.00
Circulation: 9000
Founded in 1997

18786 Millimeter Magazine
PO Box 2100
Skokie, IL 60076-7800

847-763-9504
866-505-7173; Fax: 847-763-9682
www.millimeter.com

Cynthia Wisehart, Editor

In a fast-changing and challenging industry, Millimeter anticipates the future. Its early coverage of important technology-driven trends such as 24p production, desktop post, and digital cinema has helped readers remain competitive and plan their business investments. Millimeter is an authoritative resource for professionals in production, postproduction, animation, streaming, and visual effects for motion pictures, television and commercials.
Cost: $70.00
Frequency: Monthly

18787 Movie Collectors World
Arena Publishing
PO BOX 309
Fraser, MI 48026

586-774-4311; Fax: 703-940-4566
www.mcwonline.com

Brian Bukantis, Editor

Leading collector's publication for collectors of movie memorabilia, with an emphasis on collectible movie posters. Each issue is filled with ads from dealers and collectors all over the world. In any monthly issue, you will find movie posters common and rare - everything from the 'Golden Age' to today's blockbusters.
Cost: $36.00
36-44 Pages
Frequency: Monthly
Circulation: 6000

18788 MovieMaker
MovieMaker Magazine
8328 De Soto Ave.
Canoga Park, CA 91304

310-742-7214
888-881-5861; Fax: 818-349-9922
www.moviemaker.com

Timothy Rhys, Publisher/Editor-in-Chief
Jennifer M Wood, Editor
Phillip Williams, Editor at Large
Ian Bage, New Marketing Services
Liza Kelley, Production Manager

MovieMaker is the world's most widely - read independent movie magazine that focuses on the art and business of making movies. Its editorial mix is a progressive mix of in depth interviews and criticism combined by practical techniques and advice on financing, distribution and production strategies.
Cost: $18.00
Frequency: Quarterly
Circulation: 54000
Founded in 1993
Mailing list available for rentat $175 per M

18789 Premiere Magazine
Hachette Filipacchi Media US Inc
1633 Broadway
Suite 41
New York, NY 10019-6708

212-767-6000; Fax: 212-481-6428

Jessica Letkemann, Editor
Jennifer Cooper, Producer

A magazine for young adults, which focuses on the art and commerce of the film industry. Première's feature articles, profiles and monthly columns include original photgraphy, interviews with Hollywood's A-list and up-and-coming talent, studio heads and producers.

18790 Produced By
The Producers Guild of America
8530 Wilshire Blvd
Suite 450
Beverly Hills, CA 90211-3115

310-358-9020; Fax: 310-358-9520
info@producersguild.org
www.producersguild.org

Vance Van Petter, Executive Director
Audra Whaley, Director Operations
Kyle Katz, Director Member Benefits
Chris Greenr, Director Communications
Dan Dodd, Advertising

Provided as a benefit with membership to the Producers Guild of America.
Frequency: Quarterly
Circulation: 325
Founded in 1962

18791 Producer
Testa Communications
25 Willowdale Avenue
Port Washington, NY 11050-3779

516-767-2500; Fax: 516-767-9335

Randi Altman, Editor
Sande Seidman, Advertising Manager

Magazine aimed at producers, directors and creative people in the image and sound realms, with production stories on feature films, television, commercials, documentary, and corporate video projects. Accent is on the creative application of technology, following producers into the field and onto the studio set.
Cost: $15.00
Frequency: Bi-Monthly
Circulation: 18,300

18792 SMPTE Journal
Society of Motion Picture & Television Engineers
3 Barker Ave
Sute 5
White Plains, NY 10601-1509

914-761-1100; Fax: 914-761-3115
www.smpte.org
Facebook, Twitter

Barbara Lange, Executive Director

Featuring industry-leading papers and standards, each month the Journal keeps its members on the cutting edge of the industry. Each issue provides the latest research and papers, ranging in style from technical, scientific, and tutorial, to applications/practices. Readers are kept up-to-date on events and meetings, the latest publications and brochures, and new products and developments.
Cost: $140.00
Frequency: Monthly
Circulation: 10000
Founded in 1916
Printed in on glossy stock

18793 San Francisco Cinematheque
San Francisco Cinematheque
145 Ninth Street
Suite 240
San Francisco, CA 94103

415-552-1990; Fax: 415-552-2067
sfc@sfcinematheque.org
www.sfcinematheque.org

Stephen Anker, Executive Director
Alfonso Alvarez, Board Director
Gina Basso, Board Director
Aimee Friberg, Board Director
Jeff Lambert, Board Director

Supports risk-taking art, cutting edge artists and the boundless potential of creative expression.
Cost: $15.00
Frequency: Monthly
Founded in 1961

18794 Script
Forum
5638 Sweet Air Road
Baldwin, MD 21013-9009

410-592-3466
888-245-2228; Fax: 410-592-8062
www.scriptmag.com
Facebook, YouTube, RSS

Mark Madnick, Publisher
David Geatty, Founding Publisher
Shelly Mellot, Editor-in-Chief
Andrew Schneider, Managing Editor
Maureen Green, Editor

A leading source of information on the crage and business of writing for film and television. Each issues delivers informative articles on writing, developing and marketing screenplays and television scripts. Most articles are written by working writers. Additionally, development executives, agents, managers and entertainment attorneys contribute regularly.
Cost: $24.95
Frequency: Bi-Monthly
Circulation: 12000

18795 **Starlog**
1372 Broadway
2nd Floor
New York, NY 10018

212-689-2830
800-934-6788
www.starlog.com

David McDonnel, Editor
Norman Jacobs, Founder

Information on science fiction happenings in the movies and television industries.
Cost: $56.97
Frequency: Monthly
Circulation: 350000

18796 **The Independent**

Home Page: independent-magazine.org
Facebook, Twitter

Online source of information and inspiration for independent, grassroots and activist media makers.
Founded in 2007

18797 **Variety**
Reed Business Information
5700 Wilshire Boulevard
Suite 120
Los Angeles, CA 90036-3659

323-857-6600
866-698-2743; Fax: 323-857-0494
VTCCustserv@cdsfulfillment.com
www.variety.com

Charles C Koones, Publisher
Peter Bart, Editor-in-Chief
Timothy Gray, Editor
Kathy Lyford, Managing Editor
Christopher Wessel, Circulation Director

Variety covers all aspects of film, television and cable, homevideo, music, new media and technolgy, theater and finance. Topics run from people, companies, products and performances, to development, financing, distribution, regulation and marketing.
Cost: $259.00
Frequency: Weekly
Circulation: 35168
Founded in 1905

Trade Shows

18798 **American Film Institute Festival: AFI Fest**
American Film Institute
2021 N Western Avenue
Los Angeles, CA 90027-1657

323-856-7896
866-234-3378; Fax: 323-856-9118
AFIFEST@AFI.com
www.afifest.com

Jennifer Morgerman, Publicity Director
Stacey Leinson, Publicity Manager
Lagan Sebert, Publicity Coordinator
John Wildman, Filmmaker Press Liaison
Alison Deknatel, Director Communications

A 10-day event held each November, the festival features a rich slate of films from emerging filmmakers, nightly red-carpet gala premieres and global showcases of the latest work from the great film masters. AFI runs concurrently with the American Film Market. Together, AFT Fest and AFM provide the film industry with the only concurrent festival/market event in North America.
60000 Attendees
Frequency: November
Founded in 1986

18799 **Getting Real Conference**
International Documentary Association
3470 Wilshire Boulevard
Suite 980
Los Angeles, CA 90010

213-232-1660; Fax: 213-232-1669
michael@documentary.org
www.documentary.org

Simon Kilmurry, Executive Director

A conference for documentary professionals to network and learn from colleagues.
Frequency: Annual
Founded in 1982

18800 **International Cinema Equipment (ICECO) Showest**
Magna-Tech Electronic Company
5600 NW 32nd Avenue
Miami, FL 33142

305-573-7339; Fax: 305-573-8101
www.showest.com

Steven H Krams, President
Dara Reusch, VP
Julio Urbay, VP International Sales/Marketing
Fancisco Blanco, VP Technical Services
Arturo Quintero, Architectural Design/Development

Annual convention for the Motion Picture industry. It is an international gathering devoted exclusively to the movie business. It is also the single largest international gathering of motion picture professionals and theatre owners in the world, with delegates from more than 50 countries in attendance each year.
Frequency: March
Founded in 1975

18801 **International Cinema Equipment Company ICECO Show East**
Magna-Tech Electronic Company,Inc.
1998 NE 150th Street
North Miami, FL 33181

305-573-7339; Fax: 305-573-8101
iceco@aol.com
www.iceco.com

Steven H Krams, President
Dara Reusch, VP
Julio Urbay, VP International Sales/Marketing
Francisco Blanco, VP/Technical Services
Arturo Quintero, Architectural Design & Development

This annual convention brings together over 1300 colleagues from the motion picture industry in the United States, Latin America and the Caribbean. The convention provides information on industry trends, screen films and product reels, state-of-the-art theatre equipment along with services and technologies vital to the industry.
1300 Attendees
Founded in 1975

18802 **Moondance International Film Festival**
Moondance International Film Festival
970 9th Street
Boulder, CO 80302

303-818-5771
director@moondancefilmfestival.com
www.moondancefilmfestival.com
Facebook, Twitter, LinkedIn

Elizabeth English, Festival Founder/Executive Director
Kyle/Erica Saylors, Festival Director/Event Coordinator
Karina Pyudik, Registration Coordinator
Douglis C Garvin, Special Events Coordinator
Roy Bodner, Publicist/Media Relations

The Festival's primary goal is to present films and scripts which have the power to raise awareness about vital social issues, educating writers and filmmakers, as well as festival audiences, and inspiring them to take positive action. The Festival's objective is to promote and encourage independent filmmakers, screenwriters, playwrights, and music composers and the best works in films, screenplays, stageplays, TV scripts, radioplays, film scores, lyrics, librettos, music videos, and short stor
Frequency: Annual
Founded in 1999
Mailing list available for rent

18803 **New York Film Festival**
Film Society of Lincoln Center
70 Lincoln Center Plaza
New York, NY 10023

212-875-5610
888-313-6085
www.filmlinc.com
Facebook, Twitter

Rose Kuo, Executive Director
Richard Pena, Program Director
Lesli Klainberg, Managing Director

Celebrates American and international cinema and recognizes and supports new filmmakers.
Frequency: Annual

18804 **Sundance Film Festival**
Sundance Institute
1825 Three Kings Drive
PO Box 684426
Park City, UT 84060

435-658-3456; Fax: 435-658-3457
Institute@sundance.org
www.sundance.org

Robert Redford, Founder
Keri Putnam, Executive Director
Jill Miller, Managing Director

Annual festival held in Park City, Utah as a US showcase for American and International independent film. The Institute is dedicated to the development of artists of independent vision and the exhibition of their new work. Since its inception, the Institute has grown into an internationally recognized resource for thousands of independent artists.
Frequency: January
Founded in 1981

18805 **Telluride Film Festival**
National Film Preserve
800 Jones Street
Berkeley, CA 94710

510-665-9494; Fax: 510-665-9589
mail@telluridefilmfestival.org
www.telluridefilmfestival.org

Bill Pence, Founder
Stella Pence, Founder

Well situated on the international film festival calendar, Terruride takes place in Telluride, Colorado, and is defined by sense of purity and commitment.
Founded in 1974

18806 **Toronto International Film Festival**
TIFF Bell Lightbox
350 King Street West
Toronto

888-599-8433
www.tiff.net

William Marshall, Founder
Piers Handling, Director & CEO
Noah Cowan, Artistic Director, Bell Lightbox
Cameron Bailey, Co-Director

Publicly attended film festival that takes place each September in Toronto, Ontario, Canada, showing upwards of 400 films from more than 60 countries. The festival is currently headquartered at TIFF Bell Lightbox, which opened in 2010.
Founded in 1976
Mailing list available for rent

Directories & Databases

18807 Annual Index to Motion Picture Credits
Academy of Motion Picture Arts and Sciences
8949 Wilshire Blvd
Beverly Hills, CA 90211-1972
310-247-3000; Fax: 310-271-3395
www.oscars.org
The Index is closely tied to the annual Academy Awards presentation. As part of the Academy Awards process, the Academy of Motion Picture Arts and Sciences gathers credits for each film hoping to qualify for awards. These credits, compiled and verified by the film's producer or distributor, are the core of the Annual Index and IMPC database. In addition to personal credits, IMPC also records index production and releasing dates, MPAA ratings, running times, color, language, and more.
Frequency: Annual
ISBN: 0-942102-37-1
ISSN: 0163-5123
Founded in 1934

18808 Blu-Book Production Directory
Hollywood Creative Directory
5055 Wilshire Blvd
Los Angeles, CA 90036-6103
323-525-2369
800-815-0503; Fax: 323-525-2398
Valencia McKinley, Manager
A comprehensive directory for professionals in the production and post-production industries. Provides current contact information needed to produce a film, TV program, commercial, or music video. The directory contains a special tabbed section on premier below-the-line craft professionals, along with selective credits, and has been expanded to include New York production facilities and services, making it one of the only bi-coastal resources of its kind.
Cost: $39.95
450 Pages
Frequency: Annual
ISBN: 1-928936-44-X

18809 Boxoffice: Circuit Giants
Boxoffice
PO Box 1634
Des Plains, IL 60019
212-627-7000
www.boxoffice.com
Peter Cane, Publisher
Joe Policy, CEO
Annlee Ellingson, Editor
Francesca Dinglasan, Senior Editor
Bob Vale, VP Advertising and Sales
Directory of the largest exhibition chains. Available to subscribers of Boxoffice magazine
Cost: $59.95
Frequency: Annual
Founded in 1990

18810 Boxoffice: Distributor Directory
Boxoffice
PO Box 1634
Des Plains, IL 60019
212-627-7000
www.boxoffice.com
Peter Cane, Publisher
Joe Policy, CEO
Annlee Ellingson, Editor
Francesca Dinglasan, Senior Editor
Bob Vale, VP Advertising and Sales
Listings of studio and independent film suppliers. Available to subscribers of Boxoffice magazine
Cost: $59.95
Frequency: Annual
Founded in 1990

18811 Directors Guild of America Directory of Members
Directors Guild of America
7920 W Sunset Blvd
Los Angeles, CA 90046-3347
310-289-2000
800-421-4173; Fax: 310-289-2029
www.dga.org
Jay Roth, President
Morgan Rumpf, Director Communications
Paul Zepp, Membership Administrator
Darrell L Hop, Editor DGA Monthly/Website
Michael Apted, Secretary
The DGA represents Film and Television Directors, Unit Production Managers, First Assistant Directors, Second Assistant Directors, Technical Coordinators and Tape Associate Directors, Stage Managers and Production Associates. The Directory is available in print and on-line
Cost: $25.00
Frequency: Annual

18812 Editors Guild Directory
Motion Picture Editors Guild
7715 Sunset Boulevard
Suite 200
Hollywood, CA 90046
323-876-4770
800-705-8700; Fax: 323-876-0861
info@editorsguild.com
www.editorsguild.com
Ron Kutak, Executive Director
Tomm Carroll, Publications Director
Serena Kungr, Director Membership Services
Adriana Iglesias-Dietl, Membership Administrator
Tris Carpenter, Manager
An invaluable resource for producers, directors and post production professionals alike. It lists contact, credit, award and classification information for all of the Guild's active members at the time of publication, as well as a list of Oscar and Emmy winners for every year since the awards began. It also includes a retirees section.
Cost: $25.00
Frequency: Bi-Annual
Founded in 1994

18813 Film Journal: Distribution Guide Issue
Film Journal International
770 Broadway
5th Floor
New York, NY 10003-9595
646-654-7680; Fax: 646-654-7694
www.filmjournal.com
Robert Sunshine, Publisher/Editor
Kevin Lally, Executive Editor
Rex Roberts, Associate Editor
Andrew Sunshine, Advertising Director
Katey Rich, Editorial Assistant
The International Distribution and subdistribution Guide supplements the regular monthly Buying and Booking Guide. It is designed to furnish ready reference information on the who, what, where and how of theatrical sales. It lists the names, addresses, personnel, telephone numbers and product of domestic and international distributors, both major and independent, along with similar information on regional exchanges together with national companies they handle.
Frequency: Annual

18814 Film Journal: Equipment Guide
Film Journal International
770 Broadway
5th Floor
New York, NY 10003-9595
646-654-7680; Fax: 646-654-7694
www.filmjournal.com
Robert Sunshine, Publisher/Editor
Kevin Lally, Executive Editor
Robin Klamfoth, Advertising Director
Rex Roberts, Associate Editor
Katey Rich, Editorial Assistant
The Equipment, Concessions and Services Guide is designed to provide ready reference information on the theatrical equipment and concessions industry. It lists in detail the company names, addresses, telephone numbers, personnel, affiliations and products of equipment and concession manufacturers and service companies, along with similar information on US and foreign service dealers and suppliers, arranged in alphabetical order according to state or country.
Frequency: Annual

18815 Film Journal: Exhibition Guide
Film Journal International
770 Broadway
5th Floor
New York, NY 10003-9595
212-493-4097; Fax: 646-654-7694
www.filmjournal.com
Robert Sunshine, Publisher/Editor
Kevin Lally, Executive Editor
Robin Klamfoth, Advertising Director
Rex Roberts, Associate Editor
Sarah Sluis, Editorial Assistant
The exhibition Guide is an alphabetical listing designed to provide ready reference information on the leading theatrical motion picture circuits. It lists in comprehensive detail such data as company names, addresses and phone numbers, total screens and new screens projected, division office locations, top personnel, recent circuit acquisitions, and a state-by-state breakdown of screens.
Frequency: Annual
Founded in 1934
Mailing list available for rent

18816 Film Superlist: Motion Pictures in the Public Domain
Hollywood Film Archive
8391 Beverly Blvd
Ste. 321
Los Angeles, CA 90048-2633
323-655-4968
Richard Baer, Executive Director
Created by Walter E. Hurst and updated by Richard Baer. 1992-1994. Three volumes to date, covering 50,000 films from the years 1894-1939, 1940-1949 and 1950-1959.

18817 Grey House Performing Arts Directory
Grey House Publishing
4919 Route 22
PO Box 56
Amenia, NY 12501
518-789-8700
800-562-2139; Fax: 845-373-6390
books@greyhouse.com
www.greyhouse.com
Facebook, Twitter
Leslie Mackenzie, Publisher
Richard Gottlieb, Editor
The most comprehensive resource covering the Performing Arts. This directory provides current information on over 8,500 Dance Companies, Instrumental Music Programs, Opera Companies, Choral Groups, Theater Companies, Performing Arts Series, Performing Arts Facilities and Artist

Management Groups.
Cost: $185.00
1200 Pages
Frequency: Annual
ISBN: 1-592373-76-3
Founded in 1981

18818 Grey House Performing Arts Directory - Online Database
Grey House Publishing
4919 Route 22
PO Box 56
Amenia, NY 12501
518-789-8700
800-562-2139; Fax: 518-789-0556
gold@greyhouse.com
gold.greyhouse.com
Facebook, Twitter
Leslie Mackenzie, Publisher
Richard Gottlieb, Editor
The Grey House Performing Arts Directory - Online Database provides immediate access to dance companies, orchestras, opera companies, choral groups, theater companies, series, festivals and perfoming arts facilities across the country, or in their region, state, or in your own backyard. It offers unequaled coverage of the Performing Arts - over 8,500 listings - of the major performance organization, facilities, and information resources.
Frequency: Annual
Founded in 1981

18819 International Motion Picture Alamanc
Quigley Publishing Company
64 Wintergreen Lane
Groton, MA 01450
860-228-0247
800-231-8239; Fax: 860-228-0157
quigleypub@aol.com
William J Quigley, President/Publisher
Eileen Quigley, Editor
Contains over 400 pages of biographies and 500 pages of reference material. From 1928 to the present day, the complete set contains the biography of everyone who has ever been of importance to the Industry. Each edition includes thousands of company listings, credits for current films and films released in the prior ten years, statistics and awards and complete coverage of all aspects of the indiustry, including production, distribution and exhibition.
Cost: $175.00
Frequency: Annual

18820 International Television and Video Almanac
Quigley Publishing Company
64 Wintergreen Lane
Groton, MA 01450
860-228-0247
800-231-8239; Fax: 860-228-0157
quigleypub@aol.com
William J Quigley, President/Publisher
Eileen Quigley, Editor
Each edition contains over 400 pages of biographies and an additional 500 pages of reference material on television programs, broadcast, cable and satellie, production services, the video industry, statistics and awards. Included are detailed listings for thousands of companies, as well as coverage outside the United States.
Cost: $175.00
Frequency: Annual
Founded in 1955

18821 Mini Reviews
Cineman Syndicate
31 Purchase St
Suite 203
Rye, NY 10580-3013
914-967-5353
John P McCarthy, Editor
An easy to read, easy to use guide for movie watchers updated weekly.
Frequency: Weekly
Founded in 2000

18822 Motion Picture TV and Theatre Directory
Motion Picture Enterprises
PO Box 276
Tarrytown, NY 10591-0276
212-245-0969; Fax: 212-245-0974
www.mpe.net
Neal R Pilzer, Publisher
The Guide is mailed to members of 59 trade associations, unions and professional societies; decision-makers at advertising agencies, production companies, TV stations, and government agencies; faculty and students of nearly 200 film schools; and other prime purchasers of film and TV equipment and services nationwide. Companies are listed both by category and company name. Listings include company name, address and telephone number as well as fax numbers, e-mail addresses, and web site URLs.
Cost: $18.80
335 Pages
Frequency: Annual
Circulation: 82500
Founded in 1963

18823 Movie World Almanac
Hollywood Film Archive
8391 Beverly Blvd
PMB 321
Los Angeles, CA 90048-2633
323-655-4968
Richard Baer, Executive Director
Lists over 200 major American and foreign film distributors who handle old and contemporary films.

18824 Reel Directory
Lynetta Freeman
PO Box 1910
Boyes Hot Springs, CA 95416
415-531-9760; Fax: 707-581-1725
info@reeldirectory.com
www.reeldirectory.com
Lynetta Freeman, Manager
Keith Marsalis, Director
Katie Carney, Director of Marketing
Source for Film, Video and Multimedia in Northern California.
Cost: $25.00
700 Pages
Frequency: Annual
Circulation: 5,000
Founded in 1979

18825 Studio Report: Film Development
Hollywood Creative Directory
5055 Wilshire Blvd
Los Angeles, CA 90036-6103
323-525-2369
800-815-0503; Fax: 323-525-2398
Valencia McKinley, Manager
The only directory of its kind, in print for the first time. A complete breakdown of film development project tracking. A-Z listings by title, spec screenplays sold, hot studio projects, cross-referenced by studio, production company and genre. The directory's main body consists of an alphabetical listing of all in-development projects that have achieved a forward-moving milestone some time in the last five months. Subsequent sections sort and cross-reference the information to highlight aspects
Cost: $19.95
190 Pages
ISBN: 1-928936-49-0

Industry Web Sites

18826 http://gold.greyhouse.com
G.O.L.D Grey House OnLine Databases
Grey House Publishing's online database platform, GOLD, offers Quick Search, Keyword Search and Expert Search for most business sectors including motion picture and entertainment markets. The GOLD platform makes finding the information you need quick and easy - whether you're a novice searcher or an experienced database user. All of Grey House's directory products are available for subscription on the GOLD platform.

18827 www.actioncutprint.com
Action-Cut-Print
Website for filmmakers. filmmaking resources, free ezine for directors, film and TV bookstore. The Director's Chair magazine by director Peter D. Marshall.

18828 www.artdirectors.org
Art Directors Guild
Conceive and manage the background and settings for most films and television projects.

18829 www.castingsociety.com
Casting Society of America
An organization representing casting directors.

18830 www.discoverhollywood.com
Hollywood Arts Council
Promotes, nurtures and supports the arts field in Hollywood. Discover Hollywood on line.

18831 www.documentary.org
International Documentary Association
A nonprofit association founded to promote non-fiction film and video, to support the efforts of documentary film and video makers around the world, and to increase public appreciation and demand for the documentary.

18832 www.greyhouse.com
Grey House Publishing
Authoritative reference directories for most business sectors including motion picure and entertainment markets. Users can search the online databases with varied search criteria allowing for custom searches by product category, geographic area, sales volume, keyword, subject and more. Full Grey House catalog and online ordering also available.

18833 www.iqfilm.org
International Quorum of Film and Video Producers
Fosters the exchange of information and ideas. Seeks to raise professional standards. Disseminates information on new concepts and technology.

18834 www.millimeter.com
Millimeter Magazine
Authoritative resource for more than 33,000 qualified professionals in production, postproduction, animation, streaming and visual effects for motion pictures, television and commercials.

18835 www.mpaa.org
Motion Picture Association of America

Promotes high moral and artistic standards in motion picture production. Maintains Motion Picture Association Political Action Committee.

18836 **www.nyfa.com**
New York Film Academy
Educational institution devoted to providing focused filmmaking and acting instructions. Geared to offer an intensive, hands-on experience which gives students the opportunity to develop their creative skills to the fullest extent possible.

18837 **www.oscars.org**
Academy of Motion Picture Arts and Sciences
Current information on motion pictures, the arts and sciences, events and screenings.

18838 **www.producersguild.com**
Producers Guild of America
Members are producers of motion pictures and television shows mainly in the Los Angeles area.

18839 **www.resumegenie.com**
Motion Pictures job listings, salary information and job search tips.

18840 **www.smpte.org**
Society of Motion Picture & Television Engineers
Advances the practice and theory of engineering in television and film industry.

18841 **www.stuntnet.com**
International Stunt Association
Represents those involved in stunt work for the entertainment industry.

18842 **www.stuntwomen.com**
Stuntwomen's Association of Motion Pictures
A professional association for stuntwomen and stunt coordinators which seeks to uphold professional standards and improve working conditions.

18843 **www.sundance.org**
Sundance Institute
Nonprofit corporation dedicated to the support and development of emerging screenwriters and directors of vision. Hosts the Sundance Film Festival.

18844 **www.wif.org**
Women in Film
For global entertainment,communication and media industries. Focuses on contemporary issues facing women and provides an extensive network of valuable contacts, educational programs, scholars, film finishing funds, grants, community outreach, advocacy and practical services that promote, nurture and mentor women to achieve their highest potential.

Associations

18845 American Historic Racing Motorcycle Association
309 Buffalo Run
Goodlettsville, TN 37072

615-420-6435; Fax: 615-420-6438
www.ahrma.org
Facebook

Mark Hatten, Chairman
Matthew Benson, Communications Director
Mark Hatten, Treasurer
Rob Poole, Secretary
Carl Anderson, Treasurer

For individuals interested in vintage racing motorcycles.
5M Members
Founded in 1989

18846 American Motorcyclist Association
13515 Yarmouth Dr
Pickerington, OH 43147-8273

614-856-1900
800-AMA-JOIN; Fax: 614-856-1920
tlindsay@ama-cycle.org
www.americanmotorcyclist.com
Facebook, YouTube

Rob Dingman, President
Maggie McNally, Chair
Perry King, Vice Chairman
Scott Papenfus, Marketing Director
Ken Ford, Assistant Treasurer

The association's purpose is to pursue, protect and promote the interests of motorcyclists, while serving the needs of its members.
270M Members
Founded in 1924

18847 Antique Motorcycle Club of America
PO Box 663
Huntsville, AL 35804

256-509-9095
amcaExecutiveDirector@gmail.com
antiquemotorcycle.org
Facebook, Instagram

Keith S. Kizer, Executive Director

The AMCA is the largest club of its kind in the United States.
11000 Members

18848 Breakdown & Legal Assistance for Motorcyclists
13047 Ventura Blvd
Suite 100
Studio City, CA 91604-2250

818-377-6280
800-424-5377; Fax: 818-377-6290
russbrown@russbrown.com
www.russbrown.com
Facebook, Twitter

J Russell Brown II, President

A support group for motorcyclists. Offers roadside assistance for emergencies and breakdowns. Attorney referral service specializing in motorcycle accident cases. Brochures and guest speakers available upon request, also offers a twenty-four hour toll-free hotline.
100M Members
Founded in 1983

18849 Christian Motorcyclists Association
PO Box 9
Hatfield, AR 71945

Home Page: www.cmausa.org

John Ogden Sr., Chairman & CEO

Interdenominational and evangelistic Christian ministry dedicated to reaching people for Christ through motorcycling.
Founded in 1975

18850 Combat Veterans Motorcycle Association

Home Page: www.combatvet.org

Non-profit organization of veteran motorcycle hobbyists whose charitable events raise money for veteran care facilities.
Founded in 2001

18851 Harley Owners Group
National H.O.G. Office
PO Box 453
Milwaukee, WI 53201

800-258-2464; Fax: 414-343-4515
www.harleydavidson.com
Facebook, YouTube

James L Ziemer, President/CEO

Harley Davidson established the Harley Owners Group in response to a growing desire by Harley riders for an organized way to share their passion and show their pride.
60000 Members
Founded in 1983

18852 Motorcycle & Moped Industry Council
716 Gordon Baker Road
Suite 100
North York, M2H 3B4, ON

416-491-4449
877-470-6642; Fax: 416-493-1985
info@mmic.ca
www.mmic.ca

Robert Ramsay, President

National nonprofit trade association which represents the responsible interest of the major motorcycle distributors, as well as the manufacturers, distributors and the retail outlets of motorcycle-related products and services, and individual owners and riders of motorcycles in Canada.
140 Members
Founded in 1971

18853 Motorcycle Industry Council
2 Jenner Street
Suite 150
Irvine, CA 92618

949-727-4211; Fax: 949-727-3313
memberservices@mic.org
www.mic.org

Erik Pritchard, President/CEO
Eric Barnes, VP, Technical Programs
Scott Schloegel, SVP, Government Relations

The Motorcycle Industry Council (MIC) is a non-profit, national trade association representing manufacturers and distributors of motorcycles, scooters, motorcycle/ATV parts and accessories and members of allied trades.
300 Members
Founded in 1914

18854 Motorcycle Riders Foundation
1325 G Street NW
Suite 500
Washington, DC 20005

202-546-0983; Fax: 202-546-0986
www.mrf.org

Kirk Willard, President
Mike Kerr, Vice President
Paulette Pinkham, Secretary
Chuc Coulter, Treasurer
Tiffany Latimer, Office Manager

To continue developing an aggressive, independent national advocate for the advancement of motorcycling and its associated lifestyle which is financially stable and exceeds the needs of motorcycling enthusiasts.
Founded in 1987

18855 Motorcycle Safety Foundation
2 Jenner
Suite 150
Irvine, CA 92618-3812

949-727-3227
800-446-9227; Fax: 949-727-4217
MSF@msf-usa.org
www.msf-usa.org
Facebook, Twitter, YouTube

Tim Buche, President

Founded by the five leading manufacturers and distributors of motorcycles for the purpose of public safety education.
7 Members
Founded in 1972

18856 Women in the Wind
PO Box 8392
Toledo, OH 43605-0392

becky@womeninthewind.org
www.womeninthewind.org

Becky Brown, Founder/Treasurer
Gale Collins, President
Lauranne Bailey, VP
Peggy Zeeb, Secretary

Seeks to promote a positive image for women motorcyclists. Educates members on maintenance and safety.
1000 Members
Founded in 1979

Newsletters

18857 AHRMA Newsletter
American Historic Racing Motorcycle Association
PO Box 882
Wausau, WI 54402-0882

715-842-9699; Fax: 715-842-9545
www.ahrma.org

Jeff Smith, Director
Matt Benson, Executive Director
David Lamberth, Executive Director

For individuals interested in vintage motorcycles.
Cost: $2.00
Circulation: 5,000

18858 MRF Reports
Motorcycle Riders Foundation
236 Massachusetts Ave Ne
Suite 204
Washington, DC 20002-4980

202-546-0983; Fax: 202-546-0986
www.mrf.org

Eric Hampton, Editor/Publisher
Frequency: Bi-Monthly

Magazines & Journals

18859 American Motorcyclist
American Motorcyclist Association
13515 Yarmouth Dr
Pickerington, OH 43147-8273

614-856-1900
800-262-5646; Fax: 614-856-1920
membership@ama-cycle.org
http://www.americanmotorcyclist.com

Rob Dingman, President
Bill Wood, Editor-in-Chief
Grant Parsons, Managing Editor
John Holliday, Circulation

Magazine covers every facet of motorcycling. Each monthly issue details the people, places and events - from road rallies to road races - that make up the American motorcycling experience.
Cost: $39.00
Frequency: Monthly
Circulation: 260000
Founded in 1924
Printed in 4 colors on glossy stock

18860 Biker
Paisano Publishers
PO Box 3075
Agoura Hills, CA 91376-3075

818-898-8740
800-962-985; Fax: 818-889-1252
easyridersevents.com

Joe Teresi, Publisher
Dean Shawier, Editor

Events and charity events for the motorcycle enthusiast.
Cost: $15.00
96 Pages
Founded in 1971

18861 Cycle World
Hachette Filipacchi Media US
1499 Monrovia Ave
Newport Beach, CA 92663-2752

949-720-5300; Fax: 949-631-2374
www.hfmus.com

Nancy Laporte, Executive Director
David Edwards, Editor-in-Chief

Publication for motorcycle enthusiasts.
Cost: $16.00
136 Pages
Frequency: Monthly
Circulation: 325000

18862 Cycling USA
United States Cycling Federation
1 Olympic Plz
Colorado Spring, CO 80909-5775

719-866-4581; Fax: 719-866-4628
www.usacycling.org

Gerard Bisceglia, CEO
Sean Petty, Chief of Staff
Bike racing magazine.
Cost: $10.00
24 Pages
Circulation: 3000
Founded in 1920

18863 Dealernews Magazine
Advanstar Communications
New York
New York, NY 10016-5778

212-951-6600
800-854-3112; Fax: 212-951-6793
info@advanstar.com
www.dealernews.com

Mike Vaughan, Publisher
Mary Slepicka, Associate Publisher
Arlo Redwine, Managing Editor

Written for and read by a qualified power sports dealer network and related industry associates. It features articles on merchandising, sales techniques and profiles of successful retailers. Industry trends and business conditions are monitored through exclusive industry research.
Frequency: Monthly
Circulation: 17535
Founded in 1965
Printed in 4 colors on glossy stock

18864 Easyriders
Paisano Publishers
3547 Old Conejo Rd
Suite 106
Newbury Park, CA 91320

800-962-9857
800-825-7294; Fax: 805-375-4591
info@easyridersevents.com
easyridersevents.com

Joe Teresi, Publisher
Keith Ball, Editor
John Green, President

Motorcycle magazine.
Cost: $39.95
136 Pages
Frequency: Monthly
Founded in 1971

18865 Motorcycle Dealer News
Edgell Communications
4500 Campus Drive
Suite 100
Santa Ana, CA 92705

FAX 949-252-0499

Don Emde, Publisher

For dealers of power sports equipment and supplies.
Cost: $25.00

18866 Motorcycle Industry Magazine
Industry Shopper Publishing
PO Box 160
Gardnerville, NV 89410-160

775-782-0222
800-576-4624; Fax: 775-782-0266
www.mimag.com

Rick Campbell, Publisher
Rick Campbell, Editor
Caroline Carr, Sales Manager

Provides information to the motorcycle and accessory dealer and or retailer on products, services, events and people aiming to maximize profitablity and growth, also includes personal watercraft vehicles, ATV's and snowmobiles.
Frequency: Monthly
Circulation: 14000
ISSN: 0884-626X
Founded in 1976
Printed in 4 colors on glossy stock

18867 Shootin the Breeze
Women in the Wind
PO Box 8392
Toledo, OH 43605-0392

Home Page: www.womeninthewind.org

Becky Brown, Founder
Gale Collins, President
Lauranne Bailey, VP
Peggy Zeeb, Secretary

Available to all Women in the Wind members.
Frequency: 6x/year

18868 The Antique Motorcycle
Antique Motorcycle Club of America
PO Box 3004
Westerville, OH 43086

740-803-2584
antiquemotorcycle.org

Greg Harrison, Editor
Paul Holdsworth, Director of Advertising

Official publication of The Antique Motorcycle Club of America, Inc.
Frequency: Bimonthly
Founded in 2010

18869 Upshift Magazine
Motorcycle & Moped Industry Council
3000 Steeles Avenue East
Suite 201
Markham, Ontario L3R 4T9

416-491-4449
877-470-6642; Fax: 416-493-1985
info@mmic.ca
www.mmic.ca

Steve Thornton, Producer

Features articles and information on motorcycles.
Frequency: Quarterly

Trade Shows

18870 AMA Members Tour
American Motorcyclist Association
13515 Yarmouth Drive
Pickerington, OH 43147

614-856-1900; Fax: 614-856-1920
tlindsay@ama-cycle.org
http://www.americanmotorcyclist.com

Will Stoner, Director Special Events

The goal is to spread awareness of the benefits of membership and the importance of the work of the AMA does in protecting all motorcyclists' right to ride.
Frequency: Semi-Annual, June

18871 AMA Vintage Motorcycle Days
American Motorcyclist Association
13515 Yarmouth Drive
Pickerington, OH 43147

614-856-1900; Fax: 614-856-1920
tlindsay@ama-cycle.org
www.amadirectlink.com

Will Stoner, Director Special Events

Will benefit the Motorcycle Hall of Fame Museum and will feature an exhibit of classic motorcycles and memorabilia.
Frequency: July

18872 Annual Meeting of the Minds
Motorcycle Riders Foundation
236 Massachusetts Avenue NE
Suite 510
Washington, DC 20002-4980

202-546-0983; Fax: 202-546-0986
www.mrf.org

Carol Downs, Conference Director

Designed to educate and motivate those in the motorcyclists' rights community. The premier leadership conference that boasts an audience from across the nation and around the world.
Frequency: September

18873 Beast of the East
Motorcycle Riders Foundation
236 Massachusetts Avenue NE
Suite 510
Washington, DC 20002-4980

202-546-0983; Fax: 202-546-0986
www.mrf.org

Carol Downs, Conference Director

Designed to educate and motivate those in the motorcyclists' rights community. These events are a great chance to meet other people who are as passionate about motorcyclists' rights as you are.
Frequency: April

18874 Best of the West
Motorcycle Riders Foundation

236 Massachusetts Avenue NE
Suite 510
Washington, DC 20002-4980

202-546-0983; Fax: 202-546-0986
www.mrf.org

Carol Downs, Conference Director

Designed to educate and motivate those in the motorcyclists' rights community. These events are a great chance to meet other people who are as passionate about motorcyclists' rights as you are.
Frequency: June

18875 **International Motorcycle Show**
Advanstar Communications
201 E Sandpointe
Suite 600
Santa Ana, CA 92707

714-138-8400; Fax: 714-513-8481
www.motorcycleshows.com

Jeff D'Entremont, Show Director
Leah Stevens, Account Manager
Chris Alonzo, Account Manager

Exposition for motorcyclists and enthusiasts.

18876 **Los Angeles Calendar Motorcycle Show**
Breakdown & Legal Assistance for Motorcyclists
13047 Ventura Boulevard
Suite 100
Studio City, CA 91604

323-321-1483
800-424-5377; Fax: 818-377-6290
russbrown@russbrown.com
www.russbrown.com

Russ Brown, President

Biggest custom and performance streetbike event.
Frequency: July
Founded in 1983

18877 **Motocross American Reunion and Exhibit Grand Opening**
American Motorcyclist Association
13515 Yarmouth Drive
Pickerington, OH 43147

614-856-1900
800-262-5646; Fax: 614-856-1920
americanmotorcyclist.com

Since 1924, the AMA has protected the future of motorcycling and promoted the cotorcycle lifestyle. As the world's largest motorcycling rights organization, the AMA advocates for motorcyclists' interests in the halls of local, state and federal government, the committees of international governing organizations, and the court of pulic opinion.
Frequency: July
Founded in 1924

18878 **Motorcycle and Parts**
Glahe International
PO Box 2460
Germantown, MD 20875-2460

301-515-0012; Fax: 301-515-0016
www.glahe.com

Exhibits of motorcycle equipment, supplies and services.

18879 **Summer Nationals**
Women in the Wind
PO Box 8392
Toledo, OH 43605-0392

Home Page: www.womeninthewind.org

Becky Brown, Founder/Treasurer
Gale Collins, President
Lauranne Bailey, VP
Peggy Zeeb, Secretary
Frequency: July

Directories & Databases

18880 **MSF Guide to Motorcycling Excellence**
Motorcycle Safety Foundation
2 Jenner
Irvine, CA 92618-3812

949-727-3227; Fax: 949-727-4217
www.msf-usa.org

Tim Buche, President

Covering the skills, knowledge and strategies for riding right. Subjects include: preparing yourself and your bike, developing street strategies, and advanced theory for experienced riders.
Cost: $24.95
176 Pages

18881 **MilitaryBikers.org**

Home Page: www.militarybikers.org
Facebook

Directory and discussion boards of military motorcycle clubs.

18882 **Motorcycle Statistical Annual**
Motorcycle Industry Council
2 Jenner Street
Suite 150
Irvine, CA 92618

949-727-4211; Fax: 949-727-3313
www.mic.org

Erik Pritchard, President/CEO
Eric Barnes, VP, Technical Programs
Scott Schloegel, SVP, Government Relations

This industry-related directory offers statistical information on US motorcycle manufacturers and distributors, as well as national and state motorcycle associations.
Frequency: Annual
ISSN: 0149-3027

Industry Web Sites

18883 **http://gold.greyhouse.com**
G.O.L.D Grey House OnLine Databases

Grey House Publishing's online database platform, GOLD, offers Quick Search, Keyword Search and Expert Search for most business sectors including motorcycle and biking markets. The GOLD platform makes finding the information you need quick and easy - whether you're a novice searcher or an experienced database user. All of Grey House's directory products are available for subscription on the GOLD platform.

18884 **www.ahrma.org**
American Historic Racing Motorcycle Association

For individuals interested in vintage racing motorcycles.

18885 **www.amadirectlink.com**
American Motorcyclist Association

Covers every facet of motorcycling: the people, places and events that make up the American motorcycling experience. In addition, this award winning website offers profiles of issues affecting everyone who rides, and provides tools that help motorcyclists communicate directly with legislators, business leaders and the news media.

18886 **www.greyhouse.com**
Grey House Publishing

Authoritative reference directories for most business sectors including motocycle and biking markets. Users can search the online databases with varied search criteria allowing for custom searches by product category, geographic area, sales volume, keyword, subject and more. Full Grey House catalog and online ordering also available.

18887 **www.mic.org**
Motorcycle Industry Council

Nonprofit national trade association created to represent the motorcycle industry.

18888 **www.mmic.ca**
Motorcycle & Moped Industry Council

National nonprofit trade association which represents the responsible interest of the major motorcycle distributors, as well as the manufacturers, distributors and the retail outlets of motorcycle related products and services, and individual owners and riders of motorcycles in Canada.

18889 **www.msf-usa.org**
Motorcycle Safety Foundation

Founded by the five leading manufacturers and distributors of motorcycles for the purpose of public safety education.

18890 **www.russbrown.com**
Breakdown & Legal Assistance for Motorcyclists

A support group for motorcyclists. Offers roadside assistance for emergencies and breakdowns. Attorney referral service specializing in motorcycle accident cases. Brochures and guest speakers available upon request, also offers a twenty-four hour toll-free hotline.

Associations

18891 AERA Engine Builders Association
500 Coventry Lane
Suite 180
Crystal Lake, IL 60014

815-526-7600
888- 26-2372; Fax: 815-526-7601
info@aera.org
www.aera.org
Facebook, Twitter

Rex B. Crumpton, Chairman
Steve Edmondson, First Vice Chairman
Bobby Kammerer, Second Vice Chairman
Steve Schoeben, Treasurer
Kevin Frische, Director

A specialized network of professional engine builders, rebuilders, production engine remanufacturers and installers.
Founded in 1922

18892 Advocates for Highway and Auto Safety
750 1st St NE
Suite 901
Washington, DC 20002

202-408-1711; Fax: 202-408-1699
advocates@saferoads.org
www.saferoads.org
Facebook, Twitter

Judith Lee Stone, President
Jacqueline Gillan, VP
Judie Pasquini, Director

An organization whose members advocate the support and advancement of highway and auto safety through the implementation of state and federal laws, programs and policies.
Founded in 1989

18893 Alliance of Automobile Manufacturers
803 7th Street, N.W
Suite 300
Washington, DC 20001

202-326-5500
www.autoalliance.org
Facebook, Twitter, YouTube, Google+, RSS

Mitch Bainwol, President/ CEO

An association of 12 of the largest car manufacturers, and is the leading advocacy group for the auto industry.

18894 Alliance of State Automotive Aftermarket Associations
5330 Wall Street
Suite 100
Madison, WI 53718

608-240-2066; Fax: 608-240-2069
www.asaaa.com
Facebook, Twitter, Google+, Pinterest

Skip Potter, President
Randy Lisk, VP
Gary Manke, Executive Director
Ben Welch-Bolen, CEO & Co-Owner
Tom Sepper, Chief Operating Officer

ASAAA consists of more than 10,000 members from both regional and state associations that support and represent the automotive aftermarket industry including that of parts and accessories, supplies and services.
10000 Members
Founded in 1953

18895 American Association of Motor Vehicle Administrators
4301 Wilson Blvd
Suite 400
Arlington, VA 22203

703-522-4200; Fax: 703-522-1553
info@aamva.org
www.aamva.org
Facebook, Twitter, LinkedIn, YouTube, Flickr

Neil D Schuster, President
Mark Saitta, VP
Claire O'Brian, Marketing

A nonprofit association that supports both state and provincial official members throughout North America who oversee the administration and enforcement of motor vehicle laws. Services include development and research in motor vehicle administration, law enforcement and highway safety as well as being an information clearinghouse.
Founded in 1933

18896 American Autoimmune Related Diseases Association
22100 Gratiot Ave.
Eastpointe, MI 48021

586-776-3900
800-598-4668; Fax: 586-776-3900
www.aarda.org
Twitter, LinkedIn, YouTube

Betty Diamond, Chairperson
Noel R. Rose, Chairman Emeritus
Stanley M. Finger, Vice Chairperson
Virginia T. Ladd, President
John Kaiser, Treasurer

Includes patient information about autoimmunity and autoimmune related diseases.
Founded in 1991

18897 American Automobile Association
1000 AAA Drive
Heathrow, FL 32746

407-444-4240
800-222-4357; Fax: 800-444-4247
www.aaa.com

Robert Darbelnet, President
Jerry Cheske, Director Public Relations

Nation's largest motoring and leisure travel organization. AAA provides travel, insurance, financial and automotive related services. The not-for-profit, fully tax paying AAA has been a leader and advocate for the safety and security of all travelers.
45MM Members
Founded in 1902

18898 American Automotive Leasing Association
675 North Washington Street
Suite 410
Alexandria, VI 22314

703-548-0777; Fax: 703-548-1925
sederholm@aalafleet.com
www.aalafleet.com

Pamela Sederholm, Executive Director
Traci Peters, Account Manager
Courtney Groff, Legislative Associate

A national industry association composed of commercial automotive fleet leasing and management companies.
Founded in 1955

18899 American Bus Association
111 K Street NE
9th Floor
Washington, DC 20002

202-842-1645
800-283-2877; Fax: 202-842-0850
abainfo@buses.org
www.buses.org
Facebook, Twitter, LinkedIn, YouTube

Thomas JeBran, Chair
John Meier, Vice Chair
Peter Pantuso, President & CEO
Frank Henry, Secretary/Treasurer

ABA supports 3,800 members consisting of motorcoach and tour companies in addition to organizations that represent the tourism and travel industry. ABA strives to educate consumers on the importance of highway and motorcoach safety.
Founded in 1926

18900 American Coatings Association
1500 Rhode Island Ave., NW
Washington, DC 20005

202-462-6272; Fax: 202-462-8549
members@paint.org
www.paint.org
Facebook, Twitter, LinkedIn, Hangout

18901 American Highway Users Alliance
1101 14th St NW
Suite 750
Washington, DC 20005-5608

202-857-1200; Fax: 202-857-1220
info@highways.org
www.highways.org
Facebook, Twitter

Bill Graves, Chairman
Richard A. Coon, Vice Chairman
Thomas F. Jensen, Secretary
Roy E.ÿ Littlefield, Treasurer

A nonprofit trade association that actively advocates and promotes safe and uncongested highways and America's freedom of mobility.
Founded in 1932

18902 American International Automobile Dealers Association
500 Montgomery Street
Suite 800
Alexandria, VA 22314

703-519-7800
800-462-4232; Fax: 703-519-7810
goaiada@aiada.org
www.aiada.org
Facebook, Twitter, LinkedIn, YouTube

Jenell Rose, Chairwoman
Larry Kull, Chairman Elect
Bradley Hoffman, Vice Chair
Greg Kaminsky, Secretary/Treasurer

Lobbying and communications organization for American automobile dealerships that sell and service international nameplate brands.
11000 Members
Founded in 1970

18903 American Public Transportation Association
1300ÿlÿStreet NW
Suite 1200 East
Washington, DC 20005

202-496-4800; Fax: 202-496-4324
meetings2@apta.com
www.apta.com
Facebook, Twitter, YouTube, Flickr, Blog

Michael Melaniphy, President & CEO
Petra Mollet, Chief of Staff
Rosemary Sheridan, VP, Marketing
Jeff Popovich, Chief Information Officer
Mary L. Childress, Chief Financial Officer

APTA is an international organization that supports and represents the transportation industry. Membership benefits include an annual association meeting, an international expo, membership directory, access to online publications, newsletters and electronic news service.
Founded in 1882

18904 **American Society for Quality**
600 N Plankinton Avenue
Milwaukee, WI 53203
414-272-8575
800-248-1946; Fax: 414-272-1734
help@asq.org
asq.org
Facebook, Twitter, LinkedIn
Elmer Corbin, Chair
Bill Troy, CEO
Brian Savoie, Chief Financial Officer
Andrew Baines, Managing Director, Global
Ann Jordan, General Counsel
The association's mission is to facilitate continuous improvement and customer satisfaction in manufacturing by sharing ideas, tools, standards and expertise on quality management.
80K Members
Founded in 1946

18905 **American Society of Body Engineers**
2122 15 Mile Rd
Suite F
Sterling Height, MI 48310-4853
586-268-8360; Fax: 586-268-2187
www.asbe.com
William Bonner, President
Jeff Grundy, Director
The American Society of Body Engineers is a non-profit corporation consisting of about 1,000 members within the industry including engineers, designers and suppliers. The organization strives to keep members current on the latest technological advancements within the field of automotive body engineering.
1000 Members
Founded in 1945

18906 **American Trucking Association**
950 North Glebe Road
Suite 210
Arlington, VA 22203-4181
media@trucking.org
www.trucking.org
Facebook, Twitter, YouTube, Flickr
Duane Long, Chairman
Pat Thomas, First Vice Chairman
Kevin W. Burch, Second Vice Chairman
Barry Pottle, Vice Chairman
Bill Graves, President
Founded in 1933

18907 **Antique Automobile Club of America**
501 W. Governor Rd
P.O. Box 417
Hershey, PA 17033
717-534-1910; Fax: 717-534-9101
www.aaca.org
Facebook, YouTube
Don Barlup, President
Bob Parrish, Executive Vice President
Micky Bohne, Immediate Past President
John McCarthy, VP - Finance & Budget
Mel Carson, Secretary / Treasurer
America's premiere resource for the collectible vehicle community—includes publications, calendars, membership information, merchandise, photos, and forum.
Founded in 1935

18908 **Antique Truck Club of America**
85 South Walnut Street
PO Box 31
Boyertown, PA 19512
610-367-2567; Fax: 610-367-9712
office@antiquetruckclub.org
www.antiquetruckclub.org
Facebook
Fred Chase, President
Stephen Skurnowicz, Vice President
Tom Oehme, Treasurer
Mike Fowler, Secretary
An organization of persons who own or have an interest in antique commercial vehicles, and who wish to promote the preservation, restoration, operation and history of antique commercial vehicles.
Cost: $36.00
Frequency: Membership Fee
Founded in 1971

18909 **Association for the Advancement of Automotive Medicine**
35 E Wacker Drive
Ste. 850ÿ
Chicago, IL 60601
847-844-3880; Fax: 312-644-8557
info@aaam.org
www.aaam.org
LinkedIn
Frank A. Pintar, President
Brian N. Fildes, Immediate Past President
Gary A. Smith, President-Elect
Federico E. Vaca, Secretary
Kristy B. Arbogast, Treasurer
A professional multidisciplinary organization dedicated to limiting injuries from motor vehicle crashes.
Founded in 1957

18910 **Association for the Advancement of**
PO Box 4176
Barrington, IL 60011-4176
847-844-3880; Fax: 847-844-3884
info@aaam.org
www.aaam.org
Frank A. Pintar, President
Gary A Smith, President Elect
Federico E Vaca, Secretary
Kristy B Arbogast, Treasurer
Founded in 1957

18911 **Association of Diesel Specialists**
400 Admiral Boulevard
Kansas City, MO 64106
816-285-0810
888-401-1616; Fax: 847-770-4952
info@diesel.org
www.diesel.org
Chuck Oliveros, President
Carl Fergueson, VP
Al Roerts, Secretary
Laura Roundtree, Treasurer
The worldwide diesel industry's leading trade association, dedicated to the highest level of service on diesel fuel injection and related systems.
700+ Members
Founded in 1956

18912 **Association of International Automobile Manufacturers**
1050 K Street, NW
Suite 650
Washington, DC 20001
202-650-5555; Fax: 703-525-8817
info@globalautomakers.org
www.globalautomakers.org
Facebook, Twitter, RSS
Michael J Stanton, President
Ellen J Gleberman, Vice President/General Counsel
Jim Lentz, Chairman
John Mendel, Vice Chairman
Scott Becker, Treasurer
An international trade association that supports original equipment suppliers, automobile trade organizations and motor vehicle manufacturers. AIAM monitors government regulations and provides information and advocacy support relative to regulatory and legislative issues that directly affect the auto industry.

18913 **Auto Body Parts Association**
400 Putnam Pike
Suite J 503
Smithfield, RI 02917-2442
401-531-0809
800-323-5832; Fax: 401-262-0193
info@autobpa.com
www.autobpa.com
Dan Morrissey, Chairman
Jim Smith, President
Eric Taylor, Vice President
Michael Koren, Secretary
Dolores Richardson, Treasurer
An association of manufacturers, distributors, insurance and repair professionals which provide the collision repair industry with quality replacement parts.
140 Members
Founded in 1980

18914 **Auto Care Association**
7101 Wisconsin Avenue
Bethesda, MD 20814
301-654-6664; Fax: 301-654-3299
info@autocare.org
www.autocare.org
Facebook, Twitter, Google+, YouTube
Bill Hanvey, President/CEO
Provides advocacy, educational, networking, technology, market intelligence and communications resources on auto care to its members. Formerly known as the Automotive Aftermarket Industry Association.
23000 Members
Founded in 1999

18915 **Auto International Association**
7101 Wisconsin Avenue
Suite 1300
Bethesda, MD 20814
301-654-6664; Fax: 301-654-3299
www.aiaglobal.org
Facebook, Twitter, LinkedIn
Steve Bearden, Chair
Peter Klotz, Vice Chair
The Auto International Association (AIA) segment of the Automotive Aftermarket Industry Association promotes global trade in automotive products by providing a bridge between the international automotive community and the North American aftermarket.
Founded in 1981

18916 **Automatic Transmission Rebuilders Association**
2400 Latigo Avenue
Oxnard, CA 93030
805-604-2000
866-464-2872; Fax: 805-604-2003
webmaster@atra.com
www.atra.com
Facebook, Twitter, Google+
Dennis Madden, CEO
Jim Lyons, VP
Lance Wiggins, Director
Not-for-profit professional organization dedicated to the improvement and welfare of the automatic transmission repair industry for the benefit of the motoring public.
2000 Members
Founded in 1954

18917 **Automotive Aftermarket Industry Association**
7101 Wisconsin Avenue
Bethesda, MD 20814
301-654-6664; Fax: 301-654-3299
info@autocare.org
www.autocare.org
Facebook, Twitter, LinkedIn, Google+
Kathleen Schmatz, President
Susan Medick, COO & CFO
Rich White, Senior VP
Aaron Lowe, AAP, SVP, Regulatory & Gov. Affairs
Paul Fiore, Director, Government Affairs
A trade association consisting of more than 23,000 member companies and affiliates representing over 100,000 repair shops, distribution outlets, and parts stores.
23000 Members
Founded in 1999

18918 **Automotive Aftermarket Suppliers Association**
PO Box 13966
Research Triangle Park, NC 27709-3966
919-549-4800; Fax: 919-549-4824
media@mema.org
www.aftermarketsuppliers.org
Steve Handschuh, President
Bill Hanvey, Senior Vice President
Chris Gardner, Vice President
Ann Wilson, Senior Vice President
Margaret Beck, Senior Director
Automotive aftermarket supplier industry that provides a forum to address issues and resources that highlight the importance of purchasing quality parts backed by full-service suppliers.
Founded in 1971

18919 **Automotive Body Parts Association**
400 Putnam Pike
Suite J 503
Smithfield, RI 02917-2442
401-531-0809
800-323-5832; Fax: 401-262-0193
info@autobpa.com
www.autobpa.com
Dan Morrissey, Chairman
Jim Smith, President
Eric Taylor, Vice President
Michael Koren, Secretary
Dolores Richardson, Treasurer
Members are companies that distribute, supply or manufacture automotive replacement body parts.
140 Members
Founded in 1980

18920 **Automotive Consulting Group**
Automotive Consulting Group
4370 Varsity Dr.
Suite D
Ann Arbor, MI 48108
734-973-1110; Fax: 734-973-1118
acg@autoconsulting.com
www.autoconsulting.com
Dennis Virag, President
Management consulting firm providing top line and bottom line business performance improvement services to the worldwide automotive industry.
Founded in 1986

18921 **Automotive Engine Rebuilders Association**
500 Coventry Ln
Suite 180
Crystal Lake, IL 60014
815-526-7600
888-326-2372; Fax: 815-526-7601
info@aera.org
www.aera.org
Facebook, Twitter
Rex B. Crumpton, Chairman
Steven Edmondson, First VC
Paul Hauglie, President
Steve Schoeben, Treasurer
Dwayne J. Dugas, Advisory Board Chairman
Network of specialists including production engine remanufacturers, installers, and professional engine rebuilders, provide services and support for the engine rebuilding industry.
Founded in 1922

18922 **Automotive Fleet and Leasing Association**
N83 W13410 Leon Road
Menomonee Falls, WI 53051
414-386-0366; Fax: 414-359-1671
info@afla.org
www.afla.org
Facebook, LinkedIn
Bill Elliott, Executive Director
Michael Bieger, President
Mary Sticha, Executive Vice President
Greg Haag, Communications & PR Manager
An organization consisting of more than 300 members that provides information, education and research on the fleet industry. Member benefits include annual conferences, educational seminars, the AFLA membership directory and more. The best source of information and contacts for automotive fleet and leasing professionals.
400 Members
Founded in 1969

18923 **Automotive Industry Action Group**
26200 Lahser Road
Suite 200
Southfield, MI 48033-7100
248-358-3003; Fax: 248-799-7995
www.aiag.org
Facebook, Twitter
John Batchik, Chairman
David Kneisler, Vice Chairman
Scot Sharland, Executive Director
Composed of major North American vehicle manufacturers and their suppliers. Provides an open forum where members cooperate to develop and promote solutions that enhance prosperity in the automotive industry.
1000 Members
Founded in 1982

18924 **Automotive Lift Institute**
80 Wheeler Ave
PO Box 85
Cortland, NY 13045
607-756-7775; Fax: 607-756-0888
info@autolift.org
www.autolift.org
Facebook, Twitter, YouTube
Bob O'Gorman, President
Jeff Kritzer, Board of Directors
An association of manufacturers and distributors of automotive lifts used to raise motor vehicles for undercarriage work. Promotes awareness of safety measures used in operating lifts.
20 Members
Founded in 1945

18925 **Automotive Maintenance & Repair Association**
725 E Dundee Road
Suite 206
Arlington Heights, IL 60004
847-947-2650; Fax: 202-318-0378
amra.org
Facebook
Bill Ihnken, CEO
Chuck Abbott, Vice President, US Sales
Greg Dunkin, Vice President, Key Accounts
Amy Bonder, Vice President of Sales
Dennis Johndrow, Director of Compliance
A nonprofit trade association formally organized to represent the interests, common policies, and purposes of companies engaged in providing automotive maintenance and repair services, their suppliers, and related companies in the automotive industry when dealing with consumers.
Founded in 1994

18926 **Automotive Oil Change Association**
330 North Wabash Avenue
Suite 2000
Chicago, IL 60611
312-321-5132
800-230-0702; Fax: 312-673-6832
info@aoca.org
www.aoca.org
Facebook
Bryan White, President
David Haney, President
Dave Jensen, Vice President
Jim Grant, Secretary
Bob Falter, Treasurer
AOCA is a non-profit trade association that supports and represents more than 3,500 member facilities within the convenient automotive service industry. AOCA strives to educate consumers on the benefits of preventative auto maintenance, and the reliability of fast lube service centers.
3500 Members
Founded in 1987

18927 **Automotive Parts Manufacturers' Association**
10 Four Seasons Place
Suite 801
Toronto, ON M9B 6H7
416-620-4220; Fax: 416-620-9730
apma.ca
Facebook, Twitter, LinkedIn, Google+
Flavio Volpe, President
Jonathon Azzopardi, Director
Mike Bilton, Director
Lisa T. Boulton, Director
Fred di Tosto, Director
Canadian association representing suppliers of parts, equipment, tools, supplies, and services for the automotive industry. The association offers its members supports such as publications, industry events and news.
Founded in 1952

18928 **Automotive Parts Remanufacturers Association**
7250 Heritage Village Plaza
Suite 201
Gainesville, VA 20155
703-968-2772; Fax: 703-968-2878
info@apra.org
www.apra.org
Facebook, Twitter, LinkedIn, YouTube
Omar Cueto, Chairman
Jay Robie, Vice President
Joe Kripli, President
Mission is to address the needs of the automotive and truck parts remanufacturing industry and to serve members by providing a wide range of quality products, services, workshops and educa-

tion, through legislative advocacy, offering technical services, as well as arranging many networking opportunities for members of the remanufacturing community.
1000 Members
Founded in 1941

18929 Automotive Public Relations Council
Original Equipment Suppliers Association (OESA)
25925 Telegraph Rd.
Ste. 350
Southfield, MI 48033-2553

248-952-6401; Fax: 248-952-6404
info@oesa.org
www.oesa.org

Neil De Koker, President & CEO
Greg Janicki, Executive Director, Marketing

APRC is a professional organization for those within public relations that work in the automotive industry. Member benefits include access to industry news, discounted vendor services, and APRC conferences where members have the opportunity to meet and network with colleagues and practitioners in the automotive industry.
Founded in 1998

18930 Automotive Recyclers Association
9113 Church St.
Manassas, VA 20110

571-208-0428
888-385-1005; Fax: 571-208-0430
www.a-r-a.org
Facebook, Twitter, Blog

Ricky Young, President
Mike Swift, First Vice President
RD Hooper, Second Vice President
Michael E. Wilson, Chief Executive
David Gold, Secretary

ARA is an international non-profit trade association with more than 3,000 members that supply equipment and services within the automotive recycling industry.
1000 Members
Founded in 1943

18931 Automotive Service Association
8209 Mid Cities Blvd.
Suite 100
North Richland Hill, TX 76182-4712

817-514-2900
800-272-7467; Fax: 817-514-0770
asainfo@ASAshop.org
www.asashop.org
Facebook, Twitter, LinkedIn

Donny Seyfer, AAM, Chairman
Roy Schnepper, Chairman Elect
Bill Moss, AAM, Secretary/Treasurer
Darrell Amberson, AAM, Immediate Past Chairman
John Cochrane, General Director

Leading organization for owners and managers of independent automotive service businesses that strive to deliver excellence in service and repairs to consumers.
8000 Members
Founded in 1951

18932 Automotive Specialty Products Alliance
1667 K Street
NW Suite 300
Washington, DC 20006

202-862-3902; Fax: 202-223-2636
www.inhalant.org
Facebook, Twitter, YouTube

Colleen Creighton, Executive Director

Provides a unified industry voice for its members engaged in the automotive chemical and vehicle appearance product markets before state, regional and federal legislators and regulators.
Founded in 1966

18933 Automotive Warehouse Distributors Association
7101 Wisconsin Ave.
Bethesda, MD 20814

301-654-6664; Fax: 301-654-3299
info@autocare.org
www.autocare.org
Facebook, Twitter, LinkedIn, YouTube, WordPress

Bill Hanvey, President/CEO

A trade association consisting of more than 600 members who are manufacturers and warehouse distributors, affiliates, marketing associations and others actively involved in the production, distribution and installation of motor vehicle parts, tools, services, accessories, equipment, materials and supplies. A segment of the Automotive Aftermarket Industry Association.
600 Members
Founded in 1947

18934 AutomotiveOEM, Inc.
200 East Big Beaver Road
Troy, MI 48083

248-368-0200; Fax: 248-368-0202
info@automotiveoem.com
www.automotiveoem.com

David M. Bennett, Managing Director

Publishes an automotive original equipment database for users by a wide range of industry professionals including top executives, site managers, engineers, buyers, consultants and researchers. The comprehensive directory covers the automotive manufacturing supply chain comprised of Tier I, II and III suppliers of parts, components, assemblies and related services.
Founded in 1999
Mailing list available for rent

18935 Bearing Specialists Association
630-858-3838; Fax: 630-790-3095
info@bsahome.org
www.bsahome.org
Twitter, LinkedIn, RSS

Jim Scardina, President
Michel Bouchard, Vice President

BSA is a not-for-profit association that consists of companies that distribute factory-warranted ball, roller, and anti-friction bearings through authorized dealers. BSA provides members with the opportunity to network with others in the industry through meetings, seminars and educational programs at their annual convention.
100 Members
Founded in 1966

18936 Brake Manufacturers Council
PO Box 13966
Research Triangle Park, NC 27709-3966

919-549-4800; Fax: 919-549-4824
media@mema.org
www.aftermarketsuppliers.org

Frank Oliveto, Chairman
Walt Britland, Vice Chair
Terry Heffelfinger, Second Vice Chair
Jack Carney, Secretary
Bob Wilkes, Immediate Past Chairman

Obtaining and disseminating to members information on topics of interest to the brake parts industry.
Founded in 1971

18937 California Autobody Association
P.O. Box 660607
Sacramento, CA 95866-0607

916-557-8100; Fax: 916-405-3529
www.calautobody.com
Facebook, LinkedIn

David Picton, 1st VP
Chuck Reyes, President

CAA is a non-profit trade association consisting of more than 1,000 members that support collision repair industry training and education with the goal of providing quality consumer repairs at reasonable prices.
1000+ Members
Founded in 1967

18938 Car Care Council
7101 Wisconsin Ave
Suite 1300
Bethesda, MD 20814

240-333-1088; Fax: 301-654-3299
www.carcare.org
Facebook, Twitter, Pinterest, Instagram

Rich White, Executive Director
Ruth Elhinger, President

A nonprofit 501 (c) (3) educational foundation whose purpose is to educate motorists about the importance of maintenance repairs and entertainment for safer, cleaner, better-performing vehicles. Provides editorial and public service material for media use.
2000 Members
Founded in 1968

18939 Center for Auto Safety
1825 Connecticut Ave NW
Suite 330
Washington, DC 20009-5708

202-328-7700; Fax: 202-387-0140
www.autosafety.org

Clarence M Ditlow III, Executive Director

Provides consumers with advocacy support in Washington for auto quality and safety in addition to helping owners of unreliable vehicles by providing information relative to lemon laws, recalls, defect investigations, legislative issues in Congress and more.
15000 Members
Founded in 1970

18940 Driving School Association of the Americas
506 A Deklab Pike
North Wales, PA 19454

800-270-3722; Fax: 215-699-3015
info@thedsaa.org
www.thedsaa.org
Facebook, Twitter

Robert Gillmer, President
Nina Saint, Administrative VP
Bridget Johns, Executive VP
Jill Chauncy, Treasurer
Dave Haley, Secretary

A nonprofit organization for the purpose of raising the standards of educational methods in teaching drivers education, to promote traffic safety on the highways and streets, to publicize, inform and educate the general public to the need for more intensive driver training, safer roadways and all things relating there to.
500 Members
Founded in 1973

18941 Electric Auto Association
PO Box 639
Los Altos, CA 94024-0639

831-688-8669; Fax: 831-688-8669
freund.ron@gmail.com

www.electricauto.org
Facebook, Twitter, LinkedIn

Ron Freund, Chairman
Guy Hall, Secretary
Gint Federas, Treasurer
Will Beckett, Membership
Carl Vogel, Board Member

Nonprofit educational organization promoting the advancement and adoption of electric vehicles by educating the public on the benefits of this alternative.
Founded in 1967

18942 Filter Manufacturers Council
10 Laboratory Drive
PO Box 13966
Research Triangle Park, NC 27709-3966

919-406-8846; Fax: 919-549-4824
jburkhart@mema.org
www.aftermarketsuppliers.org
Facebook

Steve Handschuh, President
Jack Cameron, VP

For manufacturers of vehicular and industrial filtration products in North America. Active in efforts to educate people on proper disposal of used oil filters.
Founded in 1971

18943 Ford Dealers Alliance
401 Hackensack Avenue
Continental Plaza
Hackensack, NJ 07601

201-342-4542; Fax: 201-342-3997
www.allianceford.com

A Michell Van Vorst, Executive Director
Edwin Mullane, President

Organization that strives to protect dealers against factory encroachment into retail.
15000 Members
Founded in 1969

18944 Formula & Automobile Racing Association
786-571-6965
info@farausa.com
www.farausa.com
Facebook, Twitter, YouTube, Instagram

Reinaldo "Tico Almeida, President
Carlos Mendez, Chief Operating Officer
Victor Leo, Driver Academy Director
Randy Almeida, Vice President
Bob Van Epps, Race Director

Provider of motorsports events for auto enthusiasts.

18945 Global Auto Makers
1050 K Street, NW
Suite 650
Washington, DC 20001

202-650-5555
info@globalautomakers.org
www.globalautomakers.org
Facebook, Twitter, RSS

Michael J Stanton, President & CEO
Ellen J Gleberman, Vice President/General Counsel
Scott Becker, Treasurer
David Zuchowski, Secretary
Michael J. Stanton, President & CEO

Working with industry leaders, legislators, regulators, and other stakeholders to create the kind of public policy that improves vehicle safety, encourages technological innovation, and protects the planet. Goal is to foster an open and competitive automotive marketplace that encourages investment, job growth, and development of more vehicles that enhance Americans' quality of life.
Founded in 1961

18946 Global Automakers
1050 K Street, NW
Suite 650
Washington, DC 20001

202-650-5555
info@globalautomakers.org
www.globalautomakers.org
Facebook, Twitter, RSS

Jim Lentz, Chairman
John Mendel, Vice Chairman
John Bozella, Chief Executive Officer
David Zuchowski, Secretary
Scott Becker, Treasurer

A Washington, D.C.-based trade association and Lobby group whose members include international automobile and light duty truck manufacturers that design, build, and sell products in the United States.

18947 Golden Era Automobile Association
18021-150th Avenue East
Orting
Washington 98360

360-893-4227
AGW1886@aol.com

Henry Moebius, President

A car club that celebrates original cars, trucks, and motorcycles from 1915-1942 and World War II.

18948 Heavy Duty Manufacturers Association
10 Laboratory Drive
PO Box 13966
Research Triangle Park, NC 27709-3966

919-549-4800; Fax: 919-506-1465
info@hdma.org
www.hdma.org

Timothy R. Kraus, President
Jennifer Hjalmquist, Senior Director
Beth Barkovich, Director
Richard Anderson, Senior Market Research Analyst
Katelyn Litalien, Manager

Represents companies participating in the classes 4-8 medium and heavy truck original equipment and aftermarket parts manufacturing industry.
Founded in 1983

18949 Independent Automotive Damage Appraisers Association
P.O. Box 12291
Columbus, GA 31917-2291

800-369-IADA; Fax: 888-IAD- NOW
admin@iada.org
www.iada.org

Mark Nathan, President
Bill Ambrosino, First Vice President
Michael E. Sellman, Secretary/ Treasurer
John Williams, Executive Vice President

Leader in the insurance/automotive industry in providing its members and the entire industry a forum for exchange of ideas and solutions to common problems in automotive appraisal and repair.
Founded in 1947

18950 International Association of Auto Theft Investigators
PO Box 223
PO Box 223
Clinton, NY 13323-0223

315-853-1913; Fax: 315-883-1310
www.iaati.org

John P O Byrne, President
John V Abounader, Executive Director
John V. Abounader, Executive Director

Formed to improve communication and coordination among the growing family of professional auto theft investigators.
4904 Members
Founded in 1952

18951 International Automotive Technician's Network
640 W Lambert Road
Brea, CA 92821

714-257-1335
dmca-copyright@iatn.net
www.iatn.net
Facebook, Twitter, LinkedIn

Monica Buchholz, Marketing

A group of professional automotive technicians from 153 countries who exchange technical knowledge and information with other members from around the world.
64601 Members

18952 International Carwash Association
230 East Ohio Street
uite 603
Chicago, IL 60611

888-422-8422
info@carwash.org
www.carwash.org
Facebook, Twitter, LinkedIn

Gary Dennis, President
Pam Piro, Vice President
Eric Wulf, Chief Executive Officer
Claire Moore, Chief Operating Officer
Charnann Cox, Treasurer

A nonprofit trade group representing the retail and supply segmentsof the professional car wash industry in North America and around the globe.

18953 International Motor Press Association
4 Park Street
Harrington Park, NJ 07640

201-750-3533; Fax: 201-750-2010
www.impa.org
Facebook, Twitter

David Kiley, President
Mike Allen, First VP
Karl Greenberg, Second VP
Lisa Barrow, Secretary
Mike Geylin, Treasurer

Professional group of writers and editors producing auto articles for the press, radio or TV.

18954 International Show Car Association
1092 Centre Rd
Auburn Hills, MI 48326-2657

248-373-1700
www.theisca.com
Facebook, Twitter

Bob Larivee, Owner
Bob Millard, General Manager

An organization of automotive enthusiasts who enjoy building, showing and viewing customs (cars, bikes and trucks), hot rods, competition cars, street machines and antique/restored vehicles.
Founded in 1963

18955 Manufacturers of Emission Controls Association
2200 Wilson Blvd
Suite 310
Arlington, VA 22201

202-296-4797; Fax: 202-331-1388
asantos@meca.org
www.meca.org

Joseph Kubsh, Executive Director
Dr. Rasto Brezny, Deputy Director

Nonprofit association of the world is leading manufacturers of mobile source emission control

manufacturers. Serves as a source of technical information on motor vehicle emission control technology.
Founded in 1976

18956 **Metropolitan Parking Association**
299 Broadway
New York, NY 10007
212-406-3590

To promote and encourage ethical business practices among the operators of parking facilities, and to instill in public and non-public users of parking services confidence in the integrity and skills of parking operators.
400 Members
Founded in 1981

18957 **Micro-Reality Motorsports**
PO 25 102 South Main Street
Cumberland, IA 50843

712-774-2577; Fax: 712-243-8552
www.microreality.com

Kerry Namanny, President

Manufactures and promotes NASCAR micro-reality racing centers, plus several other sports and entertainment/promotions.
321 Members
Founded in 1986

18958 **Mobile Air Conditioning Society Worldwide**
225 S. Broad Street
P.O. Box 88
Lansdale, PA 19446

215-631-7020; Fax: 215-631-7017
macsworldwide@macsw.org
www.macsw.org
Facebook, Twitter, LinkedIn, YouTube, Google+

Elvis Hoffpauir, President/COO
Marion Posen, VP Marketing/Membership

Provides technical training, information and communication for the professionals in the automotive air conditioning industry.
1700 Members
Founded in 1981

18959 **Motor & Equipment Manufacturers Association**
10 Laboratory Drive
PO Box 13966
Research Triangle Park, NC 27709-3966

919-549-4800; Fax: 919-406-1465
info@mema.org
www.mema.org
Flickr

Steve Handschuh, President
Wendy Earp, Senior Vice President
Paul McCarthy, Vice President
Jo Anne Farr, Vice President
Leigh Merino, Senior Director

Represents more than 1,000 companies that manufacture motor vehiclecomponents and systems for the original equipment and aftermarket segments of the light vehicle and heavy-duty industries.

18960 **Motor & Equipment Remanufacturers Association**
25925 Telegraph Road
Suite 350
Southfield, MI 48033

248-750-1280; Fax: 248-750-1281
info@mera.org
www.mera.org
Twitter, LinkedIn, YouTube, Instagram, Flickr

Shawn K. Zwicker, Chairman
Peter M. Butterfield, Vice Chairman
Michael Cardone Jr, Immediate Past Chairman
John R. Chalifoux, President & COO
Jack Vollbrecht, Senior Vice President

A trade group of many businesses, both large and small, in the remanufacturing industry.
Founded in 1904

18961 **Motor and Equipment Manufacturers Association**
10 Laboratory Drive
PO Box 13966
Research Triangle Park, NC 27709-3966

919-549-4800; Fax: 919-406-1465
info@mema.org
www.mema.org
Facebook, Twitter, LinkedIn, Flickr

Steve Handschuh, President
Robert E McKenna, CEO
Wendy Earp, CFO, Treasurer & Senior VP
Jo Ann Farr, VP, Human Resource

Serves manufacturers of all types of automotive and truck products through market research, legislative and regulatory representation and reporting, information services, industry networking and commercial services.
2000 Members
Founded in 1904

18962 **Motorcycle Industry Council**
2 Jenner Street
Suite 150
Irvine, CA 92618

949-727-4211; Fax: 949-727-3313
memberservices@mic.org
www.mic.org

Erik Pritchard, President/CEO
Eric Barnes, VP, Technical Programs
Scott Schloegel, SVP, Government Relations

The Motorcycle Industry Council (MIC) is a nonprofit, national trade association representing manufacturers and distributors of motorcycles, scooters, motorcycle/ATV parts and accessories and members of allied trades.
300 Members
Founded in 1914

18963 **NAFA Fleet Management Association**
125 Village Boulevard Princeton Forrestal Villa
Suite 200
Princeton, NJ 08540

609-720-0882; Fax: 609-452-8004
info@nafa.org
www.nafa.org
Facebook, Twitter, LinkedIn

Cluade T Masters, President
Ruth A Wolfson, Senior VP
Joanne Marsh, Director Marketing & Communications

Serving the needs of those managing fleets of automobiles, light duty trucks and/or vans for US and Canadian organizations. Offers statistical research, publications, including NAFA's Fleet Executive monthly magazine, regional meetings, government representation, conferences, trade shows and seminars.
3000+ Members
Founded in 1957

18964 **NARSA - The International Heat Transfer Association**
3000 Village Run Road
Suite 103
Wexford, PA 15090-6315

724-799-8415; Fax: 724-799-8416
info@narsa.org
www.narsa.org

Maarten Taal, Chairman
Pat O' Connor, President
Mark Hicks, Vice President
Darlene Barlow, Secretary
Angelo Miozza, Treasurer

An association that has provided focus for the business of thermal management for transportation by providing commercial and technical forums that lead business development and product innovation for more than 58 years.
Founded in 1954

18965 **National Association of Automobile Museums**
P.O. Box 271
Auburn, IN 46706

260-925-1444; Fax: 260-925-6266
www.naam.museum

Terry Ernest, President
Mary Ann Porinchak, President Elect
Matthew G. Anderson, Secretary
Judy Endelman, Treasurer
Laura Brinkman, Executive Director

A professional center for automobile museums and affiliated organizations that supports, educates, and encourages members to operate according to professional standards of the museum industry.
Founded in 1994

18966 **National Auto Auction Association**
5320 Spectrum Dr
Suite D
Frederick, MD 21703

301-696-0400; Fax: 301-631-1359
naaa@naaa.com
www.naaa.com
Facebook, Twitter

Jack Neshe, President
Ellie Johnson, President-Elect
Mike Browning, Vice President
Frank Hackett, CEO
Steve McCannoughey, CFO

NAAA represents more then 317 auto auctions both domestic and international. With more than 8.9 million units sold each year. If there is one dominant theme that runs through the colorful history and phenomenal success of this entrepreneurial industry it is that auction business is all about people. NAAA is the net result of the people who pioneered and built it into one of the most respected trade associations in the world.
Founded in 1948

18967 **National Auto Body Council**
7044 S. 13th St.
Oak Creek, WI 53154

414-908-4957; Fax: 414-768-8001
www.nationalautobodycouncil.org
Facebook, Twitter, YouTube

Nick Notte, President
Elizabeth Stein, Vice President
Brandon Devis, Past President
Rick E. Tuuri, Treasurer
Elizabeth Clark, Vice President

A nonprofit organization dedicated to promoting the professionalismand integrity of the collision industry through community service initiatives.
Founded in 1990

18968 **National Auto Sport Association**
P.O. Box 2366
Napa Valley, CA 94558

510-232-6272; Fax: 510-277-0657
www.nasaproracing.com

An American motorsports organization promoting road racing and high-performance driver education.
Founded in 1991

18969 National Automobile Dealers Association
8400 Westpark Drive
McLean, VA 22102
703-821-7000
800-252-6232
help@nada.org
www.nada.org
Facebook, Twitter, LinkedIn, YouTube, Flickr
Forest McConnell, Chairman
William C Fox, Vice Chairman
Peter K Welch, President
Jeffrey B. Carlson, Secretary
George E. Nahas, Treasurer
Represents more than 19,700 new car and truck dealers, both domestic and international, with more than 43,000 separate franchises.
Founded in 1917

18970 National Automotive Finance Association
7037 Ridge Road
Suite 300
Hanover, MD 21076-1343
410-712-4036
800-463-8955; Fax: 410-712-4038
inquire@nafassociation.com
www.nafassociation.com
LinkedIn
Asbel Perez-Viciedo, Chairman
Steve Hall, President
Scot Seagrave, Vice President
Ian Anderson, Vice President
Laurie Kight, Secretary
Founded in 1996

18971 National Automotive Radiator Service Association
3000 Villiage Run Road
Suite 103, #221
Wexford, PA 15090-6315
724-799-8415
800-551-3232; Fax: 724-799-8416
info@narsa.org
www.narsa.org
Wayne Juchno, Executive Director
Douglas Shymoniak, Manager, Sales & New Business
Laressa Davis, Member Services Coordinator
Trade association serving the cooling system service industry and the public.
1500 Members
Founded in 1953

18972 National Glass Association
1945 Old Gallows Rd
Suite 750
Vienna, VA 22182
703-442-4890
866-342-5642; Fax: 703-442-0630
www.glass.org
Facebook, Twitter, LinkedIn
Nicole Harris, President & CEO
Nicole Harris, Vice President/Publisher
Tom Howhannesian, Chairman-Elect
Ken Mairotti, Treasurer
Michael Albert, Chairman
Provides information and education, as well as promote quality workmanship, ethics, and safety in the architectural, automotive and window and door glass industries. Acts as a clearinghouse for industry information, a catalyst in education and training matters, and a powerful voice on behalf of the members.
4000 Members
Founded in 1948

18973 National Independent Automobile Dealers Association
2521 Brown Boulevard
Arlington, TX 76006-5203
817-492-2377
800-682-3837; Fax: 817-649-5866
mike@naida.com
www.niada.com
Karen Barbee, President
Michael R Linn, President
Steve Jordan, COO
Representing quality independent automobile dealers for almost 60 years. NIADA is here to assist members in becoming more successful within the used motor vehicle industry.
19000 Members
Founded in 1946

18974 National Locksmith Automobile Association
630-837-2044
customerservice@thenationallocksmith.com
www.thenationallocksmith.com
Facebook
An organization of automotive specialists that service mechanical locks, produce duplicate keys of all types, and program transponders.

18975 National Motorists Association
402 W 2nd St
Waunakee, WI 53597
608-849-6000
800-882-2785; Fax: 888-787-0381
nma@motorists.org
www.motorists.org
Facebook, Twitter
James Baxter, President
Gary Biller, Executive Director
Advocates, represents and protects the interests of North American motorists.
Cost: $35.00
Frequency: Annual Membership Dues
Founded in 1982

18976 National Parking Association
1112 16th St NW
Suite 840
Washington, DC 20036
202-296-4336
800-647-7275; Fax: 202-296-3102
info@weareparking.org
weareparking.org
Facebook, Twitter, LinkedIn, YouTube
Alan B. Lazowski, Chairman
Nicolle Judge, Chair Elect
Robert A. Zuritsky, Vice Chair
Frank Ching, Secretary
Christine Banning, President
Members are comprised of parking professionals in both the public and private sectors from across the country and around the world. NPA members are private operators, parking consultants, colleges and universities, municipalities, parking authorities, hospitals and medical centers and industry vendors.
2500 Members
Founded in 1951

18977 National Truck Equipment Association
37400 Hills Tech Dr
Farmington Hill, MI 48331-3414
248-489-7090
800-441-6832; Fax: 248-489-8590
info@ntea.com
www.ntea.com
Facebook, Twitter, LinkedIn, YouTube, Flickr, Instagram
James Carney, Executive Director
Frank Livas, First Vice President
Represents small to mid-sized companies that manufacture, distribute, install, buy, sell and repair commercial trucks, truck bodies, truck equipment, trailers and accessories.
1600 Members
Founded in 1964

18978 National Wheel and Rim Association
3943-2 Baymeadows Road
Jacksonville, FL 32217
904-737-2900; Fax: 904-636-9881
www.nationalwheelandrim.org
Dave Willis, President
Edward Neeley, Vice President
Andy Robblee, Treasurer
Angelo Volpe, Secretary/Executive VP
Represents warehouse distributors of wheels, rims and related parts.
230 Members
Founded in 1924

18979 North American Automobile Trade Association
10 Four Seasons Place
10th Floor
Etobicoke, ON M9B 6H7
877-227-8878
naata.org
Facebook, Twitter, LinkedIn, Flickr
Tahverlee Dunlop, President/ CEO
George Sahakian, Vice President
Andrew Pilsworth, Director
Jan Zurek, Director
Wouter VanEssen, Treasurer
Promotes the export of motor vehicles.
Founded in 1996

18980 North American Council of Automotive Teachers (NACAT)
1820 Shiloh Road
Suite 1403
Tyler, TX 75703
903-747-8234; Fax: 843-556-7068
office@nacat.com
www.nacat.com
Facebook, LinkedIn
Curt Ward, President
Patrick Brown-Harrison, Vice President/President Elect
Jim Voth, Secretary
Randy Nussler, Treasurer
Supports all educators in the automotive industry, with training and education, publications and seminars.
750 Members
Founded in 1974

18981 Original Equipment Suppliers Association
25925 Telegraph Rd
Ste. 350
Southfield, MI 48033-2553
248-952-6401; Fax: 248-952-6404
info@oesa.org
www.oesa.org
Facebook, LinkedIn, RSS
Julie A Fream, President &CEO
Neil De Koker, President Elect
Margaret Baxter, Senior VP, Operations
Dave Andrea, Senior VP, Industry Analysis
Glenn Stevens, Senior VP, Membership & Sales
Dedicated to advancing the business interests of companies supplying components, systems, modules, equipment, materials and services used in and by the original equipment automotive industry and to engage in activities in support of the welfare of the association membership. OESA is

an affiliate of the Motor and Equipment Manufacturers Association.
340 Members
Founded in 1998

18982 Overseas Automotive Council
10 Laboratory Drive
PO Box 13966
Research Triangle Park, NC 27709-3966
919-406-8854; Fax: 919-549-4824
bbrucato@aasa.mema.org
www.aftermarketsuppliers.org
Facebook, Twitter, LinkedIn
Steve Holloway, Chairman
Daniel Tristan, 1st Vice Chair
Ben Brucato, Executive Director
Paul McCarthy, Managing Director
One of the oldest and most unique organizations in the global automotive aftermarket. Mission is to promote the sale of automotive products and services exported from North America, to enhance the prestige and goodwill of the global automotive aftermarket industry, to promote friendly trade relationships, cultural understanding and mutually beneficial cooperation among those engaged in the automotive aftermarket industry.
500+ Members
Founded in 1923

18983 Performance Warehouse Association
41-701 Corporate Way
Suite 1
Palm Desert, CA 92260
760-346-5647; Fax: 760-346-5847
www.pwa-par.org
Larry Pacey, Chairman
Ken Woomer, Chairman Elect
Trent Lowe, Treasurer
An organization of specialty automotive parts wholesalers joined together and dealing with management, financial and legislative matters.
10000 Members
Founded in 1971

18984 Production Engine Remanufacturers Association
PO Box 250
Colleyville, TX 76034-0250
817-243-2646; Fax: 417-998-5056
www.pera.org
Facebook, LinkedIn
Nancie J. Boland, Executive VP
Robert P. McGraw, President
The Production Engine Remanufacturers Association is an association of individual and firm who remanufacture internal combustion enhgines or their major components or supply necessay components, supplies and eqipment required in the manufacturing process. The goal of PERA is to provide members with the opportinity to exchange ideas, methods and procedures necessary to efficiently produce remanufactured products which are equal or superior to origianl products in quality and performance.
Founded in 1946

18985 Recreation Vehicle Dealers Association
3930 University Dr
Suite 300
Fairfax, VA 22030-2515
703-591-7130; Fax: 703-359-0152
info@rvda.org
www.rvda.org
Facebook, Twitter, LinkedIn, YouTube
Mike Molino, President
Ronnie Hepp, VP of Administration
Hank Fortune, Director of Finance
Susan Charter, Associate Services Manager
John McCluskey, Chairman
National association advances the best interests of RV retailers through education, services, leadership and programs of market expansion that promote increased use and sale of RVs while enhancing their image.

18986 Recreational Vehicle Aftermarket Association
54 Westerly Road
Camp Hill, PA 17011
717-730-0300; Fax: 630-544-5055
Ellen Kietzmann, President
Ron Dempster, VP
Jess Fowler, Secretary
Bill Fudale, Treasurer
An organization for the suppliers, distributors and agents that represent the aftermarket segment of the RV industry.
110 Members
Founded in 1969

18987 Retread and Repair Information Bureau
1013 Birch Street
Falls Church, VA 22046
703-533-7677
877-394-6811; Fax: 703-533-7678
info@retread.org
www.retread.org
Facebook, Twitter, LinkedIn
David Stevens, Managing Director
Bob Majewski, President
Serving as the public relations arm of the retread industry. Gathering and disseminating information on retread passenger and truck tires to members and the general public.
500 Members
Founded in 1973

18988 Rubber Manufacturers Association
1400 K St NW
Suite 900
Washington, DC 20005
202-682-4800; Fax: 202-682-4854
info@rma.org
www.rma.org
Facebook, Twitter, YouTube
Charlie Cannon, President, CEO
Tracey Norberg, Senior VP
Dan Zielinski, Senior VP
National trade association for makers of tires and other rubber products.
100 Members

18989 Service Specialists Association
1221 Candlewick Drive NW
Poplar Grove, IL 61065
224-990-1005
service.specialists@outlook.com
www.truckservice.org
Jim Parsons, President
Craig Fry, Executive Director
Toni Nastali, Treasurer
Billy Burkholder, Director
Mark Broem, Director
Association whose members are persons, firms or corporations that operate a full line heavy duty repair service shop related to trucking.

18990 Society of Automotive Engineers
SAE Automotive Headquarters
755 W Big Beaver
Suite 1600
Troy, MI 48084-4906
724-776-4841
877-606-7323; Fax: 248-273-2494
CustomerService@sae.org
www.sae.org
Facebook, Twitter, LinkedIn, Google+
Donald J Hillebrand, President
Mircea Gradu, VP, Automotive
Carol Story, Treasurer
David Schutt, CEO
Offers automotive engineers the technical information and expertise used in building, maintaining and operating self propelled vehicles for use on land, sea, air or space.
84000 Members
Founded in 1905

18991 Society of Automotive Historians
webmaster@autohistory.org
www.autohistory.org
Louis F Fourie, President
Edward Garten, Vice President
Robert Casey, Secretary
Robert G. Barr, Director
Vince Wright, Director
Encourages research, preservation, recording, compilation, and publication of historical facts concerning the development of the automobile and related items throughout the world.
Founded in 1969

18992 Society of Collision Repair Specialists
PO Box 909
Prosser, WA 99350
877-841-0660
877-841-0660; Fax: 877-851-0660
info@scrs.com
www.scrs.com
Facebook, Twitter
Andy Dingman, Chairman
Kye Yeung, Vice Chair
Bruce Halcro, Treasurer
Brett Bailey, Secretary
Aaron Schulenburg, Executive Director
For owners and managers of auto collision repair shops, suppliers, insurance and educational associates and suppliers in the US, Canada, Australia and New Zealand. Distributes technical, management, marketing and sales information. Works to promote professionalism within the collision repair industry.
Founded in 1983

18993 Society of Independent Gasoline Marketers of America
3930 Pender Drive
Suite 340
Fairfax, VA 22030
703-709-7000; Fax: 703-709-7007
sigma@sigma.org
www.sigma.org
Kenneth Doyle, Executive VP
Thomas Schmidt, First VP
Brian Beaver, Second VP
Supports independent fuel marketers and suppliers, providing training and education, publications and seminars.
250 Members
Founded in 1958

18994 Specialty Equipment Market Association
1575 South Valley Vista Drive
Diamond Bar, CA 91765-0289
909-610-2030; Fax: 909-860-0184
sema@sema.org
www.sema.org
Facebook, Twitter, Google+, Tumblr
Doug Evans, Chairman
Wade Kawasaki, Chair Elect
Christopher J Kirsting, President & CEO
This trade association consists of a diverse group of manufacturers, distributors, retailers,

publishing companies, auto restorers, street rod builders, restylers, car clubs, race teams and more.
5700+ Members
Founded in 1963

18995 The Aluminum Association
1400 Crystal Dr.
Suite 430
Arlington, CA 22202

703-358-2960
info@aluminum.org
www.aluminum.org
Facebook, Twitter, LinkedIn

Heidi Brock, President
Karen Bowden, VP, Finance & Administration
Joe Quinn, VP, Public Affairs
Charles Johnson, VP, Policy
Ryan Olsen, VP, Business Info. & Statistics

The Aluminum Association's Aluminum Transportation Group promotes the use of aluminum in automobile and commercial vehicle manufacturing.

18996 The Recreation Vehicle Industry Association
1896 Preston White Drive
Reston, VA 20191

703-620-6003; Fax: 703-620-5071
www.rvia.org

Derald Bontrager, Chairman
Robert L. Parish, First Vice Chairman
Garry Enyart, Second Vice Chairman
Kevin Phillips, Secretary
Matthew Miller, Treasurer
Founded in 1963

18997 Tire Industry Association
1532 Pointer Ridge Place
Suite G
Bowie, MD 20716-1883

301-430-7280
800-876-8372; Fax: 301-430-7283
info@tireindustry.org
www.tireindustry.org
Facebook, Twitter, LinkedIn, Instagram

Roy Littlefield, CEO

TIA is an international association representing all segments of the tire industry, including those that manufacture, repair, recycle, sell, service or use new or retreaded tires, and also those suppliers or individuals who furnish equipment, material or services to the industry. TIA was formed by the July 2002 merger of the International Tire & Rubber Association (ITRA) and the Tire Association of North America (TANA).
7000+ Members
Founded in 2002

18998 Tire and Rim Association
175 Montrose West Ave
Suite 150
Copley, OH 44321-2793

330-666-8121; Fax: 330-666-8340
tra@us-tra.org
www.us-tra.org

Joseph Pacuit, Executive VP

Technical standardizing organization for tire, rim and valve manufacturers.
110 Members
Founded in 1903

18999 Triangle Electric Auto Association
3702 Burwell Rollins CIR
Raleigh, NC 27612-5239

Home Page: www.rtpnet.org

An association focused on the conversion of gas cars into electric cars.
Founded in 1990

19000 United States Auto Club
USAC National Office
4910 West 16th Street
Speedway, IN 46224-0001

317-247-5151; Fax: 317-248-5584
www.usacracing.com
Facebook, Twitter

Kevin Miller, President

Supports all driving professionals and consumers with education, publications, driving and vacation tips. Publishes monthly magazine.

19001 United States Council for Automotive Research
1000 Town Center Drive
Suite 300
Southfield, MI 48075

248-223-9000
www.uscar.org

Steve Zimmer, Executive Director
Matt Liddane, Vice President
Paul Mascarenas, Chief Technical Officer
Jon Lauckner, Council Member

The collaborative automotive technology company for Chrysler Group LLC, Ford Motor Company, and General Motors.
Founded in 1992

19002 Womens Automotive Association International
PO Box 2535
Birmingham, MI 48012

248-646-5250; Fax: 248-387-3550
lhswaai@aol.com
www.waai.com

Lorraine H Schultz, Founder/CEO
Lynn M. Wilhelm, Executive Director
Jennifer Michael, Treasurer
Ellen Mckoy, Vice President
Jody DeVere, Vice President

Dedicated to the development and advancement of women as automotive industry leaders. Today, the organization continues to thrive throughout the United States and Canada as the leading women's global organization dedicated to this purpose.
600 Members
Founded in 1995

Newsletters

19003 AIAG e-News Brief
Automotive Industry Action Group
26200 Lahser Road
Suite 200
Southfield, MI 48033-7100

248-358-3570; Fax: 248-358-3253
www.aiag.org

John Batchik, Chairman
David Kneisler, Vice Chairman
J. Scot Sharland, Executive Director

Global automotive industry news, member succes stories and need to know information on AIAG products and events.
1000 Members
Frequency: Monthly
Founded in 1982

19004 APMA Newsletter
Automotive Parts Manufacturers' Association
10 Four Seasons Place
Suite 801
Toronto, ON M9B 6H7

416-620-4220; Fax: 416-620-9730
apma.ca/apma-newsletter

Flavio Volpe, President
Jonathon Azzopardi, Director
Mike Bilton, Director
Lisa T. Boulton, Director
Fred di Tosto, Director

Newsletter featuring news items on activities and events of the Automotive Parts Manufacturers' Association.
Founded in 1952

19005 Automotive Market Report
Automotive Auction Publishing
607 Laurel Drive
Monroeville, PA 15146-4405

412-373-6383; Fax: 412-373-6388

Clyde K Hillwig, Publisher

News items pertinent to auto auctions and the auto industry.
Frequency: BiWeekly
Circulation: 10000

19006 Automotive Week: Greensheet
Molinaro Communications
PO Box 355
Munroe Falls, OH 44262-0355

330-688-4960
877-694-6076; Fax: 866-926-0452
gary@thegreensheetonline.com
www.thegreensheetonline.com

Gary Molinaro, Publisher/Editor
Marc Vincent, Managing Editor

Intelligence concerning the $270 billion independent automotive aftermarked. Breaking news & analysis not available anywhere else in the industry. Key moves in the retail and wholesale distribution channels, mergers & acquisitions; financial analysis of publicly-traded entities. Classified, non-product advertising accepted.
Cost: $225.00
4 Pages
Frequency: 48 issues
ISSN: 0889-3918
Founded in 1975
Printed in on matte stock

19007 Car Dealer Insider
United Communications Group
9737 Washingtonian Blvd.
Suite 100
Gaithersburg, MD 20878-7364
301-287-2700; Fax: 301-287-2039
www.ucg.com

Jill Gardner, Publisher
Donna Lawrence, Editor
Bruce Levenson, Co-Founder
Nancy Becker, Partner, President

Marketing intelligence for new car dealers includes dealer-tested tactics, best management practices and breaking news stories.
Frequency: Bi-Monthly
Founded in 1977

19008 Chek-Chart Service Bulletin
Motor Information Systems/Chek-Chart
1301 W Long Lake Rd
Suite 200
Troy, MI 48098-6349

248-828-0000
800-426-6867; Fax: 248-828-0215

Paul M Eckstein, Manager
Anthony Mattar, Owner

Up-to-date information on all the new automotive developments from the car manufacturers. Information bulletin for service station dealers, mechanics, and instructors. Chek/Chart is part of MotorInformation Systems.

19009 **Electric Auto Association News**
Electric Auto Association
PO Box 639
Los Altos, CA 94024-0639

831-688-8669; Fax: 831-688-8669
freund.ron@gmail.com
www.electricauto.org
Facebook, Twitter, LinkedIn

Ron Freund, Chairman
Guy Hall, Secretary
Gint Federas, Treasurer
Will Beckett, Membership
Carl Vogel, Board Member

News about current events relevant to those interested in promoting the use of electric vehicles.
Founded in 1967

19010 **EngiNEWS**
Production Engine Remanufacturers Association
28203 Woodhaven Road
Edwards, MO 65326

417-998-5057; Fax: 417-998-5056
www.pera.org
Facebook, LinkedIn

Nancie J. Boland, Exutive VP
Robert P. McGraw, President

An semi-annual e-newsletter covering problems from airline fees to the amount of cars on the road and postives of new businesses involved in remanufacturing.
Frequency: Quarterly
Founded in 1946
Mailing list available for rent: 200 names

19011 **Executive Directors Report**
Society of Collision Repair Specialists
PO Box 909
Prosser, WA 99350

509-735-0607
877-841-0660; Fax: 877-851-0660
info@scrs.com
www.scrs.com

Aaron Schulenburg, Executive Director
Luis Alonso, Treasurer
Linda Atkins, Administrative Assistant

Newsletter for owners and managers of auto collision repair shops, suppliers, insurance and educational associates and suppliers in the US, Canada, Australia and New Zealand. Technical, management, marketing and sales information. Free to members.
Frequency: Bi-Annually
Circulation: 6000
Founded in 1982

19012 **FirstUp: Daily News**
American Int'l Automobile Dealers Association
211 N Union St
Suite 300
Alexandria, VA 22314-2643

703-519-7800
800-462-4232; Fax: 703-519-7810
goaiada@aiada.org
www.aiada.org
Twitter

Jim Smail, Chairman
Ray Mungenast, Chairman-Elect
Jenell Ross, Vice Chair
Larry Kull, Secretary/ Treasurer
Cody Lusk, President

Conveys the day's auto-related news quickly, concisely, and accurately. Topics covered in FirstUp range from new vehicle releases, to the latest legislation concerning the auto industry.
11M+ Members
Frequency: Daily
Circulation: 30000
Founded in 1970

19013 **Fleet Administration News**
PO Box 159
Litchfield Park, AZ 85340

623-772-9096; Fax: 623-772-9098
ncsfa.wildapricot.org

Joe O'Neill, Executive Director

NCSFA members are state government administrators responsible for vehicle fleet management.
Cost: $50.00
Frequency: Quarterly
Printed in on matte stock

19014 **Fleet Perspectives**
National Association of Fleet Administrators
125 Village Boulevard
Suite 200
Princeton, NJ 08540

609-720-0882; Fax: 609-452-8004
info@nafa.org
www.nafa.org
Facebook, Twitter, LinkedIn

Phillip E. Russo, Executive Director
Patrick McCarron, Deputy Executive Director
Joanne Marsh, Director Marketing & Communications

Official e-newsletter for Public Service and Corporate fleet managers. Contains special profiles on NAFA Members, important fleet news, and informative articles that won't be found anywhere else.
3000+ Members
Frequency: Quarterly
Founded in 1957

19015 **FleetFOCUS**
National Association of Fleet Administrators
125 Village Boulevard
Suite 200
Princeton, NJ 08540

609-720-0882; Fax: 609-452-8004
info@nafa.org
www.nafa.org
Facebook, Twitter, LinkedIn

Phillip E. Russo, Executive Director

The focus for quick-reading highlights designed to give professional fleet managers the latest industry news.
2600+ Members
Frequency: Bi-Weekly

19016 **Highway & Vehicle/Safety Report**
Stamler Publishing Company
178 Thimble Island Road
PO Box 3367
Branford, CT 06405-1967

203-488-9808
800-422-4121; Fax: 203-488-3129

S Paul Stamler, Publisher
Suzanne Reutenauer, Circulation Manager

Business to business newsletter on the latest developments in transportation safety, regulations and new legislation, and new technology in the automotive industry.
Cost: $467.00
Frequency: Monthly
Founded in 1973

19017 **Highway Users In Action**
American Highway Users Alliance
1101 14th St NW
Suite 750
Washington, DC 20005

202-857-1200; Fax: 202-857-1220
info@highways.org
www.highways.org
Facebook, Twitter, YouTube

Bill Graves, Chairman
Richard A. Coon, Vice Chairman
Thomas F. Jensen, Secretary
Roy E. Littlefield, Treasurer

e-Newsletter with the latest, most recent Highway Users work on behalf of membership. Offers information affecting members.
Frequency: Bi-Annually
Founded in 1932

19018 **Hybrid & Electric Vehicle Progress**
Alexander Communications Group
1916 Park Ave
8th Floor
New York, NY 10037-3733

212-281-6099
800-232-4317; Fax: 212-283-7269
www.evprogress.com

Romauld Alexander, Owner
Laurence Alexander, CEO

News of hybrid and electric vehicle commercialization. Worldwide coverage focuses on news and data on both the technical and business aspects of the hybrid or electric vehicle industry.
Cost: $477.00
8 Pages
Frequency: Fortnightly
Circulation: 800
ISSN: 0190-4175
Founded in 1954
Printed in 2 colors on matte stock

19019 **IMPACT**
International Motor Press Association
4 Park Street
Harrington Park, NJ 07640

201-750-3533; Fax: 201-750-2010
www.impa.org

Mike Spinelli, President
John Matras, First VP
Mike Allen, Second VP
Frequency: Monthly

19020 **Independent Gasoline Marketing (IGM)**
Soc. of Independent Gasoline Marketers of America
3930 Pender Drive
Suite 340
Fairfax, VA 22030

703-709-7000; Fax: 703-709-7007
sigma@sigma.org
www.sigma.org

Kenneth Doyle, Executive VP
Marilyn Selvitelle, VP

Information for independent fuel marketers and suppliers on legislative issues, new market trends, equipment use and management techniques.
32 Pages
Circulation: 4000
Founded in 1958
Printed in 4 colors on glossy stock

19021 **Lemon Times**
Center for Auto Safety
1825 Connecticut Ave NW
Suite 330
Washington, DC 20009-5725

202-328-7700; Fax: 202-387-0140
www.autosafety.org

Clarence M Ditlow III, Executive Director
Sanja Pesek, Editor

Reports on the auto safety world of CAS, as well as covering safety litigation, secret warranties, crash tests, lemon laws, recalls, federal and state

investigations.
Cost: $20.00
15000 Members
Frequency: Quarterly
Founded in 1970

19022 **Market Watch**
AIADA
211 N Union St
Suite 300
Alexandria, VA 22314-2643

800-462-4232; Fax: 703-519-7810
goaiada@aiada.org
www.aiada.org
Twitter

Jim Smail, Chairman
Ray Mungenast, Chairman-Elect
Jenell Ross, Vice Chair
Larry Kull, Secretary/ Treasurer
Cody Lusk, President

Emailed report providing a succinct rundown of the latest industry sales numbers and data. A summary of monthly trends, accompanied by easy-to-read charts and graphs, allows readers to track trends, note milestones, and react quickly to a shifting auto market.
11M+ Members
Frequency: Monthly
Founded in 1970

19023 **Motor**
Hearst Business Communications
567 Robbins Dr
Suite 200
Troy, MI 48083-4515

248-585-1700; Fax: 248-828-7004
jlypen@motor.com
www.motor.com

Duane Harrison, Owner
Kevin Carr, President
Paul Moszak, Vice President/General Manager
Lori Aemiseqqer, Marketing
Richard Laimbeer, Publisher

Articles to keep readers up to date on the latest diagnostic techniques and service procedures. Management articles to help shop owners increase profitability, latest tools available, new products and industry news.
Cost: $48.00
Frequency: Monthly
Circulation: 138941
Founded in 1903

19024 **NACAT News**
North American Council of Automotive Teachers
PO Box 80010
Charleston, SC 29416

843-556-7068; Fax: 843-556-7068
office@nacat.com
www.nacat.com

Patrick Brown Harrison, President
Rob Thompson, Vice President

Cutting edge automotive information for automotive educators. Also news of the organization and the automotive industry.
Circulation: 750
Founded in 1974

19025 **NAFA Fleetfocus**
National Association of Fleet Administrators
125 Village Boulevard
Suite 200
Princeton, NJ 08540

609-720-0882; Fax: 732-494-6789
info@nafa.org
www.nafa.org

Philip Russo, Executive Director
Patrick McCarren, Deputy Executive Director
Joanne Marsh, Director Marketing

The focus for quick rading highlights designed to give professional fleet managers the latest industry news.
3000+ Members
Frequency: Weekly
Circulation: 3600
Founded in 1946
Printed in one color on matte stock

19026 **NPA NewsBrief**
National Parking Association
1112 - 16th St NW
Suite 840
Washington, DC 20036-4880

202-296-4336
800-647-7275; Fax: 202-296-3102
info@weareparking.org
weareparking.org

Weekly newsletter offering updates and industry news for members.
Frequency: Weekly

19027 **NPA eNews**
National Parking Association
1112 - 16th St NW
Suite 840
Washington, DC 20036-4880

202-296-4336
800-647-7275; Fax: 202-296-3102
info@weareparking.org
weareparking.org

Montly electronic newsletter providing information on industry meetings, leadership opportunities, and industry updates and news.
Frequency: Monthly

19028 **News & Views**
Bearing Specialists Association

630-858-3838; Fax: 630-790-3095
info@bsahome.org
www.bsahome.org
LinkedIn

Jim Scardina, President
Michel Bouchard, Vice President

Monthly newlsetter of BSA, the forum to enhance networking and knowledge sharing to promote the sale of bearings through authorized distributors. Available to members only.
100 Members
Frequency: E-Newlsetter for Members
Circulation: 400
Founded in 1966

19029 **Nozzle Chatter**
Association of Diesel Specialists
400 Admiral Boulevard
Kansas City, MO 64106

816-285-0810; Fax: 847-770-4952
info@diesel.org
www.diesel.org
Facebook, LinkedIn

Chuck Hess, President
Andy Girres, Vice President
Chuck Oliveros, Treasurer
Carl Fergueson, Secretary
David Fehling, Executive Director

Member benefit focusing on a variety of news, tips and information on the diesel industry. Contains information that will encourage the exchange of ideas among members; provides a forum for discussion and debate; allow for the fostering of new relationships and contacts; provide members with the knowledge and expertise of colleagues; and provide immediate access to information concerning training materials and publications through monthly reviews.
700+ Members
Frequency: Monthly
Founded in 1956

19030 **OAC Global Report**
Overseas Automotive Council
10 Laboratory Drive
PO Box 13966
Research Triangle Park, NC 27709-3966

919-406-8854; Fax: 919-549-4824
www.aftermarketsuppliers.org

Ben Brucato, Executive Director
Paul McCarthy, Managing Director

Free to members.
Frequency: Monthly
Founded in 1923

19031 **Passenger Transport**
American Public Transit Association
1666 K St NW
Suite 1100
Washington, DC 20006-1215

202-496-4800; Fax: 202-496-4324
ptsubscriptions@apta.com
www.apta.com

Michael Melaniphy, President/CEO
Petra Mollet, VP
Rosemary Sherid, Marketing

Information on federal legislative, administrative and regulatory developments, management and operations, new technology, and state and local developments in public transit.
Frequency: Bi-Weekly
Circulation: 5000
Founded in 1882

19032 **Power Report**
JD Power and Associates Publications Division
2625 Townsgate Rd
Suite 100
Westlake Villag, CA 91361-5737

805-418-8000
888-537-6937; Fax: 805-418-8900
information@jdpa.com
www.jdpower.com

Finbarr O'Neill, CEO
Mary Ann Maskery, Editor
JD Power, Chairman

Focuses on what car buyers and owners feel about their current vehicles.
Cost: $299.00
Frequency: Monthly
Founded in 1968

19033 **Quality**
BNP Media Company
155 N. Pfingsten Rd.
Suite 205
Deerfield, IL 60015

847-405-4044; Fax: 248-358-1024
dalpozzod@bnpmedia.com
www.qualitymag.com
Twitter

Taggart Henderson, Co-CEO
Darrell O. Dal Pozzo, Group Publisher
Chistopher Sheehy, Senior Audience Development Manager

A monthly business publication serving the quality assurance and process improvement needs of more than 64,000 manufacturing professionals. the magazine reports on the use of sound metrology methods, statistical analysis and process improvement techniques to significantly improve quality on the shop floor and in manufacturing planning.
1000 Members
Frequency: Monthly
Founded in 1962

19034 **Safety & Environment/ Working Conditions**
Automotive Industry Action Group

26200 Lahser Road
Suite 200
Southfield, MI 48033-7100

248-358-3570; Fax: 248-358-3253
www.aiag.org

John Batchik, Chairman
David Kneisler, Vice Chairman
J. Scot Sharland, Executive Director

Addresses emerging and global issues in safety, health and the environment affecting member companies and employees worldwide.
1000 Members
Frequency: Monthly
Founded in 1982

19035 **Service Executive**
Automotive Week Publishing
PO Box 3495
Wayne, NJ 07474-3495

973-694-7792
www.auto-week.com

Marketing information for the independent automotive aftermarket. Fast-breaking news of new market entries and strategies; key retail and wholesale developments; merger, acquisition, bankruptcy reports; regular charts of the Top 25 market leaders in various segments (parts, chains, tune-up specialists, brake specialists, tire, fast lube, etc.). The market's sole weekly. Classified non-product advertising accepted.
Cost: $130.00
4 Pages
Frequency: Monthly
Founded in 1975
Printed in on matte stock

19036 **Shop Talk**
IMACA Education Foundation
6410 Southwest Boulevard
Suite 212
Fort Worth, TX 76109-3920

817-732-4600; Fax: 817-732-9610
www.imaca.org

Joan M Jones, Circulation Director

Technical and industry information for the mobile air conditioning industry.
Cost: $20.00
Founded in 1958

19037 **Show Stopper**
International Show Car Association
1092 Centre Rd
Auburn Hills, MI 48326-2657

248-373-1700
www.theisca.com

Bob Larivee, Owner

Car association report about shows.

19038 **Supply Chain Solutions**
Automotive Industry Action Group
26200 Lahser Road
Suite 200
Southfield, MI 48033-7100

248-358-3570; Fax: 248-358-3253
www.aiag.org

John Batchik, Chairman
David Kneisler, Vice Chairman
J. Scot Sharland, Executive Director

Important information on customs and supply chain security regulation; materials management and logistics best practices; and automatic identifications/ RFID standards.
1000 Members
Frequency: Monthly
Founded in 1982

19039 **The Insider**
American Bus Association
111 K Street NE
9th Floor
Washington, DC 20002

202-842-1645; Fax: 202-842-0850
abainfo@buses.org
www.buses.org
Facebook, Twitter, LinkedIn

James Jalbert, Chairman
Thomas JeBran, Vice Chairman
Frank Henry, Secretary/ Treasurer
Peter Pantuso, President & CEO
Brandon Buchanan, Director of Operations

First source of information for bus and tour operators, travel partners, manufacturers, suppliers, and policy-makers seeking original coverage on the motorcoach, tous, and travel industry, from legislation and regulation to news to grow readers' business.
Frequency: Bi-Monthly
Circulation: 10000
Founded in 1926

19040 **Tire Business**
Crain Communications Inc
1725 Merriman Rd
Suite 300
Akron, OH 44313-5283

330-836-9180; Fax: 330-836-2831
info@crain.com
www.crain.com

William Morrow, Executive VP, Operations
Peter Brown, VP

Besides reporting on breaking news, Tire Business also compiles numerous rankings and industry statistics relating to the North American tire and automotive service markets, independent tire dealers, tire manufacturers, tire retreaders and the global tire market.
Frequency: Bi-Weekly
Circulation: 30000
Founded in 1983

19041 **UPdate: Society of Automotive Engineers**
Society of Automotive Engineers
400 Commonwealth Dr
Warrendale, PA 15086-7511

724-776-4841
877-606-7323; Fax: 724-776-5760
update@sae.org

Richard O Schaum, President
Martha Schanno, Circulation Manager

Published to enhance communications with and among SAE members on such non-technical issues as society activities, meetings and members. Recruitment advertising is accepted.
Frequency: Monthly
Circulation: 65000
Founded in 1905
Printed in 2 colors on newsprint stock

19042 **USAC News**
United States Auto Club
PO Box 24001
Indianapolis, IN 46224-0001

317-247-5151; Fax: 317-247-0123
www.usacracing.com

Kevin Miller, President

Contains schedules and news from USAC divisions.
8 Pages
Frequency: Monthly
Founded in 1982

19043 **Ward's Automotive Reports**
Ward's Communications
3000 Town Center
Suite 2750
Southfield, MI 48075-1245

248-799-2622
877-825-1815; Fax: 248-357-9747
wards@wardsauto.com
www.wardsauto.com

Tom Duncan, Publisher
Steve Finlay, Senior Editor
Jim Bush, Business Manager
Chris Lamphear, Marketing Manager

Automotive sales, production and inventory statistics, news and analysis.
Cost: $1195.00
8 Pages
Frequency: Weekly
Founded in 1924
Printed in 2 colors on matte stock

19044 **Ward's Dealer Business**
PRIMEDIA Intertec-Technology & Transportation
3000 Town Center
Suite 2750
Southfield, MI 48075-1245

248-799-2622
877-778-2512; Fax: 248-357-9747
wards@wardsauto.com
www.wardsauto.com

Thomas Duncan, Group Publisher
Steve Finlay, Senior Editor
Steve Sindly, Editor
James Bush, Managing Director

Information for the management of US new car dealerships by covering profit building techniques and business expansions. Includes analysis of current automotive trends.
Cost: $36.00
Frequency: Monthly
Circulation: 32635

19045 **Ward's Engine and Vehicle Technology Update**
Ward's Communications
3000 Town Center
Suite 2750
Southfield, MI 48075-1245

248-799-2622; Fax: 248-357-9747
wards@wardsauto.com
www.wardsauto.com

Thomas Duncan, Group Publisher
Steve Finlay, Senior Editor
Barbara McClellan, Senior International Edit
James Bush, Managing Director
John Sousanis, Publication Manager

Review of the latest advances in engine and vehicle technology.
Cost: $935.00
8 Pages
Printed in 2 colors on ³ stock

Magazines & Journals

19046 **ACtion Magazine**
Mobile Air Conditioning Society Worldwide
225 S. Broad Street
P.O. Box 88
Lansdale, PA 19446

215-631-7020; Fax: 215-631-7017
macsworldwide@macsw.org
www.macsw.org

Elvis Hoffpauir, President/COO
Marion Posen, VP Marketing/Membership

A trade association news magazine for the Mobile Air Conditioning Society (MACS) Worldwide.
Frequency: 8x Yearly
Circulation: 13000
Founded in 1981

19047 **AGRR**
Key Communications
PO Box 569
Garrisonville, VA 22463
540-720-5584; Fax: 540-720-5687
news@glassbytes.com
www.agrrmag.com
Debra Levy, Publisher
Charles Cumpston, Editor
Source of unbiased, accurate information about the auto glass repair and replacement industry.
Frequency: Monthly
Circulation: 10,000
Founded in 2001

19048 **Accident Analysis & Prevention**
AAAM
PO Box 4176
Barrington, IL 60011-4176
847-844-3880; Fax: 847-844-3884
info@aaam.org
www.aaam.org
Brian N. Fildes, Ph.D, President
Mary Pat McKay, MD, President-Elect
Kristy B. Arbogast, Ph.D, Secretary
Frances D. Bents, Treasurer
Provides wide coverage of the general areas relating to accidental injury and damage, including the pre-injury and immediate post-injury phases. Published papers deal with medical, legal, economic, educational, behavioral, theoretical or empirical aspects of transportation accidents, as well as with accidents at other sites.
Frequency: 6x Yearly
Founded in 1957

19049 **Aftermarket Business Magazine**
Advanstar Communications
6200 Canoga Avenue
2nd Floor
Woodland Hills, CA 91367
81 -22 -403; Fax: 818-593-5020
jsavas@advanstar.com
aftermarketbusiness.com
Larry Silvey, Editor
Jim Savas, VP
Specializing in providing news, trends, research and analysis on aftermarket auto parts
Cost: $5.00
Frequency: Monthly
Circulation: 41,077
Founded in 1936
Printed in on glossy stock

19050 **Alt Fuels Advisor**
Alexander Communications Group
1916 Park Ave
8th Floor, Suite 501
New York, NY 10037-3733
212-281-6099
800-232-4317; Fax: 212-283-7269
www.altfuels.com
Romauld Alexander, Owner
Laurence Alexander, CEO
News and developments in alternative fuel vehicles, including natural gas, propane, CNG, ethanol, electric, hybrid and fuel cells. Alt Fuels brings together news of technical and business developments, usage, infrastructure and regulations for all types of alternative and clean fuel vehicles.
Cost: $367.00
Frequency: Monthly
ISSN: 1528-6746

19051 **American Rodder**
Buckaroo Communications
701 Arcturus Avenue
Oxnard, CA 93033
805-986-0400
866-515-5600; Fax: 810-735-6765
www.superrod.com
Gerry Burgel, Editor
Debby Wheeler, Customer Service
Covers the street-rod and custom-car industries. Accepts advertising.
Cost: $39.99
100 Pages

19052 **Auto Laundry News**
EW Williams Publications
2125 Center Ave
Suite 305
Fort Lee, NJ 07024-5898
201-592-7007; Fax: 201-592-7171
Andrew Williams, President
Stefan Budricks, Editor
Janys Kuznier, Circulation Director
Provides technical, operational, marketing, advertising, and managerial information for owners, operators, and investors in self services and automatic carwashes, as well as auto detailing information.
Cost: $56.00
Frequency: Monthly
Circulation: 17292
Founded in 1953

19053 **Auto Remarketing**
Cherokee Publishing Company
301 Cascade Pointe Ln
Cary, NC 27513-5778
919-674-6020
800-608-7500; Fax: 919-674-6027
www.autoremarketing.com
Ron Smith, CEO
Reports on changes in the automotive industry and their effects on the buying and selling of cars.
Cost: $24.95
Frequency: Monthly
Circulation: 22000
Founded in 1990

19054 **Auto Rental News**
Bobit Business Media
3520 Challenger St
Torrance, CA 90503-1640
310-533-2400; Fax: 310-533-2500
www.bobit.com
Edward J Bobit, CEO
Cathy Stephens, Executive Editor
For those involved in the renting of cars and trucks.
Cost: $30.00
Frequency: Monthly
Circulation: 16000

19055 **Auto Trim and Restyling News**
Bobit Publishing
3520 Challenger St
Torrance, CA 90503-1640
310-533-2400
800-241-9034; Fax: 310-533-2500
www.bobit.com
Edward J Bobit, CEO
Travis Weeks, Group Publisher
Latest information on enhancing the appearance of cars with new upholstery, convertible tops and more.
Cost: $19.95
Frequency: Monthly
Founded in 1955

19056 **AutoDealer**
AIADA
211 N Union St
Suite 300
Alexandria, VA 22314-2643
800-462-4232; Fax: 703-519-7810
goaiada@aiada.org
www.aiada.org
Twitter
Jim Smail, Chairman
Ray Mungenast, Chairman-Elect
Jenell Ross, Vice Chair
Larry Kull, Secretary/ Treasurer
Cody Lusk, President
Offers members an in-depth look at America's international auto industry and provides thoughtful analysis of everything from cutting edge vehicle technology to legislation making its way through the halls of Congress. Features include exclusive interviews with auto executives, detailed political coverage, vehicle reviews, and member spotlights.
11M+ Members
Frequency: Quarterly
Founded in 1970

19057 **AutoInc**
Automotive Service Association
8191 Precinct Line Road
Suite 100
Colleyville, TX 76034-7675
817-514-2900
800-272-7467; Fax: 817-514-0770
asainfo@ASAshop.org
www.asashop.org
Ron Nagy, Chairman
Darrell Amberson, Chairman-Elect
Frequency: Monthly
Founded in 1951

19058 **AutoSmart**
Aegis Group-Publishers
30400 Van Dyke Avenue
Warren, MI 48093-2368
586-574-3400; Fax: 248-447-7566
campbell-ewald@c-e.com
www.campbell-ewald.com
Jim Palmer, President
Bill Ludwig, Chairman, CEO
Jeremy Morris, Publisher
Published for Delco Electronics for car company decision makers who deal with such systems.
Frequency: Monthly

19059 **Autoglass**
National Glass Association
1945 Old Gallows Rd
Suite 750
Vienna, VA 22182
703-442-4890
866-342-5642; Fax: 703-442-0630
nicole@glass.org
www.glass.org
Phil James, CEO
Nancy Davis, Editor-in-Chief
Forum for owners, managers and distributors in glass replacement, repair, tinting, and also auto security fields. News and reports on insurance and legislative regulations. New product updates, news and technology information.
Cost: $24.95
Circulation: 7000
ISSN: 1047-2061
Founded in 1948

19060 **Automotive Cooling Journal**
National Automotive Radiator Service Association

3000 Villiage Run Road
Suite 103, #221
Wexford, PA 15090-6315

724-799-8415
800-551-3232; Fax: 724-799-8416
info@narsa.org
www.narsa.org

Wayne Juchno, Executive Director
Douglas Shymoniak, Manager
Maarten Taal, President
Pat O'Connor, Vice President
Darlene Barlow, Secretary

Auto cooling system service data. Free to members.
Cost: $30.00
60 Pages
Frequency: Monthly
Circulation: 10000
Founded in 1956

19061 Automotive Design & Production
Gardner Publications
705 S Main St
Suite 200
Plymouth, MI 48170-2089

734-416-9705; Fax: 734-416-9707
www.adp.com

Mike Vohland, Publisher
Lawrence S Gould, Contributing Editor
Rick Kline Jr, Publisher

Coverage of the automotive industry: suppliers, manufacturers from design through delivery.
Cost: $65.00
Frequency: Monthly
Circulation: 60,404
Founded in 1928

19062 Automotive Engineering International Magazine
Society of Automotive Engineers
400 Commonwealth Dr
Warrendale, PA 15096-0001

724-772-8509
877-606-7323; Fax: 724-776-9765
customerservice@sae.org
www.sae.org

David Schutt, CEO
Kevin Jost, Editor
Brian Kaleida, Chief Information Officer

Cars, aircraft, trucks, off highway equipment, engines, materials, manufacturing and fuels have the Society of Engineers in common. The SAE is your one stop resource for technical information and expertise used in building, maintaining and operating self propelled vehicles for use on land, sea, air or space.
Cost: $120.00
125 Pages
Frequency: Monthly
Circulation: 124451
Founded in 1905

19063 Automotive Executive Magazine
National Auto Dealers Association
8400 Westpark Dr
Mc Lean, VA 22102-3591

703-821-7150
800-252-6232; Fax: 703-821-7234
msaldana@nada.org
www.aemag.com

Tom Choy, Owner
Mark Stertz, President

Devoted exclusively to the automotive executive. Features that take on the new topics in the industry, and columns filled with practical, solid business advice for each dealership department.
Cost: $24.00
40 Pages
Frequency: Monthly
Circulation: 23000
Founded in 1917

19064 Automotive Fleet
Bobit Publishing Company
3520 Challenger St
Torrance, CA 90503-1640

310-533-2400
847-647-9780; Fax: 310-533-2500
Bobitpubs@halldata.com
www.bobit.com

Edward J Bobit, CEO
Ty Bobit, President

Improvements in operational, purchasing and management responsibilities.
Cost: $35.00
Frequency: Monthly
Circulation: 21037
Founded in 1961

19065 Automotive Industries
Worldwide Purchasing Ltd
Versailles, KY 40383

313-262-5702
jal@autoindustry.us
www.ai-online.com

John Larkin, Publisher
Ed Richardson, Editor
Ben Adler, Finance
Nick Palmen, Associate Publisher

Offers information for vehicle producers and suppliers worldwide.
Cost: $70.00
Frequency: Monthly
Circulation: 85000
Founded in 1895
Printed in on glossy stock

19066 Automotive Manufacturing & Production
Gardner Publications
6915 Valley Ln
Cincinnati, OH 45244-3153

513-527-8800
800-950-8020; Fax: 513-527-8801
rkline2@autofieldguide.com
www.gardnerweb.com

Rick Kline Sr, CEO/Publisher
Richard Kline, VP

For engineers and managers who are concerned with improving manufacturing.
Cost: $89.00
110 Pages
Frequency: Monthly
Founded in 1934

19067 Automotive News
Crain Communications
1155 Gratiot Ave
Detroit, MI 48207-2732

313-446-0450
877-812-1584; Fax: 313-446-1680
customerservice@autonews.com
www.autonews.com

Richard Johnson, Managing Editor
Jason Stein, Editor
Tony Merpi, Director Of Marketing
Victor Galvan, Web Editor

Covers the manufacturing side of the automotive industry, including engineering, design, production and suppliers, with equal emphasis on the retail side of the industry, including the marketing, sales, service and resale of vehicles.
Frequency: Weekly
Circulation: 79000

19068 Automotive Recycling
Automotive Recyclers Association
9113 Church Street
Suite 1
Manassas, VA 20110-5457

571-208-0428
888-385-1005; Fax: 571-208-0430
michael@a-r-a.org
www.a-r-a.org

Michael E Wilson, CEO
Linda Pitman, President
Randy Reitman, Secretary

Offers information on the recycling of automobiles and automotive parts.
Cost: $40.00
Frequency: Bi-Monthly
Circulation: 1100
ISSN: 1058-9376
Founded in 1943
Printed in on glossy stock

19069 Body Language
Automotive Body Parts Association
1510 Eldridge Parkway
Suite 110-168
Houston, TX 77077

281-531-0809
800-323-5832; Fax: 281-531-9411
info@autobpa.com
www.autobpa.com

Stanley Rodman, Executive Director
Nicholas Scheid, President

Published six times per year by the Automotive Body Parts Association, this newsletter keeps body shop operators and insurance industry executives up-to-date on the latest information concerning the manufacturing, distribution and importing of aftermarket body parts.
Cost: $80.00
146 Members
167 Pages
Circulation: 400
Founded in 1980

19070 BodyShop Business
Babcox Publications
3550 Embassy Pkwy
Akron, OH 44333-8318

330-670-1234; Fax: 330-670-0874
www.babcox.com

Bill Babcox, Owner
Georgina Carson, Editor
Bob Bissler, Senior Editor

Devoted to helping collision-repair shop owners and managers run more profitable businesses. Editorially, BodyShop business covers all aspects of collision repair, with a focus on how-to topics include management, dimensioning, straightening, welding, refinishing, law and technology.
Cost: $64.00
Frequency: Monthly
Circulation: 60145
Founded in 1920

19071 Brake & Front End
Babcox Publications
3550 Embassy Pkwy
Akron, OH 44333-8318

330-670-1234; Fax: 330-670-0874
amarkel@babcox.com
www.babcox.com

Bill Babcox, Owner
Andrew Markel, Editor
Brad Mitchell, Circulation/IT Director

Has monthly service articles that feature the latest information on brake, chassis, exhaust, front end, front-wheel drive and wheel alignment. Each issue also profiles the newest product and service offerings from aftermarket suppliers.
Cost: $64.00
Frequency: Monthly
Circulation: 40,310
Founded in 1920

19072 Cars & Parts
Amos Press

PO Box 4129
Sidney, OH 45365-4129

937-498-2111
800-448-3611; Fax: 937-498-0807
www.amospress.com

Bruce D Boyd, CEO
Margie Bruns, Advertising Manager
Mark Kaufman, Associate Publisher

Focused to the serious collector car lobbyist. Each issue has an array of how-to articles, detailed coverage of feature cars and intriguing historical views of the auto companies and their most influential players. Additionally there are reports on major collector car shows and auctions including analysis of price trends on major categories of cars. Also included is a calendar of upcoming events: shows, auctions and swap meets. Finally, each issue has an extensive classified section.
Cost: $31.95
124 Pages
Frequency: Monthly
Founded in 1957
Printed in 4 colors on glossy stock

19073 **Counterman**
Babcox Publications
3550 Embassy Pkwy
Akron, OH 44333-8318

330-670-1234; Fax: 330-670-0874
www.babcox.com

Bill Babcox, Owner
Jon Owens, Publisher

Targeted at the needs of the jobber sales team — those who buy and sell parts, services, equipment, build brand awareness, preference and loyalty by recommending parts to the DIY customer and professional technician.
Cost: $ 110.00
Frequency: Monthly
Circulation: 50,000
Founded in 1920

19074 **Dealer**
Horizon Communications
5201 Great America Pkwy
Floor 20, Suite 320
Santa Clara, CA 95054-1122

408-969-4888; Fax: 408-969-4895
jh@horizonpr.com
www.horizonpr.com

Mike Roscoe, Publisher

Information for automobile dealers on service, parts, used car merchandising, financing, body shop, planning and risk management.
Cost: $35.00
Frequency: Monthly
Circulation: 21178
Founded in 1995

19075 **Destinations**
American Bus Association
111 K Street NE
9th Floor
Washington, DC 20002

202-842-1645; Fax: 202-842-0850
abainfo@buses.org
www.buses.org

Peter J Pantuso, CEO
Brandon Buchanan, Director of Operations
Clyde J. Hart Jr, Senior Vice President
Eric Braendel, CFO

Motorcoach travel across North America and Association news.
80 Pages
Frequency: Monthly
Circulation: 6000
Founded in 1926
Printed in 4 colors on glossy stock

19076 **Diesel Progress: North American Edition**
Diesel & Gas Turbine Publications
20855 Watertown Rd
Suite 220
Waukesha, WI 53186-1873

262-754-4100; Fax: 262-754-4175
mosenga@dieselpub.com
www.dieselspec.com

Michael Osenga, President
S Bollwahn, Circulation Manager

Geared towards readers interested in state-of-the-art systems technology. Features include new product listings, systems design, research and product testing as well as systems maintenance and rebuilding.
Frequency: Monthly
Circulation: 26,011
Founded in 1837

19077 **Double Clutch**
Antique Truck Club of America
PO Box 31
85 South Walnut Street
Boyertown, PA 19512

610-367-2567; Fax: 610-367-9712
office@antiquetruckclub.org
www.antiquetruckclub.org
Facebook

Fred Chase, President
Stephen Skurnowicz, Vice President
Tom Oehme, Treasurer
Mike Fowler, Secretary

Magazine for antique truck enthusiasts.
Cost: $50.00
Frequency: Bimonthly
Founded in 1971

19078 **Dual News Magazine**
Driving School Association of the Americas
506 A Deklab Pike
North Wales, PA 19454

800-270-3722; Fax: 215-699-3015
info@thedsaa.org
www.thedsaa.org

Robert Gillmer, President
Nina Saint, Administrative VP
Bridget Johns, Executive VP
Jill Chauncy, Treasurer
Dave Haley, Secretary

Keeping all driving school professionals informed of upcoming educational seminars, sharing ideas & opinions and introducing products and the like to driving educators. Represents a continuing commitment to the driving school industry.
Founded in 1973

19079 **Engine Builder**
Babcox Publications
3550 Embassy Pkwy
Akron, OH 44333-8318

330-670-1234; Fax: 330-670-0874
www.babcox.com

Bill Babcox, Owner
Doug Kaufman, Editor

Business magazine serving the machine shop, custom engine, production engine and small parts rebuilding markets. It delivers editorial excellence that reflects the growing sophistication of the rebuilding industry and aids its readers in the profitable operation of their businesses.
Cost: $64.00
72 Pages
Frequency: Monthly
Circulation: 19500
Founded in 1920
Printed in 4 colors on glossy stock

19080 **Engine Professional**
Automotive Engine Rebuilders Association
500 Coventry Ln
Suite 180
Crystal Lake, IL 60014-7592

815-526-7600
866-326-2372; Fax: 815-526-7601
info@aera.org
www.aera.org
Facebook, Twitter

David Bianchi, Chairman
John Goodman, President
Dean Yatchyshyn, Treasurer
Dwayne J. Dugas, 1st Vice Chairman
Ron McMorris, 2nd Vice Chairman

Packed with highly technical, application-driven articles that will help you and your business thrive.
Frequency: Quarterly
Founded in 1922

19081 **FLEETSolutions**
National Association of Fleet Administrators
125 Village Boulevard
Suite 200
Princeton, NJ 08540

609-720-0882; Fax: 609-452-8004
info@nafa.org
www.nafa.org
Facebook, Twitter, LinkedIn

Phillip E. Russo, Executive Director

Contains educational articles based on the eight disciplines of the fleet management profession.
2600+ Members
Frequency: Bi-Monthly

19082 **Family Motor Coaching Magazine**
8291 Clough Pike
Cincinnati, OH 45244-2796

513-474-3622
800-543-3622; Fax: 513-474-2332
membership@fmca.com
www.fmca.com

Don Eversman, Executive Director

Official publication of the Family Motor Coach Association, an organization for owners of self-contained motor homes. Publishes articles regarding motor home maintenance and repair, new products, travel destinations of interest to RV travelers and association news.
Cost: $24.00
Frequency: Monthly
Circulation: 98000

19083 **Fleet Financials**
Bobit Publishing Company
23210 Crenshaw Blvd
Suite 101
Torrance, CA 90505-3181

310-539-1969; Fax: 310-539-4329
mike.antich@bobit.com
www.fleet-central.com

John Bebout, Owner

Features profiles of successfully managed fleets and analysis of lease verses company ownership.
Cost: $28.00
Frequency: Monthly
Circulation: 15500

19084 **Global Insight**
Motor and Equipment Manufacturers Association

10 Laboratory Drive
PO Box 13966
Research Triangle Park, NC 27709-3906

919-549-4800; Fax: 919-406-1465
info@mema.org
www.mema.org

Bob McKenna, President
Wendy Earp, VP
Frank Hampshire, Marketing

Member publication examines critical issues and challenges facing today's original equipment, aftermarket and heavy duty suppliers. Subscriptions and advertising available.
Frequency: Quarterly
Circulation: 2400
Founded in 1904

19085 Hemmings Classic Car
Hemmings Motor News
PO Box 4317
Bennington, VT 05201

802-442-3101
800-227-4373; Fax: 802-447-9631
hmnmail@hemmings.com
www.hemmings.com

Formerly the Special Interest Auto magazine, features contemporary road tests and in-depth automobile profiles, automotive design, engineering, styling and historical exposes, how-to restoration and technical articles, and profiles on specialists and shops specializing in the collector-car industry.
Frequency: Monthly
Founded in 1954

19086 Hemmings Motor News
PO Box 100
Bennington, VT 05201

802-442-3101
800-227-4373; Fax: 802-447-9631
hmnmail@hemmings.com
www.hemmings.com

Terry Ehrich, Publisher
Eileen Desmarais, Marketing

The bible of the car collector, this monthly magazine serves to enhance the experience of the car collector-enthusiast. Regular departments include vehicle and parts search, price checkers, dealers tips, hobby directory and more.
Cost: $31.95
Frequency: Monthly
Circulation: 210000
Founded in 1954

19087 ImportCar
Babcox Publications
3550 Embassy Pkwy
Akron, OH 44333-8318

330-670-1234; Fax: 330-670-0874
mdellavalle@babcox.com
www.babcox.com

Bill Babcox, Owner
David Wooldridge, Publisher

Complete import service magazine. It is geared exclusively to the vehicle repair needs of import specialist technicians. The in-depth, technical nature of the magazine's editorial content helps technicians of all abilities do their jobs more efficiently and effectively.
Cost: $64.00
Frequency: Monthly
Circulation: 29190
Founded in 1979

19088 Independent Battery Manufacturers
401 North Michigan Avenue
24th Floor
Chicago, IL 60611

312-644-6610; Fax: 312-527-6640
www.thebatteryman.com

Founded in 1921

19089 International Collision Parts Industry Suppliers Guide
Automotive Body Parts Association
1510 Eldridge Parkway
Suite 110-168
Houston, TX 77077

281-531-0809
800-323-5832; Fax: 281-531-9411
info@autobpa.com
www.autobpa.com

Stanley Rodman, Executive Director
Nicholas Scheid, President

Covers the collision replacement parts industry.
146 Members
64 Pages
Frequency: Quarterly
Circulation: 2300
Founded in 1980
Printed in 4 colors on glossy stock

19090 Journal of Quality Technology
American Society for Quality
600 N Plankinton Avenue
Milwaukee, WI 53203

414-272-8575
800-248-1946; Fax: 414-272-1734
help@asq.org
asq.org/pub/jqt/index.html

Elmer Corbin, Chair
Bill Troy, CEO
Brian Savoie, Chief Financial Officer
Andrew Baines, Managing Director, Global
Ann Jordan, General Counsel

Published by the American Society for Quality, the Journal of Quality Technology is a quarterly, peer-reviewed journal that focuses on the subject of quality control and the related areas of reliability and similar disciplines.
80K Members
Frequency: Quarterly
Founded in 1946

19091 LCT Magazine
Bobit Publishing Company
3520 Challenger St
Torrance, CA 90503-1640

310-533-2400
800-380-8335; Fax: 310-533-2500
webmaster@bobit.com
www.bobit.com

Edward J Bobit, CEO

Serves the limousine agency owner.
Cost: $28.00
Frequency: Monthly
Circulation: 10000
Founded in 1961

19092 Lead, Reach and Connect
Automotive Parts Manufacturers' Association
10 Four Seasons Place
Suite 801
Toronto, ON M9B 6H7

416-620-4220; Fax: 416-620-9730
accounting@matrixgroupinc.net
apma.ca/lead-reach-and-connect

Flavio Volpe, President
Jonathon Azzopardi, Director
Shoshana Weinberg, Customer Service Liaison
Alexandra Walld, Editor

The official magazine of the Automotive Parts Manufacturers' Association, providing the Canadian automotive industry with current information on business. Some subjects covered include automotive intelligence, industry events and industry standards.
Founded in 1952

19093 Limousine Digest
Digest Publications
29 Fostertown Road
Medford, NJ 08055

609-953-4900; Fax: 609-953-4905
info@limodigest.com
www.limodigest.com

Chris Weiss, Publisher
Susan Rose, Assistant Publisher
Iric Cohen, President

Information for owners and operators of limousine, livery and transportation fleets, including day to day operational information, industry trends, product reviews, technical advances, as well as success stories.
Cost: $24.95
100 Pages
Frequency: Monthly
Circulation: 12500
ISSN: 1095-8436
Founded in 1990
Printed in 4 colors on glossy stock

19094 Locator
John Holmes Publishing Company
521 Main Street
PO Box 286
Whiting, IA 51063

712-458-2213
800-831-0820; Fax: 712-458-2687
sales@partslocator.com
www.partslocator.com

John Holmes, President
Charis Lloyd, VP
Wendy Lloyd, Marketing Director
Stacy Phillips, Editor

Nation's leading auto and truck parts magazine.
Cost: $29.00
250 Pages
Frequency: Monthly
Circulation: 18500
Founded in 1957
Printed in 4 colors on newsprint stock

19095 Lubes-N-Greases
LNG Publishing Company
6105 Arlington Blvd
Suite G
Falls Church, VA 22044-2708

703-536-0800; Fax: 703-536-0803
info@Lngpublishing.com
www.lngpublishing.com

Gloria Stienberg Briskin, Advertising Director
Nancy DeMarco, Publisher
Lisa Tocci, Managing Editor

The magazine of industry in motion.
Frequency: Monthly
Circulation: 17300
ISSN: 1080-9449
Founded in 1995
Printed in 4 colors on glossy stock

19096 Lubricants World
4545 Post Oak Place
Suite 230
Houston, TX 77027

713-840-0378; Fax: 713-840-8585

Kathryn B Carnes, Editor

Professional journal for those in the oil and grease industry.

19097 MOVE
AAMVA

4301 Wilson Blvd
Suite 400
Arlington, VA 22203-1867

703-522-4200; Fax: 703-522-1553
info@aamva.org
www.aamva.org

Neil D. Schuster, President & CEO
Marc Saitta, Vice President & CFO

Provides members with practical and in-depth how-to information on a wide range of topics. Provides feature articles and departments that tackle issues facing today's administrators.
Frequency: Quarterly
Founded in 1933
Printed in 4 colors

19098 MOVE Magazine
American Assn. of Motor Vehicle Administrators
Executive Plaza, 11350 McCormick Rd
Suite 900
Hunt Valley, MD 21031

410-584-1955; Fax: 410-584-1998
www.aamva.org

Linda Lewis-Pickett, President/CEO
Bonnie L Rutledge, Editor

Journal of the voluntary, nonprofit, educational organization. AAMVA represents the state and provincial officials in the US, Canada and Mexico, who are responsible for the administration and enforcement of laws pertaining to the motor vehicle and its use.
Cost: $26.00
Frequency: Quarterly
Circulation: 32000
Founded in 1996
Printed in 4 colors on glossy stock

19099 Market Analysis
Motor and Equipment Manufacturers Association
10 Laboratory Drive
PO Box 13966
Research Triangle Park, NC 27709-3966

919-549-4800; Fax: 919-406-1465
info@mema.org
www.mema.org

Bob McKenna, President
Wendy Earp, VP
Frank Hampshire, Marketing

Provides an analysis of how the vehicles parts industry is affected by the economy including informative news topics such as producer price indexes for parts and accessories, market data and more.
Frequency: Monthly
Founded in 1904

19100 Modern Car Care
Virgo Publishing LLC
3300 N Central Ave
Suite 300
Phoenix, AZ 85012-2532

480-990-1101; Fax: 480-990-0819
jsiefert@vpico.com
www.vpico.com

John Seifert, CEO
Kelly Ridley, Executive VP, CFO
Heather Wood, VP,Human Resources

Magazine for automotive professionals.
Frequency: Monthly
Circulation: 20000
Founded in 1986

19101 Motor Age
Chilton Company
300 Park Ave
Suite 19
New York, NY 10022-7409

212-751-3596
888-527-7008; Fax: 212-371-4058
info@advanstar.com
www.chiltonfunds.com

Richard L Chilton Jr, Chairman, CEO
Michael Clark, President, COO

Features developments in the auto industry.
Cost: $14.00
Frequency: Monthly
Circulation: 143,000
Founded in 1992

19102 Motor Magazine
Hearst Business Communications
1301 Long Lake Road
Suite 300
Troy, MI 48098

248-585-1700
800-288-6828; Fax: 248-879-8603
motorbookscallcenter@motor.com
www.motor.com

Duane Harrison, Owner
John Lypen, Editor
Richard Laimbeer, Publisher

Emphasis on repair and service end of automobile business for owners and managers.
Cost: $63.00
Frequency: Monthly
Circulation: 140000
Founded in 1903

19103 Motor Trend
Primedia
6420 Wilshire Boulevard
Los Angeles, CA 90048-5502

323-822-2201; Fax: 323-782-2467
www.motortrend.com

Tom Rogers, CEO
Eric Schwab, Advertising Manager
Peter Clancey, Marketing Executive

Comprehensive magazine offers the latest information and news on the automotive industry.
Cost: $47.88
Frequency: Monthly
Circulation: 999999
Founded in 1988
Printed in 4 colors on glossy stock

19104 NADA'S Automotive Executive
National Automobile Dealers Association
8400 Westpark Dr
9th Floor, Suite 1
Mc Lean, VA 22102-3591

703-821-7000
800-252-6232; Fax: 703-821-7075
nadainfo@nada.org
www.nada.org

Phillip D Brady, President
Rick Wagoner, CEO

Provides up to the minute legislative, regulatory and state association news, also includes product development and implementation, labor relations and the economic climate.
Cost: $24.00
Frequency: Monthly
Circulation: 21850
Founded in 1975

19105 NAPA Outlook
National Auto Parts Association
2999 Circle 75 Pkwy SE
Atlanta, GA 30339-3050

770-956-2200
877-794-9511; Fax: 770-956-2211
customersupport@napaonline.com
www.napaautocare.com

Thomas C Gallagher, CEO

Ideas for business procedures for jobber store owners.
28 Pages
Frequency: Monthly
Founded in 1925

19106 NASCAR Performance
Babcox Publications
3550 Embassy Pkwy
Akron, OH 44333-8318

330-670-1234; Fax: 330-670-0874
dkaufman@babcox.com
www.babcox.com

Bill Babcox, Owner
Doug Kaufman, Editor

Focuses on what goes on behind the scenes in NASCAR racing, and how that advanced technology transfers to automotive aftermarket applications. Professional NASCAR Garage is a quarterly supplement to all Babcox publications.
Founded in 1920

19107 National Oil & Lube News
National Oil & Lube News
4418 74th St
Suite 66
Lubbock, TX 79424-2336

806-762-4464
800-796-2577; Fax: 806-762-4023
info@noln.net
www.noln.net

Garrett McKinnon, Editor
Steve Hurt, Co Publisher

Geared towards fast oil change and lubrication shop owners and managers. Information on the latest technology and environment concerns, also provides a link between shops and suppliers.
Cost: $29.00
76 Pages
Frequency: Monthly
Circulation: 17000
ISSN: 1071-1260
Founded in 1986
Printed in 4 colors on glossy stock

19108 New England Automotive Report
Thomas Greco Publications
PO Box 734
Neptune, NJ 07753

732-922-8909; Fax: 732-922-9821
setlit4u@msn.com
www.aaspnj.org

Thomas Greco, Owner
Alicia D'Aquila, Editor
Charles Bryant, Executive Director

Provides reports on ideas, products and services to enhance collision repair productivity, also identifies insurance issues.
Cost: $48.00
85 Pages
Frequency: Monthly
Circulation: 4500
Founded in 1996
Printed in 4 colors on glossy stock

19109 Old Cars Weekly
F+W Media
38 E. 29th Street
New York, NY 10016

212-447-1400; Fax: 212-447-5231
contact_us@fwmedia.com

Jim Ogle, CFO
Sara Domville, President
Chad Phelps, Chief Digital Officer
David Nussbaum, CEO

Covers the entire field of collectible automobiles - from classic touring cars and roadsters of the early 1900s to the popular muscle cars of the 1960s and 1970s. Includes historical perspectives and facts on cars and their manufacturers, and reports on attractions at upcoming shows.

Regular columns include 'New Products,' 'Questions & Answers,' 'Show Biz,' 'Bookmobile,' 'Restoration Basics,' and an extensive classified word ad section. Hundreds of car show listings are included.
Cost: $41.98
64 Pages
Frequency: Weekly
Circulation: 63104
Founded in 1971

19110 **PWA Conference**
Performance Warehouse Association
41-701 Corporate Way
Suite 1
Palm Desert, CA 92260

760-346-5647; Fax: 760-346-5847
donnie@pedistributors.com
www.pwa-par.org

Donnie Eatherly, President
John Towle, Executive Director
Larry Pacey, Chairman
Trent Lowe, Treasurer
Frequency: September

19111 **Parking Magazine**
National Parking Association
1112 16th St NW
Suite 840
Washington, DC 20036-4880

202-296-4336
800-647-7275; Fax: 202-296-3102
info@weareparking.org
weareparking.org

Alan B. Lazowski, Chairman
Nicolle Judge, Chair Elect
Christine Banning, President
Alison Bibb-Carson, Managing Editor

Published by the National Parking Association.
Cost: $99.00
2500 Members
Frequency: Monthly
Circulation: 4000
ISSN: 0031-2193
Founded in 1952
Mailing list available for rent: 2600 names at $250 per M
Printed in 4 colors

19112 **Parts & People**
Automotive Counseling & Publishing
899 Logan Street
Denver, CO 80203

303-765-4664; Fax: 303-765-4650
www.partsandpeople.com

Lance Buchner, Owner
Rob Merwin, Editor

Collision and mechanical local and national news.
Cost: $36.00
Frequency: Monthly
Circulation: 59000
Founded in 1986

19113 **Parts Plus Magazine**
3085 Fountainside Drive
#210
Germantown, TN 38138

901-727-8112
800-727-8112; Fax: 901-682-9098
info@networkhq.org
www.partsplus.com

Alan Bostwick, Executive VP

Published by the Association of Automotive Aftermarkets Distributors.
Cost: $29.95
Frequency: Monthly
Circulation: 5000
Founded in 1965

19114 **Professional Carwashing and Detailing**
National Trade Publications
19 British American Blvd. West
Latham, NY 12110-2197

518-783-1281; Fax: 518-783-1386
www.carwash.com

Tracy Aston-Martin, Vice President
Sandy Murphy, Publisher

Provides technical and marketing information to professional vehicle washing owners, managers and investors. Accepts advertising.
Cost: $42.00
76 Pages
Frequency: Monthly
Circulation: 19000
Founded in 1976
Mailing list available for rent: 18M names at $125 per M
Printed in 4 colors on matte stock

19115 **Professional Tool & Equipment News**
1233 Janesville Avenue
Fort Atkinson, WI 53538

920-563-6388
888-966-3976; Fax: 920-563-1699
www.vehicleservicepros.com

Larry Greenberger, Publisher
Jacques Gordon, Editor
Sara Shelstrom, Publisher

Information for personnel and owners of general and specialty repair shops, including buying tools and equipment, technological innovations, new systems, time saving ideas and product releases.
Cost: $32.00
Frequency: Monthly
Circulation: 105044
Founded in 1996

19116 **Quality Engineering**
American Society for Quality
600 N Plankinton Avenue
Milwaukee, WI 53203

414-272-8575
800-248-1946; Fax: 414-272-1734
help@asq.org
asq.org/pub/qe/index.html

Elmer Corbin, Chair
Bill Troy, CEO
Brian Savoie, Chief Financial Officer
Andrew Baines, Managing Director, Global
Ann Jordan, General Counsel

Co-published by Taylor and Francis, this journal is for professional practitioners and researchers in quality engineering improvement and solutions. Subjects include quality assurance management, physical technology, statistical tools and more.
80K Members
Frequency: Quarterly
Founded in 1946

19117 **RV Trade Digest**
Cygnus Publishing
1233 Janesville Avenue
Fort Atkinson, WI 53538

920-000-1111
800-547-7377; Fax: 920-563-1699

John French, CEO
Tom Kohn, Executive Vice President
Paul Caplan, Senior Vice President
Paul Bonaiuto, CFO

Offers in-depth information to a trade audience of business professionals actively engaged in the manufacture, distribution and sales of RVs, supplies and accessories.
Cost: $40.00
Frequency: 9 issues (1year
Circulation: 16055
Founded in 1966
Printed in 4 colors on glossy stock

19118 **Recyclers Power Source**
PO Box 556
Spirit Lake, IA 51360

712-336-5614
800-336-5614; Fax: 712-336-5617
jstahly@qwestoffice.net
www.rpowersource.com

Laura Kabele
Julie Stahly

Purchasing guide for automotive recycling.
Frequency: Monthly

19119 **Reman Connection**
Automotive Parts Remanufacturers Association
7250 Heritage Village Plaza
Suite 201
Gainesville, VA 20155

703-968-2772; Fax: 703-968-2878
info@apra.org
www.apra.org

Omar Cueto, Chairman
Jay Robie, Vice President
Joe Kripli, President

Association magazine (replacing Global Connections) offers information on the remanufacturing industry including product updates, news features and more.
Cost: $35.00
1000 Members
Frequency: Monthly
Circulation: 10000+
Founded in 1941

19120 **SAE Off-Highway Engineering**
Society of Automotive Engineers
400 Commonwealth Dr
Warrendale, PA 15096-0001

724-776-4841
877-606-7323; Fax: 724-776-0790
sohe@sae.org
www.sae.org

David Schutt, CEO
Brian Kaleida, Chief Information Officer

Member services and news, as well as activities including meetings, professional development seminars, publication introductions and education programs.
Cost: $70.00
Frequency: Monthly
Circulation: 58263
Founded in 1905

19121 **SEMA News**
Performance Aftermarket Publishers
1575 South Valley Vista Drive
Diamond Bar, CA 91765

909-860-2030; Fax: 909-860-0184
www.sema.org

Christopher Kersting, President
Peter MacGillivray, VP Communications

Covers specialty and performance segment of autos with the Auto Aftermarket, Specialty Equipment and Marketing Association.
Cost: $39.95
96 Pages
Frequency: Monthly
Circulation: 35000
Founded in 1988
Printed in 4 colors on matte stock

19122 **School Bus Fleet**
Bobit Publishing Company
3520 Challenger Street
Torrance, CA 90503-1640

310-533-2400; Fax: 310-533-2500
sbf@bobit.com

www.bobitbusinessmedia.com
Facebook, Twitter, LinkedIn

Richard Rivera, CEO
Mark Hollenbeck, Associate Publisher
Frank DiGiacomo, Vice President Emeritus
James Blue, General Manager/Publisher

Published for persons involved with the transportation of school children grades K-12, includes articles on lowering costs, improving fleet operations, scheduling techniques, vehicle maintenance and federal regulatory issues.
Cost: $25.00
Frequency: Monthly
Circulation: 22000
Founded in 1961

19123 Specialty Automotive Magazine
Meyers Publishing
799 Camarillo Springs Rd
Camarillo, CA 93012-9468

805-445-8881; Fax: 805-445-8882
www.meyerspublishing.com

Len Meyers, Owner
Len Meyers, Publisher
Andrew Meyers, Associate Publisher
Harriet Kaplan, Assistant Editor

For accessories and performance specialists, dedicated for car and truck product suppliers and installers. Various fatermaker segments are covered: street, track, van, truck, and off-road. Features cover: technology and trends, performance retailing, new product showcases, upgrade news, trade shows, legislation, advertising, OEM's industry news, and people on the move.
Cost: $10.00
Frequency: Monthly
Circulation: 25000
ISSN: 0894-7414
Founded in 1983
Printed in 4 colors on glossy stock

19124 Sport Truck & SUV Accessory Business
Cygnus Publishing
1233 Janesville Avenue
Fort Atkinson, WI 53538

920-000-1111
800-547-7377; Fax: 920-563-1699

John French, CEO
Pat Walker, Editor
Tom Kohn, Executive Vice President
Founded in 1966

19125 Supercharger
Detroit Section Society of Automotive Engineers
28535 Orchard Lake Road
Suite 200
Farmington Hills, MI 48334

248-324-4445; Fax: 248-324-4449
www.sae-detroit.org

Charon Morgan, Chair
Terry Rhoades, Treasurer

The official publication of SAE Detroit Section that brings members together with news of upcoming tours, technical meetings, events and more.
Circulation: 16000
Printed in on glossy stock

19126 Tire Retread Information Packet & Buyers Guide
Tire Retread and Repair Information Bureau
1013 Birch Street
Falls Church, VA 22046

703-533-7677
877-394-6811; Fax: 703-533-7678
info@retread.org
www.retread.org

David Stevens, Managing Director
Bob Majewski, President
Eddie Burleson, Vice President
Phil Boarts, Secretary/Treasurer
Norm Ball, Director

Published by the Tire Retread Information Bureau.
380 Pages
Frequency: Weekly
Founded in 1972

19127 Tire Review
Babcox Publications
3550 Embassy Pkwy
Akron, OH 44333-8318

330-670-1234; Fax: 330-670-0874
bbabcox@babcox.com
www.babcox.com

Bill Babcox, Owner
David Modiz, Group Publisher
Dave Wooldridge, Publisher

Designed to assist the independent retail tire dealer in his number one concern—profitability. It focuses on pricing strategies, marketing and effective advertising to meet the challenges of today's industry.
Cost: $64.00
84 Pages
Frequency: Monthly
Founded in 1902

19128 Tow Times
TT Publications
203 West SR 434
Winter Springs, FL 32708

407-327-4817
800-308-3745; Fax: 407-327-2603
news@towtimes.com
www.towtimes.com

Clarissa Powell, Publisher
Tim Jackson, Editor
Dave Jones, President

Edited to review various aspects of the towing and road services. Accepts advertising.
Cost: $34.00
56 Pages
Frequency: Monthly
Founded in 1983

19129 Toy Cars & Models
F+W Media
38 E. 29th Street
New York, NY 10016

212-447-1400; Fax: 212-447-5231
contact_us@fwmedia.com
www.fwcommunity.com

Jim Ogle, CFO
Sara Domville, President
Chad Phelps, Chief Digital Officer
David Nussbaum, CEO

Provides comprehensive coverage of the model car hobby without bias toward scale, subject, manufacturer or material. Offers columns and news stories featuring models made of die-cast, white metal, plastic, resin and more while getting readers in touch with the manufacturers, distributors and retailers who sell these model cars. Monthly giveaways, reader polls and an active letters column give readers a chance to participate in their hobby.
Cost: $29.98
88 Pages
Frequency: Monthly
Circulation: 17916
Founded in 1998

19130 Traffic Injury Prevention
AAAM
PO Box 4176
Barrington, IL 60011-4176
847-844-3880; Fax: 847-844-3884
info@aaam.org
www.aaam.org

Brian N. Fildes, Ph.D, President
Mary Pat McKay, MD, President-Elect
Kristy B. Arbogast, Ph.D, Secretary
Frances D. Bents, Treasurer

Bridging the disciplines of medicine, engineering, public health and traffic safety in order to foster the science of traffic injury prevention. The journal focuses on research, interventions and evaluations within the areas of traffic safety, crash causation, injury prevention and treatment.
Frequency: 6x Yearly
ISSN: 1538-9588
Founded in 1957

19131 Truck & SUV Performance
Bobit Publishing Company
3520 Challenger St
Torrance, CA 90503-1640

310-533-2400; Fax: 310-533-2500
www.bobit.com

Edward J Bobit, CEO
John Jeffries, Editor
Circulation: 32,000
Founded in 1961

19132 Underhood Service
Babcox Publications
3550 Embassy Pkwy
Akron, OH 44333-8318
330-670-1234; Fax: 330-670-0874
bbabcox@babcox.com
www.babcox.com

Bill Babcox, CEO
Jeff Stankard, VP/ Group Publisher
Jennifer McMullen, Managing Editor

Meets the special needs of those technicians where most of their jobs involve the service and repair of under-the-hood systems. Answers the challenge of a continuing expansion of automotive technology.
Cost: $64.00
Frequency: Monthly
Circulation: 40500
Founded in 1920

19133 Used Car Dealer Magazine
Nat'l Independent Automobile Dealers Association
2521 Brown Boulevard
Arlington, TX 76006-5203

817-492-2377
800-682-3837; Fax: 817-649-5866
www.niada.com/

Michael R Linn, CEO/Publisher
Michael Harbour, Editor
Angela Ledbetter, Executive Assistant
Adrianne Argumaniz, Publication Manager

Information on auctions, profit center opportunities, trends in used car market, and updates on legislation. Coverage on association membership and the entire used vehicle industry.
Cost: $36.00
Circulation: 15000
Founded in 1946
Printed in 4 colors on glossy stock

19134 Ward's Autoworld
Ward's Communications

3000 Town Center
Suite 2750
Southfield, MI 48075-1245

248-799-2622; Fax: 248-357-9747
wards@wardsauto.com
www.wardsauto.com

Thomas Duncan, Publisher
Drew Winter, Editor

News and analysis for automotive OEM professionals.
Cost: $55.00
130 Pages
Frequency: Monthly
Circulation: 102000
ISSN: 0043-0315
Founded in 1924
Mailing list available for rent: 99,000 names
Printed in 4 colors on glossy stock

19135 **Ward's Dealer Business**
Ward's Communications
3000 Town Center
Suite 2750
Southfield, MI 48075-1245

248-799-2622; Fax: 248-357-9747
wards@wardsauto.com
www.wardsdealer.com

Thomas Duncan, Group Publisher
Drew Winter, Editor
Tony Noland, CEO
James Bush, Managing Director

News and analysis for auto dealership professionals.
80 Pages
Frequency: Monthly
Circulation: 27000
ISSN: 1086-1629
Founded in 1924
Mailing list available for rent: 98,861 names
Printed in 4 colors

Trade Shows

19136 **AAIW: Automotive Aftermarket Industry Week Expo**
Overseas Automotive Council
10 Laboratory Drive
PO Box 13966
Reserach Triangle, NC 27709-3966

919-406-8854; Fax: 919-549-4824
bbrucato@aasa.mema.org
www.aftermarketsuppliers.org

Ben Brucato, Executive Director
Paul McCarthy, Managing Director

Containing 2,500 exhibits.
100M+ Attendees
Frequency: November

19137 **AAMVA Annual International Conference**
American Assoc. of Motor Vehicle Administrators
4301 Wilson Boulevard
Suite 400
Arlington, VA 22203

703-522-4200; Fax: 703-522-1553
info@aamva.org
www.aamva.org

Neil D Schuster, President
Marc Saitta, VP &CFO
Kathy King, Director Business Services

The annual conference of the American Association of Motor Vehicle Administrators during August that provides numerous exhibits, programs and presentations and the opportunity for members to meet and network with colleagues.
800 Attendees
Frequency: August
Founded in 1933

19138 **ABPA Trade Show Fair**
Automotive Body Parts Association
1510 Eldridge Parkway
Suite 110-168
Houston, TX 77077

281-531-0809
800-323-5832; Fax: 281-531-9411
info@autobpa.com
www.autobpa.com

Stanley Rodman, Executive Director
Dolores Richardson, President

Trade show with 35 exhibitors and over 43 booths.
146 Members
Frequency: September
Founded in 1980

19139 **AFLA Annual Meeting and Conference**
Automotive Fleet and Leasing Association
N83 W13410 Leon Road
Menomonee Falls, WI 53051

414-386-0366; Fax: 414-359-1671
info@afla.org
www.afla.org
Facebook, LinkedIn

Bill Elliott, Executive Director
Michael Bieger, President
Mary Sticha, Executive Vice President
Greg Haag, Communications & PR Manager

Providing the opportunity and a forum for the exchange of information and ideas between related segments of the fleet industry.
400 Members
Frequency: Annual
Founded in 1969

19140 **AIAG AutoTech Conference**
Automotive Industry Action Group
26200 Lahser Road
Suite 200
Southfield, MI 48033

248-358-3003; Fax: 248-799-7995
www.aiag.org

Jhon Batchik, Chairman
David Kneisler, Vice Chairman

It's a venue where the collaboration between OEMs and suppliers is showcased through educational sessions, product and service exhibits and demonstrations, and networking opportunities.
3000 Attendees
Founded in 1982

19141 **APMA Annual Conference & Exhibition**
Automotive Parts Manufacturers' Association
10 Four Seasons Place
Suite 801
Toronto, ON M9B 6H7

416-620-4220; Fax: 416-620-9730
apma.ca

Flavio Volpe, President
Jonathon Azzopardi, Director
Mike Bilton, Director
Lisa T. Boulton, Director
Fred di Tosto, Director

Event for automotive equipment suppliers, focusing on key issues facing the industry.
Founded in 1952

19142 **ARA Annual Convention & Exposition**
Automotive Recyclers Association
9113 Church Street
Manassas, VA 20110

571-208-0428
888-385-1005; Fax: 571-208-0430
michael@a-r-a.org
www.a-r-a.org

Michael Wilson, CEO
Kim Glasscock, Meetings & Expositions

Automotive recycling trade show. Containing over 150 booths and more than 100 exhibits. The 2006 trade show is scheduled for September 27th to September 30th in Indianapolis, Indiana and the 2007 trade show is scheduled for September 26th to September 29th in Orlando, Florida.
800 Attendees
Frequency: Annual/September

19143 **ARTA Powertrain Expo**
Automatic Transmission Rebuilders Association
2400 Latigo Avenue
Oxnard, CA 93030

805-604-2000
866-464-2872; Fax: 805-604-2003
dmadden@atra.com
www.atra.com

Dennis Madden, CEO
Jim Lyons, VP
Lance Wiggins, Director

Speakers on many subjects, providing information and tips for those within the transmission repair industry. Event provides the opportunity for members to meet and network.
2000 Members
Frequency: September
Founded in 1954

19144 **ASA Annual Convention**
Automotive Service Association
8190 Precinct Line Road
Suite 100
Colleyville, TX 76034-7675

817-514-2900
800-272-7467; Fax: 817-514-0770
asainfo@ASAshop.org
www.asashop.org

Ron Pyle, President/Chief Staff Executive
Toni Slanton, Executive Director
Jhon Scully, Senior Vice President
Linda Ferguson, Program Administrator
Frequency: April/May

19145 **American Engine Rebuilders Association Expo**
American Engine Rebuilders Association
500 Coventry Lane
Suite 180
Crystal Lake, IL 60014

815-526-7600
888-326-2372; Fax: 815-526-7601
info@aera.org
www.aera.org

John Goodman, President
Dwayne J. Dugas, Chairman
Ron McMorris, First Vice Chairman
David Bianchi, Treasurer

550 exhibits with automotive services equipment, parts, tools, supplies and services. Seminar and dinner also offered.
6000 Attendees
Frequency: Annual
Founded in 1974

19146 **American Public Transportation Association Expo**
American Public Transit Association

1666 K Street NW
Suite 1100
Washington, DC 20006

202-496-4800; Fax: 202-496-4324
meetings2@apta.com
www.apta.com

Michael Melaniphy, President
Gary Thomas, Chair
Rosemary Sherid, Marketing
Karen W. Harvey, Director Human Resources

Industry leaders from around the globe attend to meet suppliers of the latest public transportation products, services, and technologies designed to enhance the passenger experience and make your transit system more efficient and profitable.
15000 Attendees
Frequency: October 2008/2011
Founded in 1882

19147 **Atlantic City Classic Car Show & Auction**
Atlantic City Convention Center
One Convention Center Boulevard
Atlantic City, NJ 04801

609-449-2000; Fax: 609-449-2090
www.acclassiccars.com
Facebook, Twitter

Held annually, the AC Classic Car Show and Auction is the east coast's largest classic car show and auction.
60000 Attendees

19148 **Auto Remarketing Convention**
Auto Remarketing
Westview At Weston
301 Cascade Pointe Lane # 101
Cary, NC 27513

800-608-7500; Fax: 919-674-6027
www.autoremarketing.com

Ron Smith, President

Executive conference focused on remarketing strategies for manufacturer, bank, finance, commercial and rental fleet/lease vehicles.
Frequency: February
Founded in 1996

19149 **Automotive Aftermarket Products Expo (AAPEX)**
Auto Care Association
7101 Wisconsin Avenue
Bethesda, MD 20814

301-654-6664; Fax: 301-654-3299
info@autocare.org
www.autocare.org

Bill Hanvey, President/CEO
Largest aftermarket trade show in North America, featuring over 1700 exhibitors of auto parts, accessories and services.
Frequency: November

19150 **Automotive Engine Rebuilders Association Expo**
Automotive Engine Rebuilders Association
500 Coventry Lane
Suite 180
Crystal Lake, IL 60014-7592

815-526-7600
888-326-2372; Fax: 815-526-7601
info@aera.org
www.aera.org

John Goodman, President
Dwayne J. Dugas, Chairman
Ron McMorris, First Vice Chairman
David Bianchi, Treasurer

Demonstrations of the industry's latest technology in equipment, tools, supplies, parts, and services for automotive, heavy-duty, industrial, high-performance, marine, and specialty engines. Featuring the leading national and international companies showcasing the latest new products and services in the world of engine building, remanufacturing, and installation.

19151 **BSA Convention**
Bearing Specialists Association

630-858-3838; Fax: 630-790-3095
info@bsahome.org
www.bsahome.org
LinkedIn

Jim Weihsmann, President
Michel Bouchard, Vice President

The world's premier bearing industry event for authorized distributors of bearing products and services and the manufacturers of those products.
100 Members
Frequency: Annual
Founded in 1966

19152 **BSA Winter Meeting**
Bearing Specialists Association

630-858-3838; Fax: 630-790-3095
info@bsahome.org
www.bsahome.org

Jim Scardina, President
Michel Bouchard, Vice President

BSA committees address many important issues and association projects at the Winter Meeting.
Frequency: Annual

19153 **Chicago Auto Show**
Chicago Automobile Trade Association
McCormick Place
2301 S Lake Shore Drive
Chicago, IL 60616

630-495-2282; Fax: 630-495-2260
www.chicagoautoshow.com
Facebook, Twitter, YouTube

Paul Brian, Director of Communications, CATA
Mark Bilek, Internet Director, CATA
Michelle Ferm, Communications Specialist, CATA
Dave Sloan, Auto Show General Manager
Sandi Potempa, Dir., Special Events & Exhibits

The Chicago Auto Show is the largest auto show in North America and has been held more times than any other auto exposition on the continent.
Frequency: Annual
Founded in 1901

19154 **Convergence Conference and Exhibition**
Society of Automotive Engineers
755 W Big Beaver
Suite 1600
Troy, MI 48084

248-273-2455; Fax: 24- 27- 249
pkreh@sae.org
www.sae.org/convergence

Patti Kreh, Meetings, Exhibits Contact
Nori Fought, Meetings, Exhibits Contact
David Schutt, Chief Executive Officer

Serving the automotive and transportation electronics community by delivering relevant technology solutions and an electrifying line-up invited speakers and presenters.
8900+ Attendees
Frequency: October

19155 **DSAA Fall Conference**
Driving School Association of the Americas
506 A Deklab Pike
North Wales, PA 19454

800-270-3722; Fax: 215-699-3015
info@thedsaa.org
www.thedsaa.org

Robert Gillmer, President
Nina Saint, Administrative VP
Bridget Johns, Executive VP
Jill Chauncy, Treasurer
Dave Haley, Secretary

A conference for DSAA members to network with colleagues.
Frequency: Annual/Fall
Founded in 1973

19156 **DSAA Spring Conference**
Driving School Association of the Americas
506 A Deklab Pike
North Wales, PA 19454

800-270-3722; Fax: 215-699-3015
info@thedsaa.org
www.thedsaa.org

Robert Gillmer, President
Nina Saint, Administrative VP
Bridget Johns, Executive VP
Jill Chauncy, Treasurer
Dave Haley, Secretary

A conference for DSAA members to network with colleagues.
Frequency: Annual/Spring
Founded in 1973

19157 **Dayton Auto Show**
Hart Productions
60 N Second Street
Batavia, OH 45103

513-797-7900
877-704-8190; Fax: 513-797-1013
vicki@hartproductions.com
www.hartproductions.com

Chip Hart, Show Management
Vicki Hart, Show Management
Vicki Diebold, Show Management
Trisha Marshall, Production Assistant
Victoria Hart, CFO

Annual auto show presented by the Dayton area Auto Dealers Association.
Frequency: March

19158 **Heavy Duty Aftermarket Week**
Association of Diesel Specialists
400 Admiral Boulevard
Kansas City, MO 64106

816-285-0810; Fax: 847-770-4952
info@diesel.org
www.diesel.org
Facebook, LinkedIn

Chuck Hess, President
Andy Girres, Vice President
Chuck Oliveros, Treasurer
Carl Fergueson, Secretary
David Fehling, Executive Director

A distributor-focused business conference created by the industry's leading trade associations and marketing groups with a long-term goal of consolidating the many annual events on the industry calendar and to create the most valuable annual event for the heavy duty aftermarket. Heavy Duty Aftermarket Week is the largest North American gathering of the independent heavy-duty industry.
700+ Members
1800+ Attendees
Frequency: Annual/January
Founded in 1956

19159 **IAATI Annual Training Seminar**
International Association of Auto Theft Investigators
PO Box 223
Clinton, NY

315-853-1913; Fax: 315-883-1310
jvabounader@iaati.org
www.iaati.org
LinkedIn

Joe Broslus, President
John O'Byrne, VP
John V. Abounader, Executive Director
Marianne Finney, Marketing

Provides members who are auto theft investigators with resources to develop and maintain professional standards within the industry. Some of the topics covered range from arson and marine investigations to staged accident investigations. The 2012 seminar is in Kansas City, MO.
4904 Members
350 Attendees
Founded in 1952

19160 **International Autobody Congress and Exposition**
Hanley-Wood
8600 Freeport Parkway
Suite 200
Irving, TX 75063
972-366-6324
888-529-1641; Fax: 972-536-6445
www.naceexpo.com
Linsay Roberts, Director
Ellen Pipkin, Show Manager
Specifically created for professionals involved in all aspects of the collision repair industry.
15M Attendees
Frequency: November

19161 **International Big R Show**
Automotive Parts Remanufacturers Association
7250 Heritage Village Plaza
Suite 201
Gainesville, VA 20155
703-968-2772; Fax: 703-968-2878
info@apra.org
www.apra.org
Omar Cueto, Chairman
Jay Robie, Vice President
Joe Kripli, President
Designed to attract rebuilders of a wide range of automotive and truck parts, exposing them to the key suppliers in this industry. Rebuilders specializing in electrical, c.v. joints, brake, clutch, transmissions, mechanical hydraulic, fuel systems, rack and pinion and air conditioning products will visit the show.
1000 Members
3000 Attendees
Frequency: Annual
Founded in 1941

19162 **LA Auto Show**
Los Angeles Convention Center
1201 S Figueroa Street
Los Angeles, CA 90015
213-741-1151
www.laautoshow.com
The Los Angeles Auto Show is one of the top automotive events worldwide, bringing together the latest new vehicles from auto manufacturers around the world.

19163 **MACS Convention and Trade Show**
Mobile Air Conditioning Society Worldwide
225 S. Broad Street
P.O. Box 88
Lansdale, PA 19446
215-631-7020; Fax: 215-631-7017
macsworldwide@macsw.org
www.macsw.org
Marion Posen, VP Marketing/Membership
Elvis Hoffpauir, President/COO
2000 Attendees
Frequency: Annual
Founded in 1981

19164 **NAAA Annual Conference**
National Auto Auction Association
5320 Spectrum Drive
Suite D
Frederick, MD 21703
301-696-0400; Fax: 301-631-1359
naaa@naaa.com
www.naaa.com
Frank Hackett, Executive Director
Tom Dozier, Meetings Manager
Annual convention and exhibits of automobile and truck auction equipment, supplies and services.
Frequency: Fall

19165 **NADA Convention & Expo**
National Automobile Dealers Association
8400 Westpark Drive
Mc Lean, VA 22102-3522
703-217-7000
800-252-6232; Fax: 703-821-7075
nadainfo@nada.org
www.nada.org
Gary Heimes, Convention Director
Stephen R Pitt, Executive Director, Convention
Phillip Brady, President
Providing automobile dealers with the latest in cutting edge technology, products and services they need to impact the future success of their businesses.
25000 Attendees
Frequency: January/February

19166 **NAFA Fleet Management Seminar**
National Association of Fleet Administrators
125 Villiage Boulevard
Suite 200
Princeton, NJ 08540
609-720-0882; Fax: 609-452-8004
info@nafa.org
www.nafa.org
Phillip E Russo, Executive Director
Patrick McCarren, Deputy Executive Director
Joanne Marsdh, Director Marketing & Membership
Designed to provide comprehensive education to fleet managers like you who seek the fundamental principles and practices of successful fleet management.
3000+ Members
Founded in 1957
Printed in on glossy stock

19167 **NAFA Institute & Expo**
National Association of Fleet Administrators
125 Villiage Boulevard
Suite 200
Princeton, NJ 08540
609-720-0882; Fax: 609-452-8004
info@nafa.org
www.nafa.org
Phillip E Russo, Executive Director
Patrick McCarren, Deputy Executive Director
Joanne Marsh, Director Marketing & Communications
To provide attendees and exhibitors alike with a more dynamic interaction on the exhibit hall floor and within concurrent sessions. An excellent opportunity to attend valuable education courses designed to benefit the veteran fleet professional as well as challenge first-time attendees!
3000+ Members
Frequency: April
Founded in 1957
Printed in on glossy stock

19168 **NARSA Annual Convention & Trade Show**
National Automotive Radiator Service Association
3000 Villiage Run Road
Suite103, #221
Wexford, PA 15090-6315
724-799-8415
800-551-3232; Fax: 724-799-8416
www.narsa.org
Wayne Juchno, Executive Director
Douglas Shymoniak, Manager, Sales & New Business
Maarten Taal, President
Pat O'Connor, Vice President
Angelo Miozza, Treasurer
180 booths featuring seminars and workshops of parts, equipment and supplies.
1.8M Attendees
Frequency: Annual/November

19169 **NPA Annual Convention & Expo**
National Parking Association
1112 16th Street NW
Suite 300
Washington, DC 20036
202-296-4336
800-647-7275; Fax: 202-296-3102
info@weareparking.org
weareparking.org
Christine Banning, President
Christina Garneski, Vice President, Marketing & Comms
Stacy Hudson, Director, Business Development
Bringing together parking professionals from around the world with leading experts from business and industry to explore the latest trends and developments. The Convention also affords members an opportunity to share ideas and experiences and to explore the latest equipment and technologies at the Exposition.
Frequency: Annual
Founded in 1955
Mailing list available for rent: 1700 names at $250 per M

19170 **National Auto Glass Conference & Expo**
National Glass Association
1945 Old Gallows Rd
Suite 750
Vienna, VA 22182
703-442-4890; Fax: 703-442-0630
attend@glass.org
www.glass.org
Phil James, President/CEO
Visit with over 50 companies and get informed about the latest technology and see products demonstrated live. Get answers to your technical questions and find out which solutions are right for your business.
800 Attendees
Frequency: Annual/May

19171 **National Independent Automobile Dealers Association Convention & Expo**
National Independent Automobile Dealers Assoc.
2521 Brown Boulevard
Arlington, TX 76006-5203
817-492-2377
800-682-3837; Fax: 817-649-5866
kimberly@niada.com
www.niada.com
Ginger Barrientez, Director of Events
Michael R Linn, President/CEO
Steven Jordan, COO
75 booths including automobile aftermarkets and finance companies.
Frequency: June

19172 New York International Auto Show
Jacob Javits Center
655 West 34th Street
New York, NY 10001

718-746-5300
800-282-3336; Fax: 718-746-9333
www.autoshowny.com
Facebook, Twitter, YouTube

The show offers virtually every make and model vehicle sold in the US under one roof giving consumers the unique opportunity to see everything the auto industry has to offer. From fuel-sipping economy cars to million dollar supercars, NYIAS has something for everyone.
Frequency: Annual

19173 North American Council of Automotive Teachers International Conference
North American Council of Automotive Teachers
PO Box 80010
Charleston, SC 29416

843-556-7068; Fax: 843-556-7068
office@nacat.com
www.nacat.com

Patrick Brown Harrison, President
Rob Thompson, Vice President
Curt Ward, Secretary
Chuck Ginther, Treasurer

Annual show of 70 exhibits and 50 seminars, suppliers, distributors, publishing companies and other trade organizations.
Frequency: July
Mailing list available for rent: 750 names at $165 per M

19174 North American International Auto Show
Detroit Auto Dealers Association
1900 W Big Beaver
Troy, MI 48084

248-643-0250; Fax: 248-637-0784
www.naias.com

Rod Alberts, Executive Director
William Perkins, Chair

Annual show and exhibits of new automobiles and trucks, concept cars and van conversions.
808M Attendees
Frequency: January
Founded in 1907

19175 PERA Annual Conference
Production Engine Remanufacturers Association
28203 Woodhave Road
Edwards, MO 65326

417-998-5057; Fax: 417-998-5056
www.pera.org
Facebook, LinkedIn

Nancie J. Boland, Executive VP
Robert P. McGraw, President

An opportunity to exchange ideas, methods and procedures necessary to efficiently produce remanufactured products which are equal or superior to original products in quality and performance. PERA adheres to and supports the premise that its members are dedicated to the highest business ethics, customer satisfaction, employee consideration and to the continual up-grading of the engine remanufacturing industry.
150 Attendees
Frequency: September / Seatle, WA
Founded in 1946

19176 PWA Annual Conference
Performance Warehouse Association
41-701 Corporate Way
Suite 1
Palm Desert, CA 92260

760-346-5647; Fax: 760-346-5847
www.pwa-par.org

John Towle, President
Larry Pacey, Chairman
Trent Lowe, Treasurer

This is an exclusive opportunity for manufacturers and distributors to meet in a private, business-like environment to discuss sales and marketing policies and programs.
165 Attendees
Frequency: Annual/September
Founded in 1974

19177 Performance Racing Industry Trade Show
Performace Racing Industry
31706 South Coast Highway
Laguna Beach, CA 92651

949-499-5413; Fax: 949-499-0410
mail@performanceracing.com
www.performanceracing.com

John Kilroy, Publisher/General Manager
Dan Schechner, Editor
Merredith Kaplan Burns, Managing Editor

Annual show. Features the latest in motorsports technology from 1400 companies with 4000 booths.
42000 Attendees
Frequency: Annual

19178 Philadelphia Auto Show
Philadelphia Convention Center
1101 Arch Street
Philadelphia, PA 19107

215-418-4700
www.phillyautoshow.com
Facebook, Twitter

Recognized by the industry as one of the top shows in the country, the Philly Auto Show displays more than 700 vehicles from a variety of manufacturers.
Frequency: Annual

19179 RV Dealers International Convention & Expo
Recreation Vehicle Dealers Association
3930 University Drive
Fairfax, VA 22030-2515

703-591-7130; Fax: 703-359-0152
info@rvda.org
www.rvda.org

Mike Molino, CAE, President
Mary Anne Shreve, Editor

For RV retailers from across the U.S. and Canada.
Frequency: September
Mailing list available for rent: 1500 names

19180 RVAA Executive Conference
Recreational Vehicle Aftermarket Association
1833 Centre Point Circle
Suite 123
Naperville, IL 60563-9306

630-596-9004
Facebook, Twitter

Patrick Farrey, Executive Director
Laura Hallen, Account Executive
Michael Greskiewicz, Expo Sales Manager
Meg Pawelski, Events & Awards Manager
Danielle Griffin, Communications Manager

An event which allows members to meet with each other to develop strategies for the coming year. It's the perfect opportunity for you to make the contacts and have the important face to face meeting time, with the potential partners that will enhance your success.
Frequency: October
Founded in 1969

19181 SAE International Truck & Bus Meeting and Exhibition
Society of Automotive Engineers
755 W Big Beaver
Suite 1600
Troy, MI 48084

248-273-2455
877-606-7323; Fax: 248-273-2494
automotive_hq@sae.org
www.sae.org
Facebook, Twitter, LinkedIn, YouTube, Google +

Dr. Rodica Baranescu, President
David Schutt, CEO
Nori Fought, Conference Service Representative
John Miller, Program Developer
Jack Pokrzywa, Operations Director

100 booths featuring suppliers of parts and components.
2.5M Attendees
Frequency: November

19182 SEMA International Auto Salon Trade Show
Specialty Equipment Market Association
1575 South Valley Vista Drive
Diamond Bar, CA 91765

909-610-2030
showinfo@sema.org
www.sema.org
Facebook, Twitter, Google+

Christopher Kersting, President and CEO
Gary Vigil, Trade Show Director
Marel Del Rio, Trade Show Coordinator

When the sport-compact scene was just beginning, the show was launched to educate members about the growing market and to bring new buyers and opportunities to manufacturers.
Frequency: May
Founded in 1998

19183 SEMA Offroad Convention
Specialty Equipment Market Association
1575 South Valley Vista Drive
Diamond Bar, CA 91765-0910

909-610-2030
sema@sema.org
www.phillyautoshow.com

Chris Kersting, President/CEO
Geoege Afremow, Vice President & CFO
Scooter Brothers, Chairman

Designed as a companion event to the well established SEMA Spring Expo, and as an extension of the SEMA Show, will target companies serving the recreational and performance off-road segments and aims to create new opportunities for this growing market.
Frequency: February

19184 SEMA Show
Specialty Equipment Market Association
1575 South Valley Vista Drive
Diamond Bar, CA 91765-0910

909-610-2030; Fax: 909-860-0184
sema@sema.org
www.sema.org

Chris Kersting, President/CEO
Geoege Afremow, Vice President & CFO
Scooter Scooter, Chairman

The premier automotive specialty performance products trade event in the world featuring performance, accessories, restoration and motorsports products.
100M Attendees
Frequency: November

19185 SEMA Spring Expo
Specialty Equipment Market Association
1575 South Valley Vista Drive
Diamond Bar, CA 91765-0910

909-610-2030
sema@sema.org
www.sema.org

Chris Kersting, President/CEO
Geoege Afremow, Vice President & CFO
Scooter Scooter, Chairman

The only trade show delivering the SEMA Show experience to the doorsteps of regional auto and truck parts and accessory businesses. We feature the leading companies that produce truck caps and accessories, automotive trim and restyling products, wheels and tires, gauges and instruments, performance parts and more.
Frequency: February

19186 SIGM Annual Meeting
Society of Independent Gasoline Marketers
3930 Pender Drive
Suite 340
Fairfax, VA 22030

703-709-7000; Fax: 703-709-7007
sigma@sigma.org
www.sigma.org

Kenneth Doyle, Executive Vice President
Susan Crosby, Director, Communication & Education
Mary Alice Kutyn, Director of Meetings
Nancy Muskett, Director, Advertising & Sponsorship
Marilyn Selvitelle, Director, Business Development

SIGMA meetings are valuable and varied, addressing topics of interest for branded or unbranded motor fuel marketers, those interested in alternative fuels, fuel suppliers, and of course administrative and financial discussions for all types of organizations.
Frequency: October

19187 SOUTHCON
Wescon
1230 Rosecrans Avenue
Suite 100
Manhattan Beach, CA 90266

310-524-4100
800-877-2668; Fax: 310-643-7328

Joey Quesada Cruz, Show Management
Rod Mann, Conference Management

Issues that concern design, manufacturing and test departments. Instructors are leading experts in the topics they present.
10M Attendees
Frequency: February

19188 School Bus Fleet ConneX Conference
School Bus Fleet/Bobit Publishing Comany
3520 Challenger Street
Torrance, CA 90503-1640

310-533-2400; Fax: 310-533-2500
sbf@bobit.com
www.schoolbusfleetconnex.com

Richard Rivera, CEO
Mark Hollenbeck, Associate Publisher
James Blue, General Manager/Publisher

An opportunity to network and buld relationships with other action-minded individuals involved in school transportation.
Frequency: Annual
Founded in 1961

19189 Supernationals Custom Auto Show
TNT Promotions Inc
PO Box 50386
Albuquerque, NM 87181-0386

505-480-0056
800-300-9381
www.thesupernationals.com

The premier annual automotive event in New Mexico. Attracts prominent street rods and customs from throughout the country, as well as local and regional vehicles for both show and competition display.
25000 Attendees
Frequency: Annual/February
Founded in 1992

19190 TIA Global Tire Expo
Tire Industry Association
1532 Pointer Ridge Place
Suite G
Bowie, MD 20716-1883

301-430-7280
800-876-8372; Fax: 301-430-7283
info@tireindustry.org
www.tireindustry.org

Roy Littlefield, CEO

Providing an ideal forum for diverse individuals to meet, network and advance new business and marketing opportunities. This world-class exhibition is the number one showcase dedicated to those who have an interest in tire, rubber and transportation services.

19191 WMDA Mega Show Annual Convention
WMDA Service Station & Automotive Repair Assoc.
1532 Pointer Ridge Place
Suite G
Bowie, MD 20716

301-390-0900
800-492-0329; Fax: 301-390-3161
www.wmda.net
Facebook

Rick Agoris, President
Marta Gates, Director of Operations
Kirk McCauley, Director of Member Relations
Tirika Williams, Director of Finance

Featuring Over 225 Exhibits for the service station, automotive repair, car wash, convenience store & tire industries.
1500 Attendees

19192 iFlex Annual Conference
Automotive Oil Change Association
330 North Wabash Avenue
Suite 2000
Chicago, IL 60611

312-321-5132
800-230-0702; Fax: 312-673-6832
info@aoca.org
www.aoca.org

Bryan White, Executive Director
David Haney, President
Dave Jensen, Vice President
Bob Falter, Treasurer
Jim Grant, Secretary

Brings hundreds of vendors offering thousands of products and services to the fast lube industry and ancillary profit centers.
3000 Members
Frequency: Annual/April-May
Founded in 1987

Directories & Databases

19193 American Bus Association's Motorcoach Marketer
American Bus Association
111 K Street NE
9th Floor
Washington, DC 20002

202-842-1645; Fax: 202-842-0850
abainfo@buses.org
www.buses.org

Thomas JeBran, President
John Meier, Vice Chairman
Frank Henry, Secretary/Treasurer

This directory is a comprehensive guide of the bus and travel industry offering information on hotels and sightseeing services, attractions, museums, restaurants and more.
500 Pages
Frequency: Annual
Founded in 1926

19194 American Public Transit Association Membership Directory
American Public Transit Association
1666 K St NW
Suite 1100
Washington, DC 20006-1215

202-496-4800; Fax: 202-496-4324
hbrett@apta.com
www.apta.com

Michael Melaniphy, President/CEO
Petra Mollet, VP
Rosemary Sheridan, VP Communications and Marketing

A who's who directory of services and supplies within the public transportation industry.
Founded in 1882

19195 Automotive Aftermarket Suppliers
Automotive Aftermarket Suppliers Association
10 Laboratory Drive
PO Box 13966
Research Triangle Park, NC 27709-3966

919-549-4800; Fax: 919-549-4824
media@mema.org
www.aftermarketsuppliers.org

Steve Handschuh, President
Chris Gardner, VP
Margaret Beck, Marketing and Communications

Directory of automotive supply chains and jobbers/retailers in North America. Also, warehouse distributors and major programmed distribution groups.
Founded in 1974

19196 Automotive Parts Remanufacturers Association Membership Directory
Automotive Parts Remanufacturers Association
7250 Heritage Village Plaza
Suite 201
Gainesville, VA 20155

703-968-2772; Fax: 703-968-2878
info@apra.org
www.apra.org

Omar Cueto, Chairman
Joe Kripli, President

Lists member companies and their products, addresses, phone and fax numbers, key personnel and sometimes even internet information. Keep this directory, your network resource for the automotive parts rebuilding industry, on your desk throughout the year.
Cost: $35.00
Frequency: Annual
Founded in 1941

19197 Canadian Automotive Sourcing Guide
Automotive Parts Manufacturers' Association

10 Four Seasons Place
Suite 801
Toronto, ON M9B 6H7

416-620-4220; Fax: 416-620-9730
canadianautomotivesourcingguide.com

Flavio Volpe, President
Jonathon Azzopardi, Director
Mike Bilton, Director
Lisa T. Boulton, Director
Fred di Tosto, Director

Directory of products and information for auto parts manufacturers and other industry professionals.
Founded in 1952

19198 ELM Guide to Automakers in North America
ELM International
PO Box 1740
East Lansing, MI 48826-1740

517-332-4900; Fax: 517-351-3032

The third edition of this guide contains more than 400 profiles that highlight the North American manufacturing operations of Chrysler, Ford, GM and all of the foreign owned automakers.
Cost: $350.00
Frequency: Semiannual

19199 ELM Guide to Japanese Affiliated Suppliers in North America
ELM International
PO Box 1740
East Lansing, MI 48826-1740
517-332-4900; Fax: 517-351-3032
www.automotivesuppliers.com

Mark Santucci

Offers information on approximately 290 Japanese owned automotive original equipment components manufacturers that operate in North America.
Cost: $350.00

19200 ELM Guide to US Automotive Sourcing
ELM International
PO Box 1740
East Lansing, MI 48826-1740

517-332-4900; Fax: 517-351-3032

Mark Santucci, Executive Director

Two volumes offering information on automotive original equipment manufacturer parts and components suppliers and profiles of plants belonging to 576 companies.
Cost: $775.00
1200 Pages

19201 NAFA's Professional Directory
National Association of Fleet Administrators
125 Village Boulevard
Suite 200
Princeton, NJ 08540

609-720-0882; Fax: 609-452-8004
info@nafa.org
www.nafa.org
Facebook, Twitter, LinkedIn

Phillip E. Russo, Executive Director
Patrick McCarren, Executive Director
Mary Sticha, Vice President
Joanne Marsh, Director of Marketing
Gladys Reyes, Meeting & Event Planners

NAFA Member and Affiliate contact information.
2600+ Members
Frequency: Quarterly

19202 Old Cars Price Guide
F+W Media
38 E. 29th Street
New York, NY 10016

212-447-1400; Fax: 212-447-5231
contact_us@fwmedia.com

Rick Groth, Publisher
Ron Kowalke, Editor
David Nussbaum, CEO
Sara Domville, President

The nation's most respected authority for pricing antique and collectible automobiles. The extensive price-guide section covers makes and models of domestic cars, from AMC to Willys, from model years 1901 to 1994. Also included are light-duty trucks and selected makes of imported cars. Cars are valued in six conditions - from 'Excellent' down to 'Parts Car.' Also includes columns and features on collectible cars.
Cost: $19.98
148 Pages
Frequency: Monthly
Circulation: 61000
Founded in 1978

19203 PXN Parts Exchange New
15030 Avenue of Science
Suite 100
San Diego, CA 92128

858-946-1900
800-669-4237; Fax: 858-946-1073
www.adpclaims.com
Facebook, Twitter, LinkedIn, YouTube

Tony Aquila, Chairman, President & CEO
Jack Sanders, COO
Kamal Hamid, Director Investor Relations
Lisa Collins, Marketing Coordinator

Provides an electronic link from your ADP estimating system to comprehensive database of new replacement parts. Data on over three and a half million parts facilitates the writing of complete, cost-effective damage reports.

19204 RV Trade Digest
Cygnus Publishing
1233 Janesville Avenue
Fort Atkinson, WI 53538

920-000-1111
800-547-7377; Fax: 920-563-1699
info@cygnus.com
www.cygnus.com

John French, CEO
Paul Bonaiuto, CFO
Ed Wood, VP, HR and Communications
Kris Flitcroft, EVP-Residential, Construction, Mfg.
Blair Johnson, SVP, Business Development

Propriety BASE technology connecting businesses with multi-media content.
Cost: $40.00
40 Pages
Frequency: Bi-Monthly
Circulation: 15,000
Founded in 1983
Printed in 4 colors on glossy stock

19205 Transmission Digest Buyer's Guide Issue
MD Publications
PO Box 2210
3057 E Cairo Street
Springfield, MO 65801-2210

417-866-3917
800-274-7890; Fax: 417-866-2781
www.mdpublications.com

Carol Langsford, President
Michelle Dickeman, Vice President
Bob Mace, Publisher
Gary Sifford, Editor
Mike Anderson, Advertising Sales

List of over 500 manufacturers and distributors of products and services for the motor vehicle transmission repair industry.
Cost: $15.00
Printed in 4 colors on glossy stock

19206 Ward's Automotive Yearbook
Ward's Communications
3000 Town Center
Suite 2750
Southfield, MI 48075-1245

248-799-2622; Fax: 248-357-9747
tduncan@wardsauto.com
www.wardsauto.com
Facebook, Twitter

Thomas Duncan, Group Publisher
James Bush, Managing Editor
David Zoia, Editorial Director
Drew Winter, Senior Editor
Chris Lamphear, Marketing Director

Directory of suppliers to the vehicle manufacturing industry. New vehicle sales, production and inventory data and new vehicle product information and statistics.
Cost: $475.00
500 Pages
Frequency: Annual
Circulation: 26,000
ISBN: 0-910589-15-1
Founded in 1938

19207 Who Makes It and Where Directory
Tire Guides
1101 S Rogers Circle
Suite 6
Boca Raton, FL 33487-2748

561-997-9229; Fax: 561-997-9233
tireinfo@tireguides.com
www.tireguides.com

Nancy Garfield, Owner
James Garfield, Editor-in-Chief
Al Snyder, Contributing Editor
Jeff Chychrun, Associate Editor

Brand listings with manufacturer & distributor information; worldwide listing of web site addresses, fax numbers & U.S. toll free numbers.
Cost: $7.00
62 Pages
Frequency: Annual
Founded in 1950

19208 Worldwide Automotive Supplier Directory
Society of Automotive Engineers
400 Commonwealth Drive
Warrendale, PA 15086-7511

724-776-4841
877-606-7323; Fax: 724-776-0790
customerservice@sae.org
www.sae.org
Facebook, Twitter, LinkedIn, YouTube, Google+

David Schutt, President
Michael Thompson, Publisher
Melissa Bachman, Marketing
Peggy Bartlett, Corporate Sales

Directory features 10,000+ supplier listings from every major vehicle-producing region. And, it is the ONLY directory to provide information on a company's technical capabilities.
Cost: $329.00
Frequency: Annual
Circulation: 60,550
ISBN: 0-768015-36-7

Industry Web Sites

19209 **apma.ca**
Automotive Parts Manufacturers' Association
Facebook, Twitter, LinkedIn, Google+
Canadian association representing suppliers of parts, equipment, tools, supplies, and services for the automotive industry.

19210 **http://gold.greyhouse.com**
G.O.L.D Grey House OnLine Databases
Grey House Publishing's online database platform, GOLD, offers Quick Search, Keyword Search and Expert Search for most business sectors including automotive and transportation markets. The GOLD platform makes finding the information you need quick and easy - whether you're a novice searcher or an experienced database user. All of Grey House's directory products are available for subscription on the GOLD platform.

19211 **www.aaam.org**
Assn for the Advancement of Automotive Medicine
A professional multidisciplinary organization dedicated entirely to motor vehicle crash prevention and control.

19212 **www.aamva.org**
American Assn. of Motor Vehicle Administrators
Nonprofit organization represents state and provincial officials in the US and Canada who administer and enforce motor vehicle laws. Strives to develop model programs in motor vehicle administration, police traffic services and highway safety.

19213 **www.aiada.org**
American Int'l Automobile Dealers Assocation
Lobbying and communications organization for American automobile dealerships that sell and service international nameplate brands.

19214 **www.aiag.org**
Automotive Industry Action Group
Composed of major North American vehicle manufacturers and their suppliers. Provides an open forum where members cooperate to develop and promote solutions that enhance prosperity in the automotive industry.

19215 **www.aoca.org**
Automotive Oil Change Association
Representing the convenient automotive service industry. Dedicated to enhancing the competency of fast lube owners, educating the public about services our members offer and maintaining a favorable business environment for the industry as a whole.

19216 **www.apra.org**
Automotive Parts Rebuilders Association
Association of more than 1,500 member companies engaged in the rebuilding of automotive related hard parts, including starters, alternators, clutches, transmissions, brakes, drive shafts and other parts for passenger cars, trucks, off road, equipment and industrial uses.

19217 **www.autobpa.com**
Automotive Body Parts Association
Members are companies that distribute, supply or manufacture automotive replacement body parts.

19218 **www.autocare.org**
Auto Care Association
Provides advocacy, educational, networking, technology, market intelligence and communications resources on auto care to its members. Formerly known as the Automotive Aftermarket Industry Association.

19219 **www.autoconsulting.com**
Automotive Consulting Group
Management consulting firm providing top line and bottom line business performance improvement services to the worldwide automotive industry.

19220 **www.awda.org**
Automotive Warehouse Distributors Association
A trade association consisting of more than 600 members who are manufacturers and warehouse distributors, affiliates, marketing associations and others actively involved in the production, distribution and installation of motor vehicle parts, tools, services, accessories, equipment, materials and supplies. A segment of the Automotive Aftermarket Industry Association.

19221 **www.buses.org**
American Bus Association
Trade association for the North American bus industry.

19222 **www.carcare.org**
Car Care Council
A nonprofit 501 (c) (3) educational foundation whose purpose is to educate motorists about the importance of maintenance repairs and entertainment for safer, cleaner better performing vehicles. Provides editorial and public service material for media use.

19223 **www.classiccar.com**
ClassicCar.Com
Offers classic car enthusiasts around the world an online community with chats, forums and discussion groups.

19224 **www.diesel.org**
Association of Diesel Specialists
The worldwide diesel industry's leading trade association, dedicated to the highest level of service on diesel fuel injection and related systems.

19225 **www.edmunds.com**
Edmunds.Com
Founded in 1966 for the purpose of publishing new and used automotive pricing guides for automobile buyers.

19226 **www.filtercouncil.org**
Filter Manufacturers Council
For manufacturers of vehicular and industrial filtration products in North America. Active in efforts to educate people on proper disposal of used oil filters.

19227 **www.forecastinternational.com**
Forecast International
An electronic information/data service sourced from thousands of worldwide publications, in 15 languages. Provides concise passenger vehicles e-mail news and analysis summaries, news, trends and contract information with hyper-links to the source or a related website. Delivered 100 times a year.

19228 **www.greyhouse.com**
Grey House Publishing
Authoritative reference directories for most business sectors including automotive and transportation markets. Users can search the online databases with varied search criteria allowing for custom searches by product category, geographic area, sales volume, keyword, subject and more. Full Grey House catalog and online ordering also available.

19229 **www.hemmings.com**
Hemmings Motor News
Hemmings Motor News for the car collector and enthusiast.

19230 **www.iaati.org**
Int'l Association of Auto Theft Investigators
To improve communication and coordination among the growing family of professional auto theft investigators.

19231 **www.impa.org**
International Motor Press Association
Professional group of writers and editors producing auto articles for the press, radio or TV.

19232 **www.macsw.org**
Mobile Air Conditioning Society Worldwide
Provides technical training, information and communication for the professionals in the automotive air conditioning industry.

19233 **www.mema.org**
Motor and Equipment Manufacturers Association
Serves manufacturers of all types of automotive and truck products through market research, legislative and regulatory representation and reporting, information services, EDI network and credit reporting.

19234 **www.naaa.com**
National Auto Auction Association
Represents dealer wholesale auto auctions. Promotes exchange of ideas and public relations in the used car merchandising industry.

19235 **www.nada.com**
National Automobile Dealers Association
Provides representation for franchised new car and truck dealers in government, industry and public affairs. Provides counsel on legal and regulatory and political representation on Capital Hill.

19236 **www.nafa.org**
National Association of Fleet Administrators
Serving the needs of those managing fleets of automobiles, light duty trucks and/or vans for US and Canadian organizations. Offers statistical research, publications, regional meetings, government representation, conferences, trade shows and seminars.

19237 **www.narsa.org**
National Automotive Radiator Service Association
Trade association serving the cooling system service industry and the public.

19238 **www.nascar.com**
Turner Sports Interactive
Providing up-to-the-minute coverage on a 24-hour basis, NASCAR.COM delivers news, statistics and information on races, drivers, teams and industry events.

19239 **www.nationalwheelandrim.org**
National Wheel and Rim Association
Represents warehouse distributors of wheels, rims and related parts in the US and Canada.

19240 **www.ntea.com**
National Truck Equipment Association
Represents small to mid-sized companies that manufacture, distribute, install, buy, sell and re-

pair commercial trucks, truck bodies, truck equipment, trailers and accessories.

19241 **www.partsplus.com**
Association of Automotive Aftermarkets
Purchases and markets automotive replacement parts. Headquarters office for Parts Plus program distributors.

19242 **www.pera.org**
Production Engine Remanufacturers Association
The goal of the Production Engine Remanufacturers Association is to provide it's members with the opportunity to exchange the ideas, methods and procedures necessary to efficiently produce remanufactured products which are equal or superior to original products in quality and performance.

19243 **www.pwa-par.com**
Performance Warehouse Association
An organization of specialty automotive parts wholesalers joined together and dealing with management, financial and legislative matters.

19244 **www.retread.org**
Tire Retread Information Bureau
Serving as the public relations arm of the retread industry. Gathering and disseminating information on retread passenger and truck tires to members and the general public.

19245 **www.rma.org**
Rubber Manufacturers Association
National trade association for makers of tires and other rubber products.

19246 **www.rvda.org**
National RV Dealers Association
National association advances the best interests of RV retailers through education, services, leadership and programs of market expansion that promote increased use and sale of RVs as well as enhancement of the RV's image.

19247 **www.scrs.com**
Society of Collision Repair Specialists
For owners and managers of auto collision repair shops, suppliers, insurance and educational associates and suppliers in the US, Canada, Australia and New Zealand. Distributes technical, management, marketing and sales information. Works to promote professionalism within the collision repair industry.

19248 **www.theautochannel.com**
Auto Channel
Auto news, commentary and other useful information.

Associations

19249 **Academy of Country Music**
5500 Balboa Blvd
Suite 200
Encino, CA 91316-1505

818-788-8000; Fax: 818-788-0999
info@acmcountry.com
www.acmcountry.com

Drain Murphy, Chairman
David Young, Director Operations
Tiffany Moon, Secretary
Brandi Brammer, Project Manager
Tree Paine, Director Marketing

Involved in numerous events and activities promoting country music. Presents annual awards.
4M Members
Founded in 1964

19250 **Accordian Federation of North America**
14126 E Rosencrans Boulevard
Santa Fe Springs, CA 90670

562-921-5058
afna@musician.org
Facebook, Twitter, Google+

Madeleine D'Ablaing, President
Debbie Gray, VP
Oakley Yale, Secretary
Prisscilla Martinez, Treasurer
Larry Demian, Parliamentarian

Members are primarily teachers and music school owners with the primary purpose to encourage young people to pursue their music study. Holds festivals and competitions
75 Members
Founded in 1972

19251 **Accordionists & Teachers Guild International**
813 West Lakeshore Drive
O'Fallon, IL 62269-1216

618-632-2859
amyjo@apci.net
www.accordions.com/atg

Amy Jo Sawyer, President
Joe Natole, First Vice President
Liz Finch, Second Vice President
Joan C. Sommers, Executive Secretary

ATG members are accordion teachers and professionals committed to furthering the progress of the accordion by improving teaching standards, music and all phases of music education.
Founded in 1940

19252 **Acoustical Society of America**
1305 Walt Whitman Road
Suite 300
Melville, NY 11747-4300

516-576-2360; Fax: 631-923-2875
asa@acousticalsociety.org
www.acousticalsociety.org

Christy K. Holland, President
Lily M. Wang, Vice President
David Feit, Treasurer
Christopher J. Struck, Standards Director
Susan E. Fox, Executive Director

Premier international scientific society in acoustics, dedicated to increasing and diffusing the knowledge of acoustics and its practical applications.

19253 **American Choral Directors Association**
545 Couch Drive
PO Box 2720
Oklahoma City, OK 73101-2720

405-232-8161; Fax: 405-232-8162
www.acdaonline.org

Timothy Sharp, Executive Director
Jerry Mccoy, President
Haiary Aphelstadt, VP
Jo-Ann Miller, Treasurer

Nonprofit music-education organization whose central purpose is to promote excellence in choral music through performance, composition, publication, research and teaching. In addition, ACDA strives to elevate choral music's position in American society through arts advocacy. Holds annual convention.
Cost: $90.00
19500 Members
Founded in 1959

19254 **American College of Musicians**
PO Box 1807
Austin, TX 78767

512-478-5775; Fax: 512-478-5843
ngpt@pianoguild.com
www.pianoguild.com

Richard Allison, President
Julia Kruger, VP

Provides student awards and teachers benefits.
Founded in 1931

19255 **American Composers Alliance**
PO Box 1108
New York, NY 10040

212-568-0036
info@composers.com
composers.com
Facebook, Twitter, YouTube

Gina Genova, Director

Music publisher and licensor representing Americans composing in the classical style.
Founded in 1937

19256 **American Federation of Musicians of the United States and Canada**
1501 Broadway
Suite 600
New York, NY 10036-5501

212-869-1330; Fax: 212-764-6134
info@afm.org
www.afm.org
Facebook, Twitter, YouTube

Thomas Lee, President
Linda Patterson, Executive Secreatry to President

AFM is an association of professional musicians united through their locals so that they can live and work in dignity; produce work that will be fulfilling and compensated fairly; have a meaningful voice in decisions that affect them; have the opportunity to develop their talents and skills; whose collective voice and power will be realized in a democratic and progressive union; and who oppose the forces of exploitation through their union solidarity.
10K Members
Founded in 1896

19257 **American Federation of Violin and Bow Makers**
1121 East Avenue
Red Wing, MN 55066

929-216-0720
info@afvbm.org
www.afvbm.org

David Bonsey, President
Dan Weisshaar, Vice President
Yung Chin, Treasurer
Lisbeth Nelson Butler, Secretary

Members are those with recognized professional abilities and experience in either making or repairing violins and bows. They are elected to the Federation and are entitled to all privileges and duties of membership. The Federation has designed programs to held develop the technical skills and knowledge of the membership through seminars and regular meeting events. The Federation sponsors exhibitions as a forum for makers,musicians and the general public.
Founded in 1980

19258 **American Gamelan Institute**

603-448-6060; Fax: 603-448-6060
agi@gamelan.org
www.gamelan.org

Founded in 1983

19259 **American Guild of Music**
PO Box 599
Warren, MI 48090

248-686-1975
agm@americanguild.org
www.americanguild.org

Barry Carr, President
Joanne Darby, Treasurer
Lorelei Eccleston Dart, First VP
Steve Petrunak, Second VP

The world's oldest international music organization. Its membership is open to independent music teachers, music store owners and their teaching staffs, music publishers and instrument manufacturers and music students.
6000 Members

19260 **American Guild of Musical Artists**
1430 Broadway
14th Floor
New York, NY 10018-3308

212-265-3687; Fax: 212-262-9088
agma@musicalartists.org
www.musicalartists.org
Facebook, Twitter

Leonard Egert, National Executive Director
Gerry Angel, Director of Operations
Deborah Allton-Maher, Associate Executive Director

AGMA is a labor union. It negotiates collective bargaining agreements for its members that provide them with these vital benefits: guaranteed salaries; rehearsal and overtime pay; regulated work hours; vacation and sick pay; access to low-cost health benefits; good-faith resolution of disputes; and protection of their legal and contractual rights.
5700 Members
Founded in 1936

19261 **American Guild of Organists**
475 Riverside Drive
Suite 1260
New York, NY 10115-0055

212-870-2310; Fax: 212-870-2163
info@agohq.org
www.agohq.org
Facebook, Twitter, LinkedIn, Google+

James Thomashower, Executive Director
Marcia Van Oyen, Director

Membership in the American Guild of Organists is primarily through local chapters, which hold regular meetings featuring performances, lectures, seminars, and discussions on a wide variety of topics. Many chapters also offer monthly newsletters, scholarship programs, musician placement services, and substitute referrals to employing institutions. Membership can also be without chapter affiliation.
20000 Members
Founded in 1896

19262 **American Harp Society**
PO Box 278
Greenfield Center, NY 12833
518-893-7495
www.harpsociety.org
Ann Yeung, President
Barbara Lepke Sims, 1st VP
Carolyn Munford, 2nd VP
Erin Wood, Secretary
Ashanti Pretlow, Executive Secretary
Promotes and fosters the appreciation of the harp as a musical instrument, to encourage the composition of music for the harp and to improve the quality of performance of harpists.
Cost: $50.00
3000 Members
Founded in 1962

19263 **American Music Therapy Association**
8455 Colesville Rd
Suite 1000
Silver Spring, MD 20910-3392
301-589-3300; Fax: 301-589-5175
info@musictherapy.org
www.musictherapy.org
Facebook, Twitter, YouTube
Andrea Farbman, Executive Director
Brian Abrams, Mid Atlantic Region President
The mission of the American Music Therapy Association is to advance public awareness of the benefits of music therapy and increase access to quality music therapy services in a rapidly changing world.
3800 Members
Founded in 1998

19264 **American Musical Instrument Society**
1106 Garden Street
Hoboken, NJ 07030
201-656-0107
amis@guildassoc.com
www.amis.org
Facebook
Albert R Rice, President
Carolyn Bryant, Vice-President
Deborah Check Reeves, Secretary
Joanne Kopp, Treasurer
Promotes better understanding of all aspects of history, design, construction, restoration, and usage of musical instruments in all cultures and from all periods. The membership of AMIS includes collectors, historians, curators, performers, instrument makers, restorers, dealers, conservators, teachers, students, and many institutional members.
Founded in 1971

19265 **American Musicological Society**
194 Mercer St. Room 404
New York, NY 10012-1502
212-992-6340
877-679-7648; Fax: 212-885-4022
ams@ams-net.org
www.ams-net.org
Facebook, Twitter, YouTube
Robert Judd, Executive Director
Al Hipkins, Office Manger
Melissa Kapocius, Secretary
A spcoety of professional musicologist and university educators. The annual meetings are held in the fall each year; 1007-Quebec; 2008-Nashville; 2009-Philedelphia.
3600 Members
Founded in 1934

19266 **American Orff-Schulwerk Association**
PO Box 391089
Cleveland, OH 44139-8089
440-543-5366; Fax: 440-600-7332
info@aosa.org
www.aosa2.org
Katharine P. Johnson, Executive Director
Jo Ella Hug, President
Julie Scott, VP
Jennifer Hartman, Treasurer
Professional organization of music and movement educators dedicated to the creative teaching approach developed by Carl Orff and Gunild Keetman.
Cost: $70.00

19267 **American School Band Directors Association**
227 N 1st Street
PO Box 696
Guttenberg, IA 52052-0696
563-252-2500; Fax: 563-252-2500
asbda@alpinecom.net
www.asbda.com
Facebook
Blair Callaway, President
Susan Barrett, Secretary
Blair Callaway, Treasurer
Dennis Hanna, Manager
Russ Hilton, Treasurer
Nationwide organization dedicated to the support of professional and college band conductors. Membership by invitation only.
1200 Members
Founded in 1953

19268 **American Society of Composers, Authors and Publishers (ASCAP)**
1 Lincoln Plaza
New York, NY 10023-7097
212-621-6000; Fax: 212-621-8453
info@ascap.com
www.ascap.com
Facebook, Twitter, LinkedIn, YouTube
Paul Williams, President/Chairman
James M Kendrick, Treasurer
Caroline Bienstock, Secretary
John Lofrumento, CEO
Performing rights organization created and controlled by composers, songwriters and music publishers. Protects the rights of its members by licensing and distributing royalties for the non-dramatic public performances of their copyrighted works. An online newsletter is also available filled with the most up-to-date information about professional opportunities, legislative issues, member benefits and more.
26000 Members
Founded in 1914

19269 **American Society of Music Arrangers and Composers**
5903 Noble Ave
Van Nuys, CA 91411-3026
818-994-4661; Fax: 818-994-6181
asmac@theproperimageevents.com
www.asmac.org
Facebook, Twitter, LinkedIn, Youtube
Scherr Lillico, Executive Director
Duane L Tatro, Vice President
Ray Charles, Vice President
Professional society for arrangers, composers, orchestrators, and musicians. Monthly meetings with great speakers from the music industry.
500 Members
Founded in 1938

19270 **American Song Writers Association**
205-815-8180
www.americansongwritersassociation.com
Facebook, Twitter, Pinterest

19271 **American String Teachers Association**
4155 Chain Bridge Rd
Fairfax, VA 22030-4102
703-279-2113; Fax: 703-279-2114
asta@astaweb.com
www.astaweb.com
Donna Hale, Executive Director
Beth Danner-Knight, Deputy Director
Mary Jane Dye, Deputy Director
A membership organization for string and orchestra teachers and players, helping them to develop and refine their careers. Members range from budding student teachers to artist-status performers, businesses who supply goods and services to the string and orchestra world plus colleges, universities, music programs and conservatories.
11300 Members
Founded in 1946

19272 **American Union of Swedish Singers**
president@auss.org
www.auss.org
500+ Members

19273 **American Viola Society**
14070 Proton Rd
Suite 100
Dallas, TX 75244-3601
972-233-9107; Fax: 972-490-4219
info@avsnationaloffice.org
www.americanviolasociety.org
Facebook, Twitter
Nokunthula Ngwenyama, President
Madeline Crouch, General Manager
Karin Brown, Secretary
Michelle Sayles, Treasurer
An association for the promotion of viola performance and research. AVS membership is accompanied by two print issues of the Journal of the American Viola Society (JAVS) each year.
1000 Members

19274 **Americana Music Association**
The Factory at Franklin
PO Box 628
Franklin, TN 37065
615-386-6936; Fax: 615-386-6937
press@americanamusic.org
www.americanamusic.org
Facebook, Twitter, Pinterest, YouTube
Jed Hilly, Executive Director
Danna Strong, Director
Michelle Aquilato, Director of Marketing
Sarah Comardelle, Manager of Marketingÿ
Whitney Holmes, Manager of Member Relations

19275 **Association for Electronic Music**
membership@afemorg.net
www.associationforelectronicmusic.orgÿ
Facebook, Twitter
Greg Marshall, General Manager
Melissa Sutton, Events & Communications Manager
Mark Lawrence, Advisor
The AFEM is a non-profit trade association working for the benefit of companies and individuals involved in Electronic Music as a business.
195+ Members

19276 Association of Concert Bands
6613 Cheryl Ann Drive
Independence, OH 44131-3718
800-726-8720; Fax: 216-524-1897
www.acbands.org
Facebook
Allen Beck, President
Nada Vencl, Secretary
Mike Montgomery, CIO
Howard Habenicht, Treasurer
The purpose of ACB is to encourage and foster adult concert community, municipal, and civic bands and to promote the performance of the highest quality traditional and contemporary literature for band.
750 Members
Founded in 1977

19277 Blues Foundation
421 S.Main St
Memphis, TN 38103-4464
901-527-2583; Fax: 901-529-4030
jay@blues.org
www.blues.org
Facebook, Twitter, LinkedIn, YouTube, RSS
Jay Sieleman, President
Joey Whitmer, DeputuDirector
Cindy James, Membership
Chadd Webb, Treasurer
A nonprofit corporation which serves as the hub for the worldwide passion for Blues Music.
Founded in 1980

19278 Carnatic Music Association of North America
P O Box 234
Fords, NJ 8863
908-521-0500
800-362-6137
webmaster@cmana.org
www.cmana.org
Aravind Narasimhan, President
Chithra Krishnan, Vice President
Rajesh Nathan, Secretary
Rhama Narayanan, Treasurer

19279 Chamber Music America
99 Madison Avenue
5th Floor
New York, NY 10016
212-242-2022; Fax: 646-430-5667
www.chamber-music.org
Susan Dadian, Program Director
Margaret M Lioi, CEO
Louise Smith, Chair
Promotes artistic excellence and economic stability within the profession and to ensure that chamber music is a vital part of American life. Their vision is that chamber music serves as a model of cooperation and collaboration, that audiences become more committed to supporting chamber music and the professionals who devote their lives to this art form, and that opportunities for the performance of chamber music increase in traditional concert venues and beyond.
Founded in 1977

19280 Chinese Arts and Music Association
P.O. Box 50531
Seattle, WA 98015-0531
206-817-6888
chinamusic@comcast.net
www.uschinamusic.org
Warren Chang, President
Angel Yan, Board Member
Janelle Yeung, Board Member
Minghwa Chiem, Board Member
Buyun Zhao, Director
Dedicated to promoting Chinese classical music in the United States.

19281 Chorus America
1156 15th St NW
Suite 310
Washington, DC 20005-1747
202-331-7577; Fax: 202-331-7599
service@chorusamerica.org
www.chorusamerica.org
Facebook, Twitter, Youtube
Ann Meier Baker, President & Chief Executive Officer
Rollo Dilworth, Chairman
David C. Howse, Treasurer
Mary Lou Lyons, Secretary
Gayle M. Ober, Immediate Past Chair
Chorus America's mission is to build a dynamic and inclusive choral community so that more people are enriched by the beauty and power of choral singing.
2100 Members
Founded in 1977

19282 Church Music Association of America
P.O. Box 4344
Roswell, NM 88202-4344
505-263-6298
contact@musicasacra.com
www.musicasacra.comÿ
Facebook, Twitter, Google+
Founded in 1964

19283 College Music Society
312 E Pine St
Missoula, MT 59802-4624
406-721-9616; Fax: 406-721-9419
cms@music.org
www.music.org
Facebook, Twitter, LinkedIn, YouTube, Google+
Robby D Gunstream, Executive Director
David B. Williams, President
A consortium of college, conservatory, university and independent musicians and scholars interested in all disciplines of music. Its mission is to promote music teaching and learning, musical creativity and expression, research and dialogue, and diversity and interdisciplinary interaction.
9500 Attendees
Founded in 1958

19284 Conductors Guild
719 Twinridge Ln
Richmond, VA 23235
804-553-1378; Fax: 804-553-1876
guild@conductorsguild.org
www.conductorsguild.org
Facebook, Twitter, LinkedIn
Amanda Burton Winger, Executive Director
Scott Winger, Assistant Director
David Leibowitz, Editor
Rufus Jones Jr, Editor
The Conductors Guild is the only music service organization devoted exclusively to the advancement of the art of conducting and to serving the artistic and professional needs of conductors.
1850+ Members
Founded in 1975

19285 Contemporary Record Society
724 Winchester Road
Broomall, PA 19008
610-205-9897; Fax: 707-549-5920
crsnews@verizon.net
www.crsnews.org
Caroline Hunt, Contact
John Russo, Artistic Director
Promotes both a fellowship in the musical arts between artists, composers and presenters and commercial recordingsa of participants in this endeavor. The intent of the Society is to advance the cause of music in the United States and throughout the world, promoting an association among its constituents. The scope of the Society's repertoire includes the musical masterworks of both well-known and relatively unknown composers of all periods.
Cost: $45.00
20000 Members
Founded in 1981

19286 Country Music Association
One Music Circle S
Nashville, TN 37203
615-244-2840; Fax: 615-242-4783
www.cmaworld.com
Facebook, Twitter, YouTube, Instagram
Gary Overton, Chairman
Troy Tomlison, President
Jessie Schmidt, Secretary/Treasurer
Steve Moore, CEO
CMA is dedicated to bringing the poetry and emotion of Country Music to the World. They will continue a tradition of leadership and professionalism, promotoing the music and recognizing excellence in all its forms. They foster a spirit of community and sharing, and respect and encourage creativity and the unique contributions of everyone. It is a place to have fun and celebrate success.
5000+ Members
Founded in 1958

19287 Country Radio Broadcasters
1009 16th Avenue South
Nashville, TN 37212
615-327-4487; Fax: 615-329-4492
news@crb.org
www.countryradioseminar.com/
Facebook, Twitter
RJ Curtis, Executive Director
Chasity Crouch, Business Manager
Heather Martin, Director, Logistics & Events
Darcie Van Etten, Director, Marketing
Ashley Bourque, Project Manager
A nonprofit eductional organization. It is the principal entity that brings Country radio together with the Country music industry for learning opportunities that promote growth.
Founded in 1969

19288 Creative Musicians Coalition
PO Box 6205
Peoria, IL 61601-6205
309-685-4843
800-882-4262; Fax: 309-685-4879
aimcmc@aol.com
www.creativemusicianscoalition.com
Ronald Wallace, Founder/President
An international organization dedicated to the advancement of new music and the success of independent musicians.
1000 Members
Founded in 1984

19289 East-2-West Marketing & Promotion
559 Wanamaker Road
Jenkintown, PA 19046-2219
215-884-3308; Fax: 215-884-1083
www.musiciansnetwork.com
Jackie Paul, President/CEO
Marketing and promotion.
Mailing list available for rent

19290 Folk Alliance International
509 Delaware
#101
Kansas City, MO 64105
901-522-1170; Fax: 816-221-3658
fa@folk.org
www.folk.org/
Facebook, Twitter, YouTube, Instagram
Lewis Meyers, Executive Director
Mary Sue Twohy, VP
Alan Korolenko, Secretary
Donald Davidoff, Treasurer
Lisa Schwartz, Secretary
The service association for the field, working on behalf of the folk music and dance industry year round. They offer a business directory of contacts for members, and a non-profit group exemption program for US-based organizations.
Cost: $70.00
Founded in 1989

19291 Folklife Center Of International House
3701 Chestnut Street
Philadelphia, PA 19104
215-387-5125; Fax: 215-895-6550
Osagie Imasogie, President
Tanya Steinberg, Executive Director
William Parker, Director Of Communications Events
To present the highest caliber of traditional arts.

19292 Freelance Musicians' Association
info@freelancemusicians.org
www.freelancemusicians.org

19293 Gospel Music Association
741 cool Springs Blvd.
Franklin, TN 37067
615-242-0303; Fax: 615-254-9755
service@gospelmusic.org
www.gospelmusic.org
Facebook, Twitter, LinkedIn, Youtube
John Styll, President
Scott Brickell, Director
Charles Dorris, Founder/Chairman
Ed Harper, Director
Ed Leonard, Director
Our mission is to expose, promote and celebrate the gospel through music. GMA serves as a voice for the Christian music community. It provides an atmosphere in which artists, industry leaders, retail stores, radio stations, concert promoters and local churches can coordinate their efforts for the purpose of benefitting the industry as a whole, while remaining true to the purpose of communicating the gospel message.
Cost: $85.00
5000 Members
Founded in 1964

19294 Guitar Accessory and Marketing Association (GAMA)
Po Box 757
New York, NY 10033
212-795-3630; Fax: 212-795-3630
www.discoverguitar.com
Membership is comprised of guitar and guitar accessory manufacturers and various consumer magazines.
Founded in 1933

19295 Guitar Foundation of America
PO Box 2900
Palos Verdes Peninsula, CA 78717
877-570-1651; Fax: 877-570-3409
info@guitarfoundation.org
www.guitarfoundation.org
Facebook, Twitter
Dr. Martha Masters, President
Jill Winchell, Operations Manager
Martha Masters, Executive VP
Jeff Cogan, VP
Robert Lane, Vice President/Secretary
Provides its members the combined advantages of a guitar society, a library, a publisher, a continuing education resource, and an artis council. The GFA is a non-profit educational and literacy organization devoted to furthering the knowledge of and interest in the guitar and its music.
Cost: $40.00
Founded in 1973

19296 International Association for the Study of Popular Music
Home Page: www.iaspm.net
Founded in 1981

19297 International Association of Electronic Keyboard Manufacturers
305 Maple Avenue
Wyncote, PA 19095-3228
617-747-2816
www.iaekm.org
An association that comprises the global manufacturers of electronic keyboards and affiliated software and publications.

19298 International Association of Jazz Education
PO Box 724
Manhattan, KS 66505
785-776-8744; Fax: 785-776-6190
www.iaje.org
Bill McFarlin, Executive Director
Chuck Owen, President
Ronald Carter, VP
Laura Johnson, Treasurer
Brian Coyle, Secretary
To ensure the continued development and growth of jazz through education and outreach.
Cost: $70.00
8000 Members
Founded in 1989

19299 International Bluegrass Music Association
608 West, Irish Drive
Nashville, TN 37204
615-256-3222
888-438-4262; Fax: 615-256-0450
info@ibma.org
www.ibma.org
Facebook, Twitter, LinkedIn, Youtube
Dan Hayes, Executive Director
Stan Zdonik, Vice Chair/Associations
Peter D'Addario, Treasurer
Lee Michael Demsey, Secretary
IBMA works together for high standards of professionalism, a greater appreciation for our music, and the success of the worldwide bluegrass community.

19300 International Clarinet Association
14070 Proton Rd
Suite 100 LB9
Dallas, TX 75244
972-233-9107; Fax: 972-490-4219
www.clarinet.org
Twitter
John Cipolla, President
Tod Kerstetter, Treasurer
Caroline Hartig, Secretary
So Rhee, Executive Director
A community of clarinetists and clarinet enthusiasts that supports projects that will benefit clarinet performance; provides opportunities for the exchange of ideas, materials and information among its members; fosters the composition, publication, recording, and distribution of music for the clarinet; encourages the research and manufacture of a more definitive clarinet; and encourages and promotes the perfomance and teaching of a wide variety of repertoire for the clarinet.
4000 Members
Founded in 1990

19301 International Computer Music Association
1819 Polk St.
Suite 330
San Francisco, CA 94109
FAX 734-878-3031
icma@umich.edu
www.computermusic.org
Tom Erbe, President
Michael Gurevitchÿ, VP, Membership
Margaret Schedel, VP, Conferences
Chryssie Nanou, Treasurer, Secretary
Christopher Haworth, Array Editor
Founded in 1974

19302 International Horn Society
exec-secretary@hornsociety.org
www.hornsociety.org
Jeffrey L. Snedeker, President
Kristina Mascher-Turner, Vice President
Annie Bosler, Secretary/Treasurer
Heidi Vogel, Executive Director
Cost: $35.00
3500+ Members
Founded in 1970

19303 International Piano Guild
PO Box 1807
Austin, TX 78767
512-478-5775
ngpt@pianoguild.com
www.pianoguild.com
Richard Allison, President
A division of the American College of Musicians Professional society of piano teachers and music faculty members. Its primary function is to establish definite goals and awards for students of all levels, from the earliest beginner to the gifted prodigy. Its purpose is to encourage growth and enjoyment through the study of piano.
118m Members
Founded in 1929

19304 International Polka Association
4608 S Archer Ave
Chicago, IL 60632-2932
773-254-7771
800-867-6552
ipa@internationalpolka.com
www.internationalpolka.com
Facebook, YouTube
Dave Ulczycki, President
Rick Rzeszutko, First VP
Fred Kenzierski, Second VP
Marlene Gill, Secretary
Linda Niewierowski, Treasurer
An educational and charitable organization for the preservation, promulgation and advancement of polka music and to promote, maintain and advance public interest in polka entertainment; to advance mutual interests and encourage greater cooperation among its members who are engaged in polka entertainment; and to encourage and pursue the study of polka music, dancing and traditional folklore. Responsible for the continued operation and growth of the Polka Music Hall of

Fame and Museum.
Cost: $15.00
8M Members
Founded in 1968

19305 International Society of Folk Harpers and Craftsmen
1614 Pittman Drive
Missoula, Mt 59803
406-542-1976
harps@thorharp.com
www.folkharpsociety.org

Dave Kolacny, President
Timothy Habinski, First VP
Verlene Schermer, Second VP
Alice Williams, Secretary
Barbra Bailey Bradley, Treasurer

The mission of the ISFHC is: to promote the playing and enjoyment of the folk harp by all; to promote education, creation and development in the building of the folk harp; to increase awareness of professional folk harpers; and to increase public awareness of the music and joys of the folk harp.
Cost: $30.00
Founded in 1985

19306 Keyboard Teachers Association International
361 Pin Oak Lane
Westbury, NY 11590-1941
516-333-3236; Fax: 516-997-9531
www.musiciansnetwork.com

Dr. Albert DeVito, President

19307 League of American Ochestras
33 W 60th Street
New York, NY 10023-7905
212-262-5161; Fax: 212-262-5198
www.americanorchestras.org

Henry Fogel, CEO
Jesse Rosen, President/CEO
Aja Stephens, Assistant to President
Steven C. Parrish, Vice Chair
Heather Noonan, Vice Chair

Provides leadership and service to American orchestras while communicating to the public the value and importance of orchestras and the music they perform. The League links a national network of thousands of musicians, conductors, managers, board members, volunteers, staff members and business partners, providing a wealth of services, information, and educational opportunities to its members.
1200 Members
Founded in 1942
Mailing list available for rent

19308 Metropolitan Opera Guild
70 Lincoln Center Plz
New York, NY 10023-6593
212-769-7000; Fax: 212-769-7007
info@metguild.org
www.metoperafamily.org/guild/
Facebook, Twitter, LinkedIn, YouTube, Instagram

David Dik, Manager

Seeks to encourage the appreciation of opera and to support the Metorpolitan Opera. The guild provides programs and services in many areas designed to further these goals. Publishes monthly magazine and organizes special events throughout the year to raise funds.
100M Members
Founded in 1935

19309 Midland Center For The Arts Midland Music And Concert Series
1801 W. St Andrews Road
Midland, MI 48640
989-631-8250; Fax: 989-631-7890
www.mcfta.org
Facebook, Twitter, LinkedIn, Youtube

Michael Tiknis, President
James Hohmeyer, Artistic Director
Robb Wouose, Managing Director
Mark Bachman, Director
David Blakemore, Director

encourage concert audiences; Providing students with opportunities to experience professional performances.

19310 Music Business Association
1 Eves Drive
Suite 138
Marlton, NJ 8053
856-596-2221; Fax: 856-596-7299
www.musicbiz.org
Facebook, Twitter, RSS

Fred Beteille, Chairman
Steve Harkins, Vice Chairman
John Trickett, Treasurer
Ryan Redington, Secretary
James Donio, President

Membership organization promoting music commerce.

19311 Music Critics Association of North America
722 Dulaney Valley Rd.
#259
Baltimore, MD 21204
410-435-3881
info@mcana.org
www.mcana.org

Barbara Jepson, President
John Fleming, Vice President
James Bash, Treasurer
Roy C. Dicks, Secretary
Robert Leininger, Managing Director

An association for the promotion of high standards in classical music criticism.

19312 Music Library Association
1600 Aspen Commons
Suite 100
Middleton, WI 53562
608-836-5825; Fax: 608-831-8200
mla@areditions.com
www.musiclibraryassoc.org
Facebook, Twitter

Michael Colby, President
Pamela Bristah, Secretary
Paul Cary, Admin Officer
Linda W.Blair, Admin Officer

Provides a forum for issues surrounding music, music in libraries, and music librarianship.
Cost: $90.00
Founded in 1931

19313 Music Performance Fund
1501 Broadway
Suite 600
New York, NY 10036
212-391-3950; Fax: 212-221-2604
sramos@musicpf.org
www.musicpf.org
Facebook

Den Beck, Trustee
Al Elvin, Director of Finance
Linda Williamson, Manager

A nonprofit public service organization headquartered in New York City. MPF is the world's largest sponsor of live, admission-free musical programs.
Founded in 1948

19314 Music Performance Trust Funds
1501 Broadway
Suite 600
New York, NY 10036
212-391-3950; Fax: 212-221-2604
sramos@musicpf.org
www.musicpf.org
Facebook

Dan Beck, Trustee
Vidrey Blackburn, Grant Review Process
Al Elvin, Director of Finance
Samantha Ramos, Team Member
Founded in 1948

19315 Music Publishers Association
243 5th Ave
Suite 236
New York, NY 10016-8728
212-675-7354; Fax: 212-675-7381
www.mpa.org

Kathleen Marsh, President
Bryndon Bay, Treasurer
Todd Vunderink, Secretary
Lauren Keiser, Second VP
75 Members
Founded in 1895

19316 Music Publishers Association of the United States
243 5th Ave.
Suite 236
New York, NY 10016
212-675-7354; Fax: 212-675-7381
admin@mpa.org
www.mpa.org

Kathleen Marsh, President
Sean Patrick Flahaven, Vice President
Lauren Keiser, Second Vice President
Sonya Kim, Secretary
Erin Rogers, Treasurer

The MPA fosters communication among publishers, dealers, music educators, and all ultimate users of music. It is a nonprofit association which addresses itself to issues pertaining to every area of music publishing with an emphasis on the issues relevant to the publishers of print music for concert and educational purposes.
75 Members
Founded in 1895

19317 Music Teachers National Association
1 W. 4th Street
Suite 1550
Cincinnati, OH 45202
513-421-1420
888-512-5278; Fax: 513-421-2503
mtnanet@mtna.org
www.mtna.org
Facebook, Twitter, LinkedIn, YouTube, Instagram, Pinterest

Gary L. Ingle, Executive Director & CEO
Brian Shepard, Chief Operating Officer
Scott McBride Smith, President
Madeleine Lovett, Marketing & PR

Music Teachers National Association is the preeminent source for music teacher support, where members embody like-minded values and commitment to their students, colleagues and society as a whole, while reaping the rewards of collaboration, continuity and connection throughout the lifetime of their careers. Comprised of over 20,000 members, Music Teachers National Association seeks to advance the value of music study and music making and

to support the professionalism of music teachers.
20000 Members
Founded in 1876
Mailing list available for rent: 20,000 names at $85 per M

19318 **Music Video Production Associationÿ**

infomvpa@gmail.com
www.mvpa.com

Coleen Haynes, President
Missy Galanadia, Vice President
Kim Dellara, Vice President
Grant Cihlar, Treasurer
Amanda Fox, Board of Director

19319 **Music for All Foundation**
39 W Jackson Place
Suite 150
Indianapolis, IN 46225

317-636-2263; Fax: 317-524-6200
www.musicforall.org

Eric Martin, President/CEO
Nancy H.Carlson, Executive VP/CFO
Carolyn Ealy, Education and Office Manager
Tonya Bullock, Accounting manager
Gayle W. Doster, Chairman

Committed to expanding the role of music and the arts in education, to heightening the public's appreciation of the value of music and arts education, and to creating a positive environment for the arts through societal changes.
Founded in 1975
Mailing list available for rent

19320 **Musical Box Society International**
MBSI Member Registration
PO Box 10196
Springfield, MO 65808-0196

FAX 417-886-8839
www.mbsi.org
Facebook, Twitter, Digg, Yahoo, Reddit, StumbleUp

A nonprofit organization dedicated to the enjoyment, sstudy and preservation of all automatic musical instruments. Members receive the bimonthly scholarly journal, Mechanical Music, covering educational articles, relevant events, activities, news, information, and advertisements and the biennial, Directory of Members, Museums and Dealers. Hosts annual convention.
Cost: $55.00
2.8M Members
Founded in 1949

19321 **Musicians Foundation**
875 Sixth Avenue
Suite 2303
New York, NY 10001-3507

212-239-9137; Fax: 212-239-9138
info@musiciansfoundation.org
www.musiciansfoundation.org
Facebook, Twitter

BC Vermeersch, Executive Director
Hans E Tausig, President
Joseph Hertzberg, Treasurer

Representing interests on the condition and social welfare of professional musicians and their families. Provides emergency financial assistance to meet current living, medical and allied expenses.
Founded in 1914

19322 **National Academy of Recording Arts and Sciences**
3030 Olympic Blvd.ÿ
Santa Monica, CA 90404

310-392-3777; Fax: 310-392-2188
www.grammy.org
Facebook, Twitter, YouTube, Instagram

Ryan Seacrest, Honorary Chair
Tim Bucher, Chair
Geoff Cottrillÿ, Vice Chair
Rachna Bhasin, Secretary/Treasurer
Rusty Rueff, Chair Emeritus
Founded in 1988

19323 **National Association for Music Education MENC**
1806 Robert Fulton Drive
Reston, VA 20191

703-860-4000
800-336-3768; Fax: 703-860-1531
Facebook, Twitter, LinkedIn, Google+, Pinterest

John J Mahlmann, Executive Director
Lynn Brinckmeyer, President

Mission is to advance music education by encouraging the study and making of music by all.
Founded in 1907

19324 **National Association of Band Instrument Manufacturers**
2026 Eagle Road
PO Box 51
Normal, IL 61761

309-452-4257; Fax: 309-452-4825
napbirt@napbirt.org
www.napbirt.org
Facebook

Jerome Hershman, Contact
Bill Mathwes, Executive Director
Ross, Watkins

A trade association of band instrument manufacturers, importers and distributors including accessories selling to the trade only.
34 Members
Founded in 1976

19325 **National Association of College Wind and Percussion Instructor**
Division of Fine Arts
Truman State University
Kirksville, MO 63501

660-785-4442; Fax: 660-785-7463
cmoore@fsu.edu
www.nacwpi.org
Facebook

Chris Moore, President
Michael Dean, VP
Richard K Weerts, Executive Secretary/Treasurer

A forum for communication within the profession of applied music on the college campus. The Association is composed of university, college, and conservatory teachers.
Cost: $35.00
600 Members
Founded in 1951

19326 **National Association of Composers**
P.O. Box 49256
Barrington Station
Los Angeles, CA 90049

Home Page: www.music-usa.org/nacusa

Greg A. Steinke, Ph.D., President/ Chair
Wieslaw V Rentowski ÿ, Vice President
Sylvia ÿ Constantinidis, M.M., Secretary
Joe L. Alexander, Treasurer
Daniel Kessner, Past President
Founded in 1933

19327 **National Association of Music Merchants**
5790 Armada Dr.
Carlsbad, CA 92008

760-438-8001
800-767-6266; Fax: 760-438-7327
info@namm.org
www.namm.org
Facebook, Twitter, YouTube, Instagram

Joe Lamond, President & CEO

Association of music products industry professionals.
3.6M Members
Founded in 1901

19328 **National Association of Negro Musicians Inc**
931 Monroe Drive NE
Suite A102-159
Atlanta, GA 30308

404-647-7217; Fax: 404-745-0128
www.nanm.org
Facebook, Twitter

Byron J. Smith, President
Geraldine Boone, First VP
Sylvia Turner Hollified, Second VP
Marydith Lawson, Executive Secretary
Daniel.J Long, Treasurer

Dedicated to the preservation, encouragement and advocacy of all genres of the music of African Americans. Holds a national convention in a different city eac year, offering a chance to participate in workshops, seminars, lectures and performances. NANM invites the professional artists, the educator, the student, the amateur, the lover of music to become a part of this organization's 'Pride in a Cultural Heritage.'
2.5M Members
Founded in 1919

19329 **National Association of Pastoral Musicians**
962 Wayne Ave
Suite 210
Silver Spring, MD 20910-4461

240-247-3000
855-207-0293; Fax: 240-247-3001
npmsing@npm.org
www.npm.org

Richard B. Hilgartner, President
Kathleen Haley, Director Membership Services
Peter S. Maher, Chief Operating Officer
Paul Lagoy, Secretary & Mil Clerk

Fosters the art of musical liturgy. The members of NPM serve the Catholic Church in the United States as musicians, clergy, liturgists, and other leaders of prayer.
5000 Members
Founded in 1976

19330 **National Association of Professional Band Instrument Repair Technicians**
2026 Eagle Road
PO Box 51
Normal, IL 61761

309-452-4257; Fax: 309-452-4825
napbirt@napbirt.org
www.napbirt.org
Facebook

Bill Mathews, Executive Director
Ross Watkins, Admin. Manager

A nonprofit international educational association dedicated to the advancement of the craft of band instrument repair. Their mission is to promote the highest possible standards of band instrument repair, restoration and maintenance by providing members with multi-level professional development by offering technical training, continuing education and the publication of their

bi-monthky trade journal.
Cost: $95.00
1300 Members
Founded in 1976

19331 **National Association of Recording Merchandisers**
1 Eves Drive
Suite 138
Marlton, NJ 08053-3130

856-596-2221; Fax: 856-596-7299
donio@narm.com
www.musicbiz.org/
Facebook, Twitter, RSS

Fred Beteille, Chair
Steve Harkins, Vice Chairman
John Trickett, Treasurer
Ryan Redington, Secretary
Jim Donio, President

A not-for-profit trade association that serves the music retailing community in the areas of networking, advocacy, information, education and promotion. Membership includes music and other entertainment retailers, wholesalers, distributorsm record labels, multimedia suppliers, and suppliers of related products and services, as well as individual professionals and educators in the music business field.
Founded in 1958

19332 **National Association of Schools of Music**
11250 Roger Bacon Drive
Suite 21
Reston, VA 20190-5248

703-437-0700; Fax: 703-437-6312
info@arts-accredit.org
www.arts-accredit.org

Don Gibson, President
Mark Wait, VP
Mellasenah Y Morris, Treasurer

An organization of schools, conservatories, colleges and universities. NASM provides information to potential students and parents, consultations, stastistical information, professional development and policy analysis. It is the national accrediting agency for music and music-related disciplines.
635 Members
Founded in 1924

19333 **National Association of Teachers of Singing**
9957 Moorings Drive
Suite 401
Jacksonville, FL 32257-2416

904-992-9101; Fax: 904-262-2587
info@nats.org
www.nats.org
Facebook, Twitter, LinkedIn, YouTube, Pintrest, Flickr

Allen Henderson, Executive Director
Deborah Guess, Director of Operations
Amandia Camahan, Membership Services Coordinator
Bob Bryan, Director, Development
Beth Buchanan, Manager, Marketing & Communications

To encourage the highest standards of the vocal art and of ethical principles in the teaching of singing; and to promote vocal education and research at all levels, both for the enrichment of the general public and for the professional advancement of the talented.
7000 Members
Founded in 1944

19334 **National Ballroom and Entertainment Association**
PO Box 274
Decorah, IA 52101-7600

563-382-3871
www.nbea.com
Facebook

Larry Bowers, President
Pat Brannon, Vice President
John Matter, Executive Director
Ken Paulsen, Treasurer

National nonprofit association which advocates that social dancing is a life-long activity that contributes to the physical, mantal, and social well-being of an individual. They believe that social dancing should be preserved for current and future generations and introduced to today's youth as an alternate form of social interaction.
450 Members
Founded in 1947

19335 **National Band Association**
Membership Office
745 Chastain Road-Ste 1140
PO Box 102
Kennesaw, GA 30144

601-297-8168; Fax: 601-266-6185
info@nationalbandassociation.org
www.nationalbandassociation.org
Facebook, Twitter, RSS

Richard Good, President
Scott Casagrande, First VP
Scott Tobias, Second VP
Linda Moorehouse, Secretary/Treasurer
David Gregory, Advisor to the President

The purpose of the NBA to promote the musical and educational significance of bands and is dedicated to the attainment of a high level of excellence for bands and band music. It is open to anyone and everyone interested in bands, regardless of the length if his/her experience, type of position held, or the specific area at which he/she works. The membership roster includes men and women from every facet of the band world.
3M Members
Founded in 1960

19336 **National Endowment for the Arts**
400 7th Street, SW
Washington, DC 20506-0001

202-682-5400
webmgr@arts.gov
www.arts.gov

Jane Chu, Chairman
Laura Callanan, Senior Deputy Chairman
Beth Bienvenu, Accessibility Director
Wendy Clark, Director of Museums
Ayanna N. Hudson, Arts Education Director

Independent federal agency that works with state arts agencies, local leaders, philanthropists and other federal agencies to give Americans opportunities to participate in the arts.

19337 **National Federation of Music Clubs**
1646 W Smith Valley Rd
Greenwood, IN 46142-1550

317-882-4003; Fax: 317-882-4019
info@nfmc-music.org
www.nfmc-music.org
Facebook, Twitter, LinkedIn, Youtube

Carolyn Nelson, President
Michael Edwards, First VP
Kay Hawthorne, Secretary
Barbara Hildebrand, Treasurer
Jennifer Keller, Administrative Manager

NFMC provides opportunities for musical study, performance and appreciation to more than 200,000 senior, student and junior members in 6,500 music-related clubs and organizations nationwide. Members are professional and amateur musicians, vocalists, composers, dancers, performing artists, arts and music educators, music students, generous music patrons and benefactors, and music lovers of all ages.
170M Members
Founded in 1898

19338 **National Music Council of the United States**
425 Park Street
Montclair, NJ 07043ÿ

973-655-7974
sandersd@mail.montclair.edu
www.musiccouncil.org

Michael Butera, President
Carolyn Nelson, First Vice President
Paul Williams, Second Vice President
Del R. Bryant, Third VP
Linda Lorence, Treasurer
Founded in 1940

19339 **National Opera Association**
PO Box 60869
Canyon, TX 79016-0869

806-651-2857; Fax: 806-651-2958
www.noa.org
Facebook

David Holley, President
Ruth Dobson, Vice President for Conventions
Paul Houghtaling, Vice President for Regions
Carol Ann Modesitt, Treasurer
Robert Hansen, Executive Director

The NOA seeks to promote a greater appreciation of opera and music theatre, to enhance pedagogy and performing activities, and to increase performance opportunities by supporting projects that improve the scope and quality of opera. Members in the United States, Canada, Europe, Asia and Australia participate in a wide array of activities in support of this mission.
775 Members
Founded in 1955
Mailing list available for rent

19340 **North American Basque Organizations**

info@naBASQUE.org
www.nabasque.org

Valerie Arrechea, President
Mary Gaztambide, Vice President
Grace Mainvil, Treasurer
Marisa Espinalÿ, Secretary
Kate Camino, Administrator
Founded in 1973

19341 **Opera America**
330 7th Ave
16th Floor
New York, NY 10001-5248

212-796-8620; Fax: 212-796-8621
Info@operaamerica.org
www.operaamerica.org

Marc A Scorca, President
Frayda B. Lindemann, Chairman
Timothy O'Leary, Treasurer
James W Wright, Secretary
Rebecca Ackerman, Membership Manager

Opera America serves and strengthens the field of opera by providing a variety of informational, technical, and administrative resources to the greater opera community. Its fundamental mission is to promote opera as exciting and accessible to individuals from all walks of life.

19342 Organization of American Kodaly Educators
10801 National Blvd
Suite 405
Los Angeles, CA 90064

310-441-3555; Fax: 310-441-3577
info@oake.org
www.oake.org
Facebook, Twitter, Google+

Joan Dahlin, Manager
Kevin Pearson, VP
Mary Neeley Stevens, Secretary
Kathy Hickey, Treasurer
Gary Shields, Administrative Director

The purpose of this organization is to promote Zoltan Kodaly's concept of Music for Everyone, through the improvment of music education in schools.
Founded in 1973

19343 Pedal Steel Guitar Association
PO Box 20248
Floral Park, NY 11002-0248

516-616-9214; Fax: 516-616-9214
bobpsga@optonline.net
www.psga.org

Kelly Foster Griffin, President
Jane Smith, VP
Kathy Hickey, Treasurer
David Gadberry, Secretary
Doug Mack, Newsletter Editor

A nonprofit organization whose primary purpose is to share information on playing the steel guitar and in particular the pedal steel guitar. Publishes the Pedal Steel Newsletter ten times per year
1540 Members
Founded in 1973

19344 Percussive Arts Society
110 W Washington Street
Suite A
Indianapolis, IN 46204

317-974-4488; Fax: 317-974-4499
percarts@pas.org
www.pas.org
Facebook, Twitter, Instagram

Julie Hill, President
Georgr Barrett, VP
Dr. Chris Hanning, Secretary
Michael Balter, Treasurer
Jeffery Hartsough, Executive Director

A music service organization promoting percussion education, research, performance and appreciation throughout the world. Offers two print publications, the Percussive Arts Society International Headquarters/Museum and the annual Percussive Arts Society International Convention.
Cost: $85.00
7000 Members
Founded in 1961

19345 Piano Technicians Guild
4444 Forest Ave
Kansas City, KS 66106

913-432-9975; Fax: 913-432-9986
ptg@ptg.org
www.ptg.org
Facebook, Twitter, YouTube

Barbara Cassaday, Executive Director
Phil Bondi, RPT, President
Paul Brown, RPT, VP
Paul Adams, RPT, Secretary-Treasurer

A nonprofit organization serving piano tuners, technicians, and craftsmen throughout the world, organized to promote the highest possible service and technical standards among piano tuners and technicians.
4100 Members
Founded in 1957

19346 Positive Music Association
Home Page:
www.positivemusicassociation.comÿ

Sambodhiÿ Prem, Composer/ Guitarist
400 Members
Founded in 2003

19347 Production Music Association
9220 Sunset Blvd.
Suite 220
Los Angeles, CA 90069

Home Page: www.pmamusic.com
Facebook, Twitter, YouTube
Randy Thornton, Chairman
Adam Taylor, Vice Chairman
Ivy Tombak, Treasurer
Ron Mendelsohn, Secretary
Joel Goodman, Board Member
Founded in 1997

19348 Recording Industry Association of America
1025 F ST N.W.
10th Floor
Washington, DC 20004

202-775-0101
www.riaa.com

Mitch Glazier, Sr. Executive Vice President
Steven M. Marks, Chief, Digital Business

19349 Retail Print Music Dealers Association
2650 Midway Rd
Suite 230
Carrolton, TX 75006

972-818-1333; Fax: 214-483-7004
cwilbur@penders.com
www.printmusic.org

Madeleine Crouch, Owner
Myrna Sislen, VP/Secretary
Christie Smith, VP/Treasurer

A professional trade organization founded to address the special needs and interests of the print music industry. RPMDA provides a common meeting ground for the congenial interchange of ideas among print music dealers; promotes ethical standards and policies in dealing with music publishers; promotes better dealer/publisher relations; serves the public and encourages music education; provides association-sponsored activities and publications that help its members prepare for future trends.
275 Members
Founded in 1976

19350 Rhythm and Blues Foundation
P.O.Box 22438
Philadelphia, PA 19101

215-985-4822; Fax: 215-985-1195
www.rhythm-n-blues.org

Patricia Wilson Aden, Executive Director
Jim Fifield, Vice Chairman
Jeff Harleston, Treasurer
Kenneth Gamble, Secretary

Nonprofit service organization dedicated to the historical and cultural preservation of Rhythm and Blues music. The Foundation provides financial support, medical assistance and educational outreach through various grants and programs to support R&B amd Motown artists of the 40s, 50s, 60s and 70s.
Founded in 1988

19351 Society of Professional Audio Recording Services
9 Music Square S
Suite 222
Nashville, TN 37203

800-771-7727; Fax: 214-722-1422
spars@spars.com
www.spars.com
Facebook, Twitter, YouTube

Avatar Studios, President
Eric W Johnson, Secretary
Jessica Dally, Treasurer
Sherri Tantleff, Director

SPARS is dedicated to excellence through innovation, education and communication.
200 Members
Founded in 1979
Mailing list available for rent

19352 Songwriters Guild of America, Inc.
210 Jamestown Park Road
Suite 100
Brentwood, TN 37027

615-742-9945
800-524-6742; Fax: 615-630-7501
corporate@songwritersguild.com
www.songwritersguild.com
Facebook, Twitter, LinkedIn, RSS

Joe Whitt, Manager

An educational and legislative advocacy organization to protect and defend the rights of songwriters.
4000 Members
Founded in 1931

19353 Sweet Adelines International
9110 S. Toledo
Tulsa, OK 74147-0168

918-622-1444
800-992-7464; Fax: 918-665-0894
admin@sweetadelineintl.org
www.sweetadelineintl.org
Facebook, Twitter, YouTube, Pinterest

Donna Kerley, Dicector Finance/Administration
Kelly Kirchoff, Director Communications
Jane Hanson, Marketing/Membership Coordinator
Kelly Bailey, Chief Executive Officer
Tammy Talbot, Chief Operating Officer

A worldwide organization of women singers committed to advancing the musical art form of barbershop harmony through education and performances. Their motto is to 'Harmonize the World.'
27000 Members
Founded in 1945

19354 The Society for American Music
Stephen Foster Memorial
University of Pittsburgh
Pittsburgh, PA 15260

412-624-3031
sam@american-music.org
www.american-music.org
Facebook

Judy Tsouÿ, Board of Trustee/ President
Kay Norton, Board of Trustee, VP
Sabine Feisst, Treasurer
Mariana Whitmer, Executive Director
Neil Lerner, Secretary
Founded in 1975

19355 United States Germanic Music Association

mikesurrattmusic@gmail.com
www.usgma.us

19356 **World Piano Competition/AMSA**
441 Vine St
Suite 1030
Cincinnati, OH 45202-2832

513-421-5342; Fax: 513-421-2672
www.amsa-wpc.org

Gloria Ackerman, Founder, CEO
William Selnick, Treasurer
Stanley Aronoff, Event Chair
Leon Fleisher, President

Provides an continuum of services and role models to assist youth in need. Their task is to provide a venue of excitement and compassion to teach them to do their best to prepare for the enormous challenges they will face as they approach adulthood.
2.5M Members
Founded in 1956

Newsletters

19357 **American Guild Associate News Newsletter**
American Guild of Music
PO Box 599
Warren, MI 48090-4905

248-686-1975; Fax: 630-968-0197
agm@americanguild.org
www.americanguild.org

Richard Chizmadia, Editor-in-Chief

Offers information and news for professionals in the music profession.
Cost: $25.00
5000 Members
Frequency: Quarterly
Founded in 1901

19358 **American Music Center Opportunity Update**
American Music Center
322 8th Ave
Suite 1001
New York, NY 10001-6774

212-366-5263; Fax: 212-366-5265
center@amc.net
www.amc.net

Joanne Cossa, Executive Director

A listing of composition competitions, calls for scores, workshops, and other opportunities delivered every month via e-mail to members of the American Music Center.
Frequency: Monthly
Founded in 1939

19359 **American Musical Instrument Society Newsletter**
AMIS
1106 Garden Street
Hoboken, NJ 07030

201-656-0107
amis@guildassoc.com
www.amis.org

Albert R Rice, President
Carolyn Bryant, Vice-President
Deborah Check Reeves, Secretary
Joanne Kopp, Treasurer

Official notices and news of the Society's activites; short articles and communications; recent acquisition lists from member institutions; news of members; and classified ads.
Frequency: 2x/Year

19360 **American Musicological Society Inc**
20 Cooper Square
Floor 2
New York, NY 10003

212-992-6340; Fax: 877-679-7648
ams@amsmusicology.org
www.amsmusicology.org
Facebook, Twitter, YouTube

Robert Judd, Executive Director

Members of the society receive three editions annually of the Journal of the American Musicological Society and two editions of the AMS Newsletter, published semi-annually in February and August.
Frequency: Semi-Annually
Founded in 1934

19361 **American School Band Directors Association Newsletter**
American School Band Directors Association
227 N 1st Street
PO Box 696
Guttenberg, IA 52052-0696

563-252-2500; Fax: 563-252-2500
asbda@alpinecom.net
www.asbda.com

Monte Dunnum, President
Valerie Gaffney, Secretary
Blair Callaway, Treasurer

Reports and information for members of the ASBDA
Frequency: Quarterly
Founded in 1953
Printed in 2 colors on matte stock

19362 **American Viola Society Newsletter**
American Viola Society
14070 Proton Rd
Suite 100
Dallas, TX 75244-3601

972-233-9107; Fax: 972-490-4219
stemple@comcast.net
www.madcrouch.com

Madeleine Crouch, President

A monthly e-newsletter. It contains announcements from the AVS, upcoming local chapter events, and other important items.
Frequency: Monthly

19363 **Banjo Newsletter**
PO Box 3418
Annapolis, MD 21403-0418

800-759-7425; Fax: 410-263-6503
bnl@infionline.net
www.banjonews.com

Newletter focusing on Bluegrass banjo music.
Mailing list available for rent

19364 **Bluegrass Music Profiles**
Bluegrass Publications
PO Box 850
Nicholasville, KY 40340-0850

859-333-6456
Facebook, Twitter

Information on Bluegrass music.

19365 **Bluegrass Now**
PO Box 2020
Rolla, MO 65402

573-341-7335
www.bluegrassnow.com

Information on Bluegrass music.

19366 **Bluegrass Unlimited**
PO Box 771
Warrenton, VA 20188-0771

540-349-8181
800-258-4727
info@bluegrassmusic.com
www.bluegrassmusic.com

Information on Bluegrass music.
Mailing list available for rent

19367 **Brooklyn Institute for Studies in American Music**
Brooklyn College
2900 Bedford Ave
Brooklyn, NY 11210-2889

718-951-5000

Karen L Gould, President

Music news and Academy activities.
Frequency: Semi-Annual
Founded in 1861

19368 **CMS Newsletter**
College Music Society
312 E Pine Street
Missoula, MT 59802

406-721-9616; Fax: 406-721-9419
cms@music.org
www.music.org

Robby D Gunstream, Executive Director

19369 **Dirty Linen**
PO Box 6660
Baltimore, MD 21239-6600

410-583-7973
www.dirtylinen.com

Information on Bluegrass music.

19370 **Early Music Newsletter**
New York Recorder Guild
145 W 93 Street
New York, NY 10025-7559

212-662-2946
mzumoff@nyc.rr.com
www.priceclan.com/nyrecorderguild/

Michael Zumoff, Executive Director

A publication of the New York Recorder Guild
10 Pages
Frequency: Monthly

19371 **Flatpicking Guitar**
High View Publications
PO Box 2160
Pulaski, VA 24301

540-980-0338
800-413-8296; Fax: 540-980-0557
www.flatpick.com

Information on Bluegrass music and the Flatpick guitar.
Mailing list available for rent

19372 **GMA Update**
Gospel Music Association
PO Box 22697
Nashville, TN 37202

615-242-0303; Fax: 615-254-9755
info@gospelmusic.org
www.gospelmusic.org

John Styll, President
Jackie Patillo, Executive Director

GMA's industry e-newsletter available to any non-GMA member who wishes to receive it. Sent out once a month, GMA Update contains the latest news about the Christian music industry and valuable information about the GMA.
Frequency: Monthly
Mailing list available for rent

19373 **GMAil**
Gospel Music Association
PO Box 22697
Nashville, TN 37202

615-242-0303; Fax: 615-254-9755
www.gospelmusic.org

John Styll, President

E-newsletter sent weekly to GMA members. Includes weekly music sales, charts, news, links to valuable resources, and information about upcoming GMA and industry events.
Frequency: Weekly
Founded in 1964

19374 **Girl Groups Gazette**
PO Box 69A04
Department HSND
West Hollywood, CA 90069-0066
Louis Wendruck, Editor/Publisher

For fans of girl groups and female singers of the 1960's and 70's including photos, discographies, records, t-shirts, postcards, and videos.
Cost: $20.00
Frequency: Quarterly
Founded in 1988

19375 **In the Groove**
Michigan Antique Phonograph Society
60 Central St
Battle Creek, MI 49017-3704

269-968-1299
antiquephono.org

Phil Stewart, Editor
Eileen Stewart, Editor

The Newsletter of the Michigan Antique Phonograph Society. Includes show, sales and auction announcements, MAPS chapter news, President's message, monthly feature articles, letters to the editor, and swap shop.
Cost: $25.00
24 Pages
Frequency: Monthly
Founded in 1976

19376 **International Bluegrass Music Association**
IBMA
2 Music Cir S
Suite 100
Nashville, TN 37203-4381

615-256-3222
888-438-4262; Fax: 615-256-0450
info@ibma.org
www.ibma.org

Dan Hays, Executive Director

Information on Bluegrass music from the IBMA

19377 **Music for the Love of It**
67 Parkside Drive
Berkeley, CA 94705-2409

510-654-9134; Fax: 510-654-4656
www.musicfortheloveofit.com

Edgar Rust, Publisher/Editor
Janet Telford, Co-Editor

A newsletter for people everywhere who love making music. Every issues brings new enthusiasm, new ideas and new opportunities for making music.
Frequency: Bi-Monthly
ISSN: 0898-8757
Founded in 1988
Printed in on matte stock

19378 **National Music Museum Newsletter**
National Music Museum
414 E Clark St
Vermillion, SD 57069-2307

605-677-5306; Fax: 605-677-6995
www.usd.edu/smm/

Andre Larson, Director

Quarterly Newletter which includes feature articles written by the curatorial staff and lists recent acquisitions. Published in February, May, August and November. It is available with basic museum membership.
Cost: $35.00
Printed in 4 colors

19379 **No Depression**
908 Halcyon Avenue
Nashville, TN 37204

615-292-7084
www.nodepression.net

Information on Bluegrass music
Founded in 1995

19380 **Notes a Tempo**
West Virginia University
Fairmount State University
1201 Locust Avenue
Fairmont, WV 26554

304-293-4841

David Bess, Co-Editor
Becky Terry, Co-Editor

The official publication of the West Virginia Music Educators. Published Fall, Winter and Spring
20-32 Pages
Frequency: 3 per year
Circulation: 1115

19381 **Old Time Herald**
P.O.Box 61679
Durham, NC 27715-1679

919-286-2041
info@oldtimeherald.org
www.oldtimeherald.org

Sarah Bryan, Editor-in-chief
Peter Honig, Business Director

Information on Bluegrass music
Mailing list available for rent

19382 **Pedal Steel Newsletter**
Pedal Steel Guitar Association
PO Box 20248
Floral Park, NY 11002-0248

516-616-9214; Fax: 516-616-9214
bobpsga@optonline.net
www.psga.org

Doug Mack, Editor
Bob Maickel, President

Dedicated to the art of playing pedal steel guitar. Every issue contains tablature arrangements of songs for the steel guitar as well as coming events, record reviews, product reports and news concerning the instrument.
Frequency: 10 x Per Year
ISSN: 1088-7954
Founded in 1973
Mailing list available for rent

19383 **Percussion News**
Percussive Arts Society
110 W Washington Street
Suite A
Indianapolis, IN 46204

317-974-4488; Fax: 317-974-4499
percarts@pas.org
www.pas.org

Rick Mattingly, Editor
Hillary Henry, Art Director
Lisa Rogers, President

Newsletter devoted to membership activities. This colorful newsletter also features a Classified Advertising section. Percussion News is published in January, March, May, July, September and November.
Frequency: 6 Editions Per Year
Founded in 1961
Mailing list available for rent

19384 **Rolling Stone**
Rolling Stone Magazine
1290 Ave of the Americas
2nd Floor
New York, NY 10104-0298

212-484-1616
800-283-1549; Fax: 212-484-1771
www.rssoundingboard.com
Facebook, Twitter, YouTube, RSS, Foursqare

Jann Wenner, President

A monthly newsletter geared for marketing, advertising and music exexecutives. It includes information on such matters as rock tours and musician endorsements, ad campaigns and rock contests.
Cost: $50.00
Frequency: Monthly
Founded in 1967
Mailing list available for rent

19385 **Roots and Rhythm Newsletter**
Roots and Rhythm
PO Box 837
El Cerrito, CA 94530

510-526-8373
888-766-8766; Fax: 510-526-9001
roots@toast.net
www.rootsandrhythm.com

Frank Scott, Owner
Nancy Scott-Noennig, Co-Owner

Lists, reviews and makes available for sale, recordings of blues, rhythm and blues, rockabilly, country, folk, ethnic, nostalgia and jazz music. Each newsletter reviews about 400 items and lists another 500 without reviews.
Frequency: Bi-Monthly
Circulation: 10000
Founded in 1974
Printed in 2 colors on newsprint stock

19386 **Sing Out!**
PO Box 5460
Bethlehem, PA 18015-0460

610-865-5366; Fax: 215-895-3052
info@singout.org
www.singout.org

Information on Bluegrass music
Mailing list available for rent

19387 **Tempo**
Academy of Country Music
5500 Balboa Blvd
Suite 200
Encino, CA 91316-1505

818-788-8000; Fax: 818-788-0999
info@acmcountry.com
www.acmcountry.com

Butch Waugh, Chairman

Devoted exclusively to the country music industry.
12 Pages
Frequency: Quarterly
Circulation: 4500
Founded in 1964

19388 The Voice
1156 15th St NW
Suite 310
Washington, DC 20005-1747

202-331-7577; Fax: 202-331-7599
service@chorusamerica.org
www.chorusamerica.org

Ann Meier Baker, President & Chief Executive Officer
1600 Members
Frequency: Quarterly
Circulation: 5000
ISSN: 1074-0805
Founded in 1977

19389 Westfield Center
Westfield Center for Early Keyboard Studies
726 University Ave,Room 102
Cornell University
Ithaca, NY 14850-3914

607-255-3065
info@westfield.org
www.westfield.org

Annette Richards, Executive Director
Maja Anderson, Program Coordinator
Evan Cortens, Administrative Assistant

E-newsletter providing information to professional keyboard musicians.
12 Pages
Frequency: Monthly
Founded in 1979

19390 Women in Bluegrass Newsletter
PO Box 2498
Winchester, VA 22604

800-227-2357
www.murphymethod.com/womeninbluegrass.cfm

Information on women in bluegass music

Magazines & Journals

19391 AfterTouch: New Music Discoveries
Music Discovery Network
PO Box 6205
Peoria, IL 61601-6205

309-685-4843
800-882-4262; Fax: 309-685-4878
aimcmc@aol.com
www.musicdiscoveries.com

Ronald Wallace, Editor

A magazine for music lovers who would like to experience new sights and sounds and would like to keep their fingers on the pulse of the music industry.
Frequency: Annual
Circulation: 10,000
Founded in 1984
Printed in on glossy stock

19392 American Music
University of Illinois Press
1325 South Oak Street
MC-566
Champaign, IL 61820-6903

217-244-0626
866-244-0626; Fax: 217-244-8082
journals@uillinois.edu
www.press.uillinois.edu

Michael Pisani, Editor
Jeff McArdle, Journals Marketing/Advertising Mgr.

Publishes articles on American composers, performers, publishers, institutions, events, and the music industry as well as book and recording reviews, bibliographies, and discographies.
Cost: $45.00
Frequency: Quarterly
Circulation: 1650
ISSN: 0734-4392
Founded in 1981
Mailing list available for rent: 1,650 names at $100 per M
Printed in 2 colors on glossy stock

19393 American Music Teacher
Music Teachers National Association
1 W. 4th Street
Suite 1550
Cincinnati, OH 45202

513-421-1420
888-512-5278; Fax: 513-421-2503
mtnanet@mtna.org
www.mtna.org

Gary L. Ingle, Executive Director & CEO
Brian Shepard, Chief Operating Officer
Scott McBride Smith, President
Madeleine Lovett, Marketing & PR

Provides articles, reviews and regular columns that inform, educate and challenge music teachers and foster excellence in the music teaching profession.
Cost: $30.00
Circulation: 35000
Founded in 1876
Mailing list available for rent: 20000 names at $85 per M
Printed in 4 colors on glossy stock

19394 American Organist
American Guild of Organists
475 Riverside Dr
Suite 1260
New York, NY 10115-0055

212-870-2310
800-246-5115; Fax: 212-870-2163
info@agohq.org
www.agohq.org
Facebook

James Thomashower, Executive Director

Most widely read journal devoted to organ and choral music in the world. Officialjournal of the American Guild of Organists, the Royal Canadian College of Organists, and the Associated Pipe Organ Builders of America.
Cost: $ 52.00
Frequency: Monthly
Circulation: 24000
ISSN: 0164-3150
Founded in 1967

19395 American String Teachers Journal
American String Teachers Association
4155 Chain Bridge Rd
Fairfax, VA 22030-4102

703-279-2113; Fax: 703-279-2114
asta@astaweb.com
www.astaweb.com

Donna Hale, Executive Director
Beth Danner-Knight, Deputy Director

Available to members. Provides an overview of current articles featured in the journal. Also answers questions about content, advertising, and contact information.
Cost: $90.00
Frequency: Quarterly
Circulation: 11,300
Mailing list available for rent: 10M+ names

19396 American Viola Society Journal
American Viola Society
14070 Proton Rd
Suite 100LB
Dallas, TX 75244-3601

972-233-9107; Fax: 972-490-4219
info@avsnationaloffice.org
www.americanviolasociety.org

Nokuthula Ngwenyama, President
Karin Brown, Secretary
Michelle Sayles, Treasurer
Kathryn Steely, Webmaster

Peer reviewed journal which promotes interest in the viola.
Cost: $42.00
Frequency: Annually
Circulation: 1500
Founded in 1984

19397 BMI Musicworld
Broadcast Music
7 World Trade Center
250 Greenwich Street
New York, NY 10007-0030

212-220-3000; Fax: 212-246-2163
www.bmi.com

Del Bryant, CEO
John E Cody, COO/EVP

Performing rights organization. Articles of interest to the songwriting community.
Founded in 1985

19398 Billboard Magazine
Prometheus Global Media
770 Broadwaye Blvd.
New York, NY 10003-9595

212-493-4100; Fax: 646-654-5368
www.prometheusgm.com
Facebook, Twitter

Richard D. Beckman, CEO
James A. Finkelstein, Chairman
Madeline Krakowsky, Vice President Circualtion
Tracy Brater, Executive Director Creative Service

Packed with in-depth music and entertainment features including the latest in new media and digital music, global coverage, music and money, touring, new artists, radio news and retail reports.
Cost: $149.00
Frequency: Weekly
Founded in 1894

19399 CCM Magazine
Salem Publishing
402 BNA Drive
Suite 400
Nashville, TN 37217

615-386-3011; Fax: 615-386-3380
www.ccmmagazine.com
Facebook, Twitter, RSS

Jim Cumbee, President

The voice of Contemporary Christian Music. Each monthly issue features music news, exclusive interviews, and an in-depth look at the spiritual lives of today's leading Christian music artists.
Cost: $19.95
Frequency: Monthly
Founded in 1978
Printed in 4 colors on glossy stock

19400 Chamber Music Magazine
Chamber Music America
UPS Box 458
243 Fifth Avenue
New York, NY 10016

212-242-2022; Fax: 212-242-7955
www.chamber-music.org

Susan Dadian, Program Director
Margaret M Lioi, CEO

Louise Smith, Chair
Cost: $5.95
Frequency: Bi-Monthly
Circulation: 6000
Founded in 1977

19401 Choral Journal
American Choral Directors Association
545 Couch Drive
Oklahoma City, OK 73102

405-232-8161; Fax: 405-232-8162
www.acdaonline.org

Carroll Gonzo, Editor
Ron Granger, Managing Editor

Contains articles and columns of a scholarly and practical nature in addition to reviews of newly released CD recordings, books, and printed music.
Frequency: Monthly

19402 Clarinet Journal
International Clarinet Society
PO Box 5039
Wheaton, IL 60189-5039

630-665-3602; Fax: 630-665-3848
www.clarinet.org

James Gillespie, Editor
So Rhee, Executive Director
Maxine Ramey, President
Caroline Hartig, Secretary
Tod Kerstetter, Treasurer

Contains articles in wide variety of areas written by performers and scholars.
Cost: $25.00
Frequency: Quarterly
Circulation: 3000

19403 Clavier
Instrumentalist Publishing Company
200 Northfield Road
Northfield, IL 60093-3390

847-446-5000
888-446-6888; Fax: 847-446-6263
editor@theinstrumentalist.com
www.instrumentalistmagazine.com
Facebook

James Rohner, Publisher
Judy Nelson, Editor

Provides new ideas and advice for piano teachers from leading educators. The focus of each issue is to offer practical advice for teachers. Articles include interviews with prominent performers, teachers and composers, the latest teaching methods, tributes to great artists of the past, and reviews of newly publshed music, educational software and videos.
Cost: $17.00
Frequency: 10X Per Year
Circulation: 16000
Founded in 1965
Mailing list available for rent

19404 Close Up Magazine
Country Music Association
One Music Circle S
Nashville, TN 37203

615-244-2840; Fax: 615-242-4783
international@cmaworld.com
www.cmaworld.com

Profiles of country music artists, various songwriters and industry news. Members of the Association receive the magazine as a benefit of their membership.
Circulation: 8000
Founded in 1958

19405 Country Weekly Magazine
American Media Inc
1000 American Media Way
T-Rex Technology Center
Boca Raton, FL 33464-1000

561-997-7733; Fax: 561-989-1298
www.nationalenquirer.com

David J Pecker, CEO

Devoted to country music and entertainment. Packed with feature articles and photos of country music personalities, music and video reviews, tour dates and late breaking news from the world of country music.
Cost: $34.95
Frequency: Bi-Weekly

19406 DJ Times
Testa Communications
25 Willowdale Avenue
Port Washington, NY 11050-3779

516-767-2500
800-937-7678; Fax: 516-767-9335
djtimes@testa.com
www.djtimes.com

Jim Tremayne, Editor-in-Chief
Steve Thorakos, Production Manager

Colorful tabloid magazine dedicated to professional mobile and club DJs. Specialized music sections, new product departments for sound and lighting, record reviews, business columns, informative entertainer profiles and more.
Cost: $19.40
Frequency: Monthly
Circulation: 30000
Founded in 1988

19407 Diapason
Scranton Gillette Communications
3030 W Salt Creek Lane
Suite 201
Arlington Heights, IL 60005-5025

847-391-1000; Fax: 847-390-0408
jbutera@sgcmail.com
www.thediapason.com

Jerome Butera, Editor/Publisher
Joyce Robinson, Associate Editor

Devoted to the organ, the harpischord, the carillon, and church music. Includes feature articles, reviews, reports, news, organ specifications, and a calendar, as well as classified advertisements.
Cost: $35.00
Frequency: Monthly
ISSN: 0012-2378
Founded in 1909

19408 Discoveries
700 East State Street
Ioal, WI 54990-0001

715-445-2214
800-258-0929; Fax: 715-445-4087

Mark Willliams, Publisher
Wayne Youngblood, Editorial Director
Cathy Bernardy, Associate Editor
Todd Whitesel, Associate Editor
Trevor Lauber, Advertising Sales Manager

Keeps close watch on market trends for collectible records, CDs and memorabilia. The Market Watch pages serve to interpret the mass of information available online and break it down to the most useful data collectors need. Each monthly issue is full of personality and opinion, with many reviews to help you determine where to spend your money. Coverage includes rock 'n' roll, rhythm &'blues, pop, doo-wop, classic jazz and country western recordings.
Cost: $28.00
Frequency: Monthly
Circulation: 10,859
Founded in 1988

19409 Downbeat
102 N Haven Road
PO Box 906
Elmhurst, IL 60126

630-941-2030
800-554-7470; Fax: 630-941-3210
service@downbeat.com
www.downbeat.com

Kevin Maher, CEO

Monthly magazine includes such features as Readers Poll results, festival reviews, CD reviews, feature articles and more.
Cost: $29.95
Frequency: Monthly
Mailing list available for rent

19410 Electronic Musician
PRIMEDIA
6400 Hollis Street
Suite 12
Emeryville, CA 94608-1086

510-653-3307
emeditorial@prismb2b.com
www.emusician.com
Facebook, Twitter

Steve Oppenheimer, Editor-in-Chief
Joe Perry, Associate Publisher
Marie Briganti, List Manager

Magazine for musicians recording and producing music in a home or personal studio environment. They are a source of user-friendly technical information for musicans. Features include: Tech Page, ProFile, Working Musician, Sound Design Workshop, Making Tracks, Square One, Reviews, What's New, Master Class, Final Mix, and Editors Choice Awards.
Cost: $23.97
Frequency: Monthly
Circulation: 61102
Founded in 1986
Mailing list available for rent

19411 Flute Talk
Instrumentalist Company
200 Northfield Road
Northfield, IL 60093-3390
847-446-5000
888-446-6888; Fax: 847-446-6263
www.instrumentalistmagazine.com
Facebook

Flute Talk is written for professional flute players, teachers, and advanced students. Frequent topics include performance analyses of flute repertoire, current teaching techniques, piccolo articles, interviews with prominent performers and teachers, and reviews of new music, recordings, and books for flutists.
Cost: $13.00
Frequency: 10 x Per Year
Circulation: 12000
Founded in 1981

19412 Goldmine
700 E State Street
Iola, WI 54990-0001

715-445-2214
800-258-0929; Fax: 715-445-4087
www.goldminemag.com
Facebook, YouTube, RSS, Pinterest

Jeff Pozorski, Publisher
Brian Earnest, Editorial Director
Peter Lindblad, Associate Editor
Tim Neely, Research Director
Trevor Lauber, Advertising Sales Manager

The world's largest marketplace for collectible records, CDs, and music memorabilia covering Rock N' Roll, Blues, Country, Folk, and Jazz. Large volumes of For Sale and Wanted ads are placed by collectors and dealers. Includes articles on recording stars of the past and present with discographies listing all known releases, a

listing of upcoming record-and-CD-collector conventions, album reviews, hobby and music news, a collecting column, a letters section, and Collector Mania (Q&A).
Cost: $39.95
Frequency: Bi-Weekly
Circulation: 17026
Founded in 1974
Mailing list available for rent

19413 **Guitar One**
Cherry Lane Magazines
6 E 32nd St
Suite 11
New York, NY 10016-5422
212-561-3000
800-825-4942; Fax: 212-447-6885
www.guitarmag.com
Peter W Primont, CEO
Jonathan Simpson-Bint, President
Holly Klingel, VP Circulation
Steve Aaron, Publishing Director
Greg Di Benedetto, Publisher
Information on everything from the guitar equipment evaluations to news on the latest trends and technological developments to special insider pieces covering the sound secrets of today's top players.
Cost: $24.95
Frequency: Monthly
Circulation: 105,000
Founded in 1985

19414 **Guitar Review**
Albert Augustine Limited
151 W 26th St
Suite 4
New York, NY 10001-6810
917-661-0220; Fax: 917-661-0223
www.albertaugustine.com
Steven Griesgraber, President
Eliot Fisk, Associate Editor
David Starobin, Associate Editor
Ian Gallagher, Music Editor
Matthew Hough, Circulation
Scholarly articles related to the classical guitar.
Cost: $28.00
48 Pages
Frequency: Quarterly
Circulation: 4000
Founded in 1946

19415 **HipHop Weekly**
Z & M Media
401 Broadway
New York, NY
212-696-0831
www.hiphopweekly.com
Facebook, Twitter
Covers the entire hip hop culture.

19416 **Instrumentalist**
Instrumentalist Company
200 Northfield Road
Northfield, IL 60093-3390
847-446-5000
888-446-6888; Fax: 847-446-6263
www.instrumentalistmagazine.com
Facebook
A magazine school band and orchestra directors can depend on for practical information to use for then ensembles. The articles written by veteran directors and performers cover a wide range of topics, including rehearsal techniques, conducting tips, programming ideas, instrument clinics, repertoire analyses, and much more. Monthly new music reviews guide directors to selecting the best music for their students.
Cost: $21.00
Frequency: Monthly
Circulation: 16,000
Founded in 1945
Printed in 4 colors

19417 **International Musician**
American Federation of Musicians
1501 Broadway
Suite 600
New York, NY 10036-5501
212-869-1330; Fax: 212-764-6134
info@afm.org
www.afm.org
Thomas Lee, President
Delivers the latest happenings in music. Focuses on the overall well-being of all musicians. Provides news pertaining to symphonic, rock, freelance, recording and touring musicians. IM features aricles on pressing issues sich as piracy, legislation, on-the-job struggles, and the effects of technology.
Cost: $25.00
Frequency: Monthly
Circulation: 110000
Founded in 1896
Printed in on n stock

19418 **JAMIA**
American Musical Instrument Society
389 Main Street
Suite 202
Malden, MA 02148
781-397-8870; Fax: 781-397-8887
amis@guildassoc.com
www.amis.org
Stewart Carter, President
Joanne Kopp, Treasurer
Presents peer-reviewed articles that assist in both professionals and students to develop and apply biomedical and health informatics to patient care, teaching, research, and health care administration.
Frequency: Bi-Monthly
Founded in 1971

19419 **Jazz Education Journal**
JazzTimes Magazine,Madavor Media
85 Quincy Ave
Suite 2
Quincy, MA 02169
617-706-9110; Fax: 617-536-0102
www.jazztimes.com
Leslie M Sabina, Editor
Karen Mayse, Advertising
Provides news and information in the field of jazz education. Contains information of today's top jazz artists, reviews, transcriptions, industry news, and articles on improvisation, teaching techniques, history, performance, composition, arranging and music business.
Cost: $23.95
100 Pages
Circulation: 10,000
Founded in 1968
Mailing list available for rent
Printed in on glossy stock

19420 **Journal of American Organbuilding**
American Institute of Organ Builders
PO Box 35306
Canton, OH 44735
330-806-9011
www.pipeorgan.org
Jeffrey L Weiler, Editor
Features technical articles, product and book reviews, and a forum for the exchange of building and service information and techniqes. Subscriptions are provided free to AIO members, and are available to non-members for $24.00 per year.
Cost: $24.00
Frequency: Quarterly
Founded in 1974
Mailing list available for rent: 350 names at $250 per M
Printed in on glossy stock

19421 **Journal of Music Theory**
Yale University
Department of Music
PO Box 208310
New Haven, CT 06520-8310
203-432-2985; Fax: 203-432-2983
jmt.editor@yale.edu
www.yale.edu/jmt/
Ian Quinn, Editor
David Clampitt, Associate Editor
Richard Cohn, Associate Editor
Daniel Harrison, Associate Editor
Patrick McCreless, Associate Editor
Publishes peer-reviewed reseach in Music Theory.
Cost: $30.00
Frequency: Annual
Founded in 1957

19422 **Journal of Music Therapy**
American Music Therapy Association
8455 Colesville Rd
Suite 1000
Silver Spring, MD 20910-3392
301-589-3300; Fax: 301-589-5175
info@musictherapy.org
www.musictherapy.org
Andrea Farbman, Executive Director
Research in the area of music therapy and rehabilitation, a forum for authoratative articles of current music therapy research and theory, use of music in the behavioral sciences, book reviews, and guest editorials.
Cost: $120.00
Frequency: Quarterly
Circulation: 6000
ISSN: 0022-2917
Founded in 1998

19423 **Journal of Research in Music Education**
MENC Subscription Office
PO Box 1584
Birmingham, AL 35201
800-633-4931
Facebook, Twitter
Keeps members informed of the latest music education research. Offers a collection of reports that includes thorough analyses of theories and projects by respected music researchers. Issued four times yearly.
Frequency: Quarterly
Founded in 1907
Printed in on matte stock

19424 **Journal of Singing**
National Association of Teachers of Singing
9957 Moorings Drive
Suite 401
Jacksonville, FL 32257-2416
904-992-9101; Fax: 904-262-2587
info@nats.org
www.nats.org
Facebook, Twitter, LinkedIn
Richard Dale Sjoerdsma, Editor-in-Chief
The official journal of NATS, offering a wealth of research and insight from scholars and experts on teaching singing, with topics ranging from history and voice science to voice pedagogy.
Frequency: 5x times/year
Founded in 1944

19425 **Journal of the American Musicological Society**
University of California Press, Journals Division

2000 Center Street Way
Suite 203
Berkeley, CA 94704-1223

510-643-7154; Fax: 510-642-9917
journals@ucpress.edu
www.ucpressjournals.com

Bruce Alan Brown, Editor
Louise Goldberg, Assistant Editor
Julie Cumming, Book Review Editor

The JAMS publishes scholarship from all fields of musical inquiry: from historical musicology, critical theory, music analysis, iconography and organology, to performance practice, aesthetics and hermeneutics, ethnomusicology, gender and sexuality, popular music and cultural studies. Each issue includes articles, book reviews, and communications.
Cost: $42.00
Frequency: Tri-Annual
Circulation: 5000
ISSN: 0003-0139
Founded in 1893

19426 Jukebox Collector Magazine
2545 SE 60th Court
Pleasant Hill, IA 50327-5099

515-265-8324; Fax: 515-265-1980
JukeboxCollector@att.net
www.alwaysjukin.com

Rick Botts, Editor

Focuses on collectors of jukeboxes from the 40's, 50's, and 60's. There are approximately 150 jukeboxes for sale each month, along with show events information. Accepts advertising.
Cost: $33.00
36 Pages
Frequency: Monthly
Circulation: 1800
Founded in 1977

19427 Live Sound International
111 Speen Street
Framingham, MA 01701

415-387-4009
800-375-8015; Fax: 866-449-3761
amclean@livesoundint.com
www.livesoundint.com

Mark Herman, Publisher
Jeff MacKay, Editor
Mitch Gallagher, Associate Editor
Sara Elliott, Advertising

The editorial focus is performance audio and event sound. Contains audio production techniques, new products, equipment applications and associated commercial concerns.
Cost: $60.00
Frequency: Monthly
Circulation: 20,000
Mailing list available for rent
Printed in on glossy stock

19428 Mix
Prism Business Media
6400 Hollis St
Suite 9
Emeryville, CA 94608-1052

510-658-3793
866-860-7087; Fax: 510-653-5142
mixeditorial@prismb2b.com
www.mixonline.com

Melinda Paras, Owner
Erika Lopez, Associate Publisher
Tom Kenny, Editor
John Pledger, Publisher
Christen Pocock, Marketing Director

Mix covers a wide range of topics including: recording, live sound and production, broadcast production, audio for film and video, and music technology. In addition, Mix includes coverage of facility design and construction, location recording, tape/disc manufacturing, education, and other topics of importanct to audio professionals. Distributed in 94 countries.
Cost: $35.97
Frequency: Monthly
Circulation: 45244
Founded in 1977

19429 Modern Drummer
Modern Drummer Publications
12 Old Bridge Rd
Cedar Grove, NJ 07009-1288

973-239-4140; Fax: 973-239-7139
mdinfo@moderndrummer.com
www.moderndrummer.com

Isabel Spagnardi, Owner
Tracy A Kearns, Associate Publisher
Bill Miller, Editor-in-Chief
Rick Van Horn, Senior Editor
Adam Budofsky, Managing Editor

Every issue of Modern Drummer includes interviews with the world's leading drummers, a full roster of columns on all facets of drumming, complete drum charts, solos and patterns performed by your favorite players, insightful reviews on the hottest new geat, the best in CDs, books, and DVDs for drummers, and giveaways worth thousands of dollars.
Cost: $29.97
Frequency: Monthly
Circulation: 6000
ISSN: 1078-1757
Founded in 1993
Mailing list available for rent
Printed in 4 colors on glossy stock

19430 Music
102 N Haven Road
PO Box 906
Elmhurst, IL 60126-2932

630-941-2030; Fax: 630-941-3210
www.musicincmag.com

Zach Phillip, Editor
Kevin Maher, CEO
John Cahill, Eastern Advertising
Tom Burns, Western Advertising
Chris Maher, Classified Ads

Offered free to those involved in music products retailing. Delivers news you can use for the musical products industry. Geared toward store owners and managers in musical product retail and repair shops in the United States and Canada.
Frequency: 11 Per Year
Circulation: 8,949
Founded in 1934

19431 Music & Sound Retailer
Testa Communications
25 Willowdale Avenue
Port Washington, NY 11050

516-767-2500
800-937-7678; Fax: 516-767-9335
testa@testa.com
www.testa.com

Brian Berk, Editor

News magazine serving owners, managers and sales personnel in retail musical-instument and sound-product dealershops. The magazine's emphasis is on full-line and combo dealerships offering guitars, drums, electronic keyboards and digital pianos, recording and sound-reinforcement products, lighting, DJ equipment, software, print and accessories. Recurring features include 'MI Spy,' 'Top Ten,' 'Veddatorial,' 'Selling Points,' and editor's letter
Cost: $18.00
Frequency: Monthly
Circulation: 11000
Founded in 1985

19432 Music Row
1231 17th Avenue S
PO Box 158542
Nashville, TN 37215-8542

615-321-3617; Fax: 615-329-0852
sales@musicrow.com
www.musicrow.com

David M Ross, CEO/President

Written for people who work in the music business. Contents include record reviews, current news items, timely interviews or discovering hot talent first. Music Row subscriptions include six print issues per year, daily Afternoon News updates via e-mail and @Musicrow reports every Tuesday, Thursday and Friday via e-mail.
Cost: $159.00
Frequency: Six Per Year
Circulation: 14000
Founded in 1981
Printed in 4 colors on glossy stock

19433 Music Trades Magazine
Music Trades
80 West Street
Englewood, NJ 07631-0432

201-871-1965
800-423-6530; Fax: 201-871-0455
music@musictrades.com
www.musictrades.com

Brian Majeski, Publisher
Richard T Watson, Managing Editor
Juanita Hampton, Circulation Manager

A blend of industry news, hard sales and marketing data, trend analysis and management tips in every issue. Target audience is retailers, distributors, and manufacturers of musical instruments, professional audio equipment and related products, worldwide.
Cost: $16.00
Frequency: Monthly
Circulation: 7500
Founded in 1890
Mailing list available for rent

19434 Music and Sound Journal
912 Carlton Road
Tarpon Spring, FL 34689

727-938-0571
www.masj.com

Don Kulak, Founder/Owner

Brings readers the future of sound today, with new music, experimental sound, cutting edge audio and acoustics and alternative media. MSJ is written for people who are discriminating about music, audio, and sound - people who want to improve their sonic environments on all levels, without having to study pages of data - people who want to more fully understand the profound impact sound has on every aspect of their daily lives.
ISSN: 1541-8545
Founded in 1988

19435 Musical Merchandise Review
21 Highland Circle
Suite One
Needham, MA 02494

781-453-9310
800-964-5150; Fax: 781-453-9389
www.mmrmagazine.com

Lee Zapis, President
Sidney L Davis, Group Publisher
Richard E Kessel, Publisher/Advertising Sales
Maureen Johan, Classified Sales

Serves retailers of musical instruments, accessories, and related services as well as wholesalers, importers/exporters and manufacturers of related products. Its purpose is to communicate facts and ideas that will benefit musical merchandisers and their daily business operations as well as help

them enhance their growth. Its editorial approach includes features on industry trends and innovations, new product promotion, in-store display techniques, financing, planning and dealer surveys.
Cost: $32.00
Frequency: Monthly
Founded in 1879
Mailing list available for rentat $100 per M
Printed in 4 colors

19436 New on the Charts
Music Business Reference
70 Laurel Place
New Rochelle, NY 10801-7105

914-632-3349; Fax: 914-633-7690
lenny@notc.com
www.notc.com

Leonard Kalikow, Publisher/Editor

Circulation limited to professionals only, provides major signings, contracts and directories.
Cost: $365.00
Frequency: Monthly
Circulation: 5,000
ISSN: 0276-7031
Founded in 1976

19437 Notes
Music Library Association
8551 Research Way
Suite 180
Middleton, WI 53562

608-836-5825; Fax: 608-831-8200
mla@areditions.com
www.musiclibraryassoc.org

Michael Colby, President
Jane Gottlieb, Editor

19438 Opera America Newsline
Opera America
330 7th Ave
Suite 1600
New York, NY 10001-5248

212-796-8620; Fax: 212-796-8631
info@operaamerica.org
www.operaamerica.org

Marc Scorca, President

Provides company news from around the world, articles on issues affecting the field, professional opportunities, and updates on OPERA America programs and activities. Complimentary subscription with all membership levels, excluding stand-alone professional subscriptions.
Frequency: 10X Per Year
Founded in 1970

19439 Opera News
Metropolitan Opera Guild
70 Lincoln Center Plz
New York, NY 10023-6577

212-769-7000; Fax: 212-769-7007
info@metguild.org
www.metoperafamily.org

David Dik, Manager

Monthly magazine that reports on opera around the world. Issues include reviews of commercial recordings and live performances, profiles of artists and articles by eminent writers on the music scene.
Cost: $29.95
Frequency: Monthly
Circulation: 60000
Founded in 1883

19440 Percussive Notes
Percussive Arts Society
110 W Washington Street
Suite A
Indianapolis, IN 46204

317-974-4488; Fax: 317-974-4499
percarts@pas.org
www.pas.org

Rick Mattingly, Editor
Hillary Henry, Managing Editor

The official journal of the Percussive Arts Society. Published in February, April, June, August, October and December, this magazine features a variety of articles and advertising aimed at professional and student percussionists. Regular sections are devoted to drumset, marching percussion, world percussion, symphonic percussion, technology, keyboard, health and wellness, research and reviews.
Cost: $85.00
Frequency: 6 Times Per Year
Circulation: 8000
Founded in 1961
Mailing list available for rent

19441 Piano Guild Notes
Piano Guild Publications
PO Box 1807
Austin, TX 78767-1807

512-478-5775; Fax: 512-478-5843
ngpt@pianoguild.com
www.pianoguild.com

Richard Allison, President

Music industry publication focusing on Piano Guild members and activities.
Cost: $16.00
Frequency: Quarterly
Circulation: 11000
Founded in 1929
Printed in 2 colors

19442 Piano Technicians Journal
Piano Technicians Guild
4444 Forest Avenue
Kansas City, KS 66106

913-432-9975; Fax: 913-432-9986
ptg@ptg.org
www.ptg.org

Barbara Cassaday, Executive Director
Jim Coleman Jr RPT, President
Norman R Cantrell RPT, VP

Monthly technical magazine covering all phases of working on pianos. Articles explore new tools, industry news and organizational issues. Feature articles range from setting up a repair shop to rebuilding techniques.
Cost: $ 150.00
Frequency: Monthly
Circulation: 4300
ISSN: 0031-9562

19443 Pitch Pipe
Sweet Adelines International
9110 S Toledo
PO Box 470168
Tulsa, OK 74137-0168

918-622-1444
800-992-7464; Fax: 918-665-0894
Joey@sweetadelineintl.org
www.sweetadelineintl.org

Pat LeVezu, President
Joey Mechell Stenner, Editor
Kelly Kirchhoff, Director Communications

Official publication of Sweet Adelines International, the world's largest singing performance and music education organization for women. The Pitch Pipe informs, educates and recognizes the members who have made the organization a success. The subscription price for members is included in the annual per capita fee.
Cost: $12.00
Frequency: Quarterly
Circulation: 30,000
Founded in 1947
Mailing list available for rent: 30M names
Printed in 4 colors on glossy stock

19444 Playback
American Society of Composers, Authors & Publisher
1 Lincoln Plz
New York, NY 10023-7097

212-621-6027
800-952-7227; Fax: 212-362-7328
Playback@ascap.com
www.ascap.com

Marilyn Bergman, President
Phil Crossland, Executive Editor
Jin Moon, Deputy Editor
Mike Barsky, Advertising
David Pollard, Design

The Society's magazine is loaded with full-color photos, features the latest news on ASCAP events, new member listings, legislative updates, feature articles on members, distribution info, upcoming workshops and showcases and much more.
Cost: $12.00
Frequency: Annual
Circulation: 100,000
ISSN: 1080-1391

19445 Pro Audio Review
IMAS Publishing
28 East 28th Street
12th Floor
New York, NY 22041

212-378-0400; Fax: 212-378-0470
www.proaudioreview.com

John Gatski, Publisher/Executive Editor
Brett Moss, Managing Editor
Claudia Van Veen, Advertising

Reviews of the latest new equipment written by audio professionals in the field, from bench tests checking the specs, to new product announcements.
Cost: $24.95
Frequency: Monthly
Circulation: 26000
ISSN: 1083-6241
Founded in 1995
Mailing list available for rent: 30,000 names at $145 per M
Printed in 4 colors on glossy stock

19446 Pro Sound News
United Business Media
28 East 28th Street
12th Floor
New York, NY 10019

212-378-0400; Fax: 212-378-2160
sedorusa@optonline.net
www.governmentvideo.com

Gary Rhodes, International Sales Manager

Provides timely and accurate news, industy analysis, features and technology updates to the expanded professional audio community.
Cost: $30.00
Frequency: Monthly
Circulation: 250003
Printed in 4 colors

19447 RePlay Magazine
PO Box 572829
Tarzana, CA 91357-7004

818-776-2880; Fax: 818-776-2888
editor@replaymag.com
www.replaymag.com

Edward Adlum, President
Barry Zweben, Marketing

A trade publication for those within the coin-operated amusement machine industry, primarily distributors, manufacturers and operators of

jukeboxes and games.
Cost: $65.00
Frequency: Monthly
Circulation: 36000
ISSN: 1534-2328
Founded in 1975
Mailing list available for rent
Printed in 4 colors on glossy stock

19448 Rolling Stone Magazine
1290 Ave of the Americas
Floor 2
New York, NY 10104-0295

212-484-1616; Fax: 212-484-1771
www.rssoundingboard.com
Facebook, Twitter

Jann Wenner, President

Covers pop culture, politics etc in a massive amount of music articles, interviews, news, reviews, photos, and sound clips.

19449 Sheet Music Magazine
PO Box 58629
Boulder, CO 80323

914-244-8500
800-759-3036; Fax: 914-244-8560

Ed Shanaphy, Publisher

Features actual reproduction of popular songs, both words and music, articles on various aspects of musical performance and interest for many types of musicians, and self improvement features for keyboard and fretter instrument players. A single year's subscription brings you at least 66 great songs best-loved standards and today's most lyrical hits.
Cost: $22.97
Frequency: Bi-Monthly
Circulation: 50,000

19450 Society News
Contemporary Record Society
724 Winchester Road
Broomall, PA 19008

610-205-9897; Fax: 707-549-5920
crsnews@verizon.net
www.crsnews.org

Jack M Shusterman, Advertising

Offers opportunities to CRS consitituents, progress notes on its associates, various awards and performance possibilities. The Society News offers feature articles of renowned composers/performers and reviews of music, recordings and music books.
Founded in 1983

19451 Southwestern Musician
Texas Music Educators Association
7900 Centre Park
PO Box 140465
Austin, TX 78714-0465

512-452-0710
888-318-8632; Fax: 512-451-9213
rfloyd@tmea.org
www.tmea.org

Robert Floyd, Executive Director
Karen Kneten, Communications Manager
Tesa Harding, Advertising/Exhibit Manager
Laura Kocian, Financial Manager
Rita Ellinger, Membership Assistant

The official magazine of the TMEA. Publsihed monthly August through May. Included with membership. A President's newsletter is published each June when necessary to provide an update on TMEA activities. The purposed of this publication is to serve the music educators of Texas as a means of communication or professional philosophy and action and to promote the field of music education within the state.
Circulation: 14000
Founded in 1938

Mailing list available for rent: 10,000 names
Printed in 4 colors on glossy stock

19452 Symphony Magazine
American Symphony Orchestra League
33 W 60th St
Suite 5
New York, NY 10023-7905

212-262-0638; Fax: 212-262-5198
www.symphony.org

Henry Fogel, CEO
Stephen Alter, Advertising Manager
Michael Rush, Production Manager

Bimonthly magazine of the American Symphony Orchestra League. Discusses issues critical to the orchestra community and communicates the value and importance of orchestras and the music they perform. Publishes articles on compelling issues and trends relevant to the entire orchestra field. Its readers include professional staff, musicians, and board members in the orchestra industry and related fields; orchestra patrons and volunteers; and music critics and arts and media professionals.
Cost: $22.00
Frequency: Bi-Monthly
Circulation: 18000
Founded in 1942
Mailing list available for rent
Printed in 4 colors

19453 Symposium
312 E Pine Street
Missoula, MT 59802

406-721-9616
800-729-0235; Fax: 406-721-9419
cms@music.org
www.music.org

Robby D Gunstream, Executive Director
Cynthia Taggart, President
Glenn Stanley, Editor

Serves as a vehicle for the dissemination of information and ideas on music in higher education. The content of the publication highlights concerns of general interest and reflects the work of the Society in the areas of music represented on its Board of Directors.
Frequency: One Per Year
Circulation: 8000
Founded in 1968
Printed in one color on matte stock

19454 Vibe

vbecustserv@cdsfulfillment.com
www.vibe.com

Mimi Valdez, Editor-In-Chief

Covers the trends, the events, and culture of the urban scene. Film, fashion and art to politics and music-pop, jazz, R&B, dance, hip hop, rap, house and more.
Cost: $11.95
Frequency: Monthly

Trade Shows

19455 ASTA National Conference
American String Teachers Association
4155 Chain Bridge Road
Fairfax, VA 22030

703-279-2113; Fax: 703-279-2114
asta@astaweb.com
www.astaweb.com

Donna Sizemore Hale, Executive Director
Beth Danner-Knight, Deputy Director
Jody McNamara, Deputy Director

Recognizing the wealth of our rich traditions as well as offer members new horizons in teaching and performing strings. Cost of attendance begins at $255. 150 exhibitors.
2000 Attendees
Frequency: Annual/March

19456 ATG Annual Accordion Festival
Accordionists & Teachers Guild International
813 West Lakeshore Drive
O'Fallon, IL 62269-1216

618-632-2859
amyjo@apci.net
www.accordions.com

Amy Jo Sawyer, President
Joe Natoli, First Vice President
Liz Finch, Second Vice President
Joan C. Sommers, Executive Secretary
Frequency: Annual
Founded in 1940

19457 American Choral Directors Association National Conference
American Choral Directors Association
545 Couch Drive
Oklahoma City, OK 73102

405-232-8161; Fax: 405-232-8162
www.acdaonline.org

Dr Tim Sharp, Executive Director

4 full days of concerts, interest sessions, exhibits, and networking.
Frequency: Annual/March

19458 American Guild of Organists, National Conference
475 Riverside Drive
Suite 1260
New York, NY 10115

212-870-2310; Fax: 212-870-2163
info@agohq.org
www.agohq.org

James Thomashower, Executive Director
Jennifer Madden, Manager Membership
Harold Calhoun, Mgr Competitions

Over 20 exhibits and a workshop for professional, amatuer and student organists.
Frequency: Biennial

19459 American Harp Society National Conference
3416 Primm Lane
Birmingham, AL 35216

205-795-7130; Fax: 205-823-2760
execsecretary@harpsociety.org
www.harpsociety.org

Christa Grix, National Conference Chair
Lynne Aspnes, Conference Program Advisory Chair
Delaine Fedson, President

Conference will explore the mind-body-music connection, the creative process, and the connection between creativity and learning. The conference will include multiple disciplines including educators, composers, performers, therapists and practioners.
300 Attendees
Frequency: Annual
Founded in 1962

19460 American Institute of Organbuilders Annual Convention
American Institute of Organ Builders
PO Box 130982
Houston, TX 77219

713-529-2212; Fax: 713-529-2212

Rene Marceau, Convention Committee Chairman

Annual convention includes supplier exhibits, technical lectures, sight-seeing tours, profes-

sional examinations, lectures and organ demonstrations.
Frequency: October
Founded in 1974
Mailing list available for rent: 350 names at $250 per M

19461 **American Music Therapy Conference**
National Music Therapy Association
8445 Colesville Road
Suite 1000
Silver Spring, MD 20910

301-589-3300; Fax: 301-589-5175
www.musictherapy.org

Seminar and exhibits of publications, musical instruments, books, learning aids and recordings.
Frequency: November

19462 **American Musical Instrument Society**
1106 Garden Street
Hoboken, NJ 07030

202-656-0107
amis@guildassoc.com
www.amis.org

Susan Thompson, Program Co-Chair
Kathryn Libin, Program Co-Chair

A broad range of topics include the history, design, use, care and acoustics of musical instruments in all cultures and from all periods.
Frequency: Annual

19463 **American Musicological Society Annual Meeting**
American Musicological Society
194 Mercer St. Room 404
New York, NY 10012-1502

212-992-6340
877-679-7648; Fax: 212-995-4022
ams@ams-net.org
www.ams-net.org

Robert Judd, Executive Director

A society of professional musicologists and university educators. The annual meetings are held in the fall each year; 2007- Quebec; 2008- Nashville; 2009- Philadelphia.
2000 Attendees
Frequency: Annual
Founded in 1948
Mailing list available for rent: 3515 names at $100 per M

19464 **American Orff-Schulwerk Association National Conference**
American Orff-Schulwerk Association
PO Box 391089
Cleveland, OH 44139-8089

440-543-5366; Fax: 440-600-7332
info@aosa.org
www.aosa2.org

Karen Medley, Conference Chair

One hundred exhibits of music, music books, software, insturments, and gifts in addition to National Conference of 2000+ music educators.
2400 Attendees
Frequency: November
Founded in 1969

19465 **American Symphony Orchestra League National Conference**
33 W 60th Street
5th Floor
New York, NY 10023

212-262-5161; Fax: 212-262-5198
www.symphony.org

Stephen Alter, Advertising and Meetings Manager
Meghan Whitbeck, Advertising/Meetings Coordinator
Henry Fogel, President/CEO

Ninety booths incorporating all facets of classical music industries including industry suppliers, music publishers and computer technology.
1200 Attendees
Frequency: June

19466 **CMS National Conference**
College Music Society
312 E Pine Street
Missoula, MT 59802

406-721-9616; Fax: 406-721-9419
cms@music.org
www.music.org

Robby D Gunstream, Executive Director

Presents higher education's broadest array of topics dealing with music. Attendees are faculty, administrators, graduate students, independent scholars, composers, publishers, and music business personnel who share a common interest and dedication to the improvement of music and its relationship to the other academic disciplines of higher education.
450 Attendees
Frequency: Annual/October

19467 **Chamber Music America National Conference**
Chamber Music America
305 7th Avenue
5th Floor
New York, NY 10001

212-242-2022; Fax: 212-242-7955
www.chamber-music.org

Susan Dadian, Program Director
Margaret M Lioi, CEO
Louise Smith, Chair
700 Attendees
Frequency: Annual

19468 **Chorus America Annual Conference**
910 17th Street NW
Washington, DC 20006

202-776-0215; Fax: 202-776-0224
service@chorusamerica.org
www.chorusamerica.org

Ann Meier Baker, President/CEO
Melanie Garrett, Membership Services Manager

This four day conference offers seminars, workshops, concerts, expert consultations and peer-group meetings in a friendly, dynamic environment.
500 Attendees
Frequency: June
Printed in 2 colors on matte stock

19469 **Country Radio Seminar**
Country Radio Broadcasters
819 18th Avenue S
Nashville, TN 37203

615-327-4487; Fax: 615-329-4492
info@crb.org
www.crb.org

Ed Salamon, Executive Director
Chasity Crouch, Business Manager
Carole Bowen, Secretary

Conference attendess include major radio groups and record labels as well as independents, Features include exhibits, seminars and shows.
2300 Attendees
Frequency: Annual
Founded in 1969

19470 **Folk Alliance Annual Meeting**
Folk Alliance
510 South Main
1st Floor
Memphis, TN 38103

901-522-1170; Fax: 816-221-3658
fa@folk.org
www.folkalliance.org

200+ artists, 4 nights of show cases, four days of feature concerts, exhibit hall parties, panels, workshops, clinics and much more all under one roof.
3000 Attendees

19471 **Gospel Music Week**
Gospel Music Association
PO Box 22697
Nashville, TN 37202

615-242-0303; Fax: 615-254-9755
info@gospelmusic.org
www.gospelmusic.org

Jackie Patillo, Executive Director

Listen to new music as you experience over 100 eclectic performances throughout the week from today's top artists and tomorrow's hit-makers, invent new waysof enhancing your ministry through educational opportunities found in over 100 seminars and panels and through the sharing of your ideas with colleagues. Connect with your industry peers and friends at various networking opportunities including receptions, roundtables and more.
3,000 Attendees
Frequency: April
Founded in 1964

19472 **Gospel Music Workshop America**
PO Box 34635
Detroit, MI 48208

313-898-6900; Fax: 313-898-4520
www.gmwanational.org

Rev Albert L Jamison, Sr, Chair, Board of Directors
Sheila Smith, Director Operations
Mark Smith, Convention Manager

Conferences open with a highly spirited service including Sacraments, music from choirs within the GMWA, Psalmists and the preached Word. This is followed by lectures, speakers, preachers and over 100 courses offered during the week. Nightly musicals include chapter choirs and national recording artists. Midnight services are held which include music, preaching and various recordings by the Women's Division, Men's Division, Youth/Young Adult division and a service by Bishop Richard White.
16M Attendees
Frequency: August
Founded in 1967

19473 **International Association of Jazz Educators Conference**
International Association of Jazz Education
PO Box 724
Manhattan, KS 66505

785-776-8744; Fax: 785-776-6190
www.iaje.org

Bill McFarlin, Executive Director

This four-day conference fatures a 75,000 square-food music industry exposition, commission premieres, technology presentations, research papers, award ceremonies, and performances by over 500 of the world's most respected professional jazz groups and musicians.
8000 Attendees
Frequency: Annual

19474 **International Computer Music Conference**
International Computer Music Association

1819 Polk Street
Suite 330
San Francisco, CA 94109

FAX 734-878-3031
icma@umich.edu
www.computermusic.org
Facebook

Tae Hong Park, President
Margaret Schedel, VP of Conference
Chryssie Nanou, Treasurer/Secretary
Tom Erbe, VP, Membership
Sandra Neal, Administrative Assistant

The International Computer Music Association is an international affiliation of individuals and institutions involved in the technical, creative, and performance aspects of computer music. It serves composers, engineers, researchers and musicians who are interested in the integration of music and technology.
Founded in 1974

19475 **International Horn Competition of America**
BGSU Continuing and Extended Education
14 College Park
Bowling Green, OH 43403-0200

509-963-1226; Fax: 509-963-1239
www.ihcamerica.org

Jeffrey Snedeker, President
Andrew Pelletier, Host

International competition specifically for the horn as a solo instrument.
450 Attendees
Frequency: July

19476 **International Horn Symposium**
Central Washington University Music Department
400 E University Way
Ellensburg, WA 98926-7458

509-963-1226; Fax: 509-963-1239
gross@music.ucsb.edu
www.hornsociety.org

Jeffrey Snedeker, President
Kristina Mascher-Turner, Vice President
Annie Bosler, Secretary/Treasurer
Heidi Vogel, Executive Director

Features renowned hornists, guest ensembles, recitals and master classes
Frequency: Annual

19477 **International Steel Guitar Convention**
College Music Society
312 East Pine Street
Missoula, MT 59802

406-721-9616; Fax: 406-721-9419
cms@music.org
www.music.org
Facebook, Twitter, YouTube, RSS

Dewitt Scott Sr, President
Mary Scott, Secretary

Sixty-five booths that provide entertainment from steel guitarists and various instruments including the bass guitar.
3M Attendees
Frequency: August

19478 **Mid-South Horn Conference**
Central Washington University Music Department
400 E University Way
Ellensburg, WA 98926-7458

509-963-1226; Fax: 509-963-1239
www.hornsociety.org

Jeffrey Snedeker, President
Ellen Campbell, Event Host
Heidi Vogel, Membership Coordinator

Features renowned hornists, guest ensembles, recitals and master classes
450 Attendees
Frequency: March

19479 **Midwest International Band & Orchestra Clinic**
Midwest International Band & Orchestra Clinic
111 E Touhy Ave
Suite 250
Des Plaines, IL 60018

847-424-4163; Fax: 773-321-1509
info@midwestclinic.org
www.midwestclinic.org

The purpose to the clinic is to raise the standards of music education, to develop new teaching techniqes, to examine, analyze, analyze and appraise literature dealing with music, demonstrations for the betterment of music education. 350 exhibitors, 565 booths, 30 concerts, and 50 instructional clinics.
12000 Attendees
Frequency: December

19480 **Music Teachers National Association Conference**
Music Teachers National Association
1 W. 4th Street
Suite 1550
Cincinnati, OH 45202

513-421-1420
888-512-5278; Fax: 513-421-2503
mtnanet@mtna.org
www.mtna.org

Gary L. Ingle, Executive Director & CEO
Brian Shepard, Chief Operating Officer
Scott McBride Smith, President
Madeleine Lovett, Marketing & PR

Atendees include independent music teachers, college faculty, students and parents from all over North America.
2500 Attendees
Frequency: Annual
Founded in 1876
Mailing list available for rent: 23000 names at $85 per M

19481 **NAMM: International Music Products Association**
5790 Armada Drive
Carlsbad, CA 92008-4608

760-438-8001
800-767-6266; Fax: 760-438-7327
tradeshow@namm.com
www.thenammshow.com

Joe Lamond, President

NAMM's trade shows are all about the experience. The experience of checking out the latest gear, of networking with other music product professionals, of attending free business-boosting classes. From the cook exhibits to the sizzling hot nightlife, music and music making always take center stage.
80000 Attendees
Frequency: January

19482 **NATS National Conference**
National Association of Teachers of Singing
9957 Moorings Drive
Suite 401
Jacksonville, FL 32257-2416

904-992-9101; Fax: 904-262-2587
info@nats.org
www.nats.org
Facebook, Twitter, LinkedIn

Allen Henderson, Executive Director
Deborah Guess, Director of Operations
Beth Bryan, Marketing & Communications Manager

Gathers professionals, scholars, and experts worldwide to share ideas and participate in lectures, workshops, and demonstrations aimed at promotingvocal arts and the teaching of singing.
Frequency: June/July
Founded in 1944

19483 **National Association for Music Education Conference**
1806 Robert Fulton Drive
Reston, VA 20191-4348

703-860-4000
800-336-3768; Fax: 703-860-1531
Facebook, Twitter, LinkedIn

John J Mahlmann, Executive Director
Margaret Jamborsky, Director Meetings/Conventions
Elizabeth Lasko, Director Public Relations/Marketing
Amanda Kidwell, Membership Director

To advance music education by encouraging the study and making of music by all.
5M Attendees
Frequency: April

19484 **National Association of Schools of Music Annual Meeting**
National Association of Schools of Music
11250 Roger Bacon Drive
Suite 21
Reston, VA 20190-5248

703-437-0700; Fax: 703-437-6312
info@arts-accredit.org
www.arts-accredit.org

Don Gibson, President
Mark Wait, VP
Mellasenah Y Morris, Treasurer
Frequency: November

19485 **National Opera Association Conference**
National Opera Association
PO Box 60869
Canyon, TX 79016

806-651-2857; Fax: 806-651-2958
rhansen@mail.wtamu.edu
www.noa.org
Facebook, RSS

Robert Hansen, Executive Director
Robert Thieme, Editor

Annual conference and exhibits of opera related equipment, supplies and services.
775 Attendees
Frequency: Annual
Founded in 1954

19486 **Northeast Horn Workshop**
Central Washington University Music Department
400 E University Way
Ellensburg, WA 98926-7458

509-963-1226; Fax: 509-963-1239
rdodsonw@mansfield.edu
www.hornsociety.org

Jeffrey Snedeker, President
Rebecca Dodson, Workshop Host
Heidi Vogel, Membership Coordinator

Features renowned hornists, guest ensembles, recitals and master classes
450 Attendees
Frequency: February

19487 **Opera America Conference**
Opera America

330 7th Avenue
16th Floor
New York, NY 10001-5248

212-796-8620; Fax: 212-796-8631
www.operaamerica.org
RSS

Session topics include identifying ways to harness the power of the best new technologies, how to reach current and prospective audiences, how to gain support from donors, and how to enrich the lives of children and adults who are now downloading podcasts, reading blogs, and designing their own multimedia communications.
275 Attendees
Frequency: April

19488 **Piano Technicians Guild Annual Convention**
Piano Technicians Guild
4444 Forest Avenue
Kansas City, KS 66106

913-432-9975; Fax: 913-432-9986
ptg@ptg.org
www.ptg.org

Barbara J Cassaday, Executive Director
Jim Coleman Jr RPT, President
Norman R Cantrell RPT, VP

Come for the learning: find a hands-on class for your skill level; pick from sessions covering every type of piano service; squeeze in a mini-tech; prepare for the RPT exams; see the latest and greatest piano products.
650 Attendees
Frequency: June

19489 **Sweet Adelines International Convention**
Sweet Adelines International
PO Box 470168
Tulsa, OK 74147-0168

918-622-1444
800-992-7464; Fax: 918-665-0894
www.sweetadelineintl.org

Kathy Hayes, Director Meetings/Corporate Service
Ruth Cameron, Meetings/Exhibits Coordinator
Jane Hanson, Marketing Coordinator
Connie Heyer, Membership Registrar
Kellye Kirchhoff, Director Communications

Heart-pounding chorus competitions, the rush and excitement of the quartet competition, education classes, shopping in the Harmony Bazaars and good times with old friends and new are all included in the International Convention.
8M Attendees
Frequency: October

19490 **The NAMM Show**
National Association of Music Merchants
5790 Armada Dr.
Carlsbad, CA 92008

760-438-8001
800-767-6266; Fax: 760-438-7327
www.namm.org
Facebook, Twitter, RSS

Cindy Sample, Director, Trade Show Operations

One-on-One meeting opportunities, welcome reception, keynote speakers, marketplace exhibits, live performances, forums, receptions and awards dinner
115M Attendees

19491 **Winter Music Conference**
3450 NE
12th Terrace
Fort Lauderdale, FL 33334

954-563-4444; Fax: 954-563-1599
info@wintermusicconference.com
www.wintermusicconference.com

Regarded as the singular networking event in the dance music industry, attracting professionals from over 60 different countries.

19492 **World of Bluegrass**
International Bluegrass Music Association
2 Music Circle South
Suite 100
Nashville, TN 37203

615-256-3222
888-438-4262; Fax: 615-256-0450
info@ibma.org
www.ibma.org

Dan Hays, Executive Director
Nancy Cardwell, Special Projects Coordinator
Jill Snider, Member/Convention Services

Build relationships with event producers, record label reps, agents and managers, broadcasters, association leaders, educators, the media, instrument builders, artists and composers. Educational and networking events like seminars, facilitated discussions and workshops are the primary focus of the conference. Browse through 100+ booths in the Exhibit Hall. You will hear bluegrass music around the clock for seven days. The Highpoint of the Conference is the International Bluegrass Music Awards.
1,800 Attendees
Frequency: October

Directories & Databases

19493 **American Music Center Directory**
American Music Center
90 John Street
Suite 312
New York, NY 10038

212-645-6949; Fax: 212-366-5265
library@newmusicusa.org
www.amc.net

Joanne Cossa, Executive Director
Lyn Liston, Director New Music Information
Peter Shavitz, Director Development
Lisa Taliano, Director Information Technology
Carlos Camposeco, Director Finance and Administration

Mailing lists include all United States members; all International and United States members; Composer Members in the United States; Members in the New York City Metropolitan area; and Members in the United States and Canada.

19494 **American Society of Composers, Authors and Publishers**
American Soc. of Composers, Authors & Publishers
1 Lincoln Plz
New York, NY 10023-7097

212-621-6027; Fax: 212-621-8453
www.ascap.com

Marilyn Bergman, President
Johnny Mandel, Writer Vice Chairman
Jay Morgenstern, Publisher Vice Chairman
Arnold Broido, Treasurer
Kathy Spanberger, Secretary

ASCAP created the dial-up ACE system as a useful tool for music professionals. An enhanced World Wide Web version of this database is now available. The database contains information on all compositions in the ASCAP repertory which have appeared in any of ASCAP's domestic surveys, including foreign compositions licensed by the ASCAP in the United States.
Frequency: Annual
Founded in 1993

19495 **AudArena International Guide**
Billboard Directories
PO Box 15158
North Hollywood, CA 91615

818-487-4582
800-562-2706

Arkady Fridman, Inside Sales Manager

Complete data on over 4,400 venues worldwide, including Amphitheaters, Arenas, Stadiums, Sports Facilities, Concert Halls and New Constructions. Also includes complete listings of companies offering services to the touring industry in the Facilty Buyer's Guide. The guide features contact names, phone and fax numbers, e-mail and web site addresses, market population, facility capacities and staging configurations, and rental fees and ticketing rights.
Cost: $99.00
325 Pages
Frequency: Annual

19496 **Billboard Subscriber File**
Edith Roman Associates
PO Box 1556
Pearl River, NY 10965

845-620-9000
800-223-2194; Fax: 845-620-9035
www.edithroman.com

Steve Roberts, President
Wayne Nagrowski, E-Mail List Info Contact

Directory listees include booking agencies and agents, clubs, music publishers, promoters, radio stations, record labels, sound and lighting services, retailers, video, venues, wholesalers, equipment and manufacturing and general services.
Frequency: Annual

19497 **Bluegrass Resource Directory**
International Bluegrass Music Association
2 Music Cir S
Suite 100
Nashville, TN 37203-4381

615-256-3222
888-438-4262; Fax: 615-256-0450
info@ibma.org
www.ibma.org

Member Directory can only be accessed by IBMA members.
Cost: $25.00
88 Pages
Frequency: Annual

19498 **Gospel Music Industry Directory**
Gospel Music Association
P.O Box 22697
Nashville, TN 37202

615-242-0303; Fax: 615-254-9755
info@gospelmusic.org
www.gospelmusic.org
Facebook, YouTube

John Styll, President
Scott Brickell, Director
Ed Harper, Director

Formerly called the Networking Guide, the GMA Music Industry Directory is a comprehensive listing of Christian and Gospel music artists, managers, booking agents, record companies, publishing companies and more. Active GMA Professional members get a copy of the directory free. Associate and Student GMA members can purchase one for a discounted rate.

19499 **Grey House Performing Arts Directory**
Grey House Publishing
4919 Route 22
PO Box 56
Amenia, NY 12501

518-789-8700
800-562-2139; Fax: 845-373-6390
books@greyhouse.com
www.greyhouse.com
Facebook, Twitter

Leslie Mackenzie, Publisher
Richard Gottlieb, Editor

The most comprehensive resource covering the Performing Arts. This directory provides current information on over 8,500 Dance Companies, Instrumental Music Programs, Opera Companies, Choral Groups, Theater Companies, Performing Arts Series, Performing Arts Facilities and Artist Management Groups.
Cost: $185.00
1200 Pages
Frequency: Annual
ISBN: 1-592373-76-3
Founded in 1981

19500 **Grey House Performing Arts Directory - Online Database**
Grey House Publishing
4919 Route 22
PO Box 56
Amenia, NY 12501-0556

518-789-8700
800-562-2139; Fax: 518-789-0556
gold@greyhouse.com
gold.greyhouse.com
Facebook, Twitter

Leslie Mackenzie, Publisher
Richard Gottlieb, Editor

The Grey House Performing Arts Directory - Online Database provides immediate access to dance companies, orchestras, opera companies, choral groups, theater companies, series, festivals and perfoming arts facilities across the country, or in their region, state, or in your own backyard. It offers unequaled coverage of the Performing Arts - over 8,500 listings - of the major performance organization, facilities, and information resources.
Frequency: Annual
Founded in 1981

19501 **International Buyers Guide**
Billboard Directories
PO Box 15158
North Hollywood, CA 91615

818-487-4582
800-562-2706

Arkady Fridman, Inside Sales Manager

A must-have resource for doing business in the music industry, covers every aspect of the recording business worldwide. The latest edition includes contact information on: record labels, video and digital music companies, distributors and importers/exporters; music publishers and rights organizations - blank media manufacturers, pressing plants and services; manufacturers of jewel boxes and other packaging and equipment services; and suppliers of store fixtures, security and accessories.
Cost: $179.00
340 Pages
Frequency: Annual

19502 **International Talent and Touring Guide**
Billboard Directories
PO Box 15158
North Hollywood, CA 91615

818-487-4582
800-562-2706

Arkady Fridman, Inside Sales Manager

A reference guide for anyone who books, promotes or manages talent. Features over 30,000 listings, including 12,900 artists, managers and agents worldwide, including the USA and Canada. The guide includes contact names, phone and fax numbers, e-mail and website addresses, artists and their record labels, managers and agents, tour services and merchandise, sound and lighting vendors, equipment and instrument rentals, limo rentals, security services, plus national promoters and their key personnel
Cost: $139.00
242 Pages
Frequency: Annual

19503 **Keyboard Teachers Association International**
Dr. Albert DeVito
361 Pin Oak Lane
Westbury, NY 11590-1941

516-333-3236; Fax: 516-997-9531

Albert DeVito, President

Music teachers and those related to keeping members updated as to activity going on in music world.
Frequency: Quarterly
Founded in 1963

19504 **MLA Membership Handbook**
Music Library Association
8551 Research Way
Suite 180
Middleton, WI 53562

608-836-5825; Fax: 608-831-8200
www.musiclibraryassoc.org

Philip Vandermeer, President

A mailing list that is available for rental in a variety of formats.
Cost: $25.00
Founded in 1931

19505 **Music Library Association Membership Directory**
Music Library Association
8551 Research Way
Suite 180
Middleton, WI 53562

608-836-5825; Fax: 608-831-8200
mla@areditions.com
www.musiclibraryassoc.org

Jerry L. McBride, President

The MLA mailing list is available for rental in a variety of formats. Members include music librarians, librarians who work with music as part of their responsibilities, composers and music scholars, and others interested in the program of the association.

19506 **Musical America Directory**
Musical America
PO Box 1330
Highstown, NJ 08520

609-448- 334
800-221-5488; Fax: 609-371-7879
info@musicalamerica.com
www.musicalamerica.com
Facebook, Twitter, YouTube

Joyce Wasserman, Subscription Information
Bob Hudoba, Contact

Provides thousands of names, phone numbers, addresses, and Email and Web site addresses for manangers, orchestras, opera companies, festivals, presenters, venues and more around the world.
Cost: $125.00
Mailing list available for rent

19507 **Musician's Guide**
Billboard Directories
PO Box 15158
North Hollywood, CA 91615

818-487-4582
800-562-2706

Arkady Fridman, Inside Sales Manager

Everything the working musician needs to book gigs, contact record labels, find a manager, and locate tour services. The latest edition includes A & R Directory, Music Business Services, and City by City listings.
Cost: $15.95
170 Pages
Frequency: Annual

19508 **National Opera Association Membership Directory**
PO Box 60869
Canyon, TX 79016-0869

806-651-2857; Fax: 806-651-2958
rhansen@mail.wtamu.edu
www.noa.org
Facebook, RSS

Robert Hansen, Executive Director
JoElyn Wakefield Wright, President
Edith Kirkpatrick Vrenios, VP Resources
Philip Hageman, Treasurer
Carol Notestine, Recording Secretary

Members of the National Opera Association are entitled to receive the NOA Freelance Artists and Production Resources databases, the NOA membership directory, and access to the NOA e-mail listserve.
Frequency: Annual
Mailing list available for rent

19509 **Orion Blue Book: Guitars and Musical Instruments**
Orion Research Corporation
14555 N Scottsdale Rd
Suite 330
Scottsdale, AZ 85254-3487

480-951-1114; Fax: 480-951-1117
sales@UsedPrice.com
www.orionbluebook.com

Roger Rohrs, Owner

77,834 products listed; products listed from 1970s to present; over 450 manufacturers listed; 2 volumes - hardbound or on CD-ROM. Lists musical instruments from Accordians to Xylophones
Cost: $195.00
Frequency: Annual
Founded in 1981

19510 **Orion Blue Book: Professional Sound**
Orion Research Corporation
14555 N Scottsdale Rd
Suite 330
Scottsdale, AZ 85254-3487

480-951-1114
800-844-0759; Fax: 480-951-1117
sales@UsedPrice.com
www.orionbluebook.com

Roger Rohrs, Owner

Features over 48,964 products from the 1950's to present. Over 350 manufacturers listed. Comes in hardbound or on CD-ROM. Lists products from Cartridge Players to Wireless Microphone Systems.
Cost: $150.00
970 Pages
Frequency: Annual
Founded in 1973

19511 **Orion Blue Book: Vintage Guitar**
Orion Research Corporation
14555 N Scottsdale Rd
Suite 330
Scottsdale, AZ 85254-3487
480-951-1114
800-844-0759; Fax: 480-951-1117
sales@UsedPrice.com
www.orionbluebook.com
Roger Rohrs, Owner
Features more than 11,413 products from the 1800's to present. Over 30 manufacturers listed. Comes in hardbound or CD-ROM, Lists products from Banjos to Ukuleles.
Cost: $50.00
Frequency: Quarterly
Founded in 1990

19512 **Record Retailing Directory**
Billboard Directories
PO Box 15158
North Hollywood, CA 91615
818-487-4582
800-562-2706
Arkady Fridman, Inside Sales Manager
Over 5,500 listings covering the entire retailing community. Provides access to major chain headquarters and local outlets; complete coverage of independent retailers; hard-to-find audiobook retailers; and the booming world of online record retailing, plus store genre or specialization; executives, owners, buyers and planners; address, phone, fax, email and web.
Cost: $215.00
Frequency: Annual

19513 **Salem Press Online Platform**
Grey House Publishing
4919 Route 22
PO Box 56
Amenia, NY 12501
800-221-1592; Fax: 201-968-0511
csr@salempress.com
online.salempress.com
The new Salem Press platform houses more than 500 titles including all of Salem's Health, Literature, History and Science titles in addition to select titles from the Grey House Publishing and H.W. Wilson product lines. Online access is free with each print purchase and includes an unlimited number of simultaneous users and remote access.

19514 **Source Directory of Books, Records and Tapes**
Sutton's Super Marketplace
153 Sutton Lane
Fordsville, KY 42343
270-276-9880
Jerry Sutton, Owner/Founder
Publishers, recording studios, wholesalers, distributors, manifacturers and importers. Approximatley 450 records. Changes daily as updated.
Cost: $55.20

19515 **Source Directory of Musical Instruments**
Sutton's Super Marketplace
153 Sutton Lane
Fordsville, KY 42343
270-276-9880
Jerry Sutton, Owner/Founder
Listings in directory include names, addresses, phone and fax numbers, and product descriptions from wholesale distributors, Importers, Manufacturers, Close-out houses and Liquidators. Updated daily.
Cost: $55.20

Industry Web Sites

19516 **http://gold.greyhouse.com**
G.O.L.D Grey House OnLine Databases
Grey House Publishing's online database platform, GOLD, offers Quick Search, Keyword Search and Expert Search for most business sectors including music and performance markets. The GOLD platform makes finding the information you need quick and easy - whether you're a novice searcher or an experienced database user. All of Grey House's directory products are available for subscription on the GOLD platform.

19517 **musicbiz.org**
The Music Business Association
Membership organization serving those working in the music industry through networking events, research publications and promotional opportunities. Membership consists of music retailers, streaming services, wholesalers, major and independent labels and distributors, startups, artists, songwriters, publishers and more.

19518 **www.acmcountry.com**
Academy of Country Music
Involved in numerous events and activities promoting country music. Presents annual awards.

19519 **www.afm.org**
American Federation of Musicians of the United
States and Canada
Union representing over 100,000 professional musicians, performing in all genres of music.

19520 **www.afvbm.org**
American Federation of Violin and Bow Makers
Strives to elevate professional standards of craftmanship and ethical conduct among members. Helps members develop technical skills and knowledge.Research and study organization.

19521 **www.agohq.org**
American Guild of Organists
Promotes the organ in its historic and evolving roles and provides a forum for mutual support, inspiration, education and certification.

19522 **www.ascap.com**
American Society of Composers Authors & Publishers
Membership association of more than 260,000 US composers, song writers, lyricists and music publishers.

19523 **www.asmac.org**
American Society of Music Arrangers and Composers
Professional society for arrangers, composers, orchestrators, and musicians. Monthly meetings with great speakers from the music industry.

19524 **www.billboard.com**
The ultimate music industry research tool and information source. The Member Service database is state-of-the-art electronic information service, enabling users to efficiently access information from a variety of music industry databases via the World Wide Web.

19525 **www.chorusamerica.org**
Chorus America
National service for orchestral choruses, independent choruses and professional choruses.

19526 **www.clarinet.org**
International Clarinet Association
Seeks to focus attention on the importance of the clarinet and to foster communication of the fellowship between clarinetists.

19527 **www.cmaworld.com**
Country Music Association
Promotes and publicizes country music.

19528 **www.flmusiced.org**
Florida Music Educators Association
Florida Music Educators Association and Florida School Music Association.

19529 **www.folkharpsociety.org**
International Society of Folk Harpers and Craftsmen
Conducts technical and artistic programs and promotes craft exchange.

19530 **www.gospelmusic.org**
Gospel Music Association
Dedicated to providing leadership, direction and unity for all facets of the gospel music industry. Through education, communication, information, promotion and recognition, the GMA is striving to help those involved in gospel music.

19531 **www.greyhouse.com**
Grey House Publishing
Authoritative reference directories for most business sectors including music and performance markets. Users can search the online databases with varied search criteria allowing for custom searches by product category, geographic area, sales volume, keyword, subject and more. Full Grey House catalog and online ordering also available.

19532 **www.guitarfoundation.org**
Guitar Foundation of America
Supports the serious studies of the guitar.

19533 **www.harpsociety.org**
American Harp Society
Improves the quality of the instrument and performance.

19534 **www.hornsociety.org**
International Horn Society
A national organization that focuses on music industry news and information.

19535 **www.iaekm.org**
International Association of Electronic Keyboard
Manufacturers
Global manufacturers of electronic kayboards and affiliated software and publications.

19536 **www.ibma.org**
World of Bluegrass
IBMA: working together for high standards of professionalism, a greater appreciation for our music, and the success of the world-wide bluegrass community.

19537 **www.imeamusic.org**
Indiana Music Educators Association
Supports and advances music education in Indiana.

19538 **www.internationalpolka.com**
International Polka Association
Educational organization concerned with the preservation and advancement of polka music. Operates the Polka Music Hall of Fame and Museum, and presents the International Polka

Fesitval every year during the complete first weekend of August.

19539 **www.metguild.org**
Metropolitan Opera Guild
Seeks to promote greater understanding and interest in opera.

19540 **www.mpa.org**
Music Publishers Association of the United States
Encourages understanding of the copyright laws and works to protect musical works against infringements and piracy.

19541 **www.mtna.org**
Music Teachers National Association
This is a nonprofit organization of independent and collegiate music teachers committed to furthering the art of music through teaching, performance, composition and scholarly research.

19542 **www.music.org**
College Music Society
The Society is a national service organization for college conservatory and university music teachers.

19543 **www.musicalartists.org**
American Guild of Musical Artists
Exclusive bargaining agent for all concert musical artists.

19544 **www.musicdistributors.org**
Music Distributor Association
A trade association of 160 manufactures, importers, wholesalers of musical instruments and accessories, domestic and international selling to the trade only

19545 **www.musiclibraryassoc.org**
Music Library Association
Promotes growth and establishment in the use of music libraries, musical instruments and musical literature.

19546 **www.nacwpi.org**
National Association of College Wind and Percussion Instructors
Teachers of wind and percussion instruments in American colleges and universities.

19547 **www.napbirt.org**
National Association of Professional Band Instrument Repair Technicians
Promotes technical integrity in the craft. Surveys tools and procedures to improve work quality. Makes available emergency repair of band instruments. Provides placement services.

19548 **www.nats.org**
National Association of Teachers of Singing
Promotes and encourages the highest standards of vocal education and research at all levels, both for the enrichment of the general public and for the professional advancement of the talented.

19549 **www.nbea.com**
National Ballroom and Entertainment Association
Provides exchange for owners and operators of ballrooms.

19550 **www.noa.org**
National Opera Association
To advance the appreciation, composition and production of opera.

19551 **www.npm.org**
National Association of Pastoral Musicians
Membership organization primarily composed of musicians, musician-liturgist, clergy, and other leaders of prayer devoted to serving the life and mission of the Church through fosterering the art of musical liturgy in Roman Catholic worshiping communities in the United States.

19552 **www.nyssma.org**
New York State School Music Association
Advocates and improves the education in music of all people in New York State.

19553 **www.pas.org**
Percussive Arts Society
Promotes drums and percussion through a viable network of performers, teachers, students, enthusiasts and sustaining members. Offers publications, a worldwide network of the World Percussion Network, the Percussive Arts Society International Headquarters/Museum and the annual Percussive Arts Society International Convention.

19554 **www.pianoguild.com**
International Piano Guild
A division of the American College of Musicians Professional society of piano teachers and music faculty members. Sponsers national examinations.

19555 **www.printmusic.org**
Retail Print Music Dealers Association
The voice of the print music industry.

19556 **www.ptg.org**
Piano Technicians Guild
Conducts technical institutes at conventions and seminars. Promotes public education in piano care. Bestows awards. Publishes monthly technical journal by subscriptions.

19557 **www.spars.com**
Society of Professional Audio Recording Services
Members are individuals, companies and studios connected with the professional recording industry.

19558 **www.symphony.org**
American Symphony Orchestra League
The national nonprofit service and educational organization dedicated to strengthening symphony and chamber orchestras. It provides artistic, organizational and financial leadership and service to orchestral conductors, managers, volunteers and staff.

19559 **www.tmea.org**
Texas Music Educators Association
Promoting excellence in music education.

Associations

19560 AAEI and FTA Western Regional Conference
AAEI/FTA
Torrance, CA 90501
info@foreigntradeassociation.com
www.foreigntradeassociation.com
Facebook, Twitter, LinkedIn
Tom Gould, President
Organization promotes growth of international trade in Southern California.

19561 Alabama International Trade Center
Alabama International Trade Center
University of Alabama
Tuscaloosa, AL
205-348-7621
aitc@ua.edu
aitc.ua.edu
Facebook
Brian K. Davis, Director
Partnership between University of Alabama and U.S. Small Business Administration's export financing programs.
Founded in 1979

19562 American - Russian Business Council
800-428-9308
www.russiancouncil.org
Facebook, Twitter, LinkedIn
The Council is dedicated to promoting trade and investment between the two countries.
Founded in 1994

19563 American Association of Exporters and Impo rters (AAEI)
1717 K Street NW
Suite 1120
Washington, DC 20006
202-857-8009; Fax: 202-857-7843
www.aaei.org
Facebook, Twitter, LinkedIn
Marianne Rowden, President & CEO
Trade organization advocates on behalf of U.S. companies on trade policy issues.

19564 American Australian Association
50 Broadway
New York, NY 10004
212-338-6860; Fax: 212-338-6864
info@aaanyc.org
www.americanaustralian.org
Facebook, Twitter, Pinterest
John Berry, President
The Association is dedicated to encouraging corporate, educational, economic and cultural ties between Australia and the United States.
Founded in 1948

19565 American Foreign Service Association
2101 E St Nw
Washington, DC 20037-2990
202-338-4045; Fax: 202-338-6820
member@afsa.org
www.afsa.org
Facebook, Twitter, Youtube, RSS
Hon. Barbara Stephenson, President
Hon. Charles A Ford, Treasurer
William Haugh, Secretary
Steve Morrison, FCS Vice President
Mark Petry, FAS Vice President
Missions are to enhance the effectiveness of the Foreign Service, to protect the professional interests of its members, to ensure the maintenance of high professional standards for both career diplomats and political appointeese, and to promote understanding of the critical role of the Foreign service in promoting America's national security and economic prosperity.
11M Members
Founded in 1924

19566 Association of Fish and Wildlife Agencies
1100 First Street, NE
Suite 825
Washington, DC 20002
202-838-3474; Fax: 202-350-9869
info@fishwildlife.org
www.fishwildlife.org
Facebook, Twitter, Blogger
Ron Regan, Executive Director
Carol Bambery, Association Counsel
Kathy Boydston, Wildlife & Energy Liasion
John Bloom, Accounting Manager
Arpita Choudhury, Science & Research Liasion
The organization that represents all of North America's fish and wildlife agencies that promotes sound management and conservation, and speaks with a unified voice on important fish and wildlife issues.
Founded in 1902

19567 Brazil - U.S. Business Council
1615 H Street NW
Washington, DC 20062
202-463-5729
brazilcouncil@uschamber.com
www.brazilcouncil.org
Facebook, Twitter, LinkedIn
Cassia Carvalho, Executive Director
The Council advocates for stronger economic and commercial ties between the two countries.

19568 Bureau of Intelligence and Research (INR)
Department of State
Washington, DC
Home Page: www.state.gov/s/inr
Daniel B. Smith, Asst. Secy. of State
Intelligence bureau within U.S. Department of State supports U.S. diplomats.
Founded in 1945

19569 Business Council for International Underst anding (BCIU)
1501 Broadway
Suite 2300
New York, NY 10036
212-490-0460; Fax: 212-697-8526
www.bciu.org
Twitter, LinkedIn
Peter Tichansky, President & CEO
U.S. organization supports businesses pursuing global growth opportunities by facilitating relationships between business and government leaders worldwide.
200 Members

19570 Center for Domestic Preparedness
Federal Emergency Management Agency
61 Responder Dr.
Anniston, AL 36205
866-213-9553
Facebook, Twitter, YouTube
Mike King, Superintendent
Training center for emergency responders.
Founded in 1998

19571 Central Intelligence Agency (CIA)
George Bush Center for Intelligence
Langley, VA
703-482-0623; Fax: 571-204-3800
cia.gov
Facebook, Twitter, flickr, YouTube
John O. Brennan, Director
Civilian foreign intelligence service of the U.S. government.
Founded in 1947

19572 Citizens for Global Solutions
420 7th St SE
Washington, DC 20003-2707
202-546-3950; Fax: 202-546-3749
info@globalsolutions.org
www.globalsolutions.org
Facebook, Twitter, YouTube
Marvin Perry, CEO
Jordan Bankhead, MS, Chairman
Scott Paul,, Vice-Chair
Shirley Lee Davis, Secretary
Evan Freund, Treasurer
Nonprofit, tax deductible membership organization of 50 chapters and groups throughout the United States. We work to educate policy-makers and the American public on issues of global governance, international law and grassroots activism.
11000 Members
Founded in 1978

19573 Coast Guard Intelligence (CGI)
U.S. Coast Guard
2703 Martin Luther King Jr. Ave. SE
Washington, DC 20593-7000
Home Page: www.uscg.mil
RAdm Steven J. Andersen, Asst. Commandant
Military intelligence branch of U.S. Coast Guard and component of Central Security Service (CSS).
Founded in 1915

19574 Danish American Chamber of Commerce New Yo rk
One Dag Hammarskjold Plaza
885 Second Ave., 18th Floor
New York, NY 10017-2201
646-790-7169
daccny@daccny.com
www.daccny.com
Facebook, Twitter
Anne-Mette Andersen, Chairperson
Promotes business between Denmark and the U.S. by providing information and networking opportunities to members.

19575 Defense Intelligence Agency (DIA)
Department of Defense
Joint Base Anacostia-Bolling
Washington, DC 20340-5100
Home Page: www.dia.mil
LG Vincent R. Stewart, Director
Intelligence service specializing in foreign governments and non-state actors.
Founded in 1961

19576 Florida Foreign Trade Association
2335 NW 107 Ave.
Suite 2M30
Doral, FL 33172
305-471-0737
ffta.com
Facebook, Twitter, LinkedIn, Instagram
Rafael Puga, President

FFTA is a not-for-profit promoting information exchange expanded participation in foreign trade.
Founded in 1985

19577 **Foreign Trade Association (FTA)**
6216 E Pacific Coast Hwy.
Suite 407
Long Beach, CA 90803

888-223-6459; Fax: 310-220-4474
info@foreigntradeassociation.com
www.foreigntradeassociation.com
Facebook, Twitter, LinkedIn

Tom Gould, President

Organization promotes growth of international trade in Southern California.

19578 **Intelligence & National Security Alliance**
Arlington, VA 22203

703-224-4672
info@insaonline.org
www.insaonline.org
Facebook, Twitter, LinkedIn, YouTube, Instagram

Suzanne Wilson Heckenberg, President
Larry Hanauer, VP for Policy
Jeff Lavine, VP for Administration/Management
Toya Cribbs, Director, Meetings/Events
Lauren Parker, Membership Manager

Public, private and academic leaders collaborate on intelligence and national security issues.
160 Members

19579 **Intelligence Branch (IB)**
Federal Bureau of Investigation
Washington, DC

Home Page: www.fbi.gov

Eric Velez-Villar, Asst. Dir. for Intelligence Branch

FBI division responsible for intelligence functions including national security and homeland security.
Founded in 2005

19580 **Intelligence and National Security Summit**
Washington, DC

Home Page: events.jspargo.com/inss16

Federal agency leaders and policymakers discuss U.S. intelligence priorities, challenges and opportunities.
3000 Members

19581 **International Association of Official Human Rights Agencies**
444 N Capitol Street NW
Suite 536
Washington, DC 20001

202-624-5410; Fax: 202-624-8185
iaohra@sso.org
www.iaohra.org

Jean Kelleher Niebauer, President
Alisa Warren, 2nd Vice President
Paula Haley, Secretary
Merrill Smith, Jr., Treasurer
Robin S. Toma, First Vice-President

Private non-profit corporation consisting of human rights agencies in the US and Canada. Provides opportunities and forums for the exchange of ideas and information among human rights advocates. Also provides training opportunities for members and other concerned groups and organizations.
200 Members
Founded in 1968

19582 **International City/County Management Association (ICMA)**
777 North Capitol St. NE
Suite 500
Washington, DC 20002-4201

202-289-4262
800-745-8780; Fax: 202-962-3500
icma.org
Facebook, Twitter, LinkedIn, YouTube, Pinterest, Flickr

Robert J. O'Neill, Executive Director

A worldwide organization for the advancement of professional local government.
Founded in 1914

19583 **International Economic Development Council**
734 15th Street NW
Suite 900
Washington, DC 20005

202-223-7800; Fax: 202-223-4745
www.iedconline.org/
Facebook, Twitter, LinkedIn

Dyan Lingle Brasington, CEc, Chair
Jeff Finkle, CEcD, President/CEO
Katelyn Palomo, Executive Assistant
Swati Ghosh, Director, Research
Carrie Mulcaire, Director, Federal Grants

Nonprofit membership organization dedicated to helping economic developmers do their job more effectively and raising the profile of the profession. Members create more high-quality jobs, develop more vibrant communities, and generally improve the quality of life in their regions.
1.8M Members
Founded in 1967

19584 **International Trade Administration (ITA)**
Department of Commerce
1401 Constitution Ave. NW
Washington, DC 20230

Home Page: www.trade.gov
Facebook, Twitter, LinkedIn

Letitia A. Long, Chair
Chuck Alsup, President

Promoting fair trade and an improved global business environment.
160 Members

19585 **International Trade Club of Chicago (ITCC)**
134 North LaSalle Street
Suite 1300
Chicago, IL 60602

312-423-5250
contact@itcc.org
www.itcc.org
Twitter, LinkedIn

Fabrice Bonvoisin, President

Fosters expansion of international trade.
Founded in 1919

19586 **International Trade Commission (USITC)**
500 E Street SW
Washington, DC 20436

202-205-2000
www.usitc.gov

Rhonda K. Schmidtlein, Chair

Quasi-judicial Federal agency investigates trade matters, such as dumping, in order to facilitate a rules-based international trading system.

19587 **Interstate Council on Water Policy**
505 North Ivy Street
Arlington, VA 22220-1707

703-243-7383; Fax: 301-984-5841
www.icwp.org
Facebook, Twitter

Dru Buntin, 2nd Vice-Chairman
Ryan Mueller, Executive Director
Andrew Dehoff, Secretary & Treasurer
Jerry Schulte, 1st Vice Chairman

The ICWP is the national organization of state and regional water resources management agencies. It provides a means for members to exchange information, ideas and experience to work with federal agencies which share water management responsibilities.
70 Members
Founded in 1959

19588 **Interstate Oil and Gas Compact Commission**
900 NE 23rd Street
Oklahoma City, OK 73105

405-525-3556
800-822-4015; Fax: 405-525-3592
communications@iogcc.ok.gov
www.iogcc.state.ok.us

Mike Smith, Executive Director
Gerry Baker, Associate Executive Director
Hannah Barton, Member Services Coordinator
Amy Childers, Federal Projects Manager
Carol Booth, CommunicationsÿManager

A multi-state government agency that champions the conservation and efficient recovery of domestic oil and natural gas resources.
700 Members
Founded in 1935

19589 **Marine Corps Intelligence Activity (MCIA)**
U.S. Marine Corps
Quantico, VA

Home Page:
www.hqmc.marines.mil/intelligence/Units/MCIA
Facebook, Twitter, YouTube, flickr, Instagram

BGen Michael S. Groen, Director

Intelligence service to the Marine Corps and U.S. Intelligence Community.
Founded in 1987

19590 **National Association of Clean Air Agencies**
444 N Capitol Street NW
Suite 307
Washington, DC 20001-1506

202-624-7864; Fax: 202-624-7863
4cleanair@4cleanair.org
www.4cleanair.org

Stu A Clark, Co-President
Merlyn Hough, Co-President
Bill Becker, Executive Director
Nancy Kruger, Deputy Director
Dave Klemp, Co-Vice President

Represents state and local air pollution control officers from over 150 major metropolitan areas and 53 states and territories.

19591 **National Association of Export Companies (NEXCO)**
PO Box 3949, Grand Central Station
New York, NY 10163

646-330-5168
director@nexco.org
www.nexco.org

Barney Lehrer, Board President

Trade association serving the international business community in New York City.
4000 Members
Founded in 1963

19592 **National Association of Foreign-Trade Zone s**
National Press Building 529
14th Street NW, Suite 1071
Washington, DC 20045

202-331-1950; Fax: 202-331-1994
www.naftz.org
Facebook, Twitter, LinkedIn

Erik Autor, President

Promoter of U.S. Foreign-Trade Zones Program and its role in the changing environment of international trade.

19593 **National Emergency Management Association**
2760 Research Park Drive
Lexington, KY 40578

859-244-8000; Fax: 859-244-8239
nemaadmin@csg.org
www.nemaweb.org
Facebook

Bryan Koon, President
Wendy Smith-Reeve, Vice President
Trina R. Sheets, NEMA Executive Director
Beverly Bell, Senior Policy Analyst
Karen Cobuluis, Meeting & Marketing Coordinator

A nonpartisan, nonprofit association dedicated to enhancing public safety by improving the nation's ability to prepare for, respond to, and recover from all emergencies, disasters, and threats to our nation's security. Provides national leadership and expertise in comprehensive emergency management, serves as a vital emergency management information and assistance resource, and advances continuous improvement in emergency management.
263 Members
Founded in 1970

19594 **National Foreign Trade Council**
1625 K Street NW
Suite 200
Washington, DC 20006

202-887-0278; Fax: 202-452-8160
nftcinformation@nftc.org
www.nftc.org

Rufus H. Yerxa, President

The Council advocates for interests of American business in the world economy.

19595 **National Geospatial-Intelligence Agency (N GA)**
7500 GEOINT Dr.
Springfield, VA 22150

571-557-5400
www.nga.mil
Facebook, Twitter, LinkedIn, YouTube

Robert Cardillo, Director
Susan Gordon, Deputy Director
Ed Mornston, Chief of Staff

Geospatial intelligence and combat support.
Founded in 1996

19596 **National Reconnaissance Office (NRO)**
14675 Lee Rd.
Chantilly, VA 20151-1715

703-808-5050; Fax: 703-808-1171
publicaffairs@nro.mil
www.nro.gov
Facebook, Twitter, YouTube

Betty Sapp, Director

One of the big five intelligence agencies, NRO provides satellite, signals, imagery and measurement intelligence to the U.S. government.
Founded in 1961

19597 **National Security Agency (NSA)**
9800 Savage Rd.
Suite 6272
Ft. George G. Meade, MD 20755-6000

301-688-6524
www.nsa.gov

Adm Michael S. Rogers, Director

U.S. government organization responsible for global signals intelligence.

19598 **North American Securities Administrators Association, Inc.**
750 First Street NE
Suite 1140
Washington, DC 20002-8034

202-737-0900; Fax: 202-783-3571
www.nasaa.org
Facebook, RSS

Judith Shaw, President
Russ Iuculano, Executive Director
John H. Lynch, Deputy Executive Director
Joseph Brady, General Counsel
Michael Canning, Director of Policy

NASAA is the international organization representing securities administrators from all 50 states, the District of Columbia, Canada, Mexico and Puerto Rico, and is responsible for investor protection and education. NASAA recommends national policies in the securities industry and provides model legislation for state securities agencies to adopt affecting the regulation of broker/dealers and investment advisers. Consumers can contact NASAA to get phone numbers of state securities regulators.
66 Members
Founded in 1919

19599 **Office of Intelligence and Analysis (I&A)**
Department of Homeland Security
DHS Nebraska Ave. Complex
Washington, DC

Home Page:
www.dhs.gov/office-intelligence-and-analysis

Gen Frank Taylor, Under Secretary of Homeland Secur.

The Office tracks terrorists and terrorist networks for Homeland Security.
Founded in 2007

19600 **Office of Intelligence and Counterintellig ence (OICI)**
Department of Energy
1000 Independence Ave. SW
Washington, DC 20585

202-586-5000
www.energy.gov

Steven K. Black, Director

Intelligence gathering for the U.S. Department of Energy.
Founded in 1977

19601 **Office of National Security Intelligence (ONSI)**
Drug Enforcement Administration
Washington, DC

Home Page: www.dea.gov

Doug Poole, Chief of Intelligence
Founded in 2006

19602 **Office of Naval Intelligence (ONI)**
U.S. Navy
4251 Suitland Rd.
Washington, DC 20395-5720

301-669-3001
www.oni.navy.mil
Facebook

RAdm Robert D. Sharp, Commander

Military intelligence agency of the U.S. Navy.
Founded in 1882

19603 **Office of Terrorism and Financial Intellig ence (TFI)**
Department of the Treasury
Washington, DC

Home Page: www.treasury.gov

Leslie Ireland, Asst. Secy. for Intelligence

Treasury agency combats misuse of financial system by national security threats.
Founded in 2004

19604 **Office of the U.S. Trade Representative (U STR)**
600 17th Street NW
Washington, DC 20508

Home Page: ustr.gov

Michael Froman, United States Trade Representative

The USTR is a Cabinet-level position providing leadership on trade policy and negotiations.

19605 **Organization of Women in International Tra de (OWIT)**
OWIT International
c/o 1110 Vermont Ave. NW, Suite 715
Washington, DC 20005

info@owit.org
www.owit.org
Facebook, Twitter, LinkedIn, YouTube

Andrea Ewart, President

Professional organization supporting the advancement of women in international trade.
2000 Members
Founded in 1989

19606 **The Agribusiness Council**
P.O. Box 5565
Washington, DC 20016

202-296-4563; Fax: 202-244-4694
info@agribusinesscouncil.org
www.agribusinesscouncil.org

Nicholas E. Hollis, President/CEO
Organization dedicated to strengthening US agro-industrial competitiveness through programs which highlight international trade and development potentials as well as broad issues which encompass several individual agribusiness sectors and require a food systems approach.
Founded in 1967

19607 **The American Chamber of Commerce in New Ze aland**
P.O. Box 106002
Auckland Central
Auckland, NZ 1143

64-9-309-9140; Fax: 64-9-309-1090
amcham@amcham.co.nz
www.amcham.co.nz
Twitter, LinkedIn

Mike Hearn, Executive Director

Business networking organization that exists to promote two-way trade, investment, tourism and education between the United States and New Zealand.
500 Members
Founded in 1965

19608 The Association of Women in International Trade
c/o Affinity Strategies
100 M Street SE, Suite 600
Washington, DC 20003

202-684-3040
info@wiit.org
wiit.org
Facebook, Twitter, LinkedIn

Evelyn Suarez, President

The Association promotes the professional development of women in international trade and business.

19609 The Center for Climate & Security
1025 Connecticut Ave. NW
Suite 1000
Washington, DC 20036

202-246-8612
climateandsecurity.org
Facebook, Twitter, LinkedIn

Francesco Femia, Co-Founder & President
Caitlin Werrell, Co-Founder & President

Resource hub in the climate and security field.

19610 The International Trade Association of Gre ater Chicago (ITA/GC)
4610 N Kenton Ave.
Chicago, IL 60630

Home Page: www.itagc.org
Facebook, Twitter, LinkedIn

Arthur C. O'Meara, President

Association of manufacturers and service providers promotes international business.
500 Members
Founded in 1985

19611 Twenty-Fifth Air Force (25 AF)
U.S. Air Force
Joint Base San Antonio
Lackland, TX

Home Page: www.25af.af.mil
Facebook, Twitter

MG Bradford Shwedo, Commander

Formerly Air Force Intelligence, Surveillance and Reconnaissance Agency.
Founded in 1948

19612 US Army Intelligence and Security Command (INSCOM)
U.S. Army
Ft. Belvoir, VA

Home Page: www.army.mil/inscom
Facebook, Twitter

MG Christopher Ballard, Commander

Intelligence, security and information operations for U.S. Army and part of Central Security Service (CSS) within NSA.
Founded in 1977

19613 United States Council for International Bu siness
1212 Avenue of the Americas
New York, NY 10036

212-354-4480; Fax: 212-575-0327
www.uscib.org
Facebook, Twitter, LinkedIn, YouTube

Peter M. Robinson, President & CEO

The Council promotes American business views on international policy issues, works to harmonize international trade and commercial practices and helps shape the international regulatory environment.
300 Members
Founded in 1945

19614 Washington International Trade Association
1300 Pennsylvania Ave. NW
Suite G-329
Washington, DC 20004

202-312-1600; Fax: 202-312-1601
wita@wita.org
wita.org
Facebook, Twitter, LinkedIn, YouTube

Ken Levinson, Executive Director

Non-partisan forum for discussion of international trade and economic issues.
Founded in 1982

19615 World Trade Organization (WTO)
Geneva, Switzerland

Home Page: www.wto.org

Roberto Azevedo, Director-General

Forum for governments to negotiate trade agreements and settle trade disputes.
164 Members
Founded in 1995

Newsletters

19616 AmCham NZ Monthly Newsletter
American Chamber of Commerce in New Zealand
P.O. Box 106002
Auckland Central
Auckland, NZ 1143

64-9-309-9140; Fax: 64-9-309-1090
amcham@amcham.co.nz
www.amcham.co.nz

Mike Hearn, Executive Director

Latest news related to trade between United States and New Zealand.
Frequency: Monthly

19617 BNA's Eastern Europe Reporter
Bureau of National Affairs
1801 S Bell St
Arlington, VA 22202-4501

703-341-3000
800-372-1033; Fax: 800-253-0332
customercare@bna.com
www.bnabooks.com

Paul N Wojcik, CEO
William A. Beltz

This is just one of many biweekly notification services covering legislative, regulatory and legal developments affecting business, trade and investment in Eastern Europe and the former Soviet Union.
Cost: $1750.00
Frequency: Bi-annually

19618 EuroWatch
WorldTrade Executive
PO Box 761
Concord, MA 01742

978-287-0301; Fax: 978-287-0302
www.wtexec.com

Alison French, Production Manager

Analyzes the most recent EU judicial and legislative developments. Covers EU trade issues, labor issues, single market and currency issues, EU and individual country business law, trademark issues.
Cost: $797.00

19619 International Association of Emergency Managers
201 Park Washington Court
Falls Church, VA 22046-4513

703-538-1795; Fax: 703-241-5603
info@iaem.com
www.iaem.com

Elizabeth B Armstrong, Executive Director
Sharon L Kelly, Member Director
Elizabeth B Armstrong, CEO
Karen Thompson, Editor
Dawn Shiley, Communication Manager

Representatives of city and county government departments responsible for emergency management and disaster preparedness.
Cost: $160.00
20 Pages
Frequency: Monthly
Circulation: 2700
Founded in 1952
Printed in 2 colors on matte stock

19620 NASAA Insight
NA Securities Administrators Association
750 First Street NE
Suite 1140
Washington, DC 20002-8034

202-737-0900; Fax: 202-783-3571
www.nasaa.org
Facebook

Jack Herstein, President
Preston DuFauchard, President-Elect
Rick Hancox, Secretary
Fred J. Joseph, Treasurer

Designed to keep readers informed of recent NASAA activities.
Frequency: Quarterly
Founded in 1919

19621 World Aerospace & Defence Intelligence Newsletter
Forecast International
22 Commerce Rd.
Newtown, CT 06470

203-426-0800
800-451-4975; Fax: 203-426-0223
sales@forecast1.com
www.forecastinternational.com

Raymond Jaworowski, Senior Aerospace Analyst
Richard Pettibone, Senior Government Analyst

An e-newsletter containing the latest news on market developments, trend analysis, and contract announcements. Covers civil & military aviation, military weapons, international military markets, defence electronics, and navel and power systems worldwide.
Frequency: Twice Weekly

19622 Worldwide Government Report
Worldwide Government Directories
7979 Old Georgetown Road
Suite 900
Bethesda, MD 20814-2429

301-258-2677
800-332-3535; Fax: 301-718-8494

Jonathan Hixon, Publisher

Each issue provides detailed reports of elections, government and military turnover. Events covered include ousted heads of state, reshuffled governments, changes in ruling majorities, analyses of recent elections, outlooks for upcoming elections, and senior military appointments.
Cost: $247.00
Frequency: Monthly

Magazines & Journals

19623 **Armed Forces Journal**
6883 Commercial Dr
Springfield, VA 22159
800-368-5718
armylet@atpco.com
www.defensenews.com
Mark Winans, VP
Elaine Howard, President/CEO
Alex Neill, Managing Editor
Jim Tice, Senior Writer
David Smith, Marketing
The leading joint service monthly magazine for officers and leaders in the US military community. AFJ has been providing essential review and analysis on key defense issues for more than 140 years. Offers in-depth coverage of military technology, procurement, logistics, strategy, doctrine and tactics. Also covers special operations, US Coast Guard and US National Guard developments.
Cost: $55.00
Frequency: Monthly
Circulation: 1MM

19624 **C41SR Journal**
Defense News
6883 Commercial Dr
Springfield, VA 22159
800-368-5718
armylet@atpco.com
www.defensenews.com
Mark Winans, VP
Elaine Howard, President/CEO
Alex Neill, Managing Editor
Jim Tice, Senior Writer
David Smith, Marketing
Dedicated to the rapidly advancing, high-tech realm of military intelligence, surveillance and reconnaissance. It was the first major periodical to specifically serve this key area of military growth and development, and has a strong following in the world's network-centric warfare community.
Cost: $55.00
Frequency: Monthly
Circulation: 1MM

19625 **Defense News**
6883 Commercial Dr
Springfield, VA 22151-4202
703-750-9000
800-424-9335; Fax: 703-658-8412
armylet@atpco.com
www.defensenews.com
Mark Winans, VP
Elaine Howard, President/CEO
Alex Neill, Managing Editor
Jim Tice, Senior Writer
David Smith, Marketing
Provides the global defense community with the latest news and analysis on defense programs, policy, business and technology. With bureaus and reporters around the world, Defense News sets the standard for accuracy, credibility and timeliness in defense reporting. Circulates to top leaders and decisionmakers in North America and in Europe, Asia and the Middle East.
Cost: $55.00
Frequency: Weekly
Circulation: 1MM

19626 **Economic Development Journal**
International Economic Development Council
734 15th Street NW
Suite 900
Washington, DC 20005
202-223-7800; Fax: 202-223-4745
Jeff Finkle, President & CEO
Dennis G. Coleman, Chair
Jay C. Moon, Vice Chair
Paul Krutko, Secretary/ Treasurer
Premier publication of IEDC's diverse and dynamic discipline, featuring in-depth accounts of important programs, projects, and trends from the US and around the world.
1.8M Members
Frequency: Quarterly
Founded in 1967

19627 **Foreign Service Journal**
American Foreign Service Association
2101 E St NW
Washington, DC 20037-2990
202-338-4045
800-704-2572; Fax: 202-338-6820
member@afsa.org
www.afsa.org
Susan R. Johnson, President
Andrew Winter, Treasurer
Each issue covers foreign affairs from an insider's perspective, providing thoughtful articles on international issues, the practice of diplomacy and the US Foreign Service.
Cost: $40.00
68 Pages
Frequency: Monthly
Circulation: 12500
ISSN: 0146-3543
Founded in 1924
Printed in on glossy stock

19628 **International Debates**
Congressional Digest Corporation
4416 E West Hwy
Suite 400
Bethesda, MD 20814-4568
301-634-3113
800-637-9915; Fax: 301-634-3189
info@congressionaldigest.com
www.pro-and-con.org/
Griff Thomas, President
Page Robinson, Publisher
Independent journal featuring controversies before the United Nations and other international forums. Each issue covers an important and timely international issue and includes in-depth background information, key documents, and diverse global perspectives.
Frequency: 9x Yearly
Founded in 1921

19629 **Journal of Food Protection**
International Association for Food Protection
6200 Aurora Ave
Suite 200W
Des Moines, IA 50322-2864
515-276-3344
800-369-6337; Fax: 515-276-8655
info@foodprotection.org
www.foodprotection.org
Facebook, Twitter, LinkedIn
Lisa Hovey, Managing Editor
Didi Loynachan, Administrative Editor
Internationally recognized as the leading publication in the field of food microbiology, each issue contains scientific research and authoritative review articles reporting on a variety of topics in food science pertaining to food safety and quality.
Cost: $335.00
Frequency: Monthly
Circulation: 11000+
ISBN: 0-362028-X -
Founded in 1911
Mailing list available for rent: 3000+ names at $150 per M
Printed in 4 colors on glossy stock

19630 **Navy News and Undersea Technology**
Pasha Publications
1616 N Fort Myer Drive
Suite 1000
Arlington, VA 22209-3107
703-528-1244
800-424-2908; Fax: 703-528-1253
Harry Baisden, Group Publisher
Thomas Jandl, Editor
Tod Sedgwick, Publisher
This report on the Navy, as well as the Marine Corps and naval developments overseas. Frequently cited by experts in the field as the source for breaking developments in submarine and anti-submarine warfare technology, this newsletter sets the standard for Navy reporting.
Cost: $545.00
Frequency: Weekly

19631 **Parameters**
US Army War College
122 Forbes Ave
Suite C34
Carlisle, PA 17013-5220
717-245-3131; Fax: 717-245-3323
Robert J Ivany, Manager
Refereed journal of ideas and issues. Provides a forum for mature thought on the art and science of land warfare, joint and combined matters, national and international security affairs, military strategy, military leadership and management, military history, ethics, and other topics of significant and current interest to the US Army and the Department of Defense.
Cost: $26.00
Frequency: Quarterly
Circulation: 1300

19632 **Training & Simulation Journal**
6883 Commercial Dr
Springfield, VA 22159
800-368-5718
armylet@atpco.com
www.defensenews.com
Mark Winans, VP
Elaine Howard, President/CEO
Alex Neill, Managing Editor
Jim Tice, Senior Writer
David Smith, Marketing
About trends in the global military training and simulation market, and a forum for market leaders to obtain and exchange information on emerging issues, new technologies, and new products.
Cost: $55.00
Frequency: Bi-Monthly
Circulation: 1MM

Trade Shows

19633 **AAEI Annual Conference**
American Association of Exporters and Importers
1717 K Street NW
Suite 1120
Washington, DC 20006
202-857-8009; Fax: 202-857-7843
www.aaei.org/news/events
Facebook, Twitter, LinkedIn
Marianne Rowden, President & CEO

Association's annual education event provides the latest industry information and networking opportunities.

19634 **Climate and National Security Forum**
The Center for Climate and Security
Washington, DC

Home Page: climateandsecurity.org/category/events
Facebook, Twitter, LinkedIn

Francesco Femia, Co-Founder & President
Caitlin Werrell, Co-Founder & President

Discussions regarding risks and opportunities related to climate change and security.

19635 **Department of Commerce Trade Missions**
Department of Commerce
1401 Constitution Ave. NW
Washington, DC 20230

Home Page: www.export.gov/Trade-Missions
Facebook, Twitter, LinkedIn, YouTube

Trade missions organized by the Department of Commerce put U.S. firms in direct contact with potential clients, foreign industry executives and government officials.

19636 **Discover Global Markets**
Department of Commerce
1401 Constitution Ave. NW
Washington, DC 20230
Home Page: 2016.export.gov/discoverglobalmarkets
Facebook, Twitter, LinkedIn, YouTube

Conference series put on by the U.S. Commercial Service of the Department of Commerce, designed to help U.S. businesses grow exports.

19637 **IAEM Annual Conference**
International Association of Emergency Managers
201 Park Washington Court
Falls Church, VA 22046

703-538-1795; Fax: 703-241-5603
info@iaem.com
www.iaem.com

Provides a forum for current trends and topics, information about the latest tools and technology in emergency management and homeland security, and advances IAEM-USA committee work. Sessions encourage stakeholders at all levels of government, the private sector, public health and related professions to exchange ideas on collaborating to protect lives and property from disaster.
1000 Attendees
Frequency: Annual/November

19638 **Marine West Military Expo**
Nielsen Business Media, USA
1145 Sanctuary Parkway
Suite 355
Alpharetta

703-488-2762

Ron Bates, Event Organizer
This event is fully dedicated to the defense industry. The event will showcase the latest products and equipments used for marine and related industry at one place. The visitors will be the military professionals, equipment buyers, decision makers and the other people related to the field of defense.
Frequency: Annual/February

19639 **NEMA Mid-Year Conference**
National Emergency Management Association
PO Box 11910
Lexington, KY 40578

859-244-8000; Fax: 859-244-8239
nemaadmin@csg.org
www.nemaweb.org

Jim Mullen, President
John Madden, Vice President
Charley English, Treasurer
Tom Sands, Secretary
Brenda Bergeron, Legal Counsel
Gives the opportunity to discuss important issues in the field of emergency management and homeland security. Also hear from respected leaders working on many of these issues. Opportunities to meet and network with peers are invaluable in these times of rapid change and economic challenges.
Frequency: Annual/March

19640 **UDT: Undersea Defense Technology Conference and Exhibition**
Reed Exhibition Companies
255 Washington Street
Newton, MA 02458-1637

617-584-4900; Fax: 617-630-2222
Facebook, Twitter, LinkedIn
Elizabeth Hitchcock, International Sales
The world's leading exhibition and conference for undersea defence and security. Gain access to the latest technologies, connect with existing suppliers and create new business relationships. Gives the invaluable opportunity to network across the global maritime community. Suppliers exhibiting; UUVs and components, acoustic technologies, maritime surveillance solutions, harbour and port security products, mine detection systems, and submarine hardware and electronics.
Frequency: Annual/May

19641 **UNA-USA Annual Meeting**
United Nations Association of the USA
1800 Massachusetts Avenue NW
Suite 400
Washington, DC 20036

202-887-9040; Fax: 202-887-9021
www.unausa.org

Patrick Madden, Executive Director
Brings together UNA-USA's constituencies for a variety of skills trainings, issue briefings, networking opportunities and capacity-building.
400 Attendees
Frequency: Annual/November

Directories & Databases

19642 **Daily Defense News Capsules**
United Communications Group
11300 Rockville Pike
Suite 1100
Rockville, MD 20852-3030

301-816-8950; Fax: 301-816-8945

Greg Beaudoin, Editor
This database offers the complete text of Periscope - Daily Defense News Capsules, that provide abstracts of international press coverage of military and defense news.

19643 **Defense Industry Charts**
Carroll Publishing
4701 Sangamore Rd
Suite 155S
Bethesda, MD 20816-2532

301-263-9800
800-336-4240; Fax: 301-263-9805
info@carrollpub.com
www.carrollpub.com

Tom Carroll, President

19000 key personnel in top US defense contractors, including major aerospace, electronic, military hardware, information technology and systems integration companies. Serves as a road map to the critical players in this important industry.
Cost: $2050.00
Frequency: Quarterly

19644 **Defense Programs**
Carroll Publishing
4701 Sangamore Rd
Suite 155S
Bethesda, MD 20816-2532
301-263-9800
800-336-4240; Fax: 301-263-9805
info@carrollpub.com
www.carrollpub.com

Tom Carroll, President

Detailed description of more than 2,000 military research, development, test and evaluation programs and projects.
Cost: $1060.00
Frequency: Quarterly

19645 **Defense and Foreign Affairs Handbook**
International Strategic Studies Association
PO Box 19289
Alexandria, VA 22320-0289

703-548-1070; Fax: 703-684-7476
dfa@strategicstudies.org
www.strategicstudies.org

Gregory Copley, Editor
Important global reference encyclopedia for most world leaders .Comprehensive chapters on 238 countries and territories worldwide, with each chapter giving full cabinet and leadership listings, history, recent developments, demographics, economic statistics, political and constitutional data, news media,defense overview, defense structure.
Cost: $297.00
2500 Pages
Frequency: Monthly
Circulation: 4,000
ISBN: 1-892998-06-8
Founded in 1976

19646 **Foreign Consular Offices in the United States**
Bureau of Public Affairs/US Department of State
2201 C Street NW
Washington, DC 20520-0001

202-647-6141

A complete and official listing of the foreign consular offices in the US, and recognized consular officers. Compiled by the US Department of State, with the full cooperation of the foreign missions in Washington, it is offered as a convenience to organizations and persons who must deal with consular government agencies, state tax officials, international trade organizations, chamber of commerce, and judicial authorities.
Cost: $4.00
290 Pages
Frequency: Annual

19647 **IAEM Directory**
International Association of Emergency Managers

111 Park Pl
Falls Church, VA 22046-4513

703-538-1795; Fax: 703-241-5603
info@iaem.com
www.iaem.com

Shan Coffin, Editor
Sharon L Kelly, Circulation Director
Cost: $100.00
Circulation: 8,000

19648 Kaleidoscope: Current World Data
ABC-CLIO
PO Box 1911
Santa Barbara, CA 93102-1911

805-968-1911; Fax: 805-685-9685
CustomerService@abc-clio.com
www.abc-clio.com

Ron Boehm, CEO

This comprehensive database takes a look at all aspects of the American culture. Listings of information include statistics and factual information on the population, culture, economy, military forces, government, and political systems of countries around the world, the US States and Canadian provinces.
Frequency: Full-text

19649 Military Biographical Profiles
CTB/McGraw Hill
20 Ryan Ranch Rd
Monterey, CA 93940-5770

831-393-0700
800-538-9547; Fax: 831-393-6528
www.ctb.com

Ellen Haley, President
Sandor Nagy, Chief Operating Officer

Offers valuable information on US military officers and Department of Defense officials.
Frequency: Full-text

19650 Profiles of Worldwide Government Leaders
Worldwide Government Directories
7979 Old Georgetown Road
Suite 900
Bethesda, MD 20814-2429

301-258-2677
800-332-3535; Fax: 301-718-8494

Jonathan Hixon, Publisher

Spanning 195 countries, includes comprehensive biographical snapshots of as many as 30 or more ministers from each country. The material is obtained from primary and secondary sources including embassies, government ministries, offices of the United States government and proprietary global network of correspondents.
Cost: $297.00
850+ Pages
Frequency: Annual

19651 The World Factbook
Central Intelligence Agency
Office of Public Affairs
Washington, DC 20505

703-482-0623; Fax: 571-204-3800
cia.gov
Facebook, Twitter, flickr, YouTube

Annual publication of the CIA contains information on the history, people, government, etc., of 267 world entities.
Cost: $89.00
Frequency: Annual
Founded in 1981

19652 Worldwide Directory of Defense Attorneys
Worldwide Government Directories
7979 Old Georgetown Road
Suite 900
Bethesda, MD 20814-2429

301-258-2677
800-332-3535; Fax: 301-718-8494

Jonathan Hixon, Publisher

One-of-a-kind resource covering military and civilian defense and national security agencies from the ministry of defense down to service branches in 195 countries worldwide.
Cost: $647.00
1,100 Pages
Frequency: Annual

19653 Worldwide Government Directory
Worldwide Government Directories
7979 Old Georgetown Road
Suite 900
Bethesda, MD 20814-2429

301-258-2677
800-332-3535; Fax: 301-718-8494

Jonathan Hixon, Publisher

Offers valuable information on every senior government official in the executive, legislative, and judicial branches as well as the diplomatic and defense communities of 195 countries worldwide. Plus senior officials in over 100 international organizations. Each entry includes name, address, title, telephone, telex, facsimile number, and more. Also included are current state agencies and corporations, official forms of address, international dialing codes and central bank information.
Cost: $347.00
1,400 Pages
Frequency: Annual

19654 Worldwide Government Directory with International Organizations
1414 22nd Street NW
Washington, DC 20037-1003

202-887-8500
800-432-2250; Fax: 800-380-3810
www.cqpress.com

Linda Dziobek, Editor

Coverage includes over 1800 pages of executive, legislative and political branches; heads of state, ministers, deputies, secretaries and spokespersons as well as state agencies, diplomats and senior level defense officials. Also covers the leadership of more than 100 international organizations.
Cost: $450.00
1700 Pages
Frequency: Annually

Industry Web Sites

19655 Office of the Director of National Intelli gence
Office of the Director of National Intelligence
Washington, DC 20511

703-733-8600
www.dni.gov

James R. Clapper, Director of National Intelligence
Stephanie O'Sullivan, Principal Deputy DNI

ODNI is responsible for integrating the intelligence collection and analysis of the 16 member agencies of the Intelligence Community.

19656 export.gov
International Trade Administration
1401 Constitution Ave. NW
Washington, DC 20230

Home Page: www.export.gov
Facebook, Twitter, LinkedIn, YouTube

Market intelligence, advice and tools for U.S. companies looking to succeed in global markets.

19657 www.foodprotection.org
International Association for Food Protection

The International Association for Food Protection founded in 1911, is a nonprofit educational association with a mission to provide food safety professionals worldwide with a forum to exchange information on protecting the food supply. The Association is comprised of a cross-section of over 3,000 members from 50 nations. Affiliate chapters are located in the United States, Canada and South Korea.

19658 www.intelligencecareers.gov

Home Page: www.intelligencecareers.gov

Tool for exploring careers in the 17 federal intelligence agencies.

19659 www.iogcc.state.ok.us
Interstate Oil and Gas Compact Commission

Represents the governors of 37 states that produce virtually all the domestic oil and natural gas in the United States.

19660 www.napawash.org
National Academy of Public Administration

An independent, non-profit organization chartered by Congress to improve governance at all levels- local, regional, state, national and international.

19661 www.nasaa.org
North American Securities Administrators Assoc

NASAA is the international organization representing 66 securities administrators from all 50 states, the District of Columbia, Canada, Mexico and Puerto Rico, and is responsible for investor protection and education. NASAA recommends national policies in the securities industry and provides model legislation for state securities agencies to adopt affecting the regulation of broker/dealers and investment advisers. Consumers can contact NASAA to get phone numbers of state securities regulators.

19662 www.nbpc.net
National Border Patrol Council

A labor union representing employees of the US border patrol.

19663 www.nemaweb.org
National Emergency Management Association

Members include federal agencies, local emergency management representatives and interested individuals, associations and corporations.

19664 www.sso.org
Intl Assoc of Official Human Rights Agencies

Members are state and local government human rights and human relations agencies.

International Trade Resources

19665 **Albania to the United Nations**
320 E 79th Street
New York, NY 10075

212-249-2059; Fax: 212-535-2917
www.albania-un.org
Facebook, Twitter, LinkedIn

Ferit Hoxha, Ambassador
Petrik Jorgi, Minister Counselor
Olisa Cifligu, Second Secretary
Ermal Frasheri, Advisor, Legal Issues

19666 **United States Census Bureau**
Department of Commerce
4600 Silver Hill Rd.
Washington, DC 20233

800-923-8282
www.census.gov/foreign-trade
Facebook, Twitter, YouTube

Peter M. Robinson, President & CEO

Foreign Trade is the official source for U.S. import and export statistics and information on export regulations.
300 Members
Founded in 1945

19667 **stopfakes.gov**
International Trade Administration
Office of Intellectual Property Rights
14th St. and Constitution Ave. NW
Washington, DC 20230

866-999-4258
www.stopfakes.gov

U.S. government tools and resources on intellectual property rights help businesses secure IP rights at home and abroad.

Associations

19668 ARMA International
11880 College Boulevard
Suite 450
Overland Park, KS 66210

913-444-9174
844-565-2120; Fax: 913-257-3855
headquarters@armaintl.org
www.arma.org
Facebook, Twitter, LinkedIn

Nate Hughes, Exec. Dir, Operations
Jennifer Millett, National Account Manager
Heather Lehman, Sr. Manager, Membership

ARMA International is a not-for-profit association and a source for authoritative education, the latest legislative updates, standards & best practices. The association was established in 1955. Its approximately 27,000 members include records managers, archivists, corporate librarians, imaging specialists, legal professionals, IT managers, consultants, and educators, all of whom work in a wide variety of industries.
27000 Members
Founded in 1955

19669 Business and Institutional Furniture Manufacturers Association
678 Front Avenue NW
Suite 150
Grand Rapids, MI 49504-5368

616-285-3963; Fax: 616-285-3765
email@bifma.org
www.bifma.org
Facebook, Twitter, LinkedIn

Sylvain Garneau, President
Thomas Reardon, Executive Director
Don Van Winkle, Vice President
Franco Bianchi, Treasurer

BIFMA is a not-for-profit trade association of furniture manufacturers and suppliers, addressing issues of common concern.
245+ Members
Founded in 1973

19670 Graphic Arts Information Network
200 Deer Run Road
Sewickley, PA 15143

412-741-6860
800-910-4283; Fax: 412-741-2311
www.printing.org/
Facebook, Twitter, LinkedIn, RSS

Michael F Makin, President

Members are companies printing labels for food or consumer products.
40 Members

19671 Independent Office Products & Furniture Dealers Association
3601 E. Joppa Road
Baltimore, MD 21234

410-931-8100; Fax: 410-931-8111
info@iopfda.org
www.nopanet.org/
Twitter, LinkedIn

Mike Tucker, President
Paul Miller, Director Government Affairs
Paula Kreuzburg, M.D
Alicia Ellis, Director, Marketing

Association for independent office product and office furniture dealers. IOPFDA is comprised of the National Office Products Alliance (NOPA) and the Office Furniture Dealers Alliance (OFDA).
1500 Members
Founded in 1904

19672 National Office Products Alliance
3601 E Joppa Rd.
Baltimore, MD 21234

410-931-8100; Fax: 410-931-8111
www.nopanet.org

Paula Kreuzburg, Executive Director

Information and resources to promote the success of member dealers.

19673 Office Furniture Dealers Alliance
3601 E Joppa Rd.
Baltimore, MD 21234

410-931-8100; Fax: 410-931-8111
info@ofda.org
www.ofdanet.org
LinkedIn

Rod Manson, Chair
Paula Kreuzburg, Executive Director

The Alliance's mission is to provide independent dealers with information and tools to help them succeed in a changing industry.
1200 Members

19674 Office Furniture Distribution Association
P.O. Box 2548
Secaucus, NJ 07096

517-467-9355; Fax: 517-467-9056
theofda@yahoo.com
www.theofda.org

75 Members
Founded in 1923

19675 Office Products Representatives
3131 Elbee Road
Dayton, OH 45439

937-297-2250
800-447-1684; Fax: 937-297-2254
info@oprareps.org
www.oprareps.org

Carol Hinton, Owner
100 Members
Founded in 1974

19676 Office Products Wholesalers Association
5024 Campbell Boulevard
Baltimore, MD 21236

410-931-8100; Fax: 410-931-8111

Cal Clemons, Executive Vice President
Paula Kreuzberg, Associate Director

Members are chief executives of office product wholesalers and manufacturers.
165 Members
Founded in 1995

19677 Society for Service Professionals in Printing
433 E Monroe Ave
Alexandria, VA 22301-1645

703-684-0044
866-600-8820; Fax: 703-548-9137

Peter Colaianni, Executive Director
Marj Green, Director

Individual membership society dedicated to the needs of customer service professionals in the printing industry.
8 Members
Founded in 1993

Newsletters

19678 BTA Hotline Online
Business Technology Association
12411 Wornall Road
Suite 200
Kansas City, MO 64145

800-505-2821
info@bta.org
www.bta.org

Bob Evans, President
Brent Hoskins, Executive Director
Valerie Briseno, Marketing Director
Elizabeth Marvel, Associate Editor
Brian Smith, Membership Sales Representative

A weekly e-newsletter for members of the Business Technology Association.
Founded in 1926

19679 Digital Image Review
Buyers Laboratory
20 Railroad Avenue
Hackensack, NJ 07601-3309

201-896-6439; Fax: 201-488-0461
info@buyerslab.com
www.buyerslab.com

Daria Hoffman, Managing Editor
Michael Danziger, CEO

Devoted to digital topics, all types of digital office products, industry news and trends, trade show, pricing changes and much more.
Cost: $305.00
16 Pages
Frequency: Monthly
Founded in 1961

19680 Executary
National Association of Executive Secretaries
900 S Washington Street
Suite G13
Falls Church, VA 22046-4009

703-237-8616; Fax: 703-533-1153
headquarters@theaeap.com
www.theaeap.com
LinkedIn

Ruth Ludeman, Director

Packed with practical advice on various issues of interest to administrative professionals. Seeks to support AEAP's mission to assist members in achieving their career goals by keeping you informed of advances and changes in the administrative profession.
Frequency: 10x/Year
Mailing list available for rent: 5000 names

19681 Form & Document Industry Newsletter
1147 Fleetwood Avenue
Madison, WI 53716-1417

888-367-3078
bfma@bfma.org
www.bfma.org

Robin Miller, President
Olufunke Somefun, VP Programs
Ray Killam, VP Operations/ Acting CFO

Industry newsletter containing educational articles and rules on the latest processes, techniques, and products in the form and document industry. Library rate is $35.00 per year.
Cost: $50.00
38574 Pages
Circulation: 700
Founded in 1958
Mailing list available for rent: 1000 names at $400 per M

19682 Jot and Jolts
Economics Press

12 Daniel Road
Fairfield, NJ 07004-2565

973-227-1224
800-526-2554; Fax: 973-227-8360
www.epinc.com

Monthly planner for supervisors to the office products industry.
Cost: $16.20
26 Pages
Frequency: Monthly
Printed in on glossy stock

19683 **MFP Report**
Bissett Communications
Apt 44
20919 Bloomfield Ave
Lakewood, CA 90715-1840

562-809-8917; Fax: 562-809-1627
http://www.mfpreport.com

Brian R Bissett, Publisher

A newsletter providing information on manufacturers, suppliers, sellers, and managers of multifunction peripherals and connected office equipment of the latest MFP business, market and technology issues and their impact.
Frequency: Monthly

19684 **Scanner**
Private Label Manufacturers Association (PLMA)
630 Third Avenue
New York, NY 10017-6506

212-972-3131; Fax: 212-983-1382
info@plma.com
www.plma.com

Brian Sharoff, President
Myra Rosen, VP
Tom Prendergast, Director, Research Services

News and information for the private label industry.
3200+ Members
6 Pages
Frequency: Quarterly
Circulation: 12000
Founded in 1979

Magazines & Journals

19685 **Better Buys for Business**
Progressive Business Publications
PO Box 3019
Malvern, PA 19355-0719

610-695-0201
800-247-2185; Fax: 610-647-8098
webmaster@pbp.com
www.pbp.com

Ed Satell, CEO
Steve Hannaford, Editor

Publishes 10 non-advertising buyer's guides for office equipment (copiers, printers, fax machines and scanners), with objective, unbiased information and evaluations. Each issue includes in-depth write-ups on all manufacturers and their models, easy to read specifications and price charts to compare models and Editor's Choice selections - awarded to the best machines in each product category
Cost: $149.00
Circulation: 4,000
ISSN: 1084-2055
Founded in 1980
Printed in 4 colors on matte stock

19686 **Business Documents**
North American Publishing Company
1500 Spring Garden St
Suite 1200
Philadelphia, PA 19130-4094

215-238-5300
800-627-2689; Fax: 215-238-5342
www.napco.com

Ned S Borowsky, CEO
Brian C Ludwick, Publisher

For professional buyers of forms, labels and electronic systems. Emphasizes internal and external design, production and management of business documents either as traditionally printed forms or electronically generated documents.
Cost: $24.00
42 Pages
Frequency: Monthly
Founded in 1958
Mailing list available for rent
Printed in 2 colors on matte stock

19687 **Business Forms, Labels & Systems**
North American Publishing Company
1500 Spring Garden St
Suite 1200
Philadelphia, PA 19130-4094

215-238-5300
800-627-2689; Fax: 215-238-5342
webmaster@napco.com
www.napco.com/

Ned S Borowsky, CEO
Judith Cavaliere, Publisher
Maggie DeWitt, Senior Editor
Cynthia Graham, Associate Editor
Jennifer Hans, Associate Editor

For independent manufacturers and distributors in the forms and systems industry. Emphasizes product applications, marketing and sales ideas and new technology.
Cost: $49.00
Frequency: Monthly
Circulation: 12000
Founded in 1958
Mailing list available for rent
Printed in 4 colors on glossy stock

19688 **Business Solutions**
Corry Publishing
5539 Peach Street
Erie, PA 16506

814-380-0025
800-290-5460; Fax: 814-864-2037
editor@corrypub.com
www.corrypub.com

John Clifton, Group Publisher
Melinda Reed-Fadden, Circulation Manager
Dan Schell, Editor
Carrie Brocious, Marketing Director
Jim Roddy, President

Informative magazine including analysis of technological and marketing developments.
Frequency: Monthly
Circulation: 43000
Founded in 1980

19689 **Digital Information Network**
Buyers Laboratory
20 Railroad Avenue
Hackensack, NJ 07601-3309

201-587-0828; Fax: 201-488-0461
info@buyerslab.com
www.buyerslab.com

Daria Hoffman, Managing Editor

A comprehensive test report service which provides test reports on all the office products BLI evaluates. Subscribers will also get a sixteen page monthly newsletter called Digital Imaging Review, and will recieve a copy of BLI's Multifunctional Specification Guide, Facsimile-Based Products, Copier-Based Products and the Printer Specification Guide, as well as updated specifications throughout the term of their subscription.
Cost: $755.00

19690 **Hard Copy Supplies Journal**
Lyra Research
PO Box 9143
Newtonville, MA 02640-9143

617-454-2600; Fax: 617-454-2601
www.lyra.com

Charles LeCompte, Publisher
Frank Stefansson, CEO/President
Jim Forrest, Managing Editor
Jennifer Sprague, Vice President of Sales
Andre Rebelo, Marketing Manager

In-depth coverage of current innovations in marketing materials and media, including ink jet cartridges, toner, paper and film, and monitors the fast-moving corporate developments, such as lawsuits, mergers, distribution, tactics, and marketing campaigns.
Cost: $550.00
Frequency: Monthly
Circulation: 2,000
Founded in 1991

19691 **Information Management**
ARMA International
11880 College Boulevard
Suite 450
Overland Park, KS 66215

913-444-9174
844-565-2120; Fax: 913-257-3855
headquarters@armaintl.org
magazine.arma.org
Facebook, Twitter, LinkedIn

Nick Inglis, Exec. Dir., Content & Programming
Jeff Whited, Sr. Content Writer
Ann Snyder, Manager, Content Development

Also known as ARMA Magazine, it is a major source of information on topics and issues central to the management of records and information worldwide. Each issue features articles written by experts in the management of records and information.
61 Pages
Frequency: 6/Year
Founded in 1955

19692 **Mail: Journal of Communication Distribution**
Excelsior Publications
One Millstone Road
Gold Key Box 2425
Milford, PA 18337

570-861-1969; Fax: 570-686-3495

Francis P Ruggiero, Publsher
Circulation: 43000

19693 **Office Dealer**
Quality Publishing
252 N Main Street
Suite 200
Mount Airy, NC 27030-3810

336-783-0000; Fax: 336-783-0045
www.os-od.com/

Richard Kunkel, Publisher
Simon DeGroot, Editorial Director
Bessie Comer, Sales/Advertising Coor
Scott Cullen, Managing Editor
Debbie Hooker, Director of Publishing Services

Information including the latest industry news pertaining to resellers, plus office dealer conventions and other newsworthy events.
Circulation: 17020

19694 **Office Solutions**
Quality Publishing

252 N Main Street #200
PO Box 1028
Mount Airy, NC 27030-3810

336-783-0000; Fax: 336-783-0045
www.os-od.com

Richard Kunkel, Publisher
Simon Degroot, Editorial Director
Debbey Hooker, Circulation Manager
Bill Middleton, Marketing Manager
Scott Cullen, Managing Editor

Information on state of the art, survey and overview of articles and product offerings. Emphasis on personal computing, software, telecommunications, personnel and financial management.
Cost: $36.00
Circulation: 81250
Founded in 2003

19695 **Office Systems Research Journal**
SW Missouri Council of Governments
901 S National Avenue
Springfield, MO 65804

417-836-5000; Fax: 417-836-4146
www.smsu.edu

Diane May, Executive Director

A journal offering research and news of the office supplies and products industry.
Cost: $35.00
Circulation: 400

19696 **Office Technology**
Business Tchnology Association
12411 Wornall Rd
Suite 200
Kansas City, MO 64145-1212

816-941-3100
800-325-7219; Fax: 816-941-2829
info@bta.org
www.bta.org
Facebook, Twitter, LinkedIn

Brent Hoskins, Executive Director
Rob Richardson, President
Cost: $100.00
Frequency: Monthly
Circulation: 3500
ISBN: 1-092916-9 -
Founded in 1927
Mailing list available for rent: 1200 names

19697 **Print Solutions Magazine**
Document Management Industries Association
433 E Monroe Avenue
Alexandria, VA 22301-1693

703-836-6232; Fax: 703-549-4966
www.printsolutionsmag.com

Peter L Colaianni CAE, Editor-in-Chief

Source for marketing, management and product information.
Cost: $49.00
276 Pages
Frequency: Monthly
ISSN: 0532-1700
Printed in 4 colors on glossy stock

19698 **Recharger Magazine**
Recharger Magazine
1050 E Flamingo Rd
Suite N237
Las Vegas, NV 89119-7427

702-438-5557
877-902-9759; Fax: 702-873-9671
info@rechargermag.com
www.rechargermag.com

Phyllis Gurgevich, Publisher
Amy Turner, Managing Editor
Michael MacDonald, Graphics Director
Sara Feest, Sales Assistant
Monica Miceli, Associate Editor

Information including articles that cover business and marketing, technical updates, association and industry news, and company profiles. Related features focus on the importance of recycling, government legislation, and product comparisons.
Cost: $45.00
Frequency: Monthly
Circulation: 8000

Trade Shows

19699 **ARMA InfoCon**
ARMA International
11880 College Boulevard
Suite 450
Overland Park, KS 66210

913-444-9174
844-565-2120; Fax: 913-257-3855
headquarters@armaintl.org
www.arma.org
Facebook, Twitter, LinkedIn

Nate Hughes, Exec. Dir., Operations
Jennifer Millett, National Accounts Manager
Karen Skaggs, Sales & Event Specialist

Conference, seminar, workshop, banquet, award ceremony and 175 exhibits of micrographics, optical disk, automated document storage and retrieval systems and more technology of interest to information professionals.
3500 Attendees
Frequency: Annual
Founded in 1956

19700 **American Business Women's Association Convention**
9100 Ward Parkway
PO Box 8728
Kansas City, MO 64114

816-361-6621
800-228-0007; Fax: 816-361-4991
abwa@abwa.org
www.abwa.org

Wendy Mabrey, Corporate Sponsorship Coordinator
Carolyn Elman, Executive Director

One-hundred exhibits of equipment, supplies and services for women in business, seminar and banquet.
2000 Attendees
Frequency: November

19701 **American Society for Training & Development Conference & Exposition**
American Society for Training & Development
1640 King Street
PO Box 1443
Alexandria, VA 22313-2043

703-683-8100; Fax: 703-683-8103
customercare@astd.org
www.astd.org

Michael Neff, Executive Director
2000 Attendees

19702 **Business Show**
INPEX
217 9th Street
Pittsburgh, PA 15222-3506

412-881-1300
800-544-6739; Fax: 412-288-4546
www.inventionshow.com/

Nevin Arora, Product Manager

Annual show of 150 exhibits of office furniture, supplies and machines; computers; media; specialty items; financial services; printing services; security systems; entertainment; cellular phones and pagers; sinage; travel agencies; audio-visual equipment and car rental agencies.
5000 Attendees

19703 **Business Technology Association National Conference**
Business Technology Association
12411 Wornall Road
Suite 200
Kansas City, MO 64145

800-505-2821
info@bta.org
www.bta.org
Facebook, Twitter, LinkedIn

Brent Hoskins, Executive Director
Bob Evans, President
Valerie Briseno, Marketing Director
Elizabeth Marvel, Associate Editor
Brian Smith, Membership Sales Representative

Serving independent dealers, value-added resellers, systems integrators, manufacturers and distributors in the business equipment and systems industry. BTA helps its members profit through a wide variety of services, including free legal advice and guidance; business benchmarking studies and reports; information on the latest news, trends, and products in the industry.
Frequency: Annual
Founded in 1926
Mailing list available for rent: 1200 names

19704 **Document World/American Business Equipment and Computer Show**
Key Productions
116 Murphy Road
Hartford, CT 06114-2121

860-247-8363

Eldred Codling, Show Manager

Features exhibits of computer software, hardware, supplies and services.
6M Attendees
Frequency: April

19705 **National Stationery Show**
George Little Management
10 Bank Street
White Plains, NY 10606-1954

914-486-6070
800-272-7469; Fax: 914-948-6180
www.

Lori Robinson, VP
Kelly Bristol, Assistant Show Manager
George Little II, President

A show for greeting cards and social stationery, writing instruments and home office products, party ware and giftwrap, scrapbooking and craft supplies, albums, frames and much more.
14000 Attendees
Frequency: May

Directories & Databases

19706 **ARMA International's Buyers Guide**
ARMA International
11880 College Boulevard
Suite 450
Overland Park, KS 66215

913-444-9174
844-565-2120; Fax: 913-257-3855
headquarters@armaintl.org
armabuyersguide.org
Facebook, Twitter, LinkedIn

Nick Inglis, Exec. Dir., Content & Programming
Jeff Whited, Sr. Content Writer
Ann Snyder, Manager, Content Development

75-100 companies listed. Free.
Frequency: Annual

19707 **Directory of Mail Order Catalogs**
Grey House Publishing
4919 Route 22
PO Box 56
Amenia, NY 12501
518-789-8700
800-562-2139; Fax: 845-373-6390
books@greyhouse.com
www.greyhouse.com
Facebook, Twitter
Leslie Mackenzie, Publisher
Richard Gottlieb, Editor
The premier source of information on the mail order catalog industry. Covers over 13,000 consumer and business catalog companies with 44 different product chapters including office supplies, stationery and more.
Cost: $395.00
1900 Pages
Frequency: Annual
ISBN: 1-592373-96-8
Founded in 1981

19708 **Directory of Mail Order Catalogs - Online Database**
Grey House Publishing
4919 Route 22
PO Box 56
Amenia, NY 12501
518-789-8700
800-562-2139; Fax: 845-373-6390
gold@greyhouse.com
gold.greyhouse.com
Facebook, Twitter
Leslie Mackenzie, Publisher
Richard Gottlieb, Editor
Reach over 10,000 consumer catalog companies in one easy-to-use source with The Directory of Mail Order Catalogs - Online Database. Filled with business-building detail, each company profile gives you the information you need to access that organization quickly and easily. Listings provide key contacts, sales volume, employee size, printing information, circulation, list data, product descriptions and much more.
Frequency: Annual
Founded in 1981

19709 **Orion Blue Book: Copier**
Orion Research Corporation
14555 N Scottsdale Rd
Suite 330
Scottsdale, AZ 85254-3487
480-951-1114
800-844-0759; Fax: 480-951-1117
support@orionbluebook.com
www.orionbluebook.com/
Roger Rohrs, Owner
List of manufacturers of copiers and other office equipment.
Cost: $39.00
Frequency: Annual

Industry Web Sites

19710 **http://gold.greyhouse.com**
G.O.L.D Grey House OnLine Databases
Grey House Publishing's online database platform, GOLD, offers Quick Search, Keyword Search and Expert Search for most business sectors, including office supplies and services makrets. The GOLD platform makes finding the information you need quick and easy - whether you're a novice searcher or an experienced database user. All of Grey House's directory products are available for subscription on the GOLD platform.

19711 **www.bfma.org**
Business Forms Management Association
For form systems professionals interested in the effective capture distribution and management of information in electronic and paper forms.

19712 **www.bifma.org**
Business and Institutional Furniture Manufacturers Association
The voice of the office furniture industry, BIFMA members are manufacturers and suppliers of goods and services to the industry.

19713 **www.greyhouse.com**
Grey House Publishing
Authoritative reference directories for most business sectors including office products and services markets. Users can search the online databases with varied search criteria allowing for custom searches by product category, geographic area, sales volume, keyword, subject and more. Full Grey House catalog and online ordering also available.

19714 **www.iopfda.org**
Independent Office Products & Furniture Dealers Association
Association for independent office product and office furniture dealers. IOPFDA is comprised of the National Office Products Alliance (NOPA) and the Office Furniture Dealers Alliance (OFDA).

19715 **www.oprareps.org**
Office Products Representatives Association
Provides programs and services that promote the role of the independant manufactures' representative in the various distribution channels within the entire office products industry.

19716 **www.theofda.org**
Office Furniture Distribution Association

Associations

19717 **American Forest & Paper Association**
1111 19th St NW
Suite 800
Washington, DC 20036-3652
202-463-2700
800-878-8878; Fax: 202-463-2785
info@afandpa.org
www.afandpa.org
Facebook, Twitter, LinkedIn, YouTube
James B. Hannan, Chairman
Doyle R. Simons, 1st Vice Chairman
Alexander Toeldte, 2nd Vice Chairman
Donna A. Harman, President & CEO
Jan A. Poling, Vice President & Secretary
To provide significant value to member companies through outstanding performance in those areas that are key to members' success and where an association can be more effective than individual companies.
Founded in 1993

19718 **American Paper Machinery Association**
201 Park Washington Ct
Falls Church, VA 22046-4527
703-538-1787; Fax: 703-241-5603
apmahq@aol.com
www.papermachinery.org
Clay D Tyeryar, Chief Administrative Executive
Judith O Buzzerd, Manager Meetings
Sharon Kelly, Coordinator Member Services
To promote the global common interests, image and business relations of the membership.
35 Members
Founded in 1971

19719 **Association of Independent Corrugated Converters**
113 S. West Street
3rd floor
Alexandria, VA 22314
703-836-2422
877-836-2422; Fax: 703-836-2795
info@aiccbox.org
www.aiccbox.org
Facebook, Twitter, LinkedIn, YouTube
A Steven Young, President
Maria Frustaci, Administrative Director
David Core, CAE, Director Education
Taryn Pyle, Director Meetings
Chris Richards, Webmaster/Systems Manager
Represents and protects, the business interests of the independent sector of the corrugated packaging industry. Dedicated to strengthening the independent's position in the marketplace through programs and publications that empower our members to compete successfully in a rapidly changing industry and an increasingly competitive and global business environment.
750 Members
Founded in 1974

19720 **Fibre Box Association**
500 Park Boulevard
Suite 985
Itasca, IL 60143
847-364-9600; Fax: 847-364-9639
fba@fibrebox.org
www.fibrebox.org
LinkedIn
Bill Hoel, Chairman
Peter Watson, First Vice Chairman
Douglas Bonsik, Second Vice-Chairman
Dennis J. Colley, President
Mike Waite, Immediate Past Chairman
A non-profit association that represents and serves the corrugated industry. It also brings together the North American manufacturers to improve the overall well being of the industry and to provide an array of services that enable member companies to conduct their business more effectively , responsibly and efficiently.
170 Members
Founded in 1940

19721 **Foodservice/Packaging Institute**
7700 Leesburg Pike
Suite 421
Falls Church, VA 22043
703-592-9889; Fax: 703-592-9864
fpi@fpi.org
www.fpi.org
Facebook, Twitter, LinkedIn, Blog
Lynn Dyer, President
Natha Dempsey, VP
Caron Mason, Communications Manager
Jennifer Goldman, Manager
A national association comprised of manufacturers and suppliers of single-use foodservice packaging products.
25 Members
Founded in 1933

19722 **Forest Resources Association, Inc.**
1901 Pennsylvania Ave. NW
Suite 303
Washington, DC 20006
202-296-3937; Fax: 202-296-0562
www.forestresources.org
Facebook, Twitter, YouTube
Deb Hawkinson, President
Neil Ward, Vice President
Promotes sustainable use of forest resources in the interests of its members.

19723 **International Corrugated Packaging Foundation**
113 S West Street
Alexandria, VA 22314-2858
703-549-8580; Fax: 703-549-8670
info@icpfbox.org
www.icpfbox.org
Twitter
Steven Landal, Chairman
Richard M Flaherty, President
Thomas W.H. Walton, Vice Chairman
A Steven Young, Treasurer
Paul Vishny, Secretary
An industry led philantrophic organization dedicated to building a knowledgeable workforce for the corrugated packaging industry.
Founded in 1985

19724 **International Council of Forest and Paper Associations**
info@icfpa.org
www.icfpa.org
Elizabeth de Carvalhaes, President
Worldwide network of forest and paper associations advocates for industry at international level.

19725 **International Molded Fiber Association**
355 Lexington Avenue
Floor 15
New York, NY 10017ÿ
262-241-0522; Fax: 262-241-3766
Alan@IMFA.org
www.imfa.org
Facebook, Twitter, LinkedIn
Cassandra Niesing, Asst. Director
Joseph Grygny, Chairman
Acts as an information center for the molded fiber industry with worldwide membership of users and manufacturers of molded fiber producs. Promotes use of natural and recycled fibers.
Founded in 1996

19726 **National Council for Air and Stream Improvement**
PO Box 133138
Research Triangle Park, NC 27709-3318
919-941-6400; Fax: 919-941-6401
ryeske@ncasi.org
www.ncasi.org
NCASI's mission is to serve the forest products industry as a center of excellence for providing technical information and scientific research needed to achieve the industry's environmental goals and principles.
Founded in 1943

19727 **National Paper Trade Association**
330 North Wabash Avenue
Suite 2000
Chicago, IL 60611
312-321-4092
800-355-6782; Fax: 312-673-6736
NPTA@goNPTA.com
www.gonpta.com
Facebook, Twitter, YouTube
Bob Forsberg, Chairman
Jan Gottesman, 1st Vice Chair
Scott Hider, 2nd Vice Chair
Matthew Bruno, EVP
John Hagrove, Treasurer
Representing distributors and suppliers of paper, packaging and facility supplies companies.
2000 Members
Founded in 1903

19728 **National Paperbox Association**
1901 Pennsylvania Avenue NW
Suite 1508
Washington, DC 20006
202-466-7252; Fax: 413-747-7777
www.paperbox.org
Facebook, Twitter, LinkedIn, YouTube
Ben Markens, President
Lou Kornet, Vice President
Kim Guarnaccia, Director of Marketing
Brian Chaisson, Director of Industry Benchmarking
Jennie Markens, Director of General Leaders
Serves as the voice of the paperbox and packaging industry. Also represents the concerns of boxmaker nationally, internationally and at the local level through its Regional Divisions. Publishes bi-monthly magazine and holds an annual convention.
100 Members
Founded in 1839

19729 **Paper Distribution Council**
National Paper Trade Association
330 North Wabash Avenue
Suite 2000
Chicago, IL 60611
312-321-4092; Fax: 312-673-4092
NPTA@goNPTA.com
www.gonpta.com
Facebook, Twitter, YouTube
Bob Forsberg, Chairman
Jan Gottesman, 1st Vice Chair
Scott Hider, 2nd Vice Chair
Matthew Bruno, EVP
John Hagrove, Treasurer
Representing distributors and suppliers of paper, packaging and facility supplies companies.
35 Members
ISBN: 1-092807-3 -
Founded in 1958

19730 **Paper Industry Management Association**
15 Technology Parkway South
Norcross, GA 30092
770-209-7230; Fax: 770-209-7359
www.imaweb.com
Facebook, Twitter, Youtube
Ralph W Feck, President
Terry M Gallagher, Regional VP
Jim Weir, Executive VP/COO
Julie Weldon, Senior Manager
Patrick Andrus, Marketing Coordinator
Contributes to the strength of the international pulp and paper community by providing the means for our members to address relevant industry issues and to develop their management and leadership skills.
4500 Members
Founded in 1919

19731 **Paper Shipping Sack Manufacturers Association**
5050 Blue Church Road
Coopersburg, PA 18036
610-282-6845; Fax: 610-282-1577
admin@pssma.org
Richard E. Storat, President
Ross Barett, Chairman
Donald P Belmont, Vice Chairman
Provides its member companies with programs and services which further the industry's objectives and in doing so promote and enhance the welfare of the industry.
45 Members
Founded in 1933

19732 **Paperboard Packaging Council**
1350 Main Street
Suite 1508
Springfield, MA 01103-1670
413-686-9191; Fax: 413-747-7777
www.ppcnet.org
Facebook, Twitter, LinkedIn, YouTube
Ben Markens, President
Lou Kornet, Vice President
Members are companies making folding cartons. Provides publications and instructional materials on the paper industry and recycling.
92 Members
Founded in 1929

19733 **Technical Association of the Pulp & Paper Industry**
15 Technology Parkway South
Norcross, GA 30092
770-446-1400
800-322-8686; Fax: 770-446-6947
webmaster@tappi.org
www.tappi.org
Larry N Montague, CEO
Chris Luettgen, Chair
Paul R. Durocher, Vice Chair
To engage the people and resources of our association in providing technically sound solutions to the workplace problems and opportunities that challenge our current and future members.
12000 Members
ISSN: 0734-1415
Founded in 1915

19734 **United Paperworkers International Union**
33 Gilmer Street SE
PO Box 3967
Atlanta, GA 30303-3202
404-413-2000; Fax: 404-651-4314
www.library.gsu.edu
Facebook, Twitter, LinkedIn, YouTube, Instagram, Flickr, Vi
Mike Dees, President
Bestows awards and conducts training seminars.
Founded in 1972

Newsletters

19735 **American Forest & Paper Association Report**
American Forest & Paper Association
1111 19th St NW
Suite 800
Washington, DC 20036-3652
202-463-2700; Fax: 202-463-2785
info@afandpa.org
www.afandpa.org
Covers events of the paper, wood and forest industry. Distribution is limited to association members only.
Cost: $1200.00
4 Pages
Frequency: Weekly
Founded in 1993

19736 **Conservatree Greenline**
Greenline Publications
PO Box 590780
San Francisco, CA 94159-780
415-386-8646; Fax: 415-391-7890
www.conservatree.com
Alan Davis, Founder/Publisher
Susan Kinsella, Editor
Reports on efforts and achievements by businesses on the environmental front.
Cost: $59.00
Circulation: 25000
Founded in 1976

19737 **Essential Resources, LLC**
45 S Park Pl
Suite 330
Morristown, NJ 07960-3924
908-832-6979; Fax: 908-832-6970
Newsletters for plastic, chemical, pharmaceutical, and packaging industries.
5-15 Pages

19738 **Official Board Markets**
Advanstar Communications
2835 N Sheffield Avenue
Suite 226
Chicago, IL 60657-9213
312-553-8922; Fax: 312-553-8929
www.packaging-online.com
Mark Arzoumanian, Editor-in-Chief
Esther Durkalski, Managing Editor
Covers the corrugated container and folding carton converting industries.
Cost: $180.00
24 Pages
Frequency: Weekly
Circulation: 5900
Founded in 1915
Printed in on glossy stock

19739 **Seaboard Bulletin**
International Paper
PO Box 1200
Bucksport, ME 04416-1200
207-469-1700; Fax: 207-469-1705
David Bailey, President
Paper industry news.

Magazines & Journals

19740 **Asia Pacific PaperMaker**
Paper Industry Management Association
4700 West Lake Avenue
Glenview, IL 60025-1485
847-375-6860; Fax: 877-527-5973
www.pima-online.org
Jim Weir, Executive VP/CEO
Patrick Andrus, Marketing Coordinator
Patrick Filippelli, Sales Manager
Sarah Walsh, Administrative Assistant
Mary Cornell, Account Manager
Founded in 1919

19741 **Board Converting News**
NV Business Publishers Corporation
43 Main St
Avon By the Sea, NJ 07717-1051
732-502-0500; Fax: 732-502-9606
tvilardi@NVPublications.com
www.nvpublications.com
Ted Vilardi, Owner
Jim Curley, Editor-in-Chief
Robyn Smith, Executive Publisher
Gail Kalina, Production Manager
Dan Brunton, Managing Director
News for the corrugated box and folding carton industry along with box and carton transacted prices.
Cost: $180.00
140 Pages
Frequency: Weekly

19742 **Converting Magazine**
Reed Business Information
2000 Clearwater Dr
Oak Brook, IL 60523-8809
630-574-0825; Fax: 630-288-8781
psaran@reedbusiness.com
www.reedbusiness.com
Jeff Greisch, President
Mark Spaulding, Editor-in-Chief
Steve Reiss, VP
Frequency: Monthly
Circulation: 4000

19743 **European PaperMaker**
Paper Industry Management Association
1699 Wall Street
Suite 212
Mount Prospect, IL 60056
847-699-1706; Fax: 847-956-0520
www.pima-online.org
Mary Cornell, Account Manager

19744 **International Paper Board Industry**
Brunton Publications & NV Public
43 Main Street
Avon By The Sea, NJ 07717-1051
732-502-0500; Fax: 732-502-9606
jcurley@NVPublications.com
www.nvpublications.com
Mike Brunton, Publisher
Jim Curley, Editor-in-Chief
Gail Kalina, Production Manager
Tom Vilardi, President
Dan Brunton, Managing Director
Information on corrugated paper and converting industry, encompassing news and production worldwide.
Cost: $60.00
Frequency: Monthly
Circulation: 10021

19745 **Latin American PaperMaker**
Paper Industry Management Association

1699 Wall Street
Suite 212
Mount Prospect, IL 60056

847-956-0250; Fax: 847-956-0520
www.pima-online.org

Ralph W. Feck, President
Jim Weir, COO/Executive VP
Patrick Andrus, Marketing Coordinator
Patrick Filippelli, Sales Manager
Sarah Walsh, Administrative Assistant
Founded in 1919

19746 **Mill Trade Journal's Recycling Markets**
NV Business Publishers Corporation
43 Main St
Avon By the Sea, NJ 07717-1051

732-502-0500
800-962-3001; Fax: 732-502-9606
advertising@NVPublications.com
www.nvpublications.com

Ted Vilardi, Owner
Roy Bradbrook, Editor
Jim Curley, Editor-in-Chief
Gail Kalina, Production Manager
Robyn Smith, Executive Publisher

Information on recycling mills paper stock, scrap metal and plastics brokers and dealers used by the municipal governments and private organizations as a basis for letting contracts.
Cost: $130.00
Frequency: Fortnightly
Circulation: 3625
Founded in 1984
Printed in 2 colors on matte stock

19747 **NPTA Distribution Sales & Management**
111 Great Neck Road
Suite 418
Great Neck, NY 11021-5402

516-829-3070; Fax: 516-829-3074

19748 **North American PaperMaker**
Paper Industry Management Association
4700 West Lake Avenue
Glenview, IL 60025-1485

847-375-6860; Fax: 877-527-5973
www.pima-online.org

Jim Weir, Executive VP/COO
Pam Oddi, Administrative Assistant
Patrick Filippelli, Sales Manager
Patrick Andrus, Marketing Coordinator
Julie Weldon, Senior Manager
Founded in 1919

19749 **Paper Age Magazine**
O'Brien Publications
20 Schofield Rd
Suite 200B
Cohasset, MA 02025-1922

781-749-5255; Fax: 781-749-5896
www.paperage.com

John O'Brien, Owner
John O'Brien, Managing Editor
Michael O'Brien, Publisher

For management and supervisory personnel of pulp, paper and paperboard mills. Tabloid-sized magazine covering the pulp, paper and converting industry, with a unique mix of timely and insightful coverage of corporate strategies, mill operations, technological innovations, industry issues, as well as analysis of the latest production and marketing trends.
Cost: $90.00
Circulation: 36156
Founded in 1884

19750 **Paper Industry Equipment Magazine**
PO Box 5675
Montgomery, AL 36103

604-264-1158
888-224-6611; Fax: 604-264-1367
info@paperindustrymag.com
www.paperindustrymag.com

Tim Shaddick, Publisher
Peter N Williamson, Editor

Services and equipment for the pulp/paper industry.
Cost: $12.00
32 Pages
Circulation: 1900
Founded in 1984
Printed in 4 colors on glossy stock

19751 **Paper Stock Report: News and Trends of the Paper Recycling Markets**
McEntee Media Corporation
13727 Holland Road
Brook Park, OH 44142

216-362-7979; Fax: 216-362-6553
www.recyle.cc

Ken McEntee, President

Covers news and trends of the scrap paper markets.
Cost: $115.00
Frequency: BiWeekly
Founded in 1990

19752 **Paper, Paperboard and Wood Pulp Monthly Statistical Summary**
American Forest & Paper Association
1111 19th St NW
Suite 800
Washington, DC 20036-3652

202-463-2700
800-878-8878; Fax: 202-463-2700
info@afandpa.org
www.afandpa.org

Donna Harman, CEO
Henson Moore, President

For the pulp and paper industry.
Cost: $435.00
Frequency: Monthly
Founded in 1878

19753 **Recycled Paper News**
McEntee Media Corporation
9815 Hazelwood Ave
Strongsville, OH 44149-2305

440-238-6603; Fax: 440-238-6712
info@recycle.cc
www.recycle.cc

Ken Mc Entee, Owner

Coverage of markets and environmental issues related to recycled paper and evironmentally friendly paper making process.
Cost: $235.00
Frequency: Monthly
Founded in 1990

19754 **Solutions! for People, Processes and Paper**
TAPPI and PIMA
15 Technology Parkway S
Norcross, GA 30092

770-446-1400
800-322-8686; Fax: 770-446-6947
webmaster@tappi.org
www.tappi.org

Larry N Montague, CEO
Thomas J Garland, Vice Chairman

19755 **TAPPI Journal**
Technical Association of the Pulp & Paper Industry
15 Technology Parkway S
Norcross, GA 30092

770-446-1400
800-322-8686; Fax: 770-446-6947
webmaster@tappi.org
www.tappi.org

Larry N Montague, CEO
Thomas J Garland, Vice Chairman

Serves domestic and international pulp, paper, paperboard, packaging and converting industries; manufacturers and suppliers of machinery, equipment, chemicals and other material.
Cost: $350.00
130 Pages
Frequency: Monthly
Circulation: 40637
ISSN: 0734-1415
Founded in 1915
Printed in 4 colors on glossy stock

19756 **Walden's Paper Report**
Walden-Mott Corporation
225 N Franklin Tpke
Ramsey, NJ 07446-1600

201-818-8630
888-292-5336; Fax: 201-818-8720
editorial@walden-mott.com
www.waldenmott.com

Alfred F Walden, President
Linda Colhen, Director of Operations
Kirk Hardy, Director of Operations

Reports on company expansions and general financial notes on the manufacturers, as well as personnel changes and appointments. Concise review of news on the North American paper industry.
Cost: $240.00
8 Pages
Circulation: 500
Founded in 1884

Trade Shows

19757 **Annual Information Technology Conference**
PIMA-Paper Industry Management Association
4700 West Lake Avenue
Glenview, IL 60025-1485

847-375-6860; Fax: 877-527-5973
www.pimaweb.org

Carol Waugh, Meetings Manager

Three-day conference to bring together IT and process control professionals from around the world to share their knowledge of information technology in the pulp and paper industry and to promote systems applications. The only IT conference planned for and by IT professionals.
500 Attendees
Frequency: Annual, April

19758 **International Bioenergy and Bioproducts Conference (IBBC)**
Technical Association of the Pulp & Paper Industry
15 Technology Parkway S
Norcross, GA 30092

770-446-1400
800-322-8686; Fax: 770-446-6947
webmaster@tappi.org
www.tappi.org

Norman F. Marsolan, Chair
Thomas J. Garland, Vice Chair
Larry N. Montague, President & CEO

Focusing on technical advancements and commercialization of bioconversion technologies that leverage the forest products manufacturing infrastructure and will include technical presen-

tations, expert panels, case studies, and reports from projects that address feedstock and harvesting improvements to increase yield and quality of biomass, and much more.
500 Attendees
Frequency: Annual/October

19759 **National Stationery Show**
George Little Management
10 Bank Street
White Plains, NY 10606-1954
914-486-6070
800-272-7469; Fax: 914-948-6180
www.
Lori Robinson, VP
Kelly Bristol, Assistant Show Manager
George Little II, President
A show for greeting cards and social stationery, writing instruments and home office products, party ware and giftwrap, scrapbooking and craft supplies, albums, frames and much more.
14000 Attendees
Frequency: May

19760 **Pulp and Paper**
Glahe International
PO Box 2460
Germantown, MD 20875-2460
301-515-0012; Fax: 301-515-0016
Exhibits of equipment, supplies and services for the pulp and paper industries.

Directories & Databases

19761 **Directory of Corrugated Plants**
Fibre Box Association
2850 Golf Road
Suite 412
Rolling Meadows, IL 60008
847-364-9600; Fax: 847-364-9639
shuske@fibrebox.org
www.fibrebox.org
Sharlene Huske
Lists companies and their related plant facilities that manufacture corrugated and solid fiber paperboard products in North America.
Cost: $200.00

19762 **Grade Finder's Competitive Grade Finder**
Grade Finders
622 Exton Commons
Exton, PA 19341
610-524-7070; Fax: 610-524-8912
info@gradefinders.com
www.gradefinders.com
Mark A Subers, President
Phyllis Subers, Office Manager
List of about 5500 manufacturers and distributors of paper. Also lists 6,000 grades of paper competitive classification.
Cost: $60.00
700 Pages
Frequency: Annual April
Circulation: 13,000
ISBN: 0-929502-14-0
Founded in 1967
Printed in one color on matte stock

19763 **Grade Finder's Paper Buyers Encyclopedia**
Grade Finders
622 Exton Commons
Exton, PA 19341
610-524-7070; Fax: 610-524-8912
www.gradefinders.com
Mark Subers, President
A list of about 6,700 manufacturers, converters and suppliers to the paper industry. In addition, it lists over 4,000 grades of paper categorized into competitive classifications showing each grades rating, opacity, color availability, etc. Also contains an extensive how-to buy paper section.
Cost: $150.00
530 Pages
Frequency: Annual
Circulation: 7000

19764 **National Institute of Packaging and Handling Logistics Engineers**
5903 Ridgeway Drive
Grand Prairie, TX 75052
817-466-7490
866-464-7453; Fax: 570-523-0606
admin@niphle.com
www.niphle.com
Facebook, Twitter, LinkedIn
Richard D Owen, Executive Director
An assemblage of professionals whose interest in the complex and diverse practice of distribution and logistics is a common bond.

19765 **PIMA Buyers Guide**
Paper Industry Management Association
4700 W Lake Avenue
Glenview, IL 60025-1485
847-375-6860; Fax: 877-527-5973
www.pimaweb.org
Joseph Agnew, Editor
Pam Oddi, Editorial Support
Directory aimed at the paper and pulp industry offering various information on manufacturers of chemicals and supplies used in the manufacturing of paper.
Cost: $120.00
60 Pages
Frequency: Annual
Circulation: 2,000
Printed in on matte stock

19766 **Rauch Guide to the US and Canadian Pulp & Paper Industry**
Grey House Publishing
4919 Route 22
PO Box 56
Amenia, NY 12501
518-789-8700
800-562-2139; Fax: 845-373-6390
books@greyhouse.com
www.greyhouse.com
Facebook, Twitter
Leslie Mackenzie, Publisher
Richard Gottlieb, Editor
Provides current market information and trends; industry economics and government regulations; company share data for each of the leading product categories; technology and raw material information; industry sources of further data; and unique profiles of 500+ pulp and paper manufacturers, a section which includes all known companies with pulp and paper sales at or over $15 million annually.
Cost: $595.00; 400 Pages
ISBN: 1-592371-31-0
Founded in 1981

19767 **TAPPI Membership Directory and Company Guide**
Technical Association of the Pulp & Paper Industry
15 Technology Parkway S
Norcross, GA 30092
770-446-1400
800-322-8686; Fax: 770-446-6947
webmaster@tappi.org
www.tappi.org
Larry N Montague, CEO
Thomas J Garland, Vice Chairman
About 35,000 member executives, managers, engineers, technologists and superintendents in the pulp, paper, packaging, converting, non-wovens and allied industries.
Cost: $140.00
Frequency: October

19768 **Walden's ABC Guide and Paper Production Yearbook**
Walden-Mott Corporation
225 N Franklin Tpke
Ramsey, NJ 07446-1600
201-818-8630; Fax: 201-818-8720
www.waldenmott.com
Alfred F Walden, President
Kirk Hardy, Director of Operations
Offers a large list of manufacturers and suppliers of printing papers.
Cost: $117.50
300 Pages
Frequency: Annual January

Industry Web Sites

19769 **http://gold.greyhouse.com**
G.O.L.D Grey House OnLine Databases
Grey House Publishing's online database platform, GOLD, offers Quick Search, Keyword Search and Expert Search for most business sectors including paper and allied products markets. The GOLD platform makes finding the information you need quick and easy - whether you're a novice searcher or an experienced database user. All of Grey House's directory products are available for subscription on the GOLD platform.

19770 **www.afandpa.org**
American Forest and Paper Association
Serves forest, paper, paperboard and wood products packaging industry

19771 **www.fibrebox.org**
Fibre Box Association
For national corrigated manufacturers.

19772 **www.fpi.org**
Foodservice & Packaging Institute
Manufacturers, suppliers and distributors of one-time use products used for food service, as well as packaging products made from paper, plastic, aluminum and other materials. Membership dues based on sales.

19773 **www.gonpta.com**
National Paper Trade Association
Association for paper, packaging and applied products distribution channel.

19774 **www.greyhouse.com**
Grey House Publishing
Authoritative reference directories for most business sectors including paper and allied products markets. Users can search the online databases with varied search criteria allowing for custom searches by product category, geographic area, sales volume, keyword, subject and more. Full Grey House catalog and online ordering also available.

19775 **www.tappi.org**
Technical Association of the Pulp & Paper Industry

Associations

19776 Actors Equity Association
165 W 46th St
New York, NY 10036-2500

212-869-8530; Fax: 212-719-9815
www.actorsequity.org

Alan Eisenberg, CEO
Mark Zimmerman, President
David Lotz, National Director of Communications
Mary Lou Westerfield, Natioanl Director Policy
Flora Stamatiades, National Director Organizing

A labor union that represents Actors and Stage Managers in the United States. Seeks to advance, promote and foster the art of live theatre as an essential component of our society. Negotiates wages and working conditions and provides a wide range of benefits, including health and pension plans.
45000 Members
Founded in 1913

19777 African Performing Arts Association
PO Box 660573
Atlanta, GA 30366

Home Page: www.africanperformingarts.org

Founded in 2001

19778 Alternate ROOTS
115 Martin Luther King Jr Dr
Suite 200
Atlanta, GA 30303

404-577-1079; Fax: 404-577-7991
www.alternateroots.org
Facebook, Twitter, Flickr

19779 American Alliance for Theatre and Education
4908 Auburn Avenue
Bethesda, MD 20814-3474

301-200-1944; Fax: 301-280-1682
info@aate.com
www.aate.com
Facebook, Twitter, LinkedIn, RSS

Gary Minyard, President
Kelly Prestel, Treasurer
Amy P.Jenson, Advocacy Director
Jeremy Kisling, Communications Director
Mitch Mattson, Planning Director

The national voice for theatre and education, representing artists and educators serving young people in theatre and education. Its members play a vital role in advocating for the interests of children who benefit from theatre in their communities and classrooms. AATE embraces diversity and encourages inclusion of all races, social classes, ages, genders, religions, sexual orientations, national organizations and abilities.
700 Members
Founded in 1986

19780 American Association of Community Theatre
1300 Gendy Street
Fort Worth, TX 76107-4036

817-732-3177
866-687-2228; Fax: 817-732-3178
info@aact.org
www.aact.org
Facebook, Twitter, LinkedIn

Julie Crawford, Executive Director
Murray Chase, President
Carole Ries, Executive Vice President
Frank Peot, Secretary
Michael Fox, Treasurer

The national voice of community theatre, representing the interests of its members and over 7,000 theatres across the US and with the armed services overseas. Its mission is to foster the encouragement and development of, and commitment to, the highest standards by community theatres, including standards of excellence for production, management, governance, community relations and service.
Founded in 1986
Mailing list available for rent: 10000 names at $180 per M

19781 American Composers Forum
75 West 5th Street
Suite 522
Saint Paul, MN 55102-1439

651-228-1407; Fax: 651-291-7978
lhoeschler@gmail.com
www.composersforum.org
Facebook, Twitter

Mary Ellen Childs, Chair
Patrick Castillo, Vice Chair
Dan Thomas, Vice Chair
David Ranheim, Secretary
Sam Hsu, Treasurer
2000 Members
Founded in 1973

19782 American Dance Therapy Association
10632 Little Patuxent Pkwy
Suite 108
Columbia, MD 21044-3263

410-997-4040; Fax: 410-997-4048
info@adta.org
www.adta.org
Facebook, Twitter, Pinterest, YouTube

Gloria Farrow, Manager
Jody Wager, President
Gloria J Farrow, Operations Director
Meghan Dempsey, Treasurer
Gail Wood, Secretary

Professional organization of dance movement therapists, with members both nationally and internationally; offers training, research findings, and a newsletter. Holds annual conference.
1.1M Members
Founded in 1966

19783 American Disc Jockey Association
20118 N 67th Avenue
Suite 300-605
Glendale, AZ 85308

888-723-5776
888-723-5776; Fax: 866-310-4676
office@adja.org
www.adja.org
Facebook, Twitter, YouTube

Rob Snyder, Director

An association of professional mobile entertainers. Encourages success for its members through continuous education, camaraderie, and networking. The primary goal is to educate Disc Jockeys so that each member acts ethically and responsibly.

19784 American Federation of Musicians of the United States and Canada
1501 Broadway
Suite 600
New York, NY 10036-5501

212-869-1330; Fax: 212-764-6134
info@afm.org
www.afm.org
Facebook, Twitter, YouTube

Thomas Lee, President
Linda Patterson, Executive Secreatry to President

AFM is an association of professional musicians united through their locals so that they can live and work in dignity; produce work that will be fulfilling and compensated fairly; have a meaningful voice in decisions that affect them; have the opportunity to develop their talents and skills; whose collective voice and power will be realized in a democratic and progressive union; and who oppose the forces of exploitation through their union solidarity.
10K Members
Founded in 1896

19785 American Indian Registry for the Performing Arts
1717 N Highland
Suite 614
Los Angeles, CA 90028

213-962-6574
www.afn.org/~native/orgnztns.htm

Organization of American Indian performers and technical personnel in the entertainment field.

19786 American Institute of Organ Builders
PO Box 35306
Canton, OH 44735

330-806-9011
robert_sullivan@pipeorgan.org
www.pipeorgan.org
Twitter

Philip Parkey, President
Michael Lauffer, Vice President
Louis E Patterson, Secretary
Charles R Eames, Treasurer
Joseph O'Donnell, Secretary

Sponsors training seminars, quarterly journal and annual convention for pipe organ builders and service technicians.
385 Members
Founded in 1974
Mailing list available for rent: 350 names at $250 per M

19787 American Institute of Organbuilders
PO Box 35306
Canton, OH 44735

330-806-9011
www.pipeorgan.org
Facebook

Philip Parkey, President
Michael Lauffer, Vice President
Robert Sullivan, Executive Secretary
Joseph O'Donnell, Secretary
Charles R. Eames, Treasurer
Founded in 1974

19788 Americans for the Arts
1000 Vermont Avenue, NW
6th Floor
Washington, DC 20005

202-371-2830; Fax: 202-371-0424
www.americansforthearts.org
Facebook, Twitter, LinkedIn, YouTube, Pinterest

Abel Lopez, Chair
Ramona Baker, Vice Chair
C. Kendric Fergeson, Immediate Past Chair
Michael Spring, Secretary
Julie Muraco, Treasurer
Founded in 1960

19789 Associated Pipe Organ Builders of America
P.O. Box 8268
Erie, PA 8268

800-473-5270
800-473-5270
www.apoba.com

Bob Rusczyk, Executive Director
Richard Parsons, President
Paul Lytle, Vice President
Randall Dyer, Secretary
Seth Marshall, Treasurer

A professional association of North American firms engaged in building traditional pipe organs. Members are a select group of organbuilders who have passed stringent membership requirements which include commitment to principles regarding the use of electronic technology in organ building.
27 Members

19790 **Association for Theatre in Higher Education**
1000 Westgate Dr.
Suite 252
St. Paul, MN 55114
651-288-3430
800-918-9216; Fax: 651-290-2266
info@athe.org
www.athe.org
Facebook
Eric Ewald, Executive Director
Patricia Ybarra, President
Karen Jean Martinson, Secretary
Scott Shattuck, Treasurer
ATHE serves the interests of its diverse individual and organization members. Its vision is to advocate for the field of theatre and performance in higher education. It serves as an intellectual and artistic center for producing new knowledge about theatre and performance-related disciplines. cultivating vital alliances with other scholarly and creative disciplines, linking with professional and community-based theatres, and promoting access and equity.
1700 Members
Founded in 1986

19791 **Association of Arts Administration Educators**
Bolz Center for Arts Administration
188 Hanford Street
Columbus, OH 43206
312-469-0795; Fax: 608-265-2735
info@artsadministration.org
www.artsadministration.org
Facebook, Twitter, RSS
Andrew Taylor, President/Director
John McCann, VP
Phyllis Johnson, Treasurer
Stephen Boyle, Secretary
The Association of Administration Educators (AAAE) is an international organization incorporated as a nonprofit institution within the United States. Its mission is to represent college and university graduate and undergraduate programs in the arts administration, encompassing training in the management of visual, performing, literary, media, cultural and arts service organizations.
Founded in 1975

19792 **Association of Hispanic Arts**
P.O.Box 1169
El Barrio, NY 10029
212-876-1242
888-876-1240; Fax: 212-876-1285
www.nalac.org
Nicholas L Arture, Executive Director
Julia L Gutierrez-Rivera, Program Officer/Arts Service Coord.
Crystal Chaparro, Office Assistant
Gregory Castro, Comptroller
Brenda L Jiminez, Board Chair
A nonprofit arts service organization serving the Latino arts and cultural community. AHA was established out of the need to create funding and presenting opportunities for individual Latino artists and cultural organizations whose contributions were unrecognized and whose efforts were underserved by mainstream public and private institutions.
Founded in 1975

19793 **Association of Performing Arts Presenters**
1211 Connecticut Ave NW
Suite 200
Washington, DC 20036-2716
202-833-2787
888-820-2787; Fax: 202-833-1543
info@artspresenters.org
www.apap365.org/
Facebook, Twitter, YouTube
Sandra Gibson, President
Dr. Michael Blachly, Chair
Brain Jose, Vice Chairman
Nicole Borrelli Hearn, Vice Chair
Todd Wetzel, Treasurer
A national membership and advocacy organization dedicated to bringing performing artists and audiences together.
1900 Members
Founded in 1957

19794 **Broadcast Music Incorporated BMI**
7 World Trade Center
250 Greenwich Street
New York, NY 10007-0030
212-220-3000; Fax: 212-246-2163
newyork@bmi.com
www.bmi.com
Facebook, Twitter, LinkedIn, YouTube, Pinterest, RSS, Insta
Michael O'Neill, President & CEO
Bruce Esworthy, Senior Vice President & CFO
Mike West, SVP & Chief Information Officer
Nade Latto, VP, Human Resources
Stuart Rosen, SVP & General Counsel
American performing rights organization that represents approximately 300,000 songwriters, composers and music publishers in all genres of music. The nonprofit company collects license fees on behalf of those American creators it represents, as well as thousands of creators from around the world who chose BMI for representation in the US. These fees are then distributed as royalties to the writers, composers and copyright holders it represents.
300m Members
Founded in 1939

19795 **Chinese Music Society of North America**
PO Box 5275
Woodridge, IL 60517-0275
630-910-1551; Fax: 630-910-1561
www.chinesemusic.net
Sin-Yan Shen, President
Kok-Koon Ng, VP
Yuan-Yuan Lee, Executive Director
Billie Jefferson, Artistic Administrator
Der-Tung Yuan, Membership
A national nonprofit organization founded to increase and diffuse the knowledge of Chinese music and performing arts. Today it has grown to become the national association of Chinese musicians and scholars and National and International organization specializing in Research and Educational Material in English concerning Music/Theater/Dance and Musical Instruments from China and Non-Western Cultures.
Founded in 1969

19796 **Chorus America**
P.O. Box 2646
Suite 310
Arlington, VA 22202-0646
202-331-7577; Fax: 202-331-7599
webmaster@chorusamerica.org
www.chorusamerica.org
Facebook, Twitter, YouTube, Google+
Rollo Dilworth, Chairman
Gayle. M Ober, Immediate Past Chairman
Mitch Menchaca, Interim CEO
Michael McCarthy, Treasurer
Mary Lyons, Secretary
2000 Members
Founded in 1977

19797 **Classical Action**
165 W 46th St
Suite 1300
New York, NY 10036-2514
212-997-7717; Fax: 212-840-0551
www.classicalaction.org
Facebook, Twitter
Charles Hamlen, Founding Director
Chris Kenney, Associate Director
Since 1993, Classical Action has provided a unified voice for all those within the performing arts community to help combat HIV/AIDS and the devastating effects of this epidemic.
Founded in 1993

19798 **Conductors Guild**
719 Twinridge Ln
Richmond, VA 23235
804-553-1378; Fax: 804-553-1876
guild@conductorsguild.org
www.conductorsguild.org
Facebook, Twitter, LinkedIn
Gordon Johnson, President
Amanda Burton Winger, Executive Director
Erin Freeman, VP
Christopher Blair, Treasurer
David Leibowitz, Secretary
The Conductors Guild is the only music service organization devoted exclusively to the advancement of the art of conducting and to serving the artistic and professional needs of conductors.
1850+ Members
Founded in 1975

19799 **Congress on Research in Dance**
7044 South 13th Street
Oak Creek, WI 53154
414-908-4951; Fax: 414-768-8001
info@cordance.org
www.cordance.org
Anne Flynn, President
Helen Thomas, Chair, Editorial Board
Petri Hoppu, Vice President
Bridget Cauthery, Treasurer
A not-for-profit, interdisciplinary organization with an open, international membership. Its purposes are: to encourage research in all aspects of dance, including related fields; to foster the exchange of ideas, resources, and methodology, through publication, international and regional conferences and workshops; to promote the accessibility of research materials.
Cost: $35.00
750 Members
Founded in 1965
Mailing list available for rent

19800 **Costume Society of America**
Home Page: www.costumesocietyamerica.com
Facebook, Twitter, LinkedIn, YouTube

19801 **Country Dance & Song Society**
116 Pleasant St
Suite 345
Easthampton, MA 01027-2759
413-203-5467; Fax: 413-203-5471
office@cdss.org
www.cdss.org
Facebook, Twitter, Instagram, YouTube, Flickr
Rima Dael, Executive/Artistic Director
Carol Compton, Financial Manager
Christine Dadmun, Membership Admin
Bob Blondin, Business Manager
Robin Hayden, Development Director

A national organization dedicated to the preservation and promotion of English and Anglo-American traditional and historical folk dance, music and song. Composed of individual members and affiliate groups, it functions both as an international service bureau and as a facilitator in building and maintaining local and regional dance, music and song communities. It exists to meed needs for community-based activity, for active participation, and for sharing and keeping historical and folk
3400 Members
Founded in 1915

19802 **Dance Critics Association**
Old Chelsea Station
PO Box 1882
New York, NY 10011
732-643-4008
dancecritics@hotmail.com
www.dancecritics.org
Kena Herod, Co-Chair
Linda Traiger, Co-Chair
Encourages excellence in dance criticism through education, research and the exchange of ideas. Produces quarterly newsletter.
Cost: $50.00
300 Members
Founded in 1973

19803 **Dance Educators of America**
PO Box 740387
Suite262
Boynton Beach, FL 33474
914-636-3200
800-329-3868; Fax: 914-636-5895
info@dancedea.com
www.usadance.dancedea.com/
Facebook, Twitter, Youtube
Vickie Sheer, Executive Director
Fran Peters, President
Charles Kelley, Treasurer
Robyn Bourdeau, Chief Financial Officer
Stephen Ball, Events and DEA Coordinator
Dedicated to improving the quality and teaching abilities of its member teachers and enhancing their education of students, as well as furthering the professional and ethical standards in the performing arts and of dance in all its form. Membership is limited to qualified teachers.
Cost: $150.00
1800 Members
Founded in 1932

19804 **Dance Films Association**
252 Java Street
Suit 333
Brooklyn, NY 11222
347-505-8649; Fax: 212-727-0765
info@dancefilms.org
www.dancefilms.org
Facebook, Twitter, Vimeo
Deidra Towers, Executive Director
Latika Young, Education Director
Anna Brady Nuse, Festival Coordinator
Julian Barnett, Research/Development
Supports all those professionals in both the dance and the film community. Publishes bi-monthly magazine.
Cost: $50.00
Founded in 1956

19805 **Dance Masters of America**
PO Box 610533
Bayside, NY 11361
718-255-4013; Fax: 718-225-4293
dmamann@aol.com
www.dma-national.org
Shely Pack Manning, National President
Robert Mann, National Executive Secretary
Charleen Locascio, National Treasurer
An international organization of dance educators who have been certified by test to teach whose main focus is advancing the art of dance and improving the practice of its teaching.
2.5M Members
Founded in 1884

19806 **Dance USA**
1111 16th St NW
Suite 300
Washington, DC 20036-4830
202-833-1717; Fax: 202-833-2686
danceusa@danceusa.org
www.danceusa.org
Facebook, Twitter, YouTube, Vimeo
Amy Fitterer, Executive Director
Tom Thielen, Director Finance/Operations
Katherine Fabian, Membership Manager
Dough Singleton, Chair
Andrea Clark-Smith, Vice Chair
Provides a forum for the discussion of issues of concern to members and a support network for exchange of information.
400 Members
Founded in 1982

19807 **Dance/USA**
1111 16th Street NW Ste. 300
Washington, DC 20036
202-833-1717
www.danceusa.org
Facebook, Twitter, YouTube, Vimeo
Dough Singleton, Chair
Charlotte Ballet, Chair Elect
Andrea Clark-Smith, Vice Chair
Sarah Thompson, Secretary
Robert Dorf, Treasurer

19808 **Dramatists Guild of America**
1501 Broadway
Suite 701
New York, NY 10036-5505
212-398-9366; Fax: 212-944-0420
www.dramatistsguild.com
Ralph Sevush, Executive Director Business Affairs
Gary Garrison, Executive Director Creative Affairs
Abby Marcus, Managing Director
Roland Tec, Director of Membership
The Dramatists Guild of America was established over eighty years ago, and is the only professional association that advances the interests of playwrights, composers, lyricists and librettists writing for the living stage.
6000+ Members
Founded in 1964

19809 **Educational Theatre Association**
2343 Auburn Ave
Cincinnati, OH 45219-2819
513-421-3900; Fax: 513-421-7077
www.schooltheatre.org
Facebook, Twitter, Instagram, YouTube
Jay Seller, President
Frank Pruet, VP
Julie Woffington, Executive Director
Jim Flanagan, Director of Operations
Ginny Butsch, Community Manager
EdTA is a professional organization for theatre educators. In addition to providing professional development, advocacy, and networking support to its members, Edta oprtates the International Society, an honorary organization for high school and middle school theatre students.
4600+ Members
Founded in 1929

19810 **Esperanza Performing Arts Association**
Po Box 502591
San Diego, CA 92150
858-391-1311
www.esperanzaarts.org
Alan Cox, Executive Director
Adam Stout, Assistant Director

19811 **Fractured Atlas**
248 W. 35th Street, 10th Fl.
New York, NY 10001
888-692-7878; Fax: 212-277-8025
www.fracturedatlas.orgÿ
Facebook, Twitter, LinkedIn
Holly Sidford, Chair
Russell Wills Taylor, Vice Chair
Adam Forest Huttler, Executive Director
Adam Huttler, Secretary
Alanna Weifenbach, Treasurer
Founded in 1998

19812 **Fritz and Lavinia Jensen Foundation**
Foundation for the Carolinas
220 N Tryon Street
Charlotte, NC 28202
704-641-4691; Fax: 704-973-4599
info@jensenfoundation.org
www.jensenfoundation.org
Ann Todd, Competition Coordinator
Jane W. Pardue, President
R. Benjamin Leaptrott, Jr., Vice Presidentÿ
Oliver Worthington, Vice Presidentÿ
Gene Hoots, Trustee
Sponsors voice competitions supporting opera and other classical singers.

19813 **Gina Bachauer International Piano Foundation**
138 W Broadway
Suite 220
Salt Lake City, UT 84101-1913
801-297-4250; Fax: 801-521-9202
info@bachauer.com
www.bachauer.com
Facebook, Twitter, Flickr, Google+, YouTube
Thomas Holst, Manager
Kimi Kawashima, Manager
Arlo McGinn, Secretary
Nathan Morgan, Treasurer
Kary Billings, Chairman
The mission of the Foundation is to further the pianistic art, foster excellence in performance and teaching, develop opportunities for pianists beyond the scope of the organization and offer leadership in developing a musically-educated community.
Founded in 1976

19814 **Guild of American Luthiers**
8222 S Park Ave
Tacoma, WA 98408-5226
253-472-7853; Fax: 253-472-7853
orders@luth.org
www.luth.org
Facebook
Debra G Olsen, Executive Director
Tim Olsen, Editor
Kurt Kendall, Membership
Manufacturers and repairs stringed instruments; offers quarterly journal and triennial meeting.
Cost: $45.00
3000 Members
Founded in 1972

19815 **Institute of Outdoor Drama**
201 Erwin Building
Mail Stop 528
Greenville, NC 27858-4353

252-328-5363; Fax: 252-328-0968
www.outdoor-theatre.org
Facebook, Twitter, RSS

Michael C. Hardy, Director
Susan D. Phillips, Business Manager
Founded in 1963

19816 **International Computer Music Association**
1819 Polk Street
Suite 330
San Francisco, CA 94109

FAX 734-878-3031
icma@umich.edu
www.computermusic.org
Facebook

Tae Hong Park, President
Margaret Schedel, VP Of Conference
Michael Gurevich, Vice President for Membership
Tae Hong Park, Vice President for Preservation
Chryssie Nanou, Treasurer/Secretary

The International Computer Music Association is an international affiliaton of individuals and institutions involved in the technical, creative, and performance aspects of computer music. It serves composers, engineers, researchers and musicians who are interested in the integration of music and technology.
Cost: $63.52
450 Members

19817 **International Festivals and Events Association**
2603 W Eastover Ter
Boise, ID 83706-2800

208-433-0950; Fax: 208-433-9812
nia@ifea.com
www.ifea.com
Facebook, Twitter, LinkedIn, YouTube

Ted Baroody, Chair
Steven Wood Schmader, President & CEO
Nia Forester Hovde, VP & Dir., Marketing & Comm.
Beth Peterson, Director, Membership Services
Craig Sarton, Director, Creative & Publications

A voluntary association of events, event producers, event suppliers, and related professionals and organizations whose common purpose is the production and presentation of festivals, events, and civic and private celebrations.
2000 Members
Founded in 1956

19818 **International Performing Arts for Youth**
1315 Walnut Street
Suite 320
Philadelphia, PA 19107

267-690-1325; Fax: 267-519-3343
www.ipayweb.org

Ms. Peg Schuler-Armstrong, President
Ms. Pamela K. Lieberman, Vice President
Ms. Mary Kate Barley-Jenkins, Immediate Past President
Jeremy Boomer Stacey, Executive Director
Ms. Nadine Carew, Treasurer
Founded in 2001

19819 **International Planned Music Association**
5900 S Salina Street
Syracuse, NY 13205

315-469-7711; Fax: 315-469-8842

Bob Bobuk, President
Gary Alshouse, VP
Barb Cowsert, Secretary
Jon Baker, Treasurer
Jack Carroll, General Counsel

IPMA is a trade organization made up of providers of planned and programmed music services and key vendors. The Associatin exists to provide members with a common ground on which to share informatio about running exciting, profitable franchises and to provide associate members with opportunities to expand their sales in markets all over the world.
200 Members

19820 **International Society for the Performing Arts**
630 9th Avenue
Suite 213
New York, NY 10036-4752

212-206-8490; Fax: 212-206-8603
www.ispa.org
Facebook, Twitter, Pinterest

Anthony Sargent, Chair
Jeff Daniel, Treasurer
Margia Claudia, Secretary
Johann Zietsman, CEO
Lynne Caruso, Membership Manager

A nonprofit organization of executives and directors of concert and performance halls, festivals, performing companies, and artists competitions; government cultural officials; artists' managers; and other interested parties with a professional involvement in the performing arts around the world, and in every arts disciplie. The purpose of ISPA is to develop, nurture, energize and educate an international network of arts leaders and professionals who are dedicated to advancing its field.
600 Members
Founded in 1949

19821 **International Theatre Equipment Association**
770 Broadway
5th Floor
New York, NY 10003-9595

646-654-7680; Fax: 212-257-6428
www.itea.com

Robert Sunshine, Executive Director
Barry Ferrell, President
Jack Panzeca, VP
Joe DeMeo, Treasurer
Sarah Fuller, Secretary

Fosters and maintains professional, business and social relationships among its members within all segments of the motion picture industry. Bestows annual Teddy Award to manufacturer of the year and the annual Rodney Award to dealer of the year.
Cost: $375.00
180 Members
Founded in 1971

19822 **International Ticketing Association**
10401 N Meridian St
Suite 300
Indianapolis, IN 46290

212-629-4036; Fax: 212-629-8532
info@intix.org
www.intix.org
Facebook, Twitter, LinkedIn

Jena Hoffman, President & CEO
Tiffany Kelham, Membership Associate
Stacey Ogren, Meeting Manager
Dorothea Heck, Business Development
Christine Payne, Marketing Manager

Non-profit association committed to the improvement, progress and advancement of ticket management. Provides educational programs, trade shows, conducts surveys, conference proceedings, and its valuable membership directory.
Founded in 1982

19823 **Jazz Education**
3303 South Rice, Suite 107
PO Box 8031
Houston, TX 77056

713-839-7000; Fax: 715-839-8266
www.jazzeducation.org
Facebook, LinkedIn

Tracy Scott, Executive Director

Nonprofit music organization providing worthwhile educational activities for school-aged youth in the field of music. Includes many subjects not covered by school systems. Promotes appreciation and understanding of Jazz.
Founded in 1970

19824 **League of American Orchestras**
33 West 60th Street
New York, NY 10023

212-262-5161; Fax: 212-262-5198
member@americanorchestras.org
www.americanorchestras.org
Facebook, Twitter, YouTube

Patricia A Richards, Chair
Steven C. Parrish, Vice Chair
Jesse Rosen, President/ CEO
Barry A Sanders, Secretary
Robert A Peiser, Treasurer
800 Members
Founded in 1942

19825 **League of American Theatres and Producers**
729 Seventh Avenue
5th Floor
New York, NY 10019

212-764-1122; Fax: 212-944-2136
league@broadway.org
www.broadwayleague.com
Facebook, Twitter, LinkedIn, Pinterest, Instagram, YouTube

Charolette St Martin, Executive Director
Colin Gibson, Director Finance
Jane Svendsen, Director Marketing
Ed Sandler, Director Membership Services

National trade association for the commercial theatre industry whose principal activity is negotiation of labor contracts and government relations.
400 Members
Founded in 1930

19826 **League of Historic American Theatres**
9 Newport Drive
Suite 200
Forest Hillÿ, MD 21050

443-640-1058
877-627-0833; Fax: 443-640-1031
info@lhat.org

Frances Holden, Executive Director
Thomas Johnson, VP
Alice North, Treasurer
John Bell, Chair
Don Telford, Immediate Past Chair

The League of Historic American Theatres, a nonprofit membership association, promotes the rescue, rehabilitation and sustainable operation of historic theatres throughout North America. Founded in 1976, the League serves its members through educational programs, publications, spe-

cialized services and an annual conference and theatre tour.
500+ Members
Founded in 1976

19827 **League of Professional Theatre Women**
520 8th Ave
24th Floor
New York, NY 10018
888-297-3117
theatrewomen.org
Shellen Lubin, Co-President
Mary Hodges, Co-President
Katrin Hilbe, Executive VP
Thomas Kelso, Bookkeeper
The League's purpose is to emphasize networking in order to promote the visibility of women in all aspects of professional theatre. League members include actors, administrators, agents, directors, composers, critics, and more.

19828 **Literary Managers and Dramaturgs of the Americas**
PO Box 36
New York, NY 10129
212-561-0315
800-680-2148
lmdanyc@hotmail.com
www.lmda.org
Facebook, Twitter
Brain Quirt, Chair
Beth Blickers, President
Danielle Carroll, Administrative Director
Nichole Gantshar, Treasurer
Richard Wolfe, VP
The mission of the LMDA is to affirm the role of dramaturg, to expande the possibilities of the field to other media and institutions and to cultivate, develop and promote the function of dramaturgy and literary management.
500 Members

19829 **Mid-Atlantic Arts Foundation**
201 N Charles Street
Suite 401
Baltimore, MD 21201-4102
410-539-6656; Fax: 410-837-5517
info@midatlanticarts.org
www.midatlanticarts.org
Facebook, Twitter, YouTube, Pinterest
Alan Cooper, Executive Director
E Scott Johnson, Secretary
MAAF celebrates, promotes and supports the richness and diversity of the region's art resources and works to increase access to the arts and other cultures of the region and the world.
40000 Members
Founded in 1979
Mailing list available for rent: 30,000 names

19830 **National Alliance for Musical Theatre**
520 Eighth Avenue
Suite 301
New York, NY 10018
212-714-6668; Fax: 212-714-0469
info@namt.org
www.namt.orgÿ
Facebook, Twitter, RSS, YouTube
Michael G. Murphy, Treasurer
Paige Price, Vice President
Betsy King Militello, Executive Director
Wayne Bryan, Secretary
Jeff Loeb, President
Not-for-profit working for the advance of musical theatre.
30000 Members
Founded in 1985

19831 **National Association for Drama Therapy**
Suite 101
Suite 220
Albany, NY 12203
888-416-7167; Fax: 518-463-8656
office@nadta.org
www.nadta.org
Facebook, Twitter, YouTube, Instagram
Nadya Trytan, President
Jeremy Segall, MA, RDT, LCAT, VP
Whitney Sullivan, RDT, LCSW, Secretary
Dani York, RDT, LCAT, Treasurer
Nancy Sondag, Membership
A nonprofit association which establishes and upholds high standards of professional competence and ethics among drama therapists; to develop criteria for training and registration; to sponsor publications and conferences; and to promote the profession of drama therapy through information and advocacy.
Founded in 1979

19832 **National Association for Music Education**
1806 Robert Fulton Drive
Reston, VA 20191
703-860-4000
800-336-3768; Fax: 703-860-1531
www.nafme.org
Facebook, Twitter, LinkedIn, Google+, Pinterest
Lynn M Brinckmeyer, President
The mission of MENC is to advance music education by encouraging the study and making of music by all. MENC offers more than 100 books, videos and compact discs, as well as two general-interest magazines on music education and four more closely targeted journals.
Founded in 1907
Mailing list available for rent: 60,000 names

19833 **National Association of Latino Arts and Cultures**
1208 Buena Vista
San Antonio, TX 78207
210-432-3982; Fax: 210-432-3934
info@nalac.org
www.nalac.org
Facebook, Twitter
Maria L¢pez De L,on, Executive Director
A nonprofit dedicated exclusively to serving Latino arts communities.
Founded in 1989

19834 **National Association of Performing Arts Managers and Agents**
459 Columbus Avenue
#133
New York, NY 10024
Home Page: www.napama.org
Jerry Ross, President
David Wannen, Vice President
Jeff Laramie, Vice President
Laurelle Favreau, Secretary
Robin Pomerance, Treasurer
Founded in 1979

19835 **National Corporate Theatre Fundÿ**
505 Eighth Avenue
Suite 2303
New York, NY 10018
212-750-6895; Fax: 212-750-6977
www.theatreforward.org
Facebook, Twitter, YouTube
Richard Thomas, Honorary Chair
James S Turley, Chairman
Gretchen Shugart, President
Bruce R Ewing, Secretary
Frank Orlowski, Treasurer

19836 **National Costumers Association**
6000 E. Evans Ave.
#3-205
Denver, CO 80222ÿ
317-351-1940
800-622-1321; Fax: 317-351-1941
office@costumers.org
www.costumers.org
Janie Westendorf, President
Deborah Meredith, First Vive President
Linda Adams Foat, Second VP
Jennifer Skarstedt, Secretary/Treasurer
The objectives on the NCA are to establish and maintain professional and ethical standards of business in the costume industry. They encourage and promote a greater and more diversified use of costumes in all fields of human activity. They provide trade information, cooperation and friendship among its members together with a sound public relations policy.
400 Members
Founded in 1923

19837 **National Dance Association**
1900 Association Dr
Reston, VA 20191-1502
703-476-3400
800-213-7193; Fax: 703-476-9527
nda@aahperd.org
www.aahperd.org/nda
Facebook, Twitter
Colleen Dean, Manager
Marcey E Siegel, VP Dance Education
Mary Ann Laverty, VP Dance Performance
A nonprofit service organization dedicated to increasing knowledge, improving skills and encouraging sound professional practices in dance education while promoting and supporting creative and healthy lifestyles through high quality dance programs.
2000 Members
Founded in 1932

19838 **National Dance Education Organization**
8609 2nd Avenue
Suite 203 B
Silver Spring, MD 20910
301-585-2880; Fax: 301-585-2888
info@ndeo.org
www.ndeo.org
Susan McGreevy-Nichols, Executive Director
Patricia Cohen, Treasurer
A nonprofit organization dedicated to promoting standards of excellence in dance education.
2000 Members
Founded in 1998

19839 **National Dance Society**
852 Lincoln Drive
Fredericksburg, VA 22407
540-642-1041
info.nationaldancesociety.org
www.nationaldancesociety.org
Cheryl Stafford, Advocacy Chair
Gayle Kassing, Professional Development Chair
Barbara Hernandez, Publications Chair
Keisha Breaker, Social Media Chair
Ronelle Eddings, Dance Education Chair
The National Dance Society focuses on providing teaching resources and leadership for the delivery of dance education. They promote inclusivity in dance as they believe it to be a healthy lifelong activity, available to everyone.
Founded in 2014

19840 **National Endowment for the Arts**
1100 Pennsylvania Ave NW
Washington, DC 20506

202-682-5400; Fax: 202-682-5611
webmgr@arts.gov
www.arts.gov
Facebook, Twitter

Dana Gioia, CEO
Guilomar Barbi, Scheduler
Sarah Cook, Executive Assistant
Jon P Peede, Counselor to the Chairman
Sydney Smith, Administrative Specialist

The National Endowment for the Arts, an investment in America's living heritage, serves the public good by nurturing the expression of human creativity, supporting the cultivation of community spirit, and fostering the recognition and appreciation of the excellence and diversity of our nation's artistic accomplishments.

19841 **National Folk Organization**
NFO Membership Services
15221 N. CR 400 E.
Eaton, IN 47338

president@nfo-usa.org
nfo-usa.org
Facebook

Jeanette Gibson, President
Cricket Raybern, Vice President

The NFO is a membership-based organization connected through a love of folk dance, the cultural arts and traditions. Their purpose is to further folk dance and associated events across the United States.
Founded in 1986

19842 **National Music Publishers Association**
101 Constitution Avenue NW
Suite 705 East
Washington, DC 20001

202-742-4375; Fax: 202-393-6673
pr@nmpa.org
www.nmpa.org
Facebook, Twitter, YouTube, Instagram

Martin Bandier, President/CEO
John Eastman, Director

The NMPA is committed to promoting and advancing the interests of music publishers and their songwriting partners. Their goal is to foster a business climate that allows its members to thrive creatively and financially.
800 Members
Founded in 1917

19843 **National Performance Network**
1024 Elysian Fields Avenue
New Orleans, LA 70117

504-595-8008; Fax: 504-595-8006
info@npnweb.org
www.npnweb.org
Facebook, Twitter

Abe Rybeck, Chair
Yolanda Cesta Cursach, Vice Chair
MK Wegmann, President/ CEO
Meena Natarajan, Secretary
Shannon Daut, Treasurer
Founded in 1985

19844 **National Piano Travelers Association**
401 Sawkill Road
PO Box 2264
Kingston, NY 12401-2264

845-338-1464; Fax: 845-338-5751

Roy Chandler, President
Bob dove, VP
Dawn Demars, Secretary/Treasurer

Buys and sells pianos.
110 Members

19845 **Network of Ensemble Theaters**
PO Box 83526
Portland, OR 97283

info@ensembletheaters.net
www.ensembletheaters.net

Laurie McCants, President
August Schulenburg, Vice President
Mark Valdez, Executive Director
Cynthia Ling Lee, Secretary
Bruce Allardice, Treasurer
Founded in 1995

19846 **New England Theatre Conference**
215 Knob Hill Drive
Hamden, CT 06518

617-851-8535; Fax: 203-288-5938
mail@netconline.org
www.netconline.org

James Fergudon, President
Jeffrey Watts, Executive VP
Jamie Taylor, VP Administration/Finance
Chris Crossen-sills, Executive Secretary
Jim Quinn, Clerk of the Corporation

Non-profit corporation, composed of individuals and organizations in the six-State region of New England, who are active and interested in the performing arts. The NETC promotes excellence in theatre for their region, and supports quality theatre and performance in all of its diversity.
500 Members
Founded in 1952

19847 **New Music USA**
90 Broad St.
Suite 1902
New York, NY 10004

212-645-6949
info@newmusicusa.org
www.newmusicusa.org
Facebook, Twitter, Vimeo

Ed Harsh, President & CEO
Frederick Peters, Chair

Part of the Performing Arts Alliance, New Music USA advocates for the creation and performance of new music.

19848 **North American Drama Therapy Association**
Suite 101
Suite 220
Albany, NY 12203

888-416-7167
888-416-7167; Fax: 518-463-8656
www.nadta.org
Facebook, Twitter, YouTube, Instagram

Nadya Trytan, President
Jason Butler, President-Elect
Jeremy Segall, Vice President
Whitney Sullivan, Secretary
Dani York, Treasurer
Founded in 1979

19849 **North American Performing Arts Managers and Agents**
459 Columbus Ave
Suite 133
New York, NY 10024-5129

212-362-8304
800-867-3281
www.napama.org

Richard Baird, Owner
David Wannen, VP
Jerry Ross, VP
Susan Endrizzi Moris, Secretary
Robin Pomerance, Treasurer

National nonprofit trade association dedicated to promoting the professionalism of its members and the vitality of the performing arts. NAPAMA promotes the mutual advancement and the best interests of performing arts managers and agents; promotes open discourse among members and within the larger field; gives active consideration and expression of opinion on questions affecting the industry and develops and encourages ethical and sound business practices.
Cost: $150.00
Founded in 1979

19850 **OPERA America**
330 Seventh Avenue
New York, NY 10001

212-796-8620; Fax: 212-796-8621
Info@operaamerica.org
www.operaamerica.orgÿ
Facebook, Twitter, Google+, YouTube

Dr. Frayda B. Lindemann, Chairman
Susan F. Morris, Vice Chairman
Marc A. Scorca, President/ CEO
William Florescu, Secretary
Timothy O'Leary, Treasurer
Founded in 1973

19851 **Oratorio Society of New York**
1440 Broadway
23rd Floor
New York, NY 10018-9759

212-400-7255
president@oratoriosocietyofny.org
www.oratoriosocietyofny.org
Facebook, Twitter, Youtube

Richard A Pace, Chairman & Presidentÿ
Mary J.Knight, Vice President
Marie Gangemi, Treasurer
Jay Jacobson, Secretary
Kent Tritle, Music Director

New York City's second oldest cultural organization. On December 25, 1874 the society began what has become an unbroken tradition of annual performances of Handel's Messiah (at Carnegie Hall since its opening in 1891).
Founded in 1873

19852 **Performing Arts Alliance**
1211 Connecticut Ave. NW
Suite 200
Washington, DC 20036

202-207-3850; Fax: 202-833-1543
info@theperformingartsalliance.org
www.theperformingartsalliance.org
Facebook, Twitter

Mario Garcia Durham, Chair

The Alliance advocates for federal policy that fosters the contributions to society of America's professional nonprofit arts organizations and artists.
30K Members
Founded in 1977

19853 **Performing Arts Association**
719 Edmond St
St Joseph, MO 64501-2268

816-279-1225
info@paastjo.org
www.saintjosephperformingarts.org
Facebook, Twitter

David Cripe, President
Elaine Smith, VP
Debbie Demuth, Secretary
Kim Lueger, Treasurer
Beth Sharp, Director

Mission is to provide a diverse selection of performing arts in the St. Joseph area by presenting programs that foster, increase and promote public knowledge and appreciation of music, theatre and dance and lectures on subjects of cultural interests.
Founded in 1979

19854 Performing Arts Medicine Association
PO Box 117
Englewood, CO 80151
303-808-5643; Fax: 866-408-7069
info@artsmed.org
www.artsmed.org
Facebook, Twitter, LinkedIn
Julie Massaro, Executive Director
Mary Fletcher, Consultant
Organization for physicians and other professional persons who are involved in treatment and/or research in the field of Performing Arts Medicine.
Founded in 1989

19855 Piano Manufacturers Association
14070 Proton Road
Suite 100
Dallas, TX 75244
972-233-9107; Fax: 972-490-4219
www.pianonet.com
Donald W Dillon, Executive Director
Piano industry trade association.
Founded in 1991

19856 Piano Technicians Guild
4444 Forest Avenue
Kansas City, KS 66106
913-432-9975; Fax: 913-432-9986
ptg@ptg.org
www.ptg.org
Facebook, Twitter, YouTube
Barbara Cassaday, Executive Director
Jim Coleman, President
Norman R. Cantrell, VP
Phil A Bondi, Secretary/Treasurer
A nonprofit organization serving piano tuners, technicians, and craftsman throughout the world, organized to promote the highest possible service and technical standards among piano tuners and technicians.
4100 Members
Founded in 1957

19857 Production Music Library Association
1600 Aspen Commons
Suite 100
Middleton, WI 53562
608-836-5825; Fax: 608-831-8200
mla@areditions.com
www.musiclibraryassoc.org
Facebook, Twitter
Jerry L McBride, President
Michael Colby, VP
Pamela Bristah, Secretary
Provides a forum for issues surrounding music, music in libraries, and music librarianship. Members include music librarians, librarians who work with music as part of their responsibilities, composers and music scholars, and others interested in the program of the association.
20 Members
Founded in 1931

19858 Professional Women Singers Association
P.O. Box 29
Deer Park, NY 11729
212-969-0590; Fax: 928-395-2560
professionalwomensingers@gmail.com
www.womensingers.org
Facebook
Elissa Weiss, President
Allison Atteberry, First VP
Sarah Downs, Second VP
Ruth Ann Cunningham, Secretary
Mary Lou Zobel, Treasurer
Non-profit networking organization for professional women singers. The group sponsors concerts, master classes and seminars for both singers and the community at large.
40 Members
Founded in 1982

19859 Roundalab - International Association of Round Dance Teachers
2803 Louisiana Street
Longview, WA 98632-3536
360-423-7423
877-943-2623
roundalab@roundalab.org
www.roundalab.org
Facebook
Frank & Sandy Hartzel, General Chairman
Terri & Tim Wilaby, Vice Chairman
Mary & Bob Townsend-Manning, Marketing Membership
Supports all those involved in the field of round dancing. Publishes quarterly magazine.
Founded in 1974
Mailing list available for rent

19860 Screen Actors Guild - American Federation of Television and Radio Artists
5757 Wilshire Blvd
7th Floor
Los Angeles, CA 90036-3600
323-954-1600
855-724-2387; Fax: 323-549-6792
sagaftrainfo@sagaftra.org
www.sagaftra.org
Facebook, Twitter, Instagram, YouTube, RSS
David White, National Executive Director
Arianna Ozzanto, Chief Financial Officer
Duncan Crabtree-Ireland, Chief Operating Officer
Mary Cavallaro, Chief Broadcast Officer
Pam Greenwalt, Chief Communications & Marketing
Formerly the Screen Actors Guild. Labor union affiliated with AFL-CIO which represents actors in film, television and commercials. The Guild exists to enhance actors' working conditions, compensation and benefits and to be a powerful, unifed voice on behalf of artists' rights.

19861 Society of American Magicians
PO Box 510260
Saint Louis, MO 63151-0260
314-846-5659; Fax: 314-846-5659
rmblowers@aol.com
www.magicsam.com
Facebook, Twitter
J.Christopher Bontjes, President
Bruce Kalver, First VP
Mike Miller, Second VP
Chuck Lehr, Secretary
Mary Ann Blowers, Treasurer
Founded to promote and maintain harmonious fellowship among those interested in magic as an art, to improve ethics of the magical profession, and to foster, promote and improve the advancement of magical arts in the field of amusement and entertainment. Membership includes professional and amateur magicians, manufacturers of magical apparatus and collectors.
5.5M Members
Founded in 1902

19862 Society of Stage Directors & Choreograhers
321 W. 44th Street
Suite 804
New York, NY 10036
212-391-1070; Fax: 212-302-6195
Info@SDCweb.org
www.sdcweb.org
Facebook, Twitter, LinkedIn, Google+, Instagram
Susan H Schulman, President
John Rando, Executive Vice President
Leigh Silverman, Vice President
Oz Scott, Secretary
Ethan McSweeny, Treasurer
Founded in 1965

19863 Society of Stage Directors and Choreographers
321 W. 44th Street
Suite 804
New York, NY 10036-5653
212-391-1070
800-541-5204; Fax: 212-302-6195
Info@SDCweb.org
www.sdcweb.org
Facebook, Twitter, LinkedIn, Google+, Instagram
Susan H Schulman, President
John Rando, Executive Vice President
Leigh Silverman, Vice President
Oz Scott, Secretary
Ethan McSweeny, Treasurer
An independent labor union representing directors and choreographers in American theatre.
1700 Members
Founded in 1965
Mailing list available for rent

19864 Southeastern Theatre Conference
1175 Revolution Mill Drive
Suite 14
Greensboro, NC 27405
336-272-3645
info@setc.org
www.setc.org
Susie Prueter, Executive Director
April J'Callahan Marshall, Director, Professional Services
Connecting You to Opportunities in Theatre Nationwide. A non-profit membership organization serving Alabama, Florida, Georgia, Kentucky, Mississippi, North Carolina, South Carolina, Tennessee, Virgina, and West Virgina.
4500+ Members
Founded in 1949

19865 Southern Arts Federation
1800 Peachtree St NW
Suite 808
Atlanta, GA 30309-2512
404-874-7244; Fax: 404-873-2148
www.southarts.org
Facebook, Twitter, LinkedIn
Susie Surkamer, Executive Director
Stephanie Conner, Secretary
Ken May, Treasurer
David Batley, Marketing/Communications Director
In partnership with nine state arts agencies: promotes and supports arts regionally, nationally and internationally; enhances the artistic excellence and professionalism of Southern Arts Organizations and artists; serves the diverse population of the south.
Founded in 1975

19866 Stage Directors and Choreographers Foundation
321 W. 44th Street
Suite 804
New York, NY 10036
212-391-1070; Fax: 212-302-6195
Info@SDCweb.org
www.sdcfoundation.org

Facebook, Twitter, LinkedIn, Google+, Instagram

Susan H Schulman, President
John Rando, Executive Vice President
Leigh Silverman, Vice President
Oz Scott, Secretary
Ethan McSweeny, Treasurer
Founded in 1965

19867 The Actors' Fund
729 Seventh Avenue, 10th floor
New York, NY 10019

212-221-7300
info@actorsfund.org
www.actorsfund.org
Facebook, Twitter, LinkedIn, YouTube

Brian Stokes Mitchell, Chairmen
Philip S. Birsh, Vice Chair
Marc Grodman, Secretary
Abby Schroeder, Assistant Secretary
Steve Kalafer, Treasurer
Founded in 1882

19868 The One Club For Creativity
450 W. 31st St.
6th Floor
New York, NY 10001

212-979-1900; Fax: 212-979-5006
info@oneclub.org
www.oneclub.org
Facebook, Twitter, LinkedIn, Instagram, YouTube

Kevin Swanepoel, Chief Executive Officer
Yash Egami, VP, Content & Marketing
Lucila Lopez Travez, Director of Events & Membership
Jovanne Jerome, Inclusion & Diversity Coordinator
Crystal Ray, Financial Controller

A non-profit organization that supports and celebrates the success of the global creative community. Stimulates the intersection of art and commerce, and creates spaces for artists to grow.

19869 The United States Disc Jockey Association
Post Office Box 43252
Nottingham, ML 21236

443-903-2013
www.usdja.com
Facebook, Twitter, Vimeo

Jason Walsh, President

19870 Theatre Authority
165 West 46th Street
New York, NY 10036

212-869-8530; Fax: 212-719-9815
www.actorsequity.org/benefits/theatreauthority.asp

Presides over theatrical agencies and performing arts organizations.

19871 Theatre Bay Area
1119 Market Street
2nd Floor
San Francisco, CA 94103

415-430-1140; Fax: 415-430-1145
tba@theatrebayarea.org
www.theatrebayarea.org
Facebook, Twitter, Pinterest, YouTube

Brad Erikson, Executive Director
Dale Albright, Deputy Director
MaryAnn Grossman, Development Director
Kimberley Cohan, Programs, Awards, Publications
J Jha, Marketing Manager

Theatre Bay Area's mission is to unite, strengthen and promote the theatre community in the San Francisco Bay Area, working on behalf of their conviction that the performing arts are an essential public good, critical to a healthy and truly democratic society, and invaluable as a source of personal enrichment and growth.
2100 Members
Founded in 1976
Mailing list available for rentat $65 per M

19872 Theatre Communications Group
520 8th Ave
24th Floor
New York, NY 10018-8666

212-609-5900; Fax: 212-609-5901
www.tcg.org
Facebook, Twitter, Instagram

Theresa Eyring, Executive Director
Jennifer Cleary, Director of Membership

The mission of the TCG is to strengthen, nurture and promote the professional not-for-profit American theatre. TCG believes that their diversity as a field is their greatest strength. They celebrate differences in aesthetic, culture, organizational structure, and geography. They believe that every theatre makes a contribution to the greater field as a whole, that every performance expands the artistic vocabulary for us all, and that we all benefit from one another's presence.
Cost: $39.95
14000 Members
Frequency: Monthly
Founded in 1961

19873 Theatre Development Fund
520 Eight Avenue
Suite 801
New York, NY 10018-6507

212-912-9770
info@tdf.org
www.tdf.org
Facebook, Twitter, YouTube, Google+

Earl D. Weiner, Chairman
Sandra Kresch, Vice Chairman
Robert T. Goldm Treasurer, Deborah Hartnett Secretary

Not-for-profit service organization for the performing arts. TDF administers a wide range of audience development and financial assistance programs that encourage production of new plays and musicals and enable more New Yorkers and visitors to enjoy the riches and variety of the city's theatre, dance and music.
Cost: $25.00
Founded in 1968

19874 US Institute for Theatre Technology
315 S Crouse Ave
Suite 200
Syracuse, NY 13210-1835

315-463-6463
800-938-7488; Fax: 315-463-6525
www.usitt.org
Facebook, Twitter, LinkedIn, Instagram, Pinterest

Carol Carrigan, Manager
Patricia Dennis, Secretary
Travis DeCastro, Treasurer

Association of design, production and technology professionals in the performing arts and entertainment industry whose mission is to promote the knowledge and skills of its members. International in scope, USITT draws its board of directors from across the US and Canada. Sponsors projects, programs, research, symposia, exhibits and annual conference. Disseminates information on aesthetic and technical developments.
3700 Members
Founded in 1960

19875 USA Dance Inc
PO Box 152988
Cape Coral, FL 33915-2988

800-447-9047; Fax: 239-573-0946
central-office@usadance.org
usadance.org
Facebook, Twitter, LinkedIn, YouTube

Lydia Scardina, National President
Bill Rose, Sr.Vice President
Greg Warner, National Secretary
Esther Freeman, National Treasurer
Ken Richards, VP, Dance Sports

Nonprofit organization working to promote ballroom dancing, both as a recreational activity and as a competitive sport, and to educate the public about the mental, physical and social benefits of dance.
23000 Members
Founded in 1965

19876 United Square Dancers of America

Home Page: www.usda.org
Facebook

Mike Matsko, President
L Paul Schmidt, Vice President
Jim Maczko, Past President
Milene McCall, Secretary
Jim Taylor, Treasurer
Founded in 1981

19877 United States Association of Fringe Festivals

Home Page: www.fringefestivals.us

Association of alternative performing arts festivals.

19878 United States Institute for Theatre Technology
315 South Crouse Avenue
Suite 200
Syracuse, NY 13210

315-463-6463
800-938-7488; Fax: 800-938-7488
info@usitt.org
www.usitt.org
Facebook, Twitter, LinkedIn, Instagram, Pinterest

Lea Asbell Swanger, President
Carolyn Satter, Vice President
David Grindle, Executive Director
Jimmie Byrd, Secretary
Dan Culhane, Treasurer
Founded in 1960

19879 Voice and Speech Trainers Association

773-888-2782
president@vasta.org
www.vasta.org

Lynn Watson, President
Betty Moulton, President Elect
Mandy Rees, Past President
Melanie Julian, Secretary
Artemis Preeshl, Treasurer
Founded in 2005

19880 Women in the Arts Foundation
C/O E Butler
245 Broome Street
New York, NY 10002ÿ

212-941-0130
info@nyartistsequity.org
www.nyartistsequity.org/
Twitter, Instagram

Regina Stewart, Executive Director
Eric Butler, Executive Coordinator
Linda Butti, Executive Coordinator
Sari Menna, Financial Coordinator

WIA works to overcome discrimination against women artists. They provide information to help women function effectively as professional artists. WIA is open to all women interested in the arts.
150 Members
Founded in 1971

19881 **Writers Guild of America**
7000 West Third Street
Los Angeles, CA 90048
323-951-4000; Fax: 323-782-4800
www.wga.org
Facebook, Twitter, YouTube,RSS
Chris Keyser, President
Howard A. Rodman, Vice President
Carl Gottlieb, Secretary/ Treasurer
Billy Ray, Board of Directors
Shawn Ryan, Board of Directors
Founded in 1921

Newsletters

19882 **American Dance**
240 West 14th Street
New York, NY 10011
212-932-2789
info@americandanceguild.org
www.americandanceguild.org
Facebook
Gloria McLean, President
Tina Croll, VP
Contains articles on member news, dance, and education.
Frequency: 4 per year
Founded in 1956

19883 **Artsearch**
Theatre Communications Group
520 8th Ave
Suite 305
New York, NY 10018-4156
212-609-5900; Fax: 212-609-5901
www.tcg.org
Theresa Eyring, Executive Director
Artsearch is divided into five main categories: Administration, Artistic, Production/Design, Career Development, and Education.
Cost: $75.00
Frequency: Bi-Monthly
ISSN: 0730-9023
Founded in 1961
Printed in on newsprint stock

19884 **Broadside**
Theatre Library Association
New York Public Library for Performing Arts
40 Lincoln Center Plaza
New York, NY 10023
info@tla-online.org
www.tla-online.org/publications/broadside.htm
l
Nancy Friedland, President
Angela Weaver, VP
Rebecca Lord, Executive Secretary
Collen Reilly, Treasurer
Features articles and news items related to exhibitions and collections, information about TLA-sponsored events, book reviews, and other items of interest in the fields of theatre, film, and dance.
ISSN: 0068-2748
Founded in 1937

19885 **Country Dance and Song Society News**
Country Dance and Song Society
116 Pleasant St
Suite 345
Easthampton, MA 01027-2759
413-203-5467; Fax: 413-203-5471
news@cdss.org
www.cdss.org
Caroline Batson, Editor
Rima Dael, Executive Director
Bob Blondin, Business Manager
A selection of articles, letters and poems. CDSS News is available as a benefit of membership in the Country Dance and Song Society.
ISSN: 1070-8251
Founded in 1915

19886 **DNBulletin**
151 W 30th Street
Suite 202
New York, NY 10001
212-564-0985; Fax: 212-216-9027
dnbinfo@dancenotation.org
www.dancenotation.org
Senta Driver, Editor
Dance news for consumers and professionals.
Founded in 1940
Printed in 2 colors on matte stock

19887 **Dancedrill**
3101 Poplarwood Court
Suite 310
Raleigh, NC 27604-1010
919-872-7888; Fax: 919-872-6888
Susan Wershing, Publisher
Kay Crawford, Editor
Publication informs members of dance drill teams and their directors.
Frequency: 4 per year

19888 **Dramatists Guild Newsletter**
Dramatists Guild of America
1501 Broadway
Suite 701
New York, NY 10036-5505
212-398-9366; Fax: 212-944-0420
www.dramaguild.com
Ralph Sevush, Executive Director
Supplement to 'The Dramatist,' available only to Guild members, includes bi-monthly reports from New York and Los Angeles, advice from the Business Affairs Department, the latest information on submission and career development opportunities, and reminders of approaching deadlines.

19889 **INTIX Bulletin**
International Ticketing Association
One College Park, 8910 Purdue Road
Suite 480
Indianapolis, IN 46268
212-629-4036; Fax: 212-628-8532
info@intix.org
www.intix.org
Jena Hoffman, President & CEO
E-bulletin provides news from the International Ticketing Association including information about upcoming events, conferences and exhibitions, industry news.
1200 Members
Frequency: Monthly
ISSN: 1071-6254
Founded in 1979
Printed in 4 colors on glossy stock

19890 **In Focus**
National Association of Theatre Owners
13190 SW 68th Parkway
Suite 200
Portland, OR 97223-8368
503-207-4700
877-388-8385; Fax: 503-207-1937
http://www.infocus.com

19891 **In Theater**
Parker Publishing & Communications
214 Sullivan St
Suite 2C
New York, NY 10012-1354
212-228-1225; Fax: 212-719-4477
www.parker-publishing.com
Emily Parker, President
Offers the reader a behind-the-scenes perspective of how a show is technically conceived, rehearsed and staged. Regular departments center on drama and musical reviews, listings of shows in major cities and columnist options.
Cost: $78.00
Frequency: Weekly
Circulation: 71,068

19892 **InLEAGUE**
League of Historic American Theatres
2105 Laurel Bush Rd
Suite 201
Bel Air, MD 21015
443-640-1058
877-627-0833; Fax: 443-640-1031
info@lhat.org
www.lhat.org
Frances Holden, Executive Director
John Bell, VP
Darlene Smolik, Treasurer
Edward Kelsey, Secretary
Quarterly newsletter which reports news from historic theatre progects around the country and features articles on all facets of historic theatre restoration and operation. The newsletter solicits articles and information from the membership.
Frequency: Quarterly
Founded in 1976

19893 **Performing Arts Insider**
PAI C/O Total Theater
PO Box 31
Greeley, CO 80632
970-405-3077
totalpost@totaltheater.com
performingartsinsider.com
Facebook, Twitter
A leading source of information about the perfoming arts in New York City and around the country. Each issue includes day-by-day calendar listings of shows on broadway, off and off-off broadway, plus dance, opera, cabaret and special events. Also includes comprehensive theatre guides, listing the author, director, cast, designers, synopsis, theater and box office details, as well as contact information for producers, press agents, general managers and casting directors.
Cost: $275.00
Frequency: Monthly+9 Mid-Month Updat
Founded in 1944
Printed in on matte stock

19894 **SETC News**
Southeastern Theatre Conference

1175 Revolution Mill Drive
Suite 14
Greensboro, NC 27405

336-272-3645
info@setc.org
www.setc.org

Susie Prueter, Executive Director
April J'Callahan Marshall, Director, Professional Services

Provides news and important information to members of the Southeaster Theatre Conference on upcoming SETC events, advocacy efforts, awards and competitions as well as items of special interest to the various divisions and interest areas. In addition, SETC News publishes news about people and organizations based in the Southeast.
Frequency: Bi-Monthly
Circulation: 4000
Founded in 1949

19895 Spotlight
American Association of Community Theatre
1300 Gendy Street
Forth Worth, TX 76107

817-732-3177
866-687-2228; Fax: 817-732-3178
info@aact.org
www.aact.org
Facebook, Twitter, LinkedIn

Julie Crawford, Executive Director
Murray Chase, President
David Cockerell, Marketing/Communications Director

News and updates on issues pertinent to community theatre.
Cost: $2.00
24 Pages
Circulation: 2000
Founded in 1958
Mailing list available for rent: 9,500 names at $180 per M
Printed in on matte stock

19896 Technical Brief
Yale School of Drama
222 York Street
PO Box 208244
New Haven, CT 06520

203-432-8188; Fax: 203-432-8129
bronislaw.sammler@yale.edu
technicalbrief.com

Ben Sammler, Editor
Dan Harvey, Editor

Produced for technical managers in theater. Written by professionals for professionals, its purpose is simple: communication. Technical Brief provides a dailogue between technical practitioners from the several performing arts who all share similar problems.
Cost: $15.00
Frequency: 3 X Year
Founded in 1924

19897 Women in the Arts Bulletin
Women in the Arts Foundation
32-35 30th Street
D24
Long Island City, NY 11106

212-941-0130

Erin Butler, Editor
Regina Stewart, Executir Director
Sandra Cockerham, President

Gallery information and reviews. Women in the Arts Foundation works to overcome discrimination against women artists.
Frequency: Monthly
Founded in 1971

Magazines & Journals

19898 American Dancer
USA Dance
PO Box 152988
Cape Coral, FL 33915-2988

800-447-9047; Fax: 239-573-0946
www.usadance.org

Shawn Fisher, Editor

News of interests to dance enthusiasts.
Cost: $25.00
Frequency: Bi-Monthly
Circulation: 23000

19899 American Theatre Magazine
Theatre Communications Group
520 8th Ave
Suite 305
New York, NY 10018-8666

212-609-5900; Fax: 212-609-5901
www.tcg.org

Jim O'Quinn, Editor in Chief
Nicole Estvanik Taylor, Managing Editor
Cost: $35.00

19900 Applause Magazine
Denver Center for Performing Arts
1101 13th St
Denver, CO 80204-5319

303-893-3272
800-641-1222; Fax: 303-893-3206
www.denvercenter.org

Randy Weeks, President
Daniel L. Ritchie, Chairman &CEO

A publication of the Denver Center Theatre Company and Dever Center Attractions
Frequency: 8-10 per year
Founded in 1988
Printed in 4 colors on glossy stock

19901 Asian Pacific American Journal
Asian American Writers Workshop
16 W 32nd St
Suite 10A
New York, NY 10001-1093

212-494-0061; Fax: 212-494-0062
desk@aaww.org
www.aaww.org

Ken Chen, Executive Director
Jeannie L Wong, Adminstrative Director
Anjali Goyal, Programs Assistant
Jeffrey Lin, Designer
Hanya Yanagihara, Journal Editor

Features include short fiction, poems, essays, stage scripts, translations and artwork.
Frequency: Semi-Annual
ISSN: 1067-778X
Founded in 1992

19902 Back Stage
770 Broadway 7th Floor
New York, NY 10003

212-493-4420
800-658-8372
advertising@backstage.com
www.backstage.com

Charles Weiss, Manager
Jamie Painter Young, Editor-in-Chief
Jenelle Riley, Film/TV Editor
Leonard Jacobs, Theatre Editor
Sherry Eaker, Editor-at-Large

Four print, four interactive and two face-to-face publications. Provides casting, news, articles and other resources for working actors, cingers, dancers and behind-the-scenes staff and crew.
Cost: $84.00
Circulation: 30,000
Founded in 1960
Mailing list available for rent

19903 Bomb Magazine
New Art Publications
80 Hanson Pl
Suite 703
Brooklyn, NY 11217-1506

718-636-9100
866-354-0334; Fax: 718-636-9200
info@bombsite.com
Facebook, Twitter, YouTube

Betsy Sussler, Publisher/Editor
Mary-Ann Monforton, Associate Publisher
Nell McClister, Senior Editor
Lucy Raven, Managing Editor
Paul W Morris, Director Marketing/Special Projects

Focuses on contemporary art, literature, theater, film, music.
Cost: $495.00
Frequency: Quarterly
Circulation: 60,000
Founded in 1981
Mailing list available for rent
Printed in 4 colors on matte stock

19904 BoxOffice Magazine
BoxOffice Media
9107 Wilshire Blvd.
Suite 450
Beverly Hills, CA 90210-4241

310-876-9090
www.boxoffice.com

Peter Crane, Publisher
Kenneth James Bacon, Creative Director
Phil Contrino, Editor
Amy Nicholson, Editor

The premier trade magazine covering the latest developments in the movie industry, from films in production to digital cinema and everything in between.
Founded in 1948

19905 Callaloo
Johns Hopkins University Press
2715 N Charles St
Baltimore, MD 21218-4363

410-516-6900
800-537-5487; Fax: 410-516-6998
www.press.jhu.edu/journals/callaloo

William Brody, President
Kyle G Dargan, Managing Editor

Journal of African and African-American issues. Content includes original works by, and critical studies of, black writers worldwide. Offers a rich mixture of fiction, poetry, plays, critical essays, cultural studies, interviews, and visual art, as well as special thematic issues.
Frequency: Quarterly
Circulation: 2,500
ISSN: 0161-2492
Founded in 1976

19906 Canadian Theatre Review
University of Toronto Press
5201 Dufferin Street
Toronto, ON M3H-5T8

416-667-7810
800-221-9985; Fax: 416-667-7881
www.utpjournals.com
Facebook, Twitter, Blog

Anne Marie Corrigan, VP
Audrey Greenwood, Advertising/Marketing Coordinator

Provides critical analysis and innovative coverage of current developments in Canadian theatre. Advocates new issues and artists. Publishes at

least one significant new playscript per issue. Each issue includes at least one complete playscript related to the issue theme, insightful articles, and informative reviews.
Cost: $40.00
Frequency: Quarterly
ISSN: 0315-0836
Founded in 1974
Mailing list available for rentat $250 per M

19907 **Confrontation**
CW Post Campus English Department
720 Northern Blvd
Greenvale, NY 11548-1300
516-626-0099; Fax: 516-299-3566
Jayne Mo, Manager
Brings new talent to light in the shadows cast by well-known authors. Each issue contains orignal work by famous and by lesser known writers.
Cost: $10.00
Frequency: Twice Yearly
Founded in 1968

19908 **Contact Quarterly Journal of Dance and Improvisation**
Contact Collaborations
PO Box 603
Northampton, MA 01061
413-586-1181; Fax: 413-586-9055
info@contactquarterly.com
www.contactquarterly.com
Lisa Nelson, Co-Editor
Nancy Stark Smith, Co-Editor
Melinda Buckwalter, Associate Editor
Kristin Horrigan, Operations Manager/Advertising
Bill McCully, Development/Marketing
A journal of dance, improvisation, performance and contemporary movement arts. Presents materials that spring from the experience of doing. Encourages articulation and dialogue and stimulates activity and exploration within the field of movement and its performance.
Cost: $22.00
Frequency: BiAnnual
Founded in 1978

19909 **Cue Magazine**
PO Box 2027
Burlingame, CA 94011-2027
415-348-8004; Fax: 650-348-7781
www.cuemagazines.com
Devoted to the Northern California, Seattle and Portland commercial film, video and multimedia industries and locations that support production.
Frequency: Monthly

19910 **Dance Chronicle**
Taylor & Francis Group
270 Madison Ave
Floor 4
New York, NY 10016-0601
212-679-3853; Fax: 212-564-7854
George Dorris, Co-Editor
Jack Anderson, Co-Editor
Edwin Bayrn, Associate Editor
Covers a wide variety of topics, including dance and music, theater, film, literature, painting and aesthetics.
Cost: $465.00
Frequency: TriAnnual
ISSN: 0147-2526

19911 **Dance Magazine**
Macfadden Performing Arts Media
333 7th Avenue
11th Floor
New York, NY 10001
212-979-4800
www.dancemagazine.com
Amy Cogan, VP/Group Publisher
Karen Hildebrand, VP Editorial
Jessi Petrov, Publishing/Marketing Director
Wendy Perron, Editor-in-Chief
The must read magazine for professional and aspiring dancers. From Broadway to ballet and tap to hip hop, not other magazine keeps you in touch with what is going on in all disciplines of dance.
Cost: $34.95
Frequency: Monthly
Circulation: 300,000
ISSN: 0011-6009
Founded in 1927
Printed in 4 colors on glossy stock

19912 **Dance Research Journal**
Congress on Research in dance
7044 South 13th Street
Oak Creek, WI 53154
414-908-4951; Fax: 414-768-8001
info@cordance.org
www.cordance.org
Ann Dils, Co-Editor
Jill Green, Co-Editor
Published three times a year by the Congress on Research in Dance, this journal carries scholarly articles, book reviews, lists of books and journals received, and reports of scholarly conferences, archives and other projects of interest to the field.
Frequency: 3x/Year
Founded in 1965
Mailing list available for rent

19913 **Dance Spirit**
Macfadden Performing Arts Media, LLC
333 7th Avenue
11th Floor
New York, NY 10001
212-979-4800
www.dancespirit.com
Amy Cogan, VP/Group Publisher
Karen Hildebrand, VP Editorial
Jessi Petrov, Publishing/Marekting Director
Kayte Lydon, Editor-in-Chief
Dedicated to inspiring the next generation of dancers. Packed with expert advice on dance techniques and performing, health and nutrition tips and the latest styles to keep you looking your best from studio to stage to school.
Cost: $16.95
Frequency: 10 Per Year
Founded in 1980

19914 **Dance Teacher Magazine**
Macfadden Performing Arts Media
333 7th Avenue
11th Floor
New York, NY 10001
212-979-4800; Fax: 646-459-4900
www.dance-teacher.com
Amy Cogan, VP/Group Publisher
Karen Hildebrand, VP Editorial/Editor-in-Chief
Jessie Petrov, Publishing/Marketing Director
The only magazine written just for dance professionals. Packed with useful ideas that will help you and your students become better dancers.
Cost: $24.95
Frequency: Monthly
Circulation: 60000
Founded in 1979
Printed in 4 colors

19915 **Dance on Camera Journal**
Dance Films Association
48 W 21st St
Suite 907
New York, NY 10010-6989
212-727-0764; Fax: 212-727-0764
info@dancefilms.org
www.dancefilms.org
Facebook, Twitter
Deidra Towers, Executive Director
Marta Renzi, President
Harry Streep, VP
Amy Meharg, Treasurer
Nolini Barretto, Secretary
Subjects range from reviews and essays, news items regarding dance films, festivals, opportunites, and issues facing artists
Frequency: Bi-Monthly
Founded in 1956

19916 **Dance/USA Journal**
Dance/USA
1111 16th St Nw
Suite 300
Washington, DC 20036-4830
202-833-1717; Fax: 202-833-2686
danceusa@danceusa.org
www.danceusa.org
Andrea Snyder, Executive Director
Tom Thielen, Director Finance/Operations
Katherine Fabian, Membership Manager
The journal features articles on issues of importance to the dance community; news stories relating to arts and dance; essays from leaders in the dance field; notes on changes, transitions and opportunities in the field; calendar of up coming events; and highlights of Dance/USA sponsored events. Subscription is free to members of Dance/USA.
Cost: $40.00
28-36 Pages
Frequency: Quarterly
Founded in 1982
Printed in 2 colors on glossy stock

19917 **Descant**
50 Baldwin Street
PO Box 314 Station P
Toronto, ON M5S-2S8
416-593-2557; Fax: 416-593-9362
www.descant.ca
Facebook
Karen Mulhallen, Editor-in-Chief
Vera DeWaard, Managing Editor
Mary Newberry, Project Manager
Stacey May Fowles, Circulation Manager
Pasha Malla, Director of Outreach
A quarterly journal publishing new and established contemporary writers and visual artists from Canada and around the world. Devoted to the discovery and development of new writers, and places their work in the company of celebrated writers.
Cost: $28.00
Frequency: Quarterly
Circulation: 1200
ISSN: 0382-909X
Founded in 1970
Mailing list available for rent

19918 **Drama Review**
MIT Press
55 Hayward Street
Cambridge, MA 02142-1493
617-253-5646
800-207-8354; Fax: 617-258-6779
journals-info@mit.edu
www.mitpress.mit.edu
Facebook, Twitter, RSS
Rebbecca Mc Leod, Owner
TDR focuses on performances in their social, economic, and political conctexts. It emphasizes experimental, avant-garde, intercultural

and interdisciplinary performance. TDR covers dance, theatre, performance art, visual art, popular entertainment, media, sports, rituals, and performance in politics and everyday life.
Frequency: Quarterly
Founded in 1955

19919 **Dramatics Magazine**
Educational Theatre Association
2343 Auburn Ave
Cincinnati, OH 45219-2819

513-421-3900; Fax: 513-421-7077
jpalmarini@schooltheatre.org
schooltheatre.org
Facebook, Twitter

Donald A Corathers, Publications Director
James Palmarini, Editor

Dramatics is the only magazine that is edited exclusively for students and teachers of theatre. Contents include practical articles about acting, directing, playwriting, design, and technical theatre; interviews with working professionals that illuminate the process of becoming a theatre artist; options for higher education and training in theatre; playscripts; reports on new shows and other important events in the theatre world; book, video, and CD-ROM reviews, and more.
Cost: $27.00
4000 Members
Frequency: 9x/ A Year
Circulation: 34100
ISSN: 0012-5989
Founded in 1929

19920 **Encore Performance Publishing**
PO Box 95567
South Jordan, UT 84095-0567

801-282-8159
encoreplay@aol.com
www.encoreplay.com

Michael C Perry, President

Publishes a variety of publications for those professionals in the performing arts industry.

19921 **Gospel Today**
Gospel Today
PO Box 800
Fairburn, GA 30213

770-719-4825; Fax: 770-716-2660
admin@gospeltoday.com
www.gospeltoday.com

Dr Teresa Hairston, Publisher

To provide a quality publication to inspire, educate, inform, and empower readers towards standards of Godly excellence.
Cost: $17.97
Frequency: 8 Per Year
Circulation: 250000
Founded in 1989
Printed in 4 colors on glossy stock

19922 **Hispanic Arts News**
Association of Hispanic Arts
1025 Connecticut Ave
Suite 1000
Washington, DC 20036

202-657-5158
888-876-1240; Fax: 202-478-2767
Facebook, Twitter

Features in depth articles on the local and national arts community, including artist profiles and a calendar of events.
Frequency: 9 Per Year
Mailing list available for rent: 5000 names at $80 per M

19923 **JazzTimes**
JazzTimes Magazine
Madavor Media,85 Quincy Ave
Suite 2
Quincy, MA 02169

617-706-9110
800-437-5828; Fax: 617-536-0102
www.jazztimes.com

Glen Sabin, CEO
Eric Wynne, Consumer Advertising Director

JazzTimes contains extensive news coverage, award winning jazz journalism, hundreds of CD, Book and Video reviews, World class photography and award winning graphics, informative features and columns, special theme issues, special directories, readers poll and critic pics, and sound$weeps giveaways and prizes.
Cost: $23.95
Frequency: 10 Issues per y
Circulation: 86000
Founded in 1980

19924 **Journal of Arts Management, Law, Society**
Heldref Publishers
325 Chestnut Street
Suite 800
Philadelphia, PA 19106

215-625-8900
800-354-1420; Fax: 202-296-5149
customer.service@taylorandfrancis.com
www.heldref.org

James Denton, Executive Director

A resource for arts policymakters and analysts, sociologists, arts and cultural administrators, educators, trusteed, artists, lawyers, and citizens concerned with the performing, visual, and media arts as well as cultural affairs. Articles, commentaries, and reviews of publications address marketing, intellectual property, arts policy, arts law, governance, and cultural production and dissemination, from a variety of philosophical, disciplinary, and national and international perspectives.
Cost: $79.00
Frequency: Monthly
ISSN: 1063-2921
Founded in 1956

19925 **Journal of Dance Education**
National Dance Education Organization
8609 2nd Avenue
Suite 203 B
Silver Spring, MD 20910

301-585-2880; Fax: 301-585-2888
info@ndeo.org
www.ndeo.org
Facebook, Twitter

Susan McGreevy-Nichols, Executive Director
Jane Bonbright EdD, Executive Director
Patricia Cohen, Treasurer
Cost: $90.00
Frequency: Quarterly
Circulation: 2000
ISSN: 1529-0824

19926 **Lighting Dimensions**
Primedia Business
249 W 17th St
New York, NY 10011-5382
212-206-1894
800-827-3322; Fax: 212-514-3719

Doug MacDonald, Group Publisher
David Johnson, Associate Publisher/Editorial
Marian Sandberg-Dierson, Editor
Mark Newman, Managing Editor
Jennifer Hirst, Director

Trade publication for lighting professionals in film, theatre, television, concerts, clubs, themed environments, architecctural, commercial, and industrial lighting. Sponsors of the LDI Trade Show and the Broadway Lighting Master Classes.
Cost: $34.97
Frequency: 12/year
Circulation: 14,177
Founded in 1989

19927 **Mid-Atlantic Events Magazine**
1800 Byberry Road
Suite 901
Huntingdon Valley, PA 19006

215-947-8600
800-521-8588; Fax: 215-947-8650
editor@eventsmagazine.com
www.eventsmagazine.com
Facebook, Twitter, YouTube

Jim Cohn, Publisher
Rich Kupka, Editor
Fred Cohn, VP Sales
Katie O'Connell, Director Sales/Marketing
Dana Kurtbek, Production

Focused on Hospitality in the Mid-Atlantic area. It assists the Associations, Corporations, Government, Group and Independent Meeting, Event and Travel Planners who are responsible for arranging Conventions, Trade Shows, Hotel Accommodations, Corporate/Group Travel, Meetings, Seminars, Conferences, Symposiums, Site Selections, Special Events, Banquets, Entertainment, Corporate Golf Outings and Golf Tournaments, Company Picnics, Team Building, Retreats, Board Meetings, Training & Development.
Circulation: 26000
ISSN: 0896-3967
Founded in 1987
Mailing list available for rent
Printed in 8 colors on glossy stock

19928 **National Squares**
National Square Dance Convention
C/O Gene and Connie Triplett
2760 Polo Club Boulevard
Matthews, NC 28105

704-847-1265
Richp27890@aol.com
www.nationalsquaredanceconvention.com

Dick/Linda Peterson, Editors
Gene/Connie Triplett, Circulation Managers
Dick/Linda Peterson, Public Relations

A national square dance magazine published by the National Executive Committee of the National Square Dance Convention.
Cost: $7.00
Frequency: Quarterly

19929 **New England Theatre Journal**
New England Theatre Conference
215 Knob Hill Drive
Hamden, CT 06518

617-851-8535; Fax: 203-288-5938
mail@netconline.org
www.netconline.org

Sabine Klein, President
Jeffrey Watts, Executive VP
Charles Emmons, VP Administration/Finance

Scholarly publication produced once per year. Includes book and theatre reviews, historical analyses, and other well-written articles by noted authors. Free to NETC members. Specifically designed to provide members, and others interested in live theatre arts, with the information and resources they need to enhance their careers, promote their groups, and sharpen their theatre skills.
Cost: $10.00
Frequency: Annual
Founded in 1952

19930 **Nouveau Magazine**
Barbara Tompkins

5933 Stoney Hill Rd
New Hope, PA 18938-9602

215-794-5996; Fax: 215-794-8305
www.nouveaumagazine.com

Barbara Tompkins, Publisher

Features theater reviews.
Frequency: Monthly
Founded in 1981
Printed in 4 colors on glossy stock

19931 **OffBeat**
OffBeat
421 Frenchmen St
Suite 200
New Orleans, LA 70116-2039

504-944-4300
877-944-4300; Fax: 504-944-4306
offbeat@offbeat.com
www.offbeat.com
Facebook, Twitter, Flickr

Jan Ramsy, Publisher
Joseph L Irrera, Managing Editor
Bunny Matthews, Senior Editor
Michael Jastroch, Magazine Design/Production
Doug Jackson, Distribution Manager

Consumer-oriented music magazine focusing on New Orleans and Louisiana music. Regular columns on Cajun music, zydeco, traditional and contemporary jazz, brass band (Mardi Gras second-line music), New Orleans R & B, Louisiana and delta blues, Gospel, modern and roots rock and our internationally-appreciated culture and cusine. Information on music fairs and festivals in the region is given.
Cost: $29.00
Frequency: Monthly
Circulation: 50000
ISBN: 1-090081-0 -
Founded in 1985
Mailing list available for rent: 15000 names
Printed in 4 colors on newsprint stock

19932 **Performing Arts Insider Magazine**
PAI C/O Total Theater
PO Box 31
Greeley, CO 80632

970-405-3077
paipress@aol.com
www.performingartsinsider.com

David Lefkowitz, Publisher/Editor
Richmond Shepard, Publisher
J. Weil, Advertising Sales

Includes day-by-day calendar listings of shows on Broadway, Off and Off-Off Broadway, plus dance, opera, cabaret and special events. Also included are comprehensive theater guides, listing the author, director, cast, designers, synopsis, theater and box office details, as well as contact information for producers, press agents, general managers and casting directors.
Cost: $275.00
Frequency: Monthly+9 Updates
Circulation: 2000
Founded in 1944

19933 **Performing Arts Resources**
Theatre Library Association
New York Public Library for Performing Arts
40 Lincoln Center Plaza
New York, NY 10023

info@tla-online.org
www.tla-online.org/publications/par.html

Nancy Friedland, President
Angela Weaver, VP
Rebecca Lord, Executive Secretary
Colleen Reilly, Treasurer

Features articles on resource materials in the fields of theatre, popular entertainment, film, television and radio, information on public and private collections, and essays on conservation and collection management of theatre arts materials.
Cost: $30.00
Frequency: Irregular
Circulation: 500
ISSN: 0360-3814
Founded in 1974

19934 **Playbill**
34-15 61st Street
Woodside, NY 11377

212-557-5757; Fax: 212-682-2932
agans@playbill.com
www.playbill.com

Andrew Gans, Editor

The exclusive magazine for Broadway and Off-Broadway theatregoers, providing the information necessary for the understanding and enjoyment of each show, including features articles and columns by and about theatre personalities, entertainment, travel, fashion, dining and other editorial pieces geared to the lifestyle of the upscale, active theatre attendee. Playbill also serves New York's three most prominent performing arts venues - the Metropolitan Opera House, Lincoln Center and Carnegie Hall
Cost: $24.00
Frequency: Monthly
Founded in 1884

19935 **Plays: Drama Magazine for Young People**
Plays Magazine
PO Box 600160
Newton, MA 02460

617-630-9100
800-630-5755; Fax: 617-630-9101
www.playsmag.com

Elizabeth Preston, Editor

Includes eight to ten royalty-free one-act plays, arranged by age level. Modern and traditional plays for the celebration of all important holidays and occasions. Adaptable to all cast sizes with easy to follow instructions for settings and costumes. A complete source of original plays and programs for school-age actors and audiences.
Cost: $39.00
Frequency: 7 X Per Year
Circulation: 6000
Founded in 1940
Printed in on matte stock

19936 **Pointe Magazine**
Macfadden Performing Arts Media LLC
333 7th Avenue
11th Floor
New York, NY 10001

212-979-4800
www.pointemagazine.com

Amy Cogan, VP/Group Publisher
Karen Hildebrand, VP Editorial
Jessie Petrov, Publishing/Marketing Director

Dedicated exclusively to the world of ballet.
Frequency: Bi-Monthly
Circulation: 120000

19937 **Pollstar: Concert Hotwire**
Pollstar
4697 W Jacquelyn Ave
Fresno, CA 93722-6443

559-271-7900; Fax: 559-271-7979
info@pollstar.com
www.pollstar.com

Gary Smith, COO
Shari Rice, VP
Gary Bongiovanni, CEO

Trade publication for the concert industry offering global coverage and information including concert tour schedules, ticket sales information and more.
Cost: $449.00
Frequency: Weekly
Circulation: 20000
Printed in 4 colors

19938 **Shakespeare Bulletin**
University of North Carolina
Department of English
9201 University City Boulevard
Charlotte, NC 28223
Seymour Isenberg, Founding Editor
Andrew James Hartley, Editor
Jeremy Lopez, Theatre Review Editor
Genevieve Love, Book Review Editor
Kirk Melnikoff, Shakespeare on Film Editor

A peer-reviewed journal of performance and criticism and scholarship which provides commentary on Shakespeare and Renaissance drama through feature articles, thatre and film reviews, and book reviews. The journal is a member of the Conference of Editors of Learned Journals.
Cost: $35.00
Frequency: Quarterly
ISSN: 0748-2558
Founded in 1982
Mailing list available for rent
Printed in on matte stock

19939 **Show Music**
Po Box A
East Haddam, CT 06423-0466

860-873-8664; Fax: 860-873-2329
rklink@goodspeed.org
www.showmusic.org

Ryan Klink, Managing Editor
Maz O Preeo, Editor-In-Chief

Internationally acclaimed by professionals and fans as the premier magazine covering musical theatre around the world. Show music combines insightful interviews and reviews of productions, recordings, videos and books.

19940 **Sondheim Review**
PO Box 11213
Chicago, IL 60611-0213

773-275-4254
800-584-1020; Fax: 773-275-4254
info@sondheimreview.com

Dedicated to the work of the musical theater and Broadway's foremost composer and lyricist, Stephen Sondheim. Each issue containes news, interviews, upcoming productions in the area, puzzles and more.
Cost: $19.95
Frequency: Quarterly
Circulation: 40000
ISSN: 1076-450X
Founded in 1994
Mailing list available for rent: 6,000 names at $105 per M
Printed in on glossy stock

19941 **Southern Theatre**
Southeastern Theatre Conference
1175 Revolution Mill Drive
Suite 14
Greensboro, NC 27405

336-272-3645
info@setc.org
www.setc.org

Susie Prueter, Executive Director
April J'Callahan Marshall, Director, Professional Services

Spotlights people, places and organizations within the region that are paving new paths in theatre. Includes low-cost strategies for design success, tips on hot markets for playwrights, new books of special interest, innovative ideas for marketing theatre, inside track on new trends and some of the region's up-and-coming

theatre stars. Subscription is free with SETC membership.
Cost: $18.75
Frequency: Quarterly
Circulation: 4000+
Founded in 1949

19942 **Spectrum**
110 S Jefferson Street
Dayton, OH 45402-3412

937-220-1600
800-247-1614; Fax: 937-220-1642
www.thinktv.org
Facebook, Twitter, YouTube

Jerry Kathman, President&CEO
Brad Mays, Treasurer
Alisa Poe, Secretary

ThinkTV's monthly member magazine. Contains program listings for both ThinkTV 16 and ThinkTV14 as well as interesting feature stories, station news and more.
Frequency: Weekly
Circulation: 18000
Founded in 1959

19943 **Stage of the Art**
American Alliance for Theatre and Education
4908 Auburn Avenue
Bethesda, MD 20814-3474

301-200-1944; Fax: 301-280-1682
www.aate.com
Facebook, Twitter, RSS

David Young, Editor
JoBeth Gonzalez, Director Publications/Research

Published by the American Alliance for Theatre and Education.
Mailing list available for rent: 700 names at $150 per M

19944 **Stagebill**
Stagebill
144 E 44th Street
New York, NY 10017

212-476-0640; Fax: 212-983-5976

Fred B Tarter, Chairman/President/CEO
Gerry Byrne, Chairman/President/CEO
Ben Mattison, Editorial Contact

Publisher of the program magazines for the leading, theaters, symphonies, dance companies and performing arts centers in the United States. A national performing arts magazine.
Frequency: Monthly
Founded in 1924

19945 **Stages**
Curtains
301 W 45th Street
Apartment 5A
New York, NY 10036-3825

FAX 201-836-4107

Frank Scheck, Editor
Cost: $20.00
Frequency: Monthly
Circulation: 35,000

19946 **TD & T: Theatre Design & Technology**
US Institute for Theatre Technology
315 South Crouse Avenue
Suite 200
Syracuse, NY 13210

315-463-6525; Fax: 315-463-6525
www.usitt.org
Facebook, Twitter

David Roger, Editor
Arnold Wengrow, Book Review Editor
Michelle Smith, Membership/Advertising Manager
N Deborah Hazlett, Art Director

Published by United States Institute for Theatre Technology. Focuses on USITT's ten interest areas: architecture, costume design and technology, education, engineering, health and safety, lighting, management, scene design, sound design, and technical production.
3700 Members
Frequency: Quarterly

19947 **Teaching Theatre Journal**
Educational Theatre Association
2343 Auburn Ave
Cincinnati, OH 45219-2819

513-421-3900; Fax: 513-421-7077
jpalmarini@schooltheatre.org
schooltheatre.org
Facebook, Twitter

Donald A Corathers, Publications Director
James Palmarini, Editor

For professional theatre educators. A typical issue includes an article on acting, directing, playwriting, or technical theatre; a profile of an outstanding educationl theatre program; a piece on curriculum design, assessment, or teaching methodology; and reports on current trends or issues in the field, such as funding, standards, or certification.
4000 Members
Frequency: Quarterly
Circulation: 4000
ISSN: 1077-2561
Founded in 1929

19948 **Technical Brief**
Yale School of Drama
222 York Street
PO Box 208244
New Haven, CT 06520

203-432-8188; Fax: 203-432-8129
bronislaw.sammler@yale.edu
technicalbrief.com

Ben Sammler, Co-Editor
Don Harvey, Co-Editor

Written by professionals for professionals, providing a dialogue between technical practitioners from the several performing arts. The succinct articles, complete with mechanical drawings, represent the best solutions to recurring technical problems. Published October, January and April.
Cost: $15.00
Frequency: 3X Per Year
Founded in 1924

19949 **Theater Magazine**
Yale School of Drama
1120 Chapel Street
P.O Box 1257
New Haven, CT 06505

203-432-1234; Fax: 203-432-6423
yalerep@yale.edu
www.yale.edu/drama

Tom Sellar, Editor
Laraine Sammler, Business Manager
Alex Grennan, Director of Business/Comm

Periodicals, essays and articles of the Yale School of Drama.
Cost: $22.00
Frequency: Annual+
Circulation: 2500
Founded in 1924
Mailing list available for rent: 1.5M names
Printed in one color on matte stock

19950 **Theatre Bill**
Jerome Press
332 Congress St
Suite 2
Boston, MA 02210-1217

617-423-3400; Fax: 617-423-7108

Jerome Rosenfeld, Owner

19951 **Theatre Journal**
Johns Hopkins University Press
2715 N Charles St
Baltimore, MD 21218-4363

410-516-6900
800-537-5487; Fax: 410-516-6968
webmaster@jhupress.jhu.edu
www.press.jhu.edu

William Brody, President
David Z Saltz, Co-Editor
Sonja Arsham Kuftinec, Performance Review Editor
James Peck, Book Review Editor
Bob Kowkabany, Managing Editor

One of the most authoritative and useful publications of theatre studies available today. Theatre Journal features social and historical studies, production reviews, and theoretical inquiries that analize dramatic texts and production. Official journal of the Association for Theatre in Higher Education.
Cost: $40.00
Frequency: Quarterly
Circulation: 2492
ISSN: 0192-2882
Founded in 1878
Mailing list available for rent

19952 **Theatre Symposium**
Southeastern Theatre Conference
1175 Revolution Mill Drive
Suite 14
Greensboro, NC 27405

336-272-3645
info@setc.org
www.setc.org

Susie Prueter, Executive Director
April J'Callahan Marshall, Director, Professional Services

A publication of selected scholarly papers presented at the annual Theatre Symposium Conference. A copublication of the Southeaster Theatre Conference and Alabama Press.
Frequency: Annual

19953 **Theatre Topics**
Johns Hopkins University Press
2715 N Charles St
Baltimore, MD 21218-4363
410-516-6900
800-537-5487; Fax: 410-516-6998
webmaster@jhupress.jhu.edu
www.press.jhu.edu

William Brody, President
Sandra G Shannon, Co-Editor
DeAnna Toten Beard, Book Review Editor
Elanore Lampners, Managing Editor
Beverley Pevitts, Founding Editor

Focuses on performance studies, dramaturgy, and theatre pedagogy. Concise and timely articles on a broad array of practical, performance-oriented subjects, with special attention to topics of current interest to the profession. Keeps readers informed of the latest developments on the stage and in the classroom. The official journal of the Association for Theatre in Higher Education. Published in March and September.
Cost: $32.00
Frequency: Semi-Annually
Circulation: 1528
ISSN: 1054-8378
Founded in 1878
Mailing list available for rent

19954 **Youth Theatre Journal**
American Alliance for Theatre and Education
4908 Auburn Ave
Bethesda, MD 20814

301-200-1944; Fax: 301-235-7108
info@aate.com
www.aate.com

A scholarly journal dedicated to advancing the study and practice of theatre and drama with, for, and by the people of all ages. It is concerned with all forms of scholarship of the highest quality that inform the fields of theatre for young audiences and drama/theatre education.
Cost: $25.00
Frequency: 2x/Year
Circulation: 1000
ISSN: 0892-9092
Mailing list available for rent: 700 names at $150 per M

Trade Shows

19955 **AACT WorldFest**
American Association of Community Theatre
1300 Gendy Street
Fort Worth, TX 76107-4036

817-732-3177
866-687-2228; Fax: 817-732-3178
info@aact.org
www.aact.org
Facebook, Twitter, LinkedIn

Julie Crawford, Executive Director
Murray Chase, President
Carole Ries, Executive Vice President

The international gathering of community theatre professionals for a week-long showcase of performances from theatre troupes around the world.
Frequency: Every 4 Years

19956 **CinemaCon**
National Association of Theatre Owners
750 1st St NE
Suite 1130
Washington, DC 20002-4241

202-962-0054; Fax: 202-962-0370
nato@natodc.com
www.natoonline.org

John Fithian, President
Gary Klein, VP
Kathy Conroy, Executive Director

A gathering of cinema owners and operators.
4000 Members
Frequency: Annual/March

19957 **Community Theatre Management Conference**
American Association of Community Theatre
1300 Gendy Street
Fort Worth, TX 76107-4036

817-732-3177
866-687-2228; Fax: 817-732-3178
info@aact.org
www.aact.org
Facebook, Twitter, LinkedIn

Julie Crawford, Executive Director
Murray Chase, President

Educational conference for professionals working in theatre management.
Frequency: Annual

19958 **Congress on Research in Dance Annual Conference**
Congress on Research in Dance
7044 South 13th Street
Oak Creek, WI 53154

414-908-4951; Fax: 414-768-8001

Anne Flynn, President
Petri Hoppu, Vice President
Cindy Lemek, CORD Association Manager
Frequency: November

19959 **EdTA Thespian Festival**
Educational Theatre Association
2343 Auburn Ave
Cincinnati, OH 45219-2819

513-421-3900; Fax: 513-421-7077
www.schooltheatre.org
Facebook, Twitter

Michael Peitz, Executive Director
Gloria McIntyre, President
Jay Seller VP

The premiere showcase for high school theatre, drawing students and teachers from throughout the United States and abroad.
3000 Attendees

19960 **Educational Theatre Association Conference**
Educational Theatre Association
2343 Auburn Ave
Cincinnati, OH 45219-2819
513-421-3900; Fax: 513-421-7077
www.schooltheatre.org
Facebook, Twitter

Michael Peitz, Executive Director
Gloria McIntyre, President
Jay Seller VP
400 Attendees
Frequency: Annual

19961 **International Association of Venue Managers**
International Association of Assembly Managers
635 Fritz Drive
Suite 100
Coppell, TX 75019-4442

972-906-7441
800-935-4226; Fax: 972-906-7418
www.iaam.org

Steven Peters, President
Robyn Williams, First Vice President
Frequency: Annual

19962 **NDEO National Conference**
National Dance Education Organization
8609 2nd Avenue
Suite 203 B
Silver Spring, MD 20910

301-585-2880; Fax: 301-585-2888
info@ndeo.org
www.ndeo.org

Susan McGreevy-Nichols, Executive Director
Jane Bonbright EdD, Executive Director
Patricia Cohen, Treasurer

Provides 200+ professional development sessions for artists, educators and administrators teaching or supporting dance education programs in PreK-12, colleges/universities, private studio/schools of dance, community centers and performing arts organizations.
800 Attendees
Frequency: Annual

19963 **National AACTFest**
American Association of Community Theatre
1300 Gendy Street
Fort Worth, TX 76107-4036

817-732-3177; Fax: 817-732-3178
info@aact.org
www.aact.org

Julie Crawford, Executive Director
Murray Chase, President

National theatre festival showcasing the top acts of AACT's state and regional festivals, as well as offering theatre management conference, workshops, and social networking opportunities.
Frequency: Annual

19964 **National Black Theatre Festival**
610 Coliseum Drive
Suite 1
Winston-Salem, NC 27106

336-723-2266
nbtf@bellsouth.net
www.nbtf.org

Patrice Toney, President
Frequency: Annual, Winston-Salem

19965 **National Square Dance Convention**
PO Box 5790
Topeka, KS 66605-5790

317-635-4455
www.57nsdc.com

Ernie Stone, Executive Committee
Barbara Stone, Executive Committee

250 booths and 250 exhibitors.
20M+ Attendees
Frequency: June

19966 **New England Theatre Conference**
215 Knob Hill Drive
Hamden, CT 06518

617-851-8535; Fax: 203-288-5938
mail@netconline.org
www.netconline.org

Sabine Klein, President
Jeffrey Watts, Executive VP
Charles Emmons, VP Administration/Finance

Promoting excellence in theatre, a conference of New England's oldest, largest regional theatre association.
800+ Attendees
Frequency: November
Founded in 1952

19967 **Prescott Park Arts Festival**
105 Marcy Street
PO Box 4370
Portsmouth, NH 03802-4370

603-436-2848; Fax: 603-436-1034
info@prescottpark.org
www.prescottpark.org
Facebook

Ben Anderson, Executive Director
John Moynihan, General Manager
Catherine Wejchert, Development Coordinator

Provide a financially accessible, quality multi-arts festival to a diverse audience.

19968 **Southeastern Theatre Conference Convention**
Southeastern Theatre Conference
1175 Revolution Mill Drive
Suite 14
Greensboro, NC 27405

336-272-3645
info@setc.org
www.setc.org

Susie Prueter, Executive Director
April J'Callahan Marshall, Director, Professional Services

The annual SETC Convention brings members of the theatre community together for three and a half days of workshops, keynotes, performance festivals, auditions, college recruiting, job interviews, and more. Attendees include actors, singers, dancers, designers, technicians, stage managers, directors, playwrights, teachers, students, professionals and academicians.
5000+ Attendees
Frequency: Annual
Founded in 1949

19969 **TCG National Conference**
Theatre Communications Group
520 8th Ave
24th Floor
New York, NY 10018-4156

212-609-5900; Fax: 212-609-5901
www.tcg.org

Theresa Eyring, Executive Director
Jennifer Cleary, Membership Director

19970 **Theatre Bay Area General Auditions**
Theatre Bay Area
1119 Market St.
2nd Floor
San Francisco, CA 94103

415-430-1140; Fax: 415-430-1145
tba@theatrebayarea.org
www.theatrebayarea.org

Bryan Munar, Member Services
Brad Erikson, Executive Director

An annual event that brings together member performers and independent directors, casting directors, and 150-200 auditors representing 80-90 theatre companies.
Frequency: Annual, February

19971 **Theatre Bay Area's Annual Conference**
Theatre Bay Area
1119 Market Street
2nd Floor
San Francisco, CA 94103

415-430-1140; Fax: 415-430-1145
tba@theatrebayarea.org
www.theatrebayarea.org

Brad Erikson, Executive Director
Dale Albright, Deputy Director
MaryAnn Grossman, Development Director
Kimberley Cohan, Programs, Awards, Publications
J Jha, Marketing Manager

Theatre Bay Area's Annual Conference is an opportunity for theatre makers and leaders to gather to dicuss issues in theatre community, develop professionally, and network.
500+ Attendees
Frequency: Annual, April

19972 **US Institute for Theatre Technology Annual Conference & Stage Expo**
USITT
315 S Crouse Avenue
Suite 200
Syracuse, NY 13210

315-463-6463
800-938-7488; Fax: 315-463-6525
info@usitt.org
www.usitt.org
Facebook, Twitter, LinkedIn

Carl Lefko, President
Patricia Dennis, Secretary
Travis DeCastro, Treasurer

The Conference offers over 175 sessions featuring design, technology, costume, sound, architecture, management, engineering, and production. The Stage Expo showcases businesses, products, services, and eductional opportunities in the performing arts and entertainment industry. With over 150 exhibitors, Stage Expo provides conference attendees with the opportunity to see the newest and best products and services on the market today.
3700 Members
3800 Attendees
Frequency: March
Founded in 1960

Directories & Databases

19973 **Academy Players Directory**
2210 W Olive Avenue
Suite 320
Burbank, CA 91506

310-247-3058; Fax: 310-550-5034
info@playersdirectory.com
www.playersdirectory.com

The Players Directory appeared in 1937 as the first reliable casting directory that listed both featured stars and extras. Today, more than 16,000 actors are included.
Cost: $75.00
Founded in 1937

19974 **American Association of Community Theatre Membership Directory**
American Association of Community Theatre
1300 Gendy Street
Forth Worth, TX 76107-4036

817-732-3177
866-687-2228; Fax: 817-732-3178
info@aact.org
www.aact.org

Julie Crawford, Executive Director
Murray Chase, President
Carole Ries, Executive Vice President
David Cockerell, Marketing/Communications Director

The database includes addresses for over 7,000 community theatre organizations in the USA. Only available to members.
Founded in 1980
Mailing list available for rent: 10000 names at $180 per M

19975 **Americans for the Arts Field Directory**
Americans for the Arts
1 E 53rd St
2nd Floor
New York, NY 10022-4242

212-223-2787; Fax: 212-980-4857
www.artsactionfund.org
Facebook, Twitter, RSS, You Tube

Suzanne Niemeyer, Editor
Robert L Lynch, President/CEO
Liz Bartolomeo, Public Relations/Marketing Coord
Chad Bauman, Director Print/Multimedia
Graham Dunstan, Assoc Director Publication Sales

A must-have resource for anyone working in the arts and community development. The directory provides contact information for local, state, regional, and national arts service organizations-more than 4,000 entries broken down by state and region. Also includes contact information for professional consultants working in the nonprofit arts field. A great networking tool.
Cost: $35.00
262 Pages

19976 **Association of Performing Arts Presenters Membership Directory**
APAP
1211 Connecticut Ave NW
Suite 200
Washington, DC 20036-2716

202-833-2787
888-820-2787; Fax: 202-833-1543
info@artspresenters.org
www.artspresenters.org

Sandra Gibson, President
Sean Handerhan, Marketing

An invaluable resource for keeping in touch with colleagues. Puts more than 1,450 presenters, service organizations, artists, management companies, consultants, and vendors at your fingertips. An excellent networking tool for everyone on your staff.
1900 Members
Frequency: Annual
Founded in 1957

19977 **Complete Catalogue of Plays**
Dramatists Play Service
440 Park Ave S
New York, NY 10016-8012

212-683-8960; Fax: 212-213-1539
www.dramatists.com
Facebook

Stephen Fultan, President
Rafael J Rivera, VP Finance/Administration
Michael Q Fellmeth, VP Publications/IT
Tamra Feifer, Director Operations

The Complete Catalogue is published in odd years and the Supplement of New Plays in even years. Both books are distributed, without charge, to current customers in the Fall of each year.
412 Pages
Founded in 1936

19978 **Costume Designers Guild Directory**
Costumer Designers Guild
4730 Woodman Avenue
Suite 430
Sherman Oaks, CA 91423-2400

818-905-1557; Fax: 818-905-1560
www.costumedesignersguild.com

Rachael Stanley, Executive Director

Directory includes members' names, classification, and other statistical information.
Frequency: Annual

19979 **Dance Annual Directory**
Dance Magazine
333 7th Ave
11th Floor
New York, NY 10001-5109

212-979-4800; Fax: 212-979-4817
www.dancemagazine.com

Karla Johnson, Publisher
Emily Macel, Editor
Karen Hildebrand, Editorial Director
Wendy Perron, Editor-in-Chief
Hanna Rubin, Managing Editor

Reach 300,000+ dancers, dance teachers, and dance professionals in the dance world.
Cost: $100.00
Frequency: Annual

19980 **Dance Magazine College Guide**
Dance Magazine
333 7th Ave
11th Floor
New York, NY 10038-3900

212-979-4800; Fax: 212-979-4817
www.dancemagazine.com

Karla Johnson, President
Karen Hildebrand, Editorial Director
Wendy Perron, Editor-in-Chief
Hanna Rubin, Managing Editor
Kate Lydon, Education Editor

With over 500+ listings, Dance Magazine College Guide is a comprehensive source for dance degree programs in higher education. Find application deadlines and audition dates. Get student perspectives and career advice. Online database offers the ability to identify programs that match an individual's personal criteria for degree, type of dance, location, department size, tuition and more.
Cost: $29.95
Frequency: Annual

19981 **Dance Magazine: Summer Dance Calendar Issue**
Dance Magazine
33 W 60th Street
Floor 10
New York, NY 10023-7905
212-245-9050
800-331-1750
www.dancemagazine.com
A list of dance workshops and special programs for students are listed.
Cost: $3.95
Frequency: Annual
Circulation: 100,000

19982 **Dance/USA Annual Directory and List-Serv**
Dance/USA
1111 16th St NW
Suite 300
Washington, DC 20036-4830
202-833-1717; Fax: 202-833-2686
danceusa@danceusa.org
www.danceusa.org
Andrea Snyder, Executive Director
Tom Thielen, Director Finance/Operations
Katherine Fabian, Membership Manager
On-going list-servs keep many peer councils in touch throughout the year, by providing a quick and easy connection to peer counseling when members have an immediate question or problem. Information about dance companies, schools, presenters, service organizations and commercial suppliers is included in the annual copy of Dance Annual Directory.
Frequency: Annual
Circulation: 400+

19983 **Directory of Theatre Training Programs**
Theatre Directories
P.O.Box 2409
Manchester Center, VT 05255-2409
802-867-9333; Fax: 802-867-2297
www.theatredirectories.com
Peg Lyons, Editor
PJ Tumielewicz, Editor
Profiles admissions, tuition, faculty, curriculum, facilities, productions and philosophy of training at 475 programs in the US, Canada and abroad: Colleges, Universities, Conservatories, Undergraduate and Graduate degrees. Includes Combined Auditions information. Indexed by degrees offered in each program.
Cost: $39.50
ISBN: 0-933919-61-1

19984 **Dramatics College Theatre Directory**
Educational Theatre Association
2343 Auburn Ave
Cincinnati, OH 45219-2815
513-421-3900; Fax: 513-421-7077
www.edta.org
Facebook, Twitter
Michael Peitz, Executive Director
Gloria McIntyre, President
Jay Seller, VP
Lists more than 250 college, university, and conservatory theatre programs, offering a sketch of each based on information provided by the schools. The listings can be used to measure each school against one's own criteria for location, setting, courses of study, admission requirements, and cost. Find out which programs offer merit scholarships and grants and how those funds are awarded. Use the contact information to get in touch with the programs that seem to offer the best fit for your needs
Cost: $9.00
Frequency: Annual

19985 **Dramatics Magazine: Summer Theatre Directory**
Educational Theatre Association
2343 Auburn Ave
Cincinnati, OH 45219-2815
513-421-3900; Fax: 513-421-7077
www.edta.org
Facebook, Twitter
Michael Peitz, Executive Director
Gloria McIntyre, President
Jay Seller, VP
Lists nearly 200 summer theatre programs and stock companies, offering a sketch of each based on factual information provided by the schools, camps, and theatre companies. The listings can be used to measure each program against one's own criteria for location, setting, housing, courses of study, admission requirements and fees.
Cost: $9.00
Frequency: Annual

19986 **Dramatist's Sourcebook**
Theatre Communications Group
520 8th Ave
24th Floor
New York, NY 10018-4156
212-609-5900; Fax: 212-609-5901
www.tcg.org
Theresa Eyring, Executive Director
Kelly Haydon, Database Manager
Jennifer Cleary, Director Membership
Terence Nemeth, Publisher
Kathy Sova, Editorial Director
Completely revised, with more than 900 opportunities for playwrights, translators, composers, lyricists, and librettists, as well as opportunities for screen, radio, and television writers. Thoroughly indexed, with a calendar of deadlines. The Sourcebook contains scrip-submission procedures for more than 350 theatres seeking new plays; guidelines for more than 150 prizes; and sections on agents, fellowships and residencies.
Cost: $22.95
Frequency: Annual
ISBN: 1-559362-94-4
Founded in 1980

19987 **Dramatists Guild Annual Resource Directory**
Dramatists Guild of America
1501 Broadway
Suite 701
New York, NY 10036-5505
212-398-9366; Fax: 212-944-0420
www.dramaguild.com
Ralph Sevush, Executive Director
The Resource Directory is an annual sourcebook available only to Guild members, sent automatically as one of the privileges of Guild members. It includes lists of conferences and festivals, contests, producers, publishers, agents and attorneys, fellowships and grants, and workshops throughout the US and the world.
Frequency: Annual

19988 **Encyclopedia of Exhibition**
National Association of Theatre Owners
750 1st St Ne
Suite 1130
Washington, DC 20002-4241
202-962-0054; Fax: 202-962-0370
nato@natodc.com
www.natoonline.org
John Fithian, President
Gary Klein, VP
Kathy Conroy, Executive Director
Packed with information on film grosses, upcoming releases, and filmgoer demographics. Also features a directory of international and domestic exhibitors and distributors, cinema companies ranked by screen count, trade publications and more
Cost: $500.00
Frequency: Annual

19989 **Feedback Theatrebooks and Prospero Press**
Feedback Theatrebooks & Prospero Press
PO Box 174
Brooklin, ME 04616
207-359-2781; Fax: 207-359-5532
Publishes theatre histories, cookbooks, directories, anthologies of plays, plays published before WWII, and format guidelines for playwrights.

19990 **Grey House Performing Arts Directory**
Grey House Publishing
4919 Route 22
PO Box 56
Amenia, NY 12501
518-789-8700
800-562-2139; Fax: 845-373-6390
books@greyhouse.com
www.greyhouse.com
Facebook, Twitter
Leslie Mackenzie, Publisher
Richard Gottlieb, Editor
The most comprehensive resource covering the Performing Arts. This directory provides current information on over 8,500 Dance Companies, Instrumental Music Programs, Opera Companies, Choral Groups, Theater Companies, Performing Arts Series, Performing Arts Facilities and Artist Management Groups.
Cost: $185.00
1200 Pages
Frequency: Annual
ISBN: 1-592373-76-3
Founded in 1981

19991 **Grey House Performing Arts Directory - Online Database**
Grey House Publishing
4919 Route 22
PO Box 56
Amenia, NY 12501-0056
518-789-8700
800-562-2139; Fax: 518-789-0556
gold@greyhouse.com
gold.greyhouse.com
Facebook, Twitter
Leslie Mackenzie, Publisher
Richard Gottlieb, Editor
The Grey House Performing Arts Directory - Online Database provides immediate access to dance companies, orchestras, opera companies, choral groups, theater companies, series, festivals and perfoming arts facilities across the country, or in their region, state, or in your own backyard. It offers unequaled coverage of the Performing Arts - over 8,500 listings - of the major performance organization, facilities, and information resources.
Frequency: Annual
Founded in 1981

19992 **Money for Film and Video Artists**
Americans for the Arts
1 E 53rd St
2nd Floor
New York, NY 10022-4242

212-223-2787; Fax: 212-980-4857
www.artsactionfund.org
Facebook, Twitter, RSS, You Tube

Suzanne Niemeyer, Editor
Robert L Lynch, President/CEO
Liz Bartolomeo, Public Relations/Marketing Coord
Chad Bauman, Director Print/Multimedia
Graham Dunstan, Assoc Director Publication Sales

A comprehensive resource guide to fellowships, grants, awards, low-cost facilities, emergency assistance programs, technical assistance, and support services. Entries include contact information; type of award and/or scope of service; eligibilty requirements; application procedures; deadlines and more.
Cost: $14.95
317 Pages
ISBN: 1-879903-09-1

19993 **Money for International Exchange in the Arts**
Americans for the Arts
1 E 53rd St
2nd Floor
New York, NY 10022-4242

212-223-2787; Fax: 212-980-4857
www.artsactionfund.org
Facebook, Twitter, RSS, You Tube

Suzanne Niemeyer, Editor
Robert L Lynch, President/CEO
Liz Bartolomeo, Public Relations/Marketing Coord
Chad Bauman, Director Print/Multimedia
Graham Dunstan, Assoc Director Publication Sales

This resource includes grants, fellowships and awards for travel and work abroad; support and technical assistance for international touring and exchange; international artists' residencies; programs that support artists' professional development, and more. Indexed by region, discipline and type of support.
Cost: $14.95
122 Pages
ISBN: 1-879903-01-6

19994 **Money for Performing Artists**
Americans for the Arts
1 E 53rd St
2nd Floor
New York, NY 10022-4242

212-223-2787; Fax: 212-980-4857
www.artsactionfund.org
Facebook, Twitter, RSS, You Tube

Suzanne Niemeyer, Editor
Robert L Lynch, President/CEO
Liz Bartolomeo, Public Relations/Marketing Coord
Chad Bauman, Director Print/Multimedia
Graham Dunstan, Assoc Director Publication Sales

Lists awards, grants, fellowships, competitions, auditions, workshops, and artists' colonies, as well as emergency and technical assistance programs.
Cost: $12.00
240 Pages
ISBN: 0-915400-96-0
Founded in 1991

19995 **Money for Visual Arts**
Americans for the Arts
1 E 53rd St
2nd Floor
New York, NY 10022-4242

212-223-2787; Fax: 212-980-4857
www.artsactionfund.org
Facebook, Twitter, RSS, You Tube

Suzanne Niemeyer, Editor
Robert L Lynch, President/CEO
Liz Bartolomeo, Public Relations/Marketing Coord
Chad Bauman, Director Print/Multimedia
Graham Dunstan, Assoc Director Publication Sales

A guide to grants, fellowships, awards, artist colonies, emergency and technical assistance, and support services. Entries include contact information; type of award and/or scope of service; eligibility requirements; application procedures; deadlines, and more.
Cost: $14.95
340 Pages

19996 **Musical America International Directory of the Performing Arts**
Commonwealth Business Media
P.O. Box 1330
Highstown, NJ 08520

609-448-3346; Fax: 609-301-8433
info@musicalamerica.com
www.musicalamerica.com

Stephanie Challener, Publisher
Sedgwick Clark, Features Editor
Susan Elliot, News Editor
Bill Esposito, Data Editor

Features over 14,000 detailed listings of worldwide arts organizations, including key contact information such as name, address, phone, fax, website and e-mail addresses, budget category, type of event and seating capacity. In addition, through advertising, over 10,000 artists are indexed in the alphabetical and categorical indexes. Categories include artist managers, orchestras, opera companies, concert series, festivals, competitions, music schools and departments, record companies, and more.
Founded in 1898

19997 **NYC/On Stage**
Theatre Development Fund
520 Eight Avenue
Suite 801
New York, NY 10018-6507

212-912-9770
info@tdf.org
www.tdf.org
Facebook

Earl D. Weiner, Chair
Sandra Kresch, Vice Chairman
Robert T. Goldman, Treasurer
Deborah Hartnett, Secretary

Theater, dance, and music companies and performing arts centers in New York City.
Founded in 1995

19998 **National Network For Artist Placement**
National Network for Artist Placement
935 W Avenue 37
Los Angeles, CA 90065

323-222-4035
800-354-5348
NNAPnow@aol.com
www.americansforthearts.org

Warren Christensen, Consultant

Internship opportunities in dance, music, theatre, art and film.
Cost: $85.00
375 Pages
Frequency: Bi-Annual
ISBN: 0-945941-13-7

19999 **Opera America Membership Directory**
Opera America
330 7th Ave
16th Floor
New York, NY 10001-5248

212-796-8620; Fax: 212-796-8631
info@operaamerica.org
www.operaamerica.org
YouTube

Marc Scorca, President

Directory of Opera America's Company, Business, Library, and Affiliate Members, indexed alphabetically and geographically. Includes the Annual Report to Members, a description of Opera America's programs and services, and a list of individual members.
Cost: $25.00
Frequency: Annual

20000 **Plays and Playwrights**
International Society of Dramatists
1638 Euclid Avenue
Miami Beach, FL 33139-7744

305-882-1864
http://blog.nytesmallpress.com/

Offers valuable information on over 1,000 dramatists producing works in English.
Cost: $29.95
200 Pages
Frequency: Annual
Circulation: 10,000

20001 **Regional Theatre Directory**
Theatre Directories
P.O.Box 2409
Manchester Center, VT 05255-2409

802-867-9333; Fax: 802-867-2297
www.theatredirectories.com

Peg Lyons, Editor
PJ Tumielewicz, Editor

Profiles over 400 theatres including dinner theatres, equity and non-equity. Find out when/where auditions are held, when resumes shoul be sent, housing and transportation policy, and general description of company. If you want to find a job or an internship as an actor, designer, technician or staff in a professional regional or dinner theatre anywhere in the country, this directory can help you.
Cost: $29.50
Frequency: Annual
ISBN: 0-933919-63-8
Founded in 1984

20002 **SETC Theatre Job Board**
Southeastern Theatre Conference
1175 Revolution Mill Drive
Suite 14
Greensboro, NC 27405

336-272-3645
info@setc.org
www.setc.org

Susie Prueter, Executive Director
April J'Callahan Marshall, Director, Professional Services

Online employment listing of Classified Ads for theatrical positions, auditions, and more.
Founded in 1949

20003 **Salem Press Online Platform**
Grey House Publishing
4919 Route 22
PO Box 56
Amenia, NY 12501

800-221-1592; Fax: 201-968-0511
csr@salempress.com
online.salempress.com

The new Salem Press platform houses more than 500 titles including all of Salem's Health, Literature, History and Science titles in addition to select titles from the Grey House Publishing and H.W. Wilson product lines. Online access is free with each print purchase and includes an unlimited number of simultaneous users and remote access.

20004 **ShowBiz Bookkeeper**
Theatre Directories
P.O.Box 2409
Manchester Center, VT 05255-2409
802-867-9333; Fax: 802-867-2297
www.theatredirectories.com
The tax record-keeping system for professionals working in the arts.
Cost: $22.95

20005 **Stars in Your Eyes...Feet on the Ground**
Theatre Directories
P.O.Box 2409
Manchester Center, VT 05255-2409
802-867-9333; Fax: 802-867-2297
www.theatredirectories.com
PJ Tumielewicz, Editor
Peg Lyons, Editor
For teens who want to act...Practical advice for young actors: learning how show business works; agents and managers; local cable shows and television commercials; auditioning for stage, student films and TV; choosing a school; dealing with rejection; parental support and more. Written by a 19-year old professional actress.
Cost: $16.95
ISBN: 0-933919-42-5

20006 **Student's Guide to Playwriting Opportunities**
Theatre Directories
P.O.Box 2409
Manchester Center, VT 05255-2409
802-867-9333; Fax: 802-867-2297
www.theatredirectories.com
Michael Write, Directory Editor
Christi Pyland, Directory Editor
PJ Tumielewicz, Theatre Directories, Inc Editor
Peg Lyons, Theatre Directories, Inc Editor
An essential tool for every high shool or college student with an interest in playwriting. Comprehensive listings of 79 academic programs and another 80 professional development programs geared for the young writer. New essays on the art, process and business of playwriting.
Cost: $23.95
128 Pages
ISBN: 0-933919-53-0

20007 **Summer Theatre Directory**
Theatre Directories
P.O.Box 2409
Manchester Center, VT 05255-2409
802-867-9333; Fax: 802-867-2297
www.theatredirectories.com
Opportunities at over 350 summer theatres, theme parks, and summer training programs.
Cost: $29.50

20008 **Theatre Bay Area Sources of Publicity**
Theatre Bay Area
1119 Market Street
2nd Floor
San Francisco, CA 94103
415-430-1140; Fax: 415-430-1145
tba@theatrebayarea.org
www.theatrebayarea.org
Brad Erikson, Executive Director
Dale Albright, Deputy Director
MaryAnn Grossman, Development Director
Kimberley Cohan, Programs, Awards, Publications
J Jha, Marketing Manager
The premier guide to print, web, radio, television and social media sources of publicity in the Bay Area features up-to-date information on 270 media contacts in the Bay Area.
Cost: $150.00
500+ Attendees
Frequency: Annual

20009 **Theatre Profiles Database**
Theatre Communications Group
520 8th Ave
24th Floor
New York, NY 10018-4156
212-609-5900; Fax: 212-609-5901
www.tcg.org
Theresa Eyring, Executive Director
Kelly Haydon, Database Manager
Jennifer Cleary, Director Membership
Terence Nemeth, Publisher
Kathy Sova, Editorial Director
Online database of more than 400 theatre members in 47 states, 17,000 individual members, 100 Trustee Leadership Network members and a growing number of University, Funder and Business Affiliates.
Frequency: Annual

20010 **Whole Arts Directory**
Midmarch Arts Press
300 Riverside Dr
Apartment 8A
New York, NY 10025-5279
212-666-6990; Fax: 212-865-5510
www.midmarchartspress.org
Cynthia Navaregga, Manager
Directory to arts resources, organiztions, museums, galleries, colonies, retreats, art therapy, information services, and much more. Highly useful material for all artists, students, organizations and institutions.
Cost: $12.95
175 Pages
ISBN: 0-960247-67-x
Founded in 1987
Printed in on matte stock

Industry Web Sites

20011 **http://gold.greyhouse.com**
G.O.L.D Grey House OnLine Databases
Grey House Publishing's online database platform, GOLD, offers Quick Search, Keyword Search and Expert Search for most business sectors including performing arts markets. The GOLD platform makes finding the information you need quick and easy - whether you're a novice searcher or an experienced database user. All of Grey House's directory products are available for subscription on the GOLD platform.

20012 **www.aact.org**
American Association of Community Theatre
Non-profit corporation fostering excellence in community theatre productions and governance through community theatre festivals, educational opportunity publications, network, resources, and website.
Founded in 1980

20013 **www.aahperd.org/nda**
National Dance Association
A nonprofit service organization dedicated to increasing knowledge, improving skills and encouraging sound professional practices in dance education while promoting and supporting creative and healthy lifestyles through high quality dance programs.

20014 **www.aate.com**
American Alliance for Theatre and Education
Members are artists, teachers and professionals who serve youth theatres and theatre educational programs.

20015 **www.absolutewrite.com**
Absolute Write
Advice for writers, including playwrights.

20016 **www.actorsequity.org**
Actors Equity Association
Labor union affiliated with AFL-CIO which represents actors in film, television and commercials.

20017 **www.actorsite.com**
Actor Site
Audition and other information.

20018 **www.actorsource.com**
Actorsource
Extensive information and resources for actors.

20019 **www.actorstheatre.org**
Actors Theatre of Louisville
Supports new playwrights. For information on entering a play, click Humana Festival.

20020 **www.adta.org**
American Dance Therapy Association
Founded in 1966; professional organization of dance movement therapists, with members both nationally and internationally; offers training, research findings, and a newsletter.

20021 **www.aislesay.com**
Aislesay
Internet magazine of stage reviews and opinions.

20022 **www.americandanceguild.org**
American Dance Guild
Non-profit membership organization; sponsors professional seminars, workshops, a student scholarship and other projects and institutes programs of national significance in the field of dance.

20023 **www.americantheaterweb.com**
American Theater Web
Find theaters, Broadway shows and musicals.

20024 **www.answers4dancers.com**
Answers for Dancers
Dance Magazine sponsors this site.

20025 **www.artsmed.org**
Performing Arts Medicine Association
Organization for physicians and professionals interested in the research of Performing Arts Medicine.

20026 **www.artspresenters.org**
Association of Performing Arts Presenters
Celebrates rich and diverse performing arts to the public.

20027 **www.artstabilization.org**
National Arts Strategies
Offers training and technical assistance to arts organizations.

20028 **www.athe.org**
Association for Theatre in Higher Education
Promotes quality in theatre education.

20029 **www.bachauer.com**
Gina Bachauer International Piano Foundation

Produce a yearly piano international competition

20030 **www.backstage.com**
Backstage.com
Information for actors, casting calls, film reviews, auditions and acting jobs.

20031 **www.backstagejobs.com**
Theatre Design and Technical Jobs Page
Employment opportunities.

20032 **www.backstageworld.com**
Backstage World
Post your resume and search for design and technical job opportunities worldwide.

20033 **www.bmi.com**
BMI
Secures the rights of songwriters/composers. Collects license fees for the public performance of music and pays royalties to its copyright owners.

20034 **www.catf.org**
Contemporary American Theater Festival
Dedicated to providing and developing new American Theater.

20035 **www.cincinnatiarts.org**
Cincinnati Arts Association
Dedicated to supporting performing and visual arts.

20036 **www.classicalaction.org**
Classical Action
Provides a unified voice for all those within the performing arts community to help combat HIV/AIDS.

20037 **www.computermusic.org**
International Computer Music Association
Supports the performance aspects of computer music; publishes newsletter and holds annual conferance.

20038 **www.conductorsguild.org**
Conductors Guild
Dedicated to encouraging the highest standards in the art and profession of conducting. Founded in 1975.

20039 **www.contactimprov.net**
Contact Improv
Improvisation for dancers.

20040 **www.costume-con.org**
Costume Connections
Costume conferences.

20041 **www.costume.org**
International Costumers' Guild
An affiliation of amateur hobbyist and professional costumers.

20042 **www.costumegallery.com**
Costume Gallery
A central location on the web for fashion and costume since 1996.

20043 **www.costumers.org**
National Costumers Association
Seeks to establish and maintain professional and ethical standards of business in the costume industry.

20044 **www.costumes.org**
Costumer's Manifesto
Online book, information and links.

20045 **www.costumesocietyamerica.com**
Costume Society of America
Education, research, presentation and design.

20046 **www.creativedir.com**
Creative Directory Services
Diectory of suppliers for costumes, sets, special effects and stunts.

20047 **www.criticaldance.com**
Dance Critics Association
Critical dance forum and ballet dance magazine

20048 **www.csulb.edu/~jvancamp/copyrigh.html**
Csulb.edu
Copyrighting choreographic works.

20049 **www.csusa.org/face/index.htm**
Friends of Active Copyright Education
Playwrights should click on Words, then Copyright Basics.

20050 **www.cyberdance.org**
Cyber Dance
Collection of links to modern dance and classical ballet resources.

20051 **www.danceart.com**
Danceart.com
Ballet and dance art, features, chat and more.

20052 **www.dancenotation.org**
Dance Notation Bureau
Notation basics, Notated Theatrical Dances Catalogue and links.

20053 **www.danceusa.org**
Dance/USA
Provides a forum for the discussion of issues of concern to membersand a support network for exchange of information; also bestows awards.

20054 **www.deadance.com**
Dance Educators of America
Promotes the education of teachers in the performing arts.

20055 **www.dma-national.org**
Dance Masters of America
An organization of dance teachers.

20056 **www.dramaguild.com**
Dramatists Guild
Comprehensive organization that deals solely with Broadway and off-Broadway producers, off-off-Broadway groups, agents, theatres and sources of grants.

20057 **www.dramaleague.org**
Drama League
Seeks to strengthen American theatre through the nurturing of stage directors.

20058 **www.edta.org**
Educational Theater Association
Theater educators working to increase support for theater programs in the educational system.

20059 **www.esperanzaarts.org**
Esperanza Performing Arts Association

20060 **www.etecnyc.net**
Entertainment Technology Online
For employment in design and technical theatre, click on Classifieds. Also offers resources and buyers guides for theatrical lighting.

20061 **www.gmn.com**
Global Music Network
Go backstage, watch rehearsals, listen to performances of classical and jazz artists.

20062 **www.goldmime.com**
Goldston Mime Foundation: School for Mime
Holds summer seminars and workshops.

20063 **www.greyhouse.com**
Grey House Publishing
Authoritative reference directories for most business sectors including performing arts markets. Users can search the online databases with varied search criteria allowing for custom searches by product category, geographic area, sales volume, keyword, subject and more. Full Grey House catalog and online ordering also available.

20064 **www.harada-sound.com/sound/handbook**
Kai's Sound Handbook
Information for sound designers.

20065 **www.ifea.com**
International Festivals and Events Association
Network for planning events and exchange programs; publishes quarterly magazine.

20066 **www.intix.org**
International Ticketing Association
Not-for-profit association representing 22 countries worldwide and more than 1,200 members. Committed to the improvement, progress and advancement of ticket management, and to reach this goal provides educational programs, trade shows, conducts surveys and conference proceedings and produces a membership directory.

20067 **www.ispa.org**
International Society for the Performing Arts
Foundation
Supports international cooperation, facilitates networking and enhances professional dialogue.

20068 **www.jensenfoundation.org**
Fritz and Lavinia Jensen Foundation
Sponsors competitions.

20069 **www.lib.colum.edu/costwais.html**
Costume Image Database
Access costume images.

20070 **www.light-link.com**
Lightsearch.com
Lists of lighting equipment suppliers.

20071 **www.livebroadway.com**
League of American Theatres and Producers
National trade association for the commercial theatre industry whose principal activity is negotiation of labor contracts and government relations.

20072 **www.lmda.org**
Literary Managers and Dramaturgs of the Americas
Voluntary membership organization.

20073 **www.luth.org**
Guild of American Luthiers
Manufacturers and repairs stringed instruments; offers quarterly journal and triennial meeting.

20074 **www.lycos.com**
Lycos
Click Arts and Entertainment, then Dance, Theatre or Performing Arts.

20075 **www.magicsam.com**
Society of American Magicians
Founded to promote and maintain harmonious fellowship among those interested in magic as an art, to improve ethics of the magical profession, and to foster, promote and improve the advancement of magical arts in the field of amusement

and entertainment. Membership includes professional and amateur magicians, manufacturers of magical apparatus and collectors.

20076 www.makeupmag.com
Make-Up Artist Magazine
Make-up artist magazine online.

20077 www.members.aol.com/thegoop/gaff.html
Gaff Tape Webring
Tech theatre.

20078 www.midatlanticarts.org
Mid Atlantic Arts Foundation
Provides leadership and support for artists and arts organizations in the Mid-Atlantic region and beyond.

20079 www.milieux.com/costume
Costume Source
Provides online sources for materials, costumes, accessories and books.

20080 www.mtishows.com
Music Theatre International
Scripts, cast recordings, study guides, production slides and other resources.

20081 www.musicalamerica.com
Musicalamerica.com
Late-breaking industry news, full search capabilities, immediate interaction between Presenter and Artist Manager/Artist.

20082 www.musicianshealth.com
Chiropractic Performing Arts Association
To educate amateur and professional entertainers, musicians and dancers about reaching optimum health potential through natural, drug-free, conservative chiropractic care.

20083 www.nadt.org
National Association for Drama Therapy
Promotes the profession of Drama Therapy.

20084 www.namm.org
NAMM-International Music Products Association
Offers professional development seminars; sells musical instruments and allied products.

20085 www.napama.org
North American Performing Arts Managers and Agents
A cooperative voice in a competitive business.

20086 www.natoonline.org
National Association of Theatre Owners
Exhibition trade organization, representing more than 30,000 movie screens in all 50 states, and additional cinemas in 50 countries worldwide.

20087 www.nbtf.org
National Black Theatre Festival

20088 www.netconline.org
New England Theatre Conference
Non-profit educational corporation founded to develop, expand and assist theatre activity in community, educational and professional levels in New England. Holds annual auditions.

20089 www.nmpa.org
National Music Publishers' Association
Publishes a quarterly newsletter and holds an annual meeting.

20090 www.nyfa.org
New York Foundation for the Arts
Employment openings in the arts.

20091 www.nytimes.com
New York Times on the Web
Arts and Theatre contains play reviews.

20092 www.oobr.com
Off-Off-Broadway Review
Lists information on off-off broadway shows such as: title of show, author, director, producing company, theatre, address, box-office phone number, dates and times, admission price and contact info.

20093 www.opencasting.com
Open Casting
Bulletin board containing auditions, crew calls, casting notices and links.

20094 www.paastjo.org
Performing Arts Association
Provides a diverse selection of performing arts.

20095 www.pen.org
PEN: American Center
Site of the international literary community organization.

20096 www.performingarts.net
Performing Arts Online
Dedicated to the perpetuation of quality performing arts.

20097 www.pianonet.com
Piano Manufacturers Association International
Manufacturers and suppliers of pianos and parts; holds annual trade show.

20098 www.pipeorgan.org
American Institute of Organ Builders
Sponsers training seminars, quarterly journal and annual convention for pipe organ builders and service technicians.

20099 www.plasa.org
Professional Lighting and Sound Association
Web site for PLASA, a leading trade body for Lighting and Sound Professionals.

20100 www.playbill.com
Playbill Online
Listings for Broadway and off Broadway theatre productions. Also guides for sites, including summer stock, national touring shows and regional theatres worldwide.

20101 www.playwrights.org
Playwrights Center of San Francisco
Playwrites directory.

20102 www.playwrightshorizons.org
Playwrights Horizon
At home page click arrow. On next page click working with PH. You will see Writing Submissions.

20103 www.playwrightsproject.com
Playwrights Project
Promotes literacy, creativity and communication skills in young people through drama-based activities.

20104 www.proppeople.com
Proppeople.com
Online home for props professionals.

20105 www.renfaire.com/Language/index.html
Renfaire.com
Lessons on proper Elizabethan accents.

20106 www.rigging.net
Rigger's Page
Technical information on stage rigging equipment.

20107 www.roundalab.org
Roundalab
A professional international society of individuals who teach round dancing at any phase.

20108 www.safd.org
Society of American Fight Directors
Promotes safety in directing staged combat and theatrical violence.

20109 www.sagaftra.org

20110 www.sapphireswan.com/dance
Dance Directory
Dance resources.

20111 www.setc.org
Southeastern Theatre Conference
A non-profit membership organization serving Alabama, Florida, Georgia, Kentucky, Mississippi, North Carolina, South Carolina, Tennessee, Virgina, and West Virgina.

20112 www.sfballet.org
San Francisco Ballet Association
Provides a repertoire of classical and contemporary ballet; to provide educational opportunities for professional dancers and choreographers; to excel in ballet, artistic direction and administration.

20113 www.southarts.org
Southern Arts Federation
Serves as the leadership voice to increase the regional, national and international awareness and prominence of Southern arts. Creates mechanisms and partnerships to expand local, regional, national and international markets for Southern arts.

20114 www.spolin.com
Spolin Center
Information on improvisational theatre.

20115 www.ssdc.org
Society of Stage Directors and Choreographers
An independent labor union representing directors and choreographers in American theatre.

20116 www.stage-directions.com
Stage Directions Magazine
The practical and technical side of theatrical operations.

20117 www.stageplays.com/markets.htm
Playwrights Noticeboard
Information on contests, publishing and production opportunities.

20118 www.summertheater.com
Directory of Summer Theater in the United States
Search for summer theater opportunities by alphabetized listings or geographic region.

20119 www.talkinbroadway.com
Talkin' Broadway
Theatrical events and information on and off Broadway and other selected geographical locations.

20120 www.tcg.org
Theatre Communications Group
Supports alliances among playwrights, theatres and communities. Promotes not-for-profit theatre and offers resources to jobseekers. Offers fi-

nancial support to designers and directors through its Career Development Program.

20121 **www.tdf.org**
Theatre Development Fund

Not-for-profit service organization. Provides support for every area of the dance, music and professional theatre field. Founded 1968.

20122 **www.theatrebayarea.org**
Theatre Bay Area

Serving more than 400 member theatre companies and 3,000 individual members in the San Francisco Bay Area and Northern California, Theatre Bay Area provides monthly classes, workshops, events, information and publications.

20123 **www.theatrecrafts.com**
Theatrecrafts.com

Practical information about technical theatre techniques for theatre folk at any level.

20124 **www.theatrejobs.com**
Theatrejobs.com

Online job placement. Festival listings, summer stock, assistantships, apprenticeships, fellowships and internships.

20125 **www.thecastingnetwork.com/webring.html**
Casting Network.com

By and for actors.

20126 **www.theplays.org**
Electronic Literature Foundation

William Shakespeare's plays online.

20127 **www.tla-online.org**
Theatre Library Association

Supports librarians and archivists working in theatre, dance, performance studies, popular entertainment and broadcasting collections. The association offers publications, conferences, panels, and public events to its members.

20128 **www.top20performingarts.com**
Top 20 Performing Arts

Online directory for Perfoming Arts education.

20129 **www.towson.edu/worldmusiccongresses**
World Music Congresses

1997-2010 World Cello Congress' II-V, 2004 The First World Guitar Congress and 2008 World Guitar Congress II. Celebrations of music with international gatherings of the world's greatest musicians, composers, conductors, instrument manufacturers students, and music lovers from around the globe.

20130 **www.unc.edu/depts/outdoor**
Institute of Outdoor Drama

Summer jobs for all theatrical personnel.

20131 **www.ups.edu/professionalorgs/dramaturgy**
Dramaturgy Northwest

Relevant information for all dramaturgs.

20132 **www.urta.com**
University/Resident Theatre Association

Coalition of theatre training programs. Sponsors unified auditions.

20133 **www.usabda.org**
USA Dance

Non-profit organization working to promote ballroom dancing, both as a recreational activity and as a competetive sport.

20134 **www.usitt.org**
United States Institute for Theatre Technology

The association of design, production and technology professionals in the performing arts and entertainment industry whose mission is to promote the knowledge and skills of its members. International in scope, USITT draws its board of directors from across the US and Canada. Sponsors projects, programs, research, symposia, exhibits, and annual conference. Disseminates information on aesthetic and technical developments.

20135 **www.variety.org**
Variety

e-version of the show business newspaper.

20136 **www.vcu.edu/artweb/playwriting**
Playwriting Seminars

An opinionated web companion on the art and craft of playwriting for theatre and dance.

20137 **www.vl-theatre.com**
WWW Virtual Library

Links to theatre and drama resources. Updated daily.

20138 **www.wwar.com**
World Wide Arts Resources

Links to Theatre and Dance.

20139 **www2.sundance.org**
Sundance Institute

Information on the Sundance Theatre Laboratory summer workshop for directors, playwrights, choreographers, solo performers and composers. For information on submitting a play, click Theatre Program on home page.

Associations

20140 AAPG Foundation
PO Box 979
Tulsa, OK 74101-0979
918-560-2644
855-302-2743; Fax: 918-560-2642
foundation.aapg.org
Facebook, Twitter
David Curtiss, Executive Director
The Foundation supports the geosciences by providing funding for educational and research programs.
Founded in 1967

20141 ADSC International Association of Foundation Drilling
8445 Freeport Parkway Suite 325
Irving, TX
469-359-6000; Fax: 469-359-6007
adsc@adsc-iafd.com
www.adsc-iafd.com
Facebook, Twitter, LinkedIn
Mike Moore, CEO
Fred Miller, Chief Financial Officer
Emily Matthews, Director, Operations
Angie Elmendorf, Director, Media Relations
Rick Marshall, Director, Safety

20142 ASM International
9639 Kinsman Road
Materials Park, OH 44073-0002
440-338-5151
800-336-5152; Fax: 440-338-4634
memberservicecenter@asminternational.org
www.asminternational.org
Facebook, Twitter, LinkedIn
Zi-Kui Liu, President
Diana Essock, Vice President
Raymond V. Fryan, Treasurer
William T. Mahoney, Secretary & CEO
The society for materials engineers and scientists, a worldwide network dedicated to advancing industry, technology and applications of metals and materials. ASM provides information references, education, research and international events.
30K Members
Founded in 1913

20143 American Association of Drilling Engineers
P.O. Box 107
Houston, TX 77001
281-293-9800
info@aade.org
www.aade.org
Facebook
Geree Wald Morton, President
Randy Thomas, Vice President
Duane Halverson, Treasurer
Jannie Snelson, Secretary
Bob Vaughn, Executive Director
Founded in 1978

20144 American Association of Petroleum Geologists
1444 S. Boulder
PO Box 979
Tulsa, OK 74119
918-584-2555
800-364-2274; Fax: 918-560-2665
bulletin@aapg.org
www.aapg.org
Facebook, Twitter, LinkedIn, YouTube
Paul Weimer, President
Denise M. Cox, Secretary
Edward Beaumont, President-Elect
James S. McGhay, Treasurer
Stephen E. Laubach, Editor
Supports those professionals involved in the field of geology as it relates to petroleum, natural gas, and other energy products. Publishes monthly journal of peer-reviewed articles.
30000 Members
Founded in 1917

20145 American Association of Petroleum Geologis
P.O. Box 979
Tulsa, OK 74101-0979
918-560-2644
855-302-2743; Fax: 918-560-2642
foundation.aapg.org
Facebook, Twitter, Stumbleupon
David Curtiss, Executive Director
David E. Lange, Deputy Executive Director
April Stuart, Program Coordinator
Tamra Campbell, Administrative Assistant
Karen Piqune, Librarian
Founded in 1967

20146 American Association of Professional Landmen
800 Fournier Street ÿ
Fort Worth, TX 76102
817-847-7700; Fax: 817-847-7704
aapl@landman.org
www.landman.org
Facebook, Twitter, LinkedIn, YouTube
Jack C. Richards, President
Jim R. Dewbre, 1st Vice President
Melanie Bell,CPL, Executive VP
Bernard J. Ulicy, 2nd Vice President
C.Craig Young, Sr.Director
AAPL's mission is to promote the highest standards of performance for all land professionals, to advance their stature and to encourage sound stewardship of energy and mineral resources.
7000 Members
Founded in 1955

20147 American Fuel & Petrochemical Manufacturer s
1667 K Street NW
Ste. 700
Washington, DC 20006
202-457-0480; Fax: 202-457-0486
www.afpm.org
Facebook, Twitter, RSS
David Lamp, Chairman
Gregory J. Goff, Vice Chair
Charles T. Drevna, Executive Assistant
Rich Moskowitz, General Counsel
Diana Cronan, Communications Director
450 Members
Founded in 1902

20148 American Institute of Mining Metallurgical & Petroleum Engineers
12999 East Adam Aircraft Circle
Englewood, CO 80112
303-325-5185; Fax: 888-702-0049
aime@aimehq.org
www.aimehq.org
Facebook, LinkedIn, YouTube, RSS
Brajendra Fattahi, President
Garry W. Warren, President-Elect
Nikhil C. Trivedi, President-Elect Designate
Dale E. Heinz, Past President
Drew Meyer, Trustee
AIME is and shall be a New York State Nonprofit Corporation organized and operated to advance and disseminate, through the programs of the Member Societies, knowledge of engineering and the arts and sciences involved in the production and use of minerals, metals, energy sources and materials for the benefit of humankind, and to represent AIME and the Member Societies within the larger engineering community.
90000 Members
Founded in 1871

20149 American Oil & Gas Historical Society
1201 15th Street
Ste 300
Washington, DC 20005
Home Page: aoghs.org
Facebook, Twitter, LinkedIn, Google+
Bruce A. Wells, Executive Director
Founded in 2003

20150 American Petroleum Institute
200 Massachusetts Avenue NW
Suite 1100
Washington, DC 20001-5571
202-682-8000
www.api.org
Facebook, Twitter, YouTube, Flickr
Mike Sommers, President/CEO
Amanda Eversole, EVP/COO
Paul G. Afonso, SVP/CLO/Corporate Secretary
Megan Bloomgren, SVP, Communications
Bill Koetzle, SVP, Gov. Relations
The only national trade association that represents all aspects of America's oil and natural gas industry. Members are producers, refiners, suppliers, pipeline operators and marine transporters, as well as service and supply companies that support all segments of the industry.
600+ Members
Founded in 1919

20151 Association of Desk and Derrick Clubs
5321 South Sheridan Road
Suite 24
Tulsa, OK 74145
918-622-1749; Fax: 918-622-1675
ado@addc.org
www.addc.org
Facebook, Twitter, YouTube
Linda Rodgers, President
Connie Harrison, Vice President
Maggi Franks, Treasurer
Babara Ann Pappas, Secretary
Sheryl Minear, RP, Parliamentarian
Founded in 1949

20152 Association of Drilled Shaft Contractors
8445 Freeport Parkway
Suite 325
Irving, TX 75063
469-359-6000; Fax: 469-359-6007
adsc@adsc-iafd.com
www.adsc-iafd.com
Facebook, LinkedIn
Mike Moore, CEO
Fred Miller, Chief Financial Officer
Emily Matthews, Director, Operations
Angie Elmendorf, Director, Media Relations
Rick Marshall, Director, Safety
A professional, internationa, nonprofit trade association representing the anchored earth retention, drilled shaft, micropile, and other heavy civil construction/design industries. Members include specialty subcontractors, manufacturers and suppliers, academicians and design engineers in the private and public sectors.
Founded in 1972

20153 Association of Energy Service Companies

14531 FM 529
Suite 250
Houston, TX 77095-3528

713-781-0758
800-672-0771; Fax: 713-781-7542
www.aesc.net
Facebook, Twitter, LinkedIn

Kenny Jordan, Executive Director
Patty Jordan, Publisher/Sales Manager
Angla Fails, Administrative Manager
Roni Ashley, Director Accounting Services

Professional trade association for well-site service contractors and businesses providing goods and services to well-site contractors. Develops and sells training and safety materials.
600 Members
Founded in 1956

20154 Association of International Petroleum Negotiators

11767 Katy Freeway
Suite 412
Houston, TX 77079

281-558-7715; Fax: 281-558-7073
president@aipn.org
www.aipn.org

John Bowman, President
Judith Kim, VP - Communication
Steven Otillar, VP - Education
Kimberly Reeder, VP - Membership
Joseph Wesley, VP - Planning
Founded in 1982

20155 Association of Oil Pipe Lines

1808 Eye St NW
Suite 300
Washington, DC 20006-5423

202-408-7970; Fax: 202-280-1949
aopl@aopl.org
www.aopl.org
Facebook, Twitter

Andrew J.Black, President
Steven M.Kramer, General Counsel
John Stoody, Director
Heather Keith, Director
Rekha Chandrasekher, Industry Analyst

Acts as an information clearinghouse for the public, the media and the pipeline industry; provides coordination and leaderships for the industry's ongoing joint Environmental Safety Initiative; and represents common carrier crude and product petroleum pipleines in Congress, before regulatory agencies, and in the federal courts.
47 Members
Founded in 1947

20156 Association of Petroleum Industry Cooperative Managers

Home Page: www.apicom.org
Founded in 1972

20157 Association of Petroleum Surveying & Geomatics

Home Page: www.apsg.info
Facebook, Twitter, LinkedIn

Jackie Portsmouth, Chairman
Ashok Wadwani, Vice Chair
Kevin Crozier, Nominations Chair
Alma Alling, Communications Chair
Robert Edwards, Secretary/ Treasurer
Founded in 1998

20158 Concrete Sawing & Drilling Association

100 2nd Ave South
Ste 240N
St. Petersburg, FL 33701

727-577-5004
info@CSDA.org
www.csda.org
Facebook, Twitter, YouTube, Instagram

Judith O'Day, President
Kevin Baron, Vice President
Patrick O'Brien, Executive Director
Jim Dvoratchek, Past President
Mike Orzechowski, Secretary/ Treasurer

20159 Coordinating Research Council

5755 North Point Parkway
Suite 265
Alpharetta, GA 30022-3067

678-795-0506; Fax: 678-795-0509
jantucker@crcao.com
www.crcao.org

Brent Bailey, Executive Director
Christopher Tennant, Deputy Director
Debra Carter, Controller
Betty Taylor, Administrative Assistant
Jan Beck, Committee Coordinator and Webmaster

A nonprofit organization that directs, through committee action, engineering and environmental studies on the interaction between automotive/other mobility equipment and petroleum products.
1M Members
Founded in 1942

20160 Council of Petroleum Accountants Societies

445 Union Blvd.
Suite 207
Lakewood, CO 80228

303-300-1311
877-992-6727; Fax: 303-300-3733
www.copas.org
Facebook, Twitter, LinkedIn

Tom Wierman, Executive Director
Cheri McCallister, Administrator
Anita Hartz, Creative Specialist
Rich Moring III, President
Jeff Wright, Vice President

Members are accountants involved in, or closely related to, the oil and gas industry. Also provides ethical standards for energy accountants and is the certification organization for the Accredited Petroleum Accountant program.
3200 Members
Founded in 1961

20161 Domestic Petroleum Council

101 Constitution Avenue NW
Suite 800
Washington, DC 20001-2133

202-742-4300
www.dpcusa.org/

William F Whitsitt, President

To work constructively for sound energy, environmental and related public policies that encourage responsible exploration, development, and production of natural gas and crude oil to meet consumer needs and fuel our economy.
24 Members
Founded in 1975

20162 Drilling Engineering Association

10370 Richmond Ave, Suite 760
Houston, TX 77042

713-292-1945; Fax: 713-292-1946
dea-global.org

Ben Bloys, Chairman
David Dowell, Advisory Board Member
Glenda Wylie, Advisory Board Member
Robert Estes, Advisory Board Member
Scott Maddox, Secretary/ Treasurer

20163 Energy Security Council

9720 Cypresswood Dr.
Suite 206
Houston, TX 77070ÿ

281-587-2700; Fax: 281-807-6000
mindy@energysecuritycouncil.org
www.energysecuritycouncil.org

Rob Ream, Chairman
Rick Powers, Vice-Chairman
Butch Brazell, Director of Global Security
Clete Buckaloo, Director of Law Enforcement
Kent Chrisman, Director of Corp. Security & Admin.

Founded as Petroleum Industry Security Council and assumed its current name in 1999. Provides support to security professionals and business developers in the energy industry.
450 Members
Founded in 1976

20164 Energy Telecommunications and Electrical Association

5005 Royal Lane
Suite 116
Irving, TX 75063

888-503-8700; Fax: 972-915-6040
info@entelec.org
www.entelec.org
LinkedIn

A user association that focuses on communications and control technologies used by petroleum, natural gas, pipeline and electric utility companies. Primary goal is to provide education for its members.
Founded in 1928

20165 Energy Traffic Association

3303 Main Street Corridor
Houston, TX 77002

713-528-2868; Fax: 713-464-0702

Ralph Lopez, President
Renee Ahmed, Vice President/ Secretary
Russell Powell, Executive Director
Roger Rood, Immediate Past President
Tonya Svoboda, Board member

A nonprofit educational association of logistics professionals in the energy industry. Membership consists of managers of energy industry logistics departments and those logistics providers serving the energy industry.
100 Members
Founded in 1941

20166 Fiberglass Tank and Pipe Institute

14323 Heatherfield
Suite 101
Houston, TX 77079-7407

713-690-7777; Fax: 713-690-2842
info@fiberglasstankandpipe.com
www.fiberglasstankandpipe.com

Bobby Jin, President

The fiberglass-reinforced, thermosetting, plastic tank and pipe manufacturing industry. Members are domestic manufacturers.
5 Members
Founded in 1987

20167 Foundation Drilling Magazine

Association of Drilled Shaft Contractors

8445 Freeport Parkway
Suite 325
Irving, TX 75063

469-359-6000; Fax: 469-359-6007
adsc@adsc-iafd.com
www.adsc-iafd.com
Facebook, Twitter, LinkedIn

Mike Moore, CEO
Fred Miller, CFO

The best news source within our industry. Filled with information about design, projects and updates on what's going on where, Foundation Drilling Magazine is devoted to reporting on the drilled shaft, anchored retention, and other related industries.
Frequency: 8x Yearly
Founded in 1972

20168 Gas Research Machinery Council
3030 LBJ Freeway
Suite 1300
Dallas, TX 75234

972-620-4026; Fax: 972-620-1613
memberservices@southerngas.org
www.gmrc.org

Craig Linn, Chairman
Roland Trevino, Vice Chairman
Mike Grubb, President & CEO
Jane Butler, Vice President
Scott Schubring, Project Supervisory Committee

Members are companies in the natural gas, oil and petrochemical industries in mechanical and fluid systems design.
75 Members
Founded in 1952

20169 Independent Liquid Terminals Association
1005 N Glebe Road
Suite 600
Arlington, VA 22201

703-875-2011; Fax: 703-875-2018
info@ilta.org
www.ilta.org

Kathryn Clay, President
Andy Wright, VP, Legislative Affairs
Susan Kurdziolek, Sr. Director, Operations
Leakhena Swett, Director, Membership & Marketing
Meredith DeZemler, Director of Meetings

Represents bulk liquid terminal companies that store commercial liquids in aboveground storage tanks (ASTs) and transfer products to and from ocean going tank ships, tank barges, pipelines, tank trucks and tank rail cars. Provides members with essential informational tools to facilitate regulatory compliance and improve operations, safety and environmental performance.
400 Members
Founded in 1974

20170 Independent Lubricant Manufacturers
400 N Columbus St
Suite 201
Alexandria, VA 22314-2264

703-684-5574; Fax: 703-836-8503
ilma@ilma.org
www.ilma.org
Facebook, Twitter

Holly Alfano, Chief Executive Officer
Brenda Gillinson, Sr. Director, Communications
Tim Mack, Sr. Director, Member Engagement
Amber Lopez, Sr. Manager, Marketing & Digital
Meg Thaxton, Manager, Meetings

Independent blenders and compounders of lubricants.
Founded in 1976

20171 Independent Terminal Operators Association
1150 Connecticut Avenue NW
9th Floor
Washington, DC 20036-4129

202-828-4100; Fax: 202-828-4130
wbode@bode.com

William H Bode, Secretary & General Counsel

Represents indepedent petroleum distributors.
15 Members
Founded in 1970

20172 Institute of Gas Technology
1700 S Mount Prospect Rd
Des Plaines, IL 60018-1804

847-768-0500; Fax: 847-768-0501
publicrelations@gastechnology.org
www.gastechnology.org
Facebook, Twitter, LinkedIn, YouTube

David Carroll, President & CEO
Chris Herman, Treasurer & CFO
Paul Chromek, General Counsel & Secretary

An independent, not-for-profit center for energy and environmental research, development, education and information. Main function is to perform sponsored and in-house research, development and demonstration, provide educational programs and services, and disseminate scientific and technical information.
Founded in 1941

20173 International Association for Energy Economics
28790 Chagrin Blvd.,
Ste 350
Clevelend, OH 44122

216-464-5365
www.iaee.org

Peter R. Hartley, President
Anne Neumann, VP - Publication
Jurgis Vilemas, VP -Finance
Lori Smith Dschell, VP -Communications
Ponald D. Ripple, VP -Conferences

20174 International Association of Directional Drilling

281-288-6484
www.iadd-intl.org

Jim Oberkircher, Founder/ CEO
Arstrong Lee Agbaji, Assistant Director
Bill Bailey, Board Member
Ed Dew, Board Member
Chris McCartney, Board Member

20175 International Association of Drilling Contractors
10370 Richmond Ave
Suite 760
Houston, TX 77042-9687

713-292-1945; Fax: 713-292-1946
info@iadc.org
www.iadc.org
Facebook, Twitter, LinkedIn, RSS

Stephen Colville, President and CEO
Tap Powell, Executive VP
Mike Killalea, Group VP
Jason McFarland, Corporate Development
Mike Dubose, VP-Interantional Dept

Dedicated to enhancing the interests of the oil-and-gas and geothermal drilling and completion industry worldwide
1239 Members
Founded in 1940

20176 International Coiled Tubing Association
PO Box 1082
Montgomery, TX 77356

936-520-1549; Fax: 832-201-9977
ababin@icota.com
www.icota.com

Alan Turner, Sr.Co-Chair
Jason Skufca, Executive Director
David Larimore, Treasurer
Allison Babin, Secretary
Federico Botero, Board Member
7 Members
Founded in 1994

20177 International Energy Credit Association
1120 Route 73
Suite C
Mt. Laurel, NJ 08054

856-380-6854; Fax: 856-439-0525
ieca@ahint.com
www.ieca.net
Facebook, Twitter, LinkedIn

Zachary Starbird, President
James Hawkins, 1st VP
John Early, Treasurer
Jamie Swartz, VP Education
Steve Harwitz, Director-Environment Regulations

Members are credit and financial executives with companies whose product is a petroleum derivative.
800 Members
Founded in 1923

20178 International Geophysical Association
1225 North Loop West
Suite 220
Houston, TX 77008

713-957-8080; Fax: 713-957-0008
info@iagc.org
www.iagc.org
Facebook, Twitter, Youtube

Nikki Martin, President
Walt Rosenbusch, VP
Gail Adams, VP of Communications
Dr.Robert Gisiner, Director of Marine Environment
Criss Rennie, Director-Membership

Represents the industry that provides geophysical services to the oil and gas industry.
203 Members
Founded in 1971

20179 International Oil Scouts Association
PO Box 940310
Houston, TX 77094-7310

512-472-8138
www.oilscouts.com
Facebook

Pam Florek, President
Christi Sarat, Executive VP
Don Grimm, Second VP
Lisa Bonin, Secretary
Ty Cline, VP Finance

Compiles statistics on exploration and development wells in the United States. Offers professional development and scholarship programs.
175 Members
Founded in 1924

20180 **International Slurry Surfacing Association**
3 Church Cir
PMB 250
Annapolis, MD 21401

410-267-0023; Fax: 410-267-7546
www.slurry.org
Facebook, Twitter

Rusty Price, President
Carter Dabney, Vice President
Rex Eberly, Secretary
Eric Reimschiissel, Treasurer
Bob Jerman, Technical Director

A non profit association dedicated to the interests, education, and success of slurry surfacing professionals and corporations around the world.
200 Members
Founded in 1963

20181 **International Union of Petroleum and Industrial Workers**
8131 E Rosecrans Avenue
Paramount, CA 90723

562-630-6232
800-624-5842; Fax: 562-408-1073
petroleumworkers@aol.com
Facebook

George R Beltz, International President
Pamela Parlow, Internat'l Secretary/Tresurer
5000 Members
Founded in 1951

20182 **Interstate Natural Gas Association of America**
20 F Street, NW
Suite 450
Washington, DC 20001

202-216-5900; Fax: 202-216-0870
www.ingaa.org

Donald F. Santa, Jr., President & CEO
Richard R Hoffmann, Executive Director
Catherine J Landry, Director of Communications
James O'Bryant, Researcher & Comm Assistant
Martin E. Edwards, VP, Legislative Affairs

Trade association of natural gas pipelines in the United States, Canada, Mexico and Europe.
25 Members
Founded in 1944

20183 **Interstate Oil and Gas Compact Commission**
900 NE 23rd Street
Oklahoma City, OK 73105

405-525-3556; Fax: 405-525-3592
www.iogcc.state.ok.us

Mary Fallin, Chairman
David Porter, Vice Chairman
Michael Teague, 2nd Vice Chairman
Mike Smith, Executive Director
Gerry Baker, AssociateExecutive Director

The members are states that produce oil or gas; associate states support the conservation of America's energy resources. Also establishes rules andguidelines for the proper maintenance of wells.
700 Members
Founded in 1935

20184 **Liaison Committee of Cooperating Oil and Gas Association**
1718 Columbus Road SW
PO Box 535
Granville, OH 13023-0535

740-587-0444; Fax: 202-857-4799
www.energyconnect.com/liason

Thomas E Stewart, Secretary/Treasurer

Established to facilitate communication among state and regional oil and gas associations.
25 Members
Founded in 1957

20185 **Mid-Continent Oil and Gas Association**
730 North Blvd.
Baton Rouge, LA 70802

225-387-3205; Fax: 225-344-5502
www.lmoga.com
Facebook, Twitter, Flickr

Chris John, President
Tyler Gray, General Counsel
Brent Golleher, Director of Government
Richard Metcalf, Director of Environmental Affairs
Ashley Cain, Manager of Communications

At the forefront of the continually changing legal, legislative and regulatory issues facing a growing and diverse membership.
7.5M Members
Founded in 1917

20186 **NLGI**
249 SW Noel
Suite 249
Lee's Summit, MO 64063

816-524-2500; Fax: 816-524-2504
nlgi@nlgi.org
www.nlgi.org
LinkedIn

David J Como, Vice President
Kim Smallwood, Secretary
Joe Kaperick, Treasurer
Kimberly Hartley, Executive Director
Marilyn Brohm, Manager, Membership & Market

Members are companies that manufacture and market all types of lubricating greases, additive or equipment suppliers, and research and educational groups whose interests are primarily technical.
280 Members
Founded in 1933

20187 **NORA Association of Responsible Recyclers**
7250 Heritage Village Plaza
Suite 201
Gainesville, VA 20155

703-753-4277; Fax: 703-753-2445
sparker@noranews.org
www.noranews.org

Bill Hinton, President
Chirs Bergstrom, Executive Vice President
Roy Schumacher, Vice President
Scott D Parker, Executive Director
Casey Parker, Associate Director

Members are companies that reprocess used antifreeze, wastewater, oil filters, chemicals and companies that provide products or services to the industry.
211 Members
Founded in 1985

20188 **National Association of Convenience Stores**
1600 Duke Street
Alexandria, VA 22314

703-684-3600
800-966-6227; Fax: 703-836-4564
www.convenience.org
Facebook, Twitter, LinkedIn, YouTube, Instagram

Sandy Smith, National Sales Manager

Association supporting convenience and fuel retailing companies.
2.3M Members
Founded in 1961
Mailing list available for rent

20189 **National Association of Division Order Analysts**
PO Box 2300
Lee's Summit, MO 64063

972-715-4489
administrator@nadoa.org
www.nadoa.org
Facebook, Twitter, LinkedIn, RSS

Nancy Cemino, President
Brenda Pirrozzolo, 1st VP/Finance
Sandi Rupprecht, 2nd VP/Site Selection
Jean Hinton, Treasurer
Michele Lawton, Recording Secretary
900 Members
Founded in 1974

20190 **National Association of Oil and Energy Services Professionals**
PO Box 67
East Petersburg, PA 17520

717-625-3076
888-552-0900; Fax: 717-625-3077
jgarber@thinkoesp.org
www.naohsm.org
Facebook, Twitter, LinkedIn, YouTube

Al Breda, President
Ralph Adams, Vice-President
Mike Hodge, Treasurer
Paul Cuprewich, Secretary
George Fantacone, Vice President

Members are oil heat service managers and small business owners. Also provides members with technical tapes, books and speakers to train thei employee technicians.
1500 Members
Founded in 1952

20191 **National Association of Petroleum Investment Analysts**
415 Hayward Mill Road
Concord, MA 01742-4604

978-369-0084; Fax: 978-369-0086
dbm@napia.org
www.napia.org

Gregory B. Barnett, Membership Chairman
Michael D. Smolinski, President
D. Barry McKennitt, Executive Director
Tyler Dann II, Board Member
Nancy J. F. Prue, Board Member
Founded in 1974

20192 **National Association of Royalty Owners**
15 W 6th St
Suite 2626
Tulsa, OK 74119

918-794-1660
800-558-0557; Fax: 918-794-1662
www.naro-us.org
Facebook, Twitter

Candice Brewer, President
James Elder, Vice President
Emily Wagner, Corporate Secretary
JIm Leonard, Treasurer

Assists mineral and royalty owners in the effective management of their mineral properties. Provides information on tax, regulatory, and legislative matters. Conducts seminars and bestows awards.
5M Members
Founded in 1980

20193 National Drilling Association
3053 Nationwide Pkwy.
Brunswick, OH 44212
877-632-4748; Fax: 216-803-9900
info@nda4u.com
www.nda4u.com
Facebook, LinkedIn
Rob Caho, President
Jim Howe, Secretary/Treasurer
A non-profit trade association of contractors, manufacturers and affiliated members from the drilling industry representing the geotechnical, environmental and mineral exploration sectors of this industry.
250+ Members
Founded in 1972

20194 National Ocean Industries Association
1120 G St NW
Suite 900
Washington, DC 20005
202-347-6900; Fax: 202-347-8650
jwilliams@noia.org
www.noia.org
Facebook, Twitter, LinkedIn, YouTube, Google+
Randall Luthi, President
Franki Stunz, Sr.Vice President
Ann Chapman, VP Conferences and Events
Megan Bel Miller, VP Government Relations
Nicoltte Nye, VP Communications
Represents all facets of the domestic offshore and related industries. Member companies are dedicated to the development of offshore oil and natural gas for the continued growth and security of the US.
320+ Members
Founded in 1972

20195 National Petrochemical & Refiners Association
1667 K Street, NW
Suite 700
Washington, DC 20006
202-457-0480; Fax: 202-457-0486
info@afpm.org
www.afpm.org
Facebook, Twitter
Gregory J Goff, Chairman
Lawrence M Ziemba, Vice Chair
Chet Thompson, President
Brandon E Williams, Executive Vice President
Rebecca H Adler, Senior director, Communications
Association that represents the petrochemical and refining industries, sponsors periodic conferences, and seeks to inform policymakers and the public. Issues include the recycling of used oils and other liquid wastes.
450 Members
Founded in 1902

20196 National Petroleum Council
1625 K St NW
Suite 600
Washington, DC 20006
202-393-6100; Fax: 202-331-8539
info@npc.org
www.npc.org
Charles D. Davidson, Chair
Rex W. Tillerson, Vice Chair
Marshall W. Nichols, Executive Director
Ernest J. Moniz, Secretary
Self-supporting, federal advisory body to the Secretary of Energy established in 1946 at the request of President Truman.
191 Members
Founded in 1946

20197 National Petroleum Energy Credit Association
1302 Clayton Nolen Drive
Horseshoe Bay, TX 78657
830-220-3797; Fax: 817-796-1080
ContactUs@npeca.org
www.npeca.org
Mike Swillo, President
Mark L. Macha, 1st Vice President
Della White, 2nd Vice President
Laura Roussel, 3rd Vice President
Terry Faber, Secretary
Founded in 1935

20198 National Propane Gas Association
1899 L St NW
Suite 350
Washington, DC 20036
202-466-7200; Fax: 202-466-7205
info@npga.org
www.npga.org
Charlie Ory, Chairman
Stuart Weidie, Chairman-Elect
Jerry Brick, Vice-Chairman
Richard Roldan, President & CEO
Chris Earhart, Treasurer
Members are producers and distributors of liquified petroleum gas and equipment manufacturers.
3500 Members
Founded in 1931

20199 National Stripper Well Association
1201 15th St NW
Suite 300
Washington, DC 20005
202-857-4722; Fax: 202-857-4799
webmaster@ipaa.org
www.ipaa.org
Facebook, Twitter, LinkedIn, Youtube
Michael Watford, Chairman
Mark K.Miller, Vice Chair
Diemer True, Treasurer
Barry Russell, President & CEO
This operates under the Independent Petroleum Association, which is an informed voice for the exloration and production segment of the industry. It provides economic and statistical information, and develops investment symposia and other opportunities for its members.
1600+ Members
Founded in 1929

20200 Natural Gas Supply Association
1620 Eye St., NW
Suite 700
Washington, DC 20006
202-326-9300; Fax: 202-326-9330
www.ngsa.org
Twitter
Bill Green, Chairman
Frans Everts, Vice Chair
Dean E. Wiggins, President
A.Scott Moore, Secretary-Treasurer
Represents U.S.-based producers and marketers of natural gas on issues that affect the natural gas industry, including the residential and industrial consumers who rely on the fuel for a myriad of purposes.
14 Members
Founded in 1965

20201 Newport Associates
7400 E Orchard Road
Suite 320
Englewood, CO 80111-2528
FAX 303-779-0908
Association for over 450 oil companies in over 20 world regions.

20202 Nuclear Energy Institute
1201 F St., NW
Suite 1100
Washington, DC 20004-1218
202-739-8000; Fax: 202-785-4019
webmaster@nei.org
www.nei.org
Facebook, Twitter, LinkedIn, Google+, YouTube, Pinterest, F
Donald E. Brandt, Chairman
Christopher M. Crane, President & CEO
Marvin S. Fertel, President & CEO
Alexande W. Flint, Senior Vice President
Maria G. Korsnick, Chief Operating Officer
Members are of utilities, manufacturers of electrical generating equipment, researchers, architects, engineers, labor unions, and others interested in the generation of electricity by nuclear power.
350 Members
Founded in 1984

20203 Paper, Allied-Industrial, Chemical and Energy Workers International Union
3340 Perimeter Hill Drive
Nashville, TN 37211
615-834-8590; Fax: 615-731-6362
www.paceunion.org
Jim Pannell, VP
Lynne Baker, Associate Director Communications
Joan Hill, Director Research & Education
Elaine Piper, Owner
Work to make life better for the workers and their families.
320M Members
Founded in 1884

20204 Petroleum Equipment & Services Association
2500 Citywest Blvd
Suite 1110
Houston, TX 77042-3049
713-932-0168
info@pesa.org
pesa.org
Facebook, Twitter, LinkedIn, Google+, YouTube
Gary Halverson, Chairman
Saeid Rahimian, Vice Chairman
Burk L. Ellison, First VP
Leslie Shockley Beyer, President
Molly Smart, Vice President of Communications
200 Members
Founded in 1933

20205 Petroleum Equipment Institute
PO Box 2380
Tulsa, OK 74101-2380
918-494-9696; Fax: 918-491-9895
www.pei.org
Facebook, Twitter, LinkedIn, Google+
Scott Boorse, Dir, Technical Programs
J. Rex Brown, Dir, Information Services
Teresa Farmer, Membership Manager
Rick Long, EVP & General Counsel
Julie Shank, Marketing & Event Manager
Members are makers and distributors of equipment used in service stations, bulk plants and other petroleum marketing facilities.
1600+ Members
Founded in 1951
Mailing list available for rent: 1600 names at $275 per M

20206 **Petroleum Investor Relations Association**
2800 Post Oak Boulevard
Suite 5450
Houston, TX 77056

713-621-7800; Fax: 978-369-0086
www.rowancompanies.com

Thomas P. Burke, President
W.Matt Ralls, Executive Chairman
Stephen Butz, Executive VP & Treasurer
Mark A. Keller, Executive Vice President
Melanie M. Trent, Company Secretary

Represents investor communications professional in the peroleum and natural gas industry
100 Members
Founded in 1923

20207 **Petroleum Marketers Association**
1901 Fort Myer Dr
Suite 1200
Arlington, VA 22209-1609

703-351-8000; Fax: 703-351-9160
www.pmaa.org

Daniel F Gilligan, President
Nancy Kniher, Director Member Service
Cost: $50.00
700 Members

20208 **Petroleum Marketers Association of America**
1901 North Fort Myer Drive
Suite 500
Arlington, VA 22209

703-351-8000; Fax: 703-351-9160
info@pmaa.org
www.pmaa.org
Facebook, Twitter

Grady Gaubert, Chairman
Mike Bailey, Vice Chair
Mark Whitehead, 2nd Vice Chair
Rob Underwood, President
Sherri Stone, Vice President
Founded in 1909

20209 **Petroleum Retailers & Auto Repair Association**
1051 Brinton Road
Suite 304
Pittsburgh, PA 15221

412-241-2380; Fax: 412-241-2815
www.prara.com

Jeff Decker, President
Dennis Budzynski, 1st Vice President
Gauttam Patel, 2nd Vice President
Nancy Maricondi, Executive Director
Ray Moore, Treasurer
Founded in 1937

20210 **Petroleum Technology Transfer Council**
PO Box 710942
Oak Hill, VA 20171

703-620-4797; Fax: 571-485-8255
hq@pttc.org
www.pttc.org
Facebook

J.C. Hall, Chairman
Barry Tew, Vice Chairman
Mary Carr, Executive Director
Jeremy Viscomi, Executive Director
Kathy Chapman, Director of Operations

Fosters the effective transfer of exploration and production technology to US petroleum producers through regional resource centers, workshops, websites, publications, etc.
Founded in 1993

20211 **Pipeline Research Council International**
3141 Fairview Park Drive
Suite 525
Falls Church, VA 22042

703-205-1600; Fax: 703-205-1607
www.prci.org

Phillip DePriest, Chairman
Jeff Whiworth, Vice Chairman
Cliff Johnson, President
Michael P. Whelan, Director
Gary Choquette, Senior Program Manager

Sponsors research on technical issues facing the natural gas transmission industry. Members are companies operating pipeline systems.
78 Members
Founded in 1952
Mailing list available for rent

20212 **Rocky Mountain Oil and Gas Association**
1900 Grant Street
Denver, CO 80203

303-860-0099; Fax: 303-861-0373

Jess D Cooper, General Manager
Linda Swain, Manager

A trade association, representing oil and gas industries.
600 Members
Founded in 1920

20213 **Service Station Dealers of America**
1532 Pointer Ridge Place
Suite G
Bowie, MD 20716

301-390-4405; Fax: 301-390-3161
www.ssda-at.com
Facebook, Twitter

Peter S Kischak, President
Fred Bordoff, 1st Vice President
Billy Hillmuth, 2nd Vice President
Hugh Campbell, Treasurer

Service Station Dealers of America/National Coalition of Petroleum Retailers and Allied Trades is a national association composed of individual and state affiliate associations representing service station dealers, repair facilities, car washes and convenience stores.
Founded in 1947

20214 **Society of Independent Gasoline Marketers**
3930 Pender Drive
Suite 340
Fairfax, VA 22030

703-709-7000
sigma@sigma.org
www.sigma.org

Tom Gresham, President
David Baker, 1st Vice President
William Bradford, 2nd Vice President
Liz Menz, Education Director
Nancy Muskett, Marketing Director
260 Members
Founded in 1958

20215 **Society of Petroleum Engineers**
222 Palisades Creek Drive
Richardson, TX 75080

972-952-9393
800-456-6863; Fax: 972-952-9435
spedal@spe.org
www.spe.org
Facebook, Twitter, LinkedIn, YouTube, Instagram

Nathan Meehan, President
Janeen Judah, VP Finance
Mark A. Rubin, CEO & Executive VP
Stephen Graham, Chief Operations Officer
Cordella Wong, Managing Director

Supports those professionals involved in the field of exploration, drilling, production, and reservoir management, as well as related manufacturing and service organizations. Publishes monthly magazine.
12400 Members
Founded in 1957

20216 **Society of Petroleum Evaluation Engineers**
5535 Memorial Drive
Houston, TX 77007

713-651-1639; Fax: 713-951-9659
info@spee.org
www.spee.org

Gary Gonzenbach, President
Dee Patterson, Vice President
Floyd Siegle, Secretary/Treasurer
Brad DeWitt, Director

Members are engineers specializing in the fields of petroleum and natural gas properties.
495 Members
Founded in 1962

20217 **Society of Petrophysicists and Well Log Analysts**
8866 Gulf Freeway
Suite 320
Houston, TX 77017

713-947-8727; Fax: 713-947-7181
www.spwla.org
Facebook, Twitter, LinkedIn

Thaimar Ramirez, President
Luiz Quintero, President-Elect
Brett L.Wendt, VP Technology
Oliver Mullin, VP Publications

Provides information services to scientists in the petroleum and mineral industries, serves as a voice of shared interests in our profession, plays a major role in strengthening petrophysical education, and strives to increase the awareness of the role petrophysics has in the Oil and Gas Industry and the scientific community.
3300 Members
Founded in 1959

20218 **Southern Gas Association**
3030 LBJ Freeway
Suite 1500
Dallas, TX 75234

972-620-8505; Fax: 972-620-1613
memberservices@southerngas.org
www.southerngas.org
Facebook, Twitter, YouTube, RSS

Henry P. Linginfelter, Chairman
Frank Yoho, 1st Vice Chair
Jerry L. Morris, 2nd Vice Chair
Mike Grubb, President & CEO
Kimberly Watson, Secretary - Treasurer
116 Members
Founded in 1908

20219 **Spill Control Association of America**
103 Oronoco Street
Suite 200
Alexandria, VA 22314

571-451-0433; Fax: 443-640-1086
info@scaa-spill.org
www.scaa-spill.org

Rick Lewis, President
Devon Grennan, VP
Nelson Fetgatter, Treasurer
Robert Chambers, Secretary
John Allen, Executive Director

Members are companies concerned with cleaning up spills of oil and hazardous products and

manufacturers of specialized products for spill control.
Founded in 1973

20220 The Independent Petroleum Association of America
1201 15th St NW
Suite 300
Washington, DC 20005
202-857-4722; Fax: 202-857-4799
www.ipaa.org
Facebook, Twitter, LinkedIn, YouTube
Michael Watford, Chairman
Mark Miller, Vice Chairman
Barry Russell, President & CEO
Diemer TRUE, Treasurer
Lee O. Fuller, Executive Vice President
Members are small producers of oil and natural gas and their suppliers.
5500 Members
Founded in 1929

20221 The Linde Group
200 Somerset Blvd
Bridgewater, NJ 08807
908-464-8100; Fax: 908-771-4775
thelindegroup.us
Facebook, Twitter, LinkedIn, YouTube
Global supplier of gases to many industries.

20222 The National Petroleum Management Association
10908 Courthouse Rd
Ste 102-301
Fredericksburg, VA 22408
540-507-4371; Fax: 540-507-4372
www.npma-fuelnet.org
Jack Lavin, President
Alan Reynolds, VP - Communication
Ruth Lavin, Marketing Officer
Erin Creese, San Antonio Office Manager
Al Pond, Board Member

20223 The Society of Exploration Geophysicists
8801 South Yale
Suite 500
Tulsa, OK 74137-3575
918-497-5500; Fax: 918-497-5557
www.seg.org/seg
Facebook, Twitter, LinkedIn, YouTube, Google+, Instagram
Michael C. Forrest, Chair
Dr. John Holloway, President
Alison W. Small, Treasurer
William L. Abriel, President-Elect
Dr. Eve S. Sprunt, First Vice President

20224 Tubular Exchanger Manufacturers Association, Inc.
25 North Broadway
Tarrytown, NY 10591
914-332-0040; Fax: 914-332-1541
tema@tema.org
www.tema.org
Richard C Byrne, Secretary
Sets standards for the industry, known as TEMA Standards, which are sold to the chemical processing and petroleum refining industries
18 Members
Founded in 1939

20225 US Oil & Gas Association
1101 K Street NW
Suite 425
Washington, DC 20005
202-638-4400
www.usoga.org
Facebook, Twitter
Walter G. Mayfield, Chairman
Albert L. Modiano, President
Tim Stewart, Vice President
Founded in 1917

20226 Western Petroleum Marketers Association
PO Box 571500
Salt Lake City, UT 84157-1500
801-263-9762
888-252-5550; Fax: 801-262-9413
info@wpma.com
www.wpma.com
Facebook, Twitter, LinkedIn, YouTube
Brad Bell, President
Rick Reese, 1st Vice President
Ron Berry, 2nd Vice President
Mark Lytle, 3rd Vice President
Gregg Benson, Senior PMAA Director
Trade magazine for petroleum marketers, c-store owners, and businesses associated with petroleum marketing.
700 Members
Founded in 1953

20227 Western States Petroleum Association
1415 L St
Suite 600
Sacramento, CA 95814
916-498-9203; Fax: 916-444-5745
www.wspa.org
Facebook, Twitter
Catherine Reheis-Boyd, President
Tupper Hull, Vice President
Steven Arita, Senior Environmental Coordinator
Barbara Chichester, Bookkeeper
Trade association that represents the full spectrum of those companies that refine, produce, transport, and market petroleum and petroleum products in six western states: Arizona, California, Oregon, Nevada, Hawaii and Washington.
35 Members
Founded in 1907

Newsletters

20228 Butane-Propane News
PO Box 660698
Arcadia, CA 91066-698
626-357-2168
800-214-4386; Fax: 626-303-2854
www.bpnews.com
Natalie Peal, Publisher
Ann Rey, Editorial Director
Petroleum and propane industry news.
Cost: $32.00
Frequency: Monthly
Founded in 1939

20229 Clean-Coal/Synfuels Letter
McGraw Hill
PO Box 182604
Columbus, OH 43272
614-304-4000
877-833-5524; Fax: 614-759-3749
www.mcgraw-hill.com
Facebook, Twitter, You Tube
John Higgins, Publisher
Provides worldwide coverage of the development of clean-coal technologies.
Cost: $840.00
6 Pages
Frequency: Monthly
Founded in 1899

20230 Cold Water Oil Spills
Cutter Information Corporation
37 Broadway
Suite 1
Arlington, MA 02474-5500
781-648-1950
800-888-8939; Fax: 781-648-1950
service@cutter.com
www.cutter.com
Kim Leonard, Editor
Karen Coburn, Senior Consultant
Hillel Glazer, Senior Consultant
Ron Blitstein, Director
Clean up and control of oil spills in cold and icy waters.
Cost: $175.00
Founded in 1986

20231 Fuel Line
National Petrochemical & Refiners Association
1667 K Street, NW
Suite 700
Washington, DC 20006-1654
202-457-0480; Fax: 202-457-0486
info@npra.org
www.npra.org
Charles Drevna, President
Gerald R. Van De Velde, CFO
Rebbie J. Riley, Executive Assistant
Addresses motor fuels regulations, policy and related issues. Available online only for NPRA members.
450 Members
Frequency: Weekly

20232 Gas Daily
1200 G Street NW
#1000
Washington, DC 20005
202-383-2100
800-752-8878; Fax: 202-383-2125
support@platts.com
www.gasdaily.com
Mark Davidson, Publisher
Bill Loveless, Director
Larry Foster, Director
Dixie Barrett, Vice President
Information on spot prices cash markets and regulatory developments for the natural gas industry.
Cost: $2255.00
Frequency: Daily

20233 Gas Storage Report
Pasha Publications
1600 Wilson Boulevard
#600
Arlington, VA 22209-2510
703-528-1244; Fax: 703-528-7821
www.pasha.com
Jeff Pruzan, Editor
Detailed charts that list monthly storage activity of all interstate pipelines and covers all phases of the underground storage of natural gas.
Cost: $495.00
Frequency: Monthly

20234 Golob's Oil Pollution Bulletin
World Information Systems

PO Box 535
Cambridge, MA 02238-0535

FAX 617-492-3312

Richard S Golob, Publisher
Roger B Wilson Jr, Editor

Provides news analysis on oil pollution prevention, control and cleanup. Covers oil spills worldwide, regulations, legislation and court decisions, technical reports, new equipment and products, contract opportunities and awards, and conference notices.
Cost: $335.00
Frequency: BiWeekly
Circulation: 20,000

20235 Green Room Report
National Petrochemical & Refiners Association
1667 K Street, NW
Suite 700
Washington, DC 20006-1654

202-457-0480; Fax: 202-457-0486
info@npra.org
www.npra.org

Charles Drevna, President
Gerald R. Van De Velde, CFO
Rebbie J. Riley, Executive Assistant

Addresses current environmental and safety events, including regulation and policy issues of EPA and OSHA. Available only online to NPRA members.
450 Members
Frequency: Weekly

20236 Gulf of Mexico Newsletter
Offshore Data Services
3200 Wilcrest Dr
Suite 170
Houston, TX 77042-3366

832-463-3000; Fax: 832-463-3100
www.ods-petrodata.com

Thomas E Marsh, President
Hannah Hartland, Chairman

Aimed at the supply and service people of the off-shore oil and gas industry in the Gulf of Mexico, covers all significant industry news and events, and summarizes construction and field development activities.
Cost: $259.00
Frequency: Weekly
Circulation: 2150
Founded in 2002

20237 Hart's Renewable Fuel News
Hart Evepy Publishing LP
1201 Seven Locks Road
#300
Potomac, MD 20854

301-354-2100; Fax: 301-424-7260
www.worldfuels.com

Rachel Gantz, Editor
Robert Gaph, Executive Editor
Jack Peckham, Executive Editor
Theresa Ward, Managing Editor

Refinery updates, oxygenation schemes, capital spending, strategic alliances and essential business intelligence on corporate moves.
Cost: $1495.00
Frequency: Weekly
Founded in 1973

20238 ILMA Compoundings
Independent Lubricant Manufacturers Association
400 N Columbus St
Suite 201
Alexandria, VA 22314-2264

703-684-5574; Fax: 703-836-8503
ilma@ilma.org
www.ilma.org

Celeste Powers, Executive Director
Martha Jolkovski, Director Publications/Advertising

Focuses on legislative, regulatory, marketing and industry news of concern to independent blenders and compounders of high-quality lubricants. Accepts advertising.
Cost: $150.00
20 Pages
Frequency: Monthly
Circulation: 1800
Founded in 1948

20239 Independent Liquid Terminals Association Newsletter
Independent Liquid Terminals Association
1005 N Glebe Road
Suite 600
Arlington, VA 22201

703-875-2011; Fax: 703-875-2018
info@ilta.org
www.ilta.org

Kathryn Clay, President
Peter Lidiak, VP, Government Affairs
Andy Wright, VP, Legislative Affairs
Susan Kurdziolek, Senior Director of Operations
Meredith DeZembler, Director of Meetings

Monthly publication detailing federal, state and local legislative and regulatory action, ILTA response and ILTA events. Geared specifically to bulk liquid terminal owners/operators and establishments supplying equipment, goods and services to the bulk liquid terminaling industry.
8 Pages
Frequency: Monthly
Printed in 2 colors

20240 Institute of Gas Technology
Institute of Gas Technology
1700 S Mount Prospect Rd
Des Plaines, IL 60018-1804

847-768-0500; Fax: 847-768-0501
publicrelations@gastechnology.org
www.gastechnology.org

David Carroll, President/CEO
Edward Johnston, Managing Director
Carol Worster, Manager

Newsletter
Cost: $495.00
Founded in 1945

20241 International Directory of Oil Spills and Control Products and Services
Cutter Information Corporation
37 Broadway
Suite 1
Arlington, MA 02474-5500

781-648-8700; Fax: 781-648-8707
consortium@cutter.com
www.cutter.com
Facebook, Twitter, LinkedIn, RSS

Verna Allee, Senior Consultant

Products and services listed by category.
Cost: $75.00

20242 International Gas Technology Highlights
Institute of Gas Technology
1700 S Mount Prospect Rd
Des Plaines, IL 60018-1804

847-768-0664; Fax: 847-768-0669
www.gastechnology.org

David Carroll, President/CEO
Edward Johnston, Managing Director

A biweekly newsletter covering international developments in energy with a focus on natural gas.
Cost: $100.00
4 Pages
Circulation: 1600
Founded in 1946
Printed in 2 colors on matte stock

20243 International Oil News
William F Bland
709 Turmeric Ln
Durham, NC 27713-3103

919-544-1717; Fax: 919-544-1999
mbs@PetroChemical-News.com
www.petrochemical-news.com/pcn.htm

Susan Kensil, President
Mollie B Sandor, Circulation Director

A weekly report of current news about all areas of the international petroleum industry, exploration, production, processing, transportation and marketing.
Cost: $857.00
Frequency: Weekly
Founded in 1963

20244 International Summary and Review of Oil Spills
Cutter Information Corporation
37 Broadway
Suite 1
Arlington, MA 02474-5500

781-648-8700; Fax: 781-648-8707
www.cutter.com

Verna Allee, Senior Consultant

International coverage of the gas and oil industry.
Cost: $100.00
Frequency: Monthly
Founded in 1986

20245 LNG Observer
Institute of Gas Technology
1700 S Mount Prospect Rd
Des Plaines, IL 60018-1804

847-768-0664; Fax: 847-768-0669
www.gastechnology.org

David Carroll, President/CEO

A bimonthly publication covering the worldwide liquefied natural gas industry, including political developments, technology, economics, statistics and interviews with industry leaders.
Cost: $395.00
24 Pages
Frequency: Bi-Monthly
Circulation: 2,000
ISBN: 1-053694-9 -

20246 Leading Edge
Society of Exploration Geophysicists
PO Box 702740
Tulsa, OK 74170-2740

918-497-5500; Fax: 918-497-5557
web@seg.org
www.seg.org
Facebook, Twitter, LinkedIn

Mary Fleming, Executive Director
Vladimir Grechka, Editor
David J Monk, President
Richard D Miller, First V.P
Dennis A Cooke, Second V.P.

20247 Lundberg Letter
Lundberg Survey

911 Via Alondra
Camarillo, CA 93012-8048

805-383-2400
800-660-4574; Fax: 805-383-2424
lsi@lundbergsurvey.com
www.lundbergsurvey.com

Trilby Lundberg, President

News on the US gasoline and diesel market. Retail and wholesale prices, market shares, consumption, taxes, station populations and consumer trends.
Cost: $399.00
Founded in 1950

20248 NGI's Daily Gas Price Index
Intelligence Press
PO Box 70587
Washington, DC 20024

202-583-2596
800-427-5747; Fax: 202-318-0597
subscriptions@intelligencepress.com
intelligencepress.com

Ellen Beswick, Publisher
Mike Nazzaro, Managing Editor
Alexander Steis, Managing Editor

Gas industry news, reports and statistics.
Cost: $1045.00
Frequency: Daily

20249 National Association of Royalty Owners
12316 Andrews Drive
Suite B
Oklahoma City, OK 73120-5779

405-573-2972
800-558-0557; Fax: 405-286-9402
naro@naro-us.org
www.naro-us.org

Paul Covert, VP
Wana Box, President
David Guest, Manager

Newsletter for members. Also a book is available Look Before You Lease.
Cost: $6.50
Frequency: Monthly
Founded in 1980

20250 Natural Gas Intelligence Price Index
22648 Glenn Drive
Suite 305
Sterling, VA 20164

703-318-8848
800-427-5747; Fax: 703-318-0597
info@naturalgasintel.com
www.naturalgasintel.com
Facebook, Twitter, LinkedIn

Ellen Beswick, Founder & Editor-in-Chief
Dexter Steis, Executive Publisher
Alexander Steis, Managing Editor

Price indexes available daily and weekly. Natural Gas Intelligence (NGI) is a leading provider of natural gas and market data to the energy industry. Since the first issue of Natural Gas Intelligence was published in 1981, NGI has provided key natural gas pricing, news and analysis relied upon daily by thousands of industry participants in the Americas, Europe, and Asia.
Cost: $1195.00
Frequency: Weekly
Founded in 1981

20251 Natural Gas Week
Energy Intelligence Group
1401 New York Ave Nw
Suite 500
Washington, DC 20005-2102

202-393-5113; Fax: 202-393-5115
info@accion.org
www.accion.org

Maria Otero, President
Mike Sultan, Managing Director
John Lwande, Managing Director
Melissa Baez, Project Manager

Economics news covering the gas industry.
Cost: $1860.00
20 Pages
Frequency: Weekly
Founded in 1985
Printed in 2 colors on matte stock

20252 News Fuel & Vehicles Report
Inside Washington Publishers
1919 S Eads St
Suite 201
Arlington, VA 22202-3028

703-418-3981
800-424-9068; Fax: 703-416-8543
support@iwpnews.com
www.iwpnews.com

Latest news, research and reports on alternative fuels and vehicles development aimed toward the program managers, lobbyists, policy makers, and auto, oil and corn chemical industries.
Cost: $985.00
Founded in 1980

20253 Ocean News & Technology
Technology Systems Corporation
PO Box 1096
Palm City, FL 34991-7174

772-221-7720; Fax: 772-221-7715
www.ocean-news.com

Dan White, Editor
Sharon White, Circulation Manager

Magazine focusing on the major business areas of the ocean industry. News articles and technology developments are covered in areas including defense, offshore oil, diving, science, environment and marine.
Cost: $45.00
Founded in 1981

20254 Offshore Rig Newsletter
Offshore Data Services
3200 Wilcrest Dr
Suite 170
Houston, TX 77042-3366

832-463-3000; Fax: 832-463-3100
www.ods-petrodata.com

Thomas E Marsh, President
Barry Young, Chairman

Emerging markets, accidents, new technology, financing schemes, insurance trends, rig construction, moves, sales, and rates, labor problems, attrition, marketing strategies, and the corporate activities of drilling contractors.
Cost: $220.00
Frequency: Monthly
Circulation: 900
Founded in 1973

20255 Oil Daily
Energy Intelligence Group
1401 New York Ave Nw
Suite 500
Washington, DC 20005-2102

202-393-5113; Fax: 202-393-5115
info@accion.org
www.accion.org

Maria Otero, President
John Lwande, Managing Director
Melissa Baez, Project Manager

Magazine on the petroleum and oil industry, available on line.
Cost: $1880.00
Frequency: Daily
Circulation: 60000
Founded in 1951

20256 Oil Express
United Communications Group
11300 Rockville Pike
Street 1100
Rockville, MD 20852-3030

301-287-2700; Fax: 301-816-8945
www.ucg.com

Benny Dicecca, President

Information for gasoline marketers.
Cost: $447.00
8 Pages
Frequency: Monthly
Founded in 1977

20257 Oil Spill Intelligence Report
Aspen Publishers
111 8th Ave
Suite 700
New York, NY 10011-5207

212-771-0600
800-234-1660; Fax: 212-771-0885
www.aspenlawschool.com

Richard Kravits, Executive VP
Gerry Centrowitz, Marketing/Communications Manager

Provides timely coverage of oil spills worldwide.
Cost: $695.00
6 Pages
Frequency: Weekly
Founded in 1978

20258 Oil Spill United States Law Report
Aspen Publishers
76 Ninth Avenue
7th Floor
New York, NY 10011

212-771-0600
800-638-8437
www.aspenlawschool.com

Mark Dorman, CEO
Gustavo Dobles, VP Operations

Professionals who need to stay abreast of US federal and state regulations.
Cost: $7.67
12 Pages
Frequency: Monthly

20259 Oil, Gas and Petrochem Equipment
PennWell Publishing Company
1421 S Sheridan Rd
Tulsa, OK 74112-6619

918-835-3161
800-331-4463; Fax: 918-831-9476
www.pennwell.com

Robert Biolchini, President
Tim L Tobeck, Group Publisher
J B Avants, Publisher & Editor

The petroleum industry's only all new products and services magazine. Each month it announces the newest developments in equipment, products, systems and services for drilling, production, refining, petrochemical manufacturing, pipeline/storage and gas processing.
Cost: $35.00
Frequency: Monthly
Circulation: 32000
Founded in 1955
Mailing list available for rent: 32,000 names
Printed in 4 colors on glossy stock

20260 PIW's Oil Market Intelligence
286 Madison Ave
Suite 14
New York, NY 10017-6368

212-557-3000; Fax: 212-557-5051
www.piw.pubs.com

Offers information on oil and gas stocks and bonds.
Frequency: Monthly

20261 PTTC Network News
Petroleum Technology Transfer Council
16010 Barkers Point Lane
Suite 220
Houston, TX 77079

281-921-1720; Fax: 281-921-1723
hq@pttc.org
www.pttc.org

Kristi Lovendahl, Webmaster/Newsletter Editor
Norma Gutierrez, Circulation Director
Donald Duttlinger, Executive Director
Russell Lindsay, Advertising Sales Director

16 page newsletter with east to read summaries of new oil and natural gas technologies.
Frequency: Quarterly
Circulation: 17000
Founded in 1994

20262 PetroChemical News
William F Bland
PO Box 16666
Chapel Hill, NC 27516-6666

919-490-0700; Fax: 919-490-3002

Susan D Kensil, Editor

A fast, accurate report of significant world petrochemical developments.
Cost: $739.00
4 Pages
Frequency: Weekly

20263 Petroleum Intelligence Weekly
5 E 37th St
Suite 5
New York, NY 10016-2807

212-532-1112; Fax: 212-532-4479
info@energyintel.com
www.energyintel.com

Tom Wallin, President
Peter Kemp, Editor
Raja W. Sidawi, Chairman
Sarah Miller, Editor-at-Large

News of the oil and gas industries worldwide.
Cost: $3340.00
Frequency: Weekly
Founded in 1961

20264 Platt's Oilgram News
McGraw Hill
3333 Walnut Street
Boulder, CO 80301-2525

720-485-5000
800-752-8878; Fax: 720-548-5701
support@platts.com
www.platts.com
Facebook, Twitter, LinkedIn, YouTube,LinkedIn,RSS,Blog

O Marashian, Publisher
James Keener, Marketing
Harry Sachinsis, President

News of the oil and gas industries worldwide.
Frequency: Daily
Founded in 1888
Mailing list available for rent

20265 Public Gas News
American Public Gas Association
201 Massachusetts Ave Ne
Suite C-4
Washington, DC 20002-4957

202-464-0240; Fax: 202-464-0246
www.apga.org

Bert Kalisch, President
Bob Beauregard, Marketing
Chuck Warrington, Managing Director

Written for public gas managers to keep them apprised of industry news.
Cost: $50.00
Circulation: 1000
Founded in 1961
Printed in on matte stock

20266 Security Watch
National Petrochemical & Refiners Association
1667 K Street, NW
Suite 700
Washington, DC 20006-1654

202-457-0480; Fax: 202-457-0486
info@npra.org
www.npra.org

Charles Drevna, President
Gerald R. Van De Velde, CFO
Rebbie J. Riley, Executive Assistant

Important security-related events, announcements, and background stories from government and industry. Written for members of the refining and petrochemical industries who have facility security responsibilities.
450 Members
Frequency: Weekly

20267 Tech Update
National Petrochemical & Refiners Association
1667 K Street, NW
Suite 700
Washington, DC 20006-1654

202-457-0480; Fax: 202-457-0486
info@npra.org
www.npra.org

Charles Drevna, President
Gerald R. Van De Velde, CFO
Rebbie J. Riley, Executive Assistant

Highlights developments in safety, plant security, technology, government regulations, and NPRA technical meetings for the petroleum refining and petrochemical industries.
450 Members
Frequency: Bi-Weekly

20268 WPMA Weekly Update
Western Petroleum Marketers Association
PO Box 571500
Murray, UT 84157

801-263-9762
888-252-5550; Fax: 801-262-9413
info@wpma.com
www.wpma.com

Gene Inglesby, Executive Director
Rob Franklin, President
Bob Ogan, VP

E-newsletter.
Frequency: Weekly
Founded in 1953

20269 Washington Report
Interstate Natural Gas Association of America
555 13th St Nw
Suite 300W
Washington, DC 20004-1109

202-637-8600; Fax: 202-637-8615
www.stonebridge-international.com

Anthony S Harrington, CEO
Samuel Berger, Manager

Natural gas newsletter places a special emphasis on developments that affect the interstate pipeline industry. It covers Congress, the Federal Energy Regulatory Commission and other federal agencies, state and Canadian regulatory boards and company news.

20270 Weekly Propane Newsletter
Butane-Propane News
PO Box 660698
Arcadia, CA 91066-0698

626-357-2168; Fax: 626-303-2854
www.bpnews.com

Natalie Peal, Publisher
Kurt Ruhl, National Sales Manager

Weekly updates and rates on the propane and gas industry.
Cost: $205.00
8 Pages
Frequency: Weekly
Circulation: 2000
Founded in 1939
Printed in one color on matte stock

20271 Western Petroleum Marketers Association
PO Box 571500
Salt Lake, UT 84157-1500

801-263-9762; Fax: 801-262-9413
info@wpma.com
www.wpma.com
Facebook, Twitter

Gene Inglesby, Executive Director
Sandra Peterson, Editor
Brett Adams, President
Robert Fung, First V.P
Lary Poulton, Second V.P.

Accepts advertising.
Founded in 1953

20272 World Gas Intelligence
575 Broadway
New York, NY 10012-3230

212-941-5500; Fax: 212-941-5509
www.piw.pubs.com

Edward L Morse, Publisher
Jocelyn Strauber, Circulation Director

International coverage of the oil and gas industry.
Cost: $985.00
Frequency: SemiMonthly
Mailing list available for rent

Magazines & Journals

20273 AAPG Bulletin
American Association of Petroleum Geologists
PO Box 979
Tulsa, OK 74101-979

918-584-2555; Fax: 918-560-2632
bulletin@aapg.org
www.aapg.org

Beverly Molyneux, Managing Editor
David Curtiss, CEO/President
Larry Nations, Marketing

Peer reviewed articles that cover major extent and detailed geologic data. Information on petroleum, natural gas, and other energy products.
Cost: $305.00
Frequency: Monthly
Circulation: 30000
ISSN: 0149-1423
Founded in 1917

20274 AAPG Explorer
American Association of Petroleum Geologists

1444 S Boulder Avenue
PO Box 979
Tulsa, OK 74101-979

918-584-2555
800-288-7636; Fax: 918-560-2665
postmaster@aapg.org
www.aapg.org

Patrick J F Gratton, President
Ernest A Mancini, Editor
Brenda Merideth, Advertising Sales Manager

News for explorationists of oil, gas and minerals as well as for geologists with environmental and water well concerns.
Cost: $50.00
Frequency: Monthly
Circulation: 30000
ISBN: 0-195298-6 -
Founded in 1917
Printed in 4 colors on matte stock

20275 American Oil and Gas Reporter
National Publishers Group
PO Box 343
Derby, KS 67037

316-788-6271
800-847-8301; Fax: 316-788-7568

Charlie Cookson, Publisher
Bill Campbell, Managing Editor

The American Oil & Gas Reporter serves the exploration, drilling and production segments of the oil and gas industry.
Cost: $65.07
Frequency: Monthly
Circulation: 7384
Founded in 1958

20276 BIC - Business & Industry Connection
BIC Alliance
Po Box 3502
Covington, LA 70434

985-893-8692; Fax: 985-893-8693
bic@bicalliance.com
www.bicalliance.com

Jamie Craig, Editor
Earl Heard, CEO/President
Kathy Dugas, Administrator
Joe Storer, Manager

Information on oil and gas, refining, petrochemical, environmental, construction, engineering, pulp and paper, state agencies and municipalities business.
Cost: $45.00
Circulation: 75000

20277 Bloomberg Natural Gas Report
Bloomberg Financial Markets
100 Business Park Drive
Princeton, NJ 08542-840

609-279-3000
800-395-9403; Fax: 917-369-7000
munis@bloomberg.com
www.bloomberg.com/energy

Michael Bloomberg, Publisher
Ronald Henkoff, Editor

News, interviews, and analysis of topics of importance to all levels of the natural gas market.
12 Pages
Frequency: Weekly
Circulation: 1700
Founded in 1980

20278 Butane-Propane News
Butane-Propane News
PO Box 660698
Arcadia, CA 91006

626-357-2168
800-214-4386; Fax: 626-303-2854
www.bpnews.com

Natalie Peal, Publisher
Ann Rey, Editorial Director
Kurt Ruhl, Sales Manager

Petroleum and propane industry news.
Cost: $32.00
56 Pages
Frequency: Monthly
Circulation: 16500
Founded in 1939
Printed in 4 colors on glossy stock

20279 Coal People
Al Skinner Enterprises
PO Box 6247
Charleston, WV 25362-0247

304-342-4129
800-235-5188; Fax: 304-343-3124
cpm@newwave.net
www.coalpeople.com

A Skinner, Owner
Christina Karawan, Managing Editor
Beth Terranova, Sales Manager
Angela McNealy, Circulation Manager
C K Lane, Senior Vice President

Features special news and product sections for the coal industry.
Cost: $25.00
60 Pages
Circulation: 11500
Founded in 1976
Printed in 4 colors on glossy stock

20280 Compressor Tech Two
Diesel & Gas Turbine Publications
20855 Watertown Rd
Suite 220
Waukesha, WI 53186-1873

262-754-4100; Fax: 262-754-4175
slizdas@dieselpub.com
www.dieselspec.com

Michael Osenga, President
Brent Haight, Managing Editor
Kara Kane, Advertising Manager
Christa Johnson, Production Manager
Sheila Lizdas, Circulation Manager

Covers oil and gas exploration, drilling, oilfield contracting, gas and petrochemical pipeline and storage, as well as petrochemical, hydrocarbon and gas processing industries.
Circulation: 12000

20281 Diesel Progress: North American Edition
Diesel & Gas Turbine Publications
20855 Watertown
Suite 220
Waukesha, WI 53186-1873

262-754-4100
800-558-4322; Fax: 262-832-5075
mosenga@dieselpub.com
www.dieselspec.com

Michael Osenga, President
Sheila Lizdas, Circulation Manager
Lynne Diefenbach, Advertising Manager
Christa Johnson, Production Manager

Geared towards readers interested in state-of-the-art systems technology. Features include new product listings, systems design, research amd product testing as well as systems maintenance and rebuilding.
Frequency: Monthly
Circulation: 26011
Founded in 1969

20282 Drill Bits
National Drilling Association
3053 Nationwide Pkwy.
Brunswick, OH 44212

877-632-4748; Fax: 216-803-9900
info@nda4u.com
www.nda4u.com

Rob Caho, President
Jim Howe, Secretary/Treasurer

A non-profit trade association of contractors, manufacturers and affiliated members from the drilling industry representing the geotechnical, environmental and mineral exploration sectors of this industry.
250+ Members
Frequency: 2 X/Year
Founded in 1972

20283 Drilling Contractor
International Association of Drilling Contractors
10370 Richmond Ave
Suite 760
Houston, TX 77042-9687

713-292-1945; Fax: 713-292-1946
info@iadc.org
www.iadc.org

Lee Hunt, President
Tom Terrell, Senior VP Business Development

All drilling, all completing, all the time.
Cost: $50.00
40 Pages
Frequency: 6x/Year
Circulation: 34500
Printed in 4 colors

20284 Energy Markets
Hart Publications
4545 Post Oak Place
#210
Houston, TX 77027

713-993-9320; Fax: 713-840-8585

Linda K Rader, Editor
Robert C Jarvis, Publisher

Energy Markets serves the following energy industry business classifications: utilities, municipalities, consultants and financial services, regulators, and other companies allied to or supportive of the energy industry.
Frequency: Monthly
Circulation: 25,751
Founded in 1993

20285 Energy Network
Gulf Publishing Company
PO Box 2608
Houston, TX 77252

713-529-4301
800-231-6275; Fax: 713-520-4433
store@gulfpub.com
www.gulfpub.com
Twitter, LinkedIn, RSS, YouTube

John D Royall, President/CEO
Ron Higgins, VP Sales/Publisher

Edited for companies that sell products to the oil and gas industry.
Founded in 1916
Mailing list available for rent

20286 Fuel Oil News
Hunter Publishing Limited
3100 S King Dr
Suite 1004
Chicago, IL 60616-3483

312-567-9981; Fax: 312-846-4632
www.fueloilnews.com

Luke Hunter, Partner
Joanne Juda, Circulation Director
Kate Kenny, Publisher
Keith Reid, Senior Editor
Patricia McCartney, Associate Editor

For home heating oil retailers.
Cost: $28.00
70 Pages
Frequency: Monthly
Circulation: 18000
Founded in 1935
Printed in 4 colors on glossy stock

20287 **Gas Turbine World**
Pequot Publishing
PO Box 447
Southport, CT 36490

203-259-1812; Fax: 203-254-3431
http://www.gtwbooks.com

Robert Farmer, Editor
Victor Debiasi, Publisher
Janes Janson, Marketing
Peg Walker, Circulation Manager

Serves the electric, utility and non-untility power generation, oil/gas production and processing industries.
Cost: $135.00
Frequency: Weekly
Circulation: 11000
Founded in 1979

20288 **Gas Utility Manager**
James Informational Media
6301 Gaston Avenue
#541
Dallas, TX 75214-6204

214-827-4630; Fax: 847-391-9058
www.betterroads.com

Mike Porcaro, Publisher
Mike Porcaro, CEO/President
Carole Spohr, Marketing Manager
Stacy Stiglic, Circulation Manager
Ruth Stidger, Editor

Federal and international regulations, new supply projects, research and development projects and gas industry news.
Cost: $95.00
40 Pages
Frequency: Annual+
Circulation: 40000
Founded in 1931

20289 **Georgia Petroleum Marketer**
Georgia Oilmen Association
1775 Spectrum Drive
Suite 100
Lawrenceville, GA 30043

770-995-7570; Fax: 770-995-9757
www.georgiaoilmensassoc.com

Roger T Lane, President/Editor
Mary R Franklin, Associate Editor
100 Pages
Frequency: Annual
Circulation: 800

20290 **Hart's E & P**
Hart Publications
1616 S Voss Rd
Suite 1000
Houston, TX 77057-2641

713-993-9320; Fax: 713-840-8585
directoryeditor@hartenergy.com
www.hartenergy.com

Rich Eichler, CEO
Joe Fisher, Senior Vice President
Kristine Klavers, Senior Vice President
Frederick Potter, Executive Vice President

Technical approaches and improvements related to both offshore and land drilling and extraction of petroleum products, also new product information and personality profiles.
Cost: $59.00
Frequency: Monthly
Circulation: 25000

20291 **Hart's Gas/LPG Markets**
Hart Publications
6011 Executive Drive
#200
Rockville, MD 20852-3804

301-468-1039; Fax: 301-468-1039
www.hartpub.com

Robert Gough, Editor

Financial reports on individual natural gas and liquid gasoline companies, their stock analysis, value and future mergers or acquisitions that may affect the pricing of gasoline or companies involved in the industry.
Cost: $ 1497.00
Frequency: Monthly

20292 **Hart's Oil & Gas Interests**
Hart Publications
6011 Executive Boulevard
#200
Rockville, MD 20852-3804

301-468-1039; Fax: 301-468-1039
www.hartpub.com

Brian Crotty, Group Publisher

Designed to keep readers abreast of developments and investment ideas in the petroleum and natural gas industry.
Frequency: Monthly

20293 **Hart's Oil & Gas Investor**
Hart Publications
1616 S Voss Rd
Suite 1000
Houston, TX 77057-2641

713-993-9320
800-874-2544; Fax: 713-840-8585
directoryeditor@hartenergy.com
www.hartenergy.com

Rich Eichler, CEO
Leslie Haines, Editor-in-Chief
Nissa Darbonne, Executive Editor
Kristine Klavers, Senior Vice President
Frederick Potter, Executive Vice President

Company performance, investment forecasts, economic outlooks, management strategy reports, focusing on the financial aspects of the petroleum and natural gas industry.
Cost: $297.00
Frequency: Monthly
Circulation: 5100
Printed in 4 colors

20294 **Hart's World Refining**
Hart Publications
4545 Post Oak Place
Suite 210
Houston, TX 77027-3105

713-993-9320
800-874-2544; Fax: 713-840-8585
www.hartpub.com

David Coates, Publisher
Jeremy Grunt, Executive Editor
Terry Higgins, Executive Publisher
Robert Gough, Editorial Director
Rich Eichler, President

Covers projects, financing and market developments, along with feedstock and product supply, demand, pricing information, technical and regulatory events associated with the manufacture, supply, and use of transportation fuels refining technologies, business strategies and fuel policy legislation.
Cost: $149.00
Circulation: 15,693
Founded in 1980

20295 **Hydrocarbon Processing**
Gulf Publishing Company
PO Box 2608
Houston, TX 77252-2608

713-529-4301
800-231-6275; Fax: 713-520-4433
store@gulfpub.com
www.gulfpub.com
Twitter, LinkedIn, RSS, YouTube

John D Royall, President/CEO
Ron Higgins, VP Sales/Publisher

Concentrates on the problems facing management and technical personnel in the worldwide hydrocarbon processing industry. Accepts advertising.
Cost: $120.00
Frequency: Monthly
Circulation: 30000
Founded in 1916
Mailing list available for rent
Printed in on glossy stock

20296 **Journal of Geophysical Research**
American Geophysical Union
2000 Florida Ave Nw
Washington, DC 20009-1277

202-462-6900
800-966-2481; Fax: 202-328-0566
usaha@usaha.org
www.agu.org
Facebook, Twitter, LinkedIn, YouTube, RSS, Flickr, Blog

Randy Fisher, Executive Director
John Orcutt, Publisher

There are five sections covering soid earth, oceans, atmosphere, planets, and space physics.
Cost: $20.00
Frequency: Monthly
Circulation: 10,000
Founded in 1919

20297 **Journal of Petroleum Technology**
Society of Petroleum Engineers
PO Box 833836
Richardson, TX 75083-3836

972-952-9300
800-456-6863; Fax: 972-952-9435
service@spe.org
www.spe.org

Mark Rubin, Executive Director
Giovanni Paccaloni, President
Paul Thone, Senior Manager of Sales
Niki Bradbury, Managing Director

Journal of Petroleum Technology serves the field of exploration, drilling, production, and reservoir management as well as related manufacturing and service organizations.
98 Pages
Frequency: Monthly
Circulation: 51205
Founded in 1949
Printed in 4 colors on glossy stock

20298 **LP/Gas**
Advanstar Communications
131 W 1st St
Duluth, MN 55802-2065

218-740-7200
800-346-0085; Fax: 218-740-7079
info@advanstar.com
www.advanstar.com

Kent Akervik, Manager
Sean Carr, Publisher
Joseph Loggia, CEO
Kris Meyer, Circulation Manager
Brian Kanaba, National Sales Manager

The propane industry's premier information source.
Cost: $30.00
36 Pages
Frequency: Monthly
Circulation: 15320

ISSN: 0024-7103
Printed in 4 colors on glossy stock

20299 Landman
American Association of Professional Landmen
4100 Fossil Creek Boulevard
Fort Worth, TX 76137-2723
817-847-7700; Fax: 817-847-7704
aapl@landman.org
www.landman.org
Le'ann Callihan, Editor
Robin Forte, President
Accepts advertising.
Cost: $50.00
76 Pages
Founded in 1955

20300 Lubricants World
4545 Post Oak Place
Suite 230
Houston, TX 77027
713-840-0378; Fax: 713-840-0379
Kathryn B Carnes, Editor

20301 NLGI Spokesman
National Lubricating Grease Institute
4635 Wyandotte St
Suite 202
Kansas City, MO 64112-1537
816-931-9480; Fax: 816-753-5026
nlgi@nlgi.org
www.nlgi.org
Kim Bott, Executive Director
Kim Bott, Administrative Assistant
About 50% of technical or scientific information amied at the manufacturers, users and suppliers of lubricating grease.
Cost: $53.00
Frequency: Monthly
Circulation: 2500
Founded in 1933

20302 National Petroleum News
Bel-Av Communications
359 Galahad Rd
Bolingbrook, IL 60440-2108
Home Page: www.npnweb.com
Keith Reid, Editor-in-Chief
Debra Reschke, Managing/Research Editor
The independent voice of the petroleum industry, content is aimed at the owner, operator or senior manager-the people who make the big decisions that require capital, time and resources.
Cost: $64.00
90 Pages
Frequency: Monthly
Circulation: 38000
Founded in 1909

20303 Natural Gas Fuels
RP Publishing
2696 S Colorado Blvd
Suite 595
Denver, CO 80222-5944
303-863-0521; Fax: 303-863-1722
www.rppublishing.com
Frank Rowe, President
Technological advances, marketing strategies, legislative activities, successful applications, and corporate and government initiatives to promote natural gas-powered vehicles
Circulation: 7000
Founded in 1992

20304 O&A Marketing News
KAL Publications
559 S Harbor Blvd
Suite A
Anaheim, CA 92805-4547
714-563-9300; Fax: 714-563-9310
www.kalpub.com
Kathy Laderman, President
Doreen Philbin, Advertising Sales Manager
Jim Penn, Circulation Manager
Linda Squeo, Marketing Manager
Coverage of industry events and related shows for wholesale and retail marketers of gasoline, oil and automotive service replacement products in the thirteen Pacific-Western states.
Cost: $20.00
Circulation: 7000
Founded in 1966

20305 Offshore
PennWell Publishing Company
1421 S Sheridan Rd
Tulsa, OK 74112-6619
918-835-3161
800-331-4463; Fax: 918-831-9476
Headquarters@PennWell.com
www.pennwell.com
Robert Biolchini, President
Biol Chini, CEO
Tommie Grigg, Circulation Manager
Elbon Ball, Editor
Jayne Gilfinger, Marketing Manager
Offshore serves the international oil and gas industry in its marine/offshore operations.
Cost: $75.00
186 Pages
Frequency: Monthly
Circulation: 40000
ISSN: 0030-0608
Founded in 1910
Mailing list available for rent
Printed in 4 colors on glossy stock

20306 Oil & Gas Journal
PennWell Publishing Company
1700 West Loop S
#1000
Houston, TX 77027-3005
713-621-9720; Fax: 713-963-6285
sales@pennwell.com
www.ogjonline.com
Tom T Terrell, Publisher
Tim Sullivant, Regional Sales Manager
Mike Moss, Regional Sales Manager
Detailed interpreation and information of the world developments in the oil and gas industry
Cost: $79.00
Frequency: Weekly
Circulation: 36090
Founded in 1990
Printed in 4 colors on glossy stock

20307 Oil Spill Contingency Planning: A Global Perspective
Aspen Publishers
76 Ninth Avenue
7th Floor
New York, NY 10011
212-771-0600
800-638-8437
www.aspenlawschool.com
Mark Dorman, CEO
Gustavo Dobles, VP Operations
Hands-on guidebook to contingency planning for oil spills.
Cost: $195.00

20308 Oilheating
Industry Publications
3621 Hill Rd
Parsippany, NJ 07054-1001
973-331-9545; Fax: 973-331-9547
www.spraytechnology.com
Facebook
Cynthia Hundley, Publisher
Addresses issues on dispatching and delivery efficiency, residential and commercial fuel oil use, as well as sales and services of oilfired equipment.
Cost: $42.00
Frequency: Monthly
Circulation: 13280
ISSN: 1092-6003
Founded in 1922
Mailing list available for rent

20309 Petroleo International
Keller International Publishing Corporation
150 Great Neck Rd
Suite 400
Great Neck, NY 11021-3309
516-829-9722; Fax: 516-829-9306
www.supplychainbrain.com
Victor Prieto, Editor
Sean Noble, Publisher
Steve Kann, Circulation Manager
Jerry Keller, President
Mary Chavez, Director of Sales
Spanish language petroleum/petrochemical magazine.
100 Pages
Circulation: 10,314
Founded in 1943

20310 SPE Drilling & Completion
Society of Petroleum Engineers
PO Box 833836
Richardson, TX 75083-3836
972-529-9300
800-456-6863; Fax: 972-952-9435
service@spe.org
www.spe.org
Giovanni Paccaloni, President
Shashana Pearson, Editor
Mary Jane, Advertising Manager
Georgeann Bilich, Publisher
Niki Bradbury, Managing Director
Technical papers selected for the drilling profession reviewed by peers on topics such as casing, instrumentation, bit technology, fluids, measurment, deviation control, telemetry, completion and well control.
Cost: $60.00
Frequency: Quarterly
Circulation: 3588
Founded in 1984

20311 Sea Technology Magazine
Compass Publications, Inc.
4600 N. Fairfax Drive
Suite 304
Arlington, VA 22203-1553
703-524-3136; Fax: 703-841-0852
oceanbiz@sea-technology.com
www.sea-technology.com
Twitter
Amos Bussmann, President/Publisher
Leslie Carr, Circulation Manager
Aileen Torres-Bennett, Managing Editor
Worldwide information leader for marine/offshore business, science and engineering. Read in more than 110 countries by management, engineers, scientists and technical personnel working in industry, government and education.
Cost: $40.00
Frequency: Monthly
Circulation: 16304
ISSN: 0093-3651
Founded in 1960

Mailing list available for rentat $80 per M
Printed in 4 colors

20312 Today's Refinery
Chemical Week Associates
2 Grand Central Tower,140 East 45th Street
40th floor
New York, NY 10017
212-884-9528; Fax: 212-884-9514
ltattum@chemweek.com
www.chemweek.com
Twitter, RSS,Blog
John Rockwell, VP
Joe Minnella, Global Sales Director
LYN TATTUM, Publisher
Robert Westervelt, Editor-in-Chief
Editorials from industry leaders focusing on current problems facing the industry. Highlights on legislation, activity, government regulations,and reports on major industry meetings.
Frequency: Monthly
Circulation: 10,000
Mailing list available for rent

20313 Utility & Pipeline Industries
WMO DannHausen Corporation
330 North Wabash
Suite 3201
Chicago, IL 60611
312-628-5870; Fax: 312-628-5878
www.gasindustries.com
Bob Higgins, Publisher
Heidi Liddle, Production Manager
Karen Ebbesmeyer, Circulation Manager
Ruth W. Stidger, Editor-in-Chief
Cory Sekine Pettite, Managing Editor
Market to federal agencies, bureaus, government departments and toll authorities. Accepts advertising.
Cost: $20.00
62 Pages
Frequency: Monthly
Circulation: 10680

20314 Washington Report
National Ocean Industries Association
1120 G St Nw
Suite 900
Washington, DC 20005-3801
202-347-6900; Fax: 202-347-8650
www.noia.org
Facebook, Twitter, YouTube
Tom Fry, President
Franki K Stuntz, Director Administration
Nolty J Thuriot, Director Congressional Affairs
Frequency: Bi-Weekly

20315 Well Servicing
Workover Well Servicing Publications
10200 Richmond Avenue
Suite 275
Houston, TX 77042
713-781-0758
800-692-0771; Fax: 713-781-7542
kjordan@aesc.net
www.aesc.net
Kenny Jordan, Executive DIrector
Polly Fisk, Editor
Patty Jordan, Circulation
New products listing and reviews, field reports, and information on companies in the industry. Written and edited for energy service company professionals, and oil & gas operations.
40 Pages
Circulation: 11000
ISSN: 0043-2393
Founded in 1956

20316 Western Petroleum Marketers News Magazine
Western Petroleum Marketers Association
PO Box 571500
Murray, UT 84157
801-263-9762
888-252-5550; Fax: 801-262-9413
info@wpma.com
www.wpma.com
Gene Inglesby, Executive Director
Rob Franklin, President
Bob Ogan, VP
Frequency: Quarterly

20317 World Oil
Gulf Publishing Company
PO Box 2608
Houston, TX 77252
713-529-4301
800-231-6275; Fax: 713-520-4433
store@gulfpub.com
www.gulfpub.com
Twitter, LinkedIn, RSS, YouTube
John D Royall, President/CEO
Ron Higgins, VP Sales/Publisher
Reaches the exploration, drilling, producing, and well servicing segments of the oil and gas industry.
Cost: $34.00
100 Pages
Frequency: Monthly
Circulation: 36000
ISSN: 0043-8790
Founded in 1916
Mailing list available for rent
Printed in 4 colors on glossy stock

Trade Shows

20318 American Association of Petroleum Geologists Annual Convention/Expo
American Association of Petroleum Geologists
PO Box 979
Tulsa, OK 74119
918-584-2555
800-364-2274; Fax: 918-560-2665
convene@aapg.org
www.aapg.org
Facebook, Twitter, LinkedIn, YouTube
Randa Reeder-Briggs, Annual Meeting Manager
Melissa Howerton, Annual Meeting Assistant
Steph Benton, Exhibit Manager
Rick Fritz, Executive Director
Edward 'Ted' Beaumont, President
Exhibits of instrumentation, equipment, supplies, services and publications for petroleum geologists, geophysicists and engineers.
7000 Attendees
Frequency: Annual/April

20319 American School of Gas Measurement Technology Meeting
PO Box 3991
Houston, TX 77253-3991
903-486-7875; Fax: 512-267-9243
www.asgmt.com
Seminar, workshop, and tours, plus 95 exhibits of gas measurement, equipment, supplies and services.
600 Attendees
Frequency: Annual
Founded in 1927

20320 Asia Pacific Improved Oil Recovery Conference
Society of Petroleum Engineers-Texas
222 Palisades Creek Drive
PO Box 833836
Richardson, TX 75083-3868
972-952-9300; Fax: 972-952-9435
www.spe.org
Oil recovery exhibition.
Mailing list available for rent

20321 Beaumont Industrial Petrochemical Trade Show
Lobos Services
16016 Perkins Road
Baton Rouge, LA 70810-3631
225-751-5626
Debbie Balough, Show Manager
Informs local industry of the full array of industrial equipment for the chemical industries.
5M Attendees
Frequency: January

20322 Circum-Pacific Council Energy Mineral Resources
5100 Westheimer Road
Houston, TX 77056-5596
713-709-9071; Fax: 713-622-5360
Mary Stewart, Show Manager
Napoleon Carcamo, Owner
50 booths.
1.2M Attendees
Frequency: November

20323 Eastern Oil and Gas Equipment Show
Pennsylvania Oil and Gas Association
412 N 2nd Street
Harrisburg, PA 17101-1342
717-939-9551
Stephen Rhoads, Show Manager
175 booths displaying new technologies, products and services relating to the oil and gas industries.
1M Attendees
Frequency: June

20324 Entelec Conference & Expo
Energy Telecommunications and Electrical Assoc
5005 W Royal Lane
Suite 116
Irving, TX 75063
972-929-3169
888-503-8700; Fax: 972-915-6040
www.entelec.org
Blaine Siske, Executive Manager
Susan Joiner, Exhibits Manager
Michael Blurt, President
James C Coulter, First V.P
Kenneth Clouse, Second V.P.
To bring together communications and control technology professionals from the petroleum, natural gas, pipeline, and electric utility companies for three days of quality training, seminars, exhibits and networking.
Frequency: Annual/May
Founded in 1928

20325 Europe International Offshore Exchange
222 Palisades Creek Drive
Richardson, TX 75080-2040
Donna Anderson, Show Manager
1,100 booths.
21M Attendees
Frequency: September

20326 International Thermal Spray Conference & Exposition
ASM International

9639 Kinsman Road
Materials Park, OH 44073-0002

440-338-5151
800-336-5152; Fax: 440-338-4634
memberservicecenter@asminternational.org
www.asminternational.org

William T. Mahoney, Secretary & CEO
Lindy Good, Global Conference & Exhibit Planner

International annual conference for professional thermal spray technologists, researchers, manufacturers and suppliers.
30K Members
Frequency: Annual/May
Founded in 1913

20327 **Landman**
American Association of Petroleum Landmen
4100 Fossil Creek Boulevard
Fort Worth, TX 76137-2723

817-847-7700; Fax: 817-847-7704
http://www.landman.org

Carolyn Stephens, Editor
Le Ann Pembroke, Advertising Manager

50 booths.
1.5M Attendees
Frequency: June

20328 **Liquified Gas Association Southwest**
PO Box 9925
Austin, TX 78766-0925

FAX 512-834-0758

Cheryl Tomanetz, Show Manager

125 booths.
1.8M Attendees
Frequency: September

20329 **Liquified Natural Gas**
Reed Exhibition Companies
255 Washington Street
Newton, MA 02458-1637

617-584-4900; Fax: 617-630-2222

Elizabeth Hitchcock, International Sales

Presentation for the liquefied natural gas industry.
2.5M Attendees
Frequency: May

20330 **Liquified Petroleum Gas Exposition Midwest**
4100 Country Club Drive
Jefferson City, MO 65109-0302

573-634-5345; Fax: 573-893-2623

Emma Krommel, Show Manager

100 booths of large transport and bobtail delivery trucks.
1M Attendees
Frequency: June

20331 **Midwest Petroleum & Convenience Tradeshow**
Illinois Petroleum Marketers Association
PO Box 12020
Springfield, IL 62791-2020

217-544-4609; Fax: 217-789-0222

Bill Fleischli, Executive VP, Managing Editor

Suppliers and manufacturers to petroleum marketing and convenience store trades, including pumps, computers, trucks, safety devices, canopies, car washes and tank testing. 300 booths.
4M Attendees
Frequency: June

20332 **National Petro Refiners Association Refinery Petrochemical Plant**
1899 L Street NW
Suite 1000
Washington, DC 20036-3810

202-457-0480
http://www.npra.org

Robert Dzuiban, Show Manager
Robert Slaughter, President

A forum for the exchange of technical information and services to the petroleum industry.
1.3M Attendees
Frequency: May

20333 **Offshore Technology Conference**
222 Palisades Creek Drive, Richardson
Richardson, TX 75080-2040

972-952-9494
866-229-2386; Fax: 972-952-9435
service@spe.org
www.spe.org

Alan Wegener, Show Manager
Niki Bradbury, Managing Director

Consisting of a forum to disseminate technical information for the advancement of engineering.
30M Attendees
Frequency: May

20334 **Petroleum Computer Conference**
Society of Petroleum Engineers
222 Palisades Creek Drive
Richardson, TX 75080-2040

972-952-9300; Fax: 972-952-9435
service@spe.org
www.spe.org

Niki Bradbury, Managing Director

Annual show of 50 microcomputer manufacturers and suppliers who provide hardware and software to the petroleum industry.
650 Attendees

20335 **Petroleum Equipment Institute Convention at the NACS Show**
Petroleum Equipment Institute
PO Box 2380
Tulsa, OK 74101-2380

918-494-9696; Fax: 918-491-9895
www.pei.org

Scott Boorse, Dir, Technical Programs
J. Rex Brown, Dir, Information Services
Teresa Farmer, Membership Manager
Rick Long, EVP & General Counsel
Julie Shank, Marketing & Event Manager

Annual show of manufacturers of petroleum marketing equipment. There are 260 exhibiting companies.
4500 Attendees
Frequency: October
Founded in 1951

20336 **Society Petro Engineers Annual Meeting**
PO Box 833836
Richardson, TX 75083-3836

972-952-9300; Fax: 972-952-9435

Lois Woods, Show Manager
Mark Rubin, Executive Director

Conference with exhibits of drilling and production equipment and materials.
10M Attendees
Frequency: September

20337 **Society Petro Engineers Permian Basin Oil Gas Recovery Conference and Expo**
PO Box 833836
Richardson, TX 75083-3836

972-952-9300

Susan Bell, Event Manager

70 booths.
400 Attendees
Frequency: March

20338 **Society Petro Engineers Petroleum Computer Conference and Expo**
PO Box 833836
Richardson, TX 75083-3836

972-952-9300

Georgie Cumiskey, Event Manager

30 booths of microcomputer hardware and software for the petroleum industry.
300 Attendees
Frequency: July

20339 **Society Petro Engineers Production Operations Symposium**
PO Box 833836
Richardson, TX 75083-3836

972-952-9300

Karen Rodgers, Event Manager
Mark Rubin, Executive Director

70 booths of oil and gas industry related products and services.
1M Attendees
Frequency: March

20340 **Society Petro Engineers Rocky Mountain**
PO Box 833836
Richardson, TX 75083-3836

972-952-9300

Georgie Cumiskey, Event Manager

60 booths.
300 Attendees
Frequency: April

20341 **Society Petro Engineers Western Regional Meeting**
PO Box 833836
Richardson, TX 75083-3836

972-952-9300

Lois Woods, Exchange Manager
Mark Rubin, Executive Director

65 booths.
700 Attendees
Frequency: May

20342 **Society of Petro Engineers Eastern Regional Meeting**
PO Box 833836
Richardson, TX 75083-3836

972-952-9300

Susan Bell, Event Manager
Mark Rubin, Executive Director

Offers a forum for the exchange of ideas between petroleum and gas engineers.
500 Attendees
Frequency: October

20343 **Society of Petro Engineers Enhanced Oil Recovery Symposium and Exchange**
PO Box 833836
Richardson, TX 75083-3836

972-952-9300

Georgie Cumiskey, Event Manager
Mark Rubin, Executive Director

100 booths.
1.6M Attendees
Frequency: April

20344 **Southeast Petro Food Marketing Expo**
7300 Glenwood Avenue
Raleigh, NC 27612
919-782-4411; Fax: 919-782-4414
www.sepetro.org
Sharon Vinson, Show Manager
550 booths and 400+ exhibitors serving the petroleum and convenience store industries in the southeast.
2,000 Attendees
Frequency: March

20345 **WPMA Convention & Convenience Store Expo**
Western Petroleum Marketers Association
Po Box 571500
Salt Lake, UT 84157-1500
801-263-9762; Fax: 801-262-9413
info@wpma.com
www.wpma.com
Facebook, Twitter
Gene Inglesby, Executive Director
Jan Roothoff, Administration Director
In addition to Las Vegas entertainment and special events, the convention offers keynote speakers around current issues and topics, as well as workshops. Over 400 exhibits. Registration costs vary.
3750 Attendees
Frequency: Annual/Winter

20346 **Western Petroleum Marketers Convention & Convenience Store Expo**
Western Petroleum Marketers Association
PO Box 571500
Salt Lake, UT 84157-1500
801-263-9762
888-252-5550; Fax: 801-262-9413
info@wpma.com
www.wpma.com
Facebook, Twitter
Gene Inglesby, Executive Director
Jan Roothoff, Administration Director
Bob Ogan, VP
430 booths.
3500 Attendees
Frequency: February

Directories & Databases

20347 **API Composite List**
American Petroleum Institute
200 Massachusettes Avenue NW
Suite 1100
Washington, DC 20001-5571
202-682-8000
Facebook, Twitter, YouTube, Flickr
Mike Sommers, President/CEO
Amanda Eversole, EVP/COO
Paul G. Afonso, SVP/CLO/Corporate Secretary
Megan Bloomgren, SVP, Communications
Bill Koetzle, SVP, Gov. Relations
An online Directory of API Monogram Licensees and Management System Registered Organizations. Search by company name, certificate number, product type, key words in the registration scope, status, and more.

20348 **Africa-Middle East Petroleum Directory**
PennWell Directories
1700 West Loop S
Suite 1000
Houston, TX 77027-3005
713-621-9720
800-752-9764; Fax: 281-499-6310
www.petroleumdirectories.com
Jonelle Moore, Editor
Tim Sullivant, Manager
A directory for: associations, government agencies, drilling, exploration and production of natural gas, petrochemicals, pipeline operators etc.
Cost: $125.00
156 Pages

20349 **American Oil and Gas Reporter Directory**
Domestic Petroleum Publishers
PO Box 343
Derby, KS 67037-0343
316-788-6271; Fax: 316-788-7568
Bill Campbell, Editor
Charlie Cookson, Publisher
State oil and natural gas regulatory agencies.
Cost: $25.00
Frequency: Annual March
Circulation: 13,540

20350 **American Oil and Gas Reporter: American Drilling Rig Directory Issues**
National Publishers Group
PO Box 343
Derby, KS 67037-0343
316-788-6271; Fax: 316-788-7568
Bill Campbell, Editor
Charlie Cookson, Publisher
List of contractors engaged in onshore drilling for petroleum and gas.
Cost: $25.00
Frequency: SemiAnnual
Circulation: 13,540

20351 **American Oil and Gas Reporter: Directory of Crude Oil Purchasers Issue**
Domestic Petroleum Publishers
PO Box 343
Derby, KS 67037-0343
316-788-6271; Fax: 316-788-7568
Bill Campbell, Editor
Charlie Cookson, Publisher
List of companies buying crude oil in the US.
Cost: $25.00
Frequency: Annual July
Circulation: 13,540

20352 **Armstrong Oil Directories**
Armstrong Oil
Po Box 52106
Amarillo, TX 79159-2106
806-457-9300; Fax: 806-457-9301
www.armstrongoil.com
Alan Armstrong, Owner
Directory of services and supplies to the industry.
Cost: $53.50
300 Pages
Frequency: Annual

20353 **Brown's Directory of North American and International Gas Companies**
Advanstar Communications
131 W 1st St
Duluth, MN 55802-2065
218-740-7200
800-346-0085; Fax: 218-740-7079
info@advanstar.com
www.advanstar.com
Kent Akervik, Manager
Joseph Loggia, CEO
Operating gas companies, brokers and refineries are listed in this comprehensive directory with worldwide coverage.
Cost: $265.00
350 Pages
Frequency: Annual
Circulation: 1,000

20354 **Canadian Oil Industry Directory**
PennWell Directories
1700 West Loop S
Suite 1000
Houston, TX 77027-3005
713-621-9720
800-752-9764; Fax: 281-499-6310
www.petroleumdirectories.com
Susan Anderson, Editor
Tim Sullivant, Manager
A directory for: associations, government agencies, drilling contractors, engineering, construction, exploration, production, petrochemicals, pipeline operators, etc.
Cost: $135.00

20355 **Congress Legislative Directory**
American Gas Association
1515 Wilson Boulevard
Suite 100
Arlington, VA 22209-2469
703-841-8400
Offers information on members of both houses of the United States Congress, federal government agencies relevant to the natural gas industry.
Cost: $10.00
220 Pages
Frequency: Annual

20356 **Contracts for Field Projects & Supporting Research on Enhanced Oil Recovery**
US Department of Energy
PO Box 1398
Bartlesville, OK 74005
918-336-0307; Fax: 918-337-4418
Herbert A Tiedemann, Editor
Energy Department technical project officers and contractors.
97 Pages
Frequency: Quarterly
Founded in 1997

20357 **Crude Oil Analysis Data Bank**
PO Box 2565
Bartlesville, OK 74005-2565
918-336-2400
Contains over 9,000 analyses, obtained from the Bureau of Mines, of worldwide crude oil deposits.
Frequency: Full-text

20358 **DRI/Platt's Oil Prices**
DRI/McGraw-Hill
24 Hartwell Ave
Lexington, MA 02421-3103
781-860-6060; Fax: 781-860-6002
support@construction.com
www.construction.com
Walt Arvin, President
Database provides weekly, monthly and daily time series of worldwide petroleum product prices.

20359 **Drilling & Well Servicing Contractors**
Midwest Publishing Company

2230 E 49th Ste E
Tulsa, OK 74105-8771

918-582-2000
800-829-2002; Fax: 918-587-9349
info@midwestpub.com
www.midwestpub.com

Will L Hammack, Owner

Approximately 4,000 drilling and well servicing contractors, equipment suppliers, manufacturers and service companies.
Cost: $150.00
Frequency: Annual, September
Founded in 1943

20360 **Dwight's Offshore and Bid Data**
Dwight's Energydata
1633 Firman Drive
Suite 100
Richardson, TX 75081-6790

972-783-8002
800-468-3381; Fax: 972-783-0058

This large database offers the most current information on bids, lease ownership data, and competitive intelligence data on the petroleum industry.

20361 **Fuel Oil News-Source Book Issue**
Fuel Oil News
3496 E Lake Lansing Road
Suite 150
East Lansing, MI 48823-6223

517-337-4040
www.fueloilnews.com

Offers a list of over 600 manufacturers and suppliers of oil handling, heating and delivering companies.
Cost: $10.00
Frequency: Annual
Circulation: 17,000

20362 **GOA Membership Directory**
Georgia Oilmen Association
1775 Spectrum Drive
Suite 100
Lawrenceville, GA 30043-5745

770-995-7570; Fax: 770-995-9757
www.georgiaoilmensassoc.com

Roger T Lane, President/Editor
Mary R Franklin, Associate Editor
Karen Carter, Executive Assitant

Directory of active and associate members and other valuable information.
Cost: $250.00
42 Pages
Frequency: Monthly
Circulation: 1,300
Printed in on glossy stock

20363 **Gas and Oil Equipment Directory**
Underwriters Laboratories
2600 N.W.Lake Rd
Camas, WA 98607-8542

847-412-0136
877-854-3577; Fax: 847-272-8129
www.ul.com
Facebook, Twitter, YouTube

Keith E Williams, CEO
John Drengenberg, Manager Consumer Affairs

Companies that have qualified to use the UL listing mark or classification marking on or in connection with products that have been found to be in compliance with UL's requirements.
Cost: $9.00
Frequency: Annual October

20364 **Hart Energy Publishing**
4545 Post Oak Place Drive
Suite 210
Houston, TX 77027-3105

713-993-9320
800-874-2544; Fax: 713-840-8585
jeff@grainnet.com
www.hartenergy.com

Jeff Miller, Director Marketing
Matt Beltz, Marketing Associate
Rich Eichler, President
Kristine Klavers, Senior Vice President
Frederick Potter, Executive Vice President

Hart Energy Publishing is the worldwide leader in energy industry publishing. With fiver energy magazines, E & P, Oil and Gas investors, Pipeline gas technology, energy markets and world refining. Hart Energy Publishing also has a range of newsletters and centers devoted to the downstream Energy industry.
15 Pages
Frequency: Monthly

20365 **Hart Publications**
4545 Post Oak Place Drive
Houston, TX 77027-3105

713-993-9320
800-874-2544; Fax: 713-840-8585
www.hartpub.com

Gina Acosta, Fulfillment
Rich Eichler, President

Directories, magazines and newsletters of the oil and gas industry
15 Pages
Frequency: Annually

20366 **International Oil Spill Control Directory**
Cutter Information Corporation
37 Broadway
Suite 1
Arlington, MA 02474-5500

781-648-8700; Fax: 781-648-8707
consortium@cutter.com
www.cutter.com
Facebook, Twitter, LinkedIn, RSS

Verna Allee, Senior Consultant
Karen Coburn, President & CEO
Paul Bergeron, CFO & COO
Anne Mullaney, Vice-President

Offers valuable information on more than 1,000 suppliers of more than 3,500 oil spill cleanup, prevention and control products and services.
Cost: $95.00
225 Pages
Frequency: Annual

20367 **Marketers, Purchasers & Trading Companies**
Midwest Publishing Company
2230 E 49th Ste E
Tulsa, OK 74105-8771

918-582-2000
800-829-2002; Fax: 918-587-9349
www.midwestdirectories.com

Will Hammack, Editor

Over 5,300 purchasers, marketers and traders of refined products, crude oil and natural gas.
Cost: $145.00
Frequency: Annual October

20368 **McGraw-Hill GasWire**
DRI/McGraw-Hill
24 Hartwell Ave
Lexington, MA 02421-3103

781-860-6060; Fax: 781-860-6002
support@construction.com
www.construction.com

Walt Arvin, President

Contains news and analyses of the US natural gas market.
Frequency: Full-text

20369 **Member Directory and Oil & Gas Agencies**
Interstate Oil and Gas Compact Commission
PO Box 53127
Oklahoma City, OK 73152-3127

405-525-3556
800-822-4015; Fax: 405-525-3592

Christine Hansen, Executive Director
Alesha Leemaster, Communications Manager

About 600 state representatives to the commission from 29 oil and gas producing states and seven associate states and committee members from related industries and government agencies.
Cost: $11.00
Frequency: Annual

20370 **NOIA Leaders**
National Ocean Industries Association
1120 G St NW
Suite 900
Washington, DC 20005-3801

202-347-6900; Fax: 202-347-8650
www.noia.org
Facebook, Twitter, YouTube

Tom Fry, President
Franki K Stuntz, Director Administration
Nolty J Thuriot, Director Congressional Affairs
Frequency: Annual
Founded in 1972

20371 **National Petroleum News: Buyer's Guide Issue**
2101 S Arlington Heights Road
Arlington Heights, IL 60005-4185

847-427-9512; Fax: 847-427-2041

Jim Bursch, Publisher
Don Smith, Editor

A comprehensive listing of products and services for the petroleum industry.
Cost: $30.00
Frequency: Annual
Circulation: 18,000

20372 **National Petroleum News: Market Facts Issue**
2101 S Arlington Heights Road
Arlington Heights, IL 60005-4185

847-427-9512; Fax: 847-427-2041

Jim Bursch, Publisher
Don Smith, Editor

Offers the industry's most up-to-date compilation of petroleum/convenience store facts, figures and trends.
Cost: $75.00
Frequency: Annual
Circulation: 18,000

20373 **Natural Gas Industry Directory**
PennWell Directories
1700 West Loop S
Suite 1000
Houston, TX 77027-3005

713-621-9720
800-752-9764; Fax: 281-499-6310
www.petroleumdirectories.com

Susan Anderson, Editor
Tim Sullivant, Manager

Major divisions of the natural gas industry worldwide.
Cost: $165.00

20374 Offshore Services and Equipment Directory
Greene Dot
11686 Jocatal Center
San Diego, CA 92127-1147

858-485-0189; Fax: 858-485-5139

Renee Garza, Editor

About 5,000 suppliers of equipment and services to the offshore petroleum exploration and production industry worldwide.
Cost: $235.00
Frequency: Annual May
Circulation: 4,000

20375 Oil and Gas Directory
Geophysical Directory
Po Box 130508
Houston, TX 77219-0508

713-529-1922
800-929-2462; Fax: 713-529-3646
www.iagc.org

Stewart Schafer, Owner

Valuable information is listed on over 5,000 companies worldwide that are involved in petroleum exploration and drilling.
Cost: $130.00
700 Pages
Frequency: Annual, October
Circulation: 2,000
Founded in 1970

20376 Oil and Gas Field Code Master List
US Energy Information Administration
1000 Independence Av SW
#E1-231
Washington, DC 20585-0001

202-586-8800; Fax: 202-586-0727
www.eia.doe.gov

John H Weiner, Executive Director

All identified oil and gas fields in the US.
Cost: $27.00
Frequency: Annual December

20377 Permit Data On-Line
Petroleum Information Corporation
PO Box 2612
Denver, CO 80201-2612

303-595-7500
800-645-3282

Oil well drilling permits granted by regional governmental agencies.
Frequency: Weekly

20378 PetroProcess HSE Directory
Atlantic Communications LLC
1635 W Alabama St
Houston, TX 77006-4101

713-831-1768; Fax: 713-523-7804
info@oilonline.com

Shaun Wymes, President
Rob Garza, General Manager
Graham Thomson, General Manager
Ray Vanegas, Manager
Doug Duguid, Managing Director
Cost: $79.00
650 Pages
Frequency: Annual
Founded in 1990

20379 Petroleum Equipment Directory
Petroleum Equipment Institute
PO Box 2380
Tulsa, OK 74101-2380

918-494-9696; Fax: 918-491-9895
www.pei.org

Scott Boorse, Dir, Technical Programs
J. Rex Brown, Membership Manager
Rick Long, EVP & General Counsel
Teresa Farmer, Membership Manager

Member manufacturers, distributors and installers of petroleum marketing equipment worldwide are offered.
Cost: $50.00
395 Pages
Frequency: Annual
Circulation: 3,000

20380 Petroleum Marketers Association of America Directory
Petroleum Marketers Association of America
1901 Fort Myer Dr
Suite 500
Arlington, VA 22209-1609

703-351-8000
800-300-7622; Fax: 703-351-9160
http://www.pmaa.org

Daniel F Gilligan, President
Sarah Dodge, Director/Legislative Affairs
Patricia Murrey, Director/Administration
Holly Tuminello, VP
Izua Yang, Manager/Communications/Conferences

About 45 state and regional member associations. A national organization representing the nation's independent petroleum marketers.
Cost: $50.00
Frequency: Annual February
Circulation: 2,000

20381 Petroleum Marketing Management Buyers Guide
Graphic Concepts
1801 Rockville Pike
Suite 330
Rockville, MD 20852-1633

A list of suppliers of products, equipment and services to combination gas station owners and convenience stores.
Frequency: Annual
Circulation: 20,000

20382 Petroleum Software Directory
PennWell Publishing Company
3050 Post Oak Boulevard
Suite 200
Houston, TX 77056-6570

713-219-9720
800-752-9764; Fax: 713-963-6228
susana@pennwell.com

More than 800 companies that produce over 1,800 micro-, mini- and mainframe computer software packages designed for petroleum industry applications.
Cost: $195.00
Frequency: Annual June
Circulation: 1,000

20383 Petroleum Supply Annual
Superintendent of Documents
1000 Independence Ave SW
Washington, DC 20585

202-586-8800
http://www.eia.doe.gov/oil_gas/petroleum/data_publications/petrol

Contains information on the supply and disposition of crude oil and petroleum products. Reflects data collected by the petroleum industry during 1998 through annual and monthly surveys, it is divided in to two volumes. The first volume contains three sections, Summary Statistics, Detailed Statistics, and Refinery Capacity, each with final annual data. Volume 1 cost is $17.00, volume 2 $51.00
175 Pages
Frequency: Annual
Founded in 1999

20384 Pipeline & Gas Journal: Buyer's Guide Issue
Oildom Publishing Company of Texas
PO Box 941669
Houston, TX 77094-8669

281-558-6930; Fax: 281-558-7029
www.oildompublishing.com

Jeff Share, Editor

List of over 700 companies supplying products and services used in construction and operation of cross country pipeline and gas distribution systems.
Cost: $75.00
Frequency: May

20385 Pipeline & Gas Journal: Directory of Pipeline Operating Companies
Oildom Publishing Company of Texas
PO Box 941669
Houston, TX 77218-9368

281-558-6930; Fax: 281-558-7029
www.oildompublishing.com

Jeff Share, Editor
Oliver Klinger, Editor

List of companies operating oil and gas transmission pipelines worldwide.
Cost: $80.00
Frequency: September
Circulation: 27,000

20386 Platts Insight
The McGraw-Hill Companies
1221 Avenue of the Americas
New York, NY 10020

212-904-2000
power@platts.com
www.platts.com

Glenn Goldberg, President, Information & Media

A comprehensive look at the energy industry, with year end outlook editions on global energy, sustainability, electric power, nuclear and more.

20387 SPE: Annual Membership Directory
Society of Petroleum Engineers
PO Box 833836
Richardson, TX 75083-3836

972-952-9300
800-456-6863; Fax: 972-952-9435

Georgeann Bilich, Editor

List of 52,000 member petroleum engineers.
Cost: $150.00
Frequency: Annual May
Circulation: 5,000

20388 Supply, Distribution, Manufacturing and Service
Midwest Publishing Company
2230 E 49th Ste E
Tulsa, OK 74105-8771

918-582-2000
800-829-2002; Fax: 918-587-9349
www.midwestdirectories.com

Will Hammack, Editor

8,000 oil well supply stores, service companies and equipment manufacturers.
Cost: $165.00
Frequency: Annual, September
Founded in 1943

20389 TULSA Database
Petroleum Abstracts
101 Harwell
Tulsa, OK 74104-3189

918-631-2297
800-247-8678; Fax: 918-599-9361
www.tulsaworld.com

Pam Weaver, Assistant Director
David Brown, Assistant Director of Marketing
Pam Jenni, Managing Editor

Contains more than 700,000 citations, with abstracts, to the worldwide literature and patents on the exploration, development and production of petroleum resources.
Frequency: Weekly Updates

20390 **US Non-Utility Power Directory on CD-ROM**
PennWell Publishing Company
PO Box 1260
Tulsa, OK 74101-1260

918-835-3161
800-752-9764; Fax: 918-831-9555

Gockel Delma, Sales

Offers a unique source of information to industry professionals including a listing of over 1,423 plant locations including project names, site addresses, plant types, fuels, installed capacity, power contract information, operating control systems, ownership and more.
Cost: $695.00
Frequency: Annual

20391 **US Offshore Oil Company Contact List**
Offshore Data Services
PO Box 19909
Houston, TX 77224-1909

713-781-7094; Fax: 713-781-9594

Marie Sheffer, Editor
Linda Parino, Circulation Director

Approximately 265 oil companies with US offshore leases.
Cost: $135.00
Frequency: Annual
Circulation: 800
ISBN: 1-058587-7 -
Mailing list available for rent

20392 **USA Oil Industry Directory**
PennWell Publishing Company
3050 Post Oak Boulevard
Suite 200
Houston, TX 77056-6570

713-219-9720
800-752-9764; Fax: 713-963-6228
susana@pennwell.com

Laura Bell, Editor
Susan Anderson, Publisher

Over 3,600 independent oil producers, fund companies, petroleum marketing companies, crude oil brokers and integrated oil firms.
Cost: $165.00
Frequency: Annual October
Circulation: 5,000

20393 **USA Oilfield Service, Supply and Manufacturers Directory**
PennWell Publishing Company
3050 Post Oak Boulevard
Suite 200
Houston, TX 77056-6570

713-219-9720
800-752-9764; Fax: 713-963-6228
susana@pennwell.com

Guntis Moritis, Editor

About 3,600 companies that provide oilfield equipment, supplies and services to the oil industry.
Cost: $145.00
Frequency: Annual October
Circulation: 2,500

20394 **West Coast Petroleum Industry Directory**
Economic Insight
3004 Sw 1st Ave
Portland, OR 97201-4708

503-222-2425; Fax: 503-242-2968
info@econ.com
www.econ.com

Sam Van Vactor, President

Individuals and companies that refine, buy and sell oil and petroleum products are listed.
Cost: $85.00
204 Pages
Frequency: Quarterly

20395 **World Oil-Marine Drilling Rigs**
Gulf Publishing Company
3301 Allen Parkway
Houston, TX 77019-1896

713-294-4301

Offers information on over 600 mobile and self-contained drilling rigs including submersibles, drillships and barges.
Cost: $11.00
Frequency: Annual
Circulation: 30,000

Industry Web Sites

20396 **http://gold.greyhouse.com**
G.O.L.D Grey House OnLine Databases

Grey House Publishing's online database platform, GOLD, offers Quick Search, Keyword Search and Expert Search for most business sectors including petroleum and allied services markets. The GOLD platform makes finding the information you need quick and easy - whether you're a novice searcher or an experienced database user. All of Grey House's directory products are available for subscription on the GOLD platform.

20397 **www.aesc.net**
Association of Energy Service Companies

Professional trade association for well-site service contractors and businesses providing goods and services to well-site contractors. Develops and sells training and safety materials.

20398 **www.aopl.org**
Association of Oil Pipe Lines

Assembles statistics and other data relating to the pipeline industry for presentation to Congress, government departments, trade associations, and the public.

20399 **www.api.org**
American Petroleum Institute

The only national trade association that represents all aspects of America's oil and natural gas industry. Members are producers, refiners, suppliers, pipeline operators and marine transporters, as well as service and supply companies that support all segments of the industry.

20400 **www.bpnews.com**
Butane-Propane News

Petroleum and propane industry news.

20401 **www.entelec.org**
Energy Telecommunications and Electrical Assoc

A user association focusing on communications and control technologies used by petroleum, natural gas, pipeline and electric utility companies.

20402 **www.greyhouse.com**
Grey House Publishing

Authoritative reference directories for most business sectors including petroleum and allied products marktes. Users can search the online databases with varied search criteria allowing for custom searches by product category, geographic area, sales volume, keyword, subject and more. Full Grey House catalog and online ordering also available.

20403 **www.iadc.org**
International Association of Drilling Contractors

Conducts educational and training programs. Sponsors safety contest and bestows awards.

20404 **www.liquidrecyclers.org**
NORA, An Association of Responsible Recyclers

Members are companies that reprocess used antifreeze, wastewater, oil filters, chemicals and companies that provide products or services to the industry.

20405 **www.naro-us.org**
National Association of Royalty Owners

Assists mineral and royalty owners in the effective management of their mineral properties. Provides information on tax, regulatory, and legislative matters. Conducts seminars and bestows awards.

20406 **www.noraoil.com**
National Oil Recyclers Association

Members are companies that reprocess used oil into fuel oil or recycle antifreeze, wastewater, oil filters and companies that provide products or services to the industry.

20407 **www.npc.org**
National Petroleum Council

Self-supporting federal advisory body to the Secretary of Energy established in 1946 at the request of President Truman.

20408 **www.npga.org**
National Propane Gas Association

Members are producers and distributors of liquefied petroleum gas and equipment manufacturers.

20409 **www.oilscouts.org**
International Oil Scouts Association

Compiles statistics on exploration and development wells in the US. Offers professional development and scholarship programs.

20410 **www.pei.org**
Petroleum Equipment Institute

Members are makers and distributors of equipment used in service stations, bulk plants and other petroleum marketing facilities.

20411 **www.pttc.org**
Petroleum Technology Transfer Council

Fosters the effective transfer of exploration and production technology to US petroleum producers through regional resource centers, workshops, websites, publications, etc.

20412 **www.spwla.org**
Society of Professional Well Log Analysts

Promotes the evaluation of formations, through well logging techniques, in order to locate gas, oil and other minerals.

20413 **www.wspa.org**
Western States Petroleum Association

For companies that refine, produce, transport, and market petroleum and petroleum products in six western states: Arizona, California, Oregon, Nevada, Hawaii and Washington.

Associations

20414 ASPCA
424 E 92nd St
New York, NY 10128-6804

212-876-7566; Fax: 212-876-0014
publicinformation@aspca.org
www.aspca.org
Facebook, Twitter, Pinterest, YouTube, Google+

Tim F. Wray, Chair
Frederick Tanne, Vice- Chair
Frederik Gradin, Treasurer
Sally Spooner, Secretary
Matthew Bershadker, President & CEO

Society for the humane treatment of animals, established in 1866.
300+ Members
Founded in 1866

20415 American Animal Hospital Association
12575 W Bayaud Ave
Lakewood, CO 80228-2021

303-986-2800; Fax: 303-986-1700
www.aaha.org
Facebook, Twitter, LinkedIn, Youtube

John Albers, Executive Director
Ellin Davis, Secretary

A group of hospitals and animal practitioners serving the industry.
33000 Members
Founded in 1933

20416 American Cat Fanciers Association
PO Box 1949
Nixa, MO 65714-1949

417-725-1530; Fax: 417-725-1533
ACFA@aol.com
www.acfacat.com

Doug Blackmore, President
Alan Lanners, First VP
Donald Finger, Second VP
Cindy Skeen, Executive Director

Central registry for cats. Sanctions shows, publishes a bimonthly newsletter, offers a yearbook and maintains pedigree records.
800 Members
Founded in 1955

20417 American Farriers Association
4059 Iron Works Pkwy
Suite 1
Lexington, KY 40511

859-233-7411
877-268-4505; Fax: 859-231-7862
info@americanfarriers.org
www.americanfarriers.org
Facebook

Thomas Dubois, President
Jon Johnson, President-Elect
Dave Johnson, Vice President
Bruce Worman, Treasurer
Donnie Perkinson, Secretary

To further the professional development of farriers, to provide leadership and resource for the benefit of the farrier industry, and to improve the welfare of the horse through continuing farrier education.
2.4M Members
Founded in 1971

20418 American Federation of Aviculture
STAT Marketing
11240 Waples Mill Road
Suite 200
Fairfax, VA 22030

703-281-4043; Fax: 703-359-7562
info@aaham.org
www.aaham.org
Facebook, Twitter, LinkedIn, YouTube, Google+, Pinterest

Christine Stottlemyer, Chair
Victoria Di Tomaso, President
John Currier, First VP
Lori Sickelbaugh, Second VP
Amy Mitchell, Treasurer

Information for manufacturers, suppliers, distributors and retailers of exotic birds and related products, including feed, seeds, cages, toys, vitamins and minerals.
Founded in 1968

20419 American Humane Association
1400 16th Street NW
Suite 360
Washington, DC 20036

818-501-0123
800-227-4645; Fax: 818-762-0908
info@americanhumane.org
www.americanhumane.org
Facebook, Twitter, LinkedIn, YouTube, RSS, Pinterest

Robin R. Ganzert, President & CEO
Audrey Lang, Sr. Vice President
Cliffard Rose, Chief Financial Officer
Stephanie Carmody, General Counsel
Kwane Stewart, National Director

Protects children and animals from cruelty, neglect, abuse, and exploitation.
Founded in 1877

20420 American Kennel Club
260 Madison Ave
New York, NY 10016

212-696-8200; Fax: 212-696-8239
info@akc.org
www.akc.org
Facebook, Twitter, YouTube, Pinterest, Google+, I

Ronald Menaker, Chairman
Carl C. Ashby, Vice Chairman
Dennis B. Sprung, President
James P. Crowley, Executive Secretary
Joseph V. Baffuto Jr., Chief Financial Officer

The prinicipal registry of pure-bred dogs in the United States. More ways to enjoy your dog.
15000 Members
Founded in 1884

20421 American Morgan Horse Association
4066 Shelburne Rd
Suite 5
Shelburne, VT 05482

802-985-4944; Fax: 802-985-8897
info@morganhorse.com
morganhorse.com
Facebook, Twitter, Youtube, Pinterest

Jeff Gove, President
Kris Breyer, Vice President
Carol Fletcher, Vice President of Finance
Julie Broadway, Executive Director

Information for Morgan horse breeders and owners.
7000 Members
Founded in 1909

20422 American Paint Horse Association
2800 Meacham Boulevard
Fort Worth, TX 76137

817-834-2742; Fax: 817-834-3152
askapha@apha.com
www.apha.com
Facebook, Twitter, YouTube

Ron Shelly, President
Susie Shaw, President-Elect
George Ready, Vice President
Dr. Craig Wood, Senior Committee Member
Billy L. Smith, Executive Director

Information for owners and riders of American Paint Horses.
55000 Members
Founded in 1960

20423 American Pet Products Association
255 Glenville Rd.
Greenwich, CT 06831

203-532-0000
800-452-1225; Fax: 203-532-0551
www.americanpetproducts.org

Bob Vetere, President & CEO
Andrew Darmohraj, EVP & COO

Trade association of manufacturers, manufacturers' representatives, importers and livestock suppliers.
1200 Members
Founded in 1958

20424 American Pet Products Manufacturers Association
255 Glenville Road
Greenwich, CT 06831

203-532-0000
800-452-1225; Fax: 203-532-0551
andy@appma.org
www.americanpetproducts.org

Robert Merar, Chairman
Bob Vetere, President & CEO
Andrew Darmohraj, Executive Vice President & COO
Steve Ware, Treasurer
Edith Martingnetti, General Mgr/Exhibitor Registration

Information for manufacturers of pet products and service providers in the pet industry.
Frequency: Annual
Founded in 1958

20425 American Rabbit Breeders Association
PO Box 5667
Bloomington, IL 61702

309-664-7500; Fax: 309-664-0941
info@arba.net
arba.net

Josh Humphries, President
Randy Shumaker, VP
Eric Stewart, Executive Director
David Freeman, Treasurer
Roger Hassenpflug, Director

Information for rabbit breeders and owners.
23000 Members
Founded in 1910

20426 American Veterinary Medical Association
1931 N Meacham Rd
Suite 100
Schaumburg, IL 60173-4360

847-303-6142
800-248-2862; Fax: 847-925-1329
sgranskog@avma.org
www.avma.org
Facebook, Twitter, LinkedIn, YouTube, Flickr

Tim Frey, Manager
Michael Walters, Director Communications Division
Dr. Gail Golab, Assistant Director

Publishes various journals and information for members. Acts as a clearinghouse for veterinarians.
86500 Members
Founded in 1863

20427 **Animal Health Institute**
1325 G St NW
Suite 700
Washington, DC 20005-3127

202-637-2440; Fax: 202-393-1667
rphillips@ahi.org
www.ahi.org
Facebook, Twitter, Flickr, YouTube

Alexander S.Mathews, President & CEO
Ron Phillips, VP Legislative/Public Affairs
Dr Richard A A.Carnevale, VP, Regulator
Dr Kent McClure, General Counsel
Carolyn S Ayers, VP, Admin. & Finance

Represents manufacturers of animal health care products.
24 Members
Founded in 1941

20428 **Animal Legal Defense Fund**
170 East Cotati Avenue
Cotati, CA 94931

707-795-2533; Fax: 707-795-7280
info@aldf.org
www.aldf.org
Facebook, Twitter, YouTube, Pinterest

Sarah Luick, Chair
Marilyn Forbes, Vice- Chair
Lisa Brewer, Secretary
Jim Rockenbach, Treasurer
Stephen Wells, Executive Director

Information on animal protection, wildlife conservation and animal rights.
10000 Members
Founded in 1979

20429 **Association of Pet Dog Trainers**
The Association of Pet Dog Trainers
2365 Harrodsburg Road A325
Lexington, KY 40504

800-738-3647; Fax: 864-331-0767
education@apdt.com
www.apdt.com
Facebook, Twitter, LinkedIn

Amber Burckhalter, Board Chair
Jill-Marie O'Brien, Board Vice-Chair
Robin Bennet, Board Treasurer
Casey Lomanaco, Board Secretary
Megan Armstrong, Board Member

Enhancing the human/dog relationship by educating trainers, other animal professionals and the public and advocating dog friendly training.
6000 Members
Founded in 1993

20430 **Delta Society**
875 124th Ave NW
Suite 101
Bellevue, WA 98005

425-679-5500
800-869-6898; Fax: 425-679-5539
info@deltasociety.org
petpartners.org
Facebook, Twitter, LinkedIn, YouTube, Pinterest, Instagram

C. Annie Magnant, President & CEO
David E. Williams, Chief Medical Officer
Linda Dicus, Executive Assistant
Chris Calabro, Director of Technology
Mary M. Callahan, Senior National Director

Information on human-animal interactions. Service Dog Center provides information and advocacy for dogs trained to assist people with disabilities. Pet Partners Program trains volunteers, health professionals, animals for animal-assisted therapy and activities.
4.6M Members
Founded in 1977

20431 **International Association of Pet Cemeteries & Crematories**
4991 Peachtree Road
Atlanta, GA 30341

518-594-3000
800-952-5541; Fax: 770-457-8160
info@iaopc.com
www.iaopc.com

Angie Hansen, President
Robert Blosser, Vice President
Debra Bjorling, Treasurer
Scott Hunter, Advisory Council
Donna Bethune, Executive Administrator

Educates the public on pet burials and the disposal of sick and diseased animals to eliminate contamination of ground and water. Conducts workshops and research projects.
175 Members
Founded in 1971

20432 **International Boarding & Pet Services Asso**
1702 E Pikes Peak Avenue
Colorado Springs, CO 80909

719-667-1600; Fax: 719-667-0116
info@abka.com
www.ibpsa.com

James Krack, Executive Manager

Information about the pet industry products, including pet foods, supplements, retail supplies, construction materials, cages, computers and software.
Founded in 1977

20433 **International Professional Groomers**
6475 Wallace Rd NW
Salem, OR 97304

503-551-2397; Fax: 503-581-1220
info@ipgicmg.com
www.ipgicmg.com
Facebook, Twitter

Linda Easton, President

Represents the professional pet grooming industry, providing continuing education to members and public information on the proper care treatment. also publishes a quarterly newsletter.
500 Members
Founded in 1988

20434 **National Association of Professional Pet Care**
1120 Route 73
Suite 200
Mt. Laurel, NJ 08054

856-439-0324; Fax: 856-439-0525
napps@petsitters.org
www.petsitters.org
Facebook, Twitter, LinkedIn, Google+, Pinterest

Yvette Gonzales, President
Jessica Abernathy, President Elect
Cyndy Lippert, Secretary-Treasurer
Cathleen Delaney, Administrative Director
Kara Jenkins, Director

Nonprofit organization dedicated to serving the needs of professional pet care providers. Promotes ethical standards and fosters cooperation among members in the pet care industry.
2200+ Members
Founded in 1989

20435 **National Congress of Animal Trainers**
23675 W Chardon Rd
Grayslake, IL 60030-9584

847-546-0717; Fax: 847-546-3454

John F Cuneo, President

For trainers and breeders of rare animals.
300 Members

20436 **National Dog Groomers Association of American**
PO Box 101
Clark, PA 16113

724-962-2711; Fax: 724-962-1919
ndga@nationaldoggroomers.com
www.nationaldoggroomers.com
Facebook

Jeffrey Reynolds, Executive Director
Wendy Booth, Certification Coordinator
Sue Zecco, Contest Coordinator

To unite groomers through membership and offer optional certification testing throughout the United States.
2.4M Members
Founded in 1969

20437 **National Humane Education Society**
PO Box 340
Charles Town, WV 25414-0340

304-725-0506; Fax: 304-725-1523
information@nhes.org
www.nhes.org
Facebook, Twitter, YouTube

Anna C Briggs, Founder
James D Taylor, President
Cynthia L Taylor, Vice President
Virginia Dungan, Treasurer
Christina B Fernandez, Secretary

Mission to foster a sentiment of kindness to animals.
400M+ Members
Founded in 1948

20438 **National Pigeon Association**
17128 Colima Drive Unit 603
Hacienda Heights, CA 91745

626-820-8080
npasecretary@yahoo.com
www.npausa.com
Facebook, Twitter

Jerry Gagne, President
Lennie Mefferd, Secretary/Treasurer
Tim Stajkowski, Eastern Vise President
Roger Hansen, Western Vice President

Special information for members.
Founded in 1920

20439 **National Taxidermists Association**
PO Box 384
Pocahontas, IL 62275

618-669-2929; Fax: 618-669-2909
nationaltaxidermistassoc@frontier.com
www.nationaltaxidermists.com
Facebook, Twitter, YouTube, Google+, Pinterest

Michelle Burkholder, President
Russell Knight, Vice President
Harry Whitehead, Treasurer
Tim Thacker, Secretary
Garvice Thomas, Board of Directors

Preserving animals to their natural form.
2500 Members
Founded in 1972

20440 **PETCO Foundation**
654 Richland Hills Dr.
San Antonio, TX 78245

858-453-7845
888-824-7257; Fax: 858-909-2618
www.petco.com
Facebook, Twitter, Instagram

Brian Devine, Chairman
Charlie Piscitello, President
Judith Munoz, Vice President
Susanne Kogut, Executive Director
Rana Smith, Director

We put animals first. The Petco Foundation supports community organization and efforts that enhance the lives of companion animals.
Founded in 1999

20441 People for the Ethical Treatment of Animals (PETA)

501 Front Street
Norfolk, VA 23510

757-622-7382; Fax: 757-622-0457
info@peta.org
www.peta.org
Facebook, Twitter, Pinterest, Google+

Ingrid Newkirk, President

Opposes all forms of animal exploitation. Seeks to educate the public on what the group sees as the three major institutionalized cruelty issues: the exploitation and abuse of animals in experimentation, the manufacturing of fur apparel, and slaughtering for human consumption.
80000 Members
Founded in 1980

20442 Pet Care Services Association

2760 N Academy Boulevard
Suite 120
Colorado Springs, CO 80917

719-667-1600
877-570-7788; Fax: 719-667-0116
www.petcareservices.org

Joan Saunders, CEO

Seeks to upgrade the industry through educational programs and conventions. Promotes code of ethics and accreditation programs for kennel operators.
2400 Members
Founded in 1977

20443 Pet Food Institute

2025 M St NW
Suite 800
Washington, DC 20036

202-367-1120; Fax: 202-367-2120
info@petfoodinstitute.org
www.petfoodinstitute.org

Duane H Ekedahl, Executive Director

Represents dog and cat food manufacturers. Supporting initiative to advance the quality of dog and cat food. Supporting research in pet nutrition and the important role of pets in our society. Promoting the overall care and well-being of pets.
100 Members
Founded in 1958

20444 Pet Industry Distributors Association

3465 Box Hill Corporate Center Drive
Suite H
Abingdon, MD 21009

443-640-1060; Fax: 410-569-3340
pida@kingmgmt.org
www.pida.org
LinkedIn

Celeste Powers, President
Marci Hickey, Dir, Meetings & Member Services
Debbie Dacre, Director, Finance
Nina Bull, Association Coordinator

Represents wholesaler-distributors of pet products, providing training and education to members.
190 Members
Founded in 1968

20445 Pet Industry Joint Advisory Council

1615 Duke Street
Suite 100
Alexandria, VA 22314

202-452-1525
800-553-7387; Fax: 202-452-1516
info@pijac.org
www.pijac.org
Facebook, Twitter

Ken Oh, Chair
Andy Ponte, First Vice-Chair
Marcie Whichard, Second Vice-chair
Laura Reid, Secretary/Treasurer
Edwin Sayres, President & CEO

Monitors federal and state regulations and legislation affecting industry. Sponsors research and educational projects including certification programs in veterinary care and husbandry for companion animals, in-store training videos, etc.
1500 Members
Founded in 1971

20446 Pet Lovers Association

PO Box 145
Joppa, MD 21085

410-679-0978

Elden Harrison, President

Advises pet owners of their responsibilities.
Founded in 1983

20447 Pet Pride

P.O. Box 1055
Pacific Palisades, CA 90272

310-836-5427
www.petpride.org

Ruth Argust, President

Public education programs for proper cat care.
50000 Members
Founded in 1965

20448 Pet Sitters International

201 East King Street
King, NC 27021-9163

336-983-9222; Fax: 336-983-5266
info@petsit.com
www.petsit.com
Facebook, Twitter, LinkedIn, YouTube, Google+

Terry Chance, Marketing Director
Beth Stultz, Marketing Manager
Chris Sutphin, Member Services Manager
Patti Moran, President
Mike Moran, Vice President

Society of professional pet sitters. Membership provides valuable benefits - educational resources for those engaged in the pet-sitting industry. Also provides a forum to network with peers who share a common vision of excellence in at-home pet care.
7000 Members
Founded in 1994

20449 PetCenter.Com: Internet Animal Hospital PetFoodDirect.com

189 Main Street
Harleysville, PA 19438

215-513-1999; Fax: 215-513-7286

T J Dunn, Jr DVM, Director

Award winning virtual animal hospital for dog and cat love. Mission of providing dog and cat caretakers with a better understanding of the medical and surgical treatment of pets. Created by veterinarians under the direction of Dr T.J. Dunn, all articles are presented in non-medical terms, just as if the veterinarian was speaking to you personally in a real exam room. Associated with PetFoodDirect.com

20450 PetFoodDirect.com

189 Main St
Harleysville, PA 19438

215-513-1999
877-738-3663; Fax: 215-513-7286
www.petfooddirect.com
Facebook, Twitter

Brock Weatherup, CEO
Jon Roska, Jr, Founder & VP of Merchandising
Rose Hamilton, Chief Marketing Officer
Matthew Murray, VP, Finance
Joe Falkenstein, CFO & VP of Operations

Largest pure play entailer for premium pet food, supplies and accessories on the internet. Our customers can order from a huge selection of pet products, have access to value-added services, including information on pet healthcare and nutrition.
Founded in 1997

20451 US Animal Health Association

4221 Mitchell Ave
Saint Joseph, MO 64507

816-671-1144; Fax: 816-671-1201
usaha@usaha.org
www.usaha.org

Marty Zaluski, President
Ben Richey, Executvie Director
Kelly Janicek, Executive Assistant

Science-based, non-profit, voluntary organization. Concerning disease eradication, animal health, emerging diseases, food safety, public health, animal welfare, and international trade.
1400 Members
Founded in 1897

20452 United Kennel Club

100 E Kilgore Rd
Kalamazoo, MI 49002-5584

269-343-9020; Fax: 269-343-7037
conformation@ukcdogs.com
www.ukcdogs.com

Tanya Raab, President
Todd Kellam, Senior Vice President
Angela Smith, Senior Director of Research & Dev
Taylor Armstrong, Customer Service Manager
Allen Gingerich, Senior Director of Hunting Events

Responsible for dog pedigrees and transfer of ownership of pedigree dogs. Best registry of pure-bred dogs.
50 Members
Founded in 1898

20453 Western and English Sales Association

451 E 58th Avenue
Suite 4128
Denver, CO 80216

303-295-1040
800-295-1041; Fax: 303-295-0941
info@denver-wesa.com
wesatradeshow.com
Facebook

Gerald Adame, Chair
Jay Phillips, President
Patrick Powers, Vice President
Scott Tucker, Secretary & Treasurer

Trade association
1200 Members
Founded in 1921

20454 World Pet Association

135 West Lemon Ave.
Monrovia, CA 91016

626-447-2222; Fax: 626-447-8350
info@wpamail.org
worldpetassociation.org

Jim Boschee, Chairman
Michael Twain, CFO
Vic Mason, 1st Vice Chair
Barry Berman, 2nd Vice Chair
Pete Risano, Secretary

A non-profit, membership-controlled trade association organized to represent its members and the interests of the companion animal and product industry. America's oldest pet industry trade association. Our mission is to promote responsible pet care worldwide.

20455 **World Society for the Protection of Animals**
89 South Street
2nd Floor
Boston, MA 02111
508-879-8350
800-833-9772; Fax: 212-564-4250
wspa@wspausa.com
www.wspa-usa.org
Facebook, Twitter, YouTube
Laura Simpson, USA Director
Peter Davies, Director General
Robert S Cummings, President
John Bowen, Secretary
Carter Luke, Treasurer
International animal protection news reports. Lobbies for effective animal welfare laws and provides educational material.
12 Members

Newsletters

20456 **ASPCA Report**
424 E 92nd St
New York, NY 10128-6804
212-876-7566
www.aspca.com
Janice Borzendowski, Publisher
Ed Sayres, Director
Kathryn Investigations, Director
Bonnie Shelter, Operations Manager
Pet care news, issues, features and reviews.
Frequency: Weekly
Founded in 1866

20457 **Animals International**
World Society for the Protection of Animals
34 Deloss Street
Framingham, MA 01702
508-879-8350; Fax: 508-620-0786
wspa@wspausa.com
Laura Salter, USA Director
Susan Sherwin, Press Contact
International animal protection news reports.
Cost: $10.00
12 Pages
Frequency: Quarterly
Founded in 1981

20458 **Animals' Advocate**
Animal Legal Defense Fund
170 E Cotati Avenue
Cotati, CA 94931-4474
707-795-2533; Fax: 707-795-7280
info@aldf.org
www.aldf.org/action.htm
Stephen Wells, Executive Director
A newsletter offering information on animal protection, wildlife conservation and animal rights.
4 Pages
Frequency: Monthly

20459 **Anthrozoos**
Delta Society
875 124th Ave Ne
Suite 101
Bellevue, WA 98005-2531
425-226-7357; Fax: 425-235-1076
info@deltasociety.org
www.deltasociety.org
Lawrence Norvell, CEO
Robert T Franklin, Secretary
Stephanie LaFarge, Secretary
David BellRetired, Treasurer
Scientific journal on the interactions of people, animals and nature.
Cost: $40.00
72 Pages
Frequency: Quarterly
Circulation: 800
Founded in 1977

20460 **Association of Pet Dog Trainers Newsletter**
750 Executive Center Dr
Box 35
Greenville, SC 29615
864-331-0764
800-738-3647; Fax: 856-439-0525
information@apdt.com
www.apdt.com
Richard Spencer, Executive Director
Pat Miller, Treasurer
Sue Pearson, Treasurer
Kellyann Conway-Payne, Vice President
Pia Silvani, Secretary
Building better trainers through education.
Founded in 1993

20461 **Cat Industry Newsletter**
Good Communications
PO Box 10069
Austin, TX 78766-1069
512-454-9062
800-968-1738; Fax: 512-454-3420
www.petfoodindustry.com
Ross Becker, Editor
Business newsletter for catfood, cat products and cat litter industries. Covers business news, marketing, new products in the pipeline, industry data.
Cost: $295.00
6 Pages
Frequency: Monthly
ISSN: 1074-7788
Founded in 1992
Printed in on matte stock

20462 **Country Folks Mane Stream**
Lee Publications
6113 State Hwy. 5
P.O. Box 121
Palatine Bridge, NY 13428-0121
518-673-3237
888-596-5329; Fax: 518-673-2699
subscriptions@leepub.com
cfmanestream.com
Frederick Lee, Publsiher
Joan Kark-Wren, Editor
Bruce Button, President
Larry Price, Marketing Manager
Ian Hitchener, Sales Manager
Contents include horse & hoof care, equine events, tack and a equipment. Serves all breeds and disciplines in the Northeast and Mid-Atlantic equine markets.
Frequency: Monthly

20463 **Dog Industry Newsletter**
Good Communications
PO Box 10069
Austin, TX 78766-1069
512-454-9062
800-968-1738; Fax: 512-454-3420
www.petfoodindustry.com
Ross Becker, Editor
Business newsletter for petfood,and pet products industries.Covers business news, marketing, new products in the pipeline, industry data.
Cost: $295.00
10 Pages
Frequency: Monthly
ISSN: 1074-777X
Founded in 1990
Printed in on matte stock

20464 **Humane News**
Associated Humane Societies
124 Evergreen Ave
Newark, NJ 07114-2133
973-824-7080; Fax: 973-824-5937
associatedhumane@aol.com
www.associatedhumanesocieties.org
Roseann Trezza, Executive Director
News concerning animal welfare.
24 Pages
Frequency: Monthly
Circulation: 75000
Founded in 1906

20465 **IPG Newsletter**
International Professional Groomers
6475 Wallace Rd NW
Salem, OR 97304-9743
847-758-1938
800-258-4765; Fax: 847-758-8031
Judy Kurpiel, President
A quarterly newsletter published by the International Professional Groomers.
6 Pages
Frequency: Quarterly
Circulation: 500
Founded in 1988

20466 **International Pet Industry News**
Good Communications
PO Box 10069
Austin, TX 78766-1069
512-454-9062
800-968-1738; Fax: 512-454-3420
www.petfoods.com
Ross Becker, Editor
Business newsletter for internatioal petfood, pet products industries. Covers business news, marketing, new products in the pipeline, industry data.
Cost: $295.00
8 Pages
Frequency: Monthly
ISSN: 1074-780X
Founded in 1993
Printed in on matte stock

20467 **K-9 Courier**
PO Box 49
Jerico Springs, MO 64756
Monthly newsletter for breeders.
Frequency: Monthly

20468 **Pet Gazette**
Gazette Publishing
1309 N Halifax Avenue
Daytona Beach, FL 32118-3658
editor@petgazette.net
www.petgazette.net
Robin Nudd, Advertising Coordinator
Amy McWilliams, Circulation

Pictures, anecdotes, cartoons and more for the pet industry.
Cost: $12.50
24 Pages
Frequency: Quarterly
Circulation: 300

20469 Pet Partners Newsletter
Delta Society
875 124th Ave Ne
Suite 101
Bellevue, WA 98005-2531

425-226-7357; Fax: 425-235-1076
www.deltasociety.org

Lawrence Norvell, CEO
Stephanie LaFarge, Secretary
David BellRetired, Treasurer

How-to newsletter for pet owners who volunteer in animal-assisted therapy and activity programs.
Cost: $6.00
2 Pages
Frequency: Monthly
Circulation: 2500
Founded in 1977

20470 Pet Planet Newsletter
PO Box 150899
Denver, CO 80215-0899

303-986-2800; Fax: 303-986-1700
www.healthypet.com

John W Albers, Executive Director
Gregg Takashima, Vice President

A group of hospitals and animal practitioners serving the industry.
Cost: $60.00
64 Pages
Frequency: Bi-Monthly
Circulation: 14,000
Founded in 1985
Printed in on glossy stock

20471 Pet Stuff
Pet Stuff
608 Tumbleweed Lane
Fall Brook, CA 92028-9446

760-728-9306; Fax: 760-728-9735

Robert Tanner, Publisher

A direct co-op mailing service to the pet industry. Accepts advertising.
Frequency: BiWeekly

20472 PetLetter
Pet Industry Joint Advisory Council
1146 19th St NW
Suite 350
Washington, DC 20036-2438

202-452-1525
800-553-7387; Fax: 202-452-1516
info@pijac.org
www.pijac.org

Michael Addox, VP & General Counsel
Michael Canning, President

Contains a breadth of information on the current status of pending state and federal legislation, science and educational program news, the release of PIJAC publications, other PIJAC news, and a list of the newest Certified Anical Specialists

20473 Veterinary Industry Newsletter
Good Communications
PO Box 10069
Austin, TX 78766-1069

512-454-9062
800-968-1738; Fax: 512-454-3420

Ross Becker, Editor

Business newsletter for petfood, animal health and veterinary industries.Covers business news, marketing, new products in the pipeline, industry data.
Cost: $295.00
10 Pages
Frequency: Monthly
ISSN: 1074-7796
Founded in 1993
Printed in one color on matte stock

20474 Watchbird
PO Box 56218
Phoenix, AZ 85079

602-484-0931; Fax: 602-484-0109
webmaster@afabirds.org
www.afabirds.org/

Jerry Crowley, Executive VP
S Rosenbeltt, Circulation Director
Benny Gallaway, President

Journal on conservation, education, bird keeping and breeding.
Circulation: 6000
Founded in 1974

Magazines & Journals

20475 American Farriers Journal
Lessiter Media
P.O. Box 624
Brookfield, WI 53005-5738

262-782-4480
800-645-8455; Fax: 262-782-1252
jmcgovern@lessitermedia.com
www.americanfarriers.com
Facebook, Twitter, LinkedIn, YouTube

Frank Lessiter, Editor
Jeremy McGovern, Executive Editor/Publisher

Devoted to proper hoof care and shoeing.
Cost: $47.95
Frequency: 8/Year

20476 Animal Fair
7 Penn Plaza
11th Floor
New York, NY 10001

212-629-0392; Fax: 212-988-7486
editor@animalfair.com
www.animalfair.com

Wendy Diamond, Editorial Director
Wendy Diamond, CEO/President
Cost: $19.95
Frequency: Bi-annually
Founded in 1999

20477 Aquarium Fish Magazine
Fancy Publications
PO Box 6050
Mission Viejo, CA 92690

949-855-8822; Fax: 949-855-3045

Devoted to pet stores and readers who keep fresh-water and saltwater species of tropical fish.
Cost: $15.97
Frequency: Monthly
Circulation: 49,700
Founded in 1905

20478 Bird Talk
Fancy Publications
3 Burroughs
Irvine, CA 92618

949-855-8822; Fax: 949-855-3045
www.birdtalkmagazine.com

Edward Bauman, Editor

Pet news.
Cost: $13.99
64 Pages
Frequency: Monthly
Founded in 1983

20479 BirdTimes
Pet Publishing
7-L Dundas Circle
Greensboro, NC 27407

336-292-4047; Fax: 336-292-4272
www.petpublishing.com

Mike Hammond, Publisher
Cost: $17.97
Circulation: 50000
ISSN: 1096-7923
Founded in 1992
Printed in 4 colors on glossy stock

20480 Bloodlines
United Kennel Club
100 E Kilgore Rd
Portage, MI 49002-5584

269-343-9020; Fax: 269-343-7037
webmaster@ukcdogs.com
www.ukcdogs.com

Wayne Cavanaugh, President
Rosie Reeds, Advertising

A comprehensive publication covering breeding, showing and registering of animals.
Cost: $24.00
Frequency: Monthly
Founded in 1898

20481 Cat Fancy Magazine
Fancy Publications
3 Burroughs
Irvine, CA 92618

949-855-8822; Fax: 949-855-3045

Susan Logan, Editor
Sandy Meyer, Managing Editor

Offers information to cat owners and pet shop owners regarding cats.
Cost: $14.99
Frequency: Monthly
Founded in 1965

20482 Cats & Kittens
Pet Publishing
7-L Dundas Circle
Greensboro, NC 27407

336-292-4047; Fax: 336-292-4272
www.petpublishing.com

Mike Hammond, Publisher
Rita Davis, Editor

Cat enthusiast magazine.
Cost: $19.97
52 Pages
Circulation: 50000
ISSN: 1079-8285
Founded in 1998
Printed in 4 colors on glossy stock

20483 Cats Magazine
PRIMEDIA Enthusiast Group
3585 Engineering Drive
Suite 100
Norcross, GA 30092

678-421-3000
800-216-1423; Fax: 212-745-0121
www.primedia.com

Mike Carney, Publisher
Doug Stange, Editor
Kelly P Conlin, CEO

For cat owners.
Founded in 1989

20484 Dog & Kennel
Pet Publishing
7-L Dundas Circle
Greensboro, NC 27407

336-292-4047; Fax: 336-292-4272
www.petpublishing.com

Mike Hammond, Publisher
Rita Davis, Editor

Dog enthusiast magazine.
Cost: $4.99
64 Pages
Circulation: 50000
ISSN: 1079-8277
Founded in 1996
Printed in 4 colors on glossy stock

20485 **Dog Fancy Magazine**
Fancy Publications
3 Burroughs
Irvine, CA 92618

949-855-8822
800-546-7730; Fax: 949-855-3045

Susane Chney, Editor
Scott Montey, Publisher
Dock Style, CEO/President
Christy Chism, Circulation Manager
Steven Sapoher, Marketing Manager

A magazine covering the world of dogs.
Cost: $96.00
Frequency: Monthly

20486 **Dog World Magazine**
Charels A Tupta
3 Burroughs
Irvine, CA 92618

949-855-8822
800-361-8056; Fax: 949-855-3045

Charels A Tupta, Publisher
Donna Marcel, Chairman

Written for the serious dog enthusiast, Dog World is the authority on dog care. Special editorial on behavior, nutrition, health care and training, plus thousands of classified and display listings in every issue.
Cost: $14.99
132 Pages
Frequency: Monthly
Circulation: 64876
Founded in 1916

20487 **Dogs USA**
Fancy Publications
3 Burroughs
Irvine, CA 92618

949-855-8822; Fax: 949-855-3045

Edward Bauman, Editor

Registration, breeding, pedigree news, bloodlines, etc. for dogs.
Cost: $5.95
Frequency: Annual

20488 **Equestrian Retailer**
Morris Communications
PO Box 7980
Colorado Springs, CO 80907-5339

719-633-5524; Fax: 719-633-1392
www.equestrianretailer.com

Rick Swan, Associate Publisher
Kathy Swan, Executive Editor
William S Morris, President
Karen Ficklin, Circulation Manager
Rob Fulkerson, General Manager

Serves to promote profitablity in the equine industry.
60 Pages
Circulation: 11000
Founded in 1998
Printed in 4 colors on matte stock

20489 **Freshwater and Marine Aquarium Magazine**
RC Modeler Corporation
PO Box 487
Sierra Madre, CA 91025-0487

626-355-1476
800-523-1736; Fax: 626-355-6415

Patricia Crews, President

A magazine aimed at aquarium pertaining to fish and marine life, hobboyists.
Cost: $22.00
200 Pages
Frequency: Monthly
Circulation: 65000
Founded in 1978
Printed in 4 colors on glossy stock

20490 **Good Dog!**
PO Box 10069
Austin, TX 78766-1069

512-454-9062
800-968-1738; Fax: 512-454-3420
www.gooddogmagazine.com

Judith Becker, Editor
Ross Becker, Publisher

Consumer magazine for dog owners. Nationally known for its test reports on dog food and products for dogs. Also publishes books on dog food, puppy selection and genetics.
Cost: $12.00
36 Pages
Circulation: 40000
ISSN: 0899-6024
Founded in 1988
Printed in 4 colors

20491 **NAPPS Network**
Association of Professional Pet Sitters
15000 Commerce Parkway
Suite C
Mt Laurel, NJ 08054

856-439-0324; Fax: 856-439-0525
napps@ahint.com
www.petsitters.org

Sally Liddick, Co-Director
Charlotte Reed, Editor/Publisher
Jerry Wentz, President
Caitlin Dougherty, Manager
Kimberly Libucki, Administrative Assistant

Official publication of the Association of Professional Pet Sitters.
Frequency: Quarterly
Circulation: 1500
Founded in 1989

20492 **Pet Age Magazine**
HH Backer Associates
18 S Michigan Ave
Suite 1100
Chicago, IL 60603-3233

312-578-1818; Fax: 312-578-1819
hhbacker@hhbacker.com

Patty Backer, President
Karen MacLeod, Editor in Chief
Mark Mitera, VP
Beth Morrissey, Production Coordinator
Cathy Foster, Senior Editor

Pet AGE helps pet/pet suppliers ratailers suceed in today competive marketplace. Editorial features emphasize progressive management and trends and issues. Accepts advertising.
Cost: $70.00
80 Pages
Frequency: Monthly
Circulation: 23076
ISSN: 0098-5406
Founded in 1965
Printed in on glossy stock

20493 **Pet Business Magazine**
Pet Business
333 7th Ave
11th Floor
New York, NY 10001-5004

212-979-4861; Fax: 646-674-0102
www.petbusiness.com

Craig Rexford, VP
Mike Burnette, Founder
Jerry Thom, Founder
David Litwak, Editor In Chief
Nisa Cirulnick, Sales & Marketing Coordinator

Trade magazine for the pet industry. News, new products, animal care and legislative topics. Accepts advertising.
Cost: $49.97
Circulation: 24,000
Founded in 1973
Mailing list available for rent: 19.5M names
Printed in 4 colors on glossy stock

20494 **Pet Product News Magazine**
Fancy Publications
3 Burroughs
PO Box 6040
Irvine, CA 92618

949-855-8822; Fax: 949-855-3045

Edward Bauman, Editor

Journal focusing on new products and other industry news.

20495 **Pet Sitter's World**
Pet Sitters International
201 E King St
King, NC 27021-9161

336-983-9222; Fax: 336-983-5266
info@petsit.com
www.petsit.com

Patti Moran, President

Designed to educate pet sitters and affiliated firms on pet-sitting industry buiness practices, ideas, products, field-tested consumer tips and trends
Cost: $36.00
56 Pages
Frequency: Bimonthly
Circulation: 8500
Founded in 1985
Printed in on glossy stock

20496 **Petfood Industry**
WATT Publishing Company
303 N Main Street
Suite 500
Rockford, IL 61101

815-966-5400; Fax: 815-966-6416
www.wattnet.com

James Watt, Chairman/CEO
Greg Watt, President/COO
Jeff Swanson, Publishing Director

The leading global information source for the petfood manufacturing industry, connecting manufacturing organizations with their supplier counterparts.
Cost: $48.00
46 Pages
Frequency: Monthly
Circulation: 9795
ISSN: 0031-6245
Founded in 1959
Printed in 4 colors on glossy stock

Trade Shows

20497 **AVMA Annual Convention**
American Veterinary Medical Association
1931 N Meacham Road
Suite 100
Schaumburg, IL 60173-4360

847-036-6142
800-248-2862; Fax: 847-925-1329
www.avma.org
Facebook, Twitter, LinkedIn, YouTube

Larry Corry DVM, 2009-10 President
Larry Kornegay DVM, 2009-10 President-Elect

Seminar and more than 300 exhibits of products, materials, equipment, data, and services

for veterinary medicine. Education and hands-on labs, exhibit hall, charitable events and networking
10000 Attendees
Frequency: Annual/July

20498 **America's Family Pet Expo**
World Wide Pet Supply Association
406 S 1st Avenue
Arcadia, CA 91006-3829
626-447-2222
800-999-7295; Fax: 626-447-8350
www.wwpsa.com
Rick Newman, President
Lewis M Sutton, CFO
Steve Segner, First VP
Russ Feller, Second Vice President
Dr. Robert Bray, Equine Outreach
Brings together all elements of the companion animal world and promotes responsible pet ownership. Demonstrations, speakers, product exhibits, hobbyist shows, rides for the children, contests and more. 500 booths. April, Orange County, CA
80M Attendees
Frequency: April/September
Founded in 1990

20499 **American Animal Hospital Association Annual Meeting**
American Animal Hospital Association
12575 W Bayaud Avenue
Lakewood, CO 80228
303-986-2800; Fax: 303-986-1700
www.aahanet.org
Donna Johnson, Exhibit Coordinator
Chuck Potter, Annual Meeting Manager
John Albers, Executive Director
250 scientific displays related to small animal veterinary care, computer software, marketing consulting services and pet care products.
3000 Attendees
Frequency: Annual
Founded in 1933

20500 **American College of Veterinary Opthalmologists Conference**
2316 West Northern Avenue
Phoenix, AZ 85021
602-995-2871; Fax: 602-995-1770
Lisa Schultz, Practice Manager
Meeting and 30 exhibits of opthamology equipment and information.
400 Attendees
Frequency: Annual

20501 **American College of Veterinary Surgeons - Veterinary Symposium**
American College of Veterinary Surgeons
19785 Crystal Rock Dr,
Suite 305
Germantown, MD 20874
301-916-0200; Fax: 301-916-2287
acvs@acvs.org
www.acvs.org
Ann T Loew, Executive Director
William B Henry, VP
Mark Markel, Chair
Marvin L Olmstead, ACVS President
Ann Loew, Executive Director
Over 150 exhibits featuring veterinary equipment, supplies and services.
1500 Attendees
Frequency: October 5-7
Founded in 1965

20502 **American Federation of Aviculture Inc**
STAT Marketing
PO Box 91717
Austin, TX 78709
512-585-9800; Fax: 512-858-7029
afaoffice@afabirds.org
www.afabirds.org
Facebook, Twitter
Nancy Speed, National President
Linda Sheaffer, Chair
Jamie Whittaker, First VP
Brent Gattis, Second VP
Brent Andrus, CFO
Annual convention for manufacturers, suppliers, distributors and retailers of exotic birds and related products, including feed, seeds, cages, toys, vitamins and minerals. 65 booths.
750 Attendees
Founded in 1974

20503 **American Humane Association Annual Meeting and Training Conference**
American Humane Association
1400 16th Street NW
Suite 360
Washington, DC 20036
303-792-9900
800-227-4645; Fax: 818-762-0908
info@americanhumane.org
www.americanhumane.org
Facebook, Twitter, RSS, YouTube, Pinterest
Robert R Ganzert, President/CEO
Clifford Rose, CFO
Over 50 exhibits of animal welfare equipment, including pet food, cages, trucks, id programs and veterinary services. Breakfast, luncheon, reception.
700 Attendees
Frequency: Annual
Founded in 1982

20504 **American Morgan Horse Association Grand National Show**
3 Bostwick Road
PO Box 960
Shelburne, VT 05482-0960
802-985-4944; Fax: 802-985-8897
info@morganhorse.com
morganhorse.com
Raymond Gifford, Show Manager
Fred Braden, Executive Director
Offers you a way to enjoy your Morgan in a competitive setting, while enjoying the company of other Morgan exhibitors. 30 booths.
8M Attendees
Frequency: October

20505 **American Paint Horse Association World Championship Horse Shows**
PO Box 961023
Fort Worth, TX 76161-0023
817-834-2742; Fax: 817-834-3152
http://www.apha.com
Carl Parker, President
Richard Cox, VP
Alice Singleton, Senior Committee Member
Ed Robert, Executive Secretary
A 14 day annual event that has become the proving ground for competitors striving to show that they ride or own the best American Paint Horses in the world. 100 booths.
5M Attendees
Frequency: July

20506 **American Pet Products Manufacturers Association National Tradeshow**
255 Glenville Road
Greenwich, CT 06831
203-532-0000
800-452-1225; Fax: 203-532-0551
andy@appma.org
www.americanpetproducts.org
Bob Vetere, COO/Managing Director
Jennifer Bilbao, Marketing/PR Administrator
Andrew Darmohraj, VP/Deputy Managing Director
Jamie Cavanaugh, Trade Show Coordinator
Edith Martingnetti, General Mgr/Exhibitor Registration
Breakfast, reception, and 1400 pet products manufacturers exhibits.
Frequency: Annual
Founded in 1959

20507 **American Rabbit Breeders Association National Convention**
8 Westport Court
Bloomington, IL 61704
309-664-7500; Fax: 309-664-0941
arba.net
Glen Carr, Executive Director
Seminar, banquet, luncheon and 1500 rabbit breeders exhibits.
3000 Attendees
Frequency: Annual
Founded in 1910

20508 **American Veterinary Medical Association Annual Convention**
American Veterinary Medical Association
1931 N Meacham Road
Suite 100
Schaumburg, IL 60173
847-036-6142; Fax: 847-925-1329
convention@avma.org
www.avma.org
Dr Bonnie Beaver, President
David Little, Director
Seminar and 310 exhibits of products, materials, equipment, data, and services for veterinary medicine.
10000 Attendees
Frequency: Annual

20509 **Annual Pet Industry Trade Show**
World Wide Pet Supply Association
406 S 1st Avenue
Arcadia, CA 91006-3829
626-447-2222; Fax: 626-447-8350
www.wwpsa.com
Doug Poindexter, Executive VP
A comprehensive collection of exhibits and educational events unparalleled in the industry.

20510 **Global Pet Expo**
American Pet Products Association
255 Glenville Rd.
Greenwich, CT 06831
203-532-0000
800-452-1225; Fax: 203-532-0551
globalpetexpo@americanpetproducts.org
globalpetexpo.org
Facebook, Twitter, Flickr, YouTube
Andrew Darmohraj, Executive Vice President & COO
Tracey Wilson, Show Manager
Sarah Bopp, Associate Manager
Containing 3,600 booths and 1,174 exhibiting companies, including 300 international exhibitors.
Frequency: Annual

20511 **Global Pet Expo (PIDA)**
Pet Industry Distributors Association
3465 Box Hill Corp. Center Drive
Suite H
Abingdon, MD 21009

443-640-1060; Fax: 410-569-3340
pida@kingmgmt.org
globalpetexpo.org

Celeste Powers, President
Marci Hickey, Dir, Meetings & Member Services
Debbie Dacre, Director, Finance
Nina Bull, Association Coordinator

Containing 3,600 booths and 1,174 exhibiting companies, including 300 international exhibitors.
3000 Attendees
Frequency: March
Founded in 1968

20512 **HH Backer Pet Industry Christmas Trade Show**
HH Backer Associates
200 S Michigan Avenue
Suite 840
Chicago, IL 60604

312-663-4040; Fax: 312-663-5676
hhbacker@hhbacker.com

Patty Backer, President/Publisher
Karen Long MacLeod, Assoc Publisher/Editor in Chief
M Christopher Mitera, VP
Colette Fairchild, CMP, Trade Show Director
Julie Wichert, Sales Manager

Containing 1000 plus booths and 550 plus exhibits consisting of pet supplies, products and services.
9M Attendees
Frequency: October
Founded in 1967

20513 **HH Backer Pet Industry Spring Trade Show**
HH Backer Associates
200 S Michigan Avenue
Suite 840
Chicago, IL 60604

312-663-4040; Fax: 312-663-5676
hhbacker@hhbacker.com

Patty Backer, President/Publisher
Karen Long MacLeod, Assoc Publisher/Editor in Chief
M Christopher Mitera, VP
Collette Fairchild, CMP, Trade Show Director
Julie Wichert, Sales Manager

Containing 1000 plus booths and 550 plus exhibits consisting of pet supplies, products and services.
10M Attendees
Frequency: April
Founded in 1967

20514 **International Boarding & Pet Services Asso Annual Convention & Trade Show**
1702 E Pikes Peak Avenue
Colorado Springs, CO 80909

719-667-1600; Fax: 719-667-0116
info@abka.com
www.ibpsa.com

James Krack, Executive Manager
Kathryn Eddy, Show Manager

Annual show and exhibit of pet industry products, including pet foods, supplements, retail supplies, construction materials, cages, computers and software.
300 Attendees
Frequency: October
Founded in 1977

20515 **International Hoof-Care Summit**
Lessiter Media
P.O. Box 624
Brookfield, WI 53008-0624

262-432-0388
866-839-8455; Fax: 262-786-5564
info@americanfarriers.com
www.americanfarriers.com
Facebook, Twitter, LinkedIn, YouTube

Frank Lessiter, Owner
Jeremy McGovern, Sponsorship Opportunities
Dallas Ziebell, Group Attendance Discounts

Attendees will receive unparalleled hoof-care education through engaging general sessions, practical hoof-care classrooms, hoof-care roundtables, and how-to clinics. The summit features farriers, veterinarians, and researchers.
Frequency: Annual, January

20516 **NAPPS Annual Convention: National Assoc. of Professional Pet Sitters**
17000 Commerce Parkway
Suite C
Mt. Laurel, NJ 08054

856-439-0324; Fax: 856-439-0525
napps@ahint.com
www.petsitters.org

Felicia Lembesis, Administrative Director
Rebecca Haines, Registration Coordinator
Kelly Calzaretta, Meeting/Exhibit Manager
Cathe Delaney, Membership Coordinator
Caitlin Dougherty, Manager

Exhibits, business sessions and networking opportunities. Provide tools and support to foster the success of members' businesses. To promote the value of pet sitting to the public and the advocate the welfare of animals.
Frequency: September

20517 **National Lawn & Garden Show**
Controlled Marketing Conferences
PO Box 1771
Monument, CO 80132

719-488-0226
888-316-0226; Fax: 719-488-8168
nlginfo@nlgshow.com
www.nlgshow.com

Robert Mikulas, President
Chris Wolf, VP

This event is run in conjunction with the National Lawn and Garden Show.
3000 Attendees
Frequency: June

20518 **National Pigeon Association**
1717 SE 43rd Terrace
Topeka, KS 66609-1728

785-267-5732; Fax: 785-783-2846
secretary@npausa.com
www.npausa.com

Frank Barrachina, President
Pat Avery, Secretary, Treasurer
James Avery, Secretary/Treasurer
Jerry McCalmon, Show Manager

Special information and exhibits about our members and the hobby of pigeon raising.
500 Attendees
Frequency: January
Founded in 1920

20519 **Pet Food Institute Meeting and Trade Show**
Pet Food Institute
2025 M Street NW
Washington, DC 20036

202-367-1120; Fax: 202-367-2120
info@petfoodinstitute.org
www.petfoodinstitute.org

Stephen Payne, Public Relations Manager
Duane Ekedahl, Executive Director

Annual exhibits of equipment, supplies and services for manufacturers of commercially prepared dry, semi-moist and canned pet foods.
250 Attendees
Frequency: October

20520 **Petfood Forum**
WATT Publishing Company
303 N Main Street
Suite 500
Rockford, IL 61101

815-966-5400; Fax: 815-966-6416
www.wattnet.com

Tim Phillips, Editor
Clay Schreiber, Publisher
James Watt, Owner

A technical trade show and symposium for the pet food industry including manufacturers, suppliers to the industry as well as other pet food professsionals. Containing 143 booths.
850 Attendees
Frequency: April
Founded in 1993
Mailing list available for rent

20521 **Quest for Excellence**
Pet Sitters International
201 East King Street
King, NC 27021-9163

336-983-9222; Fax: 336-983-3755
info@petsit.com
www.petsit.com

Kay Calzemari, Operating Manager
Beth Stoltz, Member Service Coordinator
Amy Woodleaf, Manager/Membership
John Long, Public Relations Coordinator
Dotty Shantz, Member Service

Containing 20+ exhibits.
250 Attendees
Frequency: September
Founded in 1994

20522 **Super Zoo Annual WWPSA Pet Industry Trade Show**
World Wide Pet Supply Association
406 S 1st Avenue
Arcadia, CA 91006-3829

626-447-2222; Fax: 626-447-8350
www.wwpsa.com

Caryn Cohan-Bates, Manager

America's oldest pet industry trade show offering over 450 exhibitors with 850 booths. Seminars, workshops, grooming events and more are held for retailers and wholesalers.
9000 Attendees
Frequency: July
Founded in 1951

20523 **Tufts Animal Expo**
Hynes Convention Center
900 Boylston Street
Boston, MA 02115

617-954-2000
800-845-8800; Fax: 617-954-2125

Animal care professionals addressed the social and medical impact pets have on human lives.
7000 Attendees
Frequency: October

20524 **World of Private Label International Trade Show**
Private Label Manufacturers Association (PLMA)
630 Third Avenue
New York, NY 10017
212-972-3131; Fax: 212-983-1382
info@plma.com
www.plma.com
Brian Sharoff, President
Myra Rosen, VP
Tom Prendergast, Director, Research Services
This show has brought retailers together with manufacturers to help them find new products, make new contacts, and discover new ideas that will help their private label programmers succeed and grow.

Directories & Databases

20525 **American Humane Association Directory**
American Humane Association
1400 16th Street NW
Suite 360
Washington, DC 20036
303-792-9900
800-227-4645; Fax: 818-762-0908
info@americanhumane.org
www.americanhumane.org
Facebook, Twitter, RSS, YouTube,Pinterest
Robert R Ganzert, President
Clifford Rose, CFO
Animal protection agencies; Canadian and some other foreign agencies are available; national and individual state editions are available.

20526 **Directory of Animal Care and Control Agencies**
American Humane Association
63 Inverness Dr E
Englewood, CO 80112-5117
303-792-9900
800-227-4645; Fax: 303-792-5333
info@americanhumane.org
www.americanhumane.org
Marie Wheatley, President
Over 6,000 animal protection agencies; Canadian and some other foreign agencies are available; national and individual state editions are available.
Cost: $75.00

20527 **Market Research Report**
Animal Health Institute
1325 G St NW
Suite 700
Washington, DC 20005-3127
202-637-2440; Fax: 202-393-1667
amathews@ahi.org
www.ahi.org
Alexander Mathews, President
Dr Richard A Carnevale, VP Regulatory, Scientific, Int'l
Ron Phillips, VP/Legislative/Public Affairs
Sandra L Phelan, Director Regulatory Affairs
Carolyn S Ayers, VP Administration/Finance
An annual directory published by the Animal Health Institute.
Cost: $150.00
50 Pages
Frequency: Annual
Founded in 1941

20528 **Pets/Animals Forum**
CompuServe Information Service
5000 Arlington Centre Blvd
Columbus, OH 43220-5439
614-326-1002
800-848-8199
This database provides a forum for the discussion of typical house and exotic pets.
Frequency: Bulletin Board

20529 **Veterinary Economics**
Veterinary Healthcare Communications
8033 Flint
Lenexa, KS 66214
913-492-4300
800-255-6864; Fax: 913-492-4157
www.vetmedpub.com
Daniel R. Verdon Chapman, Executive Director
Ray Click, VP/General Manager
Publishes two monthly magazines, a full drug list resource, and business books; conducts the Central Veterinary Conference trade show; rents its mail lists and does custom communication projects.
Frequency: Monthly
Circulation: 52,000
Mailing list available for rent: 48M+ names
Printed in 4 colors on matte stock

Industry Web Sites

20530 **http://gold.greyhouse.com**
G.O.L.D Grey House OnLine Databases
Grey House Publishing's online database platform, GOLD, offers Quick Search, Keyword Search and Expert Search for most business sectors including pet and pet supply markets. The GOLD platform makes finding the information you need quick and easy - whether you're a novice searcher or an experienced database user. All of Grey House's directory products are available for subscription on the GOLD platform.

20531 **www.aahanet.org**
American Animal Hospital Association
A group of hospitals and animal practitioners serving the industry.

20532 **www.ahi.org**
Animal Health Institute
Resource for you to learn more about how animals health products work, how they are used and their many benefits.

20533 **www.akc.org**
American Kennel Club
The principal registry of pure-bred dogs in the US.

20534 **www.allpets.com**
Dog.com
Best selection of dog supplies and prices, news and forum about dogs, health issues, grooming and the well-being for our four-legged friends.

20535 **www.apdt.com**
Association of Pet Dog Trainers
Official web site of the association. Includes members in the news, training events, industry news, trainer search engine, conference news and merchandise.

20536 **www.aspca.org**
ASPCA
Society for the humane treatment of animals, established in 1866.

20537 **www.avma.org**
American Veterinary Medical Association
Publishes various journals and information for members. Acts as a clearinghouse for veterinarians.

20538 **www.deltasociety.org**
Delta Society
Information on human-animal interactions. Service Dog Center provides information and advocacy for dogs trained to assist people with disabilities. Pet Partners Program trains volunteers, health professionals, animals for animal-assisted therapy and activities.

20539 **www.greyhouse.com**
Grey House Publishing
Authoritative reference directories for most business sectors including pet and pet supply markets. Users can search the online databases with varied search criteria allowing for custom searches by product category, geographic area, sales volume, keyword, subject and more. Full Grey House catalog and online ordering also available.

20540 **www.nhes.org**
National Humane Education Society
Fights for the prevention of cruelty to animals in any form. Fostering a sentiment of kindness since 1948.

20541 **www.npausa.com**
National Pigeon Association
Special information for members and for the hobby of pigeon raising.

20542 **www.peta.org**
People for the Ethical Treatment of Animals (PETA)
Opposes all forms of animal exploitation. Seeks to educate the public on what the group sees as the three major institutionalized cruelty issues: the exploitation and abuse of animals in experimentation, the manufacturing of fur apparel, and slaughtering for human consumption.

20543 **www.petfoodinstitute.org**
Pet Food Institute
Represents the manufacturer of 97% of all dog and cat food produced in the US. Dedicated to promoting the overall care and well-being of pets. Research in pet nutrition, proper feedings and pet care.

20544 **www.petpride.org**
Pet Pride
Operates a no kill free shelter for the lifetime of homeless cats.

20545 **www.petsit.com**
Pet Sitters International
Society of professional pet sitters. Membership provides valuable benefits - educational resources for those engaged in the pet-sitting industry. Also provides a forum to network with peers who share a common vision of excellence in at-home pet care.

20546 **www.petsitters.org**
National Association of Professional Pet Sitters
The only non-profit organization dedicated to serving the needs of professional pet care providers. Promotes ethical standards and fosters cooperation among members in the pet care industry.

20547 **www.pida.org**
Pet Industry Distributors Association
Represents wholesaler-distributors of pet products, providing training and education to members.

20548 **www.pijac.org**
Pet Industry Joint Advisory Council

Monitors federal and state regulations and legislation affecting the industry. Sponsors research and educational projects including certification programs in veterinary care and husbandry for companion animals, in-store training videos, etc.

20549 **www.usaha.org**
United States Animal Health Association

Science-based, non-profit, voluntary organization. Members are state and federal animal health officials, universities, veterinarians, livestock producers, research scientists, and extension services all to control livestock diseases in the US.

20550 **www.wwpsa.com**
World Wide Pet Supply Association

Seeks to advance the economic interests of members. Promotes responsible pet ownership. Sponsors consumer and trade shows for the pet industry.

Associations

20551 **Academy of Managed Care Pharmacy**
100 N Pitt St
Suite 400
Alexandria, VA 22314-3141

703-683-8416
800-827-2627; Fax: 703-683-8417
sandres@amcp.org
www.amcp.org
Facebook, Twitter, LinkedIn

Judy Cahill, Executive Director
Elaine Manieri, Director
Cathryn A Carroll, PhD, Treasurer

Promotes the development and application of appropriate and accessible medication therapy. Represents professional pharmacists and associates practicing in managed care settings.
4800 Members
Founded in 1989
Mailing list available for rent

20552 **Academy of Managed Care Pharmacy (AMCP)**
100 North Pitt Street
Suite 400
Alexandria, VA 22314

703-683-8416
800-827-2627; Fax: 703-683-8417
memberservices@amcp.org
www.amcp.org
Facebook, Twitter, LinkedIn

Dana Davis McCormick, President
Raulo S Frear, President Elect
Kim A. Caldwell, Past President
Stanley E. Ferrell, Director
H Eric Cannon, Treasurer
6000 Members

20553 **Accreditation Council for Pharmacy Education**
135 S. LaSalle Street
Suite 4100
Chicago, IL 60603-4810

312-664-3575; Fax: 312-664-4652
info@acpe-accredit.org
www.acpe-accredit.org
Facebook

Janet Cline, Chair
Tian Merren Owens, Vice Chair
Stephanie F. Gardner, President
Bruce Canaday, Vice President
Michael A. Mone, Secretary/Treasurer

A nonprofit accreditation national agency.
Founded in 1932

20554 **American Association of Colleges of Pharmacy**
1727 King St
Alexandria, VA 22314-2700

703-739-2330; Fax: 703-836-8982
mail@aacp.org
www.aacp.org
Facebook, Twitter, LinkedIn, YouTube

Lucinda Maine, Executive VP
Kenneth W Miller, Senior VP
Daniel J Cassidy, COO

National organization representing the interests of pharmaceutical education and educators. Comprising all 111 US pharmacy colleges and schools including more than 5,000 faculty, 50,000 students enrolled in professional programs and 4,000 individuals pursuing graduate study. AACP is committed to excellence in pharmaceutical education.
3670 Members
Founded in 1900
Mailing list available for rent

20555 **American Association of Pharmaceutical Scientists**
2107 Wilson Blvd
Suite 700
Arlington, VA 22201-3042

703-243-2800; Fax: 703-243-9650
aaps@aaps.org
www.aaps.org
Facebook, Twitter, LinkedIn, YouTube

Gene Fiese, President
Patrick Deluca, President Elect
Peter Inchauteguiz, Director Marketing
James Greif, Communcations Specialist
Maureen Downs, Director of Finance

Aims to advance science through the open exchange of scientific knowledge, serve as an information resource and contribute to human health through pharmaceutical research and development.
11000 Members
Founded in 1986
Mailing list available for rent

20556 **American Association of Pharmacy Technicians (AAPT)**
PO Box 1447
Greensboro, NC 27402

336-333-9356
877-368-4771; Fax: 336-333-9068
aapt@pharmacytechnician.com
www.pharmacytechnician.com
Facebook, Twitter

Judy Neville, BS, CPhT, President
Susan Jeffery, VP
Danalynne Young, BS, CPhT, Secretary
Bobbie Craddock, CPhT, Treasurer

Provides leadership and represents the interests of its members to the public as well as health care organizations. Promotes safe efficacious and cost effective dispensing, distribution and use of medications. Provides continuing education programs and services to help technicians update their skills and keep pace with changes in pharmacy services. Promotes pharmacy technicians as an integral part of the patient care team.
850 Members
Founded in 1979

20557 **American Association of Pharmacy Technicia**
P.O. Box 1447
Greensboro, NC 27402

336-333-9356
877-368-4771; Fax: 336-333-9068
aapt@pharmacytechnician.com
www.pharmacytechnician.com
Facebook, Twitter

Judy Neville, BS, CPhT, President
Judy Neville, Vice President
Ann Barlow Oberg, Immediate Past President
Danalynne Young, BS, CPhT, Secretary
Bobbie Craddock, Treasurer
Founded in 1979

20558 **American Chemical Society**
1155 16th St Nw
Washington, DC 20036-4892

202-872-4600
800-333-9511; Fax: 202-872-4615
service@acs.org
www.acs.org
Facebook, Twitter, LinkedIn, Google+

Thomas Connelly, Jr., CEO
Al Horvath, Chief Financial Officer
John Sullivan, Chief Information Officer
Kate Fryer, EVP, Membership & Society Services
Flint Lewis, General Counsel

Supports scientists and other professionals working in the field of drug discovery. Publishes monthly magazine.
159K Members
Founded in 1876

20559 **American Clinical Laboratory Association**
1100 New York Ave Nw
Suite 880
Washington, DC 20005-6172

202-637-9466; Fax: 202-637-2050
info@clinical-labs.org
www.acla.com
Facebook, Twitter, RSS

Alan Mertz, President
Julie Khani, SVP
Francesca Fierro O'Reilly, Vice President Government Affairs
Thomas Sparkman, Vice President Government Affairs
Peter M Kazon, Legal Counsel

Members are clinical laboratories licensed and regulated under medicare and the interstate laboratory program.
Founded in 1971

20560 **American College of Apothecaries**
2830 Summer Oaks Dr
Bartlett, TN 38134-3811

901-383-8119; Fax: 901-383-8882
aca@acainfo.org
www.acainfo.org

D C Huffman, Executive VP
Jeffrey Denton, President
Randall S Myers, VP

Disseminates and translates knowledge, research data and recent developments in professional pharmacy practice for the benefit of pharmacists, pharmacy students and the public. This is achieved through regular distribution of periodicals, development of major publications and continuing education courses on clinical and administrative topics and conducting educational conferences.
1M Members
Founded in 1940

20561 **American College of Clinical Pharmacology**
21750 Red Rum Drive
Suite 137
Ashburn, VA 20147

571-291-3493; Fax: 571-918-4167
Info@ACCP1.org
www.accp1.org
Facebook, LinkedIn

Lisa Von Moltke, President
Krista K Levy, Executive Director
Keri J Sperry, Director of Education
Erica Serow, Manager of meetings

A national organization of clinical pharmacology healthcare professionals who seek to advance clinical pharmacology.
Founded in 1969

20562 **American College of Clinical Pharmacy**
13000 W. 87th Street Parkway
Suite 650
Lenexa, KS 66215-4530

913-492-3311; Fax: 913-492-0088
accp@accp.com
www.accp.com

Michael S Maddux, Pharm.D., FCCP, Executive Director

Professional and scientific society that provides leadership, education, advocacy and resources enabling clinical pharmacists to achieve excellence in practice and research. Membership is

composed of practitioners, scientists, educators, administrators, students, residents, fellows and others committed to excellence in clinical pharmacy and patient pharmacotherapy.
Founded in 1979

20563 American College of Medical Quality
5272 River Road
Suite 630
Bethesda, MD 20816

301-718-6516
800-924-2149; Fax: 301-656-0989
acmq@acmq.org
www.acmq.org
Facebook, LinkedIn

Prathibha Varkey, President
Mark Lyles, MD, MBA, FACMQ, President-Elect
Donald E Casey, Jr MD, MPH, VP

The mission of the American College of Medical Quality is to provide leadership and education in healthcare quality management.
900 Members
Founded in 1972

20564 American Council on Pharmaceutical Education
20 N Clark Street
Suite 2500
Chicago, IL 60602

312-664-3575; Fax: 312-664-4652

Robert Buchman, Executive Director

Promotes the education of pharmaceutical medicine.

20565 American Institute of the History of Pharmacy
777 Highland Ave
Madison, WI 53705-2222

608-262-5378; Fax: 608-262-3397
Institute@aihp.org
www.pharmacy.wisc.edu/aihp
Facebook, LinkedIn

Dr. Gregory Higby, Executive Director
Dr. Elaine C Stroud, Assistant Director
Beth D Fisher, Assoc. Dir. Curatorial Affairs
Joseph Gabriel, Ph.D., Historian
William Zellmer, President

Non-profit national organization devoted to advancing knowledge and understanding of the place of pharmacy in history. Contributes to the understanding of the development of civilization by fostering the creation, preservation, and dissemination of knowledge concerning the history and related humanistic aspects of the pharmaceutical field.
900 Members
Founded in 1941

20566 American Medical Marijuana Association
Home Page: www.ammainfo.com
Facebook

A leading organization for professionals, advocates, and those interested in the benefits, application, and proper use of medical marijuana (cannabis) in the treatment of health conditions.

20567 American Pharmacists Association
2215 Constitution Ave NW
Washington, DC 20037-2985

202-628-4410
800-237-2742; Fax: 202-783-2351
infocenter@aphanet.org
www.pharmacist.com
Facebook, Twitter, LinkedIn, YouTube, RSS

Thomas E Menighan, CEO
Elizabeth Keyes, Chief Operating Officer
Joseph J Janela, CFO

It is the largest association of pharmacists in the United States, whose mission is to provide information, education, and advocacy to empower its members to improve medication use and advance patient care.
60000 Members
Founded in 1852

20568 American Public Health Association
800 I Street NW
Washington, DC 20001

202-777-2742; Fax: 202-777-2534
comments@apha.org
www.apha.org
Facebook, Twitter

Georges C. Benjamin, Executive Director

Influencing policies and setting priorities for over 125 years. Thoughout its history it has been in the forefront of numerous efforts to prevent disease and promote health.
Founded in 1872

20569 American Society for Automation in Pharmacy
492 Norristown Road
Suite 160
Blue Bell, PA 19422

610-825-7783; Fax: 610-825-7641
www.asapnet.org

Tammy Devine, President
Tim Tannert, R.Ph, Vice President
Chuck Welch, Secretary/Treasurer

Assists its members in advancing the application of computer technology in the pharmacist's role as care giver, in the efficient operation of a pharmacy and promoting standards, legislation and guidelines.
350 Members
Founded in 1988

20570 American Society for Clinical Pharmacology and Therapeutics
528 N Washington St
Alexandria, VA 22314

703-836-6981
info@ascpt.org
www.ascpt.org
Facebook, Twitter, LinkedIn, Google+

Mario L Rocci, Jr., PhD, President
Julie A Johnson, PharmD, President Elect
Russ B. Altman, Immediate Past President
Gregory L. Kearns, Secretary/Treasurer
Sharon J. Swan, Chief Executive Officer

Focuses on improving the understanding and use of existing drug therapies and developing safe and more effective treatments for the future.
2200 Members
Founded in 1900

20571 American Society for Parenteral & Enteral Nutrition
8630 Fenton Street
Suite 412
Silver Spring, MD 20910

301-587-6315
800-727-4567; Fax: 301-587-2365
aspen@nutr.org
www.nutritioncare.org
Facebook, Twitter, LinkedIn, YouTube

Marion F Winkler, President
Vincent W Vanek, VP
Robin Kriegel, CAE, Executive Director
Joanne Kieffer, Director Finance

Promotes professional communication among and within professional disciplines in the broad field of clinical nutrition including parenteral and enteral nutrition (tube feeding) through national and regional meetings, local seminars, scientific, clinical and educational exhibits and publications.
6000 Members
Founded in 1979

20572 American Society for Pharmacy Law
3085 Stevenson Drive
Suite 200
Springfield, IL 62703

217-529-6948; Fax: 217-529-9120
info@aspl.org
www.aspl.org
LinkedIn

Laura Carpenter, President
Brian Guthrie, Director
Janet Bascom, Member Services Director
Nathela Chatara, CAE, Executive Director
Jim Boyd, Treasurer

An organization of pharmacists and lawyers who are interested in the law as it applies to the pharmacy industry.
Founded in 1974

20573 American Society of Consultant Pharmacists
1321 Duke St
Alexandria, VA 22314-3563

703-739-1300
800-355-2727; Fax: 703-739-1321
info@ascp.com
www.ascp.com
Facebook, Twitter, LinkedIn, YouTube

Frank Grosso, RPh, Executive Director and CEO
Kelly Jennings, Chief Financial Officer
Cindy S. Porter, RPh, VP Education & Foundation Dev.
Debbie Furman, VP Membership & Strategic Alliances
Arnold E. Clayman, VP Pharmacy Practice & Government

The international professional association that provides leadership, education, advocacy and resources to advance the practice of senior care pharmacy.
6500+ Members
Founded in 1969

20574 American Society of Consultant Pharmacists Foundation
1321 Duke Street
Alexandria, VA 22314-3563

703-739-1300
800-355-2727; Fax: 703-739-1500
info@ascpfoundation.org
www.ascpfoundation.org

Nancy L Losben, Chairman
Frank Grosso, Executive Director
Jan Allen, Treasurer
Carla McSpadden, Board of Trustees
Ross W. Brickley, Board of Trustees

A charitable organization affiliated with the American Society of Consultant Pharmacists. It sponsors research, administers programs, holds traineeships in pharmacy practice, and performs other educational and outreach functions.
Founded in 1982

20575 American Society of Health-System Pharmacists
7272 Wisconsin Ave
Bethesda, MD 20814-4861

301-657-3000
866-279-0681; Fax: 301-664-8877
www.ashp.org
Facebook, Twitter, LinkedIn, YouTube

John A Armitstead, President
Paul W Abramowitz, EVP/CEO

An association that brings together health-system pharmacists who practice in hospitals,

health maintenance organizations, long-term care facilities, home care, and other components of health care systems. ASHSP has a long history of medication error prevention efforts and believe the mission of pharmacists is to help people make the best use of medicines.
31M Members
Founded in 1942
Mailing list available for rent

20576 American Society of Pharmacognosy
Home Page: www.pharmacognosy.us/
Facebook, Twitter, LinkedIn, RSS
Brad Moore, Chair
Phil Crews, President
Ed Kennelly, Vice President
William J. Keller, Secretary
Jim McAlpine, Treasurer
A scientific society that promotes the growth and development of pharmacognosy through presentation of research achievements and publication of meritous research.
1100 Members
Founded in 1959

20577 Americans for Safe Access
1624 U St. NW
Suite 200
Washington, DC 20009
202-857-4272; Fax: 202-618-6977
info@safeaccessnow.org
www.safeaccessnow.org
Facebook, Twitter, Google+, Instagram, YouTube
Steph Sherer, Executive Director
Debbie Churagi, Deputy Director
Geoffrey Marshall, Office & Membership Coordinator
Reenal Doshi, Director, Outreach & Communications
David Mongone Esq., Director, Government Affairs
Works to ensure safe and legal access to cannabis for therapeutic use and research.
Founded in 2002

20578 Aspirin Foundation of America
529 14th St NW
Suite 807
Washington, DC 20045-1801
202-393-0000
800-432-3247; Fax: 202-737-8406
A non-profit educational foundation with a membership of companies engaged in the manufacture, preparation, compounding or processing of aspirin and aspirin products. AFA serves as a central source of information on the health benefits of aspirin and aspirin products, when used as directed.
Founded in 1981

20579 Association for Accessible Medicines
601 New Jersey Ave. NW
Suite 850
Washington, DC 20001
202-249-7100; Fax: 202-249-7105
info@accessiblemeds.org
www.accessiblemeds.org
Facebook, Twitter, LinkedIn, Google+, YouTube
Chester Davis, Jr., President
David Gaugh, R.Ph, Senior Vice President
Represents manufacturers and distributors of finished generic pharmaceutical products, manufacturers and distributors of bulk active pharmaceutical chemicals, and suppliers of other goods and services to the generic pharmaceutical industry.

20580 Association of Clinical Research Professionals
99 Canal Center Plaza
Suite 200
Alexandria, VA 22314
703-254-8100; Fax: 703-254-8101
office@acrpnet.org
www.acrpnet.org
Facebook, Twitter, LinkedIn, YouTube
Norbert Clemens, MD, PhD, CPI, Chair, Board of Trustees
Thomas L Adams, CAE, President/CEO
James Thomasell, Director Finance
The Academy of Clinical Research Professionals and the Academy of Pharmaceutical Physician and Investigators are affiliates of ACRP. The Academy asministers non-physician certification programs and govermmental affairs activities. APPI represents all physician members of ACRP.
21000 Members
Founded in 1976

20581 Board of Pharmacy Specialties
2215 Constitution Avenue NW
Washington, DC 20037-2985
202-429-7591; Fax: 202-429-6304
www.bpsweb.org
Facebook, Twitter, YouTube
Sharon M Durfee, Chair
William Evans, Chair Elect
A post-licensure certification agency that improves patient care bypromoting the recognition and value of specialized training, knowledge, and skills in pharmacy and specialty board certification of pharmacists.
Founded in 1973

20582 College of Psychiatric and Neurologic Pharmacists
8055 O Street
Suite S113
Lincoln, NE 68510
402-476-1677; Fax: 888-551-7617
info@cpnp.org
www.cpnp.org
Facebook, Twitter, LinkedIn, YouTube, Google+
Ray Love, President
Christopher Thomas, President-Elect
Steven Burghart, Past President
Jennifer Zacher, PharmD, BCPP, Secretary
Robert Haight, PharmD, BCPP, Treasurer
Organization that advances the reach and practice of neuropsychiatric pharmacists.
Founded in 1998

20583 Drug Information Association
800 Enterprise Road
Suite 200
Horsham, PA 19044-3595
215-442-6100; Fax: 215-442-6199
dia@diahome.org
www.diaglobal.org
Facebook, Twitter, LinkedIn
Paul Pomerantz BA MBA, Worldwide Executive Director
Lisa Zoks BA, Worldwide Dir Met/Communications
Provides a neutral global forum for the exchange and dissemination of information on the discovery, development, evaluation and utilization of medicines and related health care technologies. Through these activities the DIA provides development opportunities for its members.
20000 Members
Founded in 1964

20584 Drug, Chemical & Associated Technologies Association
One Union St
Suite 208
Robbinsville, NJ 08691-3162
609-208-1888; Fax: 609-448-1944
www.dcat.org
Margaret Timony, Executive Director
Lauryn Kuna, Director, Membership
Miriam O'Donnell, Director, Project Integration
Patricia Van Arnum, Editorial Director
Erin Sanders, Sr. Communications/Tech. Specialist
The premier business development association whose membership is comprised of companies that manufacture, distribute or provide services to the pharamceutical, chemical, nutritional and related industries.
Founded in 1890

20585 Federation of Pharmacy Networks
30131 Town Center Drive
Suite 100
Laguna Niguel, CA 92677
949-495-5257; Fax: 949-495-1258
info@fpn.org
www.fpn.org
Don Anderson, President
Tom Scono, Vice President
Carol Carlson, CEO
Cathi Clark, Secretary
Curtis Woods, Treasurer
An organization of independent pharmacy group purchasing organizations established for the purpose of providing a forum for its members to exchangeideas that promote, advance and ensure the future of independent pharmacy.

20586 Food & Drug Law Institute
1155 15th Street NW
Siute 910
Washington, DC 20005-2706
202-371-1420
800-956-6293; Fax: 202-371-0649
comments@fdli.org
www.fdli.org
Facebook, LinkedIn
Amy Comstock Rick, JD, President & CEO
Iris V. Stratton CPA, VP Finance & Administration
Michael Sprott, Membership Manager
A nonprofit, educational organization dedicated to improving the understanding of the laws, regulations, and policies affecting health care technologies, food and cosmetics. FDLI is neutral, nonpartisan and does not lobby or advocate positions on any issue.
550+ Members
Founded in 1949

20587 Food and Drug Administration
10903 New Hampshire Avenue
Silver Spring, MD 20993
888-463-6332
www.fda.gov
Facebook, Twitter, YouTube, Flickr
Margaret A Hamburg, Commissioner of Food and Drugs
Walter S Harris, Deputy Commissioner for Operations
James Tyler, Chief Financial Officer
Denise Esposito, Chief of Staff
Mitch Zeller, Director
A federal agency of the United States Department of Health and Human Services that is responsible for protecting and promoting public health through the regulation and supervision of food safety, tobacco products, dietary supplements, prescription and over-the counter medications, vaccines, animal foods, veterinary products, etc.

20588 **Healthcare Distribution Alliance**
901 N Glebe Road
Suite 1000
Arlington, VA 22203

703-787-0000; Fax: 703-812-5282
www.hda.org
Twitter, LinkedIn

Chester Davis, Jr., President/CEO
Ann W. Bittman, EVP/COO
Elizabeth Gallenagh, General Counsel/SVP, Supply Chain

A national association representing primary, full-service healthcare distributors. HDMA and its members are the vital link in the healthcare system, working daily to provide value, remove costs and develop innovative solutions.
Founded in 1876

20589 **Hematology/Oncology Pharmacy Association**
8735 W. Higgins Road
Suite 300
Chicago, IL 60631

877-467-2791
www.hoparx.org

John Kuhn, Chair
Barry Goldspiel, Vice Chair
Scott Soefge, President
Helen Marshall, Secretary
Jolynn Sessions, Treasurer

A nonprofit professional organization created to help oncology and hematology.
Founded in 1995

20590 **IAGIM**
4901 Midtown Lane PBG
Florida 33418

561-376-2224
info@iagim.org
www.iagim.org

Publishes generic pharmaceutical journals and technical handbooks.

20591 **Independent Pharmacy Cooperative**
1550 Columbus St
Sun Prairie, WI 53590-3901

608-825-9556
800-755-1531; Fax: 608-825-1535
member.services@ipcrx.com
www.ipcrx.com

Don Anderson, CEO
Gary Helgerson, COO
Chuck Benjamin, CFO

Provides member pharmacies with the lowest possible contract pricing on quality products and services.
4500 Members
Founded in 1984

20592 **Institute for Safe Medication Practices**
200 Lakeside Drive
Suite 200
Horsham, PA 19044

215-947-7797; Fax: 215-914-1492
www.ismp.org
Facebook, Twitter

Michael R Cohen, RPh, MS, ScD, President
Mark J Cziraky, PharmD, Executive Vice President
Judy Smetzer, Vice President
Susan F. Paparella, Vice President
Russell H. Jenkins, Medical Director

A nonprofit organization devoted entirely to medication error prevention and safe medication use.
Founded in 1975

20593 **International Association for Cannabinoid Medicines**
Am Mildenweg 6
59602 Ruethen
Germany

+49-2952-9708571; Fax: +49-2952-902651
info@cannabis-med.org
www.cannabis-med.org
Twitter

Franjo Grotenhermen, Executive Director
Michael Krawitz, Patient Representative, USA
Alison Myrden, Patient Representative, Canada

Advances knowledge on cannabis, cannabinoids, the endocannabinoid ystem, and related topics, especially with regard to their therapeutic potential.
Founded in 2000

20594 **International Pharmaceutical Excipients Council of the Americas**
3138 N. 10th Street
Suite 500
Arlington, VA 22201

571-814-3449; Fax: 703-525-5157
ipecamer@ipecamericas.org
www.ipecamericas.org

Kimberly Beals, Executive Director
Tammy Kramer, Office Manager
Valeria Stewart, Training Coordinator
Linda A. Herzog, Technical & Membership Operations

Members are companies with an interest in the otherwise inert chemicals used as vehicles for medicines. IPEC is a federation of three independent regional associations headquartered in the US. and Japan. Each association focuses its attention on the applicable laws, regulations, science and business practices of its region to accomplish its members goals.
300 Members
Founded in 1991

20595 **International Pharmaceutical Federation**
2517 JP The Hague
The Netherlands

170-302-1970; Fax: 170-302-1999
www.fip.org
Facebook, Twitter, LinkedIn

Luc Besancon, Chief Executive Officer
Rachel Van Kesteren, Executive Secretary
Paula Cohen, Secretary
Carola Van der Hoeff, Chief Operating Officer
Lin-Nam Wang, Communication Manager

An international federation of national organizations that represent pharmacists and pharmaceutical scientists.
Founded in 1912

20596 **International Society for Pharmacoepidemiology**
5272 River Road
Suite 630
Bethesda, MD 20816

301-718-6500; Fax: 301-656-0989
ISPE@paimgmt.com
www.pharmacoepi.org
Facebook, LinkedIn, YouTube

Sonia Hernandez-Diaz, FISPE, President
Kiyoshi Kubota, FISPE, President Elect
Alison Bourke, Vice-President Finance
Mark H. Epstein, Executive Secretary
Andrew Jerdonek, Account Manager

A nonprofit international professional membership organization dedicated to advancing the health of the public by providing a forum for the open exchange of scientific information and for the development of policy, education, and advocacy for pharmacoepidemiology, pharmacovigilance, drug use research, outcomes research, comparative effectiveness research, and therapeutic risk management.

20597 **International Society for Pharmaceutical Engineering (ISPE)**
600 N. Westshore Blvd
Suite 900
Tampa, FL 33609

813-960-2105; Fax: 813-264-2816
ask@ispe.org
www.ispe.org
Facebook, Twitter, LinkedIn, Myspace, YouTube

John Bournas, President & CEO
Victoria Smoke, CFO
Kindra Bess, Director, Event Operations
Gloria Hall, Editor & Director of Publications
Karleen Kos, VP of Member Relations

Global society for technical professionals in pharmaceutical manufacturing and drug development sectors.
2000 Members
Founded in 1980

20598 **Joint Commission on the Accreditation of Healthcare Organizations**
601 13th Street, NW
Suite 560
Washington, DC 20005

630-792-5800; Fax: 630-792-5005
www.jointcommission.org
Facebook, Twitter, LinkedIn, YouTube, Google+

Mark R Chassin, President
Anne Marie Benedicto, Executive Vice President
Ann Jacobson, Executive Director
Amy Panagopoulos, Senior Director
Anita Giuntoli, Director

A nonprofit organization that accredits and certifies more than 20,500 health care organizations and programs in the United States.
Founded in 1951

20599 **Lambda Kappa Sigma (International Professional Pharmacy Fraternity)**
P.O. Box 570
Muskego, WI 53150-0570

800-LKS-1913; Fax: 262-679-4558
www.lks.org
Facebook, Twitter

Jenny Brandt, President
Patti Lozano, Vice President
Joan Rogala, Executive Director
Kim Hancock, Secretary
Sandy Mullen, Treasurer

An international professional pharmacy fraternity open to undergraduate and graduate pharmacy students and participating pharmacists. It also provides lifelong opportunities for women in pharmacy.
25000 Members
Founded in 1913

20600 **National Alliance of State Pharmacy Associations**
2530 Professional Road
Suite 202
Richmond, VA 23235

804-285-4431
804-612-6555
rsnead@naspa.us
www.naspa.us
Facebook, Twitter, LinkedIn

Mike Larkin Kansas, President
Pat Epple Pennsylvania, President-Elect
Joni Cover Nebraska, 1st Vice President
Jon Roth, 2nd Vice President
Louise Jones Alabama, Secretary/Treasurer

Promotes leadership, sharing, learning, and policy exchange among state pharmacy associations and pharmacy leaders nationwide, and provides education and advocacy to support pharmacists, patients, and communities working together to improve public health.

Founded in 1927

20601 National Alliance of State Pharmacy

2530 Professional Rd
Suite 202
Richmond, VA 23235-3217

804-285-4431; Fax: 804-285-4227
becky@naspa.us
www.naspa.us
Twitter

Rebecca Snead, Executive Director
Joni Cover Nebraska, First VP

400 Members
Founded in 1927

20602 National Association of Boards of Pharmacy

1600 Feehanville Dr
Mount Prospect, IL 60056

847-698-6227
800-774-6227; Fax: 847-391-4502
custserv@nabp.net
www.nabp.net
RSS

Joseph L Adams, RPh, Chairperson
Edward G McGinley, MBA, RPh, President
Jeanne D Waggener, RPh, Treasurer

Serves all American boards of pharmacy in matters of interstate reciprocity of licensure and licensing as well as other matters of mutual concern.

Founded in 1904

20603 National Association of Chain Drug Stores

1776 Wilson Blvd.
Suite 200
Arlington, VA 22209

703-549-3001; Fax: 703-836-4869
contactus@nacds.org
www.nacds.org
Facebook, Twitter, LinkedIn, YouTube, Flickr

Steven C. Anderson, President & CEO

The chief purpose of NACDS is to represent the views and policy positions of member chain drug companies.

105 Members
Founded in 1933

20604 National Community Pharmacists Association

100 Daingerfield Road
Alexandria, VA 22314

703-683-8200
800-544-7447; Fax: 703-683-3619
www.ncpanet.org
Facebook, Twitter, Google+, YouTube

Bradley Arthur, President
Bruce Roberts RPh, Executive VP/CEO

Represents pharmacy owners, managers and employees of nearly 25,000 independent community pharmacies across the US.

60000 Members
Founded in 1898

20605 National Council for Prescription Drug Programs

9240 E Raintree Dr
Scottsdale, AZ 85260-7518

480-477-1000; Fax: 480-767-1042
info@ncpdp.org
www.ncpdp.org

Lee Ann Stember, President
Dennis Kitterman, Director Marketing Communications
Phillip D Scott, SVP Sales/Marketing
Joanne Longie, VP Operations

Members are computer companies, drug manufacturers, drug store chains, drug wholesalers, insurers, mail order prescription drug companies, pharmaceutical claim processors, prescription drug providers, software vendors, service organizations, government agencies and others with a interest in drug program administration standardization.

1350 Members
Founded in 1977

20606 National Institute for Pharmacist Care Outcomes

100 Daingerfield Road
Alexandria, VA 22314

703-683-8200; Fax: 703-683-3619
www.ncpanet.org
Facebook, Twitter, Google+

Kathryn Kuhn, Executive Director, NIPCO Programs
Eleanor Nespica, Coordinator, NIPCO Programs
Mike Clark, Manager
Bradley Arthur, President

The national accrediting organization for pharmacist care education and training programs leading to the pharmacist care diplomate credential. A leading authority in helping community pharmacists develop new market niches in disease management and wellness.

20607 National Pharmaceutical Alliance

427 King Street
Suite 222
Alexandria, VA 22314

703-836-8816; Fax: 919-469-5858
www.npa.org

Cristina Sizemore, Executive Director
Deborah Kline, Manager Communications

Represents the interests of small pharmaceutical companies and allied industries.

Founded in 1993

20608 National Pharmaceutical Association

107 Kilmayne Drive
Suite C
Cary, NC 27511

877-215-2091; Fax: 919-469-5858
npha@npha.net
www.npha.net
Facebook, Twitter

Dr. Carleton Maxwell, President
Erica Hanesworth, President Elect
Cornetta Levi, Immediate Past-President
Gayle Tuckett, Secretary
Joseph T. Lee, Treasurer

A nationwide, professional organization of pharmacists.

Founded in 1950

20609 National Pharmaceutical Council

1717 Pennsylvania Ave., NW
Suite 800
Washington, DC 20006

703-620-6390; Fax: 202-827-0314
info@npcnow.com
www.npcnow.org
Facebook, Twitter, LinkedIn, YouTube

Daniel Leonard, President
Pat Adams, VP Business Operations
Gary Persinger, VP Health Care Systems
Richard Levy, VP Scientific
Jeffery Warren, Senior Advisor

Represents major, research-intensive, pharmaceutical companies. Conducts national and state studies, holds educational forums and generates publications for consumer and for health care cost containment programs.

31 Members
Founded in 1953

20610 National Pharmacy Purchasing Association

4747 Morena Blvd
Suite 340
San Diego, CA 92117-3468

858-581-6373
888-544-6772; Fax: 858-581-6372
info@pharmacypurchasing.com
www.pharmacypurchasing.com
Facebook, Twitter

Dale J Kroll, President & CEO
Francine Morgano, Vice President
Michael Thomas, Event & Editorial Assistant
Debby Flannery, Advisory Board
Deb Harden, Advisory Board

An association that promotes the profession of pharmacy purchasing and offers educational opportunities for pharmacy buyers. Members include pharmacy buyers and managers from private, nonprofit, or government-run institutional facilities that work to promote the profession of pharmacy purchasing and offerseducational opportunities for pharmacy buyers.

Founded in 1991

20611 National Pharmacy Technician Association

PO BOX 683148
Houston, TX 77268

888-247-8700; Fax: 888-247-8706
mikej@pharmacytechnician.org
www.pharmacytechnician.org
Facebook, Twitter, LinkedIn, YouTube, RSS

Mike Johnston, Chairman
Robin Luke, President
Wendy Meigs, Board Member
Carol Reyes, Board Member
Rhonda Wilson, Board Member

The world's largest professional organization established specifically for pharmacy technicians.

Founded in 1999

20612 New York State Council of Health-Systems Pharmacists

210 Washington Ave
Albany, NY 12203

518-456-8819
518-456-8819; Fax: 518-456-9319
nyschpweb@nyschp.org
www.nyschp.org
Facebook, Twitter, LinkedIn

Stephanie Seyse, President
Joseph Pinto, President Elect
Monica Mehta, Vice President
Shaun C. Flynn, Executive Director
Philip Manning, Treasurer

Provides leadership and resources to promote quality pharmaceuticalservices directed at appropriate medication therapy and positive patient outcomes.

2200 Members

20613 Pan American Health Organization
525 Twenty-third Street, N.W.
Washington, DC 20037

202-974-3000; Fax: 202-974-3663
www.paho.org
Facebook, Twitter, LinkedIn, YouTube, Flickr, RSS

The world's oldest international public health agency that providestechnical cooperation and mobilizes partnerships to improve health and quality of life in the countries of the Americas.
Founded in 1902

20614 Parenteral Drug Association
3 Bethesda Metro Center
Suite 1500
Bethesda, MD 20814

301-860-0293; Fax: 301-986-0296
info@pda.org
www.pda.org
Twitter, LinkedIn, YouTube

Vince R Anicetti, Chairman
Richard Jahnson, President and CEO
Wanda Neal-Ballard, Director Programs/Meetings
Lance K Hoboy, MBA, VP Finance
Matthew Clark, Director Marketing

A non-profit international association of scientists involved in the development, manufacture, quality control and regulation of pharmaceuticals/biopharmaceuticals and related products. The association also provides educational opportunities for government and university sectors that have a vocational interest in pharmaceutical/biopharmaceutical sciences and technology.
10500 Members
Founded in 1946

20615 Pediatric Pharmacy Advocacy Group
5865 Ridgeway Center Parkway
Suite 300
Memphis, TN 38120-4014

901-820-4434; Fax: 901-767-0704
membership@ppag.org
www.ppag.org
Facebook, Twitter, LinkedIn

Jared Cash, PharmD, President
Lisa Lubsch, PharmD, President-Elect
Kimberly Novak, PharmD, Secretary
Jeffrey Low, Treasurer
Matthew R. Helms, Executive Director

A nonprofit organization that strives to improve the health of children.
800 Members
Founded in 1990

20616 Pennsylvania Pharmacists Association
508 North Third Street
Harrisburg, PA 17101

717-234-6151
ppa@papharmacists.com
www.papharmacists.com
Facebook, Twitter, LinkedIn, YouTube, Flickr

Donna Hazel, President
Eric Pusey, President-Elect
Nicholas Leon, First Vice President
Nicholas Leon, Second Vice President
Eric Esterbrook, Immediate Past President

A professional membership society of registered pharmacists, student pharmacists, pharmacy technicans, and others who reside, work, attend college,or are interested in pharmacy in Pennsylvania.
Founded in 1878

20617 Pharmaceutical Care Management Association
325 7th St. NW
9th Fl.
Washington, DC 20004

202-756-5700; Fax: 202-756-5708
www.pcmanet.org
Facebook, Twitter

Mark Merritt, President & CEO
Brenda Palmer, Chief Financial Officer
Brian McCarthy, Chief Operating Officer

National association of pharmacy benefit managers.
Founded in 2009

20618 Pharmaceutical Outsourcing Management Association
8865 W Okeechobee Boulevard
Suite 202
West Palm Beach, FL 33411

561-795-5503; Fax: 561-795-5503
www.pharmoutsourcing.com

Shannon Brome-Ward, President
Linda Wauk, VP
Charles Calvert, Treasurer
Fran Grote, Secretary

Established as a forum to exchange ideas and experiences about outsourcing in the pharmaceutical industry.
Founded in 1995

20619 Pharmaceutical Research and Manufacturers of America
950 F Street, NW
Suite 300
Washington, DC 20004

202-835-3400
newsroom@phrma.org
www.phrma.org
Facebook, Twitter, YouTube, Flickr, Google+

Kenneth C Frazier, Chairman
George A Scangos, Chairman Elect
Jack Bailey, President
Joaquin Duato, Treasurer

Mission is to conduct effective advocacy for public policies that encourage discovery of important new medicines for patients by pharmaceutical/biotechnology research companies.
Founded in 1958

20620 Pharmacy Benefit Management Institute, Inc .
2901 N Dallas Pkwy
Ste 420
Plano, TX 75093

480-730-0814; Fax: 480-222-4229
jlutz@pbmi.com
www.pbmi.com
LinkedIn

Jane Lutz, Executive Director
Kathleen Fairman, Vice President
Linda DeChant, Director of Sales
Julie Blackman, Marketing Manager
Shelly Carey, Research Director

Pharmacy benefit management education, research, and consulting.

20621 Pharmacy Technician Certification Board
2215 Constitution Avenue NW
Suite 101
Washington, DC 20037

800-363-8012; Fax: 202-888-1699
contact@ptcb.org
www.ptcb.org
Facebook, Twitter

Paul Abramowitz, Chair
Paul Abramowitz, Vice Chair
Thomas Menighan, Executive Vice President
Everett B. McAllister, Executive Director & CEO
Larry Wagenknecht, Treasurer

Develops, maintains, promotes, and administers a nationally accredited certification and recertification program for pharmacy technicians to enablethe most effective support of pharmacists to advance patient safety.
Founded in 1995

20622 Pinoy Pharmacy
Home Page: www.pinoypharmacy.com
Facebook, Twitter

An online community for Filipino pharmacy professionals around the world.

20623 Professional Compounding Centers of America
9901 South Wilcrest Drive
Houston, TX 77099

281-933-6948
800-331-2498; Fax: 281-933-6627
customerservice@pccarx.com
www.pccarx.com
Facebook, Twitter, LinkedIn, YouTube, Flickr

Provides independent pharmacists with a complete support system forcompounding unique dosage forms.
3900 Members
Founded in 1981

20624 Regulatory Affairs Professionals Society
5635 Fishers Lane
Suite 550
Rockville, MA 20852

301-770-2920; Fax: 301-770-2924
raps@raps.org
www.raps.org
Facebook, Twitter, LinkedIn, YouTube, Google+, Flickr

Donald A Middlebrook, Chairman
Rainer Voelksen, President
Martha A. Brumfield, President Elect
Salma Michor, Secretary/Treasurer
Gautam Maitra, Director

The largest global organization of and for those involved with the regulation of healthcare and related products, including medical devices, pharmaceuticals, biologics and nutritional products.
Founded in 1976

20625 Roundtable of Toxicology Consultants
P.O. Box 98224
Raleigh, NC 27624

Home Page: www.toxconsultants.com

Jane Allen, President
Joann Schuh, President Elect
Dave Hobson, Past President
Lori Dostal, Secretary
Merrill Osheroff, Treasurer

An organization of independently practicing toxicologists dedicatedto solving the problems for clients.
Founded in 1986

20626 Society for Laboratory Automation and Screening
100 Illinois Street
Ste. 242
St. Charles, IL 60174

630-256-7527
877-990-7527
slas@slas.org

www.slas.org
Facebook, Twitter, LinkedIn, YouTube

Vicki Loise, CEO
Brenda Dreier, COO
Jill Hronek, Director, Marketing & Communication
Christine Diedrich, Publishing Manager
Mary Geismann, Sr. Membership Coordinator

A global community of more than 18,000 scientists from academia, government and industry collectively focused on leveraging the power of technologyto achieve scientific objectives.
18000 Members
Founded in 2009

20627 Society of Cannabis Clinicians
6842 21st Ave. NE
Seattle, WA 98115

Home Page: www.cannabisclinicians.org
Facebook, Twitter

Ellen Kuwana, Executive Director

An educational and scientific society of qualified physicians and other professionals dedicated to the promotion, protection, and support of cannabis for medical use.
Founded in 2004

20628 Society of Critical Care Medicine
500 Midway Drive
Mount Prospect, IL 60056

847-827-6869; Fax: 847-827-6886
info@sccm.org
www.sccm.org
Twitter, Google+

J. Christopher Farmer, President
David J Martin, Chief Executive Officer
Dorothy Suwanski, Executive Assistant
Ellen Turney, Human Resources Manager
Karen Boman, Business Analyst

The largest multiprofessional organization dedicated to ensuring excellence and consistency in the practice of critical care.

20629 Southeastern Society of Health-System Pharmacists

Home Page: www.smshp.org
Facebook, Twitter

A regional association representing pharmacists and related personnel associated with organized health-care settings.

20630 Student National Pharmaceutical Association
PO Box 761388ÿ
San Antonio, TX 78245

210-383-7381; Fax: 210-579-1059
contactsnpha@snpha.org
www.snpha.org
Facebook, Twitter, YouTube, Instagram

Joshua Blackwell, PharmD, Executive Chairman
Jessie Nai Hwang, President
Gevorg Martirosyan, President Elect
Dr. Carmita Coleman, Executive Director
Kyle Brown, Vice President

An educational service association of pharmacy students who are concerned about pharmacy and healthcare related issues, and the poor minority representation in pharmacy and other health-related professions.
Founded in 1972

Newsletters

20631 AACP News
American Association of Colleges of Pharmacy
1727 King St
Suite 210
Alexandria, VA 22314-2700

703-739-2330; Fax: 703-836-8982
www.aacp.org

Lucinda Maine, Executive VP
Kenneth W Miller, Senior VP
Daniel J Cassidy, COO

Activities and issues in pharmacy education. 12 pages, free to members. Published since 1874.
Cost: $35.00
Frequency: Monthly
Circulation: 300
Founded in 1900
Mailing list available for rent: 300 names
Printed in on newsprint stock

20632 ACCP Report
American College of Clinical Pharmacy
13000 W. 87th St Parkway
Lenexa, KS 66215-4530

913-492-3311; Fax: 913-492-0088
accp@accp.com
www.accp.com

George Puiges, Publisher
Bruce Mueller, Editor
Micheal Maddux, Executive Director
Jon Poynter, Project Manager, Membership
Kimma Sheldon, Medical Editor

The American College of Clinical Pharmacy (ACCP) is a professional and scientific society that provides leadership, education, advocacy, and resources enabling clinical pharmacists to achieve excellence in practice and research.
Cost: $45.00
Frequency: Monthly
Circulation: 12000

20633 ASA Monthly Activist Newsletter
Americans for Safe Access
1624 U St. NW
Suite 200
Washington, DC 20009

202-857-4272; Fax: 202-618-6977
info@safeaccessnow.org
www.safeaccessnow.org
Facebook, Twitter, Google+, Instagram, YouTube

Steph Sherer, Executive Director
Debbie Churagi, Deputy Director
Geoffrey Marshall, Office & Membership Coordinator
Reenal Doshi, Director, Outreach & Communications
David Mongone Esq., Director, Government Affairs

A monthly newsletter bringing you the latest developments in the field of medical cannabis.
Founded in 2002

20634 Alternative Medicine Alert
American Health Consultants
3525 Piedmont Rd Ne
Building Six, Suite 400
Atlanta, GA 30305-1578

404-467-4243
800-688-2421; Fax: 404-262-7837
www.ahcpub.com

Jeff Mac Donald, CEO

Reports on studies of herbs in medicine, reactions in relation to different herbs. Studies that are out and those being done.
Cost: $299.00
Frequency: Monthly
Mailing list available for rent
Printed in 4 colors on matte stock

20635 Annals of Pharmacotherapy
Harvey Whitney Books Company
8044 Montgomery Road
PO Box 42696
Cincinnati, OH 45242-0696

513-793-3555
877-742-7631; Fax: 513-793-3600
customer-services@theannals.com
www.theannals.com

Tina Whitney, Finance Executive
Eugene Sorkin, Associate Editor
Harvey Whitney, CEO
Greg Johnson, Marketing
Ann Brandwieve, Circulation Manager

For 38 years this independent peer reviewed journal has been dedicated to the advancement of pharmacotherapy. Article categories include; original research, comprehensive reviews, case reports, editorials, and letters. special article features include new drug evaluations, therapeutic controversies, recent theraputic advances, international reports, continuing education articles, and more.
Cost: $158.00
Frequency: Monthly
Circulation: 50000
ISSN: 1060-0280
Founded in 1967
Printed in 4 colors on glossy stock

20636 Chapter News
American College of Cardiology
76 S State Street
Concord, NH 03301-3520

603-228-1231; Fax: 603-228-2118
assnrhc@aol.com

Walter Perry, Executive Director

Newsletter for cardiovascular specialists in Maine, New Hampshire and Vermont.
Frequency: Quarterly
Mailing list available for rent

20637 Clin-Alert-Newsletter
Technomic Publishing Company
300 S Riverside Plz
Suite 1200
Chicago, IL 60606-6637

312-876-0004; Fax: 312-876-1158
foodinfo@technomic.com
www.technomic.com

Ronald Paul, President
Darren Tristano, Executive Vice President
Neil Stern, Senior Partner

This unique adverse drug reaction/interaction reporting service presents-in newsletter format-a summary of adverse clinical events, collected from 103 key medical and research journals from around the world. Approximately 360 abstracts per year.
Cost: $155.00
8 Pages
Frequency: Semimonthly
ISSN: 0069-4770
Printed in 2 colors

20638 Clinical Investigator News
CTB International Publishing
PO Box 218
Maplewood, NJ 07040-218

973-966-0997; Fax: 973-966-0242
www.ctbintl.com

FG Racioppi, Marketing Director
William Robison, Circulation Manager

Alerts independent investigators to existing or emerging opportunities to participate in clinical trials of drugs and maintain a steady flow of studies. Covers preclinical development through Phase II/III, approvals and post-marketing surveillance (PMS) studies.
Cost: $647.00
48 Pages
Frequency: Monthly
Founded in 1980

Mailing list available for rent
Printed in one color on newsprint stock

20639 Clinical Trials Monitor
CTB International Publishing
PO Box 218
Maplewood, NJ 07040-218
973-966-0997; Fax: 973-379-0242
www.ctbintl.com
Oykue Brogna, Publisher
Christopher Brogna, Editor
Tracks clinical trials planned, underway, completed or abandoned. Lists the drug, the company, the indication, phase or stage, principal investigator, where and when trials will be held, enrollment plans and proposed end points. Reports results at meetings, and in journals.
Cost: $1197.00
64 Pages
Frequency: Monthly
Founded in 1985
Printed in one color on newsprint stock

20640 Consumer Pharmacist
Elba Medical Foundation
PO Box 494
Metairie, LA 70004
504-889-7070; Fax: 504-889-7060
John DiMaggio, Publisher
Drug information newsletter.
Cost: $30.00
Frequency: Monthly

20641 DIA Newsletter
Drug Information Association
800 Enterprise Rd
Suite 200
Horsham, PA 19044-3595
215-442-6100; Fax: 215-442-6199
dia@diahome.org
www.diahome.org
Facebook, Twitter, LinkedIn, YouTube
Ling Su, President
John Roberts, Treasurer
Barabara Lopez Kunz, Global Chief Executive
Association activities, technical developments, supplying, and production of drugs.
Cost: $40.00
20 Pages
Frequency: Monthly
Founded in 1964

20642 Diagnostics Intelligence
CTB International Publishing
PO Box 218
Maplewood, NJ 07040-218
973-966-0997; Fax: 973-966-0242
www.ctbintl.com
Oyque Brogna, CEO/President
F Racioppi, Marketing Director
Covers the latest in research, development, new product language, regulatory affairs, patents, litigations, opportunities and finance in the invitro diagnostics business.
Cost: $578.00
20 Pages
Frequency: Monthly
Mailing list available for rent
Printed in one color on newsprint stock

20643 Drug Development Pipeline
CTB International Publishing
PO Box 218
Maplewood, NJ 07040
973-966-0997; Fax: 973-966-0242
www.ctbintl.com/
FG Racioppi, Marketing Director
Chris Brogna, President
Laszlo Novak, Editor
Newsletter that summarizes the changes in the drug development plans of US and Canadian pharmaceutical companies. Each issue will alert the reader to more than 120 products that are moving through the pipeline.
Cost: $198.00
Frequency: Monthly
Founded in 1982
Mailing list available for rent
Printed in one color on newsprint stock

20644 Emerging Pharmaceuticals
CTB International Publishing
PO Box 218
Maplewood, NJ 07040-218
973-966-0997; Fax: 973-966-0242
www.ctbintl.com
FG Racioppi, Marketing Director
Covers the earliest stage of drug development, from discovery through preclinical trials. Alerts readers to news and insights about novel compounds, innovative screening methods and candidates for the R&D pipeline.
Cost: $542.00
14 Pages
Frequency: Monthly
Mailing list available for rent
Printed in one color on newsprint stock

20645 FDC Reports: Gold Sheet
FDC Reports
5550 Friendship Boulevard
Suite 1
Chevy Chase, MD 20815-7278
301-657-9830
800-332-2181; Fax: 301-656-3094
fdc.customer.service@elsevier.com
www.fdcreports.com
Bill Paulson, Editor
Michael Magoulias, VP Sales/Marketing
Mike Squires, CEO/President
William Paulson, Executive Editor
A specialized publication which focuses each month on important changes in FDA's policies for regulating good manufacturing practices for pharmaceutical companies and their suppliers. Since 1967, this publication has provided quality control officials with the latest useful information on state-of-the-art production and quality control techniques.
Cost: $595.00
Frequency: Monthly
ISSN: 1530-6194
Founded in 1939
Mailing list available for rent
Printed in 2 colors on matte stock

20646 FDC Reports: Green Sheet
FDC Reports
5550 Friendship Boulevard
Suite 1
Chevy Chase, MD 20815-7256
301-657-9830; Fax: 301-656-3094
www.fdcreports.com
Mike Squires, President
Michael Koppenhoffer, Editor
For nearly 40 years The Green Sheet has been an independent source of news and information on the pharmacy profession and the pharmaceutical distribution system. This four-page publication provides pharmacists, wholesalers, drugstore managers and trade relations executives with concise coverage of: professional policy; national and state pharmacy association activities; reimbursement issues; new drug introductions and pharmaceutical pricing and deals.
Cost: $65.00
4 Pages
Frequency: Weekly
Founded in 1939

20647 FDC Reports: Pink Sheet
FDC Reports
5550 Friendship Boulevard
Suite 1
Chevy Chase, MD 20815-7256
301-657-9830
800-332-2181; Fax: 301-656-3094
PinkEditor@elsevier.com
www.fdcreports.com
Wallace Werble Jr, Publisher
Janet Coleman, Editor
Mike Squires, CEO/President
Shawn Smith, Marketing
Emily Brainard, Circulation Manager
Provides in-depth weekly news and analysis about developments affecting the prescription medicines. The publication closely tracks regulatory policies and actions by FDA, FTC, HCFA, Congress, the courts and other key federal and state agencies with jurisdiction over the drug industry. Regular coverage areas include: NDA and Generic Drug approvals, FDA recalls and seizures, mergers, the R&D pipeline, biotechnology start-ups and new product activity.
Cost: $1580.00
35 Pages
Frequency: Weekly
ISSN: 1068-5324
Founded in 1939

20648 FDC Reports: Tan Sheet
FDC Reports
5550 Friendship Boulevard
Suite 1
Chevy Chase, MD 20815-7256
301-657-9830; Fax: 301-656-3094
FDC.Customer.Service@Elsevier.com
www.fdcreports.com
Mike Squires, CEO/President
Ramsey Baghdadi, Editor
Michael Magoulias, Marketing Manager
Emily Brainard, Circulation Manager
Provides in-depth coverage of nonprescription pharmaceuticals and dietary supplement/nutritionals. Spectrum of coverage includes: regulatory activities of FTC, CPSC and FDA, including monograph and non-monograph decisions, enforcement actions, advisory committee reviews and approvals; Congressional hearings and legislation; business and marketing news such as Rx-to-OTC switches, product development and new product introductions; FDA recalls and seizures and regular listing of product trademarks
Cost: $1285.00
Frequency: Weekly
ISSN: 1068-5316
Founded in 1939

20649 FDLI Prospectus
Food & Drug Law Institute
1155 15th Street NW
Suite 800
Washington, DC 20005
202-371-1420
800-956-6293; Fax: 202-371-0649
comments@fdli.org
www.fdli.org
Michael D. Levin-Epstein, Vice President, Publications
Abby C. Foster, Managing Editor
weekly e-newsletter
Frequency: Weekly

20650 Food and Drug Letter
FDAnews
300 N Washington St
Suite 200
Falls Church, VA 22046-3441
703-538-7600
888-838-5578; Fax: 703-538-7676

customerservice@fdanews.com
www.fdanews.com

Cynthia Carter, President
Michael Miven, Editor
Maritva Lizama, Marketing
J T Hrontith, Sales Director

Provides reliable, in-depth analysis of how FDA's regulations and procedures will affect your current decisions and long-term plans and gives you in-depth interpretation to tell you why FDA is making or proposing revisions.
Cost: $1095.00
8 Pages
Frequency: Annual+

20651 Health News Daily
FDC Reports
5550 Friendship Boulevard
Suite 1
Chevy Chase, MD 20815-7256

301-657-9830
800-332-2181; Fax: 301-656-3094
www.healthnewsdaily.com

Jim Chicca, Editor
Mike Squires, Executive Director

Provides up-to-the-minute coverage on a broad spectrum of health care issues including pharmaceuticals, medical devices and diagnostics, biomedical research, federal health policy and legislation, Medicare-Medicaid, technology reimbursement and cost-containment. Special emphasis is placed on federal regulatory and legislative developments. Published each business day, the publication draws on the expertise of more than 40 F-D-C reports editors and reporters.
Cost: $ 1480.00
Frequency: Daily
Founded in 1939

20652 IACM-Bulletin
International Association for Cannabinoid Medicine
Am Mildenweg 6
59602 Ruethen
Germany

+49-2952-9708571; Fax: +49-2952-902651
info@cannabis-med.org
www.cannabis-med.org
Twitter

Franjo Grotenhermen, Executive Director
Michael Krawitz, Patient Representative, USA
Alison Myrden, Patient Representative, Canada

An e-newsletter containing news on all aspects of cannabis as medicine.
Frequency: Bi-Weekly
Founded in 2000

20653 International Pharmaceutical Regulatory Monitor
Omniprint
9700 Philadelphia Ct
Lanham, MD 20706-4405

301-731-7000
800-345-2611; Fax: 301-731-7001
www.omniprint.net

Ken Kaufman, President
Stephen Brown, VP

Comprehensive reports on the world's drug and biotechnology regulations for testing and marketing; provides actual regulatory documents (English texts).
Cost: $595.00
60 Pages
Frequency: Monthly
ISSN: 0888-6393
Founded in 1973
Mailing list available for rent
Printed in 2 colors on matte stock

20654 Mealey's Emerging Drugs & Devices
LexisNexis Mealey's
555 W 5th Avenue
Los Angeles, CA 90013

213-627-1130
mealeyinfo@lexisnexis.com
www.lexisnexis.com/mealeys

Tom Hagy, VP/General Manager
Maureen McGuire, Editorial Director
Tom Moylan, Editor

The report covers cases involving a variety of prescription drug vaccines, implants and devices. Duract, Parlodel, Accutane, fen-phen, Rezulin, Propulsid, dietary supplements and blood products are among the topics tracked. Medical devices covered include heart catheters, breast implants, heart valves, intraocular lenses, jaw implants, joint replacements, latex gloves, pacemakers, pedicle screws, penile implants, and surgical lasers.
Cost: $1249.00
100 Pages
Frequency: Semi-Monthly
Founded in 1996

20655 Mealey's Litigation Report: Baycol
LexisNexis Mealey's
555 W 5th Avenue
Los Angeles, CA 90013

213-627-1130
mealeyinfo@lexisnexis.com
www.lexisnexis.com/mealeys

Tom Hagy, VP/General Manager
Maureen McGuire, Editorial Director
Dylan McGuire, Editor

This report tracks the litigation surrounding Baycol and other statin-based anti-cholesterol drug cases. Since the voluntary withdrawl of Bayer's Baycol and Lipobay brand cerivastatin anti-cholesterol drugs, numerous complaints have been filed. The report will cover hard-to-find filings, new complaints, class actions, MDL developments, trial updates and more.
Cost: $950.00
100 Pages
Frequency: Monthly
Founded in 2002

20656 Mealey's Litigation Report: Fen-Phen/Redux
LexisNexis Mealey's
555 W 5th Avenue
Los Angeles, CA 90013

213-627-1130
mealeyinfo@lexisnexis.com
www.lexisnexis.com/mealeys

Tom Hagy, VP/General Manager
Maureen McGuire, Editorial Director
Michael Lefkowitz, Editor

The report provides detailed coverage of the litigation surrounding fen-phen, Redux and other diet drugs. The report covers new filings, class actions, MDL proceedings, trials, settlements, rulings, medical studies, FDA activity and more.
Cost: $995.00
100 Pages
Frequency: Monthly
Founded in 1997

20657 NABP Newsletter
National Association of Boards of Pharmacy
700 Busse Highway
Park Ridge, IL 60068

847-698-6227
800-774-6227; Fax: 847-698-0124
custserv@nabp.net
www.nabp.net

Malcom Broussard, Chairperson
Michael Burlson, President
Joseph Adams, Treasurer

Provides coverage of issues important to those who practice pharmacy and those who regulate that practice. Information about NABP's competency assessment and licensure transfer programs, news about the boards of pharmacy, and articles that impact the practice and regulation of pharmacy appear in each issue.
Cost: $35.00
Frequency: 10 Per Year

20658 NCPA Newsletter
National Community Pharmacists Association
100 Daingerfield Road
Alexandria, VA 22314

703-683-8200
800-544-7447; Fax: 703-683-3619
www.ncpanet.org

Mike Conlan, VP Publications
Chris Linville, Managing Editor

Stay up-to-date on the latest developments in legislation, federal regulation, pharmacy news, and other important events with the NCPA Newsletter. Independent pharmacists get the information they need to understand the policies, politics, and government actions that affect independent pharmacy practice. Annual subscription is included in NCPA memership dues.
Cost: $50.00

20659 PDA Letter
Parenteral Drug Association
1894 Preston White Drive
Reston, VA 20191-5433

703-620-6390; Fax: 703-476-0904
info@npcnow.org
www.npcnow.org

Walter L Morris, III, Senior Editor

Designed to keep members informed of the latest information in the regulatory arena along with scientific happenings within the Association and the industry. It also contains details on upcoming PDA events, as well as worldwide Chapter activities.
Frequency: Monthly
Founded in 1949

20660 Pharmaceutical & Med Packaging News
Canon Communications
11444 W Olympic Blvd
Suite 900
Los Angeles, CA 90064-1555

310-445-4200; Fax: 310-445-4299
feedback@cancom.com
www.cancom.com

Klaus Weinmann, CEO
Rudolf Hotter, COO
Frequency: Monthly
Founded in 1992

20661 Pharmaceutical News Daily
CTB International Publishing
PO Box 218
Maplewood, NJ 07040

973-966-0997; Fax: 973-966-0242
www.ctbintl.com

Kris Brogina, CEO/President
Kistine Yanicek, Editor
Oykue Brogina, Publisher
T Tseng, Circulation Manager

This daily electronic newsletter updates the highly competitive pharmaceutical and biotechnology industries. Delivered by e-mail.
Cost: $279.00
Frequency: Daily
Founded in 1984
Mailing list available for rent
Printed in one color on newsprint stock

20662 **Pharmacist's Letter**
Therapeutic Research
3120 W March Lane
PO Box 8190
Stockton, CA 95208-190
209-472-2240; Fax: 209-472-2249
www.pletter.com
Jeff Jellin, Publisher
A newsletter to pharmacists offering coverage of drug development, production, distribution, legislation, safety and other issues concerning the industry.
Cost: $85.00
ISSN: 0883-0371

20663 **Pharmacy Practice News**
McMahon Group
545 W 45th St
8th Floor
New York, NY 10036-3409
646-557-0966; Fax: 646-957-7230
davidb@mcmahonmed.com
Raymond Mc Mahon, CEO
Van Velle, President
David Bronstein, Editor-in-Chief
Marsha Radebaugh, Circulation Manager
Michelle McMohan, Creative Director
Created to inform hospital pharmacists of the latest news on drugs, nutrition, research and trends in the pharmaceutical industry.
Cost: $60.00
Frequency: Monthly
Circulation: 45460
Founded in 1972

20664 **Pharmacy Student**
APLA
2215 Constitution Avenue NW
Washington, DC 20037-2977
202-429-7576
Rick Harding, Publisher
Practical information to help pharmacy students grow.
Cost: $35.00
Frequency: Monthly
Circulation: 100000

20665 **Pharmacy Today**
American Pharmacists Association
2215 Constitution Avenue NW
Washington, DC 20037-2977
202-429-7557
800-237-2742; Fax: 202-783-2351
pt@aphanet.org
www.pharmacists.org
Frank Bennicasa, Publisher
L Michael Posey, Editor
Carli Richard, Managing Editor
Offering readers profiles of practices that employ unique MTM techniques to effectively serve their patients. Readers can use these profiles as models to develop and improve their own MTM practice, increase patient adherence, and build patient loyalty.
Cost: $200.00
Frequency: Monthly
ISSN: 1042-0991
Founded in 1962

20666 **Prescriber's Letter**
Therapeutic Research
PO Box 8190
Stockton, CA 95208
209-472-2240; Fax: 209-472-2249
www.pletter.com
Jeff Jellin PharmD, Publisher
A newsletter to pharmacists offering coverage of drug development, production, distribution, legislation, safety and other issues concerning the industry.
Cost: $85.00
ISSN: 1073-7219

20667 **Preventive Medicine Update**
HealthComm International
5800 Soundview Drive
PO Box 1729
Gig Harbor, WA 98335-2000
253-858-3315
800-843-9660; Fax: 253-851-9749
Jeffrey Bland, CEO/Contact

20668 **Psoriasis Resource**
National Psoriasis Foundation
6600 Sw 92nd Ave
Suite 300
Portland, OR 97223-7195
503-244-7404
800-723-9166; Fax: 503-245-0626
www.psoriasis.org
Pam Field, CEO
Bill Taggart, Managing Editor
Gail Zimmerman, CEO
A newsletter published for members of the National Psoriasis Foundation. Highlights interesting articles on psoriasis products and medications andother health related topics. Contains advertisements for psoriasis-related products and services.
16 Pages
Circulation: 40000
Mailing list available for rent: 28000 names
Printed in 2 colors on matte stock

20669 **Results Newsletter**
American Clinical Laboratory Association
1100 New York Ave Nw
Suite 725
Washington, DC 20005-6172
202-637-9466; Fax: 202-637-2050
info@clinical-labs.org
www.acla.com
Alan Mertz, President
Frequency: Monthly
Mailing list available for rent

20670 **Rx Ipsa Loquitur**
American Society for Pharmacy Law
1224 Centre West Dr
Suite 400
Springfield, IL 62704-2184
217-698-6163; Fax: 217-698-6164
www.aspl.org
Michael Monson, Owner
Francis B Palumbo, Director
Pamela Tolson CAE, Executive Director
William Fassett, Treasurer
Featuring recent court decisions, legislative and regulatory news, and other current pharmacy law news and articles.
Frequency: Bi-Monthly

20671 **The Nation's Health**
American Public Health Association
800 I Street NW
Washington, DC 20001
202-777-2742; Fax: 202-777-2534
thenationshealth.aphapublications.org
Georges C. Benjamin, Executive Director
For the latest news on public health, public health professionals, legislators and decision-makers. This newsletter is part of APHA membership.
Cost: $50.00
Frequency: 10x/yr

20672 **Washington Drug Letter**
FDAnews
300 N Washington St
Suite 200
Falls Church, VA 22046-3441
703-538-7600
888-838-5578; Fax: 703-538-7676
customerservice@fdanews.com
www.fdanews.com
Cynthia Carter, President
Maritza Lizama, Marketing Director
Summaries of FDA regulatory changes and key legislation that affects prescription and over the counter drugs. Each weekly issue brings you up-to-date on pre approval and post approval issues that directly impact your operation.
Cost: $897.00
Frequency: Weekly

Magazines & Journals

20673 **AAPS Newsmagazine**
American Association of Pharmaceutical Scientists
2107 Wilson Blvd
Suite 700
Arlington, VA 22201-3042
703-243-2800; Fax: 703-243-9054
aaps@aaps.org
www.aaps.org
John Lisack, Executive Director
Karol Shadle, Associate Director
Maria Nadeau, Member Groups Manager
Me'Gesha Portlock, Administrative Assistant
Exclusive to AAPS members. Features expanded coverage of the industry, complete with expert information on marketplace trends, regulatory matters, and career opportunities.
Mailing list available for rent

20674 **AAPS Online Buyers Guide**
American Association of Pharmaceutical Scientists
2107 Wilson Blvd
Suite 700
Arlington, VA 22201-3042
703-243-2800; Fax: 703-243-9054
aaps@aaps.org
www.aaps.org
John Lisack, Executive Director
Karol Shadle, Associate Director
Maria Nadeau, Member Groups Manager
Me'Gesha Portlock, Administrative Assistant
comprehensive sourcebook you need as a pharmaceutical scientist. Research the more than 500 companies providing the products and service you need. You can browse the entire Online Buyers Guide or you can refine your search by Company Name, Region, Business Category, or Keyword.
Mailing list available for rent

20675 **AAPS PharmSciTech Journal**
American Association of Pharmaceutical Scientists
2107 Wilson Blvd
Suite 700
Arlington, VA 22201-3042
703-243-2800; Fax: 703-243-9054
aaps@aaps.org
www.aaps.org
John Lisack, Executive Director
Karol Shadle, Associate Director
Maria Nadeau, Member Groups Manager
Me'Gesha Portlock, Administrative Assistant
An online-only journal published and owned by the American Association of Pharmaceutical Scientists. The journal's mission is to disseminate scientific and technical information on drug product design, development, evaluation

and processing to the global pharmaceutical research community, taking full advantage of web-based publishing by presenting innovative text with 3-D graphics, interactive figures and databases, video and audio files.
ISSN: 1530-9932
Mailing list available for rent

20676 **America's Pharmacist**
National Community Pharmacists Association
100 Daingerfield Road
Alexandria, VA 22314
703-683-8200
800-544-7447; Fax: 703-683-3619
www.ncpanet.org

Mike Conlan, VP Publications/Editor
Chris Linville, Managing Editor

This informative magazine gives 25,000 independent pharmacists insight into current issues that affect independent pharmacy and NCPA's activities to address those issues. Also; it serves the readers by including monthly articles on clinical topics, a continuing education series for pharmacists who want to earn CE credit, information on how to manage finances, and proven tips on better marketing, as well as profiles of NCPA members from across the country. Annual subscription included in dues.
Cost: $50.00
Frequency: Monthly

20677 **American Institute of the History of Pharmacy**
777 Highland Ave
Madison, WI 53705-2222
608-262-5378; Fax: 608-262-3397
aihp@aihp.org
www.aihp.org/

Dr. Gregory Higby, Executive Director
Dr. Elaine Stroud, Assistant Director
Beth Fisher, Assoc. Dir. Curatorial Affairs

Articles on pharmaceutical history and usage.
Cost: $50.00
200 Pages
Frequency: Quarterly
Circulation: 1200
Founded in 1960
Printed in on glossy stock

20678 **American Journal of Health-System Pharmacy**
American Society of Health-System Pharmacists
7272 Wisconsin Ave
Bethesda, MD 20814-4861
301-657-3000
866-279-0681; Fax: 301-664-8877
ajhp@ashp.org
www.ashp.org
Facebook, Twitter, LinkedIn, YouTube

Kathryn Shultz, President
Paul Abramowitz, CEO
Philip Schneider, Treasurer

The journal for pharmacists practicing in all area's of acute care, ambulatory care, home care, long term care, HMO's, PPO's, and PBM's.
Cost: $165.00
54 Pages
Frequency: Bi-Weekly
Circulation: 42,000
ISSN: 1079-2082
Printed in 2 colors on glossy stock

20679 **American Journal of Medical Quality**
American College of Medical Quality
4334 Montgomery Ave
Suite B
Bethesda, MD 20814-4415
301-913-9149
800-924-2149; Fax: 301-913-9142
acmq@acmq.org
www.acmq.org

Bridget Brodie, Manager
Frequency: Bi-Monthly

20680 **American Journal of Pharmaceutical Education**
American Association of Colleges of Pharmacy
1727 King St
Alexandria, VA 22314-2700
703-739-2330; Fax: 703-836-8982
www.aacp.org

Lucinda Maine, Executive VP
Kenneth W Miller, Senior VP
Daniel J Cassidy, COO

Official publication of the American Association of Colleges of Pharmacy. Dedicated to all those with interest in professional, graduate, and postgraduate pharmaceutical education. Its purpose is to documnet and advance pharmaceutical education in the United States and Internationally. Features original research articles, editorials, reports on the state of pharmaceutical education, descriptions of teaching innovations, and book reviews.
Cost: $65.00
120 Pages
Frequency: Quarterly
Circulation: 3200
ISSN: 0002-9459
Founded in 1937
Printed in one color on matte stock

20681 **BioPharm**
Advanstar Communications
6200 Canoga Avenue
2nd Floor
Woodland Hills, CA 91367
818-593-5000; Fax: 818-593-5020
biopharminternational.com

Joseph Loggia, President
Chris DeMoulin, VP
Susannah George, Marketing Director

Publication taking a practical approach to the technology and business of developing and manufacturing biotechnology-derived pharmaceutical products. Regular topics include process development, downstream processing, facilities design, emerging technologies and regulatory compliance.
Cost: $64.00
Frequency: Monthly
Circulation: 29,200
ISSN: 1040-8304
Founded in 1987

20682 **Cannabinoids**
International Association for Cannabinoid Medicine
Am Mildenweg 6
59602 Ruethen
Germany
+49-2952-9708571; Fax: +49-2952-902651
info@cannabis-med.org
www.cannabis-med.org
Facebook, Twitter, LinkedIn

Franjo Grotenhermen, Executive Director & Editor
Michael Krawitz, Patient Representative, USA
Alison Myrden, Patient Representative, Canada
Mark Ware, Editor

The official journal of the IACM is peer-reviewed and published online in several languages. A source of information on medical and scientific aspects of cannabis and cannabinoids.
ISSN: 2378-8763
Founded in 2000

20683 **Cannabis and Cannabinoid Research**
International Association for Cannabinoid Medicine
Am Mildenweg 6
59602 Ruethen
Germany
+49-2952-9708571; Fax: +49-2952-902651
info@cannabis-med.org
www.cannabis-med.org
Facebook, Twitter, LinkedIn

Franjo Grotenhermen, Executive Director
Michael Krawitz, Patient Representative, USA
Alison Myrden, Patient Representative, Canada
Daniele Piomelli, PhD, PharmD, Editor-in-Chief

A peer-reviewed journal dedicated to the scientific, medical, and psychosocial exploration of clinical cannabis, cannabinoids, and the endocannabinoid system. Affiliated with the IACM.
ISSN: 2378-8763
Founded in 2000

20684 **Chain Drug Review**
Racher Press
220 5th Avenue
New York, NY 10001
212-213-6000; Fax: 212-725-3961

Kevin Burke, VP/Group Advertising
Jeff Woldt, VP/Editorial Director
David Pinto, Editor

Chain Drug Review serves the chain drug industry.
Cost: $185.00
Frequency: Bi-weekly
Circulation: 54000
Founded in 1978
Printed in 4 colors on glossy stock

20685 **Chemistry**
American Chemical Society
1155 16th St Nw
Washington, DC 20036-4892
202-872-4600
800-227-5558; Fax: 202-872-4615
help@acs.org
www.acs.org

Madeleine Jacobs, CEO
Judith L Benham, Board Chair

Published for members, student affiliates, and those interested in learning more about the chemical sciences and the American Chemical Society.

20686 **CleanRooms Magazine**
PennWell Publishing Company
98 Spit Brook Rd
Suite 100
Nashua, NH 03062-5737
603-891-0123; Fax: 603-891-9294
georgem@pennwell.com
www.pennwell.com

Christine Shaw, VP
James Enos, Publisher
Bob Johnson, Sales & Marketing Manager

Serves the contamination control and ultrapure materials and process industries. Written for readers in the microelectronics, pharmaceutical, biotech, health care, food processing and other user industries. Provides technology and business news and new product listings.
Cost: $97.00
Frequency: Monthly
Circulation: 35031
Founded in 1987

20687 **Community Pharmacist**
ELF Publications

5285 W Louisiana Ave
Lakewood, CO 80232-5976

303-975-0075
800-922-8513; Fax: 303-975-0132
www.elfpublications.com

Judy Lane, Owner
Ronald R Quam, Editor/Publisher

Pharmacy trade journal that meets the professional educational needs of today's practitioner
Cost: $12.00
40 Pages
ISSN: 1096-9179
Founded in 1972
Printed in 4 colors on glossy stock

20688 Contract Pharma
Rodman Publishing
70 Hilltop Rd
3rd Floor
Ramsey, NJ 07446-1150

201-825-2552; Fax: 201-825-0553
info@rodpub.com
www.nutraceuticalsworld.com

Rodman Zilenziger Jr, President
Matt Montgomery, VP

A global publication providing most up-to-date news, outsourcing information, business trends, commentary, and viewpoints to the Pharmaceutical and Biopharmaceutical outsourcing industry.
Frequency: Monthly
Circulation: 20026
Founded in 1999

20689 DIA Global Forum
Drug Information Association
800 Enterprise Road
Suite 200
Horsham, PA 19044-3595

215-442-6100; Fax: 215-442-6199
dia@diahome.org
www.diahome.org

Barbara Lopez Kunz, Global Chief Executive

Presents important news from DIA conferences and workshops, reports of the Board of Directors and the regional advisory councils that directly impact DIA members, as well as practical tips, regulatory and global updates, upcoming DIA events, program notes, and more.
Frequency: Bi-Monthly
Circulation: 20000
ISSN: 1944-1991
Printed in 4 colors

20690 DVM News
Advanstar Communications
8033 Flint St
Lenexa, KS 66214-3335

913-492-4300
800-255-6864; Fax: 913-492-4157
www.dvm360.com

Rebecca Turner Chapman, VP

Information from veterinary medicine covering news, features, practice management and new products and services.
Cost: $4.00
Frequency: Monthly
ISSN: 0012-7337
Founded in 1987

20691 Drug Information Journal
Drug Information Association
800 Enterprise Road
Suite 200
Horsham, PA 19044-3595

215-442-6100; Fax: 215-442-6199
dia@diahome.org
www.diahome.org

Barbara Lopez Kunz, Global Chief Executive

Purpose is to disseminate information on manual and automated drug research, development, and information systems; to foster communication between educational, research, industrial and governmental personnel engaged in drug information activities; and to provide a forum for the development of improved methods of presenting research data generated from chemical, toxicologic, pharmacologic, and clinical studies.
Frequency: Bi-Monthly
Circulation: 20000
ISSN: 0092-8615
Founded in 1964

20692 Drug Store News
Lebhar-Friedman
425 Park Ave
New York, NY 10022-3526

212-756-5088; Fax: 212-838-9487
www.drugstorenews.com

Heather Martin, Manager
J Rodger Friedman, CEO

Publication consists of merchandising trends and pharmacy developments. Provides extensive coverage of every major segment of chain drug retailing and combination stores.
Cost: $119.00
Circulation: 45000
Founded in 1925

20693 Drug Topics
Medical Economics Publishing
5 Paragon Dr
Montvale, NJ 07645-1791

973-944-7777; Fax: 973-944-7778
www.drugtopics.com

Jim Granto, Publisher
Heather Schlosser, National Account Manager

Information on the distributing and dispensing drug trade.
Cost: $61.00
Printed in 4 colors on glossy stock

20694 Food & Drug Packaging
Stagnito Publishing Group
155 Pfingston Road
Suite 205
Deerfield, IL 60015

847-205-5660; Fax: 847-205-5680
www.fdp.com
Facebook, Twitter, LinkedIn, you tube

Lisa McTigue Pierce, Editor-in-Chief
Blayne Long, Senior Marketing Manager
Geneine Van Someren, Circulation Manager
Vince Miconi, Advertising Production Manager
George Misko, Regional Sales Manager

Food and Drug Packaging serves industries engaged in packaging food, beverages, pharmaceuticals, cosmetics and consulting/engineering firms.
Frequency: Monthly
Circulation: 75140
Founded in 1959

20695 Food and Drug Law Journal
Food & Drug Law Institute
1155 15th Street NW
Suite 800
Washington, DC 20005

202-371-1420
800-956-6293; Fax: 202-371-0649
comments@fdli.org
www.fdli.org

Michael D. Levin-Epstein, Vice President, Publications
Abby C. Foster, Managing Editor

Award-winning journal offering scholarly, in-depth, analytical articles, providing insight into action of the FDA, FTC, and USDA, how the courts interpret these actions, and the reaction of the industry.
Cost: $379.00
Frequency: Quarterly
ISSN: 1064-590x

20696 Formulary
Advanstar Communications
6200 Canoga Avenue
2nd Floor
Woodland Hills, CA 91367

818-593-5000; Fax: 818-593-5020
info@advanstar.com
www.advanstar.com

Joseph Loggia, President
Chris DeMoulintein, VP
Susannah George, Marketing Director

Peer-reviewed publication providing drug information for physicians, pharmacists, and other health care professionals who influence the selection and use of drugs in hospitals, HMO's, and other managed care settings.
Cost: $61.00
Frequency: Monthly
Circulation: 51402
ISSN: 1082-801X
Founded in 1992
Mailing list available for rent

20697 HealthCare Distributor
ELF Publications
5285 W Louisiana Ave
Lakewood, CO 80232-5976

303-975-0075
800-922-8513; Fax: 303-975-0132
elfpub@qwest.net
www.elfpublications.com

Judy Lane, Owner
Ronald R Quam, Editor/Publisher
Chuck Austin, Senior Editor
Jerry Lester, Director of Sales

Multi-market publication devoted to the issues and opportunities facing the wholesale drug, chain drug, medical/surgical and home care products distribution industries
Cost: $12.00
80 Pages
Frequency: Bi-annually
Circulation: 12000
ISSN: 1096-9160
Founded in 1972
Printed in 4 colors on glossy stock

20698 Hospital Pharmacy
Facts and Comparisons
111 Westport Plz
Suite 300
St Louis, MO 63146-3011

314-216-2100
800-223-0554; Fax: 314-878-5563
service@drugfacts.com
www.factsandcomparisons.com

John Pins, VP

Provides pharmacists with peer-reviewed articles and monthly features covering clinical and administrative areas such as drug use, drug distribution systems in hospitals and health-systems, automation, medication errors and adverse events, Joint Commission drug-related material and current FDA drug information.
Cost: $124.95
Frequency: Monthly
ISSN: 0018-5787
Founded in 1965

20699 Inform
American Oil Chemists' Society
2710 S Boulder
Urbana, IL 61802-6996

217-359-2344; Fax: 217-351-8091
kheine@aocs.org

www.aocs.org
Facebook, Twitter, LinkedIn, Blog

Jody Schonfeld, Publications Director
Kimmy Farris, Production Editor
Kathy Heine, Managing Editor

Member benefit pmagazine providing international news on fats, oils, surfactants, detergents, and related materials.
Cost: $175.00
462 Pages
Frequency: Monthly
Circulation: 3700
ISSN: 0897-8026
Founded in 1909
Printed in on glossy stock

20700 International Pharmaceutical Abstracts
American Society of Health-System Pharmacists
7272 Wisconsin Ave
Bethesda, MD 20814-4861

301-657-3000
866-279-0681; Fax: 301-664-8877
www.ashp.org

Mark Woods, President

These reports offering the latest in the development of drugs overseas, clinical use, cosmetics and, alternative and herbal medicine. Reports on pharmacy practice are also included.
Cost: $240.00
Frequency: Monthly
Circulation: 31,000
ISSN: 0020-8264
Founded in 1936

20701 Journal of Managed Care Pharmacy
Academy of Managed Care Pharmacy
100 N Pitt St
Suite 400
Alexandria, VA 22314-3141

703-683-8416
800-827-2627; Fax: 703-683-8417
sandres@amcp.org
www.amcp.org
Facebook, Twitter, LinkedIn

Douglas Burgoyne, President
Robert Gregory, Treasurer

Features articles on trends and recent developments in managed care pharmacy, updates from pharmacy educators about the inclusion of managed care topics in cirricula and news and information about the academy and it's activities.
Cost: $60.00
Frequency: Bi-Monthly

20702 Journal of Parenteral and Enteral Nutrition
Amer. Society for Parenteral & Enteral Nutrition
8630 Fenton Street
Suite 412
Silver Spring, MD 20910-3803

301-587-6315
800-727-4567; Fax: 301-587-2365
jpen@nutr.org
www.nutritioncare.org
Facebook, Twitter

Is the premier scientific journal of nutrition and metabolic support. It publishes original, peer-reviewd studies that define the cutting edge of basic and clinical research in the field. It explores the science of optimizing the care of patients receiving enteral or IV therapies. This is included as benefits of membership in ASPEN.
Cost: $90.00
Frequency: Fortnightly
Circulation: 7800
ISSN: 0148-6071
Founded in 1977

20703 Journal of Pharmaceutical Innovation
Int'l Society for Pharmaceutical Engineering
3109 W Dr Martin Luther King Jr Boulevard
Suite 250
Tampa, FL 33607

813-960-2105; Fax: 813-264-2816
ask@ispe.org
www.ispe.org

Gloria N Hall, Editor & Director of Publications
Lynda Goldbach, Publications Manager
Amy Lecceardone, Publications Coordinator
Valerie Adams, Advertising Sales Coordinator
Frequency: 4/Year
Circulation: 2000

20704 Journal of Pharmaceutical Marketing and Management
Taylor & Francis Group LLC
325 Chestnut St
Suite 800
Philadelphia, PA 19106-2614

215-625-8900
800-354-1420; Fax: 215-625-2940
haworthorders@taylorandfrancis.com
www.taylorandfrancis.com

Kevin Bradley, President

The journal maintains a vigorous policy of publishing quality research reports of interest to individuals involved in the manufacturing, wholesale, institutional, retail, regulatory, organizational and academic components of the pharmaceutical industry.
Frequency: Quarterly

20705 Journal of Pharmaceutical Sciences
Wiley InterScience
350 Main St
Malden, MA 02148-5089

781-388-8250
800-835-6770; Fax: 781-388-8210
cs-journals@wiley.com
www.wiley.com

Amy Yodaniss, VP
Julie Fisher, Assistant Editor
Roger Hall, VP
Laurie Beagell, Circulation Manager

A comprehensive look at the world of drugs and pharmaceuticals.
Frequency: Monthly
Circulation: 225

20706 Journal of Pharmacy Practice
Technomic Publishing Company
PO Box 3535
Lancaster, PA 17601

717-291-5609
800-233-9936; Fax: 717-295-4538
www.techpub.com

Amy Flannery, Marketing

The journal provides useful, timely reports on the most challenging issues of pharmacy today and anticipates the unique demands of this rapidly changing field. Each issue's single-topic format and thoughtful, readable analysis gives a better grasp of difficult problems and provides immediately useful information.
Cost: $210.00
80 Pages
ISSN: 0897-1900
Printed in 2 colors on matte stock

20707 Journal of Pharmacy Technology
Harvey Whitney Books Company
PO Box 42696
Cincinnati, OH 45242-696

513-793-3555
877-742-7631; Fax: 513-793-3600
customerserv@jpharmtechnol.com
www.jpharmtechnol.com

Harvey Whitney, Publisher/Editor
Eugene Sorkin, Associate Editorial
Ann Brandewiede, Circulation Manager

Latest information on drugs, for health professionals. Topics covered include new drug profiles, education and training, legal dilemmas, drug distribution, products and equipment and continuing education.
Cost: $122.00
Circulation: 1000
ISSN: 8755-1225

20708 Journal of Surfactants and Detergents
American Oil Chemists' Society
2710 S Boulder
Urbana, IL 61802-6996

217-359-2344; Fax: 217-351-8091
general@aocs.org
www.aocs.org
Facebook, Twitter, LinkedIn, Blog

Jody Schonfeld, Publications Director
Pam Landman, Journals Coordinator
Kimmy Farris, Production Editor

Dedicated to the practical and theoretical aspects of oleochemical and petrochemical surfactants, soaps and detergents. This growing scientific journal publishes peer-reviewed research papers, and reviews related to surfactants and detergents technologies.
Cost: $457.00
Frequency: Quarterly
Founded in 1998

20709 Journal of the American Medical Marijuana Association
American Medical Marijuana Association

convention@ammainfo.com
www.ammainfo.com
Facebook

Contains scientific research, news, and current events that is of interest to professionals, advocates, and those interested in the benefits, application, and proper use of medical marijuana (cannabis) in the treatment of health conditions.
Frequency: Quarterly

20710 Journal of the American Oil Chemists' Society
American Oil Chemists' Society
2710 S Boulder
Urbana, IL 61802-6966

217-359-2344; Fax: 217-351-8091
general@aocs.org
www.aocs.org
Facebook, Twitter, LinkedIn, Blog

Jodey Schonfeld, Publications Director
Pam Landman, Journals Coordinator
Kimmy Farris, Production Editor

The leading source for technical papers related to the fats and oils industries. A peer-reviewed journal devoted to fundamental and practical research, production, processing, packaging and distribution in the growing field of fats, oils, proteins and other related substances.
Cost: $619.00
Frequency: Monthly
Founded in 1947

20711 Journal of the American Pharmacists Association
American Pharmacists Association
2215 Constitution Ave NW
Washington, DC 20037-2985

202-628-4410
800-237-2742; Fax: 202-783-2351

www.pharmacist.com
Facebook, Twitter, YouTube

L Michael Posey, Editor
L Douglas Reid, Editor-In-Chief

The official peer-reviewed journal of APhA, provides information on pharmaceutical care, drug therapy, diseases and other health issues, trends in pharmacy practice and therapeutics, informed opinion, and original research.
ISSN: 1544-3191

20712 Lipids
American Oil Chemists' Society
2710 S Boulder
Urbana, IL 61802-6996

217-359-2344; Fax: 217-351-8091
general@aocs.org
www.aocs.org
Facebook, Twitter, LinkedIn, Blog

Jody Schonfeld, Publications Director
Pam Landman, Journals Coordinator
Kimmy Farris, Production Editor

Scientific journal features full-length original research articles, short communications, methods papers and review articles on timely topics. All papers are meticulously peer-reviewed and edited by some of the foremost experts in their respective fields.
Cost: $461.00
Frequency: Monthly
Founded in 1966

20713 MPMN: Medical Product Manufacturing News
UBM Canon
2901 28th St
Ste. 100
Santa Monica, CA 90045

310-445-4200; Fax: 310-445-4299
john.bethune@cancom.com
www.devicelink.com
Twitter

Shana Leonard, Editor in Chief
Bob Michaels, Managing Editor

A product tabloid magazine that provides information on the new products and services available to medical device manufacturers.
Frequency: 10x/yr

20714 Med Ad News
Canon Communicaitons Pharmaceutical Media Group
828A Newtown Yardley Road
Newtown, PA 18940

215-944-9800; Fax: 215-867-0053
sandra.baker@cancom.com
www.pharmalive.com

Christiane Truelove, Editor

Provides extensive coverage and incisive analyses of issues, events, trends and strategies shaping pharmaceutical business, marketing and sales.
Frequency: Monthly

20715 Medical Cannabis and Cannabinoids
International Association for Cannabinoid Medicine
Am Mildenweg 6
59602 Ruethen
Germany

+49-2952-9708571; Fax: +49-2952-902651
info@cannabis-med.org
www.cannabis-med.org
Facebook, Twitter, LinkedIn

Franjo Grotenhermen, Executive Director
Michael Krawitz, Patient Representative, USA
Alison Myrden, Patient Representative, Canada
Prof. Rudolf Brenneisen, Editor-in-Chief

A peer-reviewed journal offering an international forum to present and discuss recent advances in the medical use of cannabis and cannabinoids. Affiliated with the IACM.
ISSN: 2378-8763
Founded in 2000

20716 Modern Drug Discovery
American Chemical Society
1155 16th St Nw
16th Street NW
Washington, DC 20036-4892

202-872-4600
800-227-5558; Fax: 202-872-4615
service@acs.org
www.acs.org

Madeleine Jacobs, CEO/Executive Director

Reports matters of interest to scientists and other professionals working in the field of drug discovery.
Frequency: Monthly

20717 Monitor
Association of Clinical Research Professionals
1012 14th Street NW
Suite 108
Washington, DC 20006

202-737-8100; Fax: 202-737-8101
acrp@associationhq.com
www.acrpnet.org

Sharada Gilkey, Editor-in-Chief

Features peer-reviewed articles, columns, and home study.
Frequency: Quarterly

20718 Nutrition in Clinical Practice
Amer. Society for Parenteral & Enteral Nutrition
8630 Fenton Street
Suite 412
Silver Spring, MD 20910

301-587-6315
800-727-4567; Fax: 301-587-2365
aspen@nutr.org
www.nutritioncare.org
Facebook, Twitter

Bridget Hollick, Managing Editor

This compliments the Journal of Parenteral and Enteral Nutrition with practical information and advice. It provides peer-reviewed clinical studies, reviews, techniques and procedures, teaching cases, clinical observations, and nutrition news. Included as benefits of membership is ASPEN.
Cost: $45.00
Frequency: Bi-Monthly
ISSN: 0884-5336

20719 PDA Journal of Pharmaceutical Science and Technology
Parenteral Drug Association
1894 Preston White Drive
Reston, VA 20191-5433

703-620-6390; Fax: 703-476-0904
www.npcnow.org

Lee Kirsch, Editor

One of the most relevant and outstanding peer-reviewed scientific and technical papers in the pharmaceutical/biopharmaceutical industry. The Journal is distributed to members as a membership benefit.
Frequency: Bi-Monthly

20720 Pharmaceutical & Medical Packaging News
Canon Communications
11444 W Olympic Blvd
Suite 900
Los Angeles, CA 90064-1555

310-445-4200; Fax: 310-445-4299
feedback@cancom.com
www.pmpnews.com

Charlie McCurdy, President
Daphne Allen, Editor
Justine Hamilton, Marketing Director
Peter Manfre, Account Executive

Information and news on events, new technology, industry trends, regulatory matters, and health care trade associations for professionals involved in the pharmaceutical and medical product packaging industry.
Cost: $150.00
Frequency: Monthly
Circulation: 20,000
ISSN: 1081-5481
Founded in 1978

20721 Pharmaceutical Engineering
Int'l Society for Pharmaceutical Engineering
3109 W Dr Martin Luther King Jr Boulevard
Suite 250
Tampa, FL 33607

813-960-2105; Fax: 813-264-2816
ask@ispe.org
www.ispe.org

Gloria N Hall, Editor & Director of Publications
Lynda Goldbach, Publications Manager
Amy Lecceardone, Publications Coordinator
Valerie Adams, Advertising Sales Coordinator

Journal is published bi-monthly for members only and is considered by ISPE members to be the number one member benefit. Feature articles provide practical application and specification information on the design, construction, supervision and maintenance of process equipment, plant systems, instrumentation and facilities.
Frequency: Bi-monthly
Circulation: 2000

20722 Pharmaceutical Executive
Advanstar Communications
131 W 1st St
Duluth, MN 55802-2065

218-740-7200
800-598-6008; Fax: 218-723-9537
info@advanstar.com
www.advanstar.com

Kent Akervik, Manager
Kim Brown, Producation Manager

Publication designed to meet the diverse management and marketing needs of professionals in the pharmaceutical industry worldwide. Editorial provides useful information on marketing, sales and promotion, as well as legal and regulatory issues.
Cost: $70.00
Frequency: Monthly
Circulation: 16237
ISSN: 0279-6570
Founded in 1987
Mailing list available for rent

20723 Pharmaceutical Processing
Reed Business Information
100 Enterprise drive
Suite 600
Rockaway, NJ 07866-912

973-920-7000
800-222-0289; Fax: 973-920-7531
www.reedbusiness.com

Tim Canny, Publisher
Mike Auerbach, Editor
R Reed, Owner

Contents include news on new products/equipment/services, case history and application arti-

cles focusing on equipment, instrumentation, process systems, packaging, validation and outsourcing services offered to the pharmaceutical marketplace.
Frequency: Monthly
Circulation: 31075
Founded in 1984

20724 Pharmaceutical Research
Plenum Publishing Corporation
233 Spring St
New York, NY 10013-1522
212-242-1490; Fax: 212-807-1047
www.plenum.com
Wolfgang Sadee, Editor
Research reports and summaries of the latest in development of certain drugs and pharmaceuticals.
Cost: $49.95
Frequency: Monthly
Founded in 1998

20725 Pharmaceutical Technology Magazine
Advanstar Communications
485 Route One South
Building F, First Floor
Iselin, NJ 08830
732-596-0276; Fax: 732-596-0005
mtracey@advanstar.com
www.pharmtech.com
Mike Tracey, Publisher
Douglas McCormick, Editor in Chief
Paul Milazzo, Director of Sales
Tria Deibert, Marketing Director
Provides authoritative and timely information covering all aspects of conventional and biotech pharmaceutical manufacturing including: applied research and development, drug delivery, solid dosage, manufacturing machinery and equipment, information technologies, contract services, biotechnology trends, and regulatory issues.
Frequency: Monthly
Circulation: 33691
Founded in 1987

20726 Pharmacy Times
Romaine Pierson Publishers
666 Plainsboro Rd
Plainsboro, NJ 08536
609-716-7777; Fax: 609-716-4747
www.pharmacytimes.com
Facebook, Twitter, LinkedIn, YouTube
Emilie McCardell, Editor-In-Chief
Cam Bishop, CEO
James Granato, Publisher
James Marshal, Production Director
Margaret P. Roeske, Associate Editor
News, analysis and trends in the pharmaceutical business.
Cost: $65.00
Frequency: Monthly
Circulation: 174,104
Founded in 1897

20727 Pharmacy West
Western Communications
Po Box 6020
Bend, OR 97708-6020
541-382-1811; Fax: 541-385-5802
Gordon Black, President
Distributed to pharmacies in the thirteen western states.
Cost: $18.00
Frequency: Monthly

20728 Profile of Pharmacy Faculty
American Association of Colleges of Pharmacy
1727 King St
Alexandria, VA 22314-2700
703-739-2330; Fax: 703-836-8982
www.aacp.org
Lucinda Maine, Executive VP
Kenneth W Miller, Senior VP
Daniel J Cassidy, COO
Provides statistics describing faculty at U.S. colleges and schools of pharmacy including a summary of the demographics, teaching discipline, rank, highest degree earned, tenure status, type of appointment, and salary of over 3,000 full time faculty members. Updated annually.
Cost: $25.00

20729 Scrip Magazine
1775 Broadway
Suite 511
New York, NY 10019
212-262-8230; Fax: 212-262-8234
An in-depth view of the issues and challenges facing all sectors of the pharmaceutical industry worldwide. Analytical features are written by pharmaceutical experts and opinion leaders as well as specialist journalists.
Frequency: Monthly

20730 The Consultant Pharmacist
American Society of Consultant Pharmacists
1321 Duke St
Suite 120
Alexandria, VA 22314-3563
703-739-1300
800-355-2727; Fax: 703-739-1321
info@ascp.com
www.ascp.com
Facebook, Twitter, LinkedIn, YouTube, Blogs
Frank Grosso, RPh, Executive Director & CEO
Marlene Bloom, Editor
Debbie Furman, Circulation
Official peer reviewed journal of the American Society of Consultant Pharmacists. Editorial deals with geriatric pharmacotherapy.
76 Pages
Circulation: 11000
Founded in 1969
Printed in 4 colors on glossy stock

20731 Update Magazine
Food & Drug Law Institute
1155 15th Street NW
Suite 800
Washington, DC 20005
202-371-1420
800-956-6293; Fax: 202-371-0649
comments@fdli.org
www.fdli.org
Facebook, Twitter, LinkedIn
Michael D. Levin-Epstein, Vice President, Publications
Erin M Jones, Membership and Marketing
Susan C Winckler, President & CEO
Update brings you the latest news from FDLI and the industry, featuring viewpoints on trends, artilces on topics of regulatory concern, changes at the FDA, news about FDLI activities, and recurring columns about current events in the industry. Free to individuals within FDLI member organizations.
Cost: $100.00
Frequency: Bimonthly

Trade Shows

20732 AACP Annual Meeting and Seminars
American Association of Colleges of Pharmacy
1727 King Street
Alexandria, VA 22314
703-739-2330; Fax: 703-836-8982
www.aacp.org
Lucinda L Maine, Executive VP
Kenneth W Miller, Senior VP
Daniel J Cassidy, COO
A chance to learn and exchange ideas on pharmacy education and recent innovations in health care.
Frequency: July

20733 AACP Institute
American Association of Colleges of Pharmacy
1727 King Street
Alexandria, VA 22314
703-739-2330; Fax: 703-836-8982
www.aacp.org
Lucinda L Maine, Executive VP
Kenneth W Miller, Senior VP
Daniel J Cassidy, COO
Frequency: May

20734 AAPS Annual Meeting & Expo
American AssociationOf Pharmaceutical Scientists
2107 Wilson Boulevard
Suite 700
Arlington, VA 22201-3042
703-243-2800; Fax: 703-243-9650
aaps@aaps.org
www.aaps.org
John Lisack, Executive Director
Maureen Downs, Director Finance
925 booths of raw materials, supplies and equipment, research and contract service labs, computer software, packaging and more.
Frequency: Annual November
Mailing list available for rent

20735 AAPT Annual Convention
American Association of Pharmacy Technicians
PO Box 1447
Greensboro, NC 27402
877-368-4771; Fax: 336-333-9068
aapt@pharmacytechnician.com
www.pharmacytechnician.com
Sandra Covington, President
Susan Jeffery, VP
Education programs and services to help technicians update their skills to keep pace with changes in the pharmacy services.
Frequency: August

20736 ACLA Annual Meeting
American Clinical Laboratory Association
1250 H Street NW
Suite 880
Washington, DC 20005
202-637-9466; Fax: 202-637-2050
info@clinical-labs.org
www.acla.com
Aan Mertz, President
JoAnne Glisson, VP
Jason DuBois, VP of Govt. Relations
Francesca O'Reilly, VP of Govt. Affairs
Dedicated to providing the latest information for clinical laboratories.
Frequency: January
Founded in 1971

20737 ACMP Conference
Academy of Managed Care Pharmacy

100 N Pitt Street
Suite 400
Alexandria, VA 22314-3134

703-683-8416
800-827-2627; Fax: 703-683-8417
www.amcp.org
Facebook, Twitter, LinkedIn

Aimee O'Conner, Assistant Director

Offers an exciting lineup of speakers, workshops, and topical sessions designed to meet the challenges of today's pharmacist practicing in a dynamic and constantly evolving managed care environment.
Frequency: October

20738 **AMMA Convention & Expo**
American Medical Marijuana Association

convention@ammainfo.com
www.ammainfo.com
Facebook

Offers an expo and educational courses for professionals, advocates, and those interested in the benefits, application, and proper use of medical marijuana (cannabis) in the treatment of health conditions.
Frequency: Annual

20739 **APHA Annual Meeting & Expo**
American Public Health Association
800 I Street NW
Washington, DC 20001

202-777-2742; Fax: 202-777-2534
annualmeeting@apha.org
www.apha.org

Lynn Schoen, Exhibition Manager

Five-hundred seventy exhibits of medical interest, pharmaceuticals, publishers, educational, governmental, software, helth promotion products and more. Scientific Sessions available.
13000 Attendees

20740 **ASCP Annual Meeting**
American Society of Consultant Pharmacists
1321 Duke Street
Suite 120
Alexandria, VA 22314-3563

703-739-1300
800-355-2727; Fax: 703-739-1321
info@ascp.com
www.ascp.com
Facebook, Twitter, LinkedIn, Vimeo

Jackie Hajji, Director Meetings/Conventions
Frank Grosso, RPh, Executive Director & CEO
Nicole J. Brandt, Chairman
Joseph Marek, President

Annual meeting of 300 exhibitors of pharmaceuticals, drug distribution systems, packaging equipment, computers, durable medical equipment and medical supplies.
2000 Attendees
Frequency: November
Founded in 1969
Mailing list available for rent: 6500 names

20741 **ASHP Summer Meeting**
American Society of Health-System Pharmacists
7272 Wisconsin Avenue
Bethesda, MD 20814-4836

301-657-3000
866-279-0681; Fax: 301-664-8857
www.ashp.org

Janet A Silvester R.Ph.,MBA, President

Offers a variety of programming, and delivers expertise on subject areas that are crucial to advancing a professional practice. Series programming, learning communities, and updates on hot topics, combined with exhibits and a variety of networking opportunities.
Frequency: June

20742 **ASPL Developments in Pharmacy Law Seminar**
American Society for Pharmacy Law
1224 Centre W
Suite 400B
Springfield, IL 62704

217-391-0219; Fax: 217-793-0041
www.aspl.org

Melissa Madigan, President
Francis B Paulumbo, Director
Pamela Tolson, CAE, Executive Director
William Fassett, Treasurer

An annual highlight with nationally renowned speakers and panelists discussing issues pertaining to pharmacy law. This seminar has evolved into an excellent educational opportunity for practicing pharmacists, attorneys, and academicians with the opportunity to gain both pharmacy and legal continuing education credits.
Frequency: Annual

20743 **Academy of Pharmaceutical Research and Science Convention**
American Pharmaceutical Association
2215 Constitution Avenue NW
Washington, DC 20037

202-429-7524
800-237-2742; Fax: 202-628-0443
www.aphanet.org

Windy K Christner, Meetings/Expositions

Main exhibits, pharmaceutical equipment supplies and services.
Frequency: Annual

20744 **American Association of College Pharmacies**
1727 King Street
Alexandria, VA 22314

703-739-2330; Fax: 703-836-8982
www.aacp.org

Lucinda L Maine, Executive VP
Kenneth W Miller, Senior VP
Daniel J Cassidy, COO

Educational association representing pharmacy scientists, educators and administrators.
2.3M Attendees
Frequency: July

20745 **American College of Medical Quality Annual Meeting**
American College of Medical Quality
4334 Montgomery Avenue
Suite B
Bethesda, MD 20814

301-913-9149
800-924-2149; Fax: 301-656-0989
acmq@aol.com
www.acmq.org
Facebook, Twitter, LinkedIn

Alan Krumholz, MD, President
James D. Cross, President-elect
Andrew Jerdonek, Executive Director
Donald Casey, Jr MD, Treasurer

Annual show and 10-20 exhibits of computer hardware and software, pharmaceuticals, medical publications and related equipment, supplies and services.
150 Attendees
Founded in 1973

20746 **American Pharmacists Annual Meeting & Expo**
American Pharmacists Association
2215 Constitution Avenue, NW
Washington, DC 20037

202-429-7593
800-237-2742; Fax: 203-737-3211
www.aphameeting.org

Laura Larson, Exposition & Exchange Information
Todd McDonald, Meeting Schedule Information
Lindsey Mace, General Conference Assistant
Kristen Binaso, Sponsorship Coordinator
Stacy Berkowitz, Educational Coordinator

The APhA Annual Meeting and Exposition provides information on the latest trends and best practices in pharmacy, while providing attendees the opportunity to share experiences and ideas with 7,000 pharmacy professionals from every practice setting; chain, independent, hospital, federal, long-term care, nuclear, and more.
Frequency: Annual/Spring

20747 **Annual NCPA Convention & Trade Exposition**
National Community Pharmacists Associations
100 Daingerfield Road
Alexandria, VA 22314

703-683-8200
800-544-7447; Fax: 703-683-3619
www.ncpanet.org

Litsa Deck, Director Convention/Trade Expos

Workshops and education programs pretaining to Pharmacy industry.
Frequency: October
Mailing list available for rent

20748 **Annual North American Conference and European Annual Conference**
Association of Clinical Research Professionals
1012 14th Street NW
Suite 108
Washington, DC 20006

202-737-8100; Fax: 202-737-8101
acrp@associationhq.com
www.acrpnet.org

Robin Newman, Vice Chair
Thomas L Adams, CAE, President/CEO
Larry J Medley, CAE, Director Finance
Alan Armstrong, Director Marketing/COO

The world's leading conferences for clinical research professionals, presenting diverse educational opportunities and face-to-face interactions with industry experts.
Frequency: April, September

20749 **DCAT Western Education Conference**
Drug, Chemical & Associated Technologies
1 Washington Boulevard
Suite 7
Robbinsville, NJ 08691

609-448-1000
800-640-3228; Fax: 609-448-1944
info@dcat.org
www.dcat.org
Facebook, LinkedIn

Mikaela Venice, Meeting Coordinator

Gain important insights into issues and trends that will affect the future of the nutrition and health industry. Participate in discussion on key business issues with industry experts.
Frequency: April

20750 **DIA Annual Meeting**
Drug Information Association

800 Enterprise Road
Suite 200
Horsham, PA 19044-3595

215-442-6100; Fax: 215-442-6199
dia@diahome.org
www.diahome.org

Barbara Lopez Kunz, Global Chief Executive

20751 **Distribution Management Conference & Expo**
Healthcare Distribution Alliance
900 N Glebe Road
Suite 1000
Arlington, VA 22203

703-787-0000; Fax: 703-812-5282
www.hda.org

Chester Davis, Jr., President/CEO
Ann W. Bittman, EVP/COO
Elizabeth Gallenagh, General Counsel/SVP, Supply Chain

Provides the latest information on the most important topics affecting healthcare distribution.
Frequency: Annual

20752 **FDLI & FDA Annual Conference**
Food and Drug Law Institute
1155 15th Street NW
Suite 800
Washington, DC 20005

202-371-1420
800-956-6293; Fax: 202-371-0649
comments@fdli.org
www.fdli.org

Susan C. Winckler, President & CEO
Iris V. Stratton CPA, VP Finance & Administration
Michael Sprott, Membership Manager

Bringing together high-ranking officials from the food and drug industry together with top executives.
550+ Members
Founded in 1949

20753 **HDA Business and Leadership Conference**
Healthcare Distribution Alliance
900 N Glebe Road
Suite 1000
Arlington, VA 22203

703-787-0000; Fax: 703-812-5282
www.hda.org

Chester Davis, Jr., President/CEO
Ann W. Bittman, EVP/COO
Elizabeth Gallenagh, General Counsel/SVP, Supply Chain

Provides a unique opportunity for senior-level retailer and supplier member executives to interact and discuss strategic issues.

20754 **IACM Conference**
International Association for Cannabinoid Medicine
Am Mildenweg 6
59602 Ruethen
Germany

+49-2952-9708571; Fax: +49-2952-902651
info@cannabis-med.org
www.cannabis-med.org
Twitter

Franjo Grotenhermen, Executive Director
Michael Krawitz, Patient Representative, USA
Alison Myrden, Patient Representative, Canada

A conference on cannabinoids in medicine featuring programs, lectures, and poster presentations.
Frequency: Biennial
Founded in 2000

20755 **IPC Annual Meeting**
Independent Pharmacy Cooperative
1550 Columbus Street
Sun Prairie, WI 53590

608-259-9556
800-755-1531; Fax: 800-274-5525
www.ipcrx.com

Mike Flint, President/CEO
Gary Helgerson, COO
Chuck Benjamin, CFO

A venue to provide independent pharmacies vital information to maximize their store's profitability
Frequency: July

20756 **ISPE Annual Meeting**
Int'l Society for Pharmaceutical Engineering
3109 W Dr. Martin Luther King Jr Boulevard
Suite 250
Tampa, FL 33607

813-960-2105; Fax: 813-264-2816
ask@ispe.org
www.ispe.org

Education and training on topics pretaining to the pharmaceutical manufacturing industry.
Frequency: Annual

20757 **Midyear Industry & Technology Issues Conference**
American Society for Automation in Pharmacy
492 Norristown Road
Suite 160
Blue Bell, PA 19422

610-825-7783; Fax: 310-825-7641
www.asapnet.org

WA Lockwood, Executive Director

Learn about the industry and technology issues facing the pharmacy market today.
Frequency: June

20758 **NABP's Annual Meeting**
National Association of Boards of Pharmacy
700 Busse Highway
Park Ridge, IL 60068

847-698-6227
800-774-6227; Fax: 847-698-0124
custserv@nabp.net
www.nabp.net

Carmen A Catizone, Executive Director/Secretary

Building regulatory foundation for patients safety.
Frequency: May

20759 **NABP's Fall Educational Conference**
National Association of Boards of Pharmacy
700 Busse Highway
Park Ridge, IL 60068

847-698-6227
800-774-6227; Fax: 847-698-0124
custserv@nabp.net
www.nabp.net

Malcom Broussard, Chairperson
Michael Burlson, President
Joseph Adams, Treasurer
Frequency: December

20760 **NACDS Annual Meeting**
National Association of Chain Drug Stores
1776 Wilson Blvd.
Suite 200
Arlington, VA 22209

703-549-3001; Fax: 703-836-4869
registration@nacds.org
www.nacds.org
Facebook, Twitter, LinkedIn, YouTube

This unique conference explores and evaluates current systems and emerging technologies, and helps retailers and suppliers forge stronger links through supply chain management. The exhibit hall allows leading industry consultants and vendors to demonstrate their products and services.

20761 **NCPA Annual Conference on National Legislation and Government Affairs**
National Community Pharmacists Associations
100 Daingerfield Road
Alexandria, VA 22314

703-683-8200
800-544-7447; Fax: 703-683-3619
www.ncpanet.org

Litsa Deck, Director Convention/Trade Expos

An opportunity to be an insider to discuss community pharmacy issues on Capitol Hill with the people that can make things happen. It will enhance your understanding of the political process and the many legislative issues that will have a dramatic impact on the way you deliver health care in the coming years.
Frequency: April

20762 **NCPA Annual Meeting**
National Council of State Pharmacy Association
5501 Patterson Avenue
Suite 200
Richmond, VA 23226

804-285-4145; Fax: 804-285-4227
becky@ncspae.org
www.ncspae.org

Rebecca P Snead, Executive Vice President
Brad Hall, Executive Director

Offers cutting-edge training for professionals from every facet of the pharmacy industry. Learn the latest about prescription drugs, natural products, and over-the-counter remedies. Discover new products and services from the industry's leading manufacturers, and gain knowledge and insights to better aid patients and advance your career.
Frequency: October

20763 **NCPDP's Annual Conference**
National Council for Prescription Drug Programs
9240 E Raintree Drive
Scottsdale, AZ 85260-7518

480-477-1000; Fax: 480-767-1042
ncpdp@ncpdp.org
www.ncpdp.org

Beth Fagan, Meeting Planning
Lee Ann Stember, President

Topic will be Building New Technologies. Offers educational sessions, a trade show, kenote speakers and more.
Frequency: March

20764 **National Clinical Issues Forum: Metabolic Syndrome**
American Pharmaceutical Association Foundation
2215 Constitution Avenue NW
Washington, DC 20037

202-297-7524
800-237-APHA; Fax: 202-429-6300
info@aphafoundation.org
www.aphafoundation.org

Carol Bugdalski-Stutrud, Director
Carl Emswiller, Director
Hazel Pipkin, VP
Marie Michnich, Director Health Policy Program
Michael Stewart, Director Public Relations

To provide an opportunity for the exchange of information between leading clinical pharmacists from across the U.S. who are providing innovative patient care services for people afflicted with

the co-morbidities of diabetes, hypertension and hyperlipidemia.
Frequency: May

20765 **National Community Pharmacists Association Convention and Exhibition**
National Community Pharmacists Association
100 Daingerfield Road
Alexandria, VA 22314-2833
703-683-8200
800-544-7447; Fax: 703-683-3619
www.ncpanet.org
Litsa Deck, Director Convention/Meetings
Faith James, Coordinator Convention/Meetings
Deleisa Johnson, VP Public Relations
Annual show of 450 exhibitors of pharmaceutical and related equipment, supplies and services.
Frequency: October, Florida

20766 **National Conference on Advances in Perinatal and Pediatric Nutrition**
Amer. Society for Parenteral & Enteral Nutrition
8630 Fenton Street
Suite 412
Silver Spring, MD 20910
301-587-6315
800-727-4567; Fax: 301-587-2365
aspen@nutr.org
www.nutritioncare.org
Facebook, Twitter
Marion F Winkler, President
Vincent W Vanek, VP
Robin Kriegel, CAE, Executive Director
Joanne Kieffer, Director Finance
The purpose of the conference is to increase knowledge and awareness of the nutritional requirements of these special need patients. Has been planned for dieticians, nurses, obstetricians, neonatologiests, pediatricians, pediatric gastroenterologists, pharmacists, and other health care professionals involved in the care of high risk pregnant mothers, premature infants, and pediatric patients.
Frequency: July

20767 **PCMA Annual Meeting**
Pharmaceutical Care Management Association
325 7th St. NW
9th Fl.
Washington, DC 20004
202-756-5700; Fax: 202-756-5708
www.pcmanet.org
Facebook, Twitter
Mark Merritt, President & CEO
The industry's annual event for decision makers.
Frequency: Annual
Founded in 2009

20768 **RX Expo: An Educational Forum and Buying Show**
National Community Pharmacists Association
100 Daingerfield Road
Alexandria, VA 22314-2833
703-683-8200
800-544-7447; Fax: 703-683-3619
www.ncpanet.org
Stephen Giroux PD, President
Bruce Roberts RPh, Executive VP/CEO
Annual show and exhibits of general gifts, sundries and seasonal items, over the counter products, health and beauty aids, electronic products, prescription drug products, personal care products, home health care products, IV products and related products.
1700 Attendees

20769 **USP Annual Scientific Meeting**
United States Pharmacopeial Convention
12601 Twinbrook Parkway
Rockville, MD 20852-1790
301-810-0667
800-227-8772; Fax: 301-816-8148
support@usp.org
www.usp.org
Anju K Malhotra, Manager Conferences/Meetings
Roger Williams, Executive Director
Open to the public and serves as an interactive forum where USP and its stakeholders can discuss new direction and standards that affect the pharmaceutical industry. The meeting provides attendees an opportunity to better understand the scope of USP's scientific work and provide input on key standards-setting issues.
Frequency: September

20770 **Western Section Meeting of the Triological Society**
Triological Society
555 N 30th Street
Omaha, NE 68131-2136
402-346-5500; Fax: 402-346-5300
www.triological.org
I Kaufman Arenberg, MD, Executive Director
Annual show of 30 exhibitors of medical services and supplies related to Otolaryngology.
152 Attendees
Frequency: May

Directories & Databases

20771 **American Drug Index**
Lippincott Williams & Wilkins
16522 Hunters Green Pkwy
PO Box 1600
Hagerstown, MD 21740
301-223-2300
800-638-3030; Fax: 301-223-2400
www.lww.com
Facebook, Twitter
Norman Billups, Editor
Shirley Billups, Editor
Contains more than 22,000 entries. Practical features include: alphabetically listed drug names, extensive cross-indexing, complete information on the distributor's brand name, manufacturer, generic and/or chemical names, chemical strength and much more useful information. Electronic version available.
Cost: $69.95
1088 Pages
Frequency: Annual, Hardcover
ISBN: 1-574391-33-X

20772 **Annual Meeting & Showcase**
Academy of Managed Care Pharmacy
100 N Pitt St
Suite 400
Alexandria, VA 22314-3141
703-683-8416
800-827-2627; Fax: 703-683-8417
sandres@amcp.org
www.amcp.org
Facebook, Twitter, LinkedIn
Douglas Burgoyne, President
Robert Gregory, Treasurer
Nationally reowned keynote speakers, new research presentations, achievement awards, competitions and Board inaugurations fill the agenda for managed care pharmacy's premier event.
Frequency: April

20773 **CSO Directory**
Drug Information Association
800 Enterprise Road
Suite 200
Horsham, PA 19044-3595
215-442-6100; Fax: 215-442-6199
dia@diahome.org
www.diahome.org
Barbara Lopez Kunz, Global Chief Executive
One of the industry's most respected and comprehensive reference guides, compiles company descriptions and contact information from hundreds of companies that provide services for every phase of the clinical trial and drug development process.

20774 **DCAT Digest and Directory of Membership**
Drug, Chemical & Associated Technologies
1 Washington Blvd
Suite 7
Robbinsville, NJ 08691-3162
609-448-1000
800-640-3228; Fax: 609-448-1944
info@dcat.org
www.dcat.org
Facebook, LinkedIn
Margaret Timony, Executive Director
Patricia Van Arnum, Editorial Director
Lauryn Kuna, Director, Membership
Miranda Greenberg, Editorial Coordinator
Keeping members in touch with their colleagues throughout the industry.

20775 **DIOGENES**
FOI Services
704 Quince Orchard Rd
Gaithersburg, MD 20878-1700
301-975-9400; Fax: 301-975-0702
infofoi@foiservices.com
www.foiservices.com
John Carey, President
Marlene Bobka, Vice President of Services
This comprehensive database contains citations to more than 1 million unpublished US Food and Drug Administration regulatory documents covering prescription and over-the-counter drugs.
Founded in 1975

20776 **DRUGDEX System**
Thompson Micromedex
6200 South Syracuse Way
Suite 300
Greenwood Village, CO 80111-4740
303-679-9500
800-525-9083; Fax: 303-486-6464
www.micromedex.com
Facebook
This comprehensive database covers all aspects of drugs and their use, including investigational, FDA-approved, and OTC preparations.
Frequency: Full-text

20777 **DataStat**
NDCHealth
3975 Research Park Drive
Ann Arbor, MI 48108
734-994-0540
800-225-5632; Fax: 734-663-9084
mweindorf@datastat.com
www.datastat.com
Marielle Weindorf, Senior Research Director
Ellen Johnson
Randolph Hutto, EVP Business Development
Charles W Miller, EVP Corporate Initiatives
This comprehensive database offers descriptions of drug interactions at the ingredient level

for individual drugs and therapeutic classes of drugs.
Frequency: Full-text
Founded in 1967

20778 Directory of Hospital Personnel
Grey House Publishing
4919 Route 22
PO Box 56
Amenia, NY 12501

518-789-8700
800-562-2139; Fax: 845-373-6390
books@greyhouse.com
www.greyhouse.com
Facebook, Twitter

Richard Gottlieb, President
Leslie Mackenzie, Publisher

A Who's Who of the hospital universe that makes it easy to get in touch with over 10,000 key decision makers. Comprehensive data includes listing of US hospitals, detailed contact information, number of physicians and employees, teaching affiliations, accreditation and much more.
Cost: $325.00
2300 Pages
ISBN: 1-592372-86-4
Founded in 1981

20779 Directory of Hospital Personnel - Online Database
Grey House Publishing
4919 Route 22
PO Box 56
Amenia, NY 12501

518-789-8700
800-562-2139; Fax: 845-373-6390
gold@greyhouse.com
gold.greyhouse.com
Facebook, Twitter

Richard Gottlieb, President
Leslie Mackenzie, Publisher

The DHP Online Database is the best resource you can have at your fingertips when researching or marketing a product or service to the hospital market. A 'Who's Who' of the hospital universe, this database puts you in touch with over 140,000 key decision-makers at 5,800 hospitals nationwide.
Founded in 1981

20780 Drug Store and HBC Chains
Chain Store Guide
3710 Corporex Park Dr.
Suite 310
Tampa, FL 33619-1389

813-627-6700
800-927-9292; Fax: 813-627-6888
webmaster@chainstoreguide.com
www.chainstoreguide.com

Mike Jarvis, Publisher
Chris Leedy, Advertising Sales

Tap into the lucrative drug industry with profiles on more than 1,700 US and Canadian companies operating two or more retail drug stores, deep discount stores, health and beauty care (HBC) stores, cosmetic stores or vitamin stores that have industry sales of at least $250,000. This powerful database empowers you to sell and market your products successfully by reaching more than 8,300 key decision makers.
Cost: $575.00

20781 Drug and Cosmetic Industry Catalog
Advanstar Communications
One Park Avenue
New York, NY 10016

212-797-7631; Fax: 212-951-6793
info@advanstar.com
www.advanstar.com

Eric Lisman, Executive VP

Over 1,000 manufacturers and suppliers of packaging equipment, private formulas and raw materials used in the drug and cosmetics industries are profiled.
Cost: $25.00
270 Pages
Frequency: Annual
Circulation: 4,000
Mailing list available for rent

20782 FDC Reports: The NDA Pipeline
FDC Reports
5550 Friendship Boulevard
Suite 1
Chevy Chase, MD 20815-7278

301-657-9830; Fax: 301-664-7238
fdc.customer.service@elsevier.com
www.fdcreports.com

Karl Uhlendo, Executive Editor
Mike Squires, President

The NDA Pipeline is a searchable database available through the Web that contains up-to-date coverage of over 900 companies and more than 7,00 approval records. The NDA Pipeline tracks drug and biological product research, clinical trials and approvals. It also includes a comprehensive listing of products in research, descriptions of phases of development and licensing information and linked articles from The Pink Sheet and other FDC Reports publications.
900 Pages
Frequency: Annual
ISSN: 7012-8630
Founded in 1939

20783 GAMP Good Practice Guide
Int'l Society for Pharmaceutical Engineering
3109 W Dr. Martin Luther King Jr Boulevard
Suite 250
Tampa, FL 33607

813-960-2105; Fax: 813-264-2816
ask@ispe.org
www.ispe.org

Provides new comprehensive guidance on meeting current regulatory expectations for compliant electronic records and signatures, which includes the need for record integrity, security, and availability throughout the required retention period. This is achieved by well documented, validated systems, and the application of appropriate operational controls.

20784 ISPE Good Practice Guide
Int'l Society for Pharmaceutical Engineering
3109 W Dr. Martin Luther King Jr Boulevard
Suite 250
Tampa, FL 33607

813-960-2105; Fax: 813-264-2816
ask@ispe.org
www.ispe.org

Provides a standard methodology for use in testing the containment efficiency of solids handling systems used in the pharmaceutical industry under closely defined conditions. It covers the main factors that affect the test results for specific contained solids handling systems, including material handled, room environment, air quality, ventilation and operator technique.

20785 Ident-A-Drug Reference
Therapeutic Research
3120 W March Lane
PO Box 8190
Stockton, CA 95219-0190

209-472-2240; Fax: 209-472-2249
www.pletter.com

Jeff Jellin, PharmD, Editor

It gives you all the drug identification information found on this web site for more than 30,000 entries.
Cost: $85.00
704 Pages
ISBN: 0-967613-65-5

20786 InVitro Diagnostics Industry Directory
CTB International Publishing
PO Box 218
Maplewood, NJ 07040-0218

973-966-0997; Fax: 973-966-0242
www.ctbintl.com

Lists address, phone and fax number of invitro diagnostics companies, suppliers, distributors, regulatory agencies, professional societies and trade associations worldwide and contains over 2,300 entries worldwide-more than 1,200 contact names.
Cost: $277.00
ISBN: 1-887566-17-1
Printed in one color on matte stock

20787 International Pharmaceutical Abstracts Database
Thomson Scientific
1500 Spring Garden St
Philadelphia, PA 19130-4067

215-386-0100
800-336-4474; Fax: 215-386-2911
www.thomson.com

Robert C Cullen, President/CEO
Craig Soderstrom, VP Office of CEO
Kristen McCarthy, VP Marketing/Communications
James Smith, Chief Operating Officer

These reports offering the latest in the development of drugs overseas, clinical and inventigotional use, cosmetics and, alternative and herbal medicine. Reports on pharmacy practice are also included.
ISSN: 0020-8264

20788 NABP Manual
National Association of Boards of Pharmacy
700 Busse Highway
Park Ridge, IL 60068

847-698-6227
800-774-6227; Fax: 847-698-0124
custserv@nabp.net
www.nabp.net

Malcom Broussard, Chairperson
Michael Burlson, President
Joseph Adams, Treasurer

Developed to be read in conjunction with state laws. It presents general information essential to all board of pharmacy members, and serves as a valuable reference for new board members. The manual is ideal for compiling and cross-referencing amendments and other records.
Cost: $25.00

20789 Natural Medicines Comprehensive Database
Therapeutic Research
PO Box 8190
Stockton, CA 95208-0190

209-472-2240; Fax: 209-472-2249
www.pletter.com

Jeff Jellin, PharmD, Editor

Provides you with monographs on each natural ingredient plus updated helpful charts and tables.
Cost: $85.00
2000 Pages
ISBN: 0-967613-68-X

20790 Pharma Industry Directory
CTB International Publishing

PO Box 218
Maplewood, NJ 07040

973-966-0997; Fax: 973-966-0242
www.ctbintl.com

This is divided into 4 sections. The first section contains a complete alphabetical listing of the names, addresses, and phone and fax numbers of over 1,300 companies. The other sections are alphabetical listings of the companies with tables identifying them as to the fields they are involved in. The last section is a business index.
Cost: $250.00
ISBN: 1-887566-21-X
Printed in one color on matte stock

20791 **Pharmaceutical News Index**
UMI/Data Courier
620 S 3rd Street
Suite 400
Louisville, KY 40202-2475

502-583-4111
800-626-2823; Fax: 502-589-5572

Contains the latest US and international information about pharmaceutial, cosmetics, medical devices, and related health industries.

20792 **Physicians' Desk Reference**
Thomson Medical Economics
5 Paragon Drive
Montvale, NJ 07645-1742

201-358-7500
800-442-6657; Fax: 201-573-8999
www.pdr.net

Thomas Eck, Marketing Manager

Physicians have turned to PDR for the latest word in prescription drugs for 57 years. Today, it is considered the standard prescription drug reference and can be found in virtually every phyician's office, hospital and pharmacy in the US.
Cost: $92.95
3,000 Pages
Frequency: Hardcover

20793 **Roster of Faculty and Professional Staff**
American Association of Colleges of Pharmacy
1727 King St
Suite 210
Alexandria, VA 22314-2700

703-739-2330; Fax: 703-836-8982
www.aacp.org

Lucinda Maine, Executive VP
Kenneth W Miller, Senior VP
Daniel J Cassidy, COO

A directory of more than 5,000 full and part-time pharmacy faculty members including mailing and e-mail addresses, phone and fax numbers, degrees, and disciplines. Also included is valuable information about AACP such as officers, committee members, staff, and addresses and phone numbers for affiliated associations and corporations. $10 AACP Member.
Cost: $100.00
Frequency: November
Mailing list available for rent

Industry Web Sites

20794 **http://gold.greyhouse.com**
G.O.L.D Grey House OnLine Databases

Grey House Publishing's online database platform, GOLD, offers Quick Search, Keyword Search and Expert Search for most business sectors including drug, pharmaceutical and healthcare markets. The GOLD platform makes finding the information you need quick and easy - whether you're a novice searcher or an experienced database user. All of Grey House's directory products are available for subscription on the GOLD platform.

20795 **www.aacp.org**
American Association of Colleges of Pharmacy

National organization representing the interests of pharmaceutical education and educators. Comprising all 83 US pharmacy colleges and schools including more than 4,000 faculty, 36,000 student enrolled in professional programs and 3,600 individuals pursuing graduate study, AACP is committed to excellence in pharmaceutical education.

20796 **www.aaps.org**
American Association of Pharmaceutical Scientists

Aims to advance science through the open exchange of scientific knowledge, serve as an information resource and contribute to human health through pharmaceutical reseach and development.

20797 **www.accp.com**
American College of Clinical Pharmacy

Professional and scientific society that provides leadership, education, advocacy and resources enabling clinical pharmacists to achieve excellence in practice and research.

20798 **www.acrpnet.org**
Association of Clinical Research Professionals

Provides global leadership for the clinical research profession by promoting and advancing the highest ethical standards and practices.

20799 **www.aihp.org**
American Instiute of the History of Pharmacy

Supplies information regarding pharmaceutical history and usage.

20800 **www.apha.org**
American Public Health Association

Brings together researchers, health service providers, administrators, teachers and other health workers in a unique, multidisciplinary environment of professional exchange, study and action on the effort to prevent disease and promote health.

20801 **www.asapnet.org**
American Society for Automation in Pharmacy

Is to assist its members in advancing the application of computer technology in the pharmacists role as caregiver and in the efficient operation and management of a pharmacy.

20802 **www.ashp.org**
American Society of Health-System Pharmacy

An association that brings together health-system pharmacists and addresses their concerns.

20803 **www.aspl.org**
American Society for Pharmacy Law

An organization of pharmacists and lawyers who are interested in the law as it applies to the pharmacy industry.

20804 **www.diahome.org**
Drug Information Association

Association for those interested in technical developments, supply, and production of drugs. Exchanges and disseminates information by continuing to provide a neutral forum, respecting and welcoming all participants and offering quality driven programming.

20805 **www.fdli.org**
Food and Drug Law Institute

Nonprofit educational organization dedicated to improving the understanding of the laws, regulations and policies affecting the food, drug, medical device and biologics industries. A neutral, non-partisan organization that does not lobby.

20806 **www.greyhouse.com**
Grey House Publishing

Authoritative reference directories for most business sectors including drug, pharmaceutical and healthcare markets. Users can search the online databases with varied search criteria allowing for custom searches by product category, geographic area, sales volume, keyword, subject and more. Full Grey House catalog and online ordering also available.

20807 **www.ipecamericas.org**
International Pharmaceutical Excipients Council

Members are companies with an interest in the otherwise inert chemicals used as vehicles for medicines. Federation of three independent regional industry associations headquartered in the US. Each association focuses its attention on the applicable law, regulations, science and business practices of its region. The three associations work together on excipient safety and public health issues, in connection with international trade matters, and to achieve harmonization of regulatory standards.

20808 **www.ncpanet.org**
National Community Pharmacists Association

Represents independent pharmacists, provides support for undergraduate pharmacy education.

20809 **www.npa.org**
National Pharmaceutical Alliance

Represents the interests of small pharmaceutical companies and allied industries.

20810 **www.nutritioncare.org**
American Soc. for Parenteral & Enteral Nutrition

Strives to be a conduit amoung those interested in Nutrition Support.

20811 **www.pda.org**
Parenteral Drug Association

Members are makers of parenteral (injectable) drugs and other pharmaceuticals, as well as suppliers, academia and regulatory bodies. Our mission is to advance the pharmaceutical and biopharmaceutical technology internationally by promoting scientifically sound and practical technical information and education for industry and regulatory issues.

20812 **www.pdr.net**
Thomson Medical Economics

Physicians have turned to PDR for the latest word on prescription drugs for 57 years. Today it is considered the standard prescription drug reference and can be found in virtually every phyician's office, hospital and pharmacy in the US.

20813 **www.pharmacist.com**
American Pharmacists Association

APhA was the first established national professional society of pharmacists, founded in 1852 as the American Pharamceutical Assocation. It is the largest assocation of pharamcists in the US, whose mission is to provide information, education, and advocacy to empower its members to improve medication use and advance patient care.

20814 www.pharmacytechnician.com
American Association of Pharmacy Technicians
Provides leadership and represents the interests of its members to the public as well as healthcare organizations. Promotes the safe, effectacious, and cost effective dispensing distribution and use of medications. Provides continuing education programs and services to help technicians update their skills to keep pace with changes in pharmacy services.

20815 www.safeaccessnow.org
Americans for Safe Access
Works to ensure safe and legal access to cannabis for therapeutic use and research. Home to newsletters, fact sheets, state legal manuals, reports, and booklets.

20816 www.thompson.com
Thompson Scientific and Healthcare
Professionals in business, government, law and academia have reliedon us for the most authorative, timely and practical guidance available.

20817 www.usp.org
United States Pharmacopeia
Helps to ensure that consumers recieve quality medicines by establishing state-of-the-art standards that pharmaceutical manufacturers must meet. We provide standards for more than 3,800 medicines, dietary supplements and other health care products.

Associations

20818 American Photographic Artists
5042 Wilshire Boulevard
Suite 321
Los Angeles, CA 90036

executivedirector@apanational.com
apanational.org
Facebook, Twitter, LinkedIn, Vimeo, Instagram

Tony Gale, President
R.J. Muna, Executive Vice President
Dana Hursey, Senior Vice President
Inti S. Clair, Vice President
Juliette Wolf-Robin, National Executive Director

Formerly known as Advertising Photographers of America, APA's membership includes professional photographers, photo assistants, educators, and students, as well as individuals from associated fields. APA seeks to help members navigate the world of commercial photography and run a more profitable business. Chapters are located in Atlanta, Los Angeles, Chicago, New York, San Diego, San Francisco, Charlotte, the Northwest, and Washington, DC.
Founded in 1981

20819 American Photographic Artists Guild
568 Main Street
Wilbraham, MA 01095

785-883-4166
katfalls@tdi.net

D John McCarthy, President
Joanie Ford, Historian/Merits/Degrees
Miles Andonov, Education
Lori Smith, Membership/Public Relations
Joanie Ford, Chairman

Encourages a better understanding between the photographer, the color artist and the retoucher. Conducts educational programs, sponsors competitions and bestows awards.
Founded in 1966

20820 American Photography Association
407-536-4611
877-627-2360
www.americanphotographyassociation.org
Facebook, Twitter

To promote the interest, appreciation and participation in photography by all levels of photographers.

20821 American Society for Photobiology
1313 Dolley Madison Blvd
Suite 402
McLean, VA 22101

785-865-9405
800-627-0326; Fax: 785-843-6153
headquarters@photobiology.org
www.photobiology.org
Facebook, LinkedIn

Keith Cengel, President
Georg Wondrak, President-Elect
David Drupa, Executive Secretariat
Don Forbes, Secretary
Teresa Busch, Treasurer

Founded to further the scientific study of the effects of light on all living organisms.
1600 Members
Founded in 1972

20822 American Society for Photogrammetry and Remote Sensing
5410 Grosvenor Lane
Suite 210
Bethesda, MD 20814-2160

301-493-0290; Fax: 301-493-0208
www.asprs.org
Facebook, Twitter

Dr. E. Lynn Usery, President
Dr. Charles K. Toth, President Elect
Rebecca A. Morton, Vice President
Roberta E. Lenczowski, National Director
Dr. Donald T.ÿ Lauer, Treasurer

A professional scientific association to advance the knowledge of and improve mapping sciences.
7000 Members
Founded in 1934

20823 American Society of Media Photographers
150 North 2nd Street
Philadelphia, PA 19106

215-451-2767
info@asmp.org
asmp.org
Facebook, Twitter, LinkedIn

Jenna Close, Chair
Luke Copping, Vice-Chair
Mark Green, Treasurer
Irene Owsley, Secretary
Tom Kennedy, Executive Director

A trade association which protects and promotes the interests of photographers whose work is for publication.
Founded in 1942

20824 American Society of Photographers
3120 N. Argonne Dr.
Milwaukee, WI 53222

414-871-6600; Fax: 978-272-5201
jonallyn@aol.com
www.asofp.com
Facebook, Twitter, Instagram

Randy McNeilly, Chairman of the Board
Kalen Henderson, President
Jessica Vogel, President Elect
Dennis Hammon, Vice President
Gabriel I. Alonso, Secretary Treasurer

Membership requirements include membership in Professional Photographers of America and either a Master of Photography, a Photographic Craftsmen, or a photographic specialist. Publishes a quarterly newsletter.
850 Members
Founded in 1937

20825 American Society of Picture Professionals
201 E 25th St.,
Suite 11c
New York, NY 10010

516-500-3686; Fax: 424-247-9844
aspp-ny@aspp.com
www.aspp.com
Facebook, Twitter, LinkedIn, YouTube, RSS

Sam Merrell, Executive Director
Cecilia de Querol, National President
Steve Spelman, Secretary
Mary F Loftus, Treasurer
Anita Dunca, Membership Co-Chair

Members are image producers, stock photo agencies, and image users.Provides networking and educational opportunities in the image transaction industry.
800 Members
Founded in 1969

20826 Antique and Amusement Photographers International
P.O.Box 3094
McDonough, GA 30253

860-578-2274; Fax: 877-865-1052
info@oldtimephotos.org
www.oldtimephotos.org
Facebook, Twitter, LinkedIn, Pinterest

Derrick Gillikin, President
Susan K. Crutchfield, Executive Director
Michele Powers, Secretary
Sarana Rogers, Treasurer
Trent Edwards, Vice President

Members are photography studies and photographers, primarliy in the US and Canada, specializing in costume photography and suppliers to the industry.
200 Members
Founded in 1990

20827 Association of International Photography Art Dealers
2025 M Street NW
Suite 800
Washington, DC 20036

202-367-1158; Fax: 202-367-2158
info@aipad.com
www.aipad.com
Facebook, Twitter, Instagram, Flickr, Vimeo

Catherine Edelman, President
Kraige Block, Vice President
Richard Moore, Treasurer
Larry Miller, Secretary
Meredith Y. Robertson, Executive Director

Galleries and private dealers in fine photography who have been in business for at least three years.
Founded in 1979

20828 BioCommunications Association
220 Southwind Lane
Hillsborough, NC 27278

919-245-0906
office@bca.org
www.bca.org
Facebook, Twitter, LinkedIn, YouTube

Adam Cooper, President
James Hayden, Vice President
Mardell Fosse, Director, Member Services
Danielle Edwards, Director, Communications
Connie Johansen, Director, Conferences

Made up of professionals who create and use the highest quality images and presentations in visual communications media for teaching and documentation in the life sciences and medicine.
140 Members
Founded in 1931

20829 Center for Photography at Woodstock
59 Tinker St
Woodstock, NY 12498

845-679-9957; Fax: 845-679-6337
info@cpw.org
www.cpw.org
Facebook, Twitter, Flickr, Vimeo, Instagram

Howard Greenberg, Founder, Chair
Clinton Cargill, Vice President
Jed Root, Treasurer
Andy Young, Secretary
Ariel Shanberg, Executive Director

The Center for Photography at Woodstock is a not-for-profit, artist-centered organization dedicated to supporting artists working in photography and related media and engaging audiences through opportunities in which creation, discovery, and education are made possible.
Founded in 1977

20830 Council on Fine Art Photography
5613 Johnson Ave
Bethesda, MD 20817-3503

301-897-0083

Lowell Anson Kenyon, Executive Director

Members are fine art photographers employing silver processes.
50 Members
Founded in 1982

20831 Digital Media Licensing Association
3165 S. Alma School Road
#29-261
Chandler, AZ 85248-3760

714-815-8427
cathy@digitalmedialicensing.org
www.pacaoffice.org
Facebook, Twitter, LinkedIn, RSS, Skype

Sarah Fix, President
Elena Flanagan-Eister, Vice President
Chris Carey, Treasurer
Julie Zentmaier, Secretary
Cathy Aron, Executive Director

A community of visual media licensing professionals.
100+ Members
Founded in 1951

20832 Evidence Photographers International Council
229 Peachtree St. NE
#2200
Atlanta, GA 30303

570-253-5450
800-356-3742; Fax: 404-614-6406
www.evidencephotographers.com
Facebook

Claire White, Association Director

A non profit educational and scientific organization with the primary purpose is the advancement of forensic photography/videography in civil evidence and law enforcement.
2000 Members
Founded in 1968

20833 IEEE Standards Association
445 Hoes Lane
Piscataway, NJ 08854-4141

732-981-0060; Fax: 732-562-1571
standards.ieee.org
Facebook, Twitter, LinkedIn

Bruce Kraemer, President
John Kulick, Chairman
Yatin Trivedi, Treasurer
Konstantinos Karachalios, Secretary
Phil Wennblom, Corporate Advisory Group

Formerly (1997) National Association of Photographic Manufacturers and (2001) Photographic and Imaging Maufacturers Association. The Silver Council is a program sponsored by I3A that monitors environmental regulation of commercial silver use. Membership fee varies,based on annual sales.
81 Members
Founded in 1946

20834 Independent Photo Imagers
2518 Anthem Village Drive
Suite 104
Henderson, NV 89052

702-617-1141; Fax: 702-617-1181
info@ipiphoto.com
www.ipiphoto.com
Facebook, Twitter, LinkedIn, YouTube, Pinterest, Instagram

Joel Miller, Chairman
Ron Mohney, Executive Director
T.K. Broecker, Treasurer
Koby Marowelli, Secretary
Larry Steiner, Vice Chairman

An association of independent photographers, who use various means of developing their pictures.
45 Members
Founded in 1982

20835 International Color Consortium
1899 Preston White Driveÿ
Reston, VA 20191ÿ

703-264-7200
www.color.org

Max Derhak, Co-Chair
William Li, Co-Chair
Ray Cheydleur, Vice Chair
Deborah Orf, Secretary
Phil Green, Technical Secretary

An association to promote the use and adoption of open, vendor-neutral, cross-platform color management.
Founded in 1993

20836 International Fire Photographers Association
143 40th Street
New Orleans, LA 70124

504-482-9616; Fax: 504-486-4946
ifpafirephotos.org/
Facebook, Twitter, Google+, Yahoo

Chris E Mickal, President
Michael Heller, VP

Promote professionalism in all aspects of fire photography, specifically in the fields of fire, educational, and investigative photography and the recognition of all fire photography organizations as an important tool in the fire service and law enforcement
200 Members
Founded in 1964

20837 International Graphic Arts Education Association
1899 Preston White Drive
Reston, VA 20191

703-758-0595
www.igaea.org

Monika Zarzycka, President
Kelly Glentz Brush, Secretary
Dr. Jerry Waite, Treasurer
Tony Cimaglia, First Vice-President (Publications)
Michael Williams, President-Elect

An association of educators in partnership with industry, dedicated to sharing theories, principles, techniques, and processes relating to graphic communications and imaging theory.
800 Members
Founded in 1923

20838 International Virtual Reality Professionals Association
6017 Greene Street
Philadelphia, PA 19144

Home Page: ivrpa.org
Facebook, Twitter, YouTube, Instagram

Originally known as the International QuickTime VR Association, the IVRPA is a non-profit organization of professionals who create immersive experiences, namely 360-degree images and video.
Founded in 1998

20839 Naples Art Association
The von Liebig Art Center
585 Park St.
Naples, FL 34102

239-262-6517
www.naplesart.org
Facebook, Twitter, LinkedIn, Pinterest, YouTube

Andrew Sroka, Board President
Aimee Schlehr, Executive Director
Shea Lindner, Programs Manager
Maureen Christensen, Development Director
Callie Spilane, Education Director

A nonprofit organization to promote and advance education, interest and participation in the visual arts.
Founded in 1956

20840 National Association of Photo Equipment Technicians
300 Picture Place
Jackson, MI 49201

517-788-8100; Fax: 517-788-8371
www.arcat.com

William Covey, Executive Liaison

Provides information on the photogrpahic industry to those engaged in the photographic repair.
250 Members
Founded in 1973

20841 National Association of Quick Printers (NAQP)
One Meadowlands Plaza
Suite 1511
East Rutherford, NJ 07073

201-634-9600
800-642-6275; Fax: 201-634-0324
webmaster@napl.org
www.naqp.com
Facebook, Twitter, LinkedIn, YouTube,RSS, Pinterest, Google

Joseph Truncale, President & CEO
Nigel Worme, Chairman
Willam Gavigan, Treasurer/ Secretary
Niels Winther, Vice Chairman
Mike Philie, Senior Vice President

Furthers the business of quick printers, copy shops, and small format commercial printers. Also welcomes manufacturers and suppliers of equipment and consumables, trade publications, and consultants to the quick print industry.
900 Members
Founded in 1975

20842 National Photograpic Society
15 Woodbine Farm Business Park
Threemilestone, UK

843-289-0615
www.thenps.com
Facebook, Twitter, Google+, RSS

Rod Pascoe, Chairman
Stu Cooper, Mentor and Trainer
Sarah Fitzgerald, Liaison Manager
Paul Spiers, Head of marketing
Susan Hurren, Social Media and Press

A society for both professional as well as enthusiast photographers.

20843 National Press Photographers Association
120 Hooper Street
Athens, GA 30602-3018

706-542-2506; Fax: 919-383-7261
info@nppa.org
nppa.org
Facebook, Twitter, LinkedIn, Vimeo

Akili Ramsess, Executive Director
Melissa Lyttle, President
Michael King, Vice President
Seth Gitner, Secretary
Carolyn Hall, Treasurer

Sponsors numerous, annual television and print media workshops. Conducts annual competition for news photos and television news film.

Monthly magazine job information bank given to all members.
6500+ Members
Founded in 1946

20844 National Stereoscopic Association
Portland, OR

503-771-4440
strwld@teleport.com
stereoworld.org
Facebook, LinkedIn

Russell Norton, Chairman
John Bueche, President
Barb Gauche, Vice President
David Kuntz, Treasurer
John Zelenka, Secretary

Nonprofit organization promoting research, collection and use of vintage and contempory stereoviews, stereo cameras and equipment.
1200 Members
Founded in 1974

20845 North American Nature Photography Association
6382 Charleston Road
Alma, IL 62807

618-547-7616; Fax: 618-547-7438
info@nanpa.org
www.nanpa.org
RSS

Gabby Salazar, President
Sean Fitzgerald, President-Elect
Susan Day, Executive Director
Bruce Haley, Treasurer
Clay Bolt, Board Member

Committed solely to serving the field of nature photography. Provides education, information develops standards and promotes nature photography as an art form and teaching medium.
Founded in 1993

20846 North American Nature Photography Associat ion
6382 Charleston Road
Alma, IL 62807

618-547-7616; Fax: 618-547-7438
info@nanpa.org
www.nanpa.org
Facebook, Twitter, LinkedIn, RSS, Google+

Gabby Salazar, President
Sean Fitzgerald, President Elect
Bruce Haley, Past-President, Treasurer
Clay Bolt, Board Member
Gary Farber, Board Member

An organization dedicated to photography of nature.

20847 PERA
Pera Innovation Park, Nottingham Rd.
Melton Mowbray
Leicestershire, UK LE13 0PB

166-450-1501
800-776-8616; Fax: 408-512-5254
www.pera.com
Facebook, Twitter

Glyn Goddard, Non-Executive Director
Dean Hallam, Chief Financial Officer
Alan Baxter, Non Executive Director
John Hill, Executive Chairman
Paul Trantor, Chief Executive Officer

An association for production equipment rental personnel and organizations.
75 Members
Founded in 1973

20848 Photo Chemical Machining Institute
11 Robert Toner Blvd
234
North Attleboro, MA 02763

508-385-0085; Fax: 508-232-6005
cflaherty@pcmi.org
www.pcmi.org

Catherine Flaherty, Executive Director
William Fox, President
Mike Lynch, Vice-President
Eric Kemperman, Treasurer
Philip Greiner, Secretary

Members are companies producing metal products through photo chemical machining. In addition the Institute includes companies that service the PCM industry and supply its needs.
210 Members
Founded in 1967

20849 Photo Marketing Association International
718 Jones Branch Drive
Suite 300
McLean, VA 22102

703-665-4416
800-762-9287; Fax: 703-506-3266
www.theimagingalliance.com
Facebook, Twitter, LinkedIn

Gabrielle Mullinax, President
Georgia McCabe, CEO/ Executive Director
Jerry Sullivan, Vice-President
Lisa Otto, Treasurer
Mark Klostermeyer, Sr. Vice President

A national organization of associations and manufacturers and suppliers of photographic equipment; also members of the National Association of Photo Equipment Technicians and of the Professional School Photographers of America.
18000 Members
Founded in 1924

20850 Photographic Society of America
8241 S Walker Avenue
Suite 104
Oklahoma City, OK 73139

405-843-1437
855-772-4636
www.psa-photo.org

Charlie Burke, President
Elena McTighe, Executive Vice President
Dana Cohoon, Treasurer
Stan Bormann, Secretary
Ralph Durham, Conference Vice President

Worldwide interactive organization for anyone interested in photography, professional or serious amateur. Offers a wide variety of activities, monthly magazine, photo and digital competitions, study groups via mail and Internet, how-to programs, an annal conference, and many other activites and services.
Founded in 1934

20851 Photoimaging Manufacturers and Distributor s Association
7600 Jericho Turnpike
Suite 301
Woodbury, NY 11797

516-802-0895; Fax: 516-364-0140
www.pmda.com
Facebook, Twitter, LinkedIn

Dan Unger, President
Michelle Fernandez, VP
Jay Kelbley, VP
Jim Malcolm, VP
Jerry Grossman, Executive Director

Contributes to the progress and welfare of the photoimaging industry.
Founded in 1939

20852 Picture Agency Council of America
23046 Avenida De La Carlota
Suite 600
Laguna Hills, CA 92653

714-815-8427; Fax: 949-679-8224
execdirector@pacaoffice.org
www.stockindustry.org

Cathy Aron, Executive Director
Maria Kessler, President

Trade association for stock picture companies in North America. Serves member agencies, their clients and their contributing photographers by promoting communication among photo agencies and other professional groups.
150 Members
Founded in 1951

20853 Professional Aerial Photographers' Association
12069 Cessna Place
Brookshire, TX 77423

703-887-8703; Fax: 703-281-6700
cboyle@boyleconsulting.com
professionalaerialphotographers.com

Chuck Boyleÿ, President
Laura Boyko, VP, Programs
Kent Larson, VP, Membership
John Mooney, Treasurer, Secretary
Julie Belanger, ExecutiveÿDirector

A professional trade organization for aerial photographers.
Founded in 1974

20854 Professional Photographer Magazine
229 Peachtree St NE
Suite 2200
Atlanta, GA 30303

404-522-8600
800-742-7468; Fax: 404-614-6406
ppmag@omeda.com
www.ppmag.com
Facebook, Twitter, Pinterest

David Trust, CEO
Bob Lloyd, President
Dana Groves, Marketing Executive

Portrait, commercial, wedding, industrial and specialized photographers and photographic artists.
28000 Members
Founded in 1869

20855 Professional Photographers Association
Professional Photographers Assoc. of New England
PO Box 568
Durham, NH 3824

603-868-2970; Fax: 860-423-9402
www.ppane.com
Facebook, YouTube

Lorraine Bedell, President
Steve Lourenco, President Elect
Madonna Lovett, Vice President of Programs
Fred Stiteler, Executive Secretary
Alison Miniter, Vice President of Comm
1000 Attendees
Frequency: September
Founded in 1860

20856 Professional Photographers of America
229 Peachtree St. NE
Suite 2200
Atlanta, GA 30303

404-522-8600; Fax: 404-614-6400
www.ppa.com

Facebook, Twitter, LinkedIn, Google+, Instagram, YouTube

Susan Michal, Chairman
Michael Timmons, President
Lori Craft, Vice President
Rob Behm, Treasurer
Stephen Thetford, Director

A nonprofit trade association for photographers.
Founded in 1869

20857 Professional Picture Framers Association
83 South Street Unit
#303
Freehold, NJ 7728

732-536-5160
800-762-9287; Fax: 517-788-8371
info@ppfadirectory.com
www.ppfa.com
Facebook, Twitter, LinkedIn

John Pruitt CPF, President
Fran Gray MCPF, VP

A trade association of manufacturers, wholesalers, print publishers, importers and retailers selling art, framing and related supplies.
3000 Members
Founded in 1971

20858 Professional Travelogue Sponsors
El Camino College Foundation
16007 Crenshaw Boulevard
Torrance, CA 90506

310-329-5345
800-832-5345; Fax: 310-715-7875
artstickets@elcamino.edu
www.elcamino.edu/centerforthearts
Facebook, Twitter, YouTube, Instagram, Flickr

Thomas Fallow, President
Bruce Spain, Executive Director
Rick Christophersen, Director
Sara Hamilton, Administrative Assistant
Nancy Adler, Production Manager

Currently the largest documentary Travel Film Program Sponsor and Presenter.
55 Members
Founded in 1967

20859 Professional Women Photographers
Metropolitan Opera Guild
119 W. 72nd St.
#223
New York, NY 10023

212-867-7745
pwp@pwponline.org
www.pwponline.org
Facebook, Twitter, LinkedIn, Amazon, RSS

Beth Shaw, President
Fredda Gordon, Vice President
Francoise Jeanpierre, Treasurer
Joann Frechette, Secretary
Elizabeth Currier, Membership

To support and promote the work of women photographers through the sharing of ideas, resources and experience, to provide educational forums to engourage artistic growth and photographic development, and to stimulate public interst in and support for the art of photography
170 Members
Founded in 1975
Mailing list available for rent

20860 SPIE, the international society for optics and photonics
1000 20th Street
Bellingham, WA 98225-6705

360-676-3290
888-504-8171; Fax: 360-647-1445
customerservice@spie.org
www.SPIE.org
Facebook, Twitter, LinkedIn, RSS, YouTube, Blogspot

Prof. Toyohiko Yatagai, President
Dr. Eugene G. Arthurs, CEO
Dr. Glenn D. Boreman, Vice President
Gary Spiegel, Secretary/ Treasurer
Dr. Robert A. Lieberman, President-Elect

Members are scientists, engineers, researchers and companies interested in technology and applications of optical, electro-optical, fiber-optic, laser, and photonic systems.
14000 Members
Founded in 1955

20861 Silver Users Association
3930 Walnut St.
Suite 210
Fairfax, VA 22030

703-930-7790; Fax: 703-359-7562
pmiller@mwcapitol.com
www.silverusersassociation.org
Facebook

Paul A Miller, Executive Director
Bill LeRoy, President
Mike Huber, VP
John King, Secretary
Bill Hammerle, Treasury

Represents manufacturers and distributors of products in which silver is an essential element. Works for the recognition of silver as a commodity and the removal of governmental regulations which retard its free exchange in commerce both foreign and domestic. Also helps provide a stable trading climate in the metal, it monitors the silver market to insure that silver information available to the industry and public is accurate.
45 Members
Founded in 1947

20862 Society for Photographic Education
2530 Superior Avenue
Suite 403
Cleveland, OH 44114

216-622-2733; Fax: 216-622-2712
membership@spenational.org
www.spenational.org
Facebook, Twitter, Instagram

Jeff Curto, National Board Chair
Anne Massoni, Vice-Chair
James Wyman, Executive Director
Lupita Murillo Tinnen, Treasurer
Robin Germany, Secretary

The Society for Photographic Education is a non-profit membership organization that provides a forum for the discussion of photogrphy and related media as a means of creative expression and cultural insight. Through its interdisciplinary porgrams, services and publications, the society seeks to promote a broader understanding of the medium in all its forms, and to foster the development of its practice, teaching, scholarship and criticism.
1800 Members
Founded in 1963

20863 Society of American Travel Writers
One Parkview Plaza
Suite 800
Oakbrook Terrace, IL 60181

312-420-6846; Fax: 414-359-1671
info@satw.org
www.satw.org
Facebook, Twitter, LinkedIn

Paul Lasley, President
Barbara Orr, Vice President
Peggy Bendel, Secretary
Tom Adkinson, Treasurer
Catherine Hamm, President-Elect

Photographers and 35 associate member representatives of airlines, hotels, resorts, tourist agencies and public relations firms.
Founded in 1955

20864 Student Photographic Society
229 Peachtree St. NE
Suite 2200
Atlanta, GA 30303

888-722-1334
studentphoto.com
Facebook, Twitter, Google+

Susan Michal, Chairman
Michael Timmons, President
Lori Craft, Vice President
Rob Behm, Treasurer
Stephen Thetford, Director

Provides career building resources, networking opportunities and information for photography students.
Founded in 1999

20865 Take Great Pictures
109 White Oak Lane
Suite 72F
Old Bridge, NJ 08857

732-679-3460; Fax: 516-364-0140
www.takegreatpictures.com
RSS

Willard Clark, Executive Director

Founded as Photographic Merchandising and Distributing Association and became Photographic Manufacturers and Distributors Association before assuming its present name in 1999. Membership is $500/year for associate members and $1,000/year for voting members.
20000 Members
Founded in 1939

20866 The Association of Independent Architectural Photographers
32 West 200 South
Suite 219
Salt Lake City, UT 84101

801-738-8786
www.aiap.net

A professional organization for architectural photographers.

20867 The Society for Photographic Education
2530 Superior Avenue
Suite 403
Cleveland, OH 44114

216-622-2733; Fax: 216-622-2712
membership@spenational.org
www.spenational.org
Facebook, Twitter, Instagram

Jeff Curto, National Board Chair
Anne Massoni, Vice-Chair
James Wyman, Executive Director
Lupita Murillo Tinnen, Treasurer
Robin Germany, Secretary

A nonprofit ogranization for the advancement of education in photography.
1800 Members
Founded in 1963

20868 University Photographers Association of America
SUNY Brockport
350 New Campus Drive
Brockport, NY 14420-2931

716-395-2133; Fax: 662-915-1298
jdusen@brockport.edu
www.upaa.org

Glenn Carpenter, President
Robert Jordan, VP
Nick Romanenko, Treasurer

Mark Carriveau, Secretary
Bill Bitzinger, Board Member

Members are college and university photographers who are concerned with the application and practice of photography.
250 Members
Founded in 1961

20869 Wedding & Portrait Photographers International (WPPI)
85 Broad St.
11th Floor
New York, NY 10004

646-654-4500; Fax: 310-846-4770
www.wppionline.com
Facebook, Twitter, YouTube, Instagram

Stephen Sheanin, CEO/President
John McGeary, Senior Vice President
Lauren Wendle, VP, Publisher
Neeta Lakhani, Operations Manager
Jason Groupp, Director

Promotes high artistic and technical standards. Serves as a forum for an exchange of technical knowledge. Members are offered the opportunity to purchase special products and services.
2.8M Members
Founded in 1978

20870 Wedding Photojournalist Association

Home Page: www.wpja.com

A resource of photojournalists and candid wedding photographers.
Founded in 2002

20871 White House News Photographers Association
7119 Ben Franklin Station
Washington, DC 20044-7119

202-785-5230
info@whnpa.org
www.whnpa.org
Facebook, Twitter

Whitney Shefte, President
Jim Bourg, Vice President
Jon Elswick, Treasurer
Joshua Roberts, Secretary
Dennis Brack, Ex Officio

Volunteer association of professional photographers covering the Washington political venue. Activities include educational seminars, work with high school students and an annual awards contest. Our work is seen in newspapers, magazines, television and on the Internet.
500 Members
Founded in 1941

20872 Worldwide Community of Imaging Association
2282 Springport Road
Suite F
Jackson, MI 49202ÿ

517-788-8100
800-762-9287; Fax: 517-788-8371
www.theimagingalliance.com
Facebook, Twitter, LinkedIn

Bill Eklund, President
Gabrielleÿ Mullinax, Senior Vice President
Jerry Sullivan, Vice President
Mark Klostermeyer, MCPF, Treasurer
Jim Esp, Secretary, Executive Director

United diverse professionals in the imaging industry worldwide.
Founded in 1924

Newsletters

20873 American Society of Media Photgraphers Bulletin
Photo District News
150 North Second Street
Philadelphia, PA 19106

215-451-2767; Fax: 215-451-0880
info@asmp.org
www.asmp.org
Facebook, Twitter, LinkedIn

Holly Hughes, Editor
Jeffery Roberts, President

Member publication that addresses the news and preoccupations of the photography industry.
Frequency: Quarterly
Circulation: 5500
Founded in 1944

20874 BCA News
BioCommunications Association
220 Southwind Lane
Hillsborough, NC 27278-7907

919-245-0906; Fax: 919-245-0906
khensley@mdanderson.org
www.bca.org
Facebook, Twitter, LinkedIn, Blog,Tumblr

Karen Hensley, Editor
Susanne Loomis, President
Joseph Kane, Vice-President
James Koepfler, Secretary-Treasurer

Keeps members informed about such things as annual meetings, chapter activities, awards and member updates.
Frequency: 2-3x/Year

20875 Dance on Camera Journal
Dance Films Association
48 W 21st St
Suite 907
New York, NY 10010-6989

212-727-0764; Fax: 212-727-0764
www.dancefilms.org

Deidra Towers, Executive Director
Louise Spain, CEO

The only service organization in the world dedicated to both the dance and the film community.
Cost: $45.00
Circulation: 350
Founded in 1956

20876 Future Image Report
Future Image
520 South El Camino Real
Suite 206A
San Mateo, CA 94402

650-579-0493
800-749-3572; Fax: 650-579-0566
www.futureimage.com

Alexis J Gerard, Editor/Publisher
Paul Worthington, Managing Editor
Heidy Bravo, Circulaion Manager

News and analysis of technology and market developments in photo-digital imaging, for management-level industry professionals.
Cost: $500.00
Founded in 1991

20877 Light Impressions Review
PO Box 940
Rochester, NY 14603-0940

716-271-8960

William Edwards, Publisher
Lance Speer, Director

Photography notes and news.
Cost: $15.00
16 Pages
Frequency: Monthly

20878 NTIS Alert- Photography & Recording Devices
National Technical Information Service
5285 Port Royal Rd
US Department of Commerce
Alexandria, VA 22312

703-605-6000
800-553-6847; Fax: 703-605-6900
info@ntis.gov
www.ntis.gov

Linda Davis, VP
Cost: $140.00
Founded in 1955

20879 Photo Marketing
Photo Marketing Association International
2282 Springport Road
Suite F
Jackson, MI 49202

517-788-8100
800-762-9287; Fax: 517-788-8371
www.theimagingalliance.com
Facebook, Twitter, LinkedIn

Ted Fox, CEO
Allen Showalter, President
Mark Klostermeyer, Vice-President
Robert L Hanson, Treasurer

News of interest to the photo business on both a national and international basis.
Cost: $5.00
4 Pages
Frequency: Monthly
Circulation: 12,141
Founded in 1925

20880 PhotoDaily
PhotoSource International
1910 35th Ave
Pine Lake Farm
Osceola, WI 54020-5602

715-248-3800
800-624-0266; Fax: 715-248-7394
info@photosource.com
www.photosource.com

Rohn Engh, President
Bruce Swenson, Production Manager
Jonna Zehma, Editor

Pairs photographers with the picture needs of magazine and book editors.
Cost: $330.00
Frequency: Daily
Founded in 1976

20881 Photobulletin
PhotoSource International
1910 35th Ave
Osceola, WI 54020-5602

715-248-3800
800-624-0266; Fax: 715-248-7394
info@photosource.com
www.photosource.com

Rohn Engh, President

Lists photographic needs of photobuyers buying in the top-notch markets.
Frequency: Daily
Founded in 1980
Printed in one color

20882 Photofinishing News
Photofinishing News
219 Lafeyette Avenue
Westwood, NJ 07675-904

201-819-2533
www.photo-news.com

Hans Kuhlman, Editor

Technical / marketing coverage of worldwide photography / photo-imaging industry, reviews of new products, tradeshows and market statistics.
Cost: $150.00
12 Pages
ISBN: 0-889239-3 -
ISSN: 1536-6553
Founded in 1970
Printed in one color on matte stock

20883 Photograph Collector
340 East Richardson Avenue
Suite 200
Langhorne, PA 19047-2824

215-891-0214
info@photoreview.org
www.photoreview.org

Stephen Perloff, Editor

News and analysis for collectors, curators and dealers. Current coverage of the auction market, trends, discoveries, museums and trade shows. Accepts advertising.
Cost: $149.95
8 Pages
Frequency: Monthly
ISBN: 0-271083-8 -
Founded in 1980
Printed in one color on matte stock

20884 Professional Photographers Association of New England
98 Windham Street
PO Box 316
Willimantic, CT 06226-316

203-488-2334
860-423-1402; Fax: 860-423-9402
www.ppane.com

Harvey Goldstein, Editor
Ruth Clegg, CEO/President
Circulation: 1000
Founded in 1961
Printed in on glossy stock

Magazines & Journals

20885 Advanced Imaging
Cygnus Publishing
102 Wilmont Road
Suite 470
Deerfield, IL 60015-3601
847-405-0257
larry.adams@cygnusb2b.com

Dave Brambert, Group Publisher
Larry Adams, Editor-in-Chief
Richard Reiff, President
Hank Russell, Managing Editor

Contains information on professional photographic techniques and new approaches in all forms of media.
Cost: $60.00
Frequency: Monthly
Circulation: 44009
Founded in 1966

20886 Afterimage
Visual Studies Workshop
31 Prince Street
Rochester, NY 14607-1405

585-442-8676; Fax: 585-442-1992
info@vsw.org
www.vsw.org/afterimage/index.html

Karen VanMeenen, Editor
Joanna Heatwole, Managing Editor

Geared toward media arts and photography artists, curators, academics, administrators and students. Features photography, independent film and video coverage, artist's books, alternative publishing and cultural studies issues. Also highlights conference and festival reports and scholarly feature articles.
Cost: $33.00
Circulation: 10000
Founded in 1980

20887 American Photo
1633 Broadway
43rd Floor
New York, NY 10019

212-676-6000
800-274-4514; Fax: 212-489-4217
www.hfmus.com/

David Schonauer, Editor-in-Chief
Krissa Cavouras, Associate Editor
Richard Rabinowitz, Publisher

Profiles of professional photographers and other photographic topics.
Cost: $4.99
Frequency: 6 Issues per year
Circulation: 27,733
Founded in 1888

20888 Aperture
Aperture Foundation
547 W 27th St
Suite 4
New York, NY 10001-5511

212-505-5555
800-825-0061; Fax: 212-979-7759
info@aperture.org
www.aperture.org

Michael Culloso, President
Cathy Kaplan, Vice-Chairman
Frederick Smith, Treasurer

Dedicates itself to celebrating the finest in creative photography. Through the periodicals exquisitely reproduced images, rivaling the quality of the photographers' original prints, subscribers experience a wealth of challenging, beautiful pictures on a series of significant topics. Accepts advertising.
Cost: $40.00
80 Pages
Frequency: Quarterly
Founded in 1952
Mailing list available for rent

20889 Exposure
Society for Photographic Education
2530 Superior Avenue
Suite 403
Cleveland, OH 44114

216-622-2733; Fax: 216-622-2712
membership@spenational.org
www.spenational.org

Virginia Morrison, Executive Director
Nina Barcellona, Advertising & Publications
Meghan Borato, Registrar
Carla Pasquale, Office/Accounts Manager
Cost: $15.00
Frequency: Biannual
Mailing list available for rent: 700 names

20890 History of Photography
Routledge Publishing
7625 Empire Drive
Florence, KS 41042-2919

800-354-1420
orders@taylorandfrancis.com
www.taylorandfrancis.com

Graham Smith, Editor
Ann Haddrell, Advertising Manager

An international publication devoted to the history and criticism of the basic sematic unit of all modern media.
Cost: $396.00
92 Pages
Frequency: Annual+
ISSN: 0308-7298
Founded in 1977

20891 Imaging Business
Cygnus Business Media
3 Huntington Quadrangle
Suite 301N
Melville, NY 11747-4618

631-845-2700
800-308-6397; Fax: 631-845-7109
bill.schiffner@cygnuspub.com

Bill Schiffner, Associate Publisher

Formerly called Photographic Processing. Covers photographic equipment, processing, suppliers and dealers. No longer in publication, but last six years of issues available in online archive.
Cost: $66.00
Frequency: Monthly
Circulation: 21000
ISSN: 0031-8744
Founded in 1936
Printed in 4 colors

20892 News Photographer
National Press Photographers Association
120 Hooper Street
Athens, GA 30602-3018

706-542-2506; Fax: 919-383-7261
info@nppa.org
www.nppa.org
Facebook, Twitter, LinkedIn, Vimeo

Akili Ramsess, Executive Director
Melissa Lyttle, President
Tom Burton, Interim Editor

Features articles, news and profiles about still and television news photography.
Cost: $38.00
Frequency: Monthly
Circulation: 10500
ISSN: 0199-2422
Founded in 1946
Mailing list available for rent: 9,500 names at $50 per M
Printed in 4 colors

20893 Outdoor Photographer
Werner Publshing Corporation
12121 Wilshire Blvd
Suite 1200
Los Angeles, CA 90025-1168

310-820-1500; Fax: 310-826-5008
editors@outdoorphotographer.com
www.outdoorphotographer.com
Facebook, Twitter

Steve Warner, Owner
Ibarionex Perello, Associate Editor
Cost: $14.97
Founded in 1965
Mailing list available for rent

20894 PC Photo
Werner Publishing
12121 Wilshire Blvd # 1200
12th Floor
Los Angeles, CA 90025-1168

310-820-1500; Fax: 310-826-5008
www.wernerpublishing.com

Steve Werner, Owner
Rob Shepherd, Editor

Covers the new desktop darkroom or home photo lab technologies, trends and methods. Designed to stimulate desktop photographers through the listing of new products and technologies.
Cost: $11.97
Founded in 1965

20895 PCPhoto Magazine
Werner Publishing Corporation

12121 Wilshire Blvd
Suite 1200
Los Angeles, CA 90025-1176

310-820-1500; Fax: 310-826-5008
www.wernerpublishing.com

Steve Werner, Owner

Shows you how to enjy the exciting and affordable new world of computers and photography. Features step-by-step instructions, evaluations of the latest equipment, tips from the pros, and more!
Cost: $11.97
Frequency: 9 Issues
Mailing list available for rent

20896 PHOTO Techniques
Preston Publications
6600 W Touhy Ave
Niles, IL 60714-4516

847-647-2900; Fax: 847-647-1155

Tinsley Preston, Owner
Joe White, Editor
Connie Turgon, Marketplace Advertising

PHOTO Techniques offers practical articles that help solve shooting, processing, lighting and printing problems. This is the one magazine that walks you step by step through new techniques. Every other issue contains a digital section. Departments you can rely on include; Master Printing Class, David Vestal's commentary, Photochemistry and more. There are valuable guides to cameras, papers, films, useful accessories and darkroom suppliers.
Cost: $27.99
Founded in 1979
Mailing list available for rent: 30,000 names at $145 per M

20897 Photo District News
Prometheus Global Media
770 Broadway
New York, NY 10003-9595

212-493-4100; Fax: 646-654-5368
www.prometheusgm.com

Richard D. Beckman, CEO
James A. Finkelstein, Chairman
Madeline Krakowsky, Vice President Circulation
Tracy Brator, Executive Director Creative Service

Delivers the information photographers need to survive in a competitive business from marketing and business advice to legal issues, photographic techniques, new technologies and more.
Frequency: Monthly
Founded in 1980

20898 Photo Insider
123 US Hwy 46 (West)
Fairfield, NJ 07004

973-377-2007
800-631-0300
www.photoinsider.com
Facebook, Twitter, LinkedIn, YouTube,Foursquare,Flickr,Pint

Founded in 1947

20899 Photo Lab Management
PLM Publishing
1312 Lincoln Boulevard
Santa Monica, CA 90401-1706

310-451-1344; Fax: 310-395-9058
www.plumpublishing.co.uk

Claire F Irwin, Editor
Paula L McCulloch, Publishing Director
John DH Colley, Marketing Manager

Specifically for those who work in the photo lab business. Contains articles on personnel and technical information.
Cost: $15.00
52 Pages
Frequency: Monthly
Founded in 1979

20900 Photo Marketing
Photo Marketing Association International
2282 Springport Road
Suite F
Jackson, MI 49202

517-788-8100
800-762-9287; Fax: 517-788-8371
www.theimagingalliance.com
Facebook, Twitter, LinkedIn

Ted Fox, CEO
Allen Showalter, President
Mark Klostermeyer, Vice-President
Robert L Hanson, Treasurer

Directed to the marketing and advertising professionals, offers information on marketing photography nationally and internationally.
Cost: $50.00
80 Pages
Frequency: Monthly
Circulation: 12141
Founded in 1924

20901 Photo Metro
1590 Golden Gate Avenue
San Francisco, CA 94115

415-243-9917; Fax: 415-243-9919
www.photometro.com

Henry Brimmer, Publisher

Image-oriented magazine dedicated to photography, features portfolios, interviews and book reviews. Accepts advertising.
Cost: $20.00
32 Pages
Frequency: Monthly
Founded in 1982

20902 Photo Stock News
1910 35th Road
Pine Lake Farm
Osceola, WI 54020

715-248-3800; Fax: 715-248-7394
info@photosource.com
www.photosource.com
Facebook, Twitter

Ron Engh, Editor
Angela Dober, Managing Editor

Contains information of interest to freelance stock photographers, includes the latest industry trends and strategies. Regular issue features include Electronic Highway.
Frequency: 12 per year

20903 PhotoStockNotes
PhotoSource International
1910 35th Ave
Osceola, WI 54020-5602

715-248-3800
800-624-0266; Fax: 715-248-7394
info@photosource.com
www.photosource.com

Rohn Engh, Owner
Angela Dober, Managing Editor

Trends in the editorial stock photo industry.
Cost: $36.00
3 Pages
Frequency: Monthly
Founded in 1976

20904 Photography Quarterly
Center for Photography at Woodstock
59 Tinker St
Woodstock, NY 12498-1236

845-679-9957; Fax: 845-679-6337
info@cpw.org
www.cpw.org
Facebook, Twitter

Ariel Shanberg, Executive Director
Akemi Hiatt, Program Associate
Lawrence Lewis, Operations Manager
Lindsay Stern, Education Coordinator

Founded in 1977, tthe Center for Photography at Woodstock is a not-for-profit 501 (c)3 artist-centered organization dedicated to supporting artists working in photography and related media and engaging audiences through opportunities in which creation, discovery and education are made possible.
Cost: $25.00
Frequency: Quarterly
Circulation: 2500
ISSN: 0890-4639
Founded in 1977
Printed in one color on glossy stock

20905 Photoletter
PhotoSource International
1910 35th Ave
Osceola, WI 54020-5602

715-248-3800
800-624-0266; Fax: 715-248-7394
info@photosource.com
www.photosource.com

Rohn Engh, Owner

A publication covering the world of photography.
Cost: $264.00
4 Pages
Frequency: Weekly

20906 Photopro Magazine
Patch Communications
5211 S Washington Avenue
Titusville, FL 32780-7315

321-268-5010; Fax: 321-267-1894

Christi Ashby, Publisher
Suzanne Odistro, Advertising Manager

A professional trade publication covering photography nationally and internationally.
Cost: $16.95
80 Pages
Frequency: Monthly
Founded in 1990

20907 Picture Magazine
319 Lafayette Street
No 135
New York, NY 10012

212-352-2700; Fax: 212-352-2155
picmag@aol.com
www.picturemagazine.com

Brock Wylan, Pulisher
Katherine Nguyen, Associate Editor

Phot industry trade publication.

20908 Popular Photography
Hachette Filipacchi Magazines
1633 Broadway
43rd Floor
New York, NY 10019-6708

212-767-6000
800-876-6636; Fax: 212-767-5600
popphoto@neodata.com
www.popularphotography.com

Alain Lemarchand, CEO
Tami Kelly, Founder
Nate Silver, Founder

A publication offering information and updates to the photography world.
Cost: $12.00
80 Pages
Frequency: Monthly
ISSN: 0032-4582

20909 **Popular Photography & Imaging American PHOTO Magazine**
Bonnier Corp
1633 Broadway
Suite 4200
New York, NY 10019-6708
212-767-6000; Fax: 212-767-5600
www.popphoto.com
Facebook, Twitter, RSS
Jeffrey Roberts, Publisher
Russell Brock, Associate Editor
Comprehensive coverage of the latest equipment, inspiring images by leading photographers, in-depth how-to articles and wuthoritative reports. Draws upon top professionals in the field to inform committed readers who are passionate about pictures.
Mailing list available for rent

20910 **Professional Photographer**
PPA Publications
229 Peachtree Street NE
International Tower, Suite 2200
Atlanta, GA 30303-1608
404-522-8600
800-786-6277; Fax: 404-614-6405
ppa@bframe.com
www.ppmag.com
Cameron Bishopp, Senior Manager Publications
Jeff Kent, Senior Editor
Dana Groves, Marketing Executive
Business magazine for professional photographers. Delivers valuable articles packed with money making ideas to improve photography techniques and business skills. Accepts advertising.
Cost: $27.00
80 Pages
Frequency: Monthly
Circulation: 30000
Founded in 1910

20911 **Rangefinder Magazine**
Rangefinder Publishing
6255 W Sunset Blvd
Los Angeles, CA 90028
323-817-3500; Fax: 323-817-1994
Steve Sheanin, CEO
Bill Hurter, Editor
Includes product and new equipment reviews, lighting and technical pieces, how-to's, promotion and marketing stories, portraiture tips, accessories and system round-ups, computer technology, black-and-white shooting, lens reviews, processing techniques
Frequency: Monthly

20912 **Select Magazine**
Select Worldwide
18-20 Farringdon Lane
1st Floor Clerks Court
London UK EC1R 3AU
4.40207E+12; Fax: 4.40207E+12
www.select-magazine.com
Twitter, Blog
Joe Carbonara, Managing Editor
Select is used worldwide by creative decision makers in the advertising, graphic design, fashion and retail world.
Frequency: 2x/Year
Circulation: 7500

20913 **Shutterbug**
Shutterbug
261 Madison Avenue
6th Floor
New York, NY 10016
212-915-4157
800-829-3340
editorial@shutterbug.com
www.shutterbug.com
Facebook, Twitter, Instagram
Keith Pray, Publisher
Joanne George, Advertising Representative
Genny Breslin, National Account Manager
Offers articles, insights, news, and how-tos from professional photographers to amateur and novice photographers.
Cost: $17.95
Frequency: Monthly
Founded in 1989

20914 **Stereo World Magazine**
National Stereoscopic Association
Portland, OR
503-771-4440
strwld@teleport.com
www.stereoworld.org/stereo-world-magazine
Russell Norton, Chairman
John Bueche, President
Barb Gauche, Vice President
John Dennis, Editor
Mark Wilson, Art Director
Magazine published by the National Stereoscopic Association containing news, information, research and tips on the subject of 3D products, stereoscopes and stereoview photography.
1200 Members
Founded in 1974

20915 **Studio Photography**
Cygnus Business Media
1233 Janesville Avenue
Fort Atkinson, WI 53538
631-963-6200
800-547-7377
www.imaginginfo.com/spd/
RSS
Liz Vickers, Group Publisher
Alice B Miller, Editor
Jackie Dandoy, Circulation Manager
Ashley Birkholz, Classified Sales
Barry Ancona, List Rental Manager
Formerly Studio Photography & Design. Showcases the hottest portrait, wedding, commercial, digital, and travel photographers every month. It is also supported by a selection of supplementary guides, tech tips, tutorials, and product round-ups.
Frequency: Monthly
Circulation: 50000
Founded in 1936

Trade Shows

20916 **ASPRS Annual Conference**
American Society for Photogammetry/Remote Sensing
5410 Grosvenor Lane
Suite 210
Bethesda, MD 20814-2160
301-493-0290; Fax: 301-493-0208
asprs@asprs.org
www.asprs.org
Facebook, Twitter
James Plasker, Executive Director
Kimberly A Tiley, Assistant Executive Director
Jesse Winch, Program Manager
Educational sessions and exhibits committed to advancing knowledge in the mapping sciences and promoting the responsible application of photogrammetry, remote sensing and related technologies.

20917 **BIOCOMM**
BioCommunications Association
220 Southwind Lane
Hillsborough, NC 27278-7907
919-245-0906; Fax: 919-245-0906
office@bca.org
www.bca.org
Facebook, Twitter, LinkedIn
Nancy Hurtgen, Manager Central Office
Susanne Loomis, President
Joseph Kane, Vice-President
James Koepfler, Secretary-Treasurer
Includes a packed program of seminars, workshops, a juried media salon, and commercial exhibits to provide attendees with inspiration and the latest information on visual media in the life sciences.
Frequency: Annual

20918 **PMA Annual Convention and Trade Show**
3000 Picture Place
Jackson, MI 49201
517-885-5980; Fax: 517-788-8371
www.theimagingalliance.com
Rod Folland, Trade Exhibit Sevices Executive
Mary Anne LaMarre, Operations Officer
Ted Fox, Executive Director
Formerly the Photo Marketing Association, PMA is a global forum for photo imaging industry education, networking and introductions of new products and technologies. Includes conferences and meetings of the Association of Professional Color Imagers, the Digital Imaging Marketing Association, the Photo Imaging Education Association, the Professional Picture Framers Association, the Professional Scrapbook Retailers Organization and the Professional School Photographers Association.
24M Attendees
Frequency: February/March

20919 **Photohistory**
Photographic Historical Society
PO Box 39563
Rochester, NY 14604-9563
585-461-4545
Triennial show and exhibits of cameras and photographic images.
Frequency: October, Rochester

20920 **Photovision**
Glahe International
PO Box 2460
Germantown, MD 20875-2460
301-515-0012; Fax: 301-515-0016
Exhibits of photography equipment, supplies and services.

20921 **Professional Photographer American Expo**
Professional Photographers of America
229 Peachtree Street NE
International Tower, Suite 2200
Atlanta, GA 30303-1608
404-522-8600; Fax: 404-614-6401
http://www.ppa.com
Dana Groves, Advertising Director
Devoted to new technologies in the photography field. 300 booths.
5M Attendees
Frequency: July

20922 **SPE Regional & National Conference**
Society for Photographic Education

2530 Superior Avenue
Suite 403
Cleveland, OH 44114

216-622-2733; Fax: 216-622-2712
membership@spenational.org
www.spenational.org

Virginia Morrison, Executive Director
Nina Barcellona, Advertising & Publications
Meghan Borato, Registrar
Carla Pasquale, Office/Accounts Manager
1000 Attendees
Frequency: Annual

20923 SPIE Photonics West
1000 20th Street
PO Box 10
Bellingham, WA 38227-0010

360-676-3290
888-504-8171; Fax: 360-647-1445
help@spie.org
www.SPIE.org
Facebook, Twitter, LinkedIn

Eugene G Arthurs, Executive Director

Conference proceedings, and SPIE digital library.
14000 Members
Founded in 1955

20924 WPPI Conference & Expo
Wedding & Portrait Photographers International
85 Broad St.
11th Fl.
New York, NY 10004

646-846-4500; Fax: 310-846-4770
www.wppionline.com/wppi-show.shtml

Industry event for wedding and portrait photographers and filmmakers.
13000 Attendees

Directories & Databases

20925 Complete Directory of Film & Photo Products
Sutton Family Communications & Publishing Company
920 State Route 54 East
Elmitch, KY 42343

270-276-9500

Theresa Sutton, Publisher
Lee Sutton, Editor

Print-out from database of wholesalers, manufacturers, distributors, importers and close-out houses. Database is updated daily to guarantee the most current and up-to-date sources available.
Cost: $34.50
100 Pages

20926 Directory of Free Stock Photography
Infosource Publishing
10 E 39th Street
6th Floor
New York, NY 10016-0111

212-683-8905

Offers valuable information on federal, state and local governments which will provide photographs free of charge for commercial use.
Cost: $14.50
150 Pages
Frequency: Biennial

20927 Green Book: Directory of Natural History and General Stock Photography
AG Editions
41 Union Sq W
Suite 525
New York, NY 10003-3230

212-929-0959; Fax: 212-924-4796
info@agpix.com
www.ag-editions.com

Ann Guifoyle, Editor
Sharon Powers, Manager

Over 400 photographers and photo agencies that provide stock photography.
Cost: $28.00
368 Pages
Frequency: Biennial
Circulation: 6500
Founded in 1986

20928 Guide to Photography Workshops
Shaw Guides
P.O. Box 231295
New York, NY 10023

212-799-6464; Fax: 212-724-9287
http://photoworkshops.shawguides.com

Workshops are profiled that are aimed at amateurs and professionals, including photo tours, studio intensives and specialized instruction.
Cost: $19.95
300 Pages
Frequency: Biennial

20929 Hemingway's Glamour Photographer's Resource Directory
Looking Glass Photography
5975 Keller Road
Saint Louis, MO 63128-3359

314-849-8952

Buyers of glamour photography, including film and video producers are profiled.
Cost: $40.00
200 Pages
Frequency: Biennial
Circulation: 1,000

20930 Industrial Photography: Gold Book Issue
PTN Publishing Company
445 Broadhollow Road
Melville, NY 11747-3669

516-465-7684

Steve Shaw, Editor

A list of manufacturers of photographic equipment and supplies, motion picture laboratories, videotape production facilities, equipment rental services, custom developing services and photographic repair services.
Cost: $5.75
Frequency: Annual December
Circulation: 40,000

20931 Orion Blue Book: Camera
Orion Research Corporation
14555 N Scottsdale Rd
Suite 330
Scottsdale, AZ 85254-3487

480-951-1114
800-844-0759; Fax: 480-951-1117
www.bluebook.com

Roger Rohrs, Owner

List of manufacturers of cameras.
Frequency: Annual

20932 Photographer's Complete Guide to Exhibition & Sales Spaces
Consultant Press
13 Laight St
#201
New York, NY 10013-2119

212-431-3130

Bob Speirs, Owner

Directory of services and supplies to the industry.
Cost: $24.95
280 Pages

20933 Photographic Trade News: Master Buying Guide
Cygnus Business Media
445 Broad Hollow Road
Melville, NY 11747-3669

631-845-2700; Fax: 631-845-2723
www.photolife.com

Offers a list of manufacturers and distributors of photographic equipment and photography associations.
Frequency: Annual

20934 Photography Forum
CompuServe Information Service
5000 Arlington Centre Blvd
Columbus, OH 43220-5439

614-326-1002
800-848-8199

Offers a forum for the discussion of photography on both the amateur and professional levels.
Frequency: Bulletin Board

20935 Photography RoundTable
GE Information Services
401 N Washington Street
Rockville, MD 20850-1707

301-388-8284

Cathy Ge, Owner

Provides a forum for the exchange of photography tips and information.
Frequency: Bulletin Board

20936 Who's Who in Photographic Management
Photo Marketing Association International
2282 Springport Road
Suite F
Jackson, MI 49202

517-788-8100
800-762-9287; Fax: 517-788-8371
www.theimagingalliance.com
Facebook, Twitter, LinkedIn

Ted Fox, CEO
Allen Showalter, President
Mark Klostermeyer, Vice-President
Robert L Hanson, Treasurer

Over 15,500 members of the association and manufacturers and suppliers of photographic equipment; also members of the National Association of Photo Equipment Technicians and of the Professional School Photographers of America.
Cost: $75.00
Frequency: Annual

Industry Web Sites

20937 http://gold.greyhouse.com
G.O.L.D Grey House OnLine Databases

Grey House Publishing's online database platform, GOLD, offers Quick Search, Keyword Search and Expert Search for most business sectors including photography markets. The GOLD platform makes finding the information you need quick and easy - whether you're a novice searcher or an experienced database user. All of Grey House's directory products are available for subscription on the GOLD platform.

20938 www.aspp.com
American Society of Picture Professionals

Members are image producers, stock photo agencies, and image users.Provides networking and educational opportunities in the image transaction industry.

20939 www.bca.org
BioCommunications Association

Made up of professionals who create and use the highest quality images and presentations in visual communications media for teaching and documentation in the life sciences and medicine.

20940 www.cpw.org
Center for Photography at Woodstock

Founded in 1977, the Center for Photography at Woodstock is a not-for-profit 501(c)3 artist-centered organization dedicated to supporting artists working in photography and related media and engaging audiences through opportunities in which creation, discovery and education are made possible.

20941 www.editorialphoto.com
Editorial Photographers

Internet discussion forum on business issues with more than 3000 subscribers participating from over 30 countries around the globe. Via the forum photographers exchange information on business practices, copyright and contract concerns. Useful resources such as sample business forms, publisher contract reviews and more can be found here.

20942 www.greyhouse.com
Grey House Publishing

Authoritative reference directories for most business sectors including photography markets. Users can search the online databases with varied search criteria allowing for custom searches by product category, geographic area, sales volume, keyword, subject and more. Full Grey House catalog and online ordering also available.

20943 www.nppa.org
National Press Photographers Association

Sponsors numerous annual television and print media workshops. Conducts annual competition for newsphotos and television newsfilm. Monthly magazine job information bank given to all members.

20944 www.ppa.com
Professional Photographers of America

Portrait, commercial, wedding, industrial and specialized photo- graphers and photographic artists.

20945 www.stockindustry.org
Picture Agency Council of America

The trade association for stock picture agencies in North America.

Associations

20946 ASM International
9639 Kinsman Road
Materials Park, OH 44073-0002
440-338-5151
800-336-5152; Fax: 440-338-4634
memberservicecenter@asminternational.org
www.asminternational.org
Facebook, Twitter, LinkedIn
Zi-Kui Liu, President
Diana Essock, Vice President
Raymond V. Fryan, Treasurer
William T. Mahoney, Secretary & CEO
The society for materials engineers and scientists, a worldwide network dedicated to advancing industry, technology and applications of metals and materials. ASM provides information references, education, research and international events.
30K Members
Founded in 1913

20947 American Chemistry Council
American Chemistry Council
700 Second St.,NE
Washington, DC 20002
202-249-7000; Fax: 202-249-6100
www.polyurethane.org
Facebook, Twitter, LinkedIn, RSS
Anne Womack Koltan, VP of Communications
Nacole B. Hinton, Managing Dir. Of Human Resources
Calvin M. Dooley, President and CEO
Dell Perelman, Chief of staff and General Counsel
Raymond O'Bryan, CFO & Chief Administration Officer
API is composed of companies that supply polyurethane resins or chemicals used in polyurethane resins, manufacture polyurethanes, produce machinery used in the manufacture or processing polyurethane, or engage in the business of applying polyurethane products in end use applications. API consists of several groups that focus on critical industry issues such as product stewardship, recycling, communications.
80 Members
Founded in 1977

20948 American Composites Manufacturers Association
3033 Wilson Blvd
Suite 420
Arlington, VA 22201
703-525-0511; Fax: 703-525-0743
info@acmanet.org
www.acmanet.org
Facebook, Twitter, LinkedIn, RSS
Tom Dobbins, President
Jeff Craney, Chairman
Kevin Barnett, Chairman-Elect/ Treasurer
Kimberly Howard, Secretary
Leon Garoufalis, Vice Chairman
Presents information on new technology, trends and techniques for manufacturers in the fiberglass and composites industry.
600 Members
Founded in 1979

20949 American Electroplaters and Surface Finishers Society (AESF)
1155 15th Street NW
Suite 500
Washington, DC 20005
202-457-8404; Fax: 202-530-0659
www.aesf.org
Facebook, Twitter, LinkedIn, RSS, Google+
John Flatley, Executive Director
Courtney Mariette, Bookstore/Education
Melissa Walker, Membership
Carrie Hoffman, Deputy Executive Director
AESF is an international society that advances the science of surface finishing to benefit industry and society through education, information and social involvement, as well as those who provide services, supplies and support to the industry.
5000 Members
Founded in 1909

20950 American Plastics Council
American Chemistry Council
700 Second St.,NE
Washington, DC 20002
202-249-7000
800-243-5790; Fax: 202-249-6100
www.plastics.org
Facebook, Twitter, LinkedIn, RSS
Calvin M Dooley, President
Anne Womack Koltan, VP of Communications
Nacole B. Hinton, Managing Dir. Of Human Resources
Dell Perelman, Chief of staff and General Counsel
Raymond O'Bryan, CFO & Chief Administration Officer
Major trade association for the US plastics industry. We demonstrate that plastics are a responsible choice and promote the countless ways that plastics make lives better, healthier and safer.
24 Members

20951 American Society for Plasticulture
526 Brittany Drive
State College, PA 16803
814-238-7045; Fax: 814-238-7051
www.plasticulture.org
Henry Taber, President
William Tietjen, Chairman
Patricia Heuser, Executive Director
Jodi Fleck-Arnold, VP
Promotes research, education and technology application for plastics used in agricultural and horticultural production systems. Hosts a congress every year or so; published proceedings of research presentations.
100 Members
Founded in 1962

20952 Association of Industrial Metallizers, Coaters and Laminators
201 Springs Street
Fort Mill, SC 29715
803-948-9470; Fax: 803-948-9471
aimcal@aimcal.org
www.aimcal.org
Dan Bemi, President
Danis Roy, Vice President
David Bryant, Treasurer
Craig Sheppard, Executive Director
Dante Ferrari, Directors at Large
Nonprofit trade organization for makers of coated, laminated and metalized papers. AIMCAL serves as the global forum for the flexible metallizing, coating and laminating industry by providing resources, services and information. AIMCAL collects and distributes information to increase industry knowledge, while fostering an environment that builds relationships and a spirit of cooperation between member companies worldwide.
260 Members
Founded in 1970

20953 Association of Postconsumer Plastic Recyclers
1001 G Street, NW
Suite 500 West
Washington, DC 20001
202-316-3046
www.plasticsrecycling.org
Facebook, Twitter, LinkedIn
Steve Alexander, Executive Director
Josh Standish, Technical Director
Dave Cornell, Technical Consultant
Kara Pochiro, Communications Director
Liz Bedard, Rigids Program Director
Represents companies that acquire, reprocess and sell the output of more than 90 percent of the post-consumer plastic processing capacity in North America.
Founded in 1992

20954 Association of Rotational Molders International
800 Roosevelt Rd
Suite C-312
Glen Ellyn, IL 60137
630-942-6589; Fax: 630-790-3095
info@rotomolding.org
www.rotomolding.org
Facebook, LinkedIn
Adam Webb, Managing Director
Corey Claussen, President
Dru Laws, Treasurer/Secretary
Conchita Miranda, Vice President
Rick Church, Executive Dircetor
Seeks to increase awareness of roto-molding, exchange technical information, provide education, and standardize production guidelines.
425 Members
Founded in 1976

20955 Berkshire Plastics Network
Downtown Pittsfield Office
66 Allen Street
Pittsfield, MA 01201
413-499-4000
800-438-9572; Fax: 413-447-9641
www.berkshirechamber.com
Facebook, Twitter, LinkedIn, YouTube
Linda Gaspardi Febles, Chair
Jonathan Butler, President & CEO
June Roy-Martin, VP Member Services
Lori Gazzillo, Chair-Elect
Chip Moore, Treasurer
A consortium of more than 40 independent companies, representing virtually every discipline in the design and production of molds, components and plastic products.

20956 International Association of Plastics Distribution
6734 W 121st Street
Overland Park, KS 66209
913-345-1005; Fax: 913-345-1006
iapd@iapd.org
www.iapd.org
Facebook, Twitter, LinkedIn, YouTube, Flickr
Susan E. Avery, CAE, CEO
Liz Novak, CAE, Sr. Dir., Advocacy & Publications
Dave Blackhurst, Dir., Membership & Sales
Kerrie Moore, Finance Manager
Whitney Nelson, Dir., Meetings & Events
The International Association of Plastics Distribution is an international trade association com-

prised of companies engaged in the distribution and manufacturing of plastics materials.
Founded in 1956

20957 **International Molded Fiber Association**
355 Lexington Avenue, Floor 15
New York, NY 10017

262-241-0522; Fax: 262-241-3766
Alan@IMFA.org
www.imfa.org
Facebook, Twitter, LinkedIn

Cassandra Niesing, Asst. Director
Joseph Grygny, Chairman/ Founder
Hubert Ranger, Founder

Acts as an information center for the molded fiber industry with worldwide membership of users and manufacturers of molded fiber producs. Promotes use of natural and recycled fibers.
Founded in 1997

20958 **National Association for PET Container Resources**
7310 Turfway Road
Suite 550
Florence, KY 41042

859-372-6635; Fax: 707-935-1998
n4mayshun@napcor.com
www.napcor.com
Facebook

Rick Moore, Executive Director
Resa Dimino, Director of Public Policy
Kate Eagles, Project Director

National association for the PET plastic industry. Promotes the use of PET plastic packaging and facilitates the recycling of PET containers.
13 Members
Frequency: Bi-Monthly
Founded in 1987

20959 **National Certification In Plastics (NCP)**
Society of the Plastics Industry
1667 K St NW
Suite 1000
Washington, DC 20006-1620

202-496-4400
888-627-3660; Fax: 202-496-4444

Barbara Darby, Manager Plastics Learning Network
Barry Eisenberg, Director Communications/Marketing

The National Certification in Plastics (NCP) program is a national, voluntary certification examination that tests plastics operations employees' skills and knowledge. The National Certification in Plastics exam tests the knowledge and skill level of plastics operations employees in one of the four major plastics processes - injection molding, extrusion, thermoforming or blow molding.The NCP program is sponsored by the Society of the Plastics Industry.

20960 **Plastic Pipe and Fittings Association**
800 Roosevelt Rd
Building C, Suite 312
Glen Ellyn, IL 60137

630-858-6540; Fax: 630-790-3095
www.ppfahome.org
Facebook, RSS

Richard W Church, Executive Director

The Plastic Pipe and Fittings Association (PPFA) is a national trade association comprised of member companies that manufacture plastic piping, fittings and solvent cements for plumbing and related applications, or supply raw materials, ingredients or machinery for the manufacturing process.
Founded in 1978

20961 **Plastic Shipping Container Institute**
5614 Connecticut Avenue, N.W
#284
Washington, DC 20015

202-253-4347; Fax: 202-330-5092
www.pscionline.org

David H Baker, General Counsel

The Plastic Shipping Container Institute (PSCI) is an international organization of producers of plastic pails (rigid, plastic shipping containers). The Institute's mission is to promote the common interests of, and the general well being of, the plastic shipping container industry, including consideration of local, state and federal regulatory and legislative issues and international trade issues impacting customers, suppliers and consumers.
Founded in 1967

20962 **Plastics Industry Association**
1425 K Street NW
Suite 500
Washington, DC 20005

202-974-5200
202-296-7005; Fax: 202-296-7005
www.plasticsindustry.org
Facebook, Twitter, LinkedIn, YouTube

Patricia Davitt Long, COO

Organization promoting the global competitiveness of the plastics supply chain.
Founded in 1937

20963 **Plastics Institute of America**
University of Massachusetts Lowell, Plastics Engin
Ball Hall Room 204
One University Avenue
Lowell, MA 01854

978-934-2575; Fax: 978-934-3089
contactus@plasticsinstitute.org
www.plasticsinstitute.org

Aldo Crugnola, Executive Director
Angelo Sabatalo, Chair Elect
Dan Mielcarek, Chair
Nick R. Schott, Secretary/ Director of Training
Marlene Gosling, Treasurer

The Plastics Institute of America is a not-for-profit educational and research organization dedicated to providing service to the plastics industries. We support, foster and guide plastics education and research at all levels to ensure the continued growth of the industry. Since our founding the Institute has held to this mission with ongoing educational programs and resources for skilled workers, professionals and industry executives.
Founded in 1961

20964 **Plastics Learning Network**
Society of the Plastics Industry
7 North Laurens Street
Greenville, SC 29601

864-239-2939; Fax: 864-239-0549
www.plasticsnews.com

Barbara Darby, Manager Plastics Learning Network
Barry Eisenberg, Director Communications/Marketing

Training opportunities are available for plastics employers and employees through the Plastics Learning Network (PLN) which is sponsored by the Society of the Plastics Industry's (SPI). Courses from qualified instructors are presented as on-site courses tailored to individual work schedules. Courses currently available are Operator Training in Injection Molding and Extrusion. Financial aid is available.
Founded in 2001

20965 **Plastics Pipe Institute**
105 Decker Court
Suite 825
Irving, TX 75062

469-499-1044; Fax: 469-499-1063
info@plasticpipe.org
www.plasticpipe.org
Facebook, LinkedIn, YouTube

Tony Radoszewski, President
Lance MacNevin, Director of Engineering
Sarah Patterson, Technical Director
Dana gecker, Marketing Communications Manager
Vicki Hackett, Office Manager/Executive Assistant

The major trade association representing all segments of the plastics piping industry. As an association, PPI focuses collaborative efforts to accumulate data, concentrate facts and target resources toward advancements in applications and increases in widespread usage.
300 Members
Founded in 1950

20966 **Plastics USA**
1667 K St.NW.
Suite 1000
Washington, DC 20006

202-974-5200; Fax: 202-296-7005
tradeshows@socplas.org
Facebook, Twitter, LinkedIn

Adam Krumhans, Trade Show Coordinator
Donald Duncan, President

Plastics USA, sponsored by The Society of the Plastics Industry/SPI, is held once every three years. The three-day trade show and educational program, which is sponsored by the Society of Plastics Engineers, has proven to be an ideal business forum for the North American plastics industry. Last held in Chicago in 2001, Plastics USA attracted over 15,000 attendees and the show featured 435 exhibiting companies occupying 95,000 square feet of exhibit space.
12M Members

20967 **Polymer Processing Institute**
New Jersey Institute Of Technology University Heig
Guttenberg Information Technologies Center
Suite 3901
Newark, NJ 07102-1982
973-596-5256; Fax: 973-642-4594
www.polymers-ppi.com

Ming-Wan Young, Ph.D, President
Costas G. Gogos, Ph.D, Senior Advisor/President Emeritus
Mariann Pappagallo, Administrative Consultant
Niloufar Faridi, Ph.D, Senior Technical Consultant
Linjie Zhu, Ph.D., Technical Director

The Polymer Processing Institute is an independent research corporation headquartered at New Jersey Institute of Technology, Newark, New Jersey. Its mission is to assist industry by implementing the advanced knowledge in the field of polymer technology and related areas through sponsored research, development and education, and to disseminate information via technology transfer.
Founded in 1999

20968 **Polystyrene Packaging Council (PSPC)**
American Chemistry Council
700 Second St.,NE
Washington, DC 20002

202-249-7000; Fax: 202-249-6100
www.polystyrenerecyclingnetwork.com
Facebook, Twitter, RSS

Michael H. Levy, Senior Director
Annie F. Walton, Administrative Assistant

Calvin M. Dooley, President and CEO
Dell Perelman, Chief of staff and General Counsel

PSPC, a business unit of the American Plastics Council, is a nonprofit trade association dedicated to providing accurate information on the environmental impact of polystyrene packaging, including polystyrene recycling programs. PSPC's membership includes manufacturers of polystyrene resin, polystyrene foam and rigid food service packaging.

20969 SPI
1667 K St NW
Suite 1000
Washington, DC 20006

202-974-5200
888-627-3660; Fax: 202-296-7005
www.plasticbag.com
Facebook, Twitter, LinkedIn

Donna Dempsey, Executive Director
Betsy Coleman, Assistant Director
Yvonne Wade, Assistant Manager
Jack Riopelle, Chairman
John Wilhite, Vice Chairman

Members are US and Canadian manufacturers of plastic retail bags. A business unite of the Society of the Plastics Industry, Inc. that actively promotes the growth of the plastic film and bag industry. FBF membership includes companies that are in the plastic bag segment of the industry as well as those in the film sector.
50 Members
Founded in 1937

20970 Society of Plastics Engineers
6 Berskshire Blvd
Suite 306
Bethel, CT 6801

203-775-0471; Fax: 203-775-8490
info@4spe.org
www.4spe.org
Facebook, Twitter, LinkedIn, RSS

Susan Oderwald, Executive Director
Dick Cameron, President
Dr. Jaime A. Gomez, Vice President/Treasurer
Monica Verheij, Vice President/Secretary
William De Vos, Chief Executive Officer

The premier source of peer-reviewed technical information for plastics professionals. SPE takes action every day to help individuals and companies in the plastics industry succeed by spreading knowledge, strengthening skills, and promoting plastics.
15000 Members
Founded in 1942

20971 Thermoforming Institute
1667 K St NW
Suite 240
Washington, DC 20006-1620

202-974-5200; Fax: 202-296-7005
www.thermoforminginstitute.org
Facebook, Twitter, LinkedIn

William Cartuaex, President
Gene Janders, VP Trade Shows

A business unit of the Society of the Plastics Industry, Incorporated,the Thermoforming Institute is comprised of principal officers of companies or divisions significantly engaged in the manufacture of custom thermoformed products.
1200 Members
Founded in 1937

Newsletters

20972 ACM Monthly
Composite Market Reports
PO Box 137
Gilbert, AZ 85299-0137

480-507-6882; Fax: 480-507-6986
www.compositemarketreports.com/

John R. White, Executive Director/CEO
Patricia Ryan, Operations/COO
Russell Harris, Director Financial Services
Wayne Graves, Director Information Systems
Brian Hebert, Marketing/Communications Manager

Reports on market and technology intelligence for materials suppliers.

20973 Additives for Polymers
Reed Elsevier Science Direct
9555 Springboro Pike
Miamisburg, OH 45342

937-865-6800; Fax: 937-865-1349
s.barrett@elsevier.com
www.elsevier.com

Guy Kitteringhem, Publisher
A Weawer, Editor
S. Barrett, Program Editor
Marike Westra, Director Corporate Relations
Ylann Schemm, Communications Executive

Each issue identifies and details relevant materials and products, new applications, new research and technical developments, newly issued US and British patents.
Frequency: Monthly
Founded in 1887
Printed in on matte stock

20974 Advanced Materials & Composites News
Composites Worldwide
991 C Lomas Santa Fe Drive
PMB469
Solana Beach, CA 92075-2141

858-755-1372; Fax: 858-755-5271
compositesnews@adelphia.net
www.compositesnews.com

Steve Loud, Editor
Susan Loud, Managing Editor

Focuses on the processes, applications markets, design, international activities and more related to composites and other advanced materials, particularly for civil engineering and construction, but for all markets and structural applications, including aerospace, transportation, and industrial.
Cost: $598.00
Circulation: 1000

20975 Composite Industry Monthly
Composite Market Reports
PO Box 137
Gilbert, AZ 85299

480-507-6882; Fax: 480-507-6986
www.compositemarketreports.com

William Benjamin, Publisher
John R. White, Executive Director/CEO
Patricia Ryan, Operations/COO
Wayne Graves, Director Information Systems
Russell Harris, Director Financial Services

Market and technology intelligence for users, prime and sub-contractors, universities, government and others.
Cost: $1495.00
Frequency: Monthly
Circulation: 8177
Founded in 1971

20976 Modern Plastics Worldwide
Canon Communications
11444 W Olympic Blvd
Suite 900
Los Angeles, CA 90064-1555

310-445-4200; Fax: 310-445-4299
www.modplas.com/

Charlie Mc Curdy, President
Kevin O'Grady, Publisher

Industry trends and developments. Accepts advertising.
Cost: $150.00
125 Pages
Frequency: Monthly

20977 POF Newsletter
Information Gatekeepers
PO Box 35880
Brighton, MA 02135-1000

617-782-5033
800-323-1088; Fax: 617-782-5735
info@igigroup.com
www.igigroup.com

Paul Polishuk, CEO
Bev Wilson, Managing Editor
Will Ashley, IT Director/Media Manager

Covers recent developments in the plastic optical fiber industry. Also provides updates on components, systems, applications, standards and a calendar of related events.
Cost: $395.00
Founded in 1977

20978 Plastic Focus
Plastics Connection
PO Box 814
Amherst, MA 01004-0814

413-549-5020; Fax: 413-549-9955
www.trplastics.com

Michael L Berins, Publisher
Armando Honegger, CEO

Newsletter for buyers, sellers, and users of plastic.
Cost: $275.00
Frequency: Bi-Weekly

20979 Plastics Brief Newsletter
Plastic Marketing News Brief Market Search
2727 North Holland Sylvania Road
Suite A
Toledo, OH 43615-1800

419-535-7899; Fax: 419-535-1243
www.sagepub.com

James Best, Publisher

For plastic sales and marketing executives. Covers new materials, new applications, market trends, price changes.
Cost: $249.00
Frequency: Monthly

20980 Plastics Machinery & Auxiliaries
Canon Communications
Ste 370
3300 E 1st Ave
Denver, CO 80206-5806

303-321-2322; Fax: 303-321-3552
www.pma-magazine.com/

Merle R. Snyder, Editor
Jamie Quanbeck, Online Editor
Heidi Hill, Managing Editor
Kate Hunley, Associate Editor

Plastics Machinery & Auxiliaries provides readers with a forum for learning about new products and services used in a wide range of plastics processes. Plastics Machinery & Auxiliaries is distributed free of charge to qualified professionals in the plastics processing industry, in the USA and Canada.

20981 Plastics News
Crain Communications

1725 Merriman Rd
Suite 300
Akron, OH 44313-5283

330-836-9180; Fax: 330-836-2831
info@crain.com
www.crain.com

Robert S Simmons, VP
Linda Whelan, Marketing Manager

Delivers breaking news, features, detailed rankings, economic data and materials pricing to readers around the world.
Frequency: Weekly
Circulation: 60054
Founded in 1989

20982 Plastics Recycling Update
PO Box 42270
Portland, OR 97242-0270

503-233-1305; Fax: 503-233-1356
info@resource-recycling.com
www.resource-recycling.com/rr.html
Facebook, Twitter, RSS

Jerry Powell, Editor/Publisher
Rick Downing, Advertising Director
Dylan de Thomas, Managing Editor
Mary Lynch, Assistant Publisher
Chad Powell, Director of Research

Resource Recycling is the journal of recycling and composting professionals. Each month, the latest information is provided about post-consumer waste recovery efforts including: collection system assessments; processing developments; markets analyses, and legislative and regulatory reviews. Additional features includes special commodity and regular departments on equipment, recycling and composting programs, association and state activities.
Cost: $58.00
Frequency: Monthly
ISSN: 0147-2429
Founded in 1981
Printed in 2 colors

20983 Plastics Week
Market Search
Laguna Beach, CA

949-212-7400
www.plasticsweek.com

James R Best, Publisher
Linda Best, Production Manager
Jim Best, Editor
Jim Best, CEO

Weekly newletters on plastics. Focusing on strategies, markets, technology, recycling and environmental issues.
Cost: $480.00
6 Pages
Founded in 1961

20984 Polymer Blends, Alloys, and Interpenetrating Polymer Networks
Sage Publications
2455 Teller Rd
Newbury Park, CA 91320-2234

805-499-9774
800-818-7243; Fax: 805-499-0871
info@sagepub.com
www.sagepub.com

Blaise R Simqu, CEO
David P McCune, Director

Survey and summary of the growing literature and patents in the promising area of plastics technology. Each issue provides new information on chemistry, properties and performance, testing, processing, and application.
Cost: $ 455.00
40 Pages
Frequency: Monthly
ISSN: 0893-6684
Printed in 2 colors on matte stock

20985 Rubber and Plastics News
Crain Communications
1725 Merriman Rd
Suite 300
Akron, OH 44313-5283

330-836-9180; Fax: 330-836-2831
info@crain.com
www.crain.com

Robert S Simmons, VP

It provides news, features, technical and marketing information in print and daily on the Internet to rubber manufacturers, suppliers, consultants and laboratories worldwide.
Frequency: Bi-Weekly
Circulation: 16387

Magazines & Journals

20986 Advanced Composites Monthly
Composite Market Reports
PO Box 137
Gilbert, AZ 85299-0137
480-507-6882; Fax: 480-507-6986
www.compositemarketreports.com

William Benjamin, President/Editor
Chris Red, Market Research
Cher Benjamin, VP
Joe Benjamin, Office Manager

Provides information to personnel at all levels in the advanced composite manufacturing industry.
10 Pages
Frequency: Monthly
Founded in 1975

20987 Advanced Materials & Processes
ASM International
9639 Kinsman Road
Materials Park, OH 44073-0002

440-338-5151
800-336-5152; Fax: 440-338-4634
magazines@asminternational.org
www.asminternational.org

William T. Mahoney, Secretary & CEO
Joanne Miller, Editor
Vicki Burt, Managing Editor

AM&P is the monthly technical magazine from ASM International, designed to keep readers aware of leading-edge developments and trends in engineering materials - metals and alloys, engineering polymers, advanced ceramics, and composites - and the methods used to select, process, fabricate, test, and characterize them.
30K Members
Frequency: Monthly
Circulation: 23000
Founded in 1913

20988 Digest of Polymer Developments
STR-Specialized Technology Resources
10 Springborn Ctr
Enfield, CT 06082-4814

860-749-8371; Fax: 860-749-8234
www.strlab.com

Dennis Jilot, CEO

Covers domestic and international information on new plastics applications, potential growth and market performance, as well as current events in the plastics and allied chemicals industries. Contains a cumulative index by market and another by plastics materials for quick reference.
Cost: $625.00

20989 GraFiber News
Composite Market Reports
PO Box 137
Gilbert, AZ 85299-0137

480-507-6882; Fax: 602-507-6986
www.compositemarketreports.com

William Benjamin, President/Publisher/Editor/CEO
Cher Benjamin, VP
Chris Red, Market Research
Joe Benjamin, Office Manager

Provides global coverage of the aerospace industry for advanced material suppliers.
Cost: $2556.25
10 Pages
Frequency: Monthly
ISSN: 1058-9023
Founded in 1973
Printed in 4 colors on matte stock

20990 Injection Molding Magazine
Canon Communications
11444 W Olympic Blvd
Ste.900
Los Angeles, CA 90064

310-445-4200
www.immnet.com
Facebook, Twitter, LinkedIn

Paul Miller, President/CEO
Stephen Corrick, Publisher/VP/Sales & Marketing
Jeff Tade, Publications Production Manager
Willy Bruijns-Miller, VP Circulation

Custom and captive molding operations, product design, moldmaking, processing information, new materials and equipment, and management issues are the editorial focus.
Cost: $168.57
Frequency: Monthly
Circulation: 37500
Founded in 1999

20991 Journal of Cellular Plastics
Sage Publications
2455 Teller Rd
Newbury Park, CA 91320-2234

805-499-9774
800-818-7243; Fax: 805-499-0871
journals@sagepub.com
www.sagepub.com

Blaise R Simqu, CEO

A permanent record for international achievements in the science, technology, and economics of cellular plastics. It has been a major source of information on this topic for 35 years. Each issue presents outstanding technical advances in chemistry, formulation, processing, testing, properties, performance, and applications.
Cost: $901.00
96 Pages
Frequency: Bi-Monthly
ISSN: 0021-955X
Printed in 2 colors on matte stock

20992 Journal of Composite Materials
Sage Publications
2455 Teller Rd
Newbury Park, CA 91320-2234
805-499-9774
800-818-7243; Fax: 805-499-0871
journals@sagepub.com
www.sagepub.com

Blaise R Simqu, CEO
Thomas Hahn, Editor

The leading medium for composite materials technology transfer. Featuring original studies from international material scientists, the journal seeks to emphasize practical applications with no compromise in technical integrity.
Cost: $4576.00
96 Pages
Frequency: Bi-Monthly
ISSN: 0021-9983

Founded in 1965
Printed in 2 colors on matte stock

20993 Journal of Elastomers and Plastics
Sage Publications
2455 Teller Rd
Newbury Park, CA 91320-2234

805-499-9774
800-818-7243; Fax: 805-499-0871
journals@sagepub.com
www.sagepub.com

Blaise R Simqu, CEO
S. Qutubuddin, Editorial Board

The latest contributions to the technology and properties of elastomers and related polymeric products. Major emphasis is placed on specialty and high performance elastomers. The journal regularly presents current information on the chemistry, processing, properties, and applications of recently developed and improved elastomeric materials.
Cost: $867.00
96 Pages
Frequency: Quarterly
ISSN: 0095-2443
Printed in 2 colors on matte stock

20994 Journal of Materials Engineering and Performance
ASM International
9639 Kinsman Road
Materials Park, OH 44073-0002

440-338-5151
800-336-5152; Fax: 440-338-4634
memberservicecenter@asminternational.org
www.asminternational.org

William T. Mahoney, Secretary & CEO
Rajiv Asthana, Editor

Peer-reviewed journal that publishes contributions on all aspects of materials selection, design, characterization, processing and performance testing. The journal is useful for solving day-to-day engineering challenges - especially those involving components for larger systems.
30K Members
Frequency: Bi-Monthly
Founded in 1913

20995 Journal of Materials Processing
Elsevier ScienceDirect
360 Park Ave S
New York, NY 10010-1736

212-989-5800
888-437-4636; Fax: 212-633-3990
journals@sagepub.com
www.elsevier.com

Erik Engstrom, CEO
J. Gunasekera, Regional Editor North America

Original papers developments in traditional and innovative processing technologies for metals, polymers, composites, ceramics, and specialty materials. The scope is international and interdisciplinary.
Cost: $5208.00
96 Pages
Frequency: 42 Issues Per Year
ISSN: 0924-0136
Printed in 2 colors on matte stock

20996 Journal of Phase Equilibria & Diffusion
ASM International
9639 Kinsman Road
Materials Park, OH 44073-0002

440-338-5151
800-336-5152; Fax: 440-338-4634
memberservicecenter@asminternational.org
www.asminternational.org

William T. Mahoney, Secretary & CEO
John Morral, Editor
Ursula R. Kattner, Editor
H. Okamoto, Editor

Peer-reviewed journal containing basic and applied research results, evaluated phase diagrams, a survey of current literature, and comments or other material pertinent to the previous three areas. The aim of the journal is to provide a broad spectrum of information concerning phase equilibria for the materials community.
30K Members
Frequency: Bi-Monthly
Founded in 1913

20997 Journal of Plastic Film & Sheeting
Sage Publications
2455 Teller Rd
Newbury Park, CA 91320-2234

805-499-9774
800-818-7243; Fax: 805-499-0871
journals@sagepub.com
www.sagepub.com

Blaise R Simqu, CEO

The Journal of Plastic Film and Sheeting improves communication concerning plastic film and sheeting with major emphasis on the propagation of knowledge which will serve to advance the science and technology of these products and thus better serve industry and the ultimate consumer. The journal reports on the wide variety of advances that are rapidly taking place in the technology of plastic film and sheeting.
Cost: $795.00
88 Pages
Frequency: Quarterly
ISSN: 8756-0879
Printed in 2 colors on matte stock

20998 Journal of Polymer Science
John Wiley & Sons
111 River St
Hoboken, NJ 07030-5790

201-748-6000; Fax: 201-748-6088
www.wiley.com

William J Pesce, CEO

The Journal of Polymer Science provides a continuous forum for the dissemination of thoroughly peer-reviewed, fundamental, international research into the preparation and properties of macromolecules. Part A: Polymer Chemistry is devoted to studies in fundamental organic polymer chemistry and physical organic chemistry. Polymer Physics (Part B) details contemporary research on all aspects of polymer physics.
200 Pages
Frequency: 48 Issues Per Year
ISSN: 0887-624X

20999 Journal of Reinforced Plastics and Composites
Sage Publications
2455 Teller Rd
Newbury Park, CA 91320-2234

805-499-9774
800-818-7243; Fax: 805-499-0871
journals@sagepub.com
www.sagepub.com

Blaise R Simqu, CEO
Christos C. Chamis, Editorial Board

The Journal of Reinforced Plastics and Composites presents research studies on a broad range of today's reinforced plastics and composites. The journal provides a permanent record of achievements in the science, technology, and economics of reinforced plastics and composites. Reports on special topics are regularly included such as recycling, environmental effects, novel materials, computer-aided design, predictive modelling, and composite materials.
Cost: $4509.00
Frequency: 18 Times Per Year
ISSN: 0731-6844
Founded in 1962

21000 Journal of Thermoplastic Composite Materials
Sage Publications
2455 Teller Rd
Newbury Park, CA 91320-2234

805-499-9774
800-818-7243; Fax: 805-499-0871
journals@sagepub.com
www.sagepub.com

Blaise R Simqu, CEO
M.N. Ghasemi Jejhad, Associate Editor

An international forum for the presentation of new advances in the technology of this class of materials. Emphasis is given to the fundamental areas of new material development and characterization, design, rheological behavior in short, discontinuous, and continuous fiber systems; process development, manufacturing science, matrix-fiber interphase charaterization; short and long-term performance prediction; and engineering data base assistance for thermoplastic composites.
Cost: $1186.00
96 Pages
Frequency: Bi-Monthly
ISSN: 0892-7057
Printed in 2 colors on matte stock

21001 Journal of Vinyl and Additive Technology
John Wiley & Sons
111 River St
Hoboken, NJ 07030-5790

201-748-6000; Fax: 201-748-6088
subinfo@wiley.com
www.wiley.com

William J Pesce, CEO
Elliot L. Weinberg, Associate Editor

Journal of Vinyl and Additive Technology is a peer-reviewed technical publication for new work in the fields of polymer modifiers and additives, vinyl polymers and selected review papers. Over half of all papers in JVAT are based on technology of additives and modifiers for all classes of polymers: thermoset polymers and both condensation and addition thermoplastics. Papers on vinyl technology include PVC additives.
Cost: $336.00
Frequency: Quarterly
Circulation: 625
ISSN: 1083-5601
Founded in 1942

21002 Journal of Wide Bandgap Materials
Sage Publications
2455 Teller Rd
Newbury Park, CA 91320-2234

805-499-9774
800-818-7243; Fax: 805-499-0871
journals@sagepub.com
www.sagepub.com

Blaise R Simqu, CEO
Shojiro Komatsu, Editorial Advisory Board

The Journal of Wide Bandgap Materials is an international journal publishing original peer-reviewed papers on fundamental, experimental and theoretical developments in the science and engineering of wide bandgap materials. The Journal provides a broad-based forum for the publication and sharing of ongoing research and development efforts in the field of wide bandgap materials.
Cost: $245.00
96 Pages
Frequency: Quarterly

ISSN: 1524-511X
Printed in 2 colors on matte stock

21003 Medical Plastics & Biomaterials
Canon Communications
11444 W Olympic Blvd
Suite 900
Los Angeles, CA 90064-1555

310-445-4200
800-243-9696; Fax: 310-445-4299
www.cancom.com

Charlie Mc Curdy, President
Tonna Anuligo, Technical Editor
Kevin O'Grady, Group Publisher

Technical information on the full range of plastics and biomaterials used in manufacturing and packaging medical products.
Cost: $59.00
Frequency: Monthly
Circulation: 61200
Founded in 1978

21004 Modern Plastics
Canon Communications
11444 W Olympic Blvd
Suite 900
Los Angeles, CA 90064-1555

310-445-4200; Fax: 310-445-4299
www.modplas.com/
Facebook, Twitter, LinkedIn

Charlie Mc Curdy, President
Kevin O'Grady, Publisher

Serves companies utilizing plastics. Developments in resin technology, machinery/processing techniques and additive innovation.
Cost: $59.00
Frequency: Monthly
Circulation: 50300
Founded in 1978

21005 PM/USA Green Sheet
Marketing Handbook
PO Box 243687
Boynton Beach, FL 33424-3687

561-732-5858; Fax: 561-732-2607

Lee Noe, Publisher/Editor
Bob Miller, Technical Director

For those responsible for manufacturing operations.
Cost: $45.00
Frequency: Monthly
Founded in 1972

21006 Performance Plastics Magazine
International Association of Plastics Distribution
6734 W 121st Street
Overland Park, KS 66209

913-345-1005; Fax: 913-345-1006
iapd@iapd.org
www.iapd.org

Susan E. Avery, CAE, CEO
Liz Novak, CAE, Sr. Dir., Advocacy & Publications
Dave Blackhurst, Dir., Membership & Sales
Kerrie Moore, Finance Manager
Whitney Nelson, Dir., Meetings & Events

Performance Plastics magazine provides information on the plastics industry with special emphasis on profitability and advances in technology. IAPD fosters the development of the plastics industry through the collection, production and dissemination of quality information and education, and by being a catalyst in assuring proactive representation in the governmental and public arenas.
Cost: $90.00
68 Pages
Frequency: Monthly
Circulation: 10000
Founded in 1956
Printed in 4 colors on glossy stock

21007 Plastics Business News
Plastics Universe
2727 Holland Sylvania Road
Suite A
Toledo, OH 43615

419-535-7899; Fax: 419-535-1243
mberins@javanet.com
www.plasticx.com/pub/plast_11.html

Michael L. Berins, Publisher

A weekly newsletter published for the professionals in the plastic industry. Covers advances in materials and processes, pricing, new applications and markets, international competition, etc.
Cost: $327.00
Frequency: Weekly
Founded in 1972

21008 Plastics Distributor and Fabricator Magazine
KLW Enterprises
PO Box 669
LaGrange, IL 60525-0669

708-588-1845; Fax: 708-588-1846
pdfm@plasticsmag.com
www.plasticsmag.com

David Whelan, Editor/Publisher
Riia O'Donnell, Associate Editor
Lynette Zeitler, Art Director

Contains industry and products news relevant to the manufacture, distribution and fabrication of plastic rod, sheet and tube.
Founded in 1983
Printed in 4 colors on glossy stock

21009 Plastics Engineering
Society of Plastics Engineers
13 Church Hill Rd
Newtown, CT 06470

203-775-0471; Fax: 203-775-8490
info@4spe.org
www.4spe.org

Susan Oderwald, Executive Director

Communication to SPE's global audience of plastics professionals about current developments in the industry, technology, and activities of the Society.
Frequency: Monthly
Circulation: 35000

21010 Plastics Focus
Plastics Universe
2727 Holland Sylvania Road
Suite A
Toledo, OH 43615

419-535-7899; Fax: 419-535-1243

James Best, CEO

Bi-Monthly updates on new applicationsand markets for plastics, new polymers, alloys and blends as well as machinery, processing developments, and international competitions and opportunities.
Cost: $295.00

21011 Plastics Hotline
Industry Marketing Solutions
809 Central Avenue
PO Box 893, 2nd Floor
Fort Dodge, IA 50501-1052

888-247-2006; Fax: 515-574-2237
steve@plasticshotline.com
www.plasticshotline.com
Facebook, Twitter, LinkedIn, YouTube

Steve Scanlan, Publisher
Jim Rykhus, List Marketing Specialist
Cara Jondle, Tradeshow & Marketing Manager
Jody Kirchoff, Operations

Plastics Hotline has been published since 1983. This weekly periodical continues to be the National Marketplace for Plastic Processors to buy and sell equipment, parts and services.
Cost: $69.00
Frequency: Weekly
Founded in 1990

21012 Plastics Machining & Fabricating
Onsrud Cutter
800 Liberty Dr
Libertyville, IL 60048-2374

847-362-1560; Fax: 847-362-5028
www.plasticsmachining.com

Harry Urban, Publisher

Plastics Molding & Fabricating is an online technical and management magazine dedicated to the secondary plastics processing industry. It is edited for qualified professionals whose operations include: machining, milling, fabricating, forming, bending, bonding, molding, printing and finishing of plastics. Editorial subjects include case studies, technology updates, trends & news and opinion pieces.
Frequency: Bi-Monthly
Circulation: 15,015

21013 Plastics Technology
Gardner Publications
6915 Valley Ln
Cincinnati, OH 45244-3153

513-527-8800
800-950-8020; Fax: 513-527-8801
cnorman@gardnerweb.com
www.gardnerweb.com

Rick Kline Sr, CEO
Sherry Fuchs, Managing Editor
Theresa Basso, Production Editor
Joe Grande, Senior Editor

A premier source of technical and business information for plastics processors, each issue reports on technological innovations and developments in the plastics processing market and reaches more than 47,000 processors who depend on authoritative coverage on applying new technology, evaluating products and practical manufacturing.
Frequency: Monthly
Circulation: 47559
Founded in 1928

21014 Polymer Engineering & Science
John Wiley & Sons
111 River St
Hoboken, NJ 07030-5790

201-748-6000; Fax: 201-748-6088
subinfo@wiley.com
www.wiley.com

William J Pesce, CEO
Alan J Lesser, Associate Editor
Laura Espinet, Journal Production
Kim Thompkins, Advertising/Media

Presents papers of fundamental significance to engineers and scientists interested in polmeric materials.
Cost: $545.00
Frequency: Monthly
Circulation: 86000
Founded in 1945

21015 The PLASTICS Magazine
Plastics Industry Association
1425 K Street NW
Suite 500
Washington, DC 20005

202-974-5200
www.plasticsindustry.org/resources/plastics-magazine

Features and insights from all sectors of the plastics industry.
Cost: $175.00

Trade Shows

21016 ANTEC
Society of Plastics Engineering
13 Church Hill Road
Newtown, CT 06470
203-775-0471; Fax: 203-775-8490
info@4spe.org
www.4spe.org
Susan Oderwald, Executive Director
The largest technical conference for the plastics industry

21017 AeroMat Conference and Exposition
ASM International
9639 Kinsman Road
Materials Park, OH 44073-0002
440-338-5151
800-336-5152; Fax: 440-338-4634
memberservicecenter@asminternational.org
www.asminternational.org
William T. Mahoney, Secretary & CEO
Lindy Good, Global Conference & Exhibit Planner
Focuses on innovative aerospace materials, fabrication and manufacturing methods that improve aerospace structures, performance and durability.
900 Members
Frequency: Annual/May
Founded in 1913

21018 Association of Industrial Metallizers, Coaters and Laminators
201 Springs Street
Fort Mill, SC 29715
803-948-9470; Fax: 803-948-9471
aimcal@aimcal.org
www.aimcal.org
Craig Sheppard, Executive Director
Caleb Howe, Communications Manager
Ed Cohen, Technical Consultant
Norma Bryant, Office Manager
Displays relating to coaters and laminators, metallizers and producers of metallized film and or paper on continuous rolls, suppliers of plastic films, papers and adhesives.
Frequency: Annual
Founded in 1970

21019 Health Pack Innovative Technology Conference
1833 Centre Point Circle
Suite 123
Naperville, IL 60563
630-544-5051; Fax: 630-544-5055
info@healthpack.net
www.healthpack.net
Heather Jayson, Show Coordinator
Steve Bunell, Operations Manager
Curtis Larson, Program Coordinator
John Spitzley, Program Co-Chairman
Angela Holty, Owner
Unique annual conference focuses exclusively on medical device packaging, bringing together medical device manufacturers, packaging materials suppliers and converters, contract packagers, test labs, and other service providers. Food and beverage functions served in the exhibition area provide repeated opportunities for networking between exhibitors, attendees, and conference speakers. Conference location in St. Petersburg, Florida, 20 booths.
100 Attendees
Frequency: March

21020 Heat Treating Society Conference & Expo
ASM International
9639 Kinsman Road
Materials Park, OH 44073-0002
440-338-5151
800-336-5152; Fax: 440-338-4634
memberservicecenter@asminternational.org
www.asminternational.org
William T. Mahoney, Secretary & CEO
Lindy Good, Global Conference & Exhibit Planner
Conference and expo for heat treating equipment and supplies as well as information of interest to metallurgists, maintenance supervisors and production engineering staff.
30K Members
Frequency: October
Founded in 1913

21021 IAPD Annual Convention
International Association of Plastics Distribution
6734 W 121st Street
Overland Park, KS 66209
913-345-1005; Fax: 913-345-1006
iapd@iapd.org
www.iapd.org
Susan E. Avery, CAE, CEO
Liz Novak, CAE, Sr. Dir., Advocacy & Publications
Dave Blackhurst, Dir., Membership & Sales
Kerrie Moore, Finance Manager
Whitney Nelson, Dir., Meetings & Events
This three-day convention is where the best and the brightest of the plastics distribution industry come together to focus on the future of the industry.
Frequency: Annual/September
Founded in 1956

21022 International Plastics Show
1801 K Street NW
Suite 1000
Washington, DC 20006
202-974-5200; Fax: 202-296-7005
www.npe.org
Ken Rietz, President
Brigid Hughes, Director Trade Show Promotions
Adam Krumhansl, Trade Show Coordinator
Containing 2,000 exhibits.
85M+ Attendees
Frequency: June

21023 National Agricultural Plastics Congress
American Society for Plasticulture
526 Brittany Drive
State College, PA 16803
814-238-7045; Fax: 814-238-7051
www.plasticulture.org
William Tietjen, Chairman Plastics Congress
Henry Taber, President
Jodi Fleck-Arnold, VP
Edward Carey, Secretary/Treasurer
Patricia Heuser, Executive Director
Plastic products used in agriculture. 15-25 booths.
150 Attendees
Frequency: March/November

21024 National Plastics Exposition
Plastics Industry Association
1425 K Street NW
Suite 500
Washington, DC 20005
202-974-5200; Fax: 202-296-7005
www.plasticsindustry.org/events
Facebook, Twitter, LinkedIn
Susan Krys, VP, Trade Shows and Marketing
This expo features exhibits of molded, extruded, fabricated, laminated and calendered plastics, raw materials, machinery and laboratory equipment for the industry.
55M Attendees

21025 PLASTEC East Trade Show
Canon Communications
11444 West Olympic Boulevard
Los Angeles, CA 90064-1549
310-445-4200; Fax: 310-996-9499
www.plasteceast.com
Diane O'Connor, Trade Show Director
Shannon Cleghorn, Customer & Media Coordinator
Five co-located shows, 1,750 plastic exhibitors. The Trade Show takes place every 2 years, in odd years.
32000 Attendees

21026 PLASTEC West Trade Show
Canon Communications
2901 28th Street
Suite 100
Santa Monica, CA 90405
310-445-4200; Fax: 310-996-9499
Tssalesadmin@ubm.com
www.plastecwest.com
Twitter
Diane O'Connor, Trade Show Director
Jane Sullivan, Exhibit Contact
Five co-located shows, 3,000 exhibitors, trade show features plastics, packaging and manufacturing industries.
45000 Attendees
Frequency: January/February

21027 POLYCON
International Cast Polymer Association
3033 Wilson Blvd
Suite 4200
Arlington, VA 22201
703-525-0511; Fax: 703-525-0743
www.icpa-hq.org
Jeanne McCormack, Director Conferences & Meetings
Elizabeth Cookson, Mgr Conferences & Program Dvlpmt
Debbie Cannon, President
The program includes three days of in-depth educational programming, exhibits, a product showcase, and more. Sponsored annually by the International Cast Polymer Association/ICPA, POLYCON is the largest convention and trade show for the cast polymer industry. Over 800 industry professionals attend the convention to network, attend educational sessions, and visit with over 70 exhibitors.
Frequency: Annual

21028 PPI Annual Meeting
Plastics Pipe Institute
105 Decker Court
Suite 2
Irving, TX 75062
469-499-1044; Fax: 469-499-1063
info@plasticpipe.org
www.plasticpipe.org
Tony Radoszewski, Executive Director
Camille Rubeiz, Director Engineering
Stephen Boros, Technical Director
Frequency: May

21029 **Polyurethanes Technical Conference**
Alliance for the Polyurethanes Industry
700 Second St.,NE
Arlington, VA 22209
703-741-5103; Fax: 703-741-5655
www.polyurethane.org
Richard E Mericle, Executive Director
Kaye Robinson, Conference Planning Committee
Semi-annual trade show for the polyurethanes industry in North America. International technical conference and exposition will feature technical and industry issues sessions, poster session and exhibits.
Frequency: September/October
Founded in 1977

Directories & Databases

21030 **Handbook of Plastic Compounds, Elastomers and Resins**
John Wiley & Sons
10475 Crosspoint Blvd
Indianapolis, IN 46256-3386
317-572-3000; Fax: 317-572-4000
www.wiley.com
Lou Peragallo, Manager
Michael Ash, Editor
Directory of services and supplies to the industry. A complete, accurate, and current data source on primary material tradename products for the rubber and plastic industries. This handbook gives short, easy-to-find information on over 15,000 chemical trademark products currently sold throughout the world.
Cost: $385.00
ISBN: 0-471188-30-1

21031 **IAPD Membership Directory**
International Association of Plastics Distribution
6734 W 121st Street
Overland Park, KS 66209
913-345-1005; Fax: 913-345-1006
iapd@iapd.org
www.iapd.org
Susan E. Avery, CEO
Liz Novak, CAE, Sr. Dir., Advocacy & Publications
Dave Blackhurst, Dir., Membership & Sales
Kerrie Moore, Finance Manager
Whitney Nelson, Dir., Meetings & Events
The IAPD Membership Directory lists almost 400 companies by membership category with their locations, phone and fax numbers, key personnel and plastics products. There is also a listing of companies by geographical location, as well as an alphabetical listing of individuals from the various companies.
Cost: $150.00
Frequency: Annual/May

21032 **Plastics Business News**
Plastics Universe
2727 Holland Sylvania Road
Suite A
Toledo, OH 43615
419-535-7899; Fax: 419-535-1243
mberins@javanet.com
www.plasticx.com/pub/plast_11.html
Michael L. Berins, Publisher
Offers information on the plastics industry, forecasts, mergers, and new product developments.
Cost: $327.00
Frequency: Weekly
Founded in 1972

21033 **Plastics Compounding Redbook**
Advanstar Communications
2501 Colorado Avenue
Suite 280
Santa Monica, CA 90404
310-857-7500; Fax: 310-857-7510
www.advanstar.com
Joseph Loggia, CEO
Chris DeMoulin, VP
Susannah George, Marketing Director
List of suppliers — over 1,000 — of resin, additives, fillers and other materials compounding equipment and services to the plastic industry.
Cost: $150.00
280 Pages
Frequency: Annual
Circulation: 12,000

21034 **Plastics Digest/PA Index**
IHS/Information Handling Services
15 Inverness Way E
Englewood, CO 80112-5710
303-736-3000
800-525-7052; Fax: 303-736-3150
www.ihsenergy.com
Facebook, Twitter, LinkedIn
Jerre Stead, CEO
Michael Armstrong, Director
A list of over 200 manufacturers and suppliers of plastics materials are listed in this comprehensive directory. CD format only.
Cost: $768.00

21035 **Plastics News Datebook Online**
Crain Communications
1725 Merriman Rd
Suite 300
Akron, OH 44313-5283
330-836-9180; Fax: 330-836-2831
info@crain.com
www.crain.com
Robert S Simmons, VP
Linda Whelan, Marketing Manager
This business to business buyers guide highlights products and services such as extruders, sheet manufacturers, film, rod and sheet suppliers, processors, roto-molding equipment, injection molding, polyurethane machinery, resin producers and compounders. The Plastics News Online Directory helps you, as a BtoB buyer, research products and make smart buying decisions.

21036 **Plastics News Web Watch Directory**
Crain Communications
1725 Merriman Rd
Suite 300
Akron, OH 44313-9006
330-836-9180
800-678-9595; Fax: 330-836-2831
editorial@plasticsnews.com
www.crain.com
Robert S Simmons, VP
Anthony Eagan, Publisher
Contains processors, primary equipment, auxiliary equipment, resin suppliers, compounders, recyclers, tooling and molds, design and prototyping, trade associations, industry services and more.
154 Pages
ISSN: 1042-802X
Printed in 4 colors on glossy stock

21037 **Rauch Guide to the US Adhesives & Sealants Industry**
Grey House Publishing
4919 Route 22
PO Box 56
Amenia, NY 12501
518-789-8700
800-562-2139; Fax: 845-373-6390
books@greyhouse.com
www.greyhouse.com
Facebook, Twitter
Leslie Mackenzie, Publisher
Richard Gottlieb, Editor
Contains information providing data on industry economics, government regulations, technology, raw materials, products and markets in addition to industry activities, organizations and sources of information on trade shows, exhibits, professional associations and societies. Provides unique profiles of more than 700 suppliers.
Cost: $595.00
361 Pages
ISBN: 1-592371-29-9
Founded in 1981

21038 **Rauch Guide to the US Plastics Industry**
Grey House Publishing
4919 Route 22
PO Box 56
Amenia, NY 12501-0056
518-789-8700
800-562-2139; Fax: 518-789-0556
books@greyhouse.com
www.greyhouse.com
Facebook, Twitter
Leslie Mackenzie, Publisher
Richard Gottlieb, Editor
Offers comprehensive data on the $182 billion industry, the Guide is a highly valued industry resource covering the economics, processes, materials, sales and activities of leading U.S. plastics producers. Additional features include a personnel index with key industry executives and an enhanced company listing containing detailed information indicating subsidiary, division or parent information, Internet site addresses, E-mail addresses, and key contacts.
Cost: $595.00
646 Pages
ISBN: 1-592371-28-0
Founded in 1981

21039 **Who's Who in World Petrochemicals and Plastics**
Reed Business Information
3355 West Alabama
Suite 700
Houston, TX 77098
713-523-2613
888-525-3255; Fax: 713-525-2659
csc@icis.com
www.icis.com/
Jamie Reed, Owner
Andy Soloman, Global Editorial Director
Chrissy Salisbury, Manager
More than 9,600 individuals from 3,700 petrochemical and plastic companies worldwide.
Cost: $276.00
Frequency: Annual November
Circulation: 1,500

21040 **Worldwide Petrochemical Directory**
PennWell Directories
1455 West Loop South
Suite 400
Houston, TX 77027-3005
713-621-9720
800-736-6935; Fax: 713-963-6285
billw@pennwell.com
www.pennwell.com
Bob Tippee, Editor
David Nakamura, Refining/Petrochemical Editor
Guntis Moritis, Production Editor
Tim Sullivant, Manager
2,980 operative petrochemical plants with 8,675 personnel in 4,320 locations are listed with their parent companies, plant locations, products pro-

duced, capacities, and current production volumes if available. Approximately 9,340 locations having 13,145 Email and 4,330 Website addresses are listed for engineering, construction, manufacturing, supply and service companies with a description of products and services provided. Included are 350 cross-references reflecting mergers and acquisitions.
Cost: $150.00
Frequency: Annual November
Circulation: 3,500
Mailing list available for rent

Industry Web Sites

21041 **http://gold.greyhouse.com**
G.O.L.D Grey House OnLine Databases
Grey House Publishing's online database platform, GOLD, offers Quick Search, Keyword Search and Expert Search for most business sectors including plastics markets. The GOLD platform makes finding the information you need quick and easy - whether you're a novice searcher or an experienced database user. All of Grey House's directory products are available for subscription on the GOLD platform.

21042 **www.aimcal.org**
Association of Industrial Metallizers, Coaters
and Laminators

Packaging equipment.

21043 **www.americanmanufacturers.com**
AmericanManufacturers.com
Product exchanges and electronic requests for quotes.

21044 **www.apexq.com**
American Plastics Exchange
Molders and extruders can review data sheets and bid for prime virgin resin.

21045 **www.ariba.com**
Ariba
Allows buyers and sellers to find trading partners and negotiate prices.

21046 **www.assettrade.com**
AssetTrade.com
Used equipment and machinery.

21047 **www.chematch.com**
CheMatch.com
Buyers and sellers exchange for plastic materials.

21048 **www.dovebid.com**
DoveBid
Bidding on used equipment, as well as capital assets.

21049 **www.e-resin.com**
e-Resin.com
Direct negotiation with suppliers for additives, materials and finished products.

21050 **www.efodia.com**
eFodia
Online purchasing of chemical processing, compounding and additives, other materials.

21051 **www.elastomersolutions.com**
ElastomerSolutions
Online trading for the elastomers industry.

21052 **www.ewinwin.com**
eWinWin
Associations, cooperatives, buyers and suppliers can employ an aggregation system for lower priced purchases.

21053 **www.freemarkets.com**
FreeMarkets
Reverse auction in which suppliers submit online bids for commodities, services, parts and materials.

21054 **www.getplastic.com**
GetPlastic.com
Materials designed for those who purchase resins.

21055 **www.greyhouse.com**
Grey House Publishing
Authoritative reference directories for most business sectors including plastics markets. Users can search the online databases with varied search criteria allowing for custom searches by product category, geographic area, sales volume, keyword, subject and more. Full Grey House catalog and online ordering also available.

21056 **www.i2i.com**
Industry to Industry
Buying and selling of plastics.

21057 **www.mfgconnect.com**
Mfgconnect.com
Exchange product development information and CAD files prior to bidding on contracts.

21058 **www.napcor.com**
National Association for Pet Container Resources
National trade association which promotes the recycling of pet con-tainers and the usage of pet plastic.

21059 **www.omnexus.com**
Omnexus Corporation
Trading in equipment, services, materials and tooling for central injection and blow molders.

21060 **www.onechem.com**
OneChem
Software applications and transactional storefront for global commercial transactions in plastics and chemicals.

21061 **www.packagingexchange.com**
PackagingExchange.Com
Storefront transactions and online auction for packaging products, equipment and materials.

21062 **www.packexpo.com**
Packexpo.com
Source for packaging materials, machinery, parts and services.

21063 **www.packtion.com**
Packtion Corporation
Informational tools and exchange opportunites for packaging services.

21064 **www.plasticlink.com**
PlasticLink.Com
Materials, equipment and products for thermoformers, extruders and semifinished shape processors.

21065 **www.plasticpipe.org**
Plastics Pipe Institute
The major trade association representing all segments of the plastics piping industry. As an association, PPI focuses collaborative efforts to accumulate data, concentrate facts and target resources toward advancements in applications and increases in widespread usage.

21066 **www.plastics.org**
American Plastics Council
Gateway to plastics on the internet.

21067 **www.plasticsindustry.org**
Society of the Plastics Industry
The Society of the Plastics Industry is the trade assocition representing one of the largest manufacturing industries in the US. SPI's 1,500 members represent the entire plastics industry supply chain, including processors, machinery and equipment manufacturers and raw material suppliers. The US plastics industry employs 1.5 million workers and provides $304 billon in annual shipment.

21068 **www.plasticsrecycling.org**
AssociationOd Postconsumer Plastic Recyclers
Represents companies that acquire, reprocess and sell the output of more than 90 percent of the post-consumer plastic processing capacity in North America.

21069 **www.plasticulture.com**
American Society for Plasticulture
Promotes research, education, and technology application for plastics used in agricultural and horticultural production systems. Hosts a congress every year or so; published proceedings of research presentations.

21070 **www.polyurethane.org**
Alliance for the Polyurethanes Industry
For companies that supply polyurethane resins or chemicals used in polyurethane resins, manufacture polyurethanes, produce machinery used in the manufacture or processing polyurethane, or engage in the business of applying polyurethane products in end use applications.

21071 **www.primeadvantage.com**
Prime Advantage Corporation
Buying consortium offers volume discounts on resins and components.

21072 **www.sorcity.com**
Sorcity.com
Reverse auction in which buyer files request for quote and supplier bids.

21073 **www.theplasticsexchange.com**
ThePlasticsExchange.com
Trading in commodity prime resins.

21074 **www.worldwideplastics.com**
TheBuyersNet.com
Catalog of semifinished materials.

Associations

21075 American Society of Plumbing Engineers
6400 Shafer Ct.
Suite 350
Rosemont, IL 60018-4914

847-296-0002; Fax: 847-296-2963
info@aspe.org
www.aspe.org

Billy Smith, Executive Director/CEO, Secretary
Mitch Clemente, President
David E. DeBord, Vice President, Education
Chris Graham, Treasurer
Scott Steindler, Vice President, Technical

The American Society of Plumbing Engineers (ASPE) is a professional organization dedicated to the advancement of the science of plumbing engineering, to the professional growth and advancement of its members and the health, welfare and safety of the public. The Society disseminates technical data and information, sponsors activities that facilitate interaction with fellow professionals, and, through research and education, expands the base of knowledge of the plumbing engineering industry.
6000+ Members
Founded in 1964

21076 American Society of Sanitary Engineering
18927 Hickory Creek Dr.
Suite 220
Mokena, IL 60448

708-995-3019; Fax: 708-479-6139
www.asse-plumbing.org

John F. Flader, Treasurer
Douglas A. Marian, International President
Scott Hamilton, Executive Director
Michele Kilpatrick, Administrative asst.
Dana Colombo, Vice President

Members are from all segments of the plumbing industry, including contractors, engineers, inspectors, journeymen, apprentices and others who are involved in various segments of the industry. Provides information, an opportunity to exchange ideas, solve problems and offers a forum where all sides can express their views.
300 Members
Founded in 1906

21077 American Supply Association
1200 Arlington Heights Road
Itasca, IL 60143

630-467-0000; Fax: 630-467-0001
info@asa.net
www.asa.net
Facebook, Twitter, LinkedIn

Mike Adelizzi, CEO
Aaron Scheiwe, CFO

ASA is a not-for-profit national organization serving wholesale distributors and their suppliers in the plumbing, heating, cooling and industrial and mechanical pipe, valves and fittings industries.
Founded in 1969

21078 International Association of Plumbing and Mechanical Officials (IAPMO)
4755 E Philadelphia Street
Ontario, CA 91761

909-472-4100
800-854-2676; Fax: 909-472-4150
info@iapmo.org
www.iapmo.org
Facebook, Twitter, LinkedIn

David Straub, President
David Gans, Vice Pesident
Russ Chaney, CEO
Marty Cooper, Secretary
Neil Bogatz, General Counsel

IAPMO has been protecting the public's health and safety for more than eighty years by working in concert with government and industry to implement comprehensive plumbing and mechanical systems around the world.
5000 Members
Founded in 1926

21079 Manufacturers Standardization Society
127 Park St NE
Vienna, VA 22180-4602

703-281-6613; Fax: 703-281-6671
info@msshq.org
www.mss-hq.org

Robert O'Neill, Executive Director

The Manufacturers Standardization Society (MSS) of the Valve and Fittings Industry is a non-profit technical association organized for development and improvement of industry, national and international codes and standards for valves, valve actuators, valve modifications, pipe fittings, pipe hangers, flanges, and associated seals.
Cost: $1800.00
Founded in 1924

21080 Midwest Distributors Association (MWDA)
1200 N. Arlington Heights Rd.
Suite 150
Itasca, IL 60143

630-467-0000; Fax: 312-464-0091
www.mwda.net

Dave Poteete, President
Ryan Curry, Secretary/ Treasurer
Todd Restel, President-Elect
Chris Murin, Executive Director
John Bennerotte, Director

The mission of the MWDA is to professionally promote the improvement of the industry by providing quality programs, educational and training opportunities to improve operational efficiency and marketing effectiveness, and by facilitating the exchange of ideas and information throughout the distribution channel. The MWDA serves the states of Illinois, Iowa, Kansas, Minnesota, Missouri, Nebraska, North Dakota, South Dakota, Upper Michigan and Wisconsin.
110 Members
Founded in 1942

21081 National Kitchen and Bath Association
687 Willow Grove Street
Hackettstown, NJ 07840-1731

800-843-6522
feedback@nkba.org
www.nkba.org
Facebook, Twitter, LinkedIn, Pinterest

Bill Darcy, CEO
Suzie Wiliford, EVP, Industry Relations & CSO
Pam Ryerson, Director, Marketplace
Nicole Young, Director, Finance & Administration

Protects the interests of members by fostering a better business climate. Offers Awards certification and conducts training schools and seminars.
14000 Members
Founded in 1963

21082 North Central Wholesalers Association/NCWA
7107 Crossroads Blvd
Suite 106
Brentwood, TN 37027

615-371-5004; Fax: 615-371-5444
terry@northcentralwholesalers.org
www.northcentralwholesalers.org

Howard Wolff, President
Jock Castoldi, Treasurer
Russ Visner, Director

The NCWA serves wholesale distributors of plumbing, heating, cooling and piping products in Indiana, Michigan, Ohio, Western Pennsylvania and West Virginia, sponsoring educational conferences and offering networking opportunities. During the year NCWA offers its members seminars, workshops, newsletters, industry statistics, an annual regional convention and other traditional trade association programs.
75 Members
Founded in 2003

21083 Pacific Southwest Distributors Association
7345 E Evans Rd
No. 7
Scottsdale, AZ 85260

480-991-5703; Fax: 480-991-5704
rbluth@qwestoffice.net
www.thepsda.info

Bob Bluth, Owner
Michael Adelizzi, Executive Vice President

Made up of distributors of heating, cooling and plumbing supplies.
Founded in 1946

21084 Plastic Pipe and Fittings Association
800 Roosevelt Rd
Building C, Suite 312
Glen Ellyn, IL 60137

630-858-6540; Fax: 630-790-3095
www.ppfahome.org
Facebook, RSS

Richard W Church, Executive Director

The Plastic Pipe and Fittings Association (PPFA) is a national trade association of member companies that manufacture plastic piping, fittings and solvent cements for plumbing and related applications, and supply raw materials, ingredients or machinery for the manufacturing process. The PPFA provides relevant information needed to properly design, specify and install plastic piping systems, promoting an understanding of the environmental impact and benefits of thermoplastic piping products.
78 Members
Founded in 1978

21085 Plumbing Heating Cooling Contractors Association
180 South Washington Street
Suite 100
Falls Church, VA 22046

703-237-8100
800-533-7694; Fax: 703-237-7442
naphcc@naphcc.org
www.phccweb.org
Facebook, Twitter, LinkedIn, RSS

Kevin Tindall, President-Elect
Elicia Magruder, Vice President of Communications
Michael Copp, Executive Vice President
Steven A. Rivers, President
Laurie Crigler, Secretary

National organization designed for suppliers of equipment, supplies and services for the plumbing, heating and cooling industries.
3700 Members
Founded in 1883

21086 Plumbing Manufacturers International
1921 Rohlwing Rd
Unit G
Rolling Meadows, IL 60008

847-481-5500; Fax: 847-481-5501
www.pmihome.org
Facebook, Twitter, LinkedIn, YouTube, Google+

Fernando Fernandez, President
Paul Patton, Vice- President
Barbara C. Higgens, CEO/Executive Director
Peter Jahrling, Treasurer
Tim Kilbane, Immediate Past President

The Plumbing Manufacturers Institute (PMI) is the trade association of plumbing products manufacturers. The Institute functions as a sounding board for its members, a source for industry and market information, and as a coordinating and decision-making body for dealing with industry issues. It is active in many arenas as it helps develop and maintain standards and codes, and works closely with government agencies at all levels - federal, state and local.
44 Members
Founded in 1975

21087 Plumbing and Drainage Institute
800 Turnpike Street
Suite 300
North Andover, MA 01845

978-557-0720
800-589-8956; Fax: 978-557-0721
pdi@PDIonline.org
www.pdionline.org

William Whitehead, Executive Director

An association of manufacturers of engineered plumbing products. Our members and licensees make products such as; flood drains, roof drains, sanitary floor drains, cleanouts, water hammer arresters, swimming pool drains, backwater valves, grease interceptors, fixture supports and other drainage specialties.
14 Members

21088 Plumbing and Mechanical Contractors Association of Oregon
14695 SW Millikan Way
Beaverton, OR 97006

503-626-6666; Fax: 503-626-6630
www.pmcaoregon.com

Frank Wall, Executive Director
250 Members
Founded in 1980

21089 Southern Wholesalers Association
201 Seaboard Lane
7107 Crossroads Blvd
Suite 106
Brentwood, TN 37027

615-371-5004; Fax: 615-371-5444
terry@southernwholesalers.org
www.southernwholesalers.org
Facebook

Travis Elrod, President
Brendan Donahue, First VP/ Treasurer
John Simmons, Second VP
Harry Hays, Chairman Ex-Officio
Coley Herin, Chairman of the Board

The Southern Wholesalers Association is a regional association composed of leading Wholesalers of plumbing, heating, and cooling equipment and supplies; pipe, valves and fittings; and water systems throughout the southeast, as well as, Associate Member suppliers and reps to the phcp, pvf and water systems industry.
850 Members
Founded in 1928

21090 United Association
Three Park Place
Annapolis, MD 21401

410-269-2000; Fax: 410-267-0382
www.ua.org
Facebook, Twitter, YouTube

William P. Hite, General President
Mark McManus, General Secretary-Treasurer

Union of plumbers, fitters, welders and service techs.
370K Members
Founded in 1889

21091 Valve Manufacturers Association of America (VMA)
1050 17th Street NW
Suite 280
Washington, DC 20036-5521

202-331-8105; Fax: 202-296-0378
spartyke@vma.org
www.vma.org

William S. Sandler, President
Marc Pasternak, Vice President
Malena Malone-Blevins, Meetings Manager
Judy Tibbs, Education Director
Abby Brown, Education & Training Coordinator

Trade association representing manufacturers of valves, actuators and controls. The association offers supports in the form of meetings, publications, education and networking.
100 Members
Founded in 1938

21092 Western Suppliers Association
3423 Investment Blvd
Suite 204
Hayward, CA 94545

510-670-0962
800-752-8833; Fax: 510-670-9081
info@wsagroup.org
www.westernsuppliersassociation.com

Richard Amaro, President
Frank Nisonger, Vice President
Ted Green, Treasurer
Glenn Kunishige, Director
Frank Mullin, Advisory Director

A regional office that represents various wholesalers in the heating, plumbing and piping fields.
Founded in 1952

Newsletters

21093 Plumbing Systems & Design
2980 River Rd
Des Plaines, IL 60018

847-296-0002; Fax: 773-695-9007
info@aspe.org
www.psdmagazine.com

Gretchen Pienta, Managing Editor
David Jern, Executive Publisher
Rachel Boger, Graphic Designer
Richard Albrecht, Website

Industry leading technical publication with ASPE news and features. Free to ASPE members and subscribers.
Frequency: Monthly
Circulation: 27000
Founded in 1965
Printed in on glossy stock

Magazines & Journals

21094 OFFICIAL Magazine
Int'l Assn of Plumbing & Mechanical Officials
4755 E Philadelphia Street
Ontario, CA 91761

909-472-4100
800-854-2676; Fax: 909-472-4150
info@iapmo.org
www.iapmo.org

David Straub, President
David Gans, Vice President
Russ Chaney, CEO
Marty Cooper, Secretary
Neil Bogatz, General Counsel

The nation's leading source for information about plumbing and mechanical safety codes. This publication is geared toward plumbers, mechanical contractors, manufacturers and government safety officials who need to know safety code information
Cost: $75.00
9000 Members
Frequency: Bi-Monthly
Circulation: 26000
Founded in 1958

21095 PM Engineer
Business News Publishing Company
155 N Pfingsten Rd
#205
Deerfield, IL 60015

630-377-5909; Fax: 248-502-1023
privacy@BNPMedia.com
www.pmengineer.com

Bob Miondonski, Group Publisher & Editor
Mike Miazga, Ednior Editor
Julius Ballanco, Editorial Director
Suzette Rubio, Online Editor
John Siegenthaler, Hydronics Editor

Provides technical sheets, manufacturer product brochures, news features and analysis of useful industry information on the engineering and design of plumbing, piping, hydronics, cooling/heating, and fire protection/sprinkler systems. Free to trade engineers.
80 Pages
Circulation: 25000
Printed in 4 colors on glossy stock

21096 PM Plumbing & Mechanical
Business News Publishing Company
155 N Pfingsten Rd
#205
Deerfield, IL 60015

630-377-5909; Fax: 248-502-1023
privacy@BNPMedia.com
www.pmmag.com/

Bob Miondonski, Group Publisher & Editor
Mike Miazga, Ednior Editor
Julius Ballanco, Editorial Director
Suzette Rubio, Online Editor
John Siegenthaler, Hydronics Editor

Serves plumbing, hydronic heating and mechanical contractors.
Frequency: Monthly
Circulation: 45091

21097 Plumbing Engineer
TMB Publishing
2165 Shermer Rd
Suite A
Northbrook, IL 60062-5474

847-564-1127; Fax: 847-564-1264
editor@plumbingengineer.com
www.plumbingengineer.com

John Mesenbrink, Chief Editor
Marilyn Cunningham, Assistant Editor
Cate Brown, Production Manager
Sadie Bechtold, Production Assistant
Mark Bruno, Art Director

Offers news and updates to plumbing engineers and manufacturers.
Cost: $35.00
Frequency: Monthly
Founded in 1973

21098 Plumbing Standards
American Society of Sanitary Engineering
901 Canterbury Rd
Suite A
Cleveland, OH 44145-1480
440-835-3040; Fax: 440-835-3488
www.asse-plumbing.org
James Bickford, President
Donald R Jr. Summers, First VP
Steve Silber, Second VP
Scott Hamilton, Third VP
Ron Murray, Immiate Past President
Topics include standards information, updates, water, wastewater, plumbing design guidelines, and technical information pertaining to the water industry.
Cost: $12.00
Frequency: Quarterly
Circulation: 15000
Founded in 1906

21099 Reeves Journal
23421 South Pointe Drive
Suite 280
Laguna Hills, CA 92653
949-830-0881; Fax: 949-859-7845
hendersont@bnpmedia.com
www.reevesjournal.com
Ellyn Fishman, Publisher
Kati Larson, Advertising Sales
Jack Sweet, Editor
Souzan Azar, Production
Reeves Journal, one of the oldest publications in the plumbing industry, addresses the regional opportunities and challenges facing plumbing/heating/cooling-phc contractors, wholesalers and engineers in the 14 western United States, focusing on the products, issues, codes and regulations relevant to the phc industry.
Frequency: Monthly
Founded in 1926

21100 Supply House Times
American Supply Association
2401 W Big Beaver Rd.
Suite 700
Troy, MI 48084-3333
248-362-3700; Fax: 248-362-0317
info@asa.net
www.supplyht.com
Dan Ashenden, Group Publisher
Mike Miazga, Group Editorial Director
Nadia Askar, Group Multimedia Editor
Articles on plumbing, heating, cooling, and piping products.
50 Pages
Frequency: 6x Yearly
Circulation: 2,500
Mailing list available for rent: 4,000 names
Printed in 4 colors on matte stock

21101 United Association Journal
United Association
Three Park Place
Annapolis, MD 21401
410-269-2000; Fax: 410-267-0382
www.ua.org
William P. Hite, President
Mark McManus, General Secretary/Treasurer
Official publication of the United Association of Journeymen and Apprentices of the Plumbing and Pipe Fitting Industry.
Frequency: Monthly
Circulation: 315000
ISSN: 0095-7763
Founded in 1889

21102 Valve Magazine
Valve Manufacturers Association of America
1050 17th Street NW
Suite 280
Washington, DC 20036-5521
202-331-8105; Fax: 202-296-0378
gparente@vma.org
www.valvemagazine.com
William S. Sandler, President & Publisher
Judy Tibbs, Editor-in-Chief
Genilee Parente, Managing Editor
Chris Guy, Assistant Editor
Sue Partyke, Advertising Director
Magazine promoting US and Canadian manufactured industrial valves and actuators.
100 Members
Frequency: Quarterly
Circulation: 26000
Founded in 1938

21103 Working Pressure
Int'l Assn of Plumbing & Mechanical Officials
4755 E Philadelphia Street
Ontario, CA 91761
909-472-4100
800-854-2676; Fax: 909-472-4150
info@workingpressuremag.com
www.workingpressuremag.com
Facebook, Twitter, LinkedIn, YouTube
David Straub, President
David Gans, Vice President
Russ Chaney, CEO
Marty Cooper, Secretary
Neil Bogatz, General Counsel
To cover the full demographic range of ASSE, which includes backflow prevention, plumbing'mechanical, water quality, HVAC, fire protection, medical gas, and water utility.
5000 Members
Founded in 1926

Trade Shows

21104 ASA NETWORK
American Supply Association
1200 Arlington Heights Road
Itasca, IL 60143
630-467-0000; Fax: 630-467-0001
info@asa.net
www.asa.net
Mike Adelizzi, CEO
Aaron Scheiwe, CFO
For distributors and manufacturers in the PHCP/PVF industry. Provides information and opportunities that cannot be found with other organizations or events.
Frequency: Annual

21105 ASA's Women In Industry Spring Conference
American Supply Association
1200 Arlington Heights Road
Itasca, IL 60143
630-467-0000; Fax: 630-467-0001
info@asa.net
www.asa.net
Mike Adelizzi, CEO
Aaron Scheiwe, CFO
Offers the opportunity to network with female professionals in the PHCP and industrial PVF supply chain.

21106 ASPE Engineered Plumbing Exposition
National Trade Show Productions
313 South Patrick Street
Alexandria, VA 22314-1117
703-683-8500
800-687-7469; Fax: 703-836-4486
www.ntpshow.com/ or www.aspe.org
Robert E Harar, Chairman and CEO
Karin Frendrich, Chief Operating Officer
Jennifer Hoff, Executive Director
A biennial exhibits trade show for the plumbing and engineering industry, the Engineered Plumbing Exposition, sponsored by the American Society of Plumbing Engineers/ASPE, is a gathering of plumbing, engineering and design products, equipment and services. Everything from pipes to pumps to fixtures, from compressors to computers and consulting services, is on display to allow engineers and specifiers to view the newest and most innovative design materials available to them.
7000 Attendees
Founded in 1964

21107 ASSE International Annual Business Meeting
Int'l Assn of Plumbing & Mechanical Officials
4755 E Philadelphia Street
Ontario, CA 91761
909-472-4100
800-854-2676; Fax: 909-472-4150
info@iapmo.org
www.iapmo.org
Facebook, Twitter, LinkedIn, YouTube
David Straub, President
David Gans, Vice President
Russ Chaney, CEO
Marty Cooper, Secretary
Neil Bogartz, General Counsel
5000 Members
450 Attendees
Founded in 1926

21108 Business and Education Conference
Int'l Assoc of Plumbing and Mechanical Officials
4755 E Philadelphia Street
Ontario, CA 91761
909-472-4100
800-854-2676; Fax: 909-472-4150
info@iapmo.org
www.iapmo.org
David Straub, President
David Gans, Vice President
Russ Chaney, CEO
Marty Cooper, Secretary
Neil Bogatz, General Counsel
IAPMO's annual conference brings together the public health and safety officials dedicated to plumbing and mechanical systems.
5000 Members
600 Attendees
Frequency: Annual/September
Founded in 1926

21109 MSS Annual Meeting
Manufacturers Standardization Society
127 Park St NE
Vienna, VA 22180-4602
703-281-6613; Fax: 703-281-6671
orders@mss-hq.org
www.mss-hq.org
Robert O'Neill, Executive Director
Frequency: Annual/May
Founded in 1924

21110 Mid-Atlantic Plumbing Heating Cooling Expo
Reber-Friel Company

221 King Manor Drive
Suite A
King Of Prussia, PA 19406-2500

610-272-4020; Fax: 610-272-5190

Richard Retzback, Show Manager

350 booths featuring products and services used by the plumbing, heating and cooling industries.
4.3M Attendees
Frequency: Annual/November

21111 **Spring Septic System Conference**
Granite State Designers & Installers Association
53 Regional Drive
Concord, NH 03301-3520

603-228-1231; Fax: 603-228-2118
info@gsdia.org
www.gsdia.org

Carl Hagstrom, Director
Randy Orvis, Director

Conference and trade show with 30 exhibitors and booths for septic system professionals and other allied industries.
400 Attendees
Frequency: Annual/March

21112 **Valve Industry Leadership Forum**
Valve Manufacturers Association of America
1050 17th Street NW
Suite 280
Washington, DC 20036-5521

202-331-8105; Fax: 202-296-0378
mmaloneblevins@vma.org
www.vma.org

William S. Sandler, President
Marc Pasternak, Vice President
Malena Malone-Blevins, Meetings Manager
Judy Tibbs, Education Director

Forum for the leaders of companies serving the valve industry.
100 Members
Founded in 1938

Directories & Databases

21113 **Complete Directory of Plumbing Products**
Sutton Family Communications & Publishing Company
National Fleamarketeer
155 Sutton Lane
Fordsville, KY 42343

270-740-0870
www.suttoncompliance.com

Theresa Sutton, Editor
Lee Sutton, General Manager

Print-out from database of wholesalers, manufacturers, distributors, importers and close-out houses. Database is updated daily to guarantee the most current and up-to-date sources available.
Cost: $55.20
100+ Pages

21114 **Directory of Custom Compounders**
Delphi Marketing Services
400 E 89th Street
Apartment 2J
New York, NY 10128-6728
Dr. Newman Giragosian, Editor

Offers information on manufacturers of custom mixtures of plastics and resins.
Cost: $295.00
115 Pages
Frequency: Annual

21115 **Directory of Listed Plumbing Products**
Int'l Assn of Plumbing & Mechanical Officials
4755 E Philadelphia Street
Ontario, CA 91761

909-472-4100
800-854-2676; Fax: 909-472-4150
info@iapmo.org
www.iapmo.org

David Straub, President
David Gans, Vice President
Russ Chaney, CEO
Marty Cooper, Secretary
Neil Bogatz, General Counsel

Directory of products and supplies to the plumbing industry.
Frequency: Monthly

21116 **Plumbing Engineer: Product Directory Issue**
TMB Publishing
2165 Shermer Rd
Suite A
Northbrook, IL 60062-5474

847-564-1127; Fax: 847-564-1264
www.tmbpublishing.com

John Mesenbrink, Chief Editor
Marilyn Cunningham, Assistant Editor
Cate Brown, Production Manager
Sadie Bechtold, Production Assistant
Mark Bruno, Art Director

Over 400 plumbing products from approximately 250 manufacturers.
Frequency: Annual/January
Circulation: 2,6104

21117 **VMA's Product Finder for Valves, Actuators & Controls**
Valve Manufacturers Association of America
1050 17th Street NW
Suite 280
Washington, DC 20036-5521

202-331-8105; Fax: 202-296-0378
spartyke@vma.org
www.vma.org

William S. Sandler, President
Marc Pasternak, Vice President
Sue Partyke, Advertising Director
Chris Guy, Assistant Editor, News & Products

Lists U.S. and Canadian valves, actuators and controls produced by the member companies of the Valve Manufacturers Association of America.
100 Members
Founded in 1938

21118 **Who's Who in the Plumbing-Heating-Cooling Contracting Business**
Nat'l Assn of Plumbing-Heating-Cooling Contractors
180 South Washington Street
PO Box 6808
Falls Church, VA 22046-2900

703-237-8100
800-533-7694; Fax: 703-237-7442
naphcc@naphcc.org
www.phccweb.org

Frank Maddalon, President
Keith Bienvenu, President-Elect
David Dugger, VP
Kevin Tindall, Secretary
Gerry Kennedy, Executive VP

About 6,000 professional plumbing/heating/cooling contractors and member firms.
Cost: $75.00
Frequency: Annual
Circulation: 15,000
Founded in 1883

Industry Web Sites

21119 **http://gold.greyhouse.com**
G.O.L.D Grey House OnLine Databases

Grey House Publishing's online database platform, GOLD, offers Quick Search, Keyword Search and Expert Search for most business sectors including plumbing and heating markets. The GOLD platform makes finding the information you need quick and easy - whether you're a novice searcher or an experienced database user. All of Grey House's directory products are available for subscription on the GOLD platform.

21120 **www.asa.net**
American Supply Association

ASA is a not-for-profit national organization serving wholesale distributors and their suppliers in the plumbing, heating, cooling and industrial and mechanical pipe, valves and fittings industries.

21121 **www.aspe.org**
American Society of Plumbing Engineers

Seeks to resolve professional problems in plumbing engineering. Operates a certification program.

21122 **www.asse-plumbing.org**
American Society of Sanitary Engineering

Members are from all segments of the plumbing industry, including contractors, engineers, inspectors, journeymen, apprentices and others involved in the industry. Provides information, the opportunity to exchange ideas, solve problems and offers forum where all sides can express their views.

21123 **www.construction.com**
McGraw-Hill Construction

McGraw-Hill Construction (MHC), part of The McGraw-Hill Companies, connects people and projects across the design and construction industry, serving owners, architects, engineers, general contractors, subcontractors, building product manufacturers, suppliers, dealers, distributors and adjacent markets.

21124 **www.greyhouse.com**
Grey House Publishing

Authoritative reference directories for most business sectors including plumbing and heating markets. Users can search the online databases with varied search criteria allowing for custom searches by product category, geographic area, sales volume, keyword, subject and more. Full Grey House catalog and online ordering also available.

21125 **www.iapmo.org**
Int'l Assoc of Plumbing and Mechanical Officers

IAPMO has been protecting the public's health and safety for more than eighty years by working in concert with government and industry to implement comprehensive plumbing and mechanical systems around the world.

21126 **www.pdionline.org**
Plumbing and Drainage Institute

For manufacturers of engineered plumbing products, flood drains, roof drains, sanitary floor drains, cleanouts, water hammer arresters, swimming pool drains, backwater valves, grease interceptors, fixture supports, and other drainage specialties.

21127 **www.sweets.construction.com**
McGraw Hill Construction

In depth product information that lets you find, compare, select, specify and make purchase decisions in the industrial product marketplace.

21128 **www.uboiler.com**
Uniform Boiler and Pressure Vessel Laws Society

Established to promote uniformity in rules, laws and regulations for boiler and pressure vessel safety based on the requirements of the American Society of Mechanical Engineers Boiler and Pressure Vessel Code and other related national standards.

21129 **www.vma.org**
Valve Manufacturers Association of America

Trade association representing manufacturers of valves, actuators and controls.

Associations

21130 **Amalgamated Printers Association**
3019 Elm Lane
Middleton, WI 53562

406-928-4757
TWOEMPRESS@aol.com
apa-letterpress.com
Facebook, Twitter, LinkedIn, Google+, Pinterest

Sky Shipley, President
Joe Warren, VP
Cindy Iverson, Secretary/Treasurer
Howard Gelbert, Director
David Kent, Archivist

The Amalgamated Printers' Association was organized in 1958 as a hobby printers group so that members could improve their skills, expand their knowledge, and exchange samples of their letterpress work in addition to encouraging excellence of printing content, design, and techniques.
150 Members
Founded in 1958

21131 **American Printing History Association**
PO Box 4519
Grand Central Station
New York, NY 10163

secretary@printinghistory.org
printinghistory.org

Robert McCamant, President

Membership organization promoting the study of the history of printing and related arts such as calligraphy and typography.

21132 **Association for Print Technologies**
1899 Preston White Drive
Reston, VA 20191

703-264-7200; Fax: 703-620-0994
chawkins@aptech.org
www.npes.org
Facebook, Twitter, LinkedIn

Thayer Long, President

The Association for Suppliers of Printing , Publishing and Converting Technologies is a trade association that represents manufacturers, importers and distributors of equipment, supplies, systems and software used in every printing, publishing and converting process from design to distribution. Virtually all industry products and processes are represented by the member companies, which range in size from under $1 million in annual sales revenue to more than $1 billion.
600 Members
Founded in 1933

21133 **Book Manufacturers' Institute (BMI)**
PO Box 731388
Ormond Beach, FL 32173

386-986-4552; Fax: 386-986-4553
info@bmibook.com
bomi.memberclicks.net

Matt Baehr, Executive Director

Since 1933, the Book Manufacturers' Institute, Inc. (BMI) has been the leading nationally recognized trade association of the book manufacturing industry. BMI member companies annually produce the great majority of books ordered by the U. S. book publishing industry. Today, BMI is a vital part of the industry, playing a leading role by providing an intra-industry communications link among book manufacturers, publishers, suppliers and governmental bodies.
90 Members
Founded in 1933

21134 **Center for Book Arts**
28 West 27th St
3rd Floor
New York, NY 10001

212-481-0295; Fax: 212-481-9853
info@centerforbookarts.org
centerforbookarts.org
Facebook, Twitter, YouTube, Flickr, Instagram

Andrew W Mellon, Chair
Brian Hannon, Vice Chair
Robert J. Ruben, MD & Co Chair
Nancy Macomber, Treasurer
David W. Lowden, Secretary

The Center for Book Arts is dedicated to preserving the traditional crafts of book-making, as well as exploring and encouraging contemporary interpretations of the book as an art object. Each year the Center offers three terms of courses, workshops and seminars taught by experienced book artists, and providing hands-on training in all aspects of traditional and contemporary bookmaking, including bookbinding, letterpress printing, papermaking, and other associated arts.
Founded in 1974

21135 **Flexographic Technical Association**
3920 Veterans Memorial Hwy.
Suite 9
Bohemia, NY 11716-1074

631-737-6020; Fax: 631-737-6813
memberinfo@flexography.org
www.flexography.org
Twitter, LinkedIn

Allen J. Marquardt, Chair
Jack Fulton, Vice Chair
Howard B. Vreeland, Chair-elect
Mark Cisternino, President
Dan Doherty, Treasurer

Technical society devoted exclusively to the flexographic printing industry.
1500 Members
Founded in 1958

21136 **Gravure Association of the Americas**
PO Box 25617
Rochester, NY 14625

201-523-6042; Fax: 201-523-6048
gaa@gaa.org
www.gaa.org
Facebook, LinkedIn

Pamela Schenk, Director of Planning & Admin.

The Association promotes gravure printing, a high-tech process that runs on the fastest and widest presses in the world.
Founded in 2013

21137 **In-Plant Printing and Mailing Association**
103 N Jefferson St.
Kearney, MO 64060

816-919-1691; Fax: 816-945-4505
ipmainfo@ipma.org
ipma.org
Facebook, Twitter, LinkedIn, YouTube, Google+

Mike Loyd, Executive Director

The professional association for all segments of the in-house corporate printing and mailing professionals who work for educational institutions, the government, and private industry.
600 Members
Founded in 1964

21138 **International Waterless Printing Association**
5 Southside Dr.
Unit 11-328
Clifton Park, NY 12065

518-387-9321
800-850-0660; Fax: 518-310-2383
info@waterless.org
www.waterless.org

Julie Leonhard, Acting President
Brian Amos, Secretary

Dedicated to the informational and educational needs of its printer and sponsor members. Seeks to inform designers and print buyers about the many benefits the process offers.
Founded in 1993

21139 **Printing Brokerage Buyers Association**
1530 Locust Street
Mezz. 124
Philadelphia, PA 19102

215-821-6581
866-586-9391; Fax: 561-845-7130
www.pbba.org
RSS

Vincent Mallardi, Chairman

Promotes business relationships among brokers, buying groups, manufacturers and related companies. Sets standards, codes and supplies information and referrals.

21140 **Printing Industries of America**
301 Brush Creek Road
Warrendale, PA 15086-7529

412-741-6860
800-910-4283; Fax: 412-741-2311
info@printing.org
www.printing.org
Facebook, Twitter, LinkedIn, Pinterest

Michael F. Makin, President & CEO
Nicholas G. Stratigos, CFO

A graphic arts trade association representing our members in this industry. Printing Industries of America, along with its affiliates, delivers products and services that enhance the growth, efficiency and profitability of its members and the industry through advocacy, education, research and technical information
10000 Members
Founded in 1887

21141 **Printing Industries of New England**
5 Crystal Pond Road
Southborough, MA 01772-1758

508-804-4100; Fax: 508-786-2900
chagopian04@pine.org
www.pine.org
Facebook, Twitter, LinkedIn

Christine Hagopian, President

Serves more than 450 commercial printing and graphic communications companies throughout five New England states. Provides products and services on an ongoing basis to help member companies operate more profitably.
450 Members
Founded in 1887

21142 **Printing Industry Association of the South**
305 Plus Park Blvd.
Nashville, TN 37217

615-366-1094; Fax: 615-366-4192
info@pias.org
pias.org

Ed Chalifoux, President

The Printing Industry Association of the South (PIAS), a non-profit trade association, is dedicated to assisting the entire industry to continue to expand in the region and help the industry prosper across the seven-state region of Alabama, Arkansas, Kentucky, Louisiana, Mississippi, Tennessee and West Virginia.
520 Members

21143 Specialty Graphic Imaging Association
1015 Main St.
Fairfax, VA 22031
703-385-1335
888-385-3588; Fax: 703-273-0456
www.sgia.org
Facebook, Twitter, LinkedIn, Wordpress
Participants include corporations, institutions and individuals interested in screen printing and digital imaging. Conducts technical research and training workshops.
Founded in 1986

21144 The 3D Printing Association
Silicon Valley Center
2570 N First St.
San Jose, CA 95131
408-600-2647
www.the3dprintingassociation.com
Facebook, Twitter
The Association supports and represents all interests in the 3D printing industry.
Founded in 2013

21145 The Society of Typographic Aficionados
P.O. Box 457
Jefferson, GA 30549
info@typesociety.org
www.typesociety.org
Twitter
An international not-for-profit organization dedicated to the advancement and support of the typographic arts and design education.
Founded in 1998

21146 The Type Directors Club
347 West 36th St.
Suite 603
New York, NY 10018
212-633-8943; Fax: 212-633-8944
director@tdc.org
www.tdc.org
Facebook, Twitter, LinkedIn, Instagram, YouTube, Pinterest
Carol Wahler, Executive Director
An international organization that supports excellence in typography, both in print and on screen.
Founded in 1946

Newsletters

21147 Binding Edge
Printing Industry of Illinois
200 Deer Run Road
Sewickley, PA 15143
412-741-6860
800-910-4283; Fax: 412-741-2311
www.bindingindustries.org
Facebook, Twitter, LinkedIn
Michael Makin, President/CEO
Justin Goldstein, Manager
Includes articles designed to help bindery and loose leaf facilities improve their processes and keep up on the latest technologies.
Frequency: Quarterly
Circulation: 12000

21148 Business Printing Technologies Report
DMIA
433 East Monroe Avenue
Alexandria, VA 22301-1645
703-836-6232; Fax: 703-836-2241
Timothy J Mehl, President
Peter L Colaianni, Executive VP
Brad Holt, VP Media/Publications
Robert O'Connell, Treasurer
Marj Green, VP Operations
Offers a complete overview of the printing industry.
Frequency: Annual
Circulation: 5600
Founded in 1955

21149 Economic Edge
National Association for Printing Leadership
One Meadowlands Plaza
Suite 1511
East Rutherford, NJ 07073
201-634-9600
800-642-6275; Fax: 201-634-0324
webmaster@napl.org
www.napl.org
Facebook, Twitter, LinkedIn, YouTube,RSS
Joseph Truncale, President
Timothy Fischer, Executive VP/COO
Economic analysis of the graphic arts industry.
Cost: $150.00
12 Pages
Frequency: Quarterly
Founded in 1933

21150 Footprints
Footprint Communications
1339 Massachusetts Street
Lawrence, KS 66044
800-488-8316; Fax: 785-832-0087
www.footprints.com
Dick Vinocur, Publisher
A newsletter for the printing industry reporting news, management, marketing and financial data (including industry stock indexes), product introductions, personnel changes, association affairs and recent acquisitions and mergers. Footprints also reports on exhibits, shows, meetings and conferences in the graphic arts industry.
Cost: $327.00
Frequency: Fortnightly

21151 Graphic Arts Monthly Online
Reed Business Information
4709 Golf Road
Skokie, IL 60076
800-217-7874; Fax: 630-288-8781
psaran@reedbusiness.com
www.reedbusiness.com
Jeff Greisch, President
Bill Esler, Editor-in-Chief
Lisa Cross, Web Site Editor
Stephanie Kauffman, Reprint Management Services
Mark Kelsey, CEO
Graphic Arts Monthly Online is a subscriber-based Web portal for printing professionals and print buyers featuring current and archived news, research and business tools, online classifieds, used equipment marketplace and online training and education.
Cost: $159.00
Frequency: Monthly

21152 Graphic Communicator
Graphic Communications International Union
25 Louisiana Avenue N.W
Washington, DC 20001
202-624-6800; Fax: 202-721-0600
webmessenger@gciu.org
www.gciu.org
Facebook, Twitter
James P Hoffa, President
Ken Hall, Secretary-Treasurer
Tabloid size newspaper for and about members of the GCIU. The international union represents workers in the printing/publishing industry. Members range from desktop operators to paper handler.
Cost: $12.00
Circulation: 100000
Founded in 1983

21153 NAQP Network
National Association for Printing Leadership
One Meadowlands Plaza
Suite 1511
East Rutherford, NJ 07073
201-634-9600
800-642-6275; Fax: 201-634-0324
webmaster@napl.org
www.naqp.com
Facebook, Twitter, LinkedIn, YouTube,RSS
Joseph P Truncale, President & CEO
Dean D' Ambrosi, Vice President
Carol Rocke, Marketing Coordinator
Editorial content covers technologial advances, product news, profiles on industry leaders, and club events.
Frequency: Monthly
Circulation: 900

21154 Printing News
Cygnus Publishing
3 Huntington Quadrangle
Suite 301N
Melville, NY 11747-3601
631-845-2700
800-308-6397; Fax: 631-249-5774
editor@printingnews.com
www.printingnews.com
Facebook, Twitter, LinkedIn
David Kastriner, Publisher
Michael Zerner, Associate Publisher
David Lindsay, Editor-in-Chief
Rachel Frank, Editor
Includes timely news and information on a variety of subjects including technological breakthroughs, industry trends, marketing, finance, as well as industry leader and corporate profiles.
Cost: $39.95
Frequency: Weekly
Circulation: 9000
Founded in 1928
Mailing list available for rent

21155 SGIA Journal
Specialty Graphic Imaging Association
10015 Main St
Fairfax, VA 22031-3489
703-385-1335
888-385-3588; Fax: 703-273-0456
sgia@sgia.org
www.sgia.org
Facebook, Twitter, LinkedIn
Michael Robertson, President
Sondra Fry Benoudiz, VP Membership
Lynn Krinsky, Chairman
Pete Gallo, First Vice Chairman
Tim Markley, Second Vice Chairman
Provides members with access to information relative to industry trends and the latest news such as emerging markets, government regulations, and technological developments.
Cost: $149.00
Frequency: Bi-Monthly
Circulation: 3800
Founded in 1948
Printed in 2 colors on glossy stock

21156 **Signature Service**
Signature Service Real Estate Rainier
302 Binghampton Street W
PO Box 8
Rainier, WA 98576

360-446-4646
877-446-4647; Fax: 360-446-2400
www.signatureservice.com

Peter Colaianni, Executive Director
Marj Green, Director
Kevin Cooper, Billing Coordinator
Pam Decker, Webmaster

Newsletter covering rates, service and trends in the printing industry for consumers.
Cost: $115.00
8 Pages
Frequency: Monthly
Circulation: 2000

Magazines & Journals

21157 **American InkMaker**
Cygnus Publishing
PO Box 803
Fort Atkinson, WI 53538-0803

920-000-1111
800-547-7377; Fax: 920-563-1699
Rich.Reiff@CygnusPub.com

John French, CEO
Robert Stange, Senior VP Marketing

Offers information to the professional ink manufacturer. The editorial content consists of contributed technical papers and nontechnical features about trends, technology and global happenings to help our readers to improve their profitability in addition to featuring a monthly interview with printers.
Cost: $46.00
Circulation: 3800
Founded in 1923

21158 **American Printer**
American Printer
2100 West Loop South
Suite 900
Houston, TX 77027-3515

713-300-0674
info@AmericanPrinter.com
www.americanprinter.com
Facebook, Twitter, RSS

Katherine O'Brien, Editor
Michael P Koch, Senior Art Director
Denise Kapel, Managing Editor
Carrie Cleaveland, Assistant Editor
Jill Roth, Director Brand Development

Regular issue features include new products listings, new equipment technology and reports on system developments.
Frequency: Monthly
Circulation: 86037
Founded in 1883
Mailing list available for rent

21159 **Awards & Engraving Magazine**
National Business Media
PO Box 1416
Broomfield, CO 80038-1416

303-469-0424
800-669-0424; Fax: 303-469-5730
www.nbm.com
Facebook, Twitter, LinkedIn

Bob Wieber, President
Dave Pomeroy, Publisher

Content includes a special focus, and regular articles on signage, the glass market, business management, people profiles, and advances in technology.
Cost: $38.00
Frequency: Monthly
Founded in 1985

21160 **Big Picture**
325 Public Street
Providence, RI 02905

401-752-3442
800-421-1321; Fax: 401-752-3528
webmaster@bigpicturelearning.org
www.bigpicture.org

Tedd Swormstedt, CEO
Ronald A. Wolk, Chairman

This publication reports on digital printing of visual communications with coverage of digital printing from image capture and processing to finishing and display.
Frequency: Monthly
Circulation: 48000
Founded in 1996

21161 **Dealer Communicator**
Fichera Communications
441 South State Road 7
Suite 14
Margate, FL 33068-2823

954-971-4360
800-327-8999; Fax: 954-971-4362
omike@dealercommunicator.com
www.dealercommunicator.com

Orazio Fichera, Publisher/President
Particia Leavitt, VP

Provides national and international coverage for the graphic arts and printing industries.
Cost: $30.00
32 Pages
Frequency: Monthly
Circulation: 13619
Founded in 1982
Printed in 4 colors on glossy stock

21162 **Digital Graphics**
National Business Media
PO Box 1416
Broomfield, CO 80038-1416

303-469-0424
800-669-0424; Fax: 303-465-3424
www.nbm.com
Facebook, Twitter, LinkedIn

Bob Wieber, President
Ken Mergentime, Editor

Regular departments track public stock comapnies of interest to the industry, report on international graphics news and highlight recent technological advances.
64 Pages
Frequency: Monthly
Circulation: 18583
Founded in 1985
Printed in 4 colors

21163 **Digital Output**
Rockport Custom Publishing
100 Cummings Ctr
Suite 321E
Beverly, MA 01915-6101

978-921-7850; Fax: 978-921-7870
edit@rockportpubs.com
www.rockportpubs.com

Thomas Tetreault, CEO
Lynn Weese, Account Executive

Provides case studies and trend updates, as well as discussing how and why companies integrate and coordinate their marketing strategies.
Frequency: 12 + 2 Buyers Guides

21164 **Document Processing Technology**
RB Publishing Company
2424 American Lane
PO Box 259906
Madison, WI 53725-9906

608-277-8785
800-536-1992; Fax: 608-241-8666
rbpub@rbpub.com

Ron Brent, Publisher/President
Allison Lloyd, Managing Editor
Marll Thiede, Executive Editor/VP
Rachel Spahr, Circulation Manager
Tonjia Weber, Production Manager

Covers digital printing, publishing and distribution. Feature and special topic articles focus on industry trends, technology and strategies for high-volume document processors.
Frequency: Monthly
Circulation: 10000
Founded in 1988

21165 **Electronic Publishing**
PennWell Publishing Company
1421 S Sheridan Rd
Tulsa, OK 74112-6619

918-835-3161
800-331-4463; Fax: 918-831-9476
Headquarters@PennWell.com
www.pennwell.com

Robert Biolchini, President
Courtney E Howard, Managing Editor
Frank J Romano, Sr Contributing & Founding Editor
Nancy A Hitchcock, Senior Associate Editor

For those who communicate in print, including service bureaus, printers, prepress houses and desktop publishers, it provides latest products, news and related developments.
Cost: $59.00
Frequency: Monthly
Circulation: 68441
Founded in 1910
Mailing list available for rent

21166 **Flash Magazine**
BlackLighting
252 Riddle Pond Road
West Topsham, VT 05086

800-252-2599
800-252-2599; Fax: 802-439-6462
www.flashweb.com

Walter Vose Jeffries, Publisher

Flash Magazine was started in 1989 and is all about desktop publishing, book-on-demand binding, inkjet & laser printinting, heat transfers and other topics of interest to the small time publisher and graphic artist. The Flash is filled with great how-to articles that will help you take care of your printer, do maintenance & repairs yourself, teach you about graphics, digital photography, scanning and laser etching glass and book-on-demand publishing, binding and so much more.
Cost: $20.00
Frequency: Monthly
Circulation: 112000

21167 **Flexo Magazine**
Flexographic Technical Association
3920 Veterans Memorial Highway
Suite 9
Bohemia, NY 11716

631-737-6020; Fax: 631-737-6813
membership@flexography.org
www.flexography.org
Facebook, LinkedIn

Robert Moran, Publisher
Christian Bonawandt, Editor

Trade publication for the flexographic printing industry.
1300 Members
Frequency: Monthly

21168 **Forms & Direct Mail Manufacturer's Marketplace**
Bulls-Eye Communications
211 Champion Avenue
Webster, NY 14580
585-265-3045
Marsha A Thompson, Editor
The resource magazine of business forms and direct mail printers. Spotlights news and products in the industry.
Cost: $49.00
Frequency: Bi-Monthly
Circulation: 4,870

21169 **Graphic Communications World**
Hayzlett & Associates
3313 South Western Avenue
Sioux Falls, SD 57106
605-355-5531; Fax: 605-275-2087
www.hayzlett.com/index.htm
Jeanette Clinkunbroomer, Editor
Jeff Hayzlett, Owner
Offers a comprehensive overview of the graphic arts and communications industry.
Cost: $347.00
Frequency: Monthly
Founded in 1968

21170 **Gravure**
Gravure Association of America
1200A Scottsville Road
Rochester, NY 14624-5703
585-436-2150; Fax: 585-436-7689
www.gaa.org
Laura Wayland-Smith Hatch, Editor
William Martin, President/CEO
Editorial coverage focuses on the technical developments in gravure printing, the financial performance of the industry and association member activities.
Cost: $67.00
Circulation: 3500
ISSN: 0894-4946
Founded in 1987
Printed in 4 colors on matte stock

21171 **High Volume Printing (HVP)**
Innes Publishing Company
28100 North Ashley Circle
PO Box 7280
Libertyville, IL 60048
847-816-7900
800-247-3306; Fax: 847-247-8855
www.innespub.com
Mary Ellen Innes, Publisher
Ray Roth, Editor
Barb Pettersen, Circulation Manager
Mary Ellin Innes, President
Judy Abbott, Administrative Assistant
HVP offers a strategic mix of management and production-oriented editorial content, and has consistently led in coverage of new technologies and regulatory issues. It focuses on the bottom-line realities involved in merging tomorrow's technologies with today's operating environment. Subjects include prepress, press, and postpress equipment and technology, sales and marketing management, training, regulatory issues and more.
Circulation: 39057
Founded in 1982

21172 **IPA Bulletin**
IPA: Association of Graphic Solutions Providers
7200 France Ave S
Suite 223
Edina, MN 55435-4309
952-896-1908
800-255-8141; Fax: 708-596-5112
Steven Bonnoff, Executive Director
Becky Walroth, Editorial Assistant
Steven Bonoff, President
Association news offering information on prepress and graphic arts.
Cost: $20.00
6 Pages
Circulation: 2,100
ISSN: 1539-137X
Founded in 1911
Printed in 4 colors on glossy stock

21173 **In Plant Graphics**
North American Publishing Company
1500 Spring Garden St
Suite 1200
Philadelphia, PA 19130-4094
215-238-5300; Fax: 215-238-5342
www.ipgonline.com
Ned S Borowsky, CEO
Glen Reynolds, Publisher
Dorlissa Goodrich, Production Manager
Maggie Tajack, Advertising Promotion Manager
Brian Ludwig, Group Publisher
Articles include management advice, technical information, industry news and reader profiles.
Cost: $65.00
60 Pages
Frequency: Monthly
Circulation: 20,000
ISSN: 1087-2817
Founded in 1996
Printed in 4 colors on glossy stock

21174 **In Plant Printer**
Innes Publishing Company
28100 North Ashley Circle
Suite 101
Libertyville, IL 60048
847-816-7900
800-247-3306; Fax: 847-247-8855
www.innespub.com
Mary Ellin Innes, President
Jack Klasnic, Editor
Barbara Pettersen, Circulation Manager
Teri Saeed, Production Manager
Judy Abbott, Administrative Assistant
Serves printing, graphics and typesetting facilities located in business, industry, education, government, hospitals, associations, and nonprofit organizations.
Cost: $110.00
70 Pages
Frequency: Monthly
Circulation: 247637
ISSN: 0891-8996
Founded in 1977
Printed in 4 colors on glossy stock

21175 **Ink World**
Ink World Direct Limited
108 Queens Road
Nuneaton, WI 07446-1150
800-011-2011
info@rodpub.com
www.ink-world.com
Rodman Zilenziger Jr, President
Matt Montgomery, VP
Covers the printing inks, coatings and allied industries.
64 Pages
Frequency: Monthly
Circulation: 6187
Founded in 1994
Printed in 4 colors on glossy stock

21176 **Inside Finishing Magazine**
Foil & Speciality Effects Association
2150 Southwest Wesport Drive
Suite 101
Topeka, KS 66614
785-271-5816; Fax: 785-271-6404
www.fsea.com
Jeff Peterson, Executive Director
Gayla Peterson, Sales Director
Kym Conis, Assistant Director
Eric.J Carter, Art Director & Webmaster
A quarterly magazine published by the Foil Stamping and Embossing Association, Inside Finishing has a targeted circulation of 6,000 graphic finishing decision makers. These include trade finishers, folding carton companies, greeting card manufacturers, and commercial printers with finishing/bindery operations. It also includes a small percentage of graphic designers involved in the foil stamping and embossing industry, and, of course, industry suppliers to the graphic finishing industry.
56 Pages
Frequency: 4 issues
Founded in 1994

21177 **Instant and Small Commercial Printer ISCP**
Innes Publishing Company
28100 North Ashley Circle
PO Box 7280
Libertyville, IL 60048-7280
847-816-7900
800-247-3306; Fax: 847-247-8855
www.innespub.com
Dan Innes, Publisher
Linda Casey, Editor
Barb Pettersen, Circualtion MAnager
Mary Ellin Innes, President
ISCP magazine publishes how-to articles and case histories on printing and photocopy reproduction. Emphasis on desktop publishing and short-run digital technologies reflects the growth of this service in instant printing operations. Management stories are aimed at helping the publication's largely entrepreneurial audience grapple successfully with everyday problems and spot new opportunities for growth.
Frequency: Monthly
Circulation: 413671
Founded in 1982

21178 **Label & Narrow Web Industry**
Rodman Publishing
70 Hilltop Rd
Suite 3000
Ramsey, NJ 07446-1150
201-825-2552; Fax: 201-825-0553
label@rodpub.com
www.labelandnarrowweb.com
Facebook, Twitter, LinkedIn, RSS
Rodman J. Zilenziger Jr, President
Matthew Montgomery, VP
Kathleen Scully, Publisher
Steve Katz, Editor
Catherine Diamond, Associate Editor
Label and Narrow Web serves manufacturers of label and narrow web including labels, tags, tape, materials, substrates, machinery, and equipment and others allied to the field.
80 Pages
Circulation: 11000
ISSN: 1095-3248
Founded in 1996
Mailing list available for rent
Printed in 4 colors on glossy stock

21179 **New England Printer and Publisher**
Printing Industries of New England

5 Crystal Pond Rd
Southborough, MA 01772-1758

508-804-4100
800-365-7463; Fax: 508-804-4119
www.pine.org

John Scibelli, Manager
Joe La Valla, Chairman
Brie Drummond, Production Manager
Kurt Peterson, Vice-Chairman
Bob Clement, Secretary-Treasurer

Trade magazine for printers and publishers.
Cost: $2.40
48 Pages
Frequency: Monthly
Circulation: 4000
Founded in 1938
Printed in 4 colors on matte stock

21180 New Pages: Alternatives in Print and Media
New Pages Press
PO Box 1580
Bay City, MI 48706

989-671-0081; Fax: 313-743-2730
newpagesonline@hotmail.com
www.newpages.com

Casey Hill, Publisher
Denise Hill, Editor

News and information for bookstores and libraries.
Cost: $12.00
64 Pages
Frequency: Quarterly

21181 Newspapers & Technology
Conley Magazines
1623 Blake Street
Suite 250
Denver, CO 80202

303-575-9595; Fax: 303-575-9555
www.newsandtech.com/

Mary Van Meter, Publisher
Chuck Moozakis, Editor-in-Chief
Tara McKeekin, Editor
Hays Goodman, Associate Editor/Webmaster

Newspapers & Technology is a monthly trade publication for newspaper publishers and department managers involved in applying and integrating technology. Written by industry experts, News & Tech provides regular coverage of the following departments: prepress, press, postpress and new media.
Circulation: 16,874

21182 PC Presentations Productions
Pisces Publishing Group
1400 South Nova Road
Suite 303
Daytona Beach, FL 32114-5851

203-877-1927; Fax: 203-877-1927
www.piscespub.com

Don Johnson, Editor/Publisher
Douglas Finlay, Managing Editor

PC Presentations Productions is a free online magazine intended for both the high-end professional and the student. Graphic and video tutorials for intermediate and advanced content producers are regular features as are HTML and Javascript tutorials and Website design tutorials intended for students and others wishing to add these skills.
Frequency: Weekly
ISSN: 1065-9699

21183 Package Printing
North American Publishing Company
1500 Spring Garden St
Suite 1200
Philadelphia, PA 19130-4094

215-238-5300
800-627-2689; Fax: 215-238-5342
customerservice@napco.com
www.packageprinting.com
Facebook, Twitter, LinkedIn, Yahoo,Windows Live

Ned S Borowsky, CEO
Brian Ludwick, Publisher
Robert Margulies, Sales Manager
Megan Wolf, Assistant Editor
Sean Sams, Advertising Account Manager

Trade publication serving the business and technology needs of presidents and CEOs of flexible packaging, tag and label, folding rigid boxes and directing operations.
Cost: $99.50
75 Pages
Frequency: Monthly
Circulation: 24000
Founded in 1958
Mailing list available for rent

21184 Paper Magazine
365 Broadway
6th Floor
New York, NY 10013

212-226-4405
800-829-9160; Fax: 212-226-0062
edit@papermag.com
www.papermag.com

Sharon Phair, Advertising & Marketing
Kim Hastreiter, Publisher
Alexis Swerdloff, Executive Editor
Nobu Massiah, Editor
Carol Lee, Creative Director

PAPER Magazine focuses on the latest trends in pop culture, style, music and film, including information on New York art exhibits, club listings, literary events, movie reviews and shows. Includes night-life guide.
Cost: $9.97
Frequency: 10 Issues Per Year
Circulation: 90,000
Founded in 1984

21185 Print Business Register
Cygnus Business Media
3 Huntington Quadrangle
Suite 301 North
Melville, NY 11747

631-845-2700
800-308-6397; Fax: 631-845-2741
Facebook

Michael Zerner, Publisher
Rachel Frank, Editor

Editorial material reports on mergers, acquisitions, reorganizations and major issues affecting the marketplace of the commercial printing industry.
Frequency: Weekly
Circulation: 650
Mailing list available for rent

21186 Print Magazine
RC Publications
38 east 29th street, 4th floor
New York, NY 10016

212-447-1400; Fax: 212-447-5231
info@printmag.com
www.printmag.com
Facebook, Twitter, Flickr

Joel Toner, Publisher

Regular highlights include advertising and promotion design, corporate identity, design education and film/TV production. Also covered are creative trends and technological advances in photography, printing, web design, illustration, motion graphics and packaging. Includes profiles of visual artists, ad agencies and graphic design firms.
Cost: $37.00
Frequency: Monthly
Circulation: 54149
Mailing list available for rent

21187 Print Solutions Magazine
Document Management Industries Association
330 N Wabash Ave
Suite 2000
Chicago, IL 60611

800-230-0175; Fax: 312-673-6880
www.psda.org

Peter L Colaianni CAE, Editor-in-Chief
Preeti Vasishtha, Assistant Editor
Lashell Stratton, Assistant Editor
Rebecca Trela, Assistant Editor

The independent's source for marketing, management and product information.
Cost: $49.00
276 Pages
Frequency: Monthly
Circulation: 42000
ISSN: 0532-1700
Founded in 1962
Printed in 4 colors on glossy stock

21188 Print on Demand Business
Cygnus Business Media
1233 Janesville Avenue
Fort Atkinson, WI 53538

631-845-2700
800-547-7377; Fax: 631-845-2741
info@cygnus.com
www.cygnusb2b.com/

Bob Hall, Executive Editor
Denise Gustavson, Managing Editor
Paul Bonaiuto, CFO
John French, CEO

Editorial includes a look at new products, industry news, updated technology, tips on the best equipment and a look ahead with an upcoming calendar of events.
Frequency: Bi-Monthly

21189 Printing Impressions
North American Publishing Company
1500 Spring Garden St
Suite 1200
Philadelphia, PA 19130-4094

215-238-5300
800-627-2689; Fax: 215-238-5342
mmichelson@napco.com
www.napco.com

Ned S Borowsky, CEO
Chris Bauer, Managing Editor
Tunisia Bey, Circulation Manager

Offers news, articles, updates, statistics, research reports and more for the printing industry including printers involved in commercial and newspaper printing and trades.
Frequency: Weekly
Circulation: 83035
Founded in 1958
Mailing list available for rent

21190 Printing Industry Association of the South - Magazine
Printing Industry Association of the South
PO Box 290249
Nashville, TN 37229-0249

615-366-1094; Fax: 615-366-4192
info@pias.org
www.pias.org

Ed Chalifoux, President
James Tepper, Board Member

Print industry information. Free with membership.
Frequency: Monthly
Circulation: 5000
Printed in 4 colors on glossy stock

21191 Printing Manager
National Association of Printing Leadership
One Meadowlands Plaza
Suite 1511
East Rutherford, NJ 07073
201-634-9600
800-642-6275; Fax: 201-634-0324
www.napl.org
Joseph P Truncale, President/CEO
Timothy Fischer, Executive Vp/COO
Provides current news for printing executives including the latest industry, marketing and management news.
40 Pages
Frequency: Quarterly
Circulation: 6000
Founded in 1933
Mailing list available for rent
Printed in 4 colors

21192 Printing News Magazine
Cygnus Business Media
3 Huntington Quadrangle
Suite 301N
Melville, NY 11747
631-845-2700; Fax: 631-845-2741
www.printingnews.com
Facebook, Twitter, LinkedIn, RSS
David Nathenson, Publisher
Michael Zerner, Associate Publisher
David Lindsay, Editor-in-Chief
Rachel Frank, Editor
News and information on the graphic arts industry in New York, Connecticut, New Jersey and Pennsylvania.
Cost: $39.95
44 Pages
Circulation: 7000
Founded in 1937

21193 Printing News Online
Cygnus Business Media
3 Huntingon Quadrangle
Suite 301N
Melville, NY 11747
631-845-2700
800-308-6397; Fax: 631-845-2741
www.printingnews.com
Facebook, Twitter, LinkedIn, RSS
David Nathenson, Publisher
Michael Zerner, Associate Publisher
David Lindsay, Editor-in-Chief
Rachel Frank, Editor
Includes timely news and information on a variety of subjects including technological breakthroughs, industry trends, marketing, finance, as well as industry leader and corporate profiles.

21194 Publishing Executive
North American Publishing Company
1500 Spring Garden St
Suite 1200
Philadelphia, PA 19130-4094
215-238-5300; Fax: 215-238-5342
www.printmediamag.com/
Ned S Borowsky, CEO
Noelle Skodzinski, Editor-in-Chief
Matt Steinmetz, Associate Editor
Rhoda Dixon, Circulation Manager
Candas Carmen, Associate Publisher
Publishing Executive (formerly PrintMedia) delivers information to magazine publishers, associations, corporate publishers, advertising and marketing agencies.
Circulation: 17500

21195 Quick Printing
Cygnus Business Media
3 Huntington Quadrangle
Suite 301 North
Melville, NY 11747-803
631-845-2700
800-308-6397; Fax: 631-845-2741
www.quickprinting.com
Facebook
Jann Levesque, Group Publisher
Kelley Holmes, Publisher
Bob Hall, Editor
Denise Gustavson, Managing Editor
Business journal for those in the printing business.
Cost: $66.00
Frequency: Monthly
Circulation: 48000
Founded in 1937
Mailing list available for rent

21196 SGIA Journal
Specialty Graphic Imaging Association
10015 Main St
Fairfax, VA 22031-3489
703-385-1335
888-385-3588; Fax: 703-273-0456
sgia@sgia.org
www.sgia.org
Facebook, Twitter, LinkedIn
Michael Robertson, President
Sondra Fry Benoudiz, VP Membership
Published quarterly in January, April, July and October.
Circulation: 14000
Founded in 1948

21197 Screen Printing
ST Media Group International
11262 Cornell Park Dr
Cincinnati, OH 45242-1812
513-421-2050
800-421-1321; Fax: 513-421-5144
customer@stmediagroup.com
www.stmediagroup.com
Tedd Swormstedt, CEO
Brian Foos, CFO
Mark Kissling, Director
Screen printing professionals have relied on Screen Printing for landmark coverage of the latest techniques and technologies that save time, energy and money.
Frequency: Monthly
Circulation: 17000
Founded in 1953
Mailing list available for rent: 17,000 names at $200 per M

21198 Signs of the Times & Screen Printing en Espanol
ST Media Group International
11262 Cornell Park Dr
Cincinnati, OH 45242-1812
513-421-2050
800-421-1321; Fax: 513-421-5144
www.stmediagroup.com
Tedd Swormstedt, CEO
Brian Foos, CFO
Mark Kissling, Director
Covering the industries of signmaking, screen printing and digital imaging for Spanish speaking visual communications markets.
Frequency: Monthly
Circulation: 17000
Founded in 1906
Mailing list available for rent

21199 Wide Format Imaging Magazine
Cygnus Publishing
3 Huntington Quadrangle
Suite 301 North
Melville, NY 11747
631-845-2700
800-308-6397; Fax: 631-845-2741
www.wide-formatimaging.com
Facebook, Twitter, LinkedIn, RSS
David Nathenson, Publisher
Karen Lowry-Hall, Editor
Denise M Gustavson, Managing Editor/Web Editor
Charlie Lillis, Director Content Licensing
Katie Brennan, Vice President
Wide Format Imagfiring Magazine provides information on new technologies, analysis of new products, business management tips, and profiles of significant people in the industry. The magazine is a monthly business publication serving 18,000 wide-format professionals. These mostly small business owners are responsible for wide- and large-format drawings, blueprints, soft signage, outdoor signage, posters, POP displays, digital fine art printmaking, and large trade show graphics.
Cost: $25.00
Frequency: Monthly
Mailing list available for rent

Trade Shows

21200 BIA Mid Management Conference
Printing Industry of Illinois
200 Deer Run Road
Sewickley, PA 15143
412-741-6860
800-910-4283; Fax: 412-741-2311
www.bindingindustries.org
Facebook, Twitter, LinkedIn
Michael Makin, President/CEO
Justin Goldstein, Manager
Brings together mid-managers from trade binderies, graphic finishing, information packaging, custom loose leaf manufacturing, and the suppliers to those industries.
600 Attendees
Frequency: Annual/May

21201 CMM International
Romeland house
Romeland Hill
St Albans
Herdfordshire
212-268-4160; Fax: 212-268-4178
info@mackbrooks.co.uk
www.cmmshow.com
The premier converting and package printing event for thousands of professionals.
Frequency: June4-7 Chicago
Founded in 1978

21202 Graphic Arts
Graphic Arts Show Company
1899 Preston White Drive
Reston, VA 20191-5468
703-264-7200; Fax: 703-620-9187
info@gasc.org
www.gasc.org
Chris Price, VP
Kelly Kilga, Director Operations
Ralph Nappi, President
One of America's foremost regional prepress, printing, publishing, and converting trade shows. 300 booths, 70,000 square feet.
18000 Attendees
Frequency: March
Founded in 1982

21203 Graphics of the Americas
Printing Association of Florida

6275 Hazeltine National Drive
Orlando, FL 32822

407-240-8009
800-331-0461; Fax: 407-240-8333

Bill Maguire, Chairman
Larry Kudeviz, Treasurer
Rob Hasson, First Vice Chairman
Art Abbott, Second Vice Chairman
George Ryan, CEO

We are the second largest Graphic Arts and Converting show in America. We give you two vital markets, Southeast US and Latin America: Mexico, South America, Central America and the Caribbean. Our 28 year track record reflects our success with both exhibitors and show visitors.
20000 Attendees

21204 **Gutenberg Festival**
American Printer
2100 West Loop South
Suite 900
Houston, TX 77027-3515

713-300-0674
info@AmericanPrinter.com
www.americanprinter.com
Facebook, Twitter, RSS

Kelly Kilga, Conference/Show Operations Director
Lilly Kinney, Conference Manager
Tina Scott, Exhibit Sales Director
Chrissie Hahn, Exhibit Sales Manager

The top printing event on the west coast and the only place to see live running equipment both traditional and digital.
15000 Attendees
Frequency: April
Mailing list available for rent

21205 **Interquest**
Interquest Ltd.
513-D Stewart Street
Charlottesville, VA 22902

434-979-9945; Fax: 434-979-9959
iquest@inter-quest.com
www.inter-quest.com

David Davis, Director

Interquest analysts will present key results from the company's latest research in the field.
Frequency: March

21206 **Labelexpo America**
Tarsus Group Plc

Home Page: www.labelexpo-americas.com

Label, printing, decoration, web printing and converting industry's largest expo.
Frequency: Sept, Chicago

21207 **National Association of Professional Print Buyers**
15050 Northeast 20th Avenue
Suite A
North Miami, FL 33181-1123

305-956-9563

Vincent Mallardi, Executive Director

400 booths.
2.5M Attendees
Frequency: April
Founded in 1969

21208 **Print**
Graphic Arts Show Company
1899 Preston White Drive
Reston, VA 20191-5435

703-264-7200; Fax: 703-620-9187
www.gasc.org

Ralph Nappi, President
Chris Price, Vice President
Kelly Kilga, Director Communications
Lilly Kinney, Conference Manager

This is the largest, most comprehensive event for the commercial, package printing and converting industry in the world in 2013. This huge international event held every four years offers you more running machinery under one roof than any other event anywhere.
40000 Attendees
Frequency: September/Annual
Founded in 1968
Mailing list available for rent

21209 **Print Media Conference & Expo**
c/o North American Publishing Company
1500 Spring Garden St, Suite 1200
Philadelphia, PA 19130-4094

888-627-2630; Fax: 215-409-0100

21210 **Printing for Fabrication Conference**
The Society for Imaging Science & Technology
7003 Kilworth Lane
Springfield, VA 22151-4008

703-642-9090; Fax: 703-642-9094
info@imaging.org
www.imaging.org

Steven J. Simske, President
Dietmar Wueller, Secretary
Eric Hanson, Treasurer

Annual conference and exhibits of non-impact printing equipment, supplies and services, including printer components, printer consumables, paper and document handling devices and display units.
620 Attendees

21211 **SGIA Technology Show**
Specialty Graphic Imaging Association
10015 Main Street
Fairfax, VA 22031-3489

703-385-1335
888-385-3588; Fax: 703-273-0456
sgia@sgia.org
www.sgia.org
Facebook, Twitter, LinkedIn

Michael Robertson, President/CEO
Sondra Fry Benoudiz, VP Membership

Technologies showcased include: embossing, printing, graphics, digital imaging, screen printing and embroidering.
14000 Attendees
Frequency: September
Founded in 1948

21212 **Tools of Change for Publishing Conference**
O'Reilly Media, Inc.
1005 Gravenstein Highway North
Sebastopol, CA 95472

707-827-7019
800-889-8969; Fax: 707-824-8268
orders@oreilly.com
www.oreilly.com
Facebook, Twitter, YouTube,RSS

Gina Blaber, Vice President, Conferences
Suzanne Axtell, Communications Manager
Shirley Bailes, Speaker Manager

Expect coverage with a range of practical, in-depth sessions that cover the innovations rocking every aspect of the art, craft, and business of publishing in the 21st century.
Frequency: February

21213 **TypeCon**
The Society of Typographic Aficionados
P.O. Box 457
Jefferson, GA 30549

info@typesociety.org
www.typecon.com
Twitter

Features education forums, workshops, and exhibits related to typography and design.
Frequency: Annual
Founded in 1998

21214 **Vue/Point Conference**
Graphic Arts Show Company
1189 Preston White Drive
Reston, VA 22091-4367

703-264-7200; Fax: 703-620-9187
www.gasc.org

David Poulos, Conference Coordinator

Presents topics via panel discussions composed of printing professionals who are willing to share their experiences.

Directories & Databases

21215 **Coldset Web Offset Directory**
Printing Industries of America/Graphic Arts
200 Deer Run Rd
Sewickley, PA 15143-2600

412-741-6860
800-910-4283; Fax: 412-741-2311
www.printing.org
Facebook, Twitter, LinkedIn

Michael F Makin, President
Eric Delzer, Chairman

Over 600 printing firms with more than 1,000 presses in the US, Puerto Rico and Canada are profiled.
Cost: $120.00
Frequency: BiAnnual

21216 **Corporate and Incentive Travel**
Coastal Communications Corporation
2700 N Military Trail
Suite 120
Boca Raton, FL 33431-6394

561-989-0600; Fax: 561-989-9509
www.themeetingmagazines.com

Harvey Grotsky, Publisher/Editor-In-Chief
Susan Wycoff Fell, Managing Editor
Susan S Gregg, Managing Editor
Mitch D Miller, Creative Director

Read by over 40,000 ABC audited meeting and incentive travel planners and key executives responsible for meeting decisions. Articles range monthly from in-depth how-to's, to issue oriented features, examinations of professional concerns, thoroughly researched destination reports, and columns by industry experts
Cost: $50.00
Frequency: Annual
Circulation: 60,000
Founded in 1983
Mailing list available for rent

21217 **Heatset Web Offset Directory**
Printing Industries of America/Graphic Arts
200 Deer Run Rd
Sewickley, PA 15143-2600

412-741-6860
800-910-4283; Fax: 412-741-2311
www.printing.org
Facebook, Twitter, LinkedIn

Michael Makin, President
Eric Delzer, Chairman

Offers information on nearly 500 heatset web printing firms in the United States, Puerto Rico

and Canada including products produced.
Cost: $50.00
110 Pages
Frequency: BiAnnually

21218 In Plant Reproductions: Buyer's Guide Issue
North American Publishing Company
1500 Spring Garden St
Suite 1200
Philadelphia, PA 19130-4094
215-238-5300
800-627-2689; Fax: 215-238-5342
Ned S Borowsky, CEO
Firms that manufacture or supply equipment, materials and services to printing facilities of firms or organizations, including art, paste-up and copy preparation, mailing systems, darkroom equipment, presses, paper, word processing, computerized composition and electronic publishing.
Cost: $35.00
Frequency: Annual December
Circulation: 41,000

21219 International Directory of Private Presses
Educators Research Service
2443 Fair Oaks Boulevard
Suite 316
Sacramento, CA 95825-7684
Home Page: www.briarpress.org
Offers valuable information on over 1,200 private presses and hobbyist printers worldwide.
Cost: $50.00
300 Pages
Frequency: Annual

21220 Print Image International
401 N Michigan Avenue
Suite 2100
Chicago, IL 60611-4245
312-268-8015
800-234-0640; Fax: 312-321-6869
www.printimage.org
John Giles, Editor
Steve Johnson, President
300 Pages

21221 PrintStats
Assoc for Suppliers of Printing, Publishing Tech
1896 Preston White Drive
Reston, VA 20191
703-264-7200
aptech@aptech.org
www.printtechnologies.org
Thayer Long, President
Ken Garner, SVP, Content Creation
Julie Shaffer, VP, Program Development
Sarah Markfield, VP, Marketing & Communications
Judith B. Durham, EVP, Operations
An online, freely accessible, association database of NPES member companies and more than 500 products, searchable by product category, keyword or company name.
220 Pages
Frequency: Biennial

21222 Rauch Guide to the US Ink Industry
Grey House Publishing
4919 Route 22
PO Box 56
Amenia, NY 12501-0056
518-789-8700
800-562-2139; Fax: 518-789-0556
books@greyhouse.com
www.greyhouse.com
Facebook, Twitter
Leslie Mackenzie, Publisher
Richard Gottlieb, Editor
The Guide to this complex and diffuse $4.2 billion ink industry provides market facts and figures in a highly organized format, ideal for today's busy personnel. The report serves as a ready-reference for top executives as well as the industry newcomer.
Cost: $595.00
700 Pages
ISBN: 1-592371-26-4
Founded in 1981

21223 Rauch Guide to the US and Canadian Pulp & Paper Industry
Grey House Publishing
4919 Route 22
PO Box 56
Amenia, NY 12501-0056
518-789-8700
800-562-2139; Fax: 518-789-0556
books@greyhouse.com
www.greyhouse.com
Facebook, Twitter
Leslie Mackenzie, Publisher
Richard Gottlieb, Editor
Provides current market information and trends to; industry economics and government regulations; company share data for each of the leading product categories; technology and raw material information; industry sources of further data; and unique profiles of 500+ pulp and paper manufacturers, a section which includes all known companies with pulp and paper sales at or over $15 million annually.
Cost: $595.00
400 Pages
ISBN: 1-592371-31-0
Founded in 1981

21224 Salem Press Online Platform
Grey House Publishing
4919 Route 22
PO Box 56
Amenia, NY 12501
800-221-1592; Fax: 201-968-0511
csr@salempress.com
online.salempress.com
The new Salem Press platform houses more than 500 titles including all of Salem's Health, Literature, History and Science titles in addition to select titles from the Grey House Publishing and H.W. Wilson product lines. Online access is free with each print purchase and includes an unlimited number of simultaneous users and remote access.

21225 Who's Who SGIA
Specialty Graphic Imaging Association
10015 Main St
Fairfax, VA 22031-3489
703-385-1335
888-385-3588; Fax: 703-273-0456
sgia@sgia.org
www.sgia.org
Facebook, Twitter, LinkedIn
Michael Robertson, President
Sondra Fry Benoudiz, VP Membership
Circulation: 3,800
Founded in 1948

Industry Web Sites

21226 http://gold.greyhouse.com
G.O.L.D Grey House OnLine Databases
Grey House Publishing's online database platform, GOLD, offers Quick Search, Keyword Search and Expert Search for most business sectors including printing and allied markets. The GOLD platform makes finding the information you need quick and easy - whether you're a novice searcher or an experienced database user. All of Grey House's directory products are available for subscription on the GOLD platform.

21227 www.fsea.com
Foil Stamping and Embossing Association
For companies engaged in the process of hot stamping or embossing in the graphics industry and companies that manufacture, distribute or provide services to the hot stamping/embossing industry.

21228 www.gaa.org
Gravure Association of America
Members are gravure printers, converters, suppliers and users.

21229 www.greyhouse.com
Grey House Publishing
Authoritative reference directories for most business sectors including printing and allied markets. Users can search the online databases with varied search criteria allowing for custom searches by product category, geographic area, sales volume, keyword, subject and more. Full Grey House catalog and online ordering also available.

21230 www.iaphc.org
International Assn of Printing House Craftsmen
A voluntary graphic arts organization in which many people share their knowledge and their skill with one another. Open to anyone in any part of the graphic arts community who wish technical information.

21231 www.ipa.org
International Prepress Association
Members produce pre-press material for the graphics industry.

21232 www.magazine.org
Magazine Publishers of America
Promotes magazines as an advertising medium. Provides information services and assistance to members in areas of circulation marketing.

21233 www.napim.org
National Association of Printing Ink Manufacturers
Purpose is to represent the printing ink industry in the U.S.A.

21234 www.napl.org
National Association for Printing Leadership
Promotes the interests in leadership for priniting professionals.

21235 www.pgca.org
Printing and Graphic Communications Association
Serving the graphic communications community in the Washington, D.C. metropolitan area.

21236 www.pias.org
Printing Industry Association of the South
Represents the print industry.

21237 www.pine.org
Printing Institute of New England

21238 www.printing.org
Printing Industries of America (PIA)
The largest graphic arts organization founded over 100 years ago.

21239 **www.printtechnologies.com**
Assoc for Suppliers of Printing & Publishing Tech

Members are manufacturers and distributors of graphic arts equipment, systems, software and supplies. Promotes marketing, safety and industry standards, international trade and government relations.

21240 **www.waterless.org**
Waterless Printing Association

Dedicated to the informational and educational needs of its printer and sponsor members.

Associations

21241 **ANA Business Marketing**
2801 Buford Highway, Druid Chase
Suite 375
Atlanta, GA 30329

404-641-9417
800-664-4262; Fax: 312-822-0054
info@bmaatlanta.org
bmaatlanta.org
Facebook, Twitter, LinkedIn, Google+

Moira Vetter, President
Mark Towery, President Elect
Subodh Singh, VP Member Services
Khoi Ta, VP Young Professionals
Mark Miranda, VP Sponsorship

Formerly BMA Atlanta, ANA Business Marketing includes marketing executives from a variety of industries and backgrounds including research, advertising, promotions, events, Web development, printing and more. The BMA offers an information-packed Website, online skills-building, marketing certification programs, and industry surveys and papers. In addition, members have the opportunity to interact with peers at seminars, participate in chapter training programs and th
Founded in 1922

21242 **Arthur W. Page Society**
230 Park Avenue
Suite 455
New York, NY 10169

212-400-7959; Fax: 347-474-7399
page.org
Twitter, LinkedIn, YouTube, RSS

Roger Bolton, President

Professional public relations organization with a single mission, to strengthen the management policy role of the chief public relations officer. Conducts seminars and conferences.
397 Members
Founded in 1983

21243 **Association for Women in Communications**
1717 E Republic Road
Suite A
Springfield, MO 65804

417-886-8606; Fax: 417-886-3685
chair@womcom.org
www.womcom.org
Facebook, Twitter, LinkedIn, YouTube, Google+

Anita K. Parran, Chair
Kandice Mollitiam, Data Protection Officer

Professional organization that champions the advancement of women across all communications disciplines by recognizing excellence, promoting leadership and positioning its members at the forefront of the evolving communications era. Hosts a bi-annual conference.
1000 Members
Founded in 1909
Mailing list available for rent: 1000+ names at $n/a per M

21244 **Baptist Communicators Association**
1519 Menlo Drive
Kennesaw, GA 30152

770-425-3728
www.baptistcommunicators.org
Facebook, Twitter, LinkedIn, Vimeo, Wordpress

Margaret Colson, Executive Director

PR and Journalism professionals.
300 Members
Founded in 1953

21245 **Hispanic Public Relations Association**
PO Box 86760
Los Angeles, CA 90086-0760

info@hpra-usa.org
hpra-usa.org
Facebook, Twitter

Veronica Potes, President

The HPRA's mission is the professional development and advancement of its members and the practice of Hispanic public relations.
Founded in 1984

21246 **Institute for Public Relations**
Inst. for Public Relations, Univ. of Florida
PO Box 118400
Gainesville, FL 32611-8400

352-392-0280; Fax: 352-846-1122
instituteforpr.org
Facebook, Twitter, LinkedIn, YouTube,RSS

Dr. Tina McCorkindale, President & CEO
Dr. Sarab Kochhar, Director of Research

Improving the effectiveness of organizations by advancing the professional knowledge and practice of public relations through research and education.
Founded in 1956
Mailing list available for rent

21247 **International Association of Business Communicators**
649 Mission Street
5th Floor
San Francisco, CA 94105

415-544-4700
800-776-4222; Fax: 415-544-4747
member_relations@iabc.com
www.iabc.com
Twitter, LinkedIn

Peter Finn, Executive Director
Tilden Katz, Chief Communications Officer
Buffy Levy, Event Director
Jason Meyers, Content & Editorial Director
Jeff Price, Marketing & Communications Manager

International knowledge network for professionals engaged in strategic business communication management.
12000 Members
Founded in 1970

21248 **Original Equipment Suppliers Association**
Original Equipment Suppliers Association
25925 Telegraph Rd.
Suite 350
Southfield, MI 48033-2553

248-952-6401; Fax: 248-952-6404
info@oesa.org
www.oesa.org
Facebook, Twitter, LinkedIn

Julie A. Fream, President & CEO

Provides a forum for information exchange among communication professionals with the automotive industry. Two conferences are held every year, topics are integrated marketing, communications and the automotive industry.
450 Members
Founded in 1998

Newsletters

21249 **Bulldog Reporter**
InfoCom Group
5900 Hollis Street
Suite L
Emeryville, CA 94608-2008

510-653-3035
800-959-1059; Fax: 510-596-9331
www.infocomgroup.com

James Sinkinson, Publisher
Tim Gray, President

Emphasis on placement opportunities and media profiles, as well as personnel changes at media outlets throughout the US.
Cost: $599.00
Frequency: Fortnightly
Circulation: 5000
Founded in 1980

21250 **Contacts: Media Pipeline for PR People**
Larimi Communications Association
500 Executive Boulevard
Ossining on Hudson, NY 10562-1114

914-923-9400; Fax: 914-923-9484
info@mercommawards.com
www.mercommawards.com/

Michael M Smith, Publisher
Madeleine Gillis, Editor

Provides pipeline of communications between what an editor needs and a public relations person can supply.
Cost: $287.00
1 Pages
Frequency: Weekly
Founded in 1975
Printed in one color

21251 **Downtown Promotion Reporter**
Alexander Communications Group
1916 Park Ave
Suite 501
New York, NY 10037-3733

212-281-6099
800-232-4317; Fax: 212-283-7269
info@downtowndevelopment.com
www.downtowndevelopment.com/

Romauld Alexander, President

Tested ideas for promotion, public relations, marketing, increasing business, participation, downtown image building, sales, and events.
Cost: $189.00
Frequency: Monthly
ISSN: 0363-2830

21252 **Healthcare PR & Marketing News**
Phillips Business Information
1201 Seven Locks Road
Suite 300
Potomac, MD 20854-2931

301-354-1400; Fax: 301-340-1451

Sharmi Banik, Editor
Kismet Toksu Gould, Publisher

Issues faced by health care executives in PR firms and hospitals. Regular features include industry surveys, case studies and executive profiles.
Cost: $397.00
Frequency: Bi-Monthly
Founded in 1992

21253 **High-Tech Hot Sheet**
Hot Sheet Publishing
114 Sansome Street
Suite 1224
San Francisco, CA 94104

415-421-6225; Fax: 415-421-6225

Art Gracia, Editor/Publisher

Reporting updates and changes in staff, beat assignments, new publications, suspension of pub-

lishing in high-tech media.
Cost: $395.00
Frequency: Monthly
Founded in 1987

21254 **Holmes Report**
Holmes Group
271 W 47th St
Suite 23A
New York, NY 10036-1447

212-333-2300; Fax: 212-333-2624
www.holmesreport.com

Paul Holmes, President
Greg Drury, Managing Editor
Arun Sudhaman, Managing Editor

Source of information for public relations and corporate communications professionals.
Cost: $290.00
Frequency: Weekly
Circulation: 15,000
ISBN: 0-972364-50-1
Founded in 2001
Printed in 4 colors on glossy stock

21255 **Interactive PR & Marketing News**
Phillips Publishing
1201 Seven Locks Road
#300
Potomac, MD 20854-2931

301-354-1400; Fax: 301-424-8602
www.phillips.com

Angela Duff, Publisher

Covers the latest trends and news on the World Wide Web and Internet markets and looks at their users.
Cost: $347.00
Frequency: 23 per year
Circulation: 5M

21256 **Interactive Public Relations**
Ragan Communications
316 N Michigan Ave
Suite 400
Chicago, IL 60601-3773

312-960-4100
800-493-4867; Fax: 312-960-4106
cservice@ragan.com
www.ragan.com

Jim Ylisela, Publisher
Mark ragan, CEO
Kasia Chalko, Marketing Director

Includes targeted newsletters in the areas of employment communication, Web PR, organizational writing and editing, sales and marketing, media relations, motivational management, and investor relations.
Cost: $279.00
Founded in 1970

21257 **Jack O'Dwyer's Newsletter**
JR O'Dwyer Company
271 Madison Ave
Suite 600
New York, NY 10016-1013

212-683-2750; Fax: 212-683-2750
jack@odwyerpr.com
www.odwyerpr.com

Jack O'Dwyer, President
Fay Shapiro, Publisher
Eileen Kelly, Sales Manager
John ODwyer, Advertising Sales Manager

Covers current happenings in both electronic and print media, including new PR products and accounts, PR campaigns, and books about public relations.
Cost: $295.00
Frequency: Weekly
Founded in 1970

21258 **Levin's Public Relations Report**
Levin Public Relations & Marketing
2 East Ave
Suite 201
Larchmont, NY 10538-2419

914-834-2570; Fax: 914-834-5919
www.saralevin.com

Sara B Levin, President
Sylvia Moss, Editor

Strategies, tactics for the CEO, VP Sales and Marketing seeking new marketing/public relations effectiveness.
Cost: $29.00
Frequency: Monthly
Founded in 1984

21259 **Media Relations Insider**
InfoCom Group
124 Linden Street
Oakland, CA 94607

510-596-9300
800-959-1059
www.infocomgroup.com
Facebook, Twitter, LinkedIn, RSS

Eastern and Western editions give you media news and exclusive interviews with top business journalists in your region.
Cost: $399.00
Frequency: Monthly
Mailing list available for rent

21260 **Media Relations Report**
Ragan Communications
316 N Michigan Ave
Suite 400
Chicago, IL 60601-3773

312-960-4100
800-493-4867; Fax: 312-960-4106
cservice@ragan.com
www.ragan.com

Jim Ylisela, Publisher
Mark Ragan, CEO
Cost: $28.92
Frequency: Monthly
Circulation: 1000
Founded in 1975
Mailing list available for rent
Printed in 2 colors on matte stock

21261 **MediaQuest**
MediaQuest Publishing
PO Box 9222
Boston, MA 02114-0996

617-536-5353; Fax: 617-367-9151

Barbara Kalunian, Editor/Publisher

Media placement becomes easier for PR professionals through behind the scenes interviews with leading journalists at top broadcast and print outlets.
Cost: $295.00
Frequency: Bi-Monthly
Founded in 1990

21262 **Memo to the President**
American Association State Colleges & Universities
1307 New York Ave Nw
Suite 5
Washington, DC 20005-4723

202-293-7070
800-542-2062; Fax: 202-296-5819
chilcotts@aascu.org
www.aascu.org

Edward Elnendorf, President
Susan M Chilcott, Editor
Cost: $100.00
6 Pages
Frequency: Monthly
Circulation: 1200
ISSN: 0047-6692
Founded in 1961
Printed in 2 colors on matte stock

21263 **O'Dwyers Washington Report**
JR O'Dwyer Company
271 Madison Ave
#600
New York, NY 10016-1013

212-683-2750; Fax: 212-683-2750
jack@odwyerpr.com
www.odwyerpr.com

Jack O'Dwyer, President
Kevin McCowley, Advertising Sales Manager
John ODwyer, Advertising Sales Manager

Covers Washington public relations and public affairs lobbying news.
Cost: $95.00
8 Pages

21264 **Opportunity**
Career Skills Press/Brody Communications
815 Greenwood Ave
Suite 8
Jenkintown, PA 19046-2800

215-886-1688
800-726-7936; Fax: 215-886-1699
info@brodypro.com
www.brodypro.com

Marjorie Brody, President
Miryam S Raddy, Marketing Manager

Feature products published by Career Skills Press unit.
4 Pages
Frequency: Quarterly
Circulation: 10000
Founded in 1983
Printed in 4 colors on glossy stock

21265 **PR Intelligence Report**
Lawrence Ragan Communications
316 N Michigan Ave
Suite 400
Chicago, IL 60601-3773

312-960-4100; Fax: 312-960-4106
cservice@ragan.com
www.ragan.com

Jim Ylisela, Publisher
Mark Regan, CEO

Digs below the surface to provide the details, insights and information you need to improve your career, make your next campaign a success, or avoid costly mistakes.
Cost: $279.00
8 Pages
Circulation: 1000
Founded in 1970
Printed in 2 colors on matte stock

21266 **PR News**
Phillips Business Information
4 Choke Cherry Rd
Fl 2
Rockville, MD 20850-4024

301-450-0035; Fax: 301-340-3169
www.prandmarketing.com

Matthew Schwartz, Editor
Diane Schwartz, Publisher

Briefing on the latest PR trends, what's working and what's not. We feature case studies of successful PR campaigns.
Cost: $697.00
10 Pages
Frequency: Weekly
Founded in 1944

21267 **PR Reporter**
Lawrence Ragan Communications
316 N Michigan Ave
Suite 400
Chicago, IL 60601-3773

312-960-4100
800-493-4867; Fax: 312-960-4106

cservice@ragan.com
www.ragan.com

Jim Ylisela, Publisher
Mark Ragan, President
Rebecca Anderson, Managing Editor

Weekly publication dedicated to the behavioral aspects of public relations, public affairs and communication strategies. Its quick read format keeps you up to date on the latest theories, research, public opinions, case studies and successful public relations techniques.
Frequency: Weekly
Founded in 1970

21268 PR Tactics
Public Relations Society of America
33 Maiden Ln
Suite 11
New York, NY 10038-5150

212-460-1400; Fax: 212-995-0757
helpdesk@prsa.org
www.prsa.org

Catherine Bolton, President
Philip Bonaventura, Chief Financial Officer
Cost: $75.00
32 Pages
Frequency: Monthly
Circulation: 25000
Founded in 1947
Printed in 4 colors on newsprint stock

21269 PR Watch
Center for Media and Democracy
520 University Ave
Suite 227
Madison, WI 53703-4929

608-260-9713; Fax: 608-260-9714
editor@prwatch.org
www.prwatch.org

Lisa Graves, Executive Director
Dave Ross, Secretary
Sheldon Rampton, Research Director
Kristian Knutsen, Administrative Assistant

Investigates and exposes how the public relations industry and other professional propagandists manipulate public information, perceptions and opinion on behalf of governments and special interests.
Frequency: Quarterly
Founded in 1993

21270 PR Week
114 W 26th Street
3rd Floor
New York, NY 10001

646-638-6000; Fax: 646-638-6115
www.prweek.com

Lisa Kirk, Publishing Director
Julia Hood, Editor-in-Chief

Cutting-edge newsletter of public relations.
Frequency: Weekly

21271 Partyline Publishing
PartyLine Publishing Company
35 Sutton Place
New York, NY 10022-2464

212-755-3487; Fax: 212-755-4859

Morton Yarmon, Editor
Betty Yarmon, Publisher/Editor-in-chief

Weekly media newsletter, delivered by E-mail, that informs their readers of the latest happenings in the media world...new editors, new publications, new networks, new shows on existing networks, new producers, any and all media news.
Cost: $139.50
Frequency: Weekly
Circulation: 1,400
Founded in 1960

21272 Pro Motion
Beyond the Byte
PO Box 388
Fallston, MD 21047

410-877-3524
800-861-1235; Fax: 410-877-7064

Emily Laisy, President

News of interest to Media Escort and publicists.
Cost: $12.00
4 Pages
Frequency: Quarterly
Circulation: 325
ISSN: 0886-6104
Founded in 1985
Printed in one color on matte stock

21273 Public Relations Career Opportunities
CEO Update
1575 I Street NW
#1190
Washington, DC 20005-1105

202-408-7900; Fax: 202-408-7907

James Zaniello, Editor

Public relations and publis affairs job opportunities compensating $35,000 plus nationwide.
Cost: $217.00
Frequency: Bi-Monthly
Founded in 1986

21274 Ragan's Interactive Public Relations
Lawrence Ragan Communications
316 N Michigan Ave
Suite 400
Chicago, IL 60601-3773

312-960-4100
800-878-5331; Fax: 312-960-4106
cservice@ragan.com
www.ragan.com

Jim Ylisela, Publisher

Dedicated to helping PR people navigate cyberspace.
Cost: $269.00
8 Pages
Frequency: Monthly
Circulation: 800
Founded in 1970
Printed in 2 colors on matte stock

21275 Ragan's Media Relations Report
Lawrence Ragan Communications
316 N Michigan Ave
Chicago, IL 60601-3773

312-960-4100
800-493-4867; Fax: 312-960-4106
cservice@ragan.com
www.ragan.com

Jim Ylisela, Publisher
David Murray, Editor
Diane Tillman, Marketing Manager

Content focuses on personal changes, moves and additions in various media, including television, radio and print. Offers tips on angles to take, interviews top journalists on what type of information they prefer, and continuously updates contact numbers and addresses.
Cost: $317.00
Frequency: Monthly
Founded in 1970
Printed in 2 colors on matte stock

21276 West Coast PR Newsletter
West Coast MediaNet
5928 Lindley Avenue
Encino, CA 91316-1047

818-893-3449; Fax: 818-776-1930

Darren Shuster, Publisher
Ken West, Manager

Delivers in-depth inteviews and features, new media contacts and personnel updates, tips from experts in various fields, and listings of new PR markets. Regular coverage includes media web site and book reviews, as well as how-to articles, all with a West Coast angle.
Cost: $75.00
16 Pages
Frequency: 12 issues
Circulation: 1M

Magazines & Journals

21277 ACH Product & Marketing Handbook for Financial Institutions & Companies
NACHA: The Electronic Payments Association
13450 Sunrise Valley Drive
Suite 100
Herndon, VA 20171

703-561-1100; Fax: 703-787-0996
info@nacha.org
www.nacha.org

Jane Larimer, CEO
Marcie Haitema, Chairperson

Designed for full financial institutions and companies to assist them in understanding ACH products and services-their benefits, risk management considerations, marketing techniques and FAQs from both corporate and consumer perspectives.
Cost: $70.00
Frequency: Annual+

21278 Communication World
Int'l Association of Business Communicators
601 Montgomery Street
Suite 1900
San Francisco, CA 94111

415-544-4700; Fax: 415-544-4747
cwmagazine@iabc.com
www.iabc.com

Natasha Nicholson, Executive Editor
Sue Khodarahmi, Managing Editor
Sue Cavallaro, Production Editor

Covers the latest in communication research, technology and trends through in-depth reports and insightful interviews.
Cost: $150.00
Frequency: Bi-Monthly
Founded in 1970

21279 Currents
Council for Advancement & Support of Education
1307 New York Ave Nw
Suite 1000
Washington, DC 20005-4726

202-393-1301; Fax: 202-387-4973
memberservicecenter@case.org
www.case.org

Deborah Bangiorno, Editor
Donald Falkenstein, Vice President of Finance
Will Hayden, Production Coordinator
John Lippincott, President
Marla Misek, Senior Editor

Offers information on campus fund raising, public relations,and alumni administration.
Cost: $115.00
Circulation: 15000
Founded in 1974

21280 **International Public Relations Review**
18 W Church Street
Saint Frederick, MD 31701
229-567-8074; Fax: 912-845-2991
John Reed, Publisher
Public relations international communications issues for senior level PR professionals.

21281 **Jack O'Dwyer's Services Report**
JR O'Dwyer Company
271 Madison Ave
Suite 600
New York, NY 10016-1013
212-683-2750; Fax: 212-683-2750
jack@odwyerpr.com
www.odwyerpr.com
Jack O'Dwyer, Owner
John ODwyer, Advertising Sales Manager
Eileen Kelly, Sales Manager
Information on film, videotape, database and release distribution industries which serve public relations professionals.
Cost: $45.00
Frequency: Monthly
Circulation: 4500
Founded in 1980

21282 **Jack O'Dwyers Washington Report**
JR O'Dwyer Company
271 Madison Ave
Suite 600
New York, NY 10016-1013
212-683-2750; Fax: 212-683-2750
jack@odwyerpr.com
www.odwyerpr.com
Jack O'Dwyer, Owner
John ODwyer, Advertising Sales Manager
Cost: $60.00
Frequency: Weekly
Founded in 1970

21283 **Managing Media Relations in a Crisis**
NACHA: The Electronic Payments Association
13450 Sunrise Valley Drive
Suite 100
Herndon, VA 20171
703-561-1100; Fax: 703-787-0996
info@nacha.org
www.nacha.org
Jane Larimer, CEO
Marcie B Haitema, Chairperson
This guide is designed to assist your organization to develop, test and execute a crisis communication plan. Understand how to address the issues, know whom to call and in what order to alert them, which vendors you can count on to help, and how to develop a means to track the crisis as it grows or abates.
Cost: $30.00

21284 **Public Relations Quarterly**
Howard Penn Hudson
44 W Market Street
PO Box 311
Rhinebeck, NY 12572-311
845-876-2081
800-572-3451; Fax: 845-876-2561
www.hudsonsdirectory.com
Howard Penn Hudson, Editor/Publisher
Elaine F Newman, Executive Editor
Berecah Sullivan, Circulation Manager
Nichole Latierre, Marketing Manager
Independent public relations magazine, now 48 years old, presenting articles and columns on the theory and process of public relations and communications.
Cost: $65.00
Frequency: Quarterly
ISSN: 0033-3700
Founded in 1955
Printed in on matte stock

21285 **Public Relations Review**
Elsevier
6277 Seaharbor Drive
Orlando, FL 32887
877-839-7126
www.elsevier.com
Jan D Achenbach, Editor-In-Chief
Bill Godfrey, Chief Information Officer
David Clark, Senior Vice President
Covers public relations, education, government, survey research, public policy, history and bibliographies.
Cost: $110.00
Frequency: 12 issues
Circulation: 1M
ISSN: 0363-0111

21286 **Public Relations Strategist**
Public Relations Society of America
33 Maiden Ln
Suite 11
New York, NY 10038-5150
212-460-1400; Fax: 212-995-0757
william.murray@prsa.org
www.prsa.org
Gary McCormick, Chairman/CEO
William Murray, President & COO
Philip Bonaventura, CFO
Jeneen Garcia, Vice President
With emphasis on the issues and trends affecting public relations management, it examines the changing concepts and challenges current practices with relevant, original and thought-provoking articles.
Cost: $100.00
Frequency: 4 issues per ye
Circulation: 20538
Founded in 1947

21287 **Public Relations Tactics**
Public Relations Society of America
33 Maiden Ln
Suite 11
New York, NY 10038-5150
212-460-1400; Fax: 212-995-0757
helpdesk@prsa.org
www.prsa.org
Gary McCormick, Chairman/CEO
Gale Spreter, Marketing Manager
Alison Stateman, Managing Editor
Catherine A Bolton, Executive Director
Philip Bonaventura, Chief Financial Officer
News, trends and how-to information for public relations people.
Cost: $75.00
Frequency: Monthly
Circulation: 20538
Founded in 1947

21288 **Reputation Management**
Editorial Media & Marketing International
708 3rd Avenue
Frnt 2
New York, NY 10017-4201
212-687-5260
www.prcentral.com
Kara T Ingraham, Publisher/COO
Editorial focuses on finance, marketing, human resources, government and society. Highlights domestic and international corporate news presenting observations and perspectives vital to the industry.
Cost: $52.00
Frequency: Bi-Monthly
Circulation: 12M
Founded in 1995

Trade Shows

21289 **American Society of Health Care Marketing and Public Relations Trade Show**
1 N Franklin Street
31st Floor
Chicago, IL 60606-3421
773-327-1064; Fax: 312-422-4579
Lauren Barnett, Executive Director
Sixty booths of communications, printing, computer equipment, public relations and fund raising consultants in the health care profession.
600 Attendees
Frequency: September

21290 **Arthur W Page Society**
Arthur W Page Society
317 Madison Ave
Suite 1607
New York, NY 10017-5201
212-400-7959; Fax: 347-474-7399
www.awpagesociety.com
Facebook, Twitter, YouTube,RSS
Roger Bolton, President
Gary Shepper, Chairman
Valerie Di Maria, Secretary
Frequency: Annual/September
Founded in 1986

21291 **National Hispanic Market Trade Show and Media Expo (Se Habla Espanol)**
Hispanic Business Inc
5385 Hollister Avenue
Suite 204
Santa Barbara, CA 93111
800-806-4268; Fax: 805-964-5539
www.expomediainc.com
Facebook, Twitter, LinkedIn
John Pasini, Cfo/Coo
Annual show of 100 exhibitors of market/research, media, advertising, public relations, information services and recruitment.
1500 Attendees

21292 **National School for Public Relations**
15948 Derwood Rd
Rockville, MD 20855
301-519-0496; Fax: 301-519-0494
info@nspra.org
www.nspra.org
Mildred Wainger, Administration Services
Offers information and news for professionals in the field of public relations.
600 Attendees
Frequency: July

21293 **Strategic Media Relations Conference**
Ragan Communications
316 N Michigan Avenue
Chicago, IL 60601
312-960-4100
800-878-5331; Fax: 312-960-4106
cservice@ragan.com
www.reaganfoundation.org
Showcase of best practices for winning top media coverage in a new era. Learn how peers have garnered more ink, managed crises, built their brands and gone global. Attend pre- and post-conference sessions that provide career-boosting skills in crisis survival, media training, online media relations, PR writing,

persuasive communications, PR management, digital PR and pitching stories.
Frequency: March

Directories & Databases

21294 **Adweek Directory**
Prometheus Global Media
770 Broadway
New York, NY 10003-9595

212-493-4100; Fax: 646-654-5368
www.prometheusgm.com

Richard D. Beckman, CEO
James A. Finkelstein, Chairman
Madeline Krakowsky, Vice President Circulation
Tracy Brater, Executive Director Creative Service

Adweek Directories Online is where you will find searchable databases with comprehensive information on ad agencies, brand marketers and multicultural media.
Frequency: Annual
Circulation: 800
Founded in 1981

21295 **Bacon's Newspaper & Magazine Directories**
Cision U.S., Inc.
322 South Michigan Avenue
Suite 900
Chicago, IL 60604

312-263-0070
866-639-5087
info.us@cision.com
us.cision.com

Joe Bernardo, President & CEO
Heidi Sullivan, VP & Publisher
Valerie Lopez, Research Director
Jessica White, Research Director
Rachel Farrell, Research Manager

Two volume set listing all daily and community newspapers, magazines and newsletters, news service and syndicates, syndicated columnists, complete editorial staff listings of each publication provided, covers U.S., Canada, Mexico, and Carribean.
Cost: $350.00
4,700 Pages
Frequency: Annual
ISSN: 1088-9639
Founded in 1951
Printed in one color on matte stock

21296 **Bacon's Radio/TV/Cable Directory**
Cision U.S., Inc.
332 South Michigan Avenue
Suite 900
Chicago, IL 60604

312-263-0070
866-639-5087
info.us@cision.com

Joe Bernardo, President & CEO
Heidi Sullivan, VP & Publisher
Valerie Lopez, Research Director
Jessica White, Research Director
Rachel Farrell, Research Manager

Includes comprehensive coverage for contact and programming information for more than 3,500 televsion networks, cable networks, television syndicators, television stations, and cable systems in the United States and Canada.
Cost: $350.00
Frequency: Annual
ISSN: 1088-9639
Printed in one color on matte stock

21297 **Burrelle's Media Directory**
BurrellesLuce
75 E Northfield Rd
Livingston, NJ 07039-4532

973-992-6600
800-631-1160; Fax: 973-992-7675
inquiry@burrellesluce.com
www.burrellesluce.com
Facebook, Twitter, LinkedIn, RSS

Robert C Waggoner, CEO

Approximately 60,000 media listings in North America. Listings cover newspapers, magazines (trades and consumer), broadcast, and internet outlets.
Cost: $795.00
Frequency: Annual

21298 **Corporate Yellow Book**
Leadership Directories
104 5th Ave
New York, NY 10011-6901

212-627-4140; Fax: 212-645-0931
www.leadershipdirectories.com

David Hurvitz, CEO

Contact information for over 48,000 executives at over 1,000 companies and more than 9,000 board members and their outside affiliations.
Cost: $360.00
1,400 Pages
Frequency: Quarterly
ISSN: 1058-2098
Founded in 1986

21299 **Leadership Library in Print**
Leadership Directories
104 5th Ave
New York, NY 10011-6901

212-627-4140; Fax: 212-645-0931
info@leadershipdirectories.com
www.leadershipdirectories.com

David Hurvitz, CEO

Complete set of all 14 leadership directories. Provides subscribers with complete contact information for the 400,000 individuals who constitute the institutional leadership of the US.
Cost: $2300.00
Frequency: Semiannually
Founded in 1996

21300 **O'Dwyer's Directory of Corporate Communications**
JR O'Dwyer Company
271 Madison Ave
Suite 600
New York, NY 10016-1013

212-683-2750; Fax: 212-683-2750
www.odwyerpr.com

Jack O'Dwyer, Owner
John ODwyer, Advertising Sales Manager

Public relations departments are profiled that represent the United States companies that are listed on the New York Stock Exchange.
Cost: $110.00
400 Pages
Frequency: Annual

21301 **PR News**
Phillips Business Information
7811 Montrose Road
Potomac, MD 20854
301-340-2100
feedback@healthydirections.com
www.healthydirections.com

This database offers information on public relations issues.
Cost: $597.00
Frequency: 48 issues

21302 **PR Newswire**
150 E 58th Street
31st Floor
New York, NY 10155-0002

212-355-0090; Fax: 212-832-9406

This comprehensive database offers current news, financial news, earnings statements, mergers, acquisitions, proxy contests and general features pertaining to the public relations industry.
Frequency: Directory

21303 **Public Relations Tactics**
Public Relations Society of America
33 Maiden Ln
New York, NY 10038-5150

212-460-1400; Fax: 212-995-0757
william.murray@prsa.org
www.prsa.org

Catherine Bolton, Manager

List of products and services used by public relations professionals worldwide.
Frequency: Annual June

21304 **Public Relations Tactics: Register Issue/The Blue Book**
Public Relations Society of America
33 Maiden Ln
New York, NY 10038-5150

212-460-1400; Fax: 212-995-0757
william.murray@prsa.org
www.prsa.org

Catherine Bolton, Manager

About 17,000 public relations practitioners in business government education etc., who are members.
Cost: $100.00
Frequency: Annual July

21305 **Publicity at Your Finger Tips**
Federal Systems
PO Box 298-L
Oliver Springs, TN 37840-0298

865-483-3579

Offers a comprehensive list of magazines, newspapers and other publications in the United States that provide publicity for businesses, churches and charitable organizations.
Cost: $24.95

21306 **Salem Press Online Platform**
Grey House Publishing
4919 Route 22
PO Box 56
Amenia, NY 12501

800-221-1592; Fax: 201-968-0511
csr@salempress.com
online.salempress.com

The new Salem Press platform houses more than 500 titles including all of Salem's Health, Literature, History and Science titles in addition to select titles from the Grey House Publishing and H.W. Wilson product lines. Online access is free with each print purchase and includes an unlimited number of simultaneous users and remote access.

21307 **Staffing Industry Supplier Directory and Buyers Guide**
Staffing Industry Analysts
881 Fremont Ave
Suite A3
Los Altos, CA 94024-5637

650-948-9303
800-950-9496; Fax: 650-232-2360

Ron Mester, Manager

Complete listing of suppliers and products for temporary help, placement and recruiting firms

in the staffing industry.
Cost: $89.50
295 Pages
Frequency: Annual
ISBN: 1-883814-11-1

Industry Web Sites

21308 **http://gold.greyhouse.com**
G.O.L.D Grey House OnLine Databases
Grey House Pubishing's online database platform, GOLD, offers Quick Search, Keyword Search and Expert Search for most business sectors including public relations and media markets. The GOLD platform makes finding the information you need quick and easy - whether you're a novice searcher or an experienced database user. All of Grey House's directory products are available for subscription on the GOLD platform.

21309 **www.absolutelypr.com**
Absolutely Public Relations
Results-driven media relations - local, trade, national.

21310 **www.achieva.info**
ACHIEVA

21311 **www.aem.org**
Construction Equipment Advertisers and Public
Relations Council
A council of AEM that works to promote marketing, sales and advertising of construction equipment.

21312 **www.bloomgross.com**
Bloom Gross & Associates
Executive recruitment firm with corporate communications, public relations, marketing/branding/market research, and direct marketing/sales promotion practice areas.

21313 **www.case.org**
Council for the Advancement and Support of Ed.
Offers information on campus fund raising, public relations and alumni administration.

21314 **www.cof.org**
Council on Foundations
Non profit trade association for foundations

21315 **www.greyhouse.com**
Grey House Publishing
Authoritative reference directories for most business sectors including public relations and media markets. Users can search the online databases with varied search criteria allowing for custom searches by product category, geographic area, sales volume, keyword, subject and more. Full Grey House catalog and online ordering also available.

21316 **www.iabc.com**
International Association of Business Communicators
An international association for members who are professionals in organizational communications and public relations. Accepts advertising.

21317 **www.instituteforpr.com**
Institute for Public Relations
To improve the effectiveness of organizations by advancing the professional knowledge and practice of public relations through research and education.

21318 **www.mediaaccessgroup.com**
Media Access Group

21319 **www.multicultural.com**
Multicultural Marketing Resources
A place where corporate executives can find diverse resources, experts and information on how to market to multicultural (ethnic and niche) consumer markets.

21320 **www.niri.org**
National Investor Relations Institute
Professional association of corporate officers and investors relations consultants.

21321 **www.petersgrouppr.com**
PetersGroup Public Relations
Provides a full range of marketing and public relations programs to national and international businesses. The agency works closely with technology clients ranging from Funded start-ups to Fortune 500 companies, to integrate the right mix of research, strategy, positioning and media to help customers meet their ongoing business and communication goals.

21322 **www.progressivepr.com**
PPR Communications

21323 **www.prpublishing.com**
Public Relations Publishing Company
Case studies, research and trends in public relations and information on issues of importance to PR professionals.

21324 **www.prsa.org**
Public Relations Society of America
A major professional association of public relations practitioners.

21325 **www.prweek.com**
PR Week

21326 **www.silveranvil.org**
Silver Anvil Resource Center
Online database of public relations campaigns.

21327 **www.washingtonpost.com**
Washington Post

21328 **www.wepr.org**
Women Executives in Public Relations
Provides a support network for women in public relations. Offers grants and scholarships for courses in public relations and for college students studying communications.

Associations

21329 Alliance for Audited Media
48 W. Seegers Road
Arlington Heights, IL 60005-3913

224-366-6939
800-285-2220
auditedmedia.com
Facebook, Twitter, LinkedIn, YouTube, Instagram

Tom Drouillard, President, CEO & Managing Director
Brian Condon, EVP, Commercial Development
Scott Hanson, EVP, Audit Service
Mark Wachowicz, EVP, Business Innovation

A nonprofit, member-based organization that works with media companies, advertising technology providers, ad agencies, and advertisers to provide them with independently verified data and information critical to evaluating and purchasing media.
Founded in 1914

21330 Alliance of Area Business Publishers
2512 Artesia Blvd
Suite 200
Redondo Beach, CA 90278

310-379-8261; Fax: 310-379-8283
aabpstaff@gmail.com
bizpubs.org
RSS

C. James Dowden, Executive Director

Represents metropolitan area and state wide business to business publications with conventions, newsletters, and other services.
1.2M Members
Founded in 1979

21331 American Book Producers Association
23 Waverly Place
#6B
New York, NY 10003

917-620-9440
office@abpaonline.org
abpaonline.org
Facebook

Richard Rothschild, President
Nancy Hall, Vice President
Ellen Stamper, ABPA Administrator

The trade association for independent book producers in the U.S. and Canada increases the publishing industry's awareness of members capabilities and exchanges information on improving business. Member companies develops concepts for books and other publications and produce them for publishers, corporations, nonprofits, and individuals.
Founded in 1980

21332 American Booksellers Association
333 Westchester Avenue
Suite S202
White Plains, NY 10604

800-637-0037; Fax: 914-417-4013
info@bookweb.org
www.bookweb.org
Facebook, Twitter, Instagram

Oren Teicher, CEO

Trade organization pledged to protecting the well-being of book retailers and promoting the availability of books.
2000 Members
Founded in 1900
Mailing list available for rent

21333 American Library Association
50 East Huron St.
Chicago, IL 60611-2795

312-944-6780
800-545-2433; Fax: 312-440-9374
ala@ala.org
www.ala.org
Facebook, Twitter

Sylvia Norton, Executive Director

To provide leadership for the development, promotion, and improvement of library and information services and the profession of librarianship in order to enhance learning and ensure access to information for all.
65000 Members
Founded in 1876

21334 American Society of Journalists & Authors
355 Lexington Avenue
15th Floor
New York, NY 10017-6603

212-997-0947; Fax: 212-937-2315
asjaoffice@asja.org
asja.org
Facebook, Twitter, LinkedIn

Holly Koenig, Executive Director
Gemma Rainer, Assoc. Director
1200 Members
Founded in 1948

21335 Antiquarian Booksellers Association of America
20 West 44th St
Suite 507
New York, NY 10036

212-944-8291; Fax: 212-944-8293
sbenne@abaa.org
www.abaa.org
Facebook, Twitter, RSS

Susan Benne, Executive Director
Thomas Goldwasser, President
Mary Gilliam, Vice-President/ Secretary
Charles Kutcher, Treasurer

A trade association of rare book dealers.
480 Members
Founded in 1949

21336 Associated Church Press
109 State St.
Louisville, KY 40206

503-583-8655
www.theacp.org
Facebook, Twitter

Jay Blossom, President

Aims to share ideas and concerns in religious publishing and to stimulate higher standards of religious journalism to exert a more positive influence.
240 Members
Founded in 1916

21337 Association for Information and Image Management
8403 Colesville Rd.
Suite 1100
Silver Spring, MD 20910

301-587-8202
800-477-2446; Fax: 301-587-2711
aiim@aiim.org
www.aiim.org
Facebook, Twitter, LinkedIn, Google+

Peggy Winston, President & CEO
Georgina Clellend, Chief Operating Officer
Renee Martin, Dircetor, Event Marketing
Boshia Smith, Membership Manager

Members are users and manufacturers of equipment and supplies of the information and image industry.
10M Members
Founded in 1943

21338 Association of American Publishers (AAP)
455 Massachusetts Avenue NW
Suite 700
Washington, DC 20001

202-347-3375; Fax: 202-347-3690
info@publishers.org
publishers.org
Facebook, Twitter, LinkedIn

Maria A. Pallante, President & CEO

AAP is the trade association for the US book publishers, providing advocacy and communications on behalf of the industry. AAP represents the industry's priorities on policy, legislative and regulatory issues regionally, nationally and worldwide. These include protection of intellectual property rights and worldwide copyright enforcement, digital and new technology issues, funding for education and libraries, tax and trade, censorship and literacy.
400+ Members
Founded in 1970

21339 Association of Catholic Publishers
4725 Dorsey Hall Dr.
Suite A, PMB 709
Ellicott City, MD 21042

410-988-2926; Fax: 410-571-4946
info@catholicpublishers.org
www.catholicpublishers.org

Therese Brown, Executive Director

Catholic publishers and content producers.

21340 Association of Directory Publishers
PO Box 209
Traverse City, MI 49685

800-267-9002; Fax: 770-462-0457
info@adp.org
www.adp.org
Facebook, Twitter, LinkedIn, YouTube

Cindi Aldrich, President & CEO
240 Members
Founded in 1898

21341 Association of Free Community Papers
135 Old Cove Rd.
Suite 210
Liverpool, NY 13090

877-203-2327; Fax: 781-459-7770
loren@afcp.org
www.afcp.org
Facebook, Twitter, LinkedIn, YouTube, Instagram

Loren Colburn, Executive Director

Offers national classified advertising placement services; conducts charitable programs, sponsors competition, compiles statistics.
250 Members
Founded in 1951

21342 Association of Medical Media
405 North Stanwick Rd.
Moorestown, NJ 08057

888-978-0943
info@ammonline.org
www.ammonline.org
Facebook, Twitter, LinkedIn

Todd Von Deak, Executive Director

Members of this nonprofit are medical publishing firms, content providers and others in the medical communications field.

21343 **Association of University Presses**
1412 Broadway
Suite 2135
New York, NY 10018
212-989-1010; Fax: 212-989-0275
info@aaupnet.org
www.aupresses.org
Facebook, Twitter
Peter Berkery, Executive Director
Members are university presses and a limited number of presses of non-degree-granting scholarly institutions.
125 Members
Founded in 1937
Mailing list available for rent: 2.2M names

21344 **Authors Coalition of America**
PO Box 929
Pentwater, MI 49449
231-869-2011; Fax: 313-882-3047
dkelly@authorscoalition.org
www.authorscoalition.org
Dorien Kelly, Administrator
An organization of U.S. based authors and creators united to receive and distribute non-title specific reprographic royalties to member organizations, assist in further development of collective licensing programs and act for the general benefit of authors. The ACA is an association of twenty independent authors' organizations representing text writers, songwriters, visual artists, illustrators and photographers.
80000 Members
Founded in 1994

21345 **BRB Publications, LLC**
3200 W. Pleasant Run Road
Suite 420
Lancaster, TX 75146
800-929-3811; Fax: 800-929-4981
brb@brbpublications.com
www.brbpublications.com
A premier publisher of references and websites used for locating public records. BRB's books and electronic products point the way to over 28,000 government agencies, and 3,500 public record vendors who maintain, search, or retrieve public records.

21346 **Book Industry Study Group (BISG)**
232 Madison Avenue
Suite 1400
New York, NY 10016
646-336-7141
info@bisg.org
bisg.org
Facebook, Twitter, LinkedIn
Brian O'Leary, Executive Director
US book trade association offering information, best practices standards, research and events for the US book publishing industry.
164 Members
Founded in 1975

21347 **Book Manufacturers' Institute (BMI)**
PO Box 731388
Ormond Beach, FL 32173
386-986-4552; Fax: 386-986-4553
info@bmibook.com
bomi.memberclicks.net
Matt Baehr, Executive Director
Since 1933, the Book Manufacturers' Institute, Inc. (BMI) has been the leading nationally recognized trade association of the book manufacturing industry. BMI member companies annually produce the great majority of books ordered by the U. S. book publishing industry. Today, BMI is a vital part of the industry, playing a leading role by providing an intra-industry communications link among book manufacturers, publishers, suppliers and governmental bodies.
90 Members
Founded in 1933

21348 **Community of Literary Magazines and Presses**
154 Christopher St.
Suite 3C
New York, NY 10014
212-741-9110; Fax: 212-741-9112
info@clmp.org
www.clmp.org
Facebook, Twitter
Mary Gannon, Executive Director
Organization serving independent literary publishers.
Founded in 1967

21349 **Denver Publishing Institute**
University of Denver
Sturm Hall 386
2000 East Asbury Ave.
Denver, CO 80208
303-871-2570; Fax: 303-871-2501
pi-info@du.edu
www.du.edu/publishinginstitute
Facebook, Twitter, YouTube
Jill Smith, Director
Jennifer Conder, Associate Director
Margaret Shaheen, Program Administrator
A certificate program that combines workshops in editing and marketing with lecture/teaching sessions conducted by leading experts from all areas of publishing.
Founded in 1864

21350 **Digital Content Next**
530 7th Ave.
Mezz. 1
New York, NY 10018
646-473-1000; Fax: 646-473-0200
info@digitalcontentnext.org
digitalcontentnext.org
Facebook, LinkedIn
Jason Kint, CEO
Trade association of digital content companies.
Founded in 2001

21351 **Guild of Book Workers**
521 5th Avenue
New York, NY 10175
secretary@guildofbookworkers.org
www.guildofbookworkers.org
Cheryl Ball, Membership Chair
Bex Caswell, President
Brian Beidler, Vice President
Rebecca Smyrl, Secretary
Laura Bedford, Treasurer
To broaden public awareness of the hand book arts, to stimulate commissions of fine bindings, and to stress the need for sound book conservation and restoration.
900+ Members
Founded in 1906

21352 **Idealliance**
1800 Diagonal Road
Suite 320
Alexandria, VA 22314
703-837-1070; Fax: 703-837-1072
info@idealliance.org
www.idealliance.org
Dick Ryan, CEO
David Steinhardt, Managing Director
Jordan Gorski, Senior Vice President
Tar Bowman, Director, Finance & Operations
Evelyn Helminen, Dir., Media, Marketing & Comm.
Idealliance, a global think tank, is a non-profit graphic communications industry organization with 12 strategically located offices around the world. Idealliance serves brands, content and media creators, manufacturers, service providers in print and packaging, fulfillment, mail delivery, marketing, material suppliers, and technology partners worldwide.
3000+ Members
Founded in 1966

21353 **Impact Publishers, Inc.**
5674 Shattuck Avenue
Oakland, CA 94609
800-748-6273; Fax: 800-652-1613
customerservice@newharbinger.com
www.newharbinger.com
Facebook, Twitter, LinkedIn
Offers practical, reader-friendly help on a wide variety of personal interpersonal matters: relationships, divorce recovery, parenting, stress, personal growth, and mental health.
Founded in 1973

21354 **Independent Book Publishers Association**
1020 Manhattan Beach Blvd.
Suite 204
Manhattan Beach, CA 90266
310-546-1818; Fax: 310-546-3939
info@ibpa-online.org
www.ibpa-online.org
Facebook, Twitter, LinkedIn, Pinterest
Angela Bole, Chief Executive Officer
Provides cooperative marketing programs, education and advocacy within the publishing industry.
4000+ Members
Founded in 1983

21355 **Independent Free Papers of America**
104 Westland Drive
Columbia, TN 38401
931-922-4171
www.ifpa.com
Facebook, Twitter
Douglas Fry, Executive Director
Bestows awards and compiles statistics.
300 Members
Founded in 1980

21356 **Jenkins Group**
1129 Woodmere Ave.
Suite B
Traverse City, MI 49686
231-933-0445
800-706-4636; Fax: 231-933-0448
www.bookpublishing.com
Jerrold R. Jenkins, Chairman and CEO
James J. Kalajian, President and COO
Provides comprehensive marketing and custom book publishing services for independent and small press book publishers.
160 Members
Founded in 1996

21357 **Magazine Publishers of America**
757 Third Avenue
11th Floor
New York, NY 10017
212-872-3700; Fax: 212-888-4217
mpa@magazine.org
www.magazine.org
Facebook, Twitter, LinkedIn, YouTube,Pinterest
Promotes magazines as an advertising medium. Provides information services and assistance to members in areas of circulation marketing.
240 Members
Founded in 1919

21358 National Association of Hispanic Publications
529 14th St. NW
Suite 923
Washington, DC 20045

202-662-7250
nahp.org

Fanny Miller, President

Trade advocacy organization promoting Spanish-language newspapers, magazines and related media.

21359 National Association of Publishers' Representatives
PO Box 441
New York, NY 10024

332-255-2530; Fax: 212-721-1620
info@napronline.org
www.napronline.org
Facebook, LinkedIn

Darren Dunay, President
Craig Pitcher, Vice President
Gerald Massa, Secretary
Marlys Fox, Treasurer

Provides information for publishers' representatives selling advertising space.
250 Members
Founded in 1950

21360 National Music Publishers Association
975 F Street, NW
Suite 375
Washington, DC 20004

202-393-6672; Fax: 202-393-6673
admin@mpa.org
www.nmpa.org
Facebook, Twitter, YouTube, Instagram

David Israelite, President & CEO
Danielle Aguirre, Executive Vice President
Charlotte Sellmyer, Senior Vice President

An advocate for the protection of music copyrights.
800 Members
Founded in 1917

21361 National Newspaper Association
101 S Palafox
Unit 13323
Pensacola, FL 32591

850-542-7087
membership@nna.org
www.nnaweb.org
Facebook, Twitter, RSS

Lynne Lance, Executive Director

Industry trade newspaper.
2100 Members
Founded in 1885

21362 National Paper Trade Association
330 N Wabash Avenue
Suite 2000
Chicago, IL 60611

312-321-4092
800-355-6782; Fax: 312-673-6736
npta@gonpta.com
www.gonpta.com
Twitter, LinkedIn, YouTube

Bob Forsberg, Chairman
Jan Gottesman, 1st Vice Chair
Scott Hider, 2nd Vice Chair
Matthew Bruno, EVP
John Hagrove, Treasurer

Representing distributors and suppliers of paper, packaging and facility supplies companies.
2000 Members
Founded in 1903

21363 News Media Alliance
4401 N. Fairfax Drive
Suite 300
Arlington, VA 22203

571-366-1000
info@newsmediaalliance.org
www.newsmediaalliance.org
Facebook, Twitter, LinkedIn, YouTube

David Chavern, President & CEO
Robert Walden, Chief Financial Officer
Rebecca Frank, VP, Research & Insights
Danielle Coffey, SVP & General Counsel
Paul Boyle, SVP, Public Policy

Formerly known as the Newspaper Association of America, the News Media Alliance represents large daily papers, non-daily/small-market publications, as well as digital and multiplatform products across North America.
2000 Members
Founded in 1992

21364 Science Fiction & Fantasy Writers of America
PO Box 3238
Enfield, CT 06083-3238

Home Page: www.sfwa.org
Facebook, Twitter

Kate Baker, Executive Director

Professional organization for writers of fantasy, science fiction and related genres. Host of the Nebula Awards.

21365 Society for Collegiate Journalists
610 West Fourth St.
Buena Vista University
Storm Lake, IA 50588

712-749-2023
scjnationaloffice@gmail.com
scjnational.org
Facebook, Twitter

Andrea Frantz, Executive Director

A collegiate journalism organization.
800 Members
Founded in 1909

21366 Society for Scholarly Publishing
One Parkview Plaza
Suite 800
Oakbrook Terrace, IL 60181

303-422-3914; Fax: 720-881-6102
info@sspnet.org
www.sspnet.org
Facebook, Twitter, LinkedIn, RSS

A group that represents scholarly publications, such as journals, university publications and magazines.
800 Members
Founded in 1978

21367 Software & Information Industry Association
1090 Vermont Ave NW
6th Floor
Washington, DC 20005-4905

202-289-7442
800-388-7478; Fax: 202-289-7097
piracy@siia.net
www.siia.net
Facebook, Twitter, LinkedIn

Ken Wasch, President
Tom Davin, Senior Vice President
Eric Fredell, Vice President

Members are microcomputer software firms. Services include data collection program, software protection, contracts reference disk, conferences and lobbying.
1200 Members
Founded in 1984

21368 Special Libraries Association
7918 Jones Branch Dr.
Ste. 300
McLean, VA 22102

703-647-4900; Fax: 703-506-3266
sla@sla.org
www.sla.org
Facebook, Twitter, LinkedIn, YouTube, RSS

Amy Lestition Burke, Executive Director

International association of information professionals who work in special libraries serving business, research, government and institutions that produce specialized information.
7000 Members
Founded in 1856

21369 Specialized Information Publishers Association
1090 Vermont Avenue NW
Sixth Floor
Washington, DC 20005-4095

202-289-7442
800-356-9302; Fax: 202-289-7097
www.siia.net
Facebook, Twitter, LinkedIn

Nancy Brand, Managing Director

International trade association serving the interests of publishers of newsletters and specialized information services.
450 Members
Founded in 1977
Mailing list available for rentat $65 per M

21370 The Association of Publishers for Special Sales
PO Box 9725
Colorado Springs, CO 80932-0725

719-924-5534; Fax: 719-213-2602
community.bookapss.org
Facebook, Twitter, Google+

A nonprofit trade association for independent presses and self-publishers who want to produce better books and market them successfully. SPAN offers a monthly newsletter with information-rich articles and great benefits.
1300 Members
Founded in 1996

21371 Women's National Book Association
PO Box 237
FDR Station
New York, NY 10150

212-208-4629
866-610-9622; Fax: 212-208-4629
info@wnba-books.org
wnba-books.org
Facebook, Twitter, LinkedIn, RSS

Rachelle Yousuf, President
Natalie Obando-Desai, Vice President

An organization of women and men in all occupations allied to the book industry.
800 Members
Founded in 1917

Newsletters

21372 AAP Monthly Report
Association of American Publishers
71 5th Ave
Suite 2
New York, NY 10003-3004

212-255-1407; Fax: 212-255-7007
jtagler@publishers.org
www.pspcentral.org

John Tagler, VP/Executive Director
Sara Pinto, Director
Kate Kolendo, Project Manager

A report offering information and news to the publishing community.
Cost: $800.00

21373 American Book Producers Association Newsletter
American Book Producers Association
23 Waverly Place
#6B
New York, NY 10003

917-620-9440
office@abpaonline.org
abpaonline.org

Richard Rothschild, President
Ellen Stamper, ABPA Administrator

The trade association for independent book producers in the U.S. and Canada increases the publishing industry's awareness of members capabilities and exchanges information on improving business. Member companies develops concepts for books and other publications and produce them for publishers, corporations, nonprofits, and individuals.
6 Pages
Frequency: Monthly
Circulation: 2500
Founded in 1980
Printed in 2 colors on matte stock

21374 Augsburg Fortress Newsletter for Church Leaders
Augsburg Fortress
PO Box 1209
Minneapolis, MN 55440-1209

612-330-3300
800-328-4648; Fax: 800-722-7766
www.augsburgfortress.org

Roderick Olson, Publisher

Monthly newsletter designed to equip pastors, church leaders, Christian leaders, Christian Educators and volunteers with valuable and timely resources, promotions, and ministry ideas.
Frequency: Monthly eNewsletter

21375 BISG Newsletter
Book Industry Study Group (BISG)
232 Madison Avenue
Suite 1400
New York, NY 10016

646-336-7141
info@bisg.org
bisg.org

Brian O'Leary, Executive Director

Weekly email newsletter sent to 3,800 members each Tuesday.

21376 Book Arts
Center for Book Arts
28 W 27th St
Suite 3
New York, NY 10001-6906

212-481-0295; Fax: 212-481-9853
info@centerforbookarts.org
www.centerforbookarts.org
Facebook, Twitter, YouTube,Flickr

Alexander Campos, Executive Director

Center news and activities.
Founded in 1974

21377 Book News
American Book Producers Association
23 Waverly Place
#6B
New York, NY 10003

917-620-9440
office@abpaonline.org
abpaonline.org

Richard Rothschild, President
Ellen Stamper, ABPA Administrator

Monthly newsletter is part of the membership benefits; provides a transcript of the monthly member luncheon's speaker, as well as association and member news.
6 Pages
Frequency: Monthly
Founded in 1980

21378 Bookselling This Week
American Booksellers Association
333 Westchester Avenue
Suite S202
White Plains, NY 10604

800-637-0037; Fax: 914-417-4013
info@bookweb.org
www.bookweb.org
Facebook, Twitter, Instagram

Oren Teicher, CEO
Frequency: Weekly
Circulation: 10000

21379 Educational Marketer
Simba Information
60 Long Ridge Rd
Suite 300
Stamford, CT 06902-1841

203-325-8193
888-297-4622; Fax: 203-325-8975
customerservice@simbainformation.com
www.simbanet.com/

Linda Kopp, Publisher

Reports on the entire educational publishing spectrum from el-hi to College. It covers the complete range of print and electronic tools including software, and multimedia materials. It details mergers, acquisitions, financial reports, distribution, adoption and enrollment trends, legislative issues
Cost: $650.00
8 Pages
Founded in 1989
Printed in 4 colors

21380 Exchange
Association of American University Presses
Rm 602
30 W 36th St
New York, NY 10018-8063

212-989-1010; Fax: 212-989-0275
aaupnet.org/

Hollis Holmes, Publisher
Peter J Givler, Executive Director
Rachel Weiss, Marketing Manager
Latasha Watters, Marketing Coordinator

Reports on issues relevant to scholarly publishing.
Cost: $10.00
16 Pages
Frequency: Quarterly

21381 Footprints Newsletter
Evangelical Christian Publishers Association
4816 S Ash Ave
Suite 101
Tempe, AZ 85282-7735

480-966-3998; Fax: 480-966-1944
info@ecpa.org
www.ecpa.org

Mark Kuyper, President
Kelly Gallagher, VP
Dave Bird, Marketing

An international, not-for-profit, trade organization serving its industry by promoting excellence and professionalism, sharing relevant data, stimulating Christian fellowship, raising the effectiveness of member houses, and equipping them to meet the needs of the changing marketplace.
Frequency: Monthly
Circulation: 280

21382 Fusion Magazine
Newspaper Association of America
4401 Wilson Blvd
Suite 900
Arlington, VA 22203-4195

571-366-1000; Fax: 571-366-1195
www.naa.org
Facebook, Twitter, LinkedIn, YouTube,RSS

Reggie Hall, Senior VP
James M Moroney, Chairman
Robert Dickey, Secretary
Donna Barrett, Treasurer
Robert M Nutting, Vice Chairman

This newsletter focuses on the business of diversity within the newspaper industry. In it you will find new strategies for making diversity work in advertising, news and editorial, circulation, marketing, production, human resources and the business office.
Frequency: Quarterly
Mailing list available for rent

21383 Guild of Book Workers Newsletter
Guild of Book Workers
521 5th Avenue
New York, NY 10175

Home Page: guildofbookworkers.org

Cheryl Ball, Membership Chair
Bexx Caswell-Olson, President
Brien Beidler, Vice President
Rebecca Smyrl, Secretary
Lang Ingalls, Newsletter Publisher

Information for the book arts field, including Guild of Book Workers news, conference and chapter reports, supply sales, and a calendar of events.
Frequency: Bi-Monthly
Circulation: 800
Founded in 1906

21384 Hotline
1825 Ponce de Leon
Suite 429
Coral Gables, FL 33133

703-992-9339
800-356-9302; Fax: 703-992-7512
sipa@online.com
www.hotline.com

Henry Greene, Executive Director

Furthers the professional and economic interests of members. Future plans include seminars, research and representing members before federal agencies. Available only to members.
Founded in 1977
Printed in one color on matte stock

21385 Independent Book Publishers Association Newsletter
Independent Book Publishers Association
1020 Manhattan Beach Blvd
Suite 204
Manhattan Beach, CA 90266

310-546-1818; Fax: 310-546-3939
info@ibpa-online.org
www.ibpa-online.org
Facebook, Twitter, LinkedIn, Flickr,RSS

Terry Nathan, Executive Director
Lisa Krebs, Assistant Director
Steve Mettee, Board Chair
Roy M Carlisle, Treasurer
Florrie Kichler, President

Publicity, sales, legal, and marketing opportunities and news articles for independent book publishers.
Frequency: Monthly
Circulation: 6000

21386 Independent Publishers Trade Report
PO Box 176
Southport, CT 06490-176

860-669-5848; Fax: 203-332-7629

Henry Berry, Publisher

News and information for independent publishers, monthly column in the COSMEP Newsletter.

21387 Independent Small Press Review
WHW Publishing
930 Via Fruteria
Santa Barbara, CA 93110-2322

609-408-8000
www.ifpa.com

Gary Rudy, Executive Director

Offers a comprehensive look at the concerns and issues of the small business publisher.

21388 John Kremer's Book Marketing Tip of the Week
Open Horizons Publishing
PO Box 2887
Taos, NM 87571

575-751-3398
800-796-6130; Fax: 575-751-3100
www.bookmarket.com

John Kremer, Editor
Robert Sanny, Advertising/Sales Manager

Email newletter offering new PR and sales leads and tips every week.
Frequency: Weekly
Founded in 1982
Mailing list available for rent

21389 Lifelong Learning Market Report
Simba Information
60 Long Ridge Rd
Suite 300
Stamford, CT 06902-1841

203-325-8193
888-297-4622; Fax: 203-325-8975
customerservice@simbainformation.com
www.simbanet.com

Linda Kopp, Publisher

News and analysis for content and service providers of corporate training and professional development materials. Includes news on merger and aczuisitions, industry financial performance and trends, product development and distribution.
Cost: $625.00
Founded in 1989

21390 MBR Bookwatch
Midwest Book Review
278 Orchard Drive
Oregon, WI 53575-1129

608-835-7937
mbr@execpc.com
www.midwestbookreview.com

James A Cox, Editor-in-Chief

A monthly online book review publication that will showcase the reviews and commentaries of those MBR editors and specialized reviewers who've demonstrated expertise in their field. Bookwatch will also feature author interviews and editorial observations of various aspects of the publishing world, offered by knowledgeable and articulate participants.
140 Pages
Frequency: Monthly
Circulation: 30,000
Founded in 1976

21391 National Association of Professional Print Buyers
15050 NE 20th Avenue
Suite A
North Miami, FL 33181-1123

305-956-9563

Vincent Millardi, Publisher

Accepts advertising.
Cost: $315.00
296 Pages
Frequency: Monthly

21392 NewsInc.
Cole Group
PO Box 719
Pacifica, CA 94044-719

650-557-9595; Fax: 650-475-8479
admin@colegroup.com

David M Cole, Publisher/Editor
Marge Wetmore, Circulation Manager

The weekly newsletter about the business of the newspaper business, written for media executives and the investments community. subscriptions available in digital or print formats, as well as for archive access.
Cost: $99.00
Frequency: 48/Yr, for Digital Access
Founded in 1989

21393 Newsletter on Newsletters
Newsletter on Newsletters
PO Box 348
Rhinebeck, NY 12572-0348

845-876-5222; Fax: 845-876-4943
www.newsletteronnewsletters.com

Paul Swift, Editor

Graphics, editorial, promotions, management and reports on the entire newsletter industry.
Cost: $275.00
Founded in 1970

21394 Online Publishing Update E-Newsletter
Newspaper Association of America
4401 Wilson Blvd
Suite 900
Arlington, VA 22203-4195

571-366-1000; Fax: 571-366-1195
www.naa.org
Facebook, Twitter, LinkedIn, YouTube,RSS

Reggie Hall, Senior VP
James M Moroney, Chairman
Robert Dickey, Secretary
Donna Barrett, Treasurer

A round-up of news, research, industry trends, best practices and more, focusing on items of interest to newspaper and digital media executives. Online Publishing Update e-newsletter is published every Monday, Wednesday and Friday.
Frequency: 3x/Weekly

21395 PMA Newsletter
Publishers Marketing Association
627 Aviation Way
Manhattan Beach, CA 90266-7107

310-372-2732; Fax: 310-374-3342
info@ibpa-online.org
www.atlanticpublishers.com

Terry Nathan, Executive Director

Publishing law, copyrighting, marketing, business management all directed toward the independent book publishing community.
Frequency: Monthly
Circulation: 10000
Founded in 1983

21396 Personal Composition Report
Graphic Dimensions
134 Caversham Woods
Pittsford, NY 14534-2834

585-381-3428

Michael Kleper, Publisher

Covers all aspects of electronic publishing and imaging including news, reviews and in-depth analysis. Begun in 1979 by Professor Michael Kleper of RIT, the newsletter has provided consistent, valuable information for its readers.
Cost: $100.00
16 Pages
Frequency: Annual
Printed in one color on matte stock

21397 Platform News You Can Use
Newspaper Association of America
4401 N. Fairfax Drive
Suite 300
Arlington, VA 22203

571-366-1000
info@newsmediaalliance.org
www.newsmediaalliance.org

David Chavern, President & CEO
Michael Maloon, VP, Innovation & Communications
Rebecca Frank, VP, Research & Insights
Lindsey Loving, Manager, Communications
Jennifer Peters, Reporter, Trends & Insights

Members-only e-newsletter with developments on large tech platforms and their relationships with the news industry and journalism.
Frequency: Monthly

21398 Pleasures of Publishing
Columbia University
2960 Broadway
New York, NY 10027-6900

212-854-1754; Fax: 212-749-0397
www.columbia.edu

Robert Kasdin, Executive VP
Mathew Martg, Marketing

Industry news.

21399 Professional Publishing Report
Simba Information
60 Long Ridge Rd
Suite 300
Stamford, CT 06902-1841

203-325-8193; Fax: 203-325-8915
customerservice@simbainformation.com
www.simbanet.com

Linda Kopp, Publisher
Charlie Friscia, Marketing
John Fuller, Executive Editor

Newletter focuses on the $10 billion professional publishing industry. Features in-depth analysis of each of the four major professional publishing categories: scientific/technical, medical, legal and business. Provides revenue breakdowns by media and market, merger and acquisition news, and analysis of market trends.
Cost: $715.00
Founded in 1989

21400 Publishers Monthly Domestic Sales
Association of American Publishers
50 F St Nw
Suite 400
Washington, DC 20001-1565

202-347-3375; Fax: 202-347-3690
info@publishers.org
www.publishers.org

Tom Allen, CEO
Katie Blough, Editor
Patricia Schroeder, President
Tina Jordan, Vice President
Kate Kolendo, Project Manager

Sales charts, index and rates for the publishing community.
Frequency: Monthly
Founded in 1970

21401 **Publishers Multinational Direct**
Direct International
1501 Third Avenue
New York, NY 10028-2101
212-861-4188; Fax: 212-628-5070
Alfred Goodloe, Editor
National and international coverage of the publishing community including printing, prepress and direct marketing.
Cost: $195.00
Frequency: Monthly

21402 **Publishers Report**
National Association of Independent Publishers
PO Box 430
Highland City, FL 33846-430
863-648-4420; Fax: 836-648-4420
naip@aol.com
www.publishersreport.com
Betsy A Lampe, Publisher
Provides a clearinghouse of information on small/independent publishing for its members. Accepts advertising. Departments include: 'New Books, Audios & Videos,' It's a Date,' 'NAIP Book Review,' 'New Media Sources,' 'Wanted,' 'In the Know,' 'F41,' and various others helpful for new publishers and self-publishers.

21403 **Publishers' Auxiliary**
National Newspaper Association
900 Community Drive
Springfield, IL 62703
217-241-1400; Fax: 217-241-1301
membership@nna.org
www.nnaweb.org
Facebook, Twitter
Matthew Paxton, President
Tonda Rush, Director, Public Policy
Stan Schwartz, Managing Editor
Providing personnel announcements, new technology, economic trends, and new publicaiton and distribution methods for executives in the newpaper industry.
Founded in 1865

21404 **Publishing Markets**
Reed Business Information
275 Washington St
Newton, MA 02458-1611
617-964-3030; Fax: 617-558-4327
www.designnews.com
Deborah Selsky, Publisher
San Buchan, Editor
Economic and demographic trends that affect the book publishing market.
Cost: $129.00

21405 **Publishing Poynters**
Para Publishing
PO Box 8206-240
Santa Barbara, CA 93118-8206
805-968-7277
800-727-2782; Fax: 805-968-1379
www.parapublishing.com
Facebook, Twitter
Dan Poynter, Editor
Becky Carbone, Production Manager
Book publishing news and ideas: marketing, promotion and distribution.
Cost: $9.95
20 Pages
Frequency: Monthly
Circulation: 16000
ISSN: 1530-5694
Founded in 1969
Printed in one color

21406 **Report on Preschool Programs**
Business Publishers,Inc
2222 Sedwick Drive
Durham, NC 27713
800-223-8720; Fax: 800-508-2592
custserv@bpinews.com
www.bpinews.com
The one source to turn to for timely, accurate coverage of important developments in Head Start, child care, health care, special education and much more.
Cost: $357.00
8 Pages
Founded in 1963

21407 **SPAN**
Small Publishers Association of North America
1618 W Colorado Avenue
Colorado Springs, CO 80904-4029
719-475-1726; Fax: 719-471-2182
www.spannet.org
Marilyn Ross, Editor
Cathy Bowman, Production Manager
Includes money-making articles and book industry information.
24 Pages
Frequency: Monthly
Circulation: 4000
Founded in 1996

21408 **SPAN Internet Newsletter**
Small Publishers Association of North America
PO Box 9725
Colorado Springs, CO 80932-0725
719-924-5534; Fax: 719-213-2602
www.spannet.org
Facebook, Twitter
Marilyn Ross, Executive Director/Editor
Tom Ross, VP
The SPAN Internet Newsletter features timely and useful information on many aspects of writing and the publishing industry, including articles on book marketing and publicity in addition to providing links to industry related Websites.
Frequency: Monthly
Circulation: 4000
Founded in 1996

21409 **Small Publisher Co-Op**
Nigel Maxey
1521 SE Palm Court
PO Box 1620
Stuart, FL 34994-1620
772-287-8117
spcoop@hotmail.com
www.spco-op.com
Niyel Maxey, President/Editor
Kevin Hawken, Member Service Manager
This monthly newsletter offers a guide to publishing and marketing books, reports, periodicals, etc.
Cost: $15.00
Circulation: 5900

21410 **Span Connection**
Small Publishers Association of North America
PO Box 1306
Buena Vista, CO 81211-1306
719-395-4790; Fax: 719-395-8374
www.spannet.org
Scoot Flora, Editor
Scoot Flora, CEO
Wide variety of news and information about small-scale and individual publishing.
Cost: $105.00
Frequency: Monthly
Circulation: 4000
Founded in 1996

21411 **Specialty Directory Publishing Market Forecast**
Simba Information
60 Long Ridge Rd
Suite 300
Stamford, CT 06902-1841
203-325-8193
888-297-4622; Fax: 203-325-8975
info@simbanet.com
www.simbanet.com
Kathy Mickey, Managing Editor/Analyst
David Goddard, Senior Editor/Analyst
Michael Norris, Senior Editor/Analyst
Complete market size, revenue and growth figures and forecasts including revenues driven by electronic products and exclusive reanking of leading publishers by revenue.
Cost: $495.00
Frequency: Anually
Founded in 1989

21412 **The Bookwoman**
Women's National Book Association
PO Box 237
FDR Station
New York, NY 10150
212-208-4629; Fax: 212-208-4629
www.wnba-books.org
Facebook, Twitter, LinkedIn, RSS
Joan Gelfand, President
Mary Grey James, Vice President/President-Elect
Ruth Light, Secretary
Margaret E Auer, Treasurer
Shannon Janeczek, The Bookwoman, Managing Editor
Bi-annual journal for members of the Women's National Book Association. Stories of interest for people in the world of books. Book review are includes, how-to information and chapter news from across the United States. Ad space available.
2 Pages
Frequency: Biennial
Circulation: 1000
Founded in 1917

21413 **dailyXchange**
Newspaper Association of America
4401 N. Fairfax Drive
Suite 300
Arlington, VA 22203
571-366-1000
info@newsmediaalliance.org
www.newsmediaalliance.org
David Chavern, President & CEO
Michael Maloon, VP, Innovation & Communications
Rebecca Frank, VP, Research & Insights
Lindsey Loving, Manager, Communications
Jennifer Peters, Reporter, Trends & Insights
Members-only e-newsletter with relevant Alliance and industry news from the past day.
Frequency: Daily

21414 **newsXchange**
Newspaper Association of America

4401 N. Fairfax Drive
Suite 300
Arlington, VA 22203

571-366-1000
info@newsmediaalliance.org
www.newsmediaalliance.org

David Chavern, President & CEO
Michael Maloon, VP, Innovation & Communications
Rebecca Frank, VP, Research & Insights
Lindsey Loving, Manager, Communications
Jennifer Peters, Reporter, Trends & Insights

News brief from the News Media Alliance with news media industry news, as well as information on digital, advertising, trends, and Alliance products and services.
Frequency: Weekly (Wed.)

Magazines & Journals

21415 **American Libraries Magazine**
50 East Huron Street
Chicago, IL 60611

800-545-2433; Fax: 312-944-7841
membership@ala.org
www.ala.org

Keith Fields, Publisher, ALA Executive Director
Mary Mackay, Marketing & Sales Director
Camila Alire, ALA President

News and information on legislation concerning libraries, new publications and technology issues
Cost: $70.00
Frequency: 10x/Yr $ incl in ALA dues
Circulation: 60,000
ISSN: 0002-9769
Founded in 1876

21416 **Book Dealers World**
North American Bookdealers Exchange
PO Box 606
Cottage Grove, OR 97424

541-942-7455; Fax: 541-942-7455
www.bookmarketingprofits.com

Al Galasso, Editorial Director
Steve Sherman, Publisher

The book marketing magazine for independent publishers and mail order entrepreneurs. A publication of the North American Book Dealers Exchange, an international book marketing organization, specializing in cooperative opportunities at trade shows, in mail order, press releases and more.
Cost: $45.00
32 Pages
Frequency: Quarterly
Circulation: 10000
ISSN: 1098-8521
Founded in 1980
Printed in on newsprint stock

21417 **Book Promotion Hotline**
Ad-Lib Publications
51 1/2 W Adam
PO Box 1102
Fairfield, IA 52556-3226

515-472-6617
800-669-0773; Fax: 641-472-3186

Marie Kiefer, Editor/Publisher

Provides media contacts and other marketing sources of interest to the publisher/marketing trade.
Cost: $150.00
4 Pages
Frequency: Weekly
Circulation: 1,000

21418 **Booklist**
American Library Association
50 E Huron St
Chicago, IL 60611-2788

312-280-2518
800-545-2433
kfiels@ala.org
www.ala.org

Keith Michael Fiels, Executive Director
Mary Ellen Quinn, Editor

The purpose of this guide is to provide information on materials worthy of consideration for purchase by small and medium sized public libraries.
Cost: $79.95
Founded in 1876

21419 **Christian Retailing**
Strang Communications Company
600 Rinehart Rd
Lake Mary, FL 32746-4868

407-333-0600; Fax: 407-333-7100
www.strang.com

Stephen Strang, CEO
Tircia Stafford, Circulation Director

A trade journal designed to inform Christian bookstore owners about books, music and gifts, videos, etc. Also it features topics to help retailers run a successful business.
Cost: $75.00
72 Pages
Frequency: Monthly
Circulation: 10000
Founded in 1975

21420 **Circulation Management**
PRIMEDIA Intertec-Marketing & Professional Service
PO Box 4235
Stamford, CT 06907-0235

212-475-2212; Fax: 203-358-5823
www.circman.com

Roberta Thomas, Publisher

Subscriptions, renewals, direct mail, list selection, circulation planning, data management, fulfillment and list management.
Cost: $39.00
Frequency: Monthly
Circulation: 10,000

21421 **Collegiate Journalist**
Society for Collegiate Journalists
1584 Wesleyan Drive
Virginia Wesleyan College
Virginia Beach, VA 23502-5599

757-455-3419; Fax: 757-461-5025

J D Tarpley, Publisher
William Ruehlmann, CEO/President
Adam Earnheardt, Editor

For editors of yearbooks, magazines and newspapers.
Cost: $5.00
28 Pages
Frequency: Monthly

21422 **Complete Guide to Self-Publishing**
Communication Creativity
425 Cedar
Buena Vista, CO 81211-0909

719-395-8659
800-331-8355; Fax: 719-395-8374

Marilyn Ross, Publisher
Matthew Sullivan, Editor

The most comprehensive resource available about the business of publishing. Offers everything you need to know to write, publish, promote and sell books.
Cost: $19.99
521 Pages
ISBN: 1-582970-91-2

21423 **Desktop Publishers Journal**
462 Boston Street
Topsfield, MA 01983

FAX 800-492-1014

Barry Harrigan, Contact

Offers a comprehensive array of news, analysis, features and reviews on the latest products and services on the market today.
Cost: $15.00
Frequency: 12 issues

21424 **Editor & Publisher**
Editor & Publisher International Yearbook
11 W 19th Street
10th Floor
New York, NY 10011-4234

212-291-1259; Fax: 212-691-7287
www.mediainfo.com

Michael Parker, President

Covers all facets of the newspaper business today and is regarded as the bible of the newspaper industry.
Cost: $184.00
Frequency: 46 issues
Founded in 1884

21425 **Editorial Eye**
EEI Communications
66 Canal Center Plz
Suite 200
Alexandria, VA 22314-5507

703-683-0683; Fax: 703-683-4915
www.eeicom.com

James T Degrafferei, CEO
Robin Cormier, VP
Candee Wilson, Director
Linda B. Jorgensen, Editor

Offering information on written excellence, editorial information and communication skills for readers.
Cost: $125.00
Frequency: Monthly
Founded in 1972

21426 **Electronic Publishing**
PennWell Publishing Company
10 Tara Boulevard
5th Floor
Nashua, NH 03062-2880

603-891-0123; Fax: 603-891-0539
genepri@pennwell.com
www.electronic-publishing.com

Gene Pritchard, Publisher

For those who communicate in print, including service bureaus, printers, prepress houses and desktop publishers, it provides latest products, news and related developments.
Cost: $45.00
Frequency: Monthly
Circulation: 68,441

21427 **F&W Publications**
1507 Dana Avenue
Cincinnati, OH 45207

513-396-6160; Fax: 513-531-1025
www.writersdigest.com

Jeff Lapin, President

Articles that reflect the current state of American freelance writing.
72 Pages
Frequency: 8 per year
Circulation: 85,000
ISBN: 7-148602-50-8
Founded in 1930

21428 **FLEXO Magazine**
Flexographic Technical Association Inc

900 Marconi Avenue
Ronkonkoma, NY 11779-7212

631-737-6020; Fax: 631-737-6813
www.flexography.org

Robert Moran, President
Christian Bonawandt, Editor

Up-to-date on the changes and advances in the rapidly-expanding flexographic industry.
Cost: $55.00
Frequency: Monthly

21429 **Folio: Magazine for Magazine Management**
Red 7 Media, LLC
10 Norden Place
Norwalk, CT 06855

203-854-6730; Fax: 203-854-6735
tsilber@red7media.com
www.foliomag.com

Stefanie Botelho, Associate Editor
Kerry Smith, President /CEO
Dan Trombetto, Group Creative Director
Tony Silber, General Manager
John Ellertson, Director Advertising Sales Manager

Written for the people who run the nation's magazines. Offers authoritative intelligence on the magazine market to enable industry professionals to navigate the widening range of strategic options. Every issue delivers features on the people and technologies that are transforming the magazine business, along with useful columns and departments, thought-provoking analysis and tactical advice for building successful magazines.
Cost: $96.00
Frequency: Monthly
Circulation: 11550
Founded in 1971

21430 **ForeWord Reviews**
ForeWord Magazine
425 Boardman Avenue
Traverse City, MI 49684

231-933-3699; Fax: 231-933-3899
www.forewordreviews.com

Victoria Sutherland, Owner
Stacy Price, Director Advertising Sales

Review books and other servies for authors and small publishers.
Cost: $40.00
Frequency: Monthly
Circulation: 20000
Founded in 1998
Printed in 4 colors on 6 stock

21431 **Guild of Book Workers Journal**
Guild of Book Workers
521 5th Avenue
New York, NY 10175

secretary@guildofbookworkers.org
www.guildofbookworkers.org

Cheryl Ball, Membership Chair
Bex Caswell, President
Brian Beidler, Vice President
Rebecca Smyrl, Secretary
Laura Bedford, Treasurer

Published annually by the Guild of Book Workers and contains articles that address our members' interests in the arts and crafts of the book, including traditional bookbinding, paper making and decorating, conservation and restoration, calligraphy, the making of artists' books, and printing.
900+ Members
Frequency: Annually
Founded in 1906

21432 **INFO FLEX**
Flexographic Technical Association Inc
3920 Veterans Memorial Highway
Suite 9
Bohemia, NY 11716

631-737-6020; Fax: 631-737-6813
memberinfo@flexography.org
www.flexography.org

Mark Cisternino, President
Greg Platt, Chairman
Dan Doherty, Treasurer
Jason Barrier, Director

The show floor boasts 200+ booths manned by flexography's leading suppliers, as well as a presentation theater, and educational pavilion, a social event and more
Frequency: Annual/May

21433 **Independent Publisher Magazine**
Jenkins Group
1129 Woodmere Avenue
Suite B
Traverse City, MI 49686-4275

231-933-0445
800-706-4636; Fax: 231-933-0448
www.bookpublishing.com

Jerrold R Jenkins, President
Jim Barmes, Editor
Andrew Pargel, Marketing Manager

Trade journal for the independent publishing, community, university presses, librarians, bookstores and professionals.
Cost: $40.00
Frequency: Monthly
Circulation: 8000
Founded in 1988
Mailing list available for rent: 42M names
Printed in 4 colors on glossy stock

21434 **Information Publishing: Business/ Professional Markets & Media**
Simba Information
60 Long Ridge Rd
Suite 300
Stamford, CT 06902-1841

203-325-8193; Fax: 203-325-8915
www.simbanet.com

Linda Kopp, Publisher
Donna Devall, Marketing Director
Charlie Friscia, Director of Advertising

Demonstrates how publishers are profiting from media. Discover the opportunities in newsletters, directories, books, magazines, journals and electronic information services. More than 300 pages of information and analysis, 100 tables and charts, financial and operating information on more than 50 key publishing companies, 16 principal information markets reviewed in-depth, with five year forecasts by market and by media.
Cost: $1995.00
Founded in 1989

21435 **Inside Edge**
International Publishing Management Association
1205 W College Street
Liberty, MO 64068

816-781-1111; Fax: 660-781-2790
ipmainfo@ipma.org
www.ipma.org

Larry Aaron, Executive Director
Susan Murphy, Editor
Jack Welch, CEO
Lea Holt, Director

Offers information on the association's activities, industry trends, and corporate publishing facility profiles.
Cost: $50.00
24 Pages
Frequency: Monthly
Circulation: 1500
Mailing list available for rent: 2M names

21436 **MultiMedia & Internet @Schools**
Information Today
143 Old Marlton Pike
Medford, NJ 08055-8750

609-654-6266
800-300-9868; Fax: 609-654-4309
custserv@infotoday.com
www.infotoday.com

Thomas H Hogan, President
Roger R Bilboul, Chairman Of The Board
John C Yersak, Vice President
Sue Hogan, Director
John Brokenshire, CFO

A practical guide for K-12 library media specialists, technology coordinators and other educators with information on how to get high-performance learning from technology-based school products, services and resources.
Cost: $ 39.95
Frequency: 6 issues/yr
Mailing list available for rent: 4M names
Printed in 4 colors on glossy stock

21437 **New Age Publishing and Retailing Alliance Trade Journal**
PO Box 9
Eastsound, WA 98245-0009

360-376-2702; Fax: 360-376-2704

Marilyn McGuire, Executive Director
Carole Scarfuto, Administrative Director

Covers the publishing and retailing trades.
Frequency: Bi-Monthly
Circulation: 10,000

21438 **NewsInc**
PO Box 719
Pacifica, CA 94044-719

650-557-9595; Fax: 650-557-9696

David Cole, Publisher/Editor
Cost: $147.00
Frequency: Weekly
Founded in 1989

21439 **Newspapers & Technology**
Conley Magazines
1623 Blake Street
Suite 250
Denver, CO 80202

303-575-9595; Fax: 303-575-9555
www.newsandtech.com/

Mary Van Meter, Publisher
Chuck Moozakis, Editor-in-Chief
Tara McMeekin, Editor
Hays Goodman, Associate Editor/Webmaster

Newspapers & Technology is a monthly trade publication for newspaper publishers and department managers involved in applying and integrating technology. Written by industry experts, News & Tech provides regular coverage of the following departments: prepress, press, postpress and new media.
Circulation: 16,874
Mailing list available for rent

21440 **Poets & Writer's Magazine**
Poets & Writers
150 Broadway
New York, NY 10038-4381

212-566-2424; Fax: 212-587-9673
editor@pw.org
www.pettuswilliams.com

Marvin K Pettus, President
Christine Cassidy, Marketing Director
William Hayes, Finance Executive

Interviews, essays, grants and awards, practical information for poets and writers.
Cost: $19.95
Circulation: 60000

21441 **Progressive Review**
1312 18th Street NW
5th Floor
Washington, DC 20036

202-835-0770; Fax: 202-835-0779
news@prorev.com
www.prorev.com

Sam Smith, Editor
Frequency: Monthly
Founded in 1964

21442 **Publish**
462 Boston Street
Suite 310
Topsfield, MA 01983

978-887-6855; Fax: 978-887-9245

Barry Harrigan, Owner

21443 **Publishers Weekly**
PO Box 51593
Harlan, IA 51593

800-278-2991; Fax: 712-733-8019
pwycustserv@cdsfulfillment.com
www.publishersweekly.com
Facebook, Twitter, LinkedIn, RSS

Jim Milliot, Co-Editorial Director
Michael Coffey, Co-Editorial Director
Diane Roback, Children's Book Editor
Louisa Ermelino, Reviews Director
Calvin Reid, News Editor

PW is the international journal of book publishing and bookselling including business news, reviews and bestseller lists targeted at publishers, booksellers, librarians and literary agents.
Frequency: Weekly
Founded in 1872

21444 **Publishing & Production Executive**
Mark Hertzog
1500 Spring Garden Street
Suite 1200
Philadelphia, PA 19130

215-238-5300; Fax: 215-238-5457

Allison Schill Eckel, Managing Editor
Gretchen Kirby, Editor

Addresses technological trends and issues relevant to print production managers specializing in books, magazines, catalogs, agency or corporate communications.
Frequency: 12 per year
Circulation: 30,000

21445 **Quill**
PO Box 94080
Palatine, IL 60094-v

765-653-3333
800-789-1331; Fax: 800-789-8955
www.quill.com

21446 **Searcher: Magazine for the Database Professional**
Information Today
143 Old Marlton Pike
Medford, NJ 08055-8750

609-654-6266
800-300-9868; Fax: 609-654-4309
custserv@infotoday.com
www.infotoday.com
Facebook, Twitter

Thomas H Hogan, President
Roger R Bilboul, Chairman Of The Board

Explores and deliberates on a comprehensive range of issues important to the professional database researcher. Combines evaluations of data content with discussions of delivery media.
Cost: $86.95
Frequency: 10 issues/yr
Mailing list available for rent: 4M names
Printed in 4 colors on glossy stock

21447 **Student Press Review**
Columbia University
2960 Broadway
New York, NY 10027-6900

212-854-1754; Fax: 212-749-0397
cspa@columbia.edu
www.columbia.edu

Robert Kasdin, Executive VP
Helen F Smith, Editor
Edmund J Sullivan, Publisher

Reports and advises on high school and college student media. Offers how-to articles and features to improve student newspapers, magazines and yearbooks in schools, colleges, and universities.
Frequency: Quarterly
Circulation: 2200
Founded in 1925

21448 **Volt Report on Directory Publishing**
Volt Directory Marketing
1800 Byberry Road
Suite 800
Huntingdon Valley, PA 19006-3520

800-677-3839; Fax: 215-938-5549

Kathy Wolden, Editor

As the monitor of the directory publishing industry, the Morgan report provides news on the people, companies, products and opportunities shaping the industry today. Includes practical how-to guidance on key facets of the directory publishing process as well as strategic overviews.
Cost: $95.00
12 Pages
Frequency: Monthly

21449 **Writer Magazine**
21027 Crossroads Circle
PO Box 1612
Waukesha, WI 53187-1612

262-796-8776
800-533-6644; Fax: 262-796-1615
corporate.kalmbach.com

Sylvia Burack, Publisher
Elfrieda Abbe, Executive Vice President
Chuck Croft, Executive Vice President

Practical guide to instruct, inform, and inspire writers as they work toward the goal of publication. Writers of short stories, novels, poetry, plays or science fiction, readers will find straightforward advice, up-to-date market lists and tips on manuscript submission.
Cost: $29.00
Frequency: Monthly
Circulation: 43000
Founded in 1987

21450 **Writer's Digest**
F&W Publications
4700 E Galbraith Rd
Cincinnati, OH 45236-2726

513-531-2690
800-258-0929; Fax: 513-531-1843

David Nussbaum, CEO
Jim Ogle, Chief Financial Officer
Kate Rados, Marketing Director
Stacie Berger, Communications Director

Information and how to tips for freelance writers.
Cost: $19.96
Frequency: Monthly
Founded in 1920

Trade Shows

21451 **AAP General Annual Meeting**
Association of American Publishers (AAP)
455 Massachusetts Avenue NW
Suite 700
Washington, DC 20001-2777

202-347-3375; Fax: 202-347-3690
info@publishers.org
www.publishers.org
Twitter

Karen Abramson, President & CEO
Tina Jordan, Vice President
Allan R Adler, VP for Legal & Government Affairs
Jay Diskey, Executive Director, School Division
Gail Kump, Director, Membership Marketing

Discussion topics include the state of digital content, distribution channels and copyright protection as seen through the prism of publishers and their historic partners.
200 Members
Frequency: Annual

21452 **ADP Annual Convention and Partners Trade Show**
Association of Directory Publishers
116 Cass St.
Traverse City, MI 49684

800-267-9002; Fax: 231-486-2182
adp.org/node/669
Facebook, Twitter, LinkedIn, YouTube

Cindi A. Aldrich, President & CEO
Valerie Donn, Director of Meetings & Events
Frequency: Annual

21453 **American Library Association Annual Conference**
American Library Association
50 E Huron Street
Chicago, IL 60611

800-545-2433
customerservice@ala.org
www.ala.org

Loriene Roy, President
Keith Michael Fiels, Executive Director

Annual meeting and exhibits of books, periodicals, reference works, audio visual equipment, films, data processing services, computer hardware and software, library equipment and supplies.

21454 **American Medical Publishers' Association Annual Meeting**
71 Fifth Avenue
2nd Floor
New York, NY 10003

212-255-0200; Fax: 212-255-7007
jtagler@publishers.org
www.pspcentral.org
LinkedIn

John Tagler, VP/Executive Director
Sara Pinto, Director
Kate Kolendo, Project Manager

Information provided to medical publishing field.
Frequency: Annual
Founded in 1960

21455 **Association of American University Presses Conference**
Association of American University Presses

71 W 23rd Street
Suite 901
New York, NY 10010-3264

212-989-1010; Fax: 212-989-0275
annualmeeting@aaupnet.org
www.aaupnet.org

Peter Givler, Executive Director
Timothy Muench, Assistant Director

Annual conference and exhibits of equipment, supplies and services for scholarly publishing divisions of colleges and universities.
125 Attendees
Frequency: Annual

21456 Association of College and Research Libraries
American Library Association
50 E Huron Street
Chicago, IL 60611-5295

312-280-2511
800-545-2433; Fax: 312-280-2520
customerservice@ala.org
www.ala.org/acrl

Mary Ellen Davis, Executive Director

Two hundred exhibitors with computers and web products, audiovisual products, furniture and library equipment.
3000 Attendees
Frequency: Biennial
ISSN: 0099-0086
Founded in 1978
Mailing list available for rent

21457 Association of Free Community Papers
1630 Miner Street
Suite 204, Box 1989
Idaho Springs, CO 80452

877-203-2327; Fax: 781-459-7770
www.afcp.org

Craig Mullin, Executive Director
Brianne Janes, Graphic Designer

Exhibits for publishers of free circulation papers and shopping/advertising guides.
Frequency: Annual
Founded in 1951

21458 BISG Annual Meeting
Book Industry Study Group (BISG)
232 Madison Avenue
Suite 1400
New York, NY 10016

646-336-7141
info@bisg.org
bisg.org

Brian O'Leary, Executive Director

Annual meeting of members of the Book Industry Study Group (BISG).
150 Members
Frequency: Annual/April
Founded in 1975

21459 Book Expo America
Reed Exhibitions
383 Main Avenue
Norwalk, CT 06851

203-404-4800
800-840-5614
cmuller@reedexpo.com
www.bookexpoamerica.com
Facebook, Twitter, LinkedIn, YouTube,Pinterest

Courtney Muller, Event Manager
Cathy Glickstein, Registration
Lisa Montanaro, Sales Executive

Sponsored by American Booksellers Association and Association of American Publishers. More than 2,000 exhibits, 500 authors, over 60 conference sessions as well as a special area for rights business, all the latest titles across genres, uncover hidden gems, network, and meet the industry contacts to put you instantly on top of what you need to know for your business and job.
Frequency: May/June
Founded in 2000

21460 Digital Book Printing Forum
Interquest Ltd.
513-D Stewart Street
Charlottesville, VA 22902

434-979-9945; Fax: 434-979-9959
iquest@inter-quest.com
www.inter-quest.com

David Davis, Director

Interquest analysts will present key results from the company's latest research in the field.
Frequency: March

21461 Digital Book World

FAX new

Jeremy Greenfield, Editorial Director
Raymond Kyle, Business Development Manager
Gary Lynch, Group Publisher
Amanda Malek, Online Product Development

A year-round platform offering educational and networking resoruces for consumer publishing professionals and their partners - including agents ,booksellers and technology vendors - online and in person

21462 FFTA Annual Forum & INFO FLEX Exhibition
Flexographic Technical Association Inc
3920 Veterans Memorial Highway
Suite 9
Bohemia, NY 11716

631-737-6020; Fax: 631-737-6813
memberinfo@flexography.org
www.flexography.org

Mark Cisternino, President
Joe Tuccitto, Director of Education
Doreen Monteleone, Director Environmental Affairs
Sharon Cox, Director of Marketing
Katie Dubois, Creative Services Manager

Presents the most promising technological advances and emerging market opportunities to keep you and your company up to date.
1600+ Attendees

21463 FOLIO Show
Red 7 Media, LLC
10 Norden Place
Norwalk, CT 06855

203-854-6730; Fax: 203-854-6735
www.folioshow.com/
Facebook, Twitter, LinkedIn

Tony Silberg, Publisher/General Manager
John Ellertson, Group Sales Director
Magan Sprenger, Account Executive
Tania Babiuk, Account Executive
Kerry Smith, President

Biennial show and exhibits of publishing supplies, paper, printing equipment, color separators, fulfillment houses, lists and related equipment, supplies and services to the magazine and book publishing trades.
7,000 Attendees

21464 Guild of Book Workers Standards of Excellence Seminar
Guild of Book Workers
521 5th Avenue
New York, NY 10175

secretary@guildofbookworkers.org
www.guildofbookworkers.org

Cheryl Ball, Membership Chair
Bex Caswell, President
Brian Beidler, Vice President
Rebecca Smyrl, Secretary
Laura Bedford, Treasurer

The Seminar on Standards of Excellence in Hand Bookbinding is the annual Guild of Book Workers conference where participants attend presentations by leading experts in the fields related to the book and paper arts. Tours of binderies, conservation facilities, rare book libraries and papermaking establishments are regularly arranged in conjunction with the event.
900+ Members
Frequency: Annual
Founded in 1906

21465 InfoCommerce
InfoCommerce Group Inc
2 Bala Plaza
Suite 300
Bala Cynwyd, PA 19004

610-649-1200; Fax: 610-471-0515
rchristensen@infocommercegroup.com
www.infocommercegroup.com

Roxanne Christensen, Dir Awards Conferences & Consulting

Convenes all kinds of publishers who are bound only by their ability and willingness to take risks.
Frequency: Oct, Philadelphia

21466 NCRW Annual Conference
National Council for Research on Women
11 Hanover Square
24th Floor
New York, NY 10005-2819

212-785-7335; Fax: 212-785-7350
ncrw@ncrw.org

Mariam K Chamberlain, Founding President
Linda G Basch, President
Frequency: June

21467 New England Booksellers Association Annual Trade Show
1770 Massachusetts Avenue
#332
Cambridge, MA 02140

617-576-3070
800-466-8711; Fax: 617-576-3091
www.newenglandbooks.org/

Allan Schmid, President
Dale Szczeblowski, VP

Offers the opportunity for publishers to get their products in the hands of the booksellers in an area with one of the highest concentrations of readers in the country. This traditional multi-media exhibition is the largest of the regional conference in bookseller attendance.
2M+ Attendees
Frequency: September/October

21468 Publishing Institute
Publishing Institute
University of Denver
2000 E. Asbury Ave
Denver, CO 80208

303-832-5280; Fax: 303-871-2501
pi-info@du.edu
www.du.edu/publishinginstitute

Elizabeth Geiser, Director
Joyce Meskis, Director

A certificate program that combines workshops in editing and marketing with lecture/teaching sessions conducted by leading experts from all areas of publishing.
90 Attendees
Frequency: July-August

21469 Publishing University
Independent Book Publishers Association

1020 Manhattan Beach Blvd
Suite 204
Manhattan Beach, CA 90266

310-546-1818; Fax: 310-546-3939
info@ibpa-online.org
www.ibpa-online.org

Terry Nathan, Executive Director
Lisa Krebs, Assistant Director
Steve Mettee, Board Chair
Roy M Carlisle, Treasurer
Florrie B Kichler, President

A 2-day publishing conference focusing on education and networking. 40 exhibitors.
300 Attendees
Frequency: Annual

21470 Small Press Book Fair
Small Press Center
20 W 44th Street
New York, NY 10036-6604

212-764-7021; Fax: 212-354-5365
smallpress@aol.com
www.smallpress.org

Mary Bertschmann, Chair
Lloyd Jassin, Vice Chair
Mashala Solammi, Owner

One of the major book fairs for small press. Containing 100 booths and 100 exhibits.
2,500 Attendees
Frequency: March

21471 Tools of Change for Publishing Conference
O'Reilly Media, Inc.
1005 Gravenstein Highway North
Sebastopol, CA 95472

707-827-7000
800-998-9938; Fax: 707-829-0104
conf-webmaster@oreilly.com
www.oreilly.com
Facebook, Twitter, LinkedIn, RSS

Gina Blaber, Vice President, Conferences
Suzanne Axtell, Communications Manager
Shirley Bailes, Speaker Manager

Expect coverage with a range of practical, in-depth sessions that cover the innovations rocking every aspect of the art, craft, and business of publishing in the 21st century.
Frequency: February
Mailing list available for rent

21472 Writing Academy Seminar
Writing Academy
4010 Singleton Road
Rockford, IL 61114

815-877-9675

Annual seminar and exhibits by Christian writers.

21473 Yellow Pages Publishers Association Convention
Yellow Pages Publishers Association
116 Cass Street
Traverse City, MI 49684

800-267-9002; Fax: 231-486-2182
www.adp.org/

R. Lawrence Angove, President
Bonnie Pintozzi, COO
Vernon Smith, Treasurer

Annual convention and exhibits of equipment, supplies and services for the publication of Yellow Pages telephone directories.

Directories & Databases

21474 2,224 Public Libraries Data Files
Open Horizons Publishing
PO Box 2887
Taos, NM 87571

575-751-3398
800-796-6130; Fax: 575-751-3100
www.bookmarket.com

John Kremer, Editor
Robert Sanny, Advertising/Sales Manager

Database features 2,224 general public libraries, with name and address; no phone, fax, or email. Download in your choice of formats along with an information sheet.
Cost: $40.00
Frequency: Database
Founded in 1982

21475 Advertising and Publicity Resources for Scholarly Books
Association of American University Presses
Rm 602
30 W 36th St
New York, NY 10018-8063

212-989-1010; Fax: 212-989-0275
info@aaupnet.org
www.aaupnet.org

Peter Givler, Executive Director
Timothy Muench, Marketing Coordinator
Latasha Watters, Marketing Coordinator

This comprehensive directory lists periodicals which accept advertising or review copies of scholarly publications.
Cost: $189.00
425 Pages

21476 Alternative Publications: A Guide to Directories and Other Sources
Mcfarland & Company
Po Box 611
Jefferson, NC 28640-0611

336-246-4460; Fax: 336-246-5018
info@mcfarlandpub.com
www.mcfarlandpub.com
Facebook, Twitter, LinkedIn

Robert Franklin, President

Offers indexes and abstracts, review sources and bibliographies dealing with alternative publications.
Cost: $18.95
96 Pages

21477 American Book Producers Directory
American Book Producers Association
23 Waverly Place
#6B
New York, NY 10003

917-620-9440
office@abpaonline.org
abpaonline.org

Richard Rothschild, President
Ellen Stamper, ABPA Administrator
40 Pages
Circulation: 2,000
Founded in 1980
Printed in 2 colors on matte stock

21478 American Book Trade Directory
Information Today
143 Old Marlton Pike
Medford, NJ 08055-8750
609-654-6266
800-300-9868; Fax: 609-654-4309
custserv@infotoday.com
www.infotoday.com
Facebook, Twitter

Thomas H Hogan, President
Roger R Bilboul, Chairman Of The Board

A US book trade community. Profiles 25,500 retail and antiquarian book dealers, plus 1,200 book and magazine wholesalers, distributors, and jobbers in all 50 states and US territories.
Cost: $299.00
1800 Pages
ISBN: 1-573872-12-1

21479 American Directory of Writer's Guidelines
Dustbooks
PO Box 100
Paradise, CA 95967-0100

530-877-6110
800-477-6110; Fax: 530-877-0222
directories@dustbooks.com
www.dustbooks.com

Brigitte M Phillips, Editor
Susan D Klassen, Editor
Doris Hall, Editor

These guidelines help writers target their submissions to the exact needs of the individual publisher. A compilation of information for freelancers from more than 1,500 magazine editors and book publishers.
Cost: $29.95
752 Pages
ISBN: 1-884956-40-8

21480 Association of American University Presses Directory
Association of American University Presses
Rm 602
30 W 36th St
New York, NY 10018-8063

212-989-1010; Fax: 212-989-0275
info@aaupnet.org

Peter Givler, Executive Director
Timothy Muench, Assistant Director

114 presses and affiliates worldwide.
Cost: $14.95
Frequency: Annual November

21481 Bacon's Newspaper & Magazine Directories
Cision U.S., Inc.
322 South Michigan Avenue
Suite 900
Chicago, IL 60604

312-263-0070
866-639-5087
info.us@cision.com
us.cision.com

Joe Bernardo, President & CEO
Heidi Sullivan, VP & Publisher
Valerie Lopez, Research Director
Jessica White, Research Director
Rachel Farrell, Research Manager

Two volume set listing all daily and community newspapers, magazines and newsletters, news service and syndicates, syndicated columnists, complete editorial staff listings of each publication provided, covers U.S., Canada, Mexico, and Carribean.
Cost: $350.00
4,700 Pages
Frequency: Annual
ISSN: 1088-9639
Founded in 1951
Printed in one color on matte stock

21482 Bacon's Radio/TV/Cable Directory
Cision U.S., Inc.
332 South Michigan Avenue
Suite 900
Chicago, IL 60604

312-263-0070
866-639-5087

Joe Bernardo, President & CEO
Heidi Sullivan, VP & Publisher
Valerie Lopez, Research Director
Jessica White, Research Director
Rachel Farrell, Research Manager

Includes comprehensive coverage for contact and programming information for more than 3,500 televsion networks, cable networks, television syndicators, television stations, and cable systems in the United States and Canada.
Cost: $350.00
Frequency: Annual
ISSN: 1088-9639
Printed in one color on matte stock

21483 **Book Marketing 105: Choosing a Book Distribution System**
Open Horizons Publishing
PO Box 2887
Taos, NM 87571
575-751-3398
800-796-6130; Fax: 575-751-3100
www.bookmarket.com
John Kremer, Editor
Robert Sanny, Advertising/Sales Manager
A mini-guide including criteria for deciding how to distribute books. Also includes complete information on 30 distributors, 4 library distributors, 89 book publishers who also distribute for other publishers, 3 sales reps to the chains, 27 bookstore wholesalers, 34 library wholesalers, and 23 Spanish-launguage wholesalers. Plus a sample distribution contract.
Cost: $30.00
Frequency: Ebook Download
Founded in 1982

21484 **BookStats**
Association of American Publishers (AAP)
455 Massachusetts Avenue NW
Suite 700
Washington, DC 20001-2777
202-347-3375; Fax: 202-347-3690
info@publishers.org
www.publishers.org
Twitter
Karen Abramson, President & CEO
Tina Jordan, Vice President
Allan R Adler, VP for Legal & Government Affairs
Jay Diskey, Executive Director, School Division
Gail Kump, Director, Membership Marketing
Provides a comprehensive view of the size and shape of the US book publishing industry measured by publisher net unit and dollar sales.
Frequency: Annual

21485 **Business Info USA**
InfoUSA
5711 S 86th Cir
Omaha, NE 68127-4146
402-593-4500
888-260-7943; Fax: 402-331-6287
www.infousa.com
Vinod Gupta, CEO
Karen Peters, Account Executive
Cost: $2750.00
Frequency: Monthly
Circulation: 4000000
Founded in 1972

21486 **Business Periodicals Index**
HW Wilson Company
950 Dr Martin L King Jr Blvd
Bronx, NY 10452-4297
718-588-8405
800-367-6770; Fax: 718-590-1617
www.hwwilson.com
Harold Regan, CEO
Kathleen McEvoy, Director of Public Relations
Designed for businesses, business schools and libraries, business periodicals index covers English-language business periodicals and trade journals. Users enjoy quick access to feature articles, product reviews, interviews, biographical sketches, corporate profiles, obituaries, surveys, book reviews, reports from associations, societies, trade shows and conferences, and more. The database also provides SIC codes for industries and names of corporations used as subject headings.

21487 **Catalog Sales Data Files**
Open Horizons Publishing
PO Box 2887
Taos, NM 87571
575-751-3398
800-796-6130; Fax: 575-751-3100
www.bookmarket.com
John Kremer, Editor
Robert Sanny, Advertising/Sales Manager
Database features the top 1,350 catalogs, internet bookstore sites, chain store outlets, wholesalers, distributors, and other special sales outlets. Includes catalog names, buyers, addresses, phone and fax numbers, emails, website, types of books carried, and other important details.
Cost: $30.00
Frequency: Database
Founded in 1982

21488 **Celebrate Today**
Open Horizons Publishing
PO Box 2887
Taos, NM 87571
575-751-3398
800-796-6130; Fax: 575-751-3100
www.bookmarket.com
John Kremer, Editor
Robert Sanny, Advertising/Sales Manager
Database with 18,290 holidays, special days, weeks, months and historical anniversaries. Searchable by subject interest. Includes contact info and websites in most cases. Useful for setting pub dates and doing PR tie-ins.
Cost: $30.00
Frequency: Database
Founded in 1982

21489 **Complete Directory of Large Print Books and Serials**
4919 Route 22
PO Box 56
Amenia, NY 12546
518-789-8700
800-562-2139; Fax: 518-789-0556
customerservice@greyhouse.com
www.greyhouse.com
R R Bowker
Provides nine easy to use indexes including Title, Author, General Reading Subject, Textbook Subject, Children's Subject, Serials Subject, and Serials Title. For easy acquisition, full contact information on publishers, wholesalers and distributors is provided in a separate index.
Frequency: Annual
ISBN: 0-835249-41-6

21490 **Corporate Yellow Book**
Leadership Directories
398 RXR Plaza
Uniondale, NY 11556
516-730-1900
www.corporate.yellowbook.com
David Hurvitz, CEO
Bryan Turner, CFO
Jim McCusker, President
Contact information for over 48,000 executives at over 1,000 companies and more than 9,000 board members and their outside affiliations.
Cost: $400.00
1,400 Pages
Frequency: Quarterly
ISSN: 1058-2098
Founded in 1986

21491 **Directories in Print**
Gale/Cengage Learning
10650 Toebben Drive
Independence, KY 41051
800-824-5179
800-354-9706; Fax: 800-487-8488
higheredcs@cengage.com
www.gale.com
Patrick C Sommers, President
Describes more than 16,000 active rosters, guides and other print and nonprint address lists published in the United States and worldwide.
Frequency: Annual
ISBN: 1-414421-75-3

21492 **Directory of Poetry Publishers**
Dustbooks
PO Box 100
Paradise, CA 95967-0100
530-877-6110
800-477-6110; Fax: 530-877-0222
directories@dustbooks.com
www.dustbooks.com
Len Fulton, Editor
Over 2,100 magazines, small and commercial presses and university presses that accept poetry for publication.
Cost: $25.95
300 Pages
Frequency: Annual
Circulation: 2,000
ISBN: 0-916685-47-0

21493 **Directory of Small Magazines Press Magazine Editors & Publishers**
Dustbooks
PO Box 100
Paradise, CA 95967-0100
530-877-6110
800-477-6110; Fax: 530-877-0222
directories@dustbooks.com
www.dustbooks.com
Len Fulton, Editor
This directory contains more than 7,500 listings of editors and publishers in alphabetical order, along with their associated publishing companies, their addresses, phones, e-mail addresses and Web pages. Includes self publishers.
Cost: $25.95
460 Pages
Frequency: Annual
Circulation: 1,000
ISBN: 0-913218-28-6
Founded in 1967
Mailing list available for rent

21494 **Editor & Publisher International Yearbook**
Editor & Publisher Company
770 Broadway
New York, NY 10003-9595
212-291-1259
800-336-4380; Fax: 646-654-5370
www.editorandpublisher.com
Sid Holt, Editor-in-Chief
Greg Mitchell, Editor
Michael Parker, President
Daily and Sunday newspapers in the US and Canada; weekly newspapers; foreign daily newspapers; special service newspapers; newspaper syndicates; news servides; journalism schools; foreign language and Black newspapers in the US; news, picture and press services; feature and news syndicates; comic and magazine services; advertising clubs; trade associations; clipping bureaus; house organs; journalism awards; manufacturers of equipment and supplies.
Cost: $230.00
Frequency: Annual March

21495 Editor & Publisher Market Guide
Editor & Publisher Company
770 Broadway
New York, NY 10003-9595

212-291-1259
800-336-4380; Fax: 646-654-5370
www.editorandpublisher.com

Sid Holt, Editor-in-Chief
Greg Mitchell, Editor
Michael Parker, President

More than 1,700 newspaper markets in the US and Canada.
Cost: $100.00
Frequency: Annual November
Circulation: 4,500

21496 Editor & Publisher: Journalism Awards and Fellowships Directory Issue
Editor & Publisher Company
770 Broadway
New York, NY 10003-9595

212-291-1259
800-336-4380; Fax: 646-654-5370
www.editorandpublisher.com

Sid Holt, Editor-in-Chief
Greg Mitchell, Editor
Michael Parker, President

Over 500 cash prizes, scholarships, fellowships and grants available to journalists and students for work on special subjects or in specific fields.
Cost: $4.00
Frequency: Annual December
Circulation: 28,500

21497 Grey House Publishing
4919 Route 22
PO Box 56
Amenia, NY 12546

518-789-8700
800-562-2139; Fax: 518-789-0556
books@greyhouse.com
www.greyhouse.com

Leslie Mackenzie, Publisher
Richard Gottlieb, Editor

Publishes over 100 titles including reference directories in the areas of business, education, health, statistics and demographics, as well as educational encyclopedias and business handbooks. All titles offer detailed information in well-organized formats. Many titles available online.
Founded in 1981

21498 IBPA Directory
Independent Book Publishers Association
627 Aviation Way
Manhattan Beach, CA 90266

310-318-2270; Fax: 310-374-3342
info@ibpa-online.org
www.ibpa-online.org

Terry Nathan, Executive Director
Lisa Krebs, Assistant Director

A directory of members and one of regional affiliates is available online with multi-level search options.

21499 International Directory of Little Magazines & Small Presses
Dustbooks
PO Box 100
Paradise, CA 95967-0100

530-877-6110; Fax: 530-877-0222
www.dustbooks.com

Len Fulton, Editor

Lists more than 4,000 book and magazine publishers of literary, avant garde, cutting-edge contemporary, left wing, right wing and radical chic fiction to non-fiction essays, reviews, artwork, music, satire, criticism, commentary, letters, parts of novels, longpoems, concrete art, collages, plays, news items and more.
Cost: $55.00
Frequency: Annual/Cloth
Circulation: 1,000
ISBN: 0-916685-49-7

21500 International Literary Market Place
Information Today
143 Old Marlton Pike
Medford, NJ 08055-8750

609-654-6266
800-300-9868; Fax: 609-654-4309
custserv@infotoday.com
www.infotoday.com
Facebook, Twitter

Thomas H Hogan, President
Roger R Bilboul, Chairman of the Board
John C Yersak, Vice President
John Brokenshire, CFO

The directory of the international book publishing industry with 16,500 up to date profiles with book related concerns, including trade organizations, distributors, dealers, literary associations, trade publications, book trade events, and other resources conveniently organzied in a country by counrty format
Cost: $240.00
1800 Pages
ISBN: 1-573871-75-3

21501 Livestock Publications Council Membership Directory
Livestock Publications
910 Currie Street
Fort Worth, TX 76107

817-336-1130; Fax: 817-232-4820
dianej@flash.net
www.livestockpublications.com

Offers information on over 100 US and Canadian LPC-member livestock magazines, newspapers and newsletters.
40 Pages

21502 Magazines for Libraries
R R Bowker LLC
630 Central Ave
New Providence, NJ 07974-1506

908-286-0288
888-269-5372; Fax: 908-219-0098
www.bowker.com

R R Bowker

Magazines for Libraries provides the serials information you need to build and maintain a quality collection that best meets the needs of your library's users.
Frequency: Triennial
ISBN: 1-600301-16-2

21503 National Journal
National Journal
600 New Hampshire Ave NW
Washington, DC 20037-2403

202-739-8400
800-207-8001; Fax: 202-833-8069
service@nationaljournal.com
www.nationaljournal.com

John Fox Sullivan, President
Steve Hull, Senior VP
Timothy B Clark, VP

Publishes directories in the area of government.

21504 Progressive Periodicals Directory
Progressive Education
PO Box 120574
Nashville, TN 37212-0574

615-367-1874

Craig T Canan, Editor

About 600 social-concerns periodicals.
Cost: $16.00

21505 Publishers, Distributors and Wholesalers of the United States
R R Bowker LLC
630 Central Ave
New Providence, NJ 07974-1506

908-286-0288
888-269-5372; Fax: 908-219-0098
www.bowker.com

R R Bowker

In this 2 volume set locate publishers, museum and association imprint and trade organizations that publish, software firms, audio-cassette producers and even publishers that have gone out of business.
Frequency: 2 Volumes
ISBN: 0-835249-66-9

21506 Publishing & Production Executive: Who's Who of Suppliers and Services
North American Publishing Company
1500 Spring Garden St
Suite 1200
Philadelphia, PA 19130-4094

215-238-5300
800-777-8074; Fax: 215-238-5342
customerservice@napco.com
www.napco.com

Ned S Borowsky, CEO

Directory of services and supplies to the industry.
Circulation: 30,000
Mailing list available for rent

21507 Salem Press
4919 Route 22
PO Box 56
Amenia, NY 12546

518-789-8700
800-562-2139; Fax: 518-789-0556
csr@salempress.com
www.salempress.com

Leslie Mackenzie, Publisher
Richard Gottlieb, Editor

Publishes a wide range of reference works on literature, history, science, and health topics for high school, university, community college and public libraries. All of the award-winning content is available with complimentary online access.
Founded in 1981

21508 Salem Press Online Platform
Grey House Publishing
4919 Route 22
PO Box 56
Amenia, NY 12501

800-221-1592; Fax: 201-968-0511
csr@salempress.com
online.salempress.com

The new Salem Press platform houses more than 500 titles including all of Salem's Health, Literature, History and Science titles in addition to select titles from the Grey House Publishing and H.W. Wilson product lines. Online access is free with each print purchase and includes an unlimited number of simultaneous users and remote access.

21509 Single Unit Supermarkets Operators
Chain Store Guide
3710 Corporex Park Dr.
Suite 310
Tampa, FL 33619-1389

813-627-6700
800-927-9292; Fax: 813-627-6888

webmaster@chainstoreguide.com
www.chainstoreguide.com

Mike Jarvis, Publisher
Shami Choon, Manager

Discover more than 7,100 single-unit supermarkets with annual sales topping $500,000 dollars. This comprehensive desktop reference makes it easy to reach our compiled list of 21,000 key executives and buyers, plus their primary wholesalers.
Cost: $575.00
725 Pages
Frequency: Annual

21510 **Small Publishers Association of North America (SPAN)**
PO Box 1306
Buena Vista, CO 81211-1306

719-395-4790; Fax: 719-395-8374
www.spannet.org

Marilyn Ross, Executive Director/Editor
Tom Ross, VP
Cathy Bowman, Production Manager

Online resource for book publishing know-how. Works to advance the image and profits of self publishers and independent publishers through education and marketing opportunities.

21511 **Something About the Author**
Gale/Cengage Learning
Po Box 09187
Detroit, MI 48209-0187

248-699-4253
800-877-4253; Fax: 248-699-8049
gale.galeord@cengage.com
www.gale.com

Patrick C Sommers, President

An easy to use source for librarians, students and other researchers each volume in this series provides illustrated biographical profiles of approximately 75 children's authors and artists. This critically acclaimed series covers more than 12,000 individuals, ranging from established award winners to authors and illustrators who are just beginning their careers.
ISBN: 1-414442-17-3

21512 **Standard Periodical Directory**
Oxbridge Communications
39 W. 29 St.
301
New York, NY 10001

212-741-0231
800-955-0231; Fax: 212-633-2938
custserv@mediafinder.com
www.mediafinder.com

Patricia Hagood, President

Circulation, advertising and list rental info for more than 75,000 North American periodicals.
Cost: $1495.00
2,326 Pages
Frequency: Annual
Circulation: 3,500
ISBN: 1-891783-23-8
ISSN: 0085-6630
Founded in 1964
Printed in 4 colors

21513 **Top 700 Independent Bookstores**
Open Horizons Publishing
PO Box 2887
Taos, NM 87571

641-472-6130
800-796-6130; Fax: 641-472-1560
www.bookmarket.com

John Kremer, Editor
Robert Sanny, Advertising/Sales Manager

Database of 790 stores with address, book buyer, owner, event coordinator, phone, fax, email, website and more. Lists the largest bookstores that work with authors and that buy from indy book publishers. Compiled from industry news, author and publisher recommendations, and research.The report comes as a data file download in your choice of Access, Excel, comma- or tab-delimited ASCII, d-Base or rich text format.
Cost: $40.00
Frequency: Database
Founded in 1982

21514 **Ulrich's Periodicals Directory**
R R Bowker LLC
630 Central Ave
New Providence, NJ 07974-1506

908-286-1090
888-269-5372; Fax: 908-219-0098
www.bowker.com

Michael Cairns, CEO
Annie Callanan, COO

An essential reference tool for any serials librarian the Ulrich's Periodicals Directory™ is overflowing with the latest international bibliographic information on journals, magazines and newspapers.

Industry Web Sites

21515 **abpaonline.org**
American Book Producers Association

21516 **bisg.org**
Book Industry Study Group (BISG)

US book trade association offering information, best practices standards, research and events for the US book publishing industry.

21517 **http://gold.greyhouse.com**
G.O.L.D Grey House OnLine Databases

Grey House Publishing's online database platform, GOLD, offers Quick Search, Keyword Search and Expert Search for most business sectors including publishing and allied markets. The GOLD platform makes finding the information you need quick and easy - whether you're a novice searcher or an experienced database user. All of Grey House's directory products are available for subscription on the GOLD platform.

21518 **www.2020wob.com**
Women on Boards

Nonprofit organization dedicated to advancing opportunities for women to participate in boardroom roles through the promotion of effective policies and inclusive practices.

21519 **www.abaa.org**
Antiquarian Booksellers Association of America

A trade association of rare book dealers.

21520 **www.bookmarketingprofits.com**
North American Bookdealers Exchange

Independent publishers and mail order entrepreneurs. An international book marketing organization specializing in cooperative opportunities at trade shows, in mail order, press releases, and more.

21521 **www.bookpublishing.com**
Jenkins Independent Publishers

21522 **www.catholicpress.org**
Catholic Press Association of the US and Canada

21523 **www.clmp.org**
Council of Literary Magazines and Presses

Membership is open to any noncommercial literary magazine or press that publishes at least one or more books per year.

21524 **www.du.edu/pi**
Publishing Institute

A national organization that combines workshops in editing and marketing with lecture/teaching sessions conducted by leading experts from all areas of publishing.

21525 **www.ecpa.org**
Evangelical Christian Publishers Association

Promotes excellence and professionalism, shares relevant data, and equips Christian publishers to meet the needs of the changing marketplace.

21526 **www.flexography.org**
Flexographic Technical Association

21527 **www.greyhouse.com**
Grey House Publishing

Authoritative reference directories for most business sectors including publishing and allied markets. Users can search the online databases with varied search criteria allowing for custom searches by product category, geographic area, sales volume, keyword, subject and more. Full Grey House catalog and online ordering also available.

21528 **www.hwwilsoninprint.com**
H.W. Wilson

From its foundation in 1898, H.W. Wilson has dedicated itself to providing its customers and their patrons with the best possible library experience. H.W. Wilson products have become familiar to generations of library patrons as standard tools in college, public, school, and special libraries around the world.

21529 **www.interquest.Com**

A market and technology research and consulting firm in the field of digital printing and publishing that produces studies on topics such as digital printing, transactional printing, variable imaging, etc.

21530 **www.ipma.org**
International Publishing Management Association

The professional association for in-house corporate publishing professionals who work for educational institutions, governments and private industry.

21531 **www.newsmediaalliance.org**
News Media Alliance

Formerly known as the Newspaper Association of America, the News Media Alliance represents large daily papers, non-daily/small-market publications, as well as digital and multiplatform products across North America.

21532 **www.nmpa.org**
National Music Publishers' Association

21533 **www.p3-ny.org/**
Partnership in Print Production

Promotes the interests of women.

21534 **www.pacificpress.com**
Pacific Press Publishing Association

Promotes the interests of publishing, press, and media professionals.

21535 **www.papertrade.com**
National Paper Trade Association

21536 **www.publishers.org**
Association of American Publishers

Principal trade association for the US book publishing industry members comprise most of the major commerical book publishers in the US, as well as smaller and medium-sized houses, not-for-profit publishers, university presses, and scholarly societies.

21537 **www.publishersreport.com**
National Association of Independent Publishers

Assists and educates small publishing companies. Conducts seminars on marketing strategies, target audience, and techniques of book distribution. Especially helpful for the beginning or self-publisher.

21538 **www.salempress.com**
Salem Press

Since 1949, Salem Press has been the publisher of reference works on literature, history, health and science materials suitable for adult and young adult readers spanning all educational venues. Reference materials are available in both print and electronic formats. The company distributes its work to college, school and public libraries.

21539 **www.snaponline.org**
Society of National Association Publications

Develops standards for editorial and advertising content of association and professional society magazines.

21540 **www.spannet.org**
Small Publishers Association of North America

For independent presses and self-publishers who want to produce better books and market them more successfully.

21541 **www.sspnet.org**
Society for Scholarly Publishing

A group that represents scholarly publications, such as journals, university publications and magazines.

21542 **www.theacp.org**
Associated Church Press

Aims to share ideas and concerns in religious publishing and to stimulate higher standards of religious journalism to exert a more positive influence.

21543 **www.thomson.com**
Thomson.Com

A shared Web service that provides critical tools for more than 35 publishers.

21544 **www.wpa-online.org**
Western Publications Association

Represents magazine publishing companies and companies related to publishing industry, in the western United States.

Associations

21545 **American Association of Certified Wedding Planners**
2150 W Northwest Hwy.
Ste. 114-1039
Grapevine, TX 76051

844-202-2297
president@aacwp.org
aacwp.org
Facebook, Instagram, Pinterest

Wendy Kidd, President
Sheila Rigelsky, Vice President

A national organization that offers designations to qualified appraisers, teaches courses on latest appraisal information and offers courses on home inspection.

21546 **American College of Real Estate Lawyers**
11300 Rockville Pike
Suite 903
Rockville, MD 20852

301-816-9811; Fax: 301-816-9786
acrel.site-ym.com

Jay A. Epstein, President

Members are CPAs working in the real estate field.

21547 **American Land Title Association**
1800 M Street NW
Suite 300S
Washington, DC 20036-5828

202-296-3671; Fax: 202-223-5843
service@alta.org
www.alta.org
Facebook, Twitter, LinkedIn, Pinterest, Google+

Cornelia M. Horner, Interim CEO

Trade organization for title insurers, abstractors and agents.
4600+ Members
Founded in 1907
Mailing list available for rent: 3000 names at $500 per M

21548 **American Planning Association**
205 N Michigan Ave.
Suite 1200
Chicago, IL 60601-5927

312-431-9100; Fax: 312-786-6700
www.planning.org
Facebook, Twitter, LinkedIn, Pinterest, Tumblr

Joel Albizo, CEO
Ann Simms, COO & CFO
Harriet Bogdanowicz, Chief Communications Officer
Mark Ferguson, Chief Information Officer
Liz Lang, Marketing Director

A public interest and research organization representing practicing planners, officials, and citizens involved with urban and rural planning issues. APA's objective is to encourage planning that will meet the needs of people and society more effectively.
Founded in 1978

21549 **American Real Estate and Urban Economics Association**
404 BNA Dr.
Suite 650
Nashville, TN 37217

800-242-0528; Fax: 615-367-0012
areuea@travelink.com
www.areuea.org

Lindsay Buchanan, Executive Director

The association's purpose is to address concerns in real estate development, planning and economics.
1200 Members
Founded in 1964

21550 **American Rental Association**
1900 19th Street
Moline, IL 61265

309-764-2475
800-334-2177; Fax: 309-764-1533
www.ararental.org

Benefits members (rental business owners and equipment suppliers) by promoting, representing and enhancing the rental industry, resulting in improved rental services to the public.
8600 Members
Founded in 1955

21551 **American Resort Development Association**
1201 15th Street NW
Suite 400
Washington, DC 20005-2842

202-371-6700; Fax: 202-289-8544
www.arda.org

Howard Nusbaum, President & CEO
Sandra DePoy, Senior Vice President

International trade association composed of resort developers and resort industry suppliers.
1000 Members
Founded in 1982

21552 **American Society of Appraisers**
11107 Sunset Hills Road
Suite 310
Reston, VA 20190

703-478-2228
800-272-8258; Fax: 703-742-8471
asainfo@appraisers.org
www.appraisers.org
Facebook, Twitter, LinkedIn, YouTube, Instagram

Johnnie White, Chief Executive Officer
Bonny Price, Chief Operations Officer
Joseph Noselli, Chief Financial Officer
Todd Paradis, Chief Marketing Officer
Sarah Sebastian, Director of Membership Development

Organization provides education and accreditation for appraisers.
Founded in 1939

21553 **American Society of Farm Managers and Rural Appraisers**
720 S Colorado Blvd.
Suite 360-S
Glendale, CO 80246

303-758-3513; Fax: 303-758-0190
info@asfmra.org
www.asfmra.org
Facebook, Twitter, LinkedIn, Pinterest

Brian Stockman, Executive VP/CEO
Alex Clark, Dir., Membership/Marketing/Comms.
Mya Sadler, Dir., Education
Brian Sheppelman, Dir., Finance/Admin.

The largest professional society for farm managers and rural appraisers in the United States. ASFMRA provides members with resources, information and networking that enable them to provide valuable services to the agricultural community. The focus of ASFMRA is providing education, training and accreditation opportunities for a professional group of members providing farm and ranch management, rural and real property appraising, review appraisal and more.
2100+ Members
Founded in 1929

21554 **Asian Real Estate Association of America**
3990 Old Town Avenue
C304
San Diego, CA 92110

619-795-7873; Fax: 619-795-7822
contact@areaa.org
www.areaa.org
Facebook, Twitter, LinkedIn, Instagram

Tom Truong, National President

Represents the interests of the Asian real estate market.

21555 **Building Owners and Managers Association International**
1101 15th Street NW
Suite 800
Washington, DC 20005

202-326-6300; Fax: 202-326-6377
info@boma.org
www.boma.org
Facebook, Twitter, LinkedIn, YouTube

Owners and managers of commercial office buildings.
7.5M Members
Founded in 1907

21556 **CCIM Institute**
430 N Michigan Avenue
Suite 700
Chicago, IL 60611

312-321-4460
www.ccim.com
Facebook, Twitter, LinkedIn, YouTube

David P. Wilson, President

Functions as a professional association of real estate practitioners who have successfully completed its certification program or are working toward it.
4M Members

21557 **Commercial Real Estate Women**
1201 Wakarusa Dr.
Ste. D
Lawrence, KS 66049

785-832-1808
888-866-2739; Fax: 785-832-1551
crewnetwork.org
Facebook, Twitter, LinkedIn, Instagram, YouTube

Wendy Mann, Chief Executive Officer

Provides a forum for women who are involved in commercial real estate and wish to network as well as reap the benefits of their courses.
9000 Members
Founded in 1989

21558 **Community Associations Institute**
6402 Arlington Blvd.
Suite 500
Falls Church, VA 22042

703-970-9220
888-224-4321; Fax: 703-970-9558
cai-info@caionline.org
www.caionline.org
Facebook, Twitter, LinkedIn, Vimeo

John Hammersmith, President

Composed of community and condominium associations managers, management companies and other business partners.
33500 Members
Founded in 1973

21559 **CoreNet Global**
133 Peachtree St. NE
Suite 3000
Atlanta, GA 30303

404-589-3200
800-726-8111; Fax: 404-589-3201

www.corenetglobal.org
Facebook, Twitter, LinkedIn, YouTube

Angela Cain, CEO

Formerly NACORE International.
9000 Members

21560 Counselors of Real Estate
430 N Michigan Ave
Chicago, IL 60611

312-329-8427; Fax: 312-329-8881
info@cre.org
www.cre.org

Mary Fleischmann, President & CEO

Association members provide the public with expert, objective advice on property and land related matters. Individuals invited to join are awarded the CRE designation.
1100 Members
Founded in 1953

21561 Institute for Responsible Housing Preservation
799 9th Street NW
Suite 500
Washington, DC 20001

202-737-0019; Fax: 202-737-0021
info@housingpreservation.org
www.housingpreservation.org
Facebook, Twitter, LinkedIn, YouTube, RSS

Linda Kirk, Executive Director

IRHP members are owners and managers of Low Income Housing Preservation and Resident Housing Act housing and ELIHPA housing and concerned professionals.
Founded in 1989

21562 Institute of Real Estate Management
430 N Michigan Ave.
Chicago, IL 60611

800-837-0706; Fax: 800-338-4736
getinfo@irem.org
www.irem.org
Facebook, Twitter, LinkedIn, YouTube, Instagram, Google+

Denise Froemming, Executive Vice President & CEO
Chris Migala, Chief Financial Officer

Awards property manager certificate to qualifying individuals and accreditates management organizations and management firms. Offers management courses.
40000 Members
Founded in 1976

21563 International Council of Shopping Centers
1221 Avenue of the Americas
41st Floor
New York, NY 10020-1099

646-728-3800; Fax: 732-694-1690
membership@icsc.org
www.icsc.org
Facebook, Twitter, LinkedIn, Instagram

Tom McGee, President & CEO

Fosters professional standards of performance in the development, construction, financing, leasing, management and operation of shopping centers throughout the world.
70000 Members
Founded in 1957

21564 International Real Estate Federation
530 Park Avenue
4th Floor
New York, NY 10065

917-287-7020
info@fiabci-usa.com
www.fiabciusamember.com

Barbara Schmerzier, President Elect

Encourages private ownership of real property and understanding of property rights and obligations.

21565 International Real Estate Institute
810 N Farrell Drive
Palm Springs, CA 92262

760-327-5284
877-743-6799; Fax: 760-327-5631
support@assoc-hdqts.org
www.irei-assoc.org

An organization comprised of thousands of real estate professionals from over 98 countries around the world. Acts as a voting member of, and property advisor to, the United Nations. Members specialize in real estate and property management. Arranges and promotes international educational real estate seminars.
2000 Members
Founded in 1975

21566 Maine Apartment Owners and Managers Association
PO Box 282
Bath, ME 04530

207-623-3480
800-204-4311
maoma@maoma.org
www.maineapartmentowners.com

A national organization that presents the facts and information builder/developer/owners/manager members need to keep abreast of in the world of multi-family housing. Monthly issue will bring the reader timely insight on real estate, tax news, financing techniques, and effective management procedures, and keeps readers aware of the new developments in the condominium market.

21567 Mortgage Bankers Association
1919 M Street NW
5th Floor
Washington, DC 20036

202-557-2700
800-793-6222
www.mba.org
Facebook, Twitter, LinkedIn, YouTube

Robert D. Broeksmit, President & CEO
Marcia Davies, COO
Lisa Haynes, CFO/Chief of Diversity & Inclusion
Peter Grace, SVP, Strategy & Member Services
Michael Briggs, SVP, HR & General Counsel

A national association representing the entire real estate finance industry. This association develops innovative business tools and provides education and training for industry professionals.

21568 National Affordable Housing Management Association
400 N Columbus Street
Suite 203
Alexandria, VA 22314

703-683-8630; Fax: 703-683-8634
www.nahma.org
Facebook, Twitter, LinkedIn, YouTube

Kris Cook, Executive Director
Brenda Moser, Director, Meetings & Membership
Larry Keys Jr., Director, Govt. Affairs
Rajni Agarwal, Director, Finance & Administration

Trade association representing individuals involved in the management of affordable multi-family housing.
Founded in 1990

21569 National Apartment Association
4300 Wilson Blvd.
Suite 400
Arlington, VA 22203

703-518-6141; Fax: 703-248-9440
www.naahq.org
Facebook, Twitter, LinkedIn, YouTube, Google+, Pinterest

Bob Pinnegar, CEO
Kevin Madden, COO

The largest organization dedicated solely to rental housing-serves 26,000 rental housing professionals representing 3.4 million apartments nationwide. NAA lobbies for the industry, provides education programs, publishes Units Magazine, and conducts an annual Education Conference and Trade Show.
68000 Members
Founded in 1939

21570 National Association of Home Builders
1201 15th Street NW
Washington, DC 20005

202-266-8200
800-368-5242; Fax: 202-266-8400
info@nahb.org
www.nahb.org
Facebook, Twitter, LinkedIn

Gerald M. Howard, CEO

Represents the building industry by serving its members and affiliated state and local builders associations.
1.4M Members
Founded in 1942

21571 National Association of Housing Cooperatives
1120 20th Street NW
Suite 750
Washington, DC 20036-3441
202-737-0797; Fax: 202-216-9646
info@nahc.coop
coophousing.org
Facebook, Twitter

Mik Bauer, Executive Director

A nonprofit national federation of housing cooperatives, professionals, organizations and individuals promoting the interests of cooperative housing communities. Housing cooperatives are a form of multi family home ownership.
1000 Members
Founded in 1952

21572 National Association of Real Estate Investment Trusts
1875 I Street NW
Suite 600
Washington, DC 20006

202-739-9400
800-362-7348; Fax: 202-739-9401
info@nareit.org
www.reit.com
Facebook, Twitter, LinkedIn, YouTube, RSS

Steven A. Wechsler, President & CEO
Tony M. Edwards, Executive Vice President

NAREIT is the representative voice for U.S. REITs and publicly traded real estate companies worldwide. Members are real estate investment trusts and other businesses that own, operate and finance income-producing real estate, as well as those firms and individuals who advise, study and service these businesses.

21573 National Association of Realtors
430 N Michigan Ave.
Chicago, IL 60611-4087

312-645-7730
800-874-6500; Fax: 312-329-8576

www.nar.realtor
Facebook, Twitter, LinkedIn, YouTube
John Smaby, President
Promotes education, high professional standards and modern techniques of real estate work.
1.1M Members
Founded in 1908

21574 National Association of Residential Property Managers
638 Independence Parkway
Suite 100
Chesapeake, VA 23320
757-466-3336
800-782-3452; Fax: 866-466-2776
info@narpm.org
www.narpm.org
Facebook, Twitter, LinkedIn
Gail S. Phillips, CEO
Lisa Noon, Deputy Executive Director
Provides education and publications for the single-family residential property manager.
Founded in 1987

21575 National Association of Review Appraisers and Mortgage Underwriters
810 N Farrell Drive
Palm Springs, CA 92262
760-327-5284
877-743-6805; Fax: 760-327-5631
info@assoc-hdqts.org
www.naramu.org
Conducts educational seminars. Maintains library, speakers bureau and operates a placement service.
6.5M Members
Founded in 1976

21576 National Council of Exchangors
11 West Main Street
Suite 223
Belgrade, MT 59714
858-222-1608; Fax: 928-771-2323
admin@ncexchangors.com
www.ncexchangors.com
Kara Libster, Executive Administrator
A non-profit association and is a nationwide network of real estate professionals who specilize in marketing real estate equities primarily through the medium of the real estate exchange. This network is comprised of local groups organized into regional chapters.
400+ Members

21577 National Low Income Housing Coalition
1000 Vermont Ave
Suite 500
Washington, DC 20005
202-662-1530; Fax: 202-393-1973
info@nlihc.org
nlihc.org
Facebook, Twitter, LinkedIn
Diane Yentel, President & CEO
A national nonprofit organization representing housing advocates, organizers, tenants and professionals in the housing field. The Coalition advocates, represents and educates for decent housing and neighborhoods for all low-income people. It works with Congress and the executive branch to obtain adequate Federal support for low-income housing and related programs.
Founded in 1974

21578 National Property Management Association
3525 Piedmont Road
Building 5, Suite 300
Atlanta, GA 30305
404-477-5811; Fax: 404-240-0998
hq@nmpa.org
www.npma.org
Facebook, LinkedIn, YouTube
Bill Franklin, Executive Vice President
Nonprofit professional association dedicated to the cost effective management of personal property and fixed assets.
3700 Members
Founded in 1970

21579 National Real Estate Investors Association
7265 Kenwood Rd.
Suite 210
Cincinnati, OH 45236
513-827-9563
info@nationalreia.com
nationalreia.com
Facebook, Twitter, LinkedIn, Instagram, Google+
Rebecca McLean, Executive Director
Coalition of trade associations serving real estate investors, landlords and owners. Provides education and product services for officers and members.
115 Members
Founded in 1985

21580 National Residential Appraisers Institute
2001 Cooper Foster Park Rd.
Amherst, OH 44001
440-935-1698; Fax: 888-254-5314
www.nraiappraisers.com
Brian Schreiber, President
Promotes professionalism in the evaluation of residential real estate and requires demonstration appraisals and testing for professional certification.
451 Members
Founded in 1977

21581 National Society of Professional Surveyors
5119 Pegasus Court
Suite Q
Frederick, MD 21704
240-439-4615; Fax: 240-439-4952
curtis.sumner@nsps.us.com
Facebook, Twitter, LinkedIn, YouTube
Curtis Sumner, Executive Director
Organization of professionals for networking and education in the topographical field.
5500 Members
Frequency: Annual
Founded in 1942

21582 National Trust for Historic Preservation
2600 Virginia Avenue NW
Suite 1100
Washington, DC 20037
202-588-6000
800-944-6847; Fax: 202-588-6038
info@savingplaces.org
savingplaces.org
Facebook, Twitter, Instagram, YouTube
Stephanie K. Meeks, President & CEO
A private, nonprofit membership organization dedicated to saving historic places and revitlizing America's communities. Also provides leadership, education, advocacy, and resources to save America's diverse historic places and revitalize the communities.
270k Members
Founded in 1949
Mailing list available for rent

21583 NeighborWorks America
999 North Capitol Street NE
Suite 900
Washington, DC 20002
202-760-4000
editor@nw.org
www.neighborworks.org
Facebook, Twitter, LinkedIn
Non-profit supporting community development in the US and Puerto Rico.
Founded in 1978

21584 Professional Affordable Housing Management Association
PO Box 199
Glenshaw, PA 15116-0199
412-445-8357
www.pahma.org
Facebook
Information exchange between management agents and regulatory agencies.
100 Members
Founded in 1986

21585 Real Estate Buyer's Agent Council
430 N Michigan Avenue
Chicago, IL 60611
800-648-6224; Fax: 312-329-8632
rebac@realtors.org
rebac.net
Facebook, Twitter, LinkedIn
Represents professional real estate agents who act as buyers' agents.
50000 Members
Founded in 1988
Mailing list available for rent

21586 Real Estate Educators Association
7739 E Broadway
Suite 337
Tuscon, AZ 85710
520-609-2380
kris@reea.org
www.reea.org
Facebook, Twitter, LinkedIn
Kris Inman, Executive Director
Individuals involved in training and education.
1,400 Members
Founded in 1979

21587 Real Estate Roundtable
801 Pennsylvania Avenue NW
Suite 720
Washington, DC 20004
202-639-8400; Fax: 202-639-8442
info@rer.org
www.rer.org
Jeffrey D. DeBoer, President & CEO
Actively involves public and private real estate owners, advisors, builders, investors, lenders and managers on key tax, capital and credit, energy, environmental and homeland security policy issues in Washington. Its members are senior principals from every spectrum of the commercial real estate industry and leaders of major national real estate trade associations.
230 Members
Founded in 1999

21588 Realtors Land Institute
430 N Michigan Ave.
Suite 600
Chicago, IL 60611
800-441-5263; Fax: 312-329-8633
rli@realtors.org
www.rliland.com
Facebook, Twitter, LinkedIn, Instagram
Aubrie Kobernus, CEO
Karen Calarco, Manager of Operations
Promotes competence and accredits members. Maintains educational programs for real estate brokers.
1.9M Members
Founded in 1944

21589 Residential Real Estate Council
430 N Michigan Ave
Suite 300
Chicago, IL 60611
800-462-8841; Fax: 312-994-6242
crshelp@crs.com
crs.com
Facebook, Twitter
Lana Vukovljak, CEO
Seeks to establish cooperation among brokers engaged in buying, selling, trading and leasing of real estate.
40000 Members
Founded in 1976

21590 Society of Industrial and Office Realtors
1201 New York Ave. NW
Suite 350
Washington, DC 20005-6126
202-449-8200; Fax: 202-216-9325
membership@sior.com
www.sior.com
Facebook, Twitter, LinkedIn, Pinterest, Google+, YouTube
Thomas E. McCormick III, CEO
Robert Hammond, COO
Active members are brokers, consultants and appraisers.
3100 Members
Founded in 1939

21591 SourceMedia
One State Street Plaza
27th Floor
New York, NY 10004
212-803-8200
800-803-3424; Fax: 212-843-9608
www.sourcemedia.com
Facebook, Twitter, LinkedIn, Instagram
Gemma Postlethwaite, CEO
Sean Kron, CFO
David Longobardi, EVP & Chief Content Officer
Christian Ward, Chief Digital Officer
SourceMedia provides market information, including news, analysis, and insight to the financial services and related industries such as accounting and technology, through its publications, industry-standard data applications, seminars and conferences. The informational services that SourceMedia delivers are available in print or online, including newspapers and magazines, reference directories, database products, software, web seminars and live events.

21592 Women's Council of Realtors
430 N Michigan Ave.
Chicago, IL 60611
800-245-8512; Fax: 312-329-3290
wcr@wcr.org
www.wcr.org
Facebook, Twitter, LinkedIn, Pinterest, Instagram, YouTube
Heather Ozur, President
Provides opportunities for women in real estate at the local, state and national level. Offers courses in leadership training and referral and relocation buisness.
40000 Members
Founded in 1938

Newsletters

21593 ACREL News
American College of Real Estate Lawyers
11300 Rockville Pike
Suite 903
Rockville, MD 20852-3034
301-816-9811; Fax: 301-816-9786
webmaster@acrel.org
Roger D. Winston, President
Frequency: Monthly

21594 AOMA Newsletter
Apartment Owners & Managers Assn of America
65 Cherry Avenue
Cherry Plaza
Watertown, CT 06795
FAX 860-274-2580
Robert J McGough, Editor
Pietro
Each month the AOMA newsletter presents the facts and information builder/developer/owners/manager members need to keep abreast of in the world of Multi-Family housing. Every monthly issue will bring the reader timely insight on Real Estate, tax news, financing techniques, and effective management procedures, and keeps readers aware of the new developments in the condominium market.
Cost: $125.00
Frequency: 12 issues
Circulation: 6,200
Mailing list available for rent
Printed in one color

21595 AREUEA News Bytes
The American Real Estate and Urban Economics Assoc
404 BNA Drive
Suite 650
Nashville, TN 37217
800-242-0528; Fax: 615-367-0012
areuea@travelink.com
www.areuea.org
Daniel McMillen, President
Marsha J. Courchane, Executive Vice President
Lindsay Buchanan, CMP, Executive Director
David H. Downs, Treasurer
News on the operations of the The American Real Estate and Urban Economics Association. The newsletter covers job openings, calls for papers and event announcements.
1200 Members
Founded in 1964

21596 ASFMRA Newsletter
ASFMRA
720 S. Colorado Boulevard
Suite 360-S
Glendale, CO 80246
303-758-3513; Fax: 303-758-0190
info@asfmra.org
www.asfmra.org
Brian Stockman, Executive VP/CEO
Andrew Eames, Content Coordinator
Provides professionals involved in rural property issues such as management and appraisal, with information on the industry as well as educational opportunities. includes membership and information from the American Society of Farm Manager and Rural Appraisers.
Frequency: Weekly
Founded in 1929

21597 Accredited Review Appraiser
Accredited Review Appraisers Council
303 W Cypress Street
San Antonio, TX 78212-5512
800-486-3676; Fax: 210-225-8450
arac.lincoln-grad.org
Deborah J Deane, Publisher
Rachel L Phelps, Marketing Manager
Offers information on appraisals and real estate reviews.
8 Pages
Frequency: Quarterly
Founded in 1987
Printed in one color on matte stock

21598 Advise and Counsel
National Association of Counselors
303 W Cypress St
San Antonio, TX 78212-5512
210-271-0781
800-229-6262; Fax: 210-225-8450
www.masterappraisers.org
Offers information on real estate and apprisal counseling services.
Cost: $45.00
8 Pages
Frequency: Quarterly
Circulation: 4000

21599 American Chapter News
American Chapter International Real Estate Assn
30700 Russell Ranch Road
Westlake Village, CA 91362
805-557-2300; Fax: 805-557-2680
www.realtors.com
Teresa Salmon, Publisher
International real estate news and information.
Cost: $110.00
8 Pages
Frequency: Monthly

21600 American Industrial Real Estate Association Newsletter
American Industrial Real Estate Association
700 S Flowers Street
Suite 600
Los Angeles, CA 90017
213-687-8777; Fax: 213-687-8616
support@airea.com
www.airea.com
Ron Surace, COO
6 Pages
Frequency: Quarterly
Founded in 1964
Printed in 3 colors on glossy stock

21601 American Society of Farm Managers and Rural Appraisers Newsletter
ASFMRA
720 S. Colorado Boulevard
Suite 360-S
Glendale, CO 80246
303-758-3513; Fax: 303-758-0190
info@asfmra.org
www.asfmra.org
Brian Stockman, Executive VP/CEO
Andrew Eames, Content Coordinator
Provides professionals involved in rural property issues such as management and appraisal, with information on the industry as well as educational opportunities. Includes membership and

information from the American Society of Farm Manager and Rural Appraisers.
Frequency: Weekly
Founded in 1929

21602 Andrews Report
Report Publications
9595 Whitney Drive
#100
Indianapolis, IN 46280
William Woburn, Publisher
For owners and operators of small shopping centers.
Cost: $147.00
12 Pages
Frequency: Monthly

21603 Apartment Management Newsletter
AMN Publishing
PO BOX 352
Massapequa, NY 11758
516-551-5343
amnpub@aol.com
propertymanagementnewsletters.com
Helene Mandelbaum, Editor
Vera West, Circulation Manager
News and information for apartment owners and managers, including tips and techniques for marketing, maintenance, personnel and compliance with national laws and requirements.
Cost: $6.00
Founded in 2001

21604 Apartment Management Report
Apartment Owners & Managers Assn of America
65 Cherry Avenue
Cherry Plaza
Watertown, CT 06795-238
FAX 860-274-2580
Robert J McGough, Editor
Janet Pietro, Circulation Manager
Researched and written for the owner/manager, overall property manager, and for the on site managers. Typical in depth subjects cover the nuts and bolts of every day management. Research reports on tenant renting strategies, model apartments, security, outside maintenance, how to avoid and handle tenant complaints, and more.
Cost: $72.85
6 Pages
Frequency: Monthly
Circulation: 6200
Mailing list available for rent: 6000 names
Printed in one color

21605 Asset Watch
LDI Publishing
1401 16th Street NW
Washington, DC 20036-2201
202-232-2144; Fax: 202-232-4757
Steve Sullivan, Publisher
News and analysis of federal asset sales RDIC, LRTC, HUD, etc., contracting and resolutions.
Cost: $475.00
6 Pages
Frequency: 5 per year

21606 Asset-Backed Alert
Harrison Scott Publications
5 Marine View Plz
Suite 301
Hoboken, NJ 07030-5722
201-386-1491
800-283-9363; Fax: 201-659-4141
info@hspnews.com
www.hspnews.com
Andy Albert, Chairman/Publisher
Thomas J Ferris, Director
Michelle Lebowitz, Director
A weekly update on global securitization
Cost: $2297.00
20 Pages
Frequency: Weekly
Circulation: 500
Founded in 1990
Mailing list available for rent: 900 names at $400 per M
Printed in one color on matte stock

21607 Bulletin
Property Management Association
7508 Wisconsin Ave
Suite 4
Bethesda, MD 20814-3561
301-657-9200; Fax: 301-907-9326
info@pma-dc.org
www.pma-dc.org
Tom Cohn, Executive Director
News and events surrounding the real estate industry.
Cost: $100.00
24 Pages
Frequency: Monthly

21608 Commercial Lease Law Insider
Brownstone Publishers
149 5th Ave
Suite 10
New York, NY 10010-6832
212-473-8200; Fax: 212-473-8786
vendomecs@qualitycustomercare.com
www.brownstone.com
John M Striker Esq, Publisher
Nicole Lefton Esq, Editor
Commercial leasing strategies, techniques and insights with practical aids such as model lease clauses, checklists, do's and dont's, as well as coverage of new court decisions affecting commercial leases. Readership consists of commercial property owners, managers and real estate attorneys.
Cost: $337.00
Frequency: Monthly
Mailing list available for rentat $110 per M
Printed in 2 colors on matte stock

21609 Commercial Property News
Miller Freeman Publications
600 Harrison Street
Suite 400
San Francisco, CA 94107-1391
FAX 415-905-2239
David Nussbaum, Publisher
Maxine Jaffe, Editor
Tabloid newspaper edited for commercial property professionals.
Cost: $4.00
Circulation: 34,000

21610 Commercial Real Estate Digest
Vestal Communications
334 Humphrey Drive
Evergreen, CO 80439-9655
Robert Vestal, Publisher
Master copy newsletter allowing unlimited copy additions before subscriber prints and distributes to clients.
Cost: $495.00
2 Pages
Frequency: Quarterly

21611 Community Association Law Reporter
Community Associations Institute
6402 Arlington Blvd
Suite 500
Falls Church, VA Falls Chur
Fal-s C-urch
888-224-4321; Fax: 703-970-9558
caidirect@caionline.org
www.caionline.org
Daniel Brannigan, Editor
Information on legal cases and court decisions concerning condominum, cooperative and homeowner associations.
Cost: $208.00
8 Pages
Frequency: Monthly
Founded in 1973

21612 Community Associations Institute News
Community Associations Institute
6402 Arlington Blvd
Suite 500
Falls Church, VA Falls Chur
Fal-s C-urch
888-224-4321; Fax: 703-970-9558
caidirect@caionline.org
www.caionline.org
Daniel Brannigan, Editor
Real estate news and reports.
Frequency: Monthly
Founded in 1973

21613 Community Management
Community Associations Institute
6402 Arlington Blvd
Suite 500
Falls Church, VA Falls Chur
Fal-s C-urch
888-224-4321; Fax: 703-970-9558
caidirect@caionline.org
www.caionline.org
Daniel Brannigan, Editor
Bimonthly newsletter of news, strategies and trends written especially for managers of condominium and homeowner associations. This easy to read, award-winning newsletter comes packed with how-to information on such subjects as cutting expenses, complying with federal laws, working effectively with boards of directors, ensuring community safety and resolving disputes. It often features case studies of succcessful new approaches in community association management and operations.
Cost: $59.00
8 Pages
Founded in 1973

21614 Daily Commerce
Daily Journal Corporation
PO Box 54026
Los Angeles, CA 90054-0026
213-229-5300; Fax: 213-229-5481
www.dailyjournal.com
Gerald L Salzman, CEO
Ray Chagolla, Circulation Manager
Lisa Churchill, Editor
personnel announcements, datebook information, consumer news, and the internet, information on government foreclosers, default notices, lending reports and probate estate sales.
Cost: $237.00
Frequency: Monthly
Circulation: 10000

21615 Environmental Consultant
National Society of Environmental Consultants
PO Box 12528
San Antonio, TX 78212-0528
210-225-2897
800-486-3676; Fax: 210-225-8450
nsec.lincoln-grad.org/
Deborah Deane, President

Offers information, articles and news of interest to real estate environmental site consultants.
Cost: $50.00
16 Pages
Frequency: Quarterly
Circulation: 4000
Founded in 1992

21616 Housing Affairs Letter
CD Publications
8204 Fenton St
Silver Spring, MD 20910-4571

301-588-6380
800-666-6380; Fax: 301-588-6385
www.cdpublications.com

Michael Gerecht, President
Tom Edwards, Editor

The latest news on housing activity nationwide, including private, public and subsidized housing, legislation and regulations.
Cost: $559.00
Frequency: Weekly
Founded in 1961
Mailing list available for rent: 2,000 names at $160 per M

21617 Housing the Elderly Report
CD Publications
8204 Fenton St
Silver Spring, MD 20910-4571

301-588-6380
800-666-6380; Fax: 301-588-6385
www.cdpublications.com

Michael Gerecht, President
Jeff Pines, Editor

News and advice for owners and managers of long-term care facilities on marketing and managing all types of elderly housing, with profiles of new senior housing projects, business reports and an exclusive annual salary survey.
Cost: $294.00
Frequency: Monthly
Founded in 1961
Mailing list available for rent: 2,000 names at $160 per M

21618 Inside IREM
Institute of Real Estate Management
430 N Michigan Ave
Suite 7
Chicago, IL 60611-4011

312-329-6000; Fax: 312-661-0217
www.irem.org

Russell Salzman, CEO

Membership newsletter for members of the Institute of Real Estate Management. It includes news on IREM policies, programs and new products. Federal, state and local legislative developments affecting real estate and asset management are also reported.
40000 Pages
Founded in 1976

21619 Inspector
American Society of Home Inspectors
932 Lee Street
Suite 101
Des Plaines, IL 60016-3520

847-759-2820
800-248-2744; Fax: 847-759-1620
webmaster@ashi.org
www.ashi.org

Richard Clough, Executive Director
Paul Christensen, President

Newsletter for members of New England chapter of American Society of Home Inspectors.
Cost: $250.00
Frequency: Monthly
Circulation: 6000
Founded in 1976

21620 International Real Estate Newsletter
1224 N Nokomis NE
Alexandria, MN 56308-5072

320-763-4648; Fax: 320-763-9290
iami@iami.org
www.iami.org/

David Held, Production Manager
Robert Johnson, CEO

A compilation of international real estate information which is disseminated to the International Real Estate Institute's membership and to other subscribers. This publication also reviews the latest accomplishments of the Institute and those of its high quality professional members.
Cost: $29.50
4 Pages
Frequency: Monthly
Founded in 1975
Printed in one color on newsprint stock

21621 Ledger Quarterly
Community Associations Institute
6402 Arlington Blvd
Suite 500
Falls Church, VA Falls Chur

Fal-s C-urch
888-224-4321; Fax: 703-970-9558
caidirect@caionline.org
www.caionline.org

Quarterly newsletter of financial news for condominium, cooperative and homeowner associations. If you participate in any way in the financial management of an association, this eight-page newsletter is a resource you should have. It's absolutely vital for keeping up-to-date on trends in asssociation accounting practices, calculating the best strategies to minimize association taxes, and advising the board on investments.
Cost: $67.00
Frequency: Quarterly
Circulation: 12000+
Founded in 1973

21622 Mac News
Mid-Atlantic Council of Shopping Centers
8811 Colesville Road
Silver Spring, MD 20910-4343

301-890-1467

Tom Cohn, Publisher

News of the council.
Cost: $100.00
20 Pages
Frequency: Monthly

21623 Managing Housing Letter
CD Publications
8204 Fenton St
Silver Spring, MD 20910-4571

301-588-6380
800-666-6380; Fax: 301-588-6385
www.cdpublications.com

Michael Gerecht, President
Charles Wisniowski, Editor

News and advice for owners, managers and professionals dealing with apartments and the real estate industry.
Cost: $269.00
Frequency: Monthly
Founded in 1978
Mailing list available for rent: 2,000 names at $160 per M

21624 Mobilehome Parks Report
Thomas P Kerr
3807 Pasadena Ave
Suite 100
Sacramento, CA 95821-2880

916-971-0489
800-392-5180; Fax: 916-971-1849
www.aol.com

Reports on trends, issues, court decisions, legislation, financing and other matters of concern to owners and developers of manufactured housing communities. Valuable to attorneys and others who specialize in this segment of the Housing Industry.
Cost: $125.00
8 Pages
Frequency: Monthly
Circulation: 350
Founded in 1998
Printed in one color on matte stock

21625 National Association of Neighborhoods Newsletter
1300 Pennsylvania Avenue
NW Suite 700
Washington, DC 20004

202-332-7766; Fax: 202-332-2314
www.nanworld.org

C Y Doyd, Editor
Ricardo C Byrd, President

Offers news and information to the community real estate industry.
Frequency: Quarterly
Circulation: 10,000
Founded in 1975

21626 New England Real Estate Journal
East Coast Publications
PO Box 55
Accord, MA 02018

781-878-4540
800-654-4993; Fax: 781-871-1853

Tom Murray, Publisher
David Denelle, Editor

Business publication for the commercial-industrial-investment real estate industries.
Cost: $2.00
Frequency: Weekly
Circulation: 13000
Founded in 1961
Printed in on newsprint stock

21627 Professional Apartment Management
Brownstone Publishers
149 5th Ave
Suite 10
New York, NY 10010-6832

212-473-8200
800-643-8095; Fax: 212-473-8786
custserv@brownstone.com
www.brownstone.com

Mary Lopez, Production Manager
Michael Koplin, Circulation Director

Strategies, techniques and suggestions for attracting and retaining paying tenants, and avoiding legal disputes. Includes model language for leases, sample ads, plus coverage of legal issues, recent court decisions and the like.
Cost: $217.00
Frequency: Monthly
Founded in 1972
Printed in 2 colors on matte stock

21628 Real Estate Alert
Harrison Scott Publications

5 Marine View Plz
Suite 301
Hoboken, NJ 07030-5722

201-386-1491; Fax: 201-659-4141
info@hspnews.com
www.hspnews.com

Andy Albert, Chairman/President
Michelle Lebowitz, Director

Contains information for real estate and financial professionals looking for opportunities to buy or manage assets.
Cost: $1397.00
8 Pages
Frequency: Weekly
Circulation: 300+
Founded in 1989
Printed in 4 colors

21629 Real Estate Asset Manager
Lincoln Graduate Center - Executive Offices
PO Box 12528
San Antonio, TX 78212-0528

210-225-2897
800-531-5333; Fax: 210-225-8450
www.lincoln-grad.org

Debroah Deane, President
Rachel Phelps, Marketing Manager

Offers news and information on environmental concerns, real estate and appraisals.
8 Pages

21630 Real Estate Brokers Insider
Alexander Communications Group
1916 Park Ave
Suite 501
New York, NY 10037-3733

212-281-6099
800-232-4317; Fax: 212-283-7269
info@brokersinsider.com
www.brokersinsider.com/

Romauld Alexander, President
Nadine Harris, Marketing Manager

Provides agency broker/owners with in depth information on how to run their businesses better.
Cost: $247.00
8 Pages
Frequency: Fortnightly
ISSN: 1086-2935
Founded in 1978

21631 Real Estate Investor's Monthly
John T Reed Publishing
342 Bryan Dr
Alamo, CA 94507-2858

925-820-6292; Fax: 925-820-1259
johnreed@johntreed.com
www.johntreed.com

John T Reed, President

Information for owners who manage and own their own property, suggestions for increasing their investment returns.
Cost: $125.00
8 Pages
Frequency: Monthly
Circulation: 500
Founded in 1980

21632 Tax Credit Advisor
1400 16th St Nw
Suite 420A
Washington, DC 20036-2216

202-939-1790; Fax: 202-265-4435
info@housingonline.com
www.housingonline.com

Peter Bell, President
Glenn Petherick, Executive Director
Thom Amdur, Executive Director
David Abromowitz, Secretary

Monthly newsletter providing comprehensive coverage of all aspects of the federal low-income housing tax credit program, the primary incentive for low-income apartment development. Covers legislation, IRS rules, equity and debt programs, and market trends.
Cost: $269.00
12 Pages
Frequency: Monthly
Circulation: 750

21633 Upward Directions
Community Associations Institute
6402 Arlington Blvd.
Suite 500
Falls Church, VA 22042

703-970-9220
888-224-4321; Fax: 703-970-6558
www.caionline.org

Tom Skiba, CEO

NBBC-CAM's quarterly newsletter for the further education and professional development of CMCA Certificants. Program news, updates on state credentialing activities, legislation and regulation and continuing education opportunities make this newsletter required reading for Certified Managers of Community Associations (CMCA's. Everything you need to know to earn, maintain and optimize the benefits from manager certification from the National Board of Certification.
Frequency: Quarterly

Magazines & Journals

21634 ALQ Real Estate Intelligence Report
Common Communications
PO Box 5702
Portsmouth, NH 03802-5702

800-299-9961
800-299-9961; Fax: 603-436-5202
www.reintel.com

Pat Remick, Editor
Frank Cook, Publisher

A close examination of buyer agency movement, services rendered by brokerages, the impact of technology on real estate and success stories.
Cost: $200.00
Frequency: Quarterly
Founded in 1989

21635 Affordable Housing Finance
Alexander & Edwards Publishing
33 New Montgomery St
Suite 290
San Francisco, CA 94105-4520

415-315-1241
800-989-7255; Fax: 415-315-1248
www.hanleywood.com

Rob Britt, Manager
Andre Shashaty, President
Susan Piel, Conference Director
Michael Premsrirat, Circulation Manager
Carol Yee, Office Manager

Offers practical information on obtaining debt and equality financing from federal, state, and local governments as well as private resources. In-depth coverage on the federal low-income housing tax credit program, tax-exempt bond financing, corporate tax credit investigation.
Cost: $119.00
Frequency: Monthly
Circulation: 9000

21636 Alliance
John W Yopp Publications
6540 Julian Road
Gainesville, GA 30506-5550

800-849-9677; Fax: 800-849-8418

Mary Y Cronley, Associate Pubisher/Editor
Natalie Gilmer, Accounts Manager

Articles provide news and information on topics of interest, including marketing and sales, pre-need campaigns and other operational topics.
Frequency: Monthly
Circulation: 8000
Founded in 1919

21637 American Cemetery
Kates-Boylston Publications
11300 Rockville Pike
Suite 1100
Rockville, MD 20852

800-500-4585
800-500-4585; Fax: 301-287-2150
www.kates-boylston.com

Adrian F Boylston, Publisher
Thomas Lorge, Executive Director
Thomas Parmalee, Executive Director
Amy Fidalgo, Production Manager

Features articles on cemetery administration, maintenance, sales and public relations. Also includes coverage of conventions, new cemeteries and new building ideas.
Cost: $39.95
Frequency: Monthly
Circulation: 5800

21638 Apartment Age Magazine
Apartment Association of Greater Los Angeles
621 S Westmoreland Ave
Los Angeles, CA 90005-3962

310-536-0281; Fax: 213-382-3970
www.aagla.org

Charles Isham, VP
Kevin Postema, Editor/Advertising Director
Larry Cannizzaro, President

Serving the interests of residential rental property owners.
Cost: $48.00
80 Pages
Frequency: Monthly
Circulation: 40000
ISSN: 0192-0030

21639 Apartment Finance Today Magazine
Hanley Wood LLC
One Thomas Circle, NW
Suite 600
Washington, DC 20005

202-452-0800; Fax: 202-785-1974
www.hanleywood.com

John McManus, Editorial Director
Shabnam Mogharabi, Editor-In-Chief

Provides in-depth and inbiased reporting and insightful alaysis for owners, developers and asset managers.
Cost: $29.00
80 Pages
Circulation: 11784
ISSN: 1097-4059
Founded in 1995
Printed in 4 colors on glossy stock

21640 Apartment News
Arizona Multi-Housing Consulting Corporation
5110 N 44th Street
Suite L160
Phoenix, AZ 85018-2107

602-224-0135
800-316-6403; Fax: 602-224-0657
info@azama.org
www.azama.org

Terry Feinberg, President
Mitchell McBay, Marketing Manager
Erick Richard, Editor
Wayne Kaplan, Director of Community Relations
Marilyn Everroad, Events Manager

Articles on state and national government affairs, education, marketing, crime prevention, maintenance and legal issues relating to the Arizona multihousing industry.
Cost: $50.00
Frequency: Monthly
Circulation: 2500
Founded in 1964
Printed in on glossy stock

21641 Area Development
Halcyon Business Publications
400 Post Avenue
Westbury, NY 11590-2267

516-338-0900; Fax: 516-338-0100
www.areadevelopment.com

Dennis Shea, Publisher/CEO
Geraldie Gambale, Editor
Gertrude Staudt, Circulation Manager

Focuses on the factors necessary for a successful corporate expansion or relocation, labor, taxes, incentives, quality of life, market access, and transportation.
Cost: $75.00
Circulation: 45000
Founded in 1970

21642 Brownfield Renewal
Brownfield Renewal
2200 E Devon Ave
Suite 354
Des Plains, IL 60018

312-488-4830; Fax: 312-488-4220
editorial@brownfieldrenewal.com

Steve Dwyer, Editorial Director
Monica Acuna, Circulation Director

Dedicated to the remediation, redevelopment and reuse of brownfields.
Cost: $79.95
Frequency: Bimonthly
ISSN: 1554-8791
Founded in 1999

21643 Building Operating Management
Trade Press Publishing Corporation
2100 West Florist Avenue
Milwaukee, WI 53209-3799

414-228-7701; Fax: 414-228-1134
info@tradepress.com
www.tradepress.com

Scott G Holverson, Regional Sales Manager
Edward Sullivan, Editor
Eric Muench, Director of Circulation
Bobbie Reid, Production Director
Robert Wisniewski, President/CEO

Serves the field of facilities management, encompassing commercial building: office buildings, real estate/property management firms, developers, financial institutions, insurance companies, apartment complexes, civic/convention centers, including members of the Building Owners and Managers Association
Frequency: Monthly
Circulation: 70000
Founded in 1915

21644 Business Facilities
Group C Communications
PO Box 2060
Red Bank, NJ 07701-0901

732-842-7433
800-524-0337; Fax: 732-758-6634
www.groupc.com

Edgar T Coene, President
Jim Semple, Production Manager
Mary McCandless, Production Manager
Bill MacRae, Marketing Director

Magazine covering the fields of corporation expansion, economic development and real estate.
Cost: $30.00
Frequency: Monthly
Circulation: 43500
Founded in 1968

21645 Business Journal
120 W Morehead Street
Suite 200
Charlotte, NC 28202

704-347-2340
800-948-5323; Fax: 704-973-1102
www.bizjournals.com/charlotte

Robert Morris, Editor
David Harris, Managing Editor
Kim Moser, Advertising Assistant
Megan Foley, Marketing Director
Jeannie Falknor, Publisher

Provides marketing solutions and caring service.
Cost: $82.00
Frequency: Daily

21646 CF Industrial Reporter
Clayton-Fillmore
PO Box 480894
Denver, CO 80248-894

303-663-0606; Fax: 303-663-1616

Howard Treibitz, Editor

Briefs of the markets broken down into specific cities, includes briefs of the economy and average manufacturing.
Cost: $189.00
Frequency: Monthly

21647 Commercial
Oakland Press
28 W Huron St
Pontiac, MI 48342-2100

248-745-4794
248-332-1988; Fax: 248-332-3003

Edward Moss, Owner

A showcase of available commercial properties in the region.
Cost: $18.00
Frequency: Monthly
Circulation: 30,000

21648 Common Ground
Community Associations Institute
6402 Arlington Blvd
Suite 500
Falls Church, VA Falls Chur

Fal-s C-urch
888-224-4321; Fax: 703-970-9558
caidirect@caionline.org
www.caionline.org

Dori Meinert, Editor

CAL's award-winning bimonthly magazine for condominium and homeowner associations, managers and other industry professionals. Would you like to learn how a Web site can help your community association? Or peruse tips on cutting your budget? Or find out about the New Urbanism and other community development trends? Stay informed and involved via features and departments on the legal, political mechanical, personal, and day-to-day realities of community association life.
Cost: $69.00
Frequency: Monthly
Founded in 1978

21649 Comparative Statistics of Industrial and Office Real Estate Markets
Society of Industrial & Office Realtors
1201 New York Ave NW
Suite 350
Washington, DC 20005-6126

202-449-8200; Fax: 202-216-9325
www.sior.com

Richard Hollander, Executive VP
Craig S Meyer, President

A comprehensive publication that summarizes the results of a nationwide survey of industrial and office real estate market activity.
Cost: $135.00
300 Pages
Frequency: Annual+
Circulation: 3000

21650 Connections
Women's Council of Realtors
430 N Michigan Ave
Chicago, IL 60611-4011

312-329-8483
800-462-8841; Fax: 312-329-3290
www.wcr.org

Gary Krysler, Executive Director
Carol Raabe, VP Operations

Top producers in the real estate industry share their strategies for success.
32 Pages
Circulation: 14000
Founded in 1966
Printed in 4 colors on matte stock

21651 Cooperative Housing Journal
National Association of Housing Cooperatives
630 Eye St NW
Washington, DC 20001-3736

202-289-3500; Fax: 202-289-8181
nahro@nahro.org
www.nahro.org

Saul Ramirez, Executive Director
Deniz Tunder, Editor

Articles of lasting value to leaders in cooperative housing.
Cost: $25.00
Circulation: 3000
Founded in 1933

21652 Cooperator
Yale Robbins Publications
102 Madison Ave
5th Floor
New York, NY 10016-7417

212-683-5700; Fax: 212-545-0764
www.mrofficespace.com

Yale Robbins, Owner
Pam Liebman, CEO/President
Judith C Grover, Managing Editor
George Rubin, Circulation Manager
Ellen Levy, Advertising Manager

Articles covering management, maintenance business, finance, law, interior design and related topics.
Cost: $30.00
Frequency: Monthly
Circulation: 75000
Founded in 1985
Printed in 4 colors

21653 Daily Record
11 E Saratoga St
Baltimore, MD 21202-2199

410-752-3849; Fax: 410-752-2894
editor@mddailyrecord.com
www.mddailyrecord.com

Chris Eddings, Publisher
Suzanne Fischer-Huettner, VP Sales
Christopher J Chardo, Circulation Director
Mark R Cheshire, Editor-in-Chief

Jeffrey Raymond, Editor
Cost: $190.00
Frequency: Daily
Founded in 1888

21654 Development
National Assn of Industrial & Office Properties
2201 Cooperative Way
3rd floor
Herndon, VA 20171-4583

703-904-7100
800-666-6780; Fax: 703-904-7942
feedback@naiop.org
www.naiop.org

Thomas Bisacquino, President
Shirley A Maloney, Publisher

Articles pertaining to industrial and office real estate - development, ownership, management, investment, financing, leasing, etc.
Cost: $65.00
72 Pages
Frequency: Quarterly
Circulation: 14000
ISSN: 0888-6067
Founded in 2000
Printed in 4 colors on glossy stock

21655 Developments
American Resort Development Association
1201 15th St NW
Suite 400
Washington, DC 20005-2842

202-371-6700; Fax: 202-289-8544
hnusbaum@arda.org
www.ardafoundation.org

Howard Nusbaum, President

Serves the timeshare industry.
Frequency: Monthly
Circulation: 1,000
Founded in 1978

21656 Financial Freedom Report
2450 Fort Union Boulevard
Salt Lake City, UT 84121-3337

FAX 801-944-4334

Carolyn Tice, Editor

An investor's information services company which specializes in home business start-up, analysis, acquisition and maintenance of real property.
Cost: $119.00
72 Pages
Frequency: 4 issues
Founded in 1976

21657 First Tuesday
Realty Publications
PO Box 20069
Riverside, CA 92516-69

909-781-7300; Fax: 909-781-4721

Fred Crane, Publisher

Provides practical assistance to real estate professional. Includes legal and economic updates affecting the commercial and residential developments.
Frequency: Monthly
Circulation: 5000

21658 Global Property Investor
Alexander & Edwards Publishing
220 Sansome Street
11th Floor
San Francisco, CA 94104-2326

415-151-1241
800-989-7255; Fax: 415-249-1595
www.housingfinance.com

Shabnam Mogharabi, Director
Christine Serlin, Executive Editor

Objective, independent journal covering commercial property investment and development trends with readership in Europe, Asia and North America.

21659 Hotel Journal
Stacey Horowitz
45 Research Way
Suite 106
East Setauket, NY 11733

631-246-9300; Fax: 631-246-9496
www.hoteljournal.com

Stacey Silver, Group Publisher
Stefani C O'Connor, Executive News Editor
Cathy Urell, Senior Desk Editor
Barbara Jordan, Production Manager
Hope Rosenzweig, Advertising Manager
Cost: $85.00
Frequency: Monthly

21660 In Business
Business Information
2718 Dryden Drive
Madison, WI 53704

608-246-3599; Fax: 608-246-3597

Jody Glynn Patrick, Publisher
Joseph Vanden Plas, Editor

The business magazine for the Greater Madison Market.
48 Pages
Frequency: Monthly
Circulation: 15,000
ISSN: 0192-7450

21661 Ingram's
Show-Me Publishing, Inc
PO Box 411356
Kansas City, MO 64141-1356

816-842-9994; Fax: 816-474-1111
editorial@ingramsonline.com

Joe Sweeney, Editor-in-Chief/Publisher
Jack Cashill, Executive Editor

Kansas City's business magazine.
Cost: $36.00
114 Pages
Frequency: Monthly
ISSN: 1046-9958
Printed in 4 colors on glossy stock

21662 Institutional Real Estate Letter
Institutional Real Estate
2274 Camino Ramon
San Ramon, CA 94583

925-244-0500; Fax: 925-244-0520
www.irei.com

H Lawrence Hull Jr, Chairman
Geoffrey Dohrmann CRE, Founder/President/CEO
Larry Gray, Editorial Director

Offers analysis of market trends related to pension fund investment in real estate.
Cost: $2495.00
Frequency: Monthly
Founded in 1987

21663 International Real Estate Journal
International Real Estate Institute
810 N Farrell Drive
Palm Springs, CA 92262

760-327-5284
877-743-6799; Fax: 760-327-5631
info@irei-assoc.org
www.irei-assoc.org

Roger Wood, Production Manager
James Held, Production Manager
Robert Johnson, CEO

A full color magazine dedicated to discussing and promoting real estate opportunities all over the world. The articles cover a wide array of international Real Estate topics and are written by top international professionals.
Frequency: Monthly
Circulation: 10,000
Founded in 1977

21664 Journal of Property Management
Institute of Real Estate Management
430 N Michigan Ave
Suite 7
Chicago, IL 60611-4011

312-329-6000; Fax: 312-661-0217
custserv@irem.org
www.irem.org

Russell Salzman, CEO
Anthony Smith, President

Features articles on management, leasing and development of all property types.
Cost: $69.95
Circulation: 18000
Founded in 1976

21665 Journal of Real Estate Taxation
Thomson Reuters
195 Broadway
New York, NY 10007

817-332-3709
800-431-9025; Fax: 888-216-1929
ria.thomsonreuters.com

Paul D Carman, Editor-in-Chief
Robert J Murdich JD, Managing Editor

Complete, ongoing coverage of all aspects of real estate tax planning. In-depth articles by leading attorneys, accountants, and real estate authorities keep you abreast of the latest developments and how they affect real estate tax planning.
Cost: $315.00
Frequency: Quarterly

21666 MB News
Monument Builders of North America
401 N Michigan Avenue
Suite 2200
Chicago, IL 60611-4267

800-233-4472; Fax: 312-673-6732
www.monumentbuilders.org

Greg Patzer, Executive VP
Marty Kraslen, Manager

The Monument Builders of North America represent the leading retail, wholesale and manufacturing and supply firms of the monument industry. Articles promote public interest, knowledge and appreciation of memorialization.
Cost: $70.00
Frequency: 12 issues
Circulation: 1400

21667 Midwest Real Estate News
The Law Bulletin Publishing Company
415 N State St
Suite 1
Chicago, IL 60654-8116

312-644-7800; Fax: 312-644-4255
dwalsh@lbpc.com
www.lawbulletin.com

Lanning Macfarland Jr, President
Tricia Haddon, Associate Publisher
Bob Craig, Editor
Robert Carr, Associate editor

The Midwest's only commercial real estate source.
Cost: $60.00
Frequency: Monthly
Circulation: 16914
Founded in 1854
Printed in 4 colors on glossy stock

21668 Mobility Magazine
Worldwide ERC

4401 Wilson Boulevard
Suite 510
Arlington, VA 22203

703-842-3400; Fax: 703-527-1552
webmaster@worldwideerc.org
www.worldwideerc.org

Anita Brienza GMS, SVP Communications/Marketing
Frank Mauck, Managing Editor

Relocation leaders share experiences, offer new solutions to age-old challenges, set industry trends, describe best practices and policies, as well as comment on key issues affecting the relocation profession.
Cost: $48.00
68 Pages
Frequency: Monthly
Circulation: 12500
Founded in 1960

21669 **Mortgage and Real Estate Executives Report**
PO Box 64833
Saint Paul, MN 55164-0833

212-929-7500
800-950-1205; Fax: 212-367-6718

21670 **Multifamily Executive**
MGI Publications
1 Thomas Cir NW
Suite 600
Washington, DC 20005-5803

202-452-0800; Fax: 202-785-1974
www.hanleywood.com

Ed McNeill, President
Stephanie Davis, Production Manager
Alison Rice, Editor
Nicola Pellegrini, Marketing
J Michael Boyle, Publisher

Software and technology innovations, legislation, property development, management and renovation topics. Subscription free to qualified individuals.
Frequency: Monthly
Circulation: 25000
ISSN: 1089-4721
Founded in 1976
Printed in 4 colors on glossy stock

21671 **National Real Estate Investor**
Penton Media
249 W 17th Street
New York, NY 10011

212-204-4200
www.nreionline.com

Marianne Rivera, Publisher
David Bodamer, Editorial Director
Susan Piperato, Managing Editor

The leading authority on commercial real estate trends. Readers represent a cross-section of dissciplines-brokerage, construction, owner/development, finance/investment, property managment, corporate real estate, and real estate services.
Circulation: 33000
Founded in 1939

21672 **National Relocation & Real Estate Magazine**
RISMedia, Inc
69 E Avenue
Norwalk, CT 06851

203-855-1234
800-724-6000
realestatemagazinefeedback@rismedia.com
rismedia.com

John Featherston, Publisher
Steve Empey, CEO

Information on emerging trends and important issues affecting the various industries that are involved in relocating people and the home buying process.
Cost: $42.84
Frequency: Monthly
Circulation: 34,500
Founded in 1985

21673 **New Homes Guide**
4902 Eisenhower Boulevard
Suite 216
Tampa, FL 33634

813-823-3535; Fax: 813-290-7380

Emily Boyd, Manager
Sharon Kirkbride, Contact

21674 **Office & Industrial Properties**
MGI Publications
301 Oxford Valley Road
#1301
Yardley, PA 19067-7706

215-321-5112; Fax: 215-321-5122

Edward McNeill Jr, President/Editor-in-Chief

Contains business, technology, design and financial aspects concerning large private properties.
Cost: $36.00
Frequency: Bi-Monthly
Circulation: 15,000

21675 **Office Buildings Magazine**
Yale Robbins Publications
102 Madison Ave
5 Floor
New York, NY 10016-7417

212-683-5700
800-411-2229; Fax: 212-545-0764
www.mrofficespace.com

Yale Robbins, Owner
Henry Robbins, Marketing
Debbie Estock, Editor
Dane Pedupo, Circulation

Offers information on appraising and betterment of the real estate community in major markets in the Northeast.
Cost: $675.00
Frequency: Annual+
Founded in 1982
Printed in 4 colors

21676 **Pest Control**
Questex Media
600 Superior Ave E
Suite 1100
Cleveland, OH 44114-2614

216-706-3620
800-669-1668; Fax: 216-706-3711
pestcon@questex.com
www.questex.com

Tony Davino, Executive VP
Matt Waddell, Publisher
Matt Simoni, Sales Manager
Frank Andorka, Editorial Director

Serves the structural pest control industry.
Frequency: Monthly
Circulation: 21600
ISSN: 0031-6121
Founded in 1933
Printed in 4 colors on glossy stock

21677 **Plants, Sites & Parks**
12350 NW 39th Street
Suite 101
Coral Springs, FL 33065

954-753-2660
800-753-2660; Fax: 954-755-7048

Kevin Castellani, Group Publisher
Steve Chaffin, Publisher/Editor-in-Chief
Lisa M Bouchey, Managing Editor

Industrial office and economic development, facility planning and site selection for manufacturing and service industries.
Circulation: 44,500

21678 **Professional Report**
Society of Industrial & Office Realtors
1201 New York Ave NW
Suite 350
Washington, DC 20005-6126

202-449-8200; Fax: 202-216-9325
www.sior.com

Richard Hollander, Executive VP
Craig S Meyer, President

Articles by industry experts focusing on new paradigm in the practice of commercial real estate.
Cost: $295.00
Frequency: Quarterly
Circulation: 2,200
Founded in 1991

21679 **RCI Timeshare Business**
RCI
PO Box 80229
Indianapolis, IN 46280-0229

317-805-9000; Fax: 317-805-9618
alyssa.chase@rci.com
www.rci.com

Alyssa Chase, Editor
Katherine Jones, Publisher
David Tontius, CEO/President

Serves timeshare resorts/developers, hoteliers, operations and others allied to the field.
42 Pages
Frequency: Monthly
Circulation: 9000
Founded in 1974
Printed in 4 colors on glossy stock

21680 **RCI Ventures Magazine**
RCI
9998 N Michigan Road
Carmel, IN 46032

317-059-9584; Fax: 317-805-9507
alyssa.chase@rci.com
www.rciventures.com

Alyssa Chase, Editor
Nicole Keller, Senior Editor

Gathering of more than 4,000 of timesharing's best and brightest executives.
Frequency: April
Circulation: 35000
ISSN: 1099-6753
Printed in 4 colors on 6 stock

21681 **Real Estate Business**
Realtors National Marketing Institute
430 N Michigan Avenue
#300
Chicago, IL 60611-4002

312-321-4400; Fax: 312-329-8882
www.crs.com

Sara Patterson, Editor-in-Chief
Eric Berkland, Marketing
Nina Cottrell, CEO
Ron Canning, Vice President

Information for real estate agents and brokers engaged in US residential sales activities.
Cost: $24.00
64 Pages
Circulation: 48000
Founded in 1976

21682 **Real Estate Economics**
The American Real Estate and Urban Economics Assoc

404 BNA Drive
Suite 650
Nashville, TN 37217

800-242-0528; Fax: 615-367-0012
areuea@travelink.com
www.areuea.org

Daniel McMillen, President
Sheridan Titman, First Vice President
Lindsay Buchanan, CMP, Executive Director
Sumit Agarwal, Editor
Brent Ambrose, Editor

Journal from the The American Real Estate and Urban Economics Association (AREUEA). It is an academic journal covering real estate issues such as housing prices, office markets, real estate valuation and appraisal.
Cost: $100.00
1200 Members
Frequency: Quarterly
Circulation: 8000
ISSN: 1080-8620
Founded in 1964

21683 Real Estate Executive

Sunshine Media
735 Broad Street
Suite 708
Chattanooga, TN 37402

423-266-3234
800-624-7496; Fax: 423-266-7960
info@sunshinemedia.com
www.sunshinemedia.com

Tony Young, President
Jim Martin, President/CEO
David McDonald, Publisher

About real estate professionals from real estate professionals. Reaches 100 percent of the professional real estate audience in each market it serves. Each issue profiles a leading realty executive or agency within your local real estate market, as well as an assortment of new products, services and innovations.
Cost: $36.00
Frequency: Monthly
Circulation: 3000
Founded in 1996

21684 Real Estate Finance Journal

Thomson Reuters
610 Opperman Drive
Eagan, MN 55123

652-168-7700
www.west.thomson.com

Examines the opportunities and pitfalls facing real estate owners, developers, investors and lenders. Focuses on financing, liability, investments, taxes and asset management.
Cost: $558.00
Frequency: Quarterly

21685 Real Estate Finance Today

Mortgage Bankers Association of America
1919 Pennsylvania Avenue NW
Washington, DC 20006-3404

202-557-2700
membership@mortgagebankers.org
www.mortgagebankers.org

Features inside news reports on events and trends affecting the residential and commercial mortgage markets.

21686 Real Estate Forum

Real Estate Media
120 Broadway
Suite 5
New York, NY 10271

212-929-6976
www.reforum.com

Michael G Desiato, VP/Group Publisher
Sule Aygoren Carranza, Editor
Paul Bubny, Managing Editor
Alexa Faulkner, Circulation

The one source for market intelligence and business generation.
Frequency: Monthly
Circulation: 53821
Founded in 1940

21687 Real Estate Review

Thomson Reuters
195 Broadway
Suite 4
New York, NY 10007-3124

646-822-2000
800-231-1860; Fax: 646-822-2800
trta.lei-support@thomsonreuters.com
www.ria.thomsonreuters.com

Elaine Yadlon, Plant Manager
Thomas H Glocer, CEO & Director
Robert D Daleo, Chief Financial Officer
Kelli Crane, Senior Vice President & CIO

Information on financing, mortgage banking, investments, and related legal and tax issues, also covers US commercial, indiustrial and residential development.
Frequency: Quarterly
Circulation: 5,500

21688 Real Property, Property and Trust Journal

American Bar Association
321 N Clark St
Chicago, IL 60654-7598

312-988-5000
800-285-2221; Fax: 312-988-6281
askaba@abanet.org
www.abanet.org

Tommy H Wells Jr, President
Jennifer Collins, Advertising Sales Coordinator

Scholarly articles in the fields of estate planning, trust law and real property law.
Cost: $60.00
Frequency: Quarterly
Founded in 1878

21689 Realtor Magazine

New York State Association of Realtors
430 N Michigan Avenue
Suite 430
Chicago, IL 60611-4087

800-874-6500; Fax: 312-329-5978
narpubs@realtors.org
realtormag.realtor.org

Stacey Mancrieff, Editor
Frank Sibley, Senior VP/Publisher
Christina H Spira, Managing Editor
Wanda Clark, Publications Assistant
Pamela G Kabati, Vice President / Editorial Director

The business tool for real estate professionals. The New York Report is given after page 8.
Cost: $56.00
70 Pages
Frequency: Monthly
ISSN: 1522-0842
Founded in 1908
Printed in 4 colors on glossy stock

21690 Rental Management

1900 19th Street
Moline, IL 61265-4179

309-764-2475
800-334-2177; Fax: 309-764-1533
www.ararental.org

Chris Wehrman, Executive VP
Joe Lynch, Deputy Executive VP

A monthly magazine published by the American Rental Association
Frequency: Monthly
Circulation: 18000

21691 Residential Specialist

430 N Michigan Ave
Suite 3
Chicago, IL 60611-4011

312-828-9129; Fax: 312-329-8882
www.crs.com

Nina Cottrell, CEO
Eric Berkland, Director Marketing
Carol Raabe, Vice President of Operations
Carlee Londo, Marketing Manager
Richard Lawson, Director of Products

Published by the Council of Residential Specialists.
Cost: $29.95
64 Pages
Circulation: 40000
Founded in 1976

21692 Site Selection Magazine

Conway Data
6625 the Corners Pkwy
Suite 200
Peachtree Corners, GA 30092-3334

770-446-6996; Fax: 770-263-8825
www.conway.com

Adam Jones-Kelley, Managing Director
Loura Lyne, President
Julie Clark, Circulation Manager

Focus is on political, international and quality of life issues, also provides development groups, business parks, labor factors, relevant technology, real estate and finance information.
Cost: $90.00
Frequency: Monthly
Circulation: 45000
Founded in 1954

21693 Timeshare Business

RCI
PO Box 80229
Indianapolis, IN 46280-0229

317-805-9000; Fax: 317-805-9618
alyssa.chase@rci.com
www.rci.com

Alyssa Chase, Editor
Nicole keller, Senior Associate Editor
Rita Corea, Circulation Manager

Magazine for resort developers, property managers, sales and marketing professionals, homeowners association boards, and other key personnel in the timeshare industry.
42 Pages
Frequency: Monthly
Circulation: 35000
ISSN: 1099-6753
Founded in 1974
Printed in 4 colors on 6 stock

21694 US Sites & Development

Vulcan Publications
PO Box 12846
Birmingham, AL 35202-2846

205-328-6198
www.vulcanpub.com

Val Carrier, Publisher

Includes tax laws, real estate trends, as well as labor and work force issues.

21695 Unique Homes

327 Wall St
Princeton, NJ 08540-1518

609-688-1110
877-688-1110; Fax: 609-688-0201
krussell@uniquehomes.com
www.uniquehomes.com

Kathleen Carlin-Russell, Manager
Lauren Baier Kim, Managing Editor
Cheryl Jock, Production Manager

Robert Burke, Custom Publishing Manager
Cost: $24.97
Circulation: 54,856
Founded in 1978

21696 Units Magazine
National Apartment Association
4300 Wilson Boulevard
Siote 400
Arlington, VA 22203

703-518-6141; Fax: 703-248-9440
webmaster@naahq.org
www.naahq.org

Doug Culkin, President
Paul Bergeron, Communications Director

Contains news and information essential to all facets of the apartment industry-with a focus eacho month on managemetn, marketing, maintenance and politics.
Cost: $99.00
80 Pages
Frequency: Monthly
Circulation: 80,000
Printed in on glossy stock

21697 Vacation Industry Review
Interval International
PO Box 431920
Miami, FL 33243-1920

305-666-1861; Fax: 305-663-2227
www.resortdeveloper.com

Craig M Nash, CEO
Alina Betancourt, Account Executive
Ximena Villegas, Account Executive

Vacation Industry Review is a quarterly trade publication covering the global timeshare, fractional, vacation ownership resort industry. It discusses industry issues and trends and showcases new resort developments and key markets. It also covers products and services of interest to the industry, and the activities of prominent individuals and companies.
48/64 Pages
Frequency: Quarterly
Circulation: 28,000
Founded in 1984
Printed in 4 colors on glossy stock

21698 Vacation Ownership World
CHB Company
8701 Collins Ave Ph
Miami, Fl 33154

305-864-6083; Fax: 305-864-6085
www.vomagazine.com

Jon Paulisin, Publisher/President
Lou Skidmore, Editor
Howard White, Circulation Manager

News and feature stories, in depth analysis of the issues and trends affecting the industry of global timesharing.
Founded in 1984

21699 Valuation Insights & Perspectives
Appraisal Institute
550 W Van Buren St
Suite 1000
Chicago, IL 60607-3850

312-335-4100; Fax: 312-335-4400
puborders@appraisalinstitute.org
www.appraisalinstitute.org

Fred Grubbe, CEO
Larisa Phillips, President

Offers a collection of high interest articles, and features industry and institute news section and columns on legal matters, technology, marketing and timely appraisal issues.
Cost: $48.00
18 Pages
Frequency: Quarterly
Circulation: 82000
Founded in 1996
Printed in 4 colors on glossy stock

Trade Shows

21700 AREUEA National Conference
The American Real Estate & Urban Economics Assoc
404 BNA Drive
Suite 650
Nashville, TN 37217

512-232-2787; Fax: 615-367-0012
titman@mail.utexas.edu
www.areuea.org

Daniel McMillen, President
Sheridan Titman, First Vice President
Paul Bishop, Conference Contact
Leah Brooks, Conference Contact
Mike Eriksen, Conference Contact

Conference covering the subject of real estate and related research. Topics include housing, urban economics, commercial real estate investment, finance, liabilities, and more.
1200 Members
Frequency: Annual/June
Founded in 1964

21701 ASFMRA Annual Conference
ASFMRA
720 S. Colorado Boulevard
Suite 360-S
Glendale, CO 80246

303-758-3513; Fax: 303-758-0190
info@asfmra.org
www.asfmra.org

Brian Stockman, Executive VP/CEO

A conference for anyone involved with rural property and rural property assets - managing, consulting, valuing and brokering on behalf of clients and landowners throughout the United States.
Founded in 1929

21702 American Congress on Surveying & Mapping Annual Conference
6 Montgomery Village Avenue
Suite 403
Gaithersburg, MD 20879

240-680-0765; Fax: 240-632-1321
curtis.sumner@acsm.net

Curt Sumner, Executive Director
Ilse Genovese, Communications Director
Bob Jupin, Accounting Manager

One hundred and thirty exhibits of industry related equipment, supplies and services plus workshop and conference.
2000 Attendees
Frequency: Annual
Founded in 1954

21703 American Land Tree Association Annual Convention
1828 L Street NW
Suite 705
Washington, DC 20036-5104

202-296-3671
http://www.alta.org

James Maher, VP
1M Attendees
Frequency: October

21704 American Real Estate Society Annual Meeting
American Real Estate Society
Cleveland State University-BU327
Dept. Finance, Business College
Cleveland, OH 44114

216-687-4732; Fax: 216-687-9331
www.aresnet.org

Annual meeting and 10 exhibitors that are publishers, data providers, technical foundtions. Exhibits relate to decision-making within real estate finance, real estate market analysis, investment, valuation, development and other areas related to real estate.
300 Attendees
Frequency: April

21705 American Society of Appraisers International Appraisal Conference
American Society of Appraisers
11107 Sunset Hills Road
Suite 310
Reston, VA 20190

703-478-2228
800-272-8258; Fax: 703-742-8471
asainfo@appraisers.org
www.appraisers.org
Facebook, Twitter, LinkedIn, YouTube

Johnnie White, Chief Executive Officer

Organization provides education and accreditation for appraisers.
Frequency: Annual/October
Founded in 1939

21706 Apartment Association of Greater Dallas Annual Trade Show
4230 LBJ Freeway
Suite 140
Dallas, TX 75244

972-385-9091; Fax: 972-385-9412
pkelley@aagdallas.com
www.aagdallas.com

Paula Kelley CMP, Director of Events
Gerry Henigsman, Executive Assistant
Marsha Stephenson, Executive Assistant
Bradley Elliott, Director of Communications
Donna Derden, Vice President

Tours and 240 displays of industry related supplies and services.
3000 Attendees
Frequency: April
Founded in 1963

21707 Apartment Association of Metro Denver Educational Expo and Trade Show
650 S Cherry Street
Suite 635
Denver, CO 80246

303-290-0403; Fax: 303-329-0403

Mark Williams, Executive Director

Seminar, reception and 142 exhibits of property management equipment, supplies, services and information.
1500 Attendees
Frequency: Annual

21708 BOMA Winter Business Meeting & National Issues Conference
Building Owners and Managers Association
1101-15th Street NW
Suite 800
Washington, DC 20005

202-326-6300; Fax: 202-326-6377
info@boma.org
www.boma.org

Henry Chamberlain, President/COO

Opportunity for business professionals to discuss problems, security, exchange ideas and share experience and knowledge.
Frequency: January

21709 **BUILDINGS-New York**
Reed Exhibition Companies
383 Main Avenue
Norwalk, CT 06851-1543

203-840-4800; Fax: 203-840-9570

Annual show of 425 exhibitors of products and services for the building owner, developer, manager, co-ops and superintendents in the commercial and residential real estate market, including asbestos abatement, waterproofing, restoration, financial services, utilities, laundry equipment, cleaning services, computer software, elevators, heating and air conditioning, light safety/security, renovation and restoration.
9,000 Attendees

21710 **Coldwell Bankers Annual National Show**
27271 Las Ramblas
Mission Viejo, CA 92691-6386

949-673-3650; Fax: 973-496-5784

Sandra Deering, Manager

Seventy-five booths.
4.5M Attendees

21711 **MIPIM**
Reed Exhibition Companies
255 Washington Street
Newton, MA 02458-1637

617-584-4900; Fax: 617-630-2222

Elizabeth Hitchcock, International Sales

International property market conference.
4M Attendees
Frequency: March

21712 **National Association of Realtors Meetings and Trade Show**
430 N Michigan Avenue
Chicago, IL 60611-4087

312-645-7730
800-874-6500
infocentral@realtors.org
www.realtor.org

Karen Crafton, Convention Executive Secretary
Sue Gourley, Conventions VP
Terrence McDermott, CEO
Bill Armstrong, Treasurer

Seminars and networking, plus updates in the industry. More than 200 exhibiting companies.
6500 Attendees
Frequency: May

21713 **National Association of Realtors Trade Exposition**
National Association of Realtors
430 N Michigan Avenue
Chicago, IL 60611-4002

312-645-7730; Fax: 312-329-8882
www.crs.com

Sara Patterson, Director Communications
Terrence McDermott, Vice President
Ron Canning, Vice President

Spring show of 250 exhibitors of real estate industry equipment, supplies and services, including hardware and software, marketing programs, office products, mortgage and financial services and insurance.
40000 Attendees
Founded in 1976

21714 **Old House New House Home Show**
4051 E Main Street
St Charles, IL

630-515-1160
kp@corecomm.net
www.kennedyproductions.com
Facebook

Beth Wall, Contact

Discover the latest innovations, seeing creative solutions and gathering the motivation to tackle home improvement projects.
Frequency: Sept/Oct Illinois

21715 **Real Show**
Journal of Property Management
430 N Michigan Avenue
Chicago, IL 60611-4002

312-329-6064; Fax: 312-329-8882
www.crs.com

Sara Patterson, Director Communications
Ron Canning, Vice President

A trade show with 275 exhibitors and 450 booths, for professional owners and managers of investment residential and commercial property.
40000 Attendees
Founded in 1976

21716 **Realmart**
National Association of Industrial & Office Prop.
Woodlyn Park-2201 Coop. Way
Herndon, VA 22071

703-267-6665; Fax: 703-904-7974
garvin@naiop.org

Annual show of 100 suppliers of companies catering to the commercial real estate industry.
1,000 Attendees

21717 **Realtors Conference & Expo**
National Association of Realtors
430 North Michigan Ave.
Chicago, IL 60611

800-874-6500
convinfo@realtors.org
www.realtor.org/convention.nsf
Facebook, Twitter, LinkedIn, YouTube

Dale Stinton, Chief Executive Officer
Chris Polychron, President

Networking, educational sessions on timely topics and a vendor expo.
Frequency: Annual

21718 **SourceMedia Conferences & Events**
SourceMedia
One State Street Plaza
27th floor
New York, NY 10004

212-803-6093
800-803-3424; Fax: 212-803-8515
www.sourcemedia.com/

James M Malkin, Chairman & CEO
William Johnson, CFO
Steve Andreazza, VP, Sales & Customer Service
Celie Baussan, SVP, Operations
Anne O'Brien, EVP Marketing & Strategic Planning

SourceMedia Conferences & Events attract over 20,000 attendees worldwide. The content embraces a variety of formats, including: conferences, executive roundtables, expositions, Web seminars, custom events and pod casts. With over 70 events annually, participants are provided with premier content as well as access to the industry's top solution providers. Markets served include: accounting; banking; capital markets; financial services; information technology; insurance; and real estate.
Mailing list available for rent

21719 **Trade Expo**
Professional Housing Management
PO Box 4251
Leesburg, VA 20177

703-327-6873
800-543-7188; Fax: 703-327-4005

Jon Moore, Director
Mona Pearson, Trade Expo Coordinator

At the expo there will be 230 booths with 150 exhibitors.
1,200 Attendees
Frequency: January

Directories & Databases

21720 **America's Top-Rated Cities**
Grey House Publishing
4919 Route 22
PO Box 56
Amenia, NY 12501

518-789-8700
800-562-2139; Fax: 518-789-0556
books@greyhouse.com
www.greyhouse.com
Facebook, Twitter

Leslie Mackenzie, Publisher
Richard Gottlieb, Editor

Provides current, comprehensive statistical information in one easy-to-use source on the 100 top cities that have been cited as the best for business and living in the US. Available as a four volume set or individual volumes (Southern, Western, Central and Eastern)
Cost: $225.00
2000 Pages
ISBN: 1-592373-49-6
Founded in 1981

21721 **America's Top-Rated Smaller Cities**
Grey House Publishing
4919 Route 22
PO Box 56
Amenia, NY 12501

518-789-8700
800-562-2139; Fax: 845-373-6390
books@greyhouse.com
www.greyhouse.com
Facebook, Twitter

Leslie Mackenzie, Publisher
Richard Gottlieb, Editor

America's Top-Rated Smaller Cities provides current, comprehensive data on 110 US cities, all top-ranked by population growth, median income, unemployment rate and crime rate. This informative handbook allows readers to see, at a glance, a concise social, business, economic, demographic and environmental profile of each city, including brief evaluative comments.
Cost: $195.00
1800 Pages
ISBN: 1-592372-84-8
Founded in 1981

21722 **American Resort Development Association: Membership Directory**
American Resort Development Association
1201 15th St Nw
Suite 400
Washington, DC 20005-2842

202-371-6700; Fax: 202-289-8544
hnusbaum@arda.org
www.ardafoundation.org

Howard Nusbaum, President
Lou Ann Burney, VP
Rob Dumm, Finance
Alexa Antonuk, Communications Manager

Over 800 member firms in the resort development industry, including developers, finance companies, architectural firms, audiovisual companies, direct mail companies, rental and vacation exchange companies and law firms.
Frequency: Annual Winter

21723 **American Society of Appraisers Directory**
American Society of Appraisers

11107 Sunset Hills Road
Suite 310
Reston, VA 20190

703-478-2228
800-272-8258; Fax: 703-742-8471
asainfo@appraisers.org
www.appraisers.org
Facebook, Twitter, LinkedIn, YouTube

Johnnie White, Chief Executive Officer
Todd Paradis, Chief Marketing Officer
Sarah Sebastian, Director of Membership Development

Directory of association members who are accredited appraisers.
Founded in 1939

21724 Buyers Broker Registry
Who's Who in Creative Real Estate
PO Box 23275
Ventura, CA 93002-3275

Offers valuable information on over 650 real estate agents in the United States who have met performance requirements set by the publisher.
Cost: $25.00
136 Pages
Frequency: Annual

21725 CRB/CRS Referral Directory
Realtors National Marketing Institute
430 N Michigan Avenue
Suite 300
Chicago, IL 60611-4002

FAX 312-329-8882
http://www.crs.com

Gwen Voelker, Editor

Aimed at the real estate industry, this directory lists over 32,000 real estate brokerage managers and residential sales specialists.
Cost: $45.00
776 Pages
Frequency: Annual
Circulation: 32,000

21726 CRE Member Directory
Counselors of Real Estate
430 N Michigan Ave
Chicago, IL 60611-4019

312-329-8427; Fax: 312-329-8881
www.cre.org

Mary Fleischmann, President
Frequency: Annual March

21727 Commercial Investment Real Estate
CCIM Institute
430 N Michigan Ave
Chicago, IL 60611-4011

312-321-4460; Fax: 312-321-4530
magazine@ccim.com
www.ccim.com

Jonathan Falk, Manager
Ken Setlak, Chief Financial Officer
Sara Drummond, Executive Editor

Directory of services and supplies to the industry.
40000 Pages
Founded in 1976

21728 Comparative Guide to American Suburbs
Grey House Publishing
4919 Route 22
PO Box 56
Amenia, NY 12501

518-789-8700
800-562-2139; Fax: 845-373-6390
books@greyhouse.com
www.greyhouse.com
Facebook, Twitter

Leslie Mackenzie, Publisher
Richard Gottlieb, Editor

Covers statistics on the 2,000+ suburban communities surrounding the 60 largest metropolitan areas - their population characteristics, income levels, economy, school systems and important data on how they compare to one another.
Cost: $150.00
1000 Pages
ISBN: 1-592371-80-9
Founded in 1981

21729 Crime in America's Top-Rated Cities
Grey House Publishing
4919 Route 22
PO Box 56
Amenia, NY 12501

518-789-8700
800-562-2139; Fax: 845-373-6390
books@greyhouse.com
www.greyhouse.com
Facebook, Twitter

Leslie Mackenzie, Publisher
Richard Gottlieb, Editor

Details over twenty years of crime statistics in all major crime categories: violent crimes, property crimes and total crime. Conveniently arranged by city, it offers details that compare the number of crimes and crime rates for the city, suburbs and metro area with national crime trends for violent, property and total crimes. Statistics on anti-crime programs, crime risk, hate crimes, illegal drugs, law enforcement, correctional facilities, death penalty, laws and much more.
Cost: $155.00
839 Pages
ISBN: 1-891482-84-X
Founded in 1981

21730 Crittenden's Real Estate Buyers Directory
Crittendon Research
250 Bel Marin Keys Boulevard
Novato, CA 94949-5727

415-382-2400
800-421-3483; Fax: 415-382-2476
www.crittendenonline.com

John Goodwin, Editor/Publisher
Vitlario Laeson, Marketing Director
Pati Bess, Customer Service Director

A list of over 500 real estate buyers, including private institutional investors, banks, pension funds and real estate investment trusts.

21731 Crittendon Directory of Real Estate Financing
Crittendon Research
250 Bel Marin Keys Boulevard
Novato, CA 94949-5727

415-382-7790; Fax: 415-382-2476

Listing of over 400 major lenders, investors and joint ventures enagged in commercial and residential real estate financing and investing.
Cost: $387.00
500 Pages
Frequency: Semiannual

21732 DAMAR Real Estate Information Service Online Database
3550 W Temple Street
Los Angeles, CA 90004-3620

800-873-2627

This comprehensive database offers real estate information, with an emphasis on California.
Frequency: Full-text

21733 Directory of 2,500 Active Real Estate Lenders
International Wealth Success
PO Box 186
Merrick, NY 11566-0186

516-766-5850
800-323-0548; Fax: 516-766-5919
admin@iwsmoney.com
www.iwsmoney.com

Tyler G Hicks, President

Lists 2,500 names and addresses of direct lenders or sources of information on possible lenders for real estate.
Cost: $25.00
197 Pages
Frequency: Annually
ISBN: 1-561503-37-1
Founded in 1985

21734 Directory of Accredited Real Property Appraisers
American Society of Appraisers
11107 Sunset Hills Road
Suite 310
Reston, VA 20190

202-337-0037
800-272-8258; Fax: 202-742-8471
asainfo@appraisers.org
www.appraisers.org

Johnnie White, Chief Executive Officer
Todd Paradis, Chief Marketing Officer
Sarah Sebastian, Director of Membership Development

Approximately 1,700 urban, residential, rural, ad valorem and timberland appraisers; limited international coverage.

21735 Directory of Professional Appraisal Services
American Society of Appraisers
11107 Sunset Hills Road
Suite 310
Reston, VA 20190

800-272-8258
asainfo@appraisers.org
www.appraisers.org

Johnnie White, Chief Executive Officer

21736 Directory of Real Estate Development and Related Education Programs
Urban Land Institute
625 Indiana Avenue NW
Suite 400
Washington, DC 20004-2923

202-247-7116

Over 60 programs are profiled that are currently being offered at colleges and universities in the area of real estate.
Cost: $19.00
132 Pages
Frequency: Biennial

21737 ERC Directory of Real Estate Appraisers and Brokers
Employee Relocation Council
1720 N Street NW
Washington, DC 20036-2900

202-857-0857

Tina Lung, Editor
Cost: $35.00
1,100 Pages
Frequency: Annual

21738 European Investment in United States Real Estate
Mead Ventures
PO Box 44952
Phoenix, AZ 85064-4952

Investors, developers and brokers located in Europe are the focus of this valuable directory.
Cost: $195.00
406 Pages
Frequency: Annual

21739 **Executive Guide to Specialists in Industrial and Office Real Estate**
Society of Industrial & Office Realtors
1201 New York Ave NW
Suite 350
Washington, DC 20005-6126
202-449-8200; Fax: 202-216-9325
www.sior.com
Richard Hollander, Executive VP
Craig S Meyer, President
Thousands of specialists are listed that are integrated with industrial real estate and related industries.
Cost: $60.00
210 Pages
Frequency: Annual

21740 **FDIC: Investment Properties Publication**
Federal Deposit Insurance Corporation
550 17th St Nw
Washington, DC 20429-0002
202-000-1111; Fax: 202-898-8595
Mitchell L Glassman, Plant Manager
Offers information on properties owned by the Federal Deposit Insurance Corporation, including land, commercial real estate, multifamily dwellings and hotels and motels.
200 Pages
Frequency: Quarterly

21741 **Guide to Real Estate and Mortgage Banking Software**
Real Estate Solutions
2609 Klingle Road NW
Washington, DC 20008-1202
202-362-9854
Lists approximately 500 real estate and mortgage banking computer software, hardware and products.
Cost: $49.95
640 Pages
Frequency: Biennial

21742 **Income & Cost for Organization & Servicing of 1-4 Unit Residential Loans**
Mortgage Bankers Association of America
1919 Pennsylvania Avenue NW
Washington, DC 20006-3404
202-557-2700
membership@mortgagebankers.org
www.mortgagebankers.org
Annual report provides data and analysis on the income and expenses associated with the organization, warehousing, marketing and servicing or one-to-four-unit residential marketing loans.
80 Pages
Frequency: $150 Member/$300 Non

21743 **Japanese Investment in US Real Estate Review**
Mead Ventures
PO Box 44952
Phoenix, AZ 85064-4952
FAX 602-234-0076
This is a complete database listing documenting Japanese purchases of US golf courses, houses, office buildings and industrial properties.
Frequency: Full-text

21744 **Journal of the American Society of Farm Managers and Rural Appraisers**
ASFMRA
720 S. Colorado Boulevard
Suite 360-S
Glendale, CO 80246
303-758-3513; Fax: 303-758-0190
info@asfmra.org
www.asfmra.org
Brian Stockman, Executive VP/CEO
Provides the most up-to-date studies, research, practices, and methodologies proposed by the leading academic, management, appraisal and consulting members of our professions.
Frequency: Annual
Founded in 1929

21745 **Major Cities Canada**
Grey House Publishing
4919 Route 22
PO Box 56
Amenia, NY 12501
800-562-2139; Fax: 845-373-6390; Fax: new
www.greyhouse.ca
Richard Gottlieb, President
Provides an in-depth comparison and analysis of the 50 most populated cities in Canada. Split into 4 major categories; background, study rankings, development offices, and statistical tables
Cost: $180.00
793 Pages

21746 **Million Dollar Guide to Business and Real Estate Loan Sources**
International Wealth Success
PO Box 186
Merrick, NY 11566-0186
516-766-5850
800-323-0548; Fax: 516-766-5919
admin@iwsmoney.com
www.iwsmoney.com
Tyler G Hicks, President
Lists hundreds of business and real estate lenders, giving their lending data in very brief form.
Cost: $25.00
201 Pages
Frequency: Annually
Founded in 1990

21747 **Monthly Resort Real Estate Property Index**
MDR Telecom
4742 La Villa Marina
Unit A
Marina Del Rey, CA 90292-7086
Mario Collura, Editor
Offers information on resort timeshares and resort condominiums for rent or sale.
Cost: $10.00
80 Pages
Frequency: Monthly

21748 **Mortgage Banking Performance Report**
Mortgage Bankers Association of America
1919 Pennsylvania Avenue NW
Washington, DC 20006-3404
202-557-2700
membership@mortgagebankers.org
www.mortgagebankers.org
The report includes an annual summary, is a financial statement analysis of mortgage banking company performance.
80 Pages
Frequency: $125 Member/$175 Non
Founded in 1992

21749 **Mortgage Banking Sourcebook**
Mortgage Bankers Association of America
1919 Pennsylvania Avenue NW
Washington, DC 20006-3404
202-557-2700
membership@mortgagebankers.org
www.mortgagebankers.org
Comprehensive directory to federal and state government agencies, industry trade associations colleges and universities, and other organizations and sources of information on mortgage lending, Includes an entire network of industry contact complete with addresses, telephone and fax numbers and internet website addresses.
Cost: $40.00
144 Pages
Founded in 1997

21750 **Mortgage Finance Database**
Mortgage Bankers Association of America
1919 Pennsylvania Avenue NW
Washington, DC 20006-3404
202-557-2700
www.mba.org
This database contains the most comprehensive and up-to-date collection of mortgage-related variables currently available.

21751 **National Association of Independent Fee Appraisers: Membership Directory**
National Association of Independent Fee Appraisers
7501 Murdoch Avenue
Saint Louis, MO 63119-2810
314-645-7583; Fax: 314-781-2872
Donna Walters, Publications
Five thousand and five hundred independent real estate appraisers.
Frequency: Annual January

21752 **National Association of Real Estate Appraisers**
P.O. Box 879
Palm Springs, CA 92263
76- 32- 528
877-815-4172; Fax: 760-327-5631
info@narea-assoc.org
www.narea-assoc.org
Dallas Martin, President
A complete guide to the REIT industry with approximately 240 real estate investment trusts, and over 1,000 associate members listed.
Cost: $695.00
600 Pages
Frequency: Annual

21753 **National Association of Real Estate Companies: Membership Directory**
National Association of Real Estate Companies
216 W Jackson Blvd
Suite 625
Chicago, IL 60606-6945
312-263-1755; Fax: 312-750-1203
info@narec.org
www.narec.org
Kim Klein, Administrator
About 200 real estate development companies.
Frequency: Quarterly

21754 **National Directory of Exchange Groups**
Creative Real Estate Magazine
PO Box L
Rancho Santa Fe, CA 92067-0560
858-756-1441; Fax: 818-156-1111
Lists over 125 professional real estate marketing groups practicing tax-deferred real estate

exchanges.
Cost: $72.00
48 Pages
Frequency: Monthly
Circulation: 51,000
ISBN: 0-194722-2 -

21755 National Real Estate Directory
Real Estate Publishing Company
P.O. Box 180635
Coronado, CA 92118
866-431-5223; Fax: 619-615-2350
www.national-real-estate-directory.com

Over 22,000 federal and state agencies, offices and departments related to the regulation of real estate, real estate associations and publications are listed.
Cost: $29.95
110 Pages
Frequency: Biennial

21756 National Real Estate Investor Sourcebook
Primedia
5680 Greenwood Plaza Boulevard
Suite 300
Greenwood Village, CO 80111
303-741-2901; Fax: 720-489-3101
Barbara Katinsky, Editor

List of about 7,000 companies and individuals in 18 real estate fields.
Cost: $78.95
Frequency: Annual, September
Circulation: 33,000

21757 National Referral Roster
Candy Holub
615 5th Street SE
Cedar Rapids, IA 52401-2158
319-364-6167
800-553-8878; Fax: 319-369-0029
www.roster.com
Candy Holub, Publisher
Mary Richeson, Business Developer
Joey Grim, Business Developer

Approximately 90,000 Real Estate offices nationwide. Provides an effective, comprehensive and easy-to-use tool for realtors to make successful referrals to other relators nationwide.
Cost: $95.00
936 Pages
Frequency: Annual
Circulation: 18,000
ISSN: 1075-1084
Founded in 1923
Printed in 2 colors on newsprint stock

21758 National Toll-Free 800 Guide to Real Estate Publications and Publishers
Real Estate Publishing Company
4580 Brookside Rd
Cameron Park, CA 95682-9619
530-677-3864
Joe Wgle, President

Directory of publications to the industry.
Cost: $15.95
82 Pages
Frequency: Biennial

21759 Nelson's Directory of Institutional Real Estate
Nelson Publications
2500 Tamiami Trl N
Nokomis, FL 34275-3476
941-966-9521; Fax: 941-966-2590
www.healthmgttech.com
A Verner Nelson, Owner
Marcia Boysen, Editor

Institutional investors who invest in real estate: investment managers, real estate service firms, insurance companies, plan sponsors, corporations and REIT's.
Cost: $335.00
Frequency: Annual August

21760 One List Directory
MRH Associates
365 Willard Avenue
Suite 2K
Newington, CT 06111-2373
800-727-5478

Over 700 companies and 6,000 company divisions are involved as listees in this comprehensive directory. Included is a section of over 12,000 contact personnel in the real estate and construction industry.
Cost: $545.00
750 Pages
Frequency: Annual

21761 Professional Relocation and Real Estate Services Directory
Relocation Information Service
113 Post Road E
2nd Floor
Westport, CT 06880-3410
203-256-1079; Fax: 203-227-3800

Offers over 6,000 real estate brokerage companies, appraisal firms, home inspectors and services companies.
Cost: $95.00
800 Pages
Frequency: Annual
Circulation: 35,000

21762 Profiles of America
Grey House Publishing
4919 Route 22
PO Box 56
Amenia, NY 12501
518-789-8700
800-562-2139; Fax: 845-373-6390
books@greyhouse.com
www.greyhouse.com
Facebook, Twitter
Leslie Mackenzie, Publisher
Richard Gottlieb, Editor

This four volume set details over 40,000 places, from the biggest metropolis to the smallest unincorporated hamlet and provides statistical details and information on over 50 different topics including: geography, climate, population, economy, income, taxes, education, housing, health and environment, public safety, transportation, presidential election results and more.
Cost: $795.00
10000 Pages
ISBN: 1-891482-80-7

21763 Profiles of...Series - State Handbooks
Grey House Publishing
4919 Route 22
PO Box 56
Amenia, NY 12501
518-789-8700
800-562-2139; Fax: 845-373-6390
books@greyhouse.com
www.greyhouse.com
Facebook, Twitter
Leslie Mackenzie, Publisher
Richard Gottlieb, Editor

Each state-by-state volume in this new series provides at-a-glance detailed demographic and statistical data on every populated place in the state, along with easy-to-use comparative rankings. Series includes 20 states. Additional states added each year.
Founded in 1981

21764 Real Estate & Land Use Regulation in Eastern and Central Europe
WorldTrade Executive
PO Box 761
Concord, MA 01742-0761
978-287-0301; Fax: 978-287-0302
www.wtexec.com
Alison French, Production Manager

Topics covered include: leasing in Russia: helpful hints for tenants; a guide to government agencies regulating development in Moscow and St. Petersburg; current law and practice for the Russian real estate market; the real estate lease in the Czech Republic; environmental considerations for acquisition of property in Hungary.
Cost: $135.00

21765 Real Estate Books and Periodicals in Print
Real Estate Publishing Company
PO Box 41177
Sacramento, CA 95841-0177
530-677-3864
John Johnsich, Publisher

Over 400 publishers of real estate books and periodicals and their product lines are profiled in this directory.
Cost: $29.95
256 Pages
Frequency: Annual
ISBN: 0-914256-33-5
Founded in 1975

21766 Real Estate Data
DataQuick Information Systems
9620 Towne Centre Dr
San Diego, CA 92121-1963
858-455-6900
800-863-INFO; Fax: 858-455-7848
www.dataquick.com
Sara Stephenson, Marketing

More than 12 million developed and undeveloped real properties in California, Arizona, Nevada, Oregon and Washington.
Frequency: Daily

21767 Real Estate RoundTable
GE Information Services
801 Pennsylvania Ave
NW Suite 720
Washing, DC 20004
202-639-8400; Fax: 202-639-8442
info@rer.org
www.rer.org
Cathy Ge, Owner
Clifton Rodgers, Senior Vice President

This database provides a forum for discussions between professional realtors and individuals interested in the buying and selling of residential and commercial property.
Frequency: Bulletin Board

21768 Real Estate Software Directory and Catalog
Z-Law Software
PO Box 40602
Providence, RI 02940-0602
401-273-5588
800-526-5588; Fax: 401-421-5334
www.z-law.com
Facebook
Gary L Sherman, President

A comprehensive guide to real estate and mortgage banking software. Includes IBM and MAC applications for realtors, landlords, property managers, investors, developers, attorneys, contractors, appraisers, loan agents, and anyone in real estate.
Frequency: SemiAnnual

21769 **Salem Press Online Platform**
Grey House Publishing
4919 Route 22
PO Box 56
Amenia, NY 12501
800-221-1592; Fax: 201-968-0511
csr@salempress.com
online.salempress.com
The new Salem Press platform houses more than 500 titles including all of Salem's Health, Literature, History and Science titles in addition to select titles from the Grey House Publishing and H.W. Wilson product lines. Online access is free with each print purchase and includes an unlimited number of simultaneous users and remote access.

21770 **Timeshare Multiple Listing Service**
MDR Telecom
11965 Venice Boulevard
Suite 204
Los Angeles, CA 90066-3954
323-539-9701
800-423-6377; Fax: 310-915-7212
triwest@att.net
www.triwest-timeshare.com
Mario A Collura, Production Manager
Mario A Collura, Author
Approximately 6,000 pieces of timeshare real estate in the US, Mexico, and Carribean.
Cost: $10.00
60 Pages
Frequency: Monthly
ISBN: 1-888176-11-3
Founded in 1984

21771 **Timeshare Vacation Owners HIP Resort Directory**
TRI Publishing
11965 Venice Boulevard
Suite 204
Los Angeles, CA 90066-3954
800-423-6377; Fax: 310-915-7212
www.triwest-timeshare.com
Mario A Collura, President
Viccie Mac, Managing Editor
This is the only combined resort directory for buyers, owners and industry professionals. Over 3,000 resorts.
Cost: $18.95
111 Pages
Frequency: Every 2 Years
ISBN: 1-888176-12-1
Founded in 1995

21772 **US Real Estate Register**
Barry
312 Main St
Wilmington, MA 01887-2791
978-658-7174
Joe Barry, Owner
Offers information on real estate departments of large national companies, industrial organizations and chambers of commerce involved in real estate development.
Cost: $58.00
575 Pages
Frequency: Annual

21773 **United National Real Estate Catalog**
United National Real Estate
4700 Belleview Avenue
Kansas City, MO 64112-1315
816-561-1115
800-999-1020; Fax: 816-231-5599
James Marinovich
Offers information on several thousand farms, ranches and country estates.
Cost: $4.95
200 Pages
Frequency: Semiannual

21774 **Who's Who in Luxury Real Estate**
JBL
2110 Western Avenue
Seattle, WA 98121-2110
206-441-7900
800-488-4066; Fax: 206-441-5297
Approximately 500 international luxury real estate brokers.
Cost: $19.95
Frequency: Annual

Industry Web Sites

21775 **http://gold.greyhouse.com**
G.O.L.D Grey House OnLine Databases
Grey House Publishing's online database platform, GOLD, offers Quick Search, Keyword Search and Expert Search for most business sectors including real estate and allied markets. The GOLD platform makes finding the information you need quick and easy - whether you're a novice searcher or an experienced database user. All of Grey House's directory products are available for subscription on the GOLD platform.

21776 **www.aagdallas.com**
Apartment Association of Greater Dallas

21777 **www.airea.com**
American Industrial Real Estate Association
Encourages high professional standards. Has developed industrial multiple listing system and standard lease form. Publishes a quarterly newsletter

21778 **www.americanhomeowners.org**
American Homeowners Foundation
Serves as an educational and research consumer group offering books, model contracts, special studies, home buying, selling,investing, building, financing and remodeling.

21779 **www.appraisalinstitute.org**
Appraisal Institute
Promotes a code of ethics and uniform standards of the real estate appraisal practice. Publishes periodicals, books and appraisal-related materials, and sponsors courses and seminars.

21780 **www.appraisers.org**
American Society of Appraisers
Organization provides education and accreditation for appraisers.

21781 **www.areuea.org**
The American Real Estate and Urban Economics Assoc
Association for academic and commercial concerns in real estate and commercial economics.

21782 **www.asfmra.org**
American Soc of Farm Managers and Rural Appraisers
Provides professionals involved in rural property issues such as management and appraisal, with information on the industry as well as educational opportunities. Includes membership and information from the American Society of Farm Manager and Rural Appraisers.

21783 **www.commercialsources.com**
The official commercial real state site of the National Association Of Realtors.

21784 **www.crb.com**
Council of Real Estate Brokerage Managers
Members are real estate firm owners and managers.

21785 **www.cre.org**
Couselors of Real Estate
Association members provide the public with expert, objective advice on property and land related matters. Individuals invited to join are awarded the CRE designation.

21786 **www.creonline.com**
6440 Sky Pointe Dr.
Suite 140-187
Las Vegas, NV 89131
810-793-0261
www.creonline.com
Facebook, Twitter, LinkedIn
Jeanne Ekhaml, Operations
State-by-state and county-by-county listing of real estate investment clubs.

21787 **www.erc.org**
Employee Relocation Council
A national organization that examines key issues affecting the relocation industry for the benefit of corporations, government agencies, and firms or individuals providing specific services to relocated employees and their families. Accepts advertising.

21788 **www.fiabci-usa.com**
FIABCI-USA
Encourages private ownership of real property and understanding of property rights and obligations.

21789 **www.greyhouse.com**
Grey House Publishing
Authoritative reference directories for most business sectors including real estate and allied markets. Users can search the online databases with varied search criteria allowing for custom searches by product category, geographic area, sales volume, keyword, subject and more. Full Grey House catalog and online ordering also available.

21790 **www.homestore.com**
Homestore.com's family of sites is the leading destination for the home and the real estate- related information on the Internet. Provides informatin on Finance and Insurance, Home Improvement, Decorating, Lawn and garden, Home Electronics amd more.

21791 **www.iaia.org**
International Association for Impact Assessment
IAIA provides a forum for the exchange of the ideas and experiences to stimulate innovation in assessing, managing and mitigating the consequences of development.

21792 **www.icsc.org**
International Council of Shopping Centers
Fosters professional standards of performance in the development, construction, financing, leasing, management and operation of shopping centers throughout the world.

21793 **www.nahma.org**
National Affordable Housing Management Association
Trade association representing companies and individuals involved in the management of affordable multifamily housing.

21794 **www.npma.org**
National Property Management Association

Represents asset management professionals and keeps members a breast of trends in asset accountability technologies. Sponsors seminars, training courses: certification program.

21795 **www.realtor.com**
National Association of Realtors
Seeks to establish cooperation among brokers engaged in buying, selling, trading and leasing for realestate.

21796 **www.realtylocator.com**
Realty Locator
Over 100,000 real estate links nationwide in 10,000 cities and towns in all 50 states.

21797 **www.reea.org**
Real Estate Educators Association
Individuals involved in training and education.

21798 **www.reipa.com**
Real Estate Information Providers Association
Supports professional information providers in the real estate industry.

21799 **www.relibrary.com/index.html**
Real Estate Library
Contains essential resources for buyers, sellers, home owners and real estate professionals.

Associations

21800 American Bakers Association
601 Pennsylvania Ave. NW
Suite 230
Washington, DC 20004

202-789-0300; Fax: 202-898-1164
info@americanbakers.org
www.americanbakers.org
Facebook, LinkedIn, Instagram, YouTube

Robb MacKie, President & CEO

Advocates for the interests of the wholesale baking industry before US Congress.
Founded in 1897

21801 American Culinary Federation
180 Center Place Way
St. Augustine, FL 32095

904-824-4468
800-624-9458; Fax: 904-940-0741
acf@acfchefs.net
www.acfchefs.org
Facebook, Twitter, LinkedIn, Flickr, Instagram

Heidi Cramb, Executive Director

Professional organization for chefs and cooks.
Founded in 1929

21802 American Hotel and Lodging Association
1250 I Street NW
Suite 1100
Washington, DC 20005

202-289-3100; Fax: 202-289-3199
www.ahla.com
Facebook, Twitter, LinkedIn

Katherine Lugar, President & CEO

Hospitality industry resource and advocate.

21803 American Institute of Baking
1213 Bakers Way
Manhattan, KS 66505-3999

785-537-4750
800-633-5137; Fax: 785-537-1493
sales@aibonline.org
www.aibonline.org
Facebook, Twitter, LinkedIn

Andre Biane, President & CEO

Committed to protecting the safety of the food supply chain worldwide and providing high value technical programs.
Founded in 1919

21804 American Institute of Wine and Food
P.O. Box 973
Belmont, CA 94002-0973

415-508-6790
info@aiwf.org
www.aiwf.org
Facebook

Frank Giaimo, National Chair
Mary Chamberlin, National Vice Chair
Drew Jaglom, National Secretary
George Linn, National Treasurer
Joyce Kucharvy, Director

A nonprofit organization dedicated to advancing the understanding, appreciation and quality of wine and food.
6000+ Members
Founded in 1981

21805 American Knife Manufacturers Association Association
30200 DetroitRd.
Westlake, OH 44145

440-899-0010; Fax: 440-892-1404
www.americanknife.org
Facebook, Twitter, LinkedIn, You Tube

J. Jeffery Wherry, Executive Director
Rick Joswick, VP
Alan Peppel, Treasurer
Bob Clemence, President
Gregory Borrosch, Associate Member Representative

The Corporation is organized and shall operate to promote the best interests of the machine knives and cutlery industry and its members.
23 Members
Founded in 1951

21806 American Personal & Private Chef Associati on
4572 Delaware St.
San Diego, CA 92116

619-294-2436
800-644-8389
info@personalchef.com
www.personalchef.com
Facebook, Twitter, YouTube

Candy Wallace, Founder, Executive Director

Organization for professional chefs.

21807 American Restaurant Association
PO Box 51482
Sarasota, FL 34232

941-379-2228
www.americanrestaurantassociation.com

Jerry Dalton, VP, Commodities

Provider of supply chain data intelligence for US food service industry.
Founded in 1996

21808 American Society of Baking
7809 N Chestnut Avenue
Kansas City, MO 64119

800-713-0462; Fax: 888-315-2612
info@asbe.org
www.asbe.org
Facebook, Twitter, Google+

Kent Van Amburg, Executive Director

Promoting the advancement of baking science and technology through the exchange of information and interaction among baking industry professionals.
Founded in 1924

21809 Association of Correctional Food Service Affiliates
PO Box 10065
Burbank, CA 91510

818-843-6608; Fax: 818-843-7423
www.acfsa.org
Facebook, Twitter, LinkedIn, Instagram

Jon Nichols, Executive Director

An organization dedicated to advancing all aspects of food service in correctional facilities.
Founded in 1969

21810 Commercial Food Equipment Service Association
3605 Centre Circle
Fort Mill, SC 29715

336-346-4700; Fax: 336-346-4745
cfesa.com

John Schwindt, President

An organization for certified technicians servicing food equipment.
Founded in 1963

21811 Cookware Manufacturers Association
PO Box 176
Lowell, MI 49331

616-987-3520
prosema@cookware.org
cookware.org
Facebook, Twitter, LinkedIn, Pinterest

Jay Zalinskas, President
Gene Karlson, VP
Hugh J Rushing, Executive VP

Represents manufactures of cookware and bakeware in the US and Canada. Publishes consumer guides to cookware and engineering standards for industry.
21 Members
Founded in 1920

21812 Council of State Restaurant Associations
2055 L St. NW
Washington, DC 20036

202-973-5377
admin@staterestaurantassociations.org
staterestaurantassociations.org

Stan Harris, President
Adam Mills, Vice President
Lynn Minges, Secretary/Treasurer
Anuja Miner, Executive Vice President

The Council works to promote the success of State Restaurant Associations.
Founded in 1914

21813 Foodservice Consultants Society International
PO Box 4961
Louisville, KY 40204

502-379-4122
info@fcsi.org
www.fcsi.org
Facebook, Twitter, LinkedIn

Martin Rahmann, President

A foodservice association with members in over 30 countries.
1000+ Members
Founded in 1955

21814 Green Restaurant Association
89 South Streetÿ
Suite 802
Boston, MA 02111

617-737-4422
info@dinegreen.com
www.dinegreen.com
Facebook, Twitter

Nonprofit organization that provides information and resources for making aspects of restaurants more eco-friendly.
Founded in 1990

21815 Home Baking Association
2931 SW Gainsboro Road
Topeka, KS 66614-4413

785-478-3283; Fax: 785-478-3024
hbapatton@aol.com
www.homebaking.org
Facebook, Twitter, Flickr

Eric Wall, President

National organization promoting scratch baking education and practice.
Founded in 1951

21816 **International Association of Culinary Professionals**
1221 Avenue of the Americas
42nd floor
New York, NY 10020
646-358-4957
866-358-4951; Fax: 866-358-2524
www.iacp.com
Facebook, Twitter, Vimeo, YouTube
Martha Holmberg, Chief Executive Officer
Shani Phelan, Member Programs & Operations
Margaret Crable, Communications & Marketing Manager
Glenn Mack, Chair
A not for profit organization whose members represent virtually every profession in the culinary universe: teachers, cooking school owners, caterers, writers, chefs, media cooking personalities, editors, publishers, food stylists, food photographers, restauranteurs, leaders of major food corporations and vintners. Literally a who's who of the food world. Founded in 1978.
3000 Members
Founded in 1978

21817 **International Caterers Association**
3601 East Joppa Road
Baltimore, MD 21234
410-931-8100; Fax: 410-931-8111
paulak@clemonsmgmt.com
internationalcaterers.org
Facebook, Twitter, Instagram
Robin Selden, President
Jennifer Perna, Immediate Past President
Frank Christian, Treasurer
Karen O'Connor, Treasurer
Paula Kreuzberg, Executive Director
Organization for catering professionals.

21818 **International Food Service Executives Association**
PO Box 1125
Placitas, NM 87043
855-268-1367
www.ifsea.org
Facebook
Richard Weil, Chairman
Provides education and community service to the foodservice industry.
3,000 Members
Founded in 1901

21819 **James Beard Foundation**
167 W 12th Street
New York, NY 10011
212-627-2308
info@jamesbeard.org
www.jamesbeard.org
Facebook, Twitter, Pinterest, YouTube, Instagram
Clare Reichenbach, CEO
Adam Jaffe, General Manager
Nonprofit organization dedicated to preserving the country's culinary heritage and fostering the appreciation and development of gastronomy by recognizing and promoting excellence in all aspects of the culinary arts.
Founded in 1986

21820 **National Association for Catering and Events**
10440 Little Patuxent Parkway
Suite 300
Columbia, MD 21044
410-290-5410; Fax: 410-630-5768
info@nace.net
www.nace.net
Facebook, Twitter, LinkedIn, Pinterest, YouTube, Instagram
Ed DiAntonio, President
Lawrence Leonard, Executive Director
Serves catering professionals and the vendors and suppliers that support them.
4000+ Members
Founded in 1950

21821 **National Restaurant Association**
2055 L Street NW
Suite 700
Washington, DC 20036
202-331-5900
800-424-5156; Fax: 202-331-2429
restaurant.org
Facebook, Twitter, YouTube
Dawn Sweeney, President & CEO
Foodservice trade association
500M Members
Founded in 1919

21822 **North American Association of Food Equipment Manufacturers**
161 North Clark Street
Suite 2020
Chicago, IL 60601
312-821-0201; Fax: 312-821-0202
info@nafem.org
www.nafem.org
Facebook, Twitter, LinkedIn
Deirdre Flynn, Executive Vice President
Michael L. Whiteley, President
Joseph Carlson, Secretary/ Treasurer
Kevin Fink, President-Elect
Marianne Byrne, Marketing Manager
Dealers and distributors of foodservice equipment and supplies.
700 Members
Founded in 1979

21823 **North American Association of Foodservice Equipment Manufacturers**
161 North Clark Street
Suite 2020
Chicago, IL 60601
312-821-0201; Fax: 312-821-0202
info@nafem.org
www.nafem.org
Facebook
Michael L. Whiteley, CFSP, President
Kevin Fink, CFSP, President-Elect
Joseph Carlson, CFSP, Secretary/Treasurer
Deirdre Flynn, CFSP, Executive Vice President
Charlie Souhrada, CFSP, Director, Member Services
Trade association for foodservice and food equipment manufacturers.

21824 **Restaurant Facility Management Association**
5600 Tennyson Parkway
Suite 265
Plano, TX 75024
972-805-0905; Fax: 972-805-0906
www.rfmaonline.com
Tracy Tomson, Executive Director
Association for restaurant facility management professionals.

21825 **United States Personal Chef Association**
PO Box 56
Gotha, FL 34734-7680
800-995-2138
info@uspca.com
www.uspca.com
Facebook, Twitter, LinkedIn, RSS, Google+, YouTube
Larry Lynch, President
Robert Lynch, Vice President
Organization offering all the necessary resources for those interested in starting their own personal chef business.
Founded in 1991

Newsletters

21826 **AEPMA News & Views**
American Edged Products Manufacturers Association
21165 Whitfield Pl
Suite 105
Sterling, VA 20165
703-433-9281; Fax: 703-433-0369
info@aepma.org
www.aepma.org
David Barrack, Executive Director
Robert Clemence, VP
Tom Arrowsmith, Treasurer
Serves the marketing and manufacturing of the cutlery industry.
Frequency: Twice/Year

21827 **Baker's Math**
American Bakers Institute
1300 I St Nw
Suite 700W
Washington, DC 20005-7203
202-789-0300; Fax: 202-898-1164
www.americanbakers.org
Robb Mac Kie, President

21828 **CHRIE Communique**
Int'l Council on Hotel, Restaurant Institute Edu.
2810 North Parham Road
suite 230
Richmond, VA 23294-3006
804-747-4971; Fax: 804-346-5009
publications@chrie.org
www.chrie.org
Dale Gaddy, Publisher
Mike Zema, President
Kathy McCarty, CEO
Joseph Bradley, Treasurer
Monthly newsletter offering information on industry, significant hospitality and tourism education job listings.
Cost: $65.00
Frequency: Monthly
Circulation: 1800
Founded in 1946

21829 **Cameron's Foodservice Marketing Reporter**
Cameron's Publications
5423 Sheridan Drive
PO Box 676
Williamsville, NY 14231
519-586-8785; Fax: 519-586-8816
www.cameronpub.com
Nina T Cameron, Editor
Bob McClelland, Publisher
Peggy Kelly, Circulation Manager
Successful promotion and advertising case histories for the restaurant and hotel industry.
Cost: $197.00
Frequency: Fortnightly
Founded in 1970

21830 **The Culinary Insider**
American Culinary Federation

180 Center Place Way
St. Augustine, FL 32095

904-824-4468
800-624-9458; Fax: 904-940-0741
www.acfchefs.org

Heidi Cramb, Executive Director
Edward G Leonard, President
Brent T. Frei, Director of Marketing
Kay Orde, Editor
Michael Feierstein, Administrative Assistant

The official membership newsletter of the American Culinary Federation.
Frequency: Monthly
Circulation: 21000
Founded in 1929
Printed in 2 colors on matte stock

21831 **Wine on Line Food and Wine Review**
Enterprise Publishing
PO Box 328
Blair, NE 68008-0328

402-426-2121; Fax: 402-426-2227
www.enterprisepub.com

Mark Rhoades, President
Dough Barber, Editor
Lynette Hansen, Sales Manager
Bill Smutko, Circulation Manager
Dave Smith, Production Manager

Reviews, feature articles and information on all areas of food and wine, including restaurants, hotels, trains and airlines. Accepts advertising.
Cost: $36.00
10 Pages
Circulation: 13150
Founded in 1800

Magazines & Journals

21832 **CFESA Magazine**
Commercial Food Equipment Service Association
3605 Centre Circle
Fort Mill, SC 29715

336-346-4700; Fax: 336-346-4745
cfesa.com

John Schwindt, President

Discussion forum and resource of the CFESA.

21833 **Chain Store Information Guide**
3922 Coconut Palm Dr
Tampa, FL 33619

800-778-9794; Fax: 813-627-6888
www.chainstoreguide.com

A national organization that serves the commercial and institutional food and lodging industry.
Founded in 1967

21834 **Cheers**
257 Park Avenue S
3rd Floor, Suite 303
New York, NY 10010

212-967-1551; Fax: 646-654-2099

John Eastman, Owner

Every issue is designed to help on-premise operators enhance the profitability of their beverage operations.

21835 **Chef**
Talcott Communications Corporation
20 N Wacker Dr
Suite 3900
Chicago, IL 60606-3188

312-726-2410; Fax: 312-726-2554

Laura Herold, President
Rob Benes, Senior Editor
Morgan Holzman, Contributing Editor
David Pizzimenti, Circulation Manager

Information on food production and presentation, includes chef profiles, trend studies, marketing information and restaurant profiles.
Cost: $32.00
Frequency: Monthly
Circulation: 38769
ISSN: 1087-061X
Founded in 1956
Printed in 4 colors on glossy stock

21836 **Coffee & Cuisine**
Coffee Talk
1218 3rd Avenue
#1315
Seattle, WA 98101-3021

206-521-7247; Fax: 206-623-0446
www.coffeecuisine.com

Kerri Goodman, Publisher

Covers new products, personnel moves, industry news, how to articles, education, and techniques to increase sales growth for the coffee, cold beverage and foodservice industry.
Cost: $36.00
Frequency: Monthly
Circulation: 30000

21837 **Cooking for Profit**
CP Publishing
PO Box 267
Fond du Lac, WI 54936-267

920-923-3700; Fax: 920-923-6805
comments@cookingforprofit.com
www.cookingforprofit.com

Colleen Phalen, Editor-in-Chief

Paid subscription trade magazine targeted to foodservice owners, managers and chefs. Each month features current trends in food preparation with step-by-step recipes and photographs; effective management techniques; and the latest in foodservice equipment — all written by industry experts. Also features in-depth profiles of a successful foodservice operation.
Cost: $26.00
28 Pages
Frequency: Monthly
Founded in 1932
Printed in 4 colors on glossy stock

21838 **Cornell Hotel & Restaurant Administration Quarterly**
Elsevier Science Publishing Company
537 Statler Hall
Ithaca, NY 14853-6902

607-255-9780; Fax: 607-254-2922
hosp_research@cornell.edu
www.hotelschool.cornell.edu

Dr. Michael Sturman, Editor
Glenn Withiam, Executive Editor
Nicole Roach, Marketing

A journal devoted to the development and exchange of management ideas for the hospitality industry.
Cost: $113.00
Frequency: Quarterly
Circulation: 4500
Founded in 1963

21839 **Culinary Trends**
Culinary Trends Publications
6285 E Spring Street
#107
Long Beach, CA 90808-4000

310-496-2558; Fax: 310-421-8993
www.culinarytrends.com

Fred Mensigna, Publisher
Linda Mensinga, Editor

Information for food and beverage managers along with managers of hotels and restaurants.
Cost: $21.60
Frequency: Quarterly
Circulation: 10000

21840 **El Restaurante Mexicano**
Maiden Name Press
1010 Lake St
Suite 604
Oak Park, IL 60301-1136

708-848-3200
800-407-5845; Fax: 708-445-9477
kfurore@restmex.com
www.restmex.com

Joe Madden, President
Kathleen Furore, Managing Director
Jessica Pantanini, Managing Director

A bilingual magazine featuring industry specific food news, features restaurant profiles and new product information for personnel of restaurants serving mexican/southwestern menu items nationwide.
Cost: $18.00
Circulation: 27000
Founded in 1997

21841 **FEDA News & Views**
Foodservice Equipment Distributors Association
5600 N River Road
Suite 740
Rosemont, IL 60018

224-293-6500
tracy@feda.com
www.feda.com

Tracy Mulqueen, CEO
George Maul, Director, Finance & Operations
Tim O'Connor, Communications Manager

Focus is on sales, technology, new products and other areas of benefit to dealers, as well as industry trends and news.
Cost: $150.00
Circulation: 1200
Founded in 1933

21842 **Food & Beverage News**
Food & Beverage News
1886 W Bay Drive
#E6
Largo, FL 33770-3017

727-585-7745; Fax: 727-585-7245

Dennis J Regan, Publisher

News on the latest liquor law, new products, and government legislation.
Cost: $28.00
Frequency: Monthly
Circulation: 16,880

21843 **Food Arts Magazine**
M Shanken Communications
387 Park Ave S
Suite 8
New York, NY 10016-8872

212-684-4224; Fax: 212-684-5424
www.cigaraficionado.com

Marvin Shanken, Publisher

A magazine devoted to the restaurant industry.
Cost: $40.00
Frequency: Monthly
Founded in 1988

21844 **Foodservice Equipment & Supplies Specialist**
Reed Business Information
1350 E Touhy Avenue
Des Plaines, IL 60018-3358

630-320-7000; Fax: 630-288-8686
www.reedbusiness.com

Mitchell Schechter, Editor-in-Chief
Niles Crum, Publisher

Magazine for professionals who specify, sell and distribute foodservice equipment, supplies

and furnishings.
Cost: $69.95
64+ Pages
Frequency: Monthly
Circulation: 27M
Founded in 1947
Printed in 4 colors on glossy stock

21845 Foodservice Equipment Reports
Robin Ashton
2000 Clearwater Drive
Oak Brook, IL 60523-3358

630-288-8000
800-446-6551; Fax: 630-288-8265
webmaster@reedbusiness.com
www.reedbusiness.com

Josph Carbonara, Editor-in-Chief
Maureen Slocum, Publisher
Keithy Mcnamara, Marketing
katy Tucker, Circulation Manager
Jeff Greisph, CEO

Geared toward manufacturers of foodservice equipment and their agencies.
Cost: $106.90
Frequency: Monthly
Circulation: 22719
Founded in 1947

21846 Franchise Times
2808 Anthony Lane S
Minneapolis, MN 55418

612-767-3200
800-528-3296; Fax: 612-767-3230
info@franchisetimes.com
www.franchisetimes.com

Mary Jo Larson, Publisher
Nancy Weingartner, Executive Editor
Beth Ewen, Managing Editor

Investigative pieces, analysis and profiles to help franchisors, franchisees and vendors improve their businesses.
Frequency: 10x/year

21847 Fresh Cup Magazine
Fresh Cup Publishing Company
537 SE Ash Street Suite 300
PO Box 14827
Portland, OR 97293-827

503-236-2587
800-868-5866; Fax: 503-236-3165
jan@freshcup.com
www.freshcup.com

Julie Beals, Editor
Nicole Maas, Sales/Marketing Associate
Bill Berninger, Circulation Director
Ward Barbee, Publisher
Jan Gibson, Owner
Cost: $57.00
68 Pages
Frequency: Monthly
Circulation: 14000
Founded in 1992
Printed in 4 colors on glossy stock

21848 Full-Service Restaurant

Home Page: www.fsrmagazine.com
Facebook, Twitter

Greg Sanders, Group Publisher
Connie Gentry, Editor

Ideas and insights for decision-makers in full-service restaurant industry.
Founded in 2012

21849 Gourmet News
Oser Communications Group
1877 N Kolb Road
Tucson, AZ 85715

520-721-1300
www.gourmetnews.com

Rocelle Aragon, Editor
Kate Seymour, Senior Associate Publisher

The business newspaper for the gourmet industry.
40 Pages
Frequency: Monthly
Circulation: 23381
ISSN: 1052-4630
Founded in 1991
Printed in 4 colors on glossy stock

21850 Journal of Foodservice Business Research
Taylor & Francis
325 Chestnut Street
Suite 800
Philadelphia, PA 19106

800-354-1420; Fax: 215-625-2940
www.tandf.co.uk

David A Cranage, Editor

Features articles from international experts in various disciplines, including management, marketing, finance, law, food technology, nutrition, psychology, information systems, anthropology, human resources, and more.
Cost: $ 92.00
Frequency: Quarterly
ISSN: 1537-8020
Founded in 1978

21851 Midsouthwest Restaurant
3800 North Portland Avenue
Oklahoma City, OK 73112-2982

405-942-8181
800-375-8181; Fax: 405-942-0541
www.okrestaurants.com

Jim Hopper, President/CEO
Shannon Moad, Editor
Debra Bailey, Deputy Director
Frequency: Quarterly
Circulation: 2500
Founded in 1933

21852 Nation's Restaurant News
Informa USA Inc.
101 Arthur Andersen Pkwy.
Sarasota, FL 34232-6323

508-616-6600
800-944-4676; Fax: 508-616-5522
jenna.telesca@knect365.com
www.nrn.com

Jenna Telesca, Editor-in-Chief
Kent Scholla, Director, Sales
Laura Viscusi, VP, Market Leader

Serves commercial and onsite food service and lodging establishments including restaurants, schools, universities, hospitals, nursing homes and other health and welfare facilities, hotels and motels with food service, government installations, clubs and other related firms.
Cost: $44.95
Circulation: 85999
Founded in 1925
Mailing list available for rent: 100,000 names at $100 per M
Printed in 4 colors on matte stock

21853 National Dipper
US Exposition Corporation
1028 W. Devon Avenue
Elk Grove Village, IL 60007

847-301-8400; Fax: 847-301-8402
lynda@nationaldipper.com
www.nationaldipper.com

Lynda Utterback, Publisher

Information for retail ice cream and frozen yogurt owners and operators, includes changes and developments in the business.
Cost: $55.00
Circulation: 17000
Founded in 1985
Printed in 4 colors on glossy stock

21854 Quick Service Restaurant

Home Page: www.qsrmagazine.com
Facebook, Twitter

Greg Sanders, Group Publisher
Sam Oches, Editor

Leading source of news about limited-service restaurant industry.

21855 Restaurant Digest
Panagos Publishing
3930 Knowles Avenue
#305
Kensington, MD 20895-2428

301-929-6200; Fax: 301-929-6550
www.foodservicedepot.com

Bruce Panagos, Publisher

Developments and news of interest to owners, managers, and operators of dining and entertainment establishments in the region.

21856 Restaurant Hospitality
Donohue/Meehan Publishing
1801 E 9th St
Suite 920
Cleveland, OH 44114-3103

216-931-7258; Fax: 216-696-1752
rheditor@penton.com
www.restaurant-hospitality.com

Jeff Donohoe, President
Jess Grossberg, Publisher
Gail Bellamy, Managing Editor
Sue Apple, Production Manager
Frequency: Monthly
Circulation: 117,721
Founded in 1892

21857 Restaurant Marketing
Oxford Publishing
Ste 1
1903b University Ave
Oxford, MS 38655-4150

662-236-5510
800-247-3881; Fax: 662-281-0104
www.restaurant-marketing.net

Frequency: Bi-Monthly

21858 Restaurant Wine
Wine Profits
PO Box 222
Napa, CA 94559-222

707-224-4777; Fax: 707-224-6740
www.restaurantwine.com

Ronn Wiegand, Publisher
Paul Grieco, Co-Owner

Information on the marketing of wine in restaurants, hotels and clubs, wine and food pairing ideas and review of wines.
Cost: $99.00
Frequency: Monthly
Circulation: 3000
ISSN: 1040-7030
Printed in 2 colors on matte stock

21859 Restaurants & Institutions
Reed Business Information

2000 Clearwater Dr
Oak Brook, IL 60523-8809

630-574-0825; Fax: 630-288-8781
jamie.popp@reedbusiness.com
www.reedbusiness.com

Jeff Greisch, President
Scott Hume, Managing Editor

Commercial and noncommercial foodservice establishments including restaurant, hotels, motels, fast-food chains,coffee shops, food stores with foodservice
Frequency: Monthly
Circulation: 155512
Founded in 1937
Printed in 4 colors on glossy stock

21860 **Restaurants, Resorts & Hotels**
Publishing Group
PO Box 318
Trumbull, CT 06611-0318

860-279-0149; Fax: 203-254-7104

James Martone, Publisher

Information on new products, supplies, food and equipment for those executives and managers who have responsibility for the food.
Cost: $24.00
Frequency: Monthly
Circulation: 97,000

21861 **Southeast Food Service News**
8805 Tamiami Trail N #301
Naples, FL 34108

239-514-1258
efischer@sfsn.com
www.sfsn.com
Y

Elliott R Fischer, Marketing Director
John P Hayward, Account Executive
Elsie Olson, Production Manager
Frequency: Monthly
Founded in 1977

21862 **Southwest Food Service News**
4011 W Plano Pkwy
Suite 121
Plano, TX 75093-5620

972-943-1254; Fax: 972-943-1258
www.southwestfoodservice.com

Sam Ballard, Publisher

21863 **The National Culinary Review**
American Culinary Federation
180 Center Place Way
St. Augustine, FL 32095

904-824-4468
800-624-9458; Fax: 904-940-0741
www.acfchefs.org

Heidi Cramb, Executive Director
Edward G Leonard, President
Brent T. Frei, Director of Marketing
Kay Orde, Editor
Michael Feierstein, Administrative Assistant

Flagship publication of the American Culinary Federation.
Frequency: 6x/yr
Circulation: 21000
Founded in 1932

21864 **Total Food Service**
PO Box 2507
Greenwich, CT 06836-2507

203-661-9090; Fax: 203-661-9325
www.totalfood.com

Fred Klashman, President

21865 **Yankee Food Service**
Griffin Publishing Company
201 Oak St
Suite A
Pembroke, MA 02359

781-294-4700
866-677-4700; Fax: 781-829-0134
info@griffinpublishing.net
www.griffinpublishing.net

Kevin Griffin, President
Lynda Bassett, Editor
Henry Zacchini, Associate Publisher
Karen Harty, Vice President
Julie Mignosa, Office Manager

Reports news and happenings of the food service industry in New England.
Cost: $47.00
48 Pages
Frequency: Monthly
Circulation: 26110
Founded in 1979

Trade Shows

21866 **ACF National Convention**
American Culinary Federation
180 Center Place Way
St. Augustine, FL 32095

904-824-4468
800-624-9458; Fax: 904-940-0741
acf@acfchefs.net
www.acfchefs.org

Brent Frei, Director Marketing
Michael Baskette, Administrative Assistant
Michael Feierstein, Administrative Assistant
Bryan Hunt, Graphic Designer
Patricia Carroll, Director of Communications

200 booths of products and foodstuffs for the food service industry. Seminars, workshops, cooking demos, more.

21867 **AEPMA Annual Meeting**
American Edged Products Manufacturers Association
21165 Whitfield Pl
Suite 105
Sterling, VA 20165

703-433-9281; Fax: 703-433-0369
www.aepma.org

David Barrack, Executive Director
Robert Clemence, VP
Tom Arrowsmith, Treasurer

Offering training and certificate programs, and management courses.
Frequency: Annual

21868 **Annual Hotel, Motel and Restaurant Supply Show of the Southeast**
Leisure Time Unlimited
708 Main Street
PO Box 332
Myrtle Beach, SC 29577

843-448-9483
800-261-5991; Fax: 843-626-1513
hmrss@sc.rr.com
www.hmrsss.com

Brooke P Baker, Show Director

Trade show for the hospitality industry.
23000 Attendees
Frequency: January
Founded in 1975

21869 **ChefConnect**
American Culinary Federation
180 Center Place Way
St. Augustine, FL 32095

904-824-4468
800-624-9458; Fax: 904-940-0741
acf@acfchefs.net
www.acfchefs.org

Heidi Cramb, Executive Director

Regional educational and networking events for professional chefs and cooks.

21870 **Fancy Food Show**
Specialty Food Association, Inc.
136 Madison Avenue
12th Floor
New York, NY 10016

212-482-6440; Fax: new
www.specialtyfood.com

Mike Silver, Chair
Becky Renfro Borbolla, Treasurer
Dennis Deschaine, Past Chairperson
Shawn McBride, Vice Chair
Matt Nielsen, Secretary

Over 80,000 on-trend and best-in-class products, including confections, cheese, coffee, snacks, spices, ethnic, natural, organic and more. 1,300 exhibitors representing specialty foods and beverages from across the United States and 35 countries and regions.

21871 **Hospitality Food Service Expo Southeast and Atlanta International Wine**
Reed Business Information
275 Washington Street
Boston, MA 02458

617-261-1166; Fax: 617-558-4327

Patrick Paleno, Show Manager
Barry Reed Jr, CFO
Stuart Whayman, CFO

400 booths featuring educational seminars, culinary salon, and exhibits of products and services.
12M Attendees
Frequency: October

21872 **Restaurant Innovation Summit**
National Restaurant Association
2055 L Street NW
Suite 700
Washington, DC 20036

202-331-5900
800-424-5156; Fax: 202-331-2429
www.restaurant.org/ris
Facebook, Twitter

Innovations in technology and how they may be applied to the restaurant industry.
Frequency: Annual

21873 **Year of Enchantment**
Int'l Council on Hotel, Restaurant Institute Edu.
1200 17th Street NW
Washington, DC 20036-3006

202-467-6300
publications@chrie.org
www.chrie.org

Susan Gould, Manager
Joseph Bradley, Treasurer

Containing 70+ booths and 50+ exhibits.
750 Attendees
Frequency: August
Founded in 1946

Directories & Databases

21874 **Chain Restaurant Operators Directory**
Chain Store Guide

3710 Corporex Park Dr.
Suite 310
Tampa, FL 33619-1389

813-627-6700
800-972-9292; Fax: 813-627-6888
webmaster@chainstoreguide.com
www.chainstoreguide.com

Mike Jarvis, Publisher
Arthur Sciarrotta, Senior VP

Discover more than 5,600 listings and more than 26,000 unique personnel within the Restaurant Chain, Foodservice Management, and Hotel/Motel Operator markets in the U.S. and Canada. Each company must have at least $1 million in annual sales either system wide or industry and have two or more units/accounts.
Cost: $575.00
Frequency: Annual

21875 Culinary Collection Directory
International Association/Culinary Professionals
304 W Liberty Street
Suite 201
Louisville, KY 40202

502-587-7953
800-928-4227; Fax: 502-589-3602
info@iacp.com
www.iacp.com

Kerry Edwards, Sr Member Services Representative
Trina Gribbins, Manager

Teachers, cooking school owners, caterers, writers, chefs, media cooking personalities, editors, publishers, food stylists, food photographers, restauranteurs, leaders of major food corporations and vintners. Literally a who's who of the food world.

21876 Food & Beverage Market Place
Grey House Publishing
4919 Route 22
PO Box 56
Amenia, NY 12501

518-789-8700
800-562-2139; Fax: 845-373-6390
books@greyhouse.com
www.greyhouse.com
Facebook, Twitter

Leslie Mackenzie, Publisher
Richard Gottlieb, Editor

This information packed three-volume set is the most powerful buying and marketing guide for the US food and beverage industry. Includes thousands of industry freight and transportation listings.
Cost: $595.00
2000 Pages
Frequency: Annual
ISBN: 1-592373-61-5
Founded in 1981

21877 Food & Beverage Marketplace: Online Database
Grey House Publishing
4919 Route 22
PO Box 56
Amenia, NY 12501

518-789-8700
800-562-2139; Fax: 845-373-6390
gold@greyhouse.com
gold.greyhouse.com
Facebook, Twitter

Richard Gottlieb, President
Leslie Mackenzie, Publisher

This complete updated Food & Beverage Market Place: Online Database is the go-to source for the food and beverage industry. Anyone involved in the food and beverage industry needs this 'industry bible' and the important contacts to develop critical research data that can make for successful business growth.
Frequency: Annual
Founded in 1981

21878 Getaways for Gourmets in the Northeast
Wood Pond Press
365 Ridgewood Rd
West Hartford, CT 06107-3517

860-521-0389; Fax: 860-313-0185
www.green-cuisine.com

Richard M Woodworth, Owner

Directory of services and supplies to the industry.
Cost: $14.95
514 Pages

21879 High Volume Independent Restaurants Database
Chain Store Guide
3710 Corporex Park Dr.
Suite 310
Tampa, FL 33619-1389

813-627-6700
800-927-9292; Fax: 813-627-6888
webmaster@chainstoreguide.com
www.chainstoreguide.com

Mike Jarvis, Publisher
Shami Choon, Manager

Covers this growing niche through its nearly 5,900 listings featuring casual dining, family restaurants and fine dining establishments. Plus, access to over 15,000 key personnel names puts you in contact with key decision makers.
Cost: $575.00
1,000 Pages
Frequency: Annual

21880 International Association of Culinary Professionals
1221 Avenue of the Americas
42ns Floor
New York, NY 10020

646-358-4957
866-358-4951; Fax: 866-358-2524
www.iacp.com
Facebook, Twitter, YouTube, Vimeo

Martha Homberg, Chief Executive Officer
Shani Phelan, Member Programs & Operations Mgr
Margaret Crable, Communications & Marketing

A not for profit organization whose members represent virtually every profession in the culinary universe: teachers, cooking school owners, caterers, writers, chefs, media cooking personalities, editors, publishers, food stylists, food photographers, restauranteurs, leaders of major food corporations and vintners. Literally a who's who of the food world. Founded in 1978.
3000+ Members
Founded in 1978

21881 Restaurant Hospitality: Hospitality 500 Issue
Penton Media
1166 Avenue of the Americas
New York, NY 10036

212-204-4200; Fax: 216-696-6662
information@penton.com
www.penton.com
Facebook, Twitter, LinkedIn

Jane Cooper, Marketing
Chris Meyer, Director
Bev Walter, Service Manager

500 independent restaurants selected on basis of sales.
Cost: $25.00
Frequency: Annual, June
Circulation: 123,000

21882 Restaurants and Institutions: Annual 400 Issues
Reed Business Information
1350 E Touhy Avenue
Suite 200E
Des Plaines, IL 60018-3358

847-962-2200; Fax: 630-288-8686
www.reedbusiness.com

Roland Dietz, CEO
Stuart Whayman, CFO
Cost: $25.00
Frequency: Annual
Circulation: 16,000

21883 Zagat.com Restaurant Guides
Zagat Survey
4 Columbus Cir
New York, NY 10019-1180

212-977-6000; Fax: 212-977-9760
customerservice@zagat.com
www.zagat.com

Tim Zagat, CEO

Zagat.com was launched in May of 1999 and contains the most trusted and authoritive dining information online for over 20,000 restaurants in twenty eight cities worldwide, with 17 more cities to be added shortly. Based in New York City, the Zagat survey was founded in 1979 by Tim and Nina Zagat.

Industry Web Sites

21884 http://gold.greyhouse.com
G.O.L.D Grey House OnLine Databases

Grey House Publishing's online database platform, GOLD, offers Quick Search, Keyword Search and Expert Search for most business sectors including restaurant markets. The GOLD platform makes finding the information you need quick and easy - whether you're a novice searcher or an experienced database user. All of Grey House's directory products are available for subscription on the GOLD platform.

21885 www.acfchefs.org
American Culinary Federation

Member organization of professional chefs and cooks. Certifies chefs, accredits culinary programs and promotes culinary arts.

21886 www.chefcertification.com
American Culinary Federation

Offers the required courses for ACF certification online.

21887 www.chowbaby.com

This web site is search engine for restaurants.It makes finding the perfect eatery close to your home or travel destination. Online reservations, maps, menus and more. You can search by International Location, US Location, US Map, or Cuisine type.

21888 www.chrie.org
Int'l Council on Hotel, Restaurant Institute Edu.

To enhance professionalism at all levels of the hospitality and tourism industry through education and training.

21889 www.greyhouse.com
Grey House Publishing

Authoritative reference directories for most business sectors including restaurant markets. Users can search the online databases with varied search criteria allowing for custom searches by product category, geographic area, sales volume, keyword, subject and more. Full Grey House catalog and online ordering also available.

21890 **www.iacp.com**
International Association of Culinary Professionals

A not for profit organization whose members represent virtually every profession in the culinary universe: teachers, cooking school owners, caterers, writers, chefs, media cooking personalities, editors, publishers, food stylists, food photographers, restauranteurs, leaders of major food corporations and vintners. Literally a who's who of the food world. Founded in 1978.

21891 **www.restaurant.org**
National Restaurant Association
Trends, government affairs, training, research, dining guides and links.

21892 **www.therestaurantfinder.com**
This search engine help to find restaurants by type or location.

Associations

21893 **American Beverage Licensees**
5101 River Road
Suite 108
Bethesda, MD 20816-1560

301-656-1494; Fax: 301-656-7539
info@ablusa.org
www.ablusa.org
Facebook, Twitter

John Bodnovich, Executive Director

Trade association for retail beverage alcohol license holders.
20000 Members

21894 **American Booksellers Association**
333 Westchester Avenue
Suite S202
White Plains, NY 10604

800-637-0037; Fax: 914-417-4013
info@bookweb.org
www.bookweb.org
Facebook, Twitter, Instagram

Oren Teicher, CEO

Trade organization pledged to protecting the well-being of book retailers and promoting the availability of books.
2000 Members
Founded in 1900
Mailing list available for rent

21895 **American Collegiate Retailing Association**
Loyola University/Department of Marketing
6363 Saint Charles Avenue
New Orleans, LA 70118-6195

504-865-2011; Fax: 504-865-3496
www.acraretail.org

Robert Jones, President
Patrali Chatterjee, Vice President

Organization of faculty from colleges with a background in retailing.
400 Members
Founded in 1950

21896 **American Mobile Retail Association**

213-785-4783
info@americanmra.com
www.americanmra.com
Facebook, Twitter

Stacey Jischke-Steffe, Co-Founder/President
Jeanine Romo, Co-Founder/Vice President

Support and assistance for mobile retailers.

21897 **Association for Retail Technology**
1101 New York Ave NW
Washington, DC 20005

202-783-7971
800-673-4692; Fax: 202-737-2849
arts@nrf.com
www.nrf.com
Facebook, Twitter, LinkedIn, YouTube, Instagram, Flickr

Matthew Shay, President and CEO
Carleen Kohut, COO
Mallory Duncan, SVP& General Counsel
David French, SVP, Govt. Relations
Mike Gatti, SVP, Member Relations

Subsidiary of the National Retail Federation, this is a retailer-driven membership organization dedicated to creating an international, barrier-free technology environment for retailers. ARTS was established to ensure that technology works to enhance a retailer's ability to develop store level business solutions and avoid situations that limit a retailer's ability to implement change while providing industry standards designed to provide greater value at lower costs.
175 Members
Founded in 1993

21898 **Association of Canadian Cannabis Retailers**
1863 5th Ave. W
Suite 203
Vancouver, BC V6J 1P5

info@accres.ca
www.accres.ca
Facebook, Twitter

Heather Tayler, Executive Director

Promotes a community-based approach to cannabis retail that provides access to the highest quality of products and services and empowering client care.
Founded in 2011

21899 **Black Retail Action Group**
8 West 126th Street
New York, NY 10027

212-234-3050; Fax: 212-234-3053
info@bragusa.org
www.bragusa.org
Facebook, Twitter, LinkedIn, Instagram

Nicole Cokley-Dunlap, Co-President
Shawn R. Outler, Co-President
Leslie Smith, Vice President, Finance

Not for profit prepares students of color for leadership roles in fashion.
500 Members
Founded in 1970

21900 **Comics Professional Retail Organization**
PO Box 16804
Irvine, CA 92623-6804

949-387-9599
www.comicspro.org
Facebook, Twitter

Peter Dolan, President
Marco Davanzo, Executive Director

The voice of direct-market comic book retailers.

21901 **Equipment Dealers Association**
165 North Meramec Avenue
Suite 430
St. Louis, MO 63105

636-349-5000; Fax: 636-349-5443
info@equipmentdealer.org
www.equipmentdealer.org
Facebook, Twitter, LinkedIn

Kim Rominger, President & CEO
Michael Williams, VP, Operations
Joseph Dykes, VP, Industry Relations
Doug Kreienkamp, Operations Coordinator
Alex Hoffman, Communications & Marketing Director

Nonprofit trade organization supporting equipment dealers of agriculture, construction, industrial, forestry, outdoor power, lawn and garden and turf industries. The association provides a variety of educational, financial, legislative and legal services to members.
4500 Members
Founded in 1900

21902 **Institute of Store Planners**
25 N Broadway
Tarrytown, NY 10591-3221

914-332-1806; Fax: 914-332-1541
www.retaildesigninstitute.org

Richard C Byrne, Manager
Kenneth Nisch, VP
Ronald Kline, Chairman
Richard Byrne, Manager

Provides a forum for debate and discussion by store design experts and retailers. Sponsors student design programs.
1300 Members
Founded in 1961

21903 **International Council of Shopping Centers**
1221 Avenue of the Americas
41st Floor
New York, NY 10020-1099

646-728-3800; Fax: 732-694-1690
membership@icsc.org
www.icsc.org
Facebook, Twitter, LinkedIn, Instagram

Tom McGee, President & CEO

Fosters professional standards of performance in the development, construction, financing, leasing, management and operation of shopping centers throughout the world.
70000 Members
Founded in 1957

21904 **International Franchise Association**
1900 K Street NW
Suite 700
Washington, DC 20006

202-628-8000; Fax: 202-628-0812
www.franchise.org
Facebook, Twitter, LinkedIn, YouTube, Instagram

Robert Cresanti, President

Membership consists of companies franchising the distribution of goods or services.
Founded in 1997

21905 **International Map Trade Association**
2629 Manhattan Avenue
PMB 281
Hermosa Beach, CA 90254

310-376-7731; Fax: 949-458-0300
www.imiamaps.org

Chris Knoebel, President
Sanford J Hill, Executive Director

Membership comprised of retail stores featuring maps, travel books, globes, and travel products, plus publishers and manufacturers producing these products. Publishes a monthly newsletter.
800 Members
Founded in 1981

21906 **International Premium Cigar & Pipe Retailers Association**
513 Capitol Court NE
Suite 300
Washington, DC 20002

202-621-8064
www.ipcpr.org
Facebook, Twitter, LinkedIn, YouTube

Ken Neumann, President

Trade association of high quality tobacconists.
2,350 Members
Founded in 1933

21907 **Marijuana Business Association**

info@mjba.net
www.mjba.net
Facebook, Twitter, YouTube

A leading national business-to-business organization in legal cannabis. Provides members with business intelligence, networking, and business opportunities.
Founded in 2013

21908 **Marine Retailers Association of America**
8401 73rd Avenue N
Suite 71
Minneapolis, MN 55428
763-315-8043; Fax: 708-763-9236
matt@mraa.com
www.mraa.com
Facebook, Twitter, LinkedIn
Matt Gruhn, President
Liz Walz, Vice President
Allison Gruhn, Director, Business Development
Sherri Cuvala, Membership Manager
Sarah Korbel, Events & Operation Specialist
Raising the standards of retailing within the industry. Promotes activities for the recreational boating industry and holds seminars to improve management.
2.5M Members
Founded in 1972

21909 **Museum Store Association**
2025 M Street NW
Suite 800
Washington, DC 20036
202-367-1106; Fax: 202-367-2104
info@museumstoreassociation.org
www.museumstoreassociation.org
Facebook, Twitter, LinkedIn, Pinterest
Steven Antolick, Executive Director
2500 Members
Founded in 1955

21910 **National Advisory Group**
200 Ponte Vedra Blvd.
Ponte Vedra Beach, FL 32082
440-250-1583
nagconvenience.com
Facebook
John Lofstock, Executive Director
This association represents senior level management of retail companies organized to enhance buying power, merchandising programs and an exchange of ideas.
500 Members
Founded in 1983

21911 **National Association of Chain Drug Stores**
1776 Wilson Blvd.
Suite 200
Arlington, VA 22209
703-549-3001; Fax: 703-836-4869
contactus@nacds.org
www.nacds.org
Facebook, Twitter, LinkedIn, YouTube, Flickr
Steven C. Anderson, President & CEO
The chief purpose of NACDS is to represent the views and policy positions of member chain drug companies.
105 Members
Founded in 1933

21912 **National Association of College Stores**
528 E Lorain St.
Oberlin, OH 44074
800-622-7498; Fax: 440-775-4769
webteam@nacs.org
www.nacs.org
Bob Walton, CEO
Provides educational and support services and products to college stores. Promotes business methods and ethics. Conducts manager certification, educational services and research.
3.9M Members
Founded in 1963

21913 **National Association of Convenience Stores**
1600 Duke Street
Alexandria, VA 22314
703-684-3600
800-966-6227; Fax: 703-836-4564
www.convenience.org
Facebook, Twitter, LinkedIn, YouTube, Instagram
Sandy Smith, National Sales Manager
Association supporting convenience and fuel retailing companies.
2.3M Members
Founded in 1961
Mailing list available for rent

21914 **National Association of General Merchandise Representatives**
16A Journey
Suite 200
Aliso Viejo, CA 92656
716-898-0122
marketing@nagmr.com
nagmr.com
Facebook, Twitter, Pinterest, RSS
Jordan Stone, President
A professional association of consumer product brokers representing leading manufacturers to the drug, mass merchandise and food trade.

21915 **National Association of Music Merchants**
5790 Armada Dr.
Carlsbad, CA 92008
760-438-8001
800-767-6266; Fax: 760-438-7327
info@namm.org
www.namm.org
Facebook, Twitter, YouTube, Instagram
Joe Lamond, President & CEO
Association of music products industry professionals.
3.6M Members
Founded in 1901

21916 **National Association of Resale Professionals**
PO BOX 190
St. Clair Shores, MI 48080
586-294-6700
800-544-0751; Fax: 586-588-7018
info@narts.org
www.narts.org
Adele R. Meyer, Executive Director
Gail A. Seigel, Director of Membership Services
A national trade association for owners and managers of resale thrift shops. Purpose is to provide educational networking to promote the industry.
1100+ Members
Founded in 1984

21917 **National Automatic Merchandising Association**
20 N Wacker Dr.
Suite 3500
Chicago, IL 60606
312-346-0370
800-331-8816; Fax: 312-704-4140
www.namanow.org
Facebook, Twitter, x, YouTube, Instagram
Carla Balakgie, President & CEO
Association serving the convenience services industry.
1250+ Members
Founded in 1936

21918 **National Council of Chain Restaurants**
1101 New York Ave. NW
Suite 1200
Washington, DC 20005
202-783-7971
800-673-4692; Fax: 202-737-2849
nrf.com
Facebook, Twitter, LinkedIn, YouTube, Instagram
Matthew R. Shay, President & CEO
The leading trade association exclusively representing chain restaurant companies. Working to advance sound public policy that best serves the interests of restaurant businesses and the millions of people they employ.
Founded in 1965

21919 **National Grocers Association**
1005 N Glebe Road
Suite 250
Arlington, VA 22201
703-516-0700; Fax: 703-516-0115
www.nationalgrocers.org
Facebook, Twitter, LinkedIn
Greg Ferrara, President/CEO
Works to advance understanding, trade, and cooperation in the food industry. Represents members interests before the government. Offers store planning, and engineering, training and advertising.
1.5M Members
Founded in 1982

21920 **National Ice Cream Retailers Association**
743 Spirit 40 Park Dr.
Suite 121
Chesterfield, MO 63005
636-778-1822
866-303-6960; Fax: 636-898-4326
info@nicra.org
www.nicra.org
Facebook
Steve Christensen, Executive Director
Members are in retail frozen dessert businesses. Some offer food services either full of limited and some operate convenience stores. The common denominator is that all members offer frozen desserts for take home or on site consumption.
350 Members
Founded in 1933

21921 **National Restaurant Association**
2055 L Street NW
Suite 700
Washington, DC 20036
202-331-5900
800-424-5156; Fax: 202-331-2429
restaurant.org
Facebook, Twitter, YouTube
Dawn Sweeney, President & CEO
Foodservice trade association
500M Members
Founded in 1919

21922 **National Restaurant Association Educationa l Foundation**
2055 L St. NW
Washington, DC 20036
312-715-1010
800-424-5156; Fax: 312-583-9767
chooserestaurants.org
Facebook, Twitter, YouTube, Tumblr, Pinterest
Dawn Sweeney, President & CEO
NRAEF is the philanthropic foundation of the National Restaurant Association. Committed to

enhancing the restaurant industry's service to the public through education, community engagement and promotion of career opportunities.
Founded in 1987

21923 **National Retail Federation**
1101 New York Ave NW
Washington, DC 20005

202-783-7971
800-673-4692; Fax: 202-737-2849
www.nrf.com
Facebook, Twitter, LinkedIn, YouTube, Instagram, Flickr

Matthew R. Shay, President/CEO
Mindy F. Grossman, Vice Chair
Autor Erik, Vice President
Kip Tindell, Chairman
Kip Tindell, Treasurer & Chairman of Finance

Retail trade association with membership that comprises all retail formats and channels of distribution including department, specialty, discount, catalog, Internet and independent stores. NRF members represent an industry that encompasses more than 1.4 million US retail establishments which employ more than 23 million people — about one in five American workers — and registered 2002 sales of $3.6 trillion. NRF's international members operate stores in more than 50 nations.
55M Members
Founded in 1990

21924 **National Shoe Retailers Association**
7386 N La Cholla Blvd.
Tucson, AZ 85741

520-209-1710
800-673-8446; Fax: 410-381-1167
info@nsra.org
www.nsra.org
Facebook, Twitter, Pinterest

Chuck Schuyler, President

Membership association for independent shoe ratailers. Provides busisness services such as credit-card processing and shipping at special low members only prices. Also provides educational and training programs, consulting and other services.
1400 Members
Founded in 1912

21925 **National Ski & Snowboard Retailers Association**
1601 Feehanville Dr.
Suite 300
Mount Prospect, IL 60056

847-391-9825
888-257-1168; Fax: 847-391-9827
info@nssra.com
www.nssra.com

Larry Weindruch, President

The retail voice for the ski and snowboard industries and provides information and services you need to operate more successfully.
250 Members
Founded in 1987

21926 **National Sporting Goods Association**
1601 Feehanville Dr.
Suite 300
Mount Prospect, IL 60056

847-296-6742
800-815-5422; Fax: 847-391-9827
info@nsga.org
www.nsga.org
Facebook, Twitter, LinkedIn, YouTube, flickr

Matt Carlson, President & CEO

Association of retailers, manufacturers and suppliers of sports equipment, footwear and apparel.
2000+ Members
Founded in 1929

21927 **North American Retail Dealers Association**
222 South Riverside Plaza
Suite 2100
Chicago, IL 60606

888-777-8851
www.narda.com
Facebook, LinkedIn

A national organization of association members, independent retailers selling and servicing major appliances, consumer electronics products, furniture and computers. Emphasis is placed on ideas that help readers become better, more profitable businesses. Articles are featured regularly on displays, salesmanship, financial analysis and service management.
1000 Members
Founded in 1943

21928 **Oriental Rug Importers Association**
400 Tenafly Road
Suite 699
Tenafly, NJ 07670

201-866-5054; Fax: 201-866-6169
llaufer@oria.org
oria.org

Lucille Laufer, Executive Director
Ramin Kalaty, President

Trade association of Oriental and area rug importers and manufacturers.
Founded in 1958

21929 **Planning and Visual Education**
4651 Sheridan St.
Suite 470
Hollywood, FL 33021

954-241-4834
www.paveglobal.org
Facebook, Twitter, LinkedIn, Instagram

Cindi Kato, President
Todd Dittman, Executive Director

Connects students, educators, and professionals in the retail industry. Provides students with financial support and industry exposure, connects businesses with new qualified talent, supports the continued education of industry professionals, and ensures the future of the retail industry.
Founded in 1992

21930 **Professional Sales Associates**
5045 Park Avenue W
Suite 1B
Seville, OH 44273

330-299-7343; Fax: 300-408-0075
www.profsales.com

Jim McGonigal, President

Organization representing manufacturers of dental products.
25 Members
Founded in 1969

21931 **Retail Design Institute**
126A West 14th St.
2nd Floor
Cincinnati, OH 45202

513-751-5815
www.retaildesigninstitute.org
Facebook, Twitter, LinkedIn, YouTube, Flickr

Ray Ehscheid, RDI, International President

Promotes the advancement and collaborative practice of creating selling environments. A community of the retail industry's creative professionals who share ideas, knowledge, and passion. Members include graphic designers, lighting designers, interior designs, store planners, visual merchandisers, resource designers, brand strategists, educators, trade partners, editors and publishers, and students.

21932 **Retail Industry Leaders Association**
1700 N Moore St.
Suite 2250
Arlington, VA 22209

703-841-2300; Fax: 703-841-1184
www.rila.org
Facebook, Twitter, LinkedIn

Sandy Kennedy, President

Retail Industry Leaders Association is a trade association of the lasgest and fastest growing companies in the retail industry, its members include over 400 retailers, product manufacturers, and service suppliers.
400+ Members
Founded in 1969

21933 **Retail Merchants Association**
5101 Monument Ave.
Richmond, VA 23230

804-662-5500
866-750-2532; Fax: 804-662-5507
info@retailmerchants.com
www.retailmerchants.com
Facebook, Twitter, LinkedIn

Nancy C. Thomas, President & CEO

The Association is dedicated to helping local retailers and small businesses grow.
Founded in 1906

21934 **Retail Packaging Association**
105 Eastern Ave.
Suite 104
Annapolis, MD 21403

410-940-6459; Fax: 410-263-1659
info@retailpackaging.org
www.retailpackaging.org
Facebook, Twitter, Pinterest, Instagram

Molly Alton Mullins, Executive Director

Serves its members and the entire retail packaging industry. Also organizes the largest trade show and conference of its kind in the US. A self-governed not-for-profit organization comprised of professionals involved in all facets of production and distribution of retail packaging products.
Founded in 1989

21935 **Shop! Environments Association**
4651 Sheridan Street
Suite 470
Hollywood, FL 33021

954-893-7300; Fax: 954-893-7500
welcome@shopassociation.org
www.shopassociation.org
Facebook, Twitter, LinkedIn, Instagram, Pinterest

Todd Dittman, Executive Director
Susan Kimelman, Director, Member Marketing Partners
Scott Savodnik, Director, Membership
Madeline Baumgartner, Director, Education & Research
Karen Benning, Director, Communications

Formed in the merger of the Association for Retail Environments and Point of Purchase Advertising International, Shop! is a global trade association devoted to enhancing retail environments and experiences for members through research, education, and networking.
2000 Members
Founded in 2015

21936 **Small Business Technology Council**
National Small Business Association
1156 15th Street NW
Suite 502
Washington, DC 20005

202-662-9700
800-345-6728
alec@sbtc.org

sbtc.org
Facebook, Twitter, RSS

Jere Glover, Executive Director

Organization advocates for small business in the technology industry.
120 Members
Founded in 2000

21937 **Vacuum and Sewing Dealers Trade Association**
2724 2nd Ave.
Des Moines, IA 50313-4933

515-282-9101
800-367-5651; Fax: 515-282-4483
mail@vdta.com
www.vdta.com

Judy Patterson, President

Seeks to increase the independent vacuum cleaner and sewing machine dealer market share.
20,00 Members
Founded in 1981

21938 **Wine and Spirits Guild of America**
3530 Vinings Ridge Court
Atlanta, GA 30339

770-956-8808; Fax: 770-988-8634
info@wineandspiritsguild.com
www.wineandspiritsguild.com

Gary Fisch, President
Barbara Owen, Conference & Comms. Manager

Promotes the exchange of information on merchandising, marketing and buying of wines and spirits.
40 Members
Founded in 1948

Newsletters

21939 **American Collegiate Retailing Association Newsletter**
Loyola University/Department of Marketing
PO Box 121
New Orleans, LA 70118

504-865-2011; Fax: 504-865-3851
admit@loyno.edu
www.loyno.edu

Kevin Wildes, President
Alice Glenn, Secretary
Cynthia Tucker, Editor
Mary Degnan, Marketing Manager
Janice Long, Circulation Manager

Educational retailing news and information.
Frequency: Quarterly
Founded in 1923

21940 **Bookselling This Week**
American Booksellers Association
333 Westchester Avenue
Suite S202
White Plains, NY 10604

800-637-0037; Fax: 914-417-4013
info@bookweb.org
www.bookweb.org
Facebook, Twitter, Instagram

Oren Teicher, CEO
Frequency: Weekly
Circulation: 10000

21941 **Campus Marketplace**
National Association of College Stores
528 E Lorain St.
Oberlin, OH 44074

800-622-7498; Fax: 440-775-4769
membership@nacs.org
www.nacs.org

Cindy Ruckman, Editor

Weekly newsletter covering college store industry: sales, trends, news, personnel and address changes for stores as well as vendors.
Frequency: Monthly
Circulation: 4000
Founded in 1982

21942 **Equipment Dealer News**
Equipment Dealers Association
165 North Meramec Avenue
Suite 430
St. Louis, MO 63105

636-349-5000; Fax: 636-349-5443
info@equipmentdealer.org
www.equipmentdealer.org
Facebook, Twitter

Kim Rominger, President & CEO
Michael Williams, VP, Operations
Joseph Dykes, VP, Industry Relations
Alex Hoffman, Communications & Marketing Director

Features news relevant to equipment manufacturers, as well as advocacy and government policy updates, management tips and more.
4500 Members
Founded in 1900

21943 **For the President's Eyes Only**
Bureau of Business Practice
76 Ninth Avenue
7th Floor
New York, NY 10011

212-771-0600; Fax: 212-771-0885
www.aspenlawschool.com

Robert Becker, CEO
Gustavo Dobles, VP Operations

Provides the latest information on areas of vital interest to the head of the company.
12 Pages
Frequency: 2 per year

21944 **Insider**
Trade Dimensions
45 Danbury Rd
Wilton, CT 06897-4445

203-563-3000; Fax: 203-563-3131
www.tradedimensions.com

Brain Thomas, Editor
Kristina Castle, Circulation Coordina

Shopping center weekly newsletter that profiles the latest retailer expansion plans, giving - in addition to the numbers of stores operated and planned, the areas targeted, and the type of locations sought - a thumbnail sketch of what makes the concept unique, and what the company specifically looks for in a site.
Cost: $299.00
Frequency: Weekly
Founded in 1970

21945 **International Map Trade Association**
2629 Manhattan Avenue
PMB 281
Hermosa Beach, CA 90254-2447

310-376-7731; Fax: 949-458-0300
www.imiamaps.org

Sandy Hill, Executive Director
Linda Hill, Editor

Membership comprised of retail stores featuring maps, travel books, globes, and travel products, plus publishers and manufacturers producing these products. Publishes a monthly newsletter
Cost: $60.00
20 Pages
Frequency: Monthly
ISSN: 1065-6324
Founded in 1981
Printed in on matte stock

21946 **MJ Business Week**
Marijuana Business Association

info@mjba.net
www.mjnewsnetwork.com
Facebook, Twitter, YouTube

A weekly e-newsletter bringing you the latest cannabis industry business news.
Frequency: Weekly
Founded in 2013

21947 **MJ Headline News**
Marijuana Business Association

info@mjba.net
www.mjnewsnetwork.com
Facebook, Twitter, YouTube

A daily e-newsletter bringing you the latest cannabis industry news.
Frequency: Daily
Founded in 2013

21948 **Mouser Report**
CAMCO
124 E Carolina Avenue
Crewe, VA 23930-1802

434-645-1993
800-448-8595; Fax: 434-645-8232

Charles Mouser, Publisher
Brend DeLuca, Circulation Director

Newsletter covers the latest trends in retail and advertising.
Cost: $96.00
16 Pages
Frequency: Monthly

21949 **NSSRA Newsletter**
National Ski and Snowboard Retailers Association
1604 Feehanville Dr.
Suite 300
Mount Prospect, IL 60056

847-391-9825
888-257-1168; Fax: 847-391-9827
info@nssra.com
www.nssra.com

Larry Weindruch, President

Keeps members informed on critical industry issues, such as guidelines, litigation exposure and marketing
Circulation: 1000

21950 **National Research Bureau Newsletter**
National Research Bureau
320 Valley St
Burlington, IA 52601-5513

319-752-5415; Fax: 319-752-3421
www.national-research-bureau.com

Diane M Darnall, President
William H. Wood, Founder

A newsletter is created for a company by combining a customized masthead with a four page, monthly issue of helpful information on a business field selected by the company.
4 Pages
Frequency: Daily
Founded in 1933
Printed in 3 colors

21951 **Shopping Center Management Insider**
6 East 32nd St
8th Floor
New York, NY 10016

212-812-8420
800-519-3692
info@vendomegrp.com
www.vendomegrp.com

Steven Gordon Esq, Editor

Tested management techniques, legal insights and how-to guidelines for running a shopping center or mall. Includes model notices to tenants, letters, agreements, rules, etc.
Cost: $297.00
Frequency: Monthly
Founded in 1985
Printed in 2 colors on matte stock

21952 T-Shirt Business Info Mapping Newsletter
Prosperity & Profits Unlimited
PO Box 416
Denver, CO 80201-0416

303-575-5676

A Doyle, Editor

How-to T-shirt business and information.
Cost: $8.00
8 Pages
Frequency: Annual
Circulation: 1,450
Founded in 1989
Printed in one color on matte stock

Magazines & Journals

21953 AREA Magazine
Oriental Rug Importers Association
400 Tenafly Road
Suite 699
Tenafly, NJ 07670

201-866-5054; Fax: 201-866-6169
llaufer@oria.org
oria.org/area-magazine

Lucille Laufer, Editor-in-Chief
Sally James, Editor

Official publication of the Oriental Rug Importers Association.
Cost: $10.00

21954 Accessory Merchandising
Vance Publishing
400 Knightsbridge Pkwy
Lincolnshire, IL 60069-3628

847-634-2600; Fax: 847-634-4379
mreckling@vancepublishing.com
www.vancepublishing.com

Peggy Walker, President
Chandra Palermo, Editor
Michael R. Reckling, Group Publisher
Steven J. Kulikowski, Marketing Manager
Douglas Riemer, Circulation Director

21955 Army/Navy Store & Outdoor Merchandiser
445 Broad Hollow Road
Suite 21
Melville, NY 11747

631-845-2700; Fax: 631-845-2797

Military surplus, workwear, casual apparel, camping, hunting and sporting goods, and outdoor clothing industries.
Cost: $25.00
Frequency: Monthly
Circulation: 12M

21956 Barnard's Retail Trend Report
Barnard Enterprises
17 Kenneth Road
Upper Montclair, NJ 07043-2541

973-655-8888
www.retailtrends.com

Kurt Barnard, Publisher/Editor
Jim Adamson, CEO

Forecasts market trends in the retailing industry and on consumer spending.
Cost: $179.00
10 Pages
Circulation: 1200
Founded in 1984
Printed in 2 colors on newsprint stock

21957 Casual Living
Reed Business Information
2000 Clearwater Dr
Oak Brook, IL 60523-8809

630-574-0825; Fax: 630-288-8781
www.reedbusiness.com

Jeff Greisch, President
Mark Kelsey, MD
Jeremy Knibbs, Chief Executive

21958 Chain Merchandiser
Merchandising Publications Company
PO Box 95C
Baker City, OR 97814-0095

FAX 541-523-2063

Ruth Sanders, Business Manager
Henry Von Morpurgo, Editor/Publisher

A national service and promotion program incorporating Specialty Foods and Beverages and Deli-Dairy World. Devoted to improved merchandising methods at every level of the marketing and distributing processes - from the field and factory and warehouse to retail sales persons - to provide better customer values, lower costs and greater profits.

21959 Chain Store Age
Lebhar-Friedman
425 Park Ave
Suite 6
New York, NY 10022-3526

212-756-5088
800-216-7117; Fax: 212-838-9487
www.nrn.com

Heather Martin, Manager
John Rapuzzi, Group Publisher
Antonia Peterson, Desk Editor
J Roger Friedman, President

Offers a full overview of chain stores, including management, operation, construction and modernization, store equipment, real estate and advertising.
Frequency: Monthly
Circulation: 35551
Founded in 1925

21960 College Store Executive
Executive Business Media
825 Old Country Road
PO Box 1500
Westbury, NY 11590-812

516-334-3030; Fax: 516-334-3059
ebm-mail@ebmpubs.com
www.ebmpubs.com

Ken Baglino, Editor
Nancy Wilderwith, Advertising Manager

A merchandising and news magazine edited for those responsible for buying and merchandising products for college retail stores.
Cost: $35.00
36 Pages
Circulation: 8547
ISSN: 0010-1141
Founded in 1970
Printed in 4 colors on glossy stock

21961 College Store Magazine
National Association of College Stores
500 E Lorain St.
Oberlin, OH 44074

800-622-7498; Fax: 440-775-4769
thecollegestore@nacs.org
www.nacs.org

Cindy Ruckman, Editor

Covers the college store industry's long term issues and trends, focusing on retailing, technology and serving campus communities.
Cost: $66.00
Mailing list available for rent

21962 DSN Retailing Today
Lebhar-Friedman
425 Park Ave
Suite 6
New York, NY 10022-3526

212-756-5088
800-216-7117; Fax: 212-838-9487
www.dsnretailingtoday.com

Heather Martin, Manager
Tim Craig, Editor-in-Chief
Tony Lisanti, Editorial Director
Roger Friedman, CEO

Leading international newspaper serving the growing mass market.
Frequency: Monthly
Circulation: 34000
Founded in 1925

21963 Dealerscope
North American Publishing Company
1500 Spring Garden St
Suite 1200
Philadelphia, PA 19130-4094

215-238-5300
800-818-8174; Fax: 215-238-5342
www.dealerscope.com
Facebook, Twitter, LinkedIn

Ned S Borowsky, CEO
David Dritsas, Editor-in-Chief
Eric Schwartz, President/Publishing
Rhoda Dixon, Circulation Manager
Suzanne DeFruscio, Advertising Promotion Manager

Dedicated to delivering peer-based knowledge and experience, Dealerscope is the ultimate vehicle for presenting product and service solutions to the consumer.
Founded in 1958

21964 Display & Design Ideas
Shore Varrone
6255 Barfield Road
#200
Atlanta, GA 30328-4332

404-848-0077; Fax: 404-252-4436
www.svi-atl.com

Doug Hope, Publisher
Steve Kaufman, Editor
Lee Pritcher, Owner

Product news and design solutions for those in the retail chain indusrty.
Cost: $60.00
Frequency: Monthly
Circulation: 18,039

21965 Do-It-Yourself Retailing
5822 W 74th St
Indianapolis, IN 46278-1756

317-297-1190; Fax: 317-328-4354
vecchie@sbcglobal.net
www.nrha.org

John Hammond, Executive Director
Kevin Hohman, Publisher
Frequency: Monthly
Circulation: 44333

21966 Drug Store News
Lebhar-Friedman

425 Park Ave
Suite 6
New York, NY 10022-3526

212-756-5088; Fax: 212-838-9487
www.drugstorenews.com

Heather Martin, Manager
Tony Lisanti, Editor

Publication consists of merchandising trends and pharmacy developments. Provides extensive coverage of every major segment of chain drug retailing and combination stores.
Cost: $189.00
Frequency: Weekly
Circulation: 40000
Founded in 1925

21967 **Edplay**
Fahy-Williams Publishing
PO Box 1080
Geneva, NY 14456-2137

315-789-0458
800-344-0559; Fax: 315-789-4263
www.fwpi.com

J Kevin Fahy, Publisher
Tina Manzer, Editorial Director
Jason Hagerman, Advertising Account Rep
Bradley G Gordner, Senior Editor
Tricia King, Office Manager

Serves toy manufacturers and dealers. Offers product reviews, industry profiles, and reader surveys.
Cost: $22.00
Frequency: Quarterly
Circulation: 7684

21968 **Flea Markets Magazine**
FleaMarkets.com
1156 15th St NW
Suite 1100
Washington, DC 20005-1755

202-293-8830
800-835-6728
www.fleamarkets.com

Todd McCracken, President

A quarterly magazine published by FleaMarkets.com.
Cost: $15.00
Frequency: Quarterly
Circulation: 3000
Founded in 1989

21969 **Gacs Today**
Naylor Publications
PO Box 855
Snellville, GA 30078-855

770-736-9723; Fax: 770-736-9725
www.gacs.com

Jim Tudor, CEO
Frequency: Quarterly
Circulation: 2500
Founded in 1973

21970 **Garden Center Merchandising & Management**
Branch-Smith Publishing
PO Box 1868
Fort Worth, TX 76101-1868

817-882-4110
800-433-5612; Fax: 817-882-4121

David Branch, President
Terri Smith, Director Circulation
Carol Miller, Editor
Frequency: Monthly
Circulation: 15143
Founded in 1915

21971 **Garden Center Products & Supplies**
Branch-Smith Publishing
PO Box 1868
Fort Worth, TX 76101-1868

817-882-4110
800-433-5612; Fax: 817-882-4121

David Branch, President
Patrice Kuhl, Publisher/Sales Director
Frequency: Monthly
Founded in 1910

21972 **Hearth & Home**
Village West Publishing
P.O. Box 1288
Laconia, NH 03247

603-528-4285
800-258-3772; Fax: 888-873-3610
wright@villagewest.com
www.hearthandhome.com
Facebook, LinkedIn

Richard Wright, Editor
Jackie Avignone, Advertising Director
Erica Paquette, Art Director

Information for retailers and others selling hearth products, patio furnishing, barbecues, spas, garden accessories, and other outdoor products.
Cost: $11.95
Frequency: Monthly
Circulation: 18000
ISSN: 0273-5695
Founded in 1980

21973 **International Gaming and Wagering Business**
BNP Media
PO Box 1080
Skokie, IL 60076-9785

847-763-9534; Fax: 847-763-9538
igwb@halldata.com
Facebook, Twitter, LinkedIn

James Rutherford, Editor
Lynn Davidson, Marketing
Tammie Gizicki, Director

Focuses on business strategy, legislative information, food service and promotional concerns.
Frequency: Monthly
Circulation: 25000

21974 **Journal of Shopper Research**
Shop! Environments Association
4651 Sheridan Street
Suite 470
Hollywood, FL 33021

954-893-7300; Fax: 954-893-7500
editor@journalofshopperresearch.com
www.journalofshopperresearch.com

Todd Dittman, Executive Director
Raymond Burke, Editor-in-Chief
Madeline Baumgartner, Managing Editor

Academic journal focused on the shopper's journey and behavior, with academic and commercial research.
Frequency: Quarterly

21975 **Kitchenware News**
United Publications
PO Box 1056
Yarmouth, ME 04096-2056

207-846-0600; Fax: 207-846-0657
www.kitchenwares.com

Brooke Taliaferro, President
Jim McNeil, Publisher

News and information on the latest products and equipment for the retail kitchenware industry.
Cost: $45.00
Frequency: Monthly
Circulation: 12,117

21976 **MMR/Mass Market Retailers**
Racher Press
220 5th Avenue
New York, NY 10001-7798

212-213-6000; Fax: 212-725-4594
www.massmarketretailers.com

Susan Schinitsky, Publisher
David Pinto, Editor
John Dioguardi, Director Sales/Marketing
Kevin Burke, Group Advertising Director
Pam Vandernoth, Circulation Director

News, analysis, trends, and events for drug, discount, and supermarket chain executives.
Cost: $185.00
Circulation: 21645
Founded in 1984

21977 **Magazine Retailer**
MetaMedia
124 W 24th Street
#3-D
New York, NY 1011-1920

212-989-6978; Fax: 212-255-7143

David Orlow, Publisher
Djalal Mohammadi, President

Merchandising tips, new tiles, publication changes, consumer purchasing trends, industry news and media impact on sales.
Cost: $19.00
Frequency: Quarterly
Circulation: 10,326

21978 **Mass Market Retailer**
Racher Press
220 5th Avenue
New York, NY 10001-7708

212-213-6000; Fax: 212-725-3961
www.massmarketretailers.com

Susan Schinitsky, Publisher
David Pinto, Editor
Susan Schinitsky, CEO/President
John Dioguardi, Marketing
Pam Vandernoth, Circulation Manager

News and information on the drug store chain industry.
Cost: $35.00
30 Pages
Founded in 1984

21979 **Military Market**
Gannet Company
6883 Commercial Dr
Springfield, VA 22151-4202

703-750-8643; Fax: 703-750-8717
rhynema@atpco.com
www.gannett.com

Dennis V Washburn, CEO
David Craig, Managing Editor

Provides trade information, trends, and news for military commisionary and post/base exchange managers.
Cost: $84.00
Frequency: Monthly
Circulation: 12000
Founded in 1940

21980 **Museum Store Magazine**
Museum Store Association
2025 M Street NW
Suite 800
Washington, DC 20036

202-367-1106; Fax: 202-367-2104
info@museumstoreassociation.org
www.museumstoreassociation.org

Dana Butler, Editor
Cost: $50.00
Frequency: Triannual
Circulation: 3000
ISSN: 1040-6999
Founded in 1955
Printed in 4 colors on glossy stock

21981 Museums & More Specialty Shops Product News
Museums & More Specialty Product News
PO Box 128
Sparta, Mi 49345-2122

616-887-9008; Fax: 616-887-2666
www.museumsandmore.com

Julie McCallum, Editor
Jon Kaufman, Publisher

Product highlights and marketing strategies for the owners and oporators of gift shops in museums and other public attractions.
Cost: $35.00
Frequency: Quarterly
Circulation: 28014

21982 New Age Retailer
Continuity Publishing
2183 Alpine Way
Bellingham, WA 98226-8045

360-676-0789
800-463-9243; Fax: 360-676-0932
www.newageretailer.com

Molly Trimble, CEO
Ray Hemachandra, Editor-in-Chief
Laurel Leigh, Editor
Stephanie R Hager, Circulation Manager
Ellen Koolen, Production Manager

Provides information on new products and business to business trade magazine that supports store owners by providing independent product reviews, retail advice and coverage of the new age and spirtual lviing industry.
Cost: $ 85.00
192 Pages
Circulation: 10000
Founded in 1987
Mailing list available for rent: 6,000 names at $150 per M

21983 POP Design
In-Store Marketing Institute
7400 Skokie Blvd
Skokie, IL 60077-3339

847-675-7400; Fax: 847-675-7494
www.instoremarketer.org
Facebook, Twitter, LinkedIn

Peter Hoyt, President

Serves the news and product information needs of producers and designers of instore displays, signs and fixtures. Each issue features the latest trends and technologies vital to building and designing successful instore merchandising.
Frequency: Monthly
Circulation: 18000
Printed in 4 colors on glossy stock

21984 Pollution Engineering
Reed Business Information
2000 Clearwater Dr
Oak Brook, IL 60523-8809

630-574-0825; Fax: 630-288-8781
www.reedbusiness.com
Facebook, Twitter, LinkedIn

Jeff Greisch, President
Erin Purananda, Marketing Manager
Seth Fisher, Products Editor
Mark Kelsey, Chief Executive Officer

Serves the field of pollution control in manufacturing industries, utilities, consulting engineers and constructors. Also serves government agencies including administration of federal, state and local environmental programs.
Frequency: Monthly
ISSN: 0032-3640
Founded in 1977

21985 Publishers Weekly
PO Box 51593
Harlan, IA 51593

800-278-2991; Fax: 712-733-8019
pwycustserv@cdsfulfillment.com
www.publishersweekly.com
Facebook, Twitter, LinkedIn

George Slovik, President
Michael Coffey, Co-Editorial Director
Diane Roback, Children's Book Editor
Louisa Ermelino, Reviews Director
Calvin Reid, News Editor

PW is the international journal of book publishing and bookselling including business news, reviews and bestseller lists targeted at publishers, booksellers, librarians and literary agents.
Frequency: Weekly
Founded in 1872

21986 Retail Cost of Doing Business
American Floorcovering Association
2211 E Howell Avenue
Anaheim, CA 92806-6009

714-572-8370

Offers an overview of the retail trade.
Frequency: Annual

21987 Retail Focus
National Sporting Goods Association
1601 Feehanville Drive
Suite 300
Mount Prospect, IL 60056

847-296-6742
800-815-5422; Fax: 847-391-9827
info@nsga.org
www.nsga.org

Bob Dickman, Chairman of the Board
Matt Carlson, President/CEO
Dan Kasen, Director of Information Services

Magazine for members only
Frequency: Bi-Monthly
Mailing list available for rent

21988 Retail Observer
Retail Observer
1442 Sierra Creek Way
San Jose, CA 95132-3618

408-272-8974
800-393-0509; Fax: 408-272-3344
info@retailobserver.com
www.retailobserver.com/

Chuck Edmonds, Publisher
Lee Boucher, Editor

Edited for owners, managers and retail sales personnel of appliance stores, home entertainment stores and kitchen and bath dealers.
Frequency: Monthly
Circulation: 11750

21989 Retail Systems Alert
Retail Systems Alert Group
PO Box 332
Newton Upper Falls, MA 02464-02

617-527-4626; Fax: 617-527-8102
www.retailsystems.com

Thomas H Friedman, Publisher

Provides updated information on automation news and trends, including decision systems, information systems implementation, in-store merchandise management, and case studies of retailers.
Cost: $295.00
8 Pages
Frequency: Monthly
Founded in 1988

21990 Retail Systems Reseller
Edgell Communications
4 Middlebury Boulevard
Suite 107
Randolph, NJ 07869-1111

973-252-0100; Fax: 973-252-9020

Michael Kachmar, Publisher
Joseph S King, Editor-in-Chief
Gabriele A Edgell, CEO
Dan Ligorner, Director of Marketing

Offers information to retailers, dealers, systems integraters, VARs, VADs, etc., on retail technology for small to mid-size retailers.

21991 RetailTech
770 Broadway
New York, NY 10003-9522

646-654-7480; Fax: 646-654-7568
www.retail-merchandiser.com

21992 Shop! Retail Environments Magazine
Shop! Environments Association
4651 Sheridan Street
Suite 470
Hollywood, FL 33021

954-893-7300; Fax: 954-893-7500
www.journalofshopperresearch.com

Todd Dittman, Executive Director
Jo Rossman, Publisher/Editor

Official magazine of Shop! Association, devoted to the business of the retail landscape.
Circulation: 25000

21993 Succe$$ful $ource$
Sutton Family Communications & Publishing Company
155 Sutton Lane
Fordsville, KY 42343

270-740-0870
www.suttoncompliance.com

Theresa Sutton, Publisher

The #1 trade magazine for multi-billion dollar flea market industry.
Cost: $5.00
Circulation: 100000
Founded in 1977

21994 Supermarket News
Fairchild Publications
750 3rd Ave
New York, NY 10017-2703

212-630-4000
800-204-4515; Fax: 212-630-3563
www.supermarketnews.com

Mary G Berner, CEO
David Merrefield, Editorial Director
Dan Bagan, Publishing Director
David Orgel, Editor-in-Chief
Cost: $44.50
40 Pages
Frequency: Weekly
Circulation: 36346
ISSN: 0039-5803
Founded in 1892

21995 Today's Grocers
Florida Grocer Publications
PO Box 430760
S Miami, FL 33246

305-661-0792
800-440-3067; Fax: 305-661-6720

Jack Nobles, Publisher
Dennis Kane, Editor

Provides the latest food industry news and trends to Florida, Georgia, Alabama, Louisiana, Mississippi and the Carolinas.
Cost: $29.00
24 Pages
Frequency: Monthly
Circulation: 19,000

ISSN: 1529-4420
Founded in 1956
Printed in on newsprint stock

Trade Shows

21996 **ABL Annual Meeting**
American Beverage Licensees
5101 River Road
Suite 108
Bethesda, MD 20816-1560

301-656-1494; Fax: 301-656-7539
www.ablusa.org

John Bodnovich, Executive Director

Annual show of 75 manufacturers, suppliers and distributors of alcoholic beverages.
1,000 Attendees

21997 **ASD/AMD Houston Variety Merchandise Show**
ASD/AMD Merchandise Group
2950 31st Street
Suite 100
Santa Monica, CA 90405

310-396-6006
800-421-4511; Fax: 310-399-2662

Julie Ichiba, Show Director

Our newest variety and general merchandise trade show offers buyers in the southwestern US and Mexico terrific product sourcing opportunities for all types of popular consumer goods.
12000 Attendees

21998 **ASD/AMD Las Vegas Trade Show**
ASD/AMD Merchandise Group
2950 31st Street
Suite 100
Santa Monica, CA 90405

310-396-6006
800-421-4511; Fax: 310-399-2662

Julie Ichiba, Show Director

The summer edition of the largest variety merchandise event in the US attracts over 50,000 buyers to Las Vegas. Tens of thousands of unique products in hundreds of popular consumer product categories are on display at this even
50000 Attendees
Frequency: August

21999 **ASD/AMD's Atlantic City Variety Merchandise Show**
ASD/AMD Merchandise Group
2950 31st Street
Suite 100
Santa Monica, CA 90405

310-396-6006
800-421-4511; Fax: 310-399-2662

Julie Ichiba, Show Director

Held in Atlantic City, New Jersey, this event is a popular destination for east coast retailers to make deals and place orders for variety and general merchandise in hundreds of popular consumer categories before the summer selling season begins.
10000 Attendees
Frequency: May

22000 **ASD/AMD's Fall Variety Merchandise Show**
ASD/AMD Merchandise Group
2950 31st Street
Suite 100
Santa Monica, CA 90405

310-396-6006
800-421-4511; Fax: 310-399-2662

Julie Ichiba, Show Director

The fall edition of the general merchandise event on the east coast takes place in New York City. It's the last opportunity of the year for retailers to place orders for goods before the busy holiday buying season.
12000 Attendees
Frequency: September

22001 **ASD/AMD's Las Vegas Merchandise Expo**
ASD/AMD Merchandise Group
2950 31st Street
Suite 100
Santa Monica, CA 90405

310-396-6006
800-421-4511; Fax: 310-399-2662

Julie Ichiba, Show Director

Held in Las Vegas, Nevada, this event is strategically timed for western US retailers to stock their shelves with quality, value-priced variety and general merchandise in between our larger Las Vegas Trade Shows in March and Agust.
5,000 Attendees
Frequency: June

22002 **ASD/AMD's New York Variety Merchandise Show**
ASD/AMD Merchandise Group
2950 31st Street
Suite 100
Santa Monica, CA 90405

310-396-6006
800-421-4511; Fax: 310-399-2662

Julie Ichiba, Show Director

Held in New York City, this event is the first opportunity of the New Year for variety and general merchandise retailers to stock their shelves after the holidays with popular, value-priced consumer goods in hundreds of product categories.
12500 Attendees
Frequency: January

22003 **ASD/AMD's Orlando Variety Merchandise Show**
ASD/AMD Merchandise Group
2950 31st Street
Suite 100
Santa Monica, CA 90405

310-396-6006
800-421-4511; Fax: 310-399-2662

Julie Ichiba, Show Director

Held in Orlando, Florida, this event is a popular destination for southeastern US retailers to make deals and place orders for variety and general merchandise in hundreds of popular consumer categories.
5,500 Attendees
Frequency: April

22004 **Accent on Design**
George Little Management
10 Bank Street
Suite 1200
White Plains, NY 10606-1954

914-486-6070
800-272-7469; Fax: 914-948-2867
www.nyigf.com

Elizabeth Murphy, Manager
George Little II, President

370 booths of the latest and most innovative gift lines such as decorative accessories and home furnishings.
50M Attendees
Frequency: August
Founded in 1984

22005 **Associated Surplus Dealers/Associated Merchandise Dealers Trade Show**
ASD/AMD Merchandise Group
2950 31st Street
Suite 100
Santa Monica, CA 90405

310-255-4633
800-421-4511; Fax: 310-399-3662

Sam Bundy, Group President

Gifts, souvenirs and assorted merchandise for professional buyers.
15000 Attendees
Frequency: Annual/March

22006 **Book Expo America**
Reed Exhibitions
383 Main Avenue
Norwalk, CT 06851

203-404-4800
800-840-5614
cmuller@reedexpo.com
www.bookexpoamerica.com
Facebook, Twitter, LinkedIn

Courtney Muller, Event Manager
Cathy Glickstein, Registration

Sponsored by American Booksellers Association and Association of American Publishers. More than 2,000 exhibits, 500 authors, over 60 conference sessions as well as a special area for rights business, all the latest titles across genres, uncover hidden gems, network, and meet the industry contacts to put you instantly on top of what you need to know for your business and job.
Frequency: May/June
Founded in 2000

22007 **CMM International: FLEX Expo**
Bruno Blenheim
Fort Lee Executive Park
Fort Lee, FL 07024

800-829-3976; Fax: 201-346-1602

Nick Helyer, President

Exhibits by franchisers and sellers to the franchise industry. 125 booths.
5M Attendees
Frequency: June

22008 **Green Profit's Retail Experience**
Green Profit Magazine
335 N River Street
Batavia, IL 60510

630-208-9080
888-888-0013; Fax: 630-208-9350
info@ballpublishing.com
www.ballpublishing.com/conferences

Michelle Mazza, Show Manager

Educational event and tradeshow dedicated exclusively to garden center retailing. Covers topics from store layout and design to merchandising strategies and business management. 20 booths
300 Attendees
Frequency: September
Founded in 2006

22009 **International Council of Shopping Centers Fall Convention Trade & Exposition**
International Council of Shopping Centers
1221 Avenue of the Americas
41st Floor
New York, NY 10020-1099

646-728-3800; Fax: 732-694-1690
icsc@icsc.org
www.icsc.org

Tom McGee, President & CEO

22010 International Franchise Association Expo
1501 K St NW
Suite 350
Washington, DC 20005-1412

202-628-8000; Fax: 202-628-0812

Matthew Shay, President
Patricia Langfeld, VP

75 booths.
1M Attendees
Frequency: February

22011 Internet Retailer Conference & Exhibition
Internet Retailer
300 S Wacker Drive
Suite 602
Chicago, IL 60606

FAX 312-362-9532
www.internetretailer.com
Facebook, Twitter, LinkedIn

Learn the strategies, practices and tools to lift your site into e-retailing's second decade of growth. Network with your peers in the only show serving e-retailers from all merchant channels.
Frequency: Annual

22012 Logistics
Retail Industry Leaders Association
1700 N Moore Street
Suite 2250
Arlington, VA 22209

703-841-2300; Fax: 703-841-1184
www.imra.org

Britt Wood, VP
Sean Nodland, Manager

This event brings together retailers, consumer product companies, and suppliers of goods and service logistics side of business
400 Attendees
Frequency: February

22013 Loss Prevention, Auditing & Safety Conference
Retail Industry Leaders Association
1700 N Moore Street
Suite 2250
Arlington, VA 22209

703-841-2300; Fax: 703-841-1184
Facebook, Twitter, LinkedIn

Rhett Asher

Annual information exchange.
325 Attendees
Frequency: April

22014 Marketing Conference
International Mass Retail Association
1700 N Moore Street
Suite 2250
Arlington, VA 22209

703-841-2300; Fax: 703-841-1184
www.imra.org

Peter Kim, Owner

22015 NACS Show
National Association of Convenience Stores
1600 Duke St.
Alexandria, VA 22314

703-684-3600
800-966-6227; Fax: 703-836-4564
www.nacsshow.com
Facebook, Twitter, LinkedIn, YouTube, Instagram

Regina Sheehan, Director, Convention Operations

Education and networking event for convenience and fuel retailing professionals.
Founded in 1961

22016 NARTS Annual Conference
PO BOX 190
St. Clair Shores, MI 48080

586-294-6700
800-544-0751; Fax: 586-588-7018
info@narts.org
www.narts.org

Adele R. Meyer, Executive Director
Gail A. Seigel, Director of Membership Services
1100+ Members
Founded in 1984

22017 National Lawn & Garden Controlled Marketing Conference
Controlled Marketing Conferences
PO Box 1771
Monument, CO 80132

719-488-0226
888-316-0226; Fax: 719-488-8168
www.nlgshow.com

Robert Mikulas, President
Chris Wolf, VP

This year CMC events will be linked to the National Lawn ans Garden Show - The Expo Division. Don't miss out on the industries most important lawn and garden headlines event.
3000 Attendees
Frequency: June

22018 PAVE Bash & Gala
Planning and Visual Education
4651 Sheridan St.
Suite 470
Hollywood, FL 33021

954-241-4834; Fax: 954-893-8375
www.paveglobal.org
Facebook, Twitter, LinkedIn, Instagram

Todd Dittman, Executive Director

Connects students and professionals to showcase the work of upcoming talents and highlight exciting new developmets in the worldsof retail design, retail planning, and visual merchandising.
Frequency: Annual
Founded in 1992

22019 Retail Advertising Conference: RAC
Retail Advertising & Marketing International
325 7th Street NW
Suite 1100
Washington, DC 20004

202-626-8183; Fax: 202-737-2849
www.rama-nrf.org

Mike Gatti, VP Marketing

Definitive event for retail advertising and marketing professionals each year featuring the RAC Awards gala dinner and Retail Hall of Fame induction annually.
1000 Attendees
Frequency: February

22020 Shop.org Annual Summit
Shop.org
325 7th Street NW
Suite 1100
Washington, DC 20004

202-626-8183; Fax: 202-626-8191
www.shop.org

Diane Furstenberg, COO
Lane Bryant, VP Marketing

Provides a unique opportunity for Internet and multi-channel retail industry leaders to exchange ideas, perspectives, opportunities and challenges in an intimate and comfortable setting. The Summit features dialogues with distinguished keynote speakers, provocative panels and debates on timely issues, and important original research.
600 Attendees
Frequency: September

22021 Shop.org Members' Forum
Shop.org
325 7th Street NW
Suite 1100
Washington, DC 20004

202-626-8183; Fax: 202-626-8191
www.shop.org

Diane Furstenberg, COO
Lane Bryant, VP Marketing

Attendees see presentations for an online holiday recap and new multichannel retail research sessions as well as roundtable discussions and other networking events.
350 Attendees
Frequency: January

22022 Southern Convenience Store & Petroleum Show
PO Box 855
Snellville, GA 30078

770-736-9723; Fax: 770-736-9725
jtudor@aol.com
www.gacs.com

Jim Tudor, President

Contains 250 exhibits.
3,000 Attendees
Founded in 2003

22023 Store Fixturing Show
Shore Varrone
6255 Barfield Road NE
Suite 200
Atlanta, GA 30328-4332

404-848-0077
800-241-9034; Fax: 770-252-4436

Russ Eisenhardt, VP Trade Shows
Lee Pritcher, Owner

The largest annual store design event in the world. The event also includes The Visual Merchandising Show, the Retail Operations & Construction Expo, the POPAI Expo and the Exhibit Ideas Show. 800 exhibitors in total.
15M Attendees
Frequency: April

22024 Store Operations & Human Resources Conference
International Mass Retail Association
1700 N Moore Street
Suite 2250
Arlington, VA 22209

703-841-2300; Fax: 703-841-1184
www.imra.org

This educational event provides attendees with an opportunity to learn from experts in their fields on the most pressing topics of the day

22025 VDTA-SDTA Trade Show & Convention
Vacuum and Sewing Dealers Trade Association
2724 2nd Ave.
Des Moines, IA 50313-4933

515-282-9101
800-367-5651; Fax: 515-282-4483
mail@vdta.com
www.vdta.com

Judy Patterson, President

Trade show for independent floorcare, sewing and quilting retailers..
Founded in 1981

Directories & Databases

22026 Annual Trade Show Directory
Forum Publishing Company
383 E Main St
Centerport, NY 11721-1538
631-754-5000; Fax: 631-754-0630
www.forum123.com
Martin Stevens, Owner
Over 1,800 merchandise trade shows throughout the United States and Canada.
Cost: $39.95
312 Pages
Frequency: Annual

22027 Directory of Convenience Stores
Trade Dimensions
45 Danbury Rd
Wilton, CT 06897-4445
203-563-3000; Fax: 860-563-3131
www.tradedimensions.com
Jennifer Gillbert, Editor
Lynda Guticulez, Managing Editor
The directory comprises nearly 1,500 detailed profiles on the companies you need to do business with - extensive dependable information on the grocery industry's most volatile segment.
Cost: $245.00
Frequency: Annual

22028 Directory of High Discount Merchandise Sources
B Klein Publishers
Po Box 6578
Delray Beach, FL 33482-6578
561-496-3316; Fax: 561-496-5546
Bernard Klein, Owner
Approximately 1,200 sources of products offered at high discounts.
Cost: $35.00
Frequency: Annual

22029 Directory of Mail Order Catalogs
Grey House Publishing
4919 Route 22
PO Box 56
Amenia, NY 12501
518-789-8700
800-562-2139; Fax: 845-373-6390
books@greyhouse.com
www.greyhouse.com
Facebook, Twitter
Leslie Mackenzie, Publisher
Richard Gottlieb, Editor
The premier source of information on the mail order catalog industry. Covers over 13,000 consumer and business catalog companies with 44 different product chapters from Animals to Toys and Games.
Cost: $395.00
1900 Pages
Frequency: Annual
ISBN: 1-592373-96-8
Founded in 1981

22030 Directory of Mail Order Catalogs - Online Database
Grey House Publishing
4919 Route 22
PO Box 56
Amenia, NY 12501
518-789-8700
800-562-2139; Fax: 845-373-6390
gold@greyhouse.com
gold.greyhouse.com
Facebook, Twitter
Leslie Mackenzie, Publisher
Richard Gottlieb, Editor
Reach over 10,000 consumer catalog companies in one easy-to-use source with The Directory of Mail Order Catalogs - Online Database. Filled with business-building detail, each company profile gives you the information you need to access that organization quickly and easily. Listings provide key contacts, sales volume, employee size, printing information, circulation, list data, product descriptions and much more.
Frequency: Annual
Founded in 1981

22031 Directory of Major Malls
PO Box 837
Nyack, NY 10960-0837
845-348-7000; Fax: 845-426-0802
Tama J Shor, Editor/Publisher
Murray Shor, Consulting Publisher
Contains 2865 listings with over 1800 leasing/site plans of major malls, with many showing the anchors, design layout, intersecting streets, peripheral land, and major highways.
ISBN: 0-932599-13-3

22032 Directory of Mass Merchandisers
Trade Dimensions
45 Danbury Rd
Wilton, CT 06897-4445
203-563-3000; Fax: 860-563-3131
www.tradedimensions.com
Lynda Gutierrez, Managing Editor
Jennifer Gilbert, Editor
This directory defines this complex class of retail trade. Includes profiles of the chains and leading mass merchandisers by market area. Also includes HBC suppliers and store type breakdowns by state/region.
Cost: $245.00
Frequency: Annual

22033 Discount & General Merchandising Stores
Chain Store Guide
3710 Corporex Park Dr.
Suite 310
Tampa, FL 33619-1389
813-627-6700
800-972-9292; Fax: 813-627-6888
webmaster@chainstoreguide.com
www.chainstoreguide.com
Mike Jarvis, Publisher
Shami Choon, Manager
This database is an in-depth look at the mass-merchandising segment, bringing you access to more than 7,000 listings along with over 23,000 key personnel. This report includes targeted research from sectors such as Discount Department Stores, General Merchandise Stores, Dollar Stores, Automotive Aftermarket Retailers and Computer & Consumer Electronics Chains.
Cost: $575.00
720 Pages
Frequency: Annual

22034 Discount Merchandiser
McFadden Publishing Company
233 Park Ave S
6th Floor
New York, NY 10003-1606
212-979-4800; Fax: 212-979-7342
Steven Jacober, Editor
Profiles of the top 55 chains and list of top 85 discount merchandising companies.
Cost: $40.00
Frequency: Annual June

22035 IFA Franchise Opportunities Guide
International Franchise Association
1900 K Street NW
Suite 700
Washington, DC 20006
202-628-8000; Fax: 202-628-0812
www.franchise.org
Facebook, Twitter, LinkedIn, YouTube, Instagram
Robert Cresanti, President
This directory lists over 3,000 companies offering franchises.
Cost: $12.00
300 Pages
Frequency: semi-annual

22036 Leading Chain Tenants Database
Chain Store Guide
3710 Corporex Park Dr.
Suite 310
Tampa, FL 33619-1389
813-627-6700
800-927-9292; Fax: 813-627-6888
webmaster@chainstoreguide.com
www.chainstoreguide.com
Mike Jarvis, Publisher
Arthur Sciarrotta, Senior VP
Information on more than 8,600 retailers in the U.S. and Canada with over 32,000 personnel contacts. This database will lead you to new real estate prospects across a vast range of industries. Whether you are in real estate development, leasing or sales, the opportunities are endless.
Cost: $575.00
Frequency: Annual

22037 NRB Shopping Center Directory
Trade Dimensions
45 Danbury Rd
Wilton, CT 06897-4445
203-563-3000; Fax: 860-563-3131
www.nrbonline.com
Patricia Kelly, Managing Editor
Stephanie Strano, Circulation Director
The most comprehensive book on shopping centers available. Encompassing over 37,000 centers from neighborhood to super regional, the Directory is organized into four volumes: East, Midwest, South, West. A fifth volume is dedicated exclusively to the industry's top contacts, comprising the names and contact information for anyone who owns, leases, or manages three or more centers.
Cost: $325.00
Frequency: Annual

22038 Outlet Project Directory
Value Retail News
29399 Us Highway 19 N
Suite 370
Clearwater, FL 33761-2138
727-781-7557
800-669-1020; Fax: 727-536-4389
www.valueretailnews.com
Cher Russell-Street, Editor
Factory outlet projects.
Cost: $179.00
Frequency: SemiAnnual

22039 Outlet Retail Directory
Off-Price Specialists, Value Retail News
14250 49th St N
Clearwater, FL 33762-2800
727-464-6460; Fax: 727-453-7419
James Pierce, Manager
Over 500 outlet retail chains are profiled.
280 Pages
Frequency: Semiannual

22040 **Products & Services Directory**
Value Retail News
29399 Us Highway 19 N
Suite 370
Clearwater, FL 33761-2138
727-781-7557
800-669-1020; Fax: 727-536-4389
www.valueretailnews.com
Cher Russell-Street, Editor
More than 2,000 service companies specializing in outlet or off-price retailing and development industries.
Cost: $49.00
Frequency: Annual

22041 **Productscan Online**
Marketing Intelligence Service
6473 State Route 64
Naples, NY 14512-9726
585-374-6326; Fax: 585-374-5217
Tom Vierhile, Manager
Julie Fox, Finance Executive
This database is dedicated solely to new launches of consumer packaged goods. Includes label copy, in-depth reports on innovations, and product pictures capable of statistical analysis and manufacturer history reports.
Cost: $ 3995.00

22042 **Retail Tenant Directory**
Trade Dimensions
45 Danbury Rd
Wilton, CT 06897-4445
203-563-3000; Fax: 860-563-3131
www.tradedimensions.com
Garrett Van Siclen, Publisher
Thomas Donato, Editor
Complete and accurate details for 5,000+ growing retailers that are looking for space. Holding company section lists corporate profiles for major parent companies which own two or more major retail chains in the US. Individual company profiles include retail classifications, total number of stores, operating names, sales volume, who to contact, extensive site selection criteria including demographic preferences, expansion plans, acquisitions, format changes and more.
Cost: $ 345.00
1500 Pages
Frequency: Annual
ISBN: 0-911790-29-2

22043 **Shippers Guide to Department & Chain Stores Nationwide**
Shippers Guides
PO Box 112
Duarte, CA 91009-0112
626-357-6430; Fax: 626-357-6366
Profiles over 1,000 department stores and chain stores and information about routing and freight movement.
Cost: $349.00
350 Pages
Frequency: Annual
Mailing list available for rent: 1,000 names at $299 per M

22044 **Shop! Buyer's Guide**
Shop! Environments Association
4651 Sheridan Street
Suite 470
Hollywood, FL 33021
954-893-7300; Fax: 954-893-7500
service@shopassociation.org
www.shopassociation.org
Todd Dittman, Executive Director
Jo Rossman, Publisher/Editor
Karin Pryor, Director, Marketing
Karen Benning, Director, Communications
Guide to Shop! Association members: providers of store fixtures, POP displays, retail design services, visual presentation products, signage, materials, installation, and more.
Cost: $175.00
Frequency: Annual

22045 **Shopping Center Directory**
National Research Bureau
333 W Wacker Drive
Suite 900
Chicago, IL 60606-1284
312-346-3900
This large directory offers information on over 30,000 shopping centers in four regional volumes.
Cost: $225.00
3,200 Pages
Frequency: Annual

22046 **Single Unit Supermarkets Operators**
Chain Store Guide
3710 Corporex Park Dr.
Suite 310
Tampa, FL 33619-1389
813-627-6700
800-927-9292; Fax: 813-627-6888
webmaster@chainstoreguide.com
www.chainstoreguide.com
Mike Jarvis, Publisher
Shami Choon, Manager
Discover more than 7,100 single-unit supermarkets with annual sales topping $500,000 dollars. This comprehensive desktop reference makes it easy to reach our compiled list of 21,000 key executives and buyers, plus their primary wholesalers.
Cost: $575.00
725 Pages
Frequency: Annual

22047 **Supermarket, Grocery & Convenience Stores**
Chain Store Guide
3710 Corporex Park Dr.
Suite 310
Tampa, FL 33619-1389
813-627-6700
800-927-9292; Fax: 813-627-6888
webmaster@chainstoreguide.com
www.chainstoreguide.com
Mike Jarvis, Publisher
Shami Choon, Manager
Contains information on close to 3,400 U.S. and Canadian supermarket chains, each with at least $2 million in annual sales - one of the most profitable segments in this sector of the economy. The companies in this database operate over 41,000 individual supermarket, superstore, club store, gourmet supermarkets and combo-store units. A special convenience store section profiles 1,700 convenience store chains operating over 85,000 stores.
Cost: $575.00
Frequency: Annual

22048 **Top Shopping Centers: Major Markets 1-50**
National Research Bureau
333 W Wacker Drive
Suite 900
Chicago, IL 60606-1284
312-346-3900
Cost: $895.00

22049 **US Trade Pages**
Global Source
1511 K Street NW
Washington, DC 20005-1403
Kara Kent, Editor
These directories including a volume on Brazil, Chile, Canada, Mexico, Venezuela, and Argentina list trade associations and professional services that provide information on imports and exports between the US and the above listed companies.
Cost: $59.95
Frequency: 6 Volumes

22050 **World Federation of Direct Selling Associations Directory**
WFDSA
1776 K St Nw
Washington, DC 20006-2304
202-546-5330; Fax: 202-453-9010
www.wfdsa.org
Facebook, Twitter, LinkedIn
A Harold, President
Founded in 1789

Industry Web Sites

22051 **http://gold.greyhouse.com**
G.O.L.D Grey House OnLine Databases
Grey House Publishing's online database platform, GOLD, offers Quick Search, Keyword Search and Expert Search for most business sectors including retailing markets. The GOLD platform makes finding the information you need quick and easy - whether you're a novice searcher or an experienced database user. All of Grey House's directory products are available for subscription on the GOLD platform.

22052 **www.aamp.com**
American Association of Meat Processors
Membership consists of small to medium sized meat, poultry and food businesses including, slaughterers, processors, wholesalers, home food service businesses, deli and catering operators and suppliers to the industry. AAMP is affiliated with 28 state, regional and provincial associations.

22053 **www.accres.ca**
Association of Canadian Cannabis Retailers
Provides news and resources of interest to Canadian cannabis retailers.

22054 **www.bookweb.org**
American Booksellers Association
Trade association for retail booksellers. Not for profit.

22055 **www.fdi.org**
International Center for Companies of Food Trade
and Industry/North America
Provides management research on problems related to food distribution and serves as an international forum where food chain store executives can meet to exchange ideas and information.

22056 **www.fleamarkets.org**
National Flea Market Association
Represents Flea Market and Swap Meet owners and managers and disseminates information to the general public and media regarding the flea market industry worldwide.

22057 **www.greyhouse.com**
Grey House Publishing
Authoritative reference directories for most business sectors including retail markets. Users can search the online databases with varied search criteria allowing for custom searches by product category, geographic area, sales volume, keyword, subject and more. Full Grey House catalog and online ordering also available.

22058 **www.mraa.com**
Marine Retailers Association of America
Promotes activities for the recreational boating industry and holds seminars to improve management.

22059 **www.nacs.org**
National Association of College Stores
Provides educational and support services and products to college stores. Promotes business methods and ethics. Conducts manager certification, educational services and research.

22060 **www.nag-net.com**
Convenience Stores/Petroleum Marketers Association
This association represents senior level management of retail companies organized to enhance buying power, merchandising programs and an exchange of ideas. C-Stores/Petroleum Marketers membership dues: Retail Av. $300, Assoc. $500

22061 **www.narda.com**
North American Retail Dealers Association
A national organization of association members, independent retailers selling and servicing major appliances, consumer electronics products, furniture and computers. Emphasis is placed on ideas that help readers become better, more profitable businesses. Articles are featured regularly on displays, salesmanship, financial analysis and service management.

22062 **www.nationalPawnbrokers.org**
National Pawnbrokers Association
Nonprofits organization that supports all those involved with the retail pawnbrokers.

22063 **www.nationalgrocers.org**
National Grocers Association
Works to advance understanding, trade, and cooperation in the food industry. Represents members interests before the government. Offers store planning, and engineering, training and advertising.

22064 **www.nrf.com**
National Retail Federation
Retail trade association with membership that comprises all retail formats and channels of distribution including department, specialty, discount, catalog, Internet and independent stores. NRF members represent an industry that encompasses more than 1.4 million US retail establishments which employ more than 23 million people — about one in five American workers — and registered 2002 sales of $3.6 trillion. NRF's international members operate stores in more than 50 nations.

22065 **www.nssra.com**
National Ski & Snowboard Retailers Association
The retail voice for the ski and snowboard industries and provides information and services you need to operate more successfully.

22066 **www.retailsystems.com**
Retail Systems Alert Group
For retail and supply chain professionals. Access to community centers, newsletter information, and online ordering information is also available.

22067 **www.rtda.org**
Retail Tobacco Dealers of America
Trade association of high quality tobacconists.

22068 **www.shop.org**
Shop.org
Association for retailers online. It's where professional retailerscome together to garner the insight, knowledge and intellegence to make better decisions in the evolving world of the Internet and multi-channel retailing.

Associations

22069 **ACM Special Interest Group on Artificial Intelligence**
Association for Computing Machinery
1601 Broadway
10th Floor
New York, NY 10019-7434

212-869-7440
800-342-6626; Fax: 212-944-1318
acmhelp@acm.org
sigai.acm.org

Sanmay Das, Chair
Nicholas Mattei, Vice Chair
John Dickerson, Secretary/Treasurer

ACM SIGAI is an offshoot of the Association for Computing Machinery, made up of academic and industrial researchers, practitioners, software developers, end users, and students.
Mailing list available for rent

22070 **Allen Institute for AI**
Seattle, WA

206-548-5600
ai2-info@allenai.org
allenai.org
Twitter

Oren Etzioni, Chief Executive Officer
James Allard, Chief Operating Officer

Non-profit research institute named after Microsoft co-founder Paul Allen, aiming to construct Artificial Intelligence systems with reasoning, learning, and reading capabilities.

22071 **American Association for the Advancement of Science**
1200 New York Ave NW
Washington, DC 20005

202-326-6400
www.aaas.org
Facebook, Twitter, LinkedIn, YouTube, Instagram

Alan I. Leshner, Interim Chief Executive Officer
Andrew Black, Chief of Staff & External Affairs
Michael Savelli, Chief Operating Officer
Maureen Kearney, Chief Program Officer
Tiffany Lohwater, Chief Communications Officer

A nonprofit organization that has research news, issue papers, educational programs, etc.
Founded in 1848

22072 **Association for Advancing Automation**
900 Victors Way
Suite 140
Ann Arbor, MI 48108

734-994-6088; Fax: 734-994-3338
info@a3automate.org
www.a3automate.org
Facebook, Twitter, LinkedIn, YouTube

Jeff Burnstein, President
Dana Whalls, Vice President
Bob Doyle, Vice President, RIA & A3 Mexico
Robert Huschka, Director, Education Strategies
James Hamilton, Director, Sales

A3 is the umbrella association for the Robotic Industries Association, representing automation manufacturers, component suppliers, system integrators, end users, research groups, and consulting firms internationally.
1000 Members

22073 **Association for Computing Machinery**
1601 Broadway
10th Floor
New York, NY 10019-7434

212-869-7440
800-342-6626; Fax: 212-944-1318
acmhelp@acm.org
www.acm.org
Facebook, Twitter, LinkedIn, YouTube

Vicki Hanson, Chief Executive Officer
Pat Ryan, Chief Operating Officer
John Stanik, Managing Editor
Darren Ramdin, Director, Finance
Cynthia Ryan, Associate Director, Membership

Organization serving a membership of computing educators, researchers, and professionals. The association offers relevant career development, professional networking, and education opportunities.
80000 Members
Founded in 1947

22074 **Association for the Advancement of Artificial Intelligence**
2275 East Bayshore Road
Suite 160
Palo Alto, CA 94303

650-328-3123; Fax: 650-321-4457
www.aaai.org
Twitter

Carol Hamilton, Executive Director
Young Hash, Membership Coordinator
Stephanie Le, Conference Coordinator
Emma Wishmeyer, Conference Program Associate
Diane Mela, Accountant

Nonprofit society devoted to advancing the scientific understanding of the mechanisims underlying thought and intellegent behavior and their embodiment in machines.
6000 Members
Founded in 1979
Mailing list available for rent

22075 **CIFAR**
MaRS Centre, West Tower
661 University Avenue
Suite 505
Toronto, ON M5G 1M1

416-971-4251
www.cifar.ca
Facebook, Twitter, LinkedIn, YouTube

Alan Bernstein, President & CEO

Charitable organization that looks to address important questions facing humanity, such as the risks posed by Artificial Intelligence, by gathering extraordinary individuals and allowing them to share their knowledge.
400+ Members

22076 **Canadian Artificial Intelligence Association**
Concordia University
1515 St. Catherine Street W.
Montreal, QC H3G 2W1

514-848-2424
leila.kosseim@concordia.ca
www.caiac.ca
Facebook, Twitter, LinkedIn

Leila Kosseim, President
Richard Khoury, Vice President
Xin Wang, Treasurer
Denilson Barbosa, Secretary

Formerly known as the Canadian Society for the Computational Studies of Intelligence, CAIAC seeks to further research, development and education in Canada's artificial intelligence community, through knowledge-exchange in the media and other venues.

22077 **Canadian Image Processing and Pattern Recognition Society**
York University
4700 Keele Street
Toronto, ON M3J 1P3

416-736-2100
jenkin@cse.yorku.ca
www.computerrobotvision.org
Michael Jenkin, President
Steven Waslander, Treasurer
Jim Little, Secretary

Special interest group of the Canadian Information Processing Society, and the national representative organization of the International Association of Pattern Recognition.

22078 **Center for Security and Emerging Technology**
Walsh School of Foreign Service
ICC 301, 37th & O Street NW
Washington, DC 20057

202-687-0100
cset@georgetown.edu
cset.georgetown.edu
Jason Matheny, Founding Director
Tessa Baker, Director, Operations
Ben Buchanan, Director, Cybersecurity & AI
Igor Mikolic-Torreira, Director, Analysis
Dewey Murdick, Director, Data Science

CSET studies the security impacts of emerging technologies, especially Artificial Intelligence.
Founded in 2019
Mailing list available for rent

22079 **Clinical Robotic Surgery Association**
Two Prudential Plaza
180 North Stetson
Suite 3500
Chicago, IL 60601

312-268-5754
inquiries@clinicalrobotics.com
www.clinicalrobotics.com
Facebook, LinkedIn, YouTube, Instagram

Philip Clark, Executive Managing Director
Riccardo Terrosi, Technical Director
Danielle Jacobson, Membership Coordinator

Organization of surgeons practicing in Upper GI, HPB, Thoracic, Colorectal, Vascular, Transplant, ENT and other medical areas. The association's mission is to offer clinical, educational and innovative services related to use of robotics in medical procedures.
Founded in 2009

22080 **Computing Research Association**
1828 L Street NW
Suite 800
Washington, DC 20036-4632

202-234-2111; Fax: 202-667-1066
info@cra.org
www.cra.org
Facebook, Twitter, YouTube

Andrew Bernat, Executive Director
Erik Russell, Director of Programs
Sandra Corbett, Program Manager

The CRA's mission is to seek to strengthen research and advanced education in computing and allied fields.
200 Members
Founded in 1972

22081 **Continental Automated Buildings Association (CABA)**
1173 Cyrville Road
Suite 210
Ottawa, Canada, ON K1J 7S6

613-686-1814
888-798-2222; Fax: 613-744-7833
caba@caba.org

www.caba.org
Facebook, Twitter, LinkedIn, YouTube

Ronald J Zimmer, President & CEO
Conrad McCallum, Communications Director
Greg Walker, Research Director
Andrew Glennie, Member Services Coordinator
Sashien Godakandae, Business Development Officer

CABA is an international, non-profit industry organization that promotes advanced technologies in homes and buildings.
380+ Members
Founded in 1988

22082 Eta Kappa Nu
445 Hoes Lane
Piscataway, NJ 08854

732-465-5846
800-406-2590
info@hkn.org
hkn.ieee.org

Edward Rezek, President

Eta Kappa Nu (HKN) is the electrical and computer engineering honor society of the Institute of Electrical and Electronics Engineers (IEEE).
Founded in 1904

22083 Future of Life Institute
Boston, MA

meia@futureoflife.org
futureoflife.org
Facebook, Twitter

Jaan Tallinn, Co-Founder
Max Tegmark, Co-Founder
Meia Chita-Termark, Co-Founder
Viktoriya Krakovna, Co-Founder
Anthony Aguirre, Co-Founder

Seeks to mitigate emerging risks facing humanity, especially from advanced artificial intelligence, but also including biotechnology, nuclear power, and climate change.

22084 Global Association for Vision Information
900 Victors Way
Suite 140
Ann Arbor, MI 48108

734-994-6088
www.visiononline.org
Facebook, Twitter, LinkedIn, YouTube

Jeff Burnstein, President
Alex Shikany, VP, Membership & Business
James Hamilton, Director, Sales
Robert Huschka, Director, Education Strategies
Bob McCurrach, Director, Standards Development

The AIA is dedicated to vision and imaging technologies, with members including manufacturers of vision components and systems, system integrators, distributors, OEMs, end users, consulting firms, academic institutions, and research groups.
380+ Members
Founded in 1984

22085 IEEE Circuits and Systems Society
Institute Of Electrical and Electronics Engineers
445 Hoes Lane
Piscataway, NJ 08854

Home Page: www.ieee-cas.org
Facebook, Twitter, LinkedIn

Amara Amara, President
Yoshifumi Nishio, VP, Membership
Myung Hoon Sunwoo, VP, Conferences
Guoxing Wang, VP, Financial Activities
Mohammad Sawan, VP, Publications

CASS fosters interdisciplinary and cross-disciplinary cooperation with regards to using circuits and systems to address humanity's greatest challenges.

22086 IEEE Computational Intelligence Society
445 Hoes Lane
Piscataway, NJ 08855

732-465-5892; Fax: 732-465-6435
cis-info@ieee.org
cis.ieee.org
Facebook, Twitter, LinkedIn

Bernadette Bouchon-Meunier, President
Pablo Estevez, VP, Finances
Marley Vellasco, VP, Conferences
James Keller, VP, Publications
Carlos Coello Coello, VP, Member Activities

The CIS seeks to advance computational intelligence in science and engineering.

22087 IEEE Control Systems Society
445 Hoes Lane
Piscataway, NJ 08854-1331

Home Page: ieeecss.org
Facebook, Twitter, LinkedIn

Anuradha Annaswamy, President
Jorge Cortes, Director, Operations

Subsidiary of the Institute of Electrical and Electronics Engineers dedicated to control system technology.

22088 IEEE Industrial Electronics Society
Institute Of Electrical and Electronics Engineers
445 Hoes Lane
Piscataway, NJ 08854

804-827-3999
president@ieee-ies.org
www.ieee-ies.org
Facebook, Twitter, LinkedIn, YouTube

Terry Martin, President
Thilo Sauter, VP, Publications
Juan Rodriguez-Andina, VP, Conference Activities
Kiyoshi Ohishi, VP, Workshops & Activities
Yousef Ibrahim, VP, Membership Activities

Conducts, through its members, range of technical activities dedicated to applying electronics and electrical sciences in an industrial setting, including current developments in intelligent and computer control systems, robotics, factory communications and automation, flexible manufacturing, data acquisition and signal processing, vision systems, and power electronics.

22089 IEEE Industry Applications Society
Institute Of Electrical and Electronics Engineers
445 Hoes Lane
Piscataway, NJ 08854

732-562-2663
p.mccarren@ieee.org
ias.ieee.org
Facebook, Twitter, LinkedIn

Patrick McCarren, Executive Director
Lynda Bernstein, IAS Program Specialist

Seeks to link theory and practice by advancing science and technology in the electrical and electronic systems.

22090 IEEE Intelligent Transportation Systems Society
Institute Of Electrical and Electronics Engineers
445 Hoes Lane
Piscataway, NJ 08854

Home Page: www.ieee-itss.org
Facebook, Twitter, LinkedIn

Wei-Bin Zhang, President
Lingxi Li, VP, Administrative Activities
Nobuyuki Ozaki, VP, Standards
Javier Sanchez Medina, VP, Technical Activities

ITSS seeks to advance electrical engineering & information technology as applied to intelligent transportation systems.

22091 IEEE Robotics and Automation Society
445 Hoes Lane
Piscataway, NJ

732-562-3906
ras@ieee.org
www.ieee-ras.org
Facebook, Twitter, LinkedIn, YouTube

Kathy Colabaugh, Society Operations Manager
Amy Reeder, Society Program Specialist
Alexis Simoes, Society Program Coordinator

A scientific, literary and educational society of the Institute of Electrical and Electronics Engineers, seeking to facilitate scientific and technological knowledge exchange in robotics and automation.

22092 IEEE Signal Processing Society
Institute of Electrical and Electronics Engineers
445 Hoes Lane
Piscataway, NJ 08854

732-562-3888; Fax: 732-867-9953
sp-info@ieee.org
signalprocessingsociety.org
Facebook, Twitter, LinkedIn

Rich Baseil, Executive Director
Theresa Argiropoulos, Senior Manager, Operations
Caroline Johnson, Senior Manager, Conference Services
William Colacchio, Senior Manager, Publications
Jessica Perry, Member Communications Specialist

The SPS looks to provide current scientific information and resources on signal processing, while educating professionals in the industry, and providing a venue for networking.

22093 IEEE Society on Social Implications of Technology
Institute of Electrical and Electronics Engineers
445 Hoes Lane
Piscataway, NJ 08854

r.dent@ieee.org
technologyandsociety.org
Facebook, Twitter, LinkedIn

Robert Dent, President
Lew Terman, Secretary
Howard Wolfman, Treasurer

The SSIT focuses on the following areas: Sustainable Development & Humanitarian Technology; Ethics, Human Values and Technology; Technology Benefits for All; Future Societal Impact of Technology Advances; and Protecting the Planet & Sustainable Technology

22094 IEEE Solid-State Circuits Society
Institute of Electrical and Electronics Engineers
445 Hoes Lane
Piscataway, NJ 08854

m.p.kelly@ieee.org
sscs.ieee.org
Facebook, Twitter, LinkedIn

Adam Greenberg, Executive Director
Lauren Caruso, Administrator
Abira Altvater, Technical Program Specialist
Danielle Marinese, Society Administrator

The SSCS serves members by providing them with education, communication, recognition, leadership opportunities, and networking opportunities.

22095 **IEEE Systems, Man, and Cybernetics Society**
Institute of Electrical and Electronics Engineers
445 Hoes Lane
Piscataway, NJ 08854

Home Page: www.ieeesmc.org
Facebook, Twitter, LinkedIn, Instagram

Imre Rudas, President
Sam Kwong, VP, Cybernetics
Andreas Nuernberger, VP, Conferences & Meetings
Adrian Stoica, VP, Systems Science & Engineering
Vladimir Marik, VP, Organization & Planning

Promotes all aspects of systems science and engineering, human-machine systems, and cybernetics, through conferences, publications, and other activities.

22096 **IEEE Technology & Engineering Management Society**
Institute of Electrical and Electronics Engineers
445 Hoes Lane
Piscataway, NJ 08854

Home Page: www.ieee-tems.org
Facebook, Twitter, LinkedIn

Andy Chen, President
Richard Evans, VP, Technical Activities
Sudeendra Koushik, VP, Conferences

Formerly the Engineering Management Society and the Technology Management Council, TEMS seeks to provide members with essential management and leadership knowledge and skills.
Founded in 1951

22097 **IEEE Vehicular Technology Society**
3 Parl Avenue
17th Floor
New York, NY 10016-5997

212-419-7900
oliver.holland@ieee.org
vtsociety.org
Facebook, Twitter, LinkedIn

Oliver Holland, Chapter Coordinator & Developer

VTS focuses on the theory and practice of electrical engineering with regards to land transportation, railroad and mass transit, mobile communications, vehicular electrotechnology equipment and systems, and land, airborne and maritime mobile Services.

22098 **Institute of Electrical and Electronics Engineers**
3 Park Ave.
17th Fl.
New York, NY 10016-5997

212-419-7900; Fax: 212-752-4929
www.ieee.org
Facebook, Twitter, LinkedIn, YouTube, Instagram

Toshio Fukuda, President & CEO
Stephen Welby, Executive Director & COO

Supports all those involved in the field of electrical engineering, and works to nurture technological innovation and excellence for the benefit of humanity.
422K Members
Founded in 1963

22099 **Intelligent Transportation Society of America (ITS America)**
1100 New Jersey Ave. SE
Suite 850
Washington, DC 20003

202-484-4847
800-374-8472
membership@itsa.org
www.itsa.org
Twitter, Instagram

Shailen Bhatt, President & CEO
Laura Chace, Chief Operating Officer
Carlos Alban, VP, Technical Programs
Tim Drake, VP, Policy & Regulatory Affairs
Cathy St. Denis, VP, Communications & Strategy

Organization dedicated to advancing the research, development and design of surface transportation systems.
1200+ Members
Founded in 1991

22100 **International Neural Network Society**
2800 W. Higgins Road
Suite 440
Hoffman Estates, IL 60169

833-636-0351; Fax: 847-885-8393
inns@inns.org
www.inns.org
Facebook, Twitter, LinkedIn, YouTube

Irwin King, President
Marley Vellasco, Secretary
Danil Prokhorov, Treasurer
Seiichi Ozawa, VP, Membership
Richard Duro, VP, Conferences

INNS is comprised of researchers, professors, practitioners, and learners in the field of neural networks and computational science.

22101 **Kestrel Institute**
3260 Hillview Avenue
Palo Alto, CA 94304

650-493-6871; Fax: 650-424-1807
info@kestrel.edu
www.kestrel.edu

Cordell Green, Director

Non-profit computer science research center.

22102 **Machine Intelligence Research Institute**
Berkeley, CA

contact@intelligence.org
intelligence.org
Facebook, Twitter, RSS

Nate Soares, Executive Director
Malo Bourgon, Chief Operating Officer

Uses foundational mathematics to ensure artificial intelligence systems have a positive impact.

22103 **Measurement, Control & Automation Association**
200 City Hall Avenue
Suite D
Poquoson, VA 23662

757-258-3100
automationassociation.com
Facebook, Twitter, LinkedIn, YouTube

Teresa Sebring, President
Andrea Ambrose, Director, Member Relations
Elizabeth Horton, Programs Manager
Kim Malina, Marketing Communications Manager
Rebecca Moore, Administrative Manager

The MCAA is the national trade association for manufacturers and distributors of instrumentation, systems, and software products for industrial process control and factory automation.
Founded in 1944

22104 **Motion Control & Motor Association**
900 Victors Way
Suite 140
Ann Arbor, MI 48108

734-994-6088
info@motioncontrolonline.org
www.motioncontrolonline.org
Facebook, Twitter, LinkedIn, YouTube

Matt French, Chair
Gunnar Block, Vice Chair
Paul Horvat, Vice Chair

The MCMA seeks to advance motion control and related automation technologies, and to help members and the industry grow.
Founded in 2006

22105 **OpenAI**
San Francisco, CA

Home Page: openai.com
Facebook, Twitter

Greg Brockman, Chair & CTO
Ilya Sutskever, Chief Scientist

Research organization dedicated to maintaining Artificial Intelligence as a benefit to humanity.

22106 **Partnership on AI**
115 Sansome Street
Suite 1200
San Francisco, CA 94104

Home Page: www.partnershiponai.org
Facebook, Twitter

Terah Lyons, Founding Executive Director
Samir Goswami, Chief Operating Officer
Sasha Ramsaw, Human Resources Manager
Peter Lo, Senior Communications Manager
Hudson Hongo, Writer/Editor

Seeks to advance the understanding of AI technologies including machine perception, learning, and automated reasoning for the benefit of humanity.

22107 **Robotic Industries Association**
900 Victors Way
Suite 140
Ann Arbor, MI 48108

734-994-6088; Fax: 734-994-3338
info@robotics.org
www.robotics.org
Facebook, Twitter, LinkedIn, YouTube

Jeff Burnstein, President
Dana Whalls, Vice President, A3
Clarissa Carvalho, Marketing Specialist
James Hamilton, Sales Director
Bob Doyle, Vice President

Trade group serving the robotics industry. Members include robot manufacturers, users, system integrators, component suppliers, research groups, and consulting firms. The Robotic Industries Association offers educational resources, events and news for its members.
Founded in 1974
Mailing list available for rent

22108 **Society of Robotic Surgery**
c/c Veritas Meeting Solutions
1061 E. Main Street
Suite 300
East Dundee, IL 60118

847-752-5355
info@srobotics.org
www.srobotics.org
Facebook, Twitter

Farid Gharagozloo, MD, FACS, President
Vipul R. Patel, MD, FACS, Executive Director
Sue O'Sullivan, Administrative Director

Society providing education about robotic surgery, as well as studies, funding and development events for professionals in the field.
Founded in 2009

Newsletters

22109 **AI Matters**
ACM SIGAI
1601 Broadway
10th Floor
New York, NY 10019-7434

212-869-7440
800-342-6626; Fax: 212-944-1318
acmhelp@acm.org
sigai.acm.org

Amy McGovern, Editor-in-Chief
Iolanda Leite, Editor-in-Chief

Official newsletter of the ACM Special Interest Group on Artificial Intelligence.
Frequency: Quarterly

22110 **AICan Bulletin**
CIFAR, MaRS Centre, West Tower
661 University Avenue
Suite 505
Toronto, ON M5G 1M1

416-971-4251
www.cifar.ca

Alan Bernstein, President & CEO

Newsletter of CIFAR, with new developments in Artificial Intelligence.
Frequency: Bi-Monthly

22111 **Bot Brief**
Robotic Industries Association
900 Victors Way
Suite 140
Ann Arbor, MI 48108

734-994-6088; Fax: 734-994-3338
info@robotics.org
www.robotics.org

Jeff Burnstein, President
Dana Whalls, Vice President, A3
Clarissa Carvalho, Marketing Specialist
Bob Doyle, Vice President

Weekly newsletter from the Robotic Industries Association with the latest industry news.
Frequency: Weekly
Founded in 1974

22112 **Motion Control Market Report**
Motion Control & Motor Association
900 Victors Way
Suite 140
Ann Arbor, MI 48108

734-994-6088
info@motioncontrolonline.org
www.motioncontrolonline.org

Matt French, Chair
Gunnar Block, Vice Chair
Paul Horvat, Vice Chair

Quarterly release for members.
Founded in 2006

22113 **News & Ideas**
CIFAR, MaRS Centre, West Tower
661 University Avenue
Suite 505
Toronto, ON M5G 1M1

416-971-4251
www.cifar.ca

Alan Bernstein, President & CEO

Newsletter of CIFAR, with association news, events, and new discoveries.

22114 **The CAIAC Herald**
Canadian Artificial Intelligence Association
1515 St. Catherine Street W.
Montreal, QC H3G 2W1

514-848-2424
leila.kosseim@concordia.ca
www.caiac.ca

Leila Kosseim, President
Richard Khoury, Vice President
Xin Wang, Treasurer
Denilson Barbosa, Secretary

Official newsletter of the Canadian Artificial Intelligence Association, with new developments in Artificial Intelligence.

Magazines & Journals

22115 **ACM QUEUE**
Association for Computing Machinery
1601 Broadway
10th Floor
New York, NY 10019-7434

212-869-7440
800-342-6626; Fax: 212-944-1318
acmhelp@acm.org
queue.acm.org

Jack Davidson, Co-Chair, Publications Board
Joseph A. Konstan, Co-Chair, Publications Board

Published by the Association for Computing Machinery.
Circulation: 25000
Founded in 1947

22116 **AI Magazine**
Association for the Advancement of AT
2275 East Bayshore Road
Suite 160
Palo Alto, CA 94303

650-328-3123; Fax: 650-321-4457
www.aaai.org

David Leake, Editor Emeritus
Ashok Goel, Editor-In-Chief
Carol Hamilton, Executive Director

Quarterly issued magazine, available through AAAI membership. AI Magazine features articles regarding research in the field of artificial intelligence.
128 Pages
Frequency: Quarterly
Circulation: 7000
ISSN: 0738-4602
Founded in 1980
Printed in on matte stock

22117 **AMC Inroads**
Association for Computing Machinery
1601 Broadway
10th Floor
New York, NY 10019-7434

212-869-7440
800-342-6626; Fax: 212-944-1318
acmhelp@acm.org
dl.acm.org

Vick Hanson, Chief Executive Officer
Denis Doig, Senior Editor
Diana Crawford, Deputy Director
Scott Crawford, Director, Publications

Intended for professionals interested in advancing computing education in the world.
0 Pages

22118 **Circuits and Systems Magazine**
IEEE Circuits and Systems Society
445 Hoes Lane
Piscataway, NJ 08854

chaiwahwu@ieee.org
www.ieee-cas.org

Chai Wah Wu, Editor-in-Chief
Alyssa B. Apsel, Deputy Editor-in-Chief
Mohammad Sawan, VP, Publications

Feature articles with noteworthy results, surveys, and tutorials.

22119 **Communications of the ACM**
Association for Computing Machinery
1601 Broadway
10th Floor
New York, NY 10019-7434

212-869-7440
800-342-6626; Fax: 212-944-1318
acmhelp@acm.org
cacm.acm.org

Vicki Hanson, President
Thomas Lambert, Managing Editor
Andrew Rosenbloom, Senior Editor
Scott Delman, Director, Publications

Technical magazine covering developments in computer science for the computing and information technology fields, useful for computing professionals.
Cost: $17.00
Frequency: Monthly
Circulation: 82,867

22120 **Computing Surveys**
Association for Computing Machinery
1601 Broadway
10th Floor
New York, NY 10019-7434

212-869-7440
800-342-6626; Fax: 212-944-1318
acmhelp@acm.org
www.acm.org

Vicki Hanson, President
Laura Lander, Journals Manager
Scott Delman, Director, Publications
John Stanik, Managing Editor

Carefully planned and presented introductions to complex issues in computing technology, supported by exhaustive and comprehensive notations on the relevant literature. Topics covered include image understanding, software reusability, and object and relational database topics.
Cost: $170.00
Frequency: Quarterly
ISSN: 0360-0300

22121 **IEEE Computational Intelligence Magazine**
IEEE Computational Intelligence Society
445 Hoes Lane
Piscataway, NJ 08855

732-465-5892; Fax: 732-465-6435
cis-info@ieee.org
cis.ieee.org

Bernadette Bouchon-Meunier, President
Hessein Abbass, VP, Technical Activities
James Keller, VP, Publications

CIM features peer-reviewed articles with noteworthy discoveries, insights, and tutorial surveys.

22122 **IEEE Control Systems Magazine**
IEEE Control Systems Society (CSS)
445 Hoes Lane
Piscataway, NJ 08854-1331

732-562-3937
m.david@ieee.org
www.ieee.org

Jonathan How, Editor-in-Chief
Rodolphe Sepulchre, Deputy Editor-in-Chief

Focuses on applications of technical knowledge and concentrates on industrial implementations, design tools, technology review, control education and applied research. Geared towards readers with many different responsibilities including applied research, device design, product development and design including software and semiconductor components.
Cost: $210.00
Founded in 1973
Mailing list available for rent

22123 **IEEE Industrial Electronics Magazine**
Institute Of Electrical and Electronics Engineers
445 Hoes Lane
Piscataway, NJ 08854

804-827-3999
eic-iem@ieee-ies.org
www.ieee-ies.org

Peter Palesnky, Editor-in-Chief

IEM features peer-reviewed articles presenting new trends and practices in industrial electronics research & development.

22124 **IEEE Solid-State Circuits Magazine**
IEEE Solid-State Circuits Society
445 Hoes Lane
Piscataway, NJ 08854

rjacobbaker@gmail.com
sscs.ieee.org

R. Jacob Baker, Editor-in-Chief
Rakesh Kumar, Chair, Advisory Board

Tutorial-style articles on technical achievements, trends, and future developments in the field of Integrated Circuits.
Founded in 2009

22125 **IEEE Transactions on Engineering Management**
IEEE Technology & Engineering Management Society
445 Hoes Lane
Piscataway, NJ 08854

tugrul.u.daim@pdx.edu
www.ieee-tems.org

Tugrul U. Daim, Editor-in-Chief
Alison Larkin, Peer Review Support Services
Mark Werwath, VP, Publications

Journal of the Technology and Engineering Management Society of IEEE, with peer-reviewed research on engineering, technology, and innovation management.
Frequency: Quarterly
Founded in 1954

22126 **IEEE Transactions on Industry Applications**
Institute Of Electrical and Electronics Engineers
445 Hoes Lane
Piscataway, NJ 08854

732-562-2663
t.nondahl@ieee.org
www.ieee.org

Thomas A. Nondahl, Editor-in-Chief

The development and applications of electrical systems, apparatus, devices and controls to the processes and equipment of industry and commerce.
Circulation: 5100
Founded in 1980

22127 **IEEE Vehicular Technology Magazine**
IEEE Vehicular Technology Society
3 Parl Avenue
17th Floor
New York, NY 10016-5997

212-419-7900
david@uni-kassel.de
vtsociety.org

Klaus David, Editor-in-Chief

Focus is on mobile radio, connected and automated vehicles, automotive electronics, and transportation systems.
Frequency: Quarterly

22128 **ITS Magazine**
IEEE Intelligent Transportation Systems Society
445 Hoes Lane
Piscataway, NJ 08854

Home Page: www.ieee-itss.org

Wei-Bin Zhang, President
Petros A. Ioannou, VP, Publications Activities
Ljubo Vlacic, Magazine Editor

Features peer-reviewed articles on research and applications, with case studies and examinations of challenges in the intelligent transportation system industry.

22129 **Interactions Magazine**
Association for Computing Machinery
1601 Broadway
10th Floor
New York, NY 10019-7434

212-869-7440
800-342-6626; Fax: 212-944-1318
acmhelp@acm.org
dl.acm.org

Vicki Hanson, Chief Executive Officer
Denis Doig, Senior Editor
Diane Crawford, Deputy Director
Scott Crawford, Director, Publications

Editorial content covering business, design, methods and tools, book previews, conference previews and current events pertaining to designers, developers and researchers. The focus is on human-computer interaction.
Founded in 1947

22130 **Journal of Robotic Surgery**
Society of Robotic Surgery
1061 E. Main Street
Suite 300
East Dundee, IL 60118

info@srobotics.org
link.springer.com/journal/11701

Vipul R. Patel, MD, Executive Director

Journal exploring minimally invasive surgical techniques and the role of robotics in surgery.
Cost: $99.00
Circulation: 40K+
ISSN: 1863-2483
Founded in 2009

22131 **Neural Networks**
International Neural Network Society
2800 W. Higgins Road
Suite 440
Hoffman Estates, IL 60169

833-636-0351; Fax: 847-885-8393
inns@inns.org
www.inns.org

DeLiang Wang, Editor-in-Chief
Kenji Doya, Editor-in-Chief

Archival journal of the International Neural Network Society, the European Neural Network Society, and the Japanese Neural Network Society.

22132 **RIA Tech Papers**
Robotic Industries Association
900 Victors Way
Suite 140
Ann Arbor, MI 48108

734-994-6088; Fax: 734-994-3338
info@robotics.org
www.robotics.org/Tech-Papers

Jeff Burnstein, President
Dana Whalls, Vice President, A3
Clarissa Carvalho, Marketing Specialist
Bob Doyle, Vice President

Technical papers on various subjects relating to the robotics industry, including manufacturing challenges, software and safety concerns.
Frequency: Monthly
Founded in 1974

22133 **Robotics and Autonomous Systems**
Elsevier Science
230 Park Avenue
Suite 800
New York, NY 10169

212-309-8100
www.elsevier.com

K. Berns, Editor-in-Chief
M. Gini, Editor-in-Chief
J. Ota, Editor-in-Chief

Journal with articles on developments in the field of robotics, with an emphasis on autonomous systems.
Cost: $3008.00
ISSN: 0921-8890

22134 **Robotics and Computer-Intergrated Manufacturing**
Elsevier Science
230 Park Avenue
Suite 800
New York, NY 10169

212-309-8100
www.elsevier.com

Lihui Wang, Editor-in-Chief

Journal containing original papers on theoretical, applied and experimental robotics and computer-integrated manufacturing, with emphasis on flexible manufacturing systems.
Cost: $3008.00
Circulation: 2500
ISSN: 0736-5845
Founded in 1880

22135 **SMC Magazine**
IEEE Systems, Man, and Cybernetics Society
445 Hoes Lane
Piscataway, NJ 08854

smcmagazine_eic@outlook.com
www.ieeesmc.org

Saeid Nahavandi, Editor-in-Chief
Enrique Herrera Viedma, VP, Publications

Articles relevant to the research areas of the IEEE Systems, Man, and Cybernetics Society, with information on the Society's activities, and educational material as well.

22136 **Science Robotics**
American Assn for the Advancement of Science
1200 New York Avenue NW
Washington, DC 20005-3941

202-326-6490; Fax: 202-789-4669
scieroboteditors@aaas.org
robotics.sciencemag.org

Alan I. Leshner, Interim Executive Publisher
Jeremy Berg PhD, Editor-in-Chief
Monica M. Bradford, Executive Editor

Publishes original, peer-reviewed, science- or engineering-based research articles that advance

the field of robotics. The journal also features editor-commissioned reviews.
Frequency: Monthly

22137 **Signal Processing Magazine**
IEEE Signal Processing Society
445 Hoes Lane
Piscataway, NJ 08854

732-562-3888; Fax: 732-867-9953
sp-pub-info@ieee.org
signalprocessingsociety.org
Facebook, Twitter, LinkedIn

Robert Heath, Editor-in-Chief
William Colacchio, Senior Manager, Publications

Tutorials on signal processing research and applications, as well as editorial content on matters of interest.

22138 **Technology and Society**
IEEE Society on Social Implications of Technology
445 Hoes Lane
Piscataway, NJ 08854

j.pitt@imperial.ac.uk
technologyandsociety.org
Facebook, Twitter, LinkedIn

Jeremy Pitt, Editor_in-Chief
Terri A. Bookman, Managing Editor

Flagship magazine of the IEEE Society on Social Implications of Technology, with peer-reviewed articles on the impact of technology on the world.

22139 **The Bridge**
IEEE-Eta Kappa Nu
445 Hoes Lane
Piscataway, NJ 08854

732-465-5846
800-406-2590
info@hkn.org
hkn.ieee.org/news-and-announcements/the-bridge

Sahra Sedigh Sarvestani, Editor-in-Chief
Stephen Williams, Editor-in-Chief

The award-winning digital magazine of the IEEE-HKN.
Frequency: 3x/year

Trade Shows

22140 **A3 Business Forum**
Association for Advancing Automation
900 Victors Way
Suite 140
Ann Arbor, MI 48108

734-994-6088; Fax: 734-994-3338
info@a3automate.org
www.a3automate.org

Jeff Burnstein, President
Maria Kurple, Event Marketing Manager
Mandy Pawczuk, Administrator, Event Services

Conference for professionals working in robotics, vision & imaging, motion control, and motors industries.
550+ Attendees
Frequency: Annual/January

22141 **AAAI National Conference**
Association for the Advancement of AT
2275 East Bayshore Road
Suite 160
Palo Alto, CA 94303

650-328-3123; Fax: 650-321-4457
www.aaai.org
Twitter

Stephanie Le, Conference Coordinator
Emma Wishmeyer, Conference Program Associate

The conference provides a forum for a broad range of topics, including knowledge representation and automated reasoning, planning, machine learning and data mining, autonomous agents, robotics and machine perception, probabilistic inference, constraint satisfaction, search and game playing, natural language processing, neural networks, multi-agent systems, computational game theory and cognitive modeling.
1.2M Attendees
Frequency: Annual/July
Founded in 1980

22142 **American Association for the Advancement of Science Annual Meeting**
American Assn for the Advancement of Science
1200 New York Ave NW
Washington, DC 20005

202-326-6400
www.aaas.org

Alan I. Leshner, Interim Chief Executive Officer
Founded in 1848

22143 **Automate**
Motion Control & Motor Association
900 Victors Way
Suite 140
Ann Arbor, MI 48108

734-994-6088
info@motioncontrolonline.org
www.motioncontrolonline.org

Matt French, Chair
Gunnar Block, Vice Chair
Paul Horvat, Vice Chair

Trade show and conference on automation technologies.
20K Attendees

22144 **CABA Smart Buildings Summit**
Continental Automated Buildings Association
1173 Cyrville Road
Suite 210
Ottawa, Canada, ON K1J 7S6

613-686-1814
888-798-2222; Fax: 613-744-7833
caba@caba.org
www.caba.org
Facebook, Twitter, LinkedIn, YouTube

Ronald J Zimmer, President & CEO
Conrad McCallum, Communications Director
Greg Walker, Research Director
Andrew Glennie, Member Services Coordinator
Sashien Godakandae, Business Development Officer

Current intelligent building technologies.
380+ Members
Founded in 1988

22145 **CRSA Worldwide Congress**
Clinical Robotic Surgery Association
Two Prudential Plaza
180 North Stetson, Suite 3500
Chicago, IL 60601

312-268-5754
www.clinicalrobotics.com

Philip Clark, Executive Managing Director

The annual meeting for surgeons using robotic systems in General Surgery to discuss methods, share ideas and network.
Frequency: Annual/September

22146 **Canadian Conference on AI**
Canadian Artificial Intelligence Association
1515 St. Catherine Street W.
Montreal, QC H3G 2W1

514-848-2424
leila.kosseim@concordia.ca
www.caiac.ca

Leila Kosseim, President
Richard Khoury, Vice President
Xin Wang, Treasurer
Denilson Barbosa, Secretary

Conference on all areas of Artificial Intelligence, either theoretical or applied.

22147 **Conference on Computer and Robot Vision**
Cdn. Image Processing/Pattern Recognition Society
York University
4700 Keele Street
Toronto, ON M3J 1P3

416-736-2100
www.computerrobotvision.org

Helge Rhodin, Program Co-Chair
Liam Paul, Program Co-Chair

Takes place with the Canadian Conference on Artificial Intelligence.
Frequency: Annual
Founded in 2004

22148 **IEEE SoutheastCon**
IEEE Meeting & Conference Management (MCM)
445 Hoes Lane
Piscataway, NJ 08854

732-562-3878
800-678-4333; Fax: 732-971-1203
conference-services@ieee.org
www.ieee.org
Facebook, LinkedIn, Instagram

A student conference, technical conference, and business meeting.
800 Attendees
Frequency: Annual

22149 **International Conference on Automation Science and Engineering**
IEEE Robotics and Automation Society
445 Hoes Lane
Piscataway, NJ

732-562-3906
ras@ieee.org
www.ieee-ras.org

Kathy Colabaugh, Society Operations Manager
Amy Reeder, Society Program Specialist
Alexis Simoes, Society Program Coordinator

CASE is the flagship conference of the IEEE Robotics and Automation Society.

22150 **International Conference on Electronics, Circuits, and Systems**
IEEE Circuits and Systems Society
445 Hoes Lane
Piscataway, NJ 08854

manager@ieee-cas.org
www.ieee-cas.org

Brittian Parkinson, Operations Manager
Myung Hoon Sunwoo, VP, Conferences
Frequency: Annual

22151 **International Conference on Intelligent Robots and Systems**
Robotics and Automation Society

445 Hoes Lane
Piscataway, NJ

732-562-3906
ras@ieee.org
www.ieee-ras.org

Kathy Colabaugh, Society Operations Manager
Amy Reeder, Society Program Specialist
Alexis Simoes, Society Program Coordinator

22152 International Conference on Robotics and Automation
Robotics and Automation Society
445 Hoes Lane
Piscataway, NJ

732-562-3906
ras@ieee.org
www.ieee-ras.org

Kathy Colabaugh, Society Operations Manager
Amy Reeder, Society Program Specialist
Alexis Simoes, Society Program Coordinator

22153 International Joint Conference on Neural Networks
International Neural Network Society
2800 W. Higgins Road
Suite 440
Hoffman Estates, IL 60169

833-636-0351; Fax: 847-885-8393
inns@inns.org
www.inns.org

Richard Duro, VP, Conferences

Organized by the International Neural Network Society in cooperation with the IEEE Computational Intelligence Society, intended for researchers and other professionals in neural networks and related areas.

22154 International Symposium on Circuits and Systems
IEEE Circuits and Systems Society
445 Hoes Lane
Piscataway, NJ 08854

manager@ieee-cas.org
www.ieee-cas.org

Brittian Parkinson, Operations Manager
Myung Hoon Sunwoo, VP, Conferences
Frequency: Annual

22155 MCAA Industry Forum
Measurement, Control & Automation Association
200 City Hall Avenue
Suite D
Poquoson, VA 23662

757-258-3100
automationassociation.com

Teresa Sebring, President
Andrea Ambrose, Director, Member Relations
Elizabeth Horton, Programs Manager
Kim Malina, Marketing Communications Manager
Rebecca Moore, Administrative Manager

Education and networking event for manufacturers and distributors of instrumentation, systems, and software products for industrial process control and factory automation.
Founded in 1944

22156 MCMA TechCon
Motion Control & Motor Association
900 Victors Way
Suite 140
Ann Arbor, MI 48108

734-994-6088
info@motioncontrolonline.org
www.motioncontrolonline.org

Matt French, Chair
Gunnar Block, Vice Chair
Paul Horvat, Vice Chair

The Motion Control & Motor Association Technical Conference provides attendees with recent updates on motion control and automation.

22157 SIGAI Career Network and Conference
ACM SIGAI
1601 Broadway
10th Floor
New York, NY 10019-7434

212-869-7440
800-342-6626; Fax: 212-944-1318
acmhelp@acm.org
sigai.acm.org

Michael Rovatsos, Conference Coordination Officer

Conference for early-stage researchers in Artificial Intelligence.
Frequency: Quarterly

22158 SIGGRAPH Conference
Association for Computing Machinery
1601 Broadway
10th Floor
New York, NY 10019-7434

212-869-7440
800-342-6626; Fax: 212-944-1318
acmhelp@acm.org
www.acm.org
Facebook, Twitter, LinkedIn, Google+

Vicki Hanson, Chief Executive Officer
Irene Frawley, Prog. Mgr., Conference Operations
Hilaire Lee, Conference Financials
Diana Brantuas, Conference Budgeting

The annual conference and its year round initiatives provide a unique crossroads for a diverse community of researchers, developers, creators, educators and practitioners. The focus of the conference is the subject of computer graphics.
50000 Attendees
Frequency: July-August

22159 Society of Robotic Surgery Annual Meeting
Society of Robotic Surgery
1061 E. Main Street
Suite 300
East Dundee, IL 60118

847-752-5355
info@srobotics.org
www.srobotics.org

Vipul R. Patel, MD, Executive Director

Conference exploring issues related to robotic surgery, including protocols, furture developments, artificial intelligence, training and curriculum and more.
Frequency: Annual/June
Founded in 2009

22160 The Vision Show
Global Association for Vision Information
900 Victors Way
Suite 140
Ann Arbor, MI 48108

734-994-6088
www.visiononline.org
Facebook, Twitter

Jeff Burnstein, President
Maria Kurple, Event Marketing Manager
Mandy Pawczuk, Administrator, Event Services

North America's largest display of machine vision and imaging systems.
Frequency: June

Industry Web Sites

22161 www.a3automate.org
Association for Advancing Automation
A3 is the umbrella association for the Robotic Industries Association, representing automation manufacturers, component suppliers, system integrators, end users, research groups, and consulting firms internationally.

22162 www.aaas.org
American Association for Advancement of Science
A nonprofit organization that has research news, issue papers, educational programs, etc.

22163 www.acm.org
Association for Computing Machinery
Organization serving a membership of computing educators, researchers, and professionals. The association offers relevant career development, professional networking, and education opportunities.

22164 www.allenai.org
Allen Institute for AI
Non-profit research institute named after Microsoft co-founder Paul Allen, aiming to construct Artificial Intelligence systems with reasoning, learning, and reading capabilities.

22165 www.automationassociation.com
Measurement, Control & Automation Association
The MCAA is the national trade association for manufacturers and distributors of instrumentation, systems, and software products for industrial process control and factory automation.

22166 www.caiac.ca
Canadian Artificial Intelligence Association
Formerly known as the Canadian Society for the Computational Studies of Intelligence, CAIAC seeks to further research, development and education in Canada's artificial intelligence community, through knowledge-exchange in the media and other venues.

22167 www.cifar.ca
CIFAR
Charitable organization that looks to address important questions facing humanity, such as the risks posed by Artificial Intelligence, by gathering extraordinary individuals and allowing them to share their knowledge.

22168 www.computerrobotvision.org
Cdn. Image Processing/Pattern Recognition Society
Special interest group of the Canadian Information Processing Society, and the national representative organization of the International Association of Pattern Recognition.

22169 www.cra.org
Computing Research Association
The CRA's mission is to seek to strengthen research and advanced education in computing and allied fields.

22170 www.futureoflife.org
Future of Life Institute
Seeks to mitigate emerging risks facing humanity, especially from advanced artificial intelligence, but also including biotechnology, nuclear power, and climate change.

22171 www.ieee.org
Institute of Electrical and Electronics Engineers

Supports all those involved in the field of electrical engineering, and works to nurture technological innovation and excellence for the benefit of humanity.

22172 **www.inns.org**
International Neural Network Society
INNS is comprised of researchers, professors, practitioners, and learners in the field of neural networks and computational science.

22173 **www.intelligence.org**
Machine Intelligence Research Institute
Uses foundational mathematics to ensure artificial intelligence systems have a positive impact.

22174 **www.itsa.org**
Intelligent Transportation Society of America
Organization dedicated to advancing the research, development and design of surface transportation systems.

22175 **www.motioncontrolonline.org**
Motion Control & Motor Association
The MCMA seeks to advance motion control and related automation technologies, and to help members and the industry grow.

22176 **www.openai.com**
OpenAI
Research organization dedicated to maintaining Artificial Intelligence as a benefit to humanity.

22177 **www.robotics.org**
Robotic Industries Association
Trade group serving the robotics industry. Members include robot manufacturers, users, system integrators, component suppliers, research groups, and consulting firms. The Robotic Industries Association offers educational resources, events and news for its members.

22178 **www.visiononline.org**
Global Association for Vision Information
The AIA is dedicated to vision and imaging technologies, with members including manufacturers of vision components and systems, system integrators, distributors, OEMs, end users, consulting firms, academic institutions, and research groups.

Associations

22179 American Chemical Society: Rubber Division
306 N Cleveland Massillon Rd.
Commonwealth Square
Akron, OH 44333

330-595-5531
www.rubber.org
Twitter, LinkedIn, YouTube

Edward Miller, Executive Director

The Rubber Division of the American Chemical Society is a professional organization dedicated to providing educational programs, technical resources and other vital services for the people associated with rubber and affiliated industries.
Founded in 1909

22180 Association for Rubber Products Manufacturers
7321 Shadeland Station Way
Suite 285
Indianapolis, IN 46256

317-863-4072; Fax: 317-913-2445
www.arpminc.com

Dave Jentzsch, Director
Chris Wagner, Director
Tim Jarvis, Director
Charlie Braun, Director
Joe Walker, Director

Association dedicated to helping industry executives improve their businesses in rubber products manufacturing through waste reduction, benchmarking, networking, product standards, and educational opportunities provided to its members.
Founded in 2010

22181 International Institute of Synthetic Rubber Producers, Inc.
3535 Briapark Dr.
Suite 250
Houston, TX 77042

713-783-7511; Fax: 713-783-7253
info@iisrp.com
iisrp.com

Juan Ramon Salinas, Managing Director

International trade association for synthetic rubber producers to receive and benefit from statistical, environmental, and technical information in order to keep abreast of the world's market growth and events.
Founded in 1960

22182 North American Recycled Rubber Association
1621 McEwen Dr.
Unit 24
Whitby, ON L1N 9A5

905-433-7669; Fax: 905-433-0905
www.recycle.net

Diane Sarracini, Contact

Created to bring together the various stakeholders affiliated with the recycled rubber industry.
Founded in 1994

22183 Plastics Industry Association
1425 K Street NW
Suite 500
Washington, DC 20005

202-974-5200
www.plasticsindustry.org
Facebook, Twitter, LinkedIn, YouTube

Patricia Davitt Long, COO

Organization promoting the global competitiveness of the plastics supply chain.
Founded in 1937

22184 Polyurethane Foam Association
334 Lakeside Plaza
Loudon, TN 37774

865-657-9840; Fax: 865-381-1292
rbatson@pfa.org
www.pfa.org

Russ Batson, Executive Director
Wayne Bowman, Communications Counsel
Jim McIntyre, Legal Counsel
Kay Wright, Administrative Manager

The mission of the Polyurethane Foam Association (PFA) is to educate customers and other groups about flexible polyurethane foam (FPF) and to promote its use in manufactured and industrial products.
Founded in 1980

22185 Rubber Pavements Association
5117 E Tunder Dr.
Phoenix, AZ 85044

480-517-9944
877-517-9944; Fax: 480-517-9959
www.rubberpavements.org

Mark Belshe, Executive Director
Guadalupe Dickerson, Officer Manager
Marc Bertsch, President

Dedicated to encouraging greater usage of high quality, cost effective asphalt pavements containing recycled tire rubber.
Founded in 1985

22186 Single Ply Roofing Institute (SPRI, Inc.)
465 Waverley Oaks Road
Suite 421
Waltham, MA 02452

781-647-7026; Fax: 781-647-7222
info@spri.org
www.spri.org

SPRI represents sheet membrane and related component suppliers in the commercial roofing industry.
67 Members
Founded in 1981

22187 Tire Industry Association
1532 Pointer Ridge Place
Suite G
Bowie, MD 20716-1883

301-430-7280
800-876-8372; Fax: 301-430-7283
info@tireindustry.org
www.tireindustry.org
Facebook, Twitter, LinkedIn, Instagram

Roy Littlefield, CEO

TIA is an international association representing all segments of the tire industry, including those that manufacture, repair, recycle, sell, service or use new or retreaded tires, and also those suppliers or individuals who furnish equipment, material or services to the industry. TIA was formed by the July 2002 merger of the International Tire & Rubber Association (ITRA) and the Tire Association of North America (TANA).
7000+ Members
Founded in 2002

22188 Tire Retread and Repair Information Bureau
1013 Birch St.
Falls Church, VA 22046

703-533-7677
877-394-6811; Fax: 703-533-7678
info@retread.org
www.retread.org
Facebook, Twitter, YouTube

David Stevens, Managing Director
Tim BeVier, President

Our goal is to provide the motoring public (both in the private and public sectors) with the most up-to-date information about the economic and environmental benefits of tire retreading and tire repairing.
Founded in 1974

22189 U.S. Tire Manufacturers Association
1400 K Street NW
Suite 900
Washington, DC 20005

202-682-4800; Fax: 202-682-4854
www.ustires.org
Facebook, Twitter, YouTube

Anne Forristall Luke, President & CEO

National trade association for tire manufacturers.
100 Members
Founded in 1915

Newsletters

22190 Rubber Chemistry and Technology
Rubber Division, American Chemical Society
PO Box 499
Akron, OH 44325-3801

330-972-7883; Fax: 330-972-5269

Lu Ann Blazeff, Publisher

Information on materials and equipment pertaining to the rubber industry. Accepts advertising.
Cost: $487.50
Frequency: 5 Times per Year

22191 Rubber and Plastics News
Crain Communications
1725 Merriman Rd
Suite 300
Akron, OH 44313-5283

330-836-9180
800-678-9595; Fax: 330-836-2831
editorials@rubbernews.com
www.crain.com

Robert S Simmons, VP
Edward Noga, Editor

Discusses production, research and development, management, sales and marketing.
Cost: $79.00
24 Pages
Frequency: Monthly
Circulation: 16258
Founded in 1971
Printed in 4 colors on glossy stock

22192 Worldwide Rubber Statistics
Intl. Inst. of Synthetic Rubber Producers
3535 Briapark Dr.
Suite 250
Houston, TX 77042

713-783-7511; Fax: 713-783-7253
orderfs@iisrp.com
www.iisrp.com
Facebook, Twitter, LinkedIn

Juan Ramon Salinas, Managing Director

Guide to the synthetic and natural rubber industry, including Centrally Planned Economy Countries.
Cost: $2500.00
Founded in 1960

Magazines & Journals

22193 **Global Tire News.com**
Rubber & Plastic News
1725 Merriman Rd
Suite 300
Akron, OH 44313-5283
330-836-9180
330-836-9180; Fax: 330-836-1005
dsector@crain.com
www.rubbernews.com
Facebook, Twitter, LinkedIn
Dave Cielasko, Publisher
Don Sector, Advertising Coordinator
Mike McNulty, Rubber & Plastics News Staff Writer
Brent Weaver, Classified Coordinator
Provides rubber industry information relative to tire manufacturers; top tire company managers; plant listings and other data. Subscription to annual publication includes access to Global Tire News.com.
Cost: $79.00
Frequency: Annual

22194 **Rubber & Plastics News**
Crain Communications
1725 Merriman Rd.
Akron, OH 44313-5251
330-836-9180; Fax: 330-836-2831
www.rubbernews.com
Facebook, Twitter, LinkedIn
Domestic and international rubber industry news as well as new technology and products.
Frequency: 25x/year
Founded in 1971

22195 **Rubber Chemistry & Technology Journal**
American Chemical Society: Rubber Division
411 Wolf Ledges
Suite 201
Akron, OH 44311
330-972-7814; Fax: 330-972-5269
rct@allenpress.com
www.rubber.org/publications-rc-t-journal
Journal for the science and technology of rubber and related elastomers.
Frequency: quarterly
ISSN: 0035-9475

22196 **Rubber World**
Lippincott & Peto
PO Box 5451
Akron, OH 44334-0451
330-864-2122; Fax: 330-864-5298
jhl@rubberworld.com
www.rubberworld.com
Job Lippincott, President
Dennis Kennelly, VP Sales
Don R Smith, Editor
Darlene Ballard, Director of Marketing Services
Jill Rohrer, Managing Editor
Provides complete technical coverage to the rubber industry.
Cost: $34.00

Trade Shows

22197 **ARPM Benchmarking & Best Practices Conference**
Association for Rubber Products Manufacturers
7321 Shadeland Station Way
Suite 285
Indianapolis, IN 46256
317-863-4072; Fax: 317-913-2445
www.arpminc.com
Dave Jentzsch, Director
Chris Wagner, Director
Tim Jarvis, Director
Charlie Braun, Director
Joe Walker, Director
Conference for senior executives in the rubber manufacturing industry to exchange business information and network.
Founded in 2010

22198 **International Latex Conference**
Crain Communications
1725 Merriman Road
Suite 300
Akron, OH 44313-5283
330-836-9180; Fax: 330-836-1005
cstevens@crain.com
www.rubbernews.com
Twelve exhibitors with 12 booths.
Frequency: July

22199 **International Tire Exhibition and Conference**
Crain Communications
1725 Merriman Road
Suite 300
Akron, OH 44313-5283
330-836-9180; Fax: 330-836-1005
cstevens@crain.com
www.rubbernews.com
One-hundred and thirty exhibitors with 110 booths.
Frequency: September

22200 **Rubber Expo**
American Chemical Society-Rubber Division
PO Box 499
Akron, OH 44309-0499
330-972-7814
800-227-5558; Fax: 330-972-5269
help@acs.org
www.chemistry.org
Sherri L Poorman, Exhibition Manager
Biennial show of 300 manufacturers and suppliers of equipment, supplies and services for the rubber industry, including machinery, chemicals, raw rubber, finished rubber products, quality control equipment and related equipment.
8,000 Attendees
Frequency: October, Cleveland

22201 **Rubber Mini Expo**
American Chemical Society-Rubber Division
PO Box 499
Akron, OH 44309-0499
330-972-7814; Fax: 330-972-5269
www.rubber.org
Sue Barr, Exposition & Future Sites Manager
Biennial show of 150 manufacturers, suppliers and custom services for the rubber industry, including machinery, chemicals, raw rubber, finished rubber products, quality control equipment and related equipment.
3000 Attendees
Frequency: October

22202 **Rubber and Plastics Industry Conference of the United Steelworkers of America**
5 Gateway Center
Pittsburgh, PA 15220
412-562-6971; Fax: 412-562-6963
John Sellers, Executive VP
90M Attendees
Founded in 1935

Directories & Databases

22203 **ARPM Member Roster**
Association for Rubber Products Manufacturers
7321 Shadeland Station Way
Suite 285
Indianapolis, IN 46256
317-863-4072; Fax: 317-913-2445
www.arpminc.com
Dave Jentzsch, Director
Chris Wagner, Director
Tim Jarvis, Director
Charlie Braun, Director
Joe Walker, Director
List of members of the Association for Rubber Products Manufacturers.
Founded in 2010

22204 **DORA**
Single Ply Roofing Institute
465 Waverley Oaks Road
Suite 421
Waltham, MA 02452
781-647-7026; Fax: 781-647-7222
info@spri.org
www.spri.org
All roof assemblies are submitted by participating companies and are accompanied by supporting documentation in the form of test reports and qualified evaluations.

22205 **Rauch Guide to the US Rubber Industry**
Grey House Publishing
4919 Route 22
PO Box 56
Amenia, NY 12501
518-789-8700
800-562-2139; Fax: 845-373-6390
books@greyhouse.com
www.greyhouse.com
Facebook, Twitter
Leslie Mackenzie, Publisher
Richard Gottlieb, Editor
Provides industry structure and current market information about the $39 billion US rubber industry which faces intense inter-material competition and severe government regulation. The report contains a wealth of marketing and related technical information about the busines.
Cost: $595.00
500 Pages
ISBN: 1-592371-30-2
Founded in 1981

22206 **Rubber World Blue Book: Materials, Compounding and Machinery**
Lippincott & Peto
Po Box 5451
Akron, OH 44334-0451
330-864-2122; Fax: 330-864-5298
www.rubberworld.com
Job Lippincott, Owner
Over 850 suppliers of over 8,000 chemicals, materials and compounding ingredients for rub-

ber manufacturers.
Cost: $103.00
Frequency: Annual
Circulation: 4,000

22207 **Rubber World: Custom Mixers Directory**
Lippincott & Peto
Po Box 5451
Akron, OH 44334-0451

330-864-2122; Fax: 330-864-5298
www.rubberworld.com

Job Lippincott, Owner

A list of rubber manufacturers providing custom mixes.
Cost: $3.00
Frequency: Annual

22208 **Rubber World: Machinery Suppliers Issue**
Lippincott & Peto
Po Box 5451
Akron, OH 44334-0451

330-864-2122; Fax: 330-864-5298
www.rubberworld.com
Job Lippincott, Owner

Lists suppliers of used and rebuilt machinery and instrumentation and test equipment to the rubber industry.
Cost: $3.00
Frequency: Annual
ISBN: 0-035957-2 -

22209 **Rubber and Plastics News: Rubicana Issue**
Crain Communications
1725 Merriman Rd
Suite 300
Akron, OH 44313-5283

330-836-9180
800-678-9595; Fax: 330-836-2831
www.crain.com

Robert S Simmons, VP

A list of over 1,000 rubber product manufacturers and suppliers of equipment, services and materials.
Cost: $85.00
Frequency: Annual
Circulation: 15,000

Industry Web Sites

22210 **http://gold.greyhouse.com**
G.O.L.D Grey House OnLine Databases

Grey House Publishing's online database platform, GOLD, offers Quick Search, Keyword Search and Expert Search for most business sectors including rubber markets. The GOLD platform makes finding the information you need quick and easy - whether you're a novice searcher or an experienced database user. All of Grey House's directory products are available for subscription on the GOLD platform.

22211 **www.arpminc.com**
Association for Rubber Products Manufacturers

Association dedicated to helping industry executives improve their businesses in rubber products manufacturing.

22212 **www.greyhouse.com**
Grey House Publishing

Authoritative reference directories for most business sectors including rubber markets. Users can search the online databases with varied search criteria allowing for custom searches by product category, geographic area, sales volume, keyword, subject and more. Full Grey House catalog and online ordering also available.

22213 **www.iisrp.com**
Int'l Institute of Synthetic Rubber Producers

For manufacturers of synthetic rubber.

22214 **www.itra.com**
International Tire and Rubber Association

Information on tire retreading and repairing, new tires, scrap tire reduction and removal equipment, rubber recycling technologies, recycled rubber products and allied services including brake equipment, wheel alignment, tire balancers, tire changers, service trucks, marketing/sales and management programs and computer systems.

22215 **www.rma.org**
Scrap Tire Management Council

For tire manufacturers marketers of scrap tires.

22216 **www.rubbernews.com**
Rubber & Plastics News
1725 Merriman Rd.
Akron, OH 44313-5251

330-836-9180; Fax: 330-836-2831
www.rubbernews.com

Website of Rubber & Plastics News magazine. Updated daily with an online archive, statistics and rankings.

Associations

22217 **AAA Foundation for Traffic Safety**
607 14th Street NW
Suite 201
Washington, DC 20005

202-638-5944; Fax: 202-638-5943
info@aaafoundation.org
aaafoundation.org
Facebook, Twitter, RSS

C.Y. David Yang, Executive Director

AAA Foundation for Traffic Safety is dedicated to saving lives and reducing injuries on the roads. It is a not-for-profit, publicly-supported charitable educational and research organization.
Founded in 1947

22218 **ASIS International**
1625 Prince St.
Alexandria, VA 22314-2882

703-519-6200; Fax: 703-519-6299
pr@asisonline.org
www.asisonline.org
Facebook, Twitter, LinkedIn, YouTube

Richard E. Chase, President
Peter J. O'Neil, CEO

The largest organization for security professionals. ASIS is dedicated to increasing the effectiveness and productivity of security professionals by developing educational programs and materials that cover broad security interests, such as the ASIS Annual Seminar and Exhibits, as well as specific topics. ASIS also advocates the role and value of the security management profession to the media, governmental entities, and the public.
Founded in 1955

22219 **Academy of Security Educators & Trainers**
16 Penn Plaza
Suite 1570
New York, NY 10001

212-268-4555
800-947-5827; Fax: 212-563-4783
info@aset.com
www.academyofsecurity.org
Facebook, Twitter, LinkedIn

Dr Richard W Kobetz, Executive Director
Jerry Heying, President
Mary E Kobetz, Secretary-Treasurer

Non-profit organization of security professionals dedicated to exploring the large spectrum of issues confronting the security field. Meetings are held to discuss, design, develop, and exchange thoughts and ideas in an open forum. Awards the CST (certified security trainer) designation.
300 Members
Founded in 1980

22220 **Advanced Medical Technology Association: AdvaMed**
701 Pennsylvania Ave. NW
Suite 800
Washington, DC 20004-2654

202-783-8700; Fax: 202-783-8750
info@advamed.org
www.advamed.org
Facebook, Twitter, LinkedIn, YouTube

Scott Whitacker, President & CEO
Jen Brearey, Chief Finance Officer
Greg Crist, Chief Advocacy Officer
Andrew Fish, Chief Strategy Officer, AdvaMed
Christopher L. White, Chief Operating Officer

Dedicated to providing members with the advocacy, information, education and tangible solutions necessary for success in a world of increasingly complex medical regulations.
1300 Members
Founded in 1975

22221 **Advocates for Highway and Auto Safety**
750 First St. NE
Suite 1130
Washington, DC 20002

202-408-1711; Fax: 202-408-1699
advocates@saferoads.org
saferoads.org
Facebook, Twitter

Judith Lee Stone, President
Jacqueline Gillan, VP
Judie Pasquini, Director
Peter Kurdock, Advocates' State Coordinator

An organization whose members advocate the support and advancement of highway and auto safety through the implementation of state and federal laws, programs and policies.
Founded in 1989

22222 **American Association for Aerosol Research**
11130 Sunrise Valley Rd.
Suite 350
Reston, VA 20190

703-437-4377
800-485-3106
info@aaar.org
www.aaar.org

Bill Carney, Executive Director

AAAR is a nonprofit professional organization for scientists and engineers who wish to promote and communicate technical advances in the field of aerosol research. The Association fosters the exchange of information among members and with other disciplines through conferences, symposia and publication of a professional journal. Committed to the development of aerosol and its application to important social issues, AAAR offers an international forum for education, communication and networking.
1000 Members
Founded in 1982

22223 **American Association of Occupational Health Nurses**
2920 Brandywine Rd # 100
Suite 100
Chamblee, GA 30341-5539

770-455-7271; Fax: 850-484-8762
www.aaohn.org
Facebook, Twitter, LinkedIn

Ann Cox, Executive Director

AAOHN is a principal force in developing and promoting the profession of occupational and environmental health nursing by providing education, resources, and advocacy.
Founded in 1942

22224 **American Association of Poison Control Centers**
515 King St.
Suite 510
Alexandria, VA 22314

800-222-1222
www.aapcc.org
Facebook, Twitter

Steve Kaminski, Executive Director

Nonprofit nationwide organization of poison centers and others interested in the prevention and treatment of poisoning. Promotes the reduction of injury, illness and death from poisonings through public and professional education and scientific research. Promotes universal access to certified regional poison centers.
Founded in 1980

22225 **American Bio Recovery Association**
300 New Jersey Ave. NW
Suite 900 PMB #9031
Washington, DC 20001

419-663-2819
888-979-2272; Fax: 440-499-9959
www.americanbiorecovery.org
Facebook, LinkedIn

Thomas Licker, President

A nationwide non-profit association of crime and trauma scene recovery professionals who are dedicated to upholding the highest technical, ethical and educational guidelines of the biohazard remediation industry.

22226 **American Biological Safety Association**
1200 Allanson Rd.
Mundelein, IL 60060

847-949-1517
866-425-1385; Fax: 847-566-4580
info@absa.org
absa.org

Edward Stygar III, Executive Director

ABSA's goals are to provide a professional association that represents the interest and needs of practitioners of biological safety, and to providea forum for the continued and timely exchange of biosafety information.
Founded in 1984

22227 **American Chemical Society**
1155 16th St NW
Washington, DC 200036

202-872-4600
800-333-9511; Fax: 202-872-4615
help@acs.org
www.acs.org
Facebook, Twitter, LinkedIn, Google+

Thomas M. Connelly, CEO
Al Horvath, Chief Financial Officer
John Sullivan, Chief Information Officer
Kate Fryer, EVP, Membership & Society Services
Flint Lewis, General Counsel

Supports chemists and companies who work with chemicals and their by-products.
158 M Members
Founded in 1876

22228 **American College of Occupational and Environmental Medicine**
25 Northwest Point Blvd.
Suite 700
Elk Grove Village, IL 60007-1030

847-818-1800; Fax: 847-818-9266
acoeminfo@acoem.org
www.acoem.org
Twitter, YouTube

Bill Bruce, Executive Director

Occupational and environmental medicine is devoted to the prevention and management of occupational and injury, illness and disability, and promotion of health and productivity of workers, thier families and communities.
5000 Members
Founded in 1916

22229 **American Conference of Governmental Industrial Hygienists**
1330 Kemper Meadow Drive
Cincinnati, OH 45240

513-742-2020; Fax: 513-742-3355
mail@acgih.org
www.acgih.org
Facebook, Twitter, LinkedIn

J. Torey Nalbone, Chair
Shannon Henshaw Gaffney, Vice Chair
John S. Morawetz, Secretary/ Treasurer

A. Anthony Rizzuto, Executive Director
Susan Arnold, Director
A member-based organization and community of professionals that advances worker health and safety through education and the development and dissemination of scientific and technical knowledge.
Founded in 1938

22230 **American Correctional Association**
206 N Washington Street
Suite 200
Alexandria, VA 22314
703-224-0000; Fax: 703-224-0179
indiav@aca.org
www.aca.org
Facebook, Twitter, LinkedIn, YouTube
James A. Gondles Jr., Executive Director
Association for correctional professionals.
Founded in 1870

22231 **American Fire Sprinkler Association**
12750 Merit Dr.
Suite 350
Dallas, TX 75251
214-349-5965; Fax: 214-343-8898
afsainfo@firesprinkler.org
www.firesprinkler.org
Facebook, Twitter, LinkedIn, YouTube, Google+
Roland Huggins, Senior Vice President
Nonprofit international association representing open shop fire sprinkler contractors, dedicated to the educational advancement of its members and promotion of the use of automatic sprinkler systems. Offers a convention and exhibition, correspondence course, monthly magazine and a monthly newsletter.
900 Members
Founded in 1981

22232 **American Industrial Hygiene Association**
3141 Fairview Park Drive
Suite 777
Falls Church, VA 22042
703-849-8888; Fax: 703-207-3561
infonet@aiha.org
www.aiha.org
Facebook, Twitter, LinkedIn, YouTube, RSS
Steven E. Lacey, PhD, CIH, CSP, President
Cynthia A. Ostrowski, CIH, Vice President
J. Lindsay Cook, CIH, CSP, Treasurer
Kathleen S. Murphy, CIH, Secretary
Deborah Imel Nelson, PhD, CIH, President-Elect
AIHA promotes healthy and safe environments by advancing the science, principles, practice, and value of industrial hygiene and occupational and environmental health and safety.
10000 Members
Founded in 1939

22233 **American Insurance Association**
555 12th Street NW
Suite 550
Washington, DC 20004
202-828-7100; Fax: 202-293-1219
info@aiadc.org
www.aiadc.org
Facebook, Twitter
John Degnan, President & CEO
J. Stephen Zielezienski, SVP & General Counsel
Joseph DiGiovanni, SVP, State Affairs
A property, casualty insurance trade organization representing more than 40,000 insurers that write more than $120 billion in premiums each year. AIA member companies offer all types of property-casualty insurance, including personal and commercial auto insurance, commercial property and liability coverage for small businesses, worker's compensation, medical malpractice coverage, and product liability insurance.
320 Members
Founded in 1866

22234 **American National Standards Institute**
1899 L Street NW
11th Floor
Washington, DC 20036
202-293-8020; Fax: 202-293-9287
info@ansi.org
www.ansi.org
Facebook, Twitter, LinkedIn, YouTube, Google+, Instagram
S. Joe Bhatia, President & CEO
To enhance the global competition of business and quality of life by promoting and facilitating voluntary consensus standards and conformity assessment systems, and safeguarding their integrity.
27000 Members
Founded in 1918

22235 **American Polygraph Association**
PO Box 8037
Chattanooga, TN 37414-0037
423-892-3992
800-272-8037; Fax: 423-894-5435
manager@apapolygraph.org
www.polygraph.org
Facebook, Twitter
Steve Duncan, President
Representing experienced polygraph examiners in private business; law enforcement and government. Professional APA polygraph examiners administer hundreds of thousands of polygraph exams each year worldwide. The APA establishes standards of ethical practices, techniques, instrumentation and research, as well as provides advanced training and continuing education programs.
2700+ Members
Founded in 1966

22236 **American Public Health Association**
800 I Street NW
Washington, DC 20001
202-777-2742; Fax: 202-777-2534
comments@apha.org
www.apha.org
Facebook, Twitter
Georges C. Benjamin, Executive Director
Influencing policies and setting priorities for over 125 years. Thoughout its history it has been in the forefront of numerous efforts to prevent disease and promote health.
Founded in 1872

22237 **American Red Cross**
431 18th Street NW
Washington, DC 20006
202-303-5214
800-733-2767; Fax: 202-639-3021
www.redcross.org
Facebook, Twitter, Flickr, YouTube
Gail J. McGovern, President & CEO
Bonnie McElveen-Hunter, Chairman
Brian J. Rhoa, CFO
The American Red Cross is where people moblilze to help their neighbors across the street, across the country and across the world, in emergencies. Each year, in communities large and small, victims of some 70,000 disasters turn to the nearly one million volunteers and 35,000 employees of the Red Cross.
31000 Members
Founded in 1881

22238 **American Safety & Health Institute**
1450 Westec Dr.
Eugene, OR 97402
800-447-3177
customerservice@hsi.com
emergencycare.hsi.com
Facebook, Twitter, LinkedIn, YouTube
Nonprofit association of professional safety & health educators providing nationally recognized training programs through more than 5000 approved training centers across the US and in several foreign countries.
30000 Members
Founded in 1996

22239 **American Society for Nondestructive Testing**
PO Box 28518
1711 Arlingate Lane
Columbus, OH 43228-0518
614-274-6003
800-222-2768; Fax: 614-274-6899
www.asnt.org
Facebook, Twitter, LinkedIn, YouTube, Instagram
Neal Couture, Executive Director
Barry Schieferstein, Dir., Conferences & Meetings
Garra Liming, Dir., Marketing & Communications
Brad Pence, Director, Finance & Controller
Heather Cowles, Dir., Membership & Engagement
ASNT is the world's largest technical society for nondestructive tests (NDT) professionals.
15000 Members
Founded in 1941

22240 **American Society of Crime Laboratory Directors (ASCLD)**
65 Glen Road
Suite 123
Garner, NC 27529
919-773-2044
asclddirector@gmail.com
www.ascld.org
Facebook, Twitter, LinkedIn, RSS
Matthew Gamette, President
Jean Stover, Executive Director
Timothy Scanlan, Training & Education Chair
Rita Dyas, Treasurer
Linda Jackson, Secretary
A nonprofit professional society, composed of crime laboratory directors and forensic science managers, that aims to foster professional interests, to assist in laboratory management principles and technqiues, to maintain communication among crime laboratory directors, to disseminate and acquire forensic based information, and to promote high standards of practice within the field.
660 Members
Founded in 1974
Mailing list available for rent: 660 names at $800 per M

22241 **American Society of Criminology**
1314 Kinnear Rd
Suite 212
Columbus, OH 43212-1156
614-292-9207; Fax: 614-292-6767
asc@asc41.com
www.asc41.com
Facebook, Twitter
Ruth Peterson, President-Elect
Chris Eskridge, Executive Director
Candace Kruttscnitt, President
Eric Baumer, Vice President
Bonnie Fisher, Treasurer

The American Society of Criminology is an international organization concerned with criminology, embracing scholary, scientific and profesional knowledge concerning the etiology, prevention, control, and treatment of crime and delinquency.

22242 **American Society of Mechanical Engineers**
Two Park Avenue
New York, NY 10016-5990
973-882-1170
800-843-2763
CustomerCare@asme.org
www.asme.org
Facebook, Twitter, LinkedIn, Instagram
Bryan A. Erler, President
Thomas Costabile, Executive Director & CEO
William Garofalo, Chief Financial Officer
Allian Pratt, Managing Director, Board Operations
ASME aims to promote and enhance the technical competency and professional well-being of the members, and through quality programs and activities in mechanical engineering, better enable its practitioners to contribute to the well being of human kind.
100K+ Members
Founded in 1880

22243 **American Society of Safety Engineers**
520 N. Northwest Hwy
Park Ridge, IL 60068
847-699-2929; Fax: 847-768-3434
customerservice@asse.org
www.asse.org
Facebook, Twitter, LinkedIn, Instagram
Michael Belcher, President
Fred J. Fortman, Secretary & Executive Treasurer
Thomas F. Cecich, President-Elect
James D. Smith, Senior Vice President
Stephanie A. Helgerman, VP, Finance
The oldest and largest professional safety organization. Its members manage, supervise and consult on safety, health, and environmental issues in industry, insurance, government and education.
36000 Members
Founded in 1911

22244 **American Traffic Safety Services Association**
15 Riverside Parkway
Suite 100
Fredericksburg, VA 22406-1022
540-368-1701
800-272-8772; Fax: 540-368-1717
memberservices@atssa.com
www.atssa.com
Facebook, Twitter, YouTube
Scott Seeley, Chairman
Debra Ricker, Chairman Elect
Juan Arvizu, At-large-Director
Sue Reiss, Foundation President (Non-Voting)
Craig Sliter, Guardrail Services Div Director
The American Traffic Safety Services Association, is an international trade association founded in 1969. It has has represented companies and individuals in the traffic control and roadway safety industry.
11630 Members
Founded in 1969

22245 **American Welding Society**
8669 NW 36 St.
Suite 130
Miami, FL 33126-6672
305-443-9353
800-443-9353; Fax: 305-443-7559
info@aws.org
awsnow.org
Facebook, Twitter, Instagram
David J. Landon, President
David L. McQuaid, Vice President
John R. Bray, Vice President
Dale Flood, Vice President
Robert G. Pali, Treasurer
The mission of the American Welding Society is to advance the science, technology and application of welding and allied joining and cutting processes, including brazing, soldering and thermal spraying.
70000 Members
Founded in 1919

22246 **Associated Locksmiths of America**
3500 Easy St
Dallas, TX 75247
214-819-9733
800-532-2562; Fax: 214-819-9736
jim@aloa.org
www.aloa.org
Facebook, Twitter, LinkedIn
Mary May, Executive Director
Tom Foxwell, President
Clyde Roberson, Secretary
ALOA is an international professional organization of highly qualified security professionals engaged in consulting, sales, installation and maintenance of locks, keys, safes, premises security, access controls, alarms, and other security related endeavors.
10000 Members
Founded in 1956

22247 **Association of Air Medical Services**
909 N. Washington St.
Suite 410
Alexandria, VA 22314
703-836-8732; Fax: 703-836-8920
information@aams.org
www.aams.org
Cameron Curtis, President & CEO
Garet Turner, VP, Member Experience
Christopher Eastlee, VP, Public Affairs
Christina Childs, Director, Special Events
Diana Lundie, Tradeshow Manager
AAMS is built on the idea that representation from a variety of medical transport services and businesses can be brought together to share information, collectively resolve problems and provide leadership in the medical transport community.
581 Members
Founded in 1980

22248 **Association of Certified Fraud Examiners**
716 W. Avenue
Austin, TX 78701-2727
512-478-9000
800-245-3321; Fax: 512-478-9297
memberservices@acfe.com
www.acfe.com
Facebook, Twitter, LinkedIn, Instagram
Joseph T. Wells, Chair
Bruce Dorris, President & CEO
John D. Gill, VP, Education
John Warren, VP & General Counsel
Jeanette LeVie, VP & COO
The ACFE is reducing business fraud world-wide and inspiring public confidence in the integrity and objectivity within the profession.
85000 Members
Founded in 1988

22249 **Association of Christian Investigators**
2553 Jackson Keller
Suite 200
San Antonio, TX 78230
210-342-0509; Fax: 210-342-0731
kelmar@kelmarpi.com
www.a-c-i.org
Kelly E Riddle, President
Hugo Briseno, Director, Georgia
Timothy Friend, Director, California (Northern)
Andrew Smart, Director, Alabama
Paul Jacob, Director, Alaska
Provides a spirit-filled organization that promoste the investigative profession in a non-competitive atmosphere. Provides an environment in which investigators can create meaningful and long-term relationships with other investigators outside the professional bonds.
1000+ Members
Founded in 1996

22250 **Association of Contingency Planners**
136 Everett Road
Albany, NY 12205
414-908-4945
800-445-4227; Fax: 414-768-8001
staff@acp-international.com
www.acp-international.com
Facebook, Twitter, LinkedIn
Leo A Wrobel, President
Bonnie Canal, Chairman
Michael Carver, Treasurer
Steve Elliot, Board Member
Michael J. Morganti, Secretary
Nonprofit trade association dedicated to fostering continued professional growth and development in effective contingency and business resumption planning.
2300 Members
Founded in 1983

22251 **Association of Professional Industrial Hygienists**
2288 Gunbarrel Rd
Ste 154/364
Chattanooga, TN 37421
888-481-3006
www.apih.us
Offers credentialing to industrial hygienists.
Founded in 1994

22252 **Association of Public Safety Communication Officials-International**
351 N Williamson Boulevard
Daytona Beach, FL 32114-1112
386-322-2500
888-272-6911; Fax: 386-322-2501
apco@apcointl.org
www.apcointl.org
Facebook, Twitter, LinkedIn, psconnect
John W. Wright, Immediate Past President
Brent Lee, President
Cheryl J. Greathouse, 1st VP
Martha K. Carter, 2nd VP
Derek Poarch, Ex-Officio
The Association of Public-Safety Communications Officials International (APCO) is a member driven association of communications professionals that provides leadership; influences public safety communications decisions of government and industry; promotes professional development; and, fosters the development and use of technology for the benefit of the public.
16000 Members
Founded in 1932

22253 **Association of State Dam Safety Officials**
239 S. Limestone
Lexington, KY 40508

859-550-2788
info@damsafety.org
www.damsafety.org
Facebook, Twitter, LinkedIn, YouTube

Jim Pawloski, President
Dusty Myers, President Elect
Tom Woosley, Past President
Roger Adams, Secretary
Jon Garton, Treasurer

Organization for safety officials overseeing state dams.
3000 Members
Founded in 1983

22254 **Association of State Floodplain Managers**
575 D'Onoforio Drive
Suite 200
Madison, WI 53719

608-828-3000; Fax: 608-828-6319
asfpm@floods.org
www.floods.org
Facebook, Twitter, LinkedIn, Tumblr

Larry A Larson, DirectorEmeritus, Sr. Policy Adviso
Maria Cox Lamm, Vice Chair
Karen McHugh, Treasurer
Leslie Durham, Secretary
Ceil C. Strauss, Chair

It is the mission of the Association to mitigate the losses, costs and human suffering caused by flooding and to promote wise use of the natural and beneficial functions of floodplains.
6500 Members
Founded in 1976

22255 **Automatic Fire Alarm Association**
81 Mill Street
Suite 300
Gahanna, OH 43230

614-416-8076
844-438-2322; Fax: 614-453-8744
www.afaa.org
Facebook, Twitter, LinkedIn, Yahoo

Jack McNamara, President/Executive Director
Rick Heffernan, Secretary
Randall L. Hormann, Administrative Director
William Koffel, Vice President
Rodger Reiswig, Treasurer

Striving to be the foremost industry advocate organization dedicated to improving the quality, reliability and value of fire and life safety systems.
Founded in 1953

22256 **Aviation Safety Institute**
PO Box 2480
Carlingford, NS 2118

128-819-2455; Fax: 128-572-5248
enquiry@asi.net.au
www.asi.net.au
Twitter, LinkedIn

Edward H Wachs, President/Chair
Thomas Clevinger, VP/Treasurer
Richard Davies, Managing Director
Melinda Brennan, Manager-WHS
Kevin Mulholland, Manager-Audit

An aviation safety research center established in 1973. Studying the most overlooked, most important area of aviation safety.
Founded in 2008

22257 **Board of Certified Safety Professionals**
8645 Guion Road
Indianapolis, IN 46268

317-593-4800; Fax: 317-593-4400
bcsp@bcsp.org
www.bcsp.org
Facebook, Twitter, LinkedIn, Google+

Cece M Weldon, President
John E. Hodges, Vice President
Jack H. Dobson, Treasurer
Teresa M. Turnbeaugh, CEO, Secretary
Guy Snyder, CFO

Operating solely as a peer certification board with the purpose of certifying practitioners in the safety profession.
Founded in 1969
Mailing list available for rent: 20,000 names

22258 **Business Disaster Preparedness Council**
Lee County Emergency Management
PO Box 398
Ft. Meyers, FL 33902-398

239-399-9779; Fax: 941-477-3636
board@leegov.com

Bob Lee, Owner

Public and private partnership whose goal it is to assist business in planning for and recovering from natural disasters and emergencies.
Founded in 1998

22259 **CIFAR**
MaRS Centre, West Tower
661 University Avenue
Suite 505
Toronto, ON M5G 1M1

416-971-4251
www.cifar.ca
Facebook, Twitter, LinkedIn, YouTube

Alan Bernstein, President & CEO
Pauline Yick, COO
Catherine Riddell, VP, Strategic Communications
Sharon Hainey, Event & Meetings Coordinator
Leanne Woodcock, Financial Officer

Charitable organization that looks to address important questions facing humanity, such as the risks posed by Artificial Intelligence, by gathering extraordinary individuals and allowing them to share their knowledge.
400+ Members

22260 **CPWR: Center for Construction Research and Training**
8484 Georgia Ave
Suite 1000
Silver Spring, MD 20910

301-578-8500; Fax: 301-578-8572
cpwrwebsite@cpwr.com
www.cpwr.com
Facebook, Twitter, RSS, YouTube

Sean McGarvey, President
Richard Resnick, Vice President/ General Counsel
Chris Trahan, Deputy Director
Erich J. Stafford, Executive Director
Brent Booker, Secretary/ Treasurer

CPWR is committed to preventing illness, injury, and death in the construction industry through its safety and health research, broad network of trainers, and on-going outreach to workers and employers.
Founded in 1990

22261 **Canada Safety Council**
1020 Thomas Spratt Place
Ottawa, ON K1G 5L5

613-739-1535; Fax: 613-739-1566
canadasafetycouncil.org
Facebook, Twitter

Jack Smith, President
Raynald Marchand, General Manager, Programs
Judy Lavergne, Secretary
Peter Slivar, Manager, Finance & Administration
Lewis Smith, Communications

The Canada Safety Counil is a national, non-government, charitable organization dedicated to safety. Mission is to lead in the national effort to reduce preventable deaths, injuries and economic loss in public and private places throughout Canada.
Founded in 1968

22262 **Canadian Alarm & Security Association**
50 Acadia Avenue
Suite 201
Markham, ON L3R 0B3

905-513-0622
800-538-9919; Fax: 905-513-0624
www.canasa.org
Facebook, Twitter, LinkedIn

JF Champagne, Ex-Officio
Carl Jorgensen, Vice president
Carol Cairns, Treasurer
Kevin Hincks, Secretary
Philippe Bouchard, President

A national non-profit organization dedicated to promoting the interests of its members and the safety and security of all Canadians.
Founded in 1977

22263 **Center for Security and Emerging Technology**
Walsh School of Foreign Service
ICC 301, 37th & O Street NW
Washington, DC 20057

202-687-0100
cset@georgetown.edu
cset.georgetown.edu

Jason Matheny, Founding Director
Tessa Baker, Director, Operations
Ben Buchanan, Director, Cybersecurity & AI
Igor Mikolic-Torreira, Director, Analysis
Dewey Murdick, Director, Data Science

CSET studies the security impacts of emerging technologies, especially Artificial Intelligence.
Founded in 2019
Mailing list available for rent

22264 **Clery Center**
110 Gallagher Road
Wayne, PA 19087

484-580-8754
888-251-7959; Fax: 484-580-8759
clerycenter.org
Facebook, Twitter, LinkedIn, YouTube

Constance B. Clery, Co-Founder & Chairwoman
Howard K. Clery, Co-Founder
Benjamin F. Clery, Treasurer
Roger Carolin, Chairman
Christopher F. McConnell, Vice Chairman

A non-profit organization whose mission is to prevent violence, substance abuse and other crimes in college and university campus communities across the United States, and to compassionately assist the vicitims of these crimes.
Founded in 1987

22265 **Commercial Vehicle Safety Alliance**
6303 Ivy Lane
Suite 310
Greenbelt, MD 20770-6319

301-830-6143; Fax: 301-830-6144
cvsahq@cvsa.org
www.cvsa.org
Facebook, Twitter, LinkedIn, YouTube

Collin B. Mooney, Executive Director
Maj. Jay Thompson, President
Julius Debuschewitz, Vice President
Capt. Christoph Turner, Secretary

The Commercial Vehicle Safety Alliance (CVSA) is a nonprofit organization, established to promote an environment free of commercial vehicle accidents and incidents. Our mission is to promote commercial motor vehicle safty and security by providing leadership to enforcement, industry and policy makers.
540 Members
Founded in 1980

22266 **Computer Security Institute**
350 Hudson St.
Suite 300
New York, NY 10014

415-947-6320; Fax: 415-947-6023
Facebook, Twitter, LinkedIn

Jody Nurre, Sales Director
Mary Griffin, Membership Director
Robert Richardson, Director
Terri Curran, Director
Cheryl Jackson, Information Systems

Computer Security Institute serves the needs of information security professionals through membership, educational events, security surveys and awareness tools.
Founded in 1974

22267 **Consumer Data Industry Association**
1090 Vermont Ave NW
Suite 200
Washington, DC 20005-4964

202-371-0910; Fax: 202-371-0134
cdia@cdiaonline.org
www.cdiaonline.org

Norm Magnuson, VP
Betty Byrnes, Member Services

The Consumer Data Industry Association is an international trade association, founded in 1906, that represents consumer information companies that provide fraud prevention and risk management products, credit and mortgage reports, tenant and employment screening services, check fraud and verification services, and collection services.
140 Members
Founded in 1906

22268 **Conveyor Equipment Manufacturers Association (CEMA)**
5672 Strand Ct.
Suite 2
Naples, FL 34110

239-514-3441; Fax: 239-514-3470
kim@cemanet.org
www.cemanet.org
Facebook, Twitter, LinkedIn, YouTube

Paul Ross, President
E.A. Thompson, Vice President
Robert Reinfried, Executive Vice President
Noel Bell, Director
Bob Callahan, Director

CEMA seeks to support manufacturers of conveyors and conveying systems. The association sponsors an annual Engineering Conference that allows members to meet and develop the industry standards that affect the conveyor industry.
Founded in 1933

22269 **Council of International Investigators**
PO Box 565
Elmhurst, IL 60126-0565

630-501-1880
888-759-8884; Fax: 206-367-8777
office@cii2.org
www.cii2.org
Facebook, LinkedIn

Galen Clements, Executive Regional Director
Sheila Ponnosamy, President
Eduard Sigrist, Past president/ Treasurer
Anne Styren, Secretary
Bert Falbaum, VP/ Executive Regional Director

The Council of International Investigators was formed to encourage a greater association among owners and operators of investigation agencies while developing mutual trust and respect.
Founded in 1955

22270 **Council on Certification of Health, Environmental & Technologists**
2301 W. Bradley Avenue
Champaign, IL 61821

217-359-9263; Fax: 217-359-0055
www.cchest.org
Facebook, Twitter, LinkedIn, Google+

Angie Kluth, Chief accounting Officer
Andrea Kamradt, Examination Manager
Treasa Turnbeaugh, CEO
Robert Schneller, COO
Teresa Hasken, CFO

CCHEST is recognized as the leader in high-quality, third-party accredited health, safety, and environmental credentialing for technologists, technicians, supervisors, and workers.
3000 Members
Founded in 1969

22271 **Dangerous Goods Advisory Council**
7501 Greenway Center Drive
Suite 760
Greenbelt, MD 20770

202-289-4550; Fax: 202-289-4074
info@dgac.org
www.dgac.org
Facebook, Twitter

Del Billings, Technical director
Vaughn Arthur, Secretary & President
Barbara Lantry-Miller, Treasurer
Ben Barrett, Chair
Greg Allen, Vice Chair

DGAC fulfills its mission by providing education, technical assistance and information to the private and public sectors. Members incude shippers in the chemical, petroleum, and pharmaceutical industries, manufacturers, carriers, container manufacturers and reconditioners, emergency/waste clean-up companies, trade associations, and others involved in the transport of dangerous goods.
Founded in 1978

22272 **Electrical Safety Foundation International**
1300 N 17th Street
Suite 900
Arlington, VA 22209

703-841-3229; Fax: 703-841-3329
info@esfi.org
www.esfi.org
Facebook, Twitter, LinkedIn, YouTube

Ruppert Russoniello, Chairman
Stephen Sokolow, Immediate Past Chairman
Kevin Cosgriff, Treasurer
Lorraine Carli, Secretary

The mission of the Electrical Safety Foundation International (ESFI) is to advocate electrical safety in the home and in the workplace in order to reduce electrically-related fatalities, injuries and property loss.
Founded in 1994

22273 **Electronic Security Association**
6333 North State Highway 161
Suite 350
Irving, TX 75038

972-807-6800
888-447-1689; Fax: 972-807-6883
www.esaweb.org
Facebook, Twitter, LinkedIn

Marshall Marinace, President
Dee Ann Harn, Vice President
Merlin Guilbeau, Executive Director
Jon Sargent, Secretary
Steve Paley, Treasurer

Trade association representing the electronic security industry.
Founded in 1948

22274 **Environmental Information Association**
6935 Wisconsin Ave
Suite 306
Chevy Chase, MD 20815-6112

301-961-4999
888-343-4342; Fax: 301-961-3094
info@eia-usa.org
www.eia-usa.org
Twitter, Google+

Kevin Cannan, President
Chris Gates, President-Elect
Mike Schrum, Past President
Robert De Malo, Secretary
Kyle Burroughs, Treasurer

Nonprofit organization dedicated to providing environmental information to individuals, members and industry. Disseminates information on the abatement of asbestos and lead-based paint, indoor air quality, safety and health issues, analytical issues and environmental site assessments.

22275 **Executive Protein Institute**
Executive Protection Institute
16 Penn Plaza
Suite 1130
New York, NY 10001

212-268-4555; Fax: 212-563-4783
info@personalprotection.com
www.personalprotection.com
Facebook, LinkedIn

John Negus, Asst. Executive Director
Jerry Heying, Executive Director
Eugene R. Ferrara, Chief Instructor
John F. Musser, Chief to Staff
Ana Paula Alfonso, Operations Director

A non-profit professional society whose members include academics, trainers, students, law enforcement and government officials, self-employed professionals, security officers, directors from major intenational corporations, security service organizations, and communications, energy, retail, chemicals, insurance, petroleum and utility companies.
2800 Members
Founded in 1978

22276 **False Alarm Reduction Association**
10024 Vanderbilt Circle
Unit 4
Rockville, MD 20850

301-519-9237; Fax: 301-519-9508
info@faraonline.org
www.faraonline.org

Brad Shipp, Executive Director
Kerri McDonald, President
Nadya Morgan, Vice President-Electronics Security

Tammy Foxworth, Vice President-Fire
Steven Heggemann, Treasurer

Primarily made up of persons employed by government and public safety agencies in charge of, or working in, False Alarm Reduction Units. The goal is to assist these individuals in reducing false alarms for their jurisdiction.
Founded in 1997

22277 Federal Law Enforcement Officers Association

7945 MacArthur Blvd.
Suite 201
Cabin John, MD 20818

202-870-5503
866-553-5362; Fax: 717-932-2262
fleoa@fleoa.org
www.fleoa.org
Facebook, Twitter

Jon Adler, National President
Nate Catura, National Executive VP
Chris Schoppmeyer, Vice President-Agency Affairs
Lazaro Cosme, Vice President-Operations
Frank Terreri, Vice President-Legislative Affairs

Founded by a group of concerned federal agents from Customs, the IRS, FBI and INS, its goal is to assure that legal assistance and representation are a phone call away.
24000 Members
Founded in 1977

22278 Financial & Security Products Association

1024 Mebane Oaks Road
Suite 273
Mebane, NC 27302

919-648-0664
800-843-6082; Fax: 919-648-0670
www.fspa1.com
LinkedIn

Grant Case, Chairman
Fred Wheeler, President
B.J. Hanson, Executive Director
Bryce Good, Vice President
Dave Pepin, Secretary-Treasurer

Independent dealers, manufacturers and associates whose outstanding products and services give financial institutions a crucial edge in performance, efficiency and economy.
Founded in 1973

22279 Fire Apparatus Manufacturers' Association (FAMA)

PO Box 3065
Ocala, FL 34478

352-843-3404; Fax: 781-334-2911
www.fama.org

Harold Boer, President
Bruce Whitehouse, VP

Membership association for manufacturers of emergency vehicles and components affixed to or carried upon the vehicle.
125 Members
Founded in 1946

22280 Fire Equipment Manufacturers' Association

1300 Sumner Avenue
Cleveland, OH 44115

216-241-7333
www.femalifesafety.org
Facebook, LinkedIn, YouTube, Wikipedia, Slideshare

Bill Vegso, President

Trade association representing manufacturers of fire protection equipment. Products made by member companies include portable fire extinguishers, fire hose/interior equipment and pre-engineered fire suppression systems.
Founded in 1930

22281 Fire Suppression Systems Association

3601 East Joppa Road
Baltimore, MD 21234

410-931-8100; Fax: 410-931-8111
fssa@clemonsmgmt.com
www.fssa.net
Facebook, Twitter, LinkedIn

Scott Bailey, Director
Eric Burkland, Immediate Past President
Ray Aldridge, Vice President
Helen Lowery, Secretary/ Treasurer
Tim Carman, President

An organization of manufacturers, suppliers, and design-installers, dedicated to providing a higher level of fire protection. Members are specialists in protecting high value special hazardareas from fire.
Founded in 1982

22282 Flight Safety Foundation

801 N. Fairfax Street
Suite 400
Alexandria, VA 22314-1774

703-739-6700; Fax: 703-739-6708
wahdan@flightsafety.org
www.flightsafety.org
Facebook, Twitter, LinkedIn

Hassan Shahidi, President/CEO
Frank Jackman, VP, Communications
Louise Martin, VP, Membership
Jerry Lederer, Founder
Kenneth P. Quinn, General Counsel & Secretary

Flight Safety Foundation is an independent, nonprofit, international organization engaged in research, auditing, education, advocacy and publishing to improve aviation safety. The Foundation's mission is to pursue the continuous improvement of global aviation safety and the prevention of accidents.
1000+ Members
Founded in 1947

22283 Future of Life Institute

Boston, MA

meia@futureoflife.org
futureoflife.org
Facebook, Twitter

Jaan Tallinn, Co-Founder
Max Tegmark, Co-Founder
Meia Chita-Termark, Co-Founder
Viktoriya Krakovna, Co-Founder
Anthony Aguirre, Co-Founder

Seeks to mitigate emerging risks facing humanity, especially from advanced artificial intelligence, but also including biotechnology, nuclear power, and climate change.

22284 Homeland Security Industries Association

666 11th Street NW
Suite 315
Washington, DC 20001

202-386-6471; Fax: 202-331-8191
www.hsianet.org

Brenda Boone, Owner

Nonprofit group providing a mechanism for government and the private sector to coordinate on a wide range of homeland security issues. Monitors legislation, regulations and hearings, provides training, and develops position papers reflecting industry concerns.
200+ Members
Founded in 2002

22285 Institute for Health & Productivity Management

17470 N. Pacesetter Way
Scottsdale, AZ 85255

480-305-2100; Fax: 480-305-2189
sean@ihpm.org
www.ihpm.org

Sean Sullivan, President/CEO
Bill Williams, Senior VP & Co-Founder
Pamella Thomas, Chief Medical Officer
Steve Priddy, Executive Director
Deborah Love, EVP & COO

Nonprofit organization making employee health an investment in corporate success through enhanced workplace performance.
Founded in 1997

22286 Institute for Intergovernmental Research

PO Box 12729
Tallahassee, FL 32317-2729

850-385-0600; Fax: 850-422-3529
nygc@iir.com
www.iir.com

Keith G Burt, Advisory Board
Emory B. Williams, Chairman
John Czernis, President
Meena Harris, Executive Vice President
R. Clay Jester, Senior Vice President

22287 Insurance Institute for Highway Safety

1005 N Glebe Rd
Suite 800
Arlington, VA 22201

703-247-1500; Fax: 703-247-1588
rrader@iihs.org
www.iihs.org
Twitter, YouTube, RSS

Adrian Lund, President
Russ Rader, SVP, Communications
Eric Williams, Counsel
Shelly Shelton, Senior Legal Administrator
Brenda O'Donnell, VP, Insurer Relations

The Insurance Institute for Highway Safety is a nonprofit research and communications organization funded by auto insurers.
Founded in 1959

22288 Int'l Association for Counterterrorism & Security Professionals

PO Box 10265
Arlington, VA 22210

201-461-5422
www.iacsp.com

Steven Fustero, Executive Director

Our goals include creating a center of information and educational services for those concerned about the challenges now facing all free societies, and promoting professional ethics in the counter terrorism field.
Founded in 1992

22289 International Association For Healthcare Security and Safety

PO Box 5038
Glendale Heights, IL 60139
630-529-3913
888-353-0990; Fax: 630-529-4139
info@iahss.org
www.iahss.org
Facebook, Twitter, LinkedIn

David LaRose, President
Jeff A. Young, President Elect
Ben Scaglione, Vice President/Secretary
Colleen Kucera, Executive Director
Nancy Felesena, Executive Assistant

An association dedicated to professionals involved in managing and directing security and safety in healthcare establishments.
Founded in 1968

22290 **International Association for Identification**
2131 Hollywood Blvd.
Suite 403
Hollywood, FL 33020

954-589-0628; Fax: 954-589-0657
www.theiai.org
Facebook

Bridget Lewis, President
Harold Ruslander, 1st Vice President
Steve Johnson, Board Chair/Past President
Phyllis Karasov, legal Counsel
Glen Calhoun, COO

This is a forum where forensic specialists worldwide can interact as a whole. The main focus of any forensic organization is training and research to ensure all specialists maintain the highest levels of integrity and professionalism in order to meet the constant challenges to our individual disciplines.
Founded in 1915

22291 **International Association for Computer Systems Security**
Dix Hills, NY

Home Page: www.iacis.org

Maria Elena Corbeil, President & Director, Conferences
Kevin Floyd, Secretary & IIS Editor
Jeretta Horn Nord, Treasurer & Director, Publications
Alex Koohang, Director, Technology & Operation
Daryl Nord, Executive Director

A nonprofit association dedicated to the improvement of information systems and the education of information systems and computer professionals.
Founded in 1960

22292 **International Association for Healthcare Security and Safety**
PO Box 5038
Glendale Heights, IL 60139

630-529-3913
888-353-0990; Fax: 630-529-4139
info@iahss.org
www.iahss.org
Facebook, Twitter, LinkedIn

David LaRose, President
Richardý Dufresne, Sr., Member-at-Large
Jeff A. Young, President-Elect
Dana Frentz, VP/Treasurer
Ben Scaglione, VP/Secretary

Nonprofit professional organization of healthcare security and safety executives around the world. Works to improve and professionalize security and safety in healthcare facilities through the exchange of information and experiences among members. A magazine, newsletter and an annual meeting are benefits of membership.
1700 Members
Founded in 1968

22293 **International Association of Arson Investigators**
2111 Baldwin Ave
Suite 203
Crofton, MD 21114

410-451-3473
800-468-4224; Fax: 410-451-9049
www.firearson.com
Facebook, Twitter, LinkedIn, YouTube

Daniel Heenan, President
George Codding, 1st VP
Soctt Bennett, 2nd VP
Peter Mansi, Immediate Past President
Kevin Crawford, Director

Dedicated to improving the professional development of fire and explosion investigators by being the global resource for fire investigation, technology and research
7500 Members
Founded in 1949

22294 **International Association of Black Professional Firefighters**
1200 G St. nW
Suite 800
Washington, DC 20005

202-434-4526
877-213-2170; Fax: 202-434-8707
evpiabpff@yahoo.com
Facebook, Twitter, LinkedIn

James Hill, President
Sam Aubrey Jr., Treasurer
Kenyatta Smith, EVP
Melanie Anderson, Financial Secreatry
Freddie Jackson, Sergeant at Arms

Promotes interracial progress throughout the fire service and encourages African American firefighters to seek elevated ranks. Offers an annual convention, education courses an an online resource page.
Founded in 1970

22295 **International Association of Bomb Technicians and Investigators**
1120 International Parkway
Suite 129
Fredericksburg, VA 22406

540-752-4533; Fax: 540-752-2796
admin@iabti.org
www.iabti.org
Facebook, Twitter, LinkedIn

James T. Wooten, International Director

The IABTI is an independent, non-profit, professional association formed for countering the criminal use of explosives. This is accomplished through the exchange of training, expertise and information among personnel employed in the fields of law enforcement, emergency services, the military, forensic science and other related fields.
Founded in 1973

22296 **International Association of Campus Law Enforcement Administrators**
342 N Main Street
West Hartford, CT 06117-2507

860-586-7517; Fax: 860-586-7550
info@iaclea.org
www.iaclea.org
Facebook

Patricia Patton, Director
David L Perry, Immediate Past President
Willaim F Taylor, President
Randy A Burba, President- Elect
Jasper Cooke, VP for Finance

Advances public safety for educational institutions by providing educational resources, advocacy and professional development.
Founded in 1958

22297 **International Association of Chiefs of Police**
44 Canal Center Plaza
Suite 200
Alexandria, VA 22314

703-836-6767
800-THE-IACP; Fax: 703-836-4543
www.theiacp.org
Facebook, Twitter, LinkedIn, RSS, YouTube

Rechard Beary, President
Vincent Talucci, Executive Director/CEO
Gwen Boniface, Deputy Executive Director
John Firman, Director of Strategic Partnerships
Paul Santiago, Director of Intl. Policing Division

The association's goals are to advance the science and art of police services; to develop and disseminate improved administrative. technical and opreration practices and promote their use in police work; to foster police cooperation and the exchange of information and experience among police administrators throughout the world; to bring about recruitment and training in the police profession of qualified person.
15000 Members
Founded in 1893

22298 **International Association of Crime Analysts**
9218 Metcalf Ave.
Suite 364
Overland Park, KS 66212

919-940-3883
800-609-3419
iaca@iaca.net
www.iaca.net
Facebook, Twitter, LinkedIn, RSS

Ericka Jackson, VP, Membership
Carolyn Cassidy, President
Tony Berger, VP, Administration
Eric Drifmeyer, Treasurer
Dawn Clausius, Secretary

The International Association of Crime Analysts was formed in 1990 to help crime analysts around the world improve their skills and make valuable contacts, to help law enforcement agencies make the best use of crime analysis, and to advocate for standards of performance and technique within the profession itself. This is accomplished through training, networking, and publications.
Founded in 1990

22299 **International Association of Dive Rescue Specialists**
8103 East US Highway
36, Box 171 Avon
INDIANA, US 46123

317-464-9787
800-423-7911; Fax: 317-641-0730
dowens@iadrs.org
www.iadrs.org
Twitter

Blades Robinson, Executive Director
Steven Orusa, Operations Director
David Owens, Dir. Of communications
Fred Jackson, Advisory Board
Steve Fleming, Board of Directors

IADRS is dedicated to helping water rescue professionals stay informed about advances in training, equipment, and life saving techniques.
Founded in 1977

22300 **International Association of Fire Chiefs**
4025 Fair Ridge Drive
Suite 300
Fairfax, VA 22033-2868

703-273-0911; Fax: 703-273-9363
thicks@iafc.org
www.iafc.org
Facebook, Twitter, RSS

Mark W. Light, Executive Director
Karen Soyster Fitzgerald, Chief Operations Officer
Chief John Sinclair, President & Chairman
Chief Thomas Jenkins, First Vice President
Chief Gary Curmode, Second Vice President

Provides leadership to career and volunteer chief, chief fire officers and managers of emergency service organization throughout the inernational community through vision, information, education, services and representation to enhance their professionalsim and capabilities.
12000 Members
Founded in 1873

22301 **International Association of Firefighters**
1750 New York Ave
Nw Suite 300
Washington, DC 20006-5395

202-737-8484; Fax: 202-737-8418
pr@iaff.org
www.iaff.org
Facebook, Twitter, Youtube, Flickr, Pinterest

Harold Schaitberger, President
Jim Lee, Chief of Operations
Peter L. Gorman, Chief of Staff
Thomas H. Miller, Secretary/ Treasurer
William Romaka, 1st VP

Represents city and county firefighters and state and federal workers such as forestry firefighters and emergency medical workers at certain industrial facilities. Addressed are health and safety, labor relations, training, hazardous materials and burn injuries and education.
240k Members
Founded in 1903

22302 **International Association of Personal Protection Agents**
PO Box 266
Arlington Heights, IL 60006-0266

847-870-8007; Fax: 847-870-8990
proproserv@aol.com
www.iappa.net
Facebook

Stephen R. Barnhart, Executive Director
Charles Mallice, Operations & Training Director
Nikolai Ehlers, CCPA, Senior Security Consultant
James A. King, Chief Advisor
Arnaldo B. Merli, CCPA, International Security Consultant

Professional, nonprofit membership body open to military and civilian law enforcement personnel and people from the public and private sector who are engaged in the protection of royalty, presidential, state and diplomatic officials, government, military and corporate executives, personalities from the entertainment world and those involved in witness and prisoner protection.
Founded in 1989

22303 **International Association of Professional Security Consultants**
575 Market St.
Suite 2125
San Francisco, CA 94105

415-536-0288; Fax: 415-764-4915
iapsc@iapsc.org
www.iapsc.org
LinkedIn

Harold Gillens, President
Alan Brockbank, Vice President
Kerry Parker, Executive Director
Ken Wheatley, Secretary
Lynda Buel, Treasurer

The International Association of Professional Security Consultants (IAPSC) is a widely recognized consulting association in the security industry. Its rigid membership requirements ensure that potential clients may select from the most elite group of professional, ethical and competent security consultants available to them.
Founded in 1984

22304 **International Biometrics & Identification Association**
1090 Vermant Avenue
NW, 6th Floor
Washington, DC 20005

202-789-4452; Fax: 202-289-7097
ibia@ibia.org
www.ibia.org
Facebook, Twitter, RSS

Raffie Beroukhim, Director
Christer Bergman, Secretary
Robert Harbour, President and Chairman of the Board
Walter Hamilton, Vice Chairman
Mike DePasquale, Treasurer

IBIA provides strong and growing value to its members, expanding business opportunities for the industry, advocating government support for the useof biometrics in leading commercial and public-sector applications, and reporting on key issues of strategic importance to the membership.
Founded in 1998

22305 **International Biometrics Industry Association**
1090 Vermont Avenue,
NW, 6th Floor
Washington, DC 20005

202-789-4452; Fax: 202-289-7097
ibia@ibia.org
www.ibia.org
Facebook, Twitter, RSS

Robert Harbour, Chairman/ President
Walter Hamilton, Vice Chairman
Raffie Beroukhim, Director
Christer Bergman, Secretary
Mike DePasquale, Treasurer

Trade association representing developers, manufacturers and integrators of biometric hardware and software.
Founded in 1998

22306 **International Centre for the Prevention of Crime**
465 rue St-Jean Street
Bureau 803
Montreal, QU H2Y-2R6

514-288-6731; Fax: 514-288-8763
cipc@cipc-icpc.org
www.crime-prevention-intl.org/english
Facebook, Twitter, LinkedIn

Vincenzo Castelli, Administrator
Erich Marks, VP
Chantal Bernier, President
Elizabeth Johnston, Secretary
Paul Girard, Treasurer

The ICPC is an international forum for national government local authorities, public agencies, specialized institutions, and non-government organisations of exchange experience, consider emerging knowledge, and improve policies and programs in crime prevention and community safety. ICPC staff monitors developments, provides direct assistance to members, and contributes to public knowledge and understanding in the field.
Founded in 1994

22307 **International Consumer Product Health & Safety Organization**

Home Page: www.icphso.org
Facebook, Twitter, LinkedIn

Marc J Schoem, Executive Director

ICPHSO holds a unique position in its ability to attract the interest of a broad range of health and safety professionals and interested consumers, world-wide.
Founded in 1993

22308 **International Fire Service Training Association**
930 N Willis
Stillwater, OK 74078

405-744-5723; Fax: 405-744-8204
customer.service@osufpp.org
www.ifsta.org
Facebook, Twitter, LinkedIn

Robert Moore, State Fire Organization
Steve Ashbrock, Fire Dept.
Steve Austin, Fire Service Affiliate
Mike Wieder, Fire Organisation
Scott D. Kerwood, Fire Department

Nonprofit organization associated with Fire Protection Publications, a department of the College of Engineering, Architecture and Technology at Oklahoma State University.
Founded in 1934

22309 **International Foundation for Protection Officers**
1250 Tamiami
Tr. N Ste.206
Naples, FL 34102

239-430-0534; Fax: 239-430-0533
adminifpo@earthlink.net
www.ifpo.org
Facebook, Twitter, LinkedIn

Sandi J Davies, Executive Director
Michael Stroberger, Secretary/Treasurer
Rck Daniels, Chairman
Karl Poulin, Director
Tom M. Conley, Past Chairman

Nonprofit organization for the purpose of facilitating the training and certification needs of protection officers and security supervisors from both the commercial and proprietary sectors.
Founded in 1988

22310 **International High Technology Crime Investigation Association**
3288 Goldstone Drive
Roseville, CA 95747

916-408-1751; Fax: 916-384-2232
info@htcia.org
www.htcia.org
Facebook, Twitter, LinkedIn

Shadiÿ Hayden, President
Tom Quilty, Past President
Peter Morin, 1st Vice President
Steve Branigan, Secretary
Matt Samuelson, Treasurer

Designed to encourage, promote, aid and effect the voluntary interchange of data, information, experience, ideas and knowledge about methods, processes, and techniques relating to investigations and security in advanced technologies among its membership.
3500 Members
Founded in 1984

22311 **International Hologram Association**
2149 Cascade Ave
Suite 106
Hood River, OR 97031-1087

541-386-9449; Fax: 541-386-1564
www.hairmasterssalon.com

More than 60 of the worlds leading hologram manufacturers are members. Dedicated to promoting the interests of those quality hologram manufacturers worldwide and to helping our customers to achieve their security, packaging graphic and other objectives through the effective use of holography.
Founded in 1993

22312 **International Hologram Manufacturers Association**
4 Windmill Business Village
Brooklands Close, SU TW167DY

193-278-5680; Fax: 193-278-0790
info@ihma.org
www.ihma.orgÿ

Mike Messmer, Chairman
Nuray Yilmaz, Board Member
Umendra Gupta, ASPA Representative
Diana Newcomb, Board Member
Rajan Thomas, Asian Representative

A not for profit organization serving the hologram manufacturing industry.
Founded in 1993

22313 **International Locksmiths Association**
PO Box 9560
Naperville, IL 60567-0560

866-745-5625
www.ilanational.org

Tom Ripp, Director/Co-Chair
Larry Bowman, Vice President
Kurt Kloeckner, Treasurer
Kevin T. Piiper, National President
John Rendle, Secretary

Members are locksmiths, carpenters and building engineers who are employed by colleges, universities, hospitals, companies and government facilities. Dedicated to the education of members and the benefit of our institutions.

22314 **International Municipal Signal Association**
597 Haverty Court
Suite 100
Rockledge, FL 32955

321-392-0500
800-723-4672; Fax: 321-806-1400
info@imsasafety.org
www.imsasafety.org
Facebook, Twitter, LinkedIn

Douglas M. Aiken, Deputy Executive Director
Mike Flanigan, Past President
Hans Kristensen, President
Kan Balltrip, President-Elect
Leonard Addair, Director-at-Large

Basic purpose of the organization is to keep its members and others in the profession, up-to-date on proper procedures of construction and maintenance of signal systems and informed on new products and equipment developments.
10000 Members
Founded in 1896

22315 **International Photoluminescent Safety**
2001 Jefferson Davis Highway
Suite 1004
Arlington, VA 22202-3617

703-416-0060; Fax: 703-416-0014
info@plsafety.org
www.plsafety.org

Tom Thompson, Executive Director

A leader in the marine safety and implementation of the highest possible performance, manufacturing maintenance, service and training standards, for all lifesaving, survival and emergency rescue equipment.
131 Members
Founded in 1986

22316 **International Process Servers Association**
2854 Larimer St
Denver, CO 80205

585-232-8590
800-611-2774; Fax: 877-824-2482
richard@processservers.com
www.iprocessservers.com

Unifies process servers in the United States and throughout the world, as the single greatest resource for all process servers and private investigators.

22317 **International Safety Equipment Association**
1901 N Moore Street
Suite 808
Arlington, VA 22209-1762

703-525-1695; Fax: 703-528-2148
isea@safetyequipment.org
www.safetyequipment.org
Facebook, Twitter, LinkedIn

Daniel K Shipp, President
Nate Kogler, Public Affairs Director
Craig Wallentine, Office Services Manager
Eric Beck, Chairman
Brian Lyons, Past Chairman

Trade association in the US for companies that manufacture safety equipment. Member companies are world leaders in the design and manufacture of clothing and equipment used in factories, construction sites, hospitals and clinics, farms, schools, laboratories, and in the home — anywhere people are doing work. Our common goal is to protect the health and safety of people exposed to hazardous and potentially harmful environments.
Founded in 1933

22318 **International Security Management Association**
PO Box 623
Buffalo, IA 52728-0623

563-381-4008
800-368-1894; Fax: 563-381-4283
susan.pohlmann@isma.com
isma.com/

Tim Janes, President
Mike Howard, Executive Director
Damin Memeekin, Second VP
Mary Welsh, Deputy Executive Director

ISMA's mission is to provide and support an international forum of selected security executives whose combined expertise wil be utilized in a synergistic manner in developing, assimilating, sharing knowledge within security disciplines for the ultimate purpose of enhancing professional and business standards.
400 Members
Founded in 1983

22319 **International System Safety Society**
PO Box 70
Unionville, VA 22567-0070

540-854-8630; Fax: 540-854-4561
www.system-safety.org
Facebook, LinkedIn

Dr. Rod Simmons, President
Bob Schmedake, Immediate Past President
Pam Kniess, Executive Secretary
Chuick Muniak, Executive Vice President
Clif Ericson, Treasurer

The System Safety Society is a non-profit organization dedicated to supporting the safety professional in the application of system engineering and systems management to risk analysis. The Society is international in scope and draws members throughout the world.
4500 Members
Founded in 1962

22320 **International of Personal Protection Agents**
PO Box 266
Arlington Heights, IL 60006-0266

847-870-8007; Fax: 847-870-8990
proproserv@aol.com
www.iappa.net
Facebook

Dr. Stephen Barnhart, Executive Director
Charles Mallice, Operations &Training Director
Mr Nikolai Ehlers, Senior Security Consultant
Mr James A King, Chief Advisor
Mr Chris Menary, National Director

Professional, nonprofit membership body open to military and civilian law enforcement personnel and people from the public and private sector who are engaged in the protection of royalty, presidential, state and diplomatic officials, government, military and corporate executives, personalities from the entertainment world and those involved in witness and prisoner protection.
Founded in 1989

22321 **Investigators of America**
PO Box 4243
Downey, CA 90241

562-869-2535
877-393-7792; Fax: 562-869-5268
dkalepi@earthlink.net
www.investigatorsofamerica.com

John R. Spencer, Director
Dave Blair, Director
Roberto A. Rivera, Director
Edwin C. Hodges, Director
Steven Rambam, Director

Investigators of America is a rapidly growing association comprised of elite private investigators, insurance adjusters, and expert witnesses across the United States with affiliates in other countries.

22322 **Laser Institute of America**
13501 Ingenuity Dr
Suite 128
Orlando, FL 32826

407-380-1553
800-345-2737; Fax: 407-380-5588
lia@lia.org
www.lia.org
Facebook, Twitter, LinkedIn, Google+

Yongfeng Lu, Past President
Lin Li, President Elect
Rodert Thomas, President
Stephen Capp, Treasurer
Paul Denney, Secretary

The Laser Institute of America is the professional membership society dedicated to fostering lasers, laser applications and safety worldwide. Its mission is to foster lasers, laser applications, and laser safety worldwide. Serving the industrial, medical, research and government communities, LIA offers technical information and networking opportunities to laser users from around the globe.
1200 Members
Founded in 1968

22323 **Lifeboat Foundation**
1468 James Road
Gardnerville, NV 89460

775-409-3122; Fax: 775-409-3123
admin@lifeboat.com
lifeboat.com
Facebook, Twitter, LinkedIn, YouTube, RSS

Eric Klien, President & Founder
Chris Haley, VP & System Administrator
James Dunn, Director, Development Assistance

Non-profit, non-governmental organization encouraging scientific advancements in order to help humanity avoid existential risks from factors such as genetic engineering, nanotechnology, and robotics/AI.

22324 **Mine Safety and Health Administration**
1100 Wilson Blvd
21st Floor
Arlington, VA 22209-3939
202-693-9400
800-746-1553; Fax: 202-693-9401
www.msha.gov
Facebook, Twitter
David G Dye, Executive Director
Mission is to enforce compliance with mandatory safety and health standards as a means to eliminate fatal accidents, reduce the frequency and severity of nonfatal accidents, minimnize health hazards, and to promote improved safety and health conditions in national mines.
Founded in 1978

22325 **Motorcycle Safety Foundation**
2 Jenner
Suite 150
Irvine, CA 92618
800-446-9227
msf@msf-usa.org
www.msf-usa.orgÿ
Facebook, Twitter, YouTube
Russ Brenan, Chair
Joseph Dagley, Vice Chair
Tim Buche, President & CEO
Robert Gladden, Vice President
Steve Piehl, Secretary/ Treasurer
Provides information on rider training, licensing, and goverment relations.

22326 **National Alarm Association of America**
PO Box 3409
Dayton, OH 45401
937-461-2208
800-283-6285; Fax: 937-461-4759
www.arcat.com
Gene Riddlebaugh, President
Grant Angell, Senior VP Associate Affairs
Ricardo Gonzales, Vice President
Mission is to advance the welfare of members through the free exchange, among members of ideas and the dissemination of information concerning trade practices, business conditions, technical developments, within the industry, and any related subject of concern to the security industry.
Founded in 1984

22327 **National Association of Elevator Safety Authorities**
PO Box 640
Rochester, WA 98579
360-292-4968
800-746-2372; Fax: 360-292-4973
dotty@naesai.org
www.naesai.org
George W. Gibson, Advisor
Douglas S Warne, President
Dean G Mclellan, VP
Fredick C Slater, Treasurer
Michael Stewart, Secretary
Elevator inspector certification and continuing education.
2500 Members
Founded in 1969

22328 **National Association of Fire Equipment Distributors**
180 N. Wabash Avenue
Suite 401
Chicago, IL 60601
312-461-9600; Fax: 312-461-0777
dharris@nafed.org
www.nafed.org
Facebook, LinkedIn, YouTube
Ed Hugill, President
Danny Harris, Ex Officio
Tim Krulan, Treasurer
George Seymour, President Elect
Bill Johnson, Director
Mission is to improve the economic environment, business performance, and technical competence in the fire protection industry.
Founded in 1963

22329 **National Association of Fraud Investigators**
2519 NW 23rd St.
Suite 204
Oklahoma City, Ok 73107
405-833-2327
RBrown2150@aol.com
www.nafraud.com
Established to improve communications and expand the network of professional fraud investigators.

22330 **National Association of Legal Investigators**
235N Pine Street
Lansing, MI 48933
517-702-9835
866-520-NALI; Fax: 517-372-1501
www.nalionline.org
Facebook, Twitter
Don C. Johnson, National Director
Jayne McElfnesh, Assistant National Director
Andi Murphy, National Secretary
Julian Vail, Association Management
Nicole Bocra Gray, Regional Director- Northeast Region
Membership in NAL is open to all professional legal investigators who are actively engaged in negligence investigations for plaintiff and/or criminal defense, and who are employed by investigative firms, law firms or public defender agencies.
Founded in 1967

22331 **National Association of Safety Professionals**
1531 South
Post Road
Shelby, NC 28152
800-922-2219; Fax: 704-487-1579
www.naspweb.com
Facebook, Twitter
Eric Gislason, Executive Director
Jon Beard, IT Analyst
A nonprofit membership organization providing training, consultative services as well as certifications.
10000 Members

22332 **National Association of Security Companies**
444 North Capitol Street, NW
Suite 345
Washington, DC 20001
202-347-3257; Fax: 202-393-7006
information@nasco.org
www.nasco.org
Jim McNulty, Chair
Stephen Kasloff, 1st Vice Chair
Julie Payne, 2nd Vice Chair
Lynn Oliver, Secretary
David Buckman, Treasurer
To promote standards and professionalism for private security officers and within contract security.

22333 **National Burglar & Fire Alarm Association**
2300 Valley View Lane
Suite 230
Irving, TX 75062
214-260-5970
888-447-1689; Fax: 214-260-5979
www.alarm.org
Facebook, Twitter, YouTubee
Merlin Guilbeau, Executive Director
Georgia Calaway, Communications/PR Director
Founded in 1948

22334 **National Classification Management Society**
994 Old Eagle School Rd
Suite 1019
Wayne, PA 19087-1866
610-971-4856; Fax: 610-971-4859
info@classmgmt.com
www.classmgmt.com
Facebook, Twitter, LinkedIn
Sharon K. Tannahill, Executive Director
Mr. Dennis Arriage, President
Mrs. Aprilli Abbott, Vice President
Dean Young, Treasurer
Ms. Debbie Young, Secretary
Advancing the practice of classification management in the disiplines of industrial security, information security, government designated unclassified information, and intellectual property, and to foster the highest qualities of security professionalism among its members.
1,300 Members
Founded in 1964

22335 **National Council of Investigation & Security Services**
7501 Sparrows Point Boulevard
Baltimore, MD 21219-1927
800-445-8408; Fax: 410-388-9746
nciss@comcast.net
www.nciss.org
Carolyn Ward, Executive Director
Francie Koehler, Past President
Debbie Anderson, Secretary
Don C. Johnson, CLI
Bill Fletcher, Treasurer
A cooperative of those companies and associations responsible for providing private security and investigation services to the legal profession, business community, government and the public.
1300 Members
Founded in 1975

22336 **National Counterterrorism Center**
National Counterterrorism Center
Washington, DC 20511
703-733-8600
nctcpao@nctc.gov
www.nctc.govÿ
Facebook, Twitter, YouTube, RSS, Tumblr, Flickr
Nicholas J. Rasmussen, Director
John J. Mulligan, Deputy Director
The primary organization in the United States Government for integrating and analyzing all intelligence pertaining to counterterrorism.

22337 **National Crime Justice Association**
720 7th Street NW
Third Floor
Washington, DC 20001
202-628-8550; Fax: 202-448-1723
info@ncja.org
www.ncja.org
Facebook, Twitter, LinkedIn, Pinterest, RSS
Cabell C. Cropper, Executive Director
Lisa Nine Accordini, Senior Staff Associate

Bethany Broida, Director of Communications
Robert Greeves, Senior Policy Adviser
Janene Scelza, Web Manager

Exists to promote the developemtn of justice systems in states, tribal nations, and units of local government that enhance public saftety ; prevent and reduce the harmful effects of criminal and delinquent behavior on victims, individuals and communities; adjudicate defendants and sanction offenders fairly and justly; and that are effective and efficient.
Founded in 1971

22338 National Crime Prevention Council
1201 Connecticut Avenue, NW
Suite 200
Washington, DC 20036

202-466-6272; Fax: 202-296-1356
webmaster@ncpc.org
www.ncpc.org

David A. Dean, Chairman
Ann M. Harnkins, President & CEO
Jean Adnopoz, Secretary
John p. Box, Treasurer
Robert F. Diegelman, Vice Chair

Aids people in keeping themselves, their families, and their communities safe from crime. NCPC produces tools that communities can use to learn crime prevention strategies, engage community members, and coordinate with local agencies.
136 Members
Founded in 1979

22339 National Defense Industrial Association
2111 Wilson Blvd
Suite 400
Arlington, VA 22201-3061

703-522-1820; Fax: 703-522-1885
info@ndia.org
www.ndia.org
Facebook, Twitter, LinkedIn, YouTube, Pinterest, Google+

Mckinley Craig, President & CEO
O'Connell Cyndi, Web Operations
Barry D. Bates, VP, Operations
Goodman Will, VP, Government Policy
Dino Pignotti, VP, Advertising

A leading defense idustry association whose mission is to promote national security through a variety of means, including education, training and advocacy.
28100 Members
Founded in 1919

22340 National Electrical Manufacturers
1300 17th St N
Suite 900
Arlington, VA 22209

703-841-3200; Fax: 703-841-5900
webmaster@nema.org
www.nema.org
Facebook, Twitter, LinkedIn, RSS, YouTube, Google+

Kevin J. Cosgriff, President
Donald J. Hendler, Chairman
Maryrose Sylvester, Vice Chair
David G. Nord, Treasurer
John W. Estey, Board Committee Chairman

NEMA's mission is to promote the competitiveness of its member companies by providing quality services that will impact positively on standrds, government regulation and market economics.
400 Members
Founded in 1926

22341 National Emergency Equipment Dealers Association
8421 Frost Way
Annandale, VA 22003

703-280-4622; Fax: 703-280-0942
KentonP1@aol.com
www.femsa.org
Facebook, Twitter, LinkedIn, Pinterest, Google+, Tumblr

Kenton Pattie, Executive Director

Serves dealers who sell and service fire, rescue, and emergency rescue systems equipment and apparatus. Preserves and strengthens the free market system for dealers through advocacy, information and training. Assists dealers profitably deliver high quality products and support to the nation's emergency services.
Founded in 1915

22342 National Fire Protection Association
1 Batterymarch Park
Quincy, MA 02169-7471

617-770-3000
800-344-3555; Fax: 617-770-0700
www.nfpa.org
Facebook, Twitter, LinkedIn, YouTube, Google+, RSS, Pintere

Jim Pauley, President/CEO
Randolph W. Tucker, 1st VP
Ernest J. Grant, Chairman
Amy R. Action, Secretary
Thomas A. Lawson, Treasurer

The mission of the NFPA is to reduce the worldwide burden of fire and other hazards on the quality of life by providing and advocating consensus codes and standards, research, training and education.
75000 Members
Founded in 1896

22343 National Fire Safety Council
PO Box 378
Michigan Center, MI 49254-0378

517-764-2811
800-255-1082
nfsc.org
Facebook, Twitter, LinkedIn

Distributor of fire & burn prevention and life safety materials.
Founded in 1979

22344 National Fire Sprinkler Association
40 Jon Barrett Rd.
Patterson, NY 12563

845-878-4200; Fax: 845-878-4215
info@nfsa.org
www.nfsa.org
Facebook, Twitter, LinkedIn, YouTube, Google+

Russell P. Fleming, Executive Vice President
Alan Wiginton, Director
Dennis Coleman, Chairman
James Boulanger, Treasurer
Larry Thau, Vice Chair

The goal is to create a market for the widespread acceptance of competently installed automatic fire sprinkler systems in new and existing construction. Members are makers and installers of automatic fire sprinklers and related equipment.
Founded in 1905

22345 National Floor Safety Institute (NFSI)
PO Box 92607
Southlake, TX 76092

817-749-1700; Fax: 817-749-1702
info@nfsi.org
www.nfsi.org
Facebook, Twitter, LinkedIn

Richard Bing, Senior Marketing Manager
Russell Kendzior, President & Chairman
Howard W. Harris, Treasurer
Steven C. Spencer, Vice President
Beth B Risinger, CEO/Executive Director

Mission is to aid in the prevention of slip-and-fall accidents through education, training and recearch. The NFSI is led by a fifteen-member Board of Directors representing product manufacturers, insurance underwriters, trade associations, and independent consultants.
Founded in 1997

22346 National Institute for Occupational Safety & Health
1600 Clifton Rd
Atlanta, GA 30329-4027

404-639-3385
800-232-4636; Fax: 513-533-8573
eidtechinfo@cdc.gov
www.cdc.gov/niosh/homepage.html
Facebook, Twitter, RSS, MySpace, YouTube, Flickr

John Howard MD, Director
Hubert H Humphrey, Chief of Staff
Max Lum EdD, Assoc Director Health

To promote health and quality of life by preventing and controlling disease, injury, and disability.

22347 National Institute of Standards and Technology (NIST)
100 Bureau Dr
Stop 1070
Gaithersburg, MD 20899-1070

301-975-6478
800-877-8339; Fax: 301-948-6107
inquiries@nist.gov
www.nist.gov
Facebook, Twitter, LinkedIn, RSS, YouTube, Flickr

W. Watt Starnes, CEO
Dr. William E. May, Director
Kevin Kimball, Chief of Staff
George Jenkins, Chief Financial Officer
Heather Mayton, Executive Officer

Promotes US innovation and industrial competitiveness by advancing measurement science, standards, and technology in ways that enhance economic security and improve quality of life. It's four cooperative programs are NIST Laboratories, Baldrige National Quality Program, Manufacturing Extension Partnership, and Advanced Technology Program.
Founded in 1901

22348 National Nuclear Security Administration
1000 Independence Ave.,
S.W.
Washington, DC 20585

202-586-5000
800-342-5363; Fax: 202-586-7371
www.nnsa.energy.gov
Facebook, Twitter, YouTube, Flickr, RSS

Frank G. Klotz, Administrator
Madelyn Creedon, Principal Deputy Administrator
Annie Harrington, Deputy Administrator
Bruce Diamond, General Counsel
Deborah Wilbar, Associate Administrator

Organization for advancing nuclear sciences, technologies and engineering.
Founded in 2000

22349 National Safety Council
1121 SpringLake Dr.
Itasca, IL 60143-3201

630-285-1121
800-621-7619; Fax: 630-285-1434
customerservice@nsc.org
www.nsc.org

Facebook, Twitter, LinkedIn, YouTube, Google+
Deborah Hersman, CEO
John P. Surma, Chairman
Patrick Phelan, Chief Financial Officer
Shay Gallagher, Vice President
Jeane Wrenn, Senior Director/General Counsel
Nonprofit, nongovernmental, international public service organization dedicated to protecting life and promoting health.
48000 Members
Founded in 1913

22350 National Safety Management Society
PO Box 4460
Walnut Creek, CA 94596-0460
800-321-2910
nsmsinc@yahoo.com
www.nsms.us
Facebook, Twitter, LinkedIn, RSS
Roosevelt Smith, President
John H Bridges III, Director
Jeffery Chung, Board Member
Marilyn Clark Alston, Board Member
Charles W. McGlothlin, Board Member
Mission is to support managers and their employees in their responsibility to assure the safety of all employees.
Founded in 1966

22351 National Sheriffs' Association
1450 Duke Street
Alexandria, VA 22314
800-424-7827; Fax: 703-838-5349
mkendall@sheriffs.org
www.sheriffs.org
Facebook, Twitter, LinkedIn, Google+
John E. Aubrey, Immediate Past President
John Thompson, Interim Executive Director
Linda Foldvik, Director of Finance
Miriam Kendall, Executive Secretary
Fred G. Wilson, Director of Outreach & Law
An organization to promote criminal justice, homeland security and public safety.
Founded in 1940

22352 National Society of Professional Insurance Investigators
PO Box 88
Delaware, OH 43015
888-677-4498; Fax: 740-369-7155
nspii@nspii.com
www.nspii.com
LinkedIn, RSS
Micheal E. Jacobs, President
Jeffrey W. Ferrand, First VP
Michall Beagle, Secretary/Membership Chairman
A professional society for research and education.
590 Members
Founded in 1983

22353 National Tooling and Machining Association
1357 Rockside Road
Cleveland, OH 44134
440-799-8991
800-248-6862; Fax: 216-264-2840
info@ntma.org
www.ntma.org
Facebook, Twitter, LinkedIn, YouTube
Dave Tilstone, President
Candy Davis, Executive Assistant
Michel Conklin, NRL Program Manager
Matt Gilmore, Membership & Business Development
Doug DeRose, Chief Financial Officer
Membership association serving the precision custom manufacturing industry through business development support, education, events and advocacy.
1400 Members
Founded in 1943

22354 NationalÿAssociationÿof SchoolÿSafetyÿand Law Enforcement Officials
19411 S. W.
308thÿStreet
Homestead, FL 33030
305-905-1323; Fax: 305-247-9915
www.nassleo.org
Facebook, Twitter
Augustine Pescatore, Chairman
Larry D. Johnson, President
Chief Ian Moffett, President Elect
Hector Garcia, Secretary
Rudy Perez, Treasurer
Provides levels of resources for school law enforcement and safety officials.

22355 OpenAI
San Francisco, CA
Home Page: openai.com
Facebook, Twitter
Greg Brockman, Chair & CTO
Ilya Sutskever, Chief Scientist
Research organization dedicated to maintaining Artificial Intelligence as a benefit to humanity.

22356 Partnership on AI
115 Sansome Street
Suite 1200
San Francisco, CA 94104
Home Page: www.partnershiponai.org
Facebook, Twitter
Terah Lyons, Founding Executive Director
Samir Goswami, Chief Operating Officer
Sasha Ramsaw, Human Resources Manager
Peter Lo, Senior Communications Manager
Hudson Hongo, Writer/Editor
Seeks to advance the understanding of AI technologies including machine perception, learning, and automated reasoning for the benefit of humanity.

22357 Professional Investigators & Security Association
PO Box 3307
Fairfax, VA 22038-3307
703-818-0552; Fax: 703-818-0551
kbreenpi@yahoo.com
www.vapisa.com
Facebook, Twitter
Kristopher W. Wilgus, 1st, Vice President
Susan Spofford, 2nd Vice President
Nicole Bocra Grray, President
Vacant T.B.A., Secretary
Narma J. Duncan, Treasurer
PISA is recognized as the preeminent professional organization representing members of the Private Security Services.
Founded in 1984

22358 Professional Records & Information Service s Management
8735 W Higgins Rd
Suite 300
Chicago, IL 60631
847-375-6344
800-336-9793; Fax: 847-375-6343
info@prismintl.org
www.prismintl.org
Facebook, Twitter, LinkedIn
Dave Bergeson, Executive Director
Chad Sorrell, President
Chris Kelly, Vice President
Michael Fruchter, Secretary/ Treasurer
Chris Pearson, Asst. Secretary
A nonprofit trade association for the commercial information management industry whose vision is to be the primary global resource for commercial information management outsourcing providers.
Founded in 1930

22359 SAFE Association
PO Box 130
Creswell, OR 97426-0130
541-895-3012; Fax: 541-895-3014
safe@peak.org
www.safeassociation.com
Facebook
Barr Shope, President
Joe Spinosa, President-Elect
Mathew Wawrowski, Vice President
Jerry Ride, Treasurer
Alex Mc Gill, Secretary
Dedicated to the preservation of human life. Provides a common meeting ground for the sharing of problems, ideas and information.
Founded in 1956

22360 Safe & Vault Technicians Association
3500 Easy St
Dallas, TX 75247
214-819-9733
800-532-2562; Fax: 214-819-9736
www.savta.org
Charles Gibson, President
Provides a host of benefits to help its members stay informed, solving day to day problems, and out-performing the competition. Has helped thousands of safe and vault techicians achiveve personal and professional success.
Founded in 1986

22361 Safety Equipment Distributors Association
1901 North Moore Street
Suite 808
Arlington, VA 22209-1762
703-525-1695; Fax: 703-528-2148
safetycentral.org
Facebook, Twitter, LinkedIn
Charles D. Johnson, President
Cristine Fargo, VP, Operations & Technical Services
Dan Glucksman, Director, Public Affairs
Lydia Baugh, Director, External Affairs
Tanya Brosnan, Manager, Member Services
The Saftey Equipment Distributor's Association is the trade association comprised of companies that distribute safety equipmant and related products and services. Its member companies are leaders in the distribution of personal protective equipment to a broad spectrum of users, including general industry, construction, municipalities, utilities, schools and laboratories.
300 Members
Founded in 1968

22362 Safety Glazing Certification Council
P.O. Box 730
100 W. Main St.
Sackets Harbor, NY 13685
315-646-2234; Fax: 315-646-2297
staff@amscert.com
www.sgcc.org
John Kent, Administrative Staff
Peter Weismantle, President
Richard Paschel, Vice President
June Willcott, Secretary
Elaine S. Rodmanÿ, Treasurer
Nonprofit corporation that provides for the certifacation of safety glazing materials, comprised of safety glazing manufacturers and other

parties concerned with public safety. SGCC is managed by a board of directors comprised of representatives from the safety glazing industry and the public interest sector.
105 Members
Founded in 1971

22363 Scaffold & Access Industry Association
400 Admiral Blvd
Kansas City, MO 64106

816-595-4860
866-687-7115; Fax: 602-257-1166
www.scaffold.org
Facebook, Twitter, LinkedIn, RSS

Nonprofit organization which promotes scaffold safety and education through its publications, conventions, tradeshows and training programs.
Founded in 1972

22364 Scaffold and Access Industry Association
400 Admiral Blvd
Kansas City, MO 64106

816-595-4860; Fax: 816-472-7765
info@saiaonline.org
www.saiaonline.org
Facebook, Twitter, LinkedIn, RSS

Mike Russell, President
Paula Manning, President Elect
Ted Beville, Vice President
Colby Hubler, Secretary
Frank Frietsch, Treasurer

To promote, represent and enhance the access, scaffolding and forming industry for the benefit of its members.
Founded in 1972

22365 Security Hardware Distributors Association
105 Eastern Avenue
Suite 104
Annapolis, MD 21403

410-940-6346; Fax: 410-263-1659
info@shda.org
www.shda.org

David Swartz, President
Robert Justen, Vice President
Lance Johnsen, Treasurer
John M. Burke, Immediate Past President
Amy Luckado, Executive Director

The mission of the Security Hardware Distributors Association is to continually improve, through education and services, the proficiency of Security Distributors in order that they are the most effective and efficient conduit to the marketplace.

22366 Security Industry Association
8405 Colesville Road
Suite 500
Silver Spring, MD 20910

301-804-4700
866-817-8888; Fax: 301-804-4701
info@siaonline.org
www.siaonline.org
Facebook, Twitter, LinkedIn, YouTube

Denis Hebert, Chairman Elect
Herve Fages, Vice Chairman
Scott Schafer, Treasurer
V. John Storia, Chairman
John Romanowich, Secretary

SIA is dedicated to promoting growth, advancement, and professionalism within the security industry. Its activities fall into four core concentrations: government relations, research & technology, education & training, and standards.
510 Members
Founded in 1969

22367 Semiconductor Environmental Safety & Health Association
1313 Dolley Madison Boulevard
Suite 402
McLean, VA 22101

703-790-1745; Fax: 703-790-2672
BBurk@Burkinc.com
www.seshaonline.org
Facebook, Twitter, LinkedIn

Hilary Matthews, President
Brett J Burk, Executive Director
Steven Roberge, Treasurer
Raymond Mvdaid, Secretary
Paul M Connor, President-Elect

SESHA is the premier association serving the global semiconductor and associated technology industries by providing education and professional development.
1500 Members
Founded in 1978

22368 Society for Occupational & Environmental Health
1010 Vermont Ave., NW
Suite 513
Washington, DC 20005

202-347-4976; Fax: 202-347-4950
kkirkland@aoec.org

Ronald Denny Dobbin CIH, President
Katherine H. Kirrkland, Executive Director
Sarah Shiffert, Association Director
Mark Catlin, Governing Board

The Society plays a unique, integrating role by bringing together professionals in government, and academia. It reduces occupational and environmental hazards through the presentation of scientific data and the dynamic exchange of information across institutions and disciplines.
Founded in 1972

22369 Society of Fire Protection Engineers
9711 Washingtonian Blvd
Suite 380
Gaithersburg, MD 20878

301-718-2910; Fax: 240-328-6225
www.sfpe.org
Facebook, Twitter, LinkedIn, YouTube, RSS

Milosh Puchovsky, President-Elect
Michael Madden, President
Carl F. Baldassarra, President-Elect
Jack Poole, Secretary
Peter Willse, Vice President

The purpose of the Society is to advance the science and practice of fire protection engineering and its allied fields, to maintain a high ethical standard among its members and to foster fire protection engineering education. The Society provides a program of educational offerings and provides technical publications.
4500 Members
Founded in 1950

22370 The American Association of Safety Council s

Home Page: www.safetycouncils.orgÿ

Jim Meade, President
Darby Vorce, Vice President
Dianna Braud, Past President
Lynndee Riley, Secretary
Toni Burrows, Treasurer

An international association of safety professionals

22371 The Association of State Floodplain Managers
575 D'Onofrio Drive
Suite 200
Madison, WI 53719

608-828-3000; Fax: 608-828-6319
memberhelp@floods.org
www.floods.orgÿ
Facebook, Twitter, LinkedIn, Google+, Tumblr

Maria Cox Lamm, Vice Chair
Ceil Strauss, Chair
Chad Berginnis, Executive Director
Leslie Durham, Secretary
Karen McHugh, Treasurer

To promote education, policies and activities that mitigate current and future losses, costs and human suffering caused by flooding.

22372 The International Biometric Society
1444 I Street, NW
Suite 700
Washington, DC 20005

202-712-9049; Fax: 202-216-9646
ibs@biometricsociety.org
www.biometricsociety.org
Facebook, Twitter, LinkedIn

John Hinde, President
Elizabeth Thompson, President Elect
Dee Ann Walker, Executive Director
Jose Pinheiro, Director
James Carpenter, Secretary/ Treasurer

22373 The Monitoring Association
8150 Leesburg Pike
Suite 700
Vienna, VA 22182

703-242-4670; Fax: 703-242-4675
communications@tma.us
www.csaaintl.org
Facebook, Twitter, LinkedIn, RSS

Celia Trigo Besore, Executive Director

Represents companies offering security (alarm) monitoring systems through a central station. It also represents companies that provide services and products to the industry.
300+ Members
Founded in 1950

22374 The National Burglar & Fire Alarm
440 North Broad Street
Suite 130
Philadelphia, PA 19130

215-400-6428; Fax: 215-400-4717
secretary@nassleo.org
www.alarm.org
Facebook, Twitter, YouTube

22375 The World Institute for Security Enhancement

702-722-7779
www.worldinstitute.org

G.F. Bryant, Executive Director
Henry D Infante, Director of Operations
Rubern Bala, Director of International Marketing
M Gregory Scott, Director of Intnl. Investigations
Lisa A Kane, Director of Health

22376 Transportation Security Administration

866-289-9673
TSA-ContactCenter@tsa.dhs.gov
www.tsa.govÿ
Facebook, Twitter, LinkedIn, YouTube

Peter Neffenger, Administrator
Kenneth Fletcher, Chief Risk Officer
Thomas McDaniels, Chief of Staffs

Francine Kerner, Chief Counsel
Pat Rose, Finance
Founded in 2001

22377 **U.S. Fire Administration**
16825 S. Seton Ave.
Emmitsburg, MD 21727

301-447-1000
888-382-3827; Fax: 301-447-1441
netcadmissions@fema.dhs.gov
www.usfa.fema.gov
Facebook, Twitter, YouTube

Ernest Mitchell, US Fire Administrator
Kyle Blackman, Executive Officer
Vanetta Huff, Secretary
Angela Cunningham, Administrative Specialist
Elizabeth Miller, Budget Analysis

22378 **U.S. Security Associatesÿ**
200 Mansell Court Fifth Floor
Roswell, GA 30076

770-625-1500
800-730-9599
www.ussecurityassociates.com
Facebook, Twitter, LinkedIn, YouTube, Google+

Founded in 1993

22379 **Underwriters Laboratories**
333 Pfingsten Rd
Northbrook, IL 60062-2096

847-412-0136; Fax: 847-272-8129
www.ul.com
Facebook, Twitter, LinkedIn, YouTube, Google+, Pinterest

Christian Anschuetz, SVP & Chief Information Officer
Terry Brady, SVP & Chief Legal Officer
Adrian Groom, SVP & Chief Human Resources Officer
Michael Saltzman, SVP & CFO
Barbara Guthrie, SVP & Public Safety Officer

Underwriters Labdoratories Inc. is an independent, not-for-profit product-safty testing and certification organization, that has been testing products for safety for more than a century.
Founded in 1894

22380 **United States Association of Professional Investigators**
175 Hutton Ranch Rd
Ste 103-165
Kalispell, MO 59901

877-894-0615; Fax: 877-851-0794
infor@usapi.org
www.usapi.orgÿ
Twitter

Randy Torgerson, President
fred Ritz, Vice President
Leah Ritz, Executive Director
Stephane Juneau, CFO

22381 **United States Marine Safety Association**
5050 Industrial Road
Suite 2
Wall Township, NJ 07727

732-751-0102; Fax: 732-751-0508

Burt Thompson, Executive Director

22382 **United States Society on Damsÿ**
1616 Seventeenth Street
Suite 483
Denver, CO 80202

303-628-5430; Fax: 303-628-5431
www.ussdams.org

John S. Wolfhope, President
Dean B. Durkee, Secretary-Treasurer
Daniel L. Wade, Vice President
Larry D. Stephens, Executive Director
John D. Rice, Board of Director

22383 **Veterans of Safety**
22 Logan Street
New Bedford, MA 02740

660-543-4281
info@vetsofsafety.org
www.vetsofsafety.org

Warren K Brown, Past President
Dr Nigel Ellis, VP
Dianna Bryant, Executive Director
Wendell W. Wahlstedt, President
Christopher M Gates, Counsil of Ambassadors

Our mission is the promotion of safety, health, and environmental awareness by using and making available the lifetime experience of professionals throughout the world.
Founded in 1941

22384 **Western States Auto Theft Investigators Association Southern Chapter**
6 Hutton Centre Drive
Suite 1040
Santa Ana, CA 92707

714-434-9600
webmaster@wsati.org
www.wsati.org
Facebook, Twitter

Heather Roberts, Secretary
Brian Yori, VP
Aristeed Powell, President
Jeff Enfield, Treasurer
Richard O. Knapp, Legal Counsel

A non-profit organization that is comprised of professionals representing law enforcement, rental car and insurance companies, and other individuals whose goal is to reduce vehicle theft.
Founded in 1965

22385 **Women Investigators Association**
PO Box 18305
Encino, CA 91416

800-603-3524
www.w-i-a.org

Debra J Burdette, Executive Director
Robinette Desrochers, VP/Membership Director

Offering education and training, certification, networking, group discounts and represents women in our industry to the media.

Newsletters

22386 **ACP Sentinel**
Association of Contingency Planners
7044 S 13th St
Oak Creek, WI 53154-1429

414-768-8000
800-445-4227; Fax: 414-768-8001
www.naspa.com

Scott Sherer, Executive Director
Shirley Runnels, Membership

News and event information for national and local chapters dedicated to fostering continued professional growth and development in effective contingency and business planning.
Cost: $75.00
Frequency: Quarterly
Founded in 1983

22387 **AICan Bulletin**
CIFAR, MaRS Centre, West Tower
661 University Avenue
Suite 505
Toronto, ON M5G 1M1

416-971-4251
www.cifar.ca

Alan Bernstein, President & CEO

Newsletter of CIFAR, with new developments in Artificial Intelligence.
Frequency: Bi-Monthly

22388 **CGAA Signals**
Central Station Alarm Association
8150 Leesburg Pike
Suite 700
Vienna, VA 22182-2721

703-242-4670; Fax: 703-242-4675
communications@csaaul.org
www.csaaul.org

Stephen P Doyle, Executive VP/CEO
Celia Besore, VP Marketing & Programs
300+ Members
Frequency: Quarterly
Circulation: 1200
Founded in 1950

22389 **Councilor**
Safety & Health Council of Northern New England
57 Regional Dr
Suite 6
Concord, NH 03301-8518

603-228-1401
800-834-6472; Fax: 603-224-0998
safety@shcnne.org
www.shcnne.org

Lyman Cousens, Executive Director

Covers current regulatory issues as well as health and safety information. Free to members.
16 Pages
Frequency: Monthly
Founded in 2004
Printed in 2 colors on matte stock

22390 **Crime Lab Minute**
American Society of Crime Laboratory Directors
65 Glen Road
Suite 123
Garner, NC 27529

919-773-2044
ascldirector@gmail.com
www.ascld.org

Matthew Gamette, President
Jean Stover, Executive Director
Timothy Scanlan, Training & Education Chair
Rita Dyas, Treasurer
Linda Jackson, Secretary

Contains useful information and news to maintain and improve communications among crime laboratory directors and their staff, including updates about the association, training opportunities, job listings, and more.
Frequency: Weekly
Founded in 1974

22391 **Emergency Preparedness News**
Business Publishers
2601 University Boulevard W
#200
Silver Spring, MD 20902

301-929-5700
800-274-6737; Fax: 301-949-8844
custserv@bpinews.com
www.bpinews.com

Adam P Goldstein, Publisher
Deborah Eby, Editor
David Henderson, Director
Melissa Worcester, Service

Dedicated solely to disaster management: from securing pre-disaster mitigation and counter ter-

rorism funds, to staying prepared for hurricanes, terrorist threats, fires, floods and other natural disasters. Only available online now.
Cost: $357.00
Frequency: Monthly
ISSN: 0275-3782

22392 **FAMA Flyer**
Fire Apparatus Manufacturers' Association
PO Box 397
Lynnfield, MA 01940-0397

781-334-2911; Fax: 781-334-2911
info@fama.org
www.fama.org

Grady North, President
Greg Kozey, VP

A newsletter that is written specifically for Fire Apparatus Manufactures and Fire Associations across the United States.
Frequency: 3x/Yr
Circulation: 500

22393 **HTCIA Newsletter**
3288 Goldstone Drive
Roseville, CA 95747

916-408-1751; Fax: 916-408-7543
www.htcia.org

Carol Hutchings, Executive Director

For members only
Frequency: Quarterly

22394 **Homeland Security & Defense**
McGraw Hill
1200 G St Nw
Suite 900
Washington, DC 20005-3821

202-383-2377; Fax: 202-383-2438
www.aviationweek.com

Jennifer Michels, President
Paul Hoversten, Managing Editor
Mark Lipowicz, Publisher
Iain Blackhall, Managing Director

News items for defense and homeland security professionals. Available in print or electronically.
Cost: $595.00
Frequency: Weekly
Founded in 1920

22395 **News & Ideas**
CIFAR, MaRS Centre, West Tower
661 University Avenue
Suite 505
Toronto, ON M5G 1M1

416-971-4251
www.cifar.ca

Alan Bernstein, President & CEO

Newsletter of CIFAR, with association news, events, and new discoveries.

22396 **Nine Lives Associates: Newsletter**
Executive Protection Institute
PO Box 802
Berryville, VA 22611

540-554-2540; Fax: 540-554-2558
info@personalprotection.com
www.personalprotection.com

Ronald J. Wilczynski, President
Tom Quilty, VP
Peter Morin, Tresurer
Jose Soltero, Secretary

Personal protection news and announcements for member graduates of Executive Protection Institute.
Founded in 1980

22397 **Progress**
National Association of Elevator Safety
6957 Littlerock Road SW
Suite A
Tumwater, WA 98512

360-292-4968
800-746-2372; Fax: 360-292-4973
dotty@naesai.org
www.naesai.org
Facebook, Twitter, LinkedIn

Dotty Stanlaske, Executive Director
Dean McLellan, President
Bill Snyder, VP

Informs members of the newest developments in the elevator industry; listings of all currently-scheduled seminars, updated classes and workshops; a message from the Executive Director with news from the main office; articles addressing code questions and issues; news from around the globe and advertising opportunities.
Frequency: Monthly

22398 **Protection News**
International Foundation for Protection Officers
PO Box 771329
Naples, FL 34107-1329

239-430-0534; Fax: 239-430-0533
sandi@ifpo.com
www.ifpo.org

Sandi J Davies, Executive Director
Michael Stroberger, Secretary/Treasurer

Circulation to all IFPO members and candidates in associated programs. Publication is designed to keep professionals current on trends within the security industry and is full of valuable information and commentary pertinent to the enhancement of life, safety and property protection.
Cost: $18.00
Frequency: Quarterly
Founded in 1988

22399 **SAFE Symposium News**
SAFE Association
PO Box 130
Creswell, OR 97426

541-895-3012; Fax: 541-895-3014
safe@peak.org
www.safeassociation.com
Facebook

Al Loving, President
John Fair, President-Elect

The SAFE Association is dedicated to the preservation of human life. It provides a common meeting ground for the sharing of problems, ideas and information. SAFE is a non-profit international association headquartered in Oregon, with chapters located throughout the world. SAFE publishes a quarterly Newsletter and Proceedings of the Annual SAFE Symposium. These publications are valuable reference sources for the professional involved in all forms of safety and survival.
1100+ Attendees
Frequency: Quarterly
Founded in 1954

22400 **SIA News**
Security Industry Association
8405 Colesville Road
Suite 500
Alexandria, MD 20109

301-804-4700
866-817-8888; Fax: 301-804-4701
info@siaonline.org
www.siaonline.org

Richard Chace, CEO
Rand Price CAE, COO
Donald Erickson, Government Relations Director

Informs and educates members and prospective members of SIA activities, news, and information. Available online only.
Frequency: 2 X'S Monthly
ISSN: 1071-6713
Founded in 1969

22401 **Safety Compliance Letter**
Bureau of Business Practice
111 Eight Avenue
New York, NY 10011

800-638-8437
www.aspenlawschool.com

Alicia Pierce, Publisher
Michele Rubin, Editor

Monitors and reports on the regulatory environment and provides subscribers with up-to-date information in a concise and easy-to-read format, with references and resources (including internet addresses) to get additional help on particular topics.
Cost: $289.00
Frequency: Monthly
ISBN: 9-900003-20-0
Founded in 1920

22402 **Salt & Highway Deicing**
Salt Institute
700 N Fairfax St
Suite 600
Alexandria, VA 22314-2085

703-549-4648; Fax: 703-548-2194
info@saltinstitute.org
www.saltinstitute.org

Richard L Hanneman, President
Tammy Goodwin, Administrative Director

A quarterly e-newsletter published by the Salt Institute.
Frequency: Quarterly
Circulation: 8000
Founded in 1914
Printed in on glossy stock

22403 **Security Director's Report**
Institute of Management and Administration
1 Washington Park
Suite 1300
Newark, NJ 07102

212-244-0360; Fax: 973-622-0595
www.ioma.com

Designed to help security directors keep pace with the rapidly evolving world of corporate security. Alerts to critical news, import new security products, and up-to-date advice that you need to know to effectively manager your security department.
Cost: $419.00
Frequency: Monthly

22404 **Signal**
American Traffic Safety Services Association
15 Riverside Parkway
Suite 100
Fredericksburg, VA 22406-1022

540-368-1701
800-272-8772; Fax: 540-368-1717
www.atssa.com
Facebook, Twitter

James Baron, Communications Director

Covers legislative updates, industry news and meeting information, as well as other items of interest to the roadway safety industry as is a full-color publication.
Frequency: Quarterly

22405 **Society Update**
American Society of Safety Engineers

1800 E Oakton Street
Des Plaines, IL 60018

847-699-2929; Fax: 847-768-3434
customerservice@asse.org
www.asse.org
Facebook

Fred J Fortman, Executive Director
Jim Drzewiecki, Finance/Controller Director
Diane Hurns, Manager Public Relations Department

Membership benefit via e-mail with news, information on training, plus happenings in the 150 chapters throughout the US.
Cost: $60.00
Founded in 1911

22406 **TMA Dispatch**
The Monitoring Association
8150 Leesburg Pike
Suite 700
Vienna, VA 22182

703-242-4670; Fax: 703-242-4675
membership@tma.us
www.csaaintl.org

Celia Besore, Executive Director
Frequency: Quarterly

22407 **Workplace Substance Abuse Advisor**
LRP Publications
PO Box 24668
West Palm Beach, FL 33416-4668

561-622-6520
800-341-7874; Fax: 561-622-0757
custserve@lrp.com
www.lrp.com

Kenneth Kahn, President

Current developments affecting how your workplace deals with alcohol and drug abusing employees. Comprehensive overview of all the areas you need to know to create and maintain an effective substance abuse program in your company.
Cost: $377.00
Frequency: 2 X'S Month
Founded in 1977

Magazines & Journals

22408 **Access Control & Security Systems**
PRIMEDIA Business Magazines & Media
1166 Avenue of the Americas
Shawnee Mission, NY 10036

212-204-4200; Fax: 913-514-6895
www.penton.com

Eric Jacobson, Senior VP
Gregg Herring, Publisher
Paul Rothman, Associate Editor
Brenda Wiley, Advertising Production Manager
Marty McCallen, National Sales Manager

Product overview articles and columns cover topics on door entry, CCTV, operators and gates, sensors and perimeter security.
Frequency: Monthly
Circulation: 38000+
Founded in 1905

22409 **Business & Legal Reports**
Business & Legal Reports
PO Box 6001
Old Saybrook, CT 06475-6001

860-510-0100
800-727-5257; Fax: 860-510-7225
service@blr.com
www.blr.com

Robert L Brady, CEO
Peggy Carter-Ward, Editor-in-Chief

Provides essential tools for safety and environmental compliance and training needs.
32 Pages

22410 **Campus Safety Journal**
Bricepac
12228 Venice Boulevard Suite 541
PO Box 66515
Los Angeles, CA 90066

310-390-5277; Fax: 310-390-4777

Pat Restivo, Circualtion
John Horn, President

Provides a vehicle for communicating campus safety and security issues to all interested parties at the middle, secondary, college and university levels.
40 Pages
Frequency: Monthly
Circulation: 20000
Founded in 1992
Printed in 4 colors on glossy stock

22411 **Compliance Magazine**
Briefings Media Group
PO Box 787
Williamsport, PA 17703

800-791-8699; Fax: 570-320-2079
www.compliancemag.com

Betty Hintch, Editor
Laura Daugherity, Production Coordinator

Compliance Magazine offers the latest in government regulations, including the materials and information needed to stay in compliance, safety trends, and a complete Safety Buyers' Guide.
Frequency: Annual
Founded in 1985

22412 **Computer Fraud & Security**
Elsevier Science
360 Park Ave S
New York, NY 10010-1736

212-633-3980; Fax: 212-633-3913
www.elsevier.com

Provides practical, usable information to effectively manage and control computer and information security within commercial organizations.
Frequency: Monthly
ISSN: 1361-3723
Founded in 1979

22413 **Computer Security Journal**
Computer Security Institute
600 Harrison Street
San Francisco, CA 94107

415-947-6320; Fax: 415-947-6023
Facebook, Twitter, LinkedIn

Russell Kay, Publisher

Keeps you informed with comprehensive, practical articles, case studies, reviews and commentaries written by knowledgeable computer security professionals.
Cost: $224.00
Frequency: Quarterly
Circulation: 3000
Founded in 1974

22414 **Computers & Security**
Elsevier Science
360 Park Ave S
New York, NY 10010-1736

212-633-3980; Fax: 212-633-3913
www.elsevier.com
Facebook, Twitter, LinkedIn

Provides a blend of leading edge research and sound practical management advice.
Frequency: Monthly
ISSN: 0167-4048
Founded in 1997

22415 **Corporate Security**
Strafford Publications
PO Box 13729
Atlanta, GA 30324-0729

404-881-1141
800-926-7926; Fax: 404-881-0074
custserv@straffordpub.com
www.straffordpub.com

Richard Ossoff, President
George Coleman, Manager

Intelligence briefing on the latest security developments, best practices, the most important trends and new technolgies.
Cost: $330.00
Frequency: Bi-Monthly
ISSN: 0889-0625
Founded in 1984

22416 **EMS Product News**
Cygnus Publishing
PO Box 803
Fort Atkinson, WI 53538-0803

920-000-1111
800-547-7377; Fax: 920-563-1699
Ronnie.Garret@cygnuspub.com
Facebook, Twitter, LinkedIn

John French, CEO
Nancy Perry, Editor

Product information written with the emergency medical service professional in mind.
Cost: $53.00
Frequency: 6 Issues
Circulation: 20000

22417 **Emergency Medical Product News**
Cygnus Business Media
PO Box 803
Fort Atkinson, WI 53538-0803

920-000-1111
800-547-7377; Fax: 920-563-1699

John French, CEO
Ronnie Garrett, Director of Public Relations
Kathy Scott, Director of Public Relations
Paul Bonaiuto, CFO

A bi-monthly tabloid-sized magazine showcasing new products in the Emergengy Medical Technician's scope of use.

22418 **Emergency Medical Services**
Cygnus Business Media
PO Box 803
Fort Atkinson, WI 53538-0803

920-000-1111; Fax: 920-563-1699
scott.cravens@cygnusb2b.com
Facebook, Twitter, LinkedIn

John French, CEO
Nancy Perry, Associate Publisher

A magazine designed for both career and volunteer EMS professionals. This magazine has been rated number one for editorial quality, reader interest and advertising pages.
Frequency: Monthly

22419 **Fire & Arson Investigator Magazine**
International Association of Arson Investigators
2111 Baldwin Ave
Suite 203
Crofton, MD 21114

410-451-3473; Fax: 410-451-9049
www.firearson.com

David Nichols, President
Cost: $75.00
Frequency: Quarterly

22420 **Fire EMS**
PennWell

PO Box 1260
Tulsa, OK 74101-1260

918-835-3161
800-331-4463; Fax: 918-831-9497
headquarters@pennwell.com
www.pennwell.com
Facebook, Twitter

Robert F Biolchini, CEO
Junior Isles, Publisher/Editor

News, product information and feature articles of interest to paramedics.
Cost: $30.00
Frequency: Monthly
Printed in 4 colors on glossy stock

22421 **Fire Engineering**
PennWell
PO Box 1260
Tulsa, OK 74101-1260

918-835-3161
800-962-6484; Fax: 918-831-9497
dianef@pennwell.com
www.pennwell.com
Facebook, Twitter

Robert F Biolchini, CEO
Diane Feldman, Executive Editor
Bobby Halton, Editor-in-Chief

Provides education and training to the fire service through a hands-on, technically oriented editorial package.
Cost: $29.95
106 Pages
Frequency: Monthly
Circulation: 44824
ISSN: 0015-2587
Printed in 4 colors on glossy stock

22422 **Fire Protection Engineering**
Society of Fire Protection Engineers
7315 Wisconsin Ave
Suite 620E
Bethesda, MD 20814-3234

301-718-2910; Fax: 301-718-2242
www.sfpe.org

David D Evans, Executive Director
Rebecca Salzman, Membership Coordinator
Samuel Dannaway, Publisher
James D Mike, President

Technical magazine advancing the science and practice of fire protection and its allied fields.
Cost: $145.00
Frequency: Quarterly
Circulation: 4500
Founded in 1950

22423 **Fraud Magazine**
Association of Certified Fraud Examiners
716 W. Avenue
Austin, TX 78701-2727

512-478-9000
800-245-3321; Fax: 512-478-9297
memberservices@acfe.com
www.fraud-magazine.com

Bruce Dorris, President & CEO
Kevin Taparauskas, Director, Communications

Articles on white-collar crime and fraud examination techniques. Free for ACFE members.
Cost: $65.00
Frequency: Bi-Monthly
Founded in 1988

22424 **IMSA Journal**
International Municipal Signal Association
165 E Union Street
PO Box 539
Newark, NY 14513-0539

315-331-2182
800-723-4672; Fax: 315-331-8205
info@imsasafety.org
www.imsasafety.org

Marilyn Lawrence, Publisher & Executive Director
Sharon Earl, Editor

Each issue focuses on different topics, including Dispatch/Public Safety Telecommunications, Fire Alarm Interior, Fire Alarm Municipal, FCC Licensing, Flagging, Roadway Lighting, Signs & Markings, Traffic Signal Systems, Two-Way Radios, Wireless Data, Wireless Traffic Control, and Work Zone Safety.
Cost: $700.00
Frequency: Bimonthly
Circulation: 12,000
ISSN: 1064-2560

22425 **Industrial Hygiene News**
Rimbach Publishing
8650 Babcock Blvd
Suite 1
Pittsburgh, PA 15237-5010

412-364-5366
800-245-3182; Fax: 412-369-9720
info@rimbach.com
www.rimbach.com

Norberta Rimbach, President
Karen Galante, Circulation Manager

Articles, news and product information for professionals in Occupational Health and Industrial Hygiene.
Circulation: 60,111
Founded in 1978

22426 **Industrial Safety & Hygiene News**
Business News Publishing
2401 W Big Beaver RD
Suite 700
Troy, MI 48084

248-244-6498
800-837-7370; Fax: 248-244-6439
www.ishn.com
Facebook, Twitter, LinkedIn

Katie Rotella, President
Dave Johnson, Editor
Randy Green, Advertising Manager

Feature articles and product information for safety, health and environmental professionals. Free subscription to qualified professionals.
Cost: $58.00
Frequency: Monthly
Founded in 1926

22427 **Infection Control Today**
Virgo Publishing LLC
3300 N Central Ave
Suite 300
Phoenix, AZ 85012-2532

480-675-9925; Fax: 480-990-0819
peggyj@vpico.com
www.vpico.com

Jenny Bolton, President
Kelly Ridley, VP
Jennifer Janos, Controller

Infection Control Today provides science based articles for the general ward, operating room, sterile processing and environmental services departments of healthcare facilities as well as for the public health community.
Mailing list available for rent: 30000+ names

22428 **Journal of Fire Sciences**
Sage Publications
2455 Teller Rd
Newbury Park, CA 91320-2234

805-499-9774
800-818-7243; Fax: 805-499-0871
info@sagepub.com
www.sagepub.com
LinkedIn

Blaise R Simqu, CEO

Reporting new developments in related technology. Peer-reviewed articles by recognized specialists from around the world. In-depth articles provide new science based information useful in materials research and product development.
Cost: $1281.00
88 Pages
Frequency: Bi-Monthly
ISSN: 0734-9041
Founded in 1965
Printed in 2 colors on matte stock

22429 **Journal of Occupational and Environmental Medicine (JOEM)**
American College of Occupational/Environmental Med
25 Northwest Point Blvd
Suite 700
Elk Grove Village, IL 60007

847-818-1800; Fax: 847-818-9266
www.acoem.org

Barry Eisenberg, Executive Director
Marianne Dreger, Communications Director

The official publication of the ACOEM, the Journal provides the latest data on reseach, as well as practical information for use in everyday practice. Readers find articles, case reviews, news and calendar of events, book reviews, and information about new product offerings.
Cost: $338.00
Frequency: Monthly/Free for Members
ISSN: 1076-2752
Founded in 1916

22430 **Journal of Security Education**
Academy of Security Educators & Trainers
PO Box 802
Berryville, VA 22611

540-554-2540; Fax: 540-554-2558
www.tandfonline.com

Dr Richard W Kobetz, Executive Director
Dr HHA Cooper, President
Mary E Kobetz, Secretary-Treasurer

22431 **Law and Order Magazine**
Hendon Publications
130 Waukegan Rd
Suite 202, 2nd Floor
Deerfield, IL 60015-4912

847-444-3300
800-843-9764; Fax: 847-444-3333
info@hendonpub.com
www.hendonpub.com

Henry Kingwill, President
Henry Kingwill, Publisher
Kathryn Murnik, Director

Latest news of interest to police and law enforcement professionals. New product and service information, available in print and online.
Cost: $24.95
Frequency: Monthly
Circulation: 32304
Founded in 1953

22432 **Mechanical Engineering Magazine**
American Society of Mechanical Engineers
Two Park Avenue
New York, NY 10016-5990

973-882-1170
800-843-2763
falcionij@asme.org
www.asme.org/network/media/mechanical-engineering-magazine

John G. Falconi, Editor-in-Chief & Publisher
Chitra Sethi, Managing Editor

Flagship publication of the American Society of Mechanical Engineering.
Frequency: Monthly
Founded in 1880

22433 **National Defense Magazine**
National Defense Industrial Association
2111 Wilson Blvd
Suite 400
Arlington, VA 22201-3061
703-522-1820
703-247-9469; Fax: 703-522-1885
info@ndia.org
www.ndia.org
Lawrence Farrell, President
Sandra I Erwin, Editor
Sharon Foster, Circulation Manager
Places main focus on issues concerning the U.S. defense industry. Provides the trends in national security, including technology advancement, acquisition policy, critical industry sectors, and marketing are editorial staples.
Cost: $40.00
Frequency: Monthly
Circulation: 30000
ISSN: 0092-1491
Founded in 1946

22434 **National Fire Protection Association Newsletter**
National Fire Protection Association
1 Batterymarch Park
Quincy, MA 02169-7471
617-770-3000
800-344-3555; Fax: 617-770-0700
www.nfpa.org
James M. Shannon, President/CEO
Peg O'Brien, Administrator - Public Affairs
Sharon Gamache, Executive Director
Bruce Mullen, CFO
Paul Crossman, VP, Marketing
Written for various fire safety professionals and covers major topics in fire protection and suppression. The Journal carries investigation reports written by NFPA specialists, special NFPA statistical studies on large-loss fires, multiple deaths, fire fighter deaths and injuries and others annually and articles on fire protection advances, public education and information of interest to NFPA members.
75000 Members
Frequency: Monthly
Founded in 1896

22435 **National Locksmith**
National Publishing Company
1533 Burgundy Pkwy
Streamwood, IL 60107-1811
630-837-1250; Fax: 630-837-1210
natllock@aol.com
Marc Goldberg, Publisher
Greg Mango, Editor
New products, marketing, sales, merchandising, and the array of factors involved in successful locksmith enterprises and services. Informs professionals about the latest news and techniques in security.
Cost: $46.00
Frequency: Monthly
Circulation: 17000
Founded in 1983

22436 **Occupational Hazards**
Penton Media
1166 Avenue of the Americas
Suite 316
Cleveland, NY 10036
212-204-4200; Fax: 216-696-6662
information@penton.com
www.penton.com
Jane Cooper, Marketing
Bob Marinez, Publisher
Rob Howlette, Advertising Manager
Chris Meyer, Director
Bev Walter, Customer Service
Analysis of qualified recipients who have indicated that they recommend, select and/or buy the safety equipment, fire protection and other occupational health products.
Cost: $50.00
65 Pages
Frequency: Monthly
Circulation: 71,000
ISSN: 0029-7909
Founded in 1892
Printed in 4 colors on glossy stock

22437 **Oregon Investigator**
PO Box 2705
Portland, OR 97208
866-584-8645
www.oali.org
Ted J Tolliver, Executive Director
Patricia Vollbrect, President
Official journal of the organization setting a standard of excellence among investigators. Legislative issues and news of upcoming seminars.
Founded in 1983

22438 **Pest Control Technology**
GIE Media
4012 Bridge Avenue
Cleveland, OH 44113
216-961-4130
800-456-0707; Fax: 216-961-0364
www.pctonline.com
Dan Moreland, Publisher
Jodi Dorsch, CEO
Directed towards technological and educational advancement in the pest control industry.
Cost: $35.00
76 Pages
Frequency: Monthly
ISSN: 0730-7608
Founded in 1972
Printed in 4 colors on glossy stock

22439 **Pollution Equipment News**
Rimbach Publishing
8650 Babcock Blvd
Suite 1
Pittsburgh, PA 15237-5010
412-364-5366
800-245-3182; Fax: 412-369-9720
info@rimbach.com
Norberta Rimbach, President
Karen Galante, Circulation Manager
Paul Henderson, VP of Sales and Marketing
Richard Rimbach, Owner
Provides information to those responsible for selecting products and services for air, water, wastewater and hazardous waste pollution abatement.
Frequency: Bi-Annually
Circulation: 91000
Founded in 1968

22440 **Process Safety Progress**
John Wiley & Sons
1475 Crosspoint Boulevard
Indianapolis, IN 46256
877-762-2974; Fax: 800-597-3299
www.wiley.com
LinkedIn
D A Crowl, Editor
Joseph F Louvar, Editor
Practical information for engineering professionals. Focuses on chemical and hydrocarbon safety, loss prevention and health.
Cost: $345.00
Frequency: Quarterly
ISSN: 1066-8527
Founded in 1908

22441 **Professional Safety**
American Society of Safety Engineers
1800 E Oakton Street
Des Plaines, IL 60018
847-699-2929; Fax: 847-768-3434
customerservice@asse.org
www.asse.org
Facebook, Twitter
Fred Fortman, Executive Director
Jim Drzewiecki, Finance/Controller Director
Diane Hurns, Manager Public Relations Department
Journal of the well known professional safety, health and environmental organization. Articles provide in-depth examination of health and safety concerns.
Cost: $60.00
Frequency: Monthly
Founded in 1990

22442 **Public Safety Communications/APCO Bulletin**
Association of Public-Safety Comm Officials Int'l
351 N Williamson Boulevard
Daytona Beach, FL 32114-1112
386-322-2500
888-272-6911; Fax: 386-322-2501
apco@apcointl.org
www.apcointl.org/
Facebook, Twitter, LinkedIn, You Tube
Toni Edwards, Managing Editor
George S Rice Jr, Executive Director
Susan Stowell, Member Services Director
Garry Mendez, Marketing/Communications Director
Robert Gurss Esq., Legal/Government Affairs Director
Newsletter dedicated to the enhancement of public safety communications and to serving its more than 15,000 members, the people who use public safety communications systems and services. Subscription is a member benefit.
Frequency: Monthly
Circulation: 13000
ISSN: 1526-1646
Founded in 1935

22443 **Quality Digest**
Quality Control International
555 East Avenue
P.O. Box 1769
Chico, CA 95926
530-893-4095; Fax: 530-893-0395
qualitydigest@qualitydigest.com
www.qualitydigest.com
Facebook
Michael Richman, Managing Editor
Dirk Dusharme, Technical Editor
Scott Papon, Publisher
April Johnson, Circulation Manager
Serves the field of quality-related activites in manufacturing, financial services, communications, utilities, transportation, government, military, retail, educational institutions, health care, consulting, aerospace, software, agricultural,

forestry, fishing, mining, construction and other industries. Available in print and free online.
Cost: $59.00
Frequency: Monthly
ISSN: 1049-8699
Founded in 1981

22444 SAFE Newsletter
SAFE Association
PO Box 130
Creswell, OR 97426

541-895-3012; Fax: 541-895-3014
safe@peak.org
www.safeassociation.com

Marcia Baldwin, President
Bryan Billings, President-Elect
Frequency: 4-6x/Year
Circulation: 1000
Founded in 1957

22445 SC Magazine
Haymarket Media
161 Worcester Road
Suite 201
Framingham, MA 01701

508-879-9792; Fax: 508-879-2755
www.scmagazine.com
Facebook, Twitter, LinkedIn

Illena Armstrong, Editor-in-Chief
Gil Torren, Sales Director
Sherry Oommen, Circulation Director

Covers all industries that use information security systems. Provides data on information security products, services, market trends and industry developments.
Cost: $60.00
133 Pages
Frequency: Monthly
Circulation: 40,000
ISSN: 1096-7974
Founded in 1999
Printed in 4 colors

22446 Safe & Vault Technology
Safe & Vault Technicians Association
3500 Easy St
Dallas, TX 75247-6416

214-819-9771; Fax: 214-819-9736
www.savta.org

Charles Gibson, President
Mike Oelert, Editor

Industry news, reviews, announcements and new products of paticular interest to readers.
Cost: $45.00
Frequency: Monthly
Circulation: 3000
Founded in 1986

22447 Safety & Health
National Safety Council
PO Box 558
Itasca, IL 60143-0558

630-775-2213
800-621-7615; Fax: 630-285-1315
info@nsc.org
www.nsc.org

Alan C McMillan, CEO
Melissa J Ruminski, Managing Editor
Suzanne Powills, Publisher

Coverage of safety news and changes, trade shows and training courses.
Cost: $58.50
Frequency: Monthly
Founded in 1954
Mailing list available for rent

22448 Security Dealer
Cygnus Publishing
PO Box 803
Fort Atkinson, WI 53538-0803

920-000-1111
800-547-7377; Fax: 920-563-1699

John French, CEO
Susan Brady, Editor-in-Chief
Susan Whitehurst, Group Publisher

Trade publication for those in the electronic burglary and fire alarm system business.
Cost: $112.00
Frequency: Monthly
Circulation: 25500
Founded in 1966

22449 Security Distributing and Marketing
Business News Publishing
1050 IL Route 83
Suite 200
Bensenville, IL 60106-1096

630-377-5909; Fax: 630-227-0214
www.sdmmag.com

Katie Rotella, President
Laura Stepanek, Editor
Russ Gager, Senior Editor

Information source for the electronic security, life safety and home systems industries. Subscription free to professionals.
Frequency: Monthly
Circulation: 28000

22450 Security Industry Buyers Guide
ASIS International

22451 Security Magazine
Business News Publishing
2401 W Big Beaver Rd
Suite 700
Troy, MI 48084-3333

248-362-3700; Fax: 248-362-0317
www.bnpmedia.com

Mitchell Henderson, CEO
Mark McCourt, Publisher
Russ Gager, Senior Editor
Laura Stepanek, Editor
Mark McCourt, Pulisher

Covers all types of businesses, including industrial manufacturing, service companies, institutions and government, as well as consulting, design, and integrator firms that specify security. News, columns and security product information. No charge to professionals.
Frequency: Monthly
Circulation: 40590
Founded in 1964
Printed in 4 colors on glossy stock

22452 Security Management
American Society for Industrial Security
1625 Prince Street
Alexandria, VA 22314-2818

703-519-6200
800-368-5685; Fax: 703-519-6299
www.securitymanagement.com

Denny White, Publisher
Sherry Harowitz, Editor-in-Chief
Carlton Purvis, Associate Editor

Features, news and trends in the security world. In print and online.
Cost: $48.00
Frequency: Monthly
Founded in 1955

22453 Security Products
Stevens Publishing Corporation
5151 Belt Line Rd
10th Floor
Dallas, TX 75254-7507

972-687-6700; Fax: 972-687-6767
www.stevenspublishing.com

Craig S Stevens, President
Margaret Perry, Circulation Director
Russell Lindsay, Publisher
Ralph Jensen, Editor
Karina Sanchez, Managing Editor

Offers examples of security solutions set by such facilities as casinos and hospitals, and explores such issues as false alarm reduction and personnel training, it also highlights new technologies.
Cost: $75.00
Frequency: Monthly
Circulation: 65000
Founded in 1925

22454 Security Sales & Integration
Bobit Publishing Company
3520 Challenger St
Torrance, CA 90503-1640

310-533-2400; Fax: 310-533-2500
www.bobit.com

Edward J Bobit, CEO
Scott Goldfine, Editor-in-chief
Michael Zawinski, Publisher

News, feature articles, columnists and new products in the field ofelectronic security.
Cost: $15.00
Frequency: Monthly
Founded in 1981

22455 Security and Privacy
IEEE Computer Society
10662 Los Vaqueros Drive
PO Box 3014
Los Alamitos, CA 90720-1314

714-821-8380
800-272-6657; Fax: 714-821-4010
help@computer.org
www.computer.org/security

Angela Burgess, Publisher
Kathy Clark-Fisher, Lead Editor
Georgann Carter, Circulation Manager
George Cybenko, Editor-in-Chief

Trans-border data flow issues, protocols, database management and security. Available online to members and in print to others.
Cost: $29.00
Frequency: 6 Issues/Year
Circulation: 1600
Founded in 1979

22456 Sound & Video Contractor
Primedia
PO Box 12914
Overland Park, KS 66282

913-341-1300; Fax: 913-967-1903
www.svconline.com

Michael Goldman, Editor
Cynthia Wisehart, Editorial Director
Charissa Young, Associate Editor

Contains information on sound systems, video display, security, CCTV, home theater, and automation. Delivers in depth instruction and examples of successful installations, fundamental acoustical and video theory and news on new technologies affecting the systems contracting business.
Cost: $35.00
Frequency: Monthly
Circulation: 21000
Founded in 1983
Mailing list available for rent: 20,500 names at $110 per M

22457 **The Poison Line**
American Association of Poison Control Centers
3201 New Mexico Ave NW
Suite 310
Washington, DC 20016-2739

202-895-4259
800-222-1222; Fax: 202-362-8377
info@aapcc.org
www.poison.org

M Litovitz, Executive Director
Frequency: Biannual
Founded in 1958

22458 **Underground Focus**
Planet Underground
411 South Evergreen
Manteno, IL 60950

815-468-7814; Fax: 815-468-7644
www.underspace.com
Facebook, Twitter, LinkedIn

Ron Rosencrans, Founder
Amy Chmura, Editor

Documents the importance of careful excavation and helps them get the budgets to do the job. Powerfully dramatizes the need for underground damage prevention, excavation safety, and the hazards of not protecting the subsurface infrastructure.
Cost: $25.00
46 Pages
Circulation: 21800
ISSN: 1090-400X
Founded in 1986
Printed in 4 colors on glossy stock

Trade Shows

22459 **AAAR Annual Meeting**
American Association for Aerosol Research
15000 Commerce Parkway
Suite C
Mount Laurel, NJ 08054

856-439-9080; Fax: 856-439-0525
dbright@ahint.com

Lynn Russell, Program Chair
Melissa Baldwin, Executive Director

Exibits related to aerosol research in areas including industrial process, air pollution, and industrial hygiene. Over 600 professionals attend.
600 Attendees
Frequency: Annual, October

22460 **ACFE Global Fraud Conference**
Association of Certified Fraud Examiners
716 W. Avenue
Austin, TX 78701-2727

512-478-9000
800-245-3321; Fax: 512-478-9297
memberservices@acfe.com
www.fraudconference.com

Bruce Dorris, President & CEO
Leslie Simpson, Director, Events

A conference for professionals in the fraud industry to network with colleagues and learn new ways fraud is being committed and tactics to prevent, detect and deter it.
Cost: $1800.00
3000 Attendees
Frequency: Annual
Founded in 1988

22461 **AFSA Annual Convention & Exhibition**
American Fire Sprinkler Association
12750 Merit Dr.
Suite 350
Dallas, TX 75251

214-349-5965; Fax: 214-343-8898
afsainfo@firesprinkler.org
www.firesprinkler.org/afsa37
Facebook, Twitter, LinkedIn, YouTube, Google+

Marlene Garrett, COO, Meetings & Operations

120 exhibits of sprinkler heads, pipe, hangers, tools and other equipment. Seminar, workshop and tours. Held September in Phoenix, Arizona.
1000 Attendees
Founded in 1981

22462 **ASFPM Annual Conference**
Association of State Floodplain Managers
2809 Fish Hatchery Road
Suite 204
Madison, WI 53713

608-274-0123; Fax: 608-274-0696
asfpm@floods.org
www.floods.org

Larry Larson, Executive Director
Becky Head, Member Services Coordinator

Focus on floodproofing techniques, materials, floodproofing and elevation contractors, current issues and programs, new federal tax impications and the various means of funding floodproofing projects. implications. Held June in Norfolk, VA.
Frequency: Annual
Founded in 1951

22463 **ASME Annual Meeting**
American Society of Mechanical Engineers
Two Park Avenue
New York, NY 10016-5990

973-882-1170
800-843-2763
williamsk@asme.org
www.asme.org

Kim Williams, Meetings Manager

Forum for information exchange and professional growth for engineering professionals.

22464 **ASNT Annual Conference**
American Society for Nondestructive Testing
1711 Arlingate Lane
PO Box 28518
Columbus, OH 43228-0518

614-274-6003
800-222-2768; Fax: 614-274-6899
www.asnt.org

Neal Couture, Executive Director
Barry Schieferstein, Dir., Conferences & Meetings

Seminar, conference and 150 exhibits of nondestructive testing equipment, services, supplies and laboratory representatives. Holds a smaller conference in the spring.
3000 Attendees
Frequency: Annual

22465 **America's Fire & Security Expo**
ROC Exhibitions
1963 University Lane
Lisle, IL 60532

630-271-8210; Fax: 630-271-8234
info@rocexhibitions.com
www.americassecurity.com

Jerry Carter, Marketing Director

Annual 3 day marketplace featuring state-of-the-art security products, systems and services. Over 50 free educational sessions. Emphasis on the markets of Latin America, the Caribbean and the Southeastern US.
Frequency: July

22466 **American Biological Safety Association Conference**
1200 Allanson Road
Mundelein, IL 60060-3808

847-949-1517
847-566-4580; Fax: 847-566-4580
www.absa.org

LouAnn Burnett, Chair

Exhibits of biological safety equipment, supplies and services. Held October at the Opryland Hotel in Nashville, Tennessee.
300 Attendees
Frequency: October
Founded in 1984

22467 **American Industrial Hygiene Association Conference & Exposition**
American Industrial Hygiene Association
3141 Fairview Park Drive
Suite 777
Falls Church, VA 22042

703-849-8888; Fax: 703-207-3561
infonet@aiha.org
www.aiha.org
Facebook, Twitter, LinkedIn

Bethany Chirico, Director, Global Meetings & Expos
Alison Daniels, Manager, Expositions
Laura Cilano Garcia, Program Director
Steven E. Lacey, President

Conference for occupational and environmental health and safety professionals around the globe. Held June in Philadelphia, Pennsylvania.
10000 Members
4,000 Attendees
Frequency: Annual
Founded in 1939

22468 **American Society of Crime Laboratory Directors Annual Symposium**
65 Glen Road
Suite 123
Garner, NC 27529

919-773-2044
ascldirector@gmail.com
www.ascld.org

Matthew Gamette, President
Jean Stover, Executive Director
Timothy Scanlan, Training & Education Director
Rita Dyas, Treasurer
Linda Jackson, Secretary

Devoted to providing training in leadership and management techniques in the field of forensic science. Also offers membership the opportunity to network with other laboratory directors.
660 Members
Frequency: Annual
Founded in 1974

22469 **American Society of Safety Engineers Professional Development Conference**
American Society of Safety Engineers
1800 E Oakton Street
Des Plaines, IL 60018

847-699-2929; Fax: 847-768-3434
customerservice@asse.org
www.asse.org

Fred Fortman, Executive Director
Jim Drzewiecki, Finance/Controller Director
Diane Hurns, Manager Public Relations Department

Annual conference and expo of 250 manufacturers and suppliers of safety equipment and health products. Held June
3500 Attendees
Frequency: June

22470 **Annual American Occupational Health Conference**
American College of Occupational/Environmental Med
25 Northwest Point Blvd
Suite 700
Elk Grove Village, IL 60007
847-818-1800; Fax: 847-818-9266
www.acoem.org
Facebook, Twitter, LinkedIn, You Tube
Barry Eisenberg, Executive Director
Marianne Dreger, Communications Director
AOHC
Frequency: Annual/Spring

22471 **Applied Ergonomics Conference**
Institute of Industrial Engineers
3577 Parkway Lane
Suite 200
Norcross, GA 30092
770-449-0461
800-494-0460; Fax: 770-263-8532
cs@iienet.org
Carol LeBlanc, Conference Manager
An exclusive event for ergonomists, engineers, and safety professionals. The conference focuses on how companies have successfully implemented programs that provide excellent return on their ergonomics investment. Held May Nashville, Tennessee.
800 Attendees
Frequency: March
Founded in 1998

22472 **Associated Locksmiths of America Convention & Security Expo**
Associated Locksmiths of America
3500 Easy Street
Dallas, TX 75247-6416
214-819-9733
800-532-2562; Fax: 214-819-9736
convention@aloa.org
www.aloa.org
Facebook
Karen Lyons, Conventions/Meetings
Kim Hammond, Exhibits/Sales
Features industry innovation, training, networking and education in the security world. Over 350 exhibitors with cash and carry merchandise.
4000 Attendees
Frequency: August
Founded in 1956

22473 **BOMA International Conference & Expo**
Building Owners and Managers Association
1101-15th Street NW
Suite 800
Washington, DC 20005
202-326-6300; Fax: 202-326-6377
info@boma.org
www.boma.org
Facebook, Twitter, LinkedIn
Henry Chamberlain, President/COO
Opportunity for business professionals to discuss problems, security, exchange ideas and share experience and knowledge.
Frequency: Annual/June

22474 **Bomb Technicians & Investigators Annual Conference**
PO Box 160
Goldvein, VA 22720-0160
540-752-4533; Fax: 540-752-2796
admin@iabti.org
www.iabti.org
Ralph Way PhD, Executive Director
Speakers on the latest information on bomb and bio threats.Attendes are in the fields of law enforcement, fire and emergency services, the military, forensic science and other related fields.
Founded in 1973

22475 **CSAA Electronic Security Forum & Exposition**
Central Station Alarm Association
440 Maple Avenue E
Suite 201
Vienna, VA 22180
703-242-4670; Fax: 703-242-4675
meetings@csaaul.org
www.csaaul.org
John McDonald, Meetings/Conferences
Exhibitors, speakers and workshops for the alarm and security professional. Held May
Frequency: May

22476 **California Alarm Association Winter Convention**
3401 Pacific Avenue
Suite 1C
Marina del Rey, CA 90292
310-305-1277
800-437-7658; Fax: 310-305-2077
info@caaonline.org
www.caaonline.org
Jon Sargent, President
Jerry Lenander, Executive Director
George DeMarco, Southern VP
Ron Galippo, Secretary
Annual meeting of state trade association comprised of licensed alarm company operators and suppliers of products and services. Nearly 200 alarm companies and 50 suppliers are members. Alarm companies represent 70% of the electronic security industry in California. Held December in San Francisco, California.
Frequency: December

22477 **Campus Law Enforcement Administrators Annual Conference**
342 N Main Street
Hartford, CT 06117-2507
860-586-7517; Fax: 860-586-7550
info@iaclea.org
www.iaclea.org
Delores Stafford, President
Carol Ewing, Professional Development
Presentations on sucessful or new programs and current trends.
Frequency: June

22478 **Campus Safety Conference**
Bricepac
12228 Venice Boulevard
PO Box 66515
Los Angeles, CA 90066
310-390-5277; Fax: 800-758-0935
Sandra Watson, Conferences/Training
Training conference designed especially for campus safety professionals at both the secondary school and higher education levels. Features more than 13 seminars of critical importance to campus safety decision makers and staff.
Frequency: 2 Days/November

22479 **Card Tech/Secur Tech: CTST Conference & Exhibition**
SourceMedia
One State Street Plaza
27th Floor
New York, NY 10004
212-258-6093
800-803-3424; Fax: 212-803-8515
Facebook, Twitter, LinkedIn
Nicoal Crawford, Director of Operations
Nikole Tenbrink, Custom Events
250 booth exhibit hall, seminars, luncheons and keynote speakers in the advanced card and biometric technology field. Explores real world applications in several industries including financial services, goverment and security. Held May in San Francisco, California.
50000 Attendees
Frequency: April

22480 **Computer Security Conference & Expo**
Computer Security Institute
600 Harrison Street
San Francisco, CA 94107
415-947-6320; Fax: 415-947-6023
Facebook, Twitter
Jennifer Stevens, Conference Director
Annual event with over 150 educational sessions and exhibitor hall. Held October in Orlando, Florida.
Frequency: November

22481 **Convention & Traffic Expo**
American Traffic Safety Services Association
15 Riverside Parkway
Suite 100
Fredericksburg, VA 22406-1022
540-368-1701
800-272-8772; Fax: 540-368-1717
www.atssa.com
Joe Jeffrey, Chairman
The premier meeting place for roadway professionals around the world. The program and exhibits are dedicated to issues and products related to all aspects of temporary traffic control and roadway safety.
Frequency: Annual/February

22482 **Counterterrorism & Security Professionals Annual Conference**
PO Box 10265
Arlington, VA 22210
201-461-5422
www.iacsp.com
Steven Fustero, Executive Director
We believe that all elements of the world's societies must become better educated about the threats of terrorism as a first step toward developing innovative and effective countermeasures to combat these ongoing threats. A better informed society will result in a freer one.
Frequency: May
Founded in 1992

22483 **Crime Analysts Annual Conference**
9218 Metcalf
PMB 364
Overland Park, KS 66212
919-940-3883
nfritz@du.edu
www.iaca.net
Noah Fritz, Director
Christopher Bruce, VP Administration
Annual themed conference helping crime analysts around the world improve their skills and make valuable contacts. Aids law enforcement agencies in making the best use of crime analysis and advocates for standards of performance and technique within the profession itself.
Frequency: October
Founded in 1990

22484 **Disaster Response & Recovery Exposition NDMS Conference**
J Spargo & Associates

11208 Waples Mill Road
Suite 112
Fairfax, VA 22030

703-631-6200
800-564-4220; Fax: 703-654-6931
www.drrexpo.com
Facebook, Twitter, LinkedIn

Nathan Wills, Account Manager

Held in conjunction with the NDMS Conference; it is an opportunity for local, State and Federal public health practitioners and policy makers to discover the latest equipment, technologies and services available.
2700 Attendees
Frequency: August

22485 **Eastern Ergonomics Conference & Exposition**
Continental Exhibitions
370 Lexington Avenue
New York, NY 10017

212-370-5005
800-222-2596; Fax: 212-370-5699
information@ergoexpo.com
www.ergoexpo.com

Lenore Kolb, Vice President of Sales
Walter Chamizon, President

Learn how to use ergonomics to increase productivity and safety at over 80 educational sessions. Try new products from over 100 companies, in over 2,000 square feet of floor space.
Frequency: June

22486 **Emergency Preparedness & Response Conference & Exposition: READY**
National Trade Productions
313 S Patrick Street
Alexandria, VA 22314

703-683-8500
800-687-7469; Fax: 703-706-8234

Janie Bridgeman, Sales Director
Maria Chaloux, Industry Relations

Annual symposium and trade show for personnel from federal, state and local agencies to learn about the latest emergency response equipment, technology, strategies and applications.
Frequency: July

22487 **Emergency Response Conference & Expo**
PBI Media
1201 Seven Locks Road
Suite 300
Potomac, MD 20854

301-541-1400; Fax: 301-309-3847
www.pbimedia.com

Robert Lewis, Conference Coordinator

Annual event for first responders and the companies who support them, working together on land, air and sea to save lives and property. Conference and exhibitors.
Frequency: November

22488 **Energy Security Expo**
EJ Krause & Associates
6550 Rock Spring Drive
Suite 500
Bethesda, MD 20817-1126

301-493-5500; Fax: 301-493-5705
www.pipelinesecurity.com

Michael Rosenburg, Show Manager
Edward Krause, President

Intensive conference with workshops led by leading international experts from government and industry. Exhibit area featuring technologies, products and services for pipeline and energy infrastructure including oil, gas, electric grids, power plants and dams.
Frequency: May

22489 **Fire-Rescue International**
International Association of Fire Chiefs
4025 Fair Ridge Dr
Fairfax, VA 22033-2868
703-273-0911; Fax: 703-273-9363
www.iafc.org
Facebook, LinkedIn

Al H. Gillespie, President & Chairman of the Board
Hank Clemmensen, First Vice President
William R. Metcalf, Second Vice President
Richard Carrizzo, Treasurer
Luther L. Fincher, Jr., Director-At-Large

FRI education covers all areas of the emergency service: navigating the political environment, managing change, ethical leadership, EMS issues, career development and moor. Exhibitors showcase the newest fire service innovations in apparatus, technology, equipment, gear and more.
12000 Members
Founded in 1873

22490 **Fire-Rescue Med (FRM)**
International Association of Fire Chiefs
4025 Fair Ridge Drive
Suite 300
Fairfax, VA 22033-2868

703-273-0911; Fax: 703-273-9363
www.iafc.org

Mark Light, Executive Director & CEO
Lisa Yonkers, Director, Conferences & Education
Leanne Shroeder, Conference Manager
Shannon Gilliland, Assistant Director, Conferences

Each spring, Fire-Rescue Med is the conference for fire-based EMS leaders, providing education and training on hiring and retaining EMTs, public and private integration challenges, embracing technology, billing for services, illness prevention programs and more.
Frequency: Annual

22491 **Gov't Convention on Emerging Technologies Partnerships for Homeland Security**
National Conference Services
6440-C Dobbin Road
Columbia, MD 21045

301-596-8899
888-603-8899; Fax: 301-596-6274
www.federalevents.com

Fredrick Martin, Director
Anne Slobodien, Chief Executive Officer

Forum for representatives from federal, state and local governments, along with the private sector to collaborate on and experiment with information technology that addresses mission needs critical to homeland security. Exhibits, workshops and simulation exercises.
Frequency: January

22492 **GovSec**
National Trade Productions
313 S Patrick Street
Alexandria, VA 22314

703-838-8500; Fax: 703-836-4486
www.govsecinfo.com

Denise Medved, General Manager

Provides a full spectrum of security solutions for federal, state, and local governments tasked with developing comprehensive strategies that address physical security, information security and cyber security needs. Educational programs held in conjunction with displays of a wide variety of security products and services designed specifically for government users.
Frequency: Annual/May

22493 **HTCIA International Training Conference & Expo**
Int'l High Technnology Crime Investigation Assoc
3288 Goldstone Drive
Roseville, CA 95747

916-408-1751; Fax: 916-408-7543
www.htcia.org

Carol Hutchings, Executive Director
Ronald J Wilczysnki, First VP/Conference Chair

Intended to attract participants from all over the world to take advantage of the training and networking opportunities that is offered.
Frequency: Annual

22494 **Homeland Security Expo & Conference**
E-Gov Conferences
3141 Fairview Park Drive
Suite 777
Falls Church, VA 22042-4507

703-876-5060
800-746-0099; Fax: 703-876-5059
info@e-gov.com

Mike Smoyer, General Manager

Keynote presentations, conference sessions, plenary session and exhibition of solutions and technologies to enhance homeland security efforts.
Frequency: November/December

22495 **ICPHSO Annual Meeting and Training Symposium**
Intl. Consumer Product Health & Safety Org.

Home Page: www.icphso.org

Dedicated to the health and safety issues related to consumer products manufactured and marketed in the global marketplace. Serving both health and safety professionals and consumers by sponsoring national and regional workshops. Annual meeting and training syposium.
Frequency: Annual

22496 **IMSA Conference**
International Municipal Signal Association
165 E Union Street
PO Box 539
Newark, NY 14513-0539

315-331-2182
800-723-4672; Fax: 315-331-8205
info@imsasafety.org
www.imsasafety.org
Facebook, Twitter, LinkedIn

Marilyn Lawrence, Executive Director/Publisher
Sharon Earl, Executive Assistant/Assitant Editor

Schools, technical sessions, exhibit floor and product demos.
1300 Attendees

22497 **ISC Expo International Security Conference and Expo-Las Vegas**
Reed Exhibition Companies
383 Main Avenue
Norwalk, CT 06851

203-840-4800; Fax: 203-840-9322
inquiry@isc.reedexpo.com
www.iscwest.com
Facebook, Twitter, LinkedIn

Amie Cangelosi, Marketing Coordinator
Kara Buonanno, Marketing/Conference Manager

From around the globe, every relevant manufacturer, product, service and industry expert will be on hand for three days under one roof.
Frequency: March/April

22498 **ISC: International Security Conference & Expo**
Reed Exhibitions
383 Main Avenue
Norwalk, CT 06851

203-840-4800; Fax: 203-840-9322
inquiry@isc.reedexpo.com
www.isceast.com
Facebook, Twitter, LinkedIn

Amie Cangelosi, Marketing Coordinator
Kara Buonanno, Marketing/Conference Manager

From around the globe, relevant manufacturers, products, services and industry experts will be on hand under one roof.
Frequency: November

22499 **Inside ID: Identification Solutions Mega Show**
Inside ID
8900 Saunders Lane
Bethesda, MD 20817

301-365-0186; Fax: 301-365-2519

Ben Miller, President
Liz Wenchel, CEO

Helps define and center the evolution of the emerging disipline of Identity Management. Education and displays of new products and technologies in identification. Facilitates the marketplace of buyers and sellers, provides a broad-based forum, and gathering place for standards groups and associations around the world.

22500 **International Cargo Security Council**
1400 I Street NW
Suite 1050
Washington, DC 20005-2209

202-821-1787; Fax: 410-956-0679
icsc@cargosecurity.com
www.securecargo.org

Joe Baker Jr, Executive Director
Ellen Parkereman, Meeting Director

Workshops and 60 booth exposition for cargo transportation and security professionals from the entire spectrum of cargo security: air, truck, rail maritime and intermodal.
450 Attendees
Frequency: Annual
Founded in 1973

22501 **NAESA Annual Workshop**
National Association of Elevator Safety
6957 Littlerock Road SW
Suite A
Tumwater, WA 98512

360-292-4968
800-746-2372; Fax: 360-292-4973
dotty@naesai.org
www.naesai.org
Facebook, Twitter, LinkedIn

Dotty Stanlaske, Executive Director
Dean McLellan, President
Bill Snyder, VP
Frequency: August

22502 **National Council of Investigation & Security Annual Conference**
7501 Sparrows Point Boulevard
Baltimore, MD 21219-1927

800-445-8408; Fax: 410-388-9746
nciss@comcast.net
www.nciss.org

Carolyn Ward, Executive Director
Francie Koehler, President
Bruce Hulme, Legislative Director

State associations and firms providing contract security services and investigative services. Our cooperative effort includes a legislative watch and providing accurate information reguarding our profession.
Frequency: March

22503 **National Ergonomics Conference & Exposition**
Continental Exhibitions
370 Lexington Avenue
New York, NY 10017

212-370-5005
800-222-2596; Fax: 212-370-5699
lkolb@ergoexpo.com
www.ergoexpo.com

Lenore Kolb, Vice President of Sales
Walter Chamizon, President

Learn how to use ergonomics to increase productivity and safety at over 80 educational sessions. Try new products from over 100 companies, in over 2,000 square feet of floor space.
Frequency: December

22504 **National Fire Protection World Safety Conference & Exposition**
National Fire Protection Association
1 Batterymarch Park
Quincy, MA 02169-7471

617-770-3000
800-344-3555; Fax: 617-770-0700
www.nfpa.org

James M. Shannon, President/CEO
Peg O'Brien, Administrator - Public Affairs
Sharon Gamache, Executive Director
Bruce Mullen, CFO
Paul Crossman, VP, Marketing

Professional development, networking and hundreds of booths from key industry suppliers.
75000 Members
Frequency: May
Founded in 1896

22505 **National Safety Council Congress Expo**
National Safety Council
1121 Spring Lake Drive
Itasca, IL 60143

630-775-2213
800-621-7619; Fax: 630-285-0798
customerservice@nsc.org
http://congress.nsc.org

Nancy Gavin, Expo Manager
Christine Paplaczyk, Exhibit Sales
Alan McMillan, CEO

Annual event for safety, health and the environment.
16000 Attendees
Frequency: September

22506 **Police and Security Expo**
PO Box 20068
Sarasota, FL 34276-0368

609-466-2111
800-323-1927; Fax: 609-466-2675
www.police-security.com

Displaying goods, products and services for law enforcement and security professionals.
Frequency: June

22507 **Professional Security Consultants Annual Conference**
525 SW 5th Street
Suite A
Des Moines, IA 50309-4501

515-282-8192; Fax: 515-282-9117
iapsc@iapsc.org
www.iapsc.org

David G Aggleton, President
Robert A Schultheiss, VP
Dick Goodson, Executive Director
Harold Gillens, Secretary
Frank Pisciotta, Treasurer

Seeks to enhance members knowledge through seminars, training programs, and educational materials. Works to foster public awareness of the security consulting industry.
Frequency: April
Founded in 1984

22508 **Professional Security Alliance Conference & Exhibits**
PSA Security Network
12011 N Tejon Street
Denver, CO 80234

303-520-0137; Fax: 303-252-1741
lisa@psasecurity.com
www.psasecurity.com

Lisa Speyer, Conference/Marketing
Shelley Binder, Customer/Vendor Service
Michelle Medina, Membership

For corporate management, salespeople, project managers and other technicians for PSA member companies. Educational sessions and pavillion featuring video surveillance, access control and biometrics.

22509 **Prove It! Measuring Safety Performance Symposium**
American Society of Safety Engineers
1800 E Oakton Street
Des Plaines, IL 60018

847-699-2929; Fax: 847-768-3434
customerservice@asse.org
www.asse.org
Facebook

Terrie S. Norris, President
Richard A. Pollock, President Elect
Kathy Seabrook, Senior Vice President
Fred J. Fortman, Jr., Secretary & Executive Director
James D. Smith, Vice President, Finance

Demonstrate the performance of your safety program and the value of safety. This symposium will show you how and the rewards are great. Develop leading indicators specific to safety, learn what and how to measure, and learn to use metrics to improve safety performance.
30000 Members
Founded in 1911

22510 **Rocky Mountain Health & Safety Conference**
Colorado Safety Association
4730 Oakland Street
Suite 500
Denver, CO 80239

303-373-1937; Fax: 303-373-1955
info@coloradosafety.org
www.coloradosafety.org

Melodye Turek, President
Jan Harris, Finance Manager
Judy Sapp, Manager

Over 100 exhibitors of safety products, regulatory compliance updates and networking. Educational sessions are offered on various safety topics.
Frequency: April
Founded in 1968

22511 **SAFE Association Annual Symposium**
SAFE Association
PO Box 130
Creswell, OR 97426

541-895-3012; Fax: 541-895-3014
safe@peak.org
www.safeassociation.com
Facebook

Marcia Baldwin, President
Bryan Bailey, President-Elect

Presentation topics range from desert survival to the latest aircraft passenger egress aids, cockpit design, restraint systems, and school bus design to international symbols related to transportation and safety, and crew training. Attended by an international group of professionals who are there to share problems and solutions in the field of safety and survival.
1200+ Attendees

22512 SAFE Symposium
SAFE Association
PO Box 130
Creswell, OR 97426

541-895-3012; Fax: 541-895-3014
safe@peak.org
www.safeassociation.com
Facebook

Al Loving, President
John Fair, President-Elect

The SAFE Association is dedicated to the preservation of human life. It provides a common meeting ground for the sharing of problems, ideas and information. SAFE is a non-profit international association headquartered in Oregon, with chapters located throughout the world. SAFE publishes a quarterly Newsletter and Proceedings of the Annual SAFE Symposium. These publications are valuable reference sources for the professional involved in all forms of safety and survival.
1100+ Attendees
Frequency: Quarterly
Founded in 1954

22513 Safetech
Safe & Vault Technicians Association
3003 Live Oak Street
Dallas, TX 75204-6128

214-199-9771; Fax: 214-827-1810
www.savta.org

Joanne Mims, Conventions/Meetings Manager

Annual symposium and trade show for professionals in the valuables protection industry.
Frequency: March

22514 Securing New Ground
Securing New Ground
10100 Sherman Road
Chardon, OH 44024

440-286-4900; Fax: 440-286-9169
www.securingnewground.com

Dini Jones, Conference Coordinator
Rebecca Reed, Manager

Annual 2 day conference with influential people impacting the security industry. Learn about financing, new trends and opportunities for the security industry. Breakfast, lunch and reception included.
Frequency: October

22515 Security Canada Trade Shows
Canadian Alarm & Security Association
610 Alden Road
Suite 100
Markam, ON L3R-9Z1

905-513-0622; Fax: 905-513-0624
www.canasa.org

Tracy Cannata, Executive Director
Joyce Everton, Administrative Manager
Lynne Hewiston, Trade Show Manager

Offering four shows annually. Security Canada East is in April, Security Canada Atlantic is in September, Security Canada West is in June and Security Canada Central is in October. These gaterings offer professional development, information, networking and new products to dealers, distributors, manufacturers and monitoring companies across Canada.
Founded in 1977

22516 Sensors Expo & Conference
Advanstar Communications
1 Phoenix Mill Lane
Peterborough, NH 03458

603-924-5400; Fax: 603-924-5401
www.sensorsexpo.com

Cathy Walters, Show Director
Jeanne DuVal, Sales Manager

Informative, sensor related sessions, exhibits and special events for thousands of professionals who will help shape the future of sensing technology.
Frequency: June

22517 Texas Association of Fire Educators Annual Instructors Conference
13492 Research Boulevard
Suite 120, PMB 262
Austin, TX 78750-2254
Alan Storck, President
Tim Sendelbach, VP
Jim Lee, Secretary
Patricia Clinton, Treasurer

Annual gathering for state fire safety instructors to network and learn the latest in the industry.
Frequency: January

22518 Texas Burglar & Fire Alarm Assn. Annual Meeting, Trade Show & Golf Classic
PO Box 59982
Dallas, TX 75229-1982

877-908-2322; Fax: 877-908-2522
president@tbfaa.org
www.tbfaa.org

Rex Adams, President
JD Benfer, VP
Jan Wilson, Secretary
Malcolm Reed, Treasurer

Annual gathering of a large number of professional security and fire alarm companies that operate in the state of Texas.
Frequency: October

22519 US Maritime Security Expo
EJ Krause & Associates
6550 Rock Spring Drive
Suite 500
Bethesda, MD 20817-1126

301-493-5500; Fax: 301-493-5705
www.maritimesecurityexpo.com

Lindsey Field, Show Manager
Edward Krause, President

Annual conference and exhibitor hall attended by those who protect ports, harbors, bridges, cargo containers, power plants, off shore oil rigs, railroads, cargo and passenger ships.
Frequency: September

22520 Wildland Urban Interface Conference
International Association of Fire Chiefs
4025 Fair Ridge Drive
Suite 300
Fairfax, VA 22033-2868

703-273-0911; Fax: 703-273-9363
www.iafc.org

Mark Light, Executive Director & CEO
Lisa Yonkers, Director, Conferences & Education
Shannon Gilliland, Assistant Director, Conferences
Leanne Shroeder, Conference Manager

Brings together leaders from the local, state and federal levels to collaborate against the fastest growing fire threat in the world. From education and mitigation, suppression strategies, high-hazard operations to policy, WUI addresses the toughest challenges facing the wildland firefighting community.

Directories & Databases

22521 BCSP Directory and International Registry of Certified Safety Professionals
Board of Certified Safety Professionals
2301 W. Bradley Avenue
Champaign, IL 61874-9571

217-359-9263; Fax: 217-359-0055
bcsp@bcsp.org
www.bcsp.org

Thomas L Adams, Executive Director

Directory includes over 10,000 safety professionals holding the Certified Safety Professional (CSP) or Associate Safety Professional (ASP) designation.
Circulation: 20000
Founded in 1969
Mailing list available for rent: 20,000 names
Printed in on matte stock

22522 Business Insurance Directory of Safety Consultants & Rehabilitation Mgt.
Crain Communications
360 N Michigan Ave
Chicago, IL 60601-3800

312-649-5200; Fax: 312-649-7937
KCrain@crain.com
www.crain.com

Keith Crain, CEO
Ronnie Drachman, Director Communications

List of more than 150 employee safety consultants and over 70 employee rehabilitation management providers.
Cost: $4.00
Frequency: Annual
Circulation: 53,000

22523 Computer Security Buyers Guide
Computer Security Institute
600 Harrison Street
San Francisco, CA 94107-1387

415-947-6320
800-227-4675; Fax: 415-905-2218
wwilson@infi.com

Patrice Rapalus, Editor

About 650 suppliers and consultants of computer security products, including communications and network security, disaster recovery, media security, personnel security and security training.
Cost: $197.00
Frequency: Annual
Circulation: 4,500

22524 Directory of Mail Drop Addresses and Zip Codes
Fraud & Theft Information Bureau
8400 96th Ct S
Boynton Beach, FL 33472-4400

561-732-3653; Fax: 561-732-4928
Pat Ford, Owner
Pearl Say, Editor/VP

Identifies every one of the 35,000 mail drops used by credit card thieves to steel your merchandise. Thousands of credt card thieves use thse address, which sound like residential addresses, to hide their identity and true address while stealing from you with stolen credit card numbers.
Cost: $605.50
Frequency: Annual
ISBN: 0-914801-07-4
Founded in 1982

22525 Disaster Resource Guide
Disaster Resource Guide

PO Box 15243
Santa Ana, CA 92735

FAX 714-558-8901
www.disaster-resource.com

Articles, business resources and product information for public and private emergency preparedness. Free of charge if subscriber is registered annually.
Frequency: Annual

22526 **FEMA Educational Articles**
Fire Equipment Manufacturers' Association
1300 Sumner Avenue
Cleveland, OH 44115

216-241-7333
www.femalifesafety.org/articles.html

Bill Vegso, President

Articles from the Fire Equipment Manufacturers' Association covering information on fire equipment, safety procedures and laws.
Founded in 1930

22527 **Fire Protection Equipment Directory**
Underwriters Laboratories
333 Pfingsten Rd
Northbrook, IL 60062-2096

847-412-0136
877-854-3577; Fax: 847-272-8129
www.ul.com
Facebook, Twitter, LinkedIn, You Tube

Keith E Williams, CEO
John Drengenberg, Manager Consumer Affairs

Companies that have qualified to use the UL listing mark or classification marking on or in connection with products that have been found to be in compliance with UL's requirements.
Cost: $35.00
Frequency: February

22528 **Fire Resistance Directory**
Underwriters Laboratories
333 Pfingsten Rd
Northbrook, IL 60062-2096

847-412-0136
877-854-3577; Fax: 847-272-8129
www.ul.com
Facebook, Twitter, LinkedIn, You Tube

Keith E Williams, CEO
John Drengenberg, Manager Consumer Affairs

Companies that have qualified to use the UL listing mark or classification marking on or in connection with products that have been found to be in compliance with UL's requirements. 4 book set.
Cost: $110.00
Frequency: February

22529 **Fire Retardant Chemicals Association: Membership Directory**
Fire Retardant Chemicals Association
851 New Holland Avenue
Lancaster, PA 17601-5644

202-530-4590; Fax: 717-295-4538
www.fireretardants.org

Approximately 35 member manufacturers and distributors of chemical fire retardants and related supplies.

22530 **Fire Suppression Systems Association: Membership Directory**
Fire Suppression Systems Association
5024 Campbell Boulevard
Suite R
Baltimore, MD 21236

410-931-2374; Fax: 410-931-8111

Approximately 120 member companies that design, manufacture, distribute, install or repair and maintain fire suppression systems.
Frequency: Annual

22531 **Grey House Homeland Security Directory**
Grey House Publishing
4919 Route 22
PO Box 56
Amenia, NY 12501

518-789-8700
800-562-2139; Fax: 845-373-6390
books@greyhouse.com
www.greyhouse.com
Facebook, Twitter

Leslie Mackenzie, Publisher
Richard Gottlieb, Editor

Features the latest contact information for government and private organizations involved with Homeland Security along with the latest product information. The directory provides detailed profiles of nearly 1,500 Federal & State Organizations & Agencies and over 3,000 Officials and Key Executives involved with Homeland Security.
Cost: $195.00
800 Pages
ISBN: 1-592371-96-5
Founded in 1981

22532 **Grey House Homeland Security Directory - Online Database**
Grey House Publishing
4919 Route 22
PO Box 56
Amenia, NY 12501

518-789-8700
800-562-2139; Fax: 845-373-6390
gold@greyhouse.com
gold.greyhouse.com
Facebook, Twitter

Leslie Mackenzie, Publisher
Richard Gottlieb, Editor

This comprehensive database presents a wide range of information that is scattered and hard to find elsewhere, providing subscribers with access to the most comprehensive, up-to-date and detailed information on the nation's homeland security contacts and services. This online database contains over 1,100 profiles of Federal and State agencies and companies along with the names of 11,000 key contacts.
Founded in 1981

22533 **Grey House Safety & Security Directory**
Grey House Publishing
4919 Route 22
PO Box 56
Amenia, NY 12501

518-789-8700
800-562-2139; Fax: 845-373-6390
books@greyhouse.com
www.greyhouse.com
Facebook, Twitter

Leslie Mackenzie, Publisher
Richard Gottlieb, Editor

Comprehensive guide to the safety and security industry, including articles, checklists, OSHA regulations and product listings. Focuses on creating and maintaining a safe and secure enviroment, and dealing specifically with hazardous materials, noise and vibration, workplace preparation and maintenance, electrical and lighting safety, fire and rescue and more.
Cost: $165.00
1600 Pages
ISBN: 1-592373-75-5
Founded in 1981

22534 **Grey House Transportation Security Directory**
Grey House Publishing
4919 Route 22
PO Box 56
Amenia, NY 12501

518-789-8700
800-562-2139; Fax: 845-373-6390
books@greyhouse.com
www.greyhouse.com
Facebook, Twitter

Leslie Mackenzie, Publisher
Richard Gottlieb, Editor

Information on everything from Regulatory Authorities to Security Equipment, this top-flight database brings together the relevant information necessary for creating and maintaining a security plan for a wide range of transportation facilities.
Cost: $195.00
800 Pages
ISBN: 1-592370-75-6
Founded in 1981

22535 **Kodex Security Equipment/Systems Database**
Security Defense Systems
139 Chestnut Street
#626
Nutley, NJ 07110-2311

973-235-0606
800-325-6339; Fax: 973-235-0132
www.securitydefense.com

More than 32,000 manufacturers and distributors worldwide of home and office security equipment and systems.
Cost: $295.00
Frequency: Biennial

22536 **Material Safety Data Sheet Reference**
C&P Press
565 5th Ave
5th Floor
New York, NY 10017-2413

212-587-8620; Fax: 646-733-6010
www.pharmpress.com

Regulatory and product safety requirements. Contains full text MSDS's for products listed in the Crop Protection Reference plus additional safety information such as DOT shipping information, SARA Title III regulations, Hazardous Chemical inventory reporting information plus much more. Available in print, database, continually updated electronic version or CD-ROM.

22537 **NFPA Journal: Buyers' Guide**
National Fire Protection Association
1 Batterymarch Park
Quincy, MA 02169-7471

617-770-3000
800-344-3555; Fax: 617-770-0700
www.nfpa.org

James M. Shannon, President/CEO
Peg O'Brien, Administrator - Public Affairs
Sharon Gamache, Executive Director
Bruce Mullen, CFO
Paul Crossman, VP, Marketing

List of manufacturers and consultants of fire protection, fire safety and fire service products.
Cost: $30.00
75000 Members
Frequency: February
Circulation: 95,000
Founded in 1896

22538 **National Directory of Fire Chiefs & EMS Administrators**
National Public Safety Information Bureau

2173 Church Street, Suite 201
PO Box 365
Stevens Point, WI 54481-0365

715-345-2772
800-647-7579; Fax: 715-345-7288
info@safetysource.com
www.safetysource.com

Laura Gross, Vice President of Procurement
Steve Cywinski, Account Manager
John Diser, Account Manager
Christina Scott, Business Development Manager

Vital contact resource for busy professionals. Contact nearly every fire and emergency department in the US, nearly 35,000 departments.
Cost: $129.00
Frequency: June
Circulation: 10000
Founded in 1964

22539 **National Directory of Law Enforcement Administrators**
National Public Safety Information Bureau
2173 Church Street, Suite 201
PO Box 365
Stevens Point, WI 54481-0365

715-345-2772
800-647-7579; Fax: 715-345-7288
info@safetysource.com
www.safetysource.com

Laura Gross, Vice President of Procurement
Steve Cywinski, Account Manager
John Diser, Account Manager
Christina Scott, Business Development Manager

Listing of police departments, sheriffs, criminal prosecutors, state law enforcement, criminal investigation and homeland security agencies.
Cost: $129.00
Frequency: June
Circulation: 10000
ISBN: 1-880245-22-1
Founded in 1964

22540 **National Work Zone Safety Information Clearinghouse**
Texas Transportation Institute
3135 Tamu
College Station, TX 77843-0001

979-845-1715
888-447-5556
workzone@tamu.edu

Cooperative partnership between the American Road and Transportation Builders Association and the Texas Transportation Institute. Offers information traffic accidents and crashes, equipment and technology, legislation, research projects and training.

22541 **Security Industry Sourcebook**
PRIMEDIA Business Magazines & Media
1166 Avenue of the Americas
Shawnee Mission, NY 66282-2901

212-204-4200; Fax: 913-514-6895
www.penton.com

Eric Jacobson, Senior VP

Listings of over 600 manufacturers and distributors of security and safety products.
Frequency: Annual
Circulation: 28,400

22542 **Society of Fire Protection Engineers: Membership Roster**
Society of Fire Protection Engineers
7315 Wisconsin Ave
Suite 1225W
Bethesda, MD 20814-3234

301-718-2910; Fax: 301-718-2242
info@aiia-sfpe.org
www.sfpe.org

Pamela A Powell, Editor
Kathleen Almond, Executive Director
Allan Freedman, Executive Director
Frequency: Annual February

Industry Web Sites

22543 **http://gold.greyhouse.com**
G.O.L.D Grey House OnLine Databases
Grey House Publishing's online database platform, GOLD, offers Quick Search, Keyword Search and Expert Search for most business sectors including safety and security markets. The GOLD platform makes finding the information you need quick and easy - whether you're a novice searcher or an experienced database user. All of Grey House's directory products are be available for subscription on the GOLD platform.

22544 **www.abih.org**
American Board of Industrial Hygiene
Information on credientials for Certified Industrial Hygienist status.

22545 **www.afaa.org**
Automatic Fire Alarm Association
Members are made up of manufacturers, installers and others interested in fire alarm and detection equipment. Seminars are conducted on a national basis.

22546 **www.allbounty.com**
North American Recovery Network
Worldwide portal for agents of collateral repossession and bail bonds. Chats, forums and industry news.

22547 **www.aloa.org**
Associated Locksmiths of America
Facebook, Twitter, LinkedIn
News and event information for the locksmith industry. Maintains referral service and offers insurance and bonding programs. Holds technical training.

22548 **www.apco911.org**
Association of Public-Safety Communications
Officials International

Dedicated to the enhancement of public safety communications and to serving its more than 15,000 members, the people who use public safety communications systems and services.

22549 **www.asisonline.org**
American Society for Industrial Security
Organization which features ideas and practices for business and industrial security managers.

22550 **www.asse.org**
American Society of Safety Engineers
Information for members on upcoming meetings, training and local chapters.

22551 **www.atssa.org**
American Traffic Safety Services Association
Promotes uniform use of lights, signs, pavement markings and barricades. Distributes technical information and sponsors training courses for worksite traffic supervisors.

22552 **www.bioxs.com**
Bio XS
Biometrics newsletter updated weekly. Features company profiles and new products.

22553 **www.bls.gov**
Bureau of Labor Statistics
Provides data on workplace injuries, illnesses and fatalities.

22554 **www.buildershardware.com**
Builders Hardware Manufacturers Association
Code & life safety regulation information concerning locks and builders hardware.

22555 **www.ccohs.ca**
Canadian Centre for Occupational Safety & Health
Information on safety and industrial health topics in Canada.

22556 **www.cdc.gov/niosh/homepage.html**
National Institute for Occupational Safety/Health
Information on chemical safety, emergency response, injuries, construction, mining, agriculture concerns, respirators and much more.

22557 **www.cert.org**
Carnegie Mellon Software Engineering Institute
News, statistics and helpful articles relating to computer security.

22558 **www.cisecurity.org**
Center for Internet Security
Helps organizations around the world effectively manage the risks related to internet security.

22559 **www.csrc.nist.gov**
National Institute of Standards & Technology
Information, links and white papers from the Information Technology Laboratory, the Computer Security Division and the Computer Security Resource Center.

22560 **www.disaster-resource.com**
Disaster Resource Guide
News, articles, business resources and product highlights for security and business managers as well as contingency planners who are in charge of emergency business recovery.

22561 **www.eia-usa.org**
Environmental Information Association
Nonprofit organization dedicated to providing environmental information to individuals, members and the industry. Disseminates information on the abatement of asbestos and lead-based paint, indoor air quality, safety and health issues, analytical issues and environmental site assessments.

22562 **www.fama.org**
Fire Apparatus Manufacturers' Association
Membership association for manufacturers of emergency vehicles and components affixed to or carried upon the vehicle.

22563 **www.findbiometrics.com**
Topickz
Showcases new technologies in biometric security and provides links to companies providing them.

22564 **www.first.org**
Forum of Incident Response and Security Teams
Brings together a variety of computer security incident response teams from government, com-

mercial and academic organizations. This site encourages cooperation in incident prevention, rapid reaction to incidents and to promote information sharing.

22565 **www.fraud.org**
National Consumers League
Your source for Internet and telemarketing fraud information.

22566 **www.fssa.net**
Fire Suppression Systems Association
Association news and events for designers, suppliers and installers of special hazard fire suppression equipment, gases and detectors.

22567 **www.greyhouse.com**
Grey House Publishing
Authoritative reference directories for most business sectors including safety and security markets. Users can search the online databases with varied search criteria allowing for custom searches by product category, geographic area, sales volume, keyword, subject and more. Full Grey House catalog and online ordering also available.

22568 **www.highwaysafety.org**
Insurance Institute for Highway Safety
Vehicle safety news and statistics from traffic and motor vehicle safety organization supported by auto insurers.

22569 **www.htcia.org**
Int'l High Technology Crime Investigation Assoc
A nonprofit professional organization devoted to the prevention, investigation, and prosecution of crimes involving advanced technology.

22570 **www.imsasafety.org**
International Municipal Signal Association
Basic purpose of the organization is to keep its members and others in the profession, up-to-date on proper procedures of construction and maintenance of signal systems and informed on new products and equipment developments.

22571 **www.infoguys.com**
Spyville
Process servers associations, articles and certification information, forensic experts and a searchable database for private investigators or those seeking to hire one.

22572 **www.intsi.org**
International Security Industry Organization
Dedicated to improving effcient communication to all stakeholders in the security industries and provides them with the necessary information to be more effective in their daily tasks.

22573 **www.investigativeprofessionals.com**
Investigative Professionals
Consult with a professional investigator, accomplish a people locator search, do a background check, conduct your own investigation or get information on becoming a private investigator.

22574 **www.issa.org**
Information Systems Security Association
International computer system information from an organization of security professionals and practitioners.

22575 **www.museum-security.org**
Museum Security Network
Free internet service and mailing list for museum security professionals, curators, librarians, registrar and specialized police.

22576 **www.ndia.org**
National Defense Industrial Association
To provide legal and ethical forum for the interchange of ideas between the government and industry to resolve industrial problems of joint concern.

22577 **www.net-security.org**
Help Net Security
Daily updated security related site.

22578 **www.nfpa.org**
National Fire Protection Association
The mission of the NFPA is to reduce the worldwide burden of fire and other hazards on the quality of life by providing and advocating consensus codes and standards, research, training and education.

22579 **www.nnsa.doe.gov**
National Nuclear Security Administration
Increasing public awareness of nuclear security and current energy issues. Links to website of supporting offices.

22580 **www.nsi.org**
National Security Institute
Features industry and product news, computer alerts, travel advisories, a calender of events, a directory of products and services and access to a virtual security library.

22581 **www.osh.net**
Workcare
Links to health and safety news. Offers online newslettter free to subscribers.

22582 **www.osha.gov**
Occupational Safety & Health Administration
Regulations and standards for worker safety in the US. Also included are a searchable database of recent safety violation citations, electronic safety lessons for many industries, a spot where workers can report safety concerns, safety tipsheets and a section for Spanish speaking workers.

22583 **www.pavnet.org**
Partnership Against Violence Network
Virtual library of information about violence and youth-at-risk, representing data from seven different Federal agencies.

22584 **www.personalprotection.com**
Nine Lives Associates
Information on programs which emphasize personal survival skills and techniques for the protection of others. Information on training and list of protective agents and consultants.

22585 **www.pimall.com**
PI Mall
Information for private investigator contacts, products, training and services.

22586 **www.processservers.com**
International Process Servers Association
Resource for process servers and private investigators. Message board and searchable database by zipcode to locate a local process server.

22587 **www.ready.gov**
US Government
Updates and information on how the Department of Homeland Security is working to keep America safe.

22588 **www.rims.org**
Risk & Insurance Management Society
Information on worker's compensation, enterprise risk, risk management and financing, corporate governance and risk management.

22589 **www.safeassociation.com**
SAFE Association
Website of the nonprofit organization dedicated to the preservation of human life. It provides a common meeting ground for the sharing of problems, ideas and information.

22590 **www.saferoads.org**
Advocates for Highway and Auto Safety
Information on road safety issues, federal programs, polls, reports and helpful links for consumers, safety and law enforcement agencies, insurance agents and organizations.

22591 **www.safetycentral.org**
Safety Equipment Distributors Association
Represents wholesale-distributors of safety equipment and works to enhance and improve distribution through excellence in communications, training, education and services.

22592 **www.safetysmart.com**
Bongarde Holdings
Safety education products and information.

22593 **www.safetysource.com**
National Public Safety Information Bureau
News, events, web guide and public safety shopping for professionals in corrections, EMS, fire and police departments.

22594 **www.securityfocus.com**
Symantec
Offers a forum for objective reporting by security experts on the latest computer security threats and prevention.

22595 **www.securitysales.com**
Security Sales & Integration
Breaking news of electronic security concerns and articles from the current issue of Security Sales & Integration.

22596 **www.siaonline.org**
Security Industry Association
Promotes growth, expansion and professionalism within the security industry. Online newsletter has the daily top ten headlines in security.

22597 **www.terrorismcentral.com**
Terrorism Central
Responding to the need for a single, trusted source of information about terrorism and related security issues, this central information repository comprises original and secondary sources spanning decades of research.

22598 **www.vpppa.org**
Voluntary Protection Program Participant's Assoc.
Information on the Occupational Safety and Health Administration's Voluntary Protection Participant program for companies.

Associations

22599 American Association of Advertising Agencies
1065 Avenue of the Americas
16th Floor
New York, NY 10018
212-682-2500
www.aaaa.org
Facebook, Twitter, LinkedIn, YouTube, Instagram

Marla Kaplowitz, President & CEO
Adam Cotumaccio, COO
Alison Pepper, EVP, Government Relations
Mollie Rosen, EVP, Member Engagement & Dev.
Donna Tobin, EVP, Marketing & Communications

Dedicated to helping brands create, distribute, and measure effective and insightful advertising and marketing through the use of new technology and techniques.
600+ Members
Founded in 1917

22600 Association of National Advertisers
Association of National Advertisers
10 Grand Central, 155 E. 44th Street
New York, NY 10017
212-697-5950; Fax: 212-687-7310
info@ana.net
www.ana.net
Facebook, Twitter, LinkedIn, Instagram

Bob Liodice, Chief Executive Officer
Christine Manna, President & COO
Brian Davidson, EVP, Membership
Mark Liebert, SVP, Marketing Training & Dev.
Kathleen Hunter, EVP, Marketing Knowledge Center

The Association of National Advertisers (ANA) is the advertising industry's oldest trade association. Currently, the ANA leads the marketing community by providing its members insights, collaboration, and advocacy. ANA's membership includes 20,000 brands that collectively spend over $400 billion in marketing communications and advertising.
1000 Members
Founded in 1910

22601 EMarketing Association
251 W. 30th Street
6th Floor
New York, NY 10001
212-678-2520
www.emarketingassociation.com
Twitter, LinkedIn, YouTube

International association of eMarketing professionals committed to enriching the marketing community and its members through recognition, research, advocacy, education, and service.
Founded in 1997

22602 International Network for Social Network Analysis
2900 Delk Road
Suite 700, PMB 321
Marietta, GA 30067
678-271-0342; Fax: 404-393-9506
www.insna.org
Facebook, Twitter

Laura Koehly, President
Terry Dougherty, CMP, Sr. Association Manager

The International Network for Social Network Analysis was developed for researchers interested in social network theory and understanding the online world. Members discuss the virtual community, the virtual workplace and social support.
Founded in 1977

22603 Social Media Association
Home Page: socialmediaassoc.com
Facebook, Twitter, LinkedIn, RSS, Google+, Pinterest

Julie Allegretti, Co-President
Peter Stein, Co-President

Social Media Association brings together the media community both online and offline. Members are interested in business and innovation through social, digital and future media.

22604 Social Media Club
Post Office Box 1506
Millbrae, CA 94030
caroline@socialmediaclub.org
socialmediaclub.org
Facebook, Twitter, LinkedIn, YouTube, Google+, Pinterest

Caroline A. Jones, Executive Director
Kristie Wells, Co-Founder
Chris Heuer, Co-Founder

Social Media Club was founded to host conversations around the world that explore key issues facing society as technologies transform the way we connect, communicate, collaborate and relate to each other.
300 Members
Founded in 2006

22605 Social Media Professional Association
530 Lytton Avenue
Palo Alto, CA 94301
650-600-3844
800-123-4567
Facebook, Twitter, LinkedIn, YouTube, Google+, Pinterest

The Social Media Professional Association provides training, education, and advocacy for its members. It also offers a Social Media Marketing Certification program that aids existing business owners and entrepreneurs as they grow or start new businesses in the social media and mobile web marketing fields.

22606 Social Media Research Association
630-303-9272
kathy@smra-global.org
smra-global.org
Facebook, Twitter, LinkedIn

Kathy Doering, President

A global trade association dedicated to the advocacy, promotion and development of best practices for using social media as a source for insights and marketing efficiency. SMRA offers tools, tips, and education to help its members with Social Media Listening, Analytics and Brand Reputation Management.
Cost: $45.00
Founded in 2017

22607 The Internet Association
Washington, DC
202-869-8680
news@internetassociation.org
internetassociation.org
Facebook, Twitter, LinkedIn, RSS, Google+, Flickr, YouTube

Michael Beckerman, President & CEO
Jon Berroya, SVP & General Counsel
Mashau Daee, Dir., Communications & Operations
Kacie Hackett, Manager, Events

The Internet Association represents America's leading internet companies and their global community of users. They are dedicated to policy solutions that protect internet innovations and empowers users.

22608 The Social Network Association
Facebook, Twitter, Google+, RSS

The Social Network Association is a collaborative industry forum enabling social networking businesses and users to collectively identify and resolce common issues in a productive environment. It provides a comprehensive suite of applications and services to all its members.
Founded in 2011

22609 WebProfessionals.Org
PO Box 584
Washington, IL 61571-0584
662-493-2776
membership@webprofessionals.org
webprofessionals.org
Facebook, Twitter, LinkedIn, Instagram, Pinterest, YouTube

Mark DuBois, Executive Director & Chair

Also known as the World Organization of Webmasters, WebProfessionals.org is a non-profit professional association dedicated to the support of individuals and organizations who create, manage or market web sites including Web designers, Web developers, Webmasters and Web administrators and Search and Content Specialist.
Founded in 1996

22610 Word of Mouth Marketing Association
Home Page: www.womma.org
Founded in 2004

Newsletters

22611 NRB Today
National Religious Broadcasters
9510 Technology Dr
Manassas, VA 20110-4149
703-330-7100; Fax: 703-330-7100
info@nrb.org
www.nrb.org
Facebook

Frank Wright, President/CEO
Linda Smith, EVP/COO
Kenneth Chan, Director of Communications

This weekly newsletter by National Religious Broadcasters covers the latest news from the association and NRB's member organizations. The newsletter also serves as a source for tips, trends, and insights relevant to Christian communicators across the spectrum. Topics include audience building, branding, business strategy, innovation, job hunting, leadership, management, marketing, social media, and web strategy. NRB Today also features occasional columns, movie reviews, and product reviews.
Founded in 1944

Magazines & Journals

22612 The Social Media Monthly
Home Page: www.thesocialmediamonthly.com

A monthly magazine for all things involving social media.

Trade Shows

22613 **4A's Data Summit**
American Association of Advertising Agencies
1065 Avenue of the Americas
16th Floor
New York, NY 10018

212-682-2500
www.aaaa.org

Marla Kaplowitz, President & CEO
Mollie Rosen, EVP, Member Engagement & Dev.

One-day event exploring how data will impact the advertising industry.

22614 **4A's Talent@2030**
American Association of Advertising Agencies
1065 Avenue of the Americas
16th Floor
New York, NY 10018

212-682-2500; Fax: 212-682-8391
www.aaaa.org
Twitter, Instagram, YouTube

Marla Kaplowitz, President & CEO
Mollie Rosen, EVP, Member Engagement & Dev.

Event explores how technology, social media and data are impacting people and culture.

22615 **ANA Brand Masters Conference**
Association of National Advertisers
10 Grand Central, 155 E. 44th Street
New York, NY 10017

212-697-5950; Fax: 212-687-7310
info@ana.net
www.ana.net

Bob Liodice, Chief Executive Officer
Kristen McDonough, SVP, Conferences

Effective brand marketing approaches from CMOs and marketing leaders. Conference presented by Twitter.

22616 **ANA Digital & Social Media Conference**
Association of National Advertisers
10 Grand Central, 155 E. 44th Street
New York, NY 10017

212-697-5950; Fax: 212-687-7310
info@ana.net
www.ana.net

Bob Liodice, Chief Executive Officer
Kristen McDonough, SVP, Conferences

Discussing how to use social media and digital technology to impact consumer decisions and how to effectively partner with other companies to maximize social media reach and more.

22617 **International Conference on Social Media & Society**
Social Media Lab, Ryerson University
10 Dundas Steet E
Suite 1002
Toronto, ON M5B 2G9

ask@socialmediaandsociety.org
socialmediaandsociety.org
Facebook, Twitter, Flickr

Anatoliy Gruzd, Conference Chair
Philip Mai, M.A., J.D., Conference Chair

An annual event for the world's leading social media researchers. It is the premier venue for sharing and discovering new peer-reviewed interdisciplinary research on how social media affects society. The conference offers opportunities to exchange ideas, present original research, learn about recent and ongoing studies, and network with peers.
Founded in 2010

22618 **New York Social Media Marketing Conference**
SkillPath Seminars
6900 Sqibb Road
PO Box 2768
Mission, KS 66201-2768

913-623-3900
800-873-7545; Fax: 913-362-4241
webmaster@skillpath.com
www.skillpath.com

Steve Nichols, Customer Care Representative
Robb Garr, President

This state-of-the-art conference walks through everything needed to start using social media to drive real business results, even for someone who doesn't know the difference between a tweet and a like button. There's no reason to miss out any longer on the proven, bottom-line benefits of marketing with social media.
Frequency: Semi-Annual, April

22619 **Response Expo**
201 Sandpointe Ave
Suite 500
Santa Ana, CA 92707-8700

714-338-6700
800-854-3112; Fax: 714-513-8482
thaire@questex.com
www.responsemagazine.com
Facebook, Twitter, LinkedIn, YouTube

Thomas Haire, Editor
Don Rosenberg, VP
Kristina Kronenberg, Marketing Director

Focuses on the evolution of consumers from passive watchers to active and empowered brand evangelists. Technology and social media have enabled and encouraged consumers to engage and interact with content. Learn how to take DR marketing from traditional campaign management to the future of customer engagement.
Frequency: Monthly
Circulation: 12000
Founded in 1987

22620 **Social Media Association**

Home Page: socialmediaassoc.com/events
Facebook, Twitter, LinkedIn, RSS, Google+, Pinterest

Julie Allegretti, Co-President
Peter Stein, Co-President

Social Media Association brings together the media community both online and offline. Members are interested in business and innovation through social, digital and future media.

22621 **Social Media Club**
Post Office Box 1506
Millbrae, CA 94030

caroline@socialmediaclub.org
socialmediaclub.org/events
Facebook, Twitter, LinkedIn, YouTube, Google+, Pinterest

Caroline A. Jones, Executive Director
Kristie Wells, Co-Founder
Chris Heuer, Co-Founder

Social Media Club was founded to host conversations around the world that explore key issues facing society as technologies transform the way we connect, communicate, collaborate and relate to each other.
300 Members
Founded in 2006

22622 **Sunbelt Conference**
International Network for Social Network Analysis
2900 Delk Road
Suite 700, PMB 321
Marietta, GA 30067

678-271-0342; Fax: 404-393-9506
www.insna.org
Facebook, Twitter

Laura Koehly, President
Terry Dougherty, CMP, Sr. Association Manager

The International Network for Social Network Analysis was developed for researchers interested in social network theory and understanding the online world. Members discuss the virtual community, the virtual workplace and social support.
Founded in 1977

22623 **Word of Mouth Marketing Association**
65 E. Wacker Place
Suite #500
Chicago, IL 60601

312-853-4400; Fax: 312-275-7687
membership@womma.org
www.womma.org/events-education/events
Facebook, Twitter, LinkedIn, YouTube, Google+

Suzanne Fanning, President
Chris Spallino, Director of Marketing
Jennifer Connelly, Events Manager
Chelsea Hickey, Marketing Manager & Editor
Founded in 2004

Directories & Databases

22624 **Salem Press Online Platform**
Grey House Publishing
4919 Route 22
PO Box 56
Amenia, NY 12501

800-221-1592; Fax: 201-968-0511
csr@salempress.com
online.salempress.com

The new Salem Press platform houses more than 500 titles including all of Salem's Health, Literature, History and Science titles in addition to select titles from the Grey House Publishing and H.W. Wilson product lines. Online access is free with each print purchase and includes an unlimited number of simultaneous users and remote access.

Associations

22625 ADMA Annual Meeting
Alaskan Dog Mushers Association
PO Box 70662
Fairbanks, AK 99707-0662
907-457-6874; Fax: 907-479-3516
www.sleddog.org
Facebook
Dawn Brown, Secretary
Shannon Erhart, Trustee
Paula Ciniero, President
Casey Thompson, Vice President
Alaskan Dog Mushers Association annual meeting

22626 ATP Tour
Association of Tennis Professionals
201 ATP Tour Boulevard
Ponte Vedra Beach, FL
904-856-6400
800-527-4811; Fax: 904-285-5966
www.atptennis.com
Facebook, Twitter, Instagram, Google+, Youtube
Giorgio di Palermo, Player Representative
Mark Young, Vice Chairman
Flip Galloway, Chief Operating Officer
Chris Kermode, Executive Chairman & President
Mark Webster, Tournament Representative
Operates the official tennis computer ranking system. Administers entry system for international tennis circuit and tennis system. Membership restricted to male, touring, professional tennis players.
Founded in 1972

22627 Academy for Sports Dentistry
P.O. Box 364
Farmersville, IL 62533
800-273-1788
217-227-3431ÿ; Fax: 217-227-3438
sportsdentistry@consolidated.net
www.academyforsportsdentistry.org
Facebook, Twitter
Shelly Lott, Executive Secretary
James Lovelace, President
Wayne Nakamura, President-Ellet
E. Jan Chithalen, Treasurer
W Robert Howarth, Immediate Past President
Founded in 1983

22628 Adventure Cycling Association
150 East Pine Street
PO Box 8308
Missoula, MT 59807
406-721-1776
800-755-2453; Fax: 406-721-8754
info@adventurecycling.org
www.adventurecycling.org
Facebook, Twitter, Flickr, YouTube, Instagram, Pi
Leigh Carter, General Manager
Andy baur, Secretary
Andrew Huppert, Treasurer
Donna O'Neal, Vice- President
Wally Werner, President
Their mission is to inspire people of all ages to travel by bicycle for fitness, fun and self-discovery. A non-profit organization, it is a resource offering many programs for cyclists, including a national network of bicycle touring routes and organized trips.
42000 Members
Founded in 1972

22629 Aerobics and Fitness Association of America
15250 Ventura Blvd
Suite 200
Sherman Oaks, CA 91403-3297
818-905-0040
877-968-7263; Fax: 818-788-6301
contactafaa@afaa.com
www.afaa.com
Facebook, Twitter, LinkedIn, Google+, Pinterest, Youtube, I
Linda Pfeffer, President
Association for the education, certification and training of exercise instructors; information resource center for consumers.
Founded in 1983

22630 Amateur Athletic Union of the United States
PO Box 22409
Lake Buena Vista, FL 32830
407-934-7200
800-AAU-4USA; Fax: 407-934-7242
www.aausports.org
Facebook, Twitter, YouTube, Pinterest, Instagram
Dr. Roger Goudy, President/CEO
James Parker, Director Sports
Rachel D'Orazio, Director Marketing/Websites
Pam Marshall, Director Sponsorship
Cynthia Diaz, Director Finance
The AAU hosts the Junior Olympic Games, 30 youth sports programs, 25 adult sports programs, awards over 200,000 championship medals annually, partnered with Walt Disney World to host events at Disney's Wide World of Sports Complex, and presents an annual James E. Sullivan memorial award.
500M Members
Founded in 1888

22631 Amateur Softball Association
2801 NE 50th St.ÿ
Oklahoma City, OK 73111ÿ
405-424-5266
www.asasoftball.com
Facebook, Twitter, YouTube, Instagram
Craig Cress, Executive Director
Shirley Adkins, Executive Secretary
Mark Loehrs, Chief Financial Officer
Steve Walker, Director of Operations
Savannah Edwards, Director of I.T
Founded in 1933

22632 American Academy of Podiatric Sports Medicine
109 Greenwich Dr
Walkersville, MD 21793-9121
352-620-8562
888-854-3338
301-845-9887; Fax: 352-620-8765
info@aapsm.org
www.aapsm.org
Facebook
Rita J. Yates, Executive Director
David Jenkins, President
Maggie Fournier, Secretary-Treasurer
Alex Kor, Vice-President
Amol Saxena, Director
Serves to advance the understanding, prevention and management of lower extremity sports and fitness injuries. They believe that providing such knowledge to the profession and the public will optimize enjoyment and safe participation in sports and fitness activities. They accomplish this mission through professional education, scientific research, public awareness and membership support.
800 Members
Founded in 1970

22633 American Amateur Baseball Congress
100 W Broadway
Farmington, NM 87401
505-327-3120
800-557-3120; Fax: 505-327-3132
info@aabc.us
www.aabc.us
Richard Neely, President
Mike Diamond, Executive VP
Tedra Liessmann, Secretary/Treasurer
Rusty Hill, Legal Advisor
Provides profressive and continuous organized competition for sub teens through adults.bers.
250M Members
Founded in 1935

22634 American Association of Collegiate Registrars and Admissions Officers
One Dupont Circle NW
Suite 520
Washington, DC ÿ20036ÿ
202-293-9161
202-296-3359; Fax: 202-872-8857
www.aacrao.org
Facebook, Twitter, LinkedIn, Google+
Michael Reilly, Executive Director
Melanie Gottlieb, Deputy Director
Gene Parker, Administrative Assistant
Charles Han, Asst Director, IT
Martha Henebry, Director of Operations

22635 American Baseball Coaches Association
4101 Piedmont Parkway
Suite C
Greensboro, NC 27410
336-821-3140; Fax: 336-886-0000
abca@abca.org
www.abca.org
Facebook, Twitter, LinkedIn, Google+
Bill Arce, Director
Dave Keilitz, Executive Director
Scott Berry, Immediate Past President
Mark Johnson,, Chair
Ed BlankMeyer, President
Association of Baseball Coaches in the United States.
6500 Members
Founded in 1945

22636 American Camp Association
5000 State Road 67 N
Martinsville, IN 46151-7902
765-342-8456
800-428-2267; Fax: 765-342-2065
pr@acacamps.org
www.acacamps.org
Facebook, Twitter, LinkedIn, Google+, RSS, YouTube, Pintere
Tom Holland, CEO
Tisha Bolger, Chair
Craig whiting, Treasurer
Rue Mapp, Vice-Chair
Steve Baskin, Board Members
Formerly known as the American Camping Association, is a community of camp professionals who have joined together to share their knowledge and experience and to ensure the quality of camp programs.
6700 Members
Founded in 1910

22637 American Canoe Association
503 Sophia Street
Suite 100
Fredericksburg, VA 22401
540-907-4460; Fax: 888-229-3792
aca@americancanoe.org
www.americancanoe.org

Facebook, Twitter, LinkedIn, Google+, YouTube, Pinterest, I

Jerry Dunne, At-Large
Wade Blackwood, Executive Director
Katie Hansen, Membership
Christopher Stec, Chief Operating Officer

A nationwide non-profit organization that is in service to the broader paddling public by providing education on matters related to paddling, supporting stewardship of the paddling environment, and enabling programs and events to support paddlesport recreation.
50000 Members
Founded in 1880

22638 **American College of Sports Medicine**
401 W Michigan St
Indianapolis, IN 46202-3233

317-637-9200; Fax: 317-634-7817
publicinfo@acsm.org
www.acsm.org
Facebook, Twitter, YouTube, Pinterest, Instagram

Asker Jeukendrup, Corporate Representative
Henry S. Miller, Director
Carol Ewing Garber, President-Elect
Dave Hillery, Treasurer
James Pivarnik, Foundation President

The ACSM promotes and integrates scientific research, education, and practical applications of sports medicine and exercise science to maintain and enhance physical performance, fitness, health, and quality of life.
20000 Members
ISBN: 0-195913-1 -
Founded in 1954

22639 **American Council on Exercise**
4851 Paramount Dr
San Diego, CA 92123

858-576-6500
888-825-3636; Fax: 858-576-6564
support@acefitness.org
www.acefitness.org
Facebook, Twitter, LinkedIn, Google+, Pinterest, Youtube, R

Scott Goudeseune, President & CEO
Nancy Travanian, Chair
John Ellis, Vice Chair
Ariane Amiri, Treasurer
Michele Stanten, Secretary

A nonprofit organization committed to enriching quality of life through safe and effective physical activity. ACE protects all segments of society against ineffective fitness products, programs and trends through its ongoing public education, outreach and research. ACE further protects the public by setting certification and continuing education standards for fitness professionals.
Founded in 1985

22640 **American Cutting Horse Association**
P.O. Box 2443ÿ
Brenham, TX 77834ÿ

979-836-3370; Fax: 979-251-9971
achacutting@yahoo.com
www.achacutting.org
Facebook

Ryan Combs, Board Member
Jason Borchardtÿ, President
David Wilson, Vice-President
Cary Sims, Treasurer
Trent Bell, Board Member

22641 **American Fastpitch Association**
2926 Calle Frontera
San Clemente, CA 92673

949-291-8783; Fax: 888-630-1320
info@afasoftball.com
www.afasoftball.com
Instagram

Ron Gossmer, National Director
Clarence Davis, Fastpitch Director/UIC
Joey Markakis, Slow Pitch Director

Represents those individuals engaged in amateur softball.
250M Members
Founded in 1980

22642 **American Football Coaches Association**
100 Legends Lane
Waco, TX 76706

254-754-9900; Fax: 254-754-7373
info@afca.com
www.afca.com

Grant Teaffÿ, Executive Director
Gary Darnell, Associate Executive Director
Vince Thompson, Director of Media Relations
Adam Guess, Managing Director of Finance
Janet Robertson, Director of Conferences & Events
11,00 Members
Founded in 1921

22643 **American Greyhound Track Operators Association**
Palm Beach Kennel Club
1111 North Congress Avenue
West Palm Beach, FL 33409

561-688-5799; Fax: 801-751-2404
www.agtoa.com

Juan Fra, President
Dennis Bicsak, Office Coordinator
Sally Briggs, 1st VP
Michael Corbin, Treasurer
Harold Purnell, Counsel
Founded in 1946

22644 **American Hockey Coaches Association**
7 Concord Street
Gloucester, MA 01930

781-245-4177; Fax: 781-245-2492
ahcahockey@comcast.net
www.ahcahockey.com
Facebook, Twitter, LinkedIn, YouTube, RSS

Joe Bertagna, Executive Director
Brian Riley, President
Kathy Bertagna, Membership Administrator
Bruce Delventhal, Treasurer
Brett Peterson, Past President

Maintains the highest possible standards in hockey and the hockey profession
Founded in 1947

22645 **American Orthopaedic Society for Sports Medicine**
9400 W. Higgind Rd
Suite 300
Rosemont, IL 60018

847-292-4900
877-321-3500; Fax: 847-292-4905
aossm@aossm.org
www.sportsmed.org
Facebook, Twitter

Susan Serpico, Executice Asst.
Charles A. Bush-Joseph MD, VP
Bruce Reider MD, Journal Editor
Irvin E Bomberger, Executive Director
Camille Petrick, Managing Director

A national organization of orthopaedic surgeons specializing in sports medicine, including national and international sports medicine leaders.
2000 Members
Founded in 1972

22646 **American Running Association**
4405 East West Hwy
Suite 405
Bethesda, MD 20814

301-913-9517
800-776-2732; Fax: 301-913-9520
LinkedIn

David Watt, Executive Director
Maria Kolanowsk, Project Coordinator
Barb Baldwin, Project Consultant

A leading voice and center for information on sports' running medicine. The 'ARA Clinic' provides personal feedback from a select cadre of physicians and sports medicine personnel.
10000 Members
Founded in 1968

22647 **American Society of Golf Course Architects**
125 N Executive Dr
Suite 302
Brookfield, WI 53005

262-786-5960; Fax: 262-786-5919
info@asgca.org
www.asgca.org
Facebook, Twitter, LinkedIn

Chad Ritterbusch, Executive Director
Aileen Smith, Director, Programming
Mike Shefky, Web Master
Marc Whitney, Director, Communications

A non-profit organization comprised of leading golf course designers in North America. ASGCA is actively involved in many issues realted to the game of golf, including responsible environmental designs.
185 Members
Founded in 1946

22648 **American Spa and Health Resort**
PO Box 585
Lake Forest, IL 60045

847-234-8851; Fax: 847-295-7790
Facebook

Melanie Ruehle, Contact

Seeks to establish and maintain high standards of quality in US health spas.
Founded in 1982

22649 **American Volleyball Coaches Association**
2365 Harrodsburg Road
Suite A325
Lexington, KY 40504

859-226-4315
866-544-2822; Fax: 859-226-4338
members@avca.org
www.avca.org
Facebook, Twitter, YouTube, Pinterest

Kathy Deboer, Executive Director
Ross Brown, Assistant Executive Director
Anne Kordes, President
Kevin Hambly, President Elect
Kim Norman, NAIA Rep

To advance the development of the sport of volleyball by providing all coaches with educational programs, a forum for opinion exchange and recognition opportunities.
4900 Members
Founded in 1981

22650 **Aquatic Exercise Association**
PO Box 1609
Nokomis, FL 34274-1609

941-486-8600
888-232-9283; Fax: 941-486-8820
www.aeawave.com
Facebook

Julie See, President/ Education Director
Angie Proctor, Executive Director

Dan Yeats, Event Operations Coordinator
Troy Nelson, Administrative Services Coordinator
Donna Blackmon, Operations Administrator

A not-for-profit educational organization dedicated to the growth and development of the aquatic fitness industry and the safety of the public served.
6,000 Members
Founded in 1984
Mailing list available for rent: 85,000 names

22651 **Archery Range and Retailers Organization**
156 N Main St
Suite D
Oregon, WI 53575

608-835-9060
800-234-7499; Fax: 608-835-9360

Kent Colgrove, Secretary
Martin Stubstad, President
Ervin Wagner, Treasurer
Ron Pelkey, Director
Will Moulton, Vice President

A national organization of porfessional full time archery ranges and pro shops.
140 Members
Founded in 1968

22652 **Archery Trade Association**
PO Box 70
New Ulm, MN 56073-0070

507-233-8130
866-266-2776; Fax: 507-233-8140
info@archerytrade.org
www.archerytrade.org
Facebook, Twitter

Scoff Henrikson, President/CEO
Mark Copeland, Director of Marketing
Jeff Adee, Executive Asst. to the President
Peter Gussie, Communiactions coordinator
Benjamin Summers, Dir. Of finance & Operations

Formerly the Archery Manufacturers and Merchants Organization, provides the core funding and direction for two foundations critical to the future of archery and bowhunting.
Founded in 1947

22653 **Association for the Advancement of Applied Sports Psychology**
8365 Keystone Crossing
Suite 107
Indianapolis, IN 46240

317-205-9225; Fax: 317-205-9481
info@appliedsportpsych.org
www.appliedsportpsych.org
Facebook, Twitter, YouTube

Robert Schinke, Ed.D., President
Brent Walker, Ph.D., President-Elect
Jonathan Metzler, Ph.D., CC-AAS, Past-President Elect
Rebecca Concepcion, Ph.D., Secretary-Treasurery
Kent Lindeman, CMP, Executive Director
Founded in 1986

22654 **Association of Diving Contractors International**
5206 Fm 1960 Rd W
Suite 202
Houston, TX 77069

281-893-8388; Fax: 281-893-5118
www.adc-int.org
Facebook, Twitter, LinkedIn

Phil Newsum, Executive Director
Claudio Castro, At Large Executive Committee Member
Robbie Mistretta, Treasurer
Jay Crofton, 1st VP
Craig Fortenbery, President

The Association of Diving Contractors International, Inc. was founded in 1968 by a small group of diving companies. Their goal was to create a non-profit organization to cultivate and promote the art and science of commercial diving, establish uniform safe standards for commercial divers, and encourage industry-wide observance of these standards.
500 Members
Founded in 1968

22655 **Association of Volleyball Professionalsÿ**
2183 Fairview Road
Suite 222
Costa Mesa, CA 92627

949-646-4600
contact@avp.com
www.avp.com
Facebook, Twitter, LinkedIn, Instagram, YouTube

Founded in 1983

22656 **Athletic Equipment Managers Association**
207 E, Bodman
Bement, IL 61813

217-678-1004; Fax: 217-678-1005
www.equipmentmanagers.org
Facebook, Twitter, LinkedIn

Kelly Jones, Certification Steering Committee
Mike Royster, Executive Director
Matthew Althoff, Associate Executive Director
Dan Siermine, President
Meli Resendiz, VicePresident

The purpose of the AEMA is to promote, advance, and improve the Equipment Managers Profession in all of its many phases.
700 Members
Founded in 1973
Mailing list available for rent

22657 **Billiard and Bowling Institute of America**
PO Box 6363
West Palm Beach, FL 33405

561-835-0077; Fax: 561-659-1824
bbia@billiardandbowling.org
www.billiardandbowling.org

Jeff Mraz, President
Corey Dykstra, VP
Hank Boomershine, Secretary/ Treasurer/ Con. Chairman
Skip Nemecek, Director
Mike Judy, Director

A not-for-profit association formed to service the billiard and bowling industries. The BBIA network is uniquely structured to open channels of communication between manufacturers and distributors in order to assist and improve members' business operations. BBIA provides an innovative forum for billiard and bowling businesses to share ideas, gain information, gather feedback and explore the dynamics of the product pipeline between manufacturer and end user.
150 Members
Founded in 1940

22658 **Bowling Proprietors' Association of America**
621 Six Flags Drive
Arlington, TX 76011

817-649-5105
800-343-1329; Fax: 817-633-2940
answer@bpaa.com
www.bpaamax.com

Vladmir Wapensky, Executive Director

Supports the Bowling Proprietors' Association of American Political Action Committee.
3.6M Members
Founded in 1932

22659 **College Swimming Coaches Association of America**
1640 Maple
#803
Evanston, IL 60201

847-833-3478
r-groseth@northwestern.edu
www.cscaa.org/
Twitter, LinkedIn, YouTube

Joel Shinofield, Executive Director
Bill Wadley, President
Maureen Travers, Secretary
Chuck Knoles, Treasurer
Bob Pearson, Sergeant-At-Arms

The oldest organization of college coaches in America; a professional organization of college swimming and diving coaches dedicated to serving and providing leadership for the advancement of the sport of swimming at the collegiate level.
Founded in 1922

22660 **Corporate Esports Association**
administrator@cea.gg
cea.gg
Twitter, YouTube

Brad Tenenholtz, Chief Executive Officer
Michael Pleasant, Co-Founder & Chair
Terence Southard, Co-Founder & Board Member

Facilitates online esport tournaments for corporate professionals on Discord, to enocurage team-building and donate the proceeds to charity.

22661 **Cross Country Ski Areas Association**
P.O. Box 818
Woodstock, VT 05091

802-236-3021
reese@xcski.org
www.xcski.org
Facebook, Twitter, Instagram

Reese Brown, President/Executive Director

A non-profit organization representing member ski service providers. The association's purpose is to promote the growth and improve the quality of cross country ski operations in North America.
350 Members
Founded in 1977

22662 **Disabled Sports USA**
451 Hungerford Dr.
Suite 100
Rockville, MD 20850

301-217-0960
www.disabledsportsusa.org
Facebook, Twitter, YouTube

Kirk Bauer, Executive Director

Providing opportunities to participate in sports, regardless of ability.
Founded in 1967

22663 **Diving Equipment & Marketing Association**
858-616-6408
800-862-3483; Fax: 858-616-6495
info@dema.org
www.dema.org
Facebook, Twitter, LinkedIn, YouTube, RSS, Instagram

Tom Ingram, President & CEO
Nicole Russel, VP, Operations
Colleen Vasquez, VP, Finance
Rachelle Reimers, Communications Manager
Alicia Vasquez, Member Services Assistant

Trade association for the international scuba diving industry.
1400 Members

22664 Esports Trade Association
541 N. Fairbanks Court
Suite 2200
Chicago, IL 60611
708-680-7133
info@esportsta.org
esportsta.org
Facebook, Twitter, LinkedIn, YouTube, Instagram
Megan Van Petten, Founder & CEO
The ESTA serves the esports community by promoting, protecting, and advancing its interests through professional development programs, networking opportunities, industry research, and tools and resources for members.
Founded in 2018

22665 Fantasy Sports & Gaming Association
1818 Parmenter Street
Suite 300
Middleton, WI 53562
608-310-7540
thefsga.org
Facebook, Twitter, LinkedIn
Christina McCoy, Executive Director
Michael Fiez, Marketing
Emily Petersen, Membership
The FSGA is a national organization representing fantasy sports and gaming companies, and serving those companies and players with research and data, networking opportunities, and collective action.

22666 Football Writers Association of America (FWAA)
18652 Vista Del Sol Dr
Dallas, TX 75287-4021
972-713-6198
tigerfwaa@aol.com
www.sportswriters.net/fwaa
Twitter
Leeÿ Barfknecht, President
Steve Richardson, Executive director
George Schroeder, Board of Director
Mark Anderson, 1st VP
David Jones, 2nd VP
Established to improve working conditions in college press boxes.
900 Members
Founded in 1941
Mailing list available for rent: 800 names at $50 per M

22667 Golf Coaches Association of America
1225 West Main Street
Suite 110
Norman, OK 73069
405-329-4222
866-422-2669; Fax: 405-573-7888
info@collegiategolf.com
www.collegiategolf.com
Facebook, Twitter
Conrad Ray, President
Andrew Sapp, 1st Vice President
Ryan Klatt, Director of Operations
Gregg Grost, CEO
Todd Sattefield, Past President
Founded in 1958

22668 Golf Superintendents Association of America
1421 Research Park Dr
Lawrence, KS 66049
785-841-2240
800-472-7878; Fax: 785-832-3643
www.gcsaa.org
Facebook, Twitter
J. Rhett Evans, CEO
Keith A. Ihms, Immediate Past President
William H. Maynard, Secretary /Treasurer
Peter J Grass, Vice President
John J. O'Keefe, President
Provides education programs in formal settings and at home through videotapes and correspondence courses. Administers professional certification programs, publishes magazines and multiple newsletters, conducts and supports research, provides scholarship opportunities, offers employment assistance and career development support, promotes the image of the golf course superintendent through cable TV program 'Par For The Course' and other vehicles. Provides leadership in governmental issues.
22000 Members
Founded in 1926

22669 Harness Tracks of America
4640 E Sunrise Dr
Suite 200
Tucson, AZ 85718-4576
520-529-2525; Fax: 520-529-3235
www.harnesstracks.com
Facebook, Twitter
Paul J. Estok, Executive VP &General Counsel
Paul Fontaine, President
Hugh Mitchell, Chairman
Christopher Mcerlean, Treasurer
Jason Settlemoir, VP
Mission is to help members obtain their economic objectives by promoting live racing, enhancing and preserving the integrity and image of the sport, and providing information to members and the general public about the sport and the significant economic impact of the industry.
35 Members

22670 Ice Skating Institute
6000 Custer Rd
Bldg 9
Plano, TX 75023
972-735-8800; Fax: 972-735-8815
isi@skateisi.org
www.skateisi.org
Facebook, Twitter, LinkedIn, Pinterest, Google+
Peter Martell, Executive Director
Elizabeth Kibat, Controller
Jeff Anderson, Administrative Service Manager
Sandey Carlsen, Membership Coordinator
Angela Tooley, Administrative Assistant
Industry trade association dedicated to providing leadership, education and services to the ice skating industry.
64500 Members
Founded in 1959

22671 International Federation of American Football
79 Rateau Street
La Courneuve 93120
info@ifaf.org
www.ifaf.org
Twitter, YouTube
Makato Keneuji, Senior Vice President
Scottÿ Hallenbeck, Treasurer
Elesa Zehndorfer, Secretary
Founded in 1896

22672 International Professional Rodeo Association
1412 S Agnew Ave
Oklahoma City, OK 73108
405-235-6540; Fax: 405-235-6577
www.iprarodeo.com
Ronnie Williams, Chief Field Representative
Tom Schick, Chairman
Lindsay Whelchel, Membership/Receptionist
Dale Yerigan, General manager
Tammie Hiatt, IFR Tradshow Coordinator
Governing body for professional rodeo. 500 rodeos across USA and Canada, $5 million prize money per year, 5 million fans.
3500 Members
Founded in 1960

22673 International Sports Heritage Association
PO Box 2384
Florence, OR 97439
541-991-7315; Fax: 541-997-3871
info@sportsheritage.org
www.sportsheritage.org
Facebook, Twitter
Karen Bednarski, Executive Director
Marjorie Snyder, President
Susan Wasser, First Vice President
Paula Homan, Second Vice President
Megan Gardner, Treasurer
The mission of ISHA is to educate, promote and support organizations and individuals engaged in the celebration of sports heritage.
140+ Members
Founded in 1971

22674 Ladies Professional Golf Association
100 International Golf Dr
Daytona Beach, FL 32124-1092
386-274-6200; Fax: 386-274-1099
www.lpga.com
Facebook, Twitter, RSS, YouTube, Instagram, Pinte
Carolyn Bivens, CEO
Karen Durkin, EVP/Chief Marketing Officer
Christopher Higgs, Senior VP/COO
Ken Wooten, VP Finance
Micahael Whan, Commissioner
The LPGA is a non-profit organization involved in every facet of golf. In addition to staging the LPGA Tour, the LPGA is also committed to advancing women, youth and the sport of golf through expanding the programs of the LPGA Teaching and Club Professional Division, as well as increasing contributions of the organization and its tournaments to charity.
Founded in 1959

22675 League of American Bicyclists
1612 K Street NW
Suite 1102
Washington, DC 20006-2850
202-822-1333; Fax: 202-822-1334
bikeleague@bikeleague.org
www.bikeleague.org
Facebook, Twitter, LinkedIn, Google+
Alex Doty, Executive Director
Bill Nesper, Deputy Director, Programs & Ops
Kevin Dekkinga, Member Services Coordinator
Lorna Green, Operations, Manager
Founded in 1880, the League is the only national membership organization of bicyclists in the United States. The League works to promote and encourage bicycling for recreation and transportation, and to protect and defend the rights of bicyclists through advocacy and education.
Founded in 1880

22676 **Major League Gaming**
Home Page: www.mlg.com
Facebook, Twitter, YouTube, Instagram, Snapchat
Steve Bornstein, Chairman
Pete Vlastelica, President & CEO
Michael Sepso, Co-Founder & SVP, Media Networks
Sundance DiGiovanni, Co-Founder & VP, Brands & Content
Pavel Murnikov, VP, Technology
A professional eSports organization. MLG.tv, its free video streaming eSports showcase, attracts 27 million users per month.
Founded in 2002

22677 **Melbourne Greyhound Park**
1100 N Wickham Rd
Melbourne, FL 32935
321-259-9800; Fax: 321-259-3437
www.mgpark.com
Facebook, Twitter, YouTube, RSS
James J O'Brien, General Manager
Trade association representing the interest of and providing services to greyhound racetrack owners and operators via government advocacy, information sharing, annual conference and trade shows.
35 Members
Founded in 1971
Mailing list available for rent

22678 **National Aeronautic Association**
1 Reagan National Airport
Suite 202
Washington, DC 20001-6015
703-416-4888
800-644-9777; Fax: 703-416-4877
naa@naa.aero
www.naa-usa.org
Jonathan Gaffney, President
George Carneal, General Counsel
Walter J. Boyne, Chairman
Roy Kiefer, Treasurer
Elizabeth Matarese, Secretary
A non-profit association dedicated to the advancement of the art, sport and science of aviation in the United States. The official record-keeper for United States aviation.
3000 Members
Founded in 1922

22679 **National Amateur Baseball Association**
PO Box 705
Bowie, MD 20718
410-721-4727; Fax: 410-721-4940
nabf1914@aol.com
www.nabf.com
Facebook
Thomas Stout, Director
Derel J Topik, First VP
Glenn McNish, Second VP
Connie Brown, Third VP
Charles Blackburn Jr, Executive Director
The oldest continually operated national basesball organization in the country.
10M Members
Founded in 1914

22680 **National Archery Association (USA Archery)**
4065 Sinton Road
Suite 110
Colorado Springs, CO 80907
719-866-4576; Fax: 719-632-4733
www.usarchery.org
Facebook, Twitter, YouTube, Instagram, Google+, P
Denise Parker, CEO
Sheri Rhodes, Chairman
Denise Parker, Chief Executive Officer
Amber Hildebrand, Accounting Assistant
Cindy Clark, Office/Finance Manager
Formed to develop and promote the sport of archery. Recognized by the US Olympic committee as the national governing body for the olympic sport of archery. The NAA selects and trains mens and womens archery teams to represent the US in international, pan american and olympic competitions.
8500 Members
Founded in 1894

22681 **National Association of Basketball Coaches**
1111 Main St
Suite 1000
Kansas City, MO 64105-2136
816-878-6222; Fax: 816-878-6223
www.nabc.com
Facebook, Twitter
Paul Hewitt, 4th VP
Jeff Jones, 3rd VP
Ron Hunter, 2nd VP
Page Moir, 1st VP
Phil Martelli, President
Promotes the advancement and opportunities for coaches and teachers in the sport of basketball.
5000 Members
Founded in 1927

22682 **National Association of Collegiate Directors of Athletics**
24651 Detroit Rd
Cleveland, OH 44145
440-892-4000; Fax: 440-892-4007
www.nacda.com
Facebook, Twitter
Erin Dengler, Manager-Communications
Ryan Virtue, Manager- Affiliate Associations
Jason Galaska, Asst. Executive Director
Bob Vecchione, Executive Director
Noreen Byrne, Business Manger
Professional association for college atheltics directors, assistants and conference administrators. Provides educational opportunities and serves as a vehicle for networking and the exchange of information to others in the college sports profession.
1.5M Members
Founded in 1965

22683 **National Association of Collegiate Women Athletic Administrators**
2024 Main Street
#1W
Kansas City, MO 64108
816-389-8200; Fax: 816-389-8220
Facebook, Twitter, LinkedIn, YouTube, Pinterest
Joan McDermott, President
Lynn Hickey, President Elect
Chris Plonsky, Past President
Erin McDermott, Treasurer
Lori Mazza, Secretary

22684 **National Association of Professional Baseball Leagues**
1325 Franklin Ave.
Suite 160
Garden City, NY 11530
727-822-6937; Fax: 727-821-5819
inquire@napw.com
www.napw.com
Facebook, Twitter, LinkedIn, Pinteresr
Mike Moore, President
RJ Sparks, Promotional Director
Two hundred and seventy booths.
2.5M Members

22685 **National Association of Sporting Goods Wholesalers**
1255 SW Prairie Trail Parkway
Ankeny, IA 50023-7068
515-334-1484; Fax: 515-334-1143
info@nasgw.org
www.nasgw.org
Facebook, Twitter, Flickr
Kenyon Gleason, President
Meg Pawelski, Director, Operations & Expo Manager
Easton Kuboushek, Program Manager
Donna Donovan, Financial Manager
Gregg Alexander, Communications Manager
Non-profit trade association of wholesalers, distributors and manufacturers. Serves as a liaison with other sporting goods associations.
400 Members
Founded in 1953

22686 **National Association of Sports Commissions**
9916 Carver Rd.
Suite 100
Cincinnati, OH 45242
513-281-3888; Fax: 513-281-1765
info@SportsCommissions.org
www.sportscommissions.orgÿ
Facebook, Twitter, LinkedIn, Pinterest, YouTube, WordPress
Kevin Smith, CSEE, Chairman
Greg Ayers, CSEE, Vice Chairman/Chair-Elect
Ralph Morton, CSEE, Treasurer
Mike Anderson, CSEE, Secretary
Terry Hasseltine, CSEE, Immediate Past Chair
Founded in 1992

22687 **National Association of Sports Officials**
2017 Lathrop Ave
Racine, WI 53405
262-632-5448
800-733-6100; Fax: 262-632-5460
naso@naso.org
www.referee.com
Facebook, Twitter
Barry Mano, President
Marc Ratner, Chair
Anita Ortega, Vice Chair
Henry Zaborniak, Treasurer
Nonprofit 501(c)(3), educational association providing individual benefits such as training materials, liability and assault protection insurance and more to sports officials of all sports and every level.
16000 Members
Founded in 1976

22688 **National Association of Student Financial Aid Administrators**
1101 Connecticut AvenueÿNW
Suite 1100
Washington, DC 20036-4303
202-785-0453; Fax: 202-785-1487
www.nasfaa.org
Facebook, Twitter, LinkedIn, YouTube, Google+
Eileen O'Leary, National Chair
Dan Mann, National Chair-Elect
Craig Munier, Past National Chair
Justin Draeger, President
Lori Vedder, Treasurer

22689 National Athletic Trainers Association
1620 Valwood Parkway
Suite 115
Carrollton, TX 75006
214-637-6282
860-437-5700; Fax: 214-637-2206
webmaster@nata.org
www.nata.org
Facebook, Twitter, LinkedIn
Eve Becker-Doyle, Executive Director
Teresa Foster Welch, Assistant Executive Director
Karen Peterson, Manager Executive Operations
Ellen Satlof, Public Relations Manager
Cynthia Nadel, Marketing Coordinator
Association for professionals in athletic training.
28000 Members
Founded in 1950

22690 National Athletics Trainers' Associationÿ
1620 Valwood Parkway
Suite 115
Carrolltonÿ, TX 75006
214-637-6282
860-437-5700; Fax: 214-637-2206
www.nata.org
Facebook, Twitter, LinkedIn
Jim Thornton, MS, ATC, CES, President
MaryBeth Horodyski, EdD, Vice President
Marjorie Albohm, Past President
Tim Weston, MEd, ATC, Board of Director, District 1
Michael Goldenberg, MS, ATC, Board of Director, District 2
35,00 Members
Founded in 1950

22691 National Basketball Athletic Trainers Association
400 Colony Square
Suite 1750
Atlanta, GA 30361
404-892-8919; Fax: 404-892-8560
www.nbata.com
Tom Badenour, Chairman
A satelite of the National Athletic Trainers Association. Members are athletic trainers in the NBA.
60 Members
Founded in 1974

22692 National Bicycle Dealers Association
3972 Barranca Pkwy
Suite J-423
Irvine, CA 92606
949-722-6909
info@nbda.com
www.nbda.com
Brandee Lepak, Chairman
Kent Cranford, Vice Chair
Rachelle Schouten, Admin. Coordinator
The mission of the NBDA is to inspire and serve the specialty bicycle retailer through communicating the value and needs of the specialty bicycle retailer, enhancing the specialty bicycle retailer's profitability, and promoting the passion for cycling. The NBDA is a non-profit association promoting the interests of every specialty bicycle retailer in the United States.
2MM Members
Founded in 1946

22693 National Collegiate Athletic Associationÿ
700 W. Washington Street
P.O. Box 6222
Indianapolis, IN 46206-6222
317-917-6222; Fax: 317-917-6888
www.ncaa.org
Facebook, Twitter, YouTube, Instagram
Mark Emmert, President

22694 National Cutting Horse Association
260 Bailey Avenue
Fort Worth, TX 76107
817-244-6188; Fax: 817-244-2015
www.nchacutting.com
Facebook, Twitter, RSS
Keith Deaville, President
Ernie Beutenmiller, VP
Jeff Hooper, Executive Director
Members are individuals and organizations interested in the development of superior horses and the refinement of the cutting horse competition.
20500 Members
Founded in 1946

22695 National Fastpitch Coaches Association
2641 Grinstead Drive
Louisville, KY 40206
502-409-4600; Fax: 502-409-4622
nfca@nfca.org
www.nfca.org
Facebook, Twitter, LinkedIn
Rhonda Revelle, President
Kathryn Gleason, First VP
Kate Drohan, Second VP
The professional growth organization for fastpitch softball coaches from all competitives levels of play.
4100 Members
Founded in 1983

22696 National Golf Cart Manufacturers Association
NGCMA Attn: Fred Somers, Jr.
2 Ravinia Drive
Suite 1200
Atlanta, GA 30346
770-394-7200; Fax: 770-454-0138
www.ngcma.org
Fred L Somers, Jr, Secretary & General Counsel
Non-profit national trade association comprised of the leading golf car and personal transport vehicle manufacturers. NGCMA sponsors the development and maintenance of ANSI sanctioned standards to establish safety specifications for the design and operation of golf cars and PTVs driven by electric motors and internal combustion engines for golf cars.
Founded in 1984

22697 National Golf Foundation
501 N Highway A1A
Suite 401
Jupiter, FL 33477-4577
561-744-6006
888-275-4643; Fax: 561-744-6107
general@ngf.org
www.ngf.org
Facebook, Twitter, LinkedIn
Joseph Beditz, President/CEO
Greg Nathan, Sr. Vice President/ Membership
The National Golf Foundation, founded in 1936 and based in Jupiter, Fla., is the industry's knowledge leader on the U.S. golf economy and leading provider of golf industry databases. NGF delivers independent and objective narket intelligence, insights and trends to fulfill its mission: To Keep Golf Businesses Ahead of the Game.
4000 Members
Founded in 1936

22698 National High School Baseball Coaches Association
PO Box 12843
Tempe, AZ 85284
602-615-0571; Fax: 480-838-7133
rdavini@cox.net
www.baseballcoaches.org
Ron Davini, Executive Director
Provides services and recognition for baseball coaches and to help promote and represent high school baseball across this country.
1600 Members
Founded in 1991

22699 National Hockey League
1185 Avenue of the Americas
Floor 15
New York, NY 10036
212-789-2000; Fax: 212-789-2020
www.nhl.com
Facebook, Twitter, LinkedIn
Gary Bettman, Commissioner
William Daly, Deputy Commissioner
John Collins, COO
The NHL is one of the four major professional sports associations in North America, with 30 professional ice hockey franchises in the US and Canada.

22700 National Junior College Athletic Association
1631 Mesa Ave
Suite B
Colorado Springs, CO 80906
719-590-9788; Fax: 719-590-7324
meleicht@njcaa.org
www.njcaa.org
Facebook, Twitter, Pinterest
Mary Ellen Leicht, Executive Director
Mark Krug, Ass. Executive Director
Bryce Roderick, President
The purpose of the NJCAA is to promote and foster junior college athletics on intersectional and national levels so that results will be consistent with the total educational program of its members.
525 Members
Founded in 1938

22701 National Pro Fastpitch
3350 Hobson Pike
Hermitage, TN 37076
615-232-2900; Fax: 615-232-8880
info@profastpitch.com
www.profastpitch.com
Facebook, Twitter, YouTube, Instagram
Cheri Kempf, Commissioner
Gaye Lynn Wilson, Vice President
Ed Whipple, Supervisor of Officials
Cynthia Gerken, NPF Travel Agent
Nikki Worthman, NPF Intern

22702 National Recreation and Park Association
22377 Belmont Ridge Road
Ashburn, VA 20148-4501
703-858-0784
800-626-6772; Fax: 703-858-0794
info@nrpa.org
www.nrpa.org
Facebook, Twitter, LinkedIn, YouTube, Pinterest
Kristine Stratton, President & CEO
Autumn Saxton-Ross, Chief Equity Officer/VP, Education

Gina Mullins-Cohen, Chief Marketing Officer/VP, Comm.
Brenda Camacho, Chief Financial Officer/VP, Ops.
Julie Boland, VP, Membership & Certification
Advancing parks, recreation and environmental conservation efforts that enhance the quality of life for all people.
Founded in 1965

22703 National Rifle Association of America
11250 Waples Mill Rd
Fairfax, VA 22030-7400

703-267-1400; Fax: 703-267-3970
membership@nrahq.org
Facebook, Twitter

Oldest sportsmen's organization in the US. Maintains the NRA Political Victory Fund and supports the Institute for Legislative Action. Has an annual budget over $140 million.
4 Members
Founded in 1871

22704 National Soccer Coaches Association of America
30 W. Pershing Rd.
Suite 350
Kansas City, MO 64108

816-471-1941; Fax: 816-474-7408
info@nscaa.com
www.nscaa.com

George Perry, President
Mike Jacobs, VP, Events
Amanda Vandervort, VP, Marketing
Charlie Slagle, VP, Education
Lesle Gallimore, VP, Membership
Founded in 1941

22705 National Sporting Goods Association
1601 Feehanville Dr
Suite 300
Mt Prospect, IL 60056

847-296-6742
800-815-5422; Fax: 847-391-9827
info@nsga.org
www.nsga.org
Facebook, Twitter, LinkedIn, Flickr, YouTube

Ken Meehan, Chairman
Randy Nill, Treasurer/Chairman Elect
Matt Carlson, President
Association of retailers, manufacturers and suppliers of sports equipment, footwear, and apparel.
2000+ Members
Founded in 1929

22706 National Strength and Conditioning Association
1885 Bob Johnson Dr.
Colorado Springs, CO 80906

719-632-6722
800-815-6826; Fax: 719-632-6367
www.nsca.com

Steven J. Fleck, PhD, President
Todd Miller, PhD, Vice President
Colin Wilborn, PhD, Treasurer-Secretary
Michael Embree, Executive Director
Levi Boren, PhD, Sr. Director of Certification
Founded in 1978

22707 National Youth Sports Coaches Association
2050 Vista Parkway
West Palm Beach, FL 33411

636-797-5334
800-688-5437; Fax: 561-684-2546
nysca@nays.org
www.nays.org
Facebook, Twitter, LinkedIn, YouTube, RSS, Pinterest, Googl

Represents coaches involved in youth athletics.
Founded in 1981

22708 Outdoor Recreation Roundtable
1203 K Street NW
Suite 350
Washington, DC 20005

202-682-9530
recreationroundtable.org
Facebook, Twitter

Jessica Wahl, Executive Director
Phil Ingrassia, Chair
Frank Hugelmeyer, Vice Chair
Glenn Hughes, Treasurer
Chris Edmonston, Secretary
A non-profit Washington based federation that provides a unified voice for recreation interests to conserve their full and active participation in government policy making on issues such as public land management. ORR works to build public-private partnerships to enhance and protect outdoor recreation opportunities and resources.
100+ Members
Founded in 1979

22709 Pop Warner Little Scholars
586 Middletown Boulevard
Suite C-100
Langhorne, PA 19047-1867

215-752-2691; Fax: 215-752-2879
webmaster@popwarner.com
www.popwarner.com
Facebook, Twitter, LinkedIn, YouTube, Rss

Jon Butler, Executive Director
Mary Fitzgerald, COO
Lisa Moroski, National Cheer/Dance Commissioner
A national youth football and cheerleading organization that provides assistance to its various chapters.
400M Members
Founded in 1929

22710 Professional Association of Diving
30151 Tomas
Rcho Sta Marg, CA 92688-2125

949-858-7234
800-729-7234; Fax: 949-267-1267
webmaster@padi.com
www.padi.com
Facebook, Twitter, YouTube

Brian Cronin, CEO
Certifies scuba diving instructors. Provides education/training materials and retail support to its members.
67M Members
Founded in 1966

22711 Professional Association of Volleyball Officials
PO Box 780
Oxford, KS 67119

888-791-2074; Fax: 620-455-3800
pavo@pavo.org
www.pavo.org

Julie Voeck, President
Joan Powell, President
Crystal Lewis, Board Delegate
Ben Jordan, Director Examinations
Karen Gee, Director Finance
The Professional Association of Volleyball Officials is dedicated to improving the quality of volleyball officiating for all rules codes and skill levels. PAVO strives to increase the number of competent officials through education and mentoring and promotes involvement in the governing bodies of other volleyball officiating groups.
2M Members

22712 Professional Baseball Athletic Trainers Society
1201 Peachtree St Ne
Suite 1750
Atlanta, GA 30361-6320

404-875-7990; Fax: 410-730-2219
www.pbats.com
Facebook, Twitter, RSS

Jamie Reed, President
Jim Carroll, Director Public Relations
Serve as an educational resource for the Major League and Minor League baseball athletic trainers. Serves its members by providing for the continued education of the athletic trainer as it relates to the profession, helping improve his understanding of sports medicine so as to better promote the health of his constituency - professional baseball players.
60 Members
Founded in 1983

22713 Professional Bowlers Association
615 Second Ave
Seattle, WA 98104

206-332-9688; Fax: 206-332-9722
info@pba.com
www.pba.com
Facebook, Twitter, Youtube, RSS

Fred Schreyer, CEO
Steve Miller, Board Member
Lisa Gil, VP Brand Communications
Acts on behalf of professional bowlers.
3800 Members
Founded in 1958

22714 Professional Esports Association

pea@cloud9.gg
www.proesports.org
Facebook, Twitter, Instagram

PEA is a coalition of eSports teams aiming to advance the industry and grow the business of eSports.
Founded in 2016

22715 Professional Football Athletic Trainer Society
1201 Peachtree St Ne
Suite 1750
Atlanta, GA 30361-6320

404-875-7990; Fax: 404-892-8560
www.pfats.com
Facebook, Twitter, Youtube, RSS

Rollin E Mallernee II, President
Professional association whose members are the athletic trainers of the NFL. They provide, lead and manage helathcare for the NFL athletes, club employees and members of the NFL community. Dedicated to insuring the highest quality health care is practiced. Guided by the profesional integrity and ethical standards of its members and by the unity they share.
650 Members
Founded in 1982

22716 Professional Golfers Association (PGA)
100 Ave of the Champions
Palm Beach Gdns, FL 33418

561-624-8400; Fax: 561-624-8448
www.pga.com
Facebook, Twitter, Google+

Ted Bishop, President
Derek Sprague, Vice President
Paul Levy, Secretary
Peter Bevacqua, CEO

The world's largest working sports organization comprised of more than 25,000 men and women PGA professionals to promote the game of golf to everyone, and to promote its members as leaders in the golf industry.
28000 Members
Founded in 1916

22717 Professional Inline Hockey Association
1733 East Harrisburg Pike
Middletown, PA 17057
719-200-4208
www.thepiha.com
Charles Yoder, Founder
CJ Yoder, President
Jami Yoder, VP
Jim Vanhorn, Chief Financial Officer
Denis Jelcic, Commissioner

22718 Professional Skaters Association
3006 Allegro Park Ln Sw
Rochester, MN 55902
507-281-5122; Fax: 507-281-5491
office@skatepsa.com
www.skatepsa.com
Facebook, Twitter, LinkedIn, Pinterest, YouTube
Jimmie Santee, Executive Director
Kelley Morris, First VP
Jackie Brenner, Third VP
Donna Wells, Administrative Assistant
Barb Yackel, Marketing & Events
An international organization responsible for the education of skating coaches. Membership is offered to coaches in every discipline and at all levels, as well as to performing professionals, judges, eligible skaters and friends or patrons of the sport of figure skating.
6000 Members
Founded in 1938

22719 Roller Skating Association
6905 Corporate Dr
Indianapolis, IN 46278
317-347-2626; Fax: 317-347-2636
rsa@rollerskating.com
www.rollerskating.org
Facebook, Twitter, LinkedIn, YouTube, Pinterest, Google+
Jim McMahon, Executive Director
Tonya Crenshaw, Accountant
Lynette Rowland, Director, Communications
Angela Tanner, Assistant Executive Director
Sharon McMahon, Director, Membership Services
A trade association representing skating center owners and operators; teachers, coaches and judges of roller skating; and manufacturers and suppliers of roller skating equipment.
1000 Members
Founded in 1937

22720 Society for American Baseball Research
555 N. Central Ave.
#416
Phoenix, AZ 85004
602-496-1460
800-969-7227; Fax: 602-595-5690
info@sabr.org
www.sabr.org
Facebook, Twitter, Youtube
Vince Gennaro, President
Bill Nowlin, VP
Todd Lebowitz, Secretary
F X Flinn, Treasurer
Emily Hawks, Director
Foisters the study of baseball past and present and provides an outlet for educational, historical and research information about the game.
6700 Members
Founded in 1971
Mailing list available for rent: 25000 names at $85 per M

22721 Society of Health and Physical Educators
1900 Association Dr
Reston, VA 20191-1598
703-476-3400
800-213-7193; Fax: 703-476-9527
membership@shapeamerica.org
www.shapeamerica.org
Facebook, Twitter, Instagram
Stephanie A. Morris, Chief Executive Officer
Organization that provides educational programs, resources and support for professionals within the fields of health, physical education, recreation and dance.
25000 Members
Founded in 1885

22722 Sporting Arms and Ammunition Manufacturers Institute
11 Mile Hill Rd
Newtown, CT 06470-2359
203-426-4358; Fax: 203-426-3592
www.saami.org
Steve Sanetti, President
Rick Patterson, Managing Director
SAAMI is an association of the nation's leading manufacturers of sporting firearms, ammunition, and components.
Founded in 1926

22723 Sporting Goods Agents Association (SGAA)
PO Box 998
Morton Grove, IL 60053
847-296-3670; Fax: 847-827-0196
sgaa998@aol.com
LinkedIn
Skip Nipper, President
Lois Halinton, Chief Operating Officer
International trade association of independent and established sporting goods agents.
500 Members
Founded in 1934

22724 Sporting Goods Manufacturers Association
8505 Fenton Street
Suite 211
Silver Spring, MD 20910
301-495-6321; Fax: 301-495-6322
info@sfia.org
www.sfia.org
Tom Cove, President & CEO
Chip Baldwin, CFO
Bill Sells, VP, Government Relations
Ron Rosenbaum, SVP, Marketing & Business Dev
Jan Ciambor, Office Manager
SGMA is the trade association of North American manufacturers, producers, and distributers of sports apparel, athletic footwear, fitness, and sporting goods equipment. SGMA represents and supports its members through programs and strategies for sports participation, market intelligence, and public policy.
1000 Members
Founded in 1906

22725 Sports Turf Managers Association
805 New Hampshire St
Suite E
Lawrence, KS 66044
785-843-2549
800-323-3875; Fax: 785-843-2977
www.stma.org
Facebook, LinkedIn
Tom Cove, President
David Pinsonneault, President Elect
Rene Aspiron, VP
Allen Johnson, Secretary/Treasurer
Chip Baldwin, CFO
Grounds care for golf and athletic fields.
2500 Members
Founded in 1981

22726 Sportsplex Operators and Developers Association
Westgate Station
P.O. Box 24617
Rochester, NY 14624-0617
585-426-2215; Fax: 585-247-3112
info@sportsplexoperators.com
www.sportsplexoperators.com
John Fitzgerald, President
Diane Aselin, Executive VP
Don Aselin, National Executive Director
Steve Russell, Canadian Vice President
David Maury, Secretary
SODA was formed to meet the needs of the private concerns, public agencies, and other organizations that own or maintain sports complex facilities throughout the US and Canada.
1600 Members
Founded in 1981

22727 Tennis Industry Association
117 Executive Center
1 Corpus Christie Place
Hilton Head Island, SC 29928
843-686-3036; Fax: 843-686-3078
info@tennisindustry.org
www.tennisindustry.org
Facebook, Twitter, LinkedIn, YouTube, Google+, RSS, Pintere
Jon Muir, President
Jolyn DeBoer, Executive Director
Brian O'Donnell, National Coordinator
To educate the marketplace, fund research and market intelligence and supply this reliable industry data to our member companies. The TIA is the Information source and clearing house for positive tennis news that we supply to TIA members, tennis publications and to the mainstream media in cooperation with the USTA.
800 Members
Founded in 1974

22728 The College Golf Foundation
1225 West Main Street
Suite 110
Norman, OK 73069
405-329-4222; Fax: 405-573-7888
info@collegiategolf.com
www.collegiategolf.com
Facebook, Twitter
Conrad Ray, President
Andrew Sapp, 1st Vice President
Greg Sands, 2nd Vice President
Mark Crabtree, 3rd Vice President
Todd Sattefield, Past President
Founded in 1958

22729 The United States Association of Blind Athletes
1 Olympic Plaza
Colorado Springs, CO 80909
719-866-3224; Fax: 719-866-3400
www.usaba.org
Facebook, Twitter
Dave Bushland, President
Tracie Foster, Vice President
Gary Remensnyyder, Treasurer
Trishca Zorn-Hudson, Secretary
Mark A. Lucas, MS, Executive Director

22730 U.S. Track & Field and Cross Country Coaches Association
1100 Poydras Street
Suite 1750
New Orleans, LA 70163
504-599-8900; Fax: 504-599-8909
sam@ustfccca.org
www.ustfccca.org
Twitter, RSS
Sam Seemes, CEO
Damon Martin, President
Sandra Ford-Centonze, Secretary
Larry Cole, Treasurer
Dave Svoboda, Director of Operations
A non-profit professional organization that represents men's and women's cross country and track & field coaches in the United States.
8000 Members

22731 U.S. Track & Field and Cross Country Coach es Association
1100 Poydras Street
Suite 1750
New Orleans, LA 70163
504-599-8900; Fax: 504-599-8909
www.ustfccca.org
Facebook, RSS
Damon Martin, President
Larry Cole, Treasurer
Sandra Ford-Centonze, Secretary
Sam Seemes, Chief Executive Officer
Dave Svoboda, Director of Operations
8,000 Members

22732 US Field Hockey Association
1 Olympic Plaza
Colorado Springs, CO 80909
719-866-4567; Fax: 719-632-0979
usfha@usfieldhockey.com
www.usfieldhockey.com
Facebook, Twitter, LinkedIn, YouTube, Pinterest, Google+
Steve Looke, Executive Director
Simon Hoskins, Marketing Director
Represents field hockey, professional and amateur sports.
14000 Members
Founded in 1928

22733 US Handball Association
2333 N Tucson Blvd
Tucson, AZ 85716
520-795-0434
800-289-8742; Fax: 520-795-0465
handball@ushandball.org
www.ushandball.org
Facebook, Twitter, Vimeo
Mike Steele, President
LeaAnn Martin, VP
Tom Sove, VP
Mike Driscoll, Treasurer - Southwest Region
Vern Roberts, Executive Director
Organization that runs all the tournaments for the professional and amateur players. Home of the Handball Hall of Fame.

22734 US Lacrosse
113 W University Pkwy
Baltimore, MD 21210
410-235-6882; Fax: 410-366-6735
info@uslacrosse.org
www.uslacrosse.org
Facebook, Twitter, Youtube, Google+, Instagram
Steve Stenersen, President & CEO
Bill Schoonmaker, VP, Strategy & Business Development
Cara Morris, VP, Finance & Administration
Ann Kitt Carpenetti, VP, Lacrosse Operations
Mark Hogan, VP, Brand Marketing & Membership
The national governing body of men's and women's lacrosse. Through responsive and effective leadership, the organization provides programs and services to inspire participation while protecting the integrity of the sport. Known as the resource center for the sport, US Lacrosse is devoted to growing the game responsibly, providing programs and services to develop the game nationally, publishing Lacrosse Magazine & LaxMagazine.com, hosting events, and preserving the history of the game.
300M Members
Founded in 1998

22735 US Olympic Committee
One Olympic Plaza
Colorado Springs, CO 80909
719-632-5551
888-222-2313; Fax: 719-632-0250
www.teamusa.org
Facebook, Twitter, Youtube, Instagram
Scott Blackmun, Chief Executive Officer
Lawrence Probst, Chairman
Morane Kerek, Chief Financial Officer
Lisa Baird, Chief Marketing Officer
Larry Buendorf, Chief Security Officer
The national committee for the US handles the preparation of the US Olympic, Paralympic and Pan American Games teams.
Founded in 1978

22736 US Professional Tennis Association
3535 Briarpark Drive
Suite One
Houston, TX 77042
713-978-7782
800-877-8248; Fax: 713-978-7780
uspta@uspta.com
www.uspta.com
Facebook, Twitter, LinkedIn, YouTube, Pinterest, Google+, I
John Embree, CEO
Fred Viancos, Director of Professional Dev.
Kathy Buchanan, Director of Computer Services
Julie Myers, Director of Creative Services
Ellen Weatherford, Controller
A nonprofit association for professional tennis teachers.
14000 Members
Founded in 1927

22737 US Raquetball Association
AARA National Office
1685 W Uintah Street
Ste. 103
Colorado Springs, CO 80904-2906
719-635-5396; Fax: 719-635-0685
sczarnecki@usra.org
www.usra.org
Facebook, Twitter, YouTube, Instagram
Larry Haemmerle, President
Jason Thoerner, VP
Steve Czarnecki, Executive Director
Peggine Tellez, Manager, Sport Development
Myles Hayes, Coordinator, Membership Services
A nonprofit corporation designed to promote the development of competitive and recreational racquetball in the United States. The association offers a 'competitive license' membership for a one year term at $30.00 annually. A lifetime membership is also offered.
40M Members
Frequency: 6 Per Year
Circulation: 25,000
Founded in 1968
Mailing list available for rent

22738 US Ski & Snowboard Association
1 Victory Lane
PO Box 100
Park City, UT 84060
435-649-9090; Fax: 435-649-3613
info@ussa.org
usskiteam.com
Facebook, Twitter, YouTube, Instagram
Tiger Shaw, President/CEO
Calum Clark, Vice President, Events
Luke Bodensteiner, EVP, Athletics
Brooke McAffee, VP/CFO
Michael Jaquet, VP, Chief Marketing Officer
The national governing body for Olympic skiing and snowboarding.
30000 Members
Founded in 1904

22739 US Soccer Federation
1801 S Prairie Ave
Chicago, IL 60616
312-808-1300; Fax: 312-808-1301
www.ussoccer.com
Facebook, Twitter, YouTube, Google+, Instgram, Vi
Sunil K Gulati, President
Mike Edwards, EVP
Dan Flynn, CEO/Secretary General
The governing body of soccer in all its form in the United States. US Soccer has helped chart the course for the sport in the USA for 90 years.
Founded in 1913

22740 US Speedskating
5662 Cougar Lane
Kearns, UT 84118
801-417-5360; Fax: 801-417-5361
tmorris@usspeedskating.org
www.usspeedskating.org
Facebook, Twitter, Youtube
Ted Morris, Executive Director
Dale Schoon, Director of Finance
Matt Whewell, Communications Director
Angela Bond, Membership Coordinator
Shane Domer, Sports Science Director
Devoted to speedskating and its participants on the national and international levels.
2000 Members
Founded in 1966

22741 US Squash Racquet Association
555 Eighth Ave
Suite 1102
New York, NY 10018-4311
212-268-4090; Fax: 212-268-4091
membership@ussquash.com
www.ussquash.org
Facebook, Twitter, LinkedIn, Youtube, Flickr
John A Fry, Chair
David Keating, District Associations
F. Gilpin Lane, Athlete Representative
Michelle Quibell, Athlete Representative
Tim Wyant, Ex Officio
The USSRA is the national governing body for the sport of squash racquets in the United States. A nonprofit, service organization whose primary function is that of management and maintenance

of all squash related activities for a growing membership- driven organization.
8000 Members
Founded in 1907

22742 US Synchronized Swimming
132 E Washington Street
Suite 820
Indianapolis, IN 46204

317-237-5700; Fax: 317-237-5705
marketing@usasynchro.org
www.usasynchro.org
Facebook, Twitter, YouTube, Pinterest, Instagarm

Judy McGowan, President
Sheila McNabb, VP Competitive Operations
Krista Bessinger, VP, Education & Certification
Nancy Rosengard, VP, Marketing & Member Services
Britt Rooney, Treasurer

Dedicated to the promotion of synchronized swimming. Sanctions and governs all synchronized swimming in the US and selects and trains National and Olympic Teams to represent the US in international competitions.
6000 Members

22743 US Track and Field
132 East Washington Street,
Suite 800
Indianapolis, IN 46204

317-261-0500; Fax: 317-261-0481
www.usatf.org
Facebook, Twitter, You Tube

Max Siegel, CEO
Renee Washington, COO
Jill Geer, CPAO
Norman Wain, General Counsel
Carmen Triplet, Special Event Manager

The national governing body for track and field, long-distance running and race waling in the United States.
Founded in 1878

22744 US Volleyball Association
Suite 700
Los Gatos, CA 95031

volleyballorg@hotmail.com
www.volleyball.org

Promotes volleyball in the US trains the USA men's and women's teams promotes beach and grassroots volleyball in the United States.
140M Members
Founded in 1928

22745 USA Basketball
5465 Mark Dabling Boulevard
Colorado Springs, CO 80918-3842

719-590-4800; Fax: 719-590-4811
www.usab.com
Facebook, Twitter, Google+, YouTube

Jerry Colangelo, Chairman
Chauncey Billups, Athlete Representative
Kim Bohuny, NBA Representative
Jim Carr, National Organizations Rep.
Bob Gardner, NFHS Representative
Founded in 1934

22746 USA Deaf Sports Federation
PO Box 22011
Santa Fe, NM 87502

605-367-5760; Fax: 605-782-8441
support@usdeafsports.org
Facebook, Twitter, RSS, YouTube

Jack C. Lamberton, President
Jeffrey L.ÿ Salit, Vice President
Mark Apodaca, Chief Financial Officer
Danny Lacey, Chief Development Officer
Brianne Burger, Secretary
Founded in 1945

22747 USA Gymnastics
132 E Washington Street
Suite 700
Indianapolis, IN 46204

317-237-5050
800-345-4719; Fax: 317-237-5069
membership@usagym.org
www.usa-gymnastics.org
Facebook, Twitter, LinkedIn, YouTube, Instagram

Peter Vidmar, Chairman
Steve Penny, President
Paul Parilla, Vice Chair
Jim Morris, Treasurer
Gary Anderson, Secretary

The sole national governing body for the sport of gymnastics in the United States. USA Gymnastics creates, organizes and conducts clinics, training camps, team competitions and other aspects of athlete, coach and official selection and development.
13000 Members
Founded in 1963

22748 USA Hockey
1775 Bob Johnson Dr
Colorado Spring, CO 80906-4090

719-576-8724; Fax: 719-538-1160
usah@usahockey.org
www.usahockey.com
Facebook, Twitter, LinkedIn

Dave Ogrean, Executive Director
Mike Bertsch, Marketing & Communications
Kim Folsom, Executive Assistant
Rae Briggle, Member Services
Casey Jorgensen, General Counsel

Promotes the sport of hockey. USA Hockey is the national governing body for the sport of ice hockey in the US.
600K Members
Founded in 1937

22749 USA Roller Sports
PO Box 6579
Lincoln, NE 68506

402-483-7551; Fax: 402-483-1465
www.usarollersports.org
Facebook, Twitter, You Tube

George Kolibaba, Chairman/President
David Adamy, VP

The national governing body for all amateur skating sports including artistic, roller, and speed skating.
15K Members
Founded in 1937

22750 USA Swimming
One Olympic Plaza
Colorado Springs, CO 80909

719-866-4578
www.usaswimming.org

Chuck Wielgus, Executive Director
Pat Hogan, Club Development Managing Director
Mike Unger, Assistant Executive Director
Jim Harvey, Chief Financial Officer
Frank Busch, National Team Director

Devoted to the sport of swimming and its enjoyment nationwide. Governing body for the sport of swimming.
400,0 Members
Founded in 1844

22751 USA Table Tennis
4065 Sinton Road
Suite 120
Colorado Springs, CO 80907

719-866-4583; Fax: 719-632-6071
admin@usatt.org
www.usatt.org
Facebook, Twitter, LinkedIn, YouTube, Pinterest, Instagarm,

Gordon Kaye, CEO
Doru Gheorghe, COO/High Performance Director
Teresa Benavides, Financial Director
Andy Horn, Membership Director
Tiffany Oldland, Sanctioning & Ratings Manager

Dedicated to the promotion of the sport of table tennis and sponsors the US team. Membership dues are $40 per year for adults and $20 for those 17 years old and under.
9000+ Members
Founded in 1933

22752 USA Track & Field
USA Track & Field
132 East Washington Street, Suite 8
Indianapolis, IN 46204

317-261-0500; Fax: 317-261-0481
www.usatf.org

Max Siegel, CEO
Renee Washington, COO
Jill Geer, CPAO
Norman Wain, General Counsel
Carmen Triplet, Special Event Manager
Founded in 1878

22753 USA Water Ski Association
1251 Holy Cow Rd
Polk City, FL 33868

863-324-4341; Fax: 863-325-8259
usawaterski@usawaterski.org
www.usawaterski.org

The national governing body for organized water skiing in the United States. A member of the International Water Ski Federation (World Governing Body), the Pan American Sports Association and the United States Olympic Committee.
37500 Members
Founded in 1939

22754 USA Weightlifting
1 Olympic Plz
Colorado Spring, CO 80909-5764

719-866-4508; Fax: 719-866-4741
usaw@usaweightlifting.org
www.usaweightlifting.org

Michael Masik, CEO, General Secretary
Laurie Lopez, Director, Operations
Carissa Gump, Director, Corp. Services
Phil Andrews, Director, Events & Programs

USA Weightlifting is the National Governing Body (NGB) for the Olympic sport of weightlifting in the United States. USA weightlifting is a member of the United States Olympic Committee and a member of the International Weightlifting Federation. As the NGB, USA Weightlifting is responsible for conducting Olympic weightlifting programs throughout the country. The organization conducts a variety of programs that will ultimately develop Olympic, World Championship and Pan American Games' winners.
Cost: $20.00
4000 Members
Frequency: Quarterly
Circulation: 4500
Founded in 1981

22755 United States Amateur Boxing
1 Olympic Plz
Colorado Spring, CO 80909

719-866-2300; Fax: 719-866-2132
www.usaboxing.org

Anthony Bartkowski, Executive Director
Betsy McCallister, Executive Assistant
Brian Lawrence, CFO
Lynette Smith, Director, Membership Services

The national governing body for Olympic-style boxing. It is responsible for the administration, development and promotion of Olympic-style boxing in the United State.
7000 Members
Founded in 1981

22756 **United States Bowling Congress**
621 Six Flags Dr
Arlington, TX 76011
817-385-8200
800-514-2695; Fax: 817-385-8260
www.bowl.com
Facebook, Twitter, LinkedIn, You Tube
Andrew Cain, President
Frank Wilkinson, VP
Tamoria Adams, Director
Tim Payne, Chief Information Officer
Kevin Dornberger, Director, Team USA
Established in 2005 as the organization to serve amateur adult and youth bowlers of the United States. It resulted from the merger of the American Bowling Congress, Young American Bowling Alliance and USA Bowling. USBC is the national governing body for bowling as recognized by the United States Olympic Committee.
3 M Members
Founded in 2005

22757 **United States Canoe Association**
509 S Bishop Ave
Secane, PA 19018
610-405-5008
www.uscanoe.com
Susan Williams, President
Joan Theiss, Insurance Coordinator

22758 **United States Extreme Sports Association**
6350 Lake Oconee Parkway
Suite 102-128
Greensboro, GA 30642
877-900-8737
www.usesa.orgÿ

22759 **United States Fencing Association**
1 Olympic Plz
Colorado Spring, CO 80909-5760
719-866-4444; Fax: 719-866-4645
info@usfencing.org
www.usfencing.org
Facebook, Twitter, LinkedIn, You Tube
Donald Anthony Jr., Chairman
Sam Cheris, Treasurer
Nathan Anderson, Secretary
National Governing Body for the sport of fencing in the United States. Their mission is to develop fencers to achieve international success and to administer and promote the sport in the USA.
9M Members
Founded in 1891

22760 **United States Golf Association**
PO Box 708
Far Hills, NJ 07931
908-234-2300; Fax: 908-234-9687
mediarelations@usga.org
www.usga.org
Facebook, Twitter, LinkedIn, You Tube
Walter W Driver Jr, President
James E Reinhart, VP
David Fay, Executive Director
An association of member clubs and courses. Conducts the US Open and Women's Open Championships, the Walker and Curtis Cup matches and ten national amateur championships.
7.5M Members
Founded in 1894

22761 **United States Harness Writers Association**
PO Box 1314
Mechanicsburg, PA 17055
717-766-3219
www.ushwa.org
Steve Wolf, President
Chris Tully, First VP
Tim Bojarski, Second VP
Judy Davis-Wilson, Treasurer
Jerry Connors, Secretary
Members are media members who cover the sport of harness racing.
300 Members
Founded in 1947

22762 **United States Parachute Association**
5401 Southpoint Centre Boulevard
Fredricksburg, VA 22407
540-604-9740; Fax: 540-604-9741
uspa@uspa.org
www.uspa.org
Facebook, Twitter, LinkedIn, YouTube, RSS
Jay Stokes, President
Randy Allison, Vice President
Sherry Butcher, Secretary
Lee Schlichtemeier, Treasurer
BJ Worth, Chairman
The USPA is a voluntary membership organization of individuals who enjoy and support the sport of skydiving. The purpose of USPA is three-fold: to promote safe skydiving through training, licensing, and instructor qualification programs; to ensure skydiving's rightful place on airports and in the airspace system; and to promote competition and record-setting programs.
33000 Members
Founded in 1946

22763 **United States Racquet Stringers**
PO Box 3392
Duluth, GA 92084
760-536-1177; Fax: 760-536-1171
usra@racquettech.com
www.racquettech.com
David Bone, Executive Director
Dianne Pray, Membership Coordinator
Crawford Lindsey, Editor/Webmaster
Kristine Thom, Production Manager
Educates constituencies to better understand, service, perform with, and enjoy the technological wonders known as racquests, strings, balls, courts, shoes, and stringing machines.
7000 Members
Founded in 1975

22764 **United States Tennis Association**
70 West Red Oak Lane
White Plains, NY 10604
914-696-7000
www.usta.com
Facebook, Twitter, YouTube
Katrina Adams, Chairman, CEO & President
Andy Andrews, First Vice President
Tommy Ho, Vice President
Don Tisdel, Vice President
Patrick Galbraith, Secretary-Treasurer
Founded in 1881

22765 **United States Trotting Association**
750 Michigan Ave
Columbus, OH 43215
614-224-2291
877-800-8782; Fax: 614-224-4575
stats@ustrotting.com
www.ustrotting.com
Facebook, Twitter, LinkedIn, You Tube
Ivan L Axelrod, Chairman
E Phillip Langley, President
Russell C Williams, Vice Chair
Mike Tanner, VP
Richard Brandt Jr., Treasurer
The USTA licenses owners, trainers, drivers and officials; formulates the rules of racing; maintains and disseminates racing information and records; serves as the registry for the Standardbred breed; endeavors to ensure the integrity of harness racing; insists on the humane treatment of Standardbreds; and promotes the sport of harness racing and the Standardbred breed.
Founded in 1939

22766 **United States Water Fitness Association**
P.O. Box 243279
Boynton Beach, FL 33424-3279
561-732-9908; Fax: 561-732-0950
info@uswfa.org
www.uswfa.com
John R Spannuth, President/CEO
Marion Frega, Assistant to President
Nonprofit educational organization that promotes aquatics throughout the US and other countries. Publishes the National Aquatics Newsletter, names the 100 top programs and aquatics in the country, by state and in 25+ categories. Conducts a wide variety of national aquatics certifications including Water Fitness Instructors (primary and masters), aquatic directors, coordinators of water fitness programs. Conducts annual international aquatics conference.
Founded in 1988

22767 **United States eSports Federation**
Home Page: www.esportsfederation.org
Instagram
Vlad Marinescu, President
Robin Kent, General Secretary
Lance Mudd, Sport Director
Ryan Terao, VP, Education Commission
Robert Davidman, VP, Integrity Commission
USeF is the U.S. member organization of the International e-Sports Federation and official governing body of eSports in the U.S. Its goal is to promote eSports and protect athletes by uniting all facets of the industry: stakeholders, athletes, event organizers, technology producers, innovators and inventors, IP holders, parents, sponsors, and fans.
Founded in 2016

22768 **United States of America Cricket Association**
8461 Lake Worth Road
Suite B-1-185
Lake Worth, FL 33467
561-839-1888
lbrulport@usaca.org
www.usaca.org
Facebook, Twitter
Gladstone Dainty, President
Michael Gale, 1st Vice President
Rafey Syed, 2nd Vice President
John Thickett, Treasurer
Mascelles Bailey, Secretary

22769 **Western Fairs Association**
1776 Tribute Rd
Suite 210
Sacramento, CA 95815-4495
916-927-3100; Fax: 916-927-6397
stephenc@fairsnet.org
www.fairsnet.org
Cliff Munson, Chair
Sarah Cummings, President & CEO
Taylor Corder, Communications Manager
A non-profit association with members throughout the Western United States and Canada that strives to promote industry standards. Membership includes access to conventions and trade

shows, educational training programs as well as legislative advocacy support.
2000 Members
Founded in 1922

22770 Women's Basketball Coaches Association
4646 Lawrenceville Hwy.
Lilburn, GA 30047
770-279-8027; Fax: 770-279-8473
membership@wbca.org
www.wbca.org
Facebook, Twitter, RSS
Sue Semrau, President
Coquese Washington, VP
Charli Turner Thorne, Past President
Matthew Mitchell, Secretary
Danielle Donehew, Executive Director
Founded in 1981

22771 Women's National Basketball Associationÿ
645 Fifth Avenue
New York, NY 10022
Home Page: www.wnba.com
Facebook, Twitter, YouTube, Instagram

22772 Women's Sports Foundation
Eisenhower Park
East Meadow, NY 11554
516-542-4700
800-227-3988; Fax: 516-542-4716
info@womenssportsfoundation.org
www.womenssportsfoundation.org
Facebook, Twitter
Billie Jean King, Founder
Donna Lopiano, CEO
Allison Sawyer, Senior Communications Coordinator
Disseminates information as well as encourages girls and women in sports and physical activity. Organization offers free access to quarterly electronic newsletter, Women's Sports Experience, that provides general updates on the world of girls' and women's sports as well as the Foundation's work.
4000 Members
Circulation: 15000
Founded in 1974

22773 World Esports Association
info@wesa.gg
www.wesa.gg
Facebook, Twitter
Pietro Fringuelli, Executive Chair & Commissioner
Sebastian Weishaar, Board Member
Ulrich Schulze, Board Member
Ralf Reichert, Board Member
Alexander Muller, Board Member
WESA is an international body aiming to professionalize eSports by introducing elements common among traditional sports associations, including player representation, standardized regulations, & revenue shares for teams. It is a joint effort between eSports teams and eSports company ESL.

22774 YMCA of the USA
101 N Wacker Dr
Suite 1400
Chicago, IL 60606-1784
312-977-0031
800-872-9622
www.ymca.net
Facebook
Neil Nicoll, CEO
Provides national and state branch divisions.
20.1M Members

22775 ational Federation of State High School Associations
PO BOX 690
Indianapolis, IN 46206
317-972-6900; Fax: 317-822-5700
www.nfhs.org
Twitter
Tom Welter, President
Gary Musselman, President-Elect
Gary Ray, B.O.D., Section 2
Jerome Singleton, B.O.D., Section 3
Marty Hickman, B.O.D., Section 4
Founded in 1920

Newsletters

22776 AAPSM Newsletter
American Academy of Podiatric Sports Medicine
109 Greenwich Dr
Walkersville, MD 21793-9121
352-620-8562
888-854-3338; Fax: 352-620-8765
www.aapsm.org
Facebook
Rita Yates, Executive Director
David M Davidson, Director
A quarterly newsletter published by the American Academy of Podiatric Sports Medicine.
12 Pages
Frequency: Quarterly
Circulation: 700
Founded in 1970
Mailing list available for rent: 600 names at $125 per M

22777 BCA Newsletter
National High School Baseball Coaches Association
PO Box 12843
Tempe, AZ 85284
602-615-0571; Fax: 480-838-7133
rdavini@cox.net
www.baseballcoaches.org
Ron Davini, Executive Director

22778 Behind the Seams
National Amateur Baseball Federation
PO Box 705
Bowie, MD 20715
301-625-5005; Fax: 301-352-0214
NABF1914@aol.com
www.nabf.com
Facebook
J Patrick Eaken, Editor
Charles M Blackburn, Executive Director
The official newsletter of the National Amateur Baseball Federation. Sent to NABF league members.
Frequency: Quarterly
Founded in 1914

22779 CSCAA Newsletter
College Swimming Coaches Association of America
1640 Maple
#803
Evanston, IL 60201
847-833-3478
r-groseth@northwestern.edu
wwww.csaa.org
Bob Groseth, Executive Director
George Kennedy, President

22780 Field Hockey News
US Field Hockey Association
1 Olympic Plaza
Colorado Springs, CO 80909
719-866-4567; Fax: 719-632-0979
usfha@usfieldhockey.com
www.usfieldhockey.com
Facebook, Twitter, LinkedIn, You Tube
Steve Looke, Executive Director
Simon Hoskins, Marketing Director
Frequency: Seasonally

22781 Hunting Report for Big Game Hunters
Oxpecker Enterprises
Ste 523
9200 S Dadeland Blvd
Miami, FL 33156-2713
305-670-1361
800-272-5656; Fax: 305-716-1376
Subscriptions@HuntingReport.com
www.huntingreport.com
Facebook, Twitter, LinkedIn
Don Causey, President/Publisher
Nick Titus, Production Manager
Provides information on hunting opportunities and conditions in the US, Africa and other parts of the world.
Cost: $60.00
Frequency: Monthly
ISSN: 1052-4746
Founded in 1980

22782 Hunting Report: Birdshooters and Water
Oxpecker Enterprises
Ste 523
9200 S Dadeland Blvd
Miami, FL 33156-2713
305-670-1361; Fax: 954-370-1376
subscriptions@huntingreport.com
www.huntingreport.com
Facebook, Twitter, LinkedIn
Don Causey, Publisher
Serving the Sportsman who travels.
Cost: $45.00
14 Pages
Frequency: Monthly
Circulation: 1850
Founded in 1983
Printed in 2 colors on matte stock

22783 InBrief
Sporting Goods Manufacturers Association
8505 Fenton Street
Silver Spring, MD 20910
301-495-6321; Fax: 301-495-6322
info@sgma.com
Tom Cove, President & CEO
Bill Sells, VP Government Relations
Chip Baldwin, CFO
Mike May, Director Communications
Newsletter with information about and for manufacturers in the sporting goods industry.
Frequency: Bi-weekly

22784 International Sports Heritage Association
PO Box 2384
Florence, OR 97439
541-991-7315; Fax: 541-997-3871
info@sportsheritage.org
www.sportsheritage.org
Facebook, Twitter
Karen Bednarski, Executive Director
Mike Gibbons, President
Rick Wells, First Vice President
Meg Snyder, Second Vice President
Ben Sopp, Treasurer

E-Newsletter
140+ Members
Frequency: Quarterly
Founded in 1971

22785 Leader Board
Golf Course Superintendents Association of America
1421 Research Park Dr
Lawrence, KS 66049-3859

785-841-2240
800-472-7878; Fax: 785-832-4488
infobox@gcsaa.org
www.gcsaa.org
Facebook, Twitter

Mark Woodward, CEO
Melissa Householder, Communications Coordinator
Ed Hiscock, Editor-In-Chief

Bi-monthly newsletter for golf facility decision makers, including superintendents and their employers, presenting timely and useful informaiton about golf course management in a quick easy-to-read format.
Frequency: Monthly
Circulation: 40000
Founded in 1926

22786 Media Sports Business
Kagan Research
1 Lower Ragsdale Dr
Building One Suite 130
Monterey, CA 93940-5749

831-624-1536
800-307-2529; Fax: 831-625-3225
www.kagan.com

Tim Baskerville, President
Tom Johnson, Marketing Manager

Statistics of a different kind. How much media pay to carry sports events, the impact of media on pro sports franchises, and more. Scores big with major league and media players. Three month trial available.
Cost: $945.00
Frequency: Monthly
Founded in 1969

22787 NASGW Newsletter
National Association of Sporting Goods Wholesalers
1255 SW Prairie Trail Parkway
Ankeny, IA 50023-7068

515-334-1484; Fax: 515-334-1143
info@nasgw.org
www.nasgw.org
Facebook, LinkedIn

Kenyon Gleason, President
Meg Pawelski, Director, Operations & Expo Manager
Easton Kuboushek, Program Manager
Donna Donovan, Financial Manager
Gregg Alexander, Communications Manager

Non-profit trade association of wholesalers, distributors and manufacturers. Serves as a liason with other sporting goods associations. The NASGW is the organizer and sponser of the industry's annual meeting/expo event.
400 Members
Founded in 1953

22788 NSGA Sporting Goods Alert
National Sporting Goods Association
1601 Feehanville Dr
Suite 300
Mt Prospect, IL 60056-6035

847-296-6742; Fax: 847-391-9827
info@nsga.org
www.nsga.org

Jeff Rosenthal, Chairman of the Board
Matt Carlson, President/CEO
Dan Kasen, Director of Information Services

News and rule changes affecting team dealers. Newsletter is free to members.

22789 NSGA Team Line-Up
National Sporting Goods Association
1601 Feehanville Dr
Suite 300
Mt Prospect, IL 60056-6035

847-296-6742; Fax: 847-391-9827
info@nsga.org
www.nsga.org

Ken Meehan, Chairman of the Board
Matt Carlson, President/CEO
Dustin Dobrin, Director of Information Services

News and rule changes affecting team dealers. Newsletter is free to members.
Frequency: Weekly

22790 National High School Baseball Coaches Association
PO Box 12843
Tempe, AZ 85284

602-615-0571; Fax: 480-838-7133
rdavini@cox.net
www.baseballcoaches.org

Ron Davini, Executive Director

Association news, information, coaching articles.
Frequency: 2x/Year
Circulation: 1500+
Founded in 1991

22791 Newsline
Golf Course Superintendents Association of America
1421 Research Park Dr
Lawrence, KS 66049-3859

785-841-2240
800-472-7878; Fax: 785-832-4488
www.gcsaa.org
Facebook

Mark Woodward, CEO

Membership newsletter highlighting programs and services, and featuring news about the association, its members, the golf course management profession and industry.
Founded in 1926

22792 OOR e-Newsletter
Outdoor Recreation Roundtable
1203 K Street NW
Suite 350
Washington, DC 20005

202-682-9530
recreationroundtable.org
Facebook, Twitter

Jessica Wahl, Executive Director
Phil Ingrassia, Chair
Frank Hugelmeyer, Vice Chair
Glenn Hughes, Treasurer
Chris Edmonston, Secretary

A monthly e-newsletter distributed via e-mail.
Frequency: Monthly, e-Newsletter
Circulation: Variable

22793 Parachutist
United States Parachute Association
5401 Southpoint Centre Boulevard
Fredricksburg, VA 22407

540-604-9740; Fax: 540-604-9740
uspa@uspa.org
www.uspa.org
Facebook, Twitter, LinkedIn, YouTube, RSS

Elijah Florio, Editor in Chief
Laura Sharp, Managing Editor
Guilherme Cunha, Advertising Manager, Web Developer
David Cherry, Graphic Designer

The official newsletter of the USPA.
33000 Members
Founded in 1946

22794 Running & FitNews
American Running Association
4405 East-West Highway
Suite 405
Bethesda, MD 20814

800-776-2732
800-776-2732; Fax: 301-913-9520
Facebook, LinkedIn

David Watt, Executive Director
Barbara Baldwin, Projects Consultant
Jeff Venables, Editor
Jeff Harbison, President
Bill Young, Secretary/Treasurer

running, health and sports medicine e-newsletter.
Founded in 1968

22795 Sport Scene
North American Youth Sport Institute
4985 Oak Garden Drive
PO Box 957
Kernersville, NC 27285

336-784-4926
800-767-4916; Fax: 336-784-5546
jack@naysi.com
www.naysi.com
Facebook

Jack Hutslar, Publisher/Editor

News, features, tips, reviews, statistics, and summaries for people who work with tots, children and teens in fitness, recreation, education, sport and health with the focus on management, resources latest coaching and teaching methods, do's and dont's, safety, program ideas, legal issues, and training programs for leaders. Goal is to provide current information to improve learning while making activities more safe and positive so children can have more fun.
Cost: $ 16.00
Frequency: 6X/yr
ISBN: 0-270181-2 -
Founded in 1979

22796 Team Marketing Report
Team Marketing Report
1653 North Wells St
Suite 2F
Chicago, IL 60614-3962

312-280-2311
847-256-2564; Fax: 312-280-2322
Facebook, Twitter, LinkedIn

Becky Vallett, Executive Editor
Dan Bulla, Editor-at-Large / Director of Sales

Information on rates, ticket prices, and consumer attitudes, new ideas to help increase sales and exposure through the sports market.
Cost: $195.00
Frequency: Monthly
Founded in 1988

22797 Winning Edge Newsletter
1001 Diamond Ridge
Suite 800
Jefferson City, MO 65109

573-635-1660; Fax: 573-635-8233
hq@somo.org
www.somo.org
Facebook, Twitter, LinkedIn, YouTube, RSS

Mark Musso, President
Mandi Steward Mueller, Public Relations Coordinator
Diannah White, Chief Communications Officer
Randy Bohem, Chair
Don Spear, Member

Publication produced for the athletes, volunteers and supports of the Special Olympics.
Frequency: Quarterly
Founded in 1983

Magazines & Journals

22798 **ADDvantage**
US Professional Tennis Association
3535 Briarpark Drive
Suite 1
Houston, TX 77042-5245
713-978-7782
800-877-8248; Fax: 713-978-7780
uspta@uspta.org
www.uspta.com
Shawna Riley, Editor
Kim Forrester, Managing Editor
A monthly magazine published by the US Professional Tennis Association. Available through membership only.
36 Pages
Frequency: Monthly
Circulation: 13,000
Founded in 1927
Printed in 4 colors on glossy stock

22799 **AKWA Magazine**
Aquatic Exercise Association
201 Tamiami Trail
PO Box 1609
Nokomis, FL 34274-1609
941-486-8600
888-232-9283; Fax: 941-486-8820
www.aeawave.com
Angie Nelson, Executive Director
Julie See, President
Kim Huff, Director of Marketing
The aqautics fitness industry's leading magazine. Brings professionals the most up to date and innovative ideas in programming, management, safety and nutrition for group exercise and personal training in the pool. Available to AEA members with their $65.00 membership.
Circulation: 6000
Founded in 1987
Mailing list available for rent: 90M names
Printed in 4 colors on glossy stock

22800 **American Firearms Industry**
AFI Communications
2400 E Las Olas Boulevard
#397
Fort Lauderdale, FL 33301
954-467-9994; Fax: 954-463-2501
www.amfire.com
Facebook, Twitter, LinkedIn
Andrew Molchan, Editor
Alexandra Molchan, Circulation Manager
Kathleen Molchan, Sales Manager
A business-to-business trade magazine containing articles and information centered on the retailing of firearms and shooting products. Areas covered are: handguns, revolvers, pistols, rifles, shotguns, ammunition, rifle scopes, reloading, holsters, hunting accessories, gun parts, cutlery, knives, archery, bows, crossbows, camping, camouflage, black powder, smokeless powder, binoculars, safes, gunlocks, air guns, used gun news and political news and views relatingto firearms and the industry.
Cost: $18.00
Frequency: Monthly
Circulation: 34
Founded in 1973

22801 **American Fitness**
Aerobics and Fitness Association of America
15250 Ventura Blvd
Suite 200
Sherman Oaks, CA 91403-3297
818-905-0040
877-968-7263; Fax: 818-990-5468
contactafaa@afaa.com
www.afaa.com
Linda Pfeffer, President
Roscoe K Fawcett Jr, Publisher
The official publication of the Aerobics and Fitness Association of America. Known for reporting health-related fitness research, current trends, advances in equipment and training applications.
Cost: $27.00
Frequency: Bi-annually
Circulation: 100,000
Founded in 1983

22802 **American Hunter**
National Rifle Association
11250 Waples Mill Rd
Fairfax, VA 22030-7400
703-267-1400
877-672-2000
americanhunter.org
Facebook, Twitter, LinkedIn, YouTube, RSS
Mark A Keefe IV, Editor
American Hunter offers expertise on how and where to hunt all types of North American game and encourages readers to take advantage of the rich opportunities and to pass along the tradition to the next generation.

22803 **American Paddler**
American Canoe Association
7432 Alban Station Boulevard
Suite B-232
Springfield, VA 22150
703-451-0141; Fax: 703-451-2245
aca@americancanoe.org
www.acanet.org
Marty Bartels, Publisher

22804 **American Quarter Horse Journal**
American Quarter Horse Association
1600 Quarter Horse Drive
PO Box 200
Amarillo, TX 79104
806-764-4888; Fax: 806-349-6400
www.aqha.com
Bill Brewer, Executive VP
Jim Jennings, Publisher
Industry magazine for Quarter Horse breeders, farm managers and owners.
Cost: $25.00
550 Pages
Frequency: Monthly
Circulation: 66575
Founded in 1948
Printed in 4 colors on glossy stock

22805 **American Rifleman**
National Rifle Association
11250 Waples Mill Rd
Fairfax, VA 22030-7400
703-267-1400
800-672-3888; Fax: 703-267-3971
publications@nrahq.org
www.nrapublications.org
Facebook, Twitter, LinkedIn, YouTube, RSS
Mark Keefe IV, Editor-In-Chief
Premier magazine for shooting and firearms enthusiasts. Coverage is devoted to rifles, shotguns, handguns, ammunition, reloading, optics and shooting accessories.
Cost: $35.00
Frequency: Monthly
Circulation: 100000
Founded in 1975

22806 **Americas 1st Freedom**
National Rifle Association
11250 Waples Mill Rd
Fairfax, VA 22030-7400
703-267-1400
877-672-2000; Fax: 703-267-3971
publications@nrahq.org
www.nrapublications.org
Facebook, Twitter, LinkedIn, YouTube, RSS
Mark Keefe IV, Editor-In-Chief
NRA's pure news magazine. Its mission is to deliver professional, compelling, accurate, timely and hard-hitting journalism that tells the truth about the threats to our Second Amendment rights. Subscription complementary with membership in NRA. Otherwise $9.95
Founded in 1975

22807 **Aquatic Therapy and Fitness Research**
Aquatic Exercise Association
PO Box 1609
Nokomis, FL 34274-1609
941-486-8600
888-232-9283; Fax: 941-486-8820
www.aeawave.com
Facebook, Twitter, LinkedIn, YouTube, RSS
Angie Proctor, CEO
Julie See, President
Kim Huff, Director of Marketing
Journal. Peer-reviewed publication providing documentated opinions of industry leaders. A multidisciplinary publication, each issue includes two focus areas. Subscription included with AEA membership.
Cost: $65.00
Frequency: Monthly
Circulation: 6000
Founded in 1984

22808 **Aquatics International**
Leisure Publications
6222 Wilshire Blvd.
Los Angeles, CA 90020-4244
323-644-4801
888-269-8410; Fax: 323-964-4842
www.aquaticsintl.com
Facebook, Twitter, LinkedIn, YouTube, RSS
Garry Carter, Sales Manager
Steve Honum, Account Executive
Theresa Wrong, Sales Manager
Articles of interest to colleges and schools; municipal, county and state pool facilities; hotels, resorts and country clubs; fitness clubs; rehab centers; YMCAs; military facilities; and waterparks.
Cost: $30.00
Frequency: 11X/Yr
Circulation: 30000
Mailing list available for rent

22809 **Arabian Horse World**
Arabian Horse World
624 South Main Street
Suite 201
Templeton, CA 93456
805-771-2300
800-955-9423; Fax: 805-927-6522
info@arabianhorseworld.com
www.arabianhorseworld.com
Facebook
Denise Hearst, Publisher
Mary Jane Parkinson, Editor
Kristin Youngberg, Managing Editor
Our philosophy at Arabian Horse World is to promote the Arabian - through education and entertainment - to new levels of appreciation and usefullness. Show results and breeding

farms are featured.
Cost: $40.00
Frequency: Monthly
Circulation: 15000
Founded in 1990
Printed in 4 colors on glossy stock

22810 **Archery Business Magazine**
Grand View Media Group
14505 21st Ave N
Suite 202
Plymouth, MN 55447
763-473-5800
800-766-0039; Fax: 763-473-5801
pbrady@affinitygroup.com
www.bowhuntingworld.com
Facebook

Steve Schiffman, Publisher
Mark Melotik, Editor
Patty Brady, Advertising
Steven Hedlund, President

Controlled circulation trade magazine covering the business side of bowhunting and archery: trade news, industry statistics, marketing and product trends, new product research and development, tips for better business management and effective training.
Frequency: Monthly
Circulation: 11000+
Founded in 1975

22811 **Arrow Trade Magazine**
3479 409th Avenue NW.
Braham, MN 55006-3340

320-396-3473
888-796-2083; Fax: 320-396-3206
www.arrowtrademagazine.com
Facebook, Twitter

Tim Dehn, Publisher
Matt Granger, Advertising
Rachel Givens, Subscriptions

A business magazine published for retailers, distributors, sales representatives and manufacturers of bowhunting equipment and camouflage clothing.
Founded in 1997

22812 **Athletic Management**
MAG
2488 N Triphammer Road
Ithaca, NY 14850

607-257-6970; Fax: 607-257-7328
info@athleticbid.com
www.momentummedia.com

Mark Goldberg, President
Eleanor Frankel, Editor

Free to college athletic administrators and high school athletic directors in the US and Canada. The editorial mission of Athletic Management is to help Athletic Directors enhance their operations, to share new ideas, and cover pertinent news topics. Feature stories and regular sections address the various facets of managing an athletic department.
Cost: $25.00
Frequency: Weekly
Circulation: 30200
Founded in 1988
Printed in 4 colors on glossy stock

22813 **Bass Times**
ESPN

334-272-9530
sports.espn.go.com/outdoors/bassmaster

Bass Times is packed with news and information for serious bass fishermen. The perfect compliment to Bassmaster Magazine.
Cost: $12.00
Frequency: Monthly

22814 **Bassmaster**
ESPN

334-272-9530
sports.espn.go.com/bassmaster
Facebook, Twitter, LinkedIn, YouTube, RSS

Bassmaster Magazine monthly.
Frequency: Monthly

22815 **Bicycle Friendly America Magazine**
League of American Bicyclists
1612 K St NW
Suite 1102
Washington, DC 20006-2850

202-822-1333; Fax: 202-822-1334
bikeleague@bikeleague.org
www.bikeleague.org
Facebook, Twitter, LinkedIn, YouTube, RSS

Alex Doty, Executive Director
Karen Jenkins, Chair
Lorna Green, Operations Manager

Contains cycling stories; how-to articles; health; legal and safety columns; legislative updates, fitness, cycling technique and travel.
Frequency: Bi-Monthly
Circulation: 325000

22816 **Black's Buyers Directory**
PO Box 2029
Red Bank, NJ 07701

732-224-8700
800-224-9464; Fax: 732-741-2827
www.fieldandstream.com
Facebook, Twitter, LinkedIn, YouTube, RSS

James F Black Jr, Publisher
Lois Re, Editor
Christopher Pluck, Owner

The complete buyer's guide to equipment. A one-stop source of information on anything and everything that's archery/bowhunting.
Founded in 2001

22817 **Bowlers Journal International**
Luby Publishing Company
122 S Michigan Ave
Suite 1506
Chicago, IL 60603-6148

312-341-1110; Fax: 312-341-1469
www.lubypublishing.com

Keith Hamilton, President
Mason King, Editor
Emily Kupper, Circulation Director
Bob Nieman, Editor

Information geared toward all levels of industry personnel. Regular issue features include new products listings, tournament reviews, personality profiles and proprietor workshops.
Cost: $24.00
Frequency: Monthly
Circulation: 22319
Founded in 1913

22818 **Bowling Center Management**
Bowling Proprietors Association of America
122 S Michigan Avenue
Suite 1506
Chicago, IL 60603-6107

312-341-1110; Fax: 312-341-1180
bowlctrman@aol.com
www.bcmmag.com
Facebook, Twitter, LinkedIn

Mike Panozzo, Publisher
Bob Nieman, Editor
Emily Kupper, Circulation Director
Mason King, Editor

Information designed for bowling center owners to help them in the operation and management of their centers.
Cost: $60.00
Frequency: Monthly
Circulation: 5000
Founded in 1995

22819 **By Design**
American Society of Golf Course Architects
125 N Executive Dr
Suite 302
Brookfield, WI 53005-6035

262-786-5960; Fax: 262-786-5919
info@asgca.org
www.asgca.org
Facebook, Twitter

Chad Ritterbusch, Executive Director
Mike Shefky, Web Master

E-Magazine highlighting the work of ASGCA golf course architects worldwide. Subscribe at no charge at www.asgca.org
185 Members
Frequency: Quarterly
Circulation: 6000
Founded in 1946

22820 **Camping Magazine**
American Camp Association
5000 State Road 67 N
Martinsville, IN 46151-7902

765-342-8456
800-428-2267; Fax: 765-342-2065
pr@acacamps.org
www.acacamps.org
Facebook, Twitter, LinkedIn

Peg Smith, CEO
Kim Bruno, Communication/Development Head
Terrie Nicodemus, Manager

The official publication of the American Camp Association. Experts in the camp field contribute informative articles and essays on current advances in camp management, staffing and human resources, programming, risk management, special populations and diversity, health and wellness, and more.
Cost: $24.95
Founded in 1920
Mailing list available for rent

22821 **Coaching Management**
MAG
2488 N Triphammer Road
Ithaca, NY 14850-5220

607-257-6970; Fax: 607-257-7328
info@athleticbid.com
www.momentummedia.com
Facebook, Twitter, LinkedIn

Mark Goldberg, Publisher/CEO
Eleanor Frankel, Editor
Dave Dubin, Circulation Director

Information including team equipment, apparel, injury prevention, conditioning, as well as field, stadium and court maintenance and improvement. Primary feature articles cover a wide range of coaching tools and techniques.
Frequency: Bi-annually
Circulation: 20556
Founded in 1988
Mailing list available for rent

22822 **Coaching Volleyball**
American Volleyball Coaches Association
2365 Harrodsburg Road
Suite A325
Lexington, KY 40504

859-226-4315
866-544-2822; Fax: 859-226-4338
members@avca.org

www.avca.org
Facebook, Twitter, LinkedIn, YouTube, RSS
Leah DeBoer, Executive Director
Leah Brock, Communications Manager
Frequency: Bi-Monthly

22823 Cross Country Skier
PO Box 550
Cable, WI 54821
715-798-5500
800-827-0607; Fax: 715-798-3599
info@crosscountryskier.com
www.crosscountryskier.com
Facebook, Twitter, LinkedIn
Ron Bergin, Owner
The journal of nordic skiing - destinations, news, training and technique, waxing, competition, equipment and new products, and great features on all facets of the sport of cross country skiing.

22824 Cutting Horse Chatter
National Cutting Horse Association
260 Bailey Avenue
Fort Worth, TX 76107
817-244-6188; Fax: 817-244-2015
www.nchacutting.com
Chubby Turner, President
Chris Benedict, VP
Jeff Hooper, Executive Director
Rick Ivey, Tresurer
Alan Gold, Director Marketing
Frequency: Monthly
Circulation: 20500

22825 Deer & Deer Hunting
F+W Media
38 E. 29th Street
New York, NY 10016
212-447-1400; Fax: 212-447-5231
contact_us@fwmedia.com
Hugh McAloon, Publisher
Edited for serious, year-round whitetail hunting enthusiasts and focuses on hunting techniques, deer biology and behavior, deer management, habitat requirements, the natural history of deer, and hunting ethics. Contains how-to articles designed to help hunters be successful. Regular columns and departments include book reviews, Deer Browse (unusual observations by hunters), new products, an editor's column, letters from readers, Deer Behavior, Can You Outsmart This Deer? and Q&A.
Cost: $19.99
Circulation: 212500
Founded in 1977
Mailing list available for rent

22826 Fantasy Sports
F+W Media
38 E. 29th Street
New York, NY 10016
212-447-1400; Fax: 212-447-5231
contact_us@fwmedia.com
Tom Kessenich, Editor
David Nussbaum, Chair
Jim Ogle, Finance/Administration
Sara Domville, President
Phil Graham, VP
The essential manual for those who participate in Rotisserie and other fantasy sports leagues. Reports extensive statistics to help managers in making personnel moves. Also includes recommendations on who to draft or trade. The April and May issues focus on baseball. The August and September issues focus on football. An up-to-the-minute, online version is also available fo a small fee at www.fantasysportsmag.com
Cost: $9.97
132 Pages
Frequency: 4 Per Year
Circulation: 78,767
Founded in 1989
Mailing list available for rent

22827 Fastpitch Delivery
National Fastpitch Coaches Association
2641 Grinstead Drive,
Suite D
Louisville, KY 42046
502-409-4600; Fax: 502-409-4622
nfca@nfca.org
www.nfca.org
Facebook, Twitter, LinkedIn, YouTube, RSS
Lacy Lee Baker, Executive Director
Hildred Deese, Senior Director of Events
Frequency: Monthly
Founded in 1982

22828 Fishermen's News
Philip's Publishing Group
2201 W Commodore Way
Seattle, WA 98199-1298
206-284-8285
800-258-8609; Fax: 206-284-0391
circulation@rhppublishing.com
www.pacmar.com
Peter Philips, Publisher
Lisa Albers, Managing Editor
Bill Forslund, Advertising Manager
Maggie Cheung, Circulation Manager
Sharon Adjiri, Production Manager
In addition to important fisheries news, every month they bring readers important information and lessons on Safety, entertaining pieces about commercial fishing history, a commercial listing of fishing vessels and equipment in their classified section, updated information on seafood market trends and important notices about all the meetings and conferences occurring on the West Coast.
Cost: $21.00
Frequency: Monthly
Circulation: 14,933
Founded in 1945
Printed in 4 colors on newsprint stock

22829 Fishing Tackle Retailer
ESPN Productions
3500 Blue Lake Drive
Birmingham, AL 35243
407-566-2277; Fax: 334-279-7148
www.bassmaster.com
Facebook, Twitter, LinkedIn, YouTube, RSS
Clem Dippel, Publisher
Scott Wall, Advertising Sales
Information to inform and instruct America's fishing tackle retailers, merchandisers, and distributors on merchandise and sales techniques used to sell fishing tackle.
Cost: $4.00
Frequency: 11X/yr
Circulation: 17720
Founded in 1980
Printed in 4 colors

22830 Funworld
Intl. Assn. of Amusement Parks & Attractions
1448 Duke St
Alexandria, VA 22314-3403
703-836-4800; Fax: 703-299-5749
iaapa@iaapa.org
www.iaapa.org
Facebook, Twitter, LinkedIn
Scott Fais, Managing Editor
Juanita Chavarro Arias, Assistant Editor
Funworld Magazine is a service for IAAPA members and provides discussion and illustrative examinations of the amusement and attractions industry form members to stay current and connected. The magazine contains features that analyze various aspects of the amusement business including safety, thrill rides, financial issues, event coverage and profiles of member and nonmember facilities from around the world.
Cost: $45.00
Frequency: Monthly
Circulation: 8,500
Founded in 1917

22831 Golf Business
National Golf Course Owners Association
291 Seven Farms Dr
Suite 2
Daniel Island, SC 29492-8000
843-881-9956
800-933-4262; Fax: 843-856-3288
golfbusiness@ngcoa.org
www.ngcoa.org
Facebook, Twitter, YouTube
Michael Hughes, CEO
Joe Rice, Publisher
Frank Santangelo, Manager
The official publication of the National Golf Course Owners Association. The editorial content is designed to promote the exchange of information and ideas among course owners and senior industry executives to improve the profitability of their operations. Golf Business is dedicated to serving the entire interest of the golf course operation.
Cost: $35.00
Frequency: Monthly
Circulation: 20000
Founded in 1971
Printed in 4 colors on glossy stock

22832 Golf Course Management
Golf Course Superintendents Association of America
1421 Research Park Dr
Lawrence, KS 66049-3859
785-841-2240
800-472-7878; Fax: 785-832-4488
www.gcsaa.org
Facebook, Twitter
Mark Woodward, CEO
Scott Hollistor, Editor
Bunny Smith, Managing Editor
Mark Gabrick, Sr Manager Corp Sales/Marketing
Official monthly magazine of Golf Course Superintendents Association of America and golf course management industry's leading professional journal. Includes scientific, technical and practical management articles.
Cost: $60.00
Frequency: Monthly
Circulation: 40,000
Founded in 1932

22833 Golf Course News
4012 Bridge Avenue
Cleveland, OH 44113
216-961-4130; Fax: 216-961-0364
www.golfnewsmag.com
Kevin Gilbride, Publisher
John Walsh, Editor
Richard Foster, CEO
Chris Foster, President/COO
Doug Adams, Director Marketing
Focuses on course maintenance and management, new course openings, and awards and promotions. New products related to the industry and environment and government issues.
Cost: $45.00
Circulation: 30000

22834 Golf Inc Magazine
Cypress Manazines

250 Bei Marin Key Boulevard, #A
PO Box 1150
Novato, CA 94949-5727

415-382-2400
800-436-6149; Fax: 415-382-2416
mikeb@cypressmagazines.com
www.golfincmagazine.com

Jack Crittenden, President
Kim Boalick, Advertising
Mindy Heral, Marketing
Jim Dunlap, Editor-in-Chief

Provides news, success stories and benchmark data for all aspects of the golf course industry - including development, operations, marketing, retail, turf, sales and driving range.
Cost: $65.00
Frequency: Monthly
Circulation: 15000

22835 Golf Range Times
Forecast Golf Group
P.O.Box 3106
Glen Allen, VA 23058-3106

804-379-5760; Fax: 804-378-5780
www.forecastgolf.com

James E Turner, Publisher/Editor
Betty Jo Bass, Advertising Manager

Information on Golf Range industry changes and closings, new ranges, and development information and services.
Cost: $49.95
Frequency: Monthly
Circulation: 6000
Founded in 1990

22836 Golfdom
Questex Medica Group
PO Bo 5057
Brentwood, TN 37024

615-377-3322
866-344-1315; Fax: 615-377-3322
questex@sunbeltfs.com
www.golfdom.com

Patrick Jones, Publisher
Larry Aylward, Editor

Publication is written for golf course architects, superintendents, management companies, owners, developers, consultants and others in the industry with an interest in golf course design, construction, remodeling and related business and management topics. Subscription is free to Golf course superintendents, owners and managers. Individuals who are not qualified as superintendents, owners and managers can subscribe at the current subscription rate.
Cost: $30.00
Circulation: 3000
Founded in 1927

22837 Government Recreation & Fitness
Executive Business Media
825 Old Country Road
PO Box 1500
Westbury, NY 11590

516-334-3030; Fax: 516-334-3059
ebm-mail@ebmpubs.com
www.ebmpubs.com

Murry Greenwald, Publisher
Paul Ragnoz, Managing Editor

Government Recreation and Fitness reaches recreation and fitness professionals in every department and agency of the federal government, goes directly to the people who purchase your products, and covers both appropriated and nonappropriated fund budgets. Subscription is free to managers and operators of fitness centers and recreation facilities at US military bases, federal agencies and offices as well as procurement agents for these facilities and others allied to the field
Cost: $35.00
Frequency: 15 issues per year
Circulation: 9974
ISSN: 1086-7899
Founded in 1994
Printed in 4 colors on glossy stock

22838 Gun & Knife Show Calendar
F+W Media
38 E. 29th Street
New York, NY 10016

212-447-1400; Fax: 212-447-5231
contact_us@fwmedia.com
Twitter

Hugh McAloon, Publisher
Bruce Wolberg, Ad Manager
John Koenig, Editor'

A compilation of gun shows and knife shows held throughout the country, and is intended to be used as a complete guide for anyone who attends or displays at these shows. Regular listings include the dates of the show, the address, the city, state, number of tables, and the cost of tables. For attendees, the show hours and the cost of admission are listed. Shows are listed for a full year ahead and there is no charge to list a show.
Cost: $15.95
88 Pages
Frequency: Quarterly
Circulation: 5758
Founded in 1952

22839 Hockey Business News
Straight Line Communications
12327 Santa Monica Boulevard
#202
Los Angeles, CA 90025-2552

310-207-9916; Fax: 310-442-6663
hbn@artnet.net

Mark Brown, Publisher

Features articles on ice hockey news and events, Canadian and international news, industry trends and forecasts and new products.
Cost: $60.00
Frequency: 9 per year
Circulation: 5,000

22840 Horseman's Journal
National Horsemen's Administration Corporation
870 Corporate Drive
Suite 300
Lexington, KY 40503

859-259-0451
866-245-1711; Fax: 859-259-0452
racing@hpba.org
www.hbpa.org

Richard E Glover, Editor
Sandy Erreguin, Advertising Director

Official magazine of the National Horsemen's Benevolent and Protective Association. Designed to give owners and trainers of racehorses information helpful for the running of their horse related businesses.
56 Pages
Circulation: 32,000
Founded in 1942
Printed in 4 colors on glossy stock

22841 ISI EDGE
Ice Skating Institute
600 Custer Rd
Bldg 9
Plano, TX 75023

972-735-8800; Fax: 972-735-8815
isi@skateisi.org
www.skateisi.org

Peter Martell, Executive Director

Professional journal for the ice skating industry. Focuses on the needs and interests of the industry's managers, skating and hockey directors, instructors, and builders/suppliers.
Frequency: Bi-Monthly

22842 Inside Archery
2960 N Academy Boulevard
Suite 101
Colorado Springs, CO 80917

719-495-9999; Fax: 719-495-8899
www.fieldandstream.com
Twitter, LinkedIn

Bill Krenz, President/Editor
Sherry Krenz, VP/Publisher

The Archery Industry Authority
Founded in 1997

22843 International Bowling Industry
13245 Riverside Drive
Suite 501
Sherman Oaks, CA 91423

818-789-2695; Fax: 818-789-2812
info@bowlingindustry.com
www.bowlingindustry.com
Twitter, LinkedIn

Scott Frager, Publisher & Editor
Nick West, Associate Publisher
Fred Groh, Managing Editor
Patty Heath, Office Manager

Information on customer services, new products, industry trends, new concepts in management and marketing techniques, and employee motivation.
Cost: $32.00
Frequency: Monthly
Circulation: 10,205

22844 International Gaming and Wagering Business
BNP Media
PO Box 1080
Skokie, IL 60076-9785

847-763-9534; Fax: 847-763-9538
igwb@halldata.com

James Rutherford, Editor
Lynn Davidson, Marketing
Tammie Gizicki, Director

Focuses on business strategy, legislative information, food service and promotional concerns.
Frequency: Monthly
Circulation: 25000

22845 Journal of Physical Education, Recreation & Dance (JOPERD)
Society of Health and Physical Educators
1900 Association Dr
Reston, VA 20191-1502

703-476-3400
800-213-7193; Fax: 703-476-9527
lstrecker@shapeamerica.org
www.shapeamerica.org

Stephanie A. Morris, Chief Executive Officer
Laura E. Strecker, Managing Editor

Provides a variety of information on health, physical education, recreation, and dance issues than any other publication in the field.
25000 Members
Frequency: 9/Year
Founded in 1885

22846 Journal of Sport and Social Issues
Sage Publications
2455 Teller Road
Newbury Park, CA 91320

800-818-7243; Fax: 800-583-2665
journals@sagepub.com
www.sagepublications.com
Facebook

CL Cole, Editor

Brings together the latest research, discussion and analysis on contemporary sport issues.
Cost: $552.00
Frequency: Quarterly
ISSN: 0193-7235

22847 Lacrosse Magazine
113 W University Pkwy
Baltimore, MD 21210-3301

410-235-6882; Fax: 410-366-6735
info@uslacrosse.org
Facebook, Twitter, LinkedIn, Live Blogs

Steve Stenersen, President
Bill Schoonmaker, COO
Bill Rubacky, Managing Director of Marketing
Kira Muller, Director of Advertising Sales

The most widely circulated publication for the sport of lacrosse, Lacrosse Magazine connects the sport's community, educates players, coaches and officials, entertains fans and keeps the membership of US Lacrosse informed.
Frequency: Monthly
Circulation: 300M
ISSN: 1069-5893
Founded in 1982

22848 Master Skier
PO Box 187
Escabana, MI 49829

906-789-1139
www.masterskier.com

Journal dedicated to the skiing industry. Delivered to 51,000 readers in 19 countries.
Founded in 1986
Mailing list available for rent

22849 Medicine and Science in Sports and Exercise
American College of Sports Medicine
401 W Michigan Street
PO Box 1440
Indianapolis, IN 46206

317-347-7817; Fax: 317-634-7817
msse@acsm.org
www.acsm.org

Kent B Pandolf, Editor-in-Chief
Gay Smith, Editor

Scientific research, education, and practical applications of sports medicine and exercise science to maintain and enhance physical performance, fitness, health and quality of life.
Cost: $300.00
Frequency: Monthly
Circulation: 14842
ISSN: 0195-9131
Founded in 1968
Printed in 4 colors on matte stock

22850 Military Trader
F+W Media
38 E. 29th Street
New York, NY 10016

212-447-1400; Fax: 212-447-5231
contact_us@fwmedia.com
Facebook, Twitter, LinkedIn, Live Blogs

Rick Groth, Publisher
John Adams-Graf, Editor
David Nussbaum, Chair
Jim Ogle, Finance
David Blansfield, President

For military collectors, the best monthly source of news, features, collecting advice, shows, and events. Each issue offers thousands of 'For Sale' and 'Wanted' mlitary collectibles from hundreds of dealers and collectors. This is where to go when you are trying to buy or sell vintage military uniforms, pins, medals, helmets, ammunition, firearms, flags, and other militaria.
Cost: $19.00
56 Pages
Frequency: Monthly
Circulation: 9414
Founded in 1975

22851 Military Vehicles
F+W Media
38 E. 29th Street
New York, NY 10016

212-447-1400; Fax: 212-447-5231
contact_us@fwmedia.com
Facebook, Twitter, LinkedIn, Live Blogs

Bill Reed, President
John Adams-Graf, Editor
David Nussbaum, Chair
Jim Ogle, Finance
David Blansfield, President

Each issue includes news, vintage military photos, collecting advice, market information, show listings, and extensive display and classified advertising sections offering to buy and sell hundreds of jeeps, tanks, trucks, vehicle parts, and accessories from dealers and enthusiasts all over the world. Other regular features include book and media reviews, letters to the editor, tech topics, weapons & replicas, models & toys, and internet sightings.
Cost: $23.98
176 Pages
Circulation: 19,000
Founded in 1952

22852 NJCAA Review
National Junior College Athletic Association
1631 Mesa Ave Suite B
Suite 103
Colorado Springs, CO 80920

719-590-9788; Fax: 719-590-7324
www.njcaa.org
Facebook, Twitter

Mary Ellen Leicht, Executive Director
Mark Krug, Director Sports Information/Media
Marry Elen, Director
Dee Dorus, Administrative Assistant
Cost: $30.00
Frequency: 10x/Year
Circulation: 2500
Founded in 1989

22853 NRA InSights
National Rifle Association
11250 Waples Mill Rd
Fairfax, VA 22030-7400

703-267-1400
800-672-3888
www.nrapublications.org
Twitter, LinkedIn

NRAs official publication for its Junior members. Designed to motivate its readers to participate in all aspects of the shooting sports. Features personality profiles on top junior shooters, hunting stories, how-to pieces, program announcements, product surveys, safety features and educational information about firearms. Subscription included in membership dues.

22854 Online Magazine
Information Today
143 Old Marlton Pike
Medford, NJ 08055-8750

609-654-6266
800-300-9868; Fax: 609-654-4309
custserv@infotoday.com
www.infotoday.com

Thomas H Hogan, President
Roger R Bilboul, Chairman Of The Board

Online is written for information professionals and provides articles, product reviews, case studies, evaluation and informed opinion about selecting, using and managing electronic information products, plus industry and professional information about onlline database systems.
Cost: $115.00
Frequency: Monthly
Founded in 1976

22855 Outdoors Magazine
Elk Publishing
531 Main St
Colchester, VT 05446-7222

802-879-2013
800-499-0447; Fax: 802-860-0005
www.elkpublishing.com

James Austin, Publisher

A monthly publication covering hunting, fishing and wildlife issues in Vermont, New York, Maine, Massachusetts and Connecticut.
Cost: $18.95
Frequency: Monthly
Circulation: 10000
ISSN: 1096-1976
Founded in 1996
Printed in 4 colors on matte stock

22856 PGA TOUR Partners Magazine
North American Media Group
12301 Whitewater Dr
Suite 260
Minnetonka, MN 55343-4103

952-936-9333
800-688-7611; Fax: 952-936-9169

Seth Hoyt, Publisher

An exclusive, members-only publication filled with tips and techniques that can be used to improve your game, from the first tee to the 18th green.
Frequency: Bi-Monthly
Circulation: 1.3 m
Founded in 1978

22857 Paddler
Paddle Sport Publishing
122 South Orange Av.
Steamboat Springs, CO 80477-5450

970-879-1450
888-774-7554; Fax: 970-870-1404
www.paddlermagazine.com

Eugene Buchanan, Publisher/Editor
Tom Bie, Managing Editor

Each issues is filled with stories on places to paddle, skill enhancement, gear reviews, environmental issues, industry updats and profiles of leading paddlers.
Cost: $18.00
Frequency: Monthly
Circulation: 5527
Printed in 4 colors on glossy stock

22858 Parachutist Magazine
United States Parachute Association
5401 Southpoint Centre Blvd
Fredericksburg, VA 22407-2612

540-604-9740; Fax: 540-604-9741
uspa@uspa.org
www.uspa.org
Facebook, Twitter

Ed Scott, Executive Director
Stephanie Whittaker, Director, Accounting & HR
Laura Sharp, Director, Publications

Supporting safe skydiving and those individuals who practice the sport. The magazine discusses issues dealing with training, safety, equipment, and networking the worldwide community of skydivers.
Cost: $4.50
112 Pages
Frequency: Monthly
Circulation: 35000
Founded in 1946

22859 Pool and Spa News
Leisure Publications
6222 Wilshire Blvd
Los Angeles, CA 90020-4244

323-644-4801
888-269-8410; Fax: 323-801-4986
www.poolspanews.com
Facebook, Twitter, LinkedIn

Dick Coleman, Publisher
Erika Taylor, Editor
Steve Schlange, Marketing Manager
Scot Christ, Accountant

Pool and Spa News goals are: to furnish information to help pool and spa professionals function better in their businesses; to showcase products that can be sold or used in the industry; to help make their business life easier and more rewarding.
Cost: $16.50
Frequency: Semi-Monthly
Founded in 1960
Mailing list available for rent

22860 Powersports Business
Ehlert Publishing Group
3300 Fernbrook Lane N
Suite 200
Plymouth, MN 55447

763-383-4400
800-848-6247; Fax: 763-383-4499
customerservice@powersportsbusiness.com
www.powersportsbusiness.com
Facebook, Twitter, LinkedIn

Mark Adams, CEO
Dave McMahon, Editor

Gives dealers, distributors, and manufacturers timely business news and analysis every three weeks.
Frequency: Weekly
Circulation: 18000
Founded in 1969

22861 Pro Football Weekly
302 Saunders Rd
Suite 100
Riverwoods, IL 60015-3897

847-940-1100
800-331-7529; Fax: 847-940-1108
www.profootballweekly.com
Facebook, Twitter, LinkedIn

Hub Arkush, President

Seeks to bring the best coverage in the NFL to its readers.
Cost: $49.95
Frequency: Weekly
Founded in 1967

22862 Professional Skater
Professional Skaters Association
3006 Allegro Park Ln SW
Rochester, MN 55902-4159

507-280-6812; Fax: 507-281-5491
office@skatepsa.com
www.skatepsa.com

Jimmie Santee, Executive Director

A bi-monthly magazine published by the Professional Skater Association.
Cost: $19.95
40 Pages
Frequency: Bi-Monthly
Founded in 1984

22863 QUAD Off-Road Magazine
Transworld Publishing
Ste 150
2052 Corte Del Nogal
Carlsbad, CA 92011-1491

760-722-7777; Fax: 760-722-0653
www.neodata.com

Jason Young, Publication Contact

Quad off-road magazine delivers all things ATV: Breathtaking photography, tons of practical tips, the hottest nwe products, Quad comparison tests, ARV adventure stories, and much more.
Cost: $9.97
Frequency: Monthly

22864 Quarter Horse Racing Journal
American Quarter Horse Association
PO Box 200
Amarillo, TX 79168-0001

806-376-4811; Fax: 806-349-6411
www.aqha.com
Facebook, Twitter, LinkedIn, You Tube

Jim Helzer, President

News and races, health and management, business and industry, winner's circle, the handicapper, horse health, quarter paths, sports medicine, finish line and others are featured articles.
Frequency: Monthly

22865 Racquetball Magazine
USA Racquetball
4244 Russet Court
Lilburn, GA 80904-2906

770-972-2303; Fax: 719-635-0685
rjohn@usra.org
www.racqmag.com

Jim Hiser, Executive Director
Kevin Joyce, Director Membership
Melody Weiss, Director Finance
Heather Fender, Executive Assistant/Event Coord
Ed Mazur, President

Geared toward a readership of informed, active enthusiasts who seek entertainment, instruction and accurate reporting of events. Available by subscription through the US Racquetball Association National Office.
Cost: $20.00
64 Pages
Frequency: Bi-Monthly
Circulation: 16,000
ISSN: 1060-877X
Founded in 1990
Printed in 4 colors on glossy stock

22866 Recreational Ice Skating
Ice Skating Institute
6000 Custer Rd
Bldg 9
Plano, TX 75023

972-735-8800; Fax: 972-735-8815
editor@skateisi.org
www.skateisi.org

Peter Martell, Executive Director

Distributed to ISI individual skater members, skating coaches, and rinks and pro shops worldwide. Written for and about ice skating enthusiasts and focuses on promoting ice skating as recreation and sport.
Frequency: Quarterly

22867 Referee
National Association of Sports Officials
2017 Lathrop Ave
Racine, WI 53405-3758

262-632-5448
800-733-6100; Fax: 262-632-5460
questions@referee.com
www.referee.com
Facebook, Twitter, LinkedIn

Barry Mano, President

Monthly magazine published by the National Association of Sports Officials. Containes interviews, feature articles, late-breaking news, personality profiles, investigative reports, health, legal and tax tips, and a wide range of technical information for many sports.
Cost: $44.95
80 Pages
Frequency: Monthly
Circulation: 77000
Founded in 1976
Printed in 4 colors on glossy stock

22868 Research Quarterly for Exercise and Sport
Society of Health and Physical Educators
1900 Association Dr
Reston, VA 20191-1598

703-476-3400
800-213-7193; Fax: 703-476-9527
tlawson@shapeamerica.org
www.shapeamerica.org

Stephanie A. Morris, Chief Executive Officer
Thomas F. Lawson, Managing Editor

RQES is a professional journal providing members with numerous articles and research on subjects that focus on the art and science of human movement studies.
Cost: $295.00
128 Pages
Frequency: Quarterly
Circulation: 6000
ISSN: 0270-1367
Mailing list available for rent
Printed in one color on glossy stock

22869 Ride BMX
Transworld Magazines
353 Airport Road
Oceanside, CA 92054

760-722-7777; Fax: 760-722-0653
www.neodata.com
Facebook, Twitter, LinkedIn

Jason Young, Publication Contact

Publication with information for BMX riders.
Cost: $15.97
Frequency: Monthly

22870 Rodale's Scuba Diving
F+W Media
38 E. 29th Street
New York, NY 10016

212-447-1400; Fax: 212-447-5231
contact_us@fwmedia.com
Facebook, Twitter, LinkedIn

Edited to provide information about the practice of diving, dive travel opportunities, the marine environment, the reader's health and safety and the dive equipment on which they depend. Travel editorial focuses on both domestic and international dive travel and equipment editorial offers readers comparative product reviews.
Cost: $16.97
Frequency: 11 Per Year
Circulation: 187,059
Founded in 1992

22871 Shooting Illustrated
National Rifle Association
11250 Waples Mill Rd
Fairfax, VA 22030-7400

703-267-1400
877-672-2000
www.nrapublications.org
Facebook, Twitter, LinkedIn

Aaron Carter, Associate Editor

Comprehensive, timely and all-inclusive. In its pages you will find the best gun writers in the world, assembled to bring you the latest information on rifles, pistols or shotguns. From handloading to gunsmithing to highpower competition; from varmint rifles to rifles for the world's biggest game; from competition pistols to heavy field revolvers.
Cost: $9.95

22872 **Shooting Industry**
12345 World Trade Drive
San Diego, CA 92128-3102

858-674-4898
858-605-0254; Fax: 619-297-5353
subs@shootingindustry.com
www.shootingindustry.com
Facebook, Twitter, LinkedIn

Russ Thurman, Editor
Brian Friesen, Sales Manager

A trade publication covering the hunting and shooting industries. This publication is available to select dealers and select police personnel only. Dealers must have a current Federal Firearms License and no less than two additional credentials. Police personnel must have a letter from their Police Chief or Range Officer requesting a subscription (on department letterhead).
Cost: $25.00
Frequency: Monthly
Founded in 1955

22873 **Shooting Sports Retailer**
SSR Communications
200 Croft Street
Suite 1
Birmingham, AL 35242

205-408-3766; Fax: 212-944-1884
www.shootingsportsretailer.com

Glenn Karaban, President

Features articles on shooting sports equipment, sales techniques, new products, sales aids, and potential problems for the wholesale seller of shooting equipment.
Frequency: Monthly
Circulation: 17463
Founded in 1980

22874 **Shooting Sports USA**
National Rifle Association
11250 Waples Mill Rd
Fairfax, VA 22030-7400

703-267-1400
877-672-2000
www.nrapublications.org
Facebook, Twitter

Information for the competitive shooter, from smallbore to high power, air action pistol and everything in between.
Cost: $9.95

22875 **Single Shot Rifle Journal**
American Single Shot Rifle Association
PO Box 1162
Niles, MI 49120

269-687-9550
journaleditor@assra.com
www.assra.com

Gary Staup, President
John Merz, VP
D. Wayne Stiles, Editor

The official magazine of The American Single Shot Rifle Association. Susbscription is included with membership in the ASSRA.
Cost: $35.00
60 Pages
Frequency: Bi-Monthly
Circulation: 2400
Founded in 1948
Printed in on matte stock

22876 **Ski Area Management**
Beardsley Publishing Corporation
45 Main Street North
PO Box 644
Woodbury, CT 06798

203-263-0888; Fax: 203-266-0452
news@saminfo.com
www.saminfo.com

Jennifer Rowan, Publisher
Olivia Rowan, Marketing/Associate Publisher
Donna Jacobs, V.P./Administration
Rick Kahl, Editor
Ann Hasper, Senior Editor

SAM magazine is the professional trade publication for the mountain resort market. It is a bi-monthly, all-paid publication.
Cost: $48.00
Frequency: Monthly
Circulation: 3992
Founded in 1962
Printed in 4 colors on glossy stock

22877 **Ski Magazine**
929 Pearl Street
5720 Flatiron Parkway
Boulder, CO 80301

303-448-7600
800-678-0817; Fax: 303-442-6321
www.skimag.com
Facebook, Twitter, LinkedIn, You Tube

Kendall Hamilton, Editor-In-Chief
Greg Ditrinco, Executive Editor
Kim Beekman, Managing Editor
Samantha Berman, Senior Editor

Includes information on travel, gear, instruction, snow reports, mountain cams, and gift shops.
Cost: $11.00
Frequency: 8X/year

22878 **SkiTrax Magazine**
260 Spadina Avenue
Suite 200
Toronto, Canada M5V1P9, ON

416-977-2100
866-754-8729; Fax: 416-977-9200
www.skitrax.com
Facebook, Twitter, LinkedIn, You Tube

North America's premier nordic publication is the official magazine of the USSA and CCC and offers the broadest coverage of nordic skiing available. Coverage includes comprehensive Annual North American Buyer's Guide; local touring centers and exotic backcountry hide-a-ways; complete North American and international competition coverage; regular tips on products; training, technique, telemark, masters, and waxing; extensive calendar of events; plus much more.

22879 **Soccer Journal**
National Soccer Coaches Association of America
6700 Squibb Road
Suite 215
Mission, KS 66202

913-362-1747
800-458-0678; Fax: 913-362-3439
www.nscaa.com

The official publication of the National Soccer Coaches of America. Produced exclusively for soccer coaches. Each issue contains technical and tactical articles, news and updates on important events, thoughts from opinion leaders in the sport and features on the interesting people and issues of the game. Subscription included in NSCAA membership.
Cost: $50.00
Frequency: 8X/Year
Circulation: 18000
Founded in 1941

22880 **Speedway Illustrated**
Speedway Illustrated
107 Elm St
Salisbury, MA 01952-1803

978-465-9099
888-837-3684; Fax: 978-465-9033
editorial@speedwayillustrated.com
www.speedwayillustrated.com

Dick Berggren, VP
Steve Chryssos, Advertising Manager
Lynne Henry, Advertising Sales

They'll show you how to build and race your own car, and take you inside at NASCAR's hottest teams and stars.
Cost: $19.94
Frequency: Monthly
Circulation: 150000
Founded in 2000

22881 **Sporting Goods Business**
VNU Business Publications
2900 Veterans Hwy
Bristol, PA 19007-1606

847-763-9050
800-464- 759; Fax: 847-763-9037
info@sgdealer.com
Facebook, Twitter

Michael Marchesano, President
Derek Irwin, CFO
Sid Holt, Editorial Director

Covers information on all facets of sporting goods, including industry news, sales volume analysis, market events coverage, and other statistics, also covers store operation, merchandising, pricing, promotion, cost control, and sales training.
Cost: $75.00
Frequency: Monthly
Circulation: 27,374
Founded in 1905

22882 **Sporting Goods Dealer**
VNU Publications
PO Box 1184
Skokie, IL 60076-8194

847-763-9050
800-464- 759; Fax: 847-763-9037
info@sgdealer.com
Facebook, Twitter

Michael Marchesano, President/CEO
Sid Holt, Editorial Director
Derek Irwin, CFO

Sporting Goods Dealer offers reporting on industry insiders, new products, and merchandising trends affecting team dealers and retailers that service schools, colleges, and pro and local teams.
Cost: $75.00
Circulation: 10000
Founded in 1905

22883 **Sporting News**
Sporting News Publishing Company
PO Vox 51570
Boulder, CO 80322-1510

314-997-7111
800-777-6785; Fax: 314-993-7798
www.sportingnews.com

Pete Spina, Publisher
Kathy Kinkeade, VP

A comprehensive publication covering sporting goods manufacturers, retailers, wholesalers and distributors.
Cost: $15.97
Frequency: Bi-Monthly

22884 **Sports Illustrated**
Time Life Building
New York, NY 10020-1393

212-229-9797; Fax: 212-467-4049

John Huey, Editor-in-Chief
Terry McDonell, Editor, Time Inc. Sports

Group
Paul Fichtenbaum, Managing Editor, SI.com

Sports Illustrated is the most respected voice in sports journalism, which reaches a weekly audience of nearly 21 million adults, and SI.com, the 24/7 sports news website that delivers up to the minute news, scores, statistics and in-depth analysis.
Cost: $39.95

Frequency: 56 Issues/Year

22885 Sports Illustrated for Kids
Sports Illustrated
1271 Ave of the Americas
Suite 32
New York, NY 10020-1401

212-522-1212
212-467-4049; Fax: 212-522-0318
www.sikids.com
Facebook

Bob Der, Managing Editor & Publisher
Beth Power Bugler, Creative Director
Justin Tejada, Assistant Managing Editor
Paul Ulane, Senior Producer, sikids.com

Great action photos, easy-to-read stories about star athletes, helpful instructional tips from the pros, humor, comics and activities.
Cost: $24.95

Frequency: Monthly

22886 SportsTravel Magazine
Schneider Publishing Company
11835 W Olympic Blvd
Suite 1265
Los Angeles, CA 90064-5814

310-577-3700
877-577-3700; Fax: 310-577-3715
info@schneiderpublishing.com
www.schneiderpublishing.com
Facebook, Twitter, LinkedIn

Tim Schneider, President
Lisa Furfine, Associate Publisher
Jason Gewirtz, Managing Editor/SportsTravel

SportsTravel magazine is the event organizer's guide to successfully creating and staging sports events. SportsTravel provides information on sports destinations and venues, transportation and accommodations, bidding for events, sponsorships, and marketing. SportsTravel facilitates relationships among sports governing bodies, host destinations, sponsors, and suppliers.
Cost: $48.00

Circulation: 14,000
ISSN: 1091-5354
Founded in 1997
Printed in 4 colors on glossy stock

22887 Sportsbusiness Journal
Business Journals Inc
120 W Morehead St
Suite 420
Charlotte, NC 28202-1874

704-973-1200
800-829-9389; Fax: 704-973-1201
www.citybiznetwork.com

George Conley, President

Provides important news information sports industry executives need to be successful in the fast paced world of sports business
Cost: $249.00

Frequency: 49X/Year
Circulation: 17,000
Founded in 1998

22888 Squash Magazine
23 Cynwyd Road
PO Box 1216
Bala Cynwyd, PA 19004-5216

610-667-4006; Fax: 610-667-6539
Facebook, Twitter

Craig W Brand, Executive Director
Keith Klipstein, Executive Director

Articles on the sport of squash racquets in the United States.
Cost: $35.00
Frequency: 10 per year

22889 Strategies: A Journal for Physical and Sport Educators
Society of Health and Physical Educators
1900 Association Dr
Reston, VA 20191-1502

703-476-3400
800-213-7193; Fax: 703-476-9527
lstrecker@shapeamerica.org
www.shapeamerica.org

Stephanie A. Morris, Chief Executive Officer
Laura E. Strecker, Managing Editor

Delivers practical ideas, how-to information, and tips for sport and physical educators.
Frequency: Bimonthly

22890 Synchro Swimming USA
US Synchronized Swimming
132 E Washington Street
Suite 800
Indianapolis, IN 46204-3674

317-237-5700; Fax: 317-237-5705
marketing@usasynchro.org
www.usasynchro.org

Terry Harper, Executive Director
Taylor Payne, Media Relations Director
Jordan Dillon, Business Development Director
Judy McGowan, President
Frequency: Quarterly
Circulation: 6000

22891 TEE Time Magazine
PO Box 225
Whitman, MA 02382

781-447-2299; Fax: 781-447-7773
www.teetime-mag.com
Facebook, Twitter

Mary Porter, Editor
Karen Christoforo, Sales

The Mid-Atlantics region's most comprehensive golf magazine. Each issue includes golf instruction, profiles of Mid-Atlantic personalities, course reviews and more.
Cost: $12.95
64 Pages

22892 Training & Conditioning
MAG
20 East Lake Rd.
Ithaca, NY 14850-5220

607-257-6970; Fax: 607-257-7328
info@athleticbid.com
www.momentummedia.com

Mark Goldberg, Publisher
Diedra Harkenrider, East and Southeast US Sales Rep
Pennie Small, Manager

Articles on injury protection and treatment, rehabilitation, strength and speed training, as well as cardiovascular equipment for competitive athletes.
Frequency: BiMonthly
Circulation: 27,400

22893 Transworld Motocross
Transworld Publications
353 Airport Road
Oceanside, CA 92054

760-722-7777; Fax: 760-722-0653
www.neodata.com

Jason Young, Publications Contact
Al Crolius, Manager

Magazine designed for the motocross enthusiast.
Cost: $16.97
Frequency: Monthly

22894 Transworld Skateboarding Business
Transworld Business Subscriptions
2052 Corte del Nogal
Suite 100
Carlsbad, CA 92011

760-722-7777
850-682-7644; Fax: 760-722-0653
www.twsbiz.com
Facebook, Twitter, LinkedIn

Larry Balma, Publisher
Brad McDonald, Manager

Geared toward skateboard retailers, apparel chain buyers, and manufacturers of skateboard products, includes new product information, industry news, and technical innovations.
Cost: $16.97
Frequency: Monthly
Circulation: 14500

22895 Transworld Snowboarding
Transworld Business
Ste 150
2052 Corte Del Nogal
Carlsbad, CA 92011-1491

760-722-7777
850-682-7644; Fax: 760-722-0653
www.twsnow.com
Facebook, Twitter, LinkedIn

Larry Balma, Publisher
Brad McDonald, Manager

Articles on industry news, retailer surveys, new products, and technical studies.
Cost: $14.97
Frequency: 9/Year
Circulation: 20000

22896 Transworld Surf
Transworld Publishing
Ste 150
2052 Corte Del Nogal
Carlsbad, CA 92011-1491

760-722-7777
850-682-7644; Fax: 760-722-0653
www.neodata.com
Facebook, Twitter, LinkedIn

Jason Young, Publications Contact
Brad McDonald, Manager

Magazine for surfing enthusiasts.
Cost: $12.00
Frequency: Monthly

22897 Trapper & Predator
F+W Media
38 E. 29th Street
New York, NY 10016

212-447-1400; Fax: 212-447-5231
contact_us@fwmedia.com

Hugh McAloon, Publisher
Paul Wait, Editor

Contains news, in-depth features, and how-to tips on trapping, the art of predator calling, and animal damage control. Contributors include the top names in the business. Regular columns and departments include The Fur Shed, Let's Swap Ideas, Q&A, and news from state trapping associations nationwide.
Cost: $18.95
Frequency: 10 Per Year
Circulation: 38,260
Founded in 1975

22898 **Turkey & Turkey Hunting**
F+W Media
38 E. 29th Street
New York, NY 10016
212-447-1400; Fax: 212-447-5231
Hugh McAloon, Publisher
Paul Wait, Editor
Edited for serious, technical, year-round, gun and bow turkey hunters. Features emphasize success and enjoyment of the sport. Articles focus on hunting, scouting, turkey behavior and biology, hunting ethics, new equipment, methodologies, turkey management, and current research. Columns include Tree Call,Mail Pouch, Turkey Biology, a Q&A column, Hunter's Library, Turkey Gear, and Last Call.
Cost: $15.95
Frequency: 6 Per Year
Circulation: 68,962
Founded in 1991

22899 **USA Table Tennis**
USA Table Tennis
1 Olympic Plaza
Colorado Springs, CO 80909-5746
719-866-4583; Fax: 719-632-6071
www.usatt.org
Facebook, Twitter
Michael Cavanaugh, CEO
Dedicated to providing readers with all of the tools and information necessary to follow or participate in this life-long sport.
9000 Members
Frequency: 6x/Year
Circulation: 8000
Founded in 1935

22900 **Velobusiness**
Inside Communications
1830 55th St
Boulder, CO 80301-2700
303-440-0601; Fax: 303-444-6788
Felix Magowan, President
Trends in the market, new product develoment updates and spot news reports, also includes testing and performance evaluations, as well as marketing, merchandising and sales techniques.
Cost: $35.00
Frequency: Monthly
Circulation: 10,560

22901 **Woman's Outlook**
National Rifle Association
9582 Hamilton Ave
Huntington Beach, CA 92646
800-565-6651
877-672-2000
Created especially for women. Covers topics from personal protection and home security to general firearms safety and recreation. Subscription complimentary with membership in NRA. Otherwise $9.95

22902 **Woodall's Campground Management**
Woodall Publishing Company
PO Box 8600
Ventura, CA 93002-8600
805-667-2001
877-680-6155; Fax: 805-667-4122
info@woodallpub.com
www.affinitygroup.com
Michael A Schneider, CEO
Kristopher Bunker, Editor
Terry Thompson, Advertising
Information for campground owners and managers, provides methods of management and industry trends along with reports from independent and franchise campgrounds, public parks and state associations.
Cost: $24.95
Frequency: Monthly
Circulation: 10,000
Founded in 1935

Trade Shows

22903 **AACCA Spirit Coaches Conference**
American Association of Cheerleading Coaches
6745 Lenox Center Court
Suite 318
Memphis, TN 38115
800-533-6583; Fax: 901-251-5851
www.aacca.org
Lauri Harris, Executive Director
Michle Ziegler, Instructor
The official NFHS Sprit Coaches Education Program.
Frequency: Annual
Founded in 1988

22904 **AAU Annual Convention**
Amateur Athletic Union
1910 Hotel Plaza Boulevard
PO Box 22409
Lake Buena Vista, FL 32830
407-934-7200; Fax: 407-934-7242
pam@aausports.org
www.aausports.org
Facebook, Twitter
Pam Marshall, Convention Contact
John Hodges, Exhibitor Information
Bobby Dodd, President/CEO
National Convention of the Amateur Athletic Union.

22905 **ASA Sportfishing Summit**
American Sportfishing Association
225 Reinekers Lane
Suite 420
Alexandria, VA 22314
703-519-9691; Fax: 703-519-1872
mjwilliamson@asafishing.org
www.asafishing.org
Facebook, Twitter
Mary Jane Williamson, Communications Director
Amy Yohanes, Administrative Services Manager
Gordon Robertson, VP
Patrick Egan, Manager
ASA's membership meeting and premier networking event. From special sessions, to business workshops tp association committee meeting, the Summit provides a wide-range of opportunities to gain information on the most relevant issues facing the sportfishing industry.
Frequency: October

22906 **ASGCA Meeting**
American Society of Golf Course Architects
125 N Executive Dr
Suite 302
Brookfield, WI 53005-6035
262-786-5960; Fax: 262-786-5919
info@asgca.org
www.asgca.org
Facebook, Twitter
Chad Ritterbusch, Executive Director
Aileen Smith, Director, Programming
Marc Whitney, Director, Communications
Combines golfing experiences with informational seminars and social engagements to form a trulyuniqie atmosphere that makes for both an enjoyable and educational meeting experience.
185 Members
Founded in 1946

22907 **AVCA Annual Convention**
American Volleyball Coaches Association
2365 Harrodsburg Road
Suite A325
Lexington, KY 40504
859-226-4315
866-544-2822; Fax: 859-226-4338
members@avca.org
www.avca.org
Facebook, Twitter, LinkedIn
Kathy DeBoer, Executive Director
Will Engle, Assistant Director, Events
A gathering of volleyball coaches and vendors
1700 Members
Frequency: Annual

22908 **Action Sports Retailer Trade Exhibit West Fall and Spring**
ASR Trade Expo
31910 Del Obispo
Suite 200
San Juan Capistrano, CA 92675
949-226-5744; Fax: 949-226-5659
www.asrbiz.com
Tina Middleton, Marketing Director
Lisha Steinkoenig, Registration Coordinator
Megan Lara, Expo Coordinator
Provides the ultimate showcase of the action sports and youth lifestyle market by attracting the world's largest and most powerful brands and buyers representing such diverse markets as surf, skate, swim, snow, footwear and fashion.
10M Attendees
Frequency: September/February

22909 **Allegheny Sport, Travel and Outdoor Show**
Expositions
PO Box 550
Edgewater Branch
Cleveland, OH 44107-0550
216-529-1300
800-600-0307; Fax: 216-529-0311
www.sportandtravel.com
Chris Fassnacht, Show Producer
Dedicated to hunting, shiftin and camping. Features hundreds of state-of-the-art exhibitors, dozens of live demonstrations, and a top notch line-up of seminar experts.
Frequency: Annual
Founded in 1985

22910 **Amateur Softball Association of America**
2801 NE 50th Street
Oklahoma City, OK 73111
405-424-5266; Fax: 405-424-3855
www.asasoftball.com
Bill Plummer III, Hall of Fame/Trade Show Manager
Ron Radigonda, Executive Director
Annual meeting of the Amateur Softball Association.
1000+ Attendees
Frequency: Annual/November
Founded in 1933

22911 **American Baseball Coaches Association Convention**
108 S University Avenue
Suite 3
Mount Pleasant, MI 48858-2327
989-775-3300; Fax: 989-775-3600
abca@abca.org

www.abca.org
Facebook, Twitter

Nick Phillips, Membership/Convention Coordinator
4000 Attendees
Frequency: Annual

22912 American Bowling Congress Annual Convention
United States Bowling Congress
5301 South 76th Street
Greendale, WI 53129

414-216-6400
800-514-2695; Fax: 414-421-8560
bowlinfo@bowl.com
www.bowl.com

Annual conference of the United States Bowling Congress whose mission is to ensure the integrity and protect the future of the sport by providing programs and services and enhancing the bowling experience.

22913 American Camp Association Conference & Exhibits
American Camp Association
5000 State Road 67 N
Martinsville, IN 46151-7902

765-342-8456
800-428-2267; Fax: 765-342-2065
www.aca-camps.org
Facebook, Twitter, LinkedIn

Tisher Bolger, President
Scott Brody, VP
Steve Baskin, Treasurer Board of Directors
Peg Smith, CEO

One hundred and forty to one hundred and fifty booths of arts and crafts, computer software, sporting goods, waterfront equipment and more plus a seminar and workshop.
1,200 Attendees
Frequency: Annual
Founded in 1943

22914 American College of Sports Medicine Annual Meeting
401 W Michigan Street
Indianapolis, IN 46202

317-637-9200; Fax: 317-634-7817
acsm@acsm.org
www.acsm.org
Facebook, Twitter, LinkedIn, You Tube

James R Whitehead, Executive VP
Janet Walberg Rankin, President

One hundred and eighty-five exhibits of sports equipment, publications, supplies and services, conference and banquet. CME credits available for a nominal fee at time of registration.
5000 Attendees
Frequency: Annual
Founded in 1954

22915 American Football Coaches Association Convention
American Football Coaches Association
100 Legends Lane
Waco, TX 76706

254-754-9900; Fax: 254-754-7373
www.afca.com
Facebook, Twitter

Grant Teaff, Executive Director

120 booths of equipment, supplies and services relevant to the game of football. Three-day event includees coaching clinic, awards luncheon and Coach of the Year dinner.
6000 Attendees
Frequency: Annual/January
Founded in 1921

22916 American Greyhound Track Operators Association
Palm Beach Kennel Club
1111 North Congress Avenue
West Palm Beach, FL 33409

561-688-5799; Fax: 801-754-2404
www.agtoa.com
Facebook, Twitter

Richard Winning, President
Dennis Bicsak, Managing Coordinator
Dennis Bicsak, Managing Coordinator
Michael Corbin~, Treasurer

A forum for all those affiliated with the sport to exchange ideas and to develop new techniques for the improvement and growth of the greyhound industry.
400 Attendees
Frequency: Annual/March

22917 American Hockey Coaches Association Convention
American Hockey Coaches Association
7 Concord Street
Gloucester, MA 01930

781-245-4177; Fax: 781-245-2492
ahcahockey@comcast.net
www.ahcahockey.com
Facebook, Twitter, LinkedIn

Joe Bertagna, Executive Director
George Gwozdecky, President
Kevin Sneddon, VP/Convention Planning

70 exhibits of ice hockey equipment and supplies plus worksop and banquet.
500 Attendees
Frequency: Annual/April
Founded in 1960

22918 American Orthopaedic Society for Sports Medicine Annual Meeting
American Orthopaedic Society for Sports Medicine
6300 N River Road
Suite 500
Rosemont, IL 60018-4229

847-292-4900
877-321-3500; Fax: 847-292-4905
www.sportsmed.org

Michelle Schaffer, Exhibits Coordinator
Camille Petrick, Manager

130 exhibits of equipment supplies and services for sports medicine and related fields. Banquet and tours available.
1,500 Attendees
Frequency: June/July
Founded in 1972

22919 American Swimming Coaches Association
5101 NW 21st Avenue
Suite 200
Fort Lauderdale, FL 33309

954-563-4930
800-356-2722; Fax: 954-563-9813
swimmingcoach.org
Facebook

John Leonard, Executive Director
Lori Klatt, Marketing

Annual convention
1.5M Attendees
Frequency: September

22920 American Youth Soccer Organization
12501 S Isis Avenue
Hawthorne, CA 90250

310-643-6455
800-872-2976; Fax: 310-643-5310
www.soccer.org

Rick Smith, Executive Director

The AYSO annual general meeting is your opportunity to represent your region, area or section on a national level.
800 Attendees
Frequency: Annual

22921 Archery Trade Show
Archery Trade Association
PO Box 70
Suite 310
Minnesota, UT 84107

507-233-8130
866-266-2776; Fax: 507-233-8140
info@archerytrade.org
www.archerytrade.org
Facebook, Twitter

Jay McAnich, President/CEO
Denise Parker, VP/Director Marketing
Cindy Brophy, Manager Tradeshow/Membership Svces
Kelly A. Kelly, Executive Assistant
Kurt Weber, Director of Marketing

Formerly the Archery Manufacturers and Merchants Organization (AMO), the ATA provides the core funding and direction critical to the future of archery and bowhunting. The trade show features 499 exhibitors cover 155,500 square feet.
8000 Attendees
Frequency: Annual

22922 Arnold Sports Festival
Arnold Sports Festival
1215 Worthington Woods Blvd.
Worthington, OH 43805

614-431-2600; Fax: 516-625-1023
www.arnoldsportsfestival.com
Facebook, Twitter

Lucy Pinneyr, Event Chair
Brent LaLonda, Media Contact

Five days of fitness equipment, sports entertainment, supplements, apparel and athletic stars, with more than 17,000 competitive athletes in 40 sporting events. Over 500 exhibitors and 150,000 visitors; takes place during the Arnold Sports Festival
150M+ Attendees
Frequency: March
Founded in 1976

22923 Athletic Equipment Managers Association Convention
723 Keil Ct
Bowling Green, OH 43402-2235

Home Page: www.equipmentmanagers.org

Sporting goods equipment manufacturers.
300 Attendees
Frequency: June

22924 BCA Convention
National High School Baseball Coaches Association
PO Box 12843
Tempe, AZ 85284

602-615-0571; Fax: 480-838-7133
rdavini@cox.net
www.baseballcoaches.org

Ron Davini, Executive Director

22925 Billiard & Home Leisure Expo
Billiards Congress of America
4345 Beverly Street
Suite D
Colorado Springs, CO 80918

719-264-8300; Fax: 719-264-0900
www.bcaexpo.com
Facebook, Twitter, LinkedIn

Rob Johnson, Chief Executive Officer
Lynda Bradt, Business Accountant

Shane Tyree, Membership & Communications Manager

This show hosts nearly 300 companies in 1400 booths, featuring every product line in the home recreation industry, from billiard and game tables, cues and cue accessories, cloth, balls and apparel, to spas, bowling, darts, foosball, art, home furnishings, novelty items, outdoor living, books, publications, video games, coin-op, pinball, jukeboxes, gaming and much more.
Founded in 1948

22926 **Bowling Proprieters Association of America International Bowl Expo**
615 Six Flags Drive
PO Box 5802
Arlington, TX 76011-6347

800-343-1329
888-649-5585; Fax: 817-633-2940
www.bpaa.com
Facebook, Twitter, LinkedIn

Lee Ann Norton, Director Meetings/Events
Laurie Clower, Executive Assistant~
Judy King, Director of Finance

The bowling industry's premier event. Brings together thousands of bowling industry professionals in one place. You can find the latest trends, bowling-related products and services, marketing ideas, profit center opportunities, and tools to help you spread the excitement of bowling throughout your communities. Trade show showcases the latest products and services from more than 300 companies in over 900 exhibit booths.
5000 Attendees
Frequency: June
Founded in 1932

22927 **CMAA Annual Conference**
Club Managers Association of America
1733 King Street
Alexandria, VA 22314

703-739-9500; Fax: 703-739-0124
cmaa@cmaa.org
www.smaa.org
Facebook, Twitter, LinkedIn, You Tube

Jim Singerling, Executive VP

Club Managers Association of America Annual World Conference. This International Conference brings together club industry professionals from around the world for five days of challenging education, entertaining social events and an industry trade show.
Founded in 1990

22928 **CSCAA National Convention & Clinic**
College Swimming Coaches Association of America
1640 Maple
#803
Evanston, IL 60201

847-833-3478
r-groseth@northwestern.edu
Facebook, Twitter, LinkedIn

Bob Groseth, Executive Director
George Kennedy, President
Founded in 1990

22929 **Colorado RV Adventure Travel Show**
Industrial Expositions
1675 Larimer, Suite 700
PO Box 480084
Denver, CO 80248-0084

303-892-6800
800-457-2434; Fax: 303-892-6322
www.bigasalloutdoors.com
Facebook, Twitter, LinkedIn

Jeff Haughton, President
Dianne Seymour, Expo Manager

Recreational vehicles, accessories and travel.
18000 Attendees
Frequency: Annual/January
Founded in 1990

22930 **Colorado RV, Sports, Boat and Travel Show**
Industrial Expositions
1675 Larimer Street
Suite 700
Denver, CO 80202

303-892-6800
800-457-2434; Fax: 303-892-6322
www.bigasalloutdoors.com
Facebook, Twitter, LinkedIn

Jeff Haughton, President
Dianne Seymour, Expo Manager

Annual trade show of recreational vehicles, sports, boats and travel.
Founded in 1990

22931 **Crescent Ski Council**
PO Box 17944
Greenville, SC 29606-8944

864-229-7488; Fax: 864-235-2504
www.crescentskicouncil.org
Facebook, Twitter, LinkedIn, You Tube

Michelle Shuford, Contact

Exhibits of snow ski resorts and related lodging services. 50 booths.
500 Attendees
Frequency: April
Founded in 1969

22932 **Cross Country Ski Areas Association Annual Conference**
Cross Country Ski Areas Association
P.O. Box 818
Woodstock, VT 05091

802-236-3021
reese@xcski.org
Facebook, Twitter, Instagram

Reese Brown, President/ Executive Director
Jo Jo Toeppner, Chairman

Bringing together cross country ski enthusiasts to participate in workshops and forums on topics including interactive grooming, maintenance, and snowmaking elements.
Cost: $475.00
350 Members
Frequency: Annual
Founded in 1977

22933 **DEMA Show**

858-616-6408
800-862-3483; Fax: 858-616-6495
info@dema.org
www.dema.org

Tom Ingram, President & CEO
Nicole Russel, VP, Operations

Annual trade show produced by the Diving Equipment & Marketing Association, for companies doing business in the scuba diving, ocean water sports and adventure/dive travel industries.
10M Attendees
Frequency: Annual

22934 **Eastern Fishing and Outdoor Exposition**
International Sport Show Producers Association
PO Box 4720
Portsmouth, NH 03802-4720

603-431-4315; Fax: 603-431-1971
info@sportshows.com
www.sportshows.com
Facebook, Twitter, LinkedIn, You Tube

Paul Fuller, President

Over 450 exhibitors representing the entire world of fishing and hunting.
45k Attendees
Frequency: Annual/February
Founded in 1996
Mailing list available for rent

22935 **Eastern Iowa Sportshow**
Iowa Show Productions
PO Box 2460
Waterloo, IA 50704

319-232-0218; Fax: 319-235-8932
info@iowashows.com
www.iowashows.com
Facebook, Twitter, LinkedIn

See a huge display of fishing boats, family sport boats, personal watercraft, pontoons, tent campers, travel trailers, fifth wheels, vans, and motorhomes. Plus boat accessories, truck toppers, motorcycles, ATVs, fishing camps, fly-ins, outposts, Lake Erie Walleye charters, family resorts, Lake Michigan sportfishing, houseboat rentals, Golf vacations, canoe outfitters, big game outfitters, tourism associations, campgrounds, camping gear, fishing tackle, archery equipment, targets, decoys, calls.

22936 **FSGA Winter Conference**
Fantasy Sports & Gaming Association
1818 Parmenter Street
Suite 300
Middleton, WI 53562

608-310-7540
thefsga.org
Facebook, Twitter, LinkedIn

Christina McCoy, Executive Director
Michael Fiez, Marketing
Emily Petersen, Membership

January meeting of Fantasy Sports & Gaming Association members.

22937 **Fall RV & Van Show**
O'Loughlin Trade Shows
PO Box 80750
Portland, OR 97280-1750

503-246-8291; Fax: 503-246-1066
www.oloughlintradeshows.com
Facebook, Twitter, LinkedIn

Peter O'Loughlin, Show Manager

Portland, OR. Recreational vehicles and vans
Frequency: September

22938 **Fly Fishing Show - Denver**
854 Opossum Lake Road
Carlisle, PA 17013

717-243-6733
800-420-7582; Fax: 717-243-8603
www.flyfishingshow.com
Facebook, Twitter

Barry Serviente, Executive Director

Annual fly fishing show.

22939 **Football Officials Association Southwest Convention**
Dallas Football Officials Association
2005 Fairmeadow
Richardson, TX 75080

972-235-9110; Fax: 972-235-7675
dfoasecretary@aol.com
www.dfoa.com

David Tucker, Registration
Mike Woodard, President

Texas Association of Sports Officials annual convention.
1.8M Attendees
Frequency: Annual

22940 **Fred Hall's Western Fishing Tackle & Boat Show: Delmar**
Fred Hall & Associates

PO Box 2925
Camarillo, CA 93011

805-389-3339; Fax: 805-389-1219

Bart Hall, Show Manager

Featuring all forms of outdoor recreation including boats, fishing tackle, adventure travel and recreational vehicles.

22941 **Golf Course Superintendents Association of America**
GCSAA
1421 Research Park Drive
Lawrence, KS 66049-3858

785-841-2240
800-472-7878; Fax: 785-832-4455
www.golfindustryshow.com
Facebook, Twitter, LinkedIn, You Tube

Julia Ozark, Sr Trade Show Manager
Caroline Gollier, Trade Show Project Manager
Scotti Corley, Meeting/Trade Show Coordinator
Kelly Jo Springirth, Director Exhibit Services
Steve Mona, CEO

Trade show designed for the owners/operators of golf facilities and the professional members of the golf course and club management industries. The event combines education, networking and solutions for golf course superintendents, owners/operators, general managers, chief operating officers, architects and builders.
25M Attendees
Frequency: February

22942 **Grand Center Boat Show**
Show Span
2121 Celebration Drive NE
Grand Rapids, MI 49525

616-447-2860
800-328-6550; Fax: 616-447-2861
events@showspan.com
www.showspan.com
Facebook, Twitter, LinkedIn

Carolyn Alt, Manager

Held at the Grand Center in Grand Rapids, Michigan. Every kind of boat under the sun. Over 400 boats.
82000 Attendees
Frequency: February

22943 **Great Lakes Athletic Trainers**
8015 Kersey Drive
Indianapolis, IL 46236

815-455-3860; Fax: 815-477-6907
www.glata.org
Facebook, Twitter, LinkedIn

Mark Schauer, Co Coordinator
Kevin Gerlach, Co Coordinator

Annual meeting and symposium.
1M Attendees
Frequency: March

22944 **Greater Cincinnati Golf Show**
North Coast Golf Productions
PO Box 372
Twinsburg, OH 44087-0372

330-963-6963
800-939-0040; Fax: 330-487-0352
www.cincinnatigolfshow.com
Facebook, Twitter, LinkedIn

America's favorite consumer golf show.

22945 **ICAST**
American Sportfishing Association
1001 North Fairfax Street
Suite 501
Alexandria, VA 22314

703-519-9691; Fax: 703-519-1872
mdelvalle@asafishing.org
www.asafishing.org
Facebook, Twitter, LinkedIn

Maria del Valle, ICAST Director
Kenneth Andres, ICAST Associate
Gordon Robertson, VP
Mary Jane Williamson, Communications Director

The sportfishing industry's largest trade event is a major catalyst for sales and a terrific networking opportunity for the sportfishing community
Frequency: July

22946 **ISHA Annual Conference**
International Sports Heritage Association
PO Box 2384
Florence, OR 97439

541-991-7315; Fax: 541-997-3871
info@sportsheritage.org
www.sportsheritage.org
Facebook, Twitter, LinkedIn

Karen Bednarski, Executive Director
Sheila Kelly, President
Mike Gibbons, First Vice President
Pete Fierle, Second Vice President
Ed Harris, Treasurer

Session discussions, educational sessions and speakers
140+ Members
Founded in 1971

22947 **Ice Skating Institute**
6000 Custe Rd.
Bldg. 9
Plano, TX 75023

972-735-8800; Fax: 972-735-8815
isi@skateisi.org
www.skateisi.org
Facebook

Peter Martell, Executive Director

The industry's leading trade show where you're sure to find the technical information, products and suppliers you need to run your business every day. Who should attend: Arena owners and managers; Hockey and figure skating coaches and instructors; Ice arena programming directors; Operations personnel; builders and suppliers to the industry.
Frequency: Annual/May

22948 **International Pool & Spa Expo**
PO Box 612128
Dallas, TX 75261-2128

972-536-6350
888-869-8522; Fax: 972-536-6364
www.poolandspaexpo.com

Tina Brinkley, Operations Coordinator
Kathy Ruff, Operations Manager
Tracy Beaulieu, Conference Manager
Vila Snider, Registration Manager
Donna Bellantone, Assoc Show Director

Latest trends, newest products, and innovative ways to increase sales and add profits to your business.
16M Attendees
Frequency: November

22949 **Kansas Sports, Boat and Travel Show**
Industrial Expositions
PO Box 480084
Denver, CO 80248

303-892-6800
800-457-2434; Fax: 303-892-6322
www.bigasalloutdoors.com

Jeff Haughton, President
Dianne Seymour, Expo Manager

Annual show produced by Industrial Expositions.
Frequency: Annual

22950 **Let's Play Hockey International Expo**
Let's Play Hockey
2721 East 42nd Street
Minneapolis, MN 55406

612-729-0023; Fax: 612-729-0259
letsplay@letsplayhockey.com
www.letsplayhockey.com

Doug Johnson, Contact
Doug Johnson, Publisher
Kevin Kurtt, Editor

Hockey Industry Trade Show. Five days of events. Seminars, races, tournaments, awards banquet, expo demo day, Hall of Fame display, buying group meetings and more.
Founded in 1999

22951 **Lincoln Boat, Sport and Travel Show**
Egan Enterprises
4100 North 84th Street
Lincoln, NE 68505-5465

402-466-8102; Fax: 402-467-5630
www.nebraskasportsshow.com

Pat Egan, Contact Person

Equipment and supplies for the outdoor life.
Frequency: Annual

22952 **Management Conference & Team Dealer Summit**
National Sporting Goods Association
1601 Feehanville Drive
Suite 300
Mount Prospect, IL 60056

847-966-6742
800-815-5422; Fax: 847-391-9827
conference@nsga.org
www.nsga.org

Jeff Rosenthal, Chairman of the Board
Matt Carlson, President/CEO
Dan Kasen, Director of Information Services

The Sporting Goods industry's premier educational and networking event, featuring programming aimed at ensuring business' success, brings together leaders and industry insiders for engaging conversations and stimulating presentations.

22953 **NABC Convention & MarketPlace**
National Association of Basketball Coaches
1111 Main St
Suite 1000
Kansas City, MO 64105-2116

816-878-6222; Fax: 816-878-6223
www.nabc.com

Jim Haney, Executive Director
Reggie Minton, Deputy Executive Director
Kevin Henderson, Associate Executive Director
Dottie Yearout, Director of Membership Services
Janelle Guidry, Convention Manager

The Convention offers Professional Development Clinics
Frequency: Annual/Spring

22954 **NACDA Convention**
Nat'l Assoc of Collegiate Directors of Athletics
24651 Detroit Road
Westlake, OH 44145

440-892-4000; Fax: 440-892-4007
www.nacda.com
Facebook, Twitter, LinkedIn

Michael Cleary, Executive Director

Devoted to examining contemporary problems facing today's athletics administrator. Caters to administrators in all levels of intercollegiate athletics with general sessions for the entire membership and breakout sessions which are geared to the specific needs of administrators at all levels of the NCAA, NAIA, and NJCAA

22955 **NASC Sports Event Symposium**
9916 Carver Road
Suite 100
Cincinnati, OH 45242

513-281-3888; Fax: 513-281-1765
info@nascsymposium.com
www.nascsymposium.com
Facebook, Twitter, LinkedIn

Don Schumacher, Executive Director
Beth Hecquet, Director of Meetings and Events

National Association of Sports Commissions. Representing more than 550 organizations. Attendees are provided with new ideas, practical tips and the hottest trends.
550 Members
Founded in 1992

22956 **NASGW Annual Meeting and Expo**
National Association of Sporting Goods Wholesalers
1255 SW Prairie Trail Parkway
Ankeny, IA 50023-7068

515-334-1484; Fax: 515-334-1143
info@nasgw.org
www.nasgw.org
Facebook, Twitter, LinkedIn

Kenyon Gleason, President
Meg Pawelski, Director, Operations & Expo Manager
Easton Kuboushek, Program Manager
Donna Donovan, Financial Manager
Gregg Alexander, Communications Manager

Educational, marketing and communications opportunity for the hunting and shooting sports wholesaler, manufacturer and sales professional.
400 Members
Founded in 1954

22957 **NCAA Annual Convention**

317-917-6222; Fax: 317-917-6888
www.ncaasports.com
Facebook, Twitter, LinkedIn

Trade show and convention
Frequency: January
Founded in 1915

22958 **NFCA National Convention**
National Fastpitch Coaches Association
100 G T Thames Drive
Suite D
Starkville, MS 39759

662-320-2155; Fax: 662-320-2283
nfca@nfca.org
www.nfca.org
Facebook, Twitter, LinkedIn

Lacy Lee Baker, Executive Director
Hildred Deese, Senior Director of Events
Frequency: Annual, December

22959 **NSAA National Convention and Trade Show**
National Ski Areas Association
133 S Van Gordon Street
Suite 300
Lakewood, CO 80228

303-987-1111; Fax: 303-986-2345
nsaa@nsaa.org
www.nsaa.org
Facebook, Twitter, LinkedIn

Michael Berry, President
Keri Hone, Director Events/Projects
Tom Moore, Director Conventions/Meetings
Kate Powers, Director Member Services
Amy Steele, Director Sponsorships

Annual convention of the National Ski Areas Association

22960 **National Association of Basketball Coaches Annual Convention**
1111 Main Street
Suite 1000
Kansas City, MO 64105-2136

816-878-6222; Fax: 816-878-6223
www.nabc.org
Facebook, Twitter, LinkedIn

James Haney, Executive Director
Reggie Minton, Deputy Executive Director
Kevin Henderson, Associate Executive Director

Approximately 150 booths offering services and resources for Basketball Coaches.
3M Attendees
Frequency: March/April

22961 **National Institute for Golf Management**
National Golf Foundation
1150 South US Highway One
Suite 401
Jupiter, FL 33477

561-744-6006
888-275-4643; Fax: 561-744-6107
general@ngf.org
www.ngf.org
Facebook, Twitter, LinkedIn

Annual golf institute sponsored by the National Golf Foundation.
Frequency: Annual

22962 **National Intramural Recreational Sports Association**
4185 SW Research Way
Corvallis, OR 97333-1067

541-766-8211; Fax: 541-766-8284
nirsa@nirsa.org
www.nirsa.org
Facebook, Twitter, LinkedIn

Kent Blumenthal, Executive Director
Dr. William N. Wasson, Owner

This show provides an annual marketplace for athletic and recreational equipment, supplies and services.
1.6M Attendees
Frequency: Annual/April
Founded in 1950

22963 **National Recreation and Park Association's Conference and Exposition**
National Recreation and Park Association
22377 Belmont Ridge Road
Ashburn, VA 20148

703-858-0784; Fax: 703-858-0794
info@nrpa.org
www.nrpa.org

Kristine Stratton, President & CEO

Provides targeted learning opportunities specifically for parks and recreation directors, supervisors and managers, community center directors, recreation programmers, natural resources personnel, therapeutic recreation specialists, citizen advocates and students.
4000 Attendees
Founded in 1965

22964 **National Soccer Coaches Association of America**
800 Ann Avenue
Kansas City, KS 66101

913-362-1747
800-458-0676; Fax: 913-362-3439
nscaa.com
Facebook, Twitter, LinkedIn

Joe Cummings, CEO and Executive Director
Tommy Reder, CFO

Every coach who attends will find something new to add to their soccer reperoire. The trade show consists of more than 300 companies. Attendees can examine the latest soccer-related technology and equipment.
30m Members
9000 Attendees
Frequency: Annual/January
Founded in 1941

22965 **National Trappers Association Sports Show**
2815 Washington Avenue
Bedford, IN 47421

812-277-9670
866-680-8727; Fax: 812-277-9672
ntaheadquarters@nationaltrappers.com
www.nationaltrappers.com

Kraig Kaatz, President
Chris Flynn, VP
Kraig Kaatz, General Organizer

300 booths including outdoor sports supplies and dealers.
6M Attendees
Frequency: Annual/August

22966 **New York National Boat Show**
National Marine Manufacturers Association
148 West 37th Street
11th Floor
New York, NY 10018

212-984-7007; Fax: 212-564-2728
www.nyboatshow.com
Facebook, Twitter

Jonathon Pritko, Show Manager
Bob MkAlpine, Exhibitor Relationship Manager
Dan Castellano, Exhibitor Relationships Manager
Elba-Rosales Rise, Show Administrator
Josh Rosales, Operation Coordinator

Annual boat show held at Jacob Javitz Convention Center in New York
Frequency: January

22967 **North American Society for Sport Management Conference**
North American Society for Sport Management
Slippery Rock University
West Gym 014
Slippery Rock, PA 16057

724-738-4812; Fax: 724-738-4858
www.nassm.com
Facebook, Twitter

North American Society for Sport Management annual convention and trade show.

22968 **Northwest Sportshow**
General Sports Shows
3539 Hennepin Avenue
Minneapolis, MN 55408-3830

612-827-5833
800-777-4766; Fax: 612-827-1424

David Perkins, President

Public show offering the finest presentation of outdoor recreation and marine products and services.
205M Attendees
Frequency: March

22969 **Outdoorama Family Sport and Travel Show**
Michigan United Conservation Clubs
2101 Wood Street
PO Box 30235
Lansing, MI 48909

517-371-1041
800-777-6720; Fax: 517-371-1505
membership@mucc.org

www.mucc.org
Facebook, Twitter, LinkedIn

Sam Washington, Executive Director
Kelly Snyder, Event/Fundraising Assistant
Evan Steiner, Events/Fundraising Specialist

Michigan's favorite outdoor show featuring over 200,000 square feet of exhibit space dedicated to the latest in fishing and hunting equipment, fishing and power boats, recreational vehicles, outdoor gear and vacationing destinations throughout North America. Four-hundred plus booths.
42000 Attendees
Frequency: February
Founded in 1974

22970 PTR International Tennis Symposium
Professional Tennis Registry
P.O. Box 4739
Hilton Head Island, SC 29938

843-785-7244
800-421-6289; Fax: 843-686-2033
ptr@ptrtennis.org
Facebook, Twitter, LinkedIn

Dan Santorum, Chief Executive Officer
Julie Jilly, VP Marketing & Special Events
Helma Cap, Membership Director
Peggy Edwards, Director, Communications

Symposium of professional tennis teachers and coaches. PTR has excellent relationships and partnerships with industry leaders such as the USTA, Tennis Industry Association, the ITF and many National Tennis Federations.
15000 Members
Frequency: 2x Per Year
Founded in 1976

22971 Pop Warner Little Scholars Convention
586 Middletown Boulevard
Suite C-100
Langhorne, PA 19047-1867

215-752-2691; Fax: 215-752-2879
webmaster@popwarner.com
www.popwarner.com
Facebook, Twitter

Jon Butler, Executive Director
Mary Fitzgerald, COO
Lisa Moroski, National Cheer/Dance Commissioner
1000 Attendees
Frequency: Bi-Annual

22972 Professional Golfers Association Merchandise Show
Reed Exhibitions
383 Main Avenue
Norwalk, CT 06851

203-404-4800
800-840-5628; Fax: 203-840-9628
inquiry@pga.reedexpo.com
www.pgamerchandiseshow.com
Facebook, Twitter

Kara Codio, Marketing/Conference Manager
Sherry Major, Media Relations Manager
Jay Andronaco, Event Marketing Manager

The PGA Merchandise Show provides a snap-shot of the industry as a whole and access to products and services that pertain to every aspect of the game. It is the focal point for new product introductions, professional development programs, business meetings and more.
30M Attendees
Frequency: January

22973 Professional Golfers Association Golf Show
Sydney Convention and Exhibition Centre
Darling Harbour
Sydney
Australia NSW 2000

Home Page: www.pgaexpo.com
Facebook, Twitter, LinkedIn

International PGA Golf Show. 2006 Show held in Australia
50000 Attendees
Frequency: Annual

22974 RSA Convention and Trade Show
Roller Skating Association International
6905 Corporate Drive
Indianapolis, IN 46278

317-347-2626; Fax: 317-347-2636
rsa@rollerskating.com
www.rollerskating.org
Facebook, Twitter, LinkedIn, You Tube

Jim McMahon, Executive Director

Helping roller skating industry professionals discover ways to build strong foundations for their businesses.
1000 Members
Frequency: annual
Founded in 1937

22975 Rocky Mountain Snowmobile Expo
Industrial Expositions
1675 Larimer Street
Suite 700
Denver, CO 80202

303-892-6800
800-457-2434; Fax: 303-892-6322
www.bigasalloutdoors.com
Facebook, Twitter

Jeff Haughton, President
Diane Seymour, Expo Manager

Large display of snowmobiles and accessories, meet performance experts, resorts and lodges, winter clothing, ice fishing, winter travel destinations, snowmobile adventure theatre, avalanche awareness, swap meet and more.

22976 SHAPE America National Convention & Expo
Society of Health and Physical Educators
1900 Association Drive
Reston, VA 20191

703-476-3400
800-213-7193; Fax: 703-476-9527
membership@shapeamerica.org
convention.shapeamerica.org

Stephanie A. Morris, Chief Executive Officer

National convention and exposition that features many exhibits focusing on products, services and equipment within the fields of health, physical education, recreation and dance.
5000 Attendees
Frequency: Annual/April
Founded in 1879

22977 SHOT Show: Shooting Hunting Outdoor Trade Show
Reed Exhibition Companies
28 The Quadrant
Richmond 6851

203-404-4800
800-840-5628; Fax: 203-840-9628
www.reedexpo.com

Worldwide annual gathering that unites manufacturer and retailer and all other industry stakeholders to trade, source and learn about the latest products, innovations and trends in the shooting sports industry.
15M Attendees
Frequency: January

22978 SIA Snow Show
SnowSports Industries America
8377-b Greensboro Drive
McLean, VA 22102-3587

703-556-9020; Fax: 703-821-8276
siamail@snowsports.org
Facebook, Twitter, LinkedIn, YouTube, Wikipedia, Vimeo

From fashion to skis and snowboards to Nordic, snowshoes, outdoor and basic essentials, the SIA Snow Show previews the entire winter sports market and then deads to the on-snow demo to try it all out on snow.
700+ Members
19M Attendees
Frequency: Annual/January
Founded in 1954

22979 Saltwater Fishing Expo
Eastern Fishing and Outdoor Exposition
PO Box 4720
Portsmouth, NH 03802

603-431-4315; Fax: 603-431-1971
www.sportshows.com

The Saltwater Fishing Expo is expecting over 300 exhibitors representing the entire spectrum of saltwater sportfishing. There will be dozens of seminars throughout the three days of the show, which will be presented by experts who are at the top of their game.

22980 San Mateo Inernational Sportsmen's Expo
International Sportsmen's Exposition
PO Box 2569
Vancouver, WA 98668-2569

360-693-3700
800-545-6100; Fax: 360-693-3352
www.sportsexpos.com

Brian Layng, President/CEO
Rick Flattum, Director Operations
Heidi Crannell, Marketing Coordinator
Bruce Tarbet, Sponsorship/Advertising
Brent Layng, Sales Manager

Fishing, hunting, outdoor sports and destination travel show. Connect with new dealers and network with other exhibitors.

22981 Ski Dazzle Ski Show and Snowboard Expo: Chicago
Ski Dazzle
P.O. Box 1839
Laguna Beach, CA 92651

949-497-4977; Fax: 949-497-4123
snowdog@skidazzle.com
www.skidazzle.com
Facebook, Twitter, LinkedIn, You Tube

Judy Gray, Owner
Jim Foster, Owner

Hundreds of local, national and international exhibitors including over 85 resorts, ski and snowboard retailers, manufacturers, a huge ski and snowboard sale, and lots of surprises. Over 250 exhibit booths showcasing core companies of skiing and snowboarding.

22982 Ski Dazzle: The Los Angeles Ski Show & Snowboard Expo
P.O. Box 1840
Laguna Beach, CA 92651-1839

949-497-4977; Fax: 949-497-4123
snowdog@skidazzle.com
www.skidazzle.com
Facebook, Twitter, LinkedIn, You Tube

Judy Gray, Co-Owner
Jim Foster, Owner

Consumer ski show and snowboard expo at the Los Angeles Convention Center offering 350 ski and snowboard related exhibits. Excellent spon-

sor and promotional opportunities for 18-49 demographic audience.
90000 Attendees
Frequency: November

22983 **Soaring Society of America Annual Convention**
5425 West Jack Gomez Boulevard
P.O. Box 2100
Hobbs, NM 88241
575-392-1177; Fax: 575-392-8154
feedback@ssa.org
www.ssa.org
Denise Layton, Executive Director
Annual convetion of the Soaring Society of America.

22984 **Sporting Goods Manufacturers Markets**
1150 17th Street NW
8th Floor
Washington, DC 20036-1604
202-775-1762; Fax: 202-296-7462
info@sgma.com
Tom Cove, President/CEO
Gregg Harrley, VP
Kalinda Mathis, Director Marketing
Retailers, distributors, wholesalers, importers/exporters and other buyers of sports related products come for 10,000 exhibits of sports apparel, footwear, accessories and e-commerce products and services.
80000 Attendees
Frequency: Spring/Fall

22985 **Sports Licensing & Entertainment Marketplace Tailgate Picnic Show**
Showproco, LLC
1450 NE 123rd Street
North Miami, FL 33161
305-893-8771
800-327-3736; Fax: 305-893-8783
www.showproco.com
Facebook, Twitter, LinkedIn
Tom Cove, President
Stanley Schwartz, Director
A show dedicated to sports licensed apparel & products with participation from major sports licensors and their licensees. In conjunction will be the Tailgate & Picnic Show, which will bring together all of the products sports fans want to buy. Attendees will represent everything from sporting goods stores to fan shops, grocery to gift shops, drug stores to convenience stores and more.
Frequency: November

22986 **Strictly Sail Pacific**
Jack London Square
Oakland, CA
800-817-7245; Fax: 401-847-2044
info@sailamerica.com
Facebook, Twitter, LinkedIn
Cynthia Goss, Contact
Annual Boat Show. A mix of boats and gear, seminars and special events. It will feature over 300 exhibitors from 25 states and over 90 seminars.

22987 **Surf Expo**
Surf Expo Offices
990 Hammond Drive
Suite 325
Atlanta, GA 30328
678-817-7970
800-947-7873; Fax: 404-220-3030
rturner@surfexpo.com
www.surfexpo.com
Where manufacturers and retailers in the boardsports, and swim and resort industries have come together in a business-first buying and selling environment.
8M Attendees
Frequency: Twice Annually

22988 **US Gymnastics Federation**
US Gymnastics Congress
Pam American Plaza
201 South Capitol, Suite 300
Indianapolis, IN 46225
317-237-5050; Fax: 317-692-5212
www.usagym.org
Steve Penny, President
Three days of eduction with over 135 sessions offered. Lectures given by recognized top people in the field. Sessions on coaching, judging, business, preschool, recreational, sports science, fitness, Group Gymnastics and cheerleading. The Trade Show exhibit hall will feature 200 booths of products and information from over 85 different Industry Member vendors.
2M Attendees
Frequency: Annual

22989 **US Lacrosse National Convention**
113 W University Pkwy
Baltimore, MD 21210-3301
410-235-6882; Fax: 410-366-6735
info@uslacrosse.org
www.uslacrosse.org
Facebook, Twitter
Steve Stenersen, President
Bill Schoonmaker, COO
Bill Rubacky, Managing Director of Marketing
Kira Muller, Director of Advertising Sales
Billed as the unofficial start to lacrosse season, the event gathers the best the sport has to offer; providing the largest educational opportunity with over 5,000 coaches, officials, vendors and administrators in attendance. Over 100 exhibitors
5000 Attendees
Frequency: Annual

22990 **USA Track and Field Annual Meeting**
One RCA Dome
Suite 140
Indianapolis, IN 46225
317-261-0500; Fax: 317-261-0481
membership@usatf.org
www.usatf.org
Facebook, Twitter, LinkedIn
Jill Geer, Public Relations
Annual meeting of the USA Track and Field organization.
Frequency: Annual

22991 **USTFCCCA Annual Coaches Convention**
U.S. Track & Field and Cross Country Coaches Assoc
1100 Poydras Street
Suite 1750
New Orleans, LA 70163
504-599-8900; Fax: 504-599-8909
sam@ustfccca.org
www.ustfccca.org
Facebook, Twitter, LinkedIn
Sam Seemes, CEO
Mike Corn, Assistant Director
Sylvia Kamp, Administrator
Tom Lewis, Director of Communications

22992 **Underwater Intervention**
5206 FM 1960 West
Suite 202
Houston, TX 77069
281-893-8539
800-316-2188; Fax: 281-893-5118
www.underwaterintervention.com/
Facebook, Twitter, LinkedIn
Rebecca Roberts, Show Manager
Roff Saxon, Executive Director
Conference covering all aspects of underwater operations. Next trade show is scheduled for 2007 with 200+ booths, sponsored by both the Marine Technology Society and the Association of Diving Contractors International.
2500 Attendees
Founded in 1991

22993 **WBCA National Convention**
Women's Basketball Coaches Association
4646 Lawrenceville Highway
Lilburn, GA 30047
770-279-8027; Fax: 770-279-8473
www.wbca.org
Facebook, Twitter
Beth Bass, CEO
Shannon Reynolds, COO
Seana Peck, Manager Marketing
Stephanie S Baron, Director Events
Dorinda Schremmer, Director Membership/Conventions
Women's Basketball Coaches Association national convention. Held annually.
Founded in 1981

22994 **Water Ski and Wakeboard Expo**
1251 Holy Cow Road
Polk City, FL 33868
863-324-4341; Fax: 863-325-8529
usawaterski@usawaterski.org
www.usawaterski.org
Facebook, Twitter, LinkedIn
Annual event of the USA Water Ski Organization.
Frequency: Annual

22995 **Western Fairs Association Annual Trade Show**
Western Fairs Association
1776 Tribute Road
Suite 210
Sacramento, CA 95815-4495
916-927-3100; Fax: 916-927-6397
stephenc@fairsnet.org
www.fairsnet.org
Facebook, Twitter, YouTube
Cliff Munson, Chair
Meet face to face with buyers from the Fair and Festival Industry across the Western United States. Acts, attractions, services, supplies, commericial exhibitors and more.
2000 Members
Frequency: Annual/Jan
Founded in 1922

22996 **Western States Toy and Hobby Show**
Western Toy and Hobby Representative Association
PO Box 2250
Pomona, CA 91786
909-899-3753; Fax: 951-277-1599
toyshow@wthra.com
www.wthra.com
Facebook, Twitter
Phylis St John, Show Director
If it's for kids, it's here. Show is for trade members only, not open to the public.
3000 Attendees
Frequency: March

22997 **World Fishing and Outdoor Exposition**
Eastern Fishing and Outdoor Exposition

PO Box 4720
Portsmouth, NH 03802-4720

603-431-4315; Fax: 603-431-1971
info@sportshows.com
www.sportshows.com
Facebook

You'll find the entire world of fishing and hunting and much more.
Frequency: Annual
Founded in 1978

22998 **World Fly Fishing Expo**
Eastern Fishing and Outdoor Exposition
PO Box 4720
Portsmouth, NH 03802-4720

603-431-4315; Fax: 603-431-1971
info@sportshows.com
www.sportshows.com
Facebook

This expo has all the major manufacturers of fly rods and reels, fly fishing accessories, fly tying materials, guides and lodges.
Frequency: Annual

Directories & Databases

22999 **Amusement Park Guide**
Globe Pequot Press
246 Goose Ln
Suite 200
Guilford, CT 06437-2186

203-458-4500; Fax: 203-458-4601
www.globepequot.com

James Joseph, President

The complete guide to the amusement parks in the United States and Canada gives the latest details about new rides at each park, with a special focus on roller coasters.
Cost: $14.95
ISBN: 0-762725-37-0

23000 **Athlete and Celebrity Address Directory/Autograph Hunter's Guide**
Global Sports Productions
16810 Crystal Drive East
Suite 101
Santa Monica, CA 90404-2702

310-454-9480; Fax: 310-454-6590
globalnw@earthlink.net
Facebook

Ed Kobak, Owner
Greg Andrews, VP Operations

Complete source of athlete and sports personality addresses from baseball, basketball, football, hockey, golf, tennis, soccer, boxing and autosports. Also included are television, movie and other celebrities' addresses.
Cost: $ 29.95
198 Pages
Frequency: Annual
ISBN: 0-966796-17-9
Founded in 2005

23001 **Baseball Bluebook**
8373 N Cedar Hills Lane
Fair Grove, MD 65648

417-833-6550; Fax: 417-833-9911
dj@baseballbluebook.com
www.baseballbluebook.com

Dennis Wubbena, Owner
Eric Wubbena, President

Directory of baseball club personnel at all levels of play. Spiral bound directory contains Major Leagues, Minor Leagues and Independent League Personnel, contact information and schedules
Cost: $55.00
500 Pages
Frequency: Annual
Founded in 1909

23002 **Complete Directory of Fishing Tackle**
Sutton Family Communications & Publishing Company
155 Sutton Lane
Fordsville, KY 42343

270-740-0870
www.suttoncompliance.com

Jerry Sutton, Contact

Listings in directory include names, addresses, phone and fax numbers, and product descriptions from wholesale distributors, Importers, Manufacturers, Close-out houses and liquidators.
Cost: $72.20
100+ Pages

23003 **Complete Directory of Outdoor Products**
Sutton Family Communications & Publishing Company
155 Sutton Lane
Fordsville, KY 42343

270-740-0870
www.suttoncompliance.com

Jerry Sutton, Manager

Print-out from database of wholesalers, manufacturers, distributors, importers and close-out houses. Database is updated daily to guarantee the most current and up-to-date sources available.
Cost: $95.20
100+ Pages

23004 **Complete Directory of Sporting Goods**
Sutton Family Communications & Publishing Company
155 Sutton Lane
Fordsville, KY 42343

270-740-0870
www.suttoncompliance.com

Jerry Sutton, Manager

Print-out from database of wholesalers, manufacturers, distributors, importers and close-out houses. Database is updated daily to guarantee the most current and up-to-date sources available.
Cost: $139.00
100+ Pages

23005 **Computer Sports World**
675 Grier Drive
Las Vegas, NV 89119-3738

702-735-0101
800-321-5562; Fax: 702-294-1322
www.cswstats.com

Statistical information on all aspects of the sports industry.
Frequency: Full-text
Founded in 1983

23006 **Encyclopedia of Sports Business Contacts**
Global Sports Productions
1223 Broadway
Suite 101
Santa Monica, CA 90404-2702

310-395-6533; Fax: 310-454-6590
globalnw@earthlink.net
Facebook, Twitter

Ed Kobak, President

This huge book covers the business side of sports with addresses, telephone and fax numbers, emails, websites and entire contact personnel from sports organizations, teams, leagues, publications, lawyers and agents, corporate sponsors, sports marketing and management firms and others.
Cost: $79.95
600 Pages
Frequency: Annual
Founded in 2005

23007 **Golf Traveler**
Affinity Group
64 Inverness Dr E
Englewood, CO 80112-5114

303-728-7428
800-234-3450; Fax: 303-728-7257
www.affinitygroup.com

Bruce Hoster, Manager

Golf courses and affiliated resorts are listed.
Cost: $2.50
88 Pages
Frequency: BiMonthly
Circulation: 75,000

23008 **International Sports Directory**
Global Sports Productions
1223 Broadway
Suite 101
Santa Monica, CA 90404-2702

310-395-6533; Fax: 310-454-6590
globalnw@earthlink.net

Ed Kobak, Owner

This all-in-one directory covers the entire world of sports from A to Z. Included are addresses, e-mails, websites, telephone and fax numbers and contact personnel from sports organizations, clubs, teams and publications. The most comprehensive sports directory available, covering both national and international listings.
Cost: $29.95
500 Pages
Frequency: Annual
ISBN: 1-891655-02-7
Founded in 1980

23009 **Motor Sports Forum**
Racing Information Systems
2314 Harriman Ln
Unit A
Redondo Beach, CA 90278-4426

310-374-3750
www.motorsportsforum.com

Michael F Hollander, Editor-in-Chief
Bab Karambelas, Senior Editor

This database contains information on auto racing in the United States and Canada.
Frequency: Bulletin Board

23010 **News/Retrieval Sports Report**
Dow Jones & Company
1155 Avenue of the Americas
New York, NY 10036-2717

212-597-5756; Fax: 212-416-4348
www.dowjones.com

Offers information on sports news stories and statistics from United Press International.
Frequency: Full-text

23011 **Orion Blue Book: Guns and Scopes**
Orion Research Corporation
14555 N Scottsdale Rd
Suite 330
Scottsdale, AZ 85254-3487

480-951-1114
800-844-0759; Fax: 480-951-1117
www.orionbluebook.com

Roger Rohrs, Owner

List of manufacturers of guns. Current issue contains 18,543 products. Lists products from

1800's to present. Over 300 manufacturers listed.
Cost: $45.00
480 Pages
Frequency: Annual
Founded in 1992

23012 **Parks Directory of the United States**
Omnigraphics
615 Griswold Street
Detroit, MI 48226
313-961-1340
800-234-1340; Fax: 313-961-1383
editorial@omnigraphics.com
www.omnigraphics.com
Darren L Smith, Editor
Covers nearly 5,000 national and state parks, and other designated recreational, scenic, and historic areas in the United States and Canada. It provides up-to-date contact and descriptive information for every national and state park in the U.S.
Cost: $185.00
1,100 Pages
Frequency: Biennial
ISBN: 0-780806-63-8

23013 **Q&A Booklets**
Sporting Goods Agents Association
14555~N~Scottsdale~Rd
Scottsdale~, AZ 60053
847-296-3670; Fax: 847-827-0196
sgaa998@aol.com
Skip Nipper, President
Lois Halinton, Chief Operating Officer
Sporting Goods Agents Association booklets for manufacturers and agents. Answers questions such as: Why should I use an independent agent rather than hire my own salespeople? What are the most important aspects to examine when I interview an agency? What are independent sporting goods agents and what do they do? What factors should be considered when forming a territory to cover. And more.
Cost: $15.00

23014 **Recreation Facilities Products & Services**
Sutton Family Communications & Publishing Company
155 Sutton Lane
Fordsville, KY 42343
270-740-0870
www.suttoncompliance.com
Jerry Sutton, Manager
Print-out from database of wholesalers, manufacturers, distributors, importers and close-out houses. Database is updated daily to guarantee the most current and up-to-date sources available. Accepts advertising.
Cost: $97.20
100+ Pages

23015 **Recreational Sports Directory**
National Intramural Recreational Sports Assn
4185 Sw Research Way
Corvallis, OR 97333-1067
541-766-8211; Fax: 541-766-8284
nirsa@nirsa.org
www.nirsa.org
Kent Blumenthal, Executive Director
Directory of services and supplies to the industry.
Cost: $20.00
400 Pages
Frequency: Annual
Circulation: 1,500

23016 **Salem Press Online Platform**
Grey House Publishing
4919 Route 22
PO Box 56
Amenia, NY 12501
800-221-1592; Fax: 201-968-0511
csr@salempress.com
online.salempress.com
The new Salem Press platform houses more than 500 titles including all of Salem's Health, Literature, History and Science titles in addition to select titles from the Grey House Publishing and H.W. Wilson product lines. Online access is free with each print purchase and includes an unlimited number of simultaneous users and remote access.

23017 **Sporting News Baseball Guide**
Sporting News Publishing Company
10176 Corporate Square Drive
Suite 200
Saint Louis, MO 63132-2924
314-997-7111; Fax: 314-993-7798
www.sportingnews.com
Jim Nuckols, CEO
A list of National and American League and their affiliate minor leagues.
Cost: $12.95
Frequency: Annual

23018 **Sporting News Football Register**
Sporting News Publishing Company
10176 Corporate Square Drive
Suite 200
Saint Louis, MO 63132-2924
314-997-7111; Fax: 314-993-7798
www.sportingnews.com
Jim Nuckols, CEO
Directory of services and supplies to the industry.
Cost: $12.95
430 Pages
Frequency: Annual

23019 **Sports Address Bible and Almanac**
Global Sports Productions
1223 Broadway
Suite 101
Santa Monica, CA 90404-2702
310-395-6533; Fax: 310-454-6590
globalnw@earthlink.net
Ed Kobak, Owner
Greg Andrews, VP Operations
Over 7,500 sports listings from professional, semi-pro, Olympic and amateur, collegiate and interscholastic sports organizations, leagues, teams, halls of fame, media outlets and more.
Cost: $34.95
505 Pages
Frequency: Biennial
ISBN: 1-891655-11-6
ISSN: 0743-4561
Founded in 1998

23020 **Sports Market Place Directory**
Grey House Publishing
4919 Route 22
PO Box 56
Amenia, NY 12501
518-789-8700
800-562-2139; Fax: 845-373-6390
books@greyhouse.com
www.greyhouse.com
Facebook, Twitter
Leslie Mackenzie, Publisher
Richard Gottlieb, Editor
For over 20 years, this comprehensive, up-to-date directory has offered direct access to the Who, What, When & Where of the Sports Industry. With this directory on your desk, you have a comprehensive tool providing current key information about the people, organizations and events involving the explosive sports industry at your fingertips.
Cost: $225.00
1800 Pages
Frequency: Annual
ISBN: 1-592373-48-8
Founded in 1981

23021 **Sports Market Place Directory - Online Database**
Grey House Publishing
4919 Route 22
PO Box 56
Amenia, NY 12501
518-789-8700
800-562-2139; Fax: 845-373-6390
gold@greyhouse.com
gold.greyhouse.com
Facebook, Twitter
Leslie Mackenzie, Publisher
Richard Gottlieb, Editor
For over 20 years, this comprehensive, up-to-date directory provides current key information about the people, organizations and events involving the sports industry including, contact information and key executives for single sports organizations, multi-sport organizations, media, sponsors, college sports, manufacturers, trade shows and more.
Founded in 1981

23022 **Sports RoundTable**
GE Information Services
401 N Washington Street
Rockville, MD 20850-1707
301-388-8284
Cathy Ge, Owner
This database provides coverage of major professional, amateur and collegiate sports including football, basketball, baseball, and hockey.
Frequency: Full-text

23023 **SportsAlert**
Comtex Scientific Corporation
911 Hope Street
#4838
Stamford, CT 06907-2318
FAX 203-358-0236
This database contains sports news and statistics providing real-time coverage of US and international professional, collegiate and amateur athletic events.
Frequency: Full-text

23024 **Tennis-Places to Play: Camps and Clinics Issue**
Golf Digest Tennis NY Times Magazine Group
5520 Park Avenue
Trumbull, CT 06611-3400
203-373-7000; Fax: 203-371-2162
Directory of services and supplies to the industry.
Cost: $2.50
Frequency: Annual
Circulation: 800,000

Industry Web Sites

23025 **http://gold.greyhouse.com**
G.O.L.D Grey House OnLine Databases
Grey House Publishing's online database platform, GOLD, offers Quick Search, Keyword Search and Expert Search for most business sectors including sports and recreation markets. The GOLD platform makes finding the information you need quick and easy - whether you're a novice searcher or an experienced database user. All of Grey House's directory prod-

ucts are available for subscription on the GOLD platform.

23026 **usskiandsnowboard.org**
US Ski & Snowboard Association
Association for skiing and snowboarding nationwide.

23027 **www.aahperd.org**
American Alliance for Hlth, Phys. Edu. Rec. Dance

23028 **www.aahperd.org/uawgs**
National Association for Girls and Women in Sports
A non-profit organization serving the needs of teachers, coaches and participants of sports programs for girls and women.

23029 **www.aapsm.org**
American Academy of Podiatric Sports Medicine
The American Academy of Podiatric Sports Medicine was founded in San Francisco by a group of podiatric sports physicians who had the insight to realize the need for a podiatric sports medicine association devoted to the treatment of athletic injuries. Today the AAPSM has over 500 members.

23030 **www.aausports.org**
Amateur Athletic Union of the United States

23031 **www.abca.org**
American Baseball Coaches Association
Formerly called the American Association of College Baseball Coaches.

23032 **www.aca-camps.org**
American Camping Association
Educational programs. Legislative monitoring, child and youth development.

23033 **www.acanet.org**
American Canoe Association
Promotes the sport of canoeing and its safety, recreational and conservation

23034 **www.acsm.org**
American College of Sports Medicine
The ACSM promotes and integrates scientific research, education, and practical applications of sports medicine and exercise science to maintain and enhance physical performance, fitness, health, and quality of life.

23035 **www.adventurecycling.org**
Adventure Cycling Association
Developes road and mountain bike routes, runs bike tours and eventsand also acts as information resource for bicyclists planning trips.

23036 **www.aeawave.com**
Aquatic Exercise Association
Covers topics relating to aquatic fitness and therapy including industry trends, research, programs, exercises and products.

23037 **www.afaa.com**
Aerobics and Fitness Association of America
Association for the education, certification and training of exercise instructors; information resource center for consumers.

23038 **www.ahcahockey.com**
American Hockey Coaches Association
Helps maintain the highest possible standards in hockey and the hockey profession.

23039 **www.asgca.org**
American Society of Golf Course Architects
A non-profit organization comprised of leading golf course designers in North America. ASGCA is actively involved in many issues realted to the game of golf, including responsible environmental designs.

23040 **www.athleticclubs.com**
Athletic Net
Click on links to find fitness, sports medicine, general health and wellness, government sites, directories, nutrition and newsgroups.

23041 **www.avca.org**
American Volleyball Coaches Association
To develop and grow the sport of volleyball

23042 **www.baseballcoaches.org**
National High School Baseball Coaches Association
Provides services and recognition for baseball coaches and to help promote and represent high school baseball across the country.

23043 **www.bikeleague.org**
League of American Bicyclists

23044 **www.greyhouse.com**
Grey House Publishing
Authoritative reference directories for most business sectors including sports and recreation markets. Users can search the online databases with varied search criteria allowing for custom searches by product category, geographic area, sales volume, keyword, subject and more. Full Grey House catalog and online ordering also available.

23045 **www.iprarodeo.com**
International Professional Rodeo Association
Governing body for professional rodeo. 500 rodeos across USA and Canada, $5 million prize money per year, 5 million fans.

23046 **www.lpga.com**
Ladies Professional Golf Association
For women and youth golfers.

23047 **www.naa-usa.org**
National Aeronautic Association
Members include aerospace corporations, aero clubs, affiliates and major national sporting aviation organizations.

23048 **www.nabc.com**
National Association of Basketball Coaches
Promotes the advancement and opportunities for coaches and teachers in the sport of basketball.

23049 **www.nabf.com**
National Amateur Baseball Association
Promotes amateur baseball and the industry in general.

23050 **www.nacola.com**
Nat'l Assoc of Collegiate Directors of Athletics
Professional association for college atheltics directors, assistants and conference administrators. Provides educational opportunities and serves as a vehicle for networking and the exchange of information to others in the college sports profession.

23051 **www.nasgw.org**
National Association of Sporting Goods
Non-profit trade association of wholesalers, distributors and manufacturers. Serves as a liason with other sporting goods associations.

23052 **www.naso.org**
National Association of Sports Officials
Not-for-profit 501(c)(3) educational association providing individual benefits such as training materials, liability and assault protection insurance and more to sports officials of all sports and every level.

23053 **www.nauticalworld.com**
Nautical World
Dedicated to bringing all related web sites within easy access to watersports enthusiasts. This search engine has been designed to locate advertiser's information within Nautical World but will also offer access to other watersport related web sites as well. Offers sections on marine electronics and hardware, sailing, boats, boat supplies, fishing accessories, diving accessories, industry news, watersports, weather forecasting and more.

23054 **www.nays.org**
National Youth Sports Coaches Association
Represents coaches involved in youth athletics.

23055 **www.nfca.org**
National Fastpitch Coaches Association
The professional growth organization for fastpitch softball coaches from all competitives levels of play.

23056 **www.nflalumni.org**
National Football League Alumni
Provides a forum for those individuals retired from the NFL but still playing an active role.

23057 **www.ngf.org**
National Golf Foundation
Provides market research and serves as an information clearinghouse for the industry. Conducts seminars for golf teachers, coaches and professionals. Conducts golf course development feasibility studies for developers.

23058 **www.njcaa.org**
National Junior College Athletic Association
NJCAA members are two year institutions recognized by the American Association of Community and Junior Colleges.

23059 **www.nra.org**
National Rifle Association
Oldest sportsmen's organization in the US. Maintains the NRA Political Victory Fund and supports the Institute for Legislative Action.

23060 **www.nsga.org**
National Sporting Goods Association
Association of retailers, manufacturers and suppliers of sports equipment, footwear, and apparel.

23061 **www.pga.com**
Professional Golfers Association of America
The world's largest working sports organization comprised of more than 25,000 men and women PGA professionals to promote the game of golf to everyone, and to promote its members as leaders in the golf industry.

23062 **www.popwarner.com**
Pop Warner Little Scholars
A national youth football and cheerleading organization that provides assistance to its various chapters.

23063 **www.r-sports.com**
Sporting Goods Agents Association
International trade association of independent and established sporting goods agents.

23064 **www.restaurantreport.com/top100**
Resturant Report On-Line

Includes top 100 food sites, feature stories, newsletters, buyer's guide, marketplace, hospitality jobs.

23065 **www.rollerskating.com**
Roller Skating Association
Exists for private businessmen and women engaged in the enterprise of roller skating.

23066 **www.rollerskating.org**
Roller Skating Association International
A trade association representing skating center owners, operators; teachers, coaches and judges of roller skating; and manufacturers and suppliers of roller skating equipment.

23067 **www.sabr.org**
Society for American Baseball Research
Membership association whose purpose is to facilitate and disseminate baseball research.

23068 **www.skateisi.org**
Ice Skating Institute
Industry trade association dedicated to providing leadership, education and services to the ice skating industry.

23069 **www.sportsheritage.org**
International Sports Heritage Association
The mission of ISHA is to educate, promote and support organizations and individuals engaged in the celebration of sports heritage.

23070 **www.sportsmed.org**
American Orthopaedic Society for Sports Medicine
Promotes the prevention, recognition and orthopedic treatment of sports injuries.

23071 **www.sportsplexoperators.com**
Sportsplex Operators and Developers of Association
SODA was formed to meet the needs of the private concerns, public agencies, and other organizations that own or maintain sports complex facilities.

23072 **www.teamusa.org**
US Olympic Committee
The national committee for the US. Handles the preparation of the US Olympic, Paralympic and Pan American Games teams.

23073 **www.tennisindustry.org**
Tennis Industry Association
To educate the marketplace, fund research and market intelligence and supply this reliable industry data to our member companies. The TIA is the Information source and clearing house for positive tennis news that we supply to TIA members, tennis publications and to the mainstream media in cooperation with the USTA.

23074 **www.usarchery.org**
National Archery Association
Supports archers while aiming to advance the sport of archery in the US. Monthly newsletter, Nock-Nock, provides communication among the NAA office, NAA clubs, state associations and the individual members of the NAA. Provides members with news and tournament results ranging from the local and state level to international competition.

23075 **www.usaswimming.org**
USA Swimming
National governing body for the sport of swimming, promoting the culture by supporting swimmers and coaches through events and education.

23076 **www.usatt.org**
USA Table Tennis
Dedicated to the promotion of the sport of table tennis and sponsors the US team. Membership dues are $30 per year for adults and $20 for those 18 years old and under.

23077 **www.usawaterski.org**
USA Water Ski Association
Encourages interest in the sport as well as training and safety.

23078 **www.usaweightlifting.org**
USA Weightlifting
USA Weightlifting is the National Governing Body (NGB) for the Olympic sport of weightlifting in the United States. USA weightlifting is a member of the United States Olympic Committee and a member of the International Weightlifting Federation. As the NGB, USA Weightlifting is responsible for conducting Olympic weightlifting programs throughout the country. The organization conducts a variety of programs that will ultimately develop Olympic, World Championship and Pan American Games' winners.

23079 **www.usfencing.org**
United States Fencing Association
Promotes the sport of fencing in the US.

23080 **www.usfieldhockey.com**
US Field Hockey Association
Represents field hockey, professional and amateur sports.

23081 **www.ushandball.org**
US Handball Association
Organization that runs all the tournaments for the professional and amateur players. Home of the Handball Hall of Fame.

23082 **www.uspa.org**
United States Parachute Association
A not-for-profit membership association dedicated to the promotion of safe skydiving and the support of those who enjoy it. Sponsors Instructor Rating Program to train and certify instructors, jump masters and examiners.

23083 **www.usra.org**
US Raquetball Association
A nonprofit corporation designed to promote the development of competitive and recreational racquetball in the United States. The association offers a 'competitive license' membership for a one year term at $15.00 annually, or at discounted longer term rates. A lifetime membership is also offered. A 'Club Recreational Membership' program is offered for an annual fee of $150.00 with a reduced AARA recreational membership available to club members for $3.00 per player.

23084 **www.usspeedskating.org**
US Speedskating
Devoted to speedskating and its participants on the national and international levels.

23085 **www.ustfccca.org**
U.S. Track & Field and Cross Country Coaches Assoc
A non-profit professional organization that represents men's and women's cross country and track & field coaches in the United States.

23086 **www.uswfa.com**
United States Water Fitness Association
Nonprofit educational organization that promotes aquatics throughout the United States and other countries. Publishes the National Aquatics Newsletter, names the 100 top US water fitness programs and program 5 aquatics in the country, by state and in 25+ categories. Conducts a wide variety of national aquatics certifications including Water Fitness Instructors (primary and masters), aquatic directors, coordinators of water fitness programs. Conducts annual international aquatics conference.

23087 **www.volleyball.org**
US Volleyball Association
Promotes volleyball in the US trains the USA men's and women's teams promotes beach and grassroots voleyball in the United States.

23088 **www.ymca.net**
YMCA of the USA
Provides national and state branch divisions.

Associations

23089 **Allied Stone Industries**
PO Box 288145
Chicago, IL 60628-8145
773-928-4800; Fax: 773-928-4129
www.alliedstone.com
Facebook, Twitter
Gary Ballerini, President
Pam Pine, VP
Brundene Van Ness, President-Elect
Butch Coleman, Treasurer
Bill Halquist, Secretary
Quarries, fabricators and dealers in stone and concrete.
55 Members
Founded in 1950

23090 **American Concrete Institute**
38800 Country Club Drive
PO Box 9094
Farmington Hills, MI 48331
248-848-3700; Fax: 248-848-3701
ron.burg@concrete.org
www.concrete.org
Facebook, Twitter, LinkedIn, Youtube
Anne M Ellis, President
William B Rushing, VP
Sharon L Wood, VP
Ronald G Burg, Executive VP
ACI is a scientific and educational society representing the interests of concrete users concerned with the design, construction, or maintenance of concrete structures. Conventions and meetings, monthly periodicals and special publications; chapter activities; and technical committees all provide a forum for concrete interests to discuss problems relating to concrete.
20000 Members
Founded in 1904

23091 **American Concrete Pavement Association**
9450 W Bryn Mawr Ave.
Suite 150
Rosemont, IL 60018
847-966-2272; Fax: 847-966-9970
acpa@acpa.org
www.pavement.com
Facebook, Twitter, LinkedIn, Youtube
Jerry Voigt, CEO & President
Mike Lipps, Chairman
Steve Jackson, Vice Chairman
Lori Tiefenthaler, 2nd Vice Chair
Glenn Eder, Treasurer
ACPA is committed to promoting the quality and superiority of concrete pavements. It leads and assists its members in market development, technical expertise, design innovation, research, and public relations. ACPA's membership includes contractors, cement companies, material suppliers, equipment manufacturers and suppliers, ready mix producers, allied associations, bonding and insurance companies, and consulting firms.
Founded in 1963

23092 **American Concrete Pipe Association**
8445 Freeport Parkway
Suite 350
Irving, TX 75063-2595
972-506-7216; Fax: 972-506-7682
info@concrete-pipe.org
www.concrete-pipe.org
Facebook, Twitter, LinkedIn, Youtube, Pinterest
Michael D. Kusch, Chairman
A. C. Gossett, III, Vice Chairman
Darren Wise, Secretary
Brian Rhees, Treasurer
Matt Childs, P.E., President
The American Concrete Pipe Association (ACPA) is a nonprofit organization, composed primarily of manufacturers of concrete pipe and related conveyance products located throughout the United States, Canada and in over 40 foreign countries.
145 Members
Founded in 1907

23093 **American Natural Soda Ash Corporation**
15 Riverside Avenue
2nd Floor
Westport, CT 06880
203-226-9056; Fax: 203-227-1484
www.ansac.com
Facebook, Twitter
Donna McSwain-Santos, Marketing
ANSAC markets, sells and distributes high quality soda ash to over 40 countries around the world.
Founded in 1984

23094 **American Society of Concrete Contractors**
2025 S Brentwood Blvd
Suite 105
St Louis, MO 63144-1850
314-962-0210
866-788-2722; Fax: 314-968-4367
questions@ascconline.org
www.ascconline.org
Facebook, Twitter, LinkedIn, Pinterest
Beverly Garnant, Executive Director
Becky Finch, Director, Member Engagement
Shreya Arora, Manager, Meetings & Events
Mary Anderson, Accounting & Finance
Bruce Suprenant, Technical Director
The American Society of Concrete Contractors/ASCC seeks to continually advance the qualifications of concrete constructors and encourage greater interaction between designer and constructor. Publishes the Contactor's Guide to Quality Concrete Construction jointly with ACI. Issues Safety Alerts, Safety Bulletins, and a Safety Manual as well as a troubleshooting newsletter, management reports, and a members bulletin.

23095 **Concrete Foundations Association**
113 W First Street
PO Box 204
Mount Vernon, IA 52314
319-895-6940; Fax: 320-213-5556
info@cfawalls.org
www.cfawalls.org
David Martinson, President
Dennis Purinton, Vice-President
Phillip Marone, Secretary
Doug Herbert, Treasurer
Jim Bartley, Past-President
Members are residential foundation contractors and their suppliers. The association produces promotional, marketing and technical materials for members' potential customers; provides its members with newsletters, industry publications, and seminar and trade show opportunities; develops specifications, technical information, and safety programs; and represents its members on national code bodies.
300 Members
Founded in 1975

23096 **Concrete Polishing Association of America**
38800 Country Club Dr.
Farmington Hills, MI 48331
443-249-7919
www.cpaa-us.org
Facebook, Twitter
Chad Gill, President
Supporting and shaping the concrete polishing industry.
Founded in 2009

23097 **Concrete Promotion Council of Northern California**
6966 Sunrise Boulevard
Suite 329
Citrus Heights, CA 95610
916-952-0437
888-633-0393; Fax: 831-302-7330
Paulette.Salisbury@cncement.org
www.cpcnc.org
Paulette Salisbury, Interim Director
Bill Albanese, President Board of Directors
Jeff Nehmens, Treasurer Board of Directors
Dave Bearden, Member Board of Directors
Curt Higgins, Member Board of Directors
A member of the Pacific Southwest Concrete Alliance, composed of companies from all parts of the Northern Californian concrete industry including ready mix suppliers, cement producers, admixture manufacturers, concrete contractors as well as members of the public and private design committees. Their mission is to increase the quantity and diversity of quality concrete projects in Northern California through providing educational opportunities to the Professional Design Community.

23098 **Concrete Reinforcing Steel Institute**
933 N Plum Grove Road
Schaumburg, IL 60173-4758
847-517-1200; Fax: 847-517-1206
www.crsi.org
Facebook, Twitter, LinkedIn
David McDonald, President
Joe Culligan, Chief Financial Officer
Steven Hawkins, Sr., VP, Marketing
David McDonald, Managing Director
Barbara Burchett, Government Affairs
Conducts research and provides technical information on reinforced concrete design and construction practices.
1600 Members
Founded in 1924

23099 **Concrete Sawing and Drilling Association**
100 2nd Avenue South
Suite 402N
St. Petersburg, FL 33701
727-577-5004; Fax: 727-577-5012
info@csda.org
www.csda.org
Facebook, Twitter, LinkedIn, Flickr, YouTube
Patrick O'Brien, Executive Director
Erin O'Brien, Assistant to Executive Director
Russell Hitchen, Training Coordinator & Editor
Jacqueline Takach, Member Service Coordinator
An association promoting professional specialty sawing and drilling contractors and their methods.
500 Members
Founded in 1972

23100 Expanded Shale Clay and Slate Institute
35 E Wacker Drive
Suite 850
Chicago, IL 60601

801-272-7070; Fax: 312-644-8557
info@escsi.org
www.escsi.org
LinkedIn, Youtube

John Riese, President

Sponsors research at engineering schools, educational seminars and develops industry standards.
Founded in 1908

23101 Indiana Limestone Institute of America
1502 I Street
Suite 400
Bedford, IN 47421

812-275-4426; Fax: 812-279-8682
www.iliai.com

Jim Owens, Technical Director
Todd Schnatzmeyer, Executive Director
Dave Morthland, Office Manager

The trade association which represents quarries and fabricators of Indiana Limestone, as well as associate members who supply goods or services to the industry, ILIA's charte is to eductate and promote
90 Members
Founded in 1928

23102 International Cast Polymer Alliance
3033 Wilson Blvd
Suite 420
Arlington, VA 22201

703-525-0511; Fax: 703-525-0743
www.icpa-hq.org

Debbie Cannon, President
John Webster, President Elect
Jack Simmons, Secretary
Jamie Myers, Immediate Past President

Formerly known as the Cultured Marble Institute, is a nonprofit organization representing over 300 members including manufacturers, suppliers, fabricators, and installers of cultured marble, cultured granite, cultured onyx, and solid surface kitchen and bath products.

23103 Marble Institute of America
380 E. Lorain Street
Suite 100
Oberlin, OH 44074

440-250-9222; Fax: 440-774-9222
miainfo@marble-institute.com
www.marble-institute.com
Facebook, Twitter, LinkedIn, Youtube

Jonathan Zanger, President
Tony Malisani, VP
Dan Rea, Secretary
David Castelucci, Treasurer

The Marble Institute of America (MIA) is the authoritative source of information on standards of natural stone workmanship and practice and the suitable application of natural stone products.
2000 Members
Founded in 1907

23104 Masonry Society
105 S Sunset St.
Suite Q
Longmont, CO 80501-6172

303-939-9700; Fax: 303-541-9215
info@masonrysociety.org
www.masonrysociety.org
LinkedIn

Christine Subasic, Chair

Dedicated to the advancement of scientific engineering, architectural and construction knowledge of masonry. Promotes research and education and disseminates information on masonry materials, design, construction. Publishes newsletters, codes & specifications and material on masonry design.
450 Members
Founded in 1977
Mailing list available for rent: 4200 names

23105 National Concrete Burial Vault Association
136 South Keowee Street
Dayton, OH 45402

407-788-1996
888-88 -NCBV; Fax: 937-222-5794
info@ncbva.org
www.ncbva.org

Jerry Russell, President
Mark Bates, President Elect
Steve Handley, Secretary/Treasurer
Michael Crummitt, Immediate Past President
Ed Bruns, Director

A voluntary nonprofit organization of concrete burial vault manufacturers throughout the United States and Canada. The purpose of the organization is to provide a unified voice for the concrete burial vault industry regardless of product affiliation, brand recognition or location.
350 Members
Founded in 1930

23106 National Concrete Masonry Association
13750 Sunrise Valley Dr
Herndon, VA 20171-4662

703-713-1900; Fax: 703-713-1910
info@ncma.org
www.ncma.org
Facebook, Twitter, LinkedIn, Pinterest

Thomas Finch, Chair

The national trade association representing the concrete masonry industry. The association is involved in a broad range of technical, research, marketing, government relations and community activities.
Founded in 1918

23107 National Lime Association
200 N Glebe Rd
Suite 800
Arlington, VA 22203-3728

703-243-5463; Fax: 703-243-5489
wcherz@lime.org
www.lime.org
Facebook

William C Herz, Executive Director
Jonathan De'Ath, Director
Hunter L. Prillaman, Director, Govt. Affairs
Lori D Oney, Director, Finance, Administration
Robert A. Hirsch, Director, Environment

Trade association for US and Canadian manufacturers of high calcium quicklime, dolomitic quicklime and hydrated lime, collectively referred to as lime. NLA represents the interests of its members in Washington, provides input on standards and specifacations for lime, and funds and manages research on current and new uses for lime.
Founded in 1902

23108 National Precast Concrete Association
200 North Glebe
Suite 200
Arlington, IN 46032

317-571-9500
800-366-7731; Fax: 317-571-0041
npca@precast.org
www.precast.org
Facebook, Twitter, LinkedIn, Youtube, RSS, Flickr

William C. Herz, MPH, Executive Director
Phillip Cutler, VP, Technical Services
Lori D. Oney, VP, Finance & Administration
Brenda Ibitz, VP, Development & Member Services
Bob Whitmore, VP, Communications & Public Affairs

An international trade organization, NPCA represents manufacturers of plant produced precast concrete products and companies that provide the equipment, supplies and services to make these products. NPCA also provides technical information throught nine product committees, which consist of members who concentrate on specific product lines within the precast industry.
1100 Members
Founded in 1965

23109 National Ready Mixed Concrete Association
900 Spring St
Silver Spring, MD 20910-4015

301-587-1400
888-846-7622; Fax: 301-585-4219
info@nrmca.org
www.nrmca.org
Facebook, Twitter, LinkedIn, Youtube

Michael Phillips, President
Nicole Maher, Chief Operating Officer
Joe Roche, Chief Financial Officer
Alex Land, Director, Membership Engagement
Frank Cavaliere, Director, Special Programs & Comm.

NRMCA represents its membership of ready mixed concrete producrs in market development, technical research, engineering advances, government relations, and regulatory issues. In addition to conducting educational seminars, workshops, conferences and trade shows, NRMCA disseminates a wide variety of publications for its members, ranging from Congressional digests and promotion pointers to driver education.
Founded in 1930

23110 Ornamental Concrete Producers Association
759 Phelps Johnson Rd
Leitchfield, KY 42754

270-879-6319; Fax: 218-751-2186
delpreus@paulbunyan.net

Del Preuss, Executive Director
Robert Garbini, President
Shawnita Dickens, Manager

An international nonprofit educational association comprised of producers and suppliers.
Cost: $50.00
500 Members
Founded in 1991

23111 Portland Cement Association
5420 Old Orchard Road
Skokie, IL 60077-1083

847-966-6200; Fax: 847-966-9781
info@cement.org
www.cement.org
Facebook, Twitter, LinkedIn, YouTube

Michael Ireland, Chief Executive Officer
Joe Roche, Chief Financial Officer
Edward Sullivan, SVP & Chief Economist
Sean O'Neill, SVP, Government Affairs
Nick Ferrari, SVP, Membership & Admin. Affairs

The Portland Cement Association represents cement companies in the United States and Canada. It conducts market development, engineer-

ing, research, education, and public affairs programs.
Founded in 1916

23112 **Post-Tensioning Institute**
Bldg Main
38800 Country Club Dr
Farmington Hills, MI 48331-3439
248-848-3180; Fax: 248-848-3181
info@post-tensioning.org
www.post-tensioning.org
Facebook, Twitter, LinkedIn
Theodore L Neff, Executive Director
Robert Sward, President
David Martin, VP
Guy Cloutier, Secretary
Marc Khoury, Past President
Provides research, technical development, marketing and promotional activities for companies engaged in post-tensioned prestressed construction. Members include fabricators and manufacturers.
900 Members
Founded in 1976

23113 **Refractories Institute**
1300 Sumner Avenue
PO Box 8439
Cleveland, OH 44115
216-241-7333; Fax: 216-241-0105
www.refractoriesinstitute.org
Robert Crolius, President
A trade association which promotes the interests of the refractories industry. TRI has a long tradition of providing support and services to manufacturers of refractory materials and products and suppliers of raw materials, equipment, and services to the refractories industry.
80 Members
Founded in 1951

23114 **Specialty Minerals**
Minerals Technology
405 Lexington Ave
New York, NY 10174-0002
212-986-2486
800-801-1031; Fax: 610-882-8726
www.mineralstech.com
Joseph C Muscari, Executive Chairman
Robert S Wetherbee, President & CEO
Douglas T Dietrich, Senior VP/CFO
D J Monagle III, Senior VP/Managing Director
Thomas J Meek, Senior VP/General Counsel/Secretary
A subsidiary of Minerals Technology, Inc., a resource and technology based organization that develops and produces performance-enhancing minerals, mineral-based and synthetic mineral products for the paper, steel, polymer, healthcare and other manufacturing industries on a worldwide basis.
Founded in 1992

23115 **Tilt-Up Concrete Association**
113 First Street W
PO Box 204
Mount Vernon, IA 52314-0204
319-895-6911; Fax: 320-213-5555
info@tilt-up.org
www.tilt-up.org
Facebook, Twitter, LinkedIn, You Tube
Kimberley Corwin, President
Shane Miller, President Elect
Andrew S McPherson, Treasurer
James M Williams, Secretary
TCA members include contractors, suppliers, architects, and engineers dedicated to the advancement of quality tilt-up concrete construction. Activities include a national promotional program, information clearinghouse, educational seminars, referral service, achievement awards program, development of codes and standards, and a quarterly magazine.
Founded in 1986

Newsletters

23116 **Cutting Edge**
Marble Institute of America
28901 Clemens Road
Suite 100
Cleveland, OH 44145
440-250-9222; Fax: 440-250-9223
miainfo@marble-institute.com
www.marble-institute.com
Gary Distelhorst, Executive VP/CEO
Helen Distelhorst, Director Meetings/Special Events
Jim Hieb, VP
Frequency: Monthly
Circulation: 1500

23117 **Refractory News**
Refractories Institute
630 Smithfield Street
Suite 1160
Pittsburgh, PA 15222-3907
412-281-6787; Fax: 412-281-6881
triassn@aol.com
www.refractoriesinstitute.org
Facebook, Twitter
Flo Story, Editor
A monthly newsletter featuring timely industry news, information on federal regulations, member updates, announcements on seminars, and the latest refractory information and statistics.
Cost: $24.00
4 Pages
Frequency: Monthly
Circulation: 700
Founded in 1951
Mailing list available for rent
Printed in 2 colors on matte stock

Magazines & Journals

23118 **ACI Materials Journal**
American Concrete Institute
38800 Country Club Drive
PO Box 9094
Farmington Hills, MI 48333-9094
248-848-3700; Fax: 248-848-3701
shannon.hale@concrete.org
www.concrete.org/pubs/journals/mjhome.asp
Shannon M Hale, Technical Editor
Carl R Bischof, Senior Editor Publishing Services
Renee J Lewis, Publishing & Event Services
Douglas J Sordyl, Marketing/Sales/Industry Relations
Donna G Halstead, Finance & Administration
ACI Materials Journal contains individually authored papers as well as papers developed for convention sessions. These papers address structural research, materials research, design theory, structural analysis, and state-of-the-art reviews.
Founded in 1904
Mailing list available for rent

23119 **ACI Structural Journal**
American Concrete Institute
38800 Country Club Drive
PO Box 9094
Farmington Hills, MI 48333-9094
248-848-3700; Fax: 248-848-3701
shannon.hale@concrete.org
www.concrete.org/pubs/journals/sjhome.asp
Shannon M Hale, Technical Editor
Carl R Bischof, Senior Editor Publishing Services
Renee J Lewis, Publishing & Event Services
Douglas J Sordyl, Marketing/Sales/Industry Relations
Donna G Halstead, Finance & Administration
ACI Structural Journal contains individually authored papers as well as papers developed for convention sessions. These papers address structural research, materials research, design theory, structural analysis, and state-of-the-art reviews.
Founded in 1904
Mailing list available for rent

23120 **Cement Americas**
Primedia
11555 Central Parkway
10th Floor
Chicago, IL 60606
312-726-2802; Fax: 312-726-2574
www.cementamericas.com
Steven Prokopy, Editor
Norm Rose, Sales
Cement Americas provides comprehensive coverage of the North and South American cement markets from raw materials extraction to delivery and transportation to the end user. Production-oriented articles focus on areas where the market activity is at its greatest. Coverage of new ideas, technological improvements, industry trends, and views from leading figures in the cement industry ensure that Cement Americas remains the cement industry journal of the Americas.
ISSN: 0035-7464
Printed in 4 colors on glossy stock

23121 **Concrete InFocus**
Naylor Publications
5950 NW 1st Pl
Gainesville, FL 32607-6018
352-332-1252
800-369-6220; Fax: 352-331-3525
chodges@naylor.com
www.naylor.com
Facebook, Twitter, LinkedIn, You Tube
Michael Moss, President
Magazine that's mailed to 5,000+ industry personnel.

23122 **Concrete International**
American Concrete Institute
38800 Country Club Drive
PO Box 9094
Farmington Hills, MI 48333-9094
248-848-3700; Fax: 248-848-3701
ron.burg@concrete.org
www.concrete.org
Carl R Bischof, Senior Editor
Ronald G Burg, Executive Vice President
The circulation is concentrated among the most important professionals in the concrete field; the engineers, architects, contractors, manufacturers, and technicians largely responsible for the advancement of concrete technology and practice.
Frequency: Monthly
Circulation: 20000

23123 **Concrete Masonry Designs**
NCMA

13750 Sunrise Valley Dr
Herndon, VA 20171-4662

703-713-1900; Fax: 703-713-1910
ncma@ncma.org
www.ncma.org

Robert Thomas, President
Ron Churchill, Director Of Sales

Highlights concrete masonry applications, best practice tips, specifications and details. Also showcases concrete masonry landscape products.
Cost: $1.00
Frequency: Monthly
Circulation: 25000
Founded in 1918
Printed in 4 colors on glossy stock

23124 **Concrete Openings**
Concrete Sawing and Drilling Association
100 2nd Avenue South
Suite 402N
St. Petersburg, FL 33701

727-577-5004; Fax: 727-577-5012
info@csda.org
www.concreteopenings.com

Patrick O'Brien, Executive Director
Erin O'Brien, Assistant to Executive Director
Russell Hitchen, Training Coordinator & Editor
Jacqueline Takach, Member Service Coordinator

Newsletter by the Concrete Sawing and Drilling Association (CSDA), containing information relevant to the profession of concrete sawing and drilling. Some topics include wall sawing, wire sawing, polishing techniques, GPR Imaging and more.
500 Members
Frequency: Quarterly
Circulation: 17000
Founded in 1972

23125 **Concrete Producer**
Hanley Wood
426 S Westgate
Addison, IL 60101

630-543-0870; Fax: 847-564-9287
ryelton@hanleywood.com
www.theconcreteproducer.com

Richard Yelton, Editor-in-Chief
Tom Bagsarian, Managing Editor
Chari O'Rourke, Circulation Manager

Written for decision-making professionals who buy and specify materials, plant equipment, accessories, trucks, and related products used in the major concrete-producing market segments. Each issue offers money saving operational tips, management advice, new products and technology, and solutions to complex concrete-production questions.

23126 **Contemporary Stone & Tile Design**
Business News Publishing Company
299 Market Street
Suite 320
Saddle Brook, NJ 07663

201-845-5035; Fax: 201-291-9002
www.stoneworld.com

Alex Backrach, Publisher
Michael Reis, Editor

Promotes the benefits of natural stone and ceramic tile to a readership of architects, interior designers, specifiers and consumers. Practical tips and commentary on stone and tile design are included, featuring interviews with architects and designers from the world's leading firms.
Cost: $125.00
Frequency: Quarterly
Circulation: 21000
Founded in 1987

23127 **MC**
National Precast Concrete Association
10333 N Meridian St
Suite 272
Indianapolis, IN 46290-1081

317-571-9500
800-366-7731; Fax: 317-571-0041
rhyink@precast.org
www.precast.org

Ty Gable, President
Brenda Ibitz, Manager Advertising

MC magazine features detailed articles about the latest industry technologies and developments, perspectives on current industry events, profiles on leading precast concrete companies and case studies of various manufactured concrete applications.
Frequency: Bi-Monthly

23128 **Masonry Construction**
Hanley Wood
426 S Westgate
Addison, IL 60101

630-543-0870; Fax: 847-564-9287
www.masonryconstruction.com
Facebook, Twitter

Richard Yelton, Editor-in-Chief
Ron Holzhauer, Deputy Editor
Kari Moosman, Associate Editor
Ted Worthington, Managing Editor
Chari O'Rourke, Circulation Manager

Masonry Construction brings together the complex and fragmented components of the masonry industry—contractors, general contractors, architects, engineers, and producers—providing technical advice, innovative methods and materials, state-of-the-art projects, and essential product information.

23129 **Precast**
National Precast Concrete Association
1320 City Center Drive
Suite 200
Carmel, IN 46032

317-571-9500
800-366-7731; Fax: 317-571-0041
npca@precast.org
www.precast.org

Ty Gable, President
Brenda Ibitz, VP Development and Member Services
Frequency: Bi-Monthly
Circulation: 5000

23130 **Professional Builder**
Reed Business Information
8878 Barrons Blvd
Littleton, CO 80129-2345

303-470-4000
800-446-6551; Fax: 303-470-4691
subsmail@reedbusiness.com
www.reedbusiness.com

Tim Myers, Executive
Stuart Whayman, Finance
Nathan Cahill, HR

The magazine for professionals within the residential building industry. Articles cover industry news, company profiles, market reports, construction technology and merchandising information needed to successfully complete each job.
Frequency: Monthly
Founded in 1977

23131 **Rock Products**
Primedia
29 N Wacker Drive
10th Floor
Chicago, IL 60606

312-726-2802; Fax: 312-726-2574
www.rockproducts.com

Rick Markley, Editor
Scott Bieda, Publisher
Sean ~ Carr, Sales Manager

The aggregate industry's journal of applied technology.
Frequency: Monthly
ISSN: 0035-7464
Founded in 1905

23132 **Stone World**
BNP Media
210 E State Rt 4
Suite 203
Paramus, NJ 07652-5103

201-291-9001; Fax: 201-291-9002
info@stoneworld.com
www.stoneworld.com

Alex Bachrach, Publisher

A source of information on stone use in architecture and interior design as well as stone production, distribution, installationm and maintenance.

Trade Shows

23133 **CSDA Convention and Tech Fair**
Concrete Sawing and Drilling Association
100 2nd Avenue South
Suite 402N
St. Petersburg, FL 33701

727-577-5004; Fax: 727-577-5012
info@csda.org
www.csda.org

Patrick O'Brien, Executive Director
Erin O'Brien, Assistant to Executive Director
Russell Hitchen, Training Coordinator & Editor
Jacqueline Takach, Member Service Coordinator

Convention for professionals working in the concrete cutting industry, including sawing and drilling contractors, concrete polishers and GPR imaging contractors.
500 Members
300 Attendees
Frequency: Annual
Founded in 1972

23134 **Composites and Polycon Convention**
American Composites Manufacturers Association
1010 North Glebe Road
Suite 450
Arlington, VA 22201

703-525-0511; Fax: 703-525-0743
info@acmanet.org
www.acmanet.org

Three-day convention. Attendees will have the opportunity to choose from 100 presentations, live demonstrations and technical papers. Covering every level of expertise from beginer to advanced, industry experts will address dozens of subject areas in the most striking detail, from technical to production to regulatory to management and more.
Frequency: Annual

23135 **Manufactured Concrete Products Exposition**
National Concrete Masonry Association

13750 Sunrise Valley Drive
Herndon, VA 20171-4662

703-713-1900; Fax: 703-713-1910
ncma@ncma.org
www.ncma.org

Mark Hogan, President
Ron Churchill, Director Of Sales

The Manufactured Concrete Products Exposition is brought to you by a partnership between the National Concrete Masonry Association, the Interlocking Concrete Paving Institute and the American Concrete Pipe Association.
Frequency: Annual

23136 **National Concrete Burial Vault Association Convention**
NCBVA
195 Wekiva Springs Road
Suite 200
Longwood, FL 32779

407-788-1996; Fax: 407-774-6751
www.ncbva.org

Thomas A Monahan, Executive Director
Heather Jones, Conventions/Event Planning

Convention held annually. Includes awards banquet, installation of officers and more.
Frequency: Annual

23137 **PTI Technical Conference and Exhibition**
Post-Tensioning Institute
38800 Country Club Drive~
Farmington Hills, MI 48331

248-848-3180; Fax: 248-848-3181
info@post-tensioning.org
www.post-tensioning.org

Ted Neff, Executive Director
Larry Krauser, President
Marc Khoury, VP
Robert Sward, Secretary

Earn CEUs, attend technical sessions, awards events, exhibits, and ask-the-expert forum.
Frequency: May

23138 **Precast Show**
National Precast Concrete Association
1320 City Center Drive
Suite 200
Carmel, IN 46032-1074

317-571-9500
800-366-7731; Fax: 317-571-0041
npca@precast.org
www.precast.org
Facebook, Twitter, LinkedIn, You Tube

Ty Gable, President
Erica Wells, Director Meetings

Trade show for the precast concrete industry, containing 300 booths and 300 exhibits.
3000 Attendees
Frequency: Annual

23139 **StonExpo**
Marble Institute of America
28901 Clemens Road
Suite 100
Cleveland, OH 44145

440-250-9222; Fax: 440-250-9223
www.marble-institute.com

Gary Distelhorst, EVP/CEO
Helen Distelhorst, Meetings/Special Events Director

Where fabricators, installers and distributors can experience everything from natural stone extracted from quarries around the world, to the most technologically advanced fabricating machinery, to the beautiful finished product: exquisite countertops that are installed in both residential and commercial properties today.
Frequency: Annual/January

23140 **World of Concrete Exposition**
Post Tensioning Institute
8601 North Black Canyon Highway
Suite 103
Phoenix, AZ 85021

602-870-7540; Fax: 602-870-7541
info@post-tensioning.org
www.post-tensioning.org

Seminars, exhibits and trade shows. Sponsored by the Post-Tensioning Institute.
36M Attendees
Frequency: January/Febuary

Directories & Databases

23141 **CSDA Membership Directory**
Concrete Sawing and Drilling Association
100 2nd Avenue South
Suite 402N
St. Petersburg, FL 33701

727-577-5004; Fax: 727-577-5012
info@csda.org
www.csda.org

Patrick O'Brien, Executive Director
Erin O'Brien, Assistant to Executive Director
Russell Hitchen, Training Coordinator & Editor
Jacqueline Takach, Member Service Coordinator

Contains listings of contractors offering services in cutting, polishing, imaging and selective demolition.
Founded in 1972

23142 **CSDA Resource Guide**
Concrete Sawing and Drilling Association
100 2nd Avenue South
Suite 402N
St. Petersburg, FL 33701

727-577-5004; Fax: 727-577-5012
info@csda.org
www.csdabuyersguide.org

Patrick O'Brien, Executive Director
Erin O'Brien, Assistant to Executive Director
Jacqueline Takach, Member Service Coordinator

The resource guide is a directory of companies, distributers, manufacturers and contractors offering concrete sawing and drilling services.
500 Members
Founded in 1972

23143 **Dimension Stone Design Manual**
Marble Institute of America
28901 Clemens Rd
Suite 100
Cleveland, OH 44145-1166

440-250-9222; Fax: 440-250-9223
mia@marble-institute.com
www.marble-institute.com

Gary Distelhorst, Executive VP
Helen Distelhorst, Director Meetings/Special Events
Jim Hieb, VP
Michael A. Twiss, President

An authoritative source for guidelines on using natural stone in architectural designs. Contents include sections on granite, marble, limestone, serpentine, travertine, quartz-based stone and slate with product descriptions and technical data; general installation guidelines; guidelines and typical detailing for horizontal surfaces, vertical surfaces, wet areas, furniture and countertops; maintenance of exterior/ interior stone installations; and a glossary of terms relating to dimension stone.
Cost: $90.00
350 Pages
Founded in 1960

23144 **Dimension Stones of the World: Book of Color Plates**
Marble Institute of America
28901 Clemens Rd
Suite 100
Cleveland, OH 44145-1166

440-250-9222; Fax: 440-250-9223
mia@marble-institute.com
www.marble-institute.com

Gary Distelhorst, Executive VP
Helen Distelhorst, Director Meetings/Special Events
Jim Hieb, VP
Michael A. Twiss, President

This set contains over 600 full color reproductions of granites, limestones, marbles, onyx, quartz based stone, slate and travertine. On the reverse side of each page are the ASTM test values for absorbption, density, compressive strength, hardness and flexural strength. Also listed for each stone are primary name, country of origin, quarry location, geological age, color range, recommended usage and available sizes.
Cost: $330.00
Founded in 1960

23145 **Online MCP**
American Concrete Institute
38800 Country Club Drive
PO Box 9094
Farmington Hills, MI 48333-9094

248-483-3700; Fax: 248-848-3801
shannon.hale@concrete.org
www.concrete.org

William R Tolley, Executive VP
Douglas J Sordyl, Marketing/Sales/Industry Relations
Donna G Halstead, Finance/Administration
Shannon M Hale, Technical Editor
Carl R Bischof, Senior Editor Publishing Services

Contains all of the ACI documents you need to answer your questions about code requirements, specifications, tolerance, concrete proportions, construction methods, evaluations of test results, and many more topics.
Founded in 1994
Mailing list available for rent

23146 **Stone World Annual Buyer's Guide**
Stone World Magazine
210 Route 4 East
Suite 311
Paramus, NJ 90001

201-291-9001; Fax: 201-291-2002
info@stoneworld.com
www.stoneworld.com
Facebook, Twitter

Alex Bachrach, Publisher
Michael Reis, Senior Editor/Associate Publisher

Comprised of six sections covering: stone suppliers, fabricating equipment and suppliers, installation and stone care materials and supplies, associations, services, trade shows and organizers.
Cost: $6.00
Frequency: Annual
Circulation: 22,000
Founded in 1984

Industry Web Sites

23147 **http://gold.greyhouse.com**
G.O.L.D Grey House OnLine Databases

Grey House Publising's online database platform, GOLD, offers Quick Search, Keyword Search and Expert Search for most business sectors including stone and concrete markets. The GOLD platform makes finding the information you need quick and easy - whether you're a novice searcher or an experienced database user. All of Grey House's directory products are available for subscription on the GOLD platform.

23148 **www.construction.com**
McGraw-Hill Construction

McGraw-Hill Construction (MHC), part of The McGraw-Hill Companies, connects people and projects across the design and construction industry, serving owners, architects, engineers, general contractors, subcontractors, building product manufacturers, suppliers, dealers, distributors and adjacent markets.

23149 **www.crsi.org**
Concrete Reinforcing Steel Institute

Conducts research and provides technical information on reinforced concrete design and construction practices.

23150 **www.csda.org**
Concrete Sawing and Drilling Association

Facebook, Twitter, LinkedIn, Flickr, YouTube

Association committed to promoting professional specialty sawing and drilling contractors and their services.

23151 **www.greyhouse.com**
Grey House Publishing

Authoritative reference directories for most business sectors including stone and concrete markets. Users can search the online databases with varied search criteria allowing for custom searches by product category, geographic area, sales volume, keyword, subject and more. Full Grey House catalog and online ordering also available.

23152 **www.icri.org**
International Concrete Repair Institute

To improve the quality of repair, restoration, and protection of concrete and other structures.

23153 **www.marble-institute.com**
Marble Institute of America

Importers, finishers, wholesalers, fabricators, quarriers and exporters of stone for both interior and exterior application as well as suppliers of machines, tools and services.

23154 **www.masonryinstitute.org**
1315 Storm Pkwy.
Torrance, CA 90501-5041

310-257-9000; Fax: 310-257-1942
www.masonryinstitute.org

Source for contacts and publications in the masonry industry.
Founded in 1957

23155 **www.post-tensioning.org**
Post-Tensioning Institute

Provides research, technical development, marketing and promotional activities for companies engaged in post-tensioned prestressed construction. Members include fabricators and manufacturers.

23156 **www.precast.org**
National Precast Concrete Association

23157 **www.sweets.construction.com**
McGraw Hill Construction

In depth product information that lets you find, compare, select, specify and make purchase decisions in the industrial product marketplace.

Associations

23158 **4G Americas**
1750 - 112th Avenue NE, Suite B220
Bellevue, WA 98004

425-372-8922; Fax: 425-372-8923
vicki.livingston@4gamericas.org
www.4gamericas.org
Facebook, Twitter, LinkedIn

Chris Pearson, President
Vicki Livingston, Head of Comm./Analyst Relations
Jose Otero, Director
Paul Mankiewich, Director
Bob Suffern, Director

23159 **Advanced Television Systems Committee**
1776 K St. NW
8th Floor
Washington, Dc 20006-2340

202-872-9160; Fax: 202-872-9161
www.atsc.org
Facebook, Twitter

Madeleine Noland, President
Jerry Whitaker, Vice President
Daro Bruno, Director, Operations
Founded in 1982

23160 **American Radio Relay League**
225 Main St
Newington, CT 06111-1494

860-594-0200
888-277-5289; Fax: 860-594-0259
www.arrl.org
Facebook, Twitter, Youtube, RSS

David Sumner, CEO
Joel Harrison, President
Barry Shelley, CFO
Harold Kramer, COO

National membership association for amateur radio operators.
170m Members
Founded in 1914

23161 **Antenna Measurement Techniques Association**
6065 Roswell Road
Atlanta, GA 30328

770-864-3488; Fax: 770-864-3491
president@amta.org
www.amta.org
LinkedIn, RSS

Peter Collins, President
John Demas, VP
Dennis Lewis, Secretary
Dave Pinnell, Treasurer

Nonprofit professional organization open to individuals with an interest in antenna measurements. Areas of interest include: measurement facilities, unique or innovative measurement techniques, test instrumentation and systems, RCS measurements, compact range design and evaluation, near-field techniques and their applications, and the practical aspects of measurement problems and their solutions.
400 Members
Founded in 1979

23162 **Armed Forces Communications and Electronics Association**
AFCEA International Headquarters
4400 Fair Lakes Ct
Suite 100
Fairfax, VA 22033-3899

703-631-6100
800-336-4583; Fax: 703-631-6169
service@afcea.org
www.afcea.org
Facebook, Twitter, LinkedIn, Google+, YouTube, Slideshare,

Lt. Gen. Robert Shea, USMC (Ret.), President/CEO
Pat Miorin, CPA, EVP/CFO/International Treasurer
Lt. Gen. John Wood, USA (Ret.), EVP, Defense/National Security
Beverly Cooper, VP, Comm. & Media/CKO/Publisher
James L. Griggs Jr., VP/CIO/CTO

A non-profit international association dedicated to supporting global security by providing an ethical environment that encourages a close co-operative relationship among civil government agencies, the military and industry.
Cost: $35.00
31000 Members
Founded in 1946

23163 **Assn. of Public-Safety Communications Officials International**
351 N Williamson Boulevard
Daytona Beach, FL 32114-1112

386-322-2500
888-272-6911; Fax: 386-322-2501
apco@apcointl.org
www.apcointl.org
Facebook, Twitter, LinkedIn, Youtube

Brent Lee, President
Cheryl J. Greathouse, 1St VP
Martha K. Carter, 2nd VP
Doreen Geary, Accounting
Meghan Architect, Publications

A not-for-profit professional organization dedicated to the enhancement of public safety communications. Exists to serve the people who manage, operate, maintain, and supply the communications systems used to safeguard the lives and property of citizens everywhere.
16000 Members
Founded in 1935

23164 **Association for Local Telecommunications Services**
900 17th St NW
Suite 400
Washington, DC 20006-2507

202-296-6650; Fax: 202-296-7585
membership@alts.org

Earl Comstock, CEO

COMPTEL is the leading industry accociation representing communications service providers and their supplier partners.

23165 **Association of Teleservices International**
222 South Westmonte Drive
Suite 111
Altamonte Springs, FL 32714

866-896-2874; Fax: 407-774-6440
admin@atsi.org
atsi.org
Facebook, Twitter, LinkedIn

Tifani Leal, President
Jeff Rosgen, VP-Treasurer
Susan Mealer, VP-Secretary

An international trade association established by and for entrepreneurs in the TeleServices business. It provides a wide variety of services to businesses, governmental agencies, local emergency respondents and the general public.
35000 Members
Founded in 1942

23166 **Broadcast Designers' Association International**
5700 Wilshire Blvd
Suite 275
Los Angeles, CA 90036

310-788-7600; Fax: 310-788-7616
www.promaxbda.org
Facebook, Twitter, LinkedIn, RSS

Steve Kazanjian, President
Stacy LA Cotera, General Manager
Randy Smith, CFO
Lucian Cojescu, Chief Information Officer

Association for manufacturers or suppliers of broadcast design equipment, supplies and services.

23167 **CDMA Development Group**
575 Anton Blvd.
Suite 440
Costa Mesa, CA 92626

714-545-5211
888-800-CDMA; Fax: 714-545-4601
www.cdg.org
Facebook, Twitter, RSS

Mark S. Richer, President
Jerry Whitaker, Vice President
Lindsy Shelton Gross, Director of Communications
Daro Bruno, Office Manager
Founded in 1993

23168 **Carnegie Mellon University: Information Networking Institute**
Electrical & Computer Engineering Department
4616 Henry Street
Pittsburgh, PA 15213

412-268-7195; Fax: 412-268-7196
ini@cmu.edu
www.ini.cmu.edu
Facebook, Twitter, LinkedIn, Youtube, Flickr, Google+

Dena Haritos Tsamitis, Director
Lynn Carroll, Assistant Director
Andrew Pueschel, Project Manager/Events/Marketing
Chriss Swaney, Director Public Relations
Sean O'Leary, Manager

The Information Networking Institute was established by Carnegie Mellon as the nation's first research and education center devoted to Information Networking.
Founded in 1989

23169 **Cellular Telecommunications Industry**
CTIA
1400 16th St NW
Suite 600
Washington, DC 20036-2225

202-785-0081; Fax: 202-785-0721
www.ctia.org
Facebook, Twitter, LinkedIn, Youtube, Flickr, Google+

Meredith Attwell Baker, President & CEO
Tom Power, Senior VP, General Counsel
Scott Bergmann, VP, Regulatory Affairs
Jot Carpenter, VP, Govt. Affairs
Rocco Carlitti, SVP/CFO

An international organization representing all sectors of wireless communications. As a non-profit membership organization, they represent service providers, manufacturers, wireless data and Internet companies and other contributors to the wireless universe.
Founded in 1984

23170 **Center for Strategic and International Studies**
1616 Rhode Island Avenue, NW
Washington, DC 20036
202-887-0200; Fax: 202-775-3199
www.csis.org
RSS
John J. Hamre, President and CEO
Carig Cohen, Executive Vice President
Jon B. Alterman, SVP
David J. Berteau, SVP & Director
Alice Blevins, SVP for Operations
Founded in 1962

23171 **Competitive Telecommunications Association**
1200 G St. NW, Suite 350
Washington, DC 20005
202-296-6650; Fax: 202-296-7585
www.comptel.org
Facebook, Twitter, LinkedIn
Deborah Ward, Chairwoman
Chris Murray, Vice Chairman
Jim Butman, Treasurer
Ron Beaumont, Director
Bill Barloon, Director
Founded in 1981

23172 **Enterprise Wireless Alliance**
2121 Cooperative Way
Suite 225
Herndon, VA 20171
703-528-5115
800-482-8282; Fax: 703-524-1074
Info@EnterpriseWireless.org
www.enterprisewireless.org
Mark Crosbyd, President & CEO
Bill Mulholland, Executive Director of Finance
Ila Dudley, EVP, Spectrum Operations
Andrea Cumpston, Communications Director
Donna Yudkin, Membership Manager
Formerly ITA and AMTA, works to preserve spectrum rights and access for enterprise wireless customers.
400 Members
Founded in 1985

23173 **Geospatial Information & Technology Association**
1360 University Ave. West
Suite 455
St. Paul, MN 55104-4086
president@gita.org
www.gita.org
Facebook, Twitter, LinkedIn, YouTube
Don Knox, Executive Director
Emily Dufour, Membership Specialist
Mary Fitzgerald, Conference Director
Susan Nolte, Finance Director

23174 **Kagan Research**
1 Lower Ragsdale Dr
Building One Suite 130
Monterey, CA 93940-5749
831-624-1536
800-307-2529; Fax: 831-625-3225
www.kagan.com
Facebook, Twitter, LinkedIn, Youtube, Google+
Mike Chinn, President
Tom Corbitt, Chief Administration Officer
Dan Oakey, Chief Contracts Officer
Provides knowledge, insight and industry perspectives, anticipates trends, projects revenues, tracks financing and values the debt and equity of hundreds of privately held and publicly traded media and communications companies.
Founded in 1969

23175 **National Association of Broadcastersÿ**
1771 N St. NW
Washington, DC 20036
202-429-5300
800-NAB-EXPO
nan@nab.org
www.nab.org
Facebook, Twitter, LinkedIn, YouTube
Gordon Smith, President & CEO
Curtis LeGeyt, Chief Operating Officer
Tea Gennaro, EVP, Finance & CFO
Michelle Duke, Chief Diversity Officer
Sam Matheny, Chief Technology Officer

23176 **National Cable & Telecommunications Association**
25 Massachusetts Ave. NW
Suite 100
Washington, DC 20001
202-222-2300
info@ncta.com
www.ncta.com
Facebook, Twitter, LinkedIn
Michael Powell, President & CEO
James Assey, Executive VP
K. Dane Snowden, Chief Operating Officer
Mark Kulish, SVP, Finance & Admin. & CFO
William Check, SVP, Shief Technology Officer
Trade association for U.S. cable industry.
200 Members

23177 **National Exchange Carrier Association**
80 S Jefferson Rd
Suite 1
Whippany, NJ 07981-1009
973-599-0580
800-228-8597; Fax: 973-884-8469
webmastr@neca.org
www.neca.org
Facebook, Twitter
William Hegman, CEO
Peter A Dunbar, VP/CFO
James W Frame, VP Operations
Regina McNeil, VP/General Counsel/Corp Secretary
Ed Buchanan, Chair
NECA administer's the FCCs access charge plan. They file access charge tariffs with the FCC, collect and validate cost and revenue data, ensure compliance with FCC rules, distribute revenues from access charges among pool members, process FCC regulatory fees, and offer training and education on a wide variety of telecom topics.
1500 Members
Founded in 1983

23178 **National Telephone Cooperative Association**
4121 Wilson Blvd
Suite 1000
Arlington, VA 22203-4145
703-351-2000; Fax: 703-351-2001
contact@ntca.org
www.ntca.org
Facebook, Twitter, LinkedIn, YouTube
Shirley Bloomfield, CEO
Mano Koilpillai, CFO
Les Greer, SVP, Benefits, Operations & Tech
Michael Romano, SVP, Industry Affairs
April Irwin, VP, Member Engagement
Non-profit association offering a wide array of member services including a government affairs program; expert legal and industry representation; a broad range of educational services; a comprehensive assortment of regular and special publications and public relations programs; and a well-rounded complement of national and regional meetings.
900 Members
Founded in 1954

23179 **Personal Communications Industry**
500 Montgomery Street
Suite 700
Alexandria, VA 22314
703-390-0300
800-759-0300; Fax: 703-836-1608
Facebook, Twitter, LinkedIn
Thomas A Murray, Chairman
Steven Marshall, Vice Chairman
David E. Weisman, Treasurer
Jonathan S Adelstein, President & CEO
Tim House, VP, External Relations
Represents companies that develop, own, manage and operate towers, commercial rooftops and other facilities for the provision of all types of wireless, broadcasting and telecommunication services. PCIA is dedicated to advancing an understanding of the benefits of wireless services and required infrastructure to local and federal government officials and communities at large.
3000 Members
Founded in 1949

23180 **Power and Communication Contractors Association**
1908 Mt. Vernon Ave.
2nd Floor
Alexandria, VA 22301
703-212-7734
800-542-7222; Fax: 703-548-3733
info@pccaweb.org
www.pccaweb.org
Timothy Killoren, President
Todd Myers, President-Elect
James Dillahunty, 1st Vice President
Larry Pribyl, 2nd Vice President
John Fluharty, II, Secretary
A national trade association for companies constructing electric power facilities, including transmission and distribution lines and substations and telephone, fiber optic, and cable television systems.
300 Members
Founded in 1945

23181 **Satellite Broadcasting and Communications Association**
1100 17th St. NW
Ste. 1150
Washington, DC 20036
202-349-3620
800-541-5981; Fax: 202-318-2618
info@sbca.org
www.sbca.org
Facebook, Twitter, LinkedIn, YouTube
Andrew Reinsdorf, Chairman
Jeffery Blum, Vice Chairman
Joseph Widoff, Executive Director
Benjamin Rowan, Education Manager
Abdul Salam, Sr. Director of Finance & HR
Founded in 1994

23182 **Satellite Industry Association**
Home Page: www.sia.org
LinkedIn
Bill Weller, Chairman
Stacy Fuller, Vice Chairman
Sam Black, Acting President
Dean Hirasawa, Communications Manager
Jennifer Williams, Office Manager
Founded in 1995

23183 **Society for Technical Communication**
9401 Lee Highway
Suite 300
Fairfax, VA 22031

703-522-4114; Fax: 703-522-2075
www.stc.org
Facebook, Twitter, LinkedIn, YouTube

Liz Pohland, Chief Executive Officer
Erin Gallalee, Director, Membership & Community
Elaine Gilliam, Director, Meetings & Convention Op.
Sarah Black, Publications Manager
Kira Jones, Marketing Manager
Founded in 1957

23184 **Society of Broadcast Engineers**
9102 N Meridian St
Suite 150
Indianapolis, IN 46260-1896

317-846-9000; Fax: 317-846-9120
mclappe@sbe.org
www.sbe.org
Facebook, Twitter, LinkedIn, YouTube

John Poray, Executive Director
Chris Scherer, Member Communications Director
Cathy Orosz, Education Director
Megan Clappe, Certification Director
Debbie Hennessey, Sustaining Member Manager

SBE provides members with the opportunity to network and share ideas and information in keeping current with the ongoing changes within the industry. Members can attend annual conferences and expositions, have access to educational opportunities and obtain professional certification.
5100+ Members
Founded in 1964
Mailing list available for rent: 5700 names at $170 per M

23185 **Society of Cable Telecommunications Engineers**
140 Philips Rd
Exton, PA 19341-1318

610-363-6888
800-542-5040; Fax: 610-363-5898
information@scte.org
www.scte.org
Facebook, Twitter

Tony Werner, Chairman
Bill Warga, Vice Chairman
Steve Williams, Secretary
Christine Whittaker, Treasurer
Mark Dzuban, President/CEO

A nonprofit, professional organization committed to advancing the careers of cable telecommunications professionals and serving their industry through excellence in professional development, information and standards.
15000 Members
Founded in 1969

23186 **Society of Satellite Professionals**
New York Information Technology Center
250 Park Ave
7th Floor
New York, NY 10177

212-809-5199; Fax: 212-825-0075
www.sspi.org
Facebook, Twitter, LinkedIn, YouTube

Robert Bell, Executive Director
Louis Zacharilla, Director, Development
Tamara Bond-Williams, Director, Membership
Matthew Owen, Communications Manager

A nonprofit association that serves people working in the satellite industry in countries arount the world. Professional development society of the global satellite industry.
1000 Members
Founded in 1983

23187 **Society of Telecommunications Consultants**
13275 State Highway 89
PO Box 70
Old Station, CA 96071

530-335-7313
800-782-7670; Fax: 530-335-7360
Facebook, Twitter, Pinterest

Cathy Cimaglia, Administration Manager

The STC is an international organization of independent telecommunications and information technology consultants who serve clients in business and government.
180 Members
Founded in 1976

23188 **Telecom Association**
31500 Grape Street #3-307
Lake Elsinore, CA 92532

Home Page: www.telecomassociation.com
Facebook, Twitter, LinkedIn, YouTube

Nancy Hagen Baldwin, President
Dan Baldwin, Executive Director
Kathleen Brown, Administrator
3800 Members
Founded in 1995

23189 **Telecom Pioneers**
1801 California Street
Suite 225
Denver, CO 80202-2932

303-571-1200
800-872-5995; Fax: 303-572-0520
info@telecompioneers.org
www.telecompioneers.org

Gloria Pazel, Chairman
Ann Smalley, Vice Chairman
Charlene Hill, Executive Director
Michael Sears, Past Chairman

Formerly known as the Telephone Pioneers of America, TelecomPioneers is comprised of nearly 620,000 current and retired telecommunications employees who have joined together to make their communities better places in which to live and work
Founded in 1911

23190 **Telecommunications Industry Association (TIA)**
1320 N Courthouse Rd
Suite 200
Arlington, VA 22201-3834

703-907-7700; Fax: 703-907-7727
tia@tiaonline.org
www.tiaonline.org
Facebook, Twitter

David Stehlin, Chief Executive Officer
Ken Koffman, Chief Technology Officer & VP
Andrew Kurtzman, VP & General Counsel
Dan Brown, Director, Marketing & Communication
Alia Lawson, Membership Advisor

The Telecommunications Industry Association/TIA represents providers of information, communications and entertainment technology products and services for the global marketplace through its core competencies in standards development, domestic and international policy advocacy, and facilitating member business opportunities. The association facilitates the convergence of new communications networks while working for a competitive and innovative market environment.

23191 **Telework Coalition**
204 E St Ne
Washington, DC 20002-4923

202-266-0046
info@telcoa.org
Facebook, Twitter, LinkedIn

Chuck Wilsker, President
Jack Heacock, Senior VP & Co-Founder

Enabling virtual, mobile and distributed work through education, technology and legislation.

23192 **The National Communication Association**
1765 N Street NW
Washington, DC 20036

202-464-4622; Fax: 202-464-4600
inbox@natcom.org
www.natcom.org
Facebook, Twitter, YouTube, Blog

Trevor Parry-Giles, Executive Director
Joseph Ritchie, Chief Financial Officer
Justin Danowski, Asst. Dir., Governance & Membership
LaKesha Anderson, Dir., Academic/Professional Affairs
Kristin Yednock, Asst. Dir., Conventions & Meetings
Founded in 1914

23193 **United Communications Group**
9737 Washingtonian Blvd
Suite 200
Gaithersburg, MD 20878-7364

301-287-2700; Fax: 301-287-2039
info@ucq.com
www.ucg.com

Todd Foreman, Partner-CEO
Nancy Becker, Partner-President
Steve McVearry, General Counsel
Jon Slabaugh, Managing Director, Business Dev
Chris Dingee, CFO

A portfolio of highly focused business and professional publishing companies providing guidance, information, analysis, data and solutions to over two million clients worldwide.
Founded in 1977

23194 **United States International Telecommunication Union Association**
cherie.mills@pillsburylaw.com
www.usitua.org

Audrey Allison, Chair

The USITUA is a U.S. industry forum on International Telecommunication Union policy matters.

23195 **United States Telecom Association**
607 14th St Nw
Suite 400
Washington, DC 20005-2000

202-326-7300; Fax: 202-315-3603
membership@ustelecom.org
www.ustelecom.org
Facebook, Twitter, LinkedIn, YouTube

Jonathan Spalter, President/CEO
Lorna Johnson, Chief Financial Officer
Allison Remsen, EVP & Chief of Staff
Sally Aman, SVP, Communications/Public Affairs
Brandon Heiner, SVP, Government Affairs

Trade association representing service providers and suppliers for the telecom industry.
1200 Members

23196 **Wireless Communications Alliance**
1510 Page Mill Rd.
Palo Alto, CA 94304

promote@wca.org
www.wca.org
Facebook, Twitter, LinkedIn

Founded in 1994

23197 **Wireless Internet Service Providers Association**
1095 Hilltop Drive #317
Redding, CA 96003

260-622-5776
866-317-2851
tcoffey@wispa.org
www.wispa.org
Facebook, Twitter, LinkedIn, Google+, Tumblr

Alex Phillips, President
Chuck Hogg, Vice President
Mark Radabaugh, Treasurer
Dennis Burgess, Secretary
Trina Coffey, Dir., Operations/Event Management
800 Members

Newsletters

23198 **Broadband**
IGI Group
1340 Soldiers Field Road
Suite 2
Brighton, MA 02135

617-782-5033
800-323-1088; Fax: 617-782-5735
info@igigroup.com
www.igigroup.com

Paul Polishuk, President/CEO
Hui Pan, Conference Director
Bev Wilson, Managing Editor
Will Ashley, IT Director/Media Manager

The Broadband Newsletter covers such subjects as: growth in broadband access such as ADSL, cable modems, satellite and fixed wireless; spending plans of the telcos and MSOs for broadband access; important applications that will drive the market; and growth of the internet based on fast internet access.
Cost: $695.00
Frequency: Monthly
Circulation: 1500
Founded in 1977
Mailing list available for rent

23199 **Broadband Advertising**
Kagan World Media
1 Lower Ragsdale Dr
Building One, Suite 130
Monterey, CA 93940-5749

831-624-1536
800-307-2529; Fax: 831-625-3225
www.kagan.com

Tim Baskerville, President
Tom Johnson, Marketing Manager

Provides critical information about how and where advertising sales will intersect across all broadband platforms. Includes data and analysis previously published in Internet Advertising and Cable TV advertising
Cost: $1095.00
Frequency: Monthly
Founded in 1969

23200 **Broadband Technology**
Kagan World Media
1 Lower Ragsdale Dr
Building One Suite 130
Monterey, CA 93940-5749

831-624-1536
800-307-2529; Fax: 831-625-3225
www.kagan.com

Tim Baskerville, President
Tom Johnson, Marketing Manager
Michael Schroeder, Manager

Incisive, thorough reports on deployments of bundled services, high-spped data, digital video and telephony. Analyzes and projects growth of set-top boxes, modems, switches, routers and other infrastructure. Provides data and stats on services offered and plant construction by cable, DSL, satellite, wireless and wired phone providers.
Cost: $1045.00
Frequency: Monthly
Founded in 1969

23201 **Broadcast Investor**
Kagan World Media
1 Lower Ragsdale Dr
Building One Suite 130
Monterey, CA 93940-5749

831-624-1536
800-307-2529; Fax: 831-625-3225
www.kagan.com

Tim Baskerville, President
Tom Johnson, Marketing Manager

The market's most comprehensive sourve of current and historical data on valuations, deals and finance. Trends, forecasts, data.
Cost: $1295.00
Frequency: Monthly
Founded in 1969

23202 **CBQ-Communication Booknotes Quarterly**
Lawrence Erlbaum Associates
10 Industrial Avenue
Mahwah, NJ 07430

201-258-2200; Fax: 201-760-3735
www.leaonline.com/loi/cbq

Christopher Sterling, Editor
James K Bracken, Assistant Editor

Descriptive reviews of new publications and websites.
Cost: $350.00
Frequency: Quarterly
ISSN: 1094-8007
Founded in 1969

23203 **Cable Program Investor**
Kagan World Media
1 Lower Ragsdale Dr
Building One, Suite 130
Monterey, CA 93940-5749

831-624-1536
800-307-2529; Fax: 831-625-3225
www.kagan.com

Tim Baskerville, President
Tom Johnson, Marketing Manager

Provides exclusive data and analysis, deal benchmarks and balance sheet assessments. It covers home shopping networks, programming trends, multichannel penetration by platform and ratings data.
Cost: $1045.00
Frequency: Monthly
Founded in 1969

23204 **Cable TV Investor**
Kagan World Media
1 Lower Ragsdale Dr
Building One,Suite 130
Monterey, CA 93940-5749

831-624-1536
800-307-2529; Fax: 831-625-3225
www.kagan.com

Tim Baskerville, President
Tom Johnson, Marketing Manager

Provides information on the data, the deals, the valuation metrics, the distillation of information into intelligence. The information you want and need to remain competitive
Cost: $1295.00
Frequency: Monthly
Founded in 1969

23205 **Cable TV Law Reporter**
Kagan World Media
1 Lower Ragsdale Dr
Building One Suite 130
Monterey, CA 93940-5749

831-624-1536
800-307-2529; Fax: 831-625-3225
www.kagan.com

Tim Baskerville, President
Tom Johnson, Marketing Manager

The quintessential library of cable court cases, arbitrations, legal precedents. Labeled and catalogued for easy reference. Required reading for attorneys, government regulators and top executives. Three month trial available.
Cost: $995.00
Frequency: Monthly
Founded in 1969

23206 **Communication**
National Technical Information Service
5285 Port Royal Rd
Springfield, VA 22161-0001

703-605-6000; Fax: 703-605-6900
customerservice@ntis.gov
www.ntis.gov

Linda Davis, VP
Bruce Borzino, Director

Covers common carrier and satellite communications, information theory, graphics, policies, regulations, studies, radio and television.
Founded in 1991

23207 **Communications Daily**
Warren Publishing
2115 Ward Ct Nw
Washington, DC 20037-1209

202-872-9200
800-771-9202; Fax: 202-318-8350
info@warren-news.com
www.warren-news.com

Brig Easley, Executive VP/Controller
Paul Warren, Chair/Publisher
Daniel Warren, President/Editor

Daily publication for the entire telecommunications indusrty.
Frequency: Daily
Circulation: 70000+
Founded in 1945

23208 **Fiber Optic Sensors and Systems**
IGI Group
1340 Soldiers Field Road
Suite 2
Brighton, MA 02135

617-782-5033
800-323-1088; Fax: 617-782-5735
info@igigroup.com
www.igigroup.com

Paul Polishuk, CEO
Hui Pan, Conference Director
Bev Wilson, Managing Editor

Covers procurements, contract awards, requests for qualifications and proposals, reports on

market studies, patents filed and awarded, new product announcements, new technology, market forecasts, reviews of important contracts, important conferences and trade shows, and Japanese and European developments.
Cost: $695.00
Frequency: Monthly
Founded in 1977

23209 **Fiber Optics News**
Phillips Business Information
1201 Seven Locks Road
Potomac, MD 20854-2931
301-354-1400; Fax: 301-340-0542
stephenh@pennwell.com
www.lightwaveonline.com
Ellen Hamm, Publisher
Mark Mikolas, Editor
Stephen Hardy, Editorial Director
Fiber optics in the telecommunications fields.
Cost: $37.00

23210 **Fiber Optics Weekly Update**
IGI Group
1340 Soldiers Field Road
Suite 2
Brighton, MA 02135
617-782-5033
800-323-1088; Fax: 617-782-5735
info@igigroup.com
www.igigroup.com
Paul Polishuk, CEO
Hui Pan, Conference Director
Bev Wilson, Managing Editor
Yesim Taskor, Controller
Covers procurements, new contracts, company buyouts, new products, important publications, latest news, planned projects, financial reports, market forecasts, conference and trade show reviews, joint ventures, contract awards, impact of technology, and international developments.
Cost: $695.00
Frequency: Weekly
Founded in 1977

23211 **Fiber Optics and Communications**
IGI Group
1340 Soldiers Field Road
Suite 2
Brighton, MA 02135
617-782-5033
800-323-1088; Fax: 617-783-5735
editor@igigroup.com
www.igigroup.com
Paul Polishuk, Publisher
Hui Pan, Conference Director
Bev Wilson, Managing Editor
Yesim Taskor, Controller
Fiber optics is spreading rapidly into all major high and low tech fields. This newsletter helps relieve the pressure on busy executives by reviewing over 300 sources on a regular basis and providing only the most relevant information.
Cost: $695.00
Frequency: Monthly
Founded in 1977

23212 **Fixed Wireless**
IGI Group
1340 Soldiers Field Road
Suite 2
Brighton, MA 02135
617-782-5033
800-323-1088; Fax: 617-782-5735
editor@igigroup.com
www.igigroup.com
Paul Polishuk, CEO
Hui Pan, Conference Director
Bev Wilson, Managing Editor
Yesim Taskor, Controller
Tracks technological breakthroughs, network developments, market trends, contacts and examines who the players are in this re-emerging market.
Cost: $695.00
Frequency: Monthly
Founded in 1977

23213 **Home Networks**
IGI Group
1340 Soldiers Field Road
Suite 2
Brighton, MA 02135
617-782-5033
800-323-1088; Fax: 617-782-5735
info@igigroup.com
www.igigroup.com
Paul Polishuk, Publisher/CEO
Hui Pan, Conference Director
Bev Wilson, Managing Editor
Yesim Taskor, Controller
The market for home networks is driven by the 15 million homes with two or more PCs requiring interconnection and new housing units being built for tomorrow's home network environment. This newsletter keeps you connected to this rapidly developing arena of opportunities.
Cost: $695.00
Frequency: Monthly
Founded in 1977

23214 **Interval**
Society of Cable Telecommunications Engineers
140 Philips Road
Exton, PA 19341-1318
610-363-6888
800-542-5040; Fax: 610-363-5898
scte@scte.org
www.scte.org
Mark Durbaz, President/CEO
Catty Oaks, VP
Serving the members of SCTE, Interval highlights the events of the Society and it's Chapters.
Cost: $40.00
Circulation: 15000
Founded in 1969

23215 **Kagan Media Money**
Kagan World Media
1 Lower Ragsdale Dr
Building One, Suite 130
Monterey, CA 93940-5749
831-624-1536
800-307-2529; Fax: 831-625-3225
www.kagan.com
Tim Baskerville, President
Tom Johnson, Marketing Manager
Sandie Borthwick, Executive Director
Designed to continually focus on the essential trends and hottest topics. Each issue is jammed with leading media indicators, media merger and acquisition data, handy benchmarks and reference charts and the most thought-provoking and insightful analysis.
Cost: $1245.00
Frequency: 48 issues per y
Founded in 1969

23216 **LAN Newsletter**
IGI Group
1340 Soldiers Field Road
Suite 2
Brighton, MA 02135
617-782-5033
800-323-1088; Fax: 617-782-5735
editor@igigroup.com
www.igigroup.com
Paul Polishuk, President/CEO
Hui Pan, Conference Director
Bev Wilson, Managing Editor
Yesim Taskor, Controller
Provides information on new developments and products in the LAN-local area network-industry. Discusses both foreign and domestic markets, including new LAN purchases and installation and management changes.
Cost: $695.00
Frequency: Monthly
Circulation: 12000
Founded in 1977

23217 **LAN Product News**
Worldwide Videotex
Po Box 3273
Boynton Beach, FL 33424
561-738-2276
markedit@juno.com
www.wvpubs.com
Provides news and information on the computer Local Area Network (LAN) industry. Covers new hardware and software products, as well as research and development.
Cost: $25.00
Frequency: Monthly

23218 **MIC/TECH Data Communications**
1111 Markkress Road
Cherry Hill, NJ 08003-2334
856-489-4310
800-678-4642; Fax: 856-424-1999
Lawrence Feidelman, Publisher
Michael Smith, Editor
Carol Bell, Advertising/Sales
Complete performance and pricing of modems, multiplexus, networks and processing.
Cost: $920.00
Frequency: Daily

23219 **Microcell Report**
150 E 2nd Street
New York, NY 10009-8400
800-883-8989; Fax: 212-366-9798
Roger Newell, Publisher
A monthly report on personal communication services including advanced digital mobile telephone applications. Covers regulatory, technical and communication aspects of PCS which includes wireless LANS and PBX.
Cost: $397.00
10 Pages
Frequency: Monthly

23220 **Microwave News**
Microwave News
155 East 77th Street
New York, NY 10075
212-517-2800; Fax: 212-734-0316
info@microwavenews.com
www.microwavenews.com
Twitter
Louis Slesin, Editor & Publisher
Health issues relating to non-ionizing radiation.
Frequency: 6 issues per year
Founded in 1981

23221 **Modem Users News**
Worldwide Videotex
Po Box 3273
Boynton Beach, FL 33424
561-738-2276
markedit@juno.com
www.wvpubs.com
Provides the latest news and information on software, hardware, supplies and services for individuals and companies who communicate via modems in computer and/or facsimile applications. Contains detailed information, prices, and evaluations of products ranging from protable laptop PC and fax boards, to a wide range of ac-

cessible services.
Cost: $25.00
Frequency: Monthly

23222 **Newsletter**
United Communications Group
11300 Rockville Pike
#1100
Rockville, MD 20852-3012

301-816-8950; Fax: 301-816-8945
www.ucg.com

Sean Oberle, Publisher
Todd Foreman, CEO
Jon Slabaugh, MD
Stephanie Tamburello, HR

Editorial content provides hands-on advice on how to improve their services and reduce their overall operating expenses.
Cost: $379.00
Frequency: BiMonthly

23223 **North American Telecom Newswatch**
United Communications Group
11300 Rockville Pike
Street 1100
Rockville, MD 20852-3012

301-287-2700; Fax: 301-816-8945
www.ucg.com

Benny Dicecca, President
Todd Foreman, CEO
Jon Slabaugh, MD
Stephanie Tamburello, HR

The news that impacts daily business operations, including equipment updates, regulation issues, long distance and internet useage, and wireless financials.
Founded in 1977

23224 **Online Newsletter**
Information Intelligence
PO Box 31098
Phoenix, AZ 85046-1098

602-996-2283

Richard Huleatt, Publisher/Editor

Covers all on-line services, suppliers, vendors, CD-ROM data bases, microcomputers and associated equipment.
Cost: $6.25
9 Pages
Frequency: 10 per year
Founded in 1980
Printed in on newsprint stock

23225 **Optical Networks and WDM**
IGI Group
1340 Soldiers Field Road
Suite 2
Brighton, MA 02135

617-782-5033
800-323-1088; Fax: 617-782-5735
info@igigroup.com
www.igigroup.com

Paul Polishuk, CEO
Hui Pan, Conference Director
Bev Wilson, Managing Editor
Yesim Taskor, Controller

The WDM newsletter provides worldwide coverage of technology, markets and applications. Covers such subjects as: WDM systems, MAN applications, Gigabit networks, ATM, financials reports, premise wiring, optical amplifiers, optical networks, new products, network management, standards, optical cross connects, frame relay, competitive analysis, manufacturers strategies, optical access, regulations, tariffs, technology, broadband servies, WANs, market forecasts, BOC strategies and more.
Cost: $695.00
Frequency: Monthly
Founded in 1977

23226 **Photonics Components/Subsystems**
IGI group
1340 Soldiers Field Road
Suite 2
Brighton, MA 02135

617-782-5033
800-323-1088; Fax: 617-782-5735
info@igigroup.com
www.igigroup.com

Paul Polishuk, Publisher
Hui Pan, Conference Director
Bev Wilson, Managing Editor
Yesim Taskor, Controller

Provides worldwide coverage of technology, markets, and applications. Some subjects covered include: market forecasts, product comparisons, new products, contract awards, new technologies, start-up funding, customer requirements, standards, industry trends, photonics automation, systems developments, licensing, competitive assessments, mergers and acquisitions, and pricing trends.
Cost: $695.00
Frequency: Monthly
Founded in 1977

23227 **Plastic Optical Fiber (POF)**
IGI Group
1340 Soldiers Field Road
Suite 2
Brighton, MA 02135

617-782-5033
800-323-1088; Fax: 617-782-5735
editor@igigroup.com
www.igigroup.com

Paul Polishuk, CEO
Hui Pan, Conference Director
Bev Wilson, Managing Editor
Yesim Taskor, Controller

Some of the subjects covered are: applications, products, imaging, patents, technology, market research, suppliers, publications, standards, sensors, cost analyses, mergers, audio systems, lighting/illuminations, medical acquisitions, medical, market opportunities, contracts awarded, automotive, licensing opportunities, RFPs, component costs, investments and signs.
Cost: $395.00
Frequency: 6 issues per yr
Founded in 1977

23228 **SCTE Interval**
Society of Cable Telecommunications Engineers
140 Philips Road
Exton, PA 19341-1318

610-363-6888
800-542-5040; Fax: 610-363-5898
scte@scte.org
www.scte.org

Mark Durbaz, President/CEO
Catty Oaks, VP

SCTE's monthly newsletter keeps members abreast of association events, activities and member accomplishments.
Cost: $40.00
Circulation: 15,000
Founded in 1969

23229 **Satellite News**
Phillips Publishing
7811 Montrose Road
Potomac, MD 20854

301-340-2100
866-599-9491
feedback@healthydirections.com
www.healthydirections.com

Satellite telecommunications.
Frequency: Monthly
Founded in 1985

23230 **Society of Telecommunications Consultants Newsletter**
Society of Telecommunications Consultants
13275 State Highway 89
PO Box 70
Old Station, CA 96071

530-335-7313
800-782-7670; Fax: 530-335-7360
stchdq@stcconsultants.org
www.sctcconsultants.org

Cathy Cimaglia, Administrative Manager
Mark Durbaz, President/CEO
Catty Oaks, VP

A newsletter for update and informational purposes.
Frequency: Quarterly
Founded in 1969

23231 **State & Local Communications Report**
BRP Publications
1333 H Street NW
Suite 100 E
Washington, DC 20005-4746

202-312-6060
800-822-6338; Fax: 202-842-3047

Lynn Stanton, Editor
Victoria Mason, Publisher

Premier biweekly news service covering state and local communications issues. The in-depth reporting includes regular coverage of such timely topics as legislation and regulation, new state regulatory activities and important business and industry developments in the areas of telephone, data and enhanced services.
Cost: $599.00
8 Pages
Frequency: BiWeekly

23232 **State Telephone Regulation Report**
Telecom Publishing Group
1101 King Street
Suite 444
Alexandria, VA 22314-2944

703-683-4100
800-327-7205; Fax: 703-739-6490

Chris Vestal, Publisher
Herbert Kirchoff, Editor

Analysis of state telecommunications legislation.
Cost: $535.00
12 Pages
Frequency: BiWeekly
Printed in 2 colors on matte stock

23233 **Submarine Fiber Optic Communications Systems**
IGI Group
1340 Soldiers Field Road
Suite 2
Brighton, MA 02135

617-782-5033
800-323-1088; Fax: 617-782-5735
editor@igigroup.com
www.igigroup.com

Paul Polishuk, Publisher
Hui Pan, Conference Director
Bev Wilson
Yesim Taskor, Controller

Provides a monthly market intelligence report on new developments in markets, technology and applications. Of special interest will be developments in optical amplifier technology, solutions, Wavelength Division Multiplexing and how these are having an impact on the Submarine Fiber Optic business
Cost: $695.00
Frequency: Monthly
Founded in 1977

23234 **TR Wireless News**
BRP Publications
1333 H Street NW
Suite 100 E
Washington, DC 20005-4707
202-312-6060
800-822-6338; Fax: 202-842-3047
Victoria Mason, Publisher
Andrew Kreig, President
Montiors regulatory, technological and market developments in the rapidly expanding wireless communications industry. It covers new services, corporate activity, and licensing and specturm allocation in the areas of personal communication services.
Cost: $597.00
Frequency: BiWeekly

23235 **TV Program Investor**
Kagan World Media
1 Lower Ragsdale Dr
Building One, Suite 130
Monterey, CA 93940-5749
831-624-1536
800-307-2529; Fax: 831-625-3225
www.kagan.com
Tim Baskerville, President
Tom Johnson, Marketing Manager
More than just a newsletter, practically a seminar on how much programs cost and what they are worth. Exclusive spreadsheets with estimates of what goes between the commercials. Three month trial available.
Cost: $895.00
Frequency: Monthly
Founded in 1969

23236 **Telco Competition Report**
BRP Publications
1333 H Street NW
Suite 100 E
Washington, DC 20005-4746
202-312-6060
800-822-6338; Fax: 202-842-3047
Victoria Mason, Publisher
Brian Hammond, Editor
Provides important information on events and issues surrounding the $90 billion local exchange markets. Each issues covers the continuing regulatory, financial, strategic and technological ramifications of local exchange competition, including the second and third-tier cities being targeted by competitions and strategies for success.
Cost: $596.00
20 Pages
Frequency: BiWeekly

23237 **Tele-Service News**
Worldwide Videotex
Po Box 3273
Boynton Beach, FL 33424
561-738-2276
markedit@juno.com
www.wvpubs.com
Provides news and information on the telephone industry. Covers services, products, research and development and business plans of RBOCs (Regional Bell Operating Companies), long distance carriers, and independent vendors.
Cost: $25.00
Frequency: Monthly

23238 **Telecom Daily Lead from US Telecom Association**
SmartBrief
1401 H Street
N.W, Suite 600
Washington, DC 20005
202-326-7300; Fax: 202-326-7333
webmaster@smartbrief.com
www.dailylead.com/usta
Portia Krebs, VP Communications
Jason Ross, Lead Editor
Eric Hoffman, Sales Account Director
Free daily newsbriefing, delivered by e-mail, that covers the telecom industry's top news stories.
Frequency: Daily
Circulation: 11000

23239 **Telecom Outlook**
Market Intelligence Research Company
2525 Charleston Road
Mountain View, CA 94043-1626
Wyman Bravard, Publisher
Reports on the telecommunications industry.
Frequency: Monthly

23240 **Telecom Standards**
IGI Group
1340 Soldiers Field Road
Suite 2
Brighton, MA 02135
617-782-5033
800-323-1088; Fax: 617-782-5735
editor@igigroup.com
www.igigroup.com
Paul Polishuk, President/CEO
Hui Pan, Conference Director
Bev Wilson, Managing Editor
Yesim Taskor, Controller
Provides coverage of standards activities around the world, schedules of standards meetings, the availablity of standards, and how to obtain standards, minutes of standards meetings and drafts of standards.
Cost: $695.00
Frequency: Monthly
Founded in 1977

23241 **Telecommunications Mergers and Acquisitions**
IGI group
1340 Soldiers Field Road
Suite 2
Brighton, MA 02135
617-782-5033
800-323-1088; Fax: 617-782-5735
editor@igigroup.com
www.igigroup.com
Paul Polishuk, President/CEO
Hui Pan, Conference Director
Bev Wilson, Managing Editor
Yesim Taskor, Controller
Covers worldwide developments in the telecommunications mergers and acquisitions. In addition to reporting to these activities, the newsletter analyzes potential merger and acquisition candidates, summarizes in an easy-to-read form trends by different companies and industry requirements.
Cost: $695.00
Frequency: Monthly
Founded in 1977

23242 **Telecommunications Reports International**
BRP Publications
111 Eighth Avenue
7th Floor
New York, NY 10011-4707
212-771-0600
800-234-1660; Fax: 212-771-0885
www.aspenlawschool.com
Andrew Jacobson, Publisher
George Brandon, Editor
Jim Monahan, President
Richard H Kravitz, Execitive VP
International telecom policy and trade issues, global services, satellites, tariffs and financial developments.
Cost: $1789.00
Frequency: 24 issues per y

23243 **Telemarketing Update**
Prosperity & Profits Unlimited
PO Box 416
Denver, CO 80201-0416
303-573-5564
AC Doyle, Publisher
Telemarketing script presentation suggestions and ideas.
Cost: $200.00
8 Pages
Frequency: Annual
Circulation: 2,000
Printed in on matte stock

23244 **Telemarketing Update-Catering Service Business Script Presentations**
Prosperity & Profits Unlimited
PO Box 416
Denver, CO 80201-0416
303-573-5564
A Doyle, Editor
Catering service telemarketing script presentations.
Cost: $19.95
10 Pages
Frequency: Irregular
Circulation: 2,100
Founded in 1990
Printed in one color on matte stock

23245 **VoiceNews**
Stoneridge Technical Services
PO Box 1891
Rockville, MD 20849-1891
301-424-0114; Fax: 301-424-8971
William Creitz, Publisher/Editor
Covers voice technology for telecommunications and office automation: voice messaging, voice response, speech recognition, speech synthesis.
Cost: $25.00

23246 **Why Not An Answering Service?**
Prosperity & Profits Unlimited
PO Box 416
Denver, CO 80201-0416
303-573-5564
A Doyle, Editor
Offers information and ideas on telephone answering service possibilities.
Cost: $29.95
73 Pages
Frequency: Every Five Years
Circulation: 5,000
Founded in 1989
Printed in on matte stock

23247 **Wireless Market Stats**
Kagan World Media
1 Lower Ragsdale Dr
Building One Suite 130
Monterey, CA 93940-5749
831-624-1536
800-307-2529; Fax: 831-625-3225
www.kagan.com
Tim Baskerville, President
Tom Johnson, Marketing Manager
In-depth analysis of metropolitan and rural cellular market efficiency, plus operating statistics, private deal market data, economic and demographic data for narrowband and broadband

PCS, ESMR, paging and more.
Cost: $1095.00
Frequency: Monthly
Founded in 1969

23248 Wireless Satellite and Broadcasting
IGI Group
1340 Soldiers Field Road
Suite 2
Brighton, MA 02135
617-782-5033
800-323-1088; Fax: 617-782-5735
editor@igigroup.com
www.igigroup.com
Paul Polishuk, Publisher
Hui Pan, Conference Director
Bev Wilson, Managing Editor
Subjects covered include: market opportunities, technology, international developments, regulation/policy, standards, applications, procurements, PCN, market forecasts, new products, mergers/acquisitions, joint ventures and more.
Cost: $695.00
Frequency: Monthly
Founded in 1977

23249 Wireless Telecom Investor
Kagan World Media
1 Lower Ragsdale Dr
Building One, Suite 130
Monterey, CA 93940-5749
831-624-1536
800-307-2529; Fax: 831-625-3225
www.kagan.com
Tim Baskerville, President
Tom Johnson, Marketing Manager
Exclusive analysis of private and public values of wireless telecommunications companies, including cellular telephone, ESMR and PCS. Exclusive databases of subscribers, market penetrations, market potential, industry growth. Catching super-fast growth in a capsule.
Cost: $1095.00
Frequency: Monthly
Founded in 1969

23250 Wireless Week
Chilton Company
600 S Cherry Street
Suite 400
Denver, CO 80246-1706
303-393-7449; Fax: 303-399-2034
Tom Brooksher, Publisher
Judith Lockwood, Editor
Covers the wireless telecommunications industry.
Circulation: 32,000

23251 Worldwide Videotex Update
Worldwide Videotex
Po Box 3273
Boynton Beach, FL 33424
561-738-2276
markedit@juno.com
www.wvpubs.com
Reports news and information on videotex, The Internet, online services, electronic mail, satellite communications and television related technologies, such as teleconferencing and teletext.
Cost: $25.00
Frequency: Monthly

23252 XDSL
IGI Group
1340 Soldiers Field Road
Suite 2
Boston, MA 02135
617-782-5033
800-323-1088; Fax: 617-782-5735
bmark@igigroup.com
www.igigroup.com
Paul Polishuk, President/CEO
Hui Panb, Conference Director
Bev Wilson, Managing Editor
Subjects covered include: field trials, applicatins, competition ffrom cable and satellite, new products, Telco plans, fiber optics, market forecasts, techology developments, wireless, major player strategies, cable modems, ISDN and more.
Cost: $695.00
Frequency: Monthly
Founded in 1977

Magazines & Journals

23253 ACUTA Journal of Communications Technology in Higher Education
ACUTA
152 W Zandale Drive
Suite 200
Lexington, KY 40503-2486
859-278-3338; Fax: 859-278-3268
www.acuta.org
Facebook
Pat Scott, Editor
Tamara Closs, President
Jerry A Simmer, Director
Corinne Harrison, Executive Officer
Tom Chappel, Finance & Administration
Journal is distributed to telecom, information management professionals at colleges and universities, along with industry professionals with products and services for the higher education vertical market.
Cost: $80.00
48 Pages
Frequency: Quarterly
Circulation: 2320
ISSN: 1097-8658
Founded in 1997
Mailing list available for rent: 2,300 names
Printed in 4 colors on matte stock

23254 ARRL The National Association for Amateur Radio
American Radio Relay League
225 Main St
Newington, CT 06111
860-594-0200
888-277-5289; Fax: 860-594-0259
www.arrl.org
David Sumner, CEO
Kay Craigie, President
Bob Inderbitzen, Marketing Manager
Geared at the IRF and amatuer radio operators industry, provides information on communications theory and technical advances in design and construction. The official journal of the American Radio Relay League.
Cost: $24.00
156M Members
Frequency: Monthly
Circulation: 146000
Founded in 1914

23255 America's Network
Questex Media Group
201 Sandpointe Ave
Suite 500
Santa Ana, CA 92707-8716
714-338-6700
800-854-3112; Fax: 714-513-8481
Paul Semple, Publisher
Bill Pettit, National Sales Director
Independent reporting and business analysis of telecommunications technologies for today's public network.
Cost: $100.00
Frequency: Monthly
Circulation: 60,006

23256 Audiotex Update
Worldwide Videotex
PO Box 3273
Boynton Beach, FL 33424-3273
561-738-2276
markedit@juno.com
www.wvpubs.com
Mark E Wright, Editor
Provides the latest news and infromation about the audiotex industry, including voice processing information, products, services, as well as research and development.
Cost: $165.00
Frequency: Monthly
Founded in 1981

23257 B/OSS
Virgo Publishing LLC
3300 N Central Ave
Suite 300
Phoenix, AZ 85012-2532
480-675-9925; Fax: 480-990-0819
mikes@vpico.com
www.vpico.com
Facebook, Twitter, LinkedIn
Jenny Bolton, President
John Siefert, CEO
Kelly Ridley, VP
Troy Bix, Publisher
Source for news and analysis for telecommunications support systems as they take a leading role in creating and supporting service differentiation in the communications marketplace.
Circulation: 20000
Founded in 1986
Printed in on glossy stock

23258 Business Communications Review
BCR Enterprises
Ste 200
3025 Highland Pkwy
Downers Grove, IL 60515-5668
630-986-1432
800-227-1234; Fax: 630-323-5324
www.bcr.com
Fred Knight, Publisher
Offers a complete package of the latest information for persons associated with the communications industry.
Cost: $45.00
80 Pages
Frequency: Monthly
Founded in 1971

23259 CTI the Authority on Computer, Internet, & Network Telephony
Technology Marketing Corporation
1 Technology Plz
Norwalk, CT 06854-1936
203-852-6800
800-243-6002; Fax: 203-853-2845
www.tmcnet.com
Facebook, Twitter
Rich Tehrani, CEO
Anthony Graffeo, National Advertising Sales Manager
Greg Galitzine, Editorial Director
Provides tutorials, application stories, and new product listings and reviews, as well as service information. Emphasizes furthering the development, implementation and use of CTI technology.
Frequency: Monthly
Circulation: 50256
Founded in 1998

23260 Cabling Business
Cabling Publications
12035 Shiloh Rd
Suite 350
Dallas, TX 75228-1549

214-322-8171; Fax: 214-319-6077
russell@cablingbusiness.com
www.cablingbusiness.com
Facebook, Twitter

Stephen Paulov, President
Christy Sheeran, Business Manager
Rita Paulov, Senior Sales Associate
David Deal, Webmaster
Margaret Patterson, Managing Editor

New product information, troubleshooting hints, and information on installation and repair.
Frequency: Monthly
Circulation: 24070
Mailing list available for rent

23261 Cabling Installation & Maintenance
PennWell Publishing Company
1421 S Sheridan Rd
Tulsa, OK 74112-6619

918-831-9421
800-331-4483; Fax: 918-831-9476
patrick@pennwell.com
www.pennwell.com

Robert Biolchini, President
Steve Smith, Executive Editor

Emphasizes the problem solving aspects of cable installation in telecommunications, data, and video systems.
Frequency: Monthly
Circulation: 23604
Founded in 1993

23262 Call Center Magazine
Miller Freeman Publications
11 Est 19th Street
3rd Floor
New York, NY 10011

212-600-3000
800-672-6111; Fax: 212-691-1191
www.callcentermagazine.com

Keith Dawson, Editor
Max Steiger, Sales Manager

Dedicated to providing in-depth and unbiased product and strategic information for call center executives.
Frequency: Monthly
Circulation: 32904

23263 Communication Theory
International Communication Association
U de Montreal, Department de Communication
1500 21st Street
Washington, DC 20026

202-955-1444; Fax: 202-955-1448
www.icahdq.org
Facebook, Twitter, LinkedIn

Francois Cooren, Editor

Publishes research articles, theoretical essays, and reviews on topics of broad theoretical interest from across the range of communication studies. Recognizes that approaches to theory develpment and explication are diverse.
Mailing list available for rent

23264 Communication Yearbook
International Communication Association
Ohio University, School of Communication Study
1501 21st Street
Washington, DC 20026

202-955-1445; Fax: 202-955-1449
www.icahdq.org
Facebook, Twitter, LinkedIn

Dr Christina S. Beck, Editor

Features state-of-the discipline literature reviews of communication research. Highlights reviews of research exploring communication concepts that span traditional 'division' divides, issues of central importance to the accomplishment of communication in a variety of contexts and for diverse communicators throughout the world.
Founded in 1913
Mailing list available for rent

23265 Communications Billing Report
Telecommunications Reports International
76 9th Ave. 7th fl
#100-E
Washington, NY 10011

21- 77- 071; Fax: 212-771-0732
joseph.rohaly@wolterskluwer.com
www.tr.com
Facebook, Twitter, LinkedIn

Victoria Mason, Editor-in-Chief

Content provides hard-to-find facts on such issues as developing internet electronic payment systems, keeping on top of new outsourcing opportunities, enhancing customer care and back office functions and making the most of new software developments.
Cost: $765.00
Frequency: BiWeekly

23266 Communications Crossroads
United States Telecom Association
1401 H St NW
Suite 600
Washington, DC 20005-2110

202-326-7300; Fax: 202-326-7333
Facebook, Twitter, LinkedIn, You Tube

Walter Mc Kormick, President
James Cooconi, VP
Robert Curry, Tresurer
Robert Hunt, Secretary

Dedicated to the success stories, investment opportunities and industry events that herald the future of small and rural carriers.
Cost: $60.00
Circulation: 3500
Founded in 2006

23267 Enterprise Wireless Magazine
Enterprise Wireless Association
8484 Westpark Drive
Suite 630
McLean, VA 22102-5117

703-528-5115
800-482-8282; Fax: 703-524-1074
customerservice@enterprisewireless.org
www.enterprisewireless.org
Facebook, Twitter

Mark Crosby, President/CEO
Andre Cote, Senior VP
Ila Dudley, VP Spectrum Management
Ron Franklin, VP Membership/Business Development

Covers how wireless meets the operational needs of business and industrial enterprise users. Used extensivley throughout the year by your prospects to stay informed of technical, industry and association information, and as a comprehensive buyers' guide for the products and services they use most often.
Frequency: Quarterly

23268 Global Telephony
Primedia
3585 Engineering Drive
Suite 100
Norcross,, GA 30092

678-421-3000
800-216-1423; Fax: 312-595-0295
Facebook, Twitter, LinkedIn, You Tube

Larry Lannon, Publisher
Carol Wilson, Editor

Telephony delivers timely and intelligent coverage of the news, technologies and business strategies driving the industry.
Frequency: 24/Yr
Circulation: 63,500

23269 Handbooks of Communication Series
International Communication Association
Dept of Comm, University of Colorado at Boulder
1500 21st Street
Washington, DC 20026

202-955-1444; Fax: 202-955-1448
www.icahdq.org
Facebook, Twitter, LinkedIn

Robert T Craig, Editor
Linda Bathgate, Senior Editor

Publishes research articles, theoretical essays, and reviews on topics of broad theoretical interest from across the range of communication studies. Recognizes that approaches to theory develpment and explication are diverse.
Mailing list available for rent

23270 Human Communication Research
International Communication Association
Dept of Communication Arts & Science,234 Sparks
1500 21st Street
Washington, DC 20026

202-955-1444; Fax: 202-955-1448
www.icahdq.org
Facebook, Twitter, LinkedIn

James P Dillard, Editor

Publishes research articles, theoretical essays, and reviews on topics of broad theoretical interest from across the range of communication studies. Recognizes that approaches to theory develpment and explication are diverse.
Frequency: Quarterly
Mailing list available for rent

23271 ICA Communique
International Communications Association
1500 21st St NW
1500 21st Street
Washington, DC 20026

202-955-1444; Fax: 202-955-1448
www.icahdq.org
Facebook, Twitter, LinkedIn

M Haley, Executive Director

Publishes research articles, theoretical essays, and reviews on topics of broad theoretical interest from across the range of communication studies. Recognizes that approaches to theory develpment and explication are diverse.
Cost: $135.00
Frequency: 10/Year
Mailing list available for rent

23272 IEEE MultiMedia Magazine
Institute of Electrical & Electronics Engineers
2001 L Street NW
Suite 700
Washington, DC 20036-4928

202-371-0101; Fax: 202-728-9614
publications@comsoc.org
www.computer.org
Facebook, Twitter, LinkedIn, You Tube

Melissa Russell, Executive Director
Sara Scudder, Production Manager

Robin Baldwin, Publisher
Kimberly Sperka, Publications Portfolio Manager
Debbie Sims, Senior Advertising Coordinator

Serves the community of scholars, developers, practitioners, and students who are interested in multiple media types and work in fields such as image and video processing, audio analysis, text retrieval, and data fusion. The magazine includes peer-reviewed articles, editorial comment, and conference and standards reports.
Frequency: Monthly
Circulation: 43832
Founded in 1994

23273 IEEE Network
IEEE Operations Center
PO Box 1331
Piscataway, NJ 08855-1331

732-981-0060; Fax: 732-981-1721
publications@comsoc.org

John Vig, CEO

The magazine of Global Internetworking provides the most current information for communications professionals involved with the interconnection of computing systems.
Frequency: Bi-Monthly

23274 Intele-Card News
Quality Publishing
523 N Sam Houston Parkway E
Suite 300
Houston, TX 77060

281-272-2744
800-792-6397; Fax: 281-847-5752
www.intelecard.com

Theresa Ward, Editor-in-Chief
Jo Ann Davy, Managing Editor
Laurette Veres, Owner

Reports on news and events impacting the business of telephone cards, identifies significant trends and profiles industry newsmakers.
Frequency: Monthly
Circulation: 12000
Founded in 1995

23275 Journal of Communication
International Communication Association
Department of Communication-101 Burton Hall
University of Oklahoma
Norman, OK 73019

405-325-9503
joc@ou.edu
www.icahdq.org

Michael Pfau, Editor

A general forum for communication scholarship and publishes articles and book reviews examining a broad range of issues in communication theory and research. Publishes the best available scholarship on all aspects of communication.

23276 Journal of Computer-Mediated Communication
International Communication Association
1500 21st Street
Washington, DC 20026

202-955-1444; Fax: 202-955-1448
jcmc.indiana.edu
Facebook, Twitter, LinkedIn

Susan C Herring, Editor

Publishes research articles, theoretical essays, and reviews on topics of broad theoretical interest from across the range of communication studies. Recognizes that approaches to theory develpment and explication are diverse.
Mailing list available for rent

23277 Lightwave
PennWell Publishing Company
1421 S Sheridan Rd
Tulsa, OK 74112-6619

918-831-9421
800-331-4483; Fax: 918-831-9476
stephenh@pennwell.com
www.pennwell.com

Robert Biolchini, President
Carrie Meadows, Managing Editor
Meghan Fuller, Senior News Editor
Matt Vincent, Associate Editor/Web Editor

An international journal of fiber optics that covers all applications of the technology in telecommunications, data communications, broadcast and cable TV and specialized military applications.
Cost: $137.00
224 Pages
Frequency: Monthly
ISSN: 0741-5834
Founded in 1910
Printed in 4 colors on matte stock

23278 Locating, Testing and Repairing
Stober Research and Communications
PO Box 517
McHenry, IL 60051

815-385-6123; Fax: 815-385-7151
www.ltrmag.com
Facebook, Twitter

L Jack Stober, Publisher

Information on copper and fiber optic sets available for telecommunication applications, as well as listings of companies and categories of this equipment. Regular departments contain fault locating and test equipment tips, a new product showcase and a look at new industry literature.
Cost: $100.00
Frequency: Quarterly
Circulation: 27355
Founded in 1998

23279 Mobile Communication Business
Phillips Business Information
7811 Montrose Road
Potomac, MD 20854

301-340-2100
feedback@healthydirections.com
www.healthydirections.com
Facebook, Twitter

Don Steele, Editor

Offers information and the latest technological advances in telecommunications.
Frequency: Monthly
Founded in 1985

23280 Multimedia Telecommunication News
Stoneridge Technical Services
PO Box 1891
Rockville, MD 20849-1891

301-424-0114; Fax: 301-424-8971
www.stoneridgetech.com

William W Creitz, Editor

Focuses on new products, applications, technological developments, markets and company activites.
Frequency: Monthly

23281 NTCA Exchange
National Telephone Cooperative Association
4121 Wilson Blvd
Suite 1000
Arlington, VA 22203-4145

703-351-2000; Fax: 703-351-2001
www.ntca.org

Michael E Brunner, CEO

Bi-monthly newsletter examining association and member news, including profiles, business tips and member updates.
Cost: $15.00
Frequency: Bi-Monthly
Circulation: 5100
Founded in 1980

23282 Network Magazine
CMP Media
245 Blackfriars Road
Manhasset, NY 11030

516-562-5000
866-880-8219; Fax: 516-562-7013

Art Wittmann, Editor
Paula McGinlinchey, Publisher

Network Magazine serves communications carriers, communications service providers including interexchange/PTT's/long distance carriers, business services (non-computer) and other industry organizations.
Cost: $175.00
162 Pages
Frequency: Monthly
Circulation: 125000
ISSN: 1093-8001
Founded in 1986
Printed in 4 colors on matte stock

23283 Networks Update
Worldwide Videotex
Po Box 3273
Boynton Beach, FL 33424

561-738-2276
markedit@juno.com
www.wvpubs.com
Facebook, Twitter

Provides the latest news and information about the computer network industry. This includes national, international, public, private, and military network products, services, companies, marketing strategies, and research and development.
Cost: $25.00
Frequency: Monthly

23284 Opastco Roundtable
OPASTCO
2020 K Street
Suite 700
Washington, DC 20006

202-659-5990; Fax: 202-659-4619
roundtable@opastco.org
www.opastco.org

Provides practical, how-to information that small local exchange carriers can use in their day-to-day operations, as well as plain English explanations of industry issues and technologies.
Frequency: BiMonthly

23285 Outside Plant
Practical Communications
220 N Smith St
Suite 228
Palatine, IL 60067-2488

847-202-4683; Fax: 847-639-9542
www.ospmag.com

Sharon Stober, VP/Editorial Director
Karen Adolphson, Managing Editor
Mary Beth Koelling, Executive Director Sales/Marketing

Magazine for telecom outside plant professionals. Reaches ASP engineers, planners, managers and technicians in Bell and independent phone companies.
Cost: $30.00
100 Pages
Frequency: Monthly
Circulation: 25000
Founded in 1983

23286 **POINT**
Direct Marketing Association
1120 Avenue of the Americas
New York, NY 10036-6713

212-768-7277; Fax: 212-768-4547
www.the-dma.org
Facebook, Twitter

John A. Greco Jr, President & CEO

DMA's digital magazine.

23287 **Pen Computing Magazine**
Pen Computing Publishing Office
120 Bethpage Road
Suite 300
Hicksville, NY 11801

516-433-8725; Fax: 516-433-8724
cb@pencomputing.com
www.pencomputing.com

Howard Borgen, Publisher
Lisa Krebs, VP Advertising
Wayne Laslo, Advertising Manager
Conrad H Blickenstorfer, Editor-in-Chief
David MacNeill, Executive Editor

Bi-Monthly print journal of pen-based and mobile computing. Hardware and software reviews, expert opinions, feature articles, case studies, how-to, industry news, technical primers and more.
Cost: $18.00
Frequency: Bi-Monthly
Circulation: 79515
Founded in 1993

23288 **Politically Direct**
Direct Marketing Association
1120 Avenue of the Americas
New York, NY 10036-6700

212-768-7277; Fax: 212-302-6714
customerservice@the-dma.org
www.the-dma.org

Lawrence M Kimmel, CEO

Published both in print and digital, this newsletter on DMA advocacy efforts keeps DMA members informed and involved in the politics and policies that impact them today and ahead of the curve on developments that will affect them tomorrow.
Frequency: Quarterly

23289 **RCR Wireless News**
Crain Communications
1746 Cole Blvd
Suite 150
Lakewood, CO 80401-3208

303-733-2500
888-909-9111; Fax: 303-733-9941
subs@crain.com
www.crain.com

Mary Pemberton, Marketing
Tracy Ford, Associate Publisher/Editor
Dan Meyer, Managing Editor
Pete Racelis, President

News and analysis of the wireless communications industry.
Cost: $69.00
Frequency: Weekly
Circulation: 65000
Founded in 1981
Printed in on matte stock

23290 **Satellite Business News**
Satellite Business News
1990 M Street NW
Suite 510
Washington, DC 20036-3102

202-785-0505; Fax: 202-785-9291
general.mail@satbiznews.com
www.satbiznews.com

Bob Scherman, Publisher
Jeffrey Williams, Managing Editor
Charlie Ergen, CEO/President

Up-to-date news on satellite television industry, upcoming events, and new technology for the industry.
Cost: $44.75
Frequency: Bi-annually
Circulation: 565700
Founded in 1983

23291 **Satellite News**
Phillips Business Information
6181 Executive Blvd
Rockville, MD 20852-3901

301-881-7516
866-279-1930; Fax: 301-424-2709
www.phillips.com

Donald Phelps, President
Robert Phillips, CEO

Information on satellite launches, companies rebounding from losses, blows to competitors and regulatory issues.
Frequency: Weekly
Circulation: 18000
Founded in 1974

23292 **Satellite Week**
Warren Publishing
2115 Ward Ct NW
Washington, DC 20037-1209

202-872-9200
800-771-9202; Fax: 202-318-8350
info@warren-news.com
www.warren-news.com

Brig Easley, Executive VP
Paul Warren, Chair/Publisher
Daniel Warren, President/Editor

The definitive weekly source for fast-breaking, international news on space communications policy, regularion, technology and business. Offers up-to-date, comprehensive reports on new technologies, notices of international advances, details about regulation and deregularion, satellite marketplace intelligence, news of DBS developments, and continuous coverage of what industry leaders are doing and saying.
Frequency: Weekly
Founded in 1945

23293 **Sound & Communications**
Testa Communications
25 Willowdale Avenue
Port Washington, NY 11050-3779

516-767-2500
800-937-7678; Fax: 516-767-9335
testa@testa.com
www.testacommunications.com
Facebook, Twitter

Vincent P Testa, President
David A. Silverman, Editor

Covers sound, display, security and multimedia systems, also theory and applications.
Frequency: Monthly
Circulation: 22500
Founded in 1955

23294 **Sound & Video Contractor**
Primedia
PO Box 12914
Overland Park, KS 66282

913-341-1300; Fax: 913-967-1903
www.svconline.com

Mark Johnson, Editor
Trevor Boyer, Associate Editor
Trevor Boyer, Associate Editor

Contains information on sound systems, video display, security, CCTV, home theater, and automation. Delivers in depth instruction and examples of successful installations, fundamental acoustical and video theory and news on new technologies eaffecting the systems contracting business.
Cost: $35.00
Frequency: Monthly
Circulation: 21,000
Founded in 1983
Mailing list available for rent: 20,500 names at $110 per M

23295 **Sys Admin**
CMP Media
303 Second Street
Suite 200
Lawrence, KS 94107

415-947-6000; Fax: 785-841-2047
www.sysadminmag.com

Amber Ankerhola
Deirdre Blake, MD

SYS ADMIN serves the Unix and Linux system administration market.
Cost: $39.00
100 Pages
Frequency: Monthly
Founded in 1992
Printed in on glossy stock

23296 **TELEconference Magazine**
Applied Business Telecommunications
201 Sandpoint Ave
Suite 600
Santa Ana, CA 92707-8700

714-513-8400
800-854-3112; Fax: 714-513-8680
www.advanstar.com

Keith Gallagher, Publisher
Paul DeVeaux, Editor

Devoted to the field of teleconferencing and contains in-depth articles to provide updates on audio/graphic and video teleconferencing applications, trends and developments.
Cost: $10.00
Circulation: 15000
Founded in 1992

23297 **Telecommunications**
Horizon House Publications
685 Canton St
Norwood, MA 02062-2608

781-762-1319; Fax: 781-769-5037
www.horizonhouse.com

Charles A Ayotte, CEO
Robert Bass, Production Manager
Bob Wallace, Editor
William Harrison, Manager
William Bassy, President

Communication technology and market developments for users, service providers and manufacturers worldwide.
Frequency: Monthly
Circulation: 80854
Founded in 1960

23298 **Telephone IP News**
Worldwide Videotex

Po Box 3273
Boynton Beach, FL 33424

561-738-2276
markedit@juno.com
www.wvpubs.com

Provides news and information concerning the information provider (IP) industry for telephone services and two-way paging and wireless information services. Reports on new products available to providers and monitors public service commission rulings as they aplly to information services.
Cost: $25.00
Frequency: Monthly

23299 **Telephony**
Telephony Division
One IBM Plaza
Suite 2300
Chicago, IL 10151

312-595-1080; Fax: 312-595-0296
telephony@prismb2b.com
www.primedia.com

Mark Hickey, Publisher
Dan O'Shea, Editor-in-Chief
Kim Brower, Marketing Manager

Written for professionals involved in management, construction, maintenance and marketing of modern telecommunication systems. Focus is on new, technical advances, filed applications and management techniques.
Cost: $3.00
Frequency: Weekly
Circulation: 59000
Founded in 1989

23300 **VON**
Virgo Publishing LLC
3300 N Central Ave
Suite 300
Phoenix, AZ 85012-2532

480-675-9925; Fax: 480-990-0819
mikes@vpico.com
www.vpico.com
Facebook, Twitter

Jenny Bolton, President

Global information on IP Communications strategy.
Mailing list available for rent: 22000+ names at $var per M

23301 **Wire Journal International**
Wire Association International
71 Bradley Rd. Suite 9
Madison, CT 06443

203-453-2777; Fax: 203-453-8384
mmarselli@wirenet.org
www.wirenet.org
Facebook, Twitter

The leading technical publication for the wire and cable industry. Written for executives, engineers, technical and sales professionals, and purchasing agents engaged in the manufacture of ferrous and nonferrous wire and cable; electrical wire and cable; fiber optic cable; and formed and fabricated wire products.
Frequency: Monthly
Circulation: 13434
Founded in 1930
Printed in 4 colors on glossy stock

23302 **Worldwide Telecom**
Worldwide Videotex
Po Box 3273
Boynton Beach, FL 33424

561-738-2276
www.wvpubs.com
Facebook, Twitter

Provides the latest news and information on international telecommunication products, services, and contracts. The emphasis is on U.S. telecommunications companies doing business in foreign markets and on products with a potential market overseas.
Cost: $25.00
Frequency: Monthly

23303 **Yellow Pages Industry Sourcebook**
SIMBA Information
60 Long Ridge Rd
Suite 300
Stamford, CT 06902-1841

203-325-8193; Fax: 203-325-8915
info@simbanet.com
www.simbanet.com

Linda Kopp, Publisher
Kathy Mickey, Managing Editor

Lists key officers, revenues, leading books, major accounts, sales offices and suppliers for more than 1500 firms involved in yellow pages publishing.
Cost: $99.00

23304 **xchange**
Virgo Publishing LLC
3300 N Central Ave
Suite 300
Phoenix, AZ 85012-2532

480-675-9925; Fax: 480-990-0819
mikes@vpico.com
www.vpico.com

Jenny Bolton, President
John Siefert, CEO
Kelly Ridley, VP
Katherine Clements, Publisher

Provides in-depth, executive-level news and analysis regarding strategy, technology and regulation to help communications service providers create new revenue, lower costs and achieve sustainable business models.
Frequency: Annual+
Circulation: 35,003
Founded in 1996

Trade Shows

23305 **AFCEA TechNet Asia-Pacific**
Armed Forces Communications and Electronics Assn
4400 Fair Lakes Court
Fairfax, VA 22033

703-631-6200
800-564-4220; Fax: 703-654-6931
www.afcea.org

Paul doCarmo, Assistant Director/Exhibit Sales
Connie Shaw, Exhibit Sales Account Manager
Herbert Browne, President

Military, government and industry communications and electronics professionals gather to see exhibits of communications and electronics equipment, supplies and services.
2000 Attendees
Frequency: November/Annual
Founded in 1985

23306 **AFCEA Technical Committee Tech Forum TechNet International**
AFCEA Headquarters
4400 Fair Lakes Court
Fairfax, VA 22033-3899

703-631-6100
800-336-4583; Fax: 703-631-6169
service@afcea.org
www.afcea.org

Herbert Browne, President
Paul doCarmo, Assistant Director/Exhibit Sales
Connie Shaw, Exhibit Sales Account Manager

One of the nation's largest C4I conventions and expositions and features numerous professional development opportunities and tremendous networking opportunies.
Founded in 1985

23307 **AFCEA/USNI West Conference & Exposition**
Armed Forces Communications and Electronics Assn
4400 Fair Lakes Court
Fairfax, VA 22033

703-631-6200
800-564-4220; Fax: 703-654-6931
www.afcea.org

Paul doCarmo, Assistant Director/Exhibit Sales
Connie Shaw, Exhibit Sales Account Manager
Herbert Browne, President

Over 350 of the industry's most recognized defense and technology organizations showcase their technology products and services to top decision-makers from the US Pacific Fleet, Naval Station San Diego, Space & Warfare Command, Naval Base Coronado, Camp Pendleton Marine Corps Base and many other west coast military and government facilities.
6000 Attendees
Frequency: January/Annual
Founded in 1985

23308 **AIIM Annual Conference**
Association for Information and Image Management
8403 Colesville Road
Suite 1100
Silver Spring, MD 20910

301-587-8202
800-477-2446; Fax: 301-587-2711
aiim@aiim.org
www.aiim.org
Facebook, Twitter

Peggy Winton, President & CEO
Georgina Clelland, Chief Operating Officer
June Ann Ewan, Director, Finance
Jesse Wilkins, Director, Professional Development

The largest enterprise content & document management conference and exposition showcasing the technologies and solutions that provide intelligence behind information. For more than 50 years, this annual event attracts business professionals and executive management seeking the latest technologies.
Frequency: April
Founded in 1943

23309 **APCO Annual Conference & Expo**
Assoc of Public-Safety Commun Officials Intl
351 N Williamson Boulevard
Daytona Beach, FL 32114-1112

386-322-2500
888-272-6911; Fax: 386-322-2501
apco@apcointl.org
www.apcointl.org/
Facebook

George S Rice Jr, Executive Director
Barbara Myers, Conference Services Director
Brigid Blaschak, Tradeshow Manager
Patricia Giannini, Senior Meeting Coordinator
Garry Mendez, Marketing/Communications Director

The Association of Public-Safety Communications Officials International/APCO 's Annual Conference brings together more than 300 vendors to give you hands-on demonstrations of new technologies you might use in your agency or call centers. The Conference also offers sessions on personal and professional development and a variety of technical skills. Banquet, break-

fast and exhibitors of radio, computer, and supporting equipment companies.
6000 Attendees
Frequency: Annual
Founded in 1935

23310 **Annual Conference for Catalog & Multichannel Merchants (ACCM)**
Direct Marketing Association
1120 Avenue of Americas
New York, NY 10036
212-768-7277; Fax: 212-768-4547
www.the-dma.org
Julie Hogan, SVP Conference & Events
10M Attendees

23311 **Antenna Measurement Techniques Association Show**
6065 Roswell Road
Suite 2252
Atlanta, GA 30328
770-864-3488; Fax: 770-864-3491
www.amta.org
Facebook, Twitter
Janet O'Neil, Contact
Antenna test equipment, supplies and services for government, private and institutional laboratories involved in design and development.

23312 **Association for Communications Technology Professionals in Higher Education**
ACUTA
152 W Zandale Drive
Suite 200
Lexington, KY 40503-2486
859-278-3338; Fax: 859-278-3268
www.acuta.org
Facebook, Twitter, LinkedIn, You Tube
Kellie Bowman, Registration
Jeri Semer, Executive Director
Annual conference and exhibits of educational telecommunications equipment, supplies and services. Containing 95 booths.
600 Attendees
Frequency: Annual
Founded in 1971

23313 **Association of Teleservices International Conference**
Association of Teleservices International
222 South Westmonte Drive
Suite 111
Altamonte Springs, FL 32714
866-896-2874; Fax: 407-774-6440
admin@atsi.org
www.atsi.org
Tifani Leal, President
Exhibits of interest to telephone answering and voice message providers.
800+ Attendees
Founded in 1942

23314 **Cable-Tec Expo**
Society of Cable Telecommunications Engineers
140 Philips Road
Exton, PA 19341-1318
610-524-1725
800-542-5040; Fax: 610-363-5898
info@scte.org
expo.scte.org
Facebook, Twitter, LinkedIn, You Tube
Heather Gosciniak, Director
The Society's Cable-Tec Expo is the premier industry hardware exhibition that also offers an engineering conference, workshops and meetings. Expo contains more than 500 booths and 400 exhibits.
12M Attendees
Frequency: Annual

23315 **Call Center Conference and Exposition**
CMP Media
11 West 19th Street
New York, NY 10011
888-428-3976; Fax: 212-600-3080
www.callcenterweek.com
Facebook, Twitter, LinkedIn, You Tube
Joni Mitchell, Marketing Manager
Joy Cerequas, Director Events
125 booths, plus conference covering all applications of new technologies and services in call processing, transaction processing and telemarketing.
2.5M Attendees
Frequency: February

23316 **Email Evolution Conference**
Direct Marketing Association
1120 Avenue of Americas
New York, NY 10036-6700
212-768-7277; Fax: 212-302-6714
dmaconferences@the-dma.org
www.the-dma.org
Julie A Hogan, SVP Conference/Events
Lawrence M Kimmel, CEO
Focuses on the ever-changing and evolving world of email marketing, providing you with the best ways to capitalize on the high ROI this low-cost communication tool can provide both on its own, and integrated with social, search, mobile, video and other email enhancers.
10M Attendees
Frequency: Annual/February

23317 **Entelec Conference & Expo**
Energy Telecommunications and Electrical Assoc
5005 Royal Lane
Suite 116
Irving, TX 75063
888-503-8700; Fax: 972-915-6040
info@entelec.org
www.entelec.org
Facebook, Twitter, LinkedIn
Blaine Siske, Executive Manager
Amanda Prudden, Association Manager

23318 **Enterprise Wireless**
Enterprise Wireless Alliance
8484 Westpark Drive
Suite 630
McLean, VA 22102-5117
703-528-5115; Fax: 703-524-1074
customerservice@enterprisewireless.org
www.enterprisewireless.org
Facebook, Twitter, LinkedIn
Mark Crosby, President/CEO
Andre Cote, Senior VP
Ila Dudley, VP Spectrum Management
Ron Franklin, VP Membership/Business Development
Co-hosted by AAPC and USMSS, this trade show and conference is for wireless service providers, manufacturers, systems integrators an denterprise users to showcase innovative new wireless products.

23319 **IEEE Communications Expo IEEE Globecom**
J Spargo & Associates
11208 Waples Mill Road
Suite 112
Fairfax, VA 22030
703-631-6200
800-564-4220; Fax: 703-654-6931
www.ieee.org
Connie Shaw, Exhibit Sales Account Manager
In addition to targeting IEEE Communications Society members, also draws companies from Silicon Valley, Northern California, and the Pacific Rim, who manufacture or distribute products or services to support wireless technologies, optical networking, the Internet, or the telecom marketplace.
2000 Attendees
Frequency: November

23320 **INTX**
National Cable & Telecommunications Association
25 Massachusetts Ave. NW
Suite 100
Washington, DC 20001
202-222-2300
webmaster@ncta.com
www.ncta.com
Facebook, Twitter, LinkedIn
Michael Powell, President & CEO
The Internet & Television Expo
Frequency: Annual/Spring
Founded in 2015

23321 **International Wireless Communication Expo**
6300 S Syracuse Way
Suite 650
Englewood, CO 80111-6726
303-904-0407
rugianskis@prismb2b.com
www.iwceexpo.com
Facebook, Twitter, LinkedIn
Rita Ugianskis, Group Show Director
Laura Magliola, Marketing Manager
Stacey Orlick, Director
Catherine E. Campfield, Co-ordinator
Angela Wood, Conference Program Manager
The one place where all industries and communications professionals come together to share thoughts and ideas on wireless communications technologies.
6.5M Attendees
Frequency: March

23322 **NATOA Annual Conference**
Nat'l Assn of Telecommunication Officer & Advisors
3213 Duke Street
Suite 695
Alexandria, VA 22314
703-519-8035; Fax: 703-519-7080
info@natoa.org
Facebook, Twitter
Elizabeth Beaty, Executive Director
Jennifer Harman, Manager
Tonya Rideout, Deputy
Containing 30 booths featuring telecommunications equipment and supplies. Cable operators and local governments. Educational sessions topics include technology, competitive markets, programming, and cable franchise administration.
700 Attendees
Frequency: September

23323 **NCDM Conference**
Direct Marketing Association

1120 Avenue of Americas
New York, NY 10036-6700

212-768-7277; Fax: 212-302-6714
dmaconferences@the-dma.org
www.the-dma.org

Julie A Hogan, SVP Conferences/Events
Lawrence M Kimmel, CEO

Presents industry experts and hard-hitting case studies from a variety of verticals, such as financial services, retail, automotive, publishing, non-profit and many more, who will share the latest strategies and methodologies in gathering, analyzing, leveraging and protecting your most valuable business asset - customer data.
10M Attendees
Frequency: Annual/December

23324 **NEAX 2400 IMS Users Group**
40 Marsh Wall
Columbia, CT 29221-0886

803-798-4800
Facebook, Twitter

Carlisle Reames, Contact

15 booths of educational sessions for NEC 2400 DBX systems users.
350 Attendees
Frequency: April

23325 **NXTcomm**
Telecommunications Industry Association/TIA
2500 Wilson Boulevard
Suite 300
Arlington, VA 22201-3834

703-907-7700; Fax: 703-907-7727
gseiffert@tiaonline.org
www.tiaonline.org/business/events/TIATradeshows.cfm
Facebook, Twitter, LinkedIn

Grant Seiffert, President
Mike Nunes, Government Relations Director
Lora Magruder, Member Relations Director
Daniel J. Pigott, Chairman of the Board
Thomas Stanton, Vice Chair

NXTcomm is an industry event uniting the premier information and communications technology suppliers with the world's leading communications and entertainment companies. Connect with 450+ exhibitors and 20,000+ attendees. Soak up essential knowledge during insider-led conferences. The global forces that are driving communications-based innovation are here.

23326 **National Conference on Operations & Fulfillment (NCOF)**
Direct Marketing Association
1120 Avenue of Americas
New York, NY 10036-6700

212-768-7277; Fax: 212-302-6714
dmaconferences@the-dma.org
www.the-dma.org

Julie A Hogan, SVP Conference/Educational Services
Lawrence M Kimmel, CEO

Focuses on innovative solutions for warehouse, distribution, operations, and ecommerce needs in the ever-changing world of operations and fulfillment.
10M Attendees
Frequency: Annual/April

23327 **New York Nonprofit Conference**
Direct Marketing Association
1120 Avenue of Americas
New York, NY 10036-6700

212-768-7277; Fax: 212-302-6714
dmaconferences@the-dma.org
www.the-dma.org

Julie A Hogan, SVP Conference/Events
Lawrence M Kimmel, CEO

Discover which acknowledgement programs work best-and why, increase revenue with membership options-as well as traditional fundraising appeals, learn how the internet and e-mail campaigng can improve fundraising, lower costs and increase advocac
10M Attendees

23328 **PCCA Annual Convention**
Power and Communication Contractors
1908 Mt. Vernon Ave
Suite 200
Alexandria, VA 22314

703-212-7734
800-542-7222; Fax: 703-548-3733
www.pccaweb.org
Facebook, Twitter

Kevin Mason, President
Larry Libla, President-Elect
Frequency: March

23329 **TechNet North 2006**
AFCEA Canada & AFCEA International
102 Centrepointe Drive
Ottawa, ON K2G-6B1

613-786-2619; Fax: 613-230-1554
Facebook, Twitter

Kevin d'Entremont, Exhibit Director
Rick Tachuk, Marketing & Communications Director

Delivers an inovative professional development conference and a major trade exhibition focused on the latest C4ISR solutions, products and technologies for the North American defense and security sectors.

23330 **Telecom**
607 14th Street
Suite 600
Washington, DC 20005-2164

202-547-2680; Fax: 202-326-7333
Facebook, Twitter, LinkedIn, You Tube

Walter B McCormick Jr, President/CEO
Jaonne Hovis, Chair
Tony Prez, Director

Conference and exhibition offers a variety of educational sessions, special interest seminars and keynote speakers. The show features an estimated 160 exhibitors.
1300 Attendees
Frequency: Annual

23331 **Utilities Technology Council Annual Conference and Exhibition**
Utilities Technology Council
2550 South Clark Street
Suite 960
Arlington, VA 22202

202-872-0030; Fax: 202-872-1331
www.utc.org
Facebook, Twitter, LinkedIn

Connie Durcsase, President
Mike Oldak, VP & General Counsel
Karnel Thomas, VM- Member Services
Kathleen Fitzpatric, VP- Operations

Annual conference and exhibits of telecommunications equipment and services.
1,000 Attendees
Founded in 1948

23332 **Wire Expo**
Wire Association International
71 Bradley Rd.
Suite 9
Madison, CT 06443

203-453-2777; Fax: 203-453-8384
www.wirenet.org
Facebook, Twitter

Wire Expo provides you with ready-made opportunities—including meeting with more than 450 suppliers on the show floor. You'll gain manufacturing and technical information by attending short courses and listening to some of the 75+ paper that will be presented at WCTS. Social events also provide oppertunities to make conections with other professionals in the wire industry.
4000 Attendees
Frequency: Biennial
Founded in 1930

Directories & Databases

23333 **Audiotex Directory**
ADBG Publishing
PO Box 25929
Los Angeles, CA 90025-0929

310-914-9000; Fax: 310-479-0654
Facebook, Twitter

Larry Podell, Editor

Over 1,200 product and service suppliers in the voice processing fax, and audiotex fields, including hardware, software, vendors, telephone companies, service bureaus, audio programmers, and consultants
Cost: $50.00
Frequency: Annual

23334 **Bacon's Radio/TV/Cable Directory**
Cision U.S., Inc.
332 South Michigan Avenue
Suite 900
Chicago, IL 60604

312-263-0070
866-639-5087

Joe Bernardo, President & CEO
Heidi Sullivan, VP & Publisher
Valerie Lopez, Research Director
Jessica White, Research Director
Rachel Farrell, Research Manager

Includes comprehensive coverage for contact and programming information for more than 3,500 televsion networks, cable networks, television syndicators, television stations, and cable systems in the United States and Canada.
Cost: $350.00
Frequency: Annual
ISSN: 1088-9639
Printed in one color on matte stock

23335 **Communication News: Network Access Directory**
Nelson Publishing
2500 Tamiami Trl N
Nokomis, FL 34275-3476

941-966-9521; Fax: 941-966-2590
www.healthmgttech.com
Facebook, Twitter, LinkedIn

A Verner Nelson, Owner
Cost: $7.00
Frequency: Annual, June
Circulation: 71,000
Mailing list available for rent

23336 **Communications News: Broadband Directory**
Nelson Publishing

2500 Tamiami Trl N
Nokomis, FL 34275-3476

941-966-9521; Fax: 941-966-2590
www.healthmgttech.com
Facebook, Twitter, LinkedIn

A Verner Nelson, Owner
Cost: $7.00
Frequency: Annual, December
Circulation: 71,000
Mailing list available for rent

23337 **Communications News: PBX/CTI Directory**
Nelson Publishing
2500 Tamiami Trl N
Nokomis, FL 34275-3476

941-966-9521; Fax: 941-966-2590
www.healthmgttech.com
Facebook, Twitter, LinkedIn

A Verner Nelson, Owner
Cost: $7.00
Frequency: Annual, April
Circulation: 71,000
Mailing list available for rent

23338 **Communications News: Test Directory**
Nelson Publishing
2500 Tamiami Trl N
Nokomis, FL 34275-3476

941-966-9521; Fax: 941-966-2590
www.healthmgttech.com
Facebook, Twitter, LinkedIn

A Verner Nelson, Owner
Cost: $7.00
Frequency: Annual, February
Circulation: 71,000
Mailing list available for rent

23339 **Communications News: Video/ Audioconferencing Directory**
Nelson Publishing
2500 Tamiami Trl N
Nokomis, FL 34275-3476

941-966-9521; Fax: 941-966-2590
www.healthmgttech.com
Facebook, Twitter, LinkedIn

A Verner Nelson, Owner
Cost: $7.00
Frequency: Annual, October
Circulation: 71,000
Mailing list available for rent

23340 **Communications News: Wireless Directory**
Nelson Publishing
2500 Tamiami Trl N
Nokomis, FL 34275-3476

941-966-9521; Fax: 941-966-2590
www.healthmgttech.com
Facebook, Twitter, LinkedIn

A Verner Nelson, Owner
Cost: $7.00
Frequency: Annual, August
Circulation: 71,000
Mailing list available for rent

23341 **Complete Directory of Telephones & Accessories**
Sutton Family Communications & Publishing Company
155 Sutton Lane
Fordsville, KY 42343

270-740-0870
www.suttoncompliance.com
Facebook, Twitter

Theresa Sutton, Editor
Lee Sutton, General Manager

Print-out from database of wholesalers, manufacturers, distributors, importers and close-out houses. Database is updated daily to guarantee the most current and up-to-date sources available.
Cost: $55.20
100+ Pages

23342 **Corporate Yellow Book**
Leadership Directories
104 5th Ave
New York, NY 10011-6901

212-627-4140; Fax: 212-645-0931
info@leadershipdirectories.com
www.leadershipdirectories.com
Facebook, Twitter

David Hurvitz, CEO

Contact information for over 48,000 executives at over 1,000 companies and more than 9,000 board members and their outside affiliations.
Cost: $420.00
1,400 Pages
Frequency: Quarterly
ISSN: 1058-2098
Founded in 1986

23343 **Directory of Communications Professionals**
National Assn of Regulatory Utility Commissioners
1101 Vermont Ave NW
Suite 200
Washington, DC 20005-3553

202-898-2200; Fax: 202-898-2213
www.naruc.org
Facebook, Twitter

Charles Gray, Executive Director
Philip Jones, President

Offers information on consultants and other professionals active in regulated telecommunications.
Cost: $33.00
240 Pages
Frequency: Annual

23344 **International Fiber Optics Yellow Pages**
Information Gatekeepers
214 Harvard Avenue
Suite 200
Allston, MA 02134-4641

617-232-3111
800-323-1088; Fax: 617-734-8562
webmaster@igigroup.com
www.fiberopticsyp.com
Facebook, Twitter

Will Ashley, Contact

The most extensive Fiber Optics reference volume available anywhere. This directory is still the world's only source book devoted exclusively to Fiber Optics.
Cost: $89.95
Frequency: Annual
Founded in 1977

23345 **LATA Directory**
Center for Communications Management
11300 Rockville Pike
Suite 1100
Rockville, MD 20852-3003

301-770-7490; Fax: 301-287-2445
www.lataweb.com
Facebook, Twitter

Ronald Canter, Owner

Offers information on local access transport areas by states.
Cost: $195.00
220 Pages
Frequency: Annual

23346 **Local Calling Area Directory**
Center for Communications Management
11300 Rockville Pike
Suite 1100
Rockville, MD 20852-3003

301-770-7490; Fax: 301-287-2445
www.lataweb.com
Facebook, Twitter

Ronald Canter, Owner

Offers area codes and their zones or exchanges in cities of 100,000 or more in population.
Cost: $795.00
1,050 Pages
Frequency: Annual

23347 **Lynx Global Telecom Database**
Lynx Technologies
710 Route 46 East
PO Box 368
Little Falls, NJ 07424-0368

973-256-7200; Fax: 973-882-3583
www.lynxtech.com
Facebook, Twitter

Kathleen Elsayed, Production Manager
Mike Salerno, Circulation Director

350 telecommunications carriers services in approximately 200 countries, territories and other political divisions.

23348 **Network Management Guidelines and Contact Directory**
Network Operations Forum
1200 G Street NW
Washington, DC 20005-3814

202-347-1228; Fax: 202-393-5453

Over 25 telecommunications companies.

23349 **North American Telecommunications Association - Sourcebook**
2000 P St NW
Suite 550
Washington, DC 20036-6921

202-419-0412
www.naaee.org

Brian Day, Executive Director
Sue Bumpous, Communications Manager

Offers a wide array of information on manufacturers and suppliers of non-utility telephone terminal equipment.
Cost: $53.00
208 Pages

23350 **Outside Plant: Directory of Outside Plant Contractors Issue**
Practical Communications
PO Box 183
Cary, IL 60013-0183

847-639-2200; Fax: 847-639-7598

John Saxtan, Editor

Offers a list of over 800 contractors in the telecommunications industry that specialize in outside plant projects.
Cost: $30.00
Frequency: Annual
Circulation: 20,000

23351 **Phillips Satellite Industry Directory**
Phillips Business Information
1201 Seven Locks Road
Potomac, MD 20854-2931

301-354-1400
800-777-5006; Fax: 301-309-9473

Minica Kenny, Editor
Don Pazour, CEO

Over 6,000 contacts and more than 3,800 hardware and technical service companies, transponder brokers and resellers, consultants, communications attorneys, publishers, uplinks

and downlinks, video conference suppliers, related trade associations, government agencies and satellite telecommunications carriers.
Cost: $257.00
Frequency: Annual January

23352 **Phillips Who's Who in Electronic Commerce**
Phillips Business Information
1201 Seven Locks Road
Potomac, MD 20854-2931
301-354-1400
800-777-5006; Fax: 301-309-9473
Jennifer O Newman, Editor
Don Pazour, CEO
Service providers, value-added banks and networks, software vendors, associations, user groups, consultants, business and technical services for electronic commerce industry.
Cost: $199.00
Frequency: Annual

23353 **Pocket Guides to the Internet: Terminal Connections**
Information Today
143 Old Marlton Pike
Medford, NJ 08055-8750
609-654-6266
800-300-9868; Fax: 609-654-4309
custserv@infotoday.com
www.infotoday.com
Facebook, Twitter
Thomas H Hogan, President
Roger R Bilboul, Chairman Of The Board
Unix/VMS systems and other basic terminal applications and telecommunications programs.
Cost: $9.95

23354 **Q-TEL 1000**
United Communications Group
11300 Rockville Pike
P.O Box: 217
Rockville, MD 20852-3030
301-816-8950
800-526-5307; Fax: 858-674-5491
www.qtel.qa
Facebook, Twitter
This database offers information on telecommunications charges.
Frequency: Full-text
Mailing list available for rent

23355 **RCR Publications**
RCR Publications
1746 Cole Boulevard
Suite 150
Golden, CO 80401
303-733-2500
800-678-9696; Fax: 303-733-9941
mbush@crain.com
Melodye Bush, Database Coordinator
Offers a wide variety of information on cellular and personal communications industries. Includes detailed information on carriers and vendors around the world.
Cost: $950.00
Frequency: Annual
Founded in 1991

23356 **RCR's Cellular Database**
RCR Publications
1746 Cole Boulevard
Suite 150
Golden, CO 80401
303-733-2500
800-678-9696; Fax: 303-733-9941
mbush@crain.com
Melodye Bush, Database Coordinator
Offers a wide variety of information on cellular communications industry. Includes detailed information on cellular carriers and vendors.
Cost: $300.00
Frequency: Annual
Founded in 1991

23357 **RCR's PCS Database**
RCR Publications
1746 Cole Boulevard
Suite 150
Golden, CO 80401
303-733-2500
800-678-9696; Fax: 303-733-9941
mbush@crain.com
Melodye Bush, Database Coordinator
Offers a wide variety of information on the personal communications industry. Includes detailed information on PCS carriers and vendors.
Cost: $300.00
Frequency: Annual
Founded in 1991

23358 **Satellite Industry Directory**
Phillips Business Information
1201 Seven Locks Road
Suite 300
Potomac, MD 20854-2931
301-354-1400; Fax: 301-309-9473
Monica Kenny, Editor
Profiles operational and planned satellite systems, equipment and service providers, satellite brokers, uplinkers/downlinkers and more.
Cost: $247.00
750 Pages
Frequency: Annual

23359 **Sbusiness**
AFSM International
17065 Camino San Bernardo
Suite 200
San Diego, CA 92127-1709
858-673-3055
800-333-9786; Fax: 239-275-0794
Facebook, Twitter
John Shoenewald, Executive Director
Jb Wood, President/CEO
The professional journal for customer service and support managers.
Cost: $60.00
100 Pages
Frequency: Bi-Monthly
Circulation: 10000
Founded in 1975
Mailing list available for rent

23360 **TCP/IP for the Internet**
Mecklermedia Corporation
20 Ketchum Street
Westport, CT 06880-5908
203-341-2806; Fax: 203-454-5840
Marshall Breeding, Editor
Standard network protocol for data transmission over the global internet - products and packages for Unix, DOS, Windows and Macintosh platforms.
Cost: $24.95

23361 **Telecommunications Directory**
Gale/Cengage Learning
10650 Toebben Drive
Detroit, KY 41051
248-699-4253
800-877-4253; Fax: 248-699-8049
gale.galeord@cengage.com
www.gale.com
Facebook, Twitter
Patrick C Sommers, President
Provides detailed information on telecommunications companies providing a range of products and services from cellular communications and local exchange carriers to satellite services and Internet service providers.
ISBN: 1-414419-80-5

23362 **Telecommunications Export Guide**
North American Telecommunications Association
2000 P St NW
Suite 550
Washington, DC 20036-6921
202-419-0412
www.naaee.org
Brian Day, Executive Director
Sue Bumpous, Communications Manager
Offers a list of over 135 foreign telecommunications agencies, and federal and state government agencies concerned with exports in the United States.
Cost: $103.00

23363 **Telemarketing and Call Center Solutions Buyer's Guide and Directory Issue**
Technology Marketing Corporation
800 Connecticut Ave
1st Floor East
Norwalk, CT 06854-1936
203-852-6800
800-243-6002; Fax: 203-853-2845
tmc@tmcnet.com
www.tmcnet.com
Facebook, Twitter, LinkedIn, You Tube
Rich Tehrani, CEO
Nanji Tehrani, Chair
David Rodriguez, President/Assistant Treasurer
Michael Genaro, VP
Over 1100 domestic and foreign suppliers of equipment products and services to the telecommunications/telemarketing industry.
Cost: $25.00
Frequency: Annual December
Founded in 1972

23364 **Telephone Industry Directory**
Phillips Business Information
1201 Seven Locks Road
Suite 300
Potomac, MD 20854-2931
301-354-1400; Fax: 301-349-9473
Jennifer Newman, Assistant Managing Editor
Offers valuable information on over 4,800 manufacturers, distributors and suppliers to the telecommunications industry.
Cost: $249.00
750 Pages
Frequency: Annual

23365 **Voice Mail Reference Manual and Buyer's Guide**
Robins Press
2675 Henry Hudson Parkway W
Apartment 6J
Bronx, NY 10463-7741
718-548-7245
800-238-7130; Fax: 718-548-7237
Marc Robins, Publisher
Offers information on over 60 suppliers of about 90 voice mail systems and service bureaus.
Cost: $65.00
384 Pages
Frequency: Annual
Mailing list available for rent: 10M names
Printed in 2 colors on matte stock

23366 **Voice Processing Printed Circuit Cards: A Sourcebook of Suppliers & Products**
Robins Press
2675 Henry Hudson Parkway W
Apartment 6J
Bronx, NY 10463-7741
718-548-7245
Offers a list of over 50 vendors of voice processing circuit cards and related technology worldwide.
Cost: $150.00
Frequency: Annual

23367 **World Satellite Almanac**
Phillips Business Information
1201 Seven Locks Road
Suite 300
Potomac, MD 20854-2931
301-354-1400; Fax: 301-340-1520
Monica Kenny, Editor
All commercial satellite systems and operators are profiled.
Cost: $247.00
700 Pages
Frequency: Annual

23368 **World Telecommunications Tariff Directory**
Lynx Technologies
PO Box 368
Little Falls, NJ 07424-0368
973-256-7200
A comprehensive directory of over 1,200 Local Exchange Carriers and other telecom companies make up this directory. Includes a detailed index for easy cross-referencing by company name, contacts, titles, geographical region, services provided, email and more.
Cost: $699.00
9,000 Pages

Industry Web Sites

23369 **http://gold.greyhouse.com**
G.O.L.D Grey House OnLine Databases
Grey House Publishing's online database platform, GOLD, offers Quick Search, Keyword Search and Expert Search for most business sectors including telecommunications and media markets. The GOLD platform makes finding the information you need quick and easy - whether you're a novice searcher or an experienced database user. All of Grey House's directory products are available for subscription on the GOLD platform.

23370 **www.adweek.com**
ADWEEK
Leading decision makers in the advertising and marketing field go to Adweek.Com every day for breaking news, insight, buzz, opinion, analysis, research and classifieds. The resources of all six regional editions of Adweek, as well as the national edition of Brandweek are combined with the knowledge of our online editors and the multimedia-interactive capabilities of the web to deliver vital information quickly and effectively to our target audience.

23371 **www.alts.org**
Association of Local Telecommunications Services
Represents state and local telecommunications offices.

23372 **www.amtausa.org**
American Mobile Telecommunications Association
Membership is made up of operators in the 220 MHz, 450 MHz, 800 MHz and 900 MHz bands, as well as product and service providers for the industry. Many members are exploring other areas of the mobile telecommunications industry — digital SMR, Personal Communications Services, data communications, mobile satellite, cable telephony and international wireless interests. AMTA is working with its members and with government to insure that those areas can be pursued successfully.

23373 **www.arrl.org**
American Radio Relay League
National membership association for amateur radio operators.

23374 **www.atis.org**
Alliance for Telecommunications Industry Solutions
Membership organization that provides the tools necessary for the industry to identify standards, guidelines and operating procedures that make the interoperability of existing and emerging telecommunications proiducts and services possible.

23375 **www.atsi.org**
Association of Teleservices International
Promotes fair competition through appropriate regulation and legislation; provides research and development provides support services and educational opportunities to address challenges in operating environments; in encourages and maintains the high standards of ethics and service.

23376 **www.floridapsc.com**
Telecommunications Cooperative Network
Offers group purchasing discounts on long-distance telephone services, equipment counseling, and analysis of communications needs.

23377 **www.greyhouse.com**
Grey House Publishing
Authoritative reference directories for most business sectors including telecommunications and media markets. Users can search the online databases with varied search criteria allowing for custom searches by product category, geographic area, sales volume, keyword, subject and more. Full Grey House catalog and online ordering also available.

23378 **www.icea.net**
Insulated Cable Engineers Association
Professional organization dedicated to developing cable standards for the electric power, control and telecommunications industries. Ensures safe, economical and efficient cable systems utilizing proven state-of-the-art materials and concepts. ICEA documents are of interest to cable manufacturers, architects and engineers, utility and manufacturing plant personnel, telecommunication engineers, consultants and OEMs.

23379 **www.igigroup.com**
Information Gatekeepers
Provides worldwide coverage of wireless LAN's, LAN interconnection, wireless in-building and major applications such as point-of-sales, portable computer interconnections and remote data collection.

23380 **www.imc.org**
Internet Email Consortium
Information about IMC and its members, all the internet email standards and more.

23381 **www.isoc.org**
Internet Society
International, professional membership organization focusing on standards, education and policy issues.

23382 **www.kagan.com**
Wireless/Private Cable Investor
The original bible of the wireless cable, multipoint distribution pay TV industry. Published continuously since 1972, this newsletter is the window on cable competition. Three month trial available.

23383 **www.ntca.org**
National Telephone Cooperative Association
Represents both cooperative and commercial, independent rural phone companies.

23384 **www.pcca.org**
Power and Communication Contractors
A national trade association for companies constructing electric power facilities, including transmission and distribution lines and substations and telephone, fiber optic, and cable television systems.

23385 **www.scte.org**
Society of Cable Telecommunications Engineers
For people engaged in engineering, construction, installation, manufacture, technical direction, management, regulation, or administration of broad band communications technologies.

23386 **www.telecommagazine.com**
Telecommunications Industry Association
This magazine reports on carrier class and wide area communications technologies for service providers and their corporate network customers worldwide. Coverage includes technology, product, market and application information for serious communications professionals, interexchange, cellular/wireless/satellite carriers, cable companies as well as commercial users and government agencies in the communications industry.

23387 **www.telecommute.org**
Telecommuting Advisory Council
A comprehensive monthly digest of news about employer-sponsored telecommuting programs for employers working at home or elsewhere off-site. Contains case studies, international news, technology updates, legal and regulatory news, and managerial topics.

Associations

23388 Acrylic Council
1285 Avenue of the Americas
35th Floor
New York, NY 10019

212-397-4600; Fax: 212-554-4042
www.fabriclink.com
Facebook, Twitter

Lynn Misiak, Executive Director

A business league created to provide products in facilities maintained in the US. Educates the retailer and consumer of the benefits of acrylic fiber.

23389 Amalgamated Clothing and Textile Workers Union
1710 Broadway
New York, NY 10019-5254

212-255-9655
www.acronymfinder.com
Facebook, Twitter

Jack Sheinkman, President
William Towne, Manager

Sponsors and supports the Political Action Committee in this field.
249M Members
Founded in 1976

23390 American Flock Association
PO Box 1090
Suite C
Cherryville, NC 28021

617-303-6288; Fax: 704-671-2366
info@flocking.org
www.flocking.org
LinkedIn, YouTube, Pinterest

Karl Spilhaus, President
Steve Rosenthal, Managing Director

Provides positive leadership to foster a strong flock industry in North America.
60 Members
Founded in 1984

23391 American Home Sewing & Craft Association
PO Box 369
Monroeville, PA 15146

412-372-5950; Fax: 412-372-5953
info@sewing.org
www.sewing.org

Handicraft and collectibles forum

23392 American Sheep Industry Association
9785 Maroon Circle
Suite 360
Englewood, CO 80112

303-771-3500; Fax: 303-771-8200
www.sheepusa.org
Facebook

Benny Cox, President
Susan Shultz, VP
Peter Orwick, Executive Director
Larry Kincaid, Chief Financial Officer
Rita Kourlis Samuelson, Deputy Dir. & Dir., Wool Marketing

A federation of state associations dedicated to the welfare and profitability of the sheep industry.
8000+ Members
Founded in 1865

23393 American Textile Machinery Association
201 Park Washington Ct
Falls Church, VA 22046-4527

703-538-1789; Fax: 703-241-5603
info@atmanet.org
www.atmanet.org
Facebook, Twitter

Will Motchar, Chairman
Mike Viniconis, Vice Chairman
Clay D Tyeryar, President & Assistant Treasurer
Allen Moore, Vice Chairman/Treasurer
Susan A Denston, Executive VP & Secretary

The American Textile Machinery Association/ATMA's purpose is to improve business conditions within the textile machinery industry of the United States within a global context; to encourage the use of the products of the industry; and to protect, promote, foster and advance the common interests of the members as manufacturers and distributors of textile machinery and parts and machinery accessory to textile machinery on a worldwide basis.
1.5M Members
Founded in 1933

23394 American Yarn Spinners Association
PO Box 99
Gastonia, NC 28053

704-824-3522; Fax: 704-824-0630
www.aysa.org
Facebook, Twitter

Michael Hubbard, Executive Director

Provides full service to the sales yarn industry.
100 Members
Founded in 1967

23395 Association of Georgia's Textile, Carpet, & Consumer Products Manufacturers
50 Hurt Plz Se
Suite 985
Atlanta, GA 30303-2941

404-688-0555; Fax: 404-584-0720
info@gamfg.org
www.gamfg.org
Facebook, Twitter

Lee Bryan, Chairman
Del Land, Vice Chairman
G L Bowen III, President
Kevin Thieneman, Treasurer
Charles B Jones III, VP & General Counsel
Founded in 1900

23396 Association of Knitted Fabrics
1001 Connecticut Ave NW
Suite 315
Washington, DC 20036

202-822-8028; Fax: 202-822-8029
www.nationaltextile.org
Facebook, Twitter

William L Jasper, Chairman
James C Self III, Vice Chairman
Augustine Tantillo, President
Sarah Pierce, Senior VP
Mike Hubbard, VP

Manufacturers of knitted cotton and wool products.
6 Members
Founded in 1935

23397 Carpet & Rug Institute: West
100 South Hamilton Street
Suite 3
Dalton, CA 30720

706-278-3176; Fax: 706-278-8835
www.carpet-rug.com
Facebook, Twitter, LinkedIn, Youtube, Google+

Terri Caputo, President
Founded in 1791
Mailing list available for rent

23398 Cotton Council International
1521 New Hampshire Avenue NW
Washington, DC 20036

202-745-7805; Fax: 202-483-4040
cottonuse@cotton.org
www.cottonusa.org
Facebook, Twitter, YouTube, Pinterest

James L Webb, Chairman
John A Burch, President
T Jordan Lea, First VP
Dahlen K Hancock, Second VP
Keith T Lucas, Treasurer

23399 Craft Yarn Council
3740 N. Josey Lane
Suite 102
Carrollton, TX 75007

972-325-7232; Fax: 972-215-7333
www.craftyarncouncil.com
Facebook, Youtube, Google+

Michael Hubbard, Secretary/Treasurer
Mary Colucci, Executive Director

The Craft Yarn Council represents the leading yarn companies, accessory manufacturers, magazine, book publishers, and consultants in the yarn industry.
Founded in 1981

23400 Durene Association of America
194 S South St
Gastonia, NC 28052-4125

704-865-1651; Fax: 704-824-0638

Russell Duren, President

Develops and uses tests to determine quality. Licenses manufacturers to use Durene identification on products.
4 Members
Founded in 1929

23401 Elastic Fabric Manufacturers Council
230 Congress Street
Boston, MA 02110

617-542-8220; Fax: 617-542-2199
www.textilenta.org

Provides exchange and management services, trade promotions, statistical programs and information bulletins.
32 Members
Founded in 1915

23402 Electrostatic Discharge Association
7900 Turin Road
Building 3
Rome, NY 13440-2069

315-339-6937; Fax: 315-339-6793
info@esda.org
www.esda.org
Facebook, Twitter, LinkedIn

Donn Bellmore, President
Leo G Henry, Senior VP

Professional voluntary association dedicated to advancing the theory and practice of electrostatic discharge avoidance. Initial emphasis on the effects of ESD on electronic components has broadened to include textiles, plastics, web processing, explosives, clean rooms and graphic arts. Expands ESD awareness through educational programs, development of standards, tutorials, publications, local chapters, symposia and certification.
Founded in 1982

23403 Hard Fibers Association
120 Genesee Street
Suite 601
Auburn, NY 13021-3603

315-520-0871; Fax: 315-255-3292

John Hurd, President

Importers and distributors of sisal, abaca and other hard fibers.

23404 **Home Sewing Association**
PO Box 369
Monroeville, PA 15146
412-725-5950; Fax: 412-372-5953
info@sewing.org
www.sewing.org
Joyce Perhac, Manager
Represents most facets of the home sewing industry. National trade association for independent sewing machine dealers and distributors.
1.5M Members
Founded in 1912

23405 **INDA Association of Nonwoven Fabrics**
1100 Crescent Green
Suite 115
Cary, NC 27518
919-459-3700; Fax: 919-459-3701
info@inda.org
www.inda.org
Facebook, Twitter, LinkedIn, RSS
Robert Lovegrove, Chairman
Karen Castle, Vice Chairperson Planning
Renita Jones Anderson, Vice Chairperson Finance
Todd Bassett, Past INDA Chairman
Joan Izzo, Director of Marketing
Mission is to promote the value and profitability of the global nonwovens/engineered fabrics industry to benefit the members.
300 Members
Founded in 1968

23406 **Industrial Fabrics Association International**
1801 County Road BW
Roseville, MN 55413-4061
651-222-2508
800-225-4324; Fax: 651-631-9334
generalinfo@ifai.com
www.ifai.com
Facebook, Twitter, LinkedIn, YouTube
Steve Schiffman, President & CEO
Cherie Schmit, Executive Assistant
Sheila Sumner, VP, Finance/Administration
Amy Collins, Dircetor, Sales & Marketing
Linden Wicklund, Director, Events & Member Programs
A not-for-profit trade association that represent the international specialty fabrics marketplace that facilitates the development, application and promotion of products manufactured by the diverse membership.
2000 Members

23407 **Institute of Textile Technology**
North Carolina State University
3426 College of Textiles
NSCU Centennial Campus
Raleigh, NC 27695-8301
919-513-7704
888-348-3512; Fax: 919-882-9410
www.ittorissa.org
Facebook, Twitter
W Gilbert O'Neal, President & CEO
George Edmunds, VP
A graduate school supported in part by member companies. Publishes the Textile Technology Digest.

23408 **International Textile and Apparel Association**
PO Box 70687
Knoxville, TN 37938-0687
865-992-1535
info@itaaonline.org
itaaonline.org
Facebook, Twitter
Nancy Rutherford, Executive Director
Professional association for 1,000 college professors of clothing and textile studies.
Founded in 1935
Mailing list available for rent: 950 names at $80 per M

23409 **Knitted Textile Association**
1701 K St. NW
Suite 625
Washington, DC 20006
202-822-8028; Fax: 202-822-8029
spierce@ncto.org
www.ncto.org
Facebook, Twitter, LinkedIn, YouTube
Jeffrey Price, Chairman
Rob Chapman, Vice Chairman
Augustine Tantillo, President
Sara Beatty, Secretary
Robin Haynes, Treasurer
The KTA is an active participant in the International Mechinery and Equipment exhibition that takes place in Textile Hall in Greenville, South Carolina and highlights the latest in knitting and related dying and finishing equipment.

23410 **Narrow Fabrics Institute**
1801 County Road BW
Roseville, MN 55113-4061
651-225-6920; Fax: 651-631-9334
generalinfo@ifai.com
www.narrowfabrics.org
Facebook, Twitter, LinkedIn, Youtube
Mary J Hennessy, President & CEO
Todd V Lindemann, VP, Conference Management
Pam Egan-Blahna, Director, Human Resource
Dan McCarthy, VP, Finance/CFO
Andrew M Aho, Director, Membership & Divisions
Conducts research, sells abrasior rods, and compiles statistics on narrow fabrics
40 Members
Founded in 1956

23411 **National Cotton Batting Institute**
4322 Bloombury St
Southaven, MS 38672
901-218-2393; Fax: 662-449-0046
Facebook, Twitter
Weston Arnall, President
Greg Windsperger, VP
Fred Middleton, Executive Secretary-Treasurer
NCBI respresents U.S. companies that manufacture and sell batting for use in mattresses, futons, home furnishing, and upholstered products. It provides a range of services to assist its members in expanding markets, monitoring and contributing to legislative and regulatory decisions that affect the industry, and conducting consumer education and information programs.
27 Members
Founded in 1954

23412 **National Cotton Council of America**
7193 Goodlett Farms Pkwy
Cordova, TN 38016
901-274-9030; Fax: 901-725-0510
www.cotton.org
Facebook, Twitter
Kent Fountain, Chair
Gary Adams, President & CEO
Ken Burton, Exec. Dir. US Cotton Trust Protocol
Bruce Atherley, Exec. Dir. Cotton Council Intl.
John Gibson, Vice President, Member Services
The council serves as the central forum for consensus-building among producers, ginners, warehousers, merchants, cottonseed processors/dealers, cooperatives and textile manufacturers.

23413 **National Council for Textile Education**
Georgia Institute of Technology
1701 K St. NW
Suite 625
Washington, DC 20006
202-822-8028; Fax: 202-822-8029
spierce@ncto.org
www.ncto.org
Facebook, Twitter, LinkedIn, YouTube
Jeffrey Price, Chairman
Augustine Tantillo, President
Sara Beatty, Secretary
Robin Haynes, Treasurer
Rob Chapman, Vice Chairman
Members are administrators of college textile departments whose curriculum comprise science-based programs with substantial laboratory and plant experience.

23414 **National Council of Textile Organizations**
1701 K St. NW
Suite 625
Washington, DC 20006
202-822-8028; Fax: 202-822-8029
www.ncto.org
Facebook, Twitter, LinkedIn, YouTube
Augustine Tantillo, President & CEO
Jeffrey Price, Chairman
The voice of the U.S. textile industry.

23415 **National Knitwear & Sportswear Association**
1701 K St. NW
Suite 625
Washington, DC 20006
202-822-8028; Fax: 202-822-8029
spierce@ncto.org
www.ncto.org
Facebook, Twitter, LinkedIn, YouTube
Jeffrey Price, Chairman
Rob Chapman, Vice Chairman
Augustine Tantillo, President
Sara Beatty, Secretary
Robin Haynes, Treasurer
Represents U.S. manufacturers and contractors, designing studios and related business engaged in the production of knitted sportswear and knitted products of all types.

23416 **Northern Textile Association**
1701 K St. NW
Suite 625
Washington, DC 20006
202-822-8028; Fax: 202-822-8029
spierce@ncto.org
www.ncto.org
Facebook, Twitter, LinkedIn, YouTube
Jeffrey Price, Chairman
Rob Chapman, Vice Chairman
Augustine Tantillo, President
Sara Beatty, Secretary
Robin Haynes, Treasurer
The KTA is an active participant in the International Mechinery and Equipment exhibition that takes place in Textile Hall in Greenville, South Carolina and highlights the latest in knitting and related dying and finishing equipment.

23417 **Restoration Industry Association**
2025 M Street, NW
Suite 800
Rockville, MD 20852
202-367-1180
800-272-7012; Fax: 202-367-2180
info@restorationindustry.org

www.restorationindustry.org
Facebook, Twitter, LinkedIn

Scott Stamper, President
Chuck Violand, First Vice President
Mark Springer, Vice President
Jack A. White, Secretary
Larry Holder, Treasurer

A trade association for cleaning and restoration professionals worldwide, and the foremost authority, trainer and educator in the industry.
1100 Members
Founded in 1946

23418 **Schiffi Lace & Embroidery Manufacturers Association**
26 Industrial Ave
Suite 2
Fairview, NJ 07022-1600

201-840-7611; Fax: 201-943-7793
www.schiffli.org
Facebook, Twitter

August Bischoff, President
Vincent Mesiano, VP

Crafted lace, and embroidery that adorns lingerie and dresses t towels, sheets, curtains, tablecloths, patches, logos and much more.
Founded in 1848

23419 **Secondary Materials and Recycled Textiles Association**
3465 Box Hill Corp. Center Drive
Suite H
Abingdon, MD 21009

443-640-1050; Fax: 443-640-1086
Heather@KINGmgmt.org
www.smartasn.org
Facebook, Twitter, LinkedIn, Youtube

Jeff Pearl, President
Eric Stubin, Vice President
David Bloovman, 2nd Vice President
E. Carle Shotwell, Treasurer
Lou Buty, Immediate Past President

A dynamic international association which seeks to strengthen the economic opportunities of its members. Promotes the interdependence of all its industry segments by providing a common forum for networking, education, and trade.
Founded in 1932

23420 **Shippers of Recycled Textiles**
7910 Woodmont Ave # 1405
Bethesda, MD 20814-3082

301-907-0001; Fax: 301-656-1079
smartinfo@kingmgmt.org
www.sorti.org
Facebook, Twitter

Eric Stubin, President
Robert Goode, Treasurer
Lou Buty, VP
75 Members
Founded in 1988

23421 **Southern Textile Association**
PO Box 66
Gastonia, NC 28053-0066

704-215-4543; Fax: 704-215-4160
www.southerntextile.org
Facebook, Twitter

Judson L. Boehmer, Chairman
Todd Wemyss, President
Mike Kingsmore, First VP
Carson Copeland, Second VP
Lillian G. Link, Secretary/Treasurer

Represents the textile and clothing industry in the South.
Founded in 1908

23422 **Surface Design Association**
PO Box 20430
Albuquerque, NM 87154

707-829-3110; Fax: 707-829-3285
info@surfacedesign.org
www.surfacedesign.org
Facebook, Twitter, LinkedIn

Astrid Bennett, President
Jennifer Reis, VP
Joyce Martelli, Treasurer
Tedd Milder, Secretary
Danielle Kelly, Executive Director

Aims to stimulate, promote and improve education in the area of surface design, to encourage the surface designer as an individual artist and to provide a forum for exchange of ideas through conferences and publications.
Founded in 1977
Mailing list available for rentat $75 per M

23423 **TRI/Princeton**
601 Prospect Ave
PO Box 625
Princeton, NJ 08540

609-430-4820; Fax: 609-683-7836
info@triprinceton.org
www.triprinceton.org
Facebook, Twitter, LinkedIn

Kurl L Adams, Chair
David Graham, Vice Chairman
Yash K Kamath, Research Director
Robert J. Bianchin, Chairman of the Board
Kurt L. Adams, Vice Chair

Provides advanced research and education in polymers, fibers, films, personal care and porous materials.
40 Members
Founded in 1930

23424 **Textile Care Allied Trades Association**
4023 N Armenia Avenue
Suite 270
Tampa, FL 33607

813-348-0075; Fax: 813-348-0077
luci@tcata.org
www.tcata.org
Facebook, Twitter, LinkedIn

Leslie Schaeffer, Chief Executive Officer
Luci Ward, Business Manager

The Textile Care Allied Trades Association (TCATA) is an international trade association representing manufacturers and distributors of dry-cleaning and laundry equipment and supplies. It is the only trade association dedicated exclusively to the interests of the allied trades.

23425 **Textile Rental Services Association**
1800 Diagonal Rd
Suite 200
Alexandria, VA 22314-2842

703-519-0029
877-770-9274; Fax: 703-519-0026
trsa@trsa.org
www.trsa.org
Facebook, Twitter, LinkedIn, Youtube, RSS

Covers the uniform, linen supply, health care and dust control service markets.
Founded in 1912

23426 **The Knitting Guild Association (TKGA)**
1100-H Brandywine Boulevard
Zanesville, OH 43701-7303

740-452-4541; Fax: 740-452-2552
tkga@tkga.com
tkga.org
Facebook, Twitter, Pinterest

Arenda Holladay, President & Executive Director
Leslie Gonzalez, VP, Certification
Donna Estin, VP, Public Relations

Membership organization for knitters with focus on knitting education and enhancing knitters skills.
11000 Members
Founded in 1984

Newsletters

23427 **Embroidery News**
Schiffi Lace & Embroidery Manufacturers Assn
596 Anderson Avenue
Suite 203
Cliffside Park, NJ 07010-1831

201-943-7757; Fax: 201-943-7793

Leonard Seiler, Editor
Eugene Schrouzol, Publisher

Newsletter for the embroidery industry.
Frequency: BiMonthly
Circulation: 500

23428 **Marine Textiles**
RCM Enterprises
12 Oaks Center #922
Wayzata, MN 55391

800-451-9278

Mara Sidney, Publisher
Jim Penningroth, Editor

Serves firms in the boating market who use fabrics and furnishings. Accepts advertising.
Cost: $28.00

Magazines & Journals

23429 **AATCC Review**
American Assoc Textile Chemists and Colorists
1 Davis Dr
Research Triangle Park, NC 27709-2215

919-549-8141
800-360-5380; Fax: 919-549-8933
danielsj@aatcc.org
www.aatcc.org
Facebook, Twitter, LinkedIn

John Daniels, Executive VP
Debra Hibbard, Executive Assistant
Charles E Gavin, Treasurer
Brenda Jones, Production Manager

Covers all aspects of design, dyeing, printing, finishing, and testing as they relate to textile manufacturing, including fibers, fabrics of all types, garments, carpets, home textiles, and industrial products.
Frequency: Monthly
ISSN: 1532-8813
Founded in 1997
Mailing list available for rent
Printed in 4 colors on glossy stock

23430 **Cleaning & Restoration Magazine**
Restoration Industry Association
12339 Carroll Avenue~
Suite K
Rockville, MD 20852

301-231-6505
800-272-7012; Fax: 301-231-6569
info@restorationindustry.org
www.restorationindustry.org

Kristy Cohen, Chief Executive Officer

Trade journal covering fire and water damage restoration, rug and textile cleaning, indoor air quality and business issues.
Frequency: Monthly
Circulation: 6000

23431 **Fabric Architecture**
Industrial Fabrics Association International
1801 County Road B W
Roseville, MN 55113-4061

651-222-2508
800-225-4324; Fax: 651-631-9334
bnwhite@ifai.org
www.ifai.com

Rebecca Post, Editorial Director

Strives to inform architects, designers, landscape architects, engineers and other specifiers about architectural fabric structutres, the fibers and fabrics used to make them, their design possibilities, their construction, and issues regarding their applicability and acceptance.
Cost: $39.00
Frequency: Bi-Monthly

23432 **Geosynthetics**
Industrial Fabrics Association International
1801 County Road B W
Roseville, MN 55113-4061

651-222-2508
800-225-4324; Fax: 651-631-9334
generalinfo@ifai.com
www.ifai.com

Todd Berger, Senior Editor

Peer reviewed technical journal for civil engineers using geosynthetics in road construction, errosion control, hazardous waste, drainage, containment and reinforcement.
Cost: $49.00
Circulation: 16,000
ISSN: 0882-4983
Founded in 1988
Printed in 4 colors on glossy stock

23433 **Home Textiles Today**
Reed Business Information
360 Park Ave S
New York, NY 10010-1737

646-746-6400
800-446-6551; Fax: 646-756-7583
corporatecommunications@reedbusiness.com
www.reedbusiness.com

John Poulin, CEO
Mark Fraser, Publisher

Textile industry news, reports, research and summaries for the professional.
Circulation: 8000
Founded in 1979

23434 **Impressions Magazine**
Miller Freeman Publications
13760 Noel Rd
Suite 500
Dallas, TX 75240-7336

972-239-3060
800-527-0207; Fax: 972-419-7825

Carl Piazza, Publisher
Laura Gonz, Editor

Covers the textile screen printing imprinted sportswear retailing, and commercial embroidery industry. Accepts advertising.
Cost: $36.00
250 Pages
Frequency: Annual

23435 **Industrial Fabric Products Review**
Industrial Fabrics Association International
1801 County Road B W
Roseville, MN 55113-4061

651-222-2508
800-225-4324; Fax: 651-631-9334
generalinfo@ifai.com
www.ifai.com

Jill Lafferty, Editor
Elisa Bernick, Associate Editor

Keeps individuals up to date on the information needed to keep their business growing, including reports on traditional or emerging markets and end products worldwide; forecasts and analyses of industry trends, announcements of new technologies in fibers, fabrics, equipment and treatments, and profiles of growth-oriented businesses and prodcuts.
Cost: $69.00
Frequency: Monthly
Founded in 1915

23436 **Journal of Engineered Fibers & Fabrics**
INDA Association of Nonwoven Fabrics
1100 Crescent Green
Suite 115
Cary, NC 27511

919-233-1210; Fax: 919-233-1282
www.inda.org
Facebook, Twitter, LinkedIn

Rory Holmes, President
Peggy Blake, Director of Marketing
Ian Butler, Director Market Research
Todd~ Bassett, Managing Director
Monica Moretti, Tresurer

International peer reviewed scientific eJournal that publishes original R&D on all aspects o ffabric technologies and their value chain from raw materials to end-use products.
Frequency: Quarterly
Circulation: 3000
Founded in 1968

23437 **Journal of Industrial Textiles**
851 New Holland Avenue
Suite 3535
Lancaster, PA 17604

717-291-5609
800-233-9936; Fax: 717-295-4538

23438 **Marine Fabricator**
Industrial Fabrics Association International
1801 County Road BW
Roseville, MN 55413

651-222-2508
800-225-4324; Fax: 651-631-9334
cptschida@ifai.com
www.ifai.com
Facebook, Twitter, LinkedIn

Elisa Bernick, Senior Editor

Educates and informs 5,000 marine shop professionals and also provides reportage that reflects the innovations and trends of the industry.
Cost: $34.00
Frequency: Bi-Monthly

23439 **Nonwovens Industry**
Rodman Publishing
70 Hilltop Rd
Suite 3000
Ramsey, NJ 07446-1150

201-825-2552; Fax: 201-825-0553
info@rodpub.com
www.nutraceuticalsworld.com
Facebook, Twitter, LinkedIn

Rodman Zilenziger Jr, President
Matt Montgomery, VP

Written for nonwoven roll goods producers, converters and end-use manufacturers.
70 Pages
Frequency: Monthly
Circulation: 11000
Founded in 1970

23440 **Nonwovens World**
MTS Publications
4100 S 7th Street
Kalamazoo, MI 49009-8461

269-375-1236; Fax: 269-375-6710
admin@marketingtechnologyservice.com
www.marketingtechnologyservice.com

James P Hanson, Editor
Cindy Costello, Circulation Manager
Wayne C Carter, Advertising Sales Director

Covers new products, as well as production and marketing strategies.
Circulation: 10384
Founded in 1986

23441 **Sheep Industry News**
9785 Maroon Circle
Suite 360
Englewood, CO 80112

303-771-3500; Fax: 303-771-8200
www.sheepusa.org
Facebook

Benny Cox, President
Peter Orwick, Executive Director
Kyle Partain, Editor

A federation of state associations dedicated to the welfare and profitability of the sheep industry.
Cost: $25.00
8000+ Members
Frequency: Monthly
Circulation: 8000
Founded in 1865

23442 **Surface Design Journal**
PO Box 360
Sebastopol, CA 95473-360

707-829-3110; Fax: 707-829-3285
www.surfacedesign.org
Facebook, Twitter, LinkedIn

Jason Pollen, President

Professional organization of more than 2,000 textile artists, designers for industry, and academicians.
Cost: $8.00
52 Pages
Frequency: Quarterly
Circulation: 6000
Founded in 1977

23443 **Textile Rental Magazine**
Textile Rental Services Association
1800 Diagonal Rd
Suite 200
Alexandria, VA 22314-2842

703-519-0029
877-770-9274; Fax: 703-519-0026
trsa@trsa.org
www.trsa.org
Facebook, Twitter, LinkedIn, You Tube

Roger Cocivera, President/CEO
Jack Morgan, Editor

Packed with valuable tips and ideas.
Frequency: Monthly

23444 **Textile Research Journal**
TRI Princeton
PO Box 625
Princeton, NJ 08542

609-924-3150; Fax: 609-683-7836
www.triprinceton.com

Dr. Gail R Eaton, President

Provides advanced research and education in polymers, fibers, films, personel care and porous materials.
Frequency: Monthly
Founded in 1930

Trade Shows

23445 **ATME-I/Techtextil North America**
American Textile Machinery Association
201 Park Washington Court
Falls Church, VA 22046

703-538-1789
ttnasales@usa.messefrankfurt.com
www.atmanet.org

Carina Whitaker, Operations Director
Carrie Kittrell, Sales Manager
Sarah Hatcher, Sales Associate

Show for technical textiles and nonwoven materials, exploring production, research and development.
Frequency: May
Founded in 1933

23446 **American Home Sewing & Craft Association Sewing & Craft Show: AHSCA**
American Home Sewing and Craft Association
1350 Broadway
Suite 1601
New York, NY 10018

212-714-1633; Fax: 212-714-1655
info@sewing.org
www.sewing.org

200 exhibits of fabric, notions, patterns, sewing and knitting machines, crafts and trimmings. Attended by professionals from major chain stores, independent retailers, wholesalers and manufacturers.
3000 Attendees
Frequency: Semiannual

23447 **American Textile Machinery Exhibition International**
Textile Hall Corporation
PO Box 5823
Greenville, SC 29606

864-331-2277; Fax: 864-331-2282

Butler Mullins, Director

Exhibition of machinery, supplies and services required for manufacture of yarn and fiber, for the weaving, knitting and dying/printing/finishing processes, for manufacture of non-wovens and for plant maintenance.
10000 Attendees
Frequency: September

23448 **Apparel Printing and Embroidery Expo**
Primedia
3585 Engineering Drive
Suite 100
Norcross, GA 30092

678-421-3000; Fax: 913-967-1898

Joanie Forsythe, Sales Manager
Arlene Mayfield, President
Scott Asher, VP

Semi-annual show of 200 manufacturers, suppliers and distributors of commercial screen printing and embroidery equipment and supplies, computer graphic systems and softgoods such as T-shirts, sweats, jackets and caps.
3000 Attendees

23449 **Apparel Show of the Americas**
Bobbin Publishing/Miller Freeman
PO Box 279
Euless, TX 76039

817-215-1600
800-693-1363; Fax: 817-215-1666

Betty Webb, Trade Show Director

Conference, seminar and 329 exhibits of equipment, fabrics, accessories and services for sewn products and apparel.
5790 Attendees
Frequency: Annual
Founded in 1992

23450 **Association of Specialists in Cleaning & Restoration Convention**
Restoration Industry Association
9810 Patuxent Woods Drive
Suite K
Columbia, MD 21046-1595

443-878-1000
800-272-7012; Fax: 443-878-1010
info@restorationindustry.org
www.restorationindustry.org
Facebook, Twitter, LinkedIn, You Tube

Kristy Cohen, Chief Executive Officer
Clare MacNab, Meeting Manager
Julia Vargo, Meeting Coordinator

Annual convention and exhibits of carpet, upholstery and draperies cleaning and restoration equipment, duct cleaning supplies and services, 100+ booths.
600 Attendees
Frequency: Annual
Founded in 1945

23451 **Filtration: International Conference & Exposition**
INDA Association of Nonwoven Fabrics
1100 Crescent Green
Suite 115
Cary, NC 27511

919-233-1210; Fax: 919-233-1282
www.inda.org
Facebook, Twitter, LinkedIn

Rory Holmes, President
Peggy Blake, Director of Marketing
Ian Butler, Director Market Research/Stats

The North American Show for all aspects of filter media. One-stop shopping where you can compare products and prices. See state-of-the-art products. Great networking experience.
1400 Attendees
Frequency: Annual

23452 **Geosynthetics**
Industrial Fabrics Association International
1801 County Road BW
Roseville, MN 55113

651-222-2508
800-225-4324; Fax: 651-631-9334
www.ifaiexpo.info
Facebook, Twitter, LinkedIn

Beth Wistrcill, Conference Manager

Features design, engineering strategies and cost-saving geosynthetics solutions.
Frequency: February

23453 **IDEA, International Engineered Fabrics Con ference + Expositions**
INDA Association of Nonwoven Fabrics
1100 Crescent Green
Suite 115
Cary, NC 27518

919-233-1210; Fax: 919-233-1282
www.inda.org
Facebook, Twitter, LinkedIn

Dave Rousse, President
Joan Izzo, Director of Marketing
Brad Kalil, Director Market Research/Stats

See, touch and buy state-of-the-art engineered fabrics. Compare all the components used to make first class fabrics-raw materials, chemicals, machinery and converting and finishind services.
5200 Attendees
Frequency: Triennial

23454 **IFAI Annual Expo**
Industrial Fabrics Association International
1801 County Road BW
Roseville, MN 55113

651-222-2508
800-225-4324; Fax: 651-631-9334
http://www.ifaiexpo.com

Beth Wistrcill, Conference Manager
Miller Weldmaster, Director
JoAnne Ferris, Director of Marketing

A trade event on the America's for the technical textiles and specialty fabrics industry.
Frequency: Annual/September

23455 **International Engineered Fabrics**
INDA Association of Nonwoven Fabrics
1100 Crescent Green
Suite 115
Cary, NC 27511

919-233-1210; Fax: 919-233-1282
www.inda.org
Facebook, Twitter, LinkedIn

Rory Holmes, President
Peggy Blake, Director of Marketing
Ian Butler, Director Market Research/Stats

See, touch and buy state-of-the-art engineered fabrics. Compare all the components used to make first class fabrics-raw materials, chemicals, machinery and converting and finishind services.

23456 **International Fashion and Boutique Shows**
100 Wells Avenue
#9103
Newton, MA 02459-3210

617-731-8316

Samuel Starr, Show Manager

1,800 booths.
30M Attendees
Frequency: January

23457 **International Fastener Exposition**
PEMCO
383 Main Avenue
Norwalk, CT 06851-1543

203-840-7700; Fax: 630-260-0395

Barbara Silverman, VP, Show Manager
Laura Rezek, Advertising

450 booths developed specifically for the fastener manufacturing and precision formed parts industry.
4.8M Attendees
Frequency: March

Directories & Databases

23458 **ATI's Textile Red Book: America's Textile Industries**
Billian Publishing Company
2100 Powers Ferry Rd SE
Suite 300
Atlanta, GA 30339-5055

770-955-5656
800-533-8484; Fax: 770-952-0669
www.billian.com

Jim Borneman, President
Dave Ramsays, Database Sales
Douglas Billian, Owner

Comprehensive reference guide for the textile industry. Includes over 6,000 mills in the US, Canada and Mexico. In addition to providing the complete contact information for the plant, each listing gives key personnel, products produced, fibers processed and mill equipment

used.
Cost: $160.00
Frequency: Annual
ISSN: 1047-6903

23459 America's Textiles International
Billian Publishing Company
2100 Powers Ferry Rd SE
Suite 300
Atlanta, GA 30339-5055
770-955-5656; Fax: 770-952-0669
www.billian.com
Annual directory provides the complete contact information - including Web sites and e-mail addresses for over 2,400 equipment, technology and service providers to the textile industry.
Frequency: Annual
Circulation: 32,000
ISSN: 0890-9970
Founded in 1887

23460 Davison's Textile Blue Book
Davison Publishing Company
PO Box 1289
Concord, NC 28026-1289
704-785-8700
800-328-4766; Fax: 704-785-8701
www.davisonpublishing.com
Carol Nealy, Advertising Manager
5,400 mills, dryers, finishers, in the United States, Canada, and Mexico.
Cost: $165.00
800 Pages
Frequency: Annual
ISBN: 0-875150-69-1
Founded in 1866

23461 Interior Textiles Fabric Resource Directory
Wool Bureau/Atlanta Merchandise Mart
240 Peachtree Street NW
Suite 6F11
Atlanta, GA 30303-1361
404-577-4320
Approximately 108 manufacturers and suppliers of wool and wool blend upholsteries, wallcoverings and draperies.
45 Pages

23462 International Textile & Apparel Association Membership Directory
PO Box 1360
Monument, CO 80132-1360
719-488-3716
info@itaaonline.org
www.itaaonline.org
Sandra S Hutton, Executive Director
Professional association for 1,000 college professors of clothing and textile studies.
8-12 Pages
Frequency: 6 per year
Circulation: Members
Founded in 1944

23463 Knitted Textile Association: Official Resource Guide and Fact Book
Knitted Textile Association
386 Park Avenue
New York, NY 10016-8804
212-545-9014; Fax: 212-889-6160
Peter Adelman, Editor
A list of over 150 member manufacturers, suppliers and distributors of knitted fabric products and services.
Cost: $10.00
Frequency: Annual

23464 Knitting Times: Buyers' Guide Issue
National Knitwear & Sportswear Association
386 Park Avenue S
New York, NY 10016-8804
212-545-9014; Fax: 212-532-0766
Dawne G Shink, Editor
List of about 4,500 suppliers and manufacturers of chemicals, contract, management and computer services, cutting room equipment, dyeing, finishing and printing equipment, knitted and woven fabrics, fibers and yarn, interfacing, pressing and steaming, knitting, sewing and trimming equipment, materials handling and plant control services.
Cost: $25.00
Frequency: Annual, September
Circulation: 10,000

23465 LDB Interior Textiles Buyers' Guide
EW Williams Publications
342 Madison Avenue
Room 1901
New York, NY 10173-1999
212-697-1122; Fax: 212-661-1713
ldb342@aol.com
Renee Bennett, Editor-in-Chief
Aleksandra Kazimierska, Directory Manager
Janys Kuznier, Circulation Director
Over 2,000 manufacturers, importers and suppliers of home fashions products and services, decorative fabric converters and alternative window coverings, fabricators, manufacturer's representatives and others allied to the home fashions trade.
Cost: $40.00
Frequency: Annual June
Circulation: 12,000

23466 Narrow Fabrics Institute: Buyer's Guide
Narrow Fabrics Institute
345 Cedar Street
Suite 800
Saint Paul, MN 55101-1004
800-225-4324; Fax: 651-222-8215
Approximately 34 producers of narrow fabrics for use in automotive medical, lifting, environmental safety, recreational, military, air cargo, trucks, and other fields, requiring industrial fabrics.
Frequency: Annual fall

23467 Textile Chemist and Colorist Buyers Guide
American Assoc Textile Chemists and Colorists
PO Box 12215
Research Triangle Park, NC 27709-2215
919-549-8141
800-360-5380; Fax: 919-549-8933
www.aatcc.org
John Daniels, Executive VP
Debra Hibbard, Executive Assistant
Charles E Gavin, Treasurer
Brenda Jones, Product Orders
Over 500 dye, pigments, machinery and equipment manufacturers are profiled.
ISBN: 0-040490-0 -
Founded in 1921
Mailing list available for rent

23468 Textile Technology Digest
2551 Ivy Road
Charlottesville, VA 22903
434-296-5511; Fax: 434-296-2957
www.ittorissa.org
Offers abstracts to worldwide literature from more than 1,300 sources annually such as proceedings, trade literature and other sources collected by the institutes library. The CD-ROM quarterly is available for $1,710 plus shipping. Network licenses begin at $500 for up to 10 simultaneous users.
Cost: $545.00
Frequency: Monthly
Founded in 1944

23469 Wool Source List
Kairalla Agency
27 Raymond Street
Manchester, MA 01944-1614
Eleanor Kairalla, Executive Director
Conducts trade and consumer polls on woolen apparel.
360 Pages
Founded in 1939

Industry Web Sites

23470 http://gold.greyhouse.com
G.O.L.D Grey House OnLine Databases
Grey House Publishing's online database platform, GOLD, offers Quick Search, Keyword Search and Expert Search for most business sectors including textile markets. The GOLD platform makes finding the information you need quick and easy - whether you're a novice searcher or an experienced database user. All of Grey House's directory products are available for subscription on the GOLD platform.

23471 www.aatcc.org
American Association of Textile Chemists & Colorists

23472 www.atmanet.org
American Textile Machinery Association
The association aims to improve business conditions within the US textile machinery industry.

23473 www.carpet-rug.com
Carpet & Rug Institute

23474 www.cottoninc.com
Cotton

23475 www.fibersource.com
American Fiber Manufacturers Association
Trade association for US companies that manufacture synthetic and cellulostic fibers. The industry employs 30,000 people and produces over 9 billion pounds of fiber in the US. The association maintains close ties to other manufactured fiber trade associations worldwide.

23476 www.flocking.org
American Flock Association
Fosters the use of flocked products. Strives to improve and advance flocking technology.

23477 www.greyhouse.com
Grey House Publishing
Authoritative reference directories for most business sectors including textile markets. Users can search the online databases with varied search criteria allowing for custom searches by product category, geographic area, sales volume, keyword, subject and more. Full Grey House catalog and online ordering also available.

23478 www.ifai.com
Industrial Fabrics Association International
Association of geosynthetics, fabricators, installers, equipment manufacturers, suppliers, testing firms, consultants, and educators, who produce textiles, nets, mats, grids, and other products. Industrial Fabrics Association International is the industry's first source for technical fabric resources and information.

23479 **www.inda.org**
INDA Association of Nonwoven Fabrics Industries

23480 **www.sewing.org**
Home Sewing Association

Represents most facets of the home sewing industry. National trade association for independent sewing machine dealers and distributors.

23481 **www.sleepproducts.org**
International Sleep Products Association

Maintains a strong organization to influence government actions, inform and educate the membership and act on industry issues to enhance the growth,profitability and stature of the sleep products industry. Provides members with information and services to manage their business more effectively and efficiently. Publishes a magazine devoted exclusively to the mattress industry, BEDtimes covers a broad range of issue and news important to the industry.

23482 **www.smartasn.org**
Shippers of Recycled Textiles

23483 **www.textilenta.org**
Northern Textile Association

Textile manufacturing trade association.

23484 **www.triprinceton.org**
TRI Princeton

TRI/Princeton provides advanced research and education in polymers, fibers, films, personel care, and porous materials.

Associations

23485 American Wholesale Marketers Association
11311 Sunset Hills Road
Suite 530
Reston, VA 20190

703-208-3358
800-482-2962; Fax: 703-573-5738
info@cdaweb.net
www.cdaweb.net
Facebook, Twitter, LinkedIn

Scott Ramminger, President & CEO
Chad Owen, First Vice Chairman
Susie Douglas Munson, Second Vice Chairman
Meredith Kimbrell, Director, Education
Robert Sincavich, Chairman

A trade association supporting the confectionary, tobacco and allied products industries through programs and services. members include wholesale distributors, manufacturers, and other allieds to the industry.
1000 Members
Founded in 1942

23486 Association of Dark Leaf Tobacco Dealers
2500 S Main St
Springfield, TN 37172-0638

615-384-9576; Fax: 615-384-6461
www.hailcotton.com

Mike De la Fargue, President & CEO
Tom Wilks, Executive VP
Roderick Roe, CFO
Andy Spies, Executive VP Sales
Eric Van Der Linden, Executive VP

An affiliate of Burley and Dark Leaf Tobacco Export Association.
Founded in 1902

23487 Bright Belt Warehouse Association
PO Box 120004
Raleigh, NC 27606

919-828-8988; Fax: 919-821-2092

Association of flue-cured tobacco warehousemen.

23488 Burley Stabilization Corporation
835 Bill Jones Industrial Dr.
Springfield, TN 37172

615-212-0508; Fax: 866-828-6501
burleytobacco@aol.com
www.burleystabilization.com

George Marks, President
Joe K Thomas III, VP
Charlie C Finch, Managing Director

Association of Burley tobacco warehouses in Kentucky, Tennessee, Ohio, Missouri, Indiana, Virginia, West Virginia and North Carolina.

23489 Burley Tobacco Growers Cooperative Association
620 S Broadway
Lexington, KY 40508-3149

859-252-3561; Fax: 859-231-9804
stephanie@burleytobacco.com
www.burleytobacco.com

Pat Raines, President
Eddie Warren, VP
Robert Reed Bush Sr., Secretary
Al Pedigo, Treasurer
Steve Pratt, General Manager

Burley tobacco grower cooperative

23490 Cigar Association of America
1100 G Street NW
Suite 1050
Washington, DC 20005-7405

202-223-8204
866-482-3570; Fax: 202-833-0379
www.cigarassociation.org
Facebook, Twitter, LinkedIn, Pinterest

Dan Carr, Chairman
Craig Williamson, President

Consists of cigar manufacturers, importers and major industry suppliers. Provides government relations and statistical services to the industry and promotes the image of the cigar.
60 Members
Founded in 1937

23491 Eastern Dark-Fired Tobacco
1109 S Main St
Springfield, TN 37172-3509

615-384-4543; Fax: 615-384-4545

Dan Borthick, President

Association of North Central Tennessee and South Central Kentucky growers that produce Type 22 Dark fire-cured and Type 35 Dark air-cured (one sucker) tobacco.

23492 Flue-Cured Tobacco Cooperative
1304 Annapolis Dr
Raleigh, NC 27608-2130

919-821-4560; Fax: 919-821-4564
www.ustobaccofarmer.com

Tommy Bunn, President/CEO
Stuart Thompson, CEO
Edward Kacsuta, Chief Financial Officer
Mike Lynch, Senior VP, Global Sales & Marekting
Sam Tie, Manager, Human Resource

Marketing cooperative which administers price support and provides %100 US flue-cured tobacco direct to purchasers.
Founded in 1946

23493 Friends of Tobacco
403 B East New Bern Road
Kinston, NC 20501

919-522-4769; Fax: 919-522-4769
fot@fujipub.com

Gary Corbett, President

Nonprofit organization promoting the economic importance of tobacco and freedom of choice in using tobacco products.
16000 Members
Founded in 1991

23494 Retail Tobacco Dealers of America
14611 Goodrich Dr NW
Suite 2H
Gig Harbor, WA 98329

253-857-8934; Fax: 253-857-0143
info@fujipub.com
www.rtda.org
Facebook, Twitter, LinkedIn, Youtube

Joe Row, Executive Director

Represents and assists retail tobacconists.
Founded in 1993

23495 Specialty Tobacco Council
102 W Third Street
Suite 200-B
Winston-Salem, NC 27101

336-723-4311; Fax: 336-759-0965
hroemer@specialtytobacco.org
specialtytobacco.org

Henry C Roemer III, Executive Director

Represents manufacturers and importers of specialty tobacco products.
Founded in 1984

23496 Tobacco Associates
1306 Annapolis Drive
Suite 102
Raleigh, NC 27608-2136

919-821-7670; Fax: 919-821-7674
tar@tobaccoassociatesinc.org
www.tobaccoassociatesinc.org
Kirk Wayne, President
Hank Mozingo, VP
Veronica Martins, Office Manager

Mission is to enhance understanding of US flue-cured tobacco and assist manufacturers interested in adding quality US leaf to their products.
Founded in 1947
Mailing list available for rent

23497 Tobacco Association of the United States
PO Box 8019
Princeton, NC 08543-8019

609-275-4900; Fax: 609-275-8379
tma@tma.org
www.tma.org

Tommy Bunn, Executive VP

Promotes market for US leaf tobacco.
100 Members
Founded in 1915

23498 Tobacco Growers Association of North Carolina
3901 Barrett Dr
Suite 202
Raleigh, NC 27609-6611

919-781-0066; Fax: 919-781-0066
grahamboyd@nc.rr.com
www.tganc.com

Graham Boyd, Executive VP

Commodity association for North Carolina tobacco growers.
10000 Members
Founded in 1981

23499 Tobacco Merchants Association
PO Box 8019
Princeton, NJ 08543-8019

609-275-4900; Fax: 609-275-8379
tma@tma.org
www.tma.org
Facebook, Twitter

Farrell Delman, President
Mark Schoenseld, Editor
Roberta Crosdy, Marketing Manager
Mark Schoenseld, Publisher

Tobacco trade association and source of current information on the tobacco industry.
170 Members
Founded in 1915

Newsletters

23500 Tobacco Barometer
Tobacco Merchants Association of the United States
PO Box 8019
Princeton, NJ 08543-8019

609-275-4900; Fax: 609-275-8379
tma@tma.org
www.tma.org
Facebook, Twitter

Mark Schoenseld, Editor
Roberta Crosdy, Marketing Manager
Mark Schoenseld, Farrell
Delman President

Tobacco industry news.
Frequency: Monthly
Founded in 1915

23501 Tobacco Products Litigation Reporter
TPLR
PO Box 1162
Back Bay Annex
Boston, MA 02117-1162
617-373-2026; Fax: 617-437-3672
www.tplr.com/
Richard Daynard, Publisher
Lissy Friedman, Publication Director
Mark Gottlieb, Legal Editor
Tobacco industry news.
Cost: $995.00
Frequency: 8 issues per year
Founded in 1950

23502 Tobacco on Trial
Tobacco Products Liability Project
102 The Fenway
Cushing Hall, Suite 117
Boston, MA 02115-5098
617-373-2026; Fax: 617-373-3672
www.tobacco-on-trial.com
Richard A Daynard, Publisher
Susan L Frank, Editor
Mark Gottlieb, Executive Director
Richard A Daynard, President
Tobacco industry news.
Cost: $95.00
Founded in 1979

Magazines & Journals

23503 Smokeshop
Lockwood Trade Journal
26 Broadway
Suite 9M2
New York, NY 10004-1777
212-391-2060
800-766-2633; Fax: 212-827-0945
sales@smokeshopmag.com
www.lockwoodpublications.com
Robert Lockwood, CEO
Edward Hoyt III, Editor
Bob Olesen, Advertising Sales Manager
Retail tobacco dealer's prevailing source for industry news designed to help readers operate their business more successfully.
Cost: $24.00
Founded in 1970

23504 Tobacco International
Lockwood Trade Journal
26 Broadway
Suite 9M2
New York, NY 10004-1777
212-391-2060; Fax: 212-827-0945
sales@smokeshopmag.com
www.lockwoodpublications.com
Robert Lockwood, CEO
Edward Hoyt III, Editor
Bob Olesen, Advertising Sales Manager
This trade publication offers information and news on the importing and exporting of tobacco.
Cost: $25.00
Frequency: Monthly
Founded in 1970

23505 Tobacco Reporter
SpecComm International
3000 Highwoods Boulevard
Suite 300
Raleigh, NC 27604-1029
919-878-0540; Fax: 919-876-8531
customerservice@tobaccoreporter.com
www.tobaccoreporter.com
Cost: $36.00
ISSN: 0361-5593

23506 Tobacco Retailer
Bel-Av Communications
359 Galahad Rd
Bolingbrook, IL 60440-2108
Home Page: www.tobaccoretailer.com
Charlie Forman, Group Publisher
Richard Brandes, Editor-in-Chief
Features sales, marketing and operations articles, news and new products, personnel advice, cigar reviews, updates on the National Association of Tobacco Outlets and profiles of leading retailers.
Cost: $29.00
Frequency: Bi-Monthly
Circulation: 15000
Founded in 1998

23507 Tobacco Science
2016 Fanning Bridge Road
Fletcher, NC 28732
828-684-3562; Fax: 828-684-8715
pam_puryear@ncsu.edu
Dr David Shew, Editor
Pam Puryear, Managing Editor
Scientific journal containing technical reports on tobacco and tobacco smoke.

23508 Tobacconist
SpecComm International
3101 Poplarwood Court
Suite 115
Raleigh, NC 27604-1029
919-872-5040; Fax: 919-876-6531
mjackson@speccomm.com
www.tobacconistmagazine.com
Dayton Matlick, Publisher
Ed O'Connor, Advertising/Sales Manager
Dayton Matlick, Editor
Dayton Matlick, CEO
A business publication for retail tobacconists in the United States that includes information ranging from critical issues to new products and business advice.
Cost: $28.00
Frequency: Quarterly

Trade Shows

23509 AWMA Expo
American Wholesale Marketers Association
1128 16th Street NW
Washington, DC 20036-4808
202-463-2124
800-642-2962; Fax: 202-467-0559
robertp@awmanet.org
www.cdaweb.net
Robert Pignato, VP Marketing/Industry Affairs
Annual show of 4500 manufacturers and suppliers of confectionery, tobacco, snack foods, juice, novelties and related products.

23510 Retail Tobacco Dealers of America Trade Show
4 Bradley Park Court
Suite 2H
Columbus, GA 31904-3637
706-494-1143; Fax: 706-494-1893
rtda@msn.com
www.rtda.org
Ira Fader Jr, Show Manager
Trade show for premium tobacco products. Not open to the public. For the benefit of association members only. Containing 950 booths and 6,400 exhibits.
5,500 Attendees
Frequency: July

Directories & Databases

23511 Tobacco Barometer: Cigarettes and Cigars/ Smoking, Chewing and Snuff
Tobacco Merchants Association of the United States
Po Box 8019
Princeton, NJ 08543-8019
609-275-4900; Fax: 609-275-8379
www.tma.org
Farrell Delman, President
These two databases offers information on every aspect of the tobacco industry.
Frequency: Full-text

23512 Tobacco Reporter's Global Tobacco Industry Guide
SpecComm International
3000 Highwoods Boulevard
Suite 300
Raleigh, NC 27604-1029
919-878-0540; Fax: 919-876-8531
sales@tobaccoreporter.com
www.tobaccoreporter.com
Noel Morris, Publisher
Taco Tuinstra, Managing Editor
Directory of tobacco suppliers, leaf dealers, processors, manufacturers, brokers, marketing boards and associations.
Cost: $78.00
Frequency: Annual

Industry Web Sites

23513 http://gold.greyhouse.com
G.O.L.D Grey House OnLine Databases
Grey House Publishing's online database platform, GOLD, offers Quick Search, Keyword Search and Expert Search for most business sectors including tobacco markets. The GOLD platform makes finding the information you need quick and easy - whether you're a novice searcher or an experienced database user. All of Grey House's directory products are available for subscription on the GOLD platform.

23514 www.buycheapcigarettes.com
We offer discount cigarettes and tobacco products. Cigarettes and tobacco products are for consumer use only. Minimum order is 3 Cartons.

23515 www.greyhouse.com
Grey House Publishing
Authoritative reference directories for most business sectors including tobacco markets. Users can search the online databases with varied search criteria allowing for custom searches by product category, geographic area, sales volume, keyword, subject and more. Full Grey House catalog and online ordering also available.

23516 www.paylesscigarettes.com
Sells dicount cigarettes and tobacco products.

23517 www.taxfreetobacco.com
Sells dicount cigarettess.

23518 www.thetobaccoshop.com
Offers discount cigarettes and tobacco products.

23519 www.tobaccoassociatesinc.org
Website of the association representing US flue-cured tobacco producers.

23520 www.ustobaccofarmer.com
Information of interest to tobacco farmers.

Associations

23521 ABF Freight Systems
3801 Old Greenwood Road
PO Box 10048
Fort Smith, AR 72917-0048
479-785-8700
800-610-5544; Fax: 479-785-8701
customercare@abf.com
www.abfs.com
Facebook, Twitter, LinkedIn, Google+
Robert A Davidson, CEO
Shannon Lively, Vive President of Transportation
Concentrates on national and regional transportation of general commodities freight, involving primarily LTL shipments. Mission is to provide reliable transportation services in a responsible manner to meet customers' unique needs.

23522 AIT Worldwide Logistics
701 N Rohlwing Rd
Itasca, IL 60143-1348
815-229-7700
800-669-4248; Fax: 630-766-0205
info@aitworldwide.com
www.aitworldwide.com
Facebook, Twitter, LinkedIn, You Tube
Vaughn Moore, President & CEO
Keith Tholan, Executive VP, Sales
Joe Kayser, Executive VP, Finance
Ray Fennelly, Executive VP, Global Development
Chris Jostes, Ocean Transport Coordinator
AIT Worldwide Logistics provides customers with inovative high-tech support and customization that enhances every shipment by tailoring the technology to the systems of each individual customer. AIT distinguishes itself by offering customers a variety of value-added services to enhance supply chain efficiencies: custom-built IT solutions, flexible worldwide service offerings by ground, air, ocean and rail, an extensive global network, competitive price structure, and superior customer service.

23523 APL Logistics
16220 N Scottsdale Rd
Suite 400
Scottsdale, AZ 85254-1720
602-586-4800
800-666-2723; Fax: 602-586-4585
www.apllogistics.com/wps/portal/apll
Beat Simon, President
Kurt Breinlinger, Chief Commercial Officer
Danny Goh, Chief Operations Officer
David Frentzel, VP, Contract Logistics
David Howland, VP, Land Transport Services
APL provides customers around the world with container transportation services through a network combining high-quality intermodal operations with state-of-the-art information technology.

23524 Advanced Transit Association
9019 Hamilton Drive
Fairfax, VA 22031-3075
703-591-8328
www.advancedtransit.org
Tom Richert, Chairman
Catherine G Burke, President
Bob Dunning, VP
Jerry Kieffer, Manager
Supports the transportation association.
100 Members

23525 Air Courier Conference of America
Express Delivery & Logistics Association
400 Admiral Blvd
Kansas City, MO 64106
703-998-7121
816-221-0254; Fax: 703-998-7123
www.expressassociation.org
LinkedIn
George Trapp, President
Jim Conway, Executive Director
Ken Bowman, Dir of Strategic Initiatives
Jennifer Crane, Associate Director
Air courier and air package delivery companies.

23526 Air Line Pilots Association, International
1625 Massachusetts Ave NW
Washington, DC 20036
703-689-2270
www.alpa.org
Facebook, Twitter, YouTube
Joe DePete, President
Bob Fox, First Vice President
Bill Couette, Vice President-Administration
Joseph Genovese, Jr., Vice President-Finance
Russell Sklenka, Executive Administrator
International association for airline pilots
Founded in 1931

23527 Air Transport Research Societyÿ
3433 Van Munching Hall
University of Maryland
College Park, MD 20742
301-405-2204; Fax: 301-314-1023
atrs@rhsmith.umd.edu
www.atrsworld.org
Tae H. Oum, Founder, Chair
Martin Dresner, President, CEO
Anming Zhang, VP, Research
Sveinnÿ Gudmundsson, VP, External
Christian Hofer, VP, Programs
A Society for researchers in the field of air transportation
Founded in 1995

23528 Aircraft Owners and Pilots Association (AOPA)
421 Aviation Way
Frederick, MD 21701
301-695-2000
800-872-2672; Fax: 301-695-2375
www.aopa.org
Facebook, Twitter, LinkedIn, Pinterest, Google+
Mark Baker, President & CEO
Jiri Marousek, SVP, Marketing
Erica Saccoia, SVP, Finance
For pilots and aircraft owners
Founded in 1939

23529 Airlines for America
1275 Pennsylvania Ave NW
Suite 1300
Washington, DC 20004
202-626-4000
mediarelations@airlines.org
airlines.org
Facebook, Twitter, LinkedIn, YouTube
Nicholas E Calio, President & CEO
Paul R Archambeault, SVP, CFO & COO
David A Berg, SVP, General Counsel & Secretary
Christine M Burgeson, SVP, Global Govt. Affairs
Todd Burke, SVP, Communications
Airlines for America advocates for a safe, secure and healthy U.S. airline industry.
Founded in 1936

23530 America's Independent Truckers' Association
P.O. Box 1250
Clinton, MS 39060
601-924-9606
844-464-2482
www.aitaonline.com
Facebook, Twitter
Larry Daniel, Founder
Created to serve independent owner operators and small to medium sized fleet owners.
Founded in 1997

23531 American Association of Airport Executives
601 Madison Street
Suite 400
Alexandria, VA 22314
703-824-0504; Fax: 703-820-1395
member.services@aaae.org
www.aaae.org
Facebook, Twitter, LinkedIn, RSS, Pinterest, YouTube
Jeffrey A. Mulder, Chair
Carl D. Newman, 1st Vice Chair
Scott A. Brockman, 2nd Vice Chair
Janne M. Olivier, Secretary/Treasurer
Brad Van Dam, Senior VP, Federal Affairs
The professional association that represents airport management personnel at public-use commercialand general aviation airports in the US
Founded in 1928

23532 American Association of Motor Vehicle Administrators
4401 Wilson Boulevard
Suite 700
Alexandria, VA 22203
703-522-4200
www.aamva.org
Facebook, Twitter, LinkedIn, Flickr, YouTube
Anne Ferro, President & CEOÿ
Whitney Brewster, Executive Directorÿ
Terri L. Coombesÿ, Deputy Chief of Staff
Stephen Campbell, Commissioner
Heidi Francis, Assistant Deputy Ministerÿ
Non-governmental, voluntary organization who strives to develop model programs in motor vehicle administration
Founded in 1933

23533 American Association of Port Authorities
1010 Duke Street
Alexandria, VA 22314-3589
703-684-5700; Fax: 703-684-6321
info@aapa-ports.org
www.aapa-ports.org
Facebook, Twitter, LinkedIn
Kristin Decas, Chairman
Kurt J. Nagle, President & CEO
Jean C. Godwin, Executive Vice President
Colleen O'sullivan, Finance & Human Resources
Maria Estevez, Administrative Assistant
Trade association founded in 1912 that represents over 130 port authorities in the western hemisphere
Founded in 1912

23534 American Association of Railroad Superintendents
425 Third Street SW
Washington, DC 20024
202-639-2100; Fax: 630-762-0755
media@aar.org

www.aar.org
Facebook, Twitter, LinkedIn, Youtube

Edward R. Hamberger, President
John Gray, SVP, Policy and Economics
Ian Jefferies, SVP, Government Affairs
Jeffrey Marsh, SVP, Finance and Administration
Patricia M. Reilly, SVP, Communications

Operating department officers of railroads.
500 Members
Founded in 1881

23535 **American Association of State Highway & Transportation**
444 N Capitol St NW
Suite 249
Washington, DC 20001-1539

202-624-5800; Fax: 202-624-5806
info@aashto.org
Facebook, Twitter, LinkedIn, You Tube

Bud Wright, Executive Director
Jenet Adem, Director, Finance & Administration
Clarisse Bernardes Coble, Human Resources Manager
Tony Bianchi, Associate Project Director
Belinda Bates, Senior Graphic Designer

Representing highway and transportation departments in the 50 states, the District of Columbia, and Puerto Rico. It represents all five transportation modes: air, highways, public transportation, rail ,and water. Its primary goal is to foster the development, operation, and maintenance of an integrated national transportation system.
Founded in 1981

23536 **American Association of State Highway and Transportation Officials**
444 North Capitol Street N.W.
Suite 249
Washington, DC 20001

202-624-5800; Fax: 202-624-5806
info@aashto.org
Facebook, Twitter, LinkedIn, YouTube

Bud Wright, Executive Director
Jenet Adem, Director of Financeÿ
Tony Bianchi, Associate Project Director
John Boyd, Senior Communications Editor
Lloyd Brown, Director of Communications

A standards-setting body which publishes specifications, test protocols anf guidelines used in highway design and construction across the United States

23537 **American Automobile Association**
1000 AAA Drive
Heathrow, FL 32746-5062

407-444-7966; Fax: 800-222-4357
www.aaa.com

23538 **American Bus Association**
111 K Street NE
9th Floor
Washington, DC 20002

202-842-1645
800-283-2877; Fax: 202-842-0850
abainfo@buses.org
www.buses.org
Facebook, Twitter, LinkedIn

Peter J Pantuso, President & CEO
Brandon Buchanan, Director, Operations
Clyde J Hart Jr., Senior VP, Govt. Affairs & Policy
Norm Litter, VP, Regulatory & Industry Affairs
Eric Braendel, CFO

ABA supports 3,800 members consisting of motorcoach and tour companies in addition to organizations that represent the tourism and travel industry. ABA strives to educate consumers on the importance of highway and motorcoach safety.
Founded in 1926

23539 **American Commodity and Shipping**
2102-D Gallows Rd.
Vienna, VA 22182

703-848-9422; Fax: 703-848-9424
info@americancommodity.com
www.americancommodity.com
Facebook, Twitter, LinkedIn

23540 **American Concrete Pavement Association**
9450 W Bryn Mawr Ave.
Suite 150
Rosemont, IL 60018

847-966-2272
acpa@acpa.org
www.pavement.com
Facebook, Twitter, LinkedIn, YouTube

Mike Lipps, Chairman
Steve Jackson, Vice Chairman
Lori Tiefenthaler, 2nd Vice Chair
Jerry Voigt, President, CEO
Glenn Eder, Treasurer

Trade association that exclusively represents the interests of those involved with the design, construction and preservation of concrete pavements.
Founded in 1963

23541 **American Council of Highway Advertisers**
1629 K St. NW
Washington, DC 20006

202-452-9044

A national organization representing highway users and traveler-oriented companies utilizing Out-of-Home advertising.

23542 **American Moving and Storage Association**
1611 Duke St
Alexandria, VA 22314-3406

703-683-7410; Fax: 703-683-7527
www.moving.org
Facebook, Twitter, LinkedIn, Pinterest

Linda Bauer Darr, CEO
Sandy Lynch, SVP

Represents members including interstate moving and storage companies, local movers, international movers plus industry suppliers and state association members. AMSA's chief goals include strong support for effective government regulations and policies that protect consumers while allowing members to provide quality service at compensatory prices, and ensuring that consumers understand the value of professional moving and storage services.
3200 Members
Founded in 1936

23543 **American Public Transportation Association**
1300 I Street NW
Suite 1200 East
Washington, DC 20005

202-496-4800; Fax: 202-496-4324
meetings2@apta.com
www.apta.com
Facebook, Twitter, LinkedIn, Youtube, Flickr, Blog

Michael P Melaniphy, President & CEO
Petra Mollet, Chief Of Staff
Pamela L Boswell, VP, Workforce Development
Mary Childress, CFO
Art Guzzetti, VP, Policy

APTA is an international organization that supports and represents the transportation industry. Membership benefits include an annual association meeting, an international expo, membership directory, access to online publications, newsletters and electronic news service.
Founded in 1882

23544 **American Railway Development Association**
500 New Jersey Avenue, NW
Suite 400
Washington, DC 20001

202-715-1259; Fax: 952-828-9751
info@amraildev.com
www.amraildev.com/
Facebook, Twitter, LinkedIn

Stephanie Johnson, President
Alan Sisk, First VP
Gary Rozmus, Second VP
Mark Holder, Secretary/Treasurer

Members are marketing, real estate and industrial development officers of railroads. Objectives are to foster the industrial, real estate, natural resources and market development activities of North American railroads and through the advancement of ideas and education of its members, further promote the effectiveness of railway development and related work.
200 Members
Founded in 1906

23545 **American Railway Engineering and Maintenance-of-Way Association**
4501 Forbes Blvd
Suite 130
Lanham, MD 20706-4362

301-459-3200; Fax: 301-459-8077
bcaruso@arema.org
www.arema.org
Facebook, LinkedIn

Beth Caruso, Executive Director & CEO
Vickie Fisher, Director, Finance
Stacy Spaulding, Executive & Board Operations
Janice Clements, Director, Membership
Christy Thomas, Events Manager

Fosters concern for design, construction and maintenance of bridges, buildings, water service facilities and other railway structures.
5400 Members
Founded in 1891

23546 **American Road and Transportation Builders**
1219 28th St NW
Washington, DC 20007-3389

202-289-4434; Fax: 202-289-4435
general@artba.org
www.artba.org

David S. Zachry, Chairman
Bob Alger, Senior Vice Chair
Matt Cummings, First Vice Chair
Tom Hill, Treasurer
Pete Ruane, Secretary

Offers information and resources for members associated with the transporation building industry.
Founded in 1902

23547 **American Short Line & Regional Railroad Association**
50 F Street, N.W.
Suite 7020
Washington, DC 20001

202-628-4500; Fax: 202-628-6430
lbdarr@aslrra.org
www.aslrra.org

Linda Bauer Darr, President & Treasurer
Keith T. Borman, VP, General Counsel
Kathleen M. Cassidy, VP, Member Services
Jo E. Strang, VP, Regulatory Affairs
Jenny M. Bourque, Director

An association of North American short line and regional railroads

23548 **American Short Line Railroad Association**
50 F Street NW
Suite 7020
Washington, DC 20001-1536

202-628-4500; Fax: 202-628-6430
aslrra@aslrra.org
www.aslrra.org

Linda Bauer Darr, President & Treasurer
Keith T Borman, VP, General Counsel
Jenny M Bourque, Director, Marketing
Kathleen M Cassidy, VP, Meetings & Member Services
Jenny M. Bourque, Director

Monitors and reports legislative and regulatory activities.
750 Members
Founded in 1913

23549 **American Society of Transportation & Logistics**
8430 W Bryn Mawr Ave
Suite 1000
Chicago, IL 60631

773-867-1777; Fax: 773-639-3000
www.astl.org
Facebook, Twitter, LinkedIn

George Yarusavage, CTL C.P.M., Chairman
William J. Ferreira, Vice Chairman
Laurie Denham, PLS, President
Mike A. Regan, DLP, Treasurer
Evelyn Thomchick, CTL, Secretary

Professional organization for transportation and logistics professionals.
Founded in 1946

23550 **American Space Transportation Association**
General Dynamics
1801 Alexander Bell Drive
Reston, VA 20191-4400

703-548-2723
800-548-2723; Fax: 703-295-6222
www.asce.org
Facebook, Twitter, LinkedIn, YouTube, Google+

Patrick J Natale, Executive Director
Pete Shavalay, CFO
Thomas Smith, Deputy Executive Director

The successor organization to the Ad Hoc Industry Group promoting the development of commercial space transportation in the United States.
25 Members
Founded in 1852

23551 **American Towman Network**
7 West Street
Warwick, NY 10990

201-722-3000
800-732-3869; Fax: 201-722-3010
towcrazy@wrecker.com
www.towman.com
Facebook, RSS

Jim Sorrenti, Editor
Steven Calitri, Editor in Chief
Henry Calitri, Exhibit Sales

23552 **American Traffic Safety Services Association**
15 Riverside Parkway
Suite 100
Fredericksburg, VA 22406-1022

540-368-1701
800-272-8772; Fax: 540-368-1717
www.atssa.com
Facebook, Twitter, YouTube

Scott Seeley, Chairman
Debra Ricker, Chairman Elect
Kathleen Holst, Past President
Henry Ross, Past President
Peter Speer, Past President

An international trade association with the core purpose to advance roadway safety.
Founded in 1969

23553 **American Truck Historical Society**
10380 N Ambassador Dr.
Suite 101, P.O. Box 901611
Kansas City, MO 64153

816-891-9900; Fax: 816-891-9903
www.aths.org
Facebook, Twitter, YouTube

Don Bretthauer, Executive Director
Shelley Ruhlman, Managing Director
Melinda Hunsberger, Director of Finance
Courtney Dery, Library Director
Jan Martin, Support Systems Specialist

Collects and preserves the history of antique trucks and the industry.
Founded in 1971

23554 **American Trucking Association**
950 North Glebe Road
Suite 210
Arlington, VA 22203-4181

703-838-1700
866-821-3468; Fax: 703-838-8884
atamembership@trucking.org
www.trucking.org
Twitter

Pat Thomas, Chairman
Bill Graves, President & CEO
Kevin W. Burch, ATA First Vice Chairman
David Manning, ATA Second Vice Chairman
John M Smith, Secretary

Largest national trade association for the trucking industry.
Founded in 1933

23555 **American Underground Space Association**
12999 E. Adam Aircraft Circle
Englewood, CO 80112

303-948-4200
800-763-3132; Fax: 303-973-3845
cs@smenet.org
www.auca.org
Facebook, Twitter, LinkedIn

William W Edgerton, Chair
Arthur D Silber, Vice Chairman
700 Members
Founded in 1976

23556 **American Waterways Operators**
801 N Quincy St
Suite 200
Arlington, VA 22203-1708

703-841-9300; Fax: 703-841-0389
www.americanwaterways.com
Facebook, Twitter, LinkedIn

Buckley McAllister, Chairman
Frank Morton, Vice Chairman
George Foster, Treasurer
Thomas A. Allegretti, President & CEO
Mary J. Anastacio, Manager - Finance

Members include domestic carriers transporting commodities by water, shipyards, terminals and affiliated, business.
375 Members

23557 **Association for Commuter Transportation**
1330 Braddock Place
Suite 350
Alexandria, VA 22314-6405

571-699-3064
888-719-5772
info@actweb.org
www.actweb.org
Facebook, Twitter

Caryn Souza, Director
Marlon Powell, Adminstrative Assistant
Kevin Oliff, Marketing & Outreach Specialist
Jason Pavluchuk, Govt. Relations Specialist

ACT provides you with the resources of an international organization and the support of a regional affiliate of experienced Transportation Demand Management professionals.
810 Members
Founded in 1991

23558 **Association for Women in Aviation Maintenance**
2330 Kenlee Drive
Cincinnati, OH 45230

386-416-0248; Fax: 386-236-0517
www.awam.org
Facebook, LinkedIn

Lynette Ashland, President
Jane Shelton, Vice President
Teressa Stark, Treasurer
Laura Gordon, Secretary
Anna Romer, Director | Scholarship Co-Chair

An organization formed for the purpose of championing women's professional growth and enrichment in the aviation maintenance fields.

23559 **Association of Air Medical Services**
909 N. Washington Street
Suite 410
Alexandria, VA 22314-3143

703-836-8732; Fax: 703-836-8920
information@aams.org
www.aams.org

Cameron Curtis, President & CEO
Garet Turner, VP, Member Experience
Christopher Eastlee, VP, Public Affairs
Christina Childs, Director, Special Events
Diana Lundie, Tradeshow Manager

Voluntary nonprofit organization, encourages and supports its members in maintaining a standard of performance reflecting safe operations and efficient, high quality patient care. Built on the idea that representation from a variety of medical transport services and businesses can be brought together to share information, collectively resolve problems and provide leadership in the medical transport community.

23560 **Association of American Railroads**
425 Third Street SW
Suite 114
Washington, DC 20024-3217

202-639-2100
media@aar.org
www.aar.org
Facebook, Twitter, LinkedIn, YouTube

Edward R. Hamberger, President & CEO
Patricia M. Reilly, SVP, Communications
Jeffrey Marsh, SVP, Finance & Administration
Ian Jefferies, SVP, Government Affairs
John Gray, svp, Policy and Economics

Presently serves a joint agency of its individual railroad members to ensure an efficient nationwide rail system.
Founded in 1934

23561 Association of Metropolitan Planning Organizations
444 North Capitol Street, NW
Suite 345
Washington, DC 20000

202-624-3680; Fax: 202-624-3685
www.ampo.org

Richard Perrin, President
Elaine Clegg, Vice President
R. Todd Ashby, Executive Director
Rich Denbow, Director of Technical Programs
Levon Boyagian, Policy Consultant

A nonprofit organization serving metropolitan planning organizations.
Founded in 1994

23562 Association of Railway Museums
PO Box 370
Tujunga, CA 91043-0370

818-951-9151; Fax: 818-951-9151
www.hotels-in-utah.com/railwaymuseumsorg

Ellen Fishburn, Secretary
Paul Hamond, President

The association of railway museums is for the preservation of railway equipment, artifacts and history.
125 Members
Founded in 1961

23563 Automotive Parts Remanufacturers Association
7250 Heritage Villa Plaza
Suite 201
Gainesville, VA 20155

703-968-2772; Fax: 703-753-2445
info@apra.org
www.apra.org
Facebook, Twitter, LinkedIn, YouTube

Omar Cueto, Chairman
Jay Robie, Vice President
Joe Kripli, President

Association for remanufacturers of automotive parts.
Founded in 1941

23564 BAX Global
440 Exchange
Irvine, CA 92602

602-458-6200
800-225-5229
Twitter

Joseph L Carnes, President
Jay Arnold, VP Human Resources

Specializes in managing the movement of heavy-weight packages and cargo of all shapes and sizes.

23565 Boat Owners Association of the United States
880 South Pickett Street
Alexandria, VA 22304-4606

703-461-2878
membership@boatus.com
www.boatus.com
Facebook, Twitter, YouTube, Google+

Richard Schwartz, Chairman, Founder
Margaret Podlich, President
Adam Wheeler, VP and Director of Towing
Heather Lougheed, VP, Membership
John Condon, AVP, Towing Operations

Association of boat owners offering various services, supporting recreational boat and trailer towing activities.
Founded in 1966

23566 Brotherhood of Locomotive Engineers and Trainmen
Standard Building
1370 Ontario St.
Mezzanine, OH 44113-1702

216-241-2630; Fax: 216-241-6516
PresStaff@ble-t.org
www.ble-t.org

Dennis R. Pierce, National President
E. Lee Pruitt, First Vice President
Marcus J. Ruef, VP, Director of Arbitration
Gil L. Gore, Michael D., Vice President

A trade organization for railroad workers.

23567 Brotherhood of Maintenance of Way Employee s
41475 Gardenbrook Road
Novi, MI 48375-1328

248-662-2660; Fax: 248-662-2659
www.bmwe.org

Freddie N. Simpson, National Division President
Perry Geller, National Div. Secretary-Treasurer
David R. Scoville, Vice President- Western Region
Roger Sanchez, Vice President- South Region
David D. Joynt, Vice President at Large

A national union representing the workers who build and maintain the tracks, bridges, building and other structures of the railroads.

23568 Brotherhood of Railroad Signalmen
917 Shenandoah Shores Rd
Front Royal, VA 22630-6418

540-622-6522; Fax: 540-622-6532
kelly@brs.org
www.brs.org
Facebook, Twitter, RSS

W Dan Pickett, President
Walter A Barrows, Treasurer
Floyd Mason, VP
Mike S. Baldwin, Research

National organization representing the men and women who install and maintain signal systems for most of the nation's railroads.
ISSN: 0037-5020
Founded in 1901

23569 Carrier Information Exchange
4601 N Fairfax Drive
Suite 1160
Arlington, VA 22203

703-841-6374; Fax: 703-841-6370
mcinfosupport@egov.com
www.mcinfo.org

23570 Center for Transportation and the Environment (CTE)
730 Peachtree Street
Suite 760
Atlanta, GA 30308

678-244-4150; Fax: 678-244-4151
www.cte.tv

Eric Sonnichsen, Chairman
Joe Beno, Treasurer
John Sleconich, Secretary
James B. Martin, M.C.E., P.E., Associate Director
Eugene Murray, B.A., Distance Learning Specialist

A nonprofit organization to improve the efficiency and sustainability of the energy ad transportation systems.
Founded in 1991

23571 Commercial Vehicle Safety Alliance
6303 Ivy Lane
Suite 310
Greenbelt, MD 20770-631

301-830-6144
cvsahq@cvsa.org
www.cvsa.org
Facebook, Twitter, LinkedIn, YouTube

A nonprofit organization dedicated to improving the safety of commercial vehicles.

23572 Committee for Better Transit
38 W Cliff Street
Somerville, NJ 08876

brooklynbus@hotmail.com

The Committee for Better Transit is a forty-one year old New York Metropolitan independent transit advocacy organization comprised of transit experts and users, which seeks cost effective user-friendly solutions to transit challenges.

23573 Council of Fleet Specialists
315 Delaware Street
Kansas City, MO 64105-1256

816-421-2600; Fax: 816-421-0515

UJ Reese, Executive VP

Members are distributors of parts and services for heavy-duty trucks.
210 Members
Founded in 1967

23574 Driver Employee Council of America
1001 G St Nw
Suite 500-W
Washington, DC 20001-4564

202-434-4100; Fax: 202-842-0011
info@khlaw.com
www.khlaw.com
LinkedIn, RSS

Jerome H Heckman, Partner

Members are companies leasing truck drivers to private carriers.
43 Members
Founded in 1992

23575 Energy Traffic Association
935 Eldridge Road
Suite 604
Sugar Land, TX 77478

832-474-3564

Ralph Lopez, President
Renee Ahmed, VP & Secretary
Russell Powell, Executive Director

Formed by the merger of the Oilfield Supply Traffic Association and the Shippers Oil Field Traffic Association, ETA serves the oil and gas industry in transportation, distribution and logistics. Members are energy industry transportation, distribution, purchasing and logistics managers, and transportation and logistics providers.
Founded in 1997

23576 Expediting Management Association
Livingston, TN

931-823-1122; Fax: 403-201-6402
www.expedite.org

Katherine Rench, C.E.M, President
Glenda Warman, VP
Linda Strauss, Secretary
David Kern, Treasurer
Patricia Murphy, Executive Administrator

The Expediting Management Association, Inc. will maintain a certification program for it's memebers giving them the opportunity to achieve recognition from their peers in the association and industry.
200 Members
Founded in 1972

23577 **Express Carriers Association**
9532 Liberia Ave.
Suite 752
Manassas, VA 20110

703-361-1058; Fax: 703-361-5274
eca@expresscarriers.com
www.expresscarriers.com

Paul Steffes, President
Jim Luciani, 1st VP
Mike Coyle, Second VP
Jim King, Treasurer
Jim Bernecker, Secretary

The mission of the ECA is to develop business between carriers, shippers and vendors of products and services to the transportation industry.

23578 **Fleet Management Institute (NAFA)**
125 Village Boulevard
Suite 200
Princeton, NJ 08540

609-720-0882; Fax: 609-452-8004
info@nafa.org
www.nafa.org
Facebook, Twitter, LinkedIn, YouTube

Patricia Murtaugh, Assistant Executive Director
Joanne Marsh, Manager

23579 **Flight Safety Foundation**
801 N. Fairfax Street
Suite 400
Alexandria, VA 22314-1774

703-739-6700; Fax: 703-739-6708
wahdan@flightsafety.org
flightsafety.org
Facebook, Twitter, LinkedIn

Ken Hylander, Chair
David McMillan, Past Chair
Jon Beatty, President and CEO
David Barger, Treasurer
Kenneth P. Quinn, General Counsel and Secretary

Independent, nonprofit international organization engaged in research, auditing, education, advocacy and publishing to imporove flight safety.
Founded in 1947

23580 **Gemini Shippers Group**
137 West 25th Street
3rd Floor
New York, NY 10001

212-947-3424; Fax: 212-629-0361
info@geminishippers.com
www.geminishippers.com
Facebook, Twitter, LinkedIn, Google+

Sara L. Mayes, CEO and President
Kenneth O'Brien, Chief Operating Officer
Nicole Uchrin, Managing Director
Rich Moore, Sales Director
Arlene L. Blocker, Membership Director

Shippers association with global contracts for all commodities.
200 Members
Founded in 1916

23581 **Heavy Duty Representatives Association**
160 Symphony Way
Elgin, IL 847-760-00

330-725-7160
800-763-5717; Fax: 330-725-7160
trucksvc@aol.com
www.hdra.org

Larry Rossenthal, President
Walt Sirman, Vice President
John Stojak, Secretary

Independent sales agencies which sell heavy-duty components to the trucking and aftermarket industries.

23582 **High Speed Grand Transportation**
1010 Massachusetts Avenue NW
Washington, DC 20001

202-789-8107
www.hsgt.org

23583 **Highway Users Federation for Safety and**
PO Box 6285
Olympia, WA 98507-1904

253-376-8492
www.acronymfinder.com
Facebook

Diane Steed, President

The Highway Users Federation (WHUF) is an association concerned ith increasing capacity and safer on Highways.

23584 **IEEE Intelligent Transportation Systems Society**
Institute Of Electrical and Electronics Engineers
445 Hoes Lane
Piscataway, NJ 08854

Home Page: www.ieee-itss.org
Facebook, Twitter, LinkedIn

Wei-Bin Zhang, President
Lingxi Li, VP, Administrative Activities
Nobuyuki Ozaki, VP, Standards
Javier Sanchez Medina, VP, Technical Activities

ITSS seeks to advance electrical engineering & information technology as applied to intelligent transportation systems.

23585 **IEEE Society on Social Implications of Technology**
Institute of Electrical and Electronics Engineers
445 Hoes Lane
Piscataway, NJ 08854

r.dent@ieee.org
technologyandsociety.org
Facebook, Twitter, LinkedIn

Robert Dent, President
Lew Terman, Secretary
Howard Wolfman, Treasurer

The SSIT focuses on the following areas: Sustainable Development & Humanitarian Technology; Ethics, Human Values and Technology; Technology Benefits for All; Future Societal Impact of Technology Advances; and Protecting the Planet & Sustainable Technology

23586 **IEEE Vehicular Technology Society**
3 Parl Avenue
17th Floor
New York, NY 10016-5997

212-419-7900
oliver.holland@ieee.org
vtsociety.org
Facebook, Twitter, LinkedIn

Oliver Holland, Chapter Coordinator & Developer

VTS focuses on the theory and practice of electrical engineering with regards to land transportation, railroad and mass transit, mobile communications, vehicular electrotechnology equipment and systems, and land, airborne and maritime mobile Services.

23587 **Institute of Transportation Engineers**
1627 Eye St NW
Suite 600
Washington, DC 20006

202-785-0060; Fax: 202-785-0609
ite_staff@ite.org
www.ite.org
Facebook, Twitter, LinkedIn, YouTube, Google+, Pinterest

Zaki Mustafa, President
W Hibbett Neel Jr., VP
16000 Members
Founded in 1930

23588 **Insurance Institute for Highway Safety**
988 Dairy Road
Ruckersville, VA 22968

434-985-4600; Fax: 434-985-2202
rrader@iihs.org
www.iihs.org
Twitter, RSS, YouTube

Adrian Lund, President
Russ Rader, SVP, Communications
Shelley Shelton, Sr. Legal Associate
Brenda O'Donnell, VP, Insurer Relations
Chamelle Matthew, Sr. Communications Specialist

Independent, nonprofit research and communications organization dedicated to reducing highway crash death, injuries and property damage losses.
Founded in 1959

23589 **Intelligent Transportation Society of America (ITS America)**
1100 New Jersey Ave. SE
Suite 850
Washington, DC 20003

202-484-4847
800-374-8472
membership@itsa.org
www.itsa.org
Twitter, Instagram

Shailen Bhatt, President & CEO
Laura Chace, Chief Operating Officer
Carlos Alban, VP, Technical Programs
Tim Drake, VP, Policy & Regulatory Affairs
Cathy St. Denis, VP, Communications & Strategy

Organization dedicated to advancing the research, development and design of surface transportation systems.
1200+ Members
Founded in 1991

23590 **Intermodal Association of North America**
11785 Beltsville Drive
Suite 1100
Calverton, MD 20705-4049

301-982-3400; Fax: 301-982-4815; Fax: 301-982-4815
iana@intermodal.org
www.intermodal.org
Facebook, Twitter, LinkedIn

Joanne F. Casey, President & CEO
Stephen A. Keppler, SVP, Member Services
Jon Palmbak, SVP, Digital Products & Technology

Promotes the benefits and growth of intermodal freight transportation.
1000+ Members
Founded in 1991

23591 **International Association of Structural Movers**
PO Box 2104
Neenah, WI 54956-2104

803-951-9304; Fax: 920-486-1519
info@iasm.org
www.iasm.org
Facebook, LinkedIn, YouTube, Google+

Jim Herman, President
Don Toothman, Jr., VP
Natalie Hammer, Secretaty/Treasurer

Members are movers of heavy structural products, trusses, houses, machinery and masonry structures.
385 Members
Founded in 1983

23592 International Brotherhood of Teamsters
25 Louisiana Ave Nw
Washington, DC 20001-2130

202-624-6800; Fax: 202-624-6918
www.teamster.org
Facebook, Twitter, Google+

James P Hoffa, President
Ken Hall, Secretary/Treasurer

Affiliated with the AFL-CIO.
1.3MM Members
Founded in 1954

23593 International Council of Cruise Lines
910 SE 17th Street
Suite 400
Fort Lauderdale, FL 33316

754-224-2200; Fax: 754-224-2250
info@cruising.org
www.cruising.org
Facebook, Twitter, LinkedIn, Pinterest

Cindy D'Aoust, CEO
Tom Fischetti, CFO
Bud Darr, SVP Tech & Regulatory Affairs
Lorri Christou, SVP Marketing & Communications
Mike McGarry, SVP, Public Affairs

Dedicated to the promotion and growth of the cruise industry.
Founded in 1975

23594 International Furniture Transportation and Logistics Council
PO Box 889
Gardner, MA 01440-0889

978-632-1913; Fax: 978-630-2917
jsears@iftlc.org
www.iftlc.org
Twitter

Raynard F Bohman Jr, Managing Director

Members are furniture manufacturers, retrilers, carriers, wholesalers and warehouses of allied products.
300 Members

23595 International Light Transportation Vehicle Association
5579-B Chamblee Dunwoody Road
Atlanta, GA 30338

fsomers@ILTVA.org
www.iltva.org

Caleb Chesser, President
Fred Somers, General Counsel & Secretary

Organization dedicated to ensuring best practices and safety standards for light vehicle transportation.
Founded in 1984

23596 International Marine Transit Association
34 Otis Hill Road
Hingham, MA 02043

781-749-0078; Fax: 781-749-0078
www.interferry.com
Twitter, RSS

Mike Grainger, Chairman
John Steen-Mikkelsen, President
Mike Corrigan, Treasurer
Len Roueche, Secretary

Membership includes ferry operators, naval architects, manufacturers, suppliers, and others in the ferry industry around the world.
400 Members
Founded in 1976

23597 International Parking Institute
1330 Braddock Place
Suite 350
Alexandria, VA 22314

571-699-3011; Fax: 703-566-2267
info@parking-mobility.org
www.parking-mobility.org
Facebook, Twitter, LinkedIn, YouTube, Pinterest, Instagram

Shawn D. Conrad, CAE, CEO
Rachel Yoka, CAPP, LEED AP, VP, Program Development
Bonnie Watts, CEM, VP, Sales

Organization that provides educational and technical services to parking professionals and to the public.
Founded in 1962

23598 International Road Federation
500 Montgomery Street
Fifth Floor
Alexandria, VA

703-535-1001; Fax: 703-535-1007
info@IRFnews.org
www.irfnet.org
Facebook, Twitter, LinkedIn, Flickr

A service organization for better road transportation systems.
Founded in 1948

23599 International Safe Transit Association
1400 Abbot Rd
Suite 160
East Lansing, MI 48823-1900

517-333-3437
888-367-4782; Fax: 517-333-3813
ista@ista.org
www.ista.org
Facebook, Twitter, LinkedIn

Edward A Church, President
A J Gruber, VP, Technical Services
Lisa Bonsignore, VP, Special Events
Larry Dull, VP, Sustainable Solutions
Kathy A Joneson, VP, Communications

Members are shippers, carriers, manufacturers, packagers, package designers and testing laboratories, included in transport packaging.
750 Members
Founded in 1948
Mailing list available for rent: 4000 names at $500 per M

23600 Interstate Trucking Association
Express Carriers Association
9532 Liberia Avenue
#752
Manassas, VA 20110

703-361-1058
866-322-7447; Fax: 703-361-5274
eca@expresscarriers.com
www.expresscarriers.com

Paul Steffes, President
Jim Luciani, First VP
Mike Coyle, Second VP
Jim King, Treasurer
Jim Bernecker, Secretary

Organization of newly enacted state legislation regulations having direct impact on vehicle operations, fuel taxes, registration size and weight.

23601 Lake Carriers Association
20325 Center Ridge Road
Suite 720
Rocky River, OH 44116-3508

440-333-4444; Fax: 440-333-9993
info@lcaships.com
www.lcaships.com
Twitter

James H I Weakley, President
Glen G Nekvasil, VP
Harold W Henderson, General Counsel
Thomas G. Rayburn, Director of Env.& Reg. Affairs
Katherine A. Gumeny, Secretary/Treasurer

Members are US- Flag Great Lakes vessel operators engaged in transporting iron ore, coal, grain, limestone, cement and petroleum products.
Founded in 1880

23602 Landstar Global Logistics
13410 Sutton Park Drive S
Jacksonville, FL 32224

904-398-9400
800-872-9400
corpcomm@landstar.com
www.landstar.com
Facebook, LinkedIn

Henry H Gerkens, Chairman, President & CEO
Jim B Gattoni, Executive VP, CFO
Joe Beacorn, VP & Chief Safety Operations Office
Larry S Thomas, VP/Chief Information Officer
Michael Kneller, VP, General Counsel & Secretary

Mission is to be the leading non-asset based provider of transportation capacity delivering safe, specialized transportation services to customers worldwide utilizing a network of agents, third-party capacity owners and employees.

23603 Light Truck Assessory Alliance
SEMA
1575 S.Valley Vista Drive
Diamond Bar, CA 91765-0910

909-396-0289
info@sema.org
www.sema.org
Facebook, Twitter, Google+

Nate Shelton, Chairman
Doug Evans, Chair-Elect
Christopher J Kersting, President & CEO
George Afremow, VP, CFO
Tom Myroniak, VP, Marketing & Market Research

A national organization with 150 manufacturers of truck caps and light truck accessories.

23604 Mid-West Truckers Association
2727 N Dirksen Pkwy
Springfield, IL 62702-1490

217-525-0310; Fax: 217-525-0342
info@mid-westtruckers.com
www.mid-westtruckers.com
Facebook, YouTube

Don Schaefer, Executive Vice President
Matt Wells, Associate Director
Jeanne Campo, Secretary/Treasurer
Candy Wendt, Drug & Alcohol Supervisor
Diana McMahan, Membership Coordinator

Serves the trucking industry by lobbying on their behalf, assisting with registration, license plate procurement and group insurance programs. Conducts educational programs, has own self-funded workers compensation insurance program. Trade association represents truck owners in 14 states.
3000 Members
Founded in 1962

23605 **Motor Transport Management Group**
PO Box 605
Rillito, AZ 85654
520-616-0175; Fax: 208-561-2980
Facebook

23606 **National Air Carrier Association**
1000 Wilson Boulevard
Suite 1700
Arlington, VA 22209-3928
703-358-8060; Fax: 703-358-8070
www.naca.cc
Oakley Brooks, President
Paul H Doell, Director, Govt. Affairs
George R Paul, Director Technical Services
Paul H Doell, Director Government Affairs
7 Members
Founded in 1962

23607 **National Air Traffic Controllers Association**
1325 Massachusetts Avenue N.W.
Washington, DC 20005
202-628-5451
800-266-0895; Fax: 202-628-5767
www.natca.org
Facebook, Twitter, LinkedIn, YouTube, Instagram
Dean Iacopelli, Chief Of Staff
Marguerite Graf, General Counsel
Lisa Head, Membership Services Coordinator
Preet Mohinder Singh Virk, Comptroller
Thom Metzger, Director, Public Affairs
Members are controllers in public and private sectors and Federal Aviation Administration engineers.

23608 **National Air Transportation Association**
818 Connecticut Avenue, NW
Suite 900
Washington, DC 22302-1507
202-774-1535
800-808-6282; Fax: 703-845-8176
www.nata.aero
Facebook, Twitter, LinkedIn, RSS
Timothy Obitts, President & CEO
Jason Miller, CFO & COO
Shannon Chambers, VP, Marketing & Communications
John McGraw, VP, Regulatory Affairs
Jonathon Freye, VP, Government & Public Affairs
Aggressively promotes safety and the success of aviation service businesses through its advocacy efforts before government, the media and the public as well as by providing valuable programs and forums to further its members' prosperity.
1800 Members
Founded in 1940

23609 **National Asphalt Pavement Association**
5100 Forbes Blvd
Lanham, MD 20708
301-731-4748
888-468-6499; Fax: 301-731-4621
www.asphaltpavement.org
Audrey Copeland, President & CEO
Melanie Richardson, VP, Finance & Operations
Lori Wolking, VP, Meetings & Education
Steve Shivak, Director, Membership
Kelly Kanaras, Director, Awards & Marketing
A trade association that exclusively represents the interests of the asphalt pavment matieral producer and paving contractor on the national level with Congress, government agenices and other national trade and business organizations.

23610 **National Association of Freight & Logistics**
P.O.Box 60944
Dubai
714-343-1112; Fax: 714-343-1105
www.nafl.ae
David Phillips, President
Kevin Ennis, VP
Nadia Abdul Aziz, Secretary General
Suman Chakrabarti, Treasurer
Previously the National Committee of Freight Forwarders, the NAFL brings together in one body all the major players in the freight fowarding, logistics, and shipping industries.
Founded in 1992

23611 **National Association of Rail Shippers**
77 K Street NE
8th Floor
Washington, DC 20002-4681
202-650-6500
800-432-2250; Fax: 972-644-8208
www.rollcall.com
Facebook, Twitter, LinkedIn, You Tube
Charlie Mitchell, VP
Laurie Battaglia, Publisher
Strives to provide a sound transporation system. Bestows annual Award of Excellence.
2M Members
Founded in 1937

23612 **National Association of Railroad Passengers**
505 Capitol Court NE
Suite 300
Washington, DC 20002-7706
202-408-8362; Fax: 202-408-8287
narp@narprail.org
www.narprail.org
Facebook, Twitter, Google+
Jim Mathews, President & CEO
Sean Jeans-Gail, VP
Robert J. Stewart, Chairman
Carol Haslett, Vice Chair
Stephen J. Salatti, Secretary
Seeks to increase public awareness of rail passenger service and its benefits. Works for a national transportation policy.
12M Members
Founded in 1967

23613 **National Association of Small Trucking Companies**
2054 Nashville Pike
Gallatin, TN 37066
615-451-4555
800-264-8580; Fax: 615-451-0041
david.owen@nastc.com
www.nastc.com
Twitter
David Owen, President
Buster Anderson, Executive Vice President
Dana Campbell, Vice President Of Operations
Hunter Owen, VP, Sales and Marketing
Angel Clark, Director of Safety & Compliance
Association for small trucking fleets and companies.
Founded in 1989

23614 **National Association of State Aviation Officials**
8400 Westpark Dr.
2nd Floor
McLean, VA 22102
703-454-0649
info@nasao.org
www.nasao.org
Facebook, Twitter, LinkedIn
Gary Cathey, Chairman
Brad Brandt, Vice Chairman
Ronnie Mitchell, Treasurer
Carol L. Comer, Immediate Past Chairman
Greg Principato, President/ CEO
Established to ensure uniformity of safety measures and to standardize airport regulations.
Founded in 1931

23615 **National Association of Truck Stop Operators**
1330 Braddock Place
#501
Alexandria, VA 22314-1483
703-549-2100
800-956-9160; Fax: 703-684-4525
editor@natso.com
www.natso.com
Facebook, Twitter, Youtube, RSS
Tom Heinz, Chairman
Thomas M O'Brien, Secretary/Treasurer
Lisa J Mullings, President & CEO
Taryn Brice-Rowland, Director of Member Engagement
Roger Cole, Editor, Biz Brief
NATSO is the professional association of America's $42 billion travel plaza and truckstop industry. NATSO represents the industry on legislative and regulatory matters; serves as the official source of information on the diverse travel plaza and truckstop industry; provides education to its members; conducts an annual convention and trade show; and supports efforts to generally improve the business climate in which its members operate.
1230+ Members
Founded in 1990

23616 **National Automobile Dealers Association**
8400 Westpark Dr
Mc Lean, VA 22102-3591
703-821-7000
800-252-6232; Fax: 703-821-7234
help@nada.org
www.nada.org
Facebook, Twitter, LinkedIn, Flickr, Youtube
Bill Fox, Chairman
Jeff Carlson, Vice Chairman
Peter Welch, President
Joe Cowden, EVP/COO/CFO
David Regan, EVP, Legislative Affairs
Manufacturers, suppliers and distributors of products and services designed to control dealership expenses, help merchandising or improve profitability.
19700 Members
Founded in 1917

23617 **National Business Aviation Association**
1200 G Street NW
Suite 1100
Washington, DC 20005ÿ
202-783-9000; Fax: 202-331-8364
info@nbaa.org
www.nbaa.org
Facebook, Twitter, LinkedIn
Edward Bolen, President & CEO
Dan Hubbard, SVP, Communications
Chris Strong, SVP, Conventions & Membership
Steve Brown, Chief Operating Officer
Marc Freeman, Chief Financial Officer
Promotes the aviation interests of organizations utilizing general aviation aircraft for business purposes.
Founded in 1947

23618 National Business Travel Association
123 North Pitt Street
Alexandria, VA 22314-3234
703-684-0836; Fax: 703-342-4324
info@nbta.org
www.gbta.org
Facebook, Twitter, LinkedIn, You Tube
Christle Johnson, President & CEO
Mark Ziegler, Vice President
Hema Shah, Chief Financial Officer
Hayford Mensah, CPA, Director, Finance
Getnesh Made, Manager, Finance
Offers over 1,300 corporate travel managers and allied members in the United States and Canada.
7000+ Members
Founded in 1968

23619 National Center for Bicycling and Walking
1612 K Street, NW
Suite 802
Washington, DC 20006
202-223-3621
info@bikewalk.org
www.bikewalk.org
Mark Plotz, Senior Associate / Program Manager
John Williams, CenterlinesÿEditor
Jim Johnston, Web/Systems Administrator
A resident program at the Project for Public Spaces, Inc.
Founded in 1977

23620 National Child Transport Association
Hall of States
444 N Capitol St Nw
Suite 438
Washington, DC 20001-1505
202-624-7710; Fax: 202-624-5899
www.ncsha.org
Facebook, Twitter
Barbara J Thompson, Executive Director
Cary D Knox, Executive Office Admin
Thomas R. Gleason, President
Grant S. Whitaker, Vice President
Ralph M. Perrey, Secretary/Treasurer
Thirty booths.
1.2M Members

23621 National Customs Brokers and Forwarders
1200 18th St Nw
Suite 901
Washington, DC 20036-2572
202-466-0222; Fax: 202-466-0226
www.ncbfaa.org
Facebook, Twitter, LinkedIn
Darrell Sekin, Jr., Chairman
Geoffrey Powell, President
Amy Magnus, VP
Scott E. Larson, Treasurer
William S. App, Jr., Secretary
Learn about new business leads, stay on top of Customs Service and other agency regulations that will impact your operations and provide invaluable professional development resources for your employees.
600+ Members
Founded in 1897

23622 National Defense Transportation Association (NDTA)
50 S Pickett Street
Suite 220
Alexandria, VA 22304
703-751-5011; Fax: 703-823-8761
info@ndtahq.com
www.ndtahq.com
Facebook, Twitter, LinkedIn
Mark H. Buzby RADM, USN (Ret.), President & COO
Jim Veditz COL, USA (Ret.), Senior VP Operations
Lee Matthews, VP, Marketing & Corp. Development
Patty Casidy, VP, Finance
Rebecca Jones, Executive Asst. To President
Intended as a liasion between government, military and private transportation officials.
7800 Members
Founded in 1944

23623 National Food Distributors Association
401 N. MIchigan Avenue
Suite 2200
Chicago, IL 60611-4267
312-644-6610; Fax: 212-482-6459
www.allfoodbusiness.com
An organization comprised of independent store-to-door service distributors and suppliers of specialty food items.
2100 Members
Founded in 1952

23624 National Industrial Transportation League
1700 N Moore St
Suite 1900
Arlington, VA 22209-1931
703-524-5011; Fax: 703-524-5017
info@nitl.org
www.nitl.org
Twitter
Bruce J Carlton, President & CEO
Ellie Gilanshah, VP, Finance, Admin & Membership
Doug J. Kratzberg, Chairman
Mary Pileggi, 1st Vice Chairman
Gary A. Palmer, 2nd Vice Chairman
Provides information to the industrial transportation industry, including computer services software and innovations for transportation operations.
600 Members
Founded in 1907

23625 National Institute of Certified Moving Consultants
1420 King Street
Alexandria, VA 22314-2794
703-683-7410
800-538-6672; Fax: 703-683-7527
cert@nicet.org
www.nicet.org
Facebook, LinkedIn
Michael A Clark, Chief Operating Executive
Ahmed Farouki, Senior Director, Technical Services
Regina L. Stevenson, Director, Administrative Services
Brian Gifford, Director, Quality Management
Paul L. Stockman, Manager, Certification Services
Awards the certified moving consultant designation to those who have passed an exam testing their liability.
Founded in 1961

23626 National Institute of Packaging and Handling Logistics Engineers
5903 Ridgeway Drive
Grand Prairie, TX 75052
817-466-7490
866-464-7453; Fax: 570-523-0606
admin@niphle.com
www.niphle.com
Facebook, Twitter, LinkedIn
Sean Kerins, President
An assemblage of professionals whose interest in the complex and diverse practice of distribution and logistics is a common bond.
600 Members
Founded in 1956

23627 National Marine Representatives Associatio n
PO Box 360
Gurnee, IL 60031
847-662-3167; Fax: 847-336-7126
info@nmraonline.org
www.nmraonline.org
Scott Kolodny, President
Aaron Freeman, VP
Mark Goodman, Treasurer
Craig Cochran, Secretary
A national organization serving marine industry sales representatives and the manufacturers who sell marine products.
Founded in 1960

23628 National Motor Freight Traffic Association
1001 North Fairfax Street
Suite 600
Alexandria, VA 22314-1798
703-838-1810
866-411-6632; Fax: 703-683-6296
customerservice@nmfta.org
www.nmfta.org
LinkedIn
Paul Levine, Executive Director
Joel Ringer, Chairman, CCSB
Urban Jonson, Chief Technology Officer
Leslie Tate, Finance & HR Manager
Urban Jonson, Chief Technology Officer
Provides expertise in freight classification, packaging, and transportation codes.

23629 National Parking Association
1112 16th St Nw
Suite 840
Washington, DC 20036-4880
202-296-4336
800-647-7275; Fax: 202-296-3102
info@npapark.org
www.npapark.org
Facebook, Twitter, LinkedIn, YouTube
Mark Muglich, Chairman
Alan B. Lazowski, Chair Elect
Nicolle Judge, Vice Chair
David Damus, Secretary
Robert A Zuritsky, Treasurer
Proudly serving the nation's parking industry since 1951. Our members are comprised of parking professionals in both the public and private sectors from across the country and around the world. NPA members are private operators, parking consultants, colleges and universities, municipalities, parking authorities, hospitals and medical centers and industry vendors.
2500+ Members
Founded in 1951
Mailing list available for rent

23630 National Private Truck Council
950 N Glebe Rd
Suite 530
Arlington, VA 22203-4183
703-683-1300; Fax: 703-683-1217
tmoore@nptc.org
www.nptc.org
Facebook, Twitter, LinkedIn, Youtube, Flickr, RSS
Gary S Petty, President & CEO
Tom Moore, CTP, SVP

Serena Porter, Membership Manager
George Mundell, EVP & COO
Rick Schweiter, General Counsel & Govt. Affairs

Distributors, shippers, processors, jobbers and manufacturers who transport their own goods and are owners of their own truck fleets. Sponsors national safety contests, safety seminars, management workshops, fleet management certification.
650 Members
Founded in 1939

23631 National Private Truck Councilÿ

950 N. Glebe Road
Suite 2300
Arlington, VA 22203-4183

703-683-1300; Fax: 703-683-1217
www.nptc.org
Facebook, Twitter, LinkedIn, Flickr, YouTube, RSS

Tom Moore, CTP, Senior Vice President
George Mundell, Executive Vice President & COO
Gary F. Petty, President & CEO
Serena Porter, Membership Manager
Rick Schweitzer, General Counsel & Gov. Affairs

National trade association dedicated exclusively to representing private motor carrier fleets.
Founded in 1939

23632 National School Transportation Association

122 South Royal Street
Alexandria, VA 22314

703-684-3200
800-222-6782; Fax: 703-684-3212
www.yellowbuses.org
Facebook, Twitter, LinkedIn, YouTube

Todd Monteferrario, President
Steve Hey, President Elect
Blake Krapf, Secretary/Treasurer
Ronna Weber, Executive Director
Meaghan Allain, Membership & Ops Coor.

Strives to provide safe transportation, foster safety, and an atmosphere conducive to private enterprise.
3M Members
Founded in 1964

23633 National Small Shipments Traffic

330 N Wabash Avenue
Suite 2000
Chicago, IL 60611

202-367-1174; Fax: 202-686-2877
info@nasstrac.org
www.nasstrac.org
Facebook, Twitter, LinkedIn

Doug Easley, Chairperson
Chris Norek, Ph.D., President
Terri Reid, 1st VP
Marc Feeser, 2nd VP
Tom Wenzinger, Treasurer

Members are truck, air, rail and sea shippers of freight weighing less than 10,000 pounds.
250 Members
Founded in 1952

23634 National Truck Equipment Association

37400 Hills Tech Dr
Farmington Hill, MI 48331-3414

248-489-7090
800-441-6832; Fax: 248-489-8590
info@ntea.com
www.ntea.com
Facebook, Twitter, LinkedIn, Flickr, YouTube, Instagram

Steve Carey, Executive Director
Carole Vartanian, Accounting Manager
Derek Eng, Director of Information Technology
Sheree Campbell, Executive Assistant
Michelle Kubitz, Director of Events

NTEA currently represents nearly 1,600 small to mid sized companies that manufacture, distribute, install, buy, sell and repair commercial trucks, truck bodies, truck equipment, trailers and accessories. The major commercial truck chassis manufacturers also belong to the NTEA as associate members.
1800 Members
Founded in 1964

23635 National Truck Leasing System

2651 Warrenville Road
Suite 560
Oakbrook Terrace, IL 60515

630-538-8878
800-729-6857; Fax: 630-953-0040
eventsadmin@nationalease.com
www.nationalease.com
Facebook, Twitter, LinkedIn, Google+

John Grainger, President

Members are independent truck leasing companies.
Founded in 1944

23636 National Truck and Heavy Equipment Claims Council (NTHECC)

PO Box 5928
Fresno, CA 93755-5928

559-431-3774; Fax: 559-436-4755
www.nthecc.org
Betty Clayton, President
Ed Williams, President Elect
Kelly R. Reich, Past President
Shane Carder, Secretary
Darrell W. Bickley, Treasurer

Repair and manufacturing facilities, insurance companies and adjusters concerned with insuring of heavy equipment and trucks. Promotes safety.
125 Members
Founded in 1961

23637 National Truckers Association, Inc.

info@nationaltruckers.com
www.nationaltruckers.com

Information and services for independent owner operators and small fleets.

23638 National Trucking Industrial Relations

908 King Street
Alexandria, VA 22314-3067

703-836-5506
www.all-acronyms.com
Facebook

Trucking executives and lawyers concerned with personnel and labor relations issues.
128 Members
Founded in 1987

23639 National Waterways Conference

110 N Glebe Rd.
Suite 1010
Arlington, VA 22201

703-224-8007; Fax: 866-371-1390
amy@waterways.org
www.waterways.org

Jim Oliver, Chairman
Jamie McCurry, Vice Chairman
Amy W. Larson, Esq.,, President
Randy Richardson, VP
Carole Wright, Director of Internal Operations

Dedicated to a greater understanding of the widespread public benefits of the American waterways system.
350 Members
Founded in 1960

23640 Natural Gas Vehicles for America

400 N Capitol St Nw
Washington, DC 20001-1511

202-824-7360; Fax: 202-824-7087
rkolodziej@ngvamerica.org
www.ngvamerica.org
Facebook, Twitter, LinkedIn, YouTube

Matthew Godlewski, President
Jeffrey Clarke, Gen. Counsel & Dir., Reg. Affairs
Paul Kerkhoven, Director, Government Affairs
Lucas Blanchard, Dir., Ops, Membership & Planning
Dan Bowerson, Director, Technology & Dev.

Members are organizations with an interest in encouraging the development of natural gas powered vehicles.
250 Members
Founded in 1988

23641 Network of Employers for Traffic Safety

344 Maple Avenue, West
#357
Vienna, VA 22180-5162

703-755-5350
888-221-0045
sgillies@trafficsafety.org
trafficsafety.org

Jack Hanley, Executive Director
Susan Gillies, Administrative Lead
Joseph L. McKillips, CSP, Chair

Focused on improving traffic safety.

23642 North American Shippers Association

1600 St. Georges Ave
PO Box 249
Rahway, NJ 07065

732-680-4540; Fax: 732-388-6580
www.nasaships.com

Case Pieterman, Executive Director
Stephen Ballas, President

Members are shippers of wine and alcoholic beverages.
430 Members
Founded in 1987

23643 North American Transportation Council

427 Garrison Rd.
Unit 3 & 4
Fort Erie, ON L2A 6E6

800-559-7421; Fax: 905-994-0117
www.natc.com

Dave Sirgey, President
Mary Anne Vehrs, Sales & Marketing
Julie Gauthier, Administrative Assistantÿ
Diane Sheppard, Accounting Supervisor
Jon Ainsworth, Manager, IT & Dev

Represents Canadian and US based motor carriers engaged in for-hire trucking in the North American transborder market.

23644 NorthAmerican Transportation Association
9120 Double Diamond Parkway
Ste 346
Reno, NV 89521-4842
800-805-0040
www.ntassoc.com
Facebook, Twitter, LinkedIn, YouTube
Association of transportation safety and compliance professionals serving the motor carrier industry.
Founded in 1989

23645 Owner Operator Independent Drivers
1 OOIDA Drive
Grain Valley, MO 64029-1000
816-229-5791
800-444-5791; Fax: 816-229-0518
webmaster@ooida.com
www.ooida.com
Facebook, Twitter, YouTube
Todd Spencer, President
Lewie Pugh, EVP
Terry Button, General VP
Robert Esler, Secretary
Leland Wilkins, Treasurer
National association for owner-operators, professional drivers and small fleet owners. Lobbies federal and state government and advises on all legislation affecting the trucking industry. Provides insurance, financial products and business services.
160K Members
Frequency: Monthly
Circulation: 200000
Founded in 1973

23646 Owner Operators of America
PO Box 582
Orchard Park, NY 14127-0582
Merchants providing goods and services to truck drivers, operators and owners. Seeks to protect the status, interests and image of truck drivers. Offers discounts on fuel, tires, food, repairs, parts and insurance. Provides tax filing assistance. Sponsors trade shows, conferences and public relations programs.
250 Members
Founded in 1982

23647 Passenger Vessel Association
103 Oronoco Street
Suite 200
Alexandria, VA 22314-1549
703-518-5005
800-807-8360; Fax: 703-518-5151
pvainfo@passengervessel.com
www.passengervessel.com
Facebook
Dave Anderson, President
Margo Marks, Vice President
Jeff Whitaker, Secretary/Treasurer
John Groundwater, Executive Director
Edmund Welch, Legislative Director
Represents operators of tours, excursions, ferries, charter vessels, dinner boats and other small passenger vessels.
600 Members
Founded in 1971

23648 Professional Truck Driver Institute
Express Carriers Association
555 E Barddock Road
Alexandria, VA 22314
703-647-7015
866-322-7447; Fax: 703-836-6610
dheller@truckload.org
www.ptdi.org
David Money, Chairman
Kevin Bursch, Vice Chair
Mary Beth McCollum, Secretary
David Heller, Director
Marlene Dakita, Certification Coordinator
The nation's foremost advocate of optimum standards and professionalism for entry level truck driver training.
60 Members
Founded in 1986

23649 Professional Truck Driving Institute
555 E. Braddock Road
Alexandria, VA 22314
703-647-7015; Fax: 703-846-6610
dheller@truckload.org
www.ptdi.org
David Money, Chairman
Kevin Bursch, Vice Chair
Mary Beth McCollum, Secretary
David Heller, Director
Marlene Dakita, Certification Coordinator
Advocates of truck-driver training standards, driver professionalism and safety.
Founded in 1986

23650 Professional Trucking Services Association
United Truckers Service
1001 Bayhill Drive
Suite 300
San Bruno, CA 94066
650-260-3170; Fax: 770-929-3201
www.allbusiness.com
Facebook, Twitter, Youtube, RSS, Google+
Members are service bureaus which assist trucking companies in obtaining licensing and permits.
52 Members
Founded in 1984

23651 Railway Industrial Clearance Association
8900 Eastloch Dr.
Suite 215
Spring, TX 77379
281-826-0009
www.rica.org
Rick Ford, Chairman
Kelli Collins, President
Justin Gilmet, VP
Mike Scott, Treasurer
Mark Lockwood, Secretary
Representation includes all aspects of logistics associated with the movement of dimensional cargo via rail.
400+ Members
Founded in 1969

23652 Railway Supply Institute
425 Third Street, S.W.
Suite 920
Washington, DC 20024
202-347-4664; Fax: 202-347-0047
simpson@rsiweb.org
www.rsiweb.org
Twitter, LinkedIn
Thomas D Simpson, President
Nicole B Brewin, VP, Govt. Affairs
Robyn M. Leach, VP, Administration
Amanda T. Patrick, CEM, Trade Shows & Marketing
Brian M. Kellman, Membership & Grassroots Coordinator
The railway equipment and supply industry.
300 Members
Founded in 1908

23653 Railway Systems Suppliers
13133 Professional Drive
Suite 100
Jacksonville, FL 32225
904-379-3366; Fax: 904-379-3941
rssi@rssi.org
www.rssi.org
Michael Drudy, Executive Director
Dot Frenette, Executive Assistant
A trade association serving the communication and signal segment of the rail transportation industry. Manages an annual trade show.
260+ Members
Founded in 1966

23654 Regional Airline Association
2025 M Street NW
Washington, DC 20036-3309
202-367-1170; Fax: 202-367-2170
registration@raa.org
www.raa.org
Facebook, Twitter, YouTube
Faye Malarkey Black, President
Nobuyo Reinsch, VP, Aviation Safety & Security
Michelle Cravez, Manager, Membership, Ops. & Events
Diana Lundie, Exhibit Sales & Sponsorship
Sara Haukap, Manager, Conventions
Membership consists of more than 70 airlines and 350 associate members that provide goods and services.
300 Members
Founded in 1975

23655 Shippers Oil Field Traffic Association
907 Kiowa Drive E
Gainesville, TX 76240-9575
940-668-7735; Fax: 940-668-7212
www.all-acronyms.com
Facebook, Twitter
50 Members
Founded in 1941

23656 Society of Automotive Engineers
400 Commonwealth Dr
Warrendale, PA 15096
724-776-4841
877-606-7323; Fax: 724-776-0790
customerservice@sae.org
www.sae.org
Facebook, Twitter, LinkedIn, Google+
David L. Schutt, PhD, Chief Executive Officer
Gregory L. Bradley, Esq., General Counsel
Sandra L. Dillner, Director of Human Resources
Brian Kaleida, Chief Information Officer
Frank Menchaca, Chief Product Officer
Offers automotive engineers the technical information and expertise used in building, maintaining and operating self propelled vehicles for use on land, sea, air or space.

23657 Space Transportation Association
4305 Underwood Street
University Park, MD 20782
703-855-3917
rich@spacetransportation.us
Richard Coleman, President
Ty McCoy, Chairman
Represents the interests of organizations which intend to develop, build, operate and use space transportation vehicles and systems in order to provide reliable, economical, safe and routine access to space for public and private entities.
20 Members
Founded in 1989

23658 Specialized Carriers and Rigging
5870 Trinity Parkway
Suite 200
Centreville, VA 20120

703-698-0291; Fax: 571-722-1698
info@scranet.org
www.scranet.org
Facebook, Twitter, LinkedIn

Alan Barnhart, Chairman
Bruce Forster, President
John McTyre, VP
Delynn Burkhalter, Treasurer
Terry Young, Assistant Treasurer

Members are carriers, crane and rigging operators and millwrights engaged in the transport of heavy goods.
1300 Members
Founded in 1959

23659 Taxicab, Limousine & Paratransit Association
3200 Tower Oaks Boulevard
Suite 220
Rockville, MD 20852

301-984-5700; Fax: 301-984-5703
info@tlpa.com
www.tlpa.org

Alfred La Gasse III, CEO
Harold Morgan, Executive VP
Leah New, Manager, Communications
Michelle A Jasper, Manager, Meetings
Ayesha Plaskett, Office Assistant

Members include owners of taxicab, limousine, airport shuttle, paratransit and nonemergency medical transportation fleets.
1107 Members
Founded in 1917
Mailing list available for rent: 6,000 names at $100 per M

23660 The American Road & Transportation Builders Association
1219 28th Street, N.W.ÿ
Washington, DC 20007ÿ

202-289-4434
info@artba.org
www.artba.org
Facebook, Twitter, LinkedIn, YouTube, Google+

David S. Zachry, Chairman
Bob Alger, Senior Vice Chairman
Matt Cummings, First Vice Chairman
Rob Charter, Vice Chairman At-Large
Tom Hill, Treasurer

National transportation construction trade group.
Founded in 1902

23661 The Associated General Contractors of America
2300 Wilson Blvd.
Suite 300
Arlington, VA 22201

703-548-3118
800-242-1767; Fax: 703-548-3119
info@agc.org
www.agc.org
Facebook, Twitter, LinkedIn, YouTube

Robert Lanham, Jr., President
Dan Fordice, Senior Vice President
Lester Snyder, Vice Presidentÿ
Jeffrey DiStefano, Treasurer
Stephen E. Sandherr, CEO

Trade association for the construction industry.
26000 Members
Founded in 1918

23662 The Association Of American Truckers
P.O. Box 230369
Montgomery, AL 36123-0369

800-426-6221; Fax: 334-269-1352

Provides insurance and other trucking related products for the American Trucking Associations.

23663 The Institute of Navigation
8551 Rixlew Ln.
STE 360
Manassas, VA 20109

703-366-2723; Fax: 703-366-2724
membership@ion.org
www.ion.org
Facebook, Twitter, LinkedIn, YouTube

Lisa Beaty, Executive Director
Rick Buongiovanni, IT Director
Ken Esthus, Marketing Director
Miriam Lewis, Program/Author Liaison
Megan Andrews, Senior Meeting Manager

Nonprofit professional society dedicated to the advancement of the art and sciece of positioning, radar and navigation.
Founded in 1945

23664 The National Customs Brokers & Forwarders Association of America
1200 18th Street, NW
#901
Washington, DC 20036

202-466-0222; Fax: 202-466-0226
www.ncbfaa.org
Facebook, Twitter, LinkedIn

Darrell Sekin, Jr., Chairman, Board
Geoffrey Powell, President
Scott E. Larson, Treasurer
William S. App, Jr., Secretary
Amy Magnus, VP

Represents and supports members of the US freight forwarding industry providing education and publications.
970+ Members
Founded in 1987

23665 The Trucking Industry Defense Association
3601 E. Joppa Road
Baltimore, MD 21234

410-931-8100; Fax: 410-931-8111
info@tida.org
www.tida.org
LinkedIn

Joel B. Schechter, President
Dana Hoffman, Secretary
William Schrank, General Counsel
Tim Sullivan, Treasurer
Ren,e Theragood, Executive Director

A nonprofit assocation devoted to sharing knowledge and resources for defense of the trucking industry.

23666 Transport Workers Union of America
501 3rd Street NW
9th Floor
Washington, DC 20001

202-719-3900; Fax: 202-347-0454
www.twu.org
Facebook, Twitter, Youtube, Flickr

Harry Lombardo, President
John Samuelson, Executive VP
Alex Garcia, Secretary/Treasurer

Chartered by the Congress of Industrial Organizations.
110M Members
ISBN: 0-039865-9 -
Founded in 1934

23667 Transportation Clubs International
P.O. Box 426
Union, WA 98592
877-858-8627

Members are individuals in all phases of transportation, traffic management and physical distribution.
10M Members

23668 Transportation Institute
5201 Auth Way
Camp Springs, MD 20746-4211

301-423-3335; Fax: 301-423-0634
info@trans-inst.org
www.trans-inst.org

James L Henry, Chairman & President
Jerome K Welsch Jr, COO
Robert E Johnston, Executive VP

Members are US flag shipping, towing and dredging companies.
100 Members
Founded in 1967

23669 Transportation Intermediaries Association
1625 Prince St
Suite 200
Alexandria, VA 22314-2883

703-299-5700
888-910-4747; Fax: 703-836-0123
info@tianet.org
www.tianet.org
Facebook, Twitter, LinkedIn

Robert Voltmann, President/CEO
Cindy Amos, Dir. Education & Meeting
Nancy O'Liddy, Dir. Policy & TIA Services
Valerie Sumner, Meetings Manager
Roberta Sumner, Meetings Manager

Education and policy organization for North American transportation intermediaries. The only national association representing the interests of all third party transportation service providers. Members include logistics management firms, property brokers, perishable commodities brokers, freight forwarders, intermodal marketers and ocean and air forwarders.
700 Members
Founded in 1977

23670 Transportation Loss Claim and Security
120 Main Street
Huntington, NY 11743-6906

631-549-8988; Fax: 631-549-8962
www.tlcouncil.org

Reed Tepper, Chairman
Nadia Martin, CCP, President
Phillip Lamb, Secretary/Treasurer
Curtis Hart, Vice President
Kristen Walberg, CCP, Regional Director

A nonprofit trade association dedicated to the prevention of freight loss, damage and delay, the promulgation of reasonable liability rules, laws and claim policies.
660 Members
Founded in 1974

23671 Transportation Loss Prevention & Security Association
155 Polifly Road
Hackensack, NJ 07601

732-350-3776
www.tlpsa.org

William D Bierman, Executive Director
Edward M Loughman, Assistant to Executive Director

Originally a combination of the National Freight Claim Council and the Transportation Loss Prevention and Security Council, this in-

dependent association supports all persons who have an interest in loss and damage claims and security issues. Members include carriers, shippers, vendors, law enforcement, attorneys, insurance carriers, third-party logistics, etc.
Founded in 2000

23672 **Transportation Research Board**
500 Fifth Street NW
Washington, DC 20001
202-334-2934; Fax: 202-334-2527
www.trb.org
Facebook, Twitter, LinkedIn
Janet M. McNaughton, Senior Editor
Rosa P Allen, Administrative Coordinator
Cynthia M Baker, Executive Assistant
Anthony T Bailey, Financial Associate
Thomas R. Menzies, Senior Program Officer

23673 **Transportation Research Forum**
Department 2880
PO Box 6050
Fargo, ND 58108-6050
701-231-7766; Fax: 701-231-1945
info@trforum.org
www.trforum.org
Facebook, LinkedIn
Pat McCarthy, Executive VP
David Ripplinger, President
P.S. Sriraj, VP, Membership
Marla Westervelt, VP, Public Relations
Joe Schwieterman, VP, Chapter Relations
An independent organization of transportation professionals.
300 Members
Founded in 1958

23674 **Truck Frame and Axle Repair Association**
3741 Enterprise Drive SW
Rochester, MN 55902-0122
800-232-8272; Fax: 813-626-5385
w.g.reich@att.net
www.taraassociation.com
Facebook
Paul Jones, President
Ken Dias, Consultant
Bill Hinchcliffe, Secretary/Treasurer
For operators and owners of heavy duty truck repair facilities, fleet managers, truckers and insurance damage appraisers.
110 Members
Founded in 1966

23675 **Truck Renting and Leasing Corporation**
675 N Washington Street
Suite 410
Alexandria, VA 22314
703-299-9120
800-426-1420; Fax: 703-299-9115
www.trala.org
Jack Jacoby, President & CEO
Peter Einisman, Manager of Government Relations
Shannon Davison, Director of Communications & Events
Tonya Gibbs, VP, Finance & Business Operations
Andrew Stasiowski, Director, Govt. Relations
A multi-national technology company, NRLC monitors legislation and other issues affecting the truck/trailer leasing and rental industry. It also manufacturers heavy-duty, on-and-off-road trucks worldwide.
275 Members
Founded in 1978

23676 **Truck Trailer Manufacturers Association**
7001 Heritage Village Plaza
Suite 220
Gainesville, VA 20155
703-549-3010; Fax: 703-549-3014
www.ttmanet.org
Jeff Sims, President
John Freiler, Engineering Manager
Nancy Livingston, Administration
A national organization of truck and tank trailer manufacturers and 120 suppliers to the industry.
Founded in 1941

23677 **Truck and Heavy Equipment Claims Council**
PO Box 5928
Fresno, CA 93755-5928
559-431-3774; Fax: 559-436-4755
www.nthecc.org
Betty Clayton, President
Ed Williams, President Elect
Kelly R. Reich, Past President
Shane Carder, Secretary
Darrell W. Bickley, Treasurer
Repair and manufacturing facilities, insurance companies and adjusters concerned with insuring of heavy equipment and trucks. Promotes safety.
45 Members
Founded in 1961

23678 **Truck-Frame Axle Repair Association**
Home Page: www.taraassociation.com
Facebook
Paul Jones, President
Ken Dias, Consultant
Bill Hinchcliffe, Secretary/Treasurer
Association for truck frame and axle repairers.

23679 **Trucker Buddy International**
3200 Rice Mine Rd
Tuscaloosa, A 35406
05 -48 -261
800-692-8339
info@truckerbuddy.org
www.truckerbuddy.org
Facebook, Twitter
K.C. Brau, President
Elizabeth Barna, Vice President
Brad Williamson, Secretary
Steve Sichterman, Treasurer
Randy Schwartzenburg, Executive Director
A nonprofit organization for educating and mentoring schoolchildren via trucker penpals.
Founded in 1992

23680 **Truckload Carriers Association**
555 East Braddock Road
Alexandria, VA 22314-2182
703-838-1950; Fax: 703-836-6610
tca@truckload.org
www.truckload.org
Facebook, Twitter, LinkedIn, Youtube, Flickr
Russell Stubbs, Chairman
John Lyboldt, President
William Giroux, Executive Vice President
Tomora Brown, Membership Liaison
The Truckload Carriers Association (TCA) represents nearly 700 companies working in and serving the truckload freight industry. Collectively, TCA member companies employ several hundred thousand people across the U.S. and Canada. TCA is the only national trade association whose collective sole focus is thetruckload segment of the motor carrier industry. The association represents dry van, refrigerated, flatbed, and intermodal container carriers across North America and Mexico.
800 Members
Founded in 1938

23681 **United Bus Owners of America**
113 S West Street
4th Floor
Alexandria, VA 22314-2824
703-838-8262
800-424-8262; Fax: 703-838-2950
info@uma.org
www.uma.org
Facebook, Twitter, LinkedIn, Youtube
Victor S Parra, President & CEO
Ken Presley, VP, Industry Relations & COO
Maggie Masterson, Meetings & Operations Director
Terri Tackett, Marketing & Membership Director
Brian Annett, Chairman
Serves the bus industry, with particular emphasis on group travel and tourism.
800 Members
Founded in 1971

23682 **United States Telecom Association**
607 14th St Nw
Suite 400
Washington, DC 20005-2000
202-326-7300; Fax: 202-315-3603
membership@ustelecom.org
www.ustelecom.org
Facebook, Twitter, LinkedIn, Youtube
Jonathan Spalter, President/CEO
Lorna Johnson, Chief Financial Officer
Allison Remsen, EVP & Chief of Staff
Sally Aman, SVP, Communications/Public Affairs
Brandon Heiner, SVP, Government Affairs
Trade association representing service providers and suppliers for the telecom industry.
Cost: $699.00

23683 **United Truckers Association**
9090 FM 1026
Gouldbusk, TX 76845
484-681-9283; Fax: 956-425-9350
info@utatruckers.com
Assocation for truck drivers.
Founded in 1995

23684 **Used Truck Association**
325 County Club Drive
Suite A
Stockbridge, GA 30281
817-439-3900
877-438-7882; Fax: 817-439-3609
contact@uta.org
www.uta.org
Facebook, LinkedIn
Rick Clark, President
Craig Kendall, VP
Angelique Pierce, Secretary
Brock Frederick, Treasurer
Marty Crawford, President Emeritus
Used truck manufacturers and dealerships.
800 Members
Founded in 1988

23685 **Wine and Spirits Shippers Association**
11800 Sunrise Valley Dr
Suite 332
Reston, VA 20191-5302
207-805-1664
800-368-3167; Fax: 703-860-2422
info@wssa.com
www.wssa.com
Facebook, Twitter, LinkedIn, RSS
Alison Leavitt, Managing Director
Gretchen Veevaert, Program Coordinator

Cecilia Borruso, Contract Supervisor/Pricing Analyst
Heather Randolph, Director of Operations
Louis Healey, President

Provides members with services that allow for the efficient and economical transportation of alcoholic beverages.
320 Members
Founded in 1976

23686 Women's Transportation Seminar: National
1701 K St Nw
Suite 800
Washington, DC 20006-1504

202-955-5085; Fax: 202-955-5088
membership@wtsinternational.org
www.wtsinternational.org
Facebook, Twitter, LinkedIn, Pinterest, Instagram

Beverley Swaim-Staley, Chair
Diane Woodend Jones, Vice Chairman
Felicia Boyd, Secretary
Rina Cutler, Treasurer
Marcia Ferranto, President/CEO
5000+ Members
Founded in 1977

23687 Womens Transportation Seminar
1701 K St Nw
Suite 800
Washington, DC 20006-1504

202-955-5085; Fax: 202-955-5088
membership@wtsinternational.org
www.wtsinternational.org
Facebook, Twitter, LinkedIn, Pinterest, Instagram

Beverley Swaim-Staley, Chair
Diane Woodend Jones, Vice Chairman
Felicia Boyd, Secretary
Rina Cutler, Treasurer
Marcia Ferranto, President/CEO
5000+ Members
Founded in 1977

23688 World Organization of Dredging
Post Office Box 2035
Spotsylvania, VA 22553

619-839-9474; Fax: 360-750-1445
tmverna@westerndredging.org
www.woda.org

Anders Jensen, President
Dr A Csiti, General Manager
Rashyan Allays, Secretary
Thomas M. Verna, Executive Director

Develops professionalism in individuals involved in the dredging industry.
2700 Members
Founded in 1981

Newsletters

23689 ABA Insider
American Bus Association
111 K Street NE
Suite 575
Washington, DC 20005-5923

202-842-1645; Fax: 202-842-0850
abainfo@buses.org
www.buses.org

Peter J Pantuso, CEO
Eron Shosteck, Marketing

ABA's biweekly newsletter that keeps members informed on the travel, tourism and motorcoach industry.
Frequency: Biweekly
Founded in 1926

23690 Advanced Transit News
Advanced Transit Association
PO Box 162
Palo Alto, CA 94302

800-779-0544
800-779-0544; Fax: 800-779-0544
jpaskry@davinciglobal.com
www.advancedtransit.org

Catherine G. Burke, President
Bob Dunning, VP
Lawrence Fabian, Publisher

Offers information on the American transit system.
100 Pages
Frequency: Quarterly
Founded in 1953
Printed in one color on matte stock

23691 American Trucker
PRIMEDIA Intertec-Technology & Transportation
PO Box 12901
Shawnee Mission, KS 66282-2901

913-341-1300
800-827-7468; Fax: 913-514-6895
www.trucker.com

Eric Jacobson, Senior VP
Coleen Liatch, Supervisor

Information for those interested in the truck industry. Contains articles on new and used trucks, supplies, equipment, financing, pricing, and other truck related services.
Cost: $21.00
Frequency: Monthly
Circulation: 600000
Founded in 1926

23692 Center for Microcomputers in Transportation
512 Weil Hall
PO Box 116585
Gainesville, FL 32611

352-392-7575
800-226-1013; Fax: 352-389-2324
mctrans@ce.ufl.edu

Mark Newman, Associate Director
Max Crumit, Executive Vice President
Kirk Hatfield, Director
Founded in 1986

23693 Dispatch & Division Newsletters
Taxicab, Limousine & Paratransit Association
3200 Tower Oaks Blvd
Suite 220
Rockville, MD 20852

301-984-5700; Fax: 301-984-5703
info@tlpa.org
www.tlpa.org

Alfred LaGasse, CEO
Victor Dizengoff, President

Dispatch features articles on industry business issues, provides advice on running a transportation company, and comes with division specific bi-monthly newsletters.
Frequency: Bimonthly
Circulation: 6000

23694 Dual News
Driving School Association of America
11 W Pomona Boulevard
Monterey Park, CA 91754

FAX 626-722-0485

George Hensel, Publisher

Association news for student driving instructors and educational personnel.
Frequency: BiWeekly
Circulation: 5,000

23695 Fleet Street
Greenwich Consulting
15821 Fetlock Lane
Chino Hills, CA 91709

909-606-2271; Fax: 909-597-7759

Karen Edward, Publisher

Consulting newsletter geared toward Distribution and Fleet Management Executives - Provides transportation managers with cost-cutting methodogies.
Circulation: 15500

23696 HazMat Transport News
Business Publishers
8737 Colesville Road
Suite 1100
Silver Spring, MD 20910-3925

301-876-6300
800-274-6737; Fax: 301-587-4530
custserv@bpinews.com
www.bpinews.com

Leonard A Eiserer, Publisher
Beth Early, Operations Director

Regulatory and legislative development affecting hazardous materials transportation. In-depth coverage on research and special programs administration, hazmat regulation programs and enforcement actions.
Cost: $447.00
Founded in 1963

23697 Inside DOT and Transportation Week
King of Communications Group
1325 Massachusetts Ave Nw
Suite 310
Washington, DC 20005-4194

240-455-6801
800-926-5464; Fax: 240-628-5774
www.king-com.com

F King, President
Dave Ahearn, Editor
Wenita Lhill-waddell, Marketing
Linda Gasparello, General Manager

Offers information to persons working in the transportation profession.
Cost: $1300.00
12 Pages
Frequency: Daily
Founded in 1973
Printed in one color on newsprint stock

23698 Intermodal Connections
Intermodal Association of North America
11785 Beltsville Drive
Suite 1100
Calverton, MD 20705-4049

301-982-3400; Fax: 301-982-4815
iana@intermodal.org
www.intermodal.org

Joanne F. Casey, President & CEO
Stephen A. Keppler, SVP, Member Services
Jon Palmbak, SVP, Digital Products & Technology

The official e-newsletter for the Intermodal Association of North America.
Frequency: 2x/Monthly

23699 Intermodal Edge
Intermodal Association of North America
11785 Beltsville Drive
Suite 1100
Calverton, MD 20705-4049

301-982-3400; Fax: 301-982-4815
iana@intermodal.org
www.intermodal.org/intermodal-edge

Joanne F. Casey, President & CEO
Stephen A. Keppler, SVP, Member Services

Jon Palmbak, SVP, Digital Products & Technology
The official blog for the Intermodal Association of North America.

23700 **Interstate Information Report**
Express Carriers Association
9532 Liberia Avenue,
Suite 130
Manassas, VA 20190-3233
703-361-1058
866-322-7447; Fax: 704-435-4390
www.expresscarriers.com
Carrie Ehlers, President
Stuart Hyden, First Vice President
Compilation of newly enacted state legislation regulations having direct impact on vehicle operations, fuel taxes, registration size and weight.

23701 **Legislative Alert**
Taxicab, Limousine & Paratransit Association
3200 Tower Oaks Blvd
Suite 220
Rockville, MD 20852
301-984-5700; Fax: 301-984-5703
info@tlpa.org
www.tlpa.org
Alfred LaGasse, CEO
Victor Dizengoff, President
TLPA's members-only bulletin of early alerts to critical changes in the industry, announcing threats and opportunities on issues that are before Congress and federal agencies. Organizes operators to take action, and provides knowledge and awareness.
Circulation: 6000

23702 **McTrans**
Center for Microcomputers in Transportation
512 Weil Hall
PO Box 116585
Gainesville, FL 32611
352-392-7575
800-226-1013; Fax: 352-389-2324
mctrans@ce.ufl.edu
CE Wallace, Publisher
Mark Newman, Associate Director
Max Crumit, Executive Vice President
Kirk Hatfield, Director
Information about microcomputer software and resources in transportation.
Circulation: 8,000
Founded in 1986

23703 **Owner Operator News**
PO Box 582
Orchard Park, NY 14127-0582
FAX 716-941-5582
Charles DeVaul, Publisher
Trucking news and information.
Frequency: Monthly

23704 **Passenger Transport**
American Public Transit Association
1666 K St Nw
Suite 1100
Washington, DC 20006-1215
202-496-4800; Fax: 202-496-4324
hbrett@apta.com
www.apta.com
Karol J Popkin, CEO
Petra Mollet, VP
Rosemary Sherid, Marketing
Information on federal legislative, administrative and regulatory developments, management and operations, new technology, and state and local developments in public transit.
Cost: $75.00
Frequency: B-Weekly
Circulation: 5000
Founded in 1882

23705 **Proclaim**
Slesia Companies
619 Broad Creek Dr
Fort Washington, MD 20744-5800
301-292-1970; Fax: 301-292-1787
silesia-aroma.com
Dale L Anderson, President
Covers transportation freight claims.
Frequency: Monthly

23706 **Rider's Digest**
Metropolitan Atlanta Road Transit
2424 Piedmont Rd Ne
Atlanta, GA 30324-3311
404-848-5000; Fax: 404-848-5098
schedinfo@itsmarta.com
www.itsmarta.com
Nathaniel P Ford Sr, CEO
Public transportation news.
Frequency: Monthly

23707 **TransitPulse**
Trans 21
55 Virginia St
Dorchester, MA 02125-2352
617-825-9687; Fax: 617-482-7417
Lawrence J Fabin, Publisher
Newsletters and faxed advisory service on worldwide developments in Automated People Movers.
Cost: $75.00
4 Pages
Frequency: BiMonthly
Circulation: 500
Printed in one color on matte stock

23708 **Transport Workers Union of America**
Transport Workers Union of America
1700 Broadway
Suite 2
New York, NY 10019-5905
212-259-4900; Fax: 202-347-0454
mailbox@twu.org
www.twu.org
James Little, President
David Rosen, General Counsel
Alex Garcia, Director
Chartered by the Congress of Industrial Organizations.
Frequency: Monthly
ISBN: 0-039865-9 -
Founded in 1934

23709 **Transportation Intermediaries Update**
Transportation Intermediaries Association
1625 Prince St
Suite 200
Alexandria, VA 22314-2883
703-299-5700; Fax: 703-836-0123
voltmann@tianet.org
www.tianet.org
Robert Voltmann, President
Education and policy organization for North American transportation intermediaries. TIA is the only national association representing the interests of all third party transportation service providers. The members of TIA include logistics management firms, property brokers, perishable commodities brokers, freight forwarders, intermodal marketers, ocean and air forwarders, and NVOCC's.
700 Pages
Frequency: Monthly

23710 **Truck Equipment News**
National Truck Equipment Association
37400 Hills Tech Dr
Farmington Hill, MI 48331-3414
248-489-7090
800-441-6832; Fax: 248-489-8590
info@ntea.com
www.ntea.com
James Carney, Executive Director
Dennis Jones, First Vice President
Covers NTEA and member/industry activities, business management issues, technical topics, excise tax applications, sales/marketing management topics, legislative and regulatory news, monthly new truck retail sales figures, NTEA/industry events calendar, and other current topics of interest to industry members.
Cost: $72.00
150 Pages
Frequency: Monthly
Circulation: 1600
Founded in 1964

23711 **Trucker Publications**
Trucker Publications
PO Box 3413
Little Rock, AR 72203-3413
501-666-0500; Fax: 501-666-0700
www.thetrucker.com
Ray Wittenberg, Publisher
Up to date, comprehensive coverage of news affecting both drivers and management, including regulatory issues, road conditions, fuel, and current trends in technology.
Cost: $21.50
Frequency: BiWeekly
Circulation: 27,500

23712 **Truckload Authority**
Truckload Carriers Association
555 East Braddock Road
Suite CS-4
Alexandria, VA 22314-2182
703-838-1950; Fax: 703-836-6610
tca@truckload.org
www.truckload.org
Facebook, Twitter, LinkedIn
Chris Burruss, President
Deborah Sparks, VP
Gary Salisbury, Chairman
Offers industry insights for truckload carrier executives.
850 Members
Frequency: Monthly
Founded in 1938

23713 **Truckload Carriers Report**
Truckload Carriers Association
555 E Braddock Road
Suite CS-4
Alexandria, VA 22314-2182
703-838-1950; Fax: 703-836-6610
tca@truckload.org
www.truckload.org
John Lyboldt, President
William Giroux, Executive Vice President
Russell Stubbs, Chairman
Bianca Gibson, Executive Editor
A newsletter for truckload carriers executives. Free to association members.
Frequency: Weekly
Founded in 1938
Mailing list available for rent

23714 **US Rail News**
Business Publishers

222 Sedwick Dr
Suite 101
Durham, NC 27713

800-223-8720; Fax: 800-508-2592
custserv@bpinews.com
www.bpinews.com

Reports on the trends, legislation, regulations, acquisitions, business opportunities and technological developments that directly affect the rail industry.
Cost: $437.00
Frequency: 25 per year
Founded in 1963

23715 **Urban Transport News**
Business Publishers
8737 Colesville Road
Suite 1100
Silver Spring, MD 20910-3928

301-876-6300
800-274-6737; Fax: 301-587-4530
www.bpinews.com

Leonard A Eiserer, Publisher
Beth Early, Operations Director

Comprehensive briefings on trends, regulations, legislation, business and technological developments in the mass transit area.
Cost: $437.00
Founded in 1963

Magazines & Journals

23716 **Air Medical Journal**
526 King Street
Suite 415
Alexandria, VA 22314-3143

703-836-8732
800-525-3712; Fax: 703-836-8920
information@aams.org
www.aams.org

Renee Holleran, Editor
Dawn M Mancuso, Director
John Fiegel, Director

An association of health care entities operating helicopter transport services. Magazine is published, price included in membership.
375 Pages
Founded in 1980
Printed in on glossy stock

23717 **American Journal of Transportation**
Fleur de Lis Publishing
1354 Hancock Street
Suite 300
Quincy, MA 02169

617-328-5005
800-599-6358; Fax: 617-328-5999
editorial@ajot.com
www.ajot.com/

George Lauriat, Editor
Ann Radwan, Associate Editor
William Bourbon, Publisher
Bob Kirk, Production Manager
Kristen Davis, Graphic Designer

Newspaper serving the shipping, trucking, air freight and railroad industries in the US and Canada.
Cost: $98.00
Frequency: Weekly
Circulation: 8115
ISSN: 1529-1820
Founded in 1994
Printed in on newsprint stock

23718 **American Mover**
American Movers Conference
1611 Duke St
Alexandria, VA 22314-3406

703-683-7410; Fax: 703-683-7527
info@moving.org
www.moving.org

Linda Bauer Darr, CEO
Joseph M Harrison, President
Carol Laird, Production Manager
Norma Gyovai, Advertising Manager

This publication covers the moving and storage industry.
Cost: $60.00
24 Pages
Frequency: Monthly
Circulation: 3700
Founded in 1958

23719 **American Shipper**
Howard Publications
300 W Adams Street Suite 600
PO Box 4728
Jacksonville, FL 32201-4728

904-355-2601
800-874-6422; Fax: 904-791-8836
www.americanshipper.com

Nancy Barry, Production Manager
Hayes Howard, Publisher
Kerry Cowart, Circulation Manager
James Blaeser, Sales Associate

Provides those involved in domestic and global supply chain management with news and information of a strategic nature, useful in the formation of logistics polices and partnerships.
Cost: $36.00
104 Pages
Frequency: Monthly
Circulation: 13705
ISSN: 1074-8350
Founded in 1951
Printed in 4 colors on glossy stock

23720 **American Trucker**
Primedia
7355 Woodland Drive
Indianapolis, IN 46278-1769

317-991-1350
800-827-7468; Fax: 317-299-1356
www.trucker.com

Dallas Nauert, Production Manager
Diana Starks, Circulation Director

A trade publication featuring new and used trucks, trailors,parts and services for the heavy duty trucking industry.
Cost: $21.00
Frequency: Monthly
Circulation: 930338
Founded in 1975
Printed in 4 colors on matte stock

23721 **Analysis of Class I Railroads**
Association of American Railroads
425 Third Street SW
Suite 1144
Washington, DC 20024-3217

202-639-2100
media@aar.org
www.aar.org
Facebook, Twitter, LinkedIn

Edward R. Hamberger, President & CEO
Tom White, Editor
Patricia M. Reilly, SVP, Communications

Offers information on the railroad travel industry.
Cost: $400.00
Frequency: Annual
Founded in 1934

23722 **Atlantic Northeast Rails & Ports**
162 main street
Yarmouth, ME 04096

207-846-3549; Fax: 603-215-4482
www.atlanticnortheast.com

Chop Hardenbergh, CEO/President
Cost: $375.00
Frequency: Monthly
Circulation: 300
Founded in 1994

23723 **Better Roads**
WMO DannHausen Corporation
PO Box 558
Park Ridge, IL 60068

847-696-2391; Fax: 847-696-3445

Wm O Dannhausen, Publisher

Market to federal agencies, bureaus, government departments, states, counties township road and city public works.
Cost: $26.96
Frequency: Monthly
Circulation: 38406
Founded in 1769

23724 **Brotherhood of Locomotive Engineers**
Brotherhood of Locomotive Engineers
1370 Ontario St
Cleveland, OH 44113-1701

216-241-2630; Fax: 216-241-6516
policy@ble.org
www.ble.org

Ed Rodzwicz, CEO
John Bentley, Editor

23725 **Bus Conversions Magazine**
MAK Publishing
7246 Garden Grove Boulevard
Westminster, CA 92683

714-799-0062; Fax: 714-799-0042
www.busconversions.com

Michael A Kadletz, Publisher
Rikki Gee, Publication Manager

how-to, full color, monthly magazine that includes photos, floor plans, helpful hints and guides for buying, selling, selecting, and converting a bus to an RV or executive entertainer's coach. Features pages of classified ads and valuable info on maintaining, operating and updating your coach.
Cost: $38.00
72 Pages
Circulation: 8000
ISSN: 1070-6526
Founded in 1992
Printed in 4 colors on glossy stock

23726 **Bus Ride**
Friendship Publications
4742 N 24th St
Suite 340
Phoenix, AZ 85016-4884

602-265-7600
800-541-2670; Fax: 602-277-7588
www.busride.com

Steve Kane, Publisher/Editor-in-Chief
Wayne Bryan, Editor
Donna Arnseth, Circulation Administrator
Maria Jolly, Assistant Editor
Valerie Valtierra, Production Director

Bus industry trade journal with articles about bus companies, training agencies and manufacturers and suppliers to the bus industry.
Cost: $39.00
120 Pages
Frequency: Monthly
Circulation: 16000
Founded in 1965
Printed in 4 colors on glossy stock

23727 Chief Logistics Officer
Penton Media
1166 Avenue of the Americas/10th
Suite 316
Cleveland, NY 10036

212-204-4200; Fax: 216-696-6662
information@penton.com
www.penton.com

Jane Cooper, Marketing
Perry A Trunick, Editor
Maryann Jovorek, Production Manager
Chris Meyer, Director

Magazine for supply chain leaders, supplement to Transportation and Distribution.
Cost: $50.00
48 Pages
Frequency: Quarterly
Circulation: 12M
Founded in 1960
Printed in 4 colors on glossy stock

23728 Classic Trains
James Folcum
21027 Crossroads Circle
Waukesha, WI 53187

262-796-8776; Fax: 262-796-1615
www.classictrain.com

Rob McGornigal, Editor
Mike Yuhaf, Advertising Manager

Publication features stories on antique and old trains.

23729 Commercial Carrier Journal
Randall-Reilly
3200 Rice Mine Road NE
Tuscaloosa, AL 35406

800-633-5953; Fax: 610-964-4647
www.ccjdigital.com

Jeff Crissey, Editor

Covering fleet management topics from technology to equipment.
Frequency: Monthly
Circulation: 96500
Founded in 1934

23730 Contracting for Transportation & Logistics Services
120 Main Street
Huntington, NY 11743-6906

631-270-0100; Fax: 516-549-8962
tcpc@transportlaw.com
www.transportlaw.com

William J Augello, Executive Director

Published by the Transportation Consumer Protection Council.
Cost: $48.00
Founded in 2001

23731 Corporate Procedures for Shipping & Receiving
120 Main Street
Huntington, NY 11743-6906

631-270-0100; Fax: 516-549-8962
tcpc@transportlaw.com
www.transportlaw.com

William J Augello, Executive Director

Published by the Transportation Consumer Protection Council.
Cost: $95.00
Founded in 1998

23732 Defense Transportation Journal
National Defense Transportation Association
50 S Pickett Street
Suite 220
Alexandria, VA 22304-7206

703-751-5011; Fax: 703-823-8761
info@ndtahq.com
www.ndtahq.com

LTG Kenneth Wykle, President
Karen Schmitt, Managing Editor

The official publication of the National Defense Transportation Association and the only publication for the government and military transportation industry.
Cost: $35.00
Frequency: Bi-Monthly
Circulation: 8500

23733 Destinations
American Bus Association
700 13th St NW
Suite 575
Washington, DC 20005-5923

202-842-1645
800-283-2877; Fax: 202-842-0850
abainfo@buses.org
www.buses.org

Peter J Pantuso, CEO
Eron Shosteck, Marketing

Motorcoach travel across North America and Association news.
80 Pages
Frequency: Monthly
Circulation: 6000
Founded in 1926
Printed in 4 colors on glossy stock

23734 Diesel Equipment Superintendent
Business Journals
50 Day Street
Norwalk, CT 06854-3100

203-853-6015; Fax: 203-852-8175

James Jones, Editor

Maintenance management in areas of selection, of heavy duty trucks and trailers.
Cost: $25.00
100 Pages
Frequency: Monthly
Founded in 1923

23735 Digest
American Bus Association
700 13th St NW
Suite 575
Washington, DC 20005-5923

202-842-1645
800-283-2877; Fax: 202-842-0850
abainfo@buses.org
www.buses.org

Peter J Pantuso, CEO
Judi Bredemeier, Editor
Chrystal Farmer, Marketing Manager
Michael Hayes, Publisher

Legislation news.
Cost: $150.00
Circulation: 3200
Founded in 1996
Printed in 2 colors on matte stock

23736 Direction
American Moving and Storage Association
1611 Duke St
Alexandria, VA 22314-3406

703-683-7410; Fax: 703-683-7527
www.moving.org

Matthew Hicks, Advertising
John Parkinson, Editorial
Allison Bresky, Production

Provides news and in-depth feature articles to provide members with vital information to help operate their companies more profitably.
Cost: $35.00
Frequency: Bi-Monthly
Circulation: 4000

23737 Fastline Catalog
Fastline Media Group
4900 Fox Run Road
P.O. Box 248
Buckner, KY 40010-0248

502-222-0146
800-626-6409; Fax: 502-222-0615
www.fastline.com
Facebook, Twitter

William Howard, Editor
Susan Arterburn, Marketing Director
Pat Higgins, Vice President, Sales

Nationwide and regional picture buying guides for the trucking industry.
Frequency: Monthly
Founded in 1978

23738 Fleet Equipment Magazine
Maple Publishing Company
3550 Embassy Parkway
Akron, OH 44333-8318

330-670-1234; Fax: 330-670-0874
www.truklink.com

Tom Gelinas, Editor
Bill Babcox, President
Robert Dorn, Publisher
Kelly McAleese, Ad Services Manager
Lindsey Fritz, Circulation Manager

Edited for fleet equipment managers of truck fleets.
Cost: $82.00
Frequency: Monthly
Circulation: 61,571
Founded in 1974

23739 Fleet Owner Magazine
Primedia
11 River Bend Drive South
PO Box 4949
Stamford, CT 06907-949

203-358-9900; Fax: 203-358-5811
frcs@pbsub.com
www.fleetowner.com

Thomas Duncan, Vice President
Jim Mele, Editor-in-Chief
David Cullen, Executive Editor

Monthly business magazine serving executives and managers in commercial trucking fleets.
Cost: $40.00
Frequency: Monthly
Founded in 1928

23740 Freight Claims in Plain English
120 Main Street
Huntington, NY 11743-6906

631-270-0100; Fax: 516-549-8962
tcpc@transportlaw.com
www.transportlaw.com

William J Augello, Executive Director

Published by the Transportation Consumer Protection Council.
Cost: $100.00
Founded in 1995

23741 Freight Claims: Filing & Recovery
120 Main Street
Huntington, NY 11743-6906

631-270-0100; Fax: 516-549-8962
tcpc@transportlaw.com
www.transportlaw.com

William J Augello, Executive Director

Published by the Transportation Consumer Protection Council.
Cost: $48.00
Founded in 2001

23742 **Go-West Magazine**
Motor Transport Management Group
3251 Beacon Road
West Sacramento, CA 95691-3475
916-373-3630; Fax: 916-852-5707
Jim Beach, Editor
Complete overview of the transportation industry.
Frequency: Monthly

23743 **Guide to Transportation After the Sunsetting of the ICC**
120 Main Street
Huntington, NY 11743-6906
631-270-0100; Fax: 516-549-8962
tcpc@transportlaw.com
www.transportlaw.com
William J Augello, Executive Director
Published by the Transportation Consumer Protection Council.
Cost: $75.00
Founded in 1997

23744 **Heavy Duty Trucking**
Newport Communications
38 Executive Park
Suite 300
Irvine, CA 92614-6755
949-261-1636; Fax: 949-261-2904
webmaster@truckinginfo.com
www.truckinginfo.com
Doug Condra, President
Susan Condra, Circulation Manager
Susan Patterson, Marketing
Marty Mc Collan, Publisher
National business magazine for managers of medium and heavy duty truck fleets, and manufacturers and dealers of those trucks and the components used to build them.
Cost: $65.00
Frequency: Monthly
Circulation: 90000
Founded in 1922
Printed in 4 colors on glossy stock

23745 **Hemispheres**
Pace Communications
PO Box 13607
Greensboro, NC 27415-3607
336-378-6065
800-346-1336; Fax: 336-275-2864
www.pacecommunications.com
Bonnie McElveen, CEO
Leigh Klee, Chief Financial Officer
Ed Calfo, Executive Vice President
Children's magazine for US airline fliers.
Frequency: Monthly
Circulation: 60000
Founded in 1973

23746 **High Performance Composites**
Ray Publishing
P.O.Box 992
Morrison, CO 80465-0992
303-467-1776; Fax: 303-467-1777
www.compositeworld.com
Approach is technical, offering cutting-edge design, engineering, prototyping, and manufacturing solutions for aerospace and other traditional and emerging structural applications for advanced composites.

23747 **IEEE Vehicular Technology Magazine**
IEEE Vehicular Technology Society
3 Parl Avenue
17th Floor
New York, NY 10016-5997
212-419-7900
david@uni-kassel.de
vtsociety.org
Klaus David, Editor-in-Chief
Focus is on mobile radio, connected and automated vehicles, automotive electronics, and transportation systems.
Frequency: Quarterly

23748 **ITE Journal**
Institute of Transportation Engineers
1099 14th St NW
Suite 300E
Washington, DC 20005-5924
202-289-0222; Fax: 202-289-7722
ite_staff@ite.org
www.it.org
Thomas Brahms, CEO
Shannon Gore Peters, Editor
Christina Denekas, Circulation Manager
Richard T Romer, International President
Provides timely news and information on subjects of interest to professionals responsible for traffic engineering, transportation planning, ITS, transit, safety, demand management, education etc.
Cost: $100.00
300 Pages
Frequency: Monthly
Circulation: 7500
Founded in 1930

23749 **ITS Magazine**
IEEE Intelligent Transportation Systems Society
445 Hoes Lane
Piscataway, NJ 08854
Home Page: www.ieee-itss.org
Wei-Bin Zhang, President
Petros A. Ioannou, VP, Publications Activities
Ljubo Vlacic, Magazine Editor
Features peer-reviewed articles on research and applications, with case studies and examinations of challenges in the intelligent transportation system industry.

23750 **Inbound Logistics Magazine**
Thomas Publishing Company
5 Penn Plaza
New York, NY 10001-1810
212-950-0500; Fax: 212-629-1565
editor@inboundlogistics.com
www.inboundlogistics.com
Keith Biondo, Publisher
Felecia Stratton, Editor
Carolyn Smolin, Circulation Manager
Robert Malone, Executive Editor
Accepts advertising.
Frequency: Monthly
Circulation: 55050
Founded in 1981

23751 **Institute of Transportation Engineering Journal**
Institute of Transportation Engineering
1627 Eye St. NW
Suite 600
Washington, DC 20006
202-785-0060; Fax: 202-785-0609
ite_staff@ite.org
www.ite.org
Thomas Brahms, CEO
Christina Denekas, Marketing Manager
Marianne Saglam, Communications & Media Sr. Director
Dedicated to the transportation engineering field. A journal is published for members only.
Cost: $65.00
Frequency: Monthly
Circulation: 17000
Founded in 1930

23752 **Intermodal Insights**
Intermodal Association of North America
11785 Beltsville Drive
Suite 1100
Calverton, MD 20705-4049
301-982-3400; Fax: 301-982-4815
iana@intermodal.org
www.intermodal.org
Joanne F. Casey, President & CEO
Stephen A. Keppler, SVP, Member Services
Jon Palmbak, SVP, Digital Products & Technology
The official magazine of the Intermodal Association of North America.
Frequency: Bi-Monthly

23753 **International Rail Journal**
Simmons-Boardman Publishing Corporation
345 Hudson St
Suite 1201
New York, NY 10014-7123
212-620-7200; Fax: 212-633-1165
db@railjournal.co.uk
www.simmonsboardman.com
Arthur J McGinnis Jr, President
Covers the rapidly developing railway marketplace for railway and rail transit managers and engineers, suppliers and consultants worldwide.
Frequency: Monthly
Circulation: 100960
Founded in 1960

23754 **Journal of HazMat Transportation**
Packaging Research International
404 Price St
West Chester, PA 19382-3531
610-436-8292
877-429-7447; Fax: 610-436-9422
www.hazmatship.com
Vincent A Vitollo, Owner
A professionally prepared technical reporting system, focused exlusively on explaining changes to the hazardous materials transportation regulations. Thoroughly covers and provides technical reviews of the US 49CFR, International Civil Aviation Organization Technical Instructions, the International Maritime Dangerous Goods Code, and the European Road and Rail Regulations.
Cost: $209.00
Circulation: 1000
Founded in 1990
Printed in 4 colors on matte stock

23755 **Journal of the Transportation Research Forum**
Transportation Research Forum
Department 2880
PO Box 6050
Fargo, ND 58108-6050
701-231-7766; Fax: 701-231-1945
info@trforum.org
www.trforum.org
Richard Gritta, President
Starr McMullen, VP
Contains original manuscripts which are timely in scope and germane to transportation
300 Members
Frequency: 3x/Year
Founded in 1958

23756 **Keep on Truckin' News**
Mid-West Truckers Association
2727 N Dirksen Pkwy
Springfield, IL 62702-1490

217-525-0310; Fax: 217-525-0342
info@mid-westtruckers.com
www.trucknews.com

Don Schaefer, President

For members of Mid-West Association.
64 Pages
Frequency: Monthly
Circulation: 4000
Founded in 1964
Printed in 4 colors on glossy stock

23757 **Land Line Magazine**
1 NW OOIDA Drive
Grain Valley, MO 64029-712

816-229-5791
800-444-5791; Fax: 816-443-2227
info@landlinemag.com
www.landlinemag.com

Todd Spencer, Editor-in-Chief
Sandi Soendker, Publisher
Jim Johnson, CEO/President
Mike Schermoly, Marketing
Pam Perry, Circulation Manager

Edited for the owner/operator and independent trucker and small fleet operator who drive heavy duty trucks.
13 Pages
Frequency: Monthly
Circulation: 200000+
Founded in 1973
Printed in 4 colors on glossy stock

23758 **Light & Medium Truck**
TT Publishing
2200 Mill Road
Alexandria, VA 22314-4654

703-838-1770; Fax: 703-548-3662
bharmon@trucking.org
www.ttnews.com

Bruce Harmon, Managing Editor
Debra Devine, Production Coordinator
Stanford Erickson, Associate Publisher
Scott Smith, Circulation Manager
Paul Rosenthal, Marketing Manager

Provides information for day to day management of a company using light to medium duty trucks, such as equipment safety, alternative fuels, maintenance and government regulations.
Frequency: Monthly
Circulation: 50509
Founded in 1945

23759 **Locomotive Engineers Journal**
Brotherhood of Locomotive Engineers
1370 Ontario St
Standard Building
Cleveland, OH 44113-1701

216-241-2630; Fax: 216-241-6516
execstaff@ble.org

Ed Rodzwicz, CEO
Kathleen Policy, Associate Editor
Don M Hahs, President

Designed to meet the information needs of professional engineers throughout North America, also for railroad enthusiasts.
Cost: $10.00
Frequency: Quarterly
Circulation: 54000
Founded in 1863

23760 **Logistics Management & Distribution Report**
Reed Business Information
225 Wyman St
Suite 3
Waltham, MA 02451-1216

781-734-8000
800-662-7776; Fax: 781-734-8076
lm@reedbusiness.com
www.reedbusiness.com

Mark Finklestein, President
Peter Bradley, CFO
Stuart Whayman, CFO

Logistics Management and Distribution Report is written for managers and professionals in charge of traffic, transportation, purchasing, inventory control, containerization and warehousing the functions of physical distribution and business logistics. Covers marketing and operating strategies, cost reduction opportunities and governmental regulation and law.
Frequency: Monthly
Circulation: 30,000
Founded in 1977

23761 **Marine Digest & Transportation News**
Marine Publishing
1710 South Norman Street
Seattle, WA 98144-1234

206-709-1840; Fax: 206-324-8939
www.marinedigest.com

Peter Hurme, Publisher/Senior Editor
Gary Greenewald, Circulation Manager
Tom Henning, Sales/Marketing Manager
M Daigle, Owner

Serves the maritime shipping community primarily in the western United States. Updates on new products, suppliers, legislation and insurance are featured.
Cost: $28.00
Frequency: Monthly
Circulation: 7200
Founded in 1922

23762 **Mass Transit Magazine**
Cygnus Publishing
PO Box 803
Fort Atkinson, WI 53538-0803

920-000-1111; Fax: 920-563-1699

John French, CEO
Carie Grall, Associate Publisher
Paul Bowers, Group VP
Debbie Dumke, Manager
Deb Krause, National Accounts Manager
Cost: $120.00
Frequency: Monthly
Founded in 1966

23763 **Mid-West Truck Trader**
Heartland Communications
15400 Knoll #500
Dallas, TX 75248

800-247-2000; Fax: 515-574-2213

Bruce Foval, Editor

Trucking industry news and views.
Cost: $59.00
56 Pages
Frequency: Monthly
Founded in 1976

23764 **Milk & Liquid Food Transporter**
Brady Company
N80w12878 Fond Du Lac Ave
Menomonee Falls, WI 53051-4410

262-255-0100; Fax: 262-255-3388
www.bradycorp.com

Kathy Wall, President

Information for owners, operators and managers of companies that haul milk or other liquid foods in sanitary or food grade tankers. Publication covers maintenance, association news, state of the industry, business management, and activities of independent haulers.
Cost: $12.00
Frequency: Monthly
Circulation: 4,100

23765 **Modern Bulk Transporter**
Tunnell Publications
PO Box 66010
Houston, TX 77266

713-523-8124; Fax: 713-523-8384

Charles Wilson, Editor
Robin Anderson, Advertising Director

Serves the truck industry that transports petroleum and petroleum products. Accepts advertising.
Cost: $25.00
Frequency: Monthly

23766 **Movers News**
New York State Movers & Warehousemen's Association
125 Maiden Lane
11th Floor
New York, NY 10038

212-635-0510; Fax: 212-635-0511
nymovers@msn.com

David Blake, Editor
John Palisand, President

Association news.
Cost: $24.00
Frequency: BiMonthly
ISSN: 8750-1155
Founded in 1937

23767 **NATSO Truckers News**
Newport Communications
PO Box W
Newport Beach, CA 92658-8910

949-261-1636; Fax: 949-261-2904
www.heavytruck.com

W Dewey Clower, Publisher

Provides industry news, legislation affecting drivers, product developments, and on road service.
Cost: $20.00
Frequency: Monthly
Circulation: 182,716

23768 **National Bus Trader**
National Bus Trader
9698 W Judson Rd
Polo, IL 61064-9015

815-946-2341; Fax: 815-946-2347
www.busmag.com

Larry Plachno, CEO

Equipment magazine for over-the-road and integral buses in the United States and Canada.
Cost: $25.00
Frequency: Monthly
Circulation: 7000
ISSN: 0194-939X
Founded in 1977
Printed in on glossy stock

23769 **New Equipment Digest**
Penton Media
1166 Avenue of the Americas/10th
Suite 316
New York, NY 10036

212-204-4200; Fax: 216-696-6662
information@penton.com
www.penton.com

Jane Cooper, Marketing
Tom Sockel, Associate Editor
Robert King, Editor
Sarah Hughes, Production Manager
Bobbie Macy, Circulation Manager

Serves the general industrial field which includes manufacturing, processing, engineering services, construction, transportation, mining, pub-

lic utilities, wholesale distributors, educational services, libraries and governmental establishments.
Frequency: Monthly
Circulation: 206154
Founded in 1936

23770 **Newport's Road Star**
Newport Communications
38 Executive Park
Suite 300
Irvine, CA 92614-6755

949-261-1636
800-233-1911; Fax: 949-261-2904
www.truckinginfo.com

Doug Condra, President
Faye Solem, Circulation Manager
Steve Sturgess, Editor

Monthly magazine for professional long-distance tractor-trailer drivers, who either own their own trucks or drive for trucking companies.
Frequency: Monthly
Circulation: 153000
Founded in 1898

23771 **Oklahoma Motor Carrier**
Okalhoma Trucking Association
7201 N Classen Boulevard
Suite 106
Oklahoma City, OK 73116-620

405-843-9488
800-368-9576; Fax: 405-843-7310
www.oktrucking.org

Dan Case, Executive Director
Craig Schneithorst, Chairman

Official publication of Associated Motor Carriers of Oklahoma, the state trade association for the trucking industry.
30 Pages
Frequency: Quarterly
Circulation: 3000
Founded in 1932
Printed in 4 colors

23772 **Over the Road**
Ramp Publishing Group
PO Box 549
Roswell, GA 30077

770-587-0311; Fax: 770-642-8874

Marvin Shefsky, Publisher

Information for professional truck drivers, owners, operators, and fleet drivers on current events, industry news, driver profiles, and employment opportunities.
Cost: $30.00
Frequency: Monthly
Circulation: 116624

23773 **Overdrive Magazine**
Randall Publishing Company
PO Box 2155
Tuscaloosa, AL 35403-2155

205-758-2585
800-633-5953; Fax: 205-758-2593
www.randallpub.com

Wayne Randall, President
Brad Holthaus, Publisher
Linda Longton, Editor

For the owner/operator and small fleet operator.
Cost: $30.00
Frequency: Monthly
Circulation: 104753
Founded in 1934
Printed in 4 colors on glossy stock

23774 **Owner Operator**
Reed Business Information
2000 Clearwater Dr
Oak Brook, IL 60523-8809

630-574-0825; Fax: 630-288-8781
www.reedbusiness.com

Jeff Greisch, President

For independent truckers and small fleet owners.
Frequency: Monthly

23775 **P&D Magazine**
Motor Transport Management Group
3251 Beacon Road
West Sacramento, CA 95691-3475

916-373-3630; Fax: 916-852-5707

Robert L Titus, Publisher

Edited for the needs of pick up and delivery.
Cost: $5.00
Circulation: 33,571

23776 **PC-Trans**
University of Kansas
2011 Learned Hall
Lawrence, KS 66044-7526

785-864-2700; Fax: 785-864-5655
mgivechi@ku.edu
www.ku.edu

Lisa Harris, Editor
Mehrdad Givechi, Manager
Alice Kuo, Advertising
Pat Weaver, Director

Software reviews and miscellaneous computer information for transportation professionals.
Circulation: 13000
Founded in 1872

23777 **Pro Trucker**
Ramp Publishing Group
PO Box 549
Roswell, GA 30077-549

770-587-0311
800-878-0311; Fax: 770-642-8874
www.protruckeronline.com

Greg McClendon, Sales Manager
Marvin Shefsky, Publisher

Professional truck drivers, owners, operators, and fleet drivers, information on interviews, industry news, employment information, distribution locations and leasing options for the professional drivers.
Frequency: Monthly
Circulation: 116000
Founded in 1981

23778 **Progressive Railroading**
Trade Press Publishing Corporation
PO Box 694
Milwaukee, WI 53201-694

414-271-5011; Fax: 414-228-1134
www.facilities.com

Steve Bolte, Publisher
Pat Foran, Editor
Tim Rowe, Marketing
Wendy Melnick, Production Manager
Robert J Wisniewski, CEO

Feature includes management techniques, purchasing developments, engineering innovations and general industry news.
Cost: $55.00
Frequency: Monthly
Circulation: 25,207
Founded in 1994

23779 **Protecting Shippers' Interests**
120 Main Street
Huntington, NY 11743-6906

631-270-0100; Fax: 516-549-8962
tcpc@transportlaw.com
www.transportlaw.com

William J Augello, Executive Director

Published by the Transportation Consumer Protection Council.
Cost: $75.00
Founded in 1997

23780 **RV Business**
TL Enterprises
3601 Calle Tecate
Camarillo, CA 93012-5056

805-987-1800; Fax: 805-389-0484
tlecs@magserv.com
www.rvbusiness.com

Katherine Sharma, Editor
Denielle Sternburg, Business Manager
Sherman Goldenberg, Publisher

Reports on various aspects of the recreational vehicle industry, including forecasting trends, new technologies, marketing and business concepts.
Cost: $12.00
Frequency: Monthly

23781 **Rail News Update**
Association of American Railroads
425 Third Street SW
Suite 114
Washington, DC 20024-3217

202-639-2100
www.aar.org
Facebook, Twitter, LinkedIn

Edward R. Hamberger, President & CEO
Patricia M. Reilly, SVP, Communications

Publishes pertinent new in the railroad industry especially covering Washington news. Covers Department of Transportation and Interstate Commerce activities.
Frequency: BiWeekly

23782 **Railroad Facts**
Association of American Railroads
425 Third Street SW
Suite 114
Washington, DC 20024-3217

202-639-2100
media@aar.org
www.aar.org
Facebook, Twitter, LinkedIn

Offers statistical information and research reports on railroad travel.
Cost: $60.00
Frequency: Annual
Founded in 1934

23783 **Railroad Ten-Year Trends**
Association of American Railroads
425 Third Street SW
Suite 114
Washington, DC 20024-3217

202-639-2100
media@aar.org
www.aar.org
Facebook, Twitter, LinkedIn

Edward Hamberger, President & CEO
Tom White, Editor

Offers historical facts and perspectives on America's railroad industry.
Cost: $95.00
Founded in 1934

23784 **Railway Age**
Simmons-Boardman Publishing Corporation
345 Hudson St
Suite 1201
New York, NY 10014-7123

212-620-7200; Fax: 212-633-1165
www.simmonsboardman.com

Arthur J McGinnis Jr, President

Emphasis is placed on technology, operations, strategic planning, marketing and other issues

such as legislative, labor and management developments.
Frequency: Monthly
Circulation: 260030
Founded in 1876

23785 **Railway Track and Structures**
Simmons-Boardman Publishing Corporation
345 Hudson St
Suite 1201
New York, NY 10014-7123
212-620-7200; Fax: 212-633-1165
www.simmonsboardman.com
Arthur J McGinnis Jr, President
A technical magazine designed to meet the information needs of the roadway and other civil engineering related departments of North American rail freight and passenger operators.
Frequency: Monthly
Circulation: 8541

23786 **Refrigerated Transporter**
Penton
PO Box 66010
Houston, TX 77266
713-523-8124
800-880-0368; Fax: 713-523-8384
refrigeratedtransporter.com
Ray Anderson, Publisher

23787 **Road King**
Hammock Publishing
28 White Bridge Road
Suite 209
Nashville, TN 37205
615-385-9745; Fax: 615-386-9349
www.roadking.com
Rex Hammock, President
Focuses on trucking lifestyles, achievements and interests. Offers articles on equipment and driver success.
Cost: $15.00
Frequency: BiMonthly
Circulation: 222,590

23788 **School Bus Fleet**
Bobit Publishing Company
3520 Challenger Street
Torrance, CA 90503-1640
310-533-2400; Fax: 310-533-2500
sbf@bobit.com
www.bobitbusinessmedia.com
Facebook, Twitter, LinkedIn
Richard Rivera, CEO
Mark Hollenbeck, Associate Publisher
Frank Digiacomo, Vice President Emeritus
James Blue, General Manager/Publisher
A magazine that serves the field of pupil transportation, to public and private schools and to independent contract operators transporting students.
Cost: $25.00
Frequency: Monthly
Circulation: 22000
Founded in 1961

23789 **Shippers' Domestic Truck Bill of Lading & Common Carrier Rate Agreement Kit**
Transportation & Logistics Council
120 Main Street
Huntington, NY 11743
631-549-8988; Fax: 631-549-8962
www.tlcouncil.org
Diane Smid, Membership Secretary
Judy Selvaggio, Administrative Secretary
George Pezold, Executive Director
Published by the Transportation Consumer Protection Council.
Cost: $50.00
Frequency: Monthly
Founded in 1974

23790 **Signalman's Journal**
Brotherhood of Railroad Signalmen
601 W Golf Road
Box U
Mount Prospect, IL 60056-4276
847-439-3732; Fax: 847-439-3743
signalman@brs.org
www.brs.org
W Dan Pickett, President
Walter A Barrows, Treasurer
Information concerning railroad signaling devices, equipment and apparatus, also includes current events and items pertaining to railroad signalmen.
40 Pages
Frequency: Quarterly
Circulation: 10700
ISSN: 0037-5020
Founded in 1901
Printed in 4 colors on glossy stock

23791 **Southern Motor Cargo**
477 S Shady Grove Road
Memphis, TN 38120-2512
901-346-5943; Fax: 901-276-5400
Wallace Witmer Jr, Editor
Offers information on shipping.
Cost: $30.00
66 Pages
Frequency: Monthly
Founded in 1945

23792 **Speedlines**
High Speed Grand Transportation Association
1010 Massachusetts Avenue NW, #110
Washington, DC 20001-5402
202-789-8107; Fax: 212-789-8109
www.hsgt.org
Mark Dysart, Editor
Exclusively devoted to the High Speed Ground Transportation Association covering broad policy debates, state activity reports, federal developments and technological papers.
Frequency: Quarterly
Circulation: 3,200

23793 **Structural Mover**
International Association of Structural Movers
PO Box 2637
Lexington, SC 29071-2637
803-951-9304; Fax: 803-951-9314
www.iasm.org
N Eugene Brymer, Staff Executive
A magazine written specifically for members of the International Association of Structural Movers. Subcription to quarterly magazine included in price of membership to IASM.
Frequency: Quarterly
Circulation: 500

23794 **Successful Dealer**
Kona Communications
707 Lake Cook Road
Deerfield, IL 60015
847-498-3180
800-767-5662; Fax: 847-498-3197
www.successfuldealer.com
Denise Rondini, Editorial Director
James D Moss, Publisher
James D Moss, President
Tom Cory, Circulation Manager
John S Dickson, National Sales Manager
Edited for the dealer organization covering dealerships, selling and servicing medium to heavy-duty trucks, trailers and construction equipment. Accepts advertising.
Cost: $50.00
52 Pages
Frequency: bi-monthly
Circulation: 23000
ISSN: 0161-6080
Founded in 1918
Printed in g colors on 4 stock

23795 **Teamster Magazine**
International Brotherhood of Teamsters
25 Louisiana Ave NW
Washington, DC 20001-2130
202-624-6800; Fax: 202-624-6918
communications@teamster.org
www.teamster.org
James P Hoffa Jr, President
Per Bernstein, Editor-in-Chief
Affiliated with the AFL-CIO. Magazine is published for members only of 30 pages.
Cost: $12.00
Circulation: 1.4 mill
Founded in 1903

23796 **Technology and Society**
IEEE Society on Social Implications of Technology
445 Hoes Lane
Piscataway, NJ 08854
j.pitt@imperial.ac.uk
technologyandsociety.org
Facebook, Twitter, LinkedIn
Jeremy Pitt, Editor_in-Chief
Terri A. Bookman, Managing Editor
Flagship magazine of the IEEE Society on Social Implications of Technology, with peer-reviewed articles on the impact of technology on the world.

23797 **Traffic Management**
Reed Business Information
275 Washington St
Newton, MA 02458-1611
617-964-3030; Fax: 617-630-3730
webmaster@reedbusiness.com
www.designnews.com
Mitch MacDonald, Editor
Ron Bondlow, Publisher
Accepts advertising.
100 Pages
Frequency: Monthly
Circulation: 73000
Founded in 1982

23798 **Traffic World**
Journal of Commerce
33 Washington Street
13th Floor
Newark, NJ 07102
973-848-7000
800-255-1341; Fax: 973-848-7068
William B Cassidy, Managuing Editor
Discusses all facets of the transportation industry. Also online at www.joc.com.
Cost: $174.00
Frequency: Weekly
Founded in 1907

23799 **Trailer/Body Builders**
Penton
PO Box 66010
Houston, TX 77266
713-523-8124
800-880-0368; Fax: 713-523-8384
www.trailer-bodybuilders.com
Ray Anderson, Publisher

Serves the truck trailer and truck body manufacturing industry. Accepts advertising.
Cost: $25.00
Frequency: Monthly
Circulation: 15500
Founded in 1960

23800 **Transport Fleet News**
Transport Publishing
1962 N Bissell Street
#3
Chicago, IL 60614-5015
773-058-8540
Lillana Rogala, Publisher
Industry news and product for fleet supervisors.
Circulation: 10,500

23801 **Transport Topics**
Express Carriers Association
950 N. Glebe Road
Suite 210
Arlington, VA 22203
703-838-1770
866-322-7447; Fax: 703-838-7916
habramso@ttnews.com
www.ttnews.com
Bruce harmon, Managing Editor
Neil Abt, News Editor
Nancy Baily, Copy Editor
Trucking industry news, features and analysis.

23802 **Transportation & Distribution**
Penton Media
1166 Avenue of the Americas/10th
Suite 316
New York, NY 10036
212-204-4200; Fax: 216-696-6662
editor@logisticstoday.com
www.penton.com
Jane Cooper, Marketing
Antoinette Sanchez-Perkins, Circulation Manager
Newt Barret, Publisher
Dave Blanchard, Editor
David Nussbaum, CEO
Serves the information needs of logistics professionals, identifying trends and providing expert views on strategic, management and operational subjects affecting logistics. Accepts advertising.
Cost: $60.00
78 Pages
Frequency: Monthly
Circulation: 85000
Founded in 1960
Printed in 4 colors on glossy stock

23803 **Transportation Equipment News**
Vulcan Publications
PO Box 55886
Birmingham, AL 35255
205-328-6198; Fax: 205-987-2882
www.vulcanpub.com
Ian Greenspan, Publisher
Extensive coverage of government regulations, recruiting and training issues as well as buying and leasing, maintenance and industry trade shows.

23804 **Transportation Leader**
Taxicab, Limousine & Paratransit Association
3200 Tower Oaks Blvd
Suite 220
Rockville, MD 20852
301-984-5700; Fax: 301-984-5703
info@tlpa.org
www.tlpa.org
Alfred LaGasse, CEO
Victor Dizengoff, President
Leading resource for news and information on issues, trends, and people in the private, for-hire passenger transportation industry. Provides readers with an array of features, articles, and columns that include information on managing a transportation company, industry trends, driver's tips, an industry calendar of events, coverage of TLPA events, and advertisements from the industry's leading suppliers.
Cost: $4.00
48 Pages
Frequency: Quarterly
Circulation: 6000
Founded in 1920
Mailing list available for rent: 6,000 names at $100 per M
Printed in 4 colors on glossy stock

23805 **Truck Accessory News**
Bobit Publishing
3520 Challenger St
Torrance, CA 90503-1640
310-533-2400; Fax: 310-533-2500
www.bobit.com
Edward J Bobit, CEO
Travis Weeks, Publisher
Jerry Martin, Circulation Manager
Provides information on product and merchandise trends, covers industry news on retail activities, and interviews top executives and buyers.
Cost: $37.00
Frequency: Monthly
Circulation: 10000
Founded in 1961

23806 **Trucker's Connection**
Megan Cullingford
5960 Crooked Creek Road
Suite 15
Norcross, GA 30092
770-416-0927; Fax: 770-416-1734
www.truckersconnection.com
Dan Barnhill, Editor
Reid Ramsay, Production Manager
Megan Cullingford, General Manager
David Guthrie, Advertising Sales
Published for the use of long haul, over-the-road truck drivers, owner operators, small trucking company fleet owners, safety and recruiting of personnel for trucking companies in the US and Canada.
Frequency: Monthly
Circulation: 16,5,000
Founded in 1986
Printed in 4 colors on glossy stock

23807 **Truckin'**
McMullen Argus Publishing
2400 E Katella Avenue
11th Floor
Anaheim, CA 92806-6832
714-939-2559; Fax: 714-978-6390
Steve Parr, CEO
Susan Brocett, Marketing Manager
Brad Christopher, Publisher
Steve Warner, Editor
Jerome Dziechiasz, Sales Manager
Provides information on testing new trucks, reviewing accessories and trucking' activities.
Cost: $24.95
Frequency: Monthly
Circulation: 180000

23808 **Trucking Technology**
167 Cherry Street
Suite 430
Milford, CT 06460-3466
203-882-9485

23809 **World Wide Shipping (WWS)**
World Wide Shipping Guide
16302 Byrnwyck Ln
Odessa, FL 33556-2807
813-920-4788; Fax: 813-920-8268
www.wwship.com
Lee Di Paci, Publisher
Barbara Edwards, Marketing Manager
Bob Susor, Marketing Manager
Dedicated to the interests of North American exporters, importers, distributors, freight forwarders, NVOCC's and customs brokers requiring freight tranportation services and equipment.
Cost: $32.00
32 Pages
Frequency: Fortnightly
Circulation: 9000
ISSN: 1060-7900
Founded in 1919
Printed in 4 colors on glossy stock

Trade Shows

23810 **AAR Annual Convention and Exhibit**
Railway Systems Suppliers
9306 New Lagrange Road
Suite 100
Louisville, KY 40242
502-327-7774; Fax: 502-327-0541
rssi@rssi.org
www.rssi.org
Donald Remaley, Executive Director
Franklin Brown, President
Railroad signal and communication equipment displays, annual meeting & banquet.
Frequency: Annual
Founded in 1960

23811 **AREMA Annual Conference & Exposition**
American Railway Engineering & Maintenance-of-Way
4501 Forbes Boulevard
Suite 130
Lanham, MD 20706
301-459-3200; Fax: 301-459-8077
dknight@arema.org
www.arema.org
Beth Caruso, Executive Director & CEO
Stacy Spaulding, Senior Director, Board Operations
Desiree Knight, Director, Conferences & Seminars
Approximately 198 exhibitors from all segments of the railway engineering and maintenance industry, in addition to the conference talks, seminars, and events. Advanced registration for non-members starts at $760.
1600 Attendees
Frequency: Bi-Ennial

23812 **ARTBA National Convention**
American Road and Transportation Builders Assn
1219 28th St NW
Washington, DC 20007-3389
202-289-4434; Fax: 202-289-4435
general@artba.org
www.artba.org
Pete Ruane, President
Matt Jeanneret, Sr. VP, Communications/Marketing
Jaime Mahoney, Publications Manager
Liz Cavallaro, Sales Manager
Tom Hill, Treasurer
Frequency: Annual/Fall

23813 **American Bus Marketplace**
1015 15th Street NW
Washington, DC 20005-2605

202-842-9100
800-283-2877; Fax: 202-842-0850

Katie Robbins

Sales and marketing event for the North American group travel industry. 350 booths.
2M Attendees
Frequency: December

23814 **American Car Rental Association Convention**
11250 Roger Bacon Drive
#8
Reston, VA 20190

703-787-7718; Fax: 703-435-4390
www.acraorg.com

Gwendolyn Hogan

One hundred exhibits of cars, vans, buses, computers, equipment and services for car rental company owners and officers. Conference, reception and dinner.
600 Attendees
Frequency: Annual
Founded in 1978

23815 **American Public Transportation Association Expo**
1666 K Street NW
Suite 1100
Washington, DC 20006

202-496-4800; Fax: 202-496-4324
meetings2@apta.com
www.apta.com

William W Millar, President
Petra Mollet, VP
Rosemary Sherid, Marketing

Seminar, workshop, conference, luncheon, banquet, tours and 800 exhibits for the planning designing and finance and operation of public transportation.
15000 Attendees
Frequency: October 2008/2011
Founded in 1882

23816 **American Truck Dealers Convention and Equipment Exposition**
National Automobile Dealers Association
8400 Westpark Drive
Mc Lean, VA 22102-3522

703-217-7000; Fax: 703-821-7075
www.nada.org

Gary Heimes

Annual show of 100 manufacturers, suppliers and distributors of products and services designed to control dealership expenses, help merchandising or improve profitability.
2,500 Attendees
Founded in 1963

23817 **American Trucking Association Management Conference and Exhibition**
American Trucking Association
2200 Mill Road
Alexandria, VA 22314-4677

703-838-1700
800-282-5463; Fax: 703-838-5720
www.trucking.org

Bill Graves, President

Annual show of 168 exhibitors of equipment, supplies and services related to the trucking industry.
1,500 Attendees
Frequency: Annual
Founded in 1984

23818 **Association for Commuter Transportation Convention**
808 17th Street NW
Suite 200
Washington, DC 20006-3910

202-393-3497
tmi.cob.fsu.edu/act

Elizabeth Stutts, President
Kenneth M Sufka, Executive Director
Shamus Misek, VP
Kim Tabah, Director of Development
Barbara Ash, Communications Manager

Thirty booths.
300 Attendees
Frequency: September

23819 **Association of Railway Museums Convention**
Association of Railway Museums
PO Box 370
Tujunga, CA 91043-0370

818-951-9151; Fax: 818-951-9151

Paul Hammond, President ARM

Annual show and exhibits for the preservation of railway equipment, artifacts and history. Seminar, tours, banquet and dinner.
125 Attendees
Frequency: October
Founded in 1961

23820 **Biodiesel Investor Conference**
Platts
24 Hartwell Avenue
Lexington, MA 02421

781-860-6100
866-355-2930
registration@platts.com
www.platts.com

Frequency: June Houston

23821 **ECA Shipper: Carrier Marketplace**
Express Carriers Association
9532 Liberia Avenue
Manassas, VA 20110

703-361-1058
866-322-7447; Fax: 703-361-5274
www.expresscarriers.com

Carrie Ehlers, President
Stuart Hyden, First Vice President

Premier business to business event featuring one on one interviews between shippers, carriers and vendors of products/services to the transportation industry.
300+ Attendees
Frequency: April
Founded in 1997

23822 **Education Conference & Expo**
American Moving and Storage Association
1611 Duke St
Alexandria, VA 22314-3406

703-683-7410; Fax: 703-683-7527
www.moving.org

Linda Bauer Darr, CEO
Sandy Lynch, SVP

The largest gathering of moving and storage industry professionals in the country. With more than 30 education sessions and over 10 hours of dedicated network time, the conference & expo offers countless opportunities to further your career while making new business contacts.
Frequency: Annual/March

23823 **Fleet Management Institute (NAFA) Convention**
100 Wood Avenue S
Suite 310
Iselin, NJ 08830

732-494-8100; Fax: 732-494-6789
info@nafa.org
www.nafa.org

Patricia Murtaugh, Assistant Executive Director
Joanne Marsh, Manager

Fleet management education and automobile parts and services, as well as maintenance for business and public service vehicles. 250 booths
2M Attendees
Frequency: April/May

23824 **Institute of Transportation Engineers Annual Meeting**
Institute of Transportation Engineers
525 School Street SW
Suite 410
Washington, DC 20024-2729

202-548-8050; Fax: 202-863-5486
www.ite.org

Marianne Wool, Manager
Shannon Gore Peters, Editor

Annual meeting of 100 exhibitors of transportation equipment, supplies and services.
2,000 Attendees
Frequency: Las Vegas

23825 **Intermodal EXPO**
Intermodal Association of North America
11785 Beltsville Drive
Suite 1100
Calverton, MD 20705-4049

301-982-3400; Fax: 301-982-4815
iana@intermodal.org
www.intermodal.org
Facebook, Twitter, LinkedIn

Joanne F. Casey, President & CEO
Stephen A. Keppler, SVP, Member Services
Jon Palmbak, SVP, Digital Products & Technology

Forum for information exchange on issues facing intermodal supply chain.
1800 Attendees
Founded in 1991

23826 **Intermodal Operations, Safety and Maintenance Business Meeting**
Intermodal Association of North America
11785 Beltsville Drive
Suite 1100
Calverton, MD 20705-4049

301-982-3400; Fax: 301-982-4815; Fax: 301-982-4815
iana@intermodal.org
www.intermodal.org

Joanne F. Casey, President & CEO
Stephen A. Keppler, SVP, Member Services
Jon Palmbak, SVP, Digital Products & Technology

Promotes the benefits and growth of intermodal freight transportation.
Frequency: Annual/May

23827 **International Association of Structural Movers Annual Convention**
PO Box 600
Oakton, VA 22124

703-648-3225; Fax: 503-543-6697
www.iasm.org

Containing 20 booths and 15 exhibits.

23828 **International Public Transit Expo**
Pemco/Professional Expo Management Company

191 S Gary Avenue
Carol Stream, IL 60188-2092

630-690-5600; Fax: 203-840-9662

Barbara Silverman, VP

The world's largest transit industry event offering a chance for top transit officials to meet with manufacturers from around the world.
16M Attendees
Frequency: October

23829 **International Truck and Bus Expo**
Society of Automotive Engineers
400 Commonwealth Drive
Warrendale, PA 15096-0001

724-772-8548; Fax: 724-776-0790
www.sae.org

Andrew Brown, Treasurer

23830 **Light Truck Accessory Expo**
Truck Cap and Accessory Association
6564 Loisdale Court
Suite 430
Springfield, VA 22150-1812

703-822-0707
800-283-8242; Fax: 703-922-7806

Kendra Moore, Director Meetings/Marketing

Annual show of 150 manufacturers of truck caps and light truck accessories.
2,500 Attendees

23831 **Link**
R&D Associates
16607 Blanco Road
Suite 305
San Antonio, TX 78232-1940

210-682-4302; Fax: 830-493-8036

David Dee, Editor

Articles of interest to the food, food packaging, food processing and foodservice industry. 50 booths.
300 Attendees
Frequency: Spring/Fall

23832 **Mid-West Truck & Trailer Show**
2727 N Dirksen Pkwy
Springfield, IL 62702-1490

217-525-0310; Fax: 217-525-0342
www.midwesttruckshow.com
Facebook

Don Schaefer, President

Serves trucking industry by lobbying on their behalf, assisting with registration, license plate procurement and group insurance programs. Conducts educational programs, has own self-funded workers compensation insurance program. Trade association represents truck owners in 14 states.
2700 Members
Founded in 1962

23833 **Midwest Truck Show**
Mid-West Truckers Association
2727 N Dirksen Parkway
Springfield, IL 62702

217-525-0310; Fax: 217-525-0342
info@mid-westtruckers.com
www.mid-westtruckers.com

Don Schaefer, Executive VP

Annual show and exhibits of trucks, trailers, financing information, computers, insurance information and related equipment, supplies and services. Containing 200 booths and 150 exhibitors.
6,000 Attendees
Frequency: February

23834 **NDTA Forum & Expo**
National Defense Transportation Association
50 S Pickett Street
Suite 220
Alexandria, VA 22304-7206

703-751-5011; Fax: 703-823-8761
info@ndtahq.com
www.ndtahq.com

LTG Kenneth Wykle, President
COL Dennis Edwards, VP Marketing

A key element in the Association's fulfillment of its educational and professional development missions and it also offers outstanding opportunities for networking and mentoring.
1200 Attendees
Frequency: Annual/September

23835 **National Industrial Transportation League Trade Show**
1700 N Moore St
Suite 1900
Arlington, VA 22209-1931

703-524-5011; Fax: 703-524-5017
info@nitl.org
www.nitl.org

Arthur E. Cole, President
Michael J Barr, First Vice Chairman
Peter Gatti, Executive VP

Annual show of 250 exhibitors of computer services software and innovations for transportation operations.
600 Members
Founded in 1907

23836 **National Private Truck Council Management/ Education Conference**
National Private Truck Council
66 Canal Center Plaza
Alexandria, VA 22314-1591

703-683-1300; Fax: 703-683-1217

Gary Petty, CEO

Annual conference and exhibits of equipment, supplies and services for processors, shippers, distributors and retailers who operate their own truck fleets to advance their primary nontransportation business enterprises.

23837 **North American Truck Show**
North American Expositions Company
33 Rutherford Avenue
Boston, MA 02129-3795

617-242-6092
800-225-1577; Fax: 617-242-1817
www.truckingexpo.com

Gregory Soughlin, Show Manager

Six hundred booths.
25M Attendees
Frequency: May

23838 **Railway Interchange Annual Conference**
American Railway Engineering & Maintenance-of-Way
4501 Forbes Boulevard
Suite 150
Lanham, MD 20706-4362

301-459-3200; Fax: 301-459-8077
bcaruso@arema.org
www.arema.org

Beth Caruso, Executive Director & CEO
Vickie Fisher, Director, Finance
Stace Spaulding, Executive & Board Operations
Desiree Knights, Director, Conferences & Seminars
Lindsay Hamilton, Director, Marketing & Communication

23839 **School Bus Fleet ConneX Conference**
School Bus Fleet/Bobit Publishing Company
3520 Challenger Street
Torrance, CA 90503-1640

310-533-2400; Fax: 310-533-2500
sbf@bobit.com
www.schoolbusfleetconnex.com

Richard Rivera, CEO
Mark Hollenbeck, Associate Publisher
James Blue, General Manager/Publisher

An opportunity to network and build relationships with other action-minded individuals involved in school transportation.
Frequency: Annual
Founded in 1961

23840 **TLPA Annual Convention & Trade Show**
Taxicab, Limousine & Paratransit Association
3200 Tower Oaks Boulevard
Suite 220
Rockville, MD 20852

301-984-5700; Fax: 301-984-5703
www.tlpa.org

Alfred La Gasse III, Executive VP
Victor Dizengoff, President

Shares information vital to owners or taxicab, limousine, airport shuttle, paratransit and nonemergency medical transportation fleets. 100 suppliers and exhibitors of the newest products available to the industry.
1000 Attendees
Frequency: Annual

23841 **TransComp Exhibition**
National Industrial Transportation League
1700 N Moore Street
Suite 1900
Arlington, VA 22209-1931

703-524-5011; Fax: 703-524-5017
info@nitl.org
www.nitl.org

Ellie Gilanshah, VP Finance and Membership
3000 Attendees
Frequency: November
Founded in 1907

23842 **Transportation Intermediaries Annual Convention & Trade Show**
Transportation Intermediaries Association
1625 Prince St.
Suite 200
Alexandria, VA 22314

703-299-5700; Fax: 703-836-0123
info@tianet.org
www.tianet.org

Robert Voltmann, President/CEO
Larry Fisher, Contact

Education and policy organization for North American transportation intermediaries. TIA is the only national association representing the interests of all third party transportation service providers. The members of TIA include logistics management firms, property brokers, perishable commodities brokers, freight forwarders, intermodal marketers, ocean and air forwarders, and NVOCC's.
700 Attendees
Founded in 1978

23843 **Transportation Research Forum Annual Meeting**
Transportation Research Forum

Department 2880
PO Box 6050
Fargo, ND 58108-6050

701-231-7766; Fax: 701-231-1945
info@trforum.org
www.trforum.org

Richard Gritta, President
Starr McMullen, VP
300 Members
Founded in 1958

23844 **Truck Show Las Vegas**
Independent Trade Show Management
1155 Chess Drive
Suite 102
Foster City, CA 94404-1117

650-349-4876
800-227-5992; Fax: 650-349-5169
www.truckshow.com

Sue K Fena, Sr. Show Coordinator
Roger Sherrard, President

The premier commercial truck and equipment show in the USA. Containing 2,500 booths and 350 exhibits, also offers seminars and workshops on current topics in the trucking industry.
20M Attendees
Frequency: June
Founded in 1961
Mailing list available for rent

23845 **Truckerfest**
Newport Communications
38 Executive Park
Suite 300
Irvine, CA 92614-6755

949-261-1636
800-233-1911; Fax: 949-261-2904
www.truckerfest.com

Bud Farquhar, Show Manager
BJ Iverson, Events Coordinator

Trucker appreciation event at Alamo Travel Plaza, Reno, NV. Truck Parade, trucker games, music, free dinners, truck beauty contest, and fireworks. Containing 75 booths and 60 exhibits.
10M Attendees
Frequency: August

23846 **Trucking Show Mid-America**
1404 Browns Lane
Suite E
Louisville, KY 40207

Home Page: www.truckingshow.com

Timothy Young, Show Manager

Four hundred and fifty booths displaying the latest in trucking.
35M Attendees
Frequency: March

23847 **Truckload Carriers Association Annual Convention**
Truckload Carriers Association
555 East Braddock Road
Suite CS-4
Alexandria, VA 22314-2182

703-838-1960; Fax: 703-836-6610
tca@truckload.org
www.truckload.org
Facebook, Twitter, LinkedIn, YouTube, Flickr

Russell Stubbs, Chairman
John Lyboldt, President
William Giroux, Executive Vice President
Tomora Brown, Membership Liaison

Annual convention bringing together professionals from across the truckload carrier industry for 3.5 days of networking, speakers, and exhibitors.
900 Members
Frequency: Annual/March
Founded in 1938

23848 **Women's Transportation Seminar**
Women's Transportation Seminar
1 Walnut Street
Boston, MA 02108-3616

617-367-3273; Fax: 617-227-6783

Annual seminar and exhibits of transportation equipment, supplies and services.

23849 **Work Truck Show**
National Truck Equipment Association
37400 Hills Tech Drive
Farmington Hills, MI 48331-3414

248-489-7090
800-441-6832; Fax: 248-489-8590
info@ntea.com
www.ntea.com

Tom Rawson, President
Dennis Jones, First Vice President

Annual business to business event designed to bring together distributors, upfitters, manufacturers, buyers and users of work trucks in all industries including delivery, government, construction and landscaping.
7,000 Attendees
Frequency: March

Directories & Databases

23850 **AAA Bridge and Ferry Directory**
American Automobile Association
1000 AAA Drive
Heathrow, FL 32746-5062

407-444-7966

Melanie Fuller, Highway Infoformation Coordinator

Offers information on over 500 toll facilities in the US, Canada and Mexico that enable automobiles and passengers to complete toll non-highway portions of their journey.
Cost: $12.50
103 Pages
Frequency: Annual

23851 **ARTBA Transportation Officials & Engineers Directory**
American Road and Transportation Builders Assn
1219 28th St NW
Washington, DC 20007-3389

202-289-4434; Fax: 202-289-4435
general@artba.org
www.artba.org

Pete Ruane, President
Matt Jeanneret, Sr. VP, Communications/Marketing
Jaime Mahoney, Publications Manager
Liz Cavallaro, Sales Manager
Tom Hill, Treasurer

An annual survey of local, state and federal transportation agencies offered as a pocket-sized publication and as a mergeable Excel spreadsheet. The TO&E Directory includes key information about more than 6,000 state and local transportation departments and authorities, including URLs and e-mail addresses. From $195 for members to get the pocket edition to $475 for non-members to get the Excel version.
6300 Members
Frequency: Annual
Founded in 1902

23852 **Affiliated Warehouse Companies Directory**
Affiliated Warehouse Companies, Inc
PO Box 295
Hazlet, NJ 07730-0295

732-739-2323; Fax: 732-739-4154
sales@awco.com
www.awco.com

Jim McBride, President
Patrick McBride, Vice President

Third party logistics and public warehousing, marketing and sales company. Directory is free.
Founded in 1953
Mailing list available for rent: 8,500 names at $100 per M
Printed in 4 colors

23853 **Air CargoWorld & Traffic World**
Knight-Ridder Financial
75 Wall Street
Floor 23
New York, NY 10005-2833

212-429-2307; Fax: 212-372-7148

Offers valuable information on cash, futures and options markets.

23854 **Airline, Ship & Catering: Onboard Service Buyer's Guide & Directory**
International Publishing Company of America
664 La Villa Dr
Miami Springs, FL 33166-6030

305-887-1700; Fax: 305-885-1923

Alexander Morton, Owner

Offers information on over 6,000 airlines, railroads, ship lines and termianl restaurants.
Cost: $125.00
Frequency: Annual
Circulation: 6,000

23855 **American Bus Association's Motorcoach Marketer**
American Bus Association
700 13th St NW
Suite 575
Washington, DC 20005-5923

202-842-1645; Fax: 202-842-0850
abainfo@buses.org
www.buses.org

Peter J Pantuso, CEO
Eron Shosteck, Marketing

This directory is a comprehensive guide of the bus and travel industry offering information on hotels and sightseeing services, attractions, museums, restaurants and more.
500 Pages
Frequency: Annual
Founded in 1926

23856 **American Public Transit Association Membership Directory**
American Public Transit Association
1666 K St NW
Suite 1100
Washington, DC 20006-1215

202-496-4800; Fax: 202-496-4324
hbrett@apta.com
www.apta.com

Karol J Popkin, CEO
Petra Mollet, VP
Rosemary Sherid, Marketing

A who's who directory of services and supplies within the public transportation industry.
Founded in 1882

23857 **American Shortline Railway Guide**
Kalmbach Publishing Company

Po Box 1612
Waukesha, WI 53187-1612

262-796-8776; Fax: 262-796-1615
www.trains.com

Gerald Boettcher, President

Directory of services and supplies to the industry.
Cost: $18.95
320 Pages

23858 Bus Garage Index
Friendship Publications
PO Box 1472
Spokane, WA 99210-1472

800-541-2670; Fax: 509-325-0405

Bruce Sankey, President
Leslie Maris, VP Marketing
Linda Metler, Production Manager

Offers information on over 900 garages and service centers in the United States and Canada offering services to buses on charter service and tours.
Cost: $28.00
140 Pages
Circulation: 3,000
Mailing list available for rent: 14M names
Printed in 4 colors on glossy stock

23859 Bus Industry Directory
Friendship Publications
PO Box 1472
Spokane, WA 99210-1472

800-541-2670; Fax: 509-325-0405

Bruce Sankey, President/Publisher
Leslie Maris, VP Marketing

A comprehensive list of over 4,500 intercity and charter bus companies and local transit authorities in the United States and Canada.
Cost: $78.00
500 Pages
Frequency: Annual
Mailing list available for rent: 14M names
Printed in 4 colors on glossy stock

23860 Carrier Routing Director
Transportation Technical Services
500 Lafayette Boulevard
Fredericksburg, VA 22401-6070

540-899-9872
800-666-4887; Fax: 888-665-9887

Thomas R Fugee, Executive VP

Two thousand six hundred top common and contract carriers, toll-free faxes, states served + Canadian provinces and Mexico, equipment types, commodities.
Cost: $145.00
Frequency: Annual
Founded in 1992

23861 DRI Transportation Detail
DRI/McGraw-Hill
24 Hartwell Ave
Lexington, MA 02421-3103

781-860-6060; Fax: 781-860-6002
support@construction.com
www.construction.com

Walt Arvin, President

This time series contains annual and quarterly data describing aspects of the transportation industry.

23862 Defense Transportation Journal NDTA Almanac
National Defense Transportation Association
50 S Pickett Street
Suite 220
Alexandria, VA 22304-7206

703-751-5011; Fax: 703-823-8761
info@ndtahq.com
www.ndtahq.com
Facebook, Twitter, LinkedIn, You Tube

LTG Kenneth Wykle, President
COL Dennis Edwards, VP Marketing

Reference book of Military/Government/Transportation industry companies and executives
128 Pages

23863 Directory of Shippers
Transportation Technical Services
500 Lafayette Boulevard
Fredericksburg, VA 22401-6070

540-899-9872
800-666-4887; Fax: 888-665-9887

Thomas R Fugee, Executive VP

Compilateion of 14,000 logistics executives. Key information on 13,500 companies, phone, fax-e-mail, addresses, SIC's, revenue. Great marketing sales and research tool.
Cost: $170.00
Frequency: Annual
Founded in 1992

23864 Directory of Transportation Professionals
National Assn of Regulatory Utility Commissioners
PO Box 684
Washington, DC 20044-0684

202-898-2200

Offers valuable information on over 100 regulated transportation firms and professionals.
Cost: $20.00
150 Pages
Frequency: Annual

23865 Directory of Truck Dealers
Transportation Technical Services
500 Lafayette Boulevard
Fredericksburg, VA 22401-6070

540-899-9872
800-666-4887; Fax: 888-665-9887

Thomas R Fugee, Executive VP

Unique, extensive list of 2,700 of the nation's kmid-size/heavy truck dealers. Address, brands sold, serviced, keky contacts, phone and fax.
Cost: $95.00
Frequency: Annual
Founded in 1992

23866 Fleet Owner-Specs and Buyers' Directory Issue
Primedia
1166 Avenue of the Americas/10th Fl
Shawnee Mission, NY 10036

212-204-4200; Fax: 913-514-6895
www.penton.com

Eric Jacobson, Senior VP
Tom Moore, Editor
Chris Meyer, Director

Lists of manufacturers of equipment and materials used in the operation, management and maintenance of truck and bus fleets.
Cost: $5.00
Frequency: Annual October
Circulation: 100,250

23867 Foreign Flag Merchant Ships Owned by US Parent Companies
US Department of Transportation
400 7th Street SW
Room 8117
Washington, DC 20590-0001

202-366-4000

Directory of services and supplies to the industry.
20 Pages
Frequency: SemiAnnual

23868 Greenwood's Guide to Great Lakes Shipping
Freshwater Press
1700 E 13th Street
Suite 3-R
Cleveland, OH 44114-3213

216-241-0373; Fax: 216-781-6344
www.greenwoodsguide.com

Michael Dills, VP/General Manager

Offers companies that ship water-carried commodities and service firms on the Great Lakes Seaway systems. Details of vessels, dock facilities, shipyards, etc.
Cost: $71.00
650 Pages
Frequency: Annual
Circulation: 2,500
Founded in 1960
Printed in on glossy stock

23869 Grey House Transportation Security Directory
Grey House Publishing
4919 Route 22
PO Box 56
Amenia, NY 12501

518-789-8700
800-562-2139; Fax: 845-373-6390
books@greyhouse.com
www.greyhouse.com
Facebook, Twitter

Leslie Mackenzie, Publisher
Richard Gottlieb, Editor

Provides information on everything from Regulatory Authorities to Security Equipment, this top-flight directory brings together the relevant information necessary for creating and maintaining a security plan for a wide range of transportation facilities.
Cost: $195.00
800 Pages
ISBN: 1-592370-75-6
Founded in 1981

23870 Heavy Duty Representatives Profile Directory
Heavy Duty Representatives Association
160 Symphony Way
Elgin, IL 60120

847-760-0067
800-763-5717; Fax: 330-722-5638
trucksvc@aol.com
hdra.org

Larry Rosenthal, President
Walt Sirman, Vice President
John Stojack, Secretary

About 60 independent sales agencies which sell heavy-duty components to the trucking and aftermarket industries.
Frequency: Annual January

23871 Heavy Duty Trucking: CFS Buyers Guide
Newport Communications Div.-HIC Corporation
38 Executive Park
Suite 300
Irvine, CA 92614-6755

949-261-1636; Fax: 949-261-2904

Doug Condra, Publisher

Five hundred Council of Fleet Specialists member manufacturers and wholesalers specializing in heavy-duty truck parts and repairs.
Cost: $45.00
Frequency: Annual January
Circulation: 98,502

23872 Inland River Guide
Waterways Journal

319 N 4th St
Suite 650
St Louis, MO 63102-1994

314-241-7354; Fax: 314-241-4207
info@waterwaysjournal.net
www.waterwaysjournal.net

H Nelson Spencer Iii, Publisher
John S Shoulberg, Editor/Associate Publisher
Ed Rahe, Advertising Sales
Alan Bates, Manager
Marie Rausch, Advertising Sales Director

The only directory published specifically for the benefit of the companies doing business along the inland and intracoastal waterways. It contains vital information about companies servicing all industry segments.
Cost: $65.00
600+ Pages
Frequency: Annual
Circulation: 3,000
Founded in 1972

23873 **Inland River Record**
Waterways Journal
319 N 4th St
Suite 650
St Louis, MO 63102-1994

314-241-7354; Fax: 314-241-4207
hnspencer@waterwaysjournal.net
www.waterwaysjournal.net

H Nelson Spencer III, Publisher
John S Shoulberg, Manager
Alan Bates, Manager
Marie Rausch, Advertising Sales Director

Lists in detail more than 3,500 commercial towboats and tugs, U.S. engineer vessels and Coast Guard vessels navigating the Mississippi and Ohio, their tributaries and the Gulf Intracoastal Waterway.
Cost: $37.50
475 Pages
Frequency: Annual
Circulation: 3,000

23874 **Leonard's Guide National Third Party Logistics Directory**
GR Leonard & Company
49 E Huntington Dr
Arcadia, CA 91006-3210

626-574-1800
800-574-5250
www.leonardsguide.com

David Ercolani, President

Approximately 2,000 transportation brokers and third party logistics firms and brokerages in the US and Canada.
Cost: $75.00
Frequency: Annual Spring

23875 **Light List**
United States Coast Guard
2100 2nd Street SW
Washington, DC 20593-0002

202-488-8157; Fax: 202-366-5063

Offers information to the shipping industry in the form of lights. This comprehensive directory offers a list of lights, fog signals, daybeacons, radiobeacons and LORAN stations operated or authorized by the US Coast Guard. Various volumes are offered.
Cost: $25.00
200+ Pages
Frequency: Volumes

23876 **Mass Transit: Consultants Issue**
Cygnus Publishing
Po Box 803
Fort Atkinson, WI 53538-0803

920-000-1111; Fax: 920-563-1699

John French, CEO
Kathy Scott, Director of Public Relations
Paul Bonaiuto, CFO

Offers listings of over 300 urban transportation architects, designers, engineers and other specialists serving the urban transportation industry.
Frequency: BiMonthly

23877 **Mexican Motor Carrier Directory**
Transportation Technical Services
500 Lafayette Boulevard
Fredericksburg, VA 22401-6070

540-899-9872
800-666-4887; Fax: 888-665-9887

Thomas R Fugee, Executive VP

Unique, extensive and key information on 500 Mexican carriers.
Cost: $145.00
Frequency: Annual

23878 **NARUC Compilation of Transportation Regulatory Policy**
National Assn of Regulatory Utility Commissioners
PO Box 684
Washington, DC 20044-0684

202-898-2200
http://www.naruc.org

Offers a list of over 100 regulatory agencies in the United States and Canada for the transportation industry.
Cost: $33.00

23879 **NTEA Membership Roster & Product Directory**
National Truck Equipment Association
37400 Hills Tech Dr
Farmington Hill, MI 48331-3414

248-489-7090
800-441-6832; Fax: 248-489-8590
info@ntea.com
www.ntea.com

James Carney, Executive Director
Dennis Jones, First Vice President

Over 1,600 manufacturers and distributors of commercial trucks, bodies, trailers and related equipment. Information includes: product info, membership category, affiliate membership, join date, address, phone and fax numbers, e-mail address, Web site address.
Cost: $50.00
Frequency: Annual
Founded in 1964

23880 **National Customs Brokers and Forwarders Association of America**
National Customs Brokers & Forwarders Association
1200 18th St NW
Suite 901
Washington, DC 20036-2572

202-466-0222; Fax: 202-466-0226
www.ncbfaa.org

Barbara Reilly, Executive VP

About 600 customs brokers, international air cargo agents, and freight forwarders in the United States.
Cost: $24.00
Frequency: Annual

23881 **National Industrial Transportation League Reference Manual**
National Industrial Transportation League
1700 N Moore St
Suite 1900
Arlington, VA 22209-1931

703-524-5011; Fax: 703-524-5017
info@nitl.org
www.nitl.org

Bruce J Carlton, President
Frequency: SemiAnnual

23882 **National Institute of Packaging, Handling and Logistic Engineers**
NIPHLE
5903 Ridgeway Drive
Grand Prairie, TX 75052

817-466-7490
866-464-7453; Fax: 570-523-0606
www.niphle.org

Richard D Owen, Executive Director
Founded in 1956

23883 **National Motor Carrier Directory**
Transportation Technical Services
500 Lafayette Boulevard
Fredericksburg, VA 22401-6070

540-899-9872
800-666-4887; Fax: 888-665-9887

Thomas R Fugee, Executive VP

CEO, fleet size, toll-free/fax number, revenue, SCAC, trailer type, TK or LTL, trucks plus tractors owned and leased and more.
Cost: $395.00
1982 Pages
Frequency: Annual
Founded in 1992

23884 **National Private Truck Council: Official Membership Directory**
2200 Mill Road
Suite 350
Alexandria, VA 22314

703-683-1300; Fax: 703-683-1217
www.nptc.org

Gary Petty, President/CEO
Richard LaRoche, Director Membership

The only organization that represents the interests and concerns of private fleets — companies that use in-house or dedicated truck fleets to support distribution of their products. The directory includes members listed by: company, individual and industry. Both private fleet and supplier members are listed.
Cost: $145.00
100 Pages
Frequency: Annual
Printed in 4 colors on glossy stock

23885 **Pacific Shipper's Transportation Services Directory**
PRIMEDIA Information
10 Lake Drive
Hightstown, NJ 08520-5321

609-371-7700
800-224-5488

Amy Middlebrook, Editor
John Capers III, Publisher
John Murphy, Circulation Director

Offers valuable information on coastal transportation operations and support services on the Pacific Coast.
Cost: $202.00
730 Pages
Frequency: Annual
Printed in 4 colors on newsprint stock

23886 **Private Fleet Directory**
Transportation Technical Services

500 Lafayette Boulevard
Fredericksburg, VA 22401-6070

540-899-9872
800-666-4887; Fax: 888-665-9887

Thomas R Fugee, Executive VP

Over 26,000 private fleets in the US that transport their own freight (Wal-Mart, Ace Hardware, Toys R Us).
Cost: $295.00
1,900 Pages
Frequency: Annual July
Founded in 1992

23887 **Railway Line Clearances**
Commonwealth Business Media
10 Lake Drive
Hightstown, NJ 08520-5321

609-371-7703
800-224-5488; Fax: 609-371-7830
www.cbizmedia.com

Alan Glass, Chairman/CEO
Susan Murray, Publisher
Kathy Keeney, Associate Publisher

This directory offers weight limitations, heights and widths of clearances for railroads in North America and Canada, parts of the United States, clearance contacts and AAR rules and regulation.
Cost: $200.00
Frequency: Annual
Printed in 2 colors on matte stock

23888 **Refrigerated Transporter: Warehouse Directory Issue**
Penton
PO Box 66010
Houston, TX 77266

713-523-8124
800-880-0368; Fax: 713-523-8384
refrigeratedtransporter.com

Ray Anderson, Publisher

Listing of approximately 265 refrigerated warehouses in the US and Canada.

23889 **Survey of State Travel Offices**
United States Travel Data Center
1100 New York Avenue NW
Washington, DC 20005-3934

202-326-7300; Fax: 202-408-1255

Patrick Thompson, Editor

State and territorial government agencies responsible for travel and travel promotion in their states.
Cost: $475.00
Frequency: Annual March

23890 **Transportation Management Association Directory**
Association for Commuter Transportation
1518 K St NW
Suite 503
Washington, DC 20005-1203

202-737-2926; Fax: 202-347-8847
info@nadca.com
www.nadca.com

Jodi Araujo, Chief Executive Officer

Over 50 established transportation management associations in the United States are the focus of this comprehensive directory.
123 Pages
Circulation: 400

23891 **Transportation Research Board Directory**
Transportation Research Board
2101 Constitution Ave Nw
Washington, DC 20418-0007

202-334-2933; Fax: 202-334-2527
www.nationalacademies.org/trb

Robert Skinner, CEO

Directory lists organizations and committee members with an interest in transportation. Individual affiliate information is no longer available in print or in electronic format.
Frequency: Annual

23892 **Truck Trailer Manufacturers Association: Membership Directory**
Truck Trailer Manufacturers Association
8506 Wellington Road
Suite 101
Alexandria, VA 20109

703-549-3010; Fax: 703-549-3014
www.ttmanet.org

Richard Bowling, President

About 100 truck and tank trailer manufacturers and 120 suppliers to the industry.
Cost: $135.00
Frequency: Annual

23893 **Trucksource: Sources of Trucking Industry Information**
Express Carriers Association
9532 Liberia Avenue
Suite 130
Manassas, VA 20110

703-361-1058
866-322-7447; Fax: 703-361-5274
eca@expresscarriers.org
www.expresscarriers.com

Carrie Ehlers, President
Stuart Hyden, First Vice President

Features over 1,000 sources of information on the trucking industry, including industry reports, videos, periodicals and databases about the motor carrier industry.

23894 **USTA Industry Directory**
United States Telecom Association
1401 H St NW
Suite 600
Washington, DC 20005-2110

202-326-7300; Fax: 202-326-7333

Walter McKormick, President
Joan Johnson, Secretary

Comprehensive directory of over 1200 local exchange carriers and other telecom companies make up this directory. Includes a detailed index for easy cross-referencing by company name, contacts, titles, geographical region, services provided, e-mail and more. USTA's directory is your gateway to the telecom industry.
Cost: $699.00
Frequency: Annual

23895 **Vocational Equipment Directory for GMC Truck Dealers**
Verbiest Publishing Company
1155 Henrietta Street
Birmingham, MI 48009-1906

Directory of services and supplies to the industry.
Cost: $25.00
200 Pages
Frequency: Annual
Circulation: 6,000

23896 **WESTLAW Transportation Library**
West Publishing Company
610 Opperman Drive
Eagan, MN 55123-1340

651-687-7327
www.westgroup.com

This database offers information on US transportation laws.
Frequency: Full-text

Industry Web Sites

23897 **http://gold.greyhouse.com**
G.O.L.D Grey House OnLine Databases

Grey House Publishing's online database platform, GOLD, offers Quick Search, Keyword Search and Expert Search for most business sectors including transportation markets. The GOLD platform makes finding the information you need quick and easy - whether you're a novice searcher or an experienced database user. All of Grey House's directory products are available for subscription on the GOLD platform.

23898 **www.aar.org**
Association of American Railroads

Seeks to advance knowledge of scientific and economic location, construction, maintenance and operation of railroad.

23899 **www.apta.com**
American Public Transit Association

Maintains biographical archives and operates a placement service.

23900 **www.buses.org**
American Bus Association

Trade association for the North American bus industry.

23901 **www.expedia.com**
Expedia.com

Internet travel service offers access to airlines, hotels, car rentals, vacation packages, cruises and corporate travel.

23902 **www.expresscarriers.com**

Conducts research, promotes federal standards of construction, design, use and operation of tank trucks.

23903 **www.greyhouse.com**
Grey House Publishing

Authoritative reference directories for most business markets including transportation markets. Users can search the online databases with varied search criteria allowing for custom searches by product category, geographic area, sales volume, keyword, subject and more. Full Grey House catalog and online ordering also available.

23904 **www.hotwire.com**
Hotwire.com

Internet travel service offering discounts on flights, hotels, car rentals, packages and cruises.

23905 **www.iasm.org**
International Association of Structural Movers

Members are movers of heavy structural products, trusses, houses and machinery and masonry structures.

23906 **www.iccl.org**
Internhational Council of Cruise Lines

For North American oceangoing, overnight major cruise line companies.

23907 **www.intermodal.org**
Intermodal Association of North America

Promotes the benefits and growth of intermodal freight transportation.

23908 www.ista.org
International Safe Transit Association
Members are shippers, carriers, manufacturers, packagers, package designers and testing laboratories, included in transport packaging.

23909 www.ite.org
Institute for Transportation Engineering
Dedicated to the transportation engineering field.

23910 www.moving.org
American Moving and Storage Association
Represents members including interstate moving and storage companies, local movers, international movers plus industry suppliers and state association members. AMSA's chief goals include strong support for effective government regulations and policies that protect consumers while allowing members to provide quality service at compensatory prices, and ensuring that consumers understand the value of professional moving and storage services.

23911 www.narprail.org
National Association of Railroad Passengers
Seeks to increase public awareness of rail passenger service and its benefits. Works for a national transportation policy.

23912 www.natso.com
NATSO
NATSO is the professional association of America's $42 billion travel plaza and truckstop industry. NATSO represents the industry on legislative and regulatory matters; serves as the official source of information on the diverse travel plaza and truckstop industry; provides education to its members; conducts an annual convention and trade show; and supports efforts to generally improve the business climate in which its members operate.

23913 www.ndtahq.com
National Defense Transportation Association
Intended as a liasion between government, military and private transportation officials.

23914 www.nitl.org
National Industrial Transportation League
Annual show of 250 exhibitors of computer services software and innovations for transportation operations.

23915 www.nptc.org
National Private Truck Council
Distributors, shippers, processors, jobbers and manufacturers who transport their own goods and are owners of their own truck fleets.

23916 www.ntea.com
National Truck Equipment Association
For small to mid-sized companies that manufacture, distribute, install, sell and repair commercial trucks, truck bodies, truck equipment, trailers and accessories.

23917 www.ooida.com
Owner Operator Independent Drivers Association
For owner-operators, professional drivers and small fleet owners.

23918 www.ptdi.org
Professional Truck Driver Institute
Advocate of optimum standards and professionalism for entry-level truck driver training.

23919 www.raa.org
Regional Airline Association
Membership consists of more than 70 airlines, plus 350 Associate members provide goods and services.

23920 www.rssi.org
Railway Systems Suppliers
A trade association serving the communication and signal segment of the rail transportation industry. Manages an annual trade show.

23921 www.scranet.org
Specialized Carriers and Rigging Association
Members are carriers, crane and rigging operators and millwrights engaged in the transport of heavy goods.

23922 www.teamster.org
International Brotherhood of Teamsters
Affiliated with the AFL-CIO.

23923 www.terry.org
International Marine Transit Association
Membership includes ferry operators, naval architects, manufacturers, suppliers, and others in the terry industry around the world.

23924 www.tianet.org
Transportation Intermediaries Association
For North American transportation intermediaries including logistics management firms, property brokers, perishable commodities brokers, freight forwarders, intermodal marketers, ocean and air forwarders.

23925 www.travel.yahoo.com
Yahoo.com
Internet travel service providing access to flights, hotels, car rentals, vacation packages and cruises.

23926 www.travelocity.com
Sabre Holdings
Travel service offering consumers access to hundreds of airlines and thousands of hotels, as well as cruise, last-minute and vacation packages and best-in-class car rental companies.

23927 www.truckline.com
American Trucking Association

23928 www.ttmanet.org
Truck Trailer Manufacturers Association
A national organization of truck and tank trailer manufacturers and 120 suppliers to the industry.

23929 www.waterways.org
National Waterways Conference
For shippers, barge lines and local port authorities working to promote a better understanding of the public value of the American waterways system.

23930 www.weareparking.org
National Parking Association
Facebook, Twitter, LinkedIn
For operators of public and private parking facilities, including government, hospitals, colleges, universities and others.

23931 www.woda.org
World Organization of Dredging Associations
Develops professionalism in individuals involved in the dredging industry.

Associations

23932 Adventure Travel Trade Association
14751 N Kelsey Street
Suite 105 pMB 604
Monroe, WA 98272

360-805-3131; Fax: 360-805-0649
info@adventuretravel.biz
www.adventuretravel.biz

Shannon Stowell, CEO
Casey Hanisko, President
Jason Reckers, CTO
Mira Poling Anselmi, Communication Director

Adventure Travel Trade Association is the largest global network of adventure travel leaders. Members include guides, tour operators, lodges, travel advisors, tourism boards, destination marketing and management organizations, outdoor educators, gear companies and travel media companies.
Founded in 1990

23933 American Bus Association
111 K Street NE
9th Floor
Washington, DC 20002

202-877-2208
800-283-2877; Fax: 202-842-0850
abainfo@buses.org
www.buses.org
Facebook, Twitter, LinkedIn, YouTube

Peter J Pantuso, President & CEO
Roderick Lewis, Director, Membership & BD
Suzanne Te Beau Rohde, VP, Govt. Affairs & Policy
Brandon Buchanan, Director of Regulatory Affairs
Daniel Hoff, Director, Gov Affairs & Policy

ABA supports 3,800 members consisting of motorcoach and tour companies in addition to organizations that represent the tourism and travel industry. ABA strives to educate consumers on the importance of highway and motorcoach safety.
Founded in 1926

23934 American Council of Highway Advertisers
1629 K St. NW
Washington, DC 20006

202-452-9044

A national organization representing highway users and traveler-oriented companies utilizing Out-of-Home advertising.
Founded in 1983

23935 American Society of Travel Agents (ASTA)
675 N. Washington Street
Suite 490
Alexandria, VA 22314

703-739-2782
800-275-2782; Fax: 703-684-8319
askasta@asta.org
www.asta.org
Facebook, Twitter, LinkedIn

Zane Kerby, President & CEO
Paul Ruden, EVP, Legal & Industry Affairs
Eben Peck, SVP, Government & Industry Affairs
Mark Meader, VP, Industry Affairs
Sue Sheats, VP, Business Development

Promotes and encourages travel among people of all nations. Serves as an information resource for the travel industry.
21M Members
Founded in 1931

23936 Association of Corporate Travel Executives
510 King Street
Suite 220
Alexandria, VA 22314-2964

262-763-1902
800-375-2283; Fax: 613-836-0619
info@acte.org
www.acte.org
Facebook, Twitter, LinkedIn, YouTube, RSS

Kurt Knackstedt, President
Greeley Koch, Executive Director
Jeff Kurn, Treasurer
Greeley Koch, Chief Staff Officer
Amber Kelleher, Global Engagement

Provides a forum for the discussion of ideas and information related to the corporate travel industry. Conducts educational programs and conferences.
700 Members
Founded in 1988
Mailing list available for rent

23937 Association of Group Travel Executives
AH Light Company
510 King Street
Suite 220
Alexandria, VA 22314

262-763-1902
800-375-2283; Fax: 908-273-2344
info@acte.org
www.acte.org
Facebook, Twitter, LinkedIn, YouTube, RSS

Kurt Knackstedt, President
Greeley Koch, Executive Director
Jeff Kurn, Treasurer
Greeley Koch, Chief Staff Officer
Amber Kelleher, Global Engagement

Affiliated with the Travel Industry Association of America.
675 Members
Founded in 1988

23938 Association of Retail Travel Agents
4320 North Miller Road
Scottsdale, AZ 85251

800-969-6069; Fax: 866-743-2087
www.arta.travel
Facebook, Twitter, LinkedIn, You Tube

Nancy Linares, Board of Director

Promotes the interests of retail travel agents through representation on industry councils and testimony before Congress. Conducts joint marketing and educational programs.
2800 Members
Founded in 1963

23939 Association of Travel Marketing Executives
PO Box 3176
West Tisbury, MA 02575

508-693-0550; Fax: 508-693-0115
kzern@atme.org
www.atme.org
Facebook, Twitter, LinkedIn, Flickr

Kristin Zern, Executive Director
Henry Harteveldt, Chairman
Susan Black, Vice Chairman
Jeffrey DeKorte, Secretary
Jacqueline Johnson, Treasurer
Founded in 1980

23940 Association of Travel Marketing Executives
PO Box 3176
West Tisbury, MA 02575

508-693-0550; Fax: 508-693-0115
Facebook, Twitter, LinkedIn, Flickr

Kristin Zern, Executive Director
Henry Harteveldt, Chairman
Susan Black, Vice Chairman
Jeffrey DeKorte, Secretary
Jacqueline Johnson, Treasurer

Travel and tourism reports.
Founded in 1980

23941 Brand USA
1725 Eye Street NW
8th Floor
Washington, DC 20006

202-536-2060
www.thebrandusa.com

Christopher L. Thompson, President & CEO
Thomas Garzilli, Chief Marketing Officer
Donald F. Richardson, Chief Financial Officer

Brand USA works in close partnership with the travel industry to maximize the economic and social benefits of travel. These benefits include fostering understanding between people and cultures and creating jobs essential to the economy.

23942 Caribbean Hotel Association
2655 Le Jeune Rd
Suite 910
Coral Gables, FL 33134

305-443-3040; Fax: 305-675-7977
membership@caribbeanhotelandtourism.com
www.caribbeanhotelandtourism.com
Facebook, Twitter, LinkedIn

Richard Doumeng, Chairman
Emil Lee, President
Karolin Troubetzkoy, 1st VP
Stuart Bowe, 2nd VP
Karen Whitt, 3rd VP

Mission is to optimize the full potential of the Caribbean hotel and tourism industry by serving member needs and building partnerships. It's a LLC registered in the Cayman Islands, with offices in San Juan, Puerto Rico and Miami, FL.
Founded in 1959

23943 Cruise Lines International Association
1201 F Street NW
Suite 250
Washington, DC 20004

202-759-9370
info@cruising.org
cruising.org

Kelly Craighead, President & CEO
Josh Good, SVP, Global Finances & Operations
Lawrence Kaye, General Counsel

Provides a unified voice and leading authority of the global cruise community. CLIA supports policies and practices that foster a safe, secure, healthy and sustainable cruise ship environment and is dedicated to promoting the cruise travel experience.
Founded in 1975

23944 Destinations International
2025 M Street NW
Suite 500
Washington, DC 20036

202-296-7888; Fax: 202-296-7889
info@destinationsinternational.org

destinationsinternational.org
Facebook, Twitter, LinkedIn, YouTube

Don Welsh, President & CEO
Melissa Cherry, COO
Jack Johnson, Chief Advocacy Officer
Nina Winston, EVP, Global Development & Alliances
Caitlyn Blizzard, VP, Communications

Serves destination marketing and management professionals.
650+ Members
Founded in 1914

23945 Diving Equipment & Marketing Association

858-616-6408
800-862-3483; Fax: 858-616-6495
info@dema.org
www.dema.org
Facebook, Twitter, LinkedIn, YouTube, RSS, Instagram

Tom Ingram, President & CEO
Nicole Russel, VP, Operations
Colleen Vasquez, VP, Finance
Rachelle Reimers, Communications Manager
Alicia Vasquez, Member Services Assistant

Trade association for the international scuba diving industry.
1400 Members

23946 Greater Independent Association of National Travel Services

915 Broadway
20th Floor
New York, NY 10010-7130

212-627-0001; Fax: 212-627-1110
www.giantstravel.com
Twitter, Youtube

Desiree Gruber, President
Susan Shapiro, Executive Director

Aims to establish a travel industry marketing cooperative. Holds regional workshops and seminars.
1.8M Members
Founded in 1968

23947 Hospitality Sales & Marketing Association International

7918 Jones Branch Drive
Suite 300
McLean, VA 22102

703-506-3280; Fax: 703-506-3266
info@hsmai.org
www.hsmai.org
Facebook, Twitter, LinkedIn, Flicker

Robert A. Gilbert, President & CEO
Fran Brasseux, EVP
Jason Smith, VP, Marketing & Communications
Juli Jones, Vice President
Chris Durso, VP, Content Development

Global organization of sales, marketing, and revenue management professionals involved in the hospitality industry.
5000 Members
Founded in 1927

23948 Hotel Electronic Distribution Network Association

1000 Westgate Drive
Suite 252
St. Paul, MN 55114

Home Page: www.hedna.org

Sebastien Leitner, President
Anne Cole, Vice President
Jennifer Camarota, Secretary
Nadine Pagel, Treasurer

HEDNA is a global community of hospitality professionals, technology providers, educators, and consultants passionate. Its mission is to simplify hospitality distribution.
Founded in 1991

23949 International Association of Travel

PO Box D
Hurleyville, NY 12747

845-434-7777

Promotes accurate reporting on fields of aviation, travel, tourism and airports.
50+ Members
Founded in 1988

23950 International LGBTQ Travel Association

5079 N Dixie Highway
Suite 367
Fort Lauderdale, FL 33334

954-630-1637; Fax: 954-630-1652
www.iglta.org

John Tanzella, President & CEO
LoAnn Halden, VP, Communications
Tony Warner, VP, Finance

Provides free travel resources and information while continuously working to promote equality and safety within LGBTQ+ tourism worldwide. IGLTA's members include LGBTQ+-friendly accommodations, transport, destinations, service providers, Travel Advisors, tour operators, events and travel media located in over 75 countries.
Founded in 1983

23951 National Association of Business Travel Agents

National Association of Business Travel Agents
1920 L St. NW
Suite 300
Washington, DC 20036-2365

202-463-6223; Fax: 202-463-6239
nabe@nabe.com
www.nabe.com
Twitter

Tom Beers, Executive Director
Colette Brissett, Administrative Director
Chris Jonas, Director, Comm. and Programs
Suzanne Clegg, Events Coordinator
Robert Crow, Editor, Business Economics

NBTA is a forum bringing together business travel buyer and supplier professionals from around the world. Membership includes access to the industry's premier network of corporate and government travel decision-makers and purchasers, a monthly e-newsletter as well as a quarterly publication, world-wide and local events, CTE opportunities and professional certificate programs.
Founded in 1959

23952 National Association of RV Parks and Campgrounds

9085 E. Mineral Circle
Suite 200
Centennial, CO 80112

303-681-0401
800-395-2267; Fax: 303-681-0426
info@arvc.org
www.arvc.org
Facebook, Twitter, LinkedIn, Youtube

Paul Bambei, President/CEO
Candra Talley, Membership Program Manager
Barb Youmans, Senior Director of Education
Jennifer Schwartz, Vice President, Marketing
Molly Martin, Marketing Coordinator

The association actively protects the best interests of its members on a federal level and provides awareness and assistance against government legislation & regulations at all levels(national, state and local).
3100 Members
Founded in 1966
Mailing list available for rent: 3,200 names

23953 National Tour Association

101 Prosperous Place
Suite 350
Lexington, KY 40509

859-264-6540
800-682-8886; Fax: 859-264-6570
www.ntaonline.com
Facebook, Twitter, LinkedIn, Youtube, Google+, Instagram

Catherine Prather, President
Kami Risk, President, NTA Services
Bob Rouse, VP, Communication & Marketing
Dawn Pettus, VP, Events

The National Tour Association is an organization of nearly 4,000 international tourism professionals focused on the development, promotion and increased use of tour operators packaged travel.
4000 Members
Founded in 1951
Mailing list available for rent

23954 Office of General Supply and Services

1800 F Street, NW
Washington, DC 20405

202-564-2480
866-606-8220
NCSCcustomer.service@gsa.gov
www.gsa.gov
Facebook, Twitter, Youtube, RSS

Adam Neufeld, Deputy Administrator
Denise Turner Roth, Administrator
Katy Kale, Chief Of Staff
Reginald Cardozo, Deputy Chief of Staff
Norman Dong, Public Buildings Service

The Office of General Supplies and Services (GSS) is responsible for acquisition services and comprehensive supply chain management, including excess/surplus federal property.
Founded in 1949

23955 Passenger Vessel Association

103 Oronoco Street
Suite 200
Alexandria, VA 22314-1549

703-518-5005
800-807-8360; Fax: 703-518-5151
pvainfo@passengervessel.com
www.passengervessel.com
Facebook

John Groundwater, Executive Director
Margo Marks, Vice President
Leslie Kagarise, Director of Finance
Lee Hill, Chief Financial Officer
Edmund Welch, Legislative Director

Represents operators of tours, excursions, ferries, charter vessels, dinner boats and other small passenger vessels.
600 Members
Founded in 1971

23956 Receptive Services Association

2365 Harrodsburg Road
Suite A325
Lexington, KY 40504

859-219-3545
866-939-0934; Fax: 859-226-4404
headquarters@rsaa.com
www.rsana.com
Facebook, Youtube

Matt Grayson, Executive Director
Rachel Gates, Member Services Administrator
Toby Bishop, Sales Manager
Jonathan Zuk, Chairman
Veronique Hubert, Vice Chairman

Helping receptive operators serve international tour companies through partnerships with North American suppliers.
570 Members

23957 **Recreational Vehicle Industry Association**
1896 Preston White Drive
Reston, VA 20191

703-620-6003; Fax: 703-620-5071
www.rvia.org

David Humphreys, President

The national trade association representing recreation vehicle manufacturers and their component parts suppliers who build more than 98% of all RVsproduced in the U.S.
Founded in 1963

23958 **Society of American Travel Writers**
One Parkview Plaza
Suite 800
Oakbrook Terrace, IL 60181

414-359-1671; Fax: 414-359-1671
info@satw.org
www.satw.org
Facebook, Twitter, LinkedIn

Paul Lasley, President
Annette Thompson, Immediate Past President
Barbara Orr, Vice President, Membership
Tom Adkinson, Treasurer
Peggy Bendel, Secretary

Photographers and 35 associate member representatives of airlines, hotels, resorts, tourist agencies and public relations firms.
Founded in 1955

23959 **Society of Incentive and Travel Executives**
330 N Wabash Ave
Chicago, IL 60611

312-321-5148; Fax: 312-527-6783
site@siteglobal.com
www.siteglobal.com
Facebook, Twitter, LinkedIn, Youtube

Kevin M. Hinton, CEO
Ashley Mayrisch, Marketing Coordinator
Maggie Vaulman, Membership Associate
Adrianne Stokes, Operations Associate
Murphy Goodworth, Global Conference Director

An individual membership society covering 70 countries. Members are corporate users, airlines, Tourist Boards, cruise lines, destination management companies, consultants, hotels/resorts, travel agents, incentive travel houses and publications.
2000 Members
Founded in 1973

23960 **Student & Youth Travel Association**
2776 S Arlington Mill Drive
Suite 564
Arlington, VA 22206

703-610-1263; Fax: 703-610-0270
info@syta.org
syta.org

Carylann Assante, CEO
Becky Armely, Director of Operations
Katy Summers, Sr. Manager, Education

SYTA is the non-profit, professional trade association that promotes student & youth travel and seeks to foster integrity and professionalism among student and youth travel service providers.

23961 **Travel Industry Association of America**
1100 New York Ave Nw
Suite 450
Washington, DC 20005-3934

202-408-8422; Fax: 202-408-1255

Roger J Dow, President & CEO
Todd Davidson, Treasurer & Director
Bonnie L Carlson, Secretary & Director

Members are hotels, airlines and travel agencies interested in promoting increased travel to and within the US.
2100 Members
Founded in 1941

23962 **Travel and Tourism Research Association**
5300 Lakewood Road
Whitehall, MI 49461

248-708-8872; Fax: 248-814-7150
info@ttra.com
www.ttra.com

Dan Mishell, Chairman
Jeffrey Eslinger, President
Susan Bruinzeel, 1st VP/Conference Chair
Dr. Marion Joppe, 2nd VP/Membership Chair
John Markham, Treasurer
Founded in 1970

23963 **U.S. Travel Association**
1100 New York Ave. NW
Suite 450
Washington, DC 20005

202-408-8422; Fax: 202-408-1255
feedback@ustravel.org
www.ustravel.org

Todd Davidson, Chair
Roger J. Dow, President

The Association advocates for the importance of travel, and the freedom to travel, to a healthy U.S. economy.

23964 **United States Tour Operators Association**
345 7th Avenue
Suite 1801
New York, NY 10001

212-599-6599; Fax: 212-599-6744
information@ustoa.com
ustoa.com

USTOA's goals are to educate the travel industry, government agencies, and the public about tours, vacation packages, and tour operators; protect consumers and travel advisors from financial loss in the event of a USTOA Active Member's bankruptcy, insolvency or cessation of business; foster a high level of professionalism within the tour operator industry; and promote and develop travel on a worldwide basis.
Founded in 1972

23965 **Volunteers for Peace**
7 Kilburn Street
Suite 316
Belmont, VT 05401

802-598-0052
vfp@vfp.org
www.vfp.org
Facebook, Twitter

Matt Messier, Executive Director
Alexandra Smith, International Placement Coordinator
Ton Sherman, President
Lila Hobbes, Secretary, Treasurer

A Vermont nonprofit membership organization promoting over 3000 international voluntary service projects in 100 countries. Workcamps are an affordable way to travel, live and work abroad.
2000 Members
Founded in 1982

23966 **Wellness Tourism Association**
891 14th Street
Suite 1915
Denver, CO 80202

800-450-1443
admin@wellnesstourismassociation.org
www.wellnesstourismassociation.org

Anne Dimon, President & CEO
Andrew Gibson, Chairman
Thomas Klein, Treasurer

A non-profit global network for qualifying DMOs, hotels/resorts/retreats, tour operators, travel advisors, wellness practitioners, media, partners and others in the global wellness tourism industry.
100+ Members
Founded in 2018

23967 **World Food Travel Association**
4110 SE Hawthorne Boulevard
Suite 440
Portland, OR 97214

Home Page: worldfoodtravel.org

Erik Wolf, Executive Director & Founder
Jane Connelly, Program Manager

Serving annually a community of nearly 200,000 professionals in 150 countries. Offers members tools and training help trade professionals and organizations to leverage their area's food and beverage.
Founded in 2003

Newsletters

23968 **AAA World**
2040 Market Street
Philadelphia, PA 19103

215-851-0291
800-763-9900; Fax: 215-851-0297
letters@aaaworld.com
www.aaaworld.com

Allen EeWalle, CEO
Sandy Kaden, Circulation Manager

Promotes travel destinations, gives advice on traveling and helpful automobile information.
Cost: $71.00
Circulation: 2.1 mill
Founded in 1900

23969 **ABA Insider**
American Bus Association
111 K Street NE
9th Floor
Washington, DC 20002

202-842-1645; Fax: 202-842-0850
abainfo@buses.org
www.buses.org

Peter J Pantuso, CEO
Buchcannon Brandon, Director of Operations
Hart Clyde, Senior VP of Government Affairs
Hoff Daniel, Director of ABA Foundation & Policy
Jones Patrick, Legislative & Communications Coordi

ABA's biweekly newsletter that keeps members informed on the travel, tourism and motorcoach industry.
Frequency: Biweekly
Founded in 1926

23970 **Caribbean Reporter**
Caribbean Hotel Association

18 Calle Marseilles
San Juan, PR 907-1682

787-725-2901; Fax: 787-725-9180

Beverly Telemague, Publisher

Membership news.
Cost: $4.99
Frequency: Monthly
Founded in 1959

23971 Entree Travel Newsletter
Entree Publishing
PO Box 5148
Santa Barbara, CA 93150-5148

805-969-5848; Fax: 805-969-5849
wtomicki@aol.com
www.entreenews.com

William Tomicki, Editor/Publisher

Travel, fashion and beauty ideas, sports and photography, wines and restaurants reviews new literature, music and film of interest to the travel and food enthusiast.
Cost: $75.00
Frequency: Monthly
Circulation: 8000
Printed in one color on matte stock

23972 Ocean and Cruise News
PO Box 329
Northport, NY 11768

203-329-2787; Fax: 203-329-2767
www.wocls.org/

Tom Cassidy, VP
Geroge Devol, President

Complete news on cruises.
Cost: $30.00
Frequency: Monthly
Circulation: 7000
Founded in 1980

23973 Travel Industry Association of America Newsletter
Travel Industry Association of America
1100 New York Ave Nw
Suite 450 W
Washington, DC 20005-6130

202-408-8422; Fax: 202-408-1255

Roger J Dow, CEO
C Betsi, Marketing Manager
Kathy Keefe, Editor

Travel information.
Cost: $1350.00
Frequency: Monthly
Circulation: 3500
Founded in 1941
Printed in 3 colors on glossy stock

23974 Travel Management Newsletter
Reed Travel Group
500 Plaza Dr
Secaucus, NJ 07094-3619

201-902-1800; Fax: 202-902-2053
www.tmdaily.com

Steve Bailey, Publisher

Discusses the news and views of the travel professional.
Cost: $735.00
Frequency: Weekly

23975 Travel Manager's Executive Briefing
Health Resources Publishing
1913 Atlantic Ave
Suite 200
Manasquan, NJ 08736-1067

732-292-1100
800-516-4343; Fax: 732-292-1111

Robert K Jenkins, Publisher
Lisa Mansfield, Marketing Assistant

Read by travel managers of major corporations, Fortune 500 companies and corporate travel agencies twice a month to get up to the minute developments in the important field of travel and expense cost control.
Cost: $447.00
ISSN: 0272-569x

23976 Travel Weekly
500 Plaza Drive
Secaucus, NJ 07094-3685

201-902-1696; Fax: 201-902-2053
www.travelweekly.com

William D Scott, Publisher

Industry news, articles and stories on the travel industry.
Cost: $26.00
Frequency: BiWeekly

23977 Travel and Tourism Executive Report
10200 W 44th Avenue
Suite 304
Wheat Ridge, CO 80033-2840

303-463-2887

Francine Butler, Executive Director

Established as the Travel Research Association as the result of a merger.
750 Pages

23978 Travelwriter Marketletter
21553 Center Point Circle
Ashburn, VA 20147

571-214-9086; Fax: 208-988-7672
www.travelwriterml.com

Mimi Backhausen, Editor & Publisher

A monthly newsletter for travel writers and travel photographers. It's mainly about marketing travel articles, photography and travel books; also describes free trips for professional travel writers.
Cost: $75.00
10 Pages
Frequency: Monthly
Circulation: 1000
ISSN: 0738-9093

23979 Tuesday Newsletter
National Tour Association
101 Prosperours Place
Suite 350
Lexington, KY 40509

859-264-6540
800-682-8886; Fax: 859-264-6570
chorton@multibriefs.com
ntaonline.com
Facebook, Twitter, LinkedIn

Pam Inman, President
Doug Rentz, Director, Communication & Marketing

The National Tour Association is an organization of nearly 4,000 North American tourism professionals focused on the development, promotion and increased use of tour operators packaged travel.
Cost: $36.00
Frequency: Monthly
Circulation: 5000
Founded in 1998
Mailing list available for rent: 3,800 names

Magazines & Journals

23980 ABC Preferred Flight Planner: Europe- Middle East-Africa
ABC Corporate Services/Reed Travel Group
500 Plaza Drive
Secaucus, NJ 07094-3619

201-678-8775; Fax: 201-902-2053
www.infotec-travel.com

Luis Murcia, Owner

Offers information on properties and locations of interest to corporate business travelers.
250 Pages
Frequency: SemiAnnual
Circulation: 65,000

23981 ASTA Agency Management
Miller Freeman Publications
2655 Seely Avenue
San Jose, CA 95134

408-943-1234; Fax: 408-943-0513

Mary Pat Sullivan, Publisher

Provides concise and useful information on trends in the industry and practical ideas regarding the profitable administration of travel agencies.
Cost: $36.00
Frequency: Monthly
Circulation: 35,182

23982 ASU Travel Guide
448 Ignacio Boulevard
Suite 333
San Rafael, CA 94949-5539

415-898-9500
866-459-0300; Fax: 415-898-9501
www.asutravelguide.com

Christopher Gil, Managing Editor
Hank Sousa, VP

Provides information concerning worldwide travel destinations and other locales of interest to travelers and the bargains and discounts available to airline employees.
352 Pages
Frequency: Quarterly
Circulation: 700000
Founded in 1971
Printed in 4 colors on glossy stock

23983 Bank Travel Management
Group Travel Leader
301 East High Street
Lexington, KY 40507

859-253-0455; Fax: 859-253-0499

Mac Lacy, President & Publisher
Herb Sparrow, Executive Editor
Brian Jewell, Associate Editor
Kelly Tyner, Director of Sales & Marketing
Stacey Bowman, National Account Manager

Regular sections include: The Banker's Box, managing your senior program, and marketing your trips, with special features on personal travel accounts, trends in travel and banking clubs. Subscriptions are complimentary for qualified travel planners.
Cost: $49.00
Frequency: 6/Year
Circulation: 4100
Founded in 1994

23984 Bus Tours Magazine
National Bus Trader
9698 W Judson Rd
Polo, IL 61064-9015

815-946-2341; Fax: 815-946-2347
nbt@busmag.com
www.busmag.com

Larry Plachno, President
Shaye Hall, Assistant Editor
Nancy Ann Plachno, Business Manager

Focuses on the operations, arrangements and marketing techniques used to plan these excur-

sions as well as what's new in the industry.
Cost: $10.00
Frequency: Monthly
Circulation: 7,200
Founded in 1979

23985 **Byways Magazine**
7902 Pleasant Valley Court
Louisville, KY 40291

502-785-4875
stephen.kirchner@gmail.com
bywaysmagazine.com

Stephen M. Kirchner, Editor & Publisher

Byways is a 100 percent digital publication in its 36th year of publication, featuring the destinations along the highways and byways of North America. To view all digital issues visit http://www.issuu.com/byways.
48 Pages
Frequency: Bi-Monthly
Founded in 1984
Mailing list available for rent: 6000 names

23986 **City Visitor**
Travelhost
5755 Granger Road
Independence, OH 44131

972-556-0541; Fax: 972-432-8729
www.travelhost.com

James E Buerger, President

Travelhost is an in room publisher edited for the business and vacation traveler, with news features and general information relating to travel, recreation, business, new products and services and leisure activities.
Cost: $33.00
Frequency: Monthly
Founded in 1967

23987 **Conde Nast Traveler Business Extra**
Conde Nast
4 Times Sq
14th Floor
New York, NY 10036-6561

212-286-2860; Fax: 212-286-5960
www.condenast.com

Charles H Townsend, CEO

Relates to gathering information for tourism.

23988 **Corporate & Incentive Travel**
Coastal Communications Corporation
2700 N Military Trail
Suite 120
Boca Raton, FL 33431

561-989-0600; Fax: 561-989-9509
ccceditor1@att.net
www.themeetingmagazines.com

Harvey Grotsky, Publisher/Editor-In-Chief
Susan Wyckoff Fell, Managing Editor
Susan Gregg, Managing Editor

The magazine for corporate meetings and incentive travel planners. In-depth editorial focus on site selection, accommodations and transportation, current legislation, conference, seminar and training facilities, budget and cost controls, and destination reports. Regular features highlight industry news and developments, trends and personalities, meeting values, facilities, and destinations.
Frequency: Monthly
Circulation: 40,000
Founded in 1983

23989 **Corporate and Incentive Travel**
Coastal Communications Corporation
2700 N Military Trail
Suite 120
Boca Raton, FL 33431-6394

561-989-0600; Fax: 561-989-9509
www.themeetingmagazines.com

Harvey Grotsky, President & CEO
Susan Wyckoff Fell, Managing Editor
Susan S Gregg, Managing Editor

This magazine is edited for corporate meeting planners with the responsibility for staging and planning meetings, incentive travel programs, conferences and conventions.
Frequency: Monthly
Founded in 1983

23990 **Country Discoveries**
5400 S 60th Street
Greendale, WI 53129-1404

414-423-0100
800-344-6913; Fax: 414-423-8463

Focuses on backwoods travel in both the United States and Canada.
Cost: $14.98
Founded in 1965

23991 **Courier**
National Tour Association
101 Prosperous Place
Suite 350
Lexington, KY 40509

859-264-6540
800-682-8886; Fax: 859-264-6570
questions@ntastaff.com
ntaonline.com

Pam Inman, President
Bob Rouse, Editor-in-Chief

Courier Magazine helps readers to meet their responsibilities involved with their jobs.
Cost: $36.00
Frequency: Monthly
Circulation: 6000
ISSN: 0279-4489
Founded in 1955
Printed in 4 colors on glossy stock

23992 **Cruise Industry News - Annual**
Nissel-Lie Communications
441 Lexington Avenue
Room 809
New York, NY 10017-3910

212-986-1025; Fax: 212-986-1033
info2@cruiseindustrynews.com
www.cruiseindustrynews.com

Oivind Mathisen, Editor/Publisher
Angela Mathisen, Advertising Director/Publisher
Monty Mathisen, Reporter/Web Editor

The only book of its kind, and often rated the most comprehensive information source on the industry by cruise line executives.
Cost: $575.00
Frequency: Annual+
Founded in 1988

23993 **Cruise Industry News Quarterly Magazine**
Nissel-Lie Communications
441 Lexington Avenue
Room 809
New York, NY 10017-3910

212-986-1025; Fax: 212-986-1033
info2@cruiseindustrynews.com
www.cruiseindustrynews.com

Oivind Mathisen, Editor/Publisher
Angela Mathisen, Advertising Director/Publsher
Monty Mathisen, Reporter/Web Editor

The magazine covers all aspects of cruise operations, shipbuilding, new ships, cruise companies, ship reviews, onboard services, food and beverage, and ports and destinations.
Cost: $495.00
Frequency: Quarterly
Circulation: 50000
Founded in 1991
Printed in 4 colors

23994 **Destinations**
American Bus Association
700 13th St NW
Suite 575
Washington, DC 20005-5923

202-842-1645
800-283-2877; Fax: 202-842-0850
abainfo@buses.org
www.buses.org

Peter J Pantuso, CEO
Eron Shosteck, Marketing

Motorcoach travel across North America and Association news.
80 Pages
Frequency: Monthly
Circulation: 6000
Founded in 1926
Printed in 4 colors on glossy stock

23995 **Digital Travel**
Jupiter Communications Company
475 Park Ave S
Suite 4
New York, NY 10016-6901

212-547-7900
800-481-1212; Fax: 212-953-1733

Alan Meckler, CEO
Marla Kammer, Managing Editor

Editorial includes the latest information and technology in agencies, airlines, lodging, ticketing, mapping, Web advertising, transaction processing, revenue models, demographics, and full-service sites.
Cost: $595.00
Frequency: Monthly

23996 **Family Motor Coaching Magazine**
Family Motor Coach Association
8291 Clough Pike
Cincinnati, OH 45244-2796

513-474-3622
800-543-3622; Fax: 513-474-2332
www.fmca.com

Don Eversman, Executive Director
Ranita Jones, Sales Manager
Cost: $3.99
Frequency: Monthly
Circulation: 140000

23997 **Frequent Flyer Magazine**
2000 Clearwater Drive
Oak Brook, IL 60523

630-574-6000
800-342-5674; Fax: 630-574-6565

23998 **Going on Faith**
Group Traveler Leader
301 E High Street
Lexington, KY 40507

859-253-0455
888-253-0455; Fax: 859-253-0499
www.grouptravelleader.com

Mac Lacy, Publisher
Herb Sparrow, Executive Editor
Brian Jewell, Associate Editor
Kelly Tyner, Director of Sales & Marketing
Stacey Bowman, National Account Manager

The national travel newspaper for churches, synagogues and Religious organizations. The

official newspaper for the Going on Faith Conference. Online.
Frequency: 6/Year
Circulation: 5500
Founded in 1997

23999 Group Travel Leader
Group Travel Leader
301 E High St
Lexington, KY 40507-1509
859-253-0455; Fax: 859-253-0499
www.grouptravelleader.com
Mac Lacy, President
Herb Sparrow, Executive Editor
Brian Jewell, Associate Editor
Kelly Tyner, Director of Sales & Marketing
Stacey Bowman, National Account Manager
Supplies the senior travel planner with new destinations, unique points of interest and historical venues for their group, club or organization.
Cost: $39.00
Frequency: Monthly
Circulation: 30000
Founded in 1991

24000 HSMAI Marketing Review
Hospitality Sales & Marketing Association Int'l
1760 Old Meadow Road
Suite 500
McLean, VA 22102
703-506-3280; Fax: 703-506-3266
info@hsmai.org
www.hsmai.org
Kathleen Tindell, Editor
Features in-depth information and columns on best practices, web marekting, international affairs and future forecasting.
Cost: $65.00
7000 Pages
Frequency: Quarterly
Circulation: 10000
Founded in 1927

24001 Inside Flyer
Flight Plan
1930 Frequent Flyer Point
Colorado Springs, CO 80915
719-597-8889
800-767-8896; Fax: 719-597-6855
www.insideflyer.com/
Randy Petersen, Editor/publ/CEO
Karen Heldt, Advertising Coordinator
Linda Hanwella, Managing Editor
Leading publication of information for and about frequent traveler programs.
Cost: $45.00
Frequency: Monthly
Founded in 1986
Mailing list available for rent
Printed in 4 colors on matte stock

24002 Jax Fax Travel Marketing
Jax Fax
52 West Main Street
Milford, CT 06460-3310
203-301-0255; Fax: 203-301-0250
www.jaxfax.com
Doug Cooke, President
Marc Spac, Publishing Director
Theresa Seanlon, Editor
Marjorie Vincent, Circulation Manager
Peter Badeau, Associate Publisher
Monthly travel trade magazine featuring destination information and listings of discounted airfares and tour packages.
Cost: $15.00
Frequency: Monthly
Circulation: 25000
Founded in 1973
Printed in 4 colors on glossy stock

24003 Mexico Today
2009 S 10th Street
McAllen, TX 78503-5405
956-686-0711
800-222-0158; Fax: 956-686-0732
info@sanbornsinsurance.com
www.sanbornsinsurance.com
Pete Castillo, Marketing Director
Frequency: Quarterly
Circulation: 5000
Printed in 4 colors on glossy stock

24004 Mid-Atlantic Group Tour Magazine
Shoreline Creations
PO Box 638
Yarmouth Port, MA 02675-638
508-398-0400; Fax: 616-393-0085
travel@grouptour.com
www.grouptour.com
Carl Wassink, Publisher
Carol Smith, Editor
Katie Weller, Circulation Manager
Jamie Cannon, Marketing Manager
Ruth Wassink, Vice President
Material looks at the latest offerings in tour travel including restaurants, theater, shopping, hotels, festivals, and events and activities.
Frequency: Quarterly
Circulation: 10000
Founded in 1980

24005 Midwest Traveler
12901 N Forty Drive
Saint Louis, MO 63141
314-523-6981
800-222-7623; Fax: 314-523-6982
www.autoclubmo.aaa.com
Mike Right, Editor
Cost: $3.00
Circulation: 45000
Founded in 1902

24006 Mobility
1717 Pennsylvania Avenue NW
8th Floor
Washington, DC 20006
202-293-7744; Fax: 202-659-8631

24007 NBTA Travel Quarterly
National Association of Business Travel Agents
123~North~Pitt Street
4th Floor
Alexandria, VA 22314
703-684-0836; Fax: 703-342-4324
Caleb Tiller, Sr Dir, Marketing & Communications
Wendy Santiago, Marketing Manager
Nicole Hayes, Assistant Manager, Communications
Jack Machlum, CEO
Kevin Maguire, VP/Chief Information Officer
This publication provides valuable information on NBTA, its members and the corporate travel industry, to help the professional stay connected to the industry.
Frequency: Quarterly/Members Only

24008 New England Tour Magazine
Shoreline Creations
PO Box 638
Yarmouth Port, MA 02675-638
508-398-0400; Fax: 508-398-4703
travel@grouptour.com
www.grouptour.com
Carol Smith, Editor
Carl Wassink, President
Katie Weller, Circulation Manager
Jamie Cannon, Marketing
Ruth Wassink, Executive Vice President
Promotes and covers the attractions, lodging, dining, events and other highlights of popular and less-famous travel destinations in the region.
Frequency: Quarterly
Circulation: 10000
Founded in 1925

24009 Onboard Services
International Publishing Company of America
50 Millstone Road
Building 300 Suite 110
East Windsor, NJ 08520
609-945-8000
800-280-8591; Fax: 609-945-8080
Alexander Morton, President
George Hulcher, Contributing Editor
Keeps airline, cruise ships, railroad, and terminal concessions management and purchasing departments up-to-date on all phases of passenger services.
Cost: $25.00
24 Pages
ISSN: 0892-4236
Founded in 1968
Printed in 4 colors on glossy stock

24010 Ozark Mountain Visitor
200 Industrial Park Drive
Hollister, MO 65672-5327
417-334-3161; Fax: 417-335-3933

24011 Pacific Asia Travel News
Americas Publishing Company
3657 Harriet Road
Victoria, Can, BC V8Z-3T1
250-260-1883; Fax: 250-953-5250
Malcolm Scott, Publisher
Issues include a news dateline with features on travel trends and outlooks, a special destination focus, and updates from the Pacific Asia Travel Association.
Cost: $30.00
Frequency: BiMonthly
Circulation: 24,000

24012 Practical Gourmet
Linick Group
PO Box 102
Middle Island, NY 11953-0102
631-924-3888; Fax: 631-924-3890
linickgrp@att.net
www.thepracticalgourmet.blogspot.com
Andrew S Linick, CEO
Roger Dextor, Production
Barbara Deal, Marketing Manager
The focus of this publication is light, healthy gourmet dining; includes reports on wine tasting, food festivals, contests, celebrations, cooking schools and other events.
Cost: $48.00
36 Pages
Frequency: Monthly
Circulation: 210,000
Founded in 1975
Mailing list available for rent: 210 M names at $110 per M
Printed in 4 colors on glossy stock

24013 Recommend
Worth International Communication Corp

PO Box 171070
Hialeah, FL 33017-1070

305-828-0123
800-447-0123; Fax: 305-826-6950
www.recommend.com

Laurel A Herman, Publisher
Lorri Robbins, National Director

Contains colorful information on worldwide destinations, resorts, hotels, transportation and tour operators, as well as marketing angles to help travel agents sell travel.
Cost: $48.00
Frequency: Monthly
Circulation: 60000
Founded in 1967
Printed in on glossy stock

24014 **Runzheimer Reports on Travel Management**
Runzheimer Park
Rochester, WI 53167-9999

262-712-2200
800-558-1702; Fax: 262-971-2254

Rex Runzheimer, President

24015 **Sea Mass Traveler**
PO Box 3189
Newport, RI 02840-0322

401-848-2922

24016 **Southwest Airlines Spirit**
Pace Communications
2811 McKinney Avenue
Suite 360
Dallas, TX 75204

214-580-2491; Fax: 214-580-8070

Jay Heinrichs, Editorial Director
John McAlley, Executive Editor
Frequency: Monthly
Circulation: 400088
Founded in 1971

24017 **Specialty Travel Index**
PO Box 458
San Anselmo, CA 94979

415-594-4900
888-624-4030; Fax: 415-455-1648
info@specialtytravel.com
www.specialtytravel.com

Karin Kinsey, Art Director
Stean Hansen, Circulation Manager
Andy Alpine, Marketing Manager
Risa Weinreb, Editor
Judith Alpine, Advertising Manager

Directory/magazine of adventure and specialty travel.
Cost: $10.00
Circulation: 32000
ISSN: 0889-7085
Founded in 1980
Printed in 4 colors on glossy stock

24018 **SportsTravel Magazine**
Schneider Publishing Company
11835 W Olympic Blvd
Suite 1265
Los Angeles, CA 90064-5814

310-577-3700; Fax: 310-577-3715
info@schneiderpublishing.com
www.schneiderpublishing.com
Facebook, Twitter, LinkedIn

Tim Schneider, President
Jason Gewirtz, Managing Editor/Sports Travel
Lisa Furfine, Associate Publisher
Chad Starbuck, Marketing Manager

Includes articles on travel training, sports law, event spotlights, and vital information on sites, hotels, transportation, trade shows and upcomiong events for team travel planners and event organizers.
Cost: $48.00
Frequency: Monthly
Circulation: 1400
ISSN: 1091-5354
Founded in 1997
Printed in on glossy stock

24019 **Sun Valley Magazine**
Mandala Media LLC
111 1st Avenue North #1M
Meriwether Building
Hailey, ID 83333

208-788-0770; Fax: 208-788-3881
www.sunvalleymag.com

Laurie C Sammis, Publisher/Editor-in-Chief
Mike McKenna, Editor
Julie Molema, Production Director

Articles on the arts, community, recreation, dining, shopping and real estate in the Sun Valley, Idaho area.
Cost: $22.00
Frequency: Quarterly
Circulation: 20000

24020 **Sundancer's West**
1108 Meadowview Drive
Euless, TX 76039

817-545-5265; Fax: 817-571-6481

Gerry Watkins, Webmaster/Editor/Photographer

24021 **Travel & Leisure**
American Express Publishing Corporation
1120 Avenue of the Americas
Suite 9
New York, NY 10036-6700

212-382-5600
800-888-8728; Fax: 212-382-5878
www.tlexplorer.com

Ed Kelly, CEO
Nancy Novogrod, Editor-in-Chief
Antonia LoPresti, Senior Marketing Manager
Cost: $19.95
Frequency: Monthly
Circulation: 950000

24022 **Travel Agent International**
Universal Media
PO Box 5386
Bloomington, IL 61702-5386

309-663-6327; Fax: 212-883-1244
tai@taitravelbmi.com

Richard P Friese, Publisher

Provides profiles on resorts and attractions for each given season.
Cost: $250.00
Frequency: 10 per year
Circulation: 19,100

24023 **Travel Counselor**
Miller Freeman Publications
600 Harrison Street
6th Fl
San Francisco, CA 94107

415-947-6000
800-764-759; Fax: 415-947-6055
email@travel-counselors.com
www.travel-counselors.com

Contains business information and analysis appropriate to the retail agency profession
Frequency: 7 per year
Circulation: 28,000

24024 **Travel Trends**
Meredith Corporation
125 Park Ave
New York, NY 10017-5529

212-557-6600; Fax: 212-551-7161

Peter Mason, Publisher/Editor

Information on the trends of the travel industry.
Frequency: Quarterly
Circulation: 5,000

24025 **Travel World**
East - West News Bureau
16051 W. Tampa Palms Blvd
Tampa, FL 33647

813-978-0877
800-494-3279
debbie@travelworld1.com
www.travelworld1.com

24026 **Travel World News**
Travel Industry Network
Ste 8
28 Knight St
Norwalk, CT 06851-4719

203-286-6679; Fax: 203-286-6681
editor@travelworldnews.com
www.travelworldnews.com

Charles Gatt Jr, Publisher
Peter Gatt, Associate Publisher

Monthly trade publication covering the retail travel industry. Each issue contains industry information and coverage for agents who are making recommendations and booking for their clients, including comprehensive, up to date, and worldwide product news and destination editorial coverage. Available online and in print.
Frequency: Monthly
Circulation: 22000
Founded in 1988

24027 **Travel, Food & Wine**
Punch-In-Syndicate
400 E 59th Street
Floor 9
New York, NY 10022-2342

212-755-4363
punchin@usa.net
www.punchin.com

J Walman, Editor

A magazine featuring articles and reviews on travel, food and wine, columns on airlines, hotels, cruise ships, railroads, resorts, restaurants, and spas. Also theater reviews, cinema, radio and all forms of entertainment.
Cost: $300.00
Frequency: Monthly

24028 **TravelBound!**
Group Traveler Leader
301 E High Street
Lexington, KY 40507

859-253-0455
888-253-0455; Fax: 859-253-0499
www.grouptravelleader.com
Facebook, Twitter, LinkedIn, You Tube

Mac Lacy, Publisher
Herb Sparrow, Executive Editor
Brian Jewell, Associate Editor
Kelly Tyner, Director of Sales & Marketing
Stacey Bowman, National Account Manager

The national magazine for African American Group Traveling, and the official magazine for the African American Travel Conference (AATC).
Circulation: 4500
Founded in 2001

24029 **Travelhost Magazine**
Travelhost

10701 N Stemmons Fwy
Dallas, TX 75220-2419

972-556-0541; Fax: 972-432-8729
www.travelhost.com

James E Buerger, CEO
David B Portener, Associate Publisher
Frequency: Monthly
Circulation: 60000
Founded in 1967

24030 **Vermont Green Mountain Guide**
44 Country Road
North Springfield, VT 05150-9738

802-886-3333
www.vtliving.com/newspapers/vtgreenmtnguid

Cindy Thiel, President

Trade Shows

24031 **Adventure Travel and Outdoor Show**
McRand International
1 Westminster Place
Suite 300
Lake Forest, IL 60045-1867

FAX 847-295-4419

Richard Dux, VP
Sue Wildman, VP

Exhibits by tour operators, outfitters and others geared toward soft and hard adventure travel vacations and outdoor activities.
15M Attendees
Frequency: January

24032 **American Society of Travel Agents Conference**
1101 King Street
Ste. 200
Alexandria, VA 22314-2944

703-739-2782; Fax: 703-684-8319
bdaniels@asta.org
www.asta.org

Chris Vranas, VP
Brooke Daniels, Event Manager

Gathering of travel agents, airlines, hotels and tour operators that provides the opportunity to view and discuss new products, services and trends in the industry. 700 booths.
6M Attendees
Frequency: November

24033 **American Travel Market Exhibition Company**
Reed Exhibition Companies
383 Main Avenue
Norwalk, CT 06851-1543

203-840-4800; Fax: 203-840-9628
www.reedexpo.com

Gregg Vautrin, CEO

The national event for all US travel buyers, including tour operators, travel agents, corporate travel buyers and meeting/conference planners. One of a global series of Travel Market events.
Frequency: September

24034 **Annual American and Canadian Sport, Travel and Outdoor Show**
Expositions
Edgewater Branch
PO Box 550
Cleveland, OH 44107-0550

216-529-1300; Fax: 216-529-0311
ech.case.edu

John Grabowskie, Online Editor
John Bedan, Associate Online Editor
Nathan Delany, Associate Online Editor

975 exhibits of hunting and fishing equipment, travel services, boats, recreational vehicles and related equipment, supplies and services.
300k Attendees
Frequency: Annual
Founded in 1935

24035 **Annual Boat, Vacation and Outdoor Show**
Showtime Productions
PO Box 4372
Rockford, IL 61110

815-877-8043; Fax: 815-877-9037
brenda@showtimeproduction.net
showtimeproduction.net

Duane Nichols, President
Brenda Rotoco, Event Coordinator

Boat, travel, outdoor equipment, supplies, and services plus demonstrations.
28000 Attendees
Frequency: February
Founded in 1970

24036 **Annual Capital Sport Fishing, Travel and Outdoor Show**
International Sport Show Producers Association
PO Box 4720
Portsmouth, NH 03802-4720

603-431-4315; Fax: 603-431-1971
info@sportshows.com
www.sportshows.com

Paul Fuller, President

Over 350 exhibits of sports, fishing, recreation and travel equipment, supplies and services.
45k Attendees
Frequency: Annual
Founded in 1996

24037 **Arabian Travel Market**
Reed Exhibition Companies
383 Main Avenue
PO Box 6059
Norwalk, CT 06851

203-840-4800; Fax: 203-840-9628
www.arabiantravelmarket.com

Three hundred exhibitors with travel related information, supplies and services.
5915 Attendees
Frequency: Annual

24038 **Corporate and Incentive Travel**
685 S. Washington Street
Alexandira, VA 22314

703-683-0123; Fax: 703-683-4545
info@corporateincentivetravel.net
www.corporateincentivetravel.net

Corporate travel forum.

24039 **DEMA Show**

858-616-6408
800-862-3483; Fax: 858-616-6495
info@dema.org
www.dema.org

Tom Ingram, President & CEO
Nicole Russel, VP, Operations

Annual trade show produced by the Diving Equipment & Marketing Association, for companies doing business in the scuba diving, ocean water sports and adventure/dive travel industries.
10M Attendees
Frequency: Annual

24040 **Destinations International Annual Convention**
Destinations International
2025 M St NW
Suite 500
Washington, DC 20036-3349

202-296-7888; Fax: 202-296-7889
info@destinationsinternational.org
destinationsinternational.org

Don Welsh, President & CEO
Barbra Gustis, EVP, Meetings & Event Design
1500 Attendees
Founded in 1914

24041 **Destinations Showcase**
Intl. Association of Convention/Visitors Bureaus
2025 M Street
Suite 500
Washington, DC 20036

202-296-7888; Fax: 202-296-7889
info@destinationmarketing.org
www.destinationsshowcase.com
Facebook, Twitter

Michael D Gehrisch, President/CEO

Containing 100-200 exhibits at tradeshows.
575 Attendees
Founded in 1914
Mailing list available for rent: 1200+ names at $400 per M

24042 **Discover America International Pow Wow**
Travel Industry Association of America
1100 New York Avenue NW
Suite 450
Washington, DC 20005-3934

202-408-8422; Fax: 202-408-1255
feedback@ustravel.org
www.ustravel.org

Rodger Dow, President & CEO
Siming Cao, Coordinator
Geoff Freeman, Executive Vice President and COO
Rebecca Shafer, Director of Executive Operations

Annual show of 1050 suppliers of travel products and services.
5,600 Attendees

24043 **Euro Travel Forum**
Reed Exhibition Companies
255 Washington Street
Newton, MA 02458-1637

617-584-4900; Fax: 617-630-2222

Elizabeth Hitchcock, International Sales

A mobile, multi-product and multi-destination travel trade exhibition bringing travel products from all over the world into direct contact with travel agents and travel buyers from the leisure, business and incentive products industries.
27M Attendees
Frequency: April

24044 **Family Motor Coach Association Convention**
8291 Clough Pike
Cincinnati, OH 45244-2756

513-474-3622
800-543-3622; Fax: 513-388-5286
www.fmca.com

Jerry Yeatts, Convention Director
Ranita Jones, Sales Manager
Shawna Grubbs, Sales Assistant

Convention for Motorhome enthusiasts. Includes hundreds of motorhome displays, supplier displays and component displays.
15M Attendees
Frequency: Mar/Apr/July/Aug
Founded in 1963

24045 **Heartland Travel Showcase**
Hart Productions
130 E Chestnut Street
Suite 301
Columbus, OH 43215

513-281-0022
800-896-4682; Fax: 513-281-3322
www.heartlandtravelshowcase.com

Annual show and exhibits of information from 10 midwest states and the province of Ontario on travel destinations, attractions, accommodations, activities and restaurants.
Frequency: February

24046 **Incentive Travel and Meeting Executives Show**
Hall-Erickson
98 E Naperville Road
Westmont, IL 60559-1559

630-963-9185
800-752-6312; Fax: 630-434-1216

Nancy A Petitti, Show Director
20M Attendees
Frequency: October
Founded in 1972

24047 **Motivation Show**
Hall-Erickson
98 E Naperville Road
Westmont, IL 60559-1559

630-963-9185
800-752-6312; Fax: 630-434-1216

Nancy A Petitti, Exhibit Show Manager
25M Attendees
Frequency: September
Founded in 1929

24048 **National Camping Industry Expo**
3700 W Flamingo Rd
Las Vegas, NV 22182-2240

703-932-2342; Fax: 703-734-3004
www.gocampingamerica.com

Rick Carbo, Manager
Chandana Karmarkar, Manager

National camping industry expo, only trade expo for RV parks and campground owners/operators. Containing 120 booths and 100 exhibitors.
850+ Attendees
Frequency: November
Founded in 1966
Mailing list available for rent: 3,200 names

24049 **Recreational Vehicle Industry Association National RV Trade Show**
1896 Preston White Drive
Reston, VA 20191-4325

703-206-6003

David Humphreys, President
Mary Hutya, VP

Six hundred and thirty booths.
10M Attendees
Frequency: November

24050 **Seatrade Cruise Convention**
Miller Freeman Publications
13760 Noel Road
Suite 500
Dallas, TX 75240

800-527-0207; Fax: 214-419-8855

24051 **Sport Travel Outdoor Show**
Expositions
PO Box 550
Cleveland, OH 44107-0550

216-529-1300; Fax: 330-529-0311

Judy Fassnacht, Show Manager

475 booths of products and services related to the outdoor travel industry.
93M Attendees
Frequency: February

24052 **Sports Travel and Adventure**
Show Productions
800 Roosevelt Road
Suite 407
Glen Ellyn, IL 60137-5839

630-694-4611; Fax: 630-790-0209

Sandra Lewis, Show Manager

Two hundred and fifty six booths geared toward outdoor enthusiasts.
15M Attendees
Frequency: February

24053 **Travel Exchange Annual Conference**
National Tour Association
101 Prosperous Place
Suite 350
Lexington, KY 40509

859-264-6540
800-682-8886; Fax: 859-264-6570
questions@ntastaff.com
ntaonline.com
Facebook, Twitter, LinkedIn

Pam Inman, President
Dawn Pettus, Manager, Events
Doug Rentz, Director, Communciation & Marketing

Brings together industry professionals and members to showcase ideas and products new to the travel and tourism industry.
Frequency: Annual

24054 **Travel Industry Association American Pow Wow Marketing**
1100 New York Avenue NW
Suite 450W
Washington, DC 20005

202-408-8422

Sue Elms, Show Manager
Roger Dow, CEO

Seven hundred booths where providers of US travel products promote these products.
3M Attendees
Frequency: April

24055 **Travel and Tourism Research Association Show**
546 E Main Street
Lexington, KY 40508-2342
859-226-4355; Fax: 859-226-4355
lisalcarey@aol.com
www.ttra.com

Twenty booths exhibiting information of interest to members of the Tourism Research Association.
400 Attendees
Frequency: June

24056 **TravelAge Tradeshows**
11400 West Olympic Blvd
Suite 325
Los Angeles, CA 90064

310-954-2510; Fax: 212-237-3007

Nancy Montella, Show Manager

Four hundred booths of educational and business-oriented tradeshow that provides a vehicle for various people within the travel industry to meet and exchange information on products, services and trends.
2.5M Attendees
Frequency: March

24057 **World Travel Market**
Reed Exhibition Companies
255 Washington Street
Newton, MA 02458-1637

617-584-4900; Fax: 617-630-2222
www.wtmlondon.com

Elizabeth Hitchcock, International Sales

Premium travel show.
43M Attendees
Frequency: November

Directories & Databases

24058 **ABC Cruise and Ferry Guide**
Reed Travel Group
Church Street
Hertfordshire, England, LU 5 4HB

Offers information on international shipping companies operating passenger services and cruises.
320 Pages
Frequency: Quarterly
ISBN: 0-001048-0 -

24059 **ABC Guide to International Travel**
Reed Travel Group
Church Street
Hertfordshire, England, LU 5 4HB

Offers a list of foreign consulates in London, England that offer travel information to tourists.
Frequency: Quarterly

24060 **Access Travel: Airports**
Airport Operators Council International
1220 19th Street NW
Suite 200
Washington, DC 20036-2463

202-293-8500; Fax: 202-331-1362

Information is given on over 500 airports worldwide that offer handicapped facilities.
50 Pages

24061 **Airport Hotel Directory**
3255 Wilshire Boulevard
Suite 1514
Los Angeles, CA 90010-1418

213-739-1956

Restaurants and hotels are listed that are a close proximity to major airports.
Cost: $12.00
170 Pages

24062 **American Bus Association's Motorcoach Marketer**
American Bus Association
111 K Street NE
9th Floor
Washington, DC 20002

202-842-1645; Fax: 202-842-0850
abainfo@buses.org
www.buses.org/Member-Resources/Motorcoach-Marketer

Peter J Pantuso, CEO
Eron Shosteck, Marketing

This directory is a comprehensive guide of the bus and travel industry offering information on hotels and sightseeing services, attractions, museums, restaurants and more.
500 Pages
Frequency: Annual
Founded in 1926

24063 **American Society of Travel Agents Membership Directory**
NACTA

1101 King St
Alexandria, VA 22314-2963

703-739-2782; Fax: 703-684-8319
www.nacta.com

Bill Maloney, Manager

Travel agents that represent over 17,000 agencies in the United States, Canada and overseas are the focus of this comprehensive directory.
Cost: $125.00
600 Pages
Frequency: Annual

24064 **CMP Publications Travel File**
CMP Publications
600 Community Dr
Manhasset, NY 11030-3810

516-562-5000; Fax: 516-562-5718

This large database covers the travel industry, with emphasis on news for travel agents and business travelers.
Frequency: Full-text

24065 **Club Metro**
Metro Online
1358 Hooper Avenue
Ste. 293
Toms River, NJ 08752

212-794-2664
www.clubmetrousa.com

This database contains information on travel, entertainment, and metropolitan services.
Frequency: Bulletin Board

24066 **Condo Vacations: the Complete Guide**
Lanier Publishing International
PO Box 20429
Oakland, CA 94620-0429

Condominiums that are available for vacation rentals are listed.
Cost: $14.95
320 Pages
Frequency: Annual

24067 **Cruise Industry News Annual**
Nissel-Lie Communications
441 Lexington Avenue
Suite 809
New York, NY 10017-3910

212-986-1025; Fax: 212-986-1033
info2@cruiseindustrynews.com
www.cruiseindustrynews.com

Oivind Mathisen, Editor/Publisher
Angela Mathisen, Publisher/Advertising Director
Monty Mathisen, Reporter/Web Editor

This book presents the entire worldwide cruise industry from new ships on order to supply/demand scenarios; plus reports on relevant issues, financial results, newbuilding and second-hand ship values, shipbuilding, new technology and on board services; plus exclusive reports on each sailing region, and a comprehensive directory of all cruised lines, shipyards, ports and other suppliers.
Cost: $450.00
300 Pages
Frequency: Annual
Founded in 1988

24068 **Environmental Vacations: Volunteer Projects to Save the Planet**
John Muir Publications
PO Box 613
Santa Fe, NM 87504-0613

505-466-6360; Fax: 505-988-1680

Information is given on vacations that provide opportunities to assist environmental projects.
Cost: $16.95
250 Pages

24069 **Federal Travel Directory**
Office of Federal Supply & Services
4 Crystal Mall Building
Washington, DC 20406-0001

202-564-2480

A list of airlines is offered in this directory that are under contract to the federal government.
Cost: $77.00
Frequency: Monthly

24070 **Ford's Travel Guides**
Ford's Travel Guides
19448 Londelius Street
Northridge, CA 91324-3511

818-987-1413

Offers valuable information on cruise ships and their planned cruises for one year ahead.
Cost: $14.95
200 Pages
Frequency: Quarterly
Circulation: 5,000

24071 **Foster Travel Publishing Website**
Foster Travel Publishing
Po Box 5715
Berkeley, CA 94705-0715

510-549-2202; Fax: 510-549-1131
lee@fostertravel.com
www.fostertravel.com

Lee Foster, Owner

award winning travel writing and photography on 200 worldwide locations, presented to the consumer and to the content buyer on the web or in print looking for travel writing or travel photography.
Frequency: Full-text

24072 **Free US Tourist Attractions**
Pilot Books
127 Sterling Avenue
PO Box 2102
Greenport, NY 11944

631-477-0978
800-797-4568; Fax: 631-477-0978

A directory of free family entertainment in every state of the union.
Cost: $12.95
ISBN: 0-875762-04-2

24073 **International Workcamp Directory**
VFP International Voluntary Service
7 Kilburn Street
Suite 31
Burlington, VT 05401

802-540-3060; Fax: 802-540-3061
vfp@vfp.org
www.vfp.org

Meg Brook, President
Chelsea Frisbee, Outgoing Volunteer Coordinator
Peter Coldwell, Treasurer/Founder
Scott Simpson, Board Chair
Matt Messier, Secretary

An annual booklet listing over 2400 opportunities for meaningful travel throughout Western and Easter Europe, Russia, Africa, Asia, Australia and Latin America. 2-3 week programs are $200 including room and board.
Cost: $20.00
2000 Members
289 Pages
Frequency: Annual
Circulation: 2,000
ISBN: 0-945617-20-8
ISSN: 0896-565X
Founded in 1982
Printed in 4 colors

24074 **National Bed and Breakfast Association Guide**
National Bed & Breakfast Association
2009 Family Circle
Lexington, KY 50505

859-255-0076; Fax: 859-255-0938

Phyllis Featherston, Executive Director
Cost: $17.95
600 Pages
Frequency: Every 2-3 Years
ISBN: 0-961129-86-7
Founded in 1982
Printed in 2 colors on matte stock

24075 **OAG Flights2Go**
UBM Aviation
3025 Highland Parkway
Suite 200
Downers Grove, IL 60515-5561

630-515-5300; Fax: 630-515-3251
www.oagtravel.com

Anthony Smith, Group Publisher
Jason Holland, Editor
Simon Barker, Publisher

Flights2Go provides mobile access to worldwide flight schedules in an instance direct to your mobile device. No matter where you are, you can look up flight schedules from across the globe and even check flight status.

24076 **OAG Travel Planner Pro**
UBM Aviation
3025 Highland Parkway
Suite 200
Downers Grove, IL 60515-5561

630-515-5300; Fax: 630-515-3251
www.oagtravel.com

Anthony Smith, Group Publisher
Jason Holland, Editor
Simon Barker, Publisher

OAG Travel Planner Pro is the premier online tool for travel arrangers who need to create, manage, and save complex travel plans quickly and easily.

24077 **Official Bus Guide**
Russell's Guides
834 3rd Avenue SE
Cedar Rapids, IA 52403-2408

319-364-6138; Fax: 319-364-4853

A list of 475 intercity bus companies in the United States, Canada and Mexico.
Cost: $9.90
Frequency: Monthly
Circulation: 14,000

24078 **Official Handbook of Travel Brochures**
Vacation Publications
1502 Augusta Drive
Suite 415
Houston, TX 77057-2484

713-974-6903

16 Pages
Frequency: Quarterly
Circulation: 38,000

24079 **Real Guides**
Farmers Trip & Travel
PO Box 473
Mount Morris, IL 61054-0473

FAX 815-734-1223

A series of guidebooks that list sites, attractions and events in a city or country.
Cost: $8.00
300 Pages
Frequency: Per Edition

24080 **Reed's Travel Group's Travel Agent Database**
Reed Travel Group
2000 Clearwater Dr
Oak Brook, IL 60523-8809

630-574-0825
800-424-3996; Fax: 630-288-8781
www.reedbusiness.com

Jeff Greisch, President

About 65,000 wholesale, retail and cooperative travel agencies worldwide, including tour operators.
Cost: $270.00

24081 **Society of American Travel Writers: Membership Directory**
Society of American Travel Writers
4101 Lake Boone Trail
Suite 201
Raleigh, NC 27607-7506

FAX 919-787-4916

Sarah Haw, Member Services

About 550 newspaper and magazine travel editors, writers, columnists, photo journalists and broadcasters in the US and Canada.
Cost: $95.00
Frequency: Annual February

24082 **Thomas Cook Airports Guide Europe**
Thomas Cook
Unit 11, Coningsby Road
Peterborough, England, PE 3 85B

Offers valuable information on over 75 public airports in Europe.
255 Pages
Frequency: Biennial

24083 **Thomas Cook Airports Guide International**
Thomas Cook
Unit 11, Coningsby Road
Peterborough, England, PE 3 85B

Offers valuable information on over 90 airport facilities outside of the United Kingdom.
255 Pages
Frequency: Biennial

24084 **Tours.com**
490 Post St
Suite 1701-A
San Francisco, CA 94102-1308

415-956-0111; Fax: 415-956-0117
info@tours.com
www.tours.com

Maria Polk, President/CEO/Co-Founder
Karin Wacaster, Public Relations
Marijo Douglass, Finance Executive

Home of the Worldwide Directory of Tours and Vacation Packages.
Founded in 1995

24085 **Travel Agent: Focus 500 Directory Issue**
Universal Media
801 2nd Ave
New York, NY 10017-8638

212-986-5100; Fax: 212-883-1244

Lists of attractions, restaurants, convention and visitor bureaus, hotel chains and management companies, cruise lines, state tourism offices, travel trade associations, tourist railways.
Frequency: Annual October
Circulation: 50,000

24086 **Travel Editors: US Consumer & Inflight Magazines**
Rocky Point Press
4830 Ranchito Avenue
Sherman Oaks, CA 91423-1927

FAX 818-763-4818

Listings of travel editors of US consumer and in-flight magazines.
Frequency: Annual

24087 **Travel Forum**
CompuServe Information Service
5000 Arlington Centre Blvd
Columbus, OH 43220-5439

614-326-1002
800-848-8199
www.travelforum.org

This database contains information on travel and related topics of interest, including travel planning.
Frequency: Bulletin Board

24088 **Travel Industry Association of America: Travel Media Directory**
Travel Industry Association of America
1100 New York Ave NW
Suite 450
Washington, DC 20005-6130

202-408-8422; Fax: 202-408-1255

Roger J Dow, CEO
Peter Strebel, Secretary

Travel editors of major newspapers, magazines and broadcast outlets.
Cost: $40.00
Frequency: Annual
Circulation: 3,000

24089 **Travel Insider's Guide to Alternative Accommodations**
Travel Insider
PO Box 14
Streamwood, IL 60107-0014

206-338-3381; Fax: 206-338-3381

John E Sullivan, Editor

Over 400 sources for alternative accommodations worldwide, such as farmhouses, castles, universities and country inns.
Cost: $9.95
Frequency: Annual October

24090 **Travel Photo Source Book**
Society of American Travel Writers
4101 Lake Boone Trail
Suite 201
Raleigh, NC 27607-7506

715-248-3800; Fax: 919-787-4916
www.photosource.com

Nancy Belcher, Editor

Nearly 100 member photographers and 35 associate member representatives of airlines, hotels, resorts, tourist agencies and public relations firms.
Frequency: Biennial

24091 **Travel Tips USA**
Renaissance Publications
7950 Jones Branch Drive
McLean, VA 22108-0605

614-777-1227
accuracy@usatoday.com
www.usatourist.com

Michelle Leco
Mike Leco

Amusement parks, attractions and festivals are among some of the categories listed in this travel directory.
Cost: $17.95
320 Pages

24092 **Travel World News Resource Directory**
Travel Industry Network
28 Knight Street
Norwalk, CT 06851

203-286-6679; Fax: 203-286-6681
editor@travelworldnews.com
www.travelworldnews.com

Charles Gatt Jr, Publisher
Peter Gatt, Associate Publisher

A directory by continent/region/locale of local vendors, tour operators, railways, cruise lines, and travel links.
Founded in 1988

24093 **Travel and Tourism Research Association: Membership Directory**
Travel and Tourism Research Association
546 E Main Street
Lexington, KY 40508-2342

859-226-4355; Fax: 859-226-4355
lisalcarey@aol.com

Lisa Carey, Executive Director

Over 750 state and local tourism bureaus and other federal and provincial government agencies, airlines, media, hotels, university bureaus of business research and other university departments and research and consulting firms concerned with travel research, marketing and promotion.
Cost: $50.00
Frequency: Annual June

24094 **Travel, Leisure and Entertainment News Media**
Larriston Communications
PO Box 20229
New York, NY 10025-1518

212-864-0150; Fax: 212-662-8103

Sheila Gordon, Editor

Over 350 travel and leisure magazines and daily newspapers with circulations of over 50,000 that have special leisure or entertainment sections.
Cost: $89.00
Frequency: Annual May

24095 **Traveler's Hotline Directory**
Forte Travel Lodge
Po Box 270469
San Diego, CA 92198-2469

858-487-9596
800-578-7878; Fax: 858-487-9658

Victor Ferrette, Partner

Approximately 12,000 travel services such as air couriers, auto rental agencies, campgrounds, resorts, hotels, spas, travel groups and airlines that offer toll-free domestic or international telephone numbers.
Cost: $15.95

24096 **Travelers Information RoundTable**
GE Information Services
401 N Washington Street
Rockville, MD 20850-1707

301-388-8284

Cathy Ge, Owner

Provides a forum enabling users to share information on a range of travel topics.
Frequency: Bulletin Board

24097 **West Coast Travel**
Foster Travel Publishing

Po Box 5715
Berkeley, CA 94705-0715

510-549-2202; Fax: 510-549-1131
lee@fostertravel.com
www.westcoasttravels.com

Lee Foster, Owner

This database offers information for travelers and tourists on approximately 150 locations in the western United States, Canada and Mexico.
Frequency: Full-text

24098 **Worldspan TravelShopper**
WORLDSPAN
300 Galleria Parkway
Atlanta, GA 30339

770-637-7400; Fax: 770-563-7004

Rakesh Gangwal, CEO

This database offers travel information, including 5 million domestic and international flights for every airline in the world for more than 100,000 cities.
Frequency: Directory

Industry Web Sites

24099 **http://gold.greyhouse.com**
G.O.L.D Grey House OnLine Databases

Grey House Publishing's online database platform, GOLD, offers Quick Search, Keyword Search and Expert Search for most business sectors including travel markets. The GOLD platform makes finding the information you need quick and easy - whether you're a novice searcher or an experienced database user. All of Grey House's directory products are available for subscription on the GOLD platform.

24100 **www.buses.org**
American Bus Association

Trade association for the North American bus industry.

24101 **www.gocampingamerica.com**
National Association of RV Parks and Campgrounds

Nat ARVC serves the business and legislative needs of more than 3,200 member RV parks and campgrounds.

24102 **www.goworldnet.com/cgi-bin**
Worldnet USA

States and their hotels, theaters and museums.

24103 **www.greyhouse.com**
Grey House Publishing

Authoritative reference directories for most business markets including travel markets. Users can search the online databases with varied search criteria allowing for custom searches by product category, geographic area, sales volume, keyword, subject and more. Full Grey House catalog and online ordering also available.

24104 **www.hotwire.com**
Hotwire.com

Internet travel service offering discounts on flights, hotels, car rentals, packages and cruises.

24105 **www.hsmai.org**
Hospitality Sales and Marketing Association

To provide resources to sales and marketing professionals at all levels of thier career in travel, hospitality, and tourism.

24106 **www.iacvb.org**
International Association of Convention and Visitor Bureaus

Promotes sound professional practices in the solicitation and servicing of meetings and conventions. Members represent travel/tourism-related businesses. Publications include a electronic newsletter and on-line directory.

24107 **www.nbba.com**
National Bed & Breakfast Association

Innkeepers of bed and breakfast lodgings.

24108 **www.ntaonline.com**
National Tour Association

For North American tourism professionals focused on the development, promotion and increased use of tour operators packaged travel.

24109 **www.orbitz.com**
Orbitz.com

Internet travel service offering discounts on flights, hotels, car rentals, packages and cruises.

24110 **www.rsana.com**
Receptive Services Association

Helping receptive operators serve international tour companies through partnerships with North American suppliers.

24111 **www.travel.com**
Travel.com

Internet travel service providing access to flights, hotels, car rentals, vacation packages and cruises.

24112 **www.travel.lycos.com**
Lycos.com

Internet travel service offering discounts on flights, hotels, car rentals, packages and cruises.

24113 **www.travel.yahoo.com**
Yahoo.com

Internet travel service providing access to flights, hotels, car rentals, vacation packages and cruises.

24114 **www.travelocity.com**
Sabre Holdings

Travel service offering consumers access to hundreds of airlines and thousands of hotels, as well as cruise, last-minute and vacation packages and best-in-class car rental companies.

Associations

24115 Air Conditioning Contractors of America
2800 S Shirlington Road
Suite 300
Arlington, VA 22206

703-575-4477
membership@acca.org
www.acca.org
Facebook, Twitter, LinkedIn, YouTube

Barton James, President & CEO
Samuel Awotwi, Director of Finance
Christine Gibson, VP, Marketing & Partnerships
Sean Robertson, VP, Membership/Business Operations
Kimya Bailey, Director, Events & Benchmarking

ACCA is a non-profit association serving the HVACR community, working to promote professional contracting, energy efficiency, and healthy, comfortable indoor environments.
60000 Members
Founded in 1968

24116 Air and Waste Management Association
436 7th Avenue
Suite 2100
Pittsburgh, PA 15219

412-232-3444
800-270-3444; Fax: 412-232-3450
info@awma.org
www.awma.org
Facebook, Twitter, LinkedIn

Stephanie Glyptis, Executive Director
Gerald Armstrong, Customer Service & Membership
Tracy Fedkoe, Director, Marketing/Project Mgmt.
Jeff Schurman, Manager, Exhibits & Sponsorship
Lisa Bucher, Managing Editor

Professional organization that provides training, information, and networking opportunities to environmental professionals.
5000 Members
Founded in 1907

24117 Alliance to Save Energy
1850 M Street NW
Suite 610
Washington, DC 20036

202-857-0666
www.ase.org
Facebook, Twitter, LinkedIn, YouTube, Google+, Flickr

Jason Hartke, President
Kara O'Connell, Chief Operating Officer
Ross Robinson, Chief Financial Officer
Susanna Silvan, Manager, Events/Executive Affairs
Ben Somberg, Manager, Communications

Organization that leads worldwide energy efficiency initiatives in policy advocacy, research, education and technology deployment.
Founded in 1977

24118 American Coal Ash Association
38800 Country Club Drive
Farmington Hills, MI 48331

720-870-7897; Fax: 720-870-7889
info@acaa-usa.org
www.acaa-usa.org

Thomas H. Adams, Executive Director
Alyssa Barto, Member Liaison
John Ward, Communications Coordinator

A non-profit trade association devoted to recycling the materials created from burning coal.
Founded in 1968

24119 American National Standards Institute
1899 L Street NW
11th Floor
Washington, DC 20036

202-293-8020; Fax: 202-293-9287
info@ansi.org
www.ansi.org
Facebook, Twitter, LinkedIn, YouTube, Google+, Instagram

S. Joe Bhatia, President & CEO

To enhance the global competition of business and quality of life by promoting and facilitating voluntary consensus standards and conformity assessment systems, and safeguarding their integrity.
27000 Members
Founded in 1918

24120 American Nuclear Society
555 N Kensington Avenue
La Grange Park, IL 60526

708-352-6611
800-323-3044; Fax: 708-352-0499
www.ans.org
Facebook, Twitter, LinkedIn

Serves its members in their efforts to develop and safely apply nuclear science and technology for public benefit through knowledge exchange, professional development, and enhanced public understanding.
Founded in 1954

24121 American Petroleum Institute
200 Massachusetts Avenue NW
Suite 1100
Washington, DC 20001-5571

202-682-8000
www.api.org
Facebook, Twitter, YouTube, Flickr

Mike Sommers, President/CEO
Amanda Eversole, EVP/COO
Paul G. Afonso, SVP/CLO/Corporate Secretary
Megan Bloomgren, SVP, Communications
Bill Koetzle, SVP, Gov. Relations

The only national trade association that represents all aspects of America's oil and natural gas industry. Members are producers, refiners, suppliers, pipeline operators and marine transporters, as well as service and supply companies that support all segments of the industry.
600+ Members
Founded in 1919

24122 American Public Energy Agency
P.O. Box 70
Shickley, NE 68436

Home Page: www.apea.org
Facebook

Purpose is to provide energy acquisition and energy-related services for its members and other public agencies, and to assist such agencies in acquiring stable energy supplies, reducing energy costs through group purchases, and developing enhanced energy acquisition mechanisms.
40 Members
Founded in 1995

24123 American Public Power Association
2451 Crystal Drive
Suite 1000
Arlington, VA 22202

202-467-2900
info@PublicPower.org
www.publicpower.org
Facebook, Twitter, LinkedIn, YouTube, Instagram, Pinterest

Sue Kelly, President/CEO
Michael Hyland, SVP, Engineering Services
Delia Patterson, SVP, Advocacy/Communications
Jeff Haas, VP, Membership & Strategic Devel.
Harry Olibris, Chief Financial Officer

Service association for community-owned eletric utilities.
Founded in 1940

24124 American Public Works Association
1200 Main Street
Suite 1400
Kansas City, MO 64105-2100

816-472-6100
800-848-APWA; Fax: 816-472-1610
www.apwa.net
Facebook, Twitter, LinkedIn, YouTube

Scott Grayson, Chief Executive Officer
Mary Knollmeyer, Director of Finance
Julie Bebermeyer, Director of Operations
Lysa Byous, Meeting Planner & Exhibit Manager
Tammy Bennett, Director, Membership & Engagement

International educational and professional association of public agencies, private sector companies, and individuals dedicated to providing high quality public works goods and services. AWA provides a forum in which public works professionals' competency, increase the performance of their agencies and companies, and bring important public works-related topics to public attention in local, state, and federal areas. Mailing list for members only.
30000 Members
Founded in 1937

24125 American Society of Appraisers
11107 Sunset Hills Road
Suite 310
Reston, VA 20190

703-478-2228
800-272-8258; Fax: 703-742-8471
asainfo@appraisers.org
www.appraisers.org
Facebook, Twitter, LinkedIn, YouTube

Johnnie White, Chief Executive Officer
Bonny Price, Chief Operating Officer
Joseph Noselli, Chief Financial Officer
Todd Paradis, Chief Marketing Officer
Sarah Sebastian, Director of Membership Development

Organization provides education and accreditation for appraisers.
Founded in 1939

24126 American Water Works Association
6666 W Quincy Ave.
Denver, CO 80235ÿ

303-794-7711
800-926-7337; Fax: 303-347-0804
www.awwa.org
Facebook, Twitter, LinkedIn, You Tube, RSS

Melissa Elliott, President
Aurel Arndt, Treasurer
David B. LaFrance, Chief Executive Officer

The professional society of North American drinking water experts. Develop standards and support research programs in waterworks design, construction, operation, and management. Conducts in-service training schools and offers placement service.
Founded in 1881

24127 American Wind Energy Association
1501 M Street NW
Suite 900
Washington, DC 20005

202-383-2500
engage.awea.org

Facebook, Twitter, LinkedIn, YouTube, Instagram

Tom Kiernan, Chief Executive Officer
Heather Graving, Manager, Executive Services
Joshua DeShong, Public Affairs Coordinator
Mark Bakke, Manager, Member Relations/Exhibits
Angela Bell, Manager, Member Relations

Promotes wind energy as a clean source of electricity for consumers around the world. Representing wind power project developers, equipment suppliers, services providers, parts manufacturers, utilities, researchers, and others involved in the wind industry.

24128 **Association of Energy Engineers**
3168 Mercer University Drive
Atlanta, GA 30341

770-447-5083
www.aeecenter.org

Lary Good, Dir., International Member Devel.
Stephen A. Roosa, Dir., Sustainable & Local Programs
Timohty B. Janos, Dir., Special Projects
Eric Oliver, Dir., Governmental Affairs
Albert Thumann, Executive Director

Promotes energy certification, management and education.
17500 Members
Founded in 1977

24129 **Association of Financial Guranty Insurers**
139 Lancaster Street
Albany, NY 12210-1903

518-449-4698
tcasey@mackinco.com

Bruce E. Stern, Chairman
Adam Bergonzi, Vice Chair
Cathleen Matanle, Secretary
Susan Comparato, Treasurer

Insure and reinsure municipal bonds and asset-backed securities.
Founded in 1971

24130 **Automatic Meter Reading Association**
60 Revere Dr # 500
Suite 500
Northbrook, IL 60062-1591

847-480-9628
888-612-2672; Fax: 847-480-9282
www.amra-intl.org
Facebook, Twitter, LinkedIn

John Waxman, Manager
John Waxman, Manager
Founded in 1986

24131 **Buliding Owners and Managers Association**
1101-15th Street NW
Suite 800
Washington, DC 20005

202-326-6300; Fax: 202-326-6377
info@boma.org
www.boma.org
Facebook, Twitter, LinkedIn, YouTube, Pinterest

Henry Chamberlain, Presient/COO
Luci Vallejo, Director, Executive Services
Pamela Colman, Director, Special Projects
Anita L. Smith, Director, Membership
Courtney McKay, CAE, VP, Communications & Marketing

Association for building managers and owners.
Founded in 1907

24132 **Edison Electric Institute**
701 Pennsylvania Avenue NW
Washington, DC 20004-2696

202-508-5000
feedback@eei.org
www.eei.org
Facebook, Twitter, LinkedIn, Youtube

Thomas R. Kuhn, President
John S. Schlenker, CFO/Treasurer
Jim Owen, VP, Membership & Meeting Services
Emily Sanford Fisher, General Counsel & Corp. Secretary
Stephanie Voyda, VP, Communications

Advocates public policy, expands market opportunities and provides strategic business information for the shareholder-owned electric utility industry.
Founded in 1933

24133 **Electric Power Research Institute**
3420 Hillview Avenue
Palo Alto, CA 94304

650-855-2121
800-313-3774
askepri@epri.com
www.epri.com
Facebook, Twitter, LinkedIn

Michael W. Howard, President/CEO
Pamela J. Keefe, SVP/CFO/Treasurer
Salvador A. Casente, Jr., VP/General Counsel/CCO/Secretary
Arshad Mansoor, SVP, Research/Development
Michael A. Coleman, VP, IT/CIO

Nonprofit energy research consortium for the benefit of utility members, their customers and society. Mission is to provide science and technology-based solutions to its global energy customers by managing a far-reaching program of scientific research, technology development and product implementation.
660 Members
Founded in 1965

24134 **Electric Power Supply Association**
1401 New York Ave Nw
Suite 1230
Washington, DC 20005-2110

202-628-8200; Fax: 202-628-8260
www.epsa.org
Facebook, Twitter, LinkedIn

John E Shelk, President/CEO
Nancy E Bagot, Senior Vice President
William S Burlew, VP, Govt. Affairs

24135 **Environment and Energy Study Institute**
1112 16th Street, NW
Suite 300
Washington, DC 20036

202-628-1400; Fax: 202-204-5244
info@eesi.org
www.eesi.org
Facebook, Twitter, YouTube, Google+

Jared Blum, Chairman
Carol Werner, Executive Director
David Robison, Director of Finance & Admin
Susan Williams, Director of Development
Alison Alford, Programs & Administrative Assistant

Educating Congress on energy efficiency and renewable energy, advancing innovating policy solutions.
Founded in 1984

24136 **Gas Research Institute**
1700 S Mount Prospect Road
Des Plaines, IL 60018-1804

847-768-0500; Fax: 847-768-0501
www.gastechnology.org
Facebook, Twitter

John Riordan, President/CEO

24137 **Geothermal Energy Association**
209 Pennsylvania Avenue SE
Washington, DC 20003

202-454-5261; Fax: 202-454-5265
www.geo-energy.org
Facebook, Twitter, LinkedIn, YouTube, Wordpress

Joe Greco, Chairman
Yoram Bronicki, President
Doug Glaspey, Vice President
Terryÿ Page, Secretary-Treasurer
Mihaela-Daniela Lobontiu, Business Manager

A US trade organization that supports the expanded use of geothermal energy.
Founded in 1988

24138 **Government Finance Officers Association**
203 N. LaSalle Street
Suite 2700
Chicago, IL 60601-1210

312-977-9700; Fax: 312-977-4806
www.gfoa.org
Facebook, Twitter, LinkedIn, YouTube

Marion M. Gee, President
Chris Morrill, Executive Director
Mike Mucha, Deputy Executive Director
John Jurkash, Chief Financial Officer

A professional association of finance officers.
Founded in 1906

24139 **Independent Petroleum Association of America**
1201 15th Street NW
Suite 300
Washington, DC 20005

202-857-4722; Fax: 202-857-4799
www.ipaa.org
Facebook, Twitter, LinkedIn, YouTube

Michael Watford, Chairman
Mark Miller, Vice Chairman
Barry Russell, President/CEO
Lee O. Fuller, Executive Vice President
Dan Naatz, SVP, Gov. Relations

Membership organization ensuring a strong, viable domestic oil and natural gas industry.
Founded in 1929

24140 **Institute of Industrial Engineers**
3577 Parkway Lane
Suite 200
Norcross, GA 30092

770-449-0460
800-494-0460; Fax: 770-441-3295
chapters@iienet.org
Facebook, Twitter, LinkedIn

Don Greene, CEO
Donna Calvert, COO
Monica Elliott, Director, Communications

Dedicated to supporting engineers involved in all industrial applications.

24141 **Institute of Public Utilities**
Owen Graduate Hall
735 East Shaw Lane, Room W157
East Lansing, MI 48825-1109

517-355-1876; Fax: 517-355-1854
ipu@msu.edu

ipu.msu.edu/
Facebook, Twitter, LinkedIn

Janice A Beecher, Director
Ligita Nelson, Administrative Assistant
Kenneth Rose, Ph.D., Senior Fellow
Steven Kihm, Senior Fellow (Finance)
Joydeep Mitra, Senior Faculty Associate

Research and training center at Michigan State University. Program focuses on regulation and management of energy, telecommunications and water companies.
Founded in 1965

24142 International District Energy Association (IDEA)
24 Lyman Street
Suite 230
Westborough, MA 01581

508-366-9339; Fax: 508-366-0019
idea@districtenergy.org
www.districtenergy.org
Facebook, Twitter, YouTube, Flickr, RSS

Bruce Ander, Chair
Tim Griffin, Vice Chair
Chris Lyons, 2nd Vice Chair
James Adams, Secretary/Treasurer
Ken Smith, Past Chair

IDEA fosters the success of its members as leaders in providing reliable, economical, and environmentally sound district energy services.
1780 Members
Founded in 1909

24143 International Ground Source Heat Pump Association
1201 S. Innovation Way Dr.
Suite 400'
Stillwater, OK 74074

405-744-5175
800-626-4747; Fax: 405-744-5283
www.igshpa.okstate.edu
Facebook, Twitter, YouTube, Google+

Robert Ingersoll, Director
John Turley, President
Garen Ewbank, Vice President
Jeromy Cotton, Secretary
Allan Skouby, Treasurer

A nonprofit organization to advance ground source heat pumps.
Founded in 1987

24144 International Journal of Energy Management
Association of Energy Engineers
3168 Mercer University Drive
Atlanta, GA 30341

770-447-5083
www.aeecenter.org
Facebook, Twitter, LinkedIn

Albert Thumann, Executive Director
Steven Parker, Editor

Exclusively written for engineers, energy managers, facility managers, utility professionals, VP's of operations, governmental energy managers and plant engineers involved in the design and application of energy management and facility improvement technologies.
17500 Members
Founded in 1977

24145 International Right of Way Association
19210 South Vermont Avenue
Building A Suite 100
Gardena, CA 90248

310-538-0233
888-340-4792; Fax: 310-538-1471
info@irwaonline.org
www.irwaonline.org
Facebook, Twitter, LinkedIn, YouTube

Mark Rieck, EVP
Fred Nasri, VP, CFO
Deidre C Alves, VP, Professional Development
Barbara Billitzer, VP, Publisher & Editor
Daniel M. Stekol, VP, Field Operations

Members are responsible for acquiring land over which to run utility lines, pipelines and roads.
10,00 Members
Founded in 1934

24146 Minnesota Rural Electric Association
11640 73rd Avenue N
Maple Grove, MN 55369

763-424-1020; Fax: 763-424-5820
www.mrea.org
Facebook, Twitter, LinkedIn

Darrick Moe, President & CEO
Melissa Stachovich, Director, Finance & Adminisatration
April Hildre, Executive & Membership Coordinator
Gayle Karol, Marketing & Event Coordinator
Karen Miller, Event & Membership Coordinator

The Minnesota Rural Electric Association (MREA) represents all 50 electric cooperatives in the state of Minnesota.
18M Members
Founded in 1967

24147 Municipal Waste Management Association
PO Box 1894
Guelph, ON N1H 4E9

519-823-1990; Fax: 519-823-0084
www.municipalwaste.ca

Ben Bennett, Executive Director
Melissa Campbell, Membership Co-ordinator
Karyn Hogan, Chair
Stephanie Sidler, Treasurer
Brad Whitelaw, Secretary

Concerned with the processing of municipal solid waste for the production of recyclable materials, heat, and energy. Members are local government organizations; associate members are from the private sector.
200 Members
Founded in 1987

24148 National Association of Counties
25 Massachusetts Avenue, NW
Suite 500
Washington, DC 20001ÿ

202-393-6226
888-407-6226; Fax: 202-393-2630
nacomeetings@naco.org
www.naco.org
Facebook, Twitter, LinkedIn, YouTube

Sallie Clark, President
Bryan Desloge, First Vice President
Matthew D. Chase, Executive Director
Kathy Nothstine, Program Director
Bert Jarreau, Chief Innovation Officer

The only national organization that represents county governments of the US.
Founded in 1935

24149 National Association of Energy Service Companies
1615 M St Nw
Suite 800
Washington, DC 20036-3213

202-822-0950; Fax: 202-822-0955
info@naesco.org
www.naesco.org
Facebook, LinkedIn

David Weiss, Chairman
Mike Kearney, Vice Chair
Scott Ririe, Secretary
Natasha Shah, Treasurer
Terry E. Singer, Executive Director

24150 National Association of Regulatory Utility Commissioners (NARUC)
1101 Vermont Avenue, NW
Suite 200
Washington, DC 20005

202-898-2200; Fax: 202-898-2213
admin@naruc.org
www.naruc.org
Facebook

Lisa Edgarÿ, Chairman/President
Travis Kavullaÿ, First Vice President
Robertÿ Powelson, Second Vice President
Charles Gray, Executive Director
David E. Ziegner, Treasurer

A trade association representing the state public service commissioners who regulate utility services, such as electricity, gas, telecommunication, water, and transportation throughout the country.
Founded in 1889

24151 National Association of State Energy Officials
2107 Wilson Boulevard
Suite 850
Arlington, VA 22201

703-299-8800; Fax: 703-299-6208
energy@naseo.org
www.naseo.org
Facebook, Twitter, LinkedIn, Youtube, Flickr

David Terry, Executive Director
Jeffrey C. Genzer, General Counsel
Melissa Savage, Senior Program Director
Rodney Sobin, Senior Program Director
Sandy Fazeli, Senior Program Director

The only non-profit organization that represents the Governor-designated energy officials from each state and territory. The organization was established to improve the effectiveness and quality of state energy programs and policies, provide policy input and analysis of federal energy issues and be a repository of information on energy issues of concern to the states.
56 Members
Founded in 1986

24152 National Association of State Utility
8380 Colesville Road
Suite 101
Silver Spring, MD 20910

301-589-6313; Fax: 301-589-6380
nasuca@nasuca.org
www.nasuca.org

Bill Levis, Interim Executive Director
Nicole Haslup, Deputy Director

Members are state appointed individuals that represent rate-payers in their state.
44 Members
Founded in 1979

24153 National Electrical Contractors Associatio n
3 Bethesda Metro Center
Suite 1100
Bethesda, MD 20814

301-657-3110; Fax: 301-215-4500
www.necanet.org
Facebook, Twitter, LinkedIn, YouTube, Flickr

A trade association representing electrical contractors.
Founded in 1901

24154 **National Energy Marketers Association**
3333 K Street NW
Suite 110
Washington, DC 20007
202-333-3288; Fax: 202-333-3266
www.energymarketers.com
Facebook, LinkedIn
A nonprofit trade association representing suppliers and consumers of natural energy.

24155 **National Hydropower Association**
25 Massachusetts Ave NW
Suite 450
Washington, DC 20001
202-682-1700; Fax: 202-682-9478
help@hydro.org
www.hydro.org
Facebook, Twitter
Linda Church Ciocci, Executive Director
Steve Wenke, Vice President
John McCormick, President
Debbie Mursch, Treasurer
John Suloway, Secretary
A nonprofit national association dedicated exclusively to advancing the interests of the hydropower industry. Seeks to secure hydropower's place as a climate-friendly, renewable and reliable energy source that serves national environmental and energy policy objectives.
140 Members
Founded in 1983

24156 **National Mining Association**
101 Constitution Ave. NW
Suite 500
Washington, DC 20001
202-463-2600; Fax: 202-463-2666
www.nma.org
Facebook, Twitter, LinkedIn, YouTube
Harry M. Red Conger, Chairman
Kevin Crutchfield, Vice Chairman
Hal Quinn, President & CEO
Rich Nolan, SVP, Government & Political Affairs
Bruce Watzman, SVP, Regulatory Affairs
Association for the mining industry in the US.

24157 **National Rural Electric Cooperative Association**
4301 Wilson Blvd
Suite 1
Arlington, VA 22203-1860
703-907-5500; Fax: 703-907-5526
veronica.franco@nreca.coop
www.nreca.coop
Facebook, Twitter, LinkedIn, Youtube
Jo Ann Emerson, CEO
Peter Baxter, SVP, Insurance & Financial Services
Jim Bausell, SVP, Communications
Jeffrey Connor, COO/Chief of Staff
Kirk Johnson, SVP, Government Relations
Membership consists of cooperative systems, public power and public utility districts. Annual budget of approximately $94 million. Sponsors and supports the Action for Rural Electrification Political Action Committee.
1000 Members
Founded in 1942

24158 **North American Association of Utility Distributors**
PO Box 566
Smithville, MO 64089
816-985-4997
naaud.org@gmail.com
www.naaud.org
Cathyÿ Gutierrez, Executive Director
Jim Reinhardt, President
Rick Atkinson, Vice President
A member of the National Association of Wholesaler-Distributors.

24159 **North American Electric Reliability**
3353 Peachtree Road, N.E
Suite 600, North Tower
Atlanta, GA 30326
404-446-2560; Fax: 404-467-0474
www.nerc.com
Gerry W. Cauley, President/CEO
Mark Lauby, SVP/Chief Reliability Officer
Charles A. Berardesco, SVP/General Counsel/Corp Secretary
Michael Walker, SVP/CFO/CAO/Treasurer
Stan Hoptroff, VP/CTO
Principal organization for coordinating and promoting North America's electrical supplies, demands and reliability issues.
11 Members
Founded in 1968

24160 **Northwest Public Power Association**
9817 Ne 54th St
Suite 200
Vancouver, WA 98662-6064
360-254-0109; Fax: 360-254-5731
nwppa@nwppa.org
www.nwppa.org
Facebook, Twitter
Anita J Decker, Executive Director
Debbie Kuraspediani, Communication Director
Brenda Dunn, Associate Editor/Advertising
Glenda Waite, Graphic Artist
Greg Blank, Web/IT Technician
A international training organization for electric utilities in 10 western states and 4 western Canadian provinces.
Cost: $75.00
200 Members
Frequency: Monthly/Annunal
Founded in 1940

24161 **Public Utilities Risk Management Association**
1900 West Park Drive
Suite 150
Westborough, MA 1581
508-983-1457; Fax: 508-599-3427
www.purma.org
Facebook
Wayne Doerpholz, President
Jeannine Millett, Vice President
Jeffrey Dobbins, Secretary
Gail Cohen, Treasurer
Paul Heanue, Director
Founded to provide risk management and insurance services to municipal utilities.
Founded in 1996

24162 **The Association of Businesses Advocating Tariff Equality**
151 S. Old Woodward Avenue
Suiteÿ200
Birmingham, MI 48009ÿ
248-988-5861
rstrong@clarkhill.com
abate-energy.org
Robert Strong, Legal Counsel
An organization for protecting the interests on industrial customers in energy and related matters.
Founded in 1981

24163 **U.S. Energy Information Administration**
1000 Independence Ave. SW
EI-40
Washington, DC 20585-0001
202-586-8800
infoctr@eia.gov
www.eia.gov
Facebook, Twitter, LinkedIn, YouTube, Flickr, RSS
John H. Weiner, Executive Director
The U.S. Energy Information Administration (EIA) collects, analyzes, and disseminates independent and impartial energy information to promote sound policymaking, efficient markets, and public understanding of energy and its interaction with the economy and the environment.
Founded in 1977

24164 **United States Energy Association**
1300 Pennsylvania Ave NW
Suite 550
Washington, DC 20004
202-312-1230; Fax: 202-682-1682
reply@usea.org
www.usea.org
Twitter
Barry K Worthington, Executive Director
Brian Kearns, Chief Financial Officer
Will Polen, Senior Director
U.S. member of World Energy Council represents broad interests of the U.S. energy sector.

24165 **Water Environment Federation**
601 Wythe St
Alexandria, VA 22314-1994
703-684-2400
800-666-0206; Fax: 703-684-2492
inquiry@wef.org
www.wef.org
Facebook, Twitter
Eileen O'Neill, Executive Director
Barry Liner, Director
Lisa McFadden, Sr. Program Manager
Steve Harrison, Manager-Technical Programs
Elizabeth Conway, Committee Coordinator
34000 Members
Founded in 1928

Newsletters

24166 **Clearing Up**
Energy NewsData
PO Box 900928
Seattle, WA 98109-9228
206-285-4848; Fax: 206-281-8035
newsdata@newsdata.com
www.newsdata.com
Steve Ernst, Managing Editor
Daniel Sackett, Circulation Director
Covers energy policy, resource development, public utility and energy litigation and energy marketing financing in the Pacific Northwestern United States and Western Canada.
Cost: $1199.00
14 Pages
Frequency: Weekly
ISSN: 0738-2332
Founded in 1982
Printed in one color on matte stock

24167 **Electric Utility Week**
McGraw Hill

PO Box 182604
Columbus, OH 43272

877-833-5524
800-752-8878; Fax: 614-759-3749
www.mcgraw-hill.com

Dan Tanz, Chief Editor
Paul Carlsen, Senior Editor
Harold McGraw, III, President

Provides news of significant developments affecting the electric utility industry focusing on state and federal regulation, management and bulk power markets. Publishes charts of prices utilities pay for fuels.
Cost: $2165.00
Frequency: Weekly
Founded in 1909

24168 **Energy Daily**
King Publishing Group
1325 Massachusetts Ave Nw
Suite 310
Washington, DC 20005-4194

240-455-6801
800-926-5464; Fax: 240-628-5774
www.energy-daily.com

F King, President
George Lobsenz, Editor

Information regarding energy use, supply and demand, power and heat generation, energy sources, conversion and storage, and energy and fuel conversion processes.
Cost: $1900.00
Frequency: Daily
Founded in 1974

24169 **Energy Report**
Pasha Publications
101 Second St
Suite 110
Petaluma, CA 94952

707-981-8999
800-424-2908; Fax: 707-981-8998
www.theenergyreport.com

Harry Baisden, Group Publisher
Barry Cassell, Editor

Coverage includes comprehensive policies and issues affecting oil, natural gas, electricity, cogeneration, power markets, nuclear energy, taxation, global warming and energy business opportunities.
Cost: $872.00
20 Pages
Frequency: Weekly
Founded in 1978

24170 **HydroWorld Alert**
HCI Publications
410 Archibald St
Kansas City, MO 64111-3288

816-931-1311; Fax: 816-931-2015
www.hcipub.com

Leslie Eden, President

Bi-weekly fax report on international hydroelectric project developments, business trends, and news relevant to organizations seeking business developments.
Cost: $635.00
Frequency: Weekly
Founded in 1970

24171 **Hydrowire**
HCI Publications
410 Archibald St
Kansas City, MO 64111-3288

816-931-1311; Fax: 816-931-2015
www.hcipub.com

Leslie Eden, President

Concise, bi-weekly report on major news in the hydroelectric industry. Includes timely listings of licensing for hydroelectric power projects. Also covers news and business opportunities in the North American hydroelectric industry.
Cost: $425.00
Circulation: 500
Founded in 1994

24172 **IE News: Utilities**
Institute of Industrial Engineers
3577 Parkway Lane
Suite 200
Norcross, GA 30092

770-449-0460
800-494-0460; Fax: 770-441-3295
cs@iienet.org
Facebook, Twitter, LinkedIn

Elaine Fuerst, Marketing Director
Monica Erikson, Communicaton
David Gatton, Managing Director

Association news.
4 Pages
Frequency: Quarterly
Circulation: 400
Founded in 1948

24173 **Inside Energy**
Platts, McGraw Hill Companies
1200 G St Nw
Suite 1000
Washington, DC 20005-3814

202-942-8788
800-752-8878; Fax: 202-383-2025
support@platts.com
www.platts.com

Bill Loveless, Editor
Georgia Safos, Circulation Director

Covers the Department of Energy including energy, science/technology, and environmental management programs as well as energy programs at the Interior Department.
Cost: $1810.00
16 Pages
Frequency: Weekly
Founded in 1888

24174 **NARUC Bulletin**
Nat'l Assn of Regulatory Utility Commissioners
1101 Vermont Ave Nw
Suite 200
Washington, DC 20005-3553

202-898-2200; Fax: 202-898-2213
admin@naruc.org
www.naruc.org

Charles Gray, Executive Director
Jaclyn Wintle, Publications Coordinator
Diane Munns, Publisher

A quasi-governmental nonprofit corporation composed of governmental agencies engaged in the regulation of public utilities and carriers. Its primary mission is to serve the consumer interest by seeking to improve the quality and effectiveness of public regulation in America.
Cost: $110.00
16 Pages
Frequency: Weekly
Circulation: 2000
Founded in 1889
Mailing list available for rent
Printed in one color on matte stock

24175 **National Association of Regulatory Utility Commissioners Newsletter**
Natl Assoc of Regulatory Utility Commissioners
1101 Vermont Ave Nw
Suite 200
Washington, DC 20005-3553

202-898-2200; Fax: 202-898-2213
admin@naruc.org
www.naruc.org

Charles Gray, Executive Director
Jaclyn Wintle, Publications Coordinator
Judi Sord, Circulation Manager

A national organization that offers valuable information on over 150 consultants and other professionals active in regulated water, sewer and related industries.
Cost: $125.00
Circulation: 1800
Founded in 1889

24176 **Northeast Power Report**
McGraw Hill
PO Box 182604
Columbus, OH 43272

877-833-5524
800-752-8878; Fax: 614-759-3749
www.mcgraw-hill.com
Facebook, Twitter, LinkedIn

Ron Dionne, Publisher
Rob Ingraham, Publisher
Harold McGraw, III, President
Steven H. Weiss, VP

Provides news of significant developments affecting the electric utility industry focusing on state and federal regulation, management and bulk power markets. Publishes charts of prices utilities pay for fuels.
Cost: $745.00
16 Pages
Frequency: BiWeekly
Founded in 1909

24177 **Nuclear Waste News**
Business Publishers
222 Sedwick Dr
Suite 101
Durham, NC 27713

800-223-8720; Fax: 800-508-2592
www.bpinews.com

Worldwide coverage of the nuclear waste management industry including waste generation, packaging, transport, processing and disposal.
Cost: $697.00
10 Pages
Frequency: 25 per year
Founded in 1963
Mailing list available for rent
Printed in 2 colors on matte stock

24178 **NuclearFuel**
McGraw Hill
PO Box 182605
Columbus, OH 43273

877-833-5525
800-752-8879; Fax: 614-759-3750
www.mcgraw-hill.com

Michael Knapik, Editor
Rob Ingraham, Publisher
Harold McGraw, III, President
Steven H. Weiss, VP

Provides news of significant developments affecting the electric utility industry focusing on state and federal regulation, management and bulk power markets. Publishes charts of prices utilities pay for fuels.
14 Pages
Founded in 1910

24179 **Nucleonics Week**
McGraw Hill

PO Box 182604
Columbus, OH 43272

877-833-5524
800-752-8878; Fax: 614-759-3749
support@platts.com
www.mcgraw-hill.com

Margaret Ryan, Editor

Covers all aspects of commercial nuclear power.
Cost: $2265.00
12 Pages
Frequency: Monthly
Founded in 1888

24180 **Public Gas News**
American Public Gas Association
11094 Lee Hwy
Suite 102
Fairfax, VA 22030-5034

703-352-3890; Fax: 703-352-1271
info@apga.org
www.apga.org

Robert S Cave, Executive Director

Written for public gas managers to keep them apprised of industry news.
Cost: $50.00
Circulation: 1000
Printed in 2 colors

24181 **Public Utilities**
State Capitals Newsletters
PO Box 7376
Alexandria, VA 22307-7376

703-768-9600; Fax: 703-768-9690
statecapitals.com
Cost: $345.00

Frequency: Weekly

24182 **Public Utilities: From the State Capitals**
Wakeman Walworth
300 N Washington Street
Suite 204
Alexandria, VA 22314-2530

703-689-9600; Fax: 703-549-1372

Keyes Walworth, Publisher

Covers state regulations of all forms of public utilities across the nation. It reports on new rate structures, allowable profit margins, special taxes, consumer relations, environmental legislation, nuclear plant regulations, deregulation programs and programs for low-income customers.

24183 **Utility Environment Report**
McGraw Hill
PO Box 182604
Columbus, OH 43272

877-833-5524
800-752-8878; Fax: 614-759-3749
www.mcgraw-hill.com

Rob Ingraham, Publisher
Harold McGraw, III, President
Steven H. Weiss, VP

Provides news of significant developments affecting the electric utility industry focusing on state and federal regulation, management and bulk power markets. Publishes charts of prices utilities pay for fuels.
Cost: $695.00
18 Pages
Founded in 1899

24184 **Utility Executive**
Water Environment Federation
601 Wythe St
Alexandria, VA 22314-1994

800-666-0206; Fax: 703-684-2492
www.wef.org
Facebook, Twitter

Matt Bond, President
Cordell Samuels, President-Elect
Sandra Ralston, Vice President
Chris Browning, Treasurer
Jeff Eger, Secretary and Executive Director

For managers and executives at water & wastewater treatment plants, consultants, and others interested in utility management. Focuses on such pertinent business issues as public private partnerships, capital financing options, strategic planning methods, public outreach approaches, and staff development.
79 Members
ISSN: 1044-9943
Founded in 1928

24185 **Utility Reporter: Fuels, Energy and Power**
InfoTeam
PO Box 15640
Plantation, FL 33318-5640

954-473-9560; Fax: 954-473-0544

Randy M Allen CPA, Editor

Focuses on activities involving: power generation, combustion, delivery and transmission; alternative energy devices and systems; heat transfer, storage and utilization; and myriad of related topics.
Cost: $289.00
20 Pages
Frequency: Monthly
ISBN: 0-890298-4 -
Printed in one color on matte stock

Magazines & Journals

24186 **ANS News**
American Nuclear Society
555 N Kensington Avenue
La Grange Park, IL 60526

708-352-6611
800-323-3044; Fax: 708-352-0499
www.ans.org

For personnel involved in nuclear power operation and development. Coverage includes power, plant operations and maintenance, fuel cycle, legislation, international employment and more.
Cost: $290.00
Frequency: Monthly
Circulation: 12000
Founded in 1954
Printed in on glossy stock

24187 **APWA Reporter**
American Public Works Association
1200 Main Street
Suite 1400
Kansas City, MO 64105-2100

816-472-6100
800-848-APWA; Fax: 816-472-1610
kclark@apwa.net
www.apwa.net
Facebook, Twitter, LinkedIn

Scott Grayson, Executive Director
R. Kevin Clark, Editor

Prime communication link uniting the community of public works professionals that make up APWA.
Cost: $100.00
Frequency: Monthly
Circulation: 25000
ISBN: 0-092487-3 -
Mailing list available for rent

24188 **ASH at Work**
American Coal Ash Association
38800 Country Club Drive
Farmington Hills, MI 48331

720-870-7897; Fax: 720-870-7889
info@acaa-usa.org
www.acaa-usa.org

Thomas H. Adams, Executive Director
Alyssa Barto, Member Liaison
John Ward, Communications Coordinator

The only magazine covering all facets of the coal combustion products industry. Read by ACAA members and others interested in the use and management of coal combustion products.
126 Members
Frequency: Bi-Annually
Circulation: 10000
Founded in 1968

24189 **Alternative Energy**
PWG
205 S Beverly Drive
#208
Beverly Hills, CA 90212-3827

310-273-3486; Fax: 310-858-8272
www.bp.com

Irwin Stambler, Publisher
Ahmad Taleban, President

Reports on future economic and technological trends.
Cost: $95.00
12 Pages
Frequency: Monthly
Printed in 2 colors on matte stock

24190 **American Water Works Association Journal**
American Water Works Association
6666 W Quincy Ave.
Denver, CO 80235

303-794-7711
800-926-7337; Fax: 303-347-0804
www.awwa.org

Melissa Elliott, President
David B. LaFrance, Chief Executive Officer

Journal of the professional society of North American drinking water experts. Dues cover subscription for members.
Cost: $120.00
152 Pages
Frequency: Monthly
ISSN: 0003-150X
Founded in 1935

24191 **Bulletin**
NW Public Power Association
9817 Ne 54th St
Suite 200
Vancouver, WA 98662-6064

360-254-0109; Fax: 360-254-5731
nwppa@nwppa.org
www.nwppa.org

Will Lutgen, Executive Director

Readership consists of directors, chairmen and managers of electric utilities in the ten Western States and four Canadian provinces. Provides news and events of the public power industry in the Pacific Northwest Region.
Cost: $ 32.00
32 Pages
Circulation: 6200
Printed in 4 colors

24192 **Chief Engineer**
Chief Engineers Association of Chicagoland

4701 Midlothian Turnpike
Crestwood, IL 60445

708-293-1720; Fax: 708-633-7008
www.chiefengineer.org

Ernest K Wulff, Editor

Covers building maintenance issues, laws and rulings relative to chief engineers, as well as mechanical and general HVAC equipment.
Frequency: Monthly
Circulation: 2000
Founded in 1935
Mailing list available for rent: 2K names

24193 **Cogeneration Monthly Letter**
Cogeneration Publications Company
509 Tennessee Avenue
Alexandria, VA 22305-1336

703-683-1868; Fax: 703-683-1878
www.powermarketers.com

Scott Spiewak, Publisher

Discusses new technology and legislation governing power generating facilities. Includes listings of planned projects.
Frequency: 5 per year
Circulation: 5000

24194 **Diesel & Gas Turbine Worldwide**
Diesel & Gas Turbine Publications
20855 Watertown Rd
Suite 220
Waukesha, WI 53186-1873

262-754-4100
800-558-4322; Fax: 262-832-5075
slizdas@dieselpub.com
www.dieselpub.com

Michael Osenga, President
Mark McNeely, Editor
Lynne Diefenbach, Advertising Manager
Christa Johnson, Production Manager

Focuses on the design, production, installation, operation, and maintenance of engines in the global marine, power generation, oil and gas, or railroad industries.
Frequency: bi-Monthly
Circulation: 20100
Founded in 1935

24195 **Diesel Progress: International Edition**
Diesel & Gas Turbine Publications
20855 Watertown Rd
Suite 220
Waukesha, WI 53186-1873

262-754-4100; Fax: 262-832-5075
www.dieselspec.com

Michael Osenga, President
Sue Bollwahn, Circulation Manager
Katie Evans, Sales Manager
Michael J Brezonick, Editor-in-Chief

Focuses on new products and technology that serves engineering, marketing, service and equipment, purchasing, administrative, and others allied to the field.
Circulation: 10273
Founded in 1935

24196 **District Energy**
International District Enery Association (IDEA)
24 Lyman Streetad
Suite 230
Westborough, MA 01581

508-366-9339; Fax: 508-366-0019
idea@districtenergy.org
www.districtenergy.org

Peter Myers, Editor
Rob Thornton, President

Journal of district heating and cooling industry, congeneration, physical plants and energy efficiency. Accepts advertising.
Cost: $40.00
Frequency: Quarterly

24197 **EM Magazine**
Air and Waste Management Association
436 7th Avenue
Suite 2100
Pittsburgh, PA 15219

411-232-3444
800-270-3444; Fax: 412-232-3450
info@awma.org
www.awma.org

Lisa Bucher, Managing Editor

EM Magazine is a monthly publication for environmental managers. It explores a range of issues affecting the industry with provocative articles and regular columns written by leaders in the field.
Frequency: Monthly

24198 **Electric Light & Power**
Technical Publishing
1421 S. Sheridan Road
Tulsa, OK 74112

981-831-9884; Fax: 918-831-9834
candiced@pennwell.com
www.elp.com

Wayne Beaty, Editor
Candice Doctor, Sales Director
Michael Grossman, Publisher
Teresa Hansen, Editor in Chief

Offers articles on the electric utility industry.
Cost: $38.00
84 Pages
Frequency: Monthly
Founded in 1922

24199 **Electric Perspectives**
Edison Electric Institute
701 Pennsylvania Avenue NW
Washington, DC 20004-2696

202-508-5000
feedback@eei.org
www.eei.org

Thomas R. Kuhn, President

The magazine for management in America's investor-owned electric utilities. Covers all areas of utility operations and concerns, providing detailed analyses and farsighted commentary on how issues and trends are shaping the industry today and the future impact.
Frequency: Bi-Monthly
ISSN: 0364-474X

24200 **Energy Efficiency Journal**
NAESCO
1615 M St NW
Suite 800
Washington, DC 20036-3213

202-822-0950; Fax: 202-822-0955

Terry E Singer, Executive Editor
Nina Lockhart, Senior Program Manager
Donald Gilligan, Publisher

Targets energy service companies, electric and gas utilities and other energy providers. Highlights industry news and features energy conservation.
Frequency: Quarterly
Circulation: 200

24201 **Energy Manager**
Primedia
3585 Engineering Drive
Suite 100
Norcross, GA 30092

678-421-3000; Fax: 913-514-6895
www.primedia.com

Eric Jacobson, Senior VP
Charles Stubs, President
Kim Payne, VP
Mike Barber, Accountant

Subjects include energy management systems, HVAC, automated building systems, plant and facilities control, and negotiating supplier contracts. Features include legislative news from Washington, analysis of rare updates, relevant news from around the world and new product reviews.
Frequency: 5 per year
Circulation: 50,000
Founded in 1998

24202 **Energy Today**
Trend Publishing
529 14th St NW
Suite 954
Washington, DC 20045-1925

202-662-8827; Fax: 202-662-8829

Arthur Kranish, Editor

Includes news and analysis, new regulatory and technical developments, grant and contract opportunities, investigative reports, and market studies.
Frequency: Monthly

24203 **Energy and Housing Report**
Alan L Frank Associates
9124 Bradford Road
Silverspring, MD 20901-4918

703-866-4397; Fax: 301-565-3298
homeenergy.org

Mary James, Publisher
Iain Walker, Executive Editor
Cass Duggan, Circulation Manager
Carol A. Markell, Marketing Manager
Alan Meier, President

Research in consumption with the goal of increasing energy conservation at the residential level. Follows trends in consumption and the effects of conservation efforts on energy use.
Founded in 1994

24204 **Energy in the News**
New York Mercantile Exchange
1 N End Ave
New York, NY 10282-1101

212-299-2000; Fax: 212-301-4700

Samuel Gaer, Executive VP

Covers market fundamentals, trading strategies and market conditions. Provides information that keeps future commission merchants, industry executives, options and cash market traders up-to-date with trends affecting the energy industry.
Frequency: Quarterly
Circulation: 35000

24205 **Gas Turbine World**
Pequot Publishing
PO Box 447
Southport, CT 06490-447

203-259-1812; Fax: 203-259-0532
www.business-magazines.com

Victor Debiasi, Publisher

Focuses on implementing policy, specification, design, maintenance, and modernization of the systems and equipment of electric power generation.
Cost: $135.00
Frequency: Monthly
Circulation: 10000

24206 **Generation Week**
Pasha Publications

1600 Wilson Boulevard
#600
Arlington, VA 22209-2509

703-528-1244
800-424-2908; Fax: 703-816-7821
www.pasha.com

Tod Sedgwick, Publisher

On new technology and innovative operation of power plants.
Frequency: Weekly

24207 **HRW: Hydro Review Worldwide**
HCI Publications
410 Archibald St
Kansas City, MO 64111-3288

816-931-1311; Fax: 816-931-2015
www.hcipub.com

Leslie Eden, President
Marla Barness, Editor
Bob Merrigan, Marketing

Magazine serving information needs of people associated with hydro throughout the world. Managing and improving plant operations, solving problems, financing and essential business news are covered extensively.
Cost: $44.00
Circulation: 4673
Founded in 1982

24208 **Hart's Energy Markets**
Hart Publications
4545 Post Oak Place
#210
Houston, TX 77027-3105

713-993-9320; Fax: 713-840-0983
www.hartenergy.com

Dana Griffin Smith, Publisher
Joe Fisher, Editor
Richard Eichler, President

Keeps readers abreast of trends and opportunities in the marketplace. Covers such topics as electricity deregulation, gas unbundling, rebundling of services, nuclear and renewable energy, technological developments and regulatory issues.
Frequency: Monthly
Circulation: 14000
Founded in 1973

24209 **Home Power**
PO Box 520
Ashland, OR 97520-18

541-512-0201
800-707-6585; Fax: 530-475-0836
info@homepower.com
www.homepower.com

Karen Perez, Publisher
Joe Schwartz, Manager

Covers photovoltaics, wind turbines, solar heating, methane, batteries, inverters, water pumping, electric vehicles, controls, and instruments. Examines the design and installation of balanced renewable energy systems in the home, while also reviewing products ranging from solar pumps to refrigerators.
Cost: $22.50
Circulation: 19200
Founded in 1987

24210 **Hydro Review**
HCI Publications
410 Archibald St
Kansas City, MO 64111-3288

816-931-1311; Fax: 816-931-2015
www.hcipub.com

Leslie Eden, President

Magazine providing in-depth coverage of the North American hydroelectric industry. Rehab, redevelopment, dam safety and the environment are explored.
Cost: $65.00
Circulation: 500
Founded in 1980

24211 **Independent Energy**
PennWell Publishing Company
1421 S Sheridan Rd
Tulsa, OK 74112-6619

918-831-9421
800-331-4463; Fax: 918-831-9476
www.pennwell.com

Robert Biolchini, President

Focuses on analysis and views aimed at doing business more successfully. Reports important market information, trends and equipment advances affecting power project development, financing, construction, operation and management.
Frequency: Monthly
Circulation: 10962
Founded in 1961

24212 **New Equipment Digest**
Penton Media
1300 E 9th St
Suite 316
Cleveland, OH 44114-1503

216-696-7000; Fax: 216-696-6662
information@penton.com
www.newequipment.com

Jane Cooper, Marketing
Tom Sockel, Associate Editor
Robert King, Editor
Sarah Hughes, Production Manager
Bobbie Macy, Circulation Manager

Serves the general industrial field which includes manufacturing, processing, engineering services, construction, transportation, mining, public utilities, wholesale distributors, educational services, libraries and governmental establishments.
Frequency: Monthly
Founded in 1936

24213 **Northeast Sun**
NE Sustainable Energy Association
50 Miles St
Suite 3
Greenfield, MA 01301-3255

413-774-6051; Fax: 413-774-6053
nesea@nesea.org
www.nesea.org

David Barclay, Executive Director

Addresses the current issues of solar energy and natural gas power. Also provides an exchange of ideas for those seeking other environmentally sound energy sources.
Frequency: Monthly
Circulation: 5000
Founded in 1974

24214 **Northwest Public Power Bulletin**
Northwest Public Power Association
9817 NE 54th St
Suite 200
Vancouver, WA 98662-6064

360-254-0109; Fax: 360-254-5731
nwppa@nwppa.org
www.nwppa.org

Will Lutgen, President
Brenda Dunn, Associate Editor
Debbie Kuraspediani, Director Communications

Trade publication for consumer-owned electric utilities managers, directors, commissioners and management staff.
Cost: $25.00
28 Pages
Frequency: Monthly
Circulation: 6000
Founded in 1947

24215 **Nuclear Plant Journal**
EQES
1400 Opus Place
Suite 904
Downers Grove, IL 60515

630-858-6161; Fax: 630-858-8787
michelle@goinfo.com
www.nuclearplantjournal.com

Newal Agnihotri, Publisher

Nuclear Plant Journal includes technical papers, informative articles and departments aimed at developing better methods, systems, products and services in the nuclear power industry. The Journal is compiled through the research efforts of professional engineers who are specialists in their respective fields.
Circulation: 14000
ISSN: 0892-2055
Founded in 1983
Printed in on glossy stock

24216 **Power Engineering International**
PennWell Publishing Company
1421 S Sheridan Rd
Tulsa, OK 74112-6619

918-831-9421
800-331-4463; Fax: 918-831-9476
Headquarters@PennWell.com
www.pennwell.com

Robert Biolchini, President
Candice Doctor, Regional Sales Manager
Rick Huntzicker, National Sales Manager
Junior Isles, Publisher & Editorial Director
Rafael A Junquera, Editor

A variety of topics including plant design, operations, management and applications. New products are also reviewed.
Frequency: Monthly
Circulation: 34000
Founded in 1910

24217 **Private Power Executive**
Pequot Publishing
PO Box 447
Southport, CT 06490-0447

203-259-1812; Fax: 203-259-0532

Victor de Biasi, Publisher

Written for cogenerators and developers involved in planning, design, financing, installation and operation of cogeneration plants for industrial, municipal, hospitals, and commercial district heating and cooling.
Frequency: BiMonthly
Circulation: ll,500

24218 **Public Power Magazine**
American Public Power Association
2451 Crystal Drive
Suite 1000
Arlington, VA 22202

202-467-2900
News@PublicPower.org
www.publicpower.org

Sue Kelly, President/CEO

The only national magazine published especially for policymaking and managerial personnel of local publicly owned electric systems. Public Power keeps readers abreast of policy developments, managerial techniques, new technologies, research and development and legislative issues.
ISSN: 0033-3654

24219 **Public Utilities Fortnightly**
Public Utilities Reports
8229 Boone Blvd
Suite 400
Vienna, VA 22182-2623
703-847-7720
800-368-5001; Fax: 703-917-6964

www.pur.com
Twitter

Bruce Radford, Publisher
Michael Burr, Editor-In-Chief
Philip Cross, Vice President/ Legal Editor
Joseph Paparello, Director of Sales
Jean Cole, Marketing Manager

Independent publisher for the energy industry.
Cost: $459.00
Frequency: Weekly
Founded in 1929

24220 **Public Utility Weekly**
Public Utilities Reports
8229 Boone Blvd
Suite 400
Vienna, VA 22182-2623

703-847-7720
800-368-5001; Fax: 703-917-6964
www.pur.com

Bruce Radford, President
Richard Stavros, Executive Editor
Joseph Paparello, Marketing Manager
Phillip Cross, Legal Publisher

Designed to serve as a communication forum for the utility industry covering state commission rulings and federal regulatory issues.
Founded in 1915

24221 **Transmission & Distribution World**
Primedia
PO Box 12901
Shawnee Mission, KS 66282-2901

913-341-1300
800-441-0294; Fax: 913-514-6895
www.tdworld.com
Facebook, Twitter

Eric Jacobson, Senior VP
Rick Bush, Editor
Frequency: Monthly
Circulation: 49000
Founded in 1996

24222 **Turbomachinery International**
Business Journals
PO Box 5550
Norwalk, CT 06856-5550

203-663-7814; Fax: 203-852-8175
www.turbomachinerymag.com

Richard Zanetti, Publisher

Includes updates of new approaches to energy conservation, new equipment listings and business/financial news.
Frequency: BiMonthly
Circulation: 11,100
Founded in 1959

24223 **Utilities Law Review**
John Wiley & Sons
Office A10 Spinners Court
55 West End
Witney, OX OX8 6

199-370-6183
800-825-7550; Fax: 199-370-9410
www.lawtext.com/

Nicholas Gingell, Publisher
Cosmo Graham, Editor
William J Pesce, CEO/President
Charlotte Villiers, Assistant Editor
Peter Crowther, Current Survey Editor

Edited by a team of specialist UK and European lawyers, it is the leading journal in this fast-changing field. Providing detailed coverage of electricity, gas, telecommunications, transport, water and broadcasting.
Cost: $4920.00
Frequency: Bi-Monthly
Circulation: 250
Founded in 1807

24224 **Utility & Telephone Fleets**
Practical Communications
482 Holly Ave
Saint Paul, MN 55102

651-91 -997; Fax: 651-224-2347
www.utfleets.com/

Judith F Chance, Group Publisher
Mike Domke, Publisher
Carol Birkland, Editor
Tom Gelinas, Editorial Director

The equipment, accessory and information resource for fleet professionals.
Circulation: 18,000
Founded in 1980

24225 **Utility Automation**
PennWell Publishing Company
1421 S Sheridan
PO Box 1260
Tulsa, OK 74112

918-835-3161; Fax: 918-831-9497
ua@pennwell.com
Facebook, Twitter

Shirley Wilson, Marketing Manager
Steven M Brown, Editor
Michael Grossman, Publisher
Robert F Biolchini, CEO/President
Janet Orteon, Circulation Manager

Innovative energy solutions.
Cost: $74.00
50 Pages
Circulation: 32200
ISSN: 1085-2328
Founded in 1996

24226 **Utility Automation International**
PennWell Publishing Company
1421 S Sheridan Rd
Tulsa, OK 74112-6619

918-831-9421
800-331-4463; Fax: 918-831-9476
headquarters@pennwell.com
www.pennwell.com
Facebook, Twitter

Robert Biolchini, President
Tina Jackson, Circulation Manager
Doug Pryor, Editor
Brad Dillman, Marketing
Circulation: 24002
Founded in 1910

24227 **Utility Business**
PRIMEDIA Intertec-Technology & Transportation
PO Box 12901
Shawnee Mission, KS 66282-2901

913-341-1300; Fax: 913-514-6895
barry-lecerf@intertec.com
Facebook, Twitter, LinkedIn

Eric Jacobson, Senior VP

Editorial emphasis is on providing the reader with solutions and commentary for identifying and developing company assets, realizing the impact technology has on the business, and responding to the evolving demands of the marketplace.
Frequency: 8 per year
Circulation: 50,000

24228 **Utility Contractor**
3925 Chain Bridge Road
Suite 300
Fairfax, VA 22030

703-358-9300; Fax: 703-358-9307
bill@nuca.com
www.nuca.com

Bill Hillman, CEO

Serves the underground utility construction industry, including contractors, manufacturers, suppliers, engineering firms, municipal/public/private utilities, and others allied to the field.
Frequency: Monthly
Circulation: 59329
ISSN: 1098-0342
Founded in 1963

24229 **Utility Executive**
Water Environment Federation
601 Wythe St
Alexandria, VA 22314-1994

703-684-2400
800-666-0206; Fax: 703-684-2492
csc@wef.org
www.wef.org

Bill Bertera, Executive Director
Jack Benson, Marketing Manager

Editorial focuses on issues such as continuous improvement, privatization, financial and risk management, as well as benchmarking and leadership. Problem solving strategies are included for everything from wastewater treatment efficiency to negotiation contracts and proposal evaluations, and address relevant, current issues facing utility managers today.
Cost: $33.00
Frequency: Monthly
Founded in 1928

24230 **Utility Fleet Management**
TT Publishing
2200 Mill Road
Alexandria, VA 22314-1994

703-838-1770; Fax: 703-838-6259
www.ttnews.com

Bob Raft, Publisher

Focuses on fleet management issues and new equipment.
Cost: $25.00
Frequency: Monthly
Circulation: 15,000

24231 **Western Energy**
Magellan
827 NE Oregon Street
Suite 200
Portland, OR 97232-2172

503-231-1994; Fax: 503-231-2595
www.westernenergy.org

Chuck Meyer, President
Jody Brassfield-English, Controller
Karen Himes, Webmaster

Contains technical features designed to inform and educate workers and technicians in the energy production field.
Frequency: BiMonthly
Circulation: 5,058

Trade Shows

24232 **AMRA Symposium**
Automatic Meter Reading Association
60 Revere Drive
Suite 500
Northbrook, IL 60062

847-480-9628
888-612-2672; Fax: 847-480-9282
www.amra-intl.org

Joyce Paschall, Executive Director

Gas, water and electric utilities, telephone companies and installation companies equipment and supplies for meter reading .
1600 Attendees
Frequency: Annual
Founded in 1986

24233 **AWEA CLEANPOWER**
American Wind Energy Association

1501 M Street NW
Suite 900
Washington, DC 20005

202-383-2500
conference@awea.org
engage.awea.org/events
Facebook, Twitter, LinkedIn

Tom Kiernan, Chief Executive Officer
Mark Bakke, Manager, Member Relations/Exhibits

Bringing together attendees and exhibitors from every aspect of the industry. Exhibitors display the latest industry products and services from manufacturing leaders, component suppliers, and other wind energy organizations. This conference combines education, exhibition, and networking creating a perfect venue for business development.
7000 Attendees
Frequency: Annual/June

24234 **AWEA Offshore WINDPOWER**
American Wind Energy Association
1501 M Street NW
Suite 900
Washington, DC 20005

202-383-2500
engage.awea.org/events
Facebook, Twitter, LinkedIn, YouTube, Instagram

Tom Kiernan, Chief Executive Officer
Mark Bakke, Manager, Member Relations/Exhibits

Brings together exhibitors and attendees from all over the world who are interested in becoming players in this new and highly promising market.
Frequency: Annual/October

24235 **Air and Waste Management Association Annual Conference and Exhibition**
Air and Waste Management Association
436 7th Avenue
Suite 2100
Pittsburgh, PA 15219

412-232-3444
800-270-3444; Fax: 412-232-3450
info@awma.org
www.awma.org
Facebook, Twitter, LinkedIn

Stephanie Glyptis, Executive Director
Jeff Schurman, Manager, Exhibits & Sponsorship

Environmental professionals from all sectors of the economy including colleges, universities, natural resource manufacturing and process industries, consultants, local state, provincial, regional and federal governments, construction, and utilities industries. Over 300 exhibits of environmental control products.
6000 Attendees

24236 **BOMA International Conference & Expo**
Building Owners and Managers Association
1101-15th Street NW
Suite 800
Washington, DC 20005

202-326-6300; Fax: 202-326-6377
info@boma.org
www.boma.org

Henry Chamberlain, President/COO

Opportunity for business professionals to discuss problems, security, exchange ideas and share experience and knowledge.

24237 **Buscon East/West**
Conference Management Company
200 Connecticut Avenue
Norwalk, CT 06854-1940

203-866-4400

David Caplin, Show Manager

Principal industry event for systems builders and electronics engineers.
5M Attendees

24238 **EEI Annual Convention**
Edison Electric Institute
701 Pennsylvania Avenue NW
Washington, DC 20004-2696

202-508-5000
www.eei.org

Thomas R. Kuhn, President
Lee Hutchinson, Contact

Annual event designed for CEO and other senior-level executives from the electric industry.
1000 Attendees

24239 **Engineering & Operations Conference**
American Public Power Association
2451 Crystal Drive
Suite 1000
Arlington, VA 22202

202-467-2900
info@publicpower.org
www.publicpower.org
Facebook, Twitter, LinkedIn, YouTube, Instagram, Pinterest

Sue Kelly, President/CEO
Michael Hyland, SVP, Engineering Services
Delia Patterson, SVP, Advocacy/Communications
Jeff Haas, VP, Membership & Strategic Devel.
Harry Olibris, Chief Financial Officer

A conference for public power professionals to discuss and learn about designing, developing, and maintaining the nation's electric system.
1.3M Attendees
Frequency: April

24240 **Northwest Public Power Engineering & Operations Show**
9817 NE 54th Street
Suite 200
Vancouver, WA 98662-6064

360-254-0109; Fax: 360-254-5731
nwppa@nwppa.org
www.nwppa.org

Scott Lowry, Training Manager
Debbie Kuraspediani, Director Communications
900 Attendees
Frequency: May

24241 **Public Works Expo**
American Public Works Association
1200 Main Street
Suite 1400
Kansas City, MO 64105-2100
816-472-6100
800-848-APWA; Fax: 816-472-1610
www.apwa.net
Facebook, Twitter, LinkedIn

Scott Grayson, Executive Director
Lysa Byous, Meeting Planner & Exhibit Manager

Offers the benefit of a variety of educational sessions, depth of the exhibit program and endless opportunities for networking. The latest cutting-edge technologies, managerial techniques and regulatory trends designed to keep you focused on the right solutions at the right time.
Frequency: Annual/September
ISSN: 0092-4873

24242 **Smart Energy Summitt**
Parks Associates
15950 N. Dallas Parkway
Suite 575
Dallas, TX 75248

972-490-1113
800-727-5711; Fax: 972-490-1133
info@parksassociates.com
www.parksassociates.com

Tricia Parks, Founder and CEO
Stuart Sikes, President
Farhan Abid, Research Analyst
Bill Ablondi, Director, Home Systems Research
John Barrett, Director of Research

Smart Energy Summit is an annual three-day event that examines the opportunities and technical business requirements inherent in the consumer programs and advanced systems and services made possible by Smart Grids and Residential Energy Management solutions.
Frequency: Annual
Founded in 1986

Directories & Databases

24243 **American Public Works Association Buyer's Guide**
American Public Works Association
1200 Main Street
Suite 1400
Kansas City, MO 64105-2100

816-472-6100
800-848-APWA; Fax: 816-472-1610
www.apwa.net

Scott Grayson, Executive Director
Julie Bebermeyer, Director of Operations
Tammy Bennett, Director, Membership & Engagement

International educational and professional association of public agencies, private sector companies, and individuals dedicated to providing high quality public works goods and services. AWA provides a forum in which public works professionals competency, increase the performance of their agencies and companies, and bring important public works-related topics to public attention in local, state, and federal areas. Mailing list for members only.
Cost: $100.00
Frequency: Monthly
ISSN: 0092-4873

24244 **DEED Project Database**
American Public Power Association
2451 Crystal Drive
Suite 1000
Washington, VA 22202

202-467-2900
www.publicpower.org

Sue Kelly, President/CEO

Includes over 30 years of research and development projects.

24245 **DRI Utility Cost Forecasting**
DRI/McGraw-Hill
24 Hartwell Ave
Lexington, MA 02421-3103

781-860-6060; Fax: 781-860-6002
www.construction.com

Walt Arvin, President

This large database covers the US public utility industry, including cost inputs for pumps, gas compressors, steam pipes and gas and electric meters.

24246 **Directory of Electric Power Producers and Distributors**
McGraw Hill

2 Penn Plz
5th Floor
New York, NY 10121-2298

212-760-8589; Fax: 212-904-2723
www.mcgraw-hill.com

Offers information on over 3,500 investor-owned, municipal, rural cooperative and government electric utility systems in the United States and Canada.
Cost: $395.00
1,200 Pages
Frequency: Annual

24247 **Directory of Electric Utility Company Libraries in the United States**
Library Services Committee/Edison Electric Inst
701 Pennsylvania Avenue NW
Washington, DC 20004-2608

202-347-2693

Over 90 investor-owned electric utility company libraries throughout the country are profiled.
Cost: $10.00
149 Pages
Frequency: Annual

24248 **Directory of Energy Professionals**
Assn of Regulatory Utility Commissioners
PO Box 684
Washington, DC 20044-0684

202-898-2200

Offers information on consultants and other professionals active in regulated energy utility industries.
Cost: $44.00
450 Pages
Frequency: Annual

24249 **Directory of Publicly Owned Natural Gas Systems**
American Public Gas Association
11094 Lee Hwy
Suite 102
Fairfax, VA 22030-5034

703-352-3890; Fax: 703-352-1271
info@apga.org
www.apga.org

Robert S Cave, Executive Director

A listing of all publicly owned natural gas systems in the US.
Cost: $50.00
80 Pages
Frequency: Annual
Circulation: 1,000
Printed in on matte stock

24250 **Electric Utility Cost Forecast**
WEFA Group
800 Baldwin Tower Boulevard
Eddystone, PA 19022-1368

610-490-4000; Fax: 610-490-2770
www.wefa.com

Mary Novak

This time series covers prices, construction and operating costs pertinent to the electric utilities industry.

24251 **Electric Utility Industry**
Midwest Publishing Company
2230 E 49th Ste E
Tulsa, OK 74105-8771

918-582-2000
800-829-2002; Fax: 918-587-9349
www.midwestdirectories.com

Will Hammack, Editor

Approximately 6,000 utility companies, contractors, engineering firms, equipment manufacturers and supply companies.
Cost: $155.00
Frequency: Annual February
Founded in 1943

24252 **Financial Statistics of Major Investor-Owned Electric Utilities**
US Energy Information Administration
1000 Independence Ave SW
Washington, DC 20585-0001

202-586-8800; Fax: 202-586-0727
www.eia.doe.gov

John H Weiner, Executive Director

Offers data from over 180 major investor-owned electric utilities in the United States.
Cost: $33.00
Frequency: Annual

24253 **Gas Industry Training Directory**
American Gas Association
1515 Wilson Boulevard
Suite 100
Arlington, VA 22209-2469

703-841-8400; Fax: 703-841-8406
www.ihrdc.com

David F Sullivan, Industry Training

Over 600 programs are available in this directory from gas transmission and distribution companies, manufacturers of gas-fired equipment, consultants, etc., and from gas associations.
Frequency: Annual February

24254 **Guide to Hydropower Mechanical Design**
HCI Publications
410 Archibald St
Kansas City, MO 64111-3288

816-931-1311; Fax: 816-931-2015
www.hcipub.com

Leslie Eden, President

Developed by the Hydropower Technical Committee of the American Society of Mechanical Engineers. A ready reference for individuals who design hydropower facilities and producers and distributors of electricity.
Cost: $125.00
Circulation: 4673

24255 **Handy-Whitman Index of Public Utility Construction Costs**
Whitman, Requardt and Associates
801 S Caroline St
Baltimore, MD 21231-3311

410-235-3450; Fax: 410-243-5716
www.wrallp.com

Jenny Miller, Human Resources

This database covers indexes of building costs for construction of public utilities in the United States.

24256 **International Directory of Electric Power Producers and Distributors**
McGraw Hill
1200 G St NW
Suite 250
Washington, DC 20005-3821

202-383-2377; Fax: 202-383-2438
www.aviationweek.com

Jennifer Michels, Manager

Offers valuable information on over 3,000 power generating and distribution systems in over 200 countries overseas.
Cost: $345.00

24257 **International Directory of Nuclear Utilities**
Nuexco
950 17th Street
Suite 2500
Denver, CO 80202-2825

303-534-3100

This comprehensive directory offers information on over 120 utilities in 30 countries that operate nuclear plants with a capacity of at least 100 megawatts.
Cost: $220.00
264 Pages
Frequency: Annual
Founded in 1968

24258 **Inventory of Power Plants in the United States**
US Energy Information Administration
1000 Independence Ave SW
Washington, DC 20585-0001

202-586-8800; Fax: 202-586-0727
www.eia.doe.gov

John H Weiner, Executive Director

Information is given on existing and projected and jointly-owned power plants within electric utility systems.
Cost: $23.00
393 Pages
Frequency: Annual

24259 **LEXIS Public Utilities Law Library**
Mead Data Central
9443 Springboro Pike
Dayton, OH 45401

888-223-6337; Fax: 518-487-3584
www.lexis-nexis.com

Andrew Prozes, CEO

This database contains information on public utilities-related case decisions from all state supreme courts and most state appellate courts.
Frequency: Full-text

24260 **Northwest Electric Utility Directory**
Northwest Public Power Association
9817 Ne 54th St
Suite 4576
Vancouver, WA 98662-6064

360-254-0109; Fax: 360-254-5731
www.nwppa.org

Will Lutgen, President
Randy Shipley, Project Manager

Annual directory for electric utilities in 10 western states and 4 western Canadian provinces.
Frequency: Annually

24261 **PUR Analysis of Investor-Owned Electric & Gas Utilities**
Public Utilities Reports
2111 Wilson Boulevard
Suite 200
Arlington, VA 22201-3001

Covers over 200 investor-owned electric and gas operating and holding companies.
Cost: $395.00
Frequency: Annual

24262 **Pipeline & Utilities Construction: Contractors Issue**
Oildom Publishing Company of Texas
PO Box 219368
Houston, TX 77218-9368

281-558-6930

Offers a comprehensive list of over 5,000 individual contracting firms concerned with the construction of oil and gas pipelines, water and sewer lines and gas distribution systems.
Cost: $80.00
Frequency: Annual
Circulation: 25,000

24263 **Platts UDI**
1200 G St NW
Suite 1000
Washington, DC 20005-3814

202-383-2144
800-752-8878; Fax: 202-942-8789
www.marketing.platts.com

Liane Kucher, Manager

Publisher of directories for world-wide electric power industry.

24264 **Power Engineering**
PennWell Publishing Company
1421 S Sheridan Rd
Tulsa, OK 74112-6619

918-831-9421
800-331-4463; Fax: 918-831-9476
headquarters@pennwell.com
www.power-eng.com

Rick Huntzicker, National Brand Manager
Dan Idoine, Regional Brand Manager

List of manufacturers and suppliers of products and services to the power plant and utility engineering industries.
Cost: $10.00
Frequency: Annual, September

24265 **Rural Electrification: Directory Issue**
National Rural Electric Cooperative Association
4301 Wilson Blvd
Arlington, VA 22203-1860

703-907-5500; Fax: 703-907-5526
www.nreca.org

Glenn English, CEO

Over 1,000 electric cooperatives.
Frequency: Annual July
Circulation: 35,000

24266 **The Utility Connection**

Home Page: www.utilityconnection.com

Links to more than 4,000 utilities, industry associations and organizations, news outlets and state and federal regulatory and information sites.
Founded in 1995

24267 **UDI Who's Who at Electric Power Plants**
Utility Data Institute
1200 G St NW
Suite 250
Washington, DC 20005-3814

202-942-8788

Offers valuable information on over 6,000 key personnel at over 1,200 electric utility plants.
Cost: $195.00
Frequency: Annual

24268 **US Electric Utility Industry Software Directory**
PennWell Publishing Company
PO Box 1260
Tulsa, OK 74101-1260

918-835-3161
800-752-9764; Fax: 918-831-9555
www.utilityconnection.com

Wayne Beaty, Editor
Steve Hall, Advertising/Sales

An amazing reference directory offering information on over 400 programs in 75 applications categories covering all aspects of the electric power industry.
Cost: $175.00
140 Pages
Frequency: Annual

Industry Web Sites

24269 **http://gold.greyhouse.com**
G.O.L.D Grey House OnLine Databases

Grey House Publishing's online database platform, GOLD, offers Quick Search, Keyword Search and Expert Search for most business sectors including utility markets. The GOLD platform makes finding the information you need quick and easy - whether you're a novice searcher or an experienced database user. All of Grey House's directory products are available for subscription on the GOLD platform.

24270 **www.aeecenter.org**
Association of Energy Engineers

Promotes energy certification, management and education.

24271 **www.apea.org**
American Public Energy Agency

Purpose is to provide energy acquisition and management services for public agencies.

24272 **www.apga.org**
American Public Gas Association

Association of municipal gas systems.

24273 **www.apwa.net**
American Public Works Association

International educational and professional association of public agencies, private sector companies, and individuals dedicated to providing high quality public works goods and services. AWA provides a forum in which public works professionals' competency, increase the performance of their agencies and companies, and bring important public works-related topics to public attention in local, state, and federal areas. Mailing list for members only.

24274 **www.awwa.org**
American Water Works Association

The professional society of North American drinking water experts. Develop standards and support research programs in waterworks design, construction, operation, and management. Conducts in-service training schools and offers placement service.

24275 **www.eei.org**
Edison Electric Institute

Advocates public policy, expands market opportunities and provides strategic business information for the shareholder-owned electric utility industry.

24276 **www.eia.doe.gov/**
Energy Information Administration

24277 **www.electricity-online.com**
Electricity-Online

24278 **www.electricity-online.com/**
Electricity Journal and Daily

24279 **www.energycentral.com**
Energy Central

24280 **www.energymarketers.com**
National Energy Marketers Association

24281 **www.energyonline.com**
EnergyOnLine

24282 **www.energysearch.com**
EPRI Energysearch

Provides fast, accurate search results on global energy topics, and science and technolgoy R&D for the electricity industy.

24283 **www.epri.com**
Electric Power Research Institute

Nonprofit energy research consortium for the benefit of utility members, their customers and society. Mission is to provide science and technology-based solutions to its global energy customers by managing a far-reaching program of scientific research, technology development and product implementation.

24284 **www.epsa.org**
Electric Power Supply Association

24285 **www.greyhouse.com**
Grey House Publishing

Authoritative reference directories for most business sectors including utility markets. Users can search the online databases with varied search criteria allowing for custom searches by product category, geographic area, sales volume, keyword, subject and more. Full Grey House catalog and online ordering also available.

24286 **www.hydro.org**
National Hydropower Association

For public and private utilities, developers, equipment manufacturers, engineering and design firms, environmental and hydro liscensing consultants, and legal and financial firms. Membership dues: $1,000 - $18,000.

24287 **www.icea.net**
Insulated Cable Engineers Association

Professional organization dedicated to developing cable standards for the electric power, control and telecommunications industries. Ensures safe, economical and efficient cable systems utilizing proven state-of-the-art materials and concepts. ICEA documents are of interest to cable manufacturers, architects and engineers, utility and manufacturing plant personnel, telecommunication engineers, consultants and OEMs.

24288 **www.mcgraw-hill.com**
McGraw Hill

Provides news of significant developments affecting the electric utility industry focusing on state and federal regulation, management and bulk power markets.

24289 **www.mrea.org**
Minnesota Rural Electric Association

The Minnesota Rural Electric Association (MREA) represents all 50 electric cooperatives in the state of Minnesota.

24290 **www.naesco.org**
National Association of Energy Service Companies

24291 **www.naruc.org**
National Association of Regulatory Utility Commissioners

A national organization that offers valuable information on over 150 consultants and other professionals active in regulated water, sewer and related industries.

24292 **www.naseo.org**
National Association of State Energy Officials

24293 **www.nerc.com**
North American Electric Reliability Council

Voluntary organization promoting bulk electric system reliability and security.

24294 **www.oilonline.com**
OilOnLine

24295 **www.platts.com**
Electrical World
The latest trends in utility engineering and IT, equipment and services, best business practices and critical industry thinking. For managers, engineers and technicians who plan, design, build, maintain and upgrade electric T&D systems around the world.

24296 **www.publicworks.com**
Public Works Online
For professionals in the public works industry.

24297 **www.wateronline.com**
Water Online

Associations

24298 **Allied Distribution**
Eagle River, WI 54521

559-435-5810
rob@allieddistribution.com
allieddistribution.com
Facebook, Twitter, LinkedIn

Rob Nemeth, President

A sales and marketing association representing public warehouses and distribution centers in the United States.
75 Members
Founded in 1933

24299 **American Chain of Warehouses**
225 W Vince St.
Chambersburg, PA 17201

412-441-9512
www.acwi.org
Facebook, Twitter, LinkedIn

Bill Jurus, Vice President

Sales and marketing company representing public warehouses.
50 Members
Founded in 1911

24300 **American Moving & Storage Association**
2800 Eisenhower Ave.
Suite 200
Alexandria, VA 22314

703-683-7410
membership_web@moving.org
www.moving.org

Scott Michael, President & CEO

Organization which provides information and tips to help with moving.
3500 Members
Founded in 1920

24301 **Automotive Warehouse Distributors Association**
7101 Wisconsin Avenue
Bethesda, MD 20814

301-654-6664; Fax: 301-654-3299
info@autocare.org
www.autocare.org
Facebook, Twitter, LinkedIn, Youtube, WordPress

Bill Hanvey, President/CEO

A trade association consisting of more than 600 members who are manufacturers and warehouse distributors, affiliates, marketing associations and others actively involved in the production, distribution and installation of motor vehicle parts, tools, services, accessories, equipment, materials and supplies. A segment of the Automotive Aftermarket Industry Association.
600 Members
Founded in 1947

24302 **Burley Auction Warehouse Association**
620 S Broadway STE 201
Lexington, KY 40508-3150

606-255-4504; Fax: 606-255-4534

Denny Wilson, Managing Director

Members are warehouse companies selling burley tobacco at auction in eight burley-producing states.
225 Members

24303 **Distributors & Consolidators of America**
2240 Bernays Dr.
York, PA 17404

888-519-9195
daca@comcast.net
www.dacacarriers.com

This organization helps firms and individuals active in the shipping, warehousing, receiving, distribution or consolidation of freight shipments.
39 Members
Founded in 1971

24304 **Distributors and Consolidators of America**

Home Page: dacacarriers.com
Facebook, Twitter, LinkedIn

Association for public warehousing.
Founded in 1971

24305 **Global Cold Chain Alliance**
241 18th St. S
Suite 620
Alexandria, VA 22202

703-373-4300; Fax: 703-373-4301
email@gcca.org
www.gcca.org
Facebook, Twitter, LinkedIn

Corey Rosenbusch, President and CEO

The Global Cold Chain Alliance (GCCA) is committed to building and strengthening the temperature-controlled supply chain around the world. As part of that mission, GCCA provides specialized cold chain advisory services to government agencies, organizations, and associations through its core partner, the World Food Logistics Organization (WFLO).
1300+ Members
Founded in 2007

24306 **Independent Liquid Terminals Association**
1005 N Glebe Road
Suite 600
Arlington, VA 22201

703-875-2011; Fax: 703-875-2018
info@ilta.org
www.ilta.org

Kathryn Clay, President
Andy Wright, VP, Legislative Affairs
Susan Kurdziolek, Sr. Director, Operations
Leakhena Swett, Director, Marketing & Membership
Meredith DeZemler, Director, Meetings

Represents bulk liquid terminal companies that store commercial liquids in aboveground storage tanks (ASTs) and transfer products to and from oceangoing tank ships, tank barges, pipelines, tank trucks and tank rail cars. Provides members with essential informational tools to facilitate regulatory compliance and improve operations, safety and environmental performance.
400 Members
Founded in 1974

24307 **International Association of Refrigerated Warehouses**
241 18th Street S
Suite 620
Alexandria, VA 22202

703-373-4300; Fax: 703-373-4301
email@gcca.org
www.gcca.org
Facebook, Twitter, LinkedIn

Corey Rosenbusch, President and CEO

Trade association of public refrigerated warehouses storing of all types of perishable products.
1300+ Members
Founded in 2007

24308 **International Warehouse Logistics Association**
2800 S River Road
Suite 260
Des Plaines, IL 60018

847-813-4699; Fax: 847-813-0115
mail@IWLA.com
www.iwla.com
Facebook, Twitter, LinkedIn, YouTube

Steve W. Dehaan, President & CEO
Jay D. Strother, Vice President
Jennifer Rezny, Membership Director
Hank Vaughan, Education & Meetings Director
Robert Budo, Finance & Accounting Manager

The unified voice of the global logistics outsourcing industry, representing third party warehousing, transportation and logistics service providers. Our member companies provide the most timely and cost-effective global logistics solutions for their customers and are committed to protecting the free flow of products across international borders.
500 Members
Founded in 1997

24309 **Internationl Warehouse Logistics Association**
International Warehouse Logistics Association
2800 S River Road
Suite 260
Des Plains, IL 60018-5764

847-813-4699; Fax: 847-813-0115
mail@IWLA.com
www.iwla.com
Facebook, Twitter, LinkedIn, YouTube

Rob Doyle, Chairman
Steve DeHaan, President/CEO
Mark DeFabis, Vice Chair
Clifford Otto, Treasurer
Frank Anderson, Secretary

Trade association of public warehouses.
500+ Members
Founded in 1997

24310 **Mobile Self-Storage Association**
3312 Broadway
Suite 105
Kansas City, MO 64111

816-960-6552; Fax: 816-960-6575
info@npsa.org
npsa.org

Mark DePasquale, Chief Executive Director
Joal Rathbone, Director of Operations
Kaylee Ferguson, Operations Manager

A member of the National Portable Storage Association (NPSA) with a focus on mobile self-storage units and equipment.
Founded in 2004

24311 **National Portable Storage Association**
3312 Broadway
Suite 105
Kansas City, MO 64111

816-960-6552; Fax: 816-960-6575
info@npsa.org
www.npsa.org
Facebook, Twitter, LinkedIn, YouTube

Mark DePasquale, Chief Executive Officer
Joel Rathbone, Director of Operations
Kaylee Ferguson, Operations Manager

Leading trade association for companies offering secure, portable storage containers, portable or mobile storage trailers, portable or mobile offices, portable or mobile storage units.
Founded in 2004

24312 **Outdoor Power Equipment and Engine Service Association**
37 Pratt Street
Suite 2
Essex, CT 06426-1159

860-767-1770; Fax: 860-767-7932
info@opeesa.com
www.opeesa.com
Twitter, LinkedIn

Alex Wyatt, President
Lorri Sklar, Vice President, Annual Meeting
Nancy Cueroni, Executive Director
Arin Monroe, Secretary/Treasurer

Association made up of distributors and manufacturers of outdoor power equipment and air-cooled gas and diesel engines.
100+ Members

24313 **RCS Limited**
Computer Based Training
1301 Commerce Street
Birmingham, AL 35217

205-841-9955
888-833-1970; Fax: 205-841-2106

Design and build contractor for cold storage warehouses.

24314 **Self Storage Association**
1901 N Beauregard St.
Suite 106
Alexandria, VA 22311

703-575-8000
888-735-3784; Fax: 703-575-8901
ssa@selfstorage.org
www.selfstorage.org
Facebook, Twitter, LinkedIn

Timothy J. Dietz, President & CEO
Derek E. Knights, Chief Financial Officer
Joseph L. Doherty, IV, SVP, Legal & Legislative Counsel
Ginny Stengel, SVP, Membership & Education
Mike Blackett, SVP, Marketing & Communications

Self-storage facility owners/operators and suppliers to the industry.
6000 Members
Founded in 1975

24315 **Storage Products Association**
572-B Ruger Street
San Francisco, CA 94129

415-561-6275
RSS

Association for storage manufacturers and users.

24316 **Warehousing Education and Research Council**
1100 Jorie Boulevard
Suite 170
Oak Brook, IL 60523

630-990-0001; Fax: 630-990-0256
wercoffice@werc.org
www.werc.org
Twitter, LinkedIn, YouTube

Michael J. Mikitka, CAE, Chief Executive Officer
Angie Silberhorn, CMP, VP, Event Strategy & Operations
JoAnna Leon, Membership Coordinator

Association for logistics and warehouse professionals.
Founded in 1977

24317 **World Food Logistics Organization**
Global Cold Chain Alliance
241-18th Street S
Suite 620
Arlington, VA 22202

703-373-4300; Fax: 703-373-4301
email@gcca.org
www.gcca.org/wflo

Donald Dick, Chairman
Brian Beazer, Vice Chairman
Dan Kaplan, Treasurer

Sponsors graduate-level scientific research in the refrigeration of perishable commodities. Offers annual training institute for public refrigerated warehouse personnel. Formerly known as the Refrigeration Research and Education Foundation.
1M Members
Founded in 1943

Newsletters

24318 **AUA News**
American Underground Space Association
1000 Corporate Boulevard
Linthicum, MD 21090

410-689-3700
866-746-4282; Fax: 410-689-3800
aua@AUAnet.org
www.auanet.org

Thomas O'Neil, President
Elaine Gray, Editor

Offers the latest news on underground space construction development and use in North America. Includes information on infrastructures.
Cost: $107.00
Frequency: Quarterly
Circulation: 1000
Printed in 4 colors on glossy stock

24319 **Affiliated Warehouse Companies Newsletter**
Affiliated Warehouse Companies, Inc
PO Box 295
Hazlet, NJ 07730-0295

732-739-2323; Fax: 732-739-4154
sales@awco.com
www.awco.com

Jim McBride, Publisher
Jim McBride, President
Patrick McBride, Vice President

Assists public warehouse users to gather rates and data, provides information on warehousing and distribution at no charge or obligation for over 100 public warehouse clients in the US, Canada, Mexico and Puerto Rico.
Mailing list available for rent: 8,500 names

24320 **Distribution Center Management**
Alexander Communications Group
712 Main Street~
Suite 187B
New York, NJ 07005

973-265-2300
800-232-4317; Fax: 973-402-6056
info@distributiongroup.com
www.distributiongroup.com

Romauld Alexander, President
Margaret Dewitt, Publisher/Marketing Manager

Provides practical strategies and industry news to help distribution center and warehouse professionals improve distribution center efficiency.
Cost: $199.00
8 Pages
Frequency: Monthly
ISBN: 0-894765-1 -
Founded in 1985

Magazines & Journals

24321 **Inside Self-Storage**
Virgo Publishing LLC
3300 N Central Ave
Suite 300
Phoenix, AZ 85012-2532

480-990-1101; Fax: 480-990-0819
troyb@vpico.com
www.vpico.com

Jenny Bolton, President
John Siefert, CEO & Director
Kelly Ridley, VP
John LyBarger, Director, Business Development
Troy Bix, Publications Editor

For storage professionals.
Frequency: Monthly
Circulation: 20000
Founded in 1991
Mailing list available for rent

24322 **Logistics Management & Distribution Report**
Reed Business Information
225 Wyman St
Suite 3
Waltham, MA 02451-1216

781-734-8000; Fax: 781-734-8076
fquinn@reedbusiness.com
www.reedbusiness.com

Mark Finklestein, President
Mike Levin, Group Editor-in-Chief
Frank Quinn, Editorial Director
Stephen Moylan, President, Divisions

Logistics Management and Distribution Report is written for managers and professionals in charge of traffic, transportation, purchasing, inventory control, containerization and warehousing the functions of physical distribution and business logistics. Covers marketing and operating strategies, cost reduction opportunities and governmental regulation and law.
Cost: $99.90
Frequency: Monthly
Circulation: 68000
Founded in 1977

24323 **Mini-Storage Messenger**
MiniCo
2531 W Dunlap Ave
Phoenix, AZ 85021-2730

602-870-1711
800-824-6864; Fax: 602-861-1094
publishing@minico.com
www.ministoragemessenger.com

Hardy Good, President
Denise Nunez, Director Publishing

As the industry's first trade journal, the mini-storage messenger has become the leading trade magazine for anyone involved in self-storage. This magazine covers rental rates, marketing trends, and finance.
Cost: $59.95
89 Pages
Frequency: Monthly
Founded in 1979
Printed in 4 colors on glossy stock

24324 **Refrigerated Transporter**
Penton

PO Box 66010
Houston, TX 77266
713-523-8124
800-880-0368; Fax: 713-523-8384
refrigeratedtransporter.com

Ray Anderson, Publishing
Frequency: Monthly
Circulation: 15000
Founded in 1898

24325 **Storage**
West World Productions
420 N Camden Dr
Beverly Hills, CA 90210-4507
310-276-9500; Fax: 310-276-9874
sinan@kanatsiz.com
www.wwpi.com

Yuri R Spiro, Publisher
Laura Klein, Production Manager

Storage is the unique storage-intensive magazine supplement to Computer Technology Review. It is recognized as the bible of the entire storage industry.
Cost: $10.00
72 Pages
Frequency: Quarterly
Circulation: 72000
ISSN: 0278-9647
Founded in 1981
Printed in 4 colors on glossy stock

24326 **Warehousing Management**
Reed Business Information
225 Wyman St
Suite 3
Waltham, MA 02451-1216
781-734-8000; Fax: 781-734-8076
fquinn@reedbusiness.com
www.reedbusiness.com

Mark Finklestein, President
Mike Levin, Group Editor-in-Chief
Frank Quinn, Editorial Director
Stephen Moylan, President, Divisions

Warehousing Management targets warehousing and distribution center operations managers with analysis, news, trends, equipment and events.
Circulation: 47185
Founded in 1977

Trade Shows

24327 **Eastpack**
Reed Exhibition Companies
255 Wyman Streett
Waltham, MA 02451
781-734-8000; Fax: 781-734-8076
fquinn@reedbusiness.com
www.reedbusiness.com

Mark Finklestein, President
Mike Levin, Group Editor-in-Chief
Frank Quinn, Editorial Director
Stephen Moylan, President, Divisions

275 booths.
7.5M Attendees
Frequency: March
Founded in 1977

24328 **Global Cold Chain Expo & Conference**
Global Cold Chain Alliance
241 18th St. S
Suite 620
Alexandria, VA 22202
703-373-4300; Fax: 703-373-4301
email@gcca.org
www.gcca.org

Cory Rosenbusch, President & CEO

A business-to-business networking event for operations management, engineering, plant managers, transportation directors, and others who buy or lease cold chain services.
Frequency: September

24329 **Household Goods Forwarders Association**
5904 Richman Avenue
Suite 304
Alexandria, VA 22303-4691
703-684-3780

Belvian Carpinton, Show Manager
Terry Head, President

20 tables.
1M Attendees
Frequency: September

24330 **Independent Liquid Terminals Association Annual Trade Show**
Independent Liquid Terminals Association
1005 N Glebe Road
Suite 600
Arlington, VA 22201
703-875-2011; Fax: 703-875-2018
info@ilta.org
www.ilta.org

Kathryn Clay, President
Peter Lidiak, VP, Government Affairs
Andy Wright, VP, Legislative Affairs
Susan Kurdziolek, Senior Director of Operations
Meredith DeZembler, Director of Meetings

Represents bulk liquid terminal companies that store commercial liquids in aboveground storage tanks (ASTs) and transfer products to and from ocean going tank ships, tank barges, pipelines, tank trucks and tank rail cars. Provides members with essential informational tools to facilitate regulatory compliance and improve operations, safety and environmental performance.
2,700 Attendees
Frequency: June

24331 **Inside Self-Storage World Expo**
Virgo Publishing LLC
3300 N Central Ave
Suite 300
Phoenix, AZ 85012-2532
480-675-9925; Fax: 480-990-0819
kkennedy@vpico.com
www.vpico.com

Jenny Bolton, President

The self-storage industry's largest, most comprehensive conference and tradeshow. The leading educational and networking event for facility managers, owners, developers and investors, the ISS Expo provides the resources professionals need to build, manage and market their business in a competitive environment.
Circulation: 20000
Founded in 1986
Printed in on glossy stock

24332 **International Transportation and Logistics Exhibition and Conference**
ILT
1300 Higgins Road
Suite 111
Park Ridge, IL 60068-5764
847-292-1891; Fax: 847-823-3901

Marge Whalen, Director of Sales
Regan Williams, Trade Show Coordinator

Annual conference and trade show focusing on public warehousing, distribution, transportation, logistics and systems. Containing 200 exhibits.
3,000 Attendees
Frequency: June

24333 **NORPACK**
Northern American Expositions Company
33 Rutherford Avenue
Charlestown, MA 02129
617-242-6092
800-225-1577; Fax: 617-242-1817
naexpo@hotmail.com
naexpo.com

The Northeast's premier trade show for packaging, material handling, warehouse automation, shipping/receiving, storage and bottling.
4500 Attendees

24334 **Northwest Material Handling & Packaging Show**
Professional Trade Shows-Division of Penton Media
47817 Fremont Boulevard
Fremont, CA 94538
510-651-6698; Fax: 510-354-3159
facilitiesexpo.com

5,000 Attendees
Frequency: May

24335 **Pack Expo**
Pakaging Machinery Manufacturers Institute
4350 N Fairfax Drive
Suite 600
Arlington, VA 22203
703-243-8555
888-275-7664
pmmi@pmmi.org
www.packexpo.com

Matt Crossn, Communications Director
Sara Kryder, Assistant Communications

Informational meeting and exposition held by the Packaging Machinery Manufacturers Institute.
15000 Attendees

24336 **WERC Annual Conference**
Warehousing Education and Research Concil
1100 Jorie Boulevard
Suite 170
Oak Brook, IL 60523
630-990-0001; Fax: 630-990-0256
conference@werc.org
www.werc.org
Twitter, LinkedIn

Michael J. Mikitka, CAE, Chief Executive Officer
Angie Silberhorn, CMP, VP, Event Strategy & Operations
JoAnna Leon, Membership Coordinator

The annual WERC Conference has stepped away from the traditional trade show experience, opting for a short, interactive Solutions Studio Session to facilitate discussions and learning.

24337 **Warehousing, Technology & Distribution Show**
Industrial Shows of America
164 Lake Front Drive
Hunt Valley, MD 21030-2215
410-771-1445
800-638-6396; Fax: 410-771-1158

This show will feature hands-on workshops for the practical applications of new technologies, safety issues and more all designed to improve productivity and cut losses in today's competitive market.
1500 Attendees
Frequency: April

Directories & Databases

24338 **Affiliated Warehouse Companies Database of Public Warehouse Users**
Affiliated Warehouse Companies, Inc.

PO Box 295
Hazlet, NJ 07730-0295

732-739-2323; Fax: 732-739-4154
sales@awco.com
www.awco.com

Jim McBride, President
Patrick McBride, Vice President
Jim McBride, Publisher

In excess of 8,000 listings of individuals and companies that use public warehousing, products produced and services required.
Mailing list available for rent: 8,500 names

24339 **American Chain of Warehouses Directory**
American Chain of Warehouses
225 W Vince St.
Chambersburg, PA 17201

412-441-9512
www.acwi.org

Bill Jurus, Vice President

Public warehouse listings in the United States are profiled.

24340 **American Public Warehouse Register**
Reed Business Information
2 Brandywine Way
Sicklerville, NJ 08081-0750

856-728-9745; Fax: 630-288-8686
www.reedbusiness.com

Laura Masapollo, National Sales Director
Laura MasaPollo, National Sales Director

Worldwide listings of dry, refrigerated, contract and HazMat Public Warehouses Annual.
Cost: $50.00

24341 **Associated Warehouses Directory of Services**
PO Box 471
Cedar Knolls, NJ 07927-0471

973-539-1277; Fax: 973-538-0944
www.awilogistics.com

Mark Richards, Editor
Barbara Brown, Circulation Director

A who's who directory of services to the industry.
100 Pages
Frequency: Annual

24342 **Directory of Bulk Liquid Terminal and Storage Facilities**
ITLA
1133 15th Street NW
Sutie 650
Washington, DC 20005

202-659-2301; Fax: 202-466-4166
info@ilta.org
www.ilta.org

John Prokop, President
EB Calvert, Director Administration

Locates over 480 bulk liquid terminal/storage facilities. Lists key personnel, addresses, telephone numbers. Lists products handled-petroleum products, crude oil, chemicals, animal fats and oils, vegetable oils, molasses, spirits, etc. Lists storage tanks, modes served, pipeline connections. Other services and capabilities-canning, barreling, bleaching, blending, weighing, warehousing, etc. Subc. available for Directory and Newsletter
Cost: $95.00
300 Pages
Frequency: Annual

24343 **Food & Beverage Market Place**
Grey House Publishing
4919 Route 22
PO Box 56
Amenia, NY 12501

518-789-8700
800-562-2139; Fax: 845-373-6390
books@greyhouse.com
www.greyhouse.com
Facebook, Twitter

Leslie Mackenzie, Publisher
Richard Gottlieb, Editor

This information-packed 3-volume set is the most powerful buying and marketing guide for the US food and beverage industry. Includes thousands of industry freight and transportation listings.
Cost: $595.00
2000 Pages
Frequency: Annual
ISBN: 1-592373-61-5
Founded in 1981

24344 **Food & Beverage Marketplace: Online Database**
Grey House Publishing
4919 Route 22
PO Box 56
Amenia, NY 12501

518-789-8700
800-562-2139; Fax: 845-373-6390
gold@greyhouse.com
gold.greyhouse.com
Facebook, Twitter

Richard Gottlieb, President
Leslie Mackenzie, Publisher

This complete updated Food & Beverage Market Place: Online Database is the go-to source for the food and beverage industry. Anyone involved in the food and beverage industry needs this 'industry bible' and the important contacts to develop critical research data that can make for successful business growth.
Frequency: Annual
Founded in 1981

24345 **ILTA Directory**
Independent Liquid Terminals Association
1005 N Glebe Road
Suite 600
Arlington, VA 22201

703-875-2011; Fax: 703-875-2018
info@ilta.org
www.ilta.org

Kathryn Clay, President
Peter Lidiak, VP, Government Affairs
Andy Wright, VP, Legislative Affairs
Susan Kurdziolek, Senior Director of Operations
Meredith DeZembler, Director of Meetings

The membership directories include comprehensive listings of all terminal and supplier members.

24346 **International Directory of Public Refrigerated Warehouses**
1500 King Street
Suite 201
Alexandria, VA 22314

703-373-4300; Fax: 703-373-4301

J William Hudson, President/CEO

Offers information on more than 950 member warehouses in 32 countries and on companies supplying products and services to the refrigerated warehouse industry.
Cost: $150.00
232 Pages
Frequency: Annual
Circulation: 6,000

24347 **International Warehouse Logistics Directory**
International Warehouse Logistics Association
2800 S River Road
Suite 260
Des Plaines, IL 60018

847-813-4699; Fax: 847-813-0115
mail@iwla.com
www.iwla.com

Steve W. Dehaan, President & CEO
Jay D. Strother, Vice President
Jennifer Rezny, Membership Director
Hank Vaughan, Education & Meetings Director
Robert Budo, Finance & Accounting Manager

The membership directory is published annually in January in book and CD-ROM form.
Frequency: Annually

24348 **National Refrigeration Contractors Association**
National Refrigeration Contrtactors
1900 Arch Street
Philadelphia, PA 19103-1404

215-564-3484; Fax: 215-963-9785
www.arcat.com

Elizabeth Barnett, Editor

About 100 member refrigeration contracting companies
Frequency: Annual

24349 **Transportation & Distribution Magazine's Integrated Warehousing/Storage**
Penton Media
1166 Avenue of the Americas
New York, NY 10036

212-204-4200; Fax: 216-696-6662
information@penton.com
www.penton.com

Jane Cooper, Marketing

Lists over 1,200 manufacturers of products related to the warehousing and distribution industries.
Frequency: Annual
Circulation: 71,000
Printed in 4 colors on glossy stock

24350 **Warehouses Licensed Under US Warehouse Act**
Farm Service Agency-US Dept. of Agriculture
PO Box 2415
Washington, DC 20013-2415

FAX 202-690-0014
www.fsa.usda.gov/

Agricultural warehouses voluntarily licensed under the US Warehouse Act governing public storage facilities.
Frequency: Annual

24351 **Warehousing Distribution Directory**
PRIMEDIA Information
3585 Engineering Drive
Suite 100
Norcross, GA 30092

678-421-3000
800-216-1423; Fax: 609-371-7819

Amy Middlebrook, Editor
John Capers III, Publisher

List of about 800 warehousing and consolidation companies and firms offering trucking, trailer on flatcar, container on flatcar and piggyback carrier services.
Cost: $55.00
250 Pages
Frequency: SemiAnnual
Circulation: 10,000

Founded in 1949
Printed in 4 colors on glossy stock

Industry Web Sites

24352 Www.gcca.org/wflo
World Food Logistics Organization

Sponsors graduate-level scientific research on the refrigeration of perishable commodities. Offers annual training institute for public refrigerated warehouse personnel. Formerly known as the Refrigeration Research and Education Foundation.

24353 http://gold.greyhouse.com
G.O.L.D Grey House OnLine Databases

Grey House Publishing's online database platform, GOLD, offers Quick Search, Keyword Search and Expert Search for most business sectors including warehousing and storage markets. The GOLD platform makes finding the information you need quick and easy - whether you're a novice searcher or an experienced database user. All of Grey House's directory products are available for subscription on the GOLD platform.

24354 www.awco.com
Affiliated Warehouse Companies

Assists public warehouse users to gather rates and data, provides information on warehousing and distribution at no charge or obligation for over 100 public warehouse clients in the US, Canada, Mexico, Europe and Southeast Asia.

24355 www.greyhouse.com
Grey House Publishing

Authoritative reference directories for direct marketing, demographics, business, research, health care, international trade, food industry and education. Users can search the online databases with varied search criteria allowing for custom searches by product category, geographic area, sales volume, keyword, subject and more. Full Grey House catalog and online ordering also available.

Associations

24356 **Alliance for Water Efficiency**
33 N LaSalle Street
Suite 2275
Chicago, IL 60602-3848

773-360-5100
866-730-1493; Fax: 773-345-3636
contact@a4we.org
www.allianceforwaterefficiency.org

Mary Ann Dickinson, President/CEOÿ
Bill Christiansen, Director of Programs
Jeffrey Hughes, Director of Operations
Lacey Smith, Program Planner
Liam McCarthy, Sr. Admin./Outreach Coordinator

An association for water efficient products.
Founded in 2007

24357 **American Backflow Prevention Association**
6672 S 1570 W
West Jordan, UT 84084

801-436-7238
info@abpa.org
abpa.site-ym.com

Tim Brown, International Presidentÿ
J. Frank Snyder, International Vice President
Patti Fauver, Treasurer
Mike Lueck, Director-At-Large

An association dedicated to backflow education and technical assistance.
Founded in 1984

24358 **American Fisheries Society**
425 Barlow Place
Suite 110
Bethesdaÿ, MD 20814-2144

301-897-8616; Fax: 301-897-8096
main@fisheries.org
fisheries.org
x, x, x, Pinterest, Google+, Vimeo

Douglas ÿ Austen, Executive Director
Erin Del Collo, Membership Coordinator
Katrina Dunn, Director of Development
Laura Hendee, Journals Production Manager
Shawn Johnston, Meetings Manager

Organization dedicated to strengthening the fisheries profession and advancing fisheries.
Founded in 1870

24359 **American Ground Water Trust**
50 Pleasant Street
Suite 2
Concord, NH 03301

603-228-5444
800-423-7748; Fax: 603-228-6557
trustinfo@agwt.org
www.agwt.org
x, x, x

David Kill, Chairman
Fred Rothauge, Secretary/Treasurer
Andrew Stone, Executive Director

Promotes public awareness of groundwater.
Founded in 1986

24360 **American Institute of Hydrology**
PO Box 3948
Parker, CO 80134

303-339-0523; Fax: 720-496-4974
admin@aihydrology.org
www.aihydrology.org

John L. Nieber, P.H., P.E., President
Dr. Faisal Hossain, VP for Academic Affairs
Jul, Rizzardo, VP for Institute Development
Dr. Zhuping Sheng, VP for International Affairs
Rahul Ranade, VP for Communication

Registers and certifies hydrologists and hydrogeologists, provides a forum to discuss national and international issues, and provides educational courses.
Founded in 1981

24361 **American Rivers**
1101 14th Street NW
Suite 1400
Washington, DC 20005

202-347-7550
877-347-7550
akober@americanrivers.org
www.americanrivers.org
Facebook, Twitter, YouTube, Pinterest

William Robert (Bob) Irvin, President
Kristin May, Chief Financial Officer
Amy Souers Kober, VP, Communications
Brice Leathwood, Sr. Director, Membership
Jennifer Marshall, General Counsel

Nonprofit conservation organization dedicated to protecting and restoring the rivers of America.
Founded in 1973

24362 **American Society of Irrigation Consultants**
404 E 4th Street
Royal Oak, MI 48067

508-763-8140
carolc@asic.org
www.asic.org

Carol Colein, Executive Director
Michael Krones, President
Stacy Gardner, Vice President
Janet Luehrs, Treasurer
Carly Kardon, Operations and Member Services

Promotes education skills on data exchange landscape irrigation. Members are irrigation consultants, suppliers, and manufacturers.
Founded in 1970

24363 **American Water Resources Association**
4 W. Federal Street
P.O. Box 1626
Middleburg, VA 20118-1626

540-687-8390; Fax: 540-687-8395
info@awra.orgÿ
www.awra.org
x, x, x, Blog

Kenneth D. Reid, CAEÿ, Executive Vice President
Michael J. Kowalski, CAEÿ, Director of Operations
Christine McCrehin, Membership & Marketing Director

Multi-disciplinary water resources professional association.
2000 Members
Founded in 1964

24364 **American Water Works Association**
6666 W Quincy Ave.
Denver, CO 80235

303-794-7711
800-926-7337; Fax: 303-347-0804
www.awwa.org
x, x, x, YouTube, RSS

Melissa Elliott, President
Aurel Arndt, Treasurer
David B. LaFrance, Chief Executive Officer

The professional society of North American drinking water experts. Develop standards and support research programs in waterworks design, construction, operation, and management. Conducts in-service training schools and offers placement service.
Founded in 1881

24365 **American Whitewater**
P.O. Box 1540
Cullowhee, NC 28723

828-586-1930
866-262-8429; Fax: 828-586-2840
membership@americanwhitewater.org
www.americanwhitewater.org
Facebook, Twitter, YouTube, RSS

Mark Singleton, Executive Director
Kevin Colburn, National Stewardship Director
Bob Nasdor, Northeast Stewardship Director
Evan Stafford, Communications Director
Bethany Overfield, Membership Director

Association for whitewaters and rafting.
Founded in 1954

24366 **Association of Clean Water Administrators**
1634 Eye St. NW
Suite 750
Washington, DC 20006

202-756-0605; Fax: 202-793-2600
www.acwa-us.org
Twitter

Julia Anastasio, Executive Director/ General Counsel
Sean Rolland, Deputy Director
Annette Ivey, Director of Operations
Mark Patrick McGuire, Environmental Program Manager
Jasper Hobbs, Environmental Program Manager

Association for the administrators of the clean water industry.
Founded in 1961

24367 **Association of State Drinking Water Administrators**
1401 Wilson Blvd.
Suite 1225
Arlington, VA 22209

703-812-9505; Fax: 703-812-9506
info@asdwa.org
www.asdwa.org
x, x, YouTube, Blog

Alan Roberson, Executive Director
Deirdre White, Project Manager
Wendi Wilkes, Senior Policy Analyst
Kevin Letterly, Water Policy Analyst
Anthony DeRose, Communications/IT Manager

Professional association serving state drinking water programs.
Founded in 1984

24368 **Association of State Wetland Managers**
32 Tandberg Trail
Suite 2A
Windham, ME 04062ÿ

207-892-3399; Fax: 207-894-7992
marla@aswm.org
aswm.org
x, LinkedIn, Blog

Marla J. Stelk, Executive Director
Brenda Zollitsch, Senior Policy Analyst
William Dooley, Policy Analyst
Starsha Schiller, Policy Analyst
Dawn Smith, Communications Specialist

A professional association for state wetland managers.
Founded in 1983

24369 **Clean Water Action**
1444 Eye St. NW
Suite 400
Washington, DC 20005

202-895-0420; Fax: 202-895-0438
cwa@cleanwater.org

www.cleanwateraction.org
Facebook, Twitter, YouTube, Blog

Robert Wendelgass, President/ CEO
Kathy Aterno, National Managing Director
Lynn Thorp, National Campaigns Director
Andrea Herrmann, National Development Director
Michael Kelly, National Director of Communications

A national citizen's organization working for clean, safe and affordable water and prevention of health-threatening pollution.
Founded in 1960

24370 **Coastal & Estuarine Research Federation**
2150 N 107th St.
Suite 205
Seattle, WA 98133

206-209-5262
info@cerf.science
www.cerf.science
Facebook, Twitter, Flickr, Vimeo

Jim Fourqurean, President
Susan Park, Executive Director
Louise S. Miller, Chief Operating Officer

Private nonprofit organization dedicated to advancing the understanging of coastal and estuarine ecosystems.
1650 Members
Founded in 1971

24371 **Ground Water Protection Council**
13308 N Macarthur Blvd.
Oklahoma City, OK 73142

405-516-4972
www.gwpc.org

Mike Paque, Executive Director
Dan Yates, Associate Executive Director
Paul John, Technical Director
Mike Nickolaus, Special Projects Director
Kelsey Henry, Financial Director

State ground water and underground injection control agencies whose mission is to promote the protection and conservation of ground water resources for all beneficial uses, recognizing ground water as a component of the ecosystem.
1.75M Members
Founded in 1983

24372 **Irrigation Association**
8280 Willow Oaks Corp. Dr.
Suite 400
Fairfax, VA 22031-4507

703-536-7080; Fax: 703-536-7019
info@irrigation.org
www.irrigation.org

Deborah M. Hamlin, Chief Executive Officer
Rebecca J. Bayless, Finance Director
Brad Binzer, Operations Coordinator
Anne Blankenbiller, Senior Communications Manager
Janie C. Hakim, Membership Manager

Membership organization for irrigation equipment and system manufacturers, dealers, distributors, designers, consultants, contractors and end users.
1600 Members
Founded in 1949

24373 **National Association of Clean Water Agencies**
1130 Connecticut Ave. NW
Suite 1050
Washingtonÿ, DC 20036

202-833-2672; Fax: 888-267-9505
info@nacwa.org
www.nacwa.org
Facebook, Twitter, LinkedIn, YouTube

Adam Krantz, Chief Executive Officer
Meredith Ristic, Chief Financial Officer
Nathan Gardner-Andrews, Chief Advocacy Officer
Amanda Waters, General Counsel
Kelly Brocato, Sr. Dir., Membership Development

Nationally recognized leader in environmental policy and a technical resource on water quality and ecosystem protection.
Founded in 1970

24374 **National Drilling Association**
3053 Nationwide Pkwy.
Brunswick, OH 44212

877-632-4748; Fax: 216-803-9900
info@nda4u.com
www.nda4u.com
Facebook, LinkedIn

Rob Caho, President
Jim Howe, Secretary/Treasurer

A non-profit trade association of contractors, manufacturers and affiliated members from the drilling industry representing the geotechnical, environmental and mineral exploration sectors of this industry.
250+ Members
Founded in 1972

24375 **National Environmental Services Center**
West Virginia University Energy Institute
1085 Van Voorhis Rd.
Suncrest Center, Suite 310
Morgantown, WV 26505

304-293-4191
info@mail.nesc.wvu.edu
www.nesc.wvu.edu
Facebook, Twitter, WordPress

Gerald Iwan, Ph.D., Director

Helps small, rural communities with their drinking water, wastewater and environmental training needs.
Founded in 1984

24376 **National Ground Water Association**
601 Dempsey Rd.
Westerville, OH 43081

614-898-7791
800-551-7379; Fax: 614-898-7786
ngwa@ngwa.org
www.ngwa.org
Facebook, Twitter, LinkedIn, YouTube

Terry S. Morse, Chief Executive Officer
Paul Humes, Chief Financial Officer
David Evener, Director of Operations/Technology
Erin Rodgers, Member Services Manager
Thad Plumley, Director of Publications

International nonprofit organization of groundwater professionals for the responsible use of groundwater.
Founded in 1948

24377 **National Institute for Water Resources**
University of Massachusetts
Blaisdell House
Amherst, MA 01003

413-545-2842; Fax: 413-545-2304
support@niwr.net

Brian Haggard, President
Sharon Megdal, President Elect
John Tracy, Secretary/Treasurer

Offers information on water resource directions across the nation.
54 Members
Founded in 1974

24378 **National Onsite Wastewater Recycling**
1199 N. Fairfax St.
Suite 410
Alexandria, VA 22314

703-836-1950
800-966-2942
www.nowra.org

Gregory D Graves, President
Jim Bell, President Elect/VP
Robert B Mayer MSPE, Secretary/Treasurer
Tom Fritts, Past-President

Organization dedication to onsite wastewater recycling.
Founded in 1992

24379 **National Onsite Wastewater Recycling Assoc iation**
4601 Fairfax Dr.
Suite 1200
Arlington, VA 22203

703-836-1950
800-966-2942; Fax: 703-997-5609
info@nowra.org
www.nowra.org
Facebook

Carl Thompson, President

Dedicated to educating and representing members within the onsite and decentralized industry. And also to provide leadership and promote the onsite waste water treatment and recycling through education, training, communication and quality tools to support excellence in performance.
3500 Members
Founded in 1992

24380 **National Rural Water Association**
2915 S 13th St.
Duncan, OK 73533

580-252-0629; Fax: 580-255-4476
www.nrwa.org
Facebook, Twitter, LinkedIn, YouTube

Sam Wade, Chief Executive Officer
Matt Holmes, Deputy Chief Executive Officer
Brian Churchman, Chief Financial Officer

Non-profit organization dedicated to training, supporting, and promoting the water and wastewater professionals that serve small communities across the country.
5M+ Members
Founded in 1932

24381 **National Water Research Institute**
18700 Ward St.
Fountain Valley, CA 92728

714-378-3278
admin@nwri-usa.org
www.nwri-usa.org
Facebook, Twitter, LinkedIn, YouTube

Kevin Hardy, Executive Directorÿ
Mary Collins, Communications Manager
Suzanne Sharkey, Project Manager

A nonprofit organization devoted to promoting the protection, maintenance and restoration of water supplies.
Founded in 1991

24382 **National Water Resources Association**
4 E St. SE
Washington, DC 20003

202-698-0693; Fax: 202-698-0694
nwra@nwra.org
www.nwra.org
Twitter

Cheryl Zittle, President
Ian Lyle, Executive Vice President
Abbey Linsk, Director of Government Relations

Kris Polly, Senior Advisor
John Crotty, Advisor

Dedicated to the wise management and use of the nation's water and land resources.
5M+ Members
Founded in 1932

24383 Outdoor Recreation Roundtable
1203 K St. NW
Suite 350
Washington, DC 20005

202-682-9530
recreationroundtable.org
Facebook, Twitter

Jessica Wahl, Executive Director
Phil Ingrassia, Chair
Frank Hugelmeyer, Vice Chair
Glenn Hughes, Treasurer
Chris Edmonston, Secretary

A non-profit Washington based federation that provides a unified voice for recreation interests to conserve their full and active participation in government policy making on issues such as public land management. ORR works to build public-private partnerships to enhance and protect outdoor recreation opportunities and resources.
100+ Members
Founded in 1979

24384 Soil and Water Conservation Society
945 SW Ankeny Rd.
Ankeny, IA 50023

515-289-2331; Fax: 515-289-1227
www.swcs.org

Clare Lindahl, Chief Executive Officer
Courtney Allen, Event/Professional Development Dir.
Annie Binder, Director of Publications/Editor
Erika Crady, Membership/Chapter Coordinator
Catherine DeLong, Special Projects/Policy Director

SWCS is a nonprofit scientific and educational organization that serves as an advocate for conservation professionals and for science-based conservation practice, programs, and policy.
5000+ Members
Founded in 1943

24385 Submersible Waste Water Pump Association

847-681-1868
swpaexdir@sbcglobal.net
www.swpa.org

Adam Stolberg, Executive Director

Represents and serves the manufacturers of submersible pumps for the municipal and industrial wastewater applications. Manufacturers of components and accessory items for those products and companies providing services to users of those products.
Founded in 1976

24386 WWEMA Annual Meeting
Water and Wastewater Equipment Manufacturers Assn.
540 Fort Evans Rd.
Suite 304
Leesburg, VA 20176-3379

703-444-1777
info@wwema.org
www.wwema.org

Vanessa M. Leiby, Executive Director/Corp. Secretary
Tina M. Wojnar, Prog. Mgr., Policy/Member Services
Susi Ricker, Business Operations Manager

A member-only meeting that addresses management and operational issues and trends within the water and wastewater industry.
Frequency: Annual/November
Founded in 1908

24387 WateReuse Association
1199 N Fairfax St.
Suite 900ÿ
Alexandria, VA 22314

703-548-0880; Fax: 703-548-5085
info@watereuse.org
www.watereuse.org
Facebook, Twitter, LinkedIn, YouTube

Patricia L. Sinicropi, Executive Director
Alicia Rutherford, Manager of Meetings & Events
Zachary Dorsey, Director of Communications
Carrie Capuco, Director of Strategic Operationsÿ
Erin DiMenna, Director of Membership

An association for advancing the science of water reuse and destination through research.
Founded in 1990

24388 Water Environment Federation
601 Wythe St.
Alexandria, VA 22314

800-666-0206; Fax: 703-684-2400
inquiry@wef.org
www.wef.org
Facebook, Twitter, LinkedIn

Walt Marlowe, Executive Director
Tim Williams, Deputy Executive Director
Penny Young, Chief Financial Officer

A technical and educational organization with members from varied disciplines who work toward the vision of preservation and enhancement of the global water environment.
34000 Members
Founded in 1928

24389 Water Keeper Alliance
180 Maiden Ln.
Suite 603ÿ
New York, NY 10038

212-747-0622
info@waterkeeper.org
waterkeeper.org
Facebook, Twitter, YouTube, Instagram

Marc Yaggi, Executive Director
Mary Beth Postman, Deputy Director
Rachel Cook, Finance & Operations Director
Lindsay Muzzio, Comm./Marketing Senior Coordinator
Tom Quinn, Senior Editor

An association using grassroots advocacy to achieve clean waterways.
Founded in 1996

24390 Water Quality Association
4151 Naperville Rd.
Lisle, IL 60532-3696

630-505-0160; Fax: 630-505-9637
www.wqa.org
Facebook, Twitter, LinkedIn, Youtube

Pauli Undesser, Executive Director
Tom Bruursema, Assc. Exec. Dir., Member Engagement
Wesley Bleed, Director, Marketing/Communications
LyNae Schleyer, Director, Meeting Services
Scott Freeman, Chief Financial Officer

An international, nonprofit trade association representing retail/dealers and manufacturer/suppliers in the point of use/entry water quality improvement industry. Membership benefits and services include technical and scientific information, educational seminars and home correspondence course books, professional certification and discount services.
2700+ Members
Founded in 1974

24391 Water and Wastewater Equipment Manufacturers Association
540 Fort Evans Rd.
Suite 304
Leesburg, VA 20176-3379

703-444-1777
info@wwema.org
www.wwema.org

Vanessa M. Leiby, Executive Director/Corp. Secretary
Tina M. Wojnar, Prog. Mgr., Policy/Member Services
Susi Ricker, Business Operations Manager

Represents the interests of companies that manufacture the products that are sold to the portable water and wastewater treatment industries. Also informs, educates and provides leadership on the issues which affect the worldwide water and wastewater equipment industry.
80 Members
Founded in 1908

24392 WaterJet Technology Association
906 Olive St.
Suite 1200
St. Louis, MO 63101

314-241-1445; Fax: 314-241-1449
www.wjta.org
Facebook, Twitter, LinkedIn, Google+

Bill McClister, President
Kerry Siggins, Vice President
George A. Savanick, Treasurer
Gary Noto, Secretary

A professional association of high pressure waterjet and industrial technology and industrial cleaning. Members are contractors, end users, job shops, manufacturers, researchers, and academicians.
Founded in 1983

Newsletters

24393 CERF's Up!
Coastal & Estuarine Research Federation
2150 N 107th St.
Suite 205
Seattle, WA 98133

206-209-5262
info@cerf.science
www.cerf.science

Jim Fourqurean, President
Susan Park, Executive Director
Louise S. Miller, Chief Operating Officer

Features information on conferences, affiliate society news, and other updates about the Federation.

24394 Clean Water Current
National Association of Clean Water Agencies
1130 Connecticut Ave. Nw
Suite 1050
Washington, DC 20036

202-833-2672; Fax: 888-267-9505
info@nacwa.org
www.nacwa.org

Adam Krantz, Chief Executive Officer
Meredith Ristic, Chief Financial Officer

The National Association of Clean Water Agencies' official newsletter.

24395 Drinking Water and Backflow Prevention
SFA Enterprises
18927 Hickory Creek Drive
Suite 140
Mokena, IL 60448
303-451-0978
888-367-3927; Fax: 303-452-9776
www.iapmodwbp.org/
Cindy Most, Managing Editor
Accepts advertising.
Cost: $38.00
24 Pages
Frequency: Monthly
Mailing list available for rent

24396 Jet News
WaterJet Technology Association (WJTA)
906 Olive St.
Suite 1200
St. Louis, MO 63101
314-241-1445; Fax: 314-241-1449
www.wjta.org/wjta/Newsletters.asp
Bill McClister, President
Kerry Siggins, Vice President
George A. Savanick, Treasurer
Gary Noto, Secretary
Newsletter for members of the WaterJet Technology Association. The newsletter provides the latest information on applications, equipment, news from members, new developments, meetings, conferences, and technical issues.
Frequency: Bimonthly
Founded in 1983

24397 National Association of Regulatory Utility Commisioners
Natl Assoc of Regulatory Utility Commissioner
1101 Vermont Ave Nw
Suite 200
Washington, DC 20005-3553
202-898-2200; Fax: 202-898-2213
admin@naruc.org
www.naruc.org
Charles Gray, Executive Director
Diane Munns, Publisher
A national organization that offers valuable information on over 150 consultants and other professionals active in regulated water, sewer and related industries.
Frequency: Monthly
Circulation: 1800
Founded in 1889

24398 National Water Line
National Water Resources Association
4 E St. SE
Washington, DC 20003
202-698-0693; Fax: 202-698-0694
nrwa@nrwa.org
www.nwra.org
Cheryl Zittle, President
Ian Lyle, Executive Vice President
Abbey Linsk, Director of Government Relations
Kris Polly, Senior Advisor
John Crotty, Advisor
Association news and information.
Frequency: Monthly

24399 US Water News
US Water News
230 Main St
Halstead, KS 67056-1913
316-835-2222
800-251-0046; Fax: 316-835-2223
www.uswaternews.com
Thomas Bell, President/Publisher
Mary DeSana, Editor
Reports news of current events in water resources from across the nation. Accepts advertising.
Cost: $59.00
24 Pages
Frequency: Monthly

24400 Water Newsletter
Water Information Center
1099 18th St
Suite 2600
Denver, CO 80202-1926
303-297-2600; Fax: 303-297-2750
www.rwolaw.com
Stephen L Waters, Partner
Contents include water supply and waste disposal information, and presents articles on conservation/usage.
Cost: $127.00
Frequency: Monthly
Founded in 1959

Magazines & Journals

24401 APWA Reporter
American Public Works Association
1200 Main Street
Suite 1400
Kansas City, MO 64105-2100
816-472-6100
800-848-APWA; Fax: 816-472-1610
kclark@apwa.net
www.apwa.net
Scott Grayson, Executive Director
R. Kevin Clark, Editor
Prime communication link uniting the community of public works professionals that make up APWA.
Cost: $100.00
Frequency: Monthly
ISBN: 0-092487-3 -
Mailing list available for rent

24402 AWWA Water Science
American Water Works Association
6666 W Quincy Ave.
Denver, CO 80235
303-794-7711
800-926-7337; Fax: 303-347-0804
www.awwa.org
Melissa Elliott, President
David B. LaFrance, Chief Executive Officer
Peer-reviewed research on the science, engineering, and social aspects of water.

24403 Bottled Water Reporter
International Bottled Water Association
1700 Diagonal Rd
Suite 650
Alexandria, VA 22314-2870
703-683-5213
800-928-3711; Fax: 703-683-4074
ibwainfo@bottledwater.org
www.bottledwater.org
Facebook, Twitter, LinkedIn
Joe Doss, CEO
Provides a vital source of information to bottlers and agencies, consultants and engineers. Also contains statistical data, marketing and management tips and profiles of bottled water operations and supplier companies.
Cost: $ 50.00
Circulation: 3000
Founded in 1958

24404 Cleaner Times
Advantage Publishing Company
1000 Nix Rd
Little Rock, AR 72211-3235
501-280-9111
800-525-7038; Fax: 501-280-9233
gpuls@adpub.com
www.cleanertimes.com
Charlene Yarbrough, Publisher
Gerry Puls, Circulation
Chuck Prieur, Sales Manager
Charlener Yarbrough, Publications/Premiums Marketing Mgr
Application, information, and productivity for persons engaged in the manufacturing, distribution, or the use of high pressure water systems and accessories. The emphasis is on safety, regulatory, which affect the industry as well as cleaning applications.
Cost: $18.00
72 Pages
Frequency: Monthly
Circulation: 10000
ISSN: 1073-9602
Founded in 1989
Printed in 4 colors on glossy stock

24405 Clearwaters
New York Water Environment Association
525 Plum Street
Suite 102
Syracuse, NY 13204
315-422-7811; Fax: 315-422-3851
www.nywea.org
Lois Hickey, Editor
Patricia Cerro-Reehil, Executive Director
Contains information on pollution control legislation, regulation, and compliance.
Cost: $25.00
Frequency: Quarterly
Circulation: 3000
Founded in 1929

24406 Drill Bits
National Drilling Association
3053 Nationwide Pkwy.
Brunswick, OH 44212
877-632-4748; Fax: 216-803-9900
info@nda4u.com
www.nda4u.com
Rob Caho, President
Jim Howe, Secretary/Treasurer
A non-profit trade association of contractors, manufacturers and affiliated members from the drilling industry representing the geotechnical, environmental and mineral exploration sectors of this industry.
250+ Members
Frequency: 2x/Year
Founded in 1972

24407 Estuaries and Coasts
Coastal & Estuarine Research Federation
2150 N 107th St.
Suite 205
Seattle, WA 98133
434-218-3366
estuariesandcoasts@cerf.science
www.cerf.science
Taylor Bowen, Managing Editor
The official journal published by the Coastal and Estuarine Research Federation. The publication releases original research on hydrodynamics, hydrology, among other disciplines.
Founded in 1960

24408 Ground Water
National Ground Water Association
601 Dempsey Rd.
Westerville, OH 43081
614-898-7791
800-551-7379; Fax: 614-898-7786

ngwa@ngwa.org
www.ngwa.org
Facebook, Twitter, LinkedIn, YouTube

Thad Plumley, Director of Publications

Focuses on ground water hydrogeology as a science.
Cost: $395.00
160 Pages
Circulation: 15000
ISSN: 0017-467x
Founded in 1963
Printed in one color

24409 Ground Water Monitoring & Remediation
National Ground Water Association
601 Dempsey Rd
Westerville, OH 43081

614-898-7791
800-551-7379; Fax: 614-898-7786
ngwa@ngwa.org
www.ngwa.org

Thad Plumley, Director of Publications

contains a mix of original columns authored by industry leaders, industry news, EPA updates, product and equipment news, and peer-reviewed papers.
Cost: $200.00
Frequency: Annual
Circulation: 17,000
Founded in 1981

24410 Ground Water Monitoring and Remediation
National Ground Water Association
601 Dempsey Rd.
Westerville, OH 43081

614-898-7791
800-551-7379; Fax: 614-898-7786
ngwa@ngwa.org
www.ngwa.org
Facebook, Twitter, LinkedIn, YouTube

Thad Plumley, Publications Director

Contains peer-reviewed papers, product and equipment news, EPA updates, industry news, and a mix of original columns authored by industry leaders.
Cost: $195.00
Frequency: Quarterly
Circulation: 15201
ISSN: 1069-3629
Founded in 1981

24411 Industrial Wastewater
Water Environment Federation
601 Wythe St
Alexandria, VA 22314-1994

703-684-2400; Fax: 703-684-2492
inquiry@wef.org
www.wef.org
Facebook, Twitter, LinkedIn

Bill Bertera, Executive Director

Provides the information on the practical application of science and technology in the management of water discharges, air emissions, ground water and soil remediation to the industrial personnel, consultants and other involved in all aspects of management, treatment and disposal of industrial wastewater.
Cost: $129.00
Frequency: Bi-Monthly
Circulation: 35500
ISSN: 1067-5337
Founded in 1928

24412 Journal of Soil and Water Conservation
Soil and Water Conservation Society
945 SW Ankeny Rd.
Ankeny, IA 50023

515-289-2331; Fax: 515-289-1227
pubs@swcs.org
www.swcs.org

Annie Binder, Director of Publications/Editor
Jorge A. Delgado, Research Editor
Jody Thompson, Editorial Assistant

A multidisciplinary journal of natural resource conservation research, practice, policy, and perspectives. The journal has two sections: the A Section containing various departments and features and the Research Section containing peer-reviewed research papers.
Cost: $99.00
Frequency: Bimonthly
Circulation: 2000
ISSN: 0022-4561
Founded in 1945

24413 Journal of the American Water Resources Association
American Water Resources Association
4 W. Federal Street
P.O. Box 1626
Middleburg, VA 20118-1626

540-687-8390; Fax: 540-687-8395
info@awra.org
www.awra.org

Venki Uddameri, Editor-in-Chief

Annual directory offering information on all water resources, technologies, systems and services for the water resources industry.
Frequency: Bi-Monthly
Founded in 1964

24414 Landscape & Irrigation
Adams Business Media
PO Box 17349
Chicago, IL 60617-0349

773-221-4223; Fax: 773-374-6270
www.adamsmediastore.com

Karen Adams, President

24415 National Driller
Business News Publishing Company
1050 IL Route 83
Suite 200
Bensenville, IL 60106

800-223-2194; Fax: 248-786-1358
www.nationaldriller.com

Linda Moffat, Publisher
Greg Ettling, Editor
Lisa Shroeder, Managing Editor

Provides feature articles, timely and valuable industry information, newly developed products and technologies, and quality marketing and business management advice.
Frequency: Monthly
Mailing list available for rent

24416 Operations Forum
Water Environment Federation
601 Wythe St
Alexandria, VA 22314-1994

703-684-2400
800-666-0206; Fax: 703-684-2492
www.wef.org

Bill Bertera, Executive Director

The emphasis is on process control, plant operations, collection systems and industry news.
Cost: $4995.00
Frequency: Monthly
Circulation: 17005
Founded in 1928

24417 Rural Water Magazine
National Rural Water Association
2915 S 13th St.
Duncan, OK 73533

580-252-0629; Fax: 580-255-4476
nrwa@nrwa.org
www.nrwa.org

Sam Wade, Chief Executive Officer

Targeted at the operators and board members of rural and small municipal water and wastewater utilities.
56 Pages
Frequency: Quarterly
Circulation: 22800
Founded in 1979

24418 US Water News
US Water News
230 Main St
Halstead, KS 67056-1913

316-835-2222
800-251-0046; Fax: 316-835-2223
www.uswaternews.com

Thomas Bell, President/Publisher

Reports news of current events from across the nation in the municipal and industrial water and wastewater segments of the water industry.
Cost: $59.00
28 Pages
Frequency: Monthly
Circulation: 20000
Founded in 1984
Printed in on n stock

24419 Water Conditioning and Purification Magazine
Publicom
2800 E Fort Lowell Road
Tucson, AZ 85716

520-323-6144; Fax: 520-323-7412
info@wcponline.com
www.wcponline.com

Kurt C Peterson, Publisher/Eastern Advertising Exec
Sharon M Peterson, President/Owner
Karen R Smith, Executive Editor
Margo Goldbaum, Circulation Services
Denise M Roberts, Assistant Editor

Comprehensive magazine for all aspects of the water quality improvement industry. Accepts advertising.
Cost: $49.00
100 Pages
Circulation: 20000
ISSN: 1537-1786
Founded in 1959
Mailing list available for rent: 1000 names at $250 per M
Printed in 4 colors on glossy stock

24420 Water Environment & Technology
Water Environment Federation
601 Wythe St.
Alexandria, VA 22314

800-666-0206; Fax: 703-684-2492
inquiry@wef.org
www.wef.org
Facebook, Twitter, LinkedIn

Walt Marlowe, Exeuutive Director
Tim Williams, Deputy Executive Director
Penny Young, Chief Financial Officer

Premier magazine for the water quality field. Provides information on what professionals demand; cutting-edge technologies, innovative solutions, regulatory and legislative impacts, and professional development.
Circulation: 27304

24421 Water Resources Research
American Geophysical Union

2000 Florida Ave NW
Washington, DC 20009-1231

202-462-6900
800-966-2481; Fax: 202-328-0566
service@agu.org
www.agu.org
Facebook, Twitter, LinkedIn

Fred Spilhaus, Executive Director
Karne Blaususs, Circulation Manager

Presents articles on the social, natural, and physical sciences, with emphasis on geochemistry, hydrology, and groundwater transfer technology.
Cost: $1200.00
Frequency: Monthly
Circulation: 4700
Founded in 1919

24422 **Water Technology**
National Trade Publications
19 British American Blvd. Wes
Latham, NY 12110

518-783-1281; Fax: 518-783-1386
asavino@ntpinc.com
www.watertechonline.com
Facebook, Twitter, LinkedIn

Tracy Ashton-Martin, Vice President of Business Publishi
Lisa Williman, Marketing Account Executive
Chapman Brown, Advertising Account Executive
Richard DiPaolo, Editorial Director
Jake Mastroianni, Assistant Editor

Serves the POU/POE water treatment industry. Accepts advertising.
Cost: $39.00
48 Pages
Frequency: Monthly
Circulation: 21000
Founded in 1981
Mailing list available for rent: 20000 names at $125 per M
Printed in 4 colors on glossy stock

24423 **Water Well Journal**
Ground Water Publishing Company
601 Dempsey Rd
Westerville, OH 43081-8978

614-882-8179
800-551-7379; Fax: 614-898-7786
waterwelljournal.org
Facebook, Twitter, LinkedIn

Kevin McCray, Executive Director
Jennifer Strawn, Associate Editor
Joanne Grant, Manager

A complete publication of the water supply industry. Covers technical issues related to drilling and pump installation, rig maintenance, business management and professional development, well rehabilitation, water treatment and more.
Cost: $95.00
84 Pages
Frequency: Monthly
Founded in 1948

24424 **WaterWorld**
PennNet
1421 S Sheridan Road
Tulsa, OK 74112

918-835-3161
800-331-4463; Fax: 918-831-9415
www.pennnet.com
Facebook, Twitter, LinkedIn

James Laughlin, Editor/Associate Publisher

Gives information about products and services, technology, applications, legislation and regulations to help the water industry pros successfully plan, design, operate and maintain their systems.
Frequency: Monthly
Founded in 1985

24425 **World Wastes: the Independent Voice**
Communication Channels
6151 Powers Ferry Road NW
Atlanta, GA 30339-2959

770-953-4805; Fax: 770-618-0348
Bill Wolpin, Editor
Jerrold France, President Argus Business

Reaches individuals and firms engaged in the removal and disposal of solid wastes.
Cost: $48.00
Frequency: Monthly
Circulation: 36,000

24426 **World Water**
Water Environment Federation
601 Wythe St.
Alexandria, VA 22314

800-666-0206; Fax: 703-684-2492
inquiry@wef.org
www.wef.org

Walt Marlowe, Executive Director
Tim Williams, Deputy Executive Director
Penny Young, Chief Financial Officer

International magazine for the water quality industry. Provides the most cutting-edge and helpful information on global water issues.

24427 **World Water Reuse & Desalination**
Water Environment Federation
601 Wythe St.
Alexandria, VA 22314

800-666-0206; Fax: 703-684-2492
inquiry@wef.org
www.wef.org

Walt Marlowe, Executive Director
Tim Williams, Deputy Executive Director
Penny Young, Chief Financial Officer

Becoming the global news and information resource for the water reuse and quality industries. Provides the most up-to-date and innovative information on all facets of global water reuse and desalination issues.

Trade Shows

24428 **ASDWA Annual Conference**
Association of State Drinking Water Administrators
1401 Wilson Blvd.
Suite 1225
Arlington, VA 22209

703-812-9505; Fax: 703-812-9506
info@asdwa.org
www.asdwa.org
Facebook, Twitter

Alan Roberson, Executive Director
Deidre White, Project Manager

Professional association serving state drinking water programs.
Frequency: Annual/October

24429 **AWRA Spring Conference**
American Water Resources Association
4 W. Federal Street
P.O. Box 1626
Middleburg, VA 20118-1626

540-687-8390; Fax: 540-387-8395
info@awra.org
www.awra.org

Christine McCrehin, Membership & Marketing Director
Kenneth D. Reid, CAE, Executive VP
Michael J. Kowalski, CAE, Director of Operations

Brings together a diverse group of water resource professionals from across the state and allows them to interact together.
2000 Members
Frequency: Annual/Spring
Founded in 1964

24430 **AWRA Summer Conference**
American Water Resources Association
4 W. Federal Street
P.O. Box 1626
Middleburg, VA 20118-1626

540-687-8390; Fax: 540-387-8395
info@awra.org
www.awra.org

Christine McCrehin, Membership & Marketing Director
Kenneth D. Reid, CAE, Executive VP
Michael J. Kowalski, CAE, Director of Operations

Brings together a diverse group of water resource professionals from across the state and allows them to interact together.
2000 Members
Frequency: Annual/Summer
Founded in 1964

24431 **American Backflow Prevention Association Annual Conference**
American Backflow Prevention Assocation
6672 S 1570 W
West Jordan, UT 84084

801-436-7238
info@abpa.com
abpa.site-ym.com

Tim Brown, International President
J. Frank Snyder, International Vice President
Patti Fauver, Treasurer
Mike Lueck, Director-At-Large

Gathers together professionals and experts to provide technical expertise on backflow prevention.
Frequency: Annual
Founded in 1984

24432 **American Society of Irrigation Consultants National Conference**
404 E 4th Street
Royal Oak, MI 48067

508-763-8140
carolc@asic.org
www.asic.org

Carol Colein, Executive Director
Michael Krones, President
Stacy Gardner, Vice President
Janet Luehrs, Treasurer
Carly Kardon, Operations and Member Services

Addressing major industry issues and learn from each other and leading experts in irrigation, water management and related fields. Member participate in the conference to showcase the latest in irrigation solution technology and services.
Frequency: Annual/September
Founded in 1970

24433 **American Water Resources Conference**
American Water Resources Association
4 W. Federal Street
P.O. Box 1626
Middleburg, VA 20118-1626

540-687-8390; Fax: 540-687-8395
info@awra.org
www.awra.org
Facebook, Twitter, LinkedIn

Christine McCrehin, Membership & Marketing Director
Kenneth D. Reid, CAE, Executive VP
Michael J. Kowalski, CAE, Director of Operations

Show of water resources science and technology. An opportunity for water resource practitioners from diverse disciples to gather and network among colleagues.
Frequency: Annual/November
Founded in 1964

24434 **American Water Works Association Annual Conference and Exhibition**
American Water Works Association
6666 W Quincy Ave.
Denver, CO 80235

303-794-7711
800-926-7337; Fax: 303-347-0804
www.awwa.org

Melissa Elliott, President
David B. LaFrance, Chief Executive Officer

With more than 500 exhibitors, who are a source of knowledge and information for water professionals who work to improve the supply and quality of water in North America and beyond.
12000 Attendees
Frequency: Annual, June
Founded in 1881

24435 **Biennial CERF Conference**
Coastal & Estuarine Research Federation
2150 N 107th St.
Suite 205
Seatle, WA 98133

206-209-5162
info@cerf.science
www.cerf.science

Jim Fourqurean, President
Susan Park, Executive Director
Louise S. Miller, Chief Operating Officer

Collaborate and discuss with more than 1,700 scientists and researchers during CERF's week-long conference.
Frequency: Biennial/November

24436 **Chartmaker**
American Recreation Coalition
1225 New York Avenue NW
Suite 450
Washington, DC 20005-6405

202-829-9530; Fax: 202-662-7424

Derrick Crandall, President

Triennial exhibits relating to the responsible use of US aquatic resources, including issues such as wetlands conservation, boating safety, sportfish research and enhancement and boating access improvements.

24437 **Ground Water Protection Council Annual Forum**
Ground Water Protection Council
13308 N Maccarthur Blvd.
Oklahoma City, OK 73142

405-516-4972
www.gwpc.org

Mike Paque, Executive Director
Dan Yates, Associate Executive Director
Paul Jehn, Technical Director
Mike Nickolaus, Special Projects Director
Kelsey Henry, Financial Director

State ground water and underground injection control agencies whose mission is to promote the protection and conservation of ground water resources for all beneficial uses, recognizing ground water as a component of the ecosystem.
Frequency: Annual/September

24438 **Irrigation Show & Education Conference**
6540 Arlington Boulevard
Falls Church, VA 22042-6638

703-536-7080; Fax: 703-536-7019
membership@irrigation.org
www.irrigation.org

Deborah M. Hamlin, Chief Executive Officer
Tiffany Wilson, Senior Trade Show Manager

Four hundred and twenty five booths of the newest in irrigation equipment for the agricultural industry.
3.5M Attendees
Frequency: November

24439 **Membrane Technology Conference & Exposition**
American Water Works Association
6666 W Quincy Ave.
Denver, CO 80235

303-794-7711
800-926-7337; Fax: 303-347-0804
www.awwa.org

Melissa Elliott, President
David B. LaFrance, Chief Executive Officer

Explores how the latest developments in membrane technology can enhance water reliability and quality.

24440 **National Ground Water Association Annual Convention and Exposition**
National Ground Water Association
601 Dempsey Rd.
Westerville, OH 43081

614-898-7791
800-551-7379; Fax: 614-898-7786
ngwa@ngwa.org
www.ngwa.org

Terry S. Morse, Chief Executive Officer
Paul Humes, Chief Financial Officer
David Evener, Director of Operations/Technology
Erin Rodgers, Member Services Manager

Annual show of 4600 manufacturers, suppliers, distributors, consultants and scientists, and contractors/pump installers.
5,100 Attendees
Frequency: December

24441 **National Water Resources Association Annual Conference**
National Water Resources Association
4 E St. SE
Washington, DC 20003

202-698-0693; Fax: 202-698-0694
nwra@nwra.org
www.nwra.org

Cheryl Zittle, President
Ian Lyle, Executive Vice President
Abbey Linsk, Director of Government Relations
Kris Polly, Senior Advisor
John Crotty, Advisor

Annual conference and exhibits relating to the development, control, conservation and utilization of water resources in the reclamation states.
700 Attendees
Frequency: November

24442 **North American Lake Management Society International Symposium**
North American Lake Management Society
4513 Vernon Boulevard, Suite 103
PO Box 5443
Madison, WI 53705-0443

608-233-2836; Fax: 608-233-3186
www.nalms.org

Bev Clark, President

Annual symposium and exhibits related to lake ecology and management.

24443 **Soil and Water Conservation Society Annual International Conference**
Soil and Water Conservation Society
945 SW Ankeny Rd.
Ankeny, IA 50021

515-289-2331; Fax: 515-289-1227
www.swsc.org

Clare Lindahl, Chief Executive Officer
Courtney Allen, Event/Professional Development Dir.
Catherine DeLong, Special Projects/Policy Director

Explores ways to improve the linkages among conservation science, policy and application at local, national, and international scales. The conference will provide participants an opportunity to teach skills, learn techniques, compare successes, and improve understanding.
1200 Attendees
Frequency: Annual/July

24444 **The Utility Management Conference**
Water Environment Federation
601 Wythe St.
Alexandria, VA 22314

800-666-2492; Fax: 703-684-2400
inquiry@wef.org
www.wef.org

Walt Marlowe, Executive Director
Tim Williams, Deputy Executive Director
Penny Young, Chief Financial Officer

Water and wastewater managers and professionals will gather to be part of the latest approaches, practices, and techniques in all aspects of utility management.

24445 **WJTA Expo**
WaterJet Technology Association (WJTA)
906 Olive St.
Suite 1200
St. Louis, MO 63101

314-241-1445; Fax: 314-241-1449
www.wjta.org

Bill McClister, President
Kerry Siggins, Vice President
George A. Savanick, Treasurer
Gary Noto, Secretary

Expo for professionals working in the hydroblasting, vacuum truck, industrial cleaning and waterjet markets.
Founded in 1983

24446 **Water Pro Conference**
National Rural Water Association
2915 S 13th St.
Duncan, OK 73533

580-252-0629; Fax: 580-255-4476
nwra@nrwa.org
waterproconference.org

Sam Wade, Chief Executive Officer

An industry event for networking, technology and educational sessions.
1.5M Attendees
Frequency: Annual/September

24447 **Water Quality Association Convention**
Water Quality Association
4151 Naperville Rd.
Lisle, IL 60532-3696

630-505-0160; Fax: 630-505-9637
www.wqa.org

Pauli Undesser, Executive Director
Tom Bruursema, Assc. Exec. Dir., Member Engagement
Wesley Bleed, Director, Marketing/Communications
LyNae Schleyer, Director, Meeting Services
Scott Freeman, Chief Financial Officer

Annual convention and exhibits of water treatment equipment and related articles.
4,300 Attendees
Frequency: Annual/April

Directories & Databases

24448 **American Water Works Association: Buyers' Guide**
American Water Works Association
6666 W Quincy Ave.
Denver, CO 80235

303-794-7711
800-926-7337; Fax: 303-347-0804
www.awwa.org

Melissa Elliott, President
David B. LaFrance, Chief Executive Officer

Member suppliers and distributors of water supply products and services, contractors for water supply projects and engineering consultants.
Frequency: Annual/November
Circulation: 80,000

24449 **Directory of Water/Sewer and Related Industries Professionals**
National Assn of Regulatory Utility Commissioners
1101 Vermont Ave NW
Suite 200
Washington, DC 20005-3553

202-898-2200; Fax: 202-898-2213
admin@naruc.org
www.naruc.org

Charles Gray, Executive Director

Offers valuable information on over 150 consultants and other professionals active in regulated water, sewer and related industries.
Cost: $25.00
195 Pages
Frequency: Annual

24450 **Ground Water Age: Directory of Manufacturers**
National Trade Publications
13 Century Hill Drive
Latham, NY 12110-2197

518-831-1281; Fax: 518-783-1386

Roslyn Scheib Dahl, Editor

List of over 150 companies that provide products and services to the ground water industry.
Cost: $30.00
Frequency: Annual December
Circulation: 13,448

24451 **Ground Water Monitoring & Remediation: Buyers Guide Issue**
Ground Water Publishing Company
601 Dempsey Rd
Westerville, OH 43081-8978

614-882-8179
800-332-2104; Fax: 614-898-7786
www.ngwa.org

Kevin McCray, Executive Director
Thad Plumley, Publications Director

List of companies that provide products used in the ground water monitoring and remediation industry.
Cost: $15.00
Frequency: Annual
Circulation: 12,382
Founded in 1981

24452 **Ground Water On-Line**
National Ground Water Association
601 Dempsey Rd.
Westerville, OH 43081

614-898-7791
800-551-7379; Fax: 614-898-7786
ngwa@ngwa.org
www.ngwa.org

Thad Plumley, Director of Publications

Database offers information on more than 90,000 ground water literature citations, which includes information like key words, abstracts, chemical compounds, biological factors, geographic locations, aquifer names, authors, titles, publication source names and a lot more.

24453 **Validated Water Treatment Equipment Directory**
Water Quality Association
4151 Naperville Rd
Suite 100
Lisle, IL 60532-3696

630-505-0160; Fax: 630-505-9637
www.wqa.org

Peter Censky, Manager

Over 700 water treatment products tested by the Water Quality Association and their manufacturers are listed.
Cost: $6.00
Frequency: SemiAnnual

24454 **WJTA's Directory of Products, Systems and Services**
WaterJet Technology Association (WJTA)
906 Olive St.
Suite 1200
St. Louis, MO 63101

314-241-1445; Fax: 314-241-1449
www.wjta.org

Bill McClister, President
Kerry Siggins, Vice President
George A. Savanick, Treasurer
Gary Noto, Secretary

A directory listing products, systems and services offered by members of the WaterJet Technology Association.
Founded in 1983

24455 **Water Technology: Directory of Manufacturers and Suppliers Issue**
National Trade Publications
13 Century Hill Drive
Latham, NY 12110-2197

518-783-1281; Fax: 518-783-1386
www.ntpmedia.com

Mark Wilson, Editor

List of about 250 manufacturers, distributors and other suppliers of water conditioning and treatment products.
Cost: $21.00
Frequency: Annual December
Circulation: 17,213

24456 **Water Treatability**
National Ground Water Information Center
6375 Riverside Drive
Dublin, OH 43017-5045

614-717-2770; Fax: 614-761-3446

Offers information on treatment technologies for the removal of various contaminants from water supplies.
Frequency: Full-text

24457 **Water Well Journal: Buyer's Guide Issue**
National Ground Water Association
601 Dempsey Rd.
Westerville, OH 43081

614-898-7791
800-551-7379; Fax: 614-898-7786
ngwa@ngwa.org
www.ngwa.org

Thad Plumley, Director of Publications

Feature articles, columns, and departments are authored by industry experts and professional journalists.
Frequency: Annual January
Circulation: 26,000

Industry Web Sites

24458 **http://gold.greyhouse.com**
G.O.L.D Grey House OnLine Databases

Grey House Publishing's online database platform, GOLD, offers Quick Search, Keyword Search and Expert Search for most business sectors including water supply markets. The GOLD platform makes finding the information you need quick and easy - whether you're a novice searcher or an experienced database user. All of Grey House's directory products are available for subscription on the GOLD platform.

24459 **www.greyhouse.com**
Grey House Publishing

Authoritative reference directories for most business sectors including water supply markets. Users can search the online databases with varied search criteria allowing for custom searches by product category, geographic area, sales volume, keyword, subject and more. Full Grey House catalog and online ordering also available.

24460 **www.gwpc.org**
Ground Water Protection Council

State ground water and underground injection control agencies whose mission is to promote the protection and conservation of ground water resources for all beneficial uses, recognizing ground water as a component of the ecosystem.

24461 **www.icwp.org**
Interstate Council on Water Policy

Facebook, Twitter

Association whose members are state and regional agencies concerned with water resources management and economic and environmental sustainability. Members work to conduct research.

24462 **www.nda4u.com**
National Drilling Association

A non-profit trade association of contractors, manufacturers and affiliated members from the drilling industry representing the geotechnical, environmental and mineral exploration sectors of this industry.

24463 **www.swcs.org**
Soil and Water Conservation Society

SWCS is a nonprofit scientific and educational organization that serves as an advocate for conservation professionals and for science-based conservation practice, programs, and policy.

24464 **www.wef.org**
Water Environment Federation

A not-for-profit technical and educational organization, consisting of regional association comprised of air quality professionals concerned with all types of air pollution.

24465 **www.wjta.org**
WaterJet Technology Association (WJTA)

Facebook, Twitter, LinkedIn, Google+

A professional association dedicated to high pressure waterjet/industrial technology/cleaning.

24466 www.wqa.org
Water Quality Association
An international nonprofit trade association representing retail/dealers and manufacturer/suppliers in the point of use/entry water quality improvement industry. Membership benefits and services include technical and scientific information, educational seminars and home correspondence course books, professional certification and discount services.

Associations

24467 American Association of Meat Processors
One Meating Place
Elizabethtown, PA 17022

717-367-1168
aamp@aamp.com
www.aamp.com
Facebook, Twitter, Google+, YouTube

Rick Reams, President
Chris Young, Executive Director
Diana Dietz, Communications Manager
Niki Cloud, Convention Manager
Jane Frey, Accounting Manager

Membership consists of small to medium sized meat, poultry and food businesses including, slaughterers, processors, wholesalers, home food service businesses, deli and catering operators and suppliers to the industry. AAMP is affiliated with 28 state, regional and provincial associations.
1300+ Members
Founded in 1939

24468 American Supply Association
1200 Arlington Heights Road
Itasca, IL 60143

630-467-0000; Fax: 630-467-0001
info@asa.net
www.asa.net
Facebook, Twitter, LinkedIn

Mike Adelizzi, CEO
Aaron Scheiwe, CFO

ASA is a not-for-profit national organization serving wholesale distributors and their suppliers in the plumbing, heating, cooling and industrial and mechanical pipe, valves and fittings industries.
Founded in 1969

24469 AmericanHort
2130 Stella Court
Columbus, OH 43215

614-487-1117; Fax: 614-487-1216
hello@americanhort.org
www.americanhort.org
Facebook, Twitter, Instragram

Ken Fisher, President & CEO

AmericanHort was founded through the merger of the American Nursery and Landscape Association (ANLA) and the Association of Horticultural Profressionals (OFA). AmericanHort serves firms who grow, sell, or use plants. It advocates for the industryBs interests before government officials and provides its members with business knowledge essentials to long-term growth and profitability.
Founded in 2014

24470 Appliance Parts Distributors Association
P.O. Box 31816
Charlotte, NC 28231

Home Page: www.apda.com
Facebook, Twitter, LinkedIn

Dave Cook, President
Steve Falconi, Vice President
Rachel Nystrom, Treasurer
Bob Goldberg, Legal Counsel

The APDA is an association of independent businesses that aspire to provide the highest level of quality, service, support and information to its customers and suppliers in order to make its value indispensable to the parts distribution channel.

24471 Associated Beer Distributors of Illinois
100 W Cook Street
Springfield, IL 62704

217-528-4371
abdi@abdi.org
www.abdi.org
Facebook, Twitter, LinkedIn

Bob Myers, President
Chris Coleman, VP, Government Relations
Debbie Massey, Director of Operations
Melissa Daniels, Coordinator, Member Services

The ABDI represents, maintains, and improves the interests of its members who are licensed by the State of Illinois to import and distribute beer to licensed retailers.

24472 Associated Equipment Distributors
650 E Algonquin Road
Suite 305
Schaumburg, IL 60173

630-574-0650
help@aednet.org
aednet.org
Facebook, Twitter, LinkedIn

Brian P. McGuire, President/CEO
Robert K. Henderson, EVP & Chief Operating Officer
Agnes Baczek, Director, Finance
Jon Cruthers, VP, Sales
Sara Smith, Editor-In-Chief & Marketing & Comm.

International trade association supporting companies specializing in eqipment used in construction, mining, forestry, power generation, agriculture and industrial applications.
1000 Members
Founded in 1919

24473 Association for High Technology Distribution
N19 W24400 Riverwood Drive
Waukesha, WI 53188

262-696-3645
leigha.schatzman@ahtd.org
www.ahtd.org
Facebook, Twitter, RSS

Leigha Schatzman, Executive Director
Nancy Shirley, Association Services Coordinator
Pam Estergard, Financial Services
Mara Dickson, Marketing Director

The Association for High Technology Distribution has worked to increase the productivity and profitability of the high technology Automation Solutions Providers and Manufacturers who satisfy the automation needs of general industry and OEM manufacturers.
Founded in 1984

24474 Association for Hose and Accessories Distribution
180 Admiral Cochrane Drive
Suite 370
Annapolis, MD 21401

410-940-6350
info@nahad.org
www.nahad.org
Facebook, Twitter, LinkedIn

Molly Alton Mullins, Executive Vice President
Amy Luckado, VP, Operations
Jessica Hauser Forte, Director, Conferences
Dominique Abney, Director, Marketing & Sales
Donald Smith, CFO

The mission of NAHAD is to promote a high standard of professionalism and integrity within the hose and accessories industry by providing a medium for communications, education and training, so that quality is maximized and profitability enhanced.

24475 Association for Suppliers of Printing, Publishing & Converting Tech.
1896 Preston White Drive
Reston, VA 20191

703-264-7200
aptech@aptech.org
www.printtechnologies.org

Thayer Long, President
Ken Garner, SVP, Content Creation
Julie Shaffer, VP, Program Development
Sarah Markfield, VP, Marketing & Communications
Judith B. Durham, EVP, Operations

This association is a trade association of over 400 companies that manufacture and distribute equipment, systems, software, supplies used in printing, publishing and converting.

24476 Association of Ingersoll-Rand Distributors
1300 Summer Avenue
Cleveland, OH 44115

216-241-7333
aird@aird.org
www.aird.org

The Association of Ingersoll-Rand Distributors (AIRD) was organized as a central resource for distributors of Ingersoll-Rand compressed air equipment. AIRD is chartered to promote improved business conditions affecting distributors of air compressors, further a better understanding between distributors and equipment suppliers, research ways to lower costs of distributing air compressors, collect and disseminate statistical information and conduct other beneficial activities.
Founded in 1970

24477 Association of Service and Computer Dealers International
131 NW First Avenue
Delray Beach, FL 33444

561-266-9016; Fax: 561-431-6302
www.ascdi.com
Facebook, Twitter, LinkedIn, YouTube

Joe Marion, President
Gail Goldstein, Office Manager

The ASCDI is a worldwide, nonprofit organization, made up of companies who provide technology business solutions, technical support, and value added services to the business community.
Founded in 1981

24478 Association of Woodworking and Furnishings Suppliers
2400 E Katella Avenue
Suite 340
Anaheim, CA 92806

323-838-9440
800-946-2937; Fax: 323-838-9443
angelo@awfs.org
www.awfs.org
Facebook, Twitter, LinkedIn

Daniel Hershbeger, President
Rob Howell, Secretary/Treasurer

The Association of Woodworking and Furnishings Suppliers is the largest national trade association in the U.S. representing the interests of the broad array of companies that supply the home and commercial furnishings industry.
Founded in 1911

24479 Auto Care Association
7101 Wisconsin Avenue
Bethesda, MD 20814

301-654-6664; Fax: 301-654-3299
info@autocare.org
www.autocare.org

Facebook, Twitter, LinkedIn, Youtube, WordPress
Bill Hanvey, President/CEO

Provides advocacy, educational, networking, technology, market intelligence and communications resources on auto care to its members. Formerly known as the Automotive Aftermarket Industry Association.
23000 Members
Founded in 1999

24480 Bearing Specialists Association

630-858-3838; Fax: 630-790-3095
info@bsahome.org
www.bsahome.org
Twitter, LinkedIn, RSS

Jim Scardina, President
Michel Bouchard, Vice President

BSA is a not-for-profit association that consists of companies that distribute factory-warranted ball, roller, and anti-friction bearings through authorized dealers. BSA provides members with the opportunity to network with others in the industry through meetings, seminars and educational programs at their annual convention.
100 Members
Founded in 1966

24481 Business Solutions Association

3601 E Joppa Road
Baltimore, MD 21234

410-931-8100; Fax: 410-931-8111
www.businesssolutionsassociation.com

Travis Kaste, President
Casey Avent, VP
Nick Aronis, Secretary
Marlin Wendland, Treasurer

The goal of the Business Solutions Association is to provide a forum for the development of strategic and synergistic solutions to enhance the sale and distribution of business related products and services.

24482 Ceramic Tile Distributors Association

800 Roosevelt Road
Building C, Suite 312
Glen Ellyn, IL 60137

630-545-9415; Fax: 630-790-3095
info@ctdahome.org
www.ctdahome.org
Facebook

Rudy Llerena, President
Steve Vogel, VP
Robert DeAngelis, Treasurer
Rick Church, Executive Director
Bill Ives, Legal Counsel

CTDA is an international association of distributors, manufacturers, and allied professionals of ceramic tile and related products.

24483 Cleaning Equipment Trade Association

11450 U.S. Highway 380
Suite 130, #289
Cross Roads, TX 76227

800-441-0111; Fax: 704-635-7363
info@ceta.org
www.ceta.org

Debbie Murray, Managing Director
Jim Welch, President

International nonprofit association made up of manufacturers, distributors, suppliers and contractors. CETA is dedicated to increasing the awareness and promotion of industry products, while at the same time recognizing the impact on preserving the environment and the opportunity to do business within it.
300 Members
Founded in 1990

24484 Commercial Vehicle Solutions Network

3943 Baymeadows Road
Jacksonville, FL 32217

904-737-2900
info@cvsn.org
www.cvsn.org

Sean Ryan, President
Nick Seidel, Vice President
Angelo Volpe, Executive VP
Jeff Volpe, Marketing Director

The Commercial Vehicle Solutions Network (CVSN) is an association of independent parts and service aftermarket distributors serving the transportation industry.
Founded in 2006

24485 Convenience Distribution Association

11250 Roger Bacon Drive
Suite 8
Reston, VA 20190

703-208-3358
800-482-2962; Fax: 703-573-5738
info@cdaweb.net
cdaweb.net
Facebook, Twitter, LinkedIn, RSS

Kkimberly Bolin, President & CEO
Angie Simonetti, Executive Vice President
Alex Swaim, SVP, Technology & Communications
Kimberly Kissel, Director, Education
Gene Lange, General Counsel

A trade organization supporting the confectionary, tobacco and allied industries through programs and services. Members include wholesale distributors, manufacturers and other allieds to the industry.
5300 Members
Founded in 1942

24486 Copper and Brass Servicenter Association

6734 W 121st Street
Overland Park, KS 66209

913-396-0697
cbsahq@copper-brass.org
www.copper-brass.org
Facebook, Twitter, LinkedIn, YouTube, Flickr

Susan Avery, Executive Director
Liz Novak, Senior Director

Distributors (service centers) of fabricated copper and copper alloy products (sheet, plate, coil, rod, bar tube, etc) and their brass mill suppliers.
78 Members
Founded in 1951

24487 Door & Hardware Institute

2001 K Street NW
Washington, DC 20006

202-367-1134; Fax: 202-367-2134
www.dhi.org
Facebook, Twitter, LinkedIn

Sharon Newport, CAE, Chief Executive Officer (Interim)
Laura Frye Weaver, VP, Education
Adam Berkshire, Communications/Marketing Manager

The Door & Hardware Institute (DHI) is the only professional association dedicated to the Architectural Openings Industry. DHI represents the North American openings marketplace as the advocate and primary resource for information, professional development and certification.

24488 Drycleaning & Laundry Institute International

14700 Sweitzer Lane
Laurel, MD 20707

301-622-1900
800-638-2627; Fax: 240-295-4200
techline@dlionline.org
www.dlionline.org
Facebook, Twitter, Flickr

With its education, research, testing, and professional training, DLI offers solutions that help member businesses provide expert garment care.
Founded in 1883

24489 Electrical Apparatus Service Association

1331 Baur Boulevard
St. Louis, MO 63132

314-993-2220; Fax: 314-993-1269
easainfo@easa.com
www.easa.com
Facebook, Twitter, LinkedIn, Youtube

Jerry Gray, Chair
Timothy Bieber, Vice Chair
Sid Seymour, Secretary/Treasurer
Linda J. Raynes, CAE, President/CEO
Dale Shuter, CMP, Manager, Meetings & Expositions

An international trade organization of electromechanical sales and service firms in 58 countries. Provides members with a means of keeping up to date on materials, equipment, and state of the art technology.
2000 Members
Founded in 1973

24490 Equipment Marketing & Distribution Association (EMDA)

PO Box 1347
Iowa City, IA 52244

319-354-5156
pat@emda.net
www.emda.net
Facebook, Twitter, LinkedIn

Patricia A. Collins, Executive Vice President

EMDA is the result of the 2008 merger of FEWA and AIMRA. EMDA members are devtoed to the marketing of specialized equipment: agricultural, outdoor power, light industrial, forestry, irrigation, turf and grounds maintenance, lawn and garden and parts/components for thosesegments of industry.
250 Members
Founded in 1945

24491 FPDA Motion & Control Network

180 Admiral Cochrane Drive
Suite 370
Annapolis, MD 21401

410-940-6347
info@fpda.org
www.fpda.org

Kevin Kampe, President
Amy Luckado, Executive Director
Dominique Abney, Director, Marketing/Sales
Donald Smith, Chief Financial Officer
Courtney Truelove, Manager, Membership/Programs

The FPDA Motion & Control Network is a trade association on the move, representing motion solution providers who offer fluid power, automation, and electro-mechanical technologies and distribution services to enhance customer performance and profitability. Formerly known as the Fluid Power Distributors Association.
300+ Members
Founded in 1974

24492 **Financial & Security Products Association**
1024 Mebane Oaks Road
Suite 273
Mebane, NC 27302

919-648-0664
800-843-6082; Fax: 919-648-0670
bj@fspa1.com
www.fspa1.com
LinkedIn

Grant Case, Chairman
Fred Wheeler, President
B.J. Hanson, Executive Director
Bryce Good, Vice President
Dave Pepin, Secretary-Treasurer

Independent dealers, manufacturers and associates whose outstanding products and services give financial institutions a crucial edge in performance, efficiency and economy.

Founded in 1973

24493 **Food Industry Suppliers Association**
1207 Sunset Drive
Greensboro, NC 27408

336-274-6311; Fax: 336-691-1839
stella@fisanet.org
www.fisanet.org
LinkedIn

Jason Ryan, President
Eric Perkins, Vice President
Rob Clark, Past President

Trade association dedicated to promoting distribution in serving high purity industries. Membership includes independent distributors and manufacturers who go to market through distribution. Members serve customers in food, beverage, personal care, pharmaceutical, Bio-Pharm and other high purity industries.

245 Members
Founded in 1968

24494 **Food Marketing Institute**
2345 Crystal Drive
Suite 800
Arlington, VA 22202

202-452-8444; Fax: 202-429-4519
www.fmi.org
Facebook, Twitter, LinkedIn, Youtube, RSS

Randy Edeker, Chair
Leslie G. Sarasin, President/CEO

FMI conducts programs in public affairs, food safety, research, education and industry relations on behalf of its 1,500 member companies in the United States and around the world.

1500 Members

24495 **Foodservice Equipment Distributors Association**
5600 N River Road
Suite 740
Rosemont, IL 60018

224-293-6500
info@feda.com
www.feda.com
Facebook, Twitter, LinkedIn

Tracy Mulqueen, CEO
George Maul, Director, Finance & Operations
Tim O'Connor, Communications Manager

Dealers and distributors of foodservice equipment and supplies.

300 Members
Founded in 1933

24496 **Gases and Welding Distributors Association**
1 Oakwood Boulevard
Suite 195
Hollywood, FL 33020

844-251-3219; Fax: 954-367-7790
gawda@gawda.org
www.gawda.org
Facebook, Twitter, LinkedIn, YouTube

Abydee Butler Moore, President
Robert Anders, 1st Vice President
Gary Halter, 2nd Vice President

GAWDA's mission is to promote the safe operation and economic vitality of distributors of industrial gases and related welding equipment and supplies.

775 Members
Founded in 1945

24497 **Global Market Development Center**
1115 Elkton Drive
Suite 204
Colorado Springs, CO 80907

719-576-4260
info@gmdc.org
www.gmdc.com
Facebook, Twitter, LinkedIn, YouTube, Google+, Flickr

Patrick Spear, President/CEO
Keith Wypyszynski, VP, Member Services
James Engstrom, VP, Finance & Administration
Michael Winterbottom, VP, IT/Chief Technology Officer

GMDC is the premier non-profit global trade association dedicated to serving General Merchandise and Health Beauty retailers, wholesalers and suppliers. GMDC promotes critical connectivity to grow and expand member companies by uniting members through business building events and opportunities and enriching their thinking through education and training; consumer and business insights; and information resources.

Founded in 1970

24498 **Health Industry Distributors Association**
310 Montgomery Street
Alexandria, VA 22314

703-549-4432
rowan@hida.org
www.hida.org

Matthew J. Rowan, President/CEO
Elizabeth Hilla, SVP
Linda Rouse O'Neill, VP, Govt. Affairs
Balvinder Bains, VP, Finance & Operations

HIDA keeps members current on healthcare reform, government affairs, industry trends and forecasts, provider news, and sales tips.

Founded in 1902

24499 **Healthcare Distribution Alliance**
901 N Glebe Road
Suite 1000
Arlington, VA 22203

703-787-0000; Fax: 703-812-5282
www.hda.org
Twitter, LinkedIn

Chester Davis, Jr., President/CEO
Ann W. Bittman, EVP/COO
Elizabeth A. Gallenagh, General Counsel/SVP, Supply Chain

A national association representing primary, full-service healthcare distributors. HDMA and its members are the vital link in the healthcare system, working daily to provide value, remove costs and develop innovative solutions.

Founded in 1876

24500 **Heating, Airconditioning & Refrigeration Distributors International**
445 Hutchinson Avenue
Suite 550
Columbus, OH 43235

614-345-4328
888-253-2128; Fax: 614-345-9161
www.hardinet.org
Facebook, Twitter, LinkedIn, Youtube, Instagram, Flickr

Talbot H. Gee, CEO
Emily Saving, EVP
Palmer Schoening, VP, Gov't Affairs
Alex Ayers, Director, Gov't Affairs
Eileen Mantel, Manager, Networking & Conferences

This association is a trade organization dedicated to advancing the science of wholesale distribution in the HVACR industry.

750+ Members
Founded in 1960

24501 **ISSA**
3300 Dundee Road
Northbrook, IL 60062

847-982-0800
800-225-4772; Fax: 847-982-1012
info@issa.com
www.issa.com
Facebook, Twitter, LinkedIn

John H. Barrett, Executive Director
Kim Althoff, VP, Sales/Trade Shows/Membership
Jon Adkins, VP, Divisions/Marketing/IT

The worldwide cleaning industry association.

5700+ Members
Founded in 1923

24502 **Industrial Compressor Distributor Association**
Eureka, MO

636-938-3957
margotgravel@gmail.com
www.icdaonline.com

Margot Gravel, Director

The main objectives of the ICDA are to promote for its members the highest standards of production, financial and managerial activities; to act as a vehicle for the solution of common industry problems in an effective and efficient manner; and to increase market volume and profits for its members.

24503 **Industrial Supply Association**
3435 Concord Road
Unit 21889
York, PA 17402

866-460-2360
info@isapartners.org
www.isapartners.org
Facebook, Twitter, LinkedIn, YouTube

Ed Gerber, President/CEO

The primary focus of the Industrial Supply Association is to improve the industrial supply channel through its mission-critical activities, including conventions, forums and the gathering and dissemination of critical information. The association supports distributors, manufacturers and representatives of MROP products/industrial equipment.

900+ Members
Founded in 2007

24504 **International Association of Plastics Distribution**
6734 W 121st Street
Overland Park, KS 66209
913-345-1005; Fax: 913-345-1006
iapd@iapd.org
www.iapd.org
Facebook, Twitter, LinkedIn, YouTube, Flickr
Susan E. Avery, CAE, CEO
Liz Novak, CAE, Sr. Dir., Advocacy & Publications
Dave Blackhurst, Dir., Membership & Sales
Kerrie Moore, Finance Manager
Whitney Nelson, Dir., Meetings & Events
The International Association of Plastics Distribution is an international trade association comprised of companies engaged in the distribution and manufacturing of plastics materials.
Founded in 1956

24505 **International Foodservice Distributors Association**
1660 International Drive
Suite 550
McLean, VA 22102
703-532-9400; Fax: 703-880-7117
www.ifdaonline.org
Twitter, LinkedIn
John Tracy, Chairman
Craig Hoskins, Vice Chairman
Mark Harman, Treasurer
Mark S. Allen, President/CEO
Trade association comprised of food distribution companies that supply independent grocers and food service operations throughout the US, Canada and 19 other countries.
135 Members
Founded in 2003

24506 **International Sealing Distribution Association**
180 Aadmiral Cochrane Drive
Suite 370
Annapolis, MD 21401
410-940-6344; Fax: 410-263-1659
info@isd.org
www.isd.org
Facebook, Twitter, LinkedIn
Josh Hale, President
Brian Despain, VP
Amy Luckado, Executive Director
The International Sealing Distribution Association (ISD) is a not-for-profit trade association formed to enhance the success of members through information, education, and interaction.

24507 **International Truck Parts Association**
1720 10th Avenue S
Suite 4, PMB 199
Great Falls, MT 59405
866-346-5692; Fax: 800-895-4654
info@itpa.com
www.itpa.com
Rudy Niswanger, Chairman
Ryan Hochmiller, Vice Chairman
The International Truck Parts Association was organized as a not-for-profit association to promote, foster, and improve relationships among sellers and buyers of trucks and truck surplus products and other parties.
Founded in 1974

24508 **Irrigation Association**
8280 Willow Oaks Corp. Dr.
Suite 400
Fairfax, VA 22031-4507
703-536-7080; Fax: 703-536-7019
info@irrigation.org
www.irrigation.org
Deborah Hamlin, Chief Executive Officer
Rebecca J. Bayless, Finance Director
Brad Binzer, Operations Coordinator
Anne Blankenbiller, Senior Communications Manager
Janie C. Hakim, Membership Manager
Membership organization for irrigation equipment and system manufacturers, dealers, distributors, designers, consultants, contractors and end users.
1600 Members
Founded in 1949

24509 **Jewelry Industry Distributors Association**
703 Old Route 422 West
Butler, PA 16001
jidainfo@gmail.com
www.jidainfo.com
Facebook
Bill Esslinger, President
Chris Gaber, Vice President
Richard Livesay, Treasurer
Sets standards of service and facilitates the exchange of information of all types among members in order to improve business, maximize opportunities, and minimize risks.
Founded in 1946

24510 **Machinery Dealers National Association**
315 S Patrick Street
Alexandria, VA 22314
703-836-9300
800-872-7807; Fax: 703-836-9303
office@mdna.org
www.mdna.org
Facebook, Twitter, LinkedIn
Mark Robinson, Executive Vice President
Will Keys, Accounting Manager
Joyce Fitzgerald, Administration Director
Represents dealers of used industrial equipment, providing members with business standards and development opportunities.
400 Members
Founded in 1941

24511 **Material Handling Equipment Distributors Association**
201 US Highway 45
Vernon Hills, IL 60061
847-680-3500; Fax: 847-362-6989
connect@mheda.org
www.mheda.org
Facebook, Twitter, LinkedIn, Google+
Liz Richards, CEO
Jamie Aiwohi, Financial Manager
Kathy Cotter, Membership Manager
Susan Freibrun, Education/Meeting Manager
Cindy Thoren, Project Manager
The Material Handling Equipment Distributors Association is the only national association dedicated solely to improving the proficiency of the independent material handling equipment distributor.
Founded in 1954

24512 **Metals Service Center Institute**
4201 Euclid Avenue
Rolling Meadows, IL 60008
847-485-3000; Fax: 847-485-3001
info@msci.org
www.msci.org
Facebook, Twitter, LinkedIn
MSCI is a trade association that supports and represents the elements of the metals value chain, including metals producers, distributors and processors.
400 Members
Founded in 1907

24513 **Michigan Distributors & Vendors Association**
120 N Washington Square
Suite 110 B
Lansing, MI 48933
517-372-2323; Fax: 517-372-4404
www.mdva.org
Steve LaPorte, Chairman
Polly T. Reber, President
The Michigan Distributors and Vendors Association (MDVA) is a non-profit, statewide business association representing two very significant business segments in the grocery and convenience products industry.
100 Members
Founded in 1991

24514 **Mississippi Beer Distributors Association**
4785 I-55 North, Suite 103
Jackson, MS 39206
601-987-9098
info@msbeer.com
msbeer.com
Adam Mitchell, President
The MBDA was established to represent and promote the beer wholesalers and beer industry within Mississippi.
12 Members
Founded in 1946

24515 **Motorcycle Industry Council**
2 Jenner Street
Suite 150
Irvine, CA 92618
949-727-4211; Fax: 949-727-3313
memberservices@mic.org
www.mic.org
Erik Pritchard, President & CEO
Eric Barnes, VP, Technical Programs
Scott Schloegel, SVP, Government Relations
The Motorcycle Industry Council (MIC) is a nonprofit, national trade association representing manufacturers and distributors of motorcycles, scooters, motorcycle/ATV parts and accessories and members of allied trades.
300 Members
Founded in 1914

24516 **NPTA Alliance**
330 N Wabash Avenue
Suite 2000
Chicago, IL 60611
312-321-4092
800-355-6782; Fax: 312-673-6736
npta@gonpta.com
www.gonpta.com
Twitter, LinkedIn, YouTube
Bob Forsberg, Chairman
Jan Gottesman, 1st Vice Chair
Scott Hider, 2nd Vice Chair
Matthew Bruno, EVP
John Hagrove, Treasurer
Representing distributors and suppliers of paper, packaging and facility supplies companies.
220 Members
Founded in 1903

24517 National Association of Chemical Distributors
1560 Wilson Boulevard
Suite 1100
Arlington, VA 22209

703-527-6223; Fax: 703-527-7747
www.nacd.com
Twitter, LinkedIn, Youtube

Eric R. Byer, President & CEO
Lucinda A. Schofer, COO
Lisa Vienna, Sr. Dir., Finance & Operations
Donna Thomas, Coordinator, Customer Services

The National Association of Chemical Distributors (NACD) is an international association of chemical distributor companies that purchase and take title of chemical products from manufacturers.
250 Members
Founded in 1971

24518 National Association of Electrical Distributors
1181 Corporate Lake Drive
St. Louis, MO 63132

888-791-2512
www.naed.org
Facebook, Twitter, LinkedIn, RSS, Youtube

Tom Naber, President & CEO
Michelle McNamara, COO/NAED Foundation Exec. Director
Ed Orlet, SVP, Gov't Affairs
Tim Dencker, VP, Finance

The main goal of the National Association of Electrical Distributors (NAED) is to establish the electrical distributor as an essential force in the electrical industry and the economy.
Founded in 1908

24519 National Association of Flour Distributors
nafdcontact@gmail.com
www.thenafd.com
Facebook, Twitter, LinkedIn

J. Gerard Burns, President
Nicholas DePalma, 1st VP
Ashley Koerner Turner, 2nd VP
Eric Metzendorf, Secretary/Treasurer

The mission of the NAFD is to serve the interests of its members who are engaged in the flour industry and those companies allied thereto by providing educational and networking opportunities.

24520 National Association of Sign Supply Distributors
1001 N Fairfax Street
Suite 301
Alexandria, VA 22314

703-836-4012; Fax: 703-836-8353
nassd@signs.org
www.signs.org/nassd
Facebook, Twitter, LinkedIn

Lori Anderson, President & CEO
Alicia Auerswald, VP, Marketing, Membership & Comms.
David Hickey, VP, Advocacy
Lisa Queeney, VP, Finance
Alison Kent, Director, Workforce Development

NASSD is a nonprofit trade association for organizations who are engaged in full-line sign supply distribution and who manufacture or supply commercial, neon and electrical sign products.

24521 National Association of Sporting Goods Wholesalers
1255 SW Prairie Trail Parkway
Ankeny, IA 50023-7068

515-334-1484; Fax: 515-334-1143
info@nasgw.org
www.nasgw.org
Twitter, LinkedIn, Flickr

Kenyon Gleason, President
Meg Pawelski, Director, Operations & Expo Manager
Easton Kuboushek, Program Manager
Donna Donovan, Financial Manager
Gregg Alexander, Communications Manager

Non-profit trade association of wholesalers, distributors and manufacturers. Serves as a liaison with other sporting goods associations.
400 Members
Founded in 1953

24522 National Association of Wholesaler - Distributors
1325 G Street NW
Suite 1000
Washington, DC 20005-3100

202-872-0885; Fax: 202-785-0586
naw@naw.org
www.naw.org
Facebook, Twitter, LinkedIn

Eric Hoplin, President & CEO

The NAW provides members with the opportunity for networking and benchmarking within the entire wholesale distribution industry. NAW also represents the wholesale distribution industry before Congress, the White House, and the judiciary on issues that cross the industry's many lines of trade.

24523 National Beer Wholesalers Association
1101 King Street
Suite 600
Alexandria, VA 22314

703-683-4300
800-300-6417
info@nbwa.org
www.nbwa.org
Facebook, Twitter, YouTube

Craig Purser, President/CEO
Grace Connolly, Executive Assistant
Lauren Kane, VP, Commmunications
Paul Pisano, SVP Industry Affairs & Gen. Counsel
Patti Rouzie, VP, Membership & Meetings

NBWA represents the interests of America's independent, licensed beer distributors which service every congressional district and media market in the country.
Founded in 1938

24524 National Electronics Service Dealers Association
PO Box 378
Hillsboro, TX 76645

817-921-9061
info@nesda.com
nesda.wildapricot.org

A national trade association for professionals in the business repairing consumer electronics equipment, appliances, and computers. NESDA has an e-mail group of over 600 members and manufacturers that communicate daily for information sharing.
Founded in 1950

24525 National Frozen & Refrigerated Foods Association
4755 Linglestown Road
Suite 300
Harrisburg, PA 17112

717-657-8601; Fax: 717-657-9862
nfra@nfraweb.org
www.nfraweb.org
Facebook, Twitter, LinkedIn, YouTube, Pinterest

H.V. Skip Shaw Jr., President/CEO
Jeff Rumachik, EVP/COO
Julie W. Henderson, VP, Communications
Jessica Scott, VP, Finance
Natalie Limm, Member Communications Manager

NFRA is a non-profit trade association representing all segments of the frozen and refrigerated foods industry.
450 Members
Founded in 1945

24526 National Grocers Association
1005 N Glebe Road
Suite 250
Arlington, VA 22201

703-516-0700; Fax: 703-516-0115
www.nationalgrocers.org
Facebook, Twitter, LinkedIn

Greg Ferrara, President/CEO

Works to advance understanding, trade, and cooperation in the food industry. Represents members interests before the government. Offers store planning, and engineering, training and advertising.
1.5M Members
Founded in 1982

24527 National Insulation Association
516 Herndon Parkway
Suite D
Herndon, VA 20170

703-464-6422; Fax: 703-464-5896
www.insulation.org
Facebook, Twitter, YouTube

Michele Jones, EVP/CEO
John Lamberton, President

The National Insulation Association (NIA) is a trade association representing the mechanical and specialty insulation industry.
Founded in 1953

24528 National Kitchen and Bath Association
687 Willow Grove Street
Hackettstown, NJ 07840-1731

800-843-6522
feedback@nkba.org
www.nkba.org
Facebook, Twitter, LinkedIn, Pinterest

Bill Darcy, CEO
Suzie Wiliford, EVP, Industry Relations & CSO
Pam Ryerson, Director, Marketplace
Nicole Young, Director, Finance & Administration

Protects the interests of members by fostering a better business climate. Offers Awards certification and conducts training schools and seminars.
14000 Members
Founded in 1963

24529 National Poultry and Food Distributors Association
2014 Osbourne Road
St. Marys, GA 31558

912-439-3603; Fax: 770-535-7385
cece@npfda.org
www.npfda.org
Facebook, Twitter, LinkedIn

Cece Corbin, President
Carol Lanham, Member Services & Development Dir.
Alina Cooper, Membership Relations & Comm. Dir.

A nationwide association that serves the needs of the poultry and food distribution and processing industries. Provides member services, cost cutting benefits and networking opportunities.

Sponsors Poultry Suppliers Showcase every January in Atlanta.
220 Members
Founded in 1967

24530 **National School Supply & Equipment Association**
8380 Colesville Road
Suite 250
Silver Spring, MD 20910

800-395-5550; Fax: 301-495-3330
www.edmarket.org
Facebook, Twitter, LinkedIn, Youtube

Jim McGarry, President/CEO
Adrienne Dayton, VP, Communications & Education
Karen Prince, VP, Membership & Operations
Joe Tucker, VP, Meetings & Events
Scott Beyer, Director, Sales & Development

The National School Supply and Equipment Association (NSSEA) is the leading trade organization for the educational products marketplace. NSSEA puts the collective experience of the most successful school industry business in the world at your fingertips.
1400+ Members
Founded in 1916

24531 **New York State Beer Wholesalers Association, Inc.**
119 Washington Avenue
Suite 3C
Albany, NY 12210

518-465-6115; Fax: 518-465-1907
nybeer@nybeer.org
www.nybeer.org

Bernie Schroeder, Chairman
Steven W. Harris, President
Sean Rose, Chairman Elect
Ed Keis, Treasurer
George Allen, Secretary

The New York State Beer Wholesalers Association, Inc. represents and protects the legislative and regulators interests of its members in state and local government. Their primary goal is to uphold the three-tier system in order to safeguard the industry's distribution standards.
44 Members
Founded in 1934

24532 **North American Association of Telecommunications Dealers**
131 NW First Avenue
DelRay Beach, FL 33444

561-266-9440; Fax: 561-266-9017

Rob Neuemeyer, Director
Arthur P Frierman, Associate Counsel

The North American Association of Telecommunications Dealers is a nonprofit organization of companies who provide telecom products to the business community and governments around the world. The NATD gives you access to the right kind of information, resources and business leaders, and provides you with unique opportunities to help grow your business.

24533 **North American Association of Floor Covering Distributors**
330 N Wabash Avenue
Suite 2000
Chicago, IL 60611

312-321-6836
800-383-3091; Fax: 312-673-6962
info@nafcd.org
www.nafcd.org
Facebook, Twitter, LinkedIn, Youtube

Kevin Gammonley, Executive Director
Elaura Dunning, Operations Coordinator
Lauren Willett, Marketing Manager
Robb Shrader, Sales Coordinator
Lindsey Kallai, Conference Manager

The North American Association of Floor Covering Distributors (NAFCD) was organized to foster trade and commerce for those having a business, financial or professional interest as wholesale distributors or manufacturers of floor coverings and allied products.

24534 **North American Association of Uniform Manufacturers & Distributors**
12732 Harney Street
Omaha, NE 68154

402-639-0498
www.naumd.com

Steve Zalkin, President
Kathy Fedman-Zalkin, Chief Marketing Officer
Jackie Rosselli-Verrico, Director of Communications
Rick Levine, Director of Development

The North American Association of Uniform Manufacturers & Distributors (NAUMD) is a trade association representing the interests of all parties in the uniform & image apparel industry.
Founded in 1933

24535 **North American Building Material Distribution Association**
330 N Wabash Avenue
Suite 2000
Chicago, IL 60611

312-321-6845
888-747-7862; Fax: 312-644-0310
info@nbmda.org
www.nbmda.org
Facebook, Twitter, LinkedIn, YouTube

Tom O'Neill, President
Emily Vella, President-Elect
Matt Huber, Vice President
Wayne Moriarty, Treasurer

NBMDA develops and promotes the effectiveness of distribution processes to improve member profitability and growth.
Founded in 1952

24536 **North American Meat Institute**
1150 Connecticut Ave, NW
12th floor
Washington, DC 20036

202-587-4200; Fax: 202-587-4303
info@meatinstitute.org
www.meatinstitute.org
Facebook, Twitter, LinkedIn, YouTube

Warren Panico, Chairman
Julie Anna Potts, President and CEO
Christl McCarthy, Executive Administrator
Rosemary Mucklow, Director Emeritus Consultant
William Sessions, Director, Product Marketing

Provides its members unique one-one-one assistance resolving regulatory issues. Mission is to be proactive and responsive in serving members both individually and collectively.
400 Members
Founded in 2012

24537 **North American Wholesale Lumber Association**
330 N Wabash Avenue
Suite 2000
Chicago, IL 60611

312-321-5133
800-527-8258; Fax: 312-673-6838
info@nawla.org
www.nawla.org
Facebook, Twitter, LinkedIn

Scott Parker, Executive Director
Mark Swets, Senior Manager
Elizabeth Conner, Senior Coordinator

Supports the wholesale lumber industry. Publishes monthly NAWLA Bulletin that includes industry and association news, and produces the NAWLA Traders Market, an annual trade show bringing together over 1500 manufacturers and wholesale lumber traders at the premier event in the forest products industry. NAWLA also produces a variety of educational programs designed to enhance professionalism in the lumber industry.
600+ Members
Founded in 1893

24538 **Northeast Spa & Pool Association**
6B S Gold Drive
Hamilton, NJ 08691

609-689-9111; Fax: 609-689-9110
info@nespapool.org
www.nespapool.org
Facebook, Twitter

Dominick Mondi, Executive Director
Trish McCormick, Manager, The Pool & Spa Show
Kelly McKelvey, Director, Communications/Marketing
Pat Cava, Manager, Education
B.J. Hann, Membership Director

The Northeast Spa & Pool Association offers members access to business tools, discounts, certification courses, and breaking news in the industry.
Founded in 1958

24539 **Outdoor Power Equipment Aftermarket Association**
1605 King Street
Alexandria, VA 22314

703-549-7608; Fax: 703-549-7609
infoOPEAA@opeaa.org
www.opeaa.org

Britton Harold, President
Donald (Donny) Desjarlais, Vice President
Beth Skove, Secretary/Treasurer
Brandon Martin, Director
Marla Popkin, Director

Businessmen dedicated to promoting the use of aftermarket parts in outdoor power equipment, as well as trade in the industry.
85 Members
Founded in 1986

24540 **Outdoor Power Equipment and Engine Service Association**
37 Pratt Street
Suite 2
Essex, CT 06426-1159

860-767-1770; Fax: 860-767-7932
info@opeesa.com
www.opeesa.com
Twitter, LinkedIn

Alex Wyatt, President
Lorri Sklar, Vice President, Annual Meeting
Nancy Cueroni, Executive Director
Arin Monroe, Secretary/Treasurer

Association made up of distributors and manufacturers of outdoor power equipment and air-cooled gas and diesel engines.
100+ Members

24541 **Pacific-West Fastener Association**
3020 Old Ranch Parkway
Suite 300
Seal Beach, CA 90740

562-799-5509; Fax: 562-684-0695
info@pac-west.org
www.pac-west.org
Facebook, Twitter, LinkedIn, YouTube, Instagram, Google+

Vickie Lester, Executive Director
Jamie Adams, Meetings & Events Manager
Claudia Schuetze, Membership Manager

An organization dedicated to the fastener industry.
Founded in 2009

24542 PeopleForBikes Coalition
2580 55th Street
Suite 200
Boulder, CO 80301

info@peopleforbikes.org
peopleforbikes.org

Jenn Dice, President & CEO
Erik Esborg, VP, Finance
Kerri Salazar, Manager, Membership & Development

PeopleForBikes (PFB) Coalition merged with the Bicycle Product Suppliers Association in 2019. Together, they are a coalition of supplies of bicycles, parts, accessories, and services.

24543 Pet Industry Distributors Association
3465 Box Hill Corp. Center Drive
Suite H
Abingdon, MD 21009

443-640-1060; Fax: 410-569-3340
pida@kingmgmt.org
www.pida.org
LinkedIn

Celeste Powers, President
Marci Hickey, Dir, Meetings & Member Services
Debbie Dacre, Director, Finance
Nina Bull, Association Coordinator

Represents wholesaler-distributors of pet products, providing training and education to members.
190 Members
Founded in 1968

24544 Petroleum Equipment Institute
PO Box 2380
Tulsa, OK 74101-2380

918-494-9696; Fax: 918-491-9895
www.pei.org
Facebook, Twitter, LinkedIn, Google+

Scott Boorse, Dir, Technical Programs
J. Rex Brown, Dir, Information Services
Teresa Farmer, Membership Manager
Rick Long, EVP & General Counsel
Julie Shank, Marketing & Event Manager

Members are makers and distributors of equipment used in service stations, bulk plants and other petroleum marketing facilities.
1600+ Members
Founded in 1951
Mailing list available for rent: 1600 names at $275 per M

24545 Pool & Hot Tub Alliance
2111 Eisenhower Avenue
Suite 500
Alexandria, VA 22314

703-838-0083
memberservices@phta.org
www.apsp.org
Facebook, Twitter, LinkedIn, Youtube, Flickr, RSS

Sabeena Hickman, President/CEO
Jeanne Mendelson, VP, Education & Events
Linda Beza, Sr. Director, Finance & Admin.
Jennifer Hatfield, VP, Government Affairs

The world's largest international trade association for the swimming pool, spa, and hot tub industry. It works with regulatory and legislative bodies to ensure that their codes, ordinance, and legislation are written to the safest and most current standards. The association's mission is to ensure consumer safety and enhance the business success of its members. Formerly The Association of Pool & Spa Professionals.
Founded in 1956

24546 Professional Beauty Association
7755 E Gray Road
Scottsdale, AZ 85260
480-281-0424
info@probeauty.org
www.probeauty.org
Facebook, Twitter, LinkedIn, YouTube, Instagram, Pinterest

Peggy Sue Schmoldt, Chair
Sydney Berry, Vice Chair
Steve Sleeper, Executive Director
Rachel Molepske, Manager of Leadership Operations
Steve Wilkerson, Chief Financial Officer

The Professional Beauty Association (PBA) is a nonprofit trade association that represents the interests of the professional beauty industry from manufacturers and distributors to salons and spas. PBA offers business tools, education, advocacy, networking and more to improve individual businesses and the industry as a whole.

24547 Quality Bakers of America Cooperative
1275 Glenlivet Drive
Suite 100
Allentown, PA 18106-3107
info@qba.com
www.qba.com

Don Cummings, VP, Finance
Marc Knox, EVP & COO
Jonathan J. Fink, Counsel
R. Jack Lewis, Jr., Chairman
J.R. Paterakis, President

Providing members with access to sources of appropriate services in order to maintain the highest product quality and sanitation standards.
35 Members
Founded in 1922

24548 Safety Equipment Distributors Association
1901 N Moore Street
Suite 808
Arlington, VA 22209-1762

703-525-1695; Fax: 703-528-2148
safetyequipment.org
Facebook, Twitter, LinkedIn

Charles D. Johnson, President
Cristine Fargo, VP, Operations & Technical Services
Dan Glucksman, Director, Public Affairs
Lydia Baugh, Director, External Affairs
Tanya Brosnan, Manager, Member Services

The Saftey Equipment DistributorAssociation is the trade association comprised of companies that distribute safety equipmant and related products and services. Its member companies are leaders in the distribution of personal protective equipment to a broad spectrum of users, including general industry, construction, municipalities, utilities, schools and laboratories.
300 Members
Founded in 1968

24549 Security Hardware Distributors Association
105 Eastern Avenue
Suite 104
Annapolis, MD 21403

410-940-6346; Fax: 410-263-1659
info@shda.org
www.shda.org

David Swartz, President
Robert Justen, Vice President
Lance Johnsen, Treasurer
John M. Burke, Immediate Past President
Amy Luckado, Executive Director

The mission of the Security Hardware Distributors Association is to continually improve, through education and services, the proficiency of Security Distributors in order that they are the most effective and efficient conduit to the marketplace.

24550 Souvenir Wholesale Distributors Association (SWDA)
32770 Arapahoe Road
#132-155
Lafayette, CO 80026

888-599-4474; Fax: 888-589-7610
swdabod1@gmail.com
www.souvenircentral.org
Facebook, LinkedIn

Angie Rohnke, President
Libby Smith, Vice President
Blake Shewmaker, Secretary/Treasurer
Brenda Taylor, Immediate Past President

Companies distributing local view scenic post cards and souvenirs in North America and the Caribbean.
110 Members
Founded in 1973

24551 Textile Care Allied Trades Association
4023 N Armenia Avenue
Suite 270
Tampa, FL 33607
813-348-0075; Fax: 813-348-0077
luci@tcata.org
www.tcata.org
Facebook, Twitter, LinkedIn

Leslie Schaeffer, Chief Executive Officer
Luci Ward, Business Manager

The Textile Care Allied Trades Association (TCATA) is an international trade association representing manufacturers and distributors of dry-cleaning and laundry equipment and supplies. It is the only trade association dedicated exclusively to the interests of the allied trades.

24552 The Association for Manufacturing Technology
7901 Jones Branch Drive
Suite 900
McLean, VA 22102-4206

703-893-2900
800-524-0475; Fax: 703-893-1151
amt@amtonline.org
www.amtonline.org
Facebook, Twitter, LinkedIn, YouTube

Douglas K. Woods, President
Rebecca Stahl, Chief Financial Officer
Kimberly L. Brown, Member Services Director
Peter R. Eelman, VP, Exhibitions & Business Dev
Andrea Kuchinski, Dir, Marketing & Communications

Represents and supports the U.S.-based manufacturing technology industry, including distributors, producers and service providers. The association offers essential programs and services that help its members gain global recognition.

24553 The Vision Council
225 Reinekers Lane
Suite 700
Alexandria, VA 22314

703-548-4560
866-826-0290; Fax: 703-548-4580
info@thevisioncouncil.org
www.thevisioncouncil.org
Facebook, Twitter, LinkedIn, YouTube

Kenneth T. Daley, Chair
Ashley Mills, CEO
Brian Carroll, COO/CFO
Manali Patel, Controller
Maureen Beddis, VP, Marketing & Communications

Serving as the global voice for vision care products and services, The Vision Council represents the manufacturers and suppliers of the optical industry.
263 Members
Founded in 1999

24554 **United Producers Formulators & Distributors Association**
5564 Ridgemoor Drive
Braselton, GA 30517

770-965-6972
www.upfda.com
Facebook, Twitter

Scott Riley, President
Thomas Forshaw, IV, Vice President
Cisse Spragins, Secretary & Treasurer
Karen Furgiuele, Immediate Past President

Members are firms which are directly involved in formulating and distributing products or equipment to the pest control industry.

24555 **United Veterinary Services Association**
3465 Box Hill Corp. Center Drive
Suite H
Abingdon, MD 21009

443-640-1040; Fax: 410-569-3340
casey@kingmgmt.org
www.uvsa.net
Facebook, Twitter, LinkedIn

Jackie King, Executive Director/Secretary
Heather Lester, CMP, Dir, Meetings & Member Services
Hugh Webster, Legal Counsel
Casey Joseph, Association Coordinator
Debbie Dacre, Director of Finance

The UVSA was established as the national trade organization for businesses engaged in the distribution of animal health products. Formerly known as the American Veterinary Distributors Association.
Founded in 1976

24556 **Water & Sewer Distributors of America**
7400 E Orchard Road
Suite 375S
Greenwood Village, CO 80111

303-339-0070; Fax: 720-496-4974
info@wasda.com
www.wasda.com
Facebook, Twitter, LinkedIn, YouTube

Bill Driskill, President
Kevin King, President-Elect
Nate Peirce, Secretary & Treasurer
Kevin A. Murphy, Past President
Nicole A. Singleton, Executive Director

WASDA's mission is to promote the waterworks/wastewater products distribution industry, and to further improve the image and professionalism of WASDA and its member companies.
100+ Members
Founded in 1979

24557 **Wholesale Florists and Florist Suppliers of America**
105 Eastern Avenue
Suite 104
Annapolis, MD 21403-3300

410-940-6580
info@wffsa.org
www.wffsa.org
Facebook, Twitter, LinkedIn

Patricia A Lilly, EVP

To provide networking and business opportunities to wholesale distributors and floral suppliers.
1.3M+ Members
Founded in 1926

24558 **Wine and Spirits Wholesalers of America**
805 15th Street NW
Suite 1120
Washington, DC 20005

202-371-9792; Fax: 202-789-2405
info@wswa.org
www.wswa.org
Facebook, Twitter, LinkedIn, YouTube, RSS

Michelle L. Korsmo, President/CEO
Jo Moak, SVP and General Counsel
Daweson Hobbs, SVP, Govt. Affairs
Heather Calio, VP, State Affairs
Ali Gormley, VP, Fed. Affairs

This association is comprised of wholesale distributors of domestic and imported wine and distilled spirits.
350+ Members
Founded in 1943

24559 **World Millwork Alliance**
10047 Robert Trent Jones Parkway
New Port Richey, FL 34655-4649

727-372-3665; Fax: 727-372-2879
mail@worldmillworkalliance.com
www.worldmillworkalliance.com
Twitter, LinkedIn

Rosalie Leone, President/CEO
Tim Hicks, Chair
Carl McKenzie, 1st Vice Chair
Jeff Williams, Treasurer

WWA provides leadership, education, promotion, networking, and advocacy to, and for, the millwork distribution industry.
Founded in 1963

Newsletters

24560 **AMD Insider**
10047 Robert Trent Jones Parkway
New Port Richey, FL 34655-4649

727-372-3665
800-786-7274; Fax: 727-372-2879
www.amdweb.com

Rosalie Leone, Chief Executive Officer
Terry Rodimer, Operations and Assistant to the CEO
Jeff Burton, Director of Codes & Standards
Miguel Rivera-Sanchez, Director of Education
William G Simon, Graphics Coordinator

The Association of Millwork Distributors online newsletter providing information for and about the millwork distribution industry.
Frequency: Monthly

24561 **APSP Multibrief**
Pool & Hot Tub Alliance
2111 Eisenhower Avenue
Suite 500
Alexandria, VA 22314

703-838-0083
memberservices@phta.org
www.apsp.org

Sabeena Hickman, President/CEO
Jeanne Mendelson, VP, Education & Events
Linda Beza, Sr. Director, Finance & Admin.
Jennifer Hatfield, VP, Government Affairs

APSP MultiBrief is a free weekly e-mail news service available to both APSP members and nonmembers. Each week subscribers are informed of the week's most important news stories for the pool, spa, and hot tub industry.
Frequency: Weekly
Founded in 1956

24562 **CUTTING EDGE**
Outdoor Power Equipment Aftermarket
1605 King Street
Alexandria, VA 22314

703-549-7608; Fax: 703-549-7609
infoOPEAA@opeaa.org
www.opeaa.org

Britton Harold, President

Businessmen dedicated to promoting the use of aftermarket parts in outdoor power equipment, as well as trade in the industry.
Cost: $25.00
Frequency: Quarterly
Founded in 1986

24563 **Door & Hardware IndustryWatch**
Door & Hardware Institute
2001 K Street NW
Washington, DC 20006

202-367-1134; Fax: 202-367-2134
www.dhi.org

Sharon Newport, CAE, Chief Executive Officer
Laura Frye Weaver, VP, Education
Adam Berkshire, Communications/Marketing Manager

Electronic newsletter with the latest industry news and trends.
Frequency: Biweekly

24564 **Emerging Business**
Master Security Company
PO Box 6661
Roanoke, VA 24017-0661

FAX 540-982-8407

Debra Napier, Publisher

Provides summary on articles of interest to small business owners, consultants corner, highlights services available pertaining to alternative financing of growing businesses.
6 Pages
Frequency: Quarterly

24565 **FMI Daily Lead**
Food Marketing Institute
2345 Crystal Drive
Suite 800
Arlington, VA 22202

202-452-8444; Fax: 202-425-4519
www.fmi.org
Facebook, Twitter, LinkedIn

Leslie Sarasin, President/CEO

Newsletter that provides a daily briefing on top stories in food retailing and wholesaling.
1500 Members
Frequency: Daily
Founded in 1892

24566 **GAWDA Connection**
Gases and Welding Distributors Association
1 Oakwood Boulevard
Suite 195
Hollywood, FL 33020

844-251-3219; Fax: 954-367-7790
gawda@gawda.org
www.gawda.org

Abydee Butler Moore, President
Robert Anders, 1st Vice President
Gary Halter, 2nd Vice President

Provides relevant news and technology information.
775 Members
Frequency: Quarterly
Founded in 1945

24567 **GMDC Connect Infocasts**
Global Market Development Center

1115 Elkton Drive
Suite 204
Colorado Springs, CO 80907

719-576-4260
info@gmdc.org
www.gmdc.com

Patrick Spear, President/CEO
Keith Wypyszynski, VP, Member Services
James Engstrom, VP, Finance & Administration
Michael Winterbottom, VP, IT/Chief Technology Officer

GMDC Connect Infocast addresses important General Merchandise topics, important Health Beauty Wellness topics and news from GMDC.
Frequency: Weekly
Founded in 1970

24568 **ISD Insider**
International Sealing Distribution Association
180 Admiral Cochrane Drive
Suite 370
Annapolis, MD 21401

410-940-6344; Fax: 410-263-1659
info@isd.org
www.isd.org

Josh Hale, President
Brian Despain, VP
Amy Luckado, Executive Director

The association's newsletter is devoted to topics affecting business, training, and technology within the industry, with feature articles from industry experts.
Frequency: Quarterly

24569 **Insider**
MacLean Hunter
4 Stamford Forum
Stamford, CT 06901-3253

FAX 203-325-8423

Vanessa Grey, Publisher
Adrienne Toth, Editor

A shopping center industry newsweekly. Each issue contains critical information concerning retailer news, new development items, agent announcements and new tenant listings.
Cost: $250.00
6 Pages
Frequency: Monthly

24570 **MDNA News**
Machinery Dealers National Association
315 S Patrick Street
Alexandria, VA 22314

703-836-9300
800-872-7807; Fax: 703-836-9303
office@mdna.org
www.mdna.org
Facebook, Twitter, LinkedIn

Mark Robinson, Executive Vice President
Will Keys, Accounting Manager
Joyce Fitzgerald, Administration Director

This newsletter is a valuable source of information about MDNA events and programs, industry news, updates on chapter activities, government programs, and auctions.
400 Members
Frequency: 6x/Year
Founded in 1941

24571 **MHEDA Connection**
Material Handling Equipment Distributors Assoc
201 US Highway 45
Vernon Hills, IL 60061

857-680-3500; Fax: 847-362-6989
connect@mheda.org
www.mheda.org

Liz Richards, CEO
Jamie Aiwohi, Financial Manager
Kathy Cotter, Marketing Director
Susan Freibrun, Education/Meeting Manager
Cindy Thoren, Project Manager

The MHEDA Connection is a semi-monthly newsletter distributed to members and its associates on the 1st and the 15th of the month.
Frequency: Semi-Monthly
Founded in 1954

24572 **NACD News Brief**
National Association of Chemical Distributors
1560 Wilson Boulevard
Suite 1100
Arlington, VA 22209

703-527-6223; Fax: 703-527-7747
www.nacd.com

Eric R. Byer, President/CEO
Lucinda A. Schofer, COO
Lisa Vienna, Sr. Dir., Finance & Operations
Donna Thomas, Coordinator, Customer Services

The NACD News Brief is a biweekly e-mail newsletter outlining the key legislative and regulatory actions affecting NACD members and reporting on other key industry activity.
250 Members
Frequency: Bi-Weekly
Founded in 1971

24573 **NAW Report**
National Association of Wholesalers-Distributors
1325 G Street NW
Suite 1000
Washington, DC 20005-3100

202-872-0885; Fax: 202-785-0586
naw@naw.org
www.naw.org

Eric Hoplin, President & CEO

Information on regulation, industry research and programs for distributors and wholesalers.

24574 **NBMDA Economic Outlook Report**
N.A. Building Material Distribution Association
330 N Michigan Avenue
Suite 2000
Chicago, IL 60611

312-321-6845
888-747-7862; Fax: 312-644-0310
info@nbmda.org
www.nbmda.org
Facebook, Twitter, LinkedIn

Tom O'Neill, President
Emily Vella, President-Elect
Matt Huber, Vice President
Wayne Moriarty, Treasurer

This report correlates macroeconomic data to specific product categories directly related to the building material industry
Frequency: Quarterly
Founded in 1952

24575 **NSPI News**
National Spa and Pool Institute
2111 Eisenhower Ave
Suite 500
Alexandria, VA 22314-4679

703-838-0083
800-323-3996; Fax: 703-549-0493
www.theapsp.org

Bill Weber, President
Jack Cregol, CEO

24576 **National Wholesaler Association**
251 W Renner Road
#102
Richardson, TX 75080-1318

FAX 972-470-0134

Don Akerman, Publisher

Offers products, new or old, marketing, distribution expertise, customer analysis, positioning, advertising, promotion planning. Accepts advertising.
Frequency: Quarterly

24577 **News & Views**
Bearing Specialists Association

630-858-3838; Fax: 630-790-3095
info@bsahome.org
www.bsahome.org
LinkedIn

Jim Scardina, President
Michel Bouchard, Vice President

Monthly newlsetter of BSA, the forum to enhance networking and knowledge sharing to promote the sale of bearings through authorized distributors. Available to members only.
100 Members
Frequency: E-Newlsetter for Members
Circulation: 400
Founded in 1966

24578 **North American Wholesale Lumber Association Bulletin**
North American Wholesale Lumber Association
330 N Wabash Avenue
Suite 2000
Chicago, IL 60611

312-321-5133
800-527-8258; Fax: 312-673-6838
info@nawla.org
www.nawla.org

Scott Parker, Executive Director
Mark Swets, Senior Manager
Elizabeth Conner, Senior Coordinator

Newsletter published by North American Wholesale Lumber Association.
Frequency: Monthly

24579 **Unlocked**
Security Hardware Distributors Association
105 Eastern Avenue
Suite 104
Annapolis, MD 21403

410-940-6346; Fax: 410-263-1659
info@shda.org
www.shda.org

David Swartz, President
Robert Justen, Vice President
Lance Johnsen, Treasurer
John M. Burke, Immediate Past President
Amy Luckado, Executive Director

The SHDA newsletter, Unlocked, provides members with the latest news about the association and its educational events and programs as well as trends and news about security hardware distribution.
Frequency: Monthly

24580 **Winning in Washington-NAW Annual Report**
National Association of Wholesalers-Distributors
1725 K St Nw
Washington, DC 20006-1401

202-349-7300; Fax: 202-331-7442
www.nawc.org

Peter L Cook, Executive Director

Activities of the National Association of Wholesalers and Distributors.

Magazines & Journals

24581 **AFI**
AFI Communications

2455 E Sunrise Boulevard
Suite 916
Fort Lauderdale, FL 33304-3112

FAX 954-561-4129

Andrew Molchan, President
Bob Lesmeister, Managing Editor

Edited for professional firearm retailers. Editorial emphasis is on new products, new industry and new sales programs for distributors and retailers. Also covers management level trends for manufacturers and wholesalers. Other features include New Products, Archery, Andy's Industry Insights and more.
Circulation: 23,930

24582 AQUA International Magazine
Pool & Hot Tub Alliance
2111 Eisenhower Avenue
Suite 500
Alexandria, VA 22314

703-838-0083
memberservices@phta.org
www.apsp.org

Sabeena Hickman, President/CEO
Jeanne Mendelson, VP, Education & Events
Linda Beza, Sr. Director, Finance & Admin.
Jennifer Hatfield, VP, Government Affairs

This full-color magazine is written and edited by industry experts with a keen awareness of the issues on the minds of professionals.
Frequency: Monthly
Founded in 1956

24583 ASA Materials Market Digest
American Supply Association
1200 Arlington Heights Road
Itasca, IL 60143

630-467-0000; Fax: 630-467-0001
info@asa.net
www.asa.net

Mike Adelizzi, CEO
Aaron Scheiwe, CFO

Available monthly via e-mail to all members of ASA, the ASA Materials Market Digest is designed to keep readers informed of important trends and recent changes in the industry.
Frequency: Monthly
Founded in 1969

24584 AVEM Resource Guide
Association of Vacuum Equipment Manufacturers
201 Park Washington Court
Falls Church, VA 22046-4527

703-538-3543; Fax: 703-241-5603
aveminfo@avem.org
www.avem.org

Dawn M. Shiley, Executive Director
Clay Tyeryar, Assistant Treasurer
Kim Fay, Data Analyst
Harry Buzzerd, Management Counsel

Buyers guide listing products and services offered by AVEM member companies. Items include systems, pumps, instrumentation, hardware and deposition components.
Frequency: Yearly
Founded in 1969

24585 American Wholesale Marketers Association
Ameican Wholesale Marketers Association
2750 Prosperity Ave
Suite 530
Fairfax, VA 22031-4338

703-208-3358
800-482-2962; Fax: 703-573-5738
www.cdaweb.net

Scott Ramminger, President
Traci Carneal, Editor-in-Chief
Joan Fay, Associate Publisher

Information on candy, chewing gum, tobacco, HBC, general merchandise, snack foods and related items.
Printed in 4 colors on glossy stock

24586 Beer Perspectives
National Beer Wholesalers Association
1101 King Street
Suite 600
Alexandria, VA 22314-2965

703-683-4300
info@nbwa.org
www.nbwa.org
Facebook, Twitter

Craig Purser, President/CEO

Trade association for beer wholesalers. Provides government and public affairs outreach as well as education and training for its wholesaler members.
2200 Pages
Founded in 1938

24587 Chemical Distributor
National Association of Chemical Distributors
1565 Wilson Boulevard
Suite 1100
Arlington, VA 22209

703-527-6223; Fax: 703-527-7747
www.nacd.com
Facebook, Twitter, LinkedIn, YouTube

Eric R. Byer, President/CEO
Lucinda A. Schofer, COO
Lisa Vienna, Sr. Dir., Finance & Operations
Donna Thomas, Coordinator, Customer Services

The industry's magazine that is published nine times a year and highlights members' news, Association and industry activity, and provides business information useful to chemical distributors.
250 Members
Frequency: 9x/Year
Founded in 1971

24588 Cleaner Times
Cleaning Equipment Trade Association
1000 Nix Road
Little Rock, AR 72211-3235

800-525-7038
info@adpub.com
www.cleanertimes.com

Charlene Yarbrough, Publisher
Jim McMurry, CEO
Chuck Prieur, Cleaner Times Magazine
Debbie Murray, Managing Director, CETA
Jim O'Connell, President, CETA

Magazine published by the Cleaning Equipment Trade Association for members.
Frequency: Monthly
Founded in 1990

24589 Distributor's Link
4297 Corporate Sq
Naples, FL 34104-4754

239-643-2713
800-356-1639; Fax: 239-643-5220
leojcoar@linkmagazine.com
www.linkmagazine.com

Maryann Marzocchi, President
Tracey Lumia, Advertising Sales
Michael T Wrenn, Marketing Manager

Information aimed at the fastener distributors nationwide.
Cost: $45.00
300 Pages
Frequency: Quarterly
Circulation: 50000
Founded in 1975

24590 Door Security & Safety Magazine
Door & Hardware Institute
2001 K Street NW
Washington, DC 20006

202-367-1134; Fax: 202-367-2134
www.dhi.org
Facebook, Twitter, LinkedIn

Sharon Newport, CAE, Chief Executive Officer
Laura Frye Weaver, VP, Education
Adam Berkshire, Communications/Marketing Manager

Offers information and articles from the industry's only publication dedicated solely to the architectural openings industry.
Frequency: Monthly

24591 Employment Guide
Bureau of National Affairs
1801 S Bell St
Arlington, VA 22202-4501

703-341-3000
800-372-1033; Fax: 800-253-0332
customercare@bna.com
www.bnabooks.com
Facebook, Twitter, LinkedIn

Paul N Wojcik, CEO

An easy-to-read, practical reference guide to a broad range of employment topics, designed for the small to medium sized organization.
Cost: $745.00
Founded in 1929

24592 Essentials Magazine
National School Supply & Equipment Association
8380 Colesville Road
Suite 250
Silver Spring, MD 20910

800-395-5550; Fax: 301-495-3330
www.edmarket.org
Facebook, Twitter, LinkedIn

Jim McGarry, President/CEO
Adrienne Dayton, VP, Communications & Education
Karen Prince, VP, Membership & Operations
Joe Tucker, VP, Meetings & Events
Scott Beyer, Director, Sales & Development

Essentials Magazine targets all facets of the educational industry from contemporary, bite-sized studies and statistics, to timely feature articles, as well as NSSEA member interviews, product press releases, and business updates. Mailed quarterly to over 3,000 members.
Frequency: Quarterly

24593 ISEA Protection Update
Safety Equipment Distributors Association
1901 N Moore Street
Suite 808
Arlington, VA 22209-1762

703-525-1695; Fax: 703-528-2148
lbaugh@safetyequipment.org
safetyequipment.org

Lydia Baugh, Editor

This newsletter is offered to Safety+Health readers to raise awareness about the important role products play in keeping workers safe.
Frequency: Quartely

24594 Insulation Outlook
National Insulation Association
516 Herndon Parkway
Suite D
Herndon, VA 20170

703-464-6244; Fax: 703-464-5896
editor@insulation.org
www.insulation.org

Michele Jones, EVP/CEO
John Lamberton, President

Contains information on new products, industry trends, asbestos abatement and installation practices.
Frequency: Monthly
Circulation: 7000
Founded in 1973

24595 **International Gaming and Wagering Business**
BNP Media
PO Box 1080
Skokie, IL 60076-9785

847-763-9534; Fax: 847-763-9538
igwb@halldata.com

James Rutherford, Editor
Lynn Davidson, Marketing
Tammie Gizicki, Director

Focuses on business strategy, legislative information, food service and promotional concerns.
Frequency: Monthly
Circulation: 25000

24596 **Licensing Book**
Adventure Publishing Group
1107 Broadway
Suite 1204
New York, NY 10010-1512

212-575-4510; Fax: 212-575-4521
www.licensingbook.com

Judy Basis, Publisher
Mathew C Scheiner, Editor-in-Chief
Owen Shorts, Owner

Licensing in successful retailing, licensed product merchandising in various aspects.
Cost: $48.00
40 Pages
Frequency: Monthly
Founded in 1983

24597 **Licensing International**
WFC
3000 Hadley Rd
South Plainfiel, NJ 07080-1183

908-668-4747; Fax: 732-769-1711
info@wfcinc.com
www.wfcinc.com

Theodore Pytlar, VP
Kimberly Calabrese, Production Manager

Business merchandising magazine serving the licensing industry at all levels. Publishes whole foods magazine.
Cost: $70.00
64 Pages
Frequency: Monthly
Circulation: 14,933

24598 **MHEDA Journal**
Material Handling Equipment Distributors Assoc
201 US Highway 45
Vernon Hills, IL 60061-2398

857-680-3500; Fax: 847-362-6989
connect@mheda.org
www.themhedajournal.org
Facebook, Twitter, LinkedIn

Duncan Murphy, President
Liz Richards, Executive Vice President
Kathy Cotter, Marketing Director
Natalie Cobb, Networking & Communications

The MHEDA journal is the official magazine of the association.
Frequency: Quarterly
Founded in 1954

24599 **Material Handling Wholesaler**
Specialty Publications International
801 Bluff Street
PO Box 725
Dubuque, IA 52004-725

563-557-4495
877-638-6190; Fax: 563-557-4499
circulation@mhwmag.com
www.mhwmag.com

Dean Millius, General Manager
Cathy Murphy, Editor
Sharon Dague, Account Executive
Cathy Murphy, Contributing Editor

Published for used and new material handling equipment dealers, parts suppliers, manufacturers reps, repair shops, and brokers includes articles on issues, conventions, products and people that impact the industry.
Cost: $31.00
Frequency: Monthly
Circulation: 27000
Founded in 1979
Printed in 4 colors on newsprint stock

24600 **NSPI Business Owners Journal**
National Spa and Pool Institute
2111 Eisenhower Ave
Suite 500
Alexandria, VA 22314-4679

703-838-0083
800-323-3996; Fax: 703-549-0493
www.nspi.org

Bill Weber, President

A resource service offered by the national spa and pool inst. published four times a year. Contains concise, pertinent and useful information of critical importance to business owners throughout the year, this journal delivers information that is easily applied to a business, including more than 100 action alerts and ideas, and 25 to 30 how-to articles, advisories and reports. Covers such topics as ways to cash flows; ways to save and defer taxes; how to sell and buy a business.
Founded in 1956

24601 **New Equipment Digest**
Penton Media
1300 E 9th St
Suite 316
Cleveland, OH 44114-1503

216-696-7000; Fax: 216-696-6662
information@penton.com
www.penton.com

Jane Cooper, Marketing
Dave Madonia, Associate Publisher/eMedia
Robert F King, Editor
Garnetta Russell, Ad Services Manager
Bobbie Macy, Circulation Manager

Serves the general industrial field which includes manufacturing, processing, engineering services, construction, transportation, mining, public utilities, wholesale distributors, educational services, libraries and governmental establishments.
Frequency: Monthly
Circulation: 206164
Founded in 1936

24602 **PHTA Resource Guide**
Pool & Hot Tub Alliance
2111 Eisenhower Avenue
Suite 500
Alexandria, VA 22314

703-838-0083
memberservices@phta.org
www.apsp.org

Sabeena Hickman, President/CEO
Jeanne Mendelson, VP, Education & Events
Linda Beza, Sr. Director, Finance & Admin.
Jennifer Hatfield, VP, Government Affairs

A full-colour print and digital guide to all resources and services.
Founded in 1956

24603 **Paper & Packaging**
NPTA Alliance
330 N Wabash Avenue
Suite 2000
Chicago, IL 60611

312-321-4092
800-355-6782; Fax: 312-673-6736
www.gonpta.com

Covers association news, industry news, industry reports, industry events, new products, personnel updates and business articles for management and sales representatives and much more.
Cost: $120.00
Frequency: Quarterly
Circulation: 6000

24604 **Plumbing Engineer**
TMB Publishing
1838 Techny Ct
Northbrook, IL 60062-5474

847-564-1127; Fax: 847-564-1264
www.tmbpublishing.com

Tom M Brown, President
Cate Brown, Production Manager

Over 400 plumbing products from approximately 250 manufacturers.
Frequency: Monthly
Circulation: 26104
ISSN: 0192-171X
Founded in 1973
Printed in 4 colors

24605 **Supply House Times**
Reed Business Information
1050 IL Route 83
Suite 200
Bensenville, IL 60106

630-616-0200
800-323-4958; Fax: 630-288-8686
www.supplyht.com

Patricia Lenius, Managing Editor
Scott Franz, Publisher
Kevin Hackney, Marketing Coordinator
Ashley Anderson, Associate Editor
George Zebrowski, Group Publisher

For plumbing, heating, air conditioning and piping wholesalers
Cost: $92.00
62 Pages
Frequency: Monthly
Founded in 1958
Printed in 4 colors on glossy stock

24606 **TED Magazine**
National Association of Electrical Distributors
1181 Corporate Lake Drive
St. Louis, MO 63132

888-791-2512
www.tedmag.com

Tom Naber, President/CEO
Michelle McNamara, COO/NAED Foundation Executive Dir
Ed Orlet, SVP, Gov't Affairs
Tim Dencker, VP, Finance

TED magazine (The Electrical Distributor) is NAED's premier trade publication. With the latest industry news as well as articles and research ranging from sales to voice-data-video, TED magazine is necessary reading for all electrical distributors.
Cost: $40.00
Frequency: Monthly
Founded in 1908

24607 **The MTS Journal**
American Society of Appraisers

11107 Sunset Hill Road
Suite 310
Reston, VA 20190

703-478-2228
800-272-8258; Fax: 703-742-8471
asainfo@appraisers.org
www.appraisers.org

Johnnie White, Chief Executive Officer
Bonny Price, Chief Operating Officer
Joseph Noselli, Chief Financial Officer
Todd Paradis, Chief Marketing Officer
Sarah Sebastian, Director of Membership Development

Organization provides education and accreditation for appraisers.
Cost: $45.00
48 Pages
Frequency: Quarterly
Founded in 1939

24608 Welding & Gases Today
Gases and Welding Distributors Association
1 Oakwood Blvd.
Suite 195
Hollywood, FL 33020

844-251-3219; Fax: 954-367-7790
gawda@gawda.org
gawdamedia.com

Abydee Butler Moore, President
Gary Halter, 1st Vice President
Robert Anders, 2nd Vice President

The official journal of the Gases and Welding Distributors Association.
775 Members
Frequency: Quarterly
Founded in 1945

Trade Shows

24609 AED Summit
600 22nd~Street
Suite 220
Oak Brook, IL 60523

630-574-0650
800-388-0650; Fax: 630-574-0132
info@aednet.org
www.aednet.org
Facebook, Twitter, LinkedIn

Toby Mack, President & CEO
Bob Henderson, Executive Vice President & COO
Dave Gordon, Publisher/Vice President of Sales
Kim Phelan, Executive Editor

The AED Summit provides a pure networking opportunity with both dealers and their manufacturer partners. It also offers high quality, high class, professional education content for executives and managers.
700 Members
Frequency: Annual

24610 APDA Annual Convention
Appliance Parts Distributors Association
P.O. Box 31816
Charlotte, NC 28231

Home Page: www.apda.com

Dave Cook, President
Steve Falconi, Vice President
Rachel Nystrom, Treasurer
Bob Goldberg, Legal Counsel

The APDA is an association of independent businesses that aspire to provide the highest level of quality, service, support and information to its customers and suppliers in order to make its value indispensable to the parts distribution channel.

24611 ASCDI Winter Conference
Association of Service and Computer Dealers Int'l
131 NW First Avenue
Delray Beach, FL 33444

561-266-9016; Fax: 561-431-6302
www.ascdi.com

Joe Marion, President

The ASCDI conferences provide a great forum for networking with others in the industry, meeting old friends, and making new contacts. The winter conference offers an opportunity to learn about the latest technology trends, meet with leading vendors, and gain a competitive edge in the IT market. The conference is conducted by following Green Meeting Practices.
Founded in 1981

24612 AVDA Annual Conference
2105 Laurel Bush Road
Suite 200
Bel Air, MD 21015

443-640-1040; Fax: 443-640-1086
www.avda.net
Facebook, Twitter, LinkedIn, YouTube

George Henriques, Chairman
Mary Pat Thompson, President
Ben Coe, President-Elect

The AVDA annual conference is a three-day program of information and educational sessions featuring industry and outside speakers on a variety of timely business and industry issues and topics.
Frequency: Annual
Founded in 1976

24613 AWFS Fair
Association of Woodworking & Furnishings Suppliers
2400 E Katella Avenue
Suite 340
Anaheim, CA 92806

323-838-9440
800-946-2937; Fax: 323-838-9443
www.awfs.org
Facebook, Twitter, LinkedIn, YouTube

Daniel Hershbeger, President
Rob Howell, Secretary/Treasurer

The AWFS Fair is the largest industry show in the United States.
Frequency: Biennial

24614 AWMA Real Deal Expo
American Wholesale Marketers Association
2750 Prosperity Avenue
Suite 530
Fairfax, VA 22031

703-208-3358
800-482-2962; Fax: 703-573-5738

Scott Ramminger, President/CEO
Robert Pignato, VP Marketing/Industry Affairs

Annual show of 4500 manufacturers and suppliers of confectionery, tobacco, snack foods, juice, novelties and technology and allies to the industry.
Frequency: March

24615 American Nursery & Landscape Association Convention
American Nursery & Landscape Association
1000 Vermont Avenue NW
Suite 300
Washington, DC 20005-3922

202-789-2900; Fax: 202-789-1893

Peter Orum, President
Robert J Dolibois, Executive Director

Serves firms who grow, sell or use plants. ANLA advocates the industry's interests before government and provides its members with unique business knowledge essential to long-term growth and profitability.
Frequency: July

24616 AmericanHort Cultivate
AmericanHort
2130 Stella Court
Columbus, OH 43215

614-487-1117; Fax: 614-487-1216
hello@americanhort.org
www.americanhort.org
Facebook, Twitter, Instagram

Ken Fisher, President & CEO

Cultivate is the largest all-industry trade show and conference for the horticulture industry.
Founded in 2014

24617 Annual Industry Summit
FPDA Motion & Control Network
180 Admiral Cochrane Drive
Suite 370
Annapolis, MD 21401

410-940-6347
info@fpda.org
www.fpda.org
Facebook, Twitter, LinkedIn, YouTube

Kevin Kampe, President
Amy Luckado, Executive Director
Dominique Abney, Director, Marketing/Sales
Donald Smith, Chief Financial Officer
Courtney Truelove, Manager, Membership/Programs

This conference is held each spring and is designed especially for industry decision-makers and opinion-leaders, and is focused on business opportunities, economic and industry trends, leadership development and channel efficiencies.
300+ Members
Frequency: Annual
Founded in 1974

24618 Annual Selfcare Summit
Global Market Development Center
1115 Elkton Drive
Suite 204
Colorado Springs, CO 80907

719-576-4260
info@gmdc.org
www.gmdc.com

Patrick Spear, President/CEO
Keith Wypeszynski, VP, Member Services
James Engstrom, VP, Finance & Administration
Michael Winterbottom, VP, IT/Chief Technology Officer

GMDC is the premier non-profit global trade association dedicated to serving General Merchandise and Health Beauty retailers, wholesalers and suppliers. GMDC promotes critical connectivity to grow and expand member companies by uniting members through business building events and opportunities and enriching their thinking through education and training; consumer and business insights; and information resources.
Frequency: Annual
Founded in 1970

24619 Atlantic City Pool & Spa Show
Northeast Spa & Pool Association
6B S Gold Drive
Hamilton, NJ 08691

609-689-9111; Fax: 609-689-9110
info@nespapool.org
www.nespapool.org

Dominick Mondi, Executive Director
Trish McCormick, Manager, The Pool & Spa Show
Kelly McKelvey, Director, Communications/Marketing

Pat Cava, Manager, Education
B.J. Hann, Membership Director

The Atlantic City show is one of the industry's largest, offering a large trade show and business and technical seminars.
Frequency: Annual

24620 **BSA Convention**
Bearing Specialists Association

630-858-3838; Fax: 630-790-3095
info@bsahome.org
www.bsahome.org
LinkedIn

Jim Scardina, President
Michel Bouchard, Vice President

The world's premier bearing industry event for authorized distributors of bearing products and services and the manufacturers of those products.
100 Members
Frequency: Annual
Founded in 1966

24621 **BSA Winter Meeting**
Bearing Specialists Association

630-858-3838; Fax: 630-790-3095
info@bsahome.org
www.bsahome.org
Facebook, Twitter, LinkedIn

Jim Scardina, President
Michel Bouchard, Vice President

BSA committees address many important issues and association projects at the Winter Meeting.
Frequency: Annual

24622 **CBBD Annual Convention**
1415 L Street
Suite 890
Sacramento, CA 95814

916-441-5402
800-952-8308; Fax: 916-441-0713
assn@cbbd.com
www.cbbd.com
Facebook, Twitter, LinkedIn

Victoria G Horton, President
Becky Stolberg, Vice President
Rhonda Stevenson, Marketing & Public Affairs Director

The California Beer and Beverage Distributors host this annual convention for professionals in the industry.
100+ Members
Frequency: Annual

24623 **CBSA Annual Convention**
Copper and Brass Servicenter Association
6734 W 121st Street
Overland Park, KS 66209

913-396-0697
cbsahq@copper-brass.org
www.copper-brass.org

Susan Avery, Executive Director
Liz Novak, Senior Director

Distributors (service centers) of fabricated copper and copper alloy products (sheet, plate, coil, rod, bar tube, etc) and their brass mill suppliers.
78 Members
Founded in 1951

24624 **CTDA Total Solutions Plus**
Ceramic Tile Distributors Association
800 Roosevelt Road
Building C, Suite 312
Glen Ellyn, IL 60137

630-545-9415; Fax: 630-790-3095
info@ctdahome.org
www.ctdahome.org

Rudy Llerena, President
Steve Vogel, VP
Robert DeAngelis, Treasurer
Bill Ives, Legal Counsel
Rick Church, Executive Director

The Total Solutions Plus conference was formerly known as the CTDA Management Conference between 2002 to 2009. The event is host to the biggest industry leaders and features educational sessions and exhibits.
450 Attendees
Frequency: Annual

24625 **California Compliance Symposium**
Professional Beauty Association
7755 E Gray Road
Scottsdale, AZ 85260

480-281-0424
info@probeauty.org
www.probeauty.org

Beth Hickey, Chair
Sydney Berry, Vice Chair
Steve Sleeper, Executive Director
Rachel Molepske, Manager of Leadership Operations
Steve Wilkerson, Chief Financial Officer

The California Compliance Symposium is a business education event produced for all sectors of the beauty industry.
Frequency: Annual
Founded in 1953

24626 **DHI conNextions**
Door & Hardware Institute
2001 K Street NW
Washington, DC 20006

202-367-1134; Fax: 202-367-2134
www.dhi.org

Sharon Newport, CAE, Chief Executive Officer
Laura Frye Weaver, VP, Education
Adam Berkshire, Communication/Marketing Manager

The Door & Hardware Institute (DHI) is the only professional association dedicated to the Architectural Openings Industry. DHI represents the North American openings marketplace as the advocate and primary resource for information, professional development and certification.
4200 Attendees
Frequency: Annual

24627 **Distribution Management Conference & Expo**
Healthcare Distribution Alliance
901 N Glebe Road
Suite 1000
Arlington, VA 22203

703-787-0000; Fax: 703-812-5282
www.hda.org
Facebook, Twitter, LinkedIn

Chester Davis, Jr., President/CEO
Ann W. Bittman, EVP/COO
Elizabeth A. Gallenagh, General Counsel/SVP, Supply Chain

Provides the latest information on the most important topics affecting healthcare distribution.
Frequency: Annual

24628 **EDspaces**
National School Supply & Equipment Association
8380 Colesville Road
Suite 250
Silver Spring, MD 20910

800-395-5550; Fax: 301-495-3330
www.ed-spaces.com
Facebook, Twitter, LinkedIn

Jim McGarry, President/CEO
Adrienne Dayton, VP, Communications & Education
Karen Prince, VP, Membership & Operations
Joe Tucker, VP, Meetings & Events
Scott Beyer, Director, Sales & Development

EDspaces is the country's premier event for manufacturers, distributors and service providers offering products to educational facilities.
Frequency: Annual/Oct-Nov

24629 **EMDA Industry Showcase**
FEWA-AIMRA
PO Box 1347
Iowa City, IA 52244

319-354-5156; Fax: 319-354-5157
www.edma.net
Facebook, Twitter, LinkedIn

Patricia A Collins, Executive VP

Annual convention and 130 exhibits of equipment, supplies and services for independent wholesale-distributors and independent manufacturer's representatives of shortline and specialty farm equipment, light industrial tractors, lawn and garden tractors, turf care equipment, estate and park maintenance equipment.
600 Attendees
Frequency: November

24630 **Executive Conference**
Health Industry Distributors Association
310 Montgomery Street
Alexandria, VA 22314

703-549-4432
www.hida.org

Matthew J. Rowan, President/CEO
Elizabeth Hilla, SVP
Linda Rouse O'Neill, VP, Govt. Affairs
Balvinder Bains, VP, Finance & Operations

Hundreds of distributor and manufacturer executives gather for the Executive Conference, which consists of networking, interactive education, strategic planning, and industry discussions.
Frequency: Annual
Founded in 1902

24631 **FPDA Annual Network Symposium**
FPDA Motion & Control Network
180 Admiral Cochrane Drive
Suite 370
Annapolis, MD 21401

410-940-6347
info@fpda.org
www.fpda.org

Kevin Kampe, President
Amy Luckado, Executive Director
Dominique Abney, Director, Marketing/Sales
Donald Smith, Chief Financial Officer
Courtney Truelove, Manager, Membership/Programs

This meeting is designed for key management and emerging leaders, and focuses on business and product technologies & trends, industry standards & certification, the FPDA Young Executives development and supporting the needs of participants in the FPDA E-Networks program.
300+ Members
Frequency: Annual
Founded in 1974

24632 **General Merchandise Conference**
Global Market Development Center
1115 Elkton Drive
Colorado Springs, CO 80907

719-576-4260
info@gmdc.org
www.gmdc.com

Patrick Spear, President/CEO
Keith Wypyszyski, VP, Member Services
James Engstrom, VP, Finance & Administration
Michael Winterbottom, VP, IT/Chief Technology Officer

Annual conference which has Controlled Casual Conference appointments between wholesal-

ers/retailers and the suppliers, business sessions, roundtables and workshops.
Frequency: Annual/June
Founded in 1970

24633 **Global Pet Expo (PIDA)**
Pet Industry Distributors Association
3465 Box Hill Corp. Center Drive
Suite H
Abingdon, MD 21009

443-640-1060; Fax: 410-569-1060
pida@kingmgmt.org
globalpetexpo.org

Celeste Powers, President
Marci Hickey, Dir, Meetings & Member Services
Debbie Dacre, Director, Finance
Nina Bull, Association Coordinator

Containing 3,600 booths and 1,174 exhibiting companies, including 300 international exhibitors.
3,000 Attendees
Frequency: March
Founded in 1968

24634 **IAPD Annual Convention**
International Association of Plastics Distribution
6734 W 121st Street
Overland Park, KS 66209

913-345-1005; Fax: 913-345-1006
iapd@iapd.org
www.iapd.org

Susan E. Avery, CAE, CEO
Liz Novak, CAE, Sr. Dir., Advocacy & Publications
Dave Blackhurst, Dir., Membership & Sales
Kerrie Moore, Finance Manager
Whitney Nelson, Dir., Meetings & Events

This three-day convention is where the best and the brightest of the plastics distribution industry come together to focus on the future of the industry.
Frequency: Annual/September
Founded in 1956

24635 **IFDA Distribution Solutions Conference**
1660 International Drive
Suite 550
McLean, VA 22102

703-532-9400; Fax: 703-880-7117
www.ifdaonline.org

John Tracy, Chairman
Craig Hoskins, Vice Chairman
Mark Harman, Treasurer
Mark S. Allen, President/CEO

Workshops, assemblies, facility tours and an exposition are featured. Educational programming features many practitioners who sahre knowledge to be applied to various operations. Practical information for transportation, information technology, human resources and more.
Frequency: October
Founded in 2003

24636 **ISA Product Show & Conference**
Industry Supply Association
3435 Concord Road
Unit 21889
York, PA 17402

866-460-2360
info@isapartners.org
www.isapartners.org
Facebook, Twitter, LinkedIn, YouTube

Ed Gerber, President/CEO

This is the premier event for anyone in the maintenance, repair, operations and production (MROP) industry. Any MROP distributor, manufacturer/supplier, manufacturers' representative or industry service provider is welcome to attend.
Frequency: Annual

24637 **ITPA Seasonal Meeting**
International Truck Parts Association
1720 10th Avenue S
Suite 4, PMB 199
Great Falls, MD 59405

866-346-5692; Fax: 800-895-4654
info@itpa.com
www.itpa.com
Facebook, Twitter, LinkedIn, YouTube

Rudy Niswanger, Chairman
Ryan Hochmiller, Vice Chairman

Meetings are held each Winter, Fall, and Spring and provide outstanding educational programs, one-on-one meetings with the industry's suppliers, and product trade show and excellent networking opportunities.
Founded in 1974

24638 **Industry Advancement Summit**
Security Hardware Distributors Association
105 Eastern Avenue
Suite 104
Annapolis, MD 21403

410-940-6346; Fax: 410-263-1659
info@shda.org
www.shda.org

David Swartz, President
Robert Justen, Vice President
Lance Johnsen, Treasurer
John M. Burke, Immediate Past President
Amy Luckado, Executive Director

The Annual Industry Advancement Summit is hosted by the Security Hardware Distributors Association. The four-day event offers networking opportunities, educational sessions and one-on-one appointments to exhibit recent product innovations.
Frequency: Annual
Founded in 1970

24639 **International Pool, Spa & Patio Expo**
Pool & Hot Tub Alliance
2111 Eisenhower Avenue
Alexandria, VA 22314

703-838-0083
memberservices@phta.org
www.apsp.org

Sabeena Hickman, President/CEO
Jeanne Mendelson, VP, Education & Events
Linda Beza, Sr. Director, Finance & Admin.
Jennifer Hatfield, VP, Government Affairs

The International Pool, Spa & Patio Expo is a trade show for the pool, spa and backyard living industry that provides current market updates, info on cutting edge technology and trends.
Frequency: Annual

24640 **Irrigation Show**
Irrigation Association
2880 Willow Oaks Corp. Dr.
Suite 400
Fairfax, VA 22031-4507

703-536-7080; Fax: 703-536-7019
info@irrigation.org
www.irrigation.org

Deborah M. Hamlin, Chief Executive Officer
Rebecca J. Bayless, Finance Director
Brad Binzer, Operations Coordinator
Anne Blankenbiller, Senior Communications Manager
Janie C. Hakin, Membership Manager

The Irrigation Show is the industry's one-stop event. Discover innovations on the show floor and in technical sessions, make connections with industry experts, business partners and peers; and build expertise with targeted education and certification.
1600 Members
Founded in 1949

24641 **MDVA Convention**
Michigan Distributors & Vendors Association
120 N Washington Square
Suite 110 B
Lansing, MI 48933

517-372-2323; Fax: 517-372-4404
www.mdva.org

Steve LaPorte, Chairman
Polly T. Reber, President

Annual meeting for individuals involved in the grocery and convenience products industry.
Frequency: Annual

24642 **Mid-America Pool & Spa Show**
Association of Pool & Spa Professionals
2111 Eisenhower Avenue
Alexandria, VA 22314

703-838-0083
memberservices@apsp.org
www.apsp.org

Sabeena Hickman, President/CEO
Jeanne Mendelson, VP, Education & Events
Linda Beza, Sr. Director, Finance & Admin.
Jennifer Hatfield, VP, Government Affairs

The Mid-America show offers a large trade show and business and technical seminars.
Frequency: Annual

24643 **Midwinter Executive Conference**
Food Marketing Institute
2345 Crystal Drive
Suite 800
Arlington, VA 22202

202-452-8444; Fax: 202-425-4519
www.fmi.org

Leslie Sarasin, President/CEO

The FMI Midwinter Executive Conference is an extraordinary opportunity for networking and discussion. The event is invitation-only, and it attracts food industry leaders for an outstanding program that addresses the major challenges and opportunities ahead.
1500 Members
Frequency: Annual

24644 **NACD Annual Meeting**
National Association of Chemical Distributors
1560 Wilson Boulevard
Suite 1100
Arlington, VA 22209

703-527-6223; Fax: 703-527-7747
www.nacd.com

Eric R. Byer, President/CEO
Lucinda A. Schofer, COO
Lisa Vienna, Sr. Dir., Finance & Operations
Donna Thomas, Coordinator, Customer Services

NACD's Annual Meeting is the premier meeting and annual expo for chemical distributor professionals. It provides an opportunity to exchange ideas with other top executives in the chemical distribution industry, attend sessions that focus on the latest products and trends affecting the industry, and visit with a variety of exhibitors at the Vendor Expo.
250 Members
Founded in 1971

24645 **NAFD Annual Convention**
National Association of Flour Distributors

nafdcontact@gmail.com
www.thenafd.com
Facebook, Twitter, LinkedIn

Erin M. Ruhl, Chairman
Mark R. Munroe, President
Nicholas DePalma, 1st VP
Ashley Koerner Turner, 2nd VP
Eric Metzendorf, Secretary/Treasurer

The NAFD sponsors an all-industry forum addressing strategic issues impacting the flour distribution supply chain. In addition to manufacturer and distributor decision makers, senior-level ingredient suppliers participate in the NAFD three-day meeting.
Frequency: Annual

24646 NAHAD Annual Meeting & Conference
Association For Hose and Accessories Distribution
180 Admiral Cochrane Drive
Suite 370
Annapolis, MD 21401

410-940-6350
info@nahad.org
www.nahad.org

Molly Alton Mullins, Executive Vice President
Amy Luckado, VP, Operations
Jessica Hauser Forte, Director of Conferences
Catherine Wiafe, Director, Communications/Marketing
Donald Smith, CFO

This event provides an opportunity to meet with leaders in the industry with direct purchasing power.

24647 NARM Annual Convention
National Association of Recording Merchandisers
9 Eves Drive
Suite 120
Marlton, NJ 08053-3138

856-596-2221; Fax: 856-596-3268

Linda M Still, Director Meetings/Conventions
James Donio, President

Containing 39 booths. Featuring AFIM.
2,100 Attendees
Frequency: March

24648 NASSD Distributor Management Conference
National Association of Sign Supply Distributors
1001 N Fairfax Street
Suite 301
Alexandria, VA 22314

703-836-4012; Fax: 703-836-8353
nassd@signs.org
www.signs.org/nassd
Facebook, Twitter, LinkedIn

Lori Anderson, President & CEO

Held each March, this 1-1/2 day conference features general speaker sessions and roundtable discussions. It is the perfect opportunity to get updated on the association's activities and trends in the industry.
Frequency: Annual

24649 NASSD Executive Summit
National Association of Sign Supply Distributors
1001 N Fairfax Street
Suite 301
Alexandria, VA 22314

703-836-4012; Fax: 703-836-8353
nass@signs.org
www.signs.org/nassd
Facebook, Twitter, LinkedIn

Lori Anderson, President & CEO

The meeting features distributor & manufacturer-only sessions, general speaker sessions, and roundtable discussions. A highlight of the meeting is the executive conferences which are an opportunity for distributors and manufacturers to meet one-on-one to discuss new sales and business opportunities.
Frequency: Annual

24650 NAUMD Convention & Expo
N.A. Association of Uniform Manufacturers & Dist.
336 West 37th Street
Suite 370
New York, NY 10018

212-736-3010; Fax: 212-736-3013
www.naumd.com
Facebook, Twitter, LinkedIn, you Tube

Steve Zalkin, President

The NAUMD Convention & Expo provides a tremendous opportunity for attendees to expand their horizons, sales, and profits. Attendees can find new customers and suppliers for every uniform and imagewear need.
Founded in 1933

24651 NBMDA Annual Convention
N.A. Building Material Distribution Association
300 N. Michigan Avenue
Suite 2000
Chicago, IL 60611

312-321-6845
888-747-7862; Fax: 312-644-0310
info@nbmda.org
www.nbmda.org
Facebook, Twitter, LinkedIn, you Tube

Tom O'Neill, President
Emily Vella, President-Elect
Matt Huber, Vice President
Wayne Moriarty, Treasurer

The NBMDA provides an opportunity to connect with other leaders in the Building Material Distribution industry. This annual convention is designed to be an executive-level interchange between trading partners coupled with stimulating educational opportunities.
Frequency: Annual
Founded in 1952

24652 NBWA Annual Convention
National Beer Wholesalers Association
1101 King Street
Suite 600
Alexandria, VA 22314

703-683-4300
800-300-6417
info@nbwa.org
www.nbwa.org
Facebook, Twitter

Craig Purser, President/CEO
Grace Connolly, Executive Assistant
Lauren Kane, VP, Communications
Paul Pisano, SVP Industry Affairs & Gen. Counsel
Patti Rouzie, VP, Membership & Meetings

Designed to provide valuable education programs and important networking opportunities for the beer industry. Featuring speakers and seminars on a number of topics of importance to beer distributors .
2500 Attendees
Frequency: Fall

24653 NFRA Annual Executive Conference
National Frozen & Refrigerated Foods Association
4755 Linglestown Road
Suite 300
Harrisburg, PA 17112

717-657-8601; Fax: 717-657-9862
nfra@nfraweb.org
www.nfraweb.org

H.V. Skip Shaw Jr., President/CEO
Jeff Rumachik, EVP/COO
Julie W. Henderson, VP, Communications
Jessica Scott, VP, Finance
Natalie Limm, Member Communications Manager

NFRA's annual Executive Conference brings the industry's leading decision-makers together to discuss recent industry trends, innovations, challenges and opportunities.
150 Attendees

24654 NGA Annual Convention & Supermarket Synergy Showcase
National Grocers Association
1005 North Glebe Road
Suite 250
Arlington, VA 22201

703-516-0700; Fax: 703-516-0115
www.nationalgrocers.org
Facebook, Twitter, LinkedIn, you Tube

Greg Ferrara, President/CEO

Each year, attendees are presented with timely and relevant general sessions and workshops, exciting special events and numerous networking opportunities to speak with other industry executives.
Frequency: Annual

24655 NIA Annual Convention
National Insulation Association
516 Herndon Parkway
Suite D
Herndon, VA 20170

703-464-6422; Fax: 703-464-5896
www.insulation.org
Facebook, Twitter, LinkedIn

Michele Jones, EVP/CEO
John Lamberton, President

The NIA Annual Convention is the premier gathering for the mechanical and industrial insulation industry, offering valuable and unique educational and industry sessions, networking opportunities, and entertaining evening events.
Frequency: Annual
Founded in 1953

24656 NPFDA Annual Convention & Showcase
National Poultry and Food Distributors Association
2014 Osbourne Road
St. Marys, GA 31558

912-439-3603; Fax: 770-535-7385
cece@npfda.org
www.npfda.org

Cece Corbin, Executive Director
Carol Lanham, Member Services & Development Dir.
Alina Cooper, Membership Relations & Comm. Dir.

NPFDA's largest event is held during the International production and Processing Expo (IPPE) in Atlanta, GA.
Frequency: Annual

24657 National Frozen & Refrigerated Foods Convention
4755 Linglestown Road Suite 300
PO Box 6069
Harrisburg, PA 17112

717-657-8601; Fax: 717-657-9862
info@nfraweb.org
www.nfraweb.org
Facebook, LinkedIn

H.V. Skip Shaw Jr., President/CEO
Jeff Rumachik, EVP/COO
Julie W. Henderson, VP, Communications
Jessica Scott, VP, Finance
Natalie Limm, Member Communications Manager

NFRA is a non-profit trade association representing all segments of the frozen and refrigerated foods industry.
450 Members
1200 Attendees
Founded in 1945

24658 **Paper (Conference)**
The NPTA Alliance
330 N Wabash Avenue
Suite 2000
Chicago, IL 60611

312-321-4092
800-355-6782; Fax: 312-673-6736
PaperMeets@afandpa.org
www.papermeets.com

Chandler Davis, Event Services & Information

An annual networking event for paper industry executives provides sessions on current issues and offers networking opportunities.
Frequency: Annual
Founded in 2010

24659 **Paper Distribution Conference (PDC)**
The NPTA Alliance
330 N Wabash Avenue
Suite 2000
Chicago, IL 60611

312-321-4092
800-355-6782; Fax: 312-673-6736
www.gonpta.com
Facebook, Twitter

Bob Forsberg, Chairman
Jan Gottesman, 1st Vice Chair
Scott Hider, 2nd Vice Chair
Matthew Bruno, EVP
John Hagrove, Treasurer

The annual Paper Distribution Conference is a prime opportunity to generate business leads, strengthen relationships with trading partners, develop leadership skills and more.
Frequency: Annual
Founded in 1959
Mailing list available for rent

24660 **Paper2020**
NPTA
330 N. Wabash Avenue
Suite 2000
Chicago, IL 60611

312-321-4092
800-355-6782; Fax: 312-673-6736
npta@gonpta.com
www.gonpta.com
Facebook, Twitter

Bob Forsberg, Chairman
Jan Gottesman, 1st Vice Chair
Scott Hider, 2nd Vice Chair
Matthew Bruno, EVP
John Hagrove, Treasurer

Held in conjunction with the American Forest & Paper Association, features timely sessions on emerging issues, corporate suites, and networking opportunities.
Frequency: March
Founded in 1903
Mailing list available for rent

24661 **Petroleum Equipment Institute Women Conference**
Petroleum Equipment Institute
PO Box 2380
Tulsa, OK 74101-2380

918-494-9696; Fax: 918-491-9895
www.pei.org

Scott Boorse, Dir, Technical Programs
J. Rex Brown, Dir, Information Services
Teresa Farmer, Membership Manager
Rick Long, EVP & General Counsel
Julie Shank, Marketing & Event Manager

The PEI Women annual conference provides industry insight, career leadership ideas and networking opportunities.
Frequency: Annual

24662 **Post Card & Souvenir Distributors Assocation Trade Show**
Post Card & Souvenir Distributors Association
2105 Laurel Bush Road
Suite 200
Bel Air, MD 21015

443-640-1055; Fax: 443-640-1031
www.postcardcentral.org

Maria Linton, Manager

Containing 110 booths and 80 exhibits.
175 Attendees
Frequency: September
Founded in 1973

24663 **PowerClean Trade Show and Convention**
Cleaning Equipment Trade Association
11450 U.S. Highway 380
Suite 130, #289
Cross Roads, TX 76227

800-441-0111; Fax: 704-635-7363
info@ceta.org
www.ceta.org

Debbie Murray, Managing Director
Jim Welch, President

CETA hosts the industry's premier PowerClean annual trade show and convention. PowerClean provides members with the opportunity to showcase new products, technology, and exchange ideas with industry peers, develop and present educational and certification programs, increase awareness and promotion of the industry and products and facilitate the development of unified positions when working with government agencies to set industry standards and policies.
300 Members
Founded in 1990

24664 **Read Deal Expo Convention**
American Wholesale Marketers Association
1128 16th Street NW
Washington, DC 20036-4808

202-463-2124
800-482-2962; Fax: 202-467-0559
www.cdaweb.net

Robert Pignato, VP Marketing/Industry Affairs

The AWMA Real Deal Expo and Convention is the country's oldest and largest show for distributors of confections, snacks and convenience products. The AWMA is the only national trade association working on behalf of the convenience products distribution market. AWMA members also include companies and individuals from across the distribution channel, retailers, brokers, manufacturers and others allied to the industry.
Frequency: February

24665 **Staff Development for Educators (SDE) National Conference**
National School Supply & Equipment Association
8380 Colesville Road
Suite 250
Silver Spring, MD 20910

800-395-5550; Fax: 301-495-3330
www.edmarket.org
Facebook, Twitter, LinkedIn, YouTube

Jim McGarry, President/CEO
Adrienne Dayton, VP, Communications & Education
Karen Prince, VP, Membership & Operations
Joe Tucker, VP, Meetings & Events
Scott Beyer, Director, Sales & Development

Source new products, engage in industry discussion, hear perspectives on current issues, and network with existing and potential new suppliers, distributors and purchasing influencers.
Frequency: Annual/July

24666 **Supply Chain Conference**
Food Marketing Institute
2345 Crystal Drive
Suite 800
Arlington, VA 22202

202-452-8444; Fax: 202-425-4519
www.fmi.org
Facebook, Twitter, LinkedIn

Leslie Sarasin, President/CEO

Explores the latest trends in distribution, technology and its application, supply chain collaboration, transportation efficiencies, leadership and management skills. Informal discussion groups give attendees an opportunity to discuss ideas and challenges with their peers.
Frequency: Annual

24667 **TCATA Annual Management & Educational Conference**
Textile Care Allied Trades Association
4023 N Armenia Avenue
Suite 270
Tampa, FL 33607

813-348-0075; Fax: 813-348-0077
luci@tcata.org
www.tcata.org
Facebook, Twitter, LinkedIn

Russ Poy, Conference Chair
Luci Ward, Business Manager

Trade show consisting of well-organized business programs and unique networking opportunities.
Frequency: Annual

24668 **UVSA Annual Conference**
United Veterinary Services Association
3465 Box Hill Corp. Center Drive
Suite H
Abingdon, MD 21009

443-640-1040; Fax: 410-569-3340
casey@kingmgmt.org
www.uvsa.net

Jackie King, Executive Director/Secretary
Heather Lester, CMP, Dir, Meetings & Member Services
Hugh Webster, Legal Counsel
Casey Joseph, Association Coordinator
Debbie Dacre, Director of Finance

The UVSA was established as the national trade organization for businesses engaged in the distribution of animal health products. Formerly known as the American Veterinary Distributors Association.
Founded in 1976

24669 **Washington Summit**
Health Industry Distributors Association
310 Montgomery Street
Alexandria, VA 22314

703-549-4432
rowan@hida.org
www.hida.org
Facebook, Twitter, LinkedIn

Matthew J. Rowan, President/CEO
Elizabeth Hilla, SVP
Linda Rouse O'Neill, VP, Govt. Affairs
Balvinder Bains, VP, Finance & Operations

The HIDA Washington Summit gives distributor executives and their manufacturer partners a crucial opportunity to discuss key issues of the industry with Congress.
Frequency: Annual
Founded in 1902

Directories & Databases

24670 **A-Z Wholesale Source Directory**
Sutton Family Communications & Publishing Company
155 Sutton Lane
Fordsville, KY 42343
270-740-0870
www.suttoncompliance.com
Theresa Sutton, Editor
Lee Sutton, General Manager
Print-out from database of wholesalers, manufacturers, distributors, importers and close-out houses. Database is updated daily to guarantee the most current and up-to-date sources available.
Cost: $550.00
1M Pages

24671 **American Warehouse Association and Canadian Association of Warehousing**
Association For Logistics Outsourcing
2800 South River Road
Suite 260
Chicago, IL 60018-6003
847-813-4699; Fax: 847-813-0115
email@iwla.com
www.iwla.com
Joel Hioland, President
Alex Glan, VP/CEO
Nearly 700 warehouse firms with over 2,000 locations specializing in storage, distribution, and third party logistics.

24672 **American Wholesalers and Distributors Directory**
Gale/Cengage Learning
10650 Toebben Drive
Independence, KY 41051
800-354-9706
800-877-4253; Fax: 800-487-8488
gale.galeord@cengage.com
www.gale.com
Facebook, Twitter, LinkedIn
Patrick C Sommers, President
Discover more than 27,000 large and small wholesalers and distributors throughout the US and Puerto Rico.
Frequency: Annual
ISBN: 1-414434-21-9

24673 **Complete Directory of Close-outs and Super-buys**
Sutton Family Communications & Publishing Company
155 Sutton Lane
Fordsville, KY 42343
270-740-0870
www.suttoncompliance.com
Theresa Sutton, Editor
Lee Sutton, General Manager
Print-out from database of wholesalers, manufacturers, distributors, importers and close-out houses. Database is updated daily to guarantee the most current and up-to-date sources available.
Cost: $67.50
100+ Pages

24674 **Complete Directory of General Flea Market Merchandise**
Sutton Family Communications & Publishing Company
155 Sutton Lane
Fordsville, KY 42343
270-740-0870
www.suttoncompliance.com
Theresa Sutton, Editor
Lee Sutton, General Manager
Print-out from database of wholesalers, manufacturers, distributors, importers and close-out houses. Database is updated daily to guarantee the most current and up-to-date sources available.
Cost: $289.00
100+ Pages

24675 **Complete Directory of High Profit Items**
Sutton Family Communications & Publishing Company
155 Sutton Lane
Fordsville, KY 42343
270-740-0870
www.suttoncompliance.com
Theresa Sutton, Editor
Lee Sutton, General Manager
Print-out from database of wholesalers, manufacturers, distributors, importers and close-out houses. Database is updated daily to guarantee the most current and up-to-date sources available.
Cost: $189.00
100+ Pages

24676 **Complete Directory of Importers**
Sutton Family Communications & Publishing Company
7025 N. Scottsdale Rd #320
Scottsdale, AR 85253
202-595-3101
888-843-0272; Fax: 480-245-5000
info@importgenius.com
www.importgenius.com
Theresa Sutton, Editor
Lee Sutton, General Manager
Print-out from database of wholesalers, manufacturers, distributors, importers and close-out houses. Database is updated daily to guarantee the most current and up-to-date sources available.
Cost: $109.00
100+ Pages

24677 **Complete Directory of Low-Price Merchandise**
Sutton Family Communications & Publishing Company
155 Sutton Lane
Fordsville, KY 42343
270-740-0870
www.suttoncompliance.com
Theresa Sutton, Editor
Lee Sutton, General Manager
Print-out from database of wholesalers, manufacturers, distributors, importers and close-out houses. Database is updated daily to guarantee the most current and up-to-date sources available.
Cost: $72.20
100+ Pages

24678 **Complete Directory of Promotional Products**
Sutton Family Communications & Publishing Company
155 Sutton Lane
Fordsville, KY 42343
270-740-0870
www.suttoncompliance.com
Theresa Sutton, Editor
Lee Sutton, General Manager
Print-out from database of wholesalers, manufacturers, distributors, importers and close-out houses. Database is updated daily to guarantee the most current and up-to-date sources available.
Cost: $139.00
100+ Pages

24679 **Complete Directory of Stationery Items**
Sutton Family Communications & Publishing Company
155 Sutton Lane
Fordsville, KY 42343
270-740-0870
www.suttoncompliance.com
Theresa Sutton, Editor
Lee Sutton, General Manager
Print-out from database of wholesalers, manufacturers, distributors, importers and close-out houses. Database is updated daily to guarantee the most current and up-to-date sources available.
Cost: $55.20
100+ Pages

24680 **Complete Directory of Tabletop Items**
Sutton Family Communications & Publishing Company
155 Sutton Lane
Fordsville, KY 42343
270-740-0870
www.suttoncompliance.com
Theresa Sutton, Editor
Lee Sutton, General Manager
Print-out from database of wholesalers, manufacturers, distributors, importers and close-out houses. Database is updated daily to guarantee the most current and up-to-date sources available.
Cost: $55.20
100+ Pages

24681 **Complete Directory of Unusual Items & Fads**
Sutton Family Communications & Publishing Company
155 Sutton Lane
Fordsville, KY 42343
270-740-0870
www.suttoncompliance.com
Theresa Sutton, Editor
Lee Sutton, General Manager
Print-out from database of wholesalers, manufacturers, distributors, importers and close-out houses. Database is updated daily to guarantee the most current and up-to-date sources available.
Cost: $139.00
100+ Pages

24682 **Complete Directory of Wholesale Bargains**
Sutton Family Communications & Publishing Company
155 Sutton Lane
Fordsville, KY 42343
270-740-0870
www.suttoncompliance.com
Theresa Sutton, Editor
Lee Sutton, General Manager
Print-out from database of wholesalers, manufacturers, distributors, importers and close-out houses. Database is updated daily to guarantee the most current and up-to-date sources available.
Cost: $92.70
100+ Pages

24683 **EMDA Membership Directory**
Equipment Marketing & Distribution Associaion
PO Box 1347
Iowa City, IA 52244
319-354-5156
pat@emda.net
www.emda.net
Patricia A. Collins, Executive Vice President
Annual directory of FEWA-AIMRA members, includes address, phone, fax, web, e-mail, territory covered (with map) product descriptions, key personnel, and a descriptive paragraph.
Cost: $50.00

24684 **Food & Beverage Market Place**
Grey House Publishing
4919 Route 22
PO Box 56
Amenia, NY 12501
518-789-8700
800-562-2139; Fax: 518-789-0556
gold@greyhouse.com
www.greyhouse.com
Facebook, Twitter
Leslie Mackenzie, Publisher
Richard Gottlieb, Editor
Richard Gottlieb, President
This information packed three-volume set is the most powerful buying and marketing guide for the US food and beverage industry. Includes thousands of wholesale listings.
Cost: $595.00
2000 Pages
Frequency: Annual
ISBN: 1-592373-61-5
Founded in 1981
Mailing list available for rent

24685 **Food & Beverage Marketplace: Online Database**
Grey House Publishing
4919 Route 22
PO Box 56
Amenia, NY 12501
518-789-8700
800-562-2139; Fax: 518-789-0556
gold@greyhouse.com
gold.greyhouse.com
Facebook, Twitter
Richard Gottlieb, President
Leslie Mackenzie, Publisher
Richard Gottlieb, Editor
This complete updated Food & Beverage Market Place: Online Database is the go-to source for the food and beverage industry. Anyone involved in the food and beverage industry needs this 'industry bible' and the important contacts to develop critical research data that can make for successful business growth.
Frequency: Annual
Founded in 1981
Mailing list available for rent

24686 **Global Logistics & Supply Chain Strategies**
Keller International Publishing Corporation
150 Great Neck Rd
Great Neck, NY 11021-3309
516-829-9722; Fax: 516-829-9306
www.supplychainbrain.com
Jerry Keller, President
Brad Berger, Group President/Publisher
Russell Goodman, Editor-in-Chief
Serves manufacturing, wholesale/retail trade, third party logistics, freight forwarding and transportation/warehousing firms.
Cost: $55.00
96 Pages
Frequency: 11 per year
Circulation: 40M
ISSN: 1525-4887
Founded in 1997
Printed in 4 colors on glossy stock

24687 **Membership Directory/Buyer's Guide**
Naylor Publications
5950 Nw 1st Pl
Gainesville, FL 32607-6018
352-332-1252
800-369-6220; Fax: 352-331-3525
chodges@naylor.com
www.naylor.com
Michael Moss, President
Provider of integrated communications and image-building solutions for associations.
Circulation: 1,200

24688 **Outlet Project Directory**
Off-Price Specialists, Value Retail News
29399 US Highway 19 N
Suite 370
Clearwater, FL 33761-2138
727-781-7557; Fax: 727-536-4389
www.valueretailnews.com
Linda Humphers, Editor-In-Chief
Tom Kirwan, Senior Editor
Offers valuable information on factory outlet projects.
Cost: $225.00
200 Pages
Frequency: Semiannual

24689 **Plumbing Engineer: Product Directory Issue**
TMB Publishing
1838 Techny Ct
Northbrook, IL 60062-5474
847-564-1127; Fax: 847-564-1264
www.tmbpublishing.com
Tom M Brown, Owner
Cate Brown, Production Manager
Over 400 plumbing products from approximately 250 manufacturers.
Frequency: Annual January
Circulation: 2,6104
ISBN: 0-192171-1 -

24690 **Shippers Guide to Department & Chain Stores Nationwide**
Shippers Guides
PO Box 112
Duarte, CA 91009-0112
626-357-6430; Fax: 248-786-1358
Profiles over 1,000 department stores and chain stores and their traffic managers in the United States.
Cost: $349.00
350 Pages
Frequency: Annual
Circulation: 2,000

24691 **Wholesale Grocers**
Chain Store Guide
3710 Corporex Park Dr.
Suite 310
Tampa, FL 33619-1389
813-627-6700
800-927-9292; Fax: 813-627-6888
webmaster@chainstoreguide.com
www.chainstoreguide.com
Mike Jarvis, Publisher
Shami Choon, Manager
We have uncovered the facts on more than 1,900 grocery suppliers in the U.S. and Canada in this database. This targeted database allows you to reach food wholesalers, cooperatives and voluntary group wholesalers, non-sponsoring wholesalers, and cash and carry operators who serve grocery, convenience, discount and drug stores. You will also find information regarding company headquarters, divisions, branches, and over 11,000 key executives and buyers.
Cost: $575.00
Frequency: Annual

24692 **Wholesaler**
TMB Publishing
1838 Techny Ct
Northbrook, IL 60062-5474
847-564-1127; Fax: 847-564-1264
www.tmbpublishing.com
Tom M Brown, Owner
Ranks 100 leading wholesalers of plumbing, heating, air conditioning, refrigeration equipment and industrial pipe, valves and fittings.
Cost: $25.00
Frequency: Annual July
Circulation: 30,000

24693 **Wholesaler-Wholesaling 100 Issue**
TMB Publishing
1838 Techny Ct
Northbrook, IL 60062-5474
847-564-1127; Fax: 847-564-1264
www.tmbpublishing.com
Tom M Brown, Owner
Offer information on over 100 leading wholesalers of plumbing-heating equipment and supplies.
Cost: $25.00
Circulation: 25,000

Industry Web Sites

24694 **Nesda.Wildapricot.Org**
National Electronics Service Dealers Association
Trade association for electronics repair professionals.

24695 **http://gold.greyhouse.com**
G.O.L.D Grey House OnLine Databases
Grey House Publishing's online database platform, GOLD, offers Quick Search, Keyword Search and Expert Search for most business sectors, including wholesale markets. The GOLD platform makes finding the information you need quick and easy - whether you're a novice searcher or an experienced database user. All of Grey House's directory products are available for subscription on the GOLD platform.

24696 **peopleforbikes.org**
PeopleForBikes Coalition
PeopleForBikes (PFB) Coalition merged with the Bicycle Product Suppliers Association in 2019. Together, they are a coalition of supplies of bicycles, parts, accessories, and services.

24697 **www.aamp.com**
American Association of Meat Processors
Membership consists of small to medium sized meat, poultry and food businesses including, slaughterers, processors, wholesalers, home food service businesses, deli and catering operators and suppliers to the industry. AAMP is affiliated with 28 state, regional and provincial associations.

24698 **www.adbi.org**
Associated Beer Distributors of Illinois
The ABDI represents, maintains, and improves the interests of its members who are licensed by the State of Illinois to import and distribute beer to licensed retailers.

24699 **www.aednet.org**
Associated Equipment Distributors

International trade association supporting companies specializing in eqipment used in construction, mining, forestry, power generation, agriculture and industrial applications.

24700 www.aird.org
Association of Ingersoll-Rand Distributors
The Association of Ingersoll-Rand Distributors (AIRD) was organized as a central resource for distributors of Ingersoll-Rand compressed air equipment. AIRD is chartered to promote improved business conditions affecting distributors of air compressors, further a better understanding between distributors and equipment suppliers, research ways to lower costs of distributing air compressors, collect and disseminate statistical information and conduct other beneficial activities.

24701 www.amdweb.com
Association of Millwork Distributors
AMD provides leadership, education, promotion, networking, and advocacy to, and for, the millwork distribution industry.

24702 www.apda.com
Appliance Parts Distributors Association
The APDA is an association of independent businesses that aspire to provide the highest level of quality, service, support and information to its customers and suppliers in order to make its value indispensable to the parts distribution channel.

24703 www.apsp.org
Association of Pool & Spa Professionals
The world's largest international trade association for the swimming pool, spa, and hot tub industry. It works with regulatory and legislative bodies to ensure that their codes, ordinance, and legislation are written to the safest and most current standards. The association's mission is to ensure consumer safety and enhance the business success of its members. Formerly The Association of Pool & Spa Professionals.

24704 www.asa.net
American Supply Association
ASA is a not-for-profit national organization serving wholesale distributors and their suppliers in the plumbing, heating, cooling and industrial and mechanical pipe, valves and fittings industries.

24705 www.ascdi.com
Association of Service and Computer Dealers Int'l
The ASCDI is a worldwide, nonprofit organization, made up of companies who provide technology business solutions, technical suppoer, and value added services to the business community.

24706 www.awfs.org
Association of Woodworking & Furnishings Suppliers
The Association of Woodworking and Furnishing Suppliers is the largest national trade association in the U.S. representing the interestes of the broad array of companies that supply the home and commercial furnishings industry.

24707 www.bsahome.org
Bearing Specialists Association
BSA is a not-for-profit association that consists of companies that distribute factory-warranted ball, roller, and anti-friction bearings through authorized dealers. BSA provides members with the opportunity to network with others in the industry through meetings, seminars and educational programs at their annual convention.

24708 www.cbbd.com
California Beer & Beverage Distributors
The California Beer and Beverage Distributors is a nonprofit trade association representing over 100 beer distributors and brewer/vendor members.

24709 www.ceta.org
Cleaning Equipment Trade Association
CETA is dedicated to increasing the awareness and promotion of industry products, while at the same time recognizing the impact on preserving the environment and the opportunity to do business within it.

24710 www.ctdahome.org
Ceramic Tile Distributors Association
CTDA is an international association of distributors, manufacturers, and allied professionals of ceramic tile and related products.

24711 www.cvsn.org
Commercial Vehicle Solutions Network
The Commercial Vehicle Solutions Network (CVSN) is an association of independent parts and service aftermarket distributors serving the transportation industry.

24712 www.dhi.org
Door & Hardware Institute
The Door & Hardware Institute (DHI) is the only professional association dedicated to the Architectural Openings Industry. DHI represents the North American openings marketplace as the advocate and primary resource for information, professional development and certification.

24713 www.easa.com
Electrical Apparatus Service Association
An international trade organization of electromechanical sales and service firms in 58 countries. Provides members with a means of keeping up to date on materials, equipment, and state of the art technology.

24714 www.edmarket.org
National School Supply & Equipment Association
The National School Supply and Equipment Association (NSSEA) is the leading trade organization for the educational products marketplace. NSSEA puts the collective experience of the most successful school industry business in the world at your fingertips.

24715 www.emda.net
Equipment Marketing & Distribution Association
Trade association dedicated to the marketing of specialized agricultural equipment, outdoor power equipment, light industrial equipment, and forestry equipment.

24716 www.fewa.org
Farm Equipment Wholesalers Association
International trade association of wholesale/distributors of agricultural equipment and related products.

24717 www.fmi.org
Food Marketing Institute
FMI conducts programs in public affairs, food safety, research, education and industry relations on behalf of its 1,500 member companies in the United States and around the world.

24718 www.fpda.org
Fluid Power Distributors Association
Membership is composed of distributors and manufacturers of hydraulic and pneumatic equipment.

24719 www.gawda.org
Gases and Welding Distributors Association
GAWDA's mission is to promote the safe operation and economic vitality of distributors of industrial gases and related welding equipment and supplies.

24720 www.gmdc.com
Global Market Development Center
GMDC is the premier non-profit global trade association dedicated to serving General Merchandise and Health Beauty retailers, wholesalers and suppliers. GMDC promotes critical connectivity to grow and expand member companies by uniting members through business building events and opportunities and enriching their thinking through education and training; consumer and business insights; and information resources.

24721 www.gmdc.org
General Merchandise Distributors Council
International trade association representing pharmacy products to the mass market retail industry.

24722 www.gonpta.com
NPTA Alliance
The NPTA Alliance (formerly the National Paper Trade Association, Inc.) is the association for the $60+ billion paper, packaging and supplies distribution industry. The mission of NPTA is to actively support the success of its members through the delivery of networking, industry data & research, education and advocacy that focuses on the health of the distribution channel.

24723 www.greyhouse.com
Grey House Publishing
Authoritative reference directories for most business sectors including wholesale service markets. Users can search the online databases with varied search criteria allowing for custom searches by product category, geographic area, sales volume, keyword, subject and more. Full Grey House catalog and online ordering also available.

24724 www.hardinet.org
Heating, Airconditioning & Refrigeration Dist.
This association is a trade organization dedicated to advancing the science of wholesale distribution in the HVACR industry.

24725 www.hda.org
Healthcare Distribution Alliance
The Healthcare Distribution Management Association (HDMA) is the national association representing primary, full-service heatlhcare distributors. HDMA and its members are the vital link in the healthcare system, working daily to provide value, remove costs and develop innovative solutions.

24726 www.hida.org
Health Industry Distributors Association
HIDA keeps members current on healthcare reform, government affairs, industry trends and forecasts, provider news, and sales tips.

24727 www.iapd.org
International Association of Plastics Distribution
The International Association of Plastics Distribution is an international trade association comprised of companies engaged in the distribution and manufacturing of plastics materials.

24728 www.icdaonline.com
Industrial Compressor Distributor Association
The main objetives of the ICDA are to promote for its members the highest standards of production, financial and managerial activities; to act as a vehicle for the solution of common industry

problems in an effective and efficient manner; and to increase market volume and profits for its members.

24729 **www.insulation.org**
National Insulation Association
The National Insulation Association (NIA) is a trade association representing the mechanical and specialty insulation industry.

24730 **www.irrigation.org**
Irrigation Association
Membership organization for irrigation equipment and system manufacturers, dealers, distributors, designers, consultants, contractors and end users.

24731 **www.isapartners.org**
Industrial Supply Association
The primary focus of the Industrial Supply Association is to improve the industrial supply channel through its mission-critical activities, including conventions, forums and the gathering and dissemination of critical information. The association supports distributors, manufacturers and representatives of MROP products'industrial equipment.

24732 **www.isd.org**
International Sealing Distribution Association
The International Sealing Distribution Association (ISD) is a not-for-profit trade association formed to enhance the success of members through information, education, and interaction.

24733 **www.issa.com**
International Sanitary Supply Association
Manufacturers, distributors, wholesalers, representatives and publishers engaged in the manufacture and/or distribution of cleaning and maintenance products.

24734 **www.itpa.com**
International Truck Parts Association
The International Truck Parts Association was organized as a not-for-profit association to promote, foster, and improve relationships among sellers and buyers of trucks and truck surplus products and other parties.

24735 **www.lumber.org**
North American Wholesale Lumber Association
For lumber and building distributors and manufacturers.

24736 **www.mdna.org**
Machinery Dealers National Association
Facebook, Twitter, LinkedIn
Represents dealers of used industrial equipment, providing members with business standards and development opportunities.

24737 **www.mdva.org**
Michigan Distributors & Vendors Association
The Michigan Distributors and Vendors Association (MDVA) is a non-profit, statewide business association representing two very significant business segments in the grocery and convenience products industry.

24738 **www.mheda.org**
Material Handling Equipment Distributors Assoc.
The Material Handling Equipment Distributors Association is the only national association dedicated solely to improving the proficiency of the independent material handling equipment distributor.

24739 **www.mic.org**
Motorcycle Industry Council
Nonprofit national trade association created to represent the motorcycle industry.

24740 **www.msbeer.com**
Mississippi Beer Distributors Association
The MBDA was established to represent and promote the beer wholesalers and beer industry within Mississippi.

24741 **www.msci.org**
Metal Service Center Institute (MSCI)
MSCI is the trade association that supports and represents most elements of the metals value chain, including metals producers, distributors, and processors.

24742 **www.naaud.com**
North American Association of Utility Distributors
NAAUD is comprised of select distributors who specialize in supplying products and supply chain services to the electric utility industry. The purpose of NAAUD is to discuss and promote the newest ideas and best concepts for the industry.

24743 **www.nacd.com**
National Association of Chemical Distributors
The National Association of Chemical Distributors (NACD) is an international association of chemial distributor companies that purchase and take title of chemical products from manufacturers.

24744 **www.naed.org**
National Association of Electrical Distributors
The main goal of the National Association of Electrical Distributors (NAED) is to establish the electrical distributor as an essential force in the electrical industry and the economy.

24745 **www.nafcd.org**
North American Association of Floor Covering Dist.
The North American Association of Floor Covering Distributors (NAFCD) was organized to foster trade and commerce for those having a business, financial or professional interest as wholesale distributors or manufacturers of floor coverings and allied products.

24746 **www.nationalgrocers.org**
National Grocers Association
The National Grocers Association is the national trade association representing the retail and wholesale grocers that comprise the independent sector of the food distribution industry.

24747 **www.naumd.com**
N.A. Association of Uniform Manufacturers & Dist.
An association dedicated to keeping the Uniforn & Imagewear Industry strong and healthy.

24748 **www.nbmda.org**
N.A. Building Material Distribution Association
NBMDA develops and promotes the effectiveness of distribution processes to improve member profitability and growth.

24749 **www.nbwa.org**
National Beer Wholesalers Association
Research and development, quality control and ingredients.

24750 **www.nfraweb.org**
National Frozen & Refrigerated Foods Association
NFRA is a non profit trade association comprised of 650 member companies representing all segments of the frozen and refrigerated foods industry. NFRA has been serving the frozen food industry since 1945 and just recently in 2001 began serving the refrigerated foods industry. The mission of NFRA is to promote the sales and consumption of frozen and refrigerated foods through: education, training, research, sales planning and menu development and providing a forum for industry dialogue.

24751 **www.npes.org**
NPES Association
This association is a trade association of over 400 companies that manufacture and distribute equipment, systems, software, supplies used in printing, publishing and converting.

24752 **www.npfda.org**
National Poultry & Food Distributors Association
For poultry and food distribution and processing industries. Provides member services, cost cutting benefits and networking opportunities.

24753 **www.nybeer.org**
New York State Beer Wholesalers Association
The New York State Beer Wholesalers Association, Inc. represents and protects the legislative and regulators interests of its members in state and local government. Our primary goal is to uphold the three-tier system in order to safeguard the industry's distribution standards.

24754 **www.opeesa.com**
Outdoor Power Equipment and Engine Service Assoc.
The Outdoor Power Equipment and Engine Service Association (OPEESA) consists of more than 100 members. Members include distributors and manufacturers of outdoor power equipment and air-cooled gas and diesel engines.

24755 **www.pac-west.org**
Pacific-West Fastener Association
An organization dedicated to the fastener industry.

24756 **www.pida.com**
Pet Industry Distributors Association
Represents wholesaler-distributors of pet products, providing training and education to members.

24757 **www.probeauty.org**
Professional Beauty Association
The Professional Beauty Association (PBA) is a nonprofit trade association that represents the interests of the professional beauty industry from manufacturers and distributors to salons and spas. PBA offers business tools, education, advocacy, networking and more to improve individual businesses and the industry as a whole.

24758 **www.safetycentral.org**
Safety Equipment Distributors Association
Represents wholesale-distributors of safety equipment and works to enhance and improve distribution through excellence in communications, training, education and services.

24759 **www.shda.org**
Security Hardware Distributors Association
The mission of the Security Hardware Distributors Association is to continually improve, through education and services, the proficiency of Security Distributors in order that they are the most effective and efficient conduit to the marketplace.

24760 www.signs.org/nassd
National Association of Sign Supply Distributors
NASSD is a nonprofit trade association for organizations who are engaged in full-line sign supply distribution and who manufacture or supply commercial, neon and electrical sign products.

24761 www.ssia.info
Shoe Service Institute of America
Shop to shop chat room, links and listings of manufacturers and wholesalers plus shoe care tips.

24762 www.tcata.org
Textile Care Allied Trades Association
The Textile Care Allied Trades Association (TCATA) is an international trade association representing manufacturers and distributors of drycleaning and laundry equipment and supplies. It is the only trade association dedicated exclusively to the interests of the allied trades.

24763 www.uvsa.net
United Veterinary Services Association
The UVSA was established as the national trade organization for businesses engaged in the distribution of animal health products. Formerly known as the American Veterinary Distributors Association.

24764 www.wasda.com
Water & Sewer Distributors of America
WASDA's mission is to promote the waterworks/wastewater products distribution industry, and to further improve the image and professionalism of WASDA and its member companies.

A

B

D

E

F

G

H

I

J

K

L

M

N

O

P

Q

R

S

T

U

V

W

Y

Z

A

Annual North American Waste-to-Energy Conference
Solid Waste Association of North America - SWANA, 1529

Annual Odors and Air Pollutants Conference
Water Environment Federation, 8080

Annual PPO Forum
American Assn of Preferred Provider Organizations, 13256

Annual Pet Industry Trade Show
World Wide Pet Supply Association, 20509

Annual Physical Electronics Conference
AVS Science & Technology Society, 7432

Annual Proceedings Conference
American Academy of Advertising, 523

Annual RSES Conference & Expo
Refrigeration Service Engineers Society, 7433

Annual Register of Grant Support: A Directory of Funding Ser
Information Today, 11206

Annual Renewable Energy Technology Conference & Exhibition (
American Council on Renewable Energy, 1530

Annual Repair Symposium
Aeronautical Repair Station Association, 2813

Annual Report of the Board of Governors of the Federal Reser
Board of Governors, 3195

Annual Research Program Report
National Institutes for Water Resources, 7793

Annual SWCS International Conference
Soil and Water Conservation Society, 8081

Annual Scientific & Clinical Congress
American Association of Clinical Endocrinologists, 13257

Annual Scientific Meeting and Technology Showcase
Society of Cosmetic Chemists, 5890

Annual Scientific Meeting of the Gerontological Society of A
Gerontological Society of America, 13258

Annual Scientific Seminar
Society of Cosmetic Chemists, 5891

Annual Selfcare Summit
Global Market Development Center, 24618

Annual Simulation Solutions Conference
Institute of Industrial Engineers, 7434

Annual Software Guide
Financial & Security Products Association, 3196

Annual Spring Boat Show
Southern California Marine Association, 3531

Annual Spring New Products Show
Pacific Expositions, 3532, 11701, 14971

Annual Spring-Easter Arts & Crafts Show & Sale
Finger Lakes Craftsmen Shows, 13664

Annual Statement Studies
RMA - Risk Management Association, 8596

Annual Symposium
Pedorthic Footwear Association, 11105

Annual Technical & Educational Conference
American Design Drafting Association, 2228

Annual Trade Show Directory
Forum Publishing Company, 22026

Annual Winter & Spring Conferences
Northwest Development Officers Association, 11198

Annuity Shopper
Annuity Shopper, 14241

Antenna Book
Electronic Technicians Association International, 7004

Anthrozoos
Delta Society, 20459

AntiShyster
AntiShyster, 15842

Antin Marketing Letter
Alan Antin/Antin Marketing Group, 17735

Antique Airplane Association Newsletter
Antique Airplance Association, 2648

Antique Appraisal Association of America Newsletter
Antique Appraisal Association of America, 2332

Antique Arms Show
Beinfeld Productions, 2406

Antique Trader
F+W Media, 2359

Antique Week
Mayhill Publications, 2360

Antiques and Collecting Hobbies
Lightner Publishing Corporation, 13604

Antiretroviral Resistance in Clinical Practice
National Center for Biotechnology Information, 3392

Antitrust Law Journal
American Bar Association, 15843

Antitrust and Trade Regulation Report
Bureau of National Affairs, 15635

Anvil's Ring
Artist-Blacksmith's Association of North America, 18346

Apartment Age Magazine
Apartment Association of Greater Los Angeles, 21638

Apartment Finance Today Magazine
Hanley Wood LLC, 6041, 21639

Apartment Management Newsletter
AMN Publishing, 21603

Apartment Management Report
Apartment Owners & Managers Assn of America, 21604

Apartment News
Arizona Multi-Housing Consulting Corporation, 21640

Aperture
Aperture Foundation, 20888

Appalachian Hardwood Expo
Mercer County Technical Education Center, 16619

Appalachian Hardwood Manufacturers
Appalachian Hardwood Manufacturers, 16470

Apparel Importers Trade and Transportation Conference
United States Fashion Industry Association (USFIA), 1893

Apparel Magazine
Susan S. Nichols, 1859

Apparel Printing and Embroidery Expo
Primedia, 23448

Apparel Show of the Americas
Bobbin Publishing/Miller Freeman, 1894, 23449

Apparel Specialty Stores Directory
Chain Store Guide, 1963

Applause Magazine
Denver Center for Performing Arts, 19900

Appliance
Dana Chase Publications, 2041

Appliance Design
Business News Publishing, 2042

Appliance Service News
Gamit Enterprises, 2043

Application Servers and Media Servers
Probe Research, 17736

Applications Software
Thomson Media, 5263

Applied Biochemistry and Biotechnology
Humana Press, 3393

Applied Clinical Trials
Advanstar Communications, 12825

Applied Economic Perspectives and Policy
Agricultural & Applied Economics Association, 896, 9920

Applied Engineering in Agriculture
American Society of Agricultural Engineers, 9921

Applied Ergonomics Conference
Institute of Industrial Engineers, 13259, 22471

Applied Microwave & Wireless
Noble Publishing Corporation, 6874

Applied Optics
Optical Society of America, 5361

Applied Power Electronics Conference & Exposition (APEC)
Power Sources Manufacturers Association, 6665

Applied Science & Technology Index
HW Wilson Company, 16409

Appraisers Association of America National Conference
Appraisers Association of America, 268, 8916, 14314, 14972

Aquaculture Magazine
Achill River Corporation, 9922

Aquaculture North America
Capamara Communications, 9208, 9225

Aquarium Fish Magazine
Fancy Publications, 20477

Aquatic Plant Management Society Annual Meeting
Aquatic Plant Management Society, 1116, 8082

Aquatic Plant News
Aquatic Plant Management Society, 806, 7794

Aquatic Therapy and Fitness Research
Aquatic Exercise Association, 22807

Aquatics International
Leisure Publications, 22808

Arabian Horse World
Arabian Horse World, 22809

Arabian Travel Market
Reed Exhibition Companies, 24037

Arbitration Journal
American Arbitration Association, 15844

Arbitron Radio County Coverage
Arbitron Company, 3907

Arbor Age
Green Media, 9923

Archery Business Magazine
Grand View Media Group, 22810

Archery Trade Show
Archery Trade Association, 22921

Architectural Design
John Wiley & Sons, 2181

Architectural Record
McGraw Hill, 2183
McGraw-Hill Construction, 4150

Architectural Woodwork Institute
Architectural Woodwork Institute, 16471

Architecture Magazine
American Institute of Architects, 2184

Archive Magazine
Luerzer's Archive Inc, 5051

Archives of Environmental Health
Society for Occupational and Environmental Health, 7902

Archives of Physical Medicine and Rehabilitation
American Congress of Rehabilitation Medicine, 12826

Area Development
Halcyon Business Publications, 21641

Aristos
Aristos Foundation, 2361

Armed Forces Communications and Electronics Association
AFCEA International Headquarters, 23162

Armed Forces Comptroller
American Society of Military Comptrollers, 175, 8778

Arminera
Marketing International, 18637

Armstrong Oil Directories
Armstrong Oil, 20352

Army Aviation
Army Aviation Publications, 2719

Army Aviation Association of America Convention
Army Aviation Association of America, 2814

Army Times
Army Times Publishing Company, 12055

Arnic Aviation Customer Meeting
British Telecommunications, 2815

Arnic Global Communications Workshop
British Telecommunications, 2816

Arnold Sports Festival
Arnold Sports Festival, 1895, 22922

Arrowhead Home and Builders Show
Shamrock Productions, 4293

Art & Antiques
Art & Antiques Worldwide Media LLC, 2362

B

Brahman Journal
American Brahman Breeders Association, 9942

Brain & Life
American Academy of Neurology, 12839

Brake & Front End
Babcox Publications, 19071

Branch Automation News
Phillips Publishing, 5266

Branches of Your State: Banks, Savings & Loans, Credit Union
Sheshunoff Information Services, 3200

Brand Directory
Vance Publishing, 10560

Brand Marketing
Fairchild Publications, 17869

Branding ID: Strategies to Drive Sales
Association of Sales & Marketing Companies, 10274

Brandpackaging
Independent Publishing Company, 9943

Brands and Their Companies
Gale/Cengage Learning, 580

Brandweek
Prometheus Global Media, 434, 17870

Brandwidth Supply and Demand Analysis WIT IP Traffic Demand
Probe Research, 4997

Brazil Tax, Law, & Business Briefing
WorldTrade Executive, 14724

Breakthrough Magazine
Breakthrough Magazine, 2371

Brewers Association
Brewers Association, 3610

Brewers Digest
Siebel Publishing Company, 9944

Brewers Digest: Buyers Guide and Brewery Directory
Ammark Publishing, 10561

Brewers Resource Directory
Brewers Association, 3671, 10562

Brick News
Brick Industry Association, 4107

Brick Show
Brick Industry Association, 4295

Bridge
National Academy of Engineering, 7239

Bridging the Gap
Section for Women in Public Administration, 17098

Briefs
American Institute of Fishery Research Biologists, 9209

Brilliant Ideas for Publishers
Creative Brilliance Associates, 15151

Broadband
IGI Group, 23198

Broadband Advertising
Kagan World Media, 3836, 23199

Broadband Fixed Wireless
Kagan World Media, 3779

Broadband Systems & Design
Gordon Publications, 3780

Broadband Technology
Kagan World Media, 3781, 23200

Broadband Wireless
Probe Research, 4998

Broadcast Banker/Broker
Kagan World Media, 3782, 8605

Broadcast Designers' Association International Conference &
Broadcast Designers' Association International, 3883

Broadcast Engineering
Primedia, 3837

Broadcast Engineering Conference (BEC)
Society of Broadcast Engineers, 1727, 3884

Broadcast Engineering Equipment Reference Manual
Penton, 3911

Broadcast Investor
Kagan World Media, 3783, 8606, 23201

Broadcast Stats
Kagan World Media, 3784

Broadcasting
Reed Business Information, 3838

Broadside
Theatre Library Association, 19884

Broker Magazine
Thomson Media, 3091, 8607

Broker News
Broker Publishing, 17871

Broker World
Insurance Publications, 14247

Brokerage Yacht Show
Yachting Promotions, 3539

Brooklyn Institute for Studies in American Music
Brooklyn College, 19367

Broom Brush & Mop
Rankin Publishing Company, 4807

Brotherhood of Locomotive Engineers
Brotherhood of Locomotive Engineers, 23724

Brotherhood of Traveling Jewelers
Leys, Christie & Company, 14897

Brown Swiss Bulletin
Brown Swiss Cattle Breeder's Assoc of the USA, 9748

Brown Swiss Cattle Breeders' Association Directory
Brown Swiss Cattle Breeders' Association, 10563

Brown's Directory of North American and International Gas Co
Advanstar Communications, 20353

Brownfield Renewal
Brownfield Renewal, 21642

Brushware
Brushware, 4808

BtoB Magazine
Ad Age Group/ Division of Crain Communications, 6249, 6436, 17872
Crain Communications, Inc., 435

BuSiness of Herbs
Herb Growing and Marketing Network, 9749

Budget Processors in the States
National Association of State Budge Officers, 8608

Builders Trade Show
Maryland National Capital Building Industry Assn., 4296

Building Bridges VII
American Association of Health Plans, 13270

Building Design & Construction
Reed Business Information, 2186, 4156

Building Energy
Northeast Sustainable Energy Association, 1533

Building Environment Report
IAQ Publications, 4157

Building Industry Show
Building Industry Assn. of Southern California, 4297

Building Materials Directory
Underwriters Laboratories, 4358

Building Operating Management
Trade Press Publishing Corporation, 4158, 17208, 21643

Building Products CONNECTION
Northwestern Lumber Association, 4159, 16572

Building Products News
Palgrave Macmillan, 4108

Building Stone
Building Stone Institute, 4109

Building Stone Magazine
Building Stone Institute, 4160

Building Supply Home Centers
Reed Business Information, 4161

Building and Construction Market Forecast
Reed Business Information, 4110

Buildings: Facilities Construction & Management Magazine
Stamats Communications, 4162

Buisness IP Services in Brazil
Probe Research, 14647

Bull and Bear's Directory of Investment Advisory Newsletters
Bull & Bear Financial Report, 9004

Bulldog Reporter
InfoCom Group, 21249
James Sinkinson/InfoCom Group, 15130

Bulletin
Garden Club of America, 11590
NW Public Power Association, 24191
Neighborhood Cleaners Association, 4797
Northwest Mining Association, 18578
Property Management Association, 21607

Bulletin Newsletter
EMTA - Trade Association for the Emerging Markets, 8610

Bulletin of Bibliography
Greenwood Publishing Group, 16193

Bulletin of Tau Beta Pi
Tau Beta Pi Association, 7201

Bulletin on Long-Term Care Law
Health Resources Publishing, 12747

Bulletin to Management
Bureau of National Affairs, 17099

Bulletins
World Research Foundation, 7798

Bulletproof Marketing for Small Businesses
Kay Borden/Franklin-Sarrett Publishers, 17742

Buoyant Flight
Lighter Than Air Society, 2658

Bureau of Intelligence and Research (INR)
Department of State, 19568

Burrelle's Media Directory
BurrellesLuce, 3912, 5119, 15191, 21297

Bus Conversions Magazine
MAK Publishing, 23725

Bus Garage Index
Friendship Publications, 23858

Bus Industry Directory
Friendship Publications, 23859

Bus Ride
Friendship Publications, 23726

Bus Tours Magazine
National Bus Trader, 23984

Buscon East/West
Conference Management Company, 24237

Business Journal
Business Journals of North Carolina, 17100

Business Russia
Economist Intelligence Unit, 14648

Business & Commercial Aviation
McGraw Hill, 2729

Business & Industry
Business Magazines, 13917

Business & Legal Reports
Business & Legal Reports, 22409

Business Administration Conference
National Ready Mixed Concrete Association, 4298

Business Africa
Economist Intelligence Unit, 14649

Business America: the Magazine of International Trade
US Department of Commerce, 14695

Business Asia
Economist Intelligence Unit, 14650

Business China
Economist Intelligence Unit, 14651

Business Communications Review
BCR Enterprises, 5052, 23258

Business Computer Report
Guidera Publishing Corporation, 5267

Business Credit
Assn of Executives in Finance, Credit & In'tl Bus, 3092
National Association of Credit Management, 8783

Business Credit Magazine
National Association of Credit Management, 6042

Business Crime: Criminal Liability of the Business Community
Matthew Bender and Company, 15643

Business Disaster Preparedness Council
Lee County Emergency Management, 22258

C

Catalog Connection
Holy B Pasiuk, 18021

Catalog Handbook
Enterprise Magazines, 18022

Catalog Sales Data Files
Open Horizons Publishing, 21487

Catalog Success
North American Publishing Company, 6326, 17875

Catalog in Motion
Bell Group, 14976

Catalog of Professional Testing Resources
Psychological Assessment Resources, 13365

Catalyst
Western Center for Microcomputers, 5374

Catering Service Idea Newsletter
Prosperity & Profits Unlimited, 9754

Catfish Farmers of America Annual Convention & Research Symp
Catfish Farmers of America, 9258

Catfish Journal
Catfish Farmers of America, 9228

Catholic Cemetery
National Catholic Cemetery Conference, 4166

Catholic Library Association
Catholic Library Association, 16132

Catholic Library World
Catholic Library Association, 16196

Cats & Kittens
Pet Publishing, 20482

Cats Magazine
PRIMEDIA Enthusiast Group, 20483

Cattle Guard
Colorado Cattlemen's Agricultrual Land Trust, 903

Cattle Industry Convention
Red Angus Association of America, 10279

Cattleman
Texas & Southwestern Cattle Raisers Association, 904

Cedar Shake and Shingle Bureau Membership Directory/Buyer's
Cedar Shake & Shingle Bureau, 4359, 16476, 16654

Celebrate Today
Open Horizons Publishing, 21488

Celebrity Access Directory
Celebrity Access, 1787

Celebrity Bulletin
Celebrity Service, 1659

Cellular Telecommunications Industry
CTIA, 23169

Cement Americas
Penton Media Inc, 4360
Primedia, 23120

Census and You
Census Bureau, 11978

Center for Breakthrough Thinking
Center for Breakthrough Thinking, 17005

Center for Children's Books
Center for Children's Books, 16133

Center for Childrens Books
Center for Children's Books, 16134

Center for Creative Leadership Newsletter
Center for Creative Leadership, 17006, 17104

Center for Domestic Preparedness
Federal Emergency Management Agency, 19570

Center for Environmental Design Research
University of California at Berkeley, 2128

Center for Management Effectiveness
Center for Management Effectiveness, 17007

Center for Management Systems
Center for Management Systems, 17008

Center for Professional Responsibility
American Bar Association, 15536

Center for School Mental Health Assistance National Conventi
Exhibit Promotions Plus, 13272

Center for Security and Emerging Technology
Walsh School of Foreign Service, 5194, 22078, 22263

Center for Third World Organizing
Center For Third World Organizing, 17009

Center for the Book
Library of Congress, 16357

Center on Children and the Law
American Bar Association Young Lawyers Division, 15537

Central Environmental Nursery Trade Show (CENTS)
Ohio Nursery & Landscape Association, 11636

Central Penn Business Journal
Journal Publications, 17215

Ceramic Abstracts
American Ceramic Society, 11818

Ceramic Arts Daily
Ceramic Publications Company, 11827

Ceramic Bulletin
American Ceramic Society, 11777

Ceramic Industry
Business News Publishing Company, 11778

Ceramic Interconnect and Ceramic Microsystems
International Microelectronics & Electronics, 6959

CeramicSOURCE
American Ceramic Society, 11819

Ceramics Monthly
American Ceramic Society, 11779

Cereal Chemistry
AACC International, 4588, 9951

Cereal Foods World
AACC International, 905, 9755, 9952

Certification News
Independent Community Bankers of America, 3012

Certifier
Nat'l Council of Architectural Registration Boards, 2165

Cessna Owner Magazine
Cessna Owner Organization, 2731

Chaff Newsletter
American Association of Grain Inspection, 809

Chain Drug Review
Racher Press, 20684

Chain Leader
Raymond Herrmann, 17216

Chain Merchandiser
Merchandising Publications Company, 21958

Chain Restaurant Operators Directory
Chain Store Guide, 21874

Chain Store Age
Lebhar-Friedman, 21959

Chamber Executive
American Chambers of Congress Exec Communications, 5002

Chamber Executive Magazine
Association of Chamber of Commerce Executives, 17217, 17876

Chamber Music America National Conference
Chamber Music America, 19467

Chamber Music Magazine
Chamber Music America, 19400

Champagne Wines Information Bureau
KCSA, 3628, 9756

Champion Magazine
National Association of Criminal Defense Lawyers, 15853

Channel Magazine
Semiconductor Equipment & Materials International, 6876

Channel Partners Conference & Expo
Virgo Publishing LLC, 528

Chapter 11 Update
Federal Managers Association, 15646

Chapter News
American College of Cardiology, 20636

Chapter Weekly
National Association of Tax Professionals, 104

Charitable Trust Directory
Office of the Secretary of State, 11207

Chartered Property Casualty Underwriters Society Fall Semina
Chartered Property Casualty Underwriter Society, 14321

Chartmaker
American Recreation Coalition, 24436

Cheers
Jobson Publishing Corporation, 9953
The Beverage Information Group, 3649

Cheese Market News
Quarne Publishing, 9954

Cheese Market News: Annual
Quarne Publishing, 10569

Cheese Reporter
Cheese Reporter Publishing Company, 9757

Chef
Talcott Communications Corporation, 9955, 21835

ChefConnect
American Culinary Federation, 21869

Chek-Chart Service Bulletin
Motor Information Systems/Chek-Chart, 19008

Cheklist
BKB Publications, 3013

Chem Show: Chemical Process Industries Exposition
International Exposition Company, 4665

Chem Source USA
Chemical Sources International, 4692

Chem-Distribution
PennWell Publishing Company, 4666

Chem-Safe
PennWell Conferences and Exhibitions, 4667

ChemEcology
Chemical Manufacturers Association, 4554

ChemStewards
Society of Chemical Manufacturers & Affiliates, 7802

ChemWeek Association
ChemWeek, 4555

Chemcyclopedia
American Chemical Society, 4694

Chemical & Engineering News
American Chemical Society, 7242

Chemical Abstracts
American Chemical Society, 4695

Chemical Bond
American Chemical Society, 4556

Chemical Bulletin
American Chemical Society, 4557

Chemical Distributor
National Association of Chemical Distributors, 24587

Chemical Economics Handbook Program
SRI Consulting, 4558

Chemical Engineering
Chemical Week Associates, 4589

Chemical Engineering Progress
American Institute of Chemical Engineers, 4590

Chemical Equipment
Reed Business Information, 4591

Chemical Equipment Literature Review
Reed Business Information, 4592

Chemical Exposure and Human Health
McFarland & Company Publishers, 4696

Chemical Heritage
Chemical Heritage Foundation, 4593

Chemical Industries Newsletter
SRI International, 4559

Chemical Industry Monitoring
Cyrus J Lawrence, 4560

Chemical Intelligencer
Springer Verlag, 4594

Chemical Management Review
Reed Chemical Publications, 4595

Chemical Market Reporter
Schnell Publishing Company, 4596

Chemical Processing
Putman Media, 4597

Chemical Product News
US Dept. of Commerce, Business & Defense Service, 4561

Chemical Regulation Reporter
Bureau of National Affairs, 4562

Chemical Regulations and Guidelines System
Network Management CRC Systems, 4697

Chemical Week: Financial Survey of the 300 Largest Companies
Chemical Week Associates, 4698

Chemical and Engineering News
American Chemical Society, 4563

Chemical and Pharmaceutical Press
C&P Press, 9956

Chemist
American Institute of Chemists, 4598

Chemistry
American Chemical Society, 20685

Chemistry Research in Technology
American Chemical Society, 4599

Chemweek's Business Daily
Chemical Week/Access Intelligence, 4564

Chicago Auto Show
Chicago Automobile Trade Association, 19153

Chicago Men's Collective: Winter
Merchandise Mart Properties Inc, 1898

Chicken Marketing Seminar
National Chicken Council, 10280

Chief Engineer
Chief Engineers Association of Chicagoland, 24192

Chief Executive
Chief Executive Group, 17218

Chief Executive Officers Newsletter
Center for Entreprenuel Management, 17105

Chief Logistics Officer
Penton Media, 23727

Chief Marketer
Penton Media, Inc., 6250

Chief Officers of State Library Agencies Directory
Chief Officers of State Library Agencies, 16135, 16240

Chief's Edge
International Association of Fire Chiefs, 17306

Children's Business
Fairchild Publications, 1861

Children's Writer's and Illustrator's Market
Writer's Market, 16412

Chinese Business in America
Caravel, 14726

Chinese Law and Government
ME Sharpe, 15854

Chlor-Alkali Marketwire
Chemical Week/Access Intelligence, 4565

Chlorine Institute Annual Meeting & Trade Show
Chlorine Institute, 4668

Chlorine Institute Newsletter
Chlorine Institute, 4566

Choice
Association of College and Research Libraries, 16197

Choices
Agricultural & Applied Economics Association, 906, 9957

Choral Journal
American Choral Directors Association, 19401

Christian Management Association
Christian Management Association, 17010

Christian Retailing
Strang Communications Company, 21419

Christie's International Magazine
Christies Publications, 2373

Christmas Gift & Hobby Show
HSI Show Productions, 13668

Christmas Gift and Hobby Show
HSI Show Productions, 13669

Christmas Tree Lookout
Pacific Northwest Christmas Tree Association, 907

Christmas Trees
Tree Publishers, 908

Chronos
Golden Bell Press, 14947

Cineaste
Cineaste Magazine, 18769

Cinefantastique
CFQ Media, 18770

Cinema Journal
University of Texas Press, 18772

CinemaCon
National Association of Theatre Owners, 1730, 19956

Circle of Champions
Premiere Show Group, 5900

CircuiTree
Business News Publishing Company, 5376

Circuits Assembly
Circuit Assembly, 6877

Circuits Assembly: Buyers' Guide Issue
Miller Freeman Publications, 6726

Circuits and Systems Magazine
IEEE Circuits and Systems Society, 5377, 6878, 7243, 16828, 22118

Circulation
Standard Rate & Data Services, 583

Circulation Management
PRIMEDIA Intertec-Marketing & Professional Service, 21420
Primedia, 17877

Circulation Update E-Newsletter
Newspaper Association of America, 5003

Citograph
Western Agricultural Publishing Company, 9958

Citrus & Vegetable Magazine
Vance Publishing, 909, 9959

Citrus & Vegetable Magazine: Farm Equipment Directory Issue
Vance Publishing, 1274, 10570

Citrus Expo
Southeast AgNet Publications/Citrus Industry Mag, 1126

Citrus Industry
Southeast AgNet Publications, 910

City Visitor
Travelhost, 23986

Civic.com
FCW Government Technology Group, 5378

Civil Air Patrol Annual Conference
Civil Air Patrol, 2822

Civil Aviation Medical Association Conference
Civil Aviation Medical Association, 2823

Civil Engineering
American Society of Civil Engineers, 7244

Civil RICO Report
LRP Publications, 15647

Civil Rights: From the State Capitals
Wakeman Walworth, 11979

Claim Service Guide
Bar List Publishing Company, 14378

Clarinet Journal
International Clarinet Society, 19402

Classic Trains
James Folcum, 23728

Classicist
Transaction Publishing Rutgers, 2189

Classified Exchange
Miller Publishing Corporation, 16548

Clavier
Instrumentalist Publishing Company, 19403

Clean Energy Direct
IHS, Inc., 1478

Clean Show
Riddle & Associates, 4829

Clean Water Current
National Association of Clean Water Agencies, 24394

Clean Water Report
CJE Associates, 7803

Clean-Coal/Synfuels Letter
McGraw Hill, 20229

CleanFacts Newsletter
California Cleaners Association, 4798

CleanRooms East
PennWell Conferences and Exhibitions, 17534

CleanRooms Magazine
PennWell Publishing Company, 3397, 5379, 6879, 9960, 12854, 20686

Cleaner
COLE Publishing, 4809, 13918

Cleaner Times
Advantage Publishing Company, 4810, 24404
Cleaning Equipment Trade Association, 24588

Cleanfax Magazine
National Trade Publications, 4811

Cleaning & Restoration Magazine
Restoration Industry Association, 4812, 23430

Cleaning and Maintenance Management: Buyer's Guide Directory
National Trade Publications, 4837

Cleanroom Markets Newsletter
McIlvaine Company, 6587

Cleanroom Technology Newsletter
McIlvaine Company, 6588

Clearing Up
Energy NewsData, 24166

Clearinghouse
NAGARA, 11980

Clearinghouse Reference Guide
American Bar Association, 15855

Clearwaters
New York Water Environment Association, 24405

Client Counseling Update
American Bar Association, 15648

Client Information Bulletin
WPI Communications, 105, 8616

Client Quarterly
WPI Communications, 3014

Client/Server Economics Letter
Computer Economics, 5274

Clientship
American Council of Engineering Companies, 7245

Climate Change News
Environmental & Energy Study Institute, 7804
Environmental and Energy Study Institute, 1479

Climate and National Security Forum
The Center for Climate and Security, 19634

Clin-Alert-Newsletter
Technomic Publishing Company, 20637

Clinical Advances in Periodontics
American Academy of Periodontology, 12855

Clinical Cancer Research
American Association for Cancer Research, 12856

Clinical Chemistry
American Association for Clinical Chemistry, 12857

Clinical Investigator News
CTB International Publishing, 20638

Clinical Lab Products
MWC Allied Healthcare Group, 12858

Clinical Laboratory Expo
AACC; c/o Scherago International, 13273

Clinical Laboratory Management Association Annual Conference
Clinical Laboratory Management Association, 13274

Clinical Robotic Surgery Association
Two Prudential Plaza, 16747, 22079

Clinical Trials Monitor
CTB International Publishing, 20639

Clinical and Scientific Congress of the Int'l Anesthesia Res
International Anesthesia Research Society, 13275

Clio Among the Media
Association for Education in Journalism, 15131

Close Up Magazine
Country Music Association, 19404

Clothing Manufacturers Association of the USA
Clothing Manufacturers Association of the USA, 1852
Clothing and Textile Research Journal
International Textile and Apparel Association, 1862
Club Management Magazine
Finan Publishing Company, 13783, 17219
Club Metro
Metro Online, 24065
Co-op Advertising Programs Sourcebook
National Register Publishing, 584
Coaching Management
MAG, 22821
Coaching Volleyball
American Volleyball Coaches Association, 22822
Coaching and Teambuilding Skills for Managers and Supervisor
SkillPath Seminars, 17308
Coal
MacLean Hunter, 18594
Coal Age
Primedia, 18595
Coal Data
National Coal Association, 18649
Coal Mine Directory
Primedia, 18650
Coal Outlook
Pasha Publications, 1480
Coal People
Al Skinner Enterprises, 18597, 20279
Coal Week International
McGraw Hill, 1481, 18579
Coal and Synfuels Technology
Pasha Publications, 1482
Coaldat Productivity Report
Pasha Publications, 18580
Coast Guard Intelligence (CGI)
U.S. Coast Guard, 19573
Coatings World
Rodman Publishing, 4602, 17457
Code Official
International Code Council, 12060
Coffee & Cuisine
Coffee Talk, 21836
Coffee Reporter
National Coffee Association, 9758
Coffee, Sugar and Cocoa Exchange Daily Market Report
New York Board of Trade, 9406, 9759
Coffee, Sugar and Cocoa Exchange Guide
Commerce Clearing House, 10572
Cogeneration Monthly Letter
Cogeneration Publications Company, 24193
Coherence and Electromagnetic Fields in Biological Systems
Bioelectromagnetics Society, 6668
Coil World
CJL Publishing, 18350
Coin Laundry Association of Suppliers
Coin Laundry Association, 4838
Coin Laundry Association: Journal
Coin Laundry Association, 4799
Coin Prices
F+W Media, 13608
Coin and Stamp Exposition: San Francisco
Bick International, 13670
Coins
F+W Media, 13609
Cold Regions Research and Engineering Laboratory
US Army Corps of Engineers, 7095
Cold Water Oil Spills
Cutter Information Corporation, 20230
Coldset Web Offset Directory
Printing Industries of America/Graphic Arts, 21215
Collection Agency Directory
First Detroit Corporation, 6081
Collection Agency Report
First Detroit Corporation, 6022, 8617
Collection Systems Conference
Water Environment Federation, 8086
Collections & Credit Risk
Thomson Financial Publishing, 6044, 8788
Collective Bargaining Negotiations and Contracts
Bureau of National Affairs, 15649
Collector Magazine
ACA International, 8789
College Art Association
TERRA Foundation, 2296
College Store Executive
Executive Business Media, 21960
College Store Executive: Emblematics Directory Issue
Executive Business Media, 1965
College Store Magazine
National Association of College Stores, 21961
College and University Auditor Journal
Association of College & University Auditors, 183
Collegiate Aviation Guide
University Aviation Association, 2873
Collegiate Journalist
Society for Collegiate Journalists, 21421
Collegiate Trends
Strategic Marketing, 17749
Colloquy
Frequency Marketing, 17750
Colorado RV Adventure Travel Show
Industrial Expositions, 22929
Colorado RV, Sports, Boat and Travel Show
Industrial Expositions, 22930
Colored Stone
PRIMEDIA, 14948
Columbia Journalism Review
Columbia University, 15153
Columbia Law School Magazine
Columbia Law School, 15856
Com-SAC, Computer Security, Auditing & Controls
Management Advisory Services & Publications, 5380
Combating Payments & Check Fraud Conference
Bank Administration Institute, 3149
Combustion and Flame
Combustion Institute, 4603
Comdex Spring and Fall Shows
MediaLive International, 5613
Comics & Games Retailer
F+W Media, 13610
Comics Buyer's Guide
F+W Media, 13611
CommVerge
Reed Business Information, 6880
Command, Control, Communications and Intelligence
American Defense Preparedness Association, 2660
Commercial
Oakland Press, 21647
Commercial Carrier Journal
Randall-Reilly, 23729
Commercial Carrier Journal: Buyers' Guide Issue
Reed Business Information, 11325
Commercial Carrier Journal: Top 100 Issue
Reed Business Information, 11326
Commercial Collection Guidelines for Credit Grantors
International Association of Commercial Collectors, 6045
Commercial Fisheries News
Compass Publications, 9210
Commercial Floor Care
Business News Publishing Company, 4813
Commercial Investment Real Estate
CCIM Institute, 21727
Commercial Law Journal
Commercial Law League of America, 15857
Commercial Law World Magazine
Commercial Law League of America, 15858
Commercial Laws of the World
Foreign Tax Law, 15650
Commercial Lease Law Insider
Brownstone Publishers, 21608
Commercial Marine Directory & Fish Farmers Phone Book/ Direc
Compass Publications, 9277
Commercial Mortgage Alert
Harrison Scott Publications, 8618
Commercial Mortgage Securities Association Conference
Commercial Mortgage Securities Association, 3150
Commercial Property News
Miller Freeman Publications, 21609
Commercial Real Estate Digest
Vestal Communications, 21610
Commerical Modular Construction
Emlen Publications/Modular Building Institute, 4167
Commerical Real Estate Finance/Multifamily Housing Conventio
Mortgage Bankers Association, 3151
Commission on Mental & Physical Disability Law
American Bar Association, 15539
Commitment Plus
Quality & Productivity Management Association, 17220
Commodity Classic
American Soybean Association, 10281
Commodity Classic: ASA, NWGA, NCGA, NSP, 1127
Common Ground
Community Associations Institute, 21648
Common Market Law Review
Kluwer Law and Taxation Publishers, 16011
Communication
National Technical Information Service, 23206
Communication Arts
Coyne & Blanchard, 12336
Communication Briefings
Briefings Publishing Group, 5005
Communication News: Network Access Directory
Nelson Publishing, 23335
Communication Theory
International Communication Association, 23263
Communication World
Int'l Association of Business Communicators, 5054, 21278
Communication Yearbook
International Communication Association, 23264
Communication and Agricultural Education
Oklahoma State University, 9410
Communications ASP
Technology Marketing Corporation, 5055
Communications Arts
Coyne & Blanchard, 5056
Communications Billing Report
Telecommunications Reports International, 23265
Communications Business Daily
Warren Communications News, 5006
Communications Concepts
Communication Concepts, 5007
Communications Crossroads
United States Telecom Association, 23266
Communications Daily
Warren Publishing, 5057, 23207
Communications Insights
Comquest, 17106
Communications Lawyer
American Bar Association Forum - Communication Law, 15651
Communications Marketing Association Conference
Communications Marketing Association, 5098, 17971
Communications News: Broadband Directory
Nelson Publishing, 23336
Communications News: PBX/CTI Directory
Nelson Publishing, 23337
Communications News: Test Directory
Nelson Publishing, 23338
Communications News: Video/ Audioconferencing Directory
Nelson Publishing, 23339
Communications News: Wireless Directory
Nelson Publishing, 23340

Communications and the Law
Fred B Rotham Company, 15859

Communications in Soil Science and Plant Analysis
Marcel Dekker, 9961

Communications of the ACM
Association for Computing Machinery, 5382, 22119

Communicator
American Institute of Parliamentarians, 15132
Consumer Data Industry Association, 6023
Radio Television News Directors Association, 3842

Communique
Association for Preservation Technology Int'l, 2340
CHRIE, 9760

Communiqu,
Association for Women in Communications, 5008

Community & Regional Bank Forum
Bank Insurance and Securities Association, 3152

Community Association Law Reporter
Community Associations Institute, 21611

Community Associations Institute News
Community Associations Institute, 21612

Community Bank Director's Conference
American Association of Bank Directors, 3153

Community Bank President
Siefer Consultants, 3015, 3097

Community Banking Advisory Network Super Conference
HCAA, 3154

Community College Cyber Summit (3CS)
National CyberWatch Center, 6170

Community Health Funding Report
CD Publications, 11156

Community Management
Community Associations Institute, 21613

Community Matters
Accreditation Board for Engineering & Technology, 7246

Community Pharmacist
ELF Publications, 20687

Community Radio News
National Federation of Community Broadcasting, 3792

Community Television Review
National Federation of Local Cable Programmers, 3793

Community Theatre Management Conference
American Association of Community Theatre, 19957

Commuter Flight Statistics and Online Origin & Destination D
US Department of Transportation, 2874

Comp-U-Fax Computer Trends Newsletter
Microcomputers Software and Consulting, 5275

CompTIA World
CompTIA, 6161

CompactPCI Systems
CompactPCI Systems, 5383

Company Intelligence
Information Access Company, 17343

Comparative Guide to American Suburbs
Grey House Publishing, 13366, 21728

Comparative Medicine
American Association for Laboratory Animal Science, 12860

Comparative Statistics of Industrial and Office Real Estate
Society of Industrial & Office Realtors, 21649

Compensation & Benefits for Law Offices
Institute of Management and Administration, 14203

Competitive Advantage
Competitive Advantage, 17752

Competitive Intelligence Review
John Wiley & Sons, 17221

Complete Catalogue of Plays
Dramatists Play Service, 19977

Complete Directory for Pediatric Disorders
Grey House Publishing, 13367

Complete Directory for People with Chronic Illness
Grey House Publishing, 13368, 13369

Complete Directory of Apparel Close-Outs
Sutton Family Communications & Publishing Company, 1966, 1967

Complete Directory of Baby Goods and Gifts
Sutton Family Communications & Publishing Company, 1968

Complete Directory of Belts, Buckles & Boots
Sutton Family Communications & Publishing Company, 1969

Complete Directory of Brand New Surplus Merchandise
Sutton Family Communications & Publishing Company, 1970

Complete Directory of Caps & Hats
Sutton Family Communications & Publishing Company, 1971

Complete Directory of Close-outs and Super-buys
Sutton Family Communications & Publishing Company, 24673

Complete Directory of Clothing & Uniforms
Sutton Family Communications & Publishing Company, 1972

Complete Directory of Collectibles
Sutton Family Communications & Publishing Company, 13723

Complete Directory of Concessions & Equipment
Sutton Family Communications & Publishing Company, 10573

Complete Directory of Cosmetic Specialties
Sutton Family Communications & Publishing Company, 5952

Complete Directory of Crafts and Hobbies
Sutton Family Communications & Publishing Company, 13724

Complete Directory of Cubic Zirconia Jewelry
Sutton Family Communications & Publishing Company, 15007

Complete Directory of Discount & Catalog Merchandisers
Sutton Family Communications & Publishing Company, 11460

Complete Directory of Earrings & Necklaces
Sutton Family Communications & Publishing Company, 15008

Complete Directory of Figurines
Sutton Family Communications & Publishing Company, 13725

Complete Directory of Film & Photo Products
Sutton Family Communications & Publishing Company, 20925

Complete Directory of Fishing Tackle
Sutton Family Communications & Publishing Company, 23002

Complete Directory of Food Products
Sutton Family Communications & Publishing Company, 10574

Complete Directory of Games
Sutton Family Communications & Publishing Company, 13726

Complete Directory of General Flea Market Merchandise
Sutton Family Communications & Publishing Company, 24674

Complete Directory of Giftware Items
Sutton Family Communications & Publishing Company, 11736

Complete Directory of Glassware & Glass Items
Sutton Family Communications & Publishing Company, 11820

Complete Directory of Hat Pins, Feathers and Fads
Sutton Family Communications & Publishing Company, 1973

Complete Directory of High Profit Items
Sutton Family Communications & Publishing Company, 24675

Complete Directory of Home Furnishings
Sutton Family Communications & Publishing Company, 11461

Complete Directory of Home Gardening Products
Sutton Family Communications & Publishing Company, 11660

Complete Directory of Horticulture
Sutton Family Communications & Publishing Company, 11661

Complete Directory of Importers
Sutton Family Communications & Publishing Company, 24676

Complete Directory of Jewelry Close-Outs
Sutton Family Communications & Publishing Company, 15009

Complete Directory of Jewelry: General
Sutton Family Communications & Publishing Company, 15010

Complete Directory of Kitchen Accessories
Sutton Family Communications & Publishing Company, 11462

Complete Directory of Lamps, Lamp Shades & Lamp Parts
Sutton Family Communications & Publishing Company, 11463

Complete Directory of Leather Goods & Luggage
Sutton Family Communications & Publishing Company, 15482

Complete Directory of Low-Price Merchandise
Sutton Family Communications & Publishing Company, 15011, 24677

Complete Directory of Mail Order Catalog Products
Sutton Family Communications & Publishing Company, 18023

Complete Directory of Novelties
Sutton Family Communications & Publishing Company, 13727

Complete Directory of Outdoor Products
Sutton Family Communications & Publishing Company, 23003

Complete Directory of Personal Care Items
Sutton Family Communications & Publishing Company, 5953

Complete Directory of Pewter Items
Sutton Family Communications & Publishing Company, 13728

Complete Directory of Plumbing Products
Sutton Family Communications & Publishing Company, 21113

Complete Directory of Plush and Stuffed Toys and Dolls
Sutton Family Communications & Publishing Company, 13729

Complete Directory of Posters, Buttons and Novelties
Sutton Family Communications & Publishing Company, 13730

Complete Directory of Promotional Products
Sutton Family Communications & Publishing Company, 24678

Complete Directory of Purses & Handbags
Sutton Family Communications & Publishing Company, 1974

Complete Directory of Serving Ware
Sutton Family Communications & Publishing Company, 11464

Complete Directory of Showroom Fixtures and Equipment
Sutton Family Communications & Publishing Company, 11465

Complete Directory of Small Appliances
Sutton Family Communications & Publishing Company, 2075

Complete Directory of Small Furniture
Sutton Family Communications & Publishing Company, 11466

Complete Directory of Socks & Shoes
Sutton Family Communications & Publishing Company, 11111

Complete Directory of Sporting Goods
Sutton Family Communications & Publishing Company, 23004

Complete Directory of Stationery Items
Sutton Family Communications & Publishing Company, 24679

Complete Directory of Sunglasses & Eye Weather
Sutton Family Communications & Publishing Company, 1975

D

E

G

H

Healthcare e-Business Manager
Managed Care Information Center, 12770
Healthplan
American Association of Health Plans, 12924
Healthy Buildings Conference & Exhibition
The Indoor Air Institute, 8109
Hearsay
Association of Radio Reading Services, 3797
Hearth & Home
Village West Publishing, 11607, 12409, 13506, 21972
Heartland Travel Showcase
Hart Productions, 24045
Heat Transfer Engineering
Taylor & Francis Group Ltd, 7274
Heat Treating Progress
ASM International, 18362
Heat Treating Society Conference & Expo
ASM International, 7452, 11808, 13967, 17539, 18421, 21020
Heating with Biomass;
Environmental & Energy Study Institute, 8110
Heating/Combustion and Equipment News
Business Communications Company, 13482
Heatset Web Offset Directory
Printing Industries of America/Graphic Arts, 21217
Heavy Duty Aftermarket Week
Association of Diesel Specialists, 19158
Heavy Duty Representatives Profile Directory
Heavy Duty Representatives Association, 23870
Heavy Duty Trucking
Newport Communications, 23744
Heavy Duty Trucking: CFS Buyers Guide
Newport Communications Div.-HIC Corporation, 23871
Hedge Fund Alert
Harrison Scott Publications, 8665
Heli-Expo
Helicopter Association International, 2832
Helicopter Annual
Helicopter Association International, 2878
Helicopter News
Phillips Business Information, 2665
Helicopter Safety
Flight Safety Foundation, 2666
Heller Report on Educational Technology Markets
Nelson B Heller & Associates, 5452
Heller Report on Internet Strategies for Education Markets
Nelson B Heller & Associates, 6464
Hemingway's Glamour Photographer's Resource Directory
Looking Glass Photography, 20929
Hemispheres
Pace Communications, 23745
Hemmings Classic Car
Hemmings Motor News, 19085
Hemp Industries Association Annual Confere nce
Hemp Industries Association, 1155
Hepatology
American Assn for the Study of Liver Disease, 12925
Herb Quarterly
EGW Publishing Company, 10028
Herbal Green Pages
Herb Growing and Marketing Network, 10624
Herd on the Hill
National Meat Association, 9796
Hereford World
American Hereford Association, 967, 10029
High Country News
High Country Foundation, 968
High Density Interconnect
CMP Media, 6899
High Performance Composites
Ray Publishing, 13926, 16839, 23746
High Performance Linux on Wall Street
Flagg Management, 17983
High Plains Journal/Midwest Ag Journal
High Plains Publishing Company, 969
High Tech News
Electronic Technicians Association International, 6632, 6900
High Volume Independent Restaurants Database
Chain Store Guide, 10625, 21879
High Volume Printing (HVP)
Innes Publishing Company, 21171
High Yield Report
American Banker-Bond Buyer, 8666
High-Performance Composites Directory
Ray Publishing, 6737
High-Tech Hot Sheet
Hot Sheet Publishing, 21253
High-Tech Materials Alert
John Wiley & Sons, 16810
Technical Insights, 7208
High-Volume Jeweler
Reed Business Information, 14951
Higher Education Technology News
Business Publishers, 6404
Highlights
American Association of Retired Persons, 14207
Highpoints Newsletter
American Academy of Environmental Engineers, 7209
Highway & Vehicle/Safety Report
Stamler Publishing Company, 19016
Highway Users In Action
American Highway Users Alliance, 19017
HipHop Weekly
Z & M Media, 19415
Hiring the Best
Briefings Publishing Group, 17141
Hispanic Arts News
Association of Hispanic Arts, 19922
Hispanic Business Magazine
Hispanic Business Inc, 440
Hispanic Elected Local Officials
National League of Cities, 11893
Hispanic Engineer & Information Technology
Career Communications Group, 7275
Historic New England
Soc for Preservation of New England Antiquities, 2133
History of Photography
Routledge Publishing, 20890
Hits Magazine
Color West, 3851
Hobby Industries of America Trade Show Program and Buyers Gu
Hobby Industry Association, 13735
Hobby Merchandiser
Hobby Publications, 13626
Hobby Merchandiser Annual Trade Directory
Hobby Publications, 13736
Hobby Rocketry
California Rocketry Publishing, 13627
Hobby RoundTable
GE Information Services, 13737
Hockey Business News
Straight Line Communications, 22839
Hog Producer
Farm Progress, 970
Holiday Fair
Textile Hall Corporation, 14540
Holiday Market
Gilmore Enterprises, 11706
Holiday Sample Sale
San Francisco Design Center, 1909
Hollow Metal Manufacturers Association (HMMA)
National Assn of Architectural Metal Manufacturer, 4026
Hollywood Life
Movieline Magazine, 18780
Hollywood Reporter
Prometheus Global Media, 1686, 18781
Holmes Report
Holmes Group, 21254
Holography News
Reconnaissance International Consulting, 12330
Holstein Association News
Holstein Association, 830
Holstein Pulse
Holstein Association USA, 831, 971
Holstein World
Dairy Business Communications, 972
Home Accents Today
Reed Business Information, 11420
Home Builders Magazine
Work-4 Projects, 4210
Home Business Idea Possibility Newsletter
Prosperity & Profits Unlimited, 17775
Home Center Operators & Hardware Chains
Chain Store Guide, 12422
Home Furnishing Retailer
National Home Furnishings Association, 11421
Home Furnishing Retailers
Chain Store Guide, 11469
Home Health Products
Stevens Publishing Corporation, 12926
Home Improvement & Remodeling Exposition
Dmg World Media, 4312
Home Lighting & Accessories
Doctorow Communications, 11422, 14510
Home Lighting & Accessories Suppliers Directory
Doctorow Communications, 14576
Home Medical Equipment News
United Publications, 12927, 16840
Home Networks
IGI Group, 23213
Home Office Life Underwriters Association
Minnesota Mutual Life, 14070
Home Shop Machinist
Village Press, 16841
Home Textiles Today
Reed Business Information, 23433
Home and Garden Show
Reed Exhibition Companies, 14542
Home and Outdoor Living Expo
Tower Show Productions, 11437
HomeCare
Penton Media Inc, 12928
Homeland Security & Defense
McGraw Hill, 22394
Homeland Security Expo & Conference
E-Gov Conferences, 22494
Honey Producer
American Honey Producers Association, 10030
Hong Kong Trade Development Council Newsletter
Hong Kong Trade Development Council, 14666
Hook Magazine
Tailhook Association, 2745
Hoover's Guide to Computer Companies
Hoover's, 5685
Horizons
Hobby Industry Association, 13628
Horological Times
American Watchmakers-Clockmakers Institute, 14952
Horseman's Journal
National Horsemen's Administration Corporation, 22840
Hort Expo Northwest
Mt Adams Publishing and Design, 1289, 10626
HortScience
American Society for Horticultural Science, 973, 11608
HortTechnology
American Society for Horticultural Science, 11609
Horticulture Magazine
F+W Media, 11610
Hosiery News
Home Sewing Association, 1867

I

J

K

M

N

O

P

Q

R

V

W

X

Y

Z